Who's Who in the West®

Who's Who in the West®

2002

Including Alaska, Arizona, California, Colorado, Hawaii, Idaho, Montana, Nevada, New Mexico, Oregon, Utah, Washington, and Wyoming; and in Canada, the provinces of Alberta, British Columbia, and Saskatchewan, and the Northwest and Yukon Territories.

29th Edition

07974 U.S.A.
ho.com

Who'sWho in the West®

Marquis Who's Who®

Editorial Director Fred Marks

Senior Managing Research Editor Lisa Weissbard **Managing Editor** Eileen McGuinness

Editorial

Senior Editor Donald Bunton
Associate Editor Alison C. McGowan
Assistant Editors Deanna Richmond, Kate Spirito, Laura Koserowski

Editorial Services

Senior Manager Debby Nowicki
Production Manager Paul Zema
Freelance Supervisor Mary San Giovanni
Technical Coordinator Sola Osofisan
Mail Processing Supervisor Kara A. Seitz
Mail Processing Staff Betty Gray, Hattie Walker

Creative Services

Creative Services Director Michael Noerr
Creative Services Coordinator Rose Butkiewicz
Designer William R. Miller
Production Supervisor Jeanne Danzig

Research

Senior Research Editor Musa Muromets
Associate Research Editor Jennifer Podolsky
Assistant Research Editor Willie Lee

Editorial Systems

Project Manager Helene Davis
Programmers/Analysts Sofia P. Pikulin, Tom Haggerty

Published by Marquis Who's Who, a member of the Lexis-Nexis Group.

Chief Executive Officer Andrew W. Meyer
Vice President and Publisher Randy H. Mysel
Vice President, Database Production Dean Hollister
Chief Information Officer John Roney
Vice President of Information Technology Gary Aiello

For information, contact:

Marquis Who's Who
121 Chanlon Road
New Providence, New Jersey 07974
1-908-464-6800
www.marquiswhoswho.com

WHO'S WHO IN THE WEST is a registered trademark of Reed Publishing (Nederland) B.V., used under license.
Library of Congress Catalog Card Number 49-48186
International Standard Book Number 0-8379-0933-3
International Standard Serial Number 0083-9817

Manufactured in the United States of America

Table of Contents

Preface

The 29th Edition of *Who's Who in the West* is a compilation of biographical information on men and women of distinction whose influence is concentrated in the western region of North America. Such individuals are of reference interest locally and, to a degree, nationally.

The volume contains approximately 15,000 names from the western region of the United States including Alaska, Arizona, California, Colorado, Hawaii, Idaho, Montana, Nevada, New Mexico, Oregon, Utah, Washington, and Wyoming. Also included are the Canadian provinces of Alberta, British Columbia, and Saskatchewan, and the Northwest and Yukon Territories. In some instances, persons who do not reside in the western region of the United States or Canada have also been included as Biographees. They appear in this edition because they have made significant professional or civic contributions to this region. Reviewed, revised, and amended, the 29th Edition offers current coverage of a broad range of Westerners based on position or individual achievement.

The persons sketched in this volume represent virtually every important field of endeavor. Included are executives and officials in government, business, education, medicine, religion, the press, law, and other fields. This edition also includes significant contributors in such areas as contemporary art, music, and science.

In most cases, Biographees have furnished their own data, thus assuring a high degree of accuracy. In some cases where individuals failed to supply information, Marquis staff members compiled the data through careful, independent research. Sketches compiled in this manner are denoted by an asterisk. As in previous editions, Biographees were given the opportunity to review prepublication proofs of their sketches to make sure they were correct.

The question is often asked, "How do people get into a Marquis Who's Who volume?" Name selection is based on one fundamental principle: reference value.

Biographees of *Who's Who in the West* can be classified in two basic categories: (1) Persons who are of regional reference importance to colleagues, librarians, researchers, scholars, the media, historians, biographers, participants in business and civic affairs, and others with specific or general inquiry needs; (2) Individuals of national reference interest who are also of such regional or local importance that their inclusion in the book is essential.

In the editorial evaluation that resulted in the ultimate selection of the names appearing in this directory, an individual's desire to be listed was not sufficient reason for inclusion; rather it was the person's achievement that ruled. Similarly, neither wealth nor social position was a criterion; only occupational stature or achievement in a field within the western region of North America influenced selection.

A Professional Index is again included in *Who's Who in the West.* Within the index, each Biographee is listed by occupation, and under each occupational category, names are listed alphabetically by country, state, and city. This reference tool will make it easier than ever for interested readers to find Biographees in any given profession or location.

Marquis Who's Who editors exercise the utmost care in preparing each biographical sketch for publication. Occasionally, however, errors occur. Users of this directory are requested to draw the attention of the publisher to any errors found so that corrections can be made in a subsequent edition.

The 29th Edition of *Who's Who in the West* carries on the tradition of excellence established in 1899 with the publication of the first edition of *Who's Who in America.* The essence of that tradition is reflected in our continuing effort to produce reference works that are responsive to the needs of their users throughout the world.

Board of Advisors

Marquis Who's Who gratefully acknowledges the following distinguished individuals who have made themselves available for review, evaluation, and general comment with regard to the publication of the 29th Edition of *Who's Who in the West*. The advisors have enhanced the reference value of this edition by the nomination of outstanding individuals for inclusion. However, the Board of Advisors, either collectively or individually, is in no way responsible for the final selection of names, or for the accuracy or comprehensiveness of the biographical information or other material contained herein.

Mindy Aloff
Freelance Writer

William C. Anderson
Executive Director
American Academy of Environmental Engineers
Annapolis, Maryland

Steven C. Beering
President
Purdue University
West Lafayette, Indiana

Willard L. Boyd
President Emeritus
Field Museum of Natural History

Dr. Thomas C. Dolan
President
American College of Healthcare Executives

Charles C. Eldredge
Hall Distinguished Professor of American Art
University of Kansas
Lawrence, Kansas

Barbara Haskell
Curator
Whitney Museum of American Art

Thomas R. Horton
Former Chairman
American Management Association

Jill Krementz
Author and Photographer

Charles F. Larson
President
Industrial Research Institute, Inc.

Andrew Leckey
Syndicated Financial Columnist
Tribune Media Services

Judith P. Lotas
Founding Partner
Lotas Minard Patton McIver, Inc.

Martin E. Marty
Professor Emeritus
University of Chicago Divinity School

Robert G. McKinnell
Former President
International Society of Differentiation, Inc.
University of Minnesota
St. Paul, Minnesota

Jeremiah P. Ostriker
Provost
Princeton University
Princeton, New Jersey

Louis Rukeyser
Economic Commentator
Host, Wall Street Week With Louis Rukeyser

James Bohus Sales
Former Senior Partner
Fulbright & Jaworski
Houston, Texas

Catharine R. Stimpson
University Professor
New York University

John Fox Sullivan
President and Publisher
National Journal

Elie Wiesel
Author
Professor of Philosophy
Boston University

Standards of Admission

The foremost consideration in selecting Biographees for *Who's Who in the West* is the extent of an individual's reference interest. Such reference interest is judged on either of two factors: (1) the position of responsibility held, or (2) the level of achievement attained by the individual.

Admissions based on the factor of position include:

Members of the U.S. Congress

Federal judges

Governors of states covered by this volume

Premiers of Canadian provinces covered by this volume

State attorneys general

Judges of state and territorial courts of highest appellate jurisdiction

Mayors of major cities

Heads of major universities and colleges

Heads of leading philanthropic, educational, cultural, and scientific institutions and associations

Chief ecclesiastics of the principal religious denominations

Principal officers of national and international business

Admission for individual achievement is based on objective qualitative criteria. To be selected, a person must have attained conspicuous achievement.

Key to Information

[1] ASHTON, HARDY AMES, [2] lawyer; **[3]** b. Topeka, Aug. 3, 1934; **[4]** s. Samuel Taylor and Barbara (Hanson) A.; **[5]** m. Nancy Richardson, June 20, 1955; **[6]** children: Marilyn Ashton Heim, Barbara Anne, William Marc. **[7]** BA, Pa. State U., 1955; JD, Syracuse U., 1960. **[8]** Bar: Calif. 1960, U.S. Supreme Ct. 1968. **[9]** Assoc. Prine, Belden and Coates, Sacramento, 1960-67; mem. Johnson, Randolph, Sikes and Bord, Sacramento, 1967—, ptnr., 1969-74, sr. ptnr., 1974—; **[10]** legal cons. Sacramento Urban League. **[11]** Author: Urban Renewal and the Law, 1975, Changes in California Zoning Laws: A Perspective, 1987. **[12]** Commr. Sutter County Park Dist., 1971-78; mem. planning com. Arroyo Seco Redevel. Project, Sacramento, 1980—; bd. dirs. Hargrave Inst. **[13]** Served with U.S. Army, 1956-57. **[14]** Named Man of the Yr., Sacramento C. of C., 1996. **[15]** Mem. ABA, Calif. Bar Assn., Sacramento Bar Assn., Am. Judicature Soc., Order of Coif. Clubs: Twelve Trees Country, Tuesday Luncheon. Lodge: Lions (Sacramento). **[16]** Democrat. **[17]** Episcopalian. **[18]** Home: 3080 Grant St Sacramento CA 95814 **[19]** Office: Johnson Randolph Sikes & Bord 10 Saint Paul St Sacramento CA 95822

KEY

[1]	Name
[2]	Occupation
[3]	Vital statistics
[4]	Parents
[5]	Marriage
[6]	Children
[7]	Education
[8]	Professional certifications
[9]	Career
[10]	Career-related
[11]	Writings and creative works
[12]	Civic and political activities
[13]	Military
[14]	Awards and fellowships
[15]	Professional and association memberships, clubs and lodges
[16]	Political affiliation
[17]	Religion
[18]	Home address
[19]	Office address

Table of Abbreviations

The following abbreviations and symbols are frequently used in this book.

*An asterisk following a sketch indicates that it was researched by the Marquis Who's Who editorial staff and has not been verified by the Biographee.
A Associate (used with academic degrees only)
AA, A.A. Associate in Arts, Associate of Arts
AAAL American Academy of Arts and Letters
AAAS American Association for the Advancement of Science
AACD American Association for Counseling and Development
AACN American Association of Critical Care Nurses
AAHA American Academy of Health Administrators
AAHP American Association of Hospital Planners
AAHPERD American Alliance for Health, Physical Education, Recreation, and Dance
AAS Associate of Applied Science
AASL American Association of School Librarians
AASPA American Association of School Personnel Administrators
AAU Amateur Athletic Union
AAUP American Association of University Professors
AAUW American Association of University Women
AB, A.B. Arts, Bachelor of
AB Alberta
ABA American Bar Association
ABC American Broadcasting Company
AC Air Corps
acad. academy, academic
acct. accountant
acctg. accounting
ACDA Arms Control and Disarmament Agency
ACHA American College of Hospital Administrators
ACLS Advanced Cardiac Life Support
ACLU American Civil Liberties Union
ACOG American College of Ob-Gyn
ACP American College of Physicians
ACS American College of Surgeons
ADA American Dental Association
a.d.c. aide-de-camp
adj. adjunct, adjutant
adj. gen. adjutant general
adm. admiral
adminstr. administrator
adminstrn. administration
adminstrv. administrative
ADN Associate's Degree in Nursing
ADP Automatic Data Processing
adv. advocate, advisory
advt. advertising
AE, A.E. Agricultural Engineer
A.E. and P. Ambassador Extraordinary and Plenipotentiary
AEC Atomic Energy Commission
aero. aeronautical, aeronautic
aerodyn. aerodynamic
AFB Air Force Base
AFL-CIO American Federation of Labor and Congress of Industrial Organizations
AFTRA American Federation of TV and Radio Artists
AFSCME American Federation of State, County and Municipal Employees
agr. agriculture
agrl. agricultural
agt. agent
AGVA American Guild of Variety Artists
agy. agency
A&I Agricultural and Industrial
AIA American Institute of Architects
AIAA American Institute of Aeronautics and Astronautics
AIChE American Institute of Chemical Engineers
AICPA American Institute of Certified Public Accountants
AID Agency for International Development
AIDS Acquired Immune Deficiency Syndrome
AIEE American Institute of Electrical Engineers
AIM American Institute of Management
AIME American Institute of Mining, Metallurgy, and Petroleum Engineers
AK Alaska
AL Alabama
ALA American Library Association
Ala. Alabama
alt. alternate
Alta. Alberta
A&M Agricultural and Mechanical
AM, A.M. Arts, Master of
Am. American, America
AMA American Medical Association
amb. ambassador
A.M.E. African Methodist Episcopal
Amtrak National Railroad Passenger Corporation
AMVETS American Veterans of World War II, Korea, Vietnam
ANA American Nurses Association
anat. anatomical
ANCC American Nurses Credentialing Center
ann. annual
ANTA American National Theatre and Academy
anthrop. anthropological
AP Associated Press
APA American Psychological Association
APGA American Personnel Guidance Association
APHA American Public Health Association
APO Army Post Office
apptd. appointed
Apr. April
apt. apartment
AR Arkansas
ARC American Red Cross
arch. architect
archeol. archeological
archtl. architectural
Ariz. Arizona
Ark. Arkansas
ArtsD, ArtsD. Arts, Doctor of
arty. artillery
AS American Samoa
AS Associate in Science
ASCAP American Society of Composers, Authors and Publishers
ASCD Association for Supervision and Curriculum Development
ASCE American Society of Civil Engineers
ASHRAE American Society of Heating, Refrigeration, and Air Conditioning Engineers
ASME American Society of Mechanical Engineers
ASNSA American Society for Nursing Service Administrators
ASPA American Society for Public Administration
ASPCA American Society for the Prevention of Cruelty to Animals
assn. association
assoc. associate
asst. assistant
ASTD American Society for Training and Development
ASTM American Society for Testing and Materials
astron. astronomical
astrophys. astrophysical
ATLA Association of Trial Lawyers of America
ATSC Air Technical Service Command
AT&T American Telephone & Telegraph Company
atty. attorney
Aug. August
AUS Army of the United States
aux. auxiliary
Ave. Avenue
AVMA American Veterinary Medical Association
AZ Arizona
AWHONN Association of Women's Health Obstetric and Neonatal Nurses

B. Bachelor
b. born
BA, B.A. Bachelor of Arts
BAgr, B.Agr. Bachelor of Agriculture
Balt. Baltimore
Bapt. Baptist
BArch, B.Arch. Bachelor of Architecture
BAS, B.A.S. Bachelor of Agricultural Science
BBA, B.B.A. Bachelor of Business Administration
BBB Better Business Bureau
BBC British Broadcasting Corporation
BC, B.C. British Columbia
BCE, B.C.E. Bachelor of Civil Engineering
BChir, B.Chir. Bachelor of Surgery

BCL, B.C.L. Bachelor of Civil Law
BCLS Basic Cardiac Life Support
BCS, B.C.S. Bachelor of Commercial Science
BD, B.D. Bachelor of Divinity
bd. board
BE, B.E. Bachelor of Education
BEE, B.E.E. Bachelor of Electrical Engineering
BFA, B.F.A. Bachelor of Fine Arts
bibl. biblical
bibliog. bibliographical
biog. biographical
biol. biological
BJ, B.J. Bachelor of Journalism
Bklyn. Brooklyn
BL, B.L. Bachelor of Letters
bldg. building
BLS, B.L.S. Bachelor of Library Science
BLS Basic Life Support
Blvd. Boulevard
BMI Broadcast Music, Inc.
BMW Bavarian Motor Works (Bayerische Motoren Werke)
bn. battalion
B.&O.R.R. Baltimore & Ohio Railroad
bot. botanical
BPE, B.P.E. Bachelor of Physical Education
BPhil, B.Phil. Bachelor of Philosophy
br. branch
BRE, B.R.E. Bachelor of Religious Education
brig. gen. brigadier general
Brit. British, Brittanica
Bros. Brothers
BS, B.S. Bachelor of Science
BSA, B.S.A. Bachelor of Agricultural Science
BSBA Bachelor of Science in Business Administration
BSChemE Bachelor of Science in Chemical Engineering
BSD, B.S.D. Bachelor of Didactic Science
BSEE Bachelor of Science in Electrical Engineering
BSN Bachelor of Science in Nursing
BST, B.S.T. Bachelor of Sacred Theology
BTh, B.Th. Bachelor of Theology
bull. bulletin
bur. bureau
bus. business
B.W.I. British West Indies

CA California
CAA Civil Aeronautics Administration
CAB Civil Aeronautics Board
CAD-CAM Computer Aided Design–Computer Aided Model
Calif. California
C.Am. Central America
Can. Canada, Canadian
CAP Civil Air Patrol
capt. captain
cardiol. cardiological
cardiovasc. cardiovascular
CARE Cooperative American Relief Everywhere
Cath. Catholic
cav. cavalry
CBC Canadian Broadcasting Company
CBI China, Burma, India Theatre of Operations
CBS Columbia Broadcasting Company
C.C. Community College
CCC Commodity Credit Corporation
CCNY City College of New York
CCRN Critical Care Registered Nurse
CCU Cardiac Care Unit
CD Civil Defense
CE, C.E. Corps of Engineers, Civil Engineer
CEN Certified Emergency Nurse
CENTO Central Treaty Organization
CEO chief executive officer
CERN European Organization of Nuclear Research
cert. certificate, certification, certified
CETA Comprehensive Employment Training Act
CFA Chartered Financial Analyst
CFL Canadian Football League
CFO chief financial officer
CFP Certified Financial Planner
ch. church
ChD, Ch.D. Doctor of Chemistry
chem. chemical
ChemE, Chem.E. Chemical Engineer
ChFC Chartered Financial Consultant
Chgo. Chicago
chirurg. chirurgical
chmn. chairman
chpt. chapter
CIA Central Intelligence Agency
Cin. Cincinnati
cir. circle, circuit
CLE Continuing Legal Education
Cleve. Cleveland
climatol. climatological
clin. clinical
clk. clerk
C.L.U. Chartered Life Underwriter
CM, C.M. Master in Surgery
CM Northern Mariana Islands
CMA Certified Medical Assistant
cmty. community
CNA Certified Nurse's Aide
CNOR Certified Nurse (Operating Room)
C.&N.W.Ry. Chicago & North Western Railway
CO Colorado
Co. Company
COF Catholic Order of Foresters
C. of C. Chamber of Commerce
col. colonel
coll. college
Colo. Colorado
com. committee
comd. commanded
comdg. commanding
comdr. commander
comdt. commandant
comm. communications
commd. commissioned
comml. commercial
commn. commission
commr. commissioner
compt. comptroller
condr. conductor
Conf. Conference
Congl. Congregational, Congressional
Conglist. Congregationalist
Conn. Connecticut
cons. consultant, consulting
consol. consolidated
constl. constitutional
constn. constitution
constrn. construction
contbd. contributed
contbg. contributing
contbn. contribution
contbr. contributor
contr. controller
Conv. Convention
COO chief operating officer
coop. cooperative
coord. coordinator
CORDS Civil Operations and Revolutionary Development Support
CORE Congress of Racial Equality
corp. corporation, corporate
corr. correspondent, corresponding, correspondence
C.&O.Ry. Chesapeake & Ohio Railway
coun. council
CPA Certified Public Accountant
CPCU Chartered Property and Casualty Underwriter
CPH, C.P.H. Certificate of Public Health
cpl. corporal
CPR Cardio-Pulmonary Resuscitation
C.P.Ry. Canadian Pacific Railway
CRT Cathode Ray Terminal
C.S. Christian Science
CSB, C.S.B. Bachelor of Christian Science
C.S.C. Civil Service Commission
CT Connecticut
ct. court
ctr. center
ctrl. central
CWS Chemical Warfare Service
C.Z. Canal Zone

D. Doctor
d. daughter
DAgr, D.Agr. Doctor of Agriculture
DAR Daughters of the American Revolution
dau. daughter
DAV Disabled American Veterans
DC, D.C. District of Columbia
DCL, D.C.L. Doctor of Civil Law
DCS, D.C.S. Doctor of Commercial Science
DD, D.D. Doctor of Divinity
DDS, D.D.S. Doctor of Dental Surgery
DE Delaware
Dec. December
dec. deceased
def. defense
Del. Delaware
del. delegate, delegation
Dem. Democrat, Democratic
DEng, D.Eng. Doctor of Engineering
denom. denomination, denominational
dep. deputy
dept. department
dermatol. dermatological
desc. descendant
devel. development, developmental
DFA, D.F.A. Doctor of Fine Arts
D.F.C. Distinguished Flying Cross
DHL, D.H.L. Doctor of Hebrew Literature
dir. director
dist. district
distbg. distributing
distbn. distribution
distbr. distributor
disting. distinguished
div. division, divinity, divorce
divsn. division
DLitt, D.Litt. Doctor of Literature
DMD, D.M.D. Doctor of Dental Medicine
DMS, D.M.S. Doctor of Medical Science
DO, D.O. Doctor of Osteopathy
docs. documents
DON Director of Nursing
DPH, D.P.H. Diploma in Public Health
DPhil, D.Phil. Doctor of Philosophy
D.R. Daughters of the Revolution
Dr. Drive, Doctor
DRE, D.R.E. Doctor of Religious Education
DrPH, Dr.P.H. Doctor of Public Health, Doctor of Public Hygiene
D.S.C. Distinguished Service Cross
DSc, D.Sc. Doctor of Science
DSChemE Doctor of Science in Chemical Engineering

D.S.M. Distinguished Service Medal
DST, D.S.T. Doctor of Sacred Theology
DTM, D.T.M. Doctor of Tropical Medicine
DVM, D.V.M. Doctor of Veterinary Medicine
DVS, D.V.S. Doctor of Veterinary Surgery

E, E. East
ea. eastern
E. and P. Extraordinary and Plenipotentiary
Eccles. Ecclesiastical
ecol. ecological
econ. economic
ECOSOC Economic and Social Council (of the UN)
ED, E.D. Doctor of Engineering
ed. educated
EdB, Ed.B. Bachelor of Education
EdD, Ed.D. Doctor of Education
edit. edition
editl. editorial
EdM, Ed.M. Master of Education
edn. education
ednl. educational
EDP Electronic Data Processing
EdS, Ed.S. Specialist in Education
EE, E.E. Electrical Engineer
E.E. and M.P. Envoy Extraordinary and Minister Plenipotentiary
EEC European Economic Community
EEG Electroencephalogram
EEO Equal Employment Opportunity
EEOC Equal Employment Opportunity Commission
E.Ger. German Democratic Republic
EKG Electrocardiogram
elec. electrical
electrochem. electrochemical
electrophys. electrophysical
elem. elementary
EM, E.M. Engineer of Mines
EMT Emergency Medical Technician
ency. encyclopedia
Eng. England
engr. engineer
engring. engineering
entomol. entomological
environ. environmental
EPA Environmental Protection Agency
epidemiol. epidemiological
Episc. Episcopalian
ERA Equal Rights Amendment
ERDA Energy Research and Development Administration
ESEA Elementary and Secondary Education Act
ESL English as Second Language
ESPN Entertainment and Sports Programming Network
ESSA Environmental Science Services Administration
ethnol. ethnological
ETO European Theatre of Operations
Evang. Evangelical
exam. examination, examining
Exch. Exchange
exec. executive
exhbn. exhibition
expdn. expedition
expn. exposition
expt. experiment
exptl. experimental
Expy. Expressway
Ext. Extension
F.A. Field Artillery
FAA Federal Aviation Administration
FAO Food and Agriculture Organization (of the UN)
FBA Federal Bar Association
FBI Federal Bureau of Investigation
FCA Farm Credit Administration
FCC Federal Communications Commission
FCDA Federal Civil Defense Administration
FDA Food and Drug Administration
FDIA Federal Deposit Insurance Administration
FDIC Federal Deposit Insurance Corporation
FE, F.E. Forest Engineer
FEA Federal Energy Administration
Feb. February
fed. federal
fedn. federation
FERC Federal Energy Regulatory Commission
fgn. foreign
FHA Federal Housing Administration
fin. financial, finance
FL Florida
Fl. Floor
Fla. Florida
FMC Federal Maritime Commission
FNP Family Nurse Practitioner
FOA Foreign Operations Administration
found. foundation
FPC Federal Power Commission
FPO Fleet Post Office
frat. fraternity
FRS Federal Reserve System
FSA Federal Security Agency
Ft. Fort
FTC Federal Trade Commission
Fwy. Freeway

G-1 (or other number) Division of General Staff
GA, Ga. Georgia
GAO General Accounting Office
gastroent. gastroenterological
GATE Gifted and Talented Educators
GATT General Agreement on Tariffs and Trade
GE General Electric Company
gen. general
geneal. genealogical
geod. geodetic
geog. geographic, geographical
geol. geological
geophys. geophysical
geriat. geriatrics
gerontol. gerontological
G.H.Q. General Headquarters
GM General Motors Corporation
GMAC General Motors Acceptance Corporation
G.N.Ry. Great Northern Railway
gov. governor
govt. government
govtl. governmental
GPO Government Printing Office
grad. graduate, graduated
GSA General Services Administration
Gt. Great
GTE General Telephone and ElectricCompany
GU Guam
gynecol. gynecological

HBO Home Box Office
hdqs. headquarters
HEW Department of Health, Education and Welfare
HHD, H.H.D. Doctor of Humanities
HHFA Housing and Home Finance Agency
HHS Department of Health and Human Services
HI Hawaii
hist. historical, historic
HM, H.M. Master of Humanities
HMO Health Maintenance Organization
homeo. homeopathic
hon. honorary, honorable
Ho. of Dels. House of Delegates
Ho. of Reps. House of Representatives
hort. horticultural
hosp. hospital
H.S. High School
HUD Department of Housing and Urban Development
Hwy. Highway
hydrog. hydrographic

IA Iowa
IAEA International Atomic Energy Agency
IATSE International Alliance of Theatrical and Stage Employees and Moving Picture Operators of the United States and Canada
IBM International Business Machines Corporation
IBRD International Bank for Reconstruction and Development
ICA International Cooperation Administration
ICC Interstate Commerce Commission
ICCE International Council for Computers in Education
ICU Intensive Care Unit
ID Idaho
IEEE Institute of Electrical and Electronics Engineers
IFC International Finance Corporation
IGY International Geophysical Year
IL Illinois
Ill. Illinois
illus. illustrated
ILO International Labor Organization
IMF International Monetary Fund
IN Indiana
Inc. Incorporated
Ind. Indiana
ind. independent
Indpls. Indianapolis
indsl. industrial
inf. infantry
info. information
ins. insurance
insp. inspector
insp. gen. inspector general
inst. institute
instl. institutional
instn. institution
instr. instructor
instrn. instruction
instrnl. instructional
internat. international
intro. introduction
IRE Institute of Radio Engineers
IRS Internal Revenue Service
ITT International Telephone & Telegraph Corporation

JAG Judge Advocate General
JAGC Judge Advocate General Corps
Jan. January
Jaycees Junior Chamber of Commerce
JB, J.B. Jurum Baccalaureus
JCB, J.C.B. Juris Canoni Baccalaureus
JCD, J.C.D. Juris Canonici Doctor, Juris Civilis Doctor
JCL, J.C.L. Juris Canonici Licentiatus

JD, J.D. Juris Doctor
jg. junior grade
jour. journal
jr. junior
JSD, J.S.D. Juris Scientiae Doctor
JUD, J.U.D. Juris Utriusque Doctor
jud. judicial

Kans. Kansas
K.C. Knights of Columbus
K.P. Knights of Pythias
KS Kansas
K.T. Knight Templar
KY, Ky. Kentucky

LA, La. Louisiana
L.A. Los Angeles
lab. laboratory
L.Am. Latin America
lang. language
laryngol. laryngological
LB Labrador
LDS Latter Day Saints
LDS Church Church of Jesus Christ of Latter Day Saints
lectr. lecturer
legis. legislation, legislative
LHD, L.H.D. Doctor of Humane Letters
L.I. Long Island
libr. librarian, library
lic. licensed, license
L.I.R.R. Long Island Railroad
lit. literature
litig. litigation
LittB, Litt.B. Bachelor of Letters
LittD, Litt.D. Doctor of Letters
LLB, LL.B. Bachelor of Laws
LLD, L.L.D. Doctor of Laws
LLM, L.L.M. Master of Laws
Ln. Lane
L.&N.R.R. Louisville & Nashville Railroad
LPGA Ladies Professional Golf Association
LPN Licensed Practical Nurse
LS, L.S. Library Science (in degree)
lt. lieutenant
Ltd. Limited
Luth. Lutheran
LWV League of Women Voters

M. Master
m. married
MA, M.A. Master of Arts
MA Massachusetts
MADD Mothers Against Drunk Driving
mag. magazine
MAgr, M.Agr. Master of Agriculture
maj. major
Man. Manitoba
Mar. March
MArch, M.Arch. Master in Architecture
Mass. Massachusetts
math. mathematics, mathematical
MATS Military Air Transport Service
MB, M.B. Bachelor of Medicine
MB Manitoba
MBA, M.B.A. Master of Business Administration
MBS Mutual Broadcasting System
M.C. Medical Corps
MCE, M.C.E. Master of Civil Engineering
mcht. merchant
mcpl. municipal
MCS, M.C.S. Master of Commercial Science
MD, M.D. Doctor of Medicine
MD, Md. Maryland
MDiv Master of Divinity
MDip, M.Dip. Master in Diplomacy
mdse. merchandise
MDV, M.D.V. Doctor of Veterinary Medicine
ME, M.E. Mechanical Engineer
ME Maine
M.E.Ch. Methodist Episcopal Church
mech. mechanical
MEd., M.Ed. Master of Education
med. medical
MEE, M.E.E. Master of Electrical Engineering
mem. member
meml. memorial
merc. mercantile
met. metropolitan
metall. metallurgical
MetE, Met.E. Metallurgical Engineer
meteorol. meteorological
Meth. Methodist
Mex. Mexico
MF, M.F. Master of Forestry
MFA, M.F.A. Master of Fine Arts
mfg. manufacturing
mfr. manufacturer
mgmt. management
mgr. manager
MHA, M.H.A. Master of Hospital Administration
M.I. Military Intelligence
MI Michigan
Mich. Michigan
micros. microscopic, microscopical
mid. middle
mil. military
Milw. Milwaukee
Min. Minister
mineral. mineralogical
Minn. Minnesota
MIS Management Information Systems
Miss. Mississippi
MIT Massachusetts Institute of Technology
mktg. marketing
ML, M.L. Master of Laws
MLA Modern Language Association
M.L.D. Magister Legnum Diplomatic
MLitt, M.Litt. Master of Literature, Master of Letters
MLS, M.L.S. Master of Library Science
MME, M.M.E. Master of Mechanical Engineering
MN Minnesota
mng. managing
MO, Mo. Missouri
moblzn. mobilization
Mont. Montana
MP Northern Mariana Islands
M.P. Member of Parliament
MPA Master of Public Administration
MPE, M.P.E. Master of Physical Education
MPH, M.P.H. Master of Public Health
MPhil, M.Phil. Master of Philosophy
MPL, M.P.L. Master of Patent Law
Mpls. Minneapolis
MRE, M.R.E. Master of Religious Education
MRI Magnetic Resonance Imaging
MS, M.S. Master of Science
MS, Ms. Mississippi
MSc, M.Sc. Master of Science
MSChemE Master of Science in Chemical Engineering
MSEE Master of Science in Electrical Engineering
MSF, M.S.F. Master of Science of Forestry
MSN Master of Science in Nursing
MST, M.S.T. Master of Sacred Theology
MSW, M.S.W. Master of Social Work
MT Montana
Mt. Mount
MTO Mediterranean Theatre of Operation
MTV Music Television
mus. museum, musical
MusB, Mus.B. Bachelor of Music
MusD, Mus.D. Doctor of Music
MusM, Mus.M. Master of Music
mut. mutual
MVP Most Valuable Player
mycol. mycological

N. North
NAACOG Nurses Association of the American College of Obstetricians and Gynecologists
NAACP National Association for the Advancement of Colored People
NACA National Advisory Committee for Aeronautics
NACDL National Association of Criminal Defense Lawyers
NACU National Association of Colleges and Universities
NAD National Academy of Design
NAE National Academy of Engineering, National Association of Educators
NAESP National Association of Elementary School Principals
NAFE National Association of Female Executives
N.Am. North America
NAM National Association of Manufacturers
NAMH National Association for Mental Health
NAPA National Association of Performing Artists
NARAS National Academy of Recording Arts and Sciences
NAREB National Association of Real Estate Boards
NARS National Archives and Record Service
NAS National Academy of Sciences
NASA National Aeronautics and Space Administration
NASP National Association of School Psychologists
NASW National Association of Social Workers
nat. national
NATAS National Academy of Television Arts and Sciences
NATO North Atlantic Treaty Organization
NATOUSA North African Theatre of Operations, United States Army
nav. navigation
NB, N.B. New Brunswick
NBA National Basketball Association
NBC National Broadcasting Company
NC, N.C. North Carolina
NCAA National College Athletic Association
NCCJ National Conference of Christians and Jews
ND, N.D. North Dakota
NDEA National Defense Education Act
NE Nebraska
NE, N.E. Northeast
NEA National Education Association
Nebr. Nebraska
NEH National Endowment for Humanities
neurol. neurological
Nev. Nevada
NF Newfoundland
NFL National Football League
Nfld. Newfoundland
NG National Guard

NH, N.H. New Hampshire
NHL National Hockey League
NIH National Institutes of Health
NIMH National Institute of Mental Health
NJ, N.J. New Jersey
NLRB National Labor Relations Board
NM New Mexico
N.Mex. New Mexico
No. Northern
NOAA National Oceanographic and Atmospheric Administration
NORAD North America Air Defense
Nov. November
NOW National Organization for Women
N.P.Ry. Northern Pacific Railway
nr. near
NRA National Rifle Association
NRC National Research Council
NS, N.S. Nova Scotia
NSC National Security Council
NSF National Science Foundation
NSTA National Science Teachers Association
NSW New South Wales
N.T. New Testament
NT Northwest Territories
nuc. nuclear
numis. numismatic
NV Nevada
NW, N.W. Northwest
N.W.T. Northwest Territories
NY, N.Y. New York
N.Y.C. New York City
NYU New York University
N.Z. New Zealand

OAS Organization of American States
ob-gyn obstetrics-gynecology
obs. observatory
obstet. obstetrical
occupl. occupational
oceanog. oceanographic
Oct. October
OD, O.D. Doctor of Optometry
OECD Organization for Economic Cooperation and Development
OEEC Organization of European Economic Cooperation
OEO Office of Economic Opportunity
ofcl. official
OH Ohio
OK Oklahoma
Okla. Oklahoma
ON Ontario
Ont. Ontario
oper. operating
ophthal. ophthalmological
ops. operations
OR Oregon
orch. orchestra
Oreg. Oregon
orgn. organization
orgnl. organizational
ornithol. ornithological
orthop. orthopedic
OSHA Occupational Safety and Health Administration
OSRD Office of Scientific Research and Development
OSS Office of Strategic Services
osteo. osteopathic
otol. otological
otolaryn. otolaryngological

PA, Pa. Pennsylvania
P.A. Professional Association
paleontol. paleontological
path. pathological
PBS Public Broadcasting System
P.C. Professional Corporation
PE Prince Edward Island
pediat. pediatrics
P.E.I. Prince Edward Island
PEN Poets, Playwrights, Editors, Essayists and Novelists (international association)
penol. penological
P.E.O. women's organization (full name not disclosed)
pers. personnel
pfc. private first class
PGA Professional Golfers' Association of America
PHA Public Housing Administration
pharm. pharmaceutical
PharmD, Pharm.D. Doctor of Pharmacy
PharmM, Pharm.M. Master of Pharmacy
PhB, Ph.B. Bachelor of Philosophy
PhD, Ph.D. Doctor of Philosophy
PhDChemE Doctor of Science in Chemical Engineering
PhM, Ph.M. Master of Philosophy
Phila. Philadelphia
philharm. philharmonic
philol. philological
philos. philosophical
photog. photographic
phys. physical
physiol. physiological
Pitts. Pittsburgh
Pk. Park
Pky. Parkway
Pl. Place
P.&L.E.R.R. Pittsburgh & Lake Erie Railroad
Plz. Plaza
PNP Pediatric Nurse Practitioner
P.O. Post Office
PO Box Post Office Box
polit. political
poly. polytechnic, polytechnical
PQ Province of Quebec
PR, P.R. Puerto Rico
prep. preparatory
pres. president
Presbyn. Presbyterian
presdl. presidential
prin. principal
procs. proceedings
prod. produced (play production)
prodn. production
prodr. producer
prof. professor
profl. professional
prog. progressive
propr. proprietor
pros. atty. prosecuting attorney
pro tem. pro tempore
PSRO Professional Services Review Organization
psychiat. psychiatric
psychol. psychological
PTA Parent-Teachers Association
ptnr. partner
PTO Pacific Theatre of Operations, Parent Teacher Organization
pub. publisher, publishing, published
pub. public
publ. publication
pvt. private

quar. quarterly
qm. quartermaster
Q.M.C. Quartermaster Corps
Que. Quebec

radiol. radiological
RAF Royal Air Force
RCA Radio Corporation of America
RCAF Royal Canadian Air Force
RD Rural Delivery
Rd. Road
R&D Research & Development
REA Rural Electrification Administration
rec. recording
ref. reformed
regt. regiment
regtl. regimental
rehab. rehabilitation
rels. relations
Rep. Republican
rep. representative
Res. Reserve
ret. retired
Rev. Reverend
rev. review, revised
RFC Reconstruction Finance Corporation
RFD Rural Free Delivery
rhinol. rhinological
RI, R.I. Rhode Island
RISD Rhode Island School of Design
Rlwy. Railway
Rm. Room
RN, R.N. Registered Nurse
roentgenol. roentgenological
ROTC Reserve Officers Training Corps
RR Rural Route
R.R. Railroad
rsch. research
rschr. researcher
Rt. Route

S. South
s. son
SAC Strategic Air Command
SAG Screen Actors Guild
SALT Strategic Arms Limitation Talks
S.Am. South America
san. sanitary
SAR Sons of the American Revolution
Sask. Saskatchewan
savs. savings
SB, S.B. Bachelor of Science
SBA Small Business Administration
SC, S.C. South Carolina
SCAP Supreme Command Allies Pacific
ScB, Sc.B. Bachelor of Science
SCD, S.C.D. Doctor of Commercial Science
ScD, Sc.D. Doctor of Science
sch. school
sci. science, scientific
SCLC Southern Christian Leadership Conference
SCV Sons of Confederate Veterans
SD, S.D. South Dakota
SE, S.E. Southeast
SEATO Southeast Asia Treaty Organization
SEC Securities and Exchange Commission
sec. secretary
sect. section
seismol. seismological
sem. seminary
Sept. September
s.g. senior grade
sgt. sergeant
SHAEF Supreme Headquarters Allied Expeditionary Forces
SHAPE Supreme Headquarters Allied Powers in Europe
S.I. Staten Island
S.J. Society of Jesus (Jesuit)
SJD Scientiae Juridicae Doctor
SK Saskatchewan

SM, S.M. Master of Science
SNP Society of Nursing Professionals
So. Southern
soc. society
sociol. sociological
S.P.Co. Southern Pacific Company
spkr. speaker
spl. special
splty. specialty
Sq. Square
S.R. Sons of the Revolution
sr. senior
SS Steamship
SSS Selective Service System
St. Saint, Street
sta. station
stats. statistics
statis. statistical
STB, S.T.B. Bachelor of Sacred Theology
stblzn. stabilization
STD, S.T.D. Doctor of Sacred Theology
std. standard
Ste. Suite
subs. subsidiary
SUNY State University of New York
supr. supervisor
supt. superintendent
surg. surgical
svc. service
SW, S.W. Southwest
sys. system

TAPPI Technical Association of the Pulp and Paper Industry
tb. tuberculosis
tchg. teaching
tchr. teacher
tech. technical, technology
technol. technological
tel. telephone
Tel. & Tel. Telephone & Telegraph
telecom. telecommunications
temp. temporary
Tenn. Tennessee
Ter. Territory
Ter. Terrace
TESOL Teachers of English to Speakers of Other Languages
Tex. Texas
ThD, Th.D. Doctor of Theology
theol. theological
ThM, Th.M. Master of Theology
TN Tennessee
tng. training
topog. topographical
trans. transaction, transferred
transl. translation, translated
transp. transportation
treas. treasurer
TT Trust Territory
TV television
TVA Tennessee Valley Authority
TWA Trans World Airlines
twp. township
TX Texas
typog. typographical

U. University
UAW United Auto Workers
UCLA University of California at Los Angeles
UDC United Daughters of the Confederacy
U.K. United Kingdom
UN United Nations
UNESCO United Nations Educational, Scientific and Cultural Organization
UNICEF United Nations International Children's Emergency Fund
univ. university
UNRRA United Nations Relief and Rehabilitation Administration
UPI United Press International
U.P.R.R. United Pacific Railroad
urol. urological
U.S. United States
U.S.A. United States of America
USAAF United States Army Air Force
USAF United States Air Force
USAFR United States Air Force Reserve
USAR United States Army Reserve
USCG United States Coast Guard
USCGR United States Coast Guard Reserve
USES United States Employment Service
USIA United States Information Agency
USMC United States Marine Corps
USMCR United States Marine Corps Reserve
USN United States Navy
USNG United States National Guard
USNR United States Naval Reserve
USO United Service Organizations
USPHS United States Public Health Service
USS United States Ship
USSR Union of the Soviet Socialist Republics
USTA United States Tennis Association
USV United States Volunteers
UT Utah
VA Veterans Administration
VA, Va. Virginia
vet. veteran, veterinary
VFW Veterans of Foreign Wars
VI, V.I. Virgin Islands
vice pres. vice president
vis. visiting
VISTA Volunteers in Service to America
VITA Volunteers in Technical Assistance
vocat. vocational
vol. volunteer, volume
v.p. vice president
vs. versus
VT, Vt. Vermont

W, W. West
WA Washington (state)
WAC Women's Army Corps
Wash. Washington (state)
WATS Wide Area Telecommunications Service
WAVES Women's Reserve, US Naval Reserve
WCTU Women's Christian Temperance Union
we. western
W. Ger. Germany, Federal Republic of
WHO World Health Organization
WI Wisconsin
W.I. West Indies
Wis. Wisconsin
WSB Wage Stabilization Board
WV West Virginia
W.Va. West Virginia
WWI World War I
WWII World War II
WY Wyoming
Wyo. Wyoming

YK Yukon Territory
YMCA Young Men's Christian Association
YMHA Young Men's Hebrew Association
YM & YWHA Young Men's and Young Women's Hebrew Association
yr. year
YT, Y.T. Yukon Territory
YWCA Young Women's Christian Association

zool. zoological

Alphabetical Practices

Names are arranged alphabetically according to the surnames, and under identical surnames according to the first given name. If both surname and first given name are identical, names are arranged alphabetically according to the second given name.

Surnames beginning with De, Des, Du, however capitalized or spaced, are recorded with the prefix preceding the surname and arranged alphabetically under the letter D.

Surnames beginning with Mac and Mc are arranged alphabetically under M.

Surnames beginning with Saint or St. appear after names that begin Sains, and are arranged according to the second part of the name, e.g. St. Clair before Saint Dennis.

Surnames beginning with Van, Von, or von are arranged alphabetically under the letter V.

Compound surnames are arranged according to the first member of the compound.

Many hyphenated Arabic names begin Al-, El-, or al-. These names are alphabetized according to each Biographee's designation of last name. Thus Al-Bahar, Neta may be listed either under Al- or under Bahar, depending on the preference of the listee.

Also, Arabic names have a variety of possible spellings when transposed to English. Spelling of these names is always based on the practice of the Biographee. Some Biographees use a Western form of word order, while others prefer the Arabic word sequence.

Similarly, Asian names may have no comma between family and given names, but some Biographees have chosen to add the comma. In each case, punctuation follows the preference of the Biographee.

Parentheses used in connection with a name indicate which part of the full name is usually deleted in common usage. Hence Chambers, E(lizabeth) Anne indicates that the usual form of the given name is E. Anne. In such a case, the parentheses are ignored in alphabetizing and the name would be arranged as Chambers, Elizabeth Anne. However, if the name is recorded Chambers, (Elizabeth) Anne, signifying that the entire name Elizabeth is not commonly used, the alphabetizing would be arranged as though the name were Chambers, Anne. If an entire middle or last name is enclosed in parentheses, that portion of the name is used in the alphabetical arrangement. Hence Chambers, Elizabeth (Anne) would be arranged as Chambers, Elizabeth Anne.

Where more than one spelling, word order, or name of an individual is frequently encountered, the sketch has been entered under the form preferred by the Biographee, with cross-references under alternate forms.

Who'sWho in the West®

Biographies

AALTO, MADELEINE, library director; BA, Wellesley Coll., 1964; BLS, U. Toronto, 1967. Clerical asst. Toronto Pub. Libr., 1964-66, children's libr. Parkdale br., 1968-69, collection libr. Spaced Out libr., 1969-73, br. head Annette St. br., 1973-74, coord. adult svcs., 1974-75; chief libr. East York Pub. Libr., 1975-84, Greater Victoria Pub. Libr., 1984-88; dir. Vancouver (B.C.) Pub. Libr., Can., 1988—. Contbr. intro. to A Geography for Children (Philippe du Fresnoy), 1968. Recipient Commemorative medal 125th Anniversary Confederation Can., 1993. Mem. B.C. Libr. Assn. Office: Vancouver Pub Libr 350 W Georgia St Vancouver BC Canada V6B 6B1

AARON, CYNTHIA G. judge; b. Mpls., May 3, 1957; d. Allen Harold and Barbara Lois (Perlman) A.; m. Craig D. Higgs, May 15, 1993. Student, Brandeis U., 1975-77; BA with honors and distinction, Stanford U., 1979; JD cum laude, Harvard U., 1984. Bar: Calif. 1984, U.S. Dist. Ct. (so. dist.) Calif. 1984, U.S. Ct. Appeals (9th cir.) 1984, U.S. Dist. Ct. (no. dist.) Calif. 1986, U.S. Dist. Ct. (ctrl. dist.) Calif. 1988, U.S. Supreme Ct. 1991. Rsch. asst. to Prof. Alan Dershowitz Law Sch. Harvard U., 1982-83; trial atty. Fed. Defenders San Diego, Inc., 1984-88; ptnr. Aaron & Cortez, 1988-94; U.S. magistrate judge U.S. Dist. Ct. (so. dist.) Calif., San Diego, 1994—. Instr. pacific regional program Nat. Inst. for Trial Advocacy, 1988-91, instr. deposition skills workshop, 1993; adj. prof. Calif. We. Sch. Law, San Diego, 1990-93; instr. advocacy trial skills acad. Inst. for Criminal Def., San Diego, 1992-94; adj. prof. law sch. U. San Diego, 1993, 95. Bd. dirs. San Diego Vol. Lawyer Program, 2001—. Mem. Nat. Assn. Women Judges, San Diego County Judges Assn. (pres. 2001—), Lawyers Club San Diego, City Club San Diego, Phi Beta Kappa. Office: US Dist Ct So Dist 940 Front St Ste 1185 San Diego CA 92101-8940

AARONSON, ROBERT JAY, aviation executive; b. Temple, Tex., June 8, 1942; s. Leonard and Ruth (Lader) A.; m. Louise Elaine Loia, June 6, 1967; children: Steven Bradford, Suzanne Denise. AB, Brown U., 1964; M in Govtl. Adminstrn., Wharton Sch., U. Pa., 1965. Spl. asst. Southeastern Pa. Transp. Authority, Phila., 1965-67; transp. rep. Urban Mass Transp. Adminstrn., Washington, 1967-69; transp. adviser HUD, 1969-71; aviation adminstr. Md. Dept. Transp., Balt., 1972-78; asso. adminstr. for airports FAA, Washington, 1978-81; dir. aviation Port Authority of N.Y. and N.J., N.Y.C., 1981-89; pres. Air Transport Assn. Am., Washington, 1989-92; exec. v.p. Lockheed Air Terminal, Inc., Burbank, Calif., 1993-94, Airport Group Internat., Inc., Glendale, 1995-97; pres. Strategies For Airports, Inc., Encino, 1997-98; exec. v.p. Lufthansa Cons. GmbH, Encino, 1999—. Lectr. Royal Aero. Transport Course, Oxford U. Samuel S. Fels fellow, 1964-65 Mem. Nat. Assn. State Aviation Ofcls. (pres. 1978), Airport Operators Coun. Internat. (chmn. 1987-88), Am. Assn. Airport Execs., Wings Club (pres. 1992), Mountaingate Country Club. Home: 16477 Oldham St Encino CA 91436-3701 Office: 16133 Ventura Blvd Ste 1245 Encino CA 91436-2425 E-mail: vaaronson@compuserve.com

ABADY, ARLENE, editor; Editor The Colo. Lawyer, Denver. Office: Colo Bar Assn Inc 1900 Grant St Fl 9 Denver CO 80203-4301

ABARBANEL, HENRY DON ISAAC, physicist, academic administrator; b. Washington, May 31, 1943; s. Abraham Robert and Selma Helen (Kintberger) A.; m. Gwen Lorita Lewis, May 27, 1965 (div. July 1974); m. Beth Leah Levine, Sept. 12, 1982; children: Brett Lillian, Sara Alexis. BS in Physics, Calif. Inst. Tech., 1963; PhD in Physics, Princeton U., 1966. Rsch. assoc. Stanford (Calif.) Linear Accelerator Ctr., 1967-68; asst. prof. physics Princeton (N.J.) U., 1968-72; physicist Theoretical Physics Dept. Fermi Nat. Accelerator Lab., Batavia, Ill., 1972-81; staff scientist Lawrence Berkeley Lab., 1979-82; rsch. physicist Marine Phys. Lab. Scripps Instn. Oceanography, La Jolla, Calif., 1983—; dir. Inst. for Nonlinear Sci. U. Calif. San Diego, La Jolla, 1986—, acting dir. Inst. for Nonlinear Sci., 1986, dir. Inst. for Nonlinear Sci., 1986—, prof. physics in residence, 1986-88, prof. physics, 1988—. Cons. Lockheed Palo Alto (Calif.) Rsch. Lab., 1990—; vis. scientist Ctr. Etudes Nucleaires Saclay, France, 1970, Stanford Linear Accelerator Ctr., 1971, 1975-76, Inst. Haute Études Sci., Bures-sur-Yvette, France, 1989, Inst. Applied Physics Acad. Scis. USSR, Gorky, 1990; adj. prof. physics U. Calif. San Diego, 1982; vis. prof. U. Calif., Santa Cruz, 1975-76, San Diego, 1982, 86, Japan Soc. for the Promotion Sci., 1976; vis. assoc. prof. Stanford U., 1975-76; lectr. dept. physics U. Calif., Berkeley, 1980; chmn. steering com. joint program in nonlinear sci. U. Calif.-NASA, 1987-88; lectr. U. Chgo., 1973, U. Calif., Berkeley, 1980; exchange scientist Landau Inst. for Theoretical Physics NAS, Moscow, Lenningrad, 1977; mem. U.S. Physics Del. to People's Republic China, 1973; mem. JASON, 1974—, mem. steering com., 1985-88, participant, project leader; cons. T-div. Los Alamos (N.Mex.) Nat. Sci. Lab., 1980-84; mem. bd. visitors in physics Office Naval Rsch., 1987, mem. bd. visitors in phys. oceanography, 1989-91; mem. bd. tech. advisors Program in Global Climate Change Dept. Energy, 1990—; invited speaker numerous profl. meetings. Co-editor: Encyclopedia of Chaos, 1991; editor-in-chief Springer-Verlag Series in Nonlinear Sci., 1989—; sci. referee various physics jours. Mem. Planning Commn., Del Mar, Calif., 1989-92, mem. city coun., 1992—. NSF predoctoral fellow, 1963-66, NSF postdoctoral fellow, 1966-67, Woodrow Wilson fellow (hon.); grantee Defense Advanced Rsch. and Projects Agy., 1979-83, 83-84, 86-89, 86-91, U.S. Dept. Energy, 1981-83, Office Naval Rsch., 1983-88, NASA, 1986, 88-89, 90-91, Lockheed Palo Alto Rsch. Lab., 1991—, U.S. Army Rsch. Office, 1991-94. Mem. Am. Phys. Soc., Am. Geophys. Union, Soc. for Indsl. and Applied Maths. Office: U Calif San Diego Inst Nonlinear Science Ucsd Mc # 0402 La Jolla CA 92093

ABBE, CHARLES J. manufacturing company executive; b. 1941; Sr. ptnr. McKinsey & Co., Inc., San Francisco; various sr. mgmt. positions Raychem Corp., 1989-96; v.p., gen. mgr. Santa Rosa divsn. Optical Coating Lab., Inc., 1996-98, dir., pres., CEO, 1998-2000, sr. v.p., sr. oper. officer, 2000; pres., COO JDS Uniphase Corp., San Jose, 2000—. Office: 163 Baypointe Pkwy San Jose CA 95134 Office Fax: 408-954-0760

ABBOTT, ISABELLA AIONA, retired biology educator; b. Hana, Maui, Hawaii, June 20, 1919; d. Loo Yuen and Annie Patseu (Chung) Aiona; m. Donald P. Abbott, Mar. 3, 1943 (dec.); 1 dau., Ann Kaiue Abbott. A.B., U. Hawaii, 1941; M.S., U. Mich., 1942; Ph.D., U. Calif., Berkeley, 1950. Prof. biology Stanford U., 1972-82; G.P. Wilder prof. botany U. Hawaii, 1978-98, ret., 1998. Vis. research biologist and tchr., Japan and Chile. Author: (with G.J. Hollenberg) Marine Algae of California, 1976, La'au Hawaii, traditional Hawaiian uses of plants, 1992; contbr. articles to profl. jours. Co-recipient N.Y. Bot. Garden award for best book in botany, 1978; recipient Merit award Bot. Soc. Am., 1995, G.M. Smith medal Nat. Acad. Scis., 1997. Fellow AAAS; mem. Internat. Phycological Soc. (treas. 1964-68), Western Soc. Naturalists (sec. 1962-64, pres. 1977), Phycological Soc. Am., Brit. Phycological Soc., Hawaiian Bot. Soc. Office: U Hawaii Botany Dept 3190 Maile Way Honolulu HI 96822-2232

ABBOTT, ROBERT DEAN, education scientist; b. Twin Falls, Idaho, Dec. 19, 1946; s. Charles Dean and Billie June (Moore) A.; m. Sylvia Patricia Keim, Dec. 16, 1967; children: Danielle, Matthew. B.A., Calif. Western U., San Diego, 1967; M.S., U. Wash., 1968, Ph.D., 1970. Asst. prof., assoc. prof. Calif. State U.-Fullerton, 1970-75; asst. prof., prof. ednl. psychology U. Wash., Seattle, 1975—; dir. Ctr. Inst. Devel. and Research, Seattle, 1983-92. Author: Elementary Multivariate Statistics, 1983; contbr. articles to profl. jours. Calif. State scholar, 1964-67 Fellow Am. Psychol. Assn.; mem. Am. Ednl. Research Assn., Am. Stats. Assn., Psychometric Soc. Methodist. Office: Ednl Psych 312 Miller PO Box 353600 Seattle WA 98195-3600

ABDUL-JABBAR, KAREEM (LEWIS FERDINAND ALCINDOR), retired professional basketball player, sports commentator; b. N.Y.C., Apr. 16, 1947; s. Ferdinand Lewis and Cora Alcindor; m. Habiba (Janice Brown), 1971 (div. 1973); children: Habiba, Kareem, Sultana, Amir. B.A., UCLA, 1969. Basketball player with Milw. Bucks, 1969-75, Los Angeles Lakers, 1975-89; owner Kareem Productions. Now commentator ESPN, Bristol, Ct. Became NBA all-time leading scorer, 1984; appeared on TV in episodes of Mannix, The Man from Atlantis, Diff'rent Strokes, Tales from the Darkside, Pryor's Place, The ABC Afterschool Spl.; appeared in movies: The Fish that Saved Pittsburgh, 1979, Airplane, 1980, Fletch, 1985; author: (with Peter Knobler) Giant Steps: An Autobiography of Kareem Abdul-Jabbar, 1983, (with Mignon McCarthy) Kareem, 1990. Named Rookie of Year NBA, 1970; recipient Maurice Podoloff Cup; named Most Valuable Player NBA, 1971, 72, 74, 76, 77, 80; player NBA All-Star game, 1970-87, 89; named to NBA 35th Anniversary All-Time Team, 1980; NBA Playoff Most Valuable Player, 1971, 85; mem. NBA Championship Team, 1971, 80, 82, 85, 87, 88, NCAA Championship Team, 1967, 68, 69; named NCAA Tournament Most Outstanding Player, 1967, 68, 69 Muslim. Avocation: jazz.

ABDUL-RAHIM, SHAREEF, professional basketball player; b. Dec. 11, 1976; Forward, guard Vancouver Grizzlies. Named to NBA All-Rookie Firest Team, 1996-97, Third Team All-Am., AP. Avocations: pool, collecting basketball jerseys, movies. Office: Vancouver Grizzlies 800 Griffiths Way Vancouver BC Canada V6B 6G1

ABEL, ELIZABETH A. dermatologist; b. Hartford, Conn., Mar. 16, 1940; d. Frederick A. and Rose (Borovicka) A.; m. Barton Lane; children: Barton, Geoffrey, Suzanne. Student, Colby-Sawyer Coll., 1957-60; BS, Wash. Hosp. Ctr. Sch. Med. Tech., 1961, U. Md., 1965, MD cum laude, 1967. Diplomate Am. Bd. Dermatology. Intern San Francisco Gen. Hosp., 1967-68; resident in medicine, fellow in oncology U. Calif. Med. Ctr., San Francisco, 1968-69; resident in dermatology NYU Med. Ctr., 1969-72, chief resident, 1971-72, USPHS research trainee in dermatology, 1972-73; dep. chief dept. dermatology USPHS Hosp., S.I., N.Y., 1973-74; instr. clin. dermatology Columbia U. Coll. Physicians and Surgeons, N.Y.C., 1974-75, Stanford (Calif.) U. Sch. Medicine, 1975-77, clin. asst. prof. dermatology, 1977-82, asst. prof. dermatology, 1982-90, clin. assoc. prof., 1990-96, clin. prof., 1996—. Asst. editor Jour. Am. Acad. Dermatology, 1993-98; mem. med. adv. bd. The Nat. Psoriasis Found., 1993-95. Contbr. articles to sci. jours. Mellon Found. fellow, 1983, 87. Fellow Am. Acad. Dermatology; mem. N.Am. Clin. Dermatologic Soc., San Francisco Dermatologic Soc., Internat. Soc. Dermatology Surgery, Pacific Dermatologic Assn., Women's Dermatologic Soc., Noah Worcester Dermatologic Soc., Alpha Omega Alpha. Episcopalian. Avocations: piano, golf, reading. Office: 2660 Grant Rd Ste D Mountain View CA 94040-4315

ABEL, MICHAEL L. marketing executive; b. New London, Wis., Jan. 15, 1952; s. William A. and Delores R. (Shuey) A.; m. Monica L. Miller, Dec. 18, 1971; children: Richard M., David M. AAS, Joliet (Ill.) Jr. Coll., 1975; BA in Bus. Adminstrn., Lewis U., 1977, MBA, 1979. Lab. technician No. Petrochem. Co., Morris, Ill., 1975-76, tech. specialist, 1976-80, nat. account rep. Des Plaines, 1980-82; product mgr. Enron Chem. Co., Omaha, 1982-85, mktg. mgr., 1985-87; sr. account exec. Quantum Chem. Co., Rancho Mirage, Calif., 1987-89; sr. v.p. N.Am. ops. Intac Automotive Products, Inc., Lemont, Ill., 1989—; pres., chief exec. officer Desert Leisure Devel. Corp., Palm Springs, 1991—, bd. dirs. Bd. dirs. Palm Cts. Assn., Rancho Mirage, 1988-97, The Kids Business, Inc., Rancho Mirage, 1996—. Patentee in chem. engrng. field. Pres. Palm Ct. Owners Assn., Rancho Mirage, 1988-97; mem. Rep. Presdl. Task Force, 1990—. Mem. ASTM, Soc. Automotive Engrs., Nat. Assn. Corrosion Engrs. (sec. 1981-82), Internat. Platform Assn. Republican. Lutheran. Home: 36845 Palm Ct Rancho Mirage CA 92270-2206

ABELS, ROBERT FREDERICK, tax consultant; b. West Palm Beach, Fla., Nov. 18, 1926; s. John Frederick and Nelly (Bulfin) A.; m. Shirley Mae Larsen, May 31, 1953; children: Robert Frederick, Steven John, Richard Alan. Student, U. S.C., 1946-47; ed. flight tng. program, Naval Air Sta., Pensacola, Fla., 1947-49; BS, Naval Postgrad. Sch., Monterey, Calif., 1965; MBA in Fin., U. West Fla., 1971. Enlisted USN, 1944, commd. ensign, 1949, advanced through grades to comdr., 1963, radar operator PT boats, 1945-46, radar and radio operator PT Boats World War II, aviator Republic of Korea, 1950-51, 53, Pensacola, Fla., Vietnam, 1962-63, 65-66, ret., 1969; tchr. math. and bus. Skyline H.S., Lemon Grove, Calif., 1971-83, Lemon Grove, 1983. Past ptnr., salesman area real estate co.; enrolled agent IRS, Washington, 1984. Decorated Bronze Star, Air medal, Vietnamese Cross Gallantry. Mem. Nat. Assn. Enrolled Agts., Inland Soc. Tax. Cons., Nat. Assn. Tax Consultors. Republican. Lutheran.

ABELSON, JOHN NORMAN, biology educator; b. Grand Coulee Dam, Wash., Oct. 19, 1938; B.S., Wash. State U., 1960; Ph.D., Johns Hopkins U., 1965; postgrad., Lb. Molecular Biology, Cambridge, Eng., 1965-68. Asst. prof. dept. chemistry U. Calif.-San Diego, 1968-73, assoc. prof., 1973-77, prof., 1977-82; prof. biology Calif. Inst. Tech., Pasadena, 1982—. Founding bd. dirs. Agouron Inst. (La Jolla), Calif., 1979—; co-founder Agouron Pharmaceuticals, Inc. Asst. editor: Analytical Biochemistry, 1980-87; mem. editorial bd. Jour. Biol. Chemistry, 1981-85; mem. editorial com. Ann. Rev. Inc., 1982—, Ann. Rev. Biochemistry; editor Methods in Enzymology; contbr. numerous articles to profl. jours. Mem. Am. Soc. Biol. Chemists, Am. Chem. Soc., Nat. Acad. Scis., Am. Acad. Arts and Scis. Home: 1097 Blanche St Apt 316 Pasadena CA 91106-3062 Office: Calif Inst Tech 147-75 1200 E Calif Blvd Pasadena CA 91125-0001

ABERCROMBIE, NEIL, congressman; s. G. Don and Vera June (Giersdorf) A.; m. Nancie Ellen Caraway, July 18, 1981; BA Union Coll., 1959, MA U. Hawaii, 1964, PhD in Am. Studies, 1974; Mem. Hawaii state legislature, 1974-86; elected to U.S. Congress, 1986, 91—, mem. resources com., armed svcs com., nat. security com.; mem. Honolulu City Coun., 1988-90. Democrat. *

ABERLE, DAVID FRIEND, anthropologist, educator; b. St. Paul, Nov. 23, 1918; s. David Winfield and Lisette (Friend) A.; m. Eleanor Kathleen Gough, Sept. 5, 1955 (dec. Sept. 1990); 1 son. AB summa cum laude, Harvard U., 1940; PhD in Anthropology, Columbia U., 1950; postgrad., U. N.Mex., summers 1938-40, No. Ariz. U., summers 1971, 73, Harvard U., 1946-47. Instr. dept. social rels. Harvard U., Cambridge, Mass., 1947-50, rsch. assoc. Sch. Pub. Health, 1948-50; vis. assoc. prof. Page Sch., Johns Hopkins U., Balt., 1950-52; assoc. prof., then prof. dept. sociology and dept. anthropology U. Mich., Ann Arbor, 1952-60; fellow Ctr. Advanced Study in Behavioral Scis., Stanford, Calif., 1955-56; Simon vis. prof. and hon. research assoc. dept. social anthropology Manchester U., Eng., 1960-61; prof., chmn. dept. anthropology Brandeis U., Waltham, Mass., 1961-63; prof. dept. anthropology U. Oreg., Eugene, 1963-67; prof. dept. anthropology and sociology U. B.C., Vancouver, Can., 1967-83, prof. emeritus Can., 1983—. Cons. Inst. Devel. Anthropology, Inc., Binghamton, N.Y., 1978-79; cons. to attys. Navajo Tribe, 1976-77; disting. lectr. Am. Anthrop. Assn., 1986. Author: The Peyote Religion Among the Navaho, 1966, (with Isidore Dyen) Lexical Reconstruction, the Case of the Proto-Athapaskan Kinship System, 1974; contbr. articles on anthropological theory and Navajo Indians to scholarly jours.; rev. editor: Am. Anthropologist, 1952-55. With U.S. Army, 1942-46. Recipient Social Sci. Research Council Demobilization award, 1946; Harvard U. Nat. scholar; NIMH grantee; USPHS grantee; Wenner-Gren Found. grantee, 1954-63; NSF grantee, 1965-72; Can. Council grantee, 1969-77; Social Scis. and Humanities Research Council Can., 1978-80, 84-86 Fellow Royal Soc. Can., Royal Anthropol. Inst. of Gt. Britain and Ireland; mem. Am. Anthropol. Assn. (mem. panel on Navajo-Hopi land dispute 1973-95), Am. Sociol. Assn., Soc. Applied Anthropology, Am. Ethnol. Assn., Can. Anthropology Soc., Soc. Lesbian and Gay Anthropologists, Phi Beta Kappa. Jewish. Office: U BC Dept Anthropology 6303 NW Marine Dr Vancouver BC Canada V6T 2B2

ABERMAN, HAROLD MARK, veterinarian; b. Chgo., Aug. 5, 1956; s. Howard Oscar and Goldie Esther Aberman. BS, Purdue U., 1979, MSE, 1987, BSE, 1986, DVM, 1983. NIH postdoctoral fellow Purdue U., West Lafayette, 1983-87; dir. sci. and biol. affairs Howmedica div. Pfizer, Rutherford, 1987-99; pres. Applied Biol. Concepts, Los Alamitos, Calif., 1996—; dir. devel. Orthop. Rsch. Inst., Long Beach, 1999-2001. Adj. prof. N.C. State U., Raleigh, 1988—, Miss. State U., Starkville, Miss., 1990—, Purdue U., 1991—. Contbr. articles to profl. jours. Mem. ASME, AVMA, Am. Animal Hosp. Assn., Ortho. Rsch. Soc., Soc. Biomechanics, Acad. Surg. Rsch. Jewish. Home: 14 Dewberry Way Irvine CA 92612-2711 Office: Applied Biol Concepts 12581 Silver Fox Rd Los Alamitos CA 90720-5234 E-mail: haroldabc@aol.com

ABERNATHY, SHIELDS B. allergist, immunologist, internist; b. Bronxville, N.Y., Mar. 14, 1951; m. Leslie Abernathy; children: Amelia, Camille, Lant. BA, Ohio Wesleyan U., 1973; MS, Harvard U., 1975; MD, Med. Coll. Pa., 1979. Diplomate Am. Bd. Internal Medicine, Am. Bd. Allergy and Immunology, eligible Am. Preventive Medicine, Nat. Bd. Med. Examiners; Qualified Med. Examiner Calif.; Fed. Aviation Med. Examiner; ACLS Am. Heart Assn. Intern in internal medicine L.A. County/U. So. Calif. Med. Ctr., L.A., 1979-80; resident in internal medicine Hosp. of Good Samaritan, L.A., 1980-81; resident UCLA Wadsworth VA Med. Ctr., 1981-82, fellow allergy and immunology, 1982-84. Instr. pub. edn. programs; med. philanthropic facilitator, Philippines, 2000, India, 2001, Indochina, 2001; rschr. in field. Fellow Am. Coll. Allergy and Immunology, Am. Acad. Allergy and Immunology; mem. Am. Med. Health Assn., Am. Pub. Health Assn. (internat. health sect.). Office: 1050 Las Tablas Rd Ste 3 Templeton CA 93465-9792

ABERNETHY, ROBERT JOHN, real estate developer; b. Indpls., Feb. 28, 1940; s. George Lawrence and Helen Sarah (McLandress) A. BA, Johns Hopkins U., 1962; MBA, Harvard U., 1968; cert. in real estate fin. and constrn., UCLA, 1974. Asst. to chief scientist Phoenix missile program Hughes Aircraft Co., L.A., 1968-69, asst. program mgr. Iroquois night fighter and night tracker program, 1969-71, asst. to contr. space and comm. group, 1971-72, contr. tech. divsn., 1972-74; pres. Am. Std. Devel. Co., L.A., 1974—, Transit Cmty. Devel. Corp., 1997-2001. Bd. dirs., chmn. audit com. Pub. Storage, Inc., Glendale, Calif., Marathon Nat. Bank, L.A., Tech Net, L.A. Bancorp, Met. Water Dist., So. Calif., Met. Transp. Authority, L.A. County; pres. Self Svc. Storage Assn., San Francisco, 1978-83. Asst. to dep. campaign mgr. Humphrey for Pres., Washington, 1968; commr. L.A. Planning Commn., 1984—88, L.A. Telecom. Commn., 1992—93, Calif. Transp. Commn., 1998—2001, Calif. State Bd. Edn., 2000—, Calif. Arts Coun., 2000—; vice chmn. L.A. Econ. Devel. Coun., 1988—93; chmn. Calif. Tech. Adv. Com. on Aeronautics, Ctr. for Study Dem. Inst., Santa Barbara, Calif., 1986—; bd. dirs. Met. Transp. Authority Los Angeles County, South Bay Civic Light Opera, L.A. Children's Mus., World Children's Transplant Fund, French Found. for Alzheimers Rsch., Pacific Coun. on Internat. Policy; adv. bd. mem. Peabody Conservatory, 1992—, Ctr. Talented Youth, 1992—, Nitse Sch. Advanced Internat. Studies, 1993—, Harvard Ptnrs., 1996—, Inst. Acad. Achievement of Youth, 1999—; bd. vis. Davidson Coll.; bd. dirs. L.A. Theatre Ctr., 1986—92, YMCA; trustee Johns Hopkins U., 1991—; mem. Coun. on Fgn. Rels., L.A. Com. on Fgn. Rels., Calif Arts Coun., 2001—. Lt. USNR, 1962—66. Mem. So. Calif. Planning Congress (bd. dirs.), Parker Found. (bd. dirs.), California Club, St. Francis Yacht Club, Jonathan Club, Calif. Yacht Club, Alpha Lambda. Address: 5221 W 102nd St Los Angeles CA 90045-6001 E-mail: rabernethy@pacificnet.net

ABILDSKOV, J. A. cardiologist, educator; b. Salem, Utah, Sept. 22, 1923; s. John and Annie Marie (Peterson) A.; m. Mary Helen McKell, Dec. 4, 1944; children— Becky, Alan, Mary, Marilyn B.A., U. Utah, 1944, M.D., 1946. Diplomate Am. Bd. Internal Medicine. Intern Latter-day Saints Hosp., Salt Lake City, 1947-48; resident Charity Hosp. La., New Orleans, 1948-51; instr. Tulane U., New Orleans, 1948-54; asst. prof. to prof. SUNY-Syracuse, 1955-68; prof. medicine U. Utah, Salt Lake City, 1968—. Dir. Nora Eccles Harrison Cardiovascular Rsch. and Tng. Inst., Salt Lake City, 1970-94. Contbr. articles to profl. jours. Served to capt. USAR, 1954-56 Recipient Disting. Research award U. Utah, 1976 Fellow Am. Coll. Cardiology; mem. Assn. Am. Physicians, Am. Soc. Clin. Investigation (emeritus), Assn. Univ. Cardiologists (founding), Western Assn. Physicians, Venezuelan Cardiology Soc. (hon.), Cardiology Soc. Peru (corresponding) Republican. Mormon Home: 1506 Canterbury Dr Salt Lake City UT 84108-2833 Office: U Utah Bdlg 500 Salt Lake City UT 84112

ABO, RONALD KENT, freelance/self-employed architect; b. Rupert, Idaho, July 10, 1946; s. Isamu and Ameria (Hachiya) A.; m. Lisa A. Wiesley; children: Tamiko N., Reiko D., Ryan A., Emily A. BArch, U. Colo., 1969. Lic. architect, Colo. Designer SLP & Ptnrs., Denver, 1968-71; dir. Community Design Ctr., Denver, 1971-72; assoc. Barker, Rinker, Seacat, Denver, 1972-76; pvt. practice Denver, 1976-80; pres. Abo Gude Architects, Denver, 1980-84, Ron Abo Architects, Denver, 1984-91, Abo

Architects PC, Denver, 1991-94, Abo Copeland Architecture, 1995—. Design instr., thesis advisor U. Colo., Denver. Prin. works include Morrison Horticultre Ctr., 1983 (W.O.O.D. Inc. citation 1983), Highland Square, 1982 (AIA citation 1983), Roxborough Elem. Sch., 1990, Tropical Discovery Ctr. Denver Zoo, 1992, New Denver Internat. Airport Concourse Bldgs., 1993, Nederland Middle/H.S., 1996, Julesburg Welcome Ctr., 1997, Rocky Mountain Mfg. Acad., 1998. Active Denver Comty. Leadership Forum, 1986, Colfax-on-the-Hill, 1988—, U. Colo. Alumni Bd., Workforce Devel. Bd., 1990—, Savid House. Recipient Design Excellence award W.O.O.D. Inc., Denver, 1982, Martin Luther King Bus. Social Responsibility award, 1998. Mem. AIA (bd. dirs., pres.-elect Denver chpt. 1990, pres. 1991, pres.-elect Colo. chpt. 1997, pres. 1998), Asian C. of C. (pres. 1998), Colo. Aikido Assn. (head instr. Denver Buddhist Temple Aikido), Lions Club (bd. dirs.). Democrat. Avocation: Aikido (4th degree black belt). Office: Abo Copeland Architecture 1600 Downing St Ste 700 Denver CO 80218-1540 E-mail: rka@acarch.com

ABRAHAMS, SIDNEY CYRIL, physicist, crystallographer; b. London, May 28, 1924; arrived in U.S., 1948; s. Aaron Harry and Freda (Cohen) A.; m. Rhoda Banks, May 1, 1950; children: David Mark, Peter Brian, Jennifer Anne. BS, U. Glasgow, Scotland, 1946; PhD, U. Glasgow, 1949, DSc, 1957; Fil. Dr. (hon.), U. Uppsala, Sweden, 1981; D Honoris Causa, U. Bordeaux, 1997. Rsch. fellow U. Minn., Mpls., 1949-50; mem. staff MIT, Cambridge, 1950-54; rsch. fellow U. Glasgow, 1954-57; mem. tech. staff Bell Labs., Murray Hill, N.J., 1957-82; disting. mem. tech. staff AT&T Bell Labs., Murray Hill, 1982-88; Humboldt sr. scientist Inst. Crystallography, U. Tübingen, Fed. Republic Germany, 1989-90. Guest scientist Brookhaven Nat. Lab., Upton, N.Y., 1957—; vis. prof. U. Bordeaux, France, 1979, 90; Humboldt sr. scientist U. Tübingen, Germany, 1995; adj. prof. physics So. Oreg. U., 1990—. Mem. editorial bd., Rev. Sci. Instruments, 1963-65; co-editor, Anomalous Scattering, 1975; editor, World Directory of Crystallographers, 1977; editor-in-chief Acta Crystallographica, 1978-87; book rev. editor, Ferroelectrics, 1975—. Recipient Sr. U.S. Scientist award, Alexander von Humboldt Found., 1989-90. Fellow AAAS, Am. Phys. Soc.; mem. Am. Crystallographic Assn. (pres. 1968, mng. editor 1965-90), Royal Soc. Chemistry, Am. Inst. Physics (chmn. pub. policy com. 1981-91), Internat. Union Crystallography (chmn. commn. on crystallographic apparatus 1972-75, commn. on jours. 1978-87, commn. on crystallographic nomenclature 1978—), Internat. Union Pure and Applied Chemistry (rep. interdivsnl. com. on nomenclature and symbols 1984—), Sigma Xi (founding pres. So. Oreg. State Coll. 1993-95). Avocations: photography, hiking. Home: 89 Mallard St Ashland OR 97520-7316 Office: So Oreg U Physics Dept Ashland OR 97520 E-mail: sca@sou.edu

ABRAM, DONALD EUGENE, retired federal judge; b. Des Moines, Feb. 8, 1935; s. Irwin and Freda Phyllis (Gibson) A.; m. Frances Jennette Cooley, Apr. 22, 1962; children: Karen Lynn, Susan Ann, Scott Alan, Diane Jennette. BS in Bus., U. Colo., 1957, JD, 1963. Ptnr. Phelps, Fonda, Hays, Abram and Shaw (now Peterson & Fonda, PC), Pueblo, Colo., 1963-75; dist. judge Colo. 10th Jud. Dist., Pueblo, 1975-81; chief U.S. magistrate judge U.S. Dist. Ct. State of Colo., 1981-00; ret., 2000. Lectr. law in criminal procedure U. Denver Sch. of Law, 1983-90; adj. prof. sociology, instr. bus. law U. So. Colo., Pueblo, 1977-81. Mng. editor, bd. dir. Colo. Law Review, 1961-63. Vice chmn. Pueblo County Rep. Party, 1973-75; city councilman Pueblo, 1970-73; pres. Pueblo city coun., 1972-73, Pueblo Goodwill Industries, 1965, Pueblo United Fund, 1968; chmn. consolidation planning com. Pueblo County Sch. Dists. 60, 70, 1968-70; mem. gov.'s. milit. affairs adv. com., 1975-78; mem. gov.'s commn. children and families, 1978-80. Lt. (j.g.) USN, 1957-60, capt. Res. ret. Recipient Disting. Svc. award Colo. Jaycee, 1970, Disting. Citizen Svc. award, Pueblo Rotary, 1975. Mem. Fed. Magistrate Judges Assn. (pres. 1990-91), Pueblo C. of C.(bd. dirs. 1972, chmn. edn. com. 1970-71), Colo. Bar Assn. (1st v.p. 1975-76), Nat. Coun. U.S. Magistrates (dir., officer 1984-89), Juvenile Judges Assn. Colo. (chmn. 1979-80), Colo. Navy League (state pres. 1976-78). Lutheran. Office: US Dist Ct US Courthouse C-566 1929 Stout St Denver CO 80294-1929

ABRAMOVITZ, MOSES, economist, educator; b. Bklyn., Jan. 1, 1912; s. Nathan and Betty (Goldenberg) A.; m. Carrie Glasser, June 23, 1937; 1 son, Joel Nathan. A.B., Harvard U., 1932; Ph.D., Columbia U., 1939; Ph.D. (hon.), Uppsala U., Sweden, 1985, U. Ancona, Italy, 1992. Instr. Harvard U., 1936-38; mem. research staff Nat. Bur. Econ. Research, 1938-69; lectr. Columbia U., 1940-42, 46-48; prof. econs. Stanford U., 1948—, Coe prof. Am. econ. history, exec. head dept. econs., 1963-65, 71-74. Vis. prof. U. Pa., 1955; prin. economist WPB, 1942, OSS, 1943-44; econ. adviser to U.S. rep. on Allied Commn. on Reparations, 1945-46; econ. adviser to sec.-gen. Orgn. for Econ. Coop. and Devel., 1962-63; vis. fellow All Souls Coll., Oxford, Eng., 1968 Author: Price Theory for a Changing Economy, 1939, Inventories and Business Cycles, 1950, The Growth of Public Employment in Great Britain, 1957, (with Vera Eliasberg) Thinking About Growth, 1989; also articles.; editor: Capital Formation and Economic Growth, 1955; mng. editor Jour. Econ. Lit., 1981-85. Served as lt. AUS, 1944-45. Recipient Nitti prize Accademia Nazionale Dei Lincei, Rome, 1990. Fellow Am. Acad. Arts and Scis., Am. Econ. Assn. (disting., pres. 1980), Am. Statis. Assn.; mem. Am. Econ. History Assn. (pres. 1991-92), Western Econ. Assn. (pres. 1988), Accademia Nazionale dei Lincei (fgn.), Phi Beta Kappa. Home: 762 Dolores St Stanford CA 94305-8428 Office: Stanford U Dept Econs Stanford CA 94305-6072

ABRAMS, ARTHUR JAY, physician; b. Camden, N.J., Apr. 9, 1938; s. Morris and Sophia Sarah (Kates) A.; m. Marianne Ritto Abrams, June 8, 1963; children: Suzanne Beth, Cheryl Lyn, Robert Dwight. BA, Rutgers U., Camden, N.J., 1959; MD, Hahnemann U., 1963. Diplomate Am. Bd. Dermatology. Intern Madigan Army Med. Ctr., Tacoma, 1963-64; resident, chief resident Letterman Army Med. Ctr., San Francisco, 1964-67; dermatologist, Far East cons. 249th Gen. Hosp. U.S. Army, Tokyo, 1967-69; asst. chief dermatologist Tripler Army Med. Ctr., Honolulu, 1969-70; staff dermatologist El Camino Hosp., Mountain View, Calif., 1970—; clin. assoc. prof. dermatology Stanford U. Med. Ctr., 1979—; dermatology cons. San Jose (Calif.) State U., 1994—; maj. U.S. Army, 1963-70. Mem. AMA, Calif. Med. Assn., Pacific Dermatol. Assn., San Francisco Dermatol. Soc. Avocation: volleyball, walking. Office: 763 Altos Oaks Dr Ste 4 Los Altos CA 94024-5400

ABRAMS, HERBERT KERMAN, physician, educator; b. Chgo., 1913; BS, Northwestern U.; MD, MS, U. Ill., 1940; MPH, Johns Hopkins U., 1947. Intern Cook County Hosp., Chgo., 1940-41; chief Bur. of Adult Health, Calif. Health Dept., 1947-52; dir. Chgo. Union Health Service, 1952-66; prof., chair dept. community medicine Chgo. Med. Sch.-Mt. Sinai Hosp., Chgo., 1966-68; prof., head dept. family community medicine U. Ariz., Tucson, 1968-78, prof. emeritus, 1990—; dir. Ariz. Ctr. for Occupl. Safety and Health, 1978-83. Surgeon USPHS, 1942-46. Mem. AMA, APHA (v.p. 1981-82), Ariz. Med. Assn., Assn. Tchrs. Preventive Medicine, Am. Coll. Occupational Environ. Medicine, Physicians for Social Responsibility, Internat. Physicians Prevention Nuclear War. Office: U Ariz Dept Family and Cmty Medicine PO Box 245143 Tucson AZ 85724-5143 E-mail: hka@u.arizona.edu

ABRAMS, HERBERT LEROY, radiologist, educator; b. N.Y.C., Aug. 16, 1920; s. Morris and Freda (Sugarman) A.; m. Marilyn Spitz, Mar. 23, 1943; children: Nancy, John. BA, Cornell U., 1941; MD, Downstate Med. Ctr., N.Y., 1946. Diplomate Am. Bd. Radiology. Intern L.I. Coll. Hosp., 1946-47; resident in internal medicine Montefiore Hosp., Bronx, N.Y., 1947-48; resident in radiology Stanford (Calif.) U. [illegible]; practice medicine specializing in radiology Stanford U., Calif., 1951-67, mem. faculty Sch. Medicine, 1951-67, dir. divsn. diagnostic roentgenology Sch. Medicine, 1961-67, prof. radiology Sch. Medicine, 1962-67; Philip H. Cook prof. radiology Harvard U., 1967-85, now prof. emeritus, chmn. dept. radiology, 1967-80; prof. radiology Stanford U. Sch. Medicine, 1985-90, prof. emeritus, 1990—; clin. prof. U. Calif. Sch. Medicine, San Francisco, 1986—. Radiologist-in-chief Peter Bent Brigham Hosp., Boston, 1967-80; chmn. dept. radiology Brigham and Women's Hosp., Boston, 1981-85; radiologist-in-chief Sidney Farber Cancer Inst., Boston, 1974-85; R.H. Nimmo vis. prof. U. Adelaide, Australia; mem.-in-residence Ctr. for Internat. Security and Coop. Stanford U., 1985—; mem. radiation study sect. NIH, 1962-66; cons. to hosps., profl. socs. Author: (with others) Angiocardiography in Congenital Heart Disease, 1956, Congenital Heart Disease, 1965, Coronary Arteriography: A Practical Approach, 1983, Brigham Guide to Diagnostic Imaging, 1986, Assessment of Diagnostic Technology in Health Care; editor: Abrams' Angiography, 3rd edit., 1983; author: The President Has Been Shot: Confusion, Disability and the 25th Amendment, 1992, 94, The History of Cardiac Radiology, 1996; mem. editl. bd. Investigative Radiology; editor-in-chief, founder Cardiovasc. and Interventional Radiology, 1978-88, Postgrad. Radiology, 1983-99. Nat. Cancer Inst. fellow, 1950; Spl. Rsch. fellow Nat. Heart Inst., 1960, 73-74; David M. Gould Meml. lectr. Johns Hopkins, 1964; William R. Whitman Meml. lectr., 1968; Leo G. Rigler lectr. Tel Aviv U., 1969; Holmes lectr. New England Roentgen Ray Soc., Boston, 1970; Ross Golden lectr. N.Y. Roentgen Ray Soc., N.Y.C., 1971; Stauffer Meml. lectr. Phila. Roentgen Ray Soc., 1971; J.M.T. Finney Fund lectr. Md. Radiol. Soc., Ocean City, 1972; Aubrey Hampton lectr. Mass. Gen. Hosp., Boston, 1974; Kirklin-Weber lectr. Mayo Clinic, 1974; Crookshank lectr. Royal Coll. Radiology, 1980; Alpha Omega Alpha lectr., vis. prof. U. Calif. Med. Sch., San Francisco, 1961-65; W.H. Herbert lectr. U. Calif.; Caldwell lectr. Am. Roentgen Ray Soc., 1982; Percy lectr. McMaster Med. Sch., 1983; Charles Dotter lectr. Soc. Cardiovasc. and Interventional Radiology, 1988; Philip Hodes lectr. Jefferson Med. Coll., 1988; David Gould Meml. lectr. Johns Hopkins U., 1991, Hymer Friedell lectr. Western Res. Sch. Medicine, 1993, Felix Fheischner Memmal lectr. Harvard Med. Sch., 1997, Charles Dotter Meml. lectr. Am. Heart Assn., 1998; Henry J. Kaiser sr. fellow Ctr. for Advanced Study in Behavioral Sci., 1980-81. Hon. fellow Royal Coll. Radiology (Gt. Britain), Royal Coll. Surgery (Ireland), Am. Coll. Radiology, Am. Coll. Cardiology; mem. Nat. Acad. Sci. (com. biol. effects of low-level ionizing radiation BEIR VII, 1999—), Assn. Univ. Radiologists (Gold medal 1984), Inst. Medicine, Am. Heart Assn., Am. Soc. Nephrology, Radiol. Soc. N.Am. (Gold medal 1995), N.Am. Soc. Cardiac Radiology (pres. 1979-80), Internat. Physicians for Prevention of Nuc. War (founding v.p., participant Nobel Peace prize 1985), Soc. Cardiovasc. Radiology (recipient gold medal 2000), Soc. Chmn. Acad. Radiology Depts. (pres. 1970-71), Nat. Coun. Health Tech. Assessment, Inst. of Medicine, NAS (com. on biol. effects of low level ionizing radium 1999—), NIH (chmn. consensus panel on MRI, internat. blue ribbon panel radiation effects rsch. found. Hiroshima 1996, mem. working group on disability of U.S. pres. 1995-98), Phi Beta Kappa, Alpha Omega Alpha. Home: 714 Alvarado Stanford CA 94305 Office: Stanford U Sch Medicine 300 Pasteur Dr Stanford CA 94305-5105 E-mail: hlabrams@stanford.edu

ABRAMS, MARC, lawyer, state political party executive; b. N.Y.C., Mar. 23, 1957; s. Stephen Robert and Virginia Ornstein Abrams; m. Barbara Christopher, 1981; 1 child, Lawrence Christopher. BA magna cum laude, Wesleyan U., Middletown, Conn., 1978; MA, JD, U. Mich., 1981. Bar: Conn. 1982, N.Y. 1986, D.C. 1987, Pa. 1987, Oreg. 1989, U.S. Dist Ct. (so. dist.) N.Y. 1986, U.S. Dist. Co. (ea. dist.) Pa. 1988, U.S. Dist. Ct. Mont. 1989, U.S. Cir. Ct. (3d, 4th and 9th cirs.), U.S. Dist. Ct. Oreg. 1989, U.S. Supreme Ct. Asst. prof. U. Oreg., 1981-83; exec. dir. Student Press Law Ctr., 1983-85; pvt. practice, 1985—. Co-author: Law of the Student Press, 1983, Confronting Wrongful Discharge Under Oregon and Washington Law, 1989. Vice chair Lane County (Oreg.) Dem. Ctrl. Com., 1981-82, Multnomah County (Oreg.) Dem. Ctrl. Com., 1991-92; mem. Oreg. Dem. State Ctrl. Com., 1981-82, 91—, Multnomah Edn. Svc. Dist. Bd., 1993-97, chmn., 1996-97; fin. chair Oreg. State Dem. Party, 1993-95, vice chair, 1994-97, chmn., 1997-99; mem. Portland Sch. Bd., 1995—, vice chair, 1998—; treas. Assn. State Dem. Chairs, 1998-99. Recipient Johnnie Phelps medal Vets. for Human Rights, 1995. Jewish. Office: 1753 NW Aspen Ave Portland OR 97210-1208

ABRAMS, NORMAN, law educator, university administrator; b. Chgo., July 7, 1933; s. Harry A. and Gertrude (Dick) A.; m. Toshka Alster, 1977; children: Marshall David, Julie, Hanna, Naomi. AB, U. Chgo., 1952, JD, 1955. Bar: Ill. 1956, U.S. Supreme Ct. 1967. Assoc. in law Columbia U., 1955-57; rsch. assoc. Harvard U., 1957-59; sec. Harvard-Brandeis Coop. Rsch. for Israel's Legal Devel., 1957-58, dir., 1959; mem. faculty law sch. UCLA, 1959—, prof. law, 1964—, assoc. dean law, 1989-91, vice chancellor acad. pers., 1991-2001, interim exec. v. chancellor, spring 1998, co-dir. Ctr. for internat. and strategic studies, 1982-83, chmn. steering com., 1985-87, 88-89; vis. prof. Hebrew U., 1969-70, Forchheimer vis. prof., 1986; vis. prof. Bar Ilan U., 1970-71, 78, U. So. Calif., 1972, 73, Stanford U., 1977, U. Calif. at Berkeley, 1977, Loyola U., Los Angeles, summers 1974, 75, 76, 79; spl. asst. to U.S. atty. gen., also prof.-in-residence criminal div. Dept. Justice, 1966-67. Reporter for So. Calif. indigent accused persons study Am. Bar Found., 1963; cons. Gov. Calif. Commn. L.A. Riots, 1965, Pres.'s Commn. Law Enforcement and Adminstrn. Justice, 1966-67, Nat. Commn. on Reform of Fed. Criminal Laws, 1967-69, Rand Corp., 1968-74, Ctr. for Adminstrv. Justice, ABA, 1973-77, Nat. Adv. Commn. on Criminal Justice Stds., Organized Crime Task Force, 1976; spl. hearing officer conscientious objector cases Dept. Justice, 1967-68; vis. scholar Inst. for Advanced Studies, Hebrew U., summer, 1994. Author: (with others) Evidence, Cases and Materials, 7th edit., 1983, 8th edit., 1988, 9th edit., 1997, Federal Criminal Law and Its Enforcement, 1986, 2d and 3d edits. (with S. Beale), 1993, 2000; mem. editl. bd. Criminal Law Forum, 1990—. Chmn. Jewish Conciliation Bd., L.A., 1975-81; bd. dirs. Bet Tzedek, 1975-85, L.A. Hillel Coun., 1979-82, Shalhevet High Sch., 1998—; chmn. So. Calif. region Am. Profs. for Peace in Middle East, 1981-83; bd. dirs. met. region Jewish Fedn., 1982-88, v.p. 1982-83; pres. Westwood Kehillah Congregation, 1985. Mem. Soc. for Reform of Criminal Law (mem. exec. com. 1994—), Phi Beta Kappa. Office: UCLA Law School 405 Hilgard Ave Los Angeles CA 90095-9000 E-mail: abrams@Law.UCLA.EDU

ABRAMSON, NORMAN, retired electronics executive; b. Boston, Apr. 1, 1932; s. Edward and Esther (Vaslavsky) A.; m. Joan Freulich, July 4, 1954; children: Mark David, Carin Lynn. AB, Harvard U., 1953; MA, UCLA, 1955; PhD, Stanford U., 1958. Asst. prof. Stanford (Calif.) U., from 1958, assoc. prof., to 1965; vis. prof. U. Calif., Berkeley, 1965, Harvard U., Cambridge, Mass., 1965-66; prof. U. Hawaii, Honolulu, 1966-94; v.p. Aloha Networks, Inc., San Francisco, 1994-2001. Vis. prof. MIT, 1981-82; cons. Internat. Telecom. Union, Geneva, UNESCO, Paris, UN Devel. Program, N.Y.C. Author: Information Theory and Coding, 1963; co-editor: Computer Communication Networks, [illegible], editor: Multiple Access Communications, Foundations for Emerging Technologies, 1993. Recipient Koji Kobayshi Computers and Communications award Inst. of Elec. and Electronics Engrs., 1995, Tech. award Rhein Found., 2000. Fellow IEEE, IEC, IEEE Info. Theory Soc. (Golden Jubilee award for Tech. Innovation 1998). Achievements include patents in field. [illegible] Lake St San Francisco CA 94118-1216 E-mail: norm@post.harvard.edu

ABRAVANEL, ALLAN RAY, lawyer; b. N.Y.C., Mar. 11, 1947; s. Leon and Sydelle (Berenson) A.; m. Susan Ava Paikin, Dec. 28, 1971; children: Karen, David. BA magna cum laude, Yale U., 1968; JD cum laude, Harvard U., 1971. Bar: N.Y. 1972, Oreg. 1976. Assoc. Paul, Weiss, Rifkind, Wharton & Garrison, N.Y.C., 1971-72, 74-76; fellow Internat. Legal Ctr., Lima, Peru, 1972-74; from assoc. to ptnr. Stoel, Rives, Boley, Fraser & Wyse, Portland, Oreg., 1976-83; ptnr. Perkins Coie, Portland, 1983—. Editor, pub. Abravanel Family Newsletter. Chair Oreg. Internat. Trade Com., Oreg. Dist. Export Coun. Mem. ABA, Portland Met. C. of C. Office: Perkins Coie 1211 SW 5th Ave Portland OR 97204-3713

ABSHER, DAN, construction executive; b. Apr. 30, 1958; BA in Polit. Sci., Stanford U., 1980; JD, U. Notre Dame, 1983. Pvt. practice, 1983-85; corp. atty. Absher Constrn. Co., Puyallup, 1985-90, pres., 1990—. Mediator Pierce County Small Claims Ct., 1987-89. Asst. basketball coach Mercer Island H.S., 1984-90; youth group leader St. Andrew's Cath. Ch., 1985-89, group facilitator, 1992-95; mem. Supt. Pub. Instrns. Sch. Facility Cost Adv. Bd., 1993-96. Mem. Wash. State Bar Assn. (pub. procurement and pvt. constrn. law sect.), Tacoma/Pierce County Bar Assn. (bd. mem. young lawyers divsn. 1989-91, sec. young lawyers divsn. 1990), Associated Gen. Contractors Wash. (union negotiating team 1986—, chair state facilities com. 1990-92, trustee 1990—, chair govt. affairs coun. 1992-94, pres. 1996, Contractor of the Yr. 1991), Am. Arbitration Assn. (arbitrator). Office: Absher Constrn Co 1001 Shaw Rd Puyallup WA 98372-7437

ABT, STEVEN R. civil engineering educator, dean; b. Cheyenne Wells, Colo. BCE, Colo. State U., 1973, MSCE, 1976, PhDCE, 1980. Hydraulics staff engr. Leonard Rice Engring., Denver, 1974-76; instr. Colo. State U., Ft. Collins, 1976-80, from asst. prof. to assoc. prof., 1980-88, prof., 1988—, assoc. dean rsch. and grad. studies, 1997—. Cons., Ft. Collins, 1976—. Editor, co-editor Proceedings; contbr. more than 78 articles to profl. jours. 2d lt. C.E., U.S. Army, 1973, col. USAR, 1973—. Fellow ASCE; mem. Am. Water Resource Assn., Transp. Rsch. Bd., Internat. Erosion Control Assn. Office: Colo State U Engring Rsch Ctr Fort Collins CO 80523-0001 E-mail: sabt@engr.colostate.edu

ABUL-HAJ, SULEIMAN KAHIL, pathologist; b. Palestine, Apr. 20, 1925; came to U.S., 1946, naturalized, 1955; s. Sheik Khalil and S. Buteina (Oda) Abul-H.; m. Elizabeth Abood, Feb. 11, 1948; children: Charles, Alan, Cary. BS, U. Calif., Berkeley, 1949; M.S., U. Calif., San Francisco, 1951, MD, 1955. Intern Cook County Hosp., Chgo., 1955-56; resident U. Calif. Hosp., San Francisco, 1949, Brooke Gen Hosp., 1957-59; chief clin. and anatomic pathology Walter Reed Army Hosp., Washington, 1959-62; assoc. prof. U. So. Calif. Sch. Medicine, L.A., 1963-96; sr. surg. pathologist Los Angeles County Gen. Hosp., 1963; dir. dept. pathology Cmty. Meml. Hosp., Ventura, Calif., 1964-80, Gen. Hosp. Ventura County, 1966-74; dir. Pathology Svc. Med. Group, 1970—. Cons. Calif. Tumor Tissue Registry, 1962-96, Camarillo State Hosp., 1964-70, Tripler Gen. Hosp., Hawaii, 1963-67, Armed Forces Inst. Pathology, 1960-69. Contbr. articles to profl. jours. Bd. dirs. Tri-Counties Blood Bank, Am. Cancer Soc. Maj., M.C., U.S. Army, 1956-62. Recipient Calif. Honor Soc. award, 1949, Borden award, 1955, Achievement cert. Surgeon Gen. Army, 1962. Fellow Coll. Am. Pathologists; mem. AAAS, AMA, Internat. Coll. Surgeons, World Affairs Coun. Achievements include research in cardiovascular disease, endocrine, renal, skin diseases, also cancer. Home and Office: 105 Encinal Way Ventura CA 93001-3317

ACCURSO, FRANK JOSEPH, physician, educator; b. Mt. Vernon, NY, Mar. 9, 1947; s. Joseph and Elsie A.; m. Tanya Lynn Kleen, Apr. 25, 1971; children: Aron, David. BS, CCNY, 1968; MS, U. Colo., 1971; MD, Albert Einstein Coll. Medicine, N.Y.C., 1974. Diplomate Am. Bd. Pediatrics, Am. Bd. Pediatric Pulmonology; cert. in pediatric critical care medicine. Instr. pediatrics U. Colo. Sch. Medicine, Denver, 1979-80, asst. prof. pediatrics, 1980-87, assoc. prof. pediatrics, 1987-95, prof. pediatrics, 1995—. Dir., Cystic Fibrosis Ctr., Denver, Co. Author: (with others) Alfa Clinical Series, 1994, Lange Medical Books, 1993, Marcel Dekker, 1989. Recipient Svc. award Cystic Fibrosis Found. local Denver chap., 1992, numerous clin., rsch., and tng. grants, 1986—; named to 5280 Magazine's Top Doctors, 1999. Mem. AAAS, Am. Thoracic Soc., Am. Pediatric Soc., Am. Acad. Pediatrics, Soc. Pediatric Rsch., Office: U Colo Childrens Hosp 1056 E 19th Ave # B395 Denver CO 80218-1007 E-mail: accurso.frank@tchden.org

ACHAUER, BRUCE MICHAEL, plastic surgeon; MD, Baylor U., 1967. Intern San Francisco Gen. Hosp., 1967-68; resident in gen. surgery U. Calif., Irvine, 1970-74, rsch. in plastic surgery, 1974-76, adj. prof. surgery, 1994—; fellow in plastic surgery Queen Victoria Hosp., East Grinstead, U.K., 1976; pvt. practice U. Calif. Irvine Med. Ctr., Orange, 1977—; mem. staff St. Joseph Hosp., 1977—; mem. active staff Children's Hosp. of Orange County, 1977—; pvt. practice plastic surgery Orange. Mem. courtesy staff Med. Ctr. of GGG, 1985—; dir. Am. Bd. Plastic Surgery, 1995—. Fellow Am. Acad. Pediatrics; mem. AMA, Am. Assn. Plastic Surgeons, Am. Cleft Palate Assn., Am. Soc. for Surgery of Hand, Am. Soc. Plastic and Reconstructive Surgeons (sec. ednl. found.). Office: 1140 W La Veta Ave Ste 810 Orange CA 92868-4230

ACHTEL, ROBERT ANDREW, pediatric cardiologist; b. Bklyn., May 5, 1941; s. Murray and Amelia (Ellian) A.; m. Erica Noel Woods, Mar. 10, 1963; children: Bergen Alison, Roland Hugh. BA, Adelphi U., 1963; MD, U. Cin., 1967. Diplomate Am. Bd. Pediat. Cardiology. Lic. comml. pilot FAA. Intern Cin. Children's Hosp., 1967-68; resident in pediat. Yale U., 1968-69, fellow in pediat. cardiology, 1969-71; clin. instr. pediat. U. Calif., Davis, 1972-73, asst. prof., 1977-83, U. Ky., 1973-76; dir. pediat. ICU Sutter Meml. Hosp., Sacramento, 1977-85, dir. pediat. cardiology, 1982—, chmn. instl. rev. com., 1981-85, 96—; chmn. dept. pediat. Mercy Hosp., Sacramento, 1981-83, 97—, dir. pediat. ICU, 1982-83, vice chmn. pediat., 1983-85, 95—; dir. Laurel Hills Devel. Ctr., 1985-89. Chmn. rsch. com. Sutter Inst. for Med. Rsch., 1989-98; trustee, mem. exec. com. Sutter Hosps. Found., 1988-2000, vice chmn., 1992-93; vice chmn. CEO Access Care, 1994-95; med. dir. FastServe Med. Group, 1995-97; vice chmn. dept. pediat. Mercy Hosp., 1995-97, chmn., 1997—; mem. tech. adv. com. pediat. cardiology State of Calif.; CEO Access Care, 1993-97; chmn. regional instl. rev. bd. Sutter/CHS Ctrl., 1996; mem. quality assurance com., mem. pharmacy com. Omni Health Plan, 1996-99; lectr. Mooney Aircraft Pilots Assn., FAA; bd. dirs. Mooney Aircraft Pilots Assn. Safety Found.; aviation safety counselor FAA, 1998—; ectr. Exptl. Aircraft Assn. Contbr. articles on aviation safety to cassette Pilots Audio Update; contbr. articles on cardiovasc. rsch. to profl. publs.; contbr. monthly editl. to Mooney Airplane Pilots Assn. Log. Bd. dirs. Sutter Meml. Hosp. Found., 1986-2000; bd. dirs. Sutter Found., 1989, trustee, 1989-2001. Maj. M.C., USAF, 1971-73. Grantee, U. Ky. Tobacco and Health Fsch. Found. Mem. Am. Heart Assn. (bd. dirs. Sacramento chpt., mem. couns. on congenital heart disease and atherosclerosis and cardiovasc. surgery, grantee), Am. Coll. Chest Physicians, Am. Acad. Pediat., S.W. Pediat. Cardiology Soc., So. Soc. Pediat. Rsch. Office: Perinatal & Pediatric Subspecialist Med Group 5609 J St Ste A Sacramento CA 95819-3948 E-mail: drbobar02@prodigy.net, achtelR@sutterhealth.org

ACHTENBERG, ROBERTA, former federal official; b. L.A., July 20, 1950; d. Louis and Beatrice A.; 1 child. AB, U. Calif., Berkeley, 1972; postgrad., U. Calif., San Francisco, 1972-73; JD, U. Utah, 1975. Bar: Calif., U.S. Dist. Ct. (no. dist.) Calif., U.S. Ct. Appeals (9th cir.). Exec. dir. Nat. Ctr. Lesbian Rights, 1989-90; of counsel Lilienthal & [illegible], 1992-93; asst. sec. fair housing and equal opportunity HUD, Washington, 1993-95, Sr. Adv. to Sec., 1995—; sr. v.p. pub. policy dept. San Francisco C. of C., 1995 [illegible]

Contemporary Law. Commr. San Francisco County Transp. Authority; mem. County Bd. Suprs., City and County of San Francisco; bd. dirs. Bay Area Air Quality Mgmt. Dist., 1991-93. Mem. Order of Coir, Phi Beta Kappa. Office: San Francisco C of C Pub Policy Dept 465 California St San Francisco CA 94104-1804

ACHTERMAN, GAIL LOUISE, lawyer; b. Portland, Oreg., Aug. 1, 1949; AB in Econs. with distinction, Stanford U., 1971; MS in Natural Resource Policy and Mgmt., U. Mich., 1975, JD cum laude, 1974. Bar: Oreg. 1974, U.S. Dist. Ct. Oreg. 1978, U.S. Supreme Ct. 1978, U.S. Ct. Appeals (fed. and 10th cirs.). Atty.-advisor U.S. Dept. Interior, 1975-78; asst. for natural resources Gov. Neil Goldschmidt, 1987-91; mem. Stoel Rives LLP, Portland, 1978-2000. Exec. dir. Deschutes Resources Conservancy, 2000—; adj. prof. forest policy, Coll. Forestry, Oreg. State U., 1991—. Mem. Oreg. Water Resources Commn., 1981-85, Gov.'s Growth Task Force, 1998; mem. pres.'s bd. advisors Oreg. State U., 2000—, Oreg. Transp. Commn., 2000—. Mem. bd. dirs. Sustainable Ecosystems Inst., Am. Leadership Forum, Oreg. Women's Forum, Portland C. of C. (bd. dirs. 1996-99). Office: PO Box 1560 Bend OR 97709-1560

ACKEL, RICK R. electronics manufacturing executive; Ptnr. Arthur Anderson LLP; v.p. fin., CFO Sanmina Corp., San Jose, Calif. Office: Sanmina Corp 2700 North 1st St San Jose CA 95134

ACKER, ROBERT FLINT, microbiologist; b. Chgo., Aug. 24, 1920; s. Robert Booth and Mary (Flint) A.; m. Phyllis Catharine Fry, Jan. 2, 1948; children: Catharine Elizabeth, Barbara Fenner, Robert Macdonald, James Christopher. B.A., Ind. U., 1942, M.A., 1948; Ph.D., Rutgers U., 1953. Asst. prof. Iowa State U., Ames, 1954-59; asst. chief cancer chemotherapy dept., chief quality control dept. Microbiol. Assocs., Inc., Bethesda, Md., 1959-61, chief dept. cell and media prodn., 1961-62; dir. microbiology program Office of Naval Research, Dept. Navy, Washington, 1962-69; dir. fed. program devel., asst. dean faculties for research, prof. biol. scis. Northwestern U., Evanston, Ill., 1969-74; exec. dir. Am. Soc. Microbiology, Washington, 1974-81, Nat. Found. Infectious Disease, Bethesda, Md., 1981-86; pres. Bionox Corp., Tucson, 1985-92. Author: (with R.R. Jennings) The Protistan Kingdom, 1970; editor: Proc. 24th Internat. Congress on Marine Corrosion and Fouling, 1972; editorial bd.: Applied Microbiology, 1962-73. V.p., bd. dirs. Iona House Sr. Svc. Ctr., Washington, 1978-79, pres., 1979-81; trustee Massanetta Conf. Ctr., 1983-86; bd. dirs. Am. Type Culture Collection, 1983-89; pres. Sunrise Mountain Ridge Homeowners Assn., 1994-95; bd. elders Potomac United Presbyn. Ch., Md., 1967-69, Winnetka (Ill.) Presbyn. Ch., 1972-74, Nat. Presbyn. Ch., Washington, 1983-86, St. Andrew's Presbyn. Ch., Tucson, 1989-91, 1998-2000. Eli Lilly & Co. postdoctoral fellow, 1953-54. Fellow Am. Acad. Microbiology, Soc. for Indsl. Microbiology (pres. 1986-87, Charles Porter award 2001); mem. Am. Soc. for Microbiology, Am. Inst. Biol. Sci. (coun. 1983-91), Cosmos Club. Home and Office: 6890 E Loma Del Bribon Tucson AZ 85750-6372 E-mail: rfacker@flash.net

ACKERLEY, BARRY, professional basketball team executive, communications company executive; Student, U. Iowa, 1956. Exec. v.p. Advan, Inc.; owner Golden West Outdoor Advt., 1968-75; chmn., CEO Ackerley Comm., Inc., 1975—; owner, chmn. bd. dirs. Seattle SuperSonics, 1984—. Office: Seattle SuperSonics 351 Elliott Ave W Seattle WA 98119-4101 also: Ackerley Group 1301 5th Ave Ste 4000 Seattle WA 98101-2634

ACKERMAN, MARSHALL, publishing company executive; b. N.Y.C., Jan. 22, 1925; s. Albert and Beatrice (Munstuk) A.; m. Carol Lipman, June 8, 1948; children: Stark, Scott, A. Marc. AB, Harvard U., 1949; MS in Journalism, Northwestern U., 1950. Dir. employee relations Gimbel Bros., N.Y.C., 1950-51; account exec. Leonard Wolf & Assoc. (advt. agy.), N.Y.C., 1951-54; with Rodale Press, Inc., 1954-91, exec. v.p., 1967-91, vice chmn. bd., 1978-91; pub. Prevention mag., 1977-86, Theatre Crafts mag., 1967-78, vice chmn., Western divsn., 1986-91; ind. cons. health food industry, health media, 1992—. Pres. bd. assocs. Cedar Crest Coll., Allentown, Pa., 1976-78, trustee, 1983-87; pres. Pa. Stage Co., Allentown, 1978-80; chmn. Santa Barbara chpt. Am. Inst. Wine and Food, 1998—; mem. comm. dept. adv. bd. U. Calif. Santa Barbara, 1993—, vice chmn., 1998. Charge de Presse, Confrerie de la Chaine des Rotisseurs, Bailliage de Santa Barbara, 1998—; Decorated Bronze Star, Purple Heart. Home and Office: 894 Toro Canyon Rd Santa Barbara CA 93108-1642 E-mail: mackermanm@aol.com

ACKERMAN, RICHARD C. state legislator; b. Long Beach, Calif., Dec. 5, 1942; m. Linda Ackerman; 3 children. BA, UCLA, Berkeley, 1964; JD, Hastings Sch. of Law, 1967. Ptnr. Ackerman, Murdock, Brown, AAL, 1969—; mem. Calif. Ho. of Reps. from 72nd dist., Sacramento, 1995-2000, Calif. Senate from 33rd dist., Sacramento, 2001—. Mem. Fullerton City Council (Mayor for two terms). Office: Ste 303 305 N Harbor Blvd Fullerton CA 92832

ACOBA, SIMEON RIVERA, JR. state supreme court justice, educator; b. Honolulu, Mar. 11, 1944; s. Simeon R. and Martina (Domingo) A.. BA, U. Hawaii, 1966; JD, Northwestern U., Chgo., 1969. Bar: Hawaii 1969, U.S. Dist. Ct. Hawaii, U.S. Ct. Appeals (9th cir.). Law clk. Hawaii Supreme Ct., Honolulu, 1969-70; housing officer U. Hawaii, Honolulu, 1970-71; dep. atty. gen. State of Hawaii, Honolulu, 1971-73; pvt. practice, Honolulu, 1973-80; judge 1st Circuit Ct. Hawaii, Honolulu, 1980-94, Intermediate Ct. Appeals Hawaii, Honolulu, 1994-2000; assoc. justice Hawaii Supreme Ct., 2000—. Instr. criminal law Hawaii Pacific U., 1992—; atty. on spl. contract divsn. OSHA, Dept. Labor, Honolulu, 1975—77, Pub. Utilities divsn., State of Hawaii, 1976—77; campaign spending com. State of Hawaii, 1976—; staff atty. Hawaii State Legislature, 1975. Bd. dirs. Hawaii Mental Health Assn., 1975—77, Nuuanu YMCA, 1975—78, Hawaii Youth at Risk, 1990—91; mem. Gov.'s Conf. on Yr. 2000, Honolulu, 1970, Citizens Com. on Adminstrn. of Justice, 1972, State Drug Abuse Commn., 1975—76, Com. to Consider the Adoption of ABA Model Rules of Profl. Conduct, 1989—91; mem. Judicial Edn. Com., 1992—93, Hawaii State Bar Assn. Jud. Adminstrn. Com., 1992—94, Permanent Com. Rules Penal Procedure and Cir. Ct. Rules, 1992—96; subcom. chmn. Supreme Ct. Com. Pattern Jury Instrns., 1990—91; mem. Hawaii Supreme Ct. Ad Hoc Com. Jury Master List, 1991—92. Recipient Liberty Bell award, 1964. Mem.: ABA, ATLA, Hawaii Bar Assn. (dir. young lawyers sect. 1973). Office: Hawaii Supreme Ct 417 S King St Honolulu HI 96813-2912

ACORD, LEA, dean, nursing educator; MS in Pediatric Nursing, PhD in Higher Edn. Adminstrn., U. Pitts. Asst. prof. Sch. of Nursing U. Pitts., 1972-81; exec. dir. Ill. Nurses Assn., 1981-88; dir., assoc. prof. Sch. of Nursing, U. Maine, 1988-95; dean, prof. Coll. of Nursing, Mont. State U., Bozeman. Contbr. articles to profl. publs. Recipient Peggy Mussehl award for excellence Mont. Nurses Assn., 1997, Jean McLean Nursing Edn. award Maine State Nurses Assn., 1994, Hartford Gerontol. Curriculum award Assn. of Colls. of Nursing, 1998. Mem. Sigma Theta Tau (dean's task force). Office: Mont State U Bozeman Coll Nursing PO Box 173560 Bozeman MT 59717-3560

ADAIR, ROD, state legislator; b. Durant, Okla., Nov. 19, 1953; BS in Polit. Sci., MS in Govt. Demographer; mem. N.Mex. Senate, Dist. 33, Santa Fe, 1996—; mem. edn. com., mem. rules com. N.Mex. Senate. Republican. Office: PO Box 96 Roswell NM 88202-0096 E-mail: radair@state.nm.us

ADAM, CORNEL See LENGYEL, CORNEL ADAM

ADAMEK, CHARLES ANDREW, lawyer; b. Chgo., Dec. 24, 1944; s. Stanley Charles and Virginia Marie (Budzban) A.; m. Lori Merriel Klein; children: Donald Steven, Elizabeth Jean. BA with honors, U. Mich., 1966, JD, 1969. Bar: Ill. 1969, Calif. 1978. Clk. U.S. Dist. Judge U.S. Fed. Cts., Chgo., 1969-71; assoc. atty. Lord Bissell & Brook, Chgo., 1971-77, ptnr., 1977-78, L.A., 1978—. Mem. ABA, Ill. State Bar Assn., State Bar Calif., Nat. Assn. Railroad Trial Counsel (Western Region exec. com. 1985—). Roman Catholic. Avocations: Bluegrass banjo, sr. ice hockey. Office: Lord Bissell & Brook 300 S Grand Ave Ste 800 Los Angeles CA 90071-3119 E-mail: cadamek@lordbissell.com

ADAMS, ALBERT, state legislator, management consultant; b. Kotzebue, Alaska, June 18, 1942; m. Diane Adams; children: Bart, Luke, Michelle, Herbert, Guy, Al Jr. Student, RCA Inst., U. Alaska. Past exec. v.p. Nana Regional Corp.; pres. Kikiktagruk Inupiat Corp.; pvt. practice Adams Mgmt. Svcs.; state rep. Alaska Ho. of Reps., 1981-88; mem. Alaska State Senate, 1989—. Past mem. Alcohol Beverage Control Bd.; active Alaska Native Claims Appeals Bd.; dir. rural devel. Dept. Cmty. and Regional Affairs, 1971-73. Democrat. Avocations: family activities, fishing, hunting, basketball, reading. Office: State Capitol 120 4th St Rm 417 Juneau AK 99801-1142 Fax: 907-465-4821. E-mail: adams@legis.state.ak.us

ADAMS, BRADY, state legislator; b. Portland, Oreg., Feb. 28, 1945; m. Pat Adams, 1965; children: Ted, Jennifer. BS in mktg., Portland State U. With Evergreen Fed. Savings and Loan, Grants Pass, Oreg., 1972—, now pres.; mem. Oreg. Senate, Salem, 1992—; now pres. of senate State of Oreg., 1997—. Founder Our Valley Clin.; treas. Grants Pass Cmty. Sculpture Com. Mem. Rotary (hon.). Office: Oregon State Senate State Capitol Rm S-203 Salem OR 97310-0001

ADAMS, BRYAN, vocalist, composer; b. Kingston, Ont., Can., Nov. 5, 1959; Vocalist, 1976—; composer various bands including Prism, Bachman-Turner Overdrive, Bob Welch, Kiss, 1977—. Albums include Bryan Adams, 1980, You Want It, You Got It, 1982, Cuts Like a Knife, 1983, Reckless, 1985, Into the Fire, 1987, Waking Up the Neighbors, 1991, So Far, So Good, 1993, Live! Live! Live!, 1994; singles include Straight from the Heart, Cuts Like a Knife, 1983, Heaven, One Night Love Affair, It's Only Love, 1985, Heat of the Night, Victim of Love, Only the Strong Survive, Hearts On Fire, 1987, Thought I Died and Gone to Heaven, 1991, (Everything I Do) I Do It for You (Acad. award nominee for best original song 1992), Can't Stop This Thing We Started, There Will Never Be Another Tonight, (with Michael Kamen and Robert John Lange, from Don Juan DeMarco) Have You Ever Loved a Woman, 1995 (Acad. award nominee for best original song 1996); contbr. to soundtracks: Robin Hood: Prince of Thieves, The Three Musketeers (with Rod Stewart & Sting), Don Juan DeMarco. Decorated with Order of B.C., Order of Canada; recipient multi-platinum record, #1 single in Am., Can., U.K., Sweden, Finland, Denmark, Norway; named Artist of Decade, Canadian Recording Industry; nominated for 6 Grammys and 7 Juno awards, 1992, many other awards in music.

ADAMS, BYRON, composer, conductor; b. Mar. 9, 1955; BM, Jacksonville U., 1977; MM, U. So. Calif., 1979; DMA, Cornell U., 1984. Composer-in-residence Music Ctr. U. of the South, 1979-84; lectr. Cornell U., N.Y.C., 1985-87; assoc. prof. of music U. Calif., Riverside, 1993, prof., grad. advisor. Guest composer 26th Warsaw Autumn Festival, 1983, San Francisco Conservatory, 1966. Composer: Quintet for piano and strings, 1979, Concerto for trumpet and string orch., 1983, Sonata for trumpet and piano, 1983, Concerto for violin and orch., 1984, Go Lovely Rose for male chorus, 1984, Missa Brevis, 1988, Three Epitaph, 1988; recordings include Nightingales, 1979, Serenata Aestiva, 1986; contbr. articles to music jours. Vaughan Williams Rsch. fellow Carthusian Trust, 1985; recipient Grand prize Delius Festval Composition Competition, 1977 Am. Soc. Composers, Medly P. Ray Composition award, 1985. Avocations: reading. Office: U Calif Dept Music 900 University Ave Riverside CA 92521-0001

ADAMS, CHARLES LYNFORD, English language educator; b. Joliet, Ill., May 11, 1929; s. Charles Lynford and Eloise A. (Henault) A.; m. Joan Marie Johnson, June 6, 1953; children— Rebecca Lynn, Stephen Thomas. B.A., Mich. State U., 1951; M.A., U. Ill., 1952; Ph.D., U. Oreg., 1959. Instr. English U. Ore., 1959-60; asst. prof. U. Nev., Las Vegas, 1960-65, assoc. prof., 1965-67, prof. English, 1967-96, prof. emeritus English, 1996—. Las Vegas rep. U. Nev. System Grad. Sch., 1964-66, coordinator grad. studies, 1966-68, dean grad. studies, 1968-71 Editor: Studies in Frank Waters. Mem. adv. com. Univ. Mus. Soc. Served with AUS, 1954-56. Mem. MLA, Nat. Coun. Tchrs. English, Nev. Coun. Tchrs. English, So. Nev. Coun. Tchrs. English, Rocky Mountain MLA, Conf. Coll. Composition and Comm., AAUP, Nat. Soc. Profs., Frank Waters Soc., Phi Kappa Phi. Home: 1921 E Saint Louis Ave Las Vegas NV 89104-3805 Office: 4505 S Maryland Pkwy Las Vegas NV 89154-5011 E-mail: adamsc@nevada.edu

ADAMS, CLINTON, artist, historian; b. Glendale, Calif., Dec. 11, 1918; s. Merritt Cooley and Effie (Mackenzie) A.; m. Mary Elizabeth Atchison, Jan. 9, 1943; 1 child, Michael Gerald. Ed.B., UCLA, 1940, M.A., 1942. Instr. art UCLA, 1946-48, asst. prof., 1948-54; prof. art, head dept. U. Ky.; also dir. Art Gallery, 1954-57; prof. art, head dept. U. Fla., 1957-61; dean Coll. Fine Arts, U. N.Mex., Albuquerque, 1961-76, asso. provost, dean faculties, 1976-77; dir. Tamarind Inst., 1970-85. Assoc. dir. Tamarind Lithography Workshop, Los Angeles, 1960-61, program cons., 1961-70 Represented in permanent collections Bklyn. Mus., Art. Inst. Chgo., Brit. Mus., Australian Nat. Gallery, Mus. Modern Art, Los Angeles County Art Mus., and others; author: (with Garo Antreasian) The Tamarind Book of Lithography: Art and Techniques, 1970, American Lithographers, 1900-1960: The Artists and Their Printers, 1983, (with others) Lasting Impressions: Lithography As Art, 1988, Printmaking in New Mexico, 1880-1990, 1991, Crayonstone: The Life and Work of Bolton Brown, 1993, Nineteenth-Century Lithography in Europe, 1998; editor The Tamarind Papers, 1974-90, Second Impressions: Modern Prints and Printmakers Reconsidered, 1996; subject: bibliography Clinton Adams: Paintings and Watercolors 1945-87; exhbn. catalogue Albuquerque: University of New Mexico Art Mus., 1987; biography A Spectrum of Innovation: Color in American Printmaking, 1890-1990, 1990. Recipient Gov.'s award for outstanding contbns. to arts of N.Mex., 1985, Career ACHievement awards So. Graphics Coun., 1999, U. N.Mex., 1998, N.Am. Print Conf., 2000. Mem. NAD (academician), Nat. Coun. Fine Arts Deans (chmn. 1965-67). Home: 1917 Morningside Dr NE Albuquerque NM 87110-4927 E-mail: cladams@unm.edu

ADAMS, DIRK STANDLEY, lawyer; b. Lynch, Nebr., May 19, 1951; s. Howard W. and Marilyn (Standley) A.; m. Anita Low, Feb. 14, 1984. BS, U. Tex., 1972; JD, Harvard U., 1976. Bar: N.Y. 1977, Calif. 1985. Ptnr. Sullivan, Johnson, Peters, Burns, Adams & Mullin, P.C., Rochester, N.Y., 1981-82; exec. v.p., treas., gen. counsel Suffolk County Fed. Savs & Loan Assn., Centereach, 1982; ptnr. Phillips, Lytle, Hitchcock, Blaine & Huber, Rochester, 1982-83; sr. v.p., gen. counsel, corp. sec. Fed. Home Loan Bank of San Francisco, 1983—. Acting counsel Fed. Asset Disposition Assn., San Francisco, 1985-86. Bd. dirs. Vol. Legal Services Project, Inc., Rochester, 1983. Mem. ABA (com. savs. and loan assns. sect. corp., banking and bus. 1983—), Calif. Bar Assn. (fin. instns. com. 1985). Office: Fed Home Loan Bank San Francisco 600 California St Ste 200 San Francisco CA 94108-2726

ADAMS, FRANK, education specialist; b. Cleve., Sept. 11, 1948; s. Frank Albin and Helen (Coleman) Kovacevic. BS in Bus. Adminstrn., Bowling Green (Ohio) State U., 1970, MEd in Phys. Edn., 1978. Tech. writer Soldier Phys. Fitness Sch., Ft. Ben Harrison, Ind., 1983-85; edn. specialist Directorate of Tng. and Doctrine, Ft. Huachuca, Ariz., 1985-90, Dept. Tactics Intelligence Mil. Sci., Ft. Huachuca, 1990-93, 111th Mil. Intelligence Brigade, Ft. Huachuca, 1993-97; staff 112th Mil. Intelligence Brig. U.S. Army Intelligence Ctr., 1998—. Mem. steering com. tng. and doctrine command, staff and faculty devel. divsn., El Paso, Tex., 1987. Co-author: (field manual) Physical Fitness Training, 1984, (Internet site) Total Fitness; contbr. articles to profl. jours. and local newspapers. Recipient Civilian Achievement medal Dept. Army, Ft. Huachuca 1993, Comdr.'s award, 1995, Superior Civilian Svc. award, 1999. Mem. AAHPERD (life), Mil. Intelligence Corp. Avocations: internal martial arts, reading, Reiki master-teacher. Home: 4838 Corte Vista Sierra Vista AZ 85635-5738 Office: 112th Mil Intelligence Brig Fort Huachuca AZ 85613-6000

ADAMS, GLEN CAMERON, publisher; b. Trent, Wash., June 19, 1912; s. Otto Ulysses and Mae (Cameron) A.; m. Nina Lenore Finch, Apr. 30, 1936 (div. June 1939); 1 child, Robert Glen; m. Jean Pierie Evers, June 29, 1946 (dec. 2001). BA, Ea. Wash. U., 1938; PhD (hon.), Gonzaga U., 1990. Prin. Burbank (Wash.) Sch. Dist., 1938-39; livestock breeder Fairfield, Wash., 1939-51; postmaster Fairfield Post Office, 1951-72; printer, pub. Ye Galleon Press, Fairfield, 1972—. Hon. prof. history Eastern Wash. U., Cheney, 1983. Mayor Town of Fairfield, 1974-78. Named to Wash. State Hall of Honor, Washington State Hist. Soc., Tacoma, 1983. Democrat. Presbyterian. Home: 103 Brewster St Fairfield WA 99012 Office: 103 E Main St Fairfield WA 99012

ADAMS, HAZARD SIMEON, English educator, writer; b. Cleve., Feb. 15, 1926; s. Robert Simeon and Mary (Thurness) A.; m. Diana White, Sept. 17, 1949; children: Charles Simeon, Perry White. A.B., Princeton, 1948; M.A., U. Wash., 1949, Ph.D., 1953. Instr. English Cornell U., 1952-56; asst. prof. U. Tex., 1956-59; vis. assoc. prof. Washington U., St. Louis, 1959; from assoc. prof. to prof. Mich. State U., 1959-64; Fulbright lectr. U. Dublin, 1962-63; prof. U. Calif.-Irvine, 1964-77, founding chmn. English dept., 1964-69; dean Sch. Humanities, 1970-72, vice chancellor acad. affairs, 1972-74; co-dir. Sch. Criticism and Theory, 1975-77; sr. fellow, 1975-88; hon. sr. fellow, 1988—; prof. English and comparative lit. U. Wash., Seattle, 1977-97, Byron W. and Alice L. Lockwood prof. humanities, 1988-97, prof. emeritus, 1997—. Prof. English U. Calif., Irvine, 1990-94. Author: Poems by Robert Simeon Adams, 1952, Blake and Yeats: The Contrary Vision, 1955, 2d edit., 1969, The Contexts of Poetry, 1963, William Blake: A Reading of the Shorter Poems, 1963, Poetry: An Introductory Anthology, 1968, The Horses of Instruction, 1968, Fiction as Process, 1968, The Interests of Criticism, 1969, William Blake: Jerusalem, Selected Poems and Prose, 1970, The Truth About Dragons, 1971, Critical Theory Since Plato, 1971, rev. edit., 1992, Lady Gregory, 1973, The Academic Tribes, 1976, 2d edit., 1988, Philosophy of the Literary Symbolic, 1983, Joyce Cary's Trilogies, 1983, Critical Theory Since 1965, 1986, The Book of Yeats's Poems, 1991, Antithetical Essays, 1991, Critical Essays on William Blake, 1991, The Book of Yeats's Vision, 1995,The Farm at Richwood and Other Poems, 1997, Many Pretty Toys, 1999, Home, 2001; mem. editl. bd. Epoch, 1954-56, Tex. Studies Lit. and Lang., 1957-68, Studies in Romanticism, 1966—, Blake Studies, 1969-80, Modern Lang. Quar., 1977-84. Served to 1st lt. USMC, 1943-45, 51. Guggenheim fellow, 1974-75 Mem. Internat. Assn. Univ. Profs. English, Am. Conf. for Irish Studies, Phi Beta Kappa. Home: 3930 NE 157th Pl Seattle WA 98155-6730 Office: U Wash PO Box 354338 Seattle WA 98195-4338 E-mail: hadams3048@aol.com

ADAMS, J. PHILLIP, oil industry executive; CEO Flying J. Inc., Brigham City, Utah. Office: Flying J Inc PO Box 678 Brigham City UT 84302

ADAMS, JAMES FREDERICK, psychologist, educational administrator; b. Andong, Korea, Dec. 27, 1927; s. Benjamin Nyce and Phyllis Irene (Taylor) A.; m. Carol Ann Wagner, Jan. 17, 1980; children— James Edward, Dorothy Lee Adams Vanderhorst, Robert Benjamin B.A. In Psychology, U. Calif.-Berkeley, 1950; Ed.M. in Counseling and Psychology, Temple U., 1951; Ph.D. in Exptl. Psychology, Wash. State U., 1959. Cert. psychologist, Wash., Pa.; lic. psychologist, Pa. Psychometrician Measurement and Research Ctr., Temple U., Phila., 1951-52; asst. prof. psychology Whitworth Coll., Spokane, Wash., 1952-55; teaching and research asst. State U. Wash., 1955-57; research assoc. Miami U., Oxford, Ohio, 1957-59; asst. prof. psychology Coll. Liberal Arts, Temple U., 1959-62, assoc. prof., 1962-66, prof., 1966-80, chmn. dept. counseling psychology, 1969-72; vis. prof. psychology Coll. Soc. Scis., U. P.R., Rio Piedras, 1963-64, Coll. Scis., Cath. U., Ponce, P.R., 1971-72; chmn. dept. counseling psychology Coll. Edn., Temple U., 1973-77, coordinator div. ednl. psychology, 1974-76; grad. dean, prof. psychology Grad. Coll., U. Nev., Las Vegas, 1980 85; acad. (sr.) v.p. Longwood Coll., Farmville, Va., 1985-86. Author: Problems in Counseling: A Case Study Approach, 1962, Instructors Manual for Understanding Adolescence, 1969; (exhbn. catalogue with J. D. Selig) Colonial Spanish Art of the Americas, 1976; (comml. pamphlet with C. L. Davis) The Use of the Vu-graph as an Instructional Aid, 1960; editor: Counseling and Guidance: A Summary View, 1965, Understanding Adolescence: Current Developments in Adolescent Psychology, 1968, 4th edit., 1980, Human Behavior in a Changing Society, 1973, Songs that had to be Sung (by B. N. Adams), 1979; contbr. chpts., articles, tests and book revs. to profl. publs. Served to cpl. USMC, 1945-46 Recipient Alexander Meiklejohn award AAUP, 1984; James McKean Cattell research fund grantee Miami U., Oxford, Ohio, 1958, Bolton fund research grantee Temple U., 1960, 62, faculty research grantee Temple U., 1961, 63, Commonwealth of Pa. research grantee Temple U., 1969, 70, 71, 72, summer research fellow Temple U., 1979; recipient scholarship U. Munich, 1955; James F. Adams endowment for psychology established at Wash. State U., Pullman, 2001. Fellow Am. Psychol. Assn. (divs. 26, 17); mem. Eastern Psychol. Assn., Western Psychol. Assn., Interam. Soc. Psychology, Sigma Xi, Psi Chi Avocations: art collecting; art restoring. Scholarship established in his name at U. Nev., Las Vegas. Home: 130 Palacio Rd Corrales NM 87048-9648

ADAMS, JOHN M. library director; b. Chicago, Ill., June 10, 1950; s. Merlin J. and Esther (Bohn) A.; m. Nancy Ileen Coultas, June 12, 1970; 1 child, Arwen Lee B.A. in English, U. Ill., 1972, M.L.S., 1973. Grad. asst. U. Ill. Libr., Urbana, 1972-73; libr.-reference Sherman Oaks Libr., L.A., 1973-75; libr. philosophy dept. L.A. Pub. Libr., 1975-77, head gen. reading svc., 1977-78; dir. Moline Pub. Libr., Ill., 1978-83, Tampa (Fla.)-Hillsborough County Pub. Libr. System, 1983-91; dir., county librarian Orange County (Calif.) Public Library System, 1991—. Dir. Tampa Bay Libr. Consortium, Fla., 1983-91, Santiago Libr. System, 1991—, chmn., 1999; mem. adv. com. on pub. librs. OCLC, 1992-95. Contbr. articles to profl. jours. Bd. dirs. Planned Parenthood of Tampa, 1984 Recipient Frontier award ALA Mag., 1981; named Outstanding Young Man, Moline Jaycees, 1983. Mem. ALA (J.C. Dana award 1982, 93), Calif. Libr. Assn., Calif. County Librs. Assn., Orange County C. of C. Avocations: music; tennis. Office: Orange County Pub Libr 1501 E Saint Andrew Pl Santa Ana CA 92705-4930 E-mail: jadams@ocpl.org

ADAMS, JOSEPH KEITH, lawyer; b. Provo, Utah, Apr. 3, 1949; s. Joseph S. and Marian (Bellows) A.; m. Myrle June Overly, Sept. 2, 1971; children: Derek J., Bret K., Stephanie, Julie K., Scott J., Laura. BA summa cum laude, Brigham Young U., 1973; JD, Harvard U., 1976. Bar: Utah 1976, U.S. Dist. Ct. Utah 1976, U.S. Tax Ct. 1983. Assoc. Van Cott, Bagley, Cornwall & McCarthy, Salt Lake City, 1976-82, shareholder,

1982-98; also bd. dirs. Van Cott, Bagley, et al, Salt Lake City, 1993-97, chmn. tax and estate planning sect., 1995-98; ptnr. Stoel, Rives, LLP, Salt Lake City, 1998—. Adj. faculty Brigham Young U. Law Sch., Provo, 1993. Co-author: Practical Estate Planning Techniques, 1990. Planned giving com. Restoration Cathedral Madeleine, Salt Lake City, 1991-93; pres. Utah Planned Giving Roundtable, Salt Lake City, 1994, Salt Lake City Estate Planning Coun.; planned giving com. U. Utah Hosp. Found., 1994; bd. dirs. Salt Lake C.C. Found., 1982-98; stake pres. LDS Ch. David O. Mackay scholar Brigham Young U., 1967-73. Fellow Am. Coll. Trust and Estate Counsel; mem. ABA (real property, probate and trust sect., taxation sect.), Utah State Bar (exec. com., past chmn. estate planning probate sect.), Harvard Alumni Assn. Utah (chair bd. dirs. 1980-90), Harvard Law Sch. Assn. Utah (vice chair). Republican. Mem. LDS Ch. Avocations: skiing, reading, golfing. Office: Stoel Rives LLP 201 S Main St Ste 1100 Salt Lake City UT 84111-4904 E-mail: jkadams@stoel.com

ADAMS, KENNETH ROBERT, gaming analyst, writer, consultant, historian; b. Carson City, Nev., Sept. 8, 1942; s. Maurice Adams and Gertrude Aloha (Wilson) Burke; children: John Anthony, James Joseph. Prin. Ken Adams and Assoc., Sparks, Nev., 1990—. Coord. gaming history series of the oral history program U. Nev., continuing edns. gaming mgmt. program adv. com., 1988-97, chmn., 1988. Co-author: Playing the Cards That Are Dealt, 1992, Always Bet on the Butcher, 1994, War Stories, 1995, Dwayne Kling: Luck in the Residue of Design, 2001; publ., assoc. editor: Nev. Gaming Almanac, 1991—, Nev. Gaming Directory, 1997—, The Adams Report. Chmn. mktg. com. Downtown Improvement Assn., 1994—, pres., 2001—; steering com., chmn. gaming com. Festival Reno, 1984-86; mem. adv. bd. Leadership Reno Alumni Assn., 1995-97. Mem. Internat. Platform Assn. Office: Ken Adams & Assocs 210 Marsh Ave Ste 103 Reno NV 89509-1698 Fax: 775-322-7806

ADAMS, LORETTA, marketing executive; b. Panama; BS in Internat. Mktg., Am. U., 1962; postgrad. in Econs., U. Panama, Panama City, 1963-64. Mgmt. trainee Sears Roebuck & Co., Panama City, Panama, 1962-63, mgmt. pers. Panama, 1963-65; supr. internat. advertising projects Kenyon & Eckhardt Advertising, Inc., N.Y.C., 1965-68; asst. rsch. dir. divsn. L.Am. and Far E. Richardson-Vicks Internat., Mexico City and Wilton, Conn., 1968-69, rsch. dir. divsn. Mex. and L.Am., 1969-75, mem. top mgmt. strategic planning team, 1975-78; founder, pres. Mkt. Devel., Inc., San Diego, 1978—. Contbr. articles to profl. jours. Mem. Am. Mktg. Assn., European Soc. for Opinion & Market Rsch., Advt. Rsch. Found., Coun. Am. Survey Rsch. Orgns., Market Rsch. Assn. Office: Market Devel Inc 600 B St Ste 1600 San Diego CA 92101-4584

ADAMS, MARK, artist; b. Ft. Plain, N.Y., Oct. 27, 1925; s. Earl D. and Edith (Wohlgemuth) A.; m. Beth Van Hoesen, Sept. 12, 1953. Student, Syracuse U., 1943-46, Hans Hofmann Sch. Fine Arts, 1946, 48, Jean Lurcat, 1955. Instr. San Francisco Art Inst., 1961; panelist Internat. Symposium on Tapestry, San Francisco, 1976; disting. vis. prof. U. Calif. at Davis, 1978; painter in residence Am. Acad. in Rome, 1963 Book: Mark Adams, 1985; one-man shows include deYoung Mus., San Francisco, 1959, Portland (Oreg.) Mus., 1961, Calif. Palace of Legion of Honor, San Francisco, 1961, retrospective, 1970, San Francisco Mus. Modern Art, 1962, French & Co., N.Y.C., 1964, John Berggruen Gallery, San Francisco, 1978, 80, 82, 83, 85, 87, 90, 94, Graham Modern, N.Y.C., 1981, 84, Jane Haslem Salon, Washington, 1989, Palo Alto (Calif.) Cultural Ctr., 1990; exhibited in numerous group shows including Mus. Contemporary Crafts, N.Y.C., 1957, 58, 62, 65, Dallas Mus., 1958, Internat. Biennial of Tapestry, Lausanne, Switzerland, 1962, 65, St. Louis Art Mus., 1964, Norfolk Mus., 1966; represented in permanent collections San Francisco Mus. Modern Art, Dallas Mus. Fine Arts, Chase Manhattan Bank, N.Y.C., San Francisco Pub. Library, Legion of Honor Mus., San Francisco; maj. archtl. commns. include tapestries, Bank of Calif., San Francisco, Weyerhauser Co., Tacoma, Wash., Fairmont Hotel, Dallas, San Francisco Internat. Airport, Luth. Brotherhood, Mpls., stained glass, Temple Emanu-el, San Francisco, St. Thomas More Cath. Ch., San Francisco, St. Andrews Episcopal Ch., Saratoga, Calif. Office: c/o John Berggruen Gallery 228 Grant Ave San Francisco CA 94108-4612

ADAMS, PETER FREDERICK, university president, civil engineer; b. Halifax, N.S., Can. m. Barbara Adams, Oct. 11, 1957; 3 sons. B.Eng., N.S. Tech. Coll., 1958, M.Engr., 1961; Ph.D., Lehigh U., 1966. With Internat. Nickel Co. Can., 1958-59, Dominion Bridge Co., 1974-75; mem. faculty U. Alta., Edmonton, 1960-89, prof. civil engring., 1971-89; dean Faculty of Engring., 1976-84; pres. Ctr. for Frontier Engring. Research, 1984-89, Tech. U. N.S., Halifax, 1989-92, Can. Inst. Petroleum Industry Devel. (now Can. Petroleum Inst.), Edmonton, Alta., Can., 1992—; dir. Churchill Corp., 1993—. Lectr. in field. Author: (Krentz & Kulak) Canadian Structural Steel Design, 1973, (Krentz & Kulak) Limit States Design in Structural Steel, 1977. Past pres. Aspen Gardens Community League;past chmn. Salvation Army Red Shield Appeal. Fellow Can. Soc. Civil Engring. (Sanderson award 1986), Can. Acad. Engring., Engring. Inst. Can.; mem. ASCE (A.B. Anderson award 1986), Internat. Assn. Bridge & Structural Engring. (hon.), Can. Stds. Assn., Toastmasters (past pres.). Office: Canadian Inst Petroleum 4220 98th St Edmonton AB Canada T6E 6AI

ADAMS, THOMAS MERRITT, lawyer; b. St. Louis, Sept. 27, 1935; s. Galen Edward and Chloe (Merritt) A.; m. Sarah McCardell Davis, June 6, 1959; children: Mark Merritt, John Harrison, William Shields, Thomas Bondurant. AB, Washington U., St. Louis, 1956, JD, 1960; postgrad., London Sch. Econs., 1957; LLM, George Washington U., 1966. Bar: Mo. 1960, Calif. 1971. Atty. SEC, Washington, 1964-66; asst. dir., asst. gen. counsel Investment Bankers Assn., Washington, 1966-68; pres. Transamerica Investment Mgmt., 1969-80; ptnr. Lanning Adams & Peterson, 1980—. Author: State and Local Pension Funds, 1968; contbr. articles to profl. jours. Chmn. Salina (Kans.) Community Ambassador program, 1961. Served to capt. USAF, 1960-63. Decorated Air Force Commendation medal. Mem. Phi Beta Kappa. Episcopalian. Office: Lanning Adams & Peterson 11777 San Vicente Blve #750 Los Angeles CA 90049-5067

ADAMS, WAYNE VERDUN, pediatric psychologist, educator; b. Rhinebeck, N.Y., Feb. 24, 1945; s. John Joseph and Lorena Pearl (Munroe) A.; m. Nora Lee Swindler, June 12, 1971; children: Jennifer, Elizabeth. BA, Houghton Coll., 1966; MA, Syracuse U., 1969, PhD, 1970; postgrad., U. N.C., Chapel Hill, 1975. Hon. diplomate Am. Bd. Profl. Psychology; lic. psychologist, N.Y., Del., Oreg. Asst. prof. Colgate U., Hamilton, N.Y., 1970-75; chief psychologist Alfred I. DuPont Inst., Wilmington, Del., 1976-86; dir. divsn. psychology, dept. pediat. DuPont Hosp. for Children (formerly Alfred I. DuPont Inst.), Wilmington, 1987-99; mem. Del. Bd. Licensure in Psychology, 1983-86, bd. pres., 1986; assoc. prof. pediat. Thomas Jefferson Coll. Medicine, Phila., 1995-99; prof. psychology George Fox U., Newberg, Oreg., 1999—, dept. chair grad. sch. clin. psychology, 2001—. Grant reviewer NIH, 1999—. Cons. editor Jour. Pediatric Psychology, 1980-83, guest reviewer, 1984—; co-author 4 nationally used psychol. tests in field; contbr. articles to profl. jours. Fellow APA, Nat. Acad. Neuropsychology; mem. Soc. Pediatric Psychology, Nat. Acad. Neuropsychology, Del. Psychol. Assn. (exec. com. 1979-82, pres. 1981-82), Oreg. Psychol. Assn. Office: George Fox U Dept Psychology 414 N Meridian St Newberg OR 97132-2697

ADAMS, WILLIAM B. chemical company executive; BA, Tex. Tech. U. CEO WBA Cons., Ltd., 1980-86; pres. and CEO Check Tech. Corp., 1986-88; exec. chmn. Printrak, Inc., 1989-91; chmn. bd. Chronimed, Inc., 1985-94; chmn. bd. and CEO Eco Soil Sys., Inc., [illegible] 1991—. Office: Eco Soil Sys Inc 10740 Thornmint Rd San Diego CA 92127

ADAMS, WILLIAM GILLETTE, lawyer; b. Dallas, July 26, 1940; s. Dwight B. and Ruth L. (Gillette) A.; m. Barbara A. Picoli, Jan. 24, 1970. BA in Econs., Stanford U., 1963; JD, U. Utah, 1968. Bar: Calif. 1969; registered Conseil Juridique, France. Vol. Peace Corps, Morocco, 1963-65; assoc. O'Melveny & Myers, L.A., 1968-75, ptnr. Newport Beach, Calif., 1979—, resident ptnr. Paris, 1979-84; ptnr. Erickson, Zerfas & Adams, L.A., 1975-79. Bd. dir. Valentine Enterprises, Inc., 1983—. Editor-in-chief Utah Law Rev., 1967-68 With USCG, 1957-58. Mem. ABA, Orange County Bar Assn., L.A. Bar Assn., Calif. Bar Assn., Cercle Union Interalliee, Big Canyon Country Club, Order of Coif, Phi Kappa Phi, Phi Delta Phi. Office: O'Melveny & Myers 610 Newport Center Dr Ste 1700 Newport Beach CA 92660-6429 also: 400 S Hope St Los Angeles CA 90071-2801

ADAMSON, ARTHUR WILSON, chemistry educator; b. Shanghai, China, Aug. 15, 1919; s. Arthur Quintin and Ethel (Rhoda) A.; m. Virginia Louise Dillman, Mar. 24, 1942; children: Carol Ann, Janet Louise, Jean Elizabeth B.S. with honors, U. Calif.-Berkeley, 1940; Ph.D. in Phys. Chemistry, U. Chgo., 1944; PhD (hon.), U. Ferrara, Italy, 1993. Research assoc. Manhattan Project, Oak Ridge, 1944-46; asst. prof. U. So. Calif., 1946-49, assoc. prof., 1949-53, prof., 1953-89, prof. emeritus, 1989—, chmn. dept. chemistry, 1972-75. Foster lectr. U. Buffalo, 1970; Venable lectr. U. N.C., 1975; Bikerman lectr. Case Western U., 1982; Reilly lectr. Notre Dame U., 1984. Author: Concepts of Inorganic Photochemistry, 1975, Understanding Physical Chemistry, 1980, Textbook of Physical Chemistry, 1986, Physical Chemistry of Surfaces, 1997; editor Langmuir Am. Chem. Soc., 1984-89; editor emeritus, 1990—; contbr. articles to profl. jours. Recipient Creative Scholarship and rsch. award U. So. Calif., 1971, Excellence in Teaching award, 1979, Raubenheimer award, 1984, Disting. Emeritus award, 1991; Alexander von Humboldt Sr. Scientist award, 1971, others; Gold medal Am. Inst. Chemists, 1994, Monie A. Ferst award Sigma Xi, 1999. Fellow Am. Inst. Chemists (Gold medal 1994); mem. Am. Chem Soc. (councillor So. Calif. sect. 1964-80, chmn. 1964, Tolman award 1967, Kendall award 1979, Langmuir lectr. 1981, Disting. Svc. in Inorganic Chemistry award 1982, Chem. Edn. award 1984, Agnes Ann Green Disting Svc. award 1989, Harry and Carol Mosher award 1990, Arthur W. Adamson Award for Disting. Svc. in Advancement of Surface Chemistry established in his honor 1992). Republican. Avocations: tennis; photography. Office: U So Calif Dept Chem U Park Los Angeles CA 90089-0001

ADASHI, ELI Y. obstetrician, gynecologist; MD, U. Tel Aviv, Israel, 1972. Diplomate Am. Bd. Obstetrics-Gynecology, Am. Bd. Reprodn. Endocrinology. Intern Met. Gen. Hospital, Tel Aviv, Israel, 1972-73; resident ob.-gyn. Tufts U. Sch. Medicine, Boston, 1974-77; fellow reprodn. endocrinology Johns Hopkins U., Balt., 1977-78; fellow reprodn.-endocrinology U. Calif. San Diego, La Jolla, 1978-81; mem. med. staff U. Md. Hosp., Balt., 1981-96; prof. ob.-gyn., physiology U. Md., Balt., 1981-96; pvt. practice in ob.-gyn. Balt., 1981-96; chair dept. ob-gyn. U. Utah, Salt Lake City, 1996—. ACOG, Am. Fedn. Surgeons, Endocrine Surgeons, Soc. Gastro Enterology. Office: U Utah 50 N Med Dr Ste 2b200 Salt Lake City UT 84132-0001

ADCOCK, COREY J. construction executive; CFO American West Homes, Las Vegas, Nev., 1996—. Office: American West Homes 2700 E Sunset Rd Ste 5 Las Vegas NV 89120-3507

ADDICOTT, FREDRICK TAYLOR, retired botany educator; b. Oakland, Calif., Nov. 16, 1912; s. James Edwin and Ottilia Katherine Elizabeth (Klein) A.; m. Alice Holmes Baldwin, Aug. 11, 1935; children: Donald James, Jean Alice, John Fredrick, David Baldwin. AB in Biology, Stanford U., 1934; PhD in Plant Physiology, Calif. Inst. Tech., 1939. Instr. to asst. prof. Santa Barbara (Calif.) State Coll., 1939-46; assoc. physiologist emergency rubber project USDA, Salinas, Calif., 1942-44; asst. prof. to prof. UCLA, 1946-60; prof. agronomy U. Calif., Davis, 1961-72, prof. botany, 1972-77, prof. emeritus, 1977—. Vis. prof. U. Adelaide, Australia, 1966, U. Natal, Pietermaritzburg, Republic South Africa, 1970. Author: Abscission, 1982; editor, author: Abscisic Acid, 1983; contbr. articles to profl. jours. Fulbright rsch. scholar Victoria U., N.Z., 1957, Royal Bot. Garden, U.K., 1976; vis. fellow Australian Nat. U., 1983. Fellow AAAS; mem. Am. Soc. Plant Physiologists (Charles Reid Barnes Life Membership award 1990), Australian Soc. Plant Physiologists, Bot. Soc. Am., Internat. Plant Growth Substance Assn., Internat. Soc. Plant Morphologists, South African Assn. Botanists. Avocations: backpacking, cabinet making. Home and Office: 1515 Shasta Dr Apt 3323 Davis CA 95616-6688

ADDICOTT, WARREN OLIVER, retired geologist, educator; b. Fresno, Calif., Feb. 17, 1930; s. Irwin Oliver and Astrid (Jensen) A.; m. Suzanne Aubin, Oct. 2, 1976; m. Susanne Smith, Aug. 20, 1955 (div. 1974); children: Eric Oliver, Carol. BA cum laude, Pomona Coll., Calif., 1951; MA, Stanford U., Calif., 1952; PhD, U. Calif.-Berkeley, 1956. Teaching asst. U. Calif.-Berkeley, 1952-54; paleontologist Standard Oil Co. Calif., 1953; geologist Mobil Oil Co., 1954-62; research geologist U.S. Geol. Survey, Menlo Park, Calif., 1962-94; cons. prof. Stanford U., 1970-81. Dep. chmn. Circum-Pacific Map Project, Menlo Park, Calif., 1979-82, gen. chmn., 1982-86, project advisor, 1986—; adj. prof. So. Oreg. U., 1989-97; bd. dirs. Circum-Pacific Coun. Energy and Mineral Resources, 1983-86. Contbr. articles to profl. jours. Fellow AAAS, Geol. Soc. Am., Calif. Acad. Scis., Paleontol. Soc. (pres. 1979-80), Paleontol. Res. Instn. (bd. dirs. 1980-81). Unitarian. Home: 2260 Old Siskiyou Hwy Ashland OR 97520

ADDIS, RICHARD BARTON, lawyer; b. Columbus, Ohio, April 9, 1929; s. Wilbur Jennings and Leila Olive (Grant) A.; m. Marguerite C. Christjohn, Feb. 9, 1957; children: Jacqueline Carol, Barton David. BA, Ohio State U., 1954, JD, 1955. Bar: Ohio 1956, U.S. Dist. Ct. (no. dist.) Ohio 1957, N.Mex. 1963, U.S. Dist. Ct. N.Mex. 1963, Laguna Pueblo (N.Mex.) Tribal Ct. 1986. Pvt. practice, Canton, Ohio, 1956-63, Albuquerque, 1963—, Laguna Pueblo, 1986—. Co-developer The Woodlands Subdivsn., Albuquerque; co-owner Cerro del Oro Mine, Valencia County, N.Mex., 1977—. With USMC, 1946-48, 50-52. Mem. Ohio Bar Assn., N.Mex. Bar Assn. Office: PO Box 25923 Albuquerque NM 87125-0923

ADDIS, THOMAS HOMER, III, professional golfer; b. San Diego, Nov. 30, 1945; s. Thomas H. and Martha J. (Edwards) A.; m. Susan Tera Buckley, June 13, 1966; children: Thomas Homer IV, Bryan Michael. Student, Foothill Jr. Coll., 1963, Grossmont Jr. Coll., 1965; degree in profl. golf mgmt. (hon.), Ferris State U., 1995. Head golf profl., mgr. Sun Valley Golf Course, La Mesa, Calif., 1966-67; head golf profl., dir. golf Singing Hills Country Club and Lodge, 1969-98; sr. v.p. Golfstar Mgmt., 1998-99; v.p. Full Swing Golf, San Diego, 1999-2000; pres. Medallion Golf Inc., 2000—. Gen. chmn. Nat. Jr. Golf Championship, U.S. Golf Assn., 1973-89; lectr., owner Medallion Golf Mgmt., Rocky Mountain Chocolate Factory, Mammoth; spkr. in field; instr. Profl. Golfers Career Coll. Contbr. articles to profl. jours. Chmn. Nat. Com. Liaison for Physically Challenged, 1984-88; dir. Cuyamaca Coll. Found., Burn Inst.; mem. internat. golf com. Spl. Olympics. Recipient Retailer award Golf Industry mag., 1985; named to Lady Aztec San Diego State U. Hall of Fame. Mem. PGA (pres. San Diego chpt. 1978-79, pres. sect. 1980-82, bd. dirs. sect. 1974-90, spkr., [illegible] mem. svc. com. 1980-87, bd. dirs. San Diego sect. 1974-90, assn. coord. bus. schs. and seminars, named Profl. of Yr. So. Calif. sect. 1979, 89, Horton Smith award So. Calif. sect. 1980-81, 89, PGA Golf Profl. of Yr. 1989, Nat. Horton Smith awarwd 1981, Resort Merchandiser of Yr., So. Calif. sect. 1978, 83, mem. nat. bd. control 1978-85, chmn. nat. bd. control 1991-92, membership com. 1978, 89-90, nat. [illegible] nat. bd. dirs. 1986-88, rules com. 1986-90, championship com. 1986, [illegible] mem. So. Calif. sect. and San Diego PGA,), So. Calif. PGA Hall of Fame, Nat. Golf Found. (Joe Graffis award 1988), Nat. Amputee Golf Assn. (hon.), San Diego Jr. Golf Assn. (pres. 1997-98, 2000), Assn. Golf Educators, Golf Collector's Soc., Rotary. Office: 12312A Paseo Lucido San Diego CA 92128 E-mail: taddispga@aol.com

ADELL, HIRSCH, lawyer; b. Novogrodek, Poland, Mar. 11, 1931; came to U.S., 1937; s. Nathan and Nachama (Wager) A.; m. Judith Audrey Fuss, Feb. 8, 1963; children— Jeremiah, Nikolas, Balthasar, Valentine. Student, CCNY, 1949-52; B.A., UCLA, 1955, LL.B., 1963. Bar: Cal. bar 1963. Adminstrv. asst. to State Senator Richard Richards, 1956-60; ptnr. Warren & Adell, Los Angeles, 1963-75, Reich, Adell, Crost & Cvitan, L.A., 1975—. Counsel AFTRA, Los Angeles Served with AUS, 1953-55. Mem. ABA (labor and employment law sect.) Home: 545 S Norton Ave Los Angeles CA 90020-4610 Office: Reich Adell Crost & Cvitan 501 Shatto Pl Ste 100 Los Angeles CA 90020-1792

ADELMAN, ANDREW A. city manager; married; 2 children. BS in Civil Engring., BS in Nuc. Engring., MS in Structural Engring., U. Calif.; cert. in mgmt., Harvard U. Registered profl. engr., Calif., Ariz., Nev. Engr. Impel Corp. and Quadrex Corp., San Francisco, 1979-81; lead engr. Cygna Corp., San Francisco, 1981-83; chief engr. Panel Clip/Lumberlok, Hayward, Calif., 1983-84; plans and permit divsn. mgr., chief plan check engr. City of Fremont, 1984-92; chief bldg. offcl., dep. dir. Dept. Planning Bldg. and Code Enforcement, City of San Jose, 1992-97; gen. mgr. dept. bldg. and safety City of L.A., 1997—. Adj. prof. engring. Saginaw Valley State Coll., Mich., 1982. Mem. Calif. Seismic Safety Commn., Calif. Hosp. Bldg. Safety Bd. Recipient numerous awards. Mem. Tau Beta Pi, Chi Epsilon, Delta Chi. Office: City LA Bldg & Safety Dept 201 N Figueroa St Rm 1000 Los Angeles CA 90012-2623

ADELMAN, IRMA GLICMAN, economics educator; b. Cernowitz, Rumania, Mar. 14, 1930; came to U.S., 1949, naturalized, 1955; d. Jacob Max and Raissa (Ettinger) Glicman; m. Frank L. Adelman, Aug. 16, 1950 (div. 1979); 1 son, Alexander. BS, U. Calif., Berkeley, 1950, MA, 1951, PhD, 1955. Teaching assoc. U. Calif., Berkeley, 1955-56, instr., 1956-57, lectr. with rank asst. prof., 1957-58; vis. asst. prof. Mills Coll., 1958-59; acting asst. prof. Stanford, 1959-61, asst. prof., 1961-62; assoc. prof. Johns Hopkins, Balt., 1962-65; prof. econs. Northwestern U., Evanston, Ill., 1966-72, U. Md., 1972-78; prof. econs. and agrl. econs. U. Calif. at Berkeley, 1979-94; prof. emeritus, 1994—. Cons. divsn. indsl. devel. UN, 1962-63, AID U.S. Dept. State, Washington, 1963-72, World Bank, 1968—, ILD, Geneva, 1973—. Author: Theories of Economic Growth and Development, 1961, (with A. Pepelasis and L. Mears), Economic Development: Analysis and Case Studies, 1961, (with Eric Thorbecke) The Theory and Design of Economic Development, 1966, (with C.T. Morris) Society, Politics and Economic Development— A Quantitative Approach, 1967, Practical Approaches to Development Planning-Korea's Second Five Year Plan, 1969, (with C.T. Morris) Economic Development and Social Equity in Developing Countries, 1973, (with Sherman Robinson) Planning for Income Distribution, 1977-78, (with C. T. Morris) Comparative Patterns of Economic Growth, 1850-1914, 1987, (J. Edward Taylor) Village Economies: Design, Estimation and Application of Village Wide Economic Models, 1996, Institutions and Development Strategies: Selected Essays of Irma Adelman Vol. I, 1994, Vol. II, 1994. Decorated Order of the Bronze Tower (Korea); fellow Ctr. Advanced Study Behavioral Scis., 1970-71; named Women's Hall Fame U. Calif., Berkeley, 1994. Fellow Am. Acad. Arts and Scis., Econometric Soc., Royal Soc. Encouragement Arts, Mfg. and Commerce (Berkeley citation 1996); mem. Am. Econ. Assn. (mem. exec. com., v.p. 1969-71). Office: Univ Calif Dept Agr & Natural Resources 207 Giannini Hall Spc 3310 Berkeley CA 94720-3310

ADELMAN, MARC D. lawyer; b. 1950; BA, Western Ill. U.; JD, Western State U. Bar: Calif. 1978. Pvt. practice, San Diego. Mem. ABA, Calif. State Bar Assn. (pres.). Office: 2718 5th Ave San Diego CA 92103-6329

ADELMAN, RICK, professional basketball coach; b. June 16, 1946; m. Mary Kay Adelman; children: Kathryn Mary, Laura, R.J., David. Master's, Loyola Marymount U. Profl. basketball player, San Diego, 1968-70, Portland (Oreg.) Trail Blazers, 1970-73, asst. coach, 1983-89, head coach, 1989-94; basketball player Chgo., New Orleans, Kansas City, and Omaha, 1973-75; head coach Chemeketa Community Coll., Salem, Oreg., 1975-83, Golden State Warriors, Oakland, Calif., 1995-97, Sacramento Kings, 1998—. Office: Sacramento Kings ARCO Arena One Sports Parkway Sacramento CA 95834

ADELMAN, RODNEY LEE, federal agency administrator; b. Washington, Sept. 21, 1950; s. Charles H. and Vivian Fern (Sleek) A.; widowed; 1 child. BS, U. Md., 1972. Staff Senator Robert P. Griffin, Mich., 1970-73; fin. mgr. labor mgmt. svcs. adminstrn. Dept. of Labor, 1973-78; budget officer Congress of Micronesia, 1978-79, Federated States Micronesia, 1979-80; dir. budget and grants mgmt. Trust Territory of the Pacific Islands, 1980-85; comptroller Def. Personnel Support Ctr. Def. Logistics Agy., 1985-86; dir. Washington Liaison Office, Juneau, Alaska, 1986-92; dep. asst. adminstr. Power Mktg. Liaison Office, 1992-96; Alaska power adminstr. Dept. of Energy, Juneau, 1996-99; CFO Internat. Boundary and Water Commn., El Paso, Tex.

ADELSMAN, JEAN (HARRIETTE ADELSMAN), newspaper editor; b. Indpls., Oct. 21, 1944; d. Joe and Beatrice Irene (Samuel) A. BS in Journalism, Northwestern U., 1966, MS in Journalism, 1967. Copy editor Chgo. Sun-Times, 1967-75, fin. news editor, 1975-77, entertainment editor, 1977-80, asst. mng. editor features, 1980-84; now mng. editor Daily Breeze, Torrance, Calif. Office: Daily Breeze 5215 Torrance Blvd Torrance CA 90503-4077

ADELSON, MERV LEE, entertainment and communication industry executive; b. Los Angeles, Oct. 23, 1929; s. Nathan and Pearl (Schwarzman) A.; m. Thea Nesis, May 25, 1993; 1 child, Lexi Rose; children from previous marriage: Ellen, Gary, Andrew. Student, Menlo Park Jr. Coll. Pres. Markettown Supermarket and Builders Emporium, Las Vegas, 1953-63; mng. ptnr. Paradise Devel., Las Vegas, 1958—; pres. Realty Holdings, 1962—, La Costa, Inc., 1963-87; chmn. bd. dirs. Lorimar Inc., Culver City, Calif., 1969-86; chmn. bd. dirs., chief exec. officer Lorimar Telepictures Corp., Culver City, 1986-89; vice chmn. Warner Communications, 1989—; chmn. East-West Capital Assocs., Inc. (now East-West Capital Venture Group), 1989—; bd. dirs. Time-Warner Inc. (now Warner EMI). Co-founder Nathan Adelson Hospice Found. Recipient Sherill Corwin Human Relations award Am. Jewish Com., 1987. Mem. Am. Film Inst. (trustee), Am. Mus. of Moving Images (trustee), Entertainment Industries Council (trustee), Acad. Motion Pictures Arts and Scis., Acad. TV Arts and Sciences, Nat. Acad. Cable Programming, Alliance for Capital Access (bd. dirs.), Com. Publicly Owned Cos. (bd. dirs.).

ADELSON, ROGER DEAN, history educator, editor, historian; b. Abilene, Kans., July 11, 1942; s. Orlie Austin and Winnifred Graham (McClure) A.; m. Sally Isabelle Squires, Sept. 1966 (div. Apr. 1978). BA, George Washington U., 1964, MA, Washington U., 1967, PhD, 1972; BLitt, Oxford (Eng.) U., 1970. Danforth fellow Washington U., St. Louis, 1964-67; sr. rsch. fellow St. Antony's Coll., Oxford U., 1972-73; lectr. history Harvard U., Cambridge, Mass., summer 1974; asst. prof. Ariz. State U., Tempe, 1974-78, assoc. prof., 1978-95, prof., 1996—; editor Historian, 1990-95, cons. editor, 1995—. Vis. prof. Am. Grad. Sch. [illegible] Glendale, Ariz., 1980s, Pepperdine U., Malibu, Calif., 1994, 95, 96; dir. [illegible] Project, 1995-97. Author: Mark Sykes: Portrait of an Amateur, 1975, London and the Invention of the Middle East, 1995,

Speaking of History, 1996. Founding. pres. Soc. for Internat. Devel., Ariz., 1983; charter mem. Coun. Fgn. Rels., Phoenix, 1976. Mem. Conf. Hist. Jours. (pres. 1995-97), Phi Alpha Theta (historian 1990-95). Avocations: cycling, swimming, gardening, entertaining. Office: Ariz State U Dept History PO Box 872501 Tempe AZ 85287-2501

ADELSTONE, JEFFREY ALAN, accountant, tax law specialist, educator; b. Los Angeles, Feb. 15, 1947; s. James and Joyce S. (Waldman) A.; m. E. Ruth Wilcox, Apr. 6, 1968; children: Kimberley, Stacey, Toni. BS, U. Ariz., 1969; M.Edn., 1971. Cert. Jr. Coll. Instr., Ariz; cert. instr. Ariz. Dept. Real Estate, accredited Accreditation Council for Accountancy, enrolled to practice, IRS; cert. fin. planner. Tchr., Tucson High Sch., 1969-72; instr. Pima Community Coll., Tucson, 1970-78; pres., owner Adelstone Fin. Svcs., Inc. Tucson, 1970—. Active Rep. Task Force. Named Nat. Acct. of Yr., 1985, Ariz. Acct. Advocate of the Year SBA, 1988. Mem. Nat. Soc. Pub. Accts. (mem. fed. taxation com., assoc. state dir. for Ariz. 1983-84, state dir. 1987—), Nat. Assn. Enrolled Agts., Ariz. Soc. Practicing Accountants (dir. credit union, pres. Tucson chpt., state v.p. 1983-84, state pres. 1984-86), Cen. Ariz. Soc. Enrolled Agents (dir.), Enrolled Agts. Practicing in Ariz. (state pres. 1987-88), U.S. C. of C., Ariz. C. of C., Tucson Better Bus. Bur., Nat. Fedn. Ind. Bus., Registry Fin. Planning Practioners, Inst. Cert. Fin. Planners, Internat. Assn. Fin. Planners. Contbr. articles to profl. jours. Office: Adelstone Fin Svcs Inc 1580 N Kolb Rd Ste 1W Tucson AZ 85715-4931

ADEY, WILLIAM ROSS, physician; b. Adelaide, Australia, Jan. 31, 1922; s. William James and Constance Margaret (Weston) A.; m. Alwynne Sidney Morris (div. 1970); children: John, Susan, Geoffrey. MB and BS, U. Adelaide, Australia, 1943, MD, 1949. Sr. lectr. and reader, Dept. Anatomy U. Adelaide, Australia, 1947-53; sr. lectr., Dept. Anatomy U. Melbourne, Australia, 1955-56; prof. anatomy and physiology UCLA, 1957-77; dir. Space Biology Lab UCLA Space Biology Lab., 1965-77; dir. rsch. VA Med. Ctr., Loma Linda, Calif., 1977-97; adj. prof. biochemistry U. Calif., Riverside, 1997-2000. Cons. Office of Sci. and Tech. Policy, Washington,. 1964—, NIH, 1961—, NAS, 1965—. Author: Nonlinear Electrodynamics in Biological Systems, 1984, Magnetic Resonance Imaging of the Brain, Head and Neck, 1984. Surgeon lt. Australian Navy, 1944-46, South Pacific. Fellow IEEE, Royal Soc. Medicine, Nuffield Found. (London), AAAS, Am. Electroencephalographic Soc., Royal Soc. Medicine (London), Am. Assn. Neurolog. Surgeons. Avocations: radiophysics, radioastronomy, marathon running, backpacking. Home: Rte 1 Box 615 31866 3rd Ave Redlands CA 92374-8237 E-mail: RAdey43450@aol.com

ADIZES, ICHAK, management consultant, writer; PhD, Columbia U. With Hebrew U., Jerusalem, Tel Aviv U., Stanford (Calif.) U., Columbia U., N.Y.C.; founder, profl. dir. Adizes Inst., Santa Barbara, Calif., 1975—, acad. dean. Lectr. in field. Author: Self-Management, 1975, How to Solve the Mismanagement Crisis, 1979, Corporate Lifecycles: How and Why Corporations Grow and Die and What to Do About It, 1988, Mastering Change; The power of Mutual Trust and Respect in Personal Life, Business and Society, 1992, The Pursuit of Prime, 1996, Managing Corporate Life Cycles, 1999; contbr. articles to profl. jours., newspapers. Office: Adizes Inst 2815 E Valley Rd Santa Barbara CA 93108-1611 Fax: (805) 565-0741. E-mail: adizes@adizes.com

ADJENIAN, ROBERT, publisher; Mgr. Vedanta Press, Hollywood, Calif. Office: Vedanta Press 1946 Vedanta Pl Hollywood CA 90068-3920

ADKINS, JEANNE M. state legislator; b. North Platte, Nebr., May 2, 1949; BA, U. Nebr. Journalist; mem. Colo. Ho. of Reps., chairwoman judiciary com., vice-chairwoman legal svcs. com., mem. fin. com., regional air quality control coun., state edn. accountability commn. Founding sec. Douglas County Econ. Devel. Coun., bd. dirs., 1988. Fellow Vanderbilt U. Govt., Gates fellow JFK Sch. Govt. State/Local Program, Toll fellow. Mem. Am. Soc. Newspaper Editors, Soc. Profl. Journalists, Suburban Newspaper Assn. Republican. Baptist. Home: 6517 N Pinewood Dr Parker CO 80134-6351 Office: Ho Reps State Capitol Rm 271 Denver CO 80203

ADLER, ERWIN ELLERY, lawyer; b. Flint, Mich., July 22, 1941; s. Ben and Helen M. (Schwartz) A.; m. Stephanie Ruskin, June 8, 1967; children: Lauren, Michael, Jonathan B.A., U. Mich., 1963, LL.M., 1967; J.D., Harvard U., 1966. Bar: Mich. 1966, Calif. 1967. Assoc. Pillsbury, Madison & Sutro, San Francisco, 1967-73; assoc. Lawler, Felix & Hall, L.A., 1973-76, ptnr., 1977-80, Rogers & Wells, L.A., 1981-83, Richards, Watson & Gershon, L.A., 1983—. Bd. dirs. Hollywood Civic Opera Assn., 1975-76, Children's Scholarships Inc., 1979-80 Mem. ABA (vice chmn. appellate advocacy com. 1982-87), Calif. Bar Assn., Phi Beta Kappa, Phi Kappa Phi Jewish Office: Richards Watson & Gershon 333 S Hope St Bldg 38 Los Angeles CA 90071-1406

ADLER, FRED PETER, retired electronics company executive; b. Vienna, Austria, Mar. 29, 1925; came to U.S., 1942, naturalized, 1947; s. Michael and Ellida (Bronner) A.; m. Alicia Gulkis, 1950; children; Michael Steven, Andrew David; m. Adrienne Wilcox, 1991. BSEE with honors, U. Calif., Berkeley, 1945; MEE (Charles A. Coffin fellow), Calif. Inst. Tech., 1948, PhD magna cum laude, 1950. Elec. engr. GE Rsch. and Cons. Labs., 1945-47; project engr. Jet Propulsion Lab., 1950; with Hughes Aircraft Co., 1950-70, sr. staff physicist, dept. mgr., 1954-57, mgr. advanced planning, 1957-59, dir. advanced projects labs., 1959-61, v.p., mgr. space systems div., 1961-66, v.p., asst. group exec. Aerospace Group, 1966-70; pres. Nadgeco Ltd., 1970-72, chmn. bd., 1973-77; v.p., group exec. aerospace groups Hughes Aircraft Co., 1973-81, sr. v.p., pres. electro-optical and data sys. group, 1981-87; dir. Jefferson Ctr. for Character Edn., Monvovia, Calif., 1973-99, chmn. bd., 1988-99; ret., 1999. Co-author: text Guided Missile Engineering, 1959; also articles tech. jours. Fellow AIAA; mem. N.Y. Acad. Scis., Sigma Xi, Tau Beta Pi. Home: 10811 Ashton Ave Apt 414 Los Angeles CA 90024-4887 E-mail: fredad690@cs.com

ADLER, JEFFREY D. political consultant, public affairs consultant, crisis management expert; b. Cleve., July 10, 1952; s. Bennett and Edythe Joy (Eisner) A.; m. Colleen Ann Bentley, May 29, 1983. BS in Journalism, Northwestern U., 1975. Porter, waiter, bartender Amtrak, Chgo., 1975-76; reporter Enterprise-Courier, Oregon City, Oreg., 1977, Las Vegas Sun, 1977-80, O.C. Daily Pilot, Costa Mesa, Calif., 1982-85; v.p. pub. affairs Englander Comm., Newport Beach, 1985-86; pres. Adler Wilson Campaign Svcs., Laguna Hills, 1990-95, Adler Pub. Affairs, Long Beach, 1987—. Mem. Am. Assn. Polit. Cons. Democrat. Jewish. Home: 33 Pomona Ave Long Beach CA 90803-3426 Office: Adler Pub Affairs 200 Pine Ave Ste 300 Long Beach CA 90802-3038

ADLER, LOUISE DECARL, judge; b. 1945; BA, Chatham Coll., Pitts.; JD, Loyola U., Chgo. Bar: Ill., 1970, Calif., 1972. Practicing atty., San Diego, 1972-84; standing trustee Bankruptcy Ct. So. Dist. Calif., San Diego, 1974-79, chief bankruptcy judge, 1996-2000. Mem. editorial bd. Calif. Bankruptcy Jour., 1991-92. Fellow Am. Coll. Bankruptcy; mem. San Diego County Bar Assn. (chair bus. law study sect. 1979, fed. ct. com. 1983-84), Lawyers Club of San Diego (bd. dirs. 1972-73, treas. 1972-75, sec. 1972-74, v.p. 1974-75), San Diego Bankruptcy Forum (bd. dirs. 1989-92), Nat. Conf. Bankruptcy Judges (bd. dirs. 1989-91, sec. 1992-93, v.p. 1993-94, pres. 1994-95). Office: US Bankruptcy Ct 325 W F St Rm 2 San Diego CA 92101-6017

ADLER, MICHAEL I. lawyer; b. San Francisco, May 10, 1949; BA in Polit. Sci. summa cum laude, UCLA, 1971, JD, 1976; MA, Columbia U., 1973. Bar: Calif. 1977. Extern to Hon. Matthew O. Tobriner Calif. Supreme Ct., 1975; law clerk to Hon. William B. Enright U.S. Dist. Ct. (so. dist.) Calif., 1976-77; mem. Lichter, Grossman, Nichols & Adler, Inc., L.A., 1977-97, now ptnr., 1997—. Mem. entertainment law symposium com. UCLA, 1979—; instr. UCLA Extension, 1980. Woodrow Wilson fellow, 1972; Columbia U. Presdl. fellow, 1973. Mem. ABA, State Bar Calif., L.A. County Bar Assn., Beverly Hills Bar Assn., Phi Beta Kappa, Phi Eta Sigma. Office: Lichter Grossman Nichols & Adler Inc 9200 W Sunset Blvd Ph 1200 Los Angeles CA 90069-3607 E-mail: madler@lgna.com

ADLER, NANCY ELINOR, psychologist, educator; BA, Wellesley Coll., 1968; MA, Harvard U., 1971, PhD, 1973. Asst. prof. psychology U. Calif., Santa Cruz, 1972-76, assoc. prof. psychology, 1976-77, assoc. prof. med. psychology dept. psychiatry and pediat. San Francisco, 1977-84, prof. med. psychology depts. psychiatry and pediat., 1984—, dir. health psychology program, 1988—, program dir. NIMH tng. program, 1991—, vice chair dept. psychiatry, 1994—; dir. Ctr. for Health and Cmty., 1998—. Vis. asst. rsch. psychologist Inst. Personality Assessment and Rsch., U. Calif., Berkeley, 1975; mem. peer rev. panel Ad Hoc Sci. Study Sects., Nat. Inst. Child Health and Human Devel., 1977—, Nat. Heart, Lung and Blood Inst., 1993; adv. com. for five-yr. plan Demographic and Social Scis. Br., Ctr. for Population RSch., Nat. Inst. Child Health and Human Devel., 1986-87, adv. com., 1991-2000; sr. rsch. scientist in psychology Yale U., New Haven. 1994-95; review com. Intramural Rsch. NIMH, 1997, sci. adv. bd. Ctr. Advancement Health, Washington, 1995-96, bd. trustees, 1996—; grant reviewer NSF, Social Scis. and Humanities Rsch. Coun. Can., Soc. Behavioral Medicine, March of Dimes, Ctrs. for Disease Control, Econ. and Social Rsch. Coun.; presenter in field. Author: (with others) Health Psychology-A Handbook: Theories, Applications, and Challenges of a Psychological Approach to the Health Car System, 1979, Preventing Preterm Birth: A Parent's Guide, 1988, SES & Health in Industrialized Nations, 1999; adv. bd. Ency. Mental Health, 1995—; assoc. editor Health Psychology, 1984-90, Women's Health: Research in Gender, Behavior and Policy, 1994-98; mem. editl. bd. Jour. Population and Environment, 1982-8 8, Health Psychology, 1994—; manuscript reviewer Jour. Personality and Social Psychology, Jour. Nervous and Mental Disease, Personality and Social Psychology Bull., Jour. Health and Social Behavior, Jour. Applied Social Psychology, Basic and Applied Social Psychology, Psychology Women Quarterly, The Western Jour. Medicine, Jour. Am. Med. Assn., Am. Jour. Pub. Health, many others; contbr. articles in field. Recipient Best Rsch. Paper award Soc. for Adolescent Medicine, 1984; NSF fellow, 1968-72, U. Calif. Regents Summer fellow, 1974; grantee in field. Fellow APA (sec.-treas. divsn. 34 1975-78, pres. divsn. 34 1979-80, chairperson fellow com. divsn. 34 1982-86, planning com. for nat. conf. on tng. in health psychology 1982-83, participant Arden House conf. on edn. and tng. in health psychology 1983, chairperson nominations com., mem. expert panel on psychol. effects of abortion 1989-90, task force on promotion of population psychology 1992-97), A m. Psychol. Soc., Soc. Exptl. Social Psycholgy, Internat. Assn. Applied Psychology, Soc. Advancement Social Psychology, assn. Med. Sch. Profs. Psychology, Soc. for Rsch. on Adolescence, Inst. Medicine, Sigma Xi, Phi Beta Kappa. Office: U Ca Health Psychology Program 3333 California St San Francisco CA 94118-1981 E-mail: nadler@itsa.ucsF.edu

ADRIAN, CHARLES RAYMOND, political science educator; b. Portland, Oreg., Mar. 12, 1922; s. Harry Raymond and Helen K. (Petersen) A.; m. Audrey Jean Nelson, Apr. 2, 1946; children: Kristin, Nelson. B.A., Cornell (Iowa) Coll., 1947, LL.D., 1973; M.A., U. Minn., 1948, Ph.D., 1950; postdoctoral fellow, U. Copenhagen, Denmark, 1954-55. Instr., then asst. prof. govt. Wayne State U., 1949-55; from asst. prof. to prof. polit. sci. Mich. State U., 1955-66, chmn. dept., 1963-66; dir. Inst. Community Devel., 1958-63; prof. polit. sci. U. Calif.-Riverside, 1966-88, prof. emeritus, 1988—, chmn. dept., 1966-70, acad. asst. to v.p. acad. affairs, 1973-74. Cons. fed., state and local govt. ABC; research cons. Mich. Constl. Conv., 1961-62; Adminstrv. asst. to gov. Mich., 1956-57; mem. Meridian Twp. (Mich.) Planning Commn., 1957-60 Author: (with O. P. Williams) Four Cities: A Comparative Study in Community Politics, 1963, State and Local Governments, 2d edit., 1967, 3d edit., 1971, 4th edit., 1976, (with Charles Press) American Political Process, 1965, 2d. edit., 1969, Governing Urban America, 4th edit., 1972, 5th edit., 1977, American Politics Reappraised, 1974, (with E.S. Griffith) History of American City Government 1775-1870, 1976, History of American City Government, 1920-45, 1987, (with Michael Fine) State and Local Politics, 1990; also articles. Mem. Riverside Environ. Protection Commn., 1976-78, Riverside Mayor's Charter Revision Commn., 1985. Served with USAAF, 1943-46, PTO. Faculty fellow Fund Advancement Edn., 1954-55; mem. Phi Beta Kappa. Home: 606 Peachwood Pl Riverside CA 92506-6502

AEHLERT, BARBARA JUNE, health services executive; b. San Antonio, June 17, 1956; d. Bobby Ray and Ronella Su (Light) Mahoney; m. Dean A. Aehlert, Sept. 6, 1980; children: Andrea, Sherri. AA in Nursing, Glendale (Ariz.) C.C., 1976; BS in Profl. Arts, St. Joseph's Coll., Windham, Maine, 1997. Cert. ACLS instr., affiliate faculty, BLS instr., Basic Trauma Life Support instr., emergency med. tng./paramedic instr., ATLS and PEPP course coord. Gen. mgr. Hosp. Ambulance Svc., Phoenix, 1982-83; critical care nurse Samaritan Health Svcs., Phoenix, 1978-80, coord. patient transp., 1980-82, mgr. clin. programs, 1983-92; dir. emergency med. svcs. edn. EMS Edn. and Rsch., 1992-97; pres. S.W. EMS Edn. Inc., Glendale, Ariz., 1997—. EMS coord., City of Mesa Fire Dept., 2001—. Author: ACLS Quick Review Study Guide, 2d edit., 2001, ACLS Quick Review Slide Set, 1994, ACLS Quick Review Study Cards, 1994, PALS Study Guide, 1994, ECGs Made Easy, 2d edit., 2001, ECGs Made Easy Lesson Plans, 1996, Mosby's Computerized Paramedic Test Generator, 1996, Aehlert's EMT Basic Study Guide, 1997. Republican.

AFFLECK, IAN KEITH, physics educator; b. Vancouver, B.C., Can., July 2, 1952; s. William Burchill and Evelyn Mary (Carter) A.; m. Glenda Ruth Harman, July 2, 1977; children: Geoffrey Roger, Ingrid Katherine. BS, Trent U., 1975; AM, Harvard U., 1976, PhD, 1979. Asst. prof. physics Princeton (N.J.) U., 1981-87; rsch. scientist Centre d'Etudes Nucléaire, Saclay, France, 1984-85; prof. U. B.C., Vancouver, 1987—. Contbr. articles on physics to profl. jours. Recipient Steacie prize Nat. Rsch. Coun. Can., 1988, Hertzberg medal Can. Assn. Physicists, 1990, Theoretical and Math Physics prize, 1997. Fellow Royal Soc. Can. (Rutherford medal 1991), Can. Inst. for Advanced Rsch., Harvard Soc. Fellows (jr.). Achievements include research in interface between elementary particle theory and condensed matter theory. Office: U BC Dept Physics & Astronomy 6224 Agricultural Rd Vancouver BC Canada V6T 1Z1

AFIFI, ABDELMONEM A. biostatistics educator, academic dean; b. El-Menia, Egypt, Aug. 7, 1939; came to U.S., 1960; s. Abdelaziz A. and Nazira (Afifi) A.; m. Beverly L. Coppage, June 30, 1962 (div. 1974); children: Osama A., Mostafa A.; m. Marianne H. Blimlinger, Mar. 4, 1977. BS in Math., Cairo U., 1959; MS in Stats., U. Chgo., 1962; PhD in Stats., U. Calif., Berkeley, 1965. Demonstrator math. dept. Cairo U., 1959-60; prof. biostats. Sch. Pub. Health UCLA, 1965—, dean Sch. Pub. Health, 1987—. Vis. asst. prof. U. Wis., Madison, 1965; pres. Western Consortium for Pub. Health, Berkeley, 1987—; stats. cons. numerous orgns., U.S. and abroad, 1965—. Author: Statistical Analysis, 1979, Computer Aided Multivariate Analysis, 3d edit, 1995; contbr. numerous sci. articles to jours. Fulbright scholar, 1960-64, guest scholar Internat. Inst. Systems Analysis, Laxenburg, Austria, 1974-75, 76-77. Fellow Am. Statis. Assn.; mem. Am. Pub. Health Assn. Democrat. Avocations: classical music, photography, travel. Office: UCLA Sch Pub Health PO Box 951772 Los Angeles CA 90095-1772

AGERBEK, SVEN, mechanical engineer; b. Soerabaya, Dutch Indies, Aug. 2, 1926; came to U.S., 1958, naturalized, 1964; s. Niels Magnus and Else Heidam (Nielsen) Agerbek-Poulsen; m. Helen Hadsbjerg Gerup, May 30, 1963; 1 child, Jesper. MSME, Tech. U., Denmark, 1952; LLB, LaSalle Ext. U., 1967; postgrad., UCLA, 1969. Registered profl. engr., Calif., Ohio, Fla. With Danish Refrigeration Rsch. Inst., Copenhagen, 1952; engr. B.P. Oil Co., Copenhagen, 1952-54; refrigeration insp. J. Lauritzen, Copenhagen, 1954-56; engr. Danish-Am. Gulf Oil Co., Copenhagen, 1956-58; instr. Ohio U., Athens, 1958-60; asst. prof. Calif. State Poly. U., San Luis Obispo, 1960-62; prin. engr. dept. environ. Ralph M. Parsons Co., L.A., 1962-73; engrng. supr. Bechtel Power Co., Norwalk, Calif., 1973-85; pres., owner Woodcraft Cabinets, Inc., Rancho Cordova, 1985-90; owner Acrebrook Cons., Fair Oaks, 1990—; exec. v.p. U.S.E., Inc., Incline Village, Nev., 1994—. Past mem. Luth. Ch. coun., pres. Luth. Sch. bd. With Danish underground movement, WWII. Mem. ASHRAE (mem. tech. com., author Guide on Air Conditioning of Nuclear Power Plants), Danish Engrng. Soc. Home and Office: Acrebrook Consulting 5201 Vista Del Oro Way Fair Oaks CA 95628-4148 also: USE Inc Engrng Office 9244 Old State Hwy Newcastle CA 95658-9998 E-mail: acrebrook@softcom.net

AGLER, DAVID, conductor; b. South Bend, Ind., Apr. 12, 1947; s. Wave Bloom and Doris (Sheeler) A. B.Music, Westminster Choir Coll., Princeton, N.J., 1965-70; postgrad., Phila. Coll. Performing Arts, 1973-75. Mem. faculty Westminster Choir Coll., 1970-72, Acad. Vocal Arts, Phila., 1970-72, Phila. Coll. Performing Arts, 1973-75; adminstrv. dir. Spoleto Festival, 1974-75, gen. mgr., asso. music dir., 1975-76; mem. faculty San Francisco Conservatory Music, 1980-82; dir. Am. Opera Project.; music dir. Syracuse Opera Theatre, 1978-79; music supr., resident condr. San Francisco Opera, 1979-85; prin. condr. Australian Opera, 1986-88; music dir. Vancouver (B.C.) Opera, 1992-2000. Named Exxon Arts-Endowment condr., 1979 Home: 62-1386 Nicola St Vancouver BC Canada 06G 2G2 E-mail: david_agler@compuserve.com

AGOSTA, WILLIAM CARLETON, chemist, educator; b. Dallas, Jan. 1, 1933; s. Angelo N. and Helen Carleton (Jones) A.; m. Karin Solveig Engstrom, July 2, 1958; children— Jennifer Ellen, Christopher William. BA, Rice Inst., 1954; AM, Harvard U., 1955, PhD, 1957. NRC postdoctoral fellow Oxford (Eng.) U., 1957-58; Pfizer postdoctoral fellow U. Ill., Urbana, 1958-59; asst. prof. U. Calif., Berkeley, 1959-61; liaison scientist U.S. Navy, Frankfurt, Germany, 1961-63; asst. prof. chemistry Rockefeller U., N.Y.C., 1963-67, assoc. prof., 1967-74, prof., 1974-98, prof. emeritus, 1998—. Vis. prof. U. Innsbruck, 1995, Princeton U., 1996; cons. in field; officer Chiron Press, Inc., 1977-85; mem. NRC Associateship Programs Chem. Scis. Panel, 1997—. Author: Chemical Communication, 1992, Bombardier Beetles and Fever Trees, 1996, Thieves, Deceivers, and Killers, 2001; mem. editl. adv. bd. Jour. Organic Chemistry, 1984-88; contbr. articles to profl. jours. John Angus Erskine fellow U. Canterbury (N.Z.), 1981 Fellow AAAS; mem. Chem. Soc. London, Am. Chem. Soc., Interam. Photochem. Soc., European Photochemistry Assn., Am. Soc. Photobiology, Internat. Soc. for Chem. Ecology, Phi Beta Kappa, Sigma Xi. Home: PO Box 1547 Friday Harbor WA 98250-1547 Office: U Wash Friday Harbor Labs Friday Harbor WA 98250 E-mail: agosta@fhl.washington.edu

AGOSTI, DEBORAH ANN, state supreme court justice; State supreme ct. justice Nev. Supreme Court, Carson City. Office: Supreme Ct Nev 201 S Carson St Carson City NV 89701-4702

AGUILERA, DONNA CONANT, psychologist, researcher; b. Kinmundy, Ill. d. Charles E. and Daisy L. (Frost) Conant; m. George Limon Aguilera; children: Bruce Allen, Craig Steven. B.S., UCLA, 1963, M.S., 1965; Ph.D., U. So. Calif., 1974. Teaching asst. UCLA, 1965, grad. rsch. asst., 1965-66; prof. Calif. State U., L.A., 1966-81; cons. crisis intervention Didi Hirsch Community Mental Health Ctr., L.A., 1967-82. Mem. Def. Adv. Com. Women in the Services, 1978-82; originator, project dir. Project Link Lab. U. Author: Crisis Intervention: Theory and Methodology, 1974, 9th edit., 2001 (pub. in 14 langs., braille and tapes), Review of Psychiatric Nursing, 1977, 7th edit., 1978, Crisis Intervention: Therapy for Psychological Emergencies, 1983, Clinical Depression: A Life Span Approach, 2000; contbr. articles to profl. jours. Docent Huntington Libr. San Marino, Calif. 1991-2000; mem., mgr. disaster mental health svcs. ARC. NIH fellow, 1972-75 Fellow Am. Acad. Nursing (sec. 1976-77, pres. 1977-78), Acad. Psychiat. Nurse Specialists, Internat. Acad. Eclectic Psychotherapists (pres. 1987-89); mem. Am. Nurses Assn., Faculty Women's Assn., Am. Psychol. Assn., Calif. Psychol. Assn., AAUP, Alpha Tau Delta, Sigma Theta Tau Home: 2 Mirlo Rancho Santa Margarita CA 92688-1613 Office: Ste A175 31441 Santa Margarita Pkwy Rancho Santa Margarita CA 92688-1836 Fax: 949-766-9206. E-mail: DCA1@home.com

AGUIRRE, LINDA, state senator; b. Flagstaff, Ariz., July 12, 1951; m. John Aguirre. BA, Ariz. State U., 1978, MA, 1986. Cert. elem. tchr., prin., Ariz. Dem. rep. dist. 23 Ariz. Ho. of Reps., 1983-98; Dem. senator dist. 23 Ariz. State Senate, 1998—. Mem. bd. dirs. Mountain Park Health Ctr., Legis. Svc. YMCA; pres. Nat. Hispanic Sch. Bd. Caucus; mem. fin. instns. and retirement, judiciary and rules coms. Ariz. State Senate, vice chair edn. com. County coord. ACE; coach recreational T-ball. Mem. Nat. Sch. Bd. Assn., Ariz. Sch. Bd. Assn. (legis. com.). Office: Ariz State Senate State Senate Rm 311 1700 W Washington Phoenix AZ 85007-2890 also: 1612 E Saint Ave Phoenix AZ 85040 Office Fax: 602-542-4511

AGUIRRE, VUKOSLAV ENEAS, freelance/self-employed environmental engineer; b. Santiago, Chile, Nov. 2, 1941; came to U.S., 1960; s. Eneas and Tonka (Domic) A.; m. Emma Jeannette Bendana, Nov. 15, 1970; children: Sergio Eneas, Tonka Lily. BS, U. S. Mil. Acad., 1964; MS, U. Ill., 1965, postgrad., 1966-67. Registered profl. engr. Pa., Va., Md., Mich., D.C., Colo., Ill., Utah, Wyo., Ariz., N.Mex. Project engr. Ackenheil Assocs., Pitts., 1965-69; soils specialist Harza Internat., Chgo., 1969-70; project mgr. Law Engrng. Testing, Washington, 1971-74; pres. Colo. Testing Lab., Denver, 1974-75, Geotek Inc., Denver, 1974-77; pres., owner Aguirre Engrs. Inc., Englewood, Colo., 1977—. Mem. Internat. Soc. Soil Mechanics and Found. Engrng., Internat. Soc. Soil Mechanics, ASCE, Assn. Soil and Found. Engrs., Colo. Cons. Engrs. Council. Roman Catholic. Avocation: skiing. Office: Aguirre Engrs Inc PO Box 3814 Englewood CO 80155-3814

AHART, ALAN M. judge; b. 1949; AB, U. Calif., Berkeley, 1970; JD, SUNY, 1975; LLM, U. Pa., 1979. Judge U.S. Bankruptcy Ct. Cen. Dist. Calif., L.A., 1988—. Contbr. articles to profl. jours. Office: US Bankruptcy Ct Calif Edward R Roybal Bldg 255 E Temple St Ste 1382 Los Angeles CA 90012-3332

AHERN, JOSEPH A. television station executive; Pres., gen. mgr. WLS-TV, Chgo., 1996-97; sr. v.p., mng. dir. Walt Disney Internat., London, 1997-98; pres., gen. mgr. KGO-TV, San Francisco, 1998—. Office: KGO-TV 900 Front St San Francisco CA 94111-1450

AHLEM, LLOYD HAROLD, psychologist; b. Moose Lake, Minn., Nov. 7, 1929; s. Harold Edward and Agnes (Carlson) A.; m. Anne T. Jensen, Dec. 29, 1952; children: Ted, Dan, Mary Jo, Carol, Aileen. A.A., North Park Coll., 1948; A.B., San Jose State Coll., 1952, M.A., 1955; Ed.D., U. So. Calif., 1962. Tchr. retarded children Fresno County (Calif.) Pub. Schs., 1953-54; psychologist Baldwin Park (Calif.) Sch. Dist., 1955-62; prof. psychology Calif. State U., Stanislaus (formerly Stanislaus State Coll.), Turlock, Calif., 1962-70; pres. North Park U., Chgo., 1970-79, dir., 1966-70; exec. dir. Covenant Village Retirement Center, Turlock, 1979-89; dir. spl. projects Covenant Retirement Communities, Chgo., 1989-93; dir. Emanuel Med. Ctr., Turlock, Calif., 1984-99, Merced Mut. Ins. Co., Atwater, 1993—; chmn. Capital Corp. of West, Merced, 1995-2000. Author: Do I Have To Be Me, 1974, How to Cope: Managing Change, Crisis and Conflict, 1978, Help for the Families of the Mentally Ill, 1983, Living and Growing in Later Years, 1992; columnist Covenant Companion, 1972-90. Decorated comdr. Order of Polar Star Sweden; recipient Disting. Alumnus award North Park Coll., 1966 Mem. Assn. Colls. Ill. (vice chmn. 1975-79) Mem. Covenant Ch. Club: Rotary (Paul Harris fellow 1987). Home: 2125 N Olive C-11 Turlock CA 95382

AHLERS, GUENTER, physicist, educator; b. Bremen, Germany, Mar. 28, 1934; came to U.S., 1951; s. William Carl and Ida Pauline (Cornelson) A.; m. June Bly, Aug. 24, 1964 BS, U. Calif., Riverside, 1958; PhD, U. Calif., Berkeley, 1963. Mem. tech. staff Bell Labs., Murray Hill, N.J., 1963-79; prof. physics U. Calif.-Santa Barbara, 1979—. Contbr. numerous articles to profl. jours. Recipient Fritz London award in low temperature physics, 1978 Fellow AAAS, Am. Phys. Soc.; mem. NAS. Home: 523 Carriage Hill Ct Santa Barbara CA 93110-2022 Office: U Calif Dept Physics Santa Barbara CA 93106 E-mail: guenter@stc.ucsb.edu

AHRENS, PAMELA, state government administrator; b. Portland, Oreg., Nov. 15, 1945; m. Steve Ahrens; children: Melissa Ann, Elaine, Annette, Shannon. Grad., Ea. Wash. State U. Mem. Idaho Ho. of Reps., 1980-94; dir. Idaho State Dept. Adminstrn., Boise, 1995—; past owner equipment rental bus. Chmn. Statewide Safety and Loss Control Com. Named to Hall of Fame, Idaho Rep. Party. Mem. Nat. Assn. State Chief Adminstrs. (past pres.), Idaho Hosp. Assn. (dir. polit. activities), Idaho Rep. Women's Fedn. (nat. fedn. rep. v.p.), Idaho Info. Tech. Resource Mgmt. Coun. (chair), Lincoln Day Banquet Assn. (past pres.), Rotary (pres.). Republican. Presbyterian. Home: 5186 S Farmhouse Pl Boise ID 83716-9013 Office: State Idaho Dept Adminstrn PO Box 83720 Boise ID 83720-3720

AHRENS, THOMAS J. geophysicist; b. Wichita Falls, Tex., Apr. 25, 1936; s. Eric and Therese Ahrens. BS in Geology-Geophysics, MIT, 1957; MS in Geophysics, Calif. Inst. Tech., 1958; PhD in Geophysics, Rensselaer Poly. Inst., 1962. Geophysicst Pan Am. Petroleum Corp., Menlo Park, Calif., 1958-59; geophysicist, head geophysics sect. Poulter Lab., Stanford Rsch. Inst., Pasadena, 1962-67; assoc. prof. Calif. Inst. Tech., 1967-76, W.M. Keck prof. earth scis., prof. geophysics, 1976—. Mem. earth. scis. adv. com. NSF, 1973-76, adv. com. divsn. earth scis., 1979-82; chmn. geophysics Gordon Rsch. Conf., 1974; convenor mineral physics workshop Am. Geophys. Union, 1988, chmn. Macelwane award com., 1992-94; vis. com. dept. terrestrial magnetism and geophys. lab. Carnegie Inst. Washington, 1989, dept. geology and geophysics Princeton U., 1990—, Max Planck Inst. Chemistry, Mainz, Germany, 1993—, divsn. phys. sci. U. Chgo., 1993—. Editor: AGU, Handbook of Physical Constants, Vol. I, II, III, 1995; assoc. editor Rev. Sci. Instruments, 1972-74, Jour. Geophys. Rsch., 1972-74; adv. editor Physics and Chemistry of Minerals, 1976—; mem. editl. bd. Surveys in Geophysics, 1984-94; contbr. more than 300 sci. papers to profl. publs. 1st lt. U.S. Army, 1959-60. Recipient Shock Compression Sci. award Am. Phys. Soc., 1995, Arthur L. Day medal Geol. Soc. Am., 1995, Barringer award Meteoritical Soc., 1997; Geochem. fellow Geochem. Soc. and Geochem. Soc. of Europe, 1998; asteroid named after him/Main Belt Asteroid --4739, Tomahrens, 1985 by discoverer Theodore Bowell. Fellow AAAS (Newcomb-Cleveland prize 1984), Am. Geophys. Union (Harry H. Mess medal 1996); mem. U.S. Nat. Acad. Sci. Achievements include patents in shock consolidation of cubic boron nitride with whiskers of silicon compounds; method for measuring fracture toughness of brittle media; polycrystalline diamond and method for forming same. Office: Calif Inst Tech Seismological Lab # 252-21 Pasadena CA 91125-0001

AHUJA, JAGDISH CHAND, mathematics educator; b. Rawalpindi, West Pakistan, Dec. 24, 1927; came to U.S., 1966, naturalized 1972; s. Nihal Chand and Ishwardai (Chhabra) A.; m. Sudarshan Sachdeva, May 18, 1955; children— Naina, Anita B.A., Banaras U., 1953, M.A., 1955; Ph.D., U. B.C., 1963. Sr. math. tchr. D.A.V. High Sch., Nairobi, Kenya, 1955-56; tchr. math. Tanzania, 1956-58; teaching asst. U. B.C., 1958-61, teaching fellow, 1961-63, stats. lab. instr., 1959-61, lectr. stats., 1961-63; asst. prof. math. U. Calgary, Can., 1963-66; assoc. prof. math. Portland State U., Oreg., 1966-69, prof. math., 1969—. Contbr. articles to profl. jours.; referee profl. jours., reviewer profl. jours. Mem. Inst. Math. Stats. Home: 4016 Orchard Dr Lake Oswego OR 97035-2406 Office: Portland State U Dept Math PO Box 751 Portland OR 97207-0751 E-mail: ahua@mth.pdx.edu

AIGNER, DENNIS JOHN, economics educator, consultant; b. L.A., Sept. 27, 1937; s. Herbert Lewis and Della Geraldine (Balasek) A.; m. Vernita Lynne White, Dec. 21, 1957 (div. May 1977); children: Mitchell A., Annette N., Anita L., Angela D.; m. Gretchen Camille Bertolet, Dec. 22, 1992. B.S., U. Calif.-Berkeley, 1959, M.A., 1962, Ph.D., 1963. Asst. prof. econs. U. Ill., Urbana, 1962-67; from assoc. prof. to prof. U. Wis., Madison, 1967-76; prof., chmn. dept. econs. U. So. Calif., L.A., 1976-88; dean grad. sch. mgmt. U. Calif., Irvine, 1988-97, prof. grad. sch. mgmt., 1988—, assoc. dean sch. environ. sci. and mgmt. Santa Barbara, 1998-2000, acting dean, 2000-01, dean, 2001—. Pres. Dennis Aigner Inc., L.A., 1978—; dir. Analysis Group Econs. Author: Introduction to Statistical Decision Making, 1968, Basic Econometrics, 1971; editor: Latent Variables in Socio-Economic Models, 1977; co-editor: Jour. Econometrics, 1972-91. Fulbright fellow Belgium, 1970, Israel, 1983, Bren fellow U. Calif. Santa Barbara, 1998—; NSF grantee, 1968-70, 70-72, 73-76, 79-81, 84-86. Fellow Econometric Soc.; mem. Am. Statis. Assn., Am. Econ. Assn. Office: Sch Environ Sci Mgmt U Calif Santa Barbara CA 93106 E-mail: djaigner@bren.ucsb.edu

AIKEN, ANN L. federal judge; b. Salem, Oreg., Dec. 29, 1959; m. James R. Klonoski; 5 children. MA in Polit. Sci., Rutgers U., New Brunswick, 1976; BS in Polit. Sci., U. Oreg., 1974, JD, 1979. Bar: Oreg. 1980, U.S. Dist. Ct. Oreg. 1981. Law clk. Pub. Defender Svcs., Inc., 1979-80, Office of Legal Counsel to Gov. of Oreg., 1979-80, Judge Edwin E. Allen; atty. Sahlstrom and Dugdale PC, 1980-82; chief clk. Oreg. Ho. of Reps., 1982-83; atty. Thorp, Dennett, Purdy, Golden and Jewett PC, 1983-88; judge Lane County Dist. Ct., Oreg., 1988-92, Lane County Circuit Ct., 1993-98, U.S. Dist. Ct., Eugene, Oreg., 1998—. Aald staff Betty Roberts for U.S. Senate, 1974, Kulongoski for Gov., 1982; adminstv. asst. to Oreg. speaker pro tem Albert Densmore, 1974-75, Office of Rep. James Weaver, 1976; staff Weaver for Congress com., 1976, office clk., 1976-77; mem. adv. bd. Jr. League of Eugene; bd. visitors U. Oreg. Sch. of Law, 1997—; bd. dirs. Relief Nursery, 1989—, Roland K. Rodman Inn of Court (Eugene chap.), 1990—, Lane Co. Child Advocacy Ctr., 2000; mem Nat. Chldn's. Alliance, 1998—. Eagleton fellow, 1975-76, Health, Edn. and Welfare Pubs. Svc. Edn. fellow, 1975-76. Mem. Oreg. Circuit Ct. Judges' Assn., Oreg. Jud. Conf., Oreg. Women Lawyers Assn., Oreg. State Bar Assn., Am. Leadership Forum.

AIKEN, LEWIS ROSCOE, JR. psychologist, educator; b. Bradenton, Fla., Apr. 14, 1931; s. Lewis Roscoe and Vera Irene (Hess) A.; M. Dorothy Ree Grady, Dec. 16, 1956; children: Christopher, Timothy BS, Fla. State U., Tallahassee, 1955, MA, 1956; PhD, U. N.C., 1960. Assoc. prof. psychology U. N.C., Greensboro, 1960-65; prof. Guilford Coll., Greensboro, 1966-74, Sacred Heart Coll., Belmont, N.C., 1974-76, U. Pacific, Stockton, Calif., 1977-79, Pepperdine U., Malibu, 1979. Author: General Psychology, 1969, Psychological and Educational Testing, 1971, Readings in Psychological and Educational Testing, 1973, Psychological Testing and Assessment, 1976, 10th edit., 2000, Later Life, 1978, 3rd edit., 1989, Dying, Death and Bereavement, 1985, 4th edit., 2000, Assessment of Intellectual Functioning, 1987, 96, Personality Assessment Methods and Practices, 1989, 94, 99, Personality: Theories, Research and Applications, 1993, 2000, Aging: An Introduction to Gerontology, 1994, Rating Scales and Checklists, 1996, Assessment of Adult Personality, 1997, Questionnaires and Inventories, 1997, Human Development in Adulthood, 1998, Tests and Examinations, 1998, Human Differences, 1999, Personality: Theories, Assessment, Research and Applications, 2000, Aging and Later Life, 2001; contbr. articles to profl. jours. Sgt. USMC, 1951-54 Fla. Lewis scholar, 1949-51, Gen. scholar, 1954-56; Emory U. fellow, 1957-58, U.S. Office Edn. postdoctoral fellow, 1968-69; NAS-NRC postdoctoral resident rsch. assoc., 1963-64. Fellow APA, Am. Psychol. Soc.; mem. Am. Ednl. Rsch. Assn., Sigma Xi. Fax: 805-370-8025. E-mail: laiken@prodigy.net

AIKENS, C(LYDE) MELVIN, anthropology educator, archaeologist; b. Ogden, Utah, July 13, 1938; s. Clyde Walter and Claudia Elena (Brown) A.; m. Alice Hiroko Endo, Mar. 23, 1963; children: Barton Hiroyuki, Quinn Yoshihisa. A.S., Weber Coll., 1958; B.A., U. Utah, 1960; M.A., U. Chgo., 1962, Ph.D., 1966. Curator U. Utah Mus. Anthropology, Salt Lake City, 1963-66; asst. prof. U. Nev., Reno, 1966-68; asst. prof. anthropology U. Oreg., Eugene, 1968-72, assoc. prof., 1972-78, prof., 1978—, dir. U. Oreg. Mus. Natural History, 1996—. Author: Fremont Relationships, 1966, Hogup Cave, 1970, Great Basin Archaeology, 1978, The Last 10,000 Years in Japan and Eastern North America, 1981, From Asia to America: The First Peopling of the New World, 1990, Archaeology of Oregon, 1993; co-author: Prehistory of Japan, 1982, Great Basin Numic Prehistory, 1986, Early Human Occupation in Far Western North America, 1988; editor: Archaeological Studies Willamette Valley, 1975; co-editor: Prehistoric Hunter-Gatherers in Japan, 1986, Pacific Northeast Asia in Prehistory, 1992, Archaeological Researches in the Northern Great Basin, 1994. NSF research grantee, 1970, 73, 78-80, 84; NSF Sci. Faculty fellow Kyoto U., Japan, 1971-72; Japan Found. research fellow Kyoto U., 1977-78, Tokyo U., 1986. Fellow Am. Anthrop. Assn., AAAS; mem. Soc. for Am. Archaeology Home: 3470 Mcmillan St Eugene OR 97405-3317 Office: U Oreg Museum Natural History Eugene OR 97403-1224 E-mail: maikens@oregon.uoregon.edu

AISENBERG, BENNETT S. lawyer; b. Feb. 17, 1931; s. Joseph Samuel and Minna Ruth (Cohan) A. BA, Brown U., 1952; JD, Harvard U., 1955. Bar: Mass. 1955, Colo. 1958, U.S. Dist. Ct. Colo. 1958, U.S. Ct. Appeals (10th cir.) 1958. Ptnr. Gorsuch, Kirgis, Denver, 1958-80; pvt. practice Denver, 1980—. Mem. Nat. Acad. Arbitrators, Colo. Trial Lawyers Assn. (pres. 1984-85), Denver Bar Assn. (trustee 1982-85, 86-89, pres. 1991-92), Colo. Bar Assn. (pres. 1998-99). Office: Colorado State Bank Bldg 1600 Broadway Ste 2350 Denver CO 80202-4921

AITON, JOHN W. manufacturing executive; V.p. wafer fabrication Micron Tech., Inc., Boise, Idaho, 1978—. Office: Micron Tech Inc PO Box 6 8000 S Federal Way Boise ID 83707-0006

AKAKA, DANIEL KAHIKINA, senator; b. Honolulu, Sept. 11, 1924; s. Kahikina and Annie (Kahoa) A.; m. Mary Mildred Chong, May 22, 1948; children: Millannie, Daniel, Gerard, Alan, Nicholas. BEdn, U. Hawaii, 1952, MEdn, 1966. Tchr., Hawaii, 1953-60; vice prin., then prin. Ewa Beach Elem. Sch., Honolulu, 1960-64; prin. Pohakea Elem. Sch., 1964-65, Kaneohe Elem. Sch., 1965-68; program specialist Hawaii Compensatory Edn., 1978-79, from 1985; dir. Hawaii OEO, 1971-74; spl. asst. human resources Office Gov. Hawaii, 1975-76; mem. 95th-101st Congresses from 2d Dist., Hawaii, 1977-90; U.S. senator from Hawaii, 1990—; mem. energy and natural resources com. U.S. Senate, mem. govt. affairs com., mem. Indian affairs com., mem. Indian affairs com., mem. vets. affairs com., mem. Senate dem. policy com. Chmn. Hawaii Principals' Conf. Bd. dirs. Hanahauoli Sch.; mem. Act 4 Ednl. Adv. Council, Library Adv. Council.; Trustee Kawaiahao Congl. Ch. Served with U.S. Army, 1945-47. Mem. NEA, Musicians Assn. Hawaii. Democrat. Office: US Senate 141 Hart Senate Office Bldg Washington DC 20510-0001*

AKASOFU, SYUN-ICHI, geophysicist, educator; b. Nagano-Ken, Japan, Dec. 4, 1930; came to U.S., 1958, naturalized, 1986; s. Shigenori and Kumiko (Koike) A.; m. Emiko Endo, Sept. 25, 1961; children: Ken-Ichi, Keiko. B.S., Tohoku U., 1953, M.S., 1957; Ph.D., U. Alaska, 1961. Sr. research asst. Nagasaki U., 1953-55; research asst. Geophys. Inst., U. Alaska, Fairbanks, 1958-61, mem. faculty, 1961—, prof. geophysics, 1964—, dir. Geophys. Inst., 1986-99; dir. Internat. Arctic Rsch. Ctr., U. Alaska, Fairbanks, 1998—. Author: Polar and Magnetospheric Substorms (Russian edit. 1971), 1968, The Aurora: A Discharge Phenomenon Surrounding the Earth (in Japanese), 1975, Physics of Magnetospheric Substorms, 1977, Aurora Borealis: The Amazing Northern Lights (Japanese edit. 1981), 1979; co-author: Sydney Chapman, Eighty, 1968, Solar-Terrestrial Physics (Russian edit. 1974); editor: Dynamics of the Magnetosphere, 1979; co-editor: Physics of Auroral Arc Formation, 1980—, The Solar Wind and the Earth, 1987; editorial bd.: Planet and Earth Sci; co-editor: Space Sci. Revs. Recipient Chapman medal Royal Astron. Soc., 1976, award Japan Acad., 1977; named Disting. Alumnus U. Alaska, 1980, Centennial Alumnus Nat. Assn. State Univs. and Land Grant Colls., 1987; recipient Japanese Fgn. Minister award, 1993. Fellow Am. Geophys. Union (John Adam Fleming medal 1977); mem. AAAS, Sigma Xi E-mail: sakasofu@iarc.uaf.edu

AKERS, TOM, JR. cotton broker, consultant; b. Woodford, Okla., May 1, 1919; s. George Tom and Sadie Dean (Jones) A.; m. Eleanor Hoskins, Dec. 23, 1971; children: Tom, Alyce, Peggy, John. B.S., Okla. A&M Coll., 1946; postgrad., Stanford U., 1966. Cotton classer Chickasha Cotton Oil Co., (Okla.), 1936-41; exec. v.p. Calcot. Ltd., Bakersfield, Calif., 1946-80; owner, ptnr. Tom Akers-Cotton, Bakersfield, 1980—. Cons. Algodonera Comercial Mexicana, 1980— , Central Cooperativa Nacional, Asuncion, Paraguay, 1982, Cooperativa Agropecuaria, Tegucigal, Paraguay, 1983, Algodonera Del Sur, Honduras, 1983, cons., Cotton Trading Corp., Goondiwindi, Queensland, 1990, cons. Zimbabwe Cotton Mktg. Bd., Harare, Zimbabwe, 1994, cons., ACDI/VOCA Cooperative Union Project Addis Ababa, Ethiopia, 1998. Campaign chmn. 18th Congl. Dist. Jimmy Carter for Pres., 1976-80; campaign chmn. Kern County for Tom Bradley for Gov., 1982; mem. Kern County Democratic Central Com, 1978— . Served to maj. inf. AUS, 1941-46, PTO. Named Rotarian of Yr. East Bakersfield Rotary, 1974 Mem. Nat. Cotton Mktg. Study Group of U.S. Congress, Nat. Cotton Adv. Com. Democrat. Congregationalist. Club: Bakersfield Trade (dir. 1960-70). Lodge: East Bakersfield Rotary. Home: 4 Greenfair Ct Bakersfield CA 93309-2423 Office: Tom Akers-Cotton 1716 Oak St Rm 7 Bakersfield CA 93301-3040

AKESSON, NORMAN BERNDT, agricultural engineer, emeritus educator; b. Grandin, N.D., June 12, 1914; s. Joseph Berndt and Jennie (Nonthen) A.; m. Margaret Blasing, Dec. 14, 1946; children: Thomas Ryan (dec.), Judith Elizabeth. BS in Agrl. Engring., N.D. State U., 1940; MS in Agrl. Engring, U. Idaho, 1942. Registered profl. engr., Calif. [illegible] U. Idaho, 1940-42, physicist U.S. Navy, Bremerton, Wash., 1942-47; asst. prof. agrl. engring. U. Calif., Davis, 1947-56, assoc. prof., 1956-62, prof., 1962-84, prof. emeritus, 1984—; engring. cons., 1984—. Cons. United Fruit Honduras, 1959, Israel, 1968, WHO Mosquito Control, 1969-84, FAO Aircraft in Agr., 1971-84, Japan, 1972, Egypt, 1980, China, 1985, Can. Forest Svc. Herbicide Application, 1987, U. Fla. Aircraft Application Herbicides, 1987; chmn. expert com. on vector control equipment WHO, 1976; chmn. com. on aircraft for agr. Coun. for Agrl. Sci. and Tech., 1982; pres. Calif. Weed Control Conf., 1966. Author: The Use of Aircraft in Agriculture, 1974, Pesticide Application Equipment and Techniques, 1979, Aircraft Use for Mosquito Control, 1981; contbr. over 330 articles to profl. jours. Recipient research and devel. award FAO, 1973-74, research and devel. award WHO, 1978; Fulbright fellow, Eng. and East Africa, 1957-58. Fellow Am. Soc. Agrl. Engrs. (chmn. Pacific region 1965, dir. 1972-74, assoc. editor tech. publs. 1983-93); mem. ASTM (chair E35-22 1982-84), Am. Chemical Soc., Nat. Agrl. Aviation Assn., Calif. Agrl. Aviation Assn., Nat. Mosquito Control Assn., Entomol. Soc. Am., Weed Sci. Soc. Am. (editl. bd. 1968-70), Western Weed Soc. (hon.), Calif. Weed Sci. Soc. (hon.), Farmers Club (London), Sigma Xi, Phi Kappa Phi, Alpha Zeta, Alpha Gamma Rho. Republican. Home: 1515 Shasta Dr # 1515 Davis CA 95616-6691 Office: U Calif Bio-Agr Engring Dept Davis CA 95616-5294 E-mail: NbAkesson@ucdavis.edu

AKINAKA, ASA MASAYOSHI, lawyer; b. Honolulu, Jan. 19, 1938; s. Arthur Yoshinori and Misako (Miyoshi) A.; m. Betsy Yoshie Kurata, Oct. 7, 1967; children— David Asa Yoshio, Sarah Elizabeth Sachie. B.A. magna cum laude, Yale U., 1959; postgrad. (Rotary Found. fellow), Trinity Coll., Oxford U., 1959-60, Yale Law Sch., 1960-61; LL.B., Stanford Law Sch., 1964. Bar: Hawaii bar 1964. Research asst. U.S. Senator Oren Long, Washington, 1961-62; pvt. practice law Honolulu, 1964—. Bd. visitors Stanford Law Sch., 1971-74. Mem. Am. Bar Assn., Hawaii State Bar Assn. (pres. 1977), Nat. Conf. Bar Presidents, Pacific Club, YMCA (bd. dirs., v.p. 1970-81). Democrat. Episcopalian. Office: PO Box 1035 Honolulu HI 96808-1035

AKINS, GEORGE CHARLES, accountant; b. Willits, Calif., Feb. 22, 1917; s. Guy Brookins and Eugenie (Swan) A.; A.A., Sacramento City Coll., 1941; m. Jane Babcock, Mar. 27, 1945. Accountant, auditor Calif. Bd. Equalization, Dept. Finance, Sacramento, 1940-44; controller-treas. DeVons Jewelers, Sacramento, 1944-73, v.p., controller, 1973-80, v.p., chief fin. officer, dir., 1980-84; individual accounting and tax practice, Sacramento, 1944—. Accountant, cons. Mercy Children's Hosp. Guild, Sacramento, 1957-77. Served with USAAF, 1942. Mem. Soc. Calif. Pioneers, Nat. Soc. Accts., U.S. Navy League, Calif. Hist. Soc., Drake Navigators Guild, Internat. Platform Assn., Mendocino County Hist. Soc. (life), Sacramento County Hist. Soc. (life), Northwestern Pacific Railroad Hist. Soc., Crocker Art Mus. (life). Republican. Roman Catholic. Clubs: Commonwealth of Calif., Comstock. Contbg. author: Portfolio of Accounting Systems for Small and Medium-Sized Business, 1968, rev., 1977. Home and Office: 96 S Humboldt St Willits CA 95490-3539

AKIYAMA, CAROL LYNN, motion picture industry executive; BA magna cum laude, U. So. Calif., 1968, JD, 1971. Bar: Calif. Atty. NLRB, Los Angeles, 1971-75, ABC-TV, Hollywood, Calif., 1975-79, So. Calif. Edison, Rosemead, 1980-81; asst. gen. atty. CBS Inc., Los Angeles, 1981-82; sr. v.p. Alliance of Motion Picture and TV Producers, Sherman Oaks, Calif., 1982-88; ind. producer and writer TV, motion pictures and multimedia/new techs., Woodland Hills, 1988—. Cons. entertainment industry; founding ptnr. Bierstedt, Akiyama and Assocs., Woodland Hills, 1988—. Mem. Los Angeles County Bar Assn. (chmn. labor law sect. 1981-82, exec. com. 1975-85), Phi Kappa Phi, Phi Beta Kappa. E-mail: katramber@earthlink.net

AKUTAGAWA, DONALD, psychologist, educator; b. Grace, Idaho, June 7, 1923; s. Fred T. and Shizue (Oyama) A.; children: Trina Bortko, Murray, Doran. MA, U. Chgo., 1951; PhD, U. Pitts., 1956. Group counselor Orthogenic Sch., U. Chgo., 1951-52; clin. psychologist Inst. Pa. Hosp., Phila., 1959-67; pvt. practice Phila., 1957—, Bellevue, Wash., 1968—; chief community services Eastside Community Mental Health Center, Bellevue, 1968-72; clin. prof. psychology U. Wash., Seattle, 1974-90. Served with AUS, 1944-46. Fellow Am. Orthopsychiat. Assn. Office: Family Treatment Ctr 1607 116th Ave NE Ste 110 Bellevue WA 98004-3042 Address: PMB 175 15600 NE 8th St Ste B1 Bellevue WA 98008-3958

ALARCON, ARTHUR LAWRENCE, federal judge; b. L.A., Aug. 14, 1925; s. Lorenzo Marques and Margaret (Sais) A.; m. Sandra D. Paterson, Sept. 1, 1979; children— Jan Marie, Gregory, Lance B.A. in Polit. Sci, U. So. Calif., 1949, J.D., 1951. Bar: Calif. 1952. Dep. dist. atty. L.A. County, 1952-61; exec. asst. to Gov. Pat Brown State of Calif., Sacramento, 1962-64, legal adv. to gov., 1961-62; judge L.A. Superior Ct., 1964-78; assoc. justice Calif. Ct. Appeals, L.A., 1978-79; judge U.S. Ct. Appeals for 9th Circuit, L.A., 1979-92, sr. judge, 1992—. Served with U.S. Army, 1943-46, ETO Office: US Ct Appeals 9th Cir 1607 US Courthouse 312 N Spring St Los Angeles CA 90012-4701*

ALARCON, RICHARD, state legislator, former councilman; children: Armando, Antonio, Claudia, Andrea. Sr. mgmt. analyst Criminal Justice Planning Office, L.A.; sr. personnel analyst occupl. health and safety divsn. L.A. Personnel Dept.; San Fernando Valley coord. Mayor's Office; city councilman City of L.A., 1993-98; mem. Calif. State Senate, Sacramento, 1998-, majority whip, 1998-. Chmn. housing and cmty. devel. com., vice chair joint legis. audit com., mem. edn., energy, utilities and comm., environ. quality, indsl. rels. Adminstrv. dir. Cmty. Youth Gang Svc.; chmn. N.E. Cmty. Action Project; mem. United Way, MADD, AHA, Women's Care Cottage, Habitat for Humanity, Meet Each Need With Dignity. Office: Calif State Senate 6150 Van Nuys Blvd Ste 400 Van Nuys CA 91401-3345

ALBAUGH, JAMES F. aerospace transportation executive; b. May 31, 1950; BA in Math. and Physics, Willamette U.; MCE, Columbia U. Project engr. Boeing co., Hanford, Wash., 1975, mgr. process engring., plant mgr. Tex., v.p. ops. autonetics electronic sys. divsn.; pres. Rocketdyne Propulsion & Power, Boeing Space Transp., sr. v.p., pres. space and comm., 1998—. Mem. corp. adv. com. Harvey Mudd Coll.; bd. dirs. St. Joseph Ballet. Mem. AIAA (sr.), Nat. Mgmt. Assn. (gold knight, silve knight), Interant. Cad. Astronautics. Office: Boeing Co 7755 E Marginal Way S Seattle WA 98108-4000

ALBEE, ARDEN LEROY, geologist, educator; b. Port Huron, Mich., May 28, 1928; s. Emery A. and Mildred (Tool) A.; m. Charleen H. Ettenheim, 1978; children: Janet, Margaret, Carol, Kathy, James, Ginger, Mary, George. BA, Harvard U., 1950, MA, 1951, PhD, 1957. Geologist U.S. Geol. Survey, 1950-59; prof. geology Calif. Inst. Tech., 1959—; chief scientist Jet Propulsion Lab., 1978-84, dean grad. studies, 1984-91, project scientist Mars Observer and Global Surveyor Missions, 1984—. Cons. in field, 1950; chmn. lunar sci. rev. panel NASA, 1972-77, mem. space sci. adv. com., 1976-84; mem. exam. bd. T.O.E.F.L. (Test of English as a Foreign Lang.), 1995-97; mem. Grad. Record Exam. Bd., 1995-98; mem. exec. com. Assn. Grad. Schs., 1995-97. Assoc. editor Jour. Geophys. Rsch., 1976-82, Ann. Rev. Earth Space Scis., 1978—; contbr. numerous articles to profl. jours. Bd. regents L.A. Chiropractic Coll., 1990-98. Recipient Exceptional Sci. Achievement medal NASA, 1976 Fellow Mineral Soc. Am. (assoc. editor Am. Mineralogist 1972-76), Geol. Soc. Am. (assoc. editor bull. 1972-89, councilor 1989-92), Am. Geophys. Union. Office: [illegible] Inst Tech Mail Code 150-21 Pasadena CA 91125-0001 E-mail: aalbee@gps.caltech.edu

ALBERG, TOM AUSTIN, investment company executive, lawyer; b. San Francisco, Feb. 12, 1940; s. Thomas A. and Miriam A. (Twitchell) A.; m. Mary Ann Johnke, June 8, 1963 (div. July 1989); children: Robert, Katherine, John; m. Judith Beck, Aug. 8, 1989; children: Carson, Jessica. AB, Harvard Coll., 1962; JD, Columbia U., 1965. Bar: N.Y. 1965, Wash. 1967. Assoc. Cravath, Swaine & Moore, N.Y.C., 1965-67, Perkins, Cole, Stone, Olsen & Williams, Seattle, 1967-71, ptnr., 1971-90, chmn. exec. com., 1986-90; exec. v.p. legal and corp. affairs McCaw Cellular Comm. Inc., Kirkland, Wash., 1990-95; pres., CEO, dir. Personal Connect Comm. Corp., Kirkland, 1995—; prin. Madrona Investment Group, 1996—. Pres., COO, dir. Lin Broadcasting Inc., Kirkland, 1991-95; bd. dirs. Active Voice Corp., VISIO Corp., Emeritus Corp., Amazon Com., Inc.; pres. Seattle Legal Svcs., 1973-74; lectr. on securities and fin. law. Editor Law Rev., Columbia U. Contbr. articles to profl. jours. Pres. Intiman Theatre, Seattle, 1981-83, Pacific Sci. Ctr. Found., Seattle, 1982-84; chmn. Discovery Inst., 1991—, Seattle Commons, 1991-94; trustee Children's Hosp. Found., 1992-95, Pacific Sci. Ctr., 1994—, U. Puget Sound, 1994—, Sta. KING-FM, 1994—. Stone scholar Columbia U., 1963-65. Mem. ABA, Wash. State Bar Assn. (chmn. corp. sect. 1975-76, securities com. 1974-75), Univ. Club, Seattle Yacht Club. Office: Madrona Investment Group LLC 1000 2nd Ave Ste 3700 Seattle WA 98104-1053

ALBERTINE, ANNE, corporate chef; b. Waterbury, Conn., Jan. 3, 1964; married. Grad., U. Mass., Amherst, 1987; culinary arts cert., Western Culinary Inst., Portland, Oreg., 1993. Mgr., product and culinary devel. Taco Bell Corp., Irvine, Calif. Avocation: cooking.

ALBERTS, CELIA ANNE, lawyer; b. Denver, May 3, 1953; d. Robert Edward and Barbara Ellen Alberts. BA in French, U. Colo., 1975, JD, 1979; LLM in Taxation, U. Denver, 1984. Bar: Colo. 1979, U.S. Dist. Ct. Colo. 1979, U.S. Ct. Appeals (10th cir.) 1979. Assoc. Dietze, Davis & Porter, Boulder, Colo., 1979-82; sole practice Boulder, 1983-84; assoc. Loser, Davies, Magoon & Fitzgerald, Denver, 1984-87; adj. prof. law U. Denver, 1988; v.p., sr. counsel Merrill Lynch, Denver, 1989-96; sole practice Golden, Colo., 1997—. Mem. ABA, Colo. Bar Assn., Denver Bar Assn. (estate/probate divs.). Avocations: sports, crafts, reading, music. Home and Office: 237 Lamb Ln Golden CO 80401-9426

ALBERTS, DAVID, artistic director, mime; b. Akron, Ohio, Nov. 14, 1946; married (div. 1972); 1 child, Morgan Elizabeth; married (div. 1992); children: Sarah Aimee, Samantha Kaitlin Wynne. BA in Music, Kent State U., 1972; MA in Theatre, West Va. U., 1978; PhD in Theatre, Bowling Green State U., 1989. Instr. Akron (Ohio) U., 1970-71, W.Va. U., 1978, Va. Commonwealth U., Richmond, 1979-81, Calif. State U., Turlock, Calif., 1981-83, Kent (Ohio) State U., 1986-87, Bowling Green (Ohio) State U., 1987-89; artistic dir. Theatre of the One Actor, San Diego, 1995—. Mime artist in field. Author: Pantomime: Exercises and Elements, 1971, Talking About Mime, 1994 (San Diego Book award 1994), Rehearsal Management for Directors, 1995, The Expressive Body: Physical Characterization for the Actor, 1997, (play) Death by Arrangement, 1981; contbr. articles to profl. jours. Recipient Founders award Internat. Thespian Soc., 1972, Directing award Am. Coll. Theatre Festival, 1982. Mem. Internat. Mimes and Pantomimes, Assn. for Theatre in Higher Edn., Speech Comms. Assn. E-mail: davidmime@yahoo.com

ALBERTSON, BRUCE R. computer software company executive; Various positions GE, 1973-96, v.p. worldwide mktg. and product mgmt. GE Appliances divsn., 1996-99; pres., COO Iomega Corp., Roy, Utah, 1999-2000, pres., CEO, 2000—. Office: Iomega 1821 W Iomega Way Roy UT 84067

ALBERTSON, DAVID, food products executive; V.p., treas. Ballantine Produce Co. Inc., Sanger, Calif., 1971—. Office: Ballatine Produce Co Inc 325 L St PO Box 185 Sanger CA 93657-2122

ALBINO, JUDITH ELAINE NEWSOM, university president; b. Jackson, Tenn. m. Salvatore Albino; children: Austin, Adrian. BJ, U. Tex., 1967, PhD, 1973. Mem. faculty sch. dental medicine SUNY, Buffalo, 1972-90, assoc. provost, 1984-87, dean sch. arch. and planning, 1987-89, dean grad. sch., 1989-90; v.p. acad. affairs and rsch, dean system grad. sch. U. Colo., Boulder, 1990-91, pres., 1991-95, pres. emerita, prof. psychiatry, 1995-97; pres. Calif. Sch. Profl. Psychology Alliant U., San Francisco, 1997—. Contbr. articles to profl. jours. Acad. Adminstrn. fellow Am. Coun. on Edn., 1983; grantee NIH. Fellow APA (treas., bd. dirs.); mem. Behavioral Scientists in Dental Rsch. (past pres.), Am. Assn. Dental Rsch. (bd. dirs.). Office: Calif Sch Profl Psychology Alliant U Office Pres 2728 Hyde St Ste 100 San Francisco CA 94109-1251 Fax: 415-771-5908. E-mail: jalbino@alliant.edu

ALBRECHT, RICHARD RAYMOND, retired airplane manufacturing executive, lawyer; b. Storm Lake, Iowa, Aug. 29, 1932; s. Arnold Louis and Catherine Dorothea (Boettcher) A.; m. Constance Marie Berg, June 16, 1957; children: John Justin, Carl Arnold, Richard Louis, Henry Berg. BA, U. Iowa, 1958, JD with highest honors, 1961. Bar: Wash. 1961. Assoc. Perkins, Coie, Stone, Olsen & Williams, Seattle, 1961-67, ptnr., 1968-74; gen. counsel U.S. Dept. Treasury, Washington, 1974-76; v.p., gen. counsel, sec. Boeing Co., Seattle, 1976-81, v.p. fin., contracts and internat. bus., 1981-83, v.p., gen. mgr. Everett div., 1983-84; exec. v.p. Boeing Comml. Airplane Group, Seattle, 1984-97, sr. advisor, 1997-2000. Dir. Esterline Technologies Corp. Mem. bd. regents Wash. State U., 1987-2000With AUS, 1955-58. Recipient Outstanding Citizen of Yr. award Seattle-King County Municipal League, 1968-69. Mem. ABA, Wash. State Bar Assn., Seattle-King County Bar Assn., Am. Judicature Soc., Order of St. John (officer 1992-99, comdr. 1999—), Order of Coif, Rainier Club, Broadmoor Golf Club, Seattle Tennis Club, Sigma Nu, Omicron Delta Kappa, Phi Delta Phi. Home: 1940 Shenandoah Dr E Seattle WA 98112-2326 Office: Perkins Coie LLP 1201 3rd Ave Ste 4800 Seattle WA 98101-3099

ALBRIGHT, WILLIAM ALEXANDER, JR. pharmaceutical company executive; b. Baton Rouge, May 3, 1957; s. William Alexander and Mary (Holeman) A.; m. Jeryl Lynn Hilleman, Mar. 19, 1988; children: Colin Maurice, Evan Minter. BS in Biology, Stanford U., 1979, MS in Biology, 1981; MBA, Harvard Bus. Sch., 1986. Rsch. asst. Crosby, Heafey, Roach & May, Oakland, Calif., 1980-81; sales rep., region mgr. GCA/Precision Scientific, Chgo., 1981-83, OEM prodn. mgr., 1983-84; bus. planning assoc. Eli Lilly and Co., Indpls., 1985; mgr. strategic planning IVAC, Div. of Eli Lilly and Co., San Diego, 1986-87, product mgr. disposables, 1987-89; dir. bus. devel. and fin. Genta Inc., San Diego, 1989—. Mem. Commonwealth Club Calif. Avocations: sailing, scuba diving. Home: 1398 Dana Ave Palo Alto CA 94301-3113 Office: Nexell Therapeutics Inc 9 Parker Irvine CA 92618-1605

ALBRITTON, DANIEL LEE, atmospheric scientist; b. Camden, Ala., June 8, 1936; BS in Elec. Engring., Ga. Inst. Tech., 1959, MS in Physics, 1963, PhD in Physics, 1967. Dir. Aeronomy Lab. NOAA, Boulder, Colo., 1986—. Leader atmospheric chemistry project Climate and Global Change Program NOAA; co-chmn. sci. assessments of stratospheric ozone U.N. Environ. Programme; mem. sci. working group Intergovtl. Panel on Climate Change; lectr. in atm scis. and policy/sci. interface. Former mem. editl. adv. bd. Jour. Molecular Spectroscopy; former co-editor Jour. Atmospheric Chemistry; contbr. 150 articles to profl. jours. Recipient pres. rank svc. award, 1990, gold medal Dept. Commerce, 1977, 93, sci. freedom and responsibility award AAAS, 1993, sci. assessments award Am. Meteorol. Soc., 1993, stratospheric ozone protection award EPA, 1994, UN environ. programme ozone award, 1995. Fellow Am. Phys. Soc., Am. Geophys. Union. Achievements include research in laboratory investigation of atmospheric ion-molecular reactions and theoretical studies of diatomic molecular structure, investigation of atmospheric trace-gas photochemistry, sci. advisor in ozone depletion and climate change policy. Office: NOAA Aeronomy Lab 325 Broadway St Boulder CO 80305-3337

ALCINDOR, LEWIS FERDINAND See ABDUL-JABBAR, KAREEM

ALCONE, MATT, advertising executive; b. 1953; BS in Biology, BA in Bus. Adminstrn., U. Calif. CEO Alcone Mktg. Group, Irvine, Calif., 1975—, also chmn. bd. dirs. Office: Alcone Mktg Group 15 Whatney Irvine CA 92618-2808

ALCOSSER, SANDRA BETH, English language educator, writer; b. Washington, Feb. 3, 1944; d. Karl Richard and Bernetta Elaine (Hutson) Weis; m. Philip Maechling, May 24, 1978. BA, Purdue U., 1972; MFA, U. Mont., 1982. Assoc. editor Mademoiselle Mag., N.Y.C., 1966-69; workshop dir. Lower East Side Svc. Ctr., N.Y.C., 1973-75; dir. Poets in the Park-Ctrl. Park, N.Y.C., 1975-77; solo artist Nat. Endowment for the Arts, various, 1977-85; tchg. asst. U. Mont., Missoula, 1980-82; instr. to asst. prof. English La. State U., Baton Rouge, 1982-87; assoc. prof. English San Diego State U., 1987-89, dir. creative writing program, 1988-91, 99—, prof. English, 1990—; faculty affiliate U. Mont., Missoula, 1995—, Richard Hugo writer in residence, 2000—. Vis. prof. Southern U., Baton Rouge, 1983; writer-in-residence Glacier Nat. Park, Mont., 1978, U. Mich., Ann Arbor, 1994. Author: Each Bone a Prayerpoetry, 1982, A Fish to Feed All Hunger, 1986, (Associated Writing Program award for Poetry), Sleeping Inside the Glacier, 1997, Except by Nature, 1998 (Nat. Poetry Series selection, James Laughlin award Acad. Am. Poets, William Stafford Poetry award Pacific N.W. Booksellers, Larry Levin award Va. Commonwealth U.); author: (with others) The Central Park Book, 1977, Ariadne's Thread: A Collection of Contemporary Women's Journals, 1982, Introspections: American Poets on One of their Own Poems, 1997; editor The Pushcart Prize Anthology, 1989-91; mem. editorial bd. Poetry International, 1996; contbr. poems to profl. jours. Poetry fellow Nat. Endowment for the Arts, Wash., 1985, 91, COMBO fellow San Diego Arts Council, 1987, Bread Leaf fellow Middlebury Coll., Vermont, 1992, Creative Arts fellow Mont. Arts Council, Helena, Mont., 1993-94. Mem. Poets and Writers, Associated Writing Programs. Avocations: animal rehab., environ. protection, hiking, cross-country skiing. Home: 5791 County Line Rd Florence MT 59833-6056 Office: San Diego State Dept English & Comparative Lit San Diego CA 92182 E-mail: alcosser@mail.sdsu.edu

ALDAVE, BARBARA BADER, law educator, lawyer; b. Tacoma, Dec. 28, 1938; d. Fred A. and Patricia W. (Burns) Bader; m. Ralph Theodore Aldave, Apr. 2, 1966; children— Anna Marie, Anthony John BS, Stanford U., 1960; JD, U. Calif.-Berkeley, 1966. Bar: Oreg. 1966, Tex. 1982. Assoc. law firm, Eugene, Oreg., 1967-70; asst. prof. U. Oreg., 1970-73, prof., 2000—; vis. prof. U. Calif., Berkeley, 1973-74; from vis. prof. to prof. U. Tex., Austin, 1974-89, co-holder James R. Dougherty chair for faculty excellence, 1981-82, Piper prof., 1982, Joe A. Worsham centennial prof., 1984-89, Liddell, Sapp, Zivley, Hill and LaBoon prof. banking financial and comml. law, 1989; dean Sch. Law, prof. St. Mary's U., San Antonio, 1989-98, Ernest W. Clemens prof. corp. law, 1996-98. Vis. prof. Northeastern U., 1985-88, 98; vis. prof. Boston Coll. 1999-2000; ABA rep. to Coun. Inter-ABA, 1995-99; NAFTA chpt. 19 panelist, 1994-96. Pres. NETWORK, 1985-89; chair Gender Bias Task Force of Supreme Ct. Tex., 1991-94; bd. dirs. Tex. Alliance Children's Rights, Lawyer's Com. for Civil Rights Under Law of Tex., 1995-2000; nat. chair Gray Panthers, 1999—. Recipient tchg. excellence award U. Tex. Student Bar Assn., 1976, Appreciation awards Thurgood Marshall Legal Soc. of U. Tex., 1979, 81, 85, 87, Tchg. Excellence award Chicano Law Students Assn. of U. Tex., 1984, Hermine Tobolowsky award Women's Law Caucus of U. Tex., 1985, Ethics award Kugle, Stewart, Dent & Frederick, 1988, Leadership award Women's Law Assn. St. Mary's U., 1989, Ann. Inspirational award Women's Advocacy Project, 1989, Appreciation award San Antonio Black Lawyers Assn., 1990, Spl. Recognition award Nat. Conv. Nat. Lawyers Guild, 1990, Spirit of the Am. Woman award J. C. Penney Co., 1992, Sarah T. Hughes award Women and the Law sect. State Bar Tex., 1994, Ann. Tchg. award Soc. Am. Law Tchrs., 1996, Legal Svcs. award Mexican-Am. Legal Def. and Ednl. Fund, 1996, Woman of Justice award NETWORK, 1997, Ann. Peacemaker award Camino a la Paz, 1997, Outstanding Profl. in the Cmty. award Dept. Pub. Justice, St. Mary's U., 1997, Charles Hamilton Houston award Black Allied Law Students Assn. St. Mary's U., 1998, Woman of Yr. award Tex. Women's Polit. Caucus, 1998, award Clin. Legal Edn. Assn., 1998, lifetime achievement award Jour. Law and Religion, 1998. Mem. ABA (com. on corp. laws sect., banking and bus. law 1982-88), Bexar County Women's Bar Assn. (Belva Lockwood Outstanding Lawyer award 1991), Harlan Soc., Stanford U. Alumni Assn., Tex. Appleseed, Tex.-Mexico Bar Assn., Order of Coif, Phi Delta Phi, Iota Sigma Pi, Omicron Delta Kappa, Delta Theta Phi (Outstanding Law Prof. award St. Mary's U. chpt. 1990, 91). Roman Catholic. Home: 86399 N Modesto Dr Eugene OR 97402-9031 Office: U Oreg Sch Law Eugene OR 97403-1221 E-mail: baldave@law.uoregon.edu, balaw98@aol.com

ALDEN, JOHN W. lawyer; BS, Stanford U., 1955, MS, 1956, JD, 1959. Bar: Calif. 1960. Assoc. Pillsbury, Madison & Sutro, 1959-67; assoc. gen. counsel Occidental Petroleum Corp., L.A., 1967—. Office: Occidental Petroleum Corp 10889 Wilshire Blvd Ste 1500 Los Angeles CA 90024-4216 E-mail: john_w_alden@oxy.com

ALDER, BERNI JULIAN, physicist, researcher; b. Duisburg, Germany, Sept. 9, 1925; came to U.S., 1941, naturalized, 1944; s. Ludwig and Ottilie (Gottschalk) A.; m. Esther Berger, Dec. 28, 1956; children: Kenneth, Daniel, Janet. B.S., U. Calif., Berkeley, 1947, M.S., 1948; Ph.D., Calif. Inst. Tech., 1951. Instr. chemistry U. Calif., Berkeley, 1951-54; theoretical physicist Lawrence Livermore Lab., Livermore, Calif., 1955-93; prof. dept. applied sci. U. Calif., Davis, 1987-93, prof. emeritus, 1993; van der Waals prof. U. Amsterdam, Netherlands, 1971; prof. associé U. Paris, 1972. G.N. Lewis lectr. U. Calif., Berkeley, 1984, Hinshelwood prof., Oxford, 1986, Lorentz prof., Leiden, 1990, Kistiakowsky lectr. Harvard U., 1990, Royal Soc. lectr., 1991. Author: Methods of Computational Physics, 1963; editor: Jour. Computational Physics, 1966-91. Served with USN, 1944-46. Guggenheim fellow, 1954-55; NSF sr. postdoctoral fellow, 1963-64, Japanese Promotion of Sci. fellow, 1989; Berni J. Alder prize established by European Computer Soc., 1999. Fellow Am. Phys. Soc.; mem. Nat. Acad. Scis., Am. Chem. Soc. (Hildebrand award 1985), Rare Gas Dynamics Soc. (Grad lectr. 2000, Boltzmann medal 2001). Republican. Jewish. Office: Lawrence Livermore Lab PO Box 808 Livermore CA 94551-0808 E-mail: alder1@llnl.gov

ALDERMAN, WILLIAM FIELDS, lawyer; b. Hamilton, Ohio, 1945; AB summa cum laude, Miami U., 1967; JD, Yale U., 1970. Bar: Calif. 1971. Ptnr. Orrick, Herrington & Sutcliffe, San Francisco, 1976—. Ct. apptd. arbitrator, mediator and evaluator, 1988—. Dir. Lawyers Com. for Civil Rights of the San Francisco Bay Area, 1985—, St. Thomas More Soc. San Francisco, 1987-94, pres. 1993; dir. San Francisco Neighborhood Legal Assistance Found., 1995—. Mem. Phi Beta Kappa. Office: Orrick Herrington & Sutcliffe Old Federal Reserve Bank Bldg 400 Sansome St San Francisco CA 94111-3143

ALDISERT, RUGGERO JOHN, federal judge; b. Carnegie, Pa., Nov. 10, 1919; s. John S. and Elizabeth (Magnacca) A.; m. Agatha Maria DeLacio, Oct. 4, 1952; children: Lisa Maria, Robert, Gregory. B.A., U. Pitts., 1941, J.D., 1947. Bar: Pa. bar 1947. Gen. practice law, Pitts., 1947-61; judge Ct. Common Pleas, Allegheny County, 1961-68, U.S. Ct. Appeals (3d cir.), Pitts., 1968-84, chief judge, 1984-87, sr. judge Pitts., Sanat Barbara, Calif., 1987—. Adj. prof. law U. Pitts. Sch. Law, 1964-87 ; faculty Appellate Judges Seminar, NYU, 1971-85 , asso. dir., 1979-85 ; lectr. internat. seminar legal medicine U. Rome, 1965, Law Soc. London, 1967, Internat. seminar comparative law, Rome, 1971; chmn. Fed. Appellate Judges Seminar; bd. dirs. Fed. Jud. Center, Washington, 1974-79; mem. Pa. Civil Procedural Rules Com., 1965-84 Jud. Conf. Com. on Adminstrn. Criminal Law, 1971-77; chmn. adv. com. on bankruptcy rules Jud. Conf. U.S., 1979-84; lectr. univs. in U.S. and abroad. Author: Il Ritorno al Paese, 1966-67, The Judicial Process, Readings, Materials and Cases, 1976, Logic for Lawyers: A Guide to Clear Legal Thinking, 1989, Opinion Writing, 1990, Winning on Appeal, 1992. Allegheny dist. chmn. Multiple Sclerosis Soc., 1961-68; pres. ISDA, Cultural Heritage Found., 1965-68; trustee U. Pitts., 1968— ; chmn. bd. visitors Pitts. Sch. Law, 1978—. Served to maj. USMCR, 1942-46. Recipient Outstanding Merit award Allegheny County Acad. Trial Lawyers, 1964. Mem. Inst. Jud. Adminstrn., Am. Law Inst., Italian Sons and Daus. of Am. (nat. pres. 1954-68), Italian Sons and Daus. Am. Fraternal Assn. (nat. pres. 1960-68), Phi Beta Kappa, Phi Alpha Delta, Omicron Delta Kappa. Democrat. Roman Catholic. Office: US Ct Appeals 120 Cremona Dr Ste D Santa Barbara CA 93117-5511*

ALDRICH, FRANKLIN DALTON, research physician; b. Detroit, Jan. 25, 1929; s. George Franklin and Ruth Markham (Dalton) A.; m. Margaret Joan Pearson, Mar. 22, 1952; children: Allison Aldrich Cobb, Janet D., George P.; m. Gertrude Suydam Melsom, Mar. 24, 1984. BS, Mich. State U., 1950; MA, Oreg. State U., 1953, PhD, 1954; MD, Case Western Res. U., 1962. Diplomate Am. Bd. Med. Toxicology. Intern U. Iowa Hosps., Iowa City, 1962-63; fellow in medicine U. Colo., Denver, 1964-65; resident and chief resident Lemuel Shattuck Hosp., Boston, 1969-71; physician Colo. Dept. Pub. Health, Denver, 1966-69; asst. med. dir. MIT, Cambridge, 1971-76; med. dir. Climax (Colo.) Molybdenum Co., 1976-77; health effects research mgr. IBM, Boulder, Colo., 1977-92, ret., 1992; cons. Boulder, 1992—. Mem. com. mil. environ. rsch. Nat. Acad. Scis., 1976-80; mem. toxicology adv. com. U.S. Consumer Product Safety Com., 1982-85; clin. assoc. prof. medicine U. Colo. Health Scis. Ctr., Denver. Contbr. articles to profl. jours. Served with AUS, 1954-56. Case Meml. scholar, Mich. State U., 1948. Fellow ACP (Mead Johnson resident scholar 1970), Am. Acad. Clin. Toxicology (pres. 1980-82). Avocations: fishing, amateur radio. E-mail: frank.aldrich@uchsc.edu

ALENIUS, JOHN TODD, retired insurance executive; b. Denver, Sept. 27, 1938; s. Robert and Elizabeth Frances (Todd) A.; m. Sandra Lee Mally, June 30, 1962; children: Constance, Mark, Patricia, William. BBA, Regis. Coll., 1961; postgrad., Havard U., 1971; MA in Mgmt., Webster Coll., 1979. Commd. USAF, 1962, advanced through grades to col., personnel mgr. Vietnam, 1966-67, Colorado Springs, Colo., 1962-67, systems mgr. San Antonio, 1971-75; with exchange duty Canadian Armed Forces, Ottawa, Ont., Can., 1975-77; various system mgmt. positions USAF, San Antonio, 1977-83, dir. logistic mgmt. systems Sacramento, 1983-85; v.p. info. systems Vision Service Plan, Sacramento, 1985-88, exec. v.p. ops., 1988-98, exec. v.p., 1998—, ret. Mem. Soc. Info. Mgmt., Am. Mgmt. Assn. Republican. Roman Catholic. Avocations: fishing, golf. Office: California Vision Service Inc 3333 Quality Dr Rancho Cordova CA 95670-7985

ALEXANDER, DEAN, museum director; Supt. Kalaupapa (Hawaii) Nat. Hist. Park. Office: Kalaupapa Nat Hist Park 7 Puahi St PO Box 2222 Kalaupapa HI 96742-0040

ALEXANDER, GEORGE JONATHON, law educator, former dean; b. Berlin, Germany, Mar. 8, 1931; s. Walter and Sylvia (Grill) A.; m. Katharine Violet Sziklai, Sept. 6, 1958; children: Susan Katina, George Jonathon II. AB with maj. honors, U. Pa., 1953, JD cum laude, 1959; LLM, Yale U., 1965, JSD, 1969. Bar: Ill. 1960, N.Y. 1961, Calif. 1974. Instr. law, Bigelow fellow U. Chgo., 1959-60; instr. internat. relations Naval Res. Officers Sch., Forrest Park, Ill., 1959-60; prof. law Syracuse U. Coll. Law, 1960-70, assoc. dean, 1968-69; prof. law U. Santa Clara (Calif.) Law Sch., 1970—, disting. univ. prof., 1994-95, Elizabeth H. and John A. Sutro prof. law, 1995—, pres. faculty senate, 1996-97, dean, 1970-85, dir. Inst. Internat. and Comparative Law, 1986—, dir. grad. programs, 1998-2001. Dir. summer programs at Oxford, Geneva, Strasbourg, Budapest, Tokyo, Hong Kong, Beijing, Ho Chi Minh City, Singapore, Bangkok, Kuala Lumpur, Seoul, Munich; vis. prof. law U. So. Calif., 1963; vis. scholar Stanford (Calif.) U. Law Sch., 1985-86, 92; cons. in field. Author: Civil Rights, U.S.A., Public Schools, 1963, Honesty and Competition, 1967, Jury Instructing on Medical Issues, 1966, Cases and Materials on Space Law, 1971, The Aged and the Need for Surrogate Management, 1972, Commercial Torts, 1973, 2d edit. 1988, U.S. Antitrust Laws, 1980, Writing A Living Will: Using a Durable Power of Attorney, 1988, (with Scheflin) Law and Mental Disabilities, 1998; author, editor: International Perspectives on Aging, 1992; also articles, chpts. in books, one film. Dir. Domestic and Internat. Bus. Problems Honors Clinic, Syracuse U., 1966-69, Regulations in Space Project, 1968-70; ednl. cons. Comptroller Gen. U.S., 1977—; mem. Nat. Sr. Citizens Law Ctr., 1983-89, pres., 1986-90; co-founder Am. Assn. Abolition Involuntary Mental Hospitalization, 1970, dir., 1970-83. With USN, 1953-56. U.S. Navy scholar U. Pa., 1949-52; Law Bds. scholar, 1956-59; Sterling fellow Yale, 1964-65; recipient Ralph E. Kharas Civil Liberties award, Syracuse U. Sch. Law, 1970, Owens award as Alumnus of Yr., 1984, Disting. prof. Santa Clara Univ. Faculty Senate, 1994-95, 2000 award for outstanding contbns. to cause of civil liberties Freedom of Thought Found.; named Disting. Vis. Prof. Krens Dznube U., Vienna, 2001. Mem. Internat. Acad. Law Mental Health (mem. sci. com. 1997-99), Calif. Bar Assn. (first chmn. com. legal problems of aging), Assn. Am. Law Schs., Soc. Am. Law Tchrs. (dir., pres. 1979), AAUP (chpt. pres. 1962), N.Y. Civil Liberties Union (chpt. pres. 1965, dir., v.p. 1966-70), Am. Acad. Polit. and Social Sci., Order of Coif, Justinian Honor Soc., Phi Alpha Delta (chpt. faculty adviser 1967-70) Home: 11600 Summit Wood Ct Los Altos Hills CA 94022 Office: U Santa Clara Sch Law Santa Clara CA 95053-0001 E-mail: gjalexander@aya.yale.edu

ALEXANDER, GERRY L. state supreme court chief justice; b. Aberdeen, Wash., Apr. 28, 1936; BA, U. Wash., 1958, JD, 1964. Bar: Wash. 1964. Pvt. practice, Olympia, Wash., 1964-73; judge Wash. Superior Ct., Olympia, 1973-85, Wash. Ct. Appeals Divsn. II, Tacoma, 1985-95; state supreme ct. justice Wash. Supreme Ct., Olympia, 1995-2000, state supreme ct. chief justice, 2000—. Mem. Statute Law Com. Lt. U.S. Army, 1958-61. Mem. ABA, Am. Judges Assn., Wash. State Bar Assn., Thurston-Mason County Assn. (pres. 1973), Puget Sound Inn of Ct. (pres. 1996), Bench-Bar-Press (chair), Washington Cts. Hist. Soc. Office: Temple of Justice PO Box 40929 Olympia WA 98504-0929 E-mail: j_g.alexander@courts.wa.gov

ALEXANDER, JASPER D. publishing executive; m.; 1 child. BA in English and history, Wake Forest U., 1966. Reporter Winston-Salem (N.C.) Jour., 1958-59; dir. info. Bowman Gray Sch. Medicine, Winston-Salem, 1960; from copy editor to asst. nat. editor Washington Post, 1967-74; exec. asst. to publ. N.Y.C., 1975-76; mng. editor San Diego Union, 1977-86; exec. editor Seattle Post-Intelligencer, 1986-93, editor, publ., 1993-2000; asst. to pres. Hearst Newspapers, 2000—. Lectr. in field. Founding dir. Calif. Soc. Newspaper Editors; past chmn. journalism edn. com. Pacific

N.W. Newspaper Assn.; trustee Corp. Coun. for the Arts; dir. TVW, 1999—. With USAF, 1965-65. Mem. Am. Soc. Newspaper Editors, Allied Daily Newspapers (bd. dirs.), Wash. State Hist. Soc. (trustee). Office: Hearst Newspapers Ste 603 720 Queen Anne Ave N Seattle WA 98109-4078 E-mail: jdalexander@seattle-pi.com

ALEXANDER, JOHN DAVID, JR. college administrator; b. Springfield, Tenn., Oct. 18, 1932; s. John David and Mary Agnes (McKinnon) A.; m. Catharine Coleman, Aug. 26, 1956; children: Catharine McKinnon, John David III, Julia Mary. BA, Southwestern at Memphis, 1953; student, Louisville Presbyn. Theol. Sem., 1953-54; DPhil (Rhodes Scholar), Oxford (Eng.) U., 1957; LLD, U. So. Calif., Occidental Coll., 1970, Centre Coll. of Ky., 1971, Pepperdine U., 1991, Albertson Coll. Idaho, 1992; LHD, Loyola Marymount U., 1983; LittD, Rhodes Coll., 1986, Pomona Coll., 1996. Assoc. prof. San Francisco Theol. Sem., 1957-65; pres. Southwestern at Memphis, 1965-69, Pomona Coll., Claremont, Calif., 1969-91. Am. sec. Rhodes Scholarship Trust, 1981-98; mem. commn. liberal learning Assn. Am. Colls., 1966-69, mem. commn. instl. affairs, 1971-74; mem. commn. colls. So. Assn. Colls. and Schs., 1966-69; mem. Nat. Commn. Acad. Tenure, 1971-72; dir. Am. Coun. on Edn., 1981-84, Nat. Assn. Ind. Colls. and Univs.; bd. dirs. Children's Hosp. L.A.; trustee Tchrs. Inst. and Annuity Assn., 1970—, Woodrow Wilson Nat. Fellowship Found., 1978-99, Seaver Inst., 1992—, Phi Beta Kappa Assocs., 1993—, v.p. 1998—; bd. dirs. Wenner-Gren Found. for Anthrop. Rsch., 1995—, Webb Schs. Calif., 1995—; bd. overseers Huntington Libr., 1991—. Editor: The American Oxonian, 1997-2000. Decorated Comdr. of the Order of Brit. Empire (hon.). Mem. Soc. Bib. Lit., Soc. Religion in Higher Edn., Phi Beta Kappa Alumni in So. Calif. (pres. 1974-76), Century Club, Calif. Club, Bohemian Club, Phi Beta Kappa, Omicron Delta Kappa, Sigma Nu. Office: Pomona Coll 333 N College Way Claremont CA 91711-4429 E-mail: dalexander@pomona.edu

ALEXANDER, ROBERT C. lawyer; b. Clarksville, Tenn., Aug. 7, 1947; s. Donald C. and Margaret S. Alexander; m. Rosalie Bailey, June 14, 1969. BA cum laude, Yale Coll., 1969; JD magna cum laude, Harvard U., 1972. Bar: Calif. 1972, D.C. 1973. Law clk. to Hon. Alfred T. Goodwin U.S. Ct. Appeals, 9th cir., San Francisco, 1972-73; shareholder Heller, Ehrman, White & McAuliffe, San Francisco, 1973-86, 88—; prin. Babcock & Brown, San Francisco, 1986-87. Writer in field. Mem. ABA, State Bar Calif., D.C. Bar, Internat. Fiscal Assn., Equipment Leasing Assn. Office: Heller Ehrman White & McAuliffe 333 Bush St San Francisco CA 94104-2806

ALEXANDER, VERA, dean, marine science educator; b. Budapest, Hungary, Oct. 26, 1932; came to U.S., 1950; d. Paul and Irene Alexander; div.; children: Graham Alexander Dugdale, Elizabeth Alexander. BA in Zoology, U. Wis., 1955, MS in Zoology, 1962; PhD in Marine Sci., U. Alaska, 1965; LLD, Hokkaido U., Japan, 1999. From asst. prof. to assoc. prof. marine sci. U. Alaska, Fairbanks, 1965-74, prof., 1974—, dean Coll. Environ. Scis., 1977-78, 80-81, dir. Inst. Marine Sci., 1979-93, acting dean Sch. Fisheries and Ocean Scis., 1987-89, dean, 1989—. Mem. adv. com. to ocean scis. divsn. NSF, 1980-84, chmn. adv. com., 1983-84; mem. com. to evaluate outer continental shelf environ. assessment program Minerals Mgmt. Svc., Bd. Environ. Sci. and Tech. NRC, 1987-91, mem. com. on geophys. and environ. Data, 1993-98; mem. adv. com. Office Health and Environ. Rsch., U.S. Dept. Energy, Washington, 1987-90; vice chmn. Arctic Ocean Scis. Bd., 1988-89; commr. U.S. Marine Mammal Commn., 1995—; U.S. del. North Pacific Marine Sci. Orgn., 1991—, vice-chmn., 1999—; bd. dirs. Western Regional Aquaculture Ctr.; mem. sci. adv. bd. NOAA, 1998—; bd. govs. consortium for oceanographic rsch. and edn.; mem. ocean rsch. adv. panel Nat. Oceans Leadership Coun., 1998—; mem. steering com. Census of Marine Life, 1999—; mem. Pres.'s Panel on Ocean Exloration, 2000. Editor: Marine Biological Systems of the Far North (W.L. Rey), 1989. Sec. Fairbanks Light Opera Theatre Bd., 1987-88; chairwoman Rhodes Scholar Selection Com., Alaska, 1986-95. Research grantee U. Alaska. Fellow AAAS, Arctic Inst. N.Am., Explorers Club (sec., treas. Alaska/Yukon chpt. 1987-89, 91-99, pres. 1990-91); mem. Am. Soc. Limnology and Oceanography, Am. Geophys. Union, Oceanography Soc., Am. Fisheries Soc., Nature Conservancy of Alaska (bd. dirs.), Rotary (pres. 1999-2000). Avocations: classical piano, horsemanship. Home: PO Box 80650 Fairbanks AK 99708-0650 Office: U Alaska PO Box 707220 Fairbanks AK 99775 E-mail: vera-alexander@worldnet.att.net, vera@sfos.uaf.edu

ALFARO, FELIX BENJAMIN, physician; b. Managua, Nicaragua, Oct. 22, 1939; came to U.S., 1945, naturalized, 1962; s. Agustin Jose and Amanda Julieta (Barillas) A.; m. Carmen Heide Meyer, Aug. 14, 1965; children: Felix Benjamin, Mark. Student (state scholar), U. San Francisco, 1958-59, 61-62; MD, Creighton U., 1967. Diplomate Am. Bd. Family Practice. Clk. Pacific Gas & Electric Co., San Francisco, 1960-61; intern St. Mary's Hosp., San Francisco, 1967; resident Scenic Gen. Hosp., Modesto, Calif., 1967-70; pvt. practice, Watsonville, 1971—. Active staff Watsonville Cmty. Hosp., 1971—. Capt. M.C., U.S. Army, 1968-69. Fellow Am. Acad. Family Practice; mem. AMA, Calif. Med. Assn., Santa Cruz Country Med. Soc., 38th Parallel Med. Soc. Korea, NRA, VFW. Republican. Roman Catholic. Office: 30 Brennan St Watsonville CA 95076-4303

ALFIDI, RALPH JOSEPH, radiologist, educator; b. Rome, Apr. 20, 1932; s. Luca and Angeline (Panella) A.; m. Rose Esther Senesac, Sept. 3, 1956 (div. 1991); children: Suzanne, Lisa, Christine, Katherine, Mary, John; m. Mariella Boller, Aug. 29, 1992. A.B., Ripon (Wis.) Coll., 1955; M.D., Marquette U., Milw., 1959. Intern Oakwood Hosp., Dearborn, Mich., 1959-60; resident, chief resident, A.C.S. fellow U. Va., 1960-63; practice medicine, specializing in radiology Cleve., 1965-2000; staff mem. Cleve. Clinic, 1965-78, head dept. hosp. radiology, 1968-78; dir. dept. radiology Univ. Hosps., Cleve., 1978-92; prof. radiology U. N.Mex., Albuquerque, 2000—. Cons. VA Hosp., Cleve.; chmn. dept. radiology Case Western Res. U. Sch. Medicine, 1978-92; chmn. staff Cleve. Clinic Found., 1975-76. Author: Complications and Legal Implications of Special Procedures, 1972, Computed Tomography of the Human Body: An Atlas of Normal Anatomy, 1977; editor: Whole Body Computed Tomography, 1977; contbr. articles to radiology jours. Served to capt., M.C. U.S. Army Res., 1963-65. Picker Found. grantee, 1969-70; NRC grantee, 1969-70 Mem. Radiol. Soc. N. Am., Am. Roentgen Ray Soc., Am. Heart Assn., Soc. Cardiovascular Radiology, Soc. Gastrointestinal Radiology, Soc. Computed Body Tomography (pres. 1977-78), Eastern Radiol. Soc., Cleve. Radiol. Soc. (pres. 1976-77), Las Campanas Club. Roman Catholic. Home: 81 Calle Ventoso W Santa Fe NM 87501-0141 Office: Univ Hosp Radiology Dept Lomas Blvd Albuquerque NM 87106

ALGRA, RONALD JAMES, dermatologist; b. Artesia, Calif., Feb. 23, 1949; s. Cornelius and Helena Joyce (De Boom) A.; m. Phyllis Ann Brandsma, July 31, 1970; children: Brian David, Stephanie Ann. BS in Chemistry, Calvin Coll., 1971; MD, Baylor Coll. Medicine, 1974; MBA, Pepperdine U., 1989. Diplomate Am. Bd. Dermatology. Intern Gen. Hosp. Ventura County, Ventura, Calif., 1974-75, resident in dermatology Baylor Coll. Medicine, Houston, 1975-78; pvt. practice Hawthorne, Calif., 1978-88; asst. med. dir. FHP, Inc., Fountain Valley, 1988-89, assoc. med. dir., 1990-91, med. dir., 1991-93, sr. med. dir., 1993, assoc. v.p. med. affairs, 1993-95; COO, horses, zebras & unicorns, Irvine, Calif., 1995-96; exec., med. dir. Providence Health Plans, Eugene, Oreg., 1996-98; [illegible] HealthCare Plans. Ltd., Torrance, Calif., 1999-2000; v.p., med. dir. THIPA, Torrance, 2000—. Fellow Am. Acad. Dermatolgoy; mem. Am. Med. Informatics Assn., Am. Coll. Physician Execs., Alpha Omega Alpha. Republican. Mem. Christian Reformed Ch. Avocations: computers, photography, running, gardening, hiking. Bus. Office: TMCI 2355 Crenshaw Blvd Ste 150 Torrance CA 90501 E-mail: ralgra@thipa.com, rjalgr@mindspring.com

ALHADEFF, DAVID ALBERT, economics educator; b. Seattle, Mar. 22, 1923; s. Albert David and Pearl (Taranto) A.; m. Charlotte Pechman, Aug. 1, 1948. B.A., U. Wash., 1944; M.A., Harvard U., 1948, Ph.D., 1950. Faculty U. Calif.-Berkeley, 1949-87, prof. bus. adminstrn., 1959-87, prof. emeritus, 1987—, assoc. dean Sch. Bus. Adminstrn., 1980-82, 85-86. Author: Monopoly and Competition in Banking, 1954, Competition and Controls in Banking, 1968, Microeconomics and Human Behavior, 1982; Contbr. articles to profl. jours., chpts. to books. Served with AUS, 1943-46. Recipient The Berkeley Citation U. Calif.-Berkeley, 1987. Mem. Am. Econ. Assn., Western Econ. Assn., Am. Fin. Assn. Home: 2101 Shoreline Dr Apt 456 Alameda CA 94501-6249 Office: Haas Sch Bus Berkeley CA 94720-0001

ALICH, JOHN ARTHUR, JR. manufacturing company executive; b. Cleve., Dec. 2, 1942; s. John Arthur and Jeanette Marie (Kusa) A.; m. Susan Jane Moras, May 8, 1965; children: Michelle Monet, Amy Catherine. BS in Engring., U.S. Naval Acad., 1964; MBA, U. Del., 1971. Sr. cons./dir. Stanford Rsch. Inst., Menlo Park, Calif., 1973-77; mgr. devel. Baker Hughes Inc./Envirotech Corp., Menlo Park, 1977-80; v.p. devel. Baker Hughes Inc./Eimco Mining Machinery Internat., Menlo Park, 1980-82, v.p. mktg. Salt Lake City, 1982-85; group v.p., gen. mgr. Baker Hughes Inc./Eimco Secoma, Lyon, France, 1985-87; exec. v.p. ops. Baker Hughes Inc./Eimco Jarvis Clark, Toronto, Can., 1987-88; pres. Baker Hughes Inc./Baker Hughes Mining Tools, Grand Prairie, Tex., 1988-92, Baker Hughes Inc/Envirotech Measurements and Controls, Austin, 1992-94, Thermo Instrument Controls Inc., Austin, 1994-95; bus. devel. dir. Thermo Instrument Sys. Inc., Austin, 1995-97; pres. Kevex Instruments, Valencia, Calif., 1998, Kevex Spectrace, Sunnyvale, 1999; prin. Alides, Carmel, 2000; pres., CEO Enogen, Inc., Carmel, 2000—. Bd. dirs. Serra H.S. Bd. Regents, San Mateo, Calif., 1975-77, Boys and Girls Club, Grand Prairie, 1988-92. Lt. USN, 1964-70. DuPont fellow U. Del., 1970-71. Mem. Soc. Mining Engrs., Inst. Soc. Am., Am. Nuclear Soc., Beta Gamma Sigma. Avocations: golf, running, squash, personal computers. Office: Enogen Inc 2985 Alta Ave Carmel CA 93923-9315

ALINDER, MARY STREET, writer, lecturer; b. Bowling Green, Ohio, Sept. 23, 1946; d. Scott Winfield and McDonna Matlock (Sitterle) Street; m. James Gilbert Alinder, Dec. 17, 1965; children: Jasmine, Jesse, Zachary. Student, U. Mich., 1964-65, U. N.Mex., 1966-68; BA, U. Nebr., 1976. Mgr. The Weston Gallery, Carmel, Calif., 1978-79; chief asst. Ansel Adams, Carmel, 1979-84; exec. editor, bus. mgr. The Ansel Adams Pub. Rights Trust, Carmel, 1984-87; freelance writer, lectr., curator, Gualala, Calif., 1989—; ptnr. The Alinder Gallery, Gualala, 1990-99, 2001—; selector and writer biographies Focal Press Ency., 3d edit., 1993; chief curator, editor The Edward Carter Gallery, 1999-2001. Curator Ansel Adams: 80th Birthday Retrospective, Friends of Photography, Carmel, Acad. Sci., San Francisco, Denver Mus. Natural History, Ansel Adams and the West, Calif. State Capitol, Sacto., 2001; co-curator One With Beauty, M.H. deYoung Meml. Mus., 1987, Ansel Adams: American Artist, The Ansel Adams Ctr., San Francisco; lectr. Nat. Gallery Art, Barbican Ctr., M.H. deYoung Meml. Mus., Stanford U., L.A. County Mus., U. Mich.; vis. artist and lectr. Nebr. Art Assn., 1997; Wallace Stegner meml. lectr. Peninsula Open Space Inst., Mountainview, Calif., 1998, Assn. Internat. Photographic Art Dealers, N.Y.C., 1999, Cin. Art Mus., 2000, Eiteljorg Mus., Indpls., 2001; mem. faculty Stanford U., Spring 2000. Author: Picturing Yosemite (Places), 1990, The Limits of Reality: Ansel Adams and Group f/64 (Seeing Straight), 1992, Ansel Adams, A Biography (Henry Holt), 1996, Mabel Dodge Luhan, 1997 (ViewCamera), (with others) the Scribner Encyclopedia of American Lives, 1998; co-author: Ansel Adams: An Autobiography, 1985; co-editor: Ansel Adams: Letters and Images, 1988; columnist Coast and Valley Mag., 1993-98; columnist biz travel.com, 1996-98; political landscape (civilization), 1999; contbr. articles to jours. and popular mags. Office: Alinder Gallery PO Box 1146 Gualala CA 95445-1146

ALISKY, MARVIN HOWARD, political science educator; b. Kansas City, Mo., Mar. 12, 1923; s. Joseph and Bess June (Capp) A.; m. Beverly Kay, June 10, 1955; children: Sander Michael, Joseph. BA, U. Tex., 1946, MA, 1947, PhD, 1953; cert., Instituto Tecnologico, Monterey, Mex., 1951. News corr. S.W. and Latin Am. NBC, 1947-49, news corr. Midwest, 1954-56; news corr. NBC and Christian Sci. Monitor, Latin Am., 1957-72; asst. prof. Ind. U., 1953-57; assoc. prof. journalism and polit. sci. Ariz. State U., Tempe, 1957-60, prof. polit. sci., 1960—, founding chmn. dept. mass communication (now Sch. Journalism and Telecommunications), 1957-65, founding dir. Ctr. Latin Am. Studies, 1965-72. Vis. fellow Princeton U., 1963-64, Hoover Inst., Stanford, 1978; Fulbright prof. Cath. U., Lima, Peru, 1958, U. Nicaragua, 1960; researcher U.S.-Mex. Interparliamentary Conf., Baja, Calif., 1965, Latin Am. Inst., Chinese Acad. Social Scis., Beijing, 1986, European Inst. Def. and Strategic Studies, London, 1985, Politics Inst., Copenhagen, Denmark, 1987, U. So. Calif., 1982—; U.S. del. UNESCO Conf., Quito, Ecuador, 1960; dir. Gov.'s Ariz.-Mex. Commn., 1975—; U.S. State Dept. lectr., Costa Rica, Peru, Argentina, Chile, 1983, 88; bd. dirs. Goldwater Inst. Pub. Policy Rsch., 1989— Author: Governors of Mexico, 1965, Uruguay: Contemporary Survey, 1969, The Foreign Press, 1964, 70, Who's Who in Mexican Government, 1969, Political Forces in Latin America, 1970, Government in Nuevo Leon, 1971, Government in Sonora, 1971, Peruvian Political Perspective, 1975, (digital ed. 2000), Historical Dictionary of Peru, 1979, Historical Dictionary of Mexico, 1981, 2nd ed. 2000, Latin American Media: Guidance and Censorship, 1981, Global Journalism, 1983; co-author: Political Systems of Latin America, 1970, Political Parties of the Americas, 1982, Yucatan: A World Apart, 1980, (with J.E. Katz) Arms Production in Developing Nations, 1984, Mexico: Country in Crisis, 1986, (with Phil Rosen) International Handbook of Broadcasting Systems, 1988, Dictionary Latin American Political Leaders, 1988, (with W.C. Soderlund) Mass Media and the Caribbean, 1990; columnist Thompson Corp. Newspapers in ariz., 1999—; co-editor: (with Ron Ramachena) Federal Constitution of Mexico, 1993; contbr. numerous articles to profl. jours. and mags. Bd. dirs. Phoenix Com. on Fgn. Res., 1975—, Ariz. Acad. Town Hall, 1981, Tempe Pub. Libr., 1974-80; mem. U.S. Bd. Fgn. Scholarships Fulbright Commn. Bd., 1984—, Acad. Coun. Goldwater Inst. of Pub. Policy, 1989—. Ensign USNR, 1944-45. NSF grantee, 1984, Ariz. State U. rsch. grantee, 1962, 65, 70, Southwestern Studies Ctr. rsch. grantee, 1983, Latin Am. Rsch. in China grantee, 1986, World Media Rsch. in Soviet Union grantee, 1989, rsch. grantee, London, 1992, 94, Edinburgh, 1994, 97, 99, Vancouver, 1998. Fellow Hispanic Soc. Am.; mem. Am. Polit. Sci. Assn., Western Polit. Sci. Assn., Latin Am. Studies Assn., Pacific Coast Coun. Latin Am. Studies (bd. dirs.), Inter-Am. Press Assn., Inter-Am. Broadcasters Assn. (rsch. assoc.), Assocs. Liga de Municipios de Sonora, Friends of Mex. Art, Southwestern Polit. Sci. Assn. (chmn. 1976-77), Nat. Assn. Scholars, Ariz. Assn. Scholars, Soc. Profl. Journalists (life), Tempe Rep. Men's Club, Knights of Sq. Roundtable, Sigma Delta Chi. Home: 44 W Palmdale Dr Tempe AZ 85282-2139 Office: Ariz State U Dept Political Sci Tempe AZ 85287-2001

ALJIAN, JAMES DONOVAN, investment company executive; b. Oakland, Calif., Nov. 5, 1932; s. George W. and Marguerite (Donovan) A.; m. Marjorie L. Townsend, Oct. 17, 1959; children: Mark Donovan, [illegible] Townsend. B.S., U. Calif., Berkeley, 1955; M.B.A., Golden Gate U., 1965. Office mgr. Uniroyal Co., San Francisco, 1957-60; audit supr. Ernst & Ernst, San Francisco, 1960-65; sec.-treas. Tracy Investment Co., Las Vegas, 1965-73, Internat. Leisure Corp., Las Vegas, 1967-70; sr. v.p. fin. MGM, Culver City, Calif., 1973-79; pres. Tracinda Corp., Las Vegas, 1979-82; sr. v.p. fin. planning MGM/UA Entertainment Co., Culver City, Calif., 1982-85; exec. v.p., chief fin. officer, dir. Southwest Leasing Corp., Los Angeles, 1985-87, also bd. dirs.; with Tracinda Corp., Las Vegas, Nev., 1987—. Mem. shareholder com. Daimler Chrysler AG, 1998-2000; bd. dirs. MGM Grand, Inc., Metro-Goldwyn-Mayer, Inc. Served with AUS, 1955-57. Mem. Am. Inst. C.P.A.s, Calif. Soc. C.P.A.s., Acad. Motion Picture Arts and Scis.

ALKER, HAYWARD ROSE, political science educator; b. N.Y.C., Oct. 3, 1937; s. Hayward Rose and Dorothy (Fitzsimmons) A.; m. Judith Ann Tickner, June 3, 1961; children: Joan Christina, Heather Jane, Gwendolyn Ann. BS, MIT, 1959; MS, Yale U., 1960, PhD, 1963. Instr. to assoc. prof. polit. sci. Yale U., 1963-68; vis. prof. U. Mich., 1968, others; prof. polit. sci. MIT, 1968-95; John A. McCone prof. internat. rels. U. So. Calif., L.A., 1995—. Olaf Palme vis. prof. U. Stockholm, U. Uppsala, 1989; vis. prof., scholar Brown U., 1996, 97-2000; chmn. Math. Social Scis. Bd., 1970-71. Author: (non-fiction) Mathematics and Politics, 1965; co-author: World Handbook of Political and Social Indicators, 1966; co-author: (with Russett) World Politics in the General Assembly, 1966; co-author: (with Bloomfield and Choucri) Analyzing Global Interdependence, 1974; co-author: (with Hurwitz) Resolving Prisoner's Dilemmas, 1981; co-author: Rediscoveries and Reformations, 1996, Journeys Through Conflict, 2001; editor (mem. bd.): (jour.) Jour. Interdisciplinary History, 1969—71, Internat. Orgn., 1970—76, Quality and Quantitiy, 1974—, Internat. Studies Quar., 1980—89, European Jour. Internat. Rels., 1995—99, Internat. Rels. of Asia Pacific, 2000—. Congl. intern Office of Chester Bowles, 1960. Fellow Center for Advanced Studies in Behavioral Scis., Stanford, Calif., 1967-68 Mem. Am. Polit. Sci. Assn., Internat. Polit. Sci. Assn., Internat. Peace Rsch. Assn., Internat. Studies Assn. (v.p. 1990-91, pres. 1992-93), Internat. Social Sci. Coun. (exec. com. 1990-92, coord. conflict early warning sys. rsch. program 1992-99). E-mail: alker@usc.edu

ALKIRE, JOHN D. lawyer, mediator, arbitrator; b. Seattle, Nov. 15, 1948; s. Durwood Lee and Dorys (Maryon) A.; m. Karen A. Heerensperger, May 6, 1994; children: Lauren M., Kevin G. Student, U. Calif., Berkeley, 1967-68; BA, Principia Coll., Elsah, Ill., 1970; JD, U. Wash., 1975. Bar: Wash. 1975, Washington 1977, U.S. Dist. Ct. (we. dist.) Wash., U.S. Ct. Appeals (4th, 9th and D.C. cirs.), U.S. Supreme Ct. Budget analyst Office Mgmt. and Budget, Seattle, 1970-72; law clk 9th cir. Honorable Eugene A. Wright, Seattle, 1975-76; assoc. Jones, Grey & Bayley, Seattle, 1976-77, Steptoe & Johnson, Washington, 1977-80, Perkins Coie, Seattle, 1980-85, ptnr., 1985—. Mem. ABA, Wash. State Bar Assn. Avocations: outdoor sports, major league baseball, travel, volunteer mediation. Office: Perkins Coie 1201 3rd Ave Fl 40 Seattle WA 98101-3029

ALKON, ELLEN SKILLEN, physician; b. Los Angeles, Apr. 10, 1936; d. Emil Bogen and Jane (Skillen) Rost; m. Paul Kent Alkon, Aug. 30, 1957; children: Katherine Ellen, Cynthia Jane, Margaret Elaine. BA, Stanford U., 1955; MD, U. Chgo., 1961; MPH, U. Calif., Berkeley, 1968. Diplomate Nat. Bd. Med. Examiners, Am. Bd. Pediat., Am. Bd. Preventive Medicine in Pub. Health. Chief sch. health Anne Arundel County Health Dept., Annapolis, Md., 1970-71; practice medicine specializing in pediat. Mpls. Health Dept., 1971-73, dir. MCH, 1973-75, commr. health, 1975-80; chief preventive and pub. health Coastal Region of Los Angeles County Dept. Health Svcs., 1980-81; chief pub. health West Area Los Angeles County Dept. Health Svcs., 1981-85; acting med. dir. pub. health Los Angeles County Dept. Health, 1986-87, med. dir. pub. health, 1987-93; med. dir. Coastal Cluster Health Ctrs. L.A. County Dept. Pub. Health Svcs., 1993-96, CEO, 1996-98, med. dir., 1998-2000; dir. Pub. Health Edn. in Medicine, 2000—. Adj. prof. UCLA Sch. Pub. Health, 1981—; adminstr. vis. nurses svc., Mpls., 1975-80. Fellow Am. Coll. Preventive Medicine, Am. Acad. Pediatrics; mem. So. Calif. Pub. Health Assn. (pres. 1985-86), Minn. Pub. Health Assn. (pres. 1978-79), Am. Pub. Health Assn., Calif. Conf. Local Health Officers (pres. 1990-91), Delta Omega. Office: Los Angeles County DHS 241 N Figueroa St Rm 143 Los Angeles CA 90012 E-mail: ealkon@dhs.co.la.ca.us

ALKON, PAUL KENT, English language educator; Grad., Phillips Acad., 1953; A.B., Harvard U., 1957; Ph.D. in English Lit., U. Chgo., 1962. Instr., asst. prof. English lit. U. Calif.-Berkeley, 1962-70; assoc. prof. U. Md., 1970-71; assoc. prof. English U. Minn., Mpls., 1971-73, prof., 1973-80; Leo S. Bing prof. English U. So. Calif., Los Angeles, 1980—. Vis. prof. English, Ben Gurion U. of Negev, Israel, 1977-78 Author: Samuel Johnson and Moral Discipline, 1967, Defoe and Fictional Time, 1979, Origins of Futuristic Fiction, 1987, Science Fiction Before 1900, 1994. Mem. Am. Soc. 18th Century Studies (pres. 1989-90), Société française d'Etude du 18ème Siècle, Internat. Churchill soc. Home: 17 Masongate Dr Palos Verdes Peninsula CA 90274-1560 Office: U So Calif Dept English Los Angeles CA 90089-0354 E-mail: alkon@usc.edu

ALKSNE, JOHN F. dean; Dean Sch. of Medicine U. Calif., La Jolla, 1995-2000, prof. surgery, 2000—. Office: Univ Calif San Diego 200 W Arbor Dr Dept 8893 San Diego CA 92103-8893

ALLAN, JAMES S. sales professional; b. Chgo. m. Linda Queenan; children: Scott, Mitch, Tyler, Amanda. BS, Gustavus Adolphus Coll.; MBA in Mktg., Ind. U. Dealer sales mgr. Xerox Channel Sales Orgn. Rear adm. USNR. Decorated Def. Superior Svc. medal, Def. Meritorious Svc. medal.

ALLAN, LIONEL MANNING, lawyer; b. Detroit, Aug. 3, 1943; AB cum laude, U. Mich., 1965; JD, Stanford U., 1968; student, U. Paris. BAr: Calif. 1969, U.S. Supreme Ct. 1972. Law clk. U.S. Dist. Ct. (no. dist.) Calif., 1969-70; pres. Allan Advisors, Inc., legal cons. firm. Speaker and writer in field of corp. securities and pvt. internat. law; sec. adv. com. San Jose Fed. Ct., 1969-85; mem. bd. visitors Stanford Law Sch., 1985-88; mem. com. comml. code State Bar Calif., 1974-77, corps. com., 1983-86. Co-author: How to Structure the Classic Venture Capital Deal, 1983, Equity Incentives for Start-up Companies, 1985, Master Limited Partnerships, 1987. Bd. dirs. San Jose Mus. Art, 1983-87; trustee KTEH-TV Channel 54 Found., 1987—; dir. NCCJ, 1995—, Harker Sch., 1998—. Served to capt. JAGC, USAR, 1968-74. Mem. ABA (com. on small bus. 1980—, chmn. internat. bus. subcom. 1985-88, chmn. small bus. com. 1989-93), Santa Clara Bar Assn. (chmn. fed. ct. sect. 1971, 77), Internat. Bar Assn., San Jose C. of C. (dir.), Pi Sigma Alpha, Phi Sigma Iota, Phi Delta Phi. Office: Allan Advisors Inc 18222 Seebree Ln Monte Sereno CA 95030-3135 E-mail: lonallan@launchnet.com

ALLARD, WAYNE (A. WAYNE ALLARD), senator, veterinarian; b. Dec. 12, 1943; m. Joan Malcolm, Mar. 23, 1967; children: Christie, Cheryl. DVM, Colo. State U., 1968. Veterinarian Allard Animal Hosp.; mem. Colo. State Senate, 1983-90, U.S. Ho. Reps., Washington, 1991-96; U.S. senator from Colo., 1996—. Chmn. health, environment and instn. com., chmn. senate majority caucus; mem. 102nd-104th Congresses from 4th dist., Colo., 1991-96; mem. agrl. com., 1991-92, 93-94, 95-96, mem. small bus. com., 1991-92, mem. interior and insular affairs com., 1991-92, mem. com. on coms., 1991-92, 93-94, mem. budget com., 1993-94, 95-96, mem. natural resources com., 1993-94, 95-96, mem. joint com. on reorganization of Congress, 1993-94, 95-96, chmn. subcom. of agr. conservation, forest and water, 1995-96; senator 105th Congress, 1997—, mem. banking, urban affairs com., 1997—, [illegible] environment and pub. works com., 1997—, intelligence select com., 1997—, Senate armed svcs. com., banking, housing and urban affairs com., select com. on intelligence; mem. select com. on intelligence, armed svcs. com., chmn. pers. subcom., banking, housing and urban affairs com., chmn. subcom. on housing and transp. 106th Congress; health officer, Loveland, Colo.; mem. regional adv. coun. on vet. medicine Western Interstate Commn. Higher Edn.; mem. Colo. Low-Level Radioactive Waste Adv. Com. Chmn. United Way; active 4-H Found. Mem. AVMA, Colo. Vet. Medicine Assn., Larimer County Vet. Medicine Assn. (past pres.), Bd. Vet. Practitioners (charter mem.), Am. Animal Hosp. Assn., Nat. Conf. State Legislatures (vice-chmn. human resources com. 1987—, healthcare cost containment com.), Loveland C. of C., Republican. Methodist. Home: PO Box 2405 Loveland CO 80539-2405 Office: US Senate 525 Dirksen Senate Office Bldg Washington DC 20510-0001*

ALLBEE, SANDRA MOLL, real estate broker; b. Reading, Pa., July 15, 1947; d. Charles Lewars and Isabel May (Ackerman) Frederici; m. Thomas J. Allbee, Oct. 18, 1975 (div. 1987). Exec. sec. Hamburg (Pa.) State Sch. and Hosp., 1965-73; regional mgr. Am. Bus. Service Corp., Newport Beach, Calif., 1973-78; v.p. T.A.S.A., Inc., Long Beach, 1978-86; realtor Very Important Properties, Inc., Rolling Hills Estates, 1986-90, Re/Max Palos Verdes Realty, Rolling Hills Estates, 1990—. Bd. dirs., v.p. Nat. Coun. on Alcoholism, Torrance, Calif., 1987-96; pres. Rollingwood Homeowners Assn., Rolling Hills Estates, Calif., 1985-92. Recipient 100% Club award. Mem. Palos Verdes Rep. Women's Club (bd. dirs. 1989-94). Office: Re/Max Palos Verdes Realty 4030 Palos Verdes Dr N Ste 104 Rolling Hills Estates CA 90274 E-mail: sallbee@remaxpv.com

ALLDREDGE, LEROY ROMNEY, retired geophysicist; b. Mesa, Ariz., Feb. 6, 1917; s. Leo and Ida (Romney) A.; m. Larita Williams, Dec. 27, 1940; children— Carol, David Leroy, Joseph Leo, Gary Dean, Mark Evans, Janice, Luann. B.S., U. Ariz., 1939, M.S., 1940; M.Sc. in Engring, Harvard, 1953; Ph.D., U. Md., 1955. Instr. physics U. Ariz., 1940-41; fed. radio insp. FCC, Los Angeles, also Washington, 1941-44; radio engr. dept. terrestrial magnetism Carnegie Inst. of Washington, 1944-45; chief electricity and magnetism div. Naval Ordnance Lab., White Oak, Md., 1945-55; analyst operations research office Johns Hopkins, 1955-59; research geophysicist Coast and Geodetic Survey, Dept. Commerce, Washington, 1959-66; acting dir. Inst. Earth Scis., Environmental Sci. Services Adminstrn., Boulder, Colo., 1966; dir. Earth Scis. Labs., 1967-69, Earth Sci. Lab. Nat. Oceanographic and Atmospheric Adminstrn., 1969-73; research geophysicist U.S. Geol. Survey, 1973-88; gen. sec., dir. central bur. Internat. Assn. Geomagnetism and Aeronomy, 1963-75. Asso. editor: Jour. Geophys. Research, 1966-69. Mem. Am. Geophys. Union (sect. on geomagnetism and aeronomy 1950-56, v.p. sect. 1956-59, pres. sect. 1959-61, chmn. Eastern meeting com. 1962-66), Sigma Xi, Phi Kappa Phi. Mem. Ch. of Jesus Christ of Latter-day Saints. Home and Office: 4475 Chippewa Dr Boulder CO 80303-3616

ALLEN, CHARLES RAYMOND, television station executive; Gen. mgr. KAET-Ariz. State U., Tempe. Office: KAET Ariz State U Stauffer Hall B-Wing PO Box 871405 Tempe AZ 85287-1405

ALLEN, CHARLES RICHARD, retired financial executive; b. Cleve., Mar. 10, 1926; s. Charles Ross and Jennie (Harmon) A.; m. Marion Elizabeth Taylor, Aug. 17, 1946; children: Kathleen Allen Templin, Jeanne Allen Duffy, Kenneth. Student, Occidental Coll., 1942-43; BS, UCLA, 1945. Acctg. supr. N.Am. Aviation, Inc., Los Angeles, 1946-55; div. controller TRW, Inc., Los Angeles, 1955-61, dir. fin., 1961-64, assoc. controller Cleve., 1964-66, controller, 1966-67, v.p., 1967-77, exec. v.p., 1977-86, chief fin. officer, 1967-86. Bd. dirs. Titan Corp., San Diego. Trustee Maritime Mus. San Diego; mem. San Diego World Affairs Coun. Served with USNR, 1943-46. Mem. Fin. Execs. Inst., Univ. Club, City Club of San Diego. Home: 1730 Avenida Del Mundo Coronado CA 92118-3021 E-mail: CRA1730@worldnet.att.net

ALLEN, CHARLES WILLIAM, mechanical engineering educator; b. Newbury, Eng., July 24, 1932; s. Isaac William and Emily (Butler) A.; m. Rita Joyce Pembroke, Dec. 28, 1957; children: Malcolm Charles, Verity Simone. B.S., U. London, 1957; M.S., Case Inst. Tech., 1962; Ph.D., U. Calif., Davis, 1966. Design engr. Lear Siegler, Cleve., 1957-62; group leader Aerojet Gen., Sacramento, 1962-63; assoc. engring. U. Calif., Davis, 1965-66; assoc. prof. Calif. State U., Chico, 1966-71, prof. engring., 1971-88, prof. emeritus, 1988—, head mech. engring., 1976-79, 82-84. Vis. fellow U. Leicester, Eng., 1974; vis. lectr., rschr. U. Guadalajara, Mex., 1986, guest prof., 1997. Contbr. articles to profl. jours. Fellow NASA, 1967, 68, 69 Mem. ASME. Home: 1691 Filbert Ave Chico CA 95926-1777 Office: Calif State U Dept Mech Engring Chico CA 95929 E-mail: charlesa@ecst.csuchico.edu

ALLEN, CLARENCE RODERIC, geologist, educator; b. Palo Alto, Calif., Feb. 15, 1925; s. Hollis Partridge and Delight (Wright) A. BA, Reed Coll., 1949; MS, Cal. Inst Tech., 1951, PhD, 1954. Asst. prof. geology U. Minn., 1954-55; mem. faculty Calif. Inst. Tech., 1955—, prof. geology and geophysics, 1964-91, prof. emeritus, 1991—; interim dir. Seismological Lab., 1965-67, acting chmn. division of geological scis., 1967-68. Phi Beta Kappa Disting. lectr., 1978; chmn. cons. bd. earthquake analysis Calif. Dept. Water Resources, 1965-74; chmn. geol. hazards adv. com. for program Cal. Resources Agy., 1965-66; mem. earth scis. adv. panel NSF, 1965-68, chmn., 1967-68, mem. adv. com. environmental scis., 1970-72; mem. U.S. Geol. Survey adv. panel to Nat. Center Earthquake Research, Calif. Cal. Mining and Geology Bd., 1969-75, chmn., 1975; mem. task force on earthquake hazard reduction Office Sci. and Tech., 1970-71; mem. Can. Earthquake Prediction Evaluation Council, 1983-88; vice-chmn. Nat. Acad. Sci. Com. on Advanced Study in china, 1981-85; chmn. geology sect. Nat. Acad. Sci., 1982-85, Com. on Scholarly Communication with People's Republic China, 1984-89, chmn., 1987-89; mem. Nat. Acad. Sci. Commn. on Phys. Scis., Math. and Resources; mem. Pres.'s Nuclear Waste Tech. Rev. Bd., 1989-97. Served to 1st lt. USAAF, 1943-46. Recipient G.K. Gilbert award seismic geology Carnegie Instn., 1960. Fellow Am. Geophys. Union, Geol. Soc. Am. (counselor 1968-70, pres. 1973-74), Am. Acad. Arts Scis.; mem. Nat. Acad. Scis., Earthquake Engring. Research Inst. (bd. dirs. 1985-88, Housner medal 2001), Seismological Soc. Am. (dir. 1970-76, pres. 1975-76, medal 1995), Nat. Acad. Engring., Phi Beta Kappa. Office: Calif Inst Tech Dept Geology Pasadena CA 91125-0001 E-mail: allen@gps.caltech.edu

ALLEN, D. EDGAR, state legislator; m. Pat Allen; 6 children. BA, Weber State Coll.; MD, U. Utah. Med. intern, resident Duke U., Durham, N.C.; pvt. practice in dermatology; assoc. clin. prof.; mem. Utah Senate, Dist. 18, Salt Lake City, 1998—; mem. human svcs. com., health and environ. com.; mem. health and human svcs. appropriations com. Contbr. articles to med. jours. Mem. Weber County Drug and Alcohol Mentoring Bd., Mental Health Mentoring Bd., Youth and Families with Promise Mentoring Bd.; past mem. exec. com. Utah State Dem. Party; bd. govs. Am. Legion Boys State. Mem. Am. Cancer Soc. (past pres. Weber County dist.), Weber County Med. Soc. (past pres.). Democrat. Home: 4317 Fern Dr Ogden UT 84403-3269 Fax: 801-627-0517

ALLEN, DAVID HARLOW, business educator, logistician, consultant; b. Lynn, Mass., May 26, 1930; s. Donald H. and Miriam Ellsworth (Harlow) A.; m. Roberta Arlene Miller, July 15, 1952; children: Donald Bruce, Richard Leroy, William David. BS in Gen. Edn., U. Nebr., Omaha, 1967; MBA, N.Mex. Highlands U., 1978. Cert. profl. logistician, cost analyst. Enlisted USAF, 1948-55, commd. 2d lt., 1955, advanced through grades to lt. col., 1970; instr., planner, aircraft maintenance, staff, prodn. control officer, squadron comdr., wing asst. dep. comdr. maintenance SAC, 1948-74; dir. aircraft maintenance, dir. material Air Force Inspection and Safety Ctr., San Bernardino, Calif., 1969-72; dep. dir. logistics Air Force Test and Evaluation Ctr., Albuquerque, 1974-78; ret., 1978; sr. sys. analyst, space sys. project leader Arinc Rsch. Corp., 1978-84; airborne missile system dep. program mgr. for logistics, logistics project mgr. Ventura divsn. Northrop Corp., 1984-91; assoc. prof. West Coast U. Coll. Bus. and Mgmt., L.A., 1988-97; asst. dean West Coast U., L.A., 1988-90. Com. chmn. So. Calif. Logistics Conf. and Workshop, 1989-93; program chmn. 29th Internat. Logistics Conf. and Tech. Exposition, 1994; v.p., mem. bd. govs., trustee Logistics Edn. Found., 1993-96. Contbr. articles to profl. jours. Active state and nat. Rep. orgns., 1978—; mem. Ventura County-Santa Barbara County Planning Com. for Nat. Engring. Week, 1990-98. Decorated Bronze Star. Mem. Soc. Logistics Engrs. (chmn. chpt. 1988-90, Pres.'s award for merit 1994), Logistics Edn. Found. (v.p., bd. trustees 1993-95, Pres.'s award for merit 1996), Soc. Cost Estimating and Analysis, Air Force Assn., Ret. Officers Assn., Am. Assn. Ret. Persons, Phi Kappa Phi. Avocations: racquetball, golf, swimming. Home and Office: 428 Moondance St Thousand Oaks CA 91360-1209

ALLEN, DEBBIE, actress, dancer, director, choreographer; b. Houston, Jan. 16, 1950; d. Vivian Ayers; m. Win Wilford (div.); m. Norm Nixon; 2 children: Vivian, Norman, Jr. BA, Howard U. Appeared in Broadway musicals including Purlie, 1972, West Side Story (revival), Guys and Dolls, Raisin, Aint Misbehavin, Sweet Charity, 1986 (revival, Tony Award); appeared in (play) Sweet Charity, Los Angeles, 1985, choreographer Broadway prodn. Carrie, 1988; (TV spl.) Dancing in the Wings, 1985, (TV series) Fame, 1982-87 (3 Emmys for choreography), In the House, 1995; dir. TV series A Different World, 1988-92; dir. episodes TV series Family Ties; dir., producer films including The Fish That Saved Pittsburgh, 1979, Fame, 1980, Ragtime, 1981, JoJo Dancer, Your Life is Calling, 1986, Mona Must Die, 1994, Blank Check, 1994, Out-of-Sync, 1995, Everything's Jake, 1999, (TV movie) C Bear and Jamal (voice), 1996; star, dir., prod., co-writer, choreographer The Debbie Allen Special, ABC-TV, 1988; dir., choreographer Polly (mus. version Disney's Pollyanna), 1989; dir., appeared in CBS Stompin' at the Savoy, 1992; rec. album Special Look, MCA Records, 1989; dir. pilot and 1st episode NBC series The Fresh Prince of Bel Air, 1990; dir., choreographer NBC-Disney movie Polly II, 1990; choreographer of 63d Acad. Awards, 1991, 64th Acad. Awards, 1992, 65th Acad. Awards, 1993, 66th Acad. Awards, 1994; dir. (TV) Cool Women, 2000. Mem. exec. com. dean's adv. bd. UCLA Sch. Theatre, Film and TV, 1993. Office: William Morris Agency 151 S El Camino Dr Beverly Hills CA 90212-2775

ALLEN, DELL K. industrial engineer; Dir. Wandell Graphics, North Logan, Utah. Mem. NAE. Office: Wandlell Graphics 610 E 2330 N North Logan UT 84341

ALLEN, DONALD VAIL, investment executive, writer, concert pianist; b. South Bend, Ind., Aug. 1, 1928; s. Frank Eugene and Vera Irene (Vail) A.; m. Betty Dunn, Nov. 17, 1956. BA magna cum laude, UCLA, 1972, MA, D (hon.), UCLA, 1973. Pres., chmn. bd. dirs. Cambridge Investment Corp.; music editor and critic Times-Herald, Washington; music critic L.A. Times. Lectr. George Washington U., Am. U., Washington, Pasadena City Coll. Transl. works of Ezra Pound from Italian into English; author of papers on the musical motifs in the writings of James Joyce; specialist in works of Beethoven, Chopin, Debussy, Liszt, and Scriabin; premiere performances of works of Paul Creston, Norman dello Joio, Ross Lee Finney, appearances in N.Y., L.A., Washington; represented by William Matthews Concert Agy., N.Y.C.; selected by William Steinway and Sascha Greiner of Steinway Piano Co. as an exclusive Steinway concert artist. Pres. Funds for Needy Children, 1974-76; mem. Am. Guild Organists. Mem. Ctr. for Study of Presidency, Am. Mgmt. Assn., Internat. Platform Assn., Nat. Assn. Securities Dealers, Am. Guild Organists, Chamber Music Soc., Am. Mus. Natural History. Avocations: languages, music, travel, writing, stock market. Home: 670 W Via Rancho Pkwy Escondido CA 92029-7313 E-mail: DonaldVailAllen@cs.com

ALLEN, DOUGLAS D. horticulture and products company executive; b. 1943; Pres. Hines Nurseries; chmn. Hines Horticulture, Inc., Irvine, 1995-2000, chmn. bd. emeritus, dir., 2000—. Office: Hines Horticulture Inc 12621 Jeffrey Rd Irvine CA 92620

ALLEN, EDGAR BURNS, records management professional; b. L.A., Sept. 1, 1929; s. Harry James and Hela Ruth (Graham) A.; m. Eleanor Angela Gregory, July 24, 1960; children: Linda Marie, Lisa Ann. AA, L.A. City Coll., 1958; student, Calif. State U., L.A., 1958, 81; BS, UCLA, 1985. Supr. records ctr. L.A. Dept. Water and Power, 1958-67, records mgr., 1967-76; records mgmt. officer City of L.A., 1976-85; records mgmt. cons., L.A., 1985-2000. Profl. creator records mgmt. systems, tax preparer, L.A., 1990—; established City Records Ctr. and City Archives. Chmn. Leimert Pk. Community Assn., L.A., 1972-75. Mem. Assn. Records Mgrs. and Adminstrs. (bd. dirs. 1975-76), Soc. Calif. Archivists, All Yr. Figure Skating Club (bd. dirs. 1970-79). Democrat. Roman Catholic. Avocations: bowling, walking, travel.

ALLEN, EDWARD RAYMOND, retired business educator, accountant; b. Indpls., Sept. 30, 1913; s. Edward L. and Emmeline (Rice) A.; m. Norma D.M. Brennan, May 10, 1941. BS in Commerce, Drake U., 1950, MA in Acctg., 1951. CPA, Idaho. Asst. prof. bus. adminstrn. Parsons Coll., Fairfield, Iowa, 1952-56; faculty Coll. of Idaho (now Albertson Coll. Idaho), Caldwell, 1956-73, prof. bus. adminstrn., 1956-73, head dept., 1962-70, chmn. social sci. divsn., 1972-73, emeritus, 1973—, vis. lectr., 1973-74; practicing CPA Caldwell, 1958-92; ret. Caldwell, 1992. Contbr. articles to profl. jours. Capt. AUS, 1942-46; lt. col. Res. ret. Decorated Bronze Star with 1 palm, Med. Badge. Mem. AICPA, AAUP (past pres. Coll. of Idaho chpt.), Idaho Soc. CPAs (dir., regional v.p. 1958-61, stds. of practice com. 1974-83, chmn. com. 1980-83, chmn. rels. with ednl. instns. com. 1984-86, mem. 1993—), Elks, Pi Kappa Phi. Home: PO Box 336 Caldwell ID 83606-0336

ALLEN, JEFFREY MICHAEL, lawyer; b. Chgo., Dec. 13, 1948; s. Albert A. and Miriam (Feldman) A.; m. Anne Marie Guaraglia, Aug. 9, 1975; children: Jason M., Sara M. BA in Polit. Sci. with great distinction, U. Calif., Berkeley, 1970, JD, 1973. Bar: Calif. 1973, U.S. Dist. Ct. (no. and so. dists.) Calif. 1973, U.S. Ct. Appeals (9th cir.) 1973, U.S. Dist. Ct. (ea. dist.) Calif. 1974, U.S. Dist. Ct. (cen. dist.) Calif. 1977, U.S. Dist. Ct. (so. dist.) Calif., U.S. Supreme Ct.; lic. real estate broker. Prin. Graves & Allen, Oakland, Calif., 1973—. Teaching asst. dept. polit. sci. U. Calif., Berkeley, 1970-73; lectr. St. Mary's Coll., Moraga, Calif., 1976-90; mem. faculty Oakland Coll. of Law, 1996-98; bd. dirs. Family Svcs. of the East Bay, 1987-92, 1st v.p., 1988, pres., 1988-91; mem. panel arbitrators Ala. County Superior Ct.; arbitrator comml. arbitration panel Am. Arbitration Assn. Mem. editorial bd. U. Calif. Law Rev., 1971-73, project editor, 1972-73; mem. Ecology Law Quar., 1971-72; contbr. articles to profl. jours. Mem. U.S. Youth Soccer Constl. Commn., 1997—98, U.S. Youth Soccer Bylaws Com., 1998—; mem. region 4 regional coun. U.S. Youth Soccer, 1996—99, chmn. mediation and dispute resolution com., 1999—2000; treas. Hillcrest Elem. Sch. PTA, 1984—86, pres., 1986—88; past mem. GATE adv. com., strategic planning com. on fin. and budget, dist. budget adv. com., instructional strategy counsel Oakland Unified Sch. Dist., 1986—91; mem. Oakland Met. Forum, 1987—91, Oakland Strategic Planning Com., 1988—90; mem. adv. com. St. Mary's Coll.. Paralegal Prog.; commr. Bay Oaks Youth Soccer, 1988—94; asst. dist. commr. dist. 4 Calif. Youth Soccer Assn., 1990—92, also bd. dirs., pres. dist. 4 competitive league, 1990—93, sec. bd. dirs., 1993—96, chmn. bd. dirs., 1996—99; chmn. U.S. Soccer dateabase mktg. com. Calif. Soccer Assn., 1997—99; bd. dirs. Montera Sports Complex, 1988—89, Jack London Youth Soccer League, 1988—94, Calif. Soccer Assn., 1996—99. Mem.: ABA (chmn. real property com. gen. practice sect. 1987—91, mem. programs com. 1991—93, chmn. subcom. on use of computers in real estate trans. 1985—86, adv. coord. 1993—96, sect. coun. 1994—98, mktg. bd. 1996—98, mem. 1998—99, editor Tech. and Practice Guide 1998—, editl. bd. GP Solo 1999—), Calif. Bar Assn. (mem. ADR com. 2001—), Alameda County Bar Assn. (past vice chmn. com. continuing edn., exec. com. alternative dispute resolution programs, panel mediator, arbitrator), U.S. Soccer Assn. (database mktg. com., constl. commn.), Calif. Scholarship Fedn., U.S. Soccer Fedn. (nat. C lic. coach and state referee, state referee instr. and state referee assessor), Calif. North Referee Assn. (referee adminstr. dist. 4 1992—96, state bd. dirs. 1996—), Soc. for Profls. in Dispute Resolution, Oakland C. of C., Rotary (bd. dirs. Oakland 1992—94). Avocations: reading, computers, photography, skiing, baseball, coaching and refereeing youth soccer. Office: Graves & Allen 436 14th St Ste 1400 Oakland CA 94612-2716 E-mail: jallenlaw@aol.com, jallenlaw@gravesandallen.com

ALLEN, JOHN LOGAN, geographer, department chairman; b. Laramie, Wyo., Dec. 27, 1941; s. John Milton and Nancy Elizabeth (Logan) A.; m. Anne Evelyn Gilroy, Aug. 9, 1964; children: Traci Kathleen, Jennifer Lynne. BA (Gen. Motors Corp. scholar 1959-63), U. Wyo., 1963, MA, 1964; PhD (univ. grad. fellow 1964-67), Clark U., Worcester, Mass., 1969; PhD NSF postdoctoral fellow, 1970-71. Mem. faculty U. Conn., Storrs, 1967-2000, prof. geography, 1979-2000, head dept., 1976-94, dir. grad. program in geography, 1992-2000, mem. nat. exec. com. Faculty Athletic Rep. Assn., 1987-96; parliamentarian Faculty Athletic Rep. Assn., 1996—; prof., chair dept. geography U. Wyo., Laramie, 2000—. Non-resident fellow Ctr. Great Plains Studies; cons. in field. Author: Passage Through the Garden: Lewis and Clark and the Geographical Lore of the American Northwest, 1975, Jedediah Smith and the Mountain Men of the American West, 1991, Lewis and Clark and the Images of the American Northwest, 1991, Student Atlas of World Politics, 1991, 4th edit., 1999, Atlas of Economic Development, 1997, Atlas of Environmental Issues, 1997, Student Atlas of World Geography, 1998, 2d edit., 2000; editor: (ann. edits.) Environment, 1982—, Reshaping Traditions, 1994; mem. editl bd. Jour. Hist. Geography; project dir., gen. editor North American Exploration; A Comprehensive History, 3 vols., 1997; contbr. articles to profl. jours., chpts. to books. Pres. Mansfield (Conn.) Middle Sch. Assn., 1979-80; mem. Mansfield Conservation Commn.; vice chmn. Mansfield Zoning Bd. Appeals; mem. Mansfield Planning and Zoning Commn. Recipient Meritorious Achievement award Lewis and Clark Trail Heritage Found., 1976, Excellence in Teaching award U. Conn. Alumni Assn., 1987, Outstanding Contbn. award UCONN Club, 1993, Outstanding Alumnus award U. Wyo. Coll. Arts and Scis., 1999, Spl. Recognition award U. Conn., 2000. Fellow Am. Geog. Assn., Royal Geog. Soc.; mem. Assn. Am. Geographers, Western History Assn., Soc. Historians Early Am. Republic, Soc. History Discovery (nat. councilor), AAAS, Phi Beta Kappa, Phi Kappa Phi, Omicron Delta Kappa. Democrat. Congregationalist. Clubs: Elks, Masons. Home: 2703 Leslie Ct Laramie WY 82072-2979 Office: Univ of Wyoming Dept Geography PO Box 3311 Laramie WY 82071-3311 E-mail: jlallen@wyoming.com

ALLEN, JOSE R. lawyer; b. Panama, Sept. 8, 1951; arrived in U.S., 1956; s. Joseph R. and Grace A. (Osborne) A.; m. Irvenia E. Waters, July 20, 1986; 1 child, Jeffrey Richard Allen. BA, Yale U., 1973; JD, Boston Coll., 1976. Bar: Mass. 1977, Calif. 1986. Asst. atty. gen. Mass. Atty. Gen. Office, Boston, 1976-79; trial atty. U.S. Dept. Justice, Washington, 1979-80, asst. sect. chief, 1980-82, sect. chief, 1982-85; of counsel Orrick, Herrington & Sutcliffe, San Francisco, 1985-88; ptnr. Skadden, Arps, Slate, Meagher & Flom LLP, San Francisco, 1988—. Mem. adv. com. Practicing Law Inst., N.Y.C., 1992—. Bd. dirs. San Francisco Bay Area Lawyers' Com. Urban Affairs, 1990, Legal Aid Soc. San Francisco, 1993. Mem. ABA, Bar Assn. San Francisco, Charles Houston Bar Assn., State Bar Calif. (mem. environ. law sect.). Office: Skadden Arps Slate Meagher & Flom LLP Four Embarcadero Ctr San Francisco CA 94111

ALLEN, KEITH W. actor, singer, songwriter; b. Chgo., Dec. 3, 1953; s. Grover Dean and Francis Lee (Grayson) A.; m. Lori Paulette Ferrari, June 30, 1989; 1 child, Kelly Marie. AA, Blackhawk East Coll., 1986. Chief exec. officer New Hope Films, Denver, 1987—. Producer soundtracks and actor Producers Group Studios, Colorado Springs, Colo., 1990—. Actor, songwriter singles, albums including Pools of Anger, 1990; appeared in opening acts for Lou Rawls, 1977-78, Willie Tyler & Lester, 1985, Don Rickels, 1977-78, Kenny Rogers, 1977-78, Pat Cooper, 1977-78, Joan Rivers, 1977-78, Jerry Lewis Telethon, 1977-78. With U.S. Army, 1972-73, Vietnam. Mem. Colo. Film Commn. Democrat. Methodist. Avocations: black belt karate, boxing, running, weight lifting, tennis. Office: New Hope Films Inc 4900 DTC Pky # 246 Denver CO 80237-2703

ALLEN, LOUIS ALEXANDER, management consultant; b. Glace Bay, N.S., Oct. 8, 1917; s. Israel Nathan and Emma (Greenberg) A.; m. Ruth Graham, Aug. 24, 1946; children: Michael, Steven, Ace, Terry Allen Beck, Deborah Allen. BS cum laude, Wash. State U., 1941. Cert. mgmt. cons. Asst. to dean of men Wash. State U., Pullman, 1940-42; tng. supr. Aluminum Co. Am., Pitts., 1946-49; mgr. pers. adminstrn. Koppers Co. Inc., Pitts., 1949-53; dir. rsch. projects The Conf. Bd., N.Y.C., 1953-56; dir. orgnl. planning Booz, Allen & Hamilton, Chgo., 1956-58; founder Louis Allen Assocs., Inc., Los Altos, Calif., 1958-92; ind. rschr., 1992-95. Lectr. on bus. mgmt. Stanford U., U. Chgo., NYU, Japan, China, Australia, Africa and Europe. Author: Improving Staff and Line Relationships, 1956, Preparing the Company Organization Manual, 1957, Organization of Staff Functions, 1958, Management and Organization, 1958, The Management Profession, 1964, Professional Management: New Concepts and Proven Practices, 1973, Time before Morning: Art and Myth of the Australian Aborigines, 1975, Making Managerial Planning More Effective, 1982, The Allen Guide for Management Leaders, 1989, Common Vocabulary for Management Leaders, 1989, The Louis Allen Leader's Handbook, 1995, The New Leadership, 1996; (mus. catalog) Australian Aboriginal Art, 1972; translated into Japanese, German, French, Finnish, Swedish, Dutch, Spanish, Portuguese, Bahasa; contbr. numerous articles and monographs to profl. jours. on mgmt., primitive art; exhibitor primitive art major mus. worldwide, 1969—. Maj. USAF, 1942-55, PTO. Decorated Legion of Merit; recipient McKinsey award Acad. Mgmt. Mem. Inst. Mgmt. Cons. (sr. assoc., regional pres. 1985). Avocations: hiking, theater, opera, gardening. Achievements include first to fully classify human work into categories, a typology which facilities diagnosis and correction of organizational problems. Office: Louis Allen Rsch PO Box 11 Palo Alto CA 94302-0011 E-mail: louallenresearch@prodigy.net

ALLEN, MATTHEW ARNOLD, physicist; b. Edinburgh, Scotland, Apr. 27, 1930; came to U.S., 1955; s. William Wolff and Clara (Bloch) A.; m. Marcia Harriet Katzman, Sept. 15, 1957; children: Bruce William, Peter Jonathan, David Michael. BSc in Physics, U. Edinburgh, 1951; PhD in Physics, Stanford U., 1959. Rsch. assoc. Hansen Labs., Stanford (Calif.) U., 1959-61; rsch. mgr. tube div. Microwave Assocs., Burlington, Mass., 1961-65; radio frequency group leader Stanford Linear Accelerator Ctr., 1965-82, head accelerator physics dept., 1982-84, head klystron microwave dept., 1984-90, asst. dir. for elec. and electronic systems, 1989-90, assoc. dir. lab., 1990—. Cons. Microwave Assocs. Inc., 1965-71, Aerojet Gen., Azusa, Calif., 1959-62, Bechtel Corp., San Francisco, 1965-67; mem. tech. rev. com. Synchotron Radiation Rsch. Ctr., Taipei, Taiwan, 1985-98; chmn. U.S.A. Particle Accelerator Conf., 1991. Contbr. articles to profl. jours.; patentee in field. Commr. Environ. Planning Commn., Mountain View, Calif., 1971-74; councilman Mountain View City Coun., 1974-82; mayor City of Mountain View, 1977, 81; pres. Mountain View Community

TV, 1989. Lt. British Army, 1953-55. Fellow IEEE, Am. Phys. Soc.; mem. IEEE Nuclear and Plasma Scis. Soc. (adminstrv. com. 1978-84, 98-2001), Dem. Club (bd. dirs. 1980-84), Sigma Xi. Democrat. Avocations: skiing, running, TV producing. Home: 325 Chatham Way Mountain View CA 94040-4471 Office: Stanford U Linear Accelerator Ctr Stanford CA 94309 E-mail: matthew.allen@slac.stanford.edu

ALLEN, MICHAEL JOHN BRIDGMAN, English educator; b. Lewes, Eng., Apr. 1, 1941; came to U.S., 1966; m. Elena Hirshberg; children: William, Benjamin. BA, Oxford (Eng.) U., 1964, MA, 1966, DLitt, 1987; PhD, U. Mich., 1970. Asst. prof. UCLA, 1970-74, assoc. prof., 1974-79, prof. English, 1979—, assoc. dir. Ctr. for Medieval and Renaissance Studies, 1978-88, dir., 1988-93. Editor Renaissance Quar., 1993-2001; faculty rsch. lectr. UCLA, 1998. Author: Marsilio Ficino: The Philebus Commentary, 1975, Marsilio Ficino and the Phaedran Charioteer, 1981, The Platonism of Marsilio Ficino, 1984, Icastes: Marsilio Ficino's Interpretation of Plato's "Sophist," 1989, Nuptial Arithmetic, 1994, Plato's Third Eye: Studies in Marsilio Ficino's Metaphysics and Its Sources, 1995, Synoptic Art: Marsilio Ficino on the History of Platonic Interpretation, 1998; co-author: Sources and Analogues of Old English Poetry, 1976, Marsilio Ficino: Platonic Theology, Vol. I, Books I-IV, 2001; co-editor: First Images of America, 1976, Shakespeare's Plays in Quarto, 1984, Sir Philip Sidney's Achievements, 1990. Recipient Eby award for disting. teaching UCLA, 1977; Guggenheim fellow, 1977; disting. vis. scholar Centre for Reformation and Renaissance Studies, U. Toronto, 1997. Office: UCLA 2225 Rolfe Hall 405 Hilgard Ave Los Angeles CA 90095-9000 E-mail: mjballen@humnet.ucla.edu

ALLEN, PAUL G. computer executive, professional sports team owner; Student, Wash. State U. Co-founder Microsoft Corp., Redmond, Wash., 1975, exec. v.p., 1975-83; founder Asymetrix Corp., Bellevue, 1985—, Starwave Corp., Bellevue; founder, chmn. Intervas Rsch., Palo Alto, Calif.; CEO Vulcan Ventures, Bellevue, 1987—; owner, chmn. Seattle Seahawks; owner, chmn. bd. Portland (Oreg.) Trail Blazers, 1988—. Bd. dirs. Egghead Discount Software, Microsoft Corp., Darwin Molecular, Inc.

ALLEN, REX WHITAKER, retired architect; b. San Francisco, Dec. 21, 1914; s. Lewis Whitaker and Maude Rex (Allen) A.; m. Elizabeth Johnson, Oct. 11, 1941 (div. 1949); children: Alexandra A., Frances Lambert (Mrs. Andrew Dunn); m. Ruth Batchelor, Apr. 1, 1949 (div. 1971); children: Mark B., Susan Moore (Mrs. Kofy Lechner); m. Bettie J. Crossfield, Nov. 6, 1971. A.B., Harvard U., 1936, M.Arch., 1939; student, Columbia U. Arch. Sch., 1936-37. With Research and Planning Assos., N.Y.C., 1939-42, Camloc Fastener Corp., N.Y.C., 1942-45, Isadore Rosenfield (architect), N.Y.C., 1945-48, Blanchard and Maher (architects), San Francisco, 1949-52; established pvt. practice San Francisco, 1953; pres. Rex Whitaker Allen & Assos., San Francisco, 1961-71, Archtl. Prodns., Inc., 1971-76; prin. Hugh Stubbins/Rex Allen Partnership, 1968, Rex Allen Partnership, 1971-76; pres. Rex Allen-Drever-Lechowski, Architects, 1976-85, Rex Allen/Mark Lechowski & Assocs., 1985-87; cons. architect, health facility planner, 1987—. Mem. Calif. Bldg. Safety Bd., 1973-93. Author: (with Ilona von Karolyi) Hospital Planning Handbook, 1976; Contbr. articles to profl. jours.; prin. works include French Hosp, San Francisco, Mercy Hosp, Sacramento, Roseville (Calif.) Dist. Hosp, Highland Hosp, Oakland, St. Francis Hosp, San Francisco, Dominican Hosp, Santa Cruz, Alta Bates Hosp, Berkeley, Calif., Boston City Hosp, Out-Patient bldg. Woodland (Calif.) Meml. Hosp, Stanislaus Meml. Hosp, Modesto, Calif., Madera (Calif.) Community Hosp, Sacred Heart Hosp, Eugene, Oreg., St. Joseph Hosp, Mt. Clemens, Mich., Commonwealth Health Center, Saipan, Guam Meml. Hosp. and Nursing Facility. Chmn. Mill Valley Adv. Edn. Council, 1956; mem. Blue Ribbon com. Sonoma Valley Unified Sch. Dist., 1997—. Fellow AIA (nat. pres. 1969-70, v.p. No. Calif. chpt. 1964, bd. dirs. Calif. coun. 1955-56, 1962-64); hon. fellow Royal Archtl. Inst. Can.; mem. Constrn. Specification Inst. (pres. San Francisco chpt. 1961), San Francisco Zool. Soc. (bd. dirs. 1974-86, 88-95, exhibits com. 1988—, chmn. design stds. com. Assn. Western Hosps., chmn. arch. sect. 1957-58), Calif. Hosp. Assn., Am. Hosp. Assn., Internat. Hosp. Fedn., Am. Assn. Hosp. Planning (pres. 1971-72), Union Internat. des Architectes Pub. Health Work Group (dir. 1979-80), La Sociedad de Arquitectos Mexicanos (hon. mem.), Federaciñn Panamericana de Asociaciones de Arquitectos (v.p. 1980-84), San Francisco Planning and Urban Renewal Assn., San Francisco Mus. Modern Art, Mus. Soc., San Francisco Symphony Found., Sierra Club. Club: Harvard (N.Y.C. and San Francisco). Home and Office: 411 Chestnut Ave Sonoma CA 95476-3416 E-mail: rethmore@vom.com

ALLEN, RICHARD, computer software executive; Sr. accountant Coopers & Lybrand; controller Luff Exploration Co.; exec. vp. fin./adminstrn., CFP J.D. Edwards & Co. Office: JD Edwards & Co One Technology Way Denver CO 80237

ALLEN, RICHARD GARRETT, healthcare and education consultant; b. St. Paul, July 8, 1923; s. John and Margaretta (Taggart) A.; m. Ida Elizabeth Vernon, July 5, 1944; children— Richard Garrett, Barbara Elizabeth, Julie Frances (dec.). B.S. cum laude, Trinity U., 1954; M.H.A., Baylor U., 1957; postgrad., Indsl. Coll. of Armed Forces, 1962, USAF Command and Staff Coll., 1962. Commd. 2d lt. Med. Service Corps U.S. Air Force, 1948, advanced through grades to maj., 1961; served in U.S., Pacific, Germany; ret., 1964; asst. adminstr. U. Ala. Hosp. and Clinics; dir. Ctr. for Hosp. Continuing Edn., Sch. for Health Services, U. Ala., Birmingham, 1965-68; dir. edn. New Eng. Hosp. Assembly, Inc., New Eng. Ctr. for Continuing Edn., U. N.H., Durham, 1968-74; dir. Office Health Care Edn., 1970-74; exec. v.p. Edn. and Research Found., San Francisco, 1974-77, Assn. West Hosps., 1974-77. V.p. health affairs M G & M Communications, Foster City, Calif.; pres. Calif. Coll. Podiatric Medicine; chief exec. officer Calif. Podiatry Hosp. and Outpatient Clinic, San Francisco, 1977-81; prof. health care adminstrn. St. Mary's Coll. of Calif., Moraga, 1982-85; cons. health care and edn., 1985—; owner Sleepy Hollow Books, 1985—; mem. Nat. Adv. Coun. on Vocat. Edn., 1969-71; also cons.; cons. Booz, Allen & Hamilton, Washington, Ops. Rsch., Inc., Silver Spring, Md., Republic of Korea Air Force Med. Svcs., Seoul, Bio-Dynamics, Inc., Cambridge, Mass., HEALTHSAT— Appalachia Community Svcs. Network, Washington, 1980—. Pub.: Hosp. Forum, San Francisco, 1974-77; Contbr. articles to profl. jours. Decorated Air Force Commendation medal with oak leaf cluster. Fellow Am. Coll. Hosp. Adminstrs.; mem. Am. Soc. for Health Manpower Edn. and Tng., Am. Hosp. Assn., AAUP, Am. Soc. Hosp. Edn. and Tng. (pres. 1972), Am. Assn. Colls. Podiatric Medicine (pres. 1979-81), Sherlock Holmes Soc. London Episcopalian. Lodge: Masons. Home and Office: Sleepy Hollow Books 1455 Camino Peral Moraga CA 94556-2018 E-mail: dick78@concentric.net

ALLEN, ROBERT A, wholesale distribution executive; CEO Core-Mark Internat, South San Francisco. Office: c/o Core-Mark Internat 395 Oyster Point Blvd Ste 415 South San Francisco CA 94080

ALLEN, ROBERT EUGENE BARTON, lawyer; b. Bloomington, Ind., Mar. 16, 1940; s. Robert Eugene Barton and Berth R. A.; m. Cecelia Ward Dooley, Sept. 23, 1960 (div. 1971); children: Victoria, Elizabeth, Robert, Charles, Suzanne, William; m. Judith Elaine Hecht, May 27, 1979 (div. 1984); m. Suzanne Nickolson, Nov. 18, 1995. BS, Columbia U., 1962; LLB, Harvard U., [illegible]. Bar: Ariz. [illegible], U.S. Dist. Ct. Ariz. 1965, U.S. Tax Ct., 1965, U.S. Supreme Ct. 1970, U.S. Ct. Customs and Patent Appeals 1971, U.S. Dist. Ct. D.C. 1972, U.S. Ct. Appeals (9th cir.) 1974, U.S. Ct. Appeals (10th, and D.C. cirs.) 1984, U.S. Dist. Ct. N.Mex., U.S. Dist. Ct. (no. dist.) Calif., U.S. Dist. Ct. (no. dist.) Tex. 1991, U.S. Ct. Appeals (fed. cir.) 1992, U.S. Dist. Ct. (ea. dist.) Wis. 1995. Ptnr., dir. Allen, Price & Padden, Phoenix; spl. asst. atty. gen. Ariz. Ct. Appeals 1978, judge pro-tem, 1984, 92, 99; Ptnr., dir. Allen, Price & Padden, Phoenix, 2000—. Nat. pres. Young Dems. Clubs Am., 1971-73; mem. exec. com. Dem. Nat. Com., 1972-73, Ariz. Gov.'s Kitchen Cabinet working on a wide range of state projects; bd. dirs. Phoenix Bapt. Hosp., 1981-83, Phoenix and Valley of the Sun Conv. and Visitors Bur., United Cerebral Palsy Ariz., 1984-89, Planned Parenthood of Ctrl. and No. Ariz., 1984-87, Internat. Coun. Ariz. Heart Inst. Found., 1998—, Cordell Hull Found. for Internat. Edn., 1996—; trustee Environ. Health Found., 1994-97, Friends of Walnut Canyon, 1991-94; bd. dirs. Ariz. Aviation Futures Task Force, chmn. Ariz. Airport Devel. Criteria Subcom.; mem. Apache Junction Airport Rev. Com.; Am. rep. exec. bd. Atlantic Alliance of Young Polit. Leaders, 1973-77, 77-80; trustee Am. Counsel of Young Polit. Leaders, 1971-76, 81-85; mem. Am. delegations to Germany, 1971, 72, 76, 79, USSR, 1971, 76, 88, France, 1974, 79, Belgium, 1974, 77, Can., 1974, Eng., 1975, 79, Norway, 1975, Denmark, 1976, Yugoslavia and Hungary, 1985; Am. observer European Parlimentary elections, Eng., France, Germany, Belgium, 1979, Moscow Congressional, Journalist delegation, 1989, NAFTA Trade Conf., Mexico City, 1993, Atlantic Assembly, Copenhagen, 1993. Contbr. articles on comml. litigation to profl. jours. Mem. ABA, Ariz. Bar Assn., Maricopa County Bar Assn., N.Mex. State Bar, D.C. Bar Assn., Am. Judicature Soc., Fed. Bar Assn., Am. Arbitration Assn., Phi Beta Kappa, Harvard Club. Democrat. Episcopalian (lay reader). Office: Allen Price & Padden 3131 E Camelback Rd Phoenix AZ 85016-4500

ALLEN, RONALD CARL, state legislator, computer consulting executive, visual artist; b. Salt Lake City, Mar. 25, 1953; s. Carl Franklin and Mary Jean (Benson) A.; m. Delia Ann Fordham, Nov. 15, 1974; children: Lisa, Cindy, Jeffrey. BS in Acctg., U. Utah, 1980. Owner, bus. mgr. Alinco Mfg., Salt Lake City, 1977-79; owner, pres. Comics Utah Bookstores, Salt Lake City, 1984-86; adminstrv. supr. Am. Stores, Salt Lake City, 1978-89; pres. Cons. Svcs., Salt Lake City, 1989—; fire chief No. Tooele County Fire Dept., 1987-96; mem. Utah Senate, Dist. 13, Salt Lake City, 1998—, Dem. whip, 2001—. Pres. Intermountain EDP Trainers, Salt Lake City, 1984-86. Chmn., chief North Tooele County (Utah) Fire Dept., 1987-95; U.S. Army, 1972-75. Recipient over 30 awards for visual arts, 1981—. Mem., Tooele County Chamber of Commerce. Mem. LDS Ch. Avocations: photography, sailing, golf. Office: Cons Svcs 835 Lakeview Tooele UT 84074-9613 E-mail: rallen@vonallen.com

ALLEN, RUSSELL G. lawyer; b. Ottumwa, Iowa, Nov. 7, 1946; BA, Grinnell Coll., 1968; JD, Stanford U., 1971. Bar: Calif. 1971. Ptnr. O'Melveny & Myers LLP, Newport Beach, Calif., 1975-2001; wealth advisor J.P. Morgan Chase & Co., Newport Beach, 2001—. Trustee Grinnell Coll. Capt. JAGC, USAF, 1971-75. Fellow Am. Coll. Trust and Estate Counsel; mem. ABA (real property, probate and trust law and taxation sects.), Orange County Bar Assn. (estate planning, probate and trust sects.) Office: JP Morgan Chase and Co Ste 200 888 San Clemente Dr Newport Beach CA 92660 E-mail: rallen@omm.com

ALLEN, SONNY, professional basketball coach; Student, Marshall U. Coach freshman team Marshall U., 1959-65; coach Old Dominion U., 1965-75, So. Meth. U., 1975-80, U. Nev., Reno, 1980-87, Santa Barbara Islanders, Las Vegas Silver Streaks; NBA scout Charlotte Hornets, 1990-94, Dallas Mavericks, 1994-96, asst. coach, 1996-97, Detroit Shock, 1997-98; head coach Sacramento Monarchs, 1998—. Named Coach of the Yr., AP and Nat. Assn. Basketball Coaches, 1975, Southwest Conf. coach of the Yr., 1976, big Sky Coach of the Yr. awards, 1984, 85, Coach of the Yr. , WNBA, 1990. Office: c/o Sacramento Monarchs One Sports Pkwy Sacramento CA 95834

ALLEN, TERRY, artist; b. Wichita, Kans., May 7, 1943; BFA, Chouinard Art Inst., 1966. Instr. drawing Chouinard Art Inst., L.A., 1968-69; assoc. prof. Calif. State U., Fresno, 1974-77, prof., 1978-79. Exhibitions include Joslyn Art Mus., Omaha, 1970, San Francisco Mus. Art, 1970, Chgo. Art Inst., 1975, Ft. Worth Art Mus., 1976, San Francisco Mus. Modern Art, 1978, São Paulo (Brazil) Biennial, 1985, Documenta 8, Kassal, West Germany, 1987, L.A. County Mus. Art, 1987, Kimbell Art Mus., Ft. Worth, 1991, Wexner Ctr. Visual Arts, Columbus, Ohio, 1992, Mus. Modern Art, Paris, 1982, others. Recipient Bessie award, 1986, Adaline Kent award, 1989; Guggenheim fellow, 1986, SArtists Residency fellow Wexner Ctr. Arts, 1992. Office: W Alameda RR 10 Box 88N Santa Fe NM 87501-9402

ALLEN, WILLIAM MERLE, museum director; b. San Luis Obispo, Calif., Oct. 9, 1939; s. Lloyd Marion and Berwyn Rose (Palmer) A.; m. Janet Laurentine Clayton, June 11, 1963; children: Barbara, Gregory. BA in Chemistry, La Sierra Coll., 1961; PhD in Organic Chemistry, U. Md., 1967. From instr. to asst. prof. chemistry Andrews U., Berrien Springs, Mich., 1966-68; from asst. prof. to prof. chemistry Loma Linda U., Riverside, Calif., 1968-84; sr. v.p. acad. adminstrn. So. Coll. Seventh Day Aventists, Collegedale, Tenn., 1984-87; dean grad. sch. Loma Linda U., 1987-88; dir. ctr. lifelong learning La Sierra U., Riverside, 1988-98, dir. World Mus. Nat. History, 1988—, dir. devel. for major gifts, 1998—. Chair chemistry dept. Loma Linda U., 1971-79, dir. divsn. natural sci., 1977-81; sec., trustee So. Coll. Seventh Day Adventists, 1984-87. Internet website developer. Trustee Smyrna Hosp., Atlanta, 1986-87. Republican. Avocations: gardening, racquetball, collecting autographed books. Office: La Sierra U 4700 Pierce St Riverside CA 92505-3332

ALLER, LAWRENCE HUGH, astronomy educator, researcher; b. Tacoma, Sept. 24, 1913; s. Leslie E. and Lena Belle (Davis) A.; m. Rosalind Duncan Hall; children— Hugh Duncan, Raymond Donald, Gwendolyn Jean AB, U. Calif, Berkeley, 1936; MA, Harvard U., 1938, PhD, 1943. Instr. physics Harvard U., Cambridge, Mass., 1942-43; research physicist radiation lab. U. Calif, Berkeley, 1943-45; asst. prof. astronomy Ind. U., Bloomington, 1945-48; assoc. prof. astronomy U. Mich., Ann Arbor, 1948-54, prof. astronomy, 1954-62, UCLA, 1962-84, prof. emeritus, 1984—; vis. prof. U. Tasmania, Hobart, Australia, 1969, U. Queensland, Brisbane, Australia, 1977-78, Australian Nat. U., Canberra, 1960-61, U. Toronto, Ont., Can., 1961-62, U. Sydney, New South Wales, Australia, 1968; guest investigator radiophysics CSIRO, Epping, Australia, 1968, 69, 77; vis. lectr. Raman Inst., Bangalore, India, 1978, Sch. Advanced Studies, Trieste, Italy, 1981; guest investigator Mt. Wilson Obs., Pasadena, Calif., 1949-82. Author: Atmospheres of Sun and Stars, 1953, 2d edit., 1962; Stellar Interiors, Nuclear Transformations, 1954; Gaseous Nebulae, 1956; Abundances of Elements, 1961; Atoms, Stars and Nebulae, 1971, 3d edit., 1991, Physics of Thermal Gaseous Nebulae, 1984. Editor (with Dean B. McLaughlin) Stellar Structure and Evolution, 1965; (with Barbara Middlehurst) Interstellar Medium, 1967 NSF research fellow, 1968-69, 60-61 Mem. Am. Astron. Soc. (councillor 1953-56), Internat. Astron. Union (pres. stellar-spectroscopy group 1959-64), Astron. Soc. of Pacific (bd. dirs. 1974-77), Am. Acad. Arts and Scis., Nat. Acad. Scis. Mem. Soc. of Friends. Lodge: Masons Avocations: travel; photography. Home: 18118 Kingsport Dr Malibu CA 90265-5634 Office: U Calif Astronomy Divsn Dept Physics & Astronomy Los Angeles CA 90095-0001 E-mail: aller@astro.ucla.edu

ALLERTON, SAMUEL ELLSWORTH, biochemist; b. Three Rivers, Mich., Aug. 21, 1933; s. Sanford Ellsworth and Virginia Mary (Dickenson) A.; m. [illegible], Aug. 20, 1960; children: Adam Sanford, Eve Samantha. BA summa cum laude, Kalamazoo (Mich.) Coll., 1955; PhD, Harvard U., 1962. Teaching fellow Harvard U. Med. Sch., Boston, 1957-61; rsch. assoc. Rockefeller U., N.Y.C., 1961-65; asst. prof. U. So. Calif., L.A., 1965-69, assoc. prof., 1969—. Cons. Woodroof Labs., Santa Ana, Calif., 1978-89. Contbr. articles to profl. jours. Bd. dirs. Huntington Beach (Calif.) Community Clinic, 1990-92. Named Outstanding Young Man of [illegible]. Mem. N.Y. Acad. Scis., Am. Coll. of Nutrition, Elks, Sigma Xi, Omicron Kappa Upsilon. Anglican. Achievements include rsch. on phys.-chem. characterization of proteins, tumor products, studies on absorption of copper. Office: U So Calif Dept Dentistry University Park Mc # 0641 Los Angeles CA 90089-0001

ALLERY, KENNETH EDWARD, career officer; b. Holyoke, Mass., Mar. 3, 1925; s. Alfred Edward and Anne (Millen) A.; m. Constance DuFresne, June 22, 1946; children— Katherine Ann, Kenneth Scott, Bryan Keith, David Edward. B.A., Park Coll., 1965; M.S., George Washington U., 1969; grad., Air Command and Staff Coll., 1961, Nat. War Coll., 1969. Commd. 2d lt. U.S. Army Air Force, 1944; advanced through grades to brig. gen. U.S. Air Force, 1972; insp. with Insp. Gen. Team 17th Air Force; exec. officer, ops. officer 526th Fighter Interceptor Squadron, Ramstein Air Base, Germany, 1961; sr. Air Force adviser Oreg. Air N.G., Portland Internat. Airport, 1965-67; dir. ops. and tng. 1st Air Force, Stewart AFB, N.Y., 1967-68; mem. N.Am. br. Directorate Plans and Programs, Orgn. Joint Chiefs of Staff, 1969-71; asst. dep. chief of staff for plans Aerospace Def. Command, Ent AFB, Colo., 1971-72, N.Am. Air Def. Command/Continental Air Def. Command, 1972-73, asst. dep. chief of staff for ops., 1973-74; also dep. chief of staff for ops. Aerospace Def. Command; command insp. gen. NORAD/CONAD/ADC, 1974-76; ret.; asst. to v.p. Syscon Corp., Colorado Springs, 1976-85; founder Allery Enterprises, Inc., Colorado Springs, 1996—99; bus. devel. mgr. Litton Computer Services, Colorado Springs, 1985-96; strategic planner Ensign Devel., Colorado Springs, 1999—. Bd. govs. Nat. Coll., Colorado Springs, 1993-94. Decorated D.S.M., D.F.C., Air medal with 4 oak leaf clusters, Meritorious Service medal with oak leaf cluster, Air Force Commendation medal. Office: Allery Enterprises Inc 1320 Rangely Dr Colorado Springs CO 80921-2692 E-mail: kena0325@aol.com

ALLISON, ANDREW MARVIN, church administrator; b. Long Beach, Calif., May 21, 1949; s. Howard C. and Wilma A. (Franks) A.; m. Kathleen L. Anderson, May 28, 1971; children: Rebecca, Nathan, Joanna, Spencer, Jacob, Camilla. AA, Glendale (Ariz.) C.C., 1972; BA in History, Brigham Young U., 1974; PhD of Polit. Sci., Coral Ridge U., 1993. Cert. secondary tchr., Ariz., Utah. Adminstrv. staff, editor Brigham Young U., Provo, Utah, 1972-74; adminstrv. asst. LDS Ch., Salt Lake City, 1977-79; prin., tchr. LDS Seminaries, Ariz.,Utah, 1974-77, 79-80; assoc. editor, art dir. Bookcraft Publs., Salt Lake City, 1983-85; dir. rsch. and publs. Nat. Ctr. for Constl. Studies, Salt Lake City, 1980-83, 85-91, chmn., pres. West Jordan, Utah, 1991-95; product devel. editor Deseret Book Co., Salt Lake City, 1995-96; supr. confidential applications LDS Ch., Salt Lake City, 1996-99, mgr. confidential records, 1999—. Adj. prof. polit. sci., George Wythe Coll., Cedar City, Utah, 1993—. Author: The Real Thomas Jefferson, 1982, The Real Benjamin Franklin, 1983, The Real George Washington, 1991; contbr. articles to profl. jours. Mem. West Jordan City Coun., Utah, 2000—, mayor pro-tem, 2001—. Mem. Phi Kappa Phi.

ALLISON, JAMES PATRICK, immunology educator, medical association administrator; b. Alice, Tex., Aug. 7, 1948; m. Malinda Bell. BS in Microbiology, U. Tex., 1969, PhD in Biol. Scis., 1973. Asst. biochemist and asst. prof. U. Tex., Smithville, 1977-83; asst. prof. biochemistry Grad. Sch. of Biomedical Scis., 1981-84, assoc. biochemist and assoc. prof. biochemistry, 1983-84; prof. immunology UCLA, 1985—, dir. Cancer Rsch. Lab., 1985—, interim head Divsn. Immunology, 1987-89, head divsn immunology, 1989—, co-chair and Howard Hughes prof. immunology. Adj. prof. of zoology, U. Tex., 1979-84, spl. assoc. mem. grad. faculty, 1980-84; vis. scholar Dept. of Pathology, Stanford U., 1983-84; invited participant, Dahlem Workshop on Leukemia, 1983; faculty Advanced Course in Evolution of the Immune System Am. Assn. of Immunologists, 1985, Advanced Course in Regulation of the Immune System; mem bd. Midwinter Conf. of Immunologists, 1986-89; convener Indo-U.S. Short Term Course on The Molecular and Cellular Biology of the T Lymphocyte All India Inst. of Med. Scis., New Delhi, 1987; editorial bd. Devel. Immunology, 1989—; cons. Becton-Dickinson Immunocytometry Systems, Inc., 1984—. Reviewing editor Science, 1985-87; assoc. editor Journal of Immunology, 1987—; transmitting editor International Immunology, 1988—. Recipient Postdoctoral fellowship NIH, 1974-76, Dept. of Molecular Immunology Scripps Clinic and Rsch. Found., 1974-77; O.B. Williams award of the Tex. Branch Am. Soc. Microbiology, 1971. Mem. AAAS, Am. Assn. Immunologists, Am. Assn. Cancer Rsch. Home: 920 Oxford St Berkeley CA 94707-2435 Office: U Calif Cancer Res Lab RM 3200 447 Life Science Addition Berkeley CA 94720-2751

ALLISON, MERLE LEE, geologist; b. Phila., Jan. 15, 1948; s. Merle Raymond and Lois Loretta (Lynch) A. BS, U. Calif., Riverside, 1970; MS, San Diego State U., 1974; PhD, U. Mass., 1986. Registered geologist, Calif. Oil & gas engr. Calif. Divsn. Oil & Gas, Inglewood, 1971-72; geologist Chevron Corp., San Francisco, 1974-79; consulting geologist Amherst, Mass., 1980-84; scientist II Jet Propulsion Lab.-NASA, Pasadena, Calif., 1981; geologist Sohio Petroleum-BP, Dallas & Houston, 1984-87; sr. geologist U. Utah Rsch. Inst., Salt Lake City, 1987-89; dir., state geologist Utah Geol. Survey, Salt Lake City, 1989—. Pres. Western Earth Sci. Techs. Inc., Casper, Wyo., 1988-93; chair Utah Geog. Info. Coun., Salt Lake City, 1992-93. Editor: Energy & Mineral Resources of Utah, 1991; contbr. articles to profl. jours. Press sec., mgr. Caprio for Congress, San Diego, 1972, 74; city precinct mgr. Unruh for Gov., Riverside, 1978; energy advisor Clifford for Congress, Houston, 1990. Mem. Am. Assn. Petroleum Geologists, Geol. Soc. Am., Soc. Profl. Well Log Analysts, Am. Geophys. Union, Rocky Mountain Assn. Geologists, Utah Geol. Assn., Assn. for Women Geoscientists, Wyo. Geol. Assn., Nev. Petroleum Soc. Achievements include research on geology of Ganymede; diplog interpretation, various of in-situ crustal structures. Home: 2724 Meadow Dr Lawrence KS 66047-3237 Office: Utah Geological Survey 1594 W North Temple # 3410 Salt Lake City UT 84116-3154

ALLRED, CLARK B. judge; b. Ogden, Utah, Mar. 10, 1951; BA, Utah State U., 1975; JD, Brigham Young U., 1978. Pvt. practice lawyer; part-time magistrate judge U.S. Dist. Ct., Vernal, Utah, 1997—. Mem. Utah State Bar Assn.

ALLRED, GLORIA RACHEL, lawyer; b. Phila., July 3, 1941; d. Morris and Stella Bloom; m. William Allred (div. Oct. 1987); 1 child, Lisa. BA, U. Pa., 1963; MA, NYU, 1966; JD, Loyola U., L.A., 1974; JD (hon.), U. West Los Angeles, 1981. Bar: Calif. 1975, U.S. Dist. Ct. (cen. dist.) Calif. 1975, U.S. Ct. Appeals (9th cir.) 1976, U.S. Supreme Ct. 1979. Ptnr. Allred, Maroko, Goldberg & Ribakoff (now Allred, Maroko & Goldberg), L.A., 1976—. Contbr. articles to profl. jours. Pres. Women's Equal Rights Legal Def. and Edn. Fund, L.A., 1978—, Women's Movement Inc., L.A. Recipient Commendation award L.A. Bd. Suprs., 1986, Mayor of L.A., 1986, Pub. Svc. award Nat. Assn. Fed. Investigators, 1986, Vol. Action award Pres. of U.S., 1986. Mem. ABA, Calif. Bar Assn., Nat. Assn. Women Lawyers, Calif. Women Lawyers Assn., Women Lawyers L.A. Assn., Friars (Beverly Hills, Calif.), Magic Castle Club (Hollywood, Calif.) Office: Allred Maroko & Goldberg 6300 Wilshire Blvd Ste 1500 Los Angeles CA 90048-5217

ALM, STEVE, prosecutor; m. [illegible], 1 child. MEd, U. Oreg., 1979; JD, U. Pacific, 1983. Editor West Pub. Co., 1983-85; dep. prosecuting atty. City and County of Honolulu, 1985-87, line-dep., then felony team supr., 1987-90, dir. dist. and family ct. divsn., 1990-94; U.S. atty. for Hawaii U.S. Dept. Justice, Honolulu, 1994—. Adj. prof. Richardson Sch. Law U. Hawaii. Mem. ABA (mem. gov. com. on crime), Hawaii State Bar Assn. (ex officio mem. domestic violence coordinating coun., v.p. criminal justice [illegible]). Office: US Dept Justice 300 Ala Moana Blvd Rm 6100 Honolulu HI 96850-6100

ALMOND, GABRIEL ABRAHAM, political science educator; b. Rock Island, Ill., Jan. 12, 1911; s. David Moses and Lisa (Elson) A.; m. Maria Dorothea Kaufmann, Apr. 29, 1937; children: Richard J., Peter O., Susan J. PhB, U. Chgo., 1932, PhD, 1938. Fellow Social Sci. Rsch. Coun., 1935-36, 46; instr. polit. sci. Bklyn. Coll., 1939-42; with OWI, Washington, 1942-44, War Dept., ETO, 1945; research assoc. Yale U. Inst. Internat. Studies, 1947-49, assoc. prof. polit. sci., 1949-51, prof. polit. sci., 1959-63; assoc. prof. internat. affairs Princeton, 1951-54, prof., 1954-57, prof. politics, 1957-59; prof. polit. sci. Stanford U., 1963-76; exec. head dept. polit. sci. Stanford u., 1964-68; prof. emeritus Stanford U., 1976. Cons. Air U., 1948, Dept. State, 1950, Office Naval Rsch., 1951, Rand Corp., 1954-55, sci. adv. bd. USAF, 1960-61; vis. prof. U. Tokyo, Japan, 1962, Kiev State U., USSR, 1989; Overseas fellow Churchill Coll. U. Cambridge, 1972-73; vis. fellow Australian Nat. U., 1983. Author: The American People and Foreign Policy, 1950, The Appeals of Communism, 1954, (with others) The Struggle for Democracy in Germany, 1949, The Politics of the Developing Areas, 1960, (with Sidney Verba) The Civic Culture, 1963, (with G. Bingham Powell) Comparative Politics, 1966, Political Development, 1970, (with others) Crisis, Choice and Change, 1973, Comparative Politics Today, 1974, 80, 84, 88, 92, 96, 2000, (with G. Bingham Powell) Comparative Politics: System, Process, Policy, 1978, (with Sidney Verba and others) The Civic Culture Revisited, 1980, (with others) Progress and its Discontents, 1982, A Discipline Divided, Schools and Sects in Political Science, 1990, Comparative Politics: A Theoretical Approach, 2001, (with others) Plutocracy and Politics in New York City, 1998, European Politics Today, 1999. Recipient Travel and Study award Ford Found., 1962-63; fellow Center for Advanced Study in the Behavioral Scis., 1956-57; sr. fellow Nat. Endowment for Humanities, 1972-73 Fellow Am. Acad. Arts and Scis.; mem. Nat. Acad. Scis., Am. Philos. Soc., Social Sci. Rsch. Coun. (bd. dirs., chmn. com. comparative politics), Am. Polit. Sci. Assn. (pres. 1965-66, James Madison award 1981, Frank Goodnow award 1999). Home: 4135 Old Trace Rd Palo Alto CA 94306-3728 Office: Stanford Univ Political Sci Dept Stanford CA 94305 Fax: (650) 941-2235. E-mail: almond@Leland.Stanford.edu

ALPER, MARK D. biochemist; b. Bklyn., May 14, 1945; s. Samuel and Miriam (Grifffel) A.; m. Christine Hexem, June 6, 1975; children; Samuel Andrew, Elizabeth Laura. AB, Harvard Coll., 1967; PhD, U. Calif., Berkeley, 1973. Adj. prof. dept. molecular and cell biology U. Calif., Berkeley, 1974—, dep. dir. Ctr. Advanced Materials, Lawrence Berkeley Lab., 1983—, assoc. dir. materials sci. div., 1987—, prof. biochem. molecular and cell biology dept.; dep. divsn. dri. material scis. divsn. Lawrence Berkeley Nat. Lab. Cons. various textbook pubs. Editor: Polymers for Advanced Technologies, 1989—. Mem. Materials Rsch. Soc., Am. Chem. Soc. Office: U Calif Materials Sci Div Lawrence Berkeley Lab 1 Cyclotron Rd Berkeley CA 94720-0001

ALPERS, EDWARD ALTER, history educator; b. Phila., Apr. 23, 1941; s. Bernard Jacob and Lillian (Sher) A.; m. Ann Adele Dixon, June 14, 1963; children: Joel Dixon, Leila Sher. AB magna cum laude, Harvard U., 1963; PhD, U. London, 1966. Lectr. history Univ. Coll., Dar es Salaam, Tanzania, 1966-68; from asst. prof. to prof. history UCLA, 1968—, dean divsn. honors Coll. Letters and Sci., 1985-87, dean honors and undergrad. programs, 1987-96. Author: Ivory and Slaves in East Central Africa, 1975; editor: Walter Rodney: Revolutionary and Scholar, 1982, History, Memory and Identity, 2001, (newsletter) Assn. Concerned Africa Scholars, 1983-85; contbg. editor: Comparative Studies of South Asia, Africa and the Middle East, 1997—; contbr. articles to scholarly jours. Fellow Ford Found., 1972-73, NEH, 1978-79, Fulbright Found., 1980; Conf. fellow Humanities Rsch. Ctr., Nat. Australia U., Canberra, 1998; Fundacao Calouste Gulbenkian grantee, Lisbon, Portugal, 1975. Mem. Am. Hist. Assn. (mem. com. Joan Kelly Meml. prize 1998 99, chair 2000), Africa Studies Assn. (bd. dirs. 1985-88, v.p. 1992-93, pres. 1993-94), Assn. Concerned Africa Scholars (bd. dirs. 1983-93), Alliance for Undergrad. Edn. (UCLA rep. 1987-95, co-chair 1989-92), Hist. Abstracts (adv. bd. 1994—). Office: UCLA Dept History Los Angeles CA 90095-0001

ALPERT, DEIRDRE WHITTLETON (DEDE ALPERT), state legislator; b. N.Y.C., Oct. 6, 1945; d. Harry Mark and Dorothy (Lehn) Whittleton; m. Michael Edward Alpert, Jan. 1, 1964; children: Lehn, Kristin, Alison. Student, Pomona Coll., 1963-65; LLD (hon.), Western Am. U., 1994. Mem. from 78th dist. Calif. State Assembly, Sacramento, 1990 96; mem. from 39th dist. Calif. Senate, Sacramento, 1997—. Chairwoman Women Legislators' Caucus, Sacramento, 1993, Assembly Edn. Com., 1995, Senate Revenue and Taxation Com., 1997-98, Senate Edn. Com., 1999—; Joint. Com. to Develop a Master Plan- Kindergarten through University, 1999—; active Calif. Tourism Commn., Sacramento, 1990—, Calif. Libr. Allocations Bd., Sacramento, 1993—; com. mem. Edn. Standards and Teaching Training, Appropriations Subcom. on Fiscal Oversight, Appropriations, Environ. Quality, Natural Resources, Revenue and Taxation, select com. on Calif. Fed. Water Program, Calif.'s Wine Industry, Defense Conversion, Retention, and Space Flight Industries, Econ. Devel., Family, Child and Youth Devel., Higher Edn. Admissions and Outreach, Juvenile Justice, Urban Econ. Devel., Joint Com. on Fisheries and Aquaculture, Pacific Fisheries Legis. Task Force, Calif. Commission on Status of Women. Author: Mammography Quality Assurance Act 1992, Assembly Bill 114 of 1993, Workplace Violence Safety Act, 1994, Battered Women's Protection Act, 1994, ABC, 1995, California Assessment Academic Achievement Act, 1995. Spl. advocate Voices for Children, San Diego, 1982-90; mem. bd. Solana Beach (Calif.) Sch. Bd., 1983-90, also pres.; pres. Beach and County Guild United Cerebral Palsy, San Diego, 1986. Recipient Beach and County Guild legis. award Calif. Regional Occupation Program, 1991-92, Am. Acad. Pediats., 1991-92, San Diego Psychol. Assn., 1993-94, Commitment to Children award Calif. Assn. for Edn. of Young Children, 1991-92, Legis. Commendation award Nat. Assn. for Yr.-Round Edn., 1991-92, State Commn. on Status of Women, 1993-94, Friend of Public Edn. award Calif. Sch. Bds. Assn., 1997-98, Legis. Champion award Calif. Union Safety Employees, Unsung Hero award Youth Law Ctr., 1995-96, Champion for Children award Voices for Children, 1995-96; named Friend of Yr., Children's PKU Network, 1991-92, Woman of Yr., Nat. Women's Polit. Caucus San Diego, 1991-92, Orgn. for Rehab. through Tng., 1993-94, High Tech Legislator of Yr., Am. Electronics Assn., 1991-99, Calif. Sch.-Age Consortium, 1993-94, Women of Distinction, Soroptimists Internat. of La Jolla, 1993-94, Assemblymember of Yr., Calif. Assn. Edn. Young Children, 1993-94, Calif. Tourism Hall of Fame, 1997—, Legis. of Yr., Calif. State U. Alumni Coun., 1999, Legis. of Yr., Calif. Women for Agriculture, 1999, Honored Patriot, U.S. Selective Svc. Sys., 1999, Legis. of Yr., Profl. Engrs. Calif. Govt., 1997, Outstanding Senator of Yr., Calif. Sch. Bd. Assn., 1998, Legis. of Yr., Am. Elec. Assn., 1995-96, Legis. of Yr., Calif. League Mid. Schs., 1995, Outstanding Legis. of Yr., Nat. Women's Polit. Caucus, S.D. chpt., 1995-96, Outstanding Assembly Mem. of Yr., Calif. Sch. Bds. Assn., 1994; Recognition for Outstanding Legis. Efforts, Paw PAC, 1997. Mem. Charter 100 of San Diego, Calif. Elected Women's Assn. for Edn. and Rsch. (pres. 1995-96). Democrat. Mem. Congregation Ch. Avocations: golf, reading. Office: State Capitol Bldg Rm 5114 Senate District 39 Sacramento CA 95814 also: 1557 Columbia St San Diego CA 92101-2934

ALPERT, HERB, composer, recording artist, producer, painter; b. Los Angeles, Mar. 31, 1935; s. Louis and Tillie (Goldberg) A.; m. Sharon Mae Lubin, Aug. 5, 1956 (div.); children: Dore, Eden; m. Lani Hall; 1 dau., Aria. Student, U. So. Calif. Co-owner, founder A&M Record Co., 1962-94, Rondor Music Internat., 1994—. Band leader, trumpeter, arranger producer music group Herb Alpert & The Tijuana Brass, 34 recs. including The Lonely Bull, Whipped Cream & Other Delights, Going Places, Rise, Under A Spanish Moon, Colors, 1999 (14 Platinum recs., 15 gold recs., 7 Grammy awards); prodr. Broadway shows, including Angels in America, Jelly's Last Jam, Seven Guitars. Founder Herb Alpert Found. Office: c/o No Bull Inc 1414 6th St Santa Monica CA 90401-2510

ALPERT, JOSEPH STEPHEN, physician, educator; b. New Haven, Feb. 1, 1942; s. Zelly Charles and Beatrice Ann (Kopsofsky) A.; m. Helle Mathiasen, Aug. 6, 1965; children: Eva Elisabeth, Niels David. BA magna cum laude, Yale U., 1963; MD cum laude, Harvard U., 1969. Diplomate Am. Bd. Internal Medicine (cardiovascular disease). Successively intern, resident in internal medicine, fellow in cardiovascular disease Peter Bent Brigham Hosp.-Harvard U. Med. Sch., Boston, 1969-74, dir. Samuel A. Levine cardiac unit, asst. prof. medicine, 1976-78; prof., dir. divsn. cardiovascular medicine U. Mass. Med. Sch., Worcester, 1978-92, vice-chm. dept. medicine, 1990—, Edward Budnitz prof. of cardiovascular medicine, 1988-92; Robert W. and Irene P. Flinn prof., chmn. dept. medicine U. Ariz., 1992—. Cons. W. Roxbury VA Hosp., Boston, VA Med. Ctr., Tucson; sec., treas. med. staff U. Mass. Med. Ctr., 1979-81, pres. med. staff, 1981-82; bd. dirs. Am. Bd. Internal Medicine. Author: The Heart Attack Handbook, 1978, 2d edit., 1985, 3d edit., 1993, Cardiovascular Physiopathology, 1984; co-author: Manual of Coronary Care, 1977, 80, 84, 87, 93, 2000, Manual of Cardiovascular Diagnosis and Therapy, 1980, 84, 88, 96, Valvular Heart Disease, 1981, 87, 2000, Intensive Care Medicine, 1985, 2d edit., 1991, The Clinician's Companion, 1986, Modern Coronary Care, 1990, 2d edit., 1996, Diagnostic Atlas of the Heart, 1994, Cardiology for the Primary Care Physician, 1996, 2d edit., 1998, Primary Care of Native American Patients, 1999, American Heart Association's Clinical Cardiology Consult, 2001; editor-in-chief Current Cardiology Reports, 2001—; assoc. editor: Jour. History of Medicine and Allied Scis., 1977-80; editl. cons. Little, Brown & Co., Appleton-Century Crofts; mem. editl. bd. Am. Jour. Cardiology, 1985—, Archives Internal Medicine, 1987—, Heart and Lung, 1987-90, Cardiology, 1985—, assoc. editor, 1987—, editor-in-chief, 1991—; mem. editl. bd. Geriatric Cardiovascular Medicine, 1988-89, Am. Jour. Noninvasive Cardiology, 1987-95, Am. Heart Jour., 1992-97, Internat. Jour. Cardiology, 1992—, European Heart Jour., 1995—, Heart Disease, 1999—; contbr. articles to profl. jours. Lt. comdr. USNR, 1974-76. Recipient Gold medal U. Copenhagen, 1968, Edward Rhodes Stitt award San Diego Naval Hosp., 1976, George W. Thorn award Peter Bent Bingham Hosp., 1977, Outstanding Tchr. award U. Mass. Med. Sch., 1981, 86, 87, 90, U. Ariz. Med. Sch., 1995, 97-2000; Fulbright scholar Copenhagen, 1963-64; USPHS-Mass. Heart Assn. fellow, 1971-72, NIH spl. rsch. fellow, 1972-73. Fellow ACP, Am. Coll. Cardiology (jour. editl. bd. mem. 1983-86, chmn. tng. dirs. com. 1991—, bd. trustees 1996-2001), Am. Coll. Chest Physicians (gov. for Mass. 1983-85); mem. AAAS, Am. Heart Assn. (fellow coun. clin. cardiology, vice chmn. 1991-92, chmn. 1993-95, exec. com. 1986—), Am. Assn. History of Medicine, Am. Fedn. Clin. Rsch., Assn. Univ. Cardiologists, New Eng. Cardiovascular Club, Assn. Profs. of Medicine, Danish Cardiology Assn. (hon.), Argentine Heart Assn. (fgn. corr.), Aesculapian Club, Phi Beta Kappa, Sigma Xi, Alpha Omega Alpha. Office: 1501 N Campbell Ave Tucson AZ 85724-0001

ALSENTZER, WILLIAM JAMES, JR. lawyer; b. Ravenna, Ohio, Mar. 15, 1942; s. William J. Alsentzer and Vivian (Guy) Soash; children: Lesley Joan, Michelle Guy. AB, Duke U., 1964, JD, 1966. Bar: Del. 1966, U.S. Dist. Ct. Del. 1967, Ariz. 1980, U.S. Dist. Ct. Ariz. 1980. Assoc. Wilson & Lynam, Wilmington, Del., 1967-70; ptnr. Bayard, Brill & Handelman, Wilmington, 1970-79; v.p., gen. counsel Bapt. Hosps. and Health Systems, Phoenix, 1979-2000; legal counsel BHHS Legacy Found., Phoenix, 2000—. Mem. ABA, Maricopa County Bar Assn., Am. Health Lawyers Assn., Fedn. Ins. and Corp. Counsel. Office: 2999 N 44th St Ste 530 Phoenix AZ 85018

ALSOP, MARIN, conductor; d. LaMar and Ruth A. Student, Yale Univ., Julliard Sch. Debut with Symphony Space, N.Y.C., 1984; founder, artistic dir. Concordia Chamber Orchestra, N.Y.C., 1984—; asst. condr. Richmond Symphony, Va., 1987; music dir. Eugene Symphony Orchestra, Oreg., 1989—, Long Island Philharmonic, N.Y, 1990-94; principal condr. Colorado Symphony Orchestra, Denver, 1993—, now mus. dir. Guest condr. San Francisco Symphony Orchestra, Boston Pops, Los Angeles Philharmonic Orchestra, 1991, City Ballet Orchestra, 1992; dir. Cabrillo Music Festival, Calif., 1991—; concertmaster Northeastern Pennsylvania Philharmonic, Scranton; founder, mem. String Fever (swing band), 1980—. Recipient Koussevitzky Conducting prize Tanglewood Music Festival, 1988. Office: Colo Symphony Orch Boettcher Concert Hall 821 17th St Ste 700 Denver CO 80202-3000

ALSOP, STEWART, communications executive; Ptnr. New Enterprise Assocs., Menlo Park, Calif., 1996—. Former exec. editor Inc. mag.; former exec. v.p InfoWorld Pub. Co., former editor in chief; founder P.C. Letter; columnist Fortune Mag. Office: New Enterprise Assocs 2490 Sand Hill Rd Menlo Park CA 94025-6940

ALSPACH, PHILIP HALLIDAY, manufacturing company executive; b. Buffalo, Apr. 19, 1923; s. Walter L. and Jean E. (Halliday) A.; m. Jean Edwards, Dec. 20, 1947 (dec.); children: Philip Clough, Bruce Edwards, David Christopher; m. Loretta M. Hildebrand, Aug. 1982. BME, Tulane U., 1944. Registered profl. engr., Mass., Wis., La. With Gen. Electric Co., 1945-64, mgr. indsl. electronics div. planning, 1961-64; v.p., gen. mgr. constrn. machinery div. Allis Chalmers Mfg. Co., Milw., 1964-68; exec. v.p., dir., mem. exec. com. Jeffrey Galion, Inc., 1968-69; v.p. I.T.E. Imperial Corp., Springhouse, Pa., 1969-75; pres. E.W. Bliss div. Gulf & Western Mfg. Co., Southfield, Mich., 1975-79; group v.p. Katy Industries, Inc., Elgin, Ill., 1979-85; pres. Intercon Inc., Irvine, Calif., 1985—, also bd. dirs.; pres. Intercon Publ., Irvine, 1991—. Bd. dirs. All West Plastics, Inc., D&L Sheet Metal, Inc., Fortifiber Corp.; adv. bd. Diamond Stainless, Inc., McFarlands Foods, Inc. Author: Swiss-Bernese Oberland, 1992, 2d edit., 2000; papers in field. Mem. pres.'s coun. Tulane U., 1982-90. Mem. IEEE, Soc. Automotive Engrs. (sr.), Soc. Mfg. Engrs., Internat. Forum Corp. Dirs., Inst. Dirs. (U.K.), Am. Mgmt. Assn., Chaîne des Rotisseurs (officier). Home: 23 Alejo Irvine CA 92612-2913 Office: Intercon Inc 2500 Michelson Dr Ste #125 Irvine CA 92612-1529 E-mail: intercon@att.net

ALSTROM, SVEN ERIK, architect; b. Emporia, Kans., July 27, 1951; Buddhist. s. William E. and Willa M. (Russell) A.; m. Lynn M. Mathews, June 22, 1974 (div. June 1983). B. in Gen. Studies, U. Kans., 1975; postgrad., U. Denver, 1984. Registered Calif., Colo., Kans., Mo., N. Mex., cert. Nat. Coun. Archtl. Registration Bds. Arch. PGAV Archs., Kansas City, Mo., 1972-74, Horner Blessing, Kansas City, 1977-79, MSFS Archs., Kansas City, 1979-80, Urban Design, Denver, 1981-82, Dominck Assocs., Denver, 1983-84; with C. Welton Anderson & Assocs., Aspen, Colo., 1989-90; pvt. practice Altsrom Group, Aspen, 1990-99; arch. Ecol. Archs., Aspen, 1999—. Mem. AIA (Colo.). Buddhist. Office: Ecol Arch PO Box 551 Aspen CO 81612-0551 E-mail: svenskarch@aspeninfo.com

ALSUP, WILLIAM, judge; b. June 27, 1945; BS, Miss. State U., 1967; MPP, Kennedy Sch. Govt., 1971; JD, Harvard U., 1971. Bar: Miss. 1972, Calif. 1973. Law clk. to Hon. William O. Douglas U.S. Supreme Ct., 1971-72; mem. Morrison & Foerster, San Francisco, 1972-99; asst. to solicitor gen. U.S. Dept. Justice, 1978-80; judge U.S. Dist. Ct. (no. dist.) Calif., 1999. Law del. 9th Cir. Jud. Coun., 1993-96. Mem. Am. Coll. Trial Lawyers. Office: US Dist Ct No Dist Calif 450 Golden Gate Ave San Francisco CA 94102-3482

ALTAMIRANO, BEN D. state legislator, merchant, insurance agent; b. Silver City, Oct. 17, 1930; s. Ramon and Eloisa P. (Davila) A.; m. Nina Melendrez, July 24, 1949; children: Yolanda, Benjamin, Paul. Owner, operator Benny's Market Baskets, Silver City, 1949-78, C.H. Pennington Fashions, 1971-84, Nina's Guys N Gals. Ins. agt. TBA Ins. Co., Dallas; founder, chmn. bd. Silver City Savs. & Loan Assn.; mem. N.Mex. Senate, 1970— . Mem. City Coun. Silver City; county commr. With U.S. Army, 1946-48. Democrat. Roman Catholic. Home: 1123 N Santa Rita St Silver City NM 88061-5156 Office: New Mex Senate State Capitol Rm 325 Santa Fe NM 87503-0001

ALTER, EDWARD T. state treasurer; b. Glen Ridge, N.J., July 26, 1941; s. E. Irving and Norma (Fisher) A.; m. Patricia R. Olsen, 1975; children: Christina Lyn, Ashly Ann, Darci Lee. BA, U. Utah., 1966; MBA, U. Utah, 1967. C.P.A., Calif., Utah. Sr. acct. Touche Ross & Co., Los Angeles, 1967-72; asst. treas. U. Utah, Salt Lake City, 1972-80; treas. State of Utah, Salt Lake City, 1981—; pres. Nat. Assn. State Treas., 1987-88. Bd. dirs. Utah Housing Fin. Agy., Utah State Retirement Bd., pres., 1984-93; mem. Utah State Rep. Cen. Com., 1981—, Anthony Com. on Pub. Fin., 1988-92. Sgt. USAR, 1958-66. Named to All-pro Govt. Team, City and State Mag., 1988, Outstanding CPA for 2000 Utah Assn. CPAs; recipient Jesse M. Uhruh Award for Svc. to State Treas.', 1989. Mem. AICPAs, Nat. Assn. State Treas. (past sr. v.p., pres. 1987), Utah Bond Club (pres. 1981-82), Delta Sigma Pi, Delta Phi Kappa. Club: Utah Bond (pres. 1981-82). Office: State Capitol 215 State Capitol Building Salt Lake City UT 84114-1202

ALTER, ROBERT A. hotel executive; BS in Hotel Adminstrn., Cornell U. Chmn., CEO Sunstone Hotel Investors, Inc., 1995—; chmn. Sunstone Hotel Properties, Inc., Sunstone Hotel Mgmt., Inc.; operator Sunstone Hotels. Office: Sunstone Hotel Mgmt Inc 903 Calleancincu St San Clemente CA 92674-4240

ALTER, ROBERT BERNARD, comparative literature educator, critic; b. N.Y.C., Apr. 2, 1935; s. Harry and Tillie (Zimmmerman) A.; m. Judith Berkenbilt, June 4, 1961 (div. 1973); children: Miriam, Dan; m. Carol Cosman, June 17, 1973; children: Gabriel, Micha. BA, Columbia U., 1957; MA, Harvard U., 1958, PhD, 1962; LHD (hon.), Hebrew Union Coll., 1985. Instr., then asst. prof. English Columbia U., 1962-66; mem. faculty U. Calif.-Berkeley, 1967—, prof. Hebrew and comparative lit., 1969—, chmn. dept. comparative lit., 1970-73, 88-89, class of 1937 prof., 1989—; columnist Commentary mag., 1965-73, contbg. editor, 1973-86. Author: Rogue's Progress: Studies in the Picaresque Novel, 1964, Fielding and the Nature of the Novel, 1968, After the Tradition, 1969, Partial Magic: The Novel as a Self-Conscious Genre, 1975, Defenses of the Immagination, 1977, A Lion for Love, 1979, The Art of Biblical Narrative, 1981, Motives for Fiction, 1984, The Art of Biblical Poetry, 1985; co-editor: The Literary Guide to the Bible, 1987, The Invention of Hebrew Prose, 1988, The Pleasures of Reading in an Ideological Age, 1989, Necessary Angels, 1991, The World of Biblical Literature, 1992, Hebrew and Modernity, 1994, Genesis: Translation and Commentary, 1996, The David Story: A Translation with Commentary of 1 and 2 Samuel, 1999, Canon and Creativity, 2000; contbg. editor: Tri Quarterly mag., 1975—. Recipient essay prize English Inst., 1965, Nat. Jewish Book award for Jewish thought, 1982, Present Tense award for Jewish thought, 1986, Bay Area Book Reviewers Transl. award, 1997; Guggenheim fellow, 1966-67, 78-79, sr. fellow NEH, 1972-73, fellow Inst. for Advanced Studies, Jerusalem, 1982-83; scholar Nat. Found. for Jewish Culture, 1995. Fellow Am. Acad. Arts and Scis., Am. Philosoph. Soc.; mem. Am. Comparative Lit. Assn., Council of Scholars of Library of Congress, Assn. Lit. Scholars and Critics (pres. 1996-97). Jewish. Home: 1475 Le Roy Ave Berkeley CA 94708-1911 Office: U Calif Dept Comp Lit 4408 Dwinelle Hall Berkeley CA 94720-2510 E-mail: altcos@uclink4.berkeley.edu

ALTERSITZ, JANET KINAHAN, principal; b. Orange, N.J., May 19, 1951; d. Patrick Joseph and Ida (Clamillio) K., 1 child, Jacob. AA, County Coll. Morris, 1971; BA, Glassboro State Coll., 1973; MEd, Ariz. State U., 1980. Educator Washington (N.J.) Twp. Mid. Sch., 1974-77, Deer Valley Sch. Dist., Phoenix, 1977-82; asst. prin. Desert Sky Mid. Sch., Glendale, Ariz., 1983-86, prin., 1986—. Cons. and presenter in field. Mem. ASCD, NAASP (mid. level rep. 1993—), Nat. Mid. Sch. Assn., Western Regional Mid. Level. Assn. (program chmn. 1992), Ariz. Sch. Adminstrs. (sec., treas. 1989-90, pres. 1990-91), Cen. Ariz. Mid. Level. Assn. (bd. dirs. 1989—, exec. dir. 1994—), P.O.K. Democrat. Roman Catholic. Home: 4642 W Villa Rita Dr Glendale AZ 85308-1520 Office: Desert Sky Mid Sch 5130 W Grovers Ave Glendale AZ 85308-1300 E-mail: jaltersitz@ds.dvusd.org

ALTHEIMER, BRIAN P. See TUTASHINDA, KWELI

ALTMAN, ADELE ROSENHAIN, radiologist; b. Tel Aviv, June 4, 1924; came to U.S., 1933, naturalized, 1939; d. Bruno and Salla (Silberzweig) Rosenhain; m. Emmett Altman, Sept. 3, 1944; children: Brian R., Alan L., Karen D. Diplomate Am. Bd. Radiology. Intern Queens Gen. Hosp., N.Y.C., 1949-51; resident Hosp. for Joint Diseases, N.Y.C., 1951-52, Roosevelt Hosp., N.Y.C., 1955-57; clin. instr. radiology Downstate Med. Ctr., SUNY, Bklyn., 1957-61; asst. prof. radiology N.Y. Med. Coll., N.Y.C., 1961-65, assoc. prof., 1965-68; assoc. prof. radiology U. Okla. Health Sci. Ctr., Oklahoma City, 1968-78; assoc. prof. dept. radiology U. N.Mex. Sch. Medicine, Albuquerque, 1978-85. Author: Radiology of the Respiratory System: A Basic Review, 1978; contbr. articles to profl. jours. Fellow Am. Coll. Angiology, N.Y. Acad. Medicine; mem. Am. Coll. Radiologist, Am. Roentgen Ray Soc., Assn. Univ. Radiologists, Radiol. Soc. N.Am., B'nai B'rith Anti-Defamation League (bd. dirs. N.Mex. state bd.), Hadassah Club.

ALTMAN, DREW E. foundation executive; b. Boston, Mar. 21, 1951; s. George and Harriet A.; m. Pamela Koch; children: Daniel, Jessica. BA magna cum laude, Brandeis U., 1973; MA, Brown U., 1974; PhD in Polit. Sci., MIT, 1983. Postdoctoral fellow, rsch. assoc. Harvard U. Sch. Pub. Health, Boston, 1975-76, 78-80; prin. rsch. assoc. Codman Rsch. Group, Boston, 1976-80; spl. asst. office of adminstr. Health Care Fin. Adminstrn. Dept. HHS, Washington, 1979-81; v.p. Robert Wood Johnson Found., Princeton, N.J., 1981-86; commr. N.J. Dept. Human Svcs., Trenton, 1986-89; program dir. health and human svcs. The Pew Charitable Trusts, Phila., 1989-90; pres., CEO Henry J. Kaiser Family Found., Menlo Park, Calif., 1990—. Contbr. articles to profl. jours. Mem. Inst. of Medicine, Nat. Acad. of Soc. Ins., Assn. for Health Svcs. Rsch. Office: Henry J Kaiser Family Found 2400 Sand Hill Rd Menlo Park CA 94025-6941

ALTMAN, LEO SIDNEY, lawyer; b. Denver, May 6, 1911; s. Simon and Gisela (Marmorstein) A.; m. Helen Kimball, Aug. 30, 1949 (dec. Dec. 28, 1999). JD, U. Colo., 1935. Bar: Colo. 1935. Ptnr. Koperlik & Altman, Pueblo, Colo., 1935-56, Preston & Altman, Pueblo, 1956-64, Preston, Altman & Parlapiano, Pueblo, 1964-80, Preston, Altman, Parlapiano, Keilbach & Lytle, Pueblo, 1981-94, Altman, Keilbach, Lytle & Parlapiano, Pueblo, 1994-96, Altman, Keilbach, Lytle, Parlapiano & Ware, Pueblo, 1996—. Mcpl. ct. judge, Pueblo, 1942-50; U.S. commr., Pueblo, 1937-41. V.p. Pueblo Met. Mus. Bd., 1970-76; mem. Pueblo Civic Symphony bd., 1968-69; bd. dirs. Pueblo chpt. ARC, 1959-72, chmn., 1961, resolutions com. nat. ARC, 1963, mem. We. Area adv. counsel ARC, 1970-73; pres. Temple Emanuel Congregation, 1952; pres. Allied Jewish Coun. of Pueblo, 1946-47; pres. Family Svc. Soc., 1951-52; comdr. Pueblo Post 2 Am. Legion, 1946, Dist. 8. Colo., 1948; mem. Pueblo Cmty. welfare coun., 1948. Served to lt. col. U.S. Army, 1942-46, Res., 1946-66. Fellow Am. Coll. Trust and Estate Counsel; mem. ABA, Colo. Bar Assn. (bd. govs. 1953-56, v.p. 1956), Pueblo County Bar Assn. (pres. 1952, chmn. grievance com. 1956-61), Colo. State Bd. Law Examiners (law com. 1964-68), B'nai B'rith (pres. Pueblo lodge 524 1940), Pueblo Knife and Fork Club (pres. 1946-47), Pueblo Monday Evening (pres. 1966-67), Pi Lambda Phi. Republican. Jewish. Home: 1111 Bonforte Blvd Apt 810 Pueblo CO 81001-1830 Office: Altman Keilbach Lytle Parlapiano & Ware 229 Colorado Ave Pueblo CO 81004-2003

ALTMAN, STEVEN, telecommunications executive; BS, No. Ariz. U.; JD, U. San Diego. Bus. lawyer Gray, Cary, Ware & Freidrich, San Diego; corp. counsel Qualcomm, San Diego, 1989, gen. mgr. tech. transfer and strategic alliance divsn., exec. v.p., gen. counsel, 1998—. Office: 5775 Morehouse Dr San Diego CA 92121-1714

ALTON, N. KIRBY, health facility administrator; B in Zoology, U. Ga., 1974, D in Molecular Genetics, 1981. Joined Amgen, 1981—, dir. therapeutic product devel., 1986, v.p. therapeutic product devel., 1988-92, FDA contact, 1989, sr. v.p. devel., 1992—. Achievements include research in expression of eucaryotic genes in E.coli.

ALTROCK, RICHARD CHARLES, astrophysicist; b. Omaha, Dec. 20, 1940; s. Raymond John and Ada Ann (Baumann) A.; m. Janice Carol Reed, Mar. 23, 1963 (div. 1977); children: Craig Edward and Christopher Raymond (twins); m. Sally K. Neidig, Mar. 10, 1979; children: Kristin Ann, Krystal Sara. BS in Physics and Math., U. Nebr., 1962; PhD in Astro-Geophysics, U. Colo., 1968. Air Force cert. aquisition profl. Rsch. asst. U. Nebr., Lincoln, 1959-61, teaching asst., 1962; mathematician U.S. Army Engrs., Omaha, 1962; grad. asst. High Altitude Obs., Boulder, Colo., 1963-67; astrophysicist Air Force Rsch. Lab., Nat. Solar Obs., Sunspot, N.Mex., 1967—, work unit mgr., 1976—, site mgr., 1999—; project mgr. Coronal Synoptic Program, 1976—; project scientist Solar Mass Ejection Imager Space Expt., USAF, 1986-91, co-investigator, 1991—, task scientist, 1999—, Air Force Office of Sci. Rsch. Guest investigator NASA Solar Maximum Mission, 1984-86; vis. research fellow U. Sydney, Australia, 1971-72. Editor: Solar and Stellar Coronal Structure and Dynamics, 1988; contbr. articles to profl. jours.; speaker in the field. Bd. govs. N.Mex. Civil Liberties Union, 1974-76 Recipient Sustained Superior Performance awards USAF, 1986-96, Quar. Sci. and Engring. Tech. Achievement award Air Force Systems Command, 1987; Woodrow Wilson fellow, 1962-63, High Altitude Obs. fellow, 1962-63; mem. Air Force Office of Sci. Rsch. Star Team, 1992-99. Fellow AAAS; mem. Internat. Astron. Union, Am. Astron. Soc., Am. Geophys. Union, ACLU, Sigma Xi, Pi Mu Epsilon, Phi Beta Kappa, Delta Phi Alpha, Phi Gamma Delta. Achievements include co-discovery of the bimodal nature of solar rotation in Fe XIV data, which varies from strongly-differential to rigid over a solar cycle; that CaXV emission in the solar corona is not isolated in hot knots, but is ubiquitous over large energetic chromospheric active regions; of the first evidence of possible wave signature in the variation of spectral line intensity over the lifetime of a granule; first ground-based, two-dimensional photoelectric observation of a transient in the emission-line corona; proof (with other) that ground-based observations of the solar corona could be effectively used to predict recurrent geomagnetic disturbances; demonstration that emission maxima in the corona follow an unbroken progression from the poles to the equator over approximately 18 years, thus implying the existence of overlapping solar activity cycles, (with other) of the existence of convective overshoot phenomenon in the solar atmosphere, (with other) of the lack of solar pole-equator temperature differences in the photosphere and low chromosphere that could explain solar oblateness signals; invention of a new method for obtaining source functions from solar equivalent-width data for weak photospheric lines; research on solar granulation and solar corona. Home: PO Box 645 Cloudcroft NM 88317-0645 Office: Nat Solar Obs Sunspot NM 88349

ALTSCHUL, DAVID EDWIN, record company executive, lawyer; b. N.Y.C., Apr. 8, 1947; s. Norbert and Grace (Aderer) A.; m. Margaret Berne, July 4, 1969; children: Jonathan, Jared, Eric, Emily. BA summa cum laude, Amherst Coll., 1969; JD, Yale U., 1974. Bar: Calif. 1974. Law clerk U.S. Dist. Ct. Conn., Hartford, 1974-75; assoc. Tuttle & Taylor, Los Angeles, 1975-76, Pryor, Cashman, Sherman & Flynn, Beverly Hills, Calif., 1976-77, Hardee, Barovick, Konecky & Braun, Beverly Hills, 1977-79; prin. Rosenfeld, Kassoy & Kraus, Beverly Hills, 1979-80; dir. bus. affairs Warner Bros. Records, Inc., Burbank, Calif., 1980-83, v.p. bus. and legal affairs, 1983-88, sr. v.p. bus. and legal affairs, 1988-93, gen. counsel and sr. v.p. bus. affairs, 1993-95, vice chmn., gen. counsel, 1995—. Bd. dirs. Rec. Industry Assn. Am., Reprise! Broadway's Best in Concert, 1998-99, L.A. Jewish Fedn. Music Industry Divsn.; mem. Millenium Coun., Save Ams. Treasures, 1998—. Bd. dirs. Los Encinos Sch., Encinos, Calif., 1986-93, treas., 1986-87, pres., 1987-92; bd. dirs. People for the Am. Way, 1991—, vice chmn., 1996-97, chmn., 1998—; bd. dirs. People for the Am. Way Found., 1991—, bd. dirs. exec. com., 1993—; bd. dirs. San Fernando Valley Neighborhood Legal Svcs., Inc., 1989-90, Rock the Vote, 1997-98. Mem. Phi Beta Kappa. Democrat. Jewish. Avocations: photography, reading. Office: Warner Bros Records Inc 3300 Warner Blvd Burbank CA 91505-4694

ALVARADO, LINDA G. construction company executive; Doctorate (hon.), Dowling Coll. Pres. Alvarado Constrn., Inc., Denver, 1976—. Owner Colorado Rockies franchise; corp. dir. 3M, Pepsi Bottling Group. Chmn. bd. dirs. Denver Hispanic C. of C.; dir. Nat. Hispanic Scholarship Fund; commrs. White House Initiative for Hispanic Excellence in Edn. Named Revlon Bus. Woman of Yr., 1996, Bus. Woman of Yr., U.S. Hispanic C. of C., 1996, 100 Most Influential Hispanics in Am., Hispanic Bus. Mag., others; recipient Nat. Minority Supplier Devel. Coun. Leadership award, 1996, Sara Lee Corp. Frontrunner award, Horatio Alger award, others. Office: Alvarado Construction 1266 Santa Fe Dr Denver CO 80204-3546

ÁLVAREZ, RODOLFO, sociology educator, consultant; b. San Antonio, Oct. 23, 1936; s. Ramon and Laura (Lobo) A.; m. Edna Rosemary Simons, June 25, 1960 (div. 1984); children: Ánica, Amira. BA, San Francisco State U., 1961; cert. European Studies, Inst. Am. Univs., Aix-en-Provence, France, 1960; MA, U. Wash., 1964, PhD, 1966. Teaching fellow U. Wash., Seattle, 1963-64; asst. prof. Yale U., New Haven, 1966-72; assoc. prof. sociology UCLA, 1972-80, prof., 1980—, dir. Chicano Studies Rsch. Ctr., 1972-74, chair undergrad. coun., 1995-97. Vis. lectr. Wesleyan U., Middletown, Conn., 1970; founding dir. Spanish Speaking Mental Health Research Ctr., 1973-75. Author: Discrimination in Organizations: Using Social Indicators to Manage Social Change, 1979; Racism, Elitism, Professionalism: Barriers to Community Mental Health, 1976; mem. editorial bd. Social Sci. Quar., 1971-86. Pres. ACLU So. Calif., 1980, 81, sec., treas. 1999, Westwood Dem. Club, Calif., 1977-78; trustee Inst. for Am. Univs., Aix-en-Provence, France, 1968—; bd. dirs. Mex. Am. Legal Def. and Ednl. Fund, 1975-79, 88-92; mem. adv. commn. on housing 1984 Olympic Organizing Com., 1982-84; chmn. bd. dirs. Narcotics Prevention Assn., L.A., 1974-77; mem. bilingual adv. com. Children's TV Workshop, N.Y.C., 1970-82; candidate rep. Nat. Dem. Platform Com., Washington, 1976; alt. del. Nat. Dem. Conv., N.Y.C., 1976; bd. dirs. Univ. Credit Union, 1985-92, chmn. strategic plan com., 1987-92. Sgt. USMC, 1954-57. Pres. Mgmt. fellow U. Calif., 1994-95; recipient citation meritorious service for devel. Nat. Fed. Offenders Rehab. and Rsch. Program, State of Wash., 1967. Mem. Internat. Sociol. Honor Soc. (pres. 1976-79), Am. Sociol. Assn. (mem. coun. 1982-85, chairperson sect. racial and ethnic minorities 1989-90, assoc. editor Am. Sociol. Rev. 1989-91, chairperson sect. on sociol. practice 1990-91), Soc. Study of Social Problems (bd. dirs. 1982-87, pres. 1985-86), Pacific Sociol. Assn. (mem. coun. 1979-83, 87-89, v.p. 1991-93, pres. 1996-97), Marines Meml. Club, Rotary. Office: UCLA Dept Sociology 405 Hilgard Ave Los Angeles CA 90095-9000 E-mail: alvarez@soc.ucla.edu

ALVARIÑO DE LEIRA, ANGELES (ANGELES ALVARIÑO), biologist, oceanographer; b. El Ferrol, Spain, Oct. 3, 1916; came to U.S., 1958, naturalized, 1966; d. Antonio Alvariño-Grimaldos and Carmen Gonzalez Diaz-Saavedra; m. Eugenio Leira-Manso, Mar. 16, 1940; 1 child, Angeles. BS in Letters summa cum laude, U. Santiago de Compostela (Spain), 1933; M in Natural Scis., U. Madrid, 1941, Doctorate cert., 1951, DSc summa cum laude, 1967. Cert. biologist-oceanographer, Spanish Inst. Oceanography. Prof. biology Coll. El Ferrol, Spain, 1941-48; fishery rsch. biologist dept. Sea Fisheries Spain, 1948-52; histologist Superior Coun. Sci. Rsch., 1948-52; biologist, oceanographer Spanish Inst. Oceanography, 1950-57; biologist Scripps Inst. Oceanography-U. Calif., LaJolla, 1958-69; fishery rsch. biologist Nat. Marine Fisheries Svc. S.W. Fisheries Sci. Ctr., NOAA, U.S. Dept. Commerce, La Jolla, 1970-87; emeritus scientist Nat. Marine Fisheries Svc. S.W. Fisheries Ctr., NOAA, U.S. Dept. Commerce, La Jolla, 1987—; assoc. prof. U. Nat. Autonomous Mexico, 1976, San Diego State U., 1979-82, U. San Diego, 1982—, rsch. assoc., 1982—. Vis. prof. Poly. Tech. Mexico, 1982—, U. Parana, Brazil, 1982. Author: Spain and the First Scientific Oceanic Expedition (1789-1794) Malaspina and Bustamante with the Corvettes "Descubierta" and "Atrevida", 2000; contbr. over 100 articles to profl. books and jours., chpts. in books; discovered 22 new species and the indicator species for various oceanic currents, ocean dynamics, and the study of the biotic environment of fish spawning grounds, study of plankton predators and the impact in fisheries bunch of 200 plankton populations carried by ships into exotic oceanic areas and throughout interoceanic canals. Brit. Coun. fellow, 1953-54, Fulbright fellow, 1956-57; NSF grantee, 1961-69, U.S. Office Navy grantee, 1958-69, Calif. Coop. Oceanic Fishery Investigations grantee, 1958-69, UNESCO grantee, 1979; recipient Great Silver Medal of Galicia, Spain, presented by King Juan Carlos and Queen Sofia of Spain, 1993. Fellow Am. Inst. Fishery Rsch. Biologists, San Diego Soc. Natural History; mem. Assn. Natural History Soc., Biol. Soc. Washington, Hispano-Am. Assn. Researchers on Marine Scis. Achievements include discovery of biotic differences in the habitat of various fishes; work on the fauna represented in color plates from specimens collected during oceanic sci. expedition of 1789-94. Home: 7535 Cabrillo Ave La Jolla CA 92037-5206 Office: Nat Marine Fisheries Svc SW Fisheries Sci Ctr PO Box 271 La Jolla CA 92038-0271

AMBROSE, DANIEL MICHAEL, publishing executive; b. Salem, Oreg., Nov. 1, 1955; s. Franklin Burnell and Jean Marie (Crakes) A.; m. Cynthia Barbara Friedman, Mar. 26, 1983; children: Robert Grant, Michael Bruce. BS in Polit. Sci., Lewis and Clark Coll., 1977. Mktg. mgr. Washington Monthly, 1978-79; advt. promotion mgr. Am. Film Mag., Washington, 1979-80, advt. mgr., 1980-81, advt. dir., 1981-83, Backpacker Mag., N.Y.C., 1983-84; advt. salesman House Beautiful, Hearst Mag., N.Y.C., 1984-85; corp. advt. dir. mag. div. Hearst Pub. Corp., N.Y.C., 1985-87; pub. Fathers Mag., N.Y.C., 1987-89; advt. dir. Cahners Pub. Co., N.Y.C., 1989-92; pub. Child Mag. Network Women's Mag. div. N.Y. Times Co., N.Y.C., 1992-94; mng. dir. ambro.com., N.Y.C., 1994—, DeSilva & Phillips Media Investment Bankers, N.Y.C., 1998—. Interactive media cons., investments and sales, N.Y.C., 1994—. Contbr. articles on mag. mgmt. to Folio mag. Avocation: collecting books on publishing, skiing, tennis.

AMEMIYA, TAKESHI, economist, statistician; b. Tokyo, Mar. 29, 1935; s. Kenji and Shizuko A.; m. Yoshiko Miyaki, May 5, 1969; children: Naoko, Kentaro. B.A., Internat. Christian U., 1958; M.A. in Econs., Am. U., 1961; Ph.D., Johns Hopkins U., 1964. Mem. faculty Stanford U., (Calif.), 1964-66, 68—, prof. econs., 1974-86, Edward Ames Edmonds prof. econs., 1986—. Lectr. Inst. Econ. Research, Hitotsubashi U., Tokyo, 1966-68; cons. Author books and articles; mem. editl. bd. profl. jours. Recipient U.S. Sr. Scientist award Alexander von Humboldt Found., Fed. Republic Germany, 1988; Ford Found. fellow, 1963; Guggenheim fellow, 1975; NSF grantee; fellow Japan Soc. for Promotion of Sci., 1989. Fellow Econometric Soc., Am. Acad. Arts and Scis., Am. Statis. Assn.; mem. Internat. Statis. Inst., Am. Econ. Assn., Inst. Math. Stats., Phi Beta Kappa. Home: 923 Casanueva Pl Stanford CA 94305-1001 Office: Stanford Univ Dept Econs Stanford CA 94305 E-mail: amemiya@stanford.edu

AMEND, WILLIAM JOHN CONRAD, JR. physician, educator; b. Wilmington, Del., Sept. 17, 1941; s. William John Conrad and Catherine (Broad) A.; m. Constance Roberts, Feb. 3, 1962; children— William, Richard, Nicole, Mark B.A., Amherst Coll., 1963; M.D., Cornell U., 1967. Diplomate Am. Bd. Internal Medicine. Asst. clin. prof. U. Calif. Med. Ctr., San Francisco, 1974-76, assoc. clin. prof., 1977-82, prof. clin. medicine and surgery, 1982—; acting chief divsn. nephrology U. Calif., San Francisco, 1999—; physician Falmouth Med. Assocs. Contbr. articles to med. jours. Chmn. med. adv. com. No. Calif. Kidney Found., 1987-88; mem. stewardship com. 1st Presbyn. Ch., Burlingame, Calif., 1983, 84, elder, 1982-85, 93-96. Maj. U.S. Army, 1969-71. Simpson fellow, 1963; recipient Gift of Life award No. Calif. Kidney Found., 1994. Fellow ACP; mem. Amherst Coll. Alumni Fund (class agt. 1973-83). Republican. Avocations: golf; gardening; hiking. Home: 2860 Summit Dr Burlingame CA 94010-6257 Office: U Calif Med Ctr 3rd & Parnassus San Francisco CA 94143-0001

AMES, BRUCE N(ATHAN), biochemist, molecular biologist; b. N.Y.C., Dec. 16, 1928; s. Maurice U. and Dorothy (Andres) A.; m. Giovanna Ferro-Luzzi, Aug. 26, 1960; children: Sofia, Matteo. BA, Cornell U., 1950; PhD, Calif. Inst. Tech., 1953. Chief sect. NIH, Bethesda, Md., 1962-67; prof. biochemistry and molecular biology U. Calif., Berkeley, 1968—, chmn. biochemistry dept., 1983-89. Mem. Nat. Cancer Adv. Bd., 1976-82. Research, publs. on bacterial molecular biology, histidine biosynthesis and its control, aging, mutagenesis, detection of environ. mutagens and carcinogens, genetic toxicology, oxygen radicals and disease. Recipient Flemming award, 1966, Rosensteil award, 1976, Felix Wankel award, 1978, John Scott medal, 1979, Corson medal, 1980, Mott prize GM Cancer Rsch. Found., 1983, Gairdner award, 1983, Tyler prize for environ. achievement, 1985, gold medal Am. Inst. Chemists, 1991, Glenn Found. Gerontology award, 1992, Roentgen prize Nat. Acad. Lincei, 1993, Lovelace award for excellence in environ. health rsch., 1995, Honda prize/Achievement in Excellence award Ctr. for Excellence in Edn., Messel medal, 1996, Japan prize, 1997, Kehoe award, 1997, Joseph Priestley award Dickinson Coll., 1998, The Nat. Medal of Sci., 1998, Medal City of Paris, 1998, The Linus Pauling Inst. prize for health rsch., 2001. Fellow Acad. Toxicol. Scis., Am. Acad. Microbiology, Gerontol. Soc. Am.; mem. NAS, Am. Soc. Biol. Chemists, Am. Soc. Microbiology (N.B. lectr. 1980, lifetime achievement award 2001), Environ. Mutagen Soc. (award 1977), Genetics Soc., Am. Assn. Cancer Rsch., Soc. Toxicology (Gustavus John Esselen award 1992), Am. Chem. Soc. (Eli Lilly award 1964), Royal Swedish Acad. Scis., Am. Acad. Arts and Scis. Home: 1324 Spruce St Berkeley CA 94709-1105 Office: CHORI 5700 ML King Jr Way Oakland CA 94609 E-mail: [illegible]

AMES, EDMUND DANTES, singer, actor, producer; b. Boston, July 9, 1927; s. David and Sarah (Saslavsky) Urick; m.; children— Sonja, Ronald, Linda B.A. in Theater and Cinema, UCLA, 1975. Owner, mgr. Monte Cristo Prodns., Beverly Hills, Calif.; lead baritone Ames Bros.; performances major cities U.S., 1950-60; rec. artist RCA Records, 1963—. Broadway appearances include Carnival; starring role in TV series Daniel Boone, 1963-68; starring roles in regional theatre include Fiddler on the Roof. Bd. dirs. Bowers Mus., Santa Ana, Calif. Recipient 6 Gold Records Office: ICM 8942 Wilshire Blvd Beverly Hills CA 90211-1934

AMIOKA, WALLACE SHUZO, retired petroleum company executive; b. Honolulu, June 28, 1914; s. Tsurumatsu and Reye (Yoshimura) A.; BA, U. Hawaii, 1966, MBA, 1968; m. Ellen Misao Honda, Aug. 9, 1942; children: Carol L. Amioka Price, Joanne M. Amioka Chikuma. With Shell Oil Co., 1931-77, fin. svcs. mgr., Honolulu, 1962-77; pub. affairs cons., Honolulu, 1977-87; gen. ptnr. Pub. Affairs Cons. Hawaii, 1988-94; ret., 1994; lectr. econs. U. Hawaii, 1969-79. Mem. Honolulu Police Commn., 1965-73, vice chmn., 1966, 69, chmn., 1971. Mem. City and County of Honolulu Charter Commn., 1981-82; bd. dirs. Honolulu Symphony Soc., 1968. With M.I., AUS, 1944-48, U.S. civil adm. Ryuku Islands, 1950-52. Mem. M.I. Svc. Vets. (pres. 1981-82), Hawaii C. of C. (chmn. edn. com. 1963-64, chmn. pub. health com. 1966-67), Hui 31 Club, Hui Aikane Club, Honolulu Police Old Timers Club, Phi Beta Kappa, Phi Kappa Phi. Home: 46-310 Kamehameha Hwy Kaneohe HI 96744-4041

AMMIANO, TOM, county and municipal official; life ptnr.; 1 child. BA in Communication Arts, Seton Hall U., 1963; MA in Spl. Edn., San Francisco State U., 1965. Stand-up comic, 1981—; tchr. disabled students program City Coll. San Francisco, 1991—, instr. AIDS peer edn., 1992—; San Francisco city supr. San Francisco Bd. Supt., 1994-98, pres. bd. suprs., 1998—. Community resource tchr. AIDS spl. edn. project San Francisco Unified Sch. Dist.; classroom tchr. educable mentally retarded; tchr. of English in Vietnam; with Camp Easter Seal and Rec. Ctr. for the Handicapped, San Francisco. Active Mission Coalition, Ethnic Minority Coalition, Bay Area Gay Liberation; organizer demonstrations resp. for including sexual orientation in tchr. hiring; founder Gay Tchrs. Coalition, Gay Lesbian Speakers Bur. in Schs.; mem. community group Project Ten; mem. San Francisco Bd. Edn., 1990—, pres. 1993, v.p. 1991; elected to San. Francisco Bd. Supt., 1994—. Office: San Francisco Bd Suprs City Hall 1 Dr Carlton B Goodlett Pl San Francisco CA 94102-4603

AMMON, JOHN RICHARD, anesthesiologist; b. N.Y.C., 1948; MD, U. Pa., 1974. Cert. in anesthesiology. Intern Crozer Chester Med. Ctr., 1974-75; resident in anesthesiology Mass. Gen. Hosp., Boston, 1975-77; fellow in cardiac anesthesiology Stanford (Calif.) Med. Ctr., 1977-78; dir., v.p. Am. Bd. Anesthesiology, Phoenix, 1988-99; pvt. practice Valley Anesthesiology Ltd., Phoenix, 1999—. Mem. Am. Soc. Anesthesiology, Alpha Omega Alpha. Office: Valley Anesthesiology Ltd 2200 N Central Ave Phoenix AZ 85004-1418 also: Am Bd Anesthesiology 4101 Lake Boone Trl Ste 510 Raleigh NC 27607-7506

AMOAKO, JAMES KWAKU, transportation services executive, financial analyst; b. Nkwatia, Ghana, Dec. 4, 1951; came to U.S., 1970; s. Kwame and Amma (Nyame) A.; m. Rose Tiokor; children: James Jr., Nicole, Jennifer. AS, Cosumnes River Coll., 1977; BS, Calif. State U., Sacramento, 1978; MBA, Golden Gate U., 1979; PhD, LaSalle U., 1997. Bank examiner Calif. State Banking Dept., San Francisco, 1979-80; fin. analyst Artec Internat. Corp., Mountain View, Calif., 1980-83; cost acct. Sun Microsystems, Mountain View, 1983-88; pres., CEO Alpha Transp. Corp., Phoenix, 1988—. Recipient Svc. award Am. Field Svc., 1970. Home: 8826 W Encanto Blvd Phoenix AZ 85037-3619 Office: Alpha Transp Corp 4024 S 16th St Phoenix AZ 85040-1315

AMODEI, MARK E. state legislator, lawyer; b. Carson City, Nev., June 12, 1958; m. Michelle Amodei; children: Ryanne, Erin, Brian, Melissa. BA, U. Nev., 1980; JD, U. Pacific, 1983. Atty. gen. bus., corp. and real estate practices, 1987—; mem. Nev. Senate, Capitol Dist., 1996—; mem. commerce and labor com., mem. transp. com. Nev. Senate, mem. human resources and facilities com. Mem. Carson City Master Plan Adv. Com. Capt. JAGC, U.S. Army, 1983-87. Decorated Army Commendaiton medal. Mem. ABA. Republican. Presbyterian. Address: 905 W Sunset Way Carson City NV 89703-3789

AMON, WILLIAM FREDERICK, JR. biotechnology company executive; b. Chelsea, Mass., Jan. 11, 1922; s. William Frederick and Esther H. (Rautenberg) A.; m. Barbara Marie Erlandson, Aug. 2, 1944; children— William Frederick III, Janet B., Carol J., Robert J. B.S. Ch.E., Northeastern U., 1943. Vice pres. new bus. ventures Borden Chem., N.Y.C., 1968-72; pres., chief exec. officer Electrospin Inc., Columbus, Ohio, 1972-76; v.p. Story Chem. Co., Muskegon, Mich., 1975-76, Cetus Corp., Emeryville, Calif., 1976-87; ret., cons. Danville, 1987—. Mem. Comml. Devel. Assn., Am. Chem. Soc., Soc. Indsl. Microbiology. Lutheran. Achievements include being a holder of numerous patents. Home and Office: 831 Matadera Cir Danville CA 94526-1836 E-mail: sbwg51a@msn.com

AMOROSO, FRANK, retired communication system engineer, consultant; b. Providence, July 31, 1935; s. Michele and Angela Maria Barbara (D'Uva) A. BSEE, MSEE, MIT, 1958; postgrad., Purdue U., 1958-60, U. Turin, Italy, 1964-65. Registered profl. engr., Calif. Instr. elec. engring. Purdue U., West Lafayette, Ind., 1958-60; rsch. engr. Melpar Inc., Roxbury, Mass., 1959, MIT Instrumentation Lab., Cambridge, 1960, Litton Sys. Advanced Devel. Lab., Waltham, 1960-61; engr. Melpar Applied Sci. Divsn., Watertown, 1961; mem. tech. staff RCA Labs. David Sarnoff Rsch. Ctr., Princeton, N.J., 1962-64, Mitre Corp., Bedford, Mass., 1966-67; sr. applied mathematician Collins Radio Co., Newport Beach, 1967-68; comm. sys. engr. N.Am. Rockwell Corp., El Segundo, Calif., 1968-71, Northrop Electronics Divsn., Palos Verdes Peninsula, 1971-72; comm. sys. engr., sr. staff engr. Hughes Aircraft Co., Fullerton, 1972-89; ret., 1989; cons., developer, presenter ednl. seminars, 1989—. Cons. Lincom, Inc., L.A., 1994-96; cons. client Sklar Comm. Engring., 1996-97, Mascarell Microones, S.L., Tarragona, Spain; instr. continuing engring. edn. program George Washington U., San Diego, 1993; instr. ext. short courses UCLA, 1987-89, 98—. 1st lt. U.S. Signal Corps, 1961-62. Recipient Outstanding Achievement award RCA Labs., 1964; grad. study scholar Italian Govt., 1964-66. Mem. IEEE (sr. mem., session organizer, chmn. conf. on mil. com., presenter). Achievements include patents in field. Avocations: creating various document formats for emerging micronations, free lance writing. Home and Office: Digital Data Modulation Studies 271 W Alton Ave Apt D Santa Ana CA 92707-4171

AMOS, WALLY, entrepreneur; b. Tallahassee, July 1, 1936; s. Wallace Sr. and Ruby Amos; m. Maria LaForey (div.); children: Michael, Gregory; m. Shirlee Ellis (div.), 1 child, Shawn; m. Christine Amos, 1979; 1 child, Sarah. Stockroom clk. Saks Fifth Ave., N.Y.C., 1957-58, stockroom supr., 1958-61; mail room clk. William Morris Agy., N.Y.C., 1961, sec., 1961-62, asst. agt., 1962; talent agt., 1962-67; ind personal mgr. L.A., 1967-75; founder Famous Amos Chocolate Chip Cookie Corp., Hollywood, Calif., 1975-89, Wally Amos Presents: Chip and Cookie, 1991-92, UNCLE Nonamé Cookie Co., 1992—; chmn. Uncle Wally Cookie Co. Author: The Famous Amos Story: The Face That Launched a Thousand Chips, 1983,

The Power In You: Ten Secret Ingredients for Inner Strength, 1988, Mau with No Name: Turn Lemons Into Lemonade, 1994. Nat. spokesman Literacy Vols. of Am., 1979. With USAF, 1953-57. Recipient Pres.' award for Entrepreneurial Excellence, 1986, Horatio Alger award 1987, Nat. Literacy Honors award 1990. Home and Office: Uncle Wally Cookie Co PO Box 897 Kailua HI 96734-0897

AMYLON, MICHAEL DAVID, physician, educator; b. Providence, Apr. 30, 1950; s. Sidney Robert and Mary Elisabeth (Alexander) A. AB, Brown U., 1972; MD, Stanford U., 1976. Diplomate sub-bd. hematology/oncology Am. Bd. Pediatrics. Resident physician Stanford (Calif.) U. Hosp., 1976-79; post-doctoral scholar Stanford U., 1979-81, acting asst. prof., 1981-82, asst. prof. pediat., 1982-89, assoc. prof. pediat., 1989-2001; clin. assoc. prof. pediat. U. Calif., San Francisco, 1998-2000, prof. pediatrics, 2001—. Dir. marrow transplant svc. Children's Hosp. at Stanford, Palo Alto, Calif., 1986—; coord. nat. rsch. clin. trials in treatment pediatric leukemia and lymphoma Pediatric Oncology Group, St. Louis, Chgo., 1986—. Contbr. articles to profl. jours. Bd. dirs. Touchstone Support Network, Palo Alto, 1982-98, Robert J. Sturhahn Found., Novato, Calif., 1986-93, Okizu Found., Novato, 1993—, Parents Helping Parents, 1998—; med. dir. No. Calif. Oncology Camp, Nevada City, 1986—. Recipient For Those Who Care award Sta. KRON, 1990, "Ronnie" award Ronald McDonald House, 1992-93, Koshland prize Peninsula Cmty. Found., 1995, J.C. Penney Golden Rule award, 1996. Mem. Am. Acad. Pediatrics, Am. Soc. Clin. Oncology, Am. Soc. Hematology, Am. Soc. Pediatric Hematology/Oncology, Am. Soc. Blood and Marrow Transplantation. Office: Packard Children's Hosp 725 Welch Rd Palo Alto CA 94304-1601 E-mail: amylon@stanford.edu

ANAND, SURESH CHANDRA, physician; b. Mathura, India, Sept. 13, 1931; came to U.S., 1957, naturalized, 1971; s. Satchit and Sumaran (Bai) A. m. Wiltrud, Jan. 29, 1966; children: Miriam, Michael MB, BS, King George's Coll., U. Lucknow (India), 1954; MS in Medicine, U. Colo., 1962. Diplomate Am. Bd. Allergy and Immunology. Fellow pulmonary diseases Nat. Jewish Hosp., Denver, 1957-58, resident in chest medicine, 1958-59, chief resident allergy-asthma, 1960-62; intern Mt. Sinai Hosp., Toronto, Ont., Can., 1962-63, resident in medicine Can., 1963-64, chief resident Can., 1964-65, demonstrator clin. technique Can., 1963-64, U. Toronto fellow in medicine Can., 1964-65; rsch. assoc. asthma-allergy Nat. Jewish Hosp., Denver, 1967-69; clin. instr. medicine U. Colo., 1967-69; internist Ft. Logan Mental Health Ctr., 1968-69; pres. Allergy Assocs. & Lab., Ltd., Phoenix, 1974—. Mem. staff Phoenix Bapt. Hosp., chmn. med. records com., 1987; mem. staff St. Joseph's Hosp., St. Luke's Hosp., Human Hosp., John C. Lincoln Hosp., Good Samaritan Hosp., Phoenix Children's Hosp., Tempe St. Luke Hosp., Desert Samaritan Hosp., Mesa Luth. Hosp., Scottsdale Meml. Hosp., Chandler (Ariz.) Regional Hosp., Valley Luth. Hosp., Mesa, Ariz.; mem. staff Phoenix Meml. Hosp., mem. med. com.; pres. NJH Fed. Credit Union, 1967-68. Contbr. articles to profl. jours. Mem. Camelback Hosp. Mental Health Ctr. Citizens Adv. Bd., Scottsdale, Ariz., 1974-80; mem. Phoenix Symphony Coun., 1973-90; mem. Ariz. Opera Co., Boyce Thmpson Southwestern Arboretum; mem. Ariz. Hist. Soc., Phoenix Arts. Mus., Smithsonian Inst. Fellow ACP, Am. Coll. Chest Physicians (crit. care com.), Am. Acad. Allergy (pub. edn. com.), Am. Assn. Cert. Allergists, Am. Coll. Allergy and Immunology (aerobiology com., internat. com., pub. edn. com. 1991-94); mem. AAAS, AMA, Internat. Assn. Allergy and Clin. Immunology, Ariz. Med. Assn., Ariz. Allergy Soc. (v.p. 1988-90, pres. 1990-91), Maricopa County Med. Soc. (del. ariz. Med. Assn., bd. dirs. 1996-98, exec. com. 1996-98), West Coast Soc. Allergy and Immunology, Greater Phoenix Allergy Soc. (v.p. 1984-86, pres. 1986-88, med. adv. team sports medicine Ariz. State U.), Phoenix Zoo, N.Y. Acad. Scis., World Med. Assn., Internat. Assn. Asthmology, Assn. Care of Asthma, Ariz. Thoracic Soc., Nat. Geog. Soc., Ariz. Wild Life Assn., Village Tennis Club. Office: 1006 E Guadalupe Rd Tempe AZ 85283-3047 also: 6553 E Baywood Ave Ste 201 Mesa AZ 85206-1754 also: 7331 E Osborn Dr Ste 340 Scottsdale AZ 85251-6435 also: 2248 N Alma School Rd Chandler AZ 85224-2488

ANANG, KOFI, artistic director, educator, dancer; b. Pakro, Ghana; Degree, U. Ghana, 1971. Lead dancer Profl. OBOADE African Music and Dance Co., 1972-77; instr. African dance and music U. Washington, 1973-74; instr. African games and music Everybody's Creative Arts Ctr., Oakland, Calif., 1978; instr. W. African dance and drumming Madrona Dance Studio, 1978; instr. W. African games and drumming Langston Hughes Cultural Arts Ctr., Seattle, 1978-80; artistic dir., master drummer, dancer Ocheami-Afrikan Dance Co., Seattle, 1978—. Rschr. devels. in music and dance, Ghana and Nigeria; founder Internat. Directory Black and African Choreographers; African music instr. Prescott (Ariz.) Coll., 1993, 94; dance accompanist Cornish Coll. Arts, Seattle, 1993—. Creative designer, musician (play) Sigi- Three W. African Stories, 1994; numerous appearances worldwide. Inst. African Studies scholar. Office: Ocheami Afrikan Dance Co PO Box 31635 Seattle WA 98103-1635

ANATOL, KARL W. E. provost; BA in Speech and English, Andrews U.; MA in Interpersonal Communication, Purdue U.; PhD in Speech Communications, U. So. Calif. Dean of students Caribbean Union Coll., Trinidad, 1956-60; teaching asst. Purdue U., Lafayette, Ind., 1966-69; asst. prof. Calif. State U., Long Beach, 1969-73, assoc. prof., 1975-80, assoc. dean instrnl. support, 1978-82, acting dean sch. humanities, 1982-83, dean sch. humanities, 1983-89, acting dean sch. bus., 1988—, acting provost, 1989-90, provost, 1990—, sr. v.p. acad. affairs, 1989—. Chmn. speech communications Calif. State U., Long Beach, 1977-78, acting exec. dir. libr. & learning resources, 1983-84, mem. univ. extension svcs. adv. bd.; program producer Radio Sta. WBAA Purdue U., 1969; staff assoc. Gen. Motors Inst., Mich., 1973; mem. City of Long Beach Spl. Task Force on Ednl. Redevel.; mem. adv. bd. Global Edn. Program in So. Calif.; mem. bd. advisors Am. Inst. Fgn. Study; mem. ednl. cons. team Weyerhauser Corp. Author: Fundamental Concepts in Human communication, The Process of Group Communication, Strategies for Persuasive Communication, Organizational Communication: Behavioral Perspectives, Public Communication, The Process of Group Communication, Organizational Communication: Behavioral Perspectives, Effective Oral Communication for Business and Professions, Oral Communication in Business and the Professions; contbr. articles to profl. jours. Chmn. allocations com. United Way; nat. exec. dir. Phi Beta Delta. Office: Calif State Univ 1250 Bellflower Blvd Long Beach CA 90840-0001

ANAWALT, PATRICIA RIEFF, anthropologist, researcher; b. Ripon, Calif., Mar. 10, 1924; d. Edmund Lee and Anita Esto (Capps) Rieff; m. Richard Lee Anawalt, June 8, 1945; children: David, Katherine Anawalt Arnoldi, Harmon Fred. BA in Anthropology, UCLA, 1957, MA in Anthropology, 1971, PhD in Anthropology, 1975. Cons. curator costumes and textiles Mus. Cultural History UCLA, 1975-90, dir. Ctr. for Study Regional Dress, Fowler Mus. Cultural History, 1990—; trustee S.W. Mus., L.A., 1978-92; rsch. assoc. The San Diego Mus. Man, 1980—, UCLA Inst. Archaeology, 1994—. Trustee Archaeol. Inst. Am., U.S., Can., 1983-95, 98—; traveling lectr., 1975-86, 1994-2000, Pres.'s Lectureship, 1993-94, Charles E. Norton lectureship, 1996-97; cons. Nat. Geog. Soc., 1980-82, Denver Mus. Natural History, 1992-93; apptd. by U.S. Pres. to Cultural Property Adv. Com., Washington, 1984-93; fieldwork Guatemala, 1961, 70, 72, Spain, 1975, Sierra Norte de Puebla, Mex., 1983, 85, 88, 89, 91. Author: Indian Clothing Before Cortés: Mesoamerican Costumes from the Codices, 1981, paperback edit., 1990; co-author: The Codex Mendoza, 4 vols., 1992 (winner Archaeol. Inst. Am. 1994 James Wiseman Book award), The Essential Codex Mendoza, 1996; mem. editl. bd. Ancient Mesoamerica; contbr. articles to profl. jours. Adv. com Textile Mus., Washington, 1983-87. Grantee NEH, 1990, 96, J. Paul Getty Found. 1990, Nat. Geog. Soc., 1983, 85, 88, 89, 91, Ahmanson Found., 1996; Guggenheim fellow, 1988. Fellow Am. Anthrop. Assn.; mem. Centre Internat. D'Etude Des Textiles Anciens, Am. Ethnol. Soc., Soc. Am. Archaeology, Soc. Women Geographers (Outstanding Achievement award 1993), Textile Soc. Am. (bd. dirs. 1992-96, co-coord. 1994 biennial symposium). Avocations: ballet, reading, hiking. Office: Fowler Mus Cultural History Ctr Study Of Regional Dress Los Angeles CA 90095-0001 E-mail: panawalt@arts.ucla.edu

ANAYA, RICHARD ALFRED, JR. accountant, investment banker; b. N.Y.C., Dec. 19, 1932; s. Ricardo Martinez and Clara (Chamarro) A.; m. Ninette Calandra, Sept. 8, 1957; children: Suzanne, Richard J. BBA, CCNY, 1958. CPA, N.Y. Tax acct. C.I.T. Fin. Corp., N.Y.C., 1964-67; asst. treas. Mut. Broadcasting System, Inc., N.Y.C., 1967-72; treas. Host Internat., Inc., Santa Monica, Calif., 1972-85; dir. fin. Windsor Fin. Corp, Encino, 1985; ind. cons. mergers and acquisitions A&I Investments, Inc, Century City, 1986-87, Anaya Assocs., Century City, 1987-90, CPA cons. mergers and acquisitions Woodlands Hills, 1990—. Founder retail store chain, Clear Connect Comms., LLC, 1995. Served with U.S. Navy, 1952-54. Mem. AICPA, Calif. State Soc. CPAs, N.Y. State Soc. CPAs. Roman Catholic. Office: Anaya Assocs 21550 Oxnard St Ste 960 Woodland Hills CA 91367-7145 E-mail: anayaassociates@pacbell.net

ANAYA, RUDOLFO, educator, writer; b. Pastura, N.Mex., Oct. 30, 1937; s. Martin and Rafaelita (Mares) A.; m. Patricia Lawless, July 23, 1966. BA, U. N.Mex., Albuquerque, 1963, MA, 1968; PhD (hon.), U. Albuquerque, 1982; PhD, Mary Crest Coll., 1984; LLD (hon.), U. N.Mex., 1996. Prof. U. N.Mex., Albuquerque, 1974—. Author: (novels) Bless Me Ultima, 1972 (Primo Quinto sol) Heart of Aztlan, 1976, Tortuga, 1979 (Before Columbus Found. award), Albuquerque, 1992, Zia Summer, 1995, The Farolitos of Christmas, 1995, Jalamanta, 1996, Rio Grande Fall, 1996, (children's picture book) Maya's Children, 1997, Shaman Winter, 1999, Roadrunner's Dance, 2000, Elegy for Cesar Chavex, 2000, Farolitos for Abuelo, 2000. NEA fellow. Home: 5324 Canada Vista Pl NW Albuquerque NM 87120-2412 Office: U NMex English Dept Albuquerque NM 87131-0001

ANDARY, THOMAS JOSEPH, biochemist; b. Sault Sainte Marie, Mich., Oct. 8, 1942; s. Joseph Boula and Marion (Schwifetti) A. BS, No. Mich. U., 1966, MA, 1968; PhD, Wayne State U., 1974. Instr. biology No. Mich. U., Marquette, 1967-69; rsch. assoc. physiology Wayne State U., Detroit, 1973-76; sr. rsch. scientist, mgr. coagulation research Hyland Labs., Costa Mesa, Calif., 1976-83; dir. quality control Hyland Therapeutics, Glendale, Calif., 1983-90; dir. quality assurance and regulatory affairs Baxter/Hyland Div., Glendale, 1990-91; v.p. quality assurance and regulatory affairs, 1991—, responsible head, 1993-96; cons. in regulatory affairs/quality assurance to biopharmaceutical industry, 1996—; lectr. in field. Mem. Parenteral Drug Assn. NDEA fellow, 1969-72. Mem. Am. Chem. Soc., N.Y. Acad. Sci., Internat. Assn. Biol. Standardization, Drug Info. Assn., Sigma Xi (Rsch. award 1973). Roman Catholic. Contbr. over 25 articles to profl. publs. Home and Office: 531 N Canyon Blvd Monrovia CA 91016-1707

ANDEREGG, KAREN KLOK, business executive; b. Council Bluffs, Iowa; d. George J. and Hazel E. Klok; m. George F. Anderegg, Jr., Aug. 27, 1970 (div. Dec. 1993); m. William Drake Rutherford, Jan. 2, 1994. BA, Stanford U., 1963. Copywriter Vogue mag., N.Y.C., 1963-72; copy editor Mademoiselle mag., N.Y.C., 1972-77, mng. editor, 1977-80; assoc. editor Vogue Mag., N.Y.C., 1980-85; editor-in-chief Elle mag, N.Y.C., 1985-87; pres. Clinique USA, 1987-92; mktg. cons. Portland, Oreg., 1993—. Bd. dirs. Oregon Dental Svcs. Health Plans; bus. adv. bd. Portland State U. Bd dirs. Concordia U. Mem. Cosmetics Exec. Women.

ANDERS, ALLISON, film director, screenwriter; b. Ashland, Ky., Nov. 16, 1954, ø.-dir. (film) Border Radio, 1987 (Best First Film award UCLA); writer, dir. (feature films) Gas, Food, Lodging, 1992 (Best New Dir. award N.Y. Film Critics Circle 1992), Mi Vida Loca, 1994, Four Rooms (segment "The Missing Ingredient"),1995; dir Grace of My Heart, 1996; prodr. Lover Girl, 1998; co-dir., co-writer Sugar Town, 1999. Recipient San Goldwyn 1st prize, 1986; Nicholl fellow, 1986, MacArthur fellow, 1995. Office: UTA 9560 Wilshire Blvd 5th Fl Beverly Hills CA 90212-2401

ANDERS, GEORGE CHARLES, journalist, writer; b. Chgo., Nov. 12, 1957; s. Edward and Joan Elizabeth (Fleming) A.; m. Elizabeth Anne Corcoran, Aug. 27, 1988. BA in Econs., Stanford U., 1978. Nat. copyreader Wall St. Jour., N.Y.C., 1978-81, Heard on the Street columnist, 1981-82, London bur. chief European edit., 1982-85, news editor, 1985-88, sr. spl. writer, 1988-2000; sr. editor Fast Company Mag., 2000—. Contbg. editor SmartMoney mag., N.Y.C., 1992-95. Author: Merchants of Debt, 1992, Health Against Wealth, 1996. Recipient Janus award Am. Mortgage Bankers Assn., 1987; shared in Pulitzer Prize for nat. reporting, 1997.

ANDERS, WILLIAM ALISON, aerospace and defense manufacturing executive; b. Hong Kong, Oct. 17, 1933; s. Arthur Ferdinand and Muriel Florence (Adams) A.; m. Valerie Elizabeth Hoard, June 26, 1955; children: Alan Frank, Glen Thomas, Gayle Alison, Gregory Michael, Eric William, Diana Elizabeth. BS, U.S. Naval Acad., Annapolis, 1955; MS in Nuclear Engring., U.S. Inst. Tech., Wright-Patterson AFB, 1962. Commnd. 2d lt. U.S. Air Force, 1955, pilot, engr., 1955-69; astronaut NASA-Johnson Space Ctr., Houston, 1963-69, Apollo 8, 1st lunar flight, 1968; exec. sec. Nat. Aero. and Space Council, Washington, 1963-72; commr. AEC, Washington, 1973-74; chmn. Nuclear Regulatory Comm., Washington, 1975-76; U.S. Ambassador to Norway, 1976-77; v.p., gen. mgr. nuclear energy products div. Gen. Electric Co., 1977-80, v.p., gen. mgr. aircraft equipment div. N.Y., 1980-84; sr. exec., v.p. ops. Textron Inc., Providence, 1984-89; vice chmn. Gen. Dynamics, St. Louis, 1990-91, chmn., CEO, 1991-93; chmn. bd. dirs. N000, 1993-94; pres. Apogee Group. Chmn. Heritage Flight Mus. Trustee Battell Meml. Inst., Reno Air Races Unltd. Class, 1997-99. Maj. gen. USAFR, 1983-88, ret. Decorated various mil. awards; recipient Wright, Collier, Goddard and Arnold flight awards; co-holder several world flight records; named Disting. Grad., U.S. Naval Acad., 2000. Mem. Soc. Exptl. Test Pilots , Nat. Acad. Engring., Tau Beta Pi. Office: Heritage Flight Mus PO Box 1630 Eastsound WA 98245

ANDERSEN, HANS CHRISTIAN, chemistry educator; b. Bklyn., Sept. 25, 1941; m. June Jenny, June 17, 1967; children: Hans Christian, Albert William. SB, MIT, 1962, PhD, 1966. Jr. fellow Soc. Fellows Harvard U., Cambridge, 1965-68; asst. prof. chemistry Stanford U., Calif., 1968-74, assoc. prof., 1974-80, prof., 1980—, assoc. dean Sch. Humanities and Scis., 1996-99. Vis. prof. chemistry Columbia U., N.Y.C., 1981-82; co-dir. Stanford Ctr. for Materials Rsch., 1988-89, dep. dir., 1989-95; mem. allocation com. San Diego Supercomputer Ctr., 1986-89, chmn., 1988-89; vice-chmn. Gordon Rsch. Conf. on Physics and Chemistry of Liquids, 1989, chmn. 1991. Mem. editl. com. Ann. Rev. of Phys. Chemistry, 1983-87; mem. editl. bd. Jour. Chem. Physics, 1984-86, Chem. Physics, 1986-96; mem. adv. bd. Jour. Phys. Chemistry, 1987-92. Sloan fellow, 1972-74, Guggenheim fellow, 1976-77. Fellow AAAS, Am. Acad. Arts and Scis., Am. Phys. Soc.; mem. NAS, Am. Chem. Soc. (chmn. phys. chemistry divsn. 1986, Joel Henry Hildebrand award 1988). Office: Stanford U Dept Chemistry Stanford CA 94305-5080 E-mail: hca@stanford.edu

ANDERSEN, NIELS HJORTH, chemistry educator, biophysics researcher, consultant; b. Copenhagen, Denmark, Oct. 9, 1943; came to U.S. 1949; s. Orla and Inger (Larsen) A.; m. Sidnee Lee (div. 1986); children: Marin Christine, Beth Arkady; m. Susan Howell, July 21, 1987. BA, U. Minn., 1963; PhD, Northwestern U., 1967. Rsch. assoc and fellow Harvard U., Cambridge, Mass., 1966-68; asst. prof. U. Wash., Seattle, 1968-72, assoc. prof., 1972-76, prof., 1976—; prin. scientist ALZA Corp., Palo Alto, Calif., 1970-75. Cons. Genetic Systems, Seattle, 1984-86, Bristol-Myer Squibb, Princeton, N.J., 1984-95, Amylin Pharmaceutics, San Diego, 1992-99, Receptron Corp., Mountain View, Calif., 1995—, PathoGenesis Corp., Seattle, 1997—. Contbr. articles to profl. jours. Pres. Friends of Northshore, Bothell, Wash., 1980-86. Recipient Teacher-Scholar award Dreyfus Found., 1974-79, Career Devel. award NIH, 1975-80. Mem. AAAS, Am. Chem. Soc., Am. Peptide Soc., Protein Soc. Democrat. Avocations: contemporary folk music and swing, dulcimer playing. Office: U Wash Dept Chem PO Box 351700 Seattle WA 98195-1700 E-mail: andersen@chem.washington.edu

ANDERSEN, RONALD MAX, health services educator, researcher; b. Omaha, 1939; s. Max Adolph and Evangeline Dorothy (Wobbe) A.; m. Diane Borella, June 19, 1965; 1 dau., Rachel. BS, U. Santa Clara, 1960; MS, Purdue U., 1962, PhD, 1968. Research assoc. Purdue U., West Lafayette, Ind., 1962-63; assoc. study dir. Nat. Opinion Research Ctr., Chgo., 1963-66; research assoc. U. Chgo., 1963-77, assoc. prof., then prof. Grad. Sch. Bus., 1974-90, dir. Program in Health Adminstrn. and Ctr. for Health Adminstrn. Studies, 1980-90; Wasserman prof. dept. health svcs. and sociology UCLA, 1991—, chair dept. health svcs., 1993-96. Chmn. editl. bd. Health Adminstrn. Press, Chgo., 1980-83, 88-98, Med. Care Rsch. & Rev., 1994—; mem. coms. Agy. for Health Care Policy and Rsch., Rockville, Md., 1970—. Author: A Decade of Health Services, 1967, Two Decades of Health Service, 1976, Total Survey Error, 1979, Health Services in the U.S., 1980, Ambulatory Care and Insurance Coverage in an Era of Constraint, 1987, Training Physicians, 1994, Changing the U.S. Health Care System, 1996. NIH fellow, 1960-62; grantee Robert Wood Johnson Found., 1983, Kaiser Family Found., 1983, Agy. for Health Care Policy and Rsch., 1982, WHO, 1990. Mem. APHA, Am. Sociol. Assn. (chmn. med. sociology sect. 1980-81, Disting. Med. Sociologist 1994), Nat. Acad. Scis., Nat. Inst. Medicine, Assn. for Health Services Rsch. (dir. 1981-83), Assoc. Univ. Program in Health Adminstrn. (Baxter Allegiance prize 1999), Assn. for Health Svcs. Rsch. (Disting. Career awrd 1996). Roman Catholic. Home: 10724 Wilshire Blvd Apt 312 Los Angeles CA 90024-4453 Office: UCLA Sch Pub Health Los Angeles CA 90024

ANDERSON, ARTHUR SALZNER, publishing company executive, marketing executive; b. Boise, Idaho, Jan. 17, 1923; s. Howard Ballantyne and Mildred Ina (Salzner) A.; m. Janice Virginia Jacobsen, June 21, 1948; children: Roger Bruce, Gregory Bryan, Julie Janice Olsen, Lane Jacobsen, Margaret Virginia Ence, Heidi Gail Eldredge, Steven Jacobsen. B.A., U. Utah, 1947. Sales promotion asst. Internat. Harvester Co., 1947-48, zone mgr., 1948-51; sr. v.p., dir., chmn. exec. com. Evans Communications, Inc., Salt Lake City, 1977-84, dir., chmn. exec. com., 1984-87, pres., 1984-87; chmn. bd. Panoram Prodns., 1977-82; pres. Deseret Book Co., 1975-80, dir., 1975-92; pres., chief exec. officer Anderson Mktg. Inc., Salt Lake City, 1987—. Author: By Example, 1961. Vice-pres. Salt Lake Area United Fund, 1977-80; mem. governing bd. Primary Children's Med. Ctr., 1975-2001, vice chmn., 1981-83, chmn., 1983-92; bd. dirs. Osmond Found., 1982-83. Served with AUS, 1943-46. Mem. Utah Advt. Fedn. (pres. 1967-68), Sales and Mktg. Execs. Utah (pres. 1965-66) Mem. LDS Ch. Home: 2242 Kensington Ave Salt Lake City UT 84108-2310 Office: Anderson Mktg Inc 923 Executive Park Dr Ste C Salt Lake City UT 84117-3557

ANDERSON, AUSTIN GILMAN, economics research company consultant; b. Mpls. s. Clifford Hawkins and Katharine (Irving) A.; m. Marilyn Wheeler, Mar. 17, 1968; children: Guy, Alisa, Michael, Emily. BS, Stanford U., 1964, MBA, 1966. Systems analyst Jet Propulsion Lab., Pasadena, Calif., 1966-68; assoc. Econs. Rsch. Assoc., L.A., 1968-72, sr. v.p., 1977-88, pres., chief exec. officer, 1988—; dir. rsch. Property Rsch. Corp., L.A., 1972-73; prin. Levander, Partridge & Anderson, Beverly Hills, Calif., 1973-77; v.p. Econs. Rsch. Assocs., L.A. Instr. Grad. Sch. Mgmt. UCLA, 1989, extension, 1987; bd. dirs. Crown Iron Works Co., Mpls., 1983—; mem. bd. counselors Sch. Urban and Regional Planning U. So. Calif., L.A., 1984-95; mem. bd. trustees Real Estate Investment Trust of Calif., 1994—. Mem. Urban Land Inst. Avocations: sculpting, golf. Office: Econs Rsch Assocs 10990 Wilshire Blvd Ste 1500 Los Angeles CA 90024-3917

ANDERSON, CARL WEST, retired judge; b. Monterey Park, Calif., Sept. 11, 1935; s. Carl Ejnar and Mary Madeline (West) A.; m. Margo Hart, Aug. 15, 1964; children: Thomas Hart, Marnie Marie. AB in Pol. Sci., U. Calif., Berkeley, 1957, LLB, 1962; LLM in Jud. Process, U. Va., 1992. Bar: Calif. 1963. Dep. dist. atty. Alameda County (Calif.) Dist. Atty., 1964-72, sr. dep. dist. atty., 1972-75; judge Alameda County Superior Ct., 1975-84; assoc. justice Calif. Ct. Appeals, 1st dist., divsn. 3, San Fransisco, 1984; presiding justice divsn. 4, San Francisco, 1987-97, adminstrv. presiding justice, 1987-97; ret., 1997. Pvt. judge, assoc. Am. Arbitration Assn. and alternative adjucication, 1997—; mem. appellate performance stds. com. Nat. Ctr. for State Cts. Commn., 1994-95. Pres. Piedmont (Calif.) Coun. Boy Scouts Am., 1987, 88, 93. Capt. USAR, 1957-74. Scholar U. Calif. Alumni Assn., 1953; fellow U. Calif. Sch. Law and Ctr. for Study Law and Soc., Germany, 1962-63. Fellow ABA (commn. stds. jud. adminstrn. 1992-93, appellate judges conf. exec. com. JAD 1992, 93, chair-elect 1995—, chair 1996-97), Coun. Chief Judges Cts. Appeal (pres. 1992-93). Avocations: tennis, gardening, golf. Office: Am Arbitration Assn 225 Bush St 18th Fl San Francisco CA 94104-4211 E-mail: justicecanderson@sprynet.com

ANDERSON, CHARLES ARTHUR, former research institute administrator; b. Columbus, Ohio, Nov. 14, 1917; s. Arthur E. and Huldah (Peterson) A.; m. Elizabeth Rushforth, Oct. 27, 1942; children: Peter C., Stephen E., Julia E. AB, U. Calif. at Berkeley, 1938; MBA, Grad. Sch. Bus. Adminstrn., Harvard U., 1940; LHD, Colby Coll., 1975. Asst. prof. Grad. Sch. Bus. Adminstrn., Harvard U., Boston, 1945-48; v.p. Magna Power Tool Corp., Menlo Park, Calif., 1948-58; prof., asso. dean Stanford Grad. Sch. Bus., 1959-61; v.p. Kern County Land Co., San Francisco, 1961-64; pres. Walker Mfg. Co., Racine, Wis., 1964-66, J.I. Case Co., Racine, 1966-68; pres., chief exec. officer SRI Internat., Menlo Park, 1968-79, also dir. Bd. dirs. KRI Internat., Japan, Eaton Corp., Conoco, Owens-Corning Fiberglas, NCR, Boise Cascade, Saga; mem. adv. council Bus. Sch., Stanford, 1966-72, 74-79; mem. industry adv. council Dept. Def., 1971-73 Author (with Anthony) The New Corporate Director. Mem. Menlo Park Planning Commn. and City Coun., 1955-61, Govs. Commn. on Reorgn. Wis. State Govt., 1965-67; bd. dirs. Calif. State C. of C., 1972-77, Internat. House, U. Calif., Berkeley, 1979-90; bd. dirs. Lucile Salter Packard Children's Hosp., Stanford, 1979-95, chmn., 1992-94. With USNR, 1941-45. Recipient Exceptional Service award USAF, 1965 Mem. Palo Alto Club, Pacific-Union Club, Menlo Country Club. Presbyterian. Office: 555 Byron St Apt 207 Palo Alto CA 94301-2037

ANDERSON, CHARLES WILLIAM, computer science educator; BS in Computer Sci., U. Nebr., 1978; MS in Computer and Info. Sci., U. Mass., 1982, PhD in Computer and Info. Sci., 1986. Sys. analyst AGNET U. Nebr., 1977-79; tchg. asst. U. Mass., 1979, rsch. asst., 1979-86, computer graphics cons., 1984-86; sr. mem. tech. staff GTE Labs., Waltham, Mass., 1986-90; asst. prof. computer sci. dept. Colo. State U., Ft. Collins, 1991-97, assoc. prof. computer sci., 1997—. Mem. program com. Eighth Internat. Workshop on Machine Learning, Constructive Induction, 1991, Fla. Artificial Intelligence Rsch. Symposium, 1991, 97, IEEE-Internat. Conf. on Neural Networks, 1993, IEEE Internat. Conf. on Tools with Artificial Intelligence, 1993, Neural Info. Processing Sys. Conf., 1994; NSF panel reviewer, 1994-96; lectr. in field. Mem. editl. bd. Neural

Computing Surveys; reviewer or referee for profl. jours. including Cognitive Sci. Jour., Computer and Software Engring., Connection Sci. Jour., IEEE Control Sys. Mag., IEEE Transaction on Biomed. Engring., Jour. Empirical Software Engring., Machine Learning, others; contbr. chpts. to books and articles to profl. jours. Grantee Am. Gas Assn., 1991-92, Colo. State U., 1992, NSF, 1992-95, 92-94, 95-96, 95-96, 96—. Mem. AAAI, IEEE Computer Soc. (mem. elections com. 1994-96), Assn. for Computing Machines, Internat. Neural Network Soc., Upsilon Pi Epsilon. Office: Colo State U Dept Computer Sci Fort Collins CO 80523-0001 E-mail: anderson@cs.colostate.edu

ANDERSON, CHRISTINE MARLENE, software engineer; b. Washington, Nov. 19, 1947; 2 children. BS in Math., U. Md., 1969. Mathematician Naval Oceanographic Office, Suitland, Md., 1969-71; sr. analyst, fgn. tech. divsn. Planning Rsch. Corp., Ohio, 1971-72; computer scientist USAF Avionics Lab., Wright-Patterson Air Force Base, Dayton, 1971-74; sr. analyst USAF C3 Ctr., Cheyenne Mountain, Colorado Springs, Colo., 1974-76; chief computer tech. section USAF Wright Lab./Armament Directorate, Eglin Air Force Base, Fla., 1982-92; ADA 9X project mgr. Office Sec. Defense, 1987-94; chief software tech. br. Phillips Lab., Kirtland Air Force Base, N.Mex., 1992-93, chief, space soperations and simulation divsn.oftware rsch. ctr., 1993-96, dir. space and missiles tech. directorate, 1996; mem. sr. exec. svcs., dir. space vehicles directorate Phillips Lab., Kirtland Air Force Base, Air Force Rsch. Lab., 1996—. Co-chmn. on Ada computer programming lang. Am. Nat. Standards Inst., 1989—; editor Ada standard Internat. Standards Orgn., 1991—. Co-author: Aerospace Software Engineering, 1991; contbr. articles to profl. jours. Recipient Engr. of the Year USAF Armament Lab., 1989, Software Engring. award Am. Inst. Aeronautics, 1991, Program Mgr. of the Year award USAF Armament Lab., 1992, Sec. of Defense medal for Meritorious Civilian Svc., 1996. Fellow AIAA (chair software systems tech. com. 1987-89, bd. dirs. 1989—, Aerospace Software Engring. award 1991). Office: Air Force Rsch Lab AFRL/VS Aberdeen Ave SE Kirtland AFB NM 87117-0001

ANDERSON, DANA K. real estate company executive; With Macerich Group, Santa Monica, Calif., 1965—, now COO, exec. v.p. Bd. dirs. Alvamar Devel. Corp., Goodrich 560 Corp. Office: Macerich Co 233 Wilshire Blvd Ste 700 Santa Monica CA 90401-1207

ANDERSON, DANA Z. physics educator; b. Chgo., Apr. 10, 1953; BSEE, Cornell U., 1975; PhD, U. Ariz., 1981. Rsch. assoc. U. N.Mex., 1980-81; rsch. fellow in physics Caltech, 1981-84, lectr. in physics, 1983-84; asst. prof. dept. physics U. Colo., Boulder, 1984-89, assoc. prof., 1989-95, prof., 1995—. Mem. Joint Inst. Lab. Astrophysics, U. Colo., Nat. Inst. Stds. and Tech., 1984-85, fellow, 1985—; cons. Litton Industries Guidance and Control Sys. Divsn., 1981-82, Rockwell Internat. Corp. Marine Sys. Divsn., 1982-84. Editor: Neural Information Processing Systems, 1988; guest editor IEEE Jour. Quantum Electronics, 1987; editor Neural Info. Processing Sys., 1988; mem. series adv. bd. Computation and Neural Sys.; bd. editors Jour. Neural Networks; topical editor Optics Letters; contbr. articles to profl. jours. Alfred P. Sloan Rsch. fellow, 1986-90; recipient Presdl. Young Investigator award 1985. Fellow Optical Soc. Am. (R.W. Wood prize 1994). Office: U Colo Joint Inst Lab Astrophysics Boulder CO 80309-0001

ANDERSON, DARL, retail executive; CFO Bashas', Chandler, Ariz. Office: Bashas PO Box 488 Chandler AZ 85244-0488 also: Bashas 22402 S Basha Rd Chandler AZ 85248-4908

ANDERSON, DAVID E. zoological park administrator; Student, Pfeiffer Coll., 1964-65; BS in Zoology/Psychology, Duke U., 1972, postgrad., 1973. Colony supervisor Primate Ctr. Duke U., Durham, N.C., 1972-77, asst. dir. Primate Ctr., 1977-78; curator of mammals San Francisco Zool. Gardens, 1978-81, gen. curator, 1981-87, assoc. dir., gen. curator, 1987-90, dir., 1990—. Tech. advisor Nature Conservancy La., 1987-90; animal tech. cons., mem. advisement com. La. State U.; mem. animal care com. Tulane U.; chmn. steering com. Madagascar Fauna Captive Propagation Group. Revs. editor Zoo Biology, 1982-88; contbr. articles to profl. publs. With USMC, 1965-69, Vietnam. Mem. Am. Assn. Zool. Parks and Aquariums (grad. mgmt. sch. 1982, ethics com., long range planning com., accreditation com., program chmn. Nat. Conf. 1981, others), Internat. Union Dirs. Zool. Gardens (captive breeding specialist group). Office: San Francisco Zool Gardens 1 Zoo Rd San Francisco CA 94132-1098

ANDERSON, DON LYNN, geophysicist, educator; b. Frederick, Md., Mar. 5, 1933; s. Richard Andrew and Minola (Phares) A.; m. Nancy Lois Ruth, Sept. 15, 1956; children: Lynn Ellen, Lee Weston. B.S., Rensselaer Poly. Inst., 1955; M.S., Calif. Inst. Tech., 1959, Ph.D., 1962; DSc (hon.), Rensselaer Poly. Inst., 2000. With Chevron Oil Co., Mont., Wyo., Calif., 1955-56; with Air Force Cambridge Research Center, Boston, 1956-58, Arctic Inst. N.Am., Boston, 1958; mem. faculty Calif. Inst. Tech., Pasadena, 1962—, assoc. prof. geophysics, 1964-68, prof., 1968—, dir. seismol. lab., 1967-89, Eleanor and John R. McMillan prof. of geophysics, 1990—. Prin. investigator Viking Mars Seismic Expt.; mem. various coms. NASA; chmn. geophysics rsch. forum NAS, chmn. Arthur L. Day award com. NSF, Geosci. adv. com., 1994, adv. bd. for Sch. of Earth Scis., Stanford U., chmn. 1995); also mem. adv. com. Purdue U., U. Chgo., U. Tex., Stanford U., U. Calif. Berkeley, Carnegie Instn., Washington, U. Paris, Yale U., Rice U., chmn. 1996), Consortium for High Pressure Rsch. U. Calif.-Riverside, geosci. adv. com. NSF; co-founder Inc. Rsch. insts. for Seismology. Assoc. editor Jour. Geophys. Rsch., 1965-67, Tectonophysics, 1974-77; editor Physics of the Earth and Planetary Interiors, 1984-94. Recipient Exceptional Sci. Achievement award NASA, 1977; Sloan Found. fellow, 1965-67; Emil Wiechert Medal German Geophys. Soc., 1986, Crafoord prize Royal Swedish Acad. of Scis. 1998, Nat. medal of Sci., 1998; Guggenheim fellowship, 1998. Fellow AAAS, Am. Geophys. Union (James B. Macelwane award, 1966, pres. tectonophysics sect. 1971-72, chmn. Macelwane award com. 1975, mem. Bowie medal com. 1985, chair 1994, pres.-elect 1986-88, pres. 1988-90, Bowie medal 1990), Geol. Soc. Am. (assoc. editor bull. 1971—, Arthur L. Day medal 1987, mem. Penrose medal com. 1989, Arthur L. Day medal com. 1989-90, long range planning com. 1990—); mem. NAS (chmn. seismology com. 1975, chmn. Geophysics Research Forum 1984-86), Am. Philos. Soc., Royal Astron. Soc. (Gold medal 1988), Seismol. Soc. Am., Sigma Xi. Home: 669 Alameda St Altadena CA 91001-3001 Office: Calif Inst Tech Seismol Lab 252 21 Pasadena CA 91125-0001

ANDERSON, DONALD BERNARD, oil company executive; b. Chgo., Apr. 6, 1919; s. Hugo August and Hilda (Nelson) A.; m. Patricia Gaylord, 1945 (dec. 1978); m. Sarah Midgette, 1980. BS in Mech. Engring, Purdue U., 1942. Vice pres. Hondo Oil & Gas Co. (formerly Malco Refineries, Inc.), Roswell, N.Mex.; vice pres. Hondo Oil & Gas Co. and subs. corps., Roswell, 1946-63; pres. Anderson Oil Co., Roswell, 1963—, Cotter Corp., 1966-70, chmn. bd., 1966-74; founder, pres. Anderson Drilling Co., Denver, 1974—, pres., chmn. bd., 1977—. Curator fine arts, mem. acquisitions com. Roswell Mus. and Art Center, 1949-56, trustee, 1956-85, pres. bd., 1960-85, 87—, trustee, pres. 1987-90; bd. dirs. Sch. Am. Rsch., Santa Fe, chmn. bd., 1985-88, bd. dirs. 1989—; bd. dirs. Jargon Soc., Penland, N.C.; regent Ea. N.Mex. U., 1966-72; commr. Smithsonian Instn., Nat. Mus. Am. Art, 1980-88. Lt. USNR, 1942-46. Office: PO Box 1 Roswell NM 88202-0001

ANDERSON, DONALD H. gas industry executive; b. 1948; Graduate, U. Colo., Boulder, 1970. Acct. Peat, Marwick, Mitchell Y Co., Denver, 1970-78, Western Crude Oil Inc., Denver, 1978-82; Lantern Petroleum Corp., Denver, 1983—; chmn, pres., ceo Pan Energy, Houston; vice-cmn. & CEO TransMontaigne Inc., Denver, 1999—, pres., vice-chmn. & CEO, 2000—. Office: TransMontaigne 2750 Republic Pl Denver CO 80202

ANDERSON, DONALD LLOYD, weapon systems consultant; b. Stoughton, Wis., Sept. 19, 1921; s. Carl Gustave and Bessie (Cook) A.; m. Augusta Neidermeier, Sept. 10, 1948; children: Anita Briggs, Cathrine Krakower, Christine Robertson. Student, U. Niagara, Niagara Falls, N.Y., 1960, U. Md., Sembach, Germany, 1963-64, City Coll., Riverside, Calif. Commd. USAF, 1940, advanced through grades to chief master sgt., 1963, supply supt., 1940-71; weapon systems specialist Dynalectron Corp., Norco, Calif., 1971-88, VSE Corona (Calif.), Inc., 1988-89, Dyncorp, Norco, Calif., 1989-92, cons., 1992—. Tutor Myra Linn Sch., Riverside, Calif., 1991—. Author: (tng. manual) Standard Missile Data Processing Manual, 1989, 92. Vol. info. specialist Parkview Hosp., Riverside, 1992-96; staff mem., vol. NCO Acad., March AFB, Calif., 1991-94; vol. Citizens Patrol, Riverside Police Dept.; mem. all svcs. honor guard Riverside Nat. Cemetery, 2001—. Decorated Bronze Star medal, Meritorious Svc. medal, USAF Commendation medal, Vietnam Gallantry Cross with gold palm. Mem. DAV, VFW, NCOAC (life), Bombard Soc., Phoenix Club.

ANDERSON, DONALD MEREDITH, bank executive; b. Milan, Feb. 19, 1928; s. Meredith A. and Lydia (Helseth) A.; m. Christine Skorupa; 1 child, Karen. Student, St. Olaf Coll., Northfield, Minn., 1946-48; B.A., U. Minn., 1948-50; M.B.A., Harvard U., 1952; postgrad. Grad. Banking Sch., U. Wis.-Madison, 1965-67. Factory rep. Congoleum-Nairn, Inc., 1953-56; stockbroker J.M. Dain & Co., Mpls., 1956-58; v.p. comml. lending and corr. banking Northwestern Nat. Bank of Mpls., 1958-69; v.p. lending Santa Barbara Nat. Bank, Calif., 1969-71; pres. Santa Barbara Bank & Trust, 1971-89, chmn., 1989—. Dir. Gen. Telephone Calif., 1976— , mem. audit com., 1982— ; mem. regional adv. com. Comptroller of Currency, 1975-76 Bd. dirs. Blue Cross So. Calif., 1981— ; bd. dirs. Mission council Boy Scouts Am., 1977— , v.p. 1977-80, pres. 1985; bd. dirs. Goleta Valley Hosp., 1978— , pres., 1979-80; mem. Industry Edn. Council, 1975— , chmn., 1984— ; trustee U. Calif.-Santa Barbara, 1984— ; mem. comdr.'s adv. bd. Vandenberg AFB, 1978— ; mem. adv. bd. Vis. Nurses Assn., 1983— ; past pres. bd. dirs. Trinity Lutheran Ch., United Way; bd. dirs. Santa Barbara Zoo, 1985— . Served to 1st lt. USAF, 1952-53 Mem. Calif. Bankers Assn. (dir. 1982— , chair comml. lending com. 1977), Santa Barbara C. of C. (v.p. 1979, dir. 1972, 78— , Western Ind. Bankers Assn. (pres. 1985, sec. 1983, dir. 1981—), Am. Bankers Assn. (bank investments com. 1976-79) Republican. Home: 445 Via Hierba Santa Barbara CA 93110-2214 Office: Santa Barbara Bank & Trust 1021 Anacapa St Santa Barbara CA 93101-2102

ANDERSON, DOROTHY FISHER, social worker, psychotherapist; b. Funchal, Madeira, May 31, 1924; d. Lewis Mann Anker and Edna (Gilbert) Fisher (adoptive father David Henry Fisher); m. Theodore W. Anderson, July 8, 1950; children: Robert Lewis, Janet Anderson Yang, Jeanne Elizabeth. BA, Queens Coll., 1945; AM, U. Chgo., 1947. Diplomate Am. Bd. Examiners in Clin. Social Work; lic. clin. social worker, Calif.; registered cert. social worker, N.Y. Intern Cook County (Ill.) Bur. Pub. Welfare, Chgo., 1945-46, Ill. Neuropsychiat. Inst., Chgo., 1946; clin. caseworker, Neurol. Inst. Presbyn. Hosp., N.Y.C., 1947; therapist, Mental Hygiene Clinic VA, N.Y.C., 1947-50; therapist, Child Guidance Clinic Pub. Elem. Sch. 42, N.Y.C., 1950-53; social worker, counselor Cedarhurst (N.Y.) Family Service Agy., 1954-55; psychotherapist, counselor Family Service of the Midpeninsula, Palo Alto, Calif., 1971-73, 79-86, George Hexter, M.D., Inc., 1972-83; clin. social worker Tavistock Clinic, London, 1974-75, El Camino Hosp., Mountain View, Calif., 1979; pvt. practice clin. social work, 1978-92; ret., 1992. Cons. Human Resource Services, Sunnyvale, Calif., 1981-86. Hannah G. Solomon scholar U. Chgo., 1945-46; Commonwealth fellow U. Chgo., 1946-47. Fellow Soc. Clin. Social Work (Continuing Edn. Recognition award 1980-83); mem. Nat. Assn. Social Workers (diplomate in clin. social work). Avocations: sculpture, tennis, travel, drawing, pastels.

ANDERSON, DUANE, anthropologist; b. Norton, Kans., Nov. 21, 1943; s. Charles Raymond and Leta Marie (Stapp) A.; m. Carol Sue Haloin, Jan. 25, 1944; 1 child, Diana Sue Anderson. BA, U. Colo., 1965, MA, 1967, PhD, 1972. Dir. Sanford Mus. and Planetarium, Cherokee, Iowa, 1966-75; state archaeologist U. Iowa, Iowa City, 1975-86; exec. dir. Dayton (Ohio) Mus. Natural History, 1986-92; v.p. Sch. Am. Rsch., Santa Fe, 1992—; dir. Mus. Indian Arts & Culture, Santa Fe. Co-editor, author: The Cherokee Excavations, 1980, All That Glitters, 1999; editor: Legacy, 1999. Pres. Iowa Acad. Scis., Cedar Falls, 1983-84, Plains Anthropol. Soc., Lincoln, Nebr., 1985-86, Coun. for Mus. Anthropology, Arlington, Va., 1992-94; mem. exec. com. U. Iowa Mus. Natural History, 1977-86; mem., chair Iowa State Preserves Bd., Des Moines, 1976-86; bd. dirs. N.Mex. Mus. Natural History Found., Albuquerque, 1994-97. NDEA grad. fellow, 1970; grantee NSF, 1976-77, NEH, 1976, 80, 88. Mem. Am. Anthropol. Assn., Soc. Am. Archeology, Am. Assn. Mus. (sr. examiner, accreditation), Plains Anthropol. Soc. (pres. 1985-86), Coun. for Mus. Anthropology (pres. 1992-94), Ctrl. States Anthropol. Soc. (sec. 1987-90). Avocations: travel, jewelry making. Address: MIAC/LAB PO Box 2087 Santa Fe NM 87504-2087

ANDERSON, EDWARD VIRGIL, lawyer; b. San Francisco, Oct. 17, 1953; s. Virgil P and Edna Pauline (Pedersen) A.; m. Kathleen Helen Dunbar, Sept. 3, 1983; children: Elizabeth D., Hilary J. AB in Econs., Stanford U., 1975, JD, 1978. Bar: Calif. 1978. Assoc. Pillsbury Madison & Sutro, San Francisco, 1978—, ptnr., 1987-94; mng. ptnr., mem. firm mgmt. com. Skjerven Morrill MacPherson LLP, San Jose, 1994—. Editor IP Litigator, 1995—; mem. bd. editors Antitrust Law Devel., 1983-86. Trustee Lick-Wilmerding H.S., San Francisco, 1980—, pres.; trustee Santa Clara Law Found., 1995—; trustee, v.p. Hamlin Sch. for Girls, San Francisco, 1998—, v.p. Mem. ABA, Calif. Bar Assn., San Francisco Bar Assn., Santa Clara Bar Assn. (counsel), City Club San Francisco, Stanford Golf Club, Phi Beta Kappa. Republican. Episcopal. Home: 330 Santa Clara Ave San Francisco CA 94127-2035 Office: Skjerven Morrill MacPherson Franklin and Friel 25 Metro Dr Ste 700 San Jose CA 95110-1349 E-mail: eanderson@skjerven.com

ANDERSON, FRED D. computer company executive; B in Econs., Whittier Coll.; MBA, UCLA. CPA, Calif. Mgr. consulting divsn. Coopers & Lybrand; sr. v.p., CFO MAI Sys. Corp., pres., COO; v.p., CFO Automatic Data Processing, 1992-96; exec. v.p., CFO Apple Computer, 1996—. Capt. USAF. Office: Apple Computer Inc One Infinite Loop Cupertino CA 95014

ANDERSON, GAIL V. obstetrician/gynecologist; b. Pensacola, Fla., Oct. 3, 1925; d. Parke Pleasant and Sarada M. (Thompson) A.; m. Alice Harriet Midghall, Nov. 6, 1923; children: Gail V. Jr., David C., Jerrold B., Walter P., Mark S. BA, BS, Columbia Union Coll., 1949; MD, Loma Linda U., 1953. Diplomate Am. Bd. Ob-Gyn. Resident in ob-gyn. D.C. Gen. Hosp., Washington, 1954-55, Georgetown U. Hosp., Washington, 1955-56; chief resident in ob-gyn. D.C. Gen. Hosp., Washington, 1956-57; dir. ob-gyn. L.A. County/U. So. Calif. Med. Ctr., 1958-70; prof. ob-gyn. U. So. Calif. Sch. Medicine, L.A., 1968—, prof., chmn. dept. emergency medicine, 1971—. Mem. South Pasadena Sch. Bd., 1971-77; cand. city coun. South Pasadena, 1980; dir. salerni Collegium, 1958-95, pres., 1992-93. With USN, 1943-46. Hartford Found. grantee, 1964. Fellow ACS, ACOG; mem. Am. Bd. Emergency Medicine (founder), Am. Coll. Emergency Physicians (charter). Republican. Avocations: tennis, golf, travel. Home: 217 Oaklawn Ave South Pasadena CA 91030-1828 Office: Univ So Calif Dept Emergency Medicine 1200 N State St Los Angeles CA 90033-1029

ANDERSON, GERALD VERNE, retired aerospace company executive; b. Long Beach, Calif., Oct. 25, 1931; s. Gordon Valentine and Aletha Marian (Parkins) A.; m. Judith B. Marx, May 14, 1992; children by previous marriage: Lori Jean Anderson Fronk, Gregory Verne, David Harman, Lynn Elaine Anderson Lee (dec.), Brian Earl, Michael Gordon. AA, Long Beach City Coll., 1952; BS, U. Calif., Berkeley, 1958. Registered profl. engr., Calif. Tech. specialist N. Am. Aviation Co., L.A., 1958-65; tech. specialist McDonnell Douglas Astronautics, Huntington Beach, Calif., 1965-84, mgr., 1984-87; sr. mgr. McDonnell Douglas Aerospace, Huntington Beach, 1987-94. Cons. Mitsubishi Heavy Industries, Nagoya, Japan, 1972-73, Aeritalia, Turin, Italy, 1975-76. Patentee portable vacuum chamber, electron beam welding device. Mem. Westminster (Calif.) Planning Com., 1974, Huntington Beach Citizens Adv. Com., 1975, Westminster Bicentennial Com., 1976, L.A. Classical Ballet Guild, 1992-96; vol. Long Beach Symphony, 1995—; crew top sail program L.A. Maritime Inst., 1998—. Mem. Soc. Mfg. Engrs., Soc. Automotive Engrs., Aerospace Industries Assn., AIAA. Republican. Avocations: photography, skiing, backpacking, snorkeling, writing. Home: 3452 Falcon Ave Long Beach CA 90807-4814 E-mail: GAnder1999@aol.com

ANDERSON, HERBERT HATFIELD, lawyer, farmer; b. Rainier, Oreg., Aug. 2, 1920; s. Odin A. and Mae (Hatfield) A.; m. Barbara Stuart Bastine, June 3, 1949; children— Linda, Catherine, Thomas, Amy, Elizabeth, Kenneth B.A. in Bus. Adminstrn., U. Oreg., 1940; J.D., Yale U., 1949. Exec. trainee U.S. Steel Co., San Francisco, 1940-41; assoc. Spears, Lubersky, Campbell, Bledsoe, Anderson & Young, Portland, Oreg., 1949-54; ptnr. Spears, Lubersky, Bledsoe, Anderson, Young & Hilliard, 1954-90, Lane, Powell, Spears & Lubersky, Portland, 1990—. Instr. law Lewis and Clark Coll., Portland, 1950-70. Mem. planning adv. com. Yamhill County, Oreg., 1974-82; bd. dirs. Emanuel Hosp., 1967—; bd. dirs. Flyfisher Found., 1972—, pres., 1972-84; bd. dirs. Multnomah Law Library, 1958—, sec. 1962-68, 77-95, pres., 1964-74. Served to maj., parachute inf. U.S. Army, 1942-46, ETO Fellow Am. Bar Found. (chmn. Oreg. chpt. 1988—); mem. ABA (chmn. governing com. forum on health law 1984-89, chmn. standing com. on jud. selection, tenure and compensation 1978-80, Lawyer's Conf., exec. com. 1980-94, chmn. 1989-90, judicial adminstrn. divsn. coun. 1988-94, sr. lawyer's divsn. coun. 1987-89), Am. Judicature Soc. (bd. dirs. 1981-85), Soc. Law and Medicine, Nat. Health Lawyers Assn., Am. Acad. Hosp. Attys., Oreg. Soc. Hosp. Attys. (pres. 1984-85), Multnomah Bar Found. (bd. dirs. 1955—, pres. 1959-64, 87—), Nat. Bankruptcy Conf. (conferee 1964—, exec. com. 1976-79, chmn. farmer insolvency com. 1985-88), Nat. Assn. R.R. Trial Counsel, Oreg. Bar Assn. (del. to ABA 1966-68), Multnomah Bar Assn. (pres. 1955), Western States Bar Conf. (pres. 1967), Oreg. Asian Pear Coun. (pres. 1989-91), Sigma Chi. Democrat. Lutheran. Clubs: Multnomah Athletic, Michelbook Country, Flyfishers Oreg. (pres. 1972), Willamette Amateur Field Trial (pres. 1968-72). Lodge: Masons Home: River Meadow Farm 19289 SE Neck Rd Dayton OR 97114-7815 Office: Lane Powell Spears & Lubersky 601 SW 2d Ave Ste 2100 Portland OR 97204-3158 E-mail: herband@open.org

ANDERSON, HERBERT W. consumer products company executive; b. Indpls., Oct. 1, 1939; BS in Bus. Mgmt., U. Wis. Sr. mgmt. positions McGraw-Edison, Eaton Cos.; corp. v.p., mgmt. info. svcs. Western Gear Corp.; v.p., info. rescource mgmt. Northrop Grumman Corp., 1984-90, corp. v.p., ctr. mgr., 1990-94, dep. gen. mgr., DSSD, 1994-95, corp. v.p., gen. mgr., DSSD, 1995-98, pres., CEO, Logicon, 1998—. With U.S. Army 1958-61. Office: Northrop Grumman Corp 1840 Century Park E Los Angeles CA 90067-2101

ANDERSON, HERSCHEL VINCENT, retired librarian; b. Charlotte, N.C., Mar. 14, 1932; s. Paul Kemper and Lillian (Johnson) A. B.A., Duke U., 1954; M.S., Columbia U., 1959. Library asst. Bklyn. Public Library, 1954-59; asst. bookmobile librarian King County Public Library, Seattle, 1959-62; asst. librarian Longview (Wash.) Public Library, 1962-63; librarian N.C. Mus. Art, Raleigh, 1963-64; audio-visual cons. N.C. State Library, Raleigh, 1964-68; dir. Sandhill Regional Library, Rockingham, N.C., 1968-70; asso. state librarian Tenn. State Library and Archives, Nashville, 1970-72; unit dir. Colo. State Library, Denver, 1972-73; state librarian S.D. State Library, Pierre, 1973-80; dir. Mesa (Ariz.) Public Library, 1980-99. Dir. Bibliographical Ctr. for Rsch., Denver, 1974-80, v.p. 1977; founding mem. Western Coun. St. Librs., 1975-80, v.p., 1978, pres., 1979; mem. Ariz. LSCA Adv. Coun., 1981-84, pres., 1982-83; founding mem., chief officers State Libr. Agys., 1973-80, bd. dirs.; mem. Ariz. Libr. Devel. Coun., 1991-93, Ariz. State Libr. Adv. Coun., 1998—, chair, 1999—; mem. libr. technician tng. adv. com. Mesa C.C., 1982-85, mem. commn. for excellence, 1993—; chmn. Serials On-Line in Ariz. Consortia, 1985-86; mem. libr. facilities adv. bd. Gilbert, Ariz., 1999—. Jr. warden St. Mark's Episcopal Ch., Mesa, 1985-87, vestryman, 1987-90, 95-98, sr. warden, 1996-98; del. ann. conv. Episcopal Diocese of Ariz., 1989-92, 94-98, mem. archives com., 1990-97, mem. Diocesan Coun. Episcopal, Diocese of Ariz., 1996-98; mem., treas. Maricopa County Libr. Coun., 1981-99, pres., 1983, 93; mem. City of Mesa Hist. Preservation com., 2000—; mem. Valley Citizens League, 1991—; mem. Northeast Regional Parish steering com., 1994—, chair Native Am. com., 1999—. With U.S. Army, 1955-57. Recipient Emeritus Honors Ariz. Library Friends, 1987. Mem. ALA, S.D. Libr. Assn. (hon. life, Libr. of Yr. award 1977), Mountain Plains Libr. Assn. (pres. 1974, bd. dirs. 1974-77, 86-87, Intellectual Freedom award 1979), Ariz. Libr. Assn. (exe. com. 1986-87), Kiwanis (bd. dirs. Mesa 1981-86, v.p. 1983, pres. 1985-86), Phi Kappa Psi.

ANDERSON, HOLLY GEIS, women's health facility administrator, commentator, educator; b. Waukesha, Wis., Oct. 23, 1946; d. Henry H. and Hulda S. Geis; m. Richard Kent Anderson, June 6, 1969. BA, Azusa Pacific U., 1970. CEO Oak Tree Antiques, San Gabriel, Calif., 1975-82; pres., founder, CEO Premenstrual Syndrome Treatment Clinic, Arcadia, 1982—, Breast Healthcare Ctr., 1986-89, Hormonal Treatment Ctrs., Inc., Arcadia, 1992-94; with Thyroid Ctr., 2001—. Lectr. radio and TV shows, L.A.; on-air radio personality Women's Clinic with Holly Anderson, 1990—. Author: What Every Woman Needs to Know About PMS (audio cassette), 1987, The PMS Treatment Program (video cassette), 1989, PMS Talk (audio cassette), 1989. Mem. NAFE, The Dalton Soc., Am. Hist. Soc. of Germans from Russia. Republican. Avocations: writing, genealogy, travel, hiking, boating. Office: PMS Treatment Clinic 150 N Santa Anita Ave Ste 755 Arcadia CA 91006-3148

ANDERSON, JAMES E., JR. lawyer; AB, Stanford U., 1969, JD, 1972. Bar: Calif. 1972, Tex. 1973, Tenn. 1985. Assoc. Akin, Gump, Strauss, Hauer & Feld, 1972-74, 76-78, ptnr., 1979-83, Wald, Harkrader & Ross, 1983-84, Dearborn & Ewing, 1984-91; v.p., gen. counsel Ingram Industries Inc., 1991-96; sr. v.p., sec., gen. counsel Ingram Micro, 1996—. Office: Ingram Micro 1600 E Saint Andrew Pl Santa Ana CA 92705-4926

ANDERSON, JANET ALM, librarian; b. Lafayette, Ind., Dec. 20, 1952; d. Charles Henry and Lenore Elaine Alm; m. Jay Allan Anderson, May 21, 1983. BS, Bemidji State U., 1975; MA in Folklore, Western Ky. U., 1981, MSLS in Libr. Sci., 1982; PhD in Recreation Resources Mgmt., Utah State U., 1994. Cert. elem. tchr., sch. libr. and media specialist. Storyteller, puppeteer North Country Arts Council, Bemidji, Minn., 1975-76, head children's libr. Bemidji State U., 1976-77; mid. sch. libr. Custer County Sch. Dist., Miles City, Mont., 1977-79, tchr. of gifted and talented,

1979-80; folklore archivist Western Ky. U., Bowling Green, 1981-83; head children's and young adults' svcs. Bowling Green Pub. Libr., 1983-85; head of serials Utah State U., Logan, 1986-91, campus svcs. libr., 1991—, adj. asst. prof. forestry, 1995—, chmn. adv. bd. Women's Ctr., 1988-92. Adj. instr. Miles Community Coll., 1978-80; cons. to various Am. outdoor museums; speaker Utah Endowment for the Humanities Speakers Bur., Salt Lake City, 1987-90; mem. acad. freedom and tenure com. Utah State U., 1995-97, chair, 1997-98; rsch. scientist Inst. Outdoor Recreation and Tourism, 1994—; presenter to confs. on librarianship, folklore, and natural resources. Author: (novels) Old Fred, 1972, Vendors and Library Acquisitions, 1991, Singing All the Way, 2001; co-author: (book) Advances in Serials Management, Vol. 3, 1989;contbr. book, articles to mags. and periodicals, rsch. reports; editor (assoc.): (jour.) InterpEdge; performer: (presentations on folklore and librarianship) Radio and TV. Co-founder, past pres. Rosebud chpt. Nat. Audubon Soc., Miles City, Mont., 1978-80; mem. Providence/River Hts. Libr. Bd.; trustee Cache County Libr. Bd.; bd. dirs. Denzil Stewart Nature Park; mem. adv. panel Hardware Ranch Wildlife Mgmt. Area; invited author Ky. State Book Fair, 1986, Utah Arts Festival, 1991; life mem. Women and Gender Rsch. Inst., Friends of Brooks Free Libr.; trustee Stokes Nature Ctr.; mem. adv. bd. Am. West Heritage Ctr. Recipient Exhibit and Program Grant Nat. Endowment for the Arts, Bowling Green, Ky., 1984-85. Mem. ALA, Nat. Audubon Soc. (trustee Bridgerland chpt. 1994-97), Nat. Assn. Interpretation, John Muir Assn. (founding mem. environ. ctr.), Utah Libr. Assn., Consortium of Utah Women in Higher Edn. (campus coord. 1989-91), Am. Folklore Soc., Utah Folklore Soc., Assn. Living Hist. Farms and Agrl. Mus., Visitor Studies Assn., Women and Gender Rsch. Inst. (life), Am. Assn. Mus., Assn. Coll. and Rsch. Librs., Old Main Soc., Xi Sigma Pi. Democrat. Lutheran. Home: 1090 S 400 E Providence UT 84332-9461 Office: Utah State U Merrill Libr Logan UT 84322-3000 E-mail: janand@ngw.lib.usu.edu

ANDERSON, J.C. oil and gas exploration company executive; b. Oakland, Nebr. Student, Midland Coll., Fremont, Nebr., 1949-51; BSc in Petroleum Engring., U. Tex., 1954. With Amoco Prodn. Co., various locations; chief engr. Amoco Can., Calgary, Alta., 1966-68; founder, chmn. bd., CEO Anderson Exploration Ltd., Calgary, 1968—. Bd. dirs. Investment Dealers Assn. Can., Can. Venture Exchange. With Counter-Intelligence Corps, U.S. Army, 1954-56. Mem. Assn. of Profl. Engrs., Geologists and Geophysicists of Alta., Soc. of Petroleum Engrs. Office: Anderson Exploration Ltd 1600 324 8th Ave SW Calgary AB Canada T2P 2Z5 E-mail: andersonjc@axl.ca

ANDERSON, JOHN ALBERT, physician; b. Ashtabula, Ohio, Jan. 25, 1935; s. Albert Gunnard Anderson and Martha Anetta (Bieshline) White; m. Nicole Jeanne Anderson, July 10, 1963; children: Carole Beno, John-Marc, Christopher B. BS, U. Ill., 1958, MD, 1960. Diplomate Am. Bd. Pediat., Am. Bd. Allergy and Immunology. Intern U. Ill., 1960-61, resident in pediat., 1961-62, U.S. Naval Hosp., Bethesda, Md., 1964-65; fellow in allergy and immunology Children's Hosp., Washington, 1967-69; mem. sr. staff Henry Ford Hosp., Detroit, 1969-99, dir. pediat. allergy fellowship program, 1969-77, dir. allergy and immunology program, 1977-99, head divsn. allergy and immunology, dept. pediatrics, 1977-99, chmn. dept. pediatrics, 1982-90; physician Vivra Asthma and Allergy, Tucson, 1999-2000; with VIRA Asthma and Allergy, Inc., 2000—; physician Allergy and Asthma Ctr. Ariz., Tucson, 2001—. Clin. prof. pediat., U. Mich., Ann Arbor, 1985-94; prof. pediat. Case Western Res. U., Cleve., 1994—; dir. Am. Bd. Allergy and Immunology, 1990-96, sec., 1995-96. Contbr. more than 50 articles to profl. jours. Lt. comdr. USN, 1962-66. Fellow Am. Acad. Allergy and Immunology (pres. 1990-91), Am. Acad. Pediat. (chmn. allergy sect. 1979-82), Mich. Allergy Soc. (pres. 1978-79); mem. Asthma and Allergy Found. Am. (dir. 1992-99, v.p. med. affairs 1992-95, v.p. rsch. 1995-99), Coun. Med. Speciality Soc. (bd. dirs. 1992-94), Am. Bd. Med. Specialists, Sci. Advisors Internat. Life Scis. (allergy sect. 1990—), ACGME-RRC for Allergy and Immunology. Home: 13866 N Bowcreek Springs Pl Tucson AZ 85737-5725 Office: 32 Med Sq 1601 N Tucson Blvd Tucson AZ 85716 Fax: 520-326-9276. E-mail: jonicoaz@worldnet.att.net

ANDERSON, JOHN DAVID, architect; b. New Haven, Dec. 24, 1926; s. William Edward and Norma Vere (Carson) A.; m. Florence A. Van Dyke, Aug. 26, 1950; children— Robert Stewart, David Carson. A.B. cum laude, Harvard U., 1949, M.Arch., 1952. Draftsman John K. Monroe, Architect, Denver, 1952-54; draftsman, designer, assoc. Wheeler & Lewis, Architects, Denver, 1954 60; prin. John D. Anderson, Denver, 1960-64; ptnr. Anderson, Barker Rinker, Architects, Denver, 1965-69, A-B-R Partnership, Architects, Denver, 1970-75; prin., CEO Anderson Mason Dale P.C., Denver, 1975-96, sr. v.p., 1997—. Vis. lectr. U. Colo., U. N.Mex., U. Nebr., U. Cape Town, Colo. State U., Plymouth Polytech., Eng.; chmn. Denver Bldg. Dept. Bd. Appeals, 1974-75; chmn. Colo. Gov.'s Task Force on Removal of Archtl. Barriers, 1972-74; vice chmn. Colo. Bd. Non-Residential Energy Conservation Stds., 1978 80. Prin. works include: Community Coll. Denver, North campus, Westminster, 1977, Solar Energy Rsch. Inst., Golden, 1980 (award winning solar heated structures). Served with USNR, 1944-46. Fellow AIA (pres. Colo. chpt. 1967, Western Mountain region dir. 1995-97, Silver medal, 1984, Firm of Yr. award 1986 Western Mountain region); mem. Colo. Soc. Archs. (Arch. of Yr. award 1987, pres. 1971, nat. v.p. 1999, 1st v.p. 2000, pres. 2001), Internat. Solar Energy Soc., Council Ednl. Facility Planners (internat. chmn. energy com. 1980). Republican. Congregationalist. Home: 57 S Rainbow Trail Golden CO 80401-8341 Office: Anderson Mason Dale Architects 1615 17th St Denver CO 80202-1293

ANDERSON, JOHN EDWARD, diversified holding company executive, lawyer; b. Mpls., Sept. 12, 1917; s. William Charles and Myrtle (Grosvenor) A.; m. Margaret Stewart, Sept. 14, 1942 (dec.); children: Margaret Susan, Judith Grosvenor, John Edward, Deborah Lee (dec.), William Stewart; m. Marion Redding, Mar. 3, 1967. BS cum laude, UCLA, 1940; MBA with distinction (Baker scholar), Harvard U., 1942; JD cum laude, Loyola U., 1950. Bar: Calif. 1950; CPA, Calif. Acct. Arthur Andersen & Co., Los Angeles, 1945-48; since practiced in Los Angeles, Irvine; ptnr. Kindel & Anderson, 1953-85; ceo. Topa Equities, Los Angeles, Calif. Dir. Mellon 1st Bus. Bank, Summit Health Ltd., Topa Equities, Ltd., Topa Mgmt. Co., Easton AluminumCo, Indsl. Tools, Inc., Topa Ins. Co. Trustee Claremont McKenna Coll.; trustee St. John's Hosp. and Health Center Found.; bd. dirs. YMCA Met., Los Angeles. Served to lt. USNR, 1942-45. Mem. AICPA, ABA, State Bar Calif., Calif. Soc. CPAs, L.A. Country Club, Calif. Club, Eldorado Country Club (Palm Desert, Calif.), Outrigger Canoe Club (Honolulu). Presbyterian (elder). Office: Topa Equities Ste 1400 1800 Avenue Of The Stars Los Angeles CA 90067-4216

ANDERSON, JOHN RICHARD, entomologist, educator; b. Fargo, N.D., May 5, 1931; s. John Raymond and Mary Ann (Beaulieu) A.; m. Shereen V. Erickson, Mar. 26, 1955; children: Scott F., Lisa K., Steven F. BS, Utah State U., 1957; MS, U. Wis., 1958, PhD, 1960. Asst. prof. entomology U. Calif.-Berkeley, 1961-66, assoc. prof., 1967-70, prof., 1970-93, prof. emeritus, 1993—, assoc. dean research, 1979-85. Trustee, past chmn. Alameda County (Calif.) Mosquito Abatement Dist., 1961-73, 79-93. Editoral bd.: Jour. Med. Entomology, 1968-72, Jour. Econ. Entomology, 1977-81, Thomas Say Found, 1968-72. Served with USN, 1950-54. Rsch. grantee; recipient Berkeley citation for Disting. Achievement, 1993. Fellow AAAS, Royal Entomol. Soc. (London); mem. Entomol. Soc. Am. (governing bd. 1987-90, C.W. Woodworth award Pacific br. 1988), Can. Entomol. Soc., Am. Mosquito Control Assn., Nat. Audubon Soc., Am. Mus. Natural History, Oreg. Nat. Resources Coun., Oreg. Nat. Desert Assn., High Desert Mus., Sierra Club. Home: 1283 NW Trenton Ave Bend OR 97701-1026 Office: U Calif Dept Insect Biology Berkeley CA 94720-0001

ANDERSON, JON DAVID, lawyer; b. Wichita, Kans., Oct. 29, 1952; s. Charles Henry Anderson and Patricia (Vaughan) Ross; m. Leanne Winters, Dec. 20, 1973; children: Nicklas, Scott, Brandt, Chase, Barrett, Britten, Kieryn. BA, U. Wash., Seattle, 1974; JD, Brigham Young U., 1977. Bar: Calif. 1977. Assoc. Latham & Watkins, L.A., Newport Beach, Calif., 1977-84, ptnr. Newport Beach, Costa Mesa, 1985—, mng. ptnr. Costa Mesa, Calif., 1987-93. Bd. dirs. Orange County Coun., Boy Scouts Am. Mem. Calif. Bar Assn., Orange County Bar Assn., Marbella Country Club. Republican. Ch. of Jesus Christ of Latter-day Saints. Avocations: skiing, baseball, golf. Office: Latham & Watkins 650 Town Center Dr Ste 2000 Costa Mesa CA 92626-7135 E-mail: jon.anderson@lw.com

ANDERSON, KATHRYN D. surgeon; b. Ashton-Under-Lyne, Lancashire, Eng., Mar. 14, 1939; came to U.S., 1961; m. French Anderson, June 24, 1961. BA, Cambridge (Eng.) U., 1961, MA, 1964; MD, Harvard U., 1964. Diplomate Am. Bd. Surgery with cert. in spl. competence in pediat. surgery. Intern in pediat. Children's Hosp., Boston, 1964-65; resident in surgery Georgetown U. Hosp., Washington, 1965-69, chief resident in surgery, 1969-70, attending surgeon, 1972-74; chief resident in pediat. surgery Children's Hosp., Washington, 1970-72, sr. attending surgeon, 1974-92, surgeon-in-chief L.A., 1992—; vice chmn. surgery George Washington U., Washington, 1984-92. Prof. surgery U. So. Calif. Fellow ACS (sec. 1992—), Royal Coll. Surgeons (Eng.); mem. Am. Acad. Pediatrics (sec. surg. sect. 1982-85, chmn. 1985-86), Am. Pediatric Surg. Assn. (sec. 1988-91, pres. 1999-2000), Am. Surg. Assn., Soc. Univ. Surgeons. Avocations: opera, yoga. Office: Childrens Hosp 4650 W Sunset Blvd Los Angeles CA 90027-6062

ANDERSON, KENT TAYLOR, lawyer; b. Salt Lake City, June 24, 1953; s. Neldon Leroy and Vera Minnie (Taylor) A.; m. Ellis Anderson (div. June 1979); m. Tara Dayle, Apr. 30, 1982; 1 child, Claire Marie. BA, U. Utah, 1975; JD, Georgetown U., 1978. Bar: Utah 1978, Calif. 1987. Assoc. Jones, Waldo, Holbrook & McDonough, Salt Lake City, 1978-83, ptnr., 1983-84; v.p., gen. counsel Am. Stores Properties, Inc., Salt Lake City, 1984-86; v.p., gen. counsel, asst. sec. Am. Stores Co., Salt Lake City, 1987—; sr. v.p., gen. counsel, sec. Alpha Beta Stores, Inc., Anaheim, Calif., 1986-89; exec. v.p., gen. counsel, asst. sec. Am. Stores Co., Salt Lake City, 1989-93, exec. v.p., 1993—; gen. mgr. Am. Stores Properties, Inc., Salt Lake City, 1993-95, COO strategy and devel., mem. exec. coun., 1995—. Mem. staff Georgetown Law Jour., 1976-78. Mem. Utah Bar Assn., Calif. Bar Assn., Phi Beta Kappa. Office: Am Stores Properties Inc 1654 Mohawk Way Salt Lake City UT 84108-3312

ANDERSON, LAWRENCE OHACO, magistrate judge, lawyer; b. Phoenix, Sept. 7, 1948; s. Jack M. and Viola (Ohaco) A. BS, U. San Francisco, 1971; JD, Ariz. State U., Tempe, 1974. Bar: Ariz. 1975. Prosecutor City of Phoenix, 1973-75; assoc. Jack M. Anderson, Phoenix, 1975-78; sole practice Phoenix, 1978-90; judge Superior Ct. of Ariz., Phoenix, 1990-92, judge, criminal calender, 1992-95, judge, juvenile ct., 1995-98, magistrate judge, 1998-. Natl. Wheelchair Weightlifting Championship, Spokane, Wash., 1974; Victory Achievement Award, State of Ariz., 1990. Mem. ABA, Assn. Trial Lawyers Am., Ariz. Trial Lawyers Assn. (bd. dirs. 1985—). Republic. Roman Catholic. Avocations: fishing, hunting, sports. Office: 230 N 1st Ave Phoenix AZ 85025-0230

ANDERSON, LOUIE, comedian; b. Mpls. Appeared in film Cloak & Dagger, 1984, Quick Silver, 1986, Ferris Bueller's Day Off, 1986, The Wrong Guys, 1988, Coming to America, 1988, Bebe's Kids, 1992, Mr. Wrong, 1996, (TV) Life with Louie (voice), 1995, The Louie Show, 1996; author: Dear Dad: Letters From an Adult Child, 1989; comedian: HBO Spl., host Family Feud. Recipient Daytime Emmy, 1996. Office: ICM 8942 Wilshire Blvd Beverly Hills CA 90211-1934

ANDERSON, MARILYN WHEELER, English language educator; b. Tulsa, Mar. 18, 1946; d. Robert Leslie and Lola Madelene (Offutt) Wheeler; m. Austin Gilman Anderson, Mar. 17, 1968; children: Guy, Lisa, Michael, Emily. BA, Calif. State U., L.A., 1968; MA, UCLA, 1972, Calif. State U., Dominguez Hills, 1989. Actress and dir., L.A., 1977-83; cons. Redondo Beach (Calif.) Beach City Schs., 1981-83; prof. of English El Camino Coll., Torrance, Calif., 1986—. Fine arts com. mem. El Camino Coll., 1992—, affirmative action officer, 1995-96; presenter in field. Author: (textbook) Keys to Successful Writing, 1998, 2d edit., 2001; contbr. articles to profl. jours. Vol. 1736 House/Crisis Ctr., Hermosa Beach, Calif., 1985-86; bd. dirs. Brain Injury Rsch. Ctr., UCLA, 1998—. Mem. MLA, Nat. Coun. Tchrs. of English, UCLA Alumni Assn. Democrat. Avocations: jogging, travel, hiking, book club membership. Office: El Camino Coll 16007 Crenshaw Blvd Torrance CA 90506-0001

ANDERSON, MARTIN CARL, economist; b. Lowell, Mass., Aug. 5, 1936; s. Ralph and Evelyn (Anderson) A.; m. Annelise Graebner, Sept. 25, 1965 AB summa cum laude, Dartmouth Coll., 1957, MS in Engring., MSBA; PhD in Indsl. Mgmt., MIT, 1962. Asst. to dean, instr. engring. Thayer Sch. Engring. Dartmouth Coll., Hanover, N.H., 1959; research fellow Joint Ctr. for Urban Studies MIT and Harvard U., Cambridge, 1961-62; asst. prof. fin. Grad. Sch. Bus. Columbia U., N.Y.C., 1962-65, assoc. prof. bus., 1965-68; sr. fellow Hoover Inst. on War, Revolution and Peace Stanford (Calif.) U., 1971—; spl. asst. to Pres. of U.S. The White House, 1969-70, spl. cons. for systems analysis, 1970-71, asst. for policy devel., 1981-82. Mem. Pres.' Fgn. Intelligence Adv. Bd., 1982-85, Pres.' Econ. Policy Adv. Bd., 1982-88, Pres.' Gen. Adv. Com. on Arms Control and Disarmament, 1987-93; pub. interest dir. Fed. Home Loan Bank San Francisco, 1972-79; mem. Commn. on Crucial Choices for Ams., 1973-75, Def. Manpower Commn., 1975-76, Com. on the Present Danger, 1977—. Author: The Federal Bulldozer: A Critical Analysis of Urban Renewal, 1949-62, 1964, Conscription: A Select and Annotated Bibliography, 1976, Welfare: The Political Economy of Welfare Reform in the U.S., 1978, Registration and the Draft, 1982, The Military Draft, 1982, Revolution, 1988, Impostors in the Temple, 1992, Reagan in his Own Hand, 2001; columnist Scripps-Howard News Svc., 1993-94. Dir. research Nixon presdl. campaign, 1968; policy adviser Reagan presdl. campaign, 1976, 80; del. Rep. Nat. Conv., 1992-2000; policy adviser Dole Presdl. Campaign, 1996; sr. adviser Bush presdl. campaign, 1998-2000; trustee Ronald Reagan Presdl. Found., 1985-92; mem. Calif. Gov.'s Coun. Econ. Advisors, 1993-98, chmn. Congl. Policy Adv. Bd., 1998-2001. 2d lt. AUS, 1958-59. Mem. Mont Pelerin Soc., Phi Beta Kappa. Club: Bohemian. Office: Stanford U Hoover Instn Stanford CA 94305-6010

ANDERSON, N. CHRISTIAN, III, newspaper publisher; b. Montpelier, Idaho, Aug. 4, 1950; s. Nelson C. and Esther Barbara Anderson; m. Sara Ann Coffenberry, Dec. 11, 1971 (div.); children: Ryan, Erica; m. Aletha Ann Yurewicz, May 3, 1986; children: Paul, Amanda. BA in liberal studies with honors, Ore. State U., 1972. From asst. city editor to city editor Albany (Ore.) Democrat-Herald, 1972-75; mng. editor Walla Walla (Wash.) Union Bulletin, 1975-77; assoc. mng. editor Seattle Times, 1977-80; from editor to exec. v.p., assoc. publisher The Orange County Register, Santa Ana, Calif., 1980-94; pub. Gazette Telegraph, Colorado Springs, 1994-98; pub., CEO, Orange County Register, Santa Ana, CA, 1999—; sr. v.p. Freedom Comm., Inc., 1999—. Instr. Calif. State U., Fullerton, 1983, 87, Pulitzer Prize juror, 1987, 88, 96; exec. editor Freedom Newspapers, Inc., Irvine, Calif., 1990-94; exec. v.p., CEO, Golden West Publ., Irvine, 1991-94; mem. adv. bd. Poynter Inst. for Media Studies, St. Petersburg, Fla., 1994-99, also past chmn. adv. bd.; former chmn. bd. dirs. New Directions for News, newspaper think tank; mem. nominating com. AP; bd. dirs. Robert C. Maynard Inst. for Journalism Edn. Bd. dirs. Santa Ana Rotary Found., 1984, Colorado Springs Fine Arts Ctr., 1994-98, Colorado Springs Non-Profit Ctr., 1994-98, Colorado Springs Sports Corp., 1994-98, Pike's Peak United Way, 1994-98, South Coast Repertory; bd. dirs. Econ. Devel. Corp., Colorado Springs, chmn. bd., 1996; chmn. Orange County Bus. Com. for Arts; bd. govs. Ctr. Clu; past mem. nd. dirs. Calif. First Amendment Coalition. Recipient George D. Beveridge award Nat. Press Found., 1989, named nat. newspaper editor of yr., 1989; named Calif. newspaper exec. of yr. Calif. Press. Assn., 1993. Mem. Am. Soc. Newspaper Editors (bd. dirs. 1996, treas. 1996, sec. 1997, v.p. 1998, pres. 1999), Soc. Newspaper Desirn (co-founder), Calif. Soc. Newspaper Editors (a founder, former bd. dirs. and pres.). E-mail: nca3link.freedom.com. Office: Orange County Register 625 N Grand Ave Santa Ana CA 92701-4347

ANDERSON, NORMA V. state legislator; b. Elyria, Ohio, July 6, 1932; Student, Denver U., Jones Real Estate Coll. Owner, operator KBJ Stables; office mgr. Capitol Solar; supr. Time, Inc.; mem. Colo. Ho. of Reps., Dist. 30, 1986-98; house majority leader; mem. Colo. Senate, Dist. 22, Denver, 1998—; chair bus. affairs and labor com., mem. edn. com.; mem. legis. audit com., mem. local govt. com. Mem. State Adv. Coun. on Labor Dept., State Compensation Bd., Regional Transp. Dist. Bd. Vice-chair HEWI; bd. dirs. Foothills Found.; mem. budget com. R-1 Sch. Dist. Mem. Nat. Conf. State Legislatures (energy and transp. com. chair), West Chamber (bd. mem.), Am. Cancer Soc., Edn. 2000, Bear Creek Jr. Sports Assn. Republican. Office: State Capitol 200 E Colfax Ave Ste 346 Denver CO 80203-1716

ANDERSON, NORMAN, management consultant; Grad. in geol. engring., U. Man. Joined Cominco, 1953, various positions include mine supt., mgr. Magmont operation, 1965-70; v.p., gen. mgr. Mo. Lead Operating Co. AMAX, Inc., 1970, v.p. mining and lead bus. Lead/Zinc Divsn.; CEO Fording Coal Cominco, 1973, group v.p. Potash and Nitrogen Fertilizer Ops., exec. v.p., COO, 1977, pres., COO, 1978-80, chmn., CEO, 1980-86, ret., 1986; pres. Anderson & Assocs. Internat., Vancouver, B.C., Can. Recipient INCO medal Can. Inst. Mining, Metallurgy and Petroleum, 2000. Fellow Inst. Mining and Metallurgy (chartered engr.); mem. CIM, AIME. Office: Anderson & Assocs Internat 1450 Pennyfarthing Dr #7G Vancouver BC Canada V6J 4X8

ANDERSON, PAUL IRVING, management executive; b. Portland, Oreg., Mar. 23, 1935; s. William F. and Ruth M. (Sundquist) A.; m. Lorraine A. Franz, Nov. 21, 1959; children: Todd, Susan, Cheryl, Cynthia. B.S., Oreg. State U., 1956. Various positions in mktg., sales and engring. mgmt. 3M Co., St. Paul and Boston, 1956-74, gen. mgr. Brussels, Belgium, 1974-77, group bus. planning dir. St. Paul, 1977-79; sr. v.p., gen. mgr. Rayovac Corp., Madison, Wis., 1979-82; pres. Anderson Cons. Co., Madison, 1982-83; div. v.p. RCA Corp., Indpls., 1983-84; pres. Anderson & Assocs., La Costa, Calif., 1984-87; pres., CEO Electro-Imaging Advisors, Inc., La Jolla, 1987-93; CEO Strategic Catalysts Inc., La Jolla, 1993—. Mem. Am. Mgmt. Assn., Tau Beta Pi, Pi Tau Sigma, Sigma Tau Republican. Presbyterian. Clubs: Columbia (Indpls.); Madison; Nakoma Golf (Madison). Home: 6418 Cayenne Ln Carlsbad CA 92009-4301

ANDERSON, PAUL NATHANIEL, oncologist, educator; b. Omaha, May 30, 1937; s. Nels Paul E. and Doris Marie (Chesnut) A.; m. Dee Ann Hipps, June 27, 1965; children: Mary Kathleen, Anne Christen. BA, U. Colo., 1959, MD, 1963. Diplomate Am. Bd. Internal Medicine, Am. Bd. Med. Mgmt., Am. Bd. Med. Oncology. Intern Johns Hopkins Hosp., Balt., 1963-64, resident in internal medicine, 1964-65, fellow in oncology, 1970-72; rsch. assoc., staff assoc. NIH, Bethesda, Md., 1965-70; asst. prof. medicine, oncology Johns Hopkins U. Sch. Medicine, 1972-76; attending physician Balt. City Hosps., Johns Hopkins Hosp., 1972-76; dir. dept. med. oncology Penrose Cancer Hosp., Colorado Springs, Colo., 1976-86; clin. asst. prof. dept. medicine Colo. Sch. Medicine, 1976-90, clin. assoc. prof., 1990—. Dir. Penrose Cancer Hosp., 1979-86, chief dept. medicine, 1985-86; founding dir. Cancer Ctr. of Colorado Springs, 1986-95, Pikes Peak Forum for Health Care Ethics, 1996—, Rocky Mountain Cancer Ctr., Colorado Springs, 1995—; med. dir. So. Colo. Cancer Program, 1979-86, pres., chmn. bd. dirs. Preferred Physicians, Inc., 1986-92; mem. Colo. Found. for Med. Care Health Stds. Com., 1985, sec., exec. com., 1990, bd. dirs., pres., 1992-93; mem., chmn. treatment com. Colo. Cancer Control and Rsch. Panel, 1980-83; prin. investigator Cancer Info. Svc. of Colo., 1981-87; pres., founder Timberline Med. Assocs., 1986-87, Oncology Mgmt. Network, Inc., 1985-95. Editor Advances in Cancer Control; editl. bd. Jour. Cancer Program Mgmt., 1987-92, Health Care Mgmt. Rev., 1988—; contbr. articles to med. jours. Mem. Colo. Gov.'s Rocky Flats Employee Health Assessment Group, 1983-84; mem. Gov.'s Breast Cancer Control Commn. Colo., 1984-89; founder, dir. So. Colo. AIDS project, 1986-91; mem. adv. bd. Colo. State Bd. Health Tumor Registry, 1984-87; chmn., bd. dirs. Preferred Physicians, Inc., 1986-92; bd. dirs. Share Devel. Co. of Colo. Share Health Plan of Colo., 1986-90, vice chmn., 1989-91; bd. dirs., chmn. Preferred Health Care, Inc., 1991-92; mem. health care stds. com., trustee colo. Found. for Med. Care (PRO); mem. nat. bd. med. dirs. Fox Chase Cancer Ctr. Network, Phila., 1987-89, mem. tech. expert panel Harvard Resource-Based Relative Value Scale Study for Hematology/Oncology, 1991-92. With USPHS, 1965-70. Mem. AMA (mem. practice parameters forum 1989-97, adv. com. to HCFA on uniform clin. data set), AAAS, Am. Coll. Forensic Examiners, Am. Soc. Clin. Oncology (chmn. subcom. on oncology clin. practice stds., mem. clin. practice com., rep. to AMA 1991—, mem. healthcare svcs. rsch. com., chmn. clin. guidelines subcom. 1993—), Am. Assn. Cancer Rsch., Am. Assn. Cancer Insts. (liaison mem. bd. trustees 1980-82), Am. Coll. Physician Execs., Am. Hospice Assn., Am. Soc. Internal Medicine, Nat. Cancer Inst. (com. for cmty. hosp. oncology program evaluation 1982-83), Colo. Soc. Internal Medicine, Assn. Cmty. Cancer Ctrs. (chmn. membership com. 1980, chmn. clin. rsch. com. 1983-85, sec. 1983-84, pres.-elect 1984-85, pres. 1986-87, trustee 1981-88), N.Y. Acad. Scis., Johns Hopkins Med. Soc., Colo. Med. Soc., Am. Mgmt. Assn., Am. Assn. Profl. Cons., Am. Soc. Quality, Am. Acad. Med. Dirs., Am. Coll. Physician Execs., El Paso County Med. Soc., Rocky Mountain Oncology Soc. (chmn. clin. practice com. 1989-94, pres.-elect 1990, pres. 1993-95), Acad. Hospice Physicians, Coalition for Cancer, Colorado Springs Clin. Club, Alpha Omega Alpha. Office: Rocky Mountain Cancer Ctr 3027 North Circle Dr Colorado Springs CO 80909 also: 32 Sanford Rd Colorado Springs CO 80906-4233

ANDERSON, PETER MACARTHUR, lawyer; b. New Castle, Ind., July 15, 1937; s. Earl Canute and Catherine Elizabeth (Schultz) A.; m. Ann Warren Gibson, Sept.1, 1962; children: David, Karen. AB, Dartmouth Coll., 1959; LLB, Stanford U., 1962. Bar: Calif. 1963, Wash. 1970. Assoc. O'Melveny & Myers, L.A., 1966-70, Bogle & Gates, Seattle, 1970-74, mem., 1974-99; ptnr. Preston Gates & Ellis, Seattle, 1999—. Co-chmn. equal employment law com. ABA, 1983-86. Mem. Ecumenical. Commn. for Seattle Archdiocese, St. Petersburg-Seattle Sister Chs. Com. Capt. U.S. Army, 1963-65. Fellow Coll. Labor and Employment Lawyers; mem. Phi Beta Kappa. Roman Catholic. Home: 9200 SE 57th St Mercer Island WA 98040-5005 Office: Preston Gates & Ellis LLP 701 5th Ave Ste 5000 Seattle WA 98104-7078

ANDERSON, RACHAEL KELLER, retired library administrator; b. N.Y.C., Jan. 15, 1938; d. Harry and Sarah Keller; m. Howard D. Goldwyn; children: Rebecca Anderson, Michael Goldwyn, Bryan Goldwyn, David Goldwyn. A.B., Barnard Coll., 1959; M.S., Columbia U., 1960. Librarian CCNY, 1960-62; librarian Mt. Sinai Med. Ctr., N.Y.C., 1964-73, dir. library, 1973-79; dir. Health Scis Libr. Columbia U., N.Y.C., 1979-91, acting v.p., univ. libr., 1982; dir. Ariz. Health Scis. Libr., U. Ariz., Tucson, 1991-2001; ret., 2001. Bd. dirs. Med. Libr. Ctr. of N.Y., N.Y.C., 1983-91; mem. biomed. libr. rev. com. Nat. Libr. Medicine, Bethesda, Md., 1984-88, chmn., 1987-88; mem. bd. regents Nat. Libr. Medicine, 1990-94, chmn., 1993-94; pres. Ariz. Health Info. Network, 1995. Contbr. articles to profl. jours. Mem. Med. Libr. Assn. (pres.-elect 1996-97, pres. 1997-98, bd. dirs. 1983-86, 98-99), Assn. Acad. Health Scis. Libr. Dirs. (bd. dirs. 1983-86, 90-93, pres. 1991-92). E-mail: rachaela@ahsl.arizona.edu

ANDERSON, RICHARD ERNEST, agribusiness development consultant, rancher; b. North Little Rock, Ark., Mar. 8, 1926; s. Victor Ernest and Lillian Josephine (Griffin) A.; m. Mary Ann Fitch, July 18, 1953; children: Vicki Lynn, Lucia Anita. BSCE, U. Ark., 1949; MSE, U. Mich., 1959. Registered profl. engr., Mich., Va., Tex., Mont. Commd. ensign USN, 1952, advanced through grades to capt., 1968, ret., 1974; v.p. Ocean Resources, Inc., Houston, 1974-77; mgr. maintenance and ops. Holmes & Narver, Inc., Orange, Calif., 1977-78; pres. No. Resources, Inc., Billings, Mont., 1978-81; v.p. Holmes & Narver, Inc., Orange, Calif., 1981-82; owner, operator Anderson Ranch, registered Arabian horses and comml. Murray Grey cows, Pony, Mont., 1982—; pres., dir. Carbon Resources Inc., Butte, 1983-88, Agri Resources, Inc., Butte, 1988-95, Anderson Holdings, Inc., Pony, 1995—. Trustee Lake Barcroft-Virginia Watershed Improvement Dist., 1973-74; pres. Lake Barcroft-Virginia Recreation Center, Inc., 1972-73. With USAAF, 1944-45. Decorated Silver Star, Legion of Merit with Combat V (2), Navy Marine Corps medal, Bronze Star with Combat V, Meritorious Service medal, Purple Heart; Anderson Peninsula in Antarctica named in his honor. Mem. ASCE, Soc. Am. Mil. Engrs. (Morrell medal 1965). Republican. Methodist. Office: Anderson Holdings Inc PO Box 266 Pony MT 59747-0266

ANDERSON, R(OBERT) GREGG, real estate company executive; b. St. Joseph, Mo., Oct. 3, 1928; s. Clarence William and Marie Louise (Newman) A.; m. Janice Kinrey, May 6, 2001; 1 child, Robert Gregg Jr. Student, U. Okla., 1948-49, U. Tulsa, 1950. Pres. Gregg Anderson Realty, San Diego, 1959-63; v.p. Trousdale Constrn. Co., L.A., 1963-67; pres. Amfac Properties div. Amfac, Inc., Honolulu, 1967-69; v.p. Amfac, Inc., Honolulu, 1967-69, sr. v.p., 1969-74; pres., chmn. bd. Accent Enterprises, Inc., Amfac Communities, Inc., Amfac Silverado Corp., Neilson Way Corp., 745 Fort St. Corp., Cen. Oahu Land Corp., L.A. Environ. Structures, Inc., 1969-74; chmn. bd. West Maui Properties, Inc., 1969-74; v.p. Silverado Country Club & Resort, Inc., 1969-74; pres. Gregg Anderson Realty & Devel., Inc., 1974—, Villa Pacific Bldg. Co., 1980—; gen. ptnr. Rancho Vista Devel. Co., Palmdale, Calif., 1980—; pres. Videocable, Inc., Palmdale, 1984-87; gen. ptnr. ProRep Assocs., 1991—. Bd. dirs. Antelope Valley Bd. Trade, 1991—; mem. exec. com. Gift Found. Antelope Valley Hosp. Med. Ctr., 1989-92. With USNR, 1950-54. Named Builder of Yr., Calif. Bldg. Industry Assn., 1998; inductee Calif. Bldg. Industry Hall of Fame, 1999. Mem. Bldg. Industry Assn. (bd. dirs. 1984-94), Rotary (hon.), Kiwanis (hon.). Republican. Avocations: tennis, golf, bowling. Office: Rancho Vista Devel Co Ste F-3011 3053 Rancho Vista Blvd Palmdale CA 93551-4823 E-mail: ranchvista@qnet.com

ANDERSON, ROBERT MARSHALL, retired bishop; b. S.I., N.Y., Dec. 18, 1933; s. Arthur Harold and Hazel Schneider A.; m. Mary Artemis Evans, Aug. 24, 1960; children: Martha, Elizabeth, Catherine, Thomas. BA, Colgate U., 1955; STB, Berkeley Div. Sch., 1961, DD (hon.), 1977, Seabury Western Sem., 1978, Yale U., 1977. Ordained priest Episcopal Ch. Curate St. John's Ch., Stamford, Conn., 1961-63, vicar, 1963-67, assoc. rector, 1968-72; priest in charge Middle Haddan, 1963-67; rector Middle Haddan, 1967-68; dean St. Mark's Cathedral, Salt Lake City, 1972-78; bishop Episcopal Diocese of Minn., Mpls., 1978-93; interim recotr Church of the Holy Spirit, Lake Forest, Ill., 1994-95; asst. bishop Diocese of L.A., 1995-98. Served with U.S. Army. Danforth fellow, 1959-60. Mem. Berkeley Alumni Assn. (pres. 1972-76). Democrat. Clubs: Mpls, Minikahda. Home: 65 Atterideg Rd Lake Forest IL 60045 Office: Diocese of LA PO Box 512164 Los Angeles CA 90051-0164

ANDERSON, RONALD DELAINE, education educator; b. Poplar, Wis., Aug. 25, 1937; s. Leslie A. and Linnea A. (Bergsten) A.; m. Sandra Jean Wendt, June 1, 1963; children— Debra Jean, Timothy James, Nathan David. B.S., U. Wis., 1959, Ph.D., 1964. Asst. prof. edn. Kans. State U., Manhattan, 1964-65; mem. faculty U. Colo., Boulder, 1965—, prof. edn., 1971—, asso. dean edn., 1972-78. Cons. to numerous ednl. agys. Co-author: Developing Children's Thinking Through Science, 1970, Issues of Curriculum Reform, 1994, Local Leadership for Science Education Reform, 1995, Portraits of Productive Schools, 1995, Study of Curriculum Reform, 1996; contbr. articles to profl. jours. Program dir. Nat. Sci. Found., 1989-90. Fulbright scholar, 1986-87. Fellow AAAS (chair edn. sect. 1998-99); mem. Nat. Assn. Research Sci. Teaching (pres. 1975-76), Assn. Edn. Tchrs. in Sci. (pres. 1972-73), Nat. Sci. Tchrs. Assn., Phi Delta Kappa. Home: 4800 North Creek Rd Beulah CO 81023-9601 Office: Univ Colo Sch Edn Boulder CO 80309-0001

ANDERSON, ROSS, columnist; Editorial writer, columnist The Seattle Times. Recipient Pulitzer Prize for nat. reporting, 1990. Office: The Seattle Times PO Box 70 Seattle WA 98111-0070

ANDERSON, ROSS CARL, mayor, lawyer; b. Logan, Utah, Sept. 9, 1951; s. E. LeRoy and Grace (Rasmussen) A.; 1 child, Lucas Craig Arment. BS in Philosophy magna cum laude, U. Utah, 1973; JD with honors, George Washington U., 1978. Bar: U.S. Dist. Ct. Utah 1978. Assoc. Berman & Giauque, Salt Lake City, 1978-80; v.p., ptnr. Berman & Anderson, Rooker Larsen Kimball & Parr, Salt Lake City, 1980-82; ptnr. Berman & Anderson, Salt Lake City, 1982-85; ptnr., v.p. Hansen & Anderson, Salt Lake City, 1986-89, Anderson & Watkins, Salt Lake City, 1989-92; pres. Anderson & Karrenberg, Salt Lake City, 1992-98, of counsel, 1999; mayor Salt Lake City, 1999—. Columnist Enterprise, 1997-98. Dem. candidate for Congress, Utah 2d Congl. Dist., 1996, mayor Salt Lake City, 1999—; pres. bd. dirs. Citizens for Penal Reform, 1991-94, Guadalupe Ednl. Programs, Salt Lake City, 1985-96, 97-99, ACLU of Utah, 1980-85; bd. dirs. Common Cause of Utah, 1987-89, Planned Parenthood of Utah, 1979-83; mem. Salt Lake Com. on Fgn. Rels., 1983-95. Mem. Utah State Bar Assn. Democrat. Avocations: history, fgn. affairs, skiing. Home: 418 Douglas St Salt Lake City UT 84102-3231 Office: Office Mayor 451 S State St Rm 306 Salt Lake City UT 84111-0005

ANDERSON, ROY ARNOLD, aerospace company executive; b. Ripon, Calif., Dec. 15, 1920; s. Carl Gustav and Esther Marie (Johnson) A.; m. Betty Leona Boehme, 1948; 4 children. MBA, Stanford U., 1949. Mgr. factory acctg. Westinghouse Electric Corp., 1952-56; mgr. acctg. and fin., dir. mgmt. controls Lockheed Missiles and Space Co., 1956-65; dir. finance Lockheed Ga. Co., 1965-68; asst. treas. Lockheed Aircraft Corp. (now Lockheed-Martin Corp.), 1968-69, v.p., controller, 1969-71, sr. v.p. finance, 1971-75, vice chmn. bd. dirs., chief fin. adminstrv. officer, 1975-77, chair, CEO, 1977-85, dir., chair exec. com., 1985-88, chair emeritus, 1991—; chair, CEO Weingart Found., 1994-98. Chair Oversight Bd., State of Calif., 1997-98. Avocations: tennis, golf, gardening. Home: 4367 Shepherds Ln La Canada CA 91011-3120 Office: Lockheed-Martin Corp 606 S Olive St Fl 23 Los Angeles CA 90014-1623

ANDERSON, STEPHEN HALE, federal judge; b. Salt Lake City, Jan. 12, 1932; m. Shirlee Gehring; two children. Student, Eastern Oreg. Coll. Edn., LaGrande, 1951, Brigham Young U., Provo, 1956; LLB, U. Utah, 1960. Bar: Utah 1960, U.S. Claims Ct. 1963, U.S. Tax Ct. 1967, U.S. Ct. Appeals (10th cir.) 1970, U.S. Supreme Ct. 1971, U.S. Ct. Appeals (9th cir.) 1972, various U.S. Dist. Cts. Tchr. South H.S., Salt Lake City, 1956-57; trial atty. tax div. U.S. Dept. Justice, 1960-64; ptnr. Ray Quinney & Nebeker, 1964-85; judge U.S. Ct. Appeals (10th cir.), Salt Lake City 1985—. Spl. counsel Salt Lake County Grand Jury, 1975; chmn. fed.-state jurisdiction com. Jud. Conf. U.S., 1995-98; mem. Nat. Jud. Coun. State and Fed. Cts., 1992-96; mem. ad hoc. com. on bankruptcy appellate panels 10th Cir. Jud. Coun., 1995-97; mem. various coms. U.S. Ct. Appeals (10th cir.). Editor-in-chief Utah Law Rev. Cpl. U.S. Army, 1953-55. Mem. Utah State Bar (pres. 1983-84, various offices), Salt Lake County Bar Assn. (pres. 1977-78), Am. Bar Found., Salt Lake Area C. of C. (bd. govs. 1984), U. Utah Coll. Law Alumni Assn. (trustee 1979-83, pres. 1982-83), Order of Coif. Office: US Ct Appeals 4201 Fed Bldg 125 S State St Salt Lake City UT 84138-1102

ANDERSON, THEODORE WILBUR, statistics educator; b. Mpls., June 5, 1918; s. Theodore Wilbur and Evelynn (Johnson) A.; m. Dorothy Fisher, July 8, 1950; children: Robert Lewis, Janet Lynn, Jeanne Elizabeth. BS with highest distinction, Northwestern U., 1939, DSc, 1989; MA, Princeton U., 1942, PhD, 1945; LittD, North Park U., 1988; PhD (honoris causa), U. Oslo, 1997; D (hon.), U. Athens, 1999. Asst. dept. math. Northwestern U., 1939-40; instr. math. Princeton U., 1941-43, rsch. assoc., 1943-45, Cowles Commn., U. Chgo., 1945-46; staff Columbia U., 1946-67, successively instr. math. stats., asst. prof., assoc. prof., 1946-56, prof., 1956-67, chmn. math. stats. dept., 1956-60, 64-65, acting chmn., 1950-51, 63; prof. stats. and econs. Stanford U., 1967-88, prof. stats. and econs. emeritus, 1988—. Dir. project Office Naval Rsch., 1950-82; prin. investigator NSF project, 1969-92, Army Rsch. Office project, 1982-92; vis. prof. math. U. Moscow, 1968; vis. prof. stats. U. Paris, 1968; vis. prof. econs. NYU, 1983-84; acad. visitor math. Imperial Coll. Sci. and Tech., U. London, 1967-68, London Sch. Econs. and Polit. Sci., 1974-75, U. So. Calif., 1989; C.G. Khatri Meml. lectr. Pa. State U., 1992; rsch. visitor Tokyo Inst. Tech., 1977; sabbaticant IBM Systems Rsch. Inst., 1984; rsch. assoc. Naval Postgrad. Sch., 1986-87; cons. RAND Corp., 1949-66; mem. com. on basic rsch. adv. Office Ordnance Rsch., Nat. Acad. Scis.-NRC, 1955-58; mem. panel on applied math. adv. Nat. Bur. Standards, 1964-65; chmn. com. on stats. NRC, 1961-63; mem. exec. com. Conf. Bd. Math. Scis., 1963-64; mem. com. on support rsch. in math. scis. Nat Acad. Scis., 1965-68; mem. com. Pres.'s Statis. Socs., 1962-64; sci. dir. NATO Advanced Study Inst. on Discriminant Analysis and Its Applications, 1972. Author: An Introduction to Multivariate Statistical Analysis, 1958, 2nd edit., 1984, The Statistical Analysis of Time Series, 1971, (with Somesh Das Gupta and George P.H. Styan) A Bibliography of Multivariate Statistical Analysis, 1972, (with Stanley Sclove) Introductory Statistical Analysis, 1974, An Introduction to the Statistical Analysis of Data, 1986, (with Jeremy D. Finn) The New Statistical Analysis of Data, 1996; editor: (with Krishna B. Athreya and Donald L. Iglehart) Probability, Statistics and Mathematics: Papers in Honor of Samuel Karlin, 1989, (with Kai Tai Fang) Statistical Inference in Elliptically Contoured and Related Distributions, 1990, (with K.T. Fang and I. Olkin) Multivariate Analysis and Its Applications, 1994; editor Anns. of Math. Stats., 1950-52; assoc. editor jour. Time Series Analysis, 1980-88; mem. adv. bd. Econometric Theory, 1985—, Jour. Multivariate Analysis, 1988—; mem. editl. bd. Psychometrika, 1954-72. Recipient R.A. Fisher award Pres.'s Statis. Socs., 1985, Disting. Alumnus award North Park Coll. and Theol. Sem., 1987, Minnehaha Acad., 1992, Award of Merit Northwestern U. Alumni Assn., 1989; named Wesley C. Mitchell Vis. Prof. Columbia U., 1983-84; Guggenheim fellow, 1947-48, fellow Ctr. for Advanced Study in Behavioral Scis., 1957-58; vis. scholar, 1972-73, 80; Sherman Fairchild disting. scholar Calif. Inst. Tech., 1980; vis. disting. prof. Norwegian Coun. Sci. and Indsl. Rsch. U. Oslo; Abraham Wald Meml. lectr., 1982; S.S. Wilks lectr. Princeton U., 1983, P.C. Mahalanobis Meml. lectr., 1985, S.N. Roy Meml. lectr. Calcutta U., 1985, Allen T. Craig lectr. U. Iowa, 1991, C.G. Khatri Meml. lectr. Pa. State U., 1992, George Zyskind Meml. lectr. Iowa State U., 1995. Fellow AAAS (chmn. sect. 1990-91), Am. Statis. Assn. (v.p. 1971-73, Samuel S. Wilks Meml. medal 1988, R.A. Fisher lectr. 1985), Econometric Soc., Royal Statis. Soc., Inst. Math. Stats. (pres. 1963), Am. Acad. Arts and Scis.; mem. NAS, Am. Math. Soc., Internat. Statis. Insts., Internat. Chinese Stats. Assn., Psychometric Soc. (coun. dirs.), Bernouilli Soc. for Math. Stats. and Probability, Norwegian Acad. Sci. and Letters (fgn.), Phi Beta Kappa. Achievements include research in multivariate statistical analysis, time series analysis, and econometrics. Home: 746 Santa Ynez St Stanford CA 94305-8441 Office: Stanford U Dept Stats Stanford CA 94305-4065 E-mail: twa@stat.stanford.edu

ANDERSON, BROTHER TIMOTHY MEL, academic administrator; b. Oakland, Calif., Sept. 28, 1928; BA, St. Mary's Coll., Moraga, Calif., 1952; DLitt, St. Albert's Coll., 1976; LHD, Lewis U., 1979; DHL (hon.), U. San Francisco, 1994; D in Pedagogy (hon.), Manhattan Coll., 1994. Tchr. Sacred Heart High Sch., San Francisco, 1952-56; vice prin. La Salle High Sch., Pasadena, Calif., 1956-62; prin. San Joaquin Meml. High Sch., Fresno, 1962-64; prin., superior St Mary's High Sch., Residence Sch., Grammar Sch., Berkeley, 1964-69; pres. St. Mary's Coll. of Calif., Moraga, 1969-97; dir. spl. projects Diocese of Oakland, Calif., 1999—. Trustee St. Mary's Coll., Moraga., 1968-97. Recipient Alemany award Dominican Sch. of Theology and Philosophy, 1992, Papal Pro Ecclesia medal, 1994, Disting. Lasallian Educator award, 1997; named Alumnus of Yr., St. Mary's Coll., 1987; inductee Contra Costa County Hall of Fame, 1988, Anti-Defamation League's Torch of Liberty award, 1993; named Citizen of Yr. town of Moraga, 1994. Fellow Assn. Ind. Calif. Colls. and Univs. (sr.; exec. com. 1973—, chmn. 1988, 89); mem. Regional Assn. East Bay Colls. and Univs. (chmn. 1979-81, 90-91), Fratres Scholarum Christianarum (entered order 1947). Democrat. Roman Catholic. Lodge: Rotary Internat. Avocations: photography, woodworking, travel, drama, music. Office: Oakland Diocese 2900 Lakeshore Ave Oakland CA 94610-3614

ANDERSON, W. FRENCH, biochemist, physician; b. Tulsa, Dec. 31, 1936; married, 1961. AB, Harvard U., 1958, MD, 1963; MA, Cambridge U., 1960; LHD (hon.), U. Okla., 1992. Intern pediatric medicine Children's Hosp. Med. Ctr., Boston, 1963-64; rsch. assoc. lab. biochem. genetics Nat. Heart, Lung & Blood Inst., 1965-67, rsch. med. officer, 1967-68, head sect. human biochem., 1968-71, head sect. molecular hematology, 1971-73, chief molecular hematology br., 1973-92; prof. biochemistry and pediatrics, dir. gene therapy labs. U. So. Calif. Norris Cancer Ctr., 1992—. Rsch. fellow bacteriology and immunology med. sch. Harvard U., 1964-65; prof. lectr. sch. medicine George Washington U., 1967-75; mem. faculty dept. genetics Grad. Program NIH, 1967-92, dept. medicine & physiology, 1981-92, chmn., 1984-92; mem. heart fellow bd. Nat. Heart & Lung Inst., 1968-70; mem. task force hemoglobinopathies Nat. Heart, Lung and Blood Inst. NIH, 1972, mem. nat. task group on Cooley's anemia, 1977-78, pres. assembly scientists, 1982, chmn. inter-inst. coord. com. on Cooley's anemia, 1972-77, mem. exec. com. bd. dirs. Found. Adv. Edu. in Sci., Inc., 1984-92, mem. working group human gene therapy recombinant DNA adv. com., 1984-86, mem. working group on viruses, 1985-86, hematology program dir. Lab. Molecular Hematology, 1985, mem. coord. com. human genome, 1988-92; chmn. inter-agy. coord. com. on Cooley's anemia HEW, 1975-77; mem. sr. exec. sci. svc. Dept. Health and Human Svc., 1980-92; cons. Pres. Commn. Study Ethical Problems Medicine & Biomed. Behavior Rsch., 1981-82, Human Gene Therapy Ctr. for Bioethics, Kennedy Inst. Ethics, Washington, 1982—; chmn. sci. adv. bd. Genetic Therapy Inc., Gaithersburg, Md., 1986-87, 92—; mem. sci. adv. bd. S/L Health Care Ventures, N.Y., 1986-88, 1993—; cons. human gene therapy St. Jude Childrens Rsch. Hosp., Memphis, 1990-92, U. Pitts., 1990-92; chmn. scientific adv. com. Children's Nat. Med. Ctr., Washington, 1990-92; lectr. Mider Lecture NIH, 1992, Timely Topics Lecture U.S. and Can. Acad. Pathology, 1992, Frontiers in Clin. Sci. Lecture Am. Fedn. Clin. Rsch., 1992, Myron Karon Meml. Lectureship Children's Hosp. L.A., 1992, Disting. Sci. Lecture Internat. and Am. Assns. Dental Rsch., 1993, Plenary Lecture 17th Internat. Congress of Genetics, 1993, Martin Meml. Lecture 79th Ann. Clin. Congress Am. Coll. [illegible], 1993, Plenary Lecture Am. Acad. Pediatrics, 1993. Co-editor: Fifth Cooley's Anemia Symposium, 1985. Mem. med. resources coun. Cooley's Anemia Blood & Rsch. Found for Children, 1974-77; mem. adv. bd. Cooley's Anemia Found., Inc., 1977—; mem. sci. adv. com. Children's Hosp. Rsch. Found., Cin., 1985-88. Recipient Thomas B. Cooley award Sci. Achievement Cooley's Anemia Blood & Rsch. Found. for Children, 1977, Mary Ann Liebert Biotherapeutic award, 1991, Pres. Award lectr. Am. Thoracic Soc., 1991, Maude L. Menten award U. Pitts., 1991, Ralph R. Braund award U. Tenn., 1991, Presdl. Meritorious Exec. Rank award HHS, 1991, Fed. Lab. Consortium award for Excellence in Tech. Transfer, 1992, Disting. Svc. award Nat. Ctr. Infectious Diseases, 1993, Dr. Murray Thelin award Nat. Hemophilia Found., 1993, Drew award lectr., 1993, King Faisal ibn Abdul Aziz Internat. Prize for Medicine, 1994, NORD Leadership award Nat. Orgn. Rare Disorders, 1996; named BioPharm Person of Yr. Biopharm Mag. editl. adv. bd., 1994. Fellow AAAS; mem. Assn. Am. Physicians, Am. Soc. Clin. Investigators, Am. Soc. Hematology, Am. Soc. Human Genetics, Am. Soc. Biol. Chemistry, Am. Fedn. Clin. Rsch. Achievements include research in regulation of RNA and protein synthesis, hemoglobin biosynthesis, thalassemia and hemoglobinopathies, gene expression in mammalian cells, genetic engineering of mammalian cells, human gene therapy. Office: U So Calif Sch Medicine Norris Cancer Ctr 1441 Eastlake Ave Rm 6316 Los Angeles CA 90089-0001

ANDERSON, WAYNE CARL, public affairs officer, former corporate executive; b. Sheboygan, Wis., May 5, 1935; s. Chester Phillip and Mabel Mary (Edler) A.; m. Joan Dorothy Staranick, May 18, 1963; children: David Wayne, Steven Michael, Karen Colleen. BS in Bus. Adminstrn., Upsala Coll., 1977. Cert. arbitrator, mediator. Dir. state govt. rels. Nabisco Brands Co., Parsippany, N.J., 1974-78, dir. fed. govt. rels., 1978-79, dir. govt. rels., 1979-81, v.p. govt. rels., 1981-84, v.p. govt. and cmty. rels., 1984-87, v.p. pub. affairs, 1987; non-lawyer exec. Evans Kitchel & Jenckes, P.C., 1988-89; pres., CEO Ariz. C. of C., 1990-95; exec. v.p. Americare, 1996-98; exec. emeritus Thunderbird--The Am. Grad. Sch. Internat. Mgmt., 1999—. Guest lectr. in field. Editl. adv. bd. Pub. Affairs in Rev., 1980; contbr. articles to profl. jours. Mem. Roseland (N.J.) Planning Bd., 1978-79; mem. Roseland Citizens Adv. Com., 1977-78; pres. Grace Luth. Ch., Livingston, N.J., 1980-81, chmn. bd. elders, 1981-82; trustee State Govt. Rsch. and Edn. Found., 1981-82; mem. gov.'s adv. coun. on quality, 1991-95, gov.'s commn. econ. devel., 1991-95; mem. Ariz. Space Commn., 1992-2000, commr. emeritus, 1996; bd. dirs. Quality Alliance, 1992-95, Nat. Conf. Christians and Jews, Fiesta Bowl Com., Ariz. Econ. Forum, Ariz. Utility Investors; statewide com. chmn. Superbowl XXX, 1995-96; elder Redeemer Luth. Ch., Scottsdale, Ariz., 1997-98, v.p., 1998—; chmn. adv. bd. NYU, Baruch Coll., U. N.Y.. Served with U.S. Army, 1958-60. Mem. Internat. Jaycees (senator 1989—), U.S. Jaycees (nat. dir. 1964-65), Pub. Affairs Coun. (exec. com. 1986, bd. dirs. 1988—), Nat. Fgn. Trade Coun. (dir. 1986), State Govt. Affairs Coun. (past pres. 1978-79), Ford's Theatre (bd. govs.), Acad. Polit. Sci., Pub. Affairs Profls. Ariz. (founder 1987—), World Affairs Coun. (pres. 1994-95), Thunderbird Am. Grad. Sch. Internat. Mgmt., Thunderbird Global Coun. E-mail: azwca@worldnet.att.net

ANDERSON, WHITNEY, state legislator; married; 1 child. Owner Whitney, Inc., 1961—; mem. Hawaiian Senate, Honolulu, 1994—, mem. ways and means com., mem. jud. com., mem. health and human svcs. com., mem. water, land, and Hawaiian affairs com., mem. govt. ops. and housing com. Mem. Kailua C. of C., Native Hawaiian C. of C., Portuguese C. of C., Kailua Hawaiian Civic Club, Assn. Hawaiian Civic Clubs, Elks. Republican. Office: State Capitol 415 S Beretania St Honolulu HI 96813-2407

ANDERSON, WILLIAM SCOVIL, classics educator; b. Brookline, Mass., Sept. 16, 1927; s. Edgar Weston and Katrina (Brewster) A.; m. Lorna Candee Bassette, June 12, 1954 (dec. Dec. 1977); children: Judith, Blythe, Heather, Meredith, Keith; m. Deirdre Burt, May 28, 1983. BA, Yale U., 1950, PhD, 1954; AB, Cambridge (Eng.) U., (Eng.), 1952; MA, Cambridge (Eng.) U., 1955. Prix de Rome fellow Am. Acad. in Rome, 1954-55; instr. classics Yale U., 1955-59; resident in Rome, Morse fellow, 1959-60; mem. faculty U. Calif., Berkeley, 1960-94, prof. Latin and comparative lit., 1966-94, prof. charge Intercollegiate Ctr. Classical Studies, 1967-68, chmn. classics, 1970-73. Rsch. prof. U. Melbourne, 1984; Robson lectr. Victoria Coll., Toronto, 1987; Blegen rsch. prof. Vassar Coll., 1989-90, vice chair comparative lit., 1990-93; vis. disting. prof. Fla. State U., spring 1995; Gail Burnett lectr. San Diego State U., 2001. Author: The Art of the Aeneid, 1969, Ovid, Metamorphoses, Critical Text, 1977, Essays on Roman Satire, 1982, Barbarian Play: Plautus' Roman Comedy, 1993, Ovid's Metamorphoses 1-5 Text and Commentary, 1997, Why Horace?, 1998. Served with AUS, 1946-48, Korea. Recipient Berkeley citation, 1994; NEH sr. fellow, 1973-74. Mem. Am. Philol. Assn. (pres. 1977), Danforth Assocs., Soc. Religion Episcopalian. Office: Univ Calif Dept Classics Berkeley CA 94720-0001 E-mail: wsa@socrates.berkeley.edu

ANDERSON, WILLIAM WALLACE, financial executive; b. Balt., Apr. 8, 1958; s. Joseph Merryman II and Ann Marie (Moran) Anderson; m. Marian A. Gannon, July 24, 1987; children: Ciara Ann, Deirdre Christine. BA in Acctg., U. West Fla., 1980. CPA, Md., Calif. Audit staff to supr. Coopers & Lybrand, Balt., 1980-85, audit mgr. Dublin, Ireland, 1985-87, Sacramento, 1987-89; dir. of fin. acctg. Raley's Supermarkets, Sacramento, 1989-90, dir. acctg., 1990-92, v.p., contr., 1992—. Bd. dirs., CFO Food for Families, Sacramento, 1990—. Mem. AICPA. Avocations: travel, basketball, tennis. Office: Raleys Supermarkets 500 W Capitol Ave West Sacramento CA 95605

ANDRASICK, JAMES STEPHEN, agribusiness company executive; b. Passaic, N.J., Mar. 27, 1944; s. Stephen Adam and Emily (Spolnik) A.; children: Christopher J., Gregory O.; m. Ginger Michael Simon, Feb. 22, 1997. BS, USCG Acad., 1965; MS, MIT, 1971. Commd. ensign USCG, 1965, advanced through grades to lt., 1968; assigned to Vietnam, 1967-68; resigned, 1969; sys. analyst Jamesbury Corp., 1970; corp. fin. and product devel. staffs Ford Motor Co., 1971-74; mgr. corp. devel. IU Internat. Corp., Phila., 1974-78; from v.p. planning, contr. to exec. v.p. C. Brewer & Co., Ltd., Honolulu, 1978-92, pres., 1992-2000; sr. v.p., CFO, treas. Alexander & Baldwin, Inc., Honolulu, 2000—; also bd. dirs. C. Brewer & Co., Ltd., Honolulu. Chmn. bd., mng. gen. ptnr. ML Macadamia Orchards LP, 1986-88; chmn. bd. HCPC, Olokele Sugar Co., Hawaiian Sugar and Transp. Coop., 1993-96; chmn. Hawaiian Sugar Planters Assn., 1992-93; bd. dirs. Wailuku Agribus. Co. Bd. dirs. Aloha United Way, Honolulu, 1983-89, Hawaii Opera Theater, Coast Guard Found.; treas., bd. dirs. ARC, Hawaii, 1983-94, 96—, chmn., 1989-90; bd. dirs. Hawaii Employers Coun., 1992-98, chmn., 1995-98; trustee UH Found., 1988-94, vice chmn., 1992-93, chmn., 1993-94; trustee Hawaii Maritime Ctr., 1993-98; bd. dirs. Coast Guard Found., Hawaii Opera Theater. Office: Alexander & Baldwin Inc PO Box 3440 Honolulu HI 96801-3440

ANDRE, MICHAEL PAUL, physicist, educator; b. Des Moines, Apr. 25, 1951; s. Paul Leo and Pauline (Vermie) A.; m. Janice Joan Hanecak, Mar. 12, 1988. BA, Cen. U. Iowa, 1972; postgrad., U. Ariz., 1972-73; MS, UCLA, 1975, PhD, 1980; cert., Am. Bd. Radiology, 1999. Rsch. assoc. Inst. Atmospheric Physics, Tucson, 1972-73; mem. tech. staff Hughes Aircraft Co., L.A., 1973-74, postgrad. researcher UCLA, 1974-77; cons. L.A., 1975-84; med. radiologic physicist LACO/UCLA Olive View, L.A., 1977-81; sr. radiation physicist Cedars-Sinai Med. Ctr., L.A., 1979-84; chief med. physicist Dept. Vet. Affairs, San Diego, 1981—; prof. radiology, chief divsn.Physics and Engring, sch. medicine U. Calif., La Jolla, 1981—; chief scientific officer Radco Corp., 1996—; chief med. officer Almen Labs., Inc., 1999—. Qualified expert Calif. Radiol. Health Dept., Berkeley, 1979—, chmn. Nat. Physics Conf., San Diego, 1984-89. Editor: Physics and Biology of Radiology, 1988, Investigative Radiology, 1990—; guest editor: Internat. Jour. Imaging Sci. & Tech., 1997; contbr. articles to profl. jours. Mountain guide Sierra Club, L.A., 1977-80; dir. Ariz. PIRG, Tucson, 1973; mountain guide Am. Alpine Inst., Peru, 1987-90. Rsch. grantee U. Calif.-San Diego Found., 1989—, NIH,, Nat. Cancer Inst., 1986—, VA, 1989—, U.S. Army, 1994—. Mem. Am. Assn. Physicists in Medicine, Am. Inst. Ultrasound in Medicine, San Diego Radiol. Soc., Am. Inst. Physics, Soc. Photo-Optical Inst. Engrs., Am. Coll. Radiology, Soc. of Breast Imaging. Avocation: Himalayan and Andean expeditions. Office: U Calif Dept Radiology 9114 La Jolla CA 92093 E-mail: mandre@ucsd.edu

ANDREASEN, STEVEN W. lawyer; b. Salt Lake City, Sept. 17, 1948; BA, U. Utah, 1970, JD, 1974. Bar: Washington 1974. Mem. Davis Wright Tremaine, Seattle, 1974—. Comment Editor: Utah Law Review 1973-74. Mem. Seattle Estate Planning Coun., Order of Coif, Am. Coll. Trust and Estate Counsel. Office: Davis Wright Tremaine LLP 2600 Century Sq 1501 4th Ave Ste 2600 Seattle WA 98101-1688

ANDREASON, JOHN C. state legislator; b. Idaho Falls, Idaho, Apr. 20, 1929; m. Darlene Andreason; children: Tom, Dale, Karen, Lori. Student, Idaho State U.; BS in Polit. Sci., U. Idaho. Mem. Idaho Senate, Dist. 15, Boise, 1995—; vice chair edn. com., mem. resources and environ. com. Idaho Senate, Boise, mem. commerce and human resources com. Ret. Legis. Budget Office; former mem. Arco City Coun. With USAF. Mem. Nat. Conf. State Legis. (past staff chair), Nat. Fiscal Officers Assn. (pres.), Lions (past dep. dist. gov.). Republican. Office: State Capitol PO Box 83720 Boise ID 83720-3720

ANDREESSEN, MARC, communications company executive; BS in Computer Sci., U. Ill., 1993. Co-founder, v.p. tech. Netscape Comms. Corp., Mountain View, Calif., 1994-97, co-founder, exec. v.p., 1997-99; chief tech. officer AOL, 1999; co-founder, chmn. Loudcloud, 1999—. Office: Loudcloud Inc 599 N Mathilda Ave Sunnyvale CA 94085-3545

ANDREOS, GEORGE PHILLIP, lawyer; b. Chgo., Jan. 20, 1935; s. Nicholas and Harriet (MacKenzie) A.; m. Beverly Chadwell, Aug. 28, 1965; children: Leslie, Linda, Darin, Craig. BA, U. Ill., 1957; JD, Calif. Western Sch. Law, San Diego, 1964. Bar: Calif. (so. dist., 9th cir.), 1965. Dep. city atty. City of San Diego, 1965-66; sole practitioner San Diego, 1966—. Contbr. articles to profl. jours. Bd. dirs. For Parents' and Kids' Sake, Poway, Calif., 1984-92. Capt. USMC, 1957-60. Mem. San Diego County Bar Assn. (treas. 1989, v.p. 1990, pres. 1991), Calif. Trial Lawyers Assn. (bd. govs. 1979-83), San Diego Trial Lawyers Assn. (bd. dirs. 1977-82, pres. 1981), Outstanding Trial Lawyer 1982), Consumer Attys. San Diego (bd. dirs. 2000—). Avocations: handball, hiking, avocado and grapefruit grower. Office: 11405 W Bernardo Ct Ste 203 San Diego CA 92127-1639 Fax: 858-675-8695. E-mail: GAndreos@aol.com

ANDREW, JANE HAYES, non-profit organization executive; b. Phila., Jan. 1, 1947; d. David Powell and Vivian Muriel (Seager) Hayes; m. Brian David Andrew, June 14, 1977; 1 child, Kevin Hayes. AB, Barnard Coll., 1968; grad., Harvard Arts Adminstrn. Inst., 1972; MBA, U. Wash., 1994. Mgr. theater Minor Latham Playhouse, Barnard Coll., N.Y.C., 1970-74; co. mgr. Houston Ballet, 1974-77, Ballet West, Salt Lake City, 1978-83; gen. mgr. Pacific N.W. Ballet, Seattle, 1983-87. Organizer non-profit consortium nat. ballet cos. and nat. presenting orgns., 1987; pres., exec. dir. Ballet/America, 1988-91; ind. cons. arts mgmt., 1991-94; dir. Found. for Internat. Understanding Through Students, 1995-97; panelist NEA Dance Program Presentors, 1987-88, 88-89, 89-90, Seattle Arts Commn. dance grants, 1989, 90; cons. Ariz. Arts Commn., Phoenix, 1985-86; com. mem. 25th Anniversary of World's Fair, Seattle, 1986-87; panelist NEA Local Programs, 1987; vol. Interlace H.S., 1997. Editor (directory) Philadelphia Cultural Orgns., 1977. Bd. dirs. Good Shepherd Adv. Bd., Seattle, 1985-87. Recipient Dorothy D. Spivack award Barnard Coll., 1972. Mem. Dance/USA (chmn. mgrs. coun. 1986). Home and Office: 7706 146th Ave NE Redmond WA 98052-4105

ANDREW, LUCIUS ARCHIBALD DAVID, III, bank executive; b. Mar. 5, 1938; s. Lucius Archibald David Jr. and Victoria (Rollins) A.; m. Susan Ott, June 1, 1963 (div. 1973); children: Ashley W., L.A. David IV; m. Phoebe Haffner Kellogg, Dec. 21, 1974; children: Gaylord M., Charles H., Matthew K., Louise K. BS, U. Pa., 1962; MBA, NYU, 1965. Asst. treas. The Bank of N.Y., N.Y.C., 1962-68; instl. salesman Drexel, Harriman, Ripley, N.Y.C., 1968-70; v.p., br. mgr. Drexel, Firestone, Inc., Chgo., 1970-72; ptnr., br. mgr. Fannestock & Co., Chgo., 1972-74; pres. N.E.A., Inc., 1975-85; dir. First Am. Bank Corp., Seattle, 1985—. Vice chmn. Viner's, Ltd., Sheffield, Eng., 1981-82; chmn. exec. com. Cert. Mfg. Co., Shelton, Wash., 1975-85; bd. dirs. First Am. Bank, Chgo., 1965-91, chmn., 1982-91; bd. dirs. First Am. Data Corp.; chmn. FGI, Inc., Forest Grove, Oreg., 1985-86, Union St. Capital Corp., Seattle, Wash., 1986-87, Brudi Inc., Seattle, 1988-90. Trustee Brooks Sch.; past trustee Seattle Repertory Theatre; bd. dirs The Found. for Lifetime Advocacy and Guardian Svcs., Swedish Met. Ctr. Cound., chmn. Mem. The Brook, Racquet and Tennis Club (N.Y.C.), Racquet Club (Chgo.), Rainier Club, Univ. Club, Golf Club (Seattle), Tennis Club (Seattle). Home: The Highlands Seattle WA 98177 Office: 200 1st Ave W Ste 400 Seattle WA 98119-4219

ANDREWS, CHARLES, wholesale distribution executive; Ceo, pres. Sunbelt Beverage, Lutherville, Md., 1997—; ceo Young's Market, Orange, Calif. Office: Young's Market 2164 N Batavia St Orange CA 92865-3109

ANDREWS, DAVID RALPH, lawyer; b. Oakland, Calif., Jan. 4, 1942; m. Rozan McCurdy, July 1, 1962; children: David, Linda. BA, U. Calif., Berkeley, 1968; JD, U. Calif., 1971. Bar: Calif. 1971, D.C. 1986, U.S. Dist. Ct. (no. dist.) Calif. 1971, U.S. Dist. Ct. Hawaii 1991, U.S. Supreme Ct. 1980. Assoc. McCutchen, Doyle, Brown & Enersen, San Francisco, 1971-75; regional counsel Reg. IX U.S. EPA, San Francisco, 1975-77; legal counsel and spl. asst. for policy U.S. EPA, Washington, 1977-79; dep. gen. counsel Dept. Health and Human Svcs., Washington, 1980-81; ptnr. McCutchen, Doyle, Brown & Enersen, San Francisco, 1981-97, chmn., 1991-95; legal adviser U.S. Dept. State, Washington, 1997-2000; ptnr. McCutchen, Doyle, Brown & Enersen, San Francisco, 2000—. Amb., spl. negotiator U.S./Iran Claims, 2000—; bd. dirs. Union Bank Calif., Kaiser Permanente, NetCel360 Holdings Ltd., PG&E Corp. Trustee San Francisco Mus. of Modern Art, 1988-97; bd. trustees Golden Gate Nat. Park Assn., 1992-95, Marin Cmty. Found., 1996-97; mem. U.S. Agy. for Internat. Devel. Energy Tng. Program Adv. Com. of the Inst. Internat. Edn.; mem. bd. dirs. Union Bank Calif., Kaiser Permanente and NetCel360 Holdings Ltd., 2000—. Fellow Max Planck Inst. of Pub. Internat. Law, Heidelberg, Fed. Republic of Germany, 1974. Mem. ABA (natural resources sect.), Calif. Bar Assn.), San Francisco Bar Assn. Avocations: photography, tennis, running. Office: McCutchen Doyle Brown & Enersen 3 Embarcadero Ctr San Francisco CA 94111-4003

ANDREWS, DONALD L. performing arts company executive; Pres., CEO Utah Symphony, Salt Lake City. Office: Utah Symphony Maurice Abravanel Hall 123 W South Temple Salt Lake City UT 84101-1496

ANDREWS, FRED CHARLES, mathematics educator; b. Aylesbury, Sask., Can., July 13, 1924; s. Henry Marmaduke and Margaret (Van de Bogart) A.; m. Joyce Davenny, Apr. 5, 1944; children— Linda (Mrs. Pierre Dunn), David W. (dec.), Gail E.(Mrs. Gregory Crandell). BS in Math, U. Wash., 1946, MS in Math. Statistics, 1948; PhD, U. Calif., Berkeley, 1953; PhD (hon.), U. Tampere, Finland, 1985. Research asso. Applied Math. and Statistics Lab., Stanford, 1952-54; asst. prof. math., asso. statistician U. Nebr., 1954-57; asso. prof. math. U. Oreg., 1957-66; dir. U. Oreg. (Statistics Lab. and Computing Center), 1960-69, prof. math., 1966-89, prof. emeritus math., 1989—, head dept. math., 1973-80. Vis. statistician Math Centrum, Amsterdam, The Netherlands, 1963-64; Fulbright-Hays sr. lectr. U. Tampere, Finland, 1969-70; Fulbright-Hays sr. lectr. Univ. Coll., Cork, Ireland, 1976-77; Fulbright sr. lectr. U. Jordan, Amman, 1983-84 Contbr. articles to profl. jours. Pres. Met.-Civic Club, Eugene-Springfield, 1967-68; Trustee Oreg. Grad. Center, 1967-77. Served to lt. (j.g.) USNR, 1943-46. Fellow AAAS; mem. Sigma Xi. Office: U Oreg Dept Math Eugene OR 97403

ANDREWS, J. DAVID, lawyer; b. Decatur, Ill., July 5, 1933; s. Jesse D. and Louise Glenna (Mason) A.; m. Helen Virginia Migely, July 12, 1958; children: Virginia, Robert, Michael, Betsy. BA magna cum laude, U. Ill., 1955, JD with honors, 1960. Bar: Wash. 1961. Ptnr. Perkins Coie, Seattle, 1960-96, counsel, 1997—. Bd. dirs., v.p. Am. Bar Ins. Plans Cons., Inc., 1991—, also bd. dirs.; pres. Wash. Law Fund, 1997-98; bd. dirs. Cornish Inst., Seattle, 1977-83, pres. 1981-83; bd. dirs. Am. Bar Endowment, 1981-94, pres. 1985-87; bd. visitors U. Puget Sound Law Sch., 1976-94; trustee AEF Pension Fund, 1975-79. Contbr. articles to profl. jours. Bd. dirs. Leukemia Soc. Wash., 1984-99, pres. 1985-91; nat. bd. dirs. Leukemia Soc. Am., 1992-96. Capt. USAF, 1955-57. Fellow Am. Bar Found. (bd. dirs., former treas.), Am. Coll. Trial Lawyers; mem. ABA (ho. of dels. 1967-69, 75—, asst. treas. 1972-74, treas. 1975-79, bd. govs. 1975-79, bd. dirs. Am. Bar Found., fed. judiciary standing com. 1985-90), Wash. Bar Assn. (chmn. pub. rels. com. 1971-73), Seattle-King County Bar Assn., Am. Judicature Soc. (bd. dirs. 1985-89), Phi Beta Kappa, Phi Kappa Phi, Phi Eta Sigma. Home: 9413 SW Quartermaster Dr Vashon WA 98070-7081 Office: Perkins Coie 1201 3rd Ave Ste 4000 Seattle WA 98101-3029 E-mail: daveandhelen@attglobal.net, andrj@perkinscoie.com

ANDREWS, JOHN, state legislator; b. Allegan, Mich., May 1, 1944; m. Donna Andrews. Head Independence Inst., 1985-92; mem. Colo. Senate, Dist. 27, Denver, 1998; vice-chmn. edn. com., mem. fin. com., mem. judiciary com. Republican. Home: PMB J122 8547 E Arapahoe Rd Englewood CO 80112-1436 Office: State Capitol 200 E Colfax Ave Ste 346 Denver CO 80203-1716 E-mail: andrewsjk@aol.com

ANDREWS, JOHN H. communications executive; BS in Acctg., Ariz. State U. CPA, Ariz. Prin. acctg. officer, corp. controller MicroAge Logistics Group, 1988-90, v.p., CFO, 1990-93, pres., 1993-98; exec. v.p., COO MicroAge Telesvcs., Inc., Tempe, Ariz., 1998-99, pres., 1999—. Office: MicroAge Telesvcs Inc 2400 S Microage Way Tempe AZ 85282-1896

ANDREWS, RICHARD OTIS, museum director; b. L.A., Nov. 8, 1949; s. Robert and Theodora (Hammond) A.; m. Colleen Chartier, Jan. 3, 1976; 1 child, Bryce. BA, Occidental Coll., L.A., 1971; BFA, U. Wash., 1973, MFA, 1975. Project mgr. Art in Pub. Places, Seattle Arts Commn., 1978-80, coord., 1980-84; dir. visual arts program Nat. Endowment for Arts, Washington, 1985-87; dir. Henry Art Gallery, U. Wash., Seattle, 1987—. Co-curator Art Into Life: Russian Constructivism 1914-1932; cons. pub. art program devel., 1982-84; bd. trustees Assn. Art Mus. Dirs., 1997-2000. Author: Insights/On Sites, 1984, James Turrell: Sensing Space, 1992; editor Artwork/Network, 1984; contbg. editor Going Public, 1988. Office: U Wash Henry Art Gallery PO Box 351410 Seattle WA 98195-1410

ANDREWS, ROBERT GOFF, pediatrician, medical educator; b. Mpls., Jan. 28, 1949; s. James Edward and Marie Adelaide (Jones) A.; m. Carol Ann Chellino, July 1, 1979; 1 child, Joseph Einar. AB, Amherst Coll., 1972; MD, U. Minn., 1976. Diplomate Am. Bd. Pediats., Am. Bd. Pediat. Hematology and Oncology, Nat. Bd. Med. Examiners. Intern in pediats. New Eng. Med. Ctr., Boston, 1976-77, resident in pediats., 1977-79; fellow in pediat. hematology and oncology U. Wash. Sch. Medicine and Fred Hutchinson Cancer Rsch. Ctr., Seattle, 1979-83; pediats. instr. Sch. Medicine U. Wash., Seattle, 1983-84, asst. prof. Sch. Medicine, 1984-90, assoc. prof. Sch. Medicine, 1990—; dir. transp. and stem cell biology Wash. Regional Primate Rsch. Ctr., Seattle, 2000—. Presenter more than 50 papers and abstracts at sci. and med. meetings. Contbr. more than 150 articles and abstracts to profl. jours. Grantee Am. Cancer Soc., 1979-80, among others; fellow Am. Cancer Soc., 1983-86. Office: Fred Hutchinson Cancer Rsch Ctr 1100 Fairview Ave N Seattle WA 98109-4417

ANDRUS, CECIL DALE, academic administrator; b. Hood River, Oreg., Aug. 25, 1931; s. Hal Stephen and Dorothy (Johnson) A.; m. Carol Mae May, Aug. 27, 1949; children: Tana Lee, Tracy Sue, Kelly Kay. Student, Oreg. State U., 1948-49; LLD (hon.), Gonzaga U., U. Idaho, U. N.Mex., Coll. Idaho, Idaho State U., Whitman Coll. State gen. mgr. Paul Revere Life Ins. Co., 1969-70; gov. State of Idaho, 1971-77, 87-95; sec. of interior, 1977-81; chmn. Andrus Ctr. for Pub. Policy, Boise (Idaho) State U., 1995—. Bd. dirs. KeyCorp., Albertson's, Inc., Coeur d'Alene Mines; mem. Idaho Senate, 1961-66, 69-70; mem. exec. com. Nat. Gov.'s Conf., 1971-72, chmn., 1976; chmn. Fedn. Rocky Mountain States, 1971-72. Author: Cecil Andrus: Politics Western Style, 1998. Chmn. bd. trustees Coll. of Idaho, 1985-89; bd. dirs. Sch. Forestry, Duke U. With USN, 1951-55. Recipient Disting. Citizen award Oreg. State U., 1980, Collier County Conservancy medal, 1979, Ansel Adams award Wilderness Soc., 1985, Audubon medal, 1985, Statesman of the Yr. award Idaho State U., 1990, Torch of Liberty award B'nai B'rith, 1991, William Penn Mott award, Nat. Parks Conservation Assn., 2000; named Conservationist of Yr. Nat. Wildlife Fedn., 1980, Idaho Wildlife Fedn., 1972, Man of Yr., VFW, 1959. Mem. VFW, Idaho Taxpayers Assn. (bd. dirs. 1964-66). Democrat. Office: Boise State U Andrus Ctr Pub Policy 1910 University Dr Boise ID 83725-0399

ANG, ALFREDO HUA-SING, civil engineering educator; b. Davao, The Philippines, June 4, 1930; came to U.S., 1955; s. Tiong Ang and Khio Tan; m. Myrtle Mae Ang; children: Evelyn, Irene, James. BSCE, Mapua Inst. Tech., Manila, 1954; MS, U. Ill., 1957, Phd, 1959. Registered structural engr., Ill. From asst. prof. to prof. U. Ill., Urbana, 1959-65, prof., 1965-88, U. Calif., Irvine, 1988—. Cons. NRC, Washington, 1979—, Ea. Internat. Engrs., Lafayette, Calif., 1983-90, Internat. Civil Engring Cons., Berkeley, Calif., 1992—; sr. tech. adviser Kajima Corp., Tokyo, 1984—, Tokyo Elec. Power Svcs. Co., 1987—; MCA engr. Mobil Offshore Base. Author: Probability Concepts in Engineering Planning and Design, Vol. I, 1975, Vol. II, 1984; editor Jour. Structural Engring., 1986—; mem. editorial bd. Jour. Structural Mechanics, 1971-84, Structural Safety, 1982—, Probabilistic Engring. Mechanics, 1985—, Reliability Engring. and System Safety, 1992—, Internat. Jour. Structural Engring. and Mechanics, 1992—; contbr. numerous articles to profl. jours. Recipient Sr. Rsch. award Am. Soc. Engring. Edn., 1983, Disting. Rsch. award U. Calif.-Irvine Alumni Assn., 1993. Fellow ASME, ASCE (chmn. STD EXCOM, internat. dir. 1998—, rsch. prize 1968, State-of-Art award 1973, Freudenthal medal 1982, Newmark medal 1988, hon. mem. 1991, Ernest Howard award 1996), AIAA (assoc.); mem. NAE, Earthquake Engring. Rsch. Inst., Seismol. Soc. Am., Soc. Naval Architects and Marine Engrs., Internat. Assn. for Structural Safety and Reliability (pres. 1985-89, Rsch. prize 1993). Home: 5311 154th Ave SE Bellevue WA 98006-5151 Office: U Calif Dept Civil Engring Irvine CA 92697-0001 E-mail: ahang2@aol.com

ANGEL, ARTHUR RONALD, lawyer, consultant; b. Long Beach, Calif., May 10, 1948; s. Morris and Betty Estelle (Unger) A.; 1 child, Jamie Kathryn. BA, U. Calif.-Berkeley, 1969; JD, Harvard U., 1972. Bar: Mass. 1972, D.C. 1975, Okla. 1979, Calif. 2001, U.S. Dist. Ct. (we. dist.) Okla. 1980, U.S. Dist. Ct. (no. dist.) Okla. 1981, U.S. Dist. Ct. (ctrl. dist.) Calif. 2001, U.S. Supreme Ct. 1983. Atty. FTC, Washington, 1972-78; pvt. practice Oklahoma City, 1978-87; ptnr. Angel & Ikard, Oklahoma City, 1987-93; of counsel Abel, Musser Sokolosky & Assoc., L.A., 1994-2000; ptnr. Carrick Law Group, L.A., 2001—. Mem. adv. panel on cardiovascular devices, Washington, 1979-82; cons. FTC, 1978-79; adminstrv. law judge Okla. Dept. Labor, 1999-2000; spl. mcpl. judge City of Oklahoma City, 1999-2001. Recipient Meritorious Service award FTC, Washington, 1978. Fellow Inst. Law and Social Scis.; mem. Am. Arbitration Assn., Assn. Trial Lawyers Am., Okla. Trial Lawyers Assn., Okla. Bar Assn., D.C. Bar Assn., Mass. Bar Assn. Democrat. Jewish. Home: 1236 N Fairfax Ave Los Angeles CA 90046 Office: Carrick Law Group 350 S Grand Ave Ste 2930 Los Angeles CA 90071-3406 E-mail: art@carricklawgroup.com

ANGEL, JAMES ROGER PRIOR, astronomer; b. St. Helens, Eng., Feb. 7, 1941; came to U.S., 1967; s. James Lee and Joan (Prior) A.; m. Ellinor M. Goonan, Aug. 21, 1965; children: Jennifer, James. B.A., Oxford (Eng.) U., 1963, D.Phil., 1967; M.S., Calif. Inst. Tech., 1966. From rsch. assoc. to assoc. prof. physics Columbia U., 1967-74; prof. astronomy U. Ariz., 1975—, prof. optical sci., 1984—, Regents prof., 1990—. Sloan fellow, 1970-74; hon. fellow St. Peter's Coll., Oxford U.; MacArthur fellow, 1996. Fellow Royal Soc., Royal Astron. Soc., Am. Acad. Arts and Scis.; mem. NAS, Am. Astron. Soc. (v.p. 1987-90, Pierce prize 1976). Achievements include research on white dwarf stars, quasars, the search for extra-solar planetary systems, astronomical mirrors, telescopes and their instruments, and adaptive optics. Office: Univ Ariz Steward Obs Tucson AZ 85721-0001

ANGELOFF, DANN VALENTINO, investment banking executive; b. Hollywood, Calif., Nov. 15, 1935; m. Jo Jeanne Ahlstrom, Sept. 26, 1964; children: Jennifer J., Dann V., Julie A. BS in Fin., U. So. Calif., 1958, MBA, 1963. Trainee Dean Witter & Co., Inc., L.A., 1957-60; v.p. Dempsey-Tegeler & Co., Inc., L.A., 1960-70; mng. dir. West Coast corp. fin. dept. Reynolds Securities, Inc., L.A., 1970-76; pres., bd. dirs. The Angeloff Co., L.A., 1976—. Bd. dirs. Aremissoft Corp., London, Eng., Ready Pac Produce, Irwin Dale, Calif. , Pub. Storage, Glendale, Calif., Nicholas-Applegate Fund, San Diego, Royce Med. Co., Westlake, Calif., Balboa Capital Corp., Newport Beach, Calif., XDimensionalTechs., Inc., Brea, Calif.; chmn. bd. Marshall Assocs./Univ. So. Calif. Trustee U. So. Calif., 1979-86, univ. counselor; bd. dirs., chmn. Trojan Bd. Govs., 1990-92. Mem. Bond Club L.A., Commerce Assocs. U. So. Calif., Skull and Dagger, Cardinal and Gold, Calif. Club, Pacific Club, Valley Hunt Club, San Marino City Club, Kappa Beta Phi. Office: The Angeloff Co 727 W 7th St Los Angeles CA 90017-3707

ANKA, PAUL, singer, composer; b. Ottawa, Ont., Can., July 30, 1941; came to U.S., 1959; s. Andrew Emile and Camilia (Tannis) A.; m. Anne Alison de Zogheb, Feb. 16, 1963; children: Alexandra, Amanda, Alicia, Anthea, Amelia. Grad. high sch., Ottawa; Doctorate Music (hon.), St. Johns U., N.Y.C., 1981. Owner, prin. Spanka Music Corp., 1958—, Flanka Music Corp., 1958—, Camy Prodns., Inc., 1961-66. Internat. performer, 1956— ; films include The Longest Day, 1961 (also wrote title song), Girl's Town, Look in Any Window, Captain Ron, 1992, Ordinary Magic, 1993, Shake, Rattle and Rock!, 1994, Mr. Playback: An Interactive Movie, 1995, Mad Dog Time, 1996, 3000 miles to Graceland, 1999, TV film Perry Mason: The Case of the Maligned Mobster, 1991; TV appearances include Larry King Live, Barbara Walters, The View, Ed Sullivan Show, Danny Thomas, Perry Como, Johnny Carson, Dean Martin, Hollywood Palace, Open Mind, Atlantic City U.S.A, Happy Birthday, America, 1976, Sinatra— The First Forty Years; appeared syndicated variety show, 1973; replacement in Broadway mus. What Makes Sammy Run?, 1954; appeared at Copacabana, N.Y.C., Sands Hotel, Caesars Palace, Hilton Hotel, all Las Vegas, Caribe Hilton Hotel, San Juan, P.R., Paladium, London, Olympia, Paris, Uris, N.Y.C., Waldorf Astoria, N.Y.C., Golden Nugget Hotels, Las Vegas and Atlantic City; participated San Remo Music Festival, 1964; recs. include My Way, 1968, (You're) Having My Baby, 1974, One Man Woman/One Woman Man, 1974, I Don't Like To Sleep Alone, 1975, (I Believe) There's Nothing Stronger Than Our Love, 1975, Times of Your Life, 1975, Anytime (I'll Be There), 1976, Happier, 1976, My Best Friend's Wife, 1977, Everybody Ought To Be in Love, 1977, Both Sides of Love, Headlines; wrote: (with Burt Bacharach) score for film Together?, 1979; composer Diana, 1957, Crazy Love, Lonely Boy, 1959, Put Your Head on My Shoulder, 1959, Time to Cry, 1959, The Longest Day, 1962, Ogni Volta, 1964, Do I Love You, 1971, Tonight Show theme music; others; also compositions for other artists including My Way for Frank Sinatra and She's A Lady for Tom Jones. Recipient Chevalier De l'ordre Des Arts Et Des Letters (France); named 21st most successful artist in Billboards history. Mem. Broadcast Music, Inc. (22 songwriting awards-18 for most performed songs, 4 for songs performed more than one million times). Eastern Orthodox. Club: Friars (N.Y.C.). Achievements include being a holder of 15 gold records for million dollar world-wide sellers, and having to his credit more than 42 million single sales and over 900 songs. Office: Paul Anka Productions 433 N Camden Dr Ste 960 Beverly Hills CA 90210-4413 E-mail: fan@paulanka.com

ANNAKIN, KENNETH COOPER, film director, writer; b. Beverly, Yorkshire, England; came to U.S., 1979; s. Edward C. and Hannah J. (Gains) A.; m. Pauline Mary Carter, 1960; children: Jane, Deborah. Student, Hull U., 1934-35. Dir. The Swiss Family Robinson, 1960, A Very Important Person, 1961, The Hellions, 1961, Crooks Anonymous, 1962, The Fast Lady, 1962, The Longest Day, 1962, Those Magnificent Men in Their Flying Machines, 1965, The Battle of the Bulge, 1965, The Biggest Bundle of Them All, 1967, Those Daring Young Men in Their Jaunty Jalopies, 1969, Call of the Wild, 1972, Paper Tiger, 1974, The Fifth Musketeer, 1977, The Pirate Movie, 1982, Pippi Longstocking, 1986, 99; screenwriter Coco Chanel, 1999, Chiffon, 2001, Fair Play, 2001, Yours Truly, Amelia, 2001; author (autobiography): So You Wanna Be A Director?, 2001. Office: 9233 Swallow Dr West Hollywood CA 90069-1145 E-mail: flyingmachines@earthlink.net

ANNUNZIATA, ROBERT, fiber optics company executive; Pres. AT&T, until 1999; CEO, dir. Global Crossngs Ltd., Beverly Hills, Calif., 1999—. Office: Global Crossings Ltd 360 N Crescent Dr Beverly Hills CA 90210-4802

ANSCHUTZ, PHILIP F. transportation executive, communications executive; b. Russell, Kansas, 1939; BS, Univ. Kansas, 1961. Dir. chair. QCC, 1993—, Anschutz Co., Denver, 1991—; ceo, dir. Anschutz Corp., Denver, 1992—; dir. So. Pacific Rail Corp., San Francisco, 1988-96; chair. So Pacific Rail Corp., 1988-96; vice chmn. (merger with So Pacific Rail Corp) Union Pacific, San Francisco, 1996—; dir. Forest Oil Corp., 1995—; dir., chair. Qwest Communications, 1997—; co-owner L.A. Kings, 1995—; owner L.A. Galaxy, 1996—; investor-operator Major League Soccer, 1995—. Board Mem: Am. Petroleum Inst., Nat. Petroleum Council, Nat. Hockey League, Kansas Univ. Endowment Assoc. Office: Southern Pacific Rail Corp 49 Stevenson St Fl 15 San Francisco CA 94105-2909 also: 555 17th St Ste 2400 Denver CO 80202-3941 also: Quest Communication 1801 Calif St Inglewood CA 80202

ANSELL, BENJAMIN JESSE, physician; b. Troy, N.Y., May 17, 1967; MD, UCLA, 1992. Diplomate Am. Bd. Internal Medicine. Intern UCLA Med. Ctr., 1992-93, resident, 1993-95; asst. clin. prof. UCLA, 1995—, dir. Ctr. Primary Care Based Cardiovasc. Disease Prevention. Mem. ACP, Am. Heart Assn. Office: UCLA Med Ctr 200 Med Plz Ste 365 Los Angeles CA 90095-0001

ANSELL, EDWARD ORIN, lawyer; b. Superior, Wis., Mar. 29, 1926; s. H. S. and Mollie (Rudnitzky) A.; m. Hanne B. Baer, Dec. 23, 1956; children: Deborah, William. BSEE, U. Wis., 1948; JD, George Washington U., 1955. Bar: D.C. 1955, Calif. 1960. Electronic engr. FCC, Buffalo and Washington, 1948-55; patent atty. RCA, Princeton, N.J., 1955-57; gen. mgr. AeroChem. Rsch. Labs., Princeton, 1957-58; patent atty. Aerojet-Gen. Corp., La Jolla, Calif., 1958-63, corp. patent counsel, 1963-82, asst. sec., 1970-79, sec., 1979-82, assoc. gen. counsel, 1981-82; dir. patents and licensing Calif. Inst. Tech., Pasadena, 1982-92; pvt. practice Claremont, Calif., 1992—; co-founder Gryphon Scis., South San Francisco, 1993, Ciphergen Biosystems, Fremont, 1993. Adj. prof. U. La Verne (Calif.) Coll. Law, 1972-78; spl. advisor, task force chmn. U.S. Commn. Govt. Procurement, 1971 Editor: Intellectual Property in Academe: A Legal Compendium, 1991; contbr. articles to profl. publs. Recipient Alumni Svc. award George Washington U., 1975. Mem. Am. Intellectual Property Law Assn., Assn. Corp. Patent Counsel, Ea. Bar Assn. Los Angeles County, L.A. Intellectual Property Law Assn., Assn. Univ. Tech. Mgrs., State Bar Calif. (exec. com. intellectual property sect. 1983-86), Athenaeum Club Pasadena, Univ. Club Claremont. Office: 427 N Yale Ave # 204 Claremont CA 91711 E-mail: anselaw@att.net

ANSELL, GEORGE STEPHEN, retired metallurgical engineering educator, academic administrator; b. Akron, Ohio, Apr. 1, 1934; s. Frederick Jesse and Fanny (Soletsky) A.; m. Marjorie Boris, Dec. 18, 1960; children: Frederick Stuart, Laura Ruth, Benjamin Jesse. B. in Metall. Engring., Rensselaer Poly. Inst., 1954, M. in Metall. Engring., 1955, PhD, 1960; DEng (hon.), Colo. Sch Mines, 1998. Physical metallurgist USN Research Lab., Washington, 1957-58; mem. faculty Rensselaer Poly. Inst., Troy, N.Y., 1960-84, Robert W. Hunt prof., 1965-84, chmn. materials div., 1969-74, dean engring., 1974-84; pres. Colo. Sch. Mines, Golden, 1984-98. Editor books; patentee in field; contbr. over 100 articles to profl. jours. Served with USN, 1955-58. Recipient Hardy Gold Medal AIME, 1961, Curtis W. McGraw award Am. Soc. Engring. Edn., 1971, Souzandrade Gold Medal of Univ. Merit Fed. U. Maranhao, 1986. Fellow Metall. Soc. (pres. 1986-87), Am. Soc. Metals (Alfred H. Geisler award 1964, Bradley Stoughton award 1968), Am. Soc. Engring. Edn. (Curtis W. McGraw award 1971), Sigma Xi, Tau Beta Pi, Phi Lambda Upsilon. E-mail: gansell@mines.edu

ANSELL, JULIAN S. physician, retired urology educator; b. Portland, Maine, June 30, 1922; s. Jacob M. and Anna Gertrude (Fieldman) A.; m. Eva Ruth Ballin, June 17, 1951; children: Steven, Jody, Carol, Ellen, Peter. BA, Bowdoin Coll., 1946; MD, Tufts U., 1951; PhD, U. Minn., 1959. Intern in surgery U. Minn. Hosps., Mpls., 1951-52, resident in urology, 1952-54; NIH fellow U. Minn., Mpls., 1954, instr., 1956-59; asst. prof., head urology U. Wash., Seattle, 1959-62, assoc. prof., head urology, 1962-64, prof., chair urology, 1965-87, prof. urology, 1987-92, prof. emeritus, 1992—. With U.S. Army, 1943-46. Mem. Am. Alpine Club. Office: 3827 49th Ave NE Seattle WA 98105-5233

ANSON, FRED COLVIG, chemistry educator; b. L.A., Feb. 17, 1933; m. Roxana Anson; children: Alison, Eric. BS, Calif. Inst. Tech., 1954; MS, Harvard U., 1955, PhD, 1957. Instr. chemistry Calif. Inst. Tech., Pasadena, 1957-58, asst. prof., 1958-62, assoc. prof., 1962-68, prof. chemistry, 1968—, chmn. divsn. chemistry and chem. engring., 1984-94. Contbr. numerous articles to profl. jours. Fellow J.S. Guggenheim Found., U. Brussels, 1964, Alfred P. Sloan Found., 1965-69; scholar Fulbright-Hays Found., U. Florence, Italy, 1972, A. von Humboldt Found., Fritz Haber Inst., Berlin, 1984, 86, 94; recipient award in Electrochemistry Am. Chem. Soc., 1994. Fellow Electrochem. Soc.; mem. AAAS, Nat. Acad. Sci., Am. Chem. Soc. (Award in Electrochemistry, 1994), Am. Electrochem. Soc., Internat. Soc. Electrochemistry, Soc. Electroanalytical Chemistry, Tau Beta Pi. Office: Calif Inst Tech Divsn Chemistry and Chem Engring Ms 127 72 Pasadena CA 91125-0001

ANSPAUGH, LYNN RICHARD, research biophysicist; b. Rawlins, Wyo., May 25, 1937; s. Solon Earl and Alice Henrietta (Day) A.; m. Barbara Anne Corrigan, Nov. 2, 1965 (div.); children: Gregory, Heidi; m. Larisa Fedorovna Kornushina, Sept. 27, 1993. BA, Nebr. Wesleyan U., 1959; M in Bioradiology, U. Calif., Berkeley, 1961, PhD, 1963. Biophysicist Lawrence Livermore (Calif.) Nat. Lab., 1963-74, group leader, 1974-75, sect. leader, 1976-82, div. leader, 1982-92, dir. Risk Scis. Ctr., 1992-95, dir. Dose Reconstruction program, 1995-96; rsch. prof. radiobiology divsn. Univ. Utah, Salt Lake City, 1997—. Tchr. extension U. Calif., Berkeley, 1966-69; lectr. San Jose (Calif.) State U., 1975; guest lectr. UCLA, Stanford U., U. Calif., Davis, 1992-96; faculty affiliate Colo. State U., Ft. Collins, 1979-83; cons. EPA, Washington, 1984-85, U. Utah, Salt Lake City, 1983-88, NAS/NRC, 1998; mem. U.S. del. UN Sci. Com. on Effects of Radiation, Vienna, 1987—; mem. Nat. Coun. on Radiation Protection and Measurements, 1989-2001; mem. radiation adv. com. EPA, 1999—. Contbr. articles to profl. jours. AEC fellow, 1959-61; fellow NSF, 1961-63. Fellow Health Physics Soc. (pres. environ. radiation sect. 1984-85, pres. No. Calif. chpt. 1986-87); mem. AAAS, Soc. for Risk Analysis, Internat. Union Radioecology, Radiation Rsch. Soc., Sigma Xi. Home: PO Box 171319 Salt Lake City UT 84117-1319 Office: U Utah 729 Arapeen Dr Ste 2334 Salt Lake City UT 84108-1218 E-mail: LAnspaugh@aol.com

ANSTAD, NEIL, director; Coord. humanities program Cleve. High Sch. Office: Cleve HS Humanites Program 8140 Vanalden Ave Reseda CA 91335-1136

ANTANITUS, DAVID J. career officer; b. LaSalle, Ill. BS in Math., U.S. Naval Acad., 1974. Commd. 2d lt. USN; various assignments including USS Parche (SSN 683), 1975-79; asst. dept. comdr. for readiness and tng. Comdr. Submarine Squadron Fourteen, Holy Loch, Scotland, 1979-82; exec. officer USS Boston (SSN 703), 1986-91; comdr. Pre-Commissioning Unit Hampton (SSN 767); program mgr. Deep Submergence Systems Program (PMS 395)/NAVSEA; vice-comdr., rear adm. Space and Naval Warfare Systems Command. Decorated Legion of Merit, Meritorious Svc. medal, Navy Commendation medal with four gold stars.

ANTHONY, METROPOLITAN OF THE DARDANELLES (ANTHONY EMMANUEL GERGIANNAKIS), bishop; b. Heraklion, Crete, Mar. 2, 1935; Degree in theology, Theol. Sch., Halki, Constantinople, 1960; MDiv, Yale U., 1964; postgrad., U. Chgo., 1964-73, U. Wis., 1964-73. Ordained deacon Greek Orthodox Ch., 1958, ordained priest, 1960. Priest Holy Trinity Ch., Ansonia, Conn., 1961-64, Assumption Ch., Chicago Heights, Ill., 1964-69, Madison, Wis., 1969-73; dean St. George Cathedral, Montreal, 1974-78; titular bishop Ammissos, Denver, 1978-79; bishop San Francisco, 1979—. Founder St. Nicholas Ranch and Retreat Ctr., Dunlap Calif.; elected Met. of Dardanelles and Presiding Hierarch of San Francisco by Ecumenical Patriarchate, 1997. Office: Greek Orthodox Diocese San Francisco 372 Santa Clara Ave San Francisco CA 94127-2090 E-mail: diocese@sanfran.goarch.org

ANTHONY, SUSAN [illegible] educator; [illegible] secondary geography Anchorage Sch. Dist. Recipient Disting. Tchr. K-12 award Nat. Coun. for Geog. Edn., 1992. Office: Anchorage Sch District PO Box 196614 Anchorage AK 99519-6614

ANTIN, DAVID, poet, critic; b. Bklyn., Feb. 1, 1932; s. Max and Mollie (Kitzes) A.; m. Eleanor Fineman, Dec. 16, 1961; 1 son, Blaise BA, CCNY, 1955; MA (Herbert Lehman fellow), NYU, 1966. Prof. visual art U. Calif.-San Diego, 1968—; contbg. editor Alcheringa, 1972-80, New Wilderness 1979—; editorial com. U. Calif. Press, 1972-76; prof. emeritus visual arts U. Calif.-San Diego. Author: Definitions, 1967, Autobiography, 1967, Code of Flag Behavior, 1968, Meditations, 1971, Talking, 1972, Talking at the Boundaries, 1976 , Tuning, 1984, Selected Poems 1963-73, 1991, What It Means to be Avant Garde, 1993. Recipient Creative Arts award U. Calif., 1972; Guggenheim fellow, 1976-77; Nat. Endowment Humanities fellow, 1983-84 Home: PO Box 1147 Del Mar CA 92014-1147 Office: U Calif San Diego Visual Arts Dept La Jolla CA 92037

ANTONE, DOUGLAS R. corporate executive; Former sr. v.p. worldwide sales Borland Internat.; former pres. Ingram Alliance (divsn. of Ingram Micro); former pres. Frameworks Divsn. Ingram Micro; CEO Who?Vision, Lake Forest, Calif., 1999—. Office: Who Vision Inc 16965 Allondre Dr San Diego CA 92128

ANTONIOU, ANDREAS, electrical engineering educator; b. Yerolakkos, Nicosia, Cyprus, Mar. 3, 1938; immigrated to Can., 1969; s. Antonios and Eleni (Costi Coufou) Hadjisavva; m. Rosemary C. Kennedy, Mar. 7, 1964 (dec.); children: Anthony, David, Constantine, Helen BSc with honors, U. London, 1963, PhD, 1966. Mem. sci staff GEC Ltd., London, 1966; sr. sci. officer P.O. Rsch. Dept., London, 1966-69; mem. sci. staff in R & D No. Electric Co., Ottawa, Ont., Can., 1969-70; successively asst. prof. elec. engring., assoc. prof., prof., dept. chmn. Concordia U., Montreal, Que., Can., 1970-83; prof. U. Victoria, B.C., Can., 1983—, founding chmn. elec. and computer engring. dept. Can., 1983-90. Author: Digital Filters: Analysis, Design, and Applications, 1979, 2d edit., 1993; co-author: Two-Dimensional Digital Filters, 1992; contbr. articles to profl. jours. Recipient Chmn.'s award for Career Achievement, B.C. Sci. Coun., 2000. Fellow IEEE (assoc. editor Trans. on Cirs. and Sys. jour. 1983-85, Golden Jubilee award 2000, editor 1985-87, mem. bd. govs. Cirs. and Sys. Soc.), Instn. Elec. Engrs. (Ambrose Fleming premium 1969); mem. Assn. Profl. Engrs. and Geoscientists B.C. (councilor 1988-90). Greek Orthodox. Home: 4058 Jason Pl Victoria BC Canada V8N 4T6 Office: U Victoria Dept Elec & Computer Engring PO Box 3055 STN CSC Victoria BC Canada V8W 3P6 Fax: 250-721-6052. E-mail: andreas@ece.uciv.ca

ANTONOVICH, MICHAEL DENNIS, county official; b. L.A. m. Christine Hu; children: Michael Dennis, Jr., Mary Christine. BA, Calif. State U., L.A., 1963; secondary tchg. cert., Cail. State U., 1966; MA, Calif. State U., L.A., 1967; grad., Pasadena Police Acad., 1967; postgrad., Harvard U., 1984, 87; postgrad. Hoover Inst., Stanford U., 1968-70. Govt. and history instr. L.A. Unified Sch. Dist., 1966-72; Republican whip Calif. State Assembly, 1976-78, assemblyman, 1972-78; mem. bd. suprs. 5th Dist. L.A. County, 1980—; mem. Gov. George Bush- Cheney State Steering Com., 2000. Instr. Calif. State U., 1979, 85, Pepperdine U., 1979. Trustee L.A. C.C., 1969-73; mem. Tournament of Roses Com., Glendale Symphony, L.A. Zoo. Assn., South Pasadena Police Dept. Res., Good Shepherd Luth. Home for Retarded Children; mem. Met. Transp. Authority, 1993—, chmn., 1994-95; mem. L.A. County Transp. Commn., 1980-93, chmn., 1984, 92; chmn. Calif. State Rep. Party, 1985-86; mem. L.A. Coliseum Commn., South Coast Air Quality Mgmt. Dist.; presdl. appointee U.S. Del. to UN Internat. Conf. on Indo-Chinese Refugees, Geneva, 1989, Com. on Privatization, 1987-88, U.S.-Japan Adv. Com., 1984, J. Fulbright Fgn. Scholarship Bd., 1991-93; mem. adv. bd. Atty. Gen.'s Missing Children, 1987-88; mem. delegation Rep. Nat. Com., 1972, 76, 84, 88, 92, 96, 2000, mem. platform com., 1976, co-chmn. human resources com. Recipient Pub. Ofcl. Yr., Nat. Fedn. Indian-Ams., 1989, Outstanding and Invaluable Svc. award Home Visitation Ctr., 1990, Brother's Keeper award Chaplain's Eagles, 1990, Responsible Citizen award Thomas Jefferson Rsch. Ctr., 1990, Outstanding Citizen award Internat. Footprint Assn., 1991, Recognition award Salvation Army, Leadership awards United Way, 1987, 91, 93, Hon. Svc. award PTA, 1991, San Fernando Valley Outstanding Leadership award Min.'s Fellowship and Focus 90s, 1991, Mental Health Assn. award of appreciation Antelope Valley Social Ctr., 1991, Recognition award MADD, 1992, Appreciation award Soc. Hispanic Profl. Engrs., L.A. chpt., 1992, awards Boy Scouts Am., 1992, 93, Recognition award Mex. Am. Correctional Assn., 1996; named Man of Yr. Pasadena NAACP, 1999. Mem. County Suprs. Assn. Calif. (bd. dirs.), Phila. Soc., Glendale C. of C., Blue Key, Elks, Sigma Nu. Lutheran. Office: LA County 5th Dist 869 Hall of Adminstrn 500 W Temple St Los Angeles CA 90012-2713

ANTREASIAN, GARO ZAREH, artist, lithographer, art educator; b. Indpls., Feb. 16, 1922; s. Zareh Minas and Takouhie (Daniell) A.; m. Jeanne Glascock, May 2, 1947; children: David Garo, Thomas Berj. BFA, Herron Sch. Art, 1948; DFA (hon.), Ind. U.-Purdue U. at Indpls., 1972. Instr. Herron Sch. Art, 1948-64; tech. dir. Tamarind Lithography Workshop, Los Angeles, 1960-61; prof. art U. N.Mex., 1964-87, chmn. dept. art, 1981-84; tech. dir. Tamarind Inst., U. N.Mex., 1970-72; vis. lectr., artist numerous univs. Bd. dirs. Albuquerque Mus., 1980-90; printmaker emeritus Southern Graphics Coun., 1994. Prin. author: The Tamarind Book of Lithography: Art and Techniques, 1970; one-man shows include Malvina Miller Gallery, San Francisco, 1971, Marjorie Kauffman Gallery, Houston, 1975-79, 84, 86, U. Colo., Boulder, 1972, Calif. Coll. Arts & Crafts, Oakland, 1973, Miami U., Oxford, Ohio, 1973, Kans. State U., 1973, Atlanta Coll. Art, 1974, U. Ga., Athens, 1974, Alice Simsar Gallery, Ann Arbor, 1977-79, Elaine Horwich Gallery, Santa Fe, 1977-79, Mus. of N.Mex., Santa Fe, 1979, Robischon Gallery, Denver, 1984, 86, 90, Moss-Chumley Gallery, Dallas, 1987, Rettig-Martinez Gallery, Santa Fe, 1988, 91, 92, U. N.Mex. Art Mus., 1988, Albuquerque Mus., 1988, Louis Newman Gallery, L.A., 1989, Expositum Gallery, Mexico City, 1989, State U. Coll., Cortland, N.Y., 1991, Mus. Art, U. Ariz., Tucson, 1991, Indpls. Mus. Art, 1994, Ruschmon Gallery, Indpls., 1994, Mitchell Mus. Art, Vernon, Ill., 1995, Cline-Lewallen Gallery, Santa Fe, 1997, Anderson Gallery, Albuquerque, 1997, Feenix Gallery, Taos, NM State U., Las Crucis, 1998; exhibited group shows Phila. Print Club, 1960-63, Ind. Artists, 1947-63, White House, 1966, Nat. Lithographic Exhbn. Fla. State U., 1965, Library Congress, 1961-66, Bklyn. Mus., 1958-68, 76, U.S. Pavilion Venice Biennale, 1970, Internat. Biennial, Bradford, Eng., 1972-74, Internat. Biennial, Tokyo, 1972, City Mus. Hong Kong, 1972, Tamarind UCLA, 1985, Roswell Mus., 1989, Pace Gallery, 1990, Worcester (Mass.) Art Mus., 1990, Amon Carter Mus., Ft. Worth, 1990, Albuquerque Mus., 1991, 92, Art Mus. U. N.Mex., 1991, 92, 99, Norton Simon Mus., Pasadena, Calif., 1999, U. N.H., 1999; represented in permanent collections: Albuquerque Mus., Bklyn. Mus., Guggenheim Mus., N.Y.C., Cin. Mus., Chgo. Art Inst., Ind. State Mus., Mus. Modern Art, N.Y.C., Library of Congress, Met. Mus., N.Y.C., N.Y. Pub. Libr., Mus. Fine Arts, Santa Fe, also, Boston, Indpls., Seattle, Phila., San Diego, Dallas, N.Mex., Worcester Art Museums, Los Angeles County Mus., Roswell Mus. and Art Ctr., Tucson Mus., murals, Ind. U., Butler U., Ind. State Office Bldg. Fulbright vis. lectr. U. São Paulo and Found. Armando Alvares Penteado, Brazil, 1985. Combat artist with USCGR, World War II, PTO. Recipient Distinguished Alumni award Herron Sch. Art, 1972, N.Mex. Annual Gov.'s award, 1987; Grantee Nat. Endowment for Arts, 1983. Fellow NAD; mem. World Print Coun. (bd. dirs. 1980-87), Nat. Print Coun. Am. (co-pres. [illegible]), [illegible] (bd. dirs. 1977-80). Home: 7012 Arroyo Del Oso Ave NE Albuquerque NM 87109 [illegible]

ANZAI, EARL I. state attorney general; b. Honolulu; Student, Emroy U., Oreg. State U.; BA, U. Hawaii, 1964, MA, 1966. Law clk. First Cir. Ct., Honolulu, 1983-95; dir. Dept. Budget and Fin., Honolulu, 1995-99; atty. gen. State Senate Hawaii, Honolulu, 1999—. Office: Dept Atty Gen 425 Queen St Honolulu HI 96813-2903*

ANZEL, SANFORD HAROLD, orthopedic surgeon; b. Bayonne, N.J., Feb. 17, 1929; s. Jules and Faye (Morganstein) A.; m. Darlene J. Wilson, July 14, 1937; children: Linda, Jon. BA, Yale U., 1950; MD, N.Y. Med. Coll., 1954; MS in Orthopaedic Surgery, U. Minn., 1959; cer. Cert. Am. Bd. Orthopaedic Surgery; lic. Nat. Bd. Med. Examiners, Bd. Med. Examiners, Calif., Minn. State Bd. Med. Examiners. Intern U. Calif. Med. Ctr., San Francisco, 1954-55; fellow in orthopaedic surgery Mayo Clinic, Rochester, Minn., 1955-59; chief orthopaedic surgery Orange (Calif.) County Med. Ctr., 1965-71; assoc. clin. prof. orthopaedic surgery U. Calif., Irvine, 1971-79, clin. prof., 1979—; chief orthopaedic sect. Children's Hosp. Orange County, 1977-78. State co-chmn. Orthopaedic Research and Edn. Found., 1982-84; chief orthopaedics Long Beach (Calif.) Vet's. Hosp., 1986—; cons. Baden Powell Orthopaedic Unite, Anaheim, Calif., Foothill High Sch., Katella High Sch., Univ. High Sch., Mater Dei High Sch., Los Angeles Rams; 7th ann. former alumnus vis. prof. Mayo Clinic and Found., 1975. Contbr. numerous articles to profl. jours. Served to maj. USAF, 1959-64. S.H. Anzel Soc. named in his honor, 1985. Fellow ACS (select membership com. 1969-76), Am. Acad. Orthopaedic Surgeons (regional admission com. 11 1969-76, com. ann. meeting press relations 1975-77, 82, co-vice chmn. sci. com. 1981, chmn. sci. com. 1983, bd. councilors); mem. AMA, Western Orthopaedic Assn. (membership com. 1975-78, v.p. Orange County chpt. 1976 , pres.-elect 1988-89, pres. 1988-89, 92, bd. dirs. 1985—), Calif. Med. Assn. Orange County Med. Assn., Am. Orthopaedic Soc. Sports Medicine, Arthritis Found. (Disting. Svc. award So. Calif. chpt. 1974, Humanitarian award Orange County chpt. 1968-79, Nat. Vol. Svc. Citation, 1981), Am. Soc. Shoulder and Elbow Surgeons, Am. Orthopaedic Assn., Wilson-Bost Interurban Club, Calif. Orthopedic Assn. (pres. 1994), Am. Orthopedic Assn. Office: Orthopaedic Surgery Med Group Inc 1140 W La Veta Ave Ste 850 Orange CA 92868-4218

APATOFF, MICHAEL JOHN, financial entrepreneur; b. Harvey, Ill., June 12, 1955; s. William and Frances (Brown) A. BA, Reed Coll., 1980. Chief legis. asst. to U.S. Congressman Al Ullman, Chmn. Ways and Means Com., Washington, 1978-80; spl. asst. to U.S. Congressman Tom Foley, Majority Whip, Washington, 1981-85; exec. v.p., COO Chgo. Merc. Exch., 1986-90; pres., COO Dresdner RCM Global Investors, San Francisco, 1991-98, fin. entrepreneur, 1999—. Democrat. Office: 11 Edwards Ave Sausalito CA 94965 E-mail: mapatoff@msn.com

APFEL, GARY, lawyer; b. N.Y.C., June 2, 1952; s. Willy and Jenny (Last) A.; m. Serena Jakobovits, June 16, 1980; children: Alyssa J., I. Michael, Alanna J., Stephen J., Alexander. BA, NYU magna cum laude, 1973; JD, Columbia U., 1976. Bar: N.Y. 1977, Calif. 1988, U.S. Dist. Ct. (so. and ea. dists.) N.Y. 1977, U.S. Dist. Ct. (cen. dist.) Calif. 1988, U.S. Ct. Appeals (9th cir.) 1988. Assoc. Sullivan & Cromwell, N.Y.C., 1976-80, LeBoeuf, Lamb, Leiby & MacRae, N.Y.C., 1980-84, ptnr., 1985-88, Kaye, Scholer, Fierman, Hays & Handler LLP, L.A., 1988-97, Akin, Gump, Strauss, Hauer & Feld, L.L.P., L.A., 1997—. Kent scholar Columbia U., 1976. Mem. ABA, Calif. State Bar Assn. (bus. law sect. corps. com.), Phi Beta Kappa. Office: Akin Gump Strauss Hauer & Feld LLP 2029 Century Park E Ste 2600 Los Angeles CA 90067-3012

APFEL, JOSEPH H. optical engineer, research scientist; AB in Physics, U. Calif., Berkeley, 1954, MA in Physics, 1956, PhD in Physics, 1959. With Optical Coating Lab., Inc., Santa Rosa, Calif., 1961—, former dir. corp. rsch., former v.p., chief tech. officer, now part-time staff mem. Contbr. articles to sci. jours. Recipient Joseph Fraunhofer award and Robert M. Burlez prize Optical Soc. Am., 1995. Office: Optical Coating Lab Inc 2789 Northpoint Pkwy Santa Rosa CA 95407-7397

APPEL, JOEL, household cleaner manufacturing executive; With mktg. dept. Quaker Oats; pres. Orange Glo Internat., Greenwood Village, Colo. Office: Orange Glo Internat 8765 E Orchard Rd #703 Englewood CO 80111-5009

APPENZELLER, OTTO, neurologist, researcher; b. Czernowitz, Romania, Dec. 11, 1927; came to U.S., 1963; s. Emmanuel Adam and Josephine (Metsch) A.; m. Judith Bryce, Dec. 11, 1956; children: Timothy, Martin, Peter. MBBS, Sydney U., Australia, 1957, MD, 1966; PhD, U. London, 1963. Diplomate Am. Bd. Psychiatry and Neurology. Prof. U. N. Mex., Albuquerque, 1970-90; vis. prof. McGill U., Montreal, 1977; hon. rsch. fellow U. London, 1983; vis. scientist Oxygen Transport Program Lovelace Med. Found., Albuquerque, 1990-92; pres. N.Mex. Health Enhancement and Marathon Clinics Rsch. Found., Albuquerque, 1992—; prof. exptl. neurobiology Bogomoletz Inst., Ukrainian Acad. Sci., Kiev, 1995-2000. U.S.-India exch. scientist NSF, 1992; Fogarty internat. exch. scientist, Kiev, Ukraine, 1993; rsch. com. UNESCO Internat. Coun. Sports and Phys. Edn., 1978-99; ref. Med. Rsch. Coun. New Zealand, 1986-99, reviewer, 1988-99; participant individual health scientist exch. program Fogarty Internat. Ctr., NIH to A.A. Bogomoletz Inst. Physiology, Kiev, 1993. Author: The Autonomic Nervous System, 5th edit., 1997; co-author: Headache, 1984; editor: Pathogenesis and Management of Headache, 1976, Health Aspects of Endurance Training, 1978, Sports Medicine, 3d edit., 1988, Jour. Headache, 1975-77, Annals of Sports Medicine, 1984-88; translator: Neurologic Differential Diagnosis (M. Mumentaler), 2nd edit., 1992; vol. editor: Handbook of Clinical Neurology: The Autonomic Nervous System, Parts I and II, 1998-2000; mem. editl. bd. numerous med. jours. Grantee Diabetes Rsch. and Edn. Found., 1988, Inst. C. Mondino, U. Pavia, Italy, 1992, 95-96, 2000. Fellow ACP (sr.), Am. Acad. Neurology (sr.), Royal Australasian Coll. Physicians (sr.). Achievements include discovery of disease affecting peripheral nerves of Navajo children, of release of opioids and endothelin in human circulatory system after exercise, of chronic neurodegenerative disease in human T-lymphotropic viral II (HTLV II) infection, of peptidergic innervation of blood vessels supplying blood to peripheral nerves in present day and ancient mummified tissues, of neuropathy in chronic pulmonary disease; leader of Mt. Everest research expedition in 1987, Khachenjunga research expedition, 1989, Stock Kangri research expedition, 1992, Tso Moriri Lake (Ladakh) research expedition, 1994, Cerro de Pasco research expedition, 1997, 99, 2000. E-mail: ottoarun12@aol.com

APPIER, KEVIN (ROBERT KEVIN APPIER), professional baseball player; b. Lancaster, Calif., Dec. 6, 1967; Student, Fresno State U., Antelope Valley Coll. Pitcher Kansas City Royals, 1989-99, Oakland Athletics, 1999—. Named Sporting News Rookie Pitcher of Yr., 1990; selected to Am. League All-Star Team, 1995. Office: Oakland Athletics 7677 Oakport St Ste 200 Oakland CA 94621-1933

APPLEBY, JOYCE OLDHAM, historian, educator; b. Omaha, Apr. 9, 1929; d. Junius G. and Edith (Cash) Oldham; children: Ann Lansburgh Caylor, Mark Lansburgh, Frank Bell Appleby. B.A., Stanford U., 1950; M.A., U. Calif., Santa Barbara, 1959; Ph.D., Claremont Grad. Sch., 1966. With Mademoiselle mag., 1950-52; asst. prof. history San Diego State U., [illegible], assoc. prof., 1970-73, prof. history, asso. dean Coll. Arts and Letters, 1973-75, prof., 1976-81. Vis. asso. prof. U. Calif., Irvine, 1975-76; vis. prof. UCLA, 1978-79, prof. history, 1981—; [illegible] rine's Coll., U. Oxford, 1983; Harmsworth prof. Am. History U. Oxford, 1990-91; Bd. fellows Claremont Grad. Sch. and U. Center, 1970-73

Author: Economic Thought and Ideology in Seventeenth-Century England, 1978, Capitalism and a New Social Order, 1983, Liberalism and Republicanism in the Historical Imagination, 1992; co-author: Telling the Truth about History, 1994; co-editor: Knowledge and Postmodernism in Historical Perspective, Inheriting the Revolution, 2000; mem. bd. editors Democracy, 1980-83, William and Mary Quar., 1980-83, 18th Century Studies, 1982-87, Ency. Am. Polit. History, Am. Hist. Rev., 1988—, Jour. Interdisciplinary History, 1989—, The Papers of Thomas Jefferson, 1988—, The Adams Papers, 1990—; contbr. articles to profl. jours.; mem. adv. bd. Am. Nat. Biography. Mem. Am. Acad. Arts and Scis., Am. Philos. Soc., Smithsonian Inst. (coun.), Am. Hist. Assn. (pres.), Orgn. Am. Historians (pres.), Inst. Early Am. History and Culture (coun. 1980-86, chmn. 1983-89). Home: 615 Westholme Ave Los Angeles CA 90024-3209 Office: UCLA Dept History Los Angeles CA 90024

APPLETON, JAMES ROBERT, university president, educator; b. North Tonawanda, N.Y., Jan. 20, 1937; s. Robert Martin and Emma (Mollnow) A.; m. Carol Koelsch, Aug. 8, 1959; children: Steven, Jon, Jennifer. AB in Social Sci., Wheaton Coll., 1958; MA, PhD, Mich. State U., 1965. Lectr. Mich. State U., East Lansing, 1969-72; assoc. dean students Oakland U., Rochester, Mich., 1965-68, dean student life, 1968-72, assoc. prof. behavioral scis., 1969-72, v.p., 1969-72; v.p. student affairs U. So. Calif., L.A., 1972-82, v.p. devel., 1982-87; pres., Univ. prof. U. Redlands, Calif., 1987—. Author: Pieces of Eight: Rights, Roles & Styles of the Dean; guest editor Nat. Assn. Student Pers. Adminstrs. Jour., 1971; contbr. articles to profl. jours. Bd. dirs. So. Calif. Ind. Colls.; bd. dirs., treas., mem. exe. com. Nat. Assn. Ind. Colls. and Univs.; mem. exec. com. Inland Empire Econ. Partnership; mem. nat. exec. com. Tuition Exch.; trustee San Francisco Presbyn. Sem., 1985-95. 1st lt. U.S. Army, 1958-60. Named One of 100 Emerging Young Leaders in Higher Edn., Am. Council Edn./Change, 1978; recipient Fred Turner award Nat. Assn. Student Personnel Adminstrs., 1980. Mem. NCAA (pres.'s commn.), Assn. Ind. Calif. Colls. & Univs. (govtl. rels. com.), Am. Assn. Higher Edn., Western Coll. Assn. (past pres.). Avocations: music performance and appreciation, athletics. Home: 1861 Rossmont Dr Redlands CA 92373-7219 Office: U Redlands 1200 E Colton Ave PO Box 3080 Redlands CA 92373-0999

APPLETON, STEVEN R. electronics executive; BBA, Boise State U., 1982. Fab supr., prodn. mgr., dir. mfg., v.p. mfg. Micron Tech., Inc., Boise, Idaho, 1983-91, pres., COO, 1991, now chmn., CEO, pres.; chmn., CEO Micron Semiconductor, 1992. Bd. dirs. Semiconductor Industry Asssn., St. Luke's Hosp.; trustee Boise State U.; mem. Coll. Bus. Adv. Coun., Semiconductor Tech. Coun. Office: Micron Tech PO Box 6 8000 South Federal Way Boise ID 83707

APRIL, RAND SCOTT, lawyer; b. Bklyn., Feb. 10, 1951; s. Arthur and Muriel (Marmorstein) A. BA, Northwestern U., 1972; JD, Columbia U., 1975. Bar: N.Y. 1976, U.S. Dist. Ct. (so. and ea. dists.) N.Y. 1976, Calif. 1989. Assoc. Marshall, Bratter, Greene, Allison & Tucker, N.Y.C., 1975-78, Gordon, Hurwitz, Butowsky, Baker, Weitzen & Shalov, N.Y.C., 1978-81, Skadden, Arps, Slate, Meagher & Flom, N.Y.C., 1981-83, ptnr., 1983—. Stone scholar Columbia U., 1974-75. Mem. Phi Beta Kappa. Avocation: skiing. Office: Skadden Arps Slate Meagher & Flom 300 S Grand Ave Los Angeles CA 90071-3109

APT, LEONARD, physician; b. Phila., June 28, 1922; s. Morris and Rebecca A. AB with honors, U. Pa., 1942; MD with honors, Jefferson Med. Coll., 1945. Diplomate Am. Bd. Pediat., Am. Bd. Ophthalmology. Intern Jefferson Med. Coll. Hosp., Phila., 1945-46; rsch. fellow in pathology-hematology, resident in pediat. Children's Hosp., Detroit, 1946-49, resident in pediat. Cin., 1949-50, Children's Med. Ctr., Boston, 1950-52, chief med. resident, 1952-53, asst. physician, 1953-55; resident in ophthalmology Wills Eye Hosp., Phila., 1955-57, fellow in pediat. ophthalmology rsch., 1959-61; fellow in pediat. ophthalmology NIH-Children's Hosp., Washington, 1957-59; practice medicine specializing in pediat. ophthalmology L.A., 1961—; assoc. prof. ophthalmology Sch. Medicine, UCLA, 1968-72, prof., 1972—; disting. prof. UCLA, 1993—; attending surgeon Jules Stein Eye Inst., UCLA, dir. pediat. ophthalmology, 1961-81, dir. emeritus, 1981—. Tchg. fellow in pediat. Harvard U. Med. Sch., Boston, 1950-52, instr. pediat., 1953-55; sr. physician radioisotope unit Boston VA Hosp., 1953-55; cons. pediat. ophthalmology Cedars-Sinai Med. Ctr., L.A., St. John's Hosp., Santa Monica, Calif., Bur. Maternal and Child Health, Dept. Pub. Health, Calif., Dept. Health, L.A. Contbr. numerous articles on pediatric ophthalmology to med. books; editorial bd. numerous med. jours.; author: Diagnostic Procedures in Pediatric Ophthalmology, 1963. 1st lt. M.C. U.S. Army, 1943-46. Founder L.A. Philharmonic Assn.; presdl. circle mem. L.A. County Mus. of Art; v.p. fin. UCLA Grunwald Ctr. for Graphic Arts; steering com. UCLA Performing Arts Dept.; founder John Wooden UCLA Athletic Ctr.; judge ann. Wines of Am. competition; mem. exec. coun. UCLA Divsn. of Humanities. Recipient Disting. Alumnus Achievement award Jefferson Med. Coll., 1992, 1st Escalon Sci. award, 1992, Hall of Fame Distinction award Cin. Pediatric Hist. Soc., 1994, 1st Disting. Alumni award Sch. Arts and Scis. U. Pa., 1995, Alumni Univ. Svc. award UCLA 1996, William Feinbloom 1st Disting. Achievement award, 1999, Profl. Achievement award UCLA Med. Alumni Assn., 1999, 1st Disting. Achievement award Ethicon Inc.-Johnson & Johnson Co., 1999. Mem. AMA, Am. Acad. Ophthalmology (honor award 1968), Am. Acad. Pediats. (Lifetime Achievement award 2000, annual Leonard Apt Lectureship named in his honor 2000), Am. Ophthal. Soc., Assn. for Rsch. in Ophthalmology, Soc. Pediat. Rsch., Am. Assn. Pediat. Ophthalmology and Strabismus (1st Disting. Achievement award 1995, honor award 1995), Internat. Strabismol. Assn., Pacific Coast Oto-Ophthal. Soc., Am. Med. Writers Assn., Internat. Wine and Food Soc., Confrerie de la Chaine des Rotisseurs, L'Ordre Mondial des Gourmets Deguistaeurs, Masons (32 degree), Shriner, Alpha Omega Alpha. Avocations: oenophile, gourmet food, theater, arts, sports. Office: UCLA Sch Medicine Jules Stein Eye Inst Los Angeles CA 90095-7000 Fax: 310-206-3652

ARABIAN, ARMAND, arbitrator, mediator, lawyer; b. N.Y.C., Dec. 12, 1934; s. John and Aghavnie (Yalian) A.; m. Nancy Arabian, Aug. 26, 1962; children: Allison Ann, Robert Armand. BSBA, Boston U., 1956, JD, 1961; LLM, U. So. Calif., L.A., 1970; LLD (hon.), Southwestern Sch. Law, 1990, Pepperdine U., 1990, U. West L.A., 1994, We. State U., 1997, Thomas Jefferson Sch. of Law, 1997, Am. Coll. Law, 2001. Bar: Calif. 1962, U.S. Supreme Ct. 1966. Dep. dist. atty. L.A. County, 1962-63; pvt. practice law Van Nuys, Calif., 1963-72; judge Mcpl. Ct., L.A., 1972-73, Superior Ct., L.A., 1973-83; assoc. justice U.S. Ct. Appeal, L.A., 1983-90, U.S. Supreme Ct. Calif., San Francisco, 1990-96; ret., 1996. Adj. prof. sch. law Pepperdine U., 1996—. 1st lt. U.S. Army, 1956-58. Recipient Stanley Litz Meml. award San Fernando Valley Bar Assn., 1986, Lifetime Achievement award San Fernando Valley Bar Assn., 1993; Pappas Disting. scholar Boston U. Sch. Law, 1987; Justice Armand Arabian Resource and Comm. Ctrs. named in honor of Van Nuys and San Fernando Calif. Courthouses, 1999. Republican. Office: 6259 Van Nuys Blvd Van Nuys CA 91401-2711 Fax: 818-781-6002. E-mail: honarabian@AOL.com

ARAGON, MANNY M. state legislator; b. Albuquerque, 1948; BA, JD, U. N. Mex. Mem. N.Mex. Senate from 14th Dist. Address: Pres Pro Tempore Drawer Z Albuquerque NM 87103 Office: New Mex Senate State Capitol Rm 105 Santa Fe NM 87503-0001

ARANT, EUGENE WESLEY, lawyer; b. North Powder, Oreg., Dec. 21, 1920; s. Ernest Elbert and Wanda (Haller) A.; m. Juanita Clark Flowers, Mar. 15, 1953; children: Thomas W., Kenneth E., Richard W. B.S. in Elec. Engring, Oreg. State U., 1943; J.D., U. So. Calif., 1949. Bar: Calif. 1950. Mem. engring. faculty U. So. Calif., 1947-51; practiced in Los Angeles, 1950-51; patent atty. Hughes Aircraft Co., Culver City, Calif., 1953-56; pvt. practice, L.A., 1957-97, Ventura, Calif., 1997-2001, Gleneden Beach, Oreg., 2001—. Author articles. Mem. La Mirada (Calif.) City Council, 1958-60; trustee Beverly Hills Presbyn. Ch., 1976-78. Served with AUS, 1943-46, 51-53. Mem. ABA, Am. Intellectual Property Law Assn., State Bar Calif., Ala. State Bar, Santa Barbara Rotary, Univ. Club Santa Barbara. Democrat. E-mial. Home: 100 NE Indian Shores Lincoln City OR 97367 Office: PO Box 0250 Ste A7 Gleneden Beach OR 97388 E-mail: gwapat@wcn.net

ARBIB, MICHAEL ANTHONY, neuroscientist, educator, computer scientist; b. Eastbourne, U.K., May 28, 1940; came to U.S., 1961; s. John R. and Helen (Arbib) A.; m. Prue Hassell, Dec. 29, 1965; children: Phillipa Jane, Benjamin Giles. BSc with honors, U. Sydney, 1960; PhD in Math., MIT, 1963. Mem. faculty Stanford (Calif.) U., 1965-70, assoc. prof. elec. engring., 1969-70; adj. prof. psychology, prof. computer and info. sci. U. Mass., Amherst, 1970-86, chmn. dept. computer and info. sci., 1970-75; dir. Ctr. for Systems Neurosci., 1974-86, dir. Cognitive Sci. Program, 1980-82, dir. Lab. Perceptual Robotics, 1982-86; prof. biomed. engring., neurobiology, psychology U. So. Calif., L.A., 1986-94, prof. computer sci., elec. engring., 1986—, dir. Ctr. for Neural Engring., 1987-94, dir. USC Brain Project, 1994—, chair computer sci., 1999-2000, Fletcher Jones prof. computer sci., prof., 1999—. Vis. prof. U. Western Australia, Perth, 1974, 96, 99, 2000, Technion, Israel, 1975, Washington U., St. Louis, 1976, U. Edinburgh, 1976-77, U. Calif., Irvine, 1980; vis. scientist Inst. Cybernetics, Barcelona, spring 1985, Cognitive Scis. Inst., U. Calif., San Diego, 1985-86; vis. lectr. U. New South Wales, Australia, 1962, 65, 68, Mont. State U., summers, 1963, 65, Imperial Coll. London, 1964; Gifford lectr. in natural theology U. Edinburgh, Scotland, 1983; John Douglas French lectr. Brain Rsch. Inst., UCLA, 1993; lectr. tours to U.S., USSR, Japan, Australia and China. Author: Brains, Machines and Mathematics, 1964, 2d. edit., 1987, Theories of Abstract Automata, 1969, The Metaphorical Brain, 1972, Computers and the Cybernetic Society, 1977, 2d edit., 1984, In Search of the Person, 1985, The Metaphorical Brain 2, 1989; (with others) Topics in Mathematical System Theory, 1969, System Theory, 1974, Discrete Mathematics, 1974, Conceptual Models of Neural Organization, 1974, Arrows, Structures and Functors, 1975, Design of Well-Structured and Correct Programs, 1978, A Basis for Theoretical Computer Science, 1981, A Programming Approach to Computability, 1982, Algebraic Approaches to Program Semantics, 1986, The Construction of Reality, 1986, From Schema Theory to Language, 1987, An Introduction to Formal Language Theory, 1988, Neural Organization: Structure, Function, Dynamics, 1997; editor: The Handbook of Brain Theory and Neural Networks, 1995, (with others) Algebraic Theory of Machines, Languages and Semigroups, 1968, Neural Models of Language Processes, 1982, Competition and Cooperation in Neural Nets, 1982, Adaptive Control of Ill-Defined Systems, 1983, Vision, Brain and Cooperative Computation, 1987, Dynamic Interactions in Neural Networks: Models and Data, 1988, Visuomotor Coordination: Amphibia, Comparisons, Models, and Robots, 1989, Natural and Artificial Parallel Computation, 1990, Visual Structures and Integrated Functions, 1991, Neuroscience: From Neural Networks to Artificial Intelligence, 1993, Neuroscience and the Person, 1999, Computing the Brain, A Guide to Neuroinformatics, 2001; contbr. articles to profl. jours. Mem. IEEE, AAAS, Soc. Neurosci., Neurosci. and the Person. Office: U So Calif Brain Project Los Angeles CA 90089-0001

ARBUTHNOT, ROBERT MURRAY, lawyer; b. Montreal, Quebec, Can., Oct. 23, 1936; s. Leland Claude and Winnifred Laura (Hodges) A.; m. Janet Marie O'Keefe, Oct. 6, 1968; children: Douglas, Michael, Mary Kathleen, Allison Anne. BA, Calif. State U., San Francisco, 1959; JD, U. Calif., San Francisco, 1966. Bar: Calif. 1967, U.S. Dist. Ct. (no. and cen. dists.) Calif. 1967, U.S. Ct. Appeals (9th cir.) 1967, U.S. Supreme Ct. 1975. Assoc. trial lawyer Rankin & Craddick, Oakland, Calif., 1967-69; assoc. atty. Ericksen, Arbuthnot, Brown, Kilduff & Day, Inc., San Francisco, 1970-73, ptnr., 1973-80, chmn. bd., mng. dir., 1980—. Gen. counsel CFS Ins. Svcs., San Francisco, 1990—; pro tem judge, arbitrator San Francisco Superior Ct., 1990—; lectr. in field. Bd. regents St. Mary's Coll. High Sch., Berkeley, Calif., 1988-91. With U.S. Army, 1959-62. Recipient Honors plaque St. Mary's Coll. High Sch., 1989. Mem. Internat. Assn. of Ins. Counsel, No. Calif. Assn. of Def. Counsel, Def. Rsch. Inst., Assn. Trial Lawyers Am., San Francisco Lawyers Club. Avocations: boating, family activities. Office: Ericksen Arbuthnot Kilduff Day & Lindstrom Inc 260 California St Ste 1100 San Francisco CA 94111-4300 E-mail: eakdlsf@aol.com

ARCE, PHILLIP WILLIAM, hotel and casino executive; b. N.Y.C., June 25, 1937; s. Joseph F. and Margaret (Degnan) A.; m. Dorothy Fiss, June 25, 1966; children: Joseph, William, Serena. Student, U. Notre Dame, 1955-56; AA, San Diego Jr. Coll., 1958; student, San Diego State U., 1958-60, San Diego U., 1960-62, LaSalle Law Sch., 1963-65. Various positions Del Webb Corp., Las Vegas and Reno, Nev., Oahu, Hawaii, 1963-75; exec. Caesars Palace, Las Vegas, 1975-78; pres. Frontier Hotel, Las Vegas, 1978-84; corp. v.p., v.p. mktg., sr. v.p. Dunes Hotel & Country Club, Las Vegas, 1985-88; hotel and gaming specialist Arce Cons., Las Vegas, 1988—. Tchr. hotel div. U. Nev., Las Vegas, 1966-67, 1976-77 Mem. exec. com. Boulder Dam Area coun. Boy Scouts Am., 1976-88; vice chmn. United Way So. Nev., 1968-70; founder, chmn. Las Vegas Events, Inc., 1980-89; pres. Easter Seals Nev., 1974-76, pres. first nat. telethon, 1975; bd. dirs. Air Force Acad. Found., 1982-89. Served with USMC, 1962. Recipient numerous awards including Appreciation awards Easter Seals, 1972, 73, United Way, 1975, Silver Beaver Boy Scouts Am., 1984 Mem. Am. Hotel and Motel Assn. (bd. dirs. 1979-82), Nev. Hotel and Motel Assn. (founder, pres. 1980, Hotelier of Yr. award 1981), Las Vegas C. of C. (dir. 1979-85, pres. 1984). Republican. Roman Catholic. Home: 4243 Ridgecrest Dr Las Vegas NV 89121-4949 Office: Arce Cons Hotel Gaming Ind Specialists Ste 1 4460 W Hacienda Ave Las Vegas NV 89118-4909 also: Colo Belle Hotel & Casino PO Box 77000 Laughlin NV 89028-7000

ARCHER, RICHARD JOSEPH, lawyer; b. Virginia, Minn., Mar. 24, 1922; s. William John and Margaret Leanore (Duff) A.; m. Kristina Hanson, Jan. 29, 1977 (dec.); children: Alison P., Cynthia J. A.B., U. Mich., 1947, J.D., 1948. Bar: Calif. 1949, U.S. Supreme Ct. 1962, Hawaii 1982. Partner firm Morrison and Foerster, San Francisco, 1954-71, Sullivan, Jones and Archer, San Francisco, 1971-81, Archer Rosenak & Hanson, San Francisco, 1981-85, Archer & Hanson, San Francisco, 1985—. Served with USN, 1942-45. Decorated Bronze Star. Mem. ABA, Am. Bar Found. (life), Am. Law Inst. (life). Republican. Home: 3110 Bohemian Hwy Occidental CA 95465-9113 Office: Mauka Tower Ste 2920 737 Bishop St Honolulu HI 96813-3201

ARCHER, STEPHEN HUNT, economist, educator; b. Fargo, N.D., Nov. 30, 1928; s. Clifford Paul and Myrtle Mona (Blair) A.; m. Carol Rosa Mohr, Dec. 29, 1951 (div. Feb. 1971); children— Stephen Paul, Timothy William, David Conrad; m. Lana Jo Urban, Sept. 23, 1972. B.A., U. Minn., 1949, M.S., 1953, Ph.D., 1958; postdoctoral student (Ford Found. grantee), U. Calif. at Los Angeles, 1959-60. Mgr. trader J.M. Dain Co., Mpls., 1950, account exec., 1952-53; instr. econs. U. Minn., Mpls., 1954-56; asst. prof. fin. U. Wash., Seattle, 1956-60, assoc. prof., 1960-65, prof., 1965-73, chmn. dept. fin., bus. econs. and quantitative methods, 1966-70; dean Grad. Sch. Adminstrn. Willamette U., Salem, Oreg., 1973-76, 83-85, prof., 1976-79, Guy F. Atkinson prof., 1979-96. Fulbright sr. lectr. Bocconi U., Milan, Italy, 1982; v.p. Hinton, Jones & Co., Inc. (investment brokers), Seattle, 1969-70; cons. Wash. Bankers Assn., 1971-72, Weyerhaeuser Co., 1971, Bus.-Econs. Adv. & Research Inc., 1969-77, State of Oreg., 1984, 86, 88, 91; vis. prof. Manchester Bus. Sch., Manchester, Eng., 1990-91, Aomori (Japan) Pub. coll., 2000, 01. Author: Introduction to Mathematics for Business Analysis, 1960, Business Finance: Theory and Mgmt, 1966, revised edit., 1972, The Theory of Business Finance, 1967, 2d revised edit., 1983, Portfolio Analysis, 1971, revised edit., 1979, Introduction to Financial Management, 1979, revised edit., 1983, Cases and Readings in Corporate Finance, 1988; editor Jour. Fin. and Quantitative Analysis, 1966-70, Economic Perspectives, Economica Aziendale, Jour. Bus. and Entrepreneurship. Served with USNR, 1950-52. Mem. Phi Beta Kappa, Beta Gamma Sigma.

ARCHERD, ARMY (ARMAND ARCHERD), columnist, television commentator; b. N.Y.C., 13 Jan. m. Selma Archerd. Grad., UCLA, 1941, U.S. Naval Acad. Postgrad. Sch., 1943. With Hollywood bur. AP, from 1945; columnist Herald-Express, Daily Variety, from 1953. Master of ceremonies numerous Hollywood premieres, Acad. Awards shows; co-host People's Choice Awards shows. Served to lt. USN. Recipient awards Masquers, L.A. Press Club, Hollywood Fgn. Press Club, Newsman of Yr. award Publicists Guild, 1970. Mem. Hollywood Press Club (founder). Office: Daily Variety 5700 Wilshire Blvd Ste 120 Los Angeles CA 90036-5804

ARCHIBALD, JAMES DAVID, biology educator, paleontologist; b. Lawrence, Kans., Mar. 23, 1950; s. James R. and Donna L. (Accord) A. B.S. in Geology, Kent State U., 1972; Ph.D. in Paleontology, U. Calif., Berkeley, 1977. Gibb's fellow dept. geology Yale U., New Haven, 1977-79, asst., then assoc. prof. dept. biology, 1979-83; curator of mammals Peabody Mus. Natural Hist., New Haven, 1979-83; assoc. prof., then prof. dept. biology San Diego State U., 1983—. Extensive field expeditions in Mont., Colo., N.Mex., Pakistan, and former USSR, 1973—. Author: A Study of Mammalia and Geology Across the Cretaceous-Tertiary Boundary, 1982, Dinosaur Extinction and the End of an Era: What The Fossils Say, 1996; contbr. over 100 articles to profl. jours. Past trustee San Diego Natural History Mus. Fellow Alcoa Found., U. Calif.-Berkeley, Fulbright fellow to Russia, 1996; Disting Lectr., grantee Paleontology Soc.; grantee Sigma Xi, Nat. Geog. Soc., NSF, Petroleum Research Found., San Diego State U. Mem. Soc. Vertebrate Paleontology, Geol. Soc. Am., Paleontol. Soc., Soc. Systematic Zoologists, Am. Soc. Mammalogists, Willi Hennig Soc., Soc. for Study of Evolution, Phi Beta Kappa Nu, Sigma Xi. Office: San Diego State U Dept Biology San Diego CA 92182

ARCINIEGA, TOMAS ABEL, university president; b. El Paso, Tex., Aug. 5, 1937; s. Tomas Hilario and Judith G. (Zozaya) A.; m. M. Concha Ochotorena, Aug. 10, 1957; children: Wendy M. Heredia, Lisa, Judy, Laura. BS in Tchr. Edn., N. Mex. State U., 1960; MA, U. N. Mex., 1966, PhD, 1970; postdoc., Inst. for Ednl. Mgmt., Harvard U., 1989. Asst. dean Grad. Sch. U. Tex.-El Paso, 1972-73; co-dir. Southwestern Schs. Study, U. Tex.-El Paso, 1970-73; dean Coll. Edn. San Diego State U., 1973-80; v.p. acad. affairs. Calif. State U., Fresno, 1980-83, pres. Bakersfield, 1983—. Prof. ednl. adminstrn. and supervision U. N.Mex., U. Tex.-El Paso, San Diego State U., Calif. State U., Fresno, Calif. State U., Bakersfield; cons. in edn. to state and fed. agys., instns.; USAID advisor to Dominican Republic U.S. Dept. State., 1967-68; dir. applied rsch. project U. N.Mex., 1968-69, dep. chief party AID Project, Colombia, 1969-70; cons. in field. Author: Public Education's Response to the Mexican-American, 1971, Preparing Teachers of Mexican Americans: A Sociocultural and Political Issue, 1977; co-author: Chicanos and Native Americans: The Territorial Minorities, 1973; guest editor: Calif. Jour. Tchr. Edn., 1981; editor Commn. on Hispanic Underrepresentation Reports, Hispanic Underrepresentation: A Call for Reinvestment and Innovation, 1985, 88. Trustee emeritus Carnegie Corp. N.Y.; trustee Ednl. Testing Svc., Princeton, N.J., The Aspen Inst.; bd. dirs. Math., Engring., Sci. Achievement, Berkeley, Calif.; mem. bd. dirs. Air U., Hispanic Scholarship Fund; mem. Am. Coun. on Edn.; founding mem., trustee Tomas Rivera Policy Inst.; dir. Civic Kern Citizens Effective Local Govt.; mem. adv. bd. Beautiful Bakersfield; advisor Jr. League Bakersfield. Vis. scholar Leadership Enrichment Program, 1982; recipient Legis. commendation for higher edn. Calif. Legislature, 1975-78, Meritorious Svc. award Am. Assn. Colls. Tchr. Edn., 1977 78, Meritorious Svc. award League United L.Am. Citizens, 1983, Svc. award Hispanic and Bus. Alliance for Edn., 1991, Pioneer award Nat. Assn. Bilingual Edn., 1994; named to Top 100 Acad. Leaders in Higher Edn. Change Mag., 1978, Top 100 Hispanic Influentials Hispanic Bus. Mag., 1987, 97. Mem. Am. Ednl. Rsch. Assn. (editl. com. 1979-82), Am. Assn. State Colls. and Univs. (bd. dirs.), Hispanic Assn. Colls. and Univs. (bd. dirs.), Assn. Mexican Am. Educators (various commendations), Am. Assn. Higher Edn. (instl. rep.), Western Coll. Assn. (past pres.), Rotary, Stockdale Country Club, Bakersfield Petroleum Club. Democrat. Roman Catholic. Home: 2213 Sully Ct Bakersfield CA 93311-1560 Office: Calif State U 9001 Stockdale Hwy Bakersfield CA 93311-1022

ARDANS, ALEXANDER ANDREW, veterinarian, laboratory director, educator; b. Ely, Nev., June 6, 1941; s. Jean Baptiste and Eleanora (Campbell) A.; m. Janice Gae Sanford, Dec. 23, 1961; children: Tamara Marie, Stephanie Marie, Melanie Alexandra, Angela Rosanne, Jeanette Alison. Student, U. Nev., 1959-61; BS, U. Calif., Davis, 1963, DVM, 1965; MS, U. Minn., St. Paul, 1969. Instr. Colo. State U., Ft. Collins, 1965-66, U. Minn., St. Paul, 1966-69; asst. prof., Sch. Vet. Medicine U. Calif., Davis, 1969-74, assoc. prof., 1974-80, prof., 1980—, chmn. dept. medicine, 1983-87; dir. Calif. Vet. Diagnostic Lab., U. Calif., Davis, 1987—. Recipient Outstanding Tchr. award U. Calif.-Davis Sch. Vet. Medicine, 1970, 73, Alumni award Sch. Vet. Med. U. Calif. Davis, 2000. Mem. Nat. Acad. Practitioners, AVMA, Am. Assn. Vet. Lab. Diagnosticians (Pope award 2000), Calif. Vet. Med. Assn., Conf. Rsch. Workers in Animal Disease. Republican. Roman Catholic. Avocations: swimming, fishing, hunting. Office: Univ Calif Sch Vet Medicine Vet Diag Lab Sys Davis CA 95616

ARDANTZ, HENRI, agricultural products executive; b. 1936; Student, Fresno State Coll. With Ferini & Ardantz, Santa Maria, Calif., 1958-63; ptnr. Betteravia Farms, Santa Maria, 1963—. Office: Betteravia Farms PO Box 5079 Santa Maria CA 93456-5079

AREIAS, JOHN, state agency administrator; BA, Calif. State U., Chico; grad., Harvard U. Mem. Calif. Assembly, 1982-95, chmn. calif. coastal commn., 1995-99; dir. State Calif., Dept. Parks and Recreation, 1999—. Office: State Calif Dept Parks & Rec 1416 9th St Dept Parks& Sacramento CA 95814-5511 also: PO Box 942896 Sacramento CA 94296-0001 Fax: 916-657-3903

ARENBERG, IRVING KAUFMAN KARCHMER, surgeon, educator, entrepeneur; b. East Chicago, Ind., Jan. 10, 1941; s. Harry and Gertrude (Field) Kaufman; divorced; children: Daniel Kaufman, Michael Harrison, Julie Gayle. BA in Zoology, U. Mich., Ann Arbor, 1963; MD, U. Mich., 1967. Diplomate Am. Bd. Otolaryngology. Intern Chgo. Wesley Meml. Hosp., 1967-68; resident Barnes and Allied Hosps., St. Louis, 1969-74; asst. prof. surgery U. Wis., Madison, 1976-80, chief otolaryngology, 1976-80; clin. assoc. prof. otolaryngology U. Colo., Denver, 1980—; pres., CEO Ear Ctr. PC, Englewood, Colo., 1989-96. Pres., chmn. bd., CEO IntraEar, Neurobiometrix Inc., IEMDS, Inc., 1994-99; dir., founder Internat. Meniere's Disease Rsch. Inst., Denver, 1971—; guest of honor 39th Chinese Nat. ENT Congress, Taipei, 1985, U. Antwerp, 1995, West German ENT Soc., 1996; vis. scientist Swedish Med. Rsch. Coun., 1975-76, vis. surgeon, 1987; vis. prof. U. Mich., Ann Arbor, 1988, 94, St. Mary's Hosp. and Med. Sch., London, 1988, U. Verona (Italy) Med. Sch., 1989, U. N.C., Chapel Hill, 1989, U. Wurzburg (Germany) Med. Sch., 1989, 90, 92, U. Ark., Little Rock, 1990, 95, U. Innsbruck, Austria, 1991, U. Sydney, Australia, 1992, U. Tex., Dallas, 1993. Editor: Meniere's Disease, 1983, Inner Ear Surgery, 1991, Dizziness and Balance Disorders,

1993; assoc. editor AMA Archives of Otolaryngology, 1968-81; mem. editorial bd. Am. Jour. Otology, 1978-91, Head and Neck Surgery Jour., 1992—, Jour. Club Jour., 1993; guest editor Otolaryngologic Clinics N.Am., 1980, 83, Neurologic Clinics N.Am., 1990; editor Inner Ear Surgery, 1991; mem. rev. bd. Rev. de Laryngologie et Otology (France), 1984—; contbr. over 400 articles to profl. peer-reviewed jours. Recipient Pietro Caliceti prize and Gold Medal Honor award U. Bologna, Italy, 1983, Spl. Tchr. Investigation Tng. award NIH; fellow Barnes and Allied Hosps., 1968-69, 75, NIH, 1971-76, U. Uppsala-Royal Acad. Hosp., Sweden, 1975-76; grantee NIH, 1971-77, Deafness Rsch. Found., 1971-73. Fellow ACS, Am. Acad. Otolaryngology, Am. Soc. Neurophysiologic Monitoring; mem. AMA, Am. Neurotology Soc., Am. Soc. Laser Medicine and Surgery, Am. Acad. Otolaryngic Allergy, N.Y. Acad. Scis., Colo. Orologic Rsch. Ctr. (pres., bd. dirs. 1980-88), Internat. Meniere's Disease Rsch. Inst. (founder, dir. 1971—), Internat. ECoG Monitoring Correspondence Group (founder), Internat. Electric Response Audiometry Study Group, Assn. Rsch. in Otolaryngology, Barany Soc., Triological Soc., Politzer Soc., Prosper Meniere Soc. (founder, exec. dir. 1981-99), Children's Deafness Found. (pres., bd. dirs. 1983-88), Acoustical Soc. Am., Von Bekesy Soc., N.Am. Skull Base Soc. (founder), Ogura Soc., Sigma Xi. Avocations: skiing, golf, biking, tennis.

ARGUEDAS, CRISTINA C. lawyer; b. 1953; BA, U. N.H.; JD, Rutgers U., 1979. Bar: Calif. 1979. Dep. fed. defender U.S. Dist. Ct. (no. dist.) Calif.; ptnr. Cooper, Arguedas & Cassman, Emeryville, Calif. Lawyer rep. U.S. Ct. Appeals (9th cir.) Jud. Conf. Named one of 50 Top Lawyers Nat. Law Jour., 1998. Mem. Calif. Attys. for Criminal Justice (past pres.). Office: Cooper Arguedas & Cassman 5900 Hollis St Ste N Emeryville CA 94608-2008

ARIAS, JOE, agricultural products company executive; With subsidiaries of Valley Fresh Foods, Inc., 1966—; pres., chmn. bd. Valley Fresh Foods, Inc., Turlock, Calif., 1991—. Office: Valley Fresh Foods Inc 3600 E Linwood Ave Turlock CA 95380-9109

ARKIN, MICHAEL BARRY, lawyer, arbitrator, writer; b. Washington, Jan. 11, 1941; s. William Howard and Zenda Lillian (Liebermann) A.; children and stepchildren from previous marriages: Tracy Renee, Jeffrey Harris, Marcy Susan, Chatom Callan, Michael Edwin, Samuel Hopkins, Brandon Maddox Richards, Jessica Remaley, Brandi Remaley, Casey Remaley; m. Laura Dorene Haynes, Aug. 16, 1998. AA, George Washington U., 1961; BA in Psychology, U. Okla., 1962, JD, 1965. Bar: Okla. 1965, U.S. Ct. Claims 1968, U.S. Supreme Ct. 1968, Calif. 1970, U.S. Tax Ct. 1970, U.S. Ct. Appeals (3d, 5th, 6th, 9th, 10th cirs.) 1970, U.S. Dist. Ct. (cen. dist.) Calif. 1970, U.S. Dist. Ct. (so. dist.) Calif. 1970, U.S. Dist. Ct. (ea. dist.) Calif. 1987. Trial atty. tax divsn. U.S. Dept. Justice, 1965-68, appellate atty., 1968-69; ptnr. Surr & Hellyer, San Bernardino, Calif., 1969-79; mng. ptnr. Wied, Granby Alford & Arkin, San Diego, 1979-82, Lorenz Alhadeff Fellmeth Arkin & Multer, San Diego, 1982, Finley, Kumble, Heine, Underberg, Manley & Casey, San Diego, 1983; pvt. practice Sacramento and San Andreas (Calif.), 1984-86; ptnr. McDonough Holland & Allen, Sacramento, 1986-87; pvt. practice San Andreas, Calif., 1987—; chief counsel Calaveras County Child Protective Svcs., 1996—. Judge pro-tem Calaveras County (Calif.) Consol. Cts., 1999—. Author: History of the Bench and Bar of Calaveras County California, 1997—. Bd. dirs. San Bernardino County Legal Aid Soc., 1971-73, sec., 1971-72, pres., 1973; mem. Calaveras County Adv. Com. on Alcohol and Drug Abuse, 1985-94, pres., 1991-92; treas. Calaveras County Legal Assistance Program, 1987—; trustee Calaveras County Law Libr., 1987-98; bd. dirs. Mark Twain Hosp. Dist., 1990—, treas., 1994—; mem. Calaveras County Rep. Ctrl. Com., 1990-92, 94-96; Calaveras County chmn. Wilson for Gov., 1994. Named to Hon. Order of Ky. Cols., 1967. Mem. ABA, Calif. Bar Assn. (Wiley F. Manuel pro bono pub. svc. award 1991), San Diego County Bar Assn., San Bernardino County Bar Assn. (bd. dirs., sec.-treas. 1973-75, pilot drug abuse program 1970), Calaveras County Bar Assn. (bd. dirs., v.p. 1988-90, pres. 1990-95), Am. Arbitration Assn. (arbitrator 1987—). Republican. Jewish. Home: Fourth Mesa Murphys CA 95247 Office: PO Box 1077 1265 S Main St Angels Camp CA 95222 E-mail: markin2500@aol.com

ARLEDGE, CHARLES STONE, former aerospace executive, entrepreneur; b. Bonham, Tex., Oct. 20, 1935; s. John F. and Mary Madeline (Jones) A.; m. Barbara Jeanne Ruff, June 18, 1966; children: John Harrison, Mary Katherine. B.S., Stanford U., 1957, M.S. (Standard Oil Co. Calif. scholar 1958), 1958, M.B.A., 1966. Engr. Shell Oil Co., Los Angeles, 1958-64; with Signal Cos., La Jolla, Calif., 1966-86, v.p., 1970-79, group v.p., 1979-83, sr. v.p., 1983-86; v.p. Aerojet Gen. Corp., La Jolla, Calif., 1986-90; ptnr. Signal Ventures, 1990—. Republican. Presbyterian. Clubs: California; La Jolla Beach and Tennis. Home: PO Box 957 Rancho Santa Fe CA 92067-0957 Office: 777 S Pacific Coast Hwy Ste 107 Solana Beach CA 92075-2623

ARLIDGE, JOHN WALTER, retired utility company executive; b. Rochester, N.Y., Feb. 4, 1933; s. Harold Wesley and Grace Edith (Kempshall) A.; m. Sandra Marie Koswar, Feb. 4, 1955; children: James William, Edward John. BS, L.A. State Coll., 1962. Registered profl. engr., Calif., Nev., Utah. Comm. sys. engring. design and purchase City of L.A., 1961-62, power sys. resource planning R & D, 1962-74; asst. to v.p. Nev. Power Co., Las Vegas, 1974-82, v.p. resource planning and power dispatch, 1982-89, sr. v.p. govt. affairs, 1989-93; v.p., dir. Nev. Electric Investment Co., Las Vegas, 1982-89; cons. on energy resources and regulation, Las Vegas, 1995—. Advisor electric-lignite sector Ministry Indusry and Trade, Warsaw, Poland, 1992-95; mem. Nev. Engr.'s Adv. Com. on Geothermal Devel., 1974-76, Nev. Solar Energy Devel. Adv. Group, 1976-86; mem. energy task force WEST, 1972-84, mem. energy engring. planning com., 1978; mem. advanced energy sys. divsnl. com. Electric Power Rsch. Inst., 1973-92; mem. Western Utility Group on Fed. Land, 1977; mem. endangered species subcom., rail issues group Edison Elec. Inst., 1977; cons. on air, land and water Western Regional Coun., 1977; mem. Nev. adv. bd. U.S. Bur. Land Mgmt., 1975-77, mem. adv. coun. Las Vegas dist., 1980-92; mem. rsch. adv. bd. U. Nev.; trustee Corp. Devel. Sci. Tech. Nev. Contbr. articles on energy resources to various publs. Mem. Nev. adv. bd. Nature Conservancy; mem. Sec. Energy's Nat. Coal Coun., 1988-93. With USMC, 1950-54. Mem. IEEE, Geothermal Resources Coun. (dir.), utility Coal Gasification Assn. (chmn.), Internat. Solar Energy Assn., Nat. Coal Coun. (advisor to sec. energy), Pacific Coast Elec. Assn., So. Nev. Off-Road Vehicle Assn., Slurry Transp. Assn. (dir. 1979), Masons.

ARMACOST, MARY JANE, healthcare company executive; BA, Denison U. Bd. dirs. Mills-Peninsula Hosps., chmn. bd. dirs.; mem. governing bd. Sutter Health Inc., Sacramento, 1996—, chmn. bd. dirs., 1997—. Trustee Denison U., Ohio, 1981—; San Francisco Zool. Soc., 1985—. Office: Sutter Health Inc One Capitol Mall Sacramento CA 95814

ARMENTROUT, STEVEN ALEXANDER, oncologist; b. Morgantown, W.Va., Aug. 22, 1933; s. Walter W. and Dorothy (Gasch) A.; m. Johanna [illegible]; children: [illegible] Marc, Susan, Sandra, Nancy. A.B., U. Chgo., 1953, M.D., 1959. Intern U. Hosp., Cleve., 1959-60; resident in medicine, fellow Am. Cancer Soc. Western Res. U. Hosp., 1960-63; project dir. USPHS, 1963-65; asst. prof. Case Western Res. U. Med. Sch., 1965-71; mem. faculty U. Calif. Med. Sch., Irvine, 1971—, prof. medicine, chief divsn. hematology-oncology, 1978—, also dir. program in oncology. [illegible] staff U. Calif.-Irvine Med. Ctr., 1983-85; researcher in multiple sclerosis Mem. Am. Assn. Cancer Research, AAUP, ACP, Am. Cancer Soc. (chmn. bd. 1973, pres. Orange County chpt. 1985-86), AMA, Am. Soc. Clin. Oncology, Am. Soc. Hematology, Orange County Med. Assn., Am. Soc. Internal Medicine, Calif. Med. Assn., Cen. Soc. Clin. Research, Leukemia Soc. Am., Orange County Chief of Staff Council. Office: 101 The City Dr S Orange CA 92868-3201

ARMEY, DOUGLAS RICHARD, investment consultant; b. Fresno, Calif., Oct. 23, 1948; s. Wilbur Rutter and Mildred (Broadbent) A.; m. Jennifer Louise Armey, Sept. 23, 1972; children: Laura Elizabeth, Andrew Douglas. AA, Fresno (Calif.) City Coll., 1969; BS summa cum laude, Calif. State U., Fresno, 1971; MA, Mennonite Brethren Sem., Fresno, 1976. Ordained to ministry, Ch. of Brethren, 1973. Intern pastor The Peoples Ch. of Fresno, 1972-73; founding chaplain Fresno County Juvenile Hall, 1973; pres. Precision Parts Distbrs., Inc., Fresno, 1973-80, Rutter Armey Engine Co., Inc., Bakersfield, Calif., 1980-88; sr. pastor Fresno Ch. of the Brethren, 1988-97; investment cons., 1997—. Radio broadcaster Fresno Fellowship of Christian Athletes/KIRV Radio, 1987-96. Contbr. articles to profl. jours. and mags. Bd. dirs. Fresno Youth for Christ, 1985-87, Fellowship of Christian Athletes, 1999—. Mem. Nat. Assn. Evangelicals, Rotary, Sigma Alpha Epsilon. Republican. Ch. of the Brethren. Avocations: martial arts, snow skiing, tennis. Office: 6475 N Palm Ave Ste 101 Fresno CA 93704-1020

ARMINANA, RUBEN, academic administrator, educator; b. Santa Clara, Cuba, May 15, 1947; came to U.S., 1961; s. Aurelio Ruben and Olga Petrona (Nart) A.; m. Marne Olson, June 6, 1954; children: Cesar A. Martino, Tuly Arminana. AA, Hill Jr. Coll., 1966; BA, U. Tex., 1968, MA, 1970; PhD, U. New Orleans, 1983; postgrad. Inst. of Applied Behavioral Scis., Nat. Tng. Labs., 1971. Nat. assoc. dir. Phi Theta Kappa, Canton, Miss., 1968-69; dir. ops. and tng. Inter-Am. Ctr. Loyola U., New Orleans, 1969-71; adminstrv. analyst City of New Orleans, 1972, adminstrv. analyst and orgnl. devel. and tng. cons., 1972-78; anchor and reporter part time STA. WWL-TV, New Orleans, 1973-81; v.p. Commerce Internat. Corp., New Orleans, 1978-83; exec. asst. to sr. v.p. Tulane U., New Orleans, 1983-85, assoc. exec. v.p., 1985-87, v.p., asst. to pres., 1987-88; v.p. fin. and devel. Calif. State Poly U., Pomona, 1988-92; pres. Sonoma State U., 1992—. TV news cons., New Orleans, 1981-88; lectr. Internat. Trade Mart, New Orleans, 1983-89, U.S. Dept. Commerce, New Orleans. Co-author: Hemisphere West-El Futuro, 1968; co-editor: Colloquium on Central America-A Time for Understanding, Background Readings, 1985. Bd. dirs. Com. on Alcoholism and Substance Abuse, 1978-79, SER, Jobs for Progress, Inc., 1974-82, Citizens United for Responsive Broadcasting, Latin Am. Festival Com.; dir. bd. advisors Sta. WDSU-TV, 1974-77; mem. Bus. Govt. Rsch., 1987-88, Coun. Advancement of Support to Edn.; mem. League of United Latin Am. Citizens, Mayor's Latin Am. Adv. Com., Citizens to Preserve the Charter, Met. Area Com., Mayor's Com. on Crime. Kiwanis scholar, 1966, Books scholar, 1966. Mem. Assn. U. Related Rsch. Prks., L.A. Higher Edn. Roundtable, Soc. Coll. and U. Planning, Nat. Assn. Coll. and U. Bus. Officers Coun., Am. Econ. Assn., Assn. of Evolutionary Econs., Am. Polit. Sci. Assn., AAUP, Western Coll. Assn. (pres. 1994-95), Latin Am. C. of C. (founding dir. New Orleans and River Region 1976-83), Cuban Profl. Club, Phi Theta Kappa, Omicron Delta Epsilon, Sigma Delta Pi, Delta Sigma Pi. Democrat. Roman Catholic. Avocation: mask collecting. Office: Sonoma State U 1801 E Cotati Ave Rohnert Park CA 94928-3609 E-mail: ruben.arminana@sonoma.edu

ARMISTEAD, ROBERT ASHBY, JR. scientific research company executive; b. Roanoke, Va., Feb. 7, 1940; s. Robert Ashby and Lucille Denis (Owen) A.; m. Mona Thornhill, Dec. 26, 1965; children: Robert Ashby III, Wade Owen, Clay Thornhill. BS in Physics with highest honors, Va. Mil. Inst., 1962; MS in Physics, Carnegie Mellon U., 1963, PhD in Nuclear Sci. and Engring., 1966; MBA, U. Santa Clara, 1973. Physicist reactor divsn. Oak Ridge (Tenn.) Nat. Lab., 1964-67; nuclear weapons effects projecy officer Def. Atomic Support Agy., Washington, 1967-69; mgr. radiation physics Stanford Rsch. Inst., Menlo Park, Calif., 1969-77; pres., chmn. Advanced Rsch. and Applications Corp., Sunnyvale, 1977—. Chmn. Calif. innovation com. 1986 White House Conf. Small Bus. Contbr. articles to profl. jours.; patentee x-ray imaging. Bd. dirs. Bay Area Regional Tech. Alliance, VMI Found., bd. trustees. Capt. U.S. Army, 1967-69. Named Innovator of Yr., U.S. Small Bus. Adminstrn., 1987, San Francisco Innovation Person of Yr. Small Bus. Adminstrn., 1987; Spl. fellow Atomic Energy Commn., 1963-64, Oak Ridge Grad. fellow, 1965-66. Mem. Am. Electronics Assn. (mem. procurement com. 1986-87, bd. dirs. 1987-90, mem. exec. com. 1989-90), Nat. Innovation Network (bd. dirs.). Avocations: tennis, golf. Office: Advanced Rsch Applications 425 Lakeside Dr Sunnyvale CA 94085-4704

ARMOR, JAMES B., JR. career officer; BSc in Psychology and Elec. Engring., Lehigh U., 1973; graduate, Squadron Officer Sch., 1976; MEE, Air Force Inst. Tech., Wright-Patterson AFB, Ohio, 1977; student, Air Command and Staff Coll., 1983. Commd. 2d. lt. USAF, 1973, advanced through grades to col., 1992; sr. instr. 381st Strategic Missile Wing, McConnell AFB, Kans., 1973-76; chief Laser Signal Intelligence Branch Foreign Tech. Divsn., Wright-Patterson AFB, Ohio, 1977-81; asst. dep. for mission integration Sec. of AF Special Projects Office, L.A., 1981-86; dep. divsn. chief Headquarters USAF, Washington, 1986-89, dep. chief, 1990-92; dep. program dir. Advanced Sys. Program Office, L.A. AFB, 1992-94; program dir. Defense Dissemination Program Office, L.A. AFB, 1994-96; sys. program dir. Space and Missile Sys. Ctr., L.A. AFB, 1996—. Decorated Legion of Merit, Air Force Meritorious Svc. medal with three oak leaf clusters, Air Force Organizational Excellence award with three oak leaf clusters.

ARMSTRONG, CHARLES G. professional baseball executive, lawyer; b. Louisville, Aug. 31, 1942; m. Susan; children— Dorrie, Katherine, Chuck B.S., Purdue U., 1964; J.D., Stanford U., 1967. Bar: Calif. Practice law Hill Farrer & Burrill, Calif., 1971—; pres., chief operating officer Seattle Mariners Baseball Team, 1983—. Served with USN, 1967-70 Office: Seattle Mariners Safeco Field PO Box 4100 Seattle WA 98104-0100

ARMSTRONG, DAVID MICHAEL, biology educator; b. Louisville, July 31, 1944; s. John D. and Elizabeth Ann (Horine) A.; children: John D., Laura C. BS, Colo. State U., 1966; MA in Teaching, Harvard U., 1967; PhD, U. Kans., 1971. From asst. prof. to prof. natural sci. U. Colo., Boulder, 1971-85, prof. environ., population, and organismic biology, 1993—, assoc. chair, 1997-99; sr. scientist Rocky Mountain Biol. Lab., Gothic, Colo., 1977, 79; resident naturalist Sylvan Dale Ranch, Loveland, 1984—; acting dir. Univ. Mus., 1987-88, dir., 1989-93. Cons. ecologist. Author: Distribution of Mammals in Colorado, 1972, Rocky Mountain Mammals, 1975, 87, Mammals of the Canyon Country, 1982; co-author: Mammals of the Northern Great Plains, Mammals of the Plains States, Mammals of Colorado. Mem. non-game adv. council Colo. Div. Wildlife, 1972-76, Colo. Natural Areas Council, 1975-80. Mem. Am. Soc. Mammalogists (editor 1981-87), Southwestern Assn. Naturalists (editor 1976-80), Rocky Mountain Biol. Lab. (trustee 1979-83), The Nature Conservancy (Colo. chpt. trustee 1989-99, chair 1996-98), Colo. Wildlife Fedn. (bd. dirs. 2000—). Avocations: draft horses, conservation activities, writing. Office: U Colo EPO Biology PO Box 334 Boulder CO [illegible] E-mail: mausmann@aol.com, david.armstrong@colorado.edu

ARMSTRONG, ELIZABETH NEILSON, curator; b. Winchester, Mass., June 30, 1952; d. Douglas Byron and Ruth Mary (Publow) A.; m. Daniel Alexander Boone, Mar. 1, 1985; children: Olivia Armstrong Boone, [illegible] Boone. BA, Hampshire Coll., 1974; MA, U. Calif., Berkeley, 1982. [illegible] NEH, Washington, [illegible], rsch. asst. San Francisco Mus. Modern Art, 1979-81; cons. Lowie Mus. Anthropology, Berkeley, 1981-82; Nat. Endowment for Arts curatorial intern Walker Art Ctr., Mpls., 1982-83, asst. curator, 1983-86, assoc. curator, 1986-89, curator, 1989-96; sr. curator Mus. Contemporary Art, San Diego, 1996—. Mem. adv. bd. Capp Street Project, San Francisco, 1987; guest curator Ctr. for Book Arts, N.Y.C., 1989; panelist NEA, Washington, 1988, 89, Pew Charitable Trust, 1994; cons., reviewer Nat. Gallery Art, Washington, 1990. Author: First Impressions, 1989; author, editor: Tyler Graphics: The Extended Image, 1987, Jasper Johns: Printed Symbols, 1990, In the Spirit of Fluxus, 1993. Mem. adv. com. Minn. Percent for Art Program, St. Paul, 1987; bd. dirs. Artpaper, Mpls., 1989-93. Recipient govt. merit award for outstanding performance NEH, 1979; humanities grad. rsch. grantee U. Calif., 1981; fellow for mus. profls. Nat. Endowment for Arts, 1989. Mem. Print Coun. Am., Minn. Ctr. for Book Arts. Avocations: snorkeling, tennis, skiing. Office: San Diego Mus Contemporary Art 700 Prospect St La Jolla CA 92037-4228

ARMSTRONG, GENE LEE, systems engineering consultant, retired aerospace company executive; b. Clinton, Ill., Mar. 9, 1922; s. George Dewey and Ruby Imald (Dickerson) A. m. Lael Jeanne Baker, Apr. 3, 1946; children: Susan Lael, Roberta Lynn, Gene Lee. BS with high honors, U. Ill., 1948, MS, 1951. Registered profl. engr., Calif. With Boeing Aircraft, 1948-50, 51-52; chief engr. astronautics divsn., corp. dir. Gen. Dynamics, 1954-65; chief engr. Def. Sys. Group TRW, Redondo Beach, Calif., 1956-86, pvt. cons. sys. engring., 1986—; with Armstrong Sys. Engring. Co, Westminster. Mem. NASA Rsch. Adv. Com. on Control, Guidance & Navigation, 1959-62 Contbr. chpts. to books, articles to profl. publs. 1st lt. USAAF, 1942-45 Decorated Air medal; recipient alumni awards U. Ill., 1965, 77 Mem. Am. Math. Soc., AIAA, Nat. Mgmt. Assn., Am. Def. Preparedness Assn., Masons. Home: 5242 Bryant Cir Westminster CA 92683-1713 Office: Armstrong Sys Engring Co 5242 Bryant Cir Westminster CA 92683

ARMSTRONG, LLOYD, JR. university official, physics educator; b. Austin, Tex., May 19, 1940; s. Lloyd and Beatrice (Jackson) A.; m. Judith Glantz, July 9, 1965; 1 son, Wade Matthew. BS in Physics, MIT, 1962; PhD in Physics, U. Calif., Berkeley, 1966. Postdoctoral physicist Lawrence Berkeley (Calif.) Lab., 1965-66, cons., 1976; sr. physicist Westinghouse Research Labs., Pitts., 1967-68, cons., 1968-70; research asso. Johns Hopkins U., 1968-69, asst. prof. physics, 1969-73, assoc. prof., 1973-77, prof., 1977-93, chmn. dept. physics and astronomy, 1985-87, dean Sch. Arts and Scis., 1987-93; provost, sr. v.p. for acad. affairs U. So. Calif., L.A., 1993—, prof. physics, 1993—. Assoc. rsch. scientist Nat. Ctr. Sci. Rsch. (CNRS), Orsay, France, 1972-73; vis. fellow Joint Inst. Lab. Astrophysics, Boulder, Colo., 1978-79; program officer NSF, 1981-83, mem. adv. com. for physics, 1985-87, mem. visitors com. physics divsn., 1991; chmn. com. atomic and molecular scis. NAS/NRC, 1985-88, mem. bd. physics and astronomy, 1989-96; mem. adv. bd. Inst. for Theoretical Physics, Santa Barbara, 1992-96, chmn., 1994-95, Inst. Theoretical Atomic and Molecular Physics, Cambridge, Mass., 1994-97, Rochester Theory Ctr. for Optical Sci. and Enging., 1996—, chmn., 1997—; bd. dirs. So. Calif. Econ. Partnership, 1994—, Calif. Coun. on Sci. and Tech., 1994—, Pacific Coun. on Internat. Policy, 1996—. Author: Theory of Hyperfine Structure of Free Atoms, 1971; contbr. articles to profl. jours. NSF grantee, 1972-90; Dept. Energy grantee, 1975-82 Fellow Am. Phys. Soc. Office: U So Calif Office Provost University Park Los Angeles CA 90089-0001

ARMSTRONG, MARY M. insurance company executive; Various positions Safeco Corp, Seattle, 1973-94, v.p., chief info. officer, 1994—. Office: SAFECO Corp SAFECO Plaza Seattle WA 98185

ARMSTRONG, NELSON WILLIAM, JR. gaming company executive; b. Port Huron, Mich., Mar. 5, 1941; s. Nelson William and Kathryn J. (Clarke) A.; m. Judith A. Roth, Sept. 05, 1964; children: Nelson William III, Tad John. BA, Mich. State U., 1964—64. Acct. Gen. Motors Corp., Warren, Mich., 1964—66; in acctg. and fin. Consumers Power Co., Jackson, 1966—73; dir acctg. Ramada Inns, Inc., Phoenix, 1973—77; asst. contr. %, %, 1977—79, v.p. audit svcs., 1979—82, corp. contr., 1982—85, v.p. adminstrn., 1985—, v.p. audit and adminstrv. svcs., 1985—, v.p. corp. contr., 1987—90; v.p. adminstrn., sec. Aztar Corp., %, 1990. Mem.: Fin. Execs. Inst. Republican. Office: Aztar Corp 2390 E Camelback Rd Phoenix AZ 85016-3448

ARMSTRONG, SAUNDRA BROWN, federal judge; b. Oakland, Calif., Mar. 23, 1947; d. Coolidge Logan and Pauline Marquette Brown; m. George Walter Armstrong, Apr. 18, 1982 B.A., Calif. State U.-Fresno, 1969; J.D. magna cum laude, U. San Francisco, 1977. Bar: Calif. 1977, U.S. Supreme Ct. 1984. Policewoman Oakland Police Dept., 1970-77; prosecutor, dep. dist. atty. Alameda County Dist. Atty., Oakland, 1978-79, 80-82; staff atty. Calif. Legis. Assembly Com. on Criminal Justice, Sacramento, 1979-80; trial atty. Dept. Justice, Washington, 1982-83; vice chmn. U.S. Consumer Product Safety Commn., Washington, 1984-86; commr. U.S. Parole Commn., Washington, 1986-89; judge Alameda Superior Ct., 1989-91, U.S. Dist. Ct. (no. dist.) Calif., San Francisco, 1991—. Recipient commendation Calif. Assembly, 1980 Mem. Nat. Bar Assn., ABA, Calif. Bar Assn., Charles Houston Bar Assn., Black C. of C., Phi Alpha Delta Republican. Baptist Office: US Dist Ct N Calif 1301 Clay St Rm 390C Oakland CA 94612-5217

ARNBERGER, ROBERT, federal agency administrator; Supt. Grand Canyon Nat. Park, Ariz. Office: Grand Canyon Nat Park PO Box 129 Grand Canyon AZ 86023-0129

ARNELL, WALTER JAMES WILLIAM, mechanical engineering educator, consultant; b. Farnborough, Eng., Jan. 9, 1924; came to U.S., 1953, naturalized, 1960; s. James Albert and Daisy (Payne) A.; m. Patricia Catherine Cannon, Nov. 12, 1955; children: Sean Paul, Victoria Clare, Sarah Michele Arnell Aero. Engr., Royal Aircraft Establishment, 1946; BSc, U. London, 1953, PhD, 1967; MA, Occidental Coll., L.A., 1956; MS, U. So. Calif., 1958. Lectr. Poly. and Northampton Coll. Advance Tech., London, 1948-53; instr. U. So. Calif., L.A., 1954-59; asst. prof. mech. engring. Calif. State U., Long Beach, 1959-62, assoc. prof., 1962-66, prof., 1966-71, chmn. dept. mech. engring., 1964-65, acting chmn. divsn. engring., 1964-66, dean engring., 1967-69, rschr.; affiliate faculty dept. ocean engring. U. Hawaii, 1970-74; adj. prof. systems and insdl. engring. U. Ariz., 1981—; pres. Lenra Assocs. Ltd., 1973—; chmn., project mgr. Hawaii Environ. Simulation Lab., 1971-72. Contbr. articles to profl. jours. Trustee Rehab. Hosp. of the Pacific, 1975-78. Fellow Ergonomics Soc.; mem. Royal Aero. Soc., AIAA, IEEE Systems Man and Cybernetics Soc., AAUP, Am. Psychol. Assn., Soc. Engring., Psychology, Human Factors and Ergonomics Soc., Psi Chi, Alpha Pi Mu, Tau Beta Pi, Phi Kappa Phi, Pi Tau Sigma. Home: 4491 E Fort Lowell Rd Tucson AZ 85712-1106

ARNN, LARRY PAUL, former foundation executive, editor; b. Borger, Tex., Oct. 8, 1952; s. Robert Paul and Georgia (Asberry) A.; m. Penelope Margaret Carus Houghton, Oct. 20, 1979; children: Katy, Henry, Alice. BA in Polit. Sci., Ark. State U., 1974; MA in Govt., Claremont (Calif.) U., 1976, PhD, 1985. Dir. rsch. Winston Churchill Biography, Oxford, Eng., 1977-80; treas. Claremont Inst., Montclair, Calif., 1980-85, pres., 1985-98; editor Pub. Rsch., Syndicated, Montclair, 1980-85, pres., 1985—. Exec. dir. Aequus Inst., Montclair, 1985—; bd. dirs. North Cen. Life Ins. Co., chair various profl. panels; mem. Nat. Commn. on Regulatory Barriers to Affordable Housing, [illegible] Winston Churchill. Editor The Claremont Letter, 1981-83; pub. Claremont Review of Books, [illegible] Contbr. numerous articles to profl. jours. Mem. planning com. United Way,

Upland, Calif., 1990. Fellow Earhart Found., 1978-80, Rotary Found. fellow, 1977-78, Alcoa Found. fellow, 1972-74, Ark. State U. fellow, 1971-72, Richard M. Weaver fellow Intercollegiate Studies Inst., 1975. Mem. Am. Polit. Sci. Assn., Winston S. Churchill Assn. U.S. (fellow 1977-80), Western Polit. Sci. Assn., Phila. Soc., Pi Sigma Alpha. Republican. Episcopal. Avocation: tennis. Home: 189 Hillsdale St Hillsdale MI 49242-1244 Office: Claremont Inst 250 W 1st St Ste 330 Claremont CA 91711-4744

ARNOLD, DENNIS B. lawyer; b. Apr. 25, 1950; BA magna cum laude, SUNY Buffalo, 1972; JD, Yale U., 1975. Bar: Calif. 1976. Asst.-in-instrn. Yale Law Sch., New Haven, 1974-75; law clk. to Hon. Murray M. Schwartz U.S. Dist. Ct., Del., 1975-76; ptnr. Irell & Manella, 1980-88, Gibson, Dunn & Crutcher LLP, L.A., 1988—. Adj. assoc. prof. law Southwestern U. Sch. Law, 1980-82; advisor Restatement of Law, 2d edit., Suretyship and Guaranty, Am. Law Inst., 1989-95. Contbr. articles to profl. jours. Mem. ABA, Am. Law Inst., State Bar Calif. (standing joint com. anti-deficiency laws 1985-89, real property and bus. law sect. 1978—), L.A. County Bar Assn. (exec. com. commercial law and bankruptcy sect. 1987-90, 96—, exec. com. real property sect. 1987-92, steering com. real estate fin. subsect. 1987—), Fin. Lawyers Conf. (bd. govs. 1986-89, 92-95, 96—), Am. Coll. Real Estate Lawyers. Office: Gibson Dunn & Crutcher LLP 333 South Grand Ave Los Angeles CA 90071-3197

ARNOLD, J. KELLEY, magistrate; b. Lewiston, Idaho, Oct. 3, 1937; m. Diane Louise Jenkins. Student, Wash. State U., 1955-58; LLB, U. Idaho, 1961. Bar: Wash. 1961. Dep. pros. atty. Pierce County, 1963-64; atty., 1965-82; judge Wash. Superior Ct. Pierce County, Tacoma, 1982-94; magistrate judge for western Wash., U.S. Dist. Ct., Tacoma, 1994—. With U.S. Army, 1961-63. Office: US Ct 1717 Pacific Ave Rm 3409 Tacoma WA 98402-3234 E-mail: kelley_arnold@wawd.uscourts.gov

ARNOLD, JAMES RICHARD, chemist, educator; b. New Brunswick, N.J., May 5, 1923; s. Abraham Samuel and Julia (Jacobs) A.; m. Louise Clark, Oct. 11, 1952; children: Robert C., Theodore J., Kenneth C. AB, Princeton U., 1943, MA, 1945, PhD, 1946. Fellow Inst. Nuclear Studies, U. Chgo., 1946-47, faculty, 1948-55; NRC fellow Harvard U., 1947-48; faculty chemistry Princeton U., 1955-58; assoc. prof. chemistry U. Calif., San Diego, 1958-60, prof., 1960-92, Harold C. Urey prof., 1983-92, chmn. dept. chemistry, 1960-63. Assoc. Manhattan Project, 1943-46; dir. Calif. Space Inst., 1980-89, interim dir., 1996-97; prin. investigator Calif. Space Grant Consortium, 1989—; mem. various bds. NASA, 1959—; space sci. bd. NAS, 1970-74, com. on sci. and pub. policy, 1970-77. Mem. editl. bd. Ann. Rev. Nuclear Chemistry, 1972, Revs. Geophysics and Space Physics, 1972-75, Moon, 1972—; contbr. articles to profl. jours. Pres. Torrey Pines Elem. Sch. PTA, 1964-65; pres. La Jolla Democratic Club, 1965-66; nat. council World Federalists-U.S.A., 1970-72. Recipient E.O. Lawrence medal AEC, 1968, Leonard medal Meteoritical Soc., 1976, Kuiper award Am. Astron. Soc., 1993; asteroid 2143 named Jimarnold in his honor, 1980; Guggenheim fellow, India, 1972-73. Mem. Nat. Acad. Sci., Am. Acad. Arts and Scis., Internat. Acad. Astronautics, Am. Chem. Soc., AAAS, Fedn. Am. Scientists, World Federalist Assn. Office: U Calif San Diego Dept Chemistry Code 0524 La Jolla CA 92093 E-mail: jarnold@ucsd.edu

ARNOLD, JEANNE ELOISE, anthropologist, archaeologist, educator; b. Cleve., July 9, 1955; d. Lawrence Fred and Marybelle Eloise Arnold. BA, U. Mich., 1976; MA, U. Calif., Santa Barbara, 1979, PhD, 1983. Prof. anthropology U. No. Iowa, Cedar Falls, 1984-88, UCLA, 1988—, assoc. dir. Inst. Archaeology, 1988-99. Vis. instr. anthropology Rice U., Houston, 1981; vis. prof. anthropology Oreg. State U., Corvallis, 1983-84; sr. archaeologist Infotec Rsch., Inc., Sonora, Calif., 1986-87; cons. in field. Author 4 books; contbr. more than 45 articles and revs. to profl. jours. and over 25 chpts. to books. Rsch. grantee NSF, 1988-91, 95-99, 98-01; Rsch. and Ednl. grantee UCLA and Santa Barbara, 1977—. Mem. Am. Anthropol. Assn., Soc. Am. Archaeology, Soc. Calif. Archaeology, Cotsen Inst. Archaeology (mem. editorial bd. 1988—), Sigma Xi, Phi Beta Kappa. Avocations: photography, cinema, collecting ethnographic arts. Office: UCLA Dept Anthropology Box 951553 Haines Hall Los Angeles CA 90095-1553 E-mail: jearnold@ucla.edu

ARNOLD, JOHN DAVID, management counselor, catalyst; b. Boston, May 14, 1933; s. Israel and Edith (Gordon) A.; children by previous marriage: Derek, Keith, Craig; m. Diane Summers, Sept. 1994. BA cum laude in Social Rels., Harvard U., 1955. Prodn. supr., dealer svc. mgr. Arnold Stretch Mates Corp., Boston, 1957-59; asst. dir. manpower and orgn. devel. Polaroid Corp., Waltham, Mass., 1959-63; dir. internat. ops. Kepner-Tregoe & Assocs., Princeton, N.J., 1963-68; pres. John Arnold ExecuTrak Sys. Inc., Boston, 1968—. Merger integration catalyst, conflict resolution/prevention counselor, conf. leader numerous firms; speaker in field; bd. dirs. World Music. Author: Make Up Your Mind, 1978, The Art of Decision Making, 1978, Shooting the Executive Rapids, 1981, How To Make the Right Decisions, 1982, Trading Up-A Career Guide: How To Get Ahead without Getting Out, 1984, How To Protect Yourself Against a Takeover, 1986, The Complete Problem Solver! A Total System of Competitive Decision Making, 1992, When the Sparks Fly: Resolving Organizational Conflict, 1993; contbr. articles to bus. mags. Bd. dirs. Orange County Philharm. Soc., 2001. 1st lt. U.S. Army, 1955-57. Office: John Arnold ExecuTrak Sys 32031 Point Pl Laguna Beach CA 92651-6862 Fax: 949-499-7608. E-mail: jarnold917@aol.com

ARNOLD, KEN, state legislator; m. Marilyn Arnold. Ret. maj. state patrol; mem. Colo. Senate, Dist. 23, Denver, 1996—; mem. appropriations com., chair edn. com.; mem. joint capital devel. com., vice-chair judicary com. Republican. Home: 10187 Julian Way Westminster CO 80031-6734 Office: State Capitol 200 E Colfax Ave Ste 346 Denver CO 80203-1716 Fax: 303-439-7987

ARNOLD, MICHAEL NEAL, real property appraiser, consultant; b. Madera, Calif., June 6, 1947; s. John Patrick and Patricia (Neal) A.; m. Suzanne Elizabeth Badal, Aug. 31, 1968; children: C. Matthew Neal Arnold, Nathaniel T. Badal Arnold, Andrew T. White Arnold, Thomas A. Badal Arnold. BA in Geography, U. Calif., Santa Barbara, 1974. Cert. appraiser. Assoc. R.W. Raymond & Co., Santa Barbara, 1974; appraiser Madera County Assessor Office, 1975; assoc. Pickthorne & Assocs., San Bruno, Calif., 1975-76; ptnr. Hammock, Arnold, Smith & Co., Santa Barbara, 1976—. Instr. Santa Barbara City Coll., 1980-85, 99. Contbr. articles to profl. jours. Coach AYSO, Santa Barbara, 1978—; cub master Boy Scouts Am., Santa Barbara, 1985; mem. vestry, parish coun. Trinity Ch. Mem. Appraisal Inst., Vieja Valley Site Coun., Santa Barbara Coun. Real Estate Appraisers (founder, sec., speaker bur.), Appraisal Inst. (instr. 1990—, grader, com. chair, officer, chpt. pres.), Amateurs Club, Santa Barbara City Coll. (adv. coun. mem.). Episcopalian. Avocations: reading, walking, skiing, talking, genealogy. Home: 521 N Ontare Rd Santa Barbara CA 93105-2540 Office: Hammock Arnold Smith & Co 215 W Figueroa St Fl 2 Santa Barbara CA 93101-3602

ARNOLD, ROBERT MORRIS, banker; b. Seattle, June 6, 1928; s. Lawrence Moss and Grace Elizabeth (Heffernan) A.; children: Grace Allen Arnold, Lauren McLellan Gorter. BA in Fin. and Bus. Adminstrn., Yale U., 1951; grad., Pacific Coast Sch. Banking, 1963. With Seattle-1st Nat. Bank, 1951, 1955—, v.p., 1965-73, mgr. nat. accounts dept., 1969-73, sr. v.p., mgr. corp. bus. devel., 1973-99, also bd. dirs. Bd. dirs. Seafirst Corp. Bank of Am. Bd. dirs. Centrum Found., Fred C. Hutchinson Cancer Rsch.; trustee Poncho; bd. dirs., exec. com., fin. com. Seattle Art Mus., also mem., joint founder its Contemporary Art Coun. Officer USNR, 1951-55. Mem. Am. Inst. Banking, Mcpl. League Seattle, Yale Assn. Western Wash., Newcomen Soc. (treas. Pacific N.W. com.), Seattle Golf Club, Seattle Tennis Club, Seattle Yacht Club, University Club (Seattle), Bohemian Club (San Francisco), Thunderbird Golf Club (Palm Springs, Calif.), O'Donnell Golf Club (Palm Springs), Mission Hills Country Club (Palm Springs). Home: 1535 Parkside Dr E Seattle WA 98112-3719 Office: 1001 4th Ave Ste 4710 Seattle WA 98154-1198 also: 50 Hilton Head Dr Rancho Mirage CA 92270-1607

ARNOLD, ROY GARY, academic administrator; b. Lyons, Nebr., Feb. 20, 1941; m. Jane Kay Price, 1963; children: Jana Lynn Hoffman, Julie Kay Salvi. BS with distinction, U. Nebr., 1962; MS, Oreg. State U., 1965, PhD in Food Sci. and Tech., 1967. Research and devel. project leader Fairmont Foods Co., Omaha, 1962-63; asst. prof. food sci. and tech. U. Nebr., Lincoln, 1967-71, assoc. prof., 1971-74, asst. dir. resident instrn., 1971-72, acting dir. resident instrn., 1972-73, prof., 1974-87, head dept. food sci. and tech., 1973-79, coordinator food protein research group, 1975-79, dean, dir. agrl. expt. sta., 1980-82, vice chancellor inst. agr. and natural resources, 1982-87; dean Coll. Agrl. Scis. Oregon State U., Corvallis, 1987-91, provost, exec. v.p., 1991-2000; exec. assoc., dean Coll. Argl. Scis., Corvallis, 2000—. Del., devel. com. Imo (Nigeria) State U., 1981; mem. Ralston Purina Grad. Food Sci. Fellowship com., 1976-78, rev. team dept. food sci. U. Ill., 1979, adminstrv. site visit com. to Mid-Am. Internat. Agriculture Consortium Agy. for Internat. Devel. Morocco project, 1983, exec. com. agr. 2001 com. U. Nebr. Bd. Regents, 1982-83; program chmn. corn and sorghum industry research conf. Am. Seed Trade Assn., 1985. Mem. editorial bd. Jour. Dairy Sci., 1976-82, Jour, Agrl. and Food Chemistry, 1978-81; contbr. numerous articles to profl jours.; patentee in field. Mem. adminstrv. bd. St. Mark's United Meth. Ch., Lincoln, 1975-78, chmn. long range planning com., 1977-78, chmn. bldg. com. 1978-82. Grantee Nutrition Found., FDA, Nebr. Soybean Bd., Am. Soybean Assn. Research Found., Am. Egg Bd; Gen. Foods fellow, 1963-66. Fellow AAAS; mem. Inst. Food Technologists (nat. orgn. chmn. forward planning subcom. of exec. com. 1976-79, expert panel food safety and nutrition 1979-82, chmn. 1980-81, nominations and elections com. 1981-83, exec. com. 1985-88, 93-96, pres.-elect 1993-94, pres. 1994-95, William V. Cruess award 1980, Carl R. Fellers award 1998; Ak-Sar-Ben sect. past treas., sec., chmn.-elect, chmn. nat. councilor), Nat. Assn. Colls. and Tchrs. Agr., Univ. Assn. Adminstrv. Devel. (exec. com. 1973-74, 76-77, pres. 1978-79), MidAm. Internat. Agrl. Consortium (bd. dirs. 1982-87, chmn. 1986-87), N. Cen. Adminstrv. Heads Agr. (chmn.-elect 1985-86), Nat. Assn. State Univs. and Land Grant Colls. (divsn. agr. coun. adminstrv. heads agr. exec. com. 1985-87), Coll. Agr. Alumni Assn. (v.p. 1977-79), Innocents Soc. (pres. 1961-62), Sigma Xi (Nebr. chpt. sec. 1979-81), Phi Kappa Phi, Alpha Zeta, Gamma Sigma Delta (Nebr. chpt. past treas., sec., v.p., pres., Merit Tchg. award 1975), Phi Tau Sigma, FarmHouse Frat. (Doane award Nebr. chpt. 1962). Club: Crucibles (Lincoln). Office: Oreg State Univ 126 Strand Ag Hall Corvallis OR 97331-8521

ARNOLD, STANLEY NORMAN, manufacturing consultant; b. Cleve., May 26, 1915; s. Morris L. and Mildred (Stearn) A.; m. Barbara Anne Laing, Aug. 31, 1946; 1 child, Jennifer Laing B.S. in Econs., U. Pa., 1937. Co-founder, exec. v.p. Pick-N-Pay Supermarkets, Cleve., 1937-51; exec. v.p., dir. Cottage Creamery Co., Cleve., 1937-51; dir. sales promotion div. Young & Rubicam, N.Y.C., 1952-58; founder, pres. Stanley Arnold & Assocs., Inc., N.Y.C., 1958—. Cons. Ford Motor Co., United Airlines, Gen. Electric, Nat. Cash Register, IBM, Philip Morris, Am. Express, Bank of America, DuPont, Goodyear, Quaker Oats, Readers Digest, Continental Can, Hunt Foods, Moet-Hennessy, Seagram, Pan Am, Chrysler Corp., Pillsbury, Coca Cola, Gen. Mills, Lever Bros., Exxon, Arco, Hallmark, others; mem. adv. bd. Bank of Palm Springs div. Bank of Calif. subs. Mitsubishi Corp., 1989—; vis. exec. prof. Freeman Sch. Bus., Tulane U., 1998—. Author: Tale of the Blue Horse, 1968; Magic Power of Putting Yourself Over with People, 1961; I Ran Against Jimmy Carter, 1977. Syndicated daily columnist, 1943-48. Architect of plan to install new office of v.p. in White House. Contbr. articles to profl. jours. Pres. Ind. Sch. Fund of N.Y.C., 1960-66; mem. fund raising com. U.S. Olympic Team, 1984. Founding mem. Nat. Businessmen for Humphrey, 1968, Nat. Citizens for Humphrey, 1968; candidate for Dem. nomination for v.p. U.S., 1972; chmn. White House Libr. Fund Raising Com., 1961-63; corp. sponsor for The Rose as Nat. Flower, 1983-86; nat. chmn. Golf's Tribute to Ike, 1980; mem. Clinton adv. com., 1991-92. Recipient Sales Exec. award Sales Exec. Club N.Y., 1965; Wisdom award of Honor Wisdom Soc., 1979 Clubs: Les Amis D'Escoffier, Doubles, Dutch Treat (N.Y.C.); 7 Lakes Country, La Quinta Country, Racquet, Tennis, Indian Wells Racquet, Desert Riders, La Quinta Fishing, Oasis Water Park (Palm Springs, Calif.); Balboa Bay (Newport Beach, Calif.), Outrigger Canoe Club of Honolulu. Home: 162 Desert Lakes Dr Palm Springs CA 92264-5521 also: 2895 Kalakaua Ave Honolulu HI 96815-4003 Office: Stanley Arnold & Assocs Inc PO Box 2865 Palm Springs CA 92263-2865 also: 375 Park Ave New York NY 10152-0002

ARNOTT, ROBERT DOUGLAS, investment company executive; b. Chgo., June 29, 1954; s. Robert James Arnott and Catherine (Bonnell) Cameron; children: Robert Lindsay, Sydney Allison. BA, U. Calif., Santa Barbara, 1977. V.p. Boston Co., 1977-84; pres., chief exec. officer TSA Capital Mgmt., L.A., 1984-87; v.p., strategist Salomon Bros. Inc., N.Y.C., 1987-88; mng. ptnr. First Quadrant L.P., Morristown, N.J., Pasadena, Calif., and London, 1988-96, First Quadrant, L.P., Pasadena, London, Boston, 1996—. Mem. chmn.'s adv. coun. Chgo. Bd. Options Exch., 1989—; bd. dirs. Internat. Faculty in Fin.; mem. product adv. bd. Chgo. Mercantile Exch., 1990—; vis. prof. UCLA, 2001—. Editor: Asset Allocation, 1988, Active Asset Allocation, 1992, Handbook of Equity Style Management, 1997; mem. editorial bd. Jour. of Investing, 1990—, Jour. Portfolio Mgmt., 1984—, Jour. Wealth Mgmt., 1997—; contbr. articles to profl. jours. and chpts. to books. Mem. Inst. Internat. Rsch. (adv. bd. 1990—), Assn. for Investment Mgmt. and Rsch., Inst. Quantitative Rsch. in Fin., Toronto Stock and Futures Exch. (adv. coun. 1992—). Avocations: motorcycling, astrophotography, billiards, sommelier, travel. Office: 1st Quadrant LP 800 E Colorado Blvd Ste 900 Pasadena CA 91101-2141

ARO, GLENN SCOTT, environmental and safety executive; b. Balt., Jan. 18, 1948; s. Raymond Charles Sr. and Elizabeth Virginia (Coppage) A.; m. Marlene Rose Lefler, Jan. 8, 1972 (div. June 1987); children: Vincent Wade, Marlena Irene; m. Rosie Ann Lucero, Nov. 22, 1994. BS in Mech. Engrng., Gen. Motors Inst., Flint, Mich., 1972; MBA in Fin., Wayne State U., 1980. Registered environmental assessor, Calif. From engr. to supr. GM, Detroit, Balt., L.A., 1966-84; environ. specialist New United Motor, Fremont, Calif., 1984-86; environ. engrng. mgr. Def. Systems FMC Corp., San Jose, 1986-89; cons./exec. sales rep. Gaia Systems, Menlo Park, 1990; corp. environ. & safety mgr. Ampex Corp., Redwood City, 1990-92; gen. ops. mgr. Hughes Environ. Systems, El Segundo, 1992-98; corp. EHS and ethics mgr. Hughes Electronics Corp., El Segundo, 1998—. Lectr. colls. and seminars Environ. Regulatory Issues, 1988—. Author: Developing a National Environmental Policy in a Global Market, 1989; contbd. articles to profl. jours. Panel mem. Toxics Awareness Project, San Francisco, 1989—; com. mem. Environ. Working Group, Sacramento, 1986-88. Mem. Peninsula Indsl. & Bus. Assn. (bd. dirs., v.p. 1988-91). Republican. Roman Catholic. Avocations: running, reading, travel, baseball, basketball. Home: 241 Palos Verdes Dr W Apt 203 Palos Verdes Estates CA 90274

AROESTY, SIDNEY A. medical diagnostic manufacturing company executive; b. Rochester, N.Y., Nov. 20, 1946; s. Albert S. and Marilyn Jo (Stolnitz) A.; m. Craol Jean Hopper, Dec. 31, 1970; children: Jason David, Michael Jonathan. BS, U. Rochester, 1972. Lab. supr. Strong Meml. Hosp., Rochester, 1971-73; dir. spl. determinations lab. Highland Hosp., Rochester, 1973-78; exec. v.p. Diagnostic Products Corp., L.A., 1978-88, pres., 1988-94, sr. v.p., COO, 1997—, also bd. dirs. Contbr. articles to profl. jours. Sgt. USAF, 1967-71. Home: 12 Mile Post Ln Pittsfield NY 14534 Office: Diagnostic Products Corp 5700 W 96th St Los Angeles CA 90045-5597 E-mail: saroesty@dpconline.com

ARONOWITZ, JOEL ALAN, plastic and reconstructive surgeon; b. Memphis, Dec. 5, 1956; MD, Baylor Coll. Medicine, 1982. Intern in gen. surgery Baylor Coll. Medicine, 1982-83, resident in plastic surgery, 1983-87; attending plastic surgeon Cedars Sinai Med. Ctr., 1987—, vice chmn. plastic surgery divsn., 1997—. Office: 8635 W 3rd St Ste 1090 Los Angeles CA 90048-6104

ARONS, ARNOLD BORIS, physicist, educator; b. Lincoln, Nebr., Nov. 23, 1916; s. Solomon and Esther (Rosen) A.; m. Jean M. Rendall, Aug. 17, 1942; children: Marion, Janet, Kenneth, Paul. ME, Stevens Inst. Tech., 1937, MS, 1940; PhD, Harvard U., 1943; MA (hon.), Amherst (Mass.) Coll., 1953; DE (hon.), Stevens Inst. Tech., 1982. Rsch. scientist Woods Hole (Mass.) Oceanographic Inst., 1942-68; from asst. to assoc. prof. Stevens Inst. Tech., Hoboken, N.J., 1946-52; prof. physics Amherst Coll., 1952-68, U. Wash., Seattle, 1968-82, prof. emeritus, 1982—. Cons. in field, 1946-65; mem. Commn. on Coll. Physics, 1962-68. Author: A Guide to Introductory Physics Teaching, 1990, Teaching Introductory Physics, 1997; contbr. articles to profl. jours. Guggenheim Found. fellow, 1957-58, NSF fellow, 1962-63. Fellow AAAS, Am. Phys. Soc.; mem. Am. Assn. Physics Tchrs. (pres. 1966-67, Oersted medal 1972), Am. Geophys. Union, Nat. Sci. Tchrs. Assn. Achievements include patent for piezoelectric guage for explosion pressure measurement, experimental and theoretical work on phase distortion of acoustic pulses reflected from the sea bed; research on model of abyssal oceanic circulation, cognitive development, teaching and learning of physics. Home: 10313 Lake Shore Blvd NE Seattle WA 98125-8160 Office: U Wash Dept Physics PO Box 351560 Seattle WA 98195-1560 E-mail: arons@phys.washington.edu

AROVA, SONIA, artistic director, ballet educator; b. Sofia, Bulgaria, June 20, 1928; came to U.S., 1954; d. Albert and Rene (Melamedoff) Errio; m. Thor Sutowski, Mar. 11, 1965; 1 child, Arlane. Grad., Fine Arts Sch., Paris, 1940, Fine Arts Sch., Eng., 1944. Ballerina Internat. Ballet, London, 1944-47, Rambert Ballet, London, 1947-50, Festival Ballet, London, 1950-54, Am. Ballet Theater, N.Y.C., 1954-58, Ballet deChamps-Elysees, Paris, 1958-60, Ballet Russe, 1960-62, Royal Ballet, London, 1962-63; artistic dir. Nat. Ballet, Oslo, 1964-70, Hamburg (Germany) Ballet, 1970-71; co-dir. San Diego Ballet, 1971-75; dir. State of Ala. Ballet, 81-96, Ballet South, Birmingham, 1981-86; artistic advisor Calif. Ballet, San Diego, 1996—. Instr. Sch. Fine Arts, 1975-96; guest tchr. Australian Ballet, 1993, 94, Bayerische Staatsballet, Munich, Germany, 1994. Recipient World Championship of Dance award Ballet Jury, Paris, 1939; decorated knight of First Order, King Olav of Norway, 1971. Office: Calif Ballet 8276 Ronson Rd San Diego CA 92111-2015

ARROW, KENNETH JOSEPH, economist, educator; b. N.Y.C., Aug. 23, 1921; s. Harry I. and Lillian (Greenberg) A.; m. Selma Schweitzer, Aug. 31, 1947; children: David Michael, Andrew. BS in Social Sci., CCNY, 1940; MA, Columbia U., 1941, PhD, 1951, DSc (hon.), 1973; LLD (hon.), U. Chgo., 1967, CUNY, 1972, Hebrew U. Jerusalem, 1975, U. Pa., 1976, Washington U., St. Louis, 1989, Harvard U., , 1999; D. Social and Econ. Scis. (hon.), U. Vienna, Austria, 1971; LLD (hon.), Ben-Gurion U. of the Negev, 1992; D. Social Scis. (hon.), Yale, 1974; D (hon.), Université René Descartes, Paris, 1974, U. Aix-Marseille III, , 1985, U. Cattolica del Sacro Cuore, Milan, Italy, 1994, U. Uppsala, , 1995, U. Buenos Aires, 1999, U. Cyprus, 2000; Dr.Pol., U. Helsinki, 1976; MA (hon.), Harvard U., 1968; DLitt, Cambridge U., Eng., 1985; LLD (hon.), Harvard U., 1999; PhD (hon.), Tel Aviv U., 2001. Rsch. assoc. Cowles Commn. for Research in Econs., 1947-49; asst. prof. econs. U. Chgo., 1948-49; acting asst. prof. econs. and stats. Stanford, 1949-50, assoc. prof., 1950-53, prof. econs., stats. and ops. rsch., 1953-68; prof. econs. Harvard, 1968-74, James Bryant Conant univ. prof., 1974-79; exec. head dept. econs. Stanford U., 1954-56, acting exec. head dept., 1962-63, Joan Kenney prof. econs. and prof. ops. rsch., 1979-91, prof. emeritus, 1991—. Economist Coun. Econ. Advisers, U.S. Govt., 1962; cons. RAND Corp.; Fulbright prof. U. Siena, 1995; vis. fellow All Souls Coll., Oxford, 1996; overseas rsch. fellow Churchill Coll., Cambridge, 1963-64, 70, 73, 80. Author: Social Choice and Individual Values, 1951, Essays in the Theory of Risk Bearing, 1971, The Limits of Organization, 1974, Collected Papers, Vols. I-VI, 1983-85; co-author: Mathematical Studies in Inventory and Production, 1958, Studies in Linear and Nonlinear Programming, 1958, Time Series Analysis of Inter-industry Demands, 1959, Public Investment, The Rate of Return and Optimal Fiscal Policy, 1971, General Competitive Analysis, 1971, Studies in Resource Allocation Processes, 1977, Social Choice and Multicriterion Decision Making, 1985. Served as capt. AUS, 1942-46. Recipient Alfred Nobel Meml. prize in econ. scis. Swedish Acad. Scis., 1972, Kempé de Feriet medal, 1998, medal U. Paris, 1998; Social Sci. Rsch. fellow, 1952; fellow Ctr. for Advanced Study in the Behavioral Scis., 1956-57, Churchill Coll., Cambridge, Eng., 1963-64, 70, 73, 86; Guggenheim fellow, 1972-73. Fellow AAAS (chmn. sect. K. 1983), Am. Acad. Arts and Scis. (v.p. 1979-81, 91-93), Econometric Soc. (v.p. 1955, pres. 1956), Am. Statis. Assn., Inst. Math. Stats., Am. Econ. Assn. (exec. com. 1967-69, pres. 1973, John Bates Clark medal 1957), Internat. Soc. Inventory Rsch. (pres. 1983-90); mem. NAS (mem. coun. 1990-93), Inst. Medicine (sr.), Internat. Econs. Assn. (pres. 1983-86), Am. Philos. Soc., Inst. Mgmt. Scis. (pres. 1963, chmn. coun. 1964, Von Neumann prize 1986), Finnish Acad. Scis. (fgn. hon.), Brit. Acad. (corr.), Western Econ. Assn. (pres. 1980-81), Soc. Social Choice and Welfare (pres. 1991-93), Pontifical Acad. Social Scis., Game Theory Soc. Office: Stanford U Dept Econs Stanford CA 94305-6072 Fax: 650-725-5702. E-mail: arrow@leland.stanford.edu

ARTHUR, MICHAEL ELBERT, lawyer, financial advisor; b. Seattle, Oct. 9, 1952; s. Theodore E. and Gladys L. (Jones) A.; m. Claire C. Meeker, Dec. 23, 1974; children: Christine, Conor. BA, U. Calif., Santa Barbara, 1974; JD, Stanford U., 1977. Bar: Oreg. 1977, U.S. Dist. Ct. Oreg. 1977, U.S. Ct. Appeals (9th cir.) 1984. Assoc. Miller Nash LLP, Portland, Oreg., 1977-84, ptnr., 1984-2001; fin. advisor Spence Partners at UBS/Paine Webber, Portland, 2001—. Trustee Chiles Found. Mem. Oreg. Bar Assn., Wash. Bar Assn., Order of Coif, Phi Beta Kappa. Home: 13535 NW Lariat Ct Portland OR 97229-7001 Office: UBS Paine Webber 805 SW Broadway Ste 2600 Portland OR 97205-3365 E-mail: mike.arthur@ubspainewebber.com

ARTHUR, PAUL KEITH, electronic engineer; b. Kansas City, Mo., Jan. 14, 1931; s. Walter B. and Frieda J. (Burckhardt) A.; m. Joy N. Lim, Apr. 26, 1958; children: Gregory V., Lia F. Student, Ohio No. U., 1947, Taylor U., Upland, Ind., 1948-49; BSEE, Purdue U., 1956; postgrad., N.Mex. State U., 1957-78. Registered profl. engr., N.Mex.; cert. army acquisition profl.; cert. Naval engrng. duty officer, Navy material profl. With White Sands Missile Range, N.Mex., 1956—; electronic engr. field engrng., group missile flight surveillance office, 1956-60; chief field engrng group, 1960-62; project engr. Pershing Weapon Sys. Army Missile Test and Evaluation Directorate, 1962-74; chief high altitude air def. projects br., 1974-82; chief air def. materiel test divsn., 1982-91; dep dir. Materiel Test Directorate, 1991-95; dir., 1995-98; exec. dir. Nat. Range, 1998-99; dep. comdr. White Sands Test Ctr., 1999—. Mem. N.Mex. Spaceport Commn., 1994-95, Southwest Regional Space Task Force, Metro Planning Orgn.; past pres. missile range pioneer group; bd. dirs. Dagupan Electric Corp. of the Philippines. Author numerous plans and reports on weapon systems test and evaluation and topics in naval engrng. Chmn. adminstrv. bd. Meth. Ch., 1992-95. Served with USN, 1949-53, USNR, 1954-87, rear adm. and sr. engring. duty officer, 1984-87. Decorated Legion of Merit, Meritorious Svc. medal, Navy Achievement medal, Mil. Order St. Barbara, others. Mem. AIAA (past vice chmn.), Internat. Test and Evaluation Assn., Am. Def. Preparedness Assn. (past pres.), Assn. Old Crows, Naval Res. Assn., Res. Officers Assn. (pres. 1983-85), United Vets. Coun. (chmn. 1984-85), Am. Soc. Naval Engrs., Naval Inst., Navy League, Surface Navy Assn., Assn. U.S. Army, U.S. Field Arty. Assn., Purdue U. Alumni Assn. (past pres.), N.Mex. State U. Alumni Assn., Mesilla Valley Track Club, Bujutsukan Acad. Martial Arts. Home: 2050 San Acacio St Las Cruces NM 88001-1570 Office: Nat Range White Sands Missile Range NM 88002

ARUM, ROBERT, lawyer, sports events promoter; b. N.Y.C., Dec. 8, 1931; s. Samuel and Celia (Baumgarten) A.; m. Barbara Mandelbaum, July 2, 1960 (div. 1977); children: John, Richard, Elizabeth; m. Sybil Ann Hamada, Dec. 18, 1977 (div. 1991); m. Lovee Hazan Du Boef, Sept. 14, 1991. BA, NYU, 1953; JD cum laude, Harvard U., 1956. Bar: N.Y. 1956. Atty. firm Root, Barrett, Cohen, Knapp & Smith, N.Y.C., 1956-61; asst. U.S. atty., chief tax sect. U.S. Atty.'s Office, So. Dist. N.Y., 1961-64; partner firm Phillips, Nizer, Benjamin, Krim & Ballon, N.Y.C., 1964-72, Arum & Katz, N.Y.C., 1972-79; chmn. Top Rank, Inc.; Promoter Ali-Frazier Super Fight II, 1974, Evel Knievel Snake River Canyon Jump, 1974, Ali-Norton World Heavyweight Championship, 1976, Monzon-Valdez World Middleweight Championships, 1976, 77, Ali-Spinks Championships, 1978, Leonard-Duran Championships, 1980, 89, Top Rank/ESPN Boxing Series, 1980—, Arguello-Pryor Championship, 1983, Moore-Duran Championship, 1983, Hagler-Duran Championship, 1983, Hagler-Hearns Championship, 1985, Hagler-Leonard Superfight Championship, 1987, Leonard-Hearns "The War" Championship, 1989-91, Holyfield-Foreman World Heavyweight Championship, 1991, Holyfield-Holmes World Heavyweight Championship, 1992, Foreman/Morrison Heavyweight Championship, 1993, De la Hoya/Whitaker, 1997, De la Hoya/Chavez, 1996, 98, De la Hoya/Quartey, 1999, De la Hoya/Trinidad, 1999. Elected to Boxing Hall of Fame, 1999. Mem. Friars Club. Home: 36 Gulf Stream Ct Las Vegas NV 89113-1354 Office: 3980 Howard Hughes Pkwy Las Vegas NV 89109-0992 E-mail: erroa@aol.com

ARUNDEL, JAMES D. lawyer; b. Omaha, July 30, 1947; BA, U. Nebr., 1969; JD, U. Chgo., 1972. Bar: Nebr. 1972, Colo. 1981. Mng. ptnr. Kutak Rock, Denver. Mem. Nebr. State Bar Assn., Colo. State Bar Assn., Omaha Bar Assn., Denver Bar Assn., Phi Beta Kappa. Office: Kutak Rock 717 17th St Ste 2900 Denver CO 80202-3329

ARVESON, WILLIAM BARNES, mathematics educator; b. Oakland, Calif., Nov. 22, 1934; s. Ronald Magnus and Audrey Mary (Hichens) A.; m. Lee A. Kaskutas. B.S. in Math, Calif. Inst. Tech., 1960; M.A., UCLA, 1963, Ph.D., 1964. Benjamin Peirce instr. Harvard U., 1965-68; lectr. dept. math. U. Calif., Berkeley, 1968-69, assoc. prof., 1969-74, prof., 1974—, Miller rsch. prof., 1985-86, 99—. Author: An Invitation to C*-algebras, 1976; assoc. editor: Duke Math. Jour., 1975-86, Jour. of Operator Theory, 1977-87, editor, 1987—; contbr. articles to math. jours. Served with U.S. Navy, 1952-55. John Simon Guggenheim fellow, 1976-77 Mem. Am. Math. Soc. (assoc. editor bulletin 1988-91), Edinburgh Math. Soc. (assoc. editor proceedings 1989—). Office: U Calif Dept Math Berkeley CA 94720-0001

ARZBERGER, GUS, state legislator, retired farmer and rancher; m. Marsha Daniels; two children; two stepchildren. Student, Air Force U. Mem. Ariz. Ho. of Reps., 1985-88, Ariz. State Senate, 1989—, mem. natural resources com., mem. transp. com., mem. agr. and environment com., mem. appropriations com., mem. govt. reform com., others. Supporter S.E. Ariz. Food Bank Warehouse; active Ariz. Civil Air Patrol; bd. dirs. Cochise County Sheriff's Posse; pres. Willcox Dem. Club; Dem. precinct committeeman; ex-officio mem. Ariz. Aero. Bd. Infantry platoon sgt. U.S. Army, WWII, ETO. Mem. VFW (bd. dirs.), Farm Bur., Ariz. Cotton Growers, Ariz. Grain Growers, Cochise-Graham County Cattle Growers Assn., Willcox C. of C. and Agr., Gila Valley Econ. Devel. Assn., Willcox Elks Lodge (charter), Vets. Club (bd. dirs.). Democrat. Office: State Capitol Bldg 1700 W Washington St Ofc 310 Phoenix AZ 85007-2812 E-mail: garzberg@azleg.state.az.us

ARZBERGER, MARSHA, state senator; b. St. Joseph, Mo. m. Gus Arzberger; 2 children; 2 step-children. BS in Edn. with honors, N.W. Mo. State U.; MPA with distinction, postgrad. in Polit. Sci., Ariz. State U. Cert. tchr., Okla., Ariz.; registered med. lab. technologist; lic. pilot. Tchr. Okla. Sch. Bus. and Tech., Tulsa; substitute tchr. Willcox (Ariz.) H.S.; dean Draughon's Bus. Coll., Kansas City, Mo.; ptnr. ranch; owner, mgr. apt. complexes Willcox and Benson, Ariz.; asst. for spl. projects Ariz. Bd. Regents; Dem. senator dist. 8 Ariz. State Senate. Author novel; contbr. articles to profl. jours. Mem. cmty. com. Willcox Schs.; pilot Civil Air Patrol, group comdr. S.E. Ariz., search pilot, Search and Rescue Mission comdr.; campaign mgr. Senator Gus Arzberger; organizer Town Halls in Dist. 8 for 3 state legislators; precinct committeeperson; del. State Dem. Caucus; mem. Cochise Coll. Found. Bd., Farm Bur., Cattle Growers, Friends of Libr., Sulphur Springs Hist. Soc., Cochise County Dems., LWV, Cowbelles. Recipient State Comdr.'s commendation Civil Air Patrol. Mem. AAUW, AARP, Bus. and Profl. Women, Western Writers Assn., Aircraft Owners and Pilots Assn. Office: Ariz State Senate State Capitol Rm 313 1700 W Washington Phoenix AZ 85007 E-mail: marzberg@azleg.state.az.us

ASCHAFFENBURG, WALTER EUGENE, composer, music educator; b. Essen, Germany, May 20, 1927; came to U.S., 1938, naturalized, 1944; s. William Arthur and Margarete (Herz) A.; m. Nancy Dandridge Cooper, Aug. 14, 1951 (div.); children: Ruth Margareta, Katherine Elizabeth; m. Rayna Klatzkin Barroll, Aug. 5, 1987. Diploma, Hartford Sch. Music, 1945; BA, Oberlin Coll., 1951; MA, Eastman Sch. Music, 1952. Prof. composition and music theory, former chmn. composition dept. Oberlin (Ohio) Coll. Conservatory of Music, 1952-87, prof. emeritus, 1987—, also former chmn. dept. music theory., 1952-87. Composer: FANTASY for Brass Ensemble, 1950, TRIO for piano, violin, cello, 1951, Divertimento for Trumpet, Horn, Trombone 1952, Chaconne for Brass Ensemble, 1952, Ozymandias-Symphonic Reflections for Orch., 1952, Cello Sonata, 1953, Sonata for Solo Violin, 1954, Piano Sonatina, 1954, String Quartet, 1955, Bartleby-opera, 1962, Elegy for Strings, 1961, The 23d Psalm for chorus, tenor solo, and oboe, 1963, Three Dances for Orch., 1966, Three Shakespeare Sonnets for tenor and piano, 1967, Quintet for Winds, 1967, Proem for Brass and Percussion, 1969, Blossom Music Ctr. Fanfare, 1970, Duo for Violin and Cello, 1971, Conversations-Six Pieces for Piano, 1973, Summit Records, 1994, A Slight Music for Clarinet, Bassoon and Tuba, 1975, Libertatem Appellant for Tenor, Baritone and Orch., 1976, Carrousel*24 Pieces for Piano, 1980, Concertino for Violin, Ten Winds and Contrabass, 1981, Laughing Time for Mixed Chorus, 1983, Festive Fanfare and Hymn for Brass and Percussion, 1983, Concerto for Oboe and Orch., 1985, New World Records, 1997. From South Mountain for Brass Quintet, 1987, Coalescence for Oboe and Cello, 1989, Sonata for the Fortepiano or Pianoforte, 1990, Parings for Clarinet and Piano, 1993. Served with AUS, 1945-47. Recipient award Fromm Music Found., 1953; Nat. Inst. Arts and Letters award, 1966; Cleve. arts prize, 1980; Guggenheim fellow, 1955-56, 73-74 Mem. ASCAP, Soc. Composers, Am. Music Ctr., Soc. Music Theory. Home: 4639 E Monte Way Phoenix AZ 85044-[illegible]

ASCHENBRENNER, FRANK ALOYSIOUS, former diversified manufacturing company executive; b. Ellis, Kans., June 26, 1924; s. Philip A. and Rose E. Aschenbrenner; m. Gertrude Wilhelmina DeBie, Nov. 15, 1946; children: Richard David, Robert Wayne, Mary Lynne BS with high honors, Kans. State U., 1950; PhD in Physics, M.I.T., 1954. Mgr. physics and math. Gen. Electric, Cin., 1958-61; asst. dir. space div. Rockwell Internat., Downey, Calif., 1961-69, corp. dir. tech. Pitts., 1969-71, v.p., gen. mgr. div. yarn machinery Charlotte, N.C., 1971-75; pres. COR, Inc., Charlotte, 1975-77; v.p. research and devel. and engring. Ball Corp., Muncie, Ind., 1977-86; pvt. bus. cons. Poway, Calif., 1986—. Chmn. bd. RAMZ Corp., Dunkirk, Ind., 1985—; nat. bd. advisors Rose-Hulman Inst., Terre Haute, Ind., 1984—, U. Tenn. Space Inst., Tullahoma, 1982—. Served with USN, 1943-47 Mem. AIAA, Am. Phys. Soc., Naval Res. Assn., San Diego Venture Group Achievements include design of measurement technique which was needed to determine threshold energy for nuclear fission in order to improve efficiency of nuclear bombs; pioneering of computerized nuclear radiation shielding design and analysis for nuclear reactors. Home and Office: 14258 Palisades Dr Poway CA 92064-6443

ASH, ROY LAWRENCE, business executive; b. Los Angeles, Oct. 20, 1918; s. Charles K. and Fay E. (Dickinson) A.; m. Lila M. Hornbek., Nov. 13, 1943; children— Loretta Ash Danko, James, Marilyn Ash Hanna, Robert, Charles. M.B.A., Harvard, 1947. Chief fin. officer Hughes Aircraft Co., 1949-53; co-founder Litton Industries, Inc., Beverly Hills, Calif., 1953-72, dir., 1953-72, pres., 1961-72; chmn. Pres.'s Adv. Coun. on Exec. Orgn., 1969-71; asst. to Pres. U.S.; dir. Office Mgmt. and Budget, Washington, 1973-75; chmn. bd., chief exec. officer AM Internat., 1976-81. Co-chmn. Japan-Calif. Assn., 1965-72, 80-81; mem. vis. com. Harvard U. Kennedy Sch. Govt., 1992—; mem. Bus. Roundtable, 1977-81. Vice chmn. Los Angeles Olympic Organizing Com., 1980-85, chmn. fin. com.; trustee Calif. Inst. Tech., 1967-72, Com. for Econ. Devel., 1970-72, 75— ; dir. Los Angeles World Affairs Council, 1968-72, 78— , pres., 1970-72; chmn. adv. council on gen. govt. Rep. Nat. Com., 1977-80; chmn. L.A. Music Ctr. Opera Assn., 1988-93. From pvt. to capt. Army Air Corps, 1942-46. Mem. C. of C. U.S. (bd. dirs. 1979-85, chmn. internat. policy com. 1979-85). Clubs: Bel Air Country, Harvard, California (Los Angeles). Office: Ste 1600 1900 Avenue Of The Stars Los Angeles CA 90067-4407

ASHDOWN, FRANKLIN DONALD, physician, composer; b. Logan, Utah, May 2, 1942; s. Donald and Theresa Marie (Hill) A. BA, Tex. Tech. U., 1963; MD, U. Tex., 1967. Chief of med. Holloman Air Force Base, New Mexico, 1971-73; chief of staff Gerald Champion Mem. Hosp., Alamogordo, N.M., 1976, 91, 92; pvt. practice Alamogordo, 1973—; pres. Otero County Concerts Assn., Alamogordo, 1985-94, Otero County Med. Soc., Alamogordo, 1986. Cons. New Mexico Sch. for Visually Handicapped, Alamogordo, 1973-76. Composer of more than 80 published and recorded works. Bd. dirs. Otero County Mental Health Assn., Alamogordo, 1973-77, Flickinger Found. for Performing Arts, 1995; bd. trustees Gerald Champion Meml. Hosp., 1992. Mem. Gerald Champion Mem. Hosp., N.M. Med. Soc., Am. Soc. Internal Med., ASCAP (Standard Panel award 2000, 2001). Republican. Office: 1301 Cuba Ave Alamogordo NM 88310-5727

ASHFORD, CLINTON RUTLEDGE, judge; b. Honolulu, Mar. 23, 1925; s. Huron Kanoelani and Lillian Radcliffe (Cooke) A.; m. Joan Beverly Schumm, Aug. 24, 1951; children: Marguerite, Frank, Bruce, James B.A., U. Calif.-Berkeley, 1945; J.D., U. Mich., 1950. Bar: Hawaii 1950, U.S. Supreme Ct. 1967, Republic of Marshall Islands 1985. Ptnr. Lee & Ashford, Honolulu, 1951-53; dep. atty. gen. Hawaii, 1953-55; ptnr. Ashford & Wriston, Honolulu, 1955-89, of counsel, 1990—; chief justice Supreme Ct., Republic of Marshall Islands, 1989-96. Bd. dirs. Child and Family Svc., Honolulu, 1967-73, pres., 1971; bd. dirs. Health and Cmty. Svcs. Coun., 1973-75, Mediation Ctr. of the Pacific, 1995-2000, Aloha United Way, 1975-81, exec. com., 1977-79; bd. dirs. Hawaii Justice Found., 1994-99, pres., 1996. With USNR, 1943-46, res., 1950-64, ret. lt. comdr. emeritus. Fellow Am. Bar Found. (emeritus), Am. Coll. Trust and Estate Counsel, Am. Coll. Real Estate Lawyers, Am. Coll. Trial Lawyers, Am. Acad. Appellate Lawyers, Coll. Law Office Mgmt.; mem. ABA (bd. govs. 1979-82, exec. com. 1981-82), Hawaii Bar Assn. (pres. 1972), Am. Law Inst., Am. Judicature Soc. (bd. dirs. 1981-86, chpt. bd. dirs. 1998-2001), Internat. Acad. Estate and Trust Law, Order of Coif, Lambda Alpha (Aloha chpt.). Avocations: amateur radio operator, blue water sailor. Home: 45-628 Halekou Pl Kaneohe HI 96744-5203 Office: Ashford & Wriston PO Box 131 1099 Alakea St Fl 14 Honolulu HI 96813-4500 E-mail: cashford@awlaw.com

ASHMAN, STUART, museum director; b. N.Y.C., Apr. 10, 1948; BA, CUNY, 1972. Mus. intern in mus. studies and cinematography Staten Island (N.Y.) Inst. Arts and Scis., 1970-72; with Apeiron Workshops in Photography, Rochester Inst. Tech., 1972-78; gallery dir., visual arts coord. Armory for the Arts, Santa Fe, 1978-80; art instr. Santa Fe Preparatory Sch., 1980-82; artist in residence N.Mex. rural pub. schs., 1982-84; art instr. Penitentiary of N.Mex., 1984-86; studio artist Santa Fe, 1986-90; founder, coord. Mus. on Wheels program Santa Fe Children's Mus., 1990-92; Art with Elders coord. Open Hands Inc., 1990-92; artist in residence N.Mex. Arts Divsn., Santa Fe, 1990-92; curator/dir. The Gov.'s Gallery Mus. Fine Arts, Mus. N.Mex., Santa Fe, 1992-95, dir., 1995—; exec. dir. Spanish Colonial Arts Soc. Mus., Santa Fe, 2000—. Chmn. acquisitions com. Mus. N.Mex.; adv. bd. Georgia O'Keeffe Mus., SITE Santa Fe; bd. dirs. N.Mex. Counseling and Therapy Bd., Art Therapy Standards Com., Capitol Arts Found., Santa Fe Children's Mus. Mem. Am. Assn. Muss., Am. Fedn. Arts, Mus. N.Mex. Found., Friends of Contemporary Art, Folk Art Soc. Am. Home: 10 Angelitis Rd Santa Fe NM 87501 Office: Spanish Colonial Arts Soc Mus PO Box 1611 Santa Fe NM 87504 E-mail: sashman@spanishcolonial.org

ASHMEAD, ALLEZ MORRILL, speech, hearing, and language pathologist, orofacial myologist, consultant; b. Provo, Utah, Dec. 18, 1916; d. Laban Rupert and Zella May (Miller) M.; m. Harvey H. Ashmead, 1940; children: Harve DeWayne, Sheryl Mae Harames, Zeltha Janeel Henderson, Emma Allez Broadfoot. BS, Utah State U., 1938; MS summa cum laude, U. Utah, 1952, PhD summa cum laude, 1970; postgrad., Idaho State U., Oreg. State Coll., U. Denver, U. Utah, Brigham Young U., Utah State U., U. Washington, U. No. Colo. Cert. secondary edn., remedial reading, spl. edn., learning disabilities; cert. ASHA clin. competence speech pathology and audiology; profl. cert. in orofacial myology. Tchr. pub. schs., Utah, Idaho, 1938-43; speech and hearing pathologist Bushnell Hosp., Brigham City, Utah, 1943-45; sr. speech correctionist Utah State Dept. Health, Salt Lake City, 1945-52; dir. speech and hearing dept. Davis County Sch. Dist., Farmington, Utah, 1952-65; clin., field supr. U. Utah, Salt Lake City, 1965-70, 75-78; speech pathologist Box Elder Sch. Dist., Brigham City, 1970-75, 78-84. Teaching specialist Brigham Young U., Provo, 1970-73; speech pathologist Primary Children's Med. Ctr., Salt Lake City, 1975-77; pvt. practice speech pathology and orofacial myology, 1970-88; del. USSR Profl. Speech Pathology seminar, 1984, 86; participant numerous internat. seminars. Author: Physical Facilities for Handicapped Children, 1957, A Guide for Training Public School Speech and Hearing Clinicians, 1965, A Guide for Public School Speech Hearing Programs, 1959, Impact of Orofacial Myofunctional Treatment on Orthodontic Correction, 1982, Meeting Needs of Handicapped Children, 1975, Relationship of Trace Minerals to Disease, 1972, Macro and Trace Minerals in Human Metabolism, 1971, Electromotive Potential Differences Between Stutterers and Non-stutterers, 1970, Learning Disability, An Educational Adventure, 1969, New Horizons in Special Education, 1969, Developing Speech and Language in the Exceptional Child, 1961, [illegible] Primary Stuttering, 1951, numerous others; contbr. research articles to profl. jours. Student Placement chair Am. Field Service, Kaysville, Utah, 1962-66; ednl. del. Women's State Legis. Council, Salt Lake City, 1958-70; chairwoman fund raising Utah Symphony Orch., Salt Lake City, 1970-71; sec., treas. Utah chpt. U.S. Council for Exceptional Children, 1958-62, membership com. chair, 1962-66, program com. chair, 1966-68 Recipient Scholarship award for Higher Edn. U. Utah, Salt Lake City, 1969; Phi Kappa Phi scholar, Delta Kappa Gamma scholar, 1968; rsch. grantee Utah Dept. Edn., 1962. Mem. NEA, Utah Ednl. Assn., Am. Speech, Lang. Hearing Assn. (life, continuing edn. com. 1985, Ace award for Continuing Edn. 1984), Western Speech Assn., Internat. Assn. Orofacial Myology (life, bd. examiners, Sci. Contribution award 1982), Utah Speech, Hearing and Lang. Assn. (life, sec., treas. 1956-60), AAUW (Utah state bd. chair status of women 1959-62, Kaysville br. 1957-60, bd. dirs. Kaysville-Davis br. 1987-92, chair internat. rels. 1987-91, chair cultural interests Kaysville-Davis br. 1991-92), Delta Kappa Gamma (state scholarship award 1968, del. Woman's State Legis. Coun. 1958-70, profl. affairs chair 1963-67, tchr. of yr. award 1978), AAUW (bd. dirs. internat. rels. Kaysvile-Davis br., 1988-91), Daus. Utah Pioneers (parliamentarian Kaysville 1980-92, historian 1974-80, lesson leader 1992-95, capt. 1996-98), Soroptimists (charter, bd. dirs. 1954-56, pres. Davis County chpt. 1965-69, Rocky Mountain regional bd. dirs. 1965-70, cmty. svc. award 1968, pub. svc. award 1970), Sigma Alpha Eta, Theta Alpha Phi, Psi Chi, Zeta Phi Eta, Phi Kappa Phi. Republican. Mem. LDS Ch. Avocations: international travel, reading, boating, sports, fine and performing arts. Home: 719 E Center St Kaysville UT 84037-2138

ASHTON, RICK JAMES, librarian; b. Middletown, Ohio, Sept. 18, 1945; s. Ralph James and Lydia Marie (Thornbery) A.; m. Marcia K. Zuroweste, Dec. 23, 1966; children: Jonathan Paul, David Andrew. AB, Harvard U., 1967; MA, Northwestern U., 1969, PhD, 1973; MA, U. Chgo., 1976. Instr., asst. prof. history Northwestern U., Evanston, Ill., 1972-74; curator local and family history Newberry Libr., Chgo., 1974-77; asst. dir. Allen County Pub. Libr., Ft. Wayne, Ind., 1977-80, dir., 1980-85; city libr. Denver Pub. Libr., 1985—. Mem. Ind. Coop Libr. Svcs. Authority, 1980-85, pres., 1984-85; cons. NEH, Nat. Ctr. Edn. Stats., Northwestern U. Office Estate Planning, Snowbird Leadership Inst. Author: The Life of Henry Ruiter, 1742-1819, 1974, The Genealogy Beginner's Manual: A New Edition, 1977, Stuntz, Fuller, Kennard and Cheadle Ancestors, 1987 (with others) Trends in Urban Library Management, 1989, Intelligent Library Buildings, 1999. Bd. dirs. Cmty. Coordinated Child Care, Evanston, 1972-74, Three Rivers Montessori Sch., Ft. Wayne, 1977-80; bd. dirs., sec. Allen County-Ft. Wayne Hist. Soc., 1977-83; trustee Iliff Sch. Theology, 2000—; conscientious objector. Recipient Old City Hall Hist. Svc. award, 1985, Phil Milstein award Denver AIA, 1998; NDEA fellow, 1967-69, Downtown Denver award, 1996, 97; Woodrow Wilson fellow, 1971-72. Mem. ALA, Colo. Libr. Assn. (Libr. of Yr. 2000), Colo. Alliance Rsch. Librs. (pres. 1987-88, sec. 1993-95, chmn. 1995-2000), Urban Librs. Coun., Cactus Club. Home: 217 S Jackson St Unit A Denver CO 80209-3132 Office: Denver Pub Libr 10 W 14th Avenue Pkwy Denver CO 80204-2731 E-mail: rashton@denver.lib.co.us

ASKIN, WALTER MILLER, artist, educator; b. Pasadena, Calif., Sept. 12, 1929; s. Paul Henry and Dorothy Margaret (Miller) A.; child from previous marriage, Nancy Carol Oudegeest; m. Elise Anne Doyle, Apr. 17, 1993. B.A., U. Calif.-Berkeley, 1951, M.A., 1952; postgrad., Ruskin Sch. Drawing and Fine Art, Oxford. Asst. curator edn. Legion of Honor Mus., San Francisco, 1953-54; prof. art Calif. State U., Los Angeles, 1956-92; pub. Nose Press, Pasadena, Calif., 1984—; vis. artist Pasadena Art Mus., 1962-63, U. N.Mex., 1972, Calif. State U.-Long Beach, 1974-75, Cranbrook Acad. Art, Mich., 1978, Ariz. State U., Tempe, 1979, Art Ctr. Athens Sch. Fine Arts, Mykonos, Greece, 1973, Kelpra Studio, London, 1969, 73. Chief reader Advanced Placement Program Ednl. Testing Service, 1982-85; chmn. visual arts panel Art Recognition and Talent Search Nat. Found. Advancement in Arts-Commn. on Presdl. Scholars; mem. advanced placement studio art examinaton com. Coll. Bd., 1985-96, chmn., 1992-96; mem. Commn. of Future of Advanced Placement Program, The Coll. Bd., 1999-2001; mem. acad. coun. Coll. Bd., 1989-94, chair arts adv. com., 1987-93; adj. prof. Ariz. State U., 1986-90; artist-in-residence Ragdale Found., Lake Forest, Ill., 1986, John Michael Kohler Art Ctr., Sheboygan, Wis., 1987, Hambidge Ctr. for Arts & Sci., Georgia , 1991, Vt. Studio Colony, 1988; co-dir. 1st Internat. Conf. on Humor in Art, Chateau de la Bretsche, Brittany, France, 1989, 92; spkr., juror nat. travel show So. Graphics Coun. Conf., Ohio U., Athens, 1998; artist-in-residence U. Dallas, 2001; vis. prof. Ariz. State U., Tempe, 2001; invited artist 12 lithos Hullaballoo in Winter in collaboration with Wayne Kimball, Brigham Young U., 2001; historian art alumni group U. Calif., Berkeley, 2001—. Numerous exhbns. including one-man shows, Kunstlerhaus, Vienna, Austria, 1981, Santa Barbara Mus. Art, 1966, Hellenic-Am. Union, Athens, Greece, 1973, Hank Baum Gallery, San Francisco, 1970, 74, 76, Ericson Gallery, N.Y.C., 1978, Abraxas Gallery, Calif., 1979, 80, 81, Fla. State U., Tallahassee, 1988, Lizardi/Harp Gallery, Pasadena, 1988, 91, 95, L.A. Valley Coll., 1989, U. Dallas, 2001; one-man traveling show U.S. Info. Agy., Yugoslavia, 1985-86, 15th Internat. Biennale of Prints and Drawings, Taipei Mus. Art, 1998; Pasadena's choice exhbn., Armory Ctr. for Arts, 1991, Contemporary Art in Pasadena, 1960-74, Norton Simon Museum, 1999, Taipei Fine Arts Mus., 1999, Gertrude Herbert Art Inst., Ga., 1999, Schafler Gallery, Pratt Inst., Bklyn., 1999, Kittredge Gallery, U. Puget Sound, Tacoma, Wash., 1999, Cmty. Visual Art Assn., Jackson Hole, Wyo., 1999, Wayland Bapt. U., Plainview, Tex., 1999, From Paris to Pasadena exhbn. Norton Simon Mus., 2000, Artists Do Opera exhbn. Brand Libr., Glendale, Calif., 2001, print and drawing exhbn. Bradley U., Peoria, Ill., 2000, others; author: A Briefer History of the Greeks, 1983, Another Art Book to Cross Off Your List, 1984, Modern Manifesto Match Game, 1998, Hidedous Headlines, 1998, Womsters and Foozlers, 1998, On Becoming an Artist, 1999, (calendar) Man, Dog, Bone Artists' Calendar; contbr. articles to profl. jours. and mags. Trustee Pasadena Art Mus., 1963-68; bd. dirs. Los Angeles Inst. Contemporary Art., 1978-81, Pasadena Gallery Contemporary Arts; bd. govs. Baxter Art Gallery, Calif. Inst. Tech., 1980-86; bd. dirs. The Calif. Artist, Book Program, 1985-2000; dir. The Visual Humor Project, 1989—. Recipient Outstanding Prof. award Calif. State U., 1973, Artists award Pasadena Arts Council, 1970, award 61st ann. exhbn. N.W. Watercolor Soc., 2001, Past Pres.' award 80th ann. exhbn. Nat. Watercolor Soc., 2000, Purchase prize 3d nat. print biennial Frederick R. Weisman Mus., Mpls., 2001; named Disting. Alumnus, Pasadena City Coll.; Ruth G. Jansen Edn. Meml. grantee, grantee Pasadena Arts Commn., 1990; also over 50 awards in competitive exhbns. art. Mem. Coll. Art Assn. Am., Nat. Watercolor Soc., L.A. Printmaking Soc. (founding mem.) Home and Office: PO Box D South Pasadena CA 91031-0120

ASMUS, JOHN FREDRICH, physicist; b. Pasadena, Calif., Jan. 20, 1937; s. William F. and Eleanor E. (Kocher) A.; m. Barbara Ann Flaherty, Feb. 23, 1963; children— Joanne M., Rosemary H. BSEE, Calif. Inst. Tech., 1958, MSEE, 1959, PhDEE and Physics, 1965. Head optical systems dept. Aero Geo Astro Corp., Alexandria, Va., 1960-64; head laser dept. Gulf Gen. Atomic, San Diego, 1964-69; research staff Inst. Def. Analyses, Arlington, Va., 1969-71; v.p., bd. mem. Sci. Applications, Inc., Albuquerque, 1971-73; lectr. U. Calif., Davis, 1974, research physicist, co-founder art and sci. center San Diego, 1973—. Co-dir. JASON nat. laser program study Office of Pres. of U.S., 1971; cons. in field; mem. adv. group on electron devices Smithsonian Assocs.; featured cable, PBS TV documentaries, 1975—; conf. lectr. San Diego, 1999. Contbr. sci. articles to profl. jours.; patentee metallic vapor laser, embedded pinch laser, plasma pinch annealing system, chemical decontamination with ultraviolet; introduced laser, ultrasonic and computer image enhancement techniques to art conservation, introduced laser cleaning to the field of paleontology, and revealed new features of da Vinci's Mona Lisa; restored Cremona Cathedral, Calif. State Capital, White House mural, Washington, Arches Nat. Pk. Pictograph, Venice Ducal Palace Sculpture, office of Galileo in U. Padova using laser radiation; development of laser-robotic technique for the decontamination of the Hanford nuclear weapons facility of the U.S. Dept. of Energy; laser, flashlamp and pinchlamp systems for depainting stealth aircraft and decontaminating the JET TOKAMAK thermonuclear fusion reactor, Culham Laboratory, United Kingdom; laser system for branding bowhead whales at a distance. Recipient Rolex Laureate for Enterprise award for restoration Xian terra cotta warriors Montres Rolex SA, Geneva, 1990, Best Scholarly Article award Soc. for Tech. Com., 1988; named George Eastman lectr. Optical Soc. Am., 1994; winner IBM Supercomputing Competition for Image Enhancement of Mona Lisa, 1989; Schlumberger fellow, 1959-60, Tektronix fellow, 1960-61, Getty fellow, 1989, Oberlin Coll. fellow, 1990, Explorers Club fellow, 1997; decorated knight of Holy Sepulchre of Jerusalem, 1993. Mem. Internat. Inst. Conservation of Historic and Artistic Works, IEEE, Am. Inst. Conservation, Nat. Trust Historic Preservation, Venice Soc., Bay Area Art Conservation Guild, Soc. Photo-Optical Instrumentation Engrs., Lasers for the Conservation of Artworks (sci. bd. mem.), Sigma Xi, Tau Beta Pi. Home: 8239 Sugarman Dr La Jolla CA 92037-2222 Office: IPAPS 0360 U Calif San Diego 9500 Gilman Dr La Jolla CA 92093-5004 E-mail: jfasmus@ucsd.edu

ASTIN, ALEXANDER WILLIAM, education educator; b. Washington, May 30, 1932; s. Allen Varley and Margaret L. (Mackenzie) A.; m. Helen Stavridou, Feb. 11, 1956; children: John Alexander, Paul Allen. AB, Gettysburg (Pa.) Coll., 1953, LittD (hon.), 1981; MA, U. Md., 1956, PhD, 1958; LLD (hon.), Alderson-Broaddus Coll., 1982, Whitman Coll., 1986; LHD, Chapman Coll., 1987, Am. Coll. Switzerland, 1989, SUNY, 1989; D of Pedagogy, R.I. Coll., 1987; DSc, Thomas Jefferson U., 1990; EdD (hon.), Merrimack Coll., 1993; LLD (hon.), Pepperdine U., 1993. Dep. chief psychology service USPHS Hosp., Lexington, Ky., 1957-59; dep. chief psychology research unit VA Hosp., Balt., 1959-60; research asso., dir. research Nat. Merit Scholar Corp., Evanston, Ill., 1960-64; dir. research Am. Council Edn., Washington, 1965-73; Allan M. Cartter prof. edn. UCLA, 1973—; pres. Higher Edn. Research Inst., Los Angeles, 1973—. Author: The College Environment, 1968, The Educational and Vocational Development of College, 1971, The Power of Protest, 1975, Preventing Students from Dropping Out, 1975, Four Critical Years, 1977, Maximizing Leadership Effectiveness, 1980, Minorities in American Higher Education, 1982, Achieving Educational Excellence, 1985, Assessment for Excellence, 1991, What Matters in College?, 1993, others. Trustee St. Xavier Coll., Chgo., Marjorie Webster Jr. Coll., Washington, Gettysburg Coll., 1983-86, Eckerd Coll., Fla., 1986-91. Recipient Disting. Research award Am. Personnel and Guidance Assn., 1965, Disting. Research award Nat. Assn. Student Personnel Adminstrs., 1976, Outstanding Service award Am. Coll. Personnel Assn., 1978, Lindquist award for outstanding research on college students Am. Ednl. Research Assn., 1983, Excellence in Edn. award Nat. Assn. Coll. Admissions Counselors, 1985, Outstanding Research award Am. Coll. Personnel Assn., 1985, Outstanding Service award Council of Ind. Colls., 1986, Outstanding Research award Assn. for Study of Higher Edn., 1987, Roll of Svc. award Nat. Assn. Student Fin. Aid Adminstrs., 1991, Extended Rsch. award AACD, 1992, Sidney Suslow award Assn. for Instl. Rsch., 1992; fellow Center Advanced Study Behavioral Sci. Fellow Am. Psychol. Assn., AAAS; mem. Am. Assn. Higher Edn. (dir.) Office: UCLA Grad Sch Edn Higher Edn Rsch Inst 3005 Moore Hall Box 951521 Los Angeles CA 90095-9000

ASTON, EDWARD ERNEST, IV, dermatologist; b. Jersey City, Jan. 14, 1944; m. Kirsten Anita. B.A., U. Md.-College Park, 1968; M.D., U. Md.-Balt., 1969. Diplomate Am. Bd. Dermatology. Intern, Orange County Med. Ctr., Orange, Calif., 1969-70; resident U. Calif.-Irvine-Orange County Med. Ctr., 1971-74; practice medicine specializing in dermatology Fullerton Med. Clinic of Dermatology, Calif., 1974— . Office: 301 W Bastanchury Rd Ste 220 Fullerton CA 92835-3424

ASURA, JOHN F. paper company executive; BA, U. Scranton; MBA, U. Pa. CFO Sunshine Biscuits, Inc., 1995-96, CFO Consumer Banking PNC Bank, 1997-98, CEO of credit card subsidiary, 1998-99; prin. Crossroads LLC, 2000; interim CEO, dir. Day Runner Inc., Irvine, Calif., 2000—. Fulbright-Hayes grant U. Bonn. Office: Day Runner Inc 15295 Alton Pkwy Irvine CA 92618

ATAIE, ATA JENNATI, oil products marketing executive; b. Mashad, Iran, Mar. 15, 1934; came to U.S., 1957, naturalized, 1969; s. Hamid Jennati and Mohtaram (Momeni) A.; m. Judith Garrett Bush, Oct. 7, 1961; children: Ata Jennati, Andrew J. BS in Agr., Fresno State U., 1964; BA in Econs., San Francisco State U., 1966. Mktg. exec. Shell Oil Co., Oakland, Calif., 1966-75; pres. A.J. Ataie &Cos., Danville, 1975—, Am. Value Inc., 1976—. 2d lt. Iranian Army, 1953. Mem. Nat. Petroleum Retailers Assn. Democrat.

ATCHESON, SUE HART, business educator; b. Dubuque, Iowa, Apr. 12, 2000; d. Oscar Raymond and Anna (Cook) Hart; m. Walter Clark Atcheson (div.); children: Christine A. Hischar, Moffet Zoe Onofrei, Claye Williams. BBA, Mich. State U.; MBA, Calif. State Poly. U., Pomona, 1973. Cert. tchr. and adminstr. Instr. Mt. San Antonio Coll., Walnut, Calif., 1968-90. Bd. dirs. faculty assn. Mt. San Antonio Coll.; mem. acad. senate Mt. San Antonio Coll.; originator vol. income tax assistance Mt. San Antonio Coll.; speaker in field; adj. lectr. in bus. mgmt. Calif. State Polytech U., Pomona, 1973-75. Author: Fractions and Equations on Your Own, 1975. Charter mem. Internat. Commn. on Monetary and Econ. Reform; panelist infrastructure funding reform, Freeport, Ill., 1989. Mem. Cmty. Concert Assn. Inland Empire (bd. dirs.), Scripps Coll. Fine Arts Found., Recyclers Club (pres. 1996). E-mail: sueatch@amigo.net

ATKIN, J. MYRON, science educator; b. Bklyn., Apr. 6, 1927; s. Charles Z. and Esther (Jaffe) A.; m. Ann Spiegel, Dec. 25, 1947; children— David, Ruth, Jonathan. B.S., CCNY, 1947; M.A., NYU, 1948, Ph.D., 1956. Tchr. sci. Ramaz High Sch., N.Y.C., 1948-50; tchr. elem. sch. sci. Great Neck (N.Y.) pub. schs., 1950-55; prof. sci. edn. Coll. Edn., U. Ill., Urbana, 1955-79, assoc. dean, 1966-70, dean, 1970-79; prof. Sch. Edn., Stanford (Calif.) U., 1979—, dean, 1979-86. Cons. OECD, Paris, Nat. Inst. Edn.; mem. edn. adv. bd. NSF, 1973-76, 84-86, vice-chmn., 1984-85, sr. advisor, 1986-87; mem. Ill. Tchr. Certification Bd., 1973-76; Sir John Adams lectr. U. London Inst. Edn., 1980, vis. scholar com. scholarly commn. Nat. Acad. Scis., People's Republic China, 1987; math. sci. edn. bd. NRC, 1985-89, nat. com. sci. edn. standards and assessment, 1992-96, com. on sci. edn. K-12, 1996—, vice chair, 1998, chair, 1999—; invited lectr. Nat. Sci. Coun., Taiwan, 1989—; resident Rockefeller Found., Bellagio Ctr., 1999. Author children's sci. textbooks. Served with USNR, 1945-46. Fellow AAAS (v.p. sect. Q 1973-74); mem. Coun. Elem. Sci. Internat. (pres. 1969-70), Am. Ednl. Rsch. Assn. (exec. bd. 1972-75, chmn. govt. and profl. liaison com.), Sigma Xi (chair com. on sci., math. and engring. edn.). Office: Stanford U Sch Edn Stanford CA 94305-3084 E-mail: atkin@stanford.edu

ATKINSON, JASON A. state senator; b. Sacramento, Nov. 6, 1970; m. Stephanie Atkinson. BS, So. Oreg. State Coll., 1992; MBA, Willamette U., 1997. Pres. Atkinson Mgmt. Group; morning news co-anchor, talk show prodr. Dove Comm., Medford, Oreg., 1991-93; Rep. rep. dist. 51 Oreg. Ho. of Reps., 1998-2000; Rep. senator dist. 25 Oreg. State Senate, 2000—. Ski instr., coach, supr., 1989-98; mem. bus. and consumer affairs and water and environ. coms. Oreg. Ho. of Reps., vice chair gen. govt. com., chair trade/econ. devel. com. Mem. Athletes in Action Internat. Cycling Team. Presbyterian. Office: Oreg State Senate H-389 State Capitol Salem OR 97310 Fax: 541 899-6948. E-mail: atkinson.rep@state.or.us

ATKINSON, PATRICIA, government official; b. Biggar, Sask., Can., Sept. 27, 1952; d. Robert Roy and Edna (Aylward) A. BA with honors, B of Edn., U. Sask., 1976. Min. social svcs. Govt. of Sask., Can., 1992-93, min. edn., tng. & employment Can., 1993-95, min. edn. Can., 1995-98, min. health, 1998-2001, min. hwys. and transp., min. rural revitalization, 2001—, dep. govt. house leader, 2001—. Active Big Sisters; mem. Nutana Neighbor to Neighbor Program; past v.p. Saskatoon Cmty. Clinic; founding dir. Coop Housing Assn.; former Sask. rep. to Can. Daycare Advocacy Assn. Mem. Pub. Rels. Com. Avocations: hiking, Irish music, restoration of antique furniture and early 1900's home. Home and Office: Govt Sask Legis Bldg Regina SK Canada S4S 0B3

ATKINSON, PERRY, political organization administrator; Chair Oreg. Rep. Party, Beaverton. Office: Oreg Rep Party PO Box 789 Salem OR 97308-0789 Fax: 503-587-9244

ATKINSON, RICHARD CHATHAM, university president; b. Oak Park, Ill., Mar. 19, 1929; s. Herbert and Margaret Atkinson; m. Rita Loyd, Aug. 20, 1952; 1 dau., Lynn Loyd. Ph.B., U. Chgo., 1948; Ph.D., Ind. U., 1955. Lectr. applied math. and stats. Stanford (Calif.) U., 1956-57, assoc. prof. psychology, 1961-64, prof. psychology, 1964-80; asst. prof. psychology UCLA, 1957-61; dep. dir. NSF, 1975-76, acting dir., 1976, dir., 1976-80; chancellor, prof. cognitive sci. U. Calif., San Diego, 1980-95; pres. U. Calif. Sys., 1995—. Author: (with Atkinson, Smith and Bem) Introduction to Psychology, 13th edit., 2000, Computer Assisted Instruction, 1969, An Introduction to Mathematical Learning Theory, 1965, Contemporary Developments in Mathematical Psychology, 1974, Mind and Behavior, 1980, Stevens' Handbook of Experimental Psychology, 1988. Served with AUS, 1954-56. Guggenheim fellow, 1967; fellow Ctr. for Advanced Study in Behavioral Scis., 1963; recipient Distinguished Research award Social Sci. Research Council, 1962. Fellow APA (Disting. Sci. Contbn. award 1977, Thorndike award 1980), AAAS (pres. 1989-90), Am. Psychol. Soc. (William James fellow 1985), Am. Acad. Arts and Scis.; mem. NAS, Soc. Exptl. Psychologists, Am. Philos. Soc., Nat. Acad. Edn., Inst. of Medicine, Cosmos Club (Washington), Explorer's Club (N.Y.C.). Home: 70 Rincon Rd Kensington CA 94707-1047 Office: U Calif Office Pres 1111 Franklin St Oakland CA 94607-5201 E-mail: richard.atkinson@ucop.edu

ATLAS, JAY DAVID, philosopher, consultant, linguist; b. Houston, Feb. 1, 1945; s. Jacob Henry and Babette Fancile (Friedman) A. AB summa cum laude, Amherst (Mass.) Coll., 1966; PhD, Princeton (N.J.) U., 1976. Mem. common rm. Wolfson Coll., Oxford, Eng., 1978, 80; vis. fellow Princeton U., 1979; rsch. assoc. Inst. for Advanced Study, Princeton, 1982-84; vis. lectr. U. Hong Kong, 1986; prof. Pomona Coll., Claremont, Calif., 1989—. Sr. assoc. Jurecon, Inc., L.A.; lectr. 2d European Summer Sch. in Logic, Lang. and Info., 1990; examiner U. Edinburgh, Scotland, 1993, U. Groningen, The Netherlands, 1991, 93-97, vis. rsch. prof., 1995; vis. prof. UCLA, 1988-95, Max. Planck Inst. for Psycholinguistics, Nijmegen, The Netherlands, 1997. Author: Philosophy Without Ambiguity, 1989, Logic, Meaning, and Conversation, 2002; contbr. to PC Laptop Computer Mag., 1994, articles to profl. jours. Mem. Am. Philos. Assn., Linguistic Soc. Am. Office: Pomona Coll 551 N College Ave Claremont CA 91711-4410 E-mail: jatlas@alumni.princeton.edu

ATLURI, SATYA N(ADHAM), aerospace engineering educator; b. Gudivada, Andhra, India, Oct. 7, 1945; came to U.S., 1966, naturalized, 1976; s. Tirupati Rao and Tulasi (Devi) A.; m. Revati Adusumilli, May 17, 1972; children: Neelima, Niroupa. B.E., Andhra U., Vizag, 1964; M.E., Indian Inst. Sci., Bangalore, India, 1966; DSc, MIT, 1969; DSc honoris causa, Nat. U. Ireland, Dublin, 1989. Researcher MIT, Cambridge, 1966-71, Jerome Clarke Hunsaker vis. prof. aeronautics and astronautics, 1990-91; asst. prof. U. Wash., Seattle, 1971-74; assoc. prof. engring. sci. and mech. Ga. Inst. Tech., Atlanta, 1974-77, prof., 1977-79, Regents' prof. mechanics, 1979-98, dir. Ctr. for Advancement Computational Mechanics, 1980-98, inst. prof., 1991-98, Regents' prof. aerospace engring., 1991-98; White House nominee Com. for Evaluation Nat. Medal of Tech. Dept. Commerce, 1992—; mem. rsch., engring. & devel. adv. com. FAA, Washington, 1994—; dir. Ctr. for Aerospace Rsch. and Edn. UCLA, 1998—. Co-chmn. Internat. Conf. on Computational Engring. Sci., Tokyo, 1986, Atlanta, 1988, Melbourne, Australia, 1991, Patras, Greece, 1991, Hong Kong, 1992, Hawaii, 1995; gen. lectr., invited keynote speaker over 250 internat. tech. confs.; adv. prof. Southwestern Jiaotong U., Emei, Sichuan, China, 1988; bd. dirs. FAA Ctr. for Excellence in Computational Modeling of Aerospace Structures, Ga. Inst. Tech., 1992; White House nominee Evaluation Com. for Nat. Medal of Tech., U.S. Dept. Commerce, 1992; mem. adv. com. rsch., engring. and devel. FAA, 1995—. Contbr. over 500 articles to profl. jours.; gen. editor: Springer Verlag Series on Computational Mechanics, 1988-91, 91, Structural Intgegrity of Aging Airplanes, 1991, Frontiers in Computational Mechanics, 1989—; author 25 books, including Computational Methods in the Mechanics of Solids and Structures, 1984; editor: books including Hybrid and Mixed Finite Element Methods, 1983, Computational Methods in the Mechanics of Fracture, 1985 (Russian transl. 1989), Handbook of Finite Elements, 1986, Dynamic Fracture Mechanics, 1986, Computational Mechanics 86, 1986, Large-Space-Structures: Dynamics and Control, 1987, Computational Mechanics '88, 1988, Computational Mechanics '91, 1991, Frontiers in Computational Mechanics, 1989, Computational Mechanics '91, 1991, Structural Integrity of Aging Airplanes, 1991, Durability of Metal Aircraft Structures., 1992, Nonlinear Computational Mechanics in Aerospace Engineering, 1992; editor-in-chief Internat. Jour. Computational Mechanics, Computer Modeling and Simulation in Engineering; mem. editorial bd. Computers and Structures, Engring. Fracture Mechanics, Internat. Jour. Plasticity, Internat. Jour. for Numerical Methods in Engring., Acta Mecanica Solida Sinica, also others. Grantee NSF, 1975—, USAF Office Sci. Research, 1973—, Office Naval Research, 1978—, Air Force Rocket Propulsion Lab., 1976-79, NASA, 1980—, NRC, 1978-80, Dept. Transp., 1987—, ARO, 1988—, FAA, 1991—, Dept. Energy, 1994—; recipient V.K. Murti Gold medal Andhra U., India, 1964, Roll of Honors award Indian Inst. Sci., 1966, Disting. Alumnus award, 1991, Class of 1934 Disting. Prof. award for 1986 Ga. Inst. Tech., Outstanding Faculty Research award Ga. Inst. Tech., 1986, 91, Survey Paper Citation AIAA Jour., 1988, Monie Ferst Meml. award for Sustained Research, Sigma Xi, 1988, Outstanding Rsch. award, 1991, Tech. Achievement award Nat. Acad. Engring., 1995; fellow Japan Soc. for Promotion Sci., 1987—, Computational Mechanics Div. medal Japan Soc. Mech. Engrs., 1991, ICES Gold medal, 1992, A.C. Eringen medal of the Soc. of Engring. Sci., 1995; named Southwest Mechanics lectr., 1987, Midwestern Mechanics lectr., 1988. Fellow Internat. Congress on Fracture (hon.), ASME (chmn. com. computing in applied mechanics 1983-85, assoc. editor Applied Mech. Revs.), AIAA (assoc. editor AIAA Jour. 1983—, Structures Dynamics and Materials award 1988), Am. Acad. Mechanics, Aero. Soc. India, U.S. Assn. Computational Mechanics (founder, mem. exec. com.); mem. ASCE (assoc. editor Jour. Engring. Mechanics 1982-84, mem. exec. com., Aerospace Structures and Materials award 1986), U.S. Nat. Acad. Engring., Internat. Assn. for Computational Mechanics (founding mem., exec. coun.), Internat. Assn. Boundary Element Methods (mem. exec. com.). Home: 326 Lakeview Dr Palmdale CA 93551-7934 Office: UCLA Ctr Aerospace Rsch Ctr Computational Modeling 7704 Boelter Hl Los Angeles CA 90095-0001

ATTARDI, GIUSEPPE M. biology educator; b. Vicari, Italy, Sept. 14, 1923; came to U.S., 1957, naturalized, 1974; s. Luigi and Saveria (Goteri) A. M.D., U. Padua, Italy, 1947. Asst. prof. biology U. Padua, Italy, 1947-57; research fellow Washington U., St. Louis, 1957-59, Calif. Inst. Tech., Pasadena, 1959-60; chargé de recherches Lab. Enzymologie, Gif-Sur-Yvette, France, 1961-62; assoc. prof. biology Calif. Inst. Tech., Pasadena, 1963-67, prof. biology, 1967-84, G.C. Steele prof. molecular biology, 1985—. Editor: Mitochondrial Genes, 1982; editorial bd.: Jour. Molecular Biology, 1969-72; Plasmid, 1977-86. Contbr. articles to profl. jours. Fulbright fellow, 1957-60; Guggenheim fellow, 1970-71, 86. Mem. Nat. Acad. Scis. Office: Calif Inst Tech Dept Biology Pasadena CA 91125-0001

ATTEBERY, LOUIE WAYNE, English language educator, folklorist; b. Weiser, Idaho, Aug. 14, 1927; s. John Thomas Attebery and Tressie Mae (Blevins) Attebery Miller; m. Barbara Phyllis Olson, Dec. 31, 1947; children: Bobby Lou, Brian Leonard. BA, Albertson Coll. of Idaho, 1950; MA, U. Mont., 1951; PhD, U. Denver, 1961. Tchr. Middleton H.S., Idaho, 1949-50, Payette H.S., 1951-52, Nyssa H.S., Oreg, 1952-55, East H.S., Denver, 1955-61; prof. English Albertson Coll. Idaho, Caldwell, 1961-99, holder Eyck-Berringer chair English, 1987-98, acting acad. v.p., 1983-84; pres. West Shore Press, 1998—. Vis. fellow Harvard U., Cambridge, Mass., 1993-94. Author: The College of Idaho, 1981-91, A Centennial History, 1991, Sheep May Safely Graze: A Personal Essay on Tradition and A Contemporary Sheep Ranch, 1993, The Most of What We Spend, 1998, Albertson College of Idaho: The Second Hundred Years, 1999, J.R. Simplot: A Billion the Hard Way, 2000; editor: Idaho Folklife: Homesteads to Headstones, 1985; editor Northwest Folklore, 1985-91; gen. editor U. Idaho Northwest Folklife series, 1991—. Trustee Idaho Hist. Soc., 1984-91. With USN, 1945-46. Bruern fellow U. Leeds, Eng., 1971-72. Mem. Western Lit. Assn. (exec coun. 1964-65), Assn. Lit. Scholars and Critics, 1995—. Methodist. E-mail: lattebery@albertson.edu

ATTIYEH, RICHARD EUGENE, economics educator; b. Bklyn., Oct. 8, 1937; s. Semeer Mathew and Dorothy (Krentz) A.; m. Jessica Falikman, July 20, 1958; children: Michael Richard, Amy Lauren, Gregory Moss. BA, Williams Coll., 1958; PhD, Yale U., 1966. Staff economist Pres.'s Council of Econ. Advisers, Washington, 1961-62; asst. prof. econs. Stanford U., Palo Alto, Calif., 1962-64, Yale U., New Haven, 1964-67; from assoc. prof. to prof. U. Calif.-San Diego, La Jolla, 1967—, dean grad. studies and research, 1982-94, vice chancellor for rsch., dean grad. studies, 1994—, interim sr. vice chancellor acad. affairs, 1996-97. Active Grad. Record Examinations Bd., 1987-92, chmn., 1990; bd. dirs. Coun. Grad. Schs., 1990-93, chmn., 1992. Mem. Am. Econ. Assn., Assn. Grad. Schs. (pres. 1996), Calif. Biomed. Rsch. Assn. (bd. chmn. 1997-99), Calif. Soc. for Biomed. Rsch. (treas. 1998-99). Office: U Calif San Diego Office Grad Studies La Jolla CA 92093 E-mail: rattiyeh@ucsd.edu

ATTWOOD, DAVID THOMAS, physicist, educator; b. N.Y.C., Aug. 15, 1941; s. David Thomas and Josephine (Banks) A.; divorced; children: Timothy David, Courtney Catherine, Kevin Richard; m. Linda Jean Geniesse, Aug. 3, 1991. BS, Hofstra U., 1963; MS, Northwestern U., 1964; D in Engring. Sci., NYU, 1972. Physicist Lawrence Livermore Nat. Lab., Livermore, Calif., 1972-83, Lawrence Berkeley Nat. Lab., Berkeley, 1983—; prof. in residence dept. elec. engring. and computer sci. U. Calif., Berkeley, 1989—, chair applied sci. and tech., 1991-94. Founder, dir. Ctr. for X-ray Optics Lawrence Berkeley Lab. Author: Soft X-Rays and Extreme Ultraviolet Radiation: Principles and Applications, 1999; editor: (with B.L. Henke) X-Ray Diagnostics, (with J. Bokor) Short Wavelength Coherent Radiation, (with F. Zernike) Extreme Ultraviolet Lithography, (with W. Meyer-Ilse and T. Warwick) X-Ray Microscopy; reviewer numerous sci. jours.; contbr. numerous articles to profl. publs. Fellow Optical Soc. Am.; mem. AAAS, NRC (com. on optical sci. and engring.), Am. Phys. Soc. Achievements include research on x-ray optics, extreme ultraviolet lithography, synchrotrons, and partially coherent x-rays, and laser-plasma interactions. Office: Lawrence Berkeley Nat Lab Ctr X-ray Optics Berkeley CA 94720

ATWATER, TANYA MARIA, marine geophysicist, educator; b. Los Angeles, Aug. 27, 1942; d. Eugene and Elizabeth Ruth (Ransom) A.; 1 child, Alyosha Molnar. Student, MIT, 1960-63; BA, U. Calif., Berkeley, 1965; PhD, Scripps Inst. Oceanography, 1972. Vis. earthquake researcher U. Chile, 1966; research assoc. Stanford U., 1970-71; asst. prof. Scripps Inst. Oceanography, 1972-73; U.S.-USSR Acad. Scis. exchange scientist, 1973; asst. prof. MIT, 1974-79, assoc. prof., 1979-80, research assoc., 1980-81; prof. dept. geoscis. U. Calif., Santa Barbara, 1980—. Chairperson ocean margin drilling Ocean Crust Planning Adv. Com.; mem. pub. adv. com. on law of sea U.S. Dept. State, 1979-83; mem. tectonics panel Ocean Drilling Project, 1990-93; Sigma Xi lectr., 1975-76. Sci. cons.: Planet Earth: Continents in Collision (R. Miller), 1983; contbr. articles to profl. jours. Sloan fellow, 1975-77; recipient Newcomb Cleveland prize AAAS, 1980; named Scientist of Yr. World Book Ency., 1980. Fellow Am. Geophys. Union (fellows com. 1980-81, 94-95, Ewing award subcom. 1980., McElwane award subcom. 1994), Geol. Soc. Am. (Penrose Conf. com. 1978-80); mem. AAAS, Assn. Women in Sci, Am. Geol. Inst., Nat. Acad. Scis., Phi Beta Kappa, Eta Kappa Nu. Office: U Calif Dept Geoscis Santa Barbara CA 93106

ATWOOD, MARY SANFORD, writer; b. Mt. Pleasant, Mich., Jan. 27, 1935; d. Burton Jay and Lillian Belle (Sampson) Sanford; B.S., U. Miami, 1957; m. John C. Atwood, III, Mar. 23, 1957. Author: A Taste of India, 1969. Mem. San Francisco/N. Peninsula Opera Action, Hillsborough-Burlingame Newcomers, Suicide Prevention and Crisis Center, DeYoung Art Mus., Internat. Hospitality Center, Peninsula Symphony, San Francisco Art Mus., World Affairs Council, Mills Hosp. Assos. Mem. AAUW, Suicide Prevention Aux. Republican. Club: St. Francis Yacht. Office: 40 Knightwood Ln Hillsborough CA 94010-6132

AU, WHITLOW W.L. acoustician; b. Honolulu, July 31, 1940; s. Tai Hing and Violet (Chun) A.; m. Dorothy E. Wagner, Sept. 3, 1966; children: Wagner, WaiLani, Wesley, WaiNani. BS, U. Hawaii, 1962; MS, Wash. State U., 1964, PhD, 1970. Scientist Naval Command Control and Ocean Surveillance Ctr., San Diego, 1970-71, sr. scientist Kaneohe, Hawaii, 1971-93; chief scientist marine mammal rsch. project Hawaii Inst. Marine Biology, Kaneohe, 1993—. Author: Sonar of Dolphins, 1993; contbr. articles to profl. jours. Recipient Meritorious Civilian Svc. award USN, 1986. Fellow Acoustical Soc. Am. (tech. com. animal bioacoustics 1989—); mem. IEEE. Roman Catholic. Achievements include patents for broadband sonar signal processor and target recognition system, simulated echo transponder for training marine mammals, and marine mammal guidance device. Home: 251 Kakahiaka St Kailua HI 96734-3461 Office: Hawaii Inst Marine Biology PO Box 1346 Kaneohe HI 96744-1346

AUCHINLECK, RICHARD H. exploration company executive; b. Vancouver; married; 1 child. B.Applied Sci. in Chem. Engring., U. B.C., 1976. With Gulf Canada Resources Ltd., Calgary, Alta, 1976—, gas utilization engr., supt. heavy oil ops., joint interest coord., mgr. engring., mgr. fin. (major projects group), gen. mgr. north bus. unit, 1991-93, v.p., 1993-95, sr. v.p. internat. and exploration, 1995-97, COO, 1997-98, pres., CEO, 1998—; CEO Gulf Indonesia Resources, 1997-98. Bd. dirs. Gulf Indonesia Resources, Canadian Energy Rsch. Inst. Mem. Assn. Profl. Engrs., Geologists and Geophysicists of Alta., Canadian Heavy Oil Assn. (life, hon. dir.). Avocations: restoring and driving vintage sports cars, skiing, music. Office: Gulf Canada Resources Ltd 401 9th Ave SW PO Box 130 Calgary AB Canada T2P 2H7

AUDETTE, DONALD, professional hockey player; b. Laval, Que., Can., Sept. 23, 1969; m. Manon Audette; children: Ketherine, Daniel. Right wing Buffalo Sabres, 1989-98, Los Angeles KIngs, 1998-99, 99—, Atlanta Thrashers, 1999. Spokespersons First Night Buffalo. Winner Fred T. Hunt Meml. Trophy as Sabres Rookie of the Year., 1991-92, Dudley "Red" Garrett award Am. Hockey League's Rookie of the Yr., 1989-90, Guy Lafleur trophy, 1988-89. Office: Los Angeles Kings Staples Ctr 1111 S Figueroa St Los Angeles CA 90015

AUERBACH, ALAN JEFFREY, economist, educator; b. N.Y.C., Sept. 27, 1951; s. William and Tess (Kasper) A.; m. Gay Cameron Quimby, June 25, 1978; children: Ethan, Andrew. BA, Yale U., 1974; PhD, Harvard U., 1978. Asst. prof. dept. econs. Harvard U., Cambridge, Mass., 1978-82, assoc. prof., 1982-83; assoc. prof. dept. econs. U. Pa., Phila., 1983-85, prof., 1985-94, chmn. dept., 1988-90, prof. Sch. Law, 1990-94; Robert D. Burch prof. of tax policy and pub. fin. U. Calif., Berkeley, 1994—. Author: The Taxation of Capital Income, 1983 (David A. Wells prize); co-author: Dynamic Fiscal Policy, 1987, Macroeconomics: An Integrated Approach, 1995, Generational Accounting Around the World, 1999; editor: Corporate Takeovers, 1988, Mergers and Acquisitions, 1988, Fiscal Policy: Lessons from Economic Research, 1997; co-editor: Handbook of Public Economics, Vol. I, 1985, Vol. II, 1987, Demographic Change and Fiscal Policy, 2001; editor jour. Econ. Perspectives, 1995-96. Fellow Am. Acad. Arts and Scis., Econometric Soc.; mem. Am. Econ. Assn. (exec. com. 1992-94, v.p. 1999), Phi Beta Kappa. Home: 110 El Camino Real Berkeley CA 94705-2823 Office: U Calif Berkeley Dept Econs 549 Evans Hall Berkeley CA 94720-1775 E-mail: auerbach@econ.berkeley.edu

AUERBACK, SANDRA JEAN, social worker; b. San Francisco, Feb. 21, 1946; d. Alfred and Molly Loy (Friedman) A. BA, U. Calif., Berkeley, 1967; MSW, Hunter Sch. Social Work, 1972. Diplomate clin. social work. Clin. social worker Jewish Family Services, Bklyn., 1972-73, clin. social worker Hackensack, N.J., 1973-78; pvt. practice psychotherapy San Francisco, 1978—; dir. intake adult day care Jewish Home for the Aged, San Francisco, 1979-91. Mem. NASW (cert., bd. dirs. Bay Area Referral Svc. 1983-87, chmn. referral svc. 1984-87, state practice com. 1987-91, regional treas. 1989-91, rep. to Calif. Coun. Psychiatry, Psychology, Social Work and Nursing, 1987-95, chmn. 1989, 93, v.p. cmty. svcs. 1991-93, chair Calif. polit. action com. 1993-95, v.p. profl. stds. 2000), Am. Group Psychotherapy Assn., Mental Health Assn. San Francisco (trustee 1987-95). Home: 1100 Gough St Apt 8C San Francisco CA 94109-6638 Office: 450 Sutter St San Francisco CA 94108-4206

AUGENSTEIN, BRUNO W. research scientist, researcher; b. Germany, Mar. 16, 1923; came to U.S., 1927, naturalized, 1935; s. Wilhelm C. and Emma (Mina) A.; m. Kathleen Greenlaw, May 27, 1950; children: Karen, Eric, Christopher. Sc.B. in Physics and Math, Brown U., 1943; M.S. in Aero, Calif. Inst. Tech., 1945. Supr. N.Am. Aviation Co., 1946-48; asst. prof. Purdue U., 1948-49; Navaho project leader, 1948; sr. scientist Rand Corp., 1949-58; ICBM project leader, 1952-56; chief scientist satellite programs; dir. planning Lockheed Missiles & Space Co., 1958-61; spl. asst. for reconnaisance and intelligence, dep. dir. intelligence activities Office Sec. Def., 1961-65; now cons.; rsch. adviser Inst. Def. Analyses, 1965-67; v.p. research Rand Corp., Santa Monica, Calif., 1967-71, chief scientist, 1971-72, resident cons., 1972—, sr. scientist, 1976—, emeritus scientist, 1995—. Cons., NAS, Nur. Budget, 1965—, Nat. Bur. Standards, 1971—, Xerad, Inc., 1972—, Dept. Navy, NSF, NASA, 1973—, Dept. Def., 1978—, Hi Tech Investment Mgmt., Inc., 1983; chmn. naval health systems rev. com. Office Sci. Tech. Policy, 1975—, cons., 1978—; v.p. rsch., bd. dirs. Spectravision, Inc.; bd. regents, asst. chmn. Nat. Libr. Medicine, HEW, 1967-73; mem. NAS computer sci. com. Nat. Bur. Standards, 1971-79, chmn., 1973-76. Guest contbr., editor Chaos, Solitons and Fractals Jour., 1995, 99. Recipient Distinguished Pub. Service award for reconnaisance and intellignece direction Dept. Def., 1965 Mem. Am. Inst. Physics, AIAA, AAAS, IEEE, Math. Assn. Am., Am. Nuclear Soc., Philosophy of Sci. Assn., N.Y. Acad. Scis., Beta Theta Pi. Home: 1144 Tellem Dr Pacific Palisades CA 90272-2244 Office: Rand Corp 1700 Main St Santa Monica CA 90407-2138

AUGUST-DEWILDE, KATHERINE, banker; b. Bridgeport, Conn., Feb. 13, 1948; d. Edward G. and Benita Ruth (Miller) Burstein; m. David deWilde, Dec. 30, 1984; children: Nicholas Alexander, Lucas Barrymere. AB, Goucher Coll., 1969; MBA, Stanford U., 1975. Cons. McKinsey & Co., San Francisco, 1975-78; dir. fin. Itel Corp., San Francisco, 1978-79; sr. v.p., chief fin. officer PMI Group, San Francisco, 1979-85, pres., CFO, 1988-91; CEO, pres. First Republic Thrift & Loan of San Diego, 1988-96; exec. v.p. First Republic Bank, San Francisco, 1987—, sr. v.p. , chief fin. officer, 1985-87, COO, 1996—. Mem. policy adv. bd. Ctr. for Real Estate and Urban Econs., U. Calif., Berkeley, 1987—; bd. dirs. First Republic Bank, Trainer, Wortham & Co., Inc. Bd. dirs. San Francisco Zool. Soc., 1993-2001, vice-chair, 1995-2000; trustee Carnegie Found., 1999—, Town Sch. for Boys, San Francisco, 1999—. Mem. Women's Forum (bd. dirs.), Bankers Club, Belvedere Tennis Club, Univ. Club. Home: 2650 Green St San Francisco CA 94123-4607 Office: First Republic Bank 111 Pine St San Francisco CA 94111-5602

AUGUSTINE, KATHY MARIE, state controller, state legislator, secondary education educator; b. L.A., Calif., May 29, 1956; d. Philip Blase and Katherine Alice (Thompson) A.; m. Charles Francis Augustine, July 22, 1988; children: Andrea, Greg, Larry, Dallas. AB, Occidental Coll., 1977; MPA, Calif. State U., Long Beach, 1983. Flight attendant Continental Airlines, Houston, 1978-83; crew scheduler Delta Airlines, L.A., 1983-88; tchr. Diocese of Reno/Las Vegas, 1990-96; mem. Nev. Assembly, 1992-94, Nev. Senate, 1994-98. Mem. Rep. Women's Club, Las Vegas, Nev., 1992—; former coun. of State Govts. West, chair elec. restructuring. Recipient Achievement award Bank of Am., Calif., 1974, Achievement Medallion Am. Legion, 1974, Congressional Internship grantee, Washington, 1975, Distinguished Alumni award Calif. State U. Long Beach, 1997, Cmty. Appreciation award Frontier Girl Scout Coun., 1996, Svc. Excellence award Rep. Legis. of Yr., 1998. Mem. AAUV, Nat. Assn. St. Auditors (contr., treas.), Women in Govt. (former state dir.), Women Execs. in State Govt. (bd. dirs. 1999—), Nev. State Bd. Fin., Alzheimers Assn. (former bd. dirs.), Dept. Transp. (bd. dirs., exec. br. audit com.), Jr. League of Las Vegas, Clark County Panhellenic Assn. Republican. Roman Catholic. Home: 1400 Maria Elena Dr Las Vegas NV 89104-1846 E-mail: kaugust@govmail.state.nv.us

AUNG-THWIN, MICHAEL ARTHUR, history educator; b. Rangoon, Burma, 1946; BA, Doane Coll., 1969; MA, U. Ill., Urbana, 1971; PhD, U. Mich., 1976. Asst. prof. Asian history Elmira (N.Y.) Coll., 1980-87; assoc. prof. history No. Ill. U., DeKalb, 1987-95, dir. Ctr. S.E. Asian Studies Ill., 1987-95; prof. Asian Studies U. Hawaii, Honolulu, 1995—. Vis. prof. Cornell U., 1981; vis. scholar Ctr. for S.E. Asian Studies, Kyoto, Japan. Contbr. articles to profl. jours. NEH fellow, 1977-80. Mem. Assn. for Asian Studies (bd. dirs. 1980-83, mem. S.E. Asia Coun.), Burma Studies Found. (sec.-treas.). Office: U Hawaii Sch Hawaiian Asian Studies 1890 E West Rd Honolulu HI 96822-2318 E-mail: aungthwin@hawaii.edu

AURAND, CHARLES HENRY, JR. music educator, educator; b. Battle Creek, Mich., Sept. 6, 1932; s. Charles Henry and Elisabeth Dirk (Hoekstra) A.; m. Donna Mae Erb, June 19, 1954; children: Janice, Cheryl, Sandra, Charles III, William. MusB, Mich. State U., 1954, MusM, 1958; PhD, U. Mich., 1971. Cert. tchr., Mich., Ohio. Asst. prof. music Hiram Coll., Ohio, 1958-60; dean, prof. music Youngstown State U., 1960-73; dean No. Ariz. U., Flagstaff, 1973-88, prof. music, 1988-94, prof. emeritus 1994—. Chmn. Ariz. Alliance for Arts Edn., 1974-77; solo clarinetist Flagstaff Symphony; solo, chamber music and orch. musician, 1973-86; fine arts cons. Miami U. of Ohio, 1982 Author: Selected Solos, Methods, 1963. Elder Presbyterian Ch., 1965; chmn. Boy Scouts Am., Coconino dist., 1974-78; bd. dirs. Ariz. Com. Arts for the Handicapped, 1982-88, Flagstaff Symphony Orch., 1973-85, Flagstaff Festival of Arts, 1973-89; bd. dirs. Sedona Chamber Mus. Soc., 1989-99, Sedona Med. Ctr., 1998—; conf. dir. Internat. Clarinet Soc., 1991; pres. Citizens for an Alt. Rt., 1995-98; mem. Ariz. Town Hall, 1996—; bd. dirs. Sedona Med. Ctr. Found., 1998—; mem. Ariz. Town Hall, 1996—. 1st lt. USAF,1955-57 Recipient award of merit Boy Scouts Am., 1977; cert. appreciation John F. Kennedy Ctr. Performing Arts, 1985. Mem. Am. Assn. Higher Edn., Ariz. Humanities Assn., Music Educators Nat. Conf., State Adminstrs. of Music Schs. (chmn. 1971-73), Internat. Clarinet Soc./ClariNetwork Internat. (conf. dir. 1991), No. Ariz. U. Retirees Assn. (pres. 1997-98). Republican. Presbyterian. Lodge: Kiwanis (pres. 1984-85). Avocations: golf, tennis, bridge. Home: 140 Fairway Oaks Ln Sedona AZ 86351-8835 Office: No Ariz U PO Box 6040 Flagstaff AZ 86011-0001

AUST, STEVEN DOUGLAS, biochemistry, biotechnology and toxicology educator; b. South Bend, Wash., Mar. 11, 1938; s. Emil and Helen Mae (Crawford) A.; m. Nancy Lee Haworth, June 5, 1960 (dec.); children: Teresa, Brian. BS in Agr., Wash. State U., 1960, MS in Nutrition, 1962; PhD in Dairy Sci., U. Ill., 1965. Postdoctoral fellow dept. toxicology Karolinska Inst., Stockholm, 1966; N.Z. facial exzema sr. postdoctoral fellow Ruakura Agrl. Research Ctr., Hamilton, 1975-76; mem. faculty dept. biochemistry Mich. State U., East Lansing, 1967-87, prof., 1977-87, assoc. dir. Ctr. for Environ. Toxicology, 1980-85, dir. Ctr. for the Study of Active Oxygen, 1985-87; dir. biotech. ctr. Utah State U., Logan, 1987-91, prof. chem. biochemistry, 1987—. Dir. basic rsch. and tng. program Superfund Nat. Inst. Environ. Health Scis., 1988-96; mem. toxicology study sect. NIH, 1979-83; mem. environ. measurements com., mem. sci. adv. bd. EPA, 1980-83; mem. toxicology data bank, mem. peer rev. com. Nat. Libr. Medicine, 1983-85; mem. Mich. Toxic Substance Control Commn., 1979-82, chmn., 1981-82; pres., founder Intech One-Eighty Corp., North Logan Utah, 1993-99, pres. 1999—; mem. adv. panel for metabolic biochemistry program NSF, 1998; mem. EPA/DOE/NSF/ONR Joint Program on Bioremediation, 1998. Contbr. articles to profl. jours. Recipient Nat. Rsch. Svc. award NIH, USPHS, Dupont Sci. and Engring. award, 1988, Alumni Achievement award Wash. State U., 1998; NRC facial eczema fellow Ruakura Agrl. Rsch. Ctr., Hamilton, New Zealand, 1975. Fellow Acad. Toxicology Scis., Oxygen Soc.; mem. Am. Soc. Biol. Chemists, Am. Soc. Pharmacology and Exptl. Therapeutics, Soc. Toxicology, Am. Soc. Photobiology, Am. Soc. Microbiology. Office: Utah State U Biotech Ctr Logan UT 84322-4705 also: Intech One-Eighty Corp PO Box 6218 North Logan UT 84341-6218 E-mail: sdaust@cc.usu.edu

AUSTERMAN, ALAN, state senator; b. Everett, Wash., May 23, 1943; m. Virginia Austerman; children: Carol, Dawn. Grad., Kodiak (Alaska) H.S., 1961. Print shop owner, 1975-88; newspaper owner Kadiak Times, 1976-83; owner Austerman's Office Supply, 1979-88; owner hunting and fishing lodge, 1985-90; mem. Kodiak Island Borough Assembly, 1985-90, 92-94; Rep. rep. Alaska Ho. of Reps., 1994-2000; Rep. senator dist. C Alaska State Senate, 2000—. Mem. legis. fin. com. Alaska Ho. of Reps., chmn. legis. fisheries com.; chair Pacific Fisheries Legis. Task Force. Exec. dir. KICVB, 1993-94. Pres. bd. dirs. Kodiak Jaycees; co-founder Kodiak Alaska State Pks. Adv. Com.; police officer City of Kodiak; mem. Kodiak Island Borough Pks. and Recreation; mem. personnel bd. City of Kodiak; mem. Kodiak Sch. Budget Review Com., Cmty. Coll. Adv. Bd., Hosp. Adv. Bd., Kiwanis. Sgt. Alaska Army N.G. Mem. Kodiak Island Sportsman Assn., Kodiak Rodeo Assn. (co-founder), Ducks Unltd. (chmn.), Kodiak C. of C. (pres. bd. dirs.), Elks, NRA, Pioneers of Alaska, Toastmasters. Avocations: hunting, fishing, photography, hiking. Office: Alaska State Senate State Capitol Rm 417 Juneau AK 99801-1182 Office Fax: 907 465-4956. E-mail: Alanaust@ptialaska.net, Senator_Alan_Austerman@legis.state.ak.us

AUSTIN, H(ARRY) GREGORY, lawyer; b. N.Y.C., Mar. 18, 1936; s. Harry Gregory and Pauline (Moore) A.; m. Deanna Ruth Anderson, Nov. 28, 1970; children: Sabrina Elizabeth, Harry Gregory III, Anne Catherine. BE, Yale U., 1957, postgrad., 1958; JD, U. Mich., 1961; LLD (hon.), Lincoln U., 1976. Bar: Colo. 1961, U.S. Supreme Ct. 1974. Assoc., then ptnr. Holland & Hart, Denver, 1962-73, ptnr., 1977—; gen. counsel SBA, Washington, 1973-75; solicitor, gen. counsel U.S. Dept. Interior, Washington, 1975-77. Trustee Colo. Legal Aid Found., Denver, 1984-91, chmn., 1988-91; bd. dirs. Children's Hosp., Denver, 1985-97; mem. adv. com. Colo. Sec. State, 1996—. 1st lt. USAR, 1957-64. Fellow Am. Bar Found.; mem. Am. Law Inst., Colo. Bar Assn. (chmn. bus. entities subsect. bus. law sect. 1987-89, vice chmn. bus. law sect. 1989-91, chmn. 1991-93, chmn. partnership laws com. 1993—), Denver Bar Assn., Metro Denver C. of C. (bd. dirs., sec. 1995-97). Republican. Office: Holland & Hart 555 17th St Ste 2900 Denver CO 80202-3979 E-mail: gaustin@hollandhart.com

AUSTIN, JOAN D. personal care industry executive; Grad. h.s. V.p., treas. A-dec Inc., Newberg, Oreg., 1963—; pres. Austin Industries, Newberg. Chmn. bd. Drug and Alcohol Treatment Ctr. at Springbrook N.W., Newberg. Mem. Internat. Women's Forum, Found. for Women's Resources Office: A-dec Inc 2601 Crestview Dr Newberg OR 97132-9529

AUTH, JUDITH, library director; BA in English Lit., U. Calif., Riverside, 1968, grad. advanced mgmt. program, 1990; MLS, UCLA, 1971. Children's libr. Marcy br. Riverside City & County Pub. Libr., 1971-73, ctrl. libr. children's rm., 1973-75, coord. children's svcs., 1975-80, area br. supr., 1980-85, head ctrl. libr., 1985-87, acting head tech. svcs., 1987-88, asst. libr. dir., 1988-91, libr. dir., 1991—. Asst. to city mgr. in charge of entrepreneurial mgmt. program City of Riverside, 1988-91. Mem. ALA, Am. Soc. Pub. Adminstrn., Calif. Libr. Assn. (leadership inst. task force 1992-93, mem. assembly 1994), Calif. County Librs. Assn. (sec. 1992-94), So. Calif. Coun. Lit. for Children and Young People (bd. dirs. 1975-90). Office: Riverside City & County Libr 3581 Mission Inn Ave Riverside CA 92501-3306

AUTIO, RUDY, artist, educator; b. Butte, Mont., Oct. 8, 1926; BS, Mont. State U., 1950; MFA, Wash. State U., 1952; DFA, Md. Inst. Coll. Art, Balt., 1986. Resident artist dir. Archie Bray Found., 1952-56; asst. curator Mont. Mus. Hist. Soc., 1955; prof. ceramics and sculpture U. Mont., 1957-84. Author: About Drawing, 1985; one-man shows include Henry Gallery, U. Wash., Seattle, 1963, Toledo Art Mus., 1965, Retrospectives, Am. Crafts Mus., N.Y., 1983, John Michael Kohler Art Mus., Sheboygan, Wis., 1983, Bellevue Art Mus., Wash., 1983, Mont. Horses, Ryijy Tapestry, Taideteollisuusmuseo, Helsinki, 1985, Everson Mus., Syracuse, 1964; group shows include Chgo. Art Mus., 1968, Am. Studio Potters & Victoria & Albert Mus., London, 1972, San Francisco Mus. Modern Art, 1972, Mus. Contemporary Crafts, N.Y., 1974, Seattle Art Mus., 1979; retrospectives includes Am. Crafts Mus., N.Y. and Bellevue Mus. Seattle, 1984, Western States Arts Found. 3d Ann. Exhbn. Bklyn. Mus., 1986, Contemporary Am. Ceramics, Nat. Mus. Modern Art, Seoul, 1987; prin. works exhibited Renwick Gallery, Smithsonian Mus., Everson Mus., Syracuse, N.Y., Victoria & Albert Mus., London, Nat. Mus. Stockholm, Taideteollisuusmuseo, Helsinki. Recipient Tiffany Found. award, 1963, Purchase award Everson Mus., 1964, Ceramic Art award, Am. Ceramic Soc., 1978, NEA, 1980, 1st Gov.'s award in Visual Arts' Most Outstanding Artist, 1980, Disting. scholar award U. Mont., 1984. Fellow Am. Craftsmen Coun. (gold medal 1999), Archie Bray Found. (trustee 1974), Internat. Ceramic Soc. Geneva; mem. Nat. Coun. Edn. Ceramic Arts. Office: Missoula Art Mus Pattee St at Pine Missoula MT 59802

AUTOLITANO, ASTRID, consumer products executive; b. Havana, Cuba, Aug. 25, 1938; came to U.S., 1966; d. Manuel and Efigenia (Giquel) Rodriguez; m. Dominick Autolitano, July 23, 1977; children: Astrid Martinez, Manuel Martinez. Student, U. Havana, 1962-64, El Camino Coll., Torrance, Calif., 1968-71, UCLA, Westwood, 1973-75, Columbia U., , 1983. Multi-lingual sec. Mattel Toys, Hawthorne, Calif., 1966-69, coord. internat. sales, 1969-73, mgr. Pan Am. sales, 1973-78, dir. export sales and licensees, 1978-83, v.p. Latin Am., 1983-89, sr. v.p. Latin Am. El Segundo, 1989-95, exec. v.p. Latin Am., 1995-96, exec. v.p. Ams., 1996, pres. internat., 1996—. Office: Mattel Toys 333 Continental Blvd El Segundo CA 90245-5012

AVAKOFF, JOSEPH CARNEGIE, medical and legal consultant; b. Fairbanks, Alaska, July 15, 1936; s. Harry B. and Margaret (Adams) A.; m. Teddy I. Law, May 7, 1966; children: Caroline, Joey, John. AA, U. Calif., Berkeley, 1956, AB, 1957; MD, U. Calif., San Francisco, 1961; JD, Santa Clara U., 1985. Bar: Calif. 1987; diplomate Am. Bd. Surgery, Am. Bd. Plastic Surgery. Physicist U.S. Naval Radiol. Def. Lab., San Francisco, 1957, 59; intern So. Pacific Gen. Hosp., San Francisco, 1961-62; resident in surgery Kaiser Found. Hosp., San Francisco, 1962-66; resident in plastic surgery U. Tex. Sch. Medicine, San Antonio, 1970-72; pvt. practice specializing in surgery Sacramento, 1966-70; pvt. practice specializing in plastic surgery Los Gatos and San Jose, Calif., 1972-94; cons. to med. and legal professions, 1994—. Clin. instr. surgery U. Calif. Sch. Medicine, Davis, 1967-70; chief dept. surgery Mission Oaks Hosp., Los Gatos, 1988-90; chief divsn. plastic surgery Good Samaritan Hosp., San Jose, 1989-91; expert med. reviewer Med. Bd. Calif., 1995—; spl. cons. Calif. Dept. Corps., 1997—; presenter numerous med. orgns. Contbr. numerous articles to med. jours. Mem. San Jose Adv. Commn. on Health, 1975-82; bd. govs. San Jose YMCA, 1977-80. Mem. AMA, Calif. Med. Assn., Santa Clara County Bar Assn., Santa Clara County Med. Assn., Union Am. Physicians and Dentists, Phi Beta Kappa, Phi Eta Sigma. Republican. Presbyterian. Avocations: music, photography, computer programming. Home: 6832 Rockview Ct San Jose CA 95120-5607

AVERY, STEPHEN NEAL, playwright, author; b. Hot Springs, Ark., Mar. 20, 1955; s. Leo A. Avery and Dedette Carol (Miles) Andree; m. Kathleen Annette Twin, Sept. 7, 1979. Free-lance reporter Hot Springs Sentinel-Record and New Era, 1970-73. Author: Hungry: 3 Plays, 1991, Because, 1991, Insidious, 1992, Burning Bridges, 1999. With USN, 1973-77. Mem. Dramatists Guild Inc., Authors League of Am., Theatre Comms. Group, The Drama League. Avocations: museum and gallery exhbns.

AVERY, SUSAN KATHRYN, electrical engineering educator, research administrator; b. Detroit, Jan. 5, 1950; d. Theodore Peter and Alice Jane (Greene) Rykala; m. James Paul Avery, Aug. 12, 1972; 1 child, Christopher Scott. BS in Physics, Mich. State U., 1972; MS in Physics, U. Ill., 1974, PhD in Atmospheric Sci., 1978. Asst. prof. elec. engring. U. Ill., Urbana, 1978-83; fellow CIRES U. Colo., Boulder, 1982—, assoc. prof. elec. engring., 1985-92, assoc. dean rsch. and grad. edn. Coll. Engring., 1989-92, prof. elec. engring., 1992—, dir. CIRES, 1994—; sec. USNC/URSI NRC, 1994—. Adv. com. chair Elec. and Communications Div. NSF, Washington, 1991-93, adv. panel atmospheric scis. program, 1985-88, steering com. CEDAR program, 1986-87, adv. com. engring. directorate, 1991-93, vis. professorship, 1982-83; working group ionosphere, thermosphere, mesosphere NASA, Washington, 1991—; mem.-at-large USNC/URSI NRC, Washington, 1991-93, com. on solar-terrestrial rsch., 1987-90; trustee Univ. Corp. for Atmospheric Rsch., 1991—, vice chair bd. trustees, 1993, sci. programs evaluation com., 1989-91; working group on tides in mesosphere and lower thermosphere Internat. Commn. Meteorology of Upper Atmosphere, 1981-86; mesosphere-lower thermosphere network steering com. Internat. STEP Program, 1989—, equatorial mid. atmosphere dynamics steering com., 1990—. Contbr. articles to Radio Sci., Adv. Space Rsch., Jour. Atmosphere Terrestrial Physics, Jour. Geophys. Rsch., others. Recipient Faculty Award for Women, NSF, 1991, Outstanding Publ. award NCAR, 1990; faculty fellow U. Colo., 1994; vis. fellow Coop. Inst. for Rsch. in Environ. Scis., 1982-83. Fellow Am. Meteorological Soc. (com. on mid. atmosphere 1990—); mem. IEEE, Am. Geophys. Union (com. edn. and human resources 1988-92), Am. Soc. Engring. Edn., Sigma Xi. Achievements include research on the dynamics of the mesosphere, stratosphere and troposphere with emphasis on unifying observational analyses and theoretical studies, on wave dynamics including the coupling of the atmosphere/ocean and interactions between large-scale and small-scale motions, on the use of ground-based doppler radar techniques for observing the clear-air atmosphere and use of new signal processing algorithms for radar data analysis. Office: U Colo Cires Cb 216 Boulder CO 80309-0001

AVIDA, DAN, printing company executive; Project mgr. Electronics for Imaging, Inc., Foster City, Calif., 1989-91, v.p., 1991-94, pres., COO, 1994-99, chmn., 2000—. Office: Electronics for Imaging Inc 303 Velocity Way Foster City CA 94404

AVRIT, RICHARD CALVIN, defense consultant, career officer; b. Tilamook, Oreg., Feb. 18, 1932; s. Roy Calvin and Mary Louise (Morgan) A.; m. Alice Jane Tamminga, July 10, 1959; 1 dau., Tamra Jane. B.S. in Engring, U.S. Naval Acad., 1953; M.S. in Engring. Electronics, U.S. Naval Postgrad. Sch., 1960; postgrad., U.S. Naval War Coll., 1971-72. Commd. ensign U.S. Navy, 1953, advanced through grades to rear adm., 1979; served weapons dept. U.S.S. George K. Mackenzie, 1953-54; ops. dept. U.S.S. Willis A. Lee, 1954-57; comdg. officer U.S.S. Sumner County, 1960-63; project officer, staff of comdr. Operational Test and Evaluation Force, Key West, Fla., 1963-66; exec. officer U.S.S. Berkeley, 1966-68; ops. officer, AAW project officer Comdr. Cruiser Destroyer Florilla Nine, 1968-70; comdg. officer U.S.S. Sellers, 1970-71; mil. asst. for surface guns and missiles to asst. dir. Ocean Control Directorate, Def. Research and Engring., Office Sec. of Def., 1972-76; comdg. officer U.S.S. Harry E. Yarnell, 1976-78; chief of staff, comdr. Naval Surface Force U.S. Atlantic Fleet, 1978-79; project mgr. for Saudi Naval Expansion Program, Naval Material Command, Washington, 1979-82; dir. navy logistics plans Office Chief of Naval Ops., Washington, 1982-84; cons. Info. Spectrum, Inc., 1984-88; pres. Mil. Data Corp., Arlington, Va., 1989-91; small bus. cons., 1992—. Decorated D.S.M., Legion of Merit (3), Bronze Star with Combat V, Meritorious Service Medal (2). Mem. Naval Inst., IEEE. Methodist. Home: 4839 Keswick Ct Dumfries VA 22026-1084 Office: 1254 W Cedar Ave Denver CO 80223-1728 E-mail: dick-a-keswick@worldnet.att.net

AXELSON, JOSEPH ALLEN, professional athletics executive, publisher; b. Peoria, Dec. 25, 1927; s. Joseph Victor Axelson and Florence (Ealen) Massey; m. Malcolm Rae Smith, Oct. 7, 1950 (dec.); children: David Allen, Mark Stephen, Linda Rae. B.S., Northwestern U., 1949. Sports info. dir. Ga. So. U., Statesboro, 1957-60, Nat. Assn. Intercollegiate Athletics, Kansas City, Mo., 1961-62; tournament dir. Bowling Proprs. Assn. Am., Park Ridge, Ill., 1963-64; asst. exec. sec. Nat. Assn. Intercollegiate Athletics, Kansas City, Mo., 1964-68; exec. v.p., gen. mgr. Cin. Royals Profl. Basketball Team, Cin., 1969-72; mgr. Cin. Gardens, 1970-72; pres., gen. mgr. Kansas City Kings Profl. Basketball Team, Kansas City, Mo., 1972-79, 82-85, Sacramento Kings Profl. Basketball Team, 1985-88, exec. v.p., 1988-90; pres. Arco Arena, Sacramento, 1985-88; exec. v.p. Sacramento Sports Assn., Arco Sports Complex, 1988-90, Profl. Team Publs., Inc., Stamford, Conn., 1991-92; pub. Between The Vines Newsletter, 1993—. Exec. v.p. ops. NBA, N.Y.C., 1979-82, chmn. competition and rules com., 1975-79; trustee Naismith Basketball Hall of Fame; co-host The Sports Page, Sta. KFMB-AM, San Diego, 1994-97. Author: Basketball Basics, 1987. Mem. Emil Verban Meml. Soc., Washington. Capt. Signal

Corps. AUS, 1949-54. Named Nat. Basketball Exec. of Yr. The Sporting News, St. Louis, 1973, Sportsman of Yr., Rockne Club, Kansas City, 1975; recipient Annual Dirs. award Downtown, Inc., Kansas City, Mo., 1979, Nat. Assn. Intercollegiate Athletics Frank Cramer Nat. Svc. award, 1983, Man of Yr. award Sacramento (Calif.) C. of C., 1986, Sacramento Bus. Cmty. award, 1986; named to Ga. So. U. Sports Hall of Fame, 1990. Mem. Am. Philatelic Soc., Phi Kappa Psi. Republican. Presbyterian.

AXON, DONALD CARLTON, architect; b. Haddonfield, N.J., Feb. 27, 1931; s. William Russell Sr. and Gertrude L. (Ellis) A.; m. Rosemary Smith, Sept. 1952 (div. Oct. 1967); children: Donald R., James K., Marianne Axon Flannery, Darren H., William R. II; m. Janice Jacobs, Mar. 16, 1968; stepchildren: Jonathan Lee, Elise Marie. BArch, Pratt Inst., 1954; MS in Arch., Columbia U., 1966. Registered architect, N.Y., Pa., Calif. Designer, drafter Keith Hibner, Assoc., Hicksville, N.Y., 1954-56; designer Charles Wood, Riverhead, 1956-59; architect, prin Donald C. Axon, Assoc., Wantaugh, 1959; ptnr. Bailey-Axon & Assoc., Long Beach, 1960-66; project mgr. Caudill Rowlett Scott, Houston, 1966-69; in-house architect Kaiser Permanente Hosp., L.A., 1969-75; dir. med. facilities Daniel Mann Johnson Mendenhall, L.A., 1975-78, Lyon Assocs., L.A., 1979-80; pres. Donald C. Axon, FAIA, Inc., L.A., 1980—. Tchr. bldg. sci. program U. So. Calif., 1978-82; lectr. in field; profl. advisor dept. architecture U. Tex., 1968-69; advisor to chmn. Sch. Architecture Rice U., Houston, 1968-69; profl. dir. Future Architect Am., 1965-66. Mem. Crestwood Hills Assn., bd. dirs. 1971-75, pres., 1973-75, archtl. rev. com., 1987—; bd. dirs. Brentwood Community Fedn., 1973-75, v.p., 1974-75. Recipient L.A. Beautiful award KPH Norwalk Hosp. Fellow AIA (Calif. regional bd. dirs. 1987-89, mem. various subcoms., chair steering com. 1980, liaison 1991—, bd. dirs. L.A. chpt. 1983-84, pres. 1986, chair com. on architecture for health 1974, chair health facilities com. Calif. coun. 1975, Disting. Svc. citation 1992), Royal Soc. Health, Health Facilities Inst., Hosp. Facilities Inst.; mem. Archtl. Found. L.A. (founding, v.p. 1985-89, pres. 1989-90), Internat. Conf. Bldg. Ofcls., Am. Hosp. Assn., Forum for Health Care Planning (bd. dirs. 1982—, pres. 1993-94). Office: 24302 Carlton Ct Laguna Niguel CA 92677-3718 Fax: 949-360-8114. E-mail: donaxon@aol.com

AXSON, HARRY B., JR. career officer; BA, Mil. Coll. S.C., The Citadel, 1971, MEd, 1979; grad., Army Command Gen. Staff Coll., Army War Coll. Commd. 2d lt. U.S. Army, 1971, advanced through grades to brig. gen., assignments include platoon leader, co. comdr., bn. comdr., comdr. 2d bn. 504th infantry, 82d airborne divsn. Panama, 1989-90, bn. comdr. airborne divsn. Ops. Desert shield/Desert Storm Iraq and Saudi Arabia, 1990-91; exec. officer to Comdr. in chief U.S. Spl. Ops. Command, MacDill AFB, Fla., 1992-99; comdr. Jt. Task Force - Full Acctg. U.S. Army, Camp H.M. Smith, Hawaii, 1999—. Decorated Legions of Merit (2), bronze star (2), Def. Meritorious Svc. medal (2), Meritorious svc. medals (3), others. Master parachutist.

AYALA, FRANCISCO JOSÉ, geneticist, educator; b. Madrid, Mar. 12, 1934; came to U.S., 1961, naturalized, 1971; s. Francisco and Soledad (Pereda) A.; m. Hana Lostakova, Mar. 8, 1985; children by previous marriage: Francisco José, Carlos Alberto. BS, Universidad de Madrid, 1954, D. honoris causa, 1986; MA, Columbia U., 1963, Ph.D., 1964; D. honoris causa, Universidad de León (Spain), 1982, Universidad de Barcelona, Spain, 1986, U. Athens, Greece, 1991, U. Vigo, Spain, 1996, U. Islas, Baleares, Spain, 1998, U. Valencia, Spain, 1999, U. Bologna, Italy, 2001. Research assoc. Rockefeller U., 1964-65; asst. prof. Providence Coll., 1965-67, Rockefeller U., 1967-71; assoc. prof. to prof. genetics U. Calif., Davis, 1971-87, disting. prof. biology Irvine, 1987-89; Donald Bren prof. of Biol. scis., 1989—. Bd. dirs. basic biology NRC, 1982-91, chmn., 1984-91, mem. commn. on life scis., 1982-91, mem. nat. adv. coun. Nat. Inst. Gen. Med. Scis.; mem. exec. com. EPA, 1979-80; mem. adv. com. directorate sci. and engring. edn. NSF, 1989-91; mem. nat. adv. coun. for human genome rsch. NIH, 1990-93; mem. Pres. com. advisors sci. and tech., 1994-2001. Author: Population and Evolutionary Genetics, 1982, Modern Genetics, 1980, 2d edit., 1984, Evolving: the Theory and Processes of Organic Evolution, 1979, Evolution, 1977, Molecular Evolution, 1976, Studies in the Philosophy of Biology, 1974. Recipient medal Coll. de France, 1979, Mendel medal Czech Republic Acad. Scis., 1994, Hon. Gold medal Acad. Nat. dei Lincei, Rome, 2000, William Proctor prize, Sigma Xi, 2000; Guggenheim fellow, Fulbright fellow. Fellow AAAS (Sci. Freedom and Responsibility award 1987, bd. dirs. 1989-93, pres.-elect 1993-94, pres. 1994-95, chmn. of bd. 1995-96, chmn. com. on health of sci. enterprise 1991—, mem. nat. coun. for sci. and edn. for phase II, project 2061 1990—); mem. NAS (sect. population biology evolution and ecology chmn. 1983-86, councillor 1986-89, bd. dirs. Nat. Acad. Corp. 1990—), Am. Acad. Arts and Scis., Am. Soc. Naturalists (sec. 1973-76), Genetics Soc. Am., Am. Genetic Assn. (hon. life, Wilhelmine E. Key award), Ecology Soc. Am., Am. Philos. Soc., Soc. Study Evolution (pres. 1979-80), Royal Acad. Scis. Spain (fgn. mem.), Russian Acad. Natural Scis. (fgn. mem.), Mex. Acad. Scis. (fgn. mem.), Acad. Nat. dei Lincei (Rome) (fgn.). Home: 2 Locke Ct Irvine CA 92612-4034 Office: U Calif Dept Ecology & Evolution Irvine CA 92697-0001 E-mail: fjayala@uci.edu

AYALA, JOHN, librarian, dean; b. Long Beach, Calif., Aug. 28, 1943; s. Francisco and Angelina (Rodriguez) Ayala; m. Patricia Marie Dozier, July 11, 1987 (dec. Nov. 19, 2001); children: Juan, Sara. BA in History, Calif. State U., Long Beach, 1970, MPA, 1981; MLS, Immaculate Heart Coll., L.A., 1971. Library paraprofl. Long Beach Pub. Library, 1963-70; librarian L.A. County Pub. Libr., 1971-72, Long Beach City Coll., 1972-90, assoc. prof., 1972-90, pres. acad. senate, 1985-87; dean, Learning Resources Fullerton (Calif.) Coll., 1990—, evening/weekend supr., 1997—. Chmn. Los Angeles County Com. to Recruit Mexican-Am. Librs., 1971-74; mem. acad. senate Calif. Cmty. Colls., 1985-90; pres. Latino Faculty/Staff Assn., NOCCD, 1993-2000. Editor Calif. Librarian, 1971. Served with USAF, 1966-68, Vietnam. U.S. Office Edn. fellow for library sci., 1970-71. Mem. ALA (com. mem. 1971—, Melvil Dewey award com. 1998—), Calif. Libr. Assn., REFORMA Nat. Assn. to Promote Spanish Speaking Libr. Svc. (founding mem., v.p., pres. 1973-76). Democrat. Roman Catholic. Office: Fullerton College Library 321 E Chapman Ave Fullerton CA 92832-2011

AYLING, HENRY FAITHFUL, writer, editor, consultant; b. Bklyn., Dec. 30, 1931; s. Albert Edward John and Mina Campbell McCurdy (Lindsay) A.; m. Julia Corinne Gornto, 1954; children: Campbell, Eben, Corey, Harry, Faith. BA, Grinnell Coll., 1953; MA, Columbia U., Calif. State U., Carson, 1984; 2 grad. teaching certs., Calif. State U., Carson, 1985. Asst to registrar Columbia U., N.Y.C., 1958-59; supr. crew scheduling Pan Am World Airways, Jamaica, N.Y., 1959-62, supr. payload control, 1963-65; mgr. crew scheduling Seabd. World Airlines, Jamaica, 1962-63, 65-68, mgr. system control, 1968-80; mgr. ops. control Flying Tiger Line, 1980-84; instr. English, ESL Long Beach (Calif.) City Coll., 1984-85; mng. editor IEEE Expert, IEEE Computing Futures IEEE Computer Soc., Los Alamitos, Calif., 1985-90, editorial dir. Computer Soc. Press, 1990-93; writer, editor, cons., 1993—. Mem. editorial bd. Expert Mag., 1986-90, CamAm Programming Inc., 1987-88; columnist Mag. Design and Prodn. mag., 1988-89; contbr. articles to profl. mags. and tech. books; contbr. poetry to various mags. and anthologies. Bd. dirs. Playa Serena Home Owners Assn., Playa Del Rey, Calif., 1983-85. Recipient Maggie awards Western Publs. Assn., 1988-89, IEEE Computer Soc. Golden Core award, 1997. Mem. IEEE Computer Soc. Avocations: music, fine arts. Home and Office: 78291 Allegro Dr Palm Desert CA 92211-1894 E-mail: Jcayling@compaq.net

AYRES, JANICE RUTH, social service executive; b. Idaho Falls, Idaho, Jan. 23, 1930; d. Low Ray and Frances Mae (Salem) Mason; m. Thomas Woodrow Ayres, Nov. 27, 1953 (dec. 1966); 1 child, Thomas Woodrow Jr. (dec.). MBA, U. So. Calif., 1952, M in Mass Comms., 1953. Asst. mktg. dir. Disneyland, Inc., Anaheim, Calif., 1954-59; gen. mgr. Tamasha Town & Country Club, Anaheim, 1959-65; dir. mktg. Am. Heart Assn., Santa Ana, 1966-69; state exec. dir. Nev. Assn. Mental Health, Las Vegas, 1969-71; exec. dir. Clark Co. Easter Seal Treatment Ctr., Las Vegas, 1971-73; mktg. dir., fin devel. officer So. Nev. Drug Abuse Coun., Las Vegas, 1973-74; exec. dir. Nev. Assn. Retarded Citizens, Las Vegas, 1974-75; assoc., cons. Don Luke & Assocs., Phoenix, 1976-77; program dir. Inter-Tribal Coun. Nev., Reno, 1977-79; exec. dir. Ret. Sr. Vol. Program, Carson City, Nev., 1979—. Chair sr. citizen summit State of Nev., 1996; apptd. Nev. Commn. Aging Gov. Guinn, 2001; presenter in field. Bd. suprs., Carson City, Nev., 1992—; commr. Carson City Parks and Recreation, 1993—; obligation bond com., legis. chair Carson City; bd. dirs. Nev. Dept. Transp., 1993; active No. Corp. for Nat. and Cmty. Svc. by Gov., 1994, V&TRR Commn., 1993, chair, 1995; vice-chair, chair pub. rels. com., bd. dirs. Hist. V&TRR Bd.; chair PR Cmty./V&RR Commn. Nev. Home Health Assn.; appointed liaison Carson City Sr. Citizens Bd., 1995; chair summit Rural Nev. Sr. Citizens , Carson City; pres. No. Nev. R.R. Found., 1996—; chair Tri-Co-R.R. Commn., 1995, Gov.'s Nev. Commn. for Corp. in Nat. and Comty. Svc., 1997—, pres., 1998, Carson City Pub. Transp. Commn., 1998—; Carson City Commn. for Clean Groundwater Act, 1998—; chairperson Celebrate Svc. Conf. Americore, 2000; appointed by Gov. of Nev. Commn. on Aging, 2001—; appointed by Nev. Spkr. of the Ho. to new Nev. Commn. to Restructure the Historic V&T R.R. Named Woman of Distinction, Soroptimist Club, 1988, Outstanding Dir. of Excellence, Gov. State of Nev., 1989, Outstanding Dir., Vol. Action Ctr., J.C. Penney Co., Outstanding Nev. Women's Role Model Nev. A.G., 1996; recipient Gold award Western Fairs Assn., 2000; invitee to White House for outstanding contbns. to Am. Mem. AAUW, Am. Mgmt. Assn. (bd. dirs.), Am. Mktg. Assn. (bd. dirs. 1999—), Internat. Platform Assn., Pub. Rels. Soc. Am. (chpt. pres., Silver Spike award 1996), Women Radio and TV, Nat. Soc. Fund Raising Execs., Nev. Fair and Rodeo Assn. (pres.), Nev. Assn. Transit Svcs. (bd. dirs., legis. chmn.), Nev. Women's Polit. Caucus, Nat. Women's Polit. Caucus, Am. Soc. Assn. Execs., No. Nev. Railroad found. (pres. 1996). E-mail: branded@rsvp.carson_city_nv.us. Home: 1762 Montelena Ct Carson City NV 89703-8376 Office: Ret Sr Vol Program 501 E Caroline St Carson City NV 89701-4054

AZARNOFF, DANIEL LESTER, pharmaceutical company consultant; b. Bklyn., Aug. 4, 1926; s. Samuel J. and Kate (Asarnow) A.; m. Joanne Stokes, Dec. 26, 1951; children: Rachel, Richard, Martin. BS, Rutgers U., 1947, MS, 1948; MD, U. Kans., 1955. Asst. instr. anatomy U. Kans. Med. Sch., 1949-50, research fellow, 1950-52, intern, 1955-56, resident, Nat. Heart Inst. research fellow, 1956-58, asst. prof. medicine, 1962-64, assoc. prof., 1964-68, dir. clin. pharmacology study unit, 1964-68, assoc. prof. pharmacology, 1965-68, prof. medicine and pharmacology, 1968, dir. Clin. Pharmacology-Toxicology Ctr., 1967-78, Disting. prof., 1973-78, also prof. medicine, 1965-67, pres. Sigma Xi Club, 1968-69, clin. prof. medicine, 1982-96; Nat. Inst. Neurol. Diseases and Blindness spl. trainee Washington U. Sch. Medicine, St. Louis, 1958-60; asst. prof. medicine St. Louis U. Sch. Medicine, 1960-62; sr. v.p. worldwide R&D, G.D. Searle & Co., Skokie, 1978; pres. Searle R&D, Skokie, 1979-85, Azarnoff Assocs., Inc., Evanston, Ill., 1986-87, D.L. Azarnoff Assocs., So. San Francisco, Calif., 1987—; prof. pathology, clin. prof. pharmacology Northwestern U. Med. Sch., 1978-85; sr. v.p. clin. regulatory affairs Cellegy Pharms., 1999—; commr. Nat. Commn. on Orphan Diseases, 1985-87; chmn. bd. dirs. Alpha RX Corp., South San Francisco, Calif., 1992-94; clin. prof. med. Stanford U. Sch. Med., 1998—. Professorial lectr. U. Chgo., 1978-86; dir. Second Workshop on Prins. Drug Evaluation in Man, 1970; chmn. com. on problems of drug safety NRC-NAS, 1972-76; chmn. bd. dirs. Oread, Inc., Lawrence, Kans., 1998-99; CEO Cibus Pharms., Burlingame, Calif., 1996-97; cons. numerous govt. agys.; chmn. bd. dirs. Cibus Pharm., Inc., 1996-97. Editor: Devel. of Drug Interactions, 1974-77, Yearbook of Drug Therapy, 1977-79; series editor: Monographs in Clin. Pharmacology, 1977-84; mem. editl. bd. Drug Investigation, Brit. Jour. Clin. Pharmacology, Clin. Pharmacol. Therapy, Clin. Pharmacokinetics, Clin. Drug Investigation, 1989—, others. Served with U.S. Army, 1945-46. Recipient Ginsburg award in phys. diagnosis U. Kanas. Med. Ctr., 1953, Outstanding Intern award, 1956, Ciba award for gerontol. rsch., 1958, Rectors medal U. Helsinki, 1968; named Disting. Med. Alumnus, U. Kans. Coll. Health Sci., 1995; John and Mary R. Markle scholar, 1964, William N. Creasy vis. prof. clin. pharmacology Med. Coll. Va., 1975; Bruce Hall Meml. lectr. St. Vincents Hosp., Sydney, 1976, 7th Sir Henry Hallett Dale lectr. Johns Hopkins U. Med. Sch., 1978; Fulbright scholar Karolinska Inst., Stockholm, 1968. Fellow ACP, N.Y. Acad. Scis., Am. Assn. Pharm. Scientists (Rsch. Achievement award in clin. scis. 1995); AAAS (chmn. elect pharm. sect. 2001), mem. Am. Soc. Clin. Nutrition, Am. Nutrition Instn., Am. Soc. Pharmacology and Exptl. Therapeutics (chmn. clin. pharmacology divsn. 1969-71, mem. exec. com. 1966-73, 78-81, del. 1975-78, bd. publ. trustees), Am. Soc. Clin. Pharmacology and Therapeutics (Oscar B. Hunter Meml. award 1995), Am. Fedn. Clin. Rsch., Brit. Pharmacol. Soc., AMA (vice chmn. coun. on drugs 1971-72, editl. bd. jour.), Ctrl. Soc. Clin. Rsch., Royal Soc. for Promotion Health, Inst. Medicine of Nat. Acad. Scis., Soc. Exptl. Biology and Medicine (councillor 1976-80), Internat. Union Pharmacologists (sec. clin. pharmacology sect. 1975-81, internat. adv. com. Paris Congress 1978), GPIA (blue ribbon com. on generic medicine 1990), Sigma Xi. E-mail: dazarnoff@earthlink.com

AZIZ, KHALID, petroleum engineering educator; b. Bahawalpur, Pakistan, Sept. 29, 1936; came to U.S., 1952; s. Aziz Ul and Rshida (Atamohammed) Hassan; m. Mussarrat Rizwani, Nov. 12, 1962; children: Natasha, Imraan. BS in Mech. Engring., U. Mich., 1955; BSc in Petroleum Engring., U. Alta., 1958, MSc in Petroleum Engring., 1961; PhD in Chem. Engring., Rice U., 1966. Jr. design engr. Massey-Ferguson, 1955-56; various position to asst. prof. petroleum engring. U. Alta., 1960-62; various positions, chmn. bd. Neotech. Cons. Ltd., 1972-85; mgr., dir. Computer Modelling Group, Calgary, Alta., 1977-82; various positions to chief engr. Karachi (Pakistan) Gas Co., 1958-59, 62-63; various positions to prof. chem. and petroleum engring. U. Calgary, 1965-82; hon. prof., 1994—; prof. petroleum engring. dept. Stanford (Calif.) U., 1982—, assoc. dean rsch. Sch. Earth Scis., 1983-86, chmn. petroleum engring. dept., 1986-91, 94-95, Otto N. Miller prof. in earth scis., 1989—. Hon. prof. chem. and petroleum engring. U. Calgary, 1994—. Co-author: Flow of Complex Mixtures in Pipes, 1972, Petroleum Reservoir Simulation, 1979; contbr. articles to profl. jours. Recipient Diploma of Honor, Pi Epsilon Tau, 1991; Chem. Inst. Can. fellow, 1974, Killam Resident fellow U. Calgary, 1977. Mem. AIME (hon.), AAAS, European Assn. Geoscientists and Engrs., Soc. Petroleum Engrs. (disting. mem., Ferguson award 1979, Reservoir Engring. award 1987, Lester C. Uren award 1988, Disting. Achievement award for Petroleum Engring. Faculty 1990, hon. mem. 1996), Soc. Indsl. and Applied Math., Assn. Profl. Engrs. Geologists, Geophysicists (Alta., Can.), Nat. Acad. Engring., Russian Acad. Natural Scis. (fgn.), Sigma Xi. Muslim. Achievements include rsch. in multiphase flow of oil/gas mixtures & steam in pipes & wells, multiphase flow in porous media, reservoir simulation (black-oil, compositional, thermal, geothermal), natural gas engring., hydrocarbon fluid phase behavior. Home: 112 Peter Coutts Cir Stanford CA 94305-2517 Office: Stanford U Dept Petroleum Engring Stanford CA 94305-2220 E-mail: aziz@stanford.edu

BAAB, CARLTON, advertising executive; COO, CFO CKS Ptnr., Cupertino, Calif., 1994-98; COO & CFO RemarQ Communities, San Jose, CA, 1999—. Mem. bd. dirs., Peoplesoft, 1999— Office: RemarQ Communities 55 S Market St Ste 1080 San Jose CA 95113-2386

BAACK, BRET ROLYN, plastic surgeon; b. Albuquerque, July 27, 1958; s. Rolyn Ernest and Karen Lee (Engelbert) B.; m. Elena Lisa Sandoval, Feb. 14, 1987; children: Amy, David. BS in Chemistry, BA in Biology, U. N.Mex., 1979, MD, 1983. Diplomate Am. Bd. Plastic Surgery. From asst. to assoc. prof. U. N.Mex., 1990—. Fellow ACS; mem. Am Soc. Plastic and Reconstructive Surgeons (socioecon. com. 1993—), Alpha Omega Alpha, Phi Beta Kappa. Luth. Avocations: keyboards, golf. Office: Univ Hosp Dept Surg-ACC-2 2211 Lomas Blvd NE Albuquerque NM 87106-2745

BAAS, JACQUELYNN, museum consultant, art historian; b. Grand Rapids, Mich., Feb. 14, 1948; BA in History of Art, Mich. State U.; Ph.D. in History of Art, U. Mich. Registrar U. Mich. Mus. Art, Ann Arbor, 1974-78, asst. dir., 1978-82; editor Bull. Museums of Art and Archaeology, U. Mich., 1976-82; chief curator Hood Mus. Art, Dartmouth Coll., Hanover, N.H., 1982-84, dir., 1985-89, U. Calif. Berkeley Art Mus. and Pacific Film Archive, Calif., 1989-99, emeritus dir., 1999—. Cons. in field; organizer exhbns.; ind. art historian. Contbr. articles and essays to jours. and books. NEH fellow, 1972-73; Nat. Endowment Arts fellow, 1973-74, 87-88. Mem. Coll. Art Assn. Am., Am. Assn. Mus. Address: 225 Alvarado Rd Berkeley CA 94705-1512

BABAYANS, EMIL, financial planner; b. Tehran, Iran, Nov. 9, 1951; came to U.S., 1969; s. Hacob and Jenik (Khatchatourian) B.; m. Annie Ashjian. B.S., U. So. Calif., 1974, M.S., 1976; Cert. fin. planner; chartered life underwriter, fin. cons. Pres. Babtech Internat., Inc., Sherman Oaks, Calif., 1975-85; sr. ptnr. Emil Babayans & Assocs., Woodland Hills, Calif., 1985—. Mem. Am. Mgmt. Assn., Nat. Assn. Life Underwriters, Inst. Cert. Fin. Planners, Internat. Assn. Fin. Planners, Am. Soc. CLU and Chartered Fin. Cons., Million Dollar Round Table. Armenian Orthodox. Office: 21700 Oxnard St Ste 1100 Woodland Hills CA 91367-7574

BABCOCK, BARBARA ALLEN, law educator, lawyer; b. Washington, July 6, 1938; d. Henry Allen and Doris Lenore (Moses) B.; m. Thomas C. Grey, Aug. 19, 1979. AB, U. Pa., 1960; LLB, Yale U., 1963. Bar: Md. 1963, D.C. 1964, JD (hon.), U. San Diego 1983, U. Puget Sound, 1988. Law clk. U.S. Ct. Appeals D.C., 1963; assoc. Edward Bennett Williams, 1964-66; staff atty. Legal Aid Agy., Washington, 1966-68; dir. Pub. Defender Svc. (formerly Legal Aid Agy.), 1968-72; assoc. prof. Stanford U., 1972-77, prof., 1977—; asst. atty. gen. U.S. Dept. Justice, 1977-79. Ernest W. McFarland Prof. Law, 1986-97; Judge John Crown Prof. of Law, 1997—. Democrat. Author: (with others) Sex Discrimination and The Law: History, Theory and Practice, 1996; (with Massaro) Civil Procedure: Problems and Cases, 2001; contbr. articles to profl. jours. E-mail: bbabcock@stanford.edu. Home: 835 Mayfield Ave Palo Alto CA 94305-1052 Office: Stanford U Sch Law Stanford CA 94305

BABCOCK, HORACE W. retired astronomer; b. Pasadena, Calif., Sept. 13, 1912; s. Harold Delos and Mary Geddie (Henderson) B.; children: Ann Lucille, Bruce Harold, Kenneth L. B.S., Calif. Inst. Tech., 1934; Ph.D., U. Calif., 1938; D.Sc. (hon.), U. Newcastle-upon-Tyne (Eng.), 1965. Asst. Lick Obs., Mt. Hamilton, Calif., 1938-39; instr. Yerkes and McDonald Obs., Williams Bay, Wis., Ft. Davis, Tex., 1939-41; with Radiation Lab., MIT, 1941-42, Rocket Project, Calif. Inst. Tech., 1942-45; staff mem. Mt. Wilson and Palomar Obs., Carnegie Instn. of Washington, Calif. Inst. Tech., Pasadena, 1946-80; dir. Mt. Wilson and Palomar Obs., 1964-78. Author sci. and tech. papers in profl. jours. Recipient USN Bur. Ordnance Devel. award, 1946, Draper medal NAS, 1957, Eddington medal Royal Astron. Soc., 1958, gold medal, 1970, Bruce medal Astron. Soc. Pacific, 1969, Rank award in opto-electronics, 1993. Mem. NAS (councilor 1973-76), Royal Astron. Soc. (assoc.), Societé Royale des Sciences de Liege (corr. mem.), Am. Philos. Soc., Am. Acad. Arts and Scis., Am. Astron. Soc. (councilor 1956-58, George Ellery Hale award 1990), Astron. Soc. Pacific, Internat. Astron. Union. Home: 867 Windsor Way Santa Barbara CA 93105-2231 Office: Obs of Carnegie Instn 813 Santa Barbara St Pasadena CA 91101-1232

BABCOCK, LEWIS THORNTON, federal judge; b. Rocky Ford, Colo., Apr. 4, 1943; m. Judith S. Babcock; two children. BA cum laude, U. Denver, 1965, JD, 1968; LLM, U. Va., 1968. Ptnr. Mitchell and Babcock, Rocky Ford, Colo., 1968-76; atty. City Las Animas, 1969-74, City Rocky Ford, 1970-76; asst. dist. atty. 11th Jud. Cir., La Junta, Colo., 1973-76, dist. judge, 1978-83; judge Colo. Ct. Appeals, 1983-88, U.S. Dist. Ct. Colo., Denver, 1988—. Escrow and loan closing agt. FHA, Rocky Ford, 1973-76. Bd. dirs. Colo. Rural Legal Svcs. Inc., 1974-76. With Colo. N.G., 1968-74. Named to Order St. Ives. Mem. ABA, Colo. Bar Assn., Denver Bar Assn., Colo. Bar Found., North Ind. Dist. Bar Assn. Office: US Dist Ct C236 US Courthouse 1929 Stout St Rm 236 Denver CO 80294-1929

BABCOCK, WALTER CHRISTIAN, JR. membrane company executive; b. Oakland, Calif., Oct. 20, 1947; s. Walter Christian and Beatrice Alice (Sommerfield) B.; m. Jacqueline Ann Mills, Dec. 30, 1971; children: Jennifer Suzanne, Rebecca Christine. BS, U. Calif., San Diego, 1969; MS, U. Oreg., 1970, PhD, 1976. V.p. Rsch. Cons. and Design, La Jolla, Calif., 1970-71; rsch. chemist Bend (Oreg.) Rsch. Inc., 1976-81, dir. separations div., 1981-86, v.p., 1983-87, pres., 1987—, chief oper. officer, 1987-89, chief exec. officer, 1989—, pres. Bd. dirs. Consep Membranes, Bend. Contbr. articles to profl. jours. Bd. dirs. St. Charles med. Ctr., Bend, 1986. Mem. Am. Chem. Soc., N.Am. Membrane Soc., Oreg. Biotech. Assn. (bd. dirs. 1990-91). Republican. Avocations: sailing, horseback riding. Office: Bend Rsch Inc 64550 Research Rd Bend OR 97701-8599

BABICK, DON, newspaper executive; b. Montreal, Que., Can., Jan. 18, 1942; s. George and Elizabeth (Ferguson) B.; m. Jacqueline, Oct. 30, 1966; children: Nancy, Todd. Student, Ryerson Poly Inst. Pres., pub. Southam Inc., 1996—; advt. mgr. Montreal Gazette, 1969-77; advt. dir. Montreal Star, 1977-79; advt. mgr. Vancouver Sun, 1980-83; mktg. dir. Calgary Herald, 1983-88; v.p. mktg. Southam Newspaper Group, Toronto, 1988-90; pres., pub. Edmonton Jour., 1990-92, Pacific Press, 1992—. Office: Vancouver Province 200 Granville St Vancouver BC Canada V6H 3N3

BABIUK, LORNE ALAN, virologist, immunologist, research administrator; b. Canora, Sask., Can., Jan. 25, 1946; s. Paul and Mary (Mayden) B.; m. Betty Lou Carol Wagar, Sept. 29, 1973; children: Shawn, Kimberley. BSA, U. Sask., Saskatoon, 1967, MSc, 1969, DSc, 1987; PhD, U. B.C., Vancouver, 1972. Postdoctoral fellow U. Toronto, Ont., Can., 1972-73; asst. prof. We. Coll. Vet. Medicine, Saskatoon, Sask., 1973-75, assoc. prof., 1975-79, prof., 1979—; assoc. dir. rsch. Vet. Infectious Disease Orgn., Saskatoon, 1984-93, dir., 1993—. Cons. Molecular Genetics, Mpls., 1980-84, Genetech., San Francisco, 1981-84, Ciba Geigy, Basel, Switzerland, 1984-91. Contbr. some 300 articles to refereed publs., 60 chpts. to books. Recipient award Can. Soc. Microbiology, 1990, Am. Vet. Immunology, 1992, Xerox-Can. Forum., 1993, Emerging Sci. and Tech. award for innovation, 1995, Pfizer award in animal health 1998, Nat. Merit award 1998, Bill Snowden Meml. award, 2000. Fellow Infectious Disease Soc. Am., Royal Soc. Can.; mem. Internat. Soc. Interferon Rsch., Am. Soc. Microbiology, Am. Soc. Virology, Can. Soc. Microbiology, Soc. Gen. Microbiology, Internat. Soc. Antiviral Rsch. Achievements include 17 patents in field. Home: 245 East Pl Saskatoon SK Canada S7J 2Y1 Office: Vet Infectious Disease Orgn 120 Veterinary Rd Saskatoon SK S7N 5E3 Canada S7N 5E3 E-mail: babiuk@sask.usask.ca

BABULA, WILLIAM, university dean; b. Stamford, Conn., May 19, 1943; s. Benny F. and Lottie (Zajkowski) B.; m. Karen L. Gemi, June 19, 1965; children: Jared, Joelle. BA, Rutgers U., 1965; MA, U. Calif., Berkeley, 1967, PhD, 1969. Asst. prof. English U. Miami, Coral Gables, Fla., 1969-75, assoc. prof., 1975-77, prof., 1977-81, chmn. dept. Eng., 1976-81; dean of arts and humanities Sonoma State U., Rohnert Park, Calif., 1981—. Author: Shakespeare and the Tragicomic Archetype, 1975, Shakespeare in Production, 1935-79, 1981; (short stories) Motorcycle, 1982, Quarterback Sneak, 1983, The First Edsel, 1983, Ransom, 1983, The Last Jogger in Virginia, 1983, The Orthodontist and the Rock Star, 1984, Greenearth, 1984, Football and Other Seasons, The Great American Basketball Shoot, 1984, Ms. Skywriter, Inc., 1987; (plays) The Fragging of Lt. Jones (1st prize Gualala Arts Competition, 1983), Creatures (1st prize Jacksonville U. competition 1987), The Winter of Mrs. Levy (Odyssey Stage Co., New Play Series 1988), Nat. Playwright's Showcase, 1988, Theatre Americana, 1990 (James Ellis award), Basketball Jones, Black Rep of Berkeley, 1988, West Coast Ensemble, Festival of One Acts, 1992, Mark Twain Masquers, 9th Ann. Festival One Act Plays, 1994 (2d Place award), The Last Roundup, 1991 (Odyssey Stage Co.); (novels) The Bombing of Berkeley and Other Pranks (1st prize 24th Ann. Deep South Writers' Conf. 1984), St. John's Baptism, 1988, According to St. John, 1989, St. John and the Seven Veils, 1991, St. John's Bestiary, 1994, St. John's Bread, 1999; contbr. articles to profl. pubs. and short stories to lit. mags. Mem. Dramatists Guild, Assoc. Writing Programs, Mystery Writers Am., Phi Beta Kappa. Office: Sonoma State U Sch Arts and Humanities Rohnert Park CA 94928

BACA, JIM, mayor; BSBA, U. N.Mex. Mayor City of Albuquerque, 1997—. Former dir. alcohol and beverage control State of N.Mex., press sec. to gov., commr. pub. lands; past asst. to mayor, gen. mgr. Rio Grande Conservancy Dist.; former dir. Fed. Bur. Land Mgmt.; nat. cons. pub. land and conservation issues. Served with USAF. Office: Mayors Office PO Box 1293 Albuquerque NM 87103-1293

BACA, JOE, congressman; m. Barbara Baca; children: Joe Jr., Jeremy, Natalie, Jennifer. BS in Sociology, Calif. State U., L.A. Ptnr. Interstate World Travel, San Bernardino, Calif.; formerly with cmty. rels. divsn. GTE; spkr. pro tempore Calif. State Assembly, Sacramento, 1992-97, asst. spkr. pro tempore, spkr.'s fed. govt. liaison, mem. rules com., 1997-98; mem. rules com., vet. affairs com., pub. employment and ret. com., energy, utilities and comm. com., local govt. com., govtl. orgn. com. Calif. State Senate, 1998-99; mem. U.S. Congress from 42nd Calif. Dist., Washington, 1999—; mem. agriculture and sci. coms. U.S. Ho. Reps. Trustee San Bernardino Valley Coll. Dist., 1979—. With U.S. Army, 1966-68, Vietnam. Named Citizen of Distinction San Bernardino Area LWV, Kiwanian of Yr. Greater San Bernardino Kiwanis Club, Disting. Citizen Inland Empire Dist. Boy Scouts Am., Outstanding Legislator Calif. Rifle and Pistol Assn., VFW, 1994-95, Legislator of Yr. Am. Legion, Dept. Calif.; recipient Minority Male of Yr. award Greater Riverside Area Urban League. Democrat. Office: US Ho Reps 1133 Longworth Ho Office Bldg Washington DC 20515-0001 also: 201 N E St Ste 206 San Bernardino CA 92401-1520*

BACA, JOSEPH FRANCIS, state supreme court justice; b. Albuquerque, Oct. 1, 1936; s. Amado and Inez (Pino) B.; m. Dorothy Lee Burrow, June 28, 1969; children: Jolynn, Andrea, Anna Marie. BA in Edn., U. N.Mex., 1960; JD, George Washington U., 1964; LLM, U. Va., 1992. Asst. dist. atty. 1st Jud. Dist., Santa Fe, 1965-66; pvt. practice Albuquerque, 1966-72; dist. judge 2d Jud. Dist., Albuquerque, 1972-88; state supreme ct. justice N.Mex. Supreme Ct., Santa Fe, 1989—, chief justice, 1995-97. Spl. asst. to atty. gen. Office of N.Mex. Atty. Gen., Albuquerque, 1966-71. Dem. precinct chmn., albuquerque, 1968; del. N.Mex. Constl. Conv., Santa Fe, 1969; bd. dirs. State Justice Inst., 1994—, V.Chmn. 1999—. Recipient Judge of Yr. award Peoples Commn. for Criminal Justice, 1989, Quincentennial Commemoration Achievement award La Hispanidad Com., 1992, Luchando por la Justicia award Mex. Am. Law Students Assn. U. N.Mex. Law Sch., 1993; J. William Fulbright Disting. Pub. Svc. award George Washington U. Alumni Assn., 1994, Recognition and Achievement award Commn. on Opportunities for Minorities in the Profession, 1992, others; named one of 100 most influential Hispanics Hispanic Bus. Mag., 1997, 98. Mem. ABA, Hispanic Nat. Bar Assn. (Lincoln-Juarez award 2000), N.Mex. Bar Assn. (outstanding jud. svc. award 1998), Am. Law Inst., Scribes (bd. dirs. 1998—), Am. Jud. Soc. (bd. dirs. 1999—), Albuquerque Bar Assn., Santa Fe Bar Assn., N.Mex. Hispanic Bar Assn. (Outstanding Hispanic Atty. award 2000), Alumni Assn. (pres. 1980-81), Kiwanis (pres. Albuquerque chpt. 1984-85), KC (dep. grand knight 1968). Roman Catholic. Avocation: reading history. Office: Supreme Ct NMex Supreme Court Bldg PO Box 848 Santa Fe NM 87504-0848

BACA ARCHULATA, MARGIE, city clerk; b. Albuquerque, May 18, 1948; City clk. Office of Mayor, Albquerque, 1997—. Office: Office of City Clk/Govt Bld 1 Civic Plz NW Rm 11110 Albuquerque NM 87102-2167

BACCIGALUPPI, ROGER JOHN, agricultural company executive; b. N.Y.C., Mar. 17, 1934; s. Harry and Ethel (Hutcheon) B.; m. Patricia Marie Wier, Feb. 6, 1960 (div. 1978); children: John, Elisabeth, Andrea; m. Iris Christine Walfridson, Feb. 3, 1979; 1 child, Jason. B.S., U. Calif., Berkeley, 1956; M.S., Columbia U., 1957. Asst. sales promotion mgr. Maco Mag. Corp., N.Y.C., 1956-57; merchandising asst. Honig, Cooper & Harrington, San Francisco and L.A., 1957-58, 1958-60, asst. dir. merchandising, 1960-61; sales rep. Blue Diamond Growers (formerly Calif. Almond Growers Exch.), Sacramento, 1961-64, mgr. advt. and sales promotion, 1964-70, v.p. mktg., 1970-73, sr. v.p. mktg., 1973-74, exec. v.p., 1974-75, pres., 1975-91; founder RB Internat., Sacramento, 1992—. Vice chmn., bd. dirs. Agrl. Coun. Calif., 1975-91; mem. consumer-prodr. com., adminstrn. com.; mem. U.S. adv. com. Trade Policy and Negotiations, 1983—; mem. U.S. adv. bd. Rabobank Nederlands, 1988-91; mem. Calif. World Trade Commn., 1993—; mem. adv. coun. Nat. Ctr. for Food and Agr. Policy Resources for Future, 1990-99. Vice chmn. Calif. State R.R. Mus. Found.; chmn. Cmty. Colls. Found.; vice chmn. Grad. Inst. Cooperative Leadership, 1986-87, chair, 1987-89. With AUS, 1957. Mem. Calif. C. of C. (chmn. internat. trade com. 1988-94, bd. dirs. 1988—, vice chmn. bd. 1992-94, chmn. bd. 1995, Sacramento Host Com. (chmn. 1997, 98), Calif. for Higher Edn., Grad. Inst. Coop. Leadership (chmn., trustee), Grocery Mfrs. Am., Inc. (bd. dirs. 1988-91), Sutter Club. Office: RB Internat 777 Campus Commons Rd Ste 200 Sacramento CA 95825-8343

BACHMAN, BRIAN RICHARD, former electronics executive; b. Aurora, Ill., Jan. 14, 1945; BS, U. Ill., 1967; MBA, U. Chgo., 1969. With Gen. Electric, Syracuse, N.Y., 1982-85, TRW, Schaumburg, Ill., 1985-87; pres. Gen. Semiconductor Industries, Tempe, Ariz., 1987-90; group gen. mgr. ITT Cannon, Santa Ana, Calif., 1990-91; v.p., group gen. mgr. Philips Semiconductor, Sunnyvale, 1991. Office: Philips Semiconductors 811 E Arques Ave Sunnyvale CA 94085-4523

BACHRACH, CHARLES LEWIS, advertising agency executive; b. N.Y.C., Feb. 22, 1946; s. Herbert and Lilla Clare (Blumberg) B.; m. Lois Susan Davis, Sept. 12, 1968; 1 dau., Jennifer Leigh. B.S., Ithaca (N.Y.) Coll., 1968. Assoc. producer MPO Sports Co., N.Y.C., 1968-69; unit mgr. NBC, N.Y.C., 1969; with Ogilvy & Mather, Inc., N.Y.C., 1969—, sr. v.p. broadcast, 1978-83, dir. Network and Programming Dept; sr. v.p. network and programming Western Internat. Media, 1983-89, exec. v.p., 1989—; pres. Western Internat. Syndication, 1983—; sr. v.p., dir. network and program purchasing Rubin Postaer & Assocs., L.A., 1990-92, exec. v.p., dir. media and resources and programming, 1992—. Vis. prof. Ithaca Coll. Sch. Communications; vis. lectr. New Sch.; guest lectr. UCLA, Calif. State, L.A., Marymount Coll.; guest commentator NPR, CNN, NBC. Contbr. articles to profl. publs. Judge Internat. Emmy Awards.; Lobbyist N.Y. State pvt. colls.; bd. dirs. Caption Ctr., 1992. Recipient Disting. Alumni award Ithaca Coll., 1980, Aid to Advt. Edn. award Am. Advt. Fedn., 1986, Media Maven award Advt. Age, 1996; named One of Top 100 Young People in Advt., 1985. Mem. AAAA (com. broadcast network and programming), TV Acad. Arts and Scis., L.A. Advt. Club (bd. dirs. 1989). Home: 3121 Dona Marta Dr Studio City CA 91604-4327 Office: Rubin Postaer and Assocs 1333 2d St Santa Monica CA 90401-1100

BACKER, MATTHIAS, JR. obstetrician/gynecologist; b. St. Louis, Dec. 19, 1926; s. Matthias Henry Sr. and Louise (Jokisch) B.; m. Laverne Elizabeth Knapp, June 4, 1949 (dec. Oct. 15, 1992); m. Georgia Lynn Garrison, Apr. 28, 1997; children: Mary Kathryn, Matt III, Marilyn Ann, Mary Lou, Donald, Robert, Edward, Mary Susan, Mary Carol, Mary Patrice, Joseph, Brian, Denis. MD, St. Louis U., 1950. Diplomate Am. Bd. Ob-Gyn. (examiner 1986-93), Nat. Bd. Med. Examiners. Intern Nat. Naval Med. Ctr., Bethesda, Md., 1950-51; resident in ob-gyn St. Louis U. Hosps., 1951-54; practice medicine specializing in ob-gyn St. Louis, 1954-85; instr. ob-gyn St. Louis U. Sch. Medicine, 1954-60, sr. instr., 1960-63, asst. clin. prof., 1963-66, assoc. clin. prof., 1966-72, clin. prof., 1972-85, prof. ob-gyn., chmn. dept., 1985-92, prof. and chmn. emeritus, 1992—, dir. ob-gyn outpatient clinic, 1967-69, mem. com. faculty appointments and promotions, 1972-81, mem. exec. com. faculty, 1972-76, mem. faculty affairs com., 1975-78, dir. residency program, 1985-92; staff cons. tchg., rsch, patient care Naval Med. Ctr., San Diego; adj. prof. ob-gyn. Uniformed Svc. Univ. of the Health Scis., 1994—. Chief ob-gyn St. Joseph's Hosp., Kirkwood,, 1959-62, St. Anthony's, St. Louis, Hosp., 1966-69; pres. St. Louis U. Hosps. Med. Staff, 1968-69; mem. governing bd. St. Louis U. Hosps., 1969-70; pres. med. and dental staff St. Anthony's Med. Ctr., 1984-85; lectr. Archdiocesan PreCana Council, 1955-58, Archdiocesan Sch. Commn., 1969-72; pres. Backer & Probst Inc., St. Louis, 1967-85. Contbr. numerous articles to profl. jours. Bd. dirs. St. Louis chpt. Am. Cancer Soc., 1970-76, Blue Shield Mo. Med. Svc., 1970-80; lector Our Lady of Providence Ch., St. Louis, 1969-92; guardian ad litem for unborn Mo. Supreme Ct., 1971. Served to rear adm. M.C., USNR, 1944-84. Decorated Legion of Merit, Dept. Def. Superior Service medal; recipient Backer award St. Louis U. High Sch., 1983. Fellow ACS, ACOG (Adm. Robert A. Ross award Armed Forces dist. 1993); mem. AMA, Mo. Med. Assn., St. Louis Med. Soc., Soc. Mil. Surgeons U.S., Ctrl. Assn. Obstetricians and Gynecologists, St. Louis Gynecol. Soc. (pres. 1969-70), Naval Res. Assn. (past pres. Spirit of St. Louis chpt.). Roman Catholic. Home and Office: 3903 California St Unit 5 San Diego CA 92110-2157 also: 101 Flamingo Dr Saint Louis MO 63123-1007 E-mail: mattbacker@aol.com

BACKLAR, PATRICIA, education educator; Sr. scholar Oregon Health Scis. U.; rsch. assoc. prof. biotheics dept. philosophy Portland State U., adj. asst. prof. dept. psychiatry, asst. dir. ctr. ethics in health care. Mem. Nat. Bioethics Adv. Commn., 1996—; civil commitment task force Oreg. Atty. Gen.; ethics com. Oreg. State Hosp. Author: The Family Face of Schizophrenia, 1994; contbr. articles to profl. jours.

BACKUS, GEORGE EDWARD, theoretical geophysicist; b. Chgo., May 24, 1930; s. Milo Morlan and Dora Etta (Dare) B.; m. Elizabeth Evelyn Allen, Nov. 15, 1961 (div. 1971); children: Benjamin, Brian, Emily; m. Varda Esther Peller, Jan. 8, 1977 PhB, U. Chgo., 1947, BS in Math., 1948, MS in Math. and Physics, 1950, 53, PhD in Physics, 1956; D honoris causa, Inst. de Physique de Globe, Paris, 1995. Jr. mathematician Inst. for Air Weapons, Chgo., 1951-53; physicist Project Matterhorn, Princeton, N.J., 1957-58; asst. prof. math. MIT, Cambridge, 1958-60; assoc. prof. geophysics U. Calif. San Diego, La Jolla, 1960-62, prof. geophysics, 1962-94, rsch. prof. geophysics, 1994-99, prof. geophys. emeritus, 1999—. Mem. vist. com. Institut de Physique du Globe de Paris, 1987; co-chmn. Internat. Working Group on Magnetic Field Satellites, 1983-90; chair acad. senate U. Calif., San Diego, 1992-93. Contbr. articles to profl. jours. Guggenheim Found. fellow, 1963, 71; Royal Soc. Arts fellow, London, 1970— Fellow Royal Astron. Soc. (Gold medal 1986), Am. Geophys. Union (John Adam Fleming medal 1986); mem. NAS (com. on grants and fellowships Day Fund 1974-79, com. on sci. and pub. policy 1971-74), Académie des Sciences (France), Am. Phys. Soc., Am. Math. Soc., Math. Assn. Am., Soc. for Indsl. and Applied Math., Am. Geophys. Union. Avocations: skiing; swimming; bicycling; hiking; history. Office: IGPP U Calif San Diego La Jolla CA 92093-0225 E-mail: gbackus@ucsd.edu

BACON, LEONARD ANTHONY, accounting educator; b. Santa Fe, June 10, 1931; s. Manuel R. and Maria (Chavez) Baca; m. Patricia Balzaretti; children— Bernadine M., Jerry A., Tiffany A. B.E., U. Nebr.-Omaha, 1965; M.B.A., U. of the Americas, Mexico City, 1969; Ph.D., U. Miss., 1971. CPA; cert. mgmt. acct., internal auditor. Commd. 2d lt. U.S. Army, 1951, advanced through grades to maj., 1964, served fin. and acctg. officer mainly Korea, Vietnam; ret., 1966; asst. prof. Delta State U., Cleveland, Miss., 1971-76; assoc. prof. West Tex. State U., Canyon, 1976-79; prof. acctg. Calif. State U., Bakersfield, 1979—; cons. Kershen Co. (now Atlantic Richfield Oil Co.), Canyon, 1979-80. Contbr. articles to profl. jours. U.S., Mex., Can., papers to profl. confs. Leader Delta area Boy Scouts Am., Cleveland, 1971-76; dir. United Campus Ministry, Canyon, 1976-79; min. Kern Youth Facility, Bakersfield, 1983—, Christians in Commerce, 1990—. Paratrooper Brazilian Army, 1955. Mem. Am. Acctg. Assn., Am. Inst. CPA's, Am. Assn. Spanish Speaking CPA's, Inst. Mgmt. Accts. (pres. Bakersfield chpt. 1981-82, Most Valuable Mem. award 1981), Am. Mgmt. Assn., Inst. Mgmt. Acctg., Calif. Faculty Assn., Acad. Internat. Bus., Inst. Internal Auditors, Inst. Cost Estimators and Analysts, Alpha Kappa Psi (Dedicated Service award 1979), Omicron Delta Epsilon, Beta Gamma Sigma. Clubs: Jockey (Rio de Janeiro). Lodges: Lions (v.p. Cleveland 1971-73), Kiwanis (v.p. 1974-79, A Whale of a Guy award, Cleveland 1975, Plaque of Appreciation, 1992-93). Office: Calif State U 9001 Stockdale Hwy Bakersfield CA 93311-1022

BACON, VICKY LEE, lighting services executive; b. Oregon City, Oreg., Mar. 25, 1950; d. Herbert Kenneth and Lorean Betty (Boltz) Rushford; m. Dennis M. Bacon, Aug. 7, 1971; 1 child, Randene Tess. Student, Portland Community Coll., 1974-75, Mt. Hood Community Coll., 1976, Portland State Coll., 1979. With All Electric Constrn., Milwaukie, Oreg., 1968-70, Lighting Maintenance Co., Portland, 1970-78; svc. mgr. GTE Sylvania Lighting Svcs., Portland, 1978-80, br. mgr., 1980-83; div. mgr. Christenson Electric Co. Inc., Portland, 1983-90, v.p. mktg. and lighting svcs., 1990-91, v.p. svc. ops. and mktg., 1991—. Chmn. Oreg. Ltd. Energy Com., 1993—; vice chmn. to labor commr. Oreg. State Apprenticeship Coun., 1996—. Mem. Energy Contractors Assn., Illuminating Engring. Soc., Nat. Elec. Contractors Assn. (bd. dirs. Oreg. Columbia chpt. 1997—), Nat. Assn. Lighting Maintenance Contractors, Elec. Contractors Assn.. Office: Christenson Electric Co Inc PO Box 3514 Portland OR 97208-3514 E-mail: vickyb@prodigy.net

BADASH, LAWRENCE, science history educator; b. Bklyn., May 8, 1934; s. Joseph and Dorothy (Langa) B.; children: Lisa, Bruce. BS in Physics, Rensselaer Poly. Inst., 1956; PhD in History of Sci., Yale U., 1964. Instr. Yale. U., New Haven, 1964-65, research assoc., 1965-66; from asst. to assoc. prof. U. Calif., Santa Barbara, 1966-79, prof. history of sci., 1979—. Dir. summer seminar on global security and arms control U. Calif., 1983, 86, energy rsch. group, 1992, pacific rim program mem., 1993-95; cons. Nuclear Age Peace Found., Santa Barbara, 1984-90. Author: Radioactivity in Am., 1979, Kapitza, Rutherford, and the Kremlin, 1985, Scientists and the Development of Nuclear Weapons, 1995; editor: Ruth-[illegible]wood, Letters on Radioactivity, 1969, Reminiscences of Los Alamos, 1943-45, 1980. Bd. dirs. Santa Barbara chpt. ACLU, 1971-86, 96—, pres., 1982-84, 96-98; nat. bd. dirs. Com. for a Sane Nuclear Policy, Washington, 1972-81; mem. Los Padres Search and Rescue Team, Santa Barbara, 1981-94. Lt. (j.g.) USN, 1956-59. Grantee, NSF, Cambridge, Eng., 1965-66, 69-72, 90-92, Am. Philos. Soc., New Zealand, 1979-80, Inst. on Global Conflict and Cooperation, Univ. Calif., 1983-87; J.S. Guggenheim fellow, 1984-85. Fellow AAAS (sect. mem. at large 1988-92), Am. Phys. Soc. (chmn. divsn. of history of physics 1988-89, exec. com. forum on physics and society 1991-93); mem. History of Sci. Soc. (founder West Coast chpt., chpt. bd. dirs. 1971-73, nat. coun. 1975-78). Democrat. Jewish. Avocation: backpacking. Office: Univ Calif Dept History Santa Barbara CA 93106

BADER, W(ILLIAM) REECE, lawyer; b. Portland, Oreg., Oct. 31, 1941; s. William Lange and Phyllis Harriet (Cole) B.; m. Jean McCarty, Aug. 3, 1963 (div. 1993); children: Lawson R., Cole R.; m. Alicia Spatafore, June 14, 1998. BA, Williams Coll., 1963; JD, Duke U., 1966. Bar: D.C. 1967, Calif. 1969, U.S. Dist. Ct. D.C., U.S. Dist. Ct. (no., ctrl., ea. and so. dists.) Calif., U.S. Ct. Appeals (D.C., 2d, 3d, 7th, 9th and fed. cirs.), U.S. Tax Ct., U.S. Claims Ct., U.S. Supreme Ct. Law clk. to judge U.S. Ct. Appeals (D.C. cir.), Washington, 1966-68; assoc. Orrick, Herrington & Sutcliffe LLP, San Francisco, 1968-74, ptnr., 1974—. Mem. legal adv. bd. Hastings Law Ctr. Found., 1981-87; mem. securities disputes resolution com. Ctr. for Pub. Resources, 1990—; mem. nat. arbitration and med. com. NASDR, 1994-98; mem. ad hoc com. on ct. facilities and design U.S. Jud. Conf., 1969-72, mem. adv. com. on civil rules, 1982-87, mem. standing com. on rules of practice and procedure, 1987-90; lectr., panelist Practicing Law Inst., ABA Am. Law Inst., Internat. Franchise Assn., Calif. Electronic Assn., many others; arbitrator, mediator Nat. Assn. Securities Dealers Regulation Inc., 1979—, Am. Arbitration Assn., 1979—, N.Y. Stock Exch., 1984—, Nat. Futures Assn., 1985—, Pvt. Adjudication Found., 1987-96. Mem. editl. bd. Alternatives, 1991—; editor: Securities News, 1993-94, Securities Arbitration, 1999, Private Securities Litigation Reform Act Reporter, 1996—; contbr. article to profl. jours. Trustee North Park Coll. and Theol. Sem., Chgo., 1984-89, sec., 1985-86, chmn., 1986-89. Fellow Am. Bar Found., Environ. Law Inst.; mem. ABA (litig., bus., natural resources, dispute resolution sects.), State Bar Calif. (litig., bus., environ. sects.), Securities Industry Assn. (compliance and legal divsn.), Futures Industry Assn. (compliance and legal divsn.), Bar Assn. San Francisco, D.C. Bar Assn. Avocations: collecting toy trains, squash, reading, travel. Home: 62 Lloyden Dr Atherton CA 94027-3834 Office: Orrick Herrington Sutcliffe LLP 1020 Marsh Rd Menlo Park CA 94025-1021 E-mail: wrbader@orrick.com

BADGLEY, JOHN ROY, architect; b. Huntington, W.Va., July 10, 1922; s. Roy Joseph and Fannie Myrtle (Limbaugh) B.; m. Janice Atwell, July 10, 1975; 1 child, Adam; children by previous marriage: Dan, Lisa, Holly, Marcus, Michael. AB, Occidental Coll., 1943; MArch, Harvard U., 1949; postgrad., Internat. Ctr., Vincenza, Italy, 1959. Lic. Calif. Pvt. practice, San Luis Obispo, Calif., 1952-65; chief arch., planner Crocker Land Co., San Francisco, 1965-80; v.p. Cushman & Wakefield Inc., San Francisco, 1980-84; pvt. practice, San Rafael, Calif., 1984—. Insr. Calif. State U., San Luis Obispo, 1952-65. Bd. dirs. Ft. Mason Ctr., Angel Island Assn. With USCGR, 1942-54. Mem. AIA, Am. Arbitration Assn., Golden Gate Wine Soc. Home and Office: 1356 Idylberry Rd San Rafael CA 94903-1074 E-mail: jrbadgley@mindspring.com

BADGLEY, THEODORE MCBRIDE, psychiatrist, neurologist; b. Salem, Ala., June 27, 1925; s. Roy Joseph and Fannie (Limbaugh) B.; m. Mary Bennett Wells, Dec. 30, 1945; children: Justice Badgley O'Neil, Jan Badgley, Mona Jean Badgley Covey, Jason Wells, James John, Mary Rose Badgley Bleier. Student, Occidental Coll., 1942-44; M.D., U. So. Calif., 1949. Diplomate: Am. Bd. Psychiatry and Neurology. Intern Letterman Gen. Hosp., San Francisco, 1949-50, resident in psychiatry, 1950-53; commd. capt. M.C. U.S. Army, 1950, advanced through grades to lt. col., 1967; chief mental hygiene cons. service Ft. Gordon, Ga.; and asso. clin. prof. psychiatry and neurology Med. Coll. Ga., 1954-55; resident in neurology Walter Reed Gen. Hosp., Washington, 1955-57, asst. chief psychiatry service, 1957-59, chief psychiatry service, 1959-62, asst. chief dept. psychiatry and neurology, 1962-63, dir. edn. and tng. psychiatry, 1957-63; chief dept. psychiatry and neurology U.S. Army Gen. Hosp., Landstuhl, Germany, 1963-66; chief psychiatry outpatient dept. Letterman Gen. Hosp., 1966-67; ret., 1967; dir. Kern View Mental Health Center, Bakersfield, Calif., 1967-69; pvt. practice medicine specializing in med. and forensic neuropsychiatry Bakersfield, 1967-93; pres. Sans Doloroso Inst., Bakersfield, 1969-93. Lectr. community health service orgns., profl. confs., seminars. Contbr. articles to profl. jours. Fellow Am. Psychiat. Assn. (life); mem. Kern County Psychiat. Soc. (pres. 1972-93), Kern County Med. Soc. (pres. 1981). Office: 21508 Indian Wells Dr Tehachapi CA 93561-8029

BADIE, RONALD PETER, banker; b. Elizabeth, N.J., Dec. 13, 1942; s. R. Peter and Madeline E. (Knoop) B.; m. Fabiana Duclos; children: Tracey, Tamara, Tara, Gabrielle, Alexandra. B.S., Bucknell U., 1964; M.B.A., NYU, 1971. Sr. v.p. Bankers Trust Co., N.Y.C., 1979-86, mng. dir. L.A., 1986-96; sr. mng. dir. Bankers Trust Co. Calif., L.A., 1996-99; mng. dir. Deutsche Banc Alex Brown, 1999-2001, v. chmn., 2001—. Mem. adv. bd. Green Equity Investors II; vice chair Deutsche Bank Alex Brown, 2001. Mem. adv. bd. entrepreneurial studies program UCLA Sch. Mgmt., Stonington Capital Appreciation Fund. Republican. Home: 3747 Chevy Chase Dr La Canada Flintridge CA 91011-4163 Office: Deutsche Banc Alex Brown 300 S Grand Ave Los Angeles CA 90071-3109

BAER, WALTER S. research executive; b. Chgo., July 27, 1937; s. Walter S., Jr. and Margaret S. (Mayer) B.; m. Miriam R. Schenker, June 18, 1959 (div. 1987); children: David W., Alan B.; m. Jeri Weiss, Oct. 23, 1988. B.S., Calif. Inst. Tech., 1959; Ph.D. (NSF fellow), U. Wis., 1964. Rsch. physicist Bell Telephone Labs., Murray Hill, N.J., 1964-66; White House fellow Washington, 1966-67; White House sci. adv. staff, 1967-69; cons. and sr. scientist RAND Corp., Santa Monica, Calif., 1970-81, dir. energy policy program, 1978-81; dir. advanced tech. Times Mirror Co., Los Angeles, 1981-89; deputy v.p. domestic rsch. RAND Corp., Santa Monica, Calif., 1990—. Cons. UN, maj. U.S. corps, 1970—; dir. Aspen (Colo.) Cable TV Workshop, 1972-73, L.A. Ednl. Partnership; pres. KCRW Found., Santa Monica, Calif.; adv. bd. Columbia U. Inst. Tele-Info., U.S. Com. for Internat. Inst. Applied Systems Analysis; dir. Am. Tng. Internat.; mem. gov. coun. on info. tech. State of Calif. Author: Interactive Television, 1971, Cable Television: A Handbook for Decisionmaking, 1973, also articles; editor: The Electronic Box Office, 1974, w/ RAND Cable Television Series, 1974; editorial bd.: Telecommunications Policy, 1976— , Internat. Ency. Communications. Mem. European Community Visitor, 1978. Recipient U. Wis. award for excellence in teaching, 1960; Preceptor award Broadcast Industry Conf., 1974— Fellow AAAS (chmn. Indsl. Sci. Sec. 1992-93); mem. IEEE (mem. com. on comm. and info. policy 1994—), Am. Phys. Soc., Internat. Inst. Communications, Sigma Xi. Office: RAND 1700 Main St Santa Monica CA 90401-3297

BAERWALD, SUSAN GRAD, television broadcasting company executive producer; b. Long Branch, N.J., June 18, 1944; d. Bernard John and Marian Grad; m. Paul Baerwald, July 1, 1969; children: Joshua, Samuel. Degre des Arts and Lettres, Sorbonne, Paris, 1965; BA, Sarah Lawrence Coll., 1966. Script analyst United Artists, L.A., 1978-80; v.p. devel. Gordon/Eisner Prodns., L.A., 1980-81; mgr. mini-series and novels for TV, NBC, Burbank, Calif., 1981-82, dir. mini-series and novels for TV, 1982, v.p. mini-series and novels for TV, 1982-89, [illegible] Prodns., 1989-95, Savoy Pictures TV, 1995-96, Citadel Entertainment, 1996-97. Producer TV mini-series: Blind Faith, 1990, Lucky Chances (Jackie

Collins), 1990, One Spl. Victory, 1991, Cruel Doubt, 1993, A Time to Heal, 1994, Inflammable, 1995. Bd. dirs. The Paper Bag Players, N.Y.C., 1974—; vol. L.A. Children's Mus., 1978-80; mem. awards com. Scott Newman Found., 1982-84; bd. dirs. L.A. Goal, 1996—. Recipient Vol. Incentive award NBC, 1983. Mem. ATAS (bd. govs. 1993-97, nat. awards chmn. 1997-98), Am. Film Inst., Hollywood Radio and TV Soc.

BAESEL, STUART OLIVER, architect; b. Charlotte, N.C., Feb. 5, 1925; s. Edward Franklin and Rose (Engel) B.; m. Betsey London Cordon, Nov. 23, 1949; children— Stuart Oliver, Betsey London, Cordon Telfair Student, U. N.C., 1940-42, Ecole des Beaux Arts, Fountainbleau, France, 1948; B.Arch., N.C. State U., 1950; M.Arch., Cranbrook Acad. Art, 1951. Architect A.G. Odell, Jr. & Assocs., Charlotte, 1951-55; architect-designer Skidmore, Owings, Merrill, N.Y.C., 1955-59, LBC & W Assocs., Columbia, S.C., 1959-65; dir. design J.N. Pease Assocs., Charlotte, 1965-72; mem. faculty Architecture Sch. Calif. State U., Pomona, 1972-74; prin. Stuart Baesel, Architect, Design Group, La Jolla, Calif., 1972—. Dir., sec. treas. Design World, Inc., Charlotte, 1968-72; dir., pres. Space Planning Assocs., Charlotte, 1966-72 Editor: Rev. Architecture, Columbia, S.C., 1962-65 Cons. Charlotte Planning Bd., 1954. Served with USAAF, 1943-46, PTO Recipient various profl. awards, including Honor award S.C. chpt. AIA, 1964, 65, 66, N.C. chpt. AIA, 1956, 66, 68, 69, 70, 72 Fellow AIA (bd. dirs. N.C.); mem. N.Y. Archtl. League, Phi Delta Theta Episcopalian. Club: La Jolla Beach and Tennis Home: 303 Coast Blvd Unit 1 La Jolla CA 92037-4635 Office: PO Box 1237 La Jolla CA 92038-1237 also: Les Flots Bleus 06230 Villefranche Sur Mer France

BAEZ, JOAN CHANDOS, folk singer; b. S.I., N.Y., Jan. 9, 1941; d. Albert V. and Joan (Bridge) B.; m. David Victor Harris, Mar. 1968 (div. 1973); 1 son, Gabriel Earl. Appeared in coffeehouses, Gate of Horn, Chgo., 1958, Ballad Room, Club 47, 1958-68, Newport (R.I.) Folk Festival, 1959-69, 85, 87, 90, 92, 93, 95, extended tours to colls. and concert halls, 1960s, appeared Town Hall and Carnegie Hall, 1962, 67, 68, U.S. tours, 1970—, concert tours in Japan, 1966, 82, Europe, 1970-73, 80, 83-84, 87-90, 93—, Australia, 1985; rec. artist for Vanguard Records, 1960-72, A&M, 1973-76, Portrait Records, 1977-80, Gold Castle Records, 1986-89, Virgin Records, 1990-93, Grapevine Label Records (UK), 1995—, Guardian Records, 1995—, European record albums, 1981, 83, award 8 gold albums, 1 gold single; albums include Gone From Danger, 1997, Rare, Live & Classic (box set), 1993; author: Joan Baez Songbook, 1964, (biography) Daybreak, 1968, (with David Harris) Coming Out, 1971, And a Voice to Sing With, 1987, (songbook) An Then I Wrote, 1979. Extensive TV appearances and speaking tours U.S. and Can. for anti-militarism, 1967-68; visit to Dem. Republic of Vietnam, 1972, visit to war torn Bosnia-Herzegovina, 1993; founder, v.p. Inst. for Study Nonviolence (now Resource Ctr. for Nonviolence, Santa Cruz, Calif.), Palo Alto, Calif., 1965; mem. nat. adv. coun. Amnesty Internat., 1974-92; founder, pres. Humanitas/Internat. Human Rights Com., 1979-92; condr. fact-finding mission to refugee camps, S.E. Asia, Oct. 1979; began refusing payment of war taxes, 1964; arrested for civil disobedience opposing draft, Oct., Dec., 1967. Office: Diamonds & Rust Prodns PO Box 1026 Menlo Park CA 94026-1026

BAGDIKIAN, BEN HAIG, journalist, emeritus university educator; b. Marash, Turkey, Jan. 30, 1920; came to U.S., 1920, naturalized, 1926; s. Aram Theodore and Daisy (Uvezian) B.; m. Elizabeth Ogasapian, Oct. 2, 1942 (div. 1972); children: Christopher Ben, Frederick Haig; m. Betty L. Medsger, 1973 (div.); m. Marlene Griffith, 1983 A.B., Clark U., 1941, LittD, 1963; LHD, Brown U., 1961, U. R.I., 1992. Reporter Springfield (Mass.) Morning Union, 1941-42; assoc. editor Periodical House, Inc., N.Y.C., 1946; successively reporter, fgn. corr., chief Washington corr. Providence Jour., 1947-62; contbg. editor Saturday Evening Post, 1963-67; project dir. study of future U.S. news media Rand Corp., 1967-69; asst. mng. editor for nat. news Washington Post, 1970-71, asst. mng. editor, ombudsman, 1971-72; nat. corr. Columbia Journalism Review, 1972-74; prof. Grad. Sch. Journalism U. Calif., Berkeley, 1976-90, dean, Grad. Sch. Journalism, 1985-88, prof. emeritus, Grad. Sch. Journalism, 1990—. Author: In the Midst of Plenty: The poor in America, 1964, The Information Machines: Their Impact on Men and the Media, 1971, The Shame of the Prisons, 1972, The Effete Conspiracy, 1972, Caged: Eight Prisoners and Their Keepers, 1976, The Media Monopoly, 1983, 6th edit., 2000, Double Vision: Reflections on My Heritage, Life and Profession, 1995; also pamphlets; contbr.: The Kennedy Circle, 1961; editor: Man's Contracting World in an Expanding Universe, 1959; bd. editors Jour. Investigative Reporters and Editors, 1980-88. Mem. steering com. Nat. Prison Project, 1974-82; trustee Clark U., 1964-76; bd. dirs. Nat. Capital Area Civil Liberties Union, 1964-66, Com. to Protect Journalists, 1981-88, Data Ctr., Oakland, Calif., 1990-97; pres. Lowell Mellett Fund for Free an Responsible Press, 1965-76; acad. adv. bd. Nat. Citizens Com. for Broadcasting, 1978—; judge Ten Most Censored Stories, 1976-98. Recipient George Foster Peabody award, 1951, Sidney Hillman Found. award, 1956, Most Perceptive Critic citation Am. Soc. Journalism Adminstrs., 1978, Career Achievement award Soc. Profl. Journalists, John and Catherine Zenger award, 1996, James Madison award ALA, 1998; named to R.I. Journalism Hall of Fame, 1992; fellow Ogden Reid Found., 1956, Guggenheim fellow, 1961-62. Mem. ACLU. Home: 25 Stonewall Rd Berkeley CA 94705-1414

BAGLEY, JAMES W. research company executive; B of Elec. Engring., M of Elec. Engring., Miss. State U. With Tex. Instruments, 1966-79; sr. v.p. Applied Materials, Inc., 1979-87, pres., CEO, 1987-96; CEO Lam Rsch., Fremont, Calif., 1997—. Bd. dirs. KLA-Tencor, Kulicke & Soffa Industries, Teradyne, Micron Tech., Inc., Semi/SEMATECH. Office: 4650 Cushing Pkwy Fremont CA 94538-6401

BAGLEY, WILLIAM THOMPSON, lawyer; b. San Francisco, June 29, 1928; s. Nino J. and Rita V. (Thompson) Baglietto; m. Diane Lenore Oldham, June 20, 1965; children: Lynn Lorene, William Thompson, Walter William, Shana Angela, Tracy Elizabeth. AB, U. Calif., Berkeley, 1949, JD, 1952. Bar: Calif. 1953, U.S. Supreme Ct. 1967. Atty. Pacific Gas & Electric Co., 1952-56; assoc. Gardiner, Riede & Elliott, San Rafael, Calif., 1956-60; ptnr. Bagley Bernt & Bianchi, San Rafael, 1961-74; mem. Calif. Legis., 1961-74; chmn. Commodity Futures Trading Commn., Washington, 1975-79; ptnr. Nossaman, Guthner, Knox and Elliott, San Francisco, 1980—. Mem. Calif. Pub. Utilities Commn., 1983-86; mem. Calif. Transp. Commn., 1983-89, chmn., 1987-88. Bd. editors Calif. Law Rev., 1951-52. Bd. regents U. Calif., 1989—; bd. dirs. Nat. Futures Assn., Calif. Coun. Environ. and Econ. Balance, Edmund G. Brown Inst. Govtl. Affairs, L.A.; chmn. bd. Calif. Rep. League, 1980-82. Recipient Freedom of Info. award Sigma Delta Chi, 1970, Golden Bear award Calif. Pk. Commn., 1973; named Most Effective Assemblyman, Capitol Press Corps, 1969, Legislator of Yr., Calif. Trial Lawyers Assn., 1970. Mem. ABA, Calif. State Bar Assn., World Trade Club, Elks Club (life), Phi Beta Kappa, Alpha Tau Omega. Presbyterian. E-mail: wbagley@nossaman.com

BAHR, EHRHARD, Germanic languages and literature educator; b. Kiel, Germany, Aug. 21, 1932; came to U.S., 1956; s. Klaus and Gisela (Badenhausen) B.; m. Diana Meyers, Nov. 21, 1973; stepchildren: Gary, Timothy, Christopher. Student, U. Heidelberg, Germany, 1952-53, U. Freiburg, 1953-56; M.S. Ed. (Fulbright scholar), U. Kans., 1956-58; postgrad., U. Cologne, 1959-61; Ph.D., U. Calif., Berkeley, 1968. Asst. prof. German UCLA, 1968-70, assoc. prof., 1970-72, prof., 1972—, chmn. dept. Germanic langs., 1981-84, 93-98, chair grad. council, 1988-89. Author: Irony in the Late Works of Goethe, 1972, Georg Lukacs, 1970, Ernst Bloch, 1974, Nelly Sachs, 1980; editor: Kant, What is Enlightenment?, 1974, Goethe, Wilhelm Meister's Journeyman Years, 1982, History of German Literature, 3 vols., 1987-88; co-editor: The Internalized Revolution: German Reactions to the French Revolution, 1789-1989, 1992; commentary: Thomas Mann: Death in Venice, 1991; contbr. articles to profl. jours. Author: Irony in the Late Works of Goethe, 1972, Georg Lukacs, 1970, Ernst Bloch, 1974, Nelly Sachs, 1980; editor: Kant, What is Enlightenment, 1974, Goethe, Wilhelm Meister's Journeyman Years, 1982, History of German Literature, 3 vols., 1987-88, 2nd edit., 1998-99, The Novel as Archive: The Genesis, Reception and Criticism of Goethe's Wilhelm Meisters Wanderjahre, 1998; co-editor: The Internalized Revolution: German Reactions to the French Revolution, 1789-1989, 1992; commentary: Thomas Mann: Death in Venice, 1991; contbr. articles to profl. jours. Recipient Disting. Teaching award UCLA, 1970, Humanities Inst. award, 1972, summer stipend NEH, 1978 Mem. MLA, Am. Soc. 18th Century Studies, Am. Assn. Tchrs. German, Western Soc. 18th Century Studies, German Studies Assn. (pres. 1987-88), Philol. Assn. Pacific Coast, Lessing Soc., Goethe Soc. N.Am. (exec. sec. 1979-89, pres. 1995-97). Office: UCLA Dept Germanic Langs Los Angeles CA 90095-1539 E-mail: bahr@humnet.ucla.edu

BAHR, HOWARD MINER, sociologist, educator; b. Provo, Utah, Feb. 21, 1938; s. A. Francis and Louie Jean (Miner) B.; m. Rosemary Frances Smith, Aug. 28, 1961 (div. 1985); children: Bonnie Louise, Howard McKay, Rowena Ruth, Tanya Lavonne, Christopher J., Laura L., Stephen S., Rachel M.; m. Kathleen Slaugh, May 1, 1986; children: Alden Keith, Jonathan Andrew. B.A. with honors, Brigham Young U., 1962; M.A. in Sociology, U. Tex., 1964, Ph.D., 1965. Research asso. Columbia U., N.Y.C., 1965-68; vis. lectr., summer 1968; lectr. in sociology N.Y. U., 1967-68, Bklyn. Coll., City U. N.Y., 1967; asso. prof. sociology Wash. State U., Pullman, 1968-73, prof., 1972-73, chmn. dept. rural sociology, 1971-73; prof. sociology Brigham Young U., Provo, Utah, 1973—; dir. Family Research Inst., 1977-83; fellow David M. Kennedy, 1992. Virginia F. Culter lectr., 1997; vis. prof. sociology U. Va., 1976-77, 84-85. Author: Skid Row: An Introduction to Disaffiliation, 1973, Old Men Drunk and Sober, 1974, Women Alone: The Disaffiliation of Urban Females, 1976, American Ethnicity, 1979, Sunshine Widows: Adapting to Sudden Bereavement, 1980, Middletown Families, 1982, All Faithful People: Change and Continuity in Middletown's Religion, 1983, Life in Large Families, 1983, Divorce and Remarriage: Problems, Adaptations and Adjustments, 1983, Social Science Research Methods, 1984, Recent Social Trends in the United States 1960-90, 1991, Dine' Bibliography to the 1990's, 1999; contbr. articles to profl. jours.; asso. editor: Rural Sociology, 1978-83, Jour. Marriage and the Family, 1978-83. NIMH grantee, 1968-70, 71-73; NSF grantee, 1971-72, 76-80 Mem. Soc. Applied Anthropology, Rural Sociol. Assn., Nat. Coun. Family Rels. Mem. LDS Ch. E-mial: howard. Office: Brigham Young U Dept Sociology 842 SWKT Provo UT 84602 E-mail: bahr@byu.edu

BAILEY, DAVID H. computer scientist; married; 4 children. BS in Math., Brigham Young U., 1972; PhD in Math., Stanford U., 1976. Computer scientist U.S. Govt., Fort Meade, Md., 1976-80, TRW/ESL, Inc., Sunnyvale, Calif., 1980-82, SRI Internat., Menlo Park, 1982-84, NASA Ames Rsch. Ctr., Moffett Field, 1984-98, Lawrence Berkeley Lab., Berkeley, 1998—. Mem. editl. bd , referee numerous profl. jours.; presenter in field; contbr. articles to profl. jours. Recipient Chauvenet prize Math. Assn. Am., 1993, Merten Hasse prize, 1993. Mem. IEEE Computer Soc. (Sidney Fernbach award 1993), Soc. Indsl. and Applied Math., Assn. for Computing Machinery. Office: Lawrence Berkeley Lab Mail Stop 50B 2239 Berkeley CA 94720-0001 E-mail: dhbailey@lbl.gov

BAILEY, DAVID NELSON, pathology educator, university official; b. Anderson, Ind., June 21, 1945; s. Omer Nelson and Louise Genevieve (Hurst) B. BS with high distinction, Ind. U., 1967; MD, Yale U., 1973. Diplomate Nat. Bd. Med. Examiners, Am. Bd. Pathology (Clin. and Chem. Pathology). Clin. fellow dept. lab. medicine Yale U., 1973-75; asst. resident specializing in clin. pathology Yale New Haven Hosp., 1975-76, chief resident specializing in clin. pathology, 1976-77; asst. prof. pathology U. Calif., San Diego, 1977-81, assoc. prof. pathology, 1981-86, prof. pathology, 1986—, head div. lab. medicine, 1983-89, 94-98, acting chmn., 1986-88, chmn. dept. pathology, 1988-99 2000-01; dir. toxicology lab. U. Calif. Med. Ctr., San Diego, 1977—, dir. clin. labs., 1982-99, interim vice chancellor for health scis., dean, 1999-2000, dep. vice chancellor for healthscis., dep. dean, 2001—. Mem. editorial bd. Jour. Analytical Toxicology, 1979—, Clin. Chemistry Jour., 1983-93, Am. Jour. Clin. Pathology, 1991—; contbr. articles to profl. jours. Recipient Gerald T. Evans award Acad. Clin. Lab. Physicians and Scientists, 1993; Merit scholar Ind. U., 1963-65, Arthur R. Metz scholar, 1965-67. Mem. Calif. Assn. Toxicologists (pres. 1981-82), Acad. Clin. Lab. Physicians and Scientists (pres. 1988-89), Am. Assn. Clin. Chemistry, Am. Chem. Soc., Assn. Pathology Chmn. (sec.-treas. 1996-99), Phi Lambda Upsilon, Alpha Omega Alpha. Office: U Calif San Diego Sch Medicine 9500 Gilman Dr La Jolla CA 92093-5004 E-mail: dnbailey@ucsd.edu

BAILEY, DON MATTHEW, aerospace and electronics company executive; b. Pitts., Jan. 2, 1946; s. William and Vera (Mitchell) B.; m. Linda Reed, Sept. 15, 1967; children: Don Matthew Jr., Kirsten Paige, Terrance Reed. BSME, Drexel U., 1968; MS in Ops. Rsch., U. So. Calif., 1971; MBA, Pepperdine U., 1986. Programmer Naval Air Systems Command, Washington, 1963-69; engr. Rockwell Internat., Anaheim, Calif., 1969-71; program mgr. Logicon, Inc., San Pedro, 1971-80; sec., v.p. corp. devel. Comarco, Inc., Anaheim, 1980—; pres., CEO, 1990—. Bd. dirs. Devel. Disabilities Ctr. Orange County, Anaheim, Calif., Perspective Instructional Communications, San Diego. Mem. Assn. for Corp. Growth. Office: Comarco Inc 1151 N Tustin Ave Santa Ana CA 92705

BAILEY, EXINE MARGARET ANDERSON, soprano, educator; b. Cottonwood, Minn., Jan. 4, 1922; d. Joseph Leonard and Exine Pearl (Robertson) Anderson; m. Arthur Albert Bailey, May 5, 1956. B.S., U. Minn., 1944; M.A., Columbia U., 1945; profl. diploma, 1951. Instr. Columbia U., 1947-51; faculty U. Oreg., Eugene, 1951—, prof. voice, 1966-87, coordinator voice instrn., 1969-87, prof. emeritus, 1987—; faculty dir. Salzburg, Austria, summer 1968, Europe, summer 1976. Vis. prof., head vocal instrn. Columbia U., summers 1952, 59; condr. master classes for singers, developer summer program study for h.s. solo singers, U. Oreg. Sch. Music, 1988—, mem. planning com. 1998-99 MTNA Nat. Convention. Profl. singer, N.Y.C.; appearances with NBC, ABC symphonies; solo artist appearing with Portland and Eugene (Oreg.) Symphonies, other groups in Wash., Calif., Mont., Idaho, also in concert; contbr. articles, book revs. to various mags. Del. fine arts program to Ea. Europe, People to People Internat. Mission to Russia for 1990. Recipient Young Artist award N.Y.C. Singing Tchrs., 1945, Music Fedn. Club (N.Y.C.) hon. award, 1951; Kathryn Long scholar Met. Opera, 1945 Mem. Nat. Assn. Tchrs. Singing (lt. gov. 1968-72), Oreg. Music Tchrs. Assn (pres. 1974-76), Music Tchrs. Nat. Assn. (nat. voice chmn. high sch. activities 1970-74, nat. chmn. voice 1973-75, 81-85, NW chmn. collegiate activities and artists competition 1978-80, editorial com. Am. Music Tchr. jour. 1987-89), AAUP, Internat. Platform Assn., Kappa Delta Pi, Sigma Alpha Iota, Pi Kappa Lambda. Home: 17 Westbrook Way Eugene OR 97405-2074 Office: U Oreg Sch Music Eugene OR 97403

BAILEY, HENRY JOHN, III, retired lawyer, educator; b. Pitts., Apr. 4, 1916; s. Henry J. and Lenore Powell Bailey Cahoon; m. Marjorie Jane Ebner, May 30, 1949 (dec. July 1998); children: George W., Christopher G., Barbara W., Timothy P. Student, U.S. Naval Acad., 1934-36; B.A., Pa. State U., 1939; J.D., Yale U., 1947. Bar: N.Y. 1948, Mass. 1963, Oreg. 1974. Ins. investigator Liberty Mut. Ins. Co., 1941-42; atty. Fed. Res. Bank of N.Y., N.Y.C., 1947-55; asst. v.p. Empire Trust Co., N.Y.C., 1955-56; atty., legal dept. Am. Bankers Assn., N.Y.C., 1956-62; editor Banking Law Jour., Boston, 1962-65; asso. prof. law Willamette U., Salem, Oreg., 1965-69, prof., 1969-81, prof. emeritus, 1981—, adj. prof., 1981-83, scholar in residence, 1987; counsel firm Churchill, Leonard, Brown & Donaldson, Salem, 1981-85; vis. prof. sch. law U. Akron, 1983-84; vis. prof. coll. of law Fla. State U., 1984-85; vis. prof. sch. law Rutgers U., Camden, N.J., 1985-87. Cons., lectr. to bar and banking groups; lectr. Banking Sch. of South, Baton Rouge, 1972, 73, 75. Author: Brady on Bank Checks (The Law of Bank Checks), 1960, 3d edit., 1962, 4th edit., 1969, 5th edit., 1979, 6th edit., 1987 and periodic supplements, 7th edit. (with Richard B. Hagedorn), 1992, (with Richard B. Hagedorn) rev. edit. 2 vols., 1997, periodic supplements, Uniform Commercial Code Forms, 1963, (with Clarke and Young) Bank Deposits and Collections, 1972, UCC Deskbook: A Short Course in Commercial Paper, 1973, (with Robert D. Hursh) The American Law of Products Liability, 2d edit, 1984, (with William D. Hawkland) The Sum and Substance of Commercial Paper, 1976, 80, 88, Secured Transactions in a Nutshell, 1976, 2d edit., 1981, 3d edit. (with Richard B. Hagedorn), 1988, (with Richard B. Hagedorn) 4th edit., 2000, Oregon Uniform Commercial Code, 3 vols., 1983, 84, 86, 88, 2d edit. 3 vols., 1990, New 1990 Uniform Commercial Code: Article 3, and 4, periodic supplements; contbr. articles on sales, products liability, comml. paper and secured transactions to legal jours. 1st lt. USAAF, 1942-45; lt. col. Res.; ret. Mem. Am. Bar Assn. (chmn. subcom. on comml. paper 1965-66, 79-81), Am. Law Inst. (mem. editorial bd. The Practical Lawyer 1981-93, emeritus mem. editorial bd. 1993—), Oreg. State Bar, Lambda Chi Alpha. Republican. Roman Catholic. Office: Coll Law Willamette U Salem OR 97301

BAILEY, LEONARD LEE, surgeon; b. Takoma Park, Md., Aug. 28, 1942; s. Nelson Hulburt and Catherine Effie (Long) B.; m. Nancy Ann Schroeder, Aug. 21, 1966; children: Jonathan Brooks, Charles Connor. BS, Columbia Union Coll., 1960-64; postgrad., NIH, 1965; MD, Loma Linda U., 1969. Diplomate Am. Bd. Surgery, Am. Bd. Thoracic Surgery. Intern Loma Linda U. Med. Ctr., 1969-70, resident in surgery, 1970-73, resident in thoracic and cardiovascular surgery, 1973-74; resident in pediatric cardiovascular surgery Hosp. for Sick Children, Toronto, Ont., Can., 1974-75; resident in thoracic and cardiovascular surgery Loma Linda U. Med. Sch., 1975-76, asst. prof. surgery, 1976-86, prof. surgery, 1986—, dir. pediatric cardiac surgery, 1976—, chief div. cardiothoracic surgery, 1988-92, chair dept. surgery, 1992—. Mem. ACS, Am. Assn. Thoracic Surgery, Am. Surg. Assn., Am. Coll. Cardiology, Western Thoracic Surg. Assn., Soc. Thoracic Surgery, Western Soc. Pediatric Rsch., Internat. Soc. for Heart Transplantation, Am. Heart Assn., Internat. Assn. for Cardiac Biol. Implants, Am. Soc. for Artificial Internal Organs, Pacific Coast Surg. Assn., Western Assn. Transplant Surgeons, Internat. Soc. for Cardiovascular Surgery, United Network for Organ Sharing, The Transplant Soc. Democrat. Adventist. Office: Loma Linda U Medical Ctr and Children's Hospital 11175 Campus St Ste 21120 Loma Linda CA 92350-1700 E-mail: lbailey@som.llu.edu

BAILEY, ROBERT C. opera company executive; b. Metropolis, Ill., Dec. 28, 1936; m. Sally McDermott, July 13, 1958. BA in Speech, U. Ill., 1958, MA in English, 1960; BM in Applied Voice, Eastman Sch. Music, 1965; MM in Applied Voice, New Eng. Conservatory Music, 1969. Music prodr. Nat. Pub. Radio, Washington, 1971-73, dir. cultural programming, 1973-75; mgr. Western Opera Theatre, San Francisco, 1975-79; instr. arts mgmt. Golden Gate U., San Francisco, 1977-82; cons. arts mgmt. San Francisco, 1980-82; gen. dir. Portland Opera Assn., Oreg., 1982—; dir. Opera Am., 1995—. Cons. On-Site Program Nat. Endowment Arts, Washington, 1982—; judge Met. Opera Auditions, 1977—. Recipient Chevalier in the Order of Arts and Letters French Govt., 1999. Mem. Bohemian Club (San Francisco), City Club (Portland), Arlington Club, Rotary Club. Office: Portland Opera Assn Inc 1515 SW Morrison St Portland OR 97205-1814

BAILEY, SHIRLEY M. state senator; Tchr.; Rep. senator dist. 42 N.Mex. State Senate. Mem. edn., Indian and cultural affairs coms. N.Mex. State Senate. Home: 14305 Shady Ln Hobbs NM 88242 Office: NMex State Senate State Capitol Mail Rm Dept Santa Fe NM 87503 E-mail: senate@state.nm.us

BAILEY, STEPHEN FAIRCHILD, museum director and curator, ornithologist; b. Stamford, Conn., Feb. 7, 1948; s. Edwin Montgomery and Frances (Sherman) B.; m. Karen Lynn Burtness Bailey, Aug. 18, 1971 (div. July 1987); divorced. BA in Biology magna cum laude, Beloit Coll., 1971; PhD in Zoology, U. Calif., Berkeley, 1978. Museum dir. and curator Pacific Grove Mus. of Natural Hist., Calif., 1992—. Collections mgr. for ornithology and mammalogy Calif. Acad. Scis., San Francisco, 1984-92; biological cons., 1979-92; adj. prof. biology San Francisco State U., 1986—; teaching Albany Adult Sch., Calif., 1979-85. Co-author Atlas of the Breeding Birds of Monterey County, 1993; co-author, photographer Audubon Society Master Guide to Birding 3 vols., 1983; regional editor Am. Birds, 1985-98; contrb. articles to profl. jours. Rsch. fellowship Christensen Rsch. Inst., Papua New Guinea, 1989. Mem. Am. Birding Assn. (elected), Ecological Soc. Am. (life), Am. Ornithologists Union, Cooper Ornithological Soc. (life), Pacific Seabird Group, Soc. Preservation of Natural Hist. Collections, Phi Eta Sigma, Phi Beta Kappa. Avocations: birding, travel, nature study, military history. Home: 830 Sunset Dr Apt J Pacific Grove CA 93950-4729 Office: Pacific Grove Museum Natural History 165 Forest Ave Pacific Grove CA 93950-2612

BAIN, C. RANDALL, lawyer; b. Greeley, Colo., Feb. 1, 1934; s. Walter Lockwood and Harriet Lucille (Stewart) B.; m. Joanne Berg, Aug. 4, 1956 (div.); children: Jennifer Harriet, Charles Alvin; m. Lois Jean Frazier, Feb. 1, 1973 (dec.); 1 child, Frazier; m. Anna Scalise, Dec. 16, 2000. BA, Yale U., 1955, LLB, 1960. Bar: Ariz. 1961, U.S. Dist. Ct. Ariz. 1961, U.S. Ct. Appeals (9th cir.) 1963, U.S. Supreme Ct. 1968, U.S. Ct. Appeals (fed. cir.) 1992. Ptnr. Brown & Bain, Phoenix, 1961—, pres., 1972-87, exec. v.p., 1987—. Bd. dirs. UDC Homes, Inc., Tempe, Ariz., 1974-95. Trustee Phoenix Country Day Sch., 1983-94. Mem. ABA, Ariz. Bar Assn. (chmn. fee arbitration com. 1982-86), Am. Law Inst., Yale U. Law Sch. Alumni Assn. (exec. com. 1982-85, 93-97). Office: Brown & Bain PA 2901 N Central Ave Ste 2000 Phoenix AZ 85012-2788

BAIN, DONALD KNIGHT, lawyer; b. Denver, Jan. 28, 1935; s. Francis Marion and Jean (Knight) B.; divorced; children: Stephen A., Andrew K., William B. AB, Yale U., 1957; LLB, Harvard U., 1961. Bar: Colo. 1961. From assoc. to ptnr. Holme Roberts & Owen, Denver, 1961-93, chmn. exec. com., 1988-90; ptnr. Holme Roberts & Owen LLP, Denver, 1993—; chmn. Colo. Rep. Com., 1993-97. Bd. dirs. Fairmount Cemetery Co.; mem. grievance com. Colo. Supreme Ct., 1975-80, chmn., 1980. Active Rep. Nat. Com., Washington, 1993-97; bd. dirs. Rocky Mountain Corp. Pub. Broadcasting, 1975-83, Downtown Denver, Inc., 1977—, Greater Denver Corp., 1987-91, Denver Metro C. of C., 1998—; trustee Denver Pub. Libr. Friends Found., 1978-96, Denver Found., 1989-95, chmn., 1993-95; trustee Berger Found., 1994-96; trustee, chmn. Colo. Coun. on Arts, 1999—; trustee Human Svcs., Inc., 1970-81, chmn., 1979-80; trustee Colo. Humanities Program, 1975-78; bd. dirs. Auraria Higher Edn. Ctr., 1978-89, chmn., 1986-89; bd. dirs. Auraria Found., 1986—, Legal Aid Found., Colo., 1999—; mem. Denver Pub. Libr. Commn., 1983-91; candidate for mayor of Denver, 1987, 91. Fellow Royal Geog. Soc., Am. Coll. Trial Lawyers, Explorers Club; mem. ABA, Colo. Bar Assn., Denver Bar Assn., Colo. Yale Assn. (pres. 1974-76), Assn. Yale Alumni (bd. govs. 1982-85), Selden Soc., Am. Antiquarian Soc., Internat. Wine and Food Soc., Confrerie des Chevaliers du Tastevin, Cactus Club, Denver Country Club, Mile High

Club, Denver Law Club, Grolier Club, Yale Club, Colo. Mountain Club, Capitol Hill CLub, Univ. Club (Denver). Republican. Avocations: antiquarian book collecting; mountaineering. Home: 1201 Williams # 13C Denver CO 80218 Office: Holme Roberts & Owen LLP 1700 Lincoln St Ste 4100 Denver CO 80203-4541 E-mail: baind@hro.com

BAIN, LINDA L. academic administrator; BS in Phys. Edn. summa cum laude, Ill. State U., 1962, MS in Phys. Edn., 1968; PhD in Phys. Edn. and Learning Theory, U. Wis., 1974. Instr. Lowell Elem. Sch., Wheaton, Ill., 1962-64, East Peoria (Ill.) H.S., 1964-68, U. Mich., Ann Arbor, 1968-69; asst. prof. U. Ill., Chgo., 1969-75, U. Houston, 1975-78, assoc. prof., 1978-83, prof., 1983-88, chmn. dept. health, phys. edn. and recreation, 1980-82, assoc. dean rsch. Coll. Edn., 1982-88; prof. Calif. State U., Northridge, 1988-95, dean Sch. Comm., Health and Human Svcs., 1988-95; prof. San Jose (Calif.) State U., 1995—, provost, v.p. acad. affairs, 1995—. Alderson lectr. U. Tex., 1982; Amy Morris Homans lectr. Nat. Assn. Phys. Edn. in Higher Edn., 1989; Ethel Martus Lawther lectr. U. N.C., Greensboro, 1992; Scholar lectr. Ill. State U., 1993; presenter in field. Co-author: Transition to Teaching: A Guide for the Beginning Teacher, 1983, The Curriculum Process in Physical Education, 1985, 2d edit., 1995; reviewer Rsch. Quar. for Exercise and Sport, 1977-95, Jour. Phys. Edn., Recreation and Dance, 1976-88; mem. editl. adv. bd. Youth and Soc., 1984-95, Jour. Phys. Edn., Recreation and Dance, 1984-87; editl. bd. Jour. Tchg. in Phys. Edn., 1985-95, Quest, 1991-94; book rev. editor Rsch. Quar. for Exercise and Sport, 1991-94; contbr. articles to profl. jours., chpts. to books. Bd. dirs. Am. Cancer Soc., San Fernando Valley, Calif., 1993-95; mem. health project policy bd. Calif. Phys. Edn., 1994-95; mem. met. bd. YMCA of Santa Clara Valley, 1998—; bd. dirs. Met. San Jose Collaborative for Acad. Excellence, 1998—; mem. hon. com. No. Exposure: New Art from Japan, San Jose Inst. Contemporary Art, 1999. Marie L. Carns fellow, 1972-73, Fellow AAHPERD, 1980, Am. Leadership Forum Silicon Valley, 1999; recipient Rsch. award So. Assn. Phys. Edn. of Coll. Women, 1983, Honor award AAHPERD, 1990, Jose Maria Cagigal Scholar lectr. Assn. Internat. Ecoles Superieures d'Edn. Physique, 1990, Disting. Adminstrn. award Nat. Assn. Phys. Edn. in Higher Edn., 1993, Alumni Achievement award Ill. State U., 1995, U. Wis. Sch. Edn., 1997, Tribute to Women in Industry award YWCA, Santa Clara Valley, 1999. Fellow Am. Acad. Kinesiology and Phys. Edn. Office: San Jose State U 1 Washington Sq San Jose CA 95192-0001

BAIN, WILLIAM JAMES, JR. architect; b. Seattle, June 26, 1930; s. William James and Mildred Worline (Clark) B.; m. Nancy Sanford Hill, Sept. 21, 1957; children: David Hunter, Stephen Fraser (dec.), Mark Sanford, John Worthington. BArch, Cornell U., 1953. Lic. 1st class architect, Japan, lic. architect in 18 states, Can., Guam, Eng. Ptnr. NBBJ (formerly Naramore, Bain, Brady & Johanson), Seattle. Lectr. U. Wash., Seattle, mem. affiliate program steering com. Coll. Architecture and Urban Planning, 1969-71; lectr. Wash. State U.; organizer founding bd. dirs. Pacific N.W. Bank. Prin. works include U. Wash. South Campus, U.S. Pavilion at Expo '74 Worlds Fair, Honolulu Mcpl. Bldg., Two Union Square High-Rise Office Bldg., Four Seasons Olympic Hotel and Sun Mountain Lodge, Bagley Wright Theater and Paramount Theater renovation, Saitama Prefecture Demonstration Housing, Japan, Pacific Place Retail Complex, others. Bd. dirs. Corp. Coun. for Arts, 1989—, Arboretum Found., 1971-74; bd. dirs. Downtown Seattle Assn., 1980—, 1st vice-chmn., 1990-91, chmn., 1991-92; bd. dirs. Seattle Symphony Orch., 1974-87, pres., 1977-79; mem. adv. coun. Coll. Architecture, Cornell U., 1987-91, 94—, vis. com. U. Washington, 1999—; mem. Seattle Pub. Libr. Citizen's Adv. Bd., 1997. With C.E., U.S. Army, 1953-55. Recipient Cert. of Achievement Port of Whittier, Alaska, 1955, Disting. Alumnus award Lakeside Sch., 1985. Fellow AIA (pres. Seattle chpt. 1969, chmn. N.W. regional student profl. fund 1971, pres. Wash. coun. 1974, co-commn. Seattle centennial yr., Seattle medal 1997), N.W. Regional Archtl. Found. (pres. 1975); mem. Royal Inst. Brit. Architects, Royal Archtl. Inst. Can., Seattle C. of C. (bd. dirs. 1980-83), Urban Land Inst., N.W. Real Estate Inst., N.W. Forum, Am. Arbitration Assn. (comml. panel 1975—), L'Ogive Soc., Seattle Athletic Club, Seattle Tennis Club, Rotary (bd. dirs. 1970-72, svc. found. bd. 1976-80), Lambda Alpha, Phi Delta Theta. Episcopalian. Clubs: Rainier, Wash. Athletic, Tennis (Seattle); University, Columbia Tower (founding bd. dirs.). Home: 2033 1st Ave Seattle WA 98121-2132 Office: NBBJ 111 S Jackson St Seattle WA 98104-2881

BAINES, KEVIN HAYS, planetary scientist, astronomer; b. Norwalk, Conn., Feb. 11, 1954; s. Elliot A. and Martha Ellen (Ashcroft) B.; m. Jenine Bsharah, June 4, 1982; children: Emily Ansara, Christopher Lewis. BA, Amherst Coll., 1976; MA, Washington U., St. Louis, 1978, PhD, 1982. Resident rsch. assoc. NRC-JPL, Pasadena, Calif., 1982-84; rsch. scientist Jet Propulsion Lab. Calif. Tech. Inst., Pasadena, 1984—. Co-investigator Galileo Near-Infrared Mapping Spectrometer and Cassini Visual-Infrared Mapping Spectrometer expts. Contbr. articles to profl. jours. Flight dir. Aero Assn. Calif. Tech. Inst., 1986, treas., 1987—. Virgil I. Grissom Astronaut fellow Washington U., 1976-79. Mem. AAAS (planetary scis. divsn.). Republican. Achievements include research in determination of vertical cloud/haze structures of Uranus and Neptune; determination of methane and ortho/para hydrogen above averages in Uranus and Neptune; first detection of spectrally-identifiable discrete ammonia ice clouds in Jupiter; near-infrared imagery and analysis of Jupiter's cloud structure from the Galileo spacecraft; near-infrared imagery and spectroscopy of Venus surface; role of asteroid-impact generated sulfuric gases on dinosaur extinctions; near-infrared photometry of rings and satellites of Uranus and Saturn. Avocations: flight instructor (FAA cert.), multi-engine and single-engine aircraft, airline transport and rotorcraft pilot, scuba diver (cert.). Home: 778 Forest Green Dr La Canada Flintridge CA 91011 E-mail: kbaines@aloha.jpl.nasa.gov

BAINTON, DOROTHY FORD, pathology educator, researcher; b. Magnolia, Miss., June 18, 1933; d. Aubrey Ratcliff and Leta (Brumfield) Ford; m. Cedric R. Bainton, Nov. 28, 1959; children: Roland J., Bruce G., James H. BS, Millsaps Coll., 1955; MD, Tulane U. Sch. of Medicine, 1958; MS, U. Calif., San Francisco, 1966. Postdoctoral rsch. fellow U. Calif., San Francisco, 1963-66, postdoctoral rsch. pathologist, 1966-69, asst. prof. pathology, 1969-75, assoc. prof., 1975-81, prof. pathology, 1981—, chair pathology, 1987-94, vice chancellor acad. affairs, 1994—. Mem. Inst. of Medicine, NAS, 1990—. NIH grant, 1978-98. Fellow AAAS, Am. Acad. Arts & Scis.; mem. FASEB (bd. dirs.), Am. Soc. for Cell Biology, Am. Soc. Hematology, Am. Soc. Histochemists and Cytochemists, Am. Assn. of Pathologists. Democrat. Mem. Soc. of Friends. Office: Office of Acad Affairs U Calif San Francisco Med Scis Bldg Rm 115 San Francisco CA 94143-0001 E-mail: baintond@chanoff.ucsf.edu

BAIR, WILLIAM J. radiation biologist; b. Jackson, Mich., July 14, 1924; s. William J. and Mona J. (Gamble) B.; m. Barbara Joan Sites, Feb. 16, 1952; children: William J., Michael Braden, Andrew Emil. B.A. in chemistry, Ohio Wesleyan U., 1949; Ph.D. in Radiation Biology, U. Rochester, 1954. NRC-AEC fellow U. Rochester, 1949-50, research asso. radiation biology, 1950-54; biol. scientist Hanford Labs. of Gen. Electric Co., Richland, Wash., 1954-56, mgr. inhalation toxicology sect., biology dept., 1956-65, Battelle Meml. Inst., 1965-68; mgr. biology dept. Pacific Northwest Labs., Richland, Wash., 1968-74, dir. life scis. program, 1973-75, mgr. biomed. and environ. research program, 1973-76, mgr. environ. health and safety research program, 1976-86, mgr. life scis. ctr., 1986-93, sr. advisor health protection rsch., 1993—. Demonstrated toxicology of plutonium and carcinogenisis of radioactive particles in lung; lectr. radiation biology Joint Ctr. Grad. Study, Richland, 1955-75; cons. to adv. com. on reactor safeguards Nuclear Regulatory Commn., 1971-87; mem. several coms. on plutonium toxicology; mem. subcom. inhalation hazards, com. pathologic effects atomic radiation NAS, 1957-64, mem. ad hoc com. on hot particles of subcom. biol. effects ionizing radiation NAS-NRC, 1974-76, vice chmn. com. on biol. effects of ionizing radiation, BEIR IV Alpha radiation, 1985-88, mem. battlefield radiation exposure com., 1997-99; chmn. task force on biol. effects of inhaled particles Internat. Commn. on Radiol. Protection, 1970-79, mem. com. 2 on permissible dose for internal radiation, 1973-93, chmn. task group on respiratory tract models, 1984-93; mem. Nat. Coun. on Radiation Protection and Measurements, 1974-92, hon. mem., 1992, bd. dirs., mem. com. of radionuclides on maximum permissible concentration of occupl. and nonoccupl. exposure, 1970-74, mem. com. basic radiation protection criteria, 1975-92, chmn. ad hoc com. on hot particles, 1974, chmn. ad hoc com. internal emitter activities, 1976-77, mem. com. on internal emitter stds., 1977-92; mem. radiation adv. com. and sci. adv. bd. EPA, 1993-99. Author 200 books, articles, reports, chpts. in books. With AUS, 1943-46. Decorated Bronze Star; recipient E.O. Lawrence Meml. award AEC, 1970, cert. of appreciation AEC, 1975, Alumni Disting. Achievement citation Ohio Wesleyan U., 1986. Fellow AAAS, Health Physics Soc. (bd. dirs. 1970-73, 83-86, pres. elect 1983-84, pres. 1984-85, Disting. Sci. Achievement award 1991, Herbert H. Parker award Columbia chpt. 1998); mem. Radiation Rsch. Soc., Nat. Coun. Radiation Protection measurement (hon., Lauriston S. Taylor lectr. 1997), Soc. Exptl. Biology and Medicine (vice chmn. N.W. chpt. 1967-70, 74-75), Sigma Xi, Kiwanis (dir.). Home: 578 Clermont Dr Richland WA 99352-1966 Office: Battelle Pacific NW Labs PO Box 999 Richland WA 99352-0999

BAIRD, ALAN C. screenwriter; b. Waterville, Maine, Jan. 5, 1951; s. Chester A. and Beverly E. B. BA, Mich. State U., 1973. Pres. Souterrain Teeshirts, Nice, France, 1977-78; page NBC, N.Y.C., 1979-80; producer, dir. Random Prodns., Hollywood, Calif., 1981; writer, producer Preview STV, N.Y.C., 1982-83, Sta. KCOP-TV, Hollywood, 1983-84; writer Vidiom Prodns., Hollywood, 1985-95; screenwriter, 1995—. Author: ATS Operations, 1976, Writes of Passage, 1992, 9TimeZones.com, 1999; prodr. TV script Live at the Palomino, 1981; designer Screenwright Screenplay Formatting Software, 1985; writer TV scripts Night Court, 1986, 20/60, 1986, Golden Girls, 1986, Family Ties, 1986, Max Headroom, 1987, Dave's World, 1993, movie scripts Trading Up, 1988, Merlinsky, 1989, Eleven Thousand Virgins, 1994, The Fall in Budapest, 1997; play script Twisted Pair, 1998. Crisis counselor San Francisco Suicide Prevention, 1975; prodn. asst. March of Dimes Telethon, Hollywood, 1985; escort, host, vol. Verdugo Hills Hosp., 1994-96. Recipient Harvard Book prize Harvard U., Cambridge, Mass., 1969. Avocations: flying, running, scuba diving, parachuting, competitive driving.

BAIRD, BRIAN N. congressman; b. Chama, N.Mex., Mar. 7, 1956; m. Mary Baird; 2 stepchildren BS, U. Utah, 1977; MS, U. Wyo., 1980, PhD, 1984. Mem. faculty dept. psychology Pacific Luth. U., 1986—; mem. U.S. Congress from 3d Wash. dist., 1999—; mem. transp. and infrastructure, sci., and small bus. coms. Cons. clin. psychologist St. Charles Med. Ctr., 1994-96. Mem. NOW, APA, Wash. State Psychol. Assn., Amnesty Internat. Office: US Ho of Reps 1721 Longworth Ho Office Bldg Washington DC 20515-0001*

BAIRD, LOURDES G. federal judge; b. 1935; BA with highest honors, UCLA, 1973, JD with honors, 1976. Asst. U.S. atty. U.S. Dist. Ct. (ctrl. dist.) Calif., L.A., 1977-83, U.S. atty., 1990-92; ptnr. Baird & Quadros, 1983-84, Baird, Munger & Myers, 1984-86; judge East L.A. Mcpl. Ct., 1986-87; adj. prof. law Loyola U., L.A., 1986-90; judge L.A. Mcpl. Ct., 1987-88, L.A. Superior Ct., 1988-90; U.S. atty. ctrl. dist. Calif., 1990-92; judge U.S. Dist. Ct. (ctrl. dist.) Calif., L.A., 1992—. Faculty civil RICO program Practicing Law Inst., San Francisco, 1984-85, western regional program Nat. Inst. Trial Advocacy, Berkeley, Calif., 1987-88; adj. prof. trial advocacy Loyola U., L.A., 1987-90. Recipient Silver Achievement award for the professions YWCA, 1994; named Woman of Promise, Hispanic Womens' Coun., 1991, Alumnus of Yr., UCLA Sch. Law, 1991. Mem. Mexican-Am. Bar Assn., Calif. Women Lawyers, Hispanic Nat. Bar Assn., UCLA Sch. Law alumni Assn. (pres. 1984). Office: US Dist Ct Ctrl Dist Calif Edward R Roybal Bldg 255 E Temple St Ste 770 Los Angeles CA 90012-3334

BAIRD, MELLON CAMPBELL, JR. electronics industry executive; b. Corsicana, Tex., Feb. 24, 1931; s. Mellon Campbell and Katherine (Wasson) B.; m. Mary Beth Norman, Dec. 27, 1956. BBA, North Tex. State U., 1957, MBA, 1961. Adminstrv. asst. VARO Inc., Garland, Tex., 1957-59, western region mgr. Los Angeles, 1959-61, dir. mktg. Santa Barbara, Calif., 1961-63; exec. v.p., pres. F&M Systems Co., Dallas, 1963-74; pres., bd. dirs. fed. systems group Sanders Assocs. Inc., Nashua, N.H., 1974-81; pres. def. and electronics group Eaton Corp., Cleve., 1981-86; pres., chief oper. officer, bd. dirs. Tracor Inc., Austin, 1986-87, pres., CEO, 1988-89; pres., CEO, chmn. bd. dirs. Delfin Systems, Sunnyvale, Calif., 1990—; pres., CEO TITAN Systems Corp., San Diego, 1998—. Bd. dirs. Software Spectrum Inc., Dallas, EDO Corp., College Point, N.Y., Hawker Pacific Aerospace, Sun Valley, Calif. Served with USN, 1951-55. Mem. Nat. Security Indsl. Assn. (trustee 1974—), Navy League U.S. (life), Armed Forces Comms. and Electronics Assn., Assn. Old Crows (life, tech. symposium chmn. 1987), Security Affairs Support Assn. (bd. dirs.). Home: 4204 Green Cliffs Rd Austin TX 78746-1241 Office: TITAN Corp 3033 Science Park Rd San Diego CA 92121-1199

BAIRD, PATRICIA ANN, physician, educator; b. Rochdale, Eng. came to Can., 1955; d. Harold and Winifred (Cainen) Holt; m. Robert Merrifield Baird, Feb. 22, 1964; children— Jennifer Ellen, Brian Merrifield, Bruce Andrew BSc with gen. honors in biol. sci., McGill U., 1959, MD, CM, 1963; DSc (hon.), McMaster U., 1991; D Univ. (hon.), U. Ottawa, 1991; LLD (hon.), Wilfrid Laurier U., 2000. Intern Royal Victoria Hosp., Montreal, Que., Can., 1963-64; resident, fellow in pediat. Vancouver Gen. Hosp., B.C., Can., 1964-67; instr. pediat. U. B.C., Vancouver, 1968-72, from asst. prof. to prof., 1972-94, Univ. Killam Disting. prof., 1994—; head dept. med. genetics Grace Hosp., Vancouver, 1981-89, Children's Hosp., Vancouver, 1981-89, Health Scis. Centre Hosp., 1986-89. Med. cons. B.C. Health Surveillance Registry, 1977-90; chmn. genetics grants com. Med. Rsch. Coun., Ottawa, Ont., Can., 1982-87, mem. coun., 1987-90; mem. Nat. Adv. Bd. on Sci. and Tech. to Fed. Govt., 1987-91; mem. genetic predisposition study steering com. Sci. Coun. Can., 1987-90; chair Royal Commn. on New Reproductive Technologies, 1989-93; co-chair Nat. Forum Sci. and Tech. Couns., 1991; v.p. Can. Inst. for Advanced Rsch., 1991—; bd. dirs. Biomed. Rsch. Centre, 1986-89; bd. govs. U. B.C., 1984-90; temporary cons. WHO, 1999, 2000, 01, mem. human genetics ELSI planning group, 2000—. Contbr. articles to med. jours. Bd. govs. U. B.C., 1984-90. Decorated Order B.C., 1992, Commemorative medal for Confedn. of Can., 1992. Fellow RCP Can., Royal Soc. Can., Can. Coll. Med. Geneticists (v.p. 1984-86); mem. Am. Soc. Human Genetics (chair nominating com. 1987-89), B.C. Med. Assn., Can. Med. Assn., Genetics Soc. Can., Genetic Epidemiology (adv. bd. 1991-94), Internat. Fedn. of Gyn. and Obs. (mem. ethics com. 1997-99), Order of Can. (officer). Avocations: skiing, cycling, music. Office: U BC Dept Med Genetics Vancouver BC Canada V6T 1Z3

BAIRD, WILLIAM MCKENZIE, chemical carcinogenesis researcher, biochemistry educator; b. Phila., Mar. 23, 1944; s. William Henry Jr. and Edna (McKenzie) B.; m. Elizabeth A. Myers, June 21, 1969; children: Heather Jean, Elizabeth Joanne, Scott William. BS in Chemistry, Lehigh U., 1966; PhD in Oncology, U. Wis., 1971. Postdoctoral fellow Inst. Cancer Research, London, 1971-73; from asst. to assoc. prof. biochemistry Wistar Inst., Phila., 1973-80; assoc. prof. medicinal chemistry Purdue U., West Lafayette, Ind., 1980-82, prof., 1982-97, Glenn L. Jenkins prof. medicinal chemistry, 1989-97, dir. Cancer Ctr., 1986-97; faculty participant cancer ctr., biochemistry program Purdue U., 1980-97; dir. Environ. Health Scis. Ctr., Oreg. State U., Corvallis, 1997-2000, prof. dept. environ. and molecular toxicology, 1997—, prof. dept. biochemistry and biophysics, 1997—, dir. environ. Heatlh Sci. Ctr. ; adv. com. on biochemistry and chem. carcinogenesis Am. Cancer Soc., 1983-86; mem. chem. pathology study sect. NIH, 1986-90. Contbr. articles to profl. jours.; assoc. editor Cancer Rsch. Grantee NCI. Mem. ISSX, AAAS, Am. Assn. Cancer Rsch., Am. Chem. Soc., Am. Soc. Biochemistry and Molecular Biology, Environ. Mutagen Soc., Soc. Toxicology. Office: Oreg State U Environ Health Scis Ctr 1011 ALS Bldg Corvallis OR 97331-7302

BAIREY, MARIE, principal; Prin. Sonoma Elem. Sch., Modesto, Calif., 1988-98; resource tchr. Beard Elem. Sch., Modesto, 1998—. Recipient DOE Elem. Sch. Recognition Program award, 1989-90. Office: Beard Elem Sch 915 Bowen Ave Modesto CA 95350-3096

BAKALY, CHARLES GEORGE, JR. lawyer, mediator; b. Long Beach, Calif., Nov. 15, 1927; s. Charles G. Sr. and Doris (Carpenter) B.; m. Patricia Murphey, Oct. 25, 1952; children: Charles G. III, John W., Thomas B. A.B., Stanford U., 1949; J.D., U. S.C., 1952. Assoc. O'Melveny & Myers, L.A., 1956-63, ptnr., 1963-94; mem. JAMS, L.A., 2000—. Mem. Commn. on Calif. State Govt. Orgn. and Economy, 1991-94, President's Nat. Commn. on Employment Policy, 1992-94; mem. 9th Cir. Jud. Conf. Lawyer Del. Ch., 1984-87, mem. indigent def. panel, 1992-94; chmn. Calif. Dispute Resolution Adv. Coun., 1987-88; pres. Dispute Resolution Svcs. Bd. Dirs., Calif. Dispute Resolution Coun. Author: (with Joel M. Grossman) Modern Law of Employment Relationships, 1983, 2d edit. 1989; contbr. chpts. to books. Capt. JAG, U.S. Army, 1952-56. Fellow Am. Coll. Trial Lawyers, Coll. Labor and Employment Lawyers, Internat. Acad. Mediators; mem. ABA (chmn. sect. labor and employment law 1981-82, sect. dispute resolution), L.A. County Bar Assn. (trustee, chmn. labor law sect. 1976-77, dispute resolution sect.), Lincoln Club (pres. 1989-91), Chancery Club, Valley Hunt Club (Pasadena, Calif.), Calif. Club (L.A.), Bohemian Club (San Francisco). Office: JAMS 350 S Figueroa St Ste 990 Los Angeles CA 90071-1102

BAKEMAN, CAROL ANN, travel and administrative services manager, singer; b. San Francisco; d. Lars Hartvig and Gwendolyne Beatrice (Zimmer) Bergh; m. Delbert Clifton Bakeman; children: Laurie Ann, Deborah Ann. Student, UCLA, 1954-62. Singer Roger Wagner Chorale, L.A. Master Chorale, 1964-86, The Wagner Ensemble, 1991—; libr. Hughes Aircraft Co., Culver City, Calif.; head econs. libr. Planning Rsch. Corp., L.A., 1961-63; corp. libr. Econ. Cons., Inc., L.A., 1963-68; head econs. libr. Daniel, Mann, Johnson & Mendenhall, archs. and engrs., L.A., 1969-71, corp. libr., 1971-77, mgr. info. svcs., 1978-81, mgr. info. and office svcs., 1981-83, mgr. adminstrv. svcs., 1983-96, sr. assoc., 1996-98, assoc. v.p., 1998—; travel mgr. AECOM Tech. Corp., 1996—. Assoc. v.p. Corp. Consol. Svcs., Inc., (divsn. AECOM), 1997—; pres., Creative Libr. Sys., L.A., 1974-83; libr. cons. ArchiSystems (divsn. SUMMA Corp.), L.A., 1972-81, Property Rehab. Corp., Bell Gardens, Calif., 1974-75, VTN Corp., Irvine, Calif., 1974, William Pereira & Assos., 1975; mem. office sys. and bus. edn. adv. bd. Calif. State U. Northridge, 1992. Mem. Assistance League, So. Calif., 1956-86, nat. auxilaries com., 1968-72, 75-78, nat. by-laws com., 1970-75, assoc. bd. dirs., 1966-76. Mem. AFTRA, SAG, Am. Guild Musical Artists, Adminstrv. Mgmt. Soc. (v.p. L.A. chpt. 1984-86, pres. 1986-88, internat. conf. chmn. 1988-89, internat. bd. dirs. 1988-90, internat. v.p. mgmt. edn. 1990-92), L.A. Master Chorale Assn. (bd. dirs. 1978-83), Wagner Ensemble (bd. dirs.), L.A. Bus. Travel Assn. (bd. dirs. 1995, sec. 1997, v.p. 1998, pres. 1999, past pres. 2000, bd advisor 2001—), Nat. Bus. Travel Assn. (nat. conv. seminar com. 1994-95, conv. vol. chmn. 2000, profl. svc. award 2001). Office: Daniel Mann Johnson & Mendenhall 3250 Wilshire Blvd Los Angeles CA 90010-1577

BAKER, ALTON FLETCHER, III, newspaper editor, publishing executive; b. Eugene, Oreg., May 2, 1950; s. Alton Fletcher Jr. and Genevieve B.; m. Wendy, Jan. 27, 1979; children: Benjamin A., Lindsay A. BA in Comms., Washington State U., 1972. Reporter Associated Press, 1972-79; asst. city editor The Register-Guard, Eugene, 1979-80, city editor, 1980-82, mng. editor, 1982-86, editor, 1986-87, editor, publisher, 1987—; pres. Guard Publishing Co., Eugene, 1987—. Pres. Cmty. Newspapers, Inc., Portland. Pres. YMCA, Eugene, 1989, United Way of Lane County, Eugene, 1985-01, Eugene Festival Musical Theatre, 1990-94. Avocation: golf. Office: Guard Publishing Co 3500 Chad Dr Eugene OR 97408-7348

BAKER, ANITA, singer; b. Toledo, Jan. 26, 1958; m. Walter Bridgeforth, Jr., Dec. 24, 1988; 1 child, Walter Baker Bridgeforth. Mem. funk band Chapter 8, Detroit, 1978-80; receptionist Quin & Budajh, Detroit, 1980-82; ind. singer, songwriter, 1982—. Rec. artist: (with Chapter 8) I Just Wanna Be Your Girl, 1980, (solo albums) The Songstress, 1983, Rapture, 1986 (Grammy award for best rhythm and blues vocal performance 1987), Giving You the Best That I Got, 1988 (Grammy awards for best rhythm and blues song, 1988, best rhythm and blues performance, female, single, 1988, best album, 1989), Compositions, 1990 (Grammy award for best rhythm and blues performance, 1990), Rhythm of Love, 1994 (Grammy award nominee for best album 1995, best female vocal 1995, best song 1995); songs include No More Tears, Angel, Caught Up in the Rapture, Sweet Love (Grammy award best rhythm and blues song 1987), Same Ol' Love, You Bring Me Joy, Been So Long, No One in the World. Recipient Grammy award gospel, soul, best performance, duo, group, choir or chorus, 1987, NAACP Image award, best female vocalist and best album of yr. Office: Atlantic Records # 900 9229 W Sunset Blvd # 900 West Hollywood CA 90069-3402 also: 8216 Tivoli Cove Dr Las Vegas NV 89128-7446

BAKER, CAMERON, lawyer; b. Chgo., Dec. 24, 1937; s. David Cameron and Marion (Fitzpatrick) B.; m. Katharine Julia Solari, Sept. 2, 1961; children: Cameron III, Ann, John. Student, U. Notre Dame, 1954-57; AB, Stanford U., 1958; LLB, U. Calif., Berkeley, 1961. Bar: Calif. 1962, U.S. Dist. Ct. (so. dist.) Calif. 1962, U.S. Dist. Ct. (no. dist.) Calif. 1963, U.S. Ct. Appeals (9th) 1963. With Adams, Duque & Hazeltine, Los Angeles, 1961-62, Pettit & Martin, San Francisco, 1962-95, mng. ptnr., 1972-81, 84-87, exec. com., 1971-82, 84-88; with Farella, Braun & Martel, San Francisco, 1995—. Mayor City of Belvedere, Calif., 1978-79; owner Larkmead Vineyards, Napa Valley, Calif. Dir. Lassen Nat. Park Found., 1992—. Mem. ABA (sects. on bus. law and internat. law and practice), Calif. Bar Assn. (sect. bus., real property and internat. law), Bar Assn. San Francisco (bd. dirs. 1966, 72-73), Boalt Hall Alumni Assn. (dir. 1982-84), Bohemian Club, Tiburon Peninsula Club. Home: 38 Alcatraz Ave Belvedere CA 94920-2504 Office: Farella Braun Martel LLP 235 Montgomery St Fl 30 San Francisco CA 94104-2902 E-mail: cbaker@fbm.com

BAKER, CHARLES DEWITT, research and development company executive; b. Dayton, Ohio, Jan. 5, 1932; s. Donald James and Lillian Mae (Pund) B.; m. June Thordis Tandberg, June 25, 1954; children: Charles, Robert, Thomas, Michael. AA in Elec. Engring., Long Beach City Coll., 1953; ed., Boston U., 1954, Pacific Coast U., 1963, U. Utah, 1980. Registered profl. mfg. engr., Calif. Chemist Shell Oil, Torrance, Calif., 1957-60; materials and process engr. Northrop Corp., Hawthorne, 1960-63; packaging engr. Jet Propulsion Lab., Pasadena, 1963-71; med. design engr. Utah Biomed. Test Lab., Salt Lake City, 1971-78, sect. mgr., 1978-83; v.p. Tech. Rsch. Assocs., Salt Lake City, 1983-88, pres., 1988—. Pres. Thordis Corp., 1988—. Contbr. articles to profl. jours.; 20 patents in field. Chmn.

bd. dirs. Care Holder Group, 1996—; mem. cmty. adv. com. Heart and Lung Inst., spl. study sect rev. NIH, Tech. Transfer Forum, U. Utah, 1984. Recipient Cost Reduction award NASA, 1969, New Tech. award, 1969, 71, 75. Mem. ASME, Soc. Mfg. Engrs., Utah Mfg. Assn., Acad. of Tech., Entrepreneurs and Innovators. Republican. Avocations: teaching, reading, car rebuilding.

BAKER, CHARLES LYNN, management consultant; b. Dallas, Mar. 17, 1934; s. Leonard Allan and Nellie (Boals) B.; m. Joan Heverly, June 1, 1968; 1 child, Annette Lynn. BS in Internat. Rels. summa cum laude, Syracuse U., 1967; MA in Polit. Sci. cum laude, Auburn U., 1975. Commd. USAF, advanced through grades to col., dep. inspector gen., 1975-80, retired, 1980; mng. ptnr. T.Z. Assocs., Balt., 1980-83; pres. McDermott Internat. Trading A.G., Zurich, 1983-88; mng. dir. McDermott Internat. Gen. Svcs., Hong Kong, Hong Kong, 1983-88; pres. Baker Assocs., Rancho Santa Fe, Calif., 1988—. Bd. dirs. T.Z. Assocs., Balt., Environ. Scis., San Diego, Broadleaf Industries, San Diego; adj. prof. U. Redlands Grad. Bus. Sch. Author: Strategic Planning, 1987. Pres. Redlands Ballet Co., 1987-89; chmn. Redlands Cultural Art Commn., 1988—. Mem. Am. C. of C. (v.p. Hong Kong br. 1984-86), Rotary (pres. Redlands chpt. 1989-90, bd. dirs. internat. chpt. in Hong Kong 1983-85), Pres.'s Assn. (chmn. 1988—), Calif. Cultural Arts Commn. Republican. Episcopalian. Avocations: golf, tennis, reading. Office: Baker Assocs 16047 Via Galan Rancho Santa Fe CA 92091-4014

BAKER, DANIEL NEIL, physicist; b. Postville, Iowa, Nov. 10, 1948; s. Joseph N. and Alvira H. (Amundson) B.; m. A. Victoria Vaughan, Aug. 14, 1971. BA, U. Iowa, 1969, MS, 1973, PhD, 1974. Research aide dept. physics U. Iowa, Iowa City, 1967-69, grad. research asst., 1970-74, postdoctoral research assoc., 1974-75; research fellow Calif. Inst. Tech., Pasadena, 1975-78; mem. staff Los Alamos (N.Mex.) Nat. Lab., 1978-81, group leader, 1981-87; chief Lab. for Extraterrestial Physics NASA, Goddard Space Flight Ctr., Greenbelt, Md., 1987-94; dir. Lab. for Atmospheric and Space Physics U. Colo., Boulder, 1994—. Chmn. data sys. users group NASA, Washington, 1982-90, tech. cons., 1985—, mem. space physics mgmt. and ops. com., adv. coun. Space Sci. and Applications, 1988-92, grand tour cluster mission study scientist, 1991-95; mem. com. solar and space physics NAS, Washington, 1983-86, com. data mgmt. and computation, 1986-88, space studies bd., 1995—; mem. panel on long-term observations NRC, Washington, 1985-88, commn. D Sci. Com. on Solar-Terrestrial Physics, 1986-90, U.S. coordinating com. Solar Terrestrial Energy Program, 1988—, U.S. STEP project scientist, 1990-97, chair results, analysis, modeling phase (S-Ramp), 1997—, Geospace Environ. Modeling com. NSF, 1988-91; project sci. NASA small explorer program, prin. investigator NASA rocket program, numerous NASA ESA satellite missions in field; project sci. Internat. Solar-Terrestrial Physics POLAR Spacecraft Mission, 1992-94; U.S. rep. Internat. Assn. Geomagnetism and Aeronomy, 1996—. Assoc. editor Geophys. Research Letters, Washington, 1986-88; regional editor Jour. of Atmospheric and Solar-Terrestrial Physics, 1998—; mem. space tech. rev. bd. Los Alamos Nat. Lab.; contbr. numerous articles to profl. jours. Mem. external adv. com. Boston U. Ctr. for Space Rsch., 1989-94; mem. sci. vis. com. U. Md. Inst. Phys. Sci. and Tech., 1990-94; mem. external adv. com. Solar-Terrestrial Environ. Lab., Nagoya (Japan) U., 1995-97. NSF research fellow U. Iowa, 1970-74; grantee Inst. Geophys. and Planetary Physics U. Calif., 1980-89. Fellow Am. Geophys. Union (mem. natural hazards panel 1996—, pres.-elect space physics and aeronomy sect. 2000—); mem. AAAS, Am. Geophys. Union (geomagnetism assessment panel 1987-88, sec. magnetospheric sect. 1988-90), Internat. Acad. Astronautics, Univs. Space Rsch. Assn. (chair coun. of instns. 1996-97), Sigma Xi. Avocations: jogging, creative writing, basketball, cinema.

BAKER, DIANE R.H. dermatologist; b. Toledo, Nov. 17, 1945; BS, Ohio State U., 1967, MD cum laude, 1971. Diplomate Am. Bd. Dermatology. Intern U. Wis. Hosp., Madison, 1971-72, resident in dermatology, 1972-74, Oreg. Health Sci. Ctr., Portland, 1974-76; pvt. practce, Portland, 1976—. Clin. prof. dermatology Oreg. Health Sci. U., 1986—; mem. med. staff Meridian Park Hosp., Tualatin, Oreg., 1981—; dir. Am. Bd. Dermatology, 1995—. Mem. AMA (del. 1995—), Am. Acad. Dermatology (v.p. 1990), Am. Dermatol. Assn., Oreg. Derm. Soc., Alpha Omega Alpha. Office: Dermatol Assocs 1706 NW Glisan St Ste 2 Portland OR 97209-2225

BAKER, DUSTY (JOHNNIE B. BAKER JR.), professional baseball team manager; b. Riverside, Calif., June 15, 1949; Student, Am. River Coll. Player Atlanta Braves, 1968-75, L.A. Dodgers, 1976-83, San Francisco Giants, 1984, Oakland A's, 1985-86; coach San Francisco Giants, 1988-92, mgr., 1993—. Mem. Nat. League All-Star Team, 1981-82. Recipient Silver Slugger award, 1980-81, Gold Glove, 1981; named to Sporting News All-Star Team, 1980. Office: San Francisco Giants 24 Willie Mays Plz San Francisco CA 94107-2199

BAKER, EDWIN MOODY, retired newspaper publisher; b. Cleve., Dec. 20, 1923; s. Alton Fletcher and Mildred Elizabeth (Moody) B.; m. Patricia Petersen, 1954 (dec. 1983); children: Bridget Baker Kincaid, Amanda Baker Barber, Jonathan; m. Marie Kottkamp Randall, 1984; stepchildren: Steven, Mark, Bruce Randall. BS in Bus. Adminstrn., U. Oreg., 1948. With Eugene (Oreg.) Register-Guard, 1948-88; successively advt. mgr., bus. mgr., gen. mgr., pub., pres. Guard Pub. Co., chmn. bd. Mem. exec. bd. Oreg. Trail Coun., Boy Scouts Am., 1953—, pres. 1960-61, chmn. Region XI, 1971, Area I (N.W.), pres., 1972, mem. nat. exec. bd., 1971-72, nat. adv. coun., 1972-82; trustee U. Oreg. Found., 1975-90, Lane C.C. Found. Bd.; bd. dirs. Oreg. Cmty. Found., 1982-90; Oreg. Hist. Soc., 1988-92; trustee Eugene Arts Found., 1980-85; campaign chair Eugene Performing Arts Ctr. campaign; pres. Oreg. Pacific Econ. Devel. Corp., 1984-85; 2d v.p. Eugene Springfield Mt. Ptnrship; mem. chmn. Kakegawa Sister City com., 1986-88; co-chmn. Birth to Three Capital Campaign, 1997; chmn. United Way Leadership, 1997-98; hon. co-chair Eugene Pub. Libr. Found. campaign for New Pub. Libr., 1999-2000. With AUS, WWII. Decorated Bronze Star, Purple Heart; recipient Silver Beaver award Boy Scouts Am., 1962, Silver Antelope, 1965, Pioneer award U. Oreg., 1982, Disting. Eagle Scout, 1982, Aubrey Watzig award Lewis and Clark Coll., 1988, MS Hope award for Oustanding Philanthropic Cmty. Svc. and Bus. Leadership, 2000; named Eugene First Citizen, 1983. Mem. Am. Newspaper Pus. Assn. (rsch. inst. lab. com. 1978-79), Oreg. Newspaper Pubs. Assn. (dir. 1982-90, pres. 1988-89), U. Oreg. Pres. Assocs., Nat. Assn. Fund Raising Execs. (vol. 1994, Oreg. chpt. Fund Raiser of Yr. 1993), Rotary, Eugene Country Club. Home: 2121 Kimberly Cir Eugene OR 97405-5821 Office: PO Box 10188-2188 Eugene OR 97401-3204

BAKER, EDWIN STUART, retired computer consultant; b. Ottumwa, Iowa, Feb. 14, 1944; s. Edwin Moore and Geraldine Vivian (Irby) B; m. Wilma Jeanne Parker, 1968 (div. 1970). Student, Whitman Coll., 1962-64; BS, Oreg. State U., 1978. Programmer agrl. engring. dept. Oreg. State U., Corvallis, 1977-78, rsch. asst., 1979-83, sr. rsch. asst., 1984-89; measurement standards specialist Oreg. Dept. Agr., Salem, 1990-93. Cons. in field. Mem. IEEE, Assn for Computing Machinery, Am. Legion, DAV, NRA, Nat. Intercollegiate Rodeo Assn., 59ers Svc. Club. Avocations: photography, horses. Home: PO Box 370 Lebanon OR 97355-0370 Office: Oreg Dept Agr Measurements Standards Divsn Salem OR 97310-0001

BAKER, KEITH MICHAEL, history educator; b. Swindon, Eng., Aug. 7, 1938; came to U.S., 1964; s. Raymond Eric and Winifred Evelyn (Shepherd) B.; m. Therese Louise Elzas, Oct. 25, 1961 (div. 1999); children— Julian, Felix. BA, Cambridge U., 1960, MA, 1963; postgrad., Cornell U., 1960-61; PhD, U. London, 1964. Instr. history and humanities Reed Coll., 1964-65; asst. prof. European history U. Chgo., 1965-71, assoc. prof., 1971-76, prof., 1977-89, master collegiate div. social scis., 1975-78, assoc. dean coll., 1975-78, assoc. dean div. social scis., 1975-78, chmn. commn. grad. edn., 1980-82; chmn. Council Advanced Studies in Humanities and Social Scis., 1982-86; prof. European history Stanford U., 1989—, J.E. Wallace Sterling prof. in humanities, 1992—, chair dept. history, 1994-95; Anthony P. Meier family prof. humanities, dir. Stanford Humanities Ctr., 1995-2000, cognizant dean humanities, 2000—. Vis. assoc. prof. history Yale U., 1974; mem. Inst. Advanced Study, Princeton (N.J.), 1979-80; vis. prof., dir. studies Ecole des Hautes Etudes en Scis. Sociales, Paris, 1982, 84, 91; fellow Ctr. for Advanced Study in Behavioral Scis., Stanford (Calif.) U., 1986-87; vis. prof. UCLA, 1989; vis. fellow Clare Hall, Cambridge (Eng.) U., 1994; chair scholars com. Am. Com. on the French Revolution, 1989. Author: Condorcet: From Natural Philosophy to Social Mathematics, 1975, Inventing the French Revolution, 1990; prin. author: Report Commission on Graduate Education, U. Chgo., 1982; editor: Condorcet: Selected Writings, 1977, The Political Culture of the Old Regime: The Old Regime and the French Revolution, 1987, The Terror, 1994; co-editor Jour. Modern History, 1980-89. Decorated chevalier Ordre des Palmes Académiques, 1988; elect. fellow, AAAS, 1991; elect. mem. Am. Philos. Soc., 1997, NEH fellow, 1967-68, Am. Coun. Learned Soc. Study fellow, 1972-73, Guggenheim fellow, 1979. Mem. Am. Hist. Assn. (com. on coms. 1991-94), Soc. French History Studies, Am. Soc. for 18th Century Studies (v.p. 1999, pres. 2000-2001). Office: Stanford U Dept History Stanford CA 94305 E-mail: kbaker@stanford.edu

BAKER, KENNETH, art critic, writer; b. Weymouth, Mass., May 3, 1946; s. Granville and Katherine B.; m. Tonia Aminoff, July 26, 1975. BA, Bucknell U., 1968. Freelance writer, Boston, Providence, N.Y.C., 1969-84; art critic The Boston Phoenix, 1972-84; adj. faculty Boston Coll., Chestnut Hill, 1979-84; art critic San Francisco Chronicle, 1985—. Mem. adj. faculty Stanford U., 1994, 97. Author: Minimalism, 1989, reprinted 1997. Recipient Mfrs. Hanover Trust-Art World award for newspaper criticism, 1985; Critic's fellow Nat. Endowment for Arts, 1975, 78; Critics' Workshop grantee Am. Fedn. Arts, 1970; named Newspaper All-Star, Brill's Content, 2000. Mem. PEN, Nat. Book Critics Cir., Internat. Assn. Art Critics. Avocation: aikido. Office: San Francisco Chronicle 901 Mission St San Francisco CA 94103-2905

BAKER, LUCINDA, writer; b. Atlanta, July 10, 1916; d. Hazle Howard and Adah Rebecca (Mason) B.; m. Willard Alan Greiner, June 27, 1946. Student, Ariz. State Coll., 1934-38. Author: Place of Devils, 1976, Walk the Night Unseen, 1977, Memoirs of First Baroness, 1978, The Painted Lady, 1998; contbr. short stories to mags. Mem. Author's Guild, Mystery Writers Am., Romance Writers Am.

BAKER, MALCOLM, marketing executive; Pres. BRS Group Inc., Calif. Office: BRS Group Inc 100 Shoreline Hwy Ste B325 Mill Valley CA 94941-3692

BAKER, MARI JEAN, marketing director; b. Cottage Grove, Oreg., Jan. 27, 1965; d. Cecil Arthur and Eleanor Pauline (Wolf) Latterell; m. Clay Wynter Baker, Apr. 10, 1991. BA, Stanford U., 1985. Mgr. Innovative Thought and Design, Incline Village, Nev., 1983-89; group product mgr. Intuit, Palo Alto, Calif., 1989—; mktg. assoc. EF Hutton and Co., Palo Alto, 1985-87; dir. mktg. Migent, Inc., Incline Village, Nev., 1987-89. Mem., vol. Incline Village C. of C., Catholic Charities, Sparks, Nev., 1988. Mem. Nat. Assn. for Female Execs., Nat. Assn. for Desktop Publishers. Republican. Avocations: running, scuba diving, reading, hiking. Home: 164 Springdale Way Redwood City CA 94062-3909 Office: Intuit Inc 2535 Garcia Ave Mountain View CA 94043

BAKER, PATRICIA ANN, publishing executive; b. Englewood, N.J., Apr. 3, 1939; BA, St. Mary's Coll., 1961. Prodn. designer Little, Brown Pubs., 1961-63; mktg. & promotion dir. Sunset Books, 1963-68; design & prodn. mgr. Hoover Instn. Press, Stanford, Calif., 1981-89, exec. editor, 1989—. Office: Hoover Instn Press Stanford U Stanford CA 94305-6010

BAKER, RICK, make-up artist; b. Binghamton, N.Y., Dec. 8, 1950; s. Ralph B. and Doris (Hamlin) B.; m. Elaine Parkyn (div. 1984); m. Silvia Abascal, Nov. 10, 1987. Spl. effects makeup artist on the following films: Octaman, 1971, The Thing With Two Heads, 1972, Pirahna, 1972, Bone, 1972, The Exorcist, 1973, Schlock, 1973, Live and Let Die, 1973, Hell Up in Harlem, 1973, It's Alive, 1974, Death Race 2000, 1975, Black Caesar, 1975, Squirm, 1976, Food of the Gods, 1976, King Kong, 1976, Track of the Moonbest, 1976, Zebra Force, 1976, Kentucky Fried Movie, 1977, Star Wars, 1977, The Incredible Melting Man, 1978, It's Alive 2, 1978, The Fury, 1978 Tanya's Island, 1980, The Funhouse, 1980, The Incredible Shrinking Woman, 1981, An American Werewolf in London, 1981 (Acad. award Best Makeup), Videodrome, 1983, Greystoke: The Legend of Tarzan, Lord of the Apes, 1984, Starman, 1984, My Science Project, 1985, Cocoon, 1985, Ratboy, 1986, Captain Eo, 1986, Harry and the Hendersons, 1987 (Acad. award Best Makeup), Summer School, 1987, Missing Link, 1988, Coming to America, 1988, Gorillas in the Mist, 1988 (also assoc. prodr.), Gremlins 2; The New Batch, 1990 (also co-prodr.), The Rocketeer, 1991, Ed Wood, 1994 (Acad. award Best Makeup), Wolf, 1994, Batman Forever, 1995, The Amazing Panda Adventure, 1995, Just Cause, 1995, The Nutty Professor, 1996 (Acad. awd. Best Makeup), The Frighteners, 1996, Escape from L.A., 1996, Men in Black (Acad. awd. Best Makeup), 1997, Mighty Joe Young, 1998, Life, 1999; TV work includes (movies): The Autobiography of Miss Jane Pittman, 1974 (Emmy award Best Makeup), An American Christmas Carol, 1979, Something Is Out There, 1988, Body Bags, 1993; (series) Davey and Goliath, 1960-65, Werewolf, 1987-88, Beauty and the Beast, 1987-90; designed spl. makeup effects for Michael Jackson's Thriller, 1983. The Klumps, How the Grinch Stole Christmas (Acad. awd. Best Makeup), Planet of the Apes. Office: IATSE Local 706 828 N Hollywood Way Burbank CA 91505-2831

BAKER, ROBERT FRANK, molecular biologist, educator; b. Weiser, Idaho, Apr. 9, 1936; s. Robert Clarence and Beulah (Hulet) B.; m. Mary Margaret Murphy, May 29, 1965; children: Allison Leslie, Steven Mark. B.S., Stanford U., 1959; Ph.D., Brown U., 1966. Postdoctoral rsch. assoc. Stanford (Calif.) U., 1966-68; asst. prof. dept. biol. scis. U. So. Calif., L.A., 1968-72, assoc. prof., 1972-83, prof., 1983—, dir. molecular biology div., 1978-80, mem. Comprehensive Cancer Ctr., 1984—. Vis. assoc. prof. Harvard U. Med. Sch., Boston 1975-76; mem. genetic study sect. NIH, Bethesda, Md., 1977-79, 82 Contbr. articles to profl. jours. Grantee NIH, NSF, 1968—. Mem. Am. Soc. Zoologists, Am. Soc. Microbiology, Sigma Xi. Avocations: amateur radio, electronics. Home: 607 Almar Ave Pacific Palisades CA 90272-4208 Office: U So Calif Dept Molecular Biology Mc 1340 Los Angeles CA 90089-0001

BAKER, ROLAND JERALD, educator; b. Pendleton, Oreg., Feb. 27, 1938; s. Roland E. and Theresa Helen (Forest) B.; m. Judy Lynn Murphy, Nov. 24, 1973; children: Kristen L., Kurt F., Brian H. BA, Western Wash. U., 1961; MBA, U. Mich., 1968. Cert. purchasing mgr., profl. contract mgr. Asst. dir. purchasing and stores U. Wash., Seattle, 1970-75; mgr. purchasing and material control Foss Launch & Tug Co., Seattle, 1975-79; faculty Shoreline C.C., 1972-79, 98—, Pacific Luth. U., 1977-79, Edmonds C.C., 1974-79; chmn. educators group Nat. Assn. Purchasing Mgmt., Tempe, Ariz., 1976-79, exec. v.p., 1979-98; pres. Nat. Assn. Purchasing Mgmt. Svcs., Tempe, 1989-95. Faculty Ariz. State U., Tempe, 1988-91; world bus. adv. Coun. Am. Grad. Sch. of Internat. Mgmt., Glendale, Ariz., 1994-98; adv. bd. blockbuy.com, Inc., 1999—, Perfect.com., Inc., 2000—; exec. v.p. MyGroupbuy Inc., also bd. dirs. Author: Purchasing Factomatic, 1977, Inventory System Factomatic, 1978, Policies and Procedures for Purchasing and Material Control, 1980, rev. edit., 1992. With USN, 1961-70, comdr. Res., 1969-91. Recipient Disting. Achievement award Ariz. State U. Coll. Bus., 1997; U.S. Navy postgrad. fellow, 1967. Mem. Purchasing Mgmt. Assn. Wash. (pres. 1978-79), Nat. Minority Supplier Devel. Coun. (bd. dirs.), Am. Prodn. and Inventory Control Soc., Nat. Assn. Purchasing Mgmt. (exec. v.p. 1979-97), Nat. Contract Mgmt. Assn., Internat. Fedn. Purchasing and Materials Mgmt. (exec. com. 1984-87, exec. adv. com. 1991-98). Office: Shoreline CC 16101 Greenwood Ave N Seattle WA 98133-5667

BAKER, ROSALYN HESTER, county agency administrator, former state legislator; b. El Campo, Tex., Sept. 20, 1946; BA, Southwest Tex. State U., 1968; student, U. Southwestern La., 1969. Lobbyist, asst. dir. Govt. Rels. Nat. Edn. Assn., Washington, 1969-80; owner, retail sporting goods store Maui, Hawaii, 1980-87; legis. aide to Hon. Karen Honita Hawaii Ho. of Reps., Honolulu, 1987, mem., 1989-93, house majority leader, 1993, state senator Hawaii, 1993-98, majority leader, 1995-96; dir. office econ. devel. County of Maui, Hawaii, 1999—. Co-chair ways and means com., 1998; mem. econ. devel. com., water, land and Hawaiian affairs com.; co-chair rules com. Hawaii State Dem. Conv., 1990, resolutions com. 1994. Del.-at-large Dem. Nat. Conv., 1984, 92, 96; mem. exec. com. Maui County Dem. Com., 1986-88; vice chmn. Maui Svc. Area Bd. om Mental Health and Substance Abuse; unit pres. Am. Cancer Soc. Democrat. Home: 2180 W Vineyard St Apt 304 Wailuku HI 96793-1635 Office: 200 S High St # 612 Wailuku HI 96793-2155

BAKER, VINCENT LAMONT, professional basketball player; b. Lake Wales, Fla., Nov. 23, 1971; Grad., Hartford U., 1993. Player Milw. Bucks, 1993-97, Seattle Supersonics, 1997—. Named to NBA All-Rookie First Team, 1994, All-NBA Third Team, 1996-97, All-NBA Second Team, 1997-98, NBA All Star, 1995-97. Avocation: singing. Office: c/o Seattle Supersonics 190 Queen Anne Ave N Ste 200 Seattle WA 98109-4926

BAKER, WARREN J(OSEPH), university president; b. Fitchburg, Mass., Sept. 5, 1938; s. Preston A. and Grace F. (Jarvis) B.; m. Carol Ann Fitzsimons, Apr. 28, 1962; children: Carrie Ann, Kristin Robin, Christopher, Brian. B.S., U. Notre Dame, 1960, M.S., 1962; Ph.D., U. N.Mex., 1966. Research assoc., lectr. E. H. Wang Civil Engring. Research Facility, U. N.Mex., 1962-66; assoc. prof. civil engring. U. Detroit, 1966-71, prof., 1972-79, Chrysler prof., dean engring., 1973-78, acad. v.p., 1976-79; NSF faculty fellow M.I.T., 1971-72; pres. Calif. Poly. State U., San Luis Obispo, 1979—. Mem. Bd. Internat. Food and Agrl. Devel., USAID, 1983-85; mem. Nat. Sci. Bd., 1985-94, Calif. Bus. Higher Edn. Forum, 1993-98; founding mem. Calif. Coun. on Sci. and Tech., 1989—; trustee Amigos of E.A.R.T.H. Coll., 1991-96; bd. dirs. John Wiley & Sons, Inc., 1993—; bd. regents The Am. Archtl. Found., 1995-97; co-chair Joint Policy Coun. on Agr. and Higher Edn., 1995—. Contbr. articles to profl. jours. Mem. Detroit Mayor's Mgmt. Adv. Com., 1975-76; mem. engring. adv. bd. U. Calif., Berkeley, 1984-96; bd. dirs. Calif. Coun. for Environ. and Econ. Balance, 1980-85; trustee Nat. Coop. Edn. Assn.; chmn. bd. dirs. Civil Engring. Rsch. Found., 1989-91, bd. dirs., 1991-94. Fellow Engring. Soc. Detroit; mem. ASCE (chmn. geotech. div. com. on reliability 1976-78, civil engring. edn. and rsch. policy com. 1985-89), NSPE (pres. Detroit chpt. 1976-77), Am. Soc. Engring. Edn., Am. Assn. State Colls. and Univs. (bd. dirs. 1982-84). Office: Calif Poly State U Office of Pres 1 Grand Ave San Luis Obispo CA 93407 E-mail: presidentsoffice@calpoly.edu

BAKER, WILLIAM DUNLAP, lawyer; b. St. Louis, June 17, 1932; s. Harold Griffith and Bernice (Kraft) B.; m. Kay Stokes, May 23, 1955; children: Mark William, Kathryn X., Beth Kristie, Frederick Martin. AB, Colgate U., 1954; JD, U. Calif., Berkeley, 1960. Bar: Calif. 1961, Ariz. 1961, U.S. Supreme Ct. 1969. Practice in, Coolidge, 1961, Florence, 1961-63, Phoenix, 1963—; law clk. Stokes & Moring, 1960; spl. investigator Office Pinal County Atty., 1960-61, dep. county atty., 1961-63; partner McBryde, Vincent, Brumage & Baker, 1961-63; assoc. atty. Rawlins, Ellis, Burrus & Kiewit, 1963-65, partner, 1965-81; pres., atty. Ellis & Baker, P.C., 1981-84, Ellis, Baker, Lynch, Clark & Porter P.C., 1984-86, Ellis, Baker, Clark & Porter, P.C., 1986-89, Ellis, Baker & Porter, P.C., 1989-92, Ellis Baker & Porter Ltd., Phoenix, 1992-95, Ellis, Baker & Porter, P.C., Phoenix, 1995-99, Ellis & Baker, P.C., 1999—. Referee Juvenile Ct. Maricopa County Superior Ct., 1966-85 Contbr. articles to profl. jours. Mem. Gov.'s Adv. Coun., Phoenix, 1969-71, Ariz. Environ. Planning Commn., 1974-75; bd. dirs. Agri-Bus. Coun., 1978—, sec., 1978-82; pub. mem. State Bd. Accountancy, 1995—, sec., 1998-99, treas., 1999-2000, pres., 2000—; spl. legal counsel Ariz. Com. Rep. Party, 1965-69, mem. exec. com., 1972-78; vice-chmn. Maricopa County Rep. Com., 1968-69, chmn., 1969-71; bd. dirs. San Pablo Home for Youth, 1964-72, pres., 1971; bd. dirs. Maricopa County chpt. Nat. Found. March of Dimes, 1966-71, campaign chmn., 1970; trustee St. Luke's Hosp., 1976-85, sec., 1978-82, chmn., 1982-85; bd. dirs. Luke's Men, 1971-80, pres., 1976-77; bd. dirs. Combined Health Resources, 1982-85, St. Luke's Health Sys., 1985-95, chmn., 1985-89; bd. dirs. St. Luke's Health Initiatives, 1995—, vice chair, 2000—; bd. dirs., v.p. Ariz. Anglican Cursillo Movement, 1982-86; Western dist. layman rep. Nat. Episcopal Cursillo Com., 1996-98; regional v.p. Colgate Alumni Corp., 1977-82; vice chancellor Episcopal Diocese Ariz., 1970-96; sr. warden Christ Ch. of Ascension, 1983-86, 2001—; ch. atty. Episc. Diocese Ariz., 1996—. Served to 1st lt. USAF, 1954-57. Mem. ABA, Nat. Water Resources Assn. (co-chmn. task force on reclamation law 1990-97, resolutions com. 1990-93, chmn. state caucus 1993-99, chair water policy task force 2000—), Ariz. Bar Assn., Calif. Bar Assn., State C. of C. (bd. dirs. 1988-92), Maricopa County Bar Assn., Flagstaff Golf Assn. (bd. dirs. 1992-93, 94-96, pres. 1994-95), Phoenix Country Club, Sigma Chi, Phi Delta Phi. Episcopalian. Home: 1627 E Cactus Wren Dr Phoenix AZ 85020-5550 Office: 2111 E Highland Ave Ste 355 Phoenix AZ 85016-4734 E-mail: wdb@ellisbaker.com

BAKER, WILLIAM MORRIS, cultural organization administrator; m. Robin Baker. BA in History, U. Va., 1961. With FBI, 1965-87-89-91, asst. dir. criminal investigative divsn., ret., 1991; dir. pub. affairs CIA, 1987-89; sr. v.p., dir. worldwide anti-piracy Motion Picture Assn., Encino, Calif., 1991-94, pres., COO, 1994—. Spkr. in field; guest lectr. Ctr. for Internat. Affairs Harvard U., Fed. Exec. Inst. U. Va. 1st lt. USAF, 1962-65. Named Disting. Exec. by U.S. Pres. George Bush, 1990; recipient Disting. Intelligence medal CIA, 1989, Edmund J. Randolph award U.S. Atty. Gen.'s 40th Ann. Awards Ceremony, 1992, U.S. Marshals Star for lifetime achievement in law enforcement, 1992. Avocations: reading, running, sailing, skiing, cooking. Office: Motion Picture Assn 15503 Ventura Blvd Encino CA 91436-3103

BAKER, WILLIAM P. (BILL BAKER), former congressman; b. Oakland, Calif., June 14, 1940; m. Joanne Atack; children: Todd, Mary, Billy, Robby. Grad. in Bus. and Indsl. Mgmt., San Jose State Coll. Budget analyst State Dept. Fin., Calif.; assemblyman 15th dist. State of Calif., 1980-92; mem. of Congress from 10th Calif. dist., 1993-96; ptnr. Baker, Welch & Wiens, Alamo, Calif. Vice chmn. budget writing Ways and Means Com., 1984-91 Exec. v.p. Contra Costa Taxpayers Assn.; active Contra Costa County Farm Bur. With USCG Res., 1958-65. Republican. Office: Baker Welch & Weins 3189 Danville Blvd Ste 200 Alamo CA 94507-1956*

BAKER, ZACHARY MOSHE, librarian; b. Mpls., June 8, 1950; s. Michael Harry and Margaret Esther (Zanger) B. BA, U. Chgo., 1972; MA, Brandeis U., 1974; MA in LS, UU. Minn., 1975. Head tech. svcs. Jewish Pub. Libr., Montreal, Que., Can., 1981-87; asst. libr. Yivo Inst. for Jewish Rsch., N.Y.C., 1976-80, assoc. libr., 1980-81, head libr., 1987-99; Reinhard family curator Judaica & Hebraica collections Stanford U. Libr., 1999—.

Hist. cons. Que. Inst. Rsch. on Culture, Montreal, 1983; libr. cons. U.S. Holocaust Meml. Coun., Washington, 1984-85, Fla. Atlantic U., Boca Raton, 1994, Ariz. State U., Tempe, 1998. Contbg. author: From a Ruined Garden, 1983, 98; author, contbg. editor Toledot, 1978-82, Judaica Librarianship, 1983—; editor: Yiddish Catalog and Authority File of the Yivo Library, 1990. Crown fellow Brandeis U., 1973-74; travel and rsch. grantee Andrew W. Mellon Found., 1997, Lucius N. Littauer Found., 1990, 94, 96, 98/ Mem. ALA, Assn. Jewish Librs. (pres. 1994-96), Assn. for Jewish Studies, Coun. Archives and Rsch. Libr. in Jewish Studies (pres. 1998—), Phi Beta Kappa, Beta Phi Mu. Avocations: map and atlas collecting, current events, travel. E-mail: zbaker@stanford.edu

BAKKENSEN, JOHN RESER, lawyer; b. Pendleton, Oreg., Oct. 4, 1943; s. Manley John and Helen (Reser) B.; m. Ann Marie Dahlen, Sept. 30, 1978; children: Michael, Dana, Laura. AB magna cum laude, Harvard U., 1965; JD, Stanford U., 1968. Bar: Oreg. 1969, Calif. 1969, U.S. Dist. Ct. Oreg. 1969. Ptnr. Miller, Nash, Wiener, Hager & Carlsen, Portland, Oreg., 1968-99. Lawyer del. 9th Cir. Jud. Conf., San Francisco, 1980-82. Author: (with others) Advising Oregon Businesses, 1979, Arbitration and Mediation, supplement, 2000. Past bd. dirs. Assn. for Retarded Citizens, Portland; advisor Portland Youth Shelter House; mem. and counsel to bd. dirs. Friends of Pine Mountain Observatory, Portland. Mem. ABA (forum on constrn. industry), Oreg. State Bar, Oreg. Assoc. Gen. Contractors (legal com. 1991, counsel to bd. dirs. 1992), Multnomah Athletic Club. Avocation: astronomy.

BAKKER, CORNELIS B. psychiatrist, educator; b. Rotterdam, Holland, Jan. 6, 1929; came to U.S., 1953, naturalized, 1963; s. Willem and Poulina J. (Reiff) B.; m. Marianne K. Rabdau, June 11, 1955; children: Paul, James, Gabrielle. M.D. with honors, U. Utrecht, Holland, 1952. Intern Clinics of Rotterdam, 1952-53, Sacred Heart Hosp., Spokane, 1953-54; resident in psychiatry Eastern State Hosp., Medical Lake, Wash., 1954-56, U. Utrecht, 1956-57, U. Mich. Med. Sch., 1957-59; instr., research asso. psychiatry U. Mich., Ann Arbor, 1959-60; instr. psychiatry U. Wash., Seattle, 1960-63, asst. prof., 1963-67, assoc. prof., 1967-72, prof. psychiatry, 1972-79, dir. Adult Psychiat. Inpatient Service, 1961-68; dir. Adult Devel. Program, 1968-79; prof., head dept. psychiatry U. Ill. Coll. Medicine, Peoria, 1979-84; med. dir. dept. psychiatry Sacred Heart Med. Ctr., Spokane, 1984—; clin. prof. dept. psychiatry and behavioral scis. U. Wash. Sch. Medicine, Seattle, 1985—; med. dir. Spokane Mental Health, 1999-2000. Psychiat. cons. Soc. Sec. Hearings and Appeals, 1963-79, Ketchikan Community Mental Health Center, 1972-77; assoc. residency tng. dir. dept. psychiatry and behavioral scis. U. Wash., Seattle, 1991—. Contbr. articles to profl. jours.; author: (with M.K. Bakker Rabdau) No Trespassing! - Explorations in Human Territoriality, 1973. Dutch Govt. scholar, 1951-52, 52-53; Fulbright grantee, 1953; Fogarty Sr. fellow U. Leuven, Belgium, 1977-78; recipient Significant Achievement award Am. Psychiatric Assn., 1975 Fellow Am. Psychiatric Assn., Am. Coll. Psychiatrists. Office: Sacred Heart Med Ctr Dept Psychiatry PO Box 2555 Spokane WA 99220-2555 E-mail: bakkerc@shmc.org

BAKKER, THOMAS GORDON, lawyer; b. San Gabriel, Calif., Aug. 18, 1947; s. Gordon and Eva Marie (Hoekstra) B.; m. Charlotte Anne Kamstra, Aug. 1, 1969; children: Sarah, Jonathan. AB in History, Calvin Coll., Grand Rapids, Mich., 1969; JD, U. Mich., 1973. Bar: Ariz. 1973, U.S. Dist. Ct. Ariz. 1973, U.S. Ct. Appeals (9th cir.) 1973. Staff reporter Ariz. Criminal Code Revision Com., Phoenix, 1973-75; asst. atty. gen. State of Ariz., Phoenix, 1975-77; staff atty. div. 1 Ariz. Ct. Appeals, Phoenix, 1977-79; assoc. Burch, Cracchiolo et al, Phoenix, 1979-80; from assoc. to ptnr. Olson, Jantsch, Bakker & Blakey, Phoenix, 1980—. Vice chmn. tort and ins. practice sect. Appellate Advocacy Commn., 1982-83; judge pro tem div. 1 Ariz. Ct. Appeals, 1985, 92. Served with U.S. Army, 1969-71. Fellow Ariz. Bar Found. (founding fellow); mem. Ariz. Bar Assn., Maricopa County Bar Assn., Am. Judicature Soc., Am. Health Lawyers Assn., Def. Rsch. Inst., Ariz. Assn. Def. Counsel (bd. dirs.). Mem. Christian Reformed Ch. Avocations: reading, golf, aerobics, salt water fishing. . Office: Olson Jantsch Bakker & Blakey 7243 N 16th St Phoenix AZ 85020-5203 E-mail: TGB@OJBB.com

BALANIS, CONSTANTINE APOSTLE, electrical engineering educator; b. Trikala, Thessaly, Greece, Oct. 29, 1938; came to U.S., 1955; s. Apostolos G. and Erini (Vlahocostas) B.; m. Helen Jovaras, May 21, 1972; children: Erini, Stephanie. BSEE, Va. Poly. Inst., 1964; MEE, U. Va., 1966; PhDEE, Ohio State U., 1969. Electronics engr. NASA, Hampton, Va., 1964-70; asst. professorial lectr. George Washington U. Extension, Hampton, 1968-70; vis. assoc. prof. dept. elec. engring. W.Va. U., Morgantown, 1970-72, assoc. prof., 1972-76, prof., 1976-83; prof. dept. elec. engring. Ariz. State U., Tempe, 1983-91, Regents' prof., 1991—, dir. Telecommunications Rsch. Ctr., 1988-99. Cons. Motorola Inc., Scottsdale, Ariz., 1984-94, Loral Def. Systems, Litchfield Park, Ariz., 1986-88, Gen. Dynamics, Pomona, Calif., 1986-87, Naval Air Warfare Ctr., Patuxent River, Md., 1977-90, Naval Surface Warfare Ctr., Dahlgren, Va., 1985-86, Nat. Radio Astronomy Observatory, Green Bank, W.Va., 1972-74; Boeing, Seattle, 1996, Rockwell Internat., Cedar Rapids, Iowa, 1997. Author: Antenna Theory: Analysis and Design, 1982, 2d edit., 1997, Advanced Engineering Electromagnetics, 1989; patentee in field. Recipient Halliburton Best Researcher award W.Va. U., 1983, Russ award for Rsch., Ohio U., 1984, Teaching Excellence award Ariz. State U., 1988, also Outstanding Grad. Mentor award, 1996-97; grantee and contracts NASA, Army Rsch. Office, NSF, Office Naval Rsch., Dept. of Energy, Dept. of Transp., Naval Air Warfare Ctr., Naval Surface Warfare Ctr., Motorola Inc., Gen. Dynamics, Boeing Helicopter Sys., Sikorsky Aircraft, Rockwell Internat., Boeing Helicopters, IBM, 1972—. Fellow IEEE (Individual Achievement award region 6, 1989, Spl. Engring. Professionalism award Phoenix sect. 1992, Third Millennium award 2000); mem. Am. Soc. Engring. Edn., Sigma Xi, Phi Kappa Phi, Eta Kappa Nu, Tau Beta Pi. Avocations: golf, jogging, tennis, bowling. Home: 3154 E Encanto St Mesa AZ 85213-6110 Office: Ariz State U Dept Elec Engring Tempe AZ 85287-7206

BALBOA, MARCELO, professional soccer player; b. Cerritos, Calif., Aug. 8, 1967; s. Luis B.; m. Cindy Balboa. Grad., San Diego State U., 1988. Player U.S. Nat. Team, 1988—, San Diego Nomads, APSL, 1989, San Francisco Blackhawks, APSL, 1990-91, Colo. Foxes, APSL, 1992, Leon, Mex. 1st Divsn., 1995-96, Colo. Rapids, 1996—. Mem. U.S. World Cup Team, 1994—. Named MVP World Cup, 1994, Colo. Rapids, 1997. Office: c/o Colo Rapids 555 17th St Ste 3350 Denver CO 80202-3909 also: US Soccer Fedn 1801 S Prairie Ave # 1811 Chicago IL 60616-1319

BALDESCHWIELER, JOHN DICKSON, chemist, educator; b. Elizabeth, N.J., Nov. 14, 1933; s. Emile L. and Isobel (Dickson) B.; m. Marlene R. Konnar, Apr. 15, 1991; children from previous marriage: John Eric, Karen Anne, David Russell. B. Chem. Engring., Cornell U., 1956; Ph.D., U. Calif. at Berkeley, 1959. From instr. to asso. prof. chemistry Harvard U., 1960-65; faculty Stanford (Calif.) U., 1965-71, prof. chemistry, 1967-71; chmn. adv. bd. Synchrotron Radiation Project, 1972-75; vis. scientist Synchrotron Radiation Lab., 1977; dep. dir. Office Sci. and Tech., Exec. Office Pres., Washington, 1971-73; prof. chemistry Calif. Inst. Tech., Pasadena, 1973-99, chmn. div. chemistry and chem. engring., 1973-78, prof. emeritus. OAS vis. lectr. U. Chile, 1969; spl. lectr. in chemistry U. London, Queen Mary Coll., 1970, vis. scientist Bell Labs., 1978; mem. Pres.'s Sci. Adv. Com., 1969—, vice chmn., 1970-71; mem. Def. Sci. Bd., 1973-80, vice chmn., 1974-76; mem. carcinogenesis adv. panel Nat. Cancer Inst., 1973—; mem. com. planning and instl. affairs NSF, 1973-77; adv. com. Arms Control and Disarmament Agy., 1974-76; mem. NAS Bd. Sci. and Tech. for Internat. Devel., 1974-76, ad hoc com. on fed. sci. policy 1975, task force on synfuels, 1979, Com. Internat. Security and Arms Control, 1992-95—; mem. Pres.'s Com. on Nat. Medal of Sci., 1974-76, pres., 1986-88, Pres.'s Adv. Group on Sci. and Tech., 1975-76; mem. governing bd. Reza Shah Kabir U., 1975-79; mem. Sloan Commn. on Govt. and Higher Edn., 1977-79, U.S.-USSR Joint Commn. on Sci. and Tech. Coop., 1977-79; vice chmn. del. on pure and applied chemistry to China, 1978; mem. com. on scholarly communication with China, 1978-84; chmn. com. on comml. aviation security NAS, 1988—, mem. def. sci. bd. task force on 'operation desert shield', 1990-91, mem. com. on internat. security and arms control, 1991-94—; mem. rsch. adv. coun. Ford Motor Co., 1979-94—, mem. chem. and engring. adv. bd., 1981-83; vis. lectr. Rand Afrikaans U., Johannesburg, South Africa, 1987, Found. Rsch. and Devel., Pretoria, South Africa, 1989. Mem. editorial adv. bd. Chem. Physics Letters, 1979-83, Jour. Liposome Rsch., 1986—. Served to 1st lt. AUS, 1959-60. Sloan Found. fellow, 1962-64, 64-65; recipient Fresenius award Phi Lambda Upsilon, 1968, Tolman award ACS, 1989. Mem. NAS, Am. Chem. Soc. (award in pure chemistry 1967, William H. Nichols medal 1990), Council on Sci. and Tech. for Devel., Am. Acad. Arts and Scis., Am. Philos. Soc. Office: Calif Inst Tech Divsn Chemistry & Chem Engring # 127-72 Pasadena CA 91125-0001

BALDOCK, BOBBY RAY, federal judge; b. Rocky, Okla., Jan. 24, 1936; s. W. Jay and S. Golden (Farrell) B.; m. Mary Jane (Spunky) Holt, June 2, 1956; children: Robert Jennings, Christopher Guy. Grad., N.Mex. Mil. Inst., 1956; JD, U. Ariz., 1960. Bar: Ariz. 1960, N.Mex. 1961, U.S. Dist. Ct. N.Mex., 1965. Ptnr. Sanders, Bruin & Baldock, Roswell, N.Mex., 1960-83; adj. prof. Eastern N.Mex. U., 1962-81; judge U.S. Dist. Ct. N.Mex., Albuquerque, 1983-86, U.S. Ct. Appeals (10th cir.), 1986-2001, sr. judge, 2001—. Mem. N.Mex. Bar Assn., Chaves County Bar Assn., Ariz. Bar Assn., Phi Alpha Delta. Office: US Ct Appeals PO Box 2388 Roswell NM 88202-2388*

BALDWIN, BRUCE GREGG, botany educator, researcher; b. San Luis Obispo, Calif., Oct. 24, 1957; s. Robert Lee and Sally Louise (Elrod) B. BA in Biol. Scis. with honors, U. Calif., Santa Barbara, 1981; MS in Botany, U. Calif., Davis, 1985, PhD in Botany, 1989. NSF postdoctoral fellow U. Ariz., Tucson, 1990-92; asst. prof. dept. botany Duke U., 1992-94; curator Jepson Herbarium U. Calif., Berkeley, 1994—, asst. prof. in residence dept. integrative biology, 1994-98, assoc. prof. in residence dept. integrative biology, 1998-2000, assoc. prof. dept. integrative biology, 2000—. Mellon vis. scholar Rancho Santa Ana Bot. Garden, 1994. Contbr. articles to profl. jours. and books, reviewer; chief editor Jepson Flora project, 1994—. Recipient NSF Nat. Young Investigator award, 1994; Calif. Acad. Scis. fellow, 1999—. Mem. Am. Soc. Plant Taxonomists (publicity com. 1993—), Calif. Bot. Soc. (pres. 2000—). Achievements include research in plant systematics, phylogenetics, plant cytogenetics and chromosome evolution, plant speciation, California floristics, phytogeography, insular evolution. Avocations: backpacking, canoeing, fly fishing, traveling. Home: 2408 Parker St Berkeley CA 94704-2812 Office: U Calif Berkeley Jepson Herbarium Dept Integrative Biology 1001 Valley Life Scis Bldg 2465 Berkeley CA 94720-2465

BALDWIN, DOUGLAS DANIEL, pipeline company executive; Prodn. mgr. producing dept. Exxon Corp., N.Y.C., 1983-86; v.p. bus. svcs. Esso Resources Can. Ltd., 1986-88, pres., CEO, 1988-92; sr. v.p., dir. Imperial Oil Ltd., 1992-98; pres., CEO TransCanada PipeLines Ltd., Calgary, Alta., 1999—. Bd. dirs. TransCanada, Alta. Oil Sands Tech. and Rsch. Authority, UTS Energy Corp., Calgary Airport Authority. Dir. Alta. Rsch. Coun., 1992-98; past v.p. Alta. Clean Air Strategic Alliance; past chmn. Calgary Zoo Found. Mem. Interstate Natural Gas Assn. of Am. (bd. dirs.), Canadian Petroleum Assn. (past chmn.), Canadian Oilmen's Exec. Assn. (past chmn.), Calgary Petroleum Club (past pres.). Office: Transcanada Pipe-Lines Ltd PO Box 1000 Sta M Calgary AB Canada T2P 4K5 Fax: 403-267-8534

BALDWIN, GEORGE CURRIDEN, physicist, educator; b. Denver, May 5, 1917; s. Harry Lewis and Elizabeth (Watson) B.; m. Winifred M. Gould, Apr. 27, 1952; children— George T., John E., Celia M. BA, Kalamazoo Coll., 1939; MA, U. Ill., 1941, PhD, 1943. Instr. physics U. Ill., Urbana, 1943-44; rsch. assoc. GE, Schenectady, N.Y., 1944-55, nuclear engr. Cin., 1955-57; reactor mgr. Argonne (Ill.) Nat. Lab., 1957-58; physicist Gen. Engring. Lab. GE, Schenectady, 1958-67; adj. prof. nuclear engring. and sci. Rensselaer Poly. Inst., Troy, N.Y., 1964-67, prof., 1967-77, prof. emeritus, 1977—; staff mem. Los Alamos (N.Mex.) Nat. Lab., 1975-87; vis. scientist, 1987-99; ret., 1992. Author: An Introduction to Nonlinear Optics, 1969; contbr. articles on nuclear and radiation physics to sci. publs. Councilman, Niskayuna, N.Y., 1965-69; mem. Zoning Bd., 1969-77. Recipient Disting. Alumnus award Kalamazoo Coll., 1987. Fellow Am. Phys. Soc.; mem. AAAS, Phi Beta Kappa, Sigma Xi, Phi Kappa Phi, Gamma Alpha. Achievements include discovery of nuclear giant dipole resonance; research on gamma-ray lasers; discovery of 1776 Escalante inscription. E-mail: geochaldwin@cs.com

BALDWIN, JOHN, legal association administrator, lawyer; b. Salt Lake City, Feb. 9, 1954; BA, U. Utah., 1977, JD, 1980. Bar: Utah 1980, U.S. Dist. Ct. Utah 1980, U.S. Ct. Appeals (10th cir.) 1984. Assoc. Jardine, Linebaugh, Brown & Dunn, Salt Lake City, 1980-82; asst. atty. gen. Utah Atty. Gen.'s Office, Salt Lake City, 1982-85; dir. Utah Divsn. Securities, Salt Lake City, 1985-90; exec. dir. Utah State Bar, Salt Lake City, 1990—. Adj. assoc. prof. mgmt. Eccles Sch. Bus., U. Utah. Mem. N.Am. Securities Adminstrs. Assn. (bd. dirs. 1987-90, pres. 1988-89), U. Utah Young Alumni Assn. (bd. dirs. 1987-90), U. Utah Beehive Honor Soc. (bd. dirs. 1993-97), U. Utah Alumni Assn. (bd. dirs. 1995-97). Office: Utah State Bar 645 S 200 E # 310 Salt Lake City UT 84111-3837

BALDWIN, LIONEL VERNON, retired university president; b. Beaumont, Tex., May 30, 1932; s. Eugene B. and Wanda (Wiley) B.; m. Kathleen Flanagan, Sept. 3, 1955; children: Brian, Michael, Diane, Daniel. BS, U. Notre Dame, 1954; SM, MIT, 1955; PhD, Case Inst. Tech., 1959. Rsch. engr. Nat. Adv. Com. Aeros., Ohio, 1957-59; unit head NASA, 1959-61; asso. prof. engring. Colo. State U., 1961-64; acting dean Coll. of Engring., 1964-65, dean and prof., 1966-84; pres. Nat. Tech. U., Fort Collins, 1984—; ret. Served to capt. USAF, 1955-57. Recipient award for plasma research NASA, 1964, Kenneth Andrew Roe award Am. ASsn. Engrin. Soc., 1996 Fellow AIAA, Am. Soc. Engring. Edn. (chmn. engring. deans coun.); mem. ASME, IEEE, NSPE, Sigma Xi, Tau Beta Pi, Sigma Pi Sigma. Achievements include patentee apparatus for increasing ion engine beam density. Home: 1900 Sequoia St Fort Collins CO 80525-1540 Office: Nat Tech U 700 Centre Ave Fort Collins CO 80526-1842 E-mail: Baldwin@ntu.edu

BALDWIN, ROBERT LESH, biochemist, educator; b. Madison, Wis., Sept. 30, 1927; s. Ira Lawrence and Mary (Lesh) B.; m. Anne Theodora Norris, Aug. 28, 1965; children: David Norris, Eric Lawrence. B.A., U. Wis., 1950; D.Phil. (Rhodes scholar), Oxford (Eng.) U., 1954. Asst. prof., then asso. prof. biochemistry U. Wis., 1955-59; mem. faculty Stanford, 1959—, prof. biochemistry, 1964-98, prof. emeritus, 1998—, chmn. dept., 1989-94. Vis. prof. Collège de France, Paris, 1972; mem. adv. panel biochemistry and biophysics NSF, 1974-76, NIH study sect. molecular and cellular biophysics, 1984-88. Assoc. editor Jour. Molecular Biology, 1964-68, 75-79; mem. editorial bd. Trends Biochem. Sci., 1977-84, Biochemistry, 1984—, Protein Sci., 1992-97. Mem. Searle Scholars award panel, 1993-96, 1997-98; mem. adv. panel in biophysics Burroughs-Wellcome, 1995. Recipient Wheland award in chemistry U. Chgo., 1995; Guggenheim fellow, 1958-59. Fellow Am. Biophysics Soc. (coun. 1977-81, Cole award 1999); mem. NAS, Am. Soc. Biol. Chemists (Merck award 1999), Am. Chem. Soc., Am. Acad. Arts and Scis., Protein Soc. (coun. 1993-95, Stein and Moore award 1992). Home: 1243 Los Trancos Rd Portola Valley CA 94028-8125 Office: Stanford Med Sch Dept Biochemistry Beckman Ctr Stanford CA 94305-5307 E-mail: bbaldwin@cmgm.stanford.edu

BALES, ROBERT FREED, social psychologist, educator; b. Ellington, Mo., Mar. 9, 1916; s. Columbus Lee and Ada Lois (Sloan) B.; m. Dorothy Louise Johnson, Sept. 14, 1941. B.A., U. Oreg., 1938, M.S., 1941; M.A., Harvard U., 1943, Ph.D., 1945. Research assoc. sect. on alcohol studies Yale U., 1944-45; instr. sociology Harvard U., Cambridge, Mass., 1945-47, asst. prof. sociology, research assoc. Lab. Social Relations, 1947-51, lectr. sociology, research assoc., 1951-55, assoc. prof., 1955-57, prof. social relations, 1957-86, prof. emeritus, 1986—, dir. Lab. Social Rels., 1960-67, chmn. social psychology program, dept. psychology and social rels., 1970-82; cons. psychology Harvard U. Health Svcs., 1970-82. Vis. lectr. sociology and social psychology U. Mich., summer 1949, Columbia U., summer 1950; lectr. Salzberg Austria Seminar of Am. Studies, summer 1952, 56; Mem. bd. sci. counsellors NIMH, 1957-60 Author: Interaction Process Analysis: A Method for the Study of Small Groups, 1950, The Fixation Factor in Alcohol Addiction, 1980, (with Talcott Parsons, Edward A. Shils) Working Papers in the Theory of Action, 1953, (with Talcott Parsons, et al) Family, Socialization, and Interaction Process, 1955, (with Stephen P. Cohen and Stephen A. Williamson) SYMLOG, A System for the Multiple Level Observation of Groups, 1979, SYMLOG Case Study Kit and Instructions for a Group Self Study, 1980; contbr. to Group Dynamics, Research and Theory, 1953, The SYMLOG Practitioner, 1988, Social Interaction Systems, Theory and measurement, 1999, several other compilations; editor: (with A. Paul Hare and Edgar F. Borgatta) Small Groups, Studies in Social Interaction, 1955; author various instruments and booklets, sr. rsch., cons. SYMLOG Cons. Group, 1983—. Trustee Ella L. Cabot Trust. Mem.: APA Outstanding Contbn. to Leadership and Orgnl. Excellence award Calif. chpt. divsn. of I/O psychology 1999 Disting. Contbn. to Psychology as a Profession award Calif. chpt. 2001, Am. Sociol. Assn., Eastern Sociol. Soc. (pres. 1962—63), Am. Acad. Arts and Scis., Am. Psychol. Soc., Soc. Exptl. Social Psychology, Boston Psychoanalytic Soc. (affiliate). Home and Office: 17990 Bernardo Trails Pl San Diego CA 92128-1505

BALES, ROYAL EUGENE, philosophy educator; b. Pratt, Kans., Sept. 23, 1934; s. Harold Thomas and Gladys (German) B.; m. Flossie Kathleen O'Reilly, Apr. 16, 1960; children— David Scott, Elizabeth Laurel B.Music Edn. cum laude, U. Wichita, 1956, M.A., 1960; Ph.D., Stanford U., 1968. Tchr. music Kans. Pub. Schs., 1956-57, 59-60; instr. philosophy Menlo Coll., Atherton, Calif., 1962-69, prof., 1970-2000, prof. emeritus, 2000—, chmn. social scis. and humanities, 1971-74, dean liberal arts, 1974-79, provost, 1979-87, standing mem. president's adv. council, 1971-87. Vis. fellow Harris-Manchester Coll., Oxford U., 1994, 98; Wong vis. prof. Guangdong U. of Law and Bus., Guangzhou, China, 1999. Contbr. articles to profl. jours. Pres. El Camino Youth Symphony Assn., 1985-87; bd. of govs. Manchester Coll., Oxford, 1994—. Scholar and fellow U. Wichita, 1952-60, Stanford U., 1966-67; prin. investigator NSF, Menlo Coll./Stanford, 1971-72; research grantee Stanford-Warsaw Exchange, Poland, 1969-70. Mem. Am. Philos. Assn., Soc. for Bus. Ethics, Save San Francisco Bay Assn., Phi Mu Alpha Sinfonia. Democrat. Avocations: classical music, designing and constructing furniture. Home: 1255 Sherman Ave Menlo Park CA 94025-6012 Office: Menlo Coll Florence Moore Bldg 1000 El Camino Real Atherton CA 94027-4300 E-mail: rbales@mindspring.com, ebales@menlo.edu

BALKANSKI, ALEXANDRE, investment company executive; B of Physics, Harvard Coll.; M in Bus. Econs., PhD, Harvard U. Founder, pres. Diamond Devices, Inc.; pres, CEO C-Cube Microsystems, Milpitas, Calif.; gen. ptnr. Bench Mark Capital, Menlo Park, 2000—. Office: Bench Mark Capital 2480 San Hill Rd Ste 200 Menlo Park CA 94025

BALL, LAWRENCE, retired physical scientist; b. Albion, N.Y., Aug. 10, 1933; s. Harold Witheral and Gladys (Gibbs) B.; m. Caroline Moran, June 21, 1957; children: Daniel Lawrence, Logan Edward, Stacey Laura Ball Lucero, Ryan Laird (dec.). Diploma, Williston Acad., 1952; BSME, Antioch Coll., 1957; MSc in Elec. Engring., Ohio State U., 1962. Engring. aid Wright Air Devel. Ctr., Dayton, Ohio, 1957-60; engr. Deco Electronics Inc., Boulder, Colo., 1962-66; sr. engr. Westinghouse Rsch. Labs., Boulder, 1966-73, Westinghouse Ocean Rsch. Lab., Annapolis, Md., 1973-74; program mgr. div. geothermal energy U.S. Dept. Energy, Washington, 1974-79, lab. dir. Grand Junction, Colo., 1979-93; ret., 1993; lab. dir. Armstrong Cons., Inc., Grand Junction, Colo., 2000—. Pres. Liberty Cons. Co., Grand Junction, 1984—; emergency coord. dist. 3 Amateur Radio Emergency Svcs., 1995-97. Co-inventor coal mine communications; contbr. articles to profl. jours. Mem. various vol. fire depts., 1954-79, Boulder Reserve Police, 1968-74, sr. patroller Nat. Ski Patrol Sys., Md., Colo., 1973-92, Grand Junction Safety Coun., 1992-98; sr. patroller Amateur Radio Emergency Svcs., 1995—, dist. emergency coord., 1997-99; bd. dirs. Colo. Head Injury Found., chpt. pres., 1989-91. Named Profl. Govt. Employee of Yr., Western Colo. Fed. Exec. Assn., 1991. Mem. Toastmasters Internat. (area gov. 1991-92, divsn. gov. 1992-93, Toastmaster of Yr. Western Colo. 1990, DTM & ATM-S 1994), West Slope Wheelman (charter bd. dirs. 1992-93), Western Colo. Amateur Radio Club, Inc. (pres. 1994-96, bd. dirs. 1996-98), Black Ridge Comml. Site Users Assn. (charter bd. dirs. 1995—, sec. 1997-2001, sec., treas. 1999-2001). Avocations: bicycling, scuba diving (divecon), woodworking, amateur radio (extra class), Bible archaeology.

BALLARD, CLYDE, state legislator; b. Batesville, Ark., June 8, 1936; s. Jeffery C. and Monnie F. Ballard; m. Ruth L. Guthrie, Feb. 6, 1955; children: Jeff, Shawn, Scott. Store mgr., gen. mgr. Peter Rabbit Stores, Wenatchee, Wash., 1955-66; owner Ballard Svcs., Wenatchee, 1967-87; caucus chmn., minority leader Wash. Ho. of Reps., Olympia, 1985-94, spkr. house, 1995-98, co-speaker house, 1999—. Republican. Free Methodist. Home: 1790 N Baker St East Wenatchee WA 98802-4157 Office: PO Box 40600 Olympia WA 98504-0600

BALLARD, LOUIS WAYNE, composer; b. Miami, Okla., July 8, 1931; s. Charles Guthrie and Leona Mae (Quapaw) B.; m. Ruth Sands, Dec. 6, 1965; children by previous marriage: Louis Anthony, Anne Marie, Charles Christopher. B.Mus. and Music Edn., U. Tulsa, 1954; M.Mus., 1962; D.Mus. (hon.), Coll. Santa Fe, 1973. Dir. vocal and instrumental music Nelagoney (Okla.) Public Sch., 1954-56; dir. vocal music Webster High Sch., Tulsa, 1956-58; pvt. music tchr., 1959-62; music dir. Inst. Am. Indian Arts, Santa Fe, 1962-65, dir. performing arts, 1965-69; nat. dir. music edn. curriculum and rev. Bur. Indian Affairs, Washington, 1969-79. Lectr., clinician, 1960—; pres. First Am. Indian Films, Inc., 1969—; disting. vis. prof. music Wm Jewell Coll., Liberty, Mo., 2000—. Composer, Santa Fe, 1979—; guest composer West German Music Festival, Saarbrü, 1986, Musik im 20 Jahrhundert, Ariz. State U., 1992, U. Ill. at Champagne, 1992, Ea. Music Festival, Greensboro, N.C., 1994, 95, 96; gala concert Carnegie Hall, 1992; full concert in Beethoven Chamber Music Hall, Bonn (first Am. composer), 1989; (ballet) Koshare, 1964, The Four Moons, 1967, Maid of the Mist and the Thunderbeings, 1991; (orchl. music) Fantasay Aborigine, Nos. I, II, III, IV, V; (chamber music) Rhapsody for Four Bassoons, Incident at Wounded Knee, Desert Trilogy, Ritmo Indio, Katcina Dances for cello-piano suite; (choral cantatas) The Gods Will Hear, Portrait of Will Rogers, Thus Spake Abraham; (oratorio) Dialogue Differentia text in Latin, Lakota-Sioux, English, Live On, Heart of My Nation (choral cantate with native Am. dialect), Manitoo, Gitche Manitoo (Am. Indian Doxology);

(band works) Nighthawk Keetowa; (percussion) Cecega Ayuwipi, Music for the Earth and the Sky; (guitar) Quetzalcoatl's Coattails, 1992, The Lonely Sentinel, 1993, The Fire Moon (string quartet), A City of Silver, A City of Fire, A City of Light (piano concert pieces), numerous others.; commd. writer Lila Wallace Reader's Digest Arts Ptnrs./Meet the Composer, 1991; commd. writer (opera) Ministry Lower Saxony (Germany), 1993-94; author: The American Indian Sings, Book 1, 1970, Book 2, 1991, American Indian Chants for the Classroom, Oklahoma Indian Chants for the Classroom, also articles. Recipient 1st Marion Nevins MacDowell award chamber music, 1969, Nat. Indian Achievement award, 1972, Catlin Peace Pipe award Nat. Indian Lore Assn., 1976, ASCAP award, 1966-88, Lifetime Music Achievement award First Americans in Arts, 1997; F.B. Parriott grad. fellow, 1969; grantee Ford Found., 1970; grantee Nat. Endowment Arts, 1967, 69, 76, 79; commd. by Martha B. Rockefeller Found., 1969, Am. Composers Orch., 1982, commd. by Ministry Lower Saxony for Opera in Norden Gymnasium, West Germany, 1994. Mem. ASCAP, Music Educators Nat. Conf. (chmn. minority concerns com. for N.Mex. 1976), Am. Symphony Orch. League, Internat. Soc. for Polyaesthetic Music Edn. and Performance (lectr.), Phi Beta Kappa (alumni mem. Beta chpt. Okla. 1999). Lodge: Masons, Scottish Rite (32d degree). Office: PO Box 2072 Santa Fe NM 87504-2072

BALLARD, MELVIN RUSSELL, JR. investment executive, church official; b. Salt Lake City, Oct. 8, 1928; s. Melvin Russell and Geraldine (Smith) B.; m. Barbara Bowen, Aug. 28, 1951; children: Clark, Holly, Meleea, Tamara, Stacey, Brynn, Craig. Student, U. Utah, 1946, 50-52. Sales mgr. Ballard Motor Co., Salt Lake City, 1950-54; investment counselor Salt Lake City, 1954-56; founder, owner, mgr. Russ Ballard Auto, Inc., Salt Lake City, 1956-58, Ballard-Wade Co., 1958-67; owner, mgr. Ballard Investment Co., Salt Lake City, 1962—; mem. Quorum of Twelve, 1979—. Gen. authority LDS Ch., Salt Lake City, 1976—; bd. dirs. Nate-Wade, Inc., Salt Lake City, Silver King Mines, Inc., Salt Lake City, Huntsmand Chem. Co., Salt Lake City; chmn. bd. dirs. Deseret Book Co., Salt Lake City; gen. ptnr. N & R Investment, Salt Lake City, 1958—, Ballard Investment Co., Salt Lake City, 1955—. Bd. dirs. Salt Lake Jr. Achievement, 1978-80; bd. dirs. Freedoms Found., 1978—, David O. McKay Inst. Edn., 1979—; active Coun. Twelve Apostles, 1979. 1st lt. USAR, 1950-57. Mem. Salt Lake Area C. of C. (gov. 1979—). Republican. Office: LDS Church 50 E North Temple Salt Lake City UT 84150-0002

BALLING, ROBERT C., JR. geography educator; b. 1952; Asst. prof. geography U. Nebr., 1979-84; mem. faculty Ariz. State U., 1985—, assoc. prof., prof.; dir. Office of Climatology. Lectr. greenhouse effect debate, Australia, New Zealand, Can., Kuwait, U.S. Author: The Heated Debate: Greenhouse Predictions Versus Climate Reality, 1992; contbr. articles to sci. jours. Office: Ariz State U PO Box 871508 Tempe AZ 85287-1508

BALLINGER, CHARLES KENNETH, information specialist; b. Johnstown, Pa., July 28, 1950; s. Delores Jean (Cool) B.; m. Deb C. Delger, Sept. 14, 1985. Programmer analyst Cowles Pub. Co., Spokane, Wash., 1975-78; systems analyst Old Nat. Bank, Spokane, 1978-82; software engr. ISC System, Spokane, 1982; micro computer analyst Acme Bus. Computers, Spokane, 1982-85; info. ctr. analyst Wash. Water Power Co., Spokane, 1985-92; office automation analyst EDS Corp., Spokane, 1992-96, software engr.-mini/micro, 1996-98, info. analyst for client-server human resources info. sys., 1998-2000, info. analyst for energy trading divsn., 2000—. Cons. IDP Co., Spokane, 1978—. Contbr. articles to profl. jours. Served with Signal Corps, U.S. Army, 1968-71. Mem. IEEE (assoc.), Spokane Health Users Group (pres. 1979-83). Avocations: software development, motorcycling, boating, shooting, amateur radio. Home: 3810 S Havana St Spokane WA 99223-6006 Office: Avista Energy 201 W North River Dr Spokane WA 99201 E-mail: cballin@cet.com, cballinger@avistaenergy.com

BALLINGER, JAMES K. art museum executive; b. Kansas City, Mo., July 7, 1949; s. Robert Eugene and Yvonne (Davidson) B.; m. Nina Lundgaard, Aug. 21, 1971; children— Erin, Cameron B.A., U. Kans., 1972, M.A., 1974. Gallery coordinator Tucson Art Ctr., 1973; registrar U. Kans., Lawrence, 1973-74; curator collections Phoenix Art Mus., 1974-81, asst. dir., 1981, dir., 1982—. Author: (exhbn. catalogues) Beyond the Endless River, 1980, Visitors to Arizona 1846 to 1980, 1981, Peter Hurd, 1983, The Popular West, 1982, Thomas Moran, 1986, Frederick Remington, 1989. Bd. dirs. Balboa Art Conservation Ctr. Fellow Am. Assn. Mus. Dirs. (bd. dirs.), Western Assn. Art Museums; mem. Central Ariz. Mus. Assn. (v.p. 1983) Avocations: hiking; basketball; traveling. Home: 5331 E Pinchot Ave Phoenix AZ 85018-8039 Office: Phoenix Art Mus 1625 N Central Ave Phoenix AZ 85004-1685

BALLMER, STEVE, software company executive; Degree in applied math. and econs., Harvard U.; postgrad., Stanford U. Asst. product mgr. Procter and Gamble; v.p. mktg., v.p. corp. staffs, sr. v.p. syss. software Microsoft Corp., Redmond, Wash., 1980—, exec. v.p. sales and support, CEO WA, 2000—. Mem. exec. com. Microsoft. Active bd. overseers Harvard U., adv. coun. Stanford Bus. Sch. Avocations: exercise, jogging, playing basketball. Office: Microsoft Corp 1 Microsoft Way Redmond WA 98052-8300

BALMER, THOMAS ANCIL, lawyer; b. Longview, Wash., Jan. 31, 1952; s. Donald Gordon and Elisabeth Clare (Hill) B.; m. Mary Louise McClintock, Aug. 25, 1984; children: Rebecca Louise, Paul McClintock. AB, Oberlin Coll., 1974; JD, U. Chgo., 1977. Bar: Mass. 1977, D.C. 1981, U.S. Dist. Ct. Mass. 1977, Oreg. 1982, U.S. Dist. Ct. Oreg. 1982, U.S. Ct. Appeals (9th cir.) 1982, U.S. Ct. Appeals (D.C. cir.) 1983, U.S. Supreme Ct. 1987. Assoc. Choate, Hall & Stewart, Boston, 1977-79, Wald, Harkrader & Ross, Washington, 1980-82; trial atty. antitrust div. U.S. Dept. Justice, Washington, 1979-80; assoc. Lindsay, Hart, Neil & Weigler, Portland, Oreg., 1982-84, ptnr., 1985-90, Ater Wynne LLP, Portland, 1990-93, 97—; dep. atty. gen. State of Oregon, Salem, 1993-97. Adj. prof. of law Northwestern Sch. Law Lewis and Clark Coll., 1983-84, 90-92. Contbr. articles to law jours. Active mission and outreach com. United Ch. of Christ, Portland, 1984-87, Met. Svc. Dist. Budget Com., Portland, 1988-90; bd. dirs. Multnomah County Legal Aid Svc., Inc., 1989-93, chair 1992-93; bd. dirs. Chamber Music Northwest, 1997—, Classroom Law Project, 2000—. Mem. ABA, Oreg. Bar Assn. (chmn. antitrust sect. 1986-87, mem. fed. practice and procedure com. 1999—). Democrat. Home: 2521 NE 24th Ave Portland OR 97212-4831 Office: Ater Wynne LLP 222 SW Columbia St Ste 1800 Portland OR 97201-6618

BALMUTH, MICHAEL A. retail executive; With Bamberger's, Karen Austin Petites, Bon Marche, Seattle; joined Ross Stores, 1989, various positions including sr. v.p., gen. merchandise mgr., exec. v.p. merchandising, 1993-96, CEO, vice chmn., 1996—. Office: 8333 Central Ave Newark CA 94560

BALOIAN, EDWARD, food products executive; b. 1921; With Charles Baloian Co., Fresno, Calif., 1946-86; v.p. Balo Packing Co., Inc., Fresno, 1978—; chmn. bd. dirs. Baloian Packing Co., Fresno, 1985—. Office: Baloian Packing Co 324 N Fruit Ave Fresno CA 93706-1420

BALOIAN, TIMOTHY, food products executive; b. 1952; s. Edward Baloian. Pres. Balo Packing Co., Fresno, 1978—, Baloian Packing Co., Fresno, 1985—. Office: Baloian Packing Co Inc 324 N Fruit Ave Fresno CA 93706-1420

BALSWICK, JACK ORVILLE, social science educator; Asst. prof. sociology Wis. State U., 1967, U. Ga., 1968-71, assoc. prof., 1972-78, prof., 1978-82; prof. sociology and family devel. Fuller Theol. Sem., Pasadena, Calif., dir. rsch. marriage and family ministries. Author (with wife, Judith K. Balswick): The Family, 1989, Social Problems, 1990. Office: Fuller Theol Sem Dept Marriage and Family Mins 180 N Oakland Ave Sch Psycholo Pasadena CA 91182-0001

BALTAKE, JOE, film critic; b. Camden, N.J., 16 Sept. s. Joseph John and Rose Clara (Bearint) B.; m. Susan Shapiro Hale. BA, Rutgers U., 1967. Film critic Gannett Newspapers (suburban), 1969, Phila. Daily News, 1970-85; movie editor Inside Phila., 1986—; film critic The Sacramento Bee, 1987—. Leader criticism workshop Phila. Writer's Conf., 1977-79; film critic. Contbg. editor: Screen World, 1973-87 ; author: The Films of Jack Lemmon, 1977, updated, 1986; contbr. articles to Films in Rev., 1969—, broadcast criticism for Prism Cable TV, 1985; cons. Jack Lemmon: American Film Institute Life Achievement Award, 1987, Jack Lemmon: A Life in the Movies, 1990. Recipient Motion Picture Preview Group award for criticism, 1986, citation Phila. Mag., 1985, First Pl. commentary award Soc. of Profl. Journalists, 1995. Mem. Nat. Soc. Film Critics. Office: Sacramento Bee 2100 Q St Sacramento CA 95816-6899

BALTIMORE, DAVID, university president, microbiologist, educator; b. N.Y.C., Mar. 7, 1938; s. Richard I. and Gertrude (Lipschitz) B.; m. Alice S. Huang, Oct. 5, 1968; 1 dau., Teak. BA with high honors in Chemistry, Swarthmore Coll., 1960; postgrad., MIT, 1960-61; PhD, Rockefeller U., 1964. Research assoc. Salk Inst. Biol. Studies, La Jolla, Calif., 1965-68; assoc. prof. microbiology MIT, Cambridge, 1968-72, prof. biology, 1972-95, Ivan R. Cottrell prof. molecular biology and immunology, 1994-97, inst. prof., 1995-97, Am. Cancer Soc. prof. microbiology, 1973-83, 94-97, dir. Whitehead Inst. Biomed. Rsch., 1982-90; pres. Rockefeller U., N.Y.C., 1990-91, prof., 1990-94; pres. Calif. Inst. Tech., Pasadena, 1997—. Mem. editorial bd. Jour. Molecular Biology, 1971-73, Jour. Virology, 1969-90, Sci., 1986-98, New Eng. Jour. Medicine, 1989-94. Bd. govs. Weizmann Inst. Sci., Israel; bd. dirs. Life Sci. Rsch. Found.; co-chmn. Commn. on a Nat. Strategy of AIDS; ad hoc program adv. com. on complex genome, NIH; mem. office AIDS rsch. adv. coun. NIH, chair vaccine adv. com., 1997—. Recipient Gustav Stern award in virology, 1970; Warren Triennial prize Mass. Gen. Hosp., 1971; Eli Lilly and Co. award in microbiology and immunology, 1971; Nat. Acad. Scis. U.S. Steel award in molecular biology, 1974; Gairdner Found. ann. award, 1974; Nobel prize in physiology or medicine, 1975, Nat. medal of sci., 1999, Warren Alpert Found. prize, 2000. Fellow AAAS, Am. Med. Writers Assn. (hon.), Am. Acad. Microbiology; mem. NAS, Am. Acad. Arts and Scis., Inst. Medicine, Am. Philos. Soc., Pontifical Acad. Scis., Royal Soc. (Eng.) (fgn.), French Acad. Scis. (fgn. assoc.). Office: Calif Inst Tech 1200 E California Blvd Pasadena CA 91125-0001

BALTZ, PATRICIA ANN (PANN BALTZ), elementary education educator; b. Dallas, June 20, 1949; d. Richard Parks and Ruth Eileen (Hartschuh) Langford; m. William Monroe Baltz, Sept. 6, 1969; 1 childm Kenneth Chandler. Student, U. Redlands, 1967-68; BA in English Lit. cum laude, UCLA, 1971. Cert. tchr. K-8, Calif. Tchr. 4th grade Arcadia (Calif.) Unified Sch. Dist., 1972-74, 92—, substitute tchr., 1983-85, tchr. 3dr grade, 1985-87, tchr. 6th grade, 1987-90, tchr. 4th and 5th grade multiage, 1990—. Sci. mentor tchr. Arcadia Unified Sch. Dist., 1991-94; mentor Tech. Ctr. Silicon Valley, San Jose, Calif., 1991. Tchr. rep. PTA, Arcadia, 1980-93; mem. choir, children's sermon team, elder Arcadia Presbyn. Ch., 1980-93; chaperone, vol. Pasadena (Calif.) Youth Symphony Orch., 1988-90; vol. Am. Heart Assn., 1990-92. Recipient Outstanding Gen. Elem. Tchr. award, Outstanding Tchr. of the Yr. award Disney's Am. Tchr. Awards, 1993, Calif. Tchr. of Yr. award Calif. State Dept. Edn., 1993, Georgie award Girl Scouts of Am., 1993, The Self Esteem Task Force award L.A. County Task Force to Promote Self-Esteem & Personal & Social Responsibility, 1993, Profl. Achievement award UCLA Alumni Assn.; apptd. to Nat. Edn. Rsch. Policies & Priorities Bd., U.S. Sec. Edn. Richard Riley; Pann Baltz Mission Possible Scholar named in her honor. Mem. NEA, Nat. Sci. Tchrs. Assn., Calif. Tchr. Assn., Arcadia Tchrs. Assn. Avocations: reading, singing, calligraphy, book-making, computers. Home: 1215 S 3rd Ave Arcadia CA 91006-4205 Office: Arcadia Unified Sch Dist Camino Grove Elem Sch 700 Camino Grove Ave Arcadia CA 91006-4438

BALZHISER, RICHARD EARL, research and development company executive; b. Wheaton, Ill., May 27, 1932; s. Frank E. and Esther K. (Merrill Werner) B.; m. Christine Karnuth, 1951; children: Gary, Robert, Patricia, Michele. B.S. in Chem. Engring., U. Mich., 1955, M.S. in Nuclear Engring., 1956, Ph.D. in Chem. Engring., 1961. Mem. faculty U. Mich., Ann Arbor, 1961-67; White House fellow, spl. asst. to sec. Dept. Def., Washington, 1967-68; chmn. dept. chem. engring. U. Mich., 1970-71; assoc. dir. energy, environ. and natural resources White House Office of Sci. and Tech., Washington, 1971-73; dir. fossil fuel and advanced systems Electric Power Rsch. Inst., Palo Alto, Calif., 1973-79, sr. v.p. R&D, 1979-87, exec. v.p. R&D, 1987-88, pres., chief exec. officer, 1988-96, pres. emeritus, 1996—. Bd. dirs. Reliant Energy, Electro Source, Aerospace Corp.; mem. adv. bd. Nat. Renewable Energy Lab.; mem. pres. com. on sci. and tech. energy studies I and II, Pres.'s Com. Sci. & Tech. Energy Studies, 1997-99. Co-author: Chemical Engineering Thermodynamics, 1972, Engineering Thermodynamics, 1977. Mem. Ann Arbor City Coun., 1965-67, mayor pro tem, 1967. Mem. Nat. Acad. Engring. Lutheran. Office: Electric Power Rsch Inst 3412 Hillview Ave Palo Alto CA 94304-1344 Fax: 650-855-2090. E-mail: rbalzhis@epri.com

BAMBURG, JAMES ROBERT, biochemistry educator; b. Chgo., Aug. 20, 1943; s. Leslie H. and Rose A. (Abrahams) B.; m. Alma Y. Vigo, June 7, 1970 (div. Dec. 1984); children: Eric Gregory, Leslie Ann; m. Laurie S. Minamide, June 22, 1985. BS in Chemistry, U. Ill., 1965; PhD, U. Wis., 1969. Project assoc. U. Wis., Madison, 1968-69; postdoctoral fellow Stanford U., Palo Alto, Calif., 1969-71; from asst. to full prof. Colo. State U., Ft. Collins, 1971—, acad. coordinator cell and molecular biol. program, 1975-78, interim chmn. dept. biochemistry, 1982-85, 88-89, assoc. dir. neuronal growth and devel., 1986-90, dir. neuronal growth and devel., 1990-96, assoc. chmn., 1996—. Vis. prof. MRC Molecular Biol. Lab., Cambridge, Eng., 1978-79, MRC Cell Biophysics Unit, London, 1985-86, Children's Med. Rsch. Inst., U. Sydney, Australia, 1992-93, U. Calif. San Diego, 1999-2000; mem., chmn. NIH Biomed. Scis. Study Sect., Bethesda, Md., 1980-85; ad hoc mem. Physiol. Chem. Study Sec., 1997, Molecular Devel. Cell Neurosci., 1998-99, 2001, Cell Biol. Function, 2001â; mem. adv. bd. Macromolecular Resources, 1999—, Boulder Lab. 3D Fine STructure, 1994—, Alaska Basic Neurosci. Program, 2000—. Contbr. articles to sci. jours. Fellow NSF, 1964-65, Nat. Multiple Sclerosis Soc., 1969-71, J.S. Guggenheim Found., 1978-79, Fogarty Ctr., 1985-86, 92-93, W. Evans Vis. scholar U. Otago, N.Z., 1991; recipient Disting. Svc. award Colo. State U. 1989, Outstanding Adviser award, 1996. Mem. Am. Chem. Soc., Am. Soc. Cell Biology, Am. Soc. Biochem. Mol. Biol., Internat. Neurochem. Soc., Sigma Xi (pres. CSU chpt. 1989). E-mail. Home: 2125 Sandstone Dr Fort Collins CO 80524-1825 Office: Colo State U Dept Biochemistry Mrb Rm 235 Fort Collins CO 80523-0001 E-mail: jbamburg@lamar.colostate.edu

BANCEL, MARILYN, fund raising management consultant; b. Glen Ridge, N.J., June 15, 1947; d. Paul and Joan Marie (Spangler) B.; m. Rik Myslewski, Nov. 20, 1983; children: Carolyn, Roxanne. BA in English with distinction, Ind. U., 1969. Cert. fund raising exec. Ptnr. The Sultan's Shirt Tail, Gemlik, Turkey, 1969-72; prodn. mgr. High Country Co., San Francisco, 1973-74; pub. Bay Arts Rev., Berkeley, Calif., 1976-79; dir. devel. Oakland (Calif.) Symphony Orch., 1979-81; assoc. dir. devel. Exploratorium, San Francisco, 1981-86, dir. devel., 1986-91; prin. Fund Devel. Counsel, San Francisco, 1991-93; v.p. The Oram Group, Inc., San Francisco, 1993—. Co-chmn. capital campaign com. Synergy Sch., San Francisco, 1995-2000; adj. prof. U. San Francisco, 1993—. Author: Preparing Your Capital Campaign, 2000. Mem. adv. bd. Mus. City of San Francisco, 1995—, San Francisco Bot. Gardens, 1998-99. Fellow U. Strasberg, France, 1968. Mem. Assn. Fundraising Profls. (bd. mem. Golden Gate chpt. 1996-98), Am. Assn. Fund Raising Counsel, Devel. Execs. Roundtable, Phi Beta Kappa. Democrat. Avocation: gardening. Office: The Oram Group 44 Page St Ste 604C San Francisco CA 94102-5972

BANCROFT, GEORGE MICHAEL, chemical physicist, educator; b. Saskatoon, Sask., Can., Apr. 3, 1942; s. Fred and Florence Jean B.; m. Joan Marion MacFarlane, Sept. 16, 1967; children: David Kenneth, Catherine Jean. B.Sc., U. Man., 1963; M.Sc., 1964; Ph.D., Cambridge (Eng.) U., 1967, M.A., 1970, Sc.D. (E.W. Staecie fellow), 1979. Univ. demonstrator Cambridge U.; then teaching fellow Christ Coll.; mem. faculty U. Western Ont., London, now prof. dept. chemistry; dir. Can. Light Source. Author: Mössbauer Spectroscopy, 1973; also articles in photoelectron spectroscopy, synchrotron radiation studies; revs. Mössbauer Spectroscopy. Recipient Harrison Meml. prize, 1972, Meldola medal, 1972, Rutherford Meml. medal, 1980, Alcan award, 1990, Herzberg award, 1991, Can. Inst. of Chemistry Palladium medal, 1996, Morley medal Am. Chem. Soc., 1998; Guggenheim fellow, 1982-83. Fellow Royal Soc. Can.; mem. Royal Soc. Chemistry, Can. Chem. Soc., Can. Geol. Soc., Can. Physics Soc. Mem. United Ch. Can. Clubs: Curling, Tennis (London). Office: Can Light Source 107 N Univ of Saskatchewan Saskatoon SK Canada S7N 5C6 E-mail: bancroft@cls.usask.ca

BANCROFT, JAMES RAMSEY, lawyer, business executive; b. Ponca City, Okla., Nov. 13, 1919; s. Charles Ramsey and Maude (Viersen) B.; m. Jane Marguerite Oberfell, May 28, 1944; children: John Ramsey, Paul Marshall, Sara Jane Bancroft Clair AB, U. Calif., Berkeley, 1940, MBA, 1941; JD, Hastings Coll. Law, 1949. Bar: Calif. 1950; CPA, Calif. With McLaren, Goode, West & Co., CPAs, San Francisco, 1946-50; ptnr. Bancroft, Avery & McAlister, San Francisco, 1950-86, of counsel, 1986-92; owner, mgr. Bancroft Vineyard, 1982—; of counsel Bancroft & McAlister, San Francisco, 1992—; mng. ptnr. Bancroft Investments, San Francisco, 1980—; pres. Madison Properties, Inc., San Francisco, 1967-98, Adams Properties, Inc., 1969-79, Adams-Western Inc., 1969-78; chmn. bd. Adams Capital Mgmt. Co., 1987-88, pres., 1988—; chmn. bd. UNC Resources, 1978-82, dir., 1984-85; chmn. bd. United Nuclear Corp., Falls Church, Va., 1972-82, Madison Capital Inc., San Francisco, 1986-93. Former pres. Suisun Conservation Fund; former dir. Suisun Resource Conservation Dist.; former trustee Dean Witter Found., 1952-94; pres. Harvey L. Sorensen Found.; bd. dirs. Calif. Urology Found.; former dir. San Francisco Found for Rsch. and Edn. Orthopedic Surgery; trustee, former chmn. Pacific Vascular Rsch. Found. Lt. USNR, 1942-46. Mem. ABA, Confrérie des Chevaliers du Tastevin, Bohemian Club, Pacific Union Club, Order of Golf, Phi Beta Kappa. Office: 221 Main St Ste 440 San Francisco CA 94105-1913

BANDER, MYRON, physics educator, university dean; b. Belzyce, Poland, Dec. 11, 1937; came to U.S., 1949, naturalized, 1955; s. Elias and Regina (Zielonka) B.; m. Carol Heimberg, Aug. 20, 1967. B.A., Columbia U., 1958, M.A., 1959, Ph.D., 1962. Postdoctoral fellow CERN, 1962-63; research assoc. Stanford Linear Accelerator Center, 1963-66; mem. faculty U. Calif., Irvine, 1966—, prof. physics, 1974—, dean phys. scis., 1980-86; chair dept. physics, 1992-95. Sloan Found. fellow, 1967-69 Fellow Am. Phys. Soc. Office: U Calif Irvine CA 92697-0001 E-mail: mbander@uci.edu

BANDURA, ALBERT, psychologist, educator; b. Mundare, Alta., Can., Dec. 4, 1925; came to U.S., 1949, naturalized, 1956; m. Virginia Varns; 2 children. B.A., U. B.C., 1949, D.Sc. (hon.), 1979, M.A. in Psychology, U. Iowa, 1951, Ph.D. in Psychology, 1952. Prof. psychology Stanford U., 1953—, David Starr Jordan prof. social sci. in psychology, 1973—. Author: (with R.H. Walters) Adolescent Aggression, 1959, (with R.H. Walters) Social Learning and Personality Development, 1963, Principles of Behavior Modification, 1969, Aggression, 1973, Social Learning Theory, 1977, Social Foundations of Thought and Action: A Social Cognitive Theory, 1986; editor: Psychological Modeling: Conflicting Theories, 1971, Self-Efficacy in Changing Societies, 1995, Self-Efficacy: The Exercise of Control, 1997. Guggenheim fellow, 1972 Fellow Am. Acad. Arts and Scis., Ctr. Adv. Study in Behavioral Sci.; mem. Am. Psychol. Soc. (William James award 1989), Inst. Medicine NAS, Am. Psychol. Assn. (Disting. Scientist award divsn. 12, 1972, Disting. Sci. Contbn. award 1980, pres. 1974), Calif. Psychol. Assn. (Disting. Scientist award 1973, Lifetime Disting. Contbr. award 1998), Western Psychol. Assn. (pres. 1980), Internat. Soc. Research on Aggression (Disting. Contbn. award 1980), Soc. Child Devel., Inst. of Medicine, Can. Psychol. Assn. (hon. pres. 1999). Office: Stanford U Dept Psychology Stanford CA 94305-2130 E-mail: Bandura@psych.Stanford.edu

BANGERTER, VERN, secondary education educator; Physics tchr., chmn. dept. Timpview High Sch., Provo, Utah, 1998—. Recipient Gov.'s award, 1992, Pres.'s award, 1994, Huntsman Edn. award, 1995, Disting. Physics Tchr. from Utah award Am. Phys. Soc., 1999, Golden Apple award PTA, 2000; Tandy Tech. scholar, 1992; named Utah State Tchr. of Yr., US West, 1993. Office: Timpview High Sch 3570 N 650 E Provo UT 84604-4675

BANK, RON, principal; Prin. Jacoby Creek Elem. Sch., Bayside, Calif., 1982—. Recipient Elem. Sch. Recognition award U.S. Dept. Edn., 1989-90. Office: Jacoby Creek Elem Sch 1617 Old Arcata Rd Bayside CA 95524-9301

BANKS, ERNEST (ERNIE BANKS), retired professional baseball player; b. Dallas, Jan. 31, 1931; s. Eddie B. Student, Northwestern U. Baseball player Kansas City Monarchs (Negro Am. League), 1950-51, 53, Chgo. Cubs, 1953-71, mgr. group sales, to 1982, 1st base coach, to 1989; spokesperson New World Van Lines, 1984—; now ret. Formerly co-owner, v.p. Bob Nelson-Ernie Banks Ford, Inc., Chgo.; with Associated Films Promotions, L.A., 1982-84. Author: (with Jim Enright) Mr. Cub. Past mem. bd. Chgo. Transit Authority; active Boy Scouts Am., YMCA. Served with AUS, 1951-53, Europe. Named most valuable player Nat. League, 1958, 59; recipient awards from Fans, 1969, awards from Press Club, 1969, awards from Jr. C. of C., 1971; inducted into Tex. Sports Hall Fame, 1971, Baseball Hall of Fame, 1977; mem. Nat. League All-Star Team, 1957-70; hold major league record for most career grand slam home runs. Office: Ernie Banks Internat Inc 520 Washington Blvd Ste 284 Marina Dl Rey CA 90292-5442

BANKS, JAMES ALBERT, educational research director, educator; b. Marianna, Ark., Sept. 24, 1941; s. Matthew and Lula (Holt) B.; m. Cherry Ann McGee, Feb. 15, 1969; children: Angela Marie, Patricia Ann. AA, Chgo. City Coll., 1963; BE, Chgo. State U., 1964; MA (NDEA fellow 1966-69), Mich. State U., 1967, PhD, 1969; LHD, Bank St. Coll. Edn., 1993, U. Alaska, Fairbanks, 2000. Tchr. elementary sch. Joliet, Ill., 1965, Francis W. Parker Sch., Chgo., 1965-66; asst. prof. edn. U. Wash., Seattle, 1969-71, assoc. prof., 1971-73, prof., 1973—, Russell F. Stark univ. prof., 2001—, chmn. curriculum and instrn., 1982-87; dir. Ctr. for Multicultural Edn., Seattle, 1991—. Vis. prof. edn. U. Mich., 1975, Monash U., Australia, 1985, U. Warwick, Eng., 1988, U. Minn., 1991; vis. lectr. U. Southampton, Eng., 1989, Harry F. and Alva K. Ganders disting. lectr.

Syracuse U., 1989; disting. scholar lectr. Kent State U., 1978, U. Ariz., 1979, Ind. U., 1983; vis. scholar Brit. Acad., 1983; Sachs lectr. Tchrs. Coll. Columbia U., 1996; Tyler eminent scholar chair Fla. State U., 1998; Carl and Alice Daeufer lectr. U. Hawaii, Manoa, 1999; com. examiners Ednl. Testing Svc., 1974-77; nat. adv. coun. on ethnic heritage studies, U.S. Office Edn., 1975-78; com. on fed. role in ednl. rsch. NAS, 1991-92, mem. com. on developing a rsch. agenda on edn. of ltd. proficient and bilingual students, 1995-97; mem. bd. on children, youth and families NRC and Inst. of Medicine/NAS. Author: Teaching Strategies for Ethnic Studies, 1975, 6th edit., 1997, Teaching Strategies for the Social Studies, 1973, 5th edit., 1999, Teaching the Black Experience, 1970, Multiethnic Education: Practices and Promises, 1977, An Introduction to Multicultural Education, 1994, 2d edit., 1999, Educating Citizens in A Multicultural Soc., 1997, (with Cherry Ann Banks) March Toward Freedom: A History of Black Americans, 1970, 2d edit., 1974, rev. 2nd edit., 1978, Multiethnic Education: Theory and Practice, 1981, 3rd edit., 1994, 4th edit., (new title) Cultural Diversity and Education: Foundations, Curriculum, and Teaching, 2001, (with others) Curriculum Guidlines for Multicultural Education, 1976, rev. edit., 1992, We Americans: Our History and People, 2 vols., 1982; contbg. author Internat. Ency. of Edn., 1985, Handbook of Research on Teacher Education, 1990, Handbook of Research on Social Studies Teaching and Learning, 1991, Encyclopedia of Ednl. Rsch., 1992, Handbook of Research on the Education of Young Children, 1993, Review of Research in Education, vol. 19, 1993; editor: Black Self Concept, 1972, Teaching Ethnic Studies: Concepts and Strategies, 1973, (with William W. Joyce) Teaching Social Studies to Culturally Different Children, 1971, Teaching the Language Arts to Culturally Different Children, 1971, Education in the 80's: Multiethnic Education, 1981, (with James Lynch) Multicultural Education in Western Societies, 1986, (with C. Banks) Multicultural Education: Issues and Perspectives, 1989, 3d edit., 1997, 4th edit., 2001, Handbook of Research on Multicultural Education, 1995, Multicultural Education, Transformative Knowledge, and Action, 1996; editorial bd. Jour. of Tch. Edn., 1985-89, Coun. Interracial Books for Children Bull., 1982-92, Urban Edn., 1991-96, Tchrs. Coll. Record, 1998—, Multicultural Perspectives, 2000—; contbr. articles to profl. jours. Recipient Outstanding Young Man award Wash. State Jaycees, 1975, Outstanding Service in Edn. award Seattle U. Black Student Union, 1985, Pres.'s award TESOL, 1998; Spencer fellow Nat. Acad. Edn., 1973-76; Kellogg fellow, 1980-83; Rockefeller Found. fellow, 1980 Mem. ASCD (bd dirs. 1976-79, Disting. lectr. 1986, Disting. scholar, lectr. 1994, 97), Nat. Acad. Edn., Nat. Coun. Social Studies (bd. dirs. 1973-74, 80-85, pres. 1982), Internat. Assn. Intercultural Edn. (editl. bd.), Social Sci. Edn. Consortium (bd. dirs. 1976-79), Am. Ednl. Rsch. Assn. (Disting. scholar/rschr. on minority edn. 1986, Rsch. Review award 1994, com. on role and status of minorities in edn. rsch. 1992-94, mem. publs. com. 1995-96; Disting. Career Contbn. award, 1996; pres.-elect 1996-97, pres. 1997-98, exec. bd. 1998-99), Phi Delta Kappa, Phi Kappa Phi, Golden Key Nat. Honor Soc., Kappa Delta Pi (laureate chpt.). Office: U Wash 110 Miller Hall PO Box 353600 Seattle WA 98195-3600

BANKS, ROBIN, broadcast executive; Dir. ops. Metro Network News, L.A., 1999—. Office: Metro Network News 6420 Wilshire Blvd Fl 4 Los Angeles CA 90048-5502

BANNER, BOB, television producer, director; b. Ennis, Tex., Aug. 15, 1921; s. Robert James and Viola (Culbertson) B.; m. Alice Jane Baird, Jan. 14, 1946; children— Baird Allen, Robert James, Charles Moore. B.B.A., So. Meth. U., 1943; M.A., Northwestern U., 1948. Pres. Bob Banner Assocs., 1958—. Vis. prof. So. Meth. U. Dir. Garroway-at-Large, NBC-TV; producer, dir. Fred Waring Show, CBS-TV; dir. Omnibus; TV producer, pres., Bob Banner Assos.; TV shows include (series) The Uptown Comedy Club, It's Showtime at the Apollo, Garroway At Large, Fred Waring Show, Don Ho, Omnibus, Jr. Almost Anything Goes, Almost Anything Goes, Candid Camera, Carol Burnett Show, Garry Moore Show, Dinah Shore Chevy Show, Kraft Summer Music Hall, Solid Gold, Star Search, It's Showtime at the Apollo, The Uptown Comedy Club, Real Kids, Real Adventures; (spls.) Perry Como Holiday Spls., Carnegie Hall Salutes Jack Benny, Peggy Fleming Holiday Spl., Amazing Music Spls., Happy Birthday, George Gershwin, 1996, Julie & Carol at Carnegie Hall, Ford Motor Co.'s 75th Ann., Am. West of John Ford, A Spl. Sesame St. Christmas; spls. starring Bob Hope, Julie Andrews, Andy Williams; (movies) My Sweet Charlie, My Husband is Missing, Warning Shot, Journey from Darkness, The Darker Side of Terror, If Things were Different, Yes Virginia There Is A Santa Claus, 1991, Crash Landing, 1992, With Murder In Mind, 1992, The Sea Wolf, 1993. Recipient 15 Emmy awards, 11 Christopher awards, 3 Peabody awards. Mem. Acad. of TV Arts and Scis. Presbyn. Office: 535 S Curson Ave Apt 9L Los Angeles CA 90036-5297

BANSE, KARL, retired oceanography educator; b. Koenigsberg Pr., East Prussia, Germany, Feb. 20, 1929; came to U.S., 1960, naturalized; s. Karl and Wally B. PhD in Oceanography, U. Kiel, Fed. Republic Germany, 1955; Dr. honoris causa, U. Kiel, Germany, 1995. Postdoctoral fellow in marine sci. U. Kiel, 1955-57; Govt. India scholar Central Marine Fish Research Sta., India, 1958-60; asst. prof. oceanography U. Wash., Seattle, 1960-63, assoc. prof. oceanography, 1963-66, prof. oceanography, 1966-95, retired, 1995. Recipient Lifetime Achievement award ASLO, 1998. Fellow Marine Biology Assn. India. Office: U Wash Sch Oceanography Box 357940 Seattle WA 98195-7940

BARAD, JILL ELIKANN, family products company executive; b. N.Y.C., May 23, 1951; d. Lawrence Stanley and Corinne (Schuman) Elikann; m. Thomas Kenneth Barad, Jan. 28, 1979; children: Alexander David, Justin Harris. BA English and Psychology, Queens Coll., 1973. Asst. prod. mgr. mktg. Coty Cosmetics, N.Y.C., 1976-77, prod. mgr. mktg., 1977; account exec. Wells Rich Greene Advt. Agy., L.A., 1978-79; product mgr. mktg. Mattel Toys, Inc., L.A., 1981-82, dir. mktg., 1982-83, v.p. mktg., 1983-85, sr. v.p. mktg., 1985-86, sr. v.p. product devel., 1986, exec. v.p. product design and devel., exec. v.p. mktg. and worldwide product devel., 1988-89; pres. girls and activity toys div. Mattel Toys, Inc. (name now Mattel, Inc.), L.A., 1989-90; pres. Mattel USA, 1990-92; pres., COO Mattel, Inc., 1992-97, pres., CEO, 1997, chmn., CEO, 1997-2000. Bd. dirs. Pixar Animation Studios, Leap Wireless Internat.; bd. fellows Claremont U. Ctr. and Grad. Sch. Bd. govs. Town Hall of Los Angeles; trustee emeritus Queens Coll. Found.; chair exec. adv. bd. Children Affected by AIDS Found.; bd. advs. Children's Scholarship Fund, Catalyst, The For All Kids Found., Inc. Exec. bd. Med. Scis. UCLA,

BARAN, PAUL, computer executive; b. Poland, Apr. 29, 1926; came to U.S., 1928; m. Evelyn Murphy, 1955; 1 child, David. BSEE, Drexel U., 1949; MS in Engring., UCLA, 1959; DSc in Engring. (hon.), Drexel U., 1997; PhD (hon.), RAND Grad. Sch., 2000. With Eckert Mauchly Computer Co., 1949, Rosen Engring. Products Co., 1950-54; systems group Hughes Aircraft Co., 1955-59; with RAND Corp., 1959-64; co-founder Inst. for Future, 1968; founder Cabledata Assocs., 1972; co-founder Equatorial Comm., 1978-80; founder Packet Techs., 1980, Telebit, 1980, Metricom, Inc., 1985; founder, chmn. bd. Com21, Inc., Milpitas, Calif., 1992 [illegible] 1997—; trustee IEEE History Ctr., 2000—, Charles Babbage Inst., U. Minn., 2000—. Recipient Edwin H. Armstrong award IEEE Comms. Soc., 1987, First Annual award ACM Spl. Interest Group in Comms., 1990, [illegible] Internat., 1991, Centennial 100 medal Drexel U., 1992, Pioneer award Electronic Frontier Found., 1993, Computers and Comm. Found. award 1996 award NAL, 1990, Bower award Franklin Inst., 2001; named Entrepreneur of Yr. Tech., Silicon Valley Bus. Jour., 1999. Fellow AAAS, IEEE (life, Alexander Graham Bell medal 1990, Centennial medal 2000, Internet award 2000), Franklin Inst. (2001 Bower award and prize achievement in sci. 2001). Achievements include design of first doorway gun detector; inventor packet switching. Home: 83 James Ave Atherton CA 94027-2009 E-mail: paul@baran.com

BARATTA, ROBERT M. holding company executive; b. 1930; Pres., CEO UOP, Inc.; officer Katy Industries, Inc., 1990-2000, exec. v.p., 1995-2000, pres., CEO, dir. Colo., 2000—. Office: Ste 300 6300 S Syracuse Way Englewood CO 80111-6723 Office Fax: 303-290-9344

BARBAGELATA, ROBERT DOMINIC, lawyer; b. San Francisco, Jan. 9, 1925; s. Dominic Joseph and Jane Zeffra (Frugoli) B.; m. Doris V. Chatfield, June 8, 1956; children: Patricia Victoria, Robert Norman, Michael Alan. B.S., U. San Francisco, 1947, J.D., 1950. Bar: Calif. bar 1950, U.S. Supreme Ct. bar 1964. Pvt. practice, San Francisco, 1950—; judge pro-tem San Francisco County Superior Ct., 1992-95. Lectr. U. San Francisco Law Sch., Pacific Med. Center. Contbr. to legal jours. Served with USNR, 1943-46. Mem. Calif. State Bar, Calif. Trial Lawyers Assn. (lect., v.p.), Am. Bd. Trial Advocates (nat. pres. 1981-82, Trial Lawyer of Yr. 1986-87), Assn. Trial Lawyers Am., Am. Coll. Trial Lawyers, Internat. Soc. Barristers, San Francisco Lawyers Club, Roman Catholic. Home: 819 Holly Rd Belmont CA 94002-2214 Office: 109 Geary St San Francisco CA 94108-5632

BARBAKOW, JEFFREY C. healthcare industry executive; b. 1944; BS, San Jose U.; MBA, U. So. Calif. With Merrill Lynch Capital Mkts. and several additional affiliates, 1972-88, MGM/UA Communications Inc., 1988-91, Donaldson, Lufkin & Jenrette Securities Corp., 1991; dir. Tenet Healthcare, Santa Barbara, Calif., 1990—, chmn. bd., CEO, 1993—. Office: Tenet Healthcare Inc 3820 State St Santa Barbara CA 93105-3112

BARBEE, BOB, national park administrator; m. Carol; 3 children. B of Zoology, M of Wildland Mgmt., Colo. State U. Seasonal naturalist Rocky Mountain Nat. Park, 1958; various positions Yosemite Nat. Park, Carlsbad Caverns Nat. Park, Big Bend Nat. Park, Point Reyes Nat. Park; supt. Cape Lookout and Cape Hatteras Nat. Seashores, Hawaii Volcanoes Nat. Park, Redwood Nat. Park, Yellowstone Nat. Park; regional dir. Alaska Region Nat. Pk. Svc., Anchorage, 1994-2000. Office: 2525 Gambell St Anchorage AK 99503-2827

BARBER, CLARENCE LYLE, economics educator; b. Wolseley, Sask., Can., May 5, 1917; s. Richard Edward and Lulu Pearl (Lyons) B.; m. Barbara Anne Patchet, May 10, 1947; children— Paul Edward, Richard Stephen, David Stuart, Alan Gordon. BA, U. Sask., 1939; MA, Clark U., 1941; postgrad., U. Minn., 1941-43, PhD, 1952; LLD (hon.), U. Guelph, 1988. With Stats. Can., 1945-48; mem. faculty McMaster U., 1948-49, U. Man., Winnipeg, Can., 1949-85, prof. econs., 1956-85, disting. prof., 1982-85, emeritus, 1985—, head dept., 1963-72; vis. prof. Queen's U., 1954-55, McGill U., 1964-65. Commr. Royal Commn. on Farm Machinery, 1966-71; spl. adviser on nat. income Phillipines Govt., 1959-60; commr. for study welfare policy in Man., 1972; mem. Nat. Commn. on Inflation, 1979, Royal Commn. Econ. Union and Devel. Prospects for Can., 1982-85 Author: Inventories and the Business Cycle, 1958, The Theory of Fiscal Policy as Applied to a Province, 1966, (with others) Inflation and Unemployment: The Canadian Experience, 1980, Controlling Inflation: Learning from Experience in Canada, Europe and Japan, 1982, False Promises: The Failure of Conservative Economics, 1993. Served with RCAF, 1943-45. Named Officer in Order of Can., 1987; Can. Coun. Profl. Leave fellow, 1970-71 Fellow Royal Soc. Can.; mem. Canadian Assn. U. Tchrs. (pres. 1958-59), Canadian Econ. Assn. (pres. 1971-72), Am. Econ. Assn., Royal Econ. Soc., Social Sci. Research Council Can. (mem. exec. 1972-73), U. Victoria Faculty Club. Home: 766 Richmond Ave Victoria BC Canada V8S 3Z1

BARBER, JAMES P. lawyer; b. Berkeley, Calif., Nov. 11, 1944; BA, U. Calif., Santa Barbara, 1967; JD, U. Calif., 1973. Bar: Calif. 1973. Ptnr. Hancock, Rothert & Bunshoft LLP, San Francisco, 1980—. Articles editor Hastings Law Jour., 1972-73. Mem. ABA, State Bar Calif., Bar Assn. San Francisco, Def. Rsch. Inst., Thurston Soc., Order of the Coif. Office: Hancock Rothert & Bunshoft LLP 4 Embarcadero Ctr Ste 300 San Francisco CA 94111-4174

BARBER, LLOYD INGRAM, retired university president; b. Regina, Sask., Can., Mar. 8, 1932; s. Lewis Muir and Hildred (Ingram) B.; m. Muriel Pauline MacBean, May 12, 1956; children: Muir, Brian, Kathleen, David, Susan, Patricia. BA, U. Sask., 1953, BComm, 1954; MBA, U. Calif., Berkeley, 1955; PhD, U. Wash., 1964; LLD (hon.), U. Alta., 1983, Concordia U., 1984; postgrad., U. Regina, 1993. Hon. chartered acct. Instr. commerce U. Sask., 1955-57, asst. prof., 1957-64, assoc. prof., 1964-65, prof., 1965-68, 74-76, dean commerce, 1965-68, v.p., 1968-74; pres. U. Regina, Sask., prof. adminstrn., 1976-90. Indian claims commr. Govt. of Can., 1969-76, hon. lt. col.; spl. inquirer for Elder Indian Testimony, 1977-81; bd. dirs. Bank of N.S., The Molson Cos., Cominco, Working Ventures, Inc., N.W. Co. Ltd., Can. West Global Comm. Corp., Greystone Capital Mgmt. Inc.; cons. to bus. and govt.; hon. prof. Shandong U. Trustee Inst. Rsch. on Public Policy, 1972-79; bd. dirs. Indian Equity Found., 1978-79, Can. Scholarship Trust Fund, Regina United Way, 1977-79; past bd. dirs. Wascana Centre Authority; bd. dirs. Nat. Mus. Nature, Inst. Saskatchewan Enterprise, Can. Polar Commn.; bd. dirs., past trustee Can. Scheneley Football Awards; adv. com. to Rector on pub. affairs award Concordia U., 1983; past mem. Northwest Territories Legis. Coun., 1967-70, Natural Sci. and Engring. Rsch. Coun. Officer Aboriginal Order of Can.; recipient Vanier medal, 1978; named hon. Sask. Indian Chief Little Eagle. Mem. Am. Inst. Pub. Adminstrn., Nat. Stats. Coun., Assn. Univs. and Colls. Can. (past pres.), Am. Econ. Assn., Can. Econ. Assn., Order of Can. (companion), Sask. Order of Merit, Assn. Commonwealth Univs. (coun.), Assinobia Club, Regina Beach Yacht Club, Masons. Mem. United Ch. Office: PO Box 510 Regina Beach SK Canada S0G 4C0 E-mail: barberl@uregina.ca

BARBER, PHILLIP MARK, lawyer; b. Pitts., Apr. 7, 1944; s. Armour G. and Irene Estelle (Doyle) B.; m. Barbara Jean Jennings, Aug. 6, 1966 (div. Dec. 1981); children: Heather C., Jessica L., Melissa A.; m. Penelope Louise Constantikes, Apr. 15, 1989 (div. Nov. 1991). BA, U. Mich., 1966; JD, Harvard U., 1969. Bar: Idaho 1969, Calif. 1971, U.S. Ct. Appeals (9th cir.) 1974, U.S. Supreme Ct. 1977. Law clk. Supreme Ct. Idaho, Boise, 1969-70; assoc. Nossaman, Waters, Scott, Krueger & Riordan, L.A., 1970-71; asst. atty. gen. State of Idaho, Boise, 1971-72; assoc. Elam, Burke, Jeppesen, Evans & Boyd, Boise, 1972-76, ptnr., 1977-81, Hawley, Troxell, Ennis & Hawley, Boise, 1981-99. Mem. select com. on bar examination Idaho Supreme Ct., 1973-74, select com. on appellate rules, 1976-77, standing com. 1977-84; mem. Idaho Code Commn., 1978-96. Contbr. articles to profl. jours. Chmn. rules com. Idaho Dem. Comm., 1976; chmn. Boise Area Econ. Devel. Coun., 1985-88; [illegible] N.W. Policy Ctr., 1986-97, vice chmn. N.W. Bus. Coalition, 1987-89; mem. exec. com. Idaho Bus. Coun., 1986-94. Recipient Disting. Citizen award Idaho Stateman Newspapers, 1985. Mem. ABA, Idaho State Bar (exam. com. 1983-85), State Bar Calif., Boise Bar Assn., Boise Area C. of C. (bd. dirs. 1980-81, 83-88, pres., chmn. bd. 1985). Roman Catholic. [illegible] Home: 1130 Shenandoah Dr Boise ID 83712-7451 Office: 350 N 9th St # M-202 Boise ID 83702-5459

BARBERA, JOSEPH, motion picture and television producer, cartoonist; b. N.Y.C., Mar. 24, 1911; s. Vincente and Frances Barbera; m. Sheila Holden; children: (by former marriage) Lynne Meredith, Jayne Earl, Neal Francis. Grad., Am. Inst. Banking. Banking clk. Irving Trust Co., N.Y.C., 1930-32; storyboard writer, sketch artist Van Beuren Studio, N.Y.C., 1932-34; animator Terrytoons, New Rochelle, 1934-37; head animation dept. MGM, 1955-57; co-founder with William Hanna Hanna-Barbera Prodns., 1957—. Dir. with Hanna of short animated films including Puss Gets the Boot, 1940 (Academy award nomination best animated short subject 1940), The Nightmare Before Christmas, 1941 (Academy award best animated short subject 1941), Yankee Doodle Mouse, 1943 (Academy award best animated short subject 1943), Mouse Trouble, 1944 (Academy award best animated short subject 1944), Quiet, Please!, 1945 (Academy award best animated short subject 1945), The Cat Concerto, 1946 (Academy award best animated short subject 1946), Dr. Jekyll and Mr. Mouse, 1947 (Academy award nomination best animated short subject 1947), The Little Orphan, 1948 (Academy award best animated short subject 1948), Hatch Up Your Troubles, 1949 (Academy award nomination best animated short subject 1949), Jerry's Cousin, 1950 (Academy award nomination best animated short subject 1950), The Two Mouseketeers, 1951 (Academy award best animated short subject 1951), Johann Mouse, 1952 (Academy award best animated short subject 1952), Touche, Pussy Cat, 1954 (Academy award nomination best animated short subject 1954), Good Will to Men, 1955 (Academy award nomination best animated short subject 1955), One Droopy Knight, 1957 (Academy award nomination best animated short subject 1957); animated programming series with Hanna include The Ruff and Reddy Show, 1957-60, The Huckleberry Hound Show, 1958-62 (Emmy award 1960), Yogi Bear, 1958-62, The Quick Draw McGraw Show, 1959-62, The Flintstones, 1960-66 (Golden Globe award 1965), Top Cat, 1961-62, Lippy the Lion, 1962, Touche Turtle, 1962, Wally Gator, 1962, The Jetsons, 1962-67, 69-76, 79-81, 82-83, 85, The Adventures of Jonny Quest, 1964-65, 67-72, 79, 80-81, The Magilla Gorilla Show, 1964-67, The Peter Potamus Show, 1964-67, Tom and Jerry, 1965-72, 75-78, 80-82, The Atom Ant/Secret Squirrel Show, 1965-68, Sinbad, Jr., the Sailor, 1966, The Abbott and Costello Cartoon Show, 1966, Laurel and Hardy, 1966-67, Space Kiddettes, 1966-67, Space Ghost, 1966-68, Frankenstein, Jr. and the Impossibles, 1966-68, Sampson and Goliath, 1967-68, Birdman and the Galaxy Trio, 1967-68, The Herculoids, 1967-69, Moby Dick and the Mighty Mightor, 1967-69, Shazzan!, 1967-69, The Fantastic Four, 1967-70, The Wacky Races, 1968-70, The Adventures of Gulliver, 1969-70, The Perils of Penelope Pitstop, 1969-71, The Cattanooga Cats, 1969-71, Dastardly and Muttley in Their Flying Machines, 1969-71, Scooby-Doo, Where Are You?, 1969-74, Where's Huddles?, 1970-71, The Harlem Globetrotters, 1970-73, Josie and the Pussycats, 1970-76, Pebbles and Bamm Bamm, 1971-72, Help! It's the Hair Bear Bunch, 1971-72, The Funky Phantom, 1971-72, Wait Til Your Father Gets Home, 1972, Sealab 2020, 1972-73, The Roman Holidays, 1972-73, The Amazing Chan and the Chan Clan, 1972-74, The Flintstones Comedy Hour, 1972-74, Josie and the Pussycats in Outer Space, 1972-74, Speed Buggy, 1971-74, Butch Cassidy and the Sundance Kids, 1973-74, Peter Puck, 1973-74, Inch High, Private Eye, 1973-74, Yogi's Gang, 1973-75, Jeannie, 1973-75, Goober and the Ghost Chasers, 1973-75, The Addams Family, 1973-75, Super Friends, 1973-83, Wheelie and the Chopper Bunch, 1974-75, The Partridge Family: 2200 A.D., 1974-75, Hong Kong Phooey, 1974-76, These Are the Days, 1974-76, Devlin, 1974-76, Valley of the Dinosaurs, 1974-76, The Scooby-Doo/Dynomutt Hour, 1976-77, Mumbly, 1976-77, Jabberjaw, 1976-78, The Skatebirds, 1977-78, The Tom and Jerry/Great Grape Ape Show, 1977-78, Scooby's All-Star Laff-a-Lympics, 1977-78, Fred Flintstone and Friends, 1977-78, Captain Caveman and the Teen Angels, 1980, The Scooby-Doo and Scrappy-Doo Show, 1980-82, The Drak Pack, 1980-82, Fonz and the Happy Days Gang, 1980-82, The Richie Rich Show, 1980-82, The Kwicky Koala Show, 1981-82, Trollkins, 1981-82, Laverne and Shirley in the Army, 1981-82, The Smurfs, 1981-90 (Emmy award 1982, 83), Laverne and Shirley with the Fonz, 1982-83, Scooby, Scrappy, and Yabba Doo, 1982-83, Snorks, 1984-86, The Funtastic World of Hanna-Barbera, 1986-87,87-88, Pound Puppies, 1986-87, The Flintstone Kids, 1986-87, Wildfire, 1986-87, Foofur, 1986-87, Popeye and Son, 1987-88, The Completely Mental Misadventures of Ed Grimley, 1988-89; animated spls. include Alice in Wonderland, 1966, Jack and the Beanstalk, 1967 (Emmy award 1967), Last of the Curlews, 1972 (Emmy award 1973), My Smurfy Valentine, 1982, Smurfily-Ever-After, 1985, The Flintstones' 25th Anniversary Celebration, 1986, The Jetsons Meet the Flinstones, 1987, Hanna-Barbera's 50th: A Yabba Dabba Doo Celebration, 1989, I Yabba Dabba Doo!, 1993; live action spls. include The Runaways, 1974 (Emmy award 1974); live action TV movies include Hardcase, 1972, Shootout in a One-dog Town, 1974, The Gathering, 1977 (Christopher award 1978, Emmy award 1978), The Gathering Part II, 1979, Stone Fox, 1987; animated feature films include Hey There, It's Yogi Bear, 1964, A Man Called Flintstone, 1966, Charlotte's Web, 1973 (Annie award 1977), Heidi's Song, 1982, Once Upon a Forest, 1993; live action feature films C.H.O.M.P.S., 1979, The Flinstones, 1994; co-creator Huckleberry Hound, Yogi Bear, Flintstones, Jetsons, Top Cat, Jonny Quest, Scooby-Doo; author: (with Alan Axelrod) My Life in Toons, 1994. Recipient TV Acad. Gov.'s award, 1988, Hall of Fame award Acad. Arts and Scis., 1993, Movie Guide award Tom & Jerry the Movie, 1993, The Flintstones, 1994. Home: 12003 Briarvale Ln Studio City CA 91604-4106

BARBO, DOROTHY MARIE, obstetrician/gynecologist, educator; b. River Falls, Wis., May 28, 1932; d. George William and Marie Lillian (Stelsel) B. BA, Asbury Coll., 1954; MD, U. Wis., 1958; DSc (hon.), Asbury Coll., 1981. Diplomate Am. Bd. Ob-Gyn. Resident Luth. Hosp. Milw., 1958-62; instr. Sch. Medicine Marquette U., Milw., 1962-66, asst. prof., 1966-67; assoc. prof. Christian Med. Coll. Punjab U., Ludhiana, India, 1968-72; assoc. prof. Med. Coll. Pa., Phila., 1972-87, prof., 1988-91, U. N.Mex., Albuquerque, 1991-99, prof. emeritus, 1999—; med. dir. Women's Health Ctr., Albuquerque, 1991-99. Acting dept. chair Christian Med. Coll., Punjab U., 1970; dir. Ctr. for Mature Woman Med. Coll. Pa., 1983-91; examiner Am. Bd. Ob-Gyn, 1984-97; bd. dirs. Ludhiana Christian Med. Coll., N.Y.C., Svc. Master Co. Ltd., Downers Grove, Ill., 1982-91; bd. trustees Asbury Coll., 1996—. Co-author: Care of Post Menopausal Patient, 1985; editor: Medical Clinics of N.A., vol. 71, 1987; assoc. editor, contbg. author: Textbook of Women's Health, 1998; contbr. chpt. to book. Student chpt. sponsor Christian Med. and Dental Soc., Phila., 1973-93, trustee, 1991-95, pres., chair bd. trustees, 1997-99; tchr., elder Leverington Presbyn. Ch ., Phila., 1988-91; interviewer Readers Digest Internat. fellowships, Brunswick, Ga., 1982—; bd. dirs. Phila. chpt. Am. Cancer Soc., 1980-86, vol., 1984. Named sr. clin. trainee USPHS, HEW, 1963-65, one of Best Woman Drs. in Am. Harper Bazaar, 1985. Fellow ACS (sec. Phila. chpt. 1990), ACOG, Am. Fertility Soc.; mem. Obstet. Soc. Phila. (pres. 1989-90), Phila. Colposcopy Soc. (pres. 1982-84), Philadelphia County Med. Soc. (com. chmn. 1989-90), Alpha Omega Alpha. Avocations: gardening, travel, collecting antiques.

BARBOUR, MICHAEL G(EORGE), botany educator, ecological consultant; b. Jackson, Mich., Feb. 24, 1942; s. George Jerome and Mae (Dater) B.; m. Norma Jean Yourist, Sept. 30, 1963 (div. 1981); m. Valerie Ann Whitworth, Jan. 25, 1987; children: Julie Ann, Alan Benjamin, Steven [illegible] Duke U., 1967. Asst. prof. botany U. Calif., Davis, 1967-71, assoc. prof., 1971-76, prof., 1976—, chmn., 1982-85; prof. environ. horticulture U. Calif., Davis, [illegible] Coll., Davis, [illegible]. Vis. prof. botany dept. Hebrew U., Jerusalem, 1979-81; vis. prof. marine scis. dept. La. State U., Baton Rouge, 1984; vis. prof. plant biology dept. Complutense U., Madrid, 1999. Co-author: Coastal Ecology, Bodega Head, 1973, Botany, 6th edit., 1982, Terrestrial Vegetation of California, 1977, 2d edit., 1988, Terrestrial Plant Ecology, 1980, 3d edit., 1998, North American Terrestrial Vegetation, 1988, 2d edit., 2000, California's Changing Landscapes, 1993, Plant Biology, 1998. Fulbright Found. fellow Adelaide, Australia 1964; Guggenheim Found. fellow, 1978; NSF rsch. grantee, 1968-78, MAB/NSF rsch. grantee, 1989-92, USDA rsch. grantee, 1992—. Mem. Ecol. Soc. Am., Brit. Ecol. Soc., Sigma Xi Democrat. Jewish. Office: U Calif Environ Horticulture Dept Davis CA 95616

BARCA, GEORGE GINO, winery executive, financial investor; b. Sacramento, Jan. 28, 1937; s. Joseph and Annie (Muschetto) B.; m. Maria Sclafani, Nov. 19, 1960; children: Anna, Joseph, Gina and Nina (twins). AA, Grant Jr. Coll.; student, LaSalle U., 1963. With United Vintners, U.S.A., St. Helena, Napa Valley, Calif., 1960—. Chmn., pres. Barca Internat., U.S.A., Barca Internat. Wineries & Vineyards, U.S.A., Calif. Grape Growers, U.S.A., Calif. Vintage Wines, U.S.A., Am. Vintners, U.S.A. Named Best Prodr. of Sales, United Vintners, U.S.A. Mem. KC. Roman Catholic. Achievements include development of wine trademarks and brands.

BARCA, KATHLEEN, marketing executive; b. Burbank, Calif., July 26, 1946; d. Frank Allan and Blanch Irene (Griffith) Barnes; m. Gerald Albino Barca, Dec. 8, 1967 (dec. May 1993); children: Patrick Gerald, Stacia Kathleen. Student, Pierce Coll., 1964; B in Bus., Hancock Coll., 1984. Teller Security Pacific Bank, Pasadena, Calif., 1968-69, Bank Am., Santa Maria, 1972-74; operator Gen. Telephone Co., Santa Maria, 1974-83, supr. operator, 1983-84; account exec. Radio Sta. KRQK/KLLB, Lompoc, 1984-85; owner Advt. Unltd., Orcutt, 1986-88; regional mgr. A.L. Williams Mktg. Co., Los Alamos, 1988-89; supr. Matol Botanical Internat., 1989-91; account exec. Santa Maria Times, 1989-95; owner a-garagesale.com, 2000—. Author numerous local TV and radio commercials, print advt. Activist Citizens Against Dumps in Residential Environments, Polit. Action Com., Orcutt and Santa Maria; chmn. Community Action Com., Santa Maria, Workshop EPA, Calif. Div., Dept. Health Svcs. State of Calif.; vice coord. Toughlove, Santa Maria, 1988-89; parent coord., mem. steering com. ASAP and Friends, 1988-89; mem. Sloco Access, 1997-99; mem. Friends San Luis Obispo Bot. Gardens, 1997-99; v.p. Seneca Hosp. Aux., 1998-2000; active Fire Svcs., 1998-2000. Mem. NAFE, Womens Network-Santa Maria, Ctrl. Coast Ad (recipient numerous awards), Santa Maria C. of C. (amb. representing Santa Maria Times 1990-94, asst. chief amb. 1993-94), Chester Piecemakers Quilt Club, Lake Almaner Womens Club. Democrat. Avocations: raising exotic birds, writing childrens books. E-mail: a-garagesale.com.

BARCHET, STEPHEN, physician, former naval officer; b. Annapolis, Md., Oct. 25, 1932; s. Stephen George and Louise (Lankford) B.; m. Marguerite Joan Racek, Aug. 9, 1965. Student, Brown U., 1949-52; MD, U. Md., 1956. Diplomate Am. Bd. Ob-Gyn.; cert. physician exec. Commd. ensign M.C. U.S. Navy, 1955, advanced through grades to rear adm., 1978; intern Naval Hosp., Chelsea, Mass., 1956-57, resident in ob-gyn, 1958-61, resident in gen. surgery Va., 1957-58; fellow Harvard Med. Sch., 1959-60; obstetrician-gynecologist Naval Hosp., Naples, Italy, 1961-63, Portsmouth, N.H., 1963-64, Beaufort, S.C., 1964-66, Bremerton, Wash., 1967-70, chief ob-gyn Boston, 1970-73; asst. head, tng. br. Bur. Medicine and Surgery, Washington, 1973, head, 1973-75; dep. spl. asst. to surgeon gen. Navy, 1975; assoc. dean Sch. Medicine, Uniformed Services U. Health Scis., Bethesda, Md., 1976-77, exec. sec. bd. regents, 1976-77; spl. asst. to surgeon gen. for med. dept. edn. and tng. Bur. Medicine and Surgery, Navy Dept., Washington, 1977-79, insp. gen., 1979-80; comdg. officer Naval Health Scis. and Edn. and Tng. Command, Nat. Naval Med. Center, Bethesda, 1977-79; asst. chief planning, resources BUMED, 1980-82; dep. surg. gen., dep. dir. naval medicine Dept. Navy, 1982-83; ret., 1983; with Pacific Med. Ctr., Seattle, 1985-91; cons. Mil. Health Care, Seattle, 1987—; prin. MSA Programs, Seattle, 1995—; mng. ptnr. Benefit Payment Solutions, 1998— Clin. asst. prof. Boston U. Sch. Medicine, 1971—; alt. regent Nat. Libr. Medicine, Bethesda, 1977-79; adj. prof. health care scis. George Washington U. Sch. Medicine and Health Scis., Washington, 1978—; ex officio mem. grad. med. edn. nat. adv. com. HEW, 1978-79; chmn. med.-dental com. Intersvc. Tng. Rev. Orgn., Washington, 1977-79; chmn. Washington Med. Savs. Accounts Project, 1994. Contbr. articles to med. jours. Sec. The Rainier Club, 1992-93; bd. dirs. North Seattle C.C. Found., 1992-95. Decorated Bronze star, others. Fellow Am. Coll. Obstetricians and Gynecologists, Am. Coll. Physician Execs.; mem. AMA, Md. Med. Soc., Assn. Mil. Surgeons U.S., Soc. Med. Cons. Armed Forces, Wash. State Med. Assn., King County Med. Assn., N.W. Mil. Health Benefit Assn. (exec. dir. 1991-94). Home and Office: 18601 SE 64th Way Issaquah WA 98027-8616

BARCLAY, JOHN ALLEN, lawyer; b. L.A., Feb. 14, 1951; s. George H. and Shirley Iris (Handler) B. AA, L.A. Valley Coll., 1970; BA, U. Southern Calif., 1972, JD, 1975. Bar: Calif. 1975, U.S. Dist. Ct. (cen., ea., and no. dists.) Calif. 1976, U.S. Ct. Appeals (9th cir.) 1976, U.S. Tax Ct. 1976, U.S. Ct. Claims, 1995. Prin. Barclay & Brestoff, Encino, 1978-80, Barclay & Moskatel, Beverly Hills, Calif., 1980-82, Barclay Law Corp., 1982—. Instr. U. Calif.-Irvine, 1985-87, UCLA, 1982-85, L.A. Valley Coll., Van Nuys, 1980-82. Author: Exchanging in the '80's, 1986, Accumulating Wealth, 1987, Insurance for Environmental Claims Against Bankruptcy Estates, 1992, Deducting Your Down Payment, 1984; contbr. articles to profl. jours. Mem. adv. bd. Calif. State U.; dir., sec. Orange County Nat. Conf. Christians and Jews; dir. Parent Help USA. Mem. ABA, Legion Lex (bd. dirs. Orange County chpt. 1987-95, pres. 1992), Masons (master Hollywood chpt. 1982). Jewish. Avocations: sailing, scuba. Address: PO Box 2289 Costa Mesa CA 92628-2289

BARDACH, SHELDON GILBERT, lawyer; b. Holyoke, Mass., Sept. 4, 1937; s. Arthur Everett and Ruth (Goodstein) B.; m. Martha Robson, June 7, 1970; 1 child, Noah Arthur. AB, Bklyn. Coll., 1958; JD, UCLA, 1961. Bar: Calif. 1962. Pvt. practice, Beverly Hills, Calif., 1962-67, Century City, 1967-85; sr. mem. Law Offices Sheldon G. Bardach, L.A., 1969—. Bd. dirs. Mambo Films, Inc.; arbitrator L.A. Superior Ct., 1979—; gen. counsel Century Artists, Ltd.; mem. nat. and internat. panels arbitrators Am. Arbitration Assn. Bd. editors Law in Transition Quar., 1967; contbr. articles to profl. jours. Bd. govs. Studio Watts Workshop, 1963-71; founder, bd. dirs. UCLA Sch. Law, 1968. Recipient Lubin award Sch. Law UCLA, 1961, Bancroft-Whitney award UCLA Sch. Law, , 1961. Mem. ABA, Calif. Bar Assn., Beverly Hills Bar Assn. (bd. govs. varristers 1964-69), Am. Arbitration Assn., UCLA Law Sch. Alumni Assn. (bd. dirs. 1991-94), L.A. County Bar Assn., Assn. Trial Lawyers Am., Comml. Law League Am., Vikings of Scandia, Zeta Beta Tau, Phi Alpha Delta. Democrat. Jewish. Office: 18321 Ventura Blvd Ste 915 Tarzana CA 91356-4255

BARDACKE, PAUL GREGORY, lawyer, former attorney general; b. Oakland, Calif., Dec. 16, 1944; s. Theodore Joseph and Frances (Woodward) B.; children: Julie, Brynn, Francheska, Chloe. BA cum laude, U. Calif.-Santa Barbara, 1966; JD, U. Calif.-Berkeley, 1969. Bar: Calif. 1969, N.Mex. 1970. Lawyer Legal Aid Soc., Albuquerque, 1969; assoc. firm Sutin, Thayer & Browne, Albuquerque, 1970-82; atty. gen. State of N.Mex., Santa Fe, 1982-86; ptnr. Sutin, Thayer & Browne, 1987-90, Eaves, Bardacke, Baugh, Kierst & Kiernan, P.A., 1991—. Adj. prof. N.Mex. Law Sch., Albuquerque, 1973— ; mem. faculty Nat. Inst. Trial Lawyers Advocacy, 1978— Bd. dirs. All Faiths Receiving Home, Albuquerque; bd. dirs. Friends of Art, 1974, Artspace Mag., 1979-80, Legal Aid Soc., 1970-74. Reginald Heber Smith fellow, 1969 Fellow Am. Coll. Trial Lawyers; mem. ABA, Calif. Bar Assn., N.Mex. Bar Assn., Am. Bd. Trial Advocates (pres. N.Mex. chpt. 1992-93). Democrat. Office: Eaves Bardacke Baugh Kierst & Kiernan PA PO Box 35670 Albuquerque NM 87176-5670

BARDEN, ROBERT CHRISTOPHER, lawyer, psychologist, educator, legislative analyst, speaker, writer; b. Richmond, Va., June 7, 1954; s. Elliott Hatcher and Jane Elizabeth Cole (Ferris) B.; m. Robin Jones, Nov. 14, 1987. BA summa cum laude, U. Minn., 1976, PhD in Clin. Psychology, 1982; postgrad., U. Calif., Berkeley, 1977; JD cum laude, Harvard U., 1992. Lic. cons. psychologist, Minn., Tex.; diplomate Am. Bd. Forensic Examiners. Project asst. NSF, 1978-79; intern in psychology VA Med. Ctr., Stanford Med. Ctr., Palo Alto, Calif., 1979-80; dir. psychology Internat. Craniofacial Surg. Inst., Dallas, 1980-87; corp., civil litigation, family and health law atty. Lindquist and Vennum, Mpls., 1992-96; psychologist, lawyer, expert witness, pub. policy analyst R.C. Barden & Assocs., 1996—. Asst. prof. psychology So. Meth. U., Dallas, 1980-84; asst. prof., dir. child clin. psychology U. Utah, Salt Lake City, 1984-87, rsch. faculty dept. surgery, 1987-93; vis. faculty, asst. prof. psychology Gustavus Adolphus Coll., St. Peter, Minn., 1988; pres. Optimal Performance Sys., Inc., Cambridge, 1989—; mem. Minn. Bd. Psychology, 1993-97; adj. prof. law U. Minn. Law Sch., 1995-97; cons. and spkr. in field. Consulting editor Devel. Psychology, 1989; editor Harvard Jour. Law and Pub. Policy, 1990-91; contbr. to profl. publs. Project dir. ch. cmty. svc. projects, Mpls. and Cambridge, 1988—; mem. Minn. Bd. Psychology, 1993-97, Higher Edn. Coordinating Bd., 1993-94; rep. Minn. Sixth Congl. Dist. Recipient Young Scholar award Found. for Child Devel., Faculty Scholar award W.T. Grant Found., 1987-89; NSF fellow, 1978, NIMH fellow, 1976, 77. Mem. ABA, Am. Psychol. Soc., Soc. for Rsch. in Child Devel., Internat. Soc. Clin. Hypnosis, Harvard Law Sch. Soc. Law and Medicine, Lowell House Commons Rm. Harvard U., Nat.Assn. for Consumer Protection in Mental Health Practices (pres. 1995—), Sigma Xi, Phi Beta Kappa. Avocations: church and service work, tennis, martial arts, mountain climbing, music. Home and Office: RC Barden and Assocs 1093 Duffer Ln North Salt Lake UT 84054-3313 E-mail: rcbarden@aol.com

BARDWICK, JUDITH MARCIA, management consultant; b. N.Y.C., Jan. 16, 1933; d. Abraham and Ethel (Krinsky) Hardis; m. John Bardwick, III, Dec. 18, 1954 (div.); children: Jennifer, Peter, Deborah; m. Allen Armstrong, Feb. 10, 1984 BS, Purdue U., 1954; MS, Cornell U., 1955; PhD, U. Mich., 1964. Lectr. U. Mich., Ann Arbor, 1964-67, asst. prof. psychology, 1967-71, assoc. prof., 1971-75, prof., 1975-83, assoc. dean, 1977-83; clin. prof. psychiatry U. Calif., San Diego, 1984—; pres. In Transition, Inc. (name changed to Judith M. Bardwick, PhD, Inc., 1991), 1983—. Mem. population research study group NIH, 1971-75 Author: Psychology of Women, 1971, In Transition, 1979, The Plateauing Trap, 1986, Danger in The Comfort Zone, 1991, In Praise of Good Business, 1998; co-author: Feminine Personality and Conflict, 1970; editor: Readings in the Psychology of Women, 1972; coauthor Feminine Personality and Conflict, 1970; mem. editorial bd. Women's Studies, 1973—, Psychology of Women Quar., 1975—; contbr. articles to profl. jours. Mem. social sci. adv. com. Planned Parenthood Am., 1973. Fellow APA; mem. Midwest Psychol. Assn., N.Y. Acad. Scis., Am. Psychosomatic Soc., Phi Beta Kappa. Home and Office: 1389 Caminito Halago La Jolla CA 92037-7165 E-mail: jmbwick@san.rr.com

BARGER, WILLIAM JAMES, management consultant, educator; b. Los Angeles, Nov. 1, 1944; s. James Ray and Aylene M. (Skinner) B.; m. Jane A. Cox, Jan. 30, 1988. BA, U. So. Calif., 1966; MA, Harvard U., 1970, PhD, 1972. Asst. prof econs. U. So. Calif., Los Angeles, 1971-76; v.p. Bank Am., Los Angeles, 1976-81; sr. v.p. Gibraltar Savs. Co., Beverly Hills, Calif., 1981-84, exec. v.p., 1984-88; pres. High Point Acad., Pasadena, 1995—. Mem. Phi Beta Kappa.

BARHAM, WARREN SANDUSKY, horticulturist; b. Prescott, Ark., Feb. 15, 1919; s. Clint A. and Hannah Jane (Sandusky) B.; m. Margaret Alice Kyle, Dec. 27, 1940 (dec. 1997); m. Evelyn M. Csongradi, Dec. 5, 1998; children: Barbara E., Juanita S., Margaret Ann, Robert W. BS in Agr., U. Ark., 1941; PhD, Cornell U., 1950. Grad. asst. in plant breeding Cornell U., Ithaca, N.Y., 1942-45; assoc. prof. horticulture N.C. State U., Raleigh, 1949-58; dir. raw material R & D Basic Vegetable Products, Inc., Vacaville, Calif., 1958-76; prof. Tex. A&M U., College Station, 1976-82, head dept., 1976-80; v.p. Castle & Cook Techniculture, Watsonville, Calif., 1982-84; dir. watermelon R & D Tom Castle Seed Co., Morgan Hill, 1984-86; CEO Barham Seeds Inc., Gilroy, 1987—; v.p. Kyle and Barham LLC, La Quinta, 1996—. Cons. Basic Vegetable Products, Inc., Vacaville, 1976-78, U.S. AID, Central Am., 1977, Egypt and U.S., 1980-82, Gentry Foods & Gilroy Foods, 1978-93, Fed. Republic Germany Govt., Ethiopia, 1984; industry rep. adv. com. Onion Rsch. Program USDA, 1960-70. Contbr. articles to profl. jours. Bd. dirs., pres. Vacaville Sch. Bd., 1964-74. Sgt. USAF, 1942-45, ETO. Fellow Am. Soc. Hort. Sci. (pres. 1982, bd. dirs. 1979-83); mem. Sons in Retirement (bd. dirs. 1992-95, v.p. 1993, pres. 1994), Rotary Internat. (bd. dirs. 1964), Elks Club. Achievements include development of 34 varieties and hybrids of onions, 15 triploid and 8 diploid hybrid watermelons, 2 cucumber varieties and 1 tomato variety. Home and Office: 7401 Crawford Dr Gilroy CA 95020-5421 Fax: 408-847-6706. E-mail: wsbarham@garlic.com

BARKER, CLIVE, artist, screenwriter, director, producer, writer; b. Liverpool, Eng., 1952; s. Len and Joan B. Student, U. Liverpool, Eng. Author: (plays) Incarnations (Frankenstein in Love, History of the Devil, Colossus), Forms of Heaven (Paradise Street, Subtle Bodies, Crazyface); (short story collection) Books of Blood I-VI (books IV, V, and VI released in U.S. as The Inhuman Condition, 1986, In the Flesh, 1986, Cabal; (novels) The Damnation Game, 1985, Weaveworld, 1987, Cabal, 1988, The Great and Secret Show, 1989, Imajica, 1991, The Thief of Always, 1992, Everville, 1994, Sacrament, 1996, A-Z of Horror, 1997, Galilee, 1998, The Essential Clive Barker, 1999; prodr. Hellraiser II: Hellbound, 1990, Candyman, 1992, Hellraiser III: Hell on Earth, 1992, Candyman II: Farewell to the Flesh, 1995, Hellraiser: Bloodline, 1996, Gods & Monsters, 1997, (Fox TV) Spirits and Shadows, 1997; (writer and dir. screenplays) Hellraiser, 1987, Nightbreed, 1990, Lord of Illusions, 1995, Art Exhibition, 1998.

BARKER, DEE H. chemical engineering educator; b. Salt Lake City, Mar. 28, 1921; s. John Henry and Christina Selina (Heaton) Barker; m. Catherine Thompson, Apr. 24, 1945; children: DeeAnn, Lynn, Craig, Gary, Pamela. BS, U. Utah, 1948, PhD, 1951. Research engr. E.I. DuPont de Nemours & Co., Inc., Wilmington, Del., 1951-54, reactor engr. Baton, S.C., 1954-59; prof. chem. engring. Brigham Young U., Provo, Utah, 1959—. Cons. Brila Inst. Tech. & Sci., Rajasthan, India, 1966-78; Chonnam Nat. U. fellow, 1980-81, 87; prof. emeritus Brigham Young U., Provo, 1986—. Active Boy Scouts Am., Salt Lake City. With USN, 1944-46. Fellow Am. Inst. Chem. Engrs.; mem. Am. Soc. Engring. Educators, Nat. Council Engring. Examinations, Kiwanis. Avocations: photography, reading, scouting. Home: 1398 Cherry Ln Provo UT 84604-2851

BARKER, DOUGLAS P. food products executive; b. 1935; With Sunkist Growers, Van Nuys, Calif., 1961-78, Sun World Internat. Inc., Bakersfield, 1978-81, 84—, Blue Anchor, Sacramento, 1981-84; internat. sales mgr. Primetime Internat., Coachella. Office: Primetime Internat 86705 Avenue 54 Ste A Coachella CA 92236-3814

BARKER, JOHN WILLIAM, agricultural property management; b. Oxnard, Calif., June 9, 1954; s. Robert Verne and Pauline Evelyn (Silveira) B.; m. Sharon Rose Richter, July 19, 1980; children: Teresa Marie, Daniel John, Marlena Dee. BS, Calif. State U., Northridge, 1991. Auditor Hyatt Hotels, Incline Village, Nev., 1975-77; oilwell driller Cal Pacific Drilling, Et Al, Camarillo, Calif., 1977-87; gen. ptnr. GGC Partnership, Camarillo, 1987—; trustee Manuel G. Silveria Trust, Camarillo, 1988—; gen. ptnr. Barker Farms, Camarillo, 1987—. Treas. YMCA Indian Guides, 1992. Republican. Roman Catholic. Avocations: skiing, computers, performing arts, solar eclipses. Home: 1220 Via Montoya Dr Camarillo CA 93010 Office: Barker Farms 103 Alosta Dr Camarillo CA 93010-1303

BARKER, LYNN M. executive; BS in Physics, MS in Physics, U. Ariz. Co-founder, pres. Valyn Internat., Albuquerque. Mem. Am. Phys. Soc., Soc. Exptl. Mechanics, Internat. Soc. Optical Engring., Aeriballistoc Range Assn., Sigma Pi Sigma, Pi Mu Epsilon, Phi Beta Kappa, Sigma Xi. Office: Valyn Intrnat 12514 Menaul Blvd NE Albuquerque NM 87112-2554

BARKER, ROBERT JEFFERY, financial executive; b. Glendale, Calif., Feb. 22, 1946; s. Albert and Margaret E. (Windle) B.; m. Ildiko Barker, Jan. 1, 1989; 1 child, Alexander A. BSEE, UCLA, 1968, MBA, 1970. Cert. mgmt. acctg. Cost analyst Lockheed, Sunnyvale, Calif., 1976-78; from cost acctg. supr. to fin. systems mgr. Monolithic Memories Inc., Sunnyvale, 1976-84; dir. fin. Waferscale Integration, Inc., Fremont, Calif., 1984-88, v.p. fin., CFO, 1988-94; CFO Micrel, San Jose, 1994, v.p. corp. bus. devel., 1999—. Bd. dirs., treas. Am. Electronics Assn. Credit Union, Santa Clara, Calif., 1988—, bd. chmn., 1991; dir. Monolithic Memories Integration Fed. Credit Union, Sunnyvale, 1977-84, pres. 1983-84. Dir. Vets. Task Force, Palo Alto, Calif., 1980-87, pres. 1987. Capt. USAF, 1970-74. Mem. Nat. Assn. Accts., Fin. Execs. Inst., Toastmasters (pres. 1986-87). Republican. Methodist. Avocations: beach doubles volleyball, jogging, sports. Home: 1 Winchester Dr Atherton CA 94027-4040

BARKER, ROBERT WILLIAM, television personality; b. Darrington, Wash., Dec. 12, 1923; s. Byron John and Matilda Kent (Tarleton) B.; m. Dorothy Jo Gideon, Jan. 12, 1945 (dec. Oct. 1981). BA in Econs. summa cum laude, Drury Coll., 1947. Master of ceremonies: Truth or Consequences, Hollywood, Calif., 1957-75, Price is Right, 1972—, Miss Universe Beauty Pageant, 1966-87, Miss U.S.A. Beauty Pageant, 1966-87, Pillsbury Bake-Off, 1969-85, Bob Barker Fun and Games Show, 1978—; host: Rose Parade, CBS, 1969-88; appeared in (feature film) Happy Gilmore, 1996. Served to lt. (j.g.) USNR, 1943-45. Recipient Emmy award for Best Audience Participation Host, 1981-82, 83-84, 86-87, 87-88, 89-90, 90-91, 91-92, 93-94, 94-95, 95-96, 99-2000. Mem. AGVA, AFTRA, Screen Actors Guild. Office: The Price is Right care CBS TV 7800 Beverly Blvd Los Angeles CA 90036-2112

BARKIN, ELAINE RADOFF, composer, music educator; b. N.Y.C., Dec. 15, 1932; m. George J. Barkin, Nov. 28, 1957; 3 children. BA in Music, Queens Coll., 1954, MFA in Composition, 1956; PhD in Composition and Theory, Brandeis U., 1971; Cert. in Composition and Piano, Berlin Hochschule Musik, 1957; studied with Karol Rathaus, Irving Fine, Boris Blacher, Arthur Berger. Lectr. in music Queens Coll., 1964-70, Sarah Lawrence, 1969-70; from asst. to assoc. prof. music theory U. Mich., 1970-74; from asst. prof. to prof. composition and theory U. Calif., L.A., 1974-97. Vis. asst. prof. Princeton (N.J.) U., 1974; lectr. in field. Asst. to co-editor: Perspectives of New Music, 1963-85; composer String Quartet, 1969, Sound Play for violin, 1974, String Trio, 1976, Plein Chant, alto flute, 1977, Ebb Tide, 2 vibraphones, 1977, ...the Supple Suitor...for soprano and five players, 1978, (chamber mini opera) De Amore, 1980, Impromptu for violin, cello, piano, 1981, (theatre piece) Media Speak, 1981, At the Piano, piano, 1982, For String Quartet, 1982, Quilt Piece graphic score for 7 instruments, 1984, On The Way To Becoming for 4-track Tape Collage, 1985, Demeter and Persephone for violin, tape, chamber ensemble, dancers, 1986, 3 Rhapsodies, flutes and clarinet, 1986, Encore for Javanese Gamelan Ensemble, 1986, Out of the Air for Basset Horn and Tape, 188, To Whom It May Concern 4 track tape collage, reader and 4 players, 1989, Legong Dreams, oboe, 1990, Gamélange for harp and mixed gamelan band, 1992, Five Tape Collages, Open Space CD #3, 1993, "for my friends' pleasure," soprano and harp, 1994, numerous improvised group and duo sessions on tape; produced cassette and video: New Music in Bali, 1994; "touching all bases" for electronic bass, electronic percussion, and Balinese gamelan, 1996, e: an anthology (music, texts and graphics) 1975-95, "poem" for wind ensemble, 1999, (Chamber Music Improvisations) Open Space, 2000, Strings for Violin, 2001. Recipient Fulbright award, 1957, awards NEA, 1975, 79, awards Rockefeller Found., 1980, Meet the Composer award, 1994. Home: 12533 Killion St Valley Vlg CA 91607-1533

BARKLEY, JOSEPH RICHARD, controller; b. Pa., Sept. 3, 1942; s. Joseph Harold and Rose Mary (Manger) B.; m. Diane Marie Bentivoglio, July 10, 1965; children: Christopher Michael, Patrick Joseph. BS Engring., U.S. Mil. Acad., 1965; MBA in Fin., Scranton U., 1975. Commd. 2d lt. U.S. Army, 1965, advanced through grades to maj., 1979, ret., 1979; fin. and analysis dir. Am. Express Corp., N.Y.C., 1978-82; asst. controller ops. div. Ins. Corp. N.Am., Phila., 1982-83; dir fin., adminstr. Cigna Corp., Phila., 1983-86; v.p., controller facilities div. Chase Manhattan Bank N.A., N.Y.C., 1986-88, v.p. controller Ins. Products Group, 1988—. Contbr. articles to profl. jours. Judge, Newtown Election Bd., 1980—; mem. Council Rock Sch. Br., 1983-87; mem. Newtown Planning Commn., 1982, chmn., 1990. Decorated Combat Inf. Badge, Bronze Star. Mem. West Point Soc. Phila., Fin. Exec. Inst. Republican. Roman Catholic. Avocations: skiing, running, road racing. Office: Imperial Bancorp PO Box 92991 Los Angeles CA 90009

BARKLEY, WILLIAM DONALD, retired museum administrator, consultant; b. New Westminster, B.C., Can., Apr. 4, 1941; s. Donald MacMillan and Ethel Margaret (Mines) B.; m. Helen Gayle Alanson, Aug. 29, 1964; children: Warren Vincent, Colleen Michelle. BS, U. B.C., 1964, MA, 1971. Cert. tchr. Can. Tchr. Salmon Arm (B.C.) Sr. Secondary Sch., 1965-68; wildlife biologist Wye Marsh Wildlife Ctr., Midland, Ont., Can., 1968-72; chief interpretation Can. Wildlife Svc., Ottawa, 1972-77; asst. dir. B.C. Provincial Mus., Victoria, 1977-84; CEO Royal BC Mus., Victoria, 1984-2001; cons., 2001—. Advisor cultural resource mgmt. program U. Victoria, 1985—; lectr. univs. Contbr. articles to Nat. History Interpretation mag., 1965—. Bd. dirs. Tourism Victoria, 1985—; v.p. tourism victoria chair Virtual Mus. Canada; bd. dirs. Neptune Project adv. Victoria Children's Mus. Recipient Disting. Svc. award Interpretation Can., Ottawa, 1983, Can. 125 award for svc. to mus. cmty., Miracle award, Tourism Victoria, 1998, Tourism Leader Yr. award, Tourism B.C., 1999, Outstanding Achievement award, Can. Mus. Assn., 1999, GEM award Bus. Improvement Assn., 2000. Fellow Can. Mus. Assn.; mem. Can. Mus. Assn. (pres. 1987-89), B.C. Mus. Assn., Internat. Coun. of Mus.-Can., Can. Pks. and Wilderness Soc., Can. Nature Fedn., Victoria A.M. Tourism Svcs. Assn. (treas.). Mem. United Ch. Can. Avocations: design and production stained glass, backpacking, skiing, wind surfing, numismatics. Office: Royal BC Mus 675 Belleville St Victoria BC Canada V8V 1X4

BARKSDALE, BARRY W. career officer; BS in History, USAF Acad., 1972; student pilot tng., Columbus AFB, Miss., 1972-73, Davis-Monthan AFB, Ariz., 1973, 81, 86; student, Squadron Officer Sch., 1981, USMC Command and Staff Coll., 1984, Air Command and Staff Coll., 1985, Air War Coll., 1988; MA in Mgmt., U. Phoenix, 1989, Army War Coll., 1991; student Phase II, Joint Profl. Mil. Edn., 1992. Commd. 2d lt. USAF, 1972, advanced through grades to brig. gen., 1997; aircraft comdr. 75th Tactical Fighter Squadron, England AFB, La., 1973-76; forward air controller tng. Patrick AFB, Fla., 1976-77; wing scheduler 51st Composite Wing, Osan Air Base, S. Korea, 1977-78; chief weapons and tactics then asst. ops. officer 549th Tactical Air Support Tng. Squadron, Patrick AFB, 1978-81; flight comdr. 355th Tactical Fighter Squadron, Myrtle Beach AFB, S.C., 1981-83; action officer then exec. officer to dep. chief plans Hdqs. Tactical Air Command, Langley AFB, Va., 1983-86; various positions Davis-

Monthan AFB, 1986-90, 95-97; chief detection and monitoring br., counternarcotics ops. Joint Staff, Pentagon, Washington, 1991-93; comdr. 554th Support Group, Nellis AFB, Nev., 1993-94, 57th Ops. Group, Nellis AFB, 1994-95, 37th Tng. Wing, Lackland AFB, Tex., 1997-99; vice comdr. 12th Air Force U.S. So. Com., Davis-Monthan AFB, Ariz., 1999—. Decorated Legion of Merit. Office: 12 AF Davis Monthan AFB AZ 85707

BARKSDALE, JAMES LOVE, communications company executive; b. Jackson, Miss., 1943; married. Grad., U. Miss., 1965. V.p. Cook Industries, Inc., 1973-79; former pres. ISD, Inc.; sr. v.p. info. systems, chief info. officer Fed. Express Corp., Memphis, 1979-83, exec. v.p., COO, 1983-92, also dir.; pres., COO McCaw Cellular Commns.; CEO AT&T Wireless Svcs. (merger McCaw Cellular Comms. and AT&T Wireless Svcs.); pres., CEO Netscape Comms. Corp., Mountain View, Calif., 1995—, also bd. dirs. Bd. dirs. 3Com Corp., @Home, Harrah's Entertainment, Robert Mondavi Winery. Office: Netscape Comms Corp 501 E Middlefield Rd Mountain View CA 94043-4042

BARLOW, CHARLES, oil company executive; CFO Sinclair Oil Corp., Salt Lake City. Office: Sinclair Oil Corp PO Box 30825 Salt Lake City UT 84130-0825

BARLOW, JOHN PERRY, writer; b. Wyo., 1947; m. Elaine Parker (div. 1996); children: Leah Justine, Anna Winter, Amelia. Degree in comparative religion with honors, Wesleyan U., 1969. Mgr. Bar Cross Land and Livestock Co., Cora, Wyo., 1971-88; co-founder, vice chmn. Electronic Frontier Found., 1990—. Bd. dirs. WELL; cons. Vanguard Group of CSC, Global Bus. Network. Contbg. editor numerous publs. including Comm. of the ACM, Microtimes, Mondo 2000; contbg. writer Wired; co-writer songs for The Grateful Dead, 1971—. Berkman fellow Harvard Law Sch., 1998—; named Thomas Jefferson of Cyberspace, Yahoo Mag. Internet Life, 1996, one of 25 Most Influential People in Fin. Svcs., Future Banker Mag., 1999, Office: Electronic Frontier Foundation 168 S Franklin Pinedale WY 82941-1009 E-mail: Barlow@EFF.org

BARMACK, NEAL HERBERT, neuroscientist; b. N.Y.C., Aug. 23, 1942; married, 1964; 2 children. BS, U. Mich., 1963; PhD, U. Rochester, 1970. Asst. lectr. psychology U. Rochester, 1968-69, rsch. assoc. to sr. rsch. assoc. neurophysiology dept ophthalmology, 1969-75, assoc. scientist, 1975-80; sr. scientist Neurol. Sci. Inst., Good Samaritan Hosp. and Med. Ctr., Portland, 1980-81; assoc. prof. biol. sci. U. Conn., 1981-82; sr. scientist, chmn. R.S. Dow Neurol. Sci. Inst., 1990-96; sr. scientist Neurol. Sci. Inst. Neurol. Sci. Inst., Portland, 1998—. Mem. Soc. Neurosci., Am. Physiol. Soc., Internat. Brain Rsch. Orgn., Nat. Eye Inst. Achievements include research in Neural control of eye movements; plasticity of reflexive eye movements; the cellular and biochemical basis of cerebellar modulation of reflex function. Office: Neurol Sci Inst 1120 NW 20th Ave Portland OR 97209-1539

BARNARD, KATHRYN ELAINE, nursing educator, researcher; b. Omaha, Apr. 16, 1938; d. Paul and Elsa Elizabeth (Anderson) B. BS in Nursing, U. Nebr., Omaha, 1960; MS in Nursing, Boston U., 1962; PhD, U. Wash., Seattle, 1972; DSc (hon.), U. Nebr., 1990. Acting instr. U. Nebr., Omaha, 1960-61, U. Wash., Seattle, 1963-65, asst. prof., 1965-69, prof. nursing, 1972—, assoc. dean, 1987-92. Bd. dirs. Nat. Ctr. for Clin. Infant Programs, Washington, 1980— Chmn. rsch. com. Bur. of Community Health Svcs., MCH, 1987-89. Recipient Lucille Petry award Nat. League for Nursing, 1968, Martha Mae Eliot award Am. Assn. Pub. Health, 1983, Professorship award U. Wash., 1985 Fellow Am. Acad. Nursing (bd. dirs. 1980-82); mem. Inst. Medicine; mem. Am. Nurses Assn. (chmn. com. 1980-82, Jessie Scott award 1982, Nurse of Yr. award 1984), Soc. Research in Child Devel. (bd. dirs. 1981-87), Sigma Theta Tau (founders award in research 1987). Democrat. Presbyterian. Home: 11508 Durland Ave NE Seattle WA 98125-5904 Office: University of Washington Family & Child Nursing Box 357920 Seattle WA 98195-7920

BARNARD, ROLLIN DWIGHT, retired financial executive; b. Denver, Apr. 14, 1922; s. George Cooper and Emma (Riggs) B.; m. Patricia Reynolds Bierkamp, Sept. 15, 1943; children: Michael Dana, Rebecca Susan (Mrs. Paul C. Wulfestieg), Laurie Beth (Mrs. Kenneth J. Kostelecky). BA, Pomona Coll., 1943. Clk. Morey Merc. Co., Denver, 1937-40; ptnr. George C. Barnard & Co., Denver, 1946-47; v.p. Foster & Barnard, Inc., 1947-53; instr. Denver U., 1949-53; dir. real estate U.S. P.O. Dept., Washington, 1953-55, dep. asst. postmaster gen., bur. facilities, 1955-59, asst. postmaster gen., 1959-61; pres., dir. Midland Fed. Savs. & Loan Assn., Denver, 1962-84; vice-chmn. Bank Western Fed. Savs. Bank, 1984-87; vice-chmn., pres. Western Capital Investment Corp., 1985-87. Mayor City of Greenwood Village, Colo., 1989-93, chmn. Planning and Zoning Commn., 1969-73, mem. coun., 1975-77; pres. Denver Area coun. Boy Scouts Am., 1970-71, mem. exec. bd., 1962-73; mem. adv. bd. Denver Area coun. Boy Scouts Am., 1973—; bd. dirs. Downtown Denver Improvement Assn., pres., 1965; bd. dirs. Bethesda Found., Inc., 1973-82, Children's Hosp., 1979-84, treas., 1983-84; bd. dirs. Children's Health Corp., Inc., 1982-93; trustee Mile High United Fund, 1969-72, Denver Symphony Assn., 1973-74; bd. dirs. Colo. Coun. Econ. Edn., 1971-80, chmn. 1971-76; trustee, v.p., treas. Morris Animal Found., 1969-81, pres., chmn. 1974-78, trustee emeritus, 1981—; trustee Denver Zool. Found., 1994—, exec. vice-chmn., 1996-2000, vice-chmn., 2000-01; mem. acquisitions com. Friends Found. Denver Pub. Libr., 1994—; dir. Wings over the Rockies Air & Space Mus. Found., 1998—. Named one of Ten Outstanding Young Men in Am., U.S. Jaycees, 1955, 57; recipient Disting. Svc. award Postmaster Gen. U.S., 1960; Silver Beaver award Boy Scouts Am., 1969; named Outstanding Citizen of Yr., Sertoma, 1982, Colo. Citizen of Yr., Colo. Assn. Realtors, 1982, Citizen of West, Nat. Western Stockshow, 1994. Mem. Greater Denver C. of C. (pres. 1966-67), U.S. League Savs. Instns. (bd. dirs. 1972-77, vice-chmn. 1979-80, chmn. 1980-81, mem. nat. legis. com., exec. com. 1974-77), Savs. League Colo. (exec. com. 1969-73, pres. 1971-72), Colo. Assn. Commerce and Industry (dir. 1971-76), Fellowship Christian Athletes (Denver area dir. 1963-76), Western Stock Show Assn. (dir. 1971—, exec. com. 1982-94, 1st v.p. 1985-94), Mountain and Plains Appaloosa Horse Club (pres. 1970-71), Roundup Riders of the Rockies (bd. dirs. 1979-2000, dir. emeritus 2000—, treas. 1980-87, v.p. 1987-89, pres.-elect 1989-91, pres. 1991-93). Republican. Presbyterian. Home: Surrey Ridge Estates 9902 N Heather Dr Castle Rock CO 80104-9133

BARNEA, URI N. music director, conductor, composer, violinist; b. Petah-Tikvah, Israel, May 29, 1943; came to U.S., 1971; s. Shimon and Miriam Burstein; m. Lizbeth A. Lund, Dec. 15, 1977; 2 children. Tchg. cert., Oranim Music Inst., Israel, 1966; postgrad., Hebrew U., Israel, 1969-71; MusB, Rubin Acad. Music, Israel, 1971; MA, U. Minn., 1974, PhD, 1977; D (hon.), Rocky Mountain Coll., 1999. Music dir. Jewish Cmty. Ctr., Mpls., 1971-73; condr. Youval Chamber Orch., Mpls., 1971-73; asst. condr. U. Minn. Orchs., Mpls., 1972-77; music dir., condr. Unitarian Soc., Mpls., 1973-78, Kenwood Chamber Orch., Mpls., 1974-78, Knox-Galesburg Symphony, 1978-83, Billings (Mont.) Symphony Soc., 1984—; asst. prof. Knox Coll., Galesburg, Ill., 1978-83; violinist, violist Yellowstone Chamber players, Billings, 1984—; violist Tri-City Symphony, Quad-Cities, Ill., Iowa, 1983-84; condr. Cedar Arts Forum String Camp, Cedar Falls, Iowa, 1981, 88; European conducting debut, London, Neuchatel and Fribourg, Switzerland, 1986; Can. conducting debut No. Music Festival, North Bay, Ont., 1989; Violin Concerto, 1990; Russian conducting debut Symphony Orch., Kuzbass, Kemerovo, 1993; recordings include: W. Piston's Flute and Clarinet Concertos, Mario Lombardo's Oboe Concerto, two compact discs of Am. music; composer numerous compositions including String Quartet (1st prize Aspen Composition Competition 1976), Sonata for Flute and Piano, 1975 (Diploma of Distinction 26th Viotti Internat. Competition, Italy 1975), Ruth, a ballet, 1974 (1st prize Oberhoffer Composition Contest 1976). Active in music adv. panel Ill. Arts Coun., 1980-83; v.p. Cmty. Concert Assn., Galesburg, 1980-83; bd. dirs. Knox Coll. Credit Union, Galesburg, 1982-83, Sta. KEMC Pub. Radio, Billings, 1984—, Fox Theater Corp., Billings, 1984-86. Recipient Friend of the Arts title Sigma Alpha Iota, 1982; Ill. Arts Coun. grantee, 1979; Hebrew U. Jerusalem scholar, 1972-74, Hebrew U. and Rubin Acad. Mus. scholar, 1969, 70; Individual Artist fellow Mont. Arts Coun., 1986. Mem. NEA (music adv. panel 1990-95), ASCAP, Am. Composers Forum, Condrs. Gukld, Am. String Tchrs. Assn. Office: Billings Symphony Soc 201 N Broadway Ste 350 Billings MT 59101-1936

BARNES, CHARLES ANDREW, physicist, educator; b. Toronto, Ont., Can., Dec. 12, 1921; came to U.S., 1953, naturalized, 1961; m. Phyllis Malcolm, Sept., 1950. BA, McMaster U., 1943; MA, U. Toronto, 1944; PhD, Cambridge U., 1950. Physicist Joint Brit.-Canadian Atomic Energy Project, 1944-46; instr. physics U. B.C., 1950-53, 55-56; mem. faculty Calif. Inst. Tech., 1953-55, 56—, prof. physics, 1962-92; prof. emeritus physics, 1992—. Guest prof. Niels Bohr Inst., Copenhagen, 1973-74. Editor, contbr. to profl. books and jours. Recipient medal Inst. d'Astrophysique de Paris, 1986, Alexander von Humboldt U.S. Sr. Scientist award, Fed. Republic of Germany, 1986; NSF sr. fellow Denmark, 1962-63. Fellow AAAS, Am. Phys. Soc. Office: Calif Inst Tech 1201 E California Blvd Pasadena CA 91125-0001

BARNES, CLOYD RAY, sculptor, retired engineer; b. Hartford, Ark., July 18, 1934; s. Cloyd Hiram and Esta Elizabeth (McCafferty) B.; m. Wanda Jean Carlton, Oct. 17, 1954; children: Mark E., Stephanie Barnes Veasman. BS in Physics, Tulsa U., 1968. Mem. tech. staff N.Am. Rockwell, Tulsa, 1964-68; sr. aerosystems engr. Gen. Dynamics, Alamogordo, N.Mex., 1968-72; mgr. project engring. Dynalectron Corp., Alamogordo, 1972-77, mgr. ops. dept. Alamagordo, 1977-80, tech. dir. radar backscatter divsn., 1980-84, tech. dir., site mgr., 1984-86; mgr. radio frequency test ops. Martin Marietta Denver Aerospace, 1986-89, dept. staff engr., 1989-91. Represented by Nedra Matteuccis Gallery, Santa Fe; interim instr. Denver Art Students League, 1994. Exhibited in group shows at Southeastern Wildlife Expo, Charleston, S.C., Nat. Acad. Design, N.Y.C., Audubon Show, N.Y.C., Am. Artists Profl. League, N.Y.C., (Helen G. Oehler award), 1991, Nat. Wildlife Show, Kansas City, 1993 (Best of Show), Cantigny Park, Chgo., BCCFA Show, Clifton, Tex. (Best of Show award), Western Regional Show, Cheyenne, Wyo., N.Am. Sculpture Exhibit, Golden, Colo., Rough Rider Art Show, Williston, N.D., 1993 (Grand Prize 1993), Ho. Reps. Office Bldg.-Rotunda, Washington, 1994, Am. Artists Profl. League, 1994 (Leila G. Sawyer award), Visual Individualists United, Bklyn., 1995 (Grumbacher Gold Medallion award), Pacific Rim Wildlife Art Exhbn., Seattle, Wash.; commissioned works include life-size bronze portrait figure of C.L. Tutt, Colo. Coll., Colorado Springs, 1992, monumental bronze running buffalo Buffalo Run Golf Course, Adams County, Colo., 1996; monumental 9 feet high gold mineral and pack burro installed in Colorado Springs, Colo., 1999. Fellow Am. Artists Profl. League; mem. IEEE, Rocky Mountain Elk Found. (assoc.), Allied Artists Am. (assoc.), Knickerbocker Artists (assoc.). Avocations: hunting, hiking, travel, reading. Home: 7425 S Milwaukee Way Littleton CO 80122-1951

BARNES, GERALD R. bishop; b. Phoenix, June 22, 1945; Grad., St. Leonard Sem., Dayton, Ohio; student, Assumption-St. John's Sem., San Antonio. Ordained priest Roman Cath. Ch., 1975, titular bishop of Monte Fiascone. Aux. bishop, San Bernardino, Calif., 1992-95; bishop San Bernardino, 1996—. Chmn. com. Hispanic affairs Nat. Conf. Cath. Bishops. Office: 1201 E Highland Ave San Bernardino CA 92404-4607

BARNES, KEITH LEE, electronics executive; b. San Francisco, Sept. 14, 1951; s. Arch Lee and Charlotte Mae (Sanborn) B.; m. Sharon Ann Tosaw, June 9, 1986; children: Allecia, Alexandra, Wyatt. BS, Calif. State U., San Jose, 1976. Mgr. engring. and mktg. Gould, Inc., Rolling Meadow, Ill., 1976-79; v.p., gen. mgr. Kontron Electronics, Mountain View, Calif., 1979-85; v.p. Valley Data Scis., Mountain View, 1985-86; pres., CEO Integrated Measurement Sys., Beaverton, Oreg., 1986-2000, chmn., CEO, 2000—. Bd. dirs. Data Io Corp., LWG, Inc., Clarity Visual Systems, Inc. Patentee in field. Bd. dirs. Am. Electronics Assn., 1992-93, chmn. Oreg. bd., 1993; trustee Oreg. Grad. Inst. for Sci. and Industry, 1996—; vice chair Oreg. Growth Account, 1998; regent U. Portland, 2000. Mem. IEEE, PGC. Republican. Roman Catholic. Office: Integrated Measurement Systems 9525 SW Gemini Dr Beaverton OR 97008-7149

BARNES, RAYMOND EDWARD, protective services official; b. Denver, May 1, 1950; s. Carroll E. and Margaret A. (Minckler) B.; m. Katherine Michele Sanchez, Jan. 3, 1970; 1 child, Tamara Adrienne. BS in Aerospace Tech., Bus., Edn., Met. State Coll., 1971; postgrad., Red Rocks C.C., 1974-75, U. No. Colo., 1976; grad. exec. fire officer program, Nat. Fire Acad., 1990; MPA, U. Colo., 1991. With City of Aurora (Colo.) Fire Dept., 1971—, paramedic and rescue technician, 1976-79, lt., 1979-82, capt., 1982-85, battalion chief, suppression, 1985-87, dir. tng., 1987-91, fire chief, 1991—. Adj. instr. Nat. Fire Acad., Md., 1987—; co-dir. Rocky Mountain Fire Acad.; metro co-chair Region VIII Tng. Resources and Data Exch. Active Aurora Gang Task Force; past committeeman, del. to county, state polit. assemblies Mem. Internat. Assn. Fire Chiefs (com. on terrorism), Internat. Assn. Metro Fire Chiefs (bd. mem.), Internat. Soc. Fire Svc. Instrs., Internat. Assn. Firefighters (occupl. safety and health com.), Instn. Fire Engrs., Soc. Nat. Fire Acad. Instrs., Soc. Exec. Fire Officers, Fire Dept. Safety Officers Orgn., State Fire Chiefs, Denver Metro Fire Chiefs, Aurora C. of C. (bd. dirs. leadership forum), Homeowners Assn. (past pres. bd. dirs.). Avocations: whitewater rafting, mountain biking, world travel, skiing, golf. Home: 3966 S Sable Cir Aurora CO 80014-5176 Office: City of Aurora Fire Dept 1470 S Havana St Aurora CO 80012-4090

BARNES, SUSAN LEWIS, lawyer; b. Palo Alto, Calif., June 11, 1943; d. Prof. and Mrs. L.J. Lewis; m. Sanford C. Barnes; 1 child, Jason Bullard Barnes. BS, Stanford U., 1965; JD, U. Wash., 1968. Law clk. Ariz. Ct. Appeals, Tucson, 1968-71, U.S. Atty.'s Office, Seattle, 1971-96, 1st asst. U.S. atty., 1994-96, interim U.S. Atty., 1993, 1st asst. U.S. Atty., 1991-93, chief civil divsn., 1982-91; ptnr. McKay Chadwell PLLC, Seattle, 1996—. Pres. Fed. Bar WDWN, 1995; lawyer's rep. 9th cir. Office: McKay Chadwell PLLC 701 5th Ave Ste 7201 Seattle WA 98104-7042

BARNETT, R(ALPH) MICHAEL, theoretical physicist, educational agency administrator; b. Gulfport, Miss., Jan. 25, 1944; s. Herbert Chester and Lisa Margaret (Kielley) B.; m. Suzanne Hamilton, Feb. 10, 1980; children: Leilani Pinho, Julia Alexandra, Russell Alan. BS, Antioch Coll., 1966; PhD, U. Chgo., 1971. Postdoctoral fellow U. Calif., Irvine, 1972-74; rsch. fellow Harvard U., Cambridge, Mass., 1974-76; rsch. assoc. Stanford (Calif.) Linear Accelerator Ctr., 1976-83; vis. physicist Inst. Theoretical Physics U. Calif., Santa Barbara, 1983-84; staff scientist Lawrence Berkeley Nat. Lab., 1984-89, sr. scientist and head particle data group, 1990—; co-dir. QuarkNet Ednl. Project, 1999—. V.p. Contemporary Physics Edn. Project, 1987-98, pub. info. coor. Am. Phys. Soc. Dvsn. of Particles and Fields, 1994-97; edn. coord. ATLAS experiment at CERN, Geneva; prodr. film: The Atlas Experiment, 2000. Author: Teachers' Resource Book on Fundamental Particles and Interactions, 1988, Review of Particle Physics, 1990, 6th edit., 2000, Particle Physics—One Hundred Years of Discoveries, 1996, Guide to Experimental Particle Physics Literature, 1993, 2d edit., 1996, The Charm of Strange Quarks, Mysteries and Revolutions of Particle Physics, 2000, (chart) Fundamental Particles and Interactions, 1987, 4th edit., 1999, World Wide Web feature, The Particle Adventure, 1995, rev. edit. 2000, (CD ROM) The Quark Adventure, 2000. Fellow Am. Phys. Soc. (pub. info. coord. divsn. particles and fields 1994-97, taskforce on informing the public). Achievements include research on the Standard Model and its extensions, including studies of nature and validity of quantum chromodynamics; analyses of neutral current couplings; calculations of the production of heavy quarks; predictions of properties and decays of supersymmetric particles and higgs bosons. Office: Lawrence Berkeley Nat Lab MS-50-308 1 Cyclotron Rd Berkeley CA 94720-0001 E-mail: barnett@lbl.gov

BARNHART, ARTHUR L. state official; State contr. Colo. Personnel and Gen. Support Svcs., Denver. Office: Colo Personnel and Gen Support Svcs 1525 Sherman St Ste 250 Denver CO 80203-1761

BARNHART, DOUGLAS EDWARD, construction company executive; b. Tex., Dec. 15, 1946; BSCE, Tex. Tech. U., 1969. V.p. C.E. Wylie Constrn. Co., San Diego, 1976-83; CEO Douglas E. Barnhart, Inc., San Diego, 1983—. Chmn. Calif. Contractor's State Lic. Bd.; commr. Calif. Uniform Pub. Constrn. Cost Acctg. Commn.; bd. dirs. San Diego Nat. Bank. Recipient Small Bus. Award for excellence, Bus./Industry award Greater San Diego Industry-Edn. Coun., 1994. Mem. Am. Arbitration Assn., Associated Gen. Contractors Am. (chmn., dir. Constrn. Apprenticeship Trust, dir. Constrn. Pension Trust, chmn. naval engring. com., vice-chmn. heavy indsl. divsn.), Associated Builders and Contractors, Lincoln Club San Diego, Soc. Mil. Engrs., San Diego Associated Gen. Contractors (pres. 1994). Home: Douglas E Barnhart Inc PO Box 667 Poway CA 92064 E-mail: cpernieano@debconstruct.com

BARNHOLT, EDWARD W. computer company executive; CEO Hewlett-Packard, Palo Alto, Calif., 1999-00, Agilent, Palo Alto, 2000—. Address: Agilent Technologies 3000 Hanover St Palo Alto CA 94304-1112

BARON, ROBERT CHARLES, publishing executive; b. L.A., Jan. 26, 1934; s. Leo Francis and Marietta (Schulze) B.; m. Faye Helen Rogers, Jan. 28, 1961 (div. 1984); m. Charlotte Rose Persinger, Nov. 29, 1986; stepchildren: Brett, Kristen. BS in Physics, St. Joseph's Coll., 1956. Registered profl. engr., Mass. Engr. RCA, Camden, N.J., 1955-57, Computer Control Co., Framingham, Mass., 1959-61, program mgr. Mariner II and IV space computers, 1961-65, engring. mgr., 1965-69; worldwide systems mgr. Honeywell Minicomputer, Framingham, 1970-71; founder, pres., CEO Prime Computer, Framingham, 1971-75; pvt. practice Boston, 1976-83; founder and pres. Fulcrum Pub., Golden, Colo., 1984—. Bd. dirs. Prime Computer, Framingham, Mass., Alling-Lander, Cheshire, Conn., Oxion, Hugoton, Kans., Fulcrum Pub., Golden Colo. Author: Digital Logic and Computer Operations, 1966, Micropower Electronics, 1970, America in the Twentieth Century, 1995, Footsteps on the Sands of Time, 1999; editor: The Garden and Farm Books of Thomas Jefferson, 1987, Soul of America: Documenting Our Past, 1492-1974, 1989, Colorado Rockies: The Inaugural Season, 1993, Thomas Hornsby Ferril and the American West, 1996. Trustee Lincoln Filene Ctr., Tufts U., Medford, Mass., 1982-84; vice chmn. bd. dirs. Mass. Audubon Soc., Lincoln, 1980-85; bd. dirs. Rocky Mountain Women's Inst., Denver, 1987-90; bd. dirs. Denver Pub. Libr. Friends Found., 1989-96, pres., 1994-96. Mem. Am. Antiquarian Soc. (bd. dirs., chmn. 1993—), Internat. Wilderness Leadership Found. (bd. dirs. 1990—, chmn. 1994-2000), Thoreau Soc., Mass. Hist. Soc., Western History Assn., Grolier Club, Hakluyt Soc. Avocations: writing, reading, sports, gardening, collecting clocks. Office: Fulcrum Pub Ste 300 16100 Table Mountain Pkwy Golden CO 80403-1672 E-mail: bob@fulcrum_books.com

BARONDES, SAMUEL HERBERT, psychiatrist, educator; b. Bklyn., Dec. 21, 1933; s. Solomon and Yetta (Kaplow) B.; m. Ellen Slater, Sept. 1, 1963 (dec. Nov. 22, 1971); children: Elizabeth Francesca, Jessica Gabrielle. AB, Columbia U., 1954, MD, 1958. Intern, then asst. resident in medicine Peter Bent Brigham Hosp., Boston, 1958-60; sr. asst. surgeon USPHS, NIH, Bethesda, Md., 1960-63; resident in psychiatry McLean and Mass. Gen. hosps., Boston, 1963-66; asst. prof., then assoc. prof. psychiatry and molecular biology Albert Einstein Coll. Medicine., Bronx, N.Y., 1966-69; prof. psychiatry U. Calif., San Diego, 1969-86, prof., chmn. dept. psychiatry, dir. Langley Porter Psychiat. Inst. San Francisco, 1986-94, dir. Ctr. Neurobiology and Psychiatry, 1994—, Jeanne and Sanford Robertson Prof. Neurobiol. and Psychiatry, 1996—. Pres. McKnight Endowment Fund for Neurosci., 1989-98, bd. dirs., 1987—; mem. sci. adv. com. Rsch. Am.; mem. governing coun. Internat. Brain Rsch. Orgn., 1994—; mem. bd. sci. counselors NIMH, 1997—, chair, 2000—. Author: Molecules and Mental Illness, 1993, Mood Genes, 1998; mem. editorial bds. profl. jours.; contbr. numerous articles to profl. publs. Recipient Rsch. Career Devel. award USPHS, 1967, Elliott Royer award, 1989, P.H. Stillmark medal Estonia, 1989; Fogarty Internat. scholar NIH, 1979; J. Robert Oppenheimer lectr., 2000. Fellow AAAS, Am. Psychiat. Assn., Am. Coll. Neuropsychopharmacology; mem. Inst. Medicine Nat. Acad. Sci. Office: U Calif-San Francisco Langley Porter Psychiat Ins 401 Parnassus Ave San Francisco CA 94143-0984 E-mail: barondes@socrates.ucsf.edu

BARONE, ANGELA MARIA, artist, researcher; b. Concesio, Brescia, Italy, June 29, 1957; came to U.S., 1983; d. Giuseppe and Adelmina (D'Ercole) B. Laurea cum laude in geol. scis., U. Bologna, Italy, 1981; PhD in Marine Geology, Columbia U., 1989. Cert. in profl. photography, N.Y. Inst. Photography, N.Y.C., 1992; cert. in the fine art of painting and drawing North Light Art Sch., Cin., 1993. Collaborative asst. Marine Geology Inst., Bologna, 1981-83, Inst. Geology and Paleontology, Florence, Italy, 1982-83, Sta. de Geodynamique, Villefranche, France, 1982; grad. rsch. asst. Lamont-Doherty Geol. Obs., Palisades, N.Y., 1983-89, postdoctoral rsch. asst., 1989; postgrad. rschr. Scripps Instn. of Oceanography, La Jolla, Calif., 1990-92; artist San Diego, 1993—. Contbr. articles to profl. jours. Mem. Am. Geophys. Union (co-pres. meeting session 1990), Nat. Mus. Women in Arts (assoc.). Home: 7540 Charmant Dr Apt 1222 San Diego CA 92122-5044

BARR, JAMES NORMAN, federal judge; b. Kewanee, Ill, Oct. 21, 1940; s. James Cecil and Dorothy Evelyn (Dorsey) B.; m. Trilla Anne Reeves, Oct. 31, 1964 (div. 1979); 1 child, James N. Jr.; m. Phyllis L. DeMent, May 30, 1986; children: Renae, Michele. BS, Ill. Wesleyan U., 1962; JD, Ill. Inst. Tech., 1971. Bar: Ill. 1972, Calif. 1977. Assoc. Pretzel, Stouffer, Nolan & Rooney, Chgo., 1974-76; claims counsel Safeco Title Ins. Co., L.A., 1977-78; assoc. Kamph & Jackman, Santa Ana, Calif., 1978-80; lawyer pvt. practice Law Offices of James N. Barr, Santa Ana, 1980-86; judge U.S Bankruptcy Ct. Ctrl. Dist. Calif., Santa Anna, 1987—. Adj. prof. Chapman U. Sch. Law, 1996—. Lt. USN, 1962-67, Vietnam. Mem. Fed. Bar Assn. (Orange County chpt. bd. dirs. 1996-2000), Orange County Bar Assn. (cmty. outreach com.), Nat. Conf. Bankruptcy Judges, Orange County Bankruptcy Forum (bd. dirs. 1989—), Peter M. Elliott Inn Ct. (founder, first pres. 1990-91), Warren J. Ferguson Am. Inn of Ct. (founder). Office: US Bankruptcy Ct 411 W 4th St Santa Ana CA 92701-4500

BARR, M.E. See BIGELOW, MARGARET ELIZABETH BARR

BARR, RONALD JEFFREY, dermatologist, pathologist; b. Mpls., Jan. 5, 1945; s. Maxwell Michael and Ethel Deana (Ring) B.; m. Ulla Elisabet Edstam; children: Anna, Jessica, Sara. BA, Johns Hopkins U., 1967, MD, 1970. Diplomate Am. Bd. Pathology, Am. Bd. Dermatology. Intern U. Calif., San Diego, 1970-71, resident in pathology, 1971-75, resident in dermatology Irvine, 1975-78, fellow in dermatopathology, 1975-78, asst. prof. dermatology, 1977-83, assoc. prof. dermatology and pathology, 1983-86, prof. dermatology and pathology, 1987—, dir. Dermatopathology Lab., 1979—, prof., chmn. dept. dermatology Davis, 1986-87. Bd. dirs.

Am. Bd. Dermatology, 1989—, pres., 1997. Contbr. more than 10 chpts. to books. more than 100 articles to profl. jours. Lt. USN, 1971-73. Fellow Am. Soc. Dermatopathology (pres. 1988-89); mem. Internat. Soc. Dermatopathology, Internat. Com. for Dermatopathology (sec.-treas. 1987-91, pres. 1992-93). Office: U Calif Irvine Med Ctr Dermatopathology Lab 101 The City Dr S Orange CA 92868-3201

BARR, ROSEANNE See ROSEANNE

BARRETT, BRUCE RICHARD, physics educator; b. Kansas City, Kans., Aug. 19, 1939; s. Buford Russell and Miriam Aileen (Adams) B.; m. Gail Louise Geiger, Sept. 3, 1961 (div. Aug. 1969); m. Joan Frances Livermore, May 21, 1979. BS, U. Kans., 1961; postgrad., Swiss Poly., Zurich, 1961-62; MS, Stanford U., 1964, PhD, 1967. Research fellow Weizmann Inst. Sci., Rehovot, Israel, 1967-68; postdoctoral research fellow, research assoc. U. Pitts., 1968-70; asst. prof. physics U. Ariz., Tucson, 1970-72, assoc. prof., 1972-76, prof., 1976—, assoc. chmn. dept., 1977-83, mem. faculty senate, 1979-83, 88-90, 91-97, program dir. theoretical physics NSF, 1985-87, mem. tech. transfer com., 1996-97, 98-99, mem. grad. coun., 1998-2000. Chmn. adv. com. Internat. Scholars, Tucson, 1985-96; chmn. rsch. policy com. U. Ariz. Faculty Senate, 1993-94, 95-96; affiliate prof. U. Wash.-Seattle, 2000—. Woodrow Wilson fellow, 1961-62; NSF fellow, 1962-66; Weizmann Inst. fellow, 1967-68; Andrew Mellon fellow, 1968-69; Alfred P. Sloan Found. research fellow, 1972-74; Alexander von Humboldt fellow, 1976-77; Japan Soc. for Promotion of Sci. rsch. fellow, 1998; NSF grantee, 1971-85, 87—; Netherlands F.O.M. research fellow Groningen, 1980; recipient sr. U.S. scientist award (Humboldt prize) Alexander von Humboldt Found., 1983-85. Fellow Am. Phys. Soc. (publs. com. divsn. nuclear physics 1983-86, program com. 1993-94, chmn. steering com. for Nuclear Physics Summer Sch. 1996-98, mem. exec. com. four corners sect. 1998—, vice chmn. 2000, chair elect 2001, vice chmn. forum on internat. physics 2000, chair elect 2001), Phi Beta Kappa (pres. Alpha Ariz. chpt. 1992, 00), Sigma Xi, Sigma Pi Sigma, Omicron Delta Kappa, Beta Theta Pi, Phi Beta Kappa (senate 2000—). Office: U Ariz Dept Physics PO Box 210081 Tucson AZ 85721-0081 E-mail: bbarrett@physics.arizona.edu

BARRETT, CANDICE, museum administrator; BS, Northwestern U.; postgrad., U. Minn. Past dir. theatre in edn. program So. Meth. U., Dallas; past acting and directing instr. San Francisco State U.; past exec. dir. Acad. Media and Theatre Arts, San Francisco; past live entertainment dir. Disneyland, Anaheim, Calif.; past prodr., writer, actress Children's Audio Svc., Chapel Hill, N.C.; dir., curator L.A. Children's Mus., 1998—. Past guest instr. audio prodn. tchrs. seminar Stephens Coll., Columbia, Mo.; past guest instr. Nat. Summer Drama Inst. So. Ill. U., Edwardsville; past panelist children's media NEH, Washington; past on-site reviewer theatre arts NEA, Washington; past West Coast rep. Action Children's TV; past children's media reviewer Corp. Pub. Broadcasting; past adj. prof. directing dept. theatre U. So. Calif.; past asst. agent Writers and Artists. Past edn. program cons. Joseph Campbell Found. Home: 3720 Tilden Ave Los Angeles CA 90034-6912 Office: LA Children's Mus 310 N Main St Los Angeles CA 90012-2830

BARRETT, CRAIG R. computer company executive; b. 1939; Assoc. prof. Stanford U., 1965-74; with Intel Corp., Chandler, Ariz., 1974—, v.p. components tech. and mfg. group, sr. v.p., gen. mgr. components tech. and mfg. group, exec. v.p., mgr. components tech., now pres., CEO. Mem. NAE, 1994—. Office: Intel Corp 2200 Mission College Blvd. Santa Clara CA 95052-8119*

BARRETT, CYNTHIA TOWNSEND, neonatologist; b. Santa Barbara, Calif., Sept. 8, 1937; d. George Barker and Elizabeth Louise (Magee) B. AB, Vassar Coll., 1958; MD, Harvard U., 1962. Diplomate. Am. Bd. Pediats. Intern, resident in pediats., pediat. chief resident U. Wash., 1962-66, fellow in physiology & biophysics, 1966-67; fellow in fetal cardiovascular physiology U. Calif., San Francisco, 1967-70; chief divsn. neonatology, assoc. prof. pediats. UCLA Sch. Medicine, 1970—. Mem. Internat. Newborn Intensive Care Soc., European Soc. Perinatal Rsch., Western Soc. Pediat. Rsch., Am. Thoracic Soc., Soc. Pediat. Rsch., Perinatal Rsch. Soc. Republican. Episcopalian. Home: 6778 Shearwater Ln Malibu CA 90265-4144 Office: UCLA Sch Medicine Dept Pediats Rm 12-467 Los Angeles CA 90095-0001 E-mail: cbarrett@mednet.ucla.edu

BARRETT, DOROTHY, performing arts administrator; b. L.A. d. Lester Arnold and Kathryn (Halverson) Silvera; m. Robert A.H. Cochrane, May 20, 1949 (div. Feb. 1965); 1 stepchild, Michele Cochrane Shaw. Student, LA C.C., 1937-38. Adminstrv. dir. Am. Nat. Acad. of Performing Arts, 1964—; founder, dir. Acad. Children's Workshop, 1964—. Produced, choreographed 30 Christmas shows, 1964—; tchr. of dance Barrett Sch. of the Arts, North Hollywood, 1948, Am. Nat. Acad., Studio City, 1964—, tchr. of acting, 1964—; tchr. of speech UCLA Extension, West Hollywood, 1972. Actress, dancer: (motion pictures) A Damsel in Distress, 1937, The Great Waltz, 1938, Gone with the Wind, 1939, Frisco Sal, Wizard of Oz, 1939, Juke Box Soundies, 1942, Hot Money, 1944, Monsieur Beaucaire, 1945, The Imperfect Lady, 1947, Perils of Pauline, 1945, The Stork Club, 1945, Mildred Pierce, 1945, A Bell for Adano, 1945, Weekend at the Waldorf, 1945, Blue Skies, 1946, Connecticut Yankee in King Arthur's Court, 1947, California, 1947, Samson and Deliliah, 1948, The Babe Ruth Story, 1948; (Broadway stage productions) Earl Carroll's Vanities, 1939, Buddy De Sylva's Louisiana Purchase, 1940, Billy Rose's Diamond Horseshoe, 1943, George Abbott's Beat the Band, 1942, others; (TV) co-star KTLA's Secrets of Gourmet, 1946; prodr., dir.: A Touch of Broadway, 1996, 97, (on tour) 1998, 99; author: (poetry) Between the Bookends, 1942, The Tolucan, The Legal Journal, 1959, Valley Green Sheet & Van Nuys News; contbr. articles to jours. Active Am. Women's Vol. Svc., 1942. Named Miss Culver City, 1937; recipient award ARC, 1943, Humanitarian award for work with children City of L.A., 1994. Office: Am Nat Acad Performing Arts 10944 Ventura Blvd Studio City CA 91604-3340

BARRETT, JALMA See BOERSMA, JUNE ELAINE

BARRETT, JAMES EMMETT, federal judge; b. Lusk, Wyo., Apr. 8, 1922; s. Frank A. and Alice C. (Donoghue) B.; m. Carmel Ann Martinez, Oct. 8, 1949; children: Ann Catherine Barrett Sandahl, Richard James, John Donoghue. Student, U. Wyo., 1940-42, LLB, 1949; student, St. Catherine's Coll., Oxford, Eng., 1945, Cath. U. Am., , 1946. Bar: Wyo. 1949. Mem. firm Barrett and Barrett, Lusk, 1949-67; atty. Niobrara Sch. Dist., 1950-64; county and pros. atty. Niobrara County, Wyo., 1951-62; atty. Town of Lusk, 1952-54; atty. gen. State of Wyo., 1967-71; judge U.S. Circuit Ct. Appeals (10th cir.), 1971—, now sr. judge. Active Boy Scouts Am.; sec.-treas. Niobrara County Republican Central Com.; trustee St. Joseph's Children's Home, Torrington, Wyo., 1971-85. Served as cpl. AUS, 1942-45, ETO. Recipient Distinguished Alumni award U. Wyo., 1973 Mem. VFW, Am. Legion, Order of Coif (hon. mem. Wyo. Coll. Law/U. Wyo. chpt.).

BARRETT, JANE HAYES, lawyer; b. Dayton, Ohio, Dec. 13, 1947; d. Walter J. and Jane H. Barrett BA, Calif. State U.-Long Beach, 1969; JD, U. So. Calif., 1972. Bar: Calif. 1972, U.S. Dist. Ct. (cen. dist.) Calif. 1972, U.S. Ct. Appeals (9th cir.) 1982, U.S. Supreme Ct. Assoc. Arter, Hadden, Lawler, Felix & Hall, L.A., 1972-79, ptnr., 1979-94, mng. ptnr., 1984-93; ptnr. Preston, Gates & Ellis, 1994—, mng. ptnr., 1994—. Lectr. bus. law Calif. State U., 1973-75. Mem. adv. bd. Harriet Buhai Legal Aid Ctr., 1991-96, mem. bd. pub. counsel, 1996-98; pres. Pilgrim Parents Orgn. 1990-91; chmn. fin. Our Mother Good Counsel Sch.; bd. regents Loyola H.S. Named Outstanding Grad. Calif. State U., Long Beach, 1988, Outstanding Alumnae Polit. Sci., 1993. Fellow Am. Bar Found.; mem. ABA (bd. govs. 1980-84, chmn. young lawyers divsn. 1980-81, com. on delivery of legal svcs. 1985-89, exec. coun. legal edn. and admissions sects. 1985-89, fin. sec. torts and ins. practice 1982-83, adv. mem. fed. judiciary com. 9th circuit rep. 2000—, v.p. 1997—, Am. Bar Endowment 1999, bd. dirs. 1990—, sec. 1993-95, v.p. 1998-99, pres., 1999-2000, bd. fellows young lawyers divsn. 1992—), Calif. State Bar (com. adminstrn. of justice, editl. bd. Calif. Lawyers 1981-84), Legion Lex (bd. dirs. 1990-93), Los Feliz Homeowners Assn. (bd. dirs.). Democrat E-mial. Office: Preston Gates & Ellis 725 S Figueroa St Ste 2100 Los Angeles CA 90017-5421 E-mail: janeb@prestongates.com

BARRETT, MICHAEL HENRY, civil engineer; b. Dove Creek, Colo., June 20, 1932; s. Frank Ace and Carrie Ethel (Snyder) B.; m. Barbara Jane Kreutz, Aug. 7, 1954; children: Robert, Mary, Bonnie, William. B.S. in Civil Engring, U. Colo., 1955, postgrad., 1955-64; M.B.A., U. Denver, 1979. Registered profl. engr., Colo., Calif., Fla., Wis., N.C., Minn., N.Mex., Utah. Design engr., then partner Ketchum & Konkel, Denver, 1955-69; pres. Ketchum, Konkel, Barrett, Nickel, Austin, Denver, 1969-79, chmn. bd., 1979-85, pres., chmn., 1986-88; prin., cons. Martin/Martin, 1988—; cons. MMFX Steel Co., 2000—. Dir. Testing Cons., Inc., Martin Assoc. Group; mem. faculty U. Colo., 1963-64, U. Denver, 1968-69; lectr. Civil Def., 1962-68. Patentee in field. Exec. bd. Denver Area council Boy Scouts Am., 1970— , pres., 1974-75, area v.p., 1976-82, area pres., 1982; mem. Westminster (Colo.) Planning Commn., 1971-72; chmn. bd. dirs. Denver Boys, Inc. Served with USNR, 1951-54, USAR, 1955-63. Recipient Lincoln Arc Welding award, 1966, 68, award Am. Inst. Steel Constrn., 1969, Disting. Engring. Alumnus award U. Colo., 1984, Honor award Colo. Engring. Coun., 1984, Silver Beaver award Boy Scouts Am., 1977, Silver Antelope award, 1983. Fellow ASCE (life); mem. Nat. Soc. Profl. Engrs., Am. Concrete Inst., Soc. Exptl. Stress Analysis, Profl. Engrs. Colo. (pres. 1970), Am. Cons. Engrs. Coun. (1st place award 1973, pres. Colo. chpt. 1982, Orley Phillips award 1992, com. of fellows 1993, peer reviewer 1984—, George Washington Leadership award 1998), Structural Engrs. Assn. Colo., Am. Arbitration Assn., Harvard Bus. Sch. Club, Denver C. of C., Rotary (dir. 1976-78). Office: Martin & Martin Inc 4251 Kipling St Wheat Ridge CO 80033-2896 E-mail: mbarrett@martinmartin.com

BARRETT, REGINALD HAUGHTON, biology educator, wildlife management educator; b. San Francisco, June 11, 1942; s. Paul Hutchison and Mary Lambert (Hodgkin) B.; m. Katharine Lawrence Ditmars, July 15, 1967; children: Wade Lawrence, Heather Elizabeth. BS in Game Mgmt., Humboldt State U., 1965; MS in Wildlife Mgmt., U. Mich., 1966; PhD in Zoology, U. Calif., Berkeley, 1971. Rsch. biologist U. Calif., Berkeley, 1970-71, acting asst. prof., 1971-72; rsch. scientist div. wildlife rsch. Commonwealth Scientific and Indsl. Rsch. Orgn., Darwin, Australia, 1972-75; from asst. prof. to prof. U. Calif., Berkeley, 1975—. Author: (with others) Report on the Use of Fire in National Parks and Reserves, 1977, Research and Management of Wild Hog Populations, Proceedings of a Symposium, 1977, Sitka Deer Symposium, 1979, Symposium on Ecology and Management of Barbary Sheep, 1980, Handbook of Census Methods for Birds and Mammals, 1981, Wildlife 2000: Modeling Habitat Relationships of Terrestrial Vertebrates, 1986, Translocation of Wild Animals, 1988, Wildlife 2001: Populations, 1992; contbr. articles, abstracts, reports to profl. jours. Recipient Outstanding Profl. Achievement award Humboldt State U. Alumni Assn., 1986, Bruce R. Dodd award, 1965, Howard M. Wight award, 1966; Undergrad. scholar Nat. Wildlife Fedn., 1964, NSF grad. fellow, 1965-70; Union found. Wildlife Rsch. grantee, 1968-70. Mem. The Wildlife Soc. (pres. Bay Area chpt. 1978-79, pres. western sect. 1997-98, cert. wildlife biologist, R.F. Dasmann Profl. of Yr. award western sect. 1989), Am. Soc. Mammalogists (life), Soc. for Range Mgmt. (life), Ecol. Soc. Am. (cert. sr. ecologist), Soc. Am. Foresters, Australian Mammal Soc., Am. Inst. Biol. Scis., AAAS, Calif. Acad. Scis., Internat. Union for the Conservation of Nature (life), Calif. Bot. Soc., Orgn. Wildlife Planners, Sigma Xi, Xi Sigma Pi. Episcopalian. Avocations: hunting, fishing, photography, camping, backpacking. Office: U Calif 151 Hilgard Hall Berkeley CA 94720-3111

BARRETT, RONALD W. executive; Sr. v.p. Affymas Rsch. Inst., Palo Alto, Calif. Recipient Newcomb-Cleve. prize, 1996-97. Office: Affymax Rsch Inst 4001 Miranda Ave Palo Alto CA 94304-1218

BARRETT-CONNOR, ELIZABETH LOUISE, epidemiologist, educator; b. Evanston, Ill., Apr. 8, 1935; m. James D. Connor; 3 children. BA, Mt. Holyoke Coll., 1956, DSc (hon.), 1985; MD, Cornell U., 1960; PhD (hon.), U. Utrecht, The Netherlands, 1996, U. Bergen, Norway, 1996, U. Helsinki, Finland, 2000. Diplomate Am. Bd. Internal Medicine, Nat. Bd. Med. Examiners. Instr. medicine U. Miami, Fla., 1965-68, asst. prof. medicine, 1968-70; asst. prof. community and family medicine U. Calif., San Diego, 1970-74, assoc. prof. community and family medicine, 1974-81, prof. community and family medicine, 1981—, acting chair dept. community and family medicine, 1981-82, chmn. dept. family and preventative medicine, 1982-97. Mem. hosp. infection control com. VA Med. Ctr., San Diego, 1971-81; Kelly West Meml. lectr. Am. Diabetes Assn., Indpls. 1987; vis. prof.Royal Soc. Medicine, London, 1989; John Rankin lectr. U. Wis., 1989; Don McLeod Meml. lectr., Halifax, N.S., Can., 1990; Elizabeth Blackwell lectr., Rochester, Minn., 1991; Lila Wallace vis. prof. N.Y. Hosp.-Cornell Med. Ctr., N.Y.C., 1992; Donald P. Shiley vis. lectr. Scripps Clinic and Rsch. Found., La Jolla, Calif., 1993; Leonard M. Schuman lectr. U. Mich., 1993; disting. vis. U. Western Australia, 1997; disting. lectr. geriatrics Duke U. Med. Ctr., Durham, N.C., 1998; Heath Clark lectr.,London, 1989, Pickering lectr., Cambridge, England, 2000. Contbr. articles to profl. jours. Recipient Frederick Murgatroyd prize, 1965, Kaiser award for excellence in tchg., 1982, Dr. of Yr. award San Diego Health Care Assn., 1987, merit award Nat. Inst. Aging, 1987, Making a Difference for Women's Health award Soroptimists, La Jolla, 9195, clin. svc. award Soc. for Advancement Women's Health Rsch., 1997; NIH grantee, 1970—. Fellow ACP (James D. Bruce Meml. award 1994, Masters award 2001), Am. Heart Assn. (chmn. budget com. coun. on epidemiology 1987-88, chmn. coun. on epidemiology 1988-89m Ancel Keys lectr. 1995, Elizabeth Barrett-Connor rsch. award 1995, Merit award 1998), Royal Soc. Health, Am. Coll. Preventive Medicine (Katharine Boucot Sturgis lectr. 1986, Am. Coll. Nutrition, Royal Soc. Medicine; mem. APHA (chmn. epidemiology sect. 1989-90, Wade Hampton Frost lectr. 1993), Assn. Tchrs. Preventive Medicine (bd. dirs. 1987-92, Outstanding Educator award 1992), Inst. Medicine, Soc. Epidemiol. Rsch. (pres. 1983, John Cassell Meml. lectr. 1997), Phi Beta Kappa. Office: U Calif San Diego Family and Preventative Medicine 9500 Gilman Dr # Mc0607 La Jolla CA 92093-5004

BARRICKS, MICHAEL ELI, retinal surgeon; b. Chgo., Feb. 22, 1940; s. Arthur Goetz and Ruth (Zuckerman) B.; m. Zondra Dell Natman, Jan. 18, 1992; 1 child, Charleigh Ruth. BA, Harvard Coll., 1961; MD, U. Chgo., 1965; PhD, Stanford U., 1973. Diplomate Nat. Bd. Med. Examiners; lic. physician, Calif. Intern then resident in surgery Stanford (Calif.) U., 1965-67, postdoctoral fellow, 1967-72; resident, fellow in ophthalmology Bascom Palmer Eye Inst., Miami, Fla., 1972-76; fellow in retinal surgery U. Calif., San Francisco, 1976-77; asst. prof., dir. retina svc. U. Tex., San Antonio, 1977-78; retinal surgeon, dir. retina svc. Permanente Med. Group., Oakland, Calif., 1979—. Asst. clin. prof. U. Calif., San Francisco, 1980-92, assoc. clin. prof., 1993—; bd. dirs. Barricks Mfg. Co., Gadsden, Ala. Contbr. articles to profl. jours. Recipient Gold award Am. Acad. Pediatrics, Outstanding Physician award Kaiser Hosp., 1982, Cert. of Appreciation for Outstanding Teaching, U. Calif, San Francisco; ; Nat. scholar Fisher Body Craftsmans Guild; USPHS fellow Stanford U., 1967-70, Atholl McBean fellow Stanford Rsch. Inst., 1970-71. Fellow Am. Acad. Ophthalmology; mem. Permanente Ophthalmologic Soc. (pres. 1981), Vitreous Soc., Harvard Varsity Club, Crimson Key Soc. E-mail: michael.barricks@worldnet.att.net

BARRON, STEPHANIE, curator; AB, Columbia U., 1972; student, Harvard Inst. Arts Adminstrn., 1973; MA, Columbia U., 1974; postgrad., CUNY, 1975-76. Intern, curatorial asst. Solomon R. Guggenheim Mus., 1971-72; Nat. Endowment Arts intern in edn. Toledo Mus. Art, 1973-74; exhbn. coord. Jewish Mus., N.Y.C., 1975-76; assoc. curator modern art L.A. County Mus. Art, 1976-80, curator Twentieth Century art, 1980-94, coord. curatorial affairs, 1993-96, sr. curator Twentieth Century art, 1995—, v.p. edn. and pub. programs, 1996—. Lectr., panelist in field. Contbr. articles to profl. jours. Mem. art adv. panel IRS, 1996—; advisor U.S. Holocaust Mus., 1996—; mem. bd. trustees Scripps Coll., 1996—; mem. steering com. Villa Aurora, 1994—. Recipient George L. Wittenborn award ARLIS, 1991, award for best Am. exhbn. of yr. Assn. Internat. Critics Art, 1991, 97, Theo Wormland Kunstpreis, 1992, George L. Wittenborn award, 1992, Alfred H. Barr Jr. award Coll. Art Assn., 1992, E.L. Kirchner prize, Switzerland, 1997, award for best exhbn. catalogue Assn. Internat. Art Critics Art, First Pl. award Am. Assn. Art Mus., 1998, Hon. Mention, ARLIS, 1998; named Woman of Yr., Bus. and Profl. Women of UJA, Jewish Fedn., 1991, Friends of Tel Hashomer, 1991; named to Order of Merit, Fed. Republic of Germany, 1984; fellow Nat. Endowment of Arts, 1986-87; John J. McCloy fellow in art, 1981. Fellow Am. Acad. Arts and Scis.; mem. Art Table. Office: LA County Mus Art 5905 Wilshire Blvd Los Angeles CA 90036-4597

BARROW, THOMAS FRANCIS, artist, educator; b. Kansas City, Mo., Sept. 24, 1938; s. Luther Hopkins and Cleo Naomi (Francis) B.; m. Laurie Anderson, Nov. 30, 1974; children— Melissa, Timothy, Andrew. B.F.A., Kansas City Art Inst., 1963; M.S., Ill. Inst. Tech., 1965. With George Eastman House, Rochester, N.Y., 1966-72, asst. dir., 1971-72; assoc. dir. Art Mus., U. N. Mex., Albuquerque, 1973-76; assoc. prof. U. N.Mex., 1976-81, prof., 1981—, Presdl. prof., 1985-90. Author: The Art of Photography, 1971; sr. editor: Reading into Photography, 1982; contbr. to Brit. Ency. Am. Art, 1973, A Hundred Years of Photographic History: Essays in Honor of Beaumont Newhall, 1975, Experimental Vision, 1994; forward The Valiant Knights of Daguerre, 1978; contbr. articles to profl. jours.; one-man shows include Light Gallery, N.Y.C., 1974-76, 79, 82, Amarillo Art Ctr., 1990, Andrew Smith Gallery, Santa Fe, 1992, Laurence Miller Gallery, N.Y.C., 1996, U. N.Mex. Art Mus., 1997, Richard Levy Gallery, Albuquerque, 2000; exhibited in group shows including Pace Gallery, N.Y.C., 1973, Hudson River Mus., Yonkers, N.Y., 1973, Internat. Mus. Photography, Rochester, 1975, Seattle Art Mus., 1976, Mus. Fine Arts, Houston, 1977, Retrospective exhbn. L.A. County Mus. Art, 1987—; represented in permanent collections Nat. Gallery Can., Mus. Modern Art, Getty Ctr. for Arts and Humanities. Nat. Endowment for Arts fellow, 1971, 78. Office: U NMex Dept Art Albuquerque NM 87131-0001

BARRY, JOHN MAYNARD, urologist; b. Winona, Minn., Mar. 14, 1940; MD, U. Minn., 1965. Intern SUNY, Syracuse, 1965-66; resident U. Oreg. Med. Sch., Portland, 1969-73; with U. Hosp., Portland; prof., chmn. urology Oreg. Health Sci. U., Portland, 1980—. Dir. Renal Transplantation, 1976—, chmn. abdominal organ transplantation, 2000—. Office: Oreg Health Sci Ctr U Divsn Urology 3181 SW Sam Jackson Park Rd Portland OR 97201-3011

BARRY, MARY H. college official; BS in Speech and Drama, Bowling Green State U.; M Mgmt., Northwestern U.; JD, Western State U. V.p. 1st Nat. Bank, Chgo.; dir. Citibank, S.D.; sr. v.p. Marquette Banks, until 1990; dir. Nat. Coll., 1990-91; dir. acad. affairs, adminstrn. and Calif. Ctr. Profl. Edn., U. Phoenix, 1992-98; v.p. edn. Corinthian Colls., Inc., postsecondary edn. co., Santa Ana, Calif., 1998—. Maj. USMC, 1971-79. Office: Corinthian Colls 6 Hutton Centre Dr Ste 400 Santa Ana CA 92707-5764

BARRY, RICK (RICHARD FRANCIS DENNIS BARRY III), sportscaster, retired professional basketball player, marketing professional; b. Elizabeth, N.J., Mar. 28, 1944; s. Richard Francis and Alpha Monique (Stephanovich) B.; m. Pamela Hale, June 1965 (div.); children: Richard Francis IV, Jon Alan, Brent Robert, Drew William, Shannon Leigh; m. Pamela Stenesen, Sept. 1981 (div.); m. Lynn Norenberg, Aug. 1991; 1 child, Canyon Shane. Student, U. Miami, 1961-65. Basketball player San Francisco Warriors, NBA, 1965-67, Oakland Oaks, Am. Basketball Assn., 1967-69, Washington, Am. Basketball Assn., 1969-70, Virginia Squires, 1970, N.Y. Nets, Am. Basketball Assn., 1970-72, Golden State Warriors, NBA, 1972-78, Houston Rockets, NBA, 1978-80; sports broadcaster, basketball analyst CBS Sports, 1974-81; NBA color analyst Turner Sports, 1984-91; dir. mktg. Profl. Logistics Mgmt. Inc., Lafayette, Calif., 1994—. Mem. Am. Basketball Assn. All-Star Team, 1968-72, NBA All-Star Team, 1966-67, 73-78, NBA Championship Team, 1975; named Rookie of Yr., NBA, 1966, Most Valuable Player All Star Game, 1966, Most Valuable Player Championship Series, 1975; inducted into Basketball Hall of Fame, 1986. Only player to lead NCAA, NBA and Am. Basketball Assn. in scoring; all-time leader in free throw shooting NBA.

BARRY, STEVE, sculptor, educator; b. Jersey City, June 22, 1956; s. Thomas Daniel and Lorraine (Lowery) B. BFA, Sch. Visual Arts, N.Y.C., 1980; MFA, Hunter Coll., N.Y.C., 1984. Adj. lectr. Hunter Coll., 1984-89; assoc. prof. U. N.Mex., Albuquerque, 1989—. Kohler Arts and Industry Residency, 1996; bd. dirs. Albuquerque Ctr. Contemporary Arts. Exhbns. include Bklyn. Army Terminal, N.Y.C., 1983, City Gallery, N.Y.C., 1986, 90, Storefront for Art and Architecture, 1988, Artists Space, N.Y.C., 1989, Santa Barbara Art Mus., 1990, Kohler Arts Ctr., Sheboygan, Wis., 1991, Hirshhorn Mus., Washington, 1990, Fla. State U., 1992, Contemporary Art Mus., Houston, 1992, CAFE Gallery, Albuquerque, 1993, Charolette Jackson, Santa Fe, 1993, Ctr. for Contemporary Arts, Santa Fe, 1994, U. Wyo. Art Mus., 1995, Site Santa Fe, 1996, Sheldon Art Mus., Lincoln, Nebr., 1997, U. N.Mex. Art Mus., Albuquerque, 1997, Cedar Rapids (Iowa) Mus. of Art, 1998, Albuquerque Contemporary Art Ctr., 2000, Plan B, Santa Fe, 2000. Grantee Clocktower Nat. Studio, 1985, NEA, 1986, 88, 90, N.Y. State Coun. for the Arts, 1987, N.Y. Found. for the Arts, 1988; recipient AVA award, 1990. Home: PO Box 1046 Corrales NM 87048-1046 Office: U NMex Dept Art & Art History Albuquerque NM 87131-0001

BARRY, WILLIAM PATRICK, career officer; b. Boston, Aug. 1, 1957; s. John Joseph III and Esther Marie (Doherty) B.; m. Monica Marie Fournier. BS, U.S. Air Force Acad., 1979; MA in Polit. Sci., Stanford U., 1987; DPhil in Politics, Oxford (U.K.) U., 1996. Commd. 2d lt. USAF, 1979, advanced through grades to lt. col., 1995, student pilot Ariz., 1979-80, aircraft comdr. 42d Air Refueling Squadron Loring AFB, Maine, 1980-84, instr. pilot, exec. officer 509th Air Refueling Squadron Pease AFB, N.H., 1984-86; flight examiner 380th Air Refueling Wing, Plattsburgh AFB, N.Y., 1990-92; instr. dept. polit. sci. USAF Acad., Colorado Springs, Colo., 1987-89, asst. prof. polit. sci., 1995-98; politico military affairs officer Hdqs. U.S. European Command, Stuttgart, Germany, 1998—. Named one of Outstanding Young Men of Am., Montgomery, Ala., 1986. Mem. Am. Assn. Advancement of Slavic Studies. Avocations: gardening, cross-country skiing, flying. Address: HQ Useucom Unit 30400 Box 2388 APO AE 09128-4000 E-mail: barryw@eucom.mil

BART, PETER BENTON, newspaper editor, film producer, novelist; b. N.Y.C., July 24, 1932; m. Leslie Cox; children: Colby, Dilys. BA, Swarthmore Coll., 1954; MA, London Sch. Econs., 1956. Staff reporter The Wall Street Jour., N.Y.C., 1956-57, The N.Y. Times, N.Y.C., 1957-67; v.p. Paramount Pictures, Los Angeles, 1967-74; pres. Bart Palevsky Prodn., L.A., 1974-77, Lorimar Film Co., Los Angeles, 1977-82; sr. v.p., film producer Metro Goldwyn Mayer/United Artists, L.A., 1982-85; v.p., editorial dir. Variety and Daily Variety, L.A., 1989-, editor-in-chief. Author: Destinies, 1980, Thy Kingdom Come, 1983, Fade Out: The Calamitous Final Days of MGM, 1990; prodr.: (films) Fun with Dick and Jane, Islands in the Stream, Youngblood. Office: Variety 5700 Wilshire Blvd Ste 120 Los Angeles CA 90036-3644

BARTH, DELBERT SYLVESTER, environmental studies educator; b. Lawrenceburg, Ind., June 6, 1925; BS in Mil. Engring., U.S. Mil. Acad., 1946; MS in Nuclear Physics, Ohio State U., 1952; MS in Solid State Physics, Stevens Inst. Tech., 1960; PhD in Biophysics, Ohio State U., 1962. Health physics trainee Oak Ridge Nat. Lab., Tenn., 1947-49; asst. prof. dept. physics and chemistry U.S. Mil. Acad., West Point, N.Y., 1956-60; staff officer evaluation and planning sect. rsch. br. div. radiological health U.S. Pub. Health Svc., Dept. Health, Edn. and Welfare, 1960-61; investigator, staff officer experimental radiobiolgy program rsch. br. DRH, Rockville, Md., 1962-63; dir. bioenviron. rsch. program Southwestern Radiological Health Lab., U.S. Pub. Health Svc., Las Vegas, 1963-69; dir. bur. criteria and standards Nat. Air Pollution Control Adminstrn., DHEW, Durham, N.C., 1969-71; dir. Bur. Air Pollution Scis., Research Triangle Park, 1971, Nat. Environ. Rsch. Ctr., Research Triangle Park, 1971-72, Las Vegas, 1972-76; dep. asst. adminstr. health and ecological effects ORD U.S. Environ. Protection Agy., 1976-78; vis. prof. biophysics U. Nev., Las Vegas, 1978-82, sr. scientist environ. rsch. ctr., 1982-88, dir. environ. rsch. ctr., 1989-92, prof. environ. studies program, 1992-94; prof. emeritus environ. studies program, 1994—. Mem. sub-com. on environ. effects, mem. adv. com. to fed. radiation, mem. com. on hearing, bioaccoustics, biomechs.; chmn. adv. com. Nat. Air Quality Criteria; environ. monitoring advisor, mem. environ. com. ecological scis. divsn. Inst. Environ. Scis.; mem. Army Sci. Bd., 1984-90; mem. awards bd. EPA. Recipient PHS Disting. Svc. medal. Mem. AAAS, Sigma Xi. Office: U Nev Las Vegas Environ Studies Program 4505 S Maryland Pkwy Las Vegas NV 89154-9900

BARTLETT, ARTHUR EUGENE, franchise executive; b. Glens Falls, N.Y., Nov. 26, 1933; s. Raymond Ernest and Thelma (Williams) B.; m. Collette R. Bartlett, Jan. 9, 1955; 1 dau., Stacy Lynn. Sales mgr. Forest E. Olson, Inc., 1960-64; co-founder, v.p. Four Star Realty, Inc., Santa Ana, Calif., 1964-71, v.p., sec., 1964-71; founder, pres. Comps, Inc., Tustin, 1971-81; co-founder, chmn. of bd., pres., CEO Century 21 Real Estate Corp., Tustin, 1980—; pres. Larwin Sq. LLC Shopping Ctr, Tustin, Calif., 1979—. Chmn. bd. United Western Med. Ctrs., 1981-87. Named to Internat. Franchise Assn. Hall of Fame, 1987. Mem. Internat. Franchise Assn. (v.p., bd. dirs. 1975-80). Lodge: Masons. Office: 275 Centennial Way Ste 209 Tustin CA 92780-3709

BARTLETT, DAVID CARSON, state legislator; b. New London, Conn., Feb. 2, 1944; s. Neil Riley and Susan Marion (Carson) B.; m. Barbara Hunting, July 14, 1973 (div. 1974); m. Janice Anne Wezelman, Feb. 11, 1979; children: Daniel Wezelman, Elizabeth Anne. Student, Wesleyan U., Middletown, Conn., 1962-64; BA, U. Ariz., 1966, MA, 1970; JD, Georgetown U., 1976. Teaching asst. U. Ariz., Tucson, 1967-69; program analyst U.S. Dept. Labor, Washington, 1970-76; assoc. Snell & Wilmer, Tucson, 1976-77; pvt. practice Tucson, 1976-79; assoc. Davis, Eppstein & Hall, Tucson, 1979-85; mem. Ariz. Ho. of Reps., Tucson, 1983-88, Ariz. State Senate, 1989-92; chief counsel for civil rights Ariz. Atty. Gen.'s Office, Tucson, 1993-99, spl. couns., 1999—. Democrat. Home: 3236 E Via Palos Verdes Tucson AZ 85716-5854 Office: Ariz Attorney Gen 400 W Congress St Ste 215 Tucson AZ 85701-1352

BARTLETT, DAVID FARNHAM, physics educator; b. N.Y.C., Dec. 13, 1938; s. Frederic Pearson and Margaret Mary (Boulton) B.; m. Roxana Ellen Stoessel, Nov. 19, 1960; children: Andrew, Susannah, Christopher, Jennifer AB, Harvard U., 1959; AM, Columbia U., 1961, PhD, 1965. Instr. Princeton U., N.J., 1964-67, asst. prof., 1967-71; assoc. prof. physics U. Colo., Boulder, 1971-82, prof., 1982—. Editor: The Metric Debate, General Relativity and Gravitation, 1989; contbr. articles to profl. jours. Fellow Am. Phys. Soc.; mem. Am. Assn. Physics Tchrs., Am. Geophys. Union. Democrat Home: 954 Lincoln Pl Boulder CO 80302-7234 Office: U Colo Dept Physics PO Box 390 Boulder CO 80309-0390

BARTLETT, EDWARD, lawyer, legal association administrator; b. 1945; BS, JD, U. Mont. Bar: Mont. 1970. Pvt. practice, Butte. Mem. ABA, State Bar Mont. (pres.-elect 1998-99). Office: 40 E Broadway St Butte MT 59701-9350 also: State Bar Mont PO Box 577 Helena MT 59624-0577

BARTLETT, GRANT A. professional sports team executive; b. Riverside, Nova Scoti, Can. BS with honors, Mount Allison, NYU; MS in Geology, Carleton U.; PhD, NYU. Chmn. emeritus Dominion Energy Can.; co-owner Calgary Flames; mng. dir. Apogee Capital Ltd., 1998—, pres., CEO. Mem. several Canadian and Am. profl. socs. relating to engring. and scientific rsch. Achievements include more than 25 years of diversified experience in the petroleum industry, govt. and academia. Office: Can Airlines Saddledome PO Box 1540 Station M Calgary AB Canada T2P 3B9

BARTLETT, JAMES LOWELL, III, investment company executive; b. Boston, May 26, 1945; s. James Lowell and Shirley Victoria (Wyatt) B.; m. Shannon Mara McMillion, May 4, 1979; children: James Lowell IV, Zachary Morgan, Matthew Wyatt. BS, U. Calif., Berkeley, 1967, MBA, 1968. Loan officer nat. div. Bank of Am., Los Angeles, 1968; fin. mgr. Psychology Today mag., Del Mar, Calif., 1969; pres. Forum Communications Corp.; pub. Cuisine, Politics Today, Volleyball mags., N.Y.C., 1970-82; pres. Bartlett & Co., Santa Barbara, Calif., 1982—. Commr. Internat. Volleyball Assn., 1977-80 Mem. LDS Ch. Office: 5662 Calle Real Santa Barbara CA 93117-2317

BARTLETT, LEONARD LEE, communications educator, retired advertising agency executive; b. Mountain Home, Idaho, May 31, 1930; s. Harold Roberts and Alma Martina (Nixon) B.; m. Sue Ann Kipfer, Nov. 5, 1966; children: Jennifer, Deborah; children by previous marriage: Linda Lee, Cynthia, Nancy, Pamela, William Charles. BA, Brigham Young U., Provo, Utah, 1957, MA, 1989. Advt. mgr. Steiner Co., Chgo., 1957-59; sr. v.p. Marsteller Inc., Chgo., 1959-67; vice chmn. Cole & Weber, Inc., Seattle, 1966-84; chmn. Cole & Weber Calif., San Francisco, 1984-86, Los Angeles, 1986-87; assoc. prof. communications Brigham Young U., Provo, 1989-2000; ret., 2000. Acting chmn. dept. comms. Brigham Young U., Provo, 1995-96, chmn. dept. comms., 1996-97, asst. to pres. univ. comms., 1997-2000. Served with USAF, 1951-56. Mem. Am. Assn. Advt. Agys. (chmn. Western region 1980, nat. bd. 1980-81). Republican. Mem. Ch. Jesus Christ of Latter-day Saints. Home: 1211 East 2080 North Provo UT 84604-2123 E-mail: leeb1930@aol.com

BARTLETT, NEIL, chemist, emeritus educator; b. Newcastle-upon-Tyne, Eng., Sept. 15, 1932; s. Norman and Ann Willins (Vock) B.; m. Christina Isabel Cross, Dec. 26, 1957; children: Jeremy John, Jane Ann, Christopher, Robin. B.Sc., Kings Coll., U. Durham, Eng., 1954; Ph.D. in Inorganic Chemistry, Kings Coll., U. Durham, 1957; D.Sc. (hon.), U. Waterloo, Can., 1968, Colby Coll., , 1972, U. Newcastle-upon-Tyne, 1981, McMaster U., Can., 1992; D.Univ. (hon.), U. Bordeaux, France, 1976, U. Ljubljana, Slovenia, 1989, U. Nantes, France, 1990; LLD, Simon Fraser U., Can., 1993; D.Univ. (hon.), Freie U., Berlin, 1998. Lectr. chemistry U. B.C., Vancouver, Can., 1958-63, prof., 1963-66; prof. chemistry Princeton U., N.J., 1966-69, U. Calif., Berkeley, 1969-99. Mem. adv. bd. on inorganic reactions and methods Verlag Chemie, 1978—; mem. adv. panel Nat. Measurement Lab., Nat. Bur. Stds., 1974-80; E.W.R. Steacie Meml. fellow NRC, Can., 1964-66; Miller vis. prof. U. Calif., Berkeley, 1967-68; 20th G.N. Lewis Meml. lectr., 1973; William Lloyd Evans Meml. lectr. Ohio State U., 1966; A.D. Little lectr. Northeastern U., 1969; Phi Beta Upsilon lectr. U. Nebr., 1975; Henry Werner lectr. U. Kans., 1977; Jeremy Musher Meml. lectr., Israel, 1980, Randolph T. Major Meml. lectr. U. Conn., 1985, J.C. Karcher lectr. U. Okla., 1988; Brotherton vis. prof. U. Leeds, Eng., 1981; Erskine vis. lectr. U. Canterbury, New Zealand, 1983; Wilsmore fellow Melbourne U., Australia, 1983; vis. fellow All Souls Coll., Oxford U., 1984; Miller prof. U. Calif.-Berkeley, 1986-87; George H. Cady lectr. U. Wash., Seattle, 1994; Leermakers lectr. Wesleyan U., 1995; Davis Meml. lectr. U. New Orleans, 1997, Pierre Duhem seminaires, U. Bordeaux, 1998. Bd. editors Inorganic Chemistry, 1967-79, Jour. Fluorine Chemistry, 1971-80, Synthetic Metals, Revue Chimie Minerale; mem. adv. bd. McGraw-Hill Ency. Sci. and Tech. Recipient Rsch. Corp. prize; E.W.R. Steacie prize, 1965; Elliott Cresson medal Franklin Inst., 1968; Kirkwood medal Yale U. and Am. Chem. Soc. (New Haven sect.), 1969; Dannie-Heinemann prize The Gottingen acad. 1971; Robert A. Welch award in chemistry, 1987; Alexander von Humboldt Found. award, 1977; medal Jozef Stefan Inst., Slovenia, 1980; Moissan medal, 1986; Prix Moissan, Paris, 1988; fellow Alfred P. Sloan Found., 1964-66; Bonner Chemiepries, Bonn, 1991; Berkeley citation, 1993. Fellow Royal Soc., Am. Acad. Arts and Scis., Royal Inst. Chemistry, Chem. Inst. Can. (1st Noranda lectr. 1963), Royal Soc. Can.; mem. NAS (fgn. assoc.), Leopoldina Acad. (Halle, Salle), Akademie der Wissenschaften in Gottingen, Associé Etranger, Academia Europaea, Académie des Sciences, Institut de France, Am. Chem. Soc. (chmn. divs. fluorine chemistry 1972, inorganic chemistry 1977, award in inorganic chemistry 1970, W.H. Nichols award N.Y. sect. 1983, Pauling medal of Pacific N.W. sects. 1989, Disting. Svc. award 1989, award for Creative Work in Flourine Chemistry 1992), Phi Lambda Upsilon (hon.) Home: 6 Oak Dr Orinda CA 94563-3912 Office: U Calif Dept Chemistry Berkeley CA 94720-0001 E-mail: nbartlett@lbl.gov

BARTLETT, ROBERT WATKINS, education consultant, metallurgist; b. Salt Lake City, Jan. 8, 1933; s. Charles E. and Phyllis (Watkins) B.; m. Betty Cameron, Dec. 3, 1954; children: John C., Robin Parmley, Bruce R., Susanne. BS, U. Utah, 1953, PhD, 1961. Registered profl. engr., Calif. Group leader ceramics SRI Internat., Menlo Park, Calif., 1964-67; assoc. prof. metallurgy Stanford U., Palo Alto, 1967-74; mgr. hydrometallurgy Kennecott Minerals Co., Salt Lake City, 1974-77; dir. materials lab. SRI Internat., Menlo Park, Calif., 1977-80; v.p. rsch. Anaconda Minerals Co., Tucson, 1980-85; mgr. materials tech. Idaho Sci. and Tech. Dept., Idaho Falls, 1985-87; dean Coll. Mines and Earth Resources, U. Idaho, Moscow, 1987-97. Dir. Idaho Geol. Survey, Moscow. Author approximately 100 rsch. publs. in metallurgy; 12 patents in field; 1 textbook. Served to lt. (j.g.) USN, 1953-56. Recipient Turner award Electrochem. Soc., 1965, McConnell award AIME, 1985. Mem. Nat. Acad. Engring., Metall. Soc. (pres. 1989, EPD lecturer 1997), Soc. Mining Engrs. (disting. mem., Wadsworth award 1996), Sigma Xi, Tau Beta Pi. Office: 2505 Loch Way El Dorado Hills CA 95762 E-mail: bobbartlett@cs.com

BARTLETT, SUE, state legislator; b. Billings, Mont., July 4, 1947; m. Gene Fenderson. BA, Wash. U., St. Louis. Clk., recorder Lewis and Clark County, 1983-91; asst. sec. Mont. Senate, 1991-92, mem. from dist. 27, 1992—. Mem., Child Care Partherships, Bd. of Dirs., Mont. Women's Lobby, Montana NARAL. Democrat. Home: 416 N Beattie St Helena MT 59601-3701

BARTLETT, THOMAS ALVA, educational administrator; b. Salem, Oreg., Aug. 20, 1930; s. Cleave Wines and Alma (Hanson) B.; m. Mary Louise Bixby, Mar. 20, 1954; children: Thomas Glenn, Richard A., Paul H. Student, Willamette U., 1947-49, DCL (hon.), 1986; A.B., Stanford U., 1951, Ph.D., 1959; M.A. (Rhodes scholar), Oxford U., 1953; L.H.D. (hon.), Colgate U., 1977, Mich. State U., 1978, Union Coll., 1979; D.C.L. (hon.), Pusan Nat. U., Korea, 1985, U. Ala., , 1983. Mem. U.S. Permanent Mission to UN, 1956-63; advisor Gen. Assembly Dels., 1956-63; pres. Am. U., Cairo, 1963-69, Colgate U., Hamilton, N.Y., 1969-77, Assn. Am. Univs., Washington, 1977-82; chancellor U. Ala. System, 1982-89, Oreg. State System of Higher Edn. Office, Eugene, 1989-94, SUNY, 1994-96; ret., 1996. Mem. UAR-U.S. Ednl. Exch. Commn., 1966-69; mem. Task Force on Financing Higher Edn. in N.Y. State (Keppel Commn.), 1972-73; chmn. Commn. Ind. Colls. and Univs. N.Y., 1974-76; bd. dirs. Nat. Assn. Ind. Colls. and Univs., 1975-76; trustee Univs. Field Staff Internat., 1985-87; mem. NASA Comml. Space Adv. Com., 1988-90. Mem. nat. bd. examining Chaplains Episcopal Ch., 1978-91; trustee Gen. Theol. Sem., 1977-82, Am. U. in Cairo, 1978— (vie chair 1998—), U.S.-Japan Found., 1988— (chm. 1996—), bd. mem. Internat. Assn. of Univs., 1995—. Mem. Coun. Fgn. Rels., Phi Beta Kappa, Century Assn. Home: 1209 SW 6th Ave Apt 904 Portland OR 97204

BARTNICKI-GARCIA, SALOMON, microbiologist, educator; b. Mexico City, May 18, 1935; came to U.S., 1957; s. Israel Bartnicki and Refugio Garcia; m. Ildiko Nagy, Aug. 10, 1975; children— Linda Laura, David Daniel. Bacteriological Chemist, Inst. Politecnico Nacional, Mexico City, 1957; Ph.D., Rutgers U., 1961. Rsch. assoc. microbiology Rutgers U., 1961-62; mem. faculty U. Calif., Riverside, 1962—, prof. plant pathology and microbiology, 1971-94, prof. emeritus, 1994, rsch. prof., 1994-2000, chmn. dept. plant pathology, 1989-92, dir. grad. program in microbiology, 1997-2000; sci. rschr. CICESE, Ensenada, Mex., 2000—. Vis. prof. Organic Chemistry Inst., U. Stockholm, 1969-70; selected faculty rsch. lectr. U. Calif., Riverside, 1989. Author research and rev. papers. Grantee NIH, 1963-96, NSF, 1971-96. Fellow AAAS, Am. Phytopathol. Soc. (Ruth Allen award 1983); mem. Am. Soc. Microbiology, Mycol. Soc. Am. (Disting. Mycologist award 1994), Brit. Soc. Gen. Microbiology, Brit. Mycol. Soc. (hon.), Am. Soc. Biol. Chemists. Home: 387 Elliott St San Diego CA 92106-1235 Office: U Calif Dept Plant Pathology Riverside CA 92521-0001 also: CICESE Ensenada Mexico E-mail: bart@citrus.ucr.edu

BARTO, DEBORAH ANN, physician; b. West Chester, Pa., July 27, 1948; d. Charles Guy and Jeannette Victoria (Golder) B. BA, Oberlin Coll., 1970; MD, Hahnemann U., 1974. Intern, resident Kaiser Permanente Hosp., San Francisco, 1974-77; dir. med. oncology Evergreen Hosp., Kirkland, Wash., 1980-85, head oncology quality assurance, 1992-94; med. dir. Cmty. Home Health Care Hospice, Seattle, 1981-84. Mem. hosp. ethics com. Evergreen Hosp., 1995-98, mem. integrative care com., 1996-2001. Mem. Evergreen Women's Physicians. Democrat. Buddhist. Avocation: horseback riding. Office: Evergreen Profl Plz 12911 120th Ave NE Ste E60 Kirkland WA 98034-3047

BARTOK, MICHELLE, cosmetic company executive; b. Youngstown, Ohio, Feb. 18, 1961; d. Albert James and Judith Ann (Phillips) Bartok; m. John Anthony Garruto, Apr. 2, 1988 (div. 1997); children: Catherine Michelle, Gabrielle Bartok; m. Lee Edward Dupuis, Nov. 27, 1999 (div. 2000). BS in Physiol. Psychology, U. Calif., Santa Barbara, 1983. EMT, Calif. Asst. to phys. therapist Santa Barbara Phys. Therapy, 1983-84, Escondido (Calif.) Phys. Therapy, 1984-85; regional sales rep. Ft. Dodge Labs., San Francisco, 1985-87; [illegible] Therapeutics, Oceanside, Calif., 1987-92; CEO Innovative Bioscis. Corp., Carlsbad, 1992—; owner Beaches Cafe Inc., Encinitas, 1999-2000. Mem. Soc. Cosmetic Chemists, Beauty Industry West (pub. rels. dir. 1991-92, chair symposium 1996), Internat. Spa and Fitness Assn. (sponsor Ironman competition 1989). Avocations: outriger canoes, yoga. Home: 178 Grandview St Encinitas CA 92024-1009 E-mail: michelle@innovativebodyscience.com

BARTON, ALAN JOEL, lawyer; b. N.Y.C., Sept. 2, 1938; s. Sidney and Claire (Greenfield) B.; m. Ann Rena Beral, Jan. 29, 1961; children: Donna Frieda Olsen, Brian Joseph. AB, U. Calif., Berkeley, 1960, JD, 1963. Assoc. Nossaman, Krueger & Mash, Los Angeles, 1963-70, ptnr., 1970-80, Paul, Hastings, Janofsky & Walker, Los Angeles, 1980—. Lectr. corp. and securities law U. Calif. Continuing Edn. Bar, 1980—; lectr. venture capital and securities law Practicing Law Inst., 1986—. Assoc. editor U. Calif. Law Rev., 1963. Dir. Ctr. for Study of Young People in Groups, L.A., 1988—, Planned Parenthood, L.A., 1999—; trustee Dubnoff Ctr. for Ednl. Therapy, North Hollywood, Calif., 1976-80. Mem. ABA (com. on fed. regulation of securities), Calif. Bar Assn. (com. on corps.), Order of Coif, The Calif. Club. Republican. Jewish. Avocations: movies, contemporary art, tennis, travel. Office: Paul Hastings Janofsky & Walker 555 S Flower St Fl 23 Los Angeles CA 90071-2300

BARTON, ANN ELIZABETH, retired financial executive; b. Long Lake, Mich., Sept. 8, 1923; d. John and Inez Mabel (Morse) Seaton; m. H. Kenneth Barton, Apr. 3, 1948; children: Michael, John, Nancy. Student Mt. San Antonio Coll., 1969-71, Adrian Coll., 1943, Citrus Coll., 1967, Golden Gate U., 1976, Coll. Fin. Planning, 1980-82. CFP. Tax cons., real estate broker, Claremont, Calif., 1967-72, Newport Beach, Calif., 1972-74; v.p., officer Putney, Barton, Assocs., Inc., Walnut Creek, Calif., 1975-94, ret., 1997; bd. dir. Fin. Svc. Corp. Cert. fin. planner. Mem. Internat. Assn. Fin. Planners (registered investment advisor), Calif. Soc. Enrolled Agts., Nat. Assn. Enrolled Agts., Inst. CFP.

BARTON, BABETTE B. lawyer, educator; b. Los Angeles, Apr. 30, 1930; d. Milton Vernon and Ruth (Schreiber) Barancik; children: Jeffrey B. Barton, David R. Barton, Baird R. Barton. BS, U. Calif., Berkeley, 1951, LLB, 1954. Bar: Calif., U.S. Dist. Ct., U.S. Ct. Appeals 1955. Law clk. to Hon. Phil S. Gibson Calif. Supreme Ct., San Francisco, 1954-55; lectr., acting prof. U. Calif. Sch. Law, Berkeley, 1961-72, prof., 1972-99, prof. emeritus, 1999—; Adrian A. Kragen chair U. Calif., Berkeley. Cons. Calif. Inter Agy. Task Force on Electronic Funds Transfers, 1978-79, Dept. Treasury, 1963; adv. com. Calif. Bd. Legal Specialization, 1980-83. Contbr. chpts. to books in field. Adv. com. Alameda County Dir. Welfare, 1970-73; bd. dirs. Family Service Berkeley, 1967-74, Univ. Students' Coop. Assn., 1966-74. Recipient Citation award Boalt Hall Alumni Assn., 1997. Fellow Am. Law Inst., Am. Bar Found.; mem. ABA (taxation sect. chmn. tchg. tax. com. 1994-96, real property probate and trust sect. coun. 1977-79), Calif. State Bar (chmn. taxation sect. 1976-77, Joanne M. Garvey award taxation sect. 1997), Western Regional Bar Assn. (chmn. 1978-79), Am. Coll. Tax Counsel, San Francisco Tax Club, San Francisco Estate Planning Coun., Berkeley Tennis Club (bd. dirs. 1988-90, pres. 1990-91). Home: 16 Saint James Dr Piedmont CA 94611-3533 Office: U Calif Berkeley Sch Law 691 Simon Boalt Hl Berkeley CA 94720-0001

BARTON, BILLIE L. state legislator; b. Newcastle, Wyo., Apr. 4, 1930; m. Carol Barton; 4 children; 3 stepchildren. Student, Colo. State U., 1960. Livestock and natural resource prodr., 1947-98; co-op pres., mgr., 1967-87; owner, operator trucking co., 1974-90; mem. Wyo. Senate, Cheyenne, 1994—, mem. agr., water, and natural resources com., mem. corps., elections and polit. subdivsns. com., mem. select water com., mem. oil, gas, and mineral transp. com. Weston County Commr., 1986-94; asst. pres., v.p. Wyo. County Ofcls., 1993-94; committeeman Weston County Rep. Com., 1995-98. Mem. Nat. Assn. Counties, Nat. Cattleman's Assn., Wyo. Taxpayers Assn., Farm Bur., Aircraft Owners and Pilots Assn., Wyo. County Commn. Assn., Fed. Lands Conf., Nat. Innholders Assn., Wyo. Stockgrowers Assn., Mountain State Legal Found. Republican. Office: PO Box 799 Upton WY 82730-0799 also: Wyo Senate Hitching Post Inn State Capitol Rm 345 Cheyenne WY 82002-0001 Fax: 307-777-5466

BARTON, GERALD LEE, farming company executive; b. Modesto, Calif., Feb. 24, 1934; s. Robert Paul and Alice Lee (Hall) B.; m. Janet Murray, June 24, 1955; children: Donald Lee, Gary Michael, Brent Richard. BA with distinction, Stanford U., 1955. Owner, pres. Barton Ranch, Escalon, Calif., 1961—; v.p. R.P. Barton Mfg. Co., Escalon, 1963-86; chmn. bd. Diamond Walnut Growers Inc., 1976-81, chmn. emeritus, 1981—, pres., 1986-90. Chmn. Diamond-Sunsweet Co., Stockton, Calif., 1978-80, Sun Diamond Growers, Inc., 1980-81; bd. dirs. Calif. Fin. Holding Co., Stockton, Union Safe Deposit Bank, 2000—, Stockton Savs. Bank; vice chmn. Fed. Land Bank, Modesto, Calif., 1976-81; chmn. Growers Harvesting Com., Modesto, 1976-77; mem. pomology rsch. adv. bd. U. Calif., Davis, 1968-74, Walnut Mktg. Bd., San Francisco, 1971-73, 77—; mem. Calif. Walnut Commn., 1987-99; mem. agribus. adv. bd. U. Santa Clara, 1979-89; dir. Ross Hort. Found.; mem. San Joaquin County U. Calif. Ext. Adv. Bd. Chmn. bd. edn. Escalon Unified Sch. Dist., 1963-75; vice chmn. San Joaquin County Sch. Bds. Assn., 1965; bd. dirs. St. Joseph's Healthcare Corp., 1991-95; trustee Yosemite Assn., 1999—. With AUS, 1956-58. Decorated Order of the Golden Walnut; named Outstanding Young Farmer in San Joaquin County C. of C., 1965, Farmer of Yr. Escalon C. of C.; recipient U. Calif. Friend of Extension award, 1992; named to San Joaquin County Agrl. Hall of Fame, 1993; recipient Disting. Svc. award Calif. Walnut Commn., 1998; named Co-op Farmer of Yr. Agrl. Coun. Calif., 2001. Mem. Stanford U. Alumni Assn., Delta Chi. Republican. Presbyterian. Office: 22398 Mcbride Rd Escalon CA 95320-9637 E-mail: glbarton@aol.com

BARTON, PETER RICHARD, III, communications executive; b. Washington, Apr. 6, 1951; m. Laura Perry. BA, Columbia U., 1971, MS, 1972; postgrad., Harvard U., 1979, MBA, 1982. Dept. sec. to gov. State of N.Y., 1975-80; sr. v.p. Tele-Communications Inc., Englewood, Colo., 1982-86; pres. Cable Value Network, Mpls., 1986-88; sr. v.p. Tele-Communications Inc., Englewood, CO, 1988-90; pres. Liberty Media Corp, 1990-97, Barton and Assocs., 1997—.

BARTON, RICHARD N. computer company executive; BS in Indsl. Engring., Stanford U., 1989. Strategy cons. Alliance Consulting Group, 1989-91; with Microsoft Corp., Redmond, Wash., 1991-94; gen. mgr. traveler bus. unit Microsoft Corp. (Expedia), Redmond, 1994—. Office: Microsoft Corp One Microsoft Way Redmond WA 98052-6399

BARTON, STANLEY FAULKNER, management consultant; b. Halesowen, Worcestershire, Eng., Dec. 30, 1927; came to U.S., 1957, naturalized, 1963; s. Lazarus and Alice (Faulkner) B.; m. Marion Brittain, Dec. 20, 1952; children: Carolyn Francesca, Andrea Elizabeth. B.Sc. (hons.), U. Birmingham, Eng., 1949; Ph.D., U. Birmingham, 1952. Group leader Naval Rsch. Establishment, Halifax, N.S., Can., 1953-56; project coord. Def. Rsch. Chem. Labs., Ottawa, Ont., Can., 1956-57; devel. engr. Procter & Gamble, Cin., 1957-58, R & D group leader, 1958-59, R & D sect. head, 1959-69; tech. dir. food products-natural resources ITT, N.Y.C., 1969-76; sr. v.p. tech. and quality ITT Rayonier, Inc., Stamford, Conn., 1976-90; v.p., dir. Spectrum Internat. Assocs., Inc., Tucson, 1990-92. Pres. Catalina Cons., 1990—. Mem. Am. Theater Organ Soc. Home and Office: Catalina Cons 4031 N Circulo Manzanillo Tucson AZ 85750-1879 E-mail: stanb@prodigy.net

BARTON, WILLIAM E. construction company executive; BS in Acctg. and Fin., San Jose State U.; MBA, U. Santa Clara. Various positions including cash mgr., treas., contr. Granite Constrn. Inc., Watsonville, Calif., 1980—, v.p., CFO, sr. v.p., CFO, 1999—. Bd. dirs. various non-profit orgns., Santa Cruz County. Mem. Constrn. Fin. Mgmt. Assn., Fin. Execs. Inst. Office: Granite Constrn Inc 585 W Beach St Watsonville CA 94076

BARTOSIC, FLORIAN, law educator, lawyer, arbitrator; b. Danville, Pa., Sept. 15, 1926; s. Florian W. and Elsie (Woodring) B.; m. Eileen M. Payne, 1952 (div. 1969); children: Florian, Ellen, Thomas, Stephen; m. Alberta C. Chew, 1990. B.A., Pontifical Coll., 1948; B.C.L., Coll. William and Mary, 1956; LL.M., Yale U., 1957. Bar: Va. 1956, U.S. Supreme Ct. 1959. Asst. instr. Yale U., 1956-57; assoc. prof. law Coll. William and Mary, 1957, Villanova U., 1957-59; atty. NLRB, Washington, 1956, 57, 59; counsel Internat. Brotherhood of Teamsters, Washington, 1959-71; prof. law Wayne State U., 1971-80, U. Calif., Davis, 1980-92; recalled to tchg., 1994-99; prof. emeritus law U. Calif., Davis, 1993—, dean law, 1980-90. Adj. prof. George Washington U., 1966-71, Cath. U. Am., 1960-71; mem. panel arbitrators Fed. Mediation and Conciliation Service, 1972— ; hearing officer Mich. Employment Relations Commn., 1972-80, Mich. Civil Rights Commn., 1974-80; bd. dirs. Mich. Legal Services Corp., 1973-80, Inst. Labor and Indsl. Relations, U. Mich., Wayne State U., 1976-80; mem. steering com. Inst. on Global Conflict and Cooperation, 1982-83; mem. adv. bd. Assn. for Union Democracy Inc., 1980—, adv. coms. Calif. Jud. Council, 1984-85, 87; vis. scholar Harvard Law Sch., 1987, Stanford Law Sch., 1987; sr. rsch. scholar ILO, 1990-91; acad. visitor Oxford U., London Sch. Econs., 1991; mem. exec. bd. Pub. Interest Clearinghouse, 1988-90. Co-author: Labor Relations Law in the Private Sector, 1977, 2d edit., 1986; contbr. articles to law jours. Mem. ABA (sec. labor relations law sect. 1974-75), Fed. Bar Assn., Am. Law Inst. (acad. mem. labor law adv. com. on continuing profl. edn.), Soc. Profls. in Dispute Resolution (regional v.p. 1979-80), Indsl. Rels. Rsch. Assn., Internat. Soc. Labor Law and Social Legis., Internat. Indsl. Rels. Assn., Am. Arbitration Assn., Nat Lawyers Guild, ACLU (dir. Detroit chpt. 1976-77), Order of Coif (hon.), Scribes. Home: 235 Ipanema Pl Davis CA 95616-0253 Office: U Calif Sch Law Mrak Hall Dr Davis CA 95616 E-mail: fbartosic@ucdavis.edu

BARTZ, CAROL, software company executive; b. Alma, Wis., Aug. 29, 1948; m. William Marr; 1 child. BS in Computer Sci. with honors, U. Wis., 1971; DSc (hon.), Worcester Poly. Inst.; LittD (hon.), William Woods U. With sales mgmt. dept. 3M Corp., Digital Equipment Corp., 1976-83; mgr. customer mktg. Sun Microsys., 1983-84, v.p. mktg., 1984-87, v.p. customer svc., 1987-90, v.p. worldwide field ops., exec. officer, 1990-92; chmn. bd., CEO Autodesk, Inc., San Rafael, Calif., 1992—. Pres. Sun Fed., from 1987; bd. dirs. AirTouch Comm., Bea Sys., Cadence Design Sys., Cisco Sys., Inc.; mem. President's Export Coun., 1994; adv. coun. bus. sch. Stanford U. Bd. dirs. U. Wis. Sch. Bus., Nat. Breast Cancer Rsch. Found., Found. for Nat. Medals Sci. and Tech.; mem. adv. coun. Stanford U. Bus. Sch.; mem. Com. of 200; adv. for women's health issues; former mem. Ark. of Gov.'s Econ. Summit, Little Rock. Recipient Donald C. Burnham Mfg. Mgmt. award Soc. Mfg. Engrs., 1994. Mem. Calif. C. of C. (bd. dirs.). Avocations: gardening, tennis. Office: Autodesk Inc 111 Mcinnis Pkwy San Rafael CA 94903-2700

BARZA, HAROLD A. lawyer; b. Montreal, Que., Can., July 28, 1952; came to U.S., 1969; s. Solomon A. and Evelyn (Elkin) B. BA, Boston U., 1973; JD, Columbia U., 1976. Bar: N.Y. 1977, Calif. 1978, U.S. Dist. Ct. (ctrl. dist.) Calif. 1978. Law clk. to Hon. Milton Pollack U.S. Dist. Ct. (so. dist.) N.Y., 1976-77; assoc. Munger, Tolles & Rickershauser, L.A., 1978-81; ptnr. Gelles, Singer & Johnson, L.A., 1982-83, Gelles, Lawrence & Barza, L.A., 1983-87, Loeb & Loeb, L.A., 1987-99, Quinn, Emanuel, Urquehart, Oliver and Hedges, L.A., 1999—. Adj. prof. mass comm. law Southwestern U. Sch. Law, L.A., 1979-82; judge pro tem., L.A. Mcpl. Ct., 1985—. Mem. bd. editors Columbia Law Rev., 1975-76. Mem. steering com. Jewish Nat. Fund, L.A., 1983. James Kent scholar, 1974-76, Harlan Fiske Stone scholar, 1973-74. Mem. ABA (mem. com. on antitrust litigation), Los Angeles County Bar Assn. (trial lawyers, litigation and intellectual property sects.). Office: Quinn Emanuel Urquhart Oliver and Hedges 865 S Figueroa St Los Angeles CA 90017-2543 E-mail: hab@qeuo.com

BASCH, DARLENE CHAKIN, clinical social worker; b. Bklyn., Oct. 12, 1954; d. Samuel Benedict and Vivian (Sidranski) Chakin; m. Loren Bernhardt Basch, May 31, 1982; children: Michael Oswald, Ethan Raphael. BS, Cornell U., 1976; M in Social Welfare, U. Calif., Berkeley, 1979. Lic. clin. social worker, Calif.; bd. cert. Diplomate Social Work. Cottage clin. supr. St. Vincent's Sch., San Rafael, Calif., 1979-83; program dir. Jewish Family and Children's Service, San Francisco, 1983-84, therapist, program dir. family life edn., 1985-87; pvt. practice therapist Los Angeles, Calif., 1982—; clin. soc. worker Family Friends UCLA Med. Ctr., 1988-95. Lead interviewer trainer, interviewer resources advisor, debriefing cons. Spielberg's Survivors of the Shoah Visual History Found., L.A., 1994-98; founder Descs. of The Shoah, L.A., 1995—; tchr. Rosenberg's Integrative Body Psychotherapy, 1999—. Chmn. Generation-to-Generation, San Francisco, 1979-87; sec. Holocaust Library and Research Ctr., San Francisco, 1980-87; exec. com. mem. World Gathering of Holocaust Survivors, Jerusalem, 1980-81. Mem. NASW, Soc. Clin. Social Work, Internat. Soc. Traumatic Stress Studies, Internat. Assn. Body Psychotherapy (exec. dir. 1994-97), Soc. Clin. Social Work. Avocations: singing, guitar, reading, walking, spirituality. Office: 6310 San Vicente Blvd Ste 350 Los Angeles CA 90048-5448

BASCH, PAUL FREDERICK, international health educator, parasitologist; b. Vienna, Austria, Nov. 10, 1933; came to U.S, 1939; s. Richard and Anne Herta Basch; m. Maria Natalicia Mourão, Aug. 16, 1966; children: Richard Joseph, Daniel David. BS, CCNY, 1954; MS, U. Mich., 1956, PhD, 1958; M in Pub. Health, U. Calif., Berkeley, 1967. Asst. prof. biology Kans. State Tchrs. Coll., Emporia, 1959-62; from asst. to assoc. research zoologist U. Calif., San Francisco, 1962-70; assoc. prof. internat. health Stanford (Calif.) U., 1970-83, prof., 1983-97, prof. emeritus, 1997—. Cons. WHO, Pan Am. Health Orgn., UN Indsl. Devel. Orgn., NIH, U.S. Agy. for Internat. Devel. Author: Textbook of International Health, 1990, 2d edit., 1999, Schistosome Biology, 1991, Vaccines and World Health, 1994, also numerous articles. Grantee USPHS, WHO, others. Fellow Royal Soc. Tropical Medicine and Hygiene; mem. APHA, Am. Soc. Parasitologists, Am. Soc. Tropical Medicine and Hygiene, Global Health Coun. Democrat. Office: Stanford U Sch Medicine Dept Health Rsch and Policy Stanford CA 94305-5405 E-mail: pbasch@stanford.edu

BASCH, REVA, information services company executive; b. Chgo., Aug. 1, 1947; d. Victor Hugo and Hertha (Levi) B.; m. Jerrald C. Shifman, Apr. 17, 1982. BA in English Lit. summa cum laude, U. Pa., 1969; MLS, U. Calif., Berkeley, 1971. Head libr. Cogswell Coll., San Francisco, 1971-72; tech. info. specialist Gilbert Assocs. Inc., Reading, Pa., 1973-79; tech. libr. NuTech, San Jose, Calif., 1980-81; rsch. assoc. Info. on Demand, Berkeley, 1981-82, asst. dir. rsch., 1982-83, dir. rsch., 1983-86, v.p., dir. rsch., 1985-86; software designer Mead Data Ctrl., Personal Computer Sys. Group, Menlo Park, 1986-88; pres. Aubergine Info. Svcs., The Sea Ranch, 1986—. Author: Secrets of the Super Searchers, 1993, Electronic Information Delivery: Ensuring Quality and Value, 1995, Secrets of the Super Net Searchers, 1996, Researching Online for Dummies, 1998, 2d edit., 2000; columnist Online mag., CyberSkeptic's Guide to Internet Rsch.; contbr. articles to profl. jours. Recipient award for best paper UMI/Data Courier, 1990, Online Champion award Dun & Bradstreet. Mem. Assn. of Ind. Info. Profl.(pres.1991-92), Spl. Librs. Assn., Assn. Info. and Dissemination Ctrs., So. Calif. Online Users Group. Avocations: online communications, reading, travel, cooking.

BASCOM, RUTH F. retired mayor; b. Ames, Iowa, Feb. 4, 1926; d. Frederick Charles and Doris Hays Fenton; m. John U. Bascom, June 14, 1950; children: Lucinda, Rebecca, Ellen, Thomas, Paul, Mary. BS, Kans. State U., Manhattan, 1946; MA, Cornell U., 1949. Tchr. Dickinson County Cmty. H.S., Kans., 1946-48, Nat. Coll. Edn., Chgo., 1949-51. Co-chair Cascadia High Speed Rail, 1995-98. Chair City and State Bicycle Com., 1971-83; mem., chair Met. Park Bd., Eugene, 1972-82; past bd. pres. Youth Symphony, 1962-68; city councilor City of Eugene, Oreg., 1984-92, coun. v.p., pres., 1988-90, mayor, 1993-97; v.p., pres. LWV, Eugene, 1967-69; chair, Oreg. Passenger Rail Com., 2000—; state bd. 1000 Friends of Oreg., 1999—. Recipient Gold Leaf award Internat. Soc. Arboriculture, 1993. Democrat. Congregational. Avocations: music, tree farm, bicycling. Home: 2114 University St Eugene OR 97403-1542 Office: City of Eugene 777 Pearl St Ste 105 Eugene OR 97401-2720 Fax: 541-484-2646. E-mail: jbascomr@pacinfo.com

BASCOM, WILLARD NEWELL, engineer, scientist, underwater archaeologist; b. N.Y.C., Nov. 7, 1916; s. Willard Newell and Pearle (Boyd) B.; m. Rhoda Nergaard, Apr. 15, 1946; children: Willard, Anitra. Student, Colo. Sch. Mines; D in Natural Scis. (hon.), U. Genoa, Italy, 1992. Registered profl. engr., Fla., D.C. Research engr. U. Calif., Berkeley, 1945-50, Scripps Inst. Oceanography, La Jolla, Calif., 1950-54; exec. sec., dir. Mohole Project Nat. Acad. Scis., Washington, 1954-62; pres. Ocean Sci. and Engring., Inc., Washington, 1962-72; dir. Coastal Water Research Project, Long Beach, Calif., 1973-85. Mem. plowshre com. AEC, 1962-70; mem. Naval Rsch. Adv. Com., 1971-79; mem. coastal cons. bd. U.S. Army Engrs., 1980-85; mem. Sea Grant Coll. Bd., NOAA, 1979-88; mem. ocean scis. bd. NAS, 1978-81. Author: Waves and Beaches, 1964, rev. 2d edit., 1980, A Hole in the Bottom of the Sea, 1961, Deep Water, Ancient Ships, 1976, The Crest of the Wave, 1988, Endangered, 1995, Brother Jonathan's Gold, 1999; contbr. over 100 articles to sci. jours. Recipient Disting. Achievement medal Colo. Sch. Mines, 1979, Compass Disting. Achievement award Marine Tech. Soc., 1970, John Wiley Jones award, 1978, Rolex award, 1993. Mem. Explorers Club (Explorers medal 1980), Cosmos Club, Adventurers Club. Achievements include patent for deep ocean search-recovery system; inventor first dynamic positioning for holding ships in deepwater.

BASCONCILLO, LINDY, insurance and financial services company executive; b. Honolulu, Dec. 11, 1943; s. Catalino M. and Primitiva (Barientos) B.; children: Lisa M., Rod Alan. BA, Pacific Union Coll., 1965; MA, Azusa Pacific U., 1979. CLU. Tchr., vice prin. Santa Monica (Calif.) Jr. Acad., 1965-68; tchr. Temple City (Calif.) Unified Schs., 1968-79; sales agent N.Y. Life Ins. Co., Eugene, Oreg., 1980-81, tng. mgr., 1981-87; sales mgr. MONY Fin. Svcs., Eugene, 1987-88; sr. mktg. cons. Prudential Ins. and Fin. Svcs., Woodland Hills, Calif., 1988-89, sales mgr. Sacramento, 1989-91; bus., estate, retirement specialist John Deere Life Ins. Co., Calif. and Nev., 1991-94; dist. sales mgr. Mut. of Omaha, 1994-95; mng. dir. Elite Consulting, Lincoln, Calif., 1994—; brokerage dir. Nat. Life of Vt., 1995-96; reg. rep., agy. tng. dir. MassMutual, Sacramento, 1996-2000; CSAA annuity specialist, mgr. tng. and devel. Concord, 2000—. Bus. cons. Jr. Achievement, Eugene, 1986; pres.-elect Eugene Life Underwriters Assn., 1988, v.p., 1987; chairperson Life Underwriter Tng. Coun., 1987, moderator, 1984-86. Mem. coun. for minority edn. U. Oreg., Eugene, 1986-88; mem. Lane County Tng. and Devel. Com., Eugene, 1985-87. Mem. Sacramento Chpt. CLU's (bd. dirs.), Sacramento Life Underwriters Assn. Avocations: snow skiing, golfing. Home: 1812 5th St Lincoln CA 95648-2328 Office: 2055 Meridian Park Blvd Fl 2 Concord CA 94520-5722

BASELT, RANDALL CLINT, toxicologist; b. Chgo., Feb. 12, 1944; s. Benjamin Oliver and Vivian Marie (Rende) B.; m. Lana Mak, June 11, 1966; 1 child, David. BS in Chemistry, U. Ill., 1965; PhD in Pharmacology, U. Hawaii, 1972. Cert. Am. Bd. Forensic Toxicology, Am. Bd. Clin. Chemistry, Am. Bd. Toxicology, forensic alcohol supr., clin. toxicologist technologist, clin. chemist, clin. lab. toxicologist. Forensic toxicologist Office of Coroner, County of Orange, Calif., 1965-69; rsch. fellow dept. pharmacology U. Hawaii Sch. Medicine, Honolulu, 1969-72; NIH postdoctoral rsch. fellow Medizinisch-Chemisches Inst., U. Bern (Switzerland) Sch. Medicine, 1972-73; rsch. toxicologist Office of Coroner, San Francisco, 1973-75; chief toxicologist Office of Med. Examiner, Farmington, Conn., 1975-78; dir. toxicology and drug analysis lab. U. Calif. Med. Ctr., Sacramento, 1978-84; dir. Chem. Toxicology Inst., Calif., 1984—. Asst. prof. lab. medicine U. Conn. Health Ctr., Farmington, 1975-78; assoc. prof. pathology U. Calif. Sch. Medicine, Davis, 1978-84; cons. drug abuse USN, 1983—, USAF, 1984—; accredited lab. inspector Nat. Lab. Cert. Program, 1988—. Author: Disposition of Toxic Drugs and Chemicals in Man, 5th edit., 1999, Biological Monitoring Methods for Industrial Chemicals, 3d edit., 1997, Analytical Procedures for Therapeutic Drug Monitoring and Emergency Toxicology, 2d edit., 1987, (with M. Houts and R.H. Cravey) Courtroom Toxicology, 1980; editor 7 other books; founder, editor Jour. Analytical Toxicology, 1977—; mem. editl. bd. Jour. Forensic Scis., 1983—; contbr. articles to profl. jours. Mem. Am. Acad. Clin. Toxicology, Am. Assn. for Clin. Chemistry, Am. Indsl. Hygiene Assn., Calif. Assn. Toxicologists (past pres.), Internat. Assn. Forensic Toxicologists, Jour. Am. Med. Assn. (peer rev. com. 1985—), Soc. Forensic Toxicologists (bd. dirs. 1978-80, lab. survey com. 1982-83), Soc. Toxicology, Southwestern Assn. Toxicologists. Office: Chem Toxicology Inst 1167 Chess Dr Foster City CA 94404-1151

BASHA, EDWARD N., JR. grocery chain owner; CEO, chmn. Bashas Inc, Chandler, AZ. Recipient Disting. Svc. award Nat. Art Edn. Assn., 1992. Office: Bashas Inc 22402 S Basha Rd Chandler AZ 85248

BASIL, DOUGLAS CONSTANTINE, writer, educator; b. Vancouver, C., Can., May 30, 1923; s. William and Christina (Findlay) B.; m. Evelyn Margaret Pitcairn, 1950; 1 dau., Wendy Patricia. B.Commerce, U. B.C., 1949; B.A., 1949; Ph.D., Northwestern U., 1954; postgrad., London Sch. Econs., 1950. Instr. Marquette U., 1951-54; asst. prof. Northwestern U., 1954-57; asso. prof. U. Minn., 1957-61; prof. mgmt. U. So. Calif., 1961-88, prof. emeritus, 1988—. Cons. mgmt. devel.; lectr., Brussels, Caracas, Bogota, Paris, London, others. Author: Executive Development, 1964, (Paul Cone, John Fleming) Effective Decision Making Through Simulation, 1972, Organacao E Controls Da Pequena Empresa, 1968, La Direccion de la Pequena Empresa, 1969, Managerial Skills for Executive Action, 1970, Leadership Skills for Executive Action, 1971, Women in Management: Performance, Prejudice, Promotion, 1972, Autorite Personnelle et Efficacite des Cadres, 1972, Conduccion y Liderazgo, 1973, Developing Tomorrow's Managers, 1973, Management of Change, 1974, others.; Contbr. (Paul Cone, John Fleming) articles to profl. jours. Served to capt. Canadian Army, 1943-46. Home: 2201 Warmouth St San Pedro CA 90732-4532 Office: U So Calif Grad Sch Bus Adminstrn Los Angeles CA 90007

BASILE, PAUL LOUIS, JR. lawyer; b. Oakland, Calif., Dec. 27, 1945; s. Paul Louis and Roma Florence (Paris) B.; m. Linda Lou Paige, June 20, 1970; m. 2d Diane Chierichetti, Sept. 2, 1977. BA, Occidental Coll., 1968; postgrad., U. Wash., 1969; JD, UCLA, 1971. Bar: Calif. 1972, U.S. Dist. Ct. (cen. dist.) Calif. 1972, U.S. Dist. Ct. (no. dist.) Calif. 1985, U.S. Ct. Appeals (9th cir.) 1972, U.S. Tax Ct. 1977, U.S. Ct. Claims. 1978, U.S. Customs Ct. 1979, U.S. Ct. Customs and Patent Appeals 1979, U.S. Ct. Internat. Trade 1981, U.S. Supreme Ct. 1977; cert. specialist in taxation law Bd. of Legal Specialization, State Bar of Calif. Assoc. Parker, Milliken, Kohlmeier, Clark & O'Hara, L.A., 1971-72; corp. counsel TFI Cos., Inc., Irvine, Calif., 1972-73; pvt. practice L.A., 1973-80, 90-96, 98-99; mem. Basile & Siener, L.A., 1980-86, Clark & Trevithick, L.A., 1986-90; ptnr. Wolf, Rifkin & Shapiro, L.A., 1990, of counsel, 1990-92; ptnr. Basile & Lane, LLP, L.A., 1996-97; of counsel Shaffer, Gold & Rubaum, L.L.P., L.A., 1996—; sr. ptnr. Basile & Assocs., L.A. and Pasadena, Calif., 1999—. Gen. counsel J.W. Brown, Inc., L.A., 1980—, asst. sec., 1984-92; sec., gen. counsel Souriau, Inc., Valencia, Calif., 1981-90; v.p., sec., dir., gen. counsel Pvt. Fin. Assocs., L.A., 1983-94; gen. counsel Quest Relocation Group, Toluca Lake, Calif., 1994-97, v.p. real estate, 1996—. Trustee, sec. Nat. Repertory Theatre Found., 1975-94, mem. exec. com., 1976-94, chmn. bd. dirs., 1991-94; mem. fin. com., bd. dirs. Calif. Music Theatre, 1988-92; bd. dirs. March of Dimes Birth Defects Found., Los Angeles County, 1982-87, mem. exec. com., 1983-86, sec., 1985-86; dist. fin. chmn. L.A. Area coun. Boy Scouts Am., 1982-83; trustee Occidental Coll., L.A., 1989-94; active L.A. Olympic Organizing Com., Ketchum Downtown YMCA, Vols. Am. L.A., others. Mem. ABA (taxation sect., corp. tax com., vice chmn. closely held bus. com. 1992-94, chair, 1994-96, chmn. subcom. on continuing legal edn. 1990-94, chmn. subcom. on estate planning 1992, sec. 1996-97, small firm lawyers com., bus. law sect., real property sect., probate and trust law sect., spl. problems of bus. owners com., estate planning and drafting, pre-death planning issues com.), State Bar Calif. (bus. law sect., nonprofit and unicorporated orgns. com. 1989-92, taxation sect., estate planning, trust and probate sect., taxation law adv. commn. 1994-97, vice chmn. 1995-96, chair 1996-97, mem. bd. legal specialization 1996-97), L.A. County Bar Assn. (taxation sect., com. on closely-held and pass-through entities, bus. and corps. law sect., sole practitioner section exec. com. 1995-99), Beverly Hills Bar Assn. (probate, trust & estate planning section, taxation section, vice chmn. Estate and Gift Tax Com., 1998—, law practice mgmt. section), Can. Calif. C. of C. (dir. 1980-89, 2d v.p. 1983-84, 1st v.p. 1984-85, pres. 1985-87), L.A.-Vancouver Sister City Assn. (dir., exec. com. 1987-92, treas. 1987-89, pres. 1989-92), French-Am. C. of C. (councilor 1979-84, v.p. 1980, 82-84), L.A. Area C. of C. (dir. 1980-81), Occidental Coll. Alumni Assn. (pres. 1979-80, v.p. 1978-79, alumni bd. govs. 1977-81, chmn. annual fund campaign 1990-91), Grand People (bd. dirs. 1985-92, chmn. bd. 1986-92), Rotary Club of L.A. (dir. 1994-96, sergeant-at-arms 1986-87, chmn. gateway com. 1993-94, chmn. world cmty. svc. com. 1991-93, chmn. vols. Am. of L.A. com. 1988-90, chmn. golf com. 1986-87, vice-chmn. pres. com. 1985-86), Rotary Internat. (chmn. club extension com. 1995-96, cmty. svc. dir. 1993-95, chmn. gift of life com. 1992-93), Small Bus. Coun. of Am., Inc. (legal adv. bd. 1989—), The Group, Inc., Attorneys for Family Held Enterprises. Democrat. Baptist. Home: 3937 Beverly Glen Blvd Sherman Oaks CA 91423-4404 Office: Basile and Assocs 12011 San Vicente Blvd Ste 600 Los Angeles CA 90049-4948 also: 180 S Lake Ave Ste 540 Pasadena CA 91101-2666

BASILE, RICHARD EMANUEL, retired management consultant, educator; b. Buffalo, Dec. 24, 1921; s. Giustino Gregory and Minnie (Bailey) B.; m. Mariette Ruth Borocco, Oct. 12, 1946 (dec. Feb. 1994). B.A., Washington and Lee U., 1943; postgrad., U. Mo., 1947-48, Columbia U., 1965; L.H.D., Combs Coll., Phila., 1969. Geologist U.S. Geol. Survey, 1946-49; mgr. hotel industry, 1948-51; head hotel mgmt. dept. Paul Smith's Coll., 1951-57, adminstrv. dean, 1961-66; mgr. Am. Mgmt. Assn. Acad., 1957-61; dir. devel. Aramark, Phila., 1966-67, v.p. purchasing, 1966-68, v.p., 1968-70; prof. U. Nev., Las Vegas, 1970-88, prof. emeritus, 1988—; pres. Univ. Assocs., Inc., Las Vegas, 1971-92; adv. bd. Paul Smith's (N.Y.) Coll., 1994. Instr. geology U. Mo. Sch. Mines, 1948-49; cons. Indsl. Relations Counselors, Area Redevel. Act, U.S. Govt., XIX and XXI Olympiads, 1968, 76; com. chmn. XI Internat. Congress on Nutrition, Rio de Janeiro, 1978; U.S. Dept. Commerce tech. rep. Cyprus Internat. Trade Show, Nicosia, 1982; mem. Nev. Employee-Mgmt. Relations Bd., 1981— ; treas., bd. dirs. Marriott's Camelback Inn and Resort, Scottsdale, Ariz., 1987-91; cons. to hospitality industry. Cons. editor: Restaurant Hospitality Mag. Contbr. articles to profl. jours. Sec. treas. Paradise Valley Phys. Therapy Clinic, Las Vegas, Nev., 1987—89; arbitrator Teamsters local 995, Nev. Resort Assn., Nat. Assn. Security Dealers Regulations, 1997—. With USNR, 1943—46. Paul Harris fellow, 1980—; eminent fellow Wisdom Hall of Fame, 1998; Winston Churchill medal of wisdom and eminent Churchill fellow, 1999. Mem. Utility Shareholders Assn. Nev. (bd. dirs. 1994-99, v.p. 1997-99), Am. Arbitration Assn. (panel arbitrators 1961—), Pa. Acad. Fine Arts, Vesper Club, Peale Club, Masons, K.T., Rotary (pres. 1962-63), Washington and Lee Univ. Doremus Soc., Sigma Phi Epsilon, Alpha Kappa Psi. Home: 1800 S 14th St Las Vegas NV 89104-3124 Office: 4505 S Maryland Pky Las Vegas NV 89154 9900

BASINGER, RICHARD LEE, lawyer; b. Canton, Ohio, Nov. 24, 1941; s. Eldon R. and Alice M. (Bartholomew) B.; m. Rita Evelyn Gover, May 14, 1965; children: David A., Darron M. BA in Edn., Ariz. State U., 1963; postgrad. Macalester Coll., 1968-69; JD, U. Ariz., 1973. Bar: Ariz. 1973, U.S. Dist. Ct. Ariz. 1973, U.S. Tax Ct. 1977, U.S. Ct. Appeals (6th cir.) 1975, U.S. Ct. Appeals (9th cir.) 1976, U.S. Supreme Ct. 1977; cert. arbitrator. Assoc. law offices, Phoenix, 1973-74; pvt. practice, Scottsdale, Ariz. 1974-75; pres. Basinger & Assocs., P.C., Scottsdale, 1975—, also bd. dirs. Contbr. articles to profl. jours. Bd. dirs. Masters Trail Ventures, Scottsdale, 1984-85, Here's Life, Ariz., Scottsdale, 1976—; precinct committeeman Republican Party, Phoenix, 1983—; bd. dir. Ariz. Coll. of the Bible, 1992-93. NSF grantee, 1968-69. Mem. ABA, Ariz. Bar Assn., Maricopa County Bar Assn., Ariz. State Horseman's Assn. (bd. dirs. 1984-86, 1st v.p. 1986), Scottsdale Bar Assn., Western Saddle Club (bd. dirs. 1983-86, pres. 1985-86), Scottsdale Saddle Club, Saguaro Saddle Club. Baptist. Office: Mohave County Atty Dep County Atty Civil Divsn PO Box 7000 Kingman AZ 86402-7000

BASKIN, CATHRYN, former magazine editor; BA in English, SUNY, Albany; MEd, North Adams State Coll. Feature editor Popular Computing; mng. editor Byte, Lotus, New Eng. Living, PC World, San Francisco, editor-in-chief, 1996-00. McAllister Editl. fellow Am. Bus. Press, 1995. Office: PC World 501 2d St Ste 600 San Francisco CA 94107-1496

BASKIN, RONALD JOSEPH, cell biologist, physiologist, biophysicist educator, dean; b. Joliet, Ill., Nov. 25, 1935; s. Mack Robert and Evelyn Josephine (Rudzinski) B.; m. Lydia Olga Lendl, Mar. 29, 1957; children—Ronald James, Thomas William. A.B., UCLA, 1957; M.A., 1959, Ph.D., 1960. Asst. prof. biology Rensselaer Poly. Inst., Troy, N.Y., 1961-64; asst. prof. zoology U. Calif., Davis, 1964-67, assoc. prof., 1967-71, prof., 1971—, chmn. dept. zoology, 1971-78, assoc. dean coll. letters and sci., 1986-90. Mem. editorial bd. U. Calif. Press. Contbr. articles to sci. publs. Nat. Heart Inst. predoctoral fellow, 1957-60 Mem. Biophys. Soc., Soc. Cell Biology, Am. Physiol. Soc., N.Y. Acad. Scis., Sigma Xi. Office: Molecular & Cellular Biology Sect U Calif Davis CA 95616

BASKIN, SCOTT DAVID, lawyer; b. N.Y.C., Oct. 24, 1953; s. George and Anne (Strauss) B.; m. Sherry Nahmias, Mar. 13, 1982; children: Jonathan, Felicia. BA, Stanford U., 1975; JD, Yale U., 1978. Bar: Calif. 1978, U.S. Dist. Ct. (cen., ea., so. and no. dists.) Calif. 1979, U.. Appeals (9th cir.) 1979. Law clk. Hon. Herbert Choy, 9th Cir. Ct., Honolulu, 1978-79; ptnr. Irell & Manella, Newport Beach, Calif., 1979—. Lectr. Calif. Continuing Edn. of the Bar, 1985—. Contbr. articles to profl. publs. Mem. ABA. Office: Irell & Manella 840 Newport Center Dr Ste 400 Newport Beach CA 92660-6323 E-mail: sbaskin@irell.com

BASS, CHARLES MORRIS, financial and systems consultant; b. Miami, Fla., Sept. 21, 1949; s. Benjamin and Ellen Lucille (Williams) B; children: Cheryl Ellen, Benjamin Charles. BA, U. Md., 1972; MS, Am. Coll., 1982. CLU; chartered fin. cons. Group rep. Monumental Life Ins. Co., 1972-73; agt. Equitable Life Ins. Co., N.Y., 1973-76; ptnr. Bass, Bridge and Assocs., Columbia, Md., 1976-81; pres. Multi-Fin Svc., Inc., Balt., 1981-83; gen. mgr. Mfrs. Fin. Group, Denver, 1983-85; ptnr. Regency Econometrics Group, Denver, 1985—; speaker in field. Chmn. United Way Howard County, 1977-78; mem. Econ. Devel. Adv. Coun. Howard County, 1979-83. Served with USAF, 1968-71. Mem. Million Dollar Round Table, Nat. Assn. Life Underwriters, Am. Soc. C.L.U.s, Gen. Agts. and Mgrs. Assn., Columbia Life Underwriters Assn. (pres. 1982), Estate Planning Coun., Howard County C. of C., Howard County Bus. Club, Columbia Bus. Exchange. Methodist. Home and Office: 5690 W Coal Mine Ave Littleton CO 80123-3903

BASS, HAROLD NEAL, pediatrician, medical geneticist; b. Chgo., Apr. 14, 1939; s. Louis A. and Minnie (Schachter) B.; m. Phyllis Appell, June 25, 1961; children: Laura Renee, Alana Suzanne. Student, U. Ill., 1956-59; MS in Pharmacology, MD, U. Chgo., 1963. Diplomate Am. Bd. Pediatrics, Am. Bd. Med. Genetics, Nat. Bd. Med. Examiners. Intern Children's Meml. Hosp., Chgo., 1963-64, resident, 1964-65, chief resident, 1965-66, fellow in med. genetics, 1965-66; chief pediatrics and profl. svcs. Norton AFB Hosp., Calif., 1966-68; attending pediatrician/med. geneticist Kaiser Permanente Med. Ctr., Panorama City, 1968—; dir. med. genetics prog. Kaiser Permanente Med. Care Program So. Calif., 1987—; clin. prof. pediatrics and genetics UCLA Med. Sch., 1970—. Pres. med. staff Kaiser Permanente Med. Ctr., 1989; bd. dirs. So. Calif. Permanente Med. Group, 1998—; adj. prof. biology Calif. State U., Northridge, 1995—. Contbr. articles to profl. jours. Mem. mayor's adv. com. San Fernando Valley, City of L.A., 1973-78. Capt. M.C., USAF, 1966-68. Fellow Am. Coll. Human Genetics, Western Soc. Pediat. Rsch., L.A. Pediats. Soc., San Fernando Valley Interfaith Coun., Pacific S.W. Regional Genetics Network, Brady Handgun Control, ACLU, Am. Soc. Human Genetics, Amnesty Internat. Democrat. Jewish. Avocations: civic affairs, music, writing. Home: 11922 Dunnicliffe Ct Northridge CA 91326-1324 Office: Kaiser Permanente Med Ctr 13652 Cantara St Panorama City CA 91402-5423 E-mail: harold.n.bass@kp.org

BASSETT, CAROL ANN, journalism educator, writer; b. Langley AFB, Va., Mar. 2, 1953; d. William Brainard and Genevieve (Rivaldo) B. BA summa cum laude in Humanities, Ariz. State U., 1977; MA in Journalism, U. Ariz., 1982. Ptnr. Desert West News, Tucson, 1985-90; freelance writer Tucson, 1980-95; freelance writer for mags. Missoula, Mont., 1995-98; mem. faculty Sch. Journalism U. Mont., Missoula, 1996-98; mem. faculty Sch. Journalism and Comm. U. Oreg., Eugene, 1998—. Editor Tucson Weekly, 1989-90; contbr. numerous articles to nat. and internat. mags. including N.Y. Times. Recipient 2d Place Gen. Reporting award Ariz. Press Club, 1987, Gold medal for best environ. documentary Houston Internat. Film Festival, 1990, 1st Place Gen. Reporting award Ariz. Press Club, 1992, Silver Medal for Energy Issues documentary, Houston Internat. Film Festival, 1992; co-recipient Alfred I. duPont Columbia award, 1984-85, First Place award Investigative Reporting, 1986, 1st Place Polit. Reporting, 1989, First Amendment Journalism award, 1986; grantee Fund for Investigative Journalism, 1985, 87, Corp. for Pub. Broadcasting, 1988, Oxfam Am., 1991. Address: Sch Journalism Univ Oreg Eugene OR 97403

BASSINGTHWAIGHTE, JAMES BUCKLIN, physiologist, educator, medical researcher; b. Toronto, Sept. 10, 1929; s. Ewart MacQuarrie and Velma Emeline B.; m. Joan Elizabeth Graham, June 18, 1955; children: Elizabeth Anne, Mary, Alan, Sarah, Rebecca. BA, U. Toronto, 1951, MD, 1955; postgrad., Med. Sch. London, 1957-58; PhD, Mayo Grad. Sch. Medicine U. Minn., 1964. Intern Toronto Gen. Hosp., 1955-56; physician Internat. Nickel Co., Sudbury and Matheson, Ont., 1956-57; house physician Hammersmith Hosp., London; postgrad. Med. Sch. London, 1957-58; teaching asst. physiology U. Minn., Mpls., 1961-62; fellow Mayo Grad. Sch. Medicine, Rochester, Minn., 1958-64, instr., 1964-67, asst. prof., 1967-69, assoc. prof., 1969-72; vis. prof. Pharmacology Inst., U. Bern, Switzerland, 1970-71; asso. prof. bioengring. U. Minn., 1972-75; prof. physiology Mayo Grad. Sch. Medicine, 1973-75, prof. medicine, 1975; prof. bioengring., radiology and biomath U. Wash., Seattle, 1975—; dir. Ctr. for Bioengring., 1975-80; vis. prof. medicine and physiology McGill U., 1979-81; affiliate prof. physiology Limburg U., Maastricht, The Netherlands, 1990—. Mem. study sect. NIH, 1970-74, 80-83; chmn. Biotech. Resources Adv. Com., 1977-79, chmn. 1st Gordon Rsch. Conf. on Water and Solute Transport in Microvasculature, 1976; chmn. workshop on metabolic imaging Nat. Heart, Lung and Blood Inst., 1985; Lewellen-Thomas lectr., U. Toronto, 1991; Coulter lectr. U. N.C., 1995; Oxford lectr. Internat. Soc. Magnetic Resonance Medicine, 1996. Author: (with L.S. Liebovitch and B.J. West) Fractal Physiology, 1994; contbr. over 200 articles to profl. publs. Recipient NIH Rsch. Career Devel. award, 1964-74, Louis and Artur Lucian award McGill U., 1979, Witzig award Cardiovasc. Sys. Dyamics Soc., 1982, Faculty Achievement award for outstanding rsch. U. Wash. Coll. Engring., 1993; Edmund Hustinx chair Maastricht U., 1999. Mem. AAAS, Am. Heart Assn. (coun. on circulation 1976—), Biophys. Soc. (assoc. editor Biophys. Jour. 1980-83), Biomed. Engring. Soc. (dir. 1971-74, pres. 1977-78, Alza award 1986, editor-in-chief Annals of Biomedical Engring. 1993—, Disting. Svc. award 1999), Microcirculatory Soc. (mem. coun. 1975-78, 80-83, pres. 1990-91, Landis award 1995), Nat. Acad. Engring., Am. Physiol. Soc. (mem. circulation group, editorial bd. 1972-76, 79-83, mem. edn. com.), Internat. Union Physiol. Scis. (U.S.A. nat. com. 1978-86, U.S. del. to assembly 1980, 83, 86, chmn. 1983-86, chmn. Commn. on Bioengring. and Clin. Physiology 1986-97, chmn. satellite to 30th Congress on Endothelial Transport 1986, co-chmn. satellite on microvascular networks 1989, chmn. satellite on Physiome Project 1997). Achievements include research in cardiovascular physiology and bioengineering, biomathematics and computer simulation with emphasis on ion and substrate exchange in heart, fractals in physiology, integrative biology and origination of the Physiome Project. Home: 3150 E Laurelhurst Dr NE Seattle WA 98105-5333 Office: U Wash Dept Bioengring PO Box 35-7962 Seattle WA 98195-7962 E-mail: jbb@bioeng.washington.edu

BASSO, KEITH HAMILTON, cultural anthropologist, linguist, educator; b. Asheville, N.C., Mar. 15, 1940; s. Joseph Hamilton and Etolia (Simmons) B.; div. BA, Harvard U., 1962; MA, Stanford U., 1965, PhD, 1967. Asst. prof. anthropology U. Ariz.-Tucson, 1967-71, assoc. prof., 1972-76, prof., 1977-81; prof. anthropology Yale U., 1982-88, U. NMex., Albuquerque, 1988—. Mem. Inst. Advanced Study, Princeton, N.J., 1975-76; Weatherhead fellow Sch. Am. Research, Santa Fe, N.M., 1977-78; cons. cultural and historical matters White Mountain and San Carlos Apache Tribes, Alfonso Ortiz Ctr. for Internat. Studies, 2000—, Nativz nations Inst., 2000—; mem. steering com. Nat. Coalition for Am. Indian Religious Freedom; bd. trustees Nat. Mus. of the Am. Indian, 1991-96. Author: Wisdom Sits in Places: Landscape and Language Among the Western Apache, 1996 (Western States Book award 1996, Victor Turner prize for ethnographic writing 1997, J.I. Staley award 2001), Western Apache Language and Culture: Essays in Linguistic Anthropology, 1991, Portraits of the White Man, 1979, [illegible] 1970; editor: [illegible] Place, 1996, Meaning in Anthropology, 1976, Western Apache Witchcraft, 1969. Recipient J.I. Staley prize 2001. Mem. AAAS, Assn. Am. Indian Affairs (bd. dirs. 1978-86), Am. Anthropol. Assn., Am. Ethnol. Soc. (pres. 1983-84), Linguistic Soc. Am. Democrat. Home: 12 Pool St NW Albuquerque NM 87120-1809 Office: U NMex Dept Anthropology Albuquerque NM 87131

BASSO, ROBERT J. manufacturing engineer, inventor; Degree in mech. engring., Tufts Coll. Registered profl. engr., Calif. Founder, pres. Centry Design, Inc., San Diego. Recipient Project of Yr. award San Diego Engring. Soc., 1995, Eli Whitney Productivity award Soc. Mfg. Engrs.. 1998. Achievements include patents for carbon graphite golf shafts and fishing rods; developed environmentally clean, high intensity ultraviolet curing equipment for painting finished products. Office: Century Design Inc 3635 Afton Rd San Diego CA 92123-2199

BASTIAANSE, GERARD C. lawyer; b. Holyoke, Mass., Oct. 21, 1935; s. Gerard C. and Margaret (Lally) B.; m. Paula E. Paliska, June 1, 1963; children: Elizabeth, Gerard. BSBA, Boston U., 1960; JD, U. Va., 1964. Bar: Mass. 1964, Calif. 1970. Assoc. Nutter, McClennen & Fish, Boston, 1964-65; counsel Campbell Soup Co., Camden, N.J., 1965-67; gen. counsel A&W Internat. (United Fruit Co.), Santa Monica, Calif., 1968-70; ptnr. Kindel & Anderson, Los Angeles, 1970—. Mem. ABA, Calif. Bar Assn., Mass. Bar Assn., Japan Am. Soc., Asia Soc., World Trade Ctr. Assn. Clubs: California (Los Angeles); Big Canyon Country (Newport Beach, Calif.). Home: 2 San Sebastian Newport Beach CA 92660-6828 Office: Kindel & Anderson 2030 Main St Ste 1300 Irvine CA 92614-7220

BATEMAN, DONALD, aerospace engineer; Degree in elec. engring., U. Saskatchewan. Chief engr., flight safety avionics Allied Signal Aerospace, Torrance, Calif. Recipient Electronics award Aviation Week and Space Tech., 1996. Office: Allied Signal Aerospace 2525 W 190th St Torrance CA 90504-6002

BATEMAN, MERRILL JOSEPH, university president; b. Lehi, Utah, June 19, 1936; s. Joseph Fredric and Belva (Smith) B.; m. Marilyn Scholes, Mar. 23, 1959; children: Michael, Mark, Michele, Melisa, Merilee, Matthew, McKay. BA, U. Utah, 1960; PhD, MIT, 1965. Exec. Mars, Inc., 1971-75; dean Sch. Mgmt. Brigham Young U., Provo, Utah, 1975-79, pres., 1996—; mgmt. cons. Provo, 1979-92; mem. 2d Quorum of 70 LDS Ch., Salt Lake City, 1992-94, presiding bishop, 1994-95, mem. 1st Quorum of 70, 1996—. Pres. Deseret Mgmt. Corp., Salt Lake City, 1993-95. 1st lt. USAF, 1964-67. Danforth fellow, 1960-64, Woodrow Wilson fellow, 1960-61. Mem. Am. Assn. Presidents of Colls. and Univs. (pres.), Mountain West Conf. Coun. of Presidents, Phi Kappa Phi, Phi Beta Kappa. Office: Brigham Young U PO Box 21346 Provo UT 84602-1346

BATEMAN, ROBERT MCLELLAN, artist; b. Toronto, Ont., Can., May 24, 1930; s. Joseph Wilbur and Anne (McLellan) B.; m. Suzanne Bowermann, June 1961; children: Alan, Sarah, John; m. Birgit Freybe, Aug. 1975; children: Christopher, Rob. BA in Geography with honors, U. Toronto, 1954; postgrad., Ont. Coll. Edn., 1955; DSc (hon.), Carleton U., Ottawa, 1982; LLD (hon.), Brock U., St. Catherine, Ont., 1982; D Letters for Fine Arts (hon.), McMaster U., Hamilton, Ont., Can., 1983; LLD (hon.), U. Guelph, Ont., 1984; LittD (hon.), Lakehead U., Thunder Bay, Ont., 1986; LLD (hon.), Laurentian U., Sudbury, Ont., 1987; DFA (hon.), Colby Coll., 1989, Northeastern U., 1991; DSc (hon.), McGill U., Montreal, 1995. Tchr. Nelson H.S., Burlington, Ont., 1958-63, 65-69; tchr. geography Nigeria, 1963-65; tchr. art Lord Elgin H.S., Burlington, Ont., 1970-76. One-man shows include Tryon Gallery, London, 1975, 79, Beckett Gallery, Hamilton, Ont., Can., 1978, 87, Smithsonian Instn., 1987, Nat. Mus. Natural Sci., Ottawa, 1981-82, Everard Read Gallery, Johannesburg, South Africa, 2000, also touring U.S. and Can., Can. Embassy, Tokyo, 1992; represented in permanent collections Govt. Ont. Art Collection, Toronto Bd. Trade, Hamilton Art Gallery, Leigh Yawkey Woodson Art Mus., Wausau, Wis., H.R.H. The Prince of Wales, H.R.H. Prince Phillip, The Late Princess of Monaco, Am. Artists Collection, Gilcrease Mus., Tulsa, Art Gallery of Greater Victoria; commd. World Wildlife Fund, 1971, Endangered Species Silver Bowl, 1971, Endangered Species Postage Stamp Series, 1976-81, "Northern Reflections - Loon Family", 1981, Govt. Can. wedding gift to Prince of Wales, 1981, Can. Post Office, Royal Can. Mint-Platinum Polar Bear series, 1990; subject of the Art of Robert Bateman, 1981, A Day in the Life of Robert Bateman, 1985, The World of Robert Bateman, 1985, Robert Bateman An Artist in Nature, 1990, Natural Worlds: Robert Bateman, 1996, The Life and Times of Robert Bateman, 1997, Safari, 1998, Thinking Like a Mountain, 2000. Bd. dirs. Elsa Wild Animal Appeal, Toronto, 1975—, Ecotrust, Jane Goodall Inst. Can.; hon. chmn. Harmony Found., Ottawa; hon. dir. Kenya Wildlife Fund, Long Point Bird Obs., Ont., Legal Def. Fund. Decorated Queen Elizabeth Silver Jubilee medal Govt. of Can., 1977, Officer of Order of Can., 1984; recipient award of excellence Soc. Animal Artists, 1979, 80, 86, 90, Gov. Gen. award for conservation, Quebec City, Can., 1987, Lescarbot award Can. Govt., 1992, Rachel Carson award, 1996, Golden Plate award Am. Acad. Achievement, 1998; named Artist of Yr., Am. Artist Collection, 1980, Master Artist, Leigh Yawkey Woodson Mus., Wausau, Wis., 1982, Environ. Hero, Nat. Aububon Soc., 1998, others. Mem. Order B.C., Brit. Soc. for Wildlife Artists, Jane Goodall Inst. (bd. dirs.), N.Am. Native Plant Soc. (hon. dir.), Audubon Soc. (hon. life), Royal Can. Acad. Arts, Can. Nat. Wildlife Fedn. (hon. life), Fedn. Ont. Naturalists (hon. life), Sierra Club (hon. life), Kenya Wildlife Fund (hon. dir.), Sierra Legal Def. Fund (hon. dir.). E-mail: boshkung@saltspring.com

BATES, CHARLES CARPENTER, oceanographer; b. Rockton, Ill., Nov. 4, 1918; s. Carl and Vera B.; m. Pauline Barta; children: Nancy Ann, Priscilla Jane, Sally Jean. Grad. (Rector scholar 1936-39), DePauw U., 1939; M.A., U. Calif. at Los Angeles, 1944; Ph.D. in Geol. Oceanography, Tex. A. and M. Coll., 1953; student, Cath. U., 1947-48, Johns Hopkins, 1951, George Washington U., 1954. Geophys. trainee Carter Oil Co., 1939-41; spl. asst. to pres. Am. Meteorol. Soc., 1945-46; mem. survey phys. and geol. environment Marshall Is. relative to pending Bikini atomic bomb tests, 1946; with div. oceanography U.S. Navy Hydrographic Office, 1946- 57, dept. dir. div., 1953-57; environmental surveillance coordinator Office Devel. Coordinator, Office Naval Research, 1957-60; chief underground nuclear test detection br. Advanced Research Projects Agy., Office Sec. Def., 1960-64; sci. and tech. dir. U.S. Naval Oceanographic Office, 1964-68; sci. adviser to comdt., also chief scientist Office Research and Devel., USCG, 1968-79. V.p. Spectrum Internat. Assocs., 1986-88; mem. bd. experts Civil Service Examiners, 1954-60; mem. adv. com. postdoctoral awards for Fulbright grants NRC, 1957-60; vis. geoscientist Am. Geol. Inst., 1959-60; mem. meteorology panel, space sci. bd. Nat. Acad. Sci., 1959-61; mem. Mcht. Marine Council, 1968-71, Nat. Transp. Research Bd., 1968-71; mem. sea grant adv. council La. State U. System, 1968-79; co-chmn. U.S.-Japan panel marine facilities U.S.-Japan Natural Resource Program, 1969-71. Author: Geophysics in Affairs of Man, 1982, 2nd edit., 2001, America's Weather Warriors, 1814-1985, 1986; numerous articles, reports in field. Served to capt. USAAF, 1941-45, lt. col. USAFR, 1941-65. Decorated Bronze Star; recipient U.S. Navy Meritorious Civilian award, 1962, U.S. Navy Superior Civilian Service award, 1969, U.S. Dept. Transp. Silver medal, 1973. Mem. Am. Geophys. Union (chmn. com. interaction sea and atmosphere 1950, mem. council 1964-67), Soc. Exploration Geophysicists (council 1963-67, v.p. 1965-66, hon. mem. 1981), Am. Meteorol. Soc. (chmn. com. indsl. bus. and agrl. meteorology 1946-48), Am. Assn. Petroleum Geologists (President's award 1954), Am. Mgmt. Assn. (research and devel. council 1970-79), Sigma Xi. Home and Office: 136 W La Pintura Green Valley AZ 85614-1927

BATES, CHARLES WALTER, human resources executive, lawyer; b. Detroit, June 28, 1953; s. E. Frederick and Virginia Marion (Nunneley) B. BA in Psychology and Econs. cum laude, Mich. State U., 1975, M in Labor and Indsl. Rels., 1977; postgrad., DePaul U., 1979-80; JD, William Mitchell Coll. Law, 1984. Bar: Wash. 1990, U.S. Dist. Ct. (we. dist.) Wash. 1992; [illegible] paralegal Ventura County Legal Aid Assn., Ventura, Calif., 1976-79 [illegible] Inc., Mpls., 1977-78, plant pers. asst. II Chgo., 1978-80, plant asst. pers. mgr., 1980-81, pers. mgr. consumer foods mktg. Mpls., 1981-82, pers. mgr. consumer foods mktg. divsns. and Saluto Pizza, 1982-84; human resources mgr. Western divsn. Godfather's Pizza, Inc., Costa Mesa, Calif., 1984-85, human resources mgr. western U.S. and Can. Bellevue, Wash., 1985-91; dir. human resources Royal Seafoods, Inc., Seattle, 1991-92, dir. human resources and employee rels. counsel, 1992-94, dir. human resources and counsel, 1994-95; sr. internal auditor PACCAR, Inc, Bellevue, Wash., 1995-97; dir. field human resources PACCAR Automotive, Inc., Renton, 1997-2000; dir. human resources TransAlta USA, Inc., Centralia, 2000—. Instr. employee labor rels. Lake Washington Tech. Coll., 1992-94; bd. dirs. TransAlta U.S.A., Inc., TransAlta Investments, LLC. Mem. editl. adv. bd. Recruitment Today mag., 1990-91. Candidate for lt. gov. of Minn., 1982; asst. scoutmaster Boy Scouts Am., 1971—; Sammamish Cmty. Councilmem., Bellevue, 1990-93; mem. Bellevue Civil Svc. Commn., 1997-2000, vice chmn., 1999, chmn., 2000; bd. dirs. Olympic Symphony Orch., 2001— Recipient Scouter's Tng. award Boy Scouts Am., 1979, Vantage Recruiting award Recruitment Today mag., 1989, Vigil Honor award Boy Scouts Am., 1990, Dist. Award of Merit, Boy Scouts Am., 1991. Mem. Wash. State Bar Assn. (labor and employment law sect.), Thurston County Bar Assn., Lewis County Bar Assn., Nat. Eagle Scout Assn., Soc. for Human Resources Mgmt. (South Puget Sound chpt.). Office: TransAlta USA Inc 913 Big Hanaford Rd Centralia WA 98531-9111

BATES, CRAIG DANA, curator, ethnographer, government official; b. Oakland, Calif., Aug. 2, 1952; s. Dana Raymond and June (Robinson) B.; m. Jennifer Dawn Bernido, May 12, 1973 (div. 1987); 1 child, Carson Dana. Park technician Nat. Park Svc., Yosemite National Park, Calif., 1973-76, Indian cultural specialist, 1976-80, asst. curator, 1980-82, curator ethnography, 1982—. Rsch. assoc. Santa Barbara (Calif.) Mus. Natural History, 1983—; cons. Calif. Indian exhbn. SW Mus., L.A., 1985, Culin exhbn. Bklyn. Mus., 1988-89, Lowie Mus. Anthropology, U. Calif., Berkeley, 1990. Co-author: (with Martha Lee) Tradition and Innovation: A Basket History of the Indians of the Yosemite Mono Lake Area, 1990; contbr. more than 100 articles on Am. Indian culture to profl. jours. Office: Nat Park Svc Yosemite Mus PO Box 577 Yosemite National Park CA 95389-0577

BATES, JAMES ROBERT, newspaper editor; b. Great Bend, Kans., Dec. 12, 1954; s. Robert Lane and Phyllis Fern (Koltermann) B.; m. Jennifer Petkus, Nov. 7, 1986. BS, U. Kans., 1977; postgrad., U. Colo., 1979-80. Copy editor Springfield (Mo.) Daily News, 1977-78; reporter Colo. Springs (Colo.) Sun, 1978-79, news editor, 1980-86; copy editor, asst. news editor Denver Post, 1986-87, news editor, 1987-89, exec. news editor, 1989—. Recipient design and editing awards Colo. Press Assn., Colo. AP, 1986—. Mem. Soc. Newspaper Design. Office: The Denver Post 1560 Broadway Denver CO 80202-5177

BATES, MARCIA JEANNE, information scientist educator; b. Terre Haute, Ind., July 30, 1942; d. Robert Joseph and Martha Jane B. BA, Pomona Coll., 1963; MLS, U. Calif., Berkeley, 1967; PhD, U. Calif., 1972. Peace corps vol., Saraburi, Thailand, 1963-64, Nongkhai, Thailand, 1964-65; jr. specialist Inst. Libr. Rsch., U. Calif., Berkeley, 1968; acting instr. U. Calif., Berkeley, 1969-70; asst. prof. U. Md., College Park, 1972-76, U. Wash., Seattle, 1976-80, assoc. prof., 1980-81, U. Calif., Los Angeles, 1981-91, prof., 1991—, prof. and dept. chmn. libr. and info. sci. 1993-95. Cons. U.S. Libr. Congress, Washington, 1986, 91, Getty Art Hist. Info. Program, Santa Monica, Calif., 1988-91, Info. Access Co., Foster City, Calif., 1992-95; mem. editl. bd. Jour. of Asis &T, 1989—, Libr. Quar., 1993-2001. Co-author: For Information Specialists, 1992; contbr. articles to profl. jours. Recipient Distinguished Lectureship award N.J. Am. Soc. for Info. Sci., New Brunswick, 1991. Fellow AAAS (sect. T electorate nominating com. 1980-84, chmn. 1983-84, sect. T com. mem.-at-large, 2001-04), mem. ALA (Frederick G. Kilgour award, 2001), Am. Soc. Info. Sci. and Tech. (bd. dirs. 1973-74, Best Jour. Article Yr. award, 1980, 99, Rsch. award 1998), Assn. Records Mgrs. Adminstrs., Calif. Libr. Assn. (mem. task force on future of Libr. profession, 1993-95), Phi Beta Kappa. Achievements include design of information systems and interfaces for search and subject access in information retrieval systems. Avocations: walking, photography, travel. Office: Grad Sch Edn & Info Studies UCLA 405 Hilgard Ave Los Angeles CA 90095-1520

BATES, WILLIAM, III, lawyer; b. Phila., May 1, 1949; s. William and Elizabeth (Martin) B. BA, Yale U., 1971; JD, Stanford U., 1974. Bar: Calif. 1974, U.S. Dist. Ct. (no. dist.) Calif. 1976, U.S. Dist. Ct. (ea. dist.) Calif. 1978, U.S. Dist. Ct. (ctrl. dist.) Calif. 1984, U.S. Ct. Appeals (9th cir.) 1986, U.S. Dist. Ct. (so. dist.) Calif. 1987. Law clk. to chief judge U.S. Dist. Ct. Conn., Hartford, 1974-75; assoc. McCutchen, Doyle, Brown & Enersen, San Francisco, 1975-81, ptnr., 1981—. Mem. ABA (mem. bus. bankruptcy com.), State Bar Calif. (chair rules of ct. com. 1979-80, mem. uniform comml. code com. 1985-88, mem. debtor/creditor rels. com. 1989-92), San Francisco Bar Assn. (chair comml. law and bankruptcy sect. 1991-92). Democrat. Episcopalian. Avocations: wine tasting, bicycling, travel. Office: McCutchen Doyle Brown & Enersen 3150 Porter Dr Palo Alto CA 94304-1212 E-mail: wbates@mdbe.com

BATLIN, ROBERT ALFRED, newspaper editor; b. San Francisco, Aug. 24, 1930; S. Philip Alfred and Lavenia Mary (Barnes) B.; m. Diane Elise Giblin, July 4, 1956; children— Lisa, Philippa. B.A., Stanford U., 1952, M.A., 1954. Reporter San Bruno Herald, 1952-53; copy editor, then dept. editor San Francisco News, 1956-59; dept. editor San Francisco News-Call Bull., 1959-65; feature editor San Francisco Examiner, 1965-74, arts editor, 1974-85, asst. style editor, 1985-2001; copy editor San Francisco Chronicle mag., 2001—. Served with AUS, 1954-56. Mem. Soc. of Profl. Journalists. Home: 91 Fairway Dr Daly City CA 94015-1215 Office: 110 5th St San Francisco CA 94103-2918

BATT, PHILIP E. former governor; b. Wilder, Idaho, Mar. 4, 1927; m. Jacque Fallis, 1948; children: Bill, Rebecca, Leslie. Attended, U. Idaho, 1944-48. Elected mem. Idaho State Legislature, 1965-77; lt. gov. State of Idaho, 1978-82, gov., 1995-99. First pres. Idaho Food Producers; co-chmn. Wilder United Charity Auction; mem. Idaho Potato Growers Commn.; mem. bd. dirs. Wilder Farm Labor Com.; mem. bd. trustees Coll. Idaho; past pres. Idaho Hop Growers Assn., Hop Growers of Am., Homedale PTA.

BATTAGLIA, FREDERICK CAMILLO, physician; b. Weehawken, N.J., Feb. 15, 1932; m. Jane B. Donohue; children— Susan Kate, Thomas Frederick. BA, Cornell U., 1953; MD, Yale U., 1957; DSc (hon.), U. Ind. Diplomate: Am. Bd. Pediatrics. Intern in pediatrics Johns Hopkins Hosp., 1957-58; USPHS postdoctoral fellow biochemistry Cambridge (Eng.) U., 1958-59; Josiah Macy Found. fellow in physiology Yale U. Med. Sch., 1959-60; asst. resident, fellow in pediatrics Johns Hopkins Hosp., 1960-61, resident, fellow, 1961-62; USPHS surgeon lab. perinatal physiology NIH, San Juan, P.R., 1962-64; asst. prof., Johns Hopkins Med. Sch., 1963-65; mem. faculty U. Colo. Med. Sch., Denver, 1965—, prof. pediatrics, prof. Ob-Gyn, 1969—, dir. div. perinatal medicine, 1970-74, chmn. dept. [illegible] attending pediatrician Children's, Denver Gen., Fitzsimons Gen. hosps. Assoc. editor: Pediatrics, 15th edit; med. progress contbg. editor: Jour. Pediatrics, 1966-74; mem. editorial bd.: European Jour. Ob-Gyn, 1971— ; assoc. J. Perinatal med. editor Biol. Neonate, 1979—; contbr. numerous articles med. jours. Mem. Assn. Am. Physicians, Am. Acad. Pediatrics (E. Mead Johns award 1960), Am. [illegible] Obstet. Soc., Soc. Pediatric Rsch. (pres. 1976-77), Perinatal Rsch. Soc. (pres. [illegible]), Western Soc. Pediatric Rsch. (pres. 1987—), Soc. Gynecol. Investigation, Am. Pediatric Soc. (pres. 1996), Internat. Congress Perinatal Medicine (pres. 1996), Soc. Gynecol. Investigation (coun. 1969-72), Soc. Exptl. Biology and Medicine, Inst. of Medicine, Phi Beta Kappa, Sigma Xi. Home: 2975 E Cedar Ave Denver CO 80209-3211 Office: Fitzsimons Bldg 260 Mail Stop F 441 PO Box 6508 Aurora CO 80045-0508

BATTEN, ALAN HENRY, astronomer; b. Tankerton, Kent, Eng., Jan. 21, 1933; emigrated to Can., 1959, naturalized, 1975; s. George Cuthbert and Gladys (Greenwood) B.; m. Lois Eleanor Dewis, July 30, 1960; children: Michael Henry John, Margaret Eleanor. BSc with 1st class honors, U. St. Andrews, Scotland, 1955, DSc, 1974; PhD, U. Manchester, Eng., 1958. Rsch. asst. in astronomy, jr. tutor St. Anselm Residence Hall, U. Manchester, 1958-59; postdoctoral fellow Dominion Astrophys. Obs., Victoria, B.C., Can., 1959-61, mem. staff, 1961-91, assoc. rsch. officer, 1970-76, sr. rsch. officer, 1976-91, guest scientist, 1991—. Part-time lectr. astronomy U. Victoria, 1961-64; guest investigator Vatican Obs., 1970, Inst. de Astronomia y Fisica del Espacio, Buenos Aires, 1972. Author: Binary and Multiple Systems of Stars, 1973, Resolute and Undertaking Characters: The Lives of Wilhelm and Otto Struve, 1988; editor: Extended Atmospheres and Circumstellar Matter in Spectroscoscopic Binary Systems, 1973, Algols, 1989, Astronomy for Developing Countries, 2001; sr. author: Eighth Catalogue of the Orbital Elements of Spectroscopic Binary Systems, 1989; co-editor: The Determination of Radial Velocities and Their Applications, 1967; translator: L'Observation des Etoiles Doubles Visuelles par P. Couteau, 1981; contbr. articles to profl. jours. Pres. Willows Elem. Sch. PTA, Victoria, 1971-73; mem. Anglican Ch. Can. Diocesan Synod, B.C., 1966-68, 74; mem. adv. coun. Ctr. Advanced Studies in Religion and Soc., U. Victoria, 1993—, chmn., 1997-2000. Erskine Vis. fellow U. Canterbury, New Zealand, 1995; recipient Queen's Silver Jubilee medal Can., 1977. Fellow Royal Soc. Can. (convenor interdisciplinary sect. 1980-81, mem. coun. 1980-81), Royal Astron. Soc., Explorers Club; mem. Internat. Astron. Union (v.p. 1985-91, pres. commn. 30 1976-79, pres. commn. 42 1982-85, chmn. nat. orgn. com. XVII Gen. Assembly 1975-79), Royal Astron. Soc. Can. (pres. 1976-78, hon. pres. 1993-98, editor jour. 1981-88), Astron. Soc. Pacific (v.p. 1965-68), Can. Astron. Soc. (pres. 1972-74), Am. Astron. Socs., Ancient Soc. Coll. Youths. Home: 2987 Westdowne Rd Victoria BC Canada V8R 5G1 Office: Dominion Astrophys Obs 5071 W Saanich Rd Victoria BC Canada V9E 2E7

BATTIN, JIM F. state legislator; b. Billings, Mont., 28 July; m. Mary; children: Christopher, Bailey, Kelsey. BS, U. Oreg. Exec. KMIR Television (NBC), Palm Desert; mem. Calif. Ho. Reps., Sacramento, 1994-2000, Calif. State Senate, Sacramento, 2000—. Bd. dirs. Martha's Kitchen; active Youth Edn. Motivation Program. Office: Ste 112 73710 Fred Waring Dr Palm Desert CA 92260 E-mail: jim.battin@assembly.ca.gov*

BATTS, MICHAEL STANLEY, German language educator; b. Mitcham, Eng., Aug. 2, 1929; s. Stanley George and Alixe Kathleen (Watson) B.; m. Misao Yoshida, Mar. 19, 1959; 1 dau., Anna. BA, U. London, 1952, BA with honors, 1953, LittD, 1973; PhD, U. Freiburg, Germany, 1957; M.L.S., U. Toronto, 1974. Mem. faculty U. Mainz, Germany, 1953-54, U. Basel, Switzerland, 1954-56, U. Wurzburg, Germany, 1956-58; instr. German U. Calif., Berkeley, 1958-60; mem. faculty dept. German U. B.C., Can., 1960-91, prof., 1967-91, head dept., 1968-80. Author: Die Form der Aventiuren im Nibelungenlied, 1961, Bruder Hansens Marienlieder, 1964, Studien zu Bruder Hansens Marienliedern, 1964, Das Hohe Mittelalter, 1969, Das Nibelungenlied-Synoptische Ausgabe, 1971, Gottfried von Strasburg, 1971, A Checklist of German Literature, 1945-75, 1977, The Bibliography of German Literature: An Historical and Critical Survey, 1978, A History of Histories of German Literature, 1835-1914, 1993, Germanic Studies at Canadian Universities From the Beginning to 1995, 1998; editor: Seminar, 1970-80. Served with Brit. Army, 1947-49. Alexander von Humboldt fellow, 1964-65, 83; Can. Council sr. fellow, 1964-65, 71-72; Killam fellow, 1981-82. Fellow Royal Soc. Can.; mem. Canadian Assn. Univ. Tchrs. German (pres. 1982-84), Modern Humanities Rsch. Assn., Alcuin Soc. (exec. v.p. 1972-79, pres. 1979-80), Internat. Assn. for Germanic Studies (pres. 1990-95). E-mial. Office: U Brit Columbia German Dept Vancouver BC Canada V6T 1Z1 E-mail: msb@interchange.ubc.ca

BAUCH, THOMAS JAY, financial/investment advisor, lawyer, educator, former apparel company executive; b. Indpls., May 24, 1943; s. Thomas and Violet (Smith) B.; m. Ellen L. Burstein, Oct. 31, 1982; children: Chelsea Sara, Elizabeth Tree. BS with honors, U. Wis., 1964, JD with highest honors, 1966. Bar: Ill. 1966, Calif. 1978. Assoc. Lord, Bissell & Brook, Chgo., 1966-72; lawyer, asst. sec. Marcor-Montgomery Ward, Chgo., 1973-75; spl. asst. to solicitor Dept. Labor, Washington, 1975-77; dep. gen. counsel Levi Strauss & Co., San Francisco, 1977-81, sr. v.p., gen. counsel, 1981-96, of counsel, 1996-2000; pvt. practice, Tiburon, Calif., 1996-2000; mng. dir. Laurel Mgmt. Co., L.L.C., San Francisco, 2000—. Cons. prof. Stanford (Calif.) U. Law Sch., 1997—; ptnr. Ika Enterprises. Mem. U. Wis. Law Rev., 1964-66. Bd. dirs. Urban Sch., San Francisco, 1986-91, Gateway H.S., San Francisco, Charles Armstrong Sch., Belmont, Calif., San Francisco Opera Assn., Telluride Acad., Corinthian Acad.; bd. visitors U. Wis. Law Sch., 1991-95. Mem. Am. Assn. Corp. Counsel (bd. dirs. 1984-87), Bay Area Gen. Counsel Assn. (chmn. 1994), Univ. Club, Villa Taverna Club, Corinthian Yacht Club, Order of Coif, San Francisco Yacht Club. Office: Laurel Mgmt Co LLC Ste 1450 One Maritime Plaza San Francisco CA 94111 E-mail: tbauch@laurelmanagement.com

BAUCOM, SIDNEY GEORGE, lawyer; b. Salt Lake City, Oct. 21, 1930; s. Sidney and Nora (Palfreyman) B.; m. Mary B., Mar. 5, 1954; children: Sidney, George, John JD, U. Utah, 1953. Bar: Utah 1953. Pvt. practice, Salt Lake City, 1953-55; asst. city atty. Salt Lake City Corp., 1955-56; asst. atty. Utah Power and Light Co., Salt Lake City, 1956-60, asst. atty., asst. sec., 1960-62, atty., asst. sec., 1962-68, v.p., gen. counsel, 1968-75, sr. v.p., gen. counsel, 1975-79, exec. v.p., gen. counsel, 1979-89, dir., 1979-89; of counsel Jones, Waldo, Holbrook & McDonough, Salt Lake City, 1989—. Past chmn. Utah Coordinating Coun. Devel. Svcs., Utah Taxpayers Assn.; past pres. Utah State Fair Found.; past dir. Utah Power & Light Co., El Paso Electric Co., vice chmn. Mem. Alta Club, Lions, Phi Delta Phi Mem. LDS Ch. Home: 2248 Logan Ave Salt Lake City UT 84108-2715 Office: Jones Waldo Holbrook & McDonough 1500 Wells Fargo Bank Bldg 170 S Main St Salt Lake City UT 84101-1605 E-mail: sbaucom@janeswaldo.com

BAUER, ALBERT, state legislator, educator; m. Patricia Bauer; children: Sue, Jim, Nancy. Student, Clark C.C., 1948-54; BA in Polit Sci. and History, Portland State Coll., 1957; MEd, Oreg. State Coll., 1958. Tchr. La Ctr. Sch. Dist., 1958-61, Vancouver Sch. Dist., 1961-80; Dem. caucus chmn. Wash. Legislature, Olympia, 1977-80, mem., 1981—, senate v.p. pro tempore, 1986-87, senate Dem. floor leader, 1987-90, senate Dem. dep. leader, 1991-92, senate v.p. pro tempore, 1999-2000, mem. edn. com., mem. higher edn. com., mem. rules com., chair capital budget com., mem. ways and means com., mem. joint legis. audit and rev. com., 1989—, mem. joint com. on pension policy, 1994—, mem. gov.'s higher edn. task force, 1995-98. Mem. Salmon Creek Grange, Salmon Creek Meth. Ch. With USN. Recipient UN medal, Legislator of Yr. award Wash. State Sch. Prins., Betty Sharff Meml. award, HOSTS Corp., Personal Commitment to Improve Edn. award Phi Delta Kappa, Walter G. Turner award Wash. State Ednl. Svc. Mem. Am. Legion (Post 176), Kiwanis (Greater Vancouver). Democrat. Office: 406 Legislative Bldg Olympia WA 98504-0001

BAUER, A(UGUST) ROBERT, JR. surgeon, educator; b. Phila., Dec. 23, 1928; s. A(ugust) Robert and Jessie Martha-Maynard (Monie) B.; BS, U. Mich., 1949, MS, 1950, MD, 1954; M Med. Sci.-Surgery, Ohio State U., 1960; m. Charmaine Louise Studer, June 28, 1957; children: Robert, John, William, Anne, Charles, James. Intern Walter Reed Army Med. Ctr., 1954-55; resident in surgery Univ. Hosp., Ohio State U., Columbus, also instr., 1957-61; pvt. practice medicine, specializing in surgery, Mt. Pleasant, Mich., 1962-74; chief surgery Ctrl. Mich. Community Hosp., Mt. Pleasant, 1964-65, vice chief of staff, 1967, chief of staff, 1968; clin. faculty Mich. State Med. Sch., East Lansing, 1974; mem. staff St. Mark's Hosp., Salt Lake City, 1974-91; pvt. practice surgery, Salt Lake City, 1974-91; clin. instr. surgery U. Utah, 1975-91. Trustee Rowland Hall, St. Mark's Sch., Salt Lake City, 1978-84; mem. Utah Health Planning Coun., 1979-81. Served with M.C., U.S. Army, 1954-57. Diplomate Am. Bd. Surgery. Fellow ACS, Southwestern Surg. Congress; mem. AMA, Salt Lake County Med. Soc., Utah Med. Assn. (various coms.), Utah Soc. Certified Surgeons, Salt Lake Surg. Soc., Pan Am. Med. Assn. (affiliate), AAAS (affiliate), Sigma Phi Epsilon, Phi Rho Sigma. Episcopalian. Club: Zollinger. Contbr. articles to profl. publs., researcher surg. immunology. Office: PO Box 17533 Salt Lake City UT 84117-0533 Address: 1366 Murray Holladay Rd Salt Lake City UT 84117-5050

BAUER, ERNST GEORG, physicist, educator; b. Schoenberg, Germany, Feb. 27, 1928; MS, U. Munich, 1953, PhD in Physics, 1955. Rsch. asst. U. Munich, 1955-58; head crystal physics br. Michelson Lab., China Lake, Calif., 1958-69; prof. Tech. U. Clausthal, Germany, 1969-96. Disting. rsch. prof. Ariz. State U., Tempe, 1993—. Author: Elektronenbeugung, 1958. Recipient Gaede prize German Vacuum Soc., 1988, Welch award Am. Vacuum Soc., 1992, Niedersachsenpreis, 1994. Fellow Am. Phys. Soc., Am. Vacuum Soc.; mem. Goettingen Acad. Sci., Materials Rsch. Soc., German Electron Microscopy Soc. Office: Ariz State Univ Dept Phys Astronomy Tempe AZ 85287-1504

BAUER, EUGENE ANDREW, dermatologist, educator; b. Mattoon, Ill., June 17, 1942; s. Eugene C. and Madge L. (Armer) B.; m. Gloria Anne Hehman, Feb. 19, 1966; childen: Marc A., Christine A., J. Michael, Amanda F. BS, Northwestern U., 1964, MD, 1967. Diplomate Am. Bd. Dermatology, Nat. Bd. Med. Examiners. Intern Barnes Hosp., St. Louis, 1967-68; resident, fellow div. dermatology Washington U. Med. Ctr., St. Louis, 1968-70; instr. Washington U., St. Louis, 1971-72, asst. prof. dermatology, 1974-78, assoc. prof., 1978-82, prof., 1982-88; prof., chmn. Stanford U. Sch. Medicine, 1988-95, dean, 1995-2001; program dir. Gen. Clin. Rsch. Ctr., 1990-93; v.p. med. affairs Stanford U., 1997-2000, v.p. Med. Ctr., 2000—. Mem. adv. coun. Nat. Inst. Arthritis and Musculoskeletal and Skin Diseases, 1997-2000; bd. dirs. Stanford Health Svcs., U. Calif. San Francisco-Stanford Health Care, Connetics Corp., Reconstructive Techs., Abor Vita Corp., Stanford Hosp. and Clinics, Lucile Salter Packard Children's Hosp. Contbr. numerous articles to profl. jours. Served to lt. comdr. USNR, 1972-74. Recipient Alumni Merit award Northwestern U., 1999. Fellow Am. Acad. Dermatology; mem. Am. Fedn. Clin. Rsch., Am Soc. Clin. Investigation, Am. Dermatol. Assn., Soc. Investigative Dermatology (bd. dirs. 1981-86, assoc. editor Jour. Investigative Dermatology 1982-87, pres.-elect 1994-95, pres. 1995-96), Ctrl. Soc. Clin. Rsch., Assn. Am. Physicians, Inst. of Medicine of NAS, Am. Clin. and Climatological Assn. Office: Stanford U Sch Medicine Office of the VP M121 Stanford CA 94305

BAUER, JEROME LEO, JR. chemical engineer; b. Pitts., Oct. 12, 1938; s. Jerome L. and Anna Mae (Tucker) B.; children from previous marriage: children: Lori, Trish, Jeff. BSChemE, U. Dayton, 1960; MSChemE, Pa. State U., 1963; postgrad., Ohio State U., 1969. Registered profl. engr., Ohio. Asst. prof. chem. engring. U. Dayton, Ohio, 1963-67; mgr. advanced composites dept. Ferro Corp., Cleve., 1967-72; engring. material and process specifications mgr. Lockheed Missiles & Space Co., Inc., Sunnyvale, Calif., 1972-74; gen. dynamics design specialist Convair Div., San Diego, 1974-76, project devel. engr., 1976-77; dir. research Furane div. M&T Chems. Inc., Glendale, Calif., 1980-82; mem. tech. staff Jet Propulsion Lab., Calif. Inst. Tech., Pasadena, 1977-80, 82-90; mem. tech. staff mfg. engring. The Aerospace Corp., El Segundo, 1990—, engring. specialist, 1997—. Editor: Materials Sciences for Future, 1986, Moving Foreward With 50 Years of Leadership in Advanced Materials, 1994, Materials and Processes Challenges, 1996, Evolving & Revolutionary Technologies for the New Millennium, 1999; contbr. articles to profl. jours. Jr. warden St. Luke Episcopal Ch., La Crescenta, Calif., 1980, sr. warden 1981. Fellow Internat. Electronics Packaging Soc. (pres. L.A. chpt. 1982), Soc. Advancement of Material Process Engring. (membership chmn. no. Calif. sect. 1973-74, vice chmn. San Diego sect. 1974-75, chmn. 1975-76, chmn. 1976, chmn. L.A. sect. 1977, internat. nat. treas. 1978-82, gen. chmn. 31st internat. symposium exhbn., Las Vegas, Nev., 1986, Meritorious Achievement award 1983, internat. v.p. 1987-89, internat. pres. 1989-90), Am. Inst. Chem. Engrs. (founder, chmn. Dayton sect. 1964-66, spl. projects chmn. Cleve. sect. 1968-69); mem. Phi Lambda Upsilon, Delta Sigma Epsilon. Republican. Avocations: carpentry, photography, camping. Home: PO Box 3298 El Segundo CA 90245-8398 Office: The Aerospace Corp 2350 E El Segundo Blvd El Segundo CA 90245-4691

BAUER, MARTY, talent agency executive; Pres. The Bauer Co., Beverly Hills, Calif., 1978—. Office: The Bauer Co 9465 Wilshire Blvd Ste 308 Beverly Hills CA 90212-2612

BAUER, MICHAEL, newspaper editor; Food and home editor San Francisco Chronicle. Office: San Francisco Chronicle 901 Mission St San Francisco CA 94103-2905

BAUER, RANDY MARK, management training firm executive; b. Sept. 2, 1946; s. Ralph I. and Gloria P. Bauer; m. Sue Deliva, July 4, 1975; children: Sherri, Kevin. BS summa cum laude, Ohio State U., 1968; MBA, Kent State U., 1971. Auditor Peat Marwick Mitchell & Co., Cleve., 1971-72; mgmt. devel. specialist GAO, Denver, 1972-80; adj. prof. mgmt. Columbia Coll., Denver, 1979—. Pres. Leadership Tng. Assos., Denver, 1979—; condr. exec. devel. workshops U. Colo., Denver, 1979—. Recipient Best in 1976 award GAO. Mem. Am. Soc. for Tng. and Devel., Beta Gamma Sigma. Address: 10022 Oak Tree Ct Lone Tree CO 80124-9714

BAUER, ROGER DUANE, chemistry educator, science consultant; b. Oxford, Nebr., Jan. 17, 1932; s. Albert Carl and Minnie (Lueking) B.; m. Jacquelyn True, Aug. 10, 1956; children— Lisa, Scott, Robert. BS, Beloit Coll., 1953; MS, Kans. State U., 1957, PhD, 1959. Asst. prof. chemistry Calif. State U., Long Beach, 1959-64, assoc. prof., 1964-69, prof., 1969-92; dean Calif. State U. (Sch. Natural Scis.), 1975-88. Served with U.S. Army, 1954-56. USPHS fellow, 1966; Am. Coun. on Edn. fellow, 1971 Mem. Am. Chem. Soc., Radiation Rsch. Soc., Sigma Xi, Phi Lambda Upsilon. Home: 6320 E Colorado St Long Beach CA 90803-2202 Office: Calif State U Coll Natural Sci Long Beach CA 90840-0001

BAUGH, COY FRANKLIN, corporate executive; b. Mt. Vernon, Ark., Feb. 7, 1946; s. Oather Lee Baugh and Eula Faye (Barnett) Baugh King; m. Cheryl Ann Linscott; 1 child, David F. AA, Glendale Coll., 1969; BS, Calif. State U., 1971; postgrad., Cornell U., 1978—; MBA, U. So. Calif., 1992. Sr. tax specialist Ernst & Young, 1971-74; audit supr. Amfac, Inc., San Francisco, 1974-77, v.p., treas., 1984-88; controller Fisher Cheese, Inc., Wapakoneta, Ohio, 1977-80, v.p. fin., 1980-84; v.p., treas. Furr's Inc., Lubbock, Tex., 1990-91, PacifiCare Health Sys., Inc., Cypress, Calif., 1993—. Clubs: L.A. Treasurers (pres. 1996). Office: Pacificare Health Sys PO Box 25186 Santa Ana CA 92799-5186 E-mail: coy.baugh@phs.com

BAUGH, DALE E. career officer; BS in Oceanography, U.S. Naval Acad., 1972; MS in Ocean Physics, Naval Post Grad. Sch. Commd. ensign USN, 1972, advanced through ranks ro rear adm.; various assignments to comdr. Puget Sound Naval Shipyard; dep. comdr. Logistics Maintenance and Indsl. Ops Support/Naval Sea Sys., Arlington, Va. Decorated Legion of Merit with one gold star, the Meritorious Svc. medal with two gold stars, Navy Commendation medal, others. Office: 1400 Farragut Ave Bremerton WA 98314-6001

BAUGHN, WILLIAM HUBERT, former business educator and academic administrator; b. Marshall County, Ala., Aug. 27, 1918; s. J.W. and Beatrice (Jackson) B.; m. Mary Madiera Morris, Feb. 20, 1945; children: Charles Madiera, William Marsteller. BS, U. Ala., 1940; MA, U. Va, 1941, PhD, 1948. Instr. U. Va., 1942-43, asst. prof., 1946-48; assoc. prof., then prof. econs. and bus. adminstrn. La. State U., 1948-56; prof. U. Tex., 1956-62, chmn. fin. dept., 1958-60, assoc. dean Coll. Bus. Adminstrn., 1959-62; assoc. dir. Sch. Banking of South, 1952-66; dean Coll. Bus. and Pub. Adminstrn. U. Mo., 1962-64; dean Coll. Bus. and Adminstrn. U. Colo., 1964-84, pres., 1985, acting chancellor, 1986-87; pres. U. Colo. System, Boulder, 1990-91. Pres. Am. Assembly Collegiate Schs. Bus., 1973-74; chmn. Big Eight Athletic Conf., 1970-71, 78-79, 86-87; dir. Stonier Grad. Sch. of Banking, Rutgers U., 1966-86; mem. council Nat. Collegiate Athletic Assn., 1983-86. Author: (with E.W. Walker) Financial Planning and Policy, 1961; editor: (with C.E. Walker) The Bankers' Handbook, 1966, (with C.E. Walker and T.I. Storrs) 3d rev. edit., 1988, (with D. R. Mandich) The International Banking Handbook, 1983. Served to 1st lt. USAAF, World War II; lt. col. Res. Home: 555 Baseline Rd Boulder CO 80302-7421 Office: U Colo System Boulder CO 80309-0001

BAULE, JOHN ALVIN, museum director, consultant; b. Dubuque, Iowa, July 20, 1948; s. Kenneth Edward and Edith (Stiles) B. BA in Math. and Physics summa cum laude, U. Dubuque, 1970; postgrad., Loras Coll., Dubuque, 1972-75, Coll. of St. Thomas, St. Paul, 1990; MA in History of Mus. Studies, SUNY, Oneonta, 1979. Dir. St. Lawrence County Hist. Assn., Canton, N.Y., 1976-86, Hennepin County Hist. Soc., Mpls., 1986-90; assoc. dir. Hist. Soc. Western Pa., Pitts., 1990-92; dir. Yakima (Wash.) Valley Mus., 1992—. Interpretive cons. Minn. Hist. Soc., Hennepin History Mus. and City of Mpls., 1992; mus. aid panelist N.Y. State Coun. on Arts, N.Y.C., 1983-86; grant reviewer Inst. Mus. Svcs., Washington, 1988-91; mem. long-range planning com. Am. Swedish Inst., Mpls., 1988-90; mem. St. Anthony Falls Heritage Bd., Mpls., 1988-90; founding chmn. Preservation Adv. Bd., Canton, 1978-82; trustee, mem. exec. com., workshop leader, speaker, sec. corp. Regional Conf. Hist. Agys., Manlius, N.Y., 1978-84; also others. Contbr. articles to profl. publs. Coord. 50th Anniversary Exhbn., Mpls. Aquatennial Assn., 1989; performer, treas. Grasse River Cmty. Theater, Canton, 1977-86; mem. citizens adv. group West River Parkway Task Force, Mpls., 1988-89; pres. Rivermill Townhomes Assn., 1987-90; chmn. entertainment div. 4th of July Cmty. Celebration Com., 1993—. Recipient North Country citation St. Lawrence U., Canton, 1986, pub. commendation Hennepin County Bd. Commrs., 1990; fellow Bush Found., 1990. Mem. Am. Assn. for State and Local History, Am. Assn. Mus., Mid-Atlantic Mus. Conf., Midwest Mus. Conf., Wash. Assn. Mus., Rotary. Avocations: travel, theater, hiking. Home: 3513 Highview Dr Yakima WA 98902-1531 Office: Yakima Valley Mus 2105 Tieton Dr Yakima WA 98902-3766

BAUM, CARL EDWARD, electromagnetic theorist; b. Binghamton, N.Y., Feb. 6, 1940; s. George Theodore and Evelyn Monica (Bliven) B. BS with honors, Calif. Inst. Tech., 1962, MS, 1963, PhD, 1969. Commd. 2d lt. USAF, 1962, advanced through grades to capt., 1967, resigned, 1971; project officer Air Force Rsch. Lab. (formerly Phillips Lab.), Kirtland AFB, N.Mex., 1963-71, sr. scientist for electromagnetics, 1971—; pres. SUMMA Found. U.S. del. to gen. assembly Internat. Union Radio Sci., Lima, Peru, 1975, Helsinki, Finland, 1978, Washington, 1981, Florence, Italy, 1984, Tel Aviv, 1987, Prague, Czechoslovakia, 1990, Kyoto, Japan, 1993, Lille, France, 1996, Toronto, Can., 1999; mem. Commn. B U.S. Nat. Com., 1975—, Commn. E, 1982—, Commn. A, 1990—. Author: (with others) Transient Electromagnetic Fields, 1976, Electromagnetic Scattering, 1978, Acoustic, Electromagnetic and Elastic Wave Scattering, 1980, Fast Electrical and Optical Measurements, 1986, EMP Interaction: Principles, Techniques and Reference Data, 1986, Lightning Electromagnetics, 1990, Modern Radio Science, 1990, Recent Advances in Electromagnetic Theory, 1990, Direct and Inverse Methods in Radar Polarimetry, 1992, (with A.P. Stone) Transient Lens Synthesis: Differential Geometry in Electromagnetic Theory, 1991; editor: (with H.N. Kritikos) Electromagnetic Symmetry, 1995, (with L. Carin and A.P. Stone) Ultra-Wideband, Short-Pulse Electromagnetics 3, 1997, Detection and Identification of Visually Obscured Targets, 1998; contbr. articles to profl. jours. Recipient award Honeywell Corp., 1962, R&D award USAF, 1970, Harold Brown award Air Force Systems Command, 1990; Air Force Rsch. Lab. fellow, 1996; Electromagnetic pulse fellow. Fellow IEEE (Harry Diamond Meml. award, 1987, Richard R. Stoddart award, 1984); mem. Electromagnetics Soc. (pres. 1983-85), Electromagnetics Acad., Sigma Xi, Tau Beta Pi. Roman Catholic. Home: 5116 Eastern Ave SE Apt D Albuquerque NM 87108-5618 Office: AFRL/DEHE 3550 Aberdeen Ave SE Bldg 909 Kirtland AFB NM 87117-5776

BAUM, DWIGHT CROUSE, investment banking executive; b. Syracuse, N.Y., Nov. 21, 1912; s. Dwight James and Katharine Lucia (Crouse) B.; m. Hildagarde Engelhardt, Jan. 17, 1942 (dec. Apr. 1999); children: Dwight J., John E. E.E., Cornell U., 1936; M.B.A., Harvard U., 1938. Chartered fin. analyst. Asst. to v.p. Mine Safety Appliance Co., Pitts., 1938-40; armament supply officer Brit. Air Commn., Washington, 1940-46; asst. to partner Eastman Dillon & Co., Los Angeles, 1946-47; v.p. 1st Calif. Co., Los Angeles, 1947-56; gen. partner Eastman Dillon Union Securities & Co., Los Angeles, 1956-71, sr. v.p., 1971-72, also dir., 1972-80; sr. v.p. Blyth Eastman Dillon & Co., Inc., adv. dir., 1980-83; sr. v.p. Paine Webber Inc, 1980—. Bd. dirs. Dominguez Water Corp. (now Dominguez Svcs. Corp.). Trustee Alice Lloyd Coll.; bd. dirs. Planned Parenthood-World Population, Los Angeles Decorated Order Brit. Empire Mem. Nat. Assn. Securities Dealers (bd. govs. 1976-79), Los Angeles Soc. Fin. Analysts, IEEE, Pacific Stock Exch., Inc. (vice chmn. 1980-82), Phi Delta Theta. Clubs: Calif. (Los Angeles), Bond (Los Angeles). Home: 1011 Oak Grove Ave San Marino CA 91108-1025 Office: 200 S Los Robles Ave Pasadena CA 91101-2479

BAUM, HERBERT MERRILL, consumer products company executive; b. Chgo., Dec. 6, 1936; s. Jack William and Ruth Frances (Ginsburg) B.; m. Diane Jean Kale, Nov. 1, 1975 (div. Sept. 1977); m. Karen Rochelle Oberman, Dec. 22, 1983. BSBA, Drake U., 1958. Account exec. Stern, Walters & Simmons, Chgo., 1962-66, Doyle, Dane & Bernbach, Chgo., 1966-69; v.p., account dir. Needham, Harper & Steers, Chgo., 1969-78; assoc. dir., dir. new products Campbell Soup Co., Camden, N.J., 1978, v.p. mktg., gen. mgr. soup div., 1978-84, exec. v.p. U.S. div., 1984-85; pres. Campbell USA, Camden, 1985-90, sr. v.p., 1986-89, exec. v.p., 1989-93; pres. Campbell N.Am., Camden, 1990-92, Campbell North & South Am., Camden, 1992-93; chmn., CEO Quaker State Corp., Irving, Tex., 1993-98; pres., COO Hasbro Inc., Providence, 1999-2000; chmn., CEO Dial Corp., Scottsdale, Ariz., 2000—. Bd. dirs. Grocery Mfrs. Am., Meredith Corp., Pepsi Ams. Inc., Dial Corp., Midas, Inc., Action Performance Cos. Inc., Fleming Co., Inc. With U.S. Army, 1958-59. Mem. Am. Mktg. Assn. Home: 702 Ocean Dr Juno Beach FL 33408-1911 Office: Dial Corp 15501 N Dial Blvd Scottsdale AZ 85260 E-mail: hbaum@dialcorp.com

BAUM, KERRY ROBERT, retired career officer; b. LaGrande, Oreg., May 25, 1939; s. Guy Hiatt B. and Niola (Anderson) Jones; m. Lynda Sue Christian, Dec. 18, 1964; children: Kerry Jr., Tatia D., Christian H., Buffy Jo, Patrick H., Britta Sue, Natalie A. BA in History, Brigham Young U., 1967; MBA in Mktg., Murray State U., 1978; postgrad., Webster Coll., St. Louis, 1979-80; MA in Nat. Security & Strategic Studies, US Naval War Coll., 1986. Commd. 2d lt. U.S. Army, 1957, advanced through grades to col., 1990, ret., 1991; mgr. emergency preparedness Brigham Young U., 1993—. U.S. rep. to Major NATO Comdrs. Alert Conf., 1987-90; joint staff rep LIVE OAK, 1986-90. Author, editor: NATO Alert Procedures for Joint Staff, 1988, Transfer of U.S. Forces to NATO Command, 1990, Focal Point Procedures Manual, 1989. Bishop Mormon Ch., Hopkinsville, Ky., 1974-78, councilor, bishopric, Newport, R.I., 1985-86; bishop Mormon Ch. BYU 185th Ward, 1996-99; mem. Utah Campus Safety Assn., pres.; apptd. mem. Utah Seismic Safety Commn., 2001. Decorated Bronze Star, Army Commendation medal, Air Force Commendation medal, Defense Superior Service Medal; named Utah Emer. Mgmt. Assn. Mem. of Yr., 2000; recipient certified emergency mgr. Internat. Assn. Emergency Mgrs. Mem. Res. Officers Assn., Assn. Contingency Planners (treas. Utah chpt.). Home: 10938 N 5870 W Highland UT 84003-9487 E-mail: kerry_baum@byu.edu

BAUM, MARSHA LYNN, law educator; b. Fulton, N.Y., Aug. 13, 1957; d. Warren J. and Shirley M. (Kenyon) B. BA in History, U. Rochester, 1979; MS in Libr. Sci. with honors, Columbia U., 1982; JD, SUNY, Buffalo, 1985. Bar: N.Y. Libr. asst. Ctr. for Govtl. Rsch., Rochester, N.Y., 1979-81; reference libr. SUNY-Buffalo Law Libr., 1984-85, U. Minn. Law Libr., Mpls., 1985-87; head pub. svcs. U. Conn. Law Libr., Hartford, 1987-89, dep. dir., 1989-92, acting dir., 1991; dir. law libr., assoc. prof. law U. S.C. Law Sch., Columbia, 1992-97, U. N.Mex. Law Sch., Albuquerque, 1997—. Mem. ALA, Am. Assn. Law Librs., N.Y. State Bar Assn. Office: U NMex Law Libr Albuquerque NM 87131

BAUM, PHYLLIS GARDNER, travel management consultant; b. Ashtabula, Ohio, Dec. 13, 1930; d. Charles Edward Schneider and Stella Elizabeth (Schaefer) Gardner; m. Kenneth Walter Baum, Oct. 21, 1948 (div. July 1971); children: Deidre Adair, Cynthia Gail; m. Dennis Carl Marquardt, Sept. 22, 1979 (dec. 1991). Grad. high sch., Cleve. Am. Soc. Travel Agents. Travel cons. Fredo Travel Svc., Ashland, Ohio, 1960-66; sales mgr. Travelmart, Willoughby, 1966-68, br. mgr. Mentor, 1966-68, Diners Fugazy Travel, Sun City, Ariz., 1968-69; travel cons. Jarrett's Travel Svc., Phoenix, 1969-72; sr. cons. Loyal Travel, Phoenix, 1972-74; co-mgr. Phil Carr Travel, Sun City, 1974-77; tour ops. mgr. ASL Travel, Phoenix, 1978-79; owner, mgr. Travel Temporaries, Glendale, Ariz., 1979-2000; ret. Cons. and lectr. in field. Adv. bd. mem. Small Bus. Devel. Ctr., Phoenix, 1986-2000. Mem. Pacific Asia Travel Assn. Ariz. (bd. dirs. 1986—), Ariz. Women in Travel, NAFE, Altrusa. Republican. Avocations: music, travel, tatting, knitting, horseback riding. Home and Office: Travel Temps 10249 N 45th Ave Glendale AZ 85302-1901

BAUM, STEPHEN L. utilities company executive; Grad., Harvard U.; JD, U. Va. Sr. v.p., gen. counsel N.Y. Power Authority, 1982-85; various positions with SDG&E, 1985-93, exec. v.p., 1993-96; pres., CEO Enova Corp., 1996-97, chmn., CEO, 1998; vice-chmn., pres., CEO Sempra Energy, San Diego, 1998—. Bd. dirs. Computer Sci. Corp., mem. audit com. Bd. dirs., pres. Cecil H. and Ida M. Green Found. for Earth Scis., U. Calif., San Diego; bd. dirs. Desert pacific Coun. Boy Scouts Am., Pacific Coun. on Internat. Policty; mem. San Diego Opera's Corp. Coun. Capt. USMC, 1966-69. Office: Sempra Energy 101 Ash St San Diego CA 92101-3017

BAUM, WILLIAM ALVIN, astronomer, educator; b. Toledo, Jan. 18, 1924; s. Earle Fayette and Mable (Teachout) B.; m. Ester Bru, June 27, 1961. B.A. summa cum laude, U. Rochester, 1943; Ph.D. magna cum laude, Calif. Inst. Tech., 1950. Physicist U.S. Naval Research Lab., Washington, 1946-49; astronomer Mt. Wilson and Palomar observatories, Pasadena, Calif., 1950-65; dir. Planetary Research Center, Lowell Obs., Flagstaff, Ariz., 1965-90; with astronomy dept. U. Wash., Seattle, 1990—. Adj. prof. astronomy Ohio State U., 1969-91; adj. prof. physics No. Ariz. U., 1973-91; rsch. prof. astronomy U. Wash., Seattle, 1990-97, prof. emeritus, 1997—; cons. physics, astronomy, optics; cons. U.S. Army Research Office, Durham, N.C., 1967-74; vis. prof. Am. Astronomy Soc., 1961-98; adv. com. Nat. Acad. Sci., 19 58-67; mem. optical instrumentation panel adv. Air Force, 1967-76; coms. and panels NSF and NASA Office Space Scis., 1967-91; mem. NASA Viking Orbiter Imaging Team, 1970-79, Hubble Space Telescope Camera Team, 1977-96. Contbr. articles to tech. publs. Served to lt., jr. grade USNR, 1943-46. Guggenheim fellow, 1960-61 Mem. Am. Astron. Soc. (chmn. div. planetary scis. 1976-77), Royal Astron. Soc., Astron. Soc. Pacific, Internat. Astron. Union, Phi Beta Kappa, Sigma Xi, Theta Delta Chi. Home: 2124 NE Park Rd Seattle WA 98105-2422 Office: U Wash Dept Astronomy Seattle WA 98195-0001 E-mail: baum@astro.washington.edu

BAUMAN, STEPHEN ADRIAN, lawyer; b. L.A., Jan. 25, 1935; BS in Bus. Adminstrn., UCLA, 1956; JD, Stanford U., 1959; LLM, Harvard U., 1960. Bar: Calif. 1960; cert. taxation specialist Calif. State Bar Bd. Legal Specialization. Ptnr. Seyfarth Shaw, L.A., 1987—. Lectr. tax law and estate planning U. So. Calif. Law Ctr. Advanced Profl. Program; U. So. Calif. Tax Inst., Calif. Continuing Edn. of Bar, Practising Law Inst. Mem. State Bar Calif. Office: Seyfarth Shaw 2029 Century Park E Ste 3300 Los Angeles CA 90067-3019

BAUMANN, RICHARD GORDON, lawyer; b. Chgo., Apr. 7, 1938; s. Martin M. and Harriet May (Granof) B.; m. Terrie Bemel, Dec. 18, 1971; children: Michelle, Alison. BS cum laude, U. Wis., 1960, JD, 1964. Bar: Wis. 1964, Calif. 1970, U.S. Supreme Ct. 1973. Congressional intern U.S. Senator Hubert H. Humphrey, 1959; assoc. firm Kohner, Mann & Kailas, Milw., 1964-69, Sulmeyer, Kupetz & Alberts, L.A., 1969-73; mem. firm Sulmeyer, Kupetz, Baumann & Rothman, L.A., 1973—. Judge pro tem L.A. Mcpl. Ct., 1980—. Assoc. editor Comml. Law Jour., 1991—. Fellow Comml. Law Found. (bd. dirs.); mem. Nat. Inst. on Credit Mgmt. (bd. dirs.), Am. Bd. Cert. (bd. dirs.), Acad. Comml. and Bankruptcy Law Specialists (bd. dirs.), Comml. Law League (pres. 1990-91, bd. govs. 1986-92, chmn. Western Region Mem. Assn. 1982-83). Office: 300 S Grand Ave Fl 14 Los Angeles CA 90071-3109

BAUMGARTNER, ANTON EDWARD, automotive sales professional; b. N.Y.C., May 18, 1948; s. Hans and Carmen Maria (Figueroa) B.; m. Brenda Lee Lemmon, May 24, 1969 (div. 1990); 1 child, Anton Nicholaus; m. Virginia Thiele, 1992; 1 child, Bree Alexandra. BS, Woodbury U., 1970. Sales mgr. Maywood Bell Ford, Bell, Calif., 1966-69, O.R. Haan, Inc., Santa Ana, 1969-72; pres. Parkinson Volkswagen, Placentia, 1972-77; exec. v.p. United Moped, Fountain Valley, 1975-82; pres. Automobili Intermeccanica, Fountain Valley, 1975-82; gen. mgr. Bishop (Calif.) Volkswagen-Bishop Motors, 1982-85, Beach Imports-Irvine Imports, Newport Beach, Calif., 1985-88; chmn. bd. Stan and Ollie Ins. Co., Santa Ana, 1989—; exec. v.p. Asterism, Inc., 1992-96; chmn. Marich Acceptance Inland Empire, 1996—. Mem. faculty, Automotive World Congress, Detroit, 1980. Contbr. articles to weekly serial publs. Mem. Coachbuilders Assn. N.Am. (sec. 1975-78). Office: Marich Acceptance 6 Satinbush Aliso Viejo CA 92656-1827 E-mail: tbaumgartner@sreusa.com

BAUMGARTNER, BRUCE, airport administrator; Mgr. aviation Denver Internat. Airport. Office: Denver Internat Airport Airport Office Bldg 8500 Pena Blvd Denver CO 80249-6205

BAUMHEFNER, CLARENCE HERMAN, banker; b. Lester Prairie, Minn., Apr. 1, 1912; s. Walter P. and Clare A. (Jacobs) B.; m. Virginia Haight, May 11, 1941; children— Robert, Bonnie. Grad., Am. Inst. Banking, 1940; student, Grad. Sch. Banking, Rutgers U., 1951. With Bank of Am., 1940—, Bank of Am. (inspection dept.), 1940-43, insp., 1943-47, asst. chief insp., 1947-50, asst. to cashier, 1950-56, cashier and v.p., 1956-65, sr. v.p., cashier, 1965-66, exec. v.p., 1966-70, vice chmn. bd., 1970—. Clubs: Merchants Exchange (San Francisco), Bankers (San Francisco), Bohemian (San Francisco), Pacific Union (San Francisco). Home and Office: 555 California St Ste 1100 San Francisco CA 94104-1514

BAUML, FRANZ HEINRICH, German language educator; b. Vienna, Austria, June 12, 1926; came to U.S., 1942, naturalized, 1945; s. Gustav Heinrich and Josefa B.; m. Betty Zeidner, Aug. 28, 1958; children— Carolyn, Mark, Deborah. B.S., Armstrong Coll., 1950; B.A., U. Calif., Berkeley, 1953, M.A., 1955, Ph.D., 1957. Prof. German U. Calif., Los Angeles, 1957—. Author: Rhetorical Devices and Structure in the Ackerman aus Bohmen, 1960, Kudrun: Die Handschrift, 1969, Medieval Civilization in Germany, 800-1273, 1969, A Dictionary of Gestures, 1975, A Concordance to the Nibelungenlied, 1976, Mittelalter, 1987, A Dictionary of Worldwide Gestures, 1997. Served with AUS, 1944-46; Served with U.S. Army, 1950-51. Fellow Netherlands Inst. for Advanced Study, 1991-92. Mem. Medieval Acad. Am. Office: U Calif Germanic Langs Los Angeles CA 90024

BAUMRIND, DIANA, research psychologist; b. N.Y.C., Aug. 23, 1927; A.B., Hunter Coll., 1948; M.A., U. Calif., Berkeley, 1951, Ph.D., 1955. Cert. and lic. psychologist, Calif. Project dir. psychology dept. U. Calif., Berkeley, 1955-58; project dir. Inst. of Human Devel., 1960—, also rsch. psychologist and prin. investigator family socialization and devel. competence project. Lectr. and cons. in field; referee for rsch. proposals Grant Found., NIH, 1970—, NSF, 1970—. Contbr. numerous articles to profl. jours. and books; author 2 monographs; mem. editorial bd. Devel. Psychology, 1986-90. Recipient Rsch. Scientist award, NIMH; grantee NIMH, 1955-58, 60-66, Nat. Inst. Child Health and Human Devel., 1967-74, MacArthur Found., Grant Found., 1967—. Fellow Am. Psychol. Assn., Am. Psychol. Soc. (G. Stanley Hall award 1988), Soc. Research in Child Devel. Office: U Calif Inst of Human Devel 1217 Tolman Hall Berkeley CA 94720-1691

BAUTISTA, ANTHONY HERNANDEZ, biomedical company executive; b. Palo Alto, Calif., Sept. 19, 1955; s. Anthony Hernandez and Velma Rose (Morinan) B.; m. Jill Davis, June 17, 1978; children: Evan Thomas, Laura Anne. AA in Electronic Tech., Coll. of San Mateo, 1976; BSEE, San Jose (Calif.) State U., 1994. Elec. engr. Hewlett Packard, Palo Alto, Calif., 1976-86; mfg. engring. mgr. Molecular Devices Corp., Menlo Park, 1986-91; ops. v.p. LJL Biosystems, Inc., Sunnyvale, 1991—. Mem. Toastmasters (adminstrv. v.p. 1990), Tau Beta Pi.

BAVASI, PETER JOSEPH, sports management executive; b. Bronxville, N.Y., Oct. 31, 1942; s. Emil Joseph and Evit E. (Rice) B.; m. Judith Marzonie, June 13, 1964; children: Patrick, Cristina BA in Philosophy, St. Mary's Coll., Moraga, Calif., 1964. Minor league gen. mgr. Los Angeles Dodgers, 1964-68; dir. minor league ops. San Diego Padres, 1968-73, v.p., gen. mgr., 1973-76; pres., chief exec. officer Toronto Blue Jays, Ont., Can., 1976-81; pres. Peter Bavasi Sports, Inc., Tampa, Fla., 1981-84; pres., chief operating officer Cleve. Indians, 1984-87; pres., chief exec. officer Telerate Sports and SportsTicker, Jersey City, 1987-94; pres. ESPN/SportsTicker, Jersey City, 1995-96; owner, operator Masthope Guide Svc., Lackawaxen, Pa., 1996-97; pres. Masthope West Angling Svc., La Jolla, Calif., 1997—. Office: Masthope West Angling Svc 1001 Genter St Unit 3G La Jolla CA 92037-5531 E-mail: pbavasi@aol.com

BAWDEN, GARTH LAWRY, museum director; b. Truro, Eng., Dec. 31, 1939; s. Richard Thomas and Susan Elizabeth Olga (Lawry) B.; m. Margaret Ruth Greet, Dec. 21, 1963 (div. Mar. 1978); children: Michael Greet, Teona Mary, Kerenza Elizabeth; m. Elaine Louise Comack, Oct. 26, 1978; children: Jonathan Richard, Rebecca Lawry. Diploma in phys. medicine, West Middlesex Sch. Phys. Medicine, Isleworth, Eng., 1961; BA in Art History, U. Oreg., 1970; PhD in Anthropology, Harvard U., 1977. Assoc. in archaeology Harvard U., Cambridge, Mass., 1977-81, instr., 1980-85, asst., acting dir. Peabody Mus., 1980-85; assoc. prof. U. N.Mex., Albuquerque, 1985-91; prof. U. Mex., Albuquerque, 1991—; dir. Maxwell Mus. U. N.Mex., Albuquerque, 1985—. Dir. field research project Harvard U., Galindo, Peru, 1971-74, dir. field survey Peabody Mus., Saudi Arabian Archaeol. Survey, 1978-80; field supr. Cuntisuyu Project, Moquegua, Peru, 1983-86; dir. U. N.Mex. Acheol. Project, So. Peru, 1985—. Author: (with G. Conrad) The Andean Heritage, 1982; contbr. articles on archaeology to profl. jours. Fellow Woodrow Wilson, U. Oreg., 1970, Tinker, Harvard U., 1983. Mem. Soc. Am. Archaeology, Assn. Field Archaeology, Assn. Sci. Mus. Dirs., Current Anthropology (assoc.), Phi Beta Kappa, Sigma Xi. Home: 6 Applewood Ln NW Albuquerque NM 87107-6404 Office: Univ NMex Maxwell Mus Anthropology Albuquerque NM 87131-0001

BAXTER, FRANK EDWARD, brokerage executive; b. Baxter, Calif., Nov. 20, 1936; s. Erwin Williard and Alice Mary (Byrne) B.; m. Kathrine Forest Stacey, June 9, 1962; children: Stacey, Matthew, Katherine. BA, U. Calif., Berkeley, 1961. V.p., dir. J.S. Strauss & Co., San Francisco, 1963-74; chmn., cir. Jefferies & Co., L.A., 1974—. Served with USAF, 1955-58. Mem. Security Traders Assn. N.Y., Nat. Security Traders Assn., Equity Dealers Assn., London, Siwanoy Country Club, L.A. Country Club, Regency Club, Wilshire Country Club (L.A.). E-mail: fbaxter. Office: Jefferies & Co Inc 11100 Santa Monica Blvd Los Angeles CA 90025-3384 E-mail: fbaxter@jefco.com

BAXTER, JOHN DARLING, physician, educator, health facility administrator; b. Lexington, Ky., June 11, 1940; s. William Elbert and Genevive Lockhart (Wilson) B.; m. Ethelee Davidson Baxter, Aug. 10, 1963; children: Leslie Lockhart, Gillian Booth. BA in Chemistry, U. Ky., 1962; MD, Yale U., 1966. Intern, then resident in internal medicine Yale-New Haven Hosp., 1966-68; USPHS research assoc. Nat. Inst. Arthritis and Metabolic Diseases, NIH, 1968-70; Dernham sr. fellow oncology U. Calif. Med. Sch., San Francisco, 1970-72, mem. faculty, 1972—, prof. medicine and biochemistry and biophysics, 1979—, dir., Metabolic Rsch. Unit. Dir. endocrine research Howard Hughes Med. Inst., 1976-81, investigator, 1975-81; chief div. endocrinology Moffitt Hosp., 1980— , dir. Metabolic Research Unit, 1981— ; attending physician U. Calif. Med. Center, 1972— Editor textbook of endocrinology and metabolism; Author research papers in field; mem. editorial bd. profl. jours. Recipient George W. Thorn award Howard Hughes Med. Inst., 1978, Disting. Alumni award U. Ky., 1980, Dautrebande prize for research in cellular and molecular biology, Belgium, 1985, Albion Bernstein award N.Y. Med. Soc., 1987; grantee NIH, Am. Cancer Soc., others. Mem. Am. Chem. Soc., Am. Soc. Hypertension, Am. Soc. Clin. Investigation, Am. Thyroid Assn., Assn. Am. Physicians, Am. Fedn. Clin. Research, Endocrine Soc., Western Assn. Physicians, Western Soc. Clin. Research. Office: U Calif Med Sch Box 0540 HSW 116 San Francisco CA 94143-0001

BAXTER, MARVIN RAY, state supreme court justice; b. Fowler, Calif., Jan. 9, 1940; m. Jane Pippert, June 22, 1963; children: Laura, Brent. BA in Econs., Calif. State U., 1962; JD, U. Calif.-Hasting Coll. Law, 1966. Bar: Calif. 1966. Appointments sec. to Gov. George Deukmejian, 1983-88; dep. dist. atty. Fresno County, Calif., 1967-68; assoc. Andrews, Andrews, Thaxter & Jones, 1968-70, ptnr., 1971-82; apptd. sec. to Gov. George Deukmejian, 1983-88; assoc. justice Calif. Ct. Appeal (5th dist.), 1988-90; state supreme ct. assoc. justice Calif. Supreme Ct., 1991—. Mem. Jud. Coun. of Calif., chmn. policy coord. and liaison com., 1996—. Mem. Fresno County Bar Assn. (bd. dirs. 1977-82, pres. 1981), Calif. Young Lawyers Assn. (bd. gov. 1973-76, sec.-treas. 1974-75), Fresno County Young Lawyers Assn. (pres. 1973-74), Fresno County Legal Svcs., Inc. (bd. dirs. 1973-74), Fresno State U. Alumni Assn. (pres. 1970-71), Fresno State U. Alumni Trust Coun. (pres. 1970-75). Office: Calif Supreme Ct 350 Mcallister St San Francisco CA 94102-4712

BAXTER, RALPH H., JR. lawyer; b. San Francisco, 1946; AB, Stanford U., 1968; MA, Cath. U. Am., 1970; JD, U. Va., 1974. Chmn. Orrick, Herrington & Sutcliffe LLP, San Francisco, 1990—. Mem. adv. bd. nat. Employment Law Inst. Author: Sexual Harassment in the Workplace: A Guide to the Law, 1981, 2nd. rev. edit., 1989, 94, Manager's Guide to Lawful Terminations, 1983, rev. edit., 1991; mem. editorial bd. Va. Law Rev., 1973-74; mem. editorial adv. bd. Employee Rels. Law Jour. Mem. ABA (mgmt. co-chair com. on employment rights and responsibilities in workplace labor and employment law sect. 1987=90). Office: Orrick Herrington & Sutcliffe LLP Old Fed Res Bank Bldg 400 Sansome St San Francisco CA 94111-3143

BAYDA, EDWARD DMYTRO, judge; b. Alvena, Sask, Can., Sept. 9, 1931; s. Dmytro Andrew and Mary (Bilinski) B.; m. Marie-Thérèse Yvonne Gagné, May 28, 1953; children: Paula, Christopher, Margot, Marie-Thérèse, Sheila, Kathryn. BA, U. Sask., 1951, LLB cum laude, 1953; LLD (hon.), 1989. Bar: Sask. 1954; created Queen's Counsel, Exec. Br. of Govt., 1966. Barrister, solicitor, Regina, Sask., 1953-72; sr. ptnr. Bayda, Halvorson, Scheibel & Thompson, 1966-72; justice Ct. Queen's Bench for Sask., Regina, 1972-74, Ct. Appeal for Sask., Regina, 1974-81; chief justice Sask., Regina, 1981—. Created Queen's Counsel. Roman Catholic. Home: 3000 Albert St Regina SK S4S 4H2 Canada S4S 3N7 Office: Ct Appeal Sask Courthouse 2425 Victoria Ave Regina SK Canada S4P 3V7

BAYLESS, BETSEY, state official; b. Phoenix; BA in Latin Am. Studies and Spanish, U. Ariz., 1966; MPA, Ariz. State U., 1974. V.p. pub. fin. Peacock, Hislop, Staley & Given, Inc., Phoenix; asst. dir. Ariz. Bd. Regents; acting dir. dept. revenue State of Ariz., dir. dept. adminstrn., sec. of state, 1997—. Bd. suprs. Maricopa County, 1989-97, chmn. bd., 1992, 94, vice chair, 1997. Nat. bd. advisors U. Ariz. Coll. Bus. & Pub. Adminstrn.; adv. bd. Ariz. State U. West; bd. dirs. Xavier Coll. Preparatory Found., Ariz. Ctr. for the Book; commr. Gov.'s Commn. Violence Against Women; mem. Ariz. Town Hall, Charter 100, Valley Leadership Class VI, Ariz. Rep. Caucus, Ariz. Women's Forum. Named to Hall of Fame, Ariz. State U. Coll. Pub. Programs; recipient Disting. Citizen award U. Ariz. Alumni Assn., Woman of Yr. award Capitol chpt. Bus. and Profl. Women, Disting. Achievement award NEH Fellowship, Achievement award Nat. Assn. Counties, 1993, Citizen award Bur. Reclamation, 1993, Woman of Achievement award Xavier Coll. Preparatory, 1995. Mem. Phi Beta Kappa (Freeman medal 1966). Office: State Capitol 1700 W Washington St Fl 7 Phoenix AZ 85007-2814

BAYLOR, DENIS ARISTIDE, neurobiology educator; b. Oskaloosa, Iowa, Jan. 30, 1940; s. Hugh Murray and Elisabeth Anne (Barbou) B.; m. Eileen Margaret Steele, Aug. 12, 1983; children: Denis Murray, Michael Randel; 1 stepchild, Michele Gonelli. BA in Chemistry magna cum laude, Knox Coll., 1961, DS (hon.), 1989; MD cum laude, Yale U., 1965. Post-doctoral fellow Yale Med. Sch., New Haven, 1965-68; staff assoc. Nat. Inst. Neurological Diseases and Stroke, Bethesda, 1968-70; spl. fellow USPSH Physiological Lab. Cambridge U., Eng., 1970-72; assoc. prof. physiology U. Colo. Med. Sch., Denver, 1972-74, Stanford U., Calif., 1974-75, assoc. prof. neurobiology, 1975-78, prof. neurobiology, 1978—, chmn. dept. neurobiology, 1992-95; First Annual W.S. Stiles lecturer U. Coll., London, England, 1989; Jonathan Magnes lecturer Hebrew U., Jerusalem, Israel, 1990; Woolsey lecturer U. Wis., 1992; E. Hille lectr. U. Washington, 1995. Mem. NIH Visual Scis. Study Sect., 1984-88, chmn., 1986-88; vis. com. med. scis. Harvard U., 1987-93; chmn. Summer conf. on Vision FASEB, 1989; Wellcome vis. prof. U. Miami, 1995; mem. sci. adv. com. Alcon Rsch. Inst., 1994-99; mem. HHMI Sci. adv. bd. 1997—, Med. adv. bd. 1998—; mem. sci. adv. bd. Found. Fighting Blindness, 1998—; trustee The Grass Found., 1995-99. Mem. editorial bd. Jour. Physiology, 1977-84, Neuron, 1988-93, Jour. Neurophysiology, 1989—, Visual Neurosci., 1990-93, Jour. Neurosci., 1991—; contbr. articles to profl. jours. Recipient Sinsheimer Found. award, 1975, Mathilde Solowey award, 1978, Kayser Internat. award Retina Rsch. Found., 1988, Golden Brain award Minerva Found., 1988, Merit award Nat. Eye Inst., 1990, Alcon Rsch. Inst. award, 1991; Rank Optoelectronics prize Rank Orgn., Eng., 1980; Proctor medal Assn. Rsch. Vision & Ophthalmology, 1986, Von Sallman prize in eye rsch., 1998. Fellow Am. Acad. Arts and Scis.; mem. NAS, Phi Beta Kappa, Alpha Omega Alpha. Avocations: jogging, woodworking. Office: Stanford U Sch Med Neurobiology/Fairchild D237 835 Esplanada Way Stanford CA 94305 E-mail: dbaylor@stanford.edu

BAYLOR, ELGIN GAY, professional basketball team executive; b. Washington, Sept. 16, 1934; m. Elaine; 1 dau., Krystle. Ed., Coll. Idaho, Seattle U. Profl. basketball player Los Angeles (formerly Minneapolis) Lakers, 1958-72; asst. coach New Orleans Jazz, NBA, 1974-76, coach, 1976-79; exec. v.p., gen. mgr. Los Angeles Clippers, 1986-94, v.p. basketaballops., 1994—. Most Valuable Player, NCAA Tournament, 1958; mem. NBA All-Star Team, 1959-65, 67-70; Rookie of the Yr., NBA, 1959; co-Most Valuable Player, NBA All-Star Game, 1959; named to NBA 35th Anniversary All-Time Team, 1980 Office: LA Clippers 1111 S Figueroa St Ste 1100 Los Angeles CA 90015-1300

BEACH, LEE ROY, psychologist, educator, academic administrator; b. Gallup, N.Mex., Feb. 29, 1936; s. Dearl and Lucile Ruth (Krumtum) B.; m. Barbara Ann Heinrich, Nov. 13, 1971. B.A., Ind. U., 1957; M.A., U. Colo., 1959, Ph.D., 1961. Aviation psychologist U.S. Sch. Aviation Medicine, Pensacola, Fla., 1961-63; human factors officer Office of Naval Research, Washington, 1963-64; postdoctoral research U. Mich., Ann Arbor, 1964-66; faculty dept. psychology U. Wash., Seattle, 1966-89; faculty mgmt. & policy, psychology U. Ariz., Tucson, 1990—, McClelland chair mgmt. & policy, 1989—, vice dean Sch. Bus., 1998—. Contbr. articles to profl. jours. Recipient Feldman rsch. award, 1981, Disting. Tchr. award U. Wash., 1986, Prof. of Yr. award State of Wash., 1989, nat. teaching award Coun. for Advancement and Support Edn., 1989; fellow NIMH, 1964-66. Fellow Am. Psychol. Soc. Office: Univ Arizona Coll Bus & Pub Adminstrn Tucson AZ 85721-0001

BEACH, ROGER C. retired oil company executive; b. Lincoln, Nebr., Dec. 5, 1936; s. Melvin C. and L. Mayme (Hoham) B.; m. Elaine M. Wilson, Oct. 1954 (div. 1972); children: Kristi, Mark, Anne; m. Karen Lynn Ogden, July 27, 1974. BS, Colo. Sch. Mines, 1961. Profl. petroleum refining engr., Calif. With Unocal Corp., L.A., 1961—, mgr. spl. projects Los Angeles, 1976-77, dir. planning, 1977-80, v.p. crude supply, 1980-86, pres. refining and mktg., 1986-92, corp. sr. v.p., 1987-1992, pres., 1992-94, CEO, 1994—, now chmn. and COO, 1994-98, CEO, 1998—; ret., 2000. Chmn. bd. trustees Nat. 4-H Coun. Mem. Pres.'s Interchange Exec. Alumni Assn. Office: Unocal Corp 2141 Rosecrans Ave Ste 4000 El Segundo CA 90245-4746

BEADLE, CHARLES WILSON, retired mechanical engineering educator; b. Beverly, Mass., Jan. 24, 1930; s. Thomas and Jean (Wilson) B.; m. Dorothy Elizabeth Struyk, May 5, 1956; children: Steven C., Sara E., Gordon S. BS, Tufts U., 1951; MSE, U. Mich., 1954; PhD, Cornell U., 1961. Registered mech. engr., Calif. Research engr. Gen. Motors Research Labs., Detroit, 1951-54, RCA Research Labs., Princeton, N.J., 1954-57; prof. mech. engring. U. Calif., Davis, 1961-91, ret., 1991. Contbr. articles to profl. jours. Fellow ASME. Home: 420 12th St Davis CA 95616-2023 Office: U Calif Davis Dept Mech Engring Davis CA 95616

BEAKE, JOHN, professional football team executive; m. Marcia Beake; children: Jerilyn, Chip, Christopher. Grad., Trenton (N.J.) State Coll.; M degree, Pa. State U. Asst. coach Pa. State U., 1961-62, Kansas City Chiefs, NFL, 1968-74, New Orleans Saints, NFL, 1976-77; offensive coordinator Colo. State U., 1974-76; dir. profl. personnel Denver Broncos, NFL, 1979-83, dir. football ops., 1983-84, asst. gen. mgr., 1984-85, gen. mgr., 1985-98; v.p. adminstrn. Denver Broncos, 1998—. Office: Denver Broncos 13655 Broncos Pky Englewood CO 80112-4150

BEAL, DENNIS, academic administrator; CFO Stater Bros. Market, Colton, Calif., -2000; exec. v.p., CFO Corinthian Colls., Santa Ana, 2000—. Office: Corinthian Colls 6 Hutton Centre Dr Ste 400 Santa Ana CA 92707

BEALL, BURTCH W., JR. architect; b. Columbus, Ohio, Sept. 27, 1925; s. Burtch W. and Etta (Beheler) B.; m. Susan Jane Hunter, June 6, 1949; children: Brent Hunter, Brook Waite. Student, John Carroll U., 1943; BArch, Ohio State U., 1949. Draftsman Brooks & Coddington, Architects, Columbus, 1949-51, William J. Monroe, Architects, Salt Lake City, 1951-53, Lorenzo Young, Architect, Salt Lake City, 1953-54; prin. Burtch W. Beall, Jr., Architect, Salt Lake City, 1954—. Vis. lectr. Westminster Coll., 1955; adj. prof. U. Utah, 1955-85, 92-97; treas. Nat. Coun. Archtl. Registration Bds., 1982-84. Restoration architect Salt Lake City and County Bldg; contbr. projects to: A Pictorial History of Architecture in America, America Restored, This Before Architecture. Trustee Utah Found. for Arch., 1985, pres., 1987-91; mem. Utah State Bd. Fine Arts, 1987-95, chmn., 1991-93; chmn. Utah State Capitol Adv. Com., 1986-90, Western States Art Fedn., Bd. trustees, 1991-94; mem. exec. residence com. State of Utah, 1991-97; mem. Utah: A Guide to the State Found. With USN, 1943-45. Recipient several merit and honor awards; Found. fellow Utah Heritage Found., 1985. Fellow AIA (jury mem. 2000-01); mem. Masons, Sigma Alpha Epsilon. Methodist. Home: 4644 Brookwood Cir Salt Lake City UT 84117-4908 Office: Burtch W Beall Jr Arch 2188 Highland Dr Salt Lake City UT 84106-2896

BEALL, DENNIS RAY, artist, educator; b. Chickasha, Okla., Mar. 13, 1929; s. Roy A. and Lois O. (Phillips) B.; 1 son, Garm. Musician, Okla. City U., 1950-52; B.A., San Francisco State U., 1953, M.A., 1958. Registrar Oakland (Calif.) Art Mus., 1958; curator Achenbach Found. for Graphic Arts, Calif. Palace of the Legion of Honor, San Francisco, 1958-1965; asst. prof. art San Francisco State U., 1965-69, assoc. prof., 1969-76, prof. art, 1976-92; prof. emeritus, 1992—. Numerous one-man shows of prints, 1957—, including: Award Exhbn. of San Francisco Art Commn., Calif. Coll. Arts and Crafts, 1978, San Francisco U. Art Gallery, 1978, Los Robles Galleries, Palo Alto, Calif.; numerous group shows 1960— including Mills Coll. Art Gallery, Oakland, Calif., Univ. Gallery of Calif. State U., Hayward, 1979, Marshall-Meyers Gallery, 1979, 80, Marin Civic Ctr. Art Galleries, San Rafael, Calif., 1980, San Francisco Mus. Modern Art, 1985; touring exhibit U. Mont., 1987-91, An Inner Vision, Oysterponds Hist. Soc., Orient, N.Y., 1998, Modernism in Calif. Printmaking, Annex Gallery, Santa Rosa, Calif., 1998, The Stamp of Impulse, Worcester (Mass.) Art Mus., 2001; represented in numerous permanent collections including Libr. of Congress, Washington, Mus. Modern Art, N.Y.C., Nat. Libr. of Medicine, Washington, Cleve. Mus., Whitney Mus., Phila. Mus., U.S. embassy collections, Tokyo, London and other major cities, Victoria and Albert Mus., London, Achenbach Found. for graphic Arts, Calif. Palace of Legion of Honor, San Francisco, Oakland Art Mus., Phila. Free Libr., Roanoke (Va.) Art Ctr., Worcester (Mass.) Art Mus., Whitney Mus. Am. Art, Cleve. Mus., various colls. and univs. in U.S. Served with USN, 1947-50, PTO. Office: San Francisco State Univ Art Dept 1600 Holloway Ave San Francisco CA 94132-1722 E-mail: chukar@thegrid.net

BEALL, FRANK CARROLL, science director and educator; b. Balt., Oct. 3, 1933; s. Frederick Carroll Beall and Virginia Laura (Ogier) McNally; m. Mavis Lillian Holmes, Sep. 7, 1963; children: Amanda Jane Fee, Mark Walter Beall, Alyssa Joan Beall. BS, Pa. State U., 1964; MS, Syracuse U., 1966, PhD, 1968. Rsch. technologist U.S. Forest Products Lab., Madison, Wis., 1966-68; asst., then assoc. prof. Pa. State U., University Park, 1968-75; assoc. prof. U. Toronto, Can., 1975-77; scientist, mgr. Weyerhaeuser Co., Federal Way, Wash., 1977-88; Fred E. Dickinson chair in wood sci. and tech. U. Calif. Forest Products Lab., Richmond, 1997—, prof., dir., 1988—. Contbr. articles in wood and sci. tech.; patentee for wood forming method, method of measuring content of dielectric materials, vertical progressive lumber dryer, bond strength measurement of composite panel products, hybrid pultruded products and method for their manufacture, pultrusion method for condensation resin injection, others. Fellow Acoustic Emission Working Group (chmn. 1996-98), Internat. Acad. Wood Sci. (sec.-treas. 1996—); mem. ASTM (com. DO7 on wood, chmn. 1994-98), Internat. Union Forestry Rsch. Orgns. (coord. rsch. group physiomech. properties of wood and wood-based materials), Am. Soc. for Non-destructive Testing, Forest Products Soc. (pres. 2001—), Soc. Wood Sci. and Tech. (pres. 1991-92). Office: U Calif Forest Products Lab 1301 S 46th St Richmond CA 94804-4600 E-mail: frank.beall@ucop.edu

BEAN, FRANK D(AWSON), sociology and demography educator; b. May 20, 1942; s. Frank Dawson and Alta Louzana (Scott) B.; m. Carolyn P. Boyd, Jan. 4, 1975; children: Alan McDavid, Deborah Scott, Peter Justin, Michael Franklin. Student, Oberlin Coll., 1960-62; BA, U. Ky., 1964; MA, Duke U., 1965, PhD, 1970. Asst. prof. sociology U. Tex., Austin, 1968-71, assoc. prof., 1972-78, prof., 1978-85, Ashbel Smith prof. sociology, 1986-99, dept. chmn., 1978-84; asst. prof. Ind. U., Bloomington, 1971-72; dir. Population Rsch. Ctr., U. Tex., Austin, 1995-98; prof. sociology U. Calif., Irvine, 1999—. Dir. Population Studies Ctr., The Urban Inst., Washington, 1988-89. Co-author: (with Marta Tienda) The Hispanic population of the U.S., 1989; editor: (with Jurgen Schmandt and Sidney Weintraub) Mexican and Central American Population: Implications for U.S. Immigration Policy, 1989, (with C. Vernez and C. Keely) Opening and Closing the Doors: Evaluating Immigration Reform and Control, 1989, (with B. Edmonston and J. Passel) Undocumented Migration to the United States: IRCA and the Experience of the 1980s, 1990, (with Stephanie Bell-Rose) Immigration and Opportunity: Race, Ethicity and Employment in the United States, 1999. Recipient numerous grants. Mem. Am. Sociol. Assn., Population Assn. Am., So. Sociol. Soc., Sociol. Rsch. Assn., Southwestern Social Sci. Assn. Lutheran. Office: U Calif Dept Sociology Irvine CA 92697-0001

BEAR, GREGORY DALE, writer, illustrator; b. San Diego, Aug. 20, 1951; s. Dale Franklin and Wilma (Merriman) B.; m. Astrid May Anderson, June 18, 1983; children: Erik William, Alexandra. AB in English, San Diego State U., 1973. Tech. writer, host Reuben H. Fleet Space Theater, 1973; freelance writer, 1975—. Author: Hegira, 1979, Psychlone, 1979, Beyond Heaven's River, 1980, Strength of Stones, 1981, The Wind From a Burning Woman, 1983, The Infinity Concerto, 1984, Blood Music, 1985, Eon, 1985, The Serpent Mage, 1986, The Forge of God, 1987, Eternity, 1988, Tangents, 1989, Heads, 1990, Queen of Angels, 1990, Anvil of Stars, 1992, Moving Mars, 1993 (Nebula award 1994), Songs of Earth and Power, 1993, Legacy, 1995, Slant, 1997, Dinosaur Summer, 1998 (Endeavor award 1999), Foundation and Chaos, 1998, Darwin's Radio, 1999 (Endeavor award 2000, Nebula award 2001), Rogue Planet, 2000, Vitals, 2002; short stories: Blood Music (Hugo and Nebula awards), 1983, Hardfought (Nebula award), 1993, Tangents (Hugo and Nebula awards), 1987; editor: New Legends, 1995. Cons. Citizen's Adv. Council on Nat. Space Policy, Tarzana, Calif., 1983-84 Mem. Sci. Fiction Writers of Am. (editor Forum 1983-84, chmn. grievance com. 1985-86, v.p. 1987, pres. 1988-90). Avocations: book collecting; science; music; movies, history. Home: 506 Lakeview Rd Lynnwood WA 98037-2141

BEARD, RONALD STRATTON, lawyer; b. Flushing, N.Y., Feb. 13, 1939; s. Charles Henry and Ethel Mary (Stratton) B.; m. Karin Paridee, Jan. 24, 1991; children: D. Karen, Jonathan D., Dana K. BA, Denison U., 1961; LLB, Yale U., 1964. Bar: Calif. 1964, U.S. Ct. Appeals (9th cir.) 1980, U.S. Dist. Ct. (cen. dist.) Calif. 1964. Ptnr. Gibson, Dunn & Crutcher, L.A., 1964—, mng. ptnr., 1991-97, chmn., 1991—. Trustee Denison U., Granville, Ohio, 1975—, chmn., 1998—; mem. steering com. Calif. Minority Coun. Program, 1991—; mem. Constl. Rights Found., 1994—, Orange County Art Mus., Chapman Exec. Fellows; CEO roundtable U. Calif., Irvine. Mem. ABA, Calif. Bar Assn., L.A. Bar Assn., Calif. Club, City Club, Chancery Club, Bear Creek Golf Club. Avocations: sports, travel, golf. Home: 27442 Hidden Trail Rd Laguna Hills CA 92653-5876 Office: Gibson Dunn & Crutcher 4 Park Plz Ste 1700 Irvine CA 92614-8560

BEARD, TIMOTHY R, career officer; b. Mansfield, Ohio, Apr. 12, 1944; m. Melissa Cary Martinez; children: Amanda, Emily, Sarah. Diploma, U.S. Naval Acad., 1966; MS in Aero. Engring., USAF Test Pilot Sch. Commd. ensign USN, 1966, advanced through grades to rear adm.; stationed on USS Forrestal VA-94; dept. head VA-176; with Bur. Naval Pers. Office Sec. Def.; dep. dir. programming OPNAV Staff; commdg. officer Attack Squadron 176, USS Midway Air Wing 5, USS San Diego, USS John F. Kennedy; asst. to dep. chief staff Marine Corps Aviation; comdr. Carrier Group 1 & Tng. Command U.S. Pacific Fleet, dep. comdr., chief staff, comdr., chief, 1998—. Decorated Dep. Superior Svc. Medal, Legion of Merit, Bronze Star, Meritorious Svc. Medal, 11 Strike/Flight Air Medals, others. Office: USN Nav Air Sta Bldg 465 Fallon NV 89496-0001

BEART, ROBERT W., JR. surgeon, educator; b. Kansas City, Mo., Mar. 3, 1945; s. Robert Woodward and Helen Elizabeth (Wamsley) B.; m. Cynthia Anne, Jan. 23, 1971; children: Jennifer, Kristina, Amy. AB, Princeton U., 1967; MD, Harvard U., 1971. Diplomate Am. Bd. Surgery, Am. Bd. Colon and Rectal Surgery. Intern U. Colo., 1971-72, resident, 1972-76; prof. surgery Mayo Clinic, Scottsdale, Ariz., 1976-87, Scottsdale, 1987-92, U. So. Calif., L.A., 1992—. Maj. USMC, 1972-83. Fellow Am. Soc. Colon and Rectal Surgery (pres. 1994). Office: U So Calif Dept Surgery 1450 San Pablo St # 5400 Los Angeles CA 90033-1042

BEATON, JAMES DUNCAN, soil scientist; b. Vancouver, B.C., Can., Aug. 28, 1930; s. James Andrew Beaton and Gertrude Marion Lorimer; m. Doris Irene Ford, Aug. 30, 1952; children: Barbara Ruth, Andrea Irene, Alice Shirley. BSA, U. B.C., 1951, MSA, 1953; PhD, Utah State U., 1957. Soil specialist Agriculture Can., Kamloops, B.C., 1953-57, phys. chemist Swift Current, Sask., 1959-61; instr. U. B.C., Vancouver, 1957-59; dir. agrl. rsch. The Sulphur Inst., Washington, 1968-73; head of soil sci. Cominco Ltd., Trail, B.C., 1961-65, sr. agronomist, 1965-67; regional dir. Potash & Phosphate Inst., Calgary, Alta., 1978-86, v.p., pres. Saskatoon, Sask., 1986-94; cons. soil fertility and fertilizer use Kelowna, 1994—. Hon. prof. Chinese Acad. Agrl. Scis., 1994. Co-author: Soil Fertility and Fertilizers, 4th edit., 1985, 5th edit., 1993, 6th edit., 1999. Head coach Lake Bonavista Bantam and Midget Box Lacrosse Teams, Calgary, 1973-77. Fellow Am. Soc. Agronomy (Agronomic Svc. award 1983), Soil Sci. Soc. Am., Can. Soc. Soil Sci., Agrl. Inst. Can. (AIC Fellowship award 1990); mem. Nat. Fertilizer Solutions Assn. (hon.), Western Can. Fertilizer and Chem. Dealers Assn. (hon.), Western Coop. Fertilizers Ltd. (Agronomy Merit award 1981), Western Can. Fertilizer Assn. (pres. 1977-79, Award of Merit 1993), Can. Fertilizer Inst. (hon. 1995). Achievements include development of forestry grade urea, high analysis degradeable elemental S fertilizers, urea-ammonium sulphate 40-0-0-6 (S) granular fertilizer, impregnation of granular fertilizers with herbicides. Home and Office: # 13-3888 Pinnacle Way Kelowna BC Canada V1W 3Z8 E-mail: Jim_Beaton@telus.net

BEATTIE, LANE, state legislator; b. Sept. 29, 1951; m. Joy Hadlow; 3 children. Student, U. Utah. Mem. Utah State Senate, 1988—, majority leader, 1993-94, pres., 1995-96; owner Lane Realty, West Bountiful, Utah; state olympic officer Utah State Capitol, Salt Lake City, 2000—. Co-chair state strategic planning com.; mem. various coms. including retirement, transportation and pub. safety. Toll fellow Coun. of State Govt., 1991; recipient Colleen M. Bangerter award, 1992. Mem. Utah Assn. Realtors, Nat. Assn. Realtors, Bountiful Area C. of C. Republican. Office: Lane Realty 1313 N 1100 W West Bountiful UT 84087-1830

BEATTY, JOHN CABEEN , JR. judge; b. Washington, Apr. 13, 1919; s. John Cabeen and Jean (Morrison) B.; m. Clarissa Hager, Feb. 8, 1943 (dec. Apr. 4 1996); children: John Cabeen III, Clarissa Jean; m. Virginia R. Campbell, May 10, 1997. AB, Princeton U., 1941; JD, Columbia, 1948. Bar: Oreg. 1948. Practiced law, Portland, 1948-70; ptnr. Dusenbery, Martin, Beatty, Bischoff & Templeton, 1956-70, of counsel, 1985-96; judge circuit ct., 1970-85, sr. judge, 1985—. Mem. Oreg. Bd. Bar Examiners, 1953-54; chmn. legis. com. Oreg. Jud. Conf., 1976-82; mem. Oreg. CSC, 1962-64, Oreg. Law Enforcement Council, 1974-77; vice chmn. Oreg. Commn. Jud. Br., 1979-85; vice chmn., chmn. Oreg. Criminal Justice Council, 1985-90. Mem. legis. com. Nat. Sch. Bds. Assn., 1966-68, chmn. coun. large city sch. bds., 1967-68; counsel Dem. Party Oreg., 1956-58; co-chmn. Oreg. for Kennedy Com., 1968; bd. dirs. Portland Pub. Schs., 1964-70, chmn., 1967, 69; chmn. policy adv. com. on hazardous waste Dept. Environ. Quality, 1985-86; mem. Mayor's Spl. Rev. Commn., 1986; chmn. various adv. coms. Dept. Environ. Quality, 1987-89; chmn. tech. adv. com. Willamette River Basin Water Quality Study, 1990-94; chmn. city club study Oreg. Initiative and Referendum, 1994-95; chmn. Oreg. Initiative Com., 1996—. Capt. AUS, 1941-46, ETO. Decorated Bronze Star medal; recipient City Club of Portland award, 1967 Mem. ABA, Oreg. Bar Assn., Multnomah County Bar Assn., Oreg. Hist. Soc. (dir. 1973-92), City Club (past pres., bd. govs., Portland Yacht Club, Racquet Club. Home and Office: 3331 SW Mitchell St Portland OR 97201-1260 E-mail: jcbeatty@europa.com

BEATTY, MICHAEL L. lawyer; b. 1947; s. Herbert Francis and Lola (Stuewe) B.; m. Kathleen Murphy; children: Erin, Piper. BA, U. Calif., 1969; JD, Harvard U., 1972. Bar: Tex. 1972. Assoc. mem. Vinson and Elkins, 1972-74; prof. U. Idaho, 1974-79; vis. prof. law U. Wyo., 1980-81; atty. Colo. Interstate Gas Co., 1981-84, gen. counsel, 1984-85; with The Coastal Corp., Houston, 1985-93, exec. v.p., gen. counsel, 1989-93; with Akin, Gump, Strauss, Hauer & Feld LLP, Houston, 1993-98; prin. Michael L. Beatty & Assocs., P.C., Denver, 1998—. Office: Michael L Beatty & Assocs PC 1401 17th St Ste 1600 Denver CO 80202-1253

BEAUCHAMP, JESSE LEE (JACK BEAUCHAMP), chemistry educator; b. Glendale, Calif., Nov. 1, 1942; m. Patricia Margaret Beauchamp; children: Melissa Ann, Thomas Alton, Amanda Jane, Ryan Howell, Michael Andrew. BS with honors in Chemistry, Calif. Inst. Tech., 1964; PhD in Chemistry, Harvard U., 1967. Arthur Amos Noyes instr. in Chemistry Calif. Inst Tech., Pasadena, 1967-69, asst. prof. chemistry, 1969-71, assoc. prof. chemistry, 1971-74, prof. chemistry, 1974—. Panelist chem. rsch. evaluation Directorate of Chem. Scis. Air Force Office of Sci. Rsch., 1978-81, adv. panelist high energy density materials, 1988-92; exec. com. advanced light source users, LBL, 1984-87; exptl. evaluation com. TRIUMPH, U. B.C., 1985-88; grad. fellow selection panel, NSF, 1986-89; postdoctoral selection panel NATO, 1987-89; mem. com. critical techs.: role of Chemistry and Chem. Engring. Nat. Rsch. Coun., 1991-92; chmn. com. on comml. aviation security Nat. Materials Adv. Bd., Nat. Rsch. Coun., 1994-97; commr. White House commn. on aviation safety and security, 1996-97. Mem. editorial adv. bd. Chemical Physics Letters, 1981-87, Jour. Am. Chem. Soc., 1984-87, Jour Physical Chemistry, 1984-87, Organometallics, 1989-92, Interat. Jour. Chemical Kinetics, 1990—. Woodrow Wilson fellow Harvard U., 1964-65, NSF grad. fellow, 1965-67; fellow Alfred P. Sloan Found., 1967-70; tchr.-scholar Camille and Henry Dreyfus, 1971-76; meml. fellow John Simon Guggenheim, 1976-77. Fellow AAAS; mem. NAS (com. chem. scis., chem. kinetics subgroup 1980-83), Am. Chem. Soc. (award in pure chemistry 1978, exec. com. divsn. physical chem., 1980-82, Peter Debye award in phys. chemistry 1999), Am. Assn. Mas. Spectometry, Aircraft Owners and Pilots Assn., Soc. Fellows Harvard U. Office: Calif Inst Tech Dept of Chemistry Noyes Lab 127 # 72 Pasadena CA 91125-0001

BEAUCHAMP, PATRICK L. distributing company executive; Prin., owner Beauchamp Distributing Co., Compton, Calif., 1984—. Office: Beauchamp Distributing Co 1911 S Santa Fe Ave Compton CA 90221-5306 Fax: 310-537-8641

BEAUMONT, PAMELA JO, marketing professional; b. Valentine, Nebr., July 30, 1944; d. William Henry and Phyllis Faye (Zersen) (Mott) Bostrom; m. Fred H. Beaumont, Apr. 17, 1971 (div. May 1981). BS in Bus., U. Colo., 1966, MBA, 1968. Asst. product mgr. Ore-Ida Foods, Boise, Idaho, 1969-71, product mgr., 1971-73, sr. product mgr., 1973-75, gen. mgr. sales and mktg. services, 1975; v.p. consumer affairs Albertson's Inc., Boise, 1975-76, v.p. mktg., 1976-87; ptnr. Forrest/Beaumont & Andrus, Boise, 1987—; chair Garden City Urban Renewal Agy., 1995—. Home: 9304 N Pebble Falls Ln Boise ID 83703-1759 Office: 4948 Kootenai St Ste 201 Boise ID 83705-2082 E-mail: pamb@micron.net

BEAUPREZ, BOB, political organization administrator; Ptnr. Boulder Valley Holsteins, Lafayette, Colo., 1970-89; pres. Indian Peaks, Inc., Lafayette, 1989—; pres., CEO, chmn. Heritage Bank, Louisville, 1990—; state chmn. Rep. State Ctrl. Com. of Colo., 1999—. Pres. Ind. Bankers Colo., 1997-98, chmn. 1998, bd. dirs. 1993—; bd dirs. Ind. Bankers Am., 1993—; mem. Rep. Nat. Com. Western State Chmn. Assn., 1999—. Office: 1776 S Jackson St Ste 210 Denver CO 80210-3802

BEAVER, WILLIAM HENRY, accounting educator; b. Peoria, Ill., Apr. 13, 1940; s. John W. and Ethel M. (Kostka) B.; m. Suzanne Marie Hutton, May 22, 1965; children: Marie, Sarah, David. BBA, U. Notre Dame, 1962, D (hon.), 1998; MBA, PhD, U. Chgo., 1965; D (hon.), Norwegian Sch. Econs., 1996. CPA, Ill. Asst. prof. U. Chgo., 1965-69; assoc. prof. acctg. Stanford U., 1969-72, prof., 1972—, Joan E. Horngren prof., 1977—. Adv. com. on corp. disclosure SEC, 1976-77; cons. Fin. Acctg. Standards Bd., 1980-86 Author: Financial Reporting: An Accounting Revolution, 1981, 3d edit., 1998; edit. bd.: The Acctg. Rev., 1977-80, Jour. Acctg. Rsch., 1968—, Jour. Acctg. and Econs., 1978— , Fin. Analysts Jour., 1979-98; contbr. articles to profl. Jours. Recipient Lit. award Jour. Accountancy, 1978, Faculty Excellence award Calif. Soc. CPAs, 1978, Graham and Dodd award Fin. Analysts Fedn., 1979, Notable Contbn. to Acct. Lit. award, 1969, 79, 83, Outstanding Rsch. award Inst. Quantitative Rsch. in Fin., 1981, Nat. Acctg. award Alpha Kappa Psi Found., 1982, Wildman award Am. Acctg. Assn., 1985, Disting. Teaching award Stanford U., 1985, Seminal Contbn. to Acctg. Lit. award, 1989; named to Acctg. Hall of Fame, 1996. Mem. AICPA, Am. Fin. Assn., Am. Acctg. Assn. (v.p. 1981-83, pres. elect 1986-87, pres. 1987-88, disting. internat. lectr. in acct. award 1979, outstanding educator award 1990), Fin. Acctg. Found. (trustee 1993-96), Fin. Svcs. Rsch. Initiative (co-dir. 1992-95). Home: 949 Wing Pl Palo Alto CA 94305-1028 Office: Stanford U Grad Sch Bus Stanford CA 94305

BEBOUT, ELI DANIEL, oil executive; b. Rawlings, Wyo., Oct. 14, 1946; s. Hugh and Dessie Bebout; m. Lorraine J. Tavares; children: Jordan, Jentry, Reagen, Taggert. BEE, U. Wyo., 1969. With U.S. Energy Co., Riverton, Wyo., 1974-75; field engr. Am. Bechtel Corp., Green River, 1975-76; pres. NUPEC Resources, Inc., Riverton, 1976-83, Smith-Collins Pharm. Inc., Riverton, 1976-83; cons. Nucor Inc., Riverton, 1984-2000; v.p. Nucor Drilling, Inc., Riverton, 1987—; state legislator Wyo. Assembly; pres. Nucor Oil & Gas, 1993-2000. Former mem. Wyo. Ho. of Reps., mem. rules com. mgmt. coun., majority floor leader, spkr. Republican. Office: Nucor Inc PO Box 112 Riverton WY 82501-0112

BECERRA, OCTAVIO, corporate executive chef; b. L.A., Oct. 28, 1963; married. Fine arts and photography studies, Santa Monica Coll.; culinary apprenticeship, Joachim Splichal, Calif., Michelin-Star Restaurants, France, Spain. Corp. exec. chef Patina Group LLC, L.A.

BECERRA, ROSINA MADELINE, social welfare educator; b. San Diego, Mar. 6, 1939; d. Ray and Ruth (Albanez) B. BA, San Diego State U., 1961, MSW, 1971; PhD, Brandeis U., 1975; MBA, Pepperdine U., 1981. Mathematician United Tech. Corp., Sunnyvale, Calif., 1962-63; with Peace Corps, Washington, 1963-65; probation officer San Diego County Probation Office, 1965-69; research assoc. Brandeis U., Waltham, Mass., 1973-75; assoc. prof. UCLA, 1975-81, prof., 1981—, acting dean, 1989-90, assoc. dean, 1986-89, 92; dean, 1992—. Author: Defining Child Abuse, 1979, Hispanic Veterans Seek Health Care, 1982, The Hispanic Elderly, 1984 (Choice Mag. Book award 1986); editor: Hispanic Mental Health, 1981; contbr. articles to profl. jours. Ford Found. award, 1980.

BECERRA, XAVIER, congressman, lawyer; b. Sacramento, Jan. 26, 1958; s. Manuel and Maria Teresa B.; m. Carolina Reyes, 1987. AB, Stanford U., 1980, JD, 1984. Atty., 1984—; dir. dist. office State Senator Art Torres, L.A.; dep. atty. gen. dept. justice, Calif., 1987-90; assemblyman, 59th dist. State of Calif., 1990-93; mem. U.S. Congress from 30th Calif. dist., 1993—. Mem. ways and means com.; chmn. Congl. Hispanic Caucus. Mem. Mexican-Am. Bar Assn., Calif. Bar Assn., Assn. Calif. State Attys. and Adminstrv. Law Judges. Democrat. Avocations: reading, carpentry, golf. Office: Ho of Reps 1119 Longworth Bldg Washington DC 20515-0530*

BECHTEL, RILEY PEART, engineering company executive; s. Stephen Davison Bechtel, Jr. BA in Polit. Sci., Psychology, U. Calif., Davis, 1974; JD, MBA, Stanford U., 1979. Bar: Calif. 1979. With Bechtel Group, Inc., San Francisco, 1966-79, 81—, Thelen, Marrin, Johnson & Bridges, San Francisco, 1979-81; bd. dirs. Bechtel Corp. (formerly Bechtel Group Inc.), 1987—, pres., coo, 1989-1990, chmn. exec. com., ceo, 1990—, CEO, 1993—. Mem. Bus. Coun., Bus. Roundtable policy com.; bd. dirs. J.P. Morgan Chase; adv. coun. Stanford U. Grad. Sch. of Bus.; dean's adv. coun. Stanford Law Sch. Trustee Jason Found. for Edn. Fellow Am. Acad. Arts and Scis.; mem. Am. Soc. Corp. Execs. (conservation fund corp. coun.), Am. Soc. Civil Engrs. (hon.). Office: Bechtel Group Inc PO Box 193965 San Francisco CA 94119-3965

BECHTEL, STEPHEN DAVISON , JR. engineering company executive; b. Oakland, Calif., May 10, 1925; s. Stephen Davison and Laura (Peart) B.; m. Elizabeth Mead Hogan, June 5, 1946; 5 children. Student, U. Colo., 1943-44; BS, Purdue U., 1946, D. in Engrng. (hon.), 1972; MBA, Stanford U., 1948; DSc (hon.), U. Colo., 1981. Registered profl. engr., N.Y., Mich., Alaska, Calif., Md., Hawaii, Ohio, D.C., Va., Ill. Engrng. and mgmt. positions Bechtel Corp., San Francisco, 1941-60, pres., 1960-73, chmn. of cos. in Bechtel group, 1973-80; chmn. Bechtel Group, Inc., 1980-90, chmn. emeritus, 1990—, Fremont Group, Inc. Former chmn. Remington Arms, mem. bus. coun., emeritus life councillor, past chmn. Conf. Bd. Trustee, mem., past chmn. bldg. and grounds com. Calif. Inst. Tech.; mem. pres.'s coun. Purdue U.; adv. coun. Inst. Internat. Studies, bd. visitors, former charter mem., adv. coun. Stanford U. Grad. Sch. Bus. With USMC, 1943-46. Decorated officer French Legion of Honor; recipient Disting. Alumnus award Purdue U., 1964, Ernest C. Arbuckle Disting. Alumnus award Stanford Grad. Sch. Bus., 1974, Disting. Engrng. Alumnus award U. Colo., 1979, Beta Theta Pi Oxford Cup award 1997, Engr. of Distinction award U. Colo., 2000; named Man of Yr. Engrng. News-Record, 1974, Outstanding Achievement in Constrn. award Moles, 1977, Chmn.'s award Am. Assn. Engrng. Soc., 1982, Washington award Western Soc. Engrs., 1985, Nat. Medal Tech. from Pres. Bush, 1991, Golden Beaver award 1992, Herbert Hoover medal 1980. Fellow AAAS; mem. ASCE (hon., engrng. mgmt. award 1979, pres. award 1985, OPAL award for outstanding lifetime achievement in constrn. 2000), Inst. Chem. Engrs. (U.K., hon.); mem. AIME, NSPE (hon. chmn. Nat. Engrs. Week 1990), Nat. Acad. Engrng. (past chmn., Founder's award 1999), Calif. Acad. Scis. (hon. trustee), Am. Soc. French Legion Honor (bd. dirs., disting. achievement medal 1994), Royal Acad. Engrng. (U.K., fgn. mem.), Pacific Union Club, Bohemian Club, San Francisco Golf Club, Claremont Country Club, Cypress Point Club, St. Francis Yacht Club, Bear River Club (Utah), Wild Goose Club (Calif.), Chi Epsilon, Tau Beta Pi. Office: PO Box 193965 San Francisco CA 94119-3965 Address: Fremont Grp Mgmt LP 45 Fremont Street Ste 300 San Francisco CA 94105 Fax: (415) 512-1448

BECHTLE, ROBERT ALAN, artist, educator; b. San Francisco, May 14, 1932; m. Nancy Elizabeth Dalton, 1963 (div. 1982); children: Max Robert, Anne Elizabeth; m. Whitney Chadwick, 1982. B.A., Calif. Coll. Arts and Crafts, Oakland, 1954, M.F.A., 1958; postgrad., U. Calif.-Berkeley, 1960-61. Graphic designer Kaiser Industries, Oakland, 1956-59; instr. Calif. Coll. Arts and Crafts, 1957-61, assoc. prof. to prof.; lectr. U. Calif.-Berkeley, 1965-66; vis. artist U. Calif.-Davis, 1966-68; assoc. prof. San Francisco State U., 1968-76, prof., 1976-99, prof. emeritus, 1999—. One-man shows Mus. of Art, San Francisco, 1959, 64, Berkeley Gallery, 1965, Richmond Art Ctr. (Calif.), 1965, U. Calif.-Davis, 1967, O.K. Harris Gallery, N.Y.C., 1971, 74, 76, 81, 84, 87, 92, 96, Berggruen Gallery, San Francisco, 1972, E.B. Crocker Art Mus., Sacramento, 1973, Univ. Art Mus., U. Calif.-Berkeley, 1979, Daniel Weinberg Gallery, Santa Monica, 1991, Gallery Paul Anglim, San Francisco, 1991, San Francisco Mus. Modern Art, 1991; exhibited in group shows San Francisco Art Inst., 1966, Whitney Mus. N.Y.C., 1967, Milw. Art Ctr., 1969, Mus. Contemporary Art, Chgo., 1971, Serpentine Gallery, London, 1973, Toledo Mus. Art, 1975, San Francisco Mus. Modern Art, 1976, Pushkin Fine Arts Mus., Moscow, 1978, Pa. Acad. Fine Arts, Phila., 1981, San Antonio Mus. Art, 1981, Pa. Acad. Fine Arts, Phila, 1981, Calif. Palace of Legion of Honor, San Francisco, 1983, Mus. Contemporary Art, L.A., 1984, San Francisco Mus. Modern Art, 1985, Univ. Art Mus., U. Calif., Berkeley, 1987, Whitney Mus., N.Y.C., 1991, Fine Arts Mus. San Francisco, 1995; represented in permanent collections Achenbach Found. for Graphic Arts, San Francisco, Chase Manhattan Bank, N.Y.C., E.B. Crocker Art Mus., Sacramento, Gibbes Art Gallery, S.C., High Mus. Art, Atlanta, Hunter Art Mus., Chattanooga, Library of Congress, Washington, Lowe Art Mus.-U. Miami, Coral Gables, Fla., Mills Coll., Oakland, Mus. Modern Art, N.Y.C., Met. Mus., N.Y.C., Neue Gal der Stadt Aachen, West Germany, Oakland Mus., San Francisco Mus. Modern Art, Univ. Art Mus.-U. Calif-Berkeley, Fine Arts Mus. of San Diego, Rose Art Mus., Brandeis U., Waltham, Mass., U. Nebr.-Lincoln, Whitney Mus., N.Y.C., Guggenheim Mus., N.Y.C., Nat. Academician, Nat. Acad. Design, 1993. Served with U.S. Army, 1954-56. Recipient James D. Phelan award, 1965, Acad. award Am. Acad. Arts and Letters, 1995; named Nat. Academician, Nat. Acad. Design, 1993; Nat. Endowment for Arts grantee, 1977, 83, 89, Guggenheim grantee, 1986. Office: San Francisco State U 1600 Holloway Ave Dept Art San Francisco CA 94132-1722

BECK, COLLEEN MARGUERITE, archaeologist; b. San Jose, Calif., Feb. 21, 1951; d. William Robert and Willa Rose (Moore) Beck; m. William Keith Kolb; children: William Logan Kolb, Alexa Rose Kolb. BA, U. Calif., Berkeley, 1973, MA, 1974, PhD, 1979. Dir. Agy. for Conservation Archaeology, Eastern N.Mex. U., Portales, 1980-83, asst. prof., 1983-84; rsch. assoc. Lowie Mus. Anthropology, Berkeley, 1985-89; asst. rsch. prof. Desert Rsch. Inst., Las Vegas, 1990-92, dep. dir. quaternary scis. ctr., 1992-98, assoc. rsch. prof., 1993-98, rsch. prof., exec. dir., 1999—. Postdoctoral fellow Carnegie Mus. Natural History, Pitts., 1979-80; mem. N.Mex. Hist. Preservatio Adv. Bd., Santa Fe, 1981-86; mem. San Joaquin County Historic Records Commn., Stockton, Calif., 1986-89. Author: Ancient Roads on the North Coast of Peru, 1979; editor: Views of the Jornada Mogollon, 1984; author articles. Mem. tech. adv. bd. Las Vegas Sch. Dist., 1994-96; mem. tech. adv. bd. Bur. Land Mgmt., 1995—, Las Vegas Historic Preservation Commn., 1996—. NSF fellow, 197-76; Tinker Found. grantee, 1974-77. Fellow Am. Anthropology Assn. (life); mem. Soc. for Am. Archaeology, Nev. Archaeology Assn. (bd. dirs. 1993—, pres. 1995—), Archaeo-Nev. Soc., Nat. Trust for Hist. Preservation, Inst. Andean Studies (life), Nev. State Mus. Hist. Soc. Avocation: piano playing. Office: Desert Rsch Inst 1055 E Tropicana Ave Ste 450 Las Vegas NV 89119-6644

BECK, DENNIS L. judge; b. Belen, N.Mex., Dec. 7, 1947; m. Christine T. Beck, Mar. 2, 1968. BA, Coll. William & Mary, 1969, JD, 1972. Bar: Calif. 1972, U.S. Dist. Ct. (ea. dist.) Calif. 1978, U.S. Ct. Appeals (9th cir.) Calif. 1978. Asst. dist. atty. Fresno (Calif.) County, 1972-78, 79-83, 1987-90; assoc. Crossland Crossland Caswell & Bell, Fresno, 1978-79; judge Kings County Superior Ct., Hanford, Calif., 1983-85; assoc. Thomas, Snell, et al., Fresno, 1985-87; magistrate judge U.S. Dist. Ct. (ea. dist.) Calif., Fresno, 1990—. Office: US Dist Ct 1130 O St Rm 3489 Fresno CA 93721-2201

BECK, EDWARD WILLIAM, lawyer; b. Atchison, Kans., Aug. 19, 1944; s. Russell Niles and Lucille Mae (Leighton) B.; m. Marshia Ablon, June 24, 1966; children: Michael Adam, David Gordon, Stephen Jared BA cum laude, Yale U., 1967; JD cum laude, Harvard U., 1972. Bar: Calif. 1972. Assoc. firm Pillsbury, Madison & Sutro, San Francisco, 1972-77; gen. counsel Pacific Lumber Co., San Francisco, 1977-86, sec., 1978-86, v.p., 1980-86, dir., 1985-86; v.p., gen. counsel, sec. Yamamouchi Consumer, Inc. (formerly Shaklee Corp.), Pleasanton, Calif., 1986-87, sr. v.p., gen. counsel, sec., 1987—. Bd. dirs. Shaklee Corp., 1989—. Trustee, mem. exec. com. San Francisco Conservatory Music, 1988—, co-chmn. acad. affairs com., 1989-91, chmn. presdl. search com., 1991, chair trustees and offices com., 1993-96, exec. vice chair, 1994—, chair conservatory 2006 com., 1996-99; chmn. Major Gits Com., 1999—, co-chmn. Instl. Advancement Com., 1999—, mem. bldg. com., 2000—, mem. law com. United Way of Bay Area Campaign, 1991—, chmn., 1992. Mem. ABA, Calif. Bar Assn., San Francisco Bar Assn. (bd. dirs. 1991-94, nominating com. 1993), Bay Area Gen. Counsels Group (chmn. 1991), San Francisco C. of C. (leadership coun. 1987—, gen. coun., bd. dirs., exec. com. 1993-96), San Francisco Yale Alumni Assn. (schs. com.). Office: Shaklee Corp 4747 Willow Rd Pleasanton CA 94588-2740

BECK, JOHN CHRISTIAN, physician, educator; b. Audubon, Iowa, Jan. 4, 1924; s. Wilhelm and Marie (Brandt) B. MD, McGill U., 1947, MSc, 1951, DSc (hon.), 1994; PhD (hon.), Ben Gurion U. of the Negev. Diplomate Am. Bd. Internal Medicine (chmn., dir.). Intern Royal Victoria Hosp., Montreal, 1947-48, sr. asst. resident, 1948-49, physician-in-chief, endocrinologist, 1964-74; chmn. dept. medicine, dir. Univ. Clinic McGill U., 1964-74; prof. medicine U. Calif., San Francisco, 1974-79; dir. Robert Wood Johnson Clin. Scholars Program, 1974-79; prof. geriat. medicine and gerontology UCLA, 1979—, dir. academic geriat. resource ctr., 1984-90; dir. long term car gerontology ctr. UCLA/U. So. Calif., 1980-85; dir. Calif. Geriatric Edn. Ctr., 1987-97, emeritus dir., 1993—; dir. multicampus program in geriat. medicine & gerontology UCLA, 1979-93. Pres. Am. Bd. Med. Spltys.; vis. prof. numerous univs.; Simeone lectr. Brown U., 1977; John McCreary Meml. lectr. U. B.C., 1985; Bruce Hall Meml. lectr. Garvan Inst. Med. Rsch., U. N.S.W., Sydney, Australia, 1989—; Allen T. Bailey Meml. lectr. U. Sask., Can., 1989. Mem. editl. bd. Jour. Clin. Endocrinology and Metabolism, Current Topics in Exptl. Endocrinology, Psychiatry in Medicine, Health Policy and Edn., Jour. Am. Bd. Family Practice; cons. editor Roche Lab. Series on Geriatrics and Gerontology. Recipient Lifetime award Ben Gurion U. of Negev, Israel, 1985, DSc (honoris causa) McGill U., 1994, Ann. Gerontology award in edn. Jewish Homes for the Aging, 1994, commendation City of L.A., 1994. Master ACP, fellow AAAS, Royal Coll. Physicians (Can., mem. coun., Duncan Graham award 1990), Royal Coll. Physicians (London), Royal Soc. Can., Inst. of Medicine, Internat. Soc. Endocrinology (sec.-gen.), Can. Soc. Clin. Investigation (pres.), Endocrine Soc. (v.p., chmn. postgrad. assembly), Am. Fedn. Clin. Rsch. (coun. East div.), Can. Med. Assn. (postgrad. edn. com.), Am. Diabetes Assn., Can. Diabetes Assn., McGill Osler Reporting Soc. (sec.), Montreal Physiol. Soc., Can. Physiol. Soc., Laurentian Hormone Conf. (bd. dirs.), Can. Assn. Profs. Medicine (Ronald V. Christie award 1987), Am. Clin. and Climatological Assn., Assn. Am. Med. Colls., Can. Med. Protective Assn., Internat. Soc. Neuroendocrinology, Soc. Exptl. Biology and Medicine (mem. editorial bd. jour.), Western Assn. Physicians, Am. Geriatrics Soc. (Milo F. Leavitt Meml. award 1988), Gerontol. Soc. Am. (mem. editorial bd. jour., Joseph T. Freeman award 1990), Am. Fedn. on Aging Rsch. (Irving S. Wright award 1991), Sigma Xi, Alpha Omega Alpha. Office: 1562 Casale Rd Pacific Palisades CA 90272-2714 Fax: 310-454-1944. E-mail: egebjcb@ucla.edu

BECK, JOHN ROLAND, environmental consultant; b. Las Vegas, N.Mex., Feb. 26, 1929; s. Roland L. and Betty L. (Shrock) B.; m. Doris A. Olson, Feb. 9, 1951; children: Elizabeth J., Thomas R., Patricia L., John William. BS, Okla. A&M U., 1950; MS, Okla. State U., 1957; postgrad., U. Tex., 1954, George Washington U., 1965. Registered sanitarian, Ohio, Ariz.; cert. wildlife biologist. Wildlife rschr. King Ranch, Kingsville, Tex., 1950-51; faculty U. Tenn.-Inst. Human Physiology, Martin, 1954-55; rsch. biologist FWS, USDI, Grangeville, Idaho, 1955-57; ctr. dir. Job Corps, OEO, Indiahoma, Okla., 1965-67; supr. animal control biology FWS, USDI, 1953-69; operating v.p. Bio-Svc. Corp., Troy, Mich., 1969-78; pres. Biol. Environ. Cons. Svc. Ltd., Prescott, Ariz., 1981-85; spl. asst. USDA - APHIS, Washington, 1986-87; prin. cons. Biol. Environ. Cons. Svc. Inc., Phoenix, 1978-93. Faculty assoc. Ariz. State U., Tempe, 1980-89; expert witness in bus. evaluations, 1979-98; expert witness in pesticide litigations, 1989-94; participant fin. seminars, 1980-85. Sr. author: Managing Service for Success, 1987, 2d edit., 1991; columnist mo. column on pest control in 2 mags., 1980-88; referee Internat. Health Related Jour., 1999—; contbr. articles to profl. jours. Active Humboltd Unified Sch. Bd., Yavapai County, Ariz., 2000—; life mem. Rep. Nat. Com., 1993—; active Rep. Senatorial Inner Cir., 1994—99, Rep. Presdl. Roundtable, 1995—97. Fellow Royal Soc. Health, N.Y. Explorers Soc.; mem. ASTM (chmn. pesticide com. 1979-81, chmn. vertebrate pesticides 1994-2000), Rotary (dist. treas. 1997-99), Wildlife Soc., Sigma Xi. Republican. Baptist. Avocations: botany studies, ornithology, mammalogy.

BECK, MARILYN MOHR, columnist; b. Chgo., Dec. 17, 1928; d. Max and Rose (Lieberman) Mohr; m. Roger Beck, Jan. 8, 1949 (div. 1974); children: Mark Elliott, Andrea; m. Arthur Levine, Oct. 12, 1980. AA, U. So. Calif., 1950. Free-lance writer nat. mags. and newspapers, Hollywood, Calif., 1959-63; Hollywood columnist Valley Times and Citizen News, Hollywood, 1963-65; West Coast editor Sterling Mags., Hollywood, 1963-74; free-lance entertainment writer L.A. Times, 1965-67; Hollywood columnist Bell-McClure Syndicate, 1967-72; chief Bell-McClure Syndicate (West Coast bur.), 1967-72; Hollywood columnist NANA Syndicate, 1967-72; syndicated Hollywood columnist N.Y. Times Spl. Features, 1972-78, N.Y. Times Spl. Features (United Feature Syndicate), 1978-80, United Press abroad, 1978-80, Internat. Editors News and Features, Chgo. Tribune/N.Y. Daily News Syndicate, 1980-97; Grapevine columnist TV Guide, 1989-92; creators syndicate, 1997—. Creator, host Marilyn Beck's Hollywood Outtakes spls. NBC, 1977, 78; host Marilyn Beck's Hollywood Hotline, Sta. KFI, L.A., 1975-77; Hollywood reporter Eyewitness News, Sta. KABC-TV, L.A., 1981, (TV program) PM Mag., 1983-88; on-air corr. E! TV, 1993-99, CompuServe Entertainment Authority, 1994-96, eDrive Internet Authority, 1996-97, e!online Internet Hollywood Authority, 1997—, Compuserve, 2000—, aeNTV.com, 2001—; author: (non-fiction) Marilyn Beck's Hollywood, 1973, (novel) Only Make Believe, 1988; co-author: Unfinished Lives, What If...?, 1996. Recipient Citation of Merit L.A. City Coun., 1973, Press award Pub. Guild Am., 1974, Bronze Halo award So. Calif. Motion Picture Coun., 1982. Office: PO Box 11079 Beverly Hills CA 90213-4579

BECK, TERESA, supermarket executive; BS in Fin., MS in Acctg., U. Utah. With Am. Stores Co., Salt Lake City, 1982—, v.p., contr. Alpha Beta Co. sub., v.p., contr., exec. v.p. fin., CFO, until 1998, pres., 1998-99; bd. dirs. Questar Corp., Salt Lake City, 1999—. Office: Questar Corp 180 E 100 S Salt Lake City UT 84145-0433

BECK, TOM, state legislator, rancher; b. Deer Lodge, Mont., Nov. 14, 1939; m. Kay Beck. Student, Mont. State U. Rancher; mem. Mont. Senate, Dist. 28, Helena, 1987—; chair legis. adminstrn. com.; mem. fin. and claims com., rules com., fish and game com.; mem. agr., livestock and irrigation com.; majority whip Mont. Senate, 1995. Chmn. Powell Hosp. Bd.; former Powell County Commr. Mem. Mont. Assn. Counties (pres.). Republican. Home: 792 Yellowstone Trl Deer Lodge MT 59722-8704 Office: Capitol Sta Helena MT 59620

BECKEL, CHARLES LEROY, physics educator; b. Phila., Feb. 7, 1928; s. Samuel Mercer and Katherine (Linsky) B.; m. Josephine Ann Beck, June 27, 1958; children: Amanda S., Sarah Beckel Lentz, Timothy C., Andrea C. BS, U. Scranton, 1948; PhD, Johns Hopkins U., 1954. Asst. prof. physics Georgetown U., 1953-59, assoc. prof., 1959-64; rsch. staff mem. Inst. for Defense Analyses, Arlington, Va., 1964-66; assoc. prof. physics U. N.Mex., 1966-69, prof., 1969-94, prof. emeritus, 1995—, asst. dean, 1971-72, acting v.p. rsch., 1972-73. Acting dir. Inst. Social R&D, 1972; vis. prof. theoretical chemistry Oxford U., 1973; vis. prof. chemistry and molecular scis. U. Sussex, U.K., 1987; Fulbright lectr. U. Peshawar, Pakistan, 1957-58, Cheng Kung U., Tainan, Taiwan, 1963-64; cons. Ballistics Rsch. Lab., Aberdeen Proving Ground, Md., 1955-57, Dikewood Corp., Albuquerque, 1967-72, 74-80, Albuquerque Urban Obs., 1969-71, Inst. Def. Analyses, 1962-64, 66-69, U.S. ACDA, 1981-84; phys. sci. officer U.S. Arms Control and Disarmament Agy., 1980-81; vis. prof. physics U. Scranton, 1995. Pres. Nat. Kidney Found. N.Mex. Inc., 1968-72, del. trustee, 1972-73, 76-80, exec. com., 1974-80, 83-86, v.p., 1982-83, bd. trustees, 1987-93; bd. dirs. Nat. Capitol Area Nat. Kidney Found., 1965-66, N.Mex. Combined Health Appeal, 1972-73; mem. edn. subcom. Navajo Sci. Com., 1975-82. Recipient Val. award Nat. Kidney Found. of N.Mex., 1988, Frank J. O'Hara award for disting. achievement in sci. U. Scranton Nat. Alumni Soc., 1988, U.S. Dept. Energy award in solid state physics materials scis., 1988, Outstanding Teaching award Burlington Northern Found., 1989. Mem. Am. Phys. Soc., Bioelectromagnetics Soc., Nat. Eagle Scout Assn. Office: U NMex Dept Physics And Astronomy Albuquerque NM 87131-0001 E-mail: clbeckel@unm.edu

BECKER, DONALD PAUL, surgeon, neurosurgeon; b. Cleve., 1935; MD, Case Western Res. U., 1961. Diplomate Am. Bd. Neurol. Surgery. Intern U. (Cleve.) Hosps., 1961-62, resident in surgery, 1962-63, resident in neurol. surgery, 1963-67; fellow in neurosurgery NIH, Bethesda, Md., 1966; prof. UCLA Med. Ctr., 1967-71; prof., chmn. divsn. neurol. surgery Med. Coll. Va., Richmond, 1971-85; chief neurosurgery UCLA Med. Ctr., 1985—; prof., chmn. divsn. neurol. surgery Med. Coll. Va., Richmond, 1971-85. Mem. ACS, AMA. Office: UCLA Med Ctr Divsn Neurosurgery PO Box 957039 Los Angeles CA 90095-7039

BECKER, NANCY ANNE, state supreme court justice; b. Las Vegas, May 23, 1955; d. Arthur William and Margaret Mary (McLoughlin) B. BA, U.S. Internat. U., 1976; JD, George Washington U., 1979. Bar: Nev. 1979, D.C. 1980, Md. 1982, U.S. Dist. Ct. Nev. 1987, U.S. Ct. Appeals (9th cir.) 1987. Legis. cons. D.C. Office on Aging, Washington, 1979-83; assoc. Goldstein & Ahalt, College Park, Md., 1980-82; pvt. practice Washington, 1982-83; dep. city atty., prosecutor criminal div. City of Las Vegas, 1983; judge Las Vegas Mcpl. Ct., 1987-89, Clark County Dist. Ct., Las Vegas, 1989-99; now assoc. state supreme ct. justice Nev. Supreme Ct. Cons. MADD, Las Vegas, 1983-87. Contbr. articles to profl. publs. Pres. Clark County Pro Bono Project, Las Vegas, 1984-95. Mem. So. Nev. Assn. Women Attys. (past officer), Am. Businesswomen's Assn. (treas. Las Vegas chpt. 1985-86), NCCJ, Las Vegas and Latin C. of C., Vietnam Vets Am., Soroptimist Internat. Office: Nevada Supreme Court Capital Complex 316 Bridger Ave Las Vegas NV 89101-5906

BECKER, STEPHEN A. physicist, designer; b. Evanston, Ill., Sept. 11, 1950; s. John N. and Irene A. (Wlodarski) B.; m. Wendee M. Brunish, May 30, 1980. BA, Northwestern U., 1972; MS, Case Western Res. U., 1974; PhD, U. Ill., 1979. Rsch. and teaching assoc. U. Ill., Champaign, 1979-80; postdoctoral fellow Calif. Inst. Tech., Pasadena, 1980-82; team leader Los Alamos (N.Mex.) Nat. Lab., 1983—. Contbr. articles to Astrophys. Jour. Mem. Los Alamos Cable TV Bd., 1991-97. Recipient Recognition of Excellence award U.S. Dept. Energy, 1999, R&D 100 award, 1999. Mem. Am. Astron. Soc., Internat. Astron. Union. Roman Catholic. Office: Los Alamos Nat Lab PO Box 1663 Mail Stop B220 Los Alamos NM 87545 E-mail: sab@lanl.gov

BECKER, STEPHEN ARNOLD, museum administrator; b. Redwood City, Calif., Aug. 24, 1951; s. Leo H. and May B. (Goldberg) B.; m. Beverly Nichols-Fredotovich, July 31, 1977; 1 child, Joseph Nikola. Asst. curator mus. Ind. U., Bloomington, 1973-77, lectr. folklore dept., 1975-77; historian Sacramento History Ctr., 1977-78; dir. history divsn. County Pks. Dept., Riverside, Calif., 1979-85; asst. dir. Mus. Internat. Folk Art, Santa Fe, 1985-89; dir. Mus. Indian Arts and Culture/Lab. Anthropology, Santa Fe, 1989-95; pres., CEO, Turtle Bay Mus. and Arboretum, Redding, Calif., 1995-98; mus. cons. Redding, 1998-2000; deputy dir. devel. & external affairs Lindsay Wildlife Mus., Walnut Creek, Calif., 1998—; dir. external affairs Zeum Art and Tech. Ctr., San Francisco, 2000—. Mem. Am. Assn. Museums, Am. Folklore Soc. Office: 221 4th St San Francisco CA 94103-3116 E-mail: sbecker@zeum.org

BECKERS, JACQUES MAURICE, astrophysicist; b. Arnhem, The Netherlands, Feb. 14, 1934; came to U.S., 1962; s. Wilhelmus B.H. and Maria H. (Hermans) B.; m. Gerda M. Van Vuurden, Mar. 24, 1959 (div. Aug. 1995); children: Christina M., Michael P. PhD, U. Utrecht, The Netherlands, 1959. Astrophysicist Sacramento Peak Obs., Sunspot, N.Mex., 1962-79; astrophysicist, dir. Multiple Mirror Telescope Obs., Tucson, 1979-84, Advanced Devel. program Nat. Optical Astronomy Observatories, Tucson, 1984-88; astrophysicist European So. Obs., Garching, Fed. Republic of Germany, 1988-93, VLT Program Scientist, 1991-93; dir. Nat. Solar Observatory, Tucson, 1993-98, sr. rschr. Mem. Norwegian Acad. Scis. (fgn.), Royal Netherlands Acad. Scis. (corr.). Office: Nat Solar Obs Sacramento Peak PO Box 62 Sunspot NM 88349-0062

BECKMAN, ARNOLD ORVILLE, analytical instrument manufacturing company executive; b. Cullom, Ill., Apr. 10, 1900; s. George W. and Elizabeth E. (Jewkes) B.; m. Mabel S. Meinzer, June 10, 1925; children: Gloria Patricia, Arnold Stone. BS, U. Ill., 1922, MS, 1923; PhD, Calif. Inst. Tech., 1928; DSc (hon.), Chapman Coll., 1965, Whittier Coll., 1971, Clarkson U., 1989, Rockefeller U., 1992, Scripps Rsch. Inst., 1994; LLD (hon.), U. Calif., Riverside, 1966, Loyola U., L.A., 1969, U. Ill., , 1982, Pepperdine U., 1977, Ill. Wesleyan U., 1991; DHL (hon.), Calif. State U., Fullerton, 1984, Ill. State U., , 1990. Rsch. assoc. Bell Tel. Labs., N.Y.C., 1924-26; chem. faculty Calif. Inst. Tech., 1926-39; v.p. Nat. Tech. Lab., Pasadena, Calif., 1935-39, pres., 1939-40, Helipot Corp., 1944-58, Arnold O. Beckman, Inc., South Pasadena, Calif., 1946-58; founder, chmn. Beckman Instruments, Inc., Fullerton, 1940-65, chmn. emeritus, 1988—; vice chmn. SmithKline Beckman Corp., 1984-86. Bd. dirs. Security Pacific Nat. Bank, 1956-72, adv. dir., 1972-75; bd. dirs. Continental Airlines, 1956-71, adv. dir., 1971-73; bd. dirs. So. Calif. Edison, 1957-72. Author articles in field; inventor; patentee in field. Mem. Pres.'s Air Quality Bd., 1970-74; chmn. System Devel. Found., 1970-88; chmn. bd. trustees emeritus Calif. Inst. Tech.; hon. trustee Calif. Mus. Found.; bd. overseers House Ear Inst., 1981—; trustee Scripps Clinic and Rsch. Found., 1971—; bd. dirs. Hoag Meml. Hosp.; co-founder, chmn. emeritus, bd. dirs. Beckman Laser Inst. and Med. Clinic, 1982—; mem. bd. overseers U. Calif., Irvine, 1982—; founder, chmn. emeritus, bd. dirs. Arnold and Mabel Beckman Found., 1977—. With USMC, 1918-19. Benjamin Franklin fellow Royal Soc. Arts; named to Nat. Inventors Hall of Fame, 1987; recipient Nat. Medal Tech., 1988, Presdl. Citizens medal, 1989, Nat. Medal of Sci., 1989, Order of Lincoln award State of Ill., 1991, Bower award for Bus. Leadership, 1992, Public Welfare Medal, NAS, 1999. Fellow Assn. Clin. Scientists; mem. NAM, AAAS, Am. Acad. Arts and Scis., L.A. C. of C. (bd. dir. 1954-58, pres. 1956), Calif. C. of C. (dir., pres. 1967-68), Nat. Acad. Engrng. (Disting. Honoree, 1986, Founders Award, 1987), Am. Inst. Chemists (Gold medal 1987), Instrument Soc. Am. (pres. 1952), Am. Chem. Soc., Social Sci. Rsch. Coun., Am. Assn. Clin. Chemistry (hon.), Newcomen Soc., Auto Club So. Calif. (bd. dirs. 1965-73, hon. dir. 1973—), Sigma Xi, Delta Upsilon, Alpha Chi Sigma, Phi Lambda Upsilon. Clubs: Newport Harbor Yacht, Pacific. Office: Arnold & Mabel Beckman Found 100 Academy Irvine CA 92612-3002

BECKMANN, JON MICHAEL, publishing company executive; b. N.Y.C., Oct. 24, 1936; s. John L. and Grace (Hazelton) B.; m. Barbara Ann Efting, June 26, 1965. BA, U. Pa., 1958; MA, NYU, 1961. Sr. editor Prentice-Hall Inc., Englewood Cliffs, N.J., 1964-68; v.p., editor Barre Pubs., Mass., 1970-73; pub. Sierra Club Books, San Francisco, 1973-94; pres. Beckmann Assocs. and Millennium Press, Sonoma, Calif., 1994—. Author: After-Dinner Drinks. Mem. Book Club of Calif. Office: Beckmann Assocs & Millennium Press 18185 7th St E Sonoma CA 95476-4797

BEDFORD, DANIEL ROSS, lawyer; b. Berwyn, Ill., Aug. 19, 1945; s. Fred Doyle and Nelda Elizabeth (Dittrich) B.; children: Ian, Kate. BS, Stanford U., 1967, JD, MBA, Stanford U., 1971. Bar: Calif. 1972. Assoc. Thelen & Marrin, San Francisco, 1971-78, ptnr., 1979-86, Orrick, Herrington & Sutcliffe, San Francisco, 1986—. Mem. ABA, Calif. Bar Assn., San Francisco Bar Assn., Am. Coll. of Investment Counsel. Democrat. Episcopalian. Home: 2 Townsend St Apt 1-1006 San Francisco CA 94107-2043 Office: 400 Sansome St San Francisco CA 94111-3304

BEDSWORTH, WILLIAM W. judge; b. Long Beach, Calif., Nov. 21, 1947; m. Carolyn Kelly McCourt, Mar. 28, 1999. BA cum laude, Loyola U., L.A., 1968; JD, U. Calif., Berkeley, 1971. Felony trial deputy, appellate atty., mng. atty. Orange County Dist. Atty.'s Office, Calif.; judge Orange County Superior Ct., 1986-97; assoc. justice 4th Appellate Dist., Calif. Ct. of Appeals, Santa Ana, 1997—. Adj. prof. Western State U. Coll. of Law, Chapman U. Sch. of Law, Orange, Calif., Calif. Jud. Coll., Berkeley. Author: What I Saw and Heard, 1996; author nationally syndicated column A Criminal Waste of Space; contbr. articles to profl. publs. Former bd. dirs. NCCJ, Orange County Bar Assn.; bd. dirs. Fair Share 502; goal judge Nat. Hockey League, 1993—. Named Judge of Yr., Hispanic Bar Assn., 1997. Mem. Assn. Orange County Dep. Dist. Atty. (past pres.). Avocations: softball, country music, ice hockey.

BEE, KEITH A. state legislator; b. Tucson, Dec. 5, 1965; Student, U. Ariz. Mem. Ariz. State Senate, 1992—, vice-chmn. fin. instns. and retirement, mem. health com., chmn. transp. com. Leader 4-H. Mem. Ariz. Assn. Pupil Trans. Republican. Office: State Capitol Bldg 1700 W Washington St Phoenix AZ 85007-2812 Also: 11171 E Escalante Rd Tucson AZ 85730-5604 E-mail: kbee@azleg.state.az.us

BEE, ROBERT NORMAN, banker; b. Milw., Mar. 4, 1925; s. Clarence Olson and Norma Pern (Pitt) B.; m. Dolores Marie Cappelletti, Apr. 23, 1955; children: Diane, John, Leslie. Ph.B., Marquette U., 1949; B.S. in Fgn. Service, Georgetown U., 1950, M.A., 1955. With Dept. Treasury, various locations, 1950-65; fin. attache Stockholm, 1952-54, Ankara, Turkey, 1956-60; chief fin. affairs Am. embassy, Bonn, Germany, 1960-65; dep. dir. AID, Karachi, Pakistan, 1965-67; 1st. v.p. 1st Wis. Nat. Bank, 1967-71; sr. v.p. Wells Fargo Bank; also pres. Wells Fargo Internat. Investment Corp., San Francisco, 1971-78; mng. dir., chief exec. officer London Interstate Bank Ltd., Eng., 1978-87; mng. dir. TSB Pvt. Bank Internat. SA, London, 1987-90; chmn. U.S. Fin. adv. Svc., London, 1990-91, SAJ Investments Ltd., London, 1991-95; sr. advisor Porvenir Inc., San Francisco, 1998-2000. Sr. fellow Center Internat. Banking Studies, Charlottesville, Va. Chmn. World Affairs Coun. Milw., 1970-71; bd. dirs. Adam Smith Inst., London, chmn., 1985-87; chmn. Am. Soc. in London, 1986-87. With AUS, 1943-46. Recipient Bronze Star, 1945. Mem. Bankers Assn. for Fgn. Trade (pres. 1977-78) Home and Office: 1940 Vallejo St Apt 5 San Francisco CA 94123-4918 E-mail: rnbee250ad@aol.com

BEE, TIM, state senator; Senator dist. 9 Ariz. State Senate, Phoenix, 2001—. Mem. judiciary, transp. coms. Ariz. State Senate, vice chmn. appropriations com., appropriations sub-com. on health and welfare. Office: Ariz State Senate Rm 307 1700 W Washington Phoenix AZ 85007

BEEBE, MARY LIVINGSTONE, curator; b. Portland, Oreg., Nov. 5, 1940; d. Robert and Alice Beebe. BA, Bryn Mawr Coll., 1962; postgrad., Sorbonne, U. Paris, 1962-63. Curatorial asst. Fogg Art Mus., Harvard U., Cambridge, Mass., 1966-68; apprentice Portland Art Mus., 1963-64, Boston Mus. Art, 1964-65; exec. dir. Portland Ctr. for Visual Arts, 1973-81; dir. Stuart Collection U. Calif., San Diego, 1981—. Cons. in field; mem. art steering com. Portland Devel. Commn., 1977-80; bd. dirs. Henry Gallery, U. Wash., Seattle, 1977-80; project cons. Nat. Rsch. Ctr. for Arts, N.Y.C., 1978-79; bd. dirs. Western Assn. Art Museums, Art Mus. Assn. San Francisco, 1978-84; bd. dirs., trustee Art Matters Inc., 1985-96; trustee Russell Found., 1982-94; hon. mem. bd. dirs. Portland Ctr. for Visual Arts, 1984-91; mem. arts adv. bd. Centre City Devel. Corp., San Diego, 1982-94, arts adv. bd. Port of San Diego, art adv. bd. U. Calif. San Francisco Mission Bay, 1999—; panel mem., cons. Nat. Endowment Arts; juror numerous art shows and exhbns. Nat. Endowment Arts fellow, 1979. Contbr. articles to profl. jours. Recipient Allied Professions award AIA, 1992. Office: U Calif San Diego The Stuart Collection 9500 Gilman Dr La Jolla CA 92093-5004

BEEBE, STEPHEN A. agricultural products company executive; b. 1945; JD, U. Idaho. Bar: Idaho 1969. Legal asst. U.S Dist. Judge, 1969-70; staff atty. J.R. Simplot, Co., Boise, 1970—, pres., CEO, dir., 1994—. Office: JR Simplot Co PO Box 27 Boise ID 83707-0027

BEECHAM, WILLIAM R. newspaper editor; Bur. chief AP, Salt Lake City, 1982—. Office: 30 E 1st S Salt Lake City UT 84111-1930

BEEMAN, MALINDA MARY, artist, program administrator; b. Pomona, Calif., Jan. 23, 1949; d. Earl Wilson and Mary (Alvey) B. BA, San Diego State U., 1971; MFA, San Francisco Art Inst., 1973. Area coord. printmaking U. Houston, 1985-92; program dir. Anderson Ranch Art Ctr., Snowmass Village, Colo., 1992—. Recipient Visual Artists award Nat. Endowment for Arts, 1988, 96, Covision Recognition award Colo. State Arts Coun., 1992. Office: Anderson Ranch Arts Ctr 5263 Owl Creek Rd Snowmass Village CO 81615

BEENE, RICHARD STUART, newspaper editor; b. Knoxville, Tenn., June 11, 1951; s. William Wolbach and Julia (Swysgood) B.; m. Dianne Elise Klein, May 29, 1983; children: Lauren Elizabeth, Hannah Julia. BA in History, Ga. So. U., 1973. Reporter Fort Lauderdale (Fla.) Sentinel, 1978-80; state mgr. UPI, N.Y.C., Miami & Atlanta, 1980-84, bur. chief Cairo, 1983; L.Am. corr. Dallas Times Herald, 1984-87; city editor L.A. Times, 1987-94; exec. editor Bakersfield (Calif.) Californian, 1994-98, pres., CEO, 1998—. Recipient Pulitizer, L.A. Times, 1995. Mem. Am. Soc. Newspaper Editors, Calif. Soc. Newspaper Editors, Sigma Delta Chi. Avocation: bicycle racing. Office: Bakersfield Californian 1707 Eye St Bakersfield CA 93301-5299

BEER, REINHARD, atmospheric scientist; b. Berlin, Germany, Nov. 5, 1935; came to U.S., 1963, naturalized, 1979; s. Harry Joseph and Elizabet Maria (Meister) B.; m. Margaret Ann Taylor, Aug. 11, 1960. B.Sc. with Honors, U. Manchester, Eng., 1956, Ph.D., 1960. Rsch. asst. physics U. Manchester, 1956-60, sr. asst. astronomy, 1960-63; sr. scientist Jet Propulsion Lab., Pasadena, Calif., 1963-70, group supr. tropospheric sci., 1970-90, sr. rsch. scientist, 1985—, mgr. atmospheric and oceanographic scis. sect., 1990-92, flight team leader, 1997—, prin. scientist, 1999—. Vis. assoc. prof. anstronomy U. Tex., Austin, 1974; vis. astronomer Kitt Peak Nat. Obs., 1979-81, Mauna Kea Obs., 1982-86; prin. investigator tropospheric emission spectrometer NASA Earth Observing System, 1989—, airborne emission spectrometer program NASA, 1992—; co-investigator NASA Atlas 1 mission, 1992, Atlas 2, 1993. Author: Remote Sensing by Fourier Transform Spectrometry, 1992; contbr. articles to profl. jours. Hon. Turner and Newall fellow, 1961; recipient medal for exceptional sci. achievement NASA, 1974; NASA group achievement award for Pioneer Venus, 1980, Spacelab 3 ATMOS experiment and sci., 1986. Mem. AAAS, Am. Geophys. Union, Optical Soc. Am., Internat. Astron. Union. Achievements include discovery of extra-terrestrial deuterium (heavy hydrogen), 1972, of carbon monoxide in Jupiter, 1975. Office: 183-301 Jet Propulsion Lab Pasadena CA 91109

BEESLEY, H(ORACE) BRENT, savings and loan executive; b. Salt Lake City, Jan. 30, 1946; s. Horace Pratt and Mary (Brazier) B.; m. Bonnie Jean Matheson, Dec. 20, 1980; children: Laura Jean, Sarah Janice, Mary Roslyn, Amy Elizabeth, David Brent, Katherine Ann, Daniel Pratt. BA, Brigham Young U., 1969; MBA, J.D., Harvard U., 1973. Bar: Utah 1973. Instr. U. Utah, Salt Lake City, 1973-81; ptnr. Ray, Quinney & Nebeker, Salt Lake City, 1977-81; dir. Fed. Savs. and Loan Ins. Corp., Washington, 1981-83; chmn., chief exec. officer Charter Savs. Corp., Jacksonville, Fla., 1983-86; pres., chief exec. officer Farm Credit Corp. Am., Denver, 1986-88; chmn., chief exec. officer Heritage Savs. Bank, St. George, Utah, 1988—. Bd. dirs. Fed. Home Loan Bank, Seattle, 1992-95, Savs. and Cmty. Bankers Am., 1992-96, Utah Heritage Found., 1978-81, Utah Arthritis Found., 1978-81; trustee So. Va. Coll., 1998—. Mem. Utah State Bar Assn. Club: Alta (Salt Lake City). Home: 1492 Kristianna Cir Salt Lake City UT 84103-4221 Office: 95 E Tabernacle St Saint George UT 84770-2307

BEETHAM, STANLEY WILLIAMS, management consultant; b. Montpelier, Idaho, Nov. 2, 1933; s. Harry Stanley and Mary (Williams) B.; m. Barbara Burnham, June 20, 1987; children: Lara Mary, Amii, Brett.. BA, Wesleyan U., 1956; MA, U. Amsterdam, The Netherlands, 1957; postgrad., Harvard U., 1958-59, U. Wash., 1959-60. Internat. market mgr. U.S. Rubber/Uniroyal, N.Y.C., 1960-63; corp. mktg. cons. GE, N.Y.C., 1963-65; assoc. dir. Benton & Bowles, Inc., N.Y.C., 1965-67; dir. corp. planning Esmark, Chgo., 1967-72, Consol. Packaging Co., Chgo., 1972-74; sr. cons. Booz Allen Hamilton/Hay Assocs., N.Y.C. and Phila., 1975-80; sr. v.p. U.S. Tobacco Co., Greenwich, Conn., 1981-87; pres. S.W. Beetham & Co., Seattle, 1987—. Contbr. articles to profl. jours. Candidate for U.S. Congress from 13th Ill. Dist., 1972, 74; chmn. roundtable Westchester (Conn.) Planning Forum; bd. dirs. AHA Internat., Rural Devel. Inst. Fulbright scholar, 1956, Marshall scholar, 1957; Woodrow Wilson fellow, 1958. Mem. N.Am. Soc. Corp. Planning, Nat. Assn. Bus. Economists, Coun. for Urban Econ. Devel., Internat. Soc. for Planing and Strategic Mgmt., Rainier Club, Phi Beta Kappa. Office: 1223 Spring St Apt 501 Seattle WA 98104-3572

BEEVERS, HARRY, biologist, educator; b. Shildon, Eng., Jan. 10, 1924; came to U.S., 1950, naturalized, 1958; s. Norman and Olive (Ayre) B.; m. Jean Sykes, Nov. 19, 1949; 1 child, Michael BSc, U. Durham, Eng., 1945, PhD, 1947; DSc, U. Newcastle-on-Tyne, 1974, Purdue U., 1972, Nagoya U., 1986. Research fellow Oxford U., Eng., 1946-50; asst. to prof. Purdue U., West Lafayette, Ind., 1950-69; prof. biology U. Calif., Santa Cruz, 1969-90, prof. emeritus, 1990—. Fellow Crown Coll. U. Calif., Santa Cruz, 1969— Author: Respiratory Metabolism in Plants, 1961; contbr. articles to profl. jours. Recipient von Humboldt Sr. Scientist award, 1987. Mem. NAS, Am. Soc. Plant Physiologists (Stephen Hales award 1970, pres. 1960, Barnes award 1999), Am. Soc. Biol. Chemists, Am. Acad. Arts and Scis., Accademia Nazionale dei Lincei, Deutsche Botanische Gesselschaft (hon.), Academia Europaea (fgn.), Bayerische Akademie der Wissenschaften (corr.). Home: 200 Glenwood Cir Apt 311 Monterey CA 93940-6750 Office: U Calif Santa Cruz Dept Biology Santa Cruz CA 95064 E-mail: hbeevers@webtv.net

BEEZER, ROBERT RENAUT, federal judge; b. Seattle, July 21, 1928; s. Arnold Roswell and Josephine (May) B.; m. Hazlehurst Plant Smith, June 15, 1957; children: Robert Arnold, John Leighton, Mary Allison. Student, U. Wash., 1946-48, 51; BA, U. Va., 1951, LLB, 1956. Bar: Wash. 1956, U.S. Supreme Ct. 1968. Ptnr. Schweppe, Krug, Tausend & Beezer, P.S., Seattle, 1956-84; judge U.S. Ct. Appeals (9th cir.), Seattle, 1984-96, sr. judge, 1996—. Alt. mem. Wash. Jud. Qualifications Commn., Olympia, 1981-84 1st lt. USMCR, 1951-53 Fellow Am. Coll. Trust and Estate Counsel, Am. Bar Found.; mem. ABA, Seattle-King County Bar Assn. (pres. 1975-76), Wash. Bar Assn. (bd. govs. 1980-83) Clubs: Rainier, Tennis (Seattle) E-mail: robert. Office: US Ct Appeals 802 US Courthouse 1010 5th Ave Seattle WA 98104-1195 E-mail: beezer@ca9.uscourts.gov

BEGAM, ROBERT GEORGE, lawyer; b. N.Y.C., Apr. 5, 1928; s. George and Hilda M. (Hirt) B.; m. Helen C. Clark, July 24, 1949; children— Richard, Lorinda, Michael. B.A., Yale U., 1949, LL.B., 1952. Bar: N.Y. bar 1952, Ariz. bar 1956, U.S. Dist. Ct. Ariz. 1957, U.S. Ct. Appeals (9th cir.) 1958, U.S Supreme Ct. 1973. Assoc. firm Cravath, Swaine & Moore, N.Y.C., 1952-54; spl. counsel State of Ariz., Colorado River Litigation in U.S. Supreme Ct., 1956-58; pres. Begam, Lewis Marks & Wolfe, P.A., Phoenix. Author: Fireball, 1987. Pres. Ariz. Repertory Theater, 1960—66; trustee Atla Roscoe Pound Found.; bd. dirs. Boys Clubs of Met. Phoenix; bd. govs. Welzmann Inst. Sci., Rehovot, Israel; pres. Am. Com. for Welzmann Inst. of Sci., 1996—98, chmn. fin. resource devel., 2000—; bd. dirs. Phoenix Theater Ctr., 1955—60, 1987—92, Ariz. Theatre Co., 2001—, Shakespeare-Sedona Theatre Co. Fellow: Internat. Soc. Barristers; mem.: Yale Club (N.Y.C.), Wig and Pen (London), Desert Highlands Country (Scottsdale, Ariz.), ATLA (pres. 1976—77, chmn. polit. action com. 1979—86), Western Trial Lawyers Assn. (pres. 1970), Am. Bd. Trial Advocates (bd. dirs.), State Bar Ariz. (cert. specialist in injury and wrongful death litication). Avocations: writing, theater, golf. Office: Begam Lewis Marks & Wolfe 111 W Monroe St Ste 1400 Phoenix AZ 85003-1787 E-mail: begam@fastq.com

BEGELMAN, MITCHELL CRAIG, astrophysicist, educator, writer; AB, AM, Harvard U., 1974; PhD, U. Cambridge, Eng., 1978. Asst. prof. dept. astrophys., planetary and atmospheric scis. U. Colo., Boulder, 1982-87, assoc. prof., 1987-91, prof., 1991—, assoc. chair, 1992-95, chmn., 1995-98, fellow Joint Inst. for Lab. Astrophysics, 1984—. Recipient Presdl. Young Investigator award, 1984, Sci. Writing award Am. Inst. Physics, 1996; Alfred P. Sloan Found. rsch. fellow, 1987-91; John Simon Guggenheim fellow, 1998-99. Fellow Royal Astron. Soc., Cambridge Phil. Soc.; mem. Am. Astron. Soc. (Helen B. Warner prize 1988). Office: U Colo Joint Inst Lab Astrophysics PO Box 440 Boulder CO 80309-0440

BEGGS, HARRY MARK, lawyer; b. Los Angeles, Nov. 15, 1941; s. John Edgar and Agnes (Kentro) B.; m. Sandra Lynne Mikal, May 25, 1963; children: Brendan, Sean, Corey, Michael. Student, Ariz. State U., 1959-61, Phoenix Coll., 1961; LLB, U. Ariz., 1964. Bar: Ariz. 1964, U.S. Dist. Ct. Ariz. 1964, U.S. Ct. Appeals (9th cir.) 1973, U.S. Ct. Appeals (fed. cir.) 1995, U.S. Supreme Ct. 1991. Assoc. Carson Messinger Elliott Laughlin & Ragan, Phoenix, 1964-69, ptnr., 1969-93; mem., mng. lawyer Carson Messinger Elliott Laughlin & Ragan, P.L.L.C., Phoenix, 1994—. Mem. editorial bd. Ariz. Law Rev. 1963-64; contbr. articles to profl. jours. Recipient award for highest grade on state bar exam. Atty. Gen. Ariz., 1964; Fegtly Moot Ct. award, 1963, 64; Abner S. Lipscomb scholar U. Ariz. Law Sch., 1963. Fellow Ariz. Bar Found. (founder); mem. State Bar Ariz., Ariz. Acad., Maricopa County Bar Assn. Office: PO Box 33907 Phoenix AZ 85067-3907 E-mail: hbeggs@carsonlaw-az.com

BEHIE, LEO A. engineering educator; BESc, UWO, 1968, MESc, 1969, PhD, 1972. Prof. engring. U. Calgary, Alta. Recipient Outstanding Leadership in Alta. Tech. award, 1998. Fellow Chem. Inst. Can.; mem. Assn. Profl. Engrs., Geologists and Geophysicists Alta. (Frank Spragins award 1999). Achievements include developed a new pyrolysis process for upgrading Canadian heavy oils, developed a large-scale bioreactor protocols for the production of therapeutics to treat neurodegenerative diseases such as Parkinson's disease, multiple sclerosis and Huntington's disease; research on applying basic principles of chemical reaction engineering to both the animal cell biotechnology field and the energy field; co-inventor of patented process developed specifically to upgrade Alberta heavy oils to high value products such as C2 and C3 olefins. Office: U Calgary Dept Chem Engring 2500 University Dr NW Calgary AB Canada T2N 1N4 Fax: 403-282-3945. E-mail: behie@ucalgary.ca

BEHNKE, CARL GILBERT, beverage franchise executive; b. Seattle, May 13, 1945; s. Robert Joseph and Sally (Skinner) B.; m. Reneé; children: Marisa Winifred, Merrill West. BA, Princeton, 1967; MBA, Harvard, 1973. Adminstrv. asst. ALPAC Corp., Seattle, 1973-75, v.p., 1978-84, pres., 1984-93, also bd. dirs.; sales mgr. Pepsi-Cola/7Up, Honolulu, 1974-76; chmn. bd. Skinner Corp.; pres. REB Enterprises, Seattle, 1993—; bd. dirs. Sage Terrace Inc., The Commerce Bank of Washington, Northwestern Trust, Internat. Yogurt Co. Bd. dirs. Pres.'s Club, U. Wash., 1980-84, Jr. Achievement Puget Sound, 1981—, chmn. bd., 1988; bd. dirs. United Way Washington, 1982-86; pres. Bellevue Boys and Girls Club, 1985-87; trustee U. Puget Sound, Patrons of N.W. Civic Cultural and Charitable Orgns., pres., 1990; chmn. bd. dirs. Eastside Performing Arts Ctr., 1987-90; chmn. bd. Seattle-King County Conv. and Visitors Bur., 1989; mem. exec. bd. Seattle Organizing Com./Goodwill Games, 1987; bd. dirs. Croquet Found. Am., Pacific N.W. Ballet. Named One of 100 Newsmakers of Tomorrow, Time Mag.-Seattle C. of C., 1978. Mem. Nat. Soft Drink Assn. (bd. dirs.), Wash. State Soft Drink Assn. (bd. dirs.), Pepsi-Cola Bottlers Assn. (bd. dirs. 1986), 7UP Bottlers Assn. (bd. dirs.), Young Pres's. Orgn., Cen. Park Tennis Club, Men's Univ. Club, Rainier Club, Columbia Tower Club, Puget Sound Croquet Club, Washington Athletic Club. Republican. Home: 10501 NE 47th Pl Kirkland WA 98033-7610 Office: REB Enterprises 520 Pike St Ste 2620 Seattle WA 98101-4082

BEHREND, DONALD FRASER, environmental educator, university administrator; b. Manchester, Conn., Aug. 30, 1931; s. Sherwood Martin and Margaret (Fraser) B.; m. Joan Belcher, Nov. 9, 1957; children: Andrew Fraser, Eric Hemingway, David William. BS with honors and distinction, U. Conn., 1958, MS, 1960; PhD in Forest Zoology, SUNY, Syracuse, 1966. Forest game mgmt. specialist Ohio Dept. Natural Resources, Athens, 1960; res. asst. Coll. Forestry, SUNY, Newcomb, 1960-63, res. assoc., 1963-67; dir. Adirondack ecol. ctr. Coll. Environ. Science and Forestry, SUNY, Newcomb, 1968-73; acting dean grad. studies Syracuse, 1973-74; asst. v.p. research programs, exec. dir. Inst. Environ. Program Affairs, 1974-79; v.p. acad. affairs, prof., 1979-85; prof. emeritus, 1987—; asst. prof. wildlife mgmt. U. Maine, Orono, 1967-68; provost, v.p. acad. affairs U. Alaska Statewide System, Fairbanks, 1985-87, exec. v.p., provost, 1988; chancellor U. Alaska, Anchorage, 1988-94, chancellor emeritus, 1994—. Mem. patent policy bd. SUNY, 1983-85, chmn. Res. Found. com. acad. res. devel., 1984-85; chmn. 6-Yr. planning com. U. Alaska, 1985-86; bd. dirs. Commonwealth North, 1991-92, Alaska Internat. Ednl. Found., 1997; mem. selection com. Harry S. Truman Scholarship Found.; mem. Pres.'s Commn., NCAA, 1992-95; chmn. spl. com. on student athlete welfare access and equity, 1993-95; chmn. 20th Great Alaska Shootout, 1997. Contbr. numerous articles and papers to profl. jours. Mem. Newcomb Planning Bd., 1967-69; mem., pres. Bd. Edn. Newcomb Cent. Sch., 1967-73; chmn. governing bd. N.Y. Sea Grant Inst., 1984-85; trustee U. Ala. Found., 1990-94. Served with USN, 1950-54. Mem. Alaska Internat. Edn. Found. (bd. dirs. 1997—), Wildlife Soc., Soc. Am. Foresters, AAAS, Phi Kappa Phi (hon.), Sigma Xi, Gamma Sigma Delta, Sigma Lambda Alpha (hon.). Lodges: Rotary (bd. dirs. Fairbanks club 1985-86), Lions (bd. dirs. Newcomb club 1966-67). Avocations: reading, writing, photography, fly fishing, bagpiping. Home: 333 M St Apt #403 Anchorage AK 99501-1902

BEHRENDT, JOHN CHARLES, geophysicist researcher, writer; b. Stevens Point, Wis., May 18, 1932; s. Allen Charles and Vivian Eulaine B.; m. Donna Ebben, Oct. 6, 1961 (div.); children: Kurt Allen, Marc Russell. Student, Cen. State Coll., Stevens Point, 1950-52; BS in Physics, U. Wis., Madison, 1954, MS in Geology, 1956, PhD in Geophysics, 1961. Cert. geophysicist, Calif. Asst. seismologist Arctic Inst. N.Am., Ellsworth Sta., Antarctica, 1956 58; rsch. assoc. U. Wis., Madison, 1958-64; rsch. geophysicist U.S. Geol. Survey, Denver, 1964-72, Liberia, West Africa, 1968-70, Denver, 1970-72; chief br. of Atlantic-Gulf of Mex. marine geology Woods Hole, Mass., 1974-77, research geophysicist, Antarctic coordinator U.S. Geol. Survey, 1977-95, geophysicist emeritus, 1995—; fellow Inst. Arctic and Alpine Rsch U. Colo., Boulder, 1996—; sr. rsch. assoc. Inst. of Arctic and Alpine Rsch., U. Colo., Boulder, 1996—. Frequent pub. spkr. on Antarctica and other rsch.; advisor U.S. Depts. State and Interior, Washington, 1977—; mem. U.S. del. to Antarctic Treaty Meetings, various countries, 1977-95, various working groups NAS-NRC; rsch. on Antarctic, earthquakes in ea. U.S., Rocky Mountain tectonics, Gt. Lakes geologic structure, Atlantic continental margin of N.Am. and West Africa. Author: Innocents on the Ice: A Memoir of Antarctic Exploration, 1957, 1998 (Colo. Book award for non-fiction 1999); contbr. over 200 articles to sci. jours. Recipient Antarctic Svc. medal U.S. Dept. Def., 1966, Meritorious Svc. award Dept. Interior, 1992, Filice Ippolito Gold medal for Antarctic Rsch., Italian Antarctic Rsch. Program and Acad. Nazionale dei Linceia. Fellow Geol. Soc. Am., Explorers Club; mem. Am. Geophys. Union, Soc. Exploration Geophysicists, AAAS. Avocations: photography, outdoor activities, music. E-mail: behrendj@stripe.colorado.edu

BEHRENS, BEREL LYN, physician, academic and healthcare administrator; b. New South Wales, Australia, 1940; MB, BS, Sydney (Australia) U., 1964. Cert. pediatrics, allergy and immunology. Intern Royal Prince Alfred Hosp., Australia, 1964; resident Loma Linda (Calif.) U. Med. Ctr., 1966-68; with Henrietta Egleston Hosp. for Children, Atlanta, 1968-69, T.C. Thompson Children's Hosp., Chattanooga, 1969-70; instr. pediatrics Loma Linda U., 1970-72, with dept. pediatrics, 1972—, dean Sch. Medicine, 1986-91, pres., 1990—; pres., CEO Loma Linda U. Med. Ctr., 1999—. Office: Loma Linda U Med Ctr Office Of The Pres Loma Linda CA 92350-0001 E-mail: rminor@ahs.llumc.edu

BEHRENS, M. KATHLEEN, medical researcher; PhD in Microbiology, U. Calif., Davis. With Robertson Stephens Mgmt. Co., 1983-86, gen. ptnr., 1986-93; dir. Abgenix, Inc., Fremont, Calif., 1997—. Mem. Nat. Venture Capital Assn. (pres. elect 1999—). Office: Abgenix Inc 7601 Dumbarton Cir Fremont CA 94555-3616

BEHRING, KENNETH E. professional sports team owner; b. Freeport, Ill., June 13, 1928; s. Elmer and Mae (Priewe) B.; m. Patricia Riffle, Oct. 16, 1949; children: Michael, Thomas, David, Jeffrey, Scott. Student, U. Wis., 1947. Owner Behring Motors, Monroe, Wis., 1953-56, Behring Corp., Ft. Lauderdale, Fla., 1956-72, Blackhawk Corp., Danville, Calif., 1972—, also chmn. bd. dirs.; owner Seattle Seahawks, NFL, 1988-97. Calif. land developer; mem. policy adv. bd. real estate and urban econs. U. Calif., Berkeley.; chmn. bd. dirs. Behring-Hofmann Ednl. Inst., Inc. U. Calif. Trustee U. Calif., Berkeley; regent St. Mary's Coll., Moraga, Calif., Holy Name Coll., Oakland, Calif.; hon. trustee Mt. Diablo Hosp. Found., Concord, Calif.; hon. chmn. Seattle Art Mus., Am. Cancer Soc., Muscular Dystrophy, Silverado Concours. Named Man of Yr. Boys Town Italy, Entrepreneur of Yr. INC mag. Mem. Am. Acad. Achievement (honoree 1989), Assn. Wash. Bus., Seattle Master Builders Assn., Blackhawk Club, Vintage Club, Seattle Yacht Club, Wash. Athletic Club. Office: Blackhawk Corp PO Box 807 Danville CA 94526-0807

BEIGHLE, DOUGLAS PAUL, electric power industry executive, retired; b. Deer Lodge, Mont., June 18, 1932; s. Douglas Paul Beighle and Clarice Janice (Driver) Kiefer; m. Gwendolen Anne Dickson, Oct. 30, 1954 (dec. Jan. 1996); children: Cheryl, Randall, Katherine, Douglas J. B.S. in Bus. Adminstrn., U. Mont., 1954; J.D., U. Mont, 1958; LL.M., Harvard U., 1960. Bar: Mont. 1958, Wash. 1959, U.S. Supreme Ct. 1970. Assoc. Perkins & Coie, Seattle, 1960-67, ptnr., 1967-80; v.p. contracts Boeing Co., Seattle, 1980-81, v.p. contracts, gen. counsel, sec., 1981-86, sr. v.p., 1986-97; chief legal counsel Puget Sound Energy Co., Bellevue, Wash., 1970-80, also bd. dirs., 1981—; exec. dir. Wash. State, U.S. West Comm., Denver, 1990-95, ret., 1995. Bd. dirs. Washington Mut. Inc., Seattle,

Simpson Investment Co., Seattle, Active Voice Corp., Seattle, Infrastrux Group, Bellevue, Wash.; bd. dirs. KCTS-9 TV, chair 1996—. Nat. bd. dirs. Jr. Achievement, Colorado Springs, 1981-95; bd. dirs. Greater Puget Sound Jr. Achievement, 1983—, Intiman Theatre, Seattle, 1991-93; trustee Mcpl. League Seattle, 1983-88, U. Mont. Found., Missoula, 1983-91, Mansfield Found., Missoula, 1990-95, Pacific Sci. Ctr., Seattle, 1992—, pres. 1996; trustee Corp. Coun. for the Arts, Seattle, 1994—, chair, 1995-96. 1st lt. USAF, 1954-56. Harvard U. Law Sch. fellow, 1959 Mem. ABA, Mont. Bar Assn., Wash. State Bar Assn. (chmn. adminstrv. law sect. 1979-80), Seattle-King County Bar Assn., Nat. Assn. Mfrs. (bd. dirs., regional vice chmn. 1988-93), Greater Seattle C. of C. (chair 1994-95), Rainier Club Seattle, Seattle Yacht Club. Republican. Presbyterian. Office: 1000 2nd Ave Ste 3700 Seattle WA 98104-1053

BEISTLINE, EARL HOOVER, mining consultant; b. Juneau, Alaska, Nov. 24, 1916; s. Ralph H. and Catherine (Krinach) B.; m. Dorothy Ann Hering, Aug. 24, 1946; children— Ralph Robert, William Calvin, Katherine Noreen, Lynda Marie. B. Mining Engring., U. Alaska, 1939, E.M., 1947, LL.D. (hon.), 1969. Mem. faculty U. Alaska, 1946-82, dean Sch. Mines, 1949-61, dean Coll. Earth Sci. and Mineral Industry, 1961-75, provost Coll. Earth Sci. and Mineral Industry, 1970-75, exec. officer no. region, 1970-73, dean Sch. Mineral Industry, 1975-82, dean emeritus, prof. mining engring. Sch. Mineral Industry, 1982—; mining cons. Served to maj. AUS, 1941-46. Fellow AAAS, Explorers Club; mem. NSPE, Am. Inst. Mining and Metall. Engrs., Mining and Metall. Soc. Am., Arctic Inst. N.Am., Am. Soc. Engring. Edn., N.W. Mining Assn., Alaska Mining Assn., Pioneers of Alaska. Home and Office: PO Box 80148 Fairbanks AK 99708-0148

BEIZER, LANCE KURT, lawyer; b. Hartford, Conn., Sept. 8, 1938; s. Lawrence Sidney and Victoria Merriam (Kaplan) B. BA in Sociology, Brandeis U., 1967; MA in English, San Jose State U., 1967; JD, U. San Diego, 1975. Bar: Calif. 1975. Selective svc. affairs coord. U. Calif., 1969-73, vet. affairs coord., 1973-75; vet. outreach coord. San Diego Community Coll. Dist., 1975-76; dep. dist. atty. Santa Clara County, Calif., 1976—. Bd. mgrs. Santa Clara Valley S.W. YMCA, Saratoga, Calif., 1988, chair, 1991-93; bd. dirs. The Lumen Found., San Francisco, 1985—. Bd. dirs. Fedn. Cmty. Ministries, Calif., 1992—, chair, 1996—; bd. dirs. Apistolic Cath. orthodox Ch., 1997—. Lt. USNR, 1961-65. Mem. Calif. Dist. Attys. Assn., Am. Profl. Soc. on Abuse of Children, Nat. Assn. Counsel for Children, Am. Weil Soc., Mensa, Commonwealth Club. Republican. Episcopalian. Home: 1197 Capri Dr Campbell CA 95008-6002 Office: Santa Clara County Dist Atty 70 W Hedding St San Jose CA 95110-1768 E-mail: LBeizer@yahoo.com

BEJCZY, ANTAL KÁROLY, research scientist, research facility administrator; b. Ercsi, Hungary, Jan. 16, 1930; came to U.S., 1966; s. Jenö and Erzsébet (László) B.; m. Margit Tóth, Oct. 12, 1957. BSEE, Tech. U., Budapest, Hungary, 1956; PhD in Physics, Sci. U., Oslo, 1963. Univ. lectr. Sci. U., Oslo, 1963-66; rsch. scientist Norwegian Rsch. Coun., Oslo, 1963-66; sr. rsch. fellow Calif. Inst. Tech., Pasadena, 1966-69; mem. tech. staff Jet Propulsion Lab., Pasadena, 1969-79, tech. mgr., 1979-95, sr. rsch. scientist, 1985—. Bd. dirs. Zoltán Bay Applied Scis. Found., Budapest, Hungary, 1993-98; affiliate prof. Washington U., St. Louis, 1983—. Contbr. articles on robotics and telerobotics to profl. jours.; assoc. editor Automatic Control Trans., 1982-85; mem. editl. bd. Jour. Robotic Sys., 1983—; patentee in field. Recipient Jean Vertut award Robotics Internat., 1987; NASA Exceptional Svc. medal, 1991. Fellow IEEE (Third Millenium Medal award 2000); mem. Robotics and Automation Soc. of IEEE (pres. 1986-87, adminstrv. com. 1991-99). Avocations: tennis, gardening, music. Office: Jet Propulsion Lab MS 198-219 4800 Oak Grove Dr Pasadena CA 91109-8001

BEKAVAC, NANCY YAVOR, academic administrator, lawyer; b. Pitts., Aug. 28, 1947; d. Anthony Joseph and Elvira (Yavor) B. BA, Swarthmore Coll., 1969; JD, Yale U., 1973. Bar: Calif. 1974, U.S. Dist. Ct. (cen. dist.) 1974, (no. dist.) Calif. 1975, (so. dist.) Calif. 1976, U.S. Ct. Appeals (9th cir.) 1975, (8th cir.) 1981, U.S. Supreme Ct. 1979. Law clk. at large U.S. Ct. Appeals (D.C. cir.), Washington, 1973-74; assoc. Munger, Tolles & Rickershauser, L.A., 1974-79, ptnr., 1980-85; exec. dir. Thomas J. Watson Found., Providence, 1985-87, cons., 1987-88; counselor to pres. Dartmouth Coll., Hanover, N.H., 1988-90; pres. Scripps Coll., Claremont, Calif., 1990—. Adj. prof. law UCLA Law Sch., 1982-83; mem. Calif. Higher Edn. Roundtable, 1996—; trustee Am. Coun. Edn., 1994-97. Bd. mgrs. Swarthmore Coll., 1984—; trustee Wenner-Gren Found. for Anthr. Rsch. 1987-94; bd. trustees Am. Coun. Edn., 1994-97; chair Assn. Ind. Colls. and Univs., 1996-97. Recipient Human Rights award L.A. County Commn. on Civil Rights, 1984; Woodrow Wilson fellow, Thomas J. Watson fellow, 1969. Mem. Assn. Ind. Calif. Colls. and Univs. (chair 1996), Sierra Club. Avocations: hiking, reading, traveling. Office: Scripps Coll Office of Pres 1030 Columbia Ave Claremont CA 91711-3986

BEKEY, GEORGE ALBERT, computer scientist, educator, engineer; b. Bratislava, Slovakia, June 19, 1928; came to U.S., 1945, naturalized, 1956; s. Andrew and Elizabeth B.; m. Shirley White, June 10, 1951; children: Ronald Steven, Michelle Elaine. BS with honors, U. Calif., Berkeley, 1950; MS, UCLA, 1952, PhD, 1962. Research engr. UCLA, 1950-54; mgr. computer center Beckman Instruments, L.A. and Berkeley, 1955-58; mem. sr. staff, dir. computer center TRW Systems Group, Redondo Beach, Calif., 1958-62; mem. faculty U. So. Calif., L.A., 1962—, prof. elec. and biomed. engring. and computer sci., 1968, chmn. dept. elec. engring. systems, 1978-86, dir. Robotics Lab., 1983-98, chmn. computer sci. dept., 1984-89, dir. Ctr. for Mfg. and Automation Research, 1987-94, assoc. dean Sch. Engring., 1996-2001. Chair computer sci. Gordon Marshall, 1990—; cons. to govt. agys. and indsl. orgns. Author: (with W.J. Karplus) Hybrid Computation, 1968, (with K. Goldberg) Robotics and Neural Networks, 1994; editor 6 books; mem. editorial bd. 3 profl. jours.; founding editor IEEE Trans. Robotics and Automation; editor Autonomous Robots; contbr. over 200 articles to profl. jours.; patentee in field. Served with U.S. Army, 1954-56. Recipient Disting. Faculty award, 1977, Sch. Engring. Service award U. So. Calif., 1990, Presdl. medallion, 2000, Engelberger prize in robotics, 2001. Fellow AAAS, IEEE (3d Millennium medal 2000), Am. Inst. Med. and Biol. Engring., Am. Assn. Artificial Intelligence; mem. IEEE Robotics and Automation Soc. (pres. 1996-97), NAE, Assn. for Computing Machinery, Soc. for Computer Simulation, Neural Network Soc., Biomed. Engring. Soc., World Affairs Coun., Sigma Xi, Tau Beta Pi, Eta Kappa Nu. Office: U So Calif Office Of The Dean Los Angeles CA 90089-0001

BEKEY, SHIRLEY WHITE, psychotherapist; b. L.A. d. Lawrence Francis and Alice (King) White; m. George Albert Bekey, June 10, 1951; children: Ronald S., Michelle E. BA in Psychology, Occidental Coll., L.A., 1949; MSW in Psychiat. Social Work, UCLA, 1954; PhD in Edn. Psychology, U. So. Calif., 1980. Lic. clin. social worker, Calif.; cert. in pupil pers., parent-child edn. Caseworker outpatient svcs. Calif. State Dept. Mental Health, Montebello; caseworker Lowman Sch. for Handicapped, L.A. Unified Sch. Dist., North Hollywood, Calif., 1971-72; psychotherapist Hofmann Psychiat. Clinic, Glendale (Calif.) Adventist Hosp., 1973-75; pvt. practice Encino, Calif., 1980—. Sprk. in field.; TV expert on children's emotional problems. 1st hosp. vol. candystriper in U.S., Hollywood Hosp, L.A., 1942; mem. World Affairs Coun., L.A., 1960—. Fellow Soc. for Clin. Social Work; mem. NASW, APA, Am. Ednl. Rsch. Assn., Nat. Assn. Gifted Children, Assn. Transpersonal Psychology, Inst. Noetic Sci., Assn. Ednl. Therapists, So. Calif. Soc. for Clin. Hypnosis, Analytical Psychology Club L.A., Nat. Assn. Poetry Therapy, Calif. Assn. for Gifted. Avocations: clinical hypnosis, gifted and talented, learning disabilities. Office: 4924 Balboa Blvd # 199 Encino CA 91316-3402

BEKIR, NAGWA ESMAT, electrical engineer, educator, consultant; b. Cairo, Dec. 31, 1944; came to U.S., 1972; s. Mohammed Ragab Shalaby and Kamla (Abdel Megeed) Mahmood; m. Esmat Chibl, Sept. 23, 1971; children: Ahmad C., Badr E. BSEE, Cairo U., Egypt, 1966; MSEE, U. So. Calif., 1975, PhD in EE, 1978. Rsch. and hardware engr. Egyptian Indsl. Rsch. Inst., Cairo, 1966-69; quality control engr. Nat. Egyptian Co. for TV and Electronics, Cairo, 1969-72; mem. tech. staff Axiomatics, L.A., 1978; sr. staff engr. Hughes Aircraft Co., Canoga Park, Calif., 1985, mem. tech. staff, 1978-80; assoc. prof. elec. and computer engring. dept. Calif. State U., Northridge, 1980-83, prof., 1984—, chair elec. and computer engring. dept., 1997—. Mem. tech. staff ITT Gilfillan, Van Nuys, Calif., 1984; cons. aircraft divsn. Northrop Co., El Segundo, Calif., 1987; cons. Budlong & Assocs., Inc., Agoura Hills, Calif., 1992-93; rschr. Northrop Grumman Co., El Segundo, 1994-95. Contbr. articles to profl. jours. Recipient Engring. Merit award, 1999, Meritorious Performance and Profl. Promise award Calif. State U., Northridge, 1989, Outstanding Faculty awards Sch. of Engring. and Computer Sci., 1990. Mem. IEEE (sr.), Eta Kappa Nu, Tau Beta Pi. Avocations: swimming, racquet ball. Office: Calif State U 18111 Nordhoff St Northridge CA 91330-0001

BELCHER, JENNIFER MARION, state official, consultant; b. Beckley, W.Va., Jan. 4, 1944; d. Grover Emerson and Virginia Dare (Phillips) Marion. Student, Bethany Coll., 1962-63; program for sr. execs., Harvard U., 1986. Adminstrv. sec. Planning and Community Affairs Agy. State of Wash., 1967-72; spl. asst. Office of Gov., Olympia, Wash., 1973-79; owner, pres. Mgmt. Dynamics, 1980-92; mem. Wash. Ho. of Reps., Olympia, 1982-92; bd. dirs. The Nature Conservancy Wash. State Dept. of Natural Resources, Olympia, Wash., 1988-92; commr. of pub. lands WA, Olympia, 1992—. Bd. dirs. Washington Wildlife and Recreation Coalition. Pres. Wash. State's Women's Polit. Caucus, 1979-81. Mem. Wash. Bus. and Profl. Women's Club. Democrat. Home: 323 Maple Park Ave SE Olympia WA 98501-2360 Office: Wash State Dept of Natural Resources PO Box 47000 Olympia WA 98504-7000

BELITZ, PAUL EDWARD, lawyer; b. Omaha, July 11, 1951; s. Edward Paul and Jo Anna Beverly (Brown) B.; m. Joanne Deborah Nilson, June 9, 1973; children: Nicholas P., Christopher T. BS with high distinction, U. Nebr., 1973; JD magna cum laude, Creighton U., 1976. Bar: Nebr. 1976, Colo. 1982. Assoc., then ptnr. Kutak Rock LLP, Omaha, 1976-81, ptnr. Denver, 1982—. Bd. dirs. Fleischer Found., Scottsdale, Ariz., 1986—, Fleischer Mus., Scottsdale, 1989—. Mem. ABA, Nebr. Bar Assn., Colo. Bar Assn., Denver Bar Assn. Avocations: reading, skiing, golf. Office: Kutak Rock LLP 717 17th St Ste 2900 Denver CO 80202-3329 E-mail: paul.belitz@kutakrock.com

BELJAN, JOHN RICHARD, university administrator, medical educator; b. Detroit, May 26, 1930; s. Joseph and Margaret Anne (Brozovich) B.; m. Bernadette Marie Marenda, Feb. 2, 1952; children: Ann Marie, John Richard, Paul Eric. B.S., U. Mich., 1951, M.D., 1954. Diplomate: Am. Bd. Surgery. Intern U. Mich., Ann Arbor, 1954-55, resident in gen. surgery, 1955-59; dir. med. services Stuart div. Atlas Chem. Industries, Pasadena, Calif., 1965-66; from asst. prof. to assoc. prof. surgery U. Calif. Med. Sch., Davis, 1966-74, from asst. prof. to assoc. prof. engring., 1968-74, from asst. dean to assoc. dean, 1971-74; prof. surgery, prof. biol. engring. Wright State U., Dayton, Ohio, 1974-83, dean Sch. Medicine, 1974-81, vice provost, 1974-78, v.p. health affairs, 1978-81, provost, sr. v.p., 1981-83; prof. arts and scis., assoc. v.p. med. affairs Cen. State U., Wilberforce, 1976-83; provost, v.p. acad. affairs, dean Sch. Medicine Hahnemann U., Phila., 1983-85, prof. surgery and biomed. engring., 1983-86, spl. adviser to pres., 1985-86; v.p. acad. affairs Calif. State U., Long Beach, 1986-89, prof. anat., physiology and biomed. engring., 1986-91, provost, 1989-91; pres. Northrop U., L.A., 1989-93, pres. emeritus, 1993—. Trustee Cox Heart Inst., 1975-77, Drew Health Ctr., 1977-78, Wright State U. Found., 1975-83, CSULB Found., 1986-89, 49er Athletic Found., 1986-89; trustee, regional v.p. Engring. and Sci. Inst. Hall of Fame, 1983—; bd. dirs. Miami Valley Health Sys. Agy., 1975-82, UCI Ctr. for Health Edn., 1987-90, Long Beach Rsch. Found., 1989-94; cons. in field. Author articles, revs., chpts. in books. Served with M.C. USAF, 1955-65. Decorated Commendation medal; Braun fellow, 1949; grantee USPHS, NASA, 1968—. Fellow A.C.S.; mem. Los Angeles County Med. Assn., Mich. Alumni Club (Dayton, Outstanding Alumnus award 1976), Oakwood Fur Club, Fin and Feather Club, Phi Beta Delta, Phi Beta Kappa, Alpha Omega Alpha, Phi Eta Sigma, Phi Kappa Phi, Alpha Kappa Kappa. Home and Office: 1671 Mission Hills Rd Apt 501 Northbrook IL 60062-5735

BELL, CHESTER GORDON, computer engineering company executive; b. Kirksville, Mo., Aug. 19, 1934; s. Roy Chester and Lola Dolph (Gordon) B.; m. Gwendolyn Kay Druyor, Jan. 3, 1959; children: Brigham Roy, Laura Louise. BSEE, MIT, 1956, MSEE, 1957; DEng (hon.), Worcester Poly. Inst., 1993. Engr. Speech Communication Lab., MIT, Cambridge, 1959-60; mgr. computer design Digital Equipment Corp., Maynard, Mass., 1960-66, v.p. engring., 1972-83; prof. computer sci. Carnegie-Mellon U., 1966-72; vice chmn. Encore Computer Corp., Marlboro, Mass., 1983-86; asst. dir. NSF, Washington, 1986-87; v.p. R & D Stardent Computer, Sunnyvale, Calif., 1987-89; cons. The Bell-Mason Group, 1989—. Bd. dirs. Cradle Tech., Caspian Networks; bd. dirs., trustee Computer Mus., 1982—; sr. researcher Microsoft Corp., 1995—. Author: (with Newell) Computer Structures, 1971, (with Grason, Newell) Designing Computers and Digital Systems, 1972, (with Mudge, McNamara) Computer Engineering, 1978, (with Siewiorek, Newell) Computer Structures, 1982, (with McNamara) High Tech Ventures, 1991. Recipient 6th Mellon Inst. award, 1972, Nat. Medal Tech., U.S. Dept. Commerce Tech. Adminstrn., 1991, award for greatest econ. contbn. to region Am. Electronics Assn., 1993, MCI Smithsonian award for Innovation, 1995. Fellow IEEE (McDowell award 1975, Eckert-Mauchly award 1982, von Neumann medal 1992), AAAS, Am. Acad. Arts and Scis., Assn. for Computing Machinery; mem. NAE, Eta Kappa Nu (Karapetoff and Emminent mem. awards 2001). Home and Office: 212 Widler Ave Los Gatos CA 95030

BELL, DANIEL CARROLL, realtor, community association, ranch and land manager; b. Chgo., July 17, 1940; s. Daniel Gregory and Inez Margarite (Carroll) B.; m. Elaine Paula Rhody, Feb. 1, 1960; children: Tana Lou, Daniel Arden, Andrea Jane. Student, Colo. State U., 1958-62, Reisch Coll. Auctioneering, Mason City, Iowa, 1983. Cert. assn. mgmt. specialist, ind. cmty. mgr. Mgr. ptnr. Three Bell Ranch, Ft. Collins, Colo., 1958-69; sales rep. Pacific Vegetable Oil Co., San Francisco, 1969-70; mng. dir. Paveocor A.G. subs. PVO Internat., Rotterdam, Netherlands, 1970-71; nat. sales mgr. PVO Internat., San Francisco, 1971-72; v.p. commodity trading San Pablo Mfg. Co. subs. PVO Internat., Manila, Philippines, 1972-74; v.p. Rothschild Brokerage Co., San Francisco, 1975-76; owner, prin. Feed, Etc., Harbor, Oreg., 1976-79; commodity specialist Shearson Loeb Rhodes, Medford, 1979-80; exec. v.p., gen. mgr. Superior Credit Assocs., Inc., Medford, 1981-86; mng. ptnr. Three Bell Land Co., [illegible], Colo., 1986 [illegible], ptnr. Legacy Transp. Co., 1986-93; CEO Bell & Assocs. Ltd., 1993—; gen. mgr. Greenfield Village RV Resort Assn., 1994-98; exec. dir. Sun Village HOA, 1999. Mem. Medford (Oreg.) Planning Commn., 1981-84, Medford Sister Cities Commn., 1984; treas. Jackson County Rep. Ctrl. Com., Medford, 1982-84; arbitrator Better Bus. Bur., Medford and Ft. Collins, Colo., 1984-89; candidate Oreg. Ho. Reps., 1984; mem. Mesa (Ariz.) Human Svcs. Adv. Bd., 1994-95; grad. Mesa Citizens Police Acad., 1995, v.p., 1996, pres., 1998—, facilitator, 1997-98; mem. Civilian Res. Ariz. Dept. Pub. Safety; mem. Housing and Human Svcs. Adv. Bd., Mesa, 1998-99; mem. Camp Verde Bd. Adjustments, 1999-2000; mem. Town Camp Verde Civil Enforcement Hearing Officer, 2000—; mcpl. judge pro tem, 2000—. With USAR, 1958-63, Colo. Air N.G., 1963-65. Mem. NRA, Cmty. Assn. Inst. (cert. assn. mgmt. specialist), Inst. Cmty. Mmgt. (cert. ind. cmty. mgr.), Ariz. Travel Parks Assn. (bd. dirs. 1997-99, treas.), Ariz. Magistrates Assn., Elks. Republican. Presbyterian. Avocations: fishing, golf. Office: 2034 Rustler Trail Camp Verde AZ 86322-7536 E-mail: rustler@sedona.net

BELL, DAVID GUS (BUDDY BELL), professional baseball manager; b. Pitts., Aug. 27, 1951; s. Gus B.; m. Gloria Bell; children: David, Michael, Ricky, Kristi Marie, Tracy. Player in minor leagues, 1969-71; outfielder, 3d baseman Cleve. Indians, 1972-78, minor league hitting instr., 1990, coach, 1994-95; 3d baseman Tex. Rangers, 1979-85, 89; with Cin. Reds, 1985-88; player Houston Astros, 1988; dir. minor league instrn. Chgo. White Sox, 1991-93; mgr. Detroit Tigers, 1996-98, Colo. Rockies, Denver, 1999—. Mem.: Am. League All-Star Team, 1973, 80-82, 84. Recipient Gold Glove award, 1979-84. Address: Colorado Rockies 2001 Blake St Denver CO 80205-2008

BELL, FRANK OURAY, JR. lawyer; b. San Francisco, Aug. 13, 1940; s. Frank Ouray, Sr. and Clara Belle (McClure) B.; m. Sherrie A. Levie, Mar. 29, 1981; children: Aimee, David; children from previous marriage: Carin, Laurie. AB, San Francisco State U., 1963; JD, U. Calif., San Francisco, 1966. Bar: Calif. 1966, Calif. Supreme Ct. 1966, U.S. Dist. Ct. (no. dist.) Calif. 1967, U.S. Ct. Appeals (9th cir.) 1967, U.S. Supreme Ct. 1973. Dep. atty. gen. Calif. State's Atty.'s Office, Sacramento, 1966-68; ptnr. Goorjian & Bell, San Francisco, 1968-70; chief asst. Fed. Pub. Defender's Office, San Francisco, 1970-82; dir. Calif. State Pub. Defender's Office, 1984-87; pvt. practice law San Francisco, 1982-84; sr. litigation assoc. Olimpia, Whelan & Lively, San Jose, 1987-89; sole practice San Mateo, 1989—. Mem. San Mateo County Bar Assn., Calif. Pub. Defenders Assn. (bd. dirs. 1986-87). Democrat. Jewish. Office: 177 Bovet Rd Ste 600 San Mateo CA 94402-3122 E-mail: frankbell-lawyer@home.com

BELL, GENE, newspaper publishing executive; Pres. and ceo San Diego Union-Tribune, San Diego, 1992—. Office: San Diego Union-Tribune 350 Camino De La Reina San Diego CA 92108-3003

BELL, GEORGE, media executive; m. Carrie Bell; 3 children. BA, Harvard U., 1980. Head writer, prodr. Am. Sportsman-ABC, 1980-85; prodr., writer documentaries, 1985-90; sr. v.p. Times Mirror Mags., 1991-95; CEO Excite, Inc., 1996—. Mem. exec. com. Nat. Forest Found. Recipeint Emmy award. Office: Excite Inc 555 Broadway St Redwood City CA 94063-3134

BELL, GEORGE IRVING, biophysics researcher; b. Evanston, Ill., Aug. 4, 1926; s. George Irving and Hazel (Seerley) B.; m. Virginia Lotz, Jan. 13, 1956; children— Carolyn Bell Prince, George Irving Jr. B.S. in Physics, Harvard U., 1947; Ph.D. in Theoretical Physics, Cornell U., 1951. Staff mem. Los Alamos Nat. Lab, 1951-70, assoc., alt. or acting div. leader, 1970-80, leader theroetical biology and biophysics group, 1974-90, theoretical div. leader, 1980-89; acting dir. Ctr. for Human Genome Studies, 1988-89, project mgr., functional genomics, 1998—, sr. fellow, 1990—; Gordon McKay lectr. Harvard U., Cambridge, Mass., 1962-63; mem. Basel Inst. Immunology, Switzerland, 1979-80. Scholar in human biology Eleanor Roosevelt Inst. Cancer Rsch., Denver, 1977-90; bd. sci. counselors Nat. Cancer Inst., Bethesda, 1985-89, chmn. supercomputer mgmt. oversight group, 1989-96; mem. human genome steering com. U.S. Dept. Energy, 1988-89; mem. Joint Informatics Task Force for Human Genome, 1990-92, Nat. Adv. Rsch. Resources Coun., NIH, 1992-94; sci. bd. Santa Fe Inst., 1988-99; mem. various mountaineering expeditions, 1948-60. Author (with S. Glasstone) Nuclear Reactor Theory, 1970; editor: Theoretical Immunology, 1978, Computers and DNA, 1989; contbr. articles to profl. publs. RCA Corp. fellow, 1945-47, AEC fellow, 1948-50. Fellow AAAS, Am. Phys. Soc., Am. Nuclear Soc. (cert. merit 1966); mem. Biophys. Soc., Am. Alpine Club (David A. Sowles medal 1981), Himalayan Club (India). Achievements include rsch. in nuclear reactor theory such as methods for treating effective cross sections in dense lattices, anisotropic scattering, fluctuations in neutron populations; and in theoretical biology such as theoretical models of immune system, binding of antigens to cells and cell-cell adhesion, evolution of repetitive DNA sequences, functional genomics. Office: K 710 PO Box 1663 Los Alamos NM 87545-0001

BELL, HELEN LAVIN, artist; b. Allentown, Pa. d. Thomas Joseph and Anna Helen (Miko) Lavin; m. Paul Edward Bell, June 10, 1950; children: Celine Butler, Sharon Neiman, Paul Jr., Christine Schlacter. Student, Western Md. Coll., 1945-47, Md. Inst. Art, 1947-48, Telfair Acad. Arts, 1958-59, U. Calif., Riverside, 1970-71, 80-81. Asst. art dir. Davison's, Atlanta, 1950-51. One-woman shows include Riverside (Calif.) Art Mus., 1980, Mind's Eye Gallery, Riverside, 1983, Rizzoli Internat., Costa Mesa, Calif., 1987, Zola Fine Art, Beverly Hills, Calif., 1990, others; group shows include City of Riverside, Calif., 1975, Riverside County Mus., Beaumont, Calif., 1976, 90, Calif. Poly. U., Pomona, 1987, Corp. Rental program L.A. County Mus. Art, 1989-95, Calif. Small Works, Santa Rosa, 1992, 93, Ronald McDonald House, Loma Linda, Calif., 1996, Carte Blanche, 1996, Made in Calif., Brea, 1997, Echoes and Visions II, Laguna Niguel, Calif., 1998, Millard Sheets Small Works Gallery, 2001. Event chair Nat. Charity League, Riverside, Calif., 1979-83; trustee Riverside Art Mus., 1979-82. Merit scholar Telfair Acad. Arts and Scis., Savannah, Ga., 1958. Mem. Redlands Art Assn. (trustee 1985-87, 91-95, sec.), Art Alliance (pres. 1979-80, com. chairs 1978, 81, 82, 2000), Nat. Assn. Women Artists, Inc. Republican. Roman Catholic. Avocations: swimming, traveling. Gallery: Riverside Art Mus 3425 Mission Inn Ave Riverside CA 92501-3304 Studio: Gallery Blvd 73680 El Paseo Palm Desert CA 92261

BELL, JAY STUART, baseball player; b. Eglin AFB, Fla., Dec. 11, 1965; With Cleve. Indians, 1986-88; shortstop Pitts. Pirates, 1989-96, Kansas City (Mo.) Royals, 1997, Ariz. Diamondbacks, 1997—. Mem. Nat. League All-Star Team, 1993. Named Nat. League leader short stop put-outs, 1990, 91, short stop assists, 1991, 92; Nat. League Gold Glove, 1993. Office: Ariz Diamondbacks Bank One Ballpark 401 E Jefferson St Phoenix AZ 85004-2438

BELL, LEE PHILLIP, television personality, television producer; b. Chgo. d. James A. and Helen (Novak) P.; m. William Joseph Bell, Oct. 23, 1954; children: William J., Bradley, Lauralee. B.S. in Microbiology, Northwestern U., 1950. With CBS-TV, Chgo., 1952-86; pres. Bell-Phillip TV Prodns., 1985—. Bd. dirs. William Wrigley, Jr. Co., Chgo. Bank Commerce, Phillips Flowers Inc. TV and radio shows include Lee Phillip Show, Chgo., from 1952, Lady and Tiger Show WBBM Radio, from 1962, WBBM TV from 1964; hostess Noon Break, numerous TV Spls. including Forgotten Children, The Rape of Paulette (nat. Emmy award, duPont Columbia award); Children and Divorce (Chgo. Emmmy award) co-creator (with William Bell) The Young and the Restless CBS-TV daytime drama, 1973 (Emmy award); co-creator, exec. producer The Bold and the Beautiful, 1987—. Bd. dirs. United Cerebral Palsy, Chgo. Unlimited, Northwestern U. Hosp., Chgo. Heart Assn., Nat. Com. Prevention of Child Abuse, Mental Health Assn., Children's Home and Aid Soc., Salvation Army (L.A. bd. dirs.), Family Focus; mem. Chgo. Maternity Ctr.; life mem. Northwestern U. Bd. Trustees. Recipient 16 Chgo. Emmys; Top Favorite Female award TV Guide mag., 1956, Outstanding Woman of Radio and TV award McCall's mag., 1957-58, 65, bd. govs. award Chgo. chpt. Nat. Acad. TV Arts and Scis., 1977, William Booth award for community svc. Salvation Army, 1990; named Person of Yr. Broadcast Advt. Club, Chgo., 1980. Mem. Am. Women Radio and TV (Golden Mike award 1968, Broadcaster of Yr. 1993), Acad. TV Arts and Scis. (bd. dirs.), Chgo. chpt. Acad. TV Arts and Scis., Women's Athletic Club of Chgo., Comml. Club, Delta Delta Delta. Office: CBS c/o Bold and Beautiful 7800 Beverly Blvd Los Angeles CA 90036-2188 E-mail: dianemoss@boldandbeautiful.tv

BELL, LEO S. retired physician; b. Newark, Nov. 7, 1913; s. Alexander M. and Marie (Saxon) B.; m. Edith Lewis, July 3, 1938; children; Jewyl Linn, David Alden. AB, Syracuse U., 1934, MD, 1938. Diplomate Am. Bd. Pediatrics. Intern N.Y.C. Hosp., 1938, Bklyn. Hosp., 1939-40; resident Sea View Hosp., N.Y.C., 1940-41, N.Y.C. Hosp., 1941-42; pediatrician pvt. practice, San Mateo, Calif., 1946-84. Staff mem. Mills Meml. Hosp., San Mateo, Peninsula Hosp. & Med. Ctr., Burlingame, Children's Hosp., San Francisco; assoc. clin. prof. pediatrics U. Calif. Med. Sch., San Francisco; prof. clin. emeritus Stanford Med. Sch., Palo Alto; mem. curriculum & ednl. affairs com. U. San Francisco Med. Sch., adminstrv. coun. Columnist San Mateo Times; contbr. articles to profl. jours. Bd. dirs. Mills Hosp. Found., San Mateo, U. Calif. San Francisco Hosp., San Mateo County Heart Assn., Hillsborough Schs. Found. (Calif.), 1980-83. Capt. USAAF, 1942-46. Recipient bronze and silver medals Am. Heart Assn. Fellow Am. Acad. Pediatrics, Am. Pub. Health Assn.; mem. AMA (alt. del. to ho. of dels), U. Calif. San Francisco Clin. Faculty Assn. (pres.), Calif. Fedn. Pediatric Socs. (pres.), Am. Fedn. Pediatric Socs. (pres.), Calif. Med. Assn., Am. Pub. Health Assn., Air Force Assn., Calif. Med. Assn. (ho. of dels.), San Mateo County Med. Assn. (vice chmn. quality assurance com. San Mateo county health plan), Internat. Snuff Bottle Soc., Hong Kong Snuff Bottle Soc., San Francisco Gem and Mineral Soc., World Affairs Coun. San Francisco, U. San Francisco Med. Sch. Clin. Faculty Assn. (coun., pres.), Peninsula Golf & Country Club, Commonwealth Club. Home: 220 Roblar Ave Burlingame CA 94010-6846 Office: PO Box 1877 San Mateo CA 94401-0946

BELL, MAXINE TOOLSON, state legislator, librarian; b. Logan, Utah, Aug. 6, 1931; d. John Max and Norma (Watson) Toolson; m. H. Jack Bell, Oct. 26, 1949; children: Randy J. (dec.), Jeff M., Scott Alan (dec.). Assocs. in Libr. Sci., Coll. So. Idaho; CSI, Idaho State U., 1975. Librarian Sch. Dist. 261, Jerome, Idaho, 1975-88; mem. Idaho Ho. of Reps., 1988-. Bd. dirs. Idaho Farm Bur., 1976-77; rep. western states Am. Farm Bur. Women, 1990-93, vice chmn., 1993—; vice chmn. Am. Farm Bur., 1992—; mem. Jerome County Rep. PRecinct Com., 1980-88. Home: 194 S 300 E Jerome ID 83338-6532

BELL, STOUGHTON, computer scientist, mathematician, educator; b. Waltham, Mass., Dec. 20, 1923; s. Conrad and Florence Emily (Ross) B.; m. Mary Carroll O'Connell, Feb. 26, 1949 (div. 1960); children: Karen, Mark; m. Laura Joan Bainbridge, May 24, 1963 (div. 1979); children: Nathaniel Stoughton, Joshua Bainbridge. Student, Harvard U., 1946-49; A.B., U. Calif., Berkeley, 1950, M.A., 1953, Ph.D., 1955. Mem. staff Sandia Corp., Albuquerque, 1955-66, div. supr., 1964-66; vis. lectr. U. N.Mex., 1957-66, dir. computing center, 1966-79, assoc. prof. math., 1966-71, prof. math. and computer sci., 1971-92; prof. emeritus, 1992—. Vis. lectr. N.Mex. Acad. Scis., 1965— ; nat. lectr. Assn. for Computing Machinery, 1972-74 Co-author: Linear Analysis and Generalized Functions, 1965, Introductory Calculus, 1966, Modern University Calculus, 1966, Mathelatical Analysis for Modeling, 1999. Served with AUS, 1943-44. Mem. Assn. for Computing Machinery, Am. Math. Soc., Math. Assn. Am., Soc. Indsl. and Applied Math., Am. Statis. Assn., Ops. Research Soc. Am. Office: U NMex Computer Sci Dept Albuquerque NM 87131-0001 E-mail: sto@cs.unml.edu

BELL, W. DONALD, electronics company executive; BSEE, U. AL. V.p., sales and mktg. Texas Instruments; pres and CEO Electronic Arrays (now NEC Microelectronics); sr. vp memory & microprocessors, mktg. v.p., exec. v.p. Am. Microsystems Inc.; exec. V.P. Kierulff Electronics, 1980-81, pres., 1981-86; pres and COO Docummun, Inc., 1986-88; pres., CEO, chmn. Bell Microproducts, San Jose, CA, 1988—. Mem. bd. dir. Sand Hill Capital, Eng. Leadership Bd. for the U. of AL. Disting. Eng. Fellow of U of AL. Office: Bell Microproducts 1941 Ringwood Ave San Jose CA 95131-1721

BELLAH, ROBERT NEELLY, sociologist, educator; b. Altus, Okla., Feb. 23, 1927; s. Luther Hutton and Lillian Lucille (Neelly); m. Melanie Hyman, Aug. 17, 1949; 4 children. BA, Harvard U., 1950, PhD, 1955. Rsch. assoc. Inst. Islamic Studies, McGill U., Montreal, Can., 1955-57; with Harvard U., Cambridge, Mass., 1957-67, prof., 1966-67; mem. faculty dept. sociology U. Calif., Berkeley, 1967-97, Elliott prof. emeritus, 1997—. Author: Tokugawa Religion, 1957, Beyond Belief, 1970, The Broken Covenant, 1975 (Sorokin award Am. Sociol. Assn. 1976), (with Charles Y. Glock) The New Religious Consciousness, 1976, (with Phillip E. Hammond) Varieties of Civil Religion, 1980, (with others) Habits of the Heart, 1985, (with others) The Good Society, 1991. With U.S. Army, 1945-46. Fulbright fellow, 1960-61; recipient Harbison award Danforth Found., 1971, Nat. Humanities medal, 2000. Mem. Am. Acad. Arts and Scis., Am. Sociol. Assn., Am. Acad. Religion, Am. Philos. Soc. Episcopalian. Office: U Calif Dept Sociology Berkeley CA 94720-1980

BELLAMY, PAUL, communications executive; CEO, COO, CFO healthcare, electronics and energy cos.; CEO Esquire Comms. Ltd., San Diego, 1999—. Office: Esquire Comm Ltd 750 B St Ste 2350 San Diego CA 92101

BELLARDO, BRIAN, lawyer; b. 1949; BA, Yale U.; JD, Stanford U. Bar: Calif., 1975. V.p., assoc. gen. counsel The Charles Schwab Corp., San Francisco. Mem. ABA. Office: Charles Schwab Corp 101 Montgomery St San Francisco CA 94104-4122

BELLER, GERALD STEPHEN, professional magician, former insurance company executive; b. Phila., Aug. 6, 1935; s. Nathan and Adelaide B. (Goldfarb) B.; m. Nancy R. Nelson, June 8, 1968; children: Fay A., Mark S., Royce W., Merrilee A., Marie A., Frank A. CLU, Am. Coll., Bryn Mawr, Pa., 1972. Spl. agt. Prudential Ins. Co., San Bernardino, Calif., 1959-62, div. mgr., 1962-66; agy. supr. Aetna Life & Casualty, L.A., 1966-69, gen. agt., 1969-77; rsch. analyst Investigative Svcs. Bur. San Bernadino County Sheriff's Dept., 1991-95; capt. specialized svcs. bur. San Bernardino County (Calif.) Sheriff's Dept.; profl. magician, 1982—. Mem. Magician Magic Castle, Hollywood, Calif. Mem. sheriff's coun. San Bernardino County Sheriff's Dept., Apple Valley sheriff's adv. bd. Served with USAF, 1953-57. Recipient Man of Year award, 1961; Manpower Builders award, 1966-69; Agy. Builders award, 1970-72; Pres.'s Trophy award, 1973-74 Mem. Am. Soc. CLUs, Golden Key Soc., Internat. Exec. Svc. Corps. (vol.), Acad. Magical Arts, Internat. Brotherhood of Magicians (Outstanding Magic Lectr. of Yr. 1989-90, Aldini Meml. award 1990), Soc. Am. Magicians. Home: 20625 Tonawanda Rd Apple Valley CA 92307-5736

BELLES, DONALD ARNOLD, pastoral therapist, mental health counselor; b. Sayre, Pa., Mar. 7, 1948; s. William and Alice (Arnold) B.; m. Linda Scheel, July 9, 1981. BA, St. Martin's U., 1973; MDiv, Fuller Theol. Sem., 1977; PhD, Calif. Grad. Sch. Theology, 1981; MBA, City U. Bellevue, 1994; postgrad., Seattle Pacific U., 1997—. Lic. amateur radio operator; ordained to ministry Worldwide Congl. Fellowship, 1989; cert. c.c. tchr., Calif., mental health counselor, Wash., profl. stage hypnotist. Chaplain Vols. of Am., L.A., 1976-78; therapist Greater life Found., Seattle, 1979-81; industrial engr. commercial airplane divsn. Boeing, 1979-80, program planner aerospace divsn., 1980-86, sr., lead program planner electronics divsn., 1986-89, systems analyst, contract tech. mgr., 1989-92, analyst software engring. practices, mgr. total quality improvement project, 1992-95, lead, mgr. computing infrastructure archtl. design team, 1995-98, sr. analyst/architect IT/bus. sys. integration, 1998—; therapist, dir. clinic Creative Therapies, Seattle, 1982-83; clin. dir. Applied Hypnosis, Tacoma, 1984-87; dir. Active Therapy Assoc., Tacoma, 1988-89; dean of students Coll. Therapeutic Hypnosis, Puyallup, Wash., 1989-93. Cons. theological issues, abduction rsch., psychic phenomena, paranormal events; adult edn. instr. Tacoma C.C., 1987-88, Pierce Coll., 1990-92; mem. U.S. Acad. Team to CIS, U. St. Petersburg, Russia, 1994; presenter, lectr. in field; instr. Olympia Diocese Sch. of Theology, 1995; adv. bd. mem. Software Support Profls. Orgn.; cons. Wash. State Offices Supr. of Pub. Instrn.; mem. faculty U. Phoenix, 1999—. Contbr. articles to profl. jours., prodr. hypnosis, mental health videos in field. Exec. dir. Nat. Assn. to Prevent and Eliminate Child Abuse, Tacoma, 1987-89; active Light of the Hill Ch. Maj. U.S. Army, 1969-75, USAR, 1975-92. Fellow Am. Assn. Profl. Hypnotherapists; mem. Nat. Assn. Clergy Hypnotherapists (bd. dirs. 1987-88, editor jour. 1987), Internat. Med. Dental Hypnotherapy Assn., Wash. State Head Injury Found. Avocations: backpacking, swimming, reading, amateur radio. E-mail: dbelles@technologist.com

BELLEVILLE, PHILIP FREDERICK, lawyer; b. Flint, Mich., Apr. 24, 1934; s. Frederick Charles and Sarah (Adelaine) B.; m. Geraldean Bickford, Sept. 2, 1953; children— Stacy L., Philip Frederick II, Jeffrey A. BA in Econs. with high distinction and honors, U. Mich., 1956, J.D., 1960, MS in Psychology CCU, 1997. Bar: Calif. 1961. Assoc. Latham & Watkins, LA., 1960-68, ptnr. L.A. and Newport Beach, Calif., 1968-98, chmn. litigation dept., 1973-80, ptnr. L.A., Newport Beach, San Diego, Washington, 1980-98, Chgo., 1983-98, N.Y.C., 1985-98, London and San Francisco, 1990-98, Moscow, 1992-98, Hong Kong, 1995-98, Tokyo, 1995-98, Singapore, 1997-98, Silicon Valley, 1997-98. Asst. editor Mich. Law Rev., Ann Arbor, 1959-60 Past mem. So. Calif. steering com. NAACP Legal Def. Fund, Inc., L.A.; mem. cmty. adv. bd. San Pedro Peninsula Hosp., Calif., 1980-88; mem. Harbor Interfaith Bd. James B. Angell scholar U. Mich., 1955-56 Mem. ABA (antitrust and trade regulation and bus. law sects.), L.A. County Bar Assn. (bus. trial lawyers sect.), Assn. Bus. Trial Lawyers, Order of Coif, Portuguese Bend (Calif.) Club, Palos Verdes (Calif.) Golf Club, Caballeros, Phi Beta Kappa, Phi Kappa Phi, Alpha Kappa Psi. Republican. Avocations: antique and classic autos, public service, sports, art, antiques. Office: Latham & Watkins 633 W 5th St Ste 4000 Los Angeles CA 90071-2005

BELLUZZO, RICHARD E. former computer company executive; BS in Acctg., Golden Gate State U. Acctg. positions disk memory divsn. Hewlett-Packard Co., exec. and mgmt. positions printer and peripherals ops., exec. v.p., gen. mgr. computer orgn.; chmn., CEO Silicon Graphics, Inc., 1998-99. Bd. dirs. Proxima Corp. Office: 2011 N Shoreline Blvd Mountain View CA 94043-1342

BELNAP, DAVID F. journalist; b. Ogden, Utah, July 27, 1922; s. Hyrum Adolphus and Lois Ellen B.; m. Barbara Virginia Carlberg, Jan. 17, 1947. Student, Weber Coll., Ogden, 1940. Asst. city editor Seattle Star, 1945-47; bur. chief UP Assns., Helena, Mont., 1947-50, Honolulu, 1950-52; regional exec. Pacific N.W., 1952-55, dir. Latin Am. services, 1955-67; Latin Am. corr. L.A. Times, 1967-80, asst. fgn. news editor, 1980-93. Recipient Overseas Press Club Am. award for best article on Latin Am., 1970, Maria Moors Cabot prize, 1973 Mem. Overseas Press Club Am., Greater Los Angeles Press Club, Audiophile Soc. Clubs: Am. of Buenos Aires; Phoenix of Lima (Peru). Home and Office: 1134 W Huntington Dr Arcadia CA 91007-6308

BELSON, PATRICIA A. artist; b. San Francisco, Apr. 5, 1932; d. Joseph Patrick and Norma Stephanie (Bole) Gleeson; m. Dogan E. Belson, Sept. 2, 1961 (dec. July 1991); children: Linda, Susan. Office mgr. Psychiat. Group Offices, Seattle, 1958-63; pub. rels., brochure designer, English sec. Istanbul Hilton Hotel, Turkey, 1963-64; office mgr. Psychiat. Outpatient Facility, San Francisco, 1973-76; owner Wadyacallit, Sequim, Wash., 1980-85; corp. ptnr., mktg. dir. Fantasy Prodns., Inc., Seattle, 1985-90; self employed fine artist Seattle, Sequim, 1990—. Vol. treas. Blue Whole Gallery, Sequim, 1997—98; charter mem. Artist's Coop., 1997—99, 2001—. Solo exhbns. include Istanbul (Turkey) Intercontinental Hotel, 1978, Galerie du Soleil, Sequim, 1996, Gallery at the Fifth, Sequim, 2000; exhbns. include Bechtel Corp., 1976 (3d place award), A Contemporary Theater Gallery, Seattle, 1992, Juan de Fuca Festival of Arts, 1994, (hon. mention), Clallam Art League, Port Angeles, 1994 (2d place watercolor), 95, Northwest Watercolor Soc., 1994 (hon. mention), Juan de Fuca Festival Arts, 1995 (1st place watercolor), Clallam Art League Sr. Show, 1995 (Best of Show award), 98 (Best Still life winner), 1999 (Best Seascape), Sequim Arts Mem. Show, 1997 (1st place mems. choice, 2d place pub. choice), Blue Whole Gallery, Sequim, 1997-99, Olympic Nat. Resource Ctr. U. Washington, Forks, 1997-2000, Clallam Art League Gallery, 1999—, Frye Art Museum, Seattle, 2000; also pvt. galleries, Calif., Hawaii, Oreg. and Washington, others. Vol. tourist info. ctr. Sequim/Dungeness Valley C. of C., 1994-96; pub. rels. vol. Sequim Arts, 1996-97; vol. tutor Seattle Sch. Dist., 1991-92; vol. Sequim Arts Treas., 1997-99. Recipient Best of Show award Clallam Art League Sr. Show, 1995, 1st Pl. Sequim Arts Mem. Show, 1995, Best Seascape award Clallam Sr. Show, 1999, Daler-Rowney Mdse. award N.W. Watercolor Soc., 2000. Avocations: sailing, canoeing, tennis, skiing, hiking. Home: 101 Wilcox Ln Sequim WA 98382-8904 E-mail: pen4pat2@hotmail.com

BELTRÁN, ANTHONY NATALICIO, non-commissioned officer, deacon; b. Flagstaff, Ariz., Aug. 17, 1938; s. Natalicio Torres and Mary Mercedes (Sandoval) B.; m. Patricia Emily Cañez, Nov. 18, 1962; children: Geralyn P., Bernadette M., Albert A., Catherine M., Elizabeth R., Michael J., Theresa R., Christopher M. AA, Phoenix Jr. Coll., 1971, C.C. of Air Force, 1992; grad., Def. Equal Oppty. Mgmt. Inst., 1991. Gen. clk. Blue Cross Blue Shield, Phoenix, 1958-61; enlisted Air N.G., advanced through ranks to chief master sgt.; unit clk. Ariz. Air N.G., Phoenix, 1961, personnel technician, 1962-65, adminstrv. supr., 1965-81, support services supr., 1981-88, equal employment specialist, 1988-95, state sr. enlisted advisor, 1995-98, ret., 1998. With St. Matthew Cath. Ch., Phoenix. Bd. dirs. Friendly House, Phoenix, 1982-86, mem. aux. bd., 1989-97; mem. Alma de la Gente, Phoenix, 1982-92, Chiefs Police Cmty. Adv. Group, Phoenix, 1984-85, Mayor's Task Force on Juvenile Crime, Phoenix, 1979-81; pres. IMAGE de Phoenix, 1985-87. Staff sgt. USAF, 1961-62. Recipient Community Service award Phoenix C. of C., 1982. Mem. Fed. Exec. Assn. (sec., treas. Phoenix chpt. 1985-86, 1st v.p. 1987, pres. 1987-88, Community Svc. award 1986), Am. GI Forum (sec. Sylvestre Herrera chpt. 1995-96, comdr. 1996—, state comdr. 2000—), Ariz. Hispanic Employment Program Mgrs. (treas. 1980-81, v.p. 1981-82, pres. 1982-84, named Outstanding Mem. of Yr. 1981, 83), Enlisted Assn. N.G. Ariz. (pres. Copperhead chpt. 1987-90), Non-Commd. Officers Acad. Grad. Assn. (chpt. 46 v.p. 1992-94), Ariz. ANG Copperhead Retiree Assn. (v.p. 2000—). Democrat. Avocations: permanent Deacon Roman Cath. Diocese assigned to ministry for the Spanish speaking. Home: 4109 W Monte Vista Rd Phoenix AZ 85009-2005 also: St Matthew Cath Ch 320 N 20th Dr Phoenix AZ 85009-3819

BELZBERG, SAMUEL, investment professional; b. Calgary, Alta., Can., June 26, 1928; s. Abraham and Hinda (Fishman) B.; m. Frances Cooper; children: Cheryl Rae, Marc David, Wendy Jay, Lisa. B.Comm., U. Alta., Edmonton, 1948. Chmn. Balfour Holdings, Inc., 1992-97; pres. 1st City Fin. Corp. Ltd., Vancouver, B.C., Can., 1970-83, 86-91, chmn. Can., 1983-91; pres. Gibralt Capital Corp., Vancouver, 1995—, Bel-Fran US Inc., 1997—. Bd. dirs. e-Sim Ltd., Versaware Techs., Ltd., Westminster Capital, Inc., Metromedia Asia Corp., Bar Equipment of Am. Home: 3711 Alexandra St Vancouver BC Canada V6J 4C3 Office: 1177 W Hastings St Ste 2000 Vancouver BC Canada V6E 2K3

BEN-ASHER, M. DAVID, physician; b. Newark, June 18, 1931; s. Samuel Irving and Dora Ruth (Kagan)B.; m. Bryna S. Zeller, Nov. 22, 1956 BA, Syracuse U., 1952; MD, U. Buffalo Sch. Med., 1956. Intern E.J. Meyer Mem. Hosp., Buffalo, 1956-57; resident Jersey City Med. Ctr., 1957-58; asst. chief med. service U.S. Army Hosp., Ft. McPherson, Ga., 1958-60; resident Madigan Gen. Hosp., Tacoma, 1960-62; chief gen. med. service Walson Army Hosp., Ft. Dix, N.Y., 1962-64; attending staff St. Mary's Hosp., Tucson, 1964—; pvt. practice Tucson, 1964—. Bd. dirs. Tucson Symphony, 1971-73; mem. Ariz. State Bd. Med. Examiners, 1978-88, joint bd. for regulation of physicians' assts., 1990-97; bd. trustees United Synagogue Am., 1981-87, nat. adv. bd., 1987-91. Fellow ACP; mem. AMA, Pima County Med. Soc. (bd. dirs. 1971-77, pres. 1976), Ariz. Med. Assn., Am. Soc. Nephrology. Democrat. Avocations:health club, music, computers. Home: 3401 N Tanuri Dr Tucson AZ 85750-6735 Office: So Ariz Med Specialists 4711 N 1st Ave Tucson AZ 85718-5610

BENBOW, RICHARD ADDISON, psychological counselor; b. Las Vegas, Dec. 27, 1949; s. Jules Coleman and Bonnie Ray B. BBA, U. Nev., 1972, MS in Counseling, 1974; AAS in Bus. Mgmt. & Real Estate, Clark County C.C., 1980; PhD in Clin. Psychology, U. Humanistic Studies, 1986. Cert. tchr., Nev.; cert. clin. mental health counselor, secondary sch. counselor, Nev., substance abuse counselor, Nev., substance abuse program adminstr., Nev.; nat. cert. counselor. Jud. svcs. officer Mcpl. Ct. City of Las Vegas, 1983-88, pretrial program coord., 1988—. Inmate classification technician Detention and Correctional Svcs., 1982-83; stress mgmt. cons. Mem. biofeedback Soc. Am., Assn. Humanistic Psychology, Nat. Assn. Psychotherapists, Am. Counseling Assn., Am. Mental Health Counselors Assn., Am. Acad. Crisis Interveners, Jr. C. of C., U.S. Jaycees (presdl. award of honor 1978-79), Delta Sigma Phi. Democrat. Christian Scientist.

BENDER, BYRON WILBUR, linguistics educator; b. Roaring Spring, Pa., Aug. 14, 1929; s. Ezra Clay and Gertrude Magdalene (Kauffman) B.; m. Lois Marie Graber, Aug. 25, 1950; children: Susan Alice, Sarah Marie, Catherine Anne, Judith Lee, John Richard. BA, Goshen Coll., 1949; MA, Ind. U., 1950, PhD, 1963. Edn. specialist Trust Terr. of Pacific Islands, Majuro, Marshall Island, 1953-59, Saipan, Marianas Island, 1962-64; asst. prof. Goshen (Ind.) Coll., 1960-62; assoc. prof. linguistics U. Hawaii at Manoa, Honolulu, 1964-69, prof., 1969-99, chmn. dept., 1969-95, prof. emeritus, 2000—. Bd. dirs. U. Hawaii Profl. Assembly, Honolulu, 1978-88, 92-98, pres., 1982-88. Author: Spoken Marshallese, 1969, Linguistic Factors in Maori Education, 1971, (with others) Marshallese-English Dictionary, 1976; editor Oceanic Linguistics Spl. Publs., 1965—, Studies in Micronesian Linguistics, 1984, Oceanic Linguistics, 1991—; mng. editor Oceanic Linguistics, 1965-90. Trustee Hawaii Pub. Employees Health Fund Bd., 1987-95. Recipient Merit awards U. Hawaii 1971, 76, 86. Mem. NEA (standing com. higher edn. 1985-89), Linguistic Soc. Am. (dir. Linguistic Inst. summer 1977, program com. 1987-89, parliamentarian 1994-97). Mem. Soc. of Friends. Home: Apt 1504 6710 Hawaii Kai Dr Honolulu HI 96825-1559 Office: U Hawaii Dept Linguistics 1890 E West Rd Honolulu HI 96822-2318 E-mail: bender@hawaii.edu

BENDER, CHARLES WILLIAM, lawyer; b. Cape Girardeau, Mo., Oct. 2, 1935; s. Walter William and Fern Evelyn (Stroud) B.; m. Carolyn Percy Gavagan, June 20, 1961 (div. 1983); children: Theodore Marten, Christopher Percy; m. Betty Lou Port, May 5, 1983; stepchildren: Courtney Elizabeth, Cameron Ann. AB magna cum laude, Harvard U., 1960, LLB magna cum laude, 1963. Bar: Calif. 1965, U.S. Dist. Ct. (cen. dist.) Calif. 1965, U.S. Ct. Appeals (9th cir.) 1969, U.S. Supreme Ct. 1979, D.C. 1984. Assoc. O'Melveny & Myers, Los Angeles, 1965-71, ptnr., 1972-84, mng. ptnr., 1984-92; chmn., 1993—. Editor Harvard U. Law Rev., 1961-62, articles editor, 1962-63. Advisor campaign Alan Cranston for Senator, Calif., 1968, 74, 80; mgr. campaign Jess Unruh for Gov., Calif., 1970; trustee Los Angeles Legal Aid Found., 1971, Lawyers' Com. for Civil Rights Under Law, Washington, 1985—. Served with U.S. Army, 1956-57. Sheldon Traveling fellow Harvard U., 1963-64. Mem. ABA, Calif. Bar Assn., Los Angeles Bar Assn. Democrat. Home: 2831 The Strand Hermosa Beach CA 90254-2400 Office: O'Melveny & Myers 400 S Hope St Los Angeles CA 90071-2899

BENDER, DEAN, public relations executive; Ptnr. Bender/Helper Impact (formerly Bender, Goldman & Helper), L.A. Office: Bender/Helper Impact 11500 W Olympic Blvd Ste 655 Los Angeles CA 90064-1530

BENDER, JOHN C. paper company executive; BS, U.S. Naval Acad.; MSA, George Washington U. Indsl. engr. timer and wood products divsn. Boise Cascade Corp., Yakima, Wash., 1969, v.p. opers. Boise, sr. v.p. bldg. products, 1999—. Office: Boise Cascade Corp 1111 W Jefferson St Boise ID 83728-0071

BENDER, MICHAEL LEE, state supreme court justice; b. N.Y.C., Jan. 7, 1942; s. Louis and Jean (Waterman) B.; m. Judith Jones, Feb. 27, 1967 (div. Mar. 1977); children: Jeremy, Aviva; m. Helen H. Hand, Sept. 10, 1977; children: Maryjean Hand-Bender, Tess Hand-Bender, Benjamin Hand-Bender. BA in Philosophy, Dartmoutn Coll., 1964; JD, U. Colo., 1967. Bar: Colo. 1967, D.C. 1967, U.S. Supreme Ct. 1980. Pub. defender City and County Denver, 1968-71; assoc. regional atty. EEOC, 1974-75; supr. atty. Jefferson County Pub. Defender, 1975-77; divsn. chief Denver Pub. Defender, Denver, 1977-78; atty. Gibson, Dunn & Crutcher, L.A., 1979-80; ptnr. Bender & Treece P.C., Denver, 1983-93; pres., shareholder Michael L. Bender PC, 1993-97; also pres. Bender & Treece P.C.; state supreme ct. justice Colo. Supreme Ct., 1997—. Adj. faculty U. Denver Coll. Law, 1981-86, chair. ABA Criminal Justice sect., Washington, 1990-91, NACD Lawyers Assistant Com., 1989-90; dir. Nat. Assn. Criminal Def. Lawyers, 1984-90; mem. practitioner's adv. com. U.S. Sentencing Com., 1990-91; mem. com. for Criminal Justice Act for Dist. Colo. U.S. Dist. Ct., 1991-93, domestic rels. reform com.; liason mem. Colo. Pub. Edn. com., Ct. Svcs., 1998—, atty. regulation adv. com., 1998-99; co-chair civil justice com. Supreme Ct., 1998—. Contbr. articles to profl. jours. Bd. govs. Colo. Bar, 1989-91. Recipient Fireman award Colo. State Pub., 1990; Robert C. Heeney Meml. award Nat. Assn. Criminal Def. Lawyers, 1990; named Vol. of Yr. Denver Bar Assn., 1988. Mem. Colo. Bar Assn. (ethics com. 1980—), ABA (chair criminal justice sect. 1990-91, criminal justice standards com. 1997—). Democrat. Jewish. Avocations: aerobics, skiing, bicycling, camping. Office: Colo Supreme Ct State Jud Bldg 2 E 14th Ave Fl 4 Denver CO 80203-2115

BENDER, RICHARD, university dean, architect, educator; b. N.Y.C., Jan. 19, 1930; s. Edward and Betty (Okun) B.; m. Sue Rosenfeld, Aug. 9, 1956; children: Michael, David. BCE, CCNY, 1951; MArch, Harvard U., 1956. Architect Walter Gropius, 1951-53, William Lescaze, 1958-60; with Town Planning Assocs., N.Y.C., 1960-66, ptnr., 1961-66, prin., 1966—; pvt. practice Berkeley, 1966—. Lectr. Columbia U., N.Y.C., 1957-60; asst. prof. Cooper Union, 1961; prof. architecture U. Calif., Berkeley, 1969—, chmn. dept., 1974-76; vis. prof. urban design and constrn., endowed vis.

chair U. Tokyo, 1989—; dir. bldg. rsch. bd. Nat. Acad. Sci., 1974-80, mem. adv. bd. on the built environment; adv. panels HUD, Nat. Endowment Arts; mem. design rev. bd. City of San Francisco, U. Calif., J.P. Getty Trust; cons. univ campus planning U. Calif., Berkeley, 1972—, U. Calif., San Diego, 1987-90, U. Calif., Davis, 1989-93, U. Calif., Santa Cruz, 1992-96, U. Calif., Merced, 2000—, master plan Benesse Inst. of Arts, Naoshima Island, Japan, 1993—, master plan for MediaPolis, Taipei, Taiwan, 1997—, master plan for New Town Cergy-Pontoise, France, 1993—. Author: A Crack in the Rearview Mirror, 1973. Bd. dirs. Bridge Housing, San Francisco, 1980—; trustee Mills Coll., 1993-98. With U.S. Army, 1954-55. Home: 804 Santa Barbara Rd Berkeley CA 94707-2018 Office: U Calif Coll Environ Design Berkeley CA 94720-0001

BENDIX, HELEN IRENE, lawyer; b. N.Y.C., July 24, 1952; d. Gerhard Max and Eva Gabriela (Sternberger) B.; m. John A. Kronstadt, Nov. 29, 1974; children: Jessica Claire Kronstadt, Erik Bendix Kronstadt, Nicola Eva Kronstadt. BA, Cornell U., 1973; JD, Yale U., 1976. Bar: Calif. 1976, D.C. 1978, U.S. Dist. Ct. D.C. 1980, U.S. Dist. Ct. (ctrl. dist.) Calif. 1986, U.S. Ct. Appeals (D.C. cir.) 1981, U.S. Ct. Appeals (9th cir.) 1987, U.S. Dist. Ct. (so. dist.) Calif. 1990. Law clk. to Hon. Shirley M. Hufstedler U.S. Ct. Appeals (9th cir.), L.A., 1976-77; assoc. Wilmer Cutler & Pickering, Washington, 1977-79; asst. prof. law UCLA, 1979-80; from assoc. to ptnr. Leva Hawes Symington Martin & Oppenheimer, Washington, 1980-85; of counsel Gibson Dunn & Crutcher, L.A., 1986-89; ptnr. Heller Ehrman White & McAuliffe, L.A., 1989-96; sr. v.p., gen. counsel KCET Cmty. TV of So. Calif., 1996—; judge Mcpl. Ct. L.A. Jud. Dist., 1997-2000, Superior Ct. L.A., 2000—. Vis. prof. law UCLA, 1985-86. Co-author: Moore's Federal Practice, Vols. X and XI, 1976, Vols. XII and XIII, 1979; contbr. articles to profl. jours. Violinist Palisades Symphony, Pacific Palisades, Calif., 1989—. Mem. D.C. Bar Assn., Calif. State Bar Assn. (chairperson internat. law sect. 1990-91), Calif. Judges Assn., L.A. County Bar Assn. (past pres. dispute resolution svcs.), Jud. Coun. Calif. (mem. ad hoc com. on canon 6D 1998, working group on mediator ethics 2000, mem. access and fairness adv. com.), Nat. Charity League (past chmn. 12th grade class), Chancery Club, Phi Beta Kappa. Office: Dept 18 111 N Hill St Los Angeles CA 90012-3014 E-mail: hbendix@lasc.co.la.ca.us

BEN-DOR, GISSELLE, conductor, musician; b. Montevideo, Uruguay; came to U.S., 1982; m. Eli Ben-Dor; children: Roy, Gabriel. Student, Acad. of Music, Tel Aviv; artist diploma, Rubin Acad. Music, Tel Aviv; M, Yale Sch. of Music, 1982. Music dir. Annapolis Symphony, Md., Pro Arte Chamber Orch. of Boston; condr. Norwalk (Conn.) Youth Symphony; conducting fellow L.A. Philharm. Inst., 1984, Tanglewood Music Ctr., 1985; resident condr. Houston Symphony, 1991; music dir. Santa Barbara Symphony, Calif., 1994—. Resident condr. Houston Symphony; condr. variety conducting activities including prestigious summer festivals, competitions, 1983-87, Hungarian Nat. Symphony, Budapest Philharm., others; guest condr. orchs. in Uruguay, Ea. Europe, Israel and U.S. including Barvarian Radio Orch., Boston POPS, New World Symphony, Women's Philharm, San Francisco, Minn. Orch. in Summerfest Festival, 1986, N.Y. Philharm., 1993, 95, Orquestra del Teatro Nacional, Brazil, Ulster Orch., Israel Philharm., 1991, Carnegie Hall, 1991, others; past music dir. Houston Youth Symphony; past acting orch. dir. Shepherd Sch. Music Rice U.; music dir. Boston ProArte Chamber Orch., Annapolis Symphony. Condr. Israel Philharm. Orch. (play) The Rite of Spring; recs. with London Symphony, Israel Chamber Orch., (CD) London Symphony Orch., Sofia Soloists, Boston ProArte Chamber Orch.; numerous TV appearances. Am.-Israel Cultural Found scholar, Frances Wickes scholar; Leonard Bernstein fellow; recipient Bartók prize Hungarian TV Internat. Condrs. Competition, 1986. Office: Santa Barbara Symphony Orch Arlington Theatre 1900 State St Ste G Santa Barbara CA 93101-8424 also: Del Rosenfield Assoc 714 Ladd Rd Bronx NY 10471-1204 E-mail: delrosdra@aol.com

BENEDICT, BURTON, retired museum director, anthropology educator; b. Balt., May 20, 1923; s. Burton Eli Oppenheim and Helen Blanche (Deiches) B.; m. Marion MacColl Steuber, Sept. 23, 1950; children: Helen, Barbara MacVean AB cum laude, Harvard U., 1949; PhD, U. London, 1954. Sr. rsch. fellow Inst. Islamic Studies, McGill U., Montreal, Que., Can., 1954-55; sociol. rsch. officer Colonial Office, London and Mauritius, 1955-58; sr. lectr. social anthropology London Sch. Econs., 1958-68; prof. anthropology U. Calif., Berkeley, 1968-91, prof. emeritus, 1991—, chmn. dept., 1970-71, dean social scis., 1971-74, dir. Hearst Mus. Anthropology, 1989-94; dir. emeritus Hearst Mus. Anthropology, 1994—. Dir. U. Calif. Study Ctr. for U.K. and Ireland, London, 1986-88 Author: Indians in a Plural Society, 1961; author and editor: Problems of Smaller Territories, 1967, (with M. Benedict) Men, Women & Money in Seychelles, 1982, The Anthropology of World's Fairs, 1983; contbr. numerous articles to profl. jours. Trustee East Bay Zool. Soc. Sgt. USAF, 1942-46. Recipient Western Heritage award Nat. Cowboy Hall of Fame, 1984; rsch. fellow Colonial Office, 1955-58, 60, U. Calif., Berkeley, 1974-75; grantee NEH, 1981-83. Fellow Royal Anthrop. Inst. (mem. coun. 1962-65, 67-68, 86-89), Am. Anthrop. Assn.; mem. Assn. Social Anthropologists of Brit. Commonwealth, Athenaeum Club (London) Avocations: museums, zoos, bird watching, postcards, world's fairs. Office: U Calif Berkeley Dept Anthropology Berkeley CA 94720-0001

BENET, LESLIE ZACHARY, pharmacokineticist, educator; b. Cin., May 17, 1937; s. Jonas John and Esther Racie (Hirschfeld) B.; m. Carol Ann Levin, Sept. 8, 1960; children: Reed Michael, Gillian Vivia. AB in English, U. Mich., 1959, BS in Pharmacy, 1960, MS in Pharm. Chemistry, 1962; PhD in Pharm. Chemistry, U. Calif., San Francisco, 1965; PharmD (hon.), Uppsala U., Sweden, 1987; PhD (hon.), Leiden U., The Netherlands, 1995; DSc (hon.), U. Ill., Chgo., 1997, Phila. Coll. Pharm. & Sci., , 1997, L.I. U., 1999. Asst. prof. pharmacy Wash. State U., Pullman, 1965-69; asst. prof. pharmacy and pharm. chemistry U. Calif., San Francisco, 1969-71, assoc. prof., 1971-76, prof., 1976—, vice chmn. dept. pharmacy, 1973-78, chmn. dept. pharmacy, 1978-96, dir. drug studies unit, 1977—, dir. drug kinetics and dynamics ctr., 1979-98, chmn. dept. biopharm. scis., 1996-98. Mem. pharmacology study sect. NIH, Washington, 1977-81, chmn., 1979-81, mem. pharmacol. scis. rev. com., 1984-88, chmn., 1986-88; mem. generic drugs adv. com. FDA, Washington, 1990-94, mem. Sci. Bd., 1992-98; chair external rev. com. CBER, 1998, chair expert panel on individual equivalence, 1998-2000; mem. sci. adv. bd. SmithKline Beecham Pharms., 1989-92, Pharmetrix, 1989-92, Alteon, Inc., 1993—, TheraTech, Inc., 1993-96, Roche Biosci., 1998—, Pain Therapeutics, Inc., 1999—, UMD, Inc., 1999—, Silico Insights, Inc., 2000—, InforMedix, 2001—; chmn. bd. AvMax, Inc., 1994—; bd. dirs. OxoN Medica, Inc., InforMedix, Inc., Josman Labs., Inc., Impax Pharmas., One World Health. Editor Jour. Pharmacokinetics and Biopharmaceutics, 1976-98; assoc. editor Pharmacology and Therapeutics, 1995-2000; mem. editl. bd. Pharmacology, 1979—, Pharmacy Internat., 1979-82, Pharm. Rsch., 1983-95, ISI Atlas of Sci.: Pharmacology, 1988-89, Pharm. News, 1994-98, AAPS PharmSci, 1999—, Chemistry and Pharm. Bull., 2000—, Molecular Interventions, 2000—, The Effect of Disease States on Drug Pharmacokinetics, 1976, Pharmacokinetic Basis for Drug Treatment, 1984, Pharmacokinetics: A Modern View, 1984, ISI Atlas of Sci.: Pharmacology, 1988-89, Integration of Pharmacokinetics, Pharmacodynamics and Toxicokinetics in Rational Drug Development, 1992, Clinical Applications of Mifepristone (RU486) and Other Antiprogestins, 1993; contbr. more than 400 articles to profl. jours. Appt. to Forum on Drug Devel. and Regulation, 1988. Fellow Acad. Pharm. Scis. (pres. 1985-86, chmn. basic pharmaceutics sect. 1976-77, mem.-at-large exec. com. 1979-80, [illegible] award 1982), AAAS (mem.-at-large exec. com. pharm. scis. sect. 1978-81, 91-95, chair 1996-97), Am. Assn. Pharm. Scientists (pres. 1986, treas. [illegible] 1988-93, Disting. Pharm. Scientist award 1989, Disting. Svc. award 1996, Wurster rsch. award in pharmaceutics 2000); mem. AAUP, Inst. Medicine NAS (forum on drug devel. and regulation 1988-94, chmn. com. on antiprogestins, 1993, membership com. 1994-97, chmn. other health professions sect. 1995-97, chmn. com. pharmacokinetics & drug interactions in elderly 1996-97, mem. Round Table R & D Drugs, Biologics & Med. Devices 1997-2000, bd. on health scis. policy 1999—), Am. Found. for Pharm. Edn. (bd. dirs. 1987—, Disting. Svc. "Profile" award 1993), Am. Coll. Clin. Pharmacology (Disting. Svc. award 1988), ISSX (councillor 1992-96, treas. 1998-99), Am. Pharm. Assn. (Higuchi Rsch. prize 2000), Am. Soc. Clin. Pharmacology and Therapeutics (Rawls-Palmer award and lectureship 1995), Am. Soc. for Pharmacology and Exptl. Therapeutics, Generic Pharm. Industry Assn. (mem. blue ribbon com. on generic medicines 1990), Internat. Pharm. Fedn. (bd. pharm. scis. 1988, chair 1996-2000, Host-Madsen medal 2001), Drug Info. Assn., Am. Coll. Clin. Pharmacy (therapeutic frontiers lectr. 1995), Am. Assn. Colls. Pharmacy (Volwiler Rsch. Achievement award 1991, pres. 1993-94, bd. dirs. 1992-95), Sigma Xi, Rho Chi (Ann. Lecture award 1990), Phi Lambda Sigma. Home: 601 Van Ness Ave Apt 451 San Francisco CA 94102-3259 Office: U Calif San Francisco Dept Biopharm Scis San Francisco CA 94143-0446 E-mail: benet@itsa.ucsf.edu

BENFIELD, JOHN RICHARD, surgeon, educator; b. Vienna, Austria, June 24, 1931; came to U.S., 1938, naturalized, 1945; s. Richard and Charlotte Lola Benfield; m. Joyce A. Cohler, Dec. 22, 1963; children: Richard L., Robert E., Nancy J. A.B., Columbia U., 1952; M.D., U. Chgo., 1955. Diplomate Am. Bd. Surgery, Am. Bd. Thoracic Surgery (bd. dirs. 1982-88). Intern Columbia-Presbyterian Hosp., N.Y.C., 1955-56; E.H. Andrews fellow in thoracic surgery U. Chgo., 1956-57; chief resident and instr. in surgery U. Chgo. Clinics, 1962-64, resident in surgery, 1956-57, 59-63; asst. prof. surgery U. Wis., 1964-67; asst. prof. UCLA, 1967-69, assoc. prof., 1969-73, prof., 1973-77, clin. prof., 1978-88; prof. surgery, chief cardiothoracic surgery, vice chmn. surgery U. Calif. Davis Med. Ctr., Sacramento, 1988-95, prof. surgery, chief thoracic surgery, 1995-98, prof. emeritus, 1998—; attending surgeon V.A. Martinez Med. Ctr., 1988-98; courtesy staff Kaiser Permanente Med. Ctr., Sacramento, 1988-98. James Utley prof. surgery, chmn. dept. surgery Boston U., 1977; chmn. surgery City of Hope Nat. Med. Ctr., Duarte, Calif., 1978-87; bd. dirs. Am. Bd. Thoracic Surgery, 1982-88; cons. U.S. Naval Med. Ctr., San Diego, 1968-88; mem. sr. staff VA Wadsworth Med. Ctr., L.A., 1978-88. Editor Current Problems in Cancer, 1975-86; mem. editl. bd. Annals Thoracic Surgery, 1979-2001, assoc. editor, 1987-2001; mem. editl. bd. Annals Surg. Oncology, 1994-2000; contbr. articles to prof. jours., chpts. to books. Sec., trustee Univ. Synagogue, Los Angeles. Served as capt. M.C. U.S. Army, 1957-59, Korea. Grantee Life Ins. Med. Rsch., 1962-66, Am. Heart Assn., 1968-71; USPHS, 1971-92. Mem. ACS (bd. govs. 1982-88, 92-98), Am. Surg. Assn., Am. Assn. Thoracic Surgery, Am. Assn. Cancer Rsch., Am. Med. Writers Assn., Internat. Assn. Study Lung Cancer, Internat. Soc. Surgery, Calif. Med. Soc., Ctrl. Surg. Assn., L.A. Acad. Medicine, The Royal Soc. Medicine (Gt. Britain), The Transplantation Soc., Soc. Thoracic Surgeons (v.p. 1994-95, pres. 1995-96), Soc. Univ. Surgeons, Pacific Coast Surg. Assn. (v.p. 1995-96), Soc. Surg. Oncology, Am. Coll. Chest Physicians (pres. Calif. chpt. 1996-97), Western Thoracic Surgeons Assn. (pres. 1989-90), Internat. Surg. Soc., Thoracic Surgery Dirs. Assn. (pres. 1995-97). E-mail: jbenfield@verizon.net

BENFORD, GREGORY ALBERT, physicist, writer; b. Mobile, Jan. 30, 1941; s. James Alton and Mary Eloise (Nelson) B.; m. Joan Abbe, Aug. 26, 1967; children: Alyson Rhandra, Mark Gregory. B.S., U. Okla., 1963; M.S., U. Calif., San Diego, 1965, Ph.D., 1967. Research asst. U. Calif., San Diego, 1964-67; postdoctoral fellow Lawrence (Calif.) Radiation Lab., 1967-69, research physicist, 1969-71; prof. physics U. Calif., Irvine, 1971—. Cons. in field. Author: (novels) Deeper than the Darkness, 1970, Jupiter Project, 1975, If the Stars are Gods, 1977, In the Ocean of Night, 1977, The Stars in Shroud, 1978, Find the Changeling, 1980, Timescape, 1980 (Nebula Award), Against Infinity, 1983, Across the Sea of Suns, 1984, Artifact, 1985, Heart of the Comet, 1986, In Alien Flesh, 1986, Great Sky River, 1987, Tides of Light, 1989, Beyond the Fall of Night, 1990, Chiller, 1993, Furious Gulf, 1994, Sailing Bright Eternity, 1995, (with Mark O Martin) A Darker Geometry, 1996, Foundation's Fear, 1997, Cosm, 1998, Green Rider, 1998, The Martian Race, Eater, 2000, (collections) Matter's End, 1994; editor: Far Futures, 1995, (with Martin H Greenberg) The New Hugo Winners Volume IV, 1997, Nebula Awards Showcase 2000: The Year's Best SF and Fantasy Chosen by the Science Fiction a Writers of America, 2000, (with George Zebrowski) Skylife: Space Habitats in Story and Science, 2000, Worlds Vast & Various, 2000, Deep Time, 1999, Cosm, 1999, Eater, 2000; also rsch. papers on plasma physics, astrophysics, solid state physics. Woodrow Wilson fellow, 1963-64; grantee Office Naval Research, 1975—, 82—; grantee NSF, 1972-76; grantee Army Research Orgn., 1977-82; grantee Air Force Office Sci. Research, 1982— ; grantee Calif. Space Office, 1984-85; recipient Brit. Sci. Fiction award, 1981; Australian Ditmar award for internat. novel, 1981; John W. Campbell award for best novel, 1981, Lord Found. prize, 1995. Mem. Am. Phys. Soc., Royal Astron. Soc., Sci. Fiction Writers Am. (Nebula award 1975, 81), Soc. Sci. Exploration, NASA Sci. Adv. Bd., Phi Beta Kappa. Home: 1105 Skyline Dr Laguna Beach CA 92651-1936 Office: U Calif Physics Dept Irvine CA 92717 Business E-Mail: gbenford@uci.edu

BENGIER, GARY T. online company executive; BBA in Computer Sci., Kent State U.; M in Bus. Adminstrn., Harvard Bus. Sch. Sr. fin. mgmt. Kenetech Corp., Qume Corp.; sr. fin. officer Compass Design Automation; CFO Vxtreme, eBay, Inc., San Jose, CA. Office: EBay Inc 2125 Hamilton Ave San Jose CA 95125

BENHAM, JAMES H. state official; b. Twin Falls, Idaho, July 14, 1944; s. James Henry and Matilda (Riggs) B.; m. Ann Elizabeth McIntosh, Mar. 27, 1965; 2 children. BA in Polit. Sci., Idaho State U., 1990, MPA, 1992. From police officer to chief of police Pocatello (Idaho) Police Dept., 1988-94; U.S. marshal dept. justice U.S. Dist. Idaho, Boise, 1994—. Contbr. articles to profl. jours. Bd. dirs. Nat. Criminal Justice Assn., 1992-93. Mem. Idaho Peace Officers Assn. (pres. 1986), Idaho Chief of Police Assn. (pres. 1990-91), Pocatello Police Relief Assn., Lions, Phi Kappa Phi. Methodist. Avocations: golf, fishing, exercizing, hunting, gardening. Office: US Marshal for Dist Idaho 550 W Fort St # 010 Boise ID 83724-0101

BENHAM, PRISCILLA CARLA, religious studies educator, college president; b. Berkeley, Calif., Jan. 30, 1950; d. Carl Thomas and Bebe (Harrison) Patten; m. Donald W. Benham, Mar. 30, 1986; 1 child, Charmaine P. Benham. BS summa cum laude, Patten Coll., 1969; BA in Psychology, Coll. Holy Names, 1971; MA in New Testament with honors, Wheaton Coll., 1972; PhD in New Testament, Drew U., 1976. Prof. New Testament Patten Coll., Oakland, Calif., 1975—, pres., 1983—. Coor. music Christian Cathedral, Oakland, 1989—; co-founder Christian Cathedral Chorale, Oakland, 1975—; tree planting participant David Ben Gurion Forest, Israel, 1975. Co-author: Before the Times, 1989, The World of the Early Church, 1991; mem. editorial bd. Pentecostal Theology; contbr. articles to profl. jours. Violinist Redwood Symphony. Mem. AAUP, Am. Assn. Higher Edn., Am. Assn. Pres. Ind. Colls. and Univs., Am. Coun. Edn., Assn. Ind. Calif. Colls. and Univs., Soc. Bibl. Lit., Am. Acad. Religion, Bar-Ilan Assn. of the Greater Bay Area, Western Coll. [illegible] [illegible] Colls., Regional Assn. East Bay Colls. and Univs. (mem. at-large exec. com.), Oakland C. of C., Nat. Assn. Intercollegiate Athletics, Rotary of Oakland, Phi Delta Kappa. Office: Patten Coll 2433 Coolidge Ave Oakland CA 94601-2630

BENHAMOU, ERIC A. computer company executive; MSEE, Stanford U.; diplome d'Ingenieur, Ecole Nationale Superieure d'Arts et Metiers, Paris. Project mgr., software mgr., design engr. Zilog, Inc.; v.p. Bridge Comm., 1981; chmn., chief exec. officer 3Com Corp., Santa Plz., Calif., 1990—, now pres. Bd. dirs. Smart Valley Inc., Cypress Semiconductor, Legato, Santa Clara U. Sch. Bus.; chair Am. Electronics Assn. Nat. Info. Infrastructure Task Force. Recipient Pres. Environ. and Conservation Challenge award, 1992. Office: 3COM Corp 5400 Bayfront Plz Santa Clara CA 95054-3601

BENI, GERARDO, electrical and computer engineering educator, robotics scientist; b. Florence, Italy, Feb. 21, 1946; came to U.S., 1970; s. Edoardo and Tina (Bazzanti) B.; m. Susan Hackwood, May 24, 1986; children: Catherine Elizabeth, Juliet Beatrice. Laurea in Physics, U. Firenze, Florence, Italy, 1970; PhD in Physics, UCLA, 1974. Research scientist AT&T Bell Labs., Murray Hill, N.J., 1974-77, Holmdel, 1977-82, disting. mem. tech. staff, 1982-84; prof. elec. and computer engring. U. Calif., Santa Barbara, 1984-91, dir. Ctr. for Robotic Systems in Microelectronics, 1985-91, prof. elec. engring. Riverside, 1991—, chmn. elec. engring. dept., 1997-98. Founder, editor: Jours. Robotic Systems, 1983 (Jour. of Yr. award 1984); editor: Recent Advances in Robotics, 1985, Vacuum Mechatronics, 1990; contbr. more than 130 articles to tech. jours.; 16 patents in field. Fellow AAAS, Am. Physics Soc. Office: U Calif-Riverside Coll Engring Riverside CA 92521-0001

BENJAMIN, KARL STANLEY, art educator; b. Chgo., Dec. 29, 1925; s. Eustace Lincoln and Marie (Klamsteiner) B.; m. Beverly Jean Paschke, Jan. 29, 1949; children: Beth Marie, Kris Ellen, Bruce Lincoln. Student, Northwestern U., 1943, 46; BA, U. Redlands, 1949; MA, Claremont Grad. Sch., 1960. With dept. arts Pomona Coll., Claremont, Calif., 1979-97, Loren Barton Babcock Miller prof., artist-in residence, 1978-94, prof. emeritus, 1997—; prof. art Claremont Grad. Sch. Traveling exhbns. include New Talent, Am. Fedn. Arts, 1959, 4 Abstract Classicists, Los Angeles and San Francisco museums, 1959-61, West Coast Hard Edge, Inst. Contemporary Arts, London, Eng., 1960, Purist Painting, Am. Fedn. Arts, 1960-61, Geometric Abstractions in Am, Whitney Mus., 1962, Paintings of the Pacific, U.S., Japan and Australia, 1961-63, Artists Environment, West Coast, Amon Carter Mus., Houston, 1962-63, Denver annual, 1965, Survey of Contemporary Art, Speed Mus., Louisville, 1965, The Colorists, San Francisco Mus., 1965, Art Across Am, Mead Corp., 1965-67, The Responsive Eye, Mus. Modern Art, 1965-66, 30th Biennial Exhbn. Am. Painting, Corcoran Gallery, 1967, 35th Biennial Exhbn. Am. Painting, 1977, Painting and Sculpture in California: The Modern Era, San Francisco Mus. Modern Art, 1976-77, Smithsonian Nat. Collection Fine Arts, Washington, 1976-77, Los Angeles Hard Edge: The Fifties and Seventies, Los Angeles County Mus. Art, 1977, Corcoran Gallery, Washington, Cheney Cowles Mus., Spokane, 1980, Calif. State U., Bakersfield, 1982, Henry Gallery, U. Wash., 1982, U. Calif., Santa Barbara, 1984, L.A. Mcpl. Art Galleries, Barnsdall Park, 1986, Turning the Tide: Early Los Angeles Modernists, Santa Barbara Mus. Art, Oakland Mus., others, 1989-91, L.A. County Mus. Art, 1996; rep. permanent collections, Whitney Mus., L.A. County Mus. Art, San Francisco Mus. Art, Santa Barbara (Calif.) Mus. Art, Pasadena (Calif.) Art Mus., Long Beach (Calif.) Mus. Art, La Jolla (Calif.) Mus. Art, Fine Arts Gallery San Diego, U. Redlands, Mus. Modern Art, Israel, Pomona Coll., Scripps Coll., Univ. Mus., Berkeley, Calif., Wadsworth Atheneum, Nat. Collection Fine Arts, Seattle Mus. Modern Art, Newport Harbor Mus., U. N.Mex. Mus. Art, Wash. State U., L.A. Mus. Contemporary Art; retrospective exhbn. covering yrs. 1955-87 Calif State U. at Northridge, 1989, retrospective exhbn. 1979-94, Pomona Coll., 1994, 450 year survey Calif. art Orange County Mus. Art, Newport Beach, 1998-99. Served with USNR, 1943-46. Visual Arts grantee NEA, 1983, 89. Office: Pomona Coll Dept Arts 333 N College Way Dept Arts Claremont CA 91711-4429 also: Claremont Grad U Art Dept 251 E 10th St Claremont CA 91711-3913

BENJAMIN, LORNA SMITH, psychologist; b. Rochester, N.Y., Jan. 7, 1934; d. Lloyd Albert and Esther Smith; children: Laureen, Linda. AB, Oberlin Coll., 1955; PhD, U. Wis., 1960. NIMH fellow dept. psychiatry U. Wis., 1958-62, clin. psychology intern, 1960-64, asst. prof., 1966-71, assoc. prof., 1971-77, prof. psychiatry, 1977-88; prof. psychology U. Utah, 1988—. Research asso. Wis. Psychol. Inst., Madison, 1962-66 Contbr. articles to profl. jours. Mem. Am. Psychol. Assn., Soc. Psychotherapy Research, Phi Beta Kappa. Office: Univ Utah Dept Psychology 390 S 1530 E Salt Lake City UT 84112-8934 E-mail: Benjamin@xmission.com

BENJAMIN, STEPHEN ALFRED, veterinary medicine educator, environmental pathologist, researcher; b. N.Y.C., Mar. 27, 1939; s. Frank Benjamin and Dorothy (Zweighaft) Fabricant; m. Barbara Larson, July 25, 1982; children: Jeffrey, Karen, Susan, Douglas. AB, Brandeis U., 1960; DVM, Cornell U., 1964, PhD, 1968. Diplomate Am. Coll. Vet. Pathologists. Fellow pathology Johns Hopkins U., Balt., 1966-67; asst. prof. comparative medicine M.S. Hershey (Pa.) Med. Ctr. of Pa. State U.; exptl. pathologist Inhalation Toxicology Research Inst., Albuquerque, 1970-77; prof. pathology, environ. health and radiol. health scis. Colo. State U., Ft. Collins, 1977—, dir. collaborative radiol. health lab., 1977-91, assoc. dean grad. sch., 1986-94, co-dir. ctr. for environ. toxicology and tech., 1991—, chmn. dept. microbiology, immnology and pathology, 2001—. Contbr. articles sci. articles. Mem.: Am. Vet. Med. Assn., Soc. Toxicologic Pathology, Amer. Coll. Vet. Pathol. Office: Colo State U Dept Pathology Ctr Environ Toxic Fort Collins CO 80523-0001

BENNETT, ALAN JEROME, electronics executive, physicist; b. Phila., June 13, 1941; s. Leon Martin and Reba (Perry) B.; m. Frances Kitey, June 16, 1963; children: Sarah, Rachel, Daniel. BA, U. Pa., 1962; MS, U. Chgo., 1963, PhD, 1965. Physicist R & D ctr. GE, Schenectady, N.Y., 1966-74, br. mgr. R & D ctr., 1975-79; dir. electronics lab. Gould Inc., Rolling Meadows, Ill., 1979-84; v.p. R & D Varian Assocs., Palo Alto, Calif., 1984-91; dir. program devel. Lawrence Livermore Nat. Lab., Livermore, 1992-96, dir. indsl. partnerships and commercialization, 1997—, mgr. program devel. Contbr. articles to profl. jours. Fellow NSF, 1963-65, 66. Mem. Phi Beta Kappa, Sigma Xi. Avocations: linguistics, amateur radio. Home: 233 Tennyson Ave Palo Alto CA 94301-3737 Office: Lawrence Livermore Nat Lab PO Box 808 Livermore CA 94551-0808 E-mail: Abennett@llnl.gov

BENNETT, C. FRANK, molecular pharmacologist; b. Aztec, N.Mex., Nov. 1, 1956; s. Clarence Acie Bennett and Elizabeth Lavender (Fish) Taylor; m. Paula Marie Chamberland, May 17, 1986; children: Christopher Franklin, Nicholas Dean Paul. BS in Pharmacy, U. N.Mex., 1980; PhD, Baylor U., 1985. Registered pharmacist. Staff pharmacist Hermann Hosp., Houston, 1982-85; postdoctoral fellow Smith Kline & French Labs., Phila., 1985-87, assoc. sr. investigator, 1987-89; sr. scientist ISIS Pharm., Carlsbad, Calif., 1989-90, group leader, 1990—. Dir. inflammation program ISIS Pharm., Carlsbad, 1989—. Contbr. articles to profl. jours. Grantee NIH; recipient Bristol award in Pharmacy Bristol Labs., 1980. Mem. AAAS, Am. Soc. for Cell Biology, Rho Chi. Avocations: fishing, camping. Office: ISIS Pharm Inc 2292 Faraday Ave Carlsbad CA 92008

BENNETT, CHARLES FRANKLIN, JR. biogeographer, educator; b. Oakland, Calif., Apr. 10, 1926; s. Charles Franklin and Charlotte Louise (Normand) B.; m. Carole Ann Messenger, Nov. 30, 1947; 1 child, Ashley Lynn. PhD, UCLA, 1959. Instr. UCLA, 1959-60, asst. prof., 1960-65, assoc. prof., 1965-69, prof. biogeography, 1969—; prof. emeritus, 1993—. Cons. in field. Author: Human Influences on the Biogeography of Panama, 1968, Man and Earth's Ecosystems, 1976, Conservation of Natural Resources, 1983; contbr. articles to profl. jours. Guggenheim fellow,

1970-71. Fellow AAAS, Royal Geog. Soc.; mem. Ecol. Soc. Am., Brit. Ecol. Soc., Assn. Tropical Biology, Soc. for Conservation Biology, Fauna and Flora Preservation Soc., Am. Inst. Biol. Scis. Avocation: collecting natural history books. Home: 317 S Anita Ave Los Angeles CA 90049-3805 Office: UCLA Dept Geography 405 Hilgard Ave Los Angeles CA 90095-9000 E-mail: chasben@ucla.edu

BENNETT, CHARLES LEON, vocational and graphic arts educator; b. Salem, Oreg., Feb. 5, 1951; s. Theodore John and Cora Larena (Rowland) B.; m. Cynthia Alice Hostman, June 12, 1976 (div.); m. Lynn Marie Toland, Aug. 12, 1977 (div.); children: Mizzy Marie, Charles David.; m. Christina M. Crawford, Dec. 19, 1987 (div.); m. Iris J. Perrigo, Mar. 17, 2001. AS in Vocat. Tchr. Edn., Clackamas C.C., 1977; AS in Gen. Studies, Linn Benton C.C., 1979; BS in Gen. Studies, Ea. Oreg. State Coll., 1994. Tchr. printing Tongue Point Job Corps, Astorial, Oreg., 1979-80; tchr., chmn. dept. Portland (Oreg.) Pub. Schs., 1980—; owner, mgr. printing and pub. co. Portland, 1981-87. With AUS, 1970-72. Mem. NRA, Oreg. Vocat. Trade-Tech. Assn. (cept. chmn., pres. graphic arts divsn., Indsl. Educator of Yr. 1981-82), Oreg. Vocat. Assn. (Vocat. Tchr. of Yr. 1982-83), Graphic Arts Tech. Found., In-Plant Printing Mgmt. Assn., Internat. Graphic Arts Edn. Assn. (v.p. N.W. region VI), Oreg. Assn. Manpower Spl. Needs Pers., Oreg. Indsl. Arts Assn., Internat. Platform Assn., Nat. Assn. Quick Printers, Am. Vocat. Assn., Pacific Printing and Imaging Assn., Inplant Printing Mgmt. Assn., Portland Club Lithographers and Printing House Craftsmen. Republican. Home: 20295 S Unger Rd Beavercreek OR 97004-8884 Office: 546 NE 12th Ave Portland OR 97232-2719 E-mail: cbennett@aracnet.com, cbennett@pps.k12.or.us

BENNETT, FRED GILBERT, lawyer; b. May 28, 1946; HBA magna cum laude, U. Utah, 1970; JD, U. Calif., 1973. Bar: Calif. 1974. Ptnr. Gibson, Dunn & Crutcher, L.A., 1980-98; sr. ptnr. Quinn Emanuel Urquhart Oliver & Hedges, 1998—. Mem. nat. com. on arbitration U.S. Coun. for Internat. Bus., 1984—, chmn. western subcom., 1989—; comml. and constrn. arbitrator Internat. C. of C./Am. Arbitration Assn. Large Complex Case Panel; chmn. continuing edn. com. Am. Arbitration Assn. Large Complex Case Panel. Mng. editor UCLA Law Rev., 1972-73. Mem. ABA, Internat. Bar Assn., L.A. County Bar Assn., Phi Beta Kappa. Office: Quinn Emanuel Urquhart Oliver & Hedges 865 S Figueroa St Los Angeles CA 90017-2543

BENNETT, JEAN LOUISE MCPHERSON, physicist, research scientist; b. Kensington, Md., May 9, 1930; d. Archibald Turner and Margaret Fitch (Willcox) McPherson; m. Harold Earl Bennett, Aug. 17, 1952 (div. Nov. 1984). BA summa cum laude, Mt. Holyoke Coll., 1951, DSc (hon.), 1997; MS, Pa. State U., 1953, PhD in Physics, 1955. Physicist Wright Air Devel. Ctr., Dayton, Ohio, 1955-56, Naval Ordnance Test Sta. (now Naval Air Warfare Ctr. Weapons Div.), China Lake, Calif., 1956-85, sr. research scientist, 1987-93, 95; vis. prof. U. Ala., Huntsville, 1986-87, Mt. Holyoke Coll., South Hadley, Mass., 1994-95; ret., 1996—. Mem. NRC Evaluation Panel Nat. Bur. Stds., Ctr. for Radiation Rsch., 1979-85, Nat. Inst. Stds. and Tech. Mfg. Engring. Lab., 1988-94, U.S. Nat. Com. for Internat. Commn. for Optics, 1984-85, 88-95; vis. scientist Inst. Optical Rsch., Royal Inst. Tech., Stockholm, Mar.-Sept., 1988, 98, 99, 2000, 01. Author: (with Lars Mattsson) Introduction to Surface Roughness and Scattering, 1989, revised 1999; author: Surface Finish and Its Measurement, 1992; contbr. sci. articles to profl. jours.; patentee in field. Recipient Tech. Achievement award Soc. Photo-Optical Instrumentation Engrs., 1983, L.T.E. Thompson award Naval Weapons Ctr., 1988, Women in Sci. and Engring. Lifetime Achievement award, 1993, Outstanding Sci. Alumni award Pa. State U., 1999; named sr. fellow Naval Weapons Ctr., 1989, Disting. Fellow, 1994. Fellow Optical Soc. Am. (v.p. 1984, pres.-elect 1985, pres. 1986, past pres. 1987, chmn. book publ. com. 1991-94, David Richardson medal 1990); mem. Am. Inst. Physics (subcom. on books 1990-94), Phi Beta Kappa, Sigma Xi, Sigma Delta Epsilon, Iota Sigma Pi, Pi Mu Epsilon, Sigma Pi Sigma. Achievements include being the first woman to receive PhD in Physics at Pa. State U., 1955; first woman pres. Optical Soc. of Am. Avocations: backpacking, kayaking, photography. Home: 1275 Sage Ct Ridgecrest CA 93555-2622 Office: Code 4T41A0D Michelson Lab Naval Air Warfare Ctr China Lake CA 93555 E-mail: jbennett@ridgenet.net

BENNETT, KENNETH R. oil company executive, state legislator; b. Tucson, Aug. 1, 1959; s. Archie Roy and Donna Lucille (Bulechek) B.; m. Jeanne Tenney Bennett, Mar. 13, 1982; children: Ryan, Dana, Clifton. BS, Ariz. State U., 1984. Ceo Bennett's Oil Co., 1984—; mem. Ariz. Senate, Tucson, 1998—, Ariz. St. Bd. Education, 1992-1999; councilman Prescott City, 1985-89. Mem. Ariz. State Bd. Edn., Phoenix, 1992—, pres., 1996-97; Ariz. State Bd. for Charter Schs., Phoenix, 1994—, Governor's Task Force Edn. Reform, Phoenix, 1991-92. Mayor Pro Tempore City of Prescott (Ariz.), 1988; councilman City of Prescott (Ariz.), 1985-89, scoutmaster Boy Scouts of Am., 1993—. Mem., Education Leaders Council, Washington; Ariz. St. Charter Sch. Bd. Republican. LDS. Office: Bennett Oil Co 810 E Sheldon St Prescott AZ 86301-3214

BENNETT, LAWRENCE ALLEN, psychologist, criminal justice researcher; b. Selma, Calif., Jan. 4, 1923; s. Allen Walter and Eva Eleanor (Hall) B.; m. Beth J. Thompson, Aug. 14, 1948; children: Glenn Livingston, Yvonne Irene Solis. BA, Fresno State Coll., 1949; MA, Clarement Grad. Sch., 1954, PhD, 1968. Supervising psychologist Calif. med. facility Calif. Dept. Corrections, Vacaville, 1955-60, deptl. supr. clin. psychology Sacramento, 1960-67, chief rsch., 1967-76; dir. Ctr. for Study Crime, Delinquency and Corrections, So. Ill. U., Carbondale, 1976-79; dir. Office Program Evaluation, 1979-84; dir. crime prevention and enforcement divsn. Nat. Inst. Justice, Washington, 1985-86, dir. adjudication and corrections divsn., 1987-88; criminal justice cons., Sacramento, 1988—; practice clin. psychology Sacramento, 1988-99. Mem. part-time faculty U. Calif., Davis and Berkeley, 1959-76, Calif. State U., Sacramento, 1988—; mem. bd. Calif. Crime Technol. Rsch. Found., 1970-75; mem. Calif. Interdeptl. Coordinating Coun., 1967-76, chmn., 1970; bd. dirs. Am. Justice Inst., Sacramento, 1970-79, 88—, v.p., 1989-90, pres., 1991—; project dir. San Francisco Project, 1999—; mem. juvenile adv. bd. State of Ill., 1977-79; mem. Calif. Blue Ribbon Commn. on Inmate Population Mgmt., 1988-90. With U.S. Army, 1942-45, 49-50. Author: (with Thomas S. Rosenbaum and Wayne R. McCollough) Counseling in Correctional Environments, 1978; contbr. articles to profl. jours. Decorated Bronze Star with oak leaf cluster. Mem. APA, Acad. Criminal Justice Scis., Am. Soc. Criminology, Am. Correctional Assn. (rsch. coun. 1992-95), Evaluation Rsch. Soc., Assn. for Correctional Rsch. and Info. Mgmt. (pres. 1989-90). Unitarian. Office: Am Justice Inst 1129 Rivara Cir Sacramento CA 95864-3720 E-mail: larry@thebennetts.com

BENNETT, PAUL GROVER, agribusiness executive; b. Ancon, Panama, Sept. 1, 1940; s. Arden Lamont and Mercedes (Reluz) B.; m. Diane Huarte, Dec. 17, 1967; children: Courtney, Kimberly, Christopher, Michael. BA, Northwestern U., 1962; MBA, Stanford U., 1968. Fin. analyst, rsch. supt. Std. Fruit Co. (Dole Food Co.), Limon, Costa Rica, 1968-70, rsch. dir. La Ceiba, Honduras, 1970-72, asst. gen. mgr. Guayaquil, Ecuador, 1872-73; v.p., reginal controller Castle & Cooke Foods (Dole Food Co.), San Francisco, 1973-74, v.p., gen. mgr. Davao, Philippines, 1974-76, Medellin, Colombia, 1977-78, Mauna Loa Macadamia Nut Corp., Hilo, Hawaii, 1978-81, pres., 1981-83; group v.p. diversified svcs. Inernat. Air Svc. Co. Ltd, Foster City, Calif., 1983-86; pres. Hawaiian Holiday Macadamia Nut co., Honolulu, 1986-89; sr. ptnr. Agricon Hawaii, Honolulu, 1989-91; pres., CEO Caloif. Ammonia Co., Stockton, Calif., 1981-93, Naturipe Berry Growers, Watsonville, 1993-96, Sakata Seed Am., Inc., Morgan Hill, 1997—. Dir. Am. Seed Trade Assn., Washington, 1999—, Asociacion Mexicana de Semilleros, Mexico City, 1992—95, Agrl. Coun. of Calif., 1994—96; alt. dir. Calif. Strawberry Commn.; mem. adv. bd. Food and Agribus. Inst., Sta. Clara U. Served to lt. comdr. USN, 1962—66. Mem.: Stanford Alumni Assn., Phi Gamma Delta, Stanco. Republican.

BENNETT, ROBERT F. senator; b. Salt Lake City, 1933; s. Wallace F. Bennett; m. Joyce McKay; 6 children. BS, U. of Utah, 1957. Various staff positions U.S Ho. of Reps., U.S. Senate, Washington; CEO Franklin Quest, Salt Lake City, 1984-90; senator from Utah, U.S. Senate, Washington, 1993—. Sr. Rep. mem. legis. br. appropriations subcom., sr. Rep. mem. fin. instns. subcom., mem. banking, housing, urban affairs com., appropriations com., joint econ. ic com., small bus. com.; mem. Rep. high tech. task force; lobbyist various orgns., Washington; head Dept. Transp.'s Congl. Liaison. Author: Gaining Control. Chmn. Education Strategic Planning Commn. Utah State Bd. Edn. (mem. Edn. Strategic Planning Com.). Recipient Light of Learning award for Outstanding Contbns. to Utah edn., 1989; named Entrepreneur of Yr. for Rocky Mtn. region INC. magazine, 1989. Republican. Office: US Senate Senate Mems Office 431 Dirksen Senate Ofc Bldg Washington DC 20510-0001

BENNETT, ROBERT ROYCE, engineering and management consultant; b. Spokane, Wash., May 7, 1926; s. Fred Alonzo and Rebecca Jane (Sommerville) B.; m. Margaret Stewart Keyes, Aug. 20, 1950; children: Susan Bennett Olson Nelson, Philip K., Laurie B. Mapes. BS, Calif. Inst. Tech., 1945, MS, 1947, PhD, 1949. Registered profl. engr., Oreg.; lic. surveyor, Oreg. Mem. tech. staff Hughes Aircraft, Culver City, Calif., 1949-54; v.p. TRW Systems, Redondo Beach, 1954-65; engring. mgmt. cons. Eugene, Oreg., 1965—. Contbr. articles to profl. jours.; patentee in field. Served to lt. (j.g.) USNR, 1944-54. Fellow IEEE. Republican. Presbyterian. Home and Office: 85334 S Willamette St Eugene OR 97405-9568 E-mail: bennett500@prodigy.net

BENNETT, STEPHEN M. computer company executive; b. Madison, Wis., Mar. 8, 1954; BA in Fin. and Real Estate, U. Wis., 1976. Various mgmt. positions GE Appliances, GE Med. and GE Supply; v.p. of Ams. GE Elec. Distbn. and Control; pres., CEO Vendor Fin. Svcs., GE Capital e-Business; exec. v.p., CEO GE Capital subsidiary of GE Corp.; CEO, pres. Intuit, 2000—. Office: Intuit Inc 2535 Garcia Ave Mountain View CA 94043-1111

BENNETT, THOMAS LEROY, JR. clinical neuropsychology educator; b. Norwalk, Conn., Sept. 25, 1942; s. Thomas LeRoy and Gertrude Upson (Richardson) B.; m. Jacqueline Beekman, Aug. 5, 1972; children: Dean, Shannon, Brian, Laurie. B.A., U. N. Mex., 1964, M.S., 1966, Ph.D., 1968. Diplomate Am. Bd. Profl. Neuropsychology (examiner, treas. 1993-96, pres.-elect 1995-97, pres. 1997-99), Am. Bd. Forensic Examiners, Am. Bd. Profl. Disability Cons., Am. Bd. Profl. Psychology. Asst. prof. Calif. State U., Sacramento, 1968-70; assoc. prof., then prof. psychology and physiology Colo. State U., Ft. Collins, 1970-98, coord. exptl. psychology sect., 1978-81, 92-95, prof. emeritus, 1998—; pvt. practice neuropsychology Ft. Collins, 1981—. Mem. allied health staff Poudre Valley Hosp., Ft. Collins; clin. dir. Ctr. for Neurorehab. Svcs., Ft. Collins. Author: Brain and Behavior, 1977, The Sensory World, 1978, The Psychology of Learning and Memory, 1979, Exploring the Sensory World, 1979, Introduction to Physiological Psychology, 1982, The Neuropsychology of Epilepsy, 1992, Brainwave-R: Cognitive Strategies for Brain Injury Rehabilitation, 1997, Mild Traumatic Brain Injury, 1999, Psychology Video Teaching Modules: The Brain, 2d edit., 1997, Psychology Video Teaching Modules: The Mind, 2000; also articles and book chpts.; assoc. editor Rehab. Psychology, Archives of Clinical Neuropsychology; mem. editl. bd. Cognitive Rehab., Archives Clin. Neuropsychology, Jour. Head Injury, Bull. of Nat. Acad. Neuropsychology, Neuropsychology Rev., others. Elder Timnath Presbyterian Ch. Named Outstanding Grad. Educator for Coll. Natural Scis., 1998. Fellow APA, Nat. Acad. Neuropsychology (editl. bd. Bull., bd. dirs. 1993-95, conv. chmn. 1993, 94), Am. Psychol. Soc., Am. Coll. Profl. Neuropsychology (pres. 1997-99); mem. Am. Coll. Forensic Examiners, Psychonomic Soc., Rocky Mountain Psychol. Assn., Soc. for Cognitive Rehab., Nat. Head Injury Found. (provider's coun.), Colo. Head Injury Found. (provder's coun.), Internat. Neuropsychol. Soc., Colo. Neuropsychol. Soc., Sigma Xi (named Colo. State U. Honored Scientist 1996). Home: 213 Camino Real Fort Collins CO 80524-8907 Office: Colo State U Dept Psychology Fort Collins CO 80523-0001 E-mail: brain1@frii.com, benny@frii.com

BENNETT, WILLIAM GORDON, casino executive; b. Glendale, Ariz., Nov. 16, 1924; Gen. mgr. Del Webb Corp., Las Vegas, 1965-70; with Western Equities Inc., Reno, 1971-78; chmn. Circus Circus Enterprises Inc., 1974-95, dir.; owner Sahara Hotel, Las Vegas, 1995—. Office: Sahara Hotel Casino 2535 Las Vegas Blvd S Las Vegas NV 89109-1123

BENNETT, WILLIAM MICHAEL, internist, nephrologist, educator; b. Chgo., May 6, 1938; s. Harry H. and Helen A. (Kaplan) B.; m. Sandra S. Silen, June 12, 1977; four children. Student, U. Mich., 1956-59; B.S., Northwestern U., 1960, M.D., 1963. Diplomate Am. Bd. Internal Medicine, Am. Bd. Nephrology, Am. Bd. Clin. Pharmacology. Intern U. Oreg., 1963-64; resident Northwestern U., 1964-66; practice medicine specializing in internal medicine Portland, Oreg. and; Boston; mem. staff Mass. Gen. Hosp., 1969-70; asst. prof. medicine U. Oreg. Health Scis. Center, 1970-74, asso. prof., 1974-78, prof. medicine and pharmacology, 1978-2000, ret., 2000. Author: Pharmacology and Management of Hypertension, 1994, Manual of Nephrology, 1990, Drug Therapy in Renal Failure, 1994; contbr. articles to med. jours. Served with USAF, 1967-69. Fellow ACP; mem. Am. Soc. Nephrology (pres. 1998-99), Transplantation Soc., Internat. Soc. Nephrology, Am. Soc. Pharmacology and Exptl. Therapeutics. Office: Legacy Good Samaritan Hosp NSC 430 1015 NW 22d St U Portland OR 97210 also: NW Renal Clinic 1130 NW 22d St Ste 640 Portland OR 97210 E-mail: bennettw@lhs.org

BENNION, JOHN WARREN, urban education educator; b. Salt Lake City, 25 Nov. s. M. Lynn and Katherine Bennion; m. Sylvia Lustig; children: Philip, Stanford, David, Bryan, Grant, Andrew. BS in Philosophy, English, U. Utah, 1961, MA in Edn. Adminstrn., 1962; PhD in Edn. Adminstrn., Ohio State U., 1966. Tchr. Granite High Sch., Salt Lake City, 1961-63; asst. instr. Ohio State U., Columbus, 1963-64, adminstrv. asst., 1965-66; adminstrv. intern Parma (Ohio) Sch. Dist., 1964-65; asst. supt. Elgin (Ill.) Pub. Schs., 1966-68; asst. prof. edn. adminstrn. Ind. U., Bloomington, 1968-69; supt. Brighton Cen. Schs., Rochester, N.Y., 1969-79, Bloomington (Minn.) Pub. Schs., 1979-80, Provo (Utah) Sch. Dist., 1980-85, Salt Lake City Schs., 1985-94; prof. urban edn., dir. Utah Edn. Consortium U. Utah, Salt Lake City, 1994—. Dir. Utah Urban Sch. Alliance, Salt Lake City; ednl. cons. Comprehensive Sch. Reform, Salt Lake City. Recipient Nat. Superintendent of the Yr. award, Utah, Am. Assn. of School Administrators, 1992. Mem. Assn. Supervision and Curriculum Devel., Assn. Early Childhood Edn., Am. Assn. Sch. Adminstrs., Phi Delta Kappa, Rotary. Home: 1837 Harvard Ave Salt Lake City UT 84108-1804 Office: Utah Urban Sch Alliance 1865 S Main St Ste 22 Salt Lake City UT 84115-2045

BENNION, SCOTT DESMOND, physician; b. Casper, Wyo., July 26, 1948; s. Desmond and Wanda Bennion; m. Mary Marie Blanton; children: Scott, Beau, Brandon. BS summa cum laude, U. Wyo., 1970, MS, 1972; MD, U. Utah, 1975. Diplomate Nat. Bd. Med. Examiners, Am. Bd. Internal Medicine, Am. Bd. Dermatology, Am. Bd. Dermatologic Immunology/Diagnostic and Lab. Immunology. Intern U. Rutgers Med. Sch., 1975-76, resident in internal medicine, 1976-78, chief resident dept. medicine, 1978; commd. 2d lt. U.S. Army, 1976, advanced through grades to col., 1991; resident in dermatology Fitzsimons Army Med. Sch., Denver, 1981-84, chief dept. clin. investigations, 1994-96, chmn. lab. animal use and care com., 1994-96; asst. chief dermatology svc. 98th Gen. Hosp., Nuremburg, Germany, 1986, chief dept. health clinics Germany, 1987-88; chief immunodermatology sect. dermatology svc. Fitzsimons Army MC, Aurora, Colo., 1989—; command surgeon ARTASK, Kuwait, 1992; command surgeon joint task force Kuwait and Army Ctrl. Command-Forward, 1992; dermatology cons. to the Army Surgeon Gen., 1996-99; chief Troop Med. Clin. Fitzsimmons Army Garrison, 1996-99. Asst. clin. prof. dept. dermatology U. Colo. Health Sci. Ctr., 1992-99, assoc. prof. clin. dermatology, 1999—. Contbr. chpts. to books: Military Dermatology, 1994, Secrets of Dermatology, 1996, 2d edit., 2000, Dubois Lupus, 1997, also articles to profl. publs. Pres. Nuremburg Elem. Sch. PTSA; asst. cubmaster, cubmaster, chmn. Volksmarch com. Boy Scouts Am., 1986; pres. Foxridge Improvement Assn., 1992—, pres., 1994-2001; bd. mem. Wyo. Make a Wish Found., 2000—; trustee Casper Coll., 2000—, Anam Chara Hospice, Denver, 2001—. Named to Order of Mil. Med. Merit, 1987; named Cubmaster of Yr. Bavaria dist. Boy Scouts Am., 1987; recipient Legion of Merit award, 1999. Fellow ACP, Am. Acad. Dermatology (mem. govt. medicine task force 1996-2000, Colo. Dermatology Soc. rep. to adv. bd. 1997—), Assn. Mil. Surgeons, Assn. Mil. Dermatologists (Residents award 1984, sec.-treas. 1990-96, guest editor jour. 1991, pres. 1998-99), Soc. for Investigative Dermatology, Wyo. Acad. Dermatology (sec. 1999—, rep. to AAD adv. bd.), Ctrl. Wyo. Skin Clinic, Phi Kappa Phi. Avocations: skiing, diving. Home: 1604 S Sycamore St Casper WY 82604 Office: 2241 Farnum St Ste 102 Casper WY 82609-4108

BENNIS, WARREN GAMELIEL, business administration educator, writer, consultant; b. N.Y.C., Mar. 8, 1925; s. Philip and Rachel (Landau) B.; m. Clurie Williams, Mar. 30, 1962 (div. 1983); children: Katharine, John Leslie, Will Martin; m. Mary Jane O'Donnell, Mar. 8, 1988 (div. 1991); m. Grace Gabe, Nov. 29, 1992. AB, Antioch Coll., 1951; hon. cert. econs., London Sch. Econs., 1952; PhD, MIT, 1955; LLD, Xavier U., Cin., 1972, George Washington U., , 1977; LHD (hon.), Hebrew Union Coll., 1974, Kans. State U., 1979; DSc (hon.), U. Louisville, 1977, Pacific Grad. Sch. Psychology, 1987, Gov.'s State U., 1991; LHD (hon.), Doan Coll., 1993. Diplomate Am. Bd. Profl. Psychology. Asst. prof. psychology MIT, Cambridge, 1953-56, prof., 1959-67; asst. prof. psychology and bus. Boston U., 1956-59; prof. Sloan Sch. Mgmt., 1959-67; provost SUNY-Buffalo, 1967-68, v.p. acad. devel., 1968-71; pres. U. Cin., 1971-77; U.S. prof. corps. and soc. Centre d'Etudes Industrielles, Geneva, Switzerland, 1978-79; exec.-in-residence Pepperdine U., 1978-79; George Miller Disting. prof.-in-residence U. Ill., Champaign-Urbana, 1978; Disting. prof. Bus. Adminstrn. Sch. Bus., U. So. Calif., L.A., 1980-88; univ. prof., disting. prof. bus. adminstrn. U. So. Calif., L.A., 1988—. Vis. lectr. Harvard U., 1958-59, Indian Mgmt. Inst., Calcutta; vis. prof. U. Lausanne (Switzerland), 1961-62, INSEAD, France, 1983; bd. dirs. The Foothill Group. Author: Planning of Change, 4th edit., 1985, Interpersonal Dynamics, 1963, 3d and 4th edits., 1975, Personal and Organizational Change, 1965, Changing Organizations, 1966, repub. in paperback as Beyond Bureaucracy, 1974, The Temporary Society, 1968, Organization Development, 1969, American Bureaucracy, 1970, Management of Change and Conflict, 1972, The Leaning Ivory Tower, 1973, The Unconscious Conspiracy: Why Leaders Can't Lead, 1976, Essays in Interpersonal Dynamics, 1979; (with B. Nanus): Leaders, 1985, On Becoming a Leader, 1989, (with I. Mitroff) The Unreality Industry, 1989, Why Leaders Can't Lead, 1989, Leaders on Leadership, 1992, An Invented Life: Reflections on Leadership and Change, 1993, Beyond Bureaucracy, 1993, (with J. Goldsmith) Learning to Lead, 1994, (with M. Mische) Reinventing the 21st Century, 1994, Beyond Leadership, 1994, Herding Cats: Bennis on Leadership, 1996, Organizing Genius, 1997, The Temporary Society, 1998, Co-Leaders, 1999, Old Dogs, New Tricks, 1999, (with G. Heil and D. Stephens) Douglas McGregor Re-Visited, 2000; co-leaders, 1999, Managing the Dream, 2000; cons. editor Calif. Mgmt. Rev., Mgmt. Series Jossey-Bass Pubs. Mem. Pres.' White House Task Force on Sci. Policy, 1960-70; mem. FAA study task force U.S. Dept. Transp., 1975; mem. adv. com. N.Y. State Joint Legis. Com. Higher Edn., 1970-71; mem. Ohio Gov.'s Bus. and Employment Coun., 1972-74; mem. panel on alt. approaches to grad. edn. Coun. Grad. Schs. and Grad. Record-Exam Bd., 1971-73; chmn. Nat. Adv. Commn. on Higher Edn. for Police Officers, 1976-78; adv. bd. NIH, 1978-84; trustee Colo. Rocky Mountains Sch., 1978-82; bd. dirs. Am. Leadership Forum, 1984-89; mem. vis. com. for Humanities MIT, 1975-81; trustee Antioch Coll., Salk Inst. Capt. AUS, World War II. Decorated Bronze Star, Purple Heart; recipient Dow Jones award, 1987, McKinsey Fedn. award, 1967, 68. Mem. Am. Acad. Arts and Scis. (co-chmn. policy coun. 1969-71), Am. Mgmt. Assn. (dir. 1974-77), U.S. C. of C. (adv. group scholars). Office: U So Calif Sch Bus University Park Los Angeles CA 90089-0001

BENNISON, ALLAN PARNELL, geological consultant; b. Stockton, Calif., Mar. 8, 1918; s. Ellis Norman Lambly and Cora Mae (Parnell) B.; m. DeLeo Smith, Sept. 4, 1941; children: Victor, Christina, Mary. BA, U. Calif., Berkeley, 1940. Cert. petroleum geologist, cert. profl. geologist. Geology fellow Antioch Coll., Yellow Springs, Ohio, 1940-42; photogrammetrist U.S. Geol. Survey, Arlington, Va., 1942-45; stratigrapher, asst. chief geologist Companias Unidas de Petroleos, Cartagena, Colombia, 1945-49; staff stratigrapher Sinclair Oil & Gas Co., Tulsa, 1949-69; geol. cons. Tulsa, 1969—. Cons. in field. Editor: Tulsa's Physical Environment, 1973; compiler maps; contbr. articles to profl. jours. Fellow AAAS, Geol. Soc. Am., Explorers Club; mem. Am. Assn. Petroleum Geologists (hon., trustee assoc., Disting. Svc. award 1986), Soc. Econ. Paleontologists and Mineralogists (Disting. Svc. award 1990), Tulsa Geol. Soc. (pres. 1965), Tulsa Astronomy Club (v.p. 1965), Explorers Club, Sigma Xi. Republican. Episcopalian. Avocations: photography, astronomy, reading, travel. Home and Office: 11200 Butler Rd Grass Valley CA 95945-6917

BENOLIEL, JOEL, lawyer; b. Seattle, June 11, 1945; s. Joseph H. and Rachel (Maimon) B.; m. Maureen Alhadeff, Mar. 1971; 1 child, Joseph D. BA in Polit. Sci., U. Wash., 1967, JD, 1971. Bar: Wash., U.S. Dist. Ct. (we. dist.) Wash., U.S. Ct. Appeals (9th cir.), U.S. Mil. Ct. Appeals. Assoc. atty. MacDonald, Horgue & Bayless, Seattle, 1971-73, ptnr., 1973-78; v.p., gen. counsel Jack A. Benaroya Co., Seattle, 1978-84; ptnr. Trammell Crow Co., Seattle, 1985-87, Spieker Ptnrs., Bellevue, Wash., 1987-92; sr. v.p. law and real estate, gen. counsel Price Costco, Inc., Issaquah, 1992—. Bd. dirs. Overlake Sch., Redmond, Wash., 1995—, Congregation Ezra Bessaroth, Seattle, 1992-95. With U.S. Army, 1968-74. Avocations: tennis, boating, skiing, reading fiction. Office: Price Costco Inc 999 Lake Dr Issaquah WA 98027-5367

BENSCH, KLAUS GEORGE, pathology educator; b. Miedar, Germany, Sept. 1, 1928; married; 3 children. M.D., U. Erlangen, Germany, 1953. Diplomate: Am. Bd. Pathology. Intern U. Hosps. of Erlangen, 1953-54; resident in anat. pathology U. Tex. and; M.D. Anderson Hosp., Houston, 1954-56, Yale, 1956-57; instr. pathology Yale Med. Sch., 1958-61, asst. prof., 1961-64, assoc. prof., 1964-68; prof. pathology Stanford Med. Sch., 1968—, acting chmn. dept. pathology, 1984-85, chmn. dept. pathology, 1985-99. Office: Stanford U Med Sch Dept Pathology 300 Pasteur Dr Palo Alto CA 94304-2203

BENSON, ANDREW ALM, biochemistry educator; b. Modesto, Calif., Sept. 24, 1917; s. Carl Bennett and Emma Carolina (Alm) B.; m. Ruth Carkeek, May 22, 1942 (div. 1969); children: Claudia Benson Matthews, Linnea; m. Dorothy Dorgan Neri, July 31, 1971. BS, U. Calif., Berkeley, 1939; PhD, Calif. Inst. Tech., 1942; Phil D h.c., U. Oslo., 1965; Docteur h.c., U. Paris, 1986. Instr. chemistry dept. U. Calif., Berkeley, 1942-43, asst. dir. Bio-organic group Radiation Lab., 1946-54; rsch. assoc. dept. chemistry Stanford U., 1944-45, Calif. Inst. Tech., 1945-46; assoc. prof. agrl. biol. chemistry Pa. State U., 1955-60, prof., 1960-61; prof.-in-residence biophys./physiol. chemistry UCLA, 1961-62; prof. Scripps Instn. Oceanography, U. Calif., San Diego, 1962-88, prof. emeritus, 1988—. Fulbright vis. prof. Agrl. Coll. Norway, 1951-52. Contbr. articles on biochem. rsch. on photosynthesis, lipids, coral metabolism, arsenic metabolism, methanol application in agr. to profl. jours. Trustee Found. for Ocean Rsch., San Diego, 1970-88; mem. adv. coun. The Costeau Soc., 1976—; mem. internat. adv. bd. Marine Biotech. Inst. Co. Ltd., Tokyo, 1990-98. Recipient Sugar Rsch. Found. award, 1950, Ernest Orlando Lawrence Meml. award, 1962, Rsch. award Supelco/Am. Oil Chemists Soc., 1987; Sr. Queen's fellow Australia, 1979; Eminent Scientist of RIKEN, Japan, 1995; named Hon. Citizen Alert Bay, B.C., Can., 1988. Fellow AAAS; mem. Am. Acad. Arts and Sci., NAS, Royal Norwegian Soc. Sci. and Letters, Am. Oil Chemists Soc., Am. Chem. Soc. (emeritus), Am. Soc. Plant Physiologists (Stephen Hales prize 1972), Am. Soc. Biochemistry and Molecular Biology, Inst. Marine Biology, Far East Br., Acad. Sci. Russia (hon.). Home: 6044 Folsom Dr La Jolla CA 92037-6711 Office: Scripps Instn Oceanography La Jolla CA 92093-0202

BENSON, DEE VANCE, federal judge; b. Salt Lake City, Aug. 25, 1948; s. Gilbert and Beryl Butler (Despain) B.; children: Angela, Natalie, Lucas, Katherine. BA, Brigham Young U., 1973, JD, 1976. Bar: Utah 1976, U.S. Dist. Ct. Utah 1976, U.S. Ct. Appeals (10th cir.) 1976, U.S. Supreme Ct. 1984, U.S. Ct. Appeals (5th cir.) 1988. Ptnr. Snow, Christensen & Martineau, Salt Lake City, 1976-84; legal counsel Senate Judiciary Com., Washington, 1984-86; chief of staff Senator Orrin Hatch's Office, Washington, 1986-88; legal counsel U.S. Senate Select Com., Washington, 1987; assoc. dep. atty. gen. U.S. Dept. Justice, Washington, 1988, U.S. atty. dist. Utah Salt Lake City, 1989-91; judge U.S. Dist. Ct., Salt Lake, 1991—. Legal counsel Iran-Contra Congl. Investigating Com., Washington, 1987. Contbg. author univ. law rev. Mem. ABA, Utah State Bar (com. on cts. and judges), Salt Lake County Bar Assn., Phi Alpha Delta. Mem. LDS Ch. Avocations: soccer, skiing, mountain biking, basketball, running. Office: US Dist Ct 350 S Main St Ste 251 Salt Lake City UT 84101-2106

BENSON, JOAN, musician, music educator; b. St. Paul; d. John Raymond and Frances (Ostergren) B. MusM, U. Ill., 1952; performer's cert., Ind. U., 1953; pvt. studies with Edwin Fischer, Switzerland, 1953-57; pvt. studies with Fritz Neumeyer, Fed. Republic Germany, 1958-59; pvt. studies with Santiago Kastner, Portugal, 1960. Concert musician, worldwide, 1962—; lectr. early keyboard Stanford U., Palo Alto, Calif., 1970-76; asst. prof. U. Oreg., Eugene, 1976-82. Mem. artist faculty Aston Magna Acad., Mass., 1980, 82; adj. prof. U. Oreg., 1982—; artistic advisor Boston Clavichord Soc., 1996—. Albums: Repertoire, 1962, Music of C. P. E. Bach for Piano and Clavichord, 1972, Pasquini and Haydn on Clavichords of the Boston Museum of Fine Arts, 1982, Kuhnau and C.P.E. Bach on Clavichord, 1988; contbr. music notes to Titanic and Focus record labels; contbr. articles to internat. profl. jours. Recipient Kate Nell Kinley award. Mem. Am. Musicol. Soc. Home: 2795 Central Blvd Eugene OR 97403-2528

BENSON, JOHN ALEXANDER, JR. physician, educator; b. Manchester, Conn., July 23, 1921; s. John A. and Rachel (Patterson) B.; m. Irene Zucker, Sept. 29, 1947; children: Peter M., John Alexander III, Susan Leigh, Jeremy P. BA, Wesleyan U., 1943; MD, Harvard Med. Sch., 1946. Diplomate Am. Bd. Internal Medicine (mem. 1969-91, sec.-treas. 1972-75, pres. 1975-91, pres. emeritus 1991—), Subsplty. Bd. Gastroenterology (mem. 1961-66, chmn. 1965-66). Intern Univ. Hosps., Cleve., 1946-47; resident Peter Bent Brigham Hosp., Boston, 1949-51; fellow Mass. Gen. Hosp., Boston, 1951-53; rsch. asst. Mayo Clinic, Rochester, Minn., 1953-54; asst. Mass. Gen. Hosp., 1954-59; instr. medicine Harvard U., 1956-59; head divsn. gastroenterology U. Oreg. Med. Sch., Portland, 1959-75, prof. medicine, 1965-93; prof. emeritus Oreg. Health Sci. U., Portland, 1993—, interim dean Sch. Medicine, 1991-93, dean emeritus, 1993—. Cons. VA Hosps., Madigan Gen. Army Hosp., John A. Hartford Found. Editorial bd.: Am. Jour. Digestive Diseases, 1966-73, The Pharos, 2000—; contbr. articles to profl. jours. Mem. Oreg. Med. Ednl. Found., 1967-73, dir., 1967-73, pres., 1969-72; bd. dirs. N.W. Ctr. for Physician-Patient Comm., 1994-99, Am. Acad. on Physician and Patient, 1994-99; bd. dirs. Found. for Med. Excellence, 1996—, pres., 1998-2000; trustee Oreg. Health Scis. Found., 1999—. With USNR, 1947-49. Mem. AAS, AMA, ACP (master), Am. Gastroenterol. Assn. (sec. 1970-73, v.p. 1975-76, pres.-elect. 1976-77, pres. 1977-78), Am. Clin. and Climatol. Assn. (v.p. 1997), Am. Soc. Internal Medicine, Western Assn. Physicians, North Pacific Soc. Internal Medicine, Am. Fedn. Clin. Rsch., Federated Coun. for Internal Medicine, Am. Assn. Study Liver Disease, Western Soc. Clin. Investigation, Soc. Health and Human Values, Assn. Health Svcs. Rsch., Inst. Medicine NAS (sr.), Phi Beta Kappa, Sigma Xi, Alpha Omega Alpha. Office: Oreg Health Scis U Sch Medicine L102 Portland OR 97201 E-mail: bensonj@ohsu.edu

BENSON, ROBERT EUGENE, lawyer; b. Red Oak, Iowa, Apr. 7, 1940; s. Paul J. and Frances (Sever) B.; m. Ann Marie Lucke, July 20, 1968; children: Steven J., Robert J., Katherine A. BA, U. Iowa, 1962; LLB, U. Pa., 1965. Bar: Colo. 1965. Assoc. Holland & Hart, Denver, 1965-71, ptnr., 1971—. Adj. faculty U. Denver Coll. Law, 1992. Author: The Power of Arbitrators and Courts to Order Discovery in Arbitration, 1996, Application of the Pro Rata Liability, Comparative Negligence and Contribution Statues, 1994; co-author: How to Prepare For, Take and Use a Deposition, 5th edit., 1994; editor: Colorado Construction Law, 1999; contbr. articles to profl. jours. Capt. USAF, 1965-73. Mem. ABA, Colo. Bar Assn., Denver Bar Assn. Avocations: golf, skiing. Home: 5454 Preserve Pky N Littleton CO 80121-2185 Office: Holland & Hart 555 17th St Ste 3200 Denver CO 80202-3950

BENSON, SALLY M. atmospheric scientist; Dir. earth scis. divsn. Lawrence Berkeley Lab. Dept. Energy. Office: Lawrence Berkeley Lab Earth Scis Divsn 1 Cyclotron Rd Bldg 50E Berkeley CA 94720 E-mail: smbenson@lbl.gov

BENSON, SIDNEY WILLIAM, chemistry researcher; b. N.Y.C., Sept. 26, 1918; m. Anna Bruni, 1986; 2 children. A.B., Columbia Coll., 1938; A.M., Ph.D., Harvard U., 1941; Docteur Honoris Causa, U. Nancy, France, 1989. Rsch. asst. Gen. Electric Co., 1940; rsch. fellow Harvard U., 1941-42; instr. chemistry CCNY, 1942-43; group leader Manhattan Project Kellex Corp., 1943; asst. prof. U. So. Calif., 1943-48, assoc. prof., 1948-51, prof. chemistry, 1951-64, 76-89, distng. prof., 1986—, Disting. prof. emeritus, 1989—, dir. chem. physics program, 1962-63; dir. dept. kinetics and thermochemistry Stanford Rsch. Inst., 1963-76; sci. dir. Hydrocarbon Rsch. Inst. U. So. Calif., 1977-90, sci. dir. emeritus, 1991—; rsch. assoc. dept. chemistry and chem. engring. Calif. Inst. Tech., 1957-58; vis. prof. UCLA, 1959, U. Ill., 1959; hon. Glidden lectr. Purdue U., 1961; vis. prof. chemistry Stanford U., 1966-70, 71, 73; mem. adv. panel phys. chemistry Nat. Bur. Standards, 1969-72, chmn., 1970-71; hon. vis. prof. U. Utah, 1971; vis. prof. U. Paris VII and XI, 1971-72, U. St. Andrews, Scotland, 1973, U. Lausanne, Switzerland, 1979. Frank Gucker lectr. U. Ind., 1984—; Brotherton prof. in phys. chemistry U. Leeds, 1984; cons. [illegible] lectr. U. Calif., Berkeley, 1989. Author: Foundations of Chemical Kinetics, 1960, rev. edit. 1982, Thermochemical Kinetics, 1968, 2d edit., 1976, Critical Survey of the Data of the Kinetics of Gas Phase Unimolecular Reactions, Reactions, 1970, Chemical Calculations, 3d edit., 1971, Atoms, Molecules and Chemical Reactions, 1972; founder, editor-in-chief Internat. Jour. Chem. Kinetics, 1967-83; mem. editl. [illegible] Combustion Sci. and Tech., 1973-94, Oxidation Comms., 1978—, Revs. of chem. Intermediates, 1979-87, Hydrocarbon Letters, 1980-81, Jour. Phys. Chemistry, 1981-85; sci. adv. coun. Annales Medicales de Nancy, 1993—. Recipient Polanyi medal Royal Soc. Eng., 1986; faculty rsch. award U. So. Calif., 1984, Presdl. medal, 1986, Peter Kapitsa Gold Medal award Russian Acad. Natural Sci., 1997; Guggenheim fellow, 1950-51, Fulbright fellow, France, 1950-51, fellow NSF, 1957-58, 71-72; recipient citation Chem. Rev., 2000. Fellow AAAS, Am. Phys. Soc.; mem. NAS, Am. Chem. Soc. (Tolman medal 1977, Hydrocarbon Chem. award 1977, Langmuir award 1986, Orange County award 1986), Faraday Soc., Indian Acad. Sci., Phi Beta Kappa, Sigma Xi, Pi Mu Epsilon, Phi Lambda Upsilon, Phi Kappa Phi Home: 1110 N Bundy Dr Los Angeles CA 90049-1513 Office: U So Calif University Pk Mc 1661 Los Angeles CA 90089-0001

BENSON, STEPHEN R. editorial cartoonist; BA in Polit. Sci. cum laude, Brigham Young U., 1979. With Senate Rep. Policy Com., 1979-80; cartoonist The Ariz. Republic, Phoenix, 1980-90, 91—, The Morning-News Tribune, Tacoma, 1990-91. Author: Fencin' with Benson, 1984, Evanly Days, 1988, Back at the Barb-B-Cue, 1991, Where Do You Draw the Line?, 1992. Recipient Nat. Headliner award, 1984, 1st Place Best of the West, 1991, 92, 93, Pulitzer Prize finalist editorial cartooning, 1984, 89, 92, 94, Pulitzer Prize for editorial cartooning, 1993. Office: The Ariz Republic 200 E Van Buren St Phoenix AZ 85004-2238

BENSUSSEN, GALE, health products company executive; b. 1946; BS, U. So. Calif.; JD, Southwestern U. Sch. Law. Bar: Calif. 1979. Pres. Leiner Health Products, Carson, Calif. Office: Leiner Health Products Inc 901 E 233d St Carson CA 90745

BENTER, GEORGE H., JR. banker; b. 1942; BS, San Diego State U., 1963; MBA, UCLA, 1964. With Security Pacific Nat. Bank, 1964—, exec. v.p., 1986—, Security Pacific Corp. Dir. Whittaker Corp., L.A. Office: City National Corporation 400 N Roxbury Dr Beverly Hills CA 90210

BENTLEY, PETER JOHN GERALD, forest industry company executive; b. Vienna, Mar. 17, 1930; s. Leopold Lionel Garrick and Antoinette Ruth B.; m. Sheila Farrington McGiverin, May 23, 1953; children: Michael Peter, Barbara Ruth, Susan Patricia, Joan Katherine, Lisa Marie. Ed., U. B.C. Sch. Forestry, Banff Sch. Advanced Mgmt.; LLD (hon.), U. B.C. Chmn., dir. Canfor Corp., Vancouver, B.C., Can.; co-chmn., dir. Howe Sound Pulp & Paper Gen. Ptnr. Ltd.; ret. Howe Sound Pulp & Paper Mgmt. Ltd., 1995, 1995. Bd. dirs. Bank Montreal, Can. Forest Products Ltd., Vancouver, B.C. Chem. Ltd.; gov. Olympic Trust Can.; mem. adv. bd. BuildDirect.com. Bd. dirs. Jr. Achievement of Can.; past chmn., trustee Vancouver Hosp. and Health Sci. Ctr.; bd. dirs. Can. Inst. for Advanced Rsch.; mem. adv. coun. to faculty commerce and bus. adminstrn., dir. Can. adv. bd. Carlyle Group; bd. govs. Banff Ctr. for Continuing Edn. hon.; dir. Can. Profls. Golfers Assn. Decorated officer Order of Can. Mem. B.C. Forestry Assn. (hon. life, past pres., hon. dir.), Capilano Golf and Country Club, Marine Drive Golf Club, Vancouver Club, Vancouver Lawn Tennis and Badminton Club, Thunderbird Country Club (Rancho Mirage, Calif.), Morningside Club (Rancho Mirage), Royal and Ancient Golf Club (St. Andrews, Scotland). Office: Canfor Corp POB 49420 Bentall Postal Vancouver BC Canada V7X 1B5

BENTLEY, SARA, newspaper publishing executive; Pres. Gannett Northwest Newspaper Group, Salem, Oreg., 1988-95; pub. Statesman-Jour., Salem, 1988—. Office: Statesman-Jour Co Inc 280 Church St NE Salem OR 97301-3734

BENTLEY, THOMAS ROY, English language educator, writer, consultant; b. Belfast, No. Ireland, June 5, 1931; s. Thomas and Anne (Hill) B.; m. Joan M. Williams, Dec. 24, 1955; children: Kimberley, Shannon, Carolyn. BA, U. Toronto, 1960, MA, 1966; EdB, Ont. Coll., 1961; PhD, Meml. U., Nfld., Can., 1970. Assoc. dean edn. U. B.C., Vancouver, Can., 1973-77, head lang. edn. Can., 1978-79, acting dean edn. Can., 1979-81, prof. lang. edn. Can., 1983-96, prof. emeritus Can., 1996—. Cons. to maj. cos. on comm. and transp. issues; co-founder Internat. Lifewriting Network. Author 4 books on English comms.; editor 12 books on Can. lit.; contbr. articles to profl. jours.; broadcaster numerous programs on radio and TV. Mem. Nat. Assn. Tchrs. English (chmn. internat. assembly 1981), Nat. Conf. for Rsch. in English, Can. Coun. Tchrs. English (editor, bd. dirs., 1975-78), Vancouver Club. Office: 5529 University Blvd Vancouver BC Canada V6T 1K5

BENTON, ANDREW KEITH, university administrator, lawyer; b. Hawthrone, Nev., Feb. 4, 1952; s. Darwin Keith and Nelda Lou Benton; m. Deborah Sue Strickland, June 22, 1974; children: Hailey Michelle, Christopher Andrew. BS in Am. Studies, Okla. Christian Coll., 1974; JD, Oklahoma City U., 1979. Bar: Okla. 1979, U.S. Dist. Ct. (we. dist.) Okla. 1982. Sole practice, Edmond, Okla., 1979-81, 83-84; ptnr. Benton & Thomason, Edmond, 1981-83; asst. v.p. Pepperdine U., Malibu, Calif., 1984-85, v.p., 1985-87, v.p. adminstrn., 1987-89, v.p. univ. affairs, 1989-91, exec. v.p., 1991-2000, pres., 2000—. Chmn. precinct, state conv. del. Okla. Reps., 1980. Mem. ABA (chmn. subcom. emerging land use trends 1987-88, chmn. subcom. decisional trends 1988-90), Okla. Bar Assn. (contbr. articles to ednl. community). Republican. Mem. Ch. of Christ. Office: Pepperdine U 24255 Pacific Coast Hwy Malibu CA 90263-0002

BENTON, AUBURN EDGAR, lawyer; b. Colorado Springs, Colo., July 12, 1926; s. Auburn Edgar and Ella Dot (Heyer) B.; m. Stephanie Marie Jakimowitz, June 8, 1951; children— Margrit Laura, Mary Ellen BA, Colo. Coll., 1950; LLB, Yale U., 1953. Bar: Colo. 1953, U.S. Dist. Ct. Colo. 1953, U.S. Ct. Appeals (10th cir.) 1954. Assoc. Holme Roberts & Owen, Denver, 1953-57, ptnr., 1957-91, of counsel, 1992—. Mem. Bd. Edn. Denver Pub. Schs., 1961-69; mem. Colo. Commn. Higher Edn., Denver, 1975-85; mem. Colo. Bd. Ethics, Denver, 1975-98; mem. Nat. Common Cause Bd., Washington, 1975-85; dir. soc. sci. found. U. Denver. Mem. Colo. Bar Assn., Denver Bar Assn., Cactus Club (Denver), Phi Beta Kappa. Democrat. Home: 901 Race St Denver CO 80206-3735 Office: Holme Roberts & Owen 1700 Lincoln St Ste 4100 Denver CO 80203-4541

BENTON, DONALD MARK, state legislator, political organization chairman; b. Agua Dulce, Calif., Apr. 8, 1957; s. Arlis Redford and Dorothy Helen B.; m. Mary E. Enders, Nov. 6, 1982; children Jennifer Marie, Adam Carson, Bradly, Austin. AS, Coll. of the Canyons, Valencia, Calif.; BS in Bus. Mgmt. & Comm., Concordia U., Portland, Oreg. Founder, chief exec. officer Santa Clarita Temporaries, Inc., Newhall, Calif., 1979-83; dist. mgr. Farmers Ins. Group, L.A., 1983-88; nat. sales trainer, speaker Nat. Cons. Svcs., Vancouver, Wash., 1988; founder, chief exec. officer The Benton Grp., 1988—; mem. Wash. Ho. of Reps., Olympia, 1994-96, Wash. Senate, Dist. 17, Olympia, 1996—; chair. Wash. Republican Party, 1998—. Author: How To Start a Temporary Service, 1981; inventor aerovane. Clk., trustee Santa Clarita Community Coll. Dist., Valencia, Calif., 1981-88, [illegible] trustees, 1985; pres. Santa Clarita Valley Jaycees, 1981-82; chmn. bd. dirs. Santa Clarita Valley unit ARC, 1983-86. Recipient resolution Calif. Assembly, 1981, ofcl. resolution L.A. County Bd. Suprvs., 1982, spl. recogition U.S. Congress, 1982, Outstanding Young Man award Santa Clarita Valley Jaycees, 1982. Home: 121 NE 117th Ave Vancouver WA [illegible] Wash Senate 109-B Irving R Newhouse Bldg PO Box 40417 Olympia WA [illegible]

BENTON, FLETCHER, sculptor; b. Jackson, Ohio, 1931; BFA, Miami U., Oxford, Ohio, 1956, DFA (hon.), 1993, Rio Grande U., , 1994. Mem. faculty Calif. Coll. Arts and Crafts, 1959, San Francisco Art Inst., 1964-67; prof. art Calif. State U., San Jose, 1967-81, prof., 1981-86. One-man shows include, San Francisco Mus. Modern Art, 1965, Albright-Knox Mus., Buffalo, 1970, Galeria Bonino, N.Y.C., 1969, Galerie Francoise Mayer, Brussels, San Francisco Mus. Modern Art, 1970, London Arts Gallery, Detroit, 1970, Galeria Bonino, Buenos Aires, Estudio Actual, Caracas, Venezuela, 1970, Landry-Bonino Gallery, N.Y.C., 1972, Phoenix Mus. Art, 1973, Galeria Bonino, Rio de Janiero, 1973, Calif. State U.-Berkeley, 1973, Neuberger Mus., N.Y., 1974, Hirshhorn Mus., 1974, Phila. Art Alliance, 1974, Elvehejem Mus. Art, Wis., 1976, San Francisco Modern Mus. Art, 1976, Huntsville Mus. Modern Art, Ala., 1977, Alrich Mus. Contemporary Art, Conn., John Berggruen Gallery, San Francisco, 1978, 84, 89, 96, Am. Acad. and Inst. Arts and Letters, N.Y.C., 1979, Chgo. Arts Club, 1979, Milw. Art Ctr., 1980, Suermondt-Ludwig Mus., Asschen, Fed. Republic Germany, Klingspor Mus., Offenbach, Fed. Republic Germany, 1981, 96, Kunsthandlung Brigitte Haasner, Wiesbaden, Fed. Republic Germany, 1987, 92, 96, Sung Dem Fine Arts, Seoul, Korea, 1991, Dorothy Goldeen Gallery, Santa Monica, Calif., 1988, 93, Galerie Simonne Stern, New Orleans, 1990, 93, Riva Yares Gallery, Scottsdale, 1991, Miami U., Oxford, 1993, Gallery Camino Real, Boca Raton, Fla., John Berggruen Gallery, San Francisco, 1996, Klingspor Mus., Germany, 1996, Gallery Camino Real, Boca Raton, Fla., 1996, Galerie B. Haasner, Germany, 1996, Galerie Simonne Stern, N. Orleans, 1997, Frankfurt Art Fair, Germany, 1997, numerous others; group shows include San Francisco Art Inst., 1964, San Francisco Modern Mus. Art, 1964, Calif. Pal. of Legion of Honor, 1964, Whitney Mus. Am. Art, N.Y.C., 1967, 68, Los Angeles County Mus., 1967, Phila. Art Mus., 1967, Walker Art Ctr., Mpls., 1968, Art Inst. Chgo., 1968, Internat. Mus. Fine Arts, Osaka, Japan, 1970, Hayward Gallery, London, 1970, Stanford (Calif.) Mus., 1971, Am. Acad. and Inst. Arts and Letters, N.Y.C., 1981, Amerika Haus, Frankfurt, 1981, Whitney Mus. Am. Art, N.Y.C., 1981, Oakland Mus., 1982, John Berggruen Gallery, 1983, Olympic Arts Festival, Los Angeles, France, Fed. Republic Germany, Eng., Norway, 1984, John Berggruen Gallery, 1985, 89, 92, Chapman Coll. (Calif.), 1985, The Adrich Mus. Contemporary Art, Conn., 1985, Centro de Arte Moderna, Lisbon, Portugal, 1986, Kleinewefers, Krefeld, Fed. Republic Germany, 1987, Kundsthandlung Brigitte Haasner, Wiesbaden, Fed. Republic Germany, 1987, 88, Dorothy Goldeen Gallery, Santa Monica, Calif., 1988, AndreEmmerich Gallery, 1991, 92, Rio Grande (Ohio) U., 1994, Miami Art Mus., Oxford, Ohio, 1996, numerous others; major collections Euroclear Hdqs. Brussels, Belgium, 1993, Modernesstadt Cologne, 1993, Gothaer, Cologne, Top Gallant, 1994, Pauling, N.Y., 1994; subject of book, Fletcher Benton by Paul Karlstrom and Edward Lucie-Smith, 1990. Served with USN, 1949-50. Recipient Disting. Svc. award to arts Am. Acad. and Inst. Arts and Letters, 1979, Career award Ohioana Libr. Assn., 1994; Pres.'s Scholar award San Jose State U., 1980.

BENTON, LEE F. lawyer; b. Springfield, Ohio, Feb. 18, 1944; AB, Oberlin Coll., 1966; JD, U. Chgo., 1969. Bar: Calif. 1970. Mng. ptnr. Cooley Godward LLP, Palo Alto, Calif. Teaching fellow Stanford Law Sch., 1969-70. Mem. Order Coif, Phi Beta Kappa. Office: Cooley Godward LLP 5 Palo Alto Sq 3000 El Camino Real Palo Alto CA 94306-2120

BENTON-HARDY, LISA RENEE, psychiatrist, educator; BA, Stanford U., 1988; MD, U. Calif., San Francisco, 1992. Diplomate Nat. Bd. Med. Examiners, Am. Bd. Psychaiat. and Neurology. Intern U. Calif. Davis-East Bay, Oakland, CA, 1992-93; adult psychiatry resident Stanford (Calif.) U. Med. Ctr., 1993-96, child and adolescent psychiatry fellow, 1995-97; staff psychiatrist Alliance for Cmty. Care, San Jose, Calif., 1994—. Calif. Wellness Found. Violence Prevention Initiative acad. scholar, Stanford U. Med. Ctr., 1995-97; presenter in field. Contbr. articles to profl. jours., chpt. to book. Laughlin fellow Am. Coll. Psychiatrists, 1997. Mem. AMA, Am. Psychiat. Assn. (Program for Minority Rsch. and Tng. in Psychiatry mini-fellowship award 1996), Am. Acad. Child and Adolescent Psychiatry (Presdl. Scholar award 1996, Charter fellow, leadership award 1994), No. Calif. Psychiat. Soc. Office: Childrens Hosp Oakland Dept Psychiatry 747 52nd St Oakland CA 94609-1809

BENVENUTTI, PETER J. lawyer; b. Gulfport, Miss., June 24, 1949; s. Peter J. and Elizabeth Cullen (Beyer) B.; m. Lise A. Pearlman, May 31, 1974; children: Anna B., Jamie E., Amalia R. AB, Harvard U., 1971; JD, U. Calif., Berkeley, 1974. Bar: Calif. 1974, U.S. Dist. Ct. (no. dist.) Calif. 1974, U.S. Dist. Ct. (ea. dist.) Calif. 1977, U.S. Dist. Ct. (ctrl. and so. dists.) Calif. 1989, U.S. Dist. Ct. Ariz. 1990, U.S. Ct. Appeals (9th cir.) 1984. Assoc. Dinkelspiel & Dinkelspiel, San Francisco, 1974-80, ptnr., 1981-88, Heller, Ehrman, White & McAuliffe, San Francisco, 1988—; mng. ptnr. San Francisco Office, 1995-97. Bd. dirs. ARC, 1981-83. Mem. ABA, Bar Assn. San Francisco (pres. Calif. bankruptcy forum 1993-94, lawyer rep. 9th Cir. Jud. Conf. 1994—). Democrat. Home: 1147 Clarendon Cres Oakland CA 94610-1807 Office: Heller Ehrman White & McAuliffe 333 Bush St San Francisco CA 94104-2806

BERCAW, JOHN EDWARD, chemistry educator, consultant; b. Cin., Dec. 3, 1944; s. James Witherow and Mary Josephine (Heywood) B.; m. Teresa Diane Ingram, July 10, 1965; children— David Lawrence, Karin Elizabeth B.S. in Chemistry, N.C. State U., 1967; Ph.D. in Chemistry, U. Mich., 1971. Postdoctoral U. Chgo., 1971-72; A.A. Noyes fellow Calif. Inst. Tech., Pasadena, 1972-74, asst. prof. chemistry, 1974-77, assoc. prof. chemistry, 1977-79, prof. chemistry, 1979-93, Centennial prof. chemistry, 1993—, Shell Disting. prof., 1985-90. Cons. Exxon Corp., Annandale, N.J., 1979— Fellow Am. Acad. Arts and Scis.; mem. NAS, AAAS, Am. Chem. Soc. (chmn. divsn. inorganic chemistry 1988-89, organometallic subdivsn. chair 1980, chmn. Gordon Rsch. Conf. on Organometallic Chemistry 1991, award in pure chemistry 1980, award in organometallic chemistry 1990, award for disting. svc. in inorganic chemistry 1997, George A. Olah award for hydrocarbon or petroleum chemistry 1999, Arthur C. Cope Scholar award 2000). Home: 1455 Afton St Pasadena CA 91103-2702 Office: Calif Inst Tech 1201 E California Blvd Pasadena CA 91125-0001

BERCOVICI, DAVID ANTHONY LEONARDO, geophysics educator, researcher; b. Rome, Sept. 18, 1960; came to U.S., 1964; s. Leonardo and Antonia (Maddison) B.; m. Julie Ann Jirikowic, Dec. 10, 1983; children: Sarah Kathryn, Hannah La'ia. BS, Harvey Mudd Coll., 1982; MS, UCLA, 1987, PhD, 1989. Rsch. asst. UCLA, 1985-89; postdoctoral fellow Woods Hole (Mass.) Oceanographic Instn., 1989-90; asst. prof. U. Hawaii, Honolulu, 1990-95, assoc. prof., 1995-99, prof., 1999—. Mem. Venus data analysis panel program NASA, Houston, 1992-93; NSF grand challenge panelist, Washington, 1993. Contbr. articles to Sci., Jour. Geophys. Rsch., Geophys. Rsch. Letters. Mem. U. Hawaii Profl. Assembly, Honolulu, 1990—. Named NSF Presdl. Young Investigator, 1994-99. Fellow Am. Geophys. Union (James B. Macelwane medal 1996, U. Hawaii Regents medal Excellence in Rsch.). Achievements include development of theories on how plate tectonics and continental drift are generated from thermal convection in the earth's mantle; development of theories on how buyoyant plumes in the mantle rise and evolve. Avocations: scuba diving, history, weight lifting. Office: U Hawaii Dept Geology and Geophysics Honolulu HI 96822

BERDAHL, ROBERT MAX, academic administrator, historian, educator; b. Sioux Falls, S.D., Mar. 15, 1937; s. Melvin Oliver and Mildred Alberta (Maynard) B.; m. Margaret Lucille Ogle, Aug. 30, 1958; children: [illegible] B.A., Augustana Coll., 1959; M.A., U. Ill., 1961; Ph.D., U. [illegible] history U. Mass., Boston, 1965-67; asst. prof. history U. Oreg., Eugene,

1967-72, assoc. prof., 1972-81, prof., 1981-86; dean U. Oreg. (Coll. Arts and Scis.), 1981-86; prof. U. Ill., 1986-93, vice chancellor academic affairs, 1986-93; pres. U. Tex., Austin, 1993-97; chancellor U. Calif., Berkeley, 1997—. Research asso. Inst. for Advanced Study, Princeton, 1972-73 Author: The Politics of Prussian Nobility, 1988; (with others) Klassen und Kultur, 1982; contbr. articles to profl. jours. Fulbright fellow, 1975-76; Nat. Endowment Humanities fellow, 1976-77 Office: U Calif at Berkeley 200 California Hall Spc 1500 Berkeley CA 94720-1500

BERENATO, JOSEPH C. manufacturing company executive; b. 1947; BS in Engring., U.S. Naval Acad.; MA in English, U. Va.; MBA in Fin., NYU. Various exec. mgmt. positions Mfrs. Hanover Trust Co.; v.p., CFO, treas. Ducommon Inc., L.A., 1991-95, exec. v.p., COO, 1995-96, pres., 1996—, pres., CEO, 1997—, also bd. dirs. Office: Ducommun Inc 111 W Ocean Blvd Ste 900 Long Beach CA 90802

BERENBAUM, MICHAEL GARY, theology educator; b. Newark, July 3, 1945; s. Saul Berenbaum and Rhea Kass; m. Linda Bayer, Aug. 25, 1968 (div. July 1992); children: Ilana, Lev; m. Melissa Patack, June 25, 1995; children: Joshua, Mira. Student, Jewish Theol. Sem., 1963-67, Hebrew U., 1965-66; AB in Philosophy, Queens Coll., 1967; postgrad., Boston U., 1967-69; PhD in Religion and Culture, Fla. State U., 1975; DD (honoris causa), Narazeth Coll., Rochester, N.Y., 1995; LHD (hon.), Dennison U., 2000. Instr. dept. philosophy and religion Colby-Sawyer Coll., 1969-71; adj. asst. prof. religion, Jewish chaplain Wesleyan U., 1973-80; assoc. professorial lectr. dept. religion George Washington U., 1981-83; opinion page editor Washington Jewish Week, 1983-86, acting editor, 1985; sr. scholar Religious Action Ctr., 1986-88; Hymen Goldman prof. theology Georgetown U., 1983-97; rsch. fellow U.S. Holocaust Meml. Mus., 1987-88, project dir., 1988-93, dir. U.S. Holocaust Rsch. Inst., 1993-97; pres., CEO Survivors of Shoah Visual History Found., 1997-99; prof. theology U. Judaism, 1998—; Ida E. King disting. vis. scholar of the Holocaust Richard Stockton Coll., 1999-2000; pres. Berenbaum Group, 1999—. Adj. prof. Judaic studies Am. U., 1987; assoc. dir.-Zachor: Holocaust Resource Ctr., 1978; dep. dir. Pres. Commn. on Holocaust, 1979-80; vis. prof. Hebrew Studies U. Md., 1983; assoc. Gannett Ctr. Media Studies Columbia U. Author: The Vision of the Void: Theological Reflections on the Works of Elie Wiesel, 1979, paper, 1987, reprinted as Elie Weisel: God, The Holocaust and the Children of Israel, 1994, The World Must Know: The History of the Holocaust as Told in the U.S. Holocaust Museum, After Tragedy and Triumph, 1990; editor: From Holocaust to New Life, 1985, Witness to the Holocaust, 1997, The Holocaust and History: The Known, The Unknown, The Disputed and The Reexamined, 1998; co-editor: Holocaust: Religious and Philosophical Implications, 1989, Anatomy of the Auschwitz Death Camp, 1996, What Kind of God?, 1997, The Holocaust and History, 1998, The Bombing of Auschwitz: Should the Allies Have a Attempted It?, 2001; mem. editl. bd. Tikkun, Jour. Holocaust and Genocide Studies; contbg. editor Sh'ma; editor Together, 1986-89, The Holocaust and History, 1998. Recipient Simon Rockower Meml. award in Jewish journalism for Disting. Editl. Writing by Am. Jewish Press Assn., 1986, Disting. Coverage of Arts, 1987, Silver Angel award Religion and the Media, 1981, Outstanding International Emmy award for One Survivor Remembers, 1995, Cable Ace award for One Survivor Remembers, 1996; Ezra Styles fellow Yale U., 1979, Danforth Found. Underwood fellow, 1976-77, George Wise Tel Aviv U., 1974, Charles E. Merrill fellow Fla. State U., 1972-73. Fellow Soc. Values in Higher Edn. Democrat. Home: 1124 S Orlando Los Angeles CA 90035 Address: 2101 Hillsboro Ave Los Angeles CA 90034 E-mail: michael@berenbaumgroup.com

BERENDT, PAUL, political party administrator; b. July 16, 1956; m. Beth Berendt. BA, Evergreen State Coll., 1987. Chmn. Wash. State Dem. Party, 1995—. Roman Catholic. Home: 1702 Sulenes Dr SE Olympia WA 98501-7042 Office: PO Box 4027 Seattle WA 98104-0027

BERENTSEN, KURTIS GEORGE, music educator, choral conductor; b. North Hollywood, Calif., Apr. 22, 1953; s. George O. and Eleanor J. (Johnson) B.; m. Jeanette M. Sacco, Aug., 1975 (div. 1977); m. Floy I. Griffiths, March 17, 1984; 1 child, Kendra Irene. MusB, Utah State U., 1975; MA in Music, U. Calif., Santa Barbara, 1986; cert. colloguy, Concordia Coll., 1996. Cert. cmty. coll. tchr., Calif., pub. tchr., Calif.; commd. minister Luth. Ch., Mo. Synod, 1996. Dir. music Hope Luth. Ch., Daly City, Calif., 1975-81; gen. mgr. Ostara Press, Inc., Daly City, 1975-78; condr. U. Calif., Santa Barbara, 1981-86; dir., condr. Santa Barbara oratorio Chorale, 1983-85; dir. music 1st Presbyn. Ch., Santa Barbara, 1983-84, Goleta (Calif.) Presbyn. Ch., 1984-85; minister music Trinity Luth. Ch., Ventura, 1985-92, Christ Luth. Ch. & Sch., Little Rock, 1992-98; dir. choral music Concordia U., Portland, Oreg., 1998—; instr. Ventura Coll., 1987-88; music dir., condr. Gold Coast Community Chorus, Ventura, 1988-92. Choir dir. Temple Beth Torah Jewish Community, Ventura, 1982-87; adj. prof. Pepperdine U., Malibu, Calif., 1988; chorus master Ventura Symphony Orch., 1987. Condr. oratorios Christus Am Oelberg, 1983, Elijah, 1984, Hymn of Praise, 1988, cantata Seven Last Words, 1979, 84, Paukenmesse, 1989, Mozart's Requiem, 1990, Requiem-Fauré, 1991, Judas Maccabaeus-Handel, 1992; soloist 15 major oratorio and opera roles, 1971-92, Nat. Anthem, L.A. Dodgers, 1989; dir. (with John Rutter) Gold Coast Community Chorus, Carnegie Hall, N.Y.C., 1991, Tribute to America, Lincoln Ctr. Concert, N.Y.C., 1991. Min. music, tchr. Christ Luth. Ch. and Sch., Little Rock, 1992—. First place winner baritone vocalist Idaho Fedn. Music Clubs, 1971, recital winner Utah Fedn. Music Clubs, 1974. Mem. Choral Condrs. Guild, Assn. Luth. Ch. Musicians, Am. Guild of English Handbell Ringers, Am. Choral Dirs. Assn., Music Educators Nat. Conf., Sigma Nu (sec., song leader 1973-75). Home and Office: 2811 NE Holman St Portland OR 97211-6067 E-mail: Kberentsen@cu-portland.edu

BERETTA, GIORDANO BRUNO, computer scientist, researcher; b. Brugg, Aargau, Switzerland, Apr. 14, 1951; came to U.S., 1984; PhD, ETH, Zurich, Switzerland, 1984. Mem. rsch. staff Xerox Palo Alto (Calif.) Rsch. Ctr., 1984-90; charter mem., sr. scientist Canon Info. Systems, Palo Alto, 1990-93; mem. tech. staff Hewlett-Packard Labs., 1994—. Chmn. various confs. Contbr. articles to profl. jours.; patentee digital color reprodn. and colorimetry. Fellow Soc. for Imaging Sci. and Tech. (sr., svc. award 1998, sr. membership award 2000); mem. Inter-Soc. Color Coun., Internat. Soc. for Optical Engring., Swiss Math. Soc., Alumni Orgn. Swiss Fed. Inst. Tech. Zurich. Office: Hewlett-Packard Labs 1501 Page Mill Rd Palo Alto CA 94304-1100 E-mail: beretta@hpl.hp.com, giordano.beretta@alumni.ethz.ch

BERG, ALFRED OREN, epidemiology and family practice medicine educator; b. Wichita, Kans., July 3, 1949; BA, Tabor Coll., 1970; MD, Washington U., 1974; MPH, U. Wash., 1979. Prof., chair dept. U. Wash., 1979—. Assoc. editor Jour. Am. Bd. Family Practice, 1991—. Mem. Am. Acad. Family Physicians, NAS, Soc. Tchrs. Family Medicine, Inst. Medicine.

BERG, OLENA, investment company executive, former federal official; b. Dec. 31, 1949; d. Clarence Millard and Anna Elizabeth (Schlegel) Nave; 1 child. BA in English summa cum laude, Calif. State U., 1974; MBA, Harvard U., 1984. Budget and estimates analyst State of Calif. Depts. Fin. and Benefits Payments, 1975-77; asst. to sec. State of Calif. Bus. and Transp. Agy., 1977-78; chief dep. dir. State of Calif. Dept. Housing and Community Devel., 1978-82; project mgr. McNeil Consumer Products, 1983; pres., COO Gerson Bakar and Assocs., 1984-88; exec. v.p. Lowe Assocs., 1988-91; chief dep. state treas. State of Calif., 1991-93; asst. sec. pension and welfare benefits adminstrn. Dept. of Labor, Washington, 1993-98; sr. adv. Fin. Engines Inc., Palo Alto, Calif., 1998—. Baker scholar Harvard U. Mem. Century Club. Office: Fin Engines Inc 1804 Embarcadero Rd Palo Alto CA 94303-3341

BERG, PAUL, biochemist, educator; b. N.Y.C., June 30, 1926; s. Harry and Sarah (Brodsky) B.; m. Mildred Levy, Sept. 13, 1947; 1 son, John. BS, Pa. State U., 1948; PhD (NIH fellow 1950-52), Western Res. U., 1952; DSc (hon.), U. Rochester, 1978, Yale U., 1978, Washington U., St. Louis, 1986, Oreg. State U., , 1989, Pa. State U., 1995. Postdoctoral fellow Copenhagen (Denmark) U., 1952-53; postdoctoral fellow Sch. Medicine, Washington U., 1953-54, Am. Cancer Soc. scholar cancer research dept. microbiology sch. medicine, 1954-57, from asst. to assoc. prof. microbiology, 1955-59; prof. biochemistry Sch. Medicine, Stanford (Calif.) U., from 1959, now prof. emeritus, Sam, Lulu and Jack Willson prof. biochemistry, 1970-94, Robert W. Cahill prof. cancer rsch., 1994-2000, chmn. dept. sch. medicine, 1969-74. Dir. Stanford U. Beckman Ctr. for Molecular and Genetic Medicine, 1985-2000, Affymetrix, 1993—, Nat. Found. Biomed. Rsch., 1994—; non-resident fellow Salk Inst., 1973-83; adv. bd. NIH, NSF, MIT; vis. com. dept. biochemistry and molecular biology Harvard U.; bd. sci. advisors Jane Coffin Childs Found. Med. Rsch., 1970-80; chmn. sci. adv. com. Whitehead Inst., 1984-90; bd. sci. adv. DNAX Rsch. Inst., 1981—; internat. adv. bd. Basel Inst. Immunology; chmn. nat. adv. com. Human Genome Project, 1990-92. Contbr. profl. jours.; Editor: Biochem. and Biophys. Research Communications, 1959-68; editorial bd.: Molecular Biology, 1966-69. Trustee Rockefeller U., 1990-92. Served to lt. (j.g.) USNR, 1943-46. Recipient Eli Lilly prize biochemistry, 1959; V.D. Mattia award Roche Inst. Molecular Biology, 1972; Henry J. Kaiser award for excellence in teaching, 1969, 72; Disting. Alumnus award Pa. State U., 1972; Sarasota Med. awards for achievement and excellence, 1979; Gairdner Found. annual award, 1980; Lasker Found. award, 1980; Nobel award in chemistry, 1980; N.Y. Acad. Sci. award, 1980; Sci. Freedom and Responsibility award AAAS, 1982; Nat. Medal of Sci., 1983; named Calif. Scientist of Yr. Calif. Museum Sci. and Industry, 1963; numerous disting. lectureships including Harvey lectr., 1972, Lynen lectr., 1977, Priestly lectrs. Pa. State U., 1978, Dreyfus Disting. lectrs. Northwestern U., 1979, Lawrence Livermore Dir.'s Disting. lectr., 1983, Linus Pauling lectr., 1993. Fellow AAAS; mem. NAS, Inst. Medicine, Am. Acad. Arts and Scis., Am. Soc. Biol. Chemists (pres. 1974-75), Am. Soc. Cell Biology (chmn. pub. policy com. 1994—), Am. Soc. Microbiology, Am. Philos. Soc., Internat. Soc. Molecular Biology, Japan Biochem. Soc. (elected fgn. mem. 1978), French Acad. Sci. (elected fgn. mem. 1981), Royal Soc. (elected fgn. mem. 1992). Office: Stanford Sch Medicine Beckman Ctr B-062 Stanford CA 94305-5301 E-mail: pberg@cmgm.stanford.edu

BERG, PHILIP, religious organization administrator; b. N.Y.C., Aug. 20, 1929; s. Max and Ester (Reis) B.; m. Karen Mulnick, July 2, 1971. Rabbi, Mesifta Torah Vadaath, N.Y.C., 1952; JD in Hebrew Law, Yeshiva Kol Yehuda, Tel Aviv, 1967. Spiritual leader Rsch. Ctr. Kabbalah Internat., L.A., 1962—. Home: 83-84 115th St Jamaica NY 11418-1303 Office: Rsch Ctr Kabbalah Internat 1062 S Robertson Blvd Los Angeles CA 90035-1505

BERGAMO, RON, marketing executive; b. Palm Springs, Calif., Nov. 26, 1943; s. Ralph and Dorothy (Johnson) B.; m. Jane E. Reed; children: Brad, Doug, Steve. BS, U. Ariz., 1965; MBA, Northwestern U., 1972. With Leo Burnett, 1966-68, NBC Network, 1968-69, AVCO TV Sales, 1969-72, Eller Outdoor, 1972-74, Sta. KMBC-TV Sales, 1974-77, LSM Sta. WFAA-TV, 1977-80; gen. mgr. Sta. KFDM-TV, Beaumont, Tex., 1980-82, Sta. KWCH-TV, Wichita, Kans., 1983-88; pres., gen. mgr. KSAZ-TV, Phoenix, 1988-95; exec. v.p., gen. mgr. KWBA TV58, Tucson, 1997—. Bd. dirs. Kartchner Caverns, Ariz. Arts Commn., Tucson Ad Fed, Tucson YMCA, UA Eller Sch. Bd., Insight.com Bowl, Boys/Girls Club, Fiesta Bowl. With U.S. Army NG, 1965-71. Recipient Gen. Mgr. of Yr. award Am. Women in Radio and TV, 1990, Phoenix award Pub. Rels. Soc. Am., 1992, Tucson Ad Fed. Siklver medal award, 2001; named Wichita Ad Person of Yr., 1985, Person of Yr. Phoenix Ad Club, 1993. Mem. Ariz. Broadcasters Assn. (pres. 1993), Ariz. C. of C. (bd. dirs.), Hispanic C. of C. (mem. bd.), Sigma Chi. Republican. Methodist. Avocations: reading, travel, Porsches, vintage racing. Home: 5901 E Stella Ln Paradise Vly AZ 85253-4276 Office: KWBA-TV58 3481 E Michigan St Tucson AZ 85714-2025 E-mail: rbergamo@aol.com

BERGÉ, CAROL, writer; b. N.Y.C., 1928, d. Albert and Molly Peppis; m. Jack Bergé, June 1955; 1 child, Peter. Asst. to pres. Pendray Public Relations, N.Y.C., 1955; disting. prof. lit. Thomas Jefferson Coll., Allendale, Mich., 1975-76; instr. adult degree program Goddard Coll. at Asilomar, 1976; tchr. fiction and poetry U. Calif. Extension Program, Berkeley, 1976-77; assoc. prof. U. So. Miss., Hattiesburg, 1977-78; vis. prof. Honors Ctr. and English dept. U. N.Mex., 1978-79, 87; vis. lectr. Wright State U., 1979, SUNY, Albany, 1980-81; tchr. Poets and Writers, Poets in the Schs. (N.Y. State Council on Arts), 1970-72, Poets in the Schs. (Conn. Commn. Arts). Propr. Blue Gate Gallery of Art and Antiques, 1988-2001. Author: (fiction) The Unfolding, 1969, A Couple Called Moebius, 1972, Acts of Love: An American Novel, 1973 (N.Y. State Coun. on Arts CAPS award 1974), Timepieces, 1977, The Doppler Effect, 1979, Fierce Metronome, 1981, Secrets, Gossip & Slander, 1984, Zebras, or, Contour Lines, 1991; (poetry) The Vulnerable Island, 1964, Lumina, 1965, Poems Made of Skin, 1968, The Chambers, 1969, Circles, as in the Eye, 1969, An American Romance, 1969, From a Soft Angle: Poems About Women, 1972, The Unexpected, 1976, Rituals and Gargoyles, 1976, A Song, A Chant, 1978, Alba Genesis, 1979, Alba Nemesis, 1979, (reportage) The Vancouver Report, 1965; editor Ctr. Mag., 1970-84, pub., 1991—; editor Miss. Rev., 1977-78, Subterraneans, 1975-76, Paper Branches, 1987, LIGHT YEARS: The N.Y.C. Coffeehouse Poets of the 1960s, 2002; contbg.'editor Woodstock Rev., 1977-81, Shearsman mag., 1980-82, S.W. Profile, 1981; editor, pub. CENTER Press, 1991-93; pub.: Medicine Journeys (Carl Ginsburg), Coastal Lives (Miriam Sagan), 1991; co-pub.: Zebras (Carol Berge). Nat. Endowment Arts fellow, 1979-80 Mem. Authors' League, Poets and Writers, MacDowell Fellows Assn., Nat. Press Women Home: 2070 Calle Contento Santa Fe NM 87505-5406

BERGEN, CANDICE, actress, writer, photojournalist; b. Beverly Hills, Calif., May 9, 1946; d. Edgar and Frances (Westerman) B.; m. Louis Malle, Sept. 27, 1980 (dec. 1995); 1 dau., Chloe. Ed., U. Pa. Model during coll. Films include The Group, The Sand Pebbles, The Day the Fish Came Out, Live for Life, The Magus, Soldier Blue, Getting Straight, The Hunting Party, Carnal Knowledge, T.R. Baskin, The Adventurers, 11 Harrowhouse, Bite the Bullet, The Wind and the Lion, The Domino Principle, The End of the World in Our Usual Bed in a Night Full of Rain, Oliver's Story, Starting Over, Rich and Famous, Gandhi, 1982, Stick, 1985; TV series: Murphy Brown, 1988-98 (Emmy award, Leading Actress in a Comedy Series, 1988-89, 89-90, 91-92, 93-94, 94-95); TV films Arthur the King, 1985, Murder by Reason of Insanity, 1985, Mayflower Madam, 1987, Shelley Duvall's Bedtime Stories, Vol. 7, 1993, Mary and Tim, 1996; TV miniseries Hollywood Wives, 1985, Trying Times, Moving Day; author Knockwood; photojournalist credits include articles for Life, Playboy; dramatist: (play) The Freezer (included in Best Short Plays of 1968). Recipient Emmy awards for lead actress in a comedy series, 1989, 90, 92, 94, 95.

BERGER, MITCHEL STUART, neurosurgeon; b. Miami, Fla., Jan. 1, 1953; s. Howard and Normadine (Boxer) B.; m. Joan L. Hurwitt, July 3, 1983; children: Lindsay, Alex. BA, Harvard Coll., 1975; MD, U. Miami, 1979. Intern/resident dept. neurosurgery Sch. Medicine, U. Calif., San Francisco, 1980-85, clin. instr., 1985; chief pediatric neuro-oncology Children's Hosp. Med. Ctr., Seattle, 1986—, chief N.W. neuro-oncology rsch. and therapy, 1987—, acting chief pediatric neurosurgery, 1989-90. Asst. prof. U. Hosp. Med. Ctr., Seattle, 1986-90, assoc. prof., 1990—; dir. clinic and lab program U. Wash., Seattle, 1986—, course dir. 4th year human oncology course, 1994. Author: Encyclopedia of Brain Tumors, 1994, Neoplastic Diseases in Childhood, 1994; editor: Textbook of Gliomas, 1995; guest editor: Neurosurgery Clinics of North America, 1992. Dir.-at-large Am. Cancer Soc., Seattle, 1992—. Grantee NIH, 1994; fellow Am. Cancer Soc., 1995—. Mem. Congress Neurol. Surgeons (exec. com. 1994), Am. Assn. Neurol. Surgeons (pub. rels. com. 1993-94), Puget Sound Oncology Consortium (brain tumor com.), Children's Cancer Group (neurosurgery com.). Achievements include initiation of ACUSTAR I surgical navigation system clinical studies at the University of Washington, gene therapy treatment. Office: U Calif San Francisco CA 94142

BERGER, NEWELL JAMES, JR. retired security professional; b. Pitts., Oct. 26, 1926; s. Newell James and Marjorie Ikler (Herndon) B.; m. Darlene Ingram, Sept. 6, 1950 (dec. Nov. 1990). BS, Mich. State U., 1958; grad., U.S. Army Command and Gen. Staff Coll., 1963, U.S. Army War Coll., 1972; MA, Webster U., 1993. Enlisted man U.S. Army, 1944, advanced through grades to staff sgt., 1948, commd. 2d lt., 1948, advanced through grades to col., 1970, chief corrections hdqrs., 1970-72, dir. security Office Surgeon Gen., 1972-73, dir. security Health Svcs. Command Ft. Sam Houston, Tex., 1973-78, ret., 1978; security cons. Phoenix and San Diego, 1979-84; chief plant security Teledyne Ryan Aero. Co., San Diego, 1985-86; dep. dir. security BAE Sys. Mission Solutions, San Diego, 1986-99; ret., 1999. Decorated Legion of Merit with two oak leaf clusters. Mem. Internat. Assn. Chiefs Police (life), Am. Soc. for Indsl. Security (life cert. protection profl.). Republican. Episcopalian. Avocations: music, history. Home: 11872 Caminito Corriente San Diego CA 92128-4550 Fax: 858-485-6247. E-mail: bergernj@aol.com

BERGER, PAUL ERIC, artist, photographer; b. The Dalles, Oreg., Jan. 20, 1948; s. Charles Glen and Virginia (Nunez) B. B.A., UCLA, 1970; M.F.A., SUNY-Buffalo, 1973. Vis. lectr. U. Ill., 1974-78; prof. art U. Wash.-Seattle, 1978—. Exhibited one-man shows, photographs, Art Inst. Chgo., 1975, Light Gallery, N.Y.C., 1977, Seattle Art Mus., 1980, Light Gallery, N.Y.C., 1982, Univ. Art Mus., Santa Barbara, Calif., 1984, Cliff Michel Gallery, 1989, Seattle Art Mus., 1990, Fuel Gallery, 1993, Galerie Lichtblick GFFK, Cologne, Germany, 1996, SOHO Photo, N.Y.C., 1999. NEA Photographer's fellow, 1979, NEA Visual Artist's fellow, 1986; recipient Artist's Commn., Wash. State Arts Commn., 1990. Mem. Soc. Photographic Edn. Office: U Wash Sch Art PO Box 353440 Seattle WA 98195-3440 E-mail: peberger@u.washington.edu

BERGER, STANLEY ALLAN, mechanical and biomechanical engineering educator; b. Bklyn., Aug. 9, 1934; s. Jack and Esther (Bernstein) B.; m. Anna Ofman, Jan. 30, 1966 (div. Aug. 1984); children: Shoshana, Maya. BS, Bklyn. Coll., 1955; PhD, Brown U., 1959. Rsch. assoc. Princeton U., N.J., 1959-60; from lectr. to prof. U. Calif., Berkeley, 1961—. Cons. IBM, The Rand Corp., Lockheed Missiles and Space Co., Sci. Applications, Inc., Aluminum Co. Am. Author: Laminar Wakes, 1971; editor: Introduction to Bioengineering, 1996; contbr. articles to profl. jours. Fellow AAAS, ASME, AIAA, Am. Phys. Soc., Am. Inst. Med. and Biol. Engring. Home: 899 Arlington Ave Berkeley CA 94707-1926 Office: U Calif Dept Mech Engring Berkeley CA 94720-1740 E-mail: saberger@me.berkeley.edu

BERGER, WOLFGANG H. oceanographer, marine geologist; b. Erlangen, Germany; came to U.S., 1961; MS in Geology, U. Colo., 1963; PhD in Oceanography, U. Calif., San Diego, 1968. Asst. prof. Scripps Inst. Oceanography U. Calif., La Jolla, 1971-74, assoc. prof., 1974-80, prof. oceanography, 1980—; dir. Calif. Space Inst. U. Calif., San Diego, 1998—. Co-editor: Abrupt Climatic Change, 1987, Ocean Productivity, 1989, co-author: The Sea Floor, 1993. Co-chief scientist, Ocean Drilling Prog., Leg 130 (1990), Leg 175 (1997). Recipient Bigelow medal Woods Hole (Mass.) Oceanographic Inst., 1979, Huntsman medal Bedford Oceanographic Inst., Can., 1984, Humboldt award German Sci. Found., Bonn, Germany, 1986, Albert I medal, Paris, 1991, Balzan prize, 1993, Steinmann medal Geol. Vereingung, 1998, Francis P. Shepard medal, Soc. for Sedimentary Geology, 2001; Lady Davis fellow Hebrew U., 1986. Fellow AAAS, Am. Geophysical Union (Ewing medal 1988), Geol. Soc. Am.; mem. European Geophysical Soc., Academia Europaea (fgn.). Avocation: water color. Office: U Calif San Diego Scripps Inst Oceanography SI0-UCSD-0524 La Jolla CA 92093 E-mail: wberger@ucsd.edu

BERGESON, MARVIN ERNEST, pediatrician; b. Seattle, Feb. 28, 1950; s. Ernest Axel Eugene and Martha Bergeson; m. Cindy Lewanne Little, Aug. 21, 1971; children: Bo Eric, Jon Carl, Will Ernst. BA, Augustana Coll., 1972; MD, U. Ill., Peoria, 1977. Diplomate Am. Bd. Pediat.; lic. physician, Wash., Alaska. Tchg. asst. biol. scis. U. Ill., 1972-73; intern, then residen in pediat. Madigan Army Med. Ctr., Tacoma, 1977-80; fellow in developmental pediat. Med. Sch. Harvard U., Boston, 1982; pvt. practice Tanana Valley Clinic, Fairbanks, Alaska, 1984—, also bd. dirs., mem. exec. com., 1986-93, 99—. Chmn. dept. pediat. Fairbanks Meml. Hosp., 1985-87; mem. drug utilization rev. State of Alaska, 1992-98. Co-contbr. articles to profl. jours. Bd. dirs. Alaska Crippled Children's Assn., 1983-89, v.p., 1984-85, 87, pres., 1985-87, 87-89; bd. dirs. Fairbanks Counseling and Adoption, 1985-93, v.p., 1986-87, pres., 1990-92, treas., 1992-93; mem. exec. com. Fairbanks Child Sexual Abuse Task Force, 1985-87, Midnight Sun coun. Boy Scouts Am., 1989-92; founding mem. Youth at Risk Multidisciplinary Team, 1990-93, Super Substance Use, Pregnancy, Edn. and Resources, 1990—; hon. bd. dirs. Resource Ctr. for Parents and Children, 1987—; pres. bd. dirs. Samaritan Counseling Ctr., 1996—; bd. dirs. Alaska Health Care Network, 1997—, v.p., 1999—; treas. Christ Luth. Ch., 1981-88, mem. ch. coun., 1982-85. Maj. U.S. Army, 1977-84. Recipient Leadership award Ill. Alumni Assn., 1977, Granville A. Bennett award for contbns. to med. edn., 1977, Pediat. award for Excellence, Ross Labs., 1977, Friends of Edn. award Beta chpt. Delta Kappa Gamma, 1988, award for Outstanding Cmty. Work, Resource Ctr. for Parents and Children, 1988, award for Vol. Svc. to Fairbanks Cmty., Arctic Alliance for People, 1988, Parent Support Group Cert. of Svc. award City of Fairbanks, 1993. Fellow Am. Acad. Pediat.; mem. AMA, North Pacific Pediat. Soc., Alaska State Med. Assn. (councilor 1989-91), Fairbanks Counseling and Adoption-Bishop Whelan Soc., Omicron Delta Kappa, Beta Beta Beta. Home: 1621 Gonzaga Way Fairbanks AK 99709-6764 Office: Tanana Valley Med Clinic 1001 Noble St Fairbanks AK 99701-4978

BERGESON, TERESA, state system administrator; BA in English, M in Counseling and Guidance, PhD in Edn. Tchr., j.h. sch. guidance counselor, Mass., Alaska, Wash.; exec. dir. Ctrl. Kitsap Sch. Dist., 1989-92, Wash. State Commn. on Learning, 1993-95; state supt. pub. instrn. Olympia, Wash., 1997—. Office: PO Box 47200 Olympia WA 98504-7200 Fax: 360-753-6712

BERGIN, ALLEN ERIC, clinical psychologist, educator; b. Spokane, Wash., Aug. 4, 1934; s. Bernard F. and Vivian Selma (Kullberg) B.; m. Marian Shafer, June 4, 1955; children: David, Sue, Cyndy, Kathy, Eric, Ben, Patrick, Daniel, Michael. BS, Brigham Young U., 1956, MS, 1957; PhD, Stanford U., 1960. Diplomate Am. Bd. Profl. Psychology. Fellow U. Wis., Madison, 1960-61; prof. psychology and edn. Tchrs. Coll., Columbia U., N.Y.C., 1961-72; prof. psychology Brigham Young U., Provo, Utah,

1972-99, dir. Values Inst., 1976-78, dir. clin. psychology, 1989-93; sr. rsch. fellow Nat. Inst. Health Care Rsch., 1992-2000, prof. emeritus, 1999—. Assessment officer Peace Corps, Washington, 1961-66; cons. NIMH, Rockville, Md., 1969-75, 90. Co-author: Changing Frontiers in Psychotherapy, 1972, A Spiritual Strategy for Counseling and Psychotherapy, 1997; co-editor: Handbook of Psychotherapy, 1971, 4th edit., 1994 (citation classic 1979), Handbook of Pyschotherapy and Religious Diversity, 2000. Bishop LDS Ch., Emerson, N.J., 1970-72, Provo, 1981-84, stake pres., 1992-95; mem. steering com. Utah Gov.'s Conf. on Families, Salt Lake City, 1979-80. Recipient Biggs-Pine award Am. Assn. Counseling and Devel., 1986, Maeser rsch. award Brigham Young U. Alumni Assn., 1986, exemplary paper award Templeton Found., 1996. Fellow APA (Disting. Contbn. to Knowledge award 1989, William James award div. 36 1990); mem. Am. Psychiat. Assn. (Pfister award 1998), Soc. for Psychotherapy Integration, Soc. for Sci. Study Religion, Soc. for Psychotherapy Rsch. (pres. 1974-75, Disting. Career award 1998), Assn. Mormon Counselors (pres. 1979-80). Republican. Avocations: world travel, writing.

BERGLUND, CARL NEIL, electronics company executive; b. Thunder Bay, Ont., Can., July 21, 1938; came to U.S., 1978; s. Anton Robert and Mary (Sideen) B.; m. Evelyn Jean McEvilla, Apr. 1, 1961; children: Cheryl Lynn, Gregory Neil (dec.), Carl Anton. B.S. with honors, Queen's U., Kingston, Ont., 1960; M.S. in Elec. Engring., MIT, 1961; Ph.D. in Elec. Engring., Stanford U., 1964. Mem. tech staff Bell Labs., Murray Hill, N.J., 1964-66, supr. semicond. devices, 1966-72; mgr. electronic materials Bell No. Research, Ottawa, 1972-73; v.p. tech. Microsystems Internat., Ottawa, 1973-74; dir. silicon technology Bell No. Research, Ottawa, 1974-78; dir. tech. devel. Intel Corp., Aloha, Oreg., 1978-83; pres., chief exec. officer ATEQ Corp., Beaverton, 1983-87; pres. Northwest Tech. Group, Tigard, 1987—; prof. elec. engring. and applied physics Oreg. Grad. Inst., Beaverton, 1994—. Contbr. articles to profl. jours.; patentee (in field). Fellow IEEE; mem. Electron Devices Soc. Home: 3135 NW Lacamas Dr Camas WA 98607-9147 Office: Northwest Tech Group PMB 138 Ste D-105 1901 NE 162d Ave Vancouver WA 98684-9346 E-mail: berglund@ece.ogi.edu

BERGMAN, ALAN, lyricist, writer; b. Bklyn., Sept. 11, 1925; s. Samuel and Ruth (Margulies) B.; m. Marilyn Keith, Feb. 9, 1958; 1 child, Julie Rachel. Grad., Ethical Culture Sch.; BA, U. N.C.; MA, UCLA; Doctorate (hon.), Berklee Coll. Music, 1995. TV dir. CBS, Phila., 1949-53; ind. lyricist, collaborator with Marilyn Bergman, 1956—. Compositions include numerous pop, TV theme, theatrical and film score songs including (TV themes) Bracken's World, 1969-70, The Sandy Duncan Show, 1972, Maude, 1972-78, Good Times, 1974-79, The Nancy Walker Show, 1976, The Dumplings, 1976, Alice, 1976-82, In the Heat of the Night, 1988-94, Brooklyn Bridge, 1991-93, The Powers That Be, 1993; (TV film lyrics) The Hands of Time (from Brian's Song), 1971, Queen of the Stardust Ballroom, 1975 (Emmy award best dramatic underscore 1975), (score only) Sybil, 1976 (Emmy award best dramatic underscore 1976), Too Many Springs (from Hollow Image), 1979; (theatrical scores) Something More, 1964, Ballroom, 1978 (Grammy award nominee for best cast show album 1979), The Lady and the Clarinet, 1980; (feature film songs) The Marriage-Go-Round, 1960 (from The Marriage-Go-Round), Any Wednesday, 1966 (from Any Wednesday), Make Me Rainbows, 1967 (from Fitzwilly), (score) In the Heat of the Night, 1967, The Windmills of Your Mind, 1968 (from The Thomas Crown Affair; Acad. award for best song 1968, Golden Globe award for best original song 1969), His Eyes, Her Eyes, 1968 (from The Thomas Crown Affair), You Must Believe in Spring, 1968 (from Young Girls at Rochefort), Maybe Tomorrow, 1969 (from John and Mary), Tomorrow Is My Friend, 1969 (from Gaily, Gaily), There's Enough to Go Around, 1969 (from Gaily, Gaily), A Smile, A Mem'ry and an Extra Shirt, 1969 (from A Man Called Gannon), Sugar in the Rain, 1969 (from Stiletto), What Are You Doing the Rest of Your Life?, 1969 (from The Happy Ending; Acad. award nominee for best song 1969), I Was Born in Love With You, 1970 (from Wuthering Heights), Sweet Gingerbread Man, 1970 (from The Magic Garden of Stanley Sweetheart), Nobody Knows, 1970 (from The Magic Garden of Stanley Sweetheart), Move, 1970 (from Move), Pieces of Dreams (AKA Little Boy Lost), 1970 (from Pieces of Dreams; Acad. award nominee for best song 1970), The Costume Ball, 1971 (from Doctors' Wives), All His Children, 1971 (from Sometimes a Great Notion; Acad. award nominee for best song 1971), Rain Falls Anywhere It Wants To, 1971 (from The African Elephant), The Summer Knows, 1971 (from Summer of '42; Grammy award nominee for song of the year 1972), A Face in the Crowd, 1971 (from Le Mans), Marmalade, Molasses and Honey, 1972 (from The Life and Times of Judge Roy Bean; Acad. award nominee for best song 1972), Love's the Only Game in Town, 1972 (from Pete and Tillie), Molly and Lawless John, 1972, The Way We Were, 1973 (from The Way We Were; Grammy award for song of the year 1973, Acad. award for best song 1973, Golden Globe award for best original song 1974, Grammy award for best original score 1974), Breezy's Song, 1973 (from Breezy), In Every Corner of the World, 1973 (from Forty Carats), Summer Wishes, Winter Dreams, 1973 (from Summer Wishes, Winter Dreams), Easy Baby, 1974 (from 99 and 44/100%), There'll Be Time, 1975 (from Ode to Billy Joe), Evening Sun, Morning Moon, 1975 (from The Yakuza), I Believe in Love, 1976 (from A Star is Born; Grammy award nominee for best original score 1977), I'm Harry, I'm Walter, 1976 (from Harry and Walter Go to New York), Hello and Goodbye, 1976 (from Noon to Three), Bobby Deerfield, 1977 (from Bobby Deerfield), The Last Time I Felt Like This, 1978 (from Same Time Next Year; Acad. award nominee for best song 1978), The One and Only, 1978 (from The One and Only), There's Something Funny Goin' On, 1979 (from ...And Justice For All), I'll Never Say Goodbye, 1979 (from The Promise; Acad. award nominee for best song 1979), Where Do You Catch the Bus for Tomorrow, 1980 (from A Change of Seasons), Ask Me No Questions, 1981 (from Back Roads), How Do You Keep the Music Playing?, 1982 (from Best Friends; Acad. award nominee best song 1982), Think About Love, 1982 (from Best Friends), Comin' Home to You, 1982 (from Author! Author!), Tootsie, 1982 (from Tootsie), It Might Be You, 1982 (from Tootsie; Acad. award nominee for best song 1982, Grammy award nominee for best original score 1983), If We Were in Love, 1982 (from Yes, Giorgio; Acad. award nominee for best song 1982), Never Say Never Again, 1983 (from Never Say Never Again), Papa, Can You Hear Me?, 1983 (from Yentl; Acad. award nominee best song 1983), The Way He Makes Me Feel, 1983 (from Yentl; Acad. award nominee for best song 1983), Will Someone Ever Look at Me That Way?, 1983 (from Yentl; Acad. award for best original score 1983, Grammy award nominee for best original score 1984), Little Boys, 1983 (from The Man Who Loved Women), Something New in My Life, 1984 (from Mickey and Maude), The Music of Goodbye, 1985 (from Out of Africa), I Know the Feeling, 1989 (from The January Man), The Girl Who Used to Be Me, 1989 (from Shirley Valentine; Acad. award nominee for best song 1989, Golden Globe nominee for best original song 1990, Grammy award nomination 1990), Welcome Home, 1989 (from Welcome Home), Most of All You, 1989 (from Major League), Dreamland, 1991 (from For the Boys), Places That Belong to You, 1991 (from The Prince of Tides), It's All There, 1991 (from Switch), Moonlight, 1995 (from Sabrina; Acad. award nominee for best original song 1996), Bogus, 1996; (pop songs) You Don't Bring Me Flowers (Grammy award nominee for song of the year 1978), In the Heat of the Night, The Summer Knows, Nice 'N' Easy (Grammy award nominee for song of the year 1960), Someone in the Dark, L.A. Is My Lady, After the Rain, I Was Born in Love With You, That Face, Look Around, I Love to Dance Like They Used to Dance, What Matters Most, One Day, A Child Is Born, Sleep Warm, Sentimental Baby, Live It Up, If I Close My Eyes, Yellow Bird, Like a Lover, Where Do You Start?, On My Way to You, Ordinary Miracles (Ace award and Emmy award for best original song); (albums) Never Be Afraid for Bing Crosby, The Ballad of the Blues for Jo Stafford; writer: Barbra Streisand: The Concert, 1995 (Ace nominee for writing of a spl., Emmy award for Best Music & Lyrics). Served with AUS, 1943-45. Named to Songwriters Hall of Fame, 1980; grantee Am. Film Inst., 1976; recipient Singers Salute to Songwriter award Clooney Foundation, 1986, Aggie award Songwriter's Guild, 1987. Mem. ASCAP, Motion Picture Acad. Arts and Scis. (gov.). Office: Gorfaine-Schwartz 13245 Riverside Dr Ste 450 Sherman Oaks CA 91423-2172

BERGMAN, GEORGE MARK, mathematician, educator; b. Bklyn., July 22, 1943; s. Lester V. and Sylvia G. (Bernstein) B.; m. Mary Frances Anderson, Dec. 26, 1981; stepsons: Jeff E. Watson, Michael L. Anderson; children: Clifford I. and Rebecca N. Anderson-Bergman (twins). BA, U. Calif., Berkeley, 1963; PhD, Harvard U., 1968. Asst. prof. Dept. Math. U. Calif., Berkeley, 1967-72, assoc. prof., 1972-78, prof., 1978—. Contbr. articles to profl. jours. Mem. AAUP, Am. Math. Soc. Democrat. Avocations: linguistics, folk-dancing. Office: U Calif Dept Math Berkeley CA 94720-3840

BERGMAN, MARILYN KEITH, lyricist, writer; b. Bklyn. d. Albert A. and Edith (Arkin) Katz; m. Alan Bergman, Feb. 9, 1958; 1 child, Julie Rachel. BA, NYU; DMus (hon.), Berklee Coll. Music, 1995, Trinity Coll., 1997. Lyricist, collaborator (with Alan Bergman) numerous pop, TV themes, theatrical and film score songs including (TV themes) Bracken's World, 1969-70, The Sandy Duncan Show, 1972, Maude, 1972-78, Good Times, 1974-79, The Nancy Walker Show, 1976, The Dumplings, 1976, Alice, 1976-82, In the Heat of the Night, 1988-94, Brooklyn Bridge, 1991-93, The Powers That Be, 1993; (TV film lyrics) The Hands of Time (from Brian's Song), 1971, Queen of the Stardust Ballroom, 1975 (Emmy award nominee for best dramatic underscore and best musical material 1975), (score only) Sybil, 1976 (Emmy award for best dramatic underscore 1976), Too Many Springs (from Hollow Image, 1979; (theatrical scores) Something More, 1964, Ballroom, 1978 (Grammy award nominee for best cast show album 1979), The Lady and the Clarinet, 1980; (feature film songs) The Marriage Go-Round, 1960 (from The Marriage Go-Round), Any Wednesday, 1966 (from Any Wednesday), Make Me Rainbows, 1967 (from Fitzwilly), (score) In the Heat of the Night, 1967, The Windmills of Your Mind, 1968 (from The Thomas Crown Affair, Acad. award for best song 1968, Golden Globe award best original song 1969), His Eyes, Her Eyes, 1968 (from The Thomas Crown Affair), You Must Believe in Spring, 1968 (from Young Girls at Rochefort), Maybe Tomorrow, 1969 (from John and Mary), Tomorrow Is My Friend, 1969 (from Gaily, Gaily), There's Enough to Go Around, 1969 (from Gaily, Gaily), A Smile, A Mem'ry and an Extra Shirt, 1969 (from A Man Called Gannon), Sugar in the Rain, 1969 (from Stiletto), What Are You Doing the Rest of You Life?, 1969 (from The Happy Ending; Acad. award nominee for best song 1969), I Was Born in Love With You, 1970 (from Wuthering Heights), Sweet Gingerbread Man, 1970 (from The Magic Garden of Stanley Sweetheart), Nobody Knows, 1970 (from The Magic Garden of Stanley Sweetheart), Move, 1970 (from Move), Pieces of Dreams, 1970 (from Pieces of Dreams; Academy award nominee for best song 1970), Little Boy Lost, 1970 (from Pieces of Dreams) The Costume Ball, 1971 (from Doctors' Wives), All His Children, 1971 (from Sometimes a Great Notion; Acad. award nominee for best song 1971), Rain Falls Anywhere It Wants To, 1971 (from the African Elephant), The Summer Knows, 1971 (from Summer of '42 (Grammy award nominee for song of the year 1972), A Face in the Crowd, 1971 (from Le Mans), Marmalade, Molasses and Honey, 1972 (from The Life and Times of Judge Roy Bean; Acad. award nominee for best song 1972), Love's the Only Game in Town, 1972 (from Pete and Tillie), Molly and Lawless John, 1972, The Way We Were, 1973 (from The Way We Were; Grammy award for song of the year 1973, Acad. award for best song 1973, Golden Globe award for best original song 1974, Grammy award for best original score 1974), Breezy's Song, 1973, (from Breezy), In Every Corner of the World, 1973 (from Forty Carats), Summer Wishes, Winter Dreams, 1973 (from Summer Wishes, Winter Dreams), Easy Baby, 1974 (from 99 and 44/100%), There'll Be Time, 1975 (from Ode to Billy Joe), Evening Sun, Morning Moon, 1975 (from The Yakuza), I Believe in Love, 1976 (from A Star is Born; Grammy award nomination best original score 1977), I'm Harry, I'm Walter, 1976 (from Harry and Walter Go to New York), Hello and Goodbye, 1976 (from Noon to Three), Bobby Deerfield, 1977 (from Bobby Deerfield), The Last Time I Felt Like This, 1978 (from Same Time Next Year; Acad. award nominee for best song 1978), The One and Only, 1978 (from The One and Only), There's Something Funny Goin' On, 1979 (from ...And Justice For All), I'll Never Say Goodbye, 1979 (from The Promise; Acad. award nominee for best song 1979), Where Do You Catch the Bus for Tomorrow, 1980 (from A Change of Seasons), Ask Me No Questions, 1981 (from Back Roads), How Do You Keep the Music Playing?, 1982 (from Best Friends; Acad. award nominee for best song 1982), Think About Love, 1982 (from Best Friends), Comin' Home to You, 1982 (from Author! Author!), Tootsie, 1982 (from Tootsie), It Might Be You,1982 (from Tootsie; Acad. award nominee for best song, 1982, Grammy award nominee for best original score 1983), If We Were in Love, 1982 (from Yes, Giorgio; Acad. award nominee for best song 1982), Never Say Never Again, 1983 (from Never Say Never again), Papa, Can You Hear Me?, 1983 (from Yentl; Academy award nomination best song 1983), The Way He Makes Me Feel, 1983 (from Yentl; Acad. award nominee for best song 1983), Will Someone Ever Look at Me That Way?, 1983 (from Yentl; Acad. award best original score and Grammy award nomination for best original score 1984), Little Boys, 1983 (from The Man Who Loved Women), Something New in My Life, 1984 (from Mickey and Maude), The Music of Goodbye, 1985 (from Out of Africa), I Know the Feeling, 1989 (from The January Man), The Girl Who Used to Be Me, 1989 (from Shirley Valentine; Acad. award nominee for best song 1989, Golden Globe nominee for best original song 1990, Grammy award nominee 1990), Welcome Home, 1989 (from Welcome Home), Most of All You, 1989 (from Major League), Dreamland, 1991 (from For the Boys), Places That Belong to You, 1991 (from The Prince of Tides), It's All There, 1991 (from Switch), Moonlight, 1995 (from Sabrina; Acad. award nominee for best original song 1996, Golden Globe nominee, Grammy nominee), Bogus, 1996; Love is Where You Are (from at first sight), 1998 (pop songs) You Don't Bring Me Flowers (Grammy award nominee for song of the year 1978), In the Heat of the Night, The Summer Knows, Nice 'N' Easy (Grammy award nominee for song of the year 1960), Someone in the Dark, L.A. Is My Lady, After the Rain, I Was Born in Love With You, That Face, Look Around, I Love to Dance Like They Used to Dance, What Matters Most, One Day, A Child Is Born, Sleep Warm, Sentimental Baby, Live It Up, If I Close My Eyes, Yellow Bird, Like a Lover, Where Do You Start?, On My Way to You, Ordinary Miracles (Cable Ace award and Emmy award for best original song); A Ticket to Dream (Emmy Awd. for best song), 1999 (albums) Never Be Afraid for Bing Crosby, The Ballad of the Blues for Jo Stafford, Barbra Streisand: The Concert (Ace nominee for writing of a spl.). Named to songwriters hall of Fame, 1980; grantee Am. Film Inst., 1976; recipient singers salute to songwriter award Clooney Found., 1986, Aggie award Songwriter's Guild, 1987. Mem. ASCAP (pres., chmn. bd. dirs. 1994—). Office: Gorfaine-Schwartz 13245 Riverside Dr Ste 450 Sherman Oaks CA [illegible] Office: ASCAP One Lincoln Plz New York NY 10023 Office: ASCAP 714 N Maple Drive Beverly Hills CA 90210

BERGMAN, NANCY PALM, real estate investment company executive; b. McKeesport, Pa., Dec. 3, 1938; d. Walter Vaughn and Nellie (Sullivan) Leech; m. Donald Bergman; 1 child, Tiffany Palm Taylor. Student, Mt. San Antonio Coll., 1970, UCLA, 1989-93. Corporate sec. U.S. Filter Corp., Newport Beach, Calif., 19[illegible]—. Pres. Jaguar Research Corp., Los Angeles and Atlanta, 1971— ; owner Environ. Designs, Los Angeles, 1976—; pres. Prosher Corp., Los Angeles., 1978-83; now pres., dir. Futura Investments, L.A.; CEO Rescor, Inc. Author: Resident Managers Handbook. Home: 8 Fincher Way Rancho Mirage CA 92270-3036 also: 2257 Century Hl Los Angeles CA 90067-3506 Office: PO Box 67566 Los Angeles CA 90067-0566

BERGMAN, ROBERT GEORGE, chemist, educator; b. Chgo., May 23, 1942; s. Joseph J. and Stella (Horowitz) B.; m. Wendy L. Street, June 17, 1965; children: David R., Michael S. BA cum laude in chemistry, Carleton Coll., 1963; PhD (NIH fellow), U. Wis., 1966; PhD (hon.), Carleton Coll., 1995. NATO fellow in chemistry Columbia U., N.Y.C., 1966-67; Arthur Amos Noyes instr. chemistry Calif. Inst. Tech., Pasadena, 1967-69, asst. prof. chemistry, 1969-71, assoc. prof. chemistry, 1971-73, prof., 1973-77; prof. chemistry U. Calif. at Berkeley, 1977—; asst. dean Coll. Chemistry U. Calif., Berkeley, 1987-91, 96, Miller Rsch. prof., 1982-83, 93. Sherman Fairchild Disting. scholar Calif. Inst. Tech., 1984; mem. panel NIH bioinorganic and metallobiochemistry study sect. NIH, 1977-80; cons. E.I. DuPont de Nemours, 1982-85, Chevron Rsch. Co., 1983-89, Union Carbide Corp., 1977-81, 90—; disting. vis. prof. U. N.C., Chapel Hill, 1999. Mem. editorial bd. Chem. Revs., Jour. Am. Chem. Soc., Organometallics, Tetrahedron Publs.; contbr. articles to profl. jours. Recipient Tchr. Scholar award Camille and Henry Dreyfus Found., 1970-75, Excellence in Tchg. award Calif. Inst. Tech., 1978, Merit award NIH, 1991, E.O. Lawrence award for chemistry Dept. Energy, 1993, Chem. Pioneer award Am. Inst. of Chemists, 2000; Alfred P. Sloan Found. fellow, 1970-72, Guggenheim fellow, 1999. Fellow Calif. Acad. Sci.; mem. AAAS, Nat. Acad. Scis., Am. Chem. Soc. (Organometallic Chemistry award 1986, Edward Fahs Smith award Pa. sect. 1990, Ira Remsen award Balt. sect. 1990, Arthur C. Cope award, 1996, Edward Leete award 2001, Arthur C. Cope scholar 1987), Phi Beta Kappa, Sigma Xi, Phi Lambda Upsilon. Home: 501 Coventry Rd Kensington CA 94707-1316 Office: U Calif Dept Chemistry Berkeley CA 94720-0001

BERGMAN, YAACOV, performing company executive; b. Israel; m. Joan Behrens. Degree in conducting and composition, Rubin Acad., Hebrew U., Jerusalem; studied with Herbert Westenburg, Mannes Coll. Music; studied with Charles Bruck, Leonard Bernstein. Music dir. Colorado Springs (Colo.) Symphony. Music dir. Walla Walla (Wash.) Symphony; founder, music dir., condr. Heritage Orch. N.Y.; condr. Osaka (Japan) Opera Co., 1996. Office: Colorado Springs Symphony PO Box 1692 Colorado Springs CO 80901-1692

BERGREN, SCOTT C. career officer; b. Mineola, N.Y. BA in Econ., Clemson U., 1970; student navigator tng., Mather AFB, Calif., 1970-71; student, Squadron Officer Sch., 1974; M in Polit. Sci., Auburn U., 1981; student, Air Command and Staff Coll., 1981, Air War Coll., 1990, Harvard U., 1996. Commd. 2d lt. USAF, 1970, advanced through grades to maj. gen., 1999, various F-4 Phantom assignments, 1971-76; air staff ops. officer programs and resources Air Staff Tng. program, Hdqs. USAF, Pentagon, Washington, 1976-77, asst. exec. officer to dep. chief staff programs/resources, 1976-77; instr., navigator and exchange officer 237th Operational Conversion Unit, RAFB Honington, Eng., 1977-80; dir. ops. force analysis div. then spl. asst. comdr. Hdqs. Tactical Air Command, Langley AFB, Va., 1981-85; comdr. 325th Tactical Tng. Wing's Aircraft Generation Squadron, Tyndall AFB, Fla., 1985-87, asst. dep. comdr. maintenance, 1985-87; dep. comdr. maintenance 33rd Tactical Fighter Wing, Eglin AFB, 1987-89; Air Univ. chair for chief staff of Air Force Maxwell AFB, Ala., 1990-91; various comdr. positions Nellis AFB, Nev., 1991-93; stationed at U.S. Ctrl. Command, MacDill AFB, Fla., 1994-96; vice comdr. San Antonio Air Logistics Ctr., Kelly AFB, Tex., 1996-97; comdr. 82d Tng. Wing, Sheppard AFB, 1997-99; dir. maintenance, dep. chief staff installations & logistics HQ/USAF, 1999-2000; comdr. Ogden Air Logistics Ctr., Hill AFB, Utah, 2000—. Decorated Silver Star, D.F.C. with silver oak leaf cluster, Purple Heart, Air medal with three silver oak leaf clusters and bronze oak leaf cluster, Small Arms Expert Marksmanship Ribbon, Rep. Vietnam Gallantry Cross with Palm, Rep. Vietnam Campaign medal. Office: Hill AFBM OO-ALC/CC 7981 Georgia St Hill Air Force Base UT 84056-5824

BERK, JACK EDWARD, gastroenterologist, educator; b. Phila. s. Samuel and Esther B.; m. Adeline Elizabeth Alberts, June 26, 1937; children: Philip Howard (dec.), Richard Hanna. BA, U. Pa., 1932, MSc in Medicine, 1939, DSc in Medicine, 1943; MD, Jefferson Med. Coll., 1936; postgrad., Grad. Sch. Medicine, U. Pa., 1937-38. Diplomate Am. Bd. Internal Medicine, Am. Bd. Gastroenterology. Intern Walter Reed Gen. Hosp., Washington, 1936-37; resident in medicine No. divsn. Albert Einstein Med. Ctr., Phila., 1938-39; fellow gastroenterology Grad. Hosp., U. Pa., 1939-40; Ross V. Patterson fellow physiology Jefferson Med. Coll., Phila., 1940-41; instr. gastroenterology U. Pa., 1941-46; asst. prof. medicine Sch. Medicine, Temple U., 1946-54; asst. dir. Fels Research Inst., 1946-54; assoc. prof. clin. medicine Coll. Medicine, Wayne State U., 1954-62, prof. clin. medicine, 1962-63; prof. medicine Coll. Medicine, U. Calif., Irvine, 1963-79, Disting. prof. medicine, 1979—, chmn. dept. medicine, 1963-79, head div. gastroenterology, 1963-79, asst. dean, 1979-90. Cons. VA Hosp., Long Beach, Calif., 1963-97, Cedars-Sinai Med. Ctr., 1963—, Meml. Hosp., Long Beach, 1964-97. Contbg. author: Bockus Gastroenterology, 1st and 2nd edits.; assoc. editor: Bockus Gastroenterology 3d edit., 1974, editor-in-chief 4th edit., 1985, cons. editor 5th edit., 1994; editor: Developments in Digestive Diseases, Vol. 1, 1977, Vol. 2, 1979, Vol. 3, 1980; co-editor: Gastrointestinal Symptoms: Clinical Interpretation, 1991; mem. editl. bd. 13 med. jours., various times, 1959—; delivered 14 named lectureships; contbr. 200 articles to med. jours., 108 chpts. to more than 60 books. U.S. Dept. State rep. to S.Am. countries Cultural Exchange Program, 1961. Served to maj. M.C. AUS, 1941-46. Recipient Disting. Service award Mich. Med. Soc., 1959, Faculty Community Service award U. Calif.-Irvine Alumni Assn., 1971, also Faculty Univ. Service award, 1976, Disting. Achievement award Jefferson Med. Coll. Alumni Assn., 1977, Maimonides award Maimonides Soc., 1984, Centennial award N.E. High Sch., Phila., 1990, Disting. Univ. Svc. Aldrich award U. Calif., Irvine, 1993, Bockus medal World Orgn. Gastroenterology, 1994; named Disting. Physician Nat. Found. for Ileitis and Colitis, 1980; J. Edward Berk Lectr. established U. Calif. Irvine Gastroenterology Alumni Assn., Aug., 1991, J. Edward Berk Lectr. established U. Calif. Irvine Vol. Clin. Faculty, 1991, J. Edward Berk Alumni Med. Edn. Ctr. dedicated U. Calif., Irvine, May 30, 1996. Master ACP (gov. So. Calif. region II 1976-80, Laureate award So. Calif. region 1990), Am. Coll. Gastroenterology (pres. 1975-76, Rorer award 1970, 74, 78, 79, Disting. Sci. Achievement award 1982, Clin. Achievement award 1988, Samuel Weiss award 1995); mem. Am. Gastroent. Assn. (Disting. Educator award 1992), Am. Soc. Gastrointestinal Endoscopy (pres. 1958-59, Rudolf Schindler award 1966), Am. Fedn. Clin. Research (past chmn. Eastern sect.), Bockus Internat. Soc. Gastroenerology (pres. 1967-71), AMA (chmn. sect. gastroenterology 1965-66), Detroit Gastroent. Soc. (pres. 1960-61), So. Calif. Soc. Gastroenterology (pres. 1967-68), L.A. Acad. Medicine (gov. 1981-84), So. Calif. Soc. Gastrointestinal [illegible] (hon.), Orange County Acad. Medicine, Orange County Gastroenterology Soc. (founding pres.), Interam. Gastroent. Assn. (life, hon. pres. 1981—), Sigma Xi, Alpha Omega Alpha, Fgn. Med. Soc., Acad. Med. Ecuador, Peruvian and Cuban Soc. Gastroenterology (hon.), Gastroenterology Socs. Colombia (corr.), Gastrointestinal Endoscopy Soc. Colombia (corr.), Ecuador, Venezuela and Brazilian Soc. of Gastroenterology and Nutrition. Home: 894 Ronda Sevilla Unit C Laguna Woods CA [illegible] Office: Univ Calif Irvine Med Ctr Dept of Medicine 101 The City Dr Orange CA 92868-3201 E-mail: jeberk@uci.edu

BERKLEY, JAMES DONALD, clergyman; b. Yakima, Wash., May 19, 1950; s. Donald William and Erma Ercile (Van Meter) B.; m. Deborah Milam, Aug. 18, 1974; children: Peter James, Mary Milam. BS, U. Wash., 1972; MDiv, Fuller Theol. Seminary, 1975, D Ministry, 1980. Intern First Presbyn. Ch., Yakima, Wash., 1971-73, Bel Air Presbyn. Ch., L.A., 1973-75; asst. pastor Community Presbyn Ch., Ventura, Calif., 1975-78; sr. pastor Dixon (Calif.) Community Ch., 1978-85; sr. assoc. editor Leadership jour. Christianity Today Inc., Carol Stream, Ill., 1985-90, editor Your Church, 1990-94; sr. assoc. pastor First Presbyn. Ch., Bellevue, Wash., 1994—. Author: Making the Most of Mistakes, 1987, Called into Crisis, 1988, The Dynamics of Church Finance, 2000, Essential Christianity, 2001; gen. editor: Preaching to Convince, 1986, Leadership Handbooks of Practical Theology, Vol. I, 1992, Vols. II and III, 1994; editor reNEWS, 1999—. Recipient 1st place award interview Evangelical Press Assn., 1991, 92. Republican. Avocations: bagpipes, hiking, tennis, golf, music. Home: 304 128th Ave NE Bellevue WA 98005-3242 Office: First Presbyn Ch 1717 Bellevue Way NE Bellevue WA 98004-2853

BERKLEY, ROBERT JOHN, retired federal agency professional; b. Albion, Mich., Oct. 2, 1933; s. Paul Clifford and Ina Muriel (Burroughs) B.; m. Sharon Irene Haynes, Sept. 9, 1955 (div. 1965); children: Thomas Alan, Richard Jon, Luann Michele; m. Jacquelyn Jane (Lewis) Ballou, Jan. 14, 1966. AA, Jackson (Mich.) Jr. Coll., 1953; BS in Police Adminstrn., Calif. State U., L.A., 1962. Police officer City of Claremont, Calif., 1959-62, 63-66; investigator U.S. Civil Svc. Commn., Washington and L.A., 1962-63, 66-72; spl. agt. FAA, Seattle, 1972-99, office mgr., 1973-99, ret., 1999. Local chmn. Selective Svc. Bd., Wash., 1981-2001. Sgt. USMC, 1953-56, Korea. Mem. SAR (chpt. pres. 1989-90, state sec. 1989-91, state pres. 1992, Patriots medal 1990, Law Enforcement medal 1991, 92), Am. Legion, Eastern Star (patron 1989-90), Masons (master 1984, life), Scottish Rite, Shriners. Avocations: computers, photography, camping, travel. Home: 644 Briarwood Ter East Wenatchee WA 98802-8326 E-mail: rj.berkley2@verizon.net

BERKLEY, SHELLEY, congresswoman; b. N.Y.C., Jan. 20, 1951; BA, U. NEv., 1972; JD, U. San Diego, 1976. Mem. U.S. Congress from 1st Nev. dist., 1999—; mem. transp. and infrastructure com., internat. affairs com., vet. affairs com. Democrat. Office: US Ho Reps 439 Cannon House Office Bldg Washington DC 20515-0001 also: 2340 Paseo Del Prado Ste D-106 Las Vegas NV 89102*

BERKLEY, STEPHEN MARK, computer industry entrepreneur and investor; b. N.J., 1944; s. Irving S. and Goldie A. Berkley; children: David, Michael. Student, London Sch. Econs., 1964-65; BA in Econs., Colgate U., 1966; MBA, Harvard U., 1968. Mgmt. cons. Boston Cons. Group, 1968, 71-73; mgr. strategic planning Potlatch Corp., 1973-77; v.p. bus. devel. Qume Corp. subs. ITT, Hayward, Calif., 1977-80, v.p., gen. mgr. memory products divs., 1980-81; v.p. mktg. Quantum Corp., Milpitas, Calif., 1981-83, chmn., CEO, 1987-92, chmn., 1992-93, 95-98; pres. Plus Devel. Corp. (Quantum subs.), 1983-87, chmn., CEO, 1987-92; pres. The Rosewood Found., 1991—. Bd. dirs. Quantum Corp., Edify Corp., Coactive Computing Corp.; instr. bus. and econs. E. Carolina U., 1969-71. Served to lt. USNR, 1968-71. Mem. Corp. Planners Assn. (dir.), Harvard Bus. Sch. Club No. Calif., Los Altos Golf and Country Club, The Reserve Golf Club, Phi Beta Kappa. Avocations: golf, modern art, travel. E-mail: berkleys@aol.com

BERKNER, KLAUS HANS, laboratory administrator, physicist; b. Dessau, Anhalt, Germany, Mar. 2, 1938; came to U.S., 1948; s. Hans Otto and Sigrid Erika B. SB, MIT, 1960; PhD, U. Calif., Berkeley, 1964. NSF grad. fellowship U. Calif., Berkeley, 1960-61; NSF postdoctoral fellowship Culham, Eng., 1965-66; physicist Lawrence Berkeley (Calif.) Lab., 1964-79, sr. physicist, 1979—, deputy div. dir. accelerator and fusion research, 1982-84, acting div. dir., 1984-85, div. dir., 1985-91, assoc. lab. dir. for ops., 1991-94; dep. dir. ops., 1994—. Mem. Basic Energy Scis. Adv. Com., 1991-96, co-chair, 1993-96; mem. Fusion Energy Adv. Com., 1991-93. Contbr. over 100 articles on atomic physics, accelerators and fusion research to profl. jours. Fellow Am. Phys. Soc. Office: Lawrence Berkeley Nat Lab Dep Dir Ops 1 Cyclotron Rd Berkeley CA 94720-0001 E-mail: khberkner@lbl.gov

BERKOWITZ, STEVE, publishing company executive; Staff acct. J Herbert & Co, N.Y.C., 1980-81, Paramount Pictures, N.Y.C., 1981-83; fin. analyst Macmillan Pub., N.Y.C., 1983-85, bus. mgr., 1985-88, v.p. fin., 1988-91; v.p. pub. MIS Press, N.Y.C., 1991-94; pres. IDG Books Worldwide, Foster City, Calif., 1994—.

BERKUS, DAVID WILLIAM, venture capitalist; b. Los Angeles, Mar. 23, 1941; s. Harry Jay and Clara S. (Widess) B.; m. Kathleen McGuire, Aug. 6, 1966; children: Eric, Matthew, Amy. BA, Occidental Coll., 1962. Pres. Custom Fidelity Inc., Hollywood, Calif., 1958-74, Berkus Compusystems Inc., Los Angeles, 1974-81; pres., CEO, Computerized Lodging Systems Inc. and subs., Los Angeles, 1981-93; pres. Berkus Tech. Ventures, venture capital, L.A., 1993—; mng. dir. worldwide lodging Sulcus Computer Corp., 1998-99; mng. ptnr. Kodiak Ventures, LP, L.A., 1999—. Chmn., bd. dirs. seven private and one pub. corps. Author: Better Than Money, 1994; author software Hotel Compusystem, 1979; creator 1st artificial intelligence-based yield mgmt. sys., 1987. Chmn. bd. Boy Scouts Am., San Gabriel Valley, 1986, v.p. area IV, 1993-94, pres. 1995-98, v.p. western region, 1998—; trustee Occidental Coll., L.A. Lt. USNR, 1963-72. Recipient Disting. award of Merit, Boy Scouts Am., 1986, INC. mag. 500 award, 1986, Silver Beaver award Boy Scouts Am., 1988, Silver Antelope award, 1997, Dir. of Yr. award Forum for Corp. Dirs., 1999, Alumni Seal award Occidental Coll., 2000; inducted into hospitality industry Hall of Fame, 1998. Mem. Am. Hotel-Motel Assn., Audio Engring. Soc. (chmn. Los Angeles sect. 1973-74). Office: 1430 Glencoe Dr Arcadia CA 91006-1909

BERKUS, JAMES, talent agent; Pres. United Talent Agy., Beverly Hills, Calif., chmn., 1997—. Office: United Talent Agy 9560 Wilshire Blvd Fl 5 Beverly Hills CA 90212-2400

BERLAND, JAMES FRED, software company executive; b. Chgo., July 12, 1943; s. Samuel Jesse and Lillian (Singer) B. Student, Reed Coll., 1961-64, UCLA, 1964-66; student exec. mgmt. program, Harvard U., 1980. Photographer with Elson-Alexandre, 1970-73; freelance journalist, 1970-74; pub. affairs dir. Sta. KPFK-FM-Pacifica, L.A., 1974-77; news dir., 1977-78; gen. mgr., v.p. Sta. KPFK-FM, Pacificia Found. Radio, 1978-84; pres., CEO News Wave Internat., Inc., L.A., 1984-85; CEO, Berland Techs., Inc., L.A., 1985—, CardReady Internat., Inc., 1998—. Mem. Calif. State Task Force on Telecom. Policy; active Californians for Pub. Broadcasting, chmn., 1980-81, pres., 1981-83; bd. dirs. Card Realty Internat. Mem. Assn. Calif. Pub. Radio Stas. (pres. 1980-82), Profl. Networking Group, CEO Club. Democrat. Office: 11242 Playa Ct Unit B Culver City CA 90230-6127 E-mail: Jim@berlandtech.com

BERMAN, BRUCE, entertainment company executive, television producer; b. N.Y.C., Apr. 25, 1952; Grad., Calif. Inst. Arts Film Sch.; grad. magna cum laude in history, UCLA, 1975; JD, Georgetown U., 1978. Bar: Calif. 1978. Asst. to Jack Valenti Warner Bros., Burbank, Calif.; asst. to Peter Guber Casablanca Filmworks, 1979; asst. to Sean Daniel and Joel Silver Universal Pictures, 1979, v.p. prodn., 1982, Warner Bros., 1984, sr. v.p. prodn., 1988, pres. theatrical prodn., 1991-96, chmn., CEO Village Roadshow Pictures, 1998; pres. Worldwide Prodn., 1991-96. Founder Plan B Entertainment, 1996—. Office: Village Roadshow Pictures care Warner Bros Studios 3400 W Riverside Dr Ste 900 Burbank CA 91505-4639

BERMAN, DANIEL LEWIS, lawyer; b. Washington, Dec. 14, 1934; s. Herbert A. and Ruth N. (Abramson) B.; children: Priscilla Decker, Jane, Katherine Ann, Sara Mark, Heather, Melinda. BA, Williams Coll., 1956; LLB, Columbia U., 1959. Bar: N.Y. 1960, Utah 1962. Assoc. Chadbourne, Parke, Whiteside & Wolff, N.Y.C., 1959-60; asst. prof. law U. Utah, 1960-62; pvt. practice Salt Lake City, 1962—; sr. ptnr. Berman, Gaufin, Tomsic, Savage & Campbell, Salt Lake City, 1981—. Vis. prof. U. Utah, 1970, 74, 77; mem. Utah Coordinating Coun. Higher Edn., 1965-68, Salt Lake County Merit counsel, 1974-80; mem. nominating commn. Utah Appellate Ct., 1999—. Trustee Salt Lake Art Ctr., 1978-80; Dem. candidate for U.S. Senate from Utah, 1980; mem. Utah Transity Authority, 1992-97. Mem. Am. Law Inst., Salt Lake Area C. of C. (bd. govs. 1976-79). Democrat. Jewish. Office: Berman Gaufin Tomsic Savage & Campbell 50 S Main St Ste 1250 Salt Lake City UT 84144-2073 E-mail: dberman@bgtslaw.com

BERMAN, HOWARD LAWRENCE, congressman; b. L.A., Apr. 15, 1941; s. Joseph M. and Eleanor (Schapiro) B.; m. Janis Berman, 1979; children: Brinley Ann, Lindsey Rose. BA, UCLA, 1962, LLB, 1965. Bar: Calif. 1966. Vol. VISTA, Balt., San Francisco, 1966-67; assoc. Levy, Van Bourg & Hackler, L.A., 1967-72; mem. Calif. State Assembly from 43d dist., 1972-82 (majority leader), U.S. Congress from 26th Calif. dist., Washington, 1983—. Ranking mem. com. standards of ofcl. conduct, mem. jud. com., internat. law, immigration and refugees, intellectual property and jud. adminstrn. subcoms., mem. internat. rels. com. Pres. Calif. Fedn. Young Democrats, 1967-69 (budget com.); mem. adv. bd. Jewish Fund for Justice. Office: US Ho Reps 2330 Rayburn Ho Office Bldg Washington DC 20515-0001*

BERMAN, NEIL SHELDON, chemical engineering educator; b. Milw., Sept. 21, 1933; s. Henry and Ella B.; m. Sarah Ayres, June 3, 1962; children: Jenny, Daniel. B.S., U. Wis., 1955; M.S., M.A., U. Tex., Austin, 1961, Ph.D., 1962. Engr. Standard Oil Co. Calif., Los Angeles, 1955-62; research engr. E.I. DuPont Co., Wilmington, Del., 1962-64; from asst. prof. to prof. chem. engring. Ariz. State U., 1964-2000; prof. emeritus, 2000—; Grad. Coll. Disting. Rsch. prof. Ariz. State U., 1984-85. Cons. air pollution, fluid dynamics; mem. Phoenix Air Quality Maintenance Area Task Force, 1976-77 Contbr. articles on fluid dynamics of polymer solutions, air pollution, thermodynamics and chem. engring. edn. to profl. jours. Served to capt. M.S.C. USAR, 1956-58. Recipient numerous grants for research in fluid dynamics and air pollution. Fellow Am. Inst. Chem. Engrs. (chmn. Ariz. sect. 1978-79), AAAS, Ariz.-Nev. Acad. Sci. (corr. sec. 1981-88, pres.-elect 1988-89, pres. 1989-90); mem. ASME, Am. Chem. Soc., Am. Phys. Soc., Ariz. Council Engring. and Sci. Assns. (chmn. 1980-81), Soc. Rheology, Am. Soc. Engring. Edn., Am. Acad. Mechanics, Nat. Assn. State Acads. Sci. (mem.-at-large bd. dirs.), Sigma Xi, Tau Beta Pi, Phi Kappa Phi. Home: 418 E Geneva Dr Tempe AZ 85282-3731 Office: Ariz State U Dept Chem Engring Tempe AZ 85287-6006

BERMAN, STEPHEN G. toy manufacturing executive; b. 1965; V.p., mng. dir. TH-Q Internat., Inc., 1991-95; co-founder, exec. v.p., sec. JAKKS Pacific Inc., Malibu, Calif., 1995-96, pres., COO, sec., dir., 1996—. Office: JAKKS Pacific Inc Ste 226 22761 Pacific Coast Hwy Malibu CA 90265-5064 Fax: (310) 317-8527

BERN, HOWARD ALAN, science educator, research biologist; b. Montreal, Que., Can., Jan. 30, 1920; m. Estelle Bruck, 1946; children: Alan, Lauren. BA, UCLA, 1941, MA, 1942, PhD in Zoology, 1948; D (hon.), U. Rouen, France, 1996; LLD (hon.), U. Hokkaido, Japan, 1994; DPhil (hon.), Yokohama City U., 1997; DSc (hon.), Toho U., Japan, 2001. Nat. Rsch. Coun. predoctoral fellow in biology UCLA, 1946-68; instr. in zoology U. Calif., Berkeley, 1948-50, asst. prof., 1950-56, assoc. prof., 1956-60, prof., 1960-89, prof. integrative biology, 1989-90, prof. emeritus, 1990—; rsch. endocrinologist Cancer Rsch. Lab., U. Calif., Berkeley, 1960—; chair group in endocrinology U. Calif., Berkeley, 1962-90, faculty rsch. lectr., 1988. Rsch. prof. Miller Inst. for Basic Rsch. in Sci., 1961; vis. prof. pharmacology U. Bristol, 1965-66, U. Kerala, India, 1967, Ocean Rsch. Inst., U. Tokyo, 1971, 86, U. P.R., 1973, 74, U. Tel Aviv, 1975, Nat. Mus. Natural History, Paris, 1981, Toho U., Funabashi, Japan, 1982-84, 86-89, U. Hawaii, 1986, 91-93, Hokkaido U., 1992, 94, U. Fla., 1991, 92; James vis. prof. St. Francis Xavier U., Antigonish, N.S., 1986; Walker-Ames prof. U. Wash., 1977; disting. visitor U. Alta., Edmonton, Can., 1981; John W. Cowper Disting. vis. lectr. SUNY-Buffalo, 1984; Watkins vis. prof. Wichita (Kans.) State U., 1984; vis. scholar Meiji U., Tokyo, 1986; internat. guest prof. Yokohama City U., Japan, 1988, 95; lectr., spkr. in field; mem. adv. com. on instl. rsch. grants Am. Cancer Soc., 1967-70; mem. adv. com. Nat. Cancer Inst., 1975-79; mem. NIH adv. com. in Endocrinology and Metabolism, 1978-79; mem. GM Cancer Rsch. Found., Sloan Medal Selection Com., 1984-85, Japan Internat. Prize in Biology Selection Com., 1987, 92, 96. Mem. editl. bd. Endocrinology, 1962-74, Gen. and Comparative Endocrinology, Revs. in Fish Biology and Fisheries, Jour. Exptl. Zoology, 1965-69, 86-89, Internat. Rev. Cytology, Neuroendocrinology, 1974-80, Cancer Rsch., 1975-78, Jour. Comparative Physiology B, 1977-84, Am. Zoologist, 1978-83, Acta Zoologica, 1982-96, Zool. Sci., Tokyo, Animal Biol., Italy; contbr. articles to profl. publs. Assoc. Nat. Mus. Natural History, Paris, 1980; mem. adv. com. Contra Costa Cancer Rsch. Fund, 1984-98, Stazione Zoologica Anton Dohrn de Napoli, 1987-92. Recipient Disting. Tchg. award U. Calif., Berkeley, 1972, The Berkeley Citation, 1990, Disting. Svc. award Soc. Adv. Chicanos and Native Americans in Sci., 1990, Hatai medal Sci. Coun. Japan, 2001, Beverton medal Fisheries Soc. Brit. Isles, 2001; Guggenheim fellow, 1951-52, NSF fellow U. Hawaii, 1958-59, fellow Ctr. for Advanced Study in Behavioral Scis., Stanford, 1960, NSF fellow Stazione Zoologica, Naples, 1965-66, Japan Soc. Promotion of Sci. Rsch. fellow U. Toyama, Japan, 1993. Fellow NAS, AAAS, Am. Acad. Arts and Scis., Indian Nat. Sci. Acad. (fgn.), Società Nazionale di Scienze Lettere e Arti Napoli (fgn.), Calif. Acad. Sci., Accademia Nazionale dei Lincei (fgn.); mem. Soc. Integrative Comparative Biology (hon., pres. 1967), Am. Assn. Cancer Rsch., Am. Physiol. Soc., Endocrine Soc., Internat. Soc. Neuroendocrinology (coun. 1977-80), Exptl. Biology and Medicine (coun. 1980-83), Am. Soc. Molec. Marine Biol. Biotech., Western Soc. Naturalists, Japan Soc. Zootech. Sci. (hon.), Japan Soc. Comparative Endocrinology (hon.), Cosmos Club. Home: 1010 Shattuck Ave Berkeley CA 94707-2626 Office: U Calif Dept Integrative Biology Berkeley CA 94720-3140 Fax: 510-643-6264. E-mail: bern@socrates.berkeley.edu

BERNACCHI, RICHARD LLOYD, lawyer; b. Los Angeles, Dec. 15, 1938; s. Bernard and Anne B. B.S. with honors in Commerce (Nat. Merit Found. scholar), U. Santa Clara, 1961; LL.B. with highest honors (Legion Lex scholar, Jerry Geisler Meml. scholar), U. So. Calif., 1964. Bar: Calif. 1964. Assoc. Irell and Manella, L.A., 1964-70, ptnr., 1970—; lectr. Am. Law Inst., 1972-73; lectr. data processing contracts and law U. So. Calif., L.A., 1972, 78, 81. Co-chmn. Regional Transp. Com., 1970-72; mem. adv. bd. U. So. Calif. Computer Law Inst., 1979—, Ariz. Law and Tech. Inst., 1982-86; U. Santa Clara Computer and High Tech. Law Jour., 1982-90. Author: (with Gerald H. Larsen) Data Processing Contracts and the Law, 1974, (with Frank and Statland) Bernacchi on Computer Laaw, 1986; editor-in-chief U. So. Calif. Law Rev., 1962-64; adv. bd. Computer Negotiations Report, 1983-95, Computer and Tech. Law Jour., 1984-93, Computer Law Strategist, 1984-94. Capt. AUS, 1964-66, PTO. Mem. ABA (mem. adv. com. on edn. 1973-74, chmn. subcom. taxation computer sys. of sect. sci. and tech. 1976-78), L.A. Bar Assn., Computer Law Assn. (bd. dirs. 1973-86, chmn. preconf. symposium on law and computers 1974-75, West Coast v.p. 1976-79, sr. v.p. 1979-81, pres. 1981-83, adv. bd. 1986—), Internat. Bar Assn. (co-chmn. sect. on bus. law mem. com. on internat. tech. and e-commerce law 1995-98, steering com. 1998—), Am. Fedn. Info. Processing Socs. (mem. spl. com. electronic funds transfer sys. 1974-78), Order of Coif, Scabbard and Blade, Beta Gamma Sigma, Alpha Sigma Nu. Office: Irell & Manella 1800 Avenue Of The Stars Los Angeles CA 90067-4276

BERNARD, ALEXANDER, law enforcement official; b. L.A., Apr. 23, 1952; s. Louis and Hannah (Bergman) B.; m. Diana LoRee Winstead, Dec. 17, 1976; children: Michael Alexander, Andrew Alexander. AA magna cum laude, L.A. Valley Coll., 1976; BS summa cum laude, Calif. State U., L.A., 1989. Parking meter collector L.A. City Clk.'s Office, 1973-79; police officer L.A. Airport, 1979-95, sgt. police svcs. divsn. Calif., 1995—. Mem. adv. com. Calif. Commn. on Peace Officer Stds. and Tng., 1999—, vice chmn., 2001—. Contbr. articles to profl. jours. Active Boy Scouts Am. Mem. NRA (life), Internat. Police Assn. (life), Indsl. Rels. Rsch. Assn., Calif. Peace Officers Assn., Peace Officers Rsch. Assn. Calif. (chpt. pres. 1982-84, 85-87, state bd. dirs. 1984-85, 88—, ethnic rels. com. 1993-94, exec. com. 1994—, sec. 1999—), Law Enforcement Alliance of Am. (life), L.A. Airport Peace Officers Assn. (pres. 1981-89, 94-95, bd. dirs. 1992-94), L.A. Airport Police Suprs. Assn. (bd. dirs. 1996, v.p. 1997-98, pres. 1999—), Fraternal Order of Police, Calif. Rifle and Pistol Assn. (life), Golden Key (life), Phi Kappa Phi (life). Democrat. Mem. Assemblies of God Ch. Avocations: travel, record collecting. Office: Police Svcs Divsn Ontario Internat Airport 1070 S Vineyard Ave Ontario CA 91761-8007

BERNARD, EDDIE NOLAN, oceanographer; b. Houston, Nov. 23, 1946; s. Edward Nolan and Geraldine Marie (Dempsey) B.; m. Shirley Ann Fielder, May 30, 1970; 1 child, Elizabeth Ann BS, Lamar U., 1969; MS, Tex. A&M U., 1970, PhD, 1976. Geophysicist Pan Am. Petroleum Co., 1969; rsch. asst. oceanographic rsch. Tex. A&M U., College Station, Tex., 1969-70; rschr. NOAA, 1970-73, dep. dir. pacific marine environ. lab., 1980-82; rschr. Joint Tsunami Rsch. Effort, 1973-77; dir. Nat. Tsunami Warning Ctr., 1977-80, Pacific Marine Environ. Lab., Seattle, 1982—, chmn. Nat. Tsunami Hazard Mitigation Program, 1997—. Dir. NOAA hydrothermal vents program, fisheries oceanography program; exec. com. Coop. Inst. for Marine Resource Studies Oreg. State U.; adminstrv. bd. Joint Inst. Marine and Atmospheric Rsch. U. Hawaii; mem. Washington Sea Grant Steering Com., 1987—; mem. sci. coun. Joint Inst. for Marine Observations, Scripps Instn. of Oceanography, 1992—; exec. com. Cooperative Inst. for Arctic Rsch. U. Alaska; advisor Japan Marine Sci. and Tech. Ctr., 2000—. Editor: Tsunami Hazard: A Practical Guide for Tsunami Hazard Reduction, 1991; contbr. articles to profl. jours. Recipient Best of New Generation award Esquire Mag., 1984, Meritorious Presdl. Rank award Pres. Clinton, 1993. Mem. Internat. Union of Geodesy and Geophysics (chmn. Tsunami commn. 1987-95), Am. Geophys. Union, Oceanography Soc. Office: Pacific Marine Environ Lab 7600 Sand Point Way NE Bldg 3 Seattle WA 98115-6349 E-mail: bernard@pmel.noaa.gov

BERNAU, SIMON JOHN, mathematics educator; b. Wanganui, New Zealand, June 12, 1937; came to U.S., 1969; s. Earnest Lovell and Ella Mary (Mason) B.; m. Lynley Joyce Turner, Aug. 11, 1959; children: Nicola Ann, Sally Jane. B.Sc., U. Canterbury, Christchurch, New Zealand, 1958, M.Sc., 1959; B.A., Cambridge (Eng.) U., 1961, Ph.D., 1964. Lectr. U. Canterbury, 1964-65, sr. lectr., 1965-66; prof. math. U. Otago, Dunedin, New Zealand, 1966-69; assoc. prof. U. Tex., Austin, 1969-76, prof., 1976-85; prof., head math. dept. Southwest Mo. State U., Springfield, 1986-88; prof., chmn. dept. math. scis. U. Tex., El Paso, 1988-95; dean Coll. Sci. Calif. State Poly., Pomona, 1995—. Researcher numerous publs. in field, 1964— ; referee profl. jours., 1965— . Gulbenkian jr. research fellow Churchill Coll., Cambridge U., 1963-64 Mem. Am. Math. Soc. (reviewer 1965—), Math. Assn. Am., London Math. Soc. Home: 691 W 24th St Upland CA 91784-8323 Office: Calif State Poly U Coll of Sci 3801 W Temple Ave Pomona CA 91768-2557

BERNHARD, HERBERT ASHLEY, lawyer; b. Jersey City, Sept. 24, 1927; s. Richard C. and Amalie (Lobl) B.; m. Nancy Ellen Hirschaut, Aug. 8. 1954; children: Linda, Alison, Jordan, Melissa. Student, Mexico City Coll., 1948; BEE, N.J. Inst. Tech., 1949; MA in Math., Columbia U., 1950; JD cum laude, U. Mich., 1957. Bar: Calif. 1958, U.S. Dist. Ct. (cen. dist.) Calif. 1958, U.S. Dist. Ct. (no., ea. and so. dists.) Calif. 1963, U.S. Ct. Claims 1966, U.S. Dist. Ct. (ea. dist.) Wis. 1982, U.S. Dist. Ct. (ea. and we. dists.) Ark. 1982, U.S. Dist. Ct. Nebr. 1982, U.S. Ct. Internat. Trade 1979, U.S. Tax Ct. 1969, U.S. Ct. Appeals (2d, 3d, 4th, 5th, 7th, 8th, 9th, 10th, 11th and D.C. cirs.) 1969, U.S. Supreme Ct. 1965. Research engr. Curtis-Wright Co., Caldwell, N.J., 1950-52, Boeing Aircraft Co., Cape Canaveral, Fla., 1952-55; assoc. O'Melveny & Myers, Los Angeles, 1957-62; ptnr. Greenberg, Bernhard, et al, Los Angeles, 1962-85, Jeffer, Mangels, Butler & Marmaro, Los Angeles, 1985—. Instr. math. U. Fla., Cape Canaveral, 1952-55; instr. elec. engring. U. Mich., Ann Arbor, 1955-57; referee L.A. Superior Ct., 1985—, arbitrator, 1988—, judge pro tem, 1988—; judge pro tem L.A. Mcpl. Ct., 1985—, Beverly Hills Mcpl. Ct., 1989—, Malibu Mcpl. Ct., 1994—. Contbr. articles to profl. jours. Chmn. adv. com. Skirball Mus., 1976-98; bd. overseers Hebrew Union Coll., 1976-98. With USAF, 1946-47. Recipient Disting. Achievement award N.J. Inst. Tech., 1998. Mem. Jewish Publ. Soc. (trustee 1986-96). Home: 1105 Tower Rd Beverly Hills CA 90210-2130 Office: Jeffer Mangels Butler & Marmaro 2121 Avenue Of The Stars Fl 10 Los Angeles CA 90067-5010

BERNHARD, SANDRA, actress, comedienne, singer; b. Flint, Mich., June 6, 1955; d. Jerome and Jeanette B. Stand-up comedienne nightclubs, Beverly Hills, Calif., 1974-78; films include Cheech and Chong's Nice Dreams, 1981, The King of Comedy, 1983 (Nat. Soc. Film Critics award), Sesame Street Presents: Follow That Bird, 1985, Track 29, 1988, Without You I'm Nothing, 1990, Hudson Hawk, 1991, Truth or Dare, 1991, Inside Monkey Zetterland, 1993, Dallas Doll, 1994, Unzipped, 1995, Catwalk, 1995, Plump Fiction, 1996, Somewhere in the City, 1997, Lover Girl, 1997, The Apocalypse, 1997, An Alan Smithee Film: Burn Hollywood Burn, 1997, I Woke Up Early the Day I Died, 1998, Exposé, 1998, Wrongfully Accused, 1998, Hercules: Zero to Hero (voice), 1999; also appears in Heavy Petting, 1988, Perfect, 1985, The Whoopee Boys, 1986, Casual Sex?, 1988; stage appearances (solo) Without You I'm Nothing, 1988, Giving Till It Hurts, 1992; TV appearances (host) Living in America, 1990; regular guest The Richard Pryor Show, Late Night with David Letterman; TV series Instant Comedy with the Groundlings, The Hitchhiker, The Full Wax, Tales from the Crypt, Roseanne, Space Ghost Coast to Coast, The Larry Sanders Show, Clueless, Chicago Hope, Highlander, Superman (voice), Ally McBeal, Hercules; (TV movies) Freaky Friday, 1995, The Late Shift, 1996; albums (co-author 8 songs) I'm Your Woman, 1985, Without You I'm Nothing, 1989; books include Confessions of a Pretty Lady, 1988, Love Love and Love, 1993. Office: Noe-Man Mgmt Scott Noe 26500 Agoura Rd Ste 575 Calabasas CA 91302-1952

BERNHEIMER, MARTIN, music critic; b. Munich, Germany, Sept. 28, 1936; came to U.S., 1940, naturalized, 1946; s. Paul Ernst and Louise (Nassauer) B.; m. Lucinda Pearson, Sept. 30, 1961 (div. Feb. 1989); children: Mark Richard, Nora Nicoll, Marina and Erika (twins); m. Linda Winer, Sept. 27, 1992. MusB with honors, Brown U., 1958; student, Munich Conservatory, 1958-59; MA in Musicology, NYU, 1961. Freelance music critic, 1958—; contbg. critic N.Y. Herald Tribune, 1959-62; mem. music faculty NYU, 1959-62; contbg. editor Mus. Courier, 1961-64;

temporary music critic N.Y. Post, 1961-65; N.Y. corr. for Brit. Publ. Opera, 1962-65; L.A. corr., 1965—; corr. West Coast Brit. Opera Mag., 1965—; asst. to music editor Saturday Rev., 1962-65; mng. editor Philharmonic Hall Program, N.Y.C., 1962-65; music editor, chief critic L.A. Times, 1965-96. Mem. faculty U. So. Calif., 1966-71, music faculty UCLA, 1969-75, Calif. Inst. Arts, 1975-82, Calif. State U., Northridge, 1978-81, Rockefeller Program for Tng. of Music Critics; mem. Pulitzer Prize Music Jury, 1984, 86, 90; L.A. corr. for Swiss publ. Opernwelt, 1984—. Contbg. author New Groves Dictionary; contbr. liner notes for recordings; appearances on radio and TV, Met. Opera Broadcasts; contbr. articles to Vanity Fair, Music Quar., The Critic, Opera News, Mus. Am., Fin. Times, London, Sidewalk N.Y. (internet), others; contributing feature writer Fin. Times, N.Y. Newsday; lectr., moderator, essayist on Met. Opera Broadcast. Recipient Deems Taylor award ASCAP, 1974, 78, Headliners award, 1979, Pulitzer Prize for disting. criticism, 1981, Lifetime Achievement award Svc. to Music, Calif. Assn. Profl. Music Tchrs., 1990. Mem. Nat. Opera Inst. (ind. selection com. 1980), Pi Kappa Lambda (hon.).

BERNSTEIN, ELLIOT ROY, chemistry educator; b. N.Y.C., Apr. 14, 1941; s. Leonard H. Bernstein and Geraldine (Roman) Goldberg; m. Barbara Wyman, Dec. 19, 1965; children— Jephta, Rebecca. A.B., Princeton U., 1963; Ph.D., Calif. Inst. Tech., 1967. Postdoctoral fellow U. Chgo., 1967-69; asst. prof. Princeton U., N.J., 1969-75; assoc. prof. Colo. State U., Ft. Collins, 1975-80, prof. chemistry, 1980— ; cons. Los Alamos Nat. Lab., 1975-83, Philip Morris, 1984-91, Du Pont Corp., 1985-92. Contbr. articles to profl. jours. NSF fellow, 1961-62; Woodrow Wilson fellow, 1963-64, JSPS fellow, 1996, Third Cycle in Chemistry lectr., Switzerland, 1998. Fellow Am. Phys. Soc.; mem. AAAS, Am. Chem. Soc., Sigma Xi. Office: Colo State U Dept Chemistry Condensed Matter Scis Lab Fort Collins CO 80523-0001

BERNSTEIN, GIORA, artistic director; b. Vienna, Austria; Studied with Igor Markevitch; doctorate, Boston U. Mem. Boston Symphony; founder, dir. Boston Chamber Orch., Claremont (Calif.) Music Festival; founding music dir., condr. Colo. Music Festival. Guest condr. Liege Philharmonic, Stuttgart Philharmonic, Netherlands Chamber Orch., Tonkunstler Orch. Vienna, Berlin Symphony Orch., Basel Radio Orch., St. Gallen Symphony, San Remo Symphony, Haifa Symphony Orch., Seattle Symphony Orch., Colo. Symphony Orch. Recipient Westinghouse Debut Recital award, City of Claremont commendation, County of L.A. commendation, Calif. Fedn. of Music Club award, Nat. Fedn. of Music Club award, Coleman Chamber Music award, six ASCAP awards, Excellence in the Arts award Gov. of Colo.; Internat. Acad. at Mozarteum fellow, Salzburg, Austria; Juilliard Sch. of Music scholar, Brandeis U. scholar, Boston U. scholar. Office: Colo Music Festival Orch 1525 Spruce St Ste 101 Boulder CO 80302-4256

BERNSTEIN, HAROLD SETH, pediatric cardiologist, molecular geneticist; b. N.Y.C., Oct. 6, 1959; s. Wallace Carl and Naomi (Oldak) B.; m. Patricia Margaret Foster. AB, Harvard Coll., 1982; MPhil, CUNY, 1985, PhD, 1986; MD, Mt. Sinai Sch. Med., 1990. Diplomate Nat. Bd. Med. Examiners. Postdoctoral fellow div. med. & molecular genetics Mt. Sinai, N.Y.C., 1986-88; intern U. Calif., San Francisco, 1990-91, resident in pediatrics, 1991-93; clin., rsch. fellow div. pediatric cardiology Cardiovascular Rsch. Inst., U. Calif., San Francisco, 1993—. Contbr. articles to profl. jours. Harvard Coll. scholar, 1980; NIH fellow in med. genetics, 1982-86, pediatric cardiology, 1993—; recipient Disting. Performance in Rsch. award Associated Med. Schs. N.Y., 1989, Achievement award for clin. excellence Upjohn, 1990. Fellow Am. Acad. Pediatrics; mem. AAAS, Am. Soc. Human Genetics, Am. Fedn. Clin. Rsch., Alpha Omega Alpha. Achievements include rsch. in cloning and sequencing of the first human CDNA encoding galactosidase A; first to identify molecular defect in the human galactosidase A gene resulting in Fabry Disease. Office: Univ Calif Div Pediatric Cardiology PO Box 544 San Francisco CA 94143-0001

BERNSTEIN, LESLIE, dean; BA, Univ. Calif., 1965; MS, Univ. Southern Calif., 1978, PhD, 1981. Rsch. assoc. dept. preventive medicine Univ. Southern Calif., L.A., 1981-82, asst. prof. biostatistics/epidemiology, 1982-88, assoc. prof. biostatistics/epidemiology, 1988-91, prof. biostatistics/epidemiology, 1991—, sr. assoc. dean faculty affairs, 1996—. Sci. dir. Univ. So. Calif. Cancer Surveillance program, 1988—; chair dept. def. epidemiology breast cancer rsch. program, 1994, sci. adv. panel Calif. Gov., 1989-92; mem. sci. com. Internat. Soc. Study Esophageal Diseases, 1994—; chair adv. com. L.I. Breast Cancer Cancer Study, Columbia Univ., 1994—; chair external adv. com. Nurse's Health Study Harvard Univ., 1995—; sci. adv. com. Registry for Rsch. on Transplacental Carcinogenesis, Univ. Chgo., 1997—; external adv. com. No. Calif. Cancer Ctr, Hawaii Cancer Ctr., 1997—; chair in cancer rsch. AFLAC, Inc., 1999—. Contbr. over 150 articles to profl. jours. Office: PO Box 33800 MS44 1441 Eastlake Ave Los Angeles CA 90033-1048

BERNSTEIN, MICHAEL ALAN, history educator; b. 1954; BA in Econs. magna cum laude, Yale U., 1976, MA in Econs., 1978, MPhil in Econs., 1980, PhD in Econs., 1982. Instr. for the preliminary examinations in econs. Faculty Econs. and Politics, U. Cambridge, Eng., 1976-77; staff economist Office of Integrative Analysis Energy Info. Adminstrn., U.S. Dept. Energy, Washington, 1978; lectr. in econs. Mills Coll., Oakland, Calif., 1979; acting instr. econs. Yale U., 1980, asst. prof. history and associated faculty mem. dept. econs., 1982-87; asst. prof. history U. Calif., San Diego, 1987-88, assoc. prof. history, 1988-91, assoc. prof. history, associated faculty mem. dept. econs., 1991-2000, chair dept. history, 1992-2000, prof. history, 2000—. Chair undergrad. program com. and departmental rep. dept. history Princeton U., 1983-84, 85-86, mem. priorities com. on the budget, 1985-87; co-chair Columbia U. Seminar in Econ. History, 1985-86; dir. grad. studies in U.S. history dept. history U. Calif., San Diego, 1988-89, mem. chancellor's com. on the status of women, 1989-91, mem. rep. assembly of the acad. senate, 1990-92, chair undergrad. curriculum and advising com. dept. history, 1990-92, vice-chair dept. history, 1990-92, prin. investigator Calif. History-Social Sci. Project, 1994—, mem. adv. com. Office of Sexual Harassment Prevention and Policy, 1994—; mem. steering com. U. Calif. Intercampus Group in Econ. History, 1988—. Author: The Great Depression: Delayed Recovery and Economic Change in America, 1929-39, 1987, Japanese edit., 1991; co-editor (with D. Adler) Understanding American Economic Decline, 1994; mem. editl. bd. Jour. Econ. History, 1989-94; contbr. articles to profl. jours. Fulbright scholar Christ's Coll., Cambridge, Eng., 1976-77, Univ. Grad. fellow and Falk Found. fellow in econs. Yale U., 1977-81, ACLS fellow for studies in modern soc. and values, 1985, ACLS Postdoctoral fellow for sr. scholars, 1990, Andrew E. Mellon fellow Nat. Humanities Ctr., Research Triangle Park, N.C., 1990; Hoover scholar Herbert Hoover Presdl. Libr. Assn., West Branch, Iowa, 1991; recipient Grant-in-Aid, Econ. History Assn., 1982. Mem. Am. Econs. Assn., Am. Hist. Assn. (mem. com. on the Albert J. Beveridge Award and the John H. Dunning Prize 1991-93, chair 1993), Econ. History Assn. (com. on rsch. in econ. history 1994—), Orgn. Am. Historians (mem. Ellis Hawley Prize Organizing Com. 1994—), Am. Coun. Learned Socs. (mem. acad. adv. com. of the Am. studies program 1990—). Office: U Calif San Diego Dept History 0104 9500 Gilman Dr Dept 0104 La Jolla CA 92093-5004

BERNSTEIN, SANFORD IRWIN, biology educator; b. Bklyn., June 10, 195[illegible]; s. Harold and Adele Dorothy (Kuttel) B.; m. Laurel Spear, July 10, 1983. BS, SUNY, Stony Brook, 1974; PhD, Wesleyan U., 1979. Rsch. fellow U. Va., Charlottesville, 1979-82; asst. prof. biology San Diego State U., 1983-86, [illegible] prof., 1986-90, prof., 1990—, assoc. dir. Molecular Biology Inst., 1987-92, dir. 1992-95; co-dir. DNA cert. program, 1983—, chair biology dept., 1995-2000, coord. joint doctoral program in cell and molecular biology with U. Calif. San Diego, 2000—; established investigatorship Am. Heart Assn., 1989-94; mem. grant rev. panels NIH, Am. Heart Assn. Mem. editl. bd. Devel. Biology, 1991-95; contbr. articles to profl. jours. Muscular Dystrophy Assn. fellow, 1979-82, grantee, 1984—; grantee NIH, 1983—, NSF, 1997-2000. Mem. Genetics Soc. Am., AAAS, Am. Soc. Cell Biology, Am. Soc. Biochemistry and Molecular Biology, Am. Soc. Microbiology, Biophys. Soc., Sigma Xi. Achievements include research in developmental regulation of muscle gene expression in Drosophila, muscle protein isoform function, alternative RNA splicing. Office: San Diego State U Biology Dept and Molec Bio Inst San Diego CA 92182-4614 E-mail: sanford.bernstein@sdsu.edu

BERNSTEIN, SOL, cardiologist, educator; b. West New York, N.J., Feb. 3, 1927; s. Morris Irving and Rose (Leibowitz) B.; m. Suzi Maris Sommer, Sept. 15, 1963; 1 son, Paul. AB in Bacteriology, U. Southern Calif., 1952, MD, 1956. Diplomate Am. Bd. Internal Medicine. Intern Los Angeles County Hosp., 1956-57, resident, 1957-60; practice medicine specializing in cardiology L.A., 1960—; staff physician dept. medicine Los Angeles County Hosp. U. So. Calif. Med. Center, L.A., 1960—, chief cardiology clinics, 1964, asst. dir. dept. medicine, 1965-72; chief profl. services Gen. Hosp., 1972-74; med. dir. Los Angeles County-U So. Calif. Med. Center, L.A., 1974-94; med. dir. central region Los Angeles County, 1974-78; dir. Dept. Health Services, Los Angeles County, 1978; assoc. dean Sch. Medicine, U. So. Calif., L.A., 1986-94, assoc. prof., 1968—; med. dir. Health Rsch. Assn., L.A., 1995—. Cons. Crippled Childrens Svc. Calif., 1965—. Contbr. articles on cardiac surgery, cardiology, diabetes and health care planning to med. jours. Served with AUS, 1946-47, 52-53. Fellow A.C.P., Am. Coll. Cardiology; mem. Am. Acad. Phys. Execs., Am. Fedn. Clin. Research, N.Y. Acad. Sci., Los Angeles, Am. heart assns., Los Angeles Soc. Internal Medicine, Los Angeles Acad. Medicine, Sigma Xi, Phi Beta Phi, Phi Eta Sigma, Alpha Omega Alpha. Home: 4966 Ambrose Ave Los Angeles CA 90027-1756 Office: 1640 Marengo St Los Angeles CA 90033-1036

BERNSTEIN, SUSAN See DVORA, SUSAN

BERNSTEIN, WILLIAM, film company executive; b. N.Y.C., Aug. 30, 1933; s. Philip and Sadie (Lazar) B.; m. Evelyn Pauline Schnur, Aug. 3, 1958; children: Marian Suzanne, Steven Laurence. BA, NYU, 1954; LLB, Yale U., 1959. Atty. United Artists Corp., N.Y.C., 1959-67, v.p. bus. affairs, 1967-72, sr. v.p. bus. affairs, 1972-78; exec. v.p. Orion Pictures Corp., N.Y.C., 1978-91, pres., chief exec. officer, dir., 1991-92; exec. v.p. Paramount Pictures Corp., L.A., 1992—. Mem. ABA, Acad. Motion Picture Arts and Scis. Home: 282 Bentley Cir Los Angeles CA 90049-2414 Office: Paramount Pictures Corp 5555 Melrose Ave Los Angeles CA 90038-3197

BERNSTINE, DANIEL O'NEAL, law educator, university president; b. Berkeley, Calif., Sept. 7, 1947; s. Annias and Emma (Jones) B.; m. Nancy Jean Tyler, July 27, 1971 (div. Mar. 1986); children: Quincy Tyler, Justin Tyler. BA, U. Calif., Berkeley, 1969; JD, Northwestern U., Chgo., 1972; LLM, U. Wis., 1975; LLD (hon.), Hanyang U., Seoul, Korea, 1999. Bar: D.C. 1970, Wis. 1979. Prof. law Howard U. Law Sch., Washington, 1975-78, gen. counsel, interim dean, 1987-90; prof. law U. Wis. Law Sch., Madison, 1978-97, dean, 1990-97; pres. Portland (Ore.) State Univ., 1997—. Author: Wisconsin and Federal Civil Procedure, 1986. Bd. dirs. Madison Cmty. Found., 1990-94, Portland Urban League, Legacy Health Sys., Willamette United Way, 2001—; mem. Portland Multnomah Progress Bd., 1998—, Kellogg Commn. on the Future of State and Land-Grant Univs., 1997-2000. Mem. Am. Law Inst., Portland C. of C. (bd. dirs.). Office: Portland State Univ PO Box 751 Portland OR 97207-0751

BERRING, ROBERT CHARLES, JR. law educator, law librarian, former dean; b. Canton, Ohio, Nov. 20, 1949; s. Robert Charles and Rita Pauline (Franta) B.; m. Leslie Applegarth, May 20, 1998; children: Simon Robert, Daniel Fredrick. B.A. cum laude, Harvard U., 1971; J.D., M.L.S., U. Calif.-Berkeley, 1974. Asst. prof. and reference librarian U. Ill. Law Sch., Champaign, 1974-76; assoc. librarian U. Tex. Law Sch., Austin, 1976-78; dep. librarian Harvard Law Sch., Cambridge, Mass., 1978-81; prof. law, law librarian U. Wash. Law Sch., Seattle, 1981-82, U. Calif., Boalt Hall Law Sch., Berkeley, Calif., 1982—, dean sch. library and info. scis., 1986-89, Walter Perry Johnson chair, 1998—. Mem. Westlaw Adv. Bd., St. Paul, 1984-91; cons. various law firms; mem. on Legal Exch. with China, 1983—, chmn., 1991-93.; vis. prof. U. Cologne, 1993. Author: How to Find the Law, 8th edit., 1984, 9th edit., 1989, Great American Law Revs., 1985, Finding the Law, 1999; co-author: Authors Guide, 1981; editor Legal Reference Svc. Quar., 1981—; author videotape series Commando Legal Rsch., 1989. Chmn. Com. Legal Ednl. Exch. with China, 1991-93. Robinson Cox fellow U. Western Australia, 1988; named West Publishing Co. Acad. Libr. of Yr., 1994. Mem. Am. Assn. Law Libraries (pres. 1985-86), Calif. Bar Assn., ABA, ALA, Am. Law Inst. Office: U Calif Law Sch Boalt Hl Rm 345 Berkeley CA 94720-0001

BERRY, DALE E. state legislator; b. Sidney, Mont., Feb. 6, 1939; m. Dorothy Berry; 2 children. BS in Phys. Edn., U. Mont., 1961. Lic. in real estate sales; lic. real estate broker. Tchr., football, basketball and track coach Denton H.S., 1963-67, Roundup H.S., 1967-68; tchr., basketball coach Hamilton H.S., 1968-88; broker, owner Ranch and Land Co., 1984-90, Greater Mont. Land Co., 1990—; mem. Mont. Ho. of Reps., 1998-99, Mont. Senate, Dist. 30, Helena, 1999—; mem. bus. and industry com., labor and employment rels. com.; mem. pub. health, welfare and safety com. Bd. dirs. Hamilton Schs. Found.; mem. Mont. State Bd. Realty Regulation. Named Bitterroot Valley Realtor of Yr. 1996, Bitterroot Valley Bus. Person of Yr., 1997; named to Mont. Coaches Assn. Hall of Fame, 1988. Mem. Nat. Assn. Realtors, Mont. Assn. Realtors (bd. dirs.), Bitterroot Valley Bd. Realtors (past pres., bd. dirs.), Bitterroot C. of C. (bd. dirs., govt. affairs chair, pres.). Republican. Roman Catholic. Home: 1967 N 1st St Hamilton MT 59840-3197

BERRY, GLENN, educator, artist; b. Feb. 27, 1929; s. B. Franklin and Heloise (Sloan) B. BA magna cum laude, Pomona Coll., 1951, BFA (Honnold fellow); MFA, Sch. Art Inst. Chgo., 1956. Faculty Humboldt State U., Arcata, Calif., 1956-69, prof. art, 1969-81, emeritus, 1981—. One-man shows include Ingomar Gallery, Eureka, Calif., 1968, Ankrum Gallery, L.A., 1970, Esther Bear Gallery, Santa Barbara, Calif., 1971, Coll. Redwoods, Eureka, 1989, Humboldt State U., Arcata, Calif., 1992, Morris Graves Mus. of Art, Eureka, Calif., 2000; exhibited in group shows at Palace of Legion of Honor, San Francisco, Pasadena (Calif.) Art Mus., Rockford (Ill.) Coll., Richmond (Calif.) Art Mus., Henry Gallery U. Wash., Seattle, Morris Graves Mus. Art, Eureka, 2000; represented in permanent collections Storm King Art Ctr., Mountainville, N.Y., Kaiser Aluminum & Chem. Corp., Oakland, Calif., Desert Mus., Hirshhorn Mus., Washington, others; mural Griffith Hall, Humboldt State U., 1978, Morris Graves Mus. Art, Eureka, Calif. Mem. Phi Beta Kappa. Home: PO Box 2241 Mckinleyville CA 95519

BERRY, JOHN CHARLES, clinical psychologist, educational administrator; b. Modesto, Calif., Nov. 29, 1938; s. John Wesley and Dorothy Evelyn (Harris) B.; A.B., Stanford, 1960; postgrad. Trinity Coll., Dublin, Ireland, 1960-61; Ph.D., Columbia, 1967; [illegible] Oct. [illegible], 1978; children— Elise, John Jordan, Kaitlyn. Research assoc. Judge Baker Guidance Center, Boston, 1965-66; psychology asso. Napa State Hosp., [illegible], Calif., 1966-67, staff psychologist, 1967-75, program asst., 1975-76, program [illegible] Hosp., Norwalk, Calif., 1976-77, asst. supt. Empire Union Sch. Dist., Modesto, Calif., 1977-93, dep. supt., 1993—. Mem. Am. Psychol. Assn., Assn. Calif. Sch. Adminstrs., Sigma Xi. Contbg. author: Life History Research in Psychopathology, 1970. Home: 920 Eastridge Dr Modesto CA 95355-4672 Office: Empire Union Sch Dist 116 N Mcclure Rd Modesto CA 95357-1329

BERRY, KENNETH J. sociology educator; Prof. dept. sociology Colo. State U. Recipient Banner I. Miller award Am. Meteorol. Assn., 1994. Office: Colorado St Univ Dept Sociology B258 Clark Fort Collins CO 80523-0001

BERRY, NANCY, recording industry executive; With Virgin Records, 1979—, now vice chmn., Virgin Music Group Worldwide, L.A., N.Y.C. and London. Office: Virgin Records Am Inc 338 N Foothill Rd Beverly Hills CA 90210-3611

BERRY, RICHARD LEWIS, writer, magazine editor, lecturer, programmer; b. Greenwich, Conn., Nov. 6, 1946; s. John William and Dorothy May (Buck) B.; m. Eleanor von Auw, June 7, 1968 BA, U. Va., 1968; MSc, York U., Can., 1972. Rsch. asst. MacMaster U., Hamilton, Ont., Can., 1973-74; project engr. Intraspace Internat., Toronto, 1974-75; tech. editor Astronomy mag., Milw., 1976-78, editor, 1978-82, editor-in-chief, 1982-91; editor Telescope Making Mag., Milw., 1978-92; editl. dir. Earth mag., 1990-91, cons., 1992; freelance writer, programmer, lectr., 1991—; editor Cookbook Camera Newsletter, 1994-99. Cons. editor Willmann-Bell, Richmond, Va., 1983— Author: Build Your Own Telescope, 1985, Discover the Stars, 1987, (with others) The Star Book, 1984, Introduction to Astronomical Image Processing, 1991, AIP Image Processing Software, 1991, BatchPIX Image Processing Software, 1992, Choosing and Using a CCD Camera, 1992, The CCD Camera Cookbook, 1994, The Dobsonian Telescope: A Practical Manual for Building Large Aperture Telescopes, 1997, Handbook of Astronomical Image Processing, 2000; contbg. author: Robotic Observatories, 1989, ST6PIX Image Processing Software, 1992, CB245 Image Processing Software, 1994, Multi245 Image Compositing Software, 1995, QColor Color Synthesis Software, 1997, Astronomical Image Processing for Windows, 2000; editor: Telescope Optics, Design and Evaluation, 1988. Mem. adv. bd. Global Network of Automatic Telescopes. Recipient Clifford-Holmes award Astronomy for Am., 1981, Dorothea Klumpke-Roberts award Astron. Soc. Pacific, 1990, Omega Centauri award Tex. Star Party, Clyde W. Tombaugh award for tech. innovation in astronomy Riverside Telescope Makers Conf., 1995, G. Bruce Blair award for achievement in amateur astronomy Western Amateur Astronomers, 1998, Leslie C. Peltier award for contbrns. to observational amateur astronomy Astron. League, 2001; Asteroid 3684 Berry named in his honor by Internat. Astron. Union, 1990. Mem. Internat. Amateur Profl. Photoelec. Photometry, Internat. Dark Sky Assn., Am. Astron. Soc. Avocation: photography.

BERRY, ROBERT EMANUEL, aerospace company executive; b. Atlantic City, July 4, 1928; s. Charles Allen and Anne Martha (Smith) B.; m. Dorothy Ellen Rohan, June 13, 1953; 1 child, Robert Emanuel Jr. BS in Econs./Gen. Sci., Manhattan Coll., 1953; MA in Econs., U. Pa., 1958. Instr. econs. Wharton Sch., Phila., 1956-57; mgr., engring. adminstr. GE, Phila., 1957-62; dir. advanced systems Philco-Ford Corp., Palo Alto, Calif., 1962-67, dir. Newport Beach ops. Newport Beach, 1967-69; pres., chmn. INTELCOM Industries, 1969-75; dep. dir. Dept. of Def., Washington, 1975-77; div. gen. mgr. Ford Aerospace, Palo Alto, 1977-90; pres. Space Systems/Loral, Palo Alto, 1990—. Mem. Space Systems & Technology Adv. Com., Washington, 1986—, Comml. Space Transp. Adv., Washington, 1991-93, U. San Francisco Telecommunications Adv. Bd., 1988—. Ltjg. USNR, 1953-56. Mem. AIAA (Aerospace Comm. award 1996), IEEE. Office: Space Systems/Loral 3825 Fabian Way Palo Alto CA 94303-4604

BERRY, ROBERT WORTH, lawyer, educator, retired army officer; b. Ryderwood, Wash., Mar. 2, 1926; s. John Franklin and Anita Louise (Worth) B. B.A. in Polit. Sci., Wash. State U., 1950; J.D., Harvard U., 1955; M.A., John Jay Coll. Criminal Justice, 1981. Bar: D.C. 1956, U.S. Dist. Ct. (D.C.) 1956, U.S. Ct. of Appeals (D.C. cir.) 1957, U.S. Ct. Mil. Appeals 1957, Pa. 1961, U.S. Dist. Ct. (ea. dist.) Pa. 1961, U.S. Dist. Ct. (ctrl. dist.) Calif. 1967, U.S. Supreme Ct. 1961, Calif. 1967, U.S. Ct. Claims 1975, Colo. 1997, U.S. Dist. Ct. Colo. 1997, U.S. Ct. Appeals (10th cir.) 1997, U.S. Tax Ct. 1959. Research assoc. Harvard U., 1955-56; atty. Office Gen. Counsel U.S. Dept. Def., Washington, 1956-60; staff counsel Philco Ford Co., Phila., 1960-63; dir. Washington office Litton Industries, 1967-71; gen. counsel U.S. Dept. Army, Washington, 1971-74, civilian aide to sec. army, 1975-77; col. U.S. Army, 1978-87; prof., head dept. law U.S. Mil. Acad., West Point, N.Y., 1978-86; ret. as brig. gen. U.S. Army, 1987; mil. asst. to asst. sec. of army, Manpower and Res. Affairs Dept. of Army, 1986-87; asst. gen. counsel pub. affairs Litton Industries, Beverly Hills, Calif., 1963-67; chair Coun. of Def. Space Industries Assns., 1968; resident ptnr. Quarles and Brady, Washington, 1971-74; dir., corp. sec., treas., gen. counsel G.A. Wright, Inc., Denver, 1987-92, dir., 1987-2000; pvt. practice law Fort Bragg, Calif., 1993-96; spl. counsel Messner & Reeves LLC, Denver, 1997—. Bd. dirs. G.A. Wright Mktg., Inc., Denver Mgmt. Svcs., Inc.; foreman Mendocino County Grand Jury, 1995-96. Served with U.S. Army, 1944-46, 51-53, Korea. Decorated Bronze Star, Legion of Merit, Disting. Service Medal; recipient Disting. Civilian Service medal U.S. Dept. Army, 1973, 74, Outstanding Civilian Service medal, 1977. Mem. FBA, Bar Assn. D.C., Calif. Bar Assn., Pa. Bar Assn., Colo. State Bar Assn., Denver Bar Assn., Army-Navy Club, Army-Navy Country Club, Phi Beta Kappa, Phi Kappa Phi, Sigma Delta Chi, Lambda Chi Alpha. Protestant. E-mail: rberry@mprlaw.com

BERRY, STEPHEN JOSEPH, reporter; b. Ft. Jackson, S.C., May 2, 1948; s. Charles Berry and Marjorie (Sheehan) B.; m. Cheryl C. Berry, Nov. 24, 1973; 1 child, Stephen Richard. BA in Polit. Sci., U. Montevallo, 1970; MA, U. N.C. at Greensboro, 1984. Mem. staff Dothan (Ala.) Eagle, 1970-72, Greensboro (N.C.) News & Record, 1971—, Orlando (Fla.) Sentinel, 1989-96, The L.A. Times, 1996—. Recipient Pultizer prize, 1993, Pub. Svc. award Associated Press News Execs. Coun. Calif.-Nebr., 1998, 1st pl. Soc. Profl. Journalisms Excellence award in Sports Reporting, 1994, Behjamin Fine award, 1985, N.C. Sch. Bell award, 1986. Mem. Phi Alpha Theta. Home: 6527 Ellenview Ave West Hills CA 91307-2717 Office: LA Times Times Mirror Sq Los Angeles CA 90053

BERRY, WILLIAM BENJAMIN NEWELL, geologist, educator, former museum administrator; b. Boston, Sept. 1, 1931; s. John King and Margaret Elizabeth (Newell) B.; m. Suzanne Foster Spaulding, June 10, 1961; 1 child, Bradford Brown. A.B., Harvard U., 1953, A.M., 1955; Ph.D., Yale U., 1957. Asst. prof. geology U. Houston, 1957-58; asst. prof. to prof. paleontology U. Calif., Berkeley, 1958—; prof. geology, 1991—; curator Mus. of Paleontology U. Calif., Berkeley, 1960-75, 87—, dir., 1975-87, chmn. dept. paleontology, 1975-87; marine scientist Lawrence Berkeley Lab., 1989—. Cons. U.S. Geol. Survey., Environ. Edn. to Ministry for Environ., Catalonia, Spain. Author: Growth of a Prehistoric Time Scale, 1968, revised edit., 1987, Principles of Stratigraphic Analysis, 1991; assoc. editor Paleoceanography; contbr. numerous articles on stratigraphic, paleontol. and environ. subjects to profl. jours.; editor publs. in [illegible] Guggenheim Found. fellow, 1966-67 Fellow Calif. Acad. Scis.; mem. Paleontol. Soc., Geol. Soc. Norway, Internat. Platform Assn., Explorers Club [illegible] Home: 1300 Summit Rd Berkeley CA 94708-2139 Office: U Calif Dept [illegible] 3015 McCone Hall Berkeley CA 94720 E-mail: bnberry@uclink4berkeley.edu

BERSHAD, NEIL JEREMY, electrical engineering educator; b. Bklyn., Oct. 20, 1937; s. Milton Frank and Lila (Kaplan) B.; m. Susan Goldman; children: Brian, Melissa. BEE, Rensselaer Poly. Inst., 1958, PhD EE, 1962; MSEE, U. So. Calif., 1960. Mem. tech. staff Hughes Aircraft Co., Culver City, Calif., 1958-62, staff engr., 1964-69; prof. elec. engring. U. Calif., Irvine, 1966-94, prof. emeritus, 1994—. Contbr. more than 90 articles on communication theory, signal processing and adaptive filtering to profl. jours. 1st lt. USAF, 1962-65. Fellow IEEE (assoc. editor communications jour., acoustics, speech and signal processing jour.). Office: U Calif Dept Elec/Computer Engring Irvine CA 92717 E-mail: bershad@ece.uci.edu

BERSIN, ALAN DOUGLAS, lawyer, school system administrator; b. Bklyn., Oct. 15, 1946; s. Arthur and Mildred (Laikin) B.; m. Elisabeth Van Aggelen, Aug. 17, 1975 (div. Dec. 1983); 1 child, Alissa Ida; m. Lisa Foster, July 20, 1991; children, Madeleine Foster, Amalia Rose. AB magna cum laude, Harvard U., 1968; student, Oxford U., 1968-71; JD, Yale U., 1974; LLD (hon.), U. San Diego, 1994, Calif. Western Sch. Law, 1996, Thomas Jefferson Sch. Law, 2001. Bar: Calif. 1975, U.S. Dist. Ct. (ctrl. dist.) Calif. 1975, U.S. Ct. Appeals (9th cir.) 1977, Alaska 1983, U.S. Dist. Ct. Alaska 1983, U.S. Dist. Ct. Hawaii 1992, U.S. Dist. Ct. (so. dist.) Calif. 1992, U.S. Supreme Ct., 1996. Exec. asst. Bd. Police Commrs., L.A., 1974-75; assoc. Munger, Tolles & Olson, L.A., 1975-77, ptnr., 1978-92; spl. dep. dist. atty. Counties of Imperial and San Diego, Calif., 1993-98; supt. pub. edn. San Diego City Schs., 1998—. Adj. prof. of law U. So. Calif. Law Ctr.; vis. prof. Sch. Law U. San Diego, 1992-93; named spl. rep. for U.S. s.w. border by U.S. Atty. Gen., 1995-98; mem. Atty Gen.'s adv. com. of U.S. Attys., 1995-98; tech. adv. panel Nat. Inst. of Justice Law Enforcement, adv. com. FCC/NTIA Pub. Safety Wireless; founder U.S./Mex. Binat. Lab. Program; chmn. bd. dirs. U.S. Border Rsch. Tech. Ctr., S.W. Border Coun.; chmn. Calif. Commn. on Tchr. Credentialing, 2000—. Named Rhodes scholar 1968; recipient Resolution of Merit award Mayor and City Coun. L.A., 1991, Spl. Achievement award Hispanic Urban Ctr., 1992, Peacemaker's award San Diego Mediation Assn., 1997, Morgan award San Diego LEAD, 1998. Mem. Assn. Bus. Trial Lawyers (bd. govs. 1986-88), Inner City Law Ctr. (chmn. bd. dirs. 1987-90). Democrat. Jewish. Avocations: scuba diving, skiing, travel. Fax: 619-291-7182. E-mail: abersin@mail.sandi.net

BERTHELSDORF, SIEGFRIED, psychiatrist; b. Shannon County, Mo., June 16, 1911; s. Richard and Amalia (Morschenko) von Berthelsdorf; m. Mildred Friederich, May 13, 1945; children: Richard, Victor, Dianne. BA, U. Oreg., 1934, MA, MD, 1939. Lic. psychiatrist, psychoanalyst. Intern U.S. Marine Hosp., Staten Island, N.Y., 1939-40; psychiat. intern Bellevue Hosp., N.Y.C., 1940-41; psychiat. resident N.Y. State Psychiat. Hosp., N.Y.C., 1941-42; research assoc. Columbia U. Coll. Physicians and Surgeons, N.Y.C., 1942-43; asst. physician Presbyn. Hosp. and Vanderbilt Clinic, N.Y.C., 1942-51; supervising psychiatrist Manhattan (N.Y.) State Hosp., 1946-50; asst. adolescent psychiatrist Mt. Sinai Hosp., N.Y.C., 1950-52; psychiat. cons. MacLaren Sch. for Boys, Woodburn, Oreg., 1952-84, Portland (Oreg.) Pub. Schs., 1952-67. Clin. prof. U. Oreg. Health Scis. Ctr., 1956—; tng. and supervising analyst Seattle Psychoanalytic Inst., 1970—. Author: Treatment of Drug Addiction in Psychoanalytic Study of the Child, Vol. 31, 1976, Ambivalence Towards Women in Chinese Characters and Its Implication for Feminism, American Imago, 1988, (with others) Psychiatrists Look at Aging, 1992. Bd. dirs., v.p. Portland Opera Assn., 1960-64, Portland Musical Co., 1987-92; bd. dirs., pres. Portland Chamber Orch., 1964-70, 92-94, 96-97, exec., 1997—. Maj. USAF, 1943-46. Recipient Henry Waldo Coe award U. Oreg. Med. Sch., Portland, 1939, citation Parry Ctr. for Children, Portland, 1970, Child Advocacy award ORAPT, 1998. Fellow Am. Psychiat. Assn. (life), Am. Geriatrics Soc. (founding fellow); mem. Am. Psychoanalytic Assn. (life), Portland Psychiatrists in Pvt. Practice (charter, pres. 1958), Mental Health Assn. (bd. dirs., chmn. med. adv. com. 1952-60), Multnomah County Med. Soc. (pres.'s citation 1979), Oreg. Psychoanalytic Found. (founding mem.), Am. Rhododendron Soc. (bd. dirs., v.p. Portland chpt. 1956-58, Bronze medal and citation 1974), Am. Rhododendron Species Found. (bd. dirs. 1960-75), Phi Beta Kappa, Sigma Xi, Phi Sigma, Phi Mu Alpha. Avocations: farming, music. Home: 1125 SW St Clair Ave Portland OR 97205-1127 E-mail: SiegfriedMD@aol.com

BERTIGER, BARY, electronics executive; Corp. v.p., gen. mgr. Motorola Satellite Comm. Group, Chandler, Ariz. Recipient Aerospace Laureate in Space award Aviation Week and Space Tech., 1996.

BERTIN, JOHN JOSEPH, aeronautical engineer, educator, researcher; b. Milw., Oct. 13, 1938; s. Andrea and Yolanda G. (Pasquali) B.; m. Ruth Easterbrook; children: Thomas Alexander, Randolph Scott, Elizabeth Anne, Michael Robert. BA, Rice Inst., Houston, 1960; MS, Rice U., 1962, PhD, 1966. Aerospace technologist NASA Johnson Space Ctr., Houston, 1962-66; prof. U. Tex., Austin, 1966-89; program mgr. for space initiative MTS, Sandia Nat. Labs., Albuquerque, 1989-94; vis. prof. USAF Acad., Colorado Springs, Colo., 1988-89, prof. aero. engring., 1994—. Cons. McGinnis, Lochridge & Kilgore, Austin, 1978-83, Sandia Nat. Labs., Albuquerque, 1980-89, BPD Difesa e Spazio, Rome, 1980-82, NASA, 1994-96, Sci. Applications Internat. Corp., 1996; detailed to Office of Space, U.S. Dept. Energy Hdqs., 1991-92; dir. Ctr. Excellence for Hypersonic Tng. and Rsch., 1985-89; mem. sci. adv. bd. USAF, 1989-93, mem. adv. group Flight Dynamics Labs., 1989-93; tech. chmn. Space 2000 Conf., 1998-99. Author: Engineering Fluid Mechanics, 1987, Hypersonic Aerothermodynamics, 1994; co-author: Aerodynamics for Engineers, 1997; contbg. author Letterwinner, 1999—; editor: Hypersonics, 1989, Advances in Hypersonics, 1992; assoc. editor Jour. Spacecraft and Rockets, 2000—. Pres. Western Hills Little League, Austin, 1975; mem. arts subcom. NASA, 1987-91; mem. Aerospace Engring. Bd. Panel NRC, 1996-97, USAF hypersonics program rev. com., 1997-98. Recipient Gen. Dynamics tchg. award U. Tex. Coll. Engring., 1978, Tex. Exec. tchg. award Ex-Students Assn. U. Tex., 1982, faculty award Tau Beta Pi, 1986, award for meritorious civilian svc. Dept. Air Force, 1993, Gen. Daley award USAFA, 1996, Exemplary Civilian Svc. Award medal, 1996, F.J. Seiler Rsch. award, USAFA, 1997. Fellow AIAA (dir. region IV 1983-86, Disting. Lectr., Thermophysics award 1997, publs. bd. 1998-2000). E-mail: john.bertin@usafa.af.mil

BERTOLAMI, CHARLES NICHOLAS, oral surgeon; b. Lorain, Ohio, Dec. 31, 1949; s. Salvatore Charles and Michela (Orlando) B.; m. Linda Silva, June 27, 1977; children: Michela, Joseph. AA, Lorain Community Coll., 1969; DDS, Ohio State U., 1974; DMedSci, Harvard U., 1979. Diplomate Am. Bd. Oral and Maxillofacial Surgery. Chief resident Mass. Gen. Hosp., Boston, 1979-80, asst. oral surgeon, 1983; asst. prof. U. Conn., 1980-83, Harvard Sch. Dental Medicine, Boston, 1983-89; assoc. prof. UCLA, 1989-90, prof., 1990—; chief dental svcs. UCLA Med. Ctr., 1990—. Chmn. sect. oral & maxillofacial surgery UCLA Sch. Dentistry, 1989—. Rsch. editor Jour. of Oral and Maxillofacial Surgery; contbr. articles to profl. jours. Recipient Callahan Meml. award Ohio Dental Assn., 1974; fellow Am. Cancer soc., 1984—, Am. Assn. Oral and Maxillofacial Surgery, 1975; grantee USPHS, 1983—. Fellow Am. Assn. Oral and Maxillofacial Surgeons (exec. com. 1983-84); mem. ADA, Internat. Assn. Dental Rsch. (program chmn. 1984-85). Office: U of California Dept Oral Surgery 10833 LeConte Ave Los Angeles CA 90024

BERTOZZI, CAROLYN R. chemistry educator; b. Boston, 1966; AB in Chemistry summa cum laude, Harvard U.; PhD, U. Calif., Berkeley, 1993. Summer intern Bell Labs, 1987; postdoc. fellow U. Calif., San Francisco, prof. of Chemistry Berkeley, 1996—. Contbr. articles to profl. jours. including J. Org. Chem., Chem. and Biol., Biochem. MacArthur fellow 1999—. Mem. Am. Chem. Soc. (Arthur C. Cope Scholar Award, 1999). Office: U Calif Berkeley Chemistry Dept 813A Latimer Berkeley CA 94720-0001

BERZON, MARSHA S. federal judge; BA, Radcliffe Coll., 1966; JD, Boalt Hall Sch. Law, 1973. Bar: Calif. 1973, D.C. 1975. Clerk Judge James Browning, 9th Cir., 1973-74, Justice William Brennan, 1974-75; atty. Woll & Meyer, Washington, 1975-77, Altshuler, Berzson, Nussbaum, Berzon & Rubin, San Francisco, 1978-2000; judge U.S. Ct. Appeals 9th Cir., 2000—. Office: US Ct Appeals 9th cir PO Box 193939 San Francisco CA 94119-3939

BESING, RAY GILBERT, lawyer, writer; b. Roswell, N.Mex., Sept. 14, 1934; s. Ray David and Maxine Mable (Jordan) B.; children: Christopher, Gilbert, Andrew, Paul. Student, Rice U., 1952-54; B.A., Ripon Coll., 1957; postgrad., Georgetown U., 1957; J.D., So. Methodist U., 1960. Bar: Tex. 1960. Ptnr. Geary, Brice, Barron, & Stahl, Dallas, 1960-74; sr. ptnr. Besing, Baker & Glast, Dallas, 1974-77; prin. Law Offices of Ray G. Besing, P.C., Dallas, 1977—. Lectr. trial procedures So. Meth. Sch. of Law, 1966-68; guest lectr. comm. law and policy, univs. and industry confs., 1984—; lectr. Bologna Ctr. of Johns Hopkins U., Nitze Sch. Advanced Internat. Studies, 1999. Author: Who Broke Up AT&T?: From Ma Bell to the Internet, 2000; mng. editor, So. Methodist U. Law Jour., 1959-60. Pres. Dallas Cerebral Palsy Found., 1970; bd. dirs. Dallas Symphony, 1972, Dallas Theatre Center, 1971; trustee Ripon Coll., 1969-76; mem. Tex. Gov.'s Transition Team on Telecom., 1982. Tex. Moot Ct. champion, 1958 Mem. Tex. Bar Assn., Dallas Bar Assn., Dallas Jr. C. of C. (v.p. 1964), Sigma Chi. Democrat. Episcopalian (mem. exec. council diocese Dallas, 1969-72). Home and Office: 400 Graham Ave Santa Fe NM 87501-1658 E-mail: rbesing@cybermesa.com

BEST, HOLLIS GARBER, judge; b. Curry County, N.Mex., July 10, 1926; s. Ernest and Neely Civil (Stratton) B.; m. Kathryn Jean LaFollette, Aug. 4, 1947; children: David S., Daniel E., Laura J. Best Marks, Kathryn A. AB, Fresno State U., 1948; JD, Stanford U., 1951. Bar: Calif. 1951. Dep. dist. atty. County of Fresno, Fresno, Calif., 1951-53; ptnr. Manfredo, Best & Forbes, Fresno, 1953-63, McCormick, Barstow, Sheppard, Coyle & Best, Fresno, 1963-72; judge Calif. Superior Ct., Fresno, 1972-84; assoc. justice Calif. 5th dist. Ct. Appeals, Fresno, 1984—, presiding justice, 1990-94; magistrate judge Ea. Dist. Calif., 1994—. Mem. exec. com., Conf. State Bar Dels., Calif., 1969-71; adj. prof. law, San Joaquin Coll. Law, Fresno, 1974-84. Lt. (j.g.) USNR, 1944-46, PTO. Mem. Calif. Judges Assn. (sec.-treas. 1979-80), Calif. Judges Found. (bd. dirs. 1987-90), Fresno County Bar Assn. (pres. 1963), Rotary. Republican. Avocations: golf, reading. Office: US Dist Ct Ea Dist PO Box 575 Yosemite National Park CA 95389-0575 E-mail: hbest@yosemite.court.fed.com

BEST, MELVYN EDWARD, geophysicist; b. Victoria, B.C., Can., Mar. 8, 1941; s. Herbert Best and Irene Jessie (Kelly) MacKenzie; m. Virginia Marie Pignato, July 19, 1970; children: Lisette Anne, Aaron Michael. BSc in Math. and Physics with honors, U. B.C., Vancouver, 1965, MSc in Physics, 1966; PhD in Theoretical Physics, MIT, 1970. Geophysicist mineral exploration Shell Can. Resources Ltd., Calgary, Alta., Can., 1972-77, divsn. geophysicist minerals Can., 1980-82, mgr. petroleum engring. rsch. Can., 1982-85; head non-seismic rsch. Royal Dutch Shell Exploration and Prodn. Labs., The Hague, The Netherlands, 1978-80; geophys. advisor Teknica Resource Devel. Ltd., Calgary, 1985-86; head basin analysis subdivision Atlantic Geoscience Ctr. Geol. Survey Can., Dartmouth, N.S., 1986-90, dir. Pacific Geosci. Ctr. Sidney, B.C., 1990-94, sr. rsch. scientist, 1994-97; geophys. cons. Bemex Consulting Internat., Victoria, 1997—; environ. geophys. Lockheed-Martin Corp., Edison, N.J., 2001—. Vis. lectr., rsch. assoc. dept. physics McGill U., Montreal, Que., Can., 1970-72; mem. panel Jeanne d'Arc hydrocarbon resource assessment Can. Govt., 1987-90, mem. petroleum geology working group Office Energy R&D, 1987-92; mem. oil and gas com. Can. Nfld. Offshore Petroleum Bd., 1990-94, com. for coordination of joint prospecting for mineral resources in Asian offshore waters, ofcl. Can. rep., 1992-94; sessional lectr. Ctr. for Earth and Ocean Rsch., U. Victoria, 1995—, adj. prof. earth and ocean scis., 1998—; adj .prof. geology and geophysics U. Calgary, 1998—. Author: Resistivity Mapping and Electromagnetic Imaging, 1992; editor: (with J.B. Boniwell) A Geophysical Handbook for Geologists, 1989, (with T.P. Ng) Development and Exploitation Scale Geophysics, 1995. Vol. lectr. Can. Coll. Chinese Studies, Victoria, B.C., 1995-99; vol. Victoria chpt. Habitat for Humanity, 1996-97. Recipient meritorious svc. award Can. Soc. Exploration Geophysicists, Calgary, 1996. Mem. Can. Soc. Exploration Geophysicists (chmn. continuing edn. com. 1982-85, mem. tech. com. 1985 convention, assoc. editor jour. 1986-93, 95—, editor jour. 1993-95), Soc. Exploration Geophysicists (prodn. and devel. geophysics com. 1985-88, geophys. rsch. com. 1988—, organizer workshop 1989, instr. continuing edn. 1985-2000), Soc. Environ. and Engring. Geophysics (assoc. editor jour. 1995-97, 2000—, editor 1997-2000), Assn. Profl. Engrs., Geologists and Geophysicists Alta. (cert.), Assn. Profl. Engrs. and Geoscientists B.C. (cert.). Avocations: competitive badminton, squash, tennis, hiking, sailing. Office: Bemex Cons Internat 5288 Cordova Bay Rd Victoria BC Canada V8Y 2L4

BETHUNE, DAVID ROSS, pharmaceutical executive; b. Ft. Mill, S.C., Aug. 11, 1940; s. Jacob Allen and Mary (Elliott) B.; m. Sylvia Bolick; children: David Jr., Michelle. AB, Lenoir-Rhyne Coll., 1962. Regional mgr. Lederle Labs., Chgo., 1975-78, asst. gen. mgr., Wayne, N.J., 1978-79, mgr. standard products, 1979-80, dir. prodn. mgmt., 1980-81, pres., 1988—; gen. mgr. Davis & Geck, Wayne, 1981-83, Lederle Pharms., Wayne, 1983-84; v.p., gen. mgr. G. D. Searle, Skokie, Ill., 1984-86, pres. U.S., Can. and Caribbean ops., 1986-88; pres. Lederle Labs. div. Am. Cyanamid Co., Wayne, N.J., 1988-92; group v.p. Am. Cyanamid Co., Wayne, 1992-95; pres. & CEO Aesgen, Inc., 1995-96; pharmaceutical consultant, 1996-97; pres & CEO IVAX Corp., 1997-98; vice-chmn. & CEO ATRIX Labs, Inc., Ft. Collins, Colo., 1999-2000, chmn. & CEO, 2000—. Bd. dirs. Telik, Inc., San Francisco, The Femal Health Co., Chgo. Bd. dirs. Nat. Pharm. Coun., Reston, Va., 1981—88, Elan Corp. plc, Dublin, Ireland, 1995—98; mem. La. State Univ. Healthcare Network, New Orleans; bd. dirs. Partnership for Prevention. Recipient Bus. Leader of Yr. award Jour. News, Rockland County, N.J., 1989, Humanitarian of Yr. N.J. chpt. Arthritis Found., 1989. Mem. Pharm. Mfrs. Assn., Nat. Wholesale Drug Assn., Nat. Assn. Chain Drug Stores. Republican. Baptist. Avocations: skeet shooter, photography, theater. Office: ATRIX labs Inc 2579 Midpoint Dr. Fort Collins CO 80525

BETKER, MARK ALAN, manufacturing executive; b. Milw., Oct. 5, 1950; s. Thomas and Phyllis (Ruesch) B.; m. Sandra Gillis, Sept. 1, 1975; 1 child, Courtney. BBA in Fin., U. Wis., Milw., 1978; MBA in Fin., Regis Coll., Denver, 1982. Mgr. contract sales adminstrn. Maysteel Corp., Mayville, Wis., 1975-78; v.p. ops. Markan Mfg., Arvada, Colo., 1978-83; v.p., gen. mgr. Bluebird Internat., Englewood, 1983-86; v.p. ops. Windsor Industries, Englewood, 1986—. Served with USNG, 1970-76. Mem. Am. Prodn. Inventory Control Soc. Home: 4215 Morning Star Dr Castle Rock CO 80104-9022 Office: Windsor Industries 1351 W Stanford Ave Englewood CO 80110-5545 also: KOALA CORPORATION 11600 E 53rd Ave., Unit D Denver CO 80239-2312

BETTENDORF, JERRY, retired airport administrator; AA, C.C. of Air Force, 1975. Dir. airpark Pinal County Airpark, Ariz., 1980-88; op. supr., airport mgr. Grand Canyon Nat. Park Airport, 1988-91; dir. aviation Laughlin/Bullhead Internat. Airport, Bullhead City, Ariz., 1991-99; ret., 1999. Staff sgt. USAF, 1969-80. Mem. Assn. Airport Execs. (exec. mem.), Ariz. Airport Assn. (exec. mem.). Office: Laughlin/Bullhead Internat Airport 600 Hwy 95 Bullhead City AZ 86429-5007

BETTISON, CYNTHIA ANN, museum director, archaeologist; b. St. Louis, Sept. 8, 1958; d. William Leslie and Barbara Ann (Yunker) B. BA in Anthropology and Biology, Pitzer Coll., 1980; MA in Anthropology, Eastern N.Mex. U., 1983; ABD in Anthropology, U. Calif., Santa Barbara, 1986, PhD in Anthropology, 1998. Registered profl. archaeologist. Asst. curator dept. anthropology U. Calif., Santa Barbara, 1988-89, curator dept. anthropology, 1990-91; dir. Western N.Mex. U. Mus., Silver City, 1991—. Co-dir. Western N.Mex. U. Archaeol. Field Sch., 1992, 94, 95; lectr. Western N.Mex. U., 1992, 93, adj. asst. prof. dept. social scis., 1994—; various archaeol. positions, 1981—. Contbr. articles to profl. jours. Recipient Conservation Assessment Program grant, 1994-95, NEH, 1994; Gila Nat. Forest grantee, 1992, 94, 95, Mimbres Region Art Coun. mini grantee, 1992, Silver City Lodgers Tax Bd. grantee, Andrew Isabell Meml. Fund grantee U. Calif., 1990, SIMSE grantee, 1994-95, 95-96. Mem. AAUW, Am. Assn. Mus., Am. Anthrop. Assn., Am. Soc. Conservation Archaeology, N.Mex. Mus. Assn., Soc. for Am. Archaeology, Archaeol. Soc. N.Mex., N.Mex. Archaeol. Coun. (sec. 1993-94), Coun. Mus. Anthropology (sec. 1992-94), Mountain Plains Mus. Assn., Univ. Women's Club, Univ. Club, Optimist Club (sec. Silver City chpt. 1992), Silver City Rotary Club (v.p. 1999-2000, pres. elect 2000-2001, pres. 2001-2002), Silver City Grant County C. of C., Chpt. AG PEO, Phi Kappa Phi. Office: Western NM Univ Mus 1000 W College Ave Silver City NM 88061-4158 E-mail: bettisonc@iron.wnmu.edu

BETTS, JAMES WILLIAM, JR. financial analyst, consultant; b. Oct. 11, 1923; s. James William and Cora Anna (Banta) B.; m. Barbara Stoke, July 28, 1951; 1 child, Barbara Susan (dec.). BA, Rutgers U., 1946; postgrad., New Sch. for Social Rsch., 1948-49; MA, U. Hawaii, 1957. With Dun & Bradstreet, Inc., 1946-86, svc. cons., 1963-64, reporting and svc. mgr., 1964-65, sr. fin. analyst, 1965-86; owner Portfolio Cons. of Hawaii, 1979—. Cons. Saybrook Point Investments, Old Saybrook, Conn., 1979—; owner James W. Betts and Co., 1996—. Contbr. articles to mag. With AUS, 1943. Mem. Am. Econ. Assn., Nat. Assn. Bus. Economists, Western Econ. Assn., Atlantic Econ. Soc., Col. Henry Rutgers Soc., Internat. Inst. Forecasters, Transp. Rsch. Forum. Republican. Episcopalian.

BEUTLER, ERNEST, physician, research scientist; b. Berlin, Sept. 30, 1928; came to U.S., 1936, naturalized, 1943; s. Alfred David and Kaethe (Italiener) B.; m. Brondelle Fleisher, June 15, 1950; children: Steven Merrill, Earl Bryan, Bruce Alan, Deborah Ann. Ph.B., U. Chgo., 1946, B.S., 1948, M.D., 1950; PhD (hon.), Tel Aviv U., Israel, 1993. Intern U. Chgo. Clinics, 1950-51; resident in medicine 1951-53; asst. prof. U. Chgo., 1956-59; chmn. div. medicine City of Hope Med. Ctr., L.A., 1959-78; chmn. dept. clin. rsch. The Scripps Rsch. Inst., La Jolla, Calif., 1978-82, chmn. dept. basic and clin. rsch., 1982-89, chmn. dept. molecular and exptl. medicine, 1989—. Clin. prof. medicine U. So. Calif., 1964-79, U. Calif. San Diego, 1979 ; mem. hematology study sect. NIH, 1970-74, 89-91; Spinoza Chair U. Amsterdam, 1991. Author 8 books, numerous articles in med. jours.; mem. editorial bds. profl. jours. Adv. com. Blood Products FDA, 1984-88; nat. heart, lung, and blood adv. coun. mem. NIH, 1994-97. Recipient Gairdner award, 1975, Blundell prize, 1985, Nat. Heart, Lung, and Blood Inst. Merit award NIH, 1987, 5th ann. Excellence award Gen. Clin. Rsch. Program, 1993, Nat. Acad. Clin. Biochemistry Lectureship award Kodak Instruments, 1990, Mayo Soley award Western Soc. Clin. Investigation, 1992, City of Medicine award, 1994, Outstanding Rsch. award Am. Soc. Clin. Pathologists, 2000. Mem. NAS, Am. Acad. Arts and Scis., Assn. Am. Physicians, Am. Soc. Clin. Investigation, Western Assn. Physicians (pres. 1989), Am. Soc. Hematology (mem. exec. com. 1968-72, v.p. 1977, pres. 1979), Am. Soc. Human Genetics (mem. exec. com. 1968-72) Jewish. Achievements include invention of screening tests for galactosemia and other genetic disorders; co-discovery of glucose-6-phosphate dehydrogenase deficiency; origination of X inactivation hypothesis; research on glycolipid disorders. Home: 2707 Costebelle Dr La Jolla CA 92037-3518 Office: The Scripps Rsch Inst 10550 N Torrey Pines Rd La Jolla CA 92037-1000 E-mail: beutler@scripps.edu

BEUTLER, LARRY EDWARD, psychology educator; b. Logan, Utah, Feb. 14, 1941; s. Edward and Beulah (Andrus) B.; children: Jana, Kelly, Ian David, Gail. BS, Utah State U., 1965, MS, 1966; PhD, U. Nebr., 1970. Diplomate Am. Bd. Clin. Psychology. Asst. prof. psychology Duke U., Ashville, N.C., 1970-71; asst. prof. Stephen F. Austin State U., Nacogdoches, Tex., 1971-73; assoc. prof. Baylor Coll. Medicine, Houston, 1973-79; prof. U. Ariz., Tucson, 1979-90, U. Calif., Santa Barbara, 1990—. Author: Eclectic Psychotherapy, 1983; co-author: Systematic Treatment Selection, 1990, Guidelines for the Systematic Treatment of the Depressed Patient, 2000; editor Jour. Cons. Clin. Psychology, 1990-96; editor Jour. Clin. Psychology, 1997—. Fellow Am. Psychology Assn., Am. Psychol. Soc. (pres. divsn. psychotherapy, 1997, pres. divsn. clin. psychology, 2001); mem. Soc. Psychotherapy Research (pres. 1986-88). Home: 7602 Hollister Ave Unit 301 Goleta CA 93117-2459 Office: U Calif Santa Barbara Gse Santa Barbara CA 93106 E-mail: beutler@education.ucsb.edu

BEVAN, WILLIAM ARNOLD, JR. emergency physician; b. Sault St. Marie, Mich., June 23, 1943; s. William Arnold and Syneva Lois (Martin) B.; m. Martha Lynn Peterson, Dec. 29, 1973; children: Terry Eugene, Brian William, PAtrick Jon. BS, U. Minn., 1966, MD, 1970. Diplomate Am. Bd. Family Practice, Am. Bd. Emergency Medicine. Intern U. Utah, 1970-71; family practitioner Vail Mtn. Med. Profl. Corp., Vail, Colo., 1972-83; emergency physician Vail Valley Emergency Physicians, 1983—. Dir. Vail Valley Emergency Dept., 1992—; adviser Western Eagle County Ambulance Dist., 1983—. Trustee Shattuck St. Mary's Sch., Faribault, Minn., 1977—, Vail Christian H.S., 1998—; football coach Battle Mountain H.S., Vail, 1978—. Named Man of Yr. Boy Scouts Am., 1966, 77. Fellow Am. Coll. Emergency Physicians; mem. AMA, Rocky Mountain Med. Soc., Colo. Med. Soc., U. Minn. Alumni Assn. (life). Republican. Lutheran. Home: 0025 Cottonwood Rd Eagle Vail CO 81631 Office: Vail Valley Emergency Dept 181 W Meadow Dr Vail CO 81657-5058

BEVELACQUA, JOSEPH JOHN, physicist, researcher; b. Waynesburg, Pa., Mar. 17, 1949; s. Frank and Lucy Ann B.; m. Terry Sanders, Sept. 4, 1971; children: Anthony, Jeffrey, Megan, Peter, Michael, Karen. BS in Physics, Calif. State Coll., 1970; postgrad., U. Maine, 1970-72; MS in Physics, Fla. State U., 1974, PhD, 1976. Diplomate Am. Bd. Health Physics; cert. radiol. shield survey engr.; cert. health physicist (comprehensive and power reactors), sr. reactor operator cert. Teaching/rsch. asst. U. Maine, 1970-72; tchg. and rsch. asst. Fla. State U., 1973-76; rsch. asst. NSF, 1975-76, rsch. assoc., 1976; nuclear engr. Bettis Atomic Power Lab., West Mifflin, Pa., 1973, sr. nuclear engr., 1976-78; ops. rsch. analyst U.S. Dept. Energy, Oak Ridge, 1978-80, chief physicist advanced laser isotope separation program, 1980-83; sr. radiol. engr. GPU Nuclear Corp. (Three Mile Island Sta.-Unit 2), Middletown, Pa., 1983-84; Three Mile Island emergency preparedness mgr. GPU Nuclear Corp., Middletown, 1984-86, mgr. TMI-2 safety rev. group, 1986-89, dir. radiol. controls TMI-2, 1989; supt. health physics Point Beach Nuclear Power Plant Wis. Electric Co., Two Rivers, 1989-95; prodn. planning mgr. Point Beach Nuclear Plant, 1996—; pres., CEO Bevelacqua Resources, Richland, Wash., 1993—; sr. radiol.controls tech. advisor USDOE-Office River Protection, Hanford, 1996—, acting dir. environ. divsn., 2000. Cons. U.S. Dept. Energy

Process Evaluation Bd. of Isotope Separation, Washington, 1981-82; asst. mgr. environ., safety, health, and quality USDOE- Office River Protection, Hanford. Author: Contemporary Health Physics: Problems and Solutions, 1995, Basic Health Physics: Problems and Solutions, 1999, 20 health physics tng. manuals pub. by Bevelacqua Resources, 3 CD-ROMS for health physics tng.; contbr. articles to profl. jours. including Physical Rev. Letters. Mem. Rep. Presdl. Task Force, Nat. Rep. Senatorial Com. Recipient Outstanding Performance award Dept. Energy, 1982, Profl. Excellence award U. Pa., 2000; grantee USAF, NSF; Von Humboldt fellow U. Hamburg. Mem. Am. Nuclear Soc., Am. Phys. Soc., Am. Acad. Health Physics (profl. devel. com. 1992-94, chmn. 1994, nom. com. 1994-96), Susquehanna Valley Health Physics Soc. (mem. exec. com.), N.Y. Acad. Scis., Soc. Nuclear Medicine, Nuclear Utility Coordinating Group on Emergency Preparedness Implementation, Babcock and Wilcox Owners Group on Emergency Preparedness, Profl. Reactor Operators Soc., Health Physics Soc. (placement com. 1989-92, nominating com. 1994-97), Am. Bd. Health Physics (vice chmn. comprehensive panel of examiners 1990, chmn. 1991, nat. office mem.), Oak Ridge Sportsman's Club, Sigma Pi Sigma. Republican. Lutheran. Achievements include research on theoretical studies of light nuclei, few nucleon transfer reactions, radiation shielding, laser isotope separation, neutron nuclei, symmetry violations in nuclei, grand unification theories, quark models of nuclear forces, neutrino interactions, nuclear fuel cycle, laser fusion and gravitational collapse of stars, beta dosimetry, internal dosimetry, health effects of ionizing radiation; nuclear reactor safety, radon health effects and mitigation, radioactive and mixed waste management, applied health physics, internal and external dusimetry, dark matter, strange matter, symmetry violations in nuclei, cosmology, and astrophysics, genetic approaches for cancer research, radiation induced immune system activation. Home and Office: Bevelacqua Resources 343 Adair Dr Richland WA 99352-8563 E-mail: bevelresou@aol.com

BEYER, CASEY K. legislative staff member; b. Reno, Jan. 4, 1955; BA, U. Calif., Santa Barbara, 1978; MUP, San Jose U., 1984. Staff aide Rep. Ed Zschau, 1983-86; cons. to hi-tech cos. Silicone Valley, Calif., 1987-88; dist. dir. Rep. Tom Campbell, Campbell, 1989-92, Campbell, 1996-97, chief of staff, 1997—; state adminstr. State Senator Tom Campbell, Campbell, 1993-95. Mem. exec. com. Tax and Fiscal Policy Joint Venture, 1994—, mem. working group, 1994—. Office: Office US Rep Tom Campbell 910 Campisi Way Ste 1C Campbell CA 95008-2351

BEYER, LEE LOUIS, state legislator; b. Norfolk, Nebr., June 4, 1948; s. Louis E. and Arlene (Henderson) B.; m. Elizabeth Terry Yates, July 26, 1969; children: Jonathan, Joshua, Megan. BS in Pub. Mgmt., U. Oreg., 1974. Exec. dir. Linn-Benton-Lincoln Manpower Consortium, Corvallis, Oreg., 1974-76; mgmt. analyst Oreg. State Exec. Dept., Salem, 1976-78; ops. mgr. Lane County Employment Tng. Dept., Eugene, Oreg., 1978-80; exec. dir. Eugene Pvt. Industry Coun., 1980-83; indsl. devel. mgr. City of Eugene, 1983-86; city councilor Springfield, 1986-93; mem. Oreg. Ho. of Reps., Salem, 1991-98; mem. house dem. whip Oreg. Senate, Salem, 1998-. Mem., chair Lane C.C. Vocat. Edn. Commn., Eugene, 1978-79, 83—; bd. dirs. Eugene/Springfield Visitor and Conv. Bur., Eugene, Eugene/Springfield Metro. Partnership, Eugene. Mem., chmn. Intergovtl. Met. Policy Com., Springfield, 1986—; pres., councilman City of Springfield, 1986—; mem., chair Springfield City Planning Commn., 1979-86, Springfield Budget Com., 1984—; Oreg. state rep., 1991—. With USAF, 1967-70. Democrat. Lutheran. Avocations: reading, fishing. Office: Oreg Senate S 306 State Capitol Salem OR 97310-0001

BEYER, ROGER, state senator; b. Oregon City, Oreg., Sept. 1960; m. Barbara Beyer. BS in Horticulture, Oreg. State U. Rep. rep. dist. 28 Oreg. Ho. of Reps., 1996-2000; Rep. senator dist. 15 Oreg. State Senate, 2000—. Mem. agr. and forestry and rules, elections and pub. affairs coms. Oreg. Ho. of Reps., chair bus. and consumer affairs. Mem. bd. dirs. Maple Broad Sch. Office: H-382 State Capitla Salem OR 97310 also: 39486 S Cooper Rd Molalla OR 97038 E-mail: beyer.rep@state.or.us

BEYERS, WILLIAM BJORN, geography educator; b. Seattle, Mar. 24, 1940; s. William Abraham and Esther Jakobia (Svendsen) B.; m. Margaret Lyn Rice, July 28, 1968. BA, U. Wash., 1962, PhD, 1967. Asst. prof. geography U. Wash., Seattle, 1968-74, assoc. prof., 1974-82, prof., 1982—, chmn. dept. geography, 1991-95. Mem. Assn. Am. Geographers, Regional Sci. Assn., Am. Econs. Assn., Western Regional Sci. Assn. Home: 7159 Beach Dr SW Seattle WA 98136-2077 Office: U Wash Dept Geography PO Box 353550 Seattle WA 98195-3550 Fax: 206-543-3313. E-mail: beyers@u.washington.edu

BEYLKIN, GREGORY, mathematician; b. St. Petersburg, USSR, Mar. 16, 1953; came to U.S., 1980; naturalized citizen, 1985; s. Jacob and Raya (Pripshtein) B.; m. Helen Simontov, 1974; children: Michael, Daniel. Diploma in Math., U. St. Petersburg, Leningrad, 1975; PhD in Math., NYU, 1982. Assoc. rsch. sci. NYU, 1982-83; mem. profl. staff Schlumberger-Doll Research, Ridgefield, Conn., 1983-91; prof. dept. applied math. U. Colo., Boulder, 1991—. Contbr. articles to profl. jours. Mem. Am. Math. Soc., Soc. for Indsl. and Applied Math., Soc. Exptl. Geophysicists. Home: 3897 Promontory Ct Boulder CO 80304-1053 Office: U Colo Dept Applied Math PO Box 526 Boulder CO 80309-0526 E-mail: beylkin@boulder.colorado.edu

BEYSTER, JOHN ROBERT, engineering company executive; b. Detroit, July 26, 1924; s. John Frederick and Lillian Edith (Jondro) B.; m. Betty Jean Brock, Sept. 8, 1955; children: James Frederick, Mark Daneil, Mary Ann. B.S. in Engring., U. Mich., 1945, M.S., 1948, Ph.D., 1950. Registered profl. engr., Calif. Mem. staff Los Alamos Sci. Lab., 1951-56; chmn. dept. accel. physics Gulf Gen. Atomic Co., San Diego, 1957-69; pres., chmn. bd. Sci. Applications, Inc., La Jolla, Calif., from 1969, now chmn. bd., chief exec. officer; mem. Joint Strategic Target Planning Staff, Sci. Adv. Group, Omaha, 1978—; panel mem. Nat. Measurement Lab. Evaluation panel for Radiation Research, Washington, 1983—; dir. Scripps Bancorp, La Jolla, 1983. Co-author: Slow Neutron Scattering and Thermalization, 1970. With USN, 1943-46. Fellow Am. Nuclear Soc., Am. Phys. Soc.; mem. NAE. Republican. Roman Catholic. Home: 9321 La Jolla Farms Rd La Jolla CA 92037-1126 Office: Science Applications Inter Corp 1241 Cave St La Jolla CA 92037

BEZOS, JEFFREY P. multimedia executive; Degree in elec. engring. and computer sci. summa cum laude, Princeton U., 1986. With Bankers Trust Co., N.Y., 1988-90, v.p., 1990; with D.E. Shaw & Co., 1990-94, sr. v.p., 1992-94; founder, CEO Amazon.com Inc., Seattle, 1995—. Past mem. staff FITEL, N.Y. Mem. Phi Beta Kappa. Office: Amazon com Inc 1200 12th Ave S Seattle WA 98144

BEZZONE, ALBERT PAUL, structural engineer; b. Sacramento, June 22, 1931; s. Albert Paul and Angela Edna (Nicolai) B.; m. JoAnn Karslie Walther, Aug. 4, 1951; children: Jeffrey Paul, David Ernest, Judith Eileen. Student, Sacramento City Coll., 1949-50, Calif. State U., 1952-56. Engring. technician, State of Calif., Sacramento, 1950-51; civil engr. County of Sacramento, Calif., 1951-53; with Calif. Dept. Transportation, 1953-93, chief office of structure constrn., structures div., 1977-93; cons. bridge engring. Sacramento, 1993—. Contbr. articles to profl. jours. Fellow ASCE; mem. Profl. Engrs. in Calif. Govt. Home: 829 Senior Way Sacramento CA 95831-2128 Office: PO Box 942874 [illegible] 94274-0001

BHAGWAN, SUDHIR, computer industry and research executive, consultant; b. Lahore, West Pakistan, Aug. 9, 1942; came to U.S., 1963; s. Vishan and Lakshmi Devi (Arora) B.; m. Sarita Bahl, Oct. 25, 1969; children: Sonia, Sunil. BSEE, Punjab Engring. Coll., Chandigarh, India, 1963; MSEE, Stanford U., 1964; MBA with honors, Golden Gate U., 1977. Engr. Gaylor Products, North Hollywood, Calif., 1964-68, Burroughs Corp., Pasadena, 1968-70, engring. mgr. Santa Barbara, 1970-78, Intel Corp., Hillsboro, Oreg., 1978-81, chmn. strategic planning, 1981-82, gen. mgr., 1983-88; pres., exec. dir., bd. dirs. Oreg. Advanced Computing Inst., Beaverton, 1988-90; strategic bus. mgr. INTEL Corp., Hillsboro, Oreg., 1990-92, gen. mgr. bus. multimedia products, 1992-93, bus. area mgr., 1993-94, dir. internat. mktg., 1995-99; mgr. Bhagwan Enterprises LLC, 2000—. Spkr. to high tech. industry, Oreg., 1988—; mem. organizing com. Distributed Memory Computing Conf., 1989-90, gen. chmn., 1990-91; chmn. computer tech. adv. bd. Oreg. Mus. Sci. and Industry, 1991-93; bd. advisors Ironspire, Inc., Finatus.com., CB Capital IV LLC Funds, Preusch Capital Resources, Inc. Cons. Oreg. Econ. Devel. Dept., 1988-91; bd. dirs. St. Mary's Acad., Portland, 1989-92. Mem. Am. Electronics Assn. (higher edn. com. Oreg. chpt. 1989-90, exec. com. 1990). Avocations: electronics, photography, tennis, art. Home: 13940 NW Harvest Ln Portland OR 97229-3653 E-mail: sbhagwan@att.net

BHATIA, PETER K. newspaper editor, journalist; b. Pullman, Wash., May 22, 1953; s. Vishnu N. and Ursula Jean (Dawson) B.; m. Elizabeth M. Dahl, Sept. 27, 1981; children: Megan Jean, Jay Peter. BA, Stanford U., 1975. Polit. reporter, asst. news editor Spokesman Rev., Spokane, Wash., 1975-77; news editor Dallas Times Herald, 1980-81; asst. news editor San Francisco Examiner, 1977-80, news editor, 1981-85, dep. mng. editor/news, 1985-87; mng. editor Dallas Times Herald, 1987-88; editor York Dispatch, York, Pa., 1988-89; mng. editor The Sacramento Bee, 1989-93; exec. editor The Fresno Bee, 1993; mng. editor The Oregonian, Portland, 1993-97, exec. editor, 1997—. Pulitzer Prize juror, 1992-93, 98-99; bd. dirs. Am. Press Inst. Bd. chmn. Albertina Kerr Ctrs. for Children, 2000—; chmn. bd. St. John Fisher Sch., 2000—. Mem. Stanford U. Alumni Assn. (bd. dirs. 1998-01), Am. Soc. Newspaper Editors (bd. dirs. 1997—, treas. 2000-01, sec. 2001—), AP Mng. Editors (bd. dirs. 1991-97), Asian Am. Journalists Assn., Nat. Assn. Minority Media Execs., South Asian Journalists Assn., Investigative Reporters and Editors, Sigma Delta Chi, Theta Delta Chi. Office: The Oregonian 1320 SW Broadway Portland OR 97201-3499

BHAUMIK, MANI LAL, physicist; b. Calcutta, India, Jan. 5, 1932; came to U.S., 1959, naturalized, 1968; s. Gunadhar and Lolita (Pramanik) B. B.S., U. Calcutta, 1951, M.S., 1953; Ph.D., Indian Inst. Tech., 1958, DSc (hon.), 1995. Fellow U. Calif. at Los Angeles, 1959-63; with Xerox Electro-Optical Systems, Pasadena, Calif., 1961-67, Northrop Corp. Labs., Hawthorne, 1968-71, research dir., 1971-75; mgr. Laser Tech. Lab., Northrop Research and Tech. Center, 1976-84, sr. staff scientist, 1984-86. Lectr. physics Calif. State U., Long Beach, 1967-69. Contbr. articles to profl. jours.; patentee in field. Fellow Am. Phys. Soc., IEEE. Office: Laser Tech Lab PO Box 24050 Los Angeles CA 90024-0050

BIAGI, RICHARD CHARLES, retail executive, real estate consultant; b. Crockett, Calif., Aug. 29, 1925; s. Louis Joseph and Angelina Antonette (Gambaro) B.; m. Emily Annette Gino, Aug. 7, 1949 (dec.); children: Sharon A. Biagi Juhnke, Sandra A. Biagi Ogden; m. Alice C. Mulder, Nov. 26, 1995. BSBA, U. Calif., Berkeley, 1950, cert. in real estate, 1956. Real estate analyst Safeway Stores inc., Oakland, Calif., 1953-58; real estate negotiator Lucky Stores Inc., San Leandro, 1958-60, div. real estate mgr., 1960-62, mgr. corp. real estate, v.p. corp. real estate mgr. Dublin, 1963-86; cons. real estate Alamo, 1986—. Served with USNR, 1943-46, PTO. Mem. Internat. Council Shopping Ctrs. (trustee 1971-76), U. Calif. Bus. Adminstrn. Alumni Assn. (pres. 1970), Calif. Bus. Properties Assn. (bd. dirs. 1972-92), Toastmasters (pres. San Leandro club 1959). Avocations: photography, biking, golf.

BIALOSKY, MARSHALL HOWARD, composer; b. Oct. 30, 1923; Student, Converse Coll., 1942-43, 46, Colo. Coll., 1948; MusB cum laude, Syracuse U., 1949; MusM, Northwestern U., 1950. Asst. prof. music Milton (Wis.) Coll., 1950-54; asst. condr. Milton Coll. Band, 1954; asst. prof. humanities and music U. Chgo., 1956-61; assoc. prof. music and humanities, condr. chorale SUNY, Stony Brook, 1961-64; prof., chmn. dept. fine arts Calif. State U., Dominguez Hills, 1964-77, founding chmn. dept. music, 1977-78, prof. dept. music, 1978-86, prof. emeritus dept. music, 1986—. Mem. Calif. State Coll. Employee Assn. Statewide Acad. Coun., 1968-71; mem. Calif. State Coll. Internat. Program Acad. Coun. and Exec. Com., 1967-73; bd. dirs. Monday Evening Concerts, L.A., 1966-77; dir. Saturday Conservatory Music, L.A. chpt., 1967-71; coord. humanities MA program Calif. State U., Dominguez Hills; composer-in-residence Chamber Music Conf. and Composer's Forum of the East, Bennington Coll., 1989. Performer various cities, radio stas. and schs; composer piano music including An Album for the Young, Five Western Scenes, mixed chorus including American Names, A Sight in Camp in the Daybreak Gray and Dim, Women's Chorus including American Poets Suite, At Last, Vocal Music including Two Songs to Poems of Howard Nemerov, folk songs, spirituals, Christmas music, music for wind instruments, string instruments, brass instruments, guitar and percussion instruments. Contbr. articles to jours. Fulbright award, 1954-56; Wurlitzer Found. grantee, 1979, N.Y.C. Meet-the-Composer grantee, 1984, 86; recipient Career Achievement award Profl. Fraternity Assn. Am., 1980. Mem. ASCAP (creative grant award 1976—), Coll. Music Soc., Am. Soc. Univ. Composers (nat. chmn. 1974-77), Nat. Assn. Composers U.S.A. (pres. 1978—), Soc. Composers Inc., Am. Assn. Choral Condr. Office: Nat Assoc Composer USA PO Box 49256 Los Angeles CA 90049-0256

BIANCHI, CARISA, advertising company executive; Formerly with Benton & Bowles, L.A., Doyle Dane Bernbach; with Chiat/Day L.A., 1989-97; mng. dir., pres., CEO TBWA/Chiat/Day, San Francisco, 1998—. Office: TBWA/Chiat/Day 55 Union St San Francisco CA 94111-1217

BIANCO, JAMES A. research and development executive; b. 1956; BS cum laude with honors, NYU, 1979; MD, Mt. Sinai Sch. of Medicine, 1983. Intern, then resident Mt. Sinai Med. Ctr., N.Y.C., 1983-87; fellow in oncology U. Wash., Seattle, 1987-91, asst. prof. medicine, 1991-92; dir. bone marrow transplant program VA Med. Ctr., Seattle, 1990-92; asst. mem. Fred Hutchinson Cancer Rsch. Ctr., Seattle, 1991-92; pres., CEO Cell Therapeutics, Inc., Seattle, 1992—. Mem. Alpha Omega Alpha. Office: Cell Therapeutics Inc 201 Elliott Ave W Ste 400 Seattle WA 98119-4237

BICE, SCOTT HAAS, dean, lawyer, educator; b. Los Angeles, Mar. 19, 1943; s. Fred Haas and Virginia M. (Scott) B.; m. Barbara Franks, Dec. 21, 1968. B.S., U. So. Calif., 1965, J.D., 1968. Bar: Calif. bar 1971. Law clk. to Chief Justice Earl Warren, 1968-69; asst. prof., [illegible] prof., prof. law U. So. Calif., Los Angeles, 1969-2000, assoc. dean, 1971-74, dean Law Sch., 1980-2000, Carl Mason Franklin prof., 1983-2000, Robert C. Packard prof. law, 2000—. Vis. prof. polit. sci. Calif. Inst. Tech., 1977; vis. prof. U. Va., 1978-79; bd.dirs. Western Mut. Ins. Co., Residence Mut. Ins. Co., Imagine Films Entertainment Co., Jenny Craig, Inc. Mem. editl. adv. bd. Calif. [illegible], contbr. articles to law jours. Bd. dirs. L.A. Family Housing [illegible] Child Care Programs, 1988—. Affiliated scholar Am. Bar Found., 1972-74 Fellow Am. Bar Found. (life); mem. Am. Law Inst., Calif. Bar, Los Angeles County Bar Assn., Am. Law Deans Assn. (pres. 1997-99), Am. Judicature Soc., Calif. Club, Chancery Club, Long Beach Yacht Club. Home: 787 S San Rafael Ave Pasadena CA 91105-2326 Office: U So Calif Sch Law Los Angeles CA 90089-0071 E-mail: sbice@law.usc.edu

BICHSEL, HANS, physicist, consultant, researcher; b. Basel, Switzerland, Sept. 2, 1924; came to U.S., 1951; s. Paul and Anna Maria Bichsel; m. Sue O. Greenwalt, Sept. 12, 1959; children: Elizabeth Christine, Joseph Oliver. MA, PhD, U. Basel, 1951. Rsch. asst. Princeton (N.J.) U., 1951-55; rsch. assoc. Rice U., Houston, 1955-57; asst. prof. physics U. Wash., Seattle, 1957-59; affiliate prof. physics U. Wash., Seattle, 1992—; assoc. prof., prof. radiology U. Wash., Seattle, 1969-80; asst. prof., assoc. prof. physics U. So. Calif., L.A., 1959-68; assoc. prof. U. Calif., Berkeley, 1968-69. Cons. Internat. Commn. on Radiation Units, Bethesda, Md., 1970—, Los Alamos (N.Mex.) Nat. Lab., 1978-83, IAEA, Vienna, Austria, 1990—; vis. scientist Nat. Inst. Radiol., Scis., Chiba, Japan, 1991-96, U. Sherbrooke Med. Sch., Que., Can.; rschr. Relativistic Heavy Ion Collider, Brookhaven Nat. Lab., 1999—; referee Phys. Rev., Nuclear Instruments and Methods, Physics in Medicine and Biology, also others. Contbr. articles to profl. jours. Fellow Am. Phys. Soc.; mem. Swiss Phys. Soc. Home and Office: 1211 22nd Ave E Seattle WA 98112-3534 E-mail: bichsel@npl.washington.edu

BICKART, THEODORE ALBERT, university president emeritus; b. N.Y.C., Aug. 25, 1935; s. Theodore Roosevelt and Edna Catherine (Pink) B.; m. Carol Florence Nichols, June 14, 1958 (div. Dec. 1973); children: Karl Jeffrey, Lauren Spencer; m. Frani W. Rudolph, Aug. 14, 1982; 1 stepchild, Jennifer Anne Cumming. B Engring. Sci., Johns Hopkins U., 1957, MS, 1958, DEng, 1960; D Univ. (hon.), Dneprodzerzhinst State Tech. U, Ukraine, 1996. Asst. prof. elec. and computer engring. Syracuse (N.Y.) U., 1963-65, assoc. prof., 1965-70, prof., 1970-89, assoc. to vice chancellor for acad. affairs for computer resources devel., 1983-85, dean L.C. Smith Coll. Engring., 1984-89; prof. elec. engring., dean engring. Mich. State U., East Lansing, 1989-98; pres. Colo. Sch. Mines, Golden, 1998-2000. Vis. scholar U. Calif., Berkeley, 1977; Fulbright lectr. Kiev Poly Inst., USSR, 1981; vis. lectr. Nanjing Inst. Tech., China, 1981; hon. disting. prof. Taganrog Radio Engring. Inst., Russia, 1992—; mem. Accreditation Bd. for Engring. and Tch., Engring. Accreditation Commn., exec. com., 1998-2000; chmn. Engring. Workforce Commn., 1996-98; elected-mem. Johns Hopkins U. Soc. Scholars, 2001. Co-author: Electrical Network Theory, 1969, Linear Network Theory, 1981; contbr. numerous articles to profl. jours. Served to 1st lt. U.S. Army, 1961-63 Recipient numerous rsch. grants. Fellow IEEE (best paper awards Syracuse sect. 1969, 70, 73, 74, 77, chmn. com. on engring. accreditation activities 1996-98, chmn. assn. policy coun. 2001—), Am. Soc. Engring. Edn. (v.p. 1997-99); mem. Am. Math. Soc., Assn. for Computing Machinery, Soc. for Indsl. and Applied Math., N.Y. Acad. Scis., Ukrainian Acad. Engring. Scis.), Internat. Higher Edn. Acad. Scis. (Russia), Internat. Acad. Informatics (Russia), Johns Hopkins U. Soc. Scholars. Avocations: bicycling; hiking; gardening. Home: 541 Wyoming Cir Golden CO 80403-0900 E-mail: tbickart@mines.edu

BICKEL, PETER JOHN, statistician, educator; b. Bucharest, Romania, Sept. 21, 1940; came to U.S., 1957, naturalized, 1964; s. Eliezer and P. Madeleine (Moscovici) B.; m. Nancy Kramer, Mar. 2, 1964; children: Amanda, Stephen. AB, U. Calif., Berkeley, 1960, MA, 1961, PhD, 1963; PhD (hon.), Hebrew U. Jerusalem, 1988. Asst. prof. stats. U. Calif., Berkeley, 1964-67, assoc. prof., 1967-70, prof., 1970—, chmn. dept. stats., 1976-79, dean phys. scis., 1980-86, chmn. dept. stats., 1993-97. Vis. lectr. math. Imperial Coll., London, 1965-66; fellow J.S. Guggenheim Meml. Found., 1970-71, J.D. and Catherine T. MacArthur Found., 1984-89; NATO sr. sci. fellow, 1974; chair com. on applied and theoretical stats. NRC, 1998-2000, chair bd. on math. scis., 2000—. Author: (with K. Doksum) Mathematical Statistics, 1976, 2d edit., 2000, (with C. Klaassen, Y. Ritov and J. Wellner) Efficient and Adaptive Estimation in Semiparametric Models, 1993; assoc. editor Annals of Math. Stats., 1968-76, 86-93, PNAS, 1996—, Bernouilli, 1996—, Statistics Sinica, 1996—; contbr. articles to profl. jours. Fellow J.D. and Catherine T. MacArthur Found., 1984-89. Fellow AAAS (chair sect. U 1996-97), Inst. Math. Stats. (pres. 1980), Am. Statis. Assn.; mem. NAS, Royal Statis. Soc., Internat. Statis. Inst., Am. Acad. Arts and Scis., Royal Netherlands Acad. Arts and Scis., Bernoulli Soc. (pres. 1990). Office: U Calif Dept Stats Evans Hall Berkeley CA 94720

BIDDLE, DONALD RAY, aerospace company executive; b. Alton, Mo., June 30, 1936; s. Ernest Everet and Dortha Marie (McGuire) B.; m. Nancy Ann Dunham, Mar. 13, 1955; children: Jeanne Biddle Bednash, Mitchell Lee, Charles Alan. Student, El Dorado (Kans.) Jr. Coll., 1953-55, Pratt (Kans.) Jr. Coll., 1955-56; BSME, Washington U., St. Louis, 1961; postgrad. computer sci., Pa. State U. Ext., 1963; cert. bus. mgmt., Alexander Hamilton Inst., 1958. Design group engr. Emerson Elec. Mfg., St. Louis, 1957-61; design specialist Boeing Vertol, Springfield, Pa., 1962; cons. engr. Ewing Tech. Design, Phila., 1962-66; chief engr. rotary wing Gates Learjet, Wichita, Kans., 1967-70; dir. engring., R&D, BP Chems., Inc. Advanced Material Divsn., Stockton, Calif., 1971-93; prin. Biddle & Assocs., Consulting Engrs., Stockton, 1993—; pres., CEO, Big Valley Aviation, Inc., Stockton, 1997-98; CEO, Propulsion Technologies, Inc., Stockton, 1999—, United Propeller Technologies, Inc., Stockton, 1999—. Guest lectr. on manrated structures, devel. proprietary designs, small bus. devel. to various univs. and tech. socs. Patentee landing gear designs, inflatable rescue sys., glass retention sys., adjustable jack sys., cold weather start flourescent lamp, paper honeycomb core post-process sys. Scoutmaster, counselor, instl. rep. Boy Scouts Am., St. Ann, Mo., 1956-61; mem. Springfield Sch. Bd., 1964. Mem. ASME, ASTM, AIAA, Am. Helicopter Soc. (sec.-treas. Wichita chpt. 1969), Am. Mgmt. Assn., Exptl. Pilots Assn., Soc. for Advancement of Metals and Process Engring. Republican. Methodist. E-mails: (bus.) (personal). Home: 6449 Embarcadero Dr Stockton CA 95219-3800 Office: United Propeller Tech Inc 7515 C E Dixon St Stockton CA 95206-4922 E-mail: dbiddle@UnitedPropeller.com, drbiddle@juno.com

BIDLACK, WAYNE ROSS, nutritional biochemist, toxicologist, food scientist; b. Waverly, N.Y., Aug. 12, 1944; s. Andrew L. Bidlack and Vivian Pearl Cowles Williams; m. Wei Wang, July 29, 1995. BS, Pa. State U., 1966; MS, Iowa State U., 1968; PhD, U. Calif., Davis, 1972. Postdoctoral fellow dept. pharmacology U. So. Calif., L.A., 1972-74, asst prof. sch. medicine, 1974-80, assoc. prof., 1980-92, prof., 1992—, asst. dean student affairs, 1988-91, chmn. dept. pharmacology and nutrition, 1991-92; chmn. dept. food sci. and human nutrition Iowa State U., Ames, 1992-95; dean Coll. Agr. Calif. State Poly. U., Pomona, 1995—. Assoc. editor Biochem. Medicine and Metabolic Biology, 1986-87; book reviewer, abstract editor Jour. Am. Coll. Nutrition, 1995—; assoc. editor Environ. Nutritional Interactions, 1996-2000, Toxicology, 2000—. Chmn. Greater L.A. Nutrition Coun., 1982-83, So. Calif. Inst. Food Technologists, 1988-89, Toxicology and Safety Evaluation divsn. Inst. Food Technologists, 1989-90, food sci. communicator, 1986-90; chmn. Nat. Coun. Against Health Fraud, 1983-85; [illegible] and nutrition, 1989-93. Recipient Outstanding Tchr. Award U. So. Calif., [illegible] 1987-88; Meritorious Svc. award, Calif. Dietetic Assn., 1990, Disting. Achievement award

So. Calif. Inst. Food Technologists, 1990, fellow Inst. Food Technologists, 1998. Mem. Soc. Toxicology (chair awards com. food safety sect. 1993-94, chair 1994-95), Nat. Golden Key Soc. (hon.), Gamma Sigma Delta. Republican. Avocations: golf, book collecting. Office: Calif State Polytech U Coll of Agrl 3801 W Temple Ave Pomona CA 91768-2557 E-mail: wrbidlack@csupomona.edu

BIDWILL, WILLIAM V. professional football executive; s. Charles W. and Violet Bidwill; m. Nancy Bidwill; children: William Jr., Michael, Patrick, Timothy, Nicole. Grad., Georgetown U. Co-owner St. Louis Cardinals Football Team (now Ariz. Cardinals), 1962-72, owner, 1972—, also chmn., 1972—, pres. Office: Ariz Cardinals PO Box 888 Phoenix AZ 85001-0888

BIEDERMAN, DONALD ELLIS, lawyer; b. N.Y.C., Aug. 23, 1934; s. William and Sophye (Groll) B.; m. Marna M. Leerburger, Dec. 22, 1962; children: Charles Jefferson, Melissa Anne. AB, Cornell U., 1955; JD, Harvard U., 1958; LLM in Taxation, NYU, 1970. Bar: N.Y. 1959, U.S. Dist. Ct. (so. dist.) N.Y. 1967, Calif. 1977. Assoc. Hale, Russell & Stentzel, N.Y.C., 1962-66; asst. corp. counsel City of N.Y., 1966-68; assoc. Delson & Gordon, N.Y.C., 1968-69; ptnr. Roe, Carman, Clerke, Berkman & Berkman, Jamaica, N.Y., 1969-72; gen. atty. CBS Records, N.Y.C., 1972-76; sr. v.p. legal affairs and adminstrn. ABC Records, L.A., 1977-79; ptnr. Mitchell, Silberberg & Knupp, L.A., 1979-83; exec. v.p., gen. counsel Warner/Chappell Music Inc., L.A., 1983-99, cons., 2000—. Adj. prof. Sch. Law Southwestern U., L.A., 1982-2000, prof. law, dir. entertainment and media law inst., 2000—, Pepperdine U., Malibu, Calif., 1985-87, Loyola Marymount U., L.A., 1992; lectr. Anderson Sch. Mgmt. UCLA, 1993, U. So. Calif. Law Ctr., 1995-97. Editor: Legal and Business Problems of the Music Industry, 1980; co-author: Law and Business of the Entertainment Industries, 1987, 2nd edit., 1991, 3d edit., 1995, 4th edit., 2001. Bd. dirs. Calif. Chamber Symphony Soc., L.A., 1981-92; dir. Entertainment Law Inst. U. So. Calif., 1993-2000. 1st lt. U.S. Army, 1959. Recipient Hon. Gold Record, Recording Industry Assn. Am., 1974, Trendsetter award Billboard mag., 1976, Gold Triangle award Am. Acad. Dermatology, 1999; named Entertainment Lawyer of Yr., Beverly Hills Bar Assn., 2000. Mem. N.Y. Bar Assn., Calif. Bar Assn., Riviera Country Club, Cornell Club. Democrat. Jewish. Avocations: golf, skiing, travel, reading. don. Home: 2406 Pesquera Dr Los Angeles CA 90049-1225 Office: Warner/Chappell Music Inc 10585 Santa Monica Blvd Los Angeles CA 90025-4921 E-mail: dbiederman@swlaw.edu, biederman@warnerchappell.com

BIELER, CHARLES LINFORD, zoo executive director emeritus, former development director; b. East Greenville, Pa., May 19, 1935; s. Frederick William and Emma May (Freed) B.; m. Judith L. Goodwin, Feb. 23, 1963; children: Stewart, Beatriz, Christina. BA, Gettysburg Coll., 1957. Dir. tng. Gen. Motors Corp., 1962-69; mem. staff Zool. Soc. San Diego, 1969—, exec. asst. to dir., 1972-73, dir., 1973-85, dir. devel., 1987—. Bd. dirs. San Diego Conv. and Visitors Bur., 1983-88, vice chmn., 1988, chmn., 1989. Bd. dirs. Mercy Hosp. Corp., 1988—. With U.S. Army, 1957-62. Recipient Gettysburg Coll. Disting. Alumni award, 1984 Fellow Am. Assn. Zool. Parks and Aquariums (pres. 1983-84) Home: 1915 Sunset Blvd San Diego CA 92103-1545 Office: San Diego Zoo PO Box 551 San Diego CA 92112-0551

BIENENSTOCK, ARTHUR IRWIN, physicist, educator, government official; b. N.Y.C., Mar. 20, 1935; s. Leo and Lena (Senator) B.; m. Roslyn Doris Goldberg, Apr. 14, 1957; children: Eric Lawrence, Amy Elizabeth (dec.), Adam Paul. B.S., Poly. Inst. Bklyn., 1955, M.S., 1957; Ph.D., Harvard U., 1962; PhD (hon.), Poly. U., 1998. Asst. prof. Harvard U., Cambridge, Mass., 1963-67; mem. faculty Stanford (Calif.) U., 1967—, prof. applied physics, 1972—, vice provost faculty affairs, 1972-77, dir. synchrotron radiation lab., 1978-97; assoc. dir. for sci. Office of Sci. and Tech. Policy, Washington, 1997-2001. Mem. U.S. Nat. Com. for Crystallography, 1983-88, sci. adv. com. European Synchrotron Radiation Facility, 1988-90, 93-96; mem. com. on condensed matter and materials physics NRC, 1996-97. Author papers in field. Bd. dirs. No. Calif. chpt. Cystic Fibrosis Research Found., 1970-73, mem. pres.'s adv. council, 1980-82; trustee Cystic Fibrosis Found., 1982-88. Recipient Sidhu award Pitts. Diffraction Soc., 1968, Disting. Alumnus award Poly. Inst. N.Y., 1977; NSF fellow, 1962-63 Fellow AAAS, Am. Phys. Soc. (gen. councilor 1993-96); mem. Am. Crystallographic Assn., Materials Rsch. Soc. Jewish. Home: 967 Mears Ct Stanford CA 94305 Office: Stanford Symchrotron Radiation Lab PO Box 4349 Stanford CA 94309 E-mail: a@slac.stanford.edu

BIENIAWSKI, ZDZISLAW TADEUSZ RICHARD, engineering educator emeritus, writer, consultant; b. Cracow, Poland, Oct. 1, 1936; came to U.S., 1978, naturalized; m. Elizabeth Hyslop, 1964; 3 children. Student, Gdansk (Poland) Tech. U., 1954-58; BS in Mech. Engring., U. Witwatersrand, Johannesburg, South Africa, 1961, MS in Engring. Mechanics, 1963; PhD in Rock Engring., U. Pretoria, South Africa, 1968; D in Engring. (hon.), U. Madrid, 2001. Prof. mineral engring. Pa. State U., Univ. Park, 1978-96, prof. sci., tech. & society, 1994-96, prof. emeritus, 1996—; pres. Bieniawski Design Enterprises, Prescott, Ariz., 1996—. Vis. prof. U. Karlsruhe, Germany, 1972, Stanford U., 1985, Harvard U., 1990, Cambridge (Eng.) U., 1997; chmn. U.S. Nat. Com. on Tunneling Tech., 1984-85; U.S. rep. to Internat. Tunnel Assn., 1984-85. Author: Rock Mechanics Design in Mining and Tunneling, 1984, Strata Control in Mineral Engineering, 1987, Aiming High-A Collection of Essays, 1988, Engineering Rock Mass Classifications, 1989, A Tale of Three Continents, 1991, Design Methodology in Rock Engineering, 1992, Gaudeamus Igitur Poems, 1997, Alec's Journey, 1999; editor: Tunneling in Rock, 1974, Exploration for Rock Engineering, 1976, Milestones in Rock Engring., 1996; contbr. over 160 articles to profl. jours. Recipient Mayor's Proclamation of City of State College Bieniawski Day, 1983. Mem. ASCE (rock mechanics rsch. award 1984). Avocations: genealogy, cosmology, poetry writing, financial planning. Home: The Ranch 3023 Sunnybrae Cir Prescott AZ 86303-5770 Office: PO Box 11205 Prescott AZ 86304-1205

BIERBAUM, J. ARMIN, petroleum company executive, consultant; b. Oak Park, Ill., June 29, 1924; s. Armin Walter and Harriett Cornelia (Backmann) B.; m. Janith Turnbull, Apr. 17, 1948; children: Steve, Todd, Charles, Peter, Mark. B.S., Northwestern U., 1945, M.S., 1948. Project engr. Am. Oil Co., Ind., 1948-53; sales engr. Universal Oil Products Co., Des Plaines, Ill., 1953-56; tech. dir. Nat. Coop. Refinery Assn., McPherson, Kans., 1956-58; asst. plant mgr., treas., v.p., dir. Gen. Carbon & Chem. Corp., Robinson, Ill., 1958-61; cons. Williston, N.D., 1962-64; v.p. ops. Midland Coops., Inc., Mpls., 1964-72; sr. v.p. ops. Tosco Corp., Los Angeles, 1972-77; pres., chief exec. officer Gary Energy Co., Englewood, Colo., 1977-79, U.S. Ethanol Corp., Englewood, 1979-82; cons., 1983—. Served with USNR, 1942-45. Mem. Am. Inst. Chem. Engrs., Sigma Xi, Phi Epsilon Pi. Office: 1609 Ridgecrest Dr Loveland CO 80537-9073

BIERBAUM, JANITH MARIE, artist; b. Evanston, Ill., Jan. 14, 1927; d. Gerald Percy and Lillian (Sullivan) Turnbull; m. J. Armin Bierbaum, Apr. 17, 1948; children: Steve, Todd, Chad, Peter, Mark. BA, Northwestern U., 1948; student, Mpls. Art Inst., 1964; postgrad., St. Paul Art Inst., 1969-70. Rsch. asst. AMA, Chgo., 1948-49; tchr. Chgo. high schs., 1949-51; freelance artist Larkspur, Colo., 1951—. Exhibited in group shows at Foot Hills Art Ctr., 1985, 86, 87, Palmer Lake (Colo.) Art Assn., 1986-87, 88-89, Gov.'s Mansion, Bismarck, N.D., 1960; oil painting appeared in 1989 Women in Art Nat. calendar pub. by AAUW. Recipient 1st Place Purchase award U. Minn., Mpls., 1966, Coors Classic award Coors Beer, Golden, Colo., 1987. Mem. Colo. Artist Assn. Republican. Avocations: cross-country skiing, swimming, hiking. Home and Office: 1609 Ridgecrest Dr Loveland CO 80537-9073

BIERSTEDT, PETER RICHARD, lawyer, entertainment industry consultant; b. Rhinebeck, N.Y., Jan. 2, 1943; s. Robert Henry and Betty Bierstedt; m. Carol Lynn Akiyama, Aug. 23, 1980 (div. Oct. 1995); m. Lieschen van Straaten, Aug. 11, 2000. AB, Columbia U., 1965, JD cum laude, 1969; cert., U. Sorbonne, Paris, 1966. Bar: N.Y. 1969, U.S. Supreme Ct. 1973, Calif. 1977. Atty. with firms in, N.Y.C., 1969-74; pvt. practice cons. legal and entertainment industry, 1971, 75-76, 88—; with Avco Embassy Pictures Corp., L.A., 1977-83, v.p., gen. counsel, 1978-80, sr. v.p., 1980-83, dir., 1981-83; gen. counsel New World Entertainment (formerly New World Pictures), L.A., 1984-87, exec. v.p., 1985-87, sr. exec. v.p. Office of Chmn., 1987-88, also bd. dirs.; pres. subs. New World Prodns. and New World Advt. New World Pictures, 1985-88. Guest lectr. U. Calif., Riverside, 1976-77, U. So. Calif., 1986, 91, UCLA, 1987, 95, 96; bd. dirs. New World Pictures (Australia) Ltd., FilmDallas Pictures, Inc., Cinedco, Inc. Exec. prodr. (home video series) The Comic Book Greats. Mem. Motion Picture Assn. Am. (dir. 1980-83), Acad. Motion Picture Arts and Scis. (exec. br.), N.Y. State Bar Assn., L.A. Copyright Soc., ACLU. Democrat. Avocations: astronomy, literature, tennis, scuba diving. E-mail: peter@bierstedt.com

BIGELOW, MARGARET ELIZABETH BARR (M.E. BARR), mycology educator; b. Elkhorn, Man., Can., Apr. 16, 1923; d. David Hunter and Mary Irene (Parr) Barr; m. Howard Elson Bigelow, June 9, 1956 (dec.). BA with honors, U. B.C., Vancouver, Can., 1950, MA, 1952; PhD, U. Mich., 1956. Rsch. attaché U. Montreal, Que., Can., 1956-57; instr. U. Mass., Amherst, 1957-65, asst. prof., 1965-71, assoc. prof., 1971-76, prof., 1976-89, prof. emeritus, 1989—. Author: Diaporthales in N.A., 1978, Prodromus to Loculoascomycetes, 1987, Prodromus to Nonlichenized Members of Class Hymenoascomycetes, 1990; contbr. articles to profl. jours. With Can. Women's Army Corps, 1942-46. Mem. Mycol. Soc. Am. (v.p. to pres. 1980-82, editor 1975-80, Disting. Mycologist Award, 1993), Brit. Mycol. Soc., Am. Inst. Biol. Sci. (gen. chmn. ann. meeting 1986). Avocations: gardening, reading. Home and Office: 9475 Inverness Rd Sidney BC Canada V8L 5G8

BIGGER, DAROLD F. religious studies educator; m. Barbara Bigger; children: Shannon (dec.), Hilary Catlett. BA in Theology, Walla Walla Coll., 1966, MSW, 1995; MDiv cum laude, Andrews U., 1970; PhD in Theology and Personality, Claremont Sch. Theology, 1978. Pastor Crestline (Calif.) Ch., La Sierra Univ. Ch., Riverside, Calif.; sr. pastor Walla Walla (Wash.) Coll. Ch., 1980-93, prof. religion and social work faculties, 1993, prof. religion, prof. social work. Rear adm. USNR. Decorated Meritorious Svc. medal.

BIGLAN, ANTHONY, medical educator; b. Bklyn., June 6, 1944; BA in Psychology, U. Rochester, N.Y., 1966; MA in Social Psychology, U. Ill., 1968, PhD in Social Psycology, 1971; degree in Clin. Psychology, U. Wash., 1972. Rsch. assoc., instr. dept. psychology U. Wash., 1969-72; vis. asst. prof. psychology U. Oreg., 1973-74, asst. prof., 1974-78, rsch. asst., 1977-78; psychologist Behavior Change Ctr., Springfield, Oreg., 1977-82; rsch. scientist Oreg. Rsch. Inst., Eugene, 1979—. Bd. dirs. Pacific Rsch. Inst., 1992—, bd. chmn., 1994. Contbr. numerous articles to profl. jours. including Jour. Behavioral Medicine, Drugs and Society, The Analyst, others. Bd. dirs. ACLU of Oreg., pres., 1989-91. Nat. Inst. of Drug Abuse grantee, 1991—, Nat. Cancer Inst. grantee, 1995-2000. Office: Oreg Rsch Inst 1715 Franklin Blvd Eugene OR 97403-1983

BILBRAY, BRIAN P. former congressman; b. Coronado, Calif., Jan. 28, 1951; m. Karen; 5 children. Supr.ctrl. and so. coastal regions San Diego County, Calif.; mem. U.S. Congress from 49th Calif. dist., 1995-2001; mem. commerce com. Mem. commerce, fin. & hazardous materials, health & environment, oversight & investigations coms. Avocations: sailing, surfing, horseback riding.*

BILBRAY, JAMES HUBERT, former congressman, lawyer, consultant; b. Las Vegas, May 19, 1938; s. James A. and Ann E. (Miller) B.; m. Michaelene Mercer, Jan. 1960; children: Bridget, Kevin, Erin, Shannon Student, Brigham Young U., 1957-58, U. Nev., Las Vegas, 1958-60; BA, Am. U., 1962; JD, Washington Coll. Law, 1964. Bar: Nev. 1965. Staff mem. Senator Howard Cannon U.S. Senate, 1960-64; dep. dist. atty. Clark County, Nev., 1965-68; mem. Lovell, Bilbray & Potter, Las Vegas, 1969-87, Nev. Senate, 1980-86, chmn. taxation com., 1983-86, chmn. interim com. on pub. broadcasting, 1983; mem. 100th-103rd Congresses from 1st Nev. dist., 1987-95; mem. fgn. affairs com., 1987-88; mem. house armed svs. com., mem. small bus. com., chmn. procurement, taxation and tourism subcom., 1989-95; ptnr. Alcalde & Fay, Arlington, Va., 1995—. Mem. subcoms. Africa, trade exports and tourism, select com. on intelligence, 1993-95; alt. mcpl. judge City of Las Vegas, 1987-89; del. North Atlantic Alliance, 1989-95; bd. visitors U.S. Mil. Acad., West Point, 1995-99, vice chmn., 1996-97; mem. adv. bd. Ex-Import Bank U.S., 1996-97. Bd. regents U. Nev. Sys., 1968-72; mem. Nat. Coun. State Govts. Commn. on Arts and Historic Preservation; mem. bd. visitors USAF Acad., 1991-93; mem. Dem. Nat. Com., 1996—. Named Outstanding Alumnus U. Nev., Las Vegas, 1979, Man of Yr. Am. Diabetes Assn., 1989, Man of Yr. Haddassah (Nev.), 1990 Mem. Nev. State Bar Assn., Clark county Bar Assn., U. Nev.-Las Vegas Alumni Assn. (pres. 1964-69, Humanitarian of Yr. 1984), Rotary, Phi Alpha Delta, Sigma Chi, KC Democrat. Roman Catholic.

BILES, JOHN ALEXANDER, pharmacology educator, chemistry educator; b. Del Norte, Colo., May 4, 1923; s. John Alexander and Lillie (Willis) B.; m. Margaret Pauline Off, June 19, 1943; children: Paula M. (Mrs. Patrick Murphy), M. Suzanne. B.S., U. Colo., 1944, Ph.D. (AEC fellow), 1949. Prof. pharm. chem. Midwestern U., 1949-50; asst. prof. pharm. chem. Ohio State U., 1950-52, U. So. Calif., L.A., 1952-53, assoc. prof., 1953-57, prof., 1957-98, disting. emeritus prof., 1998—, dean, prof. pharm. scis., 1968-94, John Stauffer dean's chair in pharmacy, 1988-94, John Biles professorship, 1994—. Bd. dirs. Marion Merrell Dow; cons. Allergan Pharms., 1953-68, Region IX Bur. Health Manpower Edn., Health Resources Adminstrn., 1973, Region X, 1974, Region VI, 1975, VA Ctrl. Office Pharmacy Svcs.; mem. Nat. Adv. Coun., Edn. for Health Professions, 1970-71, nat. study commn. on pharmacy, 1972-75; mem. adv. panel on pharmacy for study costs of educating profls. Nat. Acad. Scis., Inst. Medicine, 1973; mem. interdisciplinary tng. in health scis. com. Bur. Health Manpower Edn., 1972, post contrn. evaluation com., 1972, health facilities survey com., 1971; mem. adv. coun. Howard U. Coll. Pharmacy, 1985-90; bd. grants Am. Found. for Pharm. Edn., 1996—. Reviewer: Jour. of AMA, 1982-90. Bd. grants Am. Found. Pharm. Edn., 1996—, bd. dirs., 1999—, chmn. bd. grants 1998—; elder Presbyn. Ch., Pacific Palisades, Calif., 1997—. Recipient Lehn and Fink Scholarship award, 1945, S.C. Assos. award for excellence in teaching, 1962 Fellow Acad. Pharm. Scis., Am. Assn. Pharm. Scientists; mem. Am., Cal. Pharm. assns., Am. Cancer Soc. (mem. sci. adv. com. Los Angeles County), Am. Assn. Colls. Pharmacy (study commn. on pharmacy 1973-75, pres. 1990-91), Nat. Adv. Health Svcs. Coun. (bur. health svcs. rsch. 1974), Phi Kappa Phi. Office: U So Calif Sch Pharmacy 1985 Zonal Ave Los Angeles CA 90033-1039 E-mail: BilesJohn@aol.com

BILLINGS, KATHY, national monument administrator; Supt. USS Arizona Meml., Honolulu. Office: USS Arizona Meml 1 Arizona Memorial Rd Honolulu HI 96818-3145

BILLINTON, ROY, engineering educator; b. Leeds, Eng., Sept. 14, 1935; s. Edwin and Nettie (Billinton); m. Alice Joyce McKenna, July 21, 1956; children— Leslie, Kevin, Michael, Christopher, Jeffrey. B.Sc.E.E., U. Man., 1960, M.Sc., 1963; Ph.D., U. Sask., 1967, D.Sc., 1975. Journeyman electrician McCaine Electric, Winnipeg, Man., Can., 1956; mem. system operation dept. and system planning dept. Man. Hydro, from 1960; asst. prof. to prof., head dept. elec. engring. U. Sask., Saskatoon, 1964—; now assoc. dean pres. PowerComp Assocs., cons. Author: Power System Reliability Evaluation, 1970, (with R. J. Ringlee and A. J. Wood) Power System Reliability Calculations, 1973, (with C. Singh) System Reliability Modelling and Evaluation, 1977; (with R.N. Allan) Reliability Evaluation of Engineering Systems, 1983, Reliability Evaluation of Power Systems, 1984, (with R.N. Allan) Reliability of Large Electric Power Systems, 1988, (with R.N. Allan, L. Salvaderi) Applied Reliability Assessment in Electric Power Systems, 1990, (with W Li) Reliability Assessment of Electric Power Systems Using Monte Carlo Methods, 1994; also articles. Recipient Sir George Nelson award Engring. Inst. Can., 1965-67, Ross medal, 1972, Centennial Disting. Svc. award Can. Elect Assn., 1991; Disting. Researcher award U. Saskatchewan. Fellow IEEE (Outstanding Power Engring. Educator award 1992, McNaughton medal 1994, Third Millenium medal 2000, Outstanding Engr. Educator award 2001), Royal Soc. Can., Engring. Inst. Can., U.K. Safety and Reliability Soc., Can. Acad. Engring. Home: 3 McLean Crescent Saskatoon SK Canada S7J 2R6 Office: U Sask Dept Elec Engring Saskatoon SK Canada S7N 0W0

BILLS, ROBERT HOWARD, political party executive; b. North Conway, N.H., Jan. 13, 1944; s. Howard William and Mary Catherine (Jackson) B.; m. Donna Gail Florian; children: Emily Ida, Katherine Mary. Staff writer Weekly People Newspaper, Bklyn., 1970-74, Palo Alto, Calif., 1974-76; nat. sec. Socialist Labor Party, Sunnyvale, 1980—, mem. nat. exec. subcom., 1976-79. Office: Socialist Labor Party of Am PO Box 218 Mountain View CA 94042-0218

BINDER, GORDON M. venture capitalist; b. St. Louis, 1935; Degree in elec. engring., Purdue U., 1957; MBA, Harvard U., 1962. With Litton Industries, 1962-64; fin. mgmt. staff Ford Motor Co., 1964-69; CFO Sys. Devel. Corp., 1971-81; v.p., CFO Amgen, Thousand Oaks, Calif., 1982-88, CEO, 1988-2000, chmn. bd., 1990-2000; mng. dir. Coastview Capital LLC, L.A., 2001—. Baker scholar Harvard U. Office: Coastview Capital LLC Ste 1850 11111 Santa Monica Blvd Los Angeles CA 90025

BINGAMAN, JEFF, senator; b. El Paso, Tex., Oct. 3, 1943; s. Jesse and Beth (Ball) B.; m. Anne Kovacovich, Sept. 13, 1968. BA in Govt., Harvard U., 1965; JD, Stanford U., 1968. Bar: N.Mex. 1968. Asst. atty. gen., N.Mex., 1969; atty. Stephenson, Campbell & Olmsted, 1971-72; ptnr. Campbell, Bingaman & Black, Santa Fe, 1972-78; atty. gen. State of N.Mex., 1978; senator from N.Mex. U.S. Senate, mem. armed svcs. com., mem. joint econ. com., mem. Senate Dem. steering and coordination com., mem. Senate Den. tech. and comm. com., ranking minority mem., mem. energy and natural resources subcom. of energy prodn. and regulation, mem. labor and human resources com. U.S. Army Reserves, 1968-74. Democrat. Methodist. Home: PO Box 5775 Santa Fe NM 87502-5775 Office: US Senate 703 Hart Senate Bldg Washington DC 20510-0001*

BINGHAM, H. RAYMOND, software company executive; b. Heber City, Utah, Oct. 18, 1945; s. Lyman Dunbar and Thora (Murdock) B.; m. Kristin Bernadine Allgood, Oct. 10, 1968; children: Ashley Dare, Derrick, Raymond, Erin Sloan, Adam Jay, Christopher Brian. BS, Weber State College, 1970; MBA, Harvard U., 1972. V.p. N_REN Internat., Peutie, Belgium, 1975-80; asst. treas. Marriott Corp., Bethesda, Md., 1980-81; mng. dir. Agrico Overseas Investment, Tulsa, Okla., 1981-85; exec. v.p., chief fin. officer Red Lion Hotels & Inns, Vancouver, Wash., 1985-93, Cadence Design Systems, Inc., San Jose, Calif., 1993-99, pres., CEO, 1999—. Bd. dirs. WTD Industries Inc., Portland. Bd. dirs. Oreg. Pub. Broadcasting Found., Portland, 1989—, Oreg. Symphony Assn., Portland, 1989—; mem. Harvard Bus. Sch. Assn. Oreg., Portland, 1985—. Mem. Urban Land Inst., Nat. Realty Inst., Fin. Execs. Inst. Republican. Mormon. Avocations: tennis, running, skiing. Home: 1 Bridal Ln Woodside CA 94062-2599 Office: Cadence Design Systems 2655 Seely Ave Bldg 5 San Jose CA 95134-1931

BINGHAM, PAUL M. finance company executive; b. Balt., June 26, 1942; Grad. in acctg. cum laude, U. Utah, 1964. CPA, Calif. With Ernst & Young, 1964-70, Fleetwood Enterprises, Riverside, Calif., 1970—, from controller adminstrn. to v.p., controller, v.p. fin., 1987, sr. v.p. fin. Mem. AICPA. Office: PO Box 7638 Riverside CA 92513-7638

BINNIE, NANCY CATHERINE, retired nurse, educator; b. Sioux Falls, S.D., Jan. 28, 1937; d. Edward Grant and Jessie May (Martini) Larkin; m. Charles H. Binnie. Diploma, St. Joseph's Hosp. Sch. Nursing, Phoenix, 1965; BS in Nursing, Ariz. State U., 1970, MA, 1974. Intensive care charge nurse Scottsdale (Ariz.) Meml. Hosp., 1968-70, coordinator critical care, 1970-71, John C. Lincoln Hosp., Phoenix, 1971-73; prof. nursing GateWay Community Coll., Phoenix, 1974-96. Coord. part-time evening nursing programs Gateway Community Coll., 1984-97, interim dir. nursing, 1989, 91. Mem. Orgn. Advancement of Assoc. Degree Nursing, Practical and Assoc. Coun. Nursing Educators, Ariz. Coun. Nurse Educators. Avocations: gardening, golf, sewing. Office: Gateway C C 104 N 40th St Phoenix AZ 85034-1704

BINTLIFF, BARBARA ANN, law librarian, educator; b. Houston, Jan. 14, 1953; d. Donald Richard and Frances Arlene (Appling) Hay; m. Byron A. Boville, Aug. 20, 1977 (div. 1992); children: Bradley, Bruce. BA, Cen. Wash. U., 1975; JD, U. Wash., 1978, MLL, 1979. Bar: Wash. 1979, U.S. Dist. Ct. (ea. dist.) Wash. 1980, Colo. 1983, U.S. Dist. Ct. Colo. 1983. Libr. Gaddis and Fox, Seattle, 1978-79; reference libr. U. Denver Law Sch., 1979-84; assoc. libr., sr. instr. Sch. Law U. Colo., Boulder, 1984-88, assoc. prof., libr. dir., 1989—. Legal cons. Nat. Ctr. Atmospheric Rsch., Environ. and Societal Impacts Group, Boulder, 1980; vis. prof. U. Wash., Seattle, 1996. Editor: A Representative Sample of Tenure Documents for Law Librarians, 1988, 2nd edit., 1994, Chapter Presidents' Handbook, 1989, Representatives Handbook, 1990; assoc. editor: Legal Reference Svcs. Quarterly, Perspectives: Teaching Legal Research and Writing; contbr. articles to profl. jours. Recipient Boulder Faculty Assembly Excellence Svc. award, 2001; named Disting. Alumnus, Ctrl. Wash. U., 2000. Mem. Am. Assn. Law Librs. (v.p./pres.-elect 2000-01, pres. 2001—), Am. Law Inst. (elected), Colo. Bar Assn., Colo. Assn. Law Librs. (pres. 1982), Southwestern Assn. Law Librs. (pres. 1987-88, 91-92). Episcopalian. Office: U Colo Law Libr PO Box 402 Boulder CO 80309-0402

BIONDI, FRANK J., JR. entertainment company executive; b. N.Y.C., Jan. 9, 1945; s. Frank J. and Virginia (Willis) B.; m. Carol Oughton, Mar. 16, 1974; children: Anne, Jane. BA, Princeton U., 1966; MBA, Harvard U., 1968. Assoc.-corp. fin. Shearson Lehman, Inc., N.Y.C., 1970-71, Prudential Securities, N.Y.C., 1969; prin. Frank J. Biondi Jr. & Assocs., N.Y.C., 1972; dir. bus. analysis Teleprompter Corp., N.Y.C., 1972-73; asst. treas., assoc. dir. bus. affairs Children's TV Workshop, N.Y.C., 1974-78; dir. entertainment program planning HBO, N.Y.C., 1978, v.p. programming ops., 1979-82, exec. v.p. planning and adminstrn., 1982-83, pres., chief exec. officer, 1983, chmn., chief exec. officer, 1984; exec. v.p. entertainment bus. sector The Coca-Cola Co., 1985; chmn., CEO, Coca-Cola TV, 1986; pres.,

CEO, Viacom Inc, N.Y.C., 1987-96; chmn., CEO, Universal Studios, Inc., Universal City, Calif., 1996-98; pres. Biondi Reiss Capital Mgmt., N.Y.C., 1998—. Mng. dir. Waterview Advisors; bd. dirs. Bank of N.Y., Seagram Co. Ltd., Vail Resorts, Inc., USA Network Inc. Bd. dirs. Leake-Watts Svcs., Yonkers, N.Y., 1975, Mus. TV and Radio, N.Y.C., Claremont Grad. U., Princeton U. Mem. Princeton of N.Y. Club, Edgartown Yacht Club, Game Creek Club (Vail, Colo.). Office: Waterview Advisors 2425 Olympic Blvd Ste 4050W Santa Monica CA 90404-4030

BIRD, PETER, geology educator; b. Cambridge, Mass., Sept. 29, 1951; s. George Richmond and Doris (Forgue) B.; m. Jean M. Campbell, Mar. 4, 1972; 1 child, Andrew Campbell. BA in Geol. Scis., Harvard U., 1972; PhD in Earth and Planetary Scis., MIT, 1976. Asst. prof. UCLA, 1976-81, assoc. prof., 1981-85, prof., 1985—. Fellow Geol. Soc. Am., Am. Geophys. Union. Avocations: hiking, photography. Office: UCLA Dept Earth Space Scis Los Angeles CA 90095-0001

BIRDSALL, BRIAN, food products executive; b. 1956; Grad., Wash. State U., 1979. With Pannell Kerr Foster Acctg., Wenatchee, Wash., 1979-88; pres., treas. Chief Wenatchee, 1988—. Office: Chief Wenatchee 1705 N Miller St Wenatchee WA 98801-1585

BIRDSALL, CHARLES KENNEDY, electrical engineer; b. N.Y.C., Nov. 19, 1925; s. Charles and Irene (Birdsall); m. Betty Jean Hansen, 1949 (div. 1977) (dec.); children: Elizabeth (dec.), Anne, Barbara, Thomas, John; m. Virginia Anderson, Aug. 21, 1981. B.S., U. Mich., 1946, M.S., 1948; Ph.D., Stanford U., 1951. Various projects Hughes Aircraft Co., Culver City, Calif., 1951-55; leader electron physics group GE Microwave Lab., Palo Alto, 1955-59; prof. elec. engring. U. Calif., Berkeley, 1959-91, prof. Grad. Sch., 1994—. Founder Plasma Theory and Simulation Group, 1967; founder, 1st chmn. Energy and Resources Com., 1972-74; cons. to industry, Lawrence Livermore Lab. of U. Calif., 1960-86; prof. Miller Inst. Basic Rsch. in Sci., 1963-64; sr. vis. fellow U. Reading (Eng.), summer 1976; rsch. assoc. Inst. Plasma Physics, Nagoya (Japan) U., winter 1981; Chevron vis. prof. energy Calif. Inst. Tech., 1982; area coord. phys. electronics/bioelectronics, 1984-86; joint U.S.-Japan Inst. Fusion Theory vis. prof. Inst. of Plasma Physics, Nagoya U., fall 1988, co-founder computational engring. sci. undergrad. program, fall 2000; lectr. Plasma Sch., Internat. Ctr. for Theoretical Physics, Trieste, Italy, 1985-99. Author: (with W.B. Bridges) Electron Dynamics of Diode Regions, 1966, (with A.B. Langdon) Plasma Physics via Computer Simulation, 1985, 91, (with S. Kuhn) Bounded Plasmas, 1994; patentee in field. Served with USNR, 1944-46. U.S.-Japan Coop. Sci. Program grantee, 1966-67; Fulbright grantee U. Innsbruck, 1991; recipient Berkeley Citation, 1991. Fellow IEEE (1st recipient Plasma Sci. and Applications award June 1988), AAAS, Am. Phys. Soc.; mem. Sigma Xi, Tau Beta Pi, Eta Kappa Nu. Achievements include being the co-originator many-particle plasma simulations in two and three dimensions using cloud-in-cell methods, 1966. Home: 4050 Valente Ct Lafayette CA 94549-3412 Office: U Calif EECS Dept Cory Hall Berkeley CA 94720-1770 E-mail: birdsall@eecs.berkeley.edu

BIRK, DAVID R. lawyer; BA, U. Fla., 1969; JD, Cornell U., 1972. Bar: N.Y. 1973. Assoc. atty. Jacobs, Persinger & Parker, 1974-77; ptnr., atty. Burstein & Marcus, 1977-80; sr. atty. Avnet Inc., Great Neck, N.Y., 1980-89, sr. v.p., gen. counsel, 1989—. 1st lt. U.S. Army, 1972-74. Mem. N.Y. State Bar (corr. law com.), Assn. of Bar of City of N.Y. (profl. discipline com.). Office: Avnet Inc 2211 S 47th St Phoenix AZ 85034-6403

BIRKELBACH, ALBERT OTTMAR, retired oil company executive; b. Oak Park, Ill., Feb. 22, 1927; s. August and Ann B.; m. Shirley M. Spandet, Aug. 21, 1948; children: J.A., Lisa M., Grace L. Birkelbach Boland, Ann C. Birkelbach Goren. B.S.Ch.E., U. Ill., 1949. Various engring., supervisory and mgmt. positions Globe Oil & Refining Co., Lemont, Ill., 1949-53, Anderson Prichard Oil Corp., Cyril, Okla., 1953-58, Signal Oil & Gas Co., Los Angeles, 1958-64; mng. dir. Raffinerie Belge de Petroles, Antwerp, Belgium, 1964-74; v.p. Occidental Petroleum Corp., London, Eng., 1972-74; cons. in field, 1974-75; pres. ATC Petroleum Inc., N.Y.C., 1975-81, also dir.; pres. Amorient Petroleum Corp., Laguna Niguel, Calif., 1981-84; mgmt. cons., 1984-87. Served with USCG, 1945-47. Decorated knight Order Leopold Belgium). Address: PO Box 1151 Carefree AZ 85377-1151 Home: 33957 N 66th Way Scottsdale AZ 85262

BIRKINBINE, JOHN, II, philatelist; b. Chestnut Hill, Pa., Mar. 29, 1930; s. Olaf Weimer and Gertrude Marie (Tyson) B.; m. Ausencia Barrera Elen, Dec. 19, 1969; children: John III, Bayani Royd. Chmn., CEO Am. Philatelic Brokerages, Tucson, 1946—. Chmn. bd. dirs. Ariz. Philatelic Rangers, Tucson, 1987—; bd. dirs. Postal History Found. Chmn. bd. 1869 Pictorial Rsch. Assn., 1969, bd. dirs., 1970-76, chmn. Baha'i Faith Adminstrv. Body, Pima County, Ariz., 1977-81, 83-91; sheriff, chmn. Santa Catalina Corral of Westerners Internat., Tucson, 1986. Recipient Large Gold and Spl. award Spanish Soc. Internat., San Juan, P.R., 1982, New Zealand Soc. Internat., Auckland, 1990, Large Internat. Gold award Australian Soc. Internat., Melbourne, 1984, Swedish Soc. Internat., Stockholm, 1986, Singapore Soc. Internat., 1995, U.S. Soc. Internat., San Francisco, 1997, Internat. Gold award U.S. Soc. Internat., Chgo., 1986, Bulgarian Soc. Internat., Sofia, 1989. Mem. Am. Philatelic Soc. (U.S. Champion of Champions award 1985), U.S. Philatelic Classics Soc. (disting. philatelist award 1995), Am. Philatelic Congress (McCoy award 1969, 97), Scandinavian Collectors Club, Collectors Club N.Y., Western Cover Soc. Avocations: swimming, tennis, travel, music, western U.S. historical research. Office: Am Philatelic Brokerages PO Box 36657 Tucson AZ 85740-6657 E-mail: jbirkinbin@aol.com

BIRMINGHAM, RICHARD JOSEPH, lawyer; b. Seattle, Feb. 26, 1953; s. Joseph E. and Anita (Loomis) B. BA cum laude, Wash. State U., 1975; JD, Seattle U., 1978; LLM in Taxation, Boston U., 1980. Bar: Wash. 1978, Oreg. 1981, U.S. Dist. Ct. (we. dist.) Wash. 1978, U.S. Tax Ct. 1981. Ptnr. Davis Wright Tremaine, Seattle, 1982-93; shareholder Birmingham Thorson & Barnett, P.C., Seattle, 1993—. Mem. King County Bar Employee Benefit Com., Seattle, 1986, U.S. Treasury ad hoc com. employee benefits, 1988—. Contbg. editor: Compensation and Benefits Mgmt., 1985—; contbr. articles to profl. jours. Mem. ABA (employee benefits and exec. compensation com. 1982—), Wash. State Bar Assn. (speaker 1984-86, tax sect. 1982—), Oreg. State Bar Assn. (tax sect. 1982—), Western Pension Conf. (speaker 1986), Seattle Pension Round table. Democrat. Avocations: jogging, bicycling, photography. Home: 3820 49th Ave NE Seattle WA 98105-5234 Office: Birmingham Thorson & Barnett PC 3315 Two Union Square 601 Union St Seattle WA 98101-2341

BIRNBAUM, STEVAN ALLEN, investment company executive; b. L.A., Apr. 21, 1943; s. Eugene David and Bessie (Holtzman) B.; m. Barbara Patricia Ostroff, June 29, 1971 (div. Aug. 1991); children: Marc, Jill; m. Bonnie Lynn Baehr, Jan. 2, 1999. BS in Engring., UCLA, 1965; MBA, Harvard U., 1967. Dir. advanced programs Whittaker Corp., L.A., 1967-69; v.p. Hohenberg & Assocs., Beverly Hills, Calif., 1969-74; dir. adminstrv. mgmt. Dames & Moore, L.A., 1974-77; prin. Xerox Venture Capital, L.A., 1977-81; [illegible], L.A., 1981-83; prin. [illegible], Santa Monica, Calif., 1983-95. Pres. Oxcal Venture Corp., Santa Monica, 1981—; founder, bd. dirs. Brentwood Savs. Bank, 1982; bd. dirs. [illegible] Corp., Torrance, Calif. Republican. Jewish.

BIRREN, JAMES EMMETT, university research center executive; b. Chgo., Apr. 4, 1918; m. Elizabeth S., 1942; children: Barbara Ann, Jeffrey Emmett, Bruce William. Student, Wright Jr. Coll., 1938; BEd, Chgo. State U., 1941; MA, Northwestern U., 1942, PhD, 1947, ScD (hon.), 1985; postgrad., U. Chgo., 1950-51; PhD (hon.), U. Gothenberg, Sweden, 1983; LLD (hon.), St. Thomas U., Can., 1990. Tutorial fellow Northwestern U., 1941-42; research asst. project for study of fatigue Office Sci. Research and Devel., 1942; research fellow NIH, USPHS, 1946-47; research psychologist gerontology unit NIH, 1947-51; research psychologist NIMH, 1951-53, chief sect. on aging, 1953-64; dir. aging program Nat. Inst. Child Health and Human Devel., Bethesda, Md., 1964-65; dir. Gerontology Center; prof. psychology U. So. Calif., 1965-89, Disting. prof. emeritus, 1992—, dean Davis Sch. Gerontology, 1975-86, Brookdale Disting. scholar, 1986-90, dir. Inst. Advanced Study in Gerontology and Geriatrics, 1981-89; dir. Borun Ctr. Gerontol. Rsch. UCLA, 1989-93, assoc. dir. Ctr. on Aging, 1990—. Fellow Center for Advanced Study in Behavioral Scis., Stanford, Calif., 1978-79; Green vis. prof. U. B.C., 1979; vis. scientist Cambridge (Eng.) U., 1960-61; Harold E. Jones meml. lectr. U. Calif., Berkeley, 1965; mem. Los Angeles County Bd. Suprs.' Com. on Aging, 1967-69 ; sr. fellow U. So. Calif. Urban Ecology Inst., 1968-70; mem. Dean's Council, U. So. Calif., 1970-86 ; chmn. aging rev. com. Nat. Inst. Aging, 1974-75; program dir. Integration of Info. on Aging: Handbook Project, 1973-76; mem. steering com. Care of Elderly, Inst. of Medicine, 1976-77; bd. dirs. Sears Roebuck Found., 1977-80; chmn. life course prevention research rev. com. NIMH, 1985-87; cons. Roche Seminars on Aging Series, 1980-82. Author: Psychology of Aging, 1964; editor: Handbook of Aging and the Individual, 1959, (with K.W. Schaie) Handbook of the Psychology of Aging, 1996, Encyclopedia of Gerontology, 1996, (with R.B. Sloane) Handbook of Mental Health and Aging, 1992; contbr. articles to books, profl. publs.; bd. collaborators: Gerontologia, 1956-89; asst. editor: Jour. Gerontology, 1956-61, assoc. editor 1961-63, editor-in-chief 1968-74, chmn. publs. com., 1975-78, adv. editl. bd., 1956-69; bd. adv. editors: Devel. Psychobiology, 1967-69; adv. editor: Jour. Human Devel., 1957-58. Mem. adv. com. and del. White House Conf. on Aging, 1995. With USNR, 1943-46; to scientist dir. USPHS Scientist Corps, 1947-65. Recipient award for rsch. on problems of aging CIBA Found., 1956, Stratton award Am. Psychopathol. Assn., 1960, Sr. 65er award Dist. 65 Retail Workers and Dept. Store Union, Sr. 65er award AFL-CIO, 1962, medal for meritorious svc. USPHS, 1965, citation Am. Assn. Ret. Persons, 1970, Am. Pioneers in Aging award U. Mich., 1972, commendation for disting. contbns. to field of gerontology Mayor of L.A., 1968, 74, Merit award Northwestern U. Alumni Assn., 1976, Creative Scholarship and Rsch. award U. So. Calif., 1979, Disting. Educator award Assn. Gerontology in Higher Edn., 1983, Eminent Svc. award Stovall Found., 1984, award of Distinction Am. Fedn. for Aging Rsch., 1986, Sandoz prize for rsch. on aging, 1989, Can. Assn. Gerontology award, 1990, Disting. Emeritus award U. So. Calif., 1992, Pres.'s award Am. Soc. on Aging, 1996; USPHS rsch. fellow, 1946-47. Fellow AAAS, Am. Geriatrics Soc. (founding fellow Western div.), Am. Psychol. Assn. (Disting. Sci. Contbn. award 1968, chmn. membership com. 1969, Disting. Contbn. award Div. Adult Devel. and Aging 1978, pres. div. 1955-56, editor newsletter 1951-55), Gerontol. Soc. (pres. 1961-62, chmn. publs. com. 1974-77, award for meritorious research 1966, Brookdale award 1980); mem. Am. Physiol. Soc., Internat. Assn. Gerontology (chmn. exec. com. 1966-69, chmn. program com. 1968-69), Psychonomic Soc., Western Gerontol. Soc. (dir. 1965— , pres. 1968-69), Golden Key Club, Skull and Dagger Club, Sigma Xi, Phi Kappa Phi. Office: UCLA Ctr on Aging 10945 Le Conte Ave Los Angeles CA 90024-2828

BISCHEL, MARGARET DEMERITT, physician, managed care consultant; b. Moorhead, Minn., Nov. 8, 1933; d. Connie Magnus Nystrom and Harriett Grace (Petersen) Zorner; m. Raymon DeMeritt, 1953 (div. 1958); 1 child, Gregory Raymon; m. John Bischel, 1961 (div. 1964); m. Kenneth Dean Serkes, June 7, 1974. BS, U. Oreg., Eugene, 1962; MD, U. Oreg., Portland, 1965. Diplomate Am. Bd. Internal Medicine, Nat. Bd. Med. Examiners. Resident, straight med. intern Los Angeles County/U. So. Calif. Med. Ctr., 1965-68, NIH fellow nephrology, 1968-70, asst. prof. renal medicine, 1970-74; asst. prof., instr. medicine U. So. Calif., 1968-74; instr. nephrology East L.A. City Coll., 1971-74; dir. med. edn. Luth. Gen. Hosp., Park Ridge, Ill., 1974-78, dir. nephrology sect., 1977-80, pres. med. staff, 1974-88; founding mem., med. dir., dir. med. svcs. Luth. Health Plan, Park Ridge, 1983-87; clin. assoc. prof. medicine Abraham Lincoln Sch. Medicine U. Ill., 1975-80; sr. cons. Parkside Assocs., Inc., Park Ridge, 1986-88; pvt. practice Chgo., 1974-88; physician Buenaventura Med. Clinic, Ventura, Calif., 1989-94, med. dir., 1992-94; prin. Apollo Managed Care Cons., Inc., Santa Barbara, 1988—. Trustee Luth. Health Care System, Park Ridge, 1986-90, Unified Med. Group Assn., Seal Beach, Calif., 1993-94; hon. lifetime staff mem. Luth. Gen. Hosp., Park Ridge; mem. formulary com. HealthNet, 1992-94, med. adv. com. TakeCare, 1993-94, quality assurance com. PacifiCare, 1993-94; mem. doctor's adv. network AMA, 1994-96. Mem. editl. adv. bd. Managed Behavioral Health Care Man., Credentials and Privileging Manual, Capitation Mgmt. Report; contbr. articles to profl. jours., chpts. to books; editor: Med. Mgmt. Manual, Managed Care Bull. Fellow Am. Coll. Physicians (Calif. Gov.'s advisor 1993-95); mem. Am. Coll. Physicians Execs., Am. Coll. Med. Quality, Nat. Assn. Physician Hosp. Orgns., Nat. Assn. Managed Care Physicians, Sigma Xi. Avocations: real estate, gardening. Office: Apollo Managed Care Consultants Inc 860 Ladera Ln Santa Barbara CA 93108-1626 E-mail: mbischel@apollomanagedcare.com

BISCHOFBERGER, NORBERT W. medical products company executive; b. 1956; PhD in Organic Chemistry, Eidgenossische Tech Hochschule, Zurich, Switzerland. Postdoctoral rsch. in steroid chemistry Syntex; rsch. prof. in organic chemistry and enzymology Harvard U.; sr. scientist DNA chemistry Genentech DNA Sythesis Group, 1986-90; dir. organic chemistry Gilead Scis. Inc., Foster City, Calif., 1990-93, v.p. organic chemistry, 1993-98, sr. v.p. R&D, 1998-2000, exec. v.p. R&D, 2000—. Office: Gilead Scis Inc 333 Lakeside Dr Foster City CA 94404-1146 Fax: (650) 573-4800

BISHNOI, P. RAJ, engineering educator; B in Chem. Engring., Bombay, 1960, MSc, 1962; PhD, Alta., Can., 1970. Prof. chem. engring. U. Calgary, Alta., Can. Contbr. articles to profl. jours. Mem. Assn. Profl. Engrs., Geologists and Geophysicists Alta. (Frank Spragins award 1998). Achievements include research on kinetics of natural gas hydrate formation and decomposition, phase behavior of hydrocarbon and aqueous systems, equations of state and computation of thermodynamic behaviour of fluids in oil recovery methods, computer simulation of distillation/absorption towers, simulation of chemical processes. Office: U Calgary Dept Chem Engring 2500 University Dr NW Calgary AB Canada T2N 1N4 Fax: 403-284-4852. E-mail: bishnoi@acs.ucalgary.ca

BISHOP, AL, state legislator, retired lawyer; b. Laurel, Mont., Feb. 19, 1925; m. Elayne Bishop; 2 children. LLB, JD, U. Mont., 1952. Atty., ret.; mem. from 9th Dist., Mont. Senate, Billings, 1986-90, 1994—; chair pub. health, welfare and safety com., also ethics com. Mont. State Senate, Billings, vice chair judiciary com.; mem. fish and game com. Mont. Fish and Game Commr., 1977-81. Served with USAAF, 1943-45. Mem. NRA, Am. Legion, Elks, Rod and Gun Club, Petroleum Club. Republican. Roman Catholic. Home: 3020 Leeann Blvd Billings MT [illegible]

BISHOP, C. DIANE, state agency administrator, educator; b. Elmhurst, Ill., Nov. 23, 1943; d. Louis William and Constance [illegible] B. BS in Maths., U. Ariz., 1965, MS in Maths., MEd in Secondary Edn., 1972. Lic. secondary educator. Tchr. math. Tucson Unified Sch. Dist., 1966-86; [illegible] council, 1985-86, mem. maths. curriculum task teams, 1983-86; state supt. of pub. instrn. State of Ariz., 1987-95, gov.'s policy advisor for edn., 1995-97, dir. gov.'s office workforce devel. policy, 1996-2000; asst. dep. dir. Ariz. Dept. Commerce, 1997-2000; exec. dir. Gov.'s Strategic Partnership for Econ. Devel., 1997—; pres. The Vandegrift Inst., 2000—. Mem. assoc. faculty Pima C.C., Tucson, 1974-84; adj. lectr. U. Ariz., 1983, 85; mem. math. scis. edn. bd. NRC, 1987-90, mem. new standards project governing bd., 1991; dir. adv. bd. sci. and engring. ednl. panel, NSF; mem. adv. bd. for arts edn. Nat. Endowment for Arts. Active Ariz. State Bd. Edn., 1984-95, chmn. quality edn. commn., 1986-87, chmn. tchr. crt. subcom., 1984-95, mem. outcomes based edn. adv. com., 1986-87, liaison bd. dirs. essential skills subcom., 1985-87, gifted edn. com. liaison, 1985-87; mem. Ariz. State Bd. Regents, 1987-95, mem. com. on preparing for U. Ariz., 1983, mem. high sch. task force, 1984-85; mem. bd. Ariz. State Community Coll., 1987-95; mem. Ariz. Joint Legis. Com. on Revenues and Expenditures, 1989, Ariz. Joint Legis. Com. on Goals for Ednl. Excellence, 1987-89, Gov.'s Task Force on Ednl. Reform, 1991, Ariz. Bd. Regents Commn. on Higher Edn., 1992. Woodrow Wilson fellow Princeton U., summer 1984; recipient Presdl. Award for Excellence in Teaching of Maths., 1983, Ariz. Citation of Merit, 1984, Maths. Teaching award Nat. Sci. Research Soc., 1984, Distinction in Edn. award Flinn Found., 1986; named Maths. Tchr. of Yr. Ariz. Council of Engring. and Sci. Assns., 1984, named One of Top Ten Most Influential Persons in Ariz. in Field of Tech., 1998. Mem. AAUW, NEA, Nat. Coun. Tchrs. Math., Coun. Chief State Sch. Officers, Women Execs. in State Govt. (bd. dirs. 1993), Ariz. Assn. Tchrs. Math., Women Maths. Edn., Math. Assn. Am., Ednl. Commn. of the States (steering com.), Nat. Endowment Arts (adv. bd. for arts edn.), Nat. Forum Excellence Edn., Nat. Honors Workshop, Phi Delta Kappa. Republican.

BISHOP, JOEY (JOSEPH ABRAHAM GOTTLIEB), comedian; b. N.Y.C., Feb. 3, 1918; s. Jacob and Anna (Siegel) Gottlieb; m. Sylvia Ruzga, Jan. 14, 1941; 1 child, Larry. Ed. pub. schs., Phila. Comedian Ea. burlesque cir., 1938-42, Vine Gardens, N.J., 1948-49, Chez Paree, Chgo.; appeared in (films) The Deep Six, 1958, Onionhead, 1958, The Naked and The Dead, 1958, Ocean's Eleven, 1960, Pepe, 1960, Sergeants Three, 1962, Johnny Cool, 1963, Texas Across the River, 1966, A Guide for the Married Man, 1967, Valley of the Dolls, 1967, Who's Minding the Mint?, 1967, The Delta Force, 1986; (miniseries) Glory Years, 1987; (television) The Jack Paar Show, 1958-62, Keep Talking, 1959-60, The Joey Bishop Show, 1961-65, 1967-69, Celebrity Sweepstakes, 1974-76, The Tonight Show; (theatre) Who Was That Lady I Saw You With?, 1960, Sugar Babies, 1981. With U.S. Army, 1942-45. Jewish. Office: William Morris Agy Inc 151 S El Camino Dr Beverly Hills CA 90212-2775

BISHOP, JOHN MICHAEL, biomedical research scientist, educator; b. York, Pa., Feb. 22, 1936; married 1959; 2 children. AB, Gettysburg Coll., 1957; MD, Harvard U., 1962; DSc (hon.), Gettysburg Coll., 1983. Intern in internal medicine Mass. Gen. Hosp., Boston, 1962-63, resident, 1963-64; rsch. assoc. virology NIH, Washington, 1964-66, sr. investigator, 1966-68; from asst. prof. to assoc. prof. U. Calif. Med. Ctr., San Francisco, 1968-72, prof. microbiology and immunology, 1972—, prof. biochemistry and biophysics, 1982—; dir. G.W. Hooper Rsch. Found. G.W. Hooper Rsch. Found., 1981—; Univ. prof. U. Calif. Med. Ctr., San Francisco, 1994-2000; chair. Nat. Cancer Adv. Bd., San Francisco. Chancellor U. Calif. Med. Ctr., San Francisco, 1998—. Recipient Nobel prize in physiology or medicine, 1989, Biomed. Rsch. award Am. Assn. Med. Colls., 1981, Albert Lasker Basic Med. Rsch. award, 1981, Armand Hammer Cancer award, 1984, GM Found. Cancer Rsch. award, 1984, Gairdner Found. Internat. award, Can., 1984, Medal of Honor, Am. Cancer Soc., 1984; NIH grantee, 1968—. Fellow Salk Inst. (trustee 1991—); mem. NAS, Inst. Medicine, Nat. Cancer Adv. Bd. Achievements include research in biochemistry of animal viruses, replication of nucleic acids, oncogenesis, control of cell growth, and molecular genetics. Office: U Calif Hooper Rsch Found Dept Microbiology PO Box 552 San Francisco CA 94143-0001

BISHOP, LEO KENNETH, clergyman, educator; b. Britton, Okla., Oct. 11, 1911; s. Luther and Edith (Scovill) B.; m. Pauline T. Shamburg, Sept. 15, 1935; 1 dau., Linda Paulette. A.B., Phillips U., 1932; L.H.D., 1958; M.A., Columbia U., 1944; M.B.A., U. Chgo., 1957; Litt.D., Kansas City Coll. Osteopathy and Surgery, 1964. Ordained to ministry Christian Ch., 1932; asso. minister Univ. Place Ch., Oklahoma City, 1932-35; minister First Ch., Paducah, Ky., 1935-41, Central Ch., Des Moines, 1941-45; dir. St. Louis office NCCJ, 1945-48, v.p., dir. central div., 1949-63; dir. pub. affairs People-to-People, Kansas City, Mo., 1963-66; v.p. Chgo. Coll. Osteopathy, 1966-72; pres. Bishop Enterprises, Colorado Springs, Colo., 1972—; also lectr. Contbr. religious and ednl. jours.; Developed: radio series Storm Warning; TV series The Other Guy, 1954. Cons. Community Social Planning Council, Mayor's Race Relations Com., YMCA, St. Louis; Am. del. Conf. World Brotherhood, Paris, 1950; bd. dirs. Am. Heritage Found. Recipient Paducah Jr. C. of C. Most Useful Citizen award, 1937, Distinguished Service award Dore Miller Found., 1958, Freedom Found. of Valley Forge award, 1961; named Chicagoan of Year, 1960 Clubs: Rotary, Union League, Winter Night. Home and Office: Montara Meadows A342 3150 E Tropicana Ave Las Vegas NV 89121

BISHOP, ROB, political party executive; Chmn. Utah State Rep. Party, 1997—. Office: 117 E South Temple Salt Lake City UT 84111-1101

BISHOP, ROBERT, political organization administrator; Mem. Utah Ho. Reps, 1979-94, minority leader, 1990-92, spkr., 1992-94, contract lobbyist, 1995—; state chmn. Utah Rep. Party, 1997—. Mem. Utah Speech Arts Assn., 1975-87, chmn., 1981-84; mem. Utah State Ctrl. Com., 1992—; co-founder, mem. exec. bd. Western States Coalition, 1994—; chmn. Utah State Convention, 1990, chmn. Rules, Parliamentarian, 1996-97; mem. Rep. Nat. Com. Western State Chmn. Assn., 1997—. Mem. Brigham City Hist. Preservation Com., Brigham Cuty Heritage Alliance Com.; chmn. Brigham City Cmty. Theater. Office: 117 E South Temple Salt Lake City UT 84111-1101

BISHOP, ROBERT R. economist; BSc in Math. Physics with honors, U. Adelaide; MSc, NYU. Sr. exec. Digital Equip. Corp., 1968-82, Apollo Computer, Inc., 1982-86; pres. world trade corp. Silicon Graphics, Inc., 1986-95, chmn., COO, 1995—, also bd. dirs. Internat. adv. panel Multimedia Super Corridor, Malaysia; invited prof. Swiss Fed. Inst. Tech., Lausanne; adj. prof. Stockholm Sch. Econs.; lectr. U. St. Gallen, Wirtschafts Tech.; spkr. in field. Mem. Swiss Acad. Engring. Scis., Industry Adv. Commn., World Intellectual Property Orgn., Govs. World Econ. Forum Info. Techs. Office: Silicon Graphics Inc 1600 Amphitheatre Pkwy Mountain View CA 94043

BISHOP, SIDNEY WILLARD, lawyer; b. Denver, Oct. 28, 1926; s. Sidney W. and Helen (Marihugh) B.; m. Betty Lou Dolan, May 10, 1947; children— Linda, Thomas, Nancy, Joan, Ann, Mary, Elizabeth, Sidney Willard III, Jane. BS, Regis U., Denver, 1949; J.D., U. Denver, 1950. Bar: Colo. 1950, Calif. 1958. With January & Yegge, Denver, 1949-50; dep. dist. atty. Cheyenne County, Colo., 1951-56; pvt. practice Cheyenne Wells, 1950-56; with Prudential Ins. Co. Am., Los Angeles, 1956-61, 64-68; asst. counsel law dept., 1958-61; asst. gen. solicitor, 1964-66; dir. govt. relations, 1966-68; gen. counsel Am. Ins. Assn., N.Y.C., 1968-70; with firm Svenson & Garvin, Van Nuys, Calif., 1970-73; sr. v.p., gen. counsel Beneficial Standard Life Ins. Co., 1973-91; of counsel Adams, Duque [illegible], Davis, Smith & Ruddy, L.A., 1996—. Confidential asst. to postmaster gen. U.S., 1961, asst. postmaster gen. bur. facilities, 1962-63, dep. postmaster gen., [illegible] Water Devel. Com., 1959-60. Served with USNR, 1944-46. Office: 601 S Figueroa St Ste 2600 Los Angeles CA 90017-5713

BISHOP, TILMAN MALCOLM, state legislator, college administrator, retired; b. Colorado Springs, Jan. 1, 1933; m. Pat Bishop, 1951; 1 son, Barry Alan. BA, MA, U. No. Colo. Adminstr., dir. student svcs. Mesa State Coll., Grand Junction, Colo., 1962-94; mem., pres. pro tem Colo. Senate, 1971-99, ret., 1999. Bd. dirs. Rocky Mountain Pub. Broadcasting TV, Colo. Family Medicine Commn., Colo. Duck Stamp Commn. World series com. Nat. Jr. Coll. Baseball. With U.S. Army. Mem. Elks, Lions. Republican. Methodist. Avocations: fishing, small game hunting. Home: 2697 G Rd Grand Junction CO 81506-8367 E-mail: tilmanmb@aol.com

BISHOP, WILLIAM PETER, research scientist; b. Lakewood, Ohio, Jan. 18, 1940; s. William Hall and Ethel Laverle (Evans) B.; m. Sarah Gilbert, Sept. 1, 1963. BA in Chemistry with honors (Nat. Merit scholar), Coll. Wooster, Ohio, 1962; PhD (NDEA fellow), Ohio State U., 1967. Resident research assoc. Ohio State U., 1967-69; mem. staff Sandia Labs., Albuquerque, 1969-75; head nuclear waste program NRC, Washington, 1975-78; dep. dir. environ. observation div. NASA, 1978-81, dep. dir. life scis. div., 1981-83; dep. asst. adminstr. satellites NOAA, 1983-85, acting asst. adminstr. satellites and info. services, 1985-87; v.p. SAIC, Washington, 1987-89; v.p. for rsch. Desert Rsch. Inst., Las Vegas, Nev., 1989-94; assigned to U.S. Dept. of Energy, 1995-99; pres. B-plus, Inc., 1999—. Mem. Nat. Acad. Com. Earth Studies, 1989-91, Task Group on Priorities in Space Rsch., 1990-94; chair Adv. Commn. on Geoscis. NSF, 1994-97. Author articles in field. Trustee Keystone (Colo.) Ctr., 1986-95, Nev. Devel. Authority, 1989-95, Univ. Corp. for Atmospheric Rsch., 1991-97; bd. dirs. Opportunities Industrialization Ctrs., Albuquerque, 1974-75, Cave Rsch. Found., 1967-74. Recipient Meritorious Service award NRC, 1977; Spaceship Earth award NASA, 1981; Meritorious Service award U.S. Dept. Commerce, 1985 Fellow Nat. Speleological Soc. (conservation editor bull. 1974-78), Am. Astron. Soc. (v.p. tech. 1987-88); mem. AAAS, Am. Geophys. Union, AIAA, Sigma Xi, Phi Lambda Upsilon.

BISSELL, GEORGE ARTHUR, architect; b. L.A., Jan. 31, 1927; s. George Arthur and Ruby Zoe (Moore) B.; m. Laurene Conlon, Nov. 21, 1947; children: Teresa Ann, Thomas Conlon, William George, Robert Anthony, Mary Catherine. BArch, U. So. Calif., 1953. Registered architect, Calif. Ptnr. Bissell Co., Covina, Calif., 1953-57, Bissell & Durquette, A.I.A., Pasadena, 1957-61; owner George Bissell, A.I.A., Laguna Beach, 1961-65; ptnr. Riley & Bissell, A.I.A., Newport Beach, 1965-72; pres. Bissell/August, Inc., Newport Beach, 1972-83, Bissell Architects, Inc., Newport Beach, 1983—. Bd. dirs. Newport Ctr. Assn., 1973-78, Lido Isle Community Assn., Newport Beach, 1985-87, Hamilton Cove Assn., 1991-92. With U.S. Mcht. Marine, 1944-46. Fellow AIA (pres. Orange County chpt. 1975, Calif. coun. 1978, nat. bd. dirs. 1980-83, Progressive Arch. award 1974, Nat. AIA Honor award 1978, 98, Merit award Calif. Coun. 1988, AIA Calif. Coun. Lifetime Achievement award 2000); mem. Newport Harbor Yacht Club, Lido Isle Yacht Club. Avocations: sailing, skiing, travel. Home: 108 Via Havre Newport Beach CA 92663-4905 also: Hamilton Cove 27 Camino de Flores Catalina Island CA 90704 Office: Bissell Architects 446 Old Newport Blvd Newport Beach CA 92663-4246 E-mail: Bisarch@aol.com

BISSELL, JAMES DOUGAL, III, motion picture production designer; b. Charleston, S.C., Aug. 6, 1951; s. James Dougal Sr. and Elizabeth McPherson (Jones) B.; m. Teresa Ann Atkinson, June 1, 1974 (div. Sept. 1987); m. Martha Wynne Snetsinger, Oct. 22, 1995; children: James Dougal, Alexander Wynne, Elizabeth Wynne. BFA in Theatre, U. N.C., 1973. Art dir. various TV movies, L.A., 1976-81; prodn. designer E.T. The Extra-Terrestrial, L.A., 1981, Twilight Zone-The Movie, L.A., 1982, The Falcon and The Snowman, Mexico City, 1983-84; prodn. designer, 2d unit dir. The Boy Who Could Fly, Vancouver, B.C., Can., 1985, Harry and the Hendersons, L.A., 1986; prodn. designer Someone to Watch Over Me, L.A. and N.Y.C., 1986-87, Twins, L.A. and Santa Fe, 1988—. Visual cons. St. Elmo's Fire, Hollywood, 1984; title co-designer Amazing Stories, Hollywood, 1985; art dir. The Last Starfighter, Hollywood, 1983; prodn. designer, 2nd unit dir. Always, L.A., Libby Mt., Epharata, Wash., 1989; prodn. designer Arachnophobia, Venezuela, Cambria, Calif., L.A. Prodn. designer Rocketeer, 1990, The Pickle, N.Y.C. and L.A., Dennis the Menace, Chgo., 1992, Blue Chips, L.A., Chgo., New Orleans, 1993, Jumanji, Vancouver, New Eng., 1994-95, Tin Cup, Tucson, Houston, 1995, My Fellow Americans, L.A., Asheville, N.C., The Sixth Day, 1999, Cats and Dogs, 2000. Nominee Prodn. Design award Brit. Acad. Film Arts, London, 1982. Mem. Soc. Motion Picture and TV Art Dirs. (exec. bd.), Dir.'s Guild Am., Acad. Motion Picture Arts and Scis.

BISSELL, MINA J. research laboratory administrator, biochemist; b. Tehran, Iran, May 14, 1940; Student, Bryn Mawr Coll., 1959-61; AB in Chemistry cum laude, Radcliff Coll., 1963; MA in Bacteriology and Biochemistry, Harvard U., 1965, PhD in Microbiology-Molecular Genetics, 1969. Milton rsch. fellow, 1969-70; Am. Cancer Soc. rsch. fellow, 1970-72; staff biochemist Lawrence Berkeley Nat. Lab. U. Calif., Berkeley, 1972-76, mem. sr. staff, 1976—, co-dir. div. biology and medicine Lab. Cell Biology, 1980—, dir. divsn., 1988-92, coord. life scis., 1989-91, assoc. lab. dir. bioscience, 1989, dir. life scis. div. Lawrence Berkeley Nat. Lab., 1992—, mem. faculty dept. comparative biochemistry, 1979—. Vis. prof. Kettering Inst., U. Cin. Med. Schs., 1986-88; disting. vis. scientist Queensland Inst. Med. Rsch., Brisbane, Australia, 1982; mem. coun. Gordon Rsch. Conf., 1991-94; George P. Peacock lectr. pathology U. Tex., Dallas, 1992; Dean's lectr. Mt. Sinai Med. Sch., N.Y.C., 1993; presenter numerous lectures, condr. symposia; keynote spkr. Gordon Conf. on Proteoglycans, 1994, others. Mem. editl. bd. and sect. editor In Vitro Cell and Devel. Biology Rapid Comm., 1986—; mem. editl. bd. Jour. Cellular Biochemistry, 1990-92; assoc. editor In Vitro Cellular and Devel. Biology, 1990—, Molecular and Cellular Differentiation, 1992—, Molecular Carcinogensis, 1993-97, Devel. Biology, 1993—, Cancer Rsch., 1994—, Breast Jour., 1994—; contbr. numerous articles to sci. jours. Recipient 1st Joseph Sadusk award for breast cancer rsch., 1985; Fogarty sr. fellow NIH, Imperial Can. Rsch. Fund Labs., London, 1983-84, Guggenheim fellow, 1992-93, E.O. Lawrence award Dept. Energy, 1996. Fellow AAAS; mem. Am. Soc. for Cell Biology (mem. coun. 1989-91, Women in Cell Biology Career Recognition award 1993, pres. 1997), Internat. Soc. Differentiation (bd. dirs. 1990-96). Office: Lawrence Berkeley Nat Lab Div Life Scis 1 Cyclotron Rd Ms 83 101 Berkeley CA 94720-0001*

BITTERMAN, MARY GAYLE FOLEY, broadcasting executive; b. San Jose, Calif., May 29, 1944; d. John Dennis and Zoe (Hames) Foley; m. Morton Edward Bitterman, June 26, 1967; 1 child Sarah Fleming. BA, Santa Clara U., 1966; MA, Bryn Mawr Coll., 1969, PhD, 1971. Exec. dir. Hawaii Pub. Broadcasting, Honolulu, 1974-79; dir. Voice of Am., Washington, 1980-81, Dept. Commerce, Honolulu, 1981-83, E.-W. Ctr. Inst. Culture and Comm., Honolulu, 1984-88; cons. pvt. practice, Honolulu, 1989-93; pres., CEO KQED, Inc., San Francisco, 1993—. Bd. dirs. Bank of Hawaii, Honolulu, 1984—, McKesson Corp., San Francisco, 1995-99; trustee Am.'s Pub. TV Stas., 1997—; vice chmn. TIDE 2000, Tokyo, 1984-93. Producer: (film) China Visit, 1978; contbr. numerous articles on internat. telecomms. to various pubs. Bd. dirs. United Way, Honolulu, 1986-93; chmn. Kuakini Health System, Honolulu, 1991-94. Recipient Candle of Understanding award Bonneville (Utah) Internat. Corp., 1985; named hon. mem. Nat. Fedn. Press Women, 1986. Fellow Nat. Acad. Pub. Info.; mem. Pacific Forum, CSIS (bd. govs.), Bay Area Coun. (bd. dirs.), World Affairs Coun. (bd. dirs.), Commonwealth Club Calif. (bd. dirs.) Office: KQED Inc 2601 Mariposa St San Francisco CA 94110-1426 Address: 229 Kaalawai Pl Honolulu HI 96816-4435

BITTERMAN, MORTON EDWARD, psychologist, educator; b. N.Y.C., Jan. 19, 1921; s. Harry Michael and Stella (Weiss) B.; m. Mary Gayle Foley, June 26, 1967; children— Sarah Fleming, Joan, Ann B.A., NYU, 1941; M.A., Columbia U., 1942; Ph.D., Cornell U., 1945. Asst. prof. Cornell U., Ithaca, N.Y., 1945-50; assoc. prof. U. Tex., Austin, 1950-55; mem. Inst. for Advanced Study, Princeton, N.J., 1955-57; prof. Bryn Mawr Coll., Pa., 1957-70, U. Hawaii, Honolulu, 1970—; dir. Békésy Lab. Neurobiology, Honolulu, 1991—. Author: (with others) Animal Learning, 1979; editor: Evolution of Brain and Behavior in Vertebrates, 1976; co-editor: Am. Jour. Psychology, 1955-73; cons. editor Jour. Animal Learning and Behavior, 1973-76, 85-88, Jour. Comparative Psychology, 1988-92. Recipient Humboldt prize Alexander von Humboldt Found., Bonn, W.Ger., 1981; Fulbright grantee; grantee NSF, Office Naval Research, NIMH, Air Force Office Sci. Research, Deutsche Forschungsgemeinschaft. Fellow Soc. Exptl. Psychologists (Warren medal 1997), Am. Psychol. Assn., AAAS; mem. Psychonomic Soc. Home: 229 Kaalawai Pl Honolulu HI 96816-4435 Office: Univ Hawaii Bekesy Lab of Neurobiology 1993 E West Rd Honolulu HI 96822-2321

BITTERWOLF, THOMAS EDWIN, chemistry educator; b. New Orleans, Jan. 19, 1947; s. Alvin John and Naomi Mae (Hendrix) B.; m. Caroline Elizabeth Means, May 25, 1968; children: Heidi Elizabeth, Katharine Naomi. BS, Centenary Coll., 1968; PhD, W.Va. U., 1976. Commd. ensign USN, 1973, advanced through grades to comdr., 1987; instr. Naval Nuclear Power Sch., Orlando, Fla., 1973-77, U.S. Naval Acad., Annapolis, Md., 1977-82; resigned USN, 1982; asst. prof. U.S. Naval Acad., Annapolis, Md., 1982-85, assoc. prof., 1985-88; assoc. prof. chemistry U. Idaho, Moscow, 1988-91, prof. chemistry, dir. teaching enhancement, 1991-96, assoc. dean coll. letters scis., 1996-98; exit stds. commr. Idaho High Schs., 1998—. Contbr. articles to refereed jours. Mem. AAAS, Am. Chem. Soc., Royal Soc. Chemistry, Sigma Xi. Methodist. Avocation: theater. Home: PO Box 8188 Moscow ID 83843-0688 Office: U Idaho Dept Chemistry Moscow ID 83844-0001

BITTING, WILLIAM, manufacturing executive; Exec. v.p. Pabst Brewing Co., San Antonio, chmn., CEO, 1998—; CEO, co-chmn., gen. counsel S&P Co., Mill Valley, Calif. Office: S&P Co 100 Shoreline Hwy Ste 395 Mill Valley CA 94941-3645

BIVENS, DONALD WAYNE, lawyer, judge; b. Ann Arbor, Mich., Feb. 5, 1952; s. Melvin Donley and Frances Lee (Speer) B.; children: Jody, Lisa. BA magna cum laude, Yale U., 1974; JD, U. Tex., 1977. Bar: Ariz. 1977, U.S. Dist. Ct. Ariz. 1977, U.S. Ct. Appeals (9th cir.) 1977, U.S. Ct. Appeals (fed. cir.) 1984, U.S. Supreme Ct. 1982. Ptnr. Meyer, Hendricks & Bivens, P.A., Phoenix, 1977—. Judge pro tem Maricopa County Superior Ct., Ariz., 1987—, Ariz. Ct. Appeals, Phoenix, 1999—; bd. dirs. Ctr. for Law in Pub. Interest, Phoenix, 1983-85. Note & Comment editor Tex. Law Rev., Austin, 1976-77. Pres. Ariz. Young Dems., 1980-82, Scottsdale Men's League, 1980-82; v.p., bd. dirs. Phoenix Symphony Assn., 1980-86; bd. dirs. Scottsdale Arts Ctr. Assn., 1981-84, Planned Parenthood Cen. and No. Ariz., 1989-92; adv. bd. Ariz. Theater Co., 1987-88. Recipient Consul award U. Tex. Sch. Law, 1977, Three Outstanding Young Men award Phoenix Jaycees, 1981. Mem. ABA (coun. litigation sect. 1995-98, chmn. computer litigation com. 1989-92, resource devel. com. litigation sect. 1992—, tech. task force 1998—, state del. to Ho. of Dels. 1999—), Am. Bar Found., Ariz. Bar Found., State Bar Ariz. (bd. govs. 1993-2000, pres. 1998-99—, peer rev. com. 1992—), Ariz. Trial Lawyers Assn., Maricopa County Bar Assn. (bd. dirs., chmn. Trial Adv. Inst. 1986-87, Mem. of Yr. 1998), Thurgood Marshall Inn of Ct. (pres. 1992-93). Democrat. Avocations: music, theater. Home: 6311 E Naumann Dr Paradise Valley AZ 85253-1044 Office: Meyer Hendricks & Bivens PA 3003 N Central Ave Ste 1200 Phoenix AZ 85012-2921

BJORK, GORDON CARL, economist, educator; b. Seattle, Dec. 15, 1935; s. Gordon E. and Florence E. (Bloomberg) B.; m. Susan Jill Serman, Dec. 29, 1960; children: Katharine, Rebecca, Susannah, Anders. AB, Dartmouth Coll., 1957; BA (hon.), Oxford U., 1959, MA, 1963; PhD, U. Wash., 1963. Lectr. econs. U. B.C., Vancouver, Can., 1962-63; asst. prof. econs. Carleton U., Ottawa, Ont., 1963-64; assoc. prof. econs. Columbia U., N.Y.C., 1964-68; pres. Linfield Coll., McMinnville, Oreg., 1968-74; prof. econs. Oreg. State U., Corvallis, 1974-75; Lovelace prof. econs. Claremont McKenna Coll., Claremont Grad. Sch., Calif., 1975—. Henry Walker disting. vis. prof. bus. enterprise U. Hawaii, 1985-86; vis. prof. econs. Nottingham (Eng.) U., 1990. Author: Private Enterprise and Public Interest: The Development of American Capitalism, 1969, Life, Liberty and Property: The Economics and Politics of Land Use Planning and Environmental Control, 1980, Stagnation and Growth in the American Economy, 1985, The Way It Worked and Why It Won't: Structural Change and the Slowdown of U.S. Economic Growth, 1999. Lt. USCGR, 1960-68. Rhodes scholar, 1957; Battelle Inst. fellow, 1975 Mem. Phi Beta Kappa Republican. United Ch. of Christ. Home: 4609 Vista Buena Rd Santa Barbara CA 93110-1945 Office: Claremont McKenna Coll Claremont Grad Sch Dept Econs Claremont CA 91711

BJORKHOLM, JOHN ERNST, physicist; b. Milw., Mar. 22, 1939; s. Jack W. and Marion B. (Anderson) B.; m. Mary J. Durbin, June 20, 1964; children— Kristin E., Laura J. BSE in Engring. Physics highest honors, Princeton U., 1961; MS, Stanford U., 1962, PhD in Applied Physics, 1966. Mem. tech. staff Electronics Rsch. Lab. AT&T Bell Labs., Holmdel, N.J., 1966-83, disting. mem. tech. staff, 1983-94, cons. in applied physics, 1994-96; prin. scientist Components Rsch., Intel Corp., Santa Clara, Calif., 1996—. Contbr. numerous articles to profl. jours.; patentee in field Chmn. Gordon Rsch. Conf. on Nonlinear Optics and Lasers, 1977; comptr. Conf. on Lasers and Electro-Optics, 1989-91; trustee Princeton U., 1991-95. NSF fellow, 1961-62, Howard Hughes fellow, 1962-65 Fellow Am. Phys. Soc., Optical Soc. Am. (dir.-at-large 1988-90, fin. and investment com. 1988-91, exec. com. 1990, treas. 1992-96); mem. IEEE (sr.), NRC (com. on atomic, molecular and optical sci. 1988-91). Home: 408 Cabonia Ct Pleasanton CA 94566-5201 Office: Intel Corp L-395 7000 East Ave Livermore CA 94550-9516

BLACK, ARTHUR LEO, biochemistry educator; b. Redlands, Calif., Dec. 1, 1922; s. Leo M. and Marie A. (Burns) B.; m. Trudi E. McCue, Nov. 11, 1945; children;3 Teresa Townsend, Janet Carter, Patti Tleimat. BS, U. Calif., Davis, 1948, PhD, 1951. Faculty physiol. chemistry Sch. Vet. Medicine U. Calif. at Davis, 1951—, prof., 1962—, prof. emeritus, 1991—, chmn. dept. physiol. scis., 1968-75. Cons. NIH, 1970-72, U.S. Dept. Agr., 1977-80; chmn. Nutritional Scis. Tng. Com., 1971-72 Contbr. papers to profl. jours. Served to 1st lt. USAAF, 1943-46. Recipient Sci. Faculty award NSF, 1958; Acad. Senate Disting. Teaching award U. Calif., Davis, 1977; Research grantee NSF; Research grantee NIH, 1952— Fellow Am. Inst. Nutrition (Borden award 1963); mem. Am. Soc. Biol. Chemists, Am. Physiol. Soc., Am. Soc. for Nutritional Scis., Sigma Xi, Phi Beta Kappa, Phi Zeta. Home: 891 Linden Ln Davis CA 95616-1763 Office: U Calif Dept Molecular Bioscis Davis CA 95616

BLACK, BRUCE D. judge; b. Detroit, July 27, 1947; m. Mary Lou Bell. BA, Albion Coll., 1969; JD, U. Mich., 1971. Judge N.Mex. Ct. Appeals, 1991-96, U.S. Dist. Ct. N.Mex., 1996—. Office: 333 Lomas Blvd NW Albuquerque NM 87102-2272

BLACK, DONNA RUTH, lawyer; b. Yuma, Ariz., Sept. 13, 1947; d. Roy Welch and Rosalie Edith (Harrison) B.; children: Gavin Lewis, Trevor Elias. BA in History with honors, U. Ariz., 1969; JD, UCLA, 1975. Bar: Calif. 1975, D.C. 1979, U.S. Dist. Ct. (ctrl. dist.) Calif., 1975, U.S. Dist. Ct. (no. dist.) Calif. 1987, U.S. Dist. Ct. (ea. dist.) Calif. 1989, U.S. Ct. Appeals (8th cir.) 1978, U.S. Ct. Appeals (9th cir.) 1983, U.S. Supreme Ct. 1994. Equity ptnr. Baker & Hostetler, L.A., 1975-95; equity ptnr. Manatt, Phelps & Phillips, L.A., 1995—. Author/editor: California Environmental Law Handbook. Mem. ABA (chmn. sect. natural resources, energy and environ. law, mem. nominating com. ho. of dels., chmn. sect. officers' conf. adv. com.), State Bar Calif., Los Angeles County Bar Assn., UCLA Law Alumni Assn. (bd. dirs. 1996—, v.p. 1998—, pres. 1999). Avocations: music, art, travel, poetry, writing. Home: 1130 Tower Rd Beverly Hills CA 90210-2131 Office: Manatt Phelps & Phillips 11355 W Olympic Blvd Los Angeles CA 90064-1614

BLACK, FREDERICK A. prosecutor; b. July 2, 1949; s. John R. and Dorothy Black; m. Katie Black, Oct. 27, 1976; children: Shane, Shanthini, Sheena. BA, U. Calif., Berkeley, 1971; JD, Lewis and Clark Coll., 1975. Bar: Oreg. 1975, Guam 1976, U.S. Ct. Appeals (9th cir.) 1976. Dir. Office of Guam Pub. Defender, 1975-78; dep. dir. Office of Oreg. Fed. Defender, 1981-84; asst. U.S. atty. Dist. Guam and No. Mariana Islands , 1978-81, 84-89; 1st asst. U.S. atty. Dist. Guam and No. Mariana Islands, 1989-91; U.S. atty. Dept. Justice Dist. Agana, Guam and No. Mariana Islands, 1991—. Author: Oregon Search and Seizure Manual. Leader Boy Scouts Am. Recipient Spl. award Chief Postal Inspector, 1986, Drug Enforcement Adminstrn. award, 1986, 89. Mem. Guam Water Polo Team. Avocation: sailing. Office: US Atty's Office 108 Hernan Cortez Ave Ste 500 Agana GU 96910-5009*

BLACK, PETE, retired state legislator, educator; b. Ansbach, Germany, Sept. 16, 1946; came to U.S., 1948; s. Howard and Kadi (Fietz) B.; m. Ronda Williams, July 12, 1970; 1 child, Darin. BS, Idaho State U., 1975, MEd, 1998. Cert. elem. tchr. Tchr. Pocatello (Idaho) Sch. Dist., 1975—; mem. Idaho Ho. Reps., Boise, 1983-96, asst. minority leader, 1987-96; tech. tng. specialist Sch. Dist. 25, 1996—. Mem. edn. tech. coun.; mem. adv. coun. chpt. II ESEA. Bd. dirs. Arts for Idaho; mem. State Libr. Bd. With USNR, 1964. Mem. NEA, Idaho Edn. Assn. (bd. dirs.), Idaho Libr. Assn., Idaho State U. Alumni Bd., Idaho Pers. Commn. Democrat. Home: 2249 Cassia St Pocatello ID 83201-2059 Office: Idaho House of Reps Statehouse Mail Boise ID 83720-0001 E-mail: blackcat@ida.net

BLACK, RICHARD BRUCE, business executive, consultant; b. Dallas, July 25, 1933; s. James Ernest and Minerva (Braden) B.; children: Kathryn Braden, Paula Anne (dec.), Erica Lynn. BS in Engring., Tex. A&M U., 1954; MBA, Harvard U., 1958; PhD (hon.), Beloit Coll., 1997. With Vulcan Materials Co., Birmingham, Ala., 1958-62; v.p. fin. Warner Electric Brake & Clutch Co., Beloit, Wis., 1962-67, dir., 1973-85; pres. automotive group, exec. v.p. corp. Maremont Corp., Chgo., 1967-72, pres. corp., COO, 1972-76, pres., chmn., CEO, 1976-79; pres., CEO, dir. Alusuisse of Am., Inc., N.Y.C., 1979-81; chmn., CEO, dir. AM Internat., Inc., Chgo., 1981-82; owner R. Black & Assocs., 1983—; chmn. ECRM, Boston, 1983—, gen. ptnr. KBA Ptnrs., LP, 1988-98, OpNet Ptnrs., LP, 2000—; pres. Oak Technology, Inc., Sunnyvale, Calif., 1998-99, Luxcore Networks, Inc., Atlanta, 2001—. Bd. dirs. Gabelli Group Capital Ptnrs., Inc., GSI Lumonics, Inc., Oak Tech., Inc., ECRM, Inc., Applied Optoelectronics, Inc., Altigen Comms., Inc., Morgan Group Inc., Luxcore Networks, Inc., Holotek, Inc., NYST, Inc., CrossFiber, Inc., Benedetto Gartland, Inc., Photoniko, Inc., Trex Enterprises, Inc., Wave Precision, Inc., Zairmail, Inc.; lectr. econs. Beloit (Wis.) Coll., 1964-67. Author: (with Jack Pierson) Linear Polyethylene-Propylene: Problems and Opportunities, 1958. Trustee Beloit Coll., Am. Indian Coll. Fund., Denver, Teton Sci. Sch., Bard Coll. Ctr. for Curatorial Studies, Inst. for Advanced Study, Princeton, N.J., Snake River Conservancy Found.; trustee, nat. chmn. Inroads, Inc., 1973-77. 1st lt. USAF, 1954-56. Recipient Flame of Hope Lifetime Achievement award, Am. Indian Coll. Fund, 1998, Inroads Lifetime Achievement award, 1979. Mem. Am. Alpine Club, Harvard Club (N.Y.C.).

BLACK, ROBERT LINCOLN, pediatrician, educator; b. Los Angeles, Aug. 25, 1930; s. Harold Alfred and Kathryn (Stone) B.; m. Jean Wilmott McGuire, June 27, 1953; children: Donald J., Douglas L., Margaret S. A.B., Stanford U., 1952, M.D., 1955. Diplomate: Am. Bd. Pediatrics. Intern Kings County Hosp., Bklyn., 1955-56; resident and fellow Stanford U. Hosp., 1958-62; practice medicine specializing in pediatrics Monterey, Calif., 1962—. Clin. prof. Stanford U., 1962— ; cons. Calif. Dept. Health, Sacramento, 1962— ; mem. Calif. State Maternal, Child, Adolescent Health Bd., 1984-93. Author: (with others) California Health Plan for Children, 1979. Bd. dirs. Lyceum of Monterey Peninsula, 1963— ; mem. Monterey Peninsula Unified Sch., 1965-73, pres., 1968-70; mem. Mid-Coast Health System Agy., Salinas, Calif., 1975-80, pres., 1979-80; bd. dirs. Carmel Bach Festival, Calif., 1972-81. With USAF, 1956-58. Fellow Am. Acad. Pediatrics; mem. Calif. Med. Assn., Monterey County Med. Soc., Inst. Medicine Nat. Acad. Sci. Democrat. Home: 976 Mesa Rd Monterey CA 93940-4612 Office: 920 Cass St Monterey CA 93940-4507

BLACK, W. L. RIVERS, III, lawyer; b. Biloxi, Miss., Sept. 2, 1952; s. William L. Jr. and Virginia (Howell) B.; m. Lisa A. Paige, Feb. 25, 1981 (div.); children: Jordanna, Caitlin; m. Elaine Kusulos, Apr. 25, 1993; children: Aristide, Hallie. BPA, U. Miss., 1974, JD, 1977; LLM in Marine Law, U. Wash., 1982; LLM in Internat. Law, U. Brussels, 1983. Bar: Miss. 1977, U.S. Ct. Mil. Appeals 1980, Wash. 1982, U.S. Ct. Appeals (9th cir.) 1983, U.S. Ct. of Internat. Trade, 1998. Instr. U. Md., Scotland and Italy, 1978-81; ptnr. Lane Powell Spears Lubersky, Seattle, 1983-99, Cozen and O'Connor, Seattle, 2000—. Mem. editl. bd. Maritime Law Reporter. Mem. assoc. bd. Corp. Coun. for the Arts; mem. bd., Pacific Marine Rsch. With USN, 1977-81, Morocco, Scotland. Capt. JAGC, USNR, 1983—. Mem. Seattle-King Bar Assn. (chair maritime sect. 1987-88), Inter-Pacific Bar Assn. (chair maritime law com. 1994-96), Asia-Pacific Lawyers Assn. (chair maritime com. 1986-89), Maritime Law Assn. of U.S. (Proctor), Washington Athletic Club, Naval Club (London). Methodist. Avocation: sailing. Office: Cozen and O Connor 1201 3rd Ave Ste 5200 Seattle WA 98101-3071 E-mail: rblack@cozen.com

BLACK, WILFORD REX, JR. former state senator; b. Salt Lake City, Jan. 31, 1920; s. Wilford Rex and Elsie Isabell (King) B.; m. Helen Shirley Frazer; children: Susan, Janet, Cindy, Joy, Peggy, Vanna, Gayle, Rex. Student pub. schs., Utah. Locomotive engr. Rio Grande R.R., 1941-81; mem. Utah Senate, Salt Lake City, 1972-96, spkr. 3d House, 1975-76, majority whip, 1977-78, minority leader, 1981-90. Sec. Utah State Legis. Bd., United Transp.; chmn. bd. Rail Operators Credit Union , 1958—87. Mission pres. Rose Park Stake Mormon Ch. Rose Park Stake Mormon Ch.; high priest group leader Rose Park 9th Ward, 1980—83, 10th Ward, 1996—99; mem. Rose Park Stake High Coun., 1957—63. Served with USAR, 1942—45. Recipient various awards r.r. and legis. activities . Democrat. Office: 826 N 1300 W Salt Lake City UT 84116-3877

BLACKBURN, ELIZABETH HELEN, molecular biologist; b. Hobart, Australia, Nov. 26, 1948; 1 child. BS, U. Melbourne, Australia, 1970, MS, 1971; PhD in Molecular Biology, Cambridge (Eng.) U., 1975; DSc (hon.), Yale U., 1991. Fellow in biology Yale U., New Haven, 1975-77; fellow in biochemistry U. Calif., San Francisco, 1977-78, from asst. prof. to assoc. prof. molecular biology Berkeley, 1978-86; prof. molecular biology, 1986-90; prof. U. Calif., San Francisco, 1990—, chair dept. microbiology and immunology, 1993-99. Recipient Eli Lilly award in microbiology,

1988, NAS award in molecular biology, 1990. Mem. AAAS (elected 1991), NAS (fgn. assoc. 1993), Am. Soc. Cell Biology (pres. 1998, recipient Australian prize 1998, Gairdner prize 1998, Passano award 1999, Rosensteil award 1999, Keio prize 1999), Royal Soc. London. Office: U Calif Biochem and Biophys Box 0448 San Francisco CA 94143-0001 E-mail: telomer@itsa.vcsf.edu

BLACKFIELD, CECILIA MALIK, civic volunteer, educator; b. Oakland, Calif., Jan. 18, 1915; d. Benjamin Malik and Mollie Saak; m. William Blackfield, Dec. 25, 1941; children: Leland Gregory, Pamela Esther, Karen Ann. BA, U. Calif., Berkeley, 1936; MEdn., San Francisco State Tchrs. Coll., 1937. cert. elem. tchr. Calif. (lifetime). Tchr. Albany (Calif.) Sch. Dist., 1938-43. Rep. NEA, Alameda County, Calif., 1938-43. Pres. Calif. Tchrs. Assn., Alameda County, Calif., 1939; mem. (charter) Territorial Hosp. Aux., Kauikeolani Children's Hosp. (bd. dirs.); bd. dirs. Hastings Law Sch. Found., San Francisco, Calif., McCoy Pavilion Park, Honolulu, Hi., Daughters of the Nile, Honolulu, Temple Emmanuel; mem. Mayor's Citizen Advisory Com. for Diamond Head, Wakiki, Honolulu, Mayor's Adv. Com. for Community & Urban Renewal, Beautification Com., League of Women Voters; chmn. Hawaii Cancer Fund Crusade and many more; mem. master planning com. Vision for Waikiki 2020; mem. Preservation Rev. Com. Hist. Hawaii. Named Woman of the Year for Nat. Brotherhood Week, Honolulu, 1972; recipient First Honorary Alumnus award Hastings Coll. of the Law U. of Calif., 1999. Mem. Nat. Assn. Home Builders (pres. Hawaii chpt. women's aux.), Outdoor Circle (pres.), Friends of Foster Gardens, Washington Palace State Capitol, Hadassah (past pres. Oakland chpt.), Women's Com. Brandeis U. (life mem.). Avocations: bridge, orchidist. Home: 901 Kealaolu Ave Honolulu HI 96816-5416

BLACKHAM, LEONARD MOYLE, state legislator; b. Mt. Pleasant, Utah, Aug. 26, 1949; m. Laura Bagley, Feb. 20, 1970; 6 children. AS, Snow Coll., 1969; BS, Utah State U., 1971. Turkey prodr. agrl. co-op bus.; mem. Utah Ho. of Reps., 1992-94, Utah Senate, Dist. 28, Salt Lake City, 1994—; majority whip, 1995-96; mem. legis. exec. appropriations com.; mem. legis. tax and revenue standing com. Chmn. bd. dirs. Moroni Feed Co.; bd. dirs. Norbest; mem. various coms. including energy, natural resources, agrl. standing. Past county commr. Republican. Office: PO Box 394 Moroni UT 84646-0394

BLACKMAN, LEE L. lawyer; b. Phila., Aug. 28, 1950; s. Harold H. and Mary Elizabeth Blackman; m. Kathryn M. Forte, Oct. 5, 1979; 1 child, Shane Forte. BA, U. So. Calif., 1973, JD, 1975. Bar: Calif. 1975, U.S. Dist. Ct. (ctrl. dist.) Calif. 1975, U.S. Ct. Appeals (9th cir) Calif. 1977, U.S. Supreme Ct. 1980, U.S. Dist. Ct. (ea. dist.) Calif. 1984, U.S. Dist. Ct. (no. dist.) Calif. 1988. Atty. Kadison, Pfaelzer, Woodard, Quinn & Rossi, L.A., 1975-81, assoc., ptnr., 1981-87; ptnr. McDermott, Will & Emery, L.A., 1987-2000. Arbitrator L.A. Superior Ct., 1986-90; judge pro tem Superior Ct. State of Calif., 1986-92; speaker in field. Mem. editl. adv. bd. Airport Noise Report, 1989-99; article editor ABA Health Litig. Reporter, 1996-97. Mem. ABA, State Bar of Calif., Legion Lex Inn of Ct. (master bencher 1989-2000). Office: McDermott Will & Emery 1562 Granvia Altamira Palos Verdes Estates CA 90274 E-mail: llblackman1@home.com

BLACKSTOCK, JOSEPH ROBINSON, newspaper editor; b. L.A., Dec. 8, 1947; s. Joseph Richard McCall and Doris Louise (Robinson) B.; m. Nancy Ruth Frederiksen, Feb. 9, 1974; children: Miriam, Susan, Cynthia, Catherine. BA, Calif. State U., L.A., 1970, MA, 1977. Sports writer Monterey Park Californian, 1967-72; sports and news writer, mng. editor San Gabriel Valley Tribune, West Covina, Calif., 1972-89; exec. editor Pasadena (Calif.) Star-News, 1989-93; layout editor Riverside (Calif.) Press-Enterprise, 1993-98; asst. city editor Inland Valley Daily Bull., Ontario, Calif., 1998—. With USAR, 1970-78.

BLADES, RUBEN, singer, songwriter, composer; b. Panama, July 16, 1948; came to U.S., 1974; s. Ruben Dario and Anoland (Bellido De Luna) B.; m. Lisa A. Lebenzon, Dec. 13, 1986. BA, Instituto Nacional, Panama, 1966; lic. in law and polit. sci. Universidad Nacional, 1973; LLM, Harvard U., 1985. Mem. legal staff, atty. Banco Nacional, Panama, 1973-74; rec. artist, legal adv. Fania Records Inc., N.Y.C., 1974-83; rec. artist Elektra Records, N.Y.C., 1984—; albums include Siembra (with Willie Colon), 1978, Auga de Luna, Buscando America, Escenas (Grammy award for Best Tropical Latin Performance 1986), Antecedente, 1988 (Grammy award for Best Tropical Latin Performance 1988), Nothing But the Truth, 1988, Y Son del Solar, 1990, Tras la Tormenta (After the Storm), 1995, La Rosa De Los Vientos, 1996 (Grammy award for Best Tropical Latin Performance 1996); film appearances include Fatal Beauty, Critical Condition, Crossover Dreams, 1985, The Milagro Beanfield War, 1988, The Lemon Sisters, 1990, Mo' Better Blues, 1990, The Super, 1991, Life with Mikey, 1993, A Million to Juan, 1994, Color of Night, 1994, The Devil's Own, 1997, Scorpion Spring, 1997, Chinese Box, 1997, From Son to Salsa, 1997, Cradle Will Rock, 1999, All the Pretty Horses, 2000; TV appearances include Miracle on Interstate 880, 1993, Somos un solo pueblo, 1995, TV series Gideon's Crossing, 2000; author book reviews; composer songs (Grammy nomination 1983, 84); contbr. articles to profl. jours. V.p. Inter Am. Soc. Harvard Law Sch., 1984-85. Named Hon. Citizen Office of the Mayor Chgo., 1984; recipient 6 Golden Records Fania Records, 1977-83, 1 Gold Record Atlantic Records, 1984, Grammy award Nat. Acad. Rec. Arts and Scis. Mem. Colegio De Abogados, Panama, Am. Soc. Composers, Authors and Publishers, Screen Actors Guild, Nat. Acad. Recording Arts and Scis., AFTRA. Presidential candidate, 1994 Panama Election. Roman Catholic. Office: United Talent Agency 9560 Wilshire Blvd Fl 5 Beverly Hills CA 90212-2400

BLAHD, WILLIAM HENRY, physician; b. Cleve., May 11, 1921; s. Moses and Rae (Lichtenstader) B.; m. Miriam Weiss, Jan. 29, 1971; children— Andrea Margery, William Henry, Karen Ruth. Student, Western Res. U., 1939-40, U. Ariz., 1940-42; M.D., Tulane U., 1945. Diplomate Am. Bd. Nuclear Medicine (chmn. 1982, v.p. 1986-97, exec. dir. 1998—), Am. Bd. Internal Medicine (bd. govs. 1981). Resident in pathology and internal medicine VA Wadsworth Med. Center, 1948-52, ward officer metabolic research ward, 1951-52, asst. chief radioisotope service, 1952-56, chief nuclear medicine dept., 1956-97, dir. nuclear medicine dept., 1997—; exec. dir. Am. Bd. Nuclear Medicine, L.A. Prof. dept. medicine U. Calif., Los Angeles; mem. ACGME residency rev. com. for nuclear medicine, 1979-97, chmn., 1991-97; mem. Joint Rev. Com. on Ednl. Programs in Nuclear Medicine Tech., 1986-93; mem. subcom. on naturally occurring and accelerator produced radioactive materials Com. on Interagency Radiation Rsch. and Policy Coordination, 1988-92; cons. nuclear medicine; mem. adv. com. on human uses radioisotopes Calif. Dept. Health Svcs.; mem. HEW Interagy. Task Force on Ionizing Radiation, 1978; dir. nuclear medicine Mt. Sinai Hosp., L.A., 1955-76, Valley Presbyn. Med. Ctr., Van Nuys, Calif., 1959-85, St. Joseph Hosp. Med. Ctr., Burbank, Calif., 1958-83. Author 3 textbooks on nuclear medicine. Contbr. numerous articles to med. jours. Served with U.S. Army, 1946-48. Grantee Muscular Dystrophy Assn. Am., 1965-69, Nat. Cancer Inst., 1973-76; recipient Lifetime Achievement award Wadsworth Physicians and Surgeons Alumni Assn., 2000, William H. Oldendorl Lifetime Achievement award West L.A. Med. Ctr., 2000. Fellow ACP, Am. Coll. Nuclear Physicians (bd. regents 1974-80); mem. AMA, Soc. Nuc. Medicine (trustee 1966-74, pres. 1977-78, Disting. Scientist award No./So. Calif. chpts. 1975, Disting. Sci. award We. Regional chpts. 1995, Disting. Pub. Svc. Career award Fed. Exec. Bd. L.A. 1998, Presdl. Disting. Svc. award 2000), Health Physics Soc. (pres. So. Calif. chpt. 1964-66), Calif. Med. Assn. [illegible] bd. nuclear medicine 1976-[illegible], [illegible], Soc.

Exptl. Biology and Medicine, Los Angeles County, Calif. Med. Assns., We. Assn. Physicians, Am. Fedn. Clin. Rsch., Nat. Assn. VA Chiefs Nuclear Medicine (pres. 1985-87), We. Soc. Clin. Rsch., Alpha Omega Alpha. Office: Nuclear Med Dept VA Greater LA Healthcare 691/W115 11301 Wilshire Blvd Los Angeles CA 90073

BLAINE, DAVIS ROBERT, investment banker, valuation consultant executive; b. Gary, Ind., Oct. 30, 1943; s. Jack Davis and Virginia Sue (Mintzer) B.; m. Karen Ellen Levenson, Dec. 28, 1981; children: Davis Justin, Tristan D., Brittara K., Whitney K. B.A., Dartmouth Coll., 1965; M.B.A., U. Mich., 1969. Founder, sr. v.p. Am. Valuation Cons., Chgo., 1971-78, chmn. bd., 1978; exec. v.p. Valuation Research, Chgo., 1978-80, pres. Los Angeles, 1980-83; sr. v.p. Arthur D. Little Valuation, Inc., Woodland Hills, Calif., 1983-87; owner, chmn. bd. Olesen, 1989-92; founder, mng. ptnr. Profls. Network Group, 1988—. Founder, chmn. bd. The Mentor Group Inc., Los Angeles, 1981— ; founder, pres. ICS Corp., Chgo., 1976-82, v.p. bd., 1982-87. Served to lt. (j.g.) USNR, 1966-68 Mem. Beta Theta Pi. E-mail: dblaine@thementorgrp.com

BLAIR, ANDREW LANE, JR. lawyer, educator; b. Oct. 10, 1946; s. Andrew Lane and Catherine (Shaffer) B.; m. Catherine Lynn Kessler, June 21, 1969; children: Christopher Lane, Robert Brook. BA, Washington & Lee U., 1968; JD, U. Denver, 1972. Bar: Colo. 1972, U.S. Dist. Ct. Colo. 1972, U.S. Ct. Appeals (10th cir.) 1972. Assoc. Dawson, Nagel, Sherman & Howard, Denver, 1972-78; ptnr. Sherman & Howard, Denver, 1978—. Lectr. U. Denver Law Sch., 1980-83, U. Colo., Colorado Springs, 1984, U. Colo. Law Sch., Boulder, 1991. Author: Uniform Commercial Code sects. for Colorado Methods of Practice, 1982; contbr. articles to profl. jours. Mem. ABA, Colo. Bar Assn. Democrat. Methodist. Home: 1111 Humboldt St Denver CO 80218-3123 Office: Sherman & Howard 633 17th St Ste 2900 Denver CO 80202-3665 E-mail: ablair@sah.com

BLAIR, DENNIS CUTLER, career officer; m. Diane Blair; children: Duncan, Pamela. BA, U.S. Naval Acad.; postgrad., Oxford U., Eng. Commd. ensign USN, advanced through grades to vice adm.; comdr. USS Cochrane, Yokosuka, Japan, 1984-86, Naval Sta. Pearl Harbor, 1989-90, Kitty Hawk Battlegroup, 1993-95; assoc. dir. Ctrl. Intelligence Mil. Support, 1995-96; mem. staff NSC; dir. Joint Staff, 1996-99; comdr. in chief U.S. Pacific Command, Camp H.M. Smith, Hawaii, 1999—. Decorated Legion of Merit with 3 gold stars, Def. Disting. Svc. medal with 2 oak leaf clusters; Rhodes scholar Oxford U.; White Ho. fellow; Naval Ops. fellow. Office: Comdr in Chief US Pacific Command PO Box 64028 Camp H M Smith HI 96861-4028

BLAIR, DONALD W. shoe manufacturing company executive; b. West Chester, Pa., Apr. 4, 1958; BS in Econ., U. Pa., 1980, MBA, 1981. CPA, N.Y. Sr. acct. Deloitte Haskins & Sells, 1981-84; sr. fin. analyst PepsiCo, Inc., 1984-85; mgr. fin. planning Pepsi-Cola USA, 1985-86, group mgr., bus. planning, 1986-88; fin. dir. Pepsi-Cola New England, 1988-90, Pepsi-Cola Japan, Tokyo, 1990-92; v.p., fin. Pepsi-Cola Asia, Hong Kong, 1992-96; v.p., planning PepsiCo, Pizza Hut divsn., 1996-97; sr. v.p., fin. The Pepsi Bottling Group Inc., 1997-99; v.p., CFO Nike Inc., Beaverton, Oreg., 1999—. Office: Nike Inc 1 Bowerman Dr Beaverton OR 97005-6453

BLAIR, FREDERICK DAVID, interior designer; b. Denver, June 15, 1946; s. Frederick Edward and Margaret (Whitely) B. BA, U. Colo., 1969; postgrad. in French, U. Denver, 1981-82. Interior designer The Denver, 1969-76, store mgr., 1976-80; v.p. Hartley House Interiors, Ltd., Denver, 1980-83; pvt. practice interior design, Denver, 1983—. Com. mem. Ice House Design Ctr., Denver, 1985-86, Design Directory Western Region, Denver, 1986; edn. com. for ASID Nat. Conf., Denver, 1991; asst. coord. Amb. Vol. Program Denver Internat. Airport, 2000—. Designs shown in various mags. Mem. Rep. Nat. Com.; bd. dirs. One Day, orgn. for children with AIDS, Very Spl. Arts, 1993; bd. dirs. Supporters of Children, 1996—, mem. steering com., 1994, pres.-elect, 1996-97; pres., bd. dirs. Supporters of Children, 1999—. Mem. Am. Soc. Interior Designers (co-chmn. com. profl. registration 1986, edn. com. nat. conf. 1991, bd. dirs. Colo. chpt. 1990—, Humanist award 1997), Denver Art Mus., Nat. Trust Hist. Preservation, Hist. Denver. Christian Scientist. Avocations: skiing, painting, tennis.

BLAIR, M. WAYNE, lawyer; b. Spokane, Washington, Oct. 17, 1942; BS in Elec. Engr., U. Washington, 1965, JD, 1968. Bar: Wash. 1968. Mem. Wash. State Bd. for Jud. Adminstrn., 1995-2000. With USAF, 1968-72. Recipient Helen M. Geisness award, 1987, President's award, 1990. Mem. ABA (Ho. of Dels. 1988-91), Am. Judicature Soc., Washington State Bar Assn. (bd. govs. 1991-94, pres. 1998-99), Seattle-King County Bar Assn. (trustee 1981-83, pres. 1987-88). Office: 5800 Bank of America Twr 701 5th Ave Seattle WA 98104-7097

BLAIR, ROBERT, animal science administrator, educator, researcher; b. Beith, Ayrshire, Scotland, May 29, 1933; s. Samuel and Mary (McBeth) B.; m. Moreen McGhie, Apr. 5, 1958; children: Rosalind M.J., Robert S. B.Sc., U. Glasgow, 1956; Ph.D., U. Aberdeen, 1960; D.Sc., U. Sask., 1983. Prin. sci. officer Agrl. Rsch. Coun., Edinburgh, Scotland, 1966-75; dir. nutrition Swift Can. Co. Ltd., Toronto, Ont., Can., 1976-78; mem. faculty U. Sask., Saskatoon, Can., 1978-84, prof. animal sci. Can., 1984, U. B.C., Vancouver, Can., 1984-98, head dept. Can., 1984-91, prof. emeritus Can., 1998—. Mem. subcom. on vitamin tolerance NRC, Washington, 1984-87; cons. life scis. office Fedn. Am. Socs. Exptl. Biology, Bethesda, Md. Former co-editor in chief Animal Feed Sci. and Tech., Amsterdam, Netherlands; contbr. chpts. to books, articles to profl. jours. Decorated Knight Lufsensic Ursinius Order (The Netherlands). Fellow Agrl. Inst. Can.; mem. World Assn. Animal Prodn. (pres. 1988-93), Nutrition Soc. U.K., Nutrition Soc. Can., Am. Inst. Nutrition, Am. Soc. Animal Sci., Can. Soc. Animal Sci. (pres. western br. 1985-87). Home: Biltmore Phase 1 1378 S Camino Real Palm Springs CA 92264 Office: U BC Dept Animal Sci 2357 Main Mall Ste 248 Vancouver BC Canada V6T 1Z4 Fax: 604-738-1004

BLAIR, ROBERT L. technology company executive; Dir. sales Precision Monolithics, Inc.; pres. SEMAG divsn. Xidex Corp.; sr. v.p. sales and ops. Logistix Corp.; v.p. ops. ESS Tech. Inc., Fremont, Calif., 1994-97, CEO, pres., bd. dirs. Office: 48401 Fremont Blvd Fremont CA 94538

BLAIR, RUSSELL, judge; Judge Hawaii Dist. Ct. (1st cir.), Honolulu. Office: Kauikeaouli Hale 11th Fl 1111 Alakea St Honolulu HI 96813-2801

BLAIRE, STEPHEN E. bishop; b. L.A., Dec. 22, 1941; Grad., St. John's Sem., Camarillo, Calif. Ordained priest Roman Cath. Ch., 1967, ordained bishop, 1990; titular bishop of Lamzella. Aux. bishop, L.A., 1990-99; bishop Stockton, 1999—. Office: Our Lady of Angels Pastoral Ctr 1105 N Lincoln St Stockton CA 95203-2410

BLAIS, ROBERT HOWARD, lawyer; b. Muskegon, Mich., May 14, 1955; BA with high honors, Mich. State U., 1977, JD cum laude, U. Notre Dame, 1980. Ptnr. Bogle & Gates, Seattle, 1988-93; shareholder Gores & Blais, Seattle, 1993—. Adj. prof. estate and tax planning Seattle U., 1982-83; chairperson Wash. State U. Planned Giving Adv. Bd., 1989-96. Mem. ABA, Wash. State Bar Assn. (real property, probate and trust coun. 1987-88), Seattle-King County Bar Assn., Estate Planning Coun. Seattle (pres. 1996-97), Am. Coll. Trust and Estate Counsel. Office: Gores & Blais 1420 5th Ave Ste 2600 Seattle WA 98101-1357

BLAKE, D. STEVEN, lawyer; b. Saginaw, Mich., June 2, 1940; BA, Mich. State U., 1963; JD, U. Calif., Davis, 1971. Bar: Calif. 1972. Sr. ptnr. Downey, Brand, Seymour & Rohwer, Sacramento, 1971—. Adj. prof. law U. Pacific, 1998—. Co-author: California Real Estate Finance and Construction Law, 1995. Mem. ABA (bus. law sect.), Am. Arbitration Assn. (arbitrator), State Bar Calif. (chair corp. com., sect., fin. instns. com., bus. law sect., panelist, presenter numerous seminars Calif. State Bar Continuing Edn. Bar 1981-91, co-chair corps. com. bus. law sect. 1997), Yolo County Bar Assn. Office: Downey Brand Seymour & Rohwer 555 Capitol Mall Ste 1050 Sacramento CA 95814-4601

BLAKE, PATRICK H. trucking executive; b. 1949; married; two sons. Dockman Consol. Freightways, 1969, exec. v.p. ops., 1994-99, pres., 1999-2000, CEO, 2000—; pres., CEO Consol. Freightways Corp., 2000—. Office: Consol Freightways 16400 SE CF Way Vancouver WA 98683

BLAKE, RENÉE, broadcast executive; b. Yonkers, N.Y. BA, Goddard Coll., 1973. Announcer, prodr. WCBQ-AM, Oxford, NC, 1974, WANV-AM, Waynesboro, Va., 1974; talk show host, anchor WEEZ-AM, Chester, PA, 1974-75; reporter, anchor WWDB-FM, Phila., 1975, WMMR-FM, Phila., 1975-78; programming special projects Drake Chenault Enterprises, L.A., 1978-79; copywriter S.M. Newmark & Assoc., L.A., 1980-81; reporter, public affairs dir. WHLY-FM, Orlando, FL, 1981-83; news dir. WJYO-FM, Orlando, 1983-86; program dir. WKXL-AM/FM, Concord, NH, 1986-91, KXCI-FM, Tucson, 1991-93; programmer Jerrold Comm., Concord, NH, Tucson, AZ, 1990-94; reporter, anchor Metro Networks, Phoenix, 1995-97, news bureau chief Albuquerque, 1997—; owner, CEO Media IQ, Albuquerque, 1996—. Interviewer, spkr. in field. Co-editor: Westside Rapper, 1970; columnist: The Drummer, 1976-77, Steppin' Out Magazine, 1983-86; creator, prodr. Music Zone Snowbank, 1988-89 (Golden Mike Merit NH Assn. Broadcasters 1988), This Island Earth, 1990 (1st Place Golden Mike NH Assn. Broadcasters 1990), NH Veterans' Memorial Wall and Scholarship Committee, 1988-90 (1st Place Golden Mike NH Assn. Broadcasters 1989), Send Our Support Day, 1990; affiliate prodr. Human Rights Now, 1989 (1st Place Golden Mike NH Assn. Broadcasters 1989); contbr. articles to profl. jours. Avocations: animal rights, alternative health care, writing, social justice, voiceovers. Office: Media IQ 174 Calle Loma Parda NW Albuquerque NM 87120-3477 E-mail: renee_blake@yahoo.com, mediaiq@email.com

BLAKENEY, ALLAN EMRYS, Canadian government official, lawyer; b. Bridgewater, N.S., Can., Sept. 7, 1925; s. John Cline and Bertha (Davies) B.; m. Mary Elizabeth Schwartz, 1950 (dec. 1957); m. Anne Louise Gorham, May 1959; children: Barbara, Hugh, David, Margaret. BA, Dalhousie U., 1945, LLB, 1947, LLD (hon.); BA (Rhodes scholar), Oxford U., 1949, MA, 1955; DCL (hon.), Mount Allison U.; LLD (hon.), York U., Toronto, U. Western Ont., London, 1991, U. Regina, , 1993, U. Sask., 1995. Bar: N.S. 1950, Sask. 1951. Queen's counsel, 1961; sec. to govt. fin. office Govt. Sask., 1950-55; chmn. Sask. Securities Commn., 1955-58; ptnr. Davidson, Davidson & Blakeney, Regina, Sask., 1958-60, Griffin, Blakeney, Beke, Koskie & Lueck, Regina, 1964-70; premier of Sask., 1971-82; Mem. Sask. Legislature, 1960-88. Officer of the Order of Can., 1992, Saskatchewan Order of Merit, 2000; leader of the opposition Sask. Legislature, 1970-71, 82-87; prof. Osgoode Hall Law Sch., York U., 1988-90, U. Sask., 1990—; minister of edn., Sask., 1960-61, provincial treas., 1961-62, minister pub. health, 1962-64; mem. Royal Commn. on Aborginal Peoples, 1991-93. Fellow Royal Soc. Can. Home: 1752 Prince of Wales Ave Saskatoon SK Canada S7K 3E5 Office: U Saskatchewan Coll Law 15 Campus Dr Saskatoon SK Canada S7N 5A6

BLANC, MAUREEN, public relations executive; Ptnr. Blanc & Otus Pub. Rels., Inc., San Francisco. Office: Blanc & Otus Pub Rels Inc 4 Embarcadero Ctr Lbby 8 San Francisco CA 94111-4112

BLANCH, HARVEY WARREN, chemical engineering educator; BS in Chem. Engring., U. Sydney, Australia, 1968; PhD, U. NSW, 1971. Lectr. Sch. of Biol. Technology U. NSW, 1971; asst. prof. dept. chem. engring. U. Del., 1974-77, assoc. prof., 1977-78; assoc. prof. dept. chem. engring. U. Calif., Berkeley, 1978-82, prof. dept. chem. engring., 1982—, chair dept. chem. engring., 1997—. Mem. numerous adv. bds. and panels in field, including NIH Cell Culture Ctr., 1991—, rsch. program com. Dept. Energy, Basic Energy Scis., 1993; numerous univ. coms.; cons. and lectr. in field. Author: (book) Biochemical Engineering, 1995; editor: Jour. Bioprocess Engring., 1986—, The Chem. Engring. Jour./Biochem. Engring. Jour., 1985—, (books) Applied Biocatalysis, 1991, Comprehensive Biotechnology, 1980-84, others; mem. editl. bd.: Biotechnology and Bioengring., 1990—, Advances in Biochem. Engring., 1992—; author more than 250 publs. in field; patentee in field. Fellow Internat. Inst. Biotechnology, Am. Inst. for Med. and Biol. Engring. (founder); mem. Am. Inst. Chem. Engrs. (recipient Food, Pharm. and Bioengring. Divsn. award 1996), Am. Chem. Soc. (Johnson award 1995, Enzyme Engring award 1997), Am. Soc. Engring. Edn. Office: U Calif/Berkeley Chem Engrg Biochem Engring Ctr Berkeley CA 94720-0001

BLANCHARD, CHARLES ALAN, lawyer, former state senator; b. San Diego, Apr. 14, 1959; s. David Dean and Janet (Laxson) B.; m. Allison Major, 2001. BS, Lewis & Clark Coll., 1981; M of Pub. Policy, JD, Harvard U., 1985. Bar: Ariz. 1987, U.S. Dist. Ct. Ariz. 1988, U.S. Ct. Appeals (D.C. cir.) 1988, U.S. Ct. Appeals (9th cir.) 1988, U.S. Supreme Ct. 1994. Law clk. to hon. Harry T. Edwards, Washington, 1985-86; law clk. to hon. Sandra Day O'Connor U.S. Supreme Ct., Washington, 1986-87; assoc. ind. counsel Ind. Counsel James McKay, Washington, 1987-88; atty. Brown & Bain, P.A., Phoenix, 1988-97; state senator State of Ariz., Phoenix, 1991-95; dir. Office of Legal Counsel Office of Nat. Drug Control Policy, Washington, 1997-99; gen. counsel U.S. Army, 1999-2001; ptnr. Brown & Bain PA, Phoenix, 2001—. Adj. prof. Ariz. State U. Coll. Law, 1996; chmn. Senate Judiciary Com., Phoenix, 1991-93; Dem. candidate U.S. Congress, 1994. Contbr. articles to profl. jours. Bd. dirs. Florence (Ariz.) Immigrant and Refugee Rights Project, 1990-97, 2001-, Homeless Legal Assistance Project, Phoenix, 1992-97, Tempe Comty. Action Agy., 1994-97, ABA Com. on Immigration Law, 1996-98, ABA Com. on Substance Abuse, 1998—, Luth. Vol. Corps., Washington, 1986-88; state committeeman Ariz. Dem. Party, Phoenix, 1991-97; chmn. Ariz. Dem. Leadership Coun., Inc., 1992-97. Recipient Disting. Svc. award Ariz. Atty. Gen., 1992, Disting. Civilian Svc. award U.S. Army, 2001; Toll fellowship Coun. of State Govts., 1991; named Disting. Young Alumni Lewis and Clark Coll., 1987. Mem. ABA. Home: 1814 Palmcroft Dr NE Phoenix AZ 85007 Office: Brown & Bain PA PO Box 400 Phoenix AZ 85007

BLANCHARD, JAY S. state senator; b. Des Moines, 1946; married; 3 children. PhD, U. Ga., 1979. With U.S. PO; tchr.; Dem. senator dist. 30 Ariz. State Senate. Mem. faculty U. Miss., U. Ky., U. Tex.; mem. fin., transp. and ethics coms. Ariz. State Senate, vice chair rules com.; cons. in field. Author, editor 5 books on tech.; contbr. chpts. to books, articles to profl. jours. With USMC, 1971-73. Mem. APA, Am. Ednl. Rsch. Assn., Internat. Reading Assn. Office: Ariz State Senate 1700 W Washington Phoenix AZ 85007-2890 E-mail: jblancha@azleg.state.az.us

BLANCHE, JOE ADVINCULA, aerospace engineer, consultant, educator; b. Rizal, Santa, Ilocos Sur, Philippines, Sept. 11, 1954; came to U.S. 1976; s. Emilio Peralta and Concepcion (Advincula) B.; m. Albine Selerio [illegible], [illegible] Emmanuel Joseph, Earl Jordan. [illegible], U. Philippines, [illegible]; BS in Math., Adamson U., Manila, 1976; postgrad., Calif. State U., Long Beach, 1982-85; AAS in Avionics Systems

Tech., C.C. Air Force, Maxwell AFB, Ala., 1990; cert. in mgmt., Cen. Tex. Coll., 1990; PhD in Mgmt., Pacific Western U., 1993; MA in Orgnl. Mgmt., U. Phoenix, 1995. Lic. real estate broker, Calif.; registered tax preparer, Calif. Assoc. engr., scientist McDonnell Douglas Corp., Long Beach, Calif., 1981-84, engr., scientist, 1984-86, engr., scientist specialist, 1987-88, sr. engr., scientist, 1988-94; lead aerospace engr. Sikorsky Aircraft-UTC, Stratford, Conn., 1986-87; founder, pres. J. & A. Blanche Ventures', Inc., Corona Hills, Calif., 1990—. Avionics maint. inspector USAFR, 1983-97; sr. engr., cons. McDonnell Douglas Tech. Svcs. Co./Shin Maywa, 1996-97; sr. engr., scientist Boeing Co., Delta Rockets Divsn., Huntington Beach, Calif. Eucharistic min. St. Edward's Ch., Corona; mem. sch. bd. St. Edward Sch., Corona, 2000—; bd. dirs. Diocese of San Bernardino, Calif., 2000-01. With USAF, 1976-80, with Res. Bur. Forestry grantee and scholar U. Philippines, 1971-73; USVA scholar Calif. State U., 1982-85. Mem. AIAA (sr.), Nat. Notary Assn., NRA, So. Calif. Profl. Engrs. Assn., Corona-Norco Bd. Realtors, Internat. Soc. Allied Weight Engrs. (sr.), Adamson U. Alumni Assn. So. Calif. (pres., chmn. bd. 1997-2001), Santanians USA Inc. (bd. dirs. 1984-87, pres. 1994-97, chmn. bd. 1997-99), Marinduque Assn. So. Calif. (press rels. officer 1998-2000), Fil-Am. Assn. Corona (auditor 1993-94, bd. dirs. 1995-96, parliamentarian 1997-98). Republican. others. Office: J & A Blanche Ventures Inc 420 N Mckinley St Ste 111-333 Corona CA 92879-6504 E-mail: jabventuresinc@msn.com, jabventuresinc@msn.com, jabventuresinc@msn.com, jbla7127@aol.com, joe.a.blanche@boeing.com

BLAND, DOROTHY ANN, construction executive, real estate agent; b. Black Township, Pa., Jan. 12, 1945; m. Jonathan Lee Sharp, Sept. 28, 1963 (dec. Dec. 31, 1979); children: Deborah, Todd, Wade; m. Brian C. Bland, Nov. 2, 1985; stepchildren: Paulette, Kelli. Lic. Real Estate Agent, Utah. Beauty coll. recruiter, sec. Continental Coll. of Beauty, Salt Lake City, 1968-72; exec. sec. Vaughn Hansen Assoc., Salt Lake City, 1973-82; v.p., co-owner Bland Bros., Inc., West Jordan, Utah, 1985—; co-owner Blands Sand & Gravel, 1990—. Real estate agent Preferred Properties, Salt Lake City, 1982-90, Mansell, Salt Lake City, 1990—. Avocations: golf, travel. Office: Bland Brothers Inc 8630 Redwood Rd West Jordan UT 84088-9226

BLANDFORD, ROGER DAVID, astronomy educator; b. Grantham, Eng., Aug. 28, 1949; s. Jack George and Janet Margaret (Evans) B.; m. Elizabeth Kellett, Aug. 5, 1972; children: Jonathan, Edward. BA, Magdalene Coll., Cambridge U., 1970; MA, PhD, Cambridge U., 1974. Rsch. fellow St. John's Coll., Cambridge U., 1973-76; asst. prof. astronomy Calif. Inst. Tech., Pasadena, 1976-79, prof., 1979-89, Richard Chace Tolman prof. theoretical astrophysics, 1989—; mem. Inst. Advanced Study, Princeton, 1974-75. Contbr. articles to profl. publs. W.B.R. King scholar, 1967-70; Charles Kingsley Bye fellow, 1972-73; Alfred P. Sloan research fellow, 1980, Guggenheim fellow, 1988—. Fellow Royal Soc., Royal Astron. Soc. (Eddington medal 1999), Cambridge Philos. Soc.; mem. Am. Astron. Soc. (Warner prize 1982, Heineman prize 1998), Am. Acad. Arts and Scis. Office: Calif Inst Tech Dept Astrophysics Pasadena CA 91125-0001

BLANKENSHIP, ROBERT EUGENE, biochemistry educator; b. Auburn, Nebr., Aug. 25, 1948; s. George Robert and Jane (Kehoe) Leech; m. Elizabeth Marie Dorland, June 26, 1971; children: Larissa Dorland, Samuel Robert. BS, Wesleyan U., Nebr., 1970; PhD, U. Calif., Berkeley, 1975. Postdoctoral fellow Lawrence Berkeley Lab., Berkeley, 1975-76, U. Washington, Seattle, 1976-79; asst. prof. Amherst (Mass.) Coll., 1979-85; assoc. prof. Ariz. State U., Tempe, 1985-88, prof., 1988—, dir. Ctr. Study of Early Events in Photosynthesis, 1988-91. Author: Molecular Mechanisms of Photosynthesis, 2002; editor Anoxygenic Photosynthetic Bacteria, 1995; editor-in-chief Photosynthesis Rsch., 1988-99; cons. editor Advances in Photosynthesis, 1991-98; mem. editl. bd. Biophys. Jour., 2000—, Biochemistry, 2001—, Internat. Jour. Astrobiology; contbr. 180 articles to sci. jours. Recipient Alumni award Nebr. Wesleyan U., 1991, Disting. Rsch. award Ariz. State U., 1992, Mentoring award Ariz. State U., 1998. Mem. AAAS, Am. Chem. Soc., Biophys. Soc., Union of Concerned Scientists, Internat. Soc. of Photodynthesis Rsch., Internat. Soc. for Study of Origin of Life. Democrat. Avocations: hiking, cooking, travel, fossil collecting. Home: 13824 S Canyon Dr Phoenix AZ 85048-9085 Office: Ariz State U Dept Chemistry And Bio Tempe AZ 85287-1604

BLANKFORT, LOWELL ARNOLD, newspaper publisher; b. N.Y.C., Apr. 29, 1926; s. Herbert and Gertrude (Butler) B.; m. April Pemberton; 1 child, Jonathan. BA in History and Polit. Sci., Rutgers U., 1946. Reporter, copy editor L.I. (N.Y.) Star-Jour., 1947-49; columnist London Daily Mail, Paris, 1949-50; copy editor The Stars & Stripes, Darmstadt, Germany, 1950-51, Wall St. Jour., N.Y.C., 1951; bus., labor editor Cowles Mags., N.Y.C., 1951-53; pub. Pacifica (Calif.) Tribune, 1954-59; free-lance writer Europe, Asia, 1959-61; co-pub., editor Chula Vista (Calif.) Star-News, 1961-78; co-owner Paradise (Calif.) Post, 1977—. Co-owner Monte Vista (Colo.) Jour., Ctr. (Colo.) Post-Dispatch, Del Norte (Colo.) Prospector, 1978-93, Plainview (Minn.) News, St. Charles (Minn.) Press, Lewiston (Minn.) Jour., 1980-98, Summit (Colo.) Sentinel, New Richmond (Wis.) News, 1981-87, Yuba City Valley Herald, Calif., 1982-85, TV Views, Monterey, Calif., 1982-87, Summit County Jour., Colo., 1982-87, Alpine (Calif.) Sun, 1987-93, Bassics Mag., 1998—, Fingerstyle Guitar Mag., 1999—. Columnist, contbr. articles on fgn. affairs to newspapers. Active Calif. Dem. Ctrl. Com., 1963. Recipient awards Best Editls. in Calif., non-dailies, 1st or 2nd place seven consecutive years Calif. Newspaper Pub. Assn., Best Editl. in U.S., Nat. Newspaper Assn., Best Editl. U.S. Suburban Newspapers, Suburban Pubs. Newspapers Am., Headliner of Yr., San Diego Press Club, John Swett award Calif. Edn. Assn. and Citizen of the Yr. (Sweetwater Edn. Assn.), Spl. Media award Nat. Conf. Christians and Jews, for articles on South America; named Outstanding Layman of Yr., Sweetwater Edn. Assn., 1966, Citizen of Yr., City of Chula Vista, 1976, Headliner of Yr., San Diego Press Club, 1980. Mem. ACLU (pres. San Diego chpt. 1970-71), Calif. Newspaper Pubs. Assn., World Affairs Coun. San Diego (pres. 1996-99), Ctr. Internat. Policy (bd. dirs. 1991—), Internat. Ctr. Devel. Policy (nat. bd. 1985-90), UN Assn. (pres. San Diego chpt. 1991-93, nat. coun. 1992-97, nat. bd. 1997-2001), World Federalist Assn. (nat. bd. 1992-2000, pres. San Diego chpt. 1984-86), Soc. Profl. Journalists, East Meets West Found. (nat. v.p. 1992-98), Inst. of the Ams. (assoc., internat. coun. 1994—). Achievements include interviewing many heads of state including Fidel Castro in Cuba, Li Peng and Li Ziannin in China, Benezir Bhutto in Pakistan, Kim Dae Jung in Korea, Paul Kagame in Rwanda. Home: 4008 Old Orchard Ln Bonita CA 91902-2337 Office: 315 4th Ave Ste S Chula Vista CA 91910-3816

BLASCHKE, TERRENCE FRANCIS, medicine and molecular pharmacology educator; b. Rochester, Minn., Oct. 4, 1942; s. Robert Elmer and Carmella Ann (Seeby) B.; m. Jeannette F. Martin, June 8, 1968; children: Anne, John. BS in Math. cum laude, U. Denver, 1964; MD, Columbia U., 1968. Diplomate Am. Bd. Internal Medicine, Nat. Bd. Med. Examiners. Intern in medicine UCLA Ctr. for Health Scis., 1968-69, asst. resident, 1969-70; clin. assoc. metabolism br. Nat. Cancer Inst., NIH, Bethesda, Md., 1970-72; clin. rsch fellow div. clin. pharmacology dept. medicine U. Calif. Med. Ctr., San Francisco, 1972-74; asst. prof. medicine (clin. pharmacology) Stanford (Calif.) U. Sch. Medicine, 1974-81, asst. prof. pharmacology, 1978-81, assoc. prof. medicine (clin. pharmacology) and pharmacology, 1981-91, prof. medicine (clin. pharmacology)-molecular pharmacology, 1991—; v.p. Pharsight Corp., Calif., 2000—. Bd. govs. Am. Bd. Clin. Pharmacology, 1990-92; vis. worker div. molecular pharmacology Nat. Inst. for Med. Rsch., London, 1980-81, Ctr. for Biopharm. Scis., U. Leiden and dept. med. info. scis. Erasmus U., The Netherlands, 1990; mem. Medi-Cal drug use rev. bd. Calif. Dept. Health Svcs., 1993-96; chmn. generic drugs adv. com. FDA, 1990-94; mem. bd. sci. advisors Merck Sharp and Dohme Rsch. Labs., Rahway, N.J., 1986-90; mem. pharmacology study sect. NIH, 1979-83; faculty of medicine Moi U., El Doret, Kenya; vis. prof. Ctr. Drug Devel. Sci., Georgetown U., 1997-98; spl. govt. employee FDA, 1997—. Mem. editl. bd. Drug Therapeutics: Concepts for Physicians, 1978-81, Rational Drug Therapy, 1984-85, Clin. Pharmacology and Therapeutics, 1981—, Drug Interaction Facts, 1983-87, Drug Metabolism and Disposition, 1994-2000; assoc. editor Ann. Rev. Pharmacology and Toxicology, 1989—. Officer USPHS, 1970-72. Recipient faculty devel. award in clin. pharmacology Pharm. Mfrs. Assn. Found.; Burroughs-Wellcome scholar. Mem. ACP, AAAS, Am. Soc. for Clin. Pharmacology and Therapeutics (chmn. liaison com. for clin. pharmacology 1985-89, sci. program com. 1986-87, pres. 1988-89, assoc. sec.-treas. 1990-92, chmn. long range planning com. 1992-94), Am. Soc. Pharmacology and Exptl. Therapeutics (exec. com. clin. pharmacology divsn. 1986-89), Am. Fedn. Clin. Rsch., Western Soc. Clin. Investigation, Western Assn. Physicians, Western Pharmacology Soc., Phi Beta Kappa, Alpha Omega Alpha. Office: Stanford U Med Ctr Div Clin Pharmacology S-009 300 Pasteur Dr Stanford CA 94305-5130 E-mail: tblaschke@pharsight.com, blaschke@stanford.edu

BLASE, NANCY GROSS, librarian; b. New Rochelle, N.Y. d. Albert Philip and Elsie Wise (May) Gross; m. Barrie Wayne Blase, June 19, 1966 (div.); m. Charles M. Goldstein, July 25, 1999; 1 child, Eric Wayne. BA in Biology, Marietta (Ohio) Coll., 1964; MLS, U. Ill., 1965. Info. scientist brain info. svc. Biomed. Libr., UCLA, 1965-66; libr. Health Sci. Libr., U. Wash., Seattle, 1966-68, Medlars search analyst, 1970-72, coord. Medline, 1972-79, head Natural Scis. Libr., 1979—. Mem. libr. adv. com. Elizabeth C. Miller Libr., Ctr. for Urban Horticulture, Seattle, 1986-90. Contbr. articles to profl. jours. NSF fellow interdept. tng. program for sci. info. specialists U. Ill., 1964-65. Mem. Am. Soc. for Info. Sci. (pres. personal computer spl. interest group 1993-94, chair constn. and bylaws com. 1994-97, chair Spl. Interest Group/Med. Informatics, 1998-99, rsch. grantee Pacific N.W. chpt. 1984-85), Internat. Tng. in Comm. (pres. Pacific N.W. region 1994-95), Phi Beta Kappa (pres. U. Wash. chpt. 1993-97, pres. Puget Sound Assn. 2001—), Bet Chaverim (pres. 1998-00). Avocations: walking, reading. Home: 10751 Durland Ave NE Seattle WA 98125-6945 Office: U Wash Natural Scis Libr Box 352900 Seattle WA 98195-2900 E-mail: nblase@uwashington.edu

BLATT, MORTON BERNARD, medical illustrator; b. Chgo., Jan. 9, 1923; s. Arthur E. and Hazel B. Student Central YMCA Coll., 1940-42, U. Ill., 1943-46. Tchr., Ray-Vogue Art Schs., Chgo., 1946-51; med. illustrator VA Center, Wood, Wis., 1951-57, Swedish Covenant Hosp., Chgo., 1957-76; med. illustrator Laidlaw Bros., River Forest, Ill., 1956-59; cons., artist health textbooks, 1956-59; illustrator Standard Edn. Soc., Chgo., 1960; art editor Covenant Home Altar, 1972-83, Covenant Companion, 1958-82. Served with USAAF, 1943-44. Mem. Art Inst. Chgo. Club: Chgo. Press. Illustrator: Atlas and Demonstration Technique of the Central Nervous System, also numerous med. jours.; illustrator, designer Covenant Hymnal, books, record jackets. Address: 373 Eliseo Dr Greenbrae CA 94904-1326

BLATTER, FRANK EDWARD, travel agency executive; b. Denver, Jan. 9, 1939; s. Anthony John and Irene Marie (Tobin) B.; m. Barbara E. Dricth, Sept. 6, 1959; children: Dean Robert, Lisa Kay Faircloth, Paul Kelly. BS, Regis U., Denver, 1961; grad., Colo. Sch. Banking, 1966, Sch. Bank Adminstrn., 1973. CPA, Colo. Acct. McMahon, Maddox & Rodriguez (C.P.A.s), Denver, 1960-63, United Bank Denver, 1963-65; with United Banks Colo., Inc., Denver, 1965-86; pres. Cath. Cmty. Svcs., Denver, 1987, Premiere Travel and Cruises, Denver, 1988—. Mem. nat. adv. coun. and devel. com., chmn. ann. funds coun. Regis U.; chmn. adv. coun. Camp Santa Maria; crusade chmn. Am. Cancer Soc., Denver. Mem. AICPA, Tax Execs. Inst. (past pres. Denver), Colo. Soc. CPAs, Fin. Execs. Inst. (dir.), Bank Adminstrn. Inst. (dir.), Arrowhead Golf Club. Roman Catholic. Office: 3900 S Wadsworth Blvd Ste 475 Denver CO 80235-2207

BLATTNER, MEERA MCCUAIG, computer science educator; b. Chgo., Aug. 14, 1930; d. William D. McCuaig and Nina (Spertus) Klevs; m. Minao Kamegai, June 22, 1985; children: Douglas, Robert, William. BA, U. Chgo., 1952; MS, U. So. Calif., 1966; PhD, UCLA, 1973. Rsch. fellow in computer sci. Harvard U., 1973-74; asst. prof. Rice U., 1974-80; assoc. prof. applied sci. U. Calif.-Davis, Livermore, 1980-91, prof. applied sci., 1991-99, prof. emeritus, 2000—; dir. rsch. Cmty. Vision, Inc., 2000—. Adj. prof. U. Tex., Houston, 1977-99; vis. prof. U. Paris, 1980; program dir. theoretical computer sci. NSF, Washington, 1979-80. Co-editor: (with R. Dannenberg) Multimedia Interface Design, 1992; contbr. articles to profl. jours. NSF grantee, 1977-81, 93-99. Mem. Assn. Computing Machinery, Computer Soc. of IEEE. Office: Cmty Vision Inc 1231 N Town Center Dr Las Vegas NV 89144-6368 E-mail: meera.blattner@communityvision.com

BLAU, ELIZABETH ANNE, restaurant executive; b. N.Y.C., Aug. 31, 1967; BS in Govt., Georgetown U., Washington; MS in Restaurant Mktg., Cornell U. Sch. Hotel Admin., Ithaca, N.Y. Dir. devel. Le Cirque, N.Y.C.; chief confectioner, sr. mgr. Hand-Crafted Hilliards Candies, West Hartford, Conn.; scholarship program developer James Beard Found., N.Y.C.; co-owner The Butler Did It Catering, Washington; asst. catering dir. Blantyte Hotel, Lenox, Mass.; v.p. of restaurant development Mirage Resorts, Inc., Las Vegas. Avocations: hiking, climbing, horseback riding, skiing. Office: Mirage Resorts Inc PO Box 7777 Las Vegas NV 89177-0777

BLAU, HELEN MARGARET, molecular pharmacology educator; b. London, May 8, 1948; (parents Am. citizens); d. George E. and Gertrude Blau; m. David Spiegel, July 25, 1976; children: Daniel Spiegel, Julia Spiegel. BA in Biology, U. York (Eng.), 1969; MA in Biology, Harvard U., 1970, PhD in Biology, 1975. Predoctoral fellow dept. biology Harvard U., Cambridge, Mass., 1969-75; postdoctoral fellow div. med. genetics U. Calif. Dept. Biochemistry and Biophysics, San Francisco, 1975-78; asst. prof. dept. pharmacology Stanford (Calif.) U., 1978-86, assoc. prof. dept. pharmacology, 1986-91, prof. dept. molecular pharmacology, 1991—, chair dept. molecular pharmacology, 1997—, Donald E. and Delia B. Baxter prof., 1999—. Co-chmn. various profl. meetings. Mem. editorial bd. 10 jours. including Jour. Cell Biology, Somatic Cell Molecular Genetics and Exptl. Cell Rsch., Molecular and Cellular Biology; contbr. articles to profl. jours. Mem. ad hoc molecular cytology study sect. NIH, 1987-88; mem. five-yr. planning com genetics and teratology br. NICHHD/NIH, 1989. Recipient Rsch. Career Devel. award NIH, 1984-89, SmithKline & Beecham award, 1989-91, Women in Cell Biology Career Recognition award, 1992, Excellence in Sci. award FASEB, 1999, McKnight Endowment Fund for Neurosci. award, 2001; Mellon Found. faculty fellow, 1979-80, William H. Hume faculty scholar, 1981-84; grantee NIH, NSF, Muscular Dystrophy Assn., march of Dimes, 1978—; Yvette Mayent-Rothschild fellow for vis. profs. Inst. Curie, Paris, 1995. Fellow AAAS; mem. NAS (del. to China 1991), Internat. Soc. Differentiation (v.p., pres. 2000—), Am. Soc. for Cell Biology (nominating com. 1985-86, program com. 1990), Soc. for Devel. Biology (pres. 1994-95). Avocations: skiing, swimming, hiking, music, theatre. Office: Stanford U Sch Medicine Molecular Pharmacology Dept Stanford CA 94305-5175 Fax: (650) 736-0080. E-mail: hblau@cmgm.stanford.edu

BLAYLOCK, MOOKIE (DARON OSHAY BLAYLOCK), professional basketball player; b. Garland, Tex., Mar. 20, 1967; Student, Midland (tex.) Coll., Oklahoma Coll. Guard N.J. Nets, 1989-92, Atlanta Hawks, 1992-99, Golden State Warriors, Oakland, Calif., 1999—. Named to NBA All-Defensive First Team, 1994. Office: Golden State Warriors 1011 Broadway Oakland CA 94607-4027

BLENCOWE, PAUL SHERWOOD, lawyer, private investor; b. Amityville, N.Y., Feb. 10, 1953; s. Frederick Arthur and Dorothy Jeanne (Ballenger) B.; m. Mary Frances Faulk, Apr. 11, 1992; 1 child, Kristin Amanda. BA with honors, U. Wis., 1975; MBA, U. Pa., 1976; JD, Stanford U., 1979. Bar: Tex. 1979, Calif. 1989. Assoc. Fulbright & Jaworski, Houston, 1979-86, London, 1986-87, ptnr., 1988-89, Fulbright & Jaworski L.L.P., L.A., 1989-2000, of counsel, 2000—. Editor: China's Quest for Independence: Policy Evolution in the 1970s, 1980; editor-in-chief Stanford Jour. of Internat. Law, 1978-79; contbr. articles on U.S. securities and corp. law to profl. jours. Mem. ABA, The Calif. Club, Phi Beta Kappa, Phi Kappa Phi, Beta Theta Pi. Office: Fulbright & Jaworski LLP 865 S Figueroa St Fl 29 Los Angeles CA 90017-2543 E-mail: pblencowe@fulbright.com

BLESSING-MOORE, JOANN CATHERINE, allergist; b. Tacoma, Sept. 21, 1946; d. Harold R. and Mildred (Benson) Blessing; m. Robert Chester Moore; 1 child, Ahna. BA in Chemistry, Syracuse U., 1968; MD, SUNY, Syracuse, 1972. Diplomate Am. Bd. Pediatrics, Am. Bd. Allergy Immunology, Am. Bd. Pediatric Pulmonology. Pediatric intern, then resident Stanford U. Sch. Medicine, Palo Alto, Calif., 1972-75, allergy pulmonology fellow, 1975-77; co-dir. pediatric allergy pulmonology dept. Stanford U. Children's Hosp., Palo Alto, 1977-84; clin. asst. prof. dept. pediatrics Stanford U. Sch. Medicine, Palo Alto, 1977-84, co-dir. pediatric pulmonology lab., 1977-84; clin. asst. prof. dept. immunology Stanford U. Hosp., 1984—; allergist Palo Alto Med. Clinic, 1984-90; pvt. practice allergy immunology-pediatric-pulmonary Palo Alto, Calif., 1990—. Dir. ednl. program for children with asthma Camp Wheeze, Palo Alto, 1975—; cons. FDA, 1992-97; cons. in field. Author handbooks, camp program manuals; co-editor jour. supplements; mem. edit. bd. Allergy jours.; contbr. articles to sci. publs. Fellow Am. Acad. Allery, Asthma, Immunology (various offices 1980—, task force parameters of care asthma and allergy 1989-98), Am. Coll. Chest Physicians (com. mem. 1980—), Am. Coll. of Asthma, Allergy and Immunology (regent 1995-98); mem. Am. Thoracic Soc., Am. Lung Assn., No. Calif. Allergy Found. (bd. dirs., pres.), Peninsula Women's Assn., Santa Clara and San Mateo County Med. Soc., Chi Omega. Republican. Presbyterian. Avocations: music, swimming, cooking, horseback riding, scuba diving. Office: 780 Welch Rd Ste 204 Palo Alto CA 94304-1518 also: 101 S San Mateo Dr Ste 310 San Mateo CA 94401-3844 also: Stanford Univ Hosp Dept Immunology Palo Alto CA 94304

BLETHEN, FRANK A. newspaper publisher; b. Seattle, Apr. 20, 1945; B.S. in Bus., Ariz. State U. Pub. Walla Walla Union-Bulletin, Wash., 1975-79; pub., circulation mgr. Seattle Times Newspaper Co., 1985—. Chmn. Walla Walla Union-Bull., Yakima (Wash.) Herald Republic, Blethen Maine Newspapers, Portland, Augusta, Waterville; pres. Blethen Corp. Mem. pres.' adv. bd. Wash. State U. and U. Wash.; campaign chair United Way King County, 1996, 97, bd. dirs., 1996—; bd. dirs. Md. Inst. for Minority Journalism Edn., 1994—. Recipient Pulitzer prize (3) for best newspaper reporting and investigative reporting, 1997, Nat. Reports, 1991, Ida B. Wells award for lifetime achievement in advancement of minority employment, 1997, Leadership Conf. on Civil Rights Chairperson's award for spl. merit, 1999, Edward R. Murrow award Wash. State U., 1998, Weldon B. Gibson Disting. Vol. award Wash. State U., 1998; named to Wash. State Hall of Journalistic Achievement, 1998. Mem. Nat. Assn. of Minority Media Execs., Am. Newspaper Pubs. Assn. (bd. dirs., chmn. telecomm. com.), Sigma Delta Chi. Office: Seattle Times Fairview Ave N & John St PO Box 70 Seattle WA 98111-0070

BLETHEN, SANDRA LEE, pediatric endocrinologist; b. San Mateo, Calif., May 16, 1942; d. Howard Albion and Laura Katherine (Wolf) B.; m. Fred I. Chasalow, Nov. 26, 1966. SB in Biochemistry, U. Chgo., 1961; PhD in Biochemistry, U. Calif., Berkeley, 1965; MD, Yeshiva U., 1975. Diplomate Am. Bd. Pediatrics. Fellow biochemistry Brandeis U., Waltham, Mass., 1965-68; instr. biochemistry U. Calif., San Diego, 1968-69, asst. prof. San Francisco State U., 1969-71; resident in pediatrics Columbia Presbyn. Med. Ctr., N.Y.C., 1975-77; fellow pediatric endocrinology U. N.C., Chapel Hill, 1977-79; asst. prof. pediatrics Washington U., St. Louis, 1979-84; assoc. prof. pediatrics SUNY, Stony Brook, 1985-96; assoc. attending pediatrician L.I. Jewish Med. Ctr., New Hyde Park, N.Y., 1984-90; attending pediatrician Univ. Hosp., Stony Brook, 1991-96; cons. Genentech, Inc., South San Francisco, Calif., 1985-96, sr. endocrinologist, 1996—, assoc. dir. product experience, 1997-2000, sr. clin. scientist, 1999—. Cons. Diagnostic Systems Labs., Webster, Tex., 1989-96. Mem. editl. bd. Steroids, 1990—, Jour. of Endocrinology and Metabolism, 1995-98; contbr. more than 90 articles to profl. jours. Predoctoral fellow NSF, 1961-63, Postdoctoral fellow USPHS, 1965-67. Mem. Am. Pediatric Soc. (program com. 1994), Endocrine Soc., Lawson Wilkens Pediatric Endocrine Soc. (membership chair 1994-95), Soc. for Pediatric Rsch., Phi Beta Kappa, Alpha Omega Alpha. Avocation: sailing. Office: Med Affairs Genentech Inc 1 Dna Way South San Francisco CA 94080-4918 E-mail: blothen.sandra@gene.com

BLEWETT, KENNETH K. business executive; CEO Richardson & Ptnrs., Albuquerque. Office: Richardson & Ptnrs PO Box 3487 Albuquerque NM 87190-3487

BLEWETT, ROBERT NOALL, lawyer; b. Stockton, Calif., July 12, 1915; s. Stephen Noall and Bess Errol (Simard) B.; m. Virginia Weston, Mar. 30, 1940; children: Richard Weston Blewett (dec.), Carolyn Blewett Lawrence. LLB, Stanford U., 1936, JD, 1939. Bar: Calif. 1939. Dep. dist. atty. San Joaquin County, 1942-46; practice law Stockton, 1946-98; ptnr., pres. Blewett & Allen-Garibaldi, Inc., Stockton, 1971-98. Chmn. San Joaquin County chpt. ARC, 1947-49; v.p. Goodwill Industries, 1967-68; vice chmn. Stockton Sister City Commn., 1969-70; adv. bd. bus. adminstrn. dept. U. Pacific; trustee San Joaquin Pioneer and Haggin Galleries. Fellow Am. Coll. Estate and Trust Counsel, Am. Bar Found.; mem. ABA, Am. Judicature Soc., Am. Law Inst., State Bar Calif. (mem. exec. com. on conf. of dels. 1969-72, vice chmn. 1971-72), Order of the Coif, Rotary (pres. 1987-88), Yosemite Club, San Francisco Banker's Club, Masons, Shriners, Delta Theta Phi, Theta Xi. Republican. Home: 3016 Dwight Way Stockton CA 95204-1809 Office: 141 E Acacia St Stockton CA 95202-1400 E-mail: ginger21@mediaone.net

BLEY, JOHN L. state agency administrator; Dir. fin. instns. State of Wash., Olympia. Office: State of Wash Rm 300 210 11th Ave SE Fl 3 Olympia WA 98501-2242

BLICKENSDERFER, CHARLES THOMAS (TOM), state legislator, lawyer; b. Denver, June 21, 1957; m. Kristin Blickensderfer. BA in History, Colo. Coll.; JD, U. Denver. Atty.; lobbyist Colo. Arts Coun.; staff intern U.S. House of Reps., White House; mem. Colo. State Assembly, 1991-92, Colo. State Senate, 1992—, mem. joint legal svcs. com., mem. joint legis. coun. com., vice-chair svcs. com. Bd. mem. Inter Faith Task Force. Mem. Greenwood Village C. of C., South Metro C. of C., Littleton Bus. Assn., Colo. Chpt. Cities in Schs. Republican. Office: State Capitol 200 E Colfax Ave Ste 263 Denver CO 80203-1716 also: 9 Parkway Dr Englewood CO 80110-4227

BLINDER, MARTIN S. business consultant, art dealer; b. Bklyn., Nov. 18, 1946; s. Meyer and Lillian (Stein) B.; m. Janet Weiss, Dec. 10, 1983. BBA, Adelphi U., 1968. Acct. exec. Bruns, Nordeman & Co., N.Y.C., 1968-69; v.p. Blinder, Robinson & Co., Westbury, NY, 1969-73; treas. BHB Prodns., L.A., 1973-76; pres. Martin Lawrence Ltd. Edits., Van Nuys, Calif., 1976-94, chmn., 1986-94, bd. dirs., 1994—; dir. AZ/NY Gallery,

Scottsdale, Ariz., 2001—. Pres., dir. Corp. Art Inc., Visual Artists Mgmt. Corp., Art Consultants Inc.; pres., owner, founder MSB Fine Art, Phoenix, 1994—; lectr. bus. symposia. Contbr. articles to mags. and newspapers; appeared on TV and radio. Mem. Dem. Nat. Com., benefit com. AIDS project, L.A., 1988; bd. dirs. Very Spl. Arts, 1989—; chmn. visual arts Internat. Very Spl. Arts Festival, 1989; patron Guggenheim Mus., N.Y.C., Mus. Modern Art, N.Y.C., L.A. County Mus. Art, L.A. Mus. Contemporary Art (hon. founder), Whitney Mus. Am. Art, Palm Springs Mus. Art, Hirschorn Mus., Washington, Skirball Mus., L.A., Diabetes Found. of City of Hope, B'nai B'rith Anti-Defamation League, 1999, Very Spl. Arts, Scottsdale (Ariz.) Ctr. for the Arts, Scottsdale Mus. Contemporary Art (lectr. on Keith Haring); mem. Citizens for Common Sense; bd. dirs., pres. Rsch. Found. for Crohns Disease; mem. benefit com. Art Against AIDS, 1989; co-chair artists com. for Don't Bungle the Jungle Companions of Arts and Nature, 1989; prin. sponsor, ann. fundraiser AIDS Project, L.A., 1990. Recipient resolution of commendation L.A. City Coun., 1983, State of Calif. resolution for contbn. to arts in Calif., 1983, Merit award Republic Haiti for contbn. to arts, 1985, U.S. Senate commendations, 1983, County of L.A. Bd. Suprs. resolution for contbn. to arts in So. Calif., 1983, Gov. of R.I. resolution for contbns. to arts, 1985, commendation County of L.A.-Supr. Ed Edelman, 1991, commendation for contbns. to the arts and the healing arts City of L.A., 1991, commendation for contbns. to arts and philanthropy Mayor David Dinkins, N.Y.C., 1992; Nov. 18, 1985 declared Martin S. Blinder Day in L.A. in his honor by Mayor Tom Bradley, spl. award San Diego Youth and Cmty. Svcs., Bruin Bear award for establishing Blinder Rsch. Found., UCLA Sch. Medicine, 1994. Mem. Fine Art Pub.'s Assn. (bd. dirs. 1990-94), Med. Art Assn. at UCLA. Office: AZ/NY Gallery 7373 Scottsdale Mall Scottsdale AZ 85251

BLINN, JAMES F. computer scientist; BS in Physics and Comm. Sci., U. Mich., 1970, MSE in Computer, Info., Control Engring., 1972; PhD in Computer Sci., U. Utah, 1978; DFA (hon.), Parsons Sch. Design, 1995. Graphics rsch. fellow Microsoft Corp., Redmond, Wash. External adv. bd. Geometry Ctr. Contbr. articles to profl. jours. Recipient service medal NASA, 1983, Siggraph Computer Achievement award, 1983; fellow MacArthur Found., 1991. Mem. IEEE (Outstanding Contbn. award 1989, writer column Computer Graphics and Application Jour.), NAE. Office: Microsoft Corp Graphics Rsch 1 Microsoft Way Redmond WA 98052-6399

BLITZ, LEO, astronomer, educator; PhD in Astronomy, Columbia U., 1979. Postdoctoral fellow U. Calif., Berkeley, prof. astronomy, dir. Radio Astronomy Lab.; prof. astronomy U. Md., founder, dir. Lab. for Millimeter-wave Astronomy. Achievements include research on star formation, the structure and dynamics of the Milky Way, fueling of active galactic nuclei. Office: U Calif Berkeley Dept Astronomy 601 Campbell Hall Berkeley CA 94720-3411

BLITZ, STEPHEN M. lawyer; b. N.Y.C., July 29, 1941; s. Leo and Dorothy B.; m. Ellen Sue Mintzer, Sept. 23, 1962; children: Catherine Denise, Thomas Joseph. B.A., Columbia U., 1962, B.S. in Elec. Engring., 1963; LL.B., Stanford U., 1966. Bar: Calif. 1967, U.S. Dist. Ct. (cen. dist.) Calif. 1967, Colo. 1996. Law clk. to judge U.S. Dist. Ct. Central Dist. Calif., 1966-67; ptnr. Gibson, Dunn & Crutcher, L.A., 1967-96, Denver, 1996-2001, Fleishman, Sterling, Gregory & Shapiro, Denver, 2001—. Adj. prof. law U. West Los Angeles Sch. Law, 1978-80, dir. Pub. Counsel, 1981-83, 94-96. Bd. dirs. Colo. Preservation, Inc., 1999—. Mem. ABA, L.A. County Bar Assn. (exec. com. 1986-96, chmn. 1994-95, real property sect.), Order of Coif, Beta Gamma Sigma. Office: Fleishman, Sterling, Gregory and Shapiro PC 1600 Broadway Ste 2600 Denver CO 80202-4926

BLIZZARD, ALAN, artist; b. Boston, Mar. 25, 1939; s. Thomas and Elizabeth B. Student, Mass. Coll. Art; M.A., U. Ariz.; M.F.A., U. Iowa, 1963. Instr. in art U. Iowa; vis. asst. prof. art Albion Coll., U. Okla.; asso. prof. UCLA; now prof. painting Scripps Coll. and; Claremont Grad. Sch. Represented in permanent collections Bklyn. Mus., Met. Mus. Art, N.Y.C., Art Inst. Chgo., Denver Art Mus., La Jolla (Calif.) Mus. Art, Ashland U., Columbia U., McGeorge Sch. Law, Pomona Coll., Sacramento State U., Pitzer Coll., Fluor Corp., Kouri Capital Corp., N.Y.C. Office: Scripps Coll Art Dept Claremont CA 91711

BLOCH, PAUL, public relations executive; b. Bklyn., July 17, 1939; s. Edwin Lionel and Antoinette (Greenberg) B. B.B. Polit. Sci., UCLA, 1962. Publicist Rogers & Cowan, Beverly Hills, Calif., 1962-70, v.p., 1970-75, sr. v.p., ptnr., 1975-83, exec. v.p., sr. ptnr., 1983—, also vice chmn., co-chmn. Asst. Am. Cancer Soc., United Way, Am. Diabetes Assn., UNICEF, 1975—; adv. council Orange County Sheriff's Dept., 1980—. Served with U.S. Army, 1957. Recipient Les Mason award Publicity Guild Am., 1991. Mem. Publicists Guild of Am. (award for publicity campaign for Brian's Song 1972), Country Music Assn. Office: Rogers & Cowan 1888 Century Park E Fl 5 Los Angeles CA 90067-1702

BLOCK, BARBARA ANN, biology educator; b. Springfield, Mass., Apr. 25, 1958; d. Merrill and Myra (Winograd) B. BA, U. Vt., 1980; PhD, Duke U., 1986. Postdoctoral fellow U. Pa., Phila., 1986-88; asst. prof. organismal biology U. Chgo., 1988-93; asst. prof. biol. sci. Stanford U., 1993-97, assoc. prof., 1997—. Contbr. articles to profl. jours. Recipient Presdl. Young Investigator award NSF, 1989; MacArthur fellow, 1996, Pew Conservation fellow, 1997. Mem. AAAS, Am. Soc. Zoologists, Biophys. Soc. Democrat.*

BLOCK, MICHAEL KENT, economics and law educator, public policy association executive, former government official, consultant; b. N.Y.C., Apr. 2, 1942; s. Philip and Roslyn (Klein) B.; m. Carole Arline Polansky, Aug. 30, 1964 (div.); children: Robert Justin, Tamara Nicole; m. Olga Vyborna, Dec. 1, 1996. A.B., Stanford U., 1964, A.M., 1969, Ph.D., 1972. Research analyst Bank of Am., San Francisco, 1965-66; research assoc. Planning Assocs., San Francisco, 1966-67; asst. prof. econs. U. Santa Clara, 1969-72; asst. prof. econs. dept. ops. research and adminstrv. sci. Naval Postgrad. Sch., Monterey, Calif., 1972-74, assoc. prof., 1974-76; research fellow Hoover Instn., Stanford U., 1975-76, sr. research fellow, 1976-87; dir. Center for Econometric Studies of Justice System, 1977-81; ptnr. Block & Nold, Cons., Palo Alto, Calif., 1980-81; assoc. prof. mgmt., econs. and law U. Ariz., Tucson, 1982-85, prof. econs. and law, 1989—; mem. U.S. Sentencing Commn., Washington, 1985-89; exec. v.p. Cybernomics, Tucson, 1991—; pres. Goldwater Inst. for Pub. Policy, Phoenix, 1992—; sr. policy adviser State of Ariz. Gov. Symington, 1996-97. Chair Basis Sch. Bd., 1998—; mem. Ariz. Residential Utility Consumer Bd., 1995-96, chmn. Ariz. Constl. Def. Coun., 1994-97, Ariz. Juvenile Justice Adv. Coun., 1996-97; seminar dir. Econ. Devel. Inst./World Bank, 1992-95; cons. in field. Author: (with H.G. Demmert) Workbook and Programmed Guide to Economics, 1974, 77, 80, (with James M. Clabault) A Legal and Economic Analysis of Criminal Antitrust Indictments:, 1955-80; contbr. articles to profl. publs. Fellow NSF, 1965, Stanford U. Fellow Progress and Freedom Found.; mem. Am. Econ. Assn., Phi Beta Kappa. Office: U Ariz Econ Dept McClelland Hl Rm 401 Tucson AZ 85721-0001

BLOCK, ROBERT N. federal judge; b. Boston, July 27, 1950; BA, U. of Calif., L.A., 1972; JD, U. of Calif. Law Sch., L.A., 1978. Apptd. magistrate judge cen. dist. U.S. Dist. Ct. Calif., 1995. Office: 1006 US Courthouse 312 N Spring St Los Angeles CA 90012-4701 Fax: 213-894-6860

BLODGETT, ELSIE GRACE, association executive; b. Eldorado Springs, Mo., Aug. 2, 1921; d. Charles Ishmal and Naoma Florence (Worthington) Robison; m. Charles Davis Blodgett, Nov. 8, 1940; children: Carolyn Doyel, Charleen Bier, Lyndon Blodgett, Daryl (dec.). Student Warrensburg (Mo.) State Tchrs. Coll., 1939-40; BA, Fresno (Calif.) State Coll., 1953. Tchr. schs. in Mo. and Calif., 1940-42, 47-72; owner, mgr. rental units, 1965—; exec. dir. San Joaquin County (Calif.) Rental Property Assn., Stockton, 1970-81; prin. Delta Rental Property Owners and Assocs., 1981-82; propr. Crystal Springs Health World, Inc., Stockton, 1980-86; bd. dirs. Stockton Better Bus. Bur. Active local PTA, Girl Scouts U.S., Boy Scouts Am.; bd. dirs. Stockton Goodwill Industries; active Vols. in Police Svc., 1993; capt. Delaware Alpine Neighborhood Watch, 1994—. Named (with husband) Mr. and Mrs. Apt. Owner of San Joaquin County, 1977. Mem. Nat. Apt. Assn. (state treas. women's div. 1977-79), Calif. Ret. Tchrs. Assn. Republican. Methodist. Lodge: Stockton Zonta. Home and Office: 2285 W Mendocino Ave Stockton CA 95204-4005

BLODGETT, FORREST CLINTON, economics educator; b. Oregon City, Oreg., Oct. 6, 1927; s. Clinton Alexander and Mabel (Wells) B.; m. Beverley Janice Buchholz, Dec. 21, 1946; children: Cherine Eiline Klein, Candis Melis, Clinton George BS, U. Omaha, 1961; MA, U. Mo., 1969; PhD, Portland State U., 1979. Joined C.E. U.S. Army, 1946, commd. 2d lt., 1946, advanced through grades to lt. col., 1965, ret., 1968, engring. assignments Japan, 1947-49, U.K., 1950-53, Korea, 1955-56, Alaska, 1958-60, Vietnam, 1963, staff engr. 2d Army Air Def. Region Mo., 1964-66; base engr. Def. Atomic Support Agy., Sandia Base, N.Mex., 1966-68; bus. mgr., trustee, asst. prof. econs. Linfield Coll., McMinnville, Oreg., 1968-73, assoc. prof., 1973-83, prof., 1983-90, emeritus prof. econs., 1990—; pres. Blodgett Enterprises, Inc., 1983-85; founder, dir. Valley Community Bank, 1980-86, vice chmn. bd. dirs., 1985-86. Commr., Housing Authority of Yamhill County (Oreg.), chmn., 1980-83; mem. Yamhill County Econ. Devel. Com., 1978-83; bd. dirs. Yamhill County Found., 1983-91, Oreg. Internat. Coun., 1995—. Decorated Army Commendation medal with oak leaf cluster; recipient Joint Service Commendation medal Dept. of Def. Mem. Soc. Am. Mil. Engrs. (pres. Albuquerque post 1968), Am. Econ. Assn., Western Econ. Assn. Internat., Nat. Ret. Officers Assn., Res. Officers Assn. (pres. Marion chpt. 1976), SAR (pres. Oreg. soc. 1985-86, v.p. gen. Nat. Soc. 1991-93), Urban Affairs Assn., Soc. for The History of Tech., Am. Law and Econs. Assn., Pi Sigma Epsilon, Pi Gamma Mu, Omicron Delta Epsilon (Pacific NW regional dir. 1978-88), Rotary (pres. McMinnville 1983-84). Republican. Episcopalian Office: Linfield Coll 1300 NE 16th Ave #1020 Portland OR 97232-1487

BLOEDE, VICTOR CARL, lawyer, academic executive; b. Woodwardville, Md., July 17, 1917; s. Carl Schon and Eleanor (Eck) B.; m. Ellen Louise Miller, May 9, 1947; children— Karl Abbott, Pamela Elena AB, Dartmouth Coll., 1940; JD cum laude, U. Md., Balt., 1950; LLM in Pub. Law, Georgetown U., 1967. Bar: Md. 1950, Fed. Hawaii 1958, U.S. Supreme Ct. 1971. Pvt. practice, Balt., 1950-64; mem. Goldman & Bloede, Balt., 1959-64; counsel Seven-Up Bottling Co., Balt., 1958-64; dep. atty. gen. Pacific Trust Ter., Honolulu, 1952-53; asst. solicitor for ters. Office of Solicitor, U.S. Dept. Interior, Washington, 1953-54; atty. U.S. Justice, Honolulu, 1955-58; assoc. gen. counsel Dept. Navy, Washington, 1960-61, 63-64; spl. legal cons. Md. Legislature, Legis. Council, 1963-64, 66-67; assoc. prof. U. Hawaii, 1961-63, dir. property mgmt., 1964-67; house counsel, dir. contracts and grants U. Hawaii System, 1967-82; house counsel U. Hawaii Research Corp., 1970-82; legal counsel Law of Sea Inst., 1978-82; legal cons. Rsch. Corp. and grad. rsch. divsn. U. Hawaii, 1982-92. Spl. counsel to Holifield Congl. Commn. on Govt. Procurement, 1970-73. Author: Hawaii Legislative Manual, 1962, Maori Affairs, New Zealand, 1964, Oceanographic Research Vessel Operations, and Liabilities, 1972, Hawaiian Archipelago, Legal Effects of a 200 Mile Territorial Sea, 1973, Copyright-Guidelines to the 1976 Act, 1977, Forms Manual, Inventions: Policy, Law and Procedure, 1982; writer, contbr. Coll. Law Digest and other publs. on legislation and pub. law. Mem. Gov.'s Task Force Hawaii and The Sea, 1969, Citizens Housing Com. Balt., 1952-64; bd. govs. Balt. Cmty. YMCA, 1954-64; bd. dirs. U. Hawaii Press, 1964-66, Coll. Housing Found., 1968-80; appointed to internat. rev. commn. Canada-France Hawaii Telescope Corp., 1973-82, chmn., 1973, 82; co-founder, incorporator First Unitarian Ch. Honolulu. Served to lt. comdr. USNR, 1942-45, PTO. Grantee ocean law studies NSF and NOAA, 1970-80. Mem. ABA, Balt. Bar Assn., Fed. Bar Assn., Am. Soc. Internat. Law, Nat. Assn. Univ. Attys. (founder & 1st chmn. patents & copyrights sect. 1974-76). Home: 635 Onaha St Honolulu HI 96816-4918

BLOEMBERGEN, NICOLAAS, physicist, educator; b. Dordrecht, The Netherlands, Mar. 11, 1920; came to U.S., 1952, naturalized, 1958; s. Auke and Sophia M. (Quint) B.; m. Huberta D. Brink, June 26, 1950; children: Antonia, Brink, Juliana. BA, Utrecht U., 1941, MA, 1943; PhD, Leiden U., 1948; MA (hon.), Harvard U., 1951; D of Sci. (hon.), Laval U., 1987, U. Conn., 1988, U. Hartford, 1991, Moscow State U., 1997, Harvard U., 2000; LHD (hon.), U. Mass., Lowell, 1994, U. Ctrl. Fla., , 1996, N.C. State U., 1998, Harvard U., 2000. Teaching asst. Utrecht U., 1942-45; research fellow Leiden U., 1948; mem. Soc. Fellows Harvard U., 1949-51, assoc. prof., 1951-57, Gordon McKay prof. applied physics, 1957—, Rumford prof. physics, 1974, Gerhard Gade univ. prof., 1980, prof. emeritus, 1990; prof. optics U. Ariz., 2001—. Vis. prof. U. Paris, 1957, U. Calif., 1965, Collège de France, Paris, 1980, U. Ariz., 2001—; Lorentz guest prof. U. Leiden, 1973; Raman vis. prof. Bangalore, India, 1979; Fairchild Disting. scholar Calif. Inst. Tech., 1984; von Humboldt Sr. Scientist, Munich, Fed. Republic Germany; hon. prof. Fudan U., Shanghai, People's Republic of China; Disting. Vis. Prof. CREOL, U. Ctrl. Fla., 1995. Author: Nuclear Magnetic Relaxation, 1948, Nonlinear Optics, 1965, Encounters in Magnetic Resonance, 1996, Encounters in Nonlinear Optics, 1996; also articles in profl. jours. Recipient Buckley prize for solid state physics Am. Phys. Soc., 1958, Dirac medal U. New South Wales (Australia), 1983, Stuart Ballantine medal Franklin Inst., 1961, Half Moon trophy Netherlands Club N.Y., 1972, Nat. medal of Sci., 1975, Lorentz medal Royal Dutch Acad., 1978, Frederic Ives medal Optical Soc. Am., 1979; von Humboldt sr. scientist award Munich, 1980, von Humboldt medal, 1989, Nobel prize in Physics, 1981; Guggenheim fellow, 1957. Fellow Am. Phys. Soc., Am. Acad. Arts and Scis., IEEE (Morris Liebmann award 1959, Medal of Honor 1983), Indian Acad. Scis. (hon.); mem. Optical Soc. Am. (hon.), Nat. Royal Dutch Acads. Scis., Nat. Acad. Engring., Am. Philos. Soc., Deutsche Akademie der Naturforscher Leopoldina, Koninklyke Nederlandse Akademie von Wetenschappen (corr.), Paris Acad. Scis. (fgn. assoc.), Royal Norwegian Soc. Scis. and Letters (fgn.). Office: Optical Scis Ctr Univ Ariz 1630 E Univ Blvd Tucson AZ 85721 E-mail: nbloembergen@optics.arizona.edu

BLOM, DANIEL CHARLES, lawyer, investor; b. Portland, Oreg., Dec. 13, 1919; s. Charles D. and Anna (Reiner) B.; m. Ellen Lavon Stewart, June 28, 1952; children: Daniel Stewart (dec.), Nicole Jan Heath. BA magna cum laude, U. Wash., 1941, postgrad., 1941-42; JD, Harvard U., 1948; postgrad., U. Paris, 1954-55. Bar: Wash. 1949, U.S. Supreme Ct. 1970. Tchg. fellow speech U. Wash., 1941-42; law clk. to justice Supreme Ct. Wash., 1948-49; since practiced in Seattle; assoc. Graves, Kizer & Graves, 1949-51; gen. counsel Northwestern Life Ins. Co., 1952-54; ptnr. Case & Blom, 1952-54; assoc., ptnr., of counsel Ryan, Swanson & Cleveland, 1956—; exec. v.p., gen. counsel Family Life Ins. Co., 1977-85, spl. counsel, 1985-91. Vice chmn. Wash. Bd. Bar Examiners, 1970-72, chmn., 1972-75; mem. industry adv. com. Nat. Assn. Ins. Commrs., 1966-68; pres. Wash. Ins. Coun,, 1971-73, gen. counsel, 1975-78; mediator Arbitration Forums, Inc. Editor Wash. State Bar Jour., 1951-52; assoc. editor The Brief, 1978-?; author: Life Insurance Law of the State of Washington, 1980, Banking and Insurance ... Surrender, 1985, Hostile Insurance Company Takeovers: New Frontier of the Law, 1990, Administrative Finality Under the Washington Insurance Code, 1991, Business and Professionalism, 1994, The Civility Problem, 1995, Technics and the Civilization of Law Practice, 1997, Varieties of Regulatory Experience, 1998. Chmn. jury selection Wash. Gov.'s Writer's Day Awards, 1976; bd. dirs. Crisis Clinic; trustee Bush Sch., 1971-79, v.p., 1976-77; trustee, v.p. Frye Mus., Seattle, 1976-82, World Affairs Coun. Seattle, 1972-94, Friends of Seattle Pub. Libr., 1982-87; bd. visitors U. Wash. Libr., 88-92, Friends of U. Wash. Librs., bd. dirs., 1991-95, pres., 1991-92. 2d lt. AUS, 1942-45, PTO. Decorated Bronze Star; Rhodes scholarship finalist, 1949. Fellow Am. Bar Found.; mem. ABA (vice chmn. com. on life ins. law, sect. tort and ins. practice 1971-76, chmn. 1976-78, sect. program chmn. 1978-79, mem. coun. 1979-83, chmn. pub. rels. com. 1981-83, chmn. com. on profl. independence of the lawyer 1984-85, chmn. com. on scope and correlation 1985-86, chmn. com. on handbook and bylaws 1987-88, chmn. hist. com. 1991-94, del. ABA to Union Internat. Des Avocats 1986-91, policy coord. tort and ins. practice sect. 1986-90), Wash. Bar Assn. (award of merit 1975, chmn. legal edn. liason com. 1977-78), Seattle Bar Assn., Union Internat. Des Avocats (v.p. 1987-92), N.Am. Found. for Internat. Legal Practice (dir. 1987-95, pres. 1987-89, chmn. 1990-95), Am. Judicature Soc., Assn. Life Ins. Counsel, Harvard Law Sch. Assn., Am. Coun. Life Ins. (legis. com. 1982-85), Am. Arbitration Assn., Found. UIA (coun. 1990-97), Fedn. Regulatory Counsel, (dir. 1995-97), Harvard Assn. Seattle and Western Wash. (trustee 1976-77), Rainier Club, Phi Beta Kappa, Tau Kappa Alpha. Home: 100 Ward St # 602-3 Seattle WA 98109-5613 Office: Ryan Swanson & Cleveland 1201 3rd Ave Ste 3400 Seattle WA 98101-3034 E-mail: blom@ryanlaw.com

BLOMDAHL, SONJA, artist; b. Waltham, Mass., Sept. 8, 1952; BFA, Mass. Coll. Art, 1974; postgrad., Orrefors Glass Skolen, Sweden, 1976. Owner, operator glass blowing studio, Seattle, 1983—. Bd. adv. Pratt Fine Arts Ctr., Seattle, 1991—; instr. Pilchuck Sch., Stanwood, 1985, Appalachian Ctr., Smithville, Tenn., 1986, Haystack Mountain Sch., Deer Isle, Maine, 1988, 92, 98; workshop leader Urban Glass, Bklyn., 1993. One-person shows include William Traver Gallery, Seattle, 1981-99, Mus. N.W. Art, LaConner, Wash., 1999, Butters Gallery, Portland, Oreg., 1998, R. Duane Reed Gallery, St. Louis, 1998, Gump's, San Francisco, 1997, Whatcom Co. Mus, Bellingham, Wash., 1992-95; exhibited in group shows King County Arts Commn., Seattle, 1993, Boston Mus. Fine Arts, 1997, Venezia Aperto Vetro, Venice, Italy, 1998, Holter Mus., Helena, Mont., 1999, Renwick Gallery, Nat. Mus. Am. Art, Smithsonian, Washington, 1999-2000, Fresno (Calif.) Art Mus., 2000, Ky. Art and Craft Gallery, Louisville, 2000, Koganezaki Glass Mus., Shizuoka, Japan, 2000; represented in mus. collections Am. Craft Mus., N.Y.C., Corning (N.Y.) Mus. Glass, Mus. Decorative Art, Prague, Czech Republic, Mus. Fine Arts, Boston, Renwick Gallery, Nat. Mus. Am. Arts, Smithsonian Instn., Washington, White House Collection of Am. Craft, Washington. Visual Artists Fellow grantee Nat. Endowment Arts, 1986, Artist's Trust Fellow grantee, 1987. Office: c/o William Traver Gallery 110 Union St Seattle WA 98101-2099

BLOOM, FLOYD ELLIOTT, physician, research scientist; b. Mpls., Oct. 8, 1936; s. Jack Aaron and Frieda (Shochman) B.; m. D'Nell Bingham, Aug. 30, 1956 (dec. May 1973); children: Fl'Nell, Evan Russell; m. Jody Patricia Corey, Aug. 9, 1980. AB cum laude, So. Meth. U., 1956; MD cum laude, Washington U., St. Louis, 1960; DSc (hon.), So. Meth. U., 1983, Hahnemann U., 1985, U. Rochester, 1985, Mt. Sinai U. Med. Sch., 1996, Thomas Jefferson U., 1997, Washington U., 1998. Intern Barnes Hosp., St. Louis, 1960-61, resident internal medicine, 1961-62; research asso. NIMH, Washington, 1962-64; fellow depts. pharmacology, psychiatry and anatomy Yale Sch. Medicine, 1964-66, asst. prof., 1966-67, asso. prof., 1968; chief lab. neuropharmacology NIMH, Washington, 1968-75, acting dir. div. spl. mental health, 1973-75; commd. officer USPHS, 1974-75; dir. Arthur Vining Davis Center for Behavioral Neurobiology; prof. Salk Inst., La Jolla, Calif., 1975-83; dir. div. preclin. neurosci. and endocrinology Scripps Rsch. Inst., La Jolla, 1983-89, chmn. dept. neuropharmacology, 1989—; editor in chief Science Magazine, 1995-2000; chief exec. officer Neurome, Inc., 2000—. Mem. Commn. on Alcoholism, 1980-81, Nat. Adv. Mental Health Coun., 1976-80; chmn. scientific adv. bd. Pharmavene, Inc., 1994-98; bd. dirs. Alkermes, Inc.; mem. sci. adv. bd. Neurocrine, Inc., 1993-2000, Neurobiol. Tech. Inc., 1994-98, Health Care Ventures, Inc., 1998-2000. Author: (with J.R. Cooper and R.H. Roth) Biochemical Basis of Neuropharmacology, 1971, 7th edit., 1996, (with Lazerson and Hofstadter) Brain, Mind and Behavior, 1984, (with Lazerson) 2d edit., 1988, (with C.A. Nelson) 3d edit., 2000, (with W. Young and Y. Kim) Brain browser, 1989; editor: Peptides: Integrators of Cell and Tissue Function, 1980, Progress in Brain Research, vol. 199, 1994, vol. 100, 1997, (with D.J. Kupfer) Neuro-Psychopharmacology: The Fourth Generation of Progress, 1994, Handbook of Chemical Neruoanatomy, 1997, The Primate Nervous System, 1997, vol. II, 1998, vol. III, 1999; co-editor: Regulatory Peptides, 1979-90, (with M. Randolph) Funding Health Sciences Research, 1990; assoc. editor: Biological Psychiatry, 1993-95; editor-in-chief Science, 1995-2000. Trustee Washington U., St. Louis, 1998—, chmn. nat. med. coun., 2000—. Recipient A. Cressy Morrison award N.Y. Acad. Scis., 1971, A.E. Bennett award for basic rsch. Soc. Biol. Psychiatry, 1971, Arthur A. Fleming award Science mag., 1973, Mathilde Solowey award, 1973, Biol. Sci. award Washington Acad. Scis., 1975, Alumni Achievement citation Washington U., 1980, McAlpin Rsch. Achievement award Mental Health Assn., 1980, Lectr.'s medal College de France, 1979, Steven Beering medal, 1985, Janssen award World Psychiat. Assn., 1989, Passerow Found. award, 1990, Herman von Helmholtz award, 1991, Pythagora award, 1994, Presdl. award Soc. for Neurosci., 1995, Golgi prize U. Brescia, 1996, Meritorious Achievement award Coun. Biology Editors, 1999, Gold medal Soc. Biol. Psychiatry, 1997, Disting. Svc. award Am. Psychiat. Assn., 2000; Disting. fellow Am. Psychiat. Assn., 1986; named scientist of the yr. Achievement Rewards for Coll. Scientists, 1996. Fellow AAAS (bd. dirs. 1986-90, pres.-elect 2001), Am. Coll. Neuropsychopharmacology (mem. coun. 1976-78, chmn. program com. 1987, pres. 1988-89, Hoch award 1998); mem. NAS (chmn. sect. neurobiology 1979-83), Inst. Medicine (mem. coun. 1986-89, 93-95), Am. Philos. Soc., Am. Acad. Arts and Scis., Soc. Neurosci. (sec. 1973-74, pres. 1976, chmn. publs. com. 1999—), Am. Soc. Pharmacology and Exptl. Therapeutics, Am. Soc. Cell Biology, Am. Physiol. Soc., Am. Assn. Anatomists, Rsch. Soc. Alcoholism (chmn. program com. 1985-87, pres.-elect 1989-91, pres. 1991-93), Swedish Acad. Sci. (fgn. assoc. 1989). Home: 628 Pacific View Dr San Diego CA 92109-1768 Office: The Scripps Rsch Inst 10550 N Torrey Pines Rd La Jolla CA 92037-1000 E-mail: fbloom@scripps.edu

BLOOM, GARY L. database company executive; BS in Computer Sci., Calif. Poly. State U., San Luis Obispo. Various tech. positions IBM Corp., Chevron Corp.; various positions Oracle Corp., Redwood Shores, Calif., 1986—, sr. v.p. woldwide alliances and techs. divsn., sr. v.p. product and platform techs. divsn., v.p. mainframe and integration tech. divsn., v.p. massively parallel computing divsn., exec. v.p. Mem. exec. mgmt. com., mgmt. com., product devel. mgmt. com.; bd. dirs. Virata Corp., Oracle Japan. Office: Oracle Corp World Hdqs 500 Oracle Pkwy Redwood City CA 94065-1675

BLOOM, JACOB A. lawyer; b. Bklyn., Apr. 10, 1942; BA, Columbia U., 1963, LLB, 1966. Bar: Calif. 1968. Sr. ptnr. Bloom, Hergott, Diemer & Cook LLP, Beverly Hills, Calif. Champion Mast Ct. Off... Bloom Hergott Diemer & Cook LLP 150 S Rodeo Dr Fl 3 Beverly Hills CA 90212-2410

BLOOM, JOSEPH D. medical educator, psychiatrist; MD, Albert Einstein Coll. Medicine. Diplomate in psychiatry and in forensic psychiatry Am. Bd. Psychiatry and Neurology. Intern Mt. Zion Hosp. and Med. Ctr., San Francisco; resident in psychiatry Harvard U.; chief psychiat. resident Southard Clinic Mass. Mental Health Ctr.; chief mental health unit Alaska Native Health Svc. USPHS; pvt. practice Anchorage; dir. cmty. psychiatry tng. program Oreg. Health Sci. U., Portland, 1977, chmn. dept. psychiatry, 1986-94, interim dean Sch. Medicine, 1993-94, dean Sch. Medicine, 1994-2001. Office: Oreg Health Scis U Sch Medicine 3181 SW Sam Jackson Park Rd Portland OR 97201-3011 E-mail: bloomj@ohsu.edu

BLOOM, JULIAN, artist, editor; b. Cleve., May 6, 1933; s. John Bernard and Lillian Judith (Finkel) B.; m. Shirley Ann Harper, Nov. 29, 1954; children: Sandra Layne Walker, Andrea Sue Wells. AA, Cypress Coll., 1972; student, U. LaVerne (Calif.), 1983-86. Lab tech. Harvey Aluminum, Torrance, Calif., 1956-64, foreman, 1964-66; sr. draftsman Northrop Corp., Anaheim, 1966-67; designer Northrop Aircraft, Anaheim, 1967-69, facilities engr., 1969-81, design to corp. cost designer, 1982-84, mfg. engring. mgr., 1984-85, mfg. mgr., 1985-92; artist, owner Realistic Watercolors, Cypress, 1992—. Instr. watercolor Huntington Beach Art Ctr., 1997—, City of Cypress, 1998—. Featured in The Best of Watercolor, 1995; columnist Event Newspapers, 1998—. Co-chmn. Cypress (Calif.) Cultural Arts Planning Com., 1993-95; pres. Cypress Art Art League, 1993-96; commr. Cypress Cultural Arts, 1999—. Served with U.S. Army, 1954-56. Fellow Am. Artists Profl. League (Signature award 1993); mem. Nat. Watercolor Soc. (assoc. mem. 1989—, editor newsletter 1994-97), Watercolor West (bd. dirs. 1999—), Am. Soc. Marine Artists (artist mem., Signature award 2000). Republican. Jewish. Avocations: travel, computers, photography. Home and Office: 4522 Cathy Ave Cypress CA 90630-4212 E-mail: h2optr@hotmail.com

BLOOM, MYER, physicist, educator; b. Montreal, Que., Can., Dec. 7, 1928; s. Israel and Leah (Ram) B.; m. Margaret Holmes, May 29, 1954; children— David, Margot. B.Sc., McGill U., 1949, M.Sc., 1950; Ph.D., U. Ill., 1954; D (hon.), Tech. U. Denmark, 1994; DSc (hon.), U. B.C., 2000. Research fellow U. Leiden, 1954-56; faculty U. B.C., Vancouver, 1956—, assoc. prof., 1960-63, prof. physics, 1963-93; D (hon.) Concordia U., 1995. Recipient Steacie prize, 1967, Jacob Biely prize, 1968, Gold medal Can. Assn. Physicists, 1973, Sci. Coun. of B.C. Chmn.'s award for career achievement, 1992, Izaak Walton Killam Meml. prize in natural sci., 1995; Alfred P. Sloan fellow, 1961-65; John Simon Guggenheim fellow, 1964-65; Izaak Walton Killam Meml. scholar, 1978-79. Fellow Royal Soc. Can., Am. Phys. Soc., Can. Inst. for Advanced Rsch. Achievements include research in structure and molecular motion in biological and model membranes, nuclear magnetic resonance. Home: 5669 King's Rd Vancouver BC Canada V6T 1K9

BLOOM, STEPHEN MICHAEL, magistrate judge, lawyer; b. San Francisco, June 10, 1948; s. Alan I. and Wilma (Morgan) B.; m. Rebecca J. Nelson, June 19, 1976; children: Benjamin Jacob, Molly Marie, John Robert. Student, Dartmouth Coll., 1966-68; BA in English, Stanford U., 1970; student, Calif. State U., Sacramento, 1973-74; JD, Willamette Coll. Law, 1977. Bar: Oreg. 1977, U.S. Dist. Ct. Oreg. 1979. Adminstrv. asst. Calif. Dept. Edn., Sacramento, 1973-74; atty. Joyce & Harding, Corvallis, Oreg., 1977-78; dep. dist. atty. Umatilla County, Pendleton, 1978-79; atty. Morrison & Reynolds, Hermiston, 1979-81, Kottkamp & O'Rourke, Pendleton, 1981—. Appointed U.S. magistrate, 1988. Bd. dirs. Edn. Svc. Dist., Pendleton, 1982-89. Lt. (j.g.) USN, 1970-72. Mem. ABA, Oreg. Bar Assn., Rotary (pres. 1990-91, bd. dirs. 1991). Avocation: sailing. Office: US Dist Ct PO Box 490 Pendleton OR 97801-0490 also: Kottkamp & O'Rourke 331 SE 2nd St Pendleton OR 97801-2224

BLOOMBERG, STU, broadcast executive; Chmn. ABC Entertainment, co-chmn. Office: ABC Inc Exec Ste 2040 Avenue Of The Stars Los Angeles CA 90067-4785

BLOOMFIELD, ARTHUR JOHN, music critic, food writer; b. San Francisco, Jan. 3, 1931; s. Arthur L. and Julia (Mayer) B.; m. Anne Buenger, July 14, 1956; children: John, Cecily, Alison. AB, Stanford U., 1951. Music and art critic San Francisco Call-Bull., 1958-59, San Francisco News Call-Bull., 1962-65; co-music and art critic San Francisco Examiner, 1965-79; corr. Mus. Am. mag., 1958-61, 63-64, Opera mag., 1964-89; restaurant critic Focus mag., San Francisco, 1979-83; program note writer Mus. and Arts Records, 1996—. Author: The San Francisco Opera, 1923-61, 61, Fifty Years of the San Francisco Opera, 1972, Guide to San Francisco Restaurants, 1975, The San Francisco Opera 1922-78, 1978, Arthur Bloomfield's Restaurant Book, 1987. With AUS, 1953-55. Home: 2229 Webster St San Francisco CA 94115-1820

BLOYD, STEPHEN ROY, environmental manager, educator, consultant; b. Alameda, Calif., Aug. 17, 1953; s. William Allen and Alice Louella (Scott) B. Grad. high sch., Reedley, Calif., 1971. Cert. environ. mgr., Nev.; registered hazardous substances specialist. Reagent tech. Tenneco Corp., Gold Hill, Nev., 1982; environ. tech. Pierson Environ. Drilling, Modesto, Calif., 1982-84; pres. Bloyd and Assocs., Dayton, Nev., 1986—. Author: Hazardous Waste Site Operations for General Site Workers, 1992; editor: (newsletter) Pumper, 1991. Firefighter Dayton Vol. Fire Dept., 1975, capt., 1976-78, chief, 1978-83, tng. officer, 1984-96; mem. Silver City (Nev.) Fire Dept., 1996—; coord. Ctrl. Lyon County Hazardous Materials, 1997—; asst. prof. Dodd/Beals Fire Protection Tng. Acad. U. Nev., Reno, 1990-96; instr. chemistry hazardous materials Nat. Fire Acad., Emmitsburg, Md., 1989—, instr. hazardous materials incident mgmt., 1996—; mem. bylaw com. Dayton Regional Adv. Coun., 1989; instr. Emergency Response to Terrorism, 1998—; tech. assistance team mem. Fed. Emergency Mgmt. Agy. Comprehensive Hazardous Materials Emergency Response Capability Assessment Project, 2000—. Named Firefighter of Yr., City of Dayton, 1992. Mem. NRA, Nat. Environ. Tng. Assn., Nat. Environ. Health Assn., Nev. State Firemen's Assn. (1st v.p. 1992-93, 2d v.p. 1991-92, pres. 1993-94, chmn. hazardous materials com. 1987-93, legis. com. 1991, bylaws com. 1986), Nev. Fire Chief's Assn., Internat. Platform Assn., Soc. Nat. Fire Acad. Instrs. Libertarian. Avocations: fishing, motorcycles, firearms, camping, reading. Office: PO Box 113 Silver City NV 89428-0113 E-mail: hazmatpro@hotmail.com

BLUESTONE, DAVID ALLAN, pediatrician; b. Pitts., Apr. 9, 1938; s. Sam Bluestone and Sarah Cohen Sager; m. Joan Sidlow, Oct. 12, 1957 (div. 1980); children: Daniel, Bradley, Deborah; m. Leslie Florence Widson Kaplan, May 26m 1983. BA, Hamilton Coll., 1959; MD, U. Pitts., 1963. Diplomate Am. Bd. Pediatrics. Pediatric intern Health Ctr. Hosps. U. Pitts., 1963-64; pediatric resident Children's Hosp., Pitts., 1964-65, L.A., 1967-68; pediatrician Med. Arts Pediatric Med. Group, Inc., L.A., 1968—. Lt. Med. Corps USNR, 1965-67. Fellow Am. Acad. Pediat.; mem. AMA, Calif. Med. Assn., Los Angeles County Med. Assn., L.A. Pediatric Soc., Phi Delta Epsilon (pres. L.A. Grad. Club 1982-83, assoc. regional gov. 1994—), Zeta Phi. Avocations: travel, photography. Office: Med Arts Pediatric Med Group Inc 6221 Wilshire Blvd Ste 215 Los Angeles CA 90048-5201

BLUM, GERALD HENRY, department store executive; b. San Francisco, 1926; s. Abe and Mildred (Loewenthal) B.; children: Shelley, Todd, Ryan, Derek. A.B., Stanford U., 1950. Mdse. trainee Emporium, San Francisco, 1950-51; with Gottschalks Inc. (formerly E. Gottschalk & Co., Inc.), Fresno, Calif., 1951-98, v.p., 1954-63, exec. v.p., 1963-82, pres., sec., 1982-94, ret., 1998, also vice chmn. bd. dirs. Bd. dirs. Fresno Conv. Bur., 1954—, pres., 1985-87; bd. dirs. Better Bus. Bur., Fresno, 1954-77, Blue Cross, Calif. 1972-85; chmn. C.A.R.E., Fresno County, 1957—, Eagle Scout Awards Banquet, 1993, Calif. State U. Bus. Coun., Fresno, 1997-98; mem. adv. com. Fresno County Arts Ctr., 1982-85, bd. dirs., 1958-66, v.p. 1961, 88-94; mem. Area VII Calif. Vocat. Edn. Com., 1972-75, Mayor's Bi-Racial Com., 1968-69; founding v.p. Jr. Achievement, Fresno County, 1957-63; bd. dirs. Fresno Boys Club, 1958-62, Central Calif. Employers Coun., 1956-62, treas. 1958; bd. dirs. Fresno Philharm. Orch., 1954-58, Salvation Army, Fresno, 1956-67, Youth Edn. Svc., 1956-57, Fresno County Taxpayers Assn., 1954, San Joaquin Valley Econ. Edn. Project, 1953; bd. dirs., bus. adv. coun. Fresno City Coll., 1955-57; trustee Valley Children's Hosp., 1955-57, United Crusade, Fresno, 1952-62; mem. adv. bd. Liberty Mut. Ins. Co., 1990— Recipient Disting. Svc. award Fresno Jaycees, 1959; winner World's Championship Domino Tournament, 1969, 86, 88. Mem. Nat. Retail Fedn. (dir. 1978-94), Calif. Retailers Assn. (dir. 1964-94), Fresno C. of C. (dir. county, city 1955-57, Boss of Yr., Jr. C. of C. 1980), Retail Mmgt. Inst., U. Santa Clara (dir. 1986-98), Nat. Secs. Assn. (Boss of Yr. 1978), Fresno County Stanford U. Alumni Assn. (pres. 1952), Pres. Club of Calif. State U., Rotary (v.p. Fresno club 1962). Clubs: Univ. Sequoia Sunnyside, San Joaquin Country, Downtown Club (Fresno) (pres. 1978). Office: Blum Consulting 9 River Park Pl E Ste 380 Fresno CA 93720-1530 E-mail: gblum2020@aol.com

BLUM, RICHARD HOSMER ADAMS, educator, writer; b. Ft. Wayne, Ind., Oct. 7, 1927; s. Hosmer and Imogene (Heino) B. A.B. with honors magna cum laude, San Jose State Coll., 1949; Ph.D., Stanford U., 1951. Research dir. Calif. Med. Assn., San Francisco, 1956-58, San Mateo County (Calif.) Mental Health Service, San Mateo, 1958-60; lectr. Sch. Criminology, U. Calif., Berkeley, 1960-62; mem. faculty Stanford (Calif.) U., 1962-78, prof. dept. psychology, 1970-75, prof. dept. gynecology and obstetrics, 1982-97; mem. faculty Stanford (Calif.) U. Law Sch., 1975-78; chmn. bd. Am. Lives Endowment, Portola Valley, Calif., 1979—. Chmn. Intern. Rsch. Group on Drug Legis. and Programs, Geneva, 1969-78; pres. Bio-Behavioral Rsch. Group, Inc., Palo Alto, 1964-87; owner/operator Shingle Mill Ranch, 1964—; vis. fellow Wolfson Coll. U. Cambridge, 1984; vis. prof. social and polit. sci. U. Cambridge, 1997-98; dir. ethics program World Jurist Assn./World Peace Through Law Ctr., Washington, 2000—. Author 22 books in field of health, criminology, public policy, psychology; author 9 books of fiction. Served in U.S. Army, 1951-53, Korea. Fellow APHA, AAAS, APA, Am. Psychol. Soc., Am. Sociol. Assn., Soc. Advanced Legal Studies (hon., life); mem. Archaeol. Inst. Am., Sigma Xi, Cosmos Club, Athenaeum Club, San Francisco Univ. Club. Unitarian. Home and Office: PO Box 620482 Woodside CA 94062-0482

BLUMBERG, GRACE GANZ, law educator, lawyer; b. N.Y.C., Feb. 16, 1940; d. Samuel and Beatrice (Finkelstein) Ganz; m. Donald R. Blumberg, Sept. 9, 1959; 1 dau., Rachel. B.A. cum laude, U. Colo., 1960; J.D. summa cum laude, SUNY, 1971; LL.M., Harvard U., 1974. Bar: N.Y. 1971, Calif. 1989. Confidential law clk. Appellate Div., Supreme Ct., 4th Dept., Rochester, N.Y., 1971-72; teaching fellow Harvard Law Sch., Cambridge, Mass., 1972-74; prof. law SUNY, Buffalo, 1974-81, UCLA, 1981—. Reporter Am. Law Inst., Prins. of the Law of Family Dissolution. Author: Community Property in California, 1987, rev. edit., 1999, Blumberg's California Family Code Annotated (ann.); contbr. articles to profl. jours. Office: UCLA Sch Law Box 951476 Los Angeles CA 90095-1476

BLUMBERG, MARK STUART, health services consultant; b. N.Y.C., Nov. 16, 1924; s. Sydney N. and Mollie (Leshrowitz) B.; m. Luba Monasevitch, 1952; children: Bart David, Eve Luise; m. 2d Elizabeth R. Conner, 1974. Student, Johns Hopkins U., 1942-43, Harvard U., 1943-44, D.M.D., 1948, M.D., 1950, student Sch. Public Health, 1955. Intern, children's med. service Bellevue Hosp., N.Y.C., 1950-51; ops. analyst Johns Hopkins U. Ops. Research Office, Chevy Chase, Md., 1951-54; exchange analyst Army Ops. Research Group (U.K.), West Byfleet, Eng., 1953-54; staff Occupational Health Program, USPHS, Washington, 1954-56; asso. ops. analyst to dir. health econs. program Stanford (Calif.) Research Inst., 1956-66; asst. to v.p. adminstrn. to dir. health planning, office of the pres. U. Calif., Berkeley, 1966-70; corp. planning advisor to dir. spl. studies Kaiser Found. Health Plan, Inc., Oakland, Calif., 1970-94; dir. Kaiser Found. Health Plan of Conn., Hartford, 1982-94, Kaiser Found. Health Plan Mass., 1987-94; cons. risk adjusted measures Oakland, 1994—; co-founder, v.p. R&D TruRisk, 1998—. Various times cons. Pan Am. Health Orgn., Calif. State Dept. Mental Hygiene, Carnegie Commn. on Higher Edn., various agys. HHS. Contbr. writings to profl. publs. Vol. Grenfell Med. Mission, Harrington Harbour, Que., Can., summer 1948; mem. tech. adv. com. AD 524 State of Calif., 1992—. Served with USNR, 1943-45; with USPHS, 1954-56. Mem. Ops. Research Soc. Am. (past mem. council, Health Applications sect.), Hosp. Mgmt. Systems Soc. (charter), Inst. of Medicine of Nat. Acad. Scis.

BLUMBERG, NATHAN(IEL) BERNARD, journalist, educator, writer and publisher; b. Denver, Apr. 8, 1922; s. Abraham Moses and Jeannette Blumberg; m. Lynne Stout, June 1946 (div. Feb. 1970); children: Janet Leslie, Jenifer Lyn, Josephine Laura; m. Barbara Farquhar, July 1973. B.A., U. Colo., 1947, M.A., 1948; D.Phil. (Rhodes scholar), Oxford (Eng.) U., 1950. Reporter Denver Post, 1947-48; assoc. editor Lincoln (Nebr.) Star, 1950-53; asst. to editor Ashland (Nebr.) Gazette, 1954-55; asst. city editor Washington Post and Times Herald, 1956; from asst. prof. to assoc. prof. journalism U. Nebr., 1950-55; asso. prof. journalism Mich. State U., 1955-56; dean, prof. Sch. Journalism, U. Mont., 1956-68, prof. journalism, 1968-78, prof. emeritus, 1978—; pub. Wood FIRE Ashes Press, 1981—. Vis. prof. Pa. State U., 1964, Northwestern U., 1966-67, U. Calif., Berkeley, 1970; Dept. State specialist in Thailand, 1961, in Trinidad, Guyana, Surinam and Jamaica, 1964 Author: One-Party Press?, 1954; The Afternoon of March 30: A Contemporary Historical Novel, 1984, also articles in mags. and jours.; co-editor: A Century of Montana Journalism, 1971; editor: The Mansfield Lectures in International Relations, Vols. I and II, 1979; founder: Mont. Journalism Rev, 1958—; editor, pub. Treasure State Rev., 1991—. Served with arty. U.S. Army, 1943-46. Bronze Star medal. Mem. Assn. Am. Rhodes Scholars, Brasenose Soc., Kappa Tau Alpha (nat. pres. 1969-70). Home: PO Box 99 Bigfork MT 59911-0099

BLUMENAUER, EARL, congressman; b. Portland, Oreg., Aug. 16, 1948; BA, Lewis and Clark Coll., 1970, JD, 1976. Asst. to pres. Portland State U., 1971-73; mem. Oreg. Ho. of Reps., 1973-79, Multnomah County Bd. Commrs., Portland, 1979-87; commr. Portland City Coun., 1987-96; mem. U.S. Congress from 3d Oreg. dist., 1996—; mem. transp. and infrastructure com., internat. rels. com. Avocations: bicycling, running. Office: US House of Reps 1406 Longworth Ho Office Bldg Washington DC 20515-0001 also: 516 SE Morrison St Ste 250 Portland OR 97214-2342*

BLUMENFELD, CHARLES RABAN, lawyer; b. Seattle, May 24, 1944; s. Irwin S. and Freda I. (Raban) B.; m. Karla Axell; children: David, Lisa. BA, U. Wash., JD, 1969. Bar: Wash. 1969, U.S. Dist. Ct. (we. dist.) Wash. 1969, U.S. Ct. Appeals (9th cir.) 1975, U.S. Supreme Ct. 1979, U.S. Dist. Ct. D.C. 1981, U.S. Ct. Appeals (D.C. cir.) 1981. Legis. counsel U.S. Senator Henry M. Jackson, Washington, 1969-72; ptnr. Bogle & Gates, Seattle, 1973-99, PerkinsCoie, Seattle, 1999—. Mem. ABA (sect. natural resources, energy and environment). Office: PerkinsCoie 1201 3rd Ave Fl 48 Seattle WA 98101-3029

BLUMER, HARRY MAYNARD, architect; b. Stillwater, Okla., Aug. 27, 1930; s. Harry H. and Nona A. (Fitzpatrick) B.; m. C. Sue Linebaugh, Sept. 2, 1952; children: Eric W., Laura B., Martha L. BArch, Okla. State U., 1953; BS in Bus., Ariz. State U., 1976. Registered arch., Ariz., landscape arch., Ariz., arch., U.S. Govt.; cert. constrn. specifier, fallout shelter analyst, U.S. Dept. Def. Designer, draftsman Norman Byrd Architect, Oklahoma City, 1952, Overend & Boucher Architects, Wichita, Kans., 1953-54; archtl. designer, draftsman Louis G. Hesselden Architect, Albuquerque, 1956; project designer, planner, constrn. & contract adminstr. Flatow, Moore, Bryan & Fairburn Architects, Albuquerque, 1956-61; regional architect U.S. Forest Svc., Albuquerque, 1961-62; v.p. prodn. Guirey, Srnka, Arnold & Sprinkle, Phoenix, 1962-82; prin. arch. H. Maynard Blumer, FAIA, FCSI, Consulting Arch., Scottsdale, Ariz., 1982—. Lectr. architecture Ariz. State U., Tempe, 1968-69; rep. specifications consulting projects for various stuctures including Chandler Med. Office bldg., 1982, Ariz. State U. w. campus utility tunnel, 1986, Mayo Clinic consourse and parking structure, 1993, City of Tempe, Ariz. Comm. Tech. Ctr., 1997, numerous others; speaker in field. Contbr. articles to profl. publs. Bd. dirs., camping com., camp master plan design Maricopa County Coun. Campfire Girls, 1962-69; pres. N.Mex. Cactus and Succulent Soc., 1959-60; sec. Advancement Mgmt., Phoenix, 1972-73, dir., 1971-72; bd. govs. Amateur Athletic Union U.S., 1972-75, chmn. nat. conv. registration com., 1975; v.p. Ariz. Assn. Bd. MGrs., 1972-73, pres., 1973; treas. Pop Warner Football Assn., 1975; pres. parents club Scottsdale YMCA Judo Club, 1970-80; chairperson materials testing lab. citizens' rev. com. City of Phoenix, 1978, mem. arch. selection com., 1990, constrn. mediation panelist, 1995; commr. planning and zoning commn. Town of Paradise Valley, Ariz., 1994-97, mem. Hillside blding. rev. com. rotation, 1994—, mem. spl. use permit rev. com. rotation, 1994—; . 1st lt. U.S. Army Corps Engrs., 1954-56, Korea. Recipient Valley Beautiful Citizens Coun. Cmty. Recognition award 1964, 68, Outstanding Use Masonry award, Ariz. Masonry Guild, 1968, Ariz. Aggregate Assn. Spl. Recognition award, 1986, Edn. Commendation award Constrn. Specifications Inst., 1980. Fellow AIA (Honor award Ctrl. Ariz. chpt. 1967, Oustanding Svc. to Profession award 1986), Constrn. Specification Inst. (Phoenix chpt., mem. chpt. fellows com. 1973—, round-table chair, moderator 1981—, Pres.'s Disting. Svc. cert. 1968, Disting. Leadership plaque Phoenix chpt. 1968, Oustanding Profl. Mem. award, 1981, Pres.'s cert. Appreciation 1985, numerous others); mem. ASTM. Office: 8517 N 49th St Paradise Valley AZ 85253-2002

BLUNK, FORREST STEWART, lawyer; b. Doniphan, Mo., July 22, 1913; s. Forest Stanley and Margaret Anna (Stewart) B.; m. Mary Williams, July 10, 1971; children— Scott Stewart, Sally Jo. B.A., U. Mo., 1936; J.D., U. Wyo., 1940. Bar: Ill. bar 1946, Colo. bar 1953. Asso. firm Vogel & Bunge, Chgo., 1946-50; assoc. January & Yegge, Denver, 1953-55; ptnr. Blunk and Johnson, Denver, 1955—. Pres., dir. Williams Land & Livestock Co., Tie Siding, Wyo. Served with AUS, 1941-46, ETO. Mem. Fed., Am., Ill., Wyo., Colo., 5th Dist., 10th Circuit bar assns., Colo. Def. Bar Assn. (pres. 1969-70), Lawyer-Pilots Bar Assn., Internat. Assn. Ins. Counsel, Denver Bar, Am. Bd. Trial Advs. (pres. Colo. chpt. 1974-75, nat. sec. 1975-76), Legal Club Chgo. Republican. Clubs: Masons, Elks, Rotary, Ft. Collins Country, Denver Athletic. Home: 1829 Elim Ct Fort Collins CO 80524-2205 Office: 2696 S Colorado Blvd Ste 595 Denver CO 80222-5944

BOADO, RUBEN JOSE, biochemist; b. Buenos Aires, Argentina, Feb. 8, 1955; came to U.S., 1985; s. Osvaldo Ruben and Lucia B.; m. Adriana Graciela Swiecicki, Jan. 11, 1980; children: Augusto Ruben, Lucrecia Adriana. MS, U. Buenos Aires, 1979, Diploma in Biochemistry, 1980, PhD, 1982. Rsch. fellow endocrinology Nat. Coun. Scientific Rsch., Buenos Aires, 1979-81, postdoctoral rsch. fellow in endocrinology, 1981-83, established investigator, 1983-89; internat. fellow UCLA Sch. Medicine, 1985-88, asst. rsch. endocrinologist, 1988-91, asst. prof. medicine, 1991-97, assoc. prof. medicine, 1997-2000, prof. medicine, 2000—. Author numerous scientific publs. Recipient Best Scientific Paper award Internat. Assn. Radiopharmacology, Chgo., 1981, Cross-Town Endocrine Soc., L.A., 1988. Mem. AAAS, European Neurosci. Assn., Argentine Soc. Clin. Rsch., Am. Thyroid Assn. (travel award 1987), Endocrine Soc. (travel award 1984), Brain Rsch. Inst., Soc. Neurosci., Controlled Release Soc. Inc. Achievements include European patent in field. Office: UCLA Dept Medicine/Endocrin Rsch Labs C-Lot Rm 104 Los Angeles CA 90024-1682

BOAL, DEAN, retired arts center administrator, educator; b. Longmont, Colo., Oct. 20, 1931; s. Elmer C. and L. Mildred (Snodgrass) B.; m. Ellen Christine TeSelle, Aug. 23, 1957; children: Brett, Jed. B.Music, B.Music Edn., U. Colo., 1953; M.Music, Ind. U., 1956; D. Musical Arts, U. Colo., 1959. Mem. faculty Hastings (Nebr.) Coll., 1958-60; head piano dept. Bradley U., Peoria, Ill., 1960-66; dean, pianist Peabody Conservatory, Balt., 1966-70; prof. piano, chair music SUNY, Fredonia, 1970-73; pres. St. Louis Conservatory, 1973-76; dir. radio sta. KWMU, St. Louis, 1976-78; v.p., gen. mgr. Sta. WETA-FM, Washington, 1978-83; dir. arts and performance programs Nat. Pub. Radio, Washington, 1982-89; pres. Interlochen (Mich.) Ctr. for the Arts, 1989-95; pres. emeritus, 1995—. Author: Concepts and Skills for the Piano, Book I, 1969, Book II, 1970, Interlochen: A Home for The Arts, 1998; contbr. articles to profl. jours. Mem. adv. bd U. Colo. Coll. Music, 1987-2000; trustee Alma Coll., 1992-95; bd. dirs., chmn. Peak Assn. of the Arts, 1998-2000. Served with U.S. Army, 1953-55. Woodrow Wilson teaching fellow, 1983-89; recipient Disting. Alumnus award in Profl. Music Univ. Colo., 1987. Mem. Eastern Public Radio Network (chmn. 1979-82), Coll. Music Soc., Pi Kappa Lambda, Mu Phi Epsilon, Phi Mu Alpha. Presbyterian.

BOARDMAN, DAVID, newspaper editor; m. Barbara Winslow; children: Emily, Madeline. BS in Journalism, Northwestern U., 1979; M in Comm., U. Wash., 1983. Copy editor Football Weekly, Chgo., 1977-79; reporter Anacortes (Wash.) American, 1979-80, Skagit Valley Herald, Mt. Vernon, Wash., 1980-81; reporter, copy editor The News Tribune, Tacoma, 1981-83; copy editor The Seattle Times, 1983, editor, reporter, 1984, nat. editor, 1984-86, local news editor, 1986-87, asst. city editor, 1987-90, regional editor, 1990-96, metro. editor, 1997—, asst. mng. editor, 1997—. Vis. faculty Poynter Inst. Media Studies, St. Petersburg, Fla. Recipient Goldsmith Prize in Investigative Reporting JFK Sch. Govt. Harvard U., 1993, Worth Bingham prize, 1993, Investigative Reporters and Editors award, 1993, AP Mng. Editors Pub. Svc. award, 1992, 1st place nat. reporting Pulitzer Prize, 1990, lead editor Pulitzer Prize in investigative reporting, 1997; finalist Pulitzer Prize, 1993, 98, 99; juror Pulitzer Prizes, 1999-2000; fellow Japan-IBCC fellowship Ctr. Fgn. Journalists, 1995. Office: The Seattle Times PO Box 70 1120 John St Seattle WA 98109-5321 E-mail: dboardman@seattletimes.com

BOATRIGHT, CLYDE A. state legislator; b. Manzinolla, Colo., July 7, 1930; m. Karen Boatright. Student, U. Alaska. Enlisted USN, 1947, ret., 1967; realtor; mem. Idaho Senate, Dist. 2, Boise, 1994—. Mem. joint fin. and transp. coms., Idaho Senate. Former chair, bd dirs., North Idaho Fair. Mem. Shriners, Masons, Rathdrum (Idaho) C. of C., Coeur d'Alene (Idaho) C. of C. Republican. Office: State Capitol 700 W Jefferson St Boise ID 83720-0001

BOBEK, NICOLE, professional figure skater; b. Chgo., Aug. 23, 1977; Competitive history includes: mem. of 1st place team Hershey's Kisses Challenge, 1997, placed 13th in World Championships, 1997, 3rd in Nat. Sr., 1997, 2nd (team) U.S. Postal Svc. Challenge, 1996, 3rd (team) Hershey's Kisses Challenge, 1996, 10th place Centennial on Ice, 1996, 1st place Starlight Challenge, 1995, 3rd in World Championships, 1995, 1st in Nat. Sr., 1995, numerous others. Avocations: dancing, drawing, writing poetry, modeling, designing clothes. Office: USFSA 20 1st St Colorado Springs CO 80906-3624

BOBEL, MARY, video development company financial executive; Various financial positions Advanced Micro Devices, 1981-90; v.p., corp. contr. Adobe Sys., 1990-94; v.p., CFO, Ednl. Pub. Corp., 1994-96; exec. v.p., CFO, Genus, Inc., semicondr. mfrs., 1997-98; CFO, Digital Origin Inc., developer digital video, Mountain View, Calif., 1999—. Office: Digital Origin Inc 460 E Middlefield Rd Mountain View CA 94043-4037

BOBISUD, LARRY EUGENE, mathematics educator; b. Midvale, Idaho, Mar. 16, 1940; s. Walter and Ida V. (Bitner) B.; m. Helen M. Meyer, June 15, 1963. B.S., Coll. of Ida., 1961; M.A., U. N.M., 1963, Ph.D., 1966. Vis. mem. Courant Inst. Math. Scis. NYU, N.Y.C., 1966-67; prof. math. U. Idaho, Moscow, 1967—. Contbr. articles to profl. jours. Mem. Am. Math. Soc. Home: 860 N Eisenhower St Moscow ID 83843-9581 Office: Univ Idaho Dept Math Moscow ID 83844-1103 E-mail: bobisud@uidaho.edu

BOBRICK, STEVEN AARON, marketing executive; b. Denver, Apr. 11, 1950; s. Samuel Michael and Selma Gertrude (Birnbaum) B.; m. Maria Diane Boltz, Oct. 5, 1980. Attended, U. Colo., 1968-72. Registered apt. mgr. Owner Bobrick Constrn., Denver, 1969-72; with Bell Mtn. Sports, Aspen, Colo., 1972-75; mgr. Compass Imports, Denver, 1975-80, Aurora (Colo.) Bullion Exch., 1980-81; contr. Bobrick Constrn., Aurora, 1981-85; appraiser Aurora, 1985—; property mgr. Aurora (Colo) Cmty. Mental Health, 1989-98, active real estate and constrn., facilities mgr., 1989-98; exec. mgmt. asst. E-470 Pub. Hwy. Authority, 1998, mktg./pub. rels. web master, 1998-99; bus. mgr. Northwest Pkwy Pub. Hwy. Authority, 1999—. Co-author: Are You Paying Too Much in Property Taxes, 1990. Coun. mem. City of Aurora, 1981-89; chmn. Explore Commercial Opportunities, Aurora, 1986-89, bd. dirs.; bd. dirs. Adam County Econ. Devel. Commn., Northglenn, Colo., 1985-89; vice chair Aurora Urban Renewal Authority, 1982-89; chmn. Aurora Enterprise Zone Found., 1991-94; bd. dirs. Aurora Community Med. Clinic, 1987-88, Aurora Cmty. Mental Health Ctr., 2001. Avocations: sking, mountain biking, exercise. Office: 555 Eldorado Blvd 130 Broomfield CO 80021

BOBROW, MICHAEL LAWRENCE, architect; b. N.Y.C., Apr. 18, 1939; s. Jack and Ruth (Gureasko) B.; m. Julia Dessery Thomas, Mar. 24, 1980; children by previous marriage: Elizabeth, Erica, David; 1 stepchild, Leslie Thomas. BArch, Columbia U., 1963. Registered arch. Calif. Sr. arch. Office Surgeon Gen./U.S. Air Force, Washington, 1963-66; dir. arch. Med. Planning Assoc., Malibu, Calif., 1966-72; founder, chmn., design ptnr. Bobrow/Thomas & Assocs., L.A., 1972—. Founder, coord. programs in health complex facilities design UCLA Grad. Sch. Arch. and Urban Planning, 1972-80; adj. prof. UCLA Grad. Sch. Pub. Health, deans adv. bd.; chmn. UCLA, Columbia U. Internat. Hosp. Design Competition; trustee Otis Coll. Art & Design; chmn. bd. Arts and Arch. Mag. Prin. works include City of Hope Nat. Med. Ctr., Cook County Hosp., Prototype Campus Calif. State U., Channel Islands, Motion Picture and TV Hosp., Cedars Sinai Med. Ctr., Otis Coll. Art & Design, VA L.A. Clinic, St. Lukes Med. Ctr., Camp Pendleton Naval Hosp., Shriners Hosp., UCLA Arroyo Bridge, Beckman Rsch. Lab., others; contbr. articles to profl. jours. Pres. The Friends of the Schindler House, L.A., 1978-79; dir. Am. Hosp. Assn. Ann. Design Inst.; chmn. strategic planning and design com. Westwood Village Bus. Improvement Dist.; chmn. Hosp. Coun. So. Calif. Seismic Design Inst., 1994. Named one of Outstanding Architects Under 40, Bldg. Design and Constrn. Mag., 1978; recipient Preservation award L.A. Conservancy to the Friends of Schindler House, 1982. Fellow AIA (co-chmn. com. on arch. for health spl. task force on capital reimbursement 1983—, Nat. and Regional Design awards); mem. Beverly Hills Tennis Club. Office: Bobrow/Thomas & Assocs 1001 Westwood Blvd Los Angeles CA 90024-2902

BOCHY, BRUCE, professional sports team manager, coach; b. Landes de Boussac, France, Apr. 16, 1955; m. Kim B.; children: Greg, Brett. Coach San Diego Padres, 1993-94, mgr., 1994—. Office: San Diego Padres PO Box 2000 San Diego CA 92112-2000

BOCK, RUSSELL SAMUEL, writer; b. Spokane, Wash., Nov. 24, 1905; s. Alva and Elizabeth (Mellinger) B.; m. Suzanne Ray, Feb. 26, 1970; children: Beverly A. Bock Wunderlich, James Russell. B.B.A., U. Wash., 1929. Part-time instr. U. So. Calif., UCLA, 1942-50; with Ernst & Ernst, CPAs, Los Angeles, 1938, ptnr., 1951-69; cons. Ernst & Young, 1969—. Author: Guidebook to California Taxes, annually, 1950— , Taxes of Hawaii, annually, 1964— ; also numerous articles. Dir., treas. Cmty. TV So. Calif., 1964-74; dir., v.p. treas., So. Calif. Symphony-Hollywood Bowl Assn., 1964-70; bd. dirs. Claremont McKenna Coll., 1964-70, Cmty. Arts Music Assn., 1974-76, 78-84, Santa Barbara Symphony Assn., 1976-78, Santa Barbara Boys and Girls Club, 1980-93, UCSB Affiliates, 1983-85, Santa Barbara Civic Light Opera, 1995-97. Mem. Am. Inst. C.P.A.s (council 1953-57, trial bd. 1955-58, v.p. 1959-60), Calif. Soc. C.P.A.s (past pres.), Los Angeles C. of C. (dir. 1957-65, v.p. 1963), Sigma Phi Epsilon, Beta Alpha Psi, Beta Gamma Sigma. Clubs: Birnam Wood Golf, Santa Barbara Yacht. Office: 300 Hot Springs Rd Apt 190 Santa Barbara CA 93108-2069

BODDIE, LEWIS FRANKLIN, obstetrics and gynecology educator; b. Forsyth, Ga., Apr. 4, 1913; s. William F. and Luetta T. (Sams) B.; m. Marian Bernice Claytor, Dec. 27, 1941; children: Roberta Boddie Miles, Lewis Jr., Bernice B. Jackson, Pamela, Kenneth, Fredda, Margaret Boddie Lewis. BA, Morehouse Coll., 1933; MD, Meharry Med. Sch., 1938. Diplomate Am. Bd. Ob-Gyn (proctor parti exam Los Angeles area 1955-63). Intern Homer-Phillips Hosp., St. Louis, 1938-39, resident in ob-gyn, 1939-42; mem. attending staff Grace Hosp., Detroit, 1944-48, Parkside Hosp., Detroit, 1944-48, Los Angeles County Gen. Hosp., 1952-79; sr. mem. attending staff Queen of Angels Hosp., Los Angeles, 1964-91, chmn. dept. ob-gyn, 1968-70; asst. clin. prof. U. So. Calif. Sch. Medicine, L.A., 1953-79, asst. clin. prof. emeritus, 1979—; assoc. clin. prof. U. Calif., Irvine, 1956-81. Sec. Verndro Med. Corp., 1952-90. Vice chmn. bd. mgrs. 28th St. YMCA, Los Angeles 1960-75; steward African Meth. Episc. Ch., Los Angeles, 1949—. Fellow ACS (life), Am. Coll. Ob-Gyn (life), Los Angeles Ob-Gyn Soc. (life): mem. Los Angeles United Way (priorities and allocations coms., 1985-95, standards com. 1987-95, new admission com. 1988-95), Children's Home Soc. (bd. dirs. 1952-89, trustee 1989—, v.p. 1963-68, pres. 1968-70), Child Welfare League Am. (bd. dirs. 1969-76). Republican.

BODENSIECK, ERNEST JUSTUS, mechanical engineer; b. Dubuque, Iowa, June 1, 1923; s. Julius Henry and Elma (Sommer) B.; m. Margery Elenore Sande, Sept. 9, 1943; children: Elizabeth Bodensieck Eley, Stephen. BSME, Iowa State U., 1943. Registered profl. engr., Ariz. Project engr. TRW Inc., Cleve., 1943-57; supr. rocket turbomachinery Rocketdyne divsn. Rockwell Internat., Canoga Park, Calif., 1967-60, supr. nuclear turbomachinery, 1964-70; advance gear engr. Gen. Electric Co., Lynn, 1960-64; asst. mgr. engine components Aerojet Nuclear Systems Co., [illegible] Corp., Phoenix, 1971-81; transmission cons. Bodensieck Engring. Co., Scottsdale, 1981—2001. Patentee in field. Mem. ASME, AIAA, Soc. Automotive Engrs. (various coms.), Aircraft Industries Assn. (various coms.), Am. Gear Mfrs. Assn. (mem. aerospace, gear rating and enclosed epicyclic coms.), Nat. Soc. Profl. Engrs., Pi Tau Sigma, Lutheran. Home: 1640 [illegible] # 318 Lima OH 50490

BODKIN, HENRY GRATTAN, JR. lawyer; b. L.A., Dec. 8, 1921; s. Henry Grattan and Ruth May (Wallis) B.; m. Mary Louise Davis, June 28, 1943; children: Maureen L. Dixon, Sheila L. McCarthy, Timothy Grattan. B.S. cum laude, Loyola U., Los Angeles, 1943, J.D., 1948. Bar: Calif. 1948. Pvt. practice, Los Angeles, 1948-51, 53-95; ptnr. Bodkin, McCarthy, Sargent & Smith (predecessor firms), L.A.; of counsel Sullivan, Workman & Dee, L.A., 1995—. Mem. L.A. Bd. Water and Power Commrs., 1972-74, pres., 1973-74; regent Marymount Coll., 1962-67; trustee Loyola-Marymount U., 1967-91, vice chmn., 1985-86. With USNR, 1943-45, 51-53. Fellow Am. Coll. Trial Lawyers; mem. Calif. State Bar (mem. exec. com. conf. of dels. 1968-70, vice chmn. 1969-70), California Club, Riviera Tennis Club, Tuna Club, Chancery Club (pres. 1990-91), Phi Delta Phi. Republican. Roman Catholic. Home: 956 Linda Flora Dr Los Angeles CA 90049-1631 Office: Sullivan Workman & Dee 800 S Figueroa St Fl 12 Los Angeles CA 90017-2521

BOECKMANN, HERBERT F., II, automotive executive; b. Aug. 21, 1930; CEO, owner, pres. Galpin Motors, North Hills, Calif. Office: Galpin Motors Inc 15505 Roscoe Blvd North Hills CA 91343-6598

BOEDER, THOMAS L. lawyer; b. St. Cloud, Minn., Jan. 10, 1944; s. Oscar Morris and Eleanor (Gile) B.; m. Carol-Leigh Coombs, Apr. 6, 1968. BA, Yale U., 1965, LLB, 1968. Bar: Wash. 1970, U.S. Dist. Ct. (we. dist.) Wash. 1970, U.S. Dist. Ct. (ea. dist.) Wash. 1972, U.S. Ct. Appeals (9th cir.) 1970, U.S. Supreme Ct. 1974, U.S. Ct. Appeals (D.C. cir.) 1975, U.S. Ct. Appeals (10th cir.) 1993. Litigation atty. Wash. State Atty. Gen., Seattle, 1970-72, antitrust div. head, 1972-76, chief, consumer protection and antitrust, 1976-78, also sr. asst. atty. gen. and criminal enforcement, 1979-81; ptnr. Perkins Coie, Seattle, 1981—. Served with U.S. Army, 1968-70, Vietnam. Mem. ABA (antitrust sect.), Wash. State Bar Assn. (antitrust sect.). Lutheran. Office: Perkins Coie 1201 3rd Ave Fl 40 Seattle WA 98101-3029

BOEHLKE, CHRISTINE, public relations executive; b. Dover, N.J., Dec. 29, 1946; BA in Creative Writing, U. Pa., 1968. Acct. supr. D.J. Edelman, 1978-79, group v.p., 1979-81; v.p. client svcs. mgr. Burson-Marsteller, Chgo., 1981-83, v.p., gen. mgr. San Francisco, 1983-85, v.p., mgr. northern calif., 1985-86, sr. v.p. western regional mgr., 1986-87; prin. Phase Two Strategies, San Francisco, 1987—. Mem. Pub. Rels. Soc. Am. (counselor's acad.), Commonwealth Club of Calif. Office: Phase Two Strategies 170 Columbus Ave Ste 300 San Francisco CA 94133-5160

BOEHLKE, WILLIAM FREDRICK, public relations executive, consultant; b. Chgo., Dec. 16, 1946; s. William Fredrick and Cynthia Charlotte (Blackmore) B.; m. Christine Ann Chervenak, July 19, 1969. Student, Wharton Sch. Bus., Phila., 1965-69. Pres. and CEO Data Solve Corp., Chgo., 1981-84, Lati Corp. Inc., San Francisco, 1985-89; CEO Phase Two Strategies Inc., San Francisco, 1989—. Contbr. articles to profl. jours. Mem. Santa Rosa Golf & Country Club, Home House (London), Penn Club N.Y. Avocation: computer software tech. Office: Phase Two Strategies Inc 111 Pine St 8th Fl San Francisco CA 94111 E-mail: william_boehlke@p2pr.com

BOEHM, BARRY WILLIAM, computer science educator; b. Santa Monica, Calif., May 16, 1935; s. Edward G. and Kathryn G. (Kane) B.; m. Sharla Perrine, July 1, 1961; children: Romney Ann, Tenley Lynn. BA, Harvard U., 1957; PhD, UCLA, 1964; ScD (hon.), U. Mass., 2000. Programmer, analyst Gen. Dynamics, San Diego, 1955-59; head infosci. dept. Rand Corp., Santa Monica, 1959-73; chief scientist TRW Def. Sys. Group, Redondo Beach, Calif., 1973-89; dir. infosci. and tech. office Def. Advanced Rsch. Agy. Dept. Def., Arlington, Va., 1989-92, dir. software and computer tech. office, dir. def. rsch. and engring., 1992; TRW prof. software engring., dir. Ctr. for Software Engring. U. So. Calif., L.A., 1992—. Co-chmn. Fed. Coordinating Coun. Sci., Engring. and Tech. High Performance Computing WG, Washington, 1989-91; chmn. DOD Software Tech. Plan WG, Arlington, 1990-92, NASA G & C/Infosystems Adv. Com., Washington, 1973-76; guest lectr. USSR Acad. Sci., 1970; chmn. bd. visitors Carnegie Mellon U. Software Engring. Inst., 1997—; chmn. USAF-Sci. Adv. Bd. Info. Tech. Panel, 1994-97. Author: ROCKET, 1964, Software Engineering Economics, 1981; co-author: Characteristics of Software Quality, 1978, Software Risk Management, 1989, Software Cost Estimation with COCOMO II, 2000; co-editor: Planning Community Information Utilities, 1972. Recipient Warnier prize Soc. Software Analysts, 1984, Freiman award Internat. Soc. Parametric Analysts, 1988, Award for Excellence Office of Sec. of Def., 1992. Fellow Internat. Coun. on Sys. Engring., Assn. for Computing Machinery (Disting. Rsch. award in Software Engring. 1997), NAE, AIAA (chair TC computers 1968-70, Info. Sys. award 1979), IEEE (gov. bd. computer sci. 1981-82, 86-87, H.D. Mills award 2000). Office: U So Calif Computer Sci Dept Los Angeles CA 90089-0781 E-mail: boehm@sunset.usc.edu

BOEHM, ERIC HARTZELL, information management executive; b. Hof, Germany, July 15, 1918; came to U.S., 1934, naturalized, 1940; s. Karl and Bertha (Oppenheimer) B.; m. Inge Pauli, June 5, 1948; children: Beatrice (dec.), Ronald James, Evelyn (dec.), Steven David. B.A., Wooster (Ohio) Coll., 1940, Litt.D. (hon.), 1973; M.A., Fletcher Sch. Law and Diplomacy, 1942; Ph.D., Yale U., 1951. With Dept. Air Force, 1951-58; chmn. bd. ABC-CLIO, Santa Barbara, Calif., 1960—, European Bibliog. Ctr., CLIO Press, Ltd., Oxford, Eng., 1970—; pres. Internat. Sch. of Info. Mgmt., 1987-94, chmn., 1994—. Chmn. bd. dirs. Internat. Acad. at Santa Barbara, 1970—, Internat. Sch. Info. Mgmt., 1983-99; pub. Environ. Studies Inst., 1971—, Info. Inst., 1980—; cons. on bibliography, information systems. Author: We Survived, 1949; microfilm Policy-making of the Nazi Government, 1969; editor Historical Abstracts, 1955-83, cons., 1983— ; editor America: History and Life, 1964-83, cons., 1983— ; editor Bibliographies on International Relations and World Affairs, an Annotated Directory, 1965, Blueprint for Bibliography, a System for Social Sciences and Humanities, 1965, Clio Bibliography Series, 1973— ; co-editor Historical Periodicals, 1961, 2d edit., 1983-85; pub. Advanced Bibliography of Contents: Political Science, 1969— , ART Bibliographies: Modern, 1972— , Environ. Periodicals Bibliography, 1972— ; bd. advisors Info. Strategy, The Exec.'s Jour., 1984— ; contbr. articles to profl. jours. Bd. dirs. UN Assn., Santa Barbara, 1973-77, Santa Barbara's Adv. Bd. Internat. Relationships (Sister Cities), 1974, Friends of Public Library, Friends of U. Calif. at Santa Barbara Library; mem. affiliates bd. U. Calif.-Santa Barbara; vice chmn. New Directions Found., 1984-88; adv. bd. Nuclear Age Peace Found., 1985— . With USAAF, 1942-46. Recipient Disting. Alumnus award Wooster Coll., 1990. Mem. AAAS, Am. Soc. Info. Sci., Assn. Bibliography in History (v.p. 1986, pres. 1987), Calif. Library Soc., Nat. Trust Historic Preservation, Santa Barbara Com. Fgn. Rels., Am. Friends of Wilton Park, Santa Barbara C. of C. (dir. 1980-84), Univ. Club, Rotary, Phi Beta Kappa Home and Office: 800 E Micheltorena St Santa Barbara CA 93103-2220

BOEHM, FELIX HANS, physicist, educator; b. Basel, Switzerland, June 9, 1924; came to U.S., 1952, naturalized, 1964; s. Hans G. and Marquerite (Philippi) B.; m. Ruth Sommerholder, Nov. 26, 1956; children: [illegible], Claude N. MS, Inst. Tech., Zurich, 1948, PhD, 1951. Research assoc. Inst. Tech., Zurich, Switzerland, 1949-52; Boese fellow Columbia U., 1952-53; faculty Calif. Inst. Tech., Pasadena, 1953—, prof. physics, 1961—, William L. Valentine prof., 1985-94, William L. Valentine prof. emeritus, 1995—; Sloan fellow, 1962-64; NSF sr. fellow Niels Bohr Inst., Copen[illegible] Geneva, 1971-72, Laue-Langevin Inst., 1980. Recipient Humboldt award, 1980, 84. Fellow Am. Phys. Soc. (Tom W. Bonner prize 1995); mem. Nat. Acad. Scis. Achievements include research on nuclear physics, nuclear beta decay, neutrino physics, atomic physics, muonic and pionic atoms, parity and time-reversal. Home: 2510 N Altadena Dr Altadena CA 91001-2836 Office: Calif Inst Tech Mail Code 161 33 Pasadena CA 91125-0001 E-mail: boehm@caltech.edu

BOEHM, ROBERT FOTY, mechanical engineer, educator, researcher; b. Portland, Oreg., Jan. 16, 1940; s. Charles Frederick and Lufteria (Christie) B.; m. Marcia Kay Pettibone, June 10, 1961; children— Deborah, Robert Christopher B.S. in Mech. Engring., Wash. State U., Pullman, 1962, M.S., 1964; Ph.D., U. Calif., Berkeley, 1968. Registered profl. engr., Calif. With Gen. Electric Co., San Jose, Calif., 1964-66; mem. faculty U. Utah, Salt Lake City, 1968-90, prof. mech. engring., 1976-90, chmn. dept., 1981-84; Nat. Sandia Labs., Albuquerque, 1984-85; prof. U. Nev., Las Vegas, 1990—, chmn. mech. engring. dept., 1990-96, univ. sys. sr. liaison to Dept. Energy, 1994-95, dir. rsch. Coll. Engring., 1999-2001. Mem. Utah Solar Adv. Com., Utah Energy Conservation and Devel. Coun., 1980-88; dir. Energy Rsch. Ctr., 1994—. Author: Design Analysis of Thermal Systems, 1987; editor: Direct Contact Heat Exchange, 1988, Developments in the Design of Thermal Systems, 1997; tech. editor Jour. Solar Energy Engring., 1980-84; contbr. articles to profl. jours. Named Utah Engring. Educator of Yr., Utah Engrs. Coun., 1988, Disting. Tchr., U. Utah, 1989; recipient UNLV Barrick Sr. Rsch. award, 1994. Fellow ASME; mem. ASHRAE, Am. Soc. for Engring. Edn., Internat. Solar Energy Soc., Corvair Soc. Am., Vintage Chevrolet Club Am., Sigma Xi. Home: 4999 Mesa View Dr Las Vegas NV 89120-1216 Office: U Nev Mech Engring Dept PO Box 454027 Las Vegas NV 89154-4027 E-mail: boehm@me.unlv.edu

BOERSMA, JUNE ELAINE (JALMA BARRETT), writer, photographer; b. N.Y.C., Apr. 27, 1926; d. Arthur Oscar and Gertrude Ann (Connolly) Schiefer; m. Kenneth Thomas McKim, June 8. 1946 (div. 1957); chldren: Kenneth Thomas Jr., Mark Rennie; m. Lawrence Allan Boersma, Nov. 22, 1962; children: Juliana Jaye, Dirk John. Student, Edgewood Park Jr. Coll., 1944-46. Writer non-fiction; co-owner, photographer Allan/The Animal Photographers, San Diego, 1980—; co-owner Animal Art, San Diego, also Shandaken, N.Y., 1999—. Author: (series) Wildcats of North America-Bobcat, Cougar, Feral Cat, Lynx, 1998, The Dove Family Tale, A True Story, 1998, Wild Canines of North America--Coyote, Foxes, Wolf, 2000; co-author: One Day in the Life of a Little Couger, 2001, One Day in the Life of a Coyote Pup, 2001; contbr. articles to Ladies' Home Jour., Horse Illus., Cat Fancy, Dog Fancy, Popular Photography, Studio Photography, Petersen's Photographic, Dog World, others. Home: 3503 Argonne St San Diego CA 92117-1009

BOERSMA, P. DEE, zoology educator; b. Mt. Pleasant, Mich., Nov. 1, 1946; d. Henry W. and Vivian (Anspach) B. BS, Ctrl. Mich. U., 1969; PhD, Ohio State U., 1974. Asst. prof. Inst. Environ. Studies U. Wash., Seattle, 1974-80, assoc. prof., 1980-88, prof. environ. studies, 1988-93, prof. zoology, 1988—, adj. prof. women's studies, 1993—, assoc. dir., 1987-93, acting dir., 1990-91; mem. sci. adv. com. for outer continental shelf Environ. Studies Program, Dept. Interior, 1980-83; prin. investigator Magellanic Penguin Project N.Y. Zool. Soc., 1982—. Evans vis. fellow U. Otago, New Zealand, 1995, Pew fellow in conservation and the environ., 1997-2000. Assoc. editor Ecological Applications, 1998-2001; exec. editor Conservation Biology in Practice, 2000—; contbr. articles to profl. jours. Mem. adv. U.S. del. to UN Status Women Commn., N.Y.C., 1973, UN World Status Women Commn., N.Y.C., 1973, UN World Population Conf., Romania, 1974; mem. Gov. Lowry's Task Force on Wildlife, 1993; sci. adv. EcoBios, 1985-95; bd. dirs. Zero Population Growth, 1975-82, Washnigton Nature Conservancy, 1995-98; mem. adv. bd. Walt Disney World Animal Kingdom, 1993—; bd. dirs. Peregine Fund, 1995—, Bullitt Found., 1996-2000, Puget Sound Learning Ctr.; mem. scholar diplomatic program Dept. State, 1977. Recipient Outstanding Alumni award Ctrl. Mich. U., 1978, Matrix award Women in Comm., 1983; named to Kellogg Nat. Leadership Program, 1982-85; recipient Top 100 Outsiders of Yr. award Outside Mag., 1987, Outstanding Centennial Alumni award Ctrl. Mich. U., 1993; sci. fellow The Wildlife Conservation Soc., 1982—, Aldo Leopold Leadership fellow, 2000-01. Fellow AAAS, Am Ornithol. Union (regional rep. Pacific seabird group 1981-85); mem. AAAS, Ecol. Soc. Am., Wilson Ornithol. Soc., Cooper Ornithol. Soc., Soc. Am. Naturalists, Soc. for Conservation Biology (bd. govs. 1991-94, pres-elect 1995-97, pres. 1997-99, past pres. 1999-2001), Gopher Brokers Club (pres. Seattle chpt. 1982-83). Office: U Wash Dept Zoology PO Box 351800 Seattle WA 98195-1800 E-mail: boersma@u.washington.edu

BOGAARD, WILLIAM JOSEPH, mayor, lawyer, educator; b. Sioux City, Iowa, Jan. 18, 1938; s. Joseph and Irene Marie (Hensing) B.; m. Claire Marie Whalen, Jan. 28, 1961; children: Michele, Jeannine, Joseph, Matthew. BS, Loyola Marymount U., L.A., 1959; JD with honors, U. Mich., 1965. Bar: Calif. 1966, U.S. Dist. Ct. (ctrl. dist.) Calif. 1966. Ptnr. Agnew, Miller & Carlson, L.A., 1970-82; exec. v.p., gen. counsel 1st Interstate Bancorp, L.A., 1982-96; vis. prof. securities regulation and banking Mich. Law Sch., Ann Arbor, 1996-97; lectr. securities regulation and corps. U. So. Calif. Law Sch., L.A., 1997—; mayor Pasadena, Calif., 1999—. Mem. Calif. Commn. on Jud. Nominees Evaluation, 1997-99. Mem. city coun., mayor City of Pasadena, Calif., 1978-86. Capt. USAF, 1959-62. Mem. Calif. State Bar, Los Angeles County Bar Assn. (Corp. Counsel of Yr. award 1988). Avocations: jogging, French and Spanish languages, hiking. Office: Pasadena City Hall 100 N Garfield Ave Pasadena CA 91109 E-mail: bbogaard@ci.pasadena.ca.us

BOGEN, ANDREW E. lawyer; b. L.A., Aug. 23, 1941; s. David and Edith B.; m. Deborah Bogen, Oct. 10, 1970; children: Elizabeth, Michael. BA, Pomona Coll., Claremont, Calif., 1963; LLB, Harvard U, 1966. Bar: Calif. 1966. Assoc. Gibson, Dunn & Crutcher, L.A., 1966-73, ptnr., 1973—. Trustee Exceptional Children's Found., L.A., 1976-89, Weingart Found., 1999—; bd. dirs. St. Anne's Maternity Home, 1990—. Office: Gibson Dunn & Crutcher 333 S Grand Ave Ste 4400 Los Angeles CA 90071-3197

BOGER, DALE L. chemistry educator; b. Hutchinson, Kans., Aug. 22, 1953; s. Lester W. and Elizabeth (Korkish) B. BS in Chemistry, U. Kans., 1975; PhD in Chemistry, Harvard U., 1980. Asst. prof. U. Kans., Lawrence, 1979-83, assoc. prof., 1983-85, Purdue U., West Lafayette, Ind., 1985-87, prof., 1987-91; Richard and Alice Cramer chair chemistry Scripps Rsch. Inst., La Jolla, Calif., 1991—. Recipient Career Devel. award NIH, 1983-88; NSF fellow, 1975-78, Alfred P. Sloan fellow, 1985-89; Searle scholar, 1981-84. Mem. Am. Chem. Soc. (A.C. Cope scholar 1989, Aldrich creative work in organic synthesis 1999), Internat. Soc. Het. Chemistry (Katritky award 1997). Home: 2819 Via Posada La Jolla CA 92037-2205 Office: Scripps Rsch Inst 10550 N Torrey Pines Rd La Jolla CA 92037-1000

BOGGS, TEX, state legislator; Mem. Wyo. Senate, Dist. 13, Cheyenne, 1998—. Democrat. Office: 2520 College Dr Rock Springs WY 82901-5805 E-mail: [illegible]

BOGGS, WILLIAM S. lawyer; b. Toledo, May 17, 1946; AB summa cum laude, Wittenberg U., 1968; JD cum laude, Harvard U., 1972. Bar: Calif. Ptnr. Gray, Cary, Ware & Freidenrich, San Diego, 1979—. Mem. ABA, San Diego County Bar Assn., Internat. Assn. Defense Counsel, Assn. So. Calif. Defense Counsel, San Diego Defense Lawyers, Lincoln's Inn. Office: Gray Cary Ware & Freidenrich 401 B St Ste 1700 San Diego CA 92101-4297

BOGUES, MUGGSY (TYRONE CURTIS BOGUES), professional basketball player; b. Balt., Jan. 9, 1965; m. Kimberly Bogues; children: Tyeisha, Brittany, Tyrone Jr. Student, Wake Forest U., 1983-87. Guard Washington Bullets, 1987-88, Charlotte (N.C.) Hornets, 1988-97, Golden State Warriors, Oakland, Calif., 1997—. Founder "Reading and Roundball" charity basketball game, Balt.; dir. numerous basketball camps. Recipient Inspirational Trophy Jim Thorpe Pro Sports Awards, 1995; number retired at Wake Forest; all-time leader assists and steals Atlantic Coast Conf., assist to turnoer ratio NBA, assists Charlotte Hornets; named Belt/WBTV Hornets Player of Yr., 1993-94. Avocations: softball, golf. Office: Golden State Warriors 1011 Broadway Oakland CA 94607-4027

BOGUES, TYRONE CURTIS See BOGUES, MUGGSY

BOGY, DAVID B(EAUREGARD), mechanical engineering educator; b. Wabbaseka, Ark., June 4, 1936; s. Jesse C. and Dorothy (Duff) B.; m. Patricia Lynn Pizzitola, Mar. 28, 1961; children: Susan, Rebecca. B.S., Rice U., 1959, M.S., 1961; Ph.D., Brown U., 1966. Mech. engr. Shell Devel. Co., Houston, 1961-63; asst. prof. mech. engring. U. Calif., Berkeley, 1967-70, assoc. prof., 1970-75, prof., 1975—, chmn. dept. mech. engring., 1991-99, founder, dir. computer mechanics lab., William S. Floyd, Jr. Disting. prof., 1993—. Cons. IBM Rsch., 1972-83; mem. nat. com. on theoretical and applied mechanics NRC. Contbr. more than 250 articles to profl. jours. Served with C.E. U.S. Army, 1961-62. Fellow ASME, IEEE; mem. NAE. Achievements include research in static and dynamic elasticity, fluid jets and mechanics of computer disk files and printers. Home: 8531 Buckingham Dr El Cerrito CA 94530-2533 Office: U Calif 6189 Etcheverry Hall Berkeley CA 94720-1740

BOHANNON, ROBERT H. diversified services company executive; married; 2 children. BBA, Kensington U. Head consumer credit bus. Marine Midland Bank; exec. v.p. ops. Mortgage Ins. Co. subs. GE Credit Corp.; pres., CeO ops. Travelers Experss subs. VIAD, Mpls., 1993; pres., CEO, chmn. Viad, Phoenix, 1996—; COO, 1996. Office: Viad 1850 N Central Ave Phoenix AZ 85077

BOHLE, SUE, public relations executive; b. Austin, Minn., June 23, 1943; d. Harold Raymond and Mary Theresa (Swanson) Hastings; m. John Bernard Bohle, June 22, 1974; children: Jason John, Christine K. BS in Journalism, Northwestern U., 1965, MS in Journalism, 1969. Tchr. pub. high schs, Englewood, Colo., 1965-68; account exec. Burson-Marsteller Pub. Relations, Los Angeles, 1969-73; v.p., mgr. pub. relations J. Walter Thompson Co., Los Angeles, 1973-79; founder, pres. The Bohle Company, L.A., 1979—; pres., CEO The Bohle Co., L.A.; former exec. v.p. Ketchum Pub. Rels., L.A. Free-lance writer, instr. communications Calif. State U. at Fullerton, 1972-73; instr. writing Los Angeles City Coll., 1975-76; lectr. U. So. Calif., 1979—. Contbr. articles to profl. jours. Dir. pub. rels. L.A. Jr. Ballet, 1971-72; pres. Panhellenic Advisers Coun., UCLA, 1972-73; mem. adv. bd. L.A. Valley Coll., 1974-75, Coll. Communications Pepperdine U., 1981-85, Sch. Journalism U. So. Calif., 1987-95, Calif. State U., Long Beach, 1988-93; bd. visitors Medill Sch. Journalism Northwestern U., 1984—. Recipient Alumni Svc. award Northwestern U., 1995; Univ. scholar, 1961-64, Panhellenic scholar, 1964-65; named to Hall of Achievement, Medill Sch. Journalism, 1997, charter mem. Hall of Fame. Fellow Pub. Rels. Soc. Am. (bd. dirs. L.A. chpt. 1981-90, v.p. 1983, pres. 1989, del. nat. assembly 1980, 94, 95, 96, co-chmn. long-range strategic com. 1990, pres.'s adv. coun. 1991, exec. com. Counselors Acad. 1984-86, sec.-treas. 1990, chmn. 1992, sec. Coll. Fellows 1993, vice chair 1994, chmn. 1995, Silver Anvil award 1994); mem. Pub. Rels. Orgn. Internat. (U.S. founder, bd. dirs. 1994—), World Com., Women in Comm., Shi-ai, Delta Zeta (editor The Lamp 1966-68, Woman of Yr. award 1993), Kappa Alpha Tau. Office: 1900 Avenue Of The Stars # 2D Los Angeles CA 90067-4301

BOHLINGER, JOHN C. state legislator; b. Bozeman, Mont., Apr. 21, 1936; m. Bette J. Bohlinger; 6 children. BA, U. Mont., 1959. Owner women's apparel store, 1961-92; mem. Mont. Senate, Dist. 7, Helena, 1998—; mem. local govt. com., pub. health, welfare and safety com. Mont. State Senate, mem. taxation com., vice chair ethics com. Past pres., chmn. bd. Yellowstone Arts Ctr.; bd. dirs. Billings Symphony Soc., St. Vincent de Paul Soc., Mont. State U. Billings Found., Yellowstone Treatment Ctr. Served with USMC, 1954-61. Mem. Billings Rotary Cub. Republican. Roman Catholic. Home: 2233 Remington Sq Billings MT 59102-2489

BOHMONT, DALE WENDELL, agricultural consultant; b. Wheatland, Wyo., June 7, 1922; s. J.E. and Mary (Armann) B.; m. Marilyn J. Horn, Mar. 7, 1969; children: Dennis E., Craig W. B.S., U. Wyo., 1948, M.S., 1950; Ph.D., U. Nebr., 1952; M.P.A., Harvard U., 1959. Registered investment adv., SEC. Pub. sch. tchr., Rock River, Wyo., 1941-42; from research asst. to head plant scis. U. Wyo., 1946-60; assoc. dir. expt. sta. Colo. State U., 1961-63; dean, dir. agr. U. Nev., Reno, 1963-82, dean, dir. emeritus, 1982—; pres. Bohmont Cons. Inc., 1982—; mem. Brucheum Group, Waynesboro, Va., 1984; chief cons. Zygro Corp., 1999. Cons. Devel. & Resources Corp., N.Y.C., 1968—, Fredriksen, Kamine & Assocs., Sacramento, 1976, Nev. Agrl. Found., 1986—; pres. Enide Corp., Reno, 1974-80, Thermal Dynamics Internat., 1983-87, Cryabis, Inc., Reno, 1993-95; co-chmn. rsch. planning West Divsn. Agr. Expt. Stas., 1975; mem. exec. com., coun. adminstrv. heads agr. Nat. Assn. State Univ. Land Grant Colls., 1975. Author: Golden Years of Agriculture in Nevada, 1989; contbr. articles to profl. jours.; mem. editorial bd.: Crops and Soils, 1962—. Pres. Dale W. and Marilyn Horn Found., 1998—. Served with USAAF, 1942-45. Fellow AAAS, Agronomy Soc.; mem. Western Soc. Weed Scis. (hon.), Western Crop Sci. Soc. (pres. 1962-63), Nat. Expt. Sta. Dirs. Assn. (chmn. 1967-68), Am. Range Mgmt. Soc., Farm House (dir. 1962—), Weed Soc. Am. (hon.), Sigma Xi, Gamma Sigma Delta (pres. 1964-66), Alpha Zeta, Alpha Tau Alpha, Phi Kappa Phi. Lodge: Lions (v.p. 1985-86, pres. 1986-87 bd. dirs. 1985—) Home: 280 Island Ave Reno NV 89501-1844 E-mail: bohconslt@aol.com

BOHN, DENNIS ALLEN, electrical engineer, executive; b. San Fernando, Calif., Oct. 5, 1942; s. Raymond Virgil and Iris Elouise (Johnson) B.; 1 child, Kira Michelle; m. Patricia Tolle, Aug. 12, 1986. BSEE with honors, U. Calif., Berkeley, 1972, MSEE with honors, 1974. Engring. technician GE Co., San Leandro, Calif., 1964-72; research and devel. engr. Hewlett-Packard Co., Santa Clara, Calif., 1973; application engr. Nat. Semicondr. Corp., Santa Clara, 1974-76; engring. mgr. Phase Linear Corp., Lynnwood, Wash., 1976-82; v.p. rsch. and devel., ptnr. Rane Corp., Mukilteo, Wash., 1982—; founder Toleco Systems, Kingston, Wash., 1980. Suicide and crisis ctr. vol., Berkeley, 1972-74, Santa Clara, 1974-76. Served with USAF, 1960-64. Recipient Am. Spirit Honor medal USAF, 1961; Math. Achievement award Chem. Rubber Co., 1962-63. Editor: We Are Not Just Daffodils, 1975; contbr. poetry to Reason mag.; tech. editor Audio Handbook, 1976; contbr. articles to tech. jours.; columnist Polyphony mag., 1981-83; 2 patents in field. Fellow Audio Engring. Soc.; mem. IEEE, Tau Beta Pi. Office: Rane Corp 10802 47th Ave W Mukilteo WA 98275-5098

BOHN, RALPH CARL, educational consultant, retired educator; b. Detroit, Feb. 19, 1930; s. Carl and Bertha (Abrams) B.; m. Adella Stanul, Sept. 2, 1950 (dec.); children: Cheryl Ann, Jeffrey Ralph; m. JoAnn Olvera Butler, Feb. 19, 1977 (div. 1990); stepchildren: Kathryn J., Kimberly J., Gregory E.; m. Mariko Tajima, Jan. 27, 1991; 1 child, Thomas Carl; 1 stepchild, Daichi Tajima. BS, Wayne State U., 1951, EdM, 1954, EdD, 1957. Instr. part-time Wayne State U., 1954-55, summer 1956; faculty San Jose (Calif.) State U., 1955-92, prof. div. tech., 1961-92, chmn. dept. indsl. studies, 1960-69, assoc. dean ednl. svc., 1968-70, dean continuing edn., 1970-92, prof. emeritus, 1992—; cons. Calif. State U. Sys., 1992—; cons. quality edn. sys. USAF, 1992-2000; dir. nat. program on non-collegiate sponsored instrn. Calif. State Univ. Sys., 1995-2000, Calif. State U. Inst., 1997-99. Guest summer faculty Colo. State Coll., 1963, Ariz. State U., 1966, U. P.R., 1967, 74, So. Ill. U., 1970, Oreg. State U., 1971, Utah State U., 1973, Va. Poly. Inst. & State U., 1973, U. Idaho, 1978; cons. U.S. Office of Edn., 1965-70, Calif. Pub. Schs., 1960, Nat. Assessment Ednl. Progress, 1968-79, ednl. div. Philco-Ford Corp., 1970-73, Am. Inst. Rsch., 1969-83, Far West Labs for Ednl. Rsch. Devel., 1971-86; mem. adv. bd. Ctr. for Vocat. and Tech. Edn., Ohio State U., 1968-74; dir. project Vocat. Edn. Act, 1965-67, NDEA, 1967, 68; co-dir. Project Edn. Profession Devel. Act, 1969, 70; mem. commn. coll. and univ. contracts Western Assn. Schs. and Colls, 1976-78, chmn. spl. com. on off-campus instrn. and continuing edn., 1978-88; chmn. continuing edn. accreditation visit U. Santa Clara, 1976; mem. accreditation team for Azusa Pacific Coll., 1975, Portland State U., 1975, 95, Brigham Young U., 1976, 86, 96, Columbia Coll., 1977, Western Wash. U., 1978, 88, Wash. State U., 1980, 90, 99, Chapman Coll., 1980, Calif. State U., Fullerton, 1981, Westminster Coll., 1983, Columbia U., 1983, Boise State U., 1984, 94, U. Hawaii, Hilo, 1984, U. Oreg., 1987, 97, U. Mont., 1989, Calif. Poly. U., Pomona, 1990, North Island Naval Air Sta., USN, 1990, U. Calif., Irvine, 1991, Western Conservative Bapt. Sem., Oreg., 1992, US Naval Sta., Hawaii, 1992, West Coast U., 1995, Norfolk Military Educ. Stations, 1996; U. Utah, 1997, Utah State U., 1997; Golden Gate U., 1997, U. Nev., Las Vegas, 2000, Nat. U., 2000, Oreg. State U., 2001, Golden Gate U., 2001; vice chmn. accreditation team U. Guam, 1978, Pepperdine U., 1979, U. LaVerne, 1980, Azusa Pacific Coll., 1981, Nat. U., 1987, Loma Linda U., 1988, 91; chmn. accreditation team Azusa Pacific Coll, 1977, Calif. Coll. Podiatric Medicine, 1982, So. Ill. U., Carbondale, 1983, Northrup U., 1984, Cogswell Coll., 1986, chmn. of spl. USAF visitation to George AFB, 1986; chair of accreditation visits Calif. State U., Chico, 1987, Chapman Coll., 1987, Hawaii Loa Coll., 1990, Myrtle Beach Air Force Base, S.C., 1990, U. Hawaii, 1991, Homestead AFB, Fla., 1992, Nellis AFB, Nev., 1992, West Coast U., Calif., 1992, Langley AFB, 1992, Seymour Johnson AFB, N.C., 1992, 1998; Shaw AFB, S.C., 1993, 99, Tustin Marine Corps Air Sta., Calif., 1993, El Toro Marine Corps Air Sta., Calif., 1993, Yokota Air Base, Japan, 1993, 2000, Holloman AFB, 1993, Mountain Home AFB, 1994, Jacksonville NAS, 1994, Cecil NAS, 1994, Mayport NS, 1994, Rota NAS, 1994, Edwards AFB, 1994, Little Rock AFB, 1995, Fort Hood U.S. Army, 1995; Howard AFB, Panama, 1997; Hickman AFB, Hawaii, 1998; Iwakuni Marine Air Base, Japan, 1999; Camp Butler Marine Corps. Base, Okinawa, 1999, Kadena Naval Station, Ikinawa, Japan, 1999, Yokusaka Naval Sta., Japan, 2000, Atsugi Naval Air Facility, Japan, 2000, Yokota Air Base, Japan, 2000, Camp Pendleton Marine Corps Base, 2001; sr. cons. Global Partnership Devel. Calif. State U. Sys., 2000—. Author: (with G.H. Silvius) Organizing Course Materials for Industrial Education, 1961, Planning and Organizing Instruction, 1976; (with A. MacDonald) Power-Mechanics of Energy Control, 1970, 2d edit., 1983, The McKnight Power Experimenter, 1970, Power and Energy Technology, 1989, Energy Technology: Power and Transportation, 1992; (with others) Basic Industrial Arts and Power Mechanics, 1978, Technology and Society: Interfaces with Industrial Arts, 1980, Fundamentals of Safety Education, 3d edit., 1981, Energy, Power and Transportation Technology, 1986; (with A. MacDonald) Energy Technology, Power and Transportation, 1991; editor (with Ralph Norman) Graduate Study in Industrial Arts, 1961; indsl. arts editor Am. Vocat. Jour., 1963-66; editor Jour. Indsl. Tchr. Edn., 1962-64. Lt. (j.g.) USCGR, 1951-53, capt. Res. ret. Recipient award Am. Legion, 1945; Wayne State U. scholar, 1953. Mem. NEA, Nat. Assn. Indsl. Tech. (bd. accreditation), Am. Indsl. Arts. Assn. (pres. 1967-68, Ship's citation 1971), Am. Coun. Indsl. Art Tchrs. Edn. (pres. 1964-66, Man of Yr. award 1967), Nat. Univ. Continuing Edn. Assn. (chair accreditation com. 1988-91), Nat. Assn. Indsl. Tchr. Educators (past v.p.), Calif. Indsl. Edn. Assn. (State Ship's citation 1971), Am. Drive Edn. Assn., Nat. Fluid Power Soc., Am. Vocat. Assn. (svc. awards 1966, 67), N.Am. Assn. for Summer Sessions (v.p. western region 1976-78), Luth. Acad. Scholarship, Calif. Employees Assn. (pres. San Jose State Coll. chpt. 1966-67), Western Assn. Summer Session Adminstrs. (newsletter editor 1970-73, pres. 1974-75), Calif. C. of C. (edn. com 1969-77), Industry-Edn. Coun. Calif. (bd. dirs. 1974-80), Sci. and Human Values, Inc. (bd. dirs. 1974—, chmn. bd. 1976—), Tahoe Tavern (bd. dirs. 1987-91, chmn. bd. 1988-90), Seascape Lagoon Homeowners Assn. (bd. dirs. 1988-95, chmn. 1989-95), Nat. Gold Key Honors Soc. (hon. life). Home and Office: 713 Clubhouse Dr Aptos CA 95003-5431 E-mail: rmbohn@cruzio.com

BOHNEN, ROBERT FRANK, hematologist, oncologist, educator; b. Huntington, N.Y., Jan. 3, 1941; s. Oscar and Sarah Leah (Piel) B.; m. Mollyn Villareal, June 20, 1965; children: Sharon Kay, Scott Owen David, Paul Alan. BS in Zoology, Syracuse U., 1961; MD, Columbia U., 1965. Diplomate Am. Bd. Internal Medicine, Am. Bd. Med. Oncology, Am. Bd. Hematology. Intern Buffalo (N.Y.) Gen. Hosp., 1965-66; resident in medicine SUNY, Buffalo, 1968-69, U. Utah, Salt Lake City, 1969-70, clin. hematology fellow, 1970-71, med. oncology fellow, 1971-72; physician hematology and med. oncology Cons. Med. Group, Carmichael and Roseville, Calif., 1972-91, Cancer Treatment Ctr. Merle West Med. Ctr., Klamath Falls, Oreg., 1991—. Instr. medicine and hematology/oncology U. Calif., Davis, Sacramento, 1973-77, asst. clin. prof. medicine and hematology/oncology, 1977-83; clin. instr. dept. family medicine Oreg. Health Scis. U., Portland, 1994—; sr. staff Mercy Am. River Hosp., Carmichael, Calif., Mercy San Juan Hosp., Carmichael, Roseville (Calif.) Cmty. Hosp.; courtesy staff Sutter Cmty. Hosp. Sacramento; active staff Merle West Med. Ctr., Klamath Falls; med. dir. Hospice Roseville, Calif.; prin. investigator No. Calif. Oncology Group Clin. Trials; med. adv. bd. Vis. Nurses Assn.; lectr. and presenter in field. Contbr. articles to profl. jours. Chmn. Greater Sacramento Cancer Coun. Clin. Trials Com./No. Calif. Oncology Group Outreach Com.; bd. dirs., sec. Greater Sacramento Cancer Coun.; chmn. prof. edn. com., bd. dirs. Tri-County chpt. Am. Cancer Soc.; soloist Sacramento Valley Concert Choir, Klamath Chorale; active Masterworks Chorus; cast member Linkville Players and Ross Ragland Theater Prodns., Klamath Falls, 1991—; choir dir. Sacred Heart Ch., Klamath Falls, 1992—. Med. Oncology fellow Am. Cancer Soc., U. Utah Med. Ctr., 1971-72. Mem. Am. Soc. Clin. Oncology, Phi Beta Kappa. Democrat. Roman Catholic. Avocations: musical theater, photography, choral singing and directing. Office: Cancer Treatment Ctr Merle West Med Ctr 2610 Uhrmann Rd Klamath Falls OR 97601-1123 E-mail: rbohnen@mwmc.org

BOHRNSTEDT, GEORGE WILLIAM, educational researcher; b. Arcadia, Wis., Sept. 28, 1938; s. Russell Gail and Agnes (Brecht) B.; m. Josephine Orlanda, Aug. 11, 1962 (div. 1973); children— Elizabeth (dec.), Brian, Matthew; m. Jennifer Lou Cain, Sept. 28, 1980; 1 child, Kassandra Student, Winona State Coll., 1956-58; B.S., U. Wis., 1960, M.A., 1963, Ph.D., 1966. Research assoc. U. Wis., Madison, 1966-69; assoc. prof. Mpls., 1969-73, chmn. dept. sociology, 1970-73; prof. Ind. U., Bloomington, 1973-88, chmn. dept. sociology, 1982-86, dir. Inst. Social Research, 1974-79; sr. v.p., dir. Am. Inst. for Rsch., Palo Alto, Calif., 1988-96, sr. v.p. for rsch., 1996—. Author: (with others) Statistics for Social Data Analysis, 3d edit., 1994; Basic Social Statistics, 1991; editor: Sociological Methodology, 1970; editor Sociol. Methods and Rsch., 1971-79, 84-87, Social Psychology Quar., 1980-82. Served to U.S. Army, 1962 Fellow NSF, 1963, NIMH, 1964-66, Ctr. for Advanced Studies in Behavioral Scis., 1986-87; Found. for Child Devel. Belding scholar, 1976-77 Mem. Am. Sociol. Assn., Psychometric Soc., Soc. Exptl. Social Psychologists Avocation: jazz musician. Office: Am Insts Rsch Behavioral Scis John C Flanagan Rsch Ctr 1791 Arastradero Rd Palo Alto CA 94304-1337

BOIME, ALBERT ISAAC, art history educator; b. St. Louis, Mar. 17, 1933; s. Max and Dorothy (Rubin) B.; m. Myra Block, June 23, 1964; children: Robert, Eric. A.B., UCLA, 1961; M.A., Columbia U., 1963, Ph.D., 1968. Instr. social history of art Columbia U., 1966-67; assoc. prof. SUNY, Stony Brook, 1967-72, prof., chmn. dept. Binghamton, 1972-74, prof., 1974-78; prof. social history of art UCLA, 1978—. Art historian in residence Coll. Creative Studies, U. Calif.-Santa Barbara, 1973; judge NEH, Washington, 1975; mem. adv. council N.Y. Acad. Art, N.Y.C., 1981— Author: The Academy and French Painting in the 19th Century, 1971, Thomas Couture and the Eclectic Vision, 1981, the Social History of Modern Art: Vol. 1: Art in an Age of Revolution, 1987, Hollow Icons: The Politics of Sculpture in Nineteenth Century France, 1987, Vincent Van Gogh: Sternennacht, 1989, The Art of Exclusion: Representing Blacks in the Nineteenth Century, 1990, The Social History of Modern Art Vol. 2: Art in an Age of Bonapartism, 1990, The Magisterial Gaze: Manifest Destiny and American Landscape Painting (ca. 1830-1865), 1991, The Art of the Macchia and the Risorgimento, 1993, The Odyssey of Jan Stussey in Black and White, 1995, Art and the French Commune, 1995, Violence and Utopia: The Work of Jerome Boime, 1996, The Unveiling of the National Icons: A Plea for Patriotic Iconoclasm in a Nationalist Era, 1998 (Gustavus Myers Outstanding Book award 1999). Served with AUS, 1955-58. Am. Council Learned Socs. fellow, 1970-71; Guggenheim fellow, 1974-75, 84-85; Regents fellow Smithsonian Institution, 1989-90. Mem. Coll. Art Assn., Soc. Fellows Am. Acad. at Rome Office: UCLA Dept Art 405 Hilgard Ave Los Angeles CA 90095-9000

BOITANO, MARK L. state legislator; b. San Francisco, July 19, 1953; m. Cory Greene. BS, Regents Coll., 1989. Realtor, 1992—; mem. N.Mex. Senate, Dist. 18, Sante Fe, 1996—; mem. edn. com., mem. pub. affairs com. N.Mex. Senate. Mem. Albuquerque Bus. Edn. Compact; mem Albuquerque Diamond Jubilee Bicentennial Com.; chair N.Mex. Parents Day Coalition Mem. Nat. Assn. Realtors, Albuquerque Bd. Realtors (cmty. affiars com., govtl. affairs com.), Realtors Assn. N.Mex., Friends to Friends Inc. (co-founder). Republican. Office: 4810 Aspen Ct NE Albuquerque NM 87111 E-mail: mboitano@state.nm.us

BOK, DEAN, cell biologist, educator; b. Douglas County, S.D., Nov. 1, 1939; s. Kryn Arie and Rena (Van Zee) B.; m. Audrey Ann Van Diest, Aug. 21, 1964; children: Jonathan, Jeremy, James. B.A., Calvin Coll., 1960; M.A., Calif. State U., Long Beach, 1965; Ph.D., UCLA, 1968. Sci. instr. Valley Christian High Sch., Cerritos, Calif.; prof. neurobiology and Dolly Green prof. ophthalmology UCLA; asso. dir. Jules Stein Eye Inst., 1972-80. Wellcome vis. prof. biomed. scis., 1994. Mem. nat. adv. bd. Eye Coun., 1998—. Recipient disting. teaching awards UCLA, sr. sci. investigator award Rsch. To Prevent Blindness Inc., 1986, 95, Disting. Alumnus award Calif. State U., 1986, Calvin Coll., 1990; grantee Nat. Eye Inst., Nat. Retinitis Pigmentosa Soc.; William and Mary Greve internat. rsch. scholar Rsch. To Prevent Blindness Inc., 1982. Fellow AAAS; mem. Nat. Eye Inst. (bd. sci. counselors 1980-82, MERIT award 1987-96), Assn. Research in Vision and Ophthalmology (trustee 1978-82, Friedenwald award 1985, Alcon award 1985), Am. Soc. Cell Biology. Home: 2135 Kelton Ave Los Angeles CA 90025-5705 Office: UCLA Los Angeles CA 90024

BOLENDER, DAVID FRANCIS, utility company executive. Grad. Colo. Sch. of Mines, 1954. Pres. Pacific Power & Light Co., Denver. Office: ELECTRO SCIENTIFIC INDUSTRIES,INC 13900 NW SCIENCE PARK DR. Portland OR 97229-5497

BOLES, ROGER, otolaryngologist; b. Oakland, Calif., Jan. 13, 1928; s. Albert and Julia Boles; m. Marianna Reeves, June 16, 1956; children: Martin Reeves, Melissa. AB, Stanford U., 1949; postgrad., Denver U., 1950-52; MD with distinction, George Washington U., 1956. Diplomate Am. Bd. Otolaryngology, Am. Bd. Med. Specialties. Intern Fitzsimmons Army Hosp., Denver, 1956-57; asst. resident through sr. clin. instr. Mich. U. Hosp., Ann Arbor, 1959-63, faculty dept. otorhinolaryngology, 1963-74, prof., 1973-74; prof., chmn. otolaryngology U. Calif. San Francisco Sch. Medicine, 1974-89; pres. med. staff U. Calif., San Francisco, 1982-83, prof. otolaryngology, 1989-98, prof. emeritus otolargyngology, 1998—, ret., 1998. Cons. for otolaryngology to Surgeon Gen., USAF, 1975-85; mem. staff San Francisco Gen. Hosp., 1984—, Childrens Hosp. San Francisco (bd. dirs. 1987-91); cons. in otolaryngology Va. Hosp., Ann Arbor, Wayne County Hosp., Eloise, Mich., So. Mich. Prison, Jackson, Fed. Penitentiary, Milan, Mich., 1963-74, Letterman Gen. Hosp., Presidio of San Francisco, U.S. Naval Hosp., Oakland, Calif., 1974-93, Kaiser Hosp., Oakland, 1975, Va. Hosp., San Francisco; bd. dirs. Council Med. Splty. Socs., 1981-82, sec., 1982-83; bd. dirs. Am. Acad. Otolaryngology-Head and Neck Surgery, 1981-88, coord. for continuing med. edn., 1980-83, pres., 1987; mem. Accreditation Coun. for Continuing Med. Edn., 1986-92, chmn., 1990; chmn. PEPP com., 1988-89, 90, vice chmn., 1989, residency rev. com. for otolaryngology; Marshall Hale Hosp., San Francisco, 1975-83, bd. dirs., 1983-87; mem. Am. Bd. Med. Specialties, 1984-89, exec. com., 1988-89; vis. prof. various univs.; participant in confs., convs., workshops, seminars, insts. Contbr. chpts. to books, numerous revs., articles and abstracts to profl. lit. Served with M.C., AUS, 1956-59. Fellow ACS (chmn. adv. coun. for otolaryngology 1977-80, adv. com. for continuing med. edn. 1982-83), Am. Laryngol. Soc.; mem. AMA (ho. dels. 1975-82, bd. editors archives otolaryngology 1975-85, mem. reference com. on ins. and med. svc. 1978, adv. com. for continuing med. edn. 1981-87), AOA Hon. Med. Soc., Am. Acad. Opthalmology and Otolaryngology (assoc. sec. com. on continuing edn. 1974-80, chmn. manuals editorial com. 1977-80, mem. at large exec. com. div. otolaryngology 1977-78, mem. interspecialty cooperation com. med. specialty socs. 1978-88), Am. Acad. Facial Plastic and Reconstructive Surgery (co-chmn. standards com. 1977-80, med. edn. com. 1979-81—), Soc. Univ. Otolaryngologists (sec.-treas. 1973-80, chmn. com. on undergrad. curriculum 1969-74, mem. exec. council 1968-79, pres. 1978), Council Acad. Socs.-Assn. Am. Med. Colls., Assn. Acad. Depts. Otolaryngology (vice chmn. subcom. Nat. Cancer Inst. liaison com. 1977-81, chmn. edn. nominating coms. 1978-79), Am. Bronco-Esophagological Assn. (mem. council 1981-82), Am. Bd. Otolaryngology(bd. dirs. 1974-91, exec. com. 1981-88, mem. various coms. 1974-91, chmn. ad hoc com. for nomination process for membership on bd. dirs. 1976-77, pres. 1986-88), Am. Council Otolaryngology (mem. subcom. on hearing 1976-80, research adv. com. 1977-81, pres. 1978-79), Am. Laryngol., Rhinological and Otolaryn. Soc. (mem. editl. bds. transactions 1978-88, mem. council 1982-88, pres. 1986-87, historian 1994—), Am. Soc. for Neck and Head Surgery, Otosclerosis Study Group, Am. Tinnitus Assn. (sci. adv. bd. 1978-81), Pacific Coast Oto-Opthal. Soc., Soc. Med. Cons. to Armed Forces, Calif. Med. Assn. (program co-chmn. sects. on allergy and otolaryngology, neurology and otolaryngology 1977-78, chmn. adv. council of otolaryngology 1979-80), Calif. Otolaryn. Soc. (pres. 1978-80), U. Calif. San Francisco Sch. Medicine Alumni-Faculty Assn. (pres. 1978-79), Am. Otological Soc., Am. Laryngol. Assn. (coun. 1983-84), San Francisco Med. Soc. (bd. dirs. 1983-90, treas. 1989-90), Royal Coll. Surgeons in Ireland (hon.), U. Mich. Med. Ctr. Alumni Assn. (bd. govs. 1983), Gold Headed Cane Soc. (hon.), U. Calif. San Francisco Sch. Medicine. Office: Univ Calif San Francisco Dept Otolaryngology 400 Parnassus Ave # A-717 San Francisco CA 94122-2721 Home: PO Box 620203 Woodside CA 94062-0203

BOLIN, VERNON SPENCER, microbiologist, consultant; b. Parma, Idaho, July 9, 1913; s. Thadeus Howard Bolin and Jennie Bell Harm; m. Helen Epling, Jan. 5, 1948 (div. 1964); children: Rex, Janet, Mark; m. Barbara Sue Chase, Aug. 1965; children: Vladimir, Erik. BS, U. Wash., 1942; MS, U. Minn., 1949. Tchg. asst. U. Minn., Mpls., 1943-45; rsch. assoc. U. Utah, Salt Lake City, 1945-50, fellow in surgery, 1950-52; rsch.

virologist Jensen-Salsbery Labs., Inc., Kansas City, Mo., 1952-57; rsch. assoc. Wistar Inst., U. Pa., 1957-58; rsch. virologist USPHS, 1958-61; founder Bolin Labs., Phoenix, 1959—, also bd. dirs. Contbr. articles to profl. jours. Served with U.S. Army, 1931-33. Mem. N.Y. Acad. Scis., Phi Mu Chi. Home: 36629 N 19th Ave Phoenix AZ 85086-9143

BOLLES, CHARLES AVERY, librarian; b. Pine Island, Minn., Aug. 10, 1940; s. Arthur Marston and Clarice Ione (Figy) B.; m. Marjorie Elaine Hancock, May 177, 1964; children: Jason Brice, Justin Brian. BA, U. Minn., 1962, MA in Libr. Sci., 1963, PhD in Libr. Sci., 1975. Catalog and serials librarian U. Iowa, Iowa City, 1964-67; asst. prof. Emporia (Kans.) State U., 1970-76, dir. Sch. Libr. Sci., 1978-80; dir. libr. devel. divsn. Kans. State Libr., 1976-78; state librarian State of Idaho, Boise, 1980—. Mem. ALA, Chief Officers State Libr. Agys., Western Coun. State Librs. (chmn. 1985-86, 98-99), Pacific N.W. Libr. Assn. (pres. 1990-91), Idaho Libr. Assn. Office: Idaho State Libr 325 W State St Boise ID 83702-6014

BOLOCOFSKY, DAVID N. lawyer, psychology educator; b. Hartford, Conn., Sept. 29, 1947; s. Samuel and Olga Bolocofsky; m. Debra Stein, June 25, 1994; children: Vincent, Daniel, Charly. BA, Clark U., 1969; MS, Nova U., 1974, PhD, 1975; JD, U. Denver, 1988. Bar: Colo. 1988; cert. sch. psychologist, Colo. Tchr. high sch. Univ. Sch., Ft. Lauderdale, Fla., 1972-73; ednl. coord. Living and Learning Ctr., Ft. Lauderdale, 1972-75; asst. prof. U. No. Colo., Greeley, 1975-79, assoc. prof., 1979-90, dir. sch. psychology program, 1979-82; assoc. Robert T. Hinds Jr. & Assocs., Littleton, Colo., 1988-93; hearing officer State of Colo., 1991—; pres. David N. Bolocofsky, P.C., Denver, 1993—. Psychol. cons. Clin. Assocs., Englewood, Colo., 1978—. Author: Enhancing Personal Adjustment, 1986, (chpts. in books) Children and Obesity, 1987, Obtaining and Utilizing a Custody Evaluation, 1989; contbr. numerous articles to profl. jours. Mem. Douglas-Elbert Bar Assn., Arapahoe Bar Assn., Colo. Soc. Sch. Psychologists (bd. dirs. 1978-96, treas. 1993-96), Interdisciplinary Commn. on Child Custody (pro bono com. 1988-93), Colo. Bar Assn. (family law sect., sec. juvenile law sect. 1990-92), Colo. Soc. Behavioral Analysis Therapy (treas. 1990-96), Arapmhc (bd. dirs. 1993-2001, bd. pres. 1995-97). Avocations: sailing, golf, skiing. Home: 9848 E Maplewood Cir Englewood CO 80111-5401 Office: 7887 E Belleview Ave Ste 1275 Englewood CO 80111-6094 E-mail: familylawdoc@aol.com

BOLTON-HOLIFIELD, ALICE RUTH, basketball player; b. Lucedale, Miss., May 25, 1967; d. Linwood and Leola Bolton; m. Mark Holifield. B of Exercise Physiology, Auburn U., 1989. Basketball player C.A. Faenza, Italy, 1993, Erreti Faenza, Italy, 1994-95, Sacramento Monarchs, 1997—. Mem. U.S.A. Women's Nat. Basketball Team. Lead singer Antidum Tarantula, Italy. 1st lt. USAR. Recipient gold medal 1994 Goodwill Games, 1994, World Championship Qualifying Team FIBA World Championship, 1993, World Univ. Games, 1991, U.S. Olympic Fesitval, 1986; bronze medal World Championship, 1994; named USA Basketball's Female Athelete of Yr., 1991, 1st Am. woman to play profl. basketball in Hungary and Sweden, 1990-91; named to NCAA 1989 Mideast Region All-Tournament Team, 1988, 89, NCAA Final Four All Tournament Team, 1988, SEC All-Academic Team, 1988, 89, All-SEC second team, 1989; earned SEC All-Tournament Team honors, 1988, All-WNBA 1st team, 1997, named first ever WNBA player of week, 1997, mem. gold medal winning Olympic team Atlanta, 1996, mem. U.S. Basketball Women's Nat. Team, 1995-96. Office: Sacramento Monarchs Arco Arena Sacramento CA 95834

BOLTZ, GERALD EDMUND, lawyer; b. Dennison, Ohio, June 1, 1931; s. Harold E. and Margaret Eve (Hecky) B.; m. Janet Ruth Scott, Sept. 19, 1959; children: Gretchen Boltz Fields, Eric Scott, Jill Marie. BA, Ohio No. U., 1953, JD, 1955. Bar: Ohio 1955, U.S. Supreme Ct. 1964, Calif. 1978, U.S. Dist. Ct. (cen. dist.) Calif. 1978. Asst. atty. gen. State of Ohio, 1958; atty. spl. investigations unit SEC, 1959-60, legal asst. to commr., 1960-61, sr. trial and spl. counsel, 1961-66, regional adminstr. Ft. Worth, 1967-71, L.A., 1972-78; ptnr. Fine, Perzik& Friedman, L.A., 1979-83, Rogers & Wells, L.A., 1983-92, Bryan Cave, L.A., 1992—. Co-author: Securities Law Techniques. Served with U.S. Army, 1955-57. Mem. ABA, Fed. Bar Assn., L.A. Bar Assn., Ohio Bar Assn., Calif. Bar Assn., Bel Air Bay Club. Republican. Presbyn. (elder). Avocations: sailing, bridge, piano. Home: 1105 Centinela Ave Santa Monica CA 90403-2316 Office: Bryan Cave 120 Broadway Ste 300 Santa Monica CA 90401-2386 E-mail: geboltz@bryancave.com

BOMAN, MARC ALLEN, lawyer; b. Cleve., Sept. 4, 1948; s. David S. and Shirley T. (Freier) B.; m. Leah Eilenberg, June 10, 1984; children: Autumn, Heidi, Jane, David. Student, Purdue U., 1966-68; BA, Case Western Res. U., 1971, JD, 1974. Bar: Ohio 1974, Wash. 1978, D.C. 1978, U.S. Dist. Ct. (we. dist.) Wash. 1980, U.S. Ct. Appeals (9th cir.), U.S. Dist. Ct. (ea. dist.) Wash. 1985, U.S. Ct. Appeals (fed. cir.) 1986. Atty.-advisor Office of Gen. Counsel U.S. Gen. Acctg. Office, Washington, 1974-78; dep. prosecuting atty. Office of Prosecuting Atty., King County, Wash., 1978-81; assoc. Perkins Coie, Seattle, 1981-86, ptnr., 1986—. Spl. ind. dep. prosecutor ethics investigation of county execs., 1994; mem. Seattle Ethics and Elections Commn., 1995-98; spkr. in field. Bd. dirs. Perkins Coie Cmty. Svcs. Fellowship, 1987-97, co-chmn., 1994-97; former bd. dirs. Totem coun. Girl Scouts U.S., Seattle Day Ctr. for Adults, Madrona Neighborhood Coun.; trustee Herzl-Ner Tamid Congregation, 1987-98, pres., 1994-96; mem. Leadership Tomorrow, United Way King County-Seattle C. of C., 1987-88; trustee King County Bar Found., 1995-2000, v.p., 1997-98, pres., 1998-99. Recipient Pres.'s award King County Bar Assn., 1999; Mayoral proclamation declaring Marc Boman Day named in honor of contbn. to citizens of Seattle, 1998. Mem. Seattle King Bar Assn. (trustee 1986-89, chmn. divsn. young lawyers 1984-85). Office: Perkins Coie 1201 3rd Ave Fl 40 Seattle WA 98101-3029

BOMES, STEPHEN D. lawyer; b. Providence, Jan. 15, 1948; s. Edward and Lillian L. (Dick) B.; m. Barbara Jean Thomas, Feb. 4, 1989; 1 child, Laura Alexandra. BS, Boston U., 1968; JD, U. Calif., Hastings, 1971; postgrad., Columbia U., 1974; LLM, NYU, 1975. Bar: Calif. 1972, N.Y. 1975, Fla. 1975, D.C. 1975, U.S. Dist. Ct. (no. and cen. dists.) Calif. 1972, U.S. Ct. Appeals (2d and 9th cirs.). Assoc. Milbank, Tweed, Hadley & McCoy, N.Y.C., 1975-79, London, 1979-81; ptnr. Brobeck, Phleger & Harrison, San Francisco, 1981-93, Loeb and Loeb, L.A., 1994-96, Heller Ehrman White & McAuliffe, L.A., 1997—. Instr. NYU 1973-75; adj. asst. prof. CUNY, 1974; mem. Brazil Soc. No. Calif., Pan. Am. Soc. Author: The Dead Hand: The Last Grasp, 1976, (with W.F. Johnson) Real Estate Transfer, Development and Finance, Cases and Materials, 1975; co-editor: Commercial Agency and Distributions in Europe, 1992; contbr. chpts. to books. Trustee 1066 Found. NYU fellow, 1973-75; included in Euromoney's Guide to the World's Leading Banking Lawyers. Mem. L.A., Assn. of Bar of City of N.Y., Internat. Bar Assn., Jonathan Club. Office: White & McAuliffe 601 S Figueroa St Fl 40 Los Angeles CA 90017-5704 E-mail: sdbomes@aol.com, sbomes@hewm.com

BOMMER, TIMOTHY J, magistrate judge, lawyer; b. Columbus, Ohio, Dec. 9, 1940; s. Thomas F. and Susan L. (Proper) B.; children: Breton J., Kevin A., Melissa K. BA, U. Wyo., 1963, JD, 1970. Bar: Wyo. 1970, Colo. 1970. Dep. county and pros. atty., 1970-74; magistrate judge U.S. Dist. Ct., Jackson, 1976—; sole practice Jackson, 1977—. Chmn. fee arbitration com. Wyo. State Bar, 1980-84, mem. Wyo. Jud. Nominating Commn., 1984-88. Mem. ATLA, Am. Bd. Trial Advocates. Republican. Episcopalian. Avocations: boating, hunting, fishing, [illegible] PO Box 1728 Jackson WY 83001-1728

BONAPART, ALAN DAVID, lawyer; b. San Francisco, Aug. 4, 1930; s. Benjamin and Rose B.; m. Helen Sennett, Aug. 20, 1955; children— Paul S., Andrew D. A.B. with honors, U. Calif., Berkeley, 1951, J.D., 1954. Bar: Calif. 1955, U.S. Tax Ct. 1965, U.S. Supreme Ct. 1971. Assoc. Bancroft & McAlister (formerly Bancroft, Avery & McAlister), San Francisco, 1959-62; ptnr. Bancroft & McAlister, San Francisco, 1962-93, Bancroft & McAlister, A Profl. Corp., 1993-99, Bancroft & McAlister LLP, 1999—. Past trustee Bancroft and McAlister Found.; mem. adv. com. Heckerling Estate Planning Inst., U. Miami, Fla., 1974-87, 92—, mem. faculty, 1974, 91-2000; past dir. Myrtle V. Fitchen Charitable Trust. Mem. ABA, Am. Coll. Trust and Estate Counsel, Bar Assn. San Francisco, State Bar Calif. (cert. in estate planning, probate and trust law Bd. Legal Specialization 1991). Office: Bancroft & McAlister LLP Ste 120 300 Drake's Landing Rd Greenbrae CA 94904-3123 E-mail: abonapart@bamlaw.com

BONAVIA, PAUL J. lawyer; m. Patricia Sesterhenn; 2 children. BA, Drake U., 1972; law degree, U. Miami Sch. Law, 1975. V.p., gen. counsel DRI, 1991, sr. v.p., corporate, 1995—. Office: New Century Energies Inc 1225 17th St Ste 1200 Denver CO 80202-5506

BOND, DAVID F. food products executive; Fin. cons., ptnr. Deloitte & Touche, San Francisco, 1986-97; sr. v.p., fin. and control Safeway, Inc., Pleasanton, Calif., 1997—. Office: Safeway Inc PO Box 99 Pleasanton CA 94566-0009

BONDAREFF, WILLIAM, psychiatry educator; b. Washington, Apr. 29, 1930; s. Leon and Gertrude Bondareff; children by previous marriage: Hyla, Sarah; m. Rita Haber Kassoy, Jan. 2, 1988. BS in Zoology, George Washington U., 1951, MS in Zoology, 1952; PhD in Anatomy, U. Chgo., 1954; MD, Georgetown U., 1962. Diplomate Am. Bd. Psychiatry and Neurology with added qualifications in geriatric psychiatry. Rsch. assoc., instr. anatomy U. Chgo., 1955; rotating intern USPHS Hosp., Balt., 1962-63; resident in psychiatry Northwestern Meml. Hosp. Inst. Psychiatry, Chgo., 1978-80; asst. prof. anatomy Northwestern U., Evanston, Ill., 1963-65, assoc. prof., 1965-69, prof., 1969-78, chmn. dept. anatomy, 1970-78; prof. psychiatry and gerontology U. So. Calif., L.A., 1981—; mem. staff U. So. Calif. Univ. Hosp., L.A., 1991—; mem. attending staff L.A. County/U. So. Calif. Med. Ctr., L.A., 1981—; mem. Hosp. Good Samaritan, L.A., 1981-96; mem. staff Norris Cancer Hosp., 1987—. Physician/cons. VA Hosp., Downey, Ill., 1969-80, Jewish Home for Aged, Reseda, Calif., 1981-90; vis. staff mem. medicine Passavant Pavilion Northwestern Meml. Hosp., 1972-80; dir. div. geriat. psychiatry U. So. Calif., 1981—; dir. U. So. Calif.-St. Barnabas Alzheimer Disease Ctr., 1985—; acting dir. dept. Gerontology Research Inst. Andrus Gerontology Ctr.-U. So. Calif., 1982; staff psychiatrist Los Angeles County Hosp., 1981—; past holder various com. offices Northwestern U. Editor Mechanisms of Aging and Devel., 1970—; assoc. editor Am. Jour. Anatomy, 1970-76; mem. editl. bd. Alzheimer Disease and Associated Disorders-An Internat. Jour., 1985-95, Neurbiology of Aging, 1980-94, The Jour. of Gerontology, 1981-84, Internat. Rev. Jour. of Psychiatry, 1988—, Jour. Alzheimer's Disease, 1997-2001; contbr. articles to profl. jours. Mem. sci. adv. bd. Alzheimer's Disease & Related disorders Assn. L.A., bd.dirs., 1989—; mem. rsch. rev. com. treatment, devel. and assessment Nat. Inst. Mental Health, 1987-92. Served with USPHS, 1955-63. USPHS fellow, 1955, U. Cambridge Clare Hall vis. fellow, 1980, Hughes Hall vis. fellow, 1988; scholar Allergy Found., 1960, U. Chgo., 1953; recipient Career Devel. award Nat. Inst. Neurol. Disease and Blindness, 1966-69, Sesquicentennial award Hobart and William Smith Colls., 1972, Sandoz prize Internat. Assn. Gerontology, 1983, Alzheimer Disease and Related Disorders Assn. award, 1984; Fulbright Lectr., U. Goteborg, Sweden, 1967-68. Fellow AAAS (councilor 1970-74), Am. Psychiat. Assn. (geriatrics task force 1981), Gerontol. Soc.; mem. Am. Assn. Anatomists (chmn. local com. ann. meeting 1969), Electron Microscope Soc. Am., Am. Soc. Cell Biology, Am. Acad. Neurology (chmn. neuroanatomical scis. sect. 1971-77), Soc. Neurosci., Assn. Anatomy Chmn. (councilor 1975-77), Am. Assn. Geriat. Psychiatry (program com. 1984-89, bd. dirs. 1985-89), So. Calif. Psychiat. Soc., Internat. Psychogeriat. Assn., Cajal Club, Cosmos Club, Sigma Xi. Office: U So Calif Sch Medicine MOL 203 1237 N Mission Rd Los Angeles CA 90033-1018

BONDI, HARRY GENE, lawyer; b. Sheridan, Wyo., Apr. 3, 1948; s. Gene and Elizabeth (Poynter) B; divorced; 1 child, Bert Gene. BS in sci., fin., Fairfield U., 1970; JD, U. Wyo., 1974; postgrad., Georgetown U. Law Ctr., 1977. Bar: Wyo. 1974, U.S. Dist. Ct. D.C. 1976, U.S. Tax Ct. 1976, U.S. Ct. Claims 1975, U.S. Supreme Ct. 1980, D.C. 1975, Colo. 1988, U.S. Dist. Ct. Wyo. 1977, U.S. Ct. Appeals (10th cir.) 1980. Trial atty. U.S. Renegotiation Bd., Washington, 1974-77; pub. defender Wyo. State Pub. Defender Office, Casper, 1978-79; pvt. practice Harry G. Bondi, P.C., Casper, 1977—. Author: Wyoming Labor and Employment Law, 1992, Workers Compensation in Wyoming, 1993, Wrongful Discharge Claims Under Wyoming Law, 1994, 95. Chmn. City of Casper Housing and Cmty. Devel. Commn., 1977-81; past pres. Natrona County Meals of Wheels, Inc., 1988-90, Meals on Wheels Found., 1991-94; bd. dirs. Casper Jr. Baseball League, 1994-95. Mem. Wyo. Bar Assn., Natrona County Bar Assn., Am. Trial Lawyers Assn., Wyo. Trial Lawyers Assn., Wyo. Criminal Defense Lawyers Assn., Colo. Bar Assn., D.C. Bar Assn., Federal Bar Assn., Criminal Justice Adminstrn. Panel Dist. Wyo. Avocations: hiking, biking, soccer.

BONDS, BARRY LAMAR, professional baseball player; b. Riverside, Calif., July 24, 1964; s. Bobby B. Student, Ariz. State U. With Pitts. Pirates, 1985-92, San Francisco Giants, 1992—. Named MVP Baseball Writers' Assn. Am., 1990, 1992, 1993, Maj. League Player Yr. Sporting News, 1990, Nat. League Player Yr. Sporting News, 1990, 91, mem. Sporting News Coll. All-Am. team, 1985, mem. All-Star team, 1990, 1992-96; recipient Gold Glove award, 1990-94, 96, Silver Slugger award, 1990-96. Achievements include leading the Nat. League in intentional walks, 1992-94. Office: San Francisco Giants Candlestick Point 24 Willie Mays Plz San Francisco CA 94107-2199

BONESTEEL, MICHAEL JOHN, lawyer; b. L.A., Dec. 22, 1939; s. Henry Theodore Samuel Becker and Kathleen Mansfield (Nolan) B.; children: Damon Becker, Kirsten Kathleen; m. Susan Elizabeth Schaff, June 1, 1980. AB in History, Stanford U., 1961; JD, U. So. Calif., 1966. Bar: Calif. 1967, U.S. Dist. Ct. (ctrl. and so. dists.) Calif, 1967, U.S. Ct. Appeals (9th cir.) 1967, U.S. Dist. Ct. (no. dist.) Calif. 1969, U.S. Dist. Ct. (ea. dist.) Calif. 1983, U.S. Supreme Ct. 1989. Assoc. Haight, Brown & Bonesteel, and predecessors, Santa Monica, Calif., 1967-71, ptnr., 1972—. Fellow Internat. Acad. Trial Lawyers, Am. Coll. Trial Lawyers; mem. ABA, State Bar Calif., Los Angeles County Bar Assn., Def. Rsch. Inst., Assn. So. Calif. Def. Counsel, Am. Soc. Most Venerable Order of Hospitaller St. John of Jerusalem, Hospitaller Order St. Lazarus of Jerusalem, Grand Priory of Am., Bel Air Bay Club, L.A. Country Club. Office: Haight Brown & Bonesteel 1620 26th St Ste 4000N Santa Monica CA 90404-4013 E-mail: bonesteels@msn.com, bonesteel,m@hbblaw.com

BONFIELD, ANDREW JOSEPH, tax practitioner; b. London, Jan. 26, 1924; came to U.S., 1946; s. George Willliam and Elizabeth Agnes B.; m. Eleanor Ackerman, Oct. 16, 1955; children: Bruce Ian, Sandra Karen. Gen. mgr. Am. Cushion Co., L.A., 1948-50, Monson Calif. Co., Redwood City, 1951-58; mfrs. mktg. rep. San Francisco, 1958-62; tax practitioner, bus. cons. Redwood City, 1963—, San Jose, Calif., 1963—, [illegible], 1969—, Kihei, Hawaii, 1986-98, Carmel, Calif., 1998. Past treas., dir. Northwood Park Improvement Assn.; exec. bd. Santa Clara County Coun. Boy Scouts Am., 1971—, past coun. pres., mem. Nat. coun., mem. Santa Clara County [illegible] 1978-81, 82-86; mem. County Assessment Appeals Bd., 1978-86, Hawaii Bd. Taxation Review, 1992-98. With Brit. Royal Navy, 1940-46. Decorated King George VI Silver Badge; recipient Silver Beaver award, Vigil honor award Boy Scouts Am.; enrolled to practice before IRS. Mem. Nat. Assn. Enrolled Agts., Calif. Soc. Enrolled Agts., Hawaii Assn. Pub. Accts., Royal Can. Legion (past state parliamentarian, past state 1st vice comdr.), Rotary (pres. San Jose E. 1977-78, pres Kihei-Wailea 1993-94), Carmel Masonic Lodge, Aloha Temple Shriners of Honolulu (amb.). Home: 181 Hacienda Carmel Carmel CA 93923-7946 E-mail: aebonfield@aol.com

BONGIORNO, JAMES WILLIAM, electronics company executive; b. Westfield, N.Y., Apr. 2, 1943; s. Samuel Salvatore and Marjorie Ruth (Hardenburg) B. Student public schs. Profl. musician, 1961-65; engr. Hadley Labs., Pomona, Calif., 1965-66, Marantz Co., Woodside, N.Y., 1966-67; chief engr. Rectilinear Research Corp., Bklyn., 1967-68; profl. musician, writer Popular Electronics, also Audio mag., 1968-71; dir. engring. Dynaco Inc., Phila., 1972, S.A.E. Inc., Los Angeles, 1973-74; founder, pres. Gt. Am. Sound Co. Inc., Chatsworth, Calif., 1974-77; founder, 1977; pres. Sumo Electric Co. Ltd., West Hollywood, Calif., 1977—. Ind. electronic cons. Patentee class A audio amplifier, FM IF-detector. Recipient State of Art Design award Stereo Sound mag., Tokyo, 1976, 80 Mem. Audio Engring. Soc., Am. Fedn. Musicians. Republican. Home and Office: 716 N G St Apt 2 Lompoc CA 93436-4530 E-mail: sstinc@earthlink.net

BONN, ETHEL MAY, psychiatrist, educator; b. Cin., Oct. 14, 1925; d. Stanley Ervin and Ethel May (Cliffe) B. BA, U. Cin., 1947; MD, U. Chgo., 1951. Asst. chief, then chief women's neuro-psychiat. services VA Hosp., Topeka, 1956-61, chief north service, 1961-62; assoc. dir. for clin. services Ft. Logan Mental Health Ctr., Denver, 1962-67, dir., 1967-76; clin. instr. psychiatry U. Colo. Sch. Medicine, 1963-76; field rep. Joint Commn. on Accreditation of Hosps., 1976-78; assoc. clin. prof. psychiatry UCLA Sch. Medicine, 1978-81; chief of quality assurance VA Med. Ctr.-Brentwood, L.A., 1978-81; chief psychiatry service VA Med. Ctr., Albuquerque, 1981-89; assoc. prof. psychiatry U. N.Mex. Sch. Medicine, 1981-89; prof. emeritus psychiatry sch. medicine U. N.Mex., 1989—. Cons. Fitzsimons Army Hosp., Denver, 1963-67, U. Calif. Dept Biobehavioral Scis., Los Angeles, 1978-81, VA Hosps., Ft. Lyon, Colo., Sheridan, Wyo., Tuscaloosa, Ala., 1963-67. Contbr. chpts. to books, articles to profl. jours. Recipient Dirs. commendation, VA, 1962, 81, 89, Psychiat. Adminstrs. award Am. Assn. Psychiat. Adminstrs., 1976. Fellow Am. Coll. Psychiatrists (emeritus), Am. Psychiat. Assn. (life; program com. insts. for hosp. and cmty. psychiatry 1977-81), Am. Coll. Mental Health Adminstrn. (founding), Am. Coll. Utilization Rev. Physicians; mem. AMA, Am. Hosp. Assn. (chmn. psychiat. sect. 1972-74). Avocations: travel, gardening, oil and watercolor painting, collecting rocks and minerals, photography.

BONNELL, VICTORIA EILEEN, sociologist, educator; b. N.Y.C., June 15, 1942; d. Samuel S. and Frances (Nassau) B.; m. Gregory Freidin, May 4, 1971. BA, Brandeis U., 1964; MA, Harvard U., 1966, PhD, 1975. Lectr. politics U. Calif., Santa Cruz, 1972-73, 74-76, asst. prof. sociology Berkeley, 1976-82, assoc. prof., 1982-91, prof., 1991—. Chair Berkeley Ctr. for Slavic and East European Studies, U. Calif.-Berkeley, 1994—. Author: Roots of Rebellion: Workers' Politics and Organizations in St. Petersburg and Moscow, 1900-1914, 1983; editor: The Russian Worker: Life and Labor Under the Tsarist Regime, 1983, (with Ann Cooper and Gregory Freidin) Russia at the Varricades: Eyewitness Accounts of the August 1991 Coup, 1994, Iconography of Power: Soviet Political Posters Under Lenin and Stalin, 1997, Identities in Transition: Eastern Europe and Russia After the Collapse of Communism, 1996, Beyond the Cultural Turn: New Directions in the Study of Society and Cultyre, 1999; contbr. articles to profl. jours. Recipient Heldt prize in Slavic women's studies, 1991; AAUW fellow, 1979; Regents Faculty fellow, 1978, Fulbright Hays Faculty fellow, 1977, Internat. Rsch. and Exch. Bd. fellow, 1977, 88, Stanford U. Hoover Instn. nat. fellow, 1973-74, Guggenheim fellow, 1985, fellow Ctr. Advanced Study in Behavioral Scis., 1986-87, Pres.' Rsch. fellow in Humanities, 1991-92; grantee Am. Philos. Soc., 1979, Am. Coun. Learned Socs., 1976, 90-91. Mem. Am. Sociol. Assn., Am. Assn. Advancement Slavic Studies, Am. Hist. Assn.

BONNER, ROBERT CLEVE, lawyer; b. Wichita, Kans., Jan. 29, 1942; s. Benjamin Joseph and Caroline (Kirkwood) B.; m. Kimiko Tanaka, Oct. 11, 1969; 1 child, Justine M. BA magna cum laude, Md. U., 1963; JD, Georgetown U., 1966. Bar: D.C. 1966, Calif. 1967, S. Ct. Appeals (4th, 5th, 9th, 10th cirs.), U.S. Supreme Ct. Law clk. to judge U.S. Dist. Ct., L.A., 1966-67; asst. atty. U.S. Atty's Office (cen. dist.) Calif., L.A., 1971-75, U.S. atty., 1984-89; judge U.S. Dist. Ct. (cen. dist.) Calif., L.A., 1989-90; ptnr. Kadison, Pfaelzer, et al, Los Angeles, 1975-84; dir. Drug Enforcement Adminstrn., Washington, 1990-93; ptnr. Gibson, Dunn & Crutcher, L.A., 1993—. Chair Calif. Commn. on Jud. Performance, 1997-99. Served to lt. comdr. USN, 1967-70 Fellow Am. Coll. Trial Lawyers, Fed. Bar Assn. (pres. Los Angeles chpt. 1982-83); mem. L.A. C. of C. (bd. dirs. 1999—). Republican. Roman Catholic. Office: Gibson Dunn & Crutcher 333 S Grand Ave Ste 4400 Los Angeles CA 90071-3197

BONNER, ROBERT WILLIAM, lawyer, director; b. Vancouver, B.C., Can., Sept. 10, 1920; s. Benjamin York and Emma Louise (Weir) B.; m. Barbara Newman, June 16, 1942; children: Barbara Carolyn (Mrs. Massie), Robert York, Elizabeth Louise (Mrs. McPhee). B.A. in Econs. and Polit. Sci, U. B.C., 1942, LL.B., 1948. Bar: B.C. 1948, created Queen's counsel 1952. With firm Clark Wilson White Clark & Maguire, Vancouver, 1948-52; atty. gen. Province of B.C., 1952-68; sr. v.p. adminstrn. MacMillan Bloedel Ltd., 1968-70, exec. v.p. adminstrn., 1970-71, vice chmn., 1971-72, pres., chief exec. officer, 1972-73, chmn. bd., 1973-74, ret., 1974; chmn. B.C. Hydro & Power Authority, 1976-85; ptnr. Bonner & Fouks, 1974-84, Robertson, Ward, Suderman, Vancouver, 1985-89, Ward & Co., Vancouver, 1989—. Mem. B.C. Legislature, 1952-69; mem. Energy Supplies Allocation Bd., bd. dirs. Served to maj. Royal Canadian Army, 1942-45; lt. col. Res. (ret.). Mem. Canadian Bar Assn., Law Soc. B.C. (life bencher), Delta Upsilon. Mem. Social Credit Party. Clubs: Mason, Vancouver; Union (Victoria). Home: 5679 Newton Wynd Vancouver BC Canada V6T 1H6 Office: Box 18162 2225 W 41st Ave Vancouver BC Canada V6M 2A3 Fax: 604-264-6142. E-mail: rwbonner@attcanada.ca

BONNEY, JOHN DENNIS, retired oil company executive; b. Blackpool, Eng., Dec. 22, 1930; s. John P. and Isabel (Evans) B.; six children. B.A., Hertford Coll., Oxford U., Eng., 1954, M.A., 1959; LL.M., U. Calif., Berkeley, 1956. Oil adviser, Middle East, 1959-60; fgn. ops. adviser, asst. mgr., then mgr. Chevron Corp. (formerly Standard Oil Co. of Calif.), San Francisco, 1960-72, v.p., from 1972, vice chmn., dir., 1987-95. Clubs: Commonwealth; World Affairs Coun. of No. Calif., World Trade (San Francisco); Oxford and Cambridge (London). Office: 32nd Fl 575 Market St San Francisco CA 94105-[illegible]

BONNIE, SHELBY W. computer company executive; BS in Commerce with distinction, [illegible] Tiger Mgmt., CFO CNET Networks, Inc., San Francisco, 1996-97; CEO CNET Networks Inc., San Francisco, 1999—; COO CNET: The Computer Network, San Francisco, 1997-99. Office: CNET Networks Inc 150 Chestnut St San Francisco CA 94111-1004

BONO, MARY, congresswoman; b. Cleve., Oct. 24, 1961; d. Clay and Karen Whitaker; m. Sonny Bono, Feb. 1986 (dec.); children: Chesare Elan, Chianna Maria. BFA in Art History, U. So. Calif., 1984. Cert. personal fitness instr. Mem. U.S. Congress from 44th Calif. dist., 1998—; mem. energy and commerce com. Past bd. dirs. Palm Springs Internat. Film Festival; active D.A.R.E program, Olive Crest Home for Abused Children, Tiempos de Los Ninos. Named Woman of Yr., San Gorgonio (Calif.) chpt. Girl Scouts Am., 1993. Republican. Avocations: outdoor activities, computer technology. Office: US House of Reps 404 Cannon Ho Office Bldg Washington DC 20515-0001*

BONSER, QUENTIN, retired surgeon; b. Sedro Wooley, Wash., Nov. 1, 1920; s. George Wayne and Kathleen Imogene (Lynch) B.; m. Loellen Rocca, Oct. 20, 1945; children: Wayne, Gordon, Carol, Patricia Bonser Sanford. BA in Zoology, UCLA, 1943; MD, U. Calif., San Francisco, 11947. Diplomate Am. Bd. Surgery. Intern U. Calif. Hosp., San Francisco, 1947-49, resident in gen. surgery, 1949-56; pvt. practice, Placerville, Calif., from 1956; now ret. Surgeon King Faisal Splty. Hosp., Saudi Arabia, Sept.-Oct., 1984; vis. prof. surgery U. Calif., San Francisco, 1968. Vol. physician, tchr. surgery, Vietnam, 1971, 72, 73. Capt. M.C., USAF, 1950-51. Fellow ACS; mem. H.C. Naffziger Surg. Soc. (pres. 1974-75). Home: 2590 Northridge Dr Placerville CA 95667-3416 Fax: 530-622-5748. E-mail: qbonser@ns.net

BONVICINI, JOAN M. university women's basketball coach; b. Bridgeport, Conn., Oct. 10, 1953; Grad., So. Conn. State U., 1975. Coach Calif. State U., Long Beach, 1980-91; head coach U. Ariz., Tucson, 1992—. Spkr. basketball seminars and camps; mem. NCAA Rules com. Bd. dirs. Tucson Area Girl Scouts, Boys and Girls Club of Tucson. Named to Hall of Fame So. Conn. State U., 1989, Conn. Women's Basketball Hall of Fame, 1994, Hall of Fame Long Beach State U., 1996, Coach of Yr., NCAA, 1981, PAC-10, 1998. Mem. Women's Basketball Coaches Assn. (pres. 1988). Office: U Ariz 236 Mckale Ctr Tucson AZ 85721-0001

BOOCHEVER, ROBERT, federal judge; b. N.Y.C., Oct. 2, 1917; s. Louis C and Miriam (Cohen) Boochever; m. Lois Colleen Maddox, Apr. 22, 1943 (dec.); children: Barbara K, Linda Lou, Ann Paula, Miriam Deon; m. Rose Marie Borden, Aug. 31, 2001. AB, Cornell U., 1939, JD, 1941; HD (hon.), U. Alaska, 1981. Bar: N.Y. 1944, Alaska 1947. Law clk. Nordlinger, Riegel & Cooper, 1941; asst. U.S. atty. Juneau, 1946-47; partner firm Faulkner, Banfield, Boochever & Doogan, Juneau, 1947-72; asso. justice Alaska Supreme Ct., 1972-75, 78-80, chief justice, 1975-78; judge U.S. Ct. Appeals (9th cir.), Pasadena, Calif., 1980-86; sr. judge U.S. Ct. Appeals, Pasadena, 1986—. Mem. 9th cir. rules com. U.S. Ct. Appeals, 1983-85, chmn. 9th cir. libr. com., 1995-2001; chmn. Ala. Jud. Coun., 1975-78; mem. appellate judges seminar NYU Sch. Law, 1975; mem. Conf. Chief Justices, 1975-79, vice chmn., 1978-79; mem. adv. bd. Nat. Bank of Ala., 1968-72; guest spkr. Southwestern Law Sch. Disting. Lecture Series, 1992. Contbr. articles to profl. jours. Chmn. Juneau chpt. ARC, 1949-51, Juneau Planning Commn., 1956-61; mem. Alaska Devel. Bd., 1949-52, Alaska Jud. Qualification Commn., 1972-75; mem. adv. bd. Juneau-Douglas Community Coll. Served to Capt. U.S. Army, 1941-45. Named Juneau Man of Year, Rotary, 1974; recipient Disting. Alumnus award Cornell U., 1989; named in his honor The Boochever & Bird Chair for Study and Teaching of Freedom & Equality, U. Calif. Sch. Law, Davis, 2000. Fellow Am. Coll. Trial Attys.; mem. ABA, Alaska Bar Assn. (pres. 1961-62), Juneau Bar Assn. (pres. 1971-72), Am. Judicature Soc. (dir. 1970-74), Am. Law Inst., Juneau C. of C. (pres. 1952, 55), Alaskans United (chmn. 1972), Cornell Club L.A., Altadena Town and County Club. E-mail: robert. Office: US Ct Appeals PO Box 91510 125 S Grand Ave Pasadena CA 91105-1652 E-mail: boochever@ca9.uscourts.gov

BOOKIN, DANIEL HENRY, lawyer; b. Ottumwa, Iowa, Oct. 16, 1951; BA, U. Iowa, 1973; JD, Yale U., 1976. Bar: Calif. 1978. Law clk. U.S. Dist. Ct. (no. dist.) Calif., 1976-77; asst. U.S. atty. U.S. Dist. Ct. (so. dist.) N.Y., 1978-82; ptnr. O'Melveny & Myers, San Francisco, 1982—. Mem. bd. editors Yale Law Jour., 1975-76. Fellow Am. Coll. Trial Lawyers, Phi Beta Kappa. Office: O'Melveny & Myers Embarcadero Ctr W Tower 275 Battery St San Francisco CA 94111-3305

BOONE, BRET ROBERT, professional baseball player; b. El Cajon, Calif., Apr. 6, 1969; s. Bob Boone. Ed., U. So. Calif. With Seattle Mariners, 1992-93; second baseman Cin. Reds, 1994-98; infielder Atlanta Braves, 1999-2000, San Diego Padres, 2000—. Office: San Diego Padres 8800 Rio San Diego Dr Ste 400 San Diego CA 92108-1622

BOONE, LOIS RUTH, legislator; b. Vancouver, B.C., Can., Apr. 26, 1947; d. George Charles Bearne and Ruth (Lindberg) Chudley; children: Sonia, Tanis. Tchr.'s cert., Simon Fraser U., 1969. Tchr. Sch. Dist. 57, Prince George, B.C., 1969-71, Sch. Dist. 27, Williams Lake, 1971-72; office mgr. Prince George YM-YWCA, 1972-73; case aide worker Vancouver YWCA, 1973-74; adminstrv. asst. Gov. B.C., Prince George, 1978-86, mem. legis. assembly Victoria, 1986—, min. govt. svcs., 1991-93, mem. bd. Ins. Corp. of B.C., 1994-96, min. mcpl. affairs, 1996, min. transp. and hwys., 1996-98, min. children and families, 1998-2000. Trustee Sch. Dist. 57, Prince George, 1981-85. Mem. New Democratic Party. Office: Parliament Bldgs Rm 028 Victoria BC Canada V8V 1X4

BOONSHAFT, HOPE JUDITH, public relations executive; b. Phila., May 3, 1949; d. Barry and Lorelei Gail (R ienzi) B. BA, Pa. State U., 1972; postgrad. Del. Law Sch, Kellogg Inst. Mgmt. Tng. Program writer Youth Edn., N.Y.C., 1972; legal aide to judge Phila., 1975; dir. spl. projects Guiffre Med. Ctr., Phila., 1975; senatorial campaign fin. dir. Arlen Specter, Phila., 1975; presdl. campaign fin. dir. Jimmy Carter, Atlanta, 1976; dir. devel. World Jewish Congress, N.Y.C., 1978, Yeshiva U., L.A., 1979; dir. comm. Nat. Easter Seal Soc., Chgo., 1979-83; CEO Boonshaft-Lewis & Savitch Pub. Rels and Govt. Affairs, L.A., 1983-93; sr. v.p. Edelman Worldwide, 1993-95; exec. v.p. external affairs Sony Pictures Entertainement, L.A., 1995—. Spl. adv. cmty. rels. The White House, 1977-80; guest lectr. U. Ill., 1982, May Co.'s Calif. Women in Bus. Bd. dirs. L.A. Arts Coun., L.A. County Citizens for Economy and Efficiency in Govt., Calif. Film Commn., Speaker's Commn. Calif. Initiative. Home: 1967 Mandeville Canyon Rd Los Angeles CA 90049-2235 Office: Sony Pictures Entertainment 10202 Washington Blvd Culver City CA 90232-3119

BOOTH, FORREST, lawyer; b. Evanston, Ill., Oct. 31, 1946; s. Robert and Florence C. (Forrest) B.; m. Louise A. Hayes, June 14, 1980; 1 child, Kristin A. BA, Amherst Coll., 1968; JD, Harvard U., 1975. Bar: D.C. 1976, U.S. Ct. Appeals (D.C. cir.) 1976, Calif. 1977, U.S. Dist. Ct. (no. dist.) Calif. 1977, U.S. Ct. Appeals (9th cir.) 1977, U.S. Supreme Ct. 1979. Assoc. Graham & James, Washington, 1975-76, Mccutchen, Doyle, Brown & Emersen, San Francisco, 1976-78; ptnr. Hancock, Rothert & Bunshoft, San Francisco, 1978-89; sr. ptnr. Booth Banning LLP, San Francisco, 1990—. Faculty mem. S.E. Admiralty Law Inst., Savannah, Ga., 1990; chmn. Pacific Admiralty Seminar, San Francisco, 1983-97; advisor U. San Francisco Maritime Law Jour., 1992—. Contbr. articles to profl. jours. Lt. USN, 1968-72, Vietnam. Mem. Maritime Law Assn. U.S. (proctor), World Trade Club of San Francisco, Marine Club London, Assn. Average Adjusters U.K., St. Francis Yacht Club. Avocations: sailing, photography, skiing. Office: Booth Banning LLP 100 Spear St Ste 1850 San Francisco CA 94105-1570

BOOTH, JOHN NICHOLLS, minister, writer, photographer; b. Meadville, Pa., Aug. 7, 1912; s. Sydney Scott and Margaret (Nicholls) B.; m. Edith Kriger, Oct. 1, 1941 (dec. Sept. 1982); 1 child, Barbara Anne Booth Christie. BA, McMaster U., 1934; MDiv, Meadville/Lombard Theol. Sch., 1942; LittD, New Eng. Sch. Law, 1950. Ordained to ministry Unitarian Ch., 1942. Profl. magician, 1934-40; min. Unitarian Ch., Evanston, Ill., 1942-48, 1st Ch., Belmont, Mass., 1949-57, 2d Ch. (formerly Old North Ch.), Boston, 1958-64, Unitarian Ch., Long Beach, Calif., 1964-71; interim pastor N.Y.C., Gainesville, (Fla.), Detroit, 1971-73. Celebrity platform lectr., stroke performer on conjuring, 1942-58; ministerial adviser to liberal students MIT, 1958-63; mem. books selection com. Gen. Theol. Library, Boston, 1960-63. Author: Super Magical Miracles, 1930, Magical Mentalism, 1931, Forging Ahead in Magic, 1939, Marvels of Mystery, 1941, The Quest for Preaching Power, 1943, Fabulous Destinations, 1950, Story of the Second Church in Boston, 1959, The John Booth Classics, 1975, Booths in History, 1982, Psychic Paradoxes, 1984, Wonders of Magic, 1986, Dramatic Magic, 1988, Creative World of Conjuring, 1990, Conjurians' Discoveries, 1992, The Fine Art of Hocus Pocus, 1995, Keys to Magic's Inner World, 1999, Extending Magic Beyond Credibility, 2001; contbr. articles to mags. and newspapers; photographer full length feature travel documentary films for TV, lecture platforms made in India, Africa, S.Am., Indonesia, South Seas, Himalayas; presented first color travelogue on TV in U.S. over NBC in N.Y.C., 1949; panel mem. radio program Churchmen Weigh The News, Boston, 1951-52; spl. corr. in Asia for Chgo. Sun-Times, 1948-49; by-line writer Boston Globe, 1952-62; producer motion picture Heart of Africa, 1954; photographer films Golden Kingdoms of the Orient, 1957, Treasures of the Amazon, Ecuador and Peru, 1960, Adventurous Britain, 1962, South Seas Saga in Tahiti, Australia and New Guinea, summer 1966, The Amazing America of Will Rogers, 1970, Spotlight on Spain, 1975. Co-founder Japan Free Religious Assn., Tokyo, 1948; co-founder Mass. Meml. Soc., 1962, dir., 1962-64; organizer Meml. Soc. Alachua County (Fla.), 1972; pres. Long Beach Mental Health Assn., 1964-66; adv. coun. Fair Housing Found. Recipient John Nevil Maskelyne prize London Magic Cir., 1987; placed on former N.Y. Town Hall Cinematographers Wall of Fame, 1967; named Disting. Alumnae, Gallery of McMaster U.; lifetime achievement fellow Acad. Magical Arts, 1990, masters fellowship, 2001. Mem. Unitarian-Universalist Mins. Assn. (past dir.), Am. Unitarian Assn. (past com. chmn.), Unitarian Mins. Pacific S.W. Assn. (v.p.), Clergy Counseling Svc. So. Calif., Soc. Am. Magicians (inducted into Hall of Fame 1983), Magic Castle Hollywood, Internat. Brotherhood Magicians (hon. life), Internat. Motion Picture and Lectrs. Assn., L.A. Adventurers Club (pres. 1983), Evanston (Ill.) Ministerial Assn. (pres. 1947-48). Achievements include having the first regularly scheduled TV broadcasts in U.S. by clergyperson, WBKB, Chgo., mid-1940s. Home and Office: 12032 Montecito Rd Los Alamitos CA 90720-4511

BOOTMAN, J. LYLE, pharmacy educator, dean; BS, U. Ariz., 1974; MS, U. Minn., 1976, PhD, 1978. Clin. resident NIH; faculty U. Ariz., 1978—, dean Coll. Pharmacy, 1990—, founding dir. Ctr. for Pharm. Econs., exec. dir. Health Outcomes and PharmacoEconomic Rsch. Ctr. Cons. and spkr. in field. Contbr. articles to profl. jours. Named one of the 50 most influential pharmacists in Am., The American Druggist, 1997; fellow Am. Found. for Pharm. Edn., Bush Found. Fellow Am. Assn. for Pharm. Scientists; mem. NAS Inst. Medicine, Am. Pharm. Assn. (trustee, pres. 1999). Office: Coll Pharmacy Adminstrn Rm 344 Univ Ariz Tucson AZ 85721 Fax: 520-626-4063. E-mail: bootman@pharmacy.arizona.edu

BOOZE, THOMAS FRANKLIN, toxicologist; b. Denver, Mar. 4, 1955; s. Ralph Walker and Ann (McNatt) B.; children: Heather N., Ian T. BS, U. Calif., Davis, 1978; MS, Kans. State U., 1981, PhD, 1985. Registered environ assessor, Calif. Asst. instr. Kans. State U., Manhattan, 1979-85; consulting toxicologist Chevron Corp., Sacramento, 1985-92; sr. toxicologist URS/Radian Internat., Sacramento, 1992-2000; toxicologist Dept. Toxic Substances Control Calif EPA, Sacramento, 2000 . Cons. in field, Manhattan, Kans., 1981-83. Contbr. articles to profl. jours. Vol. Amigos de las Americas, Marin County, Calif., 1973, Hospice Care, Manhattan, 1985. Mem. Soc. Toxicology, Soc. for Risk Analysis, Sigma Xi. Home: 8338 Titian Ridge Ct Antelope CA 95843-5627 Office: HERD PO Box 806 Sacramento CA 95812-0806 E-mail: tbooze@dtsc.ca.gov

BORCHERDS, RICHARD EWEN, mathematics educator; b. Cape Town, South Africa, Nov. 29, 1959; BA, Cambridge U., England, 1981; PhD, Cambridge U., 1983. Rsch. fellow Trinity Coll., Cambridge, England, 1983-87; asst. prof. U. Calif., Berkeley, 1987-88, rsch. fellow Cambridge U., England, 1988-92, lectr., 1992-93; prof. U. Calif., Berkeley, 1993—, Cambridge U., 1996—. Contbr. articles to profl. jours. including J. Alg., Adv. Math., Duke Math. J. Recipient Fields medal 1998. Office: U Calif Dept Math 970 Evans Hall # 3840 Berkeley CA 94720-3841 also: U Cambridge Dept Pure Math 16 Mill Lane Cambridge CB21SB England

BORDA, DEBORAH, symphony orchestra executive; b. N.Y.C., July 15, 1949; d. William and Helene (Malloy) B. BA, Bennington Coll., 1971; postgrad., Royal Coll. Music, London, 1972-73. Program dir. Mass. Coun. Arts and Humanities, Boston, 1974-76; mgr. Boston Musica Viva, Boston, 1976-77; gen. mgr. Handel and Haydn Soc., Boston, 1977-79, San Francisco Symphony, 1979-86; pres. St. Paul Chamber Orch., 1986-88; exec. dir. Detroit Symphony Orch., 1988-90; pres. Minn. Orch., Mpls., 1990-91; exec. dir. N.Y. Philharm., N.Y.C., 1991-99; exec. v.p., mging dir. Los Angeles Philharmonic Assoc., 1999—. Office: Los Angeles Philharmonic Assn 135 N Grand Ave Los Angeles CA 90012

BORDA, RICHARD JOSEPH, management consultant; b. San Francisco, Aug. 16, 1931; s. Joseph Clement and Ethel Cathleen (Donovan) B.; m. Judith Maxwell, Aug. 30, 1953; children: Michelle, Stephen Joseph. AB, Stanford U., 1953, MBA, 1957. With Wells Fargo Bank, San Francisco, 1957-70, mgr., 1963-66, asst. v.p., 1966-67, v.p., 1967-70, exec. v.p. adminstrn., 1973-85; asst. sec. Air Force Manpower Res. Affairs, Washington, 1970-73; vice chmn., chief fin. officer Nat. Life Ins. Co., Montpelier, Vt., 1985-90, also bd. dirs.; chmn., chief exec. officer Sentinal Group Funds, Inc., 1985-90, also bd. dirs.; mgmt. cons., 1990—. Former pres. Air Force Aid Soc., Washington; mem. bd. visitors Monterey Inst. Internat. Studies; govs. coun. Boys and Girls Club of Monterey Peninsula; bd. dirs. Sunset Ctr. for the Arts Found., Marines' Meml. Assn., San Francisco; mem. internat. adv. bd. Ctr. for Nonproliferation Studies. Recipient Exceptional Civilian Svc. award, 1973, 95. Mem. USMC Res. Officers Assn., Marines Meml. Assn. (dir.), Bohemian Club, Monterey Peninsula Country Club, Old Capital Club, Air Force Aid Soc. (disting. counselor), Phi Gamma Delta. Republican. Episcopalian.

BORDALLO, MADELEINE MARY (MRS. RICARDO JEROME BORDALLO), lieutenant governor; b. Graceville, Minn., May 31, 1933; d. Christian Peter and Mary Evelyn (Roth) Zeien; m. Ricardo Jerome Bordallo, June 20, 1953; 1 dau., Deborah Josephine. Student, St Mary's Coll., South Bend, Ind., 1952; A.A., St. Katherines Coll., St. Paul, 1953; A.A. hon. degree for community service, U. Guam, 1968. Presented in voice recital Guam Acad. Music, Agana., 1951, 62; mem. Civic Opera Co., St. Paul, 1952-53; mem. staff KUAM Radio-TV sta., Agana, 1954-63; freelance writer local newspaper, fashion show commentator, coordinator, civic leader, 1963; nat. Dem. committeewoman for Guam, 1964-98; 1st lady of Guam, 1974-78, 81-85; senator 16th Guam Legislature, 1981-82, 19th Guam Legislature, 1987-88, 20th Guam Legislature, 1989-90, 21st Guam Legislature, 1991-92, 22nd Guam Legislature, 1993-94; Dem. Party candidate for Gov. of Guam, 1990, lt. gov. of Guam, 1994; lt. gov. of Guam, 1995—. Del. Nat. Dem. Conv., 1964, 68, 72, 76, 80, 84, 88-92, 96, pres. Women's Dem. Party Guam, 1967-69; rep. Presdl. Inauguration, Washington, 1965, 77, 85; del. Dem. Western States Conf., Reno, 1965, L.A., 1967, Phoenix, 1968, conf. sec., 1967-69; del. Dem. Women's Campaign Conf., Wash., 1965, Dem. Inauguration, 1992. Pres. Guam Women's Club, 1958-59; del Gen. Fedn. Women's Clubs Convs., Miami Beach, Fla., 1961, New Orleans, 1965, Boston, 1968; v.p. Fedn. Asian Women's Assn., 1964-67, pres., 1967-69, pres. 1996-98; pres. Guam Symphony Soc., 1967-73, del. convs., Manila, Philippines, 1959, Taipei, Formosa, 1960, Hong Kong, 1963, Guam, 1964, Japan, 1968, Taipei, 1973; chmn. Guam Christmas Seal Drive, 1961; bd. dirs. Guam chpt. ARC, 1963, sec., 1963-67, fund dr. chmn., 2000; pres. Marianas Assn. For Retarded Children, 1968-69, 73-74, 84—; bd. dirs. Guam Theatre Guild, Am. Cancer Soc.; mem. Guam Meml. Hosp. Vols. Assn., 1966—, v.p., 1966-67, pres., 1970-71; chmn. Hosp. Charity Ball, 1966; pres. Women for Service, 1974—, Beauty World Guam Ltd., 1981—, First Lady's Beautification Task Force of Guam, 1983-86; pres. Palace Restoration Assn., 1983—; nominee Dem. party for Gov. of Guam, 1990. Mem. Internat. Platform Assn., Guam Rehab. Assn. (assoc.), Guam Lytico and Bodig Assn. (pres. 1983-98), Spanish Club of Guam, Inetnon Famalaoan Club (pres. 1983-86), Guam Coun. of Women's Club (pres. 1993-95), Nat. Conf. Lt. Govs. (exec. com. 1998—). Home: PO Box 1458 Agana GU 96932-1458 Office: PO Box 2950 Agana GU 96932-2950

BORDEN, JOHN HARVEY, entomologist, educator; b. Berkeley, Calif., Feb. 6, 1938; s. Charles Edward Borden and Alice Victoria Witkin; m. Edna Rosalind McEachern, June 23, 1962; children: Patrick Carl, Ian McEachern. BS, Washington State U., 1963; MS, U. Calif., Berkeley, 1965, PhD, 1966. Bd. cert. entomologist Entomol. Soc. Am. Rsch. and tchg. asst. dept. entomology U. Calif., Berkeley, 1963-66; asst. prof. dept. biol. scis. Simon Fraser U., Burnaby, B.C., Can., 1966-69, assoc. prof. Can., 1969-75, prof. Can., 1975—, dir. chem. ecology rsch. group Can., 1981—, NSERC Indsl. Rsch. chair Can., 1991-2001. Vis. scientist Forestry Commn. Rsch. Sta., Alice Holt Lodge, Wrecclesham, Farnham, Surrey, Eng., 1976-77; cons. to UN Devel. Program, 1989-97. Contbr. chpts. to books and over 325 articles to profl. jours.; patentee in field. With USMC, 1957-61. Coop. Grad. fellow, NSF, 1964-66, Travelling fellow Nat. Rsch. Coun., 1976-77, Killam Rsch. fellow Can. Coun., 1990-91; recipient Gold medal Sci. Coun. B.C., 1985, Hewlett Packard Can. Forum award, 1997. Fellow Entomol. Soc. Can. (C.G. Hewitt award 1977, Gold medal 1988), Royal Soc. of Canada, Entomol. Soc. Am. (cert., J.E. Bussart Meml. award 1984); mem. Entomol. Soc. B.C. (hon. life), Nat. Assn. Advancement of Sci. (life), Can. Inst. Forestry (Sci. Achievement award 1986), Profl. Pest Mgmt. Assn. B.C. (Excellence award 1986), Internat. Soc. Chem. Ecology (life), Assn. B.C. Profl. Foresters, Assn. Profl. Biologists B.C. Office: Simon Fraser U Dept Biol Scis Burnaby BC Canada V5A 1S6

BORDEN, WESTON THATCHER, chemistry educator; b. N.Y.C., Oct. 13, 1943; s. Martin L. and Doris (Weston) B.; m. Marcia E. Robbins, May 15, 1971 (div. 1987); children: Alice, Michael. BA, Harvard U., 1964, MA, 1966, PhD, 1968. Instr. Harvard U., Cambridge, Mass., 1968-69, asst. prof., 1969-73; assoc. prof. U. Wash., Seattle, 1973-77, prof., 1977—. Author: Modern Molecular Orbital Theory, 1975; editor: Diradicals, 1982; contbr. articles to profl. jours. Bd. dirs. Itteki Zendo Assn., 1995—. Fellow Fulbright Found., Sloan Found., Guggenheim Found., Japan Soc. for Promotion of Sci.; recipient Humboldt Scientist award. Mem. AAAS, Am. Chem. Soc. Buddhist. Avocation: traditional Japanese arts. Office: U Wash Dept Chemistry Bg 10 Seattle WA 98195-0001 E-mail: borden@chem.washington.edu

BORDNER, GREGORY WILSON, chemical engineer; b. Buffalo, Aug. 16, 1959; s. Raymond Gordon and Nancy Lee (Immegart) B.; m. Margaret Patricia Toon, June 14, 1981; children: Eric Lawrence, Heather Rae. BSChemE, Calif. State Poly. U., 1982; MS in Sys. Mgmt., U. So. Calif., 1987. Registered profl. engr., Calif., Ariz., environ. assessor. Commd. 2nd lt. USAF, 1983, advanced through grades to capt., 1987; engr., mgr. various air launched missile, anti-satellite and strategic def. initiative projects Air Force Rocket Propulsion Lab., Edwards AFB, Calif., 1983-86; asst. mgr. space transp. Air Force Astronautics Lab., Edwards AFB, 1986-87; chief small intercontinental ballistic missiles ordnance firing system br. Hdqrs. Ballistic Missile Orgn., San Bernardino, Calif., 1987-90; sr. plant environ. engr. Filtrol Corp./Akzo Chems. Inc., L.A., 1991-92; water/soils project engr. TABC, Inc., Long Beach, Calif., 1992-98, prodn. engr., 1998-99, asst. project mgr., 1999—. Author: (manual) Pyrotechnic Transfer Line Evaluation, 1984, (with others) Rocket Motor Heat Transfer, 1984. Mem. AIChE, Am. Water Works Assn. Avocations: jogging, weight lifting, bowling. Home: 10841 Ring Ave Alta Loma CA 91737-4429

BOREL, JAMES DAVID, anesthesiologist; b. Chgo., Nov. 15, 1951; s. James Albert and Nancy Ann (Sieverson) B. BS, U. Wis., 1973; MD, Med. Coll. of Wis., 1977. Diplomate Am. Bd. Anesthesiology, Nat. Bd. Med. Examiners, Am. Coll. Anesthesiologists. Research asst. McArdle Lab. for Cancer Research, Madison, Wis., 1972-73, Stanford U. and VA Hosp., Palo Alto, 1976-77; intern. The Cambridge (Mass.) Hosp., 1977-78; clin. fellow in medicine Harvard Med. Sch., Boston, 1977-78, clin. fellow in anesthesia, 1978-80, clin. instr. in anaesthesia, 1980; resident in anesthesiology Peter Bent Brigham Hosp., Boston, 1978-80; anesthesiologist Mt. Auburn Hosp., Cambridge, 1980; fellow in anesthesiology Ariz. Health Scis. Ctr., Tucson, 1980-81; research assoc. U. Ariz. Coll. Medicine, Tucson, 1980-81, assoc. in anesthesiology, 1981—; active staff Mesa (Ariz.) Luth. Hosp., 1981—; courtesy staff Scottsdale (Ariz.) Meml. Hosp., 1982—. Vis. anaesthetist St. Joseph's Hosp., Kingston, Jamaica, 1980. Contbr. numerous articles to profl. jours. Mem. AMA, AAAS, Ariz. Anesthesia Alumni Assn., Ariz. Soc. Anesthesiologists, Am. Soc. Regional Anesthesia, Can. Anesthestists' Soc., Internat. Anesthesia Rsch. Soc., Am. Soc. Anesthesiologists. Office: Valley Anesthesia Cons 2200 N Central Ave Ste 203 Phoenix AZ 85004-1431

BOREN, ROGER W. judge; b. Bingham Canyon, Utah, Sept. 11, 1941; m. Winifred A. Scott, Feb. 4, 1965; 6 children. BA, U. Calif., Berkeley, 1966; MA, San Jose State U., 1968; JD, UCLA, 1973. Bar: Calif. 1973, U.S. Dist. Ct. (ctrl. dist.) Calif. 1973. Dep. atty. gen. State of Calif., 1973-84; judge Mcpl. Ct., Newhall Jud. Dist., 1973-84; judge Superior Ct., L.A. County, Calif., 1985-87; assoc. justice 2 Appellate Dist., Calif. Ct. Appeals, L.A., 1987-93, presiding justice, 1993—. Bd. dirs. Henry Mayo Newhall Meml. Hosp., 1985—. Mem. LDS Ch.

BORENSTEIN, DANIEL BERNARD, psychiatrist, educator; b. Silver City, N.Mex., Mar. 31, 1935; s. Jack and Marjorie Elizabeth (Kerr) B.; m. Bonnie Denice Ulland, June 11, 1967; 1 child, Jay Brian. BSChemE, MIT, 1957; MD, U. Colo., 1962. Diplomate Am. Bd. Psychiatry and Neurology. Intern U. Hosp. U. Ky., 1962-63; resident in psychiatry U. Colo. Med. Ctr., 1963-66; chief resident, psychiatry instr. U. Colo. Sch. Medicine, 1965-66; psychiatry instr. U. So. Calif. Sch. Medicine, 1966-67; asst. clin. prof. psychiatry UCLA Sch. Medicine, 1972-84, assoc. clin. prof., 1984-96, clin. prof., 1996—. Founder, dir. UCLA Mental Health Program for Physicians in Tng., 1980-84; clin. assoc. L.A. Psychoanalytic Soc. and Inst., 1967-71, pres. clin. assocs., 1970-71, faculty, 1973-83, sr. faculty, 1983—; pvt. practice medicine specializing in psychoanalysis and psychiatry, West L.A., 1966—; assoc. vis. psychiatrist UCLA Ctr. Health Scis., 1973-90; cons. Medicare Program, 1995—; examiner Am. Bd. Psychiatry and Neurology; reviewer Jour. Psychiat. Svcs., 1991—. Author: Manual of Psychiatric Peer Review: Prelude and Promise, 1985; contbr. articles to profl. jours. Bd. dirs. L.A. Child Devel. Ctr., 1981-85, mem. hon. adv. com., 1985-2001; founding mem., bd. dirs. Found. Advancement Psychiat. Edn. and Rsch., 1991—; bd. dirs. coop. Am. Physicians Mut. Protective Trust, 1994—. Lt. AUS, 1957-58. Fellow Am. Psychiat. Assn. (life fellow, coun. area VI 1977-79, 81-82, dep. rep. assembly dist. brs. 1981-82, rep.

1982-89, com. to rev. psychiat. news 1979-81, work group on competition and legis. 1981-83, nominating com. 1982-83, assembly liaison to peer rev. com. 1982-86, assembly liaison to fni. and mktg. com. 1986-87, assembly corr. group on subspecialization 1986-89, assembly liaison to coun. on econ. affairs, 1987-89, med. student edn. com. 1987-90, bd. trustees 1989—, bd. liaison jud. action commn. 1989-91, com. managed care 1990-92, various coms., bd. liaison to managed care com. 1992-99, bd. liaison econ. affairs coun. 1992-99, chmn. bd. ethics appeals 1995-97, sec. 1995-97, v.p. 1997-99, pres.-elect 1999-2000, pres. 2000-2001, immediate past pres. 2001-2002); mem. So. Calif. Psychiat. Soc. (Outstanding Svc. citation 1975, chmn. peer rev. com. 1974-77, exec. coun. 1976-89, ethics com. 1977-85, pres. 1978-79, chmn. fellowship and awards com. 1979-85, chmn. Commn. on Psychiatry and the Law 1980-81, 1st recipient Disting. Svc. award 1984, Appreciation award 1979, Outstanding Achievment award 1993), AMA (alt. del. Ho. Dels. 1998—), L.A. County Med Assn. (exec. coun. 1988-91, com. on well-being 1986-89, com. on substance abuse 1981-86, Bay Dist. v.p. 1985-86, pres.-elect 1986, pres. 1987-88, bd. dirs. 1981—, chmn. mental health com. 1980-85), Calif. Med. Assn. (rep. for psychiat. specialty to Ho. Dels. 1979-87, com. on mental health and mental disabilities 1979-85, 1986-88, bd. trustees 1992-2001, chmn. physicians benevolence operating com. 1996-2001, chmn. bldg. com. 1999-2001, various coms.), Calif. Psychiat. Assn. (exec. coun. 1977-79, 81-95, chmn. jud. com. 1986-88, Spl. Recognition award 1995, bd. trustees 1989-95), Los Angeles Psychoanalytic Soc. and Inst. (co-chmn. extension divsn. 1973-74, chmn. peer rev. com. 1975-78, mem. curriculum com. 1980-84), Am. Psychoanalytic Assn. (com. on confidentiality 1983-96, com. on govt. relations and ins. 1983-2000), Internat. Psychoanalytic Assn. Office: 151 N Canyon View Dr Los Angeles CA 90049-2721

BORENSTEIN, MARK A. lawyer; b. Bklyn., June 26, 1951; BA, SUNY, Buffalo, 1973; JD, George Washington U., 1976; LLM, Georgetown U., 1978. Bar: Va. 1976, D,C, 1977, Calif. 1978. Law clk. to Hon. Irving Hill U.S. Dist. Ct. (cen. dist.), Calif., 1976-77; mem. Tuttle & Taylor, L.A., 1978-2000, Shapiro, Borenstein & Dupont, Santa Monica, Calif., 2000—. Lectr. U. So. Calif., 1980-82, vis. prof. law, 1997, adj. prof., 1999-2000. Exec. editor: George Washington Law Review, 1975-76. Inst. for Pub. Interest Representation Law fellow Georgetown U. Law Ctr., 1977-78. Mem. Phi Beta Kappa, Order of the Coif. Office: Shaprio Borenstein & Dupont 233 Wilshire Blvd Ste 700 Santa Monica CA 90401 E-mail: mborenstein@shapirofirm.com

BORESI, ARTHUR PETER, writer, educator; b. Toluca, Ill. s. John Peter and Eva B.; m. Clara Jean Gordon, Dec. 28, 1946; children: Jennifer Ann Boresi Hill, Annette Boresi Pueschel, Nancy Jean Boresi Broderick. Student, Kenyon Coll., 1943-44; BSEE, U. Ill., 1948, MS in Mechanics, 1949, PhD in Mechanics, 1953. Research engr. N. Am. Aviation, 1950; materials engr. Nat. Bur. Standards, 1951; mem. faculty U. Ill., Urbana, 1953—, prof. theoretical and applied mechanics and nuclear engring., 1959-79; prof. emeritus U. Ill. at Urbana, Urbana, 1979; Disting. vis. prof. Clarkson Coll. Tech., Potsdam, N.Y., 1968-69; NAVSEA research prof. Naval Postgrad. Sch., Monterey, Calif., 1978-79; prof. civil engring. U. Wyo., Laramie, 1979-95, head, 1980-94, prof. emeritus, 1995—. Vis. prof. Naval Postgrad. Sch., Monterey, Calif., 1986-87.; cons. in field. Author: Engineering Mechanics: Statics, 2001, Engineering Mechanics: Dynamics, 2001; Elasticity in Engineering Mechanics, 4th edit., 2000, Advanced Mechanics of Materials, 5th edit., 1993, Approximate Solution Methods in Engineering Mechanics, 1991; also articles. Served with USAAF, 1943-44; Served with AUS, 1944-46. Fellow ASME, ASCE, Am. Acad. Mechanics (founding, treas.); mem. Am. Soc. Engring. Edn. (Archie Higdon Disting. Educator award 1993), Soc. Exptl. Mechanics. Office: U Wyo Box 3295 Univ Station Laramie WY 82071 E-mail: boresi@uwyo.edu

BORG, ANITA, computer scientist; b. Oak Park, Ill., Jan. 17, 1949; d. Carl Edwin and Beverly May (Borg) Naffz. BA, NYU, N.Y.C., 1973, MS, 1976, PhD, 1981. Asst. prof. N.Y. Inst. Tech., N.Y.C., 1978-80; sr. sys. designer Auragen Systems Corp., Ft. Lee, N.J., 1982-85; fault tolerant sys. cons. Nixdorf Computer, Paderborn, Germany, 1985-86; mem. rsch. staff Digital Equipment Corp., Palo Alto, Calif., 1986-97, Xerox Palo Alto Rsch. Ctr., Palo Alto, 1997—; pres. Inst. Women and Tech., Palo Alto, 1997—. Presdl. appointee Congl. Commn. on Advancement of Women and Minorities in Sci. Enring. and Tech. Co-inventor method for acquiring address traces, 1993. Founder Systers Internet, 1987, Grace Hopper Celebration of Women in Computing, Washington, 1994. Recipient World of Today and Tomorrow award Santa Clara County Girl Scouts, 1994, Pioneer award Electronic Frontier Found., 1995, Augusta Ada Lovelace award Assn. Women in Computing, 1995; inductee Women in Tech. Internat. Hall of Fame, 1998. Fellow Assn. Computing Machinery (coun. mem. 1991-95); mem. IEEE Computer Soc., Computing Rsch. Assn. (bd. dirs. 1994—). Avocations: flying, hiking, gardening, mountain biking, travel. Office: Xerox PARC 3333 Coyote Hill Rd Palo Alto CA 94304-1314

BORGATTA, EDGAR F. social psychologist, educator; b. Milan, Italy, Sept. 1, 1924; came to U.S., 1929, naturalized, 1934; s. Edgar A. and Frances (Zinelli) B.; m. Marie Lentini, Oct. 5, 1946; children: Lynn, Kim, Lee. B.A., N. Y. U., 1947, M.A., 1949, Ph.D., 1952. Cert. psychologist, N.Y., Vt., Wis. Instr. NYU, 1949-51, lectr., prof., 1954-59; lectr., research assoc. Harvard U., 1951-54; social psychologist, asst. sec. Russell Sage Found., 1954-59; prof. sociology Cornell U., Ithaca, N.Y., 1959-61; Brittingham rsch. prof. U. Wis., Madison, 1961-72, chmn. dept. sociology, 1962-65, chmn. div. social studies, 1965-68; disting. prof. sociology Queens Coll., CUNY, 1972-77, prof Grad. Ctr., 1972-82, dir. Italian Social Sci. Ctr., 1972-77; rsch. CUNY Case Ctr. for Gerontol. Studies, 1978-81; dir. data svc. CUNY Case Center for Gerontol. Studies, 1981-82; prof. sociology U. Wash., Seattle, 1981—, chmn. dept. s, 1992-93; dir Inst. on Aging U. Wash., Seattle, 1981-86. Cons. to bus. and govt., 1953—, Russell Sage Found., 1970-72; lectr., prof., adj. prof. sociology NYU, 1954-59; cons. editor Rand McNally & Co., 1961-74; chmn. bd. F.E. Peacock Pubs., Inc.; Nat. Inst. Gen. Scis.; spl. research fellow, 1972 Editor: Research on Aging, Sociol. Methodology, Sociol. Methods and Research; co-editor: Handbook of Personality Theory and Research; editor-in-chief: Encyclopedia of Sociology, 2d edit.; contbr. articles to profl. jours. Fellow Am. Psychol. Assn., Am. Psychol. Soc.; mem. Psychometric Soc., Sociol. Research Assn., Am. Sociol. Assn. (v.p. 1983), Pacific Sociol. Assn. (pres. 1985), Internat. Inst. Sociology (pres. 1984-89). Office: U Wash Dept Sociology PO Box 353340 Seattle WA 98195-3340 E-mail: edgarbee@att.net

BORGMAN, LEON E. geologist; BS in Geol. Engring., Colo. Sch. Mines, 1953; MS in Math., U. Tex., Houston, 1959; PhD in Stats., U. Calif., Berkeley, 1962. Oceanographical engr. Shell Devel. Co., Houston, 1953-59; assoc. prof. stats. U. Calif., Davis, 1961-67, assoc. prof. engring. geosci. Berkeley, 1967-70; prof. geology and stats. U. Wyo., Laramie, prof. emeritus. Cons. Shell Devel. Co., Exxon Prodn. Rsch., Chevron Oil Field [illegible] Inst., Norway, Waterways Expt. Sta., EPA, Navy Civil Engring. Lab.; tech. adv. UN. Contbr. articles to profl. jours., chpts. to books. Named Disting. lectr. Internat. Assn. Hydraulic Rsch., 1989. Mem. ASCE (tech. com. ocean engring. 1990—, Internat. Coastal Engr. award 1994), NAE, NAS (com. coastal flooding 1980-82), Am. Coun. Geostats (gov. com. 1985-90). Office: U Wyo [illegible] 1034 Laramie WY 82070

BORGNINE, TOVA, cosmetic executive; m. Ernest Borgnine. Model, actress, N.Y.C.; owner, cosmotologist Tova's Touch, N.Y.C.; pres. chair The Tova Corp, Beverly Hills, Calif. Active World Econ. Forum, Susan G. Homan Br. Cancer Found.; bd. dirs. Jr. Achievement, Am. Scandinavian Found. Office: The Tova Corp 192 N Canon Dr Beverly Hills CA 90210-5304 E-mail: dave@beautybytova.com

BORIS, RUTHANNA, dancer, choreographer, dance therapist, educator; b. Bklyn., Mar. 17, 1918; d. Joseph Jay and Frances (Weiss) B.; m. Frank W. Hobi (dec.) Student, Profl. Children's Sch., N.Y.C. Dir. Boris-Hobi Concert Co., 1955-57. Prin. dancer Am. Ballet, N.Y.C., 1934, Ballet Caravan, N.Y.C., 1936; prima ballerina Met. Opera Co., N.Y.C., 1939-41, Ballet Russe de Monte Carlo, N.Y.C., 1942-49; prima ballerina, choreographer-in-residence Royal Winnipeg Ballet of Can., 1957-59, dir. 1957-58; choreographer Ballet Russe de Monte Carlo, 1947, N.Y.C. Ballet, 1951; prof. dance U. Wash., Seattle, 1965-83, prof. emeritus, 1983—; adj. prof. psychiatry U. Wash., 1982; pres. exec. dir. Ctr. for Dance Devel. & Research, Albany, Calif., 1986— ; choreographer: Cirque de Deux, 1947, Quelques Fleurs, 1948, Cakewalk, 1951, Kaleidoscope, 1951, Will O' The Wisp, 1951, Pasticcio, 1955, Wanderling, 1957, Ragtime, 1975, Tape Suite, 1976, Four All, 1980. Mem. adv. bd. Seattle Psychoanalytic Inst., 1975-82. Mem. Am. Guild Mus. Artists (award 1964, gov. 1942-64), Am. Dance Therapy Assn. (pres. Calif. chpt. 1986-88, mem. dance therapy credentials com. 1990-92). Office: Ctr Dance Devel & Rsch 555 Pierce St Apt 1033 Albany CA 94706-1009

BORN, GEORGE H. aerospace engineer, educator; b. Westhoff, Tex., Nov. 10, 1939; s. Henry and Lydia (Schulle) B.; m. Carol Ann Leslie, Mar. 21, 1992. BS, U. Tex., 1962, MS, 1965, PhD, 1968. Engr. Ling-Temco-Vought, Dallas, 1962-63; aerospace technologist Johnson Space Ctr., Houston, 1967-70; mem. tech. staff Jet Propulsion Lab., Pasadena, Calif., 1970-83; sr. rsch. engr. U. Tex., Austin, 1983-85; prof. aerospace engring. U. Colo., Boulder, 1985—, dir. Colo. Ctr. for Astrodynamics Rsch., 1985—. Contbr. articles to profl. jours. Recipient Exceptional Svc. medal NASA, 1980, Pub Svc. medal NASA, 1994. Fellow AIAA (Mechanics and Control of Flight award 1999), Am. Astronautical Soc. (Brouwer award 1998); mem. AAAS, Am. Geophys. Union, Oceanog. Soc., Inst. Navigation, Am. Meteorol. Soc., Am. Soc. Engring. Educators, Tau Beta Pi. Office: U Colo Campus Box 431 Boulder CO 80309-0431

BORNSTEIN, ELI, artist, sculptor; b. Milw., Dec. 28, 1922; dual citizen, U.S. and Can. m. Christina Bornstein; children: Sarah, Thea. BS, U. Wis., 1945, MS, 1954; student, Art Inst. Chgo., U. Chgo., 1943, Academie Montmartre of Fernand Leger, Paris, 1951, Academie Julian, , 1952; DLitt, U. Sask., Can., 1990. Tchr. drawing, painting and sculpture Milw. Art Inst., 1943-47; tchr. design U. Wis., 1949; tchr. drawing, painting, sculpture, design and graphics U. Sask., Can., 1950-90, prof., 1963-90, prof. emeritus, 1990—, head art dept., 1963-71. Painted in France, 1951-52, Italy, 1957, Holland, 1958; exhibited widely, 1943— ; retrospective exhbn. (works 1943-64), Mendel Art Gallery, Saskatoon, 1965, one man shows, Kazimir Gallery, Chgo., 1965, 67, Saskatoon Pub. Library, 1975, Can. Cultural Center, Paris, 1976, Glenbow-Alta. Inst. Art, Calgary, 1976, Mendel Art Gallery, Saskatoon, 1982, York U. Gallery, Toronto, 1983, Confedn. Ctr. Art Gallery, Charlottetown, P.E.I., 1983, Owens Art Gallery, Mt. Allison U., Sackville, N.B., 1984, Fine Arts Gallery, U. Wis.-Milw., 1984, Mendel Art Gallery, Saskatoon, 1996; represented in numerous pvt. collections; executed marble sculpture now in permanent collection, Walker Art Center, Mpls., 1947, aluminum constrn. for Sask. Tchrs. Fedn. Bldg., 1956, structurist relief in painted wood and aluminum for, Arts and Scis. Bldg., U. Sask., 1958, structurist relief in enamelled steel for, Internat. Air Terminal, Winnipeg, Man., Can., 1962, four-part constructed relief for, Wascana Pl., Wascana Ctr. Authority, Regina, Sask., 1983; also structurist reliefs exhibited, Mus. Contemporary Art, Chgo., Herron Mus. Art, Indpls., Cranbrook Acad. Art Galleries, Mich., High Mus., Atlanta, Can. House, Cultural Centre Gallery, London, 1983, Can. Cultural Ctr., Paris, 1983, Brussels, 1983, Bonn, 1984, Milw. Art Mus., 1984; model of aluminium construction, 1956 and model version of structurist relief in 5 parts, 1962, now in collection, Nat. Gallery, Ottawa, Ont., others in numerous collections.; Co-editor: periodical Structure, 1958; founder, editor: The Structurist, ann. publ. 1960-72, biennial, 1972—; Contbr. articles, principally on Structurist art to various publs. Recipient Allied Arts medal Royal Archtl. Inst. Can., 1968; honorable mention for 3 structurist reliefs 2d Biennial Internat. Art Exhbn., Colombia, S.Am., 1970 Address: 3625 Saskatchewan Cres S Corman Park SK Canada S7T 1B7 Office: U Sask Box 378 RPO U Saskatoon SK Canada S7N 4J8 Fax: 306-966-8670. E-mail: eli.bornstein@usask.ca

BORNSTEIN, PAUL, physician, biochemist; b. Antwerp, Belgium, July 10, 1934; came to U.S., 1947, naturalized, 1952; s. Abraham and Mina (Ginsburg) B. BA, Cornell U., 1954; MD, NYU, 1958. Intern in surgery Yale-New Haven Hosp., 1958-59, intern in medicine, 1959-60, asst. resident in medicine, 1960-62; sr. fellow Arthritis Found. Pasteur Inst., Paris, 1962-63; research asso. NIH, Bethesda, Md., 1963-65, research investigator, 1965-67; asst. prof. biochemistry and medicine U. Wash., 1967-69, asso. prof., 1969-73, prof., 1973—, attending physician, 1968—. Mem. editl. bd. Jour. Biol. Chemistry, 1972-78, 80-85, Jour. Cell Biology, 1988-91, 94-97, Matrix Biology, 1993—; assoc. editor Arteriosclerosis, 1980-90, Collagen Related Rsch., 1981-88; contbr. articles to profl. jours. Served to sr. surgeon USPHS, 1963-67. Recipient Lederle Med. Faculty award USPHS, 1968; Rsch. Career Devel. award NIH, 1969; Macy Faculty Scholar award, 1975; Merit award NIH, 1989; Guggenheim fellow, 1985. Mem. Am. Soc. Clin. Investigation, Am. Soc. Biol. Chemistry, Western Soc. Clin. Rsch., Assn. Am. Physicians (pres. 2001—), Am. Soc. Matrix Biology (v.p. 2001—), Internat. Soc. Matrix Biology (pres. 2001—). Home: 602 34th Ave E Seattle WA 98112-4306 Office: U Wash Sch Medicine Dept Biochemistry PO Box 357350 Seattle WA 98195-7350 E-mail: bornsten@u.washington.edu

BOROWSKY, PHILIP, lawyer; b. Phila., Oct. 9, 1946; s. Joshua and Gertrude (Nicholson) B.; m. Judith Lee Goldwasser, Sept. 5, 1970 (div. 1996); children: Miriam Isadora, Manuel, Nora Jo. BA, UCLA, 1967; JD, U. San Francisco, 1973. Bar: Calif. Pres. and mng. ptnr. Cartwright, Slobodin, Bokelman, Borowsky, Wartnick, Moore & Harris, San Francisco, 1987-95; pres. Law Offices Philip Borowsky, Inc., San Francisco, 1996—. Mem. faculty Practicing Law Inst., N.Y.C., 1983-84; mem. adj. faculty Hastings Coll. Law, San Francisco, 1982-83; arbitrator Superior Ct., San Francisco, 1982—, Am. Arbitration Assn., 1982—, Nat. Assn. Securities Dealers, 1994—. Co-author: Unjust Dismissal and At-Will Employment, 1985; mem. bd. editl. cons. Bad Faith Law Update, 1986—. With U.S. Army, 1968-70, Vietnam. Mem. Calif. Trial Lawyers Assn. Democrat. Office: 1 Market Plz San Francisco CA 94105-1420 E-mail: borowsky@borowsky.com

BORSCH, FREDERICK HOUK, bishop; b. Chgo., Sept. 13, 1935; s. Reuben A. and Pearl Irene (Houk) B.; m. Barbara Edgeley Sampson, June 25, 1960; children: Benjamin, Matthew, Stuart. AB, Princeton U., 1957; MA, Oxford U., 1959; STB, Gen. Theol. Sem., 1960; PhD, U. Birmingham, 1966; DD (hon.), Seabury Western Theol. Sem., 1978, Gen. Theol. Sem., 1988; STD (hon.), Ch. Div. Sch. of [illegible], 1991; [illegible] Yale U., 1983. Ordained priest Episcopal Ch., 1960; curate Grace Episcopal Ch., Oak Park, Ill., 1960-63; tutor Queen's Coll., Birmingham, Eng., 1963-66; asst. prof. N.T. Seabury Western Theol. Sem., Evanston, Ill., 1966-69, assoc. prof. N.T., 1969-71; prof. N.T. Gen. Theol. Sem., N.Y.C., 1971-72; pres., dean Berk Div. Sch. Yale U., Berkeley, Calif., 1972-81; dean of chapel, prof. religion Princeton U., 1981-88, bishop Episc. Diocese, L.A., 1988—; [illegible] Hall Bd. Chs., 1979-81, mem. exec. coun. Episc. Ch., 1981-88, Anglican Cons. Coun., 1984-88; chair bd. govs. Trinity Press Internat., 1989—; bd. adv. UCLA Sch. Pub. Policy & Social Rsch., 1998—, Ctr. for the Study Religion, Princeton U., 2000—; trustee Princeton U., 1998—. Author: The Son of Man in Myth and History, 1967, The Christian and Gnostic Son of Man, 1970, God's Parable, 1976, Introducing the Lessons of the Church Year, 1978, Coming Together in the Spirit, 1980, Power in Weakness, 1983, Jesus: The Human Life of God, 1987, Many Things in Parables, 1988, Christian Discipleship and Sexuality, 1993, Outrage and Hope, 1996; editor: Anglicanism and the Bible, 1984, The Bible's Authority in Today's Church, 1993. Trustee Princeton U., 1998—. Keasbey scholar, 1957-59 Fellow Soc. Arts, Religion and Contemporary Culture; mem. Am. Acad. Religion, Soc. Bibl. Lit., Studiorum Novi Testamenti Societas, Phi Beta Kappa Home: 2930 Corda Ln Los Angeles CA 90049-1105 Office: Episcopal Diocese of LA PO Box 512164 Los Angeles CA 90051-0164 E-mail: bishop@ladiocese.org

BORSON, DANIEL BENJAMIN, physiology educator, inventor, researcher, lawyer; b. Berkeley, Calif., Mar. 24, 1946; s. Harry J. and Josephine F. Borson. BA, San Francisco State Coll., 1969; MA, U. Calif., Riverside, 1973; PhD, U. Calif., San Francisco, 1982; JD, U. San Francisco, 1995. Bar: Calif. 1997, U.S. Dist. Ct. (no. dist.) Calif. 1997, U.S. Patent and Trademark Office 1998; lic. comml. pilot, flight instr. FAA. Musician Composer's Forum, Berkeley, San Francisco, 1961-70; flight instr. Buchanan Flying Club, Concord, Oakland, Calif., 1973-77, pres., 1975-77; physiology U. Calif., San Francisco, 1984-92, asst. rsch. physiologist Cardiovascular Rsch. Inst., 1988-92; assoc. Fliesler Dubb Meyer and Lovejoy LLP, 1997—. Vis. scientist Genentech Inc., South San Francisco, Calif., 1990-92. Contbr. articles, rev. chpts. and abstracts to profl. jours., legal periodicals and law rev. Fellow NIH, 1976-84, grantee, 1988-93; fellow Cystic Fibrosis Found., 1985, grantee, 1989-91; fellow Parker B. Francis Found., 1985-87; grantee Am. Lung Assn., 1985-87. Mem.: Bay Flute Club (pres. 1978), ABA, Am. Physiol. Soc. (editl. bd. Am. Jour. Physiology 1990—92), Am. Soc. Cell Biology, Am. Chem. Soc., Am. Intellectual Property Law Assn., San Francisco Intellectual Property Law Assn., Fed. Cir. Bar Assn., No. Calif. Pharm. Discussion Group (bd. dir., chmn. 2000), State Bar Calif. (patent standing com., exec. com.). Avocations: mountain climbing, aviation, music. Office: Ste 400 4 Embarcadero Ctr San Francisco CA 94111 E-mail: dbb@fmdl.com

BORSTING, JACK RAYMOND, business administration educator; b. Portland, Oreg., Jan. 31, 1929; s. John S. and Ruth (Nelson) B.; m. Peggy Anne Nygard, Mar. 22, 1953; children: Lynn Carol, Eric Jeffrey. B.A., Oreg. State U., 1951; M.A., U. Oreg., 1952, Ph.D., 1959. Instr. math. Western Wash. Coll., 1953-54; teaching fellow U. Oreg., 1956-59; mem. faculty Naval Postgrad. Sch., 1959-80, prof. ops. research, chmn. dept., 1964-73, provost, acad. dean, 1974-80; asst. sec. def. (comptroller) Washington, 1980-83; dean Sch. Bus. U. Miami, Fla., 1983-88; Robert Dockson prof. and dean bus. adminstrn. U. So. Calif., Los Angeles, 1988-94; E. Morgan Stanley prof. bus. adminstrn. and exec. dir. Ctr. for Telecomms. Mgmt./U. So. Calif. Marshall Sch. Bus., Los Angeles, 1994—. Vis. prof. U. Colo. summers 1967, 69, 71; vis. disting. prof. Oreg. State U., summer 1968; bd. dirs. Northrop Grumman Corp., TRO Learning, Whitman Edn. Group; bd. visitors Def. Sys. Mgmt. Coll., 1985-91, chmn., 1988-91; mem. adv. bd. Naval Postgrad. Sch., 1982-86, 98—; bd. overseers Ctr. Naval Analysis, 1984-94; trustee Aerospace Corp., 1986-92, Inst. Def. Analysis, 1990—; bd. advisors Elec. Power Rsch. Inst., 1999—. Contbr. to profl. jours. Trustee Orthop. Hosp. Found., L.A., 1992—, chmn., 1996—, chmn. bd. dirs. 1999—; trustee Rose Hills Found. 1996-98; gov. Town Hall of Calif., 1988-94. Recipient Disting. Pub. Service medal Dept. Def., 1980, 82 Fellow AAAS, Mil. Ops. Rsch. Soc. (bd. dirs. 1965-72, pres. 1970-71); mem. Inst. Mgmt. Sci., Am. Statis. Soc., Ops. Rsch. Soc. Am. (mem. coun. 1969-79, sec. 1972-74, pres. 1975-76, Kimball medal 1982), Internat. Fedn. Ops. Rsch. Socs. (treas. 1980-88), Internat. Engring. Consortium, Calif. Club, 100 Club L.A., Sigma Xi, Pi Mu Epsilon, Beta Theta Pi. Episcopalian. Office: Marshall Sch Bus Dcc 217 Usc Los Angeles CA 90089-0001

BORTON, GEORGE ROBERT, retired airline captain; b. Wichita Falls, Tex., Mar. 22, 1922; s. George Neat and Travis Lee (Jones) B.; m. Anne Louise Bowling, Feb. 5, 1944 (dec.); children: Trudie T., Robert B., Bruce M. AA, Hardin Coll., Wichita Falls, 1940. Cert. airline transport pilot, FAA flight examiner. Flight sch. operator Vallejo (Calif.) Sky Harbor, 1947-48; capt. S.W. Airways, San Francisco, 1948-55; check capt. Pacific Airlines, San Francisco, 1955-68, Hughes Air West, San Francisco, 1968-71; capt. N.W. Airlines, Mpls., 1971-82, ret., 1982. Col. USAF, 1943-73, ret. Decorated Air medal. Mem. Airline Pilots Assn., Res. Officers Assn., Air Force Assn., Horseless Carriage Club, Model T of Am. Club (San Jose, Calif.). Republican. Home: 325 Denio Ave Gilroy CA 95020-9203

BORWEIN, JONATHAN MICHAEL, mathematics educator; b. St. Andrews, Scotland, May 20, 1951; arrived in Can., 1963; s. David and Bessie (Flax) B.; m. Judith Dierdre Scott Roots, Sept. 17, 1973; children: Rachel, Naomi, Tova. BA in Math. with honors, U. Western Ont., 1971; MSc, Jesus Coll. Oxford, 1972, DPhil, 1974; doctorate (hon.), U. Limoges, 1999. dir. Ctr. for Exptl. and Constructive Math., Burnaby, B.C., Can., 1993-98. Postdoctoral fellow Dalhousie U., 1974-75, from asst. prof. to assoc. prof., 1976-82, lectr., rsch. assoc., 1975-76; from asst. prof. to assoc. prof. Carnegie-Mellon U., 1980-82; assoc. prof. Dalhousie U., 1982-84, prof., 1984-93, U. Waterloo, 1991-93; Shrum prof. math. Simon Fraser U., Burnaby, B.C., 1993—. French Nat. fellow Limoges, Prof. Invité, 1985; disting. vis. prof. Ctr. Math. Rsch., U. Montreal, 1986; Sr. Killam fellow Dalhousie U., 1987-88; visitor Technion, 1990; adj. prof. dept. math., stats. and computing sci. Dalhousie U., 1993-96; mem. math. grant selection com. Natural Scis. and Engring. Rsch. Coun., 1988-91, chmn., 1989-91, com. collaborative rsch. initiatives, 1992-95; mem. Simon Fraser Ctr. for Sys. Sci., 1992—, Simon Fraser U. Rsch. Coun., 1993; dir. Simon Fraser Ctr. Exptl. & Constructive Math., 1993—. Editor: (with P. Borwein) CMS Books in Mathematics, 2000—; assoc. editor: Set-Valued Analysis, 1992, ZOR: Mathematical Methods of Operations Research, 1994—, Ramanujan Jour., 1996—, Experimental Mathematics, 1996—; mem. editl. bd. Jour. Convex Analysis, 1993—, Proc. Am. Math. Soc., 1999—; mem. editl. bd., hon. editor: Communications in Applied Nonlinear Analysis, 1993—; area editor: Dictionary of Theories, 1992—; editor: (with P. Borwein) CMS Series of Graduate Texts in Mathematics, 1990—; cons. editor for math. The Guinness Encyclopedia, 1989-92. Mem. collaborative rsch. grants com. NATO, 1997-1999, chair, 1998, phys. engring. sci. tech. panel, 1999-2001; mem. Can. Inst. for Sci. and Tech. Info. Bd., 1998—; active New Dem. Party, 1967—. Recipient Atlantic Provinces Coun. on the Scis., Fraser medal for rsch. excellence, 1988; Ont. Rhodes scholar Jesus Coll., 1971-74, U.W.O. Faculty Assn. scholar, 1971, Albert O. Jeffrey scholar, 1969, Timkins Internat. Fund scholar, 1968; Australian Rsch. Grant Coun. fellow Australian Nat. U., Newcastle, 1988. Fellow Royal Soc. Can.; mem. AAAS (Coxeter-James lectr. 1987, bd. dirs., rsch. com. 1985-88, chmn. constn. revision com. 1987-88), Can. Math. Soc., Am. Math. Soc. (editl. bd., pres.-elect 1999-2000, pres. 2000—), Math. Assn. Am. (Chauvenet prize 1993, Merten M.H. prize 1993). Avocations: swimming, theater, politics. E-mail: jborwein@cecm.sfu.ca

BORWEIN, PETER BENJAMIN, mathematician; b. St. Andrews, Scotland, May 10, 1953; s. David and Bessie (Flax) B.; m. Jennifer Elaine Moore, Nov. 29, 1980; children: Alexandra, Sophie, Theresa. BSc, U. Western Ont., London, 1974; MA, U. B.C., Vancouver, 1976, PhD, 1979. Postdoctoral fellow Oxford (Eng.) U., 1979-80; asst. prof. Dalhousie U., Halifax, N.S., Can., 1980-85, assoc. prof., 1985-90, prof., [illegible] 1990-93, Simon Fraser U., Burnaby, B.C., Can., 1993—. Site dir. Pacific Inst. Math. Co-author: Pi and the AGM, 1987, A Dictionary of Real

Numbers, 1990, Polynomials and Plynomical Inequalities, 1995, Pi: A Source Book, 1997; contbr. more than 100 articles to profl. jours. Recipient Merten Hasse prize Mathematical Assn. of Am., 1993, Faculty of Yr. BC/SCUFA, 1996. Mem. Am. Math. Soc., Can. Math. Soc., Math. Assn. Am. (Hasse prize 1993), Ctr. for Constructive and Exptl. Math. (assoc. dir. Simon Fraser U. 1993). Office: Simon Fraser U Dept Math and Statistics Burnaby BC Canada V5A 1S6

BORYSENKO, JOAN, psychologist, biologist; b. Boston, Oct. 25, 1945; d. Edward and Lillian Zakon; m. Kurt Kaltreider; children: Natalia, Justin, Andrei. BA in Biology, Bryn Mawr Coll., 1967; PhD, Harvard Med. Sch., 1972. Lic. psychologist. Asst. prof. anatomy and cellular biology Tufts U., 1973-78; instr. in medicine Harvard Med. Sch., Boston, 1981-88; pres., founder Mind/Body Health Scis., Boulder, Colo., 1988—. Author: Minding the Body, Mending the Mind, 1987, Guilt is the Teacher, Love is the Lesson, 1990, Fire in the Soul, 1993, (with Miroslav Borysenko) The Power of the Mind to Heal, 1994, Pocketful of Miracles, 1995, A Woman's Book of Life, 1996, Seven Paths to God, 1997, A Woman's Journey to God, 1999, Inner Peace for Busy People, 2001; others; mem. adv. bd. several jours. and Web sites in field; pub. Circle of Healing newsletter. Achievements include pioneering work in the study of psychoneuroimmunology. Office: Mind/Body Health Scis 393 Dixon Rd Boulder CO 80302-9769 E-mail: luziemas@aol.com

BOS, JOHN ARTHUR, retired aircraft manufacturing executive; b. Holland, Mich., Nov. 6, 1933; s. John Arthur and Annabelle (Castelli) B.; m. Eileen Tempest, Feb. 15, 1974; children: John, James, William, Tiffany. BS in Acctg., Calif. State Coll., Long Beach, 1971. Officer 1st Nat. Bank, Holland, Mich., 1954-61; dir. bus. mgmt. Boeing Commercial MD-80 and Mil. Airlift and Tanker Programs, Long Beach, 1962-99. CFO Classic of Calif. Reformed Ch. in Am., 1970—. Mem. Inst. Mgmt. Accts. (cert. mgmt. acct. 1979), Nat. Assn. Accts. Avocations: automobile marketing, golf, consulting. E-mail: bjabos@hotmail.com

BOSCH, SAMUEL HENRY, computer company executive; b. Waupun, Wis., Dec. 24, 1934; s. Henry Samuel and Emma (Elgersma) B.; m. Corinne Marilyn Aardema, June 21, 1958; children: Michelle, Jonathan, David, Sara. BS in Physics, San Diego State U., 1961; MS in Physics, UCLA, 1962. Sr. rsch. engr. Gen. Dynamics, San Diego, 1962-69; mgr. mktg. Digital Equipment Corp., Maynard, Mass., 1969-77; dir. mktg. Sys. Engrng. Lab., Ft. Lauderdale, Fla., 1977-79; mgr. mktg. Intel, Hillsboro, Oreg., 1979-81; dir. mktg. Metheus, Hillsboro, 1981-82; pres. ATM Techs., Beaverton, Oreg., 1982-86; pres., owner Peregrin Techs., Inc., Portland, 1986—, Peregrin Med. Rev. Inc., Portland, 1987—. Invited spkr. at bus. confs. Contbr. articles to profl. jours. Served with U.S. Army, 1955-57. Mem. Concord Coalition, N.W. China Coun. Mem. Oreg. Hist. Soc. Republican. Mem. Christian Ref. Ch. Home: 20055 NW Nestucca Dr Portland OR 97229-2821 Office: Peregrin Techs Inc 14279 NW Science Park Dr Portland OR 97229-5416

BOSE, ANJAN, electrical engineering educator, academic administrator; b. Calcutta, India, June 2, 1946; s. Amal Nath and Anima (Guha) B.; m. Frances Magdelen Pavlas, Oct. 30, 1976; children: Rajesh Paul, Shonali Marie, Jahar Robert. B Tech with honors, Indian Inst. Tech., Kharagpur, 1967; MS, U. Calif., Berkeley, 1968; PhD, Iowa State U., 1974. Systems planning engr. Con Edison Co., N.Y.C., 1968-70; instr., research assoc. Iowa State U., Ames, 1970-74; postdoctoral fellow IBM Sci. Ctr., Palo Alto, Calif., 1974-75; asst. prof. elec. engring. Clarkson U., Potsdam, N.Y., 1975-76; mgr. EMSD, Control Data Corp., Mpls., 1976-81; prof. elec. engring. Ariz. State U., Tempe, 1981-93; disting. prof. Wash. State U., Pullman, 1993—, dir. Sch. Elec. Engring. and Computer Sci., 1993-98, dean Coll. Engring. and Architecture, 1998—. V.p. Power Math Assocs., Tempe, 1981-84; program dir. power sys. NSF, Washington, 1988-89. Contbr. over 60 articles to engring. jours. Fellow IEEE.

BOSKOVICH, GEORGE, JR. food products executive; b. 1946; Chmn. Boskovich Farms. Office: Boskovich Farms Inc 4224 Pleasant Valley Rd Camarillo CA 93012-8533

BOSL, PHILLIP L. lawyer; b. Feb. 27, 1945; BA, U. Calif., Santa Barbara, 1968; JD, U. So. Calif., 1975. Bar: Calif. 1975. Ptnr. Gibson, Dunn & Crutcher LLP, L.A., 1983—. Mem. U. So. Calif. Law Rev., 1973-75. Officer USCG, 1969-72. Mem. ABA, Los Angeles County Bar Assn., Fed. Bar Assn., Assn. Bus. Trial Lawyers Am., Securities Industry Assn. (compliance and legal divsn.), Inst. Corp. Counsel (gov.), Nat. Assn. Securities Dealers (arbitrator), Order of Coif. Home: 6226 Napoli Ct Long Beach CA 90803-4800 Office: Gibson Dunn & Crutcher LLP 333 S Grand Ave Ste 4400 Los Angeles CA 90071-3197 E-mail: pbosl@gibsondunn.com

BOSMAJIAN, HAIG ARAM, speech communication educator; b. Fresno, Calif., Mar. 26, 1928; s. Aram and Aurora (Keosheyan) B.; m. Hamida Just, Feb. 27, 1957; 1 child, Harlan. BA, U. Calif., Berkeley, 1949; MA, U. of Pacific, 1951; PhD, Stanford U., 1960. Instr. U. Idaho, Moscow, 1959-61; asst. prof. U. Conn., Storrs, 1961-65; prof. speech comm. U. Wash., Seattle, 1965—. Author: Language of Oppression (Orwell award), 1983: editor: Censorship, Libraries and the Law, 1983; Justice Douglas, 1980, Freedom of Speech, 1983, First Amendment in the Classroom Series, 1987: vol. 1, The Freedom to Read, 1987, vol. II, The Freedom of Religion, 1987, vol. III, Freedom of Expression, 1988, vol. IV, Academic Freedom, 1989, vol. V, Freedom to Publish, 1989, Metaphor and Reason in Judicial Opinions, 1992, The Freedom Not to Speak, 1999. Recipient Bicentennial of the Bill of Rights award Western States Communication Assn., 1991.

BOSSERT, PHILIP JOSEPH, information systems executive; b. Indpls., Feb. 23, 1944; s. Alfred Joseph and Phyllis Jean (Cashen) B.; m. Jane Elisabeth Shade, June 29, 1968 (div. Dec. 1990); m. ChaoYing Deng, May 22, 1992; 1 child, Lian Brittni. BA in Econs., Rockhurst Coll., 1968; cert. in Philosophy, U. Freiburg, Fed. Republic Ger., 1970; MA in Philosophy, Washington U., St. Louis, 1972, PhD in Philosophy, 1973. Asst. prof. philosophy Hawaii Loa Coll., Honolulu, 1973-76, pres., 1978-86; dir. Hawaii com. for the humanities NEH, Honolulu, 1976-77; dir. long range planning Chaminade U., Honolulu, 1977-78; pres. Strategic Info. Solutions, Honolulu, 1986-99; mgr. strategic info. systems GTE Hawaiian Telephone, Honolulu, 1987-91; asst. supt. info. and telecom. svcs. Hawaii State Dept. Edn., 1991-94; project dir. Hawaii Edn. and Rsch. Network, 1994-97; chmn. bd. dirs., dir. Media Design & Devel., Inc., 1996-99; chmn. bd. dirs., CEO Baden Wines Internat., Ltd., 1997-2000; dep. dir. Hawaii State Dept. Bus., Econ. Devel. and Tourism, 2000-01; chmn., CEO China Hawaii Investment Corp., Honolulu, 2001—. Cons. Sangyong Bus. Group, Seoul, Korea, 1987-90, Nat. Assn. Colls. Univs. and Bus. Officers, Washington, 1980-90, Nat. Inst. for Edn. Rsch., Japan, 1999-2000. Author: Strategic Planning and Budgeting, 1989; author, editor numerous books on philosophy; contbr. articles to profl. jours. Bd. dirs. Hawaii Childrens Mus., 1994-99, Friends of the East West Ctr., 1996-2000, Hawaii Alliance for the Arts, 1996-99, Hanahaúoli Sch., 1999-2000. Fulbright-Hays fellow, 1968-70, Woodrow Wilson fellow, 1972-73, Nat. Endowment for Humanities fellow, 1976. Mem. Pacific Telecom. Coun. (bd. dirs.). Office: China Hawaii Investment Corp PO Box 673 Honolulu HI 96809 E-mail: bossertp@hawaii.rr.com

BOST, THOMAS GLEN, lawyer, educator; b. Oklahoma City, July 13, 1942; s. Burl John and Lorene Bell (Croka) B.; m. Sheila K. Pettigrew, Aug. 27, 1966; children: Amy Elizabeth, Stephen Luke, Emily Anne, Paul Alexander. BS in Acctg. summa cum laude, Abilene Christian U., 1964; JD, Vanderbilt U., 1967. Bar: Tenn. 1967, Calif. 1969. Instr. David Lipscomb Coll., Nashville, 1967; asst. prof. law Vanderbilt U., Nashville, 1967-68; ptnr. Latham & Watkins, Los Angeles, 1968-99; prof. law Pepperdine U., 2000—. Lectr. on taxation subjects. Chmn. bd. regents, law sch. bd. visitors Pepperdine U., Malibu, Calif., 1980-2000. Mem. ABA (chmn. standards of tax practice com., sec. taxation 1988-90), State Bar of Calif., Los Angeles County Bar Assn. (chmn. taxation sect. 1981-82), Calif. Club (L.A.), Beach Club (Santa Monica). Republican. Mem. Ch. of Christ.

BOSWELL, JAMES DOUGLAS, medical research executive; b. Tulsa, Feb. 12, 1942; m. Pamela Scott; children: Megan, Melanie Student, U. Okla., 1960-61; B.A., U. Tulsa, 1964, M.A., 1966. Indsl. relations rep. Trans World Airlines, 1966-68; dir. placement Skelly Oil Co., 1968-72, mgr. employee and pub. relations, 1972-75, gen. mgr. adminstrn., 1975-77; corp. mgr. human resources Getty Oil Co., 1977-81; v.p. employee and pub. relations L.A. Times, 1981-91; CEO House Ear Inst., L.A., 1991—, trustee, 1995—. Bd. dirs. Employers Group; pres. Skelly Oil Found., Tulsa, 1974-78, Getty Oil Co. Found., 1978-79. Bd. dirs. L.A. Boys and Girls Club, v.p., 1985; bd. dirs. L.A. Theatre Ctr., 1988-90, L.A. chpt. ARC; bd. dirs. L.A. Jr. Achievement, 1982-91, vice chmn. human resources, 1986; fellow Nat. Health Found., 1992, San Marino Cmty. Ch. Found., 1992-95; mem. Econ. Round Table, 1993, sec.-treas., 1995-96. Mem. Am. Soc. Personnel Adminstrn., Am. Psychol. Assn., Newspaper Personnel Relations Assn., Am. Newspaper Assn. (labor and personnel relations com. 1982-91). Avocations: tennis, skiing, golf. Home: 341 Palmetto Dr Pasadena CA 91105-1815 Office: House Ear Inst 2100 W 3rd St 5th Fl Los Angeles CA 90057-1922

BOSWELL, SUSAN G. lawyer; b. El Paso, Tex., June 26, 1945; BA, U. Ariz., 1972, JD, 1976. Bar: Ariz. 1977, Nev. 1992. Dir. Tuscon (Ariz.) office Quarles, Brady, Streich, Lang, PC (fromerly known as Streich & Lang P.C.), Phoenix, 1987—. Instr., faculty mem. Nat. Inst. Trail Advocacy, 1991; bd. vis. U. Ariz. Coll. of Law. Fellow Am. Coll. Bankruptcy; mem. State Bar of Ariz. (peer review com., assistance com.), Ariz. Women Lawyers Assn, Phi Kappa Phi. Office: Quarles Brady Streich Lang PC 1 S Church Ave Ste 1700 Tucson AZ 85701-1630

BOSWORTH, BRUCE LEIGHTON, school administrator, educator, consultant; b. Buffalo, Mar. 22, 1942; s. John Wayman and Alice Elizabeth Rodgers; children: David, Timothy, Paul, Sheri, Skyler. BA, U. Denver, 1964; MA, U. No. Colo., 1970; EdD, Walden U., 1984. Elem. tchr. Littleton (Colo.) Pub. Schs., 1964-67, 70-81; bldg. prin. East Smoky Sch. Divsn. 54, Valleyview, Alta., Can., 1967-70; pres., tchr. St. Michael's-of-the-Mountains Sch., Littleton, 1981—. Adoption cons. hard-to-place children; ednl. cons. spl. needs children Columbine United Ch. Mem. ASCD, Coun. Exceptional Children, Masons, Shriners, York Rite. Home and Office: 3500 S Lowell Blvd Apt 316 Denver CO 80236-6168 E-mail: misterb@qwest.net, misterb@yahoo.com, bosworthbruce@qwest.net

BOSWORTH, THOMAS LAWRENCE, architect, educator; b. Oberlin, Ohio, June 15, 1930; s. Edward Franklin and Imogene (Rose) B.; m. Abigail Lumbard, Nov. 6, 1954 (div. Nov. 1974); children: Thomas Edward, Nathaniel David; m. Elaine R. Pedigo, Nov. 23, 1974; stepchildren: Robert Haden Pedigo, Kevin Ian Pedigo. BA, Oberlin Coll., 1952, MA, 1954; postgrad., Princeton U., 1952-53, Harvard U., 1956-57; MArch, Yale U., 1960. Draftsman Gordon McMaster AIA, Cheshire, Conn., summer 1957-58; resident planner Tunnard & Harris Planning Cons., Newport, R.I., summer 1959; designer, field supr. Eero Saarinen & Assocs., Birmingham, Mich., 1960-61, Hamden, Conn., 1961-64; individual practice architecture Providence, 1964-68, Seattle, 1968—; asst. instr. architecture Yale U., 1962-65, vis. lectr., 1965-66; asst. prof. R.I. Sch. Design, 1964-66, asso. prof., head dept., 1966-68; prof. architecture U. Wash., Seattle, 1968-98, prof. emeritus, 1998—, chmn. dept., 1968-72; chief architecture Peace Corps Tng. Program, Tunisia, Brown U., summers 1965-66; archtl. cons., individual practice Seattle, 1972—; dir. multidisciplinary program U. Wash., Rome, Italy, 1984-86. Vis. lectr. Kobe U., Japan, Oct., 1982, Nov., 1990, Apr., 1993, May, 1995, June, 1998; Pietro Belluschi Disting. Vis. Prof. U. Oreg., 1996; dir. arch. in Rome program U. Wash., Rome, 1996. Bd. dirs. N.W. Inst. Arch. and Urban Studies, Italy, 1983-90, pres., 1983-85; dir. Pilchuch Glass Sch., Seattle, 1977-80, trustee, 1980-91, adv. coun., 1993—; mem. Seattle Model Cities Land Use Rev. Bd., 1969-70, Tech. Com. Site Selection Wash. Multi-Purpose Stadium, 1970, Medina Planning Commn., 1972-74, steering adv. com. King County Stadium, 1972-74, others; chmn. King County (Wash.) Environ. Devel. Commn., 1972-74, King County Policy Devel. Commn., 1974-77; bd. dirs. Arcade Mag., 1995—, pres. 1988—; bd. mgrs. YMCA Camping Svcs., 1998—; adv. bd. U. Wash Rome Ctr., 1999—. With U.S. Army, 1954-56. Winchester Traveling fellow Greece, 1960; assoc. fellow Ezra Stiles Coll. Yale U.; mid-career fellow in arch. Am. Acad. in Rome, 1980-81, vis. scholar, Spring 1988. Fellow AIA; mem. Archtl. Inst. Japan, Monday Club (Seattle), Bohemian Club (San Francisco), Tau Sigma Delta. Home: 2411 25th Ave E Seattle WA 98112-2610 Office: U Wash Dept Architecture PO Box 355720 Seattle WA 98195-5720

BOTELHO, BRUCE MANUEL, state attorney general, mayor; b. Juneau, Alaska, Oct. 6, 1948; s. Emmett Manuel and Harriet Iowa (Tieszen) B.; m. Guadalupe Alvarez Breton, Sept. 23, 1988; children: Alejandro Manuel, Adriana Regina. Student, U. Heidelberg, Federal Republic of Germany, 1970; BA, Willamette U., 1971, JD, 1976. Bar: Alaska 1976, U.S. Ct. Appeals (9th cir.), U.S. Supreme Ct. Asst. atty. gen. State of Alaska, Juneau, 1976-83, 87-90, dep. commr., acting commr. Dept. of Revenue, 1983-86; mayor City, Borough of Juneau, 1988-91, dep. atty. gen., 1991-94; atty. gen. State of AK, 1994—. Editor: Willamette Law Jour., 1975-76; contbr. articles profl. jours. Assembly mem. City, Borough of Juneau, 1983-86; pres. Juneau Human Rights Commn., 1978-80, Alaska Coun. Am. Youth Hostels, 1979-81, Juneau Arts and Humanities Coun., 1981-83, S.E.E Alaska Area coun. Boy Scouts Am., 1991-93, 2001—, coun. commr., 1993-2000; bd. dirs. Found. for Social Innovations, Alaska, 1990-93, Alaska Econ. Devel. Coun., 1985-87, Alaska Indsl. Devel. Corp., 1984-86; pres. Juneau World Affairs Coun., 2000—; chair adminstrv. law sect. Alaska Bar Assn., 1981-82; chair Alaska Resources Corp., 1984-86, Gov.'s Conf. on Youth and Justice, 1995-96; trustee Alaska Children's Trust, 1996-2000, Alaska Permanent Fund, 2000—; mem. exec. com. Conf. of Western Attys. Gen., 1997—, chair, 2000—; co-chair Alaska Justice Assessment Commn., 1997—, chair Gov. Task Force on Confidentiality of Chldns. Procs., 1998—; mem. Commn. for Justice Across the Atlantic, 1999—. Recipient Silver Beaver award Boy Scouts Am. Mem. Nat. Assn. Attys. Gen. (exec. com. 1998—). Democrat. Methodist. Avocation: international folk dance. Home: 401 F St Douglas AK 99824-5353 Office: State Alaska Dept Law PO Box 110300 Juneau AK 99811-0300

BOTSAI, ELMER EUGENE, architect, educator, former university dean; b. St. Louis, Feb. 1, 1928; s. Paul and Ita May (Cole) B.; m. Patricia L. Keegan, Aug. 28, 1955; children: Donald Rolf, Kurt Gregory.; m. Sharon K. Kaiser, Dec. 5, 1981; 1 dau., Kiana Michelle. AA, Sacramento Jr. Coll., 1950; AB, U. Calif., Berkeley, 1954; D of Architecture, U. Hawaii, 2000. Registered architect, Hawaii, Calif. Draftsman, then asst. to architect So. Pacific Co., San Francisco, 1953-57; designer H.K. Ferguson Co., San Francisco, 1955; project architect Anshen & Allen Architects, San Francisco, 1957-63; prin. Botsai, Overstreet & Rosenberg, Architects and Planners, San Francisco, 1963-79, Elmer E. Botsai FAIA, Honolulu, 1979—; of cousnel Groupe 70 Internat., 1998—; chmn. dept. architecture U. Hawaii, Manoa, 1976-80, dean Sch. Architecture, 1980-90, prof., 1990-99, prof. emeritus, 2000—. Lectr. U. Calif., Berkeley, 1976, dir. Nat. Archtl. Accrediting Bd., 1972-73, 79; adminstrv. and tech. cons. Wood Bldg. Rsch. Ctr., U. Calif., 1985-90, mem. profl. preparation project com. at U. Mich., Ann Arbor, 1986-87; co-author water infiltration seminar series for Bldg. Owners and Mgrs. Rsch. Ctr., 1986-87; chief investigator effects of Guatemalan earthquake for NSF and AIA, Washington, 1976; steering com. on structural failures Nat. Bur. Standards, 1982-84; chmn., dir. gen. svcs. Adv. Com. State of Calif. Co-author: Architects and Earthquake, Research Needs, 1976, ATC Seismic Standards for National Bur. of Standards, 1976, Architects and Earthquakes: A Primer, 1977, Seismic Design, 1978, Wood-Detailing for Performance, 1990, Wood as a Building Material, 2d edit., 1991; contbr. articles and reports to profl. jours.; prin. works include expansion of Nuclear Weapons Tng. Facility at Lemoore Naval Air Sta., Calif., LASH Terminal Port Facility Archtl. Phase, San Francisco, Incline Village (Nev.) Country Club, 1365 Columbus Ave. Bldg., San Francisco, modernization Stanford Ct. Hotel, San Francisco; monument area constrn. several Calif. ceneteries. With U.S. Army, 1946-48. Recipient Cert. Honor Fedn. Archtl. Colls. Mex. Republic, 1984; named to Wisdom Hall of Fame, 1998; NSF grantee for investigative workshop project, San Diego, 1974-80. Fellow AIA (bd. dirs., 1966-71, treas. No. Calif. chpt. 1968-69, pres. 1971, nat. v.p., 1975-76, nat. pres. 1978, pres. Hawaii 1985); hon. fellow Royal Can. Inst. Architects, N.Z. Inst. Architects, Royal Australian Inst. Architects, La Societed de Arquitectos Mexicano; mem. Archtl. Secs. Assn. (hon.), Soc. Wood Sci. and Tech., Internat. Conf. Bldg. Ofcls. Home: 321 Wailupe Cir Honolulu HI 96821-1524 Office: 925 Bethel St Fl 5 Honolulu HI 96813-4393

BOTSTEIN, DAVID, geneticist, educator; b. Zurich, Switzerland, Sept. 8, 1942; naturalized, 1954; AB in Biochem. Scis. cum laude, Harvard U., 1963; PhD in Human Genetics, U. Mich., 1967. Woodrow Wilson fellow, 1963; instr. dept. biology MIT, Cambridge, 1967-69, asst. prof. genetics, 1969-73, assoc. prof. genetics dept. biology, 1973-78, prof., 1978-88; v.p. sci. Genetech, Inc., 1988-90; Stanford W. Ascherman prof. Stanford U., Palo Alto, Calif., 1997—. Sci. adv. bd. Collaborative Research, Inc., 1978-87. Editor in chief Nat. Acad. Scis., 1981, Inst. Medicine, 1993, Molecular Biology of Cell, 1992—; contbr. over 230 articles to profl. jours. Recipient Career Devel. award NIH, 1972-74; Eli Lilly and Co. award in microbiology and immunology, 1978, Rosenstiel award Brandeis U., 1992, Allen award Am. Soc. of Human Genetics, 1989, Inst. of Medicine, 1993. Mem. NAS, Genetics Soc. Am. (bd. dirs. 1984), Inst. Medicine. Office: Stanford U 300 Pasteur Dr Dept Genetics Palo Alto CA 94304-2203

BOTTJER, DAVID JOHN, earth scientist, biologist, educator; b. N.Y.C., Oct. 3, 1951; s. John Henry and Marilyn (Winter) B.; m. Sarah Ranney Wright, July 26, 1973. BS, Haverford Coll., 1973; MA, SUNY, Binghamton, 1976; PhD, Ind. U., 1978. NRC postdoctoral rsch. assoc. U.S. Geol. Survey, Washington, 1978-79; asst. prof. dept. geol. scis. U. So. Calif., L.A., 1979-85, assoc. prof. dept. geol. scis., 1985-91, prof. dept. earth scis., 1991—. Rsch. assoc. L.A. County Mus. Natural History, 1979—; vis. scientist Field Mus. Natural History, Chgo., 1986; Paleontol. Soc. Disting. lectr., 1992-93; mem. Nat. Sci. Found. panel on earth systems history, 1997-99; sr. fellow UCLA Ctr. for the Study of Evolution and Origin of Life, 2000. Editor Palaios, 1989-96; assoc. editor Cretaceous Rsch., 1988-91; mem. editl. bd. Geology, 1984-89, 95-2000, Hist. Biology, 1988-93; co-editor Columbia U. Press Critical Moments and Perspectives in Paleobiology and Earth History (book series), 1990—; editor-in-chief Palaeo-3, 2000—. Fellow AAAS, Geol. Soc. Am., Geol. Soc. London; mem. Paleontol. Soc., Soc. Sediment Geology (pres. Pacific sect. 2001—), Internat. Paleontology Assn. Office: U So Calif Dept Earth Scis Los Angeles CA 90089-0001 E-mail: dbottjer@usc.edu

BOUCHARD, JOAN C. nursing association administrator; Exec. dir. Oreg. State Bd. Nursing, Portland. Office: Oreg State Bd of Nursing 800 NE Oregon St Ste 25 Portland OR 97232-2162

BOUCHARD, PAUL EUGENE, artist; b. Providence, Sept. 26, 1946; s. Marcel Paul and Anna Theresa (Dullea) B., m. Ann Marie Jones, Nov. 18, 1972 (div. 1977); 1 child Michael Paul; m. R. Jane Bouchard, Apr. 11, 1997. BFA, Calif. State U., Long Beach, 1978. Bd. dir, Angeles Gate Cultural Ctr., San Pedro, Calif., 1983-85. One-man show at Rogue Coll., Grants Pass, Oreg., 1996, El Camino Coll., 1997, City of Carlsbad, Calif. 1998; exhibited in group shows at Rental Gallery, Oakland Mus., 1984, Rental Gallery, L.A. County Mus. of Art, 1985, Sixth St. Gallery, San Pedro, Calif., Aquarius Gallery, Cambria, Calif., 1986, St. Andrew's Priory, Valyermo, Calif., Riverside (Calif.) Art Mus., Rental Gallery, 1987, Vietnam Vet.'s Art Exhibit, 1988, Coos Art Mus., Coos Bay, Oreg., 1989, Grants Pass Mus. of Art, 1991, Eastern Wash. U., 1992, Dept. Vets. Affairs Hdqrs., Sydney, Australia, 1992-93, Australian Nat. Gallery, Brisbane County Hall Gallery, Nat. Vietnam Vets. Art Mus., Chgo., others. Recipient Contribution to the Arts, City of Torrance, Calif., 1985; grantee Franklin Furnace, N.Y.C., 1989-90, Artist Space, N.Y.C., 1989-90. Home: 30268 Mersey Ct Temecula CA 92591-3820 E-mail: paulandjane@dav.net

BOUCHER, HAROLD IRVING, retired lawyer; b. Chico, Calif., June 27, 1906; s. Charles Augustus and Nina Eugenia (Knickerbocker) B.; m. Beula Blair Davis, Apr. 11, 1931. LLB, JD, U. Calif., Berkeley, 1930. Bar: Calif. 1930. Assoc. to adv. ptnr. Pillsbury, Madison & Sutro, Attys. at Law, San Francisco, 1934-93, ret. ptnr., 1993. Named to Order of British Empire Queen Elizabeth II of England, 1972. Fellow Am. Bar, Am. Coll. Probate (regent 1966), Am. Coll. Counsel (pres. 1967-68); mem. ABA, State Bar Calif., Old Capital Club. Office: care Botto Law Group 180 Montgomery St Fl 16 San Francisco CA 94104-4205

BOUDART, MICHEL, chemical engineer, chemist, educator, consultant; b. Belgium, June 18, 1924; came to U.S., 1947, naturalized, 1957; s. Francois and Marguerite (Swolfs) B.; m. Marina D'Haese, Dec. 27, 1948; children: Mark, Baudouin, Iris, Philip. BS, U. Louvain, Belgium, 1944, MS, 1947; PhD, Princeton U., 1950; D honoris causa, U. Liège, U. Notre Dame, U. Nancy, U. Ghent. Research asso. James Forrestal Research Ctr., Princeton, 1950-54; mem. faculty Princeton U., 1954-61; prof. chem. engring. U. Calif., Berkeley, 1961-64, adj. prof. chem. engring., 1994—; prof. chem. engring. and chemistry Stanford U., 1964-80, Keck prof. engring., 1980-94, Keck prof. engring. emeritus, 1994—. Adj. prof. chem. engring. U. Calif., Berkeley, 1996—; co-founder Catalytica, Inc.; mem. tech. adv. bd. Brit. Petroleum, 1992-98; mem. tech. adv. coun. Nova Chems., 1997—; Humble Oil Co. lectr., 1958; AIChE lectr., 1961; Sigma Xi nat. lectr., 1965; chmn. Gordon Rsch. Conf. Catalysis, 1962; bus. affairs com. Ann. Revs., 1982—; cons. Exxon, 1964—, Catalytica, 1974—, Symyx, 2000—. Author: Kinetics of Chemical Processes, 1968, (with G. Djéga-Mariadassou) Kinetics of Heterogenous Catalytic Reactions, 1983; editor: (with J.R. Anderson) Catalysis: Science and Technology, 11 vols., 1981-96, (with Marina Boudart and René Bryssinck) Modern Belgium, 1990; mem. adv. editl. bd. Catal. Letters, 1989—, Catalysis Rev., 1968—, Jour. Molecular Catalysis, 1995—, Cattech, 1996—. Recipient Curtis-McGraw rsch. award Am. Soc. Engring. Edn., 1962, R.H. Wilhelm award in chem. reaction engring., 1974, Chem. Pioneer award Am. Inst. Chemists, 1991; Belgium-Am. Ednl. Found. fellow, 1948, Procter fellow, 1949; Fairchild disting. scholar Calif. Tech. Inst., 1995. Fellow AAAS, Am. Acad. Arts. and Scis., Calif. Acad. Scis.; mem. NAS, NAE, Am. Chem. Soc. (Kendall award 1977, E.V. Murphee award in indsl. and engring. chemistry 1985), Catalysis Soc., Am. Inst. Chem. Engrs., Chem. Soc., Académie Royale de Belgique (fgn. assoc.), French Nat. Acad. Pharmacy (fgn.). Home: 228 Oak Grove Ave Atherton CA 94027-2218 Office: Stanford U Dept Chem Engring Stanford CA 94305 Fax: 650-723-9780. E-mail: lindi@chemeng.stanford.edu

BOULANGER, DONALD RICHARD, financial services executive; b. Berlin, May 28, 1944; s. Romeo James and Jeanette A. (Vallicre) B.; m. Wendy Elwell, Nov. 26, 1990 (div. Sept. 1996). B.A., Harvard U., 1966, Ph.D., 1972. V.p. First Interstate Bank, L.A., 1972-76, Kaufman and Broad, L.A., 1976-80, sr. v.p. Los Angeles, 1983-89; v.p. Transam. Corp., San Francisco, 1981-83; exec. v.p. Far West Savs., Newport Beach, Calif., 1983; pres. Nat. Deposit Fin. Corp., Universal City, 1989—. Bd. dirs. Nat. Deposit Life Ins. Co., Phoenix, Citadel Holding Corp, Am. Stock Exch., Glendale, Calif. Republican. Roman Catholic Avocation: scuba diving. Office: Nat Deposit Fin Corp 10 Universal City Plz North Hollywood CA 91608-1009

BOULDEN, JUDITH ANN, judge; b. Salt Lake City, Dec. 28, 1948; d. Douglas Lester and Emma Ruth (Robertson) Boulden; m. Alan Walter Barnes, Nov. 7, 1982; 1 child, Dorian Lisa. BA, U. Utah, 1971, JD, 1974. Bar: Utah 1974, U.S. Dist. Ct. Utah 1974. Law clk. to A. Sherman Christianson U.S. Cts., Salt Lake City, 1974; assoc. Roe & Fowler, Salt Lake City, 1975-81, McKay Burton Thurman & Condie, Salt Lake City, 1982-83; trustee Chpt. 7, Salt Lake City, 1976-82, Standing Chpt. 12, Salt Lake City, 1987-88, Standing Chpt. 13, Salt Lake City, 1979-88; sr. ptnr. Boulden & Gillman, Salt Lake City, 1983-88; U.S. Bankruptcy judge U.S. Cts., Salt Lake City, 1988—. Mem. Utah Bar Assn. Avocations: gardening, golf.

BOULEY, JOSEPH RICHARD, pilot; b. Fukuoka, Japan, Jan. 7, 1955; came to U.S., 1955; s. Wilfrid Arthur and Minori Cecelia (Naraki) B.; m. Sara Elizabeth Caldwell, July 6, 1991; children: Denise Marie, Janice Elizabeth, Eleanor Catherine, Rachel Margaret. BA in English, U. Nebr., 1977; MAS, Embry Riddle Aeronautical U., 1988. Commd. 2d lt. USAF, 1977, F-117A Stealth Fighter pilot Persian Gulf, 1991; ret. lt. col. USAFR, 2000; pilot United Airlines, 1992—. Ct. apptd. spl. advocate Office of Guardian Ad Litem, Salt Lake City, 1996-99. Decorated Disting. Flying Cross, Def. Meritorious Svc medal, 4 Air medals, 3 Meritorious Svc. medals, 2 Aerial Achievement medals, Joint Svc. commendation medal, 3 Air Force Commendation medals, Air Force Achievement medal; recipient Alumni Achievement award U. Nebr., 1998. Mem. VFW, Am. Legion, Disting. Flying Cross Soc., Airline Pilots Assn., Red River Valley Fighter Pilots Assn., Aircraft Owners and Pilots Assn. Roman Catholic. Avocations: flying, golf, running, photography. Home: 952 E Springwood Dr North Salt Lake UT 84054

BOUMA, JOHN JACOB, lawyer; b. Ft. Dodge, Iowa, Jan. 13, 1937; s. Jacob and Gladys Glennie (Cooper) B.; m. Bonnie Jeanne Lane, Aug. 15, 1959; children: John Jeffrey, Wendy Sue, Laura Lynne, Jennifer Ann. BA, U. Iowa, 1958, JD, 1960. Bar: Iowa 1960, Wis. 1960, Ariz. 1962, U.S. Ct. Appeals (9th cir.) 1971, U.S. Ct. Appeals (D.C. cir.) 1971, U.S. Ct. Appeals (10th cir.) 1982, U.S. Tax Ct., 1983, U.S. Supreme Ct. 1975. Assoc. Foley, Sammond & Lardner, Milw., 1960, Snell & Wilmer, Phoenix, 1962-66, ptnr., 1967—, chmn., 1983—. Contbr. articles to profl. jours. Chmn. Phoenix Human Rels. Commn., 1972-75; mem. Phoenix Commn. on LEAP, 1971-72, Phoenix Cmty. Alliance, 1991—; bd. dirs. Phoenix Legal Aid Soc., 1970-76, Ariz. Econ. Coun., 1989-93, Mountain States Legal Found., 1977-95; trustee Ariz. Opera Co., 1984—, pres., 1989-91; trustee Phoenix Art Mus., 1994-2000, pres., 1996-98. Capt. JAGC, U.S. Army, 1960-62. Recipient Walter E. Craig Disting. Svc. award, 1998, Cmty. Legal Svcs. Decade of Dedication award, 1998, Disting. Achievement medal Ariz. State U. Coll. Law, 1998. Fellow Am. Coll. Trial Lawyers; mem. ABA (Ho. of Dels. 1989—, bd. govs. 1998-2001, editl. bd. 1996-98), Maricopa County Bar Assn. (pres. 1977-78), Nat. Conf. Bar Pres. (exec. coun. 1984-91, pres. 1989-90), Ariz. Bar Assn. (pres. 1983-84), Ariz. Bar Found. (pres. 1987-88), Iowa Bar Assn., Wis. Bar Assn., Phoenix Assn. Def. Counsel (pres. 1972), Attys. Liability Assurance Soc. Ltd. (bd. dirs. 1987—), Iowa Law Sch. Found. (bd. dirs. 1986—), Phoenix C. of C. (bd. dirs. 1988-94), Ariz. State Coll. Law Soc. (bd. dirs., pres. 1997-2000), Western States Bar Conf. (pres. 1988-89), Ariz. Suprme Ct. Spl. Com. on Lawyer Discipline and Profl. Conduct, Order of Coif, Phi Beta Kappa, Phi Eta Sigma, Omicron Delta Kappa. Avocations: fishing, hunting, skiing, travel, golf. Home: 800 E Circle Rd Phoenix AZ 85020-4144 Office: Snell & Wilmer One Arizona Ctr Phoenix AZ 85004-2202

BOUQUET, FRANCIS LESTER, physicist; b. Enterprise, Oreg., Feb. 1, 1926; s. Francis Lester and Esther (Johnson) B.; m. Betty Jane Davis, Sept. 26, 1979 (dec. Aug. 15, 1989); children: Tim, Jeffrey, Janet; stepchildren: John Perry, Peggy Korv. AA, U. Calif., Berkeley, 1948, BA, 1950; MA, UCLA, 1953. Physicist U.S. Radiol. Def. Lab., San Francisco, 1953-55; engr., mgr. Lockheed Aircraft Co., Burbank, Calif., 1955-74; physicist Jet Propulsion Lab., Pasadena, 1974-88; pres. Systems Co., Graham, Wash., 1988-93, FLB Assocs., Medford, Oreg., 1994—. Cons. in field. Author: Solar Energy Simplified, 1984, 4th edit., 1994, Radiation Damage in Materials, 1985, 3d edit., 1990, Radiation Effects on Electronics, 1986, 5th edit., 1995, Introduction to Materials Engineering, 1986, 3d edit., 1990, Introduction to Seals, O-Rings and Gaskets, 1988, 2d edit., 1992, Great Chefs of the Southwest Cookbook, 1988, rev. edit., 1989 (new title Chefs of the Southwest Cookbook), Radiation Effects on Teflon, 1989, Engineering Properties of Teflon, 1989, 2d edit., 1994, Radiation Effects on Kapton, 1990, Engineering Properties of Kapton, 1990, Lake Havasu Cookbook, 1990, Spacecraft Design-Thermal and Radiation, 1991, Solar Energy Technology, 1991, Practical Guide to Autos, 1992, Starting Your Business, vols. 1 & 2, 1992, Nuclear Energy Simplified, 1992, Introduction to Biological Radiation Effects, 1992, 2d edit., 1994, Successful Decision-Making, 1993, True Life Stories, 1994, Exoatmospheric and Space Travel, 1994, Engineers' Guide to Autos, 1994, Radiation Effects on Nonelectronic Materials Handbook, 1994. Elder 1st Presbyn. Ch., Van Nuys, Calif. 1970-81. Served with U.S. Army, 1944-46, with Signal Corps U.S. Army, 1951-52, PTO. Recipient Eagle Scout award Boy Scouts Am., 1940, Performance commendations Lockheed Aircraft Co., 1964, 66, Mgmt. Achievement Program award, 1973, 20 NASA awards, 1980-92; named to Honor Roll of Inventors, 1966. Mem. N.Y. Acad. Sci., Calif. Soc. Profl. Engrs., Nat. Soc. Profl. Engrs., IEEE (chmn. Los Angeles chpt. Nuclear and Plasma Scis. Soc. 1973-74), Am. Inst. Physics, AIAA, Nat. Mgmt. Assn., Air Force Assn., Lockheed Mgmt. Club, Caltech Mgmt. Club. Republican. Office: FLB Assocs # 516 Office of the Pres 1200 Mira Mar Ave Medford OR 97504-8546

BOURGAIZE, ROBERT G. economist; BA, U. Wash., 1949. Dir., sr. v.p. Peoples Nat. Bank, Seattle; pres. Central Bank, N.A., Tacoma, University Place Water Co., Central Capital Corp., Epsilon Econ. Inc. Mem. Nat. Assn. Bus. Economists, English-Speaking Union U.S.A. (nat. dir.), Royal Commonwealth Soc., Am. Waterworks Assn. (life), Internat. Platform Assn., Pacific Northwest Writers Conf., Adam Smith Econ. Found., Adam Smith Soc. (founder 1976). Office: 3502 Bridgeport Way W University Place WA 98466

BOURNE, LYLE EUGENE, JR. psychology educator; b. Boston, Apr. 12, 1932; s. Lyle E. and Blanche (White) B. BA, Brown U., 1953; MS, U. Wis., 1955, PhD, 1956. Asst. prof. psychology U. Utah, 1956-61, assoc. prof., 1961-63; vis. assoc. prof. U. Calif.-Berkeley, 1961-62, vis. prof., 1968-69; assoc. prof. psychology U. Colo., Boulder, 1963-65, prof., 1965—, chmn. dept. psychology, 1983-91, dir. Inst. Cognitive Sci., 1979-83; clin. prof. psychiatry U. Kans. Med. Ctr., 1967-90. Vis. prof. U. Wis., 1966, U. Mont., 1967, U. Hawaii, 1969; cons. in exptl. psychology, VA, 1965-93. Author: Human Conceptual Behavior, 1966, Psychology of Thinking, 1971, Psychology: Its Principles and Meanings, rev. edits., 1976, 79 82, 85, Cognitive Processes, 1979, rev. edit., 1986, Psychology: A Concise Introduction, [illegible]; acad. editor: Basic Concept Series, Learning Cognition Series, [illegible] Pub. Co., 1970-76, Charles Merill Co., 1980-84, Advanced Psychological Texts Series, Sage Publications, 1992—; editor Jour. Exptl. Psychology: Human Learning and Memory, 1975-80; cons. editor Jour. Clin. Psychology 1975-97, Jour. Exptl. Psychology: Learning, Memory and Cognition, 1984-92, Memory and Cognition, 1984-89. Recipient Research Scientist award NIMH, 1969-74 Mem. APA (coun. editors 1975-80, bd. sci. affairs 1978-81, 89-92, chmn. early awards com. 1978-79, coun. reps. 1976-79, 86-89, pres. divsn. 3 1992, publ. and comm. bd. 1995—), Psychonomic Soc. (governing bd. 1976-81, chmn. 1980-81), Soc. Exptl. Psychologists (chmn. 1987-88), Fedn. Behavioral, Psychol. and Cognitive Scis. (v.p. 1994-95, pres. 1995-97), Rocky Mountain Psychol. Assn. (pres. 1987-88), Coun. Grad. Depts. Psychology (exec. bd. 1985-89), Sigma Xi. Home: 785 Northstar Ct Boulder CO 80304-1088

BOURQUE, LINDA ANNE BROOKOVER, public health educator; b. Indpls., Aug. 25, 1941; d. Wilbur Bone and Edna Mae (Eberhart) Brookover; m. Don Philippe Bourque, June 3, 1966 (div. Nov. 1974). BA, Ind. U., 1963; MA, Duke U., 1964, PhD, 1968. Postdoctoral researcher Duke U., Durham, N.C., 1968-69; asst. prof. sociology Calif. State U., Los Angeles, 1969-72; asst. prof. to assoc. prof. pub. health UCLA, 1972-86, prof. pub. health, 1986—, acting assoc. dir. Inst. for Social Sci. Research, 1981-82, vice chair dept. community health scis., 1991-94, chair Sch. Pub. Health Policy, 1998-2000. Author: Defining Rape, 1989, (with Virginia Clark) Processing Data: The Survey Example, 1992, (with Eve Fielder) How to Conduct Self-Administered and Mail Surveys, 1995; contbr. articles to profl. jours. Violoncellist with Santa Monica (Calif.) Symphony Orch., 1978—, Los Angeles Doctors' Symphony, 1981—. Mem. AAAS, Am. Sociol. Assn. (mem. med. sociology sect. council 1975-78, co-chmn. com. freedom research and teaching, 1975-78, cert. recognition 1980), Pacific Sociol. Assn. (co-chmn. program com. 1982, v.p. 1983), APHA (mem. standing com. on status of women 1974-76), Am. Assn. Pub. Opinion Rsch., Earthquake Engring. Rsch. Inst., Assn. Rsch. in Vision and Ophthalmology, Delta Omega, Phi Alpha Theta. Avocation: playing the violoncello. Office: UCLA Sch Pub Health PO Box 957220 Los Angeles CA 90095-7220

BOURQUE, RAY, professional hockey player; b. Montreal, Que., Can., Dec. 28, 1960; m. Chris Bourque; children: Melissa, Christopher Ray. Defenseman Boston Bruins (NHL), 1979-2000, Colo. Avalanche, 2000—. Mem. QMJHL All-Star 1st team, 1977-78, 78-79, NHL All-Star 1st team, 1979-80, 81-82, 83-84, 84-85, 86-87, 89-90, 93-94, 2nd team, 80-81, 82-85, 85-86, 88-89; player NHL All-Star game, 1981-86, 88-94. Recipient Calder NHL Rookie of Yr. trophy, 1980, Norris Outstanding Defenseman trophy, 1987, Frank. J. Selke trophy, 1978-79, Emile (Butch) Bouchard trophy, 1978-79, James Norris Meml. trophy, 1986-87, 87-88, 89-90, 90-91, 93-94, King Clancy Meml. trophy, 1991-92; named to Sporting News All-Star 2nd team, 1980-81, 82-83, 85-86, 88-89, Sporting News All-Star 1st team, 1981-82, 83-84, 86-87, 87-88, 89-90, 93-94. Office: Colo Avalanche 100 Chopper Pl Denver CO 80204

BOVEN, DOUGLAS GEORGE, lawyer; b. Holland, Mich., Aug. 11, 1943; BSE, U. Mich., 1966, JD, 1969. Bar: Calif. 1970. Dir. Crosby, Heafy, Roach & May PC, San Francisco, 1989—. Arbitrator Fed. and Superior Ct. Panel of Arbitrators, 1980—; panelist Superior Ct. Early Settlement Program, 1987. Mem. ABA (mem. bus. bankruptcy, Chpt. 11 and secured creditors coms.), Am. Bankruptcy Inst., Comml. Law League Am., State Bar Calif. (insolvency law and real estate sects.), Alameda County Bar Assn., Sonoma County Bar Assn., Bay Area Bankruptcy Forum, Bar Assn. San Francisco (comml. law and bankruptcy sect., mem. arbitrator fee disputes com. 1973—), Tau Beta Pi. Office: Crosby Heafey Roach & May PC 1999 Harrison St Oakland CA 94612-3520

BOW, STEPHEN TYLER, JR. insurance and computer industry consultant; b. Bow, Ky., Oct. 20, 1931; s. Stephen Tyler Sr. and Mary L. (King) B.; m. Kathy O'Connor, July, 1982; children: Jerry, Jon; children by previous marriage: Sandra Bow Morris, Deborah Bow Goodin, Carol, Clara. BA in Sociology, Berea (Ky.) Coll., 1953; grad. exec. program bus. adminstrn., Columbia U., 1976. CLU. With Met. Life Ins. Co., 1953-74, 76-89; agt. Lexington, Ky., 1953-55; sales mgr. Birmingham, Ala., 1955-58; field tng. cons. Birmingham, 1958-59; territorial field supr., 1959-60; dist. sales mgr. Frankfort, 1960-64, Lexington, 1964-66; exec. asst. field tng. N.Y.C., 1966-67; regional sales mgr. North Jersey, 1967-72; agy. v.p., officer-in-charge Can. hdqrs., 1972-74; exec. v.p., chmn., chief exec. officer Capital Holding Corp., Louisville, 1974-76; officer-in-charge Midwestern hdqrs. Met. Life Ins. Co., Dayton, 1976-83, sr. v.p., officer-in-charge Western Hdqrs., 1983-89; chmn., CEO Southeastern Group, Inc., Louisville, 1993-94; pres., CEO Anthem Life of Ind., Indpls., 1993-95; chmn., CEO Anthem Life Ins. Cos., 1995-96; exec. v.p. Assoc. Ins. Cos., Inc., Indpls., 1993-96; chmn. Acordia of San Francisco, 1993-96; pres., CEO Delta Dental Ky., Louisville, 1989-94, Blue Cross and Blue Shield Ky., Louisville, 1989-93; vice chmn. DeHayes Group, 1996—; pres. Steve Bow and Assocs., Inc., 1996—; chmn. Victory Tech., Inc., 1998—. Past chmn. Dayton Power and Light Audit Com. Past bd. dirs. San Francisco Visitors and Conv. Bur., 1985-87, Ind. Coll. of No. Calif., Bay Area Coun., Lindsey Wilson Coll.; bd. dirs. Bay Area Boy Scouts Am., Bay Area Council, U. San Francisco; mem. adv. bd. Hugh O'Brian Youth Found.; bd. dirs. Calif. Legis. Adv. Commn. on Life and Health Ins., Metro United Way, Ky. Health Care Access Found., Greater Louisville Econ. Devel. Coun., Leadership Ky., Greater Louisville Fund for the Arts; mem. corp. council San Francisco UN Assn.; mem. bd. dirs. Ky. Home Mut., Ky. Forward, Asian Bus. League, McLaren Coll. of Bus.; past mem. San Francisco Pvt. Industry Council; past chmn. United Negro Coll. Fund of San Francisco, 1985-86; mem. exec. com. bd. dirs., v.p. county ops. United Way of San Francisco Bay Area, 1985-87; vol. chmn. U.S. Savs. Bond Campaign, Bay Area, 1987; trustee Ky. Ind. Coll. Fund, Berea Coll.; bd. dirs. Boy Scouts Am., My Old Ky. Home Coun. Recipient Outstanding Sales Mgmt. award N.Y. Sales Congress, 1972, Frederick D. Patterson award United Negro Coll. Fund San Francisco, 1986, Outstanding County Ops. Vol. award United Way of Bay Area, 1987, Bus. Appreciation award Jeffersontown, Ky. C. of C., 1993, Pres.'s award, 1993, Leadership award Internat. Women's Forum, Washington, 1993; named Citizen of Yr. Wright State U. Med. Sch., Dayton, 1982. Mem. Nat. Assn. Life Underwriters, Gen. Agts. and Mgrs. Assn., Calif. Bus. Roundtable, Nat. Assn. Corp. Dirs. (founder, former pres.), Calif. C. of C. (bd. dirs.), Ky. C. of C., Ky. Home Life Exec. Com., Am. Cancer Soc. Republican. Methodist. Club: Lincoln of Northern Calif.; San Francisco Bankers. Avocations: golf, oil painting, reading. Home: PO Box 675905 Rancho Santa Fe CA 92067 Office: 772 W Napa St Sonoma CA 95476-6452

BOWDEN, DOUGLAS MCHOSE, neuropsychiatric scientist, educator, research center administrator; b. Durham, N.C., Apr. 7, 1937; s. Daniel Joseph and Charlotte (McHose) B.; m. Vivian Lee Bowden, 1966; children: Dana, Julie, Carlos, Luis. BA, Harvard U., 1959; MD, Stanford U., 1965. Staff assoc. NIMH, Bethesda, Md., 1966-69; asst. prof. psychiatry U. Wash., Seattle, 1969-73, assoc. prof. dept. psychiatry & behavioral scis., [illegible] core staff sci. Regional Primate Rsch. Ctr., U. Wash., 1969—, from asst. dir. to assoc. dir., 1977-88, dir., 1988-94. Adj. assoc. prof. pharmacology U. Wash., 1975-79, adj. prof. pharmacology, 1979-88; rsch. fellow Japan Soc. Promotion of Sci., Japan Assn. Animal Sci., Tokyo, Tsukuba, Inuyama/Kyoto, Japan, 1989. Author: Neuronames (c) Neuroanatomical Nomenclature, 1992; editor: Aging in Nonhuman Primates, 1979; translator Traumatic Aphasia, [illegible] Psychology and Treatment, [illegible], Primate Models of Human Neurogenic Disorders, 1976; co-author: Brain Info website, 2001-. Surgeon USPHS, 1966-69. Fellow Gerontol. Soc. Am.; mem. Am. Soc. Primatologists, Soc. Neurosci., Gerontol. Soc., Internat. Primatological Soc. Office: U Wash Regl Primate Rsch Ct Box 357330 1705 NE Pacific St Seattle WA 98195-7330 E-mail: dmbowden@u.washington.edu

BOWDEN, WILLIAM DARSIE, retired interior designer; b. Palo Alto, Calif., Aug. 11, 1920; s. Edmund Robert and Elisabeth (Darsie) B.; m. Anne Minor Lile, July 29, 1948; children: Darsie Minor, Raleigh Anne, Elsiabeth Lile. B.A., Stanford U., 1942. Jr. exec. Frederick and Nelson Dept. Store, Seattle, 1946-48; v.p., co-owner William L. Davis Co., Seattle, 1948-84. Trustee Found. for Interior Design Edn. Rsch., Plestcheeff Inst. for Decorative Arts U. Wash. Served to 1st lt. AUS, 1943-46. Fellow Am. Soc. Interior Designers (pres. Wash. chpt. 1966-67, nat. v.p. 1969-71), Furniture History Soc. (London), Phi Beta Kappa, Alpha Delta Phi. Republican. Episcopalian. Clubs: University, Wash. Athletic. Home and Office: 2030 Beans Bight Rd NE Bainbridge Island WA 98110 E-mail: alile@aol.com

BOWDON, WILLIAM G. career officer; m. Sally; children: Bill, Bob. Grad., La. State U., 1970, Amphibious Warfare Sch., Quantico, Va., 1979, Marine Corps Command and Staff, 1982. Commd. 2nd lt. USMC, 1970, advanced through grades to maj. gen., 1999; with 3rd Marine Aircraft Wing, Cherry Point, N.C., 1972, VMFA-314 MAG-11, 1973-74; flight instr. TA-4 aircraft VT-7 NAS, Meridian, Miss., 1974-77; with VMFA-232 MAG-15, Iwakuni, Japan, 1977-78, VMFA-122 MAG-31; aircraft maintenance officer VMFA-333 MAG-31; exec. officer Marine Tng. Support Group, NAS Cecil Field, Fla., VMFA-251 MAG-31; administrv. officer MAG-31, 1986-88; with Joint Staff J-4 Directorate Pentagon, Washington, 1991-94; comdr. Marine Aircraft Group 11 MCAS El Toro, 1994-96; asst. wing comdr. 2nd Marine Aircraft Wing, Cherry Point, N.C., 1996—; commanding gen. COMCAB West, 1999—. Office: COMCABWEST MCAS Miramar PO Box 452013 San Diego CA 92145-2013

BOWEN, DEBRA LYNN, lawyer, state legislator; b. Rockford, Ill., Oct. 27, 1955; d. Robert Calvin and Marcia Ann (Crittenden) Bowen. BA, Mich. State U., 1976; JD, U. Va., 1979. Bar: Ill. 1979, Calif. 1983. Assoc. Winston & Strawn, Chgo., 1979-82, Washington, 1985-86, Hughes Hubbard & Reed, Los Angeles, 1982-84; sole practice Los Angeles, 1984-93; mem. Calif. State Assembly, 1992—. Gen. counsel, State Employee's Retirement System Ill., Springfield, 1980-82; adj. prof. Watterson Coll. Sch. Paralegal Studies, 1985. Exec. editor Va. Jour. Internat. Law, 1977-78; contbr. articles to profl. jours. Mem. mental health law com. Chgo. Council Lawyers, 1980-82. Rotary Internat. fellow Internat. Christian U., Tokyo, 1975; Wigmore scholar Northwestern U. Sch. Law, Chgo., 1976; recipient James Madison Freedom of Information award No. Calif. chpt. Soc. Profl. Journalists, 1995. Mem. Calif. Bar Assn. (exec. com. pub. law sect. 1990-94), Mortar Bd., Phi Kappa Phi. Office: Calif Senate State Capitol Sacramento CA 95814-4906 also: Dist Office 2512 Artesia Blvd Ste 200 Redondo Beach CA 90278-3210

BOWEN, JAMES THOMAS, career officer; b. Mason City, Iowa, May 4, 1948; s. Stanley Thomas and Marilyn Louise (Ott) B.; m. Joyce Anne Kermabon, Sept. 10, 1977; 1 child, Steven James. BBA, U. Iowa, 1969; MS, U. So. Calif., Los Angeles, 1974. Commd. 2nd lt. USAF, 1969, advance through grades to col., 1991; student pilot 3575th Pilot Tng. Wing, Vance AFB, Okla., 1969-70; co-pilot 773rd Tactical Airlift Squadron, Clark AFB, Phillipines, 1971; pilot 6594th Test Group, Hickam AFB, Hawaii, 1971-75; acquisition program mgr. Aeronautical Systems Div., Wright-Patterson AFB, Ohio, 1976-82; chief, standoff surveillance and attack systems HQ USAF, Rsch. Devel. and Acquistion, Pentagon, Va., 1984-87; chief, acquistion plans and programs br. Air Force Inspection and Safety Ctr., Norton AFB, Calif., 1988-90; dir. projects joint tactical autonomous weapons Aero. Systems Div., Wright-Patterson AFB, Ohio, 1990-91, dir. devel. and integration F-16, 1991-94; F-16 mgmt. dir. Ogden Air Logistics Ctr., Hill AFB, Utah, 1994-95; custom sys. program mgr. Hewlett Packard and Agilent Tech. Cos., Santa Rosa, Calif., 1996-2001; site mgr. Agilent Techs., Rohnert Park, 2001—. Active Rep. ctrl. com. Sonoma County. Decorated Air medal USAF, 1972. Mem. Air Force Assn., Def. Systems Mgmt. Coll. Alumni Assn., Nat. Def. U. Alumni Assn., Am. Mgmt. Assn., Assn. Old Crows, Ret. Officers Assn., Project Mgmt. Inst. Methodist. Avocations: skiing, deep sea fishing, golf. Office: Agilent Techs 1212 Valley House Dr # Ms4ura Rohnert Park CA 94928-4902 E-mail: james_bowen@agilent.com, jbowen@pacbell.net

BOWEN, JEWELL RAY, chemical engineering educator; b. Duck Hill, Miss., Jan. 9, 1934; s. Hugh and Myrtle Louise (Stevens) B.; m. Priscilla Joan Spooner, Feb. 4, 1956; children: Jewell Ray, Sandra L., Susan E. B.S., MIT, 1956, M.S., 1957; Ph.D., U. Calif., Berkeley, 1963. Asst. prof. U. Wis., Madison, 1963-67, assoc. prof., 1967-80, prof. chem. engring., 1970-81, chmn. chem engring. dept., 1971-73, 78-81, assoc. vice chancellor, 1972-76; prof. chem. engring. U. Wash., Seattle, 1981-2000, prof. emeritus, 2001—, dean coll. engring., 1981-96. Cons. in field; adviser NSF, Dept. Def.; chmn. program com. Internat. Coloquia on Dynamics of Explosions and Reactive systems. Contbr. articles to profl. jours.; editor: 7th-10th Internat. Colloquia on Dynamics of Explosions and Reactive Systems, 1979, 81, 83, 85, chmn. program com. 18th; bd. dirs. Inst. for Dynamics of Explosions and Reactive Sys., 1989—, pres., 1989-95, treas. 1995—. Bd. dirs. Wash. Tech. Ctr., 1983-97, interim exec. dir., 1989-91; mem. Wash. High Tech. Coordinating Bd., 1983-87. Recipient SWE Rodney Chipp award, 1995; NATO-NSF postdoctoral fellow, 1962-63, sr. postdoctoral fellow, 1968; Deutsche Forschungsgemeinschaft prof., 1976-77. Fellow AIAA, AAAS (com. on coun. affairs 1995-97, sect. chmn. 1996-97), Am. Soc. Engring. Edn. (deans coun. 1985-92, chmn. 1989-91, bd. dirs. 1989-94, 1st v.p. 1991, pres.-elect 1992, pres. 1993); mem. AIAA, AIChE, Am. Phys. Soc., Combustion Inst., Inst. Dynamics of Explosions and Reactive Sys. (pres. 1989-95, treas. 1995—, bd. dirs. 1989—), Sigma Xi, Taua Beta Pi, Beta Theta Pi. Home: 5324 NE 86th St Seattle WA 98115-3922 Office: U Wash Dept Chem Engring PO Box 351750 Seattle WA 98195-1750 E-mail: bowen@engr.washington.edu

BOWEN, MELANIE, legislative staff administrator; m. Ronald S. Bowen; children: Elysa, Lindsey. BS in Polit. Sci. and History, Brigham Young U. Intern to Senator Orrin Hatch, Washington, 1977; dir. Ctrl. and Ea. Utah Office; dep. state dir., 1984; state dir.; dir. Office of Senator Hatch. Mem. U.S. Delegation Am. Swiss Leadership Conf., Geneva; co-chair State Rep. Platform com.; mem. State of Utah's Immunization Task Force, Utah Internat. Biomed. Conf. com., Utah State Vets. Nursing Home Oversight com.; chair Utah Women's and Srs. Confs. Office: Office of Senator Orrin Hatch 8402 Federal Bldg 123 S State St Salt Lake City UT 84138-1101

BOWEN, RICHARD LEE, academic administrator, political science educator; b. Avoca, Iowa, Aug. 31, 1933; s. Howard L. and Donna [illegible] B.; m. Connie [illegible] Bowen, 1976; children: James, Robert, Elizabeth, Christopher; children by previous marriage— Catherine, David, Thomas. B.A., Augustana Coll., 1957; M.A., Harvard, 1959, Ph.D., 1967. Fgn. service officer State Dept., 1959-60; research asst. to U.S. Senator Francis Case, 1960-62; legis. asst. to U.S. Senator Karl Mundt, 1962-65; minority cons. sub com. [illegible] U.S. [illegible]; assoc. prof. polit. sci. U. S.D., Vermillion, 1967-69, pres. [illegible] Dakota State Coll., Madison, 1973-76; commr. higher edn. Bd. Regents State S.D.,

Pierre, 1976-80; Disting prof. polit. sci. U. S.D., 1980-85; pres. Idaho State U., Pocatello, 1985—. Served with USN, 1951-54. Recipient Outstanding Alumnus award Augustana Coll., 1970; Woodrow Wilson fellow, 1957, Congl. Staff fellow, 1965; Fulbright scholar, 1957. Office: Idaho State U Office of Pres PO Box 8310 Pocatello ID 83209-0001

BOWENS, THELLA, senior aviation director; b. Mount Enterprise, Tex. 2 children. BA, Barnard Coll, 1970; post grad., Texas Christian U. Budget adminstr. Dallas/Ft. Worth Internat. airport; dep. dir. of aviation Kansas City Internat. airport; sr. dir. of aviation San Diego Unified Port Dist., 1996—. Bd. dirs. george Washington Carver Neighborhood Ctr. and Day Care; mem. Lejardin Sr. Citizens Home; bd. dirs. San Diego United Way; mentor for Welfare to Work Program. Mem. Am. Assn. of Airport Execs., Econ. Steering Com. for Airports Coun. Internat. North Am., Natl. Forum for Black Pub. Administr. Avocations: tennis, reading hist. novels, enjoying arts and theatre productions. Office: San Diego Unified Port Dist San Diego Internat Airport PO Box 120488 San Diego CA 92112-0488

BOWER, ALLAN MAXWELL, lawyer; b. Oak Park, Ill., May 21, 1936; s. David Robert and Frances Emily Bower; m. Deborah Ann Rottmayer, Dec. 28, 1959. BS, U. Iowa, 1962; JD, U. Miami, Fla., 1968. Bar: Calif. 1969, U.S. Supreme Ct. 1979. Internat. aviation law practice, L.A., 1969—; ptnr. Kern & Wooley, L.A., 1980-85, Bronson, Bronson & McKinnon, L.A., 1985-90, Lane Powell Spears Lubersky, L.A., 1990-99, Bailey & Marzano, Santa Monica, Calif., 1999—. Contbr. articles to profl. publs. Mem. Lawyer-Pilots Bar Assn. Republican. Presbyterian. Office: Bailey & Marzano 2nd Fl 2828 Donald Douglas Loop N Santa Monica CA 90405-2959 Fax: 310-392-8091

BOWER, CURTIS A. engineering executive; Exec. v.p., CFO, Parsons Corp., Pasadena, Calif. Office: Parsons Corp 100 W Walnut St Pasadena CA 91124-0001

BOWER, JANET ESTHER, writer, educator; b. National City, Calif., Apr. 14, 1943; d. Murvel and Esther Eva (Clark) Newlan; m. Robert S. Bower Jr., Nov. 23, 1968; children: Llance Clark, Esther Elizabeth. BA in History and Psychology, Calif. Western U., San Diego, 1965; MA in History, UCLA, 1966; MA in Edn., U.S. Internat. U., San Diego, 1970. Std. jr. coll. credential, elem. credential, Calif. Instr., mem. adj. faculty San Diego C.C. Dist., 1969—, Grossmont/Cuyamaca Coll. Dist., El Cajon, Calif., 1973, 97—, Palomar Coll. Dist., San Marcos, 1993, 97—, Midlands Tech. Coll., Columbia, S.C., 1995-96, Mira Costa Coll., 2001—. Adj. faculty mem. Nat. U., 1999—, Union Inst., 2000—; hist. cons. pub. Contbg. author: Women in the Biological Sciences, 1997; contbr. articles to periodicals; pub. editor Friends of the Internat. Ctr. Newsletter, U. Calif., San Diego, 1984-85. Bd. dirs. Women of St. Paul's Episcopal Ch., San Diego, 1983-86, Oceanids, U. Calif., San Diego, 1980-85. Grantee U.S. Dept. Edn., 1968-69. Mem. Am. Hist. Assn., Calif. Hist. Soc., Project Wildlife (hon. life mem.). Republican. Avocations: cooking, travel. E-mail: newbower@aol.com

BOWER, ROBERT W. electrical engineer; BS with hons. in Physics, U. Calif., Berkeley, 1962; MSEE, Calif. Inst. Tech., 1963, PhD in Applied Physics, 1973. Asst. mgr. MOS divsn. Hughes A.C., 1965-70; cons., 1970-75; from v.p. to pres. Mnemonics Inc., 1975-77; assoc. prof. dept. elec. sci. and engring. UCLA, 1977-78; mgr. bipolar device tech. Advanced Micro Devices Inc., 1979-85; prof. dept. elec. and computer engring. U. Calif., Davis, 1987—, prof. emeritus. Vis. scientist Tech. U. Munich, 1986-87; cons. TRW, Intel, Honeywell, GCA, AMD, Xerox, Hughes, Motorola, Datapoint, ITT, High Voltage Engring., Eurocil; presenter in field. Contbr. articles to profl. jours, chpts. to books; patentee in field. Recipient Ronald H. Brown Am. Innovator award U.S. Dept. Commerce, 1997; inductee Nat. Inventors Hall of Fame, 1997. Fellow IEEE; mem. NAE, Boehmische Phys. Soc., Phi Beta Kappa, Sigma Xi. Acheivements include research in development and invention of self assigned-gate ion-implanted MOSFET, and establishment of ion implantation to fabricate semiconductor integrated circuits. Office: U Calif Davis Dept Elec/Computer Engring Davis CA 95616

BOWERING, GEORGE HARRY, writer, English literature educator; b. Penticton, B.C., Can., Dec. 1, 1936; s. Ewart Harry and Pearl Patricia (Brinson) B.; m. Angela May Luoma, Dec. 14, 1962; 1 dau., Thea Claire. Student, Victoria Coll., 1953-54; BA, U. B.C., 1960, MA, 1963; postgrad., U. Western Ont., 1966-67. Asst. prof. Am. lit. U. Calgary, 1963-66; writer in residence Sir George Williams U., Montreal, Que., 1967-68, asst. prof., 1968-71; prof. Simon Fraser U., Burnaby, B.C., 1972—. Author: Mirror on the Floor, 1967, Autobiology, 1972, Flycatcher and Other Stories, 1974, Concentric Circles, 1977, A Short Sad Book, 1977, Protective Footwear, 1978, Another Mouth, 1979, Burning Water, 1980, A Place to Die, 1983, Caprice, 1987, Harry's Fragments, 1990, The Rain Barrel, 1994, Shoot!, 1994, Parents From Space, 1994, Piccolo Mondo, 1998, Diamondback Dog, 1998; poetry Points on the Grid, 1964, The Man in Yellow Boots, 1965, The Silver Wire, 1966, Rocky Mountain Foot, 1968, The Gangs of Kosmos, 1969, Touch, 1971, In the Flesh, 1973, The Catch, 1976, Particular Accidents: Selected Poems, 1981, Smoking Mirror, 1984, Kerrisdale Elegies, 1984, 71 Poems for People, 1985, Delayed Mercy, 1986, Sticks & Stones, 1989, Quarters, 1991, Urban Snow, 1992, George Bowering Selected, 1993, The Moustache, 1993, Blonds On Bikes, 1997; (poetry) His Life: A Poem, 2000; (essays) The Mask in Place, 1982, A Way with Words, 1982, Craft Slices, 1985, Errata, 1988, Imaginary Hand, 1988, A Magpie Life, 2001, (history) Bowering's B.C., 1996, Egotists and Autocrats, 1999; editor Taking the Field: The Best of Baseball Fiction, 1990, 92, Likely Stories: A Postmodern Sampler, 1992, And Other Stories, 2001. Served with RCAF, 1954-57. Mem. Assn. Can. TV and Radio Artists Home: 2499 W 37th Ave Vancouver BC Canada V6M 1P4 E-mail: bowering@sfu.ca

BOWERS, MICHAEL THOMAS, chemistry educator; b. Spokane, Wash., June 6, 1939; s. John W. and Fae (Scott) B.; married, Feb. 8, 1964; children: Molly, Shelia, Melissa. BS, Gonzaga U., 1962; MS, U. Ill., 1964, PhD, 1966. Asst. prof. U. Calif., Santa Barbara, 1966-73, assoc. prof., 1973-76, prof. chemistry, 1976—. Faculty rsch. lectr. faculty senate U. Calif., Santa Barbara, 1994. Editor Internat. Jour. Mass Spectrometry, 1986—; contbr. over 300 articles to profl. jours.; editor 3 books in field; assoc. editor Jour. Am. Chem. Soc. 1st lt. U.S. Army, 1966-68. Guggenheim Found. fellow, 1994. Fellow AAAS, Am. Phys. Soc.; mem. Am. Chem. Soc. (assoc. editor jour. 1989—, Nobel laureate signature award 1989, Outstanding Achievement in Mass Spectrometry award 1996), Am. Soc. Mass Spectrometry, Internat. Mass Spectrometry Soc. (Thomson gold medal 1997). Roman Catholic. Avocations: golf, running. Office: U Calif Dept Chemistry Santa Barbara CA 93106 E-mail: bowers@chem.ucsb.edu

BOWERS, PAUL D. transportation company executive; b. Rome, Aug. 28, 1948; Dir. aviation Alaska Dept. Transp. and Pub. Facilities Statewide Aviation, Anchorage, 1995—. Office: Alaska Dept Transp and Pub Facilities Statewide Aviation 4111 Aviation Dr Anchorage AK 99502-1058

BOWERS, RUSSELL W. state legislator, sculptor, painter; b. Mesa, Ariz., Oct. 20, 1952; m. Donetta Bowers. Grad., Brigham Young U.; postgrad., Mesa C.C., Ariz. State U. Mem. Ariz. Ho. of Reps., 1993-97, Ariz. Senate, Dist. 21, Phoenix, 1996—; mem. edn. com., mem. family svcs. com.; mem. govt. and environ. stewardship com. Ariz. State Senate, vice-chmn. rules com. Republican. Office: State Capitol Bldg 1700 W Washington St # 212 Phoenix AZ 85007-2812 also: 8831 E Quill St Mesa AZ 85207-9706 Fax: 602-542-4511. E-mail: rbowers@azleg.state.az.us

BOWICK, SUSAN D. computer company executive; Bus. analyst Hewlett-Packard Co., Loveland, Colo., 1972-85, pers. mgr. Lake Stevens instrument divsn. Everett, Wash., 1985-89, group pers. mgr. computer sys. orgn., 1989-93, pers. mgr., 1993-95, pers. mgr. computer orgn., 1995-98, v.p. human resources Calif. Office: Hewlett-Packard Co 3000 Hanover St Palo Alto CA 94304-1181 also: PO Box 10301 Palo Alto CA 94303-0890 Fax: 650-813-3003

BOWIE, PETER WENTWORTH, judge, educator; b. Alexandria, Va., Sept. 27, 1942; s. Beverley Munford and Louise Wentworth (Boynton) B.; m. Sarah Virginia Haught, Mar. 25, 1967; children: Heather, Gavin. BA, Wake Forest Coll., 1964; JD magna cum laude, U. San Diego, 1971. Bar: Calif. 1972, D.C. 1972, U.S. Dist. Ct. D.C. 1972, U.S. Dist. Ct. Md. 1973, U.S. Dist. Ct. (so. dist.) Calif. 1974, U.S. Ct. Appeals (D.C. cir.) 1972, U.S. Ct. Appeals (9th cir.) 1974, U.S. Supreme Ct. 1980. Trial atty. honors program Dept. of Justice, Washington, 1971-74; asst. U.S. Atty. U.S. Atty.'s Office, San Diego, 1974, asst. chief civil div., 1974-82, chief asst. U.S. atty., 1982-88; lawyer rep. U.S. Ct. Appeals (9th cir.) Jud. Conf., 1977-78, 84-87; judge U.S. Bankruptcy Ct., San Diego, 1988—. Lectr. at law Calif. Western Sch. Law, 1979-83; exec. com. mem. 9th Cir. Judicial Conf., 1991-94; mem. com. on codes of conduct Jud. Conf. of U.S., 1995—. Bd. dirs. Presidio Little League, San Diego, 1984, coach, 1983-84; mem. alumni adv. bd. Sch. Law U. San Diego, 1998—. Lt. USN, 1964-68, Vietnam. Mem. State Bar Calif. (hearing referee ct. 1982-86, mem. rev. dept. 1986-90), Fed. Bar Assn. (pres. San diego chpt. 1981-83), San Diego County Bar Assn. (chmn. fed. ct. com. 1978-80, 83-85), Assn. Bus. Trial Lawyers (bd. govs.), San Diego Bankruptcy Forum (bd. dirs.), Phi Delta Phi. Republican. Mem. Unitarian Ch. Office: US Bankruptcy Court 325 W F St San Diego CA 92101-6017

BOWIE, PHYLLIS, secondary education educator; Tchr. secondary geography S.A.V.E. High Sch., Anchorage. Recipient Disting. Tchr. K-12 award Nat. Coun. for Geog. Edn., 1992. Office: SAVE HS 410 E 56th Ave Anchorage AK 99518-1244

BOWKER, ALBERT HOSMER, retired university chancellor; b. Winchendon, Mass., Sept. 8, 1919; s. Roy C. and Kathleen (Hosmer) B.; m. Elizabeth Rempfer, June 14, 1942; children: Paul Albert, Nancy Kathleen, Caroline Anne; m. Rosedith Sitgreaves, Sept. 26, 1964. B.S., Mass. Inst. Tech., 1941; Ph.D., Columbia U., 1949; D.H.L., City U. N.Y., 1971; LL.D., Brandeis U.; D.H.L., N.Y. Bd. Regents, 1972. Asst. statistician Mass. Inst. Tech., 1941-43; asst. dir. statis. research group Columbia, 1943-45; asst. prof. statistics Stanford, 1947-50, assoc. prof., 1950-53, exec. head statistics dept., 1948-59, dean grad. div., 1959-63, prof. math. and statistics, 1953-63, dir. applied math. and statistics labs., 1951-63; chancellor City U. N.Y., 1963-71, U. Calif., Berkeley, 1971-80, chancellor emeritus, 1980—; asst. sec. for postsecondary edn. Dept. Edn., Washington, 1980-81; dean Sch. Pub. Affairs U. Md., 1981-84, exec. v.p. univ., 1984-86; v.p. research found. CUNY, 1986—. Mem. com. grad. edn. Am. Assn. Univs.; mem. Sloan Commn. on Govt. and Higher Edn.; mem. exec. com. div. math. Nat. Acad. Scis.-NRC, 1963-65 Author: (with Henry P. Goode) Sampling Inspection by Variables, 1952, (with Gerald J. Lieberman) Handbook of Industrial Statistics, 1955, Engineering Statistics, 1972; also articles profl. jours.; Asso. editor: Jour. Am. Statis. Assn, 1949-52. Mem. Corp. Mass. Inst. Tech., 1967-72; mem. Centennial Commn. Howard U., 1965; bd. dirs. San Francisco Bay Area Council, 1972-77; trustee Bennington Coll., U. Haifa. Fellow Am. Statis. Assn. (pres. 1964), Am. Soc. Quality Control, Inst. Math. Statistics (pres. 1961-62), AAAS; mem. Math. Assn. Am., Biometric Soc., Operations Research Soc. Am., Soc. for Indsl. and Applied Math., Am. Assn. Univs. (com. grad. edn.), Phi Beta Kappa (hon.), Sigma Xi (exec. com. 1963-66) Office: U Calif Dept Stats 367 Evans Hall Spc 3860 Berkeley CA 94720-3860 E-mail: bowker@stat.berkeley.edu

BOWKER, LEE HARRINGTON, academic administrator; b. Bethlehem, Pa., Dec. 19, 1940; s. Maurice H. Bowker and Blanche E. Heffner; m. Nancy Bachant, 1966 (div. 1973); 1 child, Kirsten Ruth; m. Dee C. Thomas, May 25, 1975; children: Jessica Lynn, Gwendolyn Alice. BA, Muhlenberg Coll., 1962; MA, U. Pa., 1965; PhD, Wash. State U., 1972. Instr. in Sociology Lebanon Valley Coll., Annville, Pa., 1965-66, Allbright Coll., Reading, 1966-67; assoc. prof. Whitman Coll., Walla Walla, Wash., 1967-77; prof., assoc. dean U. Wis., Milw., 1977-82; dean grad. sch. and research Ind. (Pa.) U. of Pa., 1982-85; provost, v.p. Augustana Coll., Sioux Falls, S.D., 1985-87; dean behavioral and social scis. Humboldt State U., Arcata, Calif., 1987-97, emeritus dean, prof. sociology, 1997—. Cons. various pubs., colls., univs. and state agys; expert witness. Author: over 300 papers, articles and sci. revs. and 18 books including Prison Victimization, 1980, Humanizing Institutions for the Aged, 1982, Masculinities and Violence, 1997, The Role of the Department Chair, 3d edit., 1997, Ending the Violence, 3d edit., 1998; assoc. editor Pacific Sociol. Rev., 1975-78, Justice Quar., 1983-85, Criminal Justice Policy Rev., 1984-95. Pres. Blue Mountain Action Coun., OEO, Walla Walla, 1969-71; dir. social therapy program, Wash. State penitentiary, Walla Walla, 1971-73; bd. dirs. Milw. Bur. Community Corrections, 1979-81, Sioux Falls Symphony, 1985, United Way of Humboldt County, 1988-91; expert witness in criminal and civil cases involving wife battering, rape and child abuse. Grantee NIMH 1973, 79, 81, Washington Arts Commn. 1972, Washington Office Community Devel. 1974, Fulbright Found. 1985, Nat. Retired Tchrs. Assn./Am. Assn. Retired Persons Andrus Found. 1980; Law Enforcement Assistance Adminstrn. co-grantee, 1978. Mem. Pacific Sociol. Assn., Am. Sociol. Assn. Home: 3513 H St Eureka CA 95503-5358 Office: Humboldt State U Sociology Faculty Arcata CA 95521 E-mail: LHB3@humboldt.edu

BOWLEN, PAT(RICK)(DENNIS), professional sports team executive, holding company executive, lawyer; b. Prairie du Chien, Wis., Feb. 18, 1944; s. Paul Dennis and Arvella (Woods) B. B.B.A., U. Okla., 1966, J.D., 1968. Bar: Alta. 1969. Read law Saucier, Jones, Calgary, Alta., Can., assoc. Can., 1969-70; asst. to pres. Regent Drilling Ltd., 1970-71; pres. Batoni-Bowlen Enterprises Ltd., 1971-79, Bowlen Holdings Ltd., Edmonton, Alta., Can., 1979—; pres., chief exec. officer, owner Denver Broncos, 1984—. Mem. Law Soc. Alta., Can. Bar Assn., Young Presidents Orgn., Edmonton Club Roman Catholic. Avocations: golf, skiing, surfing. Office: Denver Broncos 13655 Broncos Pkwy Englewood CO 80112-4150

BOWLES, DAVID STANLEY, engineering educator, engineering consultant; b. Romford, Essex, Eng., June 30, 1949; m. Valerie Rosina Curd; children: Penny, Simon, Amy. BSc, City U., Eng., 1972; PhD, Utah State U., 1977. Registered profl. engr., Utah; cert. profl. hydrologist. Jr. civil engr. George Wimpey & Co., Hammersmith, London, 1967-72; rsch. asst. prof. Utah State U., Logan, 1976-80, rsch. assoc. prof., 1980-81, adj. rsch. assoc. prof., 1981-83, rsch. prof., 1983-85, prof., 1985—, assoc. dir., 1986-91, dir., 1992-96. Vis. scientist Internat. Inst. Applied Systems Analysis, Laxenburg, Austria, 1979; br. mgr., engr. Law Engring., Denver, 1981-83; prin. Risk Assessment Cons. Engrs. and Economists (RAC), 1986—. Contbr. numerous articles to profl. jours. Active U.S. Soc. on Dams. Fellow ASCE, Am. Water Resources Assn.; mem. Soc. Risk Analysis, Am. Geophys. Union, Am. Inst. Hydrology, European Geophys. Union, Assn. State Dam Safety Ofcls. Home: 1520 Canyon Rd Providence UT 84332-9431 Office: Utah Water Rsch Lab Utah State Univ Logan UT 84322-8200 E-mail: bowles@cache.net

BOWLIN, MICHAEL RAY, oil company executive; b. Amarillo, Tex., Feb. 20, 1943; m. Martha Ann Rowland; 1 child, John Charles. BBA, North Tex. State U., 1965, MBA, 1967. Scheduler prodn. and transp. A. Brant Co., Ft. Worth, 1965-66; mktg. rep. R.J. Reynolds Tobacco Bo., 1967-68; personnel generalist Atlantic Richfield Co., Dallas, 1969-71, coll. relations rep. Los Angeles, 1971-72, mgr. internal profl. placement, 1973, mgr. corp. recruiting and placement, 1973-75, mgr. behavioral sci. services, 1975, sr. v.p. ARCO resources adminstrn., 1985, sr. v.p. ARCO internat. oil and gas acquisitions, 1987, sr. v.p. L.A., 1987—, employee relations mgr. Alaska, 1975-77; v.p. employee relations Anaconda Copper Co. (divsn. Atlantic Richfield Co.), Denver, 1977-81; from v.p. employee rels. to v.p. fin. planning and control ARCO Oil & Gas (div. Atlantic Richfield Co.), Dallas, 1981-84, v.p. fin. planning and control, 1982-84; sr. v.p. Atlantic Richfield Co., 1985-92; pres. ARCO Coal Co., 1985-87, ARCO Internat. Oil & Gas Co., 1987-92; CEO Atlantic Richfield Co., 1994—, chmn., CEO, 1998—; pres., COO ARCO Internat. Oil & Gas Co., 1993, pres., CEO, 1994-95, chmn., CEO, 1995-2000. Office: Atlantic Richfield Co 333 S Hope St Los Angeles CA 90071-1406

BOWLUS, BRAD A. health science association administrator; BA in Bus., Calif. (Northridge) State U.; MBA, Pepperdine U. Regional dir. WellPoint Health Networks, Inc., Calif.; v.p., So. Calif. region PacifiCare Health Systems Inc., 1994-95, pres., CEO, dental, vision, divn., 1995-96, pres., CEO, Wash., 1996-97, pres., CEO, Calif., 1997—. Bd. mem. several non-profit organs. Mem. Young Pres. Orgn. Office: PacifiCare Health Systems 3120 W Lake Center Dr Santa Ana CA 92704-6917

BOWMAN, A. BLAINE, electronics company executive; B.S. (Physics), Brigham Young U., UT; MBA, Stanford U., CA. Product engr. Motorola Semiconductor Products Divsn.; mgmt. cons. McKinsey and Co.; pres., CEO Dionex, Sunnyvale, Calif., 1977—. Office: Dionex PO Box 3603 1228 Titan Way Sunnyvale CA 94088-3603

BOWMAN, BRUCE, art educator, writer, artist; b. Dayton, Ohio, Nov. 23, 1938; s. Murray Edgar Bowman and Mildred May (Moler) Elleman; m. Julie Ann Gosselin, 1970 (div. 1980); 1 child, Carrie Lynn. AA, San Diego City Coll., 1962; BA, Calif. State U.-Los Angeles, 1964, MA, 1968. Tchr. art North Hollywood Adult Sch., Calif., 1966-68; instr. art Cypress Coll., Calif., 1976-78, West Los Angeles Coll., 1969— ; tchr. art Los Angeles City Schs., 1966—; seminar leader So. Calif., 1986—. Author: Shaped Canvas, 1976; Toothpick Sculpture and Ice Cream Stick Art, 1976; Ideas: How to Get Them, 1985, (cassette tape) Develop Winning Willpower, 1986, Waikiki, 1988. Contbr. articles to profl. jours. One-man shows include Calif. State U.-Los Angeles, 1968, Pepperdine U., Malibu, Calif., 1978; exhibited in group shows McKenzie Gallery, Los Angeles, 1968, Trebor Gallery, Los Angeles, 1970, Cypress Coll., Calif., 1977, Design Recycled Gallery, Fullerton, Calif., 1977, Pierce Coll., Woodland Hills, Calif., 1978, Leopold/Gold Gallery, Santa Monica, Calif., 1980. Served with USN, 1957-61. Avocation: karate (black belt Tang Soo Do). Home: 28322 Rey De Copas Ln Malibu CA 90265-4463

BOWMAN, JEFFREY R. protective services official; b. Akron, Ohio, Apr. 24, 1952; s. Roger Heath and Ruth Ann (Corrigan) B.; divorced; children: Katie, Andrew, Brian. BS in Orgnl. Behavior, U. San Francisco, 1986. Firefighter Anaheim (Calif.) Fire Dept., 1973-75, paramedic, 1975-79, capt., 1979-83, battalion chief, 1983-85, div. chief, 1985-86, fire chief, 1986—. Pres. bd. dirs. Anaheim Boys and Girls Club, 1988—; chmn. fundraising Boy Scouts Am., Anaheim, 1988. Mem. Internat. Assn. Fire Chiefs, Calif. Fire Chiefs Assn. Office: Anaheim Fire Dept 201 S Anaheim Blvd Ste 301 Anaheim CA 92805-3858

BOWMAN, JON ROBERT, magazine editor, film critic; b. Spokane, Wash., Nov. 9, 1954; s. Donald Ken and Carolyn Joyce (Crutchfield) B.; m. Geraldine Maria Jaramillo, Jan. 27, 1979 (div. Dec. 1985); m. Amy Farida Siswayanti, May 23, 1992 (div. Jan. 1994). BA, U. N.Mex., 1976. Reporter, arts editor, news editor N.Mex. Daily Lobo, Albuquerque, 1972 76; film critic Albuquerque Jour., 1974-76; reporter Alamogordo (N.Mex.) Daily News, 1976; sci. writer, editor Los Alamos (N.Mex.) Monitor, 1976-81; reporter, arts editor New Mexican, Santa Fe, 1981-86, film critic, 1987—; editor New Mexico Mag., Santa Fe, 1986—, Guest lectr. U. N.Mex., Coll. Santa Fe, 1976—. Author: (with others) Explore New Mexico, 1988, A New Mexico Scrapbook, 1990, Day Trip Discoveries: Selected New Mexico Excursions, 1993, The Allure of Turquoise, 1995; contbr. articles to mags. and newspapers; author salutes for Greer Garson, James Coburn, Ben Johnson, and John Huston for festivals honoring them. Vol. tchr. Albuquerque pub. schs., 1972-76; organizer film festivals Albuquerque and Santa Fe. 1972-91, benefits including Ctr. for Contemporary Arts, Santa Fe; program cons. Taos Talking Picture Festival, 1995—. Recipient Sci. Writing award AP, 1978, citation AP, 1979, others. Avocations: movies, baseball, travel. Home: 335 W Manhattan Ave Santa Fe NM 87501-2650 Office: NMex Mag Lew Wallace Bldg 495 Old Santa Fe Trl Santa Fe NM 87501-2750

BOWMAN, MICHAEL L. career officer; b. St. Joseph, Mo., June 27, 1943; Grad., Kans. State U., 1967. Commd. ensign USN, 1967, advanced through ranks to vice-adm.; various assignments to chief of Naval Air Tng. Corpus Christi, Tex., 1996-97; comdr. Naval Air Force, U.S. Pacific Fleet, San Diego, 1998—. Decorated Legion of Merit (4 times), Disting. Flying Cross, Bronze Star, Meritorious Svc. medal (3 times), Air medal.

BOWMAN, RAYMOND DEARMOND, SR. writer, music critic; b. Rockingham, Va., Sept. 4, 1917; s. Rawleigh David and Vesta Virginia (Ratliff) B.; m. Lita Salgado Santos, June 1, 1960; children: R. Christian Anderson, Leslieanne Dreith, Raymond DeArmond Jr. Student in History, Columbia U., 1945-47. Classical violinist Calif. Jr. Symphony, Long Beach Symphony, 1936-38, Long Beach Jr. Coll. Trio-Broadcasts, 1938-40; enlisted Calif. N.G., 1939; advanced through grades to master sgt. U.S. Army, 1955; lit. critic Daily Mirror News, L.A., 1949-50; classical impresario mgr./dir. West Coast Artists, Hollywood, Calif., 1954-75; co-owner Bowman-Mann Art Gallery, Beverly Hills, 1963-66; impresario "Ice House" Monday Night Concerts, Pasadena, 1966-83; writer, music critic South Bay Daily Breeze News, Torrance, 1969-87. Violinist (movie) They Shall Have Music, 1939; contbr. articles to newspapers, books and mags. Adminstr. Hollywood Am. Legion, 1953-60; coord. Civilian Def., L.A., 1950s; vol. L.A. Philharmonic Promotion, 1966-87; plank owner U.S.S. Pearl Harbor LSD #52. Recipient Eistedford medal, 1927, numerous art awards. Mem. Pearl Harbor Survivors Assn. (life). Avocations: painting, writing, book collector, reading, sports. Home: 604 E 7th Ave Escondido CA 92025-4449

BOWNE, MARTHA HOKE, publishing consultant; b. Greeley, Colo., June 9, 1931; d. George Edwin and Krin (English) Hoke; children: Gretchen, William, Kay, Judith. BA, U. Mich., 1952; postgrad., Syracuse U., 1965. Tchr. Wayne (Mich.) Pub. Schs., 1953-54, East Syracuse and Minoa Cen. Schs., Minoa, N.Y., 1965-68; store mgr. Fabric Barn, Fayetteville, 1969-77; store owner Fabric Fair, Oneida, 1978-80; producer, owner Quilting by the Sound, Port Townsend, Wash., 1987—, Quilting by the Lake, Cazenovia, N.Y., 1981—. Organizer symposium Am. Quilters Soc.; founder, pres. Quilter's Quest confs., 1994. Mem., pres. Minoa Library, 1960-75; mem. Onondaga County Library, Syracuse, 1968-71. Mem. Am. Quilters Soc. (editor Am. Quilter mag. 1985-95), New Eng. Quilt Mus. Avocations: reading, hiking, cross-country skiing, travel, bridge. Home: 478 Oden Bay Dr Sandpoint ID 83864-6499 E-mail: martyidaho@sandpoint.net

BOXER, BARBARA, senator; b. Bklyn., Nov. 11, 1940; d. Ira and Sophie (Silvershein) Levy; m. Stewart Boxer, 1962; children: Doug, Nicole. BA in Econ., Bklyn. Coll., 1962. Stockbroker, econ. rschr. N.Y. Securities Firm, N.Y.C., 1962-65; journalist, assoc. editor Pacific Sun, 1972-74; congl. aide to rep. 5th Congl. Dist. San Francisco, 1974-76; mem. Marin County Bd. Suprs., San Rafael, Calif., 1976-82, 98th-102d Congresses from 6th Calif.

dist., mem. armed services com., select com. children, youth and families; majority whip at large; co-chair Mil. Reform Caucus; chair subcom. on govt. activities and transp. of house govt. ops. com., 1990-93; senator from Calif. U.S. Senate, 1993—, mem. banking, housing and urban affairs com., mem. budget com., mem. environ. and pub. works com. Pres. Marin County Bd. Suprs., 1980-81; mem. Bay Area Air Quality Mgmt. Bd., San Francisco, 1977-82, pres., 1979-81; bd. dirs. Golden Gate Bridge Hwy. and Transport Dist., San Francisco, 1978-82; founding mem. Marin Nat. Women's Polit. Caucus; pres. Dem. New Mems. Caucus, 1983. Recipient Open Govt. award Common Cause, 1980, Rep. of Yr. award Nat. Multiple Sclerosis Soc., 1990, Margaret Sanger award Planned Parenthood, 1990, Women of Achievement award Anti-defamation League, 1990. Jewish. Office: US Senate 112 Hart Senate Office Bldg Washington DC 20510-0001*

BOXER, LESTER, lawyer; b. N.Y.C., Oct. 19, 1935; s. Samuel and Anna Lena (Samovar) B.; m. Frances Barenfeld, Sept. 17, 1961; children: Kimberly Brett, Allison Joy. AA, UCLA, 1955, BS, 1957; JD, U. So. Calif., 1961. Bar: Calif. 1962; U.S. Dist. Ct. (cen. dist.) Calif. 1962. Assoc. Bautzer & Grant, Beverly Hills, Calif., 1961-63; pvt. practice Beverly Hills, 1963-65, 69—; ptnr. Boxer & Stoll, Beverly Hills, 1965-69. Mem. Calif. Bar Assn., L.A. County Bar Assn., Beverly Hills Bar Assn. Office: 2040 Avenue Of The Stars Los Angeles CA 90067-4703

BOXER, STEVEN G. physical chemistry educator; b. N.Y.C., Oct. 18, 1947; m. 1977. BS, Tufts U., 1969; PhD in Chemistry, U. Chgo., 1976. Prof. chemistry Stanford U., 1976—, chmn. dept. physics. Recipient Presdl. Young Investigator award, Arthur C. Cope scholar award Am. Chem. Soc., 1995. Mem. Am. Soc. Photobiology. Office: Stanford U Dept of Physics Stanford CA 94305-5080

BOYAJIAN, TIMOTHY EDWARD, public health officer, educator, consultant; b. Fresno, Calif., Feb. 22, 1949; s. Ernest Adam and Marge (Medzian) B.; m. Tassanee Bootdeesri, Apr. 23, 1987. BS in Biology, U. Calif., Irvine, 1975; M of Pub. Health, UCLA, 1978. Registered environ. health specialist, Calif. Rsch. asst. UCLA, 1978-81; lectr. Chapman U., 29 Palms, Calif., 1982-84, 88-89; refugee relief vol. Cath. Relief Svcs., Surin, Thailand, 1985-86; lectr. Nat. Univ., L.A., 1989-91; environ. health specialist Riverside County Health Svcs. Agy., Palm Springs, Calif., 1991-96; sci. tchr. South Gate (Calif.) H.S., L.A. Unified Sch. Dist., 1999—. Mem. adj. faculty U. Phoenix, 1998—; cons. parasitologist S. Pacific Commn., L.A., 1979; pub. health cons. several vets. groups, L.A., 1981-84, 97—; cons. Assn. S.E. Asian Nations, Bangkok, Thailand, 1988. Veterans rights advocate, Vietnam Vet. Groups, L.A., 1981-84. With USMC, Vietnam, 1969-71. Recipient U.S. Pub. Health Traineeship, U.S. Govt., L.A., 1977-81. Mem. VFW, So. Calif. Pub. Health Assn., Calif. Environ. Health Assn. Avocation: writing. E-mail: Timothy. Home: PO Box 740 Palm Springs CA 92263-0740 E-mail: 300@aol.com

BOYAN, NORMAN J. retired education educator; b. N.Y.C., Apr. 11, 1922; s. Joseph J. and Emma M. (Pelezare) B.; m. Priscilla M. Simpson, July 10, 1943; children: Stephen J., Craig S., Corydon J. A.B., Bates Coll., Lewiston, Maine, 1943; A.M., Harvard U., 1947, Ed.D., 1951. Instr. U.S. history Dana Hall Sch., Wellesley, Mass., 1946-48; research assoc. Lab. Social Relations, Harvard U., 1950-52; asst. prin. Mineola (N.Y.) High Sch., 1952-54; prin. Wheatley Sch., East Williston, N.Y., 1954-59; assoc. prof. edn., dir. student teaching and internship U. Wis., 1959-61; assoc. prof. edn. Stanford U., 1961-67; dir. div. ednl. labs. U.S. Office Edn., 1967-68, assoc. commr. for research, 1968-69; prof. edn. Grad. Sch. Edn., U. Calif., Santa Barbara, 1969-90, prof. emeritus, 1990—, dean, 1969-80; assoc. in edn. Grad. Sch. Edn., Harvard U., 1980-81; dir. Ednl. Leadership Inst. U. Calif., 1989-91. Vis. scholar Stanford U., 1974, 86; vis. prof. U. Ark. Program in Greece, 1977, Coll. Edn., Pa. State U., summer 1981, Faculty Edn. U. B.C., summer 1983, U. Alta., 1988, UCLA, 1991; cons. numerous U.S. sch. sys., U.S. govt. and Pacific Trust Ters. Co-author: Instructional Supervision Training Program, 1978; mem. editorial bd. Harvard Edn. Rev, 1948-50, Jour. Secondary Edn, 1963-68, Jour. Edn. Research, 1967-82, Urban Edn, 1967-90; cons. editor, contbr. 5th edit. Ency. Ednl. Research, 1982; editor, contbr. Handbook Research on Ednl. Adminstrn., 1988; contbr. articles to profl. jours. Served with USAAF, 1943-46. Recipient Shankland award for advanced grad. study in ednl. adminstrn., 1950, Roald F. Campbell Lifetime Achievement award U. Coun. for Ednl. Adminstrn., 1998. Mem. Am. Ednl. Rsch. Assn. (v.p. div. A 1978-80), Phi Beta Kappa, Phi Delta Kappa. Home: Apt W11 900 Calle De Los Amigos Santa Barbara CA 93105-4439 E-mail: nboyan@aol.com

BOYCE, CAROLYN, political organization administrator; State chmn. Idaho Dem. Party. Office: Idaho Dem Party 710 W Franklin St Boise ID 83702-5527

BOYCE, RONALD N. federal judge; b. Salt Lake City, Sept. 5, 1933; BSL, U. Utah, 1966, JD, 1956. Magistrate judge U.S. Dist. Ct. Utah, Salt Lake City. Office: 403 US Courthouse 350 S Main St Salt Lake City UT 84101-2106

BOYD, CAROLYN PATRICIA, history educator; b. San Diego, June 1, 1944; d. Peter James and Patricia Mae (de Soucy) B.; m. Frank Dawson Bean, Jan. 4, 1975; children: Peter Justin Bean, Michael Franklin Bean. AB with great distinction and with honors in History, Stanford U., 1966; MA, U. Wash., 1969, PhD, 1974. Tchg. asst. dept. history U. Wash., 1970-71; from instr. to prof. dept. history U. Tex., Austin, 1973-95, prof., 1995-99, assoc. dean Office Grad. Studies, 1986-88, 90-92, chair dept. history, 1994-99; dir. univ. honors program, assoc. prof. dept. history U. Md., College Park, 1989-90; prof. dept. history U. Calif., Irvine, 1999—. Lectr. in field. Author: Praetorian Politics in Liberal Spain, 1979, La política pretoriana en el reinado de Alfonso XIII, 1990, Historia Patria: Politics, History and National Identity in Spain, 1875-1975, 1997, Spanish edit., 2000; mem. editl. bd. Essays, 1992-95; author chpts. to books; contbr. articles to profl. jours. Woodrow Wilson hon. fellow, 1966, Fulbright-Hays fellow, 1966-67, NDEA Title IV fellow, 1968-72, AAUW fellow, 1972-73, ACLS fellow, 1985; ACLS Grant-in-Aid, 1977, Am. Philos. Soc. grant, 1978, URI Rsch. grant, 1985, New Del Amo Program grant, 2000-01; recipient Summer award U. Tex. Rsch. Inst., 1977. Mem. Am. Hist. Assn. (James Harvey Robinson prize com. 1992-94, John Fagg prize com. 2001—), Soc. Spanish and Portugese Hist. Studies (gen. sec. 2000—, mem. exec. com. 1978-80, 83-85, 96-98, chair local arrangements, program chmn. conf. 1987), Coun. European Studies, Internat. Inst. in Spain. Office: U Calif Irvine Dept History Irvine CA 92697-0001 E-mail: cpboyd@uci.edu

BOYD, DAVID WILLIAM, mathematician, educator; b. Toronto, Ont., Can., Sept. 17, 1941; s. Glenn Kelvin and Rachael Cecilia (Garvock) B.; m. Mary Margaret Shields, Sept. 26, 1964; children: Deborah, Paul, Kathryn. B.S., Carleton U., 1963; M.A., Toronto U., 1964, Ph.D., 1966. Asst. prof. [illegible] Calif. Inst. Tech., 1967-70, assoc. prof., 1970-71, U. B.C., Vancouver, Can., 1971-74, prof. math., 1974—, dept. head, 1986-89. Recipient E.W.R. Steacie Prize, 1978; I.W. Killam sr. research fellow, 1976-77, 81-82, Coxeter-James prize, 1979, Jeffery-Williams prize, 2001. Fellow Royal Soc. Can.; mem. Am. Math. Soc., Can. Math. Soc. Office: Univ BC Dept Math [illegible] E-mail: boyd@math.ubc.ca

BOYD, DEAN WELDON, management consultant; b. Shreveport, La., July 15, 1941; s. Vernon Dean and Josie (Weldon) B.; m. Susan C. Wickizer; children: Jodie Boyd-Wickizer, Silas Boyd-Wickizer. BEE, MIT, 1963, MEE, 1965; PhD in Engring. Econ. systems, Stanford U., 1970. Rsch. engr. Jet Propulsion Lab., Pasadena, Calif., 1965-67; sr. decision analyst Stanford Rsch. Inst., Menlo Park, 1967-70; asst. prof. info. sci. U. Calif., Santa Cruz, 1970-75; mgr. cons. Cottage Grove, Oreg., 1975-77; founder Decision Focus, Inc., Mountain View, Calif., 1977-97, CEO, prin., pres., 1997; vice chmn. Talus Solutions (formerly Decision Focus Inc.), Mountain View, 1997—. Contbr. articles to profl. jours. Mem. Sch. Bd. South Ln. Sch. Dist., Cottage Grove, 1986—. Mem. Coun. Logistics Mgmt., Inst. Mgmt. Sci. Achievements include developing methodologies for logical selection of portfolios of interrelated activities. Avocations: hiking, gardening, travel. Office: Talus Solutions 650 Castro St Ste 300 Mountain View CA 94041-2057

BOYD, LANDIS LEE, agricultural engineer, educator; b. Orient, Iowa, Dec. 1, 1923; s. Harold Everett and Edith Elizabeth (Lauer) B.; m. Lila Mae Hummel, Sept. 7, 1946; children— Susan Lee, Barbara Edith, Shirley Rae, Carl Steven, Philip Wayne. B.S. in Agrl. Engring, Iowa State U., 1947, M.S., 1948, Ph.D. in Agrl. Engring. and Engring. Mechanics, 1959. Registered profl. engr., N.Y., Minn. Sr. research fellow Iowa State Coll., 1947-48, 54-55; from asst. prof. to prof. Cornell U., Ithaca, 1948-60, coordinator grad. instrn., 1958-64; engring. design analyst Allis-Chalmers Mfg. Co., Milw., 1962-63; mem. faculty U. Minn. at St. Paul, 1964-78, prof. agrl. enging., head dept., 1964-72, asst. dir. Agrl. Exptl. Sta., 1972-78, dir. Coll. Agr. Research Center; asso. dean Coll. Agr., Wash. State U., Pullman, 1978-85; exec. dir. Western Assn. Agrl. Expt. Sta. Dirs., Agrl. Expt. Sta. Colo. State U., Fort Collins, 1985-92, adj. prof. bioresource and chem. engring., 1985—. Vis. scholar Ctr. Study Higher Edn.; vis. faculty-in-residence, intern Office Vice Pres. for Research, U. Mich., 1968; (Fed. Exec. Inst.), 1975; Cons. FAO, La Molina, Peru, 1964, 69; part-time cons. in field, 1948— Supt. farm bldg. project N.Y. State Fair, 1956, 57. Served with USNR, 1943-45. NATO postdoctoral grantee, 1962; recipient Iowa 4-H Alumni Recognition award, 1968; profl. achievement citation in engring. Iowa State U., 1980; Japan Soc. Promotion of Sci. fellow, 1981, U. Tokyo Vis. Faculty fellow, 1993. Fellow Am. Soc. Agrl. Engrs. (grad. paper award 1949, MBMA award 1969, v.p.-regions 1970-73), Minorities in Agr., Natural Resources and Related Scis., Sigma Xi, Phi Kappa Phi, Gamma Sigma Delta, Alpha Epsilon, Kappa Sigma, Rotary (Paul Harris fellow, leader group study exch. to dist. 4850 in Argentina 1994). Methodist. Home and Office: 1725 Concord Dr Fort Collins CO 80526-1671

BOYD, LEONA POTTER, retired social worker; b. Creekside, Pa., Aug. 31, 1907; d. Joseph M. and Belle (McHenry) Johnston; m. Edgar D. Potter, July 16, 1932 (div.); m. Harold Lee Boyd, Oct. 1972. Grad., Indiana (Pa.) State Normal Sch, 1927; student, Las Vegas (N.Mex.) Normal U., 1933; student Sch. Social Work, Carnegie Inst. Tech., 1945, U. Pitts., 1956-57. Tchr. Creekside Pub. Schs., 1927-30, Papago Indian Reservation, Sells, Ariz., 1931-33; caseworker, supr. Indiana County (Pa.) Bd. Assistance, 1934-54, exec. dir., 1954-68, ret. Retired social worker; b. Creekside, Pa., Aug. 31, 1907; d. Joseph M. and Belle (McHenry) Johnston. Grad. Ind. (Pa.) State Normal Sch., 1927, student Las Vegas Normal U., N.Mex., 1933, Carnegie Inst. Tech. Sch. Social Work, 1945, U. Pitts. Sch. Social Work, 1956-57; m. Edgar D. Potter, July 16, 1932 (div.); m. Harold Lee Boyd, Oct. 1972. Tchr. Creekside (Pa.) Pub. Schs., 1927-30, Papago Indian Reservation, Sells, Ariz., 1931-33; caseworker, supr. Indiana County (Pa.) Bd. Assistance, 1934-54, exec. dir., 1954-68, ret. Bd. dirs. Indiana County Tourist Promotion, hon. life mem.; former bd. dirs. Indiana County United Fund, Salvation Army, Indiana County Guidance Ctr., Armstrong-Indiana Mental Health Bd.; cons. assoc. Community Rsch. Assocs., Inc.; mem. Counseling Ctr. Aux., Lake Havasu City, Ariz., 1978-80; former mem. Western Welcome Club, Lake Havasu City, Sierra Vista Hosp. Aux., Truth or Consequences, N.Mex. Recipient Jr. C. of C. Disting. Svc. award, Indiana, Pa., 1966, Bus. and Profl. Women's Club award, Indiana, 1965. Mem. Am. Assn. Ret. Persons, Daus. Am. Colonists. Lutheran. Bd. dirs., hon. life mem. Indiana County Tourist Promotion; former bd. dirs. Indiana County United Fund, Salvation Army, Indiana County Guidance Ctr., Armstrong-Indiana Mental Health Bd.; cons. assoc. Cmty. Rsch. Assocs., Inc.; mem. Counseling Ctr. Aux., Lake Havasu City, Ariz., 1978-80; former mem. Western Welcome Club, Lake Havasu City, Sierra Vista Hosp. Aux., Truth or Consequences, N.M. Recipient Disting. Svc. award Indiana Jaycees, 1965, Bus. and Profl. Women's Club award, 1965. Mem. AARP, Daus. Am. Colonists. Lutheran. Home: 520 S Higley Rd Unit 126 Mesa AZ 85206-2274

BOYD, MALCOLM, minister, spiritual writer; b. Buffalo, June 8, 1923; s. Melville and Beatrice (Lowrie) B.; life ptnr. Mark Thompson. B.A., U. Ariz., 1944; B.D., Ch. Div. Sch. Pacific, 1954; postgrad., Oxford (Eng.) U., 1955; S.T.M., Union Theol. Sem., N.Y.C., 1956; DD (hon.), Ch. Div. Sch. of Pacific, 1995. Ordained to ministry Episcopal Ch., 1955. V.p., gen. mgr. Pickford, Rogers & Boyd, 1949-51; rector in Indpls., 1957-59; chaplain Colo. State U., 1959-61, Wayne State U., 1961-65; nat. field rep. Episcopal Soc. Cultural and Racial Unity, 1965-68; resident fellow Calhoun Coll., Yale U., 1968-71, assoc. fellow, 1971—; writer-priest in residence St. Augustine-by-the Sea Episcopal Ch., 1982-95; chaplain to commn. on AIDS Ministries of Episcopal Diocese of L.A., 1993—. Lectr. World Council Chs., Switzerland, 1955, 64; columnist Pitts. Courier, 1962-65; resident guest Mishkenot Sha'ananim, Jerusalem, 1974; chaplain AIDS Commn. Episcopal Diocese L.A., 1989—; poet-in-residence Cathedral Ctr. of St. Paul, L.A., 1996—. Host: TV spl. Sex in the Seventies, CBS-TV, Los Angeles, 1975; author: Crisis in Communication, 1957, Christ and Celebrity Gods, 1958, Focus, 1960, rev. edit., 2001, If I Go Down to Hell, 1962, The Hunger, The Thirst, 1964, Are You Running with Me, Jesus?, 1965, rev. 25th anniversary edit., 1990, Free to Live, Free to Die, 1967, Book of Days, 1968, As I Live and Breathe: Stages of an Autobiography, 1969, The Fantasy Worlds of Peter Stone, 1969, My Fellow Americans, 1970, Human Like Me, Jesus, 1971, The Lover, 1972, When in the Course of Human Events, 1973, The Runner, 1974, The Alleluia Affair, 1975, Christian, 1975, Am I Running with You, God?, 1977, Take Off the Masks, 1978, rev. edit. 1993, Look Back in Joy, 1981, rev. edit., 1990, Half Laughing, Half Crying, 1986, Gay Priest: An Inner Journey, 1986, Edges, Boundaries and Connections, 1992, Rich with Years, 1993, Go Gentle Into That Good Night, 1998, Running with Jesus: The Prayers of Malcolm Boyd, 2000, Simple Grace: A Mentor's Guide to Growing Older, 2001, Prayers for the Later Years, 2002; plays Boy, 1961, Study in Color, 1962, The Community, 1964, others; editor: On the Battle Lines, 1964, The Underground Church, 1968, Amazing Grace: Stories of Gay and Lesbian Faith, 1991; book reviewer: Los Angeles Times.; contbg. editor The Episcopal News; columnist Modern Maturity; contbr. articles to numerous mags. including Newsday, Parade, The Advocate, also newspapers. Active voter registration, Miss., Ala., 1963, 64; mem. Los Angeles City/County AIDS Task Force Malcolm Boyd Collection and Archives established Boston U., 1973; Recipient Integrity Internat. award, 1978; Union Am. Hebrew Congregations award, 1980 Mem. Nat. Council Chs. (film awards com. 1965), P.E.N. (pres. PEN Ctr. U.S. West 1984-87), Am. Center, Authors Guild, Integrity, Nat. Gay Task Force, Clergy and Laity Concerned (nat. bd.), NAACP, Amnesty Internat., [illegible] Fellowship of Reconciliation (nat. com.). Office: PO Box 512164 Los Angeles CA 90051-0164

BOYD, WILLIAM SPROTT, lawyer; b. San Francisco, Feb. 12, 1943; s. R. Mitchell S. and Mary (Mitchell) B.; children: Mitchell Sagar, Sterling McMicking. AB, Stanford U., 1964, JD, 1971. Bar: Calif. 1972, U.S. Dist. Ct. (no. dist.) 1972, U.S. Ct. Appeals (9th cir.) 1972, U.S. Dist. Ct. (cen. dist.) Calif. 1974, U.S. Dist. Ct. (ea. dist.) Calif. 1976. Assoc. Brobeck, Phleger & Harrison, San Francisco, 1971-77, ptnr., 1977—, of counsel. Mem. Lawyers Com for Urban Affairs, San Francisco, 1979—; bd. dirs. San Francisco Legal Aid Soc., 1980-85. Lt. USNR, 1965-68, Vietnam. Mem. ABA, Calif. Bar Assn., San Francisco Bar Assn. Office: Brobeck Phleger & Harrison 1 Market Pla Spear St Tower San Francisco CA 94105

BOYDEN, JACLYNE WITTE, university vice dean; BA, Calif. State U., Hayward, 1970; MBA, Golden Gate U., 1982. Dept. mgr. dept. biochemistry and biophysics U. Calif., San Francisco, 1980-82, dept. mgr. dept. medicine, 1982-84, coord. adminstrv. policies Office of Pres., 1984-85, asst. dir. Cardiovasc. Rsch. Inst., 1985-88, vice dean for Adminstrn. and Fin. Sch. Medicine, 1992—; assoc. dean for Adminstrn. SUNY Sch. Medicine, Stony Brook, 1988-92. Mem. Med. Group Mgmt. Assn., AAMC Group on Instnl. Planning (steering com. 1991-93), AAMC Group Bus. Affairs (chmn. profl. devel. com. 1996, mem. steering com. 1997—, nat. sec. 1997, chairperson-elect 1998, chair 1999). Office: U Calif San Francisco Sch Medicine Office of Dean PO Box 410 San Francisco CA 94143-0001

BOYDSTON, JAMES CHRISTOPHER, composer; b. Denver, July 21, 1947; s. James Virgal and Mary June (Wiseman) B.; m. Ann Louise Bryant, Aug. 20, 1975. BA in Philosophy, U. Tex., 1971. Lutenist and guitarist Collegium Musicum, U. Tex., Austin, 1968-70; tchr. classical guitar Extension div. The New Eng. Conservatory of Music, Boston, 1972-73. Arranger music: S. Joplins, "The Entertainer," 1976; arranger/composer/performer cassette recording: Wedding Music for Classical Guitar, 1988; composer music: International Portraits for Classical Guitar, 1999; inventor classical guitar bridge-saddle, 1990; author original poetry included in: The World of Poetry Anthology, 1991. Avocations: astronomy, reading, building clavichords, camping. Home: 4433 Driftwood Pl Boulder CO 80301-3104

BOYER, CARL, III, non-profit organization executive, former mayor, city official, secondary education educator; b. Phila., Sept. 22, 1937; s. Carl Boyer Jr. and Elizabeth Campbell Timm; m. Ada Christine Kruse, July 28, 1962. Student, U. Edinburgh, Scotland, 1956-57; BA, Trinity U., 1959; MEd in Secondary Edn., U. Cin., 1959; postgrad., Calif. State U., Northridge, 1964-72. Tchr. Edgewood High Sch., San Antonio, 1959-60; libr. U. Cin., Cincinnati, Ohio, 1960-61; tchr. Eighth Avenue Elem. Sch., Dayton, Ky., 1961-62, Amelia High Sch., Amelia, Ohio, 1962-63; instr. Kennedy San Fernando Comm. Adult Sch., San Fernando, Calif., 1964-74, Mission Coll., San Fernando, 1971; tchr. San Fernando High Sch., San Fernando, Calif., 1963-98. Faculty chmn. San Fernando High Sch., dept. chmn.; cons. Sofia (Bulgaria) City Coun., 1991; key spkr. World Mayors' Conf., Jaipur, India, 1998. Author, compiler 17 books on genealogy and family history; contbr. articles to profl. jours. Councilman City of Santa Clarita, Calif., 1987-98, mayor pro tem, 1989-90, 94-95, mayor, 1990-91, 95-96; mem. Nat. League Cities Internat. Mcpl. Consortium, 1992-98; mem. revenue and taxation com. League Calif. Cities, 1992-95; sec. Calif. Contract Cities Assn., 1992-93; trustee Santa Clarita C.C. Dist., 1973-81, pres., 1979-81; bd. dirs. Castaic Lake Water Agy., 1982-84, pres. Newhall-Saugus-Valencia Fedn. Homeowners Assn., 1969-70, 71-72; pres. Del Prado Condo. Assn., Inc., Newhall, Calif.; exec. v.p. Canyon County Formation Com.; chmn. Santa Clarita City Formation Com., 1987; pres. Santa Clarita Valley Internat. Program, 1991-97; treas. Healing the Children Calif., 1994-96, pres., 1996-99, nat. pres., 1999-2000. Mem. United Tchrs. L.A., New Eng. Hist. Geneal. Soc. Republican. Methodist. Avocations: travel, photography. Home: PO Box 220333 Santa Clarita CA 91322-0333

BOYER, HERBERT WAYNE, retired biochemist; b. Pitts., July 10, 1936; m. Grace Boyer, 1959. BA, St. Vincent Coll., Latrobe, Pa., 1958, DSc (hon.), 1981; MS, U. Pitts., 1960, PhD, 1963. Mem. faculty U. Calif., San Francisco, 1966—, prof. biochemistry, 1976—, San Francisco, 1976-91, prof. emeritus, 1991—. Co-founder, dir. Genentech, Inc., South San Francisco, Calif. Recipient V.D. Mattai award Roche Inst., 1977; Golden Plate award Am. Acad. Achievement, 1981, Moet Hennessy-Louis Vuitton prize, 1988, Jerome H. Lemelson-MIT prize for excellence in invention and innovation, 1996; Albert and Mary Lasker award for basic med. research, 1980, Nat. Tech. medal, 1989, Nat. Sci. medal NSF, 1990. Fellow AAAS; mem. Am. Acad. Arts and Scis., Am. Soc. Biol. Chemists, Nat. Acad. Scis.*

BOYER, PAUL D. biochemist, educator; b. Provo, Utah, July 31, 1918; s. Dell Delos and Grace (Guymon) B.; m. Lyda Mae Whicker, Aug. 31, 1939; children: Gail Anne (Mrs. Denis Hayes), Marjorie Lynne, Douglas. B.S., Brigham Young U., 1939; M.S., U. Wis., 1941, Ph.D. in Biochemistry, 1943; D.Sc. (hon.), U. Stockholm, 1974. Asst. rschr. biochemistry U. Wis., 1939-43; Instr., research assoc. Stanford, 1943-45; from asst. prof. to prof. biochemistry U. Minn., 1945-56; Hill research prof. U. Minn. Med. Sch., 1956-63; prof. chemistry UCLA, 1963-89, dir. Molecular Biology Inst., 1965-83, dir. biotech. program, 1985-88, 1985-89, prof. emeritus, 1989—; chmn. biochemistry study sect. USPHS, 1962-67. Mem. U.S. Nat. Com. for Biochemistry, 1965-71 Editor: Ann. Rev. of Biochemistry, 1965-71, assoc. editor, 1972-88; editor Biochemical and Biophysical Research Communications, 1969-79, The Enzymes, 1970— ; Mem. editorial bd.: Biochemistry, 1969-76, Jour. Biol. Chemistry, 1978-83, 87—; Contbr. articles to profl. jours. Recipient McCoy award chem. rsch., 1976, Tolman award, 1984, Rose award Am. Soc. Biochem. and Molecular Biology, 1989; co-recipient Nobel prize for chemistry, 1997; Guggenheim fellow, 1955-56. Fellow AAAS (council, v.p. biol. scis. 1985-88); mem. Nat. Acad. Sci., Am. Soc. Biol. Chemists (past pres., council mem.), Am. Chem. Soc. (past div. chmn., enzyme chemistry award 1955), Biophys. Soc. Home: 1033 Somera Rd Los Angeles CA 90077-2625 Office: Dept Chem-Biochem 639A MBI Bldg 607 Charles B Young Dr E Los Angeles CA 90095-0001*

BOYLAN, MERLE NELSON, librarian, educator; b. Youngstown, Ohio, Feb. 24, 1925; s. Merle Nelson and Alma Joy (Kepple) B. B.A., Youngstown U., 1950; M.L.S., Carnegie-Mellon U., 1956; postgrad., U. Ariz., 1950-51, Ind. U., 1952. Librarian Pub. Health Library U. Calif., Berkeley, 1956-58; sci. librarian U. Ariz., Tucson, 1958-59; engring. librarian Gen. Dynamics/Convair, San Diego, 1959-61, Gen. Dynamics/Astronautics, 1961-62; assoc. librarian Lawrence Radiation Lab., U. Calif., Livermore, 1962-64, library mgr., 1964-67; chief librarian NASA Ames Research Center, Moffett Field, Calif., 1968-69; asso. dir. libraries U. Mass., Amherst, 1969-70, dir. libraries, Univ. librarian, 1970-72; dir. libraries U. Tex., Austin, 1973-77, U. Wash., Seattle, 1977-89, dir. emeritus, 1989—, prof. Sch. Librarianship, 1982-89; exec. bd. Amigos Bibliographic Council, 1974-77; mem. fin. com., governance com., user's council, computer service council Wash. Library Network, 1978—. Del. Gov.'s Conf. Libraries and Info. Services, 1979; sec. Texas State Bd. Library Examiners, 1974-77; mem. bibliographic networking and resource sharing advisory group Southwestern Library Interstate Coop. Endeavor, 1975-77; sec., chmn. exec. bd. Pacific N.W. Bibliographic Center, 1977-83; mem. com. centralized acquisitions of library materials [illegible] Center for Research Libraries.; del. OCLC Users Council, 1981-86. Sec. bd. trustees Littlefield Fund for So. History, 1974-77, Fred Meyer Charitable Trust; mem. adv. bd. Library and Info. Resources for Northwest, 1984-87. Mem. ALA, Assn. Coll. and Research Libraries (legis. com. 1977-81), Assn. Research Libraries (bibliographic control com. 1979-83), [illegible] Info. Bull., Beta Phi Mu. Home: 1334 Bellefield Park Ln Bellevue WA 98004-6854 Office: Univ of Wash Libraries Suzzallo Library Seattle WA 98195-0001

BOYLE, BARBARA DORMAN, motion picture company executive; b. N.Y.C., Aug. 11, 1935; d. William and Edith (Kleiman) Dorman; m. Kevin Boyle, Nov. 26, 1960; children: David Eric, Paul Coleman. BA in English with honors, U. Calif., Berkeley, 1957; JD, UCLA, 1960. Bar: Calif. 1961, N.Y. 1964, U.S. Supreme Ct. 1964. Atty. bus. affairs dept, corp. asst. sec. Am. Internat. Pictures, L.A., 1960-65; ptnr. Cohen & Boyle, L.A., 1967-74; exec. v.p., gen. counsel, chief op. officer New World Pictures, L.A., 1974-82; sr. v.p. prodn. Orion Pictures Corp., L.A., 1982-85; exec. v.p. prodn. RKO Pictures, L.A., 1986-87; pres. Sovereign Pictures, Inc., L.A., 1988-92, Boyle and Taylor Prodns., 1993-99, Valhalla Motion Pictures, L.A., 2000—. Lectr. in field. Exec. prodr. (film) Eight Men Out, 1987, Bottle Rocket, 1995; prodr. (films) Mrs. Munck, 1995, Phenomenon, 1996, Instinct, 1999; exec. prodr. The Hi Line, 1998. Bd. dirs. UCLA Law Fund Com., L.A. Women's Campaign Fund; pres. Ind. Feature Project/West; founding mem. entertainment adv. coun. sch. law UCLA, co-chmn. 1979-80. Named UCLA Law Sch. Alumni of Yr, 1999, Women in Film Crystal award, 2000. Mem. Acad. Motion Picture Arts and Scis., Women in Film (pres. 1977-78), Hollywood Women's Polit. Com., Calif. Bar Assn., N.Y. State Bar Assn. Office: Valhalla Motion Pictures Ste 400 8530 Wilshire Blvd Beverly Hills CA 90211

BOYLE, GERTRUDE, sportswear company executive; b. Augsberg, Germany, 1924; came to U.S., 1938; d. Paul and Marie Lanfrom; m. Neil Boyle, 1948; children: Tim, Kathy, Sally. BA in Sociology, Univ. Ariz., 1947. Pres., CEO Columbia Sportswear Co., Portland, Oreg., 1970-88, CEO, 1988-94, chair, 1994—. Named one of Best Mgrs. Bus. Week Mag., 1994, Am.'s Top 50 Women Bus. Owners Working Woman mag., Woman of Yr. Oreg. chpt. Women's Forum, 1987. Office: Columbia Sportswear Co 6600 N Baltimore Ave Portland OR 97203

BOYLE, (CHARLES) KEITH, artist, educator; b. Defiance, Ohio., Feb. 15, 1930; Student, Ringling Sch. Art; B.F.A., U. Iowa. Prof. painting and drawing Stanford U., Calif., 1962-88. Group shows include Stanford U. Mus., 1964, San Francisco Mus. Art, 1965, Ann Arbor, Mich., 1965, Joslyn Art Mus., Omaha, 1970, San Jose Mus. Art, Calif., 1978; represented in permanent collections: San Francisco Mus. Art, Stanford U. Mus., Mead paper Corp., Atlanta, Nat. Fine Arts Collection, Washington, Oakland Mus., Continental Bank, Chgo., Seton Med. Ctr., Daily City, Calif., Schneider Mus., Ashland, Oreg. Grantee NEA, 1981-82, Pew Meml. Trust, 1986-87. Address: 6285 Thompson Creek Rd Applegate OR 97530-9639

BOYLE, LARRY MONROE, federal judge; b. Seattle, June 23, 1943; s. Thomas L. and Winona (Green) B.; m. Beverly Rigby, Jan 31, 1969; children: Brian, Jeffery, Bradley, David, Melissa, Layne. BSc, Brigham Young U., 1968; JD, U. Idaho, 1972. Bar: Idaho 1973, U.S. Dist. Ct. Idaho 1973. Atty. Hansen, Boyle, Beard & Martin, P.A., Idaho Falls, Idaho, 1973-86; dist. judge 7th Jud. Dist., Idaho Falls, 1986-89; judge U.S. Supreme Ct. Idaho, Boise, 1989-92; magistrate judge U.S. Dist. Ct. Idaho, Boise, 1992—, chief magistrate judge. Office: US Courthouse Box 040 550 W Fort St Boise ID 83724-0101

BOYNTON, WILLIAM LEWIS, retired electronic manufacturing company official; b. Kalamazoo, May 31, 1928; s. James Woodbury and Cyretta (Gunther) B.; m. Kei Ouchi, Oct. 8, 1953. Asst. mgr. Speigel J&R, Kalamazoo, 1947-48; with U.S. Army, 1948-74, ret., 1974, with Rockwell/Collins div. Calif., 1974-78, supr. material, investment recovery coord., 1974-81, coord., 1981-88, investment recovery supr., coord. Rockwell/CDC Santa Ana, 1981-88, coord. investment recovery, 1982-86, shipping supr., investment recovery, environ. coord., 1982-88, 87-88, material coord., 1988, environ. coord. Rockwell/CDC Newport Beach, 1988-89, ret. Trustee Corp. Bd., 1993, pres., 1993-94, mem. exec. bd. dirs.; adv. panelist bus./econ. devel. Calif. State Legis., 1979-86; trustee Orange County Vector Control Dist., 1980—. Decorated Bronze Star,8 Mem. Assn. U.S. Army, Assn. U.S. Army, Non-Commd. Officers Assn., Mosquito and Vector Control Assn. Calif. (v.p. 1992, pres. 1993), Nat. Geog. Soc. Republican. Roman Catholic. Home: 5314 W Lucky Way Santa Ana CA 92704-1048

BOYSE, EDWARD ARTHUR, research physician; b. Worthing, Sussex, Eng., Aug. 11, 1923; came to U.S., 1960; s. Arthur and Dorothy Vera (Mellersh) B. MB, BS, U. London, 1952, MD, 1957. Mem. med. staff various hosps., Eng., 1952-57; researcher Guy's Hosp., London, 1957-60, Sch. Medicine, NYU, 1960-71, adj. prof., 1971—; prof. Cornell Grad. Sch. Med. Sci., N.Y.C., 1969-89; assoc. scientist Meml. Sloan-Kettering Inst., N.Y.C., 1962-64, assoc. mem., 1964-67, mem., 1967-89; Disting. prof. U. Ariz., Tucson, 1989-94; prof. emeritus, 1994—. Affiliated scientist Monell Chem. Senses Ctr., Phila. Contbr. articles to profl. jours. Served with RAF, 1941-46. Recipient Tumor Immunology award Cancer Research Inst., N.Y.C., 1975, Isaac Adler award Rockefeller U., Harvard U., 1976. Fellow Royal Soc., Am. Acad. Arts and Sci., Nat. Acad. Sci. Office: Dept Microbiology Immunology U Ariz PO Box 24-5049 Tucson AZ 85724-5049*

BOYSEN, THOMAS CYRIL, educational association administrator; b. Sioux Falls, S.D., Nov. 16, 1940; s. Cyril Joseph and Dolores Margaret (Parry) B.; m. PoChan Mar, Aug. 25, 1964 (div. 1980); children: Thomas C., Anne-Marie Lee; m. Laurie Louise Shaffer, June 25, 1983. BA in History, Stanford U., 1962; diploma in grad. edn., Makerere U., Kampala, Uganda, 1964; EdD in Edn. Adminstrn., Harvard U., 1969. Geography master Kabaa H.S., Thika, Kenya, 1964-66; dir. adminstrn. Bellevue (Wash.) Pub. Schs., 1968-70; supt. schs. Pasco Sch. Dist., Wash., 1970-73, Pelham (N.Y.) Pub. Schs., 1973-77, Redlands United Sch. Dist., Calif., 1977-80, Conejo Valley Unified Sch. Dist., Thousand Oaks, 1980-87, San Diego County Schs., 1987-90, Ky. Commn. Edn., 1991-95; sr. v.p. edn. Milken Family Found., Santa Monica, Calif., 1995.

BOZARTH, GEORGE S. historian, musicologist, pianist; b. Trenton, N.J., Feb. 28, 1947; MFA, Princeton U., 1973; PhD, Princeton U., 1978. Prof. music history U. Wash. Dir. Brahms Archive, Seattle, Internat. Brahms Conf., Washington, 1983; co-artistic dir. Gallery Concerts, Seattle. Editor: Johannes Brahms, Orgelwerke, The Organ Works, Munich, G Henle, 1988, J.S. Bach Cantata, Ach Gott vom Himmel sieh darein, BWV2, Neue Bach Augabe, 1/16, 1981, 84, The Correspondence of Johannes Brahms and Robert Keller, 1996, articles on Brahms' Lieder and Duets, the genesis and chronology of Brahms's works, Brahms' piano sonatas and First Piano Concerto, editl. problems, questions of authenticity, Brahms's pianos and piano music. Fullbright-Hayes scholar to Austria, 1975-77; fellow ACLS, 1982; NEH Rsch. Conf. grantee, 1983; grantee Am. Philos. Soc., 1999. Mem. Am. Brahms Soc. (exec. dir.), Am. Musicol. Soc., Early Music Am., Classical Consort. Office: U Wash Sch Music PO Box 353450 Seattle WA 98195-3450

BOZDECH, MAREK JIRI, physician, educator; b. Wildflecken, Bavaria, Federal Republic Germany, Oct. 12, 1946; s. Jiri Josef and Zofia Jadwiga (Swiatecka) B.; m. Frances Barclay Craig, Dec. 22, 1967; children: Elizabeth, Andrew, Matthew. AB, U. Mich., 1967; MD, Wayne State U., 1972. Diplomate Am. Bd. Internal Medicine, Am. Bd. Med. Oncology, Am. Bd. Hematology. Intern and resident in internal medicine U. Wis. Hosps., Madison, 1972-75, dir. clin. hematology lab., 1978-82, dir. bone marrow transplantation, 1984-85; asst. prof. medicine U. Wis., Madison, 1978-84, assoc. prof. medicine, 1984-85; clin. fellow in hematology Moffitt Hosp. U. Calif., San Francisco, 1975-76, postdoctoral fellow in hematology Cancer Research Inst., 1976-78, research assoc. Cancer Research Inst., 1977-78, assoc. prof., 1985-89; dir. adult bone marrow transplantation U. Calif. Med. Ctr., San Francisco, 1985-89; chief oncology Kaiser Permanente Med. Ctr., Santa Rosa, Calif., 1989-91; pvt. practice specializing in oncology Hematology Redwood Regional Oncology Ct., Santa Rosa, 1991—. Contbr. articles to profl. jours. Scout leader Boy Scouts Am., Novato, Calif., 1985; bd. trustees Pacific Found. Med. Care, 1995—. Recipient Nat. Research Service award NIH, 1977-78; Wayne State U. scholar, 1971. Mem. ACP, Am. Soc. Hematology, Am. Soc. Clin. Oncology, Assn. No. Calif. Oncologists (bd. dirs. 1994-97), Sonoma County Med. Assn. (bd. dirs. 1994-96). Avocations: skiing, gardening, music, tennis, theatre. Home: 50 La Placita Ct Novato CA 94945-1244 Office: U Calif Med Ctr A502 M Redwood Regional Oncology 121 Sotoyome St Ste 203 Santa Rosa CA 95405-4822 E-mail: mbozdech@mindspring.com, mbozdech@yahoo.com

BRACEWELL, RONALD NEWBOLD, electrical engineering educator; b. Sydney, Australia, July 22, 1921; s. Cecil Charles and Valerie Zilla (McGowan) B.; m. Helen Mary Lester Elliott; children: Catherine Wendy, Mark Cecil. BSc in Math. and Physics, U. Sydney, 1941, B in Engring., 1943, M. in Engring. with 1st class honors, 1948; PhD, Cambridge (Eng.) U., 1951. Sr. rsch. officer Radiophysics Lab., Commonwealth Sci. and Indsl. Rsch. Orgn., Sydney, 1949-54; vis. asst. prof. radio astronomy U. Calif., Berkeley, 1954-55; mem. elec. engring. faculty Stanford U., 1955—, Lewis M. Terman prof. and fellow in elec. engring., 1974-79, now Terman prof. emeritus elec. engring. Pollock Meml. lectr. U. Sydney, 1978; Tektronix Disting. Visitor, summer 1981; Christensen fellow St. Catherine's Coll., Oxford, autumn 1987; sr. vis. fellow Inst. Astronomy, fellow commoner Churchill Coll., Cambridge U., autumn 1988; Bunyan lectr. Stanford U., 1996; mem. adv. panels NSF, Naval Rsch. Lab., Office Naval Rsch., NAS, Nat. Radio Astronomy Obs., Jet Propulsion Lab. Adv. Group on Radio Experiments in Space, Advanced Rsch. Projects Agy. Author: The Fourier Transform and Its Applications, 1965, 3rd edit., 2000, The Galactic Club: Intelligent Life in Outer Space, 1974, The Hartley Transform, 1986, Two-Dimensional Imaging, 1995; co-author: Radio Astronomy, 1955; translator: Radio Astronomy (J.L. Steinberg and J. Lequeux); editor: Paris Symposium on Radio Astronomy, 1959; former mem. editl. bd. Internat. Jour. Imaging Sys. and Tech., Planetary and Space Sci., Proceedings of the Astron. Soc. Pacific, Cosmic Search, Jour. Computer Assisted Tomography; mem. bd. ann. rev. Astronomy and Astrophysics, 1961-68; contbr. articles and revs. to jours., chpts. to books; patentee in field. Recipient Duddell Premium, Instn. Elec. Engrs., London, 1952, Inaugural Alumni award Sydney U., 1992; Fulbright travel grantee, 1954, William Gurling Watson traveling fellow, 1978, 86. Fellow IEEE (life, Heinrich Hertz Gold medal 1994, Jim Wolfensohn Suguna award 1996), AAAS, Royal Astron. Soc., Astron. Soc. Australia; mem. Inst. Medicine of NAS (fgn. assoc.), Astron. Soc. Pacific (life), Am. Astron. Soc. (past councilor), Internat. Astron. Union, Internat. Sci. Radio Union, Order of Australia (officer). Home: 836 Santa Fe Ave Stanford CA 94305-1023 Office: Stanford U 367 Packard Stanford CA 94305-9515 E-mail: bracewell@star.stanford.edu

BRACEY, EARNEST NORTON, political science educator; b. Jackson, Miss., June 8, 1953; s. Willard and Odessa Manola (Ford) B.; m. Atsuko Konuma, Apr. 2, 1995; children: Dominique, Princess, Omar. MPA, Golden Gate U., 1979; MA, Cath. U., Washington, 1983; D of Pub. Adminstrn., George Mason U., 1993; PhD in Edn., Capella U., 1999. Commd. 2d lt. U.S. Army, 1975, advanced through grades to lt. col., 1992; ret., 1995; prof. polit. sci. C.C. of So. Nev., Las Vegas, 1996—. Adj. prof. Ctrl. Tex. Coll., Camp Zama, Japan, 1993-95; mem. Nev. faculty alliance C.C. of So. Nev., Las Vegas, 1996—. Author: Choson, 1994, Prophetic Insight, 1999. Mem. NAACP, Am. Soc. of Mil. Comptrs., Assn. of the U.S. Army, Retired Officer Assn. Avocations: jazz trumpeter, marathon runner, writing, poetry, American historian.

BRACKEN, THOMAS ROBERT JAMES, real estate investment executive; b. Spokane, Wash., Jan. 1, 1950; s. James Lucas and Frances (Cadzow) B.; m. Linda Jacobson, Sept. 9, 1972; children: Karl Forest, David Erskine. BS, Yale U., 1971; MBA, Columbia U., 1972. Sr. appraiser Prudential Ins., N.Y.C., 1972-74, mgr. real estate N.Y.C. and Newark, 1974-76, assoc. gen. mgr. Seattle, 1977-78; v.p. First City Investments, Seattle, 1978-80; pres. Fenix, Inc., Seattle, 1980-86; v.p. Washington Mortgage Corp., Seattle, 1982-85, exec. v.p., 1986-88; sr. v.p. Pioneer Bank, Lynwood, Wash., 1985-86; pres.real estate financing USL Capital, San Francisco, 1988-97; sr. v.p. real estate fin. group Orix, USA, San Francisco, 1997-98; pres. Presidio Interfunding Corp., San Francisco, 1998-99; 1st v.p. L.J. Melody & Co., San Jose, Calif., 2000—; mem. Crossbow Capital, LLC, Los Altos, 2000—. Mem. Nat. Assn. Indsl./Office Parks (v.p. Seattle chpt. 1981-83), Yale Assn. Western Wash. (pres. 1984-86), Urban Land Inst., Mortgage Bankers Assn. Presbyterian. Avocations: running, sports. Office: L J Melody Y Co 226 Airport Pkwy Ste 150 San Jose CA 95110-1024 E-mail: tom.bracken@ljmelody.com

BRACKHAUS, KARL H. technology company executive; PhD in Engring. Physics, U. B.C. Co-founder, pres., CEO Dynapro Sys. Inc., B.C., Can. Vol. Elec. Club, Min. Industry and Small Bus., Simon Fraser U. Recipient R.A. McLachlan Meml. award Assn. Profl. Engrs. and Geoscientists B.C., 1997, Entrepreneur of Yr. award Ernst & Young, 1994, Leadership award Applied Sci. and Technologists and Technicians of B.C., 1995. Mem. IEEE, Can. Coun. Profl. Engrs. (Gold medal 1998), Can. Indsl. Computer Soc. Office: Dynapro Sys 800 Carleton Ct Annacis Island BC Canada V3M 6L3

BRADBURY, WILLIAM CHAPMAN, III, state official; b. Chgo., May 29, 1949; s. William L. and Lorraine (Patterson) B.; m. Betsy Harrison (Sept. 1984); children: Abby, Zoe; m. Kathleen P. Eymann, June 7, 1986. Student, Antioch Coll., 1967-69. News reporter KQED-TV Newsroom, 1969-70; dir. pub. affairs Sta. KMPX-FM, San Francisco, 1970; mem. video prodn. group Optic Nerve, San Francisco, 1970-73; project dir. Coos Country TV, Bandon, Oreg., 1973-75; reporter, anchor Sta. KVAL-TV, Eugene, 1975-76; news dir. Sta. KCBY-TV, Coos Bay, 1976-78; prodr., writer, editor video news feature svc. Local Color, Langlois, 1978-79; field prodr. PM Mag., Sta. KGW-TV, Portland, 1979-80; mem. Oreg. Ho. of Reps., Salem, 1980-84, Oreg. Senate, Salem, 1984-95, pres., 1993-95; exec. dir. Sake of the Salmon, Gladstone, Oreg., 1995-99; sec. of state Salem, 1999—. Chmn. Western Legis. Conf., Coun. State Govs., 1991, mem. ocean resources com.; founder, former chmn. Pacific Fishery Legis. Task Force. Prodr. documentaries Gorda Ridge—Boom or Bust for the Oregon Coast?, The Tillamook Burn—From Ruin to Rejuvenation, Not Guilty by Reason of Insanity, Child as Witness, Local Color, Salmon on the Run, The First Perennial Poetic Hoohaw, TV Town Hall Meetings, Common Sense, also prodr. mktg. videos and commls. for polit. candidates, hosp. Democrat. Mem. Soc. of Friends. Avocation: white water kayaking. Home: PO Box 1499 Bandon OR 97411-1499 Office: Sec of State 136 State Capitol Bldg Salem OR 97310-0001 E-mail: bill.bradbury@state.or.us

BRADEN, GEORGE WALTER, II (BARON OF CARRIGALINE), company executive; b. L.A., Sept. 1, 1936; s. Paul Sumner and Evelyn Widney (Traver) B.; m. Trina Rose Thomas, July 3, 1964; children: Barbara Diane, Beverly Eileen Braden Christensen. BS, Calif. State U., 1963; grad. cert., U. So. Calif., 1990, Harvard U., 1991; postgrad., UCLA, 1990—; MBA, Chadwick U.; JA, Blackstone Law Sch. Mgr. western region vet. div. Bristol-Myers, Syracuse, N.Y., 1970-79; pres. Braden Sales Assocs. Internat., Apple Valley, Calif., 1980—. Mem. Friends of Hoover Inst., Stanford, Calif.; charter mem. Rep. Presdl. Task Force, Washington, 1989—; commr. Rep. Presdl. Adv. Com., Washington, 1991—; active Nat. Rep. Senatorial Com. Capt. USMB, 1985-93, maj., 1993—. Recipient Presdl. order of Merit, Heritage Found., Rep. Presdl. award, 1994, Order of St. John, 1999; numerous awards Boy Scouts of Am.; named Lord of North Bovey, Lord of Newton Bushel. Mem. Am. Mktg. Assn., Tex. A&M U. Internat. Assn. of Agri-Bus., Curia Baronis Guild for Barons, Lords of Manor, Pres.'s Club, Order of St. John. Mem. LDS Ch.

BRADEN, ROBERT, communications company executive; Sr. v.p. Centenial Comms.; v.p. bus. devel. Citizens Comms.; pres., COO and dir. Electric Lightwave, Vancouver, Wash., 2001—. Office: Electric Lightwave Inc 4400 NE 77th Ave Vancouver WA 98662

BRADFORD, DAVID S. surgeon; b. Charlotte, N.C., Oct. 15, 1936; m. Helen Gray MacKay (div.); children: David Mackay, Jennifer Sutherland, Tyler Speir; m. Sharon Hale. B.A., Davidson Coll., 1958; M.D., U. Pa., 1962. Diplomate: Am. Bd. Orthopaedic Surgeons. Intern in surgery Columbia-Presbyn. Med. Center, N.Y.C., 1962-63, resident in gen. surgery, 1965-66; resident in orthopaedic surgery N.Y. Orthopaedic Hosp., Columbia-Presbyn. Med. Center, N.Y.C., 1966-68, jr. Annie C. Kane fellow orthopaedic surgery, 1968-69; research trainee orthopaedics Nat. Inst. Arthritis and Metabolic Diseases, 1969-70; prof. orthopaedic surgery U. Minn. Hosps., Mpls., 1970-90, chief of spine surgery, 1984-90; prof., chmn. dept. orthopaedic surgery U. Calif., San Francisco, 1991—. Mem. bd. editors: Spine; contbr. articles to profl. jours. Mem. Am. Acad. Orthopaedic Surgeons, Am. Orthopaedic Assn., Assn. Bone and Joint Surgeons (past pres.), Orthopaedic Research Soc., Scoliosis Research Soc. (past pres.). Office: U of Calif San Francisco Dept Orthopedic Surgery 500 Parnassus Ave # Mu320 San Francisco CA 94143-0001

BRADLEY, CHARLES WILLIAM, podiatrist, educator; b. Fife, Tex., July 23, 1923; s. Tom and Mary Ada (Cheatham) B.; m. Marilyn A. Brown, Apr. 3, 1948 (dec. Mar. 1973); children: Steven, Gregory, Jeffrey, Elizabeth, Gerald. Student, Tex. Tech., 1940-42; D. Podiatric Medicine, Calif. Coll. Podiatric Medicine U. San Francisco, 1949, MPA, 1987, D.Sc. (hon.). Pvt. practice podiatry, Beaumont, Tex., 1950-51, Brownwood, 1951-52, San Francisco, San Bruno, Calif., 1952—; assoc. clin. prof. Calif. Coll. Podiatric Medicine, 1992-98. Chief of staff Calif. Podiatry Hosp., San Francisco; mem. surg. staff Sequoia Hosp., Redwood City, Calif.; mem. med. staff Peninsula Hosp., Burlingame, Calif.; chief podiatry staff St. Luke's Hosp., San Francisco; chmn. bd. Podiatry Ins. Co. Am.; cons. VA; assoc. prof. podiatric medicine Calif. Coll. Podiatric Medicine. Mem. San Francisco Symphony Found.; mem. adv. com. Health Policy Agenda for the Am. People, AMA; chmn. trustees Calif. Coll. Podiatric Medicine, Calif. Podiatry Coll., Calif. Podiatry Hosp.; mem. San Mateo Grand Jury, 1989. Served with USNR, 1942-45. Mem. Am. Podiatric Med. Assn. (trustee, pres. 1983-84), Calif. Podiatry Assn. (pres. No. div. 1964-66, state bd. dirs., pres. 1975-76, Podiatrist of Yr. award 1983), Nat. Coun. Edn. (vice-chmn.), Nat. Acads. Practice (chmn. podiatric med. sect. 1991-96, sec. 1996—), Am. Legion, San Bruno C. of C. (bd. dirs. 1978-91, v.p. 1992, bd. dir. grand jury assoc. 1990), Olympic Club, Commonwealth Club Calif., Elks, Lions. Home: 2965 Trousdale Dr Burlingame CA 94010-5708 Office: 560 Jenevein Ave San Bruno CA 94066-4408 E-mail: bradlee2@aol.com

BRADLEY, DONALD EDWARD, lawyer; b. Santa Rosa, Calif., Sept. 26, 1943; s. Edward Aloysius and Mildred Louise (Kelley) B.; m. Marianne Stark, Apr. 22, 1990; children: Evan Patrick, Matthew Jordan, Andrea Phelps. AB, Dartmouth Coll., 1965; JD, U. Calif., San Francisco, 1968; LLM, N.Y.U., 1972. Bar: Calif. 1968, U.S. Dist. Ct. (no. dist.) Calif. 1968, U.S. Ct. Appeals (9 cir.) 1968, U.S. Tax Ct. 1972, U.S. Ct. Claims 1973, U.S. Supreme Ct. 1981. Assoc. Pillsbury, Madison & Sutro, San Francisco, 1972-77, ptnr., 1978-84; mem. Wilson Sonsini Goodrich & Rosati, Palo Alto, Calif., 1984—. Mng. dir. Wilson Sonsini Goodrich & Rosati, Palo Alto, 1995—; adj. prof. Golden State U., San Francisco, 1973-82; pres., chmn. bd. dirs. Atty.'s Ins. Mut. Risk Retention Group, Honolulu, 1986—. Capt. U.S. Army, 1969-70. Recipient Charles M. Ruddick award N.Y.U., 1972, award Bureau of Nat. Affairs, Washington, 1968. Mem. ABA, Internat. Bar Assn., Santa Clara Bar Assn., San Francisco Bar Assn., Internat. Tax Club, Peninsula Tax Club. Office: Wilson Sonsini Goodrich & Rosati 650 Page Mill Rd Palo Alto CA 94304-1050 E-mail: dbradley@wsgr.com

BRADLEY, GILBERT FRANCIS, retired banker; b. Miami, Ariz., May 17, 1920; s. Ever and Martha (Piper) B.; m. Marion Bebb, June 21, 1941; children: Larry Paul, Richard Thomas, Steven Ever. Grad., LaSalle Extension U., 1942, U. Wash., 1953; Advanced Mgmt. Program, Harvard U. With Valley Nat. Bank, Ariz., Miami, Globe, Clifton, Nogales and Phoenix, 1937—, pres., 1973-76, chmn. bd., chief exec. officer, 1976-82, ret., 1982, dir., vice chmn. exec. com., 1982—, Valley Nat. Corp., 1982—. Mem. adv. council Fed. Res. Bd., Comptroller of the Currency, Denver; instr. Am. Inst. Banking. Mem. Tucson Airport Authority, 1960—; mem. adv. council Ariz. State U. Sch. Bus., pres. dean's adv. council; dean's adv. council U. Ariz., Tucson. Served to capt. USAAF, 1942-45. Decorated D.F.C., Air medal with three oak leaf clusters. Mem. Ariz. Bankers Assn. (pres.), Assn. Res. City Bankers, Ariz. C. of C. (v.p., dir.), Tucson C. of C. (dir.), Better Bus. Bur. (dir.), Tucson Clearing House Assn. (past pres.), Navy League, Air Force Assn., Beta Gamma Sigma. Clubs: Masons, Rotary, Phoenix Country, Ariz. Home: 5340 N La Plaza Cir Phoenix AZ 85012-1416 Office: 241 N Central Ave Phoenix AZ 85004-2225

BRADLEY, LAWRENCE D., JR. lawyer; b. Santa Monica, Calif., Feb. 19, 1920; s. Lawrence D. Bradley and Virginia L. Edwards; m. Joan Worthington, Feb. 1, 1945; children— Gary W., Brooks, Eric Scott B.S., U.S. Coast Guard Acad., 1942; LL.B., Stanford U., 1950. Bar: Calif. 1950, U.S. Dist. Ct. (cen. dist.) Calif. 1950, U.S. Dist. Ct. (so. dist.) Calif. 1967. Assoc. Pillsbury, Madison & Sutro, L.A., 1950-59, ptnr., 1959-90; of counsel Pillsbury Winthrop LLP. Lectr. admiralty and ins. law U. So. Calif., 1952-80 Pres. Stanford Law Rev., 1949-50; assoc. editor Am. Maritime Cases, 1990—. Mem. adv. bd. Tulane Admiralty Law Inst., 1990—. With USN, 1942-48; to lt. comdr. Res. Mem. ABA, Calif. Bar Assn., Maritime Law Assn. U.S. (mem. exec. com. 1974-78, chmn. cruise line com. 1991-94), Inst. Navigation, Order of Coif, Calif. Club, Chancery Club, Calif. Yacht Club, San Diego Yacht Club, Propeller Club, Transpacific Yacht Club, Tutukaka South Pacific Yacht Club. Office: Pillsbury Winthrop LLP 725 S Figueroa St Ste 1200 Los Angeles CA 90017-5443

BRADLEY, R. TODD, computer company executive; b. Balt., Nov. 29, 1958; BSBA, Towson (Md.) State U. V.p. Fed. Express; v.p., mng. dir. EMEA ops. AC Nielsen; pres. NCH Promotional Svcs. subsidiary Dun & Bradstreet Corp.; pres., CEO Transport Internat. Pool; sr. v.p. Europe, Middle East and Africa region Gateway Inc., San Diego, 1998—, sr. v.p. U.S. consumer bus., 1999—, exec. v.p. global ops., 1999—. Office: Gateway Inc 4545 Towne Ctr Ct San Diego CA 92121

BRADLEY, WALTER D. lieutenant governor, real estate broker; b. Clovis, N.Mex., Oct. 30, 1946; s. Ralph W. and M. Jo (Black) B.; m. Debbie Shelly, Sept. 17, 1977; children: Tige, Lance, Nicole, Kristin. Student, Eastern N.Mex. U., 1964—67. Supr. Tex. Instruments, Dallas, 1967—73; mgr., salesman Nat. Chemsearch, Irving, 1973—76; real estate broker Colonial Real Estate, Clovis, 1976, Realtors Assn. N.Mex., Clovis, N.Mex., 1976—; state senator Curry County, State of N.Mex., 1989—93; lt. gov. State of N.Mex., Santa Fe, 1995—; mem. N.Mex. Senate, 1989—92; % %, 1999—. V.p., bd. dirs. Clovis Indsl. Commn., 1983—86; pres. econ. devel. %, 1987; bd. dirs. United Way, Clovis, 1984—86; % Curry County Blood Adv. Bd., Clovis, 1980—85; chmn. Curry County Reps., Clovis, 1984—88; % Cosmos Soccer, Clovis, 1984. Named Man of

Yr., Progressive Farmer Mag., 1998; recipient Leadership award, Albuquerque NAACP, 1997, Disting. Svc. award, N.Mex. Farm and Livestock Bur., 1997, Leadership Beatification award, Keep N.Mex. Beautiful, 2000, Mark Weidler Disting. Pub. Servant award, N.Mex. Petroleum Marketers Assn., 2000, Outstanding N.Mex. Small Bus. Supporter, N.Mex. Small Bus. Devel. Ctr., 1997, Outstanding Leadership award, N.Mex. Cattle Growers' Assn., 1996. Mem.: Lions, Realtors Assn. N.Mex. (v.p., bd. dirs. 1982—85, v.p. 1987—88), Clovis Bd. Realtors (pres. 1982, pres. 1993), Clovis C. of C., Curry County Jaycees, N.Mex. Jaycees. Baptist. Office: Office of Lt Gov State Capitol Bldg Ste 417 Santa Fe NM 87503-0001 Office Fax: 505-827-3057

BRADSHAW, CARL JOHN, investor, lawyer, consultant; b. Oelwein, Iowa, Nov. 1, 1930; s. Carl John and Lorraine Lillian (Thiele) B.; m. Katsuko Anno, Nov. 5, 1954; children: Carla K., Arthur Herbert, Vincent Marcus. BS, U. Minn., 1952, JD, 1957; LLM, U. Mich., 1958; MJur, Keio U., Tokyo, 1962. Bar: Minn. 1960, U.S. Supreme Ct., 1981, Calif. 1985. Assoc. Graham, James & Rolph, Tokyo, 1961-63; assoc. prof. law U. Wash., Seattle, 1963-64; sr. v.p. Oak Industries, Inc., Crystal Lake, Ill., 1964-84, dir. internat. ops., 1964-70, dir. corp. devel., 1970-72, pres. communications group, 1972-78, chief legal officer, 1979-84; counsel Seki & Jarvis, L.A., 1985-87, Bell, Boyd & Lloyd, L.A., 1987; prin. The Pacific Law Group, L.A., Tokyo and Palo Alto, Calif., 1987—, The Asian Mktg. Group, Torrance, 1992—. Participant Japanese-Am. program for cooperation in legal studies, 1957-61. Contbr. articles to legal and bus. jours Bd. dirs. Japan-Am. Soc., Chgo., 1966-72; bd. dirs., fin. dir. San Diego Symphony Orch. Assn., 1980-81. Served to lt. (j.g.) USN, 1952-55 Fulbright scholar, 1958-59, Ford Found. scholar, 1960-61. Fellow Radio Club Am.; mem. Minn. Bar Assn., Calif. Bar Assn., Am. Soc. Internat. Law, Internat. Fiscal Assn., Regency Club, Order of Coif. Avocation: reading, bible study. Home: 12958 Robleda Cv San Diego CA 92128-1126 Office: Pacific Law Group 12121 Wilshire Blvd Fl 2 Los Angeles CA 90025-1123

BRADSHAW, JERALD SHERWIN, chemistry educator, researcher; b. Cedar City, Utah, Nov. 28, 1932; s. Sherwin H. and Maree (Wood) B.; m. Karen Lee, Aug. 6, 1954; children: Donna M. Webster, Melinda C. BS, U. Utah, 1955; PhD, UCLA, 1963. Postdoctoral Calif. Inst. Tech., Pasadena, 1962-63; chemist Chevron Research, Richmond, Calif., 1963-66; asst. prof. chemistry Brigham Young U., Provo, Utah, 1966-69, assoc. prof., 1969-74, prof., 1974-93, asst. chmn. chemistry dept., 1980-86, Reed M. Izatt prof., 1993-2000, emeritus prof., 2000—. Vis. prof. Nat. Acad. Sci., U. Ljubljana, Yugoslavia, 1972-73, 82, U. Sheffield, England, 1978, James Cook U., Townsville, Australia, 1988. Author 2 books; contbr. more than 400 articles to profl. jours.; patentee in field. Served with USNR, 1955-59. Recipient Gov.'s medal in sci. and tech., 1991. Mem. Am. Chem. Soc. (Utah award 1989, nat. award for separations sci. and tech. 1996), Internat. Soc. Heterocyclic Chemistry (bd. advisors 1980-82), Utah Acad. Sci., Sigma Xi (ann. lectr. 1988). Republican. Mem. LDS Ch. Avocations: stamp collecting, church activities. Office: Brigham Young U Dept Chemistry-Biochemistry Provo UT 84602 E-mail: jerald_bradshaw@byu.edu

BRADSHAW, MURRAY CHARLES, musicologist, educator; b. Hinsdale, Ill., Sept. 25, 1930; s. Murray Andrew Bradshaw and Marie (Novak) Orth; m. Doris Hogg; children: Jean Marie, Murray Edward, Thomas Andrew; m. Sharon Ann Sitton, Apr. 19, 1997. MusM in Piano, Am. Conservatory Music, Chgo., 1955, MusM in Organ, 1958; PhD in Musicology, U. Chgo., 1969. Prof. UCLA, 1966—. Organist and choirmaster various chs. in Illinois, Ind., Calif., 1948—; music critic Gary Post Tribune, Ind., 1962-64; chair dep. musicology, UCLA, 1993-95. Author: The Origin of the Toccata, 1972, The Falsobordone, 1978, Francesco Severi, 1981, Girolamo Diruta The Transylvanian, 1984, Giovanni Luca Conforti, 1985, Gabriele Fattorini, 1986, Emilio de' Cavalieri, 1990, Conforti, "Breve et facile", 1999; gen. editor Musicol. Studies and Documents and Miscellanea, 2000—; contbr. articles to profl. jours. Served with U.S. Army, 1954-56. Grantee: Am. Philos. Soc., 1987, NEH (travel), 1994. Mem. Am. Musicol. Soc. (pres. local chpt. 1979-81), Am. Guild Organists, Ctr. for Medieval and Renaissance Studies. Avocations: reading, jogging, yoga, bridge. Home: 17046 Burbank Blvd Apt 3 Encino CA 91316-1830 Office: UCLA Dept Musicology 405 Hilgard Ave Los Angeles CA 90095-9000 E-mail: mbrads3486@aol.com

BRADSHAW, PETER, engineering educator; b. Torquay, Devon, Eng., Dec. 26, 1935; came to U.S., 1988; s. Joseph Newbold and Frances Winifred (Finch) B.; m. Aline Mary Rose, July 18, 1959 (div. 1968); m. Sheila Dorothy Brown, July 20, 1968. BA, Cambridge U., Eng., 1957; DSc (hon.), Exeter U., Eng., 1990. Sci. officer Nat. Phys. Lab., Teddington, Eng., 1957-69; prof. Imperial Coll. Sci. and Tech., London, 1969-88; Thomas V. Jones prof. engring. Stanford U., 1988-95, prof. emeritus, 1995—. Cons. various engring. cos. Author: Introduction to Turbulence, 1971, Momentum Transfer, 1977, Convective Heat Transfer, 1984; author nearly 200 journ. articles on aerodynamics. Recipient Bronze medal Royal Aero. Soc., London, 1971, Busk prize, 1972, Fluid Dynamics award AIAA, 1994. Fellow Royal Soc. London. Avocations: cycling, walking. Office: Stanford U Dept Mech Engring Stanford CA 94305-3030 E-mail: bradshaw@stanford.edu

BRADSHAW, RALPH ALDEN, biochemistry educator; b. Boston, Feb. 14, 1941; s. Donald Bertram and Eleanor (Dodd) B.; m. Roberta Perry Wheeler, Dec. 29, 1961; children: Christopher Evan, Amy Dodd. BA in Chemistry, Colby Coll., 1962; PhD, Duke U., 1966. Asst. prof. Washington U., St. Louis, 1969-72, assoc. prof., 1972-74, prof., 1974-82; prof., chair dept. U. Calif., Irvine, 1982-93, prof., 1993—. Study sect. chmn. NIH, 1979, mem., 1975-79, 80-85; mem. sci. adv. bd. Hereditary Disease Found., 1983-87, ICN Nucleic Acids Rsch. Inst., 1986-87; rsch. study com. physiol. chem. Am. Heart Assn., 1984-86, mem. Coun. on Thrombosis, 1976-90; fellowship screening com. Am. Cancer Soc. Calif., 1984-87; chmn. adv. com. Western Winter Workshops, 1984-88; dir., chmn., mem. organizing com. numerous symposia, confs. in field including Proteins in Biology and Medicine, Shanghai, Peoples Republic of China, 1981, Symposium Am. Protein Chemists, San Diego, 1985, mem. exec. com. Keystone Symp. Mol. Cell. Biol., 1991-97, chmn., 1991-94, bd. dirs., 1997—, treas., 1997—; trustee Keystone Ctr., 1991-97; mem. exec. com. Internat. Union Biochem. Mol. Biol., 1991-97, U.S. Nat. Commn. Biochem., 1987-96, chmn., 1992-96; bd. dirs. Fed. Am. Soc. Exptl. Biology, 1992-96, v.p., 1994-95, pres., 1995-96. Mem. editl. bd. Archives Biochemistry and Biophysics, 1972-88, Jour. Biological Chemistry, 1973-77, 78-79, 81-86, assoc. editor, 1989—, Jour. Supramolecular Structure/Cellular Biochemistry, 1980-91, Bioscience Reports, 1980-87, Peptide and Protein Reviews, 1980-86, Jour. Protein Chemistry, 1980-90, IN VITRO Rapid Com. in Cell Biology, 1984—; editor Trends in Biochem. Scis., 1975-91, editor-in-chief, 1986-91, J. Neurochem, 1986-90, Proteins: Structure, Functions & Genetics, 1988-92; assoc. editor Growth Factors, 1989—; assoc. editor Protein Sci., 1990-92, 97—, mem. editl. bd., 1992—; mem. editl. bd. Biotech. Appl. Biochem., 1995—; co-editor-in-chief Molecular Cell Biol.-Rsch. Comms., 1998—; editor-in-chief Molecular and Cellular Proteomics, 2000—; contbr. numerous articles to sci. jours. Recipient Young Scientist award Passano Found., 1976. Fellow AAAS; mem. Am. Chem. Soc. (Sect. award 1979), Am. Soc. Biochem. Molecular Biology (coun. 1987-90, treas. 1991-97), Am. Peptide Soc., N.Y. Acad. Scis., Protein Soc. (acting pres. 1986-87), Am. Soc. for Cell Biology, Soc. for Neuroscience, The Endocrine Soc., Am. Soc. Bone Mineral Rsch., Assn. Biomolecular Rsch. Facilities, Sigma Xi. Home: 25135 Rivendell Dr Lake Forest CA 92630-4124 Office: U Calif Irvine Coll Medicine Dept Physiol & Biophysics D238 Med Sci I Irvine CA 92697-0001

BRADSHAW, RICHARD ROTHERWOOD, engineering executive; b. Phila., Sept. 12, 1916; s. Joseph Rotherwood and Rosanna (Jones) B.; m. Audrey Grace Skinn, Oct. 3, 1940 (dec. Jan. 1981); children— Linda M., Barbara A., Vicki; m. Chanin Hale, Feb. 14, 1986. B.S., Calif. Inst. Tech., 1939; M.S., U. So. Calif., 1950. Pres. Richard R. Bradshaw, Inc., Van Nuys, Calif., 1946—, pres. br. office Honolulu. Contbr. articles to tech. jours., Important works include, Disneyworld Hotels, Orlando, Fla., U.S. embassy, Warsaw, Poland, U.S. Exhbn. Bldg., Moscow USSR, Taraara Hotel, Tahiti, Gulf Life Bldg., Jacksonville, Fla., Los Angeles City Airport. Recipient Alfred Lindau award Am. Concrete Inst., 1968, many others for structural design. Mem. ASCE, Internat. Assn. Bridges and Structural Engring., Am. Seismol. Soc., Cons. Engrs. Assn., Internat. Assn. Thin Shells, Am. Concrete Inst., Am. Arbitration Assn. Office: Richard R Bradshaw Inc 17300 Ballinger St Northridge CA 91325-2005

BRADSHAW, TERRY, sports announcer, former professional football player; b. Shreveport, La., Sept. 2, 1948; Ed., La. Tech. U. With profl. football team Pitts. Steelers, 1970-84; sports analyst CBS Sports Inc NFL Today, 1987-94, Fox Sports, 1995—. Country and western singer, entertainer, appears in numerous commls., pub. speaker. Named Most Valuable Player, Super Bowl XIII, 1978, Super Bowl XIV, 1979, Most Favorite TV Sportscaster TV Guide, 1999; named to Pro Bowl, 1978, 79; inducted into Hall of Fame, 1989; recipient Emmy award for sports studio analyst, 2000; named Father of Yr. L.A., 2000. Achievements include being the quarterback in Super Bowl win, 1974, 75, 78, 79. Office: care Fox Network PO Box 900 Beverly Hills CA 90213-0900 Address: 1925 N Pearson Ln Roanoke TX 76262-9018

BRADY, CARL FRANKLIN, retired aircraft charter company executive; b. Chelsea, Okla., Oct. 29, 1919; s. Kirty A. and Pauline Ellen (Doty) B.; m. Carol Elizabeth Sprague, Mar. 29, 1941; children: Carl Franklin, Linda Kathryn, James Kenneth. Ed., U. Wash., 1940. Co-owner Aero Cafe, Yakima, Wash., 1946-47; pilot Central Aircraft, Yakima, 1947-48; partner Economy Helicopters, Inc., Yakima, 1948-60; pres. ERA Helicopters, Inc., Anchorage, 1960-85, ERA Aviation Center, Inc., 1977-85, Livingston Copters, Inc., 1977-85. Exec. v.p. Rowan Companies, Inc., Houston, 1973-85, also bd. dirs.; owner, pres. Brady Investments Ltd. Mem. Alaska Ho. of Reps., 1965-66, Alaska Senate, 1967-68; pres. Alaska Crippled Childrens Assn., 1963; mem. Nat. Advisery com. Oceans and Atmosphere, 1981-86. Served with USAAF, 1943-46. Named Alaskan of Yr., 1989; named to Alaska Bus. Hall of Fame, 1990. Mem. Helicopter Assn. Am. (pres. 1953, 57, Larry D. Bell award 1976), Anchorage C. of C. (pres. 1963-64), Alaska Air Carriers Assn., Am. Helicopter Soc., Commonwealth North, Petroleum Alaska Club, Elks. Republican. Methodist. Home: 510 L St Anchorage AK 99501-1964 also: 44-832 Santa Rosa Ct Indian Wells CA 92210-7622 Office: 1031 W 4th Ave Ste 502 Anchorage AK 99501-5906

BRADY, JOHN PATRICK, JR. electronics educator, consultant; b. Newark, Mar. 20, 1929; s. John Patrick and Madeleine Mary (Atno) B.; m. Mary Coop, May 1, 1954; children: Peter, John P., Madeleine, Dennis, Mary G. BSEE, MIT, 1952, MSEE, 1953. Registered profl. engr., Mass. Sect. mgr. Hewlett-Packard Co., Waltham, Mass., 1956-67; v.p. engring. John Fluke Mfg. Co., Inc., Mountlake Terrace, Wash., 1967-73, Dana Labs., Irvine, Calif., 1973-77; engring. mgr., tech. advisor to gen. mgr. Memron Corp., Upland, 1977-78; ptnr. Resource Assocs., Newport Beach, 1978-86; prof. electronics Orange Coast Coll., Costa Mesa, 1977-99, emeritus, 1999, faculty fellow, dean tech., 1983-84, chmn. electronics tech. dept., 1994-96, chmn. acad. rank com., 1988-98. Instr. computers and elec. engring. Calif. State U., Long Beach, 1982-84; dir. measurement sci. conf. MIT, L.A., 1982-83. Contbr. articles to profl. jours. Mem. evaluation team Accrediting Commn. for Cmty. and Jr. Colls., 1982-92; mem. blue ribbon adv. com. on oversees tech. transfer U.S. Dept. of Commerce, 1974-76. With USN, 1946-48. Mem. Eta Kappa Nu, Tau Beta Pi, Sigma Xi. Office: Orange Coast Coll Costa Mesa CA 92626

BRADY, MARY ROLFES, music educator, educator; b. St. Louis, Nov. 26, 1933; d. William Henry and Helen Dorothy (Slavick) Rolfes; m. Donald Sheridan Brady, Aug. 29, 1953; children: Joseph William, Mark David, Douglas Sheridan, John Rolfes, Todd Christopher. Student, Stanford U., 1951-54, UCLA, 1967, U. So. Calif., 1972-73; pvt. studies with, Roxanna Byers, Dorothy Desmond, and Rudolph Ganz. Pvt. piano tchr., L.A., 1955—; TV and radio performer. Pres. Jr. Philharmonic Com. L.A., 1975-76; legis. coord., bd. dirs. Philharmonic Affiliates, L.A., 1978-80. Life mem. Good Samaritan Hosp., St. Vincent Med. Ctr., L.A.; trustee St. Francis Med. Ctr., 1984-88; bd. dirs. Hollygrove-L.A. Orphans Home, Inc. Mem. Am. Coll. Musicians Club, Stanford Women's Club (past bd. dirs., pres. L.A. chpt. 1977—), The Muses, Springs Country Club.

BRADY, RODNEY HOWARD, holding company executive, broadcast company executive, former college president, former government official; b. Sandy, Utah, Jan. 31, 1933; s. Kenneth A. and Jessie (Madsen) B.; m. Carolyn Ann Hansen, Oct. 25, 1960; children: Howard Riley, Bruce Ryan, Brooks Alan. BS in Acctg. with high honors, U. Utah, MBA with high honors, 1957; DBA, Harvard U., 1966; postgrad., UCLA, 1969-70; PhD (hon.), Weber State Coll., 1986, Snow Coll., 1991, Univ. Utah, 1997. Missionary Ch. Jesus Christ of Latter-day Saints, Great Britain, 1953-55; teaching assoc. Harvard U. Bus. Sch., Cambridge, Mass., 1957-59; v.p. Mgmt. Systems Corp., Cambridge, 1962-65, Center Exec. Devel., Cambridge, 1963-64, v.p., dir. Boston, 1964-65; v.p. Tamerand Reef Corp., Christiansted, St. Croix, V.I., 1963-65; v.p., dir. Am. Inst. Execs., N.Y.C., 1963-65; v.p., mem. exec. com. aircraft div. Hughes Tool Co., Culver City, Calif., 1966-70; asst. sec. adminstrn. and mgmt. Dept. HEW, Washington, 1970-72; chmn. subcabinet exec. officers group of exec. br., 1971-72; exec. v.p., chmn. exec. com., dir. Bergen Brunswig Corp., Los Angeles, 1972-78; chmn. bd. Uni-mgrs. Internat., Los Angeles, 1974-78; pres. Weber State Coll., Ogden, Utah, 1978-85; pres., CEO Bonneville Internat. Corp., Salt Lake City, 1985-96, also dir.; pres., CEO Deseret Mgmt. Corp., Salt Lake City, 1996—. Bd. dirs. Bergen Brunswig Corp., 1st Security Bank Corp., 1985-2000, Mgmt. and Tng. Corp., Deseret Mut. Benefit Assn., chmn.; bd. dirs. Maximum Svc. Television, Inc., Intermountain Health Care Found., Nat. Assn. Broadcasters TV Bd., 1993-96, Utah Opera Co.; bd. advisors Mountain Bell Telephone, 1983-87; chmn. Nat. Adv. Com. on Accreditation and Instl. Eligibility, 1984-86, mem., 1983-87; chmn. Utah Gov.'s Blue Ribbon Com. on Tax Recodification, 1984-90; cons. Dept. Def., Dept. State, Dept. Commerce, HEW, NASA, Govt. of Can., Govt. of India (and indsl. firms), 1962—. Author: An Approach to Equipment Replacement Analysis, 1957, Survey of Management Planning and Control Systems, 1962, The Impact of Computers on Top Management Decision Making in the Aerospace and Defense Industry, 1966, (with others) How To Structure Incentive Contracts— A Programmed Text, 1965, My Missionary Years in Great Britain, 1976, An Exciting Start Along an Upward Path, 1978; contbr. articles to profl. jours. Mem. exec. com. nat. exec. bd. Boy Scouts Am., 1977—; chmn. nat. Cub Scout commn., 1977-81, pres. Western region, 1981-83, chmn. nat. ct. of honor, 1984-88; mem. adv. com. program for health sys. mgmt. Harvard U., 1973-78, mem. nat. adv. coun. U. Utah, 1971—, chairperson, 1974-76, nat. adv. bd. Coll. Bus., 1985—, chmn., 1989-93, mem. adv. com. Brigham Young U. Bus. Sch., 1972—; mem. dean's round table UCLA Grad. Sch. Mgmt., 1973-78; trustee Ettie Lee H[illegible], 19[illegible]; mem. gov. bd. McKay Dee Hosp., Ogden, Utah, 1979-87; bd. dirs. Utah Endowment for Humanities, 1978-80, Nat. Legal Ctr. for the Pub. Interest, 1991—, vice chmn., 1994-95, chmn., 1995-97, Utah [illegible] Ogden C. of C., 1978-83, bd. dirs. Utah Opera Co., 1997—. 1st lt. USAF, 1959-62. Recipient Silver Antelope award Boy Scouts Am., 1976; recipient Silver Beaver award Boy Scouts Am., 1979, Silver Buffalo award Boy Scouts Am., 1982, Disting. Alumni award U. Utah, 1990. Mem. Nat. Assn. TV Broadcasters (bd. dirs.), Am. Mgmt. Assn. (award 1969), L.A. C. of C. (tax structure com. 1969-70), Salt Lake Area C. of C. (bd. dirs. 1985-88), SAR (pres. Utah chpt. 1986-87), Sons of Utah Pioneers, Freedoms Found. at Valley Forge (nat. bd. dirs. 1986—), L.A. Country Club, Alta Club, Rotary, Phi Kappa Phi, Tau Kappa Alpha, Beta Gamma Sigma. Mem. LDS Ch. (past pres. L.A. stake). Office: Deseret Mgmt Corp Eagle Gate Tower 60 E South Temple Ste 575 Salt Lake City UT 84111-1016

BRAGG, ROBERT HENRY, physicist, educator; b. Jacksonville, Fla., Aug. 11, 1919; s. Robert Henry and Lilly Camille (McFarland) B.; m. Violette Mattie McDonald, June 14, 1947; children: Robert Henry, Pamela. BS, Ill. Inst. Tech., 1949, MS, 1951, PhD, 1960. Assoc. physicist rsch. lab. Portland Cement Assn., Skokie, Ill., 1951-56; sr. physicist physics div. Armour Rsch. Found. Ill. Inst. Tech., Chgo., 1956-61; sr. mem., mgr. phys. metallurgy dept. Lockheed Palo Alto Rsch. Lab., Palo Alto, Calif., 1961-69; prof. materials sci. U. Calif., Berkeley, 1969-87, chmn. dept. materials sci. and mineral engring., 1978-81, prof. emeritus, 1987—. Faculty sr. scientist Lawrence Berkeley Lab., 1969-87, emeritus 1987—; mem. materials rsch. adv. com. NSF, 1982-86; program dir. div. materials rsch. U.S. Dept. Energy, 1981-82; cons. IBM, Siemens-Allis, NASA, NIH, NSF, NRC; vis. prof. Musashi Inst. of Tech., Tokyo, 1989, Howard U., 1999; del. 2d Edward Bouchet Internat. Conf., Accra, Ghana, 1990. Contbr. articles to profl. jours. Pres. Palo Alto NAACP, 1967-68. With U.S. Army, 1943-46. Decorated Bronze star (2); recipient Disting. award No. Calif. sect. Am. Inst. Mining and Metall. Engrs., 1970; J. William Fulbright rsch. fellow, Nigeria, 1992-93. Fellow Nat. Soc. of Black Physicists; mem. AAUP, AAAS, Am. Phys. Soc., Am. Ceramics Soc. (chmn. No. Calif. sect. 1980), AIME (chmn. No. Calif. sect. 1970), Am. Carbon Soc., Am. Soc. Metals, No. Calif. Coun. Black Profl. Engrs., Nat. Tech. Assn., Sigma Xi, Tau Beta Pi, Sigma Pi Sigma., Am. Crystallographic Assn. Democrat. Home: 2 Admiral Dr Ste 373 Emeryville CA 94608-1502 Office: U Calif Dept Materials Sci Min Berkeley CA 94720-0001 E-mail: petebragg@aol.com, rbragg@socrates.berkeley.edu

BRAGINSKY, STANISLAV IOSIFOVICH, physicist, geophysicist, researcher; b. Moscow, Apr. 15, 1926; s. Iosif Samuilovich Braginsky and Khaya Nutovna Drikker; m. Maya Aronovna Boyarskaya, May 8, 1955; children: Galina, Leonid. Degree in engring. and physics, Moscow Inst. of Mechs., 1948; cand. sci. in physics and math., Inst. Atomic Energy, Moscow, 1953, DSc in Physics and Math., 1966. Sr. scientist I.V. Kurchatov Inst. of Atomic Energy, Moscow, 1948-78, O. Yu. Schmidt Inst. of Physics of the Earth, Moscow, 1978-88; geophysicist, researcher Inst. Geophysics/Planetary Physics UCLA, 1989—. Recipient Lenin prize for rsch. in plasma physics Acad. Sci. USSR, 1958, John Adam Fleming medal for rsch. in geomagnetism Am. Geophys. Union, 1993. Fellow Am. Geophys. Union. Achievements include development of two-temperature equations of plasma dynamics and theory of the pinch-effect in high power electrical discharges in gases; advancement of theory of hydromagnetic dynamo of the Earth and theory of geomagnetic secular variations. Office: UCLA Inst Geophys & Planetary Phys 405 Hilgard Ave Los Angeles CA 90095 E-mail: sbragins@igpp.ucla.edu

BRAHAM, RAYMOND L. pediatric dentistry educator; came to the U.S., 1968; Grad., U. London, 1957; M in Pedodontics, cert. advanced tng., Boston U., 1970. Pvt. practice dentistry, London; chief resident pedodontics Winnipeg (Can.) Children's Hosp.; pedodontic trianee Boston U. Sch. Grad. Dentistry, faculty; clin. prof. dentistry dept. pediat. Sch. Medicine U. Calif., San Francisco, clin. prof., assoc. chair clin. affairs pediat. dentistry, interim-dir. postgrad. program pediat. dentistry. Lectr. in field. Sr. author, editor: The Dental Implications of Epilepsy, 1976; editor: (with M.E. Morris) Handbook of pedoDontics-Clinical and Laboratory Techniques, 1975, Textbook of Pediatric Dentistry, 1980, Odontologia Pediatrica, 1984, Textbook of Pediatric Dentistry, 1985, 2nd edit., 1988; reviewer, cons. several nat. jours.; contbr. chpts. to books and articles to profl. jours. Fellow Am. Acad. Pediat. Dentistry, Am. Acad. Dentistry for the Handicapped (past pres.), Royal Soc. Health Eng., Royal Soc. Medicine London. Office: U Calif Sch Dentistry PO Box 438 San Francisco CA 94143-0001 Fax: 415-476-1499. E-mail: rbraham@itsa.ucsf.edu

BRAHMA, CHANDRA SEKHAR, civil engineering educator; b. Calcutta, India, Oct. 5, 1941; came to U.S., 1963; s. Nalinia Kanta and Uma Rani (Bose) B.; m. Purnima Sinha, Feb. 18, 1972; children: Charanjit, Barunashish. B in Engring., Calcutta U., 1962; MS, Mich. State U., 1965; PhD, Ohio State U., 1969. Registered profl. engr. Calif., Utah, N.H., Tex., Wis. Asst. engr. Pub. Works Dept., Calcutta, 1962-63; rsch. asst. Mich. State U., East Lansing, 1963-65; teaching and rsch. assoc. Ohio State U., Columbus, 1965-69; project engr. Frank H. Lehr Assocs., East Orange, N.J., 1969-70; sr. soils engr. John G. Reutter Assocs., Camden, 1970-72; asst. prof. Worcester (Mass.) Poly. Inst., 1972-74; prin. soils engr. Daniel, Mann, Johnson & Mendenhall, Balt., 1974-79; sr. engr. Sverdrup Corp., St. Louis, 1979-80, cons., 1980—; prof. Calif. State U., Fresno, 1980—. Cons. Expert Resources, Inc., Peoria Heights, Ill., 1981—, The Twining Labs., Inc., Fresno, 1982—, Law Offices Marderosian and Swanson, Fresno, 1985—, Law Offices Hurlbutt, Clevenger, Long and Vortmann, Visalia, Calif., 1988—, Tech. Adv. Svcs. for Attys., Blue Bell, Pa., 1992—. Author: Fundaciones y Mechanica de Suelos, 1986; contbr. articles to profl. jours. Head sci. judge Calif. Cen. Valleys Sci. and Engring. Fairs, Fresno, 1988—. Recipient Outstanding Prof. of Yr. award Calif. State U., 1989, Halliburton award Calif. State U., 1991, Calif. Ctrl. Valley Outstanding Profl. Engr. award Calif. Soc. Profl. Engrs., 1993, Disting. Svc. award, 1994, Claude C. Laval Jr. award Innovative Tech. and Rsch. Calif. State U., 1991, 92, Portrait of Success award KSEE 24, Fresno, Calif., 1997, Std. of Excellence award Tau Beta Pi, 1997, Outstanding Prof. award Tau Beta Pi, 1998, Outstanding Prof. award NSPE, 1998; Brahma St. named in City of Bakersfield, Calif., 1989; Fulbright scholar, 1984; Hugh B. William fellow, Assn. Drilled Shaft Contractors, 1986, others. Fellow ASCE (v.p. 1983-84, pres. 1984-85, Outstanding Engr. award 1985, Disting Svc. award, 1986, Outstanding Prof. award 1985, Edmund Friedman Profl. Recognition award 1993); mem. ASTM, Am. Soc. Engring. Edn. (AT&T Found. award 1991, Outstanding Tchg. award 1997, AT ANDT Found. award for excellence in tchg. and rsch. 1991), Rotary (chair Clovis club 1986—, chair pub. rels. 1987, chair youth svcs. 1989, bd. dirs. 1989). Democrat. Hindu. Avocations: swimming, tennis, music, reading. Home: 561 Houston Ave Clovis CA 93611-7032 Office: Calif State U Maple And Shaw Ave Fresno CA 93740-0001

BRAINERD, CHARLES J(ON), experimental psychologist, applied mathematician, educator; b. Lansing, Mich., July 30, 1944; emigrated to Can., 1971; s. Charles Donald and Geraldine Elaine (Leffler) B.; m. Susan Haske, Jan. 18, 1964 (div.); 1 dau., Tereasa Gail; m. Valerie Reyna, Oct. 5, 1985; 1 son, Bertrand. B.S., Mich. State U., 1966, M.A., 1968, Ph.D., 1970. Asst. prof. psychology U. Alta., Edmonton, Can., 1971-73, assoc. prof. Can., 1973-76, H.M. Tory prof. social sci. Can., 1983-86; prof. U. Western Ont., London, 1976-83, U. Ariz., Tucson, 1987—. Vis. prof. U. Minn., Mpls., 1980-81, So. Meth. U., Dallas, 1986-87. Author: Piaget's Theory of Intelligence, 1978, Origins of the Number Concept, 1979; editor: Alternatives to Piaget, 1978, Recent Advances in Cognitive Developmental Theory, 1983, Springer-Verlag Series in Cognitive Development, 1979— ; assoc. editor: Behavioral and Brain Scis., 1980— . Fellow Am. Psychol. [illegible] (pres. devel. psychology sect. 1980-81), mem. Psychonomic Soc., Soc. for Research in Child Devel. ([illegible] Child Devel. 1977-80). Office: U Ariz Coll Edn Tucson AZ 85721-0001

BRAKEBILL, JEAN NEWTON, career officer, nurse, educator; b. Mobile, Ala., Sept. 4, 1953; d. James Harold and Eleanor (Mrotek) Newton; m. James Arden Brakebill, Dec. 15, 1985; 1 child, Justin James. BS in Nursing, West Tex. State U., 1975; MS, Corpus Christi U., 1982; MBA in Health Adminstrn., Nat. U., 1987. RN, Tex. Staff nurse Southwestern Gen. Hosp., El Paso, Tex., 1975-76; commd. ensign U.S. Navy, 1976, advanced through grades to capt., 1998, staff nurse Naval Hosp. S.C., 1976-78, Okinawa, Japan, 1978-80, head nurse ICU Corpus Christi, Tex., 1980-83, head nurse, clin. cons., program adminstr. Naval Hosp. San Diego, 1983-89; div. head med. surg. ward Naval Hosp., Long Beach, Calif., 1989-90, clin. nurse specialist inpatient nursing, 1990-91, head dept. inpatient nursing, 1991-92, head dept. command edn. and tng., 1992-93; command edn. and tng. program adminstr. Naval Med. Ctr., Portsmouth, Va., 1993-95; head dept. command staff edn. and tng. Twenty-Nine Palms Naval Hosp., Marine Corps Air Ground Ctr., Calif., 1995-98; dir. nursing svcs. Twenty-Nine Palms Naval Hosp., 1998-2001; instr. first aid, CPR ARC, 1998—. Instr. trainer BLS Am. Heart Assn., various locations, 1985—; advanced trauma life support educator, San Diego, 1987-91; Red Cross nurse. Mem. Kappa Delta. Roman Catholic. Avocations: guitar, needlework, reading, swimming, art. Office: Naval Hosp Marine Corps Air Ground Combat Ctr Command Ste Twentynine Palms CA 92288 E-mail: brakebill002@earthlink.net

BRAKHAGE, JAMES STANLEY, filmmaker, educator; b. Kansas City, Mo., Jan. 14, 1933; s. Ludwig and Clara (Dubberstein) B.; m. Mary Jane Collom, Dec. 28, 1957 (div. 1987); children: Myrrena, Crystal, Neowyn, Bearthm, Rarc; m. Marilyn Jull, Mar. 30, 1989; children: Anton, Vaughn. PhD, San Francisco Art Inst., 1981; PhD (hon.), Calif. Arts, 1994, Bard Coll., 2000. Lectr. Sch. Art Inst. Chgo., 1969-81; prof. U. Colo., Boulder, 1981; mem. Filmmakers Coop., N.Y.C., Canyon Cinema Coop., San Francisco, London Filmmakers Coop., Can. Filmmakers' Distbn. Ctr., Toronto, Lightcone, Paris, France. Faculty lectr. U. Colo., 1990-91. Films include Interim, 1952, Anticipation of the Night, 1958, The Dead, 1960, Blue Moses, 1962, Dog Star Man, 1964, Songs in 8mm, 1964-69, Scenes from Under Childhood, 1967-70, The Weir Falcon Saga, 1970, The Act of Seeing with One's Own Eyes, 1971, The Riddle of Lumen, 1972, Sincerity and Duplicity, 1973-80, The Text of Light, 1974, Desert, 1976, The Governor, 1977, Burial Path, 1978, Nightmare Series, 1978, Creation, 1979, Made Manifest, 1980, Salome, 1980, Murder Psalm, 1980, Roman Numeral Series, 1979-81, the Arabic series, 1980-82, Unconscious London Strata, 1982, Tortured Dust, 1984, The Egyptian Series, 1984, The Loom, 1986, Nightmusic, 1986, The Dante Quartet, 1987, Faust, parts I-IV, 1987-89, Marilyn's Window, 1988, Visions in Meditation, 1989-90, City Streaming, 1990, Glaze of Cathexis, 1990, Babylonian Series, 1989-90, Passage Through: A Ritual, 1990, A Child's Garden and the Serious Sea, 1991, Delicacies of Molten Horror Synapse, 1991, Christ Mass Sex Dance, 1991, Crack Glass Eulogy, 1992, Boulder Blues and Pearls and For Marilyn, Interpolations 1-5, 1992, Blossom Gift Favor, The Harrowing, Tryst Haunt, Study in Color and Black and White, Stellar, Atumnal, 1993, Three Homerics, 1993, Naughts, Chartres Series, Ephemeral Solidity, Elementary Phrases, Black Ice, First Hymn to the Night—Novalis, 1994, In Consideration of Pompeii, 1994, The Mammals of Victoria, 1994, Paranoia Corridor, 1994, Can Not Exist, 1994, Can Not Exist, 1994, I Take These Truths, 1994, We Hold These, 1994, I..., 1995, Earthen Aerie, 1995, Spring Cycle, 1995, The Lost Films, 1995, The B Series, 1995, Preludes 1-24, 1995, 96, The Fur of Home, 1996, Beautiful Funerals, 1996, Polite Madness, 1996, Shockingly Hot, 1996, Sexual Saga, 1996, The Lost Films, 1996, Comingled Containers, 1996, Yggdrasill Whose Roots Are Stars in the Human Mind, 1997, Last Hymn to the Night - Novalis, 1997, I...Sleeping, 1989, Selfsong/Deathsong, 1998, "..." Reels 1-5, 1998, The Birds of Paradise, 1999, The Lion and the Zebra Make God's Raw Jewels, 1999, The Earth Song of the Cricket, 1999, Cricket Requiem, 1999, Worm and Web Love, 1999, Persian Series 1-5, 1999, Moilsome Toilsome, 1999, The Dark Tower, 1999, Cloud Chamber, 1999, The God of Day Had Gone Down Upon Him, 2000, Water for Maya, 2000, Persian Series 6-12, 2000, Jesus Trilogy and Coda, 2001, Persian Series 13-18, 2001, Dance, 2000, Occam's Thread, 2000, Rounds, 2000, Lovesong, 2001, Lovesong 2, 2001, Microgarden, 2001; author: Metaphors on Vision, 1963, A Moving Picture Giving and Taking Book, 1971, The Brakhage Lectures, 1972, Seen, 1975, Film Biographies, 1977, Brakhage Scrapbook, 1982, Film at Wits End, 1989, Phillip Taffee: A Long Conversation with Stan Brakhage, 1998, The Essential Brakhage, 2001. Recipient Brussels Worlds Fair Protest award, 1958, Brandeis citation, 1973, Colo. Gov.'s award for arts and humanities, 1974, Jimmy Ryan Morris Meml. Found. award, 1979, Telluride Film Festival medallion, 1981, Maya Deren award Am. Film Inst., 1986, medal U. Colo., 1988, Outstanding Achievement award Denver Internat. Film Festival, 1988, MacDowell medal, 1989, Libr. Congress Nat. Film Registry, 1992, Anthology Film Archives honor, 1993, The Colo. 100 Cert. of Recognition, 1993, Disting. Prof. award U. Colo., 1994; retrospective Mus. Modern Art, 1995; grantee Avon Found., 1965-69, NEA, 1974-75, 77, 80, 83, 88, U. Colo. Coun. Rsch. and Creative Work, 1983, Rocky Mountain Film Ctr., 1985; Rockefeller fellow, 1967-69, Guggenheim fellow, 1978. Democrat. Home: 2222 Walnut St # 3 Boulder CO 80302-4619 Office: U Colo Film Studies Hunter 102 PO Box 316 Boulder CO 80309-0316

BRAKKEN, WILLIAM, home improvement retail executive; Exec. v.p., CFO, sec. and treas. Lanoga Corp., Redmond, Wash. Office: Lanoga Corp PO Box 97040 Redmond WA 98073 Office Fax: (426) 882-2959

BRAMBLE, CURTIS S. state legislator; b. Chgo., Oct. 18, 1953; Mem. Utah State Senate, Salt Lake City, 2001—. Office: 3663 N 870 E Provo UT 84604 E-mail: brambleco@itsnet.com*

BRAMMER, J. WILLIAM, JR. judge, lawyer; b. Des Moines, Sept. 15, 1942; s. James W. and Mary Virginia (Steck) B.; m. Donna Crosby, June 20, 1964; children: Jill S., James W. III. BS, U. Ariz., 1964, JD, 1967. Bar: Ariz. 1967, U.S. Dist. Ct. Ariz. 1968, U.S. Ct. Appeals (9th cir.) 1970, U.S. Supreme Ct. 1970. Law clk. to judge Ariz. Ct. Appeals, Tucson, 1967-68; asst. atty. City of Tucson, 1968; from assoc. to ptnr. DeConcini, McDonald, Brammer, Yetwin & Lacy PC, Tucson, 1968-97; judge Ariz. Ct. of Appeals, Tucson, 1997—. Com. examinations Ariz. Supreme Ct., Phoenix, 1977-84, chmn. 1982-84. Bd. visitors U. Ariz. Coll. Law, Tucson, 1981-84, 88—. Fellow Ariz. Bar Found.; mem. ABA, Pima County Bar Assn. (pres. 1993-94), Law Coll. Assn. U. Ariz. (pres. 1990-91). Office: Ariz Ct Appeals 400 W Congress St Ste 302 Tucson AZ 85701-1353 E-mail: brammer@apltwo.ct.state.az.us

BRAMSON, EDWARD J. electronics corporation executive, financial executive; b. 1952; Student, London U. V.p., mng. dir. Hillside Capital, 1976—; v.p. Ampex Corp., also dir. Office: Ampex Corp 401 Broadway, MS1101 Redwood City CA 94063-3126

BRANCA, JOHN GREGORY, lawyer, consultant; b. Bronxville, N.Y., Dec. 11, 1950; s. John Ralph and Barbara (Werle) B. AB in Polit. Sci. cum laude, Occidental Coll., 1972; JD, UCLA, 1975. Bar: Calif. 1975. Assoc. Kindel & Anderson, Los Angeles, 1975-77, Hardee, Barovick, Konecky & Braun, Beverly Hills, Calif., 1977-81; ptnr. Ziffren, Brittenham, Branca & Fischer, L.A., 1981—. Cons. N.Y. State Assembly, Mt. Vernon, 1978-82, various music industry orgns., L.A., 1981—. Editor-in-Chief UCLA-Alaska Law Rev., 1974-75; contbr. articles to profl. jours. Cons., bd. trustees UCLA Law Sch. Com., UCLA Athletic Dept., Occidental Coll., Musician's Assistance Program, 1995. Recipient Bancroft-Whitney award; named Entertainment Lawyer of Yr. Am. Lawyer mag., 1981. Mem. ABA (patent trademark and copyright law sect.), Calif. Bar Assn., Beverly Hills Bar Assn. (entertainment law sect.), Phi Alpha Delta, Sigma Tau Sigma. Avocations: art, antiques, music, real estate. Office: Ziffren Brittenham Branca & Fischer 1801 Century Park W Fl 9 Los Angeles CA 90067-6406

BRANCH, W. RIC, state legislator; b. Weiser, Idaho, Aug. 5, 1955; m. Cory Branch; children: LaBree, Ross, Victoria. Student, U. Idaho, We. Coll. Auctioneering. Cattle rancher; mem. Idaho Senate, Dist. 9, Boise, 1995—. Chair agrl. affairs com., 1994—; mem. commerce and human resources, local govt. and tax., and resources and environment coms.; mem. Washington County state com., 1988—. Bd. dirs., Idaho Rural Devel. Coun.; sch. bd. trustee, 1989-95. Recipient Friend of Agr. award, Farm Bur. Fedn., 1996. Mem. NRA, Farm Bur., Idaho Cattle Assn. (chair rsch. and edn. com.), Weiser River Cattle Assn. (bd. dirs.), Indian Mountain Grazing Assn. (v.p.), Fruitland (Idaho) C. of C., Fayette (Idaho) C. of C. Republican. Protestant. Office: State Capitol PO Box 83720 Boise ID 83720-3720

BRAND, VANCE DEVOE, astronaut; b. Longmont, Colo., May 9, 1931; s. Rudolph William and Donna (DeVoe) B.; m. Joan Virginia Weninger, July 25, 1953; children: Susan Nancy, Stephanie, Patrick Richard, Kevin Stephen; m. Beverly Ann Whitnel, Nov. 3, 1979; children: Erik Ryan, Dane Vance. BS in Bus., U. Colo., 1953, BS in Aero. Engring., 1960; MBA, UCLA, 1964; grad., U.S. Naval Test Pilot Sch., Patuxent River, Md., 1963; DSc (hon.), U. Colo., 2000. With Lockheed-Calif. Co., Burbank, 1960-66, flight test engr., 1961-62, traveling engr. rep., 1962-63, engring. test pilot, 1963-66; astronaut NASA Johnson Space Ctr., Houston, 1966-92, command module pilot Apollo-Soyuz mission, 1975, comdr. STS-5 Mission, 1982, comdr. STS 41-B Mission, 1984, comdr. STS-35 Mission, 1990; chief plans Nat. Aero-Space Plane Joint Program Office, Wright-Patterson AFB, Ohio, 1992-94; asst. chief flight ops. directorate DFRC NASA, Edwards, Calif., 1994-98, dep. dir. aerospace projects, 1998—. With USMCR, 1953-57. Decorated 2 Disting. Svc. medals NASA, 2 Exceptional Svc. medals, 3 Space medals; indeucted into Internat. Space Hall of Fame, 1996, U.S. Astronaut Hall of Fame, 1997, Internat. Aerspace Hall of Fame, 2001. Fellow AIAA, Am. Astron. Soc., Soc. Exptl. Test Pilots. Office: M/S D2332 DFRC PO Box 273 Edwards CA 93523-0273

BRANDENBERG, FRANK G. electronics executive; B in Indsl. Engring., M in Ops. Rsch., Wayne State U. Various Burroughs Corp., UNISYS Corp., 1987-97; pres., CEO EA Industries, Inc., 1997-99; corp. sr. v.p., group exec. elec. components & materials Litton Industries, Inc., Woodland Hills, Calif., 1999—. Office: Litton Industries Inc 21240 Burbank Blvd Woodland Hills CA 91367-6675

BRANDES, STANLEY HOWARD, anthropology educator, writer; b. N.Y.C., Dec. 26, 1942; s. Emanuel Robert and Annette (Zalisch) B.; divorced; children: Nina Rachel, Naomi Clara. BA, U. Chgo., 1964; MA, U. Calif., Berkeley, 1969, PhD, 1971. Asst. prof. anthropology Mich. State U., East Lansing, 1971-75; asst. prof. anthropology U. Calif., Berkeley, 1975-78, assoc. prof., 1978-82, prof. anthropology, 1982—, chmn. dept., 1990-93, 97-99. Dir. Barcelona Study Ctr., U. Calif. and Ill., Spain, 1981-82, Mexico City Study Ctr., 1995-96, U. Calif. Author: Migration, Kinship and Community, 1975, Metaphors of Masculinity, 1980, Forty: The Age and the Symbol, 1985, Power and Persuasion, 1988; co-editor: Symbol as Sense, 1980. NIH fellow, 1967-71; NICHD Rsch. fellow, 1975-77; fellow John Carter Brown Libr., 1994; Am. Council Learned Socs. grantee, 1977 Fellow Am. Anthrop. Assn.; mem. Am. Ethnological Soc., Soc. for Psychol. Anthropology Office: U Calif Dept Anthropology Berkeley CA 94720-0001

BRANDHORST, BRUCE PETER, biology educator; b. Galveston, Tex., Nov. 14, 1944; s. William Schroeder Brandhorst and Emilie Pontz Pickering; m. Elaine Golds; children: Gregory, Gary. AB, Harvard U., 1966; PhD, U. Calif., San Diego, 1971. Rsch. assoc. U. Colo., Boulder, 1971-73; from asst. to assoc. to prof. McGill U., Montreal, Que., Can., 1973-89; prof., dir. Inst. Molecular Biology and Biochemistry Simon Fraser U., Burnaby, B.C., Can., 1989-99, assoc. dir. Inst. Health Rsch. Can., 2001—. Instr. embryology Marine Biol. Lab., Woods Hole, Mass., 1980-82, co-dir. embryology course, 1983-88. Mem. editorial bd. (serials) Molecular and Cellular Biology, 1985-91, Molecular Reproduction and Development, 1988—, exec. editor, 1996—. Rsch. grantee Natural Scis. and Engring. Rsch. Coun., Can., 1973—, NIH, McGill U., 1984-90. Mem. Can. Soc. for Biochemistry and Cell and Molecular Biology, Soc. for Developmental Biology, Marine Biology Lab. Corp. Achievements include research in regulation of gene expression and cellular interactions in developing embryos. Office: Simon Fraser U Inst Molecular Biol Burnaby BC Canada V5A 1S6 E-mail: brandhor@sfu.ca

BRANDLER, JONATHAN M. lawyer; b. L.A., Jan. 8, 1946; AB, U. Calif., Berkeley, 1967; JD, U. So. Calif., 1970. Bar: Calif. 1971. Ptnr. Hill, Farrer & Burrill LLP, L.A. Lectr. Inst. Bus. Law, 1981-92. Mem. State Bar Calif. (labor law sect.), L.A. County Bar Assn. (labor law sect.). Office: Hill Farrer & Burrill LLP 1 California Plaza 300 S Grand Ave Ste 37 Los Angeles CA 90071-3110 E-mail: jbrandler@hfbllp.com

BRANDON, KATHRYN ELIZABETH BECK, pediatrician; b. Sept. 10, 1916; d. Clarence M. and Hazel A. (Cutler) Beck; children: John William, Kathleen Brandon McEnulty, Karen (dec.). MD, U. Chgo., 1941; BA, U. Utah, 1937; MPH, U. Calif., Berkeley, 1957. Diplomate Am. Bd. Pediats. Intern Grace Hosp., Detroit, 1941-42; resident Children's Hosp. Med. Ctr. No. Calif., Oakland, 1953-55, Children's Hosp., L.A., 1951-53; pvt. practice La Crescentia, Calif., 1946-51, Salt Lake City, 1960-65, 86—. Med. dir. Salt Lake City public schs., 1957-60; dir. Ogden City-Weber County (Utah) Health Dept., 1965-67; pediatrician Fitzsimmons Army Hosp., 1967-68; coll. health physician U. Colo., Boulder, 1968-71; student health physician U. Utah, Salt Lake City, 1971-81; occupational health physician Hill AFB, Utah, 1981-85; child health physician Salt Lake City-County Health Dept., 1971-82; cons. in field; clin. asst. U. Utah Coll. Medicine, Salt Lake City, 1958-64; clin. asst. pediatrics U. Colo. Coll. Medicine, Denver, 1958-72; active staff emeritus Primary Children's Hosp., LDS Hosp., and Cottonwood Hosp., 1960-67. Fellow APHA, Am. Pediat. Acad., Am. Sch. Health Assn.; mem. AMA, Utah Coll. Health Assn. (pres. 1978-80), Pacific Coast Coll. Health Assn., Utah Med. Assn., Salt Lake County Med. Soc., Utah Pub. Health Assn. (sec.-treas. 1960-66), Intermountain Pediat. Soc. Home and Office: PO Box 58482 Salt Lake City UT 84158-0482

BRANDSTATER, MURRAY EVERETT, physiatrist; b. Hobart, Australia, Apr. 21, 1935; MB, BS, U. Melbourne, Australia, 1957. Cert. in Phys. Med. Rehab. Intern Box Hill Dist. Hosp., Melbourne, 1958; resident in internal medicine Alfred Hosp., Melbourne, 1959, 61-62; resident Royal Children's Hosp., Melbourne, 1960; rsch. in phys. med. rehab. Mayo Clinic, Rochester, Minn., 1964-68; prof. phys. med. rehab. McMaster U., Hamilton, Ont., Can., 1968-84; mem. staff Loma Linda (Calif.) U. Med. Ctr., 1984—; prof. phys. med. rehab. Loma Linda U., 1981—. Mem. AMA, AAEM, MRCP, RCPC. Office: Loma Linda Univ Med Ctr PO Box 2000 Dept Rehab Medicine Rm A237 Loma Linda CA 92354

BRANDT, HARRY, mechanical engineering educator; b. Amsterdam, The Netherlands, Nov. 14, 1925; came to U.S., 1946, naturalized, 1962; s. Friedrich H. and Henny (Rous) B.; m. Muriel Ruth Harman, Jan. 24, 1953; children: Joyce Estelle, Marilyn Audrey, Robert Alan. B.S., U. Calif.-Berkeley, 1949, M.S., 1950, Ph.D., 1954. Supervising research engr. Chevron Research Co., La Habra, Calif., 1954-64; lectr. UCLA, 1962-64; prof. mech. engring. U. Calif., Davis, 1964—, chmn. dept., 1969-74, 86-91; dir. Internat. Pipeline Techs. Inc., Beaverton, Oreg., 1985-91; chmn. bd. Clean Energy Systems, Inc., 1997—. Cons. Lawrence Livermore Nat. Lab., 1969—, State of Calif., 1970-87, State of Alaska, 1972, Los Alamos Nat. Lab., 1988-93. Mem. ASME, Am. Welding Soc., AIAA, Sigma Xi, Tau Beta Pi. Presbyn. Home: 26934 Middle Golf Dr El Macero CA 95618-1053 Office: U Calif Dept Mech and Aero Engring Davis CA 95616 E-mail: hbrandt@ucdavis.edu

BRANDT, PHILIP H. federal judge; b. Juneau, AK, 1944; BA in Econs., Harvard U., 1966; JD, U. Wash., 1972. Atty. U.S. Dept. Justice and Fed. Maritime Commn., 1972-73; dep. prosecuting atty. Pierce County, Wash., 1973-75; dir. stds. project Wash. Gov.'s Com. on Law and Justice, 1975-76; with LeCocq, Simonarson, et al, 1976-86, Graham & Dunn, 1986-91; apptd. bankruptcy judge U.S. Dist. Ct. (we. dist.) Wash., 1991. Mem. 9th Cir. Bankruptcy Appellate Panel, 1998—. Capt. USNR, 1966-89. Mem. ABA, Wash. State Bar, Nat. Conf. Bankruptcy Judges, Tacoma-Pierce County Bar, King County Bar. Office: Park Place Bldg Ste 315 1200 6th Ave Seattle WA 98102-3123

BRANDT, R. SKIPPER, state senator; b. Grangeville, Idaho, May 26, 1964; m. Pia Brandt; 1 child, Nicolas. Student, U. Idaho, 1982. Mgr. Stites Ace Hardware; Rep. senator dist. 7 Idaho State Senate, 2000—. Mem. coun. City of Kooskia, Idaho, 1991-95; bd. dirs. Idaho County Sheriff's Posse, 1992-97, Clearwater Resource Coalition, 1994-97; mayor City of Kooskia, 1998—. Office: PO Box 296 Kooskia ID 83539 also: Idaho State Senate State Capitol 700 W Jefferson Boise ID 83720-0081 E-mail: skip@cybrquest.com

BRANDT, RICHARD PAUL, communications and entertainment company executive; b. N.Y.C., Dec. 6, 1927; s. Harry and Helen (Satenstein) B.; m. Helen H. Kogel, May 31, 1975; children: Claudia, David, Matthew, Thomas; 1 stepdau., Jennifer. BS with high honors, Yale U., 1948. With Trans-Lux Theatres Corp., 1950-54, v.p., 1952-54; with Trans-Lux Corp., Norwalk, Conn., 1954—, v.p., 1959-62, pres., 1962-80, chmn. bd., 1974—, chief exec. officer, 1974-92; dir. Am. Book-Stratford Press, Inc., 1962-87, Brandt Theatres, Presdl. Realty Corp.; founding gov. Ind. Film Importers & Distbrs. Am., 1959-63, bd. dirs., 1959-69; v.p., mem. exec. com. Theatre Owners Am., 1962-65; mem. bill of rights com. Council Motion Picture Orgns., 1963-65; bd. dirs. Film Soc. Lincoln Ctr., 1968-71; mem. N.Y. State Bus. Adv. Com. on Mgmt. Improvement, 1966-70. Chmn. bd. Univ. Settlement Soc., 1964-66, hon. pres., bd. dirs., 1966-77; dir. Am. Theatre Wing, 1970-99, United Neighborhood Houses, 1968-73; bd. dirs., treas. Settlement House Employment Devel., 1969-72; trustee, mem. exec. com. Am. Film Inst., 1971—, vice chmn., 1980-83, chmn. bd., 1983-86, chmn. emeritus 1986—; trustee Mus. Holography, 1979-82; mem. Tony awards mgmt. com., 1986-98; founder Live Poets Soc., 1991—. Vice chmn. bd. Coll. of Santa Fe, 1987-98; trustee Maritime Ctr., Norwalk, 1991-92; treas. bd., exec. com. Coll. of Santa Fe, 1999—; bd. dirs. Taos Talking Pictures Festival, 1998—. Named Exhibitor of Yr., ShoWest, 1984. Mem. Nat. Assn. Theatre Owners (dir. 1957-78, exec. com. 1965-78, Sherrill Corwin award 1983), Phi Beta Kappa, Sigma Xi. Office: Trans-Lux Corp 433 Paseo De Peralta Santa Fe NM 87501-1941

BRANN, ALTON JOSEPH, manufacturing company executive; b. Portland, Maine, Dec. 23, 1941; s. Donald Edward and Marjorie Margaret (Curran) B. BA, U. Mass., 1969. Mgr. advanced programs Dynamics Research Corp., Wilmington, Mass., 1969-73; dir. engring. Litton Guidance & Control Systems, L.A., 1973-79, dir. program mgmt., 1979-81, v.p. engring., 1981-83, pres., 1983-86; group exec. Navigation Guidance and Control Systems Group, Beverly Hills, Calif., 1986-88; sr. v.p. Components and Indsl. Products Group Litton Industries, Beverly Hills, 1988-90, pres., COO, 1990-92, CEO, 1992-94, chmn., 1994-96; chmn., CEO Western Atlas Inc., Beverly Hills, 1994-97, UNOVA Inc., Beverly Hills, 1997—. Trustee Mfrs. Alliance Productivity and Innovation, coun. fgn. diplomacy, U.S.-Russia bus. coun. Mem. IEEE (sr. mem.), Optical Soc. Am., L.A. World Affairs Coun., Town Hall of L.A. Avocations: skiing, sailing. Office: UNOVA 21900 Burbank Blvd Ste 300 Woodland Hills CA 91367-7456

BRANNEN, JEFFREY RICHARD, lawyer; b. Tampa, Fla., Aug. 27, 1945; s. Jackson Edward and Tobiah M. (Lovitz) B.; m. Mary Elizabeth Strand, Nov. 24, 1972; 1 child, Samuel Jackson. BA in English, U. N.Mex., 1967, JD, 1970. Bar: N.Mex. 1970, U.S. Dist. Ct. N.Mex. 1970, U.S. Ct. Appeals (10th cir.) 1976, U.S. Supreme Ct. 1978. Law clk. N.Mex. State Supreme Ct., Santa Fe, 1970-71; from assoc. to pres., shareholder Montgomery & Andrews, pa, Santa Fe, 1972-93; pres. Jeffrey R. Brannen, P.A., Santa Fe, 1993—; of counsel Comeau, Maldegan, Templeman & Indall (formerly known as Carpenter, Maldegan, Templeman & Indall), Santa Fe, 1995—. Faculty Nat. Inst. Trial Advocacy, Hastings Ctr. for Trial & Appellate Advocacy, 1980-93; co-chmn. Pers. Injury Inst., Hastings, 1992. Named one of Best Lawyers in Am. for personal injury and civil litig., 2001—. Mem. ABA, Am. Bd. Trial Advocates (N.Mex. pres. 1998), Assn. Def. Trial Attys. (state chmn. 1992—), Def. Rsch. Inst. (Exceptional Performance Citation 1989), N.Mex. Def. Lawyers Assn. (pres. 1989). Democrat. Avocations: skiing, soccer, fly fishing, travel. Office: Comeau Maldegan Templeman & Indall 141 E Palace Ave Santa Fe NM 87501-2041 Fax: (505) 982-4611. E-mail: jbrannen@cmtisantafe

BRANSON, ALBERT HAROLD (HARRY BRANSON), judge, educator; b. Chgo., May 20, 1935; s. Fred Brooks and Marie (Vowell) B.; m. Siri-Anne Gudrun Lindberg, Nov. 2, 1963; children: Gunnar John, Gulliver Dean, Hannah Marie, Siri Elizabeth. BA, Northwestern U., 1957; JD, U. Chgo., 1963. Bar: Pa. 1965, Alaska 1972. Atty. Richard McVeigh law offices, Anchorage, 1972-73; ptnr. Jacobs, Branson & Guetschow, Anchorage, 1973-76, Branson & Guetschow, Anchorage, 1976-82; pvt. practice Law Offices of Harry Branson, Anchorage, 1982-84, 85-89; atty. Branson, Bazeley & Chisolm, Anchorage, 1984-85; U.S. magistrate judge U.S. Dist. Ct., Anchorage, 1989—. Instr., adj. prof. U. Alaska Justice Ctr., 1980-93; U.S. magistrate, Anchorage, 1975-76. Mem. steering com. Access to Civil Justice Task Force, 1997-98. With U.S. Army, 1957-59. Mem. Alaska Bar Assn. (bd. dirs., v.p. bd. govs. 1977-80, 83-86, pres. bd. govs. 1986, Disting. Svc. award 1992, Spl. Svc. award 1988, editor-in-chief Alaska Bar Rag 1978-86), Anchorage Bar Assn. (bd. dirs., bd. govs. 1982-86), Anchorage Inn of Ct. (pres. 1995). Democrat. Avocations: book collecting, cooking, poetry. Office: US Dist Ct 222 W 7th Ave Unit 33 Anchorage AK 99513-7504

BRANTINGHAM, BARNEY, journalist, writer; b. Chgo., Feb. 26, 1932; s. Carl Brantingham and Frances Bell; m. Angela Mendez, Oct. 30, 1957 (div.); children: Barclay Carl, Frances, Wendy, Kenneth. Grad., U. Ill., 1954. Reporter Star Newspapers, Chicago Heights, Ill., 1957-59; editor San Clemente (Calif.) Sun-Post, 1959-60; reporter Santa Barbara (Calif.) News-Press, 1960—, columnist, 1977—. Commentator Sta. KTMS, Santa Barbara, 1989-91, Sta. KIST, Santa Barbara, 1991, SAM, 1990, 92; radio sta. feature and travel commentator KQSB, 1994-97; co-host Around the World with Arthur and Barney, Sta. KTMS, 1998, KEYT-AM, 1998—; founding dir. Opinionated Traveler internet site www.opinionatedtraveler-.com. Prodr. TV program Santa Barbara Traveler; author: The Pro Football Hall of Fame, 1988, Barney's Santa Barbara, 1989, Around Santa Barbara County with Barney, 1992; co-dir. The Opinionated Traveler Internet Site. With U.S. Army, 1955-57. Mem. Internat. Food, Wine and Travel Writers Assn. (dir. 1991-95), Am. Travel Media Assn. (bd. dirs.). Avocation: travel. Office: Santa Barbara News-Press PO Box 1359 Santa Barbara CA 93102-1359 E-mail: bbrantingham@newspress.com

BRANTINGHAM, PAUL JEFFREY, criminology educator; b. Long Beach, Calif., June 29, 1943; s. Charles Ross and Lila Carolyn (Price) B.; m. Patricia Louise Matthews, Aug. 26, 1967; 1 child, Paul Jeffrey Jr. BA, Columbia U., 1965, JD, 1968; Diploma in Criminology, Cambridge U., 1970. Bar: Calif. 1969. Asst. prof. Fla. State U., Tallahassee, 1971-76, assoc. prof., 1976-77, Simon Fraser U., Burnaby, B.C., Can., 1977-85, assoc. dean faculty interdisciplinary studies Can., 1980-82, prof. Can., 1985—; dir. spl. revs. Pub. Svc. Commn. Can., Ottawa, Ont., 1985-87. Editor: Juvenile Justice Philosophy, 1974, 2d edit. 1978, Environmental Criminology, 1981, 2d edit. 1991; author: Patterns in Crime. Recipient Eisenhower Watch award Columbia U., 1966; Ford Found. fellow, 1969-70, Western Soc. Criminology fellow, 1996, Sr. fellow Fraser Inst. Mem. ABA, Calif. Bar Assn., Am. Soc. Criminology (chmn. nat. program 1978), Acad. Criminal Justice Scis., Canadian Criminal Justice Assn., Soc. for Reform of Criminal Law, Western Soc. Criminology (v.p. 2000-01, pres. 2001-02). Home: 4680 Eastridge Rd North Vancouver BC Canada V7G 1K4 Office: Simon Fraser U Sch Criminol 8888 University Dr WMC 2630 Burnaby BC Canada V5A 1S6 E-mail: branting@sfu.ca

BRASEL, JO ANNE, pediatrician, educator; b. Salem, Ill., Feb. 15, 1934; d. Gerald Nolan and Ruby Rachel (Rich) B. BA, U. Colo., 1956, MD, 1959. Diplomate in pediatrics and pediatric endocrinology Am. Bd. Pediatrics. Pediatric intern, resident Cornell U. Med. Coll.-N.Y. Hosp., N.Y.C., 1959-62; fellow in pediatric endocrine Johns hOpkions U. Sch. Medicine, Balt., 1962-65, asst. prof. pediatrics, 1965-68; asst. prof., then assoc. prof. pediatrics Cornell U. Med. Coll., N.Y.C., 1969-72; assoc. prof., then prof. pediatrics Columbia U. Phys. and Syrg., N.Y.C., 1972-79; asst. prof. pediatrics Harbor-UCLA Med. Ctr./UCLA Sch. Medicine, 1979—, program dir. Gen. Clin. Rsch. Ctr., 1979-93, prof. medicine, 1980—; Joseph W. St. Geme, Jr. prof. pediatrics UCLA Sch. Medicine, 1999&. Mem. adv. com. FDA, Rockville, Md., 1971-75; mem. nutrition study sect. NIH, Bethesda, Md., 1974-78; mem. select panel for promotion of child health HEW, Washington, 1979-80; mem. life scis. adv. screening com. Fulbrifht-Hays program, Washington, 1981-84; mem. digestive disease and nutrition grant rev. group NIADDK, 1985-89; mem. U.S. Govt. Task Force on Women, Minorities and the Handicapped in Sci. and Tech., 1987-89. Recipient Rsch. Career Devel. award NIH, 1973-77, Irma T. Hirschl Trust Career Sci. award, 1974-79, Sr. Fulbright Sabbatical Rsch. award, 1980. Mem. Soc. Pediatric Rsch. (sec.-treas. 1973-77, pres. 1978-79), Am. Fedn. Clin. Rsch., Endocrine Soc., Am. Soc. Clin. Nutrition, Am. Inst. Nutrition, Western Assn. Physicians, Lawson Wilkins Pediatric Endocrine Soc. (bd. dirs. 1972-74, pres. 1992-93), Western Soc. Pediatric Rsch., Phi Beta Kappa, Alpha Omega Alpha. Office: Harbor-UCLA Med Ctr Box 446 1000 W Carson St Torrance CA 90502-2004 E-mail: brasel@gcrc.humc.edu

BRASSWEL, KERRY, tax accountant; d. J.D. Jr. and Kathryn Elizabeth (Rimmer) Braswell. Student, Occidental Coll., L.A., 1964-66. Cert. tax profl. Am. Inst. Tax Studies; qualified Ariz. and Calif. Superior Cts. and Fed. Ct. Bus. mgr. to entertainers Segal, Skaff and Co., L.A., 1968, Cary Harwin and Assocs., Beverly Hills, Calif., 1968-72, Bisgeier, Breslauer and Co., L.A., 1972-74, M. Klaiman Accountancy Corp., Beverly Hills, 1974-75, Michael L. Laney, CPA, Beverly Hills, 1975-77; pvt. practice Tucson, 1977—. Owner Brasswel Arabians, L.A. 1966-76, KaBeAraby, Tucson, 1977—; appraiser St. Paul's Ins. Co., St. Paul, Minn.; equine, also accounting expert witness; lectr. herbal horse care. Author: Herbal Horse Handbook, 1989. Judge, leader 4-H Club, Tucson, 1981-84; travel del. Calif. Horsemans People to People Goodwill Tour, 1970. Mem. Nat. Soc. Tax Profls., Arabian Horse Registry Am., Internat. Arabian Horse Assn. (judge 1976-83), Am. Horse Show Assn. (judge 1976-83), Desert Show Horse Assn. (bd. dirs. 1980-83), So. Ariz. Arabian Horse Assn. (cert. appreciation 1978). Republican. Avocations: sidereal astrology, holistic herbalogy, organic gardening. Home and Office: 10151 W Picture Rocks Rd Tucson AZ 85743-9386 E-mail: kabearaby@surfree.com

BRATTON, HOWARD CALVIN, federal judge; b. Clovis, N.Mex., Feb. 4, 1922; s. Sam Gilbert and Vivian (Rogers) B. BA, U. N.Mex., 1941, LLB, 1971, Yale U., 1947. Bar: N.Mex. 1948. Law clk. U.S. Cir. Ct. Appeals, 1948; ptnr. Grantham & Bratton, Albuquerque, 1949-52; spl. asst. U.S. atty. charge litigation OPS, 1951-52; assoc., then ptnr. Hervy, Dow & Hinkle, Roswell, N.Mex., 1952-64; judge U.S. Dist. Ct. N.Mex., Albuquerque, 1964-87, chief judge, 1978-87, sr. judge Las Cruces, 1987—. Chmn. N.Mex. Jr. Bar Assn., 1952; pres. Chaves County (N.Mex.) Bar Assn., 1962; chmn. pub. lands com. N.Mex. Oil and Gas Assn., 1961-64, Interstate Oil Compact Commn., 1963-64; mem. N.Mex. Commn. Higher Edn., 1962-64, Jud. Conf. of U.S. Com. on Operation of Jury Sys., 1966-72, 79-85, Jud. Conf. U.S. Com. on Ethics, 1987-92; mem. Ad Hoc Com. on Internat. Jud. Rels., 1992-94; 10th cir. rep. Jud. Conf. U.S., 1984-86. Bd. regents U. N.Mex., 1958-68, pres., 1963-64; bd. dirs. Fed. Jud. Ctr., 1983-87. Served to capt. AUS, 1942-45. Mem. Trial Judges Assn. 10th Circuit (pres. 1976-78), Nat. Conf. Fed. Trial Judges (exec. com. 1977-79), Sigma Chi. Office: US Dist Ct 200 E Griggs Ave Las Cruces NM 88001-3523

BRATTSTROM, BAYARD HOLMES, biology educator; b. Chgo., July 3, 1929; s. Wilber LeRoy and Violet (Holmes) B.; m. Cecile D. Funk, June 15, 1952 (div. May 1975); children: Theodore Allen, David Arthur.; m. Martha Isaacs Marsh, July 8, 1982. B.S., San Diego State Coll., 1951; M.A., UCLA, 1953, Ph.D., 1959. Dir. edn. Natural History Mus., San Diego, 1949-51, asst. curator herpetology, 1949-51; assoc. zoology UCLA, 1954-56; research fellow paleoecology Calif. Inst. Tech., Pasadena, 1955; instr. biology Adelphi U., Garden City, N.Y., 1956-60; asst. prof. Calif. State U., Fullerton, 1960-61, assoc. prof., 1961-66, prof., 1966-94, prof. emeritus, 1994—. Co-owner Horned Lizard Ranch, Horned Lizard Press; rschr., author publs. in osteology, ecology, conservation, zoogeography of vertebrates, social behavior; hon. rsch. assoc. herpetology, vertebrate paleontology Los Angeles County Mus., 1961—; pres. Fullerton Youth Mus. and Natural Sci. Ctr., 1962-64, dir., 1962-66; assoc. prof. zoology UCLA, summers 1962-63; vis. prof. zoology Sydney U., Australia, 1978, U. Queensland, Brisbane, Australia, 1984; vis. rschr. James Cook U., Townsville, Australia, 1993-94; ecol. cons. to numerous govtl. agys. and pvt. corps. Author: (with M. A. Brattstrom) Aussie Slang, 2000, poetry The Talon Digs Deeply into My Heart, 1974; Contbr. chpts. to books. Recipient Disting. Teaching award Calif. State U., Fullerton, 1968, Dean's award for Outstanding Teaching and Rsch., 1992; Am. Philos. Soc. grantee to Mex., 1958, to Panama, 1959; NSF grantee, 1964-66; NSF fellow Monash U., Australia, 1966-67. Fellow AAAS (mem. coun. 1965-90), Herpetological League; mem. Am. Soc. Ichthyologists and Herpetologists (bd. govs. 1962-66, v.p. western div. 1965), Orange County Zool. Soc. (mem. bd. 1962-65, pres. 1962-64), So. Calif. Acad. Sci. (dir. 1964-67), Ecol. Soc. Am., Soc. for Study Evolution, Soc. Systematic Zoology, San Diego Soc. Natural History, Soc. Vertebrate Paleontology, Am. Soc. Mammalogists, Cooper Ornithol. Soc., Am. Ornithol. Soc., Am. Soc. Zoologists, Sigma Xi.

BRAUMAN, JOHN I. chemist, educator; b. Pitts., Sept. 7, 1937; s. Milton and Freda E. (Schlitt) B.; m. Sharon Lea Kruse, Aug. 22, 1964; 1 dau., Kate Andrea. BS, MIT, 1959; PhD (NSF fellow), U. Calif., Berkeley, 1963. NSF postdoctoral fellow UCLA, 1962-63; asst. prof. chemistry Stanford (Calif.) U., 1963-69, asso. prof., 1969-72, prof., 1972-80, J.G. Jackson-C.J. Wood prof. chemistry, 1980—, chmn. dept., 1979-83, 95-96, cognizant dean phys. scis. Cons. in phys. organic chemistry; adv. panel chemistry divsn. NSF, 1974-78; adv. panel NASA, AEC, ERDA, Rsch. Corp., Office Chemistry and Chem. Tech., NRC; coun. Gordon Rsch. Confs., 1989-95, trustee, 1991-95. Mem. editl. adv. bd. Jour. Am. Chem. Soc., 1976-83, Jour. Organic Chemistry, 1974-78, Nouveau Jour. de Chimie, 1977-85, Chem. Revs., 1978-80, Chem. Kinetics, 1987-89, Accts. Chem. Rsch., 1995-97, 98—; bd. trustees Ann. Revs., 1995—, mem. editl. adv. bd.; dep. editor for phys. scis. Sci., 1985—. Fellow Alfred P. Sloan, 1968-70, Guggenheim, 1978-79; Christensen, Oxford U., 1983-84. Fellow AAAS (chmn. sect. 1996-97, mem.-at-large sect. 1997—), Calif. Acad. Scis. (hon.); mem. NAS (Award in Chem. Scis. 2001), Am. Acad. Arts and Scis., Am. Chem. Soc. (award in pure chemistry 1973, Harrison Howe award, 1976, R.C. Fuson award, 1986, James Flack Norris award 1986, Arthur C. Cope scholar, 1986, exec. com. phys. chemistry divsn., com. on sci. 1992-97), Sigma Xi, Phi Lambda Upsilon. Home: 849 Tolman Dr Palo Alto CA 94305-1025 Office: Stanford U Dept Chemistry Stanford CA 94305-5080

BRAUN, DAVID A(DLAI), lawyer; b. N.Y.C., Apr. 23, 1931; s. Morris and Betty Braunstein; m. Merna Feldman, Dec. 18, 1955; children: Lloyd Jeffrey, Kenneth Franklin, Evan Albert. AB, Columbia U., 1952, LLB, 1954. Bar: N.Y. 1955, Calif. 1974. Assoc. Ellis, Ellis and Ellis, N.Y.C., 1954-56, Davis and Gilbert, 1956-57; ptnr. Pryor, Cashman, Sherman and Flynn, 1957-73, Hardee, Barovick, Konecky & Braun, N.Y.C., 1973, L.A., 1974-81; pres., CEO Polygram Records, Inc., N.Y.C., 1980-81; counsel Wyman, Bautzer, Rothman, Kuchel & Silbert, L.A., 1982-85; ptnr. Braun, Margolis, Burrill & Besser, L.A., 1985-87; counsel Silverberg, Rosen, Leon & Behr, 1987-89, Silverberg, Katz, Thompson & Braun, 1989-91; spl. counsel Proskauer, Rose, Goetz & Mendelsohn, 1991-93; ptnr. Monasch Plotkin & Braun, 1993-94; pvt. practice, 1994-98; sr. counsel Akin, Gump, Strauss, Hauer & Feld, L.L.P., 1998—. Adj. prof. U. So. Calif. Sch. Cinema-TV; guest lectr. UCLA Ext.; mem. adv. com. Ctr. for Law, Media and the ARts, Columbia U. Sch. Law; internat. adv. bd. Nat. Inst. Entertainment and Media Law, Southwestern U. Sch. Law. Bd. visitors Columbia Coll., 1980-86, Columbia Law Sch., 1992-94; bd. dirs. Reprise! Broadway's Best in Concert, Musician's Assistance Program, 1994-98, Tu 'Um EST Cmty. Drug Rehab. Ctr., Rock and Roll Hall of Fame, 1985-93. Mem. Assn. of City of N.Y., L.A. County Bar Assn., Beverly Hills Bar Assn., Nat. Acad. Arts and Scis. (pres. N.Y. chpt. 1972-73), NATAS, Am. Arbitration Assn., Hollywood Radio and TV Soc. (bd. dirs. 1983-86), Sigma Chi, Phi Alpha Delta. Jewish. Home: 211 S Spalding Dr Apt 401S Beverly Hills CA 90212-3664 Office: Akin Gump Strauss Hauer & Feld LLP 24th Fl 2029 Century Park St Los Angeles CA 90067 E-mail: dbraun@akingump.com

BRAUN, JEROME IRWIN, lawyer; b. St. Joseph, Mo., Dec. 16, 1929; s. Martin H. and Bess (Donsker) B.; children: Aaron, Susan, Daniel; m. Dolores Ferriter, Aug. 16, 1987. AB with distinction, Stanford U., 1951, LLB, 1953. Bar: Mo. 1953, Calif. 1953, U.S. Dist. Ct. (no. dist.) Calif., U.S. Tax Ct., U.S. Ct. Mil. Appeals, U.S. Supreme Ct., U.S. Ct. Appeals (9th cir.). Assoc. Long & Levit, San Francisco, 1957-58, Law Offices of Jefferson Peyser, San Francisco, 1958-62; founding ptnr. Farella, Braun & Martel (formerly Elke, Farella & Braun), San Francisco, 1962—. Instr. San Francisco Law Sch., 1958-69; mem. U.S. Dist. Ct. Civil Justice Reform Act Adv. Com., 1991—; spkr. various state bar convs. in Calif., Ill., Nev., Mont.; requent moderator/participant continuing edn. of bar programs; past chmn. 9th Cir. Sr. Adv. Bd., past chmn. lawyer reps. to 9th Cir. Jud. Conf.; mem. appellate lawyers liaison com. Calif. Ct. Appeals 1st dist.; jud.conf. U.S. Com. Long Range Planning; founder Jon Samuel Abramson Scholarship Endowment Stanford U. Law. Revising editor: Stanford U. Law Rev.; contbr. articles to profl. jours. Mem. Jewish Community Fedn. San Francisco, The Peninsula, Marin and Sonoma Counties, pres., 1979-80; past pres. United Jewish Community Ctrs. 1st lt. JAGC, U.S. Army, 1954-57, U.S. Army Res., 1957-64. Recipient Lloyd W. Dinkelspiel Outstanding Young Leader award Jewish Welfare Fedn., 1967, Professionalism award 9th cir. Am. Inns of Ct., 1999. Fellow Am. Acad. Appellate Lawyers, Am. Coll. Trial Lawyers (teaching trial and appellate advocacy com.), Am. Bar Found.; mem. ABA, Calif. Bar Assn. (chmn. adminstrn. justice com. 1977), Bar Assn. San Francisco (spl. com. on lawyers malpractice and malpractice ins.), San Francisco Bar Found. (past trustee), Calif. Acad. Appellate Lawyers (past pres., mem. U.S. Dist. Ct. Civil Justice Reform Act adv. com., Calif. Ct. of Appeals 1st Dist. Appellate Lawyers liaison com., jud. conf. of the U.S., com. on long-range planning, panelist 1994), Am. Judicature Soc. (past dir.), Stanford Law Sch. Bd. of Visitors, U.S. Dist. Ct. of No. Dist. Calif. Hist. Soc. (past pres., bd. dirs.), 9th Cir. Ct. of Appeals Hist. Soc. (past. pres.), Mex.-Am. Legal Def. Fund (honoree), Order of Coif. E-mail: jbraun@fbm.com

BRAUNSTEIN, GLENN DAVID, physician, educator; b. Greenville, Tex., Feb. 29, 1944; s. Mervin and Helen (Friedman) B.; m. Jacquelyn D. Moose, July 5, 1965; children: Scott M. Braunstein, Jeffrey T. Braunstein. BS summa cum laude, U. Calif. San Francisco, 1965, MD, 1968. Diplomate Am. Bd. Internal Medicine, subspecialty endocrinology, diabetes, metabolism. Intern, resident Peter Bent Brigham Hosp., Boston, 1968-70; clin. fellow in medicine Harvard U. Med. Sch., Boston, 1969-70; clin. assoc., reproduction rsch. br. NIH, Bethesda, Md., 1970-72; chief resident in endocrinology Harbor Gen. Hosp. UCLA, 1972-73; dir. endocrinology Cedars-Sinai Med. Ctr., L.A., 1973-86, chmn., dept. medicine, 1986—; asst. prof. medicine UCLA Sch. Medicine, 1973-77, assoc. prof., 1977-81, prof., 1981—, vice chair dept. medicine, 1986—. Cons. for AMA drug evaluations, 1990—; mem. internat. adv. com. Second World Conf. on Implantation and Early Pregnancy in Human, 1994; mem. endocrinologic and metabolic drugs adv. com. FDA, 1991-95, chmn., 1994-95, spl. advisor, 1995—; bd. mem. Am. Bd. Internal Medicine Endocrinology, Diabetes, Metabolism Subspecialty, 1991-99, chmn., 1995-99, bd. dirs., 1995-99; bd. dirs. Cedars-Sinai Med. Ctr., 1997—. Mem. editl. bd. Mt. Sinai Jour. Medicine, 1984-88, Early Pregnancy: Biology and Medicine, 1998, Am. Family Physician, 1995—, The Am. Jour. Medicine, 1996—, Clin. Endocrinology & Metabolism, 1978-80; assoc. editor Integrative Medicine: Integrating Allopathic, Alternative and Complementary Medicine, 1997-2000. Bd. dirs. Israel Cancer Rsch. Fund, 1991-94, Cedars-Sinai Med. Ctr., 1997—; mem. Jonsson Comprehensive Cancer Ctr., 1991—. Recipient Gold Headed Cane Soc. award U. Calif. San Francisco Med. Ctr., 1968, Merck scholarship, 1968, Mosby scholarship, 1968, Soc. of Hacham award Cedars-Sinai Med. Ctr., 1976, Morris Press Humanism award Cedars-Sinai Med. Ctr., 1984, outstanding achievement and cmty. svc. award Anti-Defamation League, 1997, James R. Klinerberg Chair in Medicine, 2000—. Fellow ACP (mem. adv. com. to gov., So. Calif. region 1989—, credentials com. So. Calif. region 1993); mem. AAAS, Am. Diabetes Assn., Cross Town Endocrine Club (chmn. 1982-83), Endocrine Soc. (publs. com. 1983-89, long range planning com. 1986-87, recent progress hormone rsch. com. 1993-98, ann. meeting steering com. 1993-98, spl. programs com. 1998—), Pacific Coast Fertility Soc. (pres. 1988), Western Soc. for Clin. Rsch., Am. Fedn. for Clin. Rsch., Am. Fertility Soc., Western Assn. Physicians (pres. 1998-99), Assn. Am. Physicians, Am. Soc. Clin. Investigations (mem. nominating com. 1989), USCF Sch. Medicine Alumni Faculty Assn. (regional v.p. so. Calif., mem. bd. dirs. Israel Cancer Rsch. Fund 1991-94, mem. Jonsson Comprehensive Cancer Ctr. 1991—), Phi Delta Epsilon, Alpha Omega Alpha. Office: Cedars Sinai Med Ctr Dept Med Pla Level B118 8700 Beverly Blvd Los Angeles CA 90048-1865 E-mail: braunstein@cshs.org

BRAUTIGAN, ROGER L [illegible], BD, U. Hil., Master, U. Pacific. Platoon leader 22nd Replacement Battalion, Vietnam; tng., ops., and battalion exec. officer 91st Tng. Divsn.; mobilization plans officer Fort Ord; inspector general 125th Army Reserve Command; chief of tng., chief of ops. Office of the Chief Army Reserve, The Pentagon, Washington; sr. reserve advisor to commanding general US Army Europe, Seventh Army. Maj. gen. USAR. Decorated Legion of Merit with oak leaf cluster, Bronze Star, Meritorious Svc. medal with 3 oak leaf clusters.

BRAVERMAN, ALAN N. lawyer; BA, Brandeis U., 1969; JD, Duquesne U., 1975. Bar: D.C. 1976. Assoc. Wilmer, Cutler & Pickering, 1976-82, ptnr., 1983-93; sr. v.p., gen. counsel ABC, Inc., N.Y.C., 1993-2000, exec. v.p., gen. counsel Burbank, Calif., 2000—. Office: ABC Inc 500 S Buena Vista St Burbank CA 91521-0922

BRAVMAN, JOHN COLE, materials scientist, educator; b. N.Y.C., July 24, 1957; s. Maurice Daniel and Ella Katherine (Mahnke) B.; children: Christopher Daniel, Matthew Donald. BS, Stanford U., 1979, MS, 1981, PhD, 1984. Engr. Fairchild Semiconductor, Palo Alto, Calif., 1979-84; asst. prof. Stanford U., 1985-91, assoc. prof., 1991-95, prof., 1995-99, v. provost, 1999—. Contbr. over 150 articles to sci. jours. Recipient Walter J. Gores Award for Teaching Excellence, Stanford U., 1989, Tau Beta Pi Award for Engring. Edn. Excellence, 1990, Bradley Stoughton Young Tchrs. award, ASM Internat., 1991. Mem. IEEE, Matls. Rsch. Soc., Am. Phys. Soc., ASM Internat., The Metall. Soc. Office: Stanford Univ Bldg 550 Stanford CA 94305

BRAVO, PAUL, professional soccer player; b. San Jose, Calif., July 19, 1968; Student, Santa Clara U. Midfielder San Francisco Bay Blackhawks, 1991, San Francisco Greek-Ams.; U.S. Open Cup champions, 1994; midfielder Monterey Bay Jaguars, 1995, San Jose Clash, 1996; advanced to play-offs, 1996; midfielder Colo. Rapids, Denver, 1997—; advanced to play-offs, 1997, 98. Office: c/o Colo Rapids 55517th St Ste 3350 Denver CO 80202

BRAY, ABSALOM FRANCIS, JR. lawyer; b. San Francisco, Nov. 24, 1918; s. Absalom Francis and Leila Elizabeth (Veale) E.; m. Lorraine Cerena Paule, June 25, 1949; children: Oliver, Brian, Margot. BA, Stanford U., 1940; JD, U. So. Calif., 1949. Bar: Calif. 1949, U.S. Supreme Ct. 1960. Sr. ptnr. Bray & Baldin and successive firms to Bray & Bray, Martinez, Calif., 1949—, now pres. Founder, bd. dirs. John Muir Nat. Bank, Martinez. Chmn. Martinez Recreation Commn., 1949-54; chmn. nat. bd. dirs. Camp Fire Girls, 1959-61, 69-71; pres. Contra Costa County (Calif.) Devel. Assn., 1959-60, Contra Costa County Hist. Soc., 1995-97. Lt. USNR, 1942-46. Mem. State Bar Calif. (chmn. adoption com. 1955-56), Martinez His. Soc. (pres. 1984), Mohn Muir Meml. Assn. (pres. 1989-92), Navy League U.S. (pres. Contra Costsons, Rotary (pres. Martinez 1970-71). Home: 600 Flora St Martinez CA 94553-3268 Office: Bray & Bray Ward and Ferry Sts Martinez CA 94553-1697

BRAY, R(OBERT) BRUCE, music educator; b. La Grande, Oreg., July 24, 1924; s. Ernest C. and Leta M. (Haight) B.; m. Donna Marie Siegman, July 2, 1949 (div. 1980); children: Stephen Louis, Ruth Elizabeth, Katherine Ernestine, Anne-Marie. BA, U. Oreg., 1949, MMus, 1955; postgrad., U. Strasbourg, France, 1949-50, U. Wash., , 1960-61. Music tchr. Helen McCune Jr. High Sch., Pendleton, Oreg., 1951-54; dir. choral music Albany (Oreg.) Union High Sch., 1954-56; elem. music supr. Ashland (Oreg.) Public Schs., 1956-57; asst. prof. music Cen. Wash. U., Ellensburg, 1957-60; from asst. to prof. U. Idaho, Moscow, 1961-89, prof. emeritus, 1989—. Sec. faculty U. Idaho, Moscow, 1968-88, sec. emeritus, 1988—. Editor: Oreg. Music Educator, 1954-57, Wash. Music Educator, 1957-60, U. Idaho Music, 1961-68, Idaho Music Notes, 1963-68, U. Idaho Register, 1974-88 ; editorial bd. Music Educators Jour., 1964-68. With USNR, 1942-46. Mem. Music Educators Nat. Conf. (bd. dirs., pres. N.W. divsn. 1963-65, nat. exec. com. 1964-66), Phi Mu Alpha Sinfonia. Democrat. Episcopalian. Home and Office: 2614 E Everett Ave Spokane WA 99207-6210

BRAZIER, ROBERT G. transportation executive; Student, Stanford U. With Airbone Aircraft Service Inc., 1953-63; v.p. ops. Pacific Air Freight Inc., 1963-68; sr. v.p. ops. Airbone Freight Corp., Seattle, 1968-73, exec. v.p., 1973-78, COO, 1973—, pres., dir, COO, 1978—. Office: Airborne Freight Corp PO Box 662 Seattle WA 98111-0662

BRAZIL, WAYNE D. federal judge; BA, Stanford U., 1966; MA, Harvard U., 1967, PhD, 1975; JD, U. Calif., Berkeley, 1975. Extern clk. to Hon. John J. Purchivo Calif. Superior Ct., 1973-74; extern clk. to Hon. Donald R. Wright Calif. Supreme Ct., 1975-78; with Farella, Braun & Martel, San Francisco; apptd. magistrate judge no. dist. U.S. Dist. Ct. Calif., 1984. Tchr. Vols. in Asia, 1966; tchr., counselor Upward Bound, U. Mass., 1968-69; vis. prof. law U. Ky., 1978; assoc. prof. law U. Mo., 1978-80; prof. law Hastings Coll., 1980-84. Contbr. articles to law jours. Capt. USAR, 1974. Mem. ABA, Am. Law Inst., Calif. Bar Assn., Phi Beta Kappa, Order of Coif. Office: Oakland Federal Courthouse 1301 Clay St Oakland CA 94612-5217 Fax: 510-637-3327

BRECHT, ALBERT ODELL, library and information technology administrator; b. Dallas, n, Nov. 19, 1946; BA in Govt. and Sociology, North Tex. State U., 1969; JD, U. Houston, 1972; LLM, U. Wash., 1973. Bar: Tex. 1972. Asst. law libr. U. So. Calif., L.A., 1973-74, asst. law libr. in-charge Law Libr., 1975, lab libr., asst. prof. law, 1975-77, dir. Law Libr., 1977—, assoc. prof., 1977-79, prof., 1979—, interim dep. univ. libr. for ctrl. libr. sys., 1984-85, assoc. dean Law Libr. and Info. Tech., 1996—. Pres. Libraria Sodalitas, 1980; mem. Westlaw Acad. Adv. Bd., 1988-92. Author: (with A. Holoch and K. Pecarovich) Medical Malpractice Insurance and Its Alternatives: The Legal, Medical, and Insurance Literature—A Bibliography, 1975; contbr. articles and book revs. to profl. jours. Mem. Am. Assn. Law Librs. (audio-visual com. 1975, chmn. nominations com. 1978, recruitment com. 1975-76, placement com. 1979-81, cons. law librs. of correctional instns., chmn. program com. ann. meeting 1983, v.p. 1986-87, pres. 1987-88, moderator program on law librs. 1991), Spl. Librs. Assn., So. Calif. Assn. Law Librs. (v.p. 1974-75, pres. 1975-76, bd. dirs. 1978, chmn. com. on cons. for non-law librs. 1981). Office: U So Calif Law Libr University Park Los Angeles CA 90089-0001

BRECKENRIDGE, KLINDT DUNCAN, architect; b. Iowa City, Apr. 24, 1957; s. Jack Duncan and Florence (Kmiecik) B.; m. Nancy Ann Dernier, Apr. 19, 1986; children: Wilson Reid, Lauren Alessandra. BArch, U. Ariz., 1981. Registered architect, Ariz., Calif., Nev.; cert. NCARB. Architect Finical & Dombrowski, Tucson, 1981-84; pres. The IEF Group, Inc., Tucson, 1984—. Assoc. faculty Pima Community Coll. Bd. dirs., pres. Mirical Sq. Mem. AIA (treas. So. Ariz. chpt. 1997-99, pres. 1999-2000, com. on architecture for edn., pres.-elect), Leadership Tucson Alumni (bd. dirs.). Democrat. Episcopalian. Avocation: running. Home: 5535 N Waterfield Dr Tucson AZ 85750-6473 Office: The IEF Group 705 N 7th Ave Tucson AZ 85705-8306

BRECKINRIDGE, JAMES BERNARD, optical science engineer, program manager; b. Cleve., May 27, 1939; s. Albert Coles and Catherine Rose (Wengler) B.; m. Ann Marie Yoder, July 24, 1965; children: Douglass E., John Brian. B.S. in Physics, Case Inst. Tech., 1961; M.S. in Optical Sci., U. Ariz., 1970, Ph.D. in Optical Sci., 1976. Research asst. Lick Obs., Mt. Hamilton, Calif., 1961-64; electron tube engr. Rauland Corp., Chgo., 1967; rsch. asst. Kitt Peak Nat. Obs., Tucson, full time, 1964-66, 68, 75-76, part time, 1969-74; mem. tech. staff Jet Propulsion Lab., Calif. Inst. Tech., 1976—, part-time faculty in applied physics, 1981 [illegible] 1981-94; program mgr. for innovative imaging tech. and sys. Flight Projects Office, 1994-98; leader NASA Team to Assess Optics Tech. in Former Soviet Union, 1992-97; mgmt. & tech. cons., 1994—; mgr. Innovative Imaging Sys., 1998—. Co-investigator NASA Spacelab 3; mem. adv. com. NASA, NSF, Dept. Def.; staff mem. Hubble Space Telescope Failure Bd., 1990, tech. mgr. Hubble Space Telescope Camera Optics Repair. Contbr. articles to jours. in field; 5 patents in field. Scoutmaster Boy Scouts Am.; bd. trustees United Ch. of Christ. Fellow

Optical Soc. Am. (bd. dirs.), Royal Astron. Soc., Internat. Soc. Optical Engring. (bd. govs., pres. 1994); mem. IEEE, Am. Astron. Soc., Coun. of Scientific Soc. Pres.'s (bd. dirs. 1996), Internat. Astron. Union (U.S. com. rep. to the internat. congress on optics), Astron. Soc. of Pacific. Achievements include research in remote optical and infrared sensing instrumentation, interferometry, spectroscopy, image intensifiers and image analysis. Home: 900 N Stuart St Apt 1707 Arlington VA 22203-4112 Office: JPL Caltech MS 126-244 4800 Oak Grove Dr Pasadena CA 91109-8099

BRECKNER, WILLIAM JOHN, JR. retired air force officer, corporate executive, consultant; b. Alliance, Ohio, May 25, 1933; s. William John and Frances P. (Bertchey) B.; m. Cheryl V. Carmell, Aug. 30, 1963; children: William R., Kristen C. B.A., SUNY, 1976; postgrad., Harvard U., 1980. Commd. 2d lt. USAF, 1955, advanced through grades to maj. gen., 1983, various pilot and command positions worldwide, 1955-72; comdr. USAF Interceptor Weapons Sch., 1973-75; vice commandant cadets USAF Acad., Colo., 1976-79; comdr. 82d Flying Tng. Wing Williams AFB, Ariz., 1979-80; dep. chief staff logistics Hdqrs. Air Tng. Commd., Tex., 1980-83; chief staff Hdqrs. USAF Europe, 1983-84; commdr. 17th Air Force, Sembach AFB, Germany, 1984-86; ret., 1986. Prisoner of war, Vietnam, 1972-73. Decorated D.S.M., 1986, Silver Star, 1972, Legion of Merit, 1973, Bronze Star medal, 1973, Air medal, 1968, 72, Purple Heart, 1972, 73, Republic of Vietnam Cross of Gallantry with palm, 1973 Mem. Nat. War Coll. Alumni Assn., Order Daedalians, Air Force Assn., Nam Prisoners of War Inc., Red River Valley Fighter Pilots Assn., C. of C. (chmn. mil. affairs coun. 1994-95). Lutheran Avocations: golf, skiing, tennis. Home: 17865 Fairplay Way Monument CO 80132-8581 Office: 590 Hwy 105 Ste 266 Monument CO 80132 E-mail: brexgroup@earthlink.net

BREED, MICHAEL DALLAM, environmental, population, organismic biology educator; b. Kansas City, Mo., Sept. 2, 1951; s. Laurence W. and Loree (Dallam) B.; m. Cheryl A. Ristig, Aug. 9, 1975. BA, Grinnell Coll., 1973; MA, U. Kans., 1975, PhD, 1977. Asst. prof. environ., population, organismic biology U. Colo., Boulder, 1977-83, assoc. prof., 1983-89, prof., 1989—, chmn. dept., 1986-90, 97-99, acting chmn. dept. anthropology, 1991-93, acting assoc. dean, 1991-93. Contbr. articles to sci. jours. Mem. Internat. Union for Study of Social Insects (pres. N.Am. sect. 1984, sec. gen. 1994—), Animal Behavior Soc., Internat. Bee Rsch. Assn., Entomol. Soc. Am. (officer sect. C 1992-95), Sigma Xi. Home: 700 Dahlia St Denver CO 80220-5112 Office: U Colo Dept Biology 102 Boulder CO 80309-0001

BREEN, RICHARD F., JR. law librarian, lawyer, educator; b. Providence, Aug. 1, 1940; s. Richard F. and Elizabeth (Hurlin) B.; children: Stephanie, Jonathan. AB in Econs., Dartmouth Coll., 1962; LLB, U. Maine, Portland, 1967; MLS, U. Oreg., 1973. Bar: Maine, N.H. Asst dean U. Maine Sch. Law, Portland, ., 1967-70; with firm Tesreau and Gardner, Lebanon, N.H., 1970-72; assoc. law libr., assoc. prof. law U. Maine Sch. Law, Portland, 1974-76; law libr., assoc. prof. law Willamette U. Coll. Law, Salem, Oreg., 1976-80, law libr., prof. law, 1980—, interim adminstrv. dean., law libr., 1986-87. Mem. U.S. Olympic Biathlon Tng. Team, 1963. Capt. USAR, 1962-64. Mem. Am. Assn. Law Librs., Oreg. Libr. Assn., Casque and Gauntlet Honor Soc. Democrat. Congregationalist. Avocations: cross-country skiing, hiking. Office: Willamette U Law Libr 245 Winter St SE Salem OR 97301-3916 E-mail: dbreen@willamette.edu

BREGA, CHARLES FRANKLIN, lawyer; b. Callaway, Nebr., Feb. 5, 1933; s. Richard E. and Bessie (King) B.; m. Betty Jean Witherspoon, Sept. 17, 1960; children: Kerry E., Charles D., Angie G. B.A., The Citadel, 1954; LLB, U. Colo., 1960. Bar: Colo. 1960. Assoc. firm Hindry & Meyer, Denver, 1960-62, partner, 1962-75, dir., 1975; dir. firm Roath & Brega, Denver, 1975-89, Brega & Winters, Denver, 1989—. Lectr. in field; guest prof. U. Colo., U. Denver, U. Nev. (numerous states and), Can. Trustee Pres.'s Leadership Class, U. Colo., 1977—. Served with USAF, 1954-57. Mem. Colo. Trial Lawyers Assn. (pres. 1972-73), Assn. Trial Lawyers Am. (gov. 1972-79), ABA, Am. Law Inst., Am. Bd. Trial Advs., Internat. Acad. Trial Lawyers, Internat. Soc. Barristers, Cherry Hills Country Club, Denver Athletic Club. Episcopalian. Home: 4501 S Vine Way Englewood CO 80110-6027 Office: Brega & Winters PC 1700 Lincoln St Ste 2222 Denver CO 80203-4522

BREINER, SHELDON, geophysics educator, business executive; b. Milw., Oct. 23, 1936; s. James and Fannie Breiner; m. Phyllis Farrington, Feb. 4, 1962; children— David, Michelle BS, Stanford U., 1959, MS, 1962, PhD in Geophysics, 1967. Registered geophysicist. Geologist, Calif. product mgr. Varian Assocs., 1961-68; founder, pres. Geometrics, Sunnyvale, Calif., 1969-83, Syntelligence Inc., 1984-87. Pres., founder, dir. Wireless Note Systems, Inc., 1995—; dir. Sherpa Corp., Optical Sptys. Inc., Solis Therapeudics Inc.; pres., CEO, chmn., founder Para Magnetic Logging Inc.; pres. Foothill Assocs.; cons., prof., lectr. geophysics Stanford U. and Grad. Sch. Bus.; cons. archaeol. exploration problems and search for buried objects; adv. coun. Sch. of Earth Scis., Stanford U. Author: Applications Manual for Portable Magnetometers, 1973; contbr. articles to profl. jours.; patentee in oil exploration; inventor gun detector for airports Founder, trustee Peninsula Open State Trust; bd. dirs. Resource Ctr. for Women; maj. gifts com. Stanford U. With U.S. Army, 1960. Honors scholar, 1955-56; NSF grantee for earthquake research, 1965. Fellow Explorers Club; mem. Soc. Exploration Geophysicists (Best presentation award 1985), Soc. Petroleum Engrs., Am. Geophys. Union, European Assn. Exploration Geophysicists, Stanford Assocs. Achievements include discovery of oldest monuments in Western Hemisphere (colossal Olmec heads) using magnetometers. Avocation: running Boston Marathon. Office: New Ventures West 706 Comper St 3rd Fl Palo Alto CA 94301-2128 E-mail: sheldon@breiner.com

BREITHAUPT, BRENT HENRY, museum curator; b. Milw., Jan. 11, 1956; s. Henry G. Breithaupt and Ann M. (Kluge) Catalano; m. Vicki Ann Burton, Aug. 2, 1980. BS in Geology, U. Wis., Milw., 1978; MS in Geology, U. Wyo., 1981. Mus. asst. Milw. Pub. Mus., 1975-78; curatorial asst. Geol. Mus. U. Wyo., Laramie, 1980-81, curator Geol. Mus., 1981—, instr. correspondence study, 1983—, instr. Sch. Extended Studies and Pub. Svc., 1986—. Contbr. articles to profl. jours. Mem. Paleontol. Soc., Soc. for Study of Amphibians and Reptiles, Am. Soc. Ichthyologists and Herpetologists, Herpetologists League, Colo.-Wyo. Acad. Scis., Colo.-Wyo. Assn. Mus., Soc. Vertebrate Paleontology (regional editor news bulletin 1985—), Wis. Geol. Soc. (v.p. 1976), Nat. Speleological Soc., Wyo. Geol. Soc., Sigma Xi. Avocations: fencing, running, nordic and alpine skiing, rock and ice climbing, caving, soccer. Office: U Wyo The Geol Mus Laramie WY 82071

BREITROSE, HENRY S. communications educator; b. Bklyn., July 22, 1936; s. Charles and Ruth (Leib) B.; m. Prudence Elaine Martin, Oct. 11, 1968; children— Charles Daniel, Rebecca Marjorie. B.S., U. Wis., 1958; M.A., Northwestern U., 1959; Ph.D., Stanford U., 1966. Writer Internat. Film Bur., 1958; mgr. Midwest office Contemporary Films Co., 1959; mem. faculty Stanford (Calif.) U., 1959—, prof. communication, 1975—, chmn. dept. communication, 1976-82. Vis. prof. London Sch. Econs., 1976-77; mem. public media panel NEA, 1974—; ednl. adv. com. Am. Film Inst., 1974; vice chmn. tng. for developing countries, v.p. for rsch pub. Ctr. Internat. des Liasions des Ecoles du Cinema et du TV, 1989—; Christensen vis. rsch. fellow St. Catherine's Coll., Oxford, 1996; v.p. for publs. and rsch. Ctr. Internat. des Liasons des Ecoles du Cinema et de TV. Gen. editor: Cambridge Studies in Film; mem. editorial bd. Calif. Lawyer, 1980-86; author articles, chpts. in books. Bd. dirs. Sta. KQED, San Francisco, 1985-90, vice chmn. 1988; mem. adv. bd. Sta. KCSM. Grantee Rockefeller Found., 1965-66; Lilly Endowment, 1976-77; Stanford U. fellow, 1972-74, Christensen fellow Oxford U., 1996. Mem. Univ. Film Assn. (exec. v.p. 1987-89), Broadcast Educators Assn., Internat. Documentary Assn., Internat. Communication Assn., Internat. Inst. Communications. Home: 897 Tolman Dr Stanford CA 94305-1017 Office: Stanford U Dept Communication Stanford CA 94305-2050

BREMER, RONALD ALLAN, genealogist, editor; b. South Gate, Calif., May 2, 1937; s. Carl Leonard and Lena Evelyn (Jury) B.; m. Trudy Graham; childen: Blindy, Ron, Trina, Rebecca, Aaron, Serena, Lorrie, Jennie, Elizabeth, Hans, Adam, Rachel. Student, Los Angeles Trade Tech., Cerritos Coll., Am. U., Brigham Young U.; grad., Nat. Inst. Geneal. Rsch., 1961. Prof. genealogist, 1959—; research specialist Fam. Hist. Libr., Salt Lake City, 1969-72; profl. lectr. on genealogy Salt Lake City, 1973—. Editor Genealogy Digest mag., Salt Lake City, 1983-84, Roots Digest, 1984-85; lectr. in field. Author: World's Funniest Epitaphs, 1983; Compendium of Historical Sources, 1983; (with Bill Dollarhide) America's Best Genealogy Resource Centers, 1999. Office: PO Box 345 Paradise UT 84328-0345

BREMS, DAVID PAUL, architect; b. Lehi, Utah, Aug. 10, 1950; s. D. Orlo and Gearldine (Hitchcock) B.; m. Johna Devey Brems; children: Stefan Tomas Brems, Beret Alla Brems. BS, U. Utah, 1973, MArch, 1975. Registered architect, Utah, Calif., Colo., Ariz., Wyo., N.Mex., Idaho, Mont., Tex., Wash. Draftsman Environ. Assocs., Salt Lake City, 1971-73; draftsman/architect intern Environ. Design Group, Salt Lake City, 1973-76; architect/intern Frank Fuller AIA, Salt Lake City, 1976-77; prin. Edward & Daniels, Salt Lake City, 1978-83; pres. David Brems & Assocs., Salt Lake City, 1983-86; prin. Gillies, Stransky, Brems, Smith P.C., Salt Lake City, 1986—. Adj. prof. U. Utah Grad. Sch. Architecture, 1990-93; mem. urban design com. Assist, Inc., Salt Lake City, 1982-85, Salt Lake County Planning Commn., 1991-97, chmn., 1992-96; mem. Emigration Twp. Planning Commn., 1997—, chmn. 1997-99; mem. Emigration Masterplan Adv. Com., 1997-99; invited lectr. Wyo. Soc. Archs., 1992, sch. engring. U. Utah, 1993, 95, Va., 1993, Utah Soc. Archs., 1994, Utah Power and Light, 1994, Utah Soc. Archts., 1994; juror U. Utah Grad. Sch. Architecture, 1975—, Utah Soc. Am. Planning Assn., 1994—, Sunstone Symposium, 1995, Contemporary Arts Group, 1995—; with adv. com. U. Utah Grad. Sch. Architecture, 2000—. Pub. Firm Profile Intermountain Architecture,, 1996, Web Mag., 1997; prin. works include solar twin homes Utah Holiday (Best Solar Design award), Sun Builder, Daily Jour., Salt Lake Tribune, Brian Head Day Lodge, Easton Aluminum, Four Seasons Hotel, Gore Coll. Bus., CMF Tooele, utah Regional Corrections Facility, St. Vincents De Paul Ctr., Steiner Aquatic Ctr., U. Utah Football Support Facility, Sports Medicine West, West Jordan Cmty. Water Park, Utah Nat. Guard Apache Helicopter Hangar & Armory, Kashmitter I Residences, St. Thomas More Cath. Ch., Spanish Fork Cmty. Water Park, Natures Herbs, ABC Office Bldg. Divsn. of Natural Resources Bldg., Kashmitter II Residence, Litton Residence, Elliott Residence, Utah Olympic Speed Skating Oval for 2002 Olympics, Vis. Ctr. Grand Staircase Escalante Nat. Monument, and others; ALTA Club mem., Great Salt Lake Yacht Club mem., mem. Leadership Utah; mem. 2002 Olympic Energy and Water subcom., 1996—; mem. State of Utah Divsn. of Facilities Mgmt. Com. on Energy Efficient Architecture. Active adv. com. Salt Lake City Bus. Advisory. Recipient three awards Am. Concrete Inst., 1993, Chief Engrs. Honor award U.S. Army Corps Engrs., 1994; Bronze medalist Utah Summer Games, 1991, Silver medalist, 1992, Gold medalist, 1994, Design award Dept. Def., 1995, Blue Seal award, 1995, Outstanding Project award U.S. Dept. Def., 1995, Western Mountain Region Hon. Mention St. Thomas More, 1996, Solar Today award Sun award, Energy Uses News award Dept. Natural Resources, 1996; named Best Pvt. Project by Intermountain Architecture, 1994, Salt Lake County Vol. of Yr. Salt Lake County Planning Commn., 1995, Best Recreation Project Intermountain Arch., 1995. Mem. AIA (pres. Salt Lake chpt. 1983-84, pres. Utah Soc. 1987, chmn. Western Mountain Region conf., 1986, com. on design 1990—, chmn. com. on environment AIA Utah 1993, chmn. Design for Life Workshop at Sundance 1993, Honor awards 1983, 88, Merit awards 1983, 85, 88, 93, 99, chmn. Western Mountain Regiona honor awards 1983, 88, PCI award 1988, IFRAA award 1988, 94, Juror Colo. West awards 1992, award Utah sect. IES for St. Thomas More), Am. Planning Assn. (juror awards 1994), Acorn Hills Water Assn. (pres.), Black Builder Mesa Water Assn. (sec.), Utah Soc. Architects, Am. Solar Energy Soc., Hobie Fleet 67 (commodre 1985-86), Salt Lake Olympic Com. (environ. adv. com.), Utah Open Lands (S.W. Utah br.), Illuminating Engring. Soc. (assoc.), Am. Solar Soc. Home: 119 N Young Oak Rd Salt Lake City UT 84108-1601

BREMSER, GEORGE, JR. electronics company executive; b. Newark, May 26, 1928; s. George and Virginia (Christian) B.; m. Marie Sundman, June 21, 1952 (div. July 1979); children: Christian Fredrick II, Priscilla Suzanne, Martha Anne, Sarah Elizabeth; m. Nancy Kay Woods, Oct. 27, 1983 (div. Feb. 1989); m. Betty Glover Lohse, Oct. 8, 1997. BA, Yale U., 1949; postgrad., U. Miami, 1959; MBA, NYU, 1962. With McCann-Erickson Inc., N.Y.C., 1952-61, asst. gen. mgr. Bogota, Columbia, 1955, gen. mgr. Columbia, 1955-57, account supr. N.Y.C., 1958, v.p., mgr. Miami, Fla., 1959-61; with Gen. Foods Corp., White Plains, N.Y., 1961-71; v.p., gen. mgr. internat. div. Gen. Foods Europe, White Plains, 1967; pres. Gen. Foods Internat., White Plains, 1967-71; group v.p. Gen. Foods Corp., White Plains, 1970-71; chmn., pres., chief exec. officer Textar Corp., Grand Prairie, Tex., 1971-81; exec. v.p. Shaklee Corp., San Francisco, 1981-82; chmn., pres., chief exec. officer Etak Inc., Menlo Park, 1983-88, 96, chmn., 1989-96, 97—; chmn., pres., CEO Etak, Inc., Menlo Park, 1996-97, chmn., 1997-2000, CEO, 2000-01; chief adminstrv. officer Tele Atlas N.A., Inc., 2001—. Bd. dirs. PBI Industries Inc. Trustee Union Ch., Bogota, 1956-57; Dem. county committeeman, Ridgewood, N.J., 1962-63; mem. New Canaan (Conn.) Town Council, 1969-73; founder, past pres. Citizens Com. for Conservation, New Canaan; mem. coun. Save the Redwoods League, 1987—. Served to 2d lt. USMC 1950-52, capt. Res. Mem. New Canaan Country Club, Brook Club, Yale Club (N.Y.C.), Block Island Club, Casino Club (Nantucket, Mass.), Explorers Club, Phi Beta Kappa, Beta Gamma Sigma, Beta Theta Pi. Home: 5575 Hilltop Cres Oakland CA 94618-2605 also: Mansion Beach Rd Block Island RI 02807 Office: Tele Atlas NA Inc 1605 Adams Dr Menlo Park CA 94025-1448

BREN, DONALD L. real estate company executive; b. 1932; BA in Bus., MBA, U. Wash. With Calif. Pacific Homes, Inc., Newport Beach, Calif., 1956—, chmn. bd.; founder Mission Viejo (Calif.) Co.; CEO Irvine Co., Newport Beach, chmn. bd., 1998—. With USMC, 1954-57. Office: The Irvine Co 550 Newport Center Dr Newport Beach CA 92660-7011

BRENNAN, CIARAN BRENDAN, accountant; b. Dublin, Ireland, Jan. 28, 1944; s. Sean and Mary (Stone) B. BA with honors, Univ. Coll., Dublin, 1966; MBA, Harvard U., 1973; MS in Acctg., U. Houston, 1976. Lic. real estate broker, Calif.; CPA, Tex. Auditor Coopers & Lybrand, London, 1967-70; sr. auditor Price Waterhouse & Co., Toronto, Ont., Can., 1970-71; project acctg. specialist Kerr-McGee Corp., Oklahoma City, 1976-80; contr. Cummings Oil Co., Oklahoma City, 1980-82; CFO Red Stone Energies, Ltd., 1982, Leonoco, Inc., 1982-87; treas., chief fin. officer JKJ Supply Co., 1983-87, Saturn Investments Inc., 1983-87, JFL Co., 1984-87, Little Chief Drilling & Energy Inc., 1984-85; pres. Ciaran Brennan Corp., 1990—; CFO Nationwide Industries, 1991-93; mgr. of budget Mission Foods, 1996-98; contr. Hoffy Bacon, 1998—. Bd. dirs., cons. small oil cos.; adj. faculty Oklahoma City U., 1977-86; vis. faculty Ctrl. State U., 1977-86. Contbr. articles to profl. jours. Mem. AICPA, Inst. Chartered Accts. Eng. and Wales, Inst. Chartered Accts. Can. Democrat. Roman Catholic. E-mail: ciaranrb@aol.com

BRENNAN, JOAN STEVENSON, federal judge; b. Detroit, Feb. 21, 1933; d. James and Betty (Holland) Stevenson; m. Lane P. Brennan, June 26, 1954 (div. 1970); children: Suzanne, Steven, Clayton, Elizabeth, Catherine. BA, Skidmore Coll., 1954; JD, Santa Clara U., 1973. Bar: Calif. Dep. dist. atty. Dist. Attys. Office, Santa Clara, Calif., 1974-78; legal counsel U.S. Leasing Internat., San Francisco, 1978-79; asst. U.S. atty. U.S. Dist. Ct. (no. dist.) Calif., San Francisco, 1980-82, U.S. Magistrate judge, 1982—. Mem. Nat. Assn. Women Judges, Nat. Assn. Magistrate Judges. Democrat.

BRENNEMAN, DELBERT JAY, lawyer; b. Albany, Oreg., Feb. 4, 1950; s. Calvin M. and Velma Barbara (Whitaker) B.; m. Caroline Yorke Allen, May 29, 1976; children: Mark Stuart, Thomas Allen. BS magna cum laude, Oreg. State U., 1972; JD, U. Oreg., 1976. Bar: Oreg. 1976, U.S. Dist. Ct. Oreg. 1977, U.S. Ct. Appeals (9th cir.) 1977. Assoc. Schwabe, Williamson, and Wyatt, Portland, Oreg., 1976-83, ptnr., 1984-92, Hoffman, Hart & Wagner, Portland, 1993—. Spkr. Oreg. Self-Ins., 1978, 90; seminar instr. U. Oreg. Law Sch., Eugene, 1980. Mem. ABA, Oreg. State Bar Assn., Multnomah County Bar Assn. (spkr. 1983-84), Order of Coif, Multnomah Athletic Club, Propeller Club of U.S. (bd. dirs. 1983-85), Phi Kappa Phi, Beta Gamma Sigma. Office: Hoffman Hart & Wagner 1000 SW Broadway Fl 20 Portland OR 97205-3035 E-mail: djb@hhw.com

BRENNER, ELIZABETH (BETSY BRENNER), publishing executive; BJ, MBA, Northwestern U. With mktg. dept. The New York Times; with retail advt. and circulation posts Miami Herald, Rocky Mountain News, Denver, sr. v.p. sales and mktg., 1994; pub. Bremerton Sun, 1995-98, The News Tribune, Tacoma, 1998—. Bd. dirs. Econ. Devel. Bd, Tacoma, Greater Tacoma Cmty. Found., exec. coun.; mem. U. Wash. Pres. Bus. Adv. Coun. Office: The News Tribune 1950 S State St Tacoma WA 98405-2817

BRES, PHILIP WAYNE, automotive executive; b. Beaumont, Tex., Mar. 6, 1950; s. Roland Defrance Bres and Edna Gene (Griffith) Seale; m. Janet Vivian Meyer, May 16, 1987; children: Rachel Elizabeth, Rebecca Claire. BA, Lamar U., Beaumont, Tex., 1972; MBA, Stephen F. Austin State U., 1973. Distbn. mgr., bus. mgmt. mgr. Mazda Motors of Am., Houston, 1973-75; analyst, cons. C.H. McCormack and Assocs., Houston, 1975-76; assoc. Frank Gillman Pontiac/GMC/Honda, Houston, 1976-79, David Taylor Cadillac Co., Houston, 1979-80; pres. Braintrust Inc., Houston, 1980-83; sales mgr. Mossy Oldsmobile, Inc., Houston, 1983-84; gen. mgr. Mossy Nissan/Ford, Bellevue, Wash., 1984-86; dir. ops. Mossy Co., Encinitas, Calif., 1986-91; gen. mgr. Performance Nissan, Duarte, 1991—. Seminar lectr. Rice U., Houston, 1980-83. Author: The Entrepreneurs Guide for Starting a Successful Business., 1982; contbr. (book) Business Planning for the Entrepreneur, 1983. Mem. Houston C. of C. (small bus. coun.), Opt Astron. Soc., Univ. Club, Phi Eta Sigma, Phi Kappa Phi. Office: Performance Nissan PO Box 1500 Duarte CA 91009-4500

BRESLAUER, GEORGE WILLIAM, political science educator; b. N.Y.C., Mar. 4, 1946; s. Henry Edward and Marianne (Schaeffer) B.; m. Yvette Assia, June 5, 1976; children: Michelle, David. BA, U. Mich., 1966, MA, 1968, PhD, 1973. Asst. prof. polit. sci. U. Calif., Berkeley, 1971-79, assoc. prof., 1979-90, prof., 1990—, Chancellor's prof., 1998—, chmn. dept., 1993-96, chmn. Ctr. for Slavic and East European Studies, 1982-94, dean of social scis., 1999—. Vice chmn. bd. trustees Nat. Coun. for Soviet and East European Rsch., Washington, 1988-91. Author: Khrushchev and Brezhnev as Leaders, 1982, Soviet Strategy in the Middle East, 1989; editor: Can Gorbachev's Reforms Succeed?, 1990, Learning in U.S. and Soviet Foreign Policy, 1991. Grantee Ford Found., 1982-84, Carnegie Corp., 1985-94, 97-99. Mem. Am. Assn. for Advancement Slavic Studies (bd. dirs., exec. com. 1990-93). Office: U Calif Dept Polit Sci 210 Barrows Hall Berkeley CA 94720-1950

BRESLOW, NORMAN EDWARD, biostatistics educator, researcher; b. Mpls., Feb. 21, 1941; s. Lester and Alice Jane (Philp) B.; m. Gayle Marguerite Bramwell, Sept. 7, 1963; children: Lauren Louise, Sara Jo. BA, Reed Coll., 1962; PhD, Stanford U., 1967. Trainee Stanford U., 1965-67; vis. research worker London Sch. Hygiene, 1967-68; instr. U. Wash., Seattle, 1968-69, asst. prof., 1969-72, assoc. prof., 1972-76, prof., 1976—, chmn. dept. biostats., 1983-93; statistician Internat. Agy. Research Cancer, Lyon, France, 1972-74. Mem. Hutchinson Cancer Ctr., Seattle, 1982—; statistician Nat. Wilms' Tumor Study, 1969—; cons. Internat. Agy. Research Cancer, Lyon, 1978-79; assoc. prof. U. Geneva, 1994—. Recipient Spiegelman Gold medal APHA, 1978, Preventive Oncology Acad.award, NIH, 1978-83, Snedecor award Com. of Pres.'s on Statis. Socs., 1995, R.A. Fisher lectr. and award, 1995; rsch. grantee NIH, 1984—; sr. U.S. Scientist, Alexander Humboldt Found., Fed. Republic of Germany, 1982; sr. Internat. fellowship Fogarty Ctr., 1990. Fellow AAAS, Am. Statis Assn. (com. on fellows 1996-00), Royal Statis. Soc.; mem. Internat. Statis. Inst., Inst. Medicine-Nat. Acad. Scis., Internat. Biometric Soc. (regional com. 1975-78, coun. 1994-2000, v.p. 2001). Avocations: ski mountaineering, hiking, bicycling. Office: Univ of Wash Dept Biostatistics Seattle WA 98195-7232 E-mail: norm@u.washington.edu

BRESSAN, PAUL LOUIS, lawyer; b. Rockville Centre, N.Y., June 15, 1947; s. Louis Charles Bressan and Nance Elizabeth Batteley. BA cum laude, Fordham Coll., 1969; JD, Columbia U., 1975. Bar: N.Y. 1976, Calif. 1987, U.S. Dist. Ct. (so., ea. and no. dists.) N.Y. 1976, U.S. Dist. Ct. (no. and ctrl. dists.) Calif. 1987, U.S. Ct. Appeals (2d cir.) 1980, U.S. Supreme Ct. 1980, U.S. Ct. Appeals (1st and 4th cirs.) 1981, U.S. Ct. Appeals (11th cir.) 1982, U.S. Ct. Appeals (9th cir.) 1987, U.S Ct. Appeals (7th cir.) 1991, U.S. Dist. Ct. (ea. dist.) Calif. 1995; U.S. Dist. Ct. (so. dist.) Calif. 1997. Assoc. Kelley, Drye & Warren, N.Y.C., 1975-84, ptnr. N.Y.C. and Los Angeles, 1984—. Served to lt. USNR, 1971-72. Named One of Outstanding Coll. Athletes of Am., 1969; Harlan Fiske Stone scholar Columbia Law Sch. Mem. ABA, Calif. Bar Assn., Phi Beta Kappa. Republican. Roman Catholic. Office: Kelley Drye & Warren LLP 777 S Figueroa St Ste 2700 Los Angeles CA 90017-5825 E-mail: pbressan@kelleydrye.com

BREST, PAUL A. law educator; b. Jacksonville, Fla., Aug. 9, 1940; s. Alexander and Mia (Deutsch) B.; m. Iris Lang, June 17, 1962; children: Hilary, Jeremy. AB, Swarthmore Coll., 1962; JD, Harvard U., 1965; LLD (hon.), Northeastern U., 1980, Swarthmore Coll., 1991. Bar: N.Y. 1966. Law clk. to Hon. Bailey Aldrich U.S. Ct. Appeals (1st cir.), Boston, 1965-66; atty. NAACP Legal Def. Fund, Jackson, Miss., 1966-68; law clk. Justice John Harlan, U.S. Supreme Ct., 1968-69; prof. law Stanford U., 1969—, Kenneth and Harle Montgomery Prof. pub. interest law, Richard E. Lang prof. and dean, 1987-99; pres. William and Flora Hewlett Found., Menlo Park, Calif., 1999—. Author: Processes of Constitutional Decisionmaking, 1992. Mem. Am. Acad. Arts and Scis. Home: 814 Tolman Dr Palo Alto CA 94305-1026 Office: Willian and Flora Hewlett Found 525 Middlefield Rd Menlo Park CA 94025-3460 E-mail: pbrest@hewlett.org

BRETT, STEPHEN M. lawyer, retired entertainment company executive; BS, U. Pa., 1962, JD, 1966. Bar: N.Y. 1966, Colo. 1971. Assoc. Dewey, Ballantine, Bushby, Palmer & Wood, 1966-71; ptnr. Sherman & Howard, 1971-88; exec. v.p. legal, gen. counsel, sec. United Artists Entertainment Co., Denver, 1988-91; gen. counsel, v.p., sec. Tele-Comm., Inc., Englewood, Colo., 1991—, exec. v.p., gen. counsel, 1991-2000. Office: Tele-Comm Inc 5619 Dtc Pkwy Englewood CO 80111-3013

BREUER, MELVIN ALLEN, electrical engineering educator; b. L.A., Feb. 1, 1938; s. Arthur and Bertha Helen (Friedman) B.; m. Sandra Joyce Scalir, Apr. 7, 1967; children: Teri Lynn, Jeffrey Steven. BS in Engring., UCLA, 1959, MS in Engring., 1961; PhD in Elec. Engring., U. Calif., Berkeley, 1965. Asst. prof. U. So. Calif., L.A., 1965-71, assoc. prof., 1971-80, prof., 1980—, chmn. elec. engring. systems dept., 1991-94, 2000—, chair engring. faculty coun., 1997-98, Charles Lee Powell prof., 1995—. Co-author: Diagnosis and Reliable Design, 1976, Digital Systems Testing and Testable Design, 1990; editor, co-author: Design Automation, 1972; editor: Digital Systems Design Automation, 1975; editor-in-chief Jour. Design Automation, 1980-82; co-editor: Knowledge Based Systems for Test and Diagnosis, 1990; contbr. articles to profl. jours. Recipient Assocs. award U. So. Calif., 1991; Fulbright-Hays scholar, 1972. Fellow IEEE (Taylor Booth award for edn. 1993); mem. Am. Soc. Engring. Edn., N.Y. Acad. Scis., Sigma Xi, Tau Beta Pi, Eta Kappa Nu. Democrat. Office: U So Calif University Park Los Angeles CA 90089-0001

BREUER, STEPHEN ERNEST, religious organization administrator; b. July 14, 1936; came to U.S., 1938, naturalized, 1945; s. John Hans Howard and Olga Marion (Haar) B.; m. Gail Fern Breitbart, Sept. 4, 1960 (div. 1986); children: Jared Noah, Rachel Elise; m. Nadine Bendit, Sept. 25, 1988. BA cum laude, UCLA, 1959; gen. secondary credential, 1960. Tchr. L.A. City Schs., 1960-62; dir. Wilshire Blvd. Temple Camps, L.A., 1962-86; exec. dir. Wilshire Blvd. Temple, L.A., 1980; dir. Edgar F. Magnin Religious Sch., L.A., 1970-80; instr. Hebrew Union Coll., L.A., 1965-76, L.A., 1992, U. Judaism, 1991; field instr. San Francisco State U., 1970-80, Calif. State U., San Diego, Hebrew Union Coll., 1977-81, U. of Judaism UCLA extension. V.P. L.A. Youth Programs Inc., 1967-77; youth advisor L.A. County Commn. Human Rels., 1969-72, bd. dirs. Cmty. Rels. Conf. So. Calif., 1965-85; bd. dirs. Alzheimer's Disease and Related Disorders Assn., 1984-95, v.p. L.A. County chpt., 1984-86, pres., 1986-88, nat. exec. com., 1987-95, nat. devel. chair, 1992-95, Calif. state coun. pres. 1987-92, chmn. of Calif. gov.'s adv. com. on Alzheimer's disease, 1988-97; mem. goals program City of Beverly Hills, Calif., 1985-91; bd. dirs. Pacific SW regional Union Am. Hebrew Congregations, 1985-88, mem. nat. bd., exec. com., 1993-97; bd. dirs. Echo Found., 1986-88, Mazon-Jewish Response to Hunger, 1993-97, Wilshire Stakeholders exec. com., 1987-94, Internat. Rescue Cmty. West Coast Bd., 1999—; treas. Wilshire Cmty. Prayer Alliance, 1986-88; active United Way. Recipient svc. awards L.A. County Bd. Suprs., 1982, 87, Ventura County Bd. Suprs., 1982, 87, Weinberg Chai Lifetime Achievement award Jewish Fed. Council Los Angeles, 1986, Nat. Philanthropy Day L.A. Medallion, 1993, L.A. County Redevel. Agy. recognition, 1994, L.A. Bus. Coun. award, 1997; Steve Breuer Conference Ctr. in Malibu named in his honor at Wilshire Blvd. Temple Camps, 1990. Mem. So. Calif. Cmaping Assn. (dir. 1964-82), Nat. Assn. Temple Adminstrs. (nat. bd. dirs. 1987—, v.p. 1991-93, pres. 1993-97, Svc. to Judaism award 1989, Svc. to the Cmty. award 1990), NATA (Svc. to NATA award 1997), Nat. Assn. Temple Educators (Kaminker award 1973), L.A. Assn. Jewish Edn. (dir.), Profl. Assn. Temple Adminstrs. (pres. 1985-88), Jewish Communal Profls. So. Calif., Assn. Supervision and Curriculum Devel., Am. Mgmt. Assn., So. Calif. Conf. Jewish Communal Workers, Jewish Profl. Network, Amnesty Internat., Jewish Resident Camping Assn. (pres. 1976-82), World union for Progressive Judaism, UCLA Alumni Assn., Wilderness Soc., Center for Environ. Edn., Wildlife Fedn., Living Desert, Maple Mental Health Ctr. of Beverly Hills, Los Angeles County Mus. Contemporary Art, People for the Am. Way, Assn. Reform Zionists Am. (bd. dirs. 1993—). Office: Wilshire Blvd Temple 3663 Wilshire Blvd Los Angeles CA 90010-2798

BREUER, WERNER ALFRED, retired plastics company executive; b. Sinn, Hessia, Germany, Jan. 30, 1930; came to U.S., 1959; s. Christian and Hedwig (Cunz) B.; m. Gertrud Ackermann, June 21, 1950 (dec. 1998); children: Patricia, Julia, Eva-Maria. LLB, La Salle Ext. U., 1970; BS in Human Rels. and Orgnl. Behavior, U. San Francisco, 1983; MS in Bus. Mgmt., U. La Verne, 1985, DPA, 1988. Lab. supr. Dayco Corp. (Am. latex divsn.), Hawthorne, Calif., 1959-65; tech. ops. mgr. Olin Corp., Stamford and New Haven, Conn., 1965-69; gen. mgr., exec. v.p. Expanded Rubber and Plastics Corp., Gardena, Calif., 1969-96; ret., 1996; gen. mgr. Schlobohm Co. Inc., Dominguez Hills, Calif., 1989-96; ret. Cons. human resources Stabond Corp., Gardena, 1988-95. Author/composer various popular and sacred recordings, 1970s; contbr. articles to jours. Mem. ASTM, ASCAP, Am. Soc. for Metals, Soc. for Plastics Engrs., N.Y. Acad. Scis., U. La Verne Alumni Assn. Republican. Avocations: play music, writing, horseback riding, composing, sketching. Achievements include pioneering use of plastics especially polyurethanes in defense missiles and space and communication aviation industry; defense projects for DEW Line N.A. radar defense to Stealth Fighter B-2 Project. Home: 1710 Polo Way Longmont CO 80501-9515

BREWER, JOHN CHARLES, journalist; b. Cin., Oct. 24, 1947; s. Harry Marion and Barbara Ann (Burrier) B.; m. Adeline Laude, Dec. 22, 1973 (div. 1994); children: Andrew John, Jeffrey Joseph; m. Ann Hagen Kellett, 1997. B.S., Calif. State Poly. U., Pomona, 1970. Newsman, photographer Daily Report, Ontario, Calif., 1967-69; newsman AP, L.A., 1969-74, news editor, 1974-75, asst. chief bur., 1975-76, chief of bur., 1976-82, L.A., 1982-86, gen. exec. membership dept. N.Y.C., 1986-88; exec. editor news svc. The N.Y. Times, 1988-90, editor in chief news svc., 1990-97; pres. N.Y. Times Syndication Sales Corp., 1990-97; publisher, editor Peninsula Daily News, Port Angeles, Wash., 1998—. Bd. dirs. Port Angeles C. of C.; bd. dirs. Olympic Meml. Hosp. Found. Mem. Fedn. of Fly Fishers, Northwest Steelheaders-Trout Unlimited, Nat. Steelhead Trout Assn., Rotary Internat., Kiwanis. Republican. Roman Catholic. Clubs: Northwest Steelheaders-Trout Unlimited, Nat. Steelhead Trout Assn. Office: Peninsula Daily News 305 W 1st St Port Angeles WA 98362-2205

BREWER, PETER GEORGE, ocean geochemist; b. Ulverston, Eng., Dec. 30, 1940; came to U.S., 1967, naturalized, 1982; s. Frederick and Irene (Clarkson) B.; m. Hilary Williams, Mar. 29, 1966; children: Jillian Anne, Alastair Michael, Erica Christine. BSc, Liverpool (Eng.) U., 1962, PhD, 1967. Asst. scientist Woods Hole (Mass.) Oceanographic Inst., 1967-71, assoc. scientist, 1971-78, sr. scientist, 1978-91; program dir. marine chemistry NSF, 1981-83; exec. dir. Monterey Bay Aquarium Rsch. Inst., Pacific Grove, Calif., 1991-96, sr. scientist, 1996—. Leader of ocean sci. expeditions; mem. Environ. Task Force, 1992-93, NAS Ocean Studies Bd., 1986-94, Com. on Climate Change and the Ocean, 1987-90; convenor NATO A.R.I. on Chem. Dynamics of Upper Ocean, Jouy en Jossas, France, 1983; mem. NAS panel on policy implications of greenhouse gas warming: mitigation, 1989-91; mem. NAS carbon dioxide adv. com., 1982-83; vis. prof. U. Wash., 1979; mem. GEOSECS sci. adv. com., 1972-78. Assoc. editor: Geophys. Rsch. Letters, 1977-79, Jour. Marine Rsch., 1974-81, Deep-Sea Rsch., 1984-87, Jour. of Oceanography, 1994—; contbr. articles to profl. publs. Chmn. Gordon Rsch. Conf. on Chem. Oceanography, 1980; vice-chmn. Joint Global Ocean Fluxes Com., SCOR, 1987-90; mem. adv. bd. Applied Physics Lab., U. Wash., 1991-96. Grantee NSF, NASA, Office Naval Rsch., Dept. Energy. Fellow AAAS, Am. Geophys. Union. Office: Monterey Bay Aquarium Rsch Inst 7700 Sandholdt Rd PO Box 628 Moss Landing CA 95039-0628 E-mail: grpe@mbari.org

BREWER, STANLEY R. wholesale distribution consultant; b. Preston, Idaho, Nov. 5, 1937; s. G. Stanley and Emily (Wallentine) B.; m. Diane Rose, Aug. 1, 1960; children: Dee S., Douglas R., John-David, Jennifer. AS, Weber State Coll., 1957; student, U. Utah, 1960-63. Various positions Associated Food Stores, Inc., Salt Lake City, 1960-97, sr. v.p., 1994-97; pres. S. Brewer & Co., 1997—. [illegible] Salt Lake City, 1982—; bd. dirs. Wesco Explosives, Inc., Deluxe Ice Cream Co. Chmn. Salt Lake City chpt. March of Dimes, 1998-2000; nat. trustee March of Dimes Birth Defects Found., White Plains, N.Y., 1987—; chmn. Salt Lake County Voting Dist., 1965-66, 76-78. Republican. Mem. LDS Ch. Avocations: alpine and cross country skiing, hiking, boating, jogging. E-mail: sbrewco@aol.com

BREWSTER, RUDI MILTON, judge; b. Sioux Falls, S.D., May 18, 1932; s. Charles Edwin and Wilhemina Therese (Rud) B.; m. Gloria Jane Nanson, June 27, 1954; children: Scot Alan, Lauri Diane (Alan Lee), Julie Lynn Yahnke. AB in Pub. Affairs, Princeton U., 1954; JD, Stanford U., 1960. Bar: Calif. 1960. From assoc. to ptnr. Gray, Cary, Ames & Frye, San Diego, 1960-84; judge U.S. Dist. Ct. (so. dist.) Calif., San Diego, 1994-98, sr. judge, 1998—. Served to capt. USNR, 1954-82 Ret. Fellow Am. Coll. Trial Lawyers; mem. Am. Bd. Trial Advs., Internat. Assn. Ins. Counsel, Am. Inns of Ct. Republican. Lutheran. Avocations: skiing, hunting, gardening. Office: US Dist Ct Ste 4165 940 Front St San Diego CA 92101-8902 Fax: 619-702-9927. E-mail: Rudi_Brewster@casd.uscourts.gov

BREYER, CHARLES ROBERTS, judge, lawyer; b. San Francisco, Nov. 3, 1941; s. Irving Gerald and Anne Adele (Roberts) B.; m. Sydney Rachel Goldstein, Jan. 17, 1976; children: Kate, Joseph. AB, Harvard U., 1963; JD, U. Calif., Berkeley, 1966. Bar: U.S. Dist. Ct. (no. dist.) Calif. 1976, U.S. Ct. Appeals (9th cir.) 1976. Law clk. U.S. Dist. Ct. (no. dist.) Calif., San Francisco, 1966, asst. dist. atty., 1967-72; mem. task force Watergate Spl. Pros., Washington, 1972-74, chief asst dist. atty. San Francisco, 1979; ptnr. Coblentz, Cahan, McCabe & Breyer, San Francisco, 1974-79, 80-97; judge U.S. Dist. Ct. (no Calif.), San Francisco, 1997-. Dir. Lawyers Com. in Human Rights, N.Y., 1990—. Capt. U.S. Army, 1966-72. Office: Phillip Burton Fed Bldg US Courthouse PO Box 36060 San Francisco CA 94102

BREYER, JAMES WILLIAM, venture capitalist; b. New Haven, July 26, 1961; s. John Paul and Eva Breyer; m. Susan Zaroff, June 20, 1987. BS, Stanford U., 1983; MBA, Harvard U., 1987. Sr. bus. analyst McKinsey & Co., N.Y.C., 1983-85; assoc. Accel Ptnrs., San Francisco, 1987-90, gen. ptnr., 1990-95, mng. gen. ptnr., 1995—. Bd dirs. TechNet, Silicon Valley Cmty. Ventures, Harvard Bus. Sch. Calif. Rsch. Ctr. Baker scholar Harvard U., 1987. Mem. Nat. Assn. Venture Capitalists (bd. dirs.), Western Assn. Venture Capitalists (bd. dirs.), Harvard Bus. Sch. Club of No. Calif. Office: Accel Ptnrs 428 University Ave Palo Alto CA 94301-1812

BREYNE, MATTHEW M. finance company executive; m. Cathy Breyne. B Fin., No. Ill. U., 1979. With Heller Fin., Chgo., 1987—; pres., COO Finova Group Inc., Scottsdale, Ariz., pres., CEO; also bd. dirs. Office: Finova Group Inc 4800 N Scottsdale Rd Scottsdale AZ 85251-7623

BRIAN, BRAD D. lawyer; b. Merced, Calif., Apr. 19, 1952; BA, U. Calif., Berkeley, 1974; JD magna cum laude, Harvard U., 1977. Bar: Calif. 1977, U.S. Ct. Appeals (3d cir.) 1978, U.S. Dist. Ct. (ctrl. dist.) Calif. 1978, U.S. Ct. Appeals (9th cir.) 1980. Law clk. to Hon. John J. Gibbons U.S. Ct. Appeals (3d cir.), 1977-78; asst. U.S. atty. Office U.S. Atty. (ctrl. dist.) Calif., 1978-81; hearing examiner L.A. City Police Commn., 1982; atty. Munger, Tolles & Olson, L.A., 1981—. Lectr. in law U. So. Calif. Law Ctr., 1983; instr. Nat. Inst. Trial Advocacy, 1986; guest instr. Harvard Law Sch. Trial Advocacy Program, 1983. Bd. editors Harvard Law Rev., 1975-77, mng. editor and treas., 1976-77. Mem. ABA (chmn. pre-trial practice and discovery, litigation sect. 1987-89, liaison with fed. jud. confs. 1989-91, chair task force on civil justice reform act of 1990), State Bar Calif., L.A. County Bar Assn. (mem. fed. practice standards com. 1980-82). Office: Munger Tolles & Olson 355 S Grand Ave Fl 35 Los Angeles CA 90071-1560

BRICKER, NEAL S. physician, educator; b. Denver, Apr. 18, 1927; s. Eli D. and Rose (Quiat) B.; m. Miriam Thalenberg, June 24, 1951 (dec. 1974); children: Dusty, Cary, Susan, Dan Baker; m. Ruth T. Baker, Dec. 28, 1980. B.A., U. Colo., 1946, M.D., 1949. Diplomate Am. Bd. Internal Medicine (bd. govs. 1972-79, chmn. nephrology test com. 1973-76). Intern, resident Bellevue Hosp., N.Y.C., 1949-52; sr. asst. resident Peter Bent Brigham Hosp., Boston, 1954-55, asso. dir. cardio-renal lab., 1955-56; instr. Harvard, 1955-56; fellow Howard Hughes Med. Inst., 1955-56; from asst. prof. to prof. Washington U., 1956-72, dir. renal div., 1956-72; Mem. sci. adv. bd. Nat. Kidney Found., 1962-69, chmn. research and fellowship grants com., 1964-65, mem. exec. com., 1968-71; prof. medicine, chmn. dept. Albert Einstein Coll. Medicine, 1972-76; prof. medicine U. Miami, Fla., 1976-78, vice chmn. dept., 1976-78; Disting. prof. medicine UCLA, 1978-86; disting. prof. medicine, dir. sci. and tech. planning Loma Linda (Calif.) U., 1986-92; exec. v.p. Naturon Pharm., Riverside, Calif., 1992-94; clin. prof. medicine UCR/UCLA Program in Biomed. Scis., UCR, 1996—. Cons. NIH, 1964-68, chmn. gen. medicine study sect., 1966-68, chmn. renal disease and urology tng. grants com., 1969-71; vis. investigator Inst. Biol. Chemistry, Copenhagen, 1960-61; investigator Mt. Desert Island Biol. Labs.; advisor on behalf Inst. Medicine to Sen. Lowell Weicker; clin. prof. medicine U. Calif. Riverside/UCLA program in biomed. scis., 1997—. Assoc. editor: Jour. Lab. and Clin. Medicine, 1961-67, Kidney Internat, 1972; editorial com.: Jour. Clin. Investigation, 1964-68, Physiol. Revs, 1970-76, Am. Heart Assn. Publs. Com., 1974-79, Calcified Tissue Internat., 1978-86, Proc. Soc. Exptl. Biology and Medicine, 1978-86; editor: Supplements, Circulation and Circulation Research, 1974-79; contbr. articles to profl. jours., chpts. to books. Served with USNR, 1944-45; Served with U.S. Army, 1952-54. Recipient Gold-Headed Cane award U. Colo., 1949, Silver and Gold Alumni award, 1975; USPHS Research Career award, 1964-72; Skylab Achievement award NASA, 1974; Pub. Service award, 1975; George Norlin Silver medal award U. Colo. 1982; citation Kidney Found. So. Calif., 1984. Fellow A.C.P.; mem. Am. Fedn. for Clin. Research, Central Soc. Clin. Research (council 1970-73), Assn. Am. Physicians, Am. Soc. for Clin. Investigation (pres. 1972-73, chmn. com. nat. med. policy 1973-77, Disting. Service award 1969), Internat. Soc. Nephrology (exec. com. 1966-81, v.p. 1966-69, treas. 1969-81), Internat. Congress Nephrology (pres. 1981-84), Am. Soc. Nephrology (1st pres., John Peters medal 1991), Am. Physiol. Soc., Soc. for Exptl. Biology and Medicine, Western Soc. Clin. Research, So. Soc. Clin. Investigation, Nat. Acad. Scis. (com. on space biology and medicine, ad hoc panel on renal and metabolic effects space flight 1971-72, mem. drug efficacy com. 1966-68, com. space biology, chmn. medicine in space sci. bd. 1972-81, com. chmn. 1978-81, chmn. com. renal and metabloic effects space flight 1972-74, chmn. study com. on life scis. 1976-81, mem. space sci. bd. 1977-81), Inst. Medicine of NAS, Sigma Xi, Alpha Omega Alpha. Home: 1820 Oxford Ave Claremont CA 91711-2613 Office: UCR/UCLA Riverside CA 92521-0121

BRICKNER, DAVID, religious organization administrator, consultant; b. Beverly, Mass., Sept. 29, 1958; s. Avi Stanley and Leah Esther (Kendal) B.; m. Patrice Anne Vasataro, Dec. 29, 1979; children: Isaac, Ilana. Diploma in Jewish Studies, Moody Bible Inst., 1981; BA in Jewish Studies, Northeastern Ill. U., 1986; MA in Jewish Studies, Fuller Sem., 1994. Ordained min. Bapt. Gen. Conf., 1993. Mobile team leader Jews for Jesus, USA, [illegible] chief of station N.Y.C., 1995-96, exec. dir. San Francisco, 1996—. Portfolio holder Jews for Jesus South Africa, 1988-96, bd. dirs., 1989—; pres. bd. dirs. Jews for Jesus USA, San Francisco, 1996—; bd. dirs. Jews for Jesus Europe, London, 1996—. Author: Mishpochah Matters, 1996, Future Hope, 1999. Mem. Lausaunne Consultation on Jewish Evangelism, Evangelical Theol. soc., Evangelical Missiological Soc. Office: Jews for [illegible] CA 94102-[illegible]

BRIDGE, BOBBE J. state supreme court justice; m. Jonathan J. Bridge; children: Rebecca, Don. BA magna cum laude, U. Wash; MA, PhD in Polit. Sci., U. Mich.; JD, U. Wash., 1976. Superior Ct. judge King County, Wash., 1990-1999; chief judge King County Juvenile Ct., 1994-97, asst. presiding judge, 1997-98, presiding judge, 1998-99; judge Wash. State Supreme Ct., 1999—; mem. faculty Wash. State Jud. Coll. Chmn. King County Criminal Justice Coun., King County Truancy Steerin Com., Juvenile Justice Operational Master Plan Oversight Com., Pub. Trust and Confidence Com. Bd. Jud. Adminstrn.; co-chmn. Unified Family Ct. Bench-Bar Task Force. Bd. dirs. YWCA, Seattle Children's Home, Families for Kids Permanency Oversight Com., Tech. Adv. Com. Female Juvenile Offenders, Adv. Com. Adolescent Life Skills Program, Street Youth Law Program, Northwest Mediation Svc., Woodland Pk. Zoological Soc., Wash. Coun. Crime and Delinquency, Women's Funding Alliance, Alki Found., Privacy Fund, Seattle Arts Commn., U. Wash. Arts and Sci. Devel., Greater Seattle C. of C., Metrocenter YMCA, Juvenile Ct. Conf. Com.; mem. King County Task Force on Children and Families, Wash. State's Dept. Social and Health Svcs. Children., Youth, Family Svcs. Adv. Com., Child Protection Roundtable, Govs. Juvenile Justice Adv. Com.; chmn. State Task Force on Juvenile Issues, Coun. Youth Crisis Work Group, Families-at-Risk subcom., Bd. Dirs. Ctr. Career Alternatives, Candidate Evaluation Com. Seattle-King Mcpl. League, Law and justice Com. League Women Voters; co-chmn. Govs. Coun. on Families, Youth, and Justice; pres. Seattle Women's Commn., Seattle Chpt. Am. Jewish Com.,bd. dirs., asst. sec.-treas. Jewish Fedn. Greater Seattle, chmn., vice chmn. Cmty. Rels. Coun. Named Judge of Yr. Wash. Women Lawyers, 1996; recipient Hannah G. Solomon award Nat. Coun. Jewish Women, 1996, Cmty. Catalyst award Mother's Against Violence in Am., 1997, Women Making a Difference award Youthcare, 1998; honored "woman helping women" Soroptimist Internat. of Kent, 1999. Mem. Phi Beta Kappa. Office: Wash Supreme Ct PO Box 40929 Olympia WA 98504-0929

BRIDGE, HERBERT MARVIN, jewelry executive; b. Seattle, Mar. 14, 1925; s. Ben and Sally (Silverman) B.; m. Shirley Selesnick, Jan. 25, 1948; children: Jonathan J., Daniel E. BA in Polit. Sci., U. Wash., 1947. Pres. Ben Bridge Jeweler Inc., Seattle, 1955-76, chmn., 1977—. Past pres. Downtown Seattle Assn., 1980-81, Am. Jewish Com.; bd. dirs. Naval Acad. Found., Naval Undersea Mus., Alliance for Edn.; chair Puget Sound USO; chmn. sr. adv. bd. Goodwill Games of 1990; co-chair King County chpt. United Way, 2000-01. Rear adm. USNR, 1942-85. Decorated Legion of Merit with Gold Star in lieu of 2d award; recipient Israel Bonds Masada award, 1974, Am. Jewish Com. Human Rels award, 1978, Navy League scroll hon., 1980, 96, U. Wash. Alumni Legend award, 1987, Vol. of Yr. award Jewish Fedn., 1991, Privacy Fund Humanitarian award, 1991, Heritage award Mus. History and Industry, 1993, A.K. Guy Cmty. Svc. award YMCA, 1995, Sea 1st Cmty. Svc. award, 1998, Citizen Yr. Seattle-King Co., 2001; named to Nat. Jewelers Hall of Fame, 1998, Puget Sound Bus. Hall of Fame, 1999. Mem. Am. Gem. Soc. (cert. gemnologist; trustee 1993—, chair trustees 1994-2000), Pacific N.W. Jewelers (past pres.), Greater Seattle C. of C. (past chmn. 1986-87, pres. club, past pres. 1974-75), Naval Res. Assn. (past pres.), Wash. Athletic Club (pres. 1992-93), City Club (founder), Rotary (dir. found., Seattle Rotary bd.), Shriners. Democrat. Office: PO Box 1908 Seattle WA 98111-1908

BRIDGE, JONATHAN JOSEPH, lawyer, retail executive; b. Seattle, Mar. 19, 1950; s. Herbert Marvin and Shirley Geraldine (Selesnick) B.; m. Bobbe Jean Chaback, May 20, 1978; children: Donald, Rebecca. BA with honors, U. Wash., 1972, JD, 1976. Bar: Wash. 1976, U.S. Dist. Ct. (we. dist.) Wash. 1976, U.S. Ct. Mil. Appeals 1977, U.S. Ct. Appeals (9th cir.) 1979, U.S. Supreme Ct. 1980. Legal service officer USN, Oak Harbor, Wash., 1976-79, staff judge adv. Bremerton, 1979-81; exec. v.p. Ben Bridge Jeweler, Inc., Seattle, 1981-90, vice chmn., gen. counsel, co-chief exec. officer, 1990—. Bd. dirs. Ben Bridge Corp., Seattle. Bd. dirs. King County Mental Health Bd., Seattle, 1984; mem. bd. Wash. Retail Assn., 1985-94; vice chmn. Seattle Urban League, 1986-88, chmn., 1988-89; pres. Am. Jewish Com., Seattle, 1986-88; counsel Pacific Northwest Jewelers Assn., 1988—, treas., 1990, pres., 1995-97; bd. dirs. Seattle Alliance Edn., 1990—; mem. adv. bd. Ctr. for Career Alternatives, 1981—; precinct committeeman, 1990-96. Served to lt. comdr. USN, 1972-81, Vietnam, with Res., 1981—, comdr., 1988-93, capt., 1994—. Mem. ABA, Wash. State Bar Assn., Seattle/King County Bar Assn., Judge Advocates Assn., Greater Seattle C. of C., U. Wash. Alumni Assn. (bd. dirs. 1986—), U. Wash. Law Sch. Alumni Assn. (pres. 1989-91). Democrat. Jewish. Club: Wash. Athletic (Seattle), Columbia Tower (Seattle), City (Seattle). Home: 2440 Montavista Pl W Seattle WA 98199-3723 Office: Ben Bridge Jeweler Inc PO Box 1908 Seattle WA 98111-1908

BRIDGES, B. RIED, lawyer; b. Kansas City, Mo., Oct. 20, 1927; s. Brady R. and Mary H. (Nieuwenhuis) B.; m. Lou George, Feb. 9, 1955; 1 son, Ried George. BA, U. So. Calif., 1951, LLB, 1954. Bar: Calif. 1954. Assoc. Overton, Lyman & Prince, L.A., 1956-58, ptnr., 1958-63, Bonne, Jones & Bridges, L.A., 1963-74, Bonne, Bridges, Mueller & O'Keefe, L.A., Santa Ana, Santa Barbara, Ventura, San Luis Obispo, Riverside, San Francisco, 1974—. Served with U.S. Army, 1954-56. Fellow Am. Coll. Trial Lawyers, Internat. Acad. Trial Lawyers; mem. ABA, Calif. Bar Assn., Assn. So. Calif. Def. Counsel, L.A. County Bar Assn., Santa Barbara County Bar Assn., Am. Bd. Trial Advs. (diplomate), Pacific Corinthian Yacht Club, Balboa of Mazatlan (Sinaloa, Mex.). Republican. Avocation: sportfishing. Home: 2551 Victoria Ave Oxnard CA 93035-2931 Office: Bonne Bridges Mueller O'Keefe & Nichols 3699 Wilshire Blvd 10th Flr Los Angeles CA 90010 E-mail: rbridges@bbmon.com

BRIDGES, EDWIN MAXWELL, education educator; b. Hannibal, Mo., Jan. 1, 1934; s. Edwin Otto and Radha (Maxwell) B.; m. Marjorie Anne Pollock, July 31, 1954; children: Richard, Rebecca, Brian, Bruce. BS, U. Mo., 1954; MA, U. Chgo., 1956, PhD, 1964. English tchr. Bremen Community High Sch., Midlothian, Ill., 1954-56; asst. prin. Griffith (Ind.) High Sch., 1956-60, prin., 1960-62; staff assoc. U. Chgo., 1962-64, assoc. prof., 1967-72; assoc. dir. Univ. Coun. for Edn. Adminstrn., Columbus, Ohio, 1964-65; asst. prof. Washington U., St. Louis, 1965-67; assoc. prof. U. Chgo., 1967-72; prof. U. Calif., Santa Barbara, 1972-74; prof. edn. Stanford (Calif.) U., 1974—. Mem. nat. adv. panel Ctr. for Rsch. on Ednl. Accountability and Tchr. Evaluation, 1990-95; external examiner U. Hong Kong, 1990-92; vis. prof. Chinese U., Hong Kong, 1976, 96; cons. World Bank, China, 1986, 89; dir. Midwest Adminstrn. Ctr., Chgo., 1967-72. Author: Managing the Incompetent Teacher, 1984, 2d edit., 1990, The Incompetent Teacher, 1986, 2d edit., 1991, Problem Based Learning for Administrators, 1992; co-author: Introduction to Educational Adminstration, 1977, Implementing Problem-based Leadership Development, 1995. Recipient of the R.F. Campbell Lifetime Achievement award, 1996; named Outstanding Young Man of Ind., C. of C., 1960; named hon. prof. and cert. of honor So. China Normal U., 1989, Citation of Merit for Outstanding Achievement and Meritorious Svc. in Edn., U. Mo. Coll. Edn., 1999. Mem. [illegible] Stanford U [illegible] CA 94305 E-mail: bridges@stanford.edu

BRIDGES, ROBERT LYSLE, retired lawyer; b. Altus, Ark., May 12, 1909; s. Joseph Manning and Jeffa Alice (Morrison) B.; m. Alice Marian Rodenberger, June 10, 1930; children: David Manning, James Robert, Linda Lee. AB, U. Calif., 1930, JD, 1933. Bar: Calif. 1933, U.S. Supreme Ct. 1938. Pvt. practice, San Francisco, 1933-92; assoc. firm Thelen Marrin

Johnson & Bridges, 1933-39, ptnr., 1938-92. Trustee, former chmn. U. Calif. Berkeley Found. Mem. ABA, Calif. Bar Assn., San Francisco Bar Assn., Commonwealth Club of Calif., Pacific Union Club, Claremont Country Club (Oakland). Republican. Home: 3972 Happy Valley Rd Lafayette CA 94549-2426 Office: 101 Second St Ste 1800 San Francisco CA 94105-3601

BRIDGES, WILLIAM BRUCE, electrical engineer, researcher, educator; b. Inglewood, Calif., Nov. 29, 1934; s. Newman K. and Doris L. (Brown) B.; m. Carol Ann French, Aug. 24, 1957 (div. 1986); children: Ann Marjorie, Bruce Kendall, Michael Alan; m. Linda Josephine McManus, Nov. 15, 1986. B.E.E., U. Calif. at Berkeley, 1956, M.E.E. (Gen. Electric Rice fellow), 1957, Ph.D. in Elec. Engring. (NSF fellow), 1962. Assoc. elec. engring. U. Calif., Berkeley, 1957-59, grad. rsch. engr., 1959-61; mem. tech. staff Hughes Rsch. Labs. divsn. Hughes Aircraft Co., Malibu, Calif., 1960-77, sr. scientist, 1968-77, mgr. laser dept., 1969-70; prof. elec. engring. and applied physics Calif. Inst. Tech., Pasadena, 1977—, Carl F Braun prof. engring., 1983—, exec. officer elec. engring., 1978-81. Lectr. elec. engring. U. So. Calif., L.A., 1962-64; Sherman Fairchild Disting. scholar Calif. Inst. Tech., 1974-75; bd. dirs. Uniphase Corp., 1986-98. Author: (with C.K. Birdsall) Electron Dynamics of Diode Regions, 1966; contbr. articles on gas lasers, optical systems and microwave tubes to profl. jours.; assoc. editor: IEEE Jour. Quantum Electronics, 1977-82, Jour. Optical Soc. Am., 1978-83; inventor noble gas ion laser; patentee in field. Active Boy Scouts Am., 1968-82; bd. dirs. Ventura County Campfire Girls, 1973-76; mem. Air Force Sci. Adv. Bd., 1985-89. Recipient L.A. Hyland Patent award, 1969, Arthur L. Schawlow award Laser Inst. Am., 1986, Lifetime Achievement award for excellence in tchg. Assoc. Students of Calif. Inst. Tech., 2000; named Disting. Engring. Alumnus, U. Calif., Berkeley, 1995. Fellow IEEE (Quantum Electronics award 1988), Optical Soc. Am. (objectives and policies com. 1981-86, 89-91, bd. dirs. 1982-84, v.p. 1986, pres.-elect 1987, pres. 1988, past pres. 1989), Laser Inst. Am.; mem. Nat. Acad. Engring., Nat. Acad. Scis., Am. Radio Relay League, Phi Beta Kappa, Sigma Xi, Tau Beta Pi, Eta Kappa Nu (One of Outstanding Young Elec. Engrs. for 1966). Lutheran. Achievements include invention of noble gas ion laser. Office: Calif Inst Tech Moore Bldg 136-93 Pasadena CA 91125-0001 E-mail: w6fa@caltech.edu

BRIDGFORTH, ROBERT MOORE, JR. aerospace engineer; b. Lexington, Miss., Oct. 21, 1918; s. Robert Moore and Theresa (Holder) B.; student Miss. State Coll., 1935-37; BS, Iowa State Coll., 1940; MS, MIT, 1948; postgrad. Harvard U., 1949; m. Florence Jarnberg, November 7, 1943; children: Robert Moore, Alice Theresa. Asst. engr. Standard Oil Co., of Ohio, 1940; teaching fellow M.I.T., 1940-41, instr. chemistry, 1941-43, research asst., 1943-44, mem. staff div. indsl. cooperation, 1944-47; asso. prof. physics and chemistry Emory and Henry Coll., 1949-51; rsch. engr. Boeing Airplane Co., Seattle, 1951-54, rsch. specialist 1954-55, sr. group engr., 1955-58, chief propulsion systems sect. Systems Mgmt. Office, 1958-59, chief propulsion rsch. unit, 1959-60; founder, chmn. bd. Rocket Rsch. Corp., 1960-69, Explosives Corp. Am., 1966-69. Fellow AIAA (assoc.), Brit. Interplanetary Soc., Am. Inst. Chemists; mem. AAAS, Am. Astronautical Soc. (dir.), Am. Chem. Soc., Am. Rocket Soc. (pres. Pacific NW 1955), Am. Ordnance Assn., Am. Inst. Physics, Am. Assn. Physics Tchrs., Tissue Culture Assn., Soc. for Leukocyte Biology, N.Y. Acad. Scis., Combustion Inst., Sigma Xi. Achievements include U.S. patents for rocket tri-propellants and explosives. Home: 4325 87th Ave SE Mercer Island WA 98040-4127

BRIERLEY, CORALE L. geological engineer; b. Mont. m. Jim Brierley. Student, Mont. State U.; BS in Biology, MS in Chemistry, N.Mex. Inst. Mining & Tech.; PhD in Environ. Scis., U. Tex., Dallas, 1981. With N.Mex. Bur. Mines; founder Advanced Mineral Techs., 1983-87; chief environ. process devel. Newmont Mining Co., 1989-91; founder, prin. Brierley Cons. LLC, Highlands Ranch, Colo., 1991—. Office: Brierley Consultancy LLC PO Box 260012 Highlands Ranch CO 80163-0012

BRIERLEY, JAMES ALAN, biohydrometallurgy consultant; b. Denver, Dec. 22, 1938; s. Everette and Carrie (Berg) B.; m. Corale Louise Beer, Dec. 21, 1965 BS in Bacteriology, Colo. State U., 1961; MS in Microbiology, Mont. State U., 1963, PhD, 1966. Research scientist Martin Marietta Corp., Denver, 1968-69; asst. prof. biology N.Mex. Inst. Mining and Tech., Socorro, 1966-68, from asst. prof. to prof. biology, chmn. dept. biology, 1969-83; research dir. Advanced Mineral Techs., Golden, Colo., 1983-88; chief microbiologist Newmont Metall. Svcs., Englewood, 1988-2000; chief rsch. scientist biohydrometallurgy Newmont Mining Corp., 2000-01; cons. Brierley Consultancy, LLC, Highlands Ranch, Colo., 2001—. Vis. fellow U. Warwick, Coventry, Eng., 1976, vis. prof. Catholic U., Santiago, Chile, 1983; adj. prof. dept. metallurgy U. Utah, 1994-96; cons. Mountain State Mineral Enterprises, Tucson, 1980, Sandia Nat. Lab., Albuquerque, 1976, Bechtel Civil and Minerals, Scottsdale, Ariz., 1984. Contbr. numerous articles to profl. jours.; patentee in field. Served to staff sgt. Air N.G., 1956-61. Recipient 32 research grants Fellow AAAS; mem. Am. Soc. Microbiology, Soc. Gen. Microbiology, Mining and Metall. Soc. Am. Avocations: travel, model railroading, gardening. Home: 2074 East Terrace Dr Highlands Ranch CO 80126-2692 Office: Brierley Consultancy PO Box 260012 Highlands Ranch CO 80163-0012 E-mail: j.brierley@worldnet.att.net

BRIGGS, BURTON A. medical educator; b. Orange, N.J., July 24, 1939; s. Carolyn Sue Briggs; 2 children. BS, Walla Walla Coll., 1961; MD, Loma Linda U., 1966; MA in Mgmt., Claremont Grad. Sch., 1990. Diplomate Am. Bd. Med. Examiners, Am. Bd. Anesthesiology; lic. physician, Calif., Mass. Intern Loma Linda (Calif.) U. Hosp., 1966-67; asst. resident in anesthesia Mass. Gen. Hosp., Boston, 1967-68, 69-70, clin. and rsch. fellow, 1968-69, chief resident, 1969, asst. in anesthesia, co-dir. recovery room/acute care unit, 1972-75; instr. anesthesia Harvard Med. Sch., Boston, 1972-75; asst. prof. anesthesia and surgery Loma Linda U., 1975-83, asst. prof. pediatrics, 1982-87, assoc. prof. anesthesiology and surgery, 1983-87, prof. anesthesiology, prof. surgery, 1987—. Dir. surg. intensive care Loma Linda U. Med. Ctr., 1975-92, chief sect. critical care, 1983-92, med. dir. transport svcs., 1986—, med. dir. operating room svcs., 1991—, bd. trustees, 1986-90; dir. surg. intensive care J.L. Pettis Meml. VA Hosp., 1977-78; sec.-treas. Loma Linda Anesthesiology Med. Group, Inc., 1981-95, sec., 1995—, chmn. billing and reimbursement com., 1995—; chief anesthesiology svcs. Riverside Gen. Hosp., 1985-86;vis. prof. Socieda de Brasileira de Anestesiologia, 1980, Peking (China) Union Med. Coll., 1986; oral examiner Med. Bd. of Calif., 1990—; interviewer regional area Harvard/Radcliffe Colls., 1994—; bd. dirs. faculty physicians and surgeons Loma Linda U. Sch. Medicine, 1995—. Author: Principles of Critical Care, 1987; contbr. articles and abstracts to profl. jours., chpts. to books; article reviewer New Eng. Jour. Medicine, 1973-75, Jour. Critical Care Medicine, 1975-91; examiner Am. Bd. Anesthesiology, 1983-90. With U.S. Army, 1970-71. Fellow Am. Coll. Anesthesiology, Am. Coll. Critical Care Medicine; mem. Am. Soc. Anesthesiologists, Soc. Critical Care Medicine, San Bernardino County Med. Soc., Calif. Soc. Anesthesiology (alt. del. dist. 2 1983-86), Calif. Med. Assn., Loma Linda U. Sch. Medicine Alumni Assn. (bd. dirs. 1994—, CFO 1995—), Assn. Anesthesia Clin. Dirs. (bd. dirs. 1994—), Alpha Omega Alpha. Office: Loma Linda U Dept Anesthesiology 11234 Anderson St Loma Linda CA 92354-2871

BRIGGS, WINSLOW RUSSELL, plant biologist, educator; b. St. Paul, Apr. 29, 1928; s. John DeQuedville and Marjorie (Winslow) B.; m. Ann Morrill, June 30, 1955; children: Caroline, Lucia, Marion. BA, Harvard U., 1951, MA, 1952, PhD, 1956. Instr. biol. scis. Stanford (Calif.) U., 1955-57, asst. prof., 1957-62, asso. prof., 1962-66, prof., 1966-67; prof. biology Harvard U., 1967-73, Stanford U., 1973—; dir. dept. plant biology Carnegie Instn. of Washington, Stanford, 1973-93. Author: (with others) Life on Earth, 1973; mem. editl. bd. Ann. Rev. Plant Physiology, 1961-72; contbr. articles on plant growth and devel. and photobiology to profl. jours. Recipient Alexander von Humboldt U.S. Sr. Scientist award, 1984-85, Sterling Hendricks award USDA Agrl. Rsch. Svc., 1995, DeWitt award for partnership Calif. State Pks., 2000, Finsen medal Assn. Internat. Photobiology, 2000; John Simon Guggenheim fellow, 1973-74, Deutsche Akademie der Naturforscher Leopoldina, 1986. Fellow AAAS; mem. NAS, Am. Soc. Plant Physiologists (pres. 1975-76, Stephen Hales award 1994), Calif. Bot. Soc. (pres. 1976-77), Am. Acad. Arts and Scis., Am. Inst. Biol. Scis. (pres. 1980-81), Am. Soc. Photobiology, Bot. Soc. Am., Nature Conservancy, Sigma Xi. Home: 480 Hale St Palo Alto CA 94301-2207 Office: Carnegie Inst Washington Dept Plant Biology 260 Panama St Palo Alto CA 94305-4101

BRIGHAM, SAMUEL TOWNSEND JACK, III, lawyer; b. Honolulu, Oct. 8, 1939; s. Samuel Townsend Jack, Jr. and Betty Elizabeth (McNeil) B.; m. Judith Catherine Johnson, Sept. 3, 1960; children: Robert Jack, Bradley Lund, Lori Ann, Lisa Katherine. B.S. in Bus. magna cum laude, Menlo Coll., 1963; J.D., U. Utah, 1966. Bar: Calif. 1967. Asso. firm Petty, Andrews, Olsen & Tufts, San Francisco, 1966-67; accounting mgr. Western sales region Hewlett-Packard Co., North Hollywood, Calif., 1967-68; atty. Hewlett-Packard Co., Palo Alto, 1968-70, asst. gen. counsel, 1971-73, gen. atty., asst. sec., 1974-75, sec., gen. counsel, 1975-82, v.p., gen. counsel, 1982-85, v.p. corp. affairs, gen. counsel, mgr./dir. law dept., 1985—, sr. v.p. corp. affairs, gen. counsel, mgr./dir. law dept., 1994—. Lectr. law Menlo Coll.; speaker profl. assn. seminars. Bd. dirs. Palo Alto Area YMCA, 1974-81, pres., 1978; bd. govs. Santa Clara County region NCCJ; trustee Menlo Sch. and Coll.; bd. dirs. Just Say No. Served with USMC, 1957-59. Mem. ABA, Calif. Bar Assn., Peninsula Assn. Gen. Counsel, MAPI Law Council, Am. Corp. Counsel Assn. (chmn. 1985, bd. dirs. 1983—), Am. Soc. Corp. Secs. (pres. No. Calif. Chpt. 1983—), Assn. Gen. Counsel (sec.-treas. 1991—). Home: 920 Oxford Dr Los Altos CA 94024-7032 Office: Hewlett-Packard Co 3000 Hanover St Palo Alto CA 94304-1181

BRILEY, JOHN RICHARD, writer; b. Kalamazoo, June 25, 1925; s. William Treve and Mary Stella (Daly) B.; m. Dorothy Louise Reichart, Aug. 23, 1950; children: Dennis Patrick, Paul Christian, Mary Sydney, Shaun William. BA, U. Mich., 1951, MA, 1952; PhD, U. Birmingham, Eng., 1961. Lectr. Gen. Motors, Detroit, 1947-50; dir. orientation USAF, London, 1955-60; writer MGM, Elstree, Eng., 1960-64; freelance writer Trevone Prodns. Inc., L.A. and Amersham, Eng., 1970—; Bob Shaye artist is residence U. Mich., 1995. Vis. lectr. Univ. Mich., 1969; vis. prof. U. Mich., 1998. Author: (criticism) Shakespeare Survey, 1964, (novels) The Traitors, 1968, The Last Dance, 1978, Cry Freedom, 1988, The first Stone, 1997, (plays) Seven Bob a Buck, 1964, So Who Needs Men!, 1976; screenwriter: (films) (with Jack Trevor Story) Invasion Quartet, 1961, (with Story) Postman's Knock, 1962, Children of the Damned, 1964, Pope Joan, 1972, That Lucky Touch, 1975, The Medusa Touch, 1978, Eagle's Wing, 1979, Gandhi, 1982 (Academy award best original screenplay 1982), Enigma, 1983, Marie, 1985, (with Stanley Mann) Tai-Pan, 1986, Cry Freedom, 1987, (with Cary Bates and Mario Puzo) Christopher Columbus: The Discovery, 1992, , Molokai--The Story of Father Damien, 1999, (TV series) Hits & Misses, 1962, The Airbase, 1965. Served to capt. USAF, 1943-46. Recipient Golden Globe award Fgn. Press Assn., Los Angeles, 1983, Acad. award Acad. Motion Picture Arts and Scis., Los Angeles, 1983, Christopher award St. Christopher Soc., N.Y., 1983, 85, 88. Mem. Writers Guild Great Britain (exec. com. 1975-85), Writers Guild Am., Authors Guild, Dramatists Guild. Avocations: swimming, tennis, skiing. Home: PO Box 2365 Sun Valley ID 83353-2365

BRILLIANT, ASHLEIGH ELLWOOD, writer, cartoonist, publisher, educator; b. London, Dec. 9, 1933; came to the U.S., 1956, naturalized, 1969; s. Victor and Amelia (Adler) B.; m. Dorothy Low Tucker, June 28, 1968. BA with honors, Univ. Coll., London, 1955; MA in Edn., Claremont Grad. Sch., 1957; PhD in Am. History, U. Calif., Berkeley, 1964. Tchr. English Hollywood H.S., L.A., 1956-57; tchg. asst., reader in history U. Calif., Berkeley, 1960-63; asst. prof. history Ctrl. Oreg. Coll., Bend, 1964-65, Floating Campus divsn. Chapman Coll., Orange, Calif., 1965-67; entertainer in coffeehouses, outdoor spkr. San Francisco, 1967-68; syndicated cartoonist, dir. Brilliant Enterprises, pub. and licensing, San Francisco, Santa Barbara, Calif., 1967—. Creator Pot-Shots postcards, T-shirts, cocktail napkins, tote-bags, other items; mem. faculty Sonoma State U., Santa Barbara City Coll. Author: I May Not Be Totally Perfect, But Parts of Me Are Excellent, And Other Brilliant Thoughts, 1979, I Have Abandoned My Search for Truth and Am Now Looking for a Good Fantasy, 1980, Appreciate Me Now and Avoid the Rush, 1981, I Feel Much Better Now That I've Given Up Hope, 1984, All I Want Is A Warm Bed and A Kind Word, and Unlimited Power, 1985, I Try to Take One Day At A Time, But Sometimes Several Days Attack Me At Once, 1987, The Great Car Craze: How Southern California Collided With The Automobile in the 1920's, 1989, We've Been Through So Much Together and Most of It Was Your Fault, 1990, Be A Good Neighbor and Leave Me Alone, 1992, I Want to Reach Your Mind...Where is it Currently Located, 1994, I'm Just Moving Clouds Today-Tomorrow I'll Try Mountains, 1999; founder, leader Ban Leafblowers and Save Our Town, 1996. Recipient Raymond B. Bragg award, 1987, Disting. Alumnus of Yr. award Claremont Grad. U., 2000; Claremont Grad. Sch. scholar, 1956; Haynes fellow, 1962, Panama-Pacific fellow, 1963. Mem. Newspaper Comics Coun., No. Calif. Cartoonists Assn., Mensa. Jewish. Home and Office: 117 W Valerio St Santa Barbara CA 93101-2927 E-mail: ashleigh@west.net

BRIMMER, CLARENCE ADDISON, federal judge; b. Rawlins, Wyo., July 11, 1922; s. Clarence Addison and Geraldine (Zingsheim) B.; m. Emily O. Docken, Aug. 2, 1953; children: Geraldine Ann, Philip Andrew, Andrew Howard, Elizabeth Ann. BA, U. Mich., 1944, JD, 1947. Bar: Wyo. 1948. Pvt. practice law, Rawlins, 1948-71; mcpl. judge Rawlins, 1948-54; U.S. commr., magistrate, 1963-71; atty. gen. Wyo. Cheyenne, 1971-74; U.S. atty., 1975; chief judge U.S. Dist. Ct. Wyo., Cheyenne, 1975-92, dist. judge, 1975—. Mem. panel multi-dist. litigation, 1992-2000; mem. Jud. Conf. U.S., 1994-97, exec., 1995-97. Sec. Rawlins Bd. Pub. Utilities, 1954-66; Rep. gubernatorial candidate, 1974; trustee Rocky Mountain Mineral Law Found., 1963-75. With USAAF, 1945-46. Mem. ABA, Wyo. Bar Assn., Laramie County Bar Assn., Carbon County Bar Assn., Am. Judicature Soc., Masons, Shriners, Rotary. Episcopalian. Office: US Dist Ct PO Box 985 Cheyenne WY 82003-0985

BRINKLEY, SUSAN, executive pastry chef; Student, Lynchburg Coll., 1985. Pantry position, Chapel Hill, N.C., 1985; pastry chef, 1989; exec. chef, 1990; asst. pastry chef Postrio, San Francisco, 1993, exec. pastry chef, 1998. Benefits participation in Meals on Wheels, Taste of Nations, Share Our strength, Project Open Hand. Mem. Womens Chefs and Restaurateurs, The Baker's Dozen. Office: Postrio 545 Post St San Francisco CA 94102-1228

BRINKMAN, PAUL DEL(BERT), foundation executive, university administrator; b. Olpe, Kans., Feb. 10, 1937; s. Paul Theodore and Delphine Barbara (Brown) B.; m. Evelyn Marie Lange, Aug. 5, 1961 (dec. June 1988); m. Carolyn L. Backer, July 27, 1990; children: Scott Michael, Susan Lynn. BS, Emporia State Coll., 1958; MA in Journalism (Newspaper Fund fellow), Ind. U., 1963, Ph.D. in Mass Communications (Scripps-Howard fellow), 1971. Editor, reporter Emporia (Kans.) Gazette, 1954-59; instr. journalism Leavenworth (Kans.) High Sch., 1959-62; lectr. Ind. U., Bloomington, 1962-65, 68-70; asst. prof. Kans. State U., Manhattan, 1965-68; prof., dean Sch. Journalism U. Kans., Lawrence, 1970-86, vice chancellor for acad. affairs, 1986-93; dir. journalism programs John S. and James L. Knight Found., Miami, 1993-2001; dean U. Colo. Sch. Journalism and Mass Comm., Boulder, 2001—. Balt. Sun disting. lectr. Coll. Journalism, U. Md., 1993. Bd. dirs. William Allen White Found., 1974; chmn. Big Eight Athletic Conf., 1980-81, 87-88; faculty rep. Nat. Collegiate Athletic Assn., 1978-93. Named Trayes Prof. of Yr. Mass Communications Soc. div. Assn. Edn. Journalism, 1990; recipient Disting Alumni award Emporia State Coll., 1978, Ind. U., 1986. Mem. Am. Assn. Schs. and Depts. Journalism (pres. 1977-78), Inland Daily Press Assn. (chmn. edn. com. 1980-83), Assn. Edn. Journalism (chmn. publs. com. 1974-75, pres. 1980-81), Soc. Profl. Journalists, Lawrence C. of C. (v.p. 1987-88), Rotary (pres. Lawrence chpt. 1987-88), Sigma Delta Chi, Kappa Tau Alpha. Home: The Horizons at Cross Creek 2300 Rock Creek Pkwy 11-102 Superior CO 80027 Office: U Colo Sch Journalism & Mass Comm The Armory Boulder CO 80309-0040 E-mail: delpdb@aol.com, brinkman@knightfdn.org

BRISBIN, ROBERT EDWARD, insurance agency executive; b. Bklyn., Feb. 13, 1946; m. Sally Ann Tobler-Norton. BSBA, San Fancisco State U., 1968. Cert. safety exec. Field rep. Index Research, San Mateo, Calif., 1969-82; mgr. loss control Homeland Ins. Co., San Jose, 1982-87; ins. exec. Morris and Garritano Ins. Agy., San Luis Obispo, 1987—; prin., cons. Robert E. Brisbin & Assocs., Pismo Beach, 1972—. Mgt. cons.; pres. Profl. Formulas Amino Acid Food Supplements, 1987-90. Author: (non-fiction) Amino Acids, Vitamins and Fitness, 1986, Loss Control for the Small-to Medium-Sized Business, 1989; author: ((with Carol Bayly Grant)) Workplace Wellness, 1992; author: (e-book fiction) Terminal Resolve, 2000, Proprietary Oversight, 2001, (non-fiction) ...Was Yesterday, 2000; composer: (songs) Country Songs and Broken Dreams, 1978, America the Land of Liberty, 1980. Mem. Am. Soc. Safety Engrs., World Safety Orgn. (cert. safety exec.), UN Roster Safety Cons. Republican. Avocations: photography, flying, scuba diving, musical composition. Office: PO Box 341 Pismo Beach CA 93448-0341 E-mail: bbrisbin@morrisgarritano.com

BRISCOE, JOHN, lawyer; b. Stockton, Calif., July 1, 1948; s. John Lloyd and Doris (Olsen) B.; divorced; children: John Paul, Katherine. JD, U. San Francisco, 1972. Bar: Calif. 1972, U.S. Dist. Ct. (no., ea. and ctrl. dists.) Calif. 1972, U.S. Supreme Ct. 1978, U.S. Ct. Appeals (9th cir.) 1981. Dep. atty. gen. State of Calif., San Francisco, 1972-80; ptnr. Washburn and Kemp, San Francisco, 1980-88, Washburn, Briscoe & McCarthy, San Francisco, 1988—. Bd. dirs. San Francisco Bay Planning coalition, chmn., 1990-93; bd. dirs. U. Calif. Sea Grant Program, Friends of the Bancroft Libr., St. mary's Coll. MFA Program in Creative Writing, Historical Soc. US Dist. COunt, North Dist Calif.; vis. scholar U. Calif., Berkeley, 1990—; spl. adviser UN Compensation Commn., Geneva, Switzerland, 1998-99. Author: Surveying the Courtroom, 1984, rev. edit., 1999, Falsework, 1997; editor: Reports of Special Masters, 1991; contbr. articles to profl. and lit. jours. Mem. ABA, San Francisco Bar Assn., Law of the Sea Inst. Roman Catholic. Office: Washburn Briscoe & McCarthy 55 Francisco St San Francisco CA 94133-2122

BRISCOE, LAWRENCE WINTON, brokerage house executive; b. Kansas City, Mo., June 6, 1944; m. Patricia C. Briscoe. B.S.E.E., U. Mo., 1966; M.B.A., Stanford U., 1968; M.S., U. So. Calif., 1969. Systems analyst Office of Asst. Sec. of Def., Washington, 1969-72; v.p. Blyth Eastman Dillon & Co., San Francisco, 1972-77; pres., COO & dir., BRAE Corp., San Francisco, 1977-87; v.p. corp. devel., Transamerica Corp., 1987-88; COO, U.S. Comml. Telephone Corp., 1988-90; consultant, Durkee/Sharlit Assoc., 1992-94; CFO & v.p. of fin. & adminstrn., Catalytica, Inc., 1994—. Served to capt. USAF, 1968-72. Office: Catalytica Inc 430 Ferguson Dr Mountain View CA 94043

BRITTEN, ROY JOHN, biophysicist; b. Washington, Oct. 1, 1919; s. Rollo Herbert and Marion (Hale) B.; m. Jacqueline Reid, 1986; children: Gregory, Kenneth. BS, U. Va., 1941; PhD, Princeton U., 1951. Staff mem. dept. terrestrial magnetism Carnegie Instn., Washington, 1951-89; sr. research assoc. Calif. Inst. Tech., Corona del Mar, 1973-81, disting. Carnegie sr. rsch. assoc. biology, 1981-99, emeritus, 1999—. Adj. prof. U. Calif., Irvine, 1991—; discoverer repeated DNA sequences in genomes of higher organisms. Inventor in field. Named Disting. Carnegie Sr. Research Assoc. in Biology, 1981-99. Fellow Am. Acad. Arts and Scis., AAAS; mem. Nat. Acad. Scis. Office: Calif Inst Tech Kerchkhoff Marine Lab 101 Dahlia Ave Corona Del Mar CA 92625-2814

BRITTENHAM, SKIP, lawyer; b. Port Huron, Mich. BS, USAF Acad., 1963; JD, UCLA, 1970. Bar: Calif. 1971. Sr. ptnr. Ziffren, Brittenham, Branca & Fischer, L.A., 1978—. Office: Ziffren Brittenham Branca Fischer 1801 Century Park W Los Angeles CA 90067-6406

BRITTON, DENNIS A. former newspaper editor, newspaper executive; b. Santa Barbara, 1940; m. Theresa Romero Britton; children: Robert, Patrick, Anne. Attended, San Jose State U. Joined L.A. Times, 1966, various positions, including copy editor, reporter, news editor, asst. nat. editor, nat. editor, 1977-83, then dep. mng. editor; editor Chgo. Sun-Times, 1989-96, also exec. v.p., until 1996; now editor-in-chief Denver Post, 1996-99. Mem. Nat. Assn. Hispanic Journalists. Office: Denver Post 1560 Broadway Denver CO 80202-5177

BRITTON, M(ELVIN) C(REED), JR. physician, rheumatologist; b. San Francisco, Apr. 11, 1935; s. Melvin Creed and Mathilda Carolyn (Epeneter) B.; m. Mary Elizabeth Phillips, Nov. 2, 1957; children: Elizabeth Carolynne, Lisa Marie. AB, Dartmouth Coll., 1957, MS, 1958; MD, Harvard U., 1960. Diplomate Am. Bd. Internal Medicine, Am. Bd. Rheumatology, Am. Bd. Quality Assurance. Resident Dartmouth Coll. Sch. Medicine, Hanover, N.H., 1964-67; fellow Harvard U. Sch. Medicine, Boston, 1967-69; ptnr. Palo Alto (Calif.) Med. Clinic, 1969—, chmn. dept. medicine, 1990-97. Pres. med. staff Stanford (Calif.) U. Med. Ctr., 1985-87, mem. med. staff bd., 1969-87; bd. dirs. Hosp. Conf. No. Calif., 1988-92, Inst. for Med. Quality, 1998—; mem. Relative Value Update Commn., 1996— Contbr. articles to med. jours. Pres. Found. for Med. care Santa Clara county, Campbell, 1983-89; mem. Bay Area Lupus Found., 1978—, chmn., 1987-88, 94-95; v.p. Calif. Founds. for Med. Care, 1996, pres., CEO, 1996—. Fellow ACP, Am. Coll. Rheumatology (bd. dirs. 1986-89, Paulding Phelps medal 1994, mastership), Calif. Acad. Medicine (exec. com. 1996-2000, pres. 2001—); mem. AMA (alternate del. 1988—, governing coun., speciality & svcs. soc.), Calif. Med. Assn., Santa Clara County Med. Soc. (pres. 1980-81, Bd. Svc. award 1988), Arthritis Found. No. Calif. (chmn. bd. dirs. 1984-87, Disting Svc. award 1985), Vintners Club (San Francisco, v.p. 1975-78), Commonwealth Club (San Francisco). Republican. Episcopalian. Avocations: skiing, traveling, enology. Office: Palo Alto Med Clinic 300 Homer Ave Palo Alto CA 94301-2726

BRITTON, THOMAS WARREN, JR. management consultant; b. Pawhuska, Okla., June 16, 1944; s. Thomas Warren and Helen Viola (Haynes) B.; m. Jerlyn Kay Davis, 1964 (div. 1970); 1 child, Natalie Dawn; m. Deborah Ann Mansour, Oct. 20, 1973; 1 child, Kimberly Ann. BSME, Okla. State U., 1966, MS in Indsl. Engring. and Mgmt., 1968. Cert. mgmt. cons. Cons. Arthur Young & Co., L.A., 1972-76, prin., 1976-79, ptnr., 1979-87, office dir. mgmt. svcs. dept. Orange County, Calif., 1979-99; ptnr. Price Waterhouse, ptnr.-in-charge West Coast mfg. cons. practice Nat. Aerospace and Def. Industry, ptnr.-in-charge west coast products and logistics practice, 1995—. Price Waterhouse Coopers mng. ptnr. west region MCS Products Practice, chmn. US MCS Tech. Industry Practice, chmn. Global MCS Tech. Industry Practice, 2000—, COO MCS west bus. unit, chmn. global MCS tech. industry practice; lectr. in field. Mem. creative growth bd. City of San Dimas, 1976-77, chmn. Planning Commn.,

9177-83; trustee World Affairs Coun. Orange County, 1980; benefactor, mem. founders com., v.p. ann. fund, pres., chmn. long range planning, trustee South Coast Repertory Theater, 1982-92; trustee Providence Speech and Hearing Ctr., 1985-90, Spl. Olympica So. Calif., 1995-97; mem. devel. com. U. Calif.-Irvine Med. Sch.; chmn. Costa Mesa Arts Coun. Capt. USAR, 1971-86. Mem. L.A. Inst. CPAs, Mgmt. Adv. Svcs. Com., Am. Prodn. and Inventory Control Soc., Am. Inst. Indsl. Engrs., Greater Irvine Indsl. League, Okla. State U. Alumni Assn., Jonathan Club, Ridgeline Country Club, Santa Ana Country Club, Kappa Sigma. Home: 9881 Orchard Ln Villa Park CA 92861-3105 E-mail: tom.britton@us.pwcglobal.com

BROAD, ELI, financial services executive; b. N.Y.C., June 6, 1933; s. Leon and Rebecca (Jacobson) B.; m. Edythe Lois Lawson, Dec. 19, 1954; children: Jeffrey Alan, Gary Stephen. BA in Acctg. cum laude, Mich. State U., 1954. CPA, Mich. 1956. Cert. public acct., 1954-56; asst. prof. Detroit Inst. Tech., 1956; co-founder, chmn., pres., CEO SunAmerica Life Ins. Co. (formerly Kaufman & Broad, Inc.), L.A., 1957-2001, chmn., 2001—, Nat. Anchor Nat. Life Ins. Co., First SunAmerica Life Ins. Co., CalAmerica Life Ins. Co., Kaufman and Broad Home Corp., L.A., 1989-93, chmn. exec. com., 1993-95, founder, chmn., 1993—. Chmn. Stanford Ranch Co.; mem. exec. com. adv. bd. Fed. Nat. Mortgage Assn., 1972-73; active Calif. Bus. Roundtable, 1986-2000; co-owner Sacramento Kings and Arco Arena, 1992-99; trustee Com. for Econ. Devel., 1993-95; mem. real estate adv. bd. Citibank, N.Y.C., 1976-81; bd. dirs. Am. Internat. Group, Inc., L.A. Bus. Advisors, Sacramento Kings and ARCO Arena; co-owner Sacramento Kings & Arco Arena, 1992-99. Mem. bd. dirs. L.A. World Affairs Coun., 1988—, chmn., 1994-97, DARE Am., 1989-95, hon. mem. bd. dirs. 1995—; founding trustee Windward Sch., Santa Monica, Calif., 1972-77; bd. trustees Pitzer Coll., Claremont, Calif., 1970-82, chmn. bd. trustees, 1973-79, life trustee, 1982—, Haifa U., Israel, 1972-80, Calif. State U., 1978-82, vice chmn. bd. trustees, 1979-80, trustee emeritus, 1982—, Mus. Contemporary Art, L.A., 1980-93, founding chmn., 1980, Archives Am. Art, Smithsonian Instn., Washington, 1985-98, Am. Fedn. Arts, 1988-91, Leland Stanford Mansion Found., 1992—, Calif. Inst. Tech., 1993—, Armand Hammer Mus. Art and Cultural Ctr. UCLA, 1994-99; pres. Calif. Non-Partisan Vote Registration Found., 1971-72; chancellor's assoc. UCLA, 1971—, mem. vis. com. Grad. Sch. Mgmt., 1972-90, trustee UCLA Found., 1986-96, exec. com. bd. visitors Sch. of the Arts & Architecture, 1997—; assoc. chmn. United Crusade, L.A., 1973-76; chmn. Mayor's Housing Policy Com., L.A., 1974-75; del., spkr. Fed. Econ. Summit Conf., 1974, State Econ. Summit Conf., 1974; mem. contemporary coun. L.A. County Mus. Art, 1973-79, bd. trustees acquisitions com., 1978-81, trustee, 1995—; bd. fellows, mem. exec. com. The Claremont (Calif.) Colls., 1974-79; nat. trustee Balt. Mus. Art, 1985-91; mem. adv. bd. Boy Scouts Am., 1982-85, L.A. Bus. Jour., 1986-88; mem. adv. coun. Town Hall of Calif., 1985-87; trustee Dem. Nat. Com. Victory Fund, 1988, 92, 96; mem. painting and sculpture com. Whitney Mus., N.Y.C., 1987-89; chmn. adv. bd. ART/LA, 1989; bd. overseers The Music Ctr. of L.A. County, 1991-92, mem. bd. govs., 1996-98; mem. contemporary art com. Harvard U. Art Mus., Cambridge, Mass., 1992—; mem. internat. dirs. coun. Guggenheim Mus., N.Y.C., 1993-98; active Nat. Indsl. Pollution Control Coun., 1970-73, Maeght Found., St. Paul de Vence, France, 1975-80, Mayor's Spl. Adv. Com. on Fiscal Adminstrn., L.A., 1993-94; bd. dirs. UCLA/Armand Hammer Mus. Art And Cultural Ctr., 1994—. Recipient Man of Yr. award City of Hope, 1965, Golden Plate award Am. Acad. Achievement, 1971, Housing Man of Yr. award Nat. Housing Coun., 1979, Humanitarian award NCCJ, 1977, Am. Heritage award Anti Defamation League, 1984, Pub. Affairs award Coro Found., 1987, Honors award visual arts L.A. Arts Coun., 1989; Eli Broad Coll. Bus. and Eli Broad Grad. Sch. Bus. named in his honor Mich. State U., 1991; knighted Chevalier in Nat. Order Legion of Honor, France, 1994; recipient lifetime achievement award L.A. C. of C., 1999, visionary award Harvard Bus. Sch. Assn. So. Calif., 1999, Julius award U. So. Calif. Sch. Policy, Planning and Devel., 2001, Chmn.'s award Asia Soc. So. Calif., 2000, Visionary award KCET, 1999. Mem. Beta Alpha Psi, Regency Club, Hillcrest Country Club (L.A.), California Club. Office: SunAmerica Inc 10900 Wilshire Blvd 12th Fl Los Angeles CA 90024

BROADFOOT, ALBERT LYLE, physicist; b. Milestone, Sask., Can., Jan. 8, 1930; came to U.S., 1963; s. Morris Alexander and Lydia Georgina (Jacklin) B.; m. Katherine Eileen Deacon, Sept. 26, 1964; children: Alexander Lyle, Marilyn Louise. BE in Engring., Physics, U. Sask., Saskatoon, 1956, M.Sc. in Physics, 1960, Ph.D. in Physics, 1963. Engr. Def. Rsch. Bd., Ottawa, Ont., Can., 1956-58; jr. physicist space div. Kitt Peak Nat. Obs., Tucson, 1963-64, asst. physicist, 1964-68, assoc. physicist, 1968-70, physicist, 1971-79; rsch. scientist, assoc. physicist Earth and Space Scis. Inst., U. So. Calif., 1979-82; sr. rsch. scientist Lunar and Planetary Lab., U Ariz., Tucson, 1982—. Home: 5231 E 17th St Tucson AZ 85711-4429 Office: U Ariz Lunar and Planetary Lab 901 Gould Simpson Blvd Tucson AZ 85721-0001

BROADHURST, NORMAN NEIL, food products executive; b. Chico, Calif., Dec. 17, 1946; s. Frank Spencer and Dorothy Mae (Conrad) B.; m. Victoria Rose Thomson, Aug. 7, 1976; 1 child, Scott Andrew. BS, Calif. State U., 1969; MBA, Golden Gate U., 1975. With Del Monte Corp., San Francisco, 1969-76; chmn., pres., CEO Trusted Brands, Inc., 1995-98; product mgr. Del Monte Corp., San Francisco, 1973-76; product mgr. Riviana Foods, Inc. divsn. Colgate Palmolive, Houston, 1976-78; new products brand devel. mgr. foods divsn. Coca Cola Co., Houston, 1978-79, brand mgr., 1979-82, mktg. dir., 1982-89; v.p. mktg. Beatrice Foods Co., Chgo., 1983-86; pres., COO, Famous Amos Chocolate Chip Cookie Co., Torrance, Calif., 1986-88; corp. sr. v.p., gen. mgr. Kerr Group Inc., L.A., 1988-92; corp. sr. v.p., pres. Kerr Group Consumer Products, 1992-95; chmn. dir. Double Eagle Holding, Inc., Seal Beach, Calif., 1995—; chmn., pres., CEO, Trusted Brands, Inc., 1995-98; chmn., CEO, Double Eagle Market Devel. Co., Seal Beach, 1997—. Chmn., pres. and CEO Trusted Brands, Inc., 1995-98. Chmn. youth soccer program Cystic Fibrosis Found., Houston, 1982-83; chmn., pres. South Coast Symphony, 1985-88; mem. nat. bd. dirs. Literacy Vols. Am., 1988—, vice chmn., 1993-95, chmn., 1997-99; bd. dirs. Human Options , 1997-98, mem. strategic planning and mktg. coms., 1998; trustee, bd. dirs. Laguna Presbyn. Ch., 1999—. Mem. Assoc. Sales and Mktg. Co., Am. Mktg. Assn., Am. Mgmt. Assn. E-mail: nbroadhurst@deagle2000.com

BROADWATER, BRUCE A. mayor; b. Columbus, Ohio, Sept. 1, 1938; m. Peggy Broadwater; children: Josh, Jeremy AA, East L.A. Coll.; BA in Human Rels., U. San Francisco. Owner ins. agy., Garden Grove, Calif.; consumer complaint analyst Calif. Dept. Ins.; elected Garden Grove City Coun., 1992-94; elected mayor City of Garden Grove, 1994—. Bd. dirs. Am. Host Found.; active scouting programs, Boy Scouts Am. With U.S. Army, 1957-59, Germany. Mem. Garden Grove C. of C. Office: Office of Mayor PO Box 3070 Garden Grove CA 92842-3070

BROCCHINI, RONALD GENE, architect; b. Oakland, Calif., Nov. 6, 1929; s. Gino Mario and Yoli Louise (Lucchesi) B.; m. Myra Mossman, Feb. 3, 1957; 1 child, Christopher Ronald B.A. in Architecture with honors, U. Calif., Berkeley, 1953, M.A. in Architecture with honors, 1957. Registered architect, Calif., Nev. Architect, designer SMP, Inc., San Francisco, 1948-53, designer assoc., 1956-60; assoc. architect Campbell & Wong, San Francisco, 1961-63; prin. architect Ronald G. Brocchini, Berkeley, Calif., 1964-67, Worley K Wong & Ronald G Brocchini Assocs., San Francisco, 1968-87, Brocchini Architects, Berkeley, 1987—. Lectr. Calif. Coll. Arts and Crafts, Oakland, 1981-83; commr. Calif. Bd. Archtl. Examiners, 1961-89; mem. exam. com. Nat. Coun. Archtl. Registration Bds., 1983-85. Author: Long Range Master Plan for Bodega Marine Biology U. Calif., 1982; prin. works include San Simeon Visitor Ctr. Hearst Castle, Calif., Mare Island Med.-Dental Facillity, IBM Ednl. and Data Processing Hdqrs., San Jose, Calif., Simpson Fine Arts Gallery, Calif. Coll. Arts, Ceramics and Metal Crafts, Emery Bay Pub. Market Complex, Analytical Measurement Facility, U. Calif., Berkeley, Bodega Marine Biology Campus, U. Calif., Berkeley, Fromm & Sichell (Christian Bros.) Hdqrs., The Nature Co., Corp. Offices, Berkeley, Merrill Coll., Athletic Facilities, U. Calif., Santa Cruz, Coll. III Housing, U. Calif., San Diego, Ctr. Pacific Rim Studies, U. San Francisco, married student housing Escondido II, III, IV, Stanford (Calif.) U. With U.S. Army, 1953-55. Recipient Bear of Yr. award U. Calif., Berkeley, 1987, Alumni Citation, 1988; recipient 18 Design Honor awards for architecture, Design award State of Calif. Dept. Rehab., 1995. Fellow AIA (bd. dirs. Calif. coun., pres. San Francisco chpt. 1982); mem. Bear Backers Club (bd. dirs. U. Calif.-Berkeley athletic coun.), Berkeley Breakfast Club (bd. govs.), Order of the Golden Bear, Chi Alpha Kappa. Republican. Roman Catholic. Avocations: auto restoration, photography, sports, art. Office: Brocchini Architects Inc 2748 Adeline St Berkeley CA 94703-2251 E-mail: arcbro@pacbell.net

BROCK, MARK, construction company executive; Formerly with Barratt Homes and Daiwa House; former pres. No. Calif. divsn. Shea Homes, San Jose, Calif., 1992-98, pres. San Diego divsn. Walnut, 1998—. Office: JF Shea Co Inc PO Box 489 Walnut CA 91788-0489

BROCKIE, PAMELA, motion picture executive; BA, UCLA, 1972, JD, 1975. Mem. staff MCA; sr. v.p. bus. affairs ICM, Beverly Hills, Calif., 1984—. Mem. Next Generation Coun., Motion Picture and T.V. Fund Found. Mem. Women in Film (bd. dirs.). Office: ICM 8942 Wilshire Blvd Beverly Hills CA 90211-1934

BROCKLEY, JOHN P. airport terminal executive; Dir. aviation Port of Portland, Oreg. Office: Port Portland Dir Aviation PO Box 3529 Portland OR 97208-3529

BRODERSEN, ROBERT W. engineering educator; BSEE, BS in Math., Calif. State Polytechnic U., 1966; MS in Engring., MIT, 1968, PhD in Engring., 1972. Mem. technical staff Ctrl. Rsch. Lab. Texas Instruments, 1972-76; prof. dept. elec. engring. and computer scis. U. Calif., Berkeley, 1976—, John R. Whinnery chair, 1995—. Nat. chair Info. Sci. and Tech. Study Group, 1992-94. Contbr. articles to profl. jours., chpts. to books including Anatomy of a Silicon Compiler, 1992, Low Power Digital CMOS Design, 1995; patentee in field. Recipient Best Paper award Eascon, 1973, Internat. Solid States Circuits Conf., 1975, European Solid-States Circuits Conf., 1978. Fellow IEEE (editl. bd. various jours., Morris Libermann award 1983, Solid-States Circuits award 1997); mem. Nat. Acad. Engring. Achievements include research in application of integrated circuits as applied to personal communication systems. Office: U Calif Dept EECS 402 Cory Hl # 1770 Berkeley CA 94720-0001

BRODY, ARTHUR, industrial executive; b. Newark, June 30, 1920; s. Samuel A. and Ruth (Marder) B.; m. Sophie Mark, Mar. 5, 1944; children: Janice, Donald. Student, Columbia U., 1939-42. Organizer, operator Library Service, 1940-42; exec. buyer L. Bamberger & Co., Newark, 1942-43; chmn. Brodart Co., Williamsport, Pa., 1946—, BDI Investment Corp., San Diego, Tura Inc., Lake Success, N.Y. Past mem. adv. panel study on libs. and industry Nat. Adv. Com. on Librs.; past pres. Friends of N.J. Librs. Patentee in field. Past trustee Newark Symphony Hall., Ctr. for Book, Libr. of Congress, L.A. County Libr. Found., Friends of Libr. USA, San Diego Community Found.; past commr. San Diego Pub. Libr. With AUS, 1943-46. Mem. ALA, NEA, San Diego Yacht Club, Rancho Sante Fe Golf Club, Masons, Shriners. Office: Brodart Co 990 Highland Dr Ste 100 Solana Beach CA 92075-2409

BROGDEN, STEPHEN RICHARD, library administrator; b. Des Moines, Sept. 26, 1948; s. Paul M. and Marjorie (Kueck) B.; m. Melinda L. Raine, Jan. 1, 1983; 1 child, Nathan. BA, U. Iowa, 1970, MA, 1972. Caretaker Eya Fechin Branham Ranch, Taos, N.Mex., 1970-72; dir. Harwood Found. U. N.Mex., Taos, 1972-75; vis. lectr. U. Ariz., Tucson, 1975-76; rd. mgr. Bill and Bonnie Hearne, Austin, Tex., 1976-79; head fine arts Pub. Libr. Des Moines, 1980-90; dep. dir. Thousand Oaks (Calif.) Libr., 1990-99, dir., 1999—. Chair Met. Coop. Libr. Sys., 2001. Author book revs., Annals of Iowa, 1980; columnist Taos News, 1973. Bd. dirs. Thousand Oaks Libr. Found., 1999—. Mem. Am. Libr. Assn., Calif. Libr. Assn., Films for Iowa Librs. (pres. 1983-86), Metro Des Moines Libr. Assn. (pres. 1980). Office: Thousand Oaks Libr 1401 E Janss Rd Thousand Oaks CA 91362-2199

BROGLIATTI, BARBARA SPENCER, television and motion picture executive; b. L.A., Jan. 8, 1946; d. Robert and Lottie Spencer; m. Raymond Haley Brogliatti, Sept. 19, 1970. BA in Social Scis. and English, UCLA, 1968. Asst. press. info. dept. CBS TV, L.A., 1968-69, sr. publicist, 1969-74; dir. publicity Tandem Prodns. and T.A.T. Comm. (Embassy Comm.), L.A., 1974-77, corp. v.p., 1977-82; sr. v.p. worldwide publicity, promotion and advt. Embassy Comm., L.A., 1982-85; sr. v.p. worldwide corp. comm. Lorimar Telepictures Corp., Culver City, Calif., 1985-89; pres., chmn. Brogliatti Co., Burbank, 1989-90; sr. v.p. worldwide TV publicity, promotion and advt. Lorimar TV, 1991-92; sr. v.p. worldwide TV publicity, promotion and pub. rels. Warner Bros., Burbank, 1992-97; sr. v.p. corp. comm. Warner Bros., Inc., 1997-2000, sr. v.p., chief corp. comm. officer, 2000—. Mem. bd. govs. TV Acad., L.A., 1984-86; bd. dirs. KIDSNET, Washington, 1987—, Nat. Acad. Cable Programming, 1992-94; mem. Hollywood Women's Polit. Com., 1992-93; mem. steering com. L.A. Free Clinic, 1997-98. Recipient Gold medallion Broadcast Promotion and Mktg. Execs., 1984. Mem. Am. Diabetes Assn. (bd. dirs. L.A. chpt. 1992-93), Am. Cinema Found. (bd. dirs. 1994-98), Dirs. Guild Am., Publicists Guild, Acad. TV Arts and Scis. (vice chmn. awards com.). Office: Warner Bros Studios 4000 Warner Blvd Burbank CA 91522-0002 E-mail: barbara.brogliatti@warnerbros.com

BROKAW, MEREDITH A. women's health care company director; BA, English and Comm., U. S.D.; LLD (hon.), St. John's U. Founder Penny Whistle Toys, Inc., 1978-97; dir. Women First HealthCare, Inc., San Diego, 1998—. Dir. Gannett Co., Inc. Author 8 books on parenting and children's activities. Trustee Bank Street Coll. Edn., Ednl. Broadcasting Corp., Conservation Internat. Office: Women First HealthCare Inc 12220 El Camino Real Ste 400 San Diego CA 92130-2091 Fax: 619-509-1353

BROKAW, NORMAN ROBERT, talent agency executive; b. N.Y.C., Apr. 21, 1927; s. Isadore David and Marie (Hyde) B.; children: David M., Sanford Jay, Joel S., Barbara M., Wendy E., Lauren Quincy Student pvt. schs., Los Angeles. With William Morris Agy., Inc., Beverly Hills, Calif., 1943—, sr. agt. and co. exec., 1951-74, v.p. world-wide ops., 1974-80, exec. v.p., dir., 1980—, co-chmn. bd., 1986-91, pres., CEO, 1989-91, chmn. bd., CEO, 1991-97, chmn. bd. worldide, 1997—. Pres. Betty Ford Cancer Center, Cedars-Sinai Med. Center, Los Angeles, 1978— ; bd. dirs. Cedars-Sinai Med. Center; industry chmn. United Jewish Welfare Fund, 1975. With U.S. Army, World War II. Mem. Acad. Motion Picture Arts and Scis. Clubs: Hillcrest Country (Los Angeles). Clients include former Pres. and Mrs. Gerald R. Ford, Bill Cosby, Gen. Alexander Haig Jr., Tony Randall, Donald Regan, C. Everett Koop, Priscilla Presley, Andy Griffith, Brooke Shields, Juliette Lewis, Marcia Clark, Christopher Darden. Office: William Morris Agy 1 William Morris Pl Beverly Hills CA 90212-2775 also: William Morris Agy Inc 1325 Avenue Of The Americas New York NY 10019-[illegible]

BROM, ROBERT H. bishop; b. Arcadia, Wis., Sept. 18, 1938; Ed., St. Mary's Coll., Winona, Minn., Gregorian U., Rome. Ordained priest Roman Catholic Ch., 1963, consecrated bishop, 1983. Bishop of Duluth, Minn., 1983-89; coadjutor bishop Diocese of San Diego, 1989-90, bishop, 1990—. Office: Diocese of San Diego Pastoral Ctr PO Box 85728 San Diego CA 92186-5728

BRONESKY, JOSEPH J. lawyer; b. Milw., Aug. 6, 1947; m. Jacquelin A. Medina, Mar. 15, 1985; children: Jessica, Amanda, Antoinette. BA, Marquette U., 1969; JD, U. Chicago, 1972. Bar: Wis. 1972, U.S. Ct. Mil. Appeals 1974, U.S. Supreme Ct. 1975, Colo. 1977, U.S. Dist. Ct. Colo. 1977. Law clk. to judge Latham Castle U.S. Ct. Appeals 7th cir., Chgo., 1972-73; assoc. Sherman & Howard, Denver, 1976-80, ptnr., 1980—. Asst. editor U. Chgo. Law Review, 1971-72. Bd. dirs. Camp Fire Denver area coun. 1983-86, Montessori Sch. Denver, 1992-94, Mile Hi coun. Girl Scouts U.S., Denver, 1992—, fin. com. 1989—. Lt. JAGC USN, 1973-76. Mem. ABA, Colo. Bar Assn., Colo. Trial Lawyers Assn. Roman Catholic. Avocations: skiing, bicycling, hiking. Office: Sherman & Howard 633 17th St Ste 3000 Denver CO 80202-3665

BRONSON, JOSEPH R. manufacturing company executive; BS in Acctg., Fairfield U.; MBA, U. Conn. V.p., CFO, Kubota Pacific Computer, Stardent Computer Inc.; corp. controller Applied Materials Inc., Santa Clara, Calif., 1984, v.p., gen. mgr. implant divsn., 1990, group v.p. worldwide mfg. ops., 1994, group v.p., 1996, CFO, chief adminstrv. officer, exec. v.p., 1998—. Office: Applied Materials Inc 3050 Bowers Ave Santa Clara CA 95054-3299

BRONSTEIN, ARTHUR J. linguistics educator; b. Balt., Mar. 15, 1914; s. Gershon and Bessie B.; m. Elsa Meltzer, May 15, 1941; children: Nancy Ellen, Abbot Alan. B.A., CCNY, 1934; M.A., Columbia U., 1936; Ph.D., NYU, 1949. Vis. scholar and rsch. assoc. in linguistics U. Calif., Berkeley, 1987—; prof. Queens Coll., N.Y.C., 1938-67; Fulbright prof. U. Tel Aviv, (Israel), 1967-68, U. Trondheim, (Norway), 1979; prof. linguistics Lehman Coll. and Grad. Sch., CUNY, 1968-83, prof. emeritus, 1983—; exec. officer PhD program in speech and hearing scis. CUNY, 1969-72; exec. officer Ph.D. program in linguistics Grad. Sch., CUNY, 1981-83; cons. in field; with dept. linguistics U. Calif., Berkeley. Author: Pronunciation of American English, 1960, Essays in Honor of C.M. Wise, 1970, Biographical Dictionary of the Phonetic Sciences, 1977; project dir.: Dictionary of American English Pronunciation Served with Signal Corps and AGD USAAF, 1942-46. Fellow Am. Speech and Hearing Assn., Internat. Soc. Phonetic Scis., Dictionary Soc. N.Am., N.Y. Acad. Sci.; mem. MLA, Linguistics Soc. Am., Am. Dialect Soc., Internat. Phonetic Assn., Am. Assn. Phonetic Scis., Phi Beta Kappa. Office: U Calif Dept Linguistics Berkeley CA 94720-0001 E-mail: arthurb@socrates.berkeley.edu

BRONSTEIN, PHIL, executive editor; Reporter Sta. KQED-TV, San Francisco; reporter, fgn. corr. San Francisco Examiner, 1980-90, exec. editor, 1991—. Recipient awards Overseas Press Club, AP, World Affairs Coun., Media Alliance, Pulitzer Prize finalist. Office: San Francisco Examiner 110 5th St San Francisco CA 94103-2918

BRONSTER, MARGERY S, state attorney general; b. N.Y., Dec. 12, 1957; married; 1 child. BA in Chinese Lang., Lit. and History, Brown U., 1979; JD, Columbia U., 1982. Assoc. Sherman & Sterling, N.Y., 1982-87; ptnr. Carlsmith, Ball, Wichman, Murray, Case & Ichiki, Honolulu, 1988-94; atty. gen. State of Hawaii, 1994-99; pvt. practice Honolulu, 1999—. Co-chair planning com. Citizens Conf. Judicial Selection, 1993. Mem. Am. Judicature Soc. (bd. dirs.; chair gov. com. on crime, VAWA planning com.). Office: Bronster Crabtree Hoshibata 23d Fl 1001 Biship St Pavahi Tower Honolulu HI 96813

BROOK, ROBERT HENRY, health services researcher, physician, educator; b. N.Y.C., July 3, 1943; s. Benjamin and Elizabeth (Berg) B.; m. Susan Jean Weiss, June 26, 1966 (div. 1980); children: Rebecca, Daniel; m. Jacqueline Barbara Kosecoff Plaut, Jan. 17, 1982; children— Rachel, Davida BS, U. Ariz., 1964; MD, Johns Hopkins U., 1968, ScD, 1972. Diplomate: Am. Bd. Internal Medicine. Intern Balt. City Hosp., 1968-69, resident in medicine, 1969-72; project officer Nat. Ctr. Health Svcs. Rsch., HEW, Washington, 1972-74; vice chmn. medicine UCLA, 1990-92, dir. clin. scholar program, 1974—, prof. of medicine and pub. health, 1974—; dir. health program RAND Corp., Santa Monica, Calif., 1990—, v.p., 1998—. Mem. editorial bd. Health Adminstrn. Press., 1986-92, Jour. Gen. Internal Medicine, 1987-89, Health Policy, 1986—; contbr. articles to profl. jours. Served as asst. surgeon USPHS, 1972-74. Lita Annenberg Biomed. fellow Inst. Humanistic Studies, Aspen, Colo., 1981; recipient Rsch. prize Baxter Found. Health Svcs., 1988, Glazer award Soc. Gen. Internal Medicine; selected as one of 75 pub. health heroes of Johns Hopkins, 1991. Fellow ACP (Rosenthal award); mem. Inst. Medicine, Am. Soc. Clin. Investigation, Assn. Health Svcs. Rsch. (bd. dirs. 1982-89, Disting. Health Svc. Researcher award), Assn. Am. Physicians, Johns Hopkins Soc. Scholars. Democrat. Jewish. Home: 1474 Bienveneda Ave Pacific Palisades CA 90272-2346 Office: Rand Corp 1700 Main St Santa Monica CA 90401-3297

BROOKBANK, JOHN W(ARREN), retired microbiology educator; b. Seattle, Apr. 3, 1927; s. Earl Bruce and Louise Sophia (Stoecker) B.; m. Marcia Ireland, Sept. 16, 1950 (div. 1978); children: Ursula Ireland, John W. Jr., Phoebe Bruce; m. Sally Satterberg Cahill, Aug. 6, 1983. BA, U. Wash., 1950, MS, 1953; PhD, Calif. Inst. Tech., 1955. Asst. prof. biology U. Fla., Gainesville, 1955-58, assoc. prof., 1958-68, prof. zoology and microbiology, 1972-79, prof. microbiology and cell sci., 1972-85, prof. emeritus, 1985—. Vis. assoc. prof. U. Fla. Coll. Medicine, Gainesville, 1961-63, U. Wash., Seattle, 1965; cons. in field, Friday Harbor, Wash. 1986—. Author: Developmental Biology, 1978, (with W. Cunningham) Gerontology, 1988; editor: Improving Quality of Health Care of the Elderly, 1977, Biology of Aging, 1990; contbr. articles to profl. jours. Pres. Griffin Bay Preservation Com., Friday Harbor, 1985-99, past pres., 2000; pres. Bridge Council on Narcotics Addiction, Gainesville, 1974, Marine Environ. Consortium, 1986-89, San Juan Nature Inst., 1997-98; founding pres. Gainesville Regional Council on Alcoholism, 1976; mem devel. adv. bd. U. Wash. Friday Harbor Lab., 1995-98. Research grantee NIH, 1957-80, NSF, 1972-73. Mem. Seattle Tennis Club. Republican. Episcopalian. Avocations: fishing, boating, tennis, skiing. Home: PO Box 2688 Friday Harbor WA 98250-2688 E-mail: johnb@rockisland.com

BROOKE, EDNA MAE, retired business educator; b. Las Vegas, Nev., Feb. 10, 1923; d. Alma Lyman and Leah Mae (Ketcham) Shurtliff; m. Bill T. Brooke, Dec. 22, 1949; 1 child, John C. BS in Acctg., Ariz. State U., 1965, MA in Edn., 1967, EdD, 1975. Grad. teaching asst. Ariz. State U., Tempe, 1968-69; prof. bus. Maricopa Tech. Coll., Phoenix, 1967-72, assoc. dean instl. services, 1972-74; prof. bus. and acctg. Scottsdale (Ariz.) Community Coll., 1974-93; ret., 1993. Cons. in field. Author: The Effectiveness of Three Techniques Used in Teaching First Semester Accounting Principles to Tech. Jr. College Students, 1974. Home: 1176 E Northern Hills Dr Bountiful UT 84010-1707

BROOKE, TAL (ROBERT TALIAFERRO), writer; b. Washington, Jan. 21, 1945; s. Edgar Duffield and Frances (Lea) B. BA, U. Va., 1969; M in Theology/Philosophy, Princeton (N.J.) U., 1996. [illegible] Telecom Inc., 1982-83; pres., chmn. Spiritual Counterfeits Project, Inc., Berkeley, 1989—; founder End Run Pub., 1999—. Guest lectr. Cambridge U., Eng., 1977, 80, 97, 99, Oxford and Cambridge U., 1979, 84; founder End Run Pub. Author: [illegible] of Night: Millennial Edition, 1999, Lord of the Air, 1990, When the World Will Be As One, 1989 (bestseller 1989-90), Riders of the Cosmic Circuit, 1986, Avatar of Night, 1987 (bestseller in India 1981-84), 2d edit., 1999, The Other Side of Death, Lord of the Air: The International Edition, 1976, America's Waning Light, 1994, Virtual Gods, 1997, Conspiracy to Silence the Son, 1998, One World, 2000, The Mystery of Death, 2001. Mem. Internat. Platform Assn., Authors Guild, Soc. of The Cincinnati. Office: SCP Inc PO Box 4308 Berkeley CA 94704-0308 E-mail: scp@scp-inc.org, tal7@home.com

BROOKMAN, ANTHONY RAYMOND, lawyer; b. Chgo., Mar. 23, 1922; s. Raymond Charles and Marie Clara (Alberg) B.; m. Marilyn Joyce Brookman, June 5, 1982; children: Meribeth Brookman Farmer, Anthony Raymond, Lindsay Logan Christensen. Student, Ripon Coll., 1940-41; BS, Northwestern U., 1947; JD, U. Calif., San Francisco, 1953. Bar: Calif. 1954. Law clk. to presiding justice Calif. Supreme Ct., 1953-54; ptnr. Nichols, Williams, Morgan, Digardi & Brookman, 1954-68; sr. ptnr. Brookman & Talbot, Inc. (formerly Brookman & Hoffman, Inc.), Walnut Creek, Calif., 1969-92, Brookman & Talbot Inc., Sacramento, 1992—. Pres. Young Reps. Calif., San Mateo County, 1953-54. 1st lt. USAF. Mem. ABA, Alameda County Bar Assn., State Bar Calif., Lawyers Club Alameda County, Alameda-Contra Costa County Trial Lawyers Assn., Assn. Trial Lawyers Am., Calif. Trial Lawyers Assn., Athenian Nile Club, Masons, Shriners. Republican. Office: 901 H St Ste 200 Sacramento CA 95814-1808 also: Ste B-201 675 Ygnacio Valley Rd Walnut Creek CA 94596 also: 1746 Grand Canal Blvd Ste 11 Stockton CA 95207-8111

BROOKS, CHARLES LEE, III, computational biophysicist, educator; b. Detroit, May 14, 1956; married; 2 children. BS in Chemistry and Physics, Alma (Mich.) Coll., 1978; PhD in Physical Chemistry, Purdue U., 1982. Postdoc. fellow Harvard U., Boston, 1982-85, NIH, 1983-85; from asst. prof. to prof. Carnegie Mellon U., 1985—92, prof., 1992—; prof. molecular biology Scripps Rsch. Inst., 1994—. Mem. spl. rev. panels, site visit coms., mem. reviewers reserve Cell Biology & Biophysics Divsn. A study section, NIH; reviewer, mem. cellular and molecular biophysics panel, NSF; mem. adv. bd. Nat. Biomed. Computation Resource Inst., San Diego Supercomputing Ctr., sr. fellow; presenter in field. Mem. editl. bd. Proteins, 1995—, Biochimica et Biophysica Acta, 2000—, Physical Chemistry Chemical Physics, 2000—; contbr. over 100 articles to profl. jours.; author 1 book, several book chpts. A.P. Sloan fellow, 1990-93, AAAS, 2000; grantee Swedish Rsch. Coun., 1992. Office: Scripps Rsch Inst Dept Molecular Biology TPC6 10550 N Torrey Pines Rd La Jolla CA 92037-1000

BROOKS, JOHN WHITE, lawyer; b. Long Beach, Calif., Sept. 3, 1936; s. John White and Florence Belle (O'Grady) B.; m. Elizabeth Ann Bellmore, June 21, 1958; children: Stephen Sanford, John Tinley. AB, Stanford U., 1958, LLB, 1966. Assoc. Luce, Forward, Hamilton and Scripps, San Diego, 1966-71, ptnr., 1971-81, sr. ptnr., 1981—; chmn. Internat. Svcs. Group, 1989—. Mem. Internat. Coun. Inst. Ams., Pacific Coun. Internat. Policy. 1996-98; panelist Ctr. for Internat. Comml. Arbitration, 1987—; bd. dirs. Union of Pan-Asian Communities, , 1989-98, Ctr. for Dispute Resolution, 1986—; chmn. Pacific Rim Adv. Coun., 1984-91. Author: Passport Pal, The Pacific Rim, 1996—, The Heads Up Report; contbr. articles to profl. jours. Dir. corp. fin. council of San Diego, 1977-82, chmn., 1980-81; bd. visitors Stanford Law Sch., 1978-80, mem. Commn. of the Californias, 1977-79; chair San Diego Regional Yr. 2000 Working Group, 1998—. With USN, 1958-63. Named Alfred P. Sloan scholar Stanford U., 1958, Rocky Mountain Mineral Law Found. Research scholar, 1966. Mem. ABA (bus. law sect., com. on internat. bus. law, subcom. on Asia-Pacific law and internat. bus. structures and agreements, internat. law sect., subcom. on multinat. corps., com. on internat. comml. transactions), Calif. Bar Assn. (bus. law sect. com. on corps. 1977, vice chmn. com. on internat. practice 1986-87, exec. com. internat. law sect. 1987), San Diego County Bar Assn., Internat. Bar Assn. (com. on issues and trading in securities 1980-89, com. on procedures for settling disputes 1980—, com. on bus. orgns. 1989—), Inter-Pacific Bar Assn. (com. on internat. trade), Am. Arbitration Assn. (panel of arbitrators 1975-96), State Bar Calif. Avocations: greenhouse gardening, horse competitions, wine, food. Office: Luce Forward Hamilton & Scripps 600 W Broadway Ste 2600 San Diego CA 92101-3372 E-mail: jwbrooks@luce.com

BROOKS, MEL, producer, director, writer, actor; b. June 28, 1926; Author: sketch Of Fathers and Sons in New Faces of 1952, 1957, sketch Shinbone Alley; co-author: sketch All American, 1962; writer (for TV series) Your Show of Shows; also Caesar's Hour, The Sid Caesar, Imogene Coca, Carl Reiner, Howard Morris Special, 1967 (Emmy award for outstanding writing achievement in a comedy-variety); co-creator (TV series) Get Smart; recs. include 2000 Years, 2000 and One Years, 2000 and Thirteen Years, 2000 Years Old Man in the Year 2000, 1997 (Grammy award for Best Spoken Word Album Comedy 1998); writer, dir., star motion pictures including Producers, 1968 (Acad. award for Best Original Screenplay), The Twelve Chairs, 1970; co-writer, dir., star Blazing Saddles, 1974; co-writer, dir. Young Frankenstein, 1974; co-writer, dir., prodr., star: Robin Hood: Men In Tights, 1993, Dracula: Dead and Loving It, 1995; co-writer, dir., star: Silent Movie, 1976; prodr., dir., co-writer and star: High Anxiety, 1977, Spaceballs, 1987, Life Stinks, 1991; writer, dir., prodr., star: History of the World-Part I, 1981; writer, narrator: The Critic, 1964 (Acad. award for best animated short subject); actor, prodr. To Be or Not To Be, 1983; prodr.: 84 Charing Cross Road, 1987, The Elephant Man, 1980, Frances, 1982, My Favorite Year, 1982, Fly I, 1986, Fly II, 1989; guest actor (TV show) Mad About You (Emmy award for outstanding guest actor in a comedy series 1997, 98, 99); co-writer, composer, prodr. (Broadway musical) The Producers, 2001 (3 Tony awards). Office: c/o The Culver Studios 9336 Washington Blvd Culver City CA 90232-2628

BROOKS, ROBERT EUGENE, management consultant; b. Chgo., June 13, 1946; s. Robert Eugene and Shirley Mae (Kunkel) B.; m. Tonya Thompson, Aug. 19, 1969; children: Shannon, Gabriel, Cyrus, Aleisha, Aaron, Ethan, David. AB in Arts and Scis., U. Calif., Berkeley, 1968; MA in Physics, U. Tex., 1972; PhD in Mgmt., MIT, 1975. Asst. prof. bus. U. So. Calif., Los Angeles, 1975-76; prin. Robert Brooks & Assocs., Norwalk, Calif., 1976-79; v.p. Transportation and Econ. Research Assocs., Washington, 1979-82; pres. RBA Cons., Los Angeles, 1982-84; v.p. software devel. Profit Mgmt. Devel. Inc., Los Angeles, 1984-87; ind. cons., 1987—. Cons. Arthur D. Little, Inc., Cambridge, Mass., 1972-75, Chase Econometrics, Bala Cynwyd, Pa., 1976, Mathematica, Inc., Princeton, N.J., 1977-78, 82, McDonnell-Douglas Corp., 1987-97, fed. and state govts., Washington, Sacramento, Austin, Tex., 1976-83, Logistic Solutions, 1990-95, Ventana Systems, 1987-97. Author: (computer models) GASNET, 1976, GASNET2, 1977, NETS, 1981, CMOTSIM, 1982; Profit Maker, 1986, GPCM, 1987. Mem. Inst. Mgmt. Scis. Mem. Ch. Scientology. Avocations: sports, music, new mathematics. Home: 2150 Micheltorena St Los Angeles CA 90039-3019 Office: Leahy & Associates Inc 19131 Enadia Way Reseda CA 91335-3828

BROOKS, RUBEN B. judge; b. El Paso, Tex. BA, UCLA, 1971; JD, Yale U., 1974. Assoc. Page, Polin, Busch and Boatwright, 1983-93; magistrate judge U.S. Dist. Ct. (so. dist.) Calif., San Diego, 1993—. Mem. ABA, Calif. State Bar Assn., San Diego County Bar Assn., La Raza Lawyers Assn.

BROOKS, SIDNEY B. judge; b. 1945; married; 2 children. BA in Polit. Sci., U. Colo.; JD, U. Denver Coll. Law. Assoc. atty. Nelson and Haridng, Denver, 1971-73; asst. atty. gen. Office of Atty. Gen., Denver, 1973-75; ptnr. Nelson & Harding, Denver, 1975-80, Smart DeFurio Brooks Eklund and McClure, Denver, 1980-84; pres. Brooks and Krieger P.C., 1984-87; judge U.S. Bankruptcy Ct. Colo., 1988—. Guest spkr. Russian Law Conf., Russian Rsch. Ctr., Harvard U. Law Sch., 1994, Russian Bankruptcy Conf., Moscow, 1994; participant Conf. on Chinese Bankruptcy Law Reform, Internat. Rep. Inst., Beijing, 1995; cons. World Bank Legal Advisors, USAID, Orgn. Econ. Corp. and Devel., Internat. Jud. Rels. Com. of U.S. Jud. Conf.; advisor/cons. on jud. tng. and comml. ct. programs various countries; mem. and advisor Am. Law Inst.; spkr./lectr. for Fed. Jud. Ctr., Nat. Conf. of Bankrupty Judges and Am. Bankruptcy Inst., 1997-2000. Contbr. over 50 articles to profl. jours. Office: US Bankruptcy Ct Colo 721 19th St Rm 560 Denver CO 80202-2500

BROOME, BURTON EDWARD, former insurance company executive; b. N.Y.C., July 10, 1935; s. Burton Edward and Ann Loretta (Wall) B.; m. Anne Curtis, June 21, 1974; 1 child, Chelsea Anne. BSc, Fordham U., 1963; MBA, U. Calif., Berkeley, 1964. Ins. examiner Crum & Forster, N.Y.C., 1956-60; audit mgr. Price Waterhouse, N.Y.C., 1960-74; v.p., contr. Transamerica Corp., San Francisco, 1974-99; mem. oper. com. ARC Reins. Corp., Honolulu, 1993-99; ret., 1999. Mem. profl. acctg. program U. Calif., Berkeley, 1982-99; bd. dirs. Transamerica HomeFirst Corp., San Francisco, 1994-98, River Thames Ins. Co., London, 1994-98. Chmn. adv. coun. SEC and Fin. Reporting Inst., U. So. Calif., L.A., 1982-99. With U.S. Army, 1954-55. Mem. Fin. Exec. Inst.

BROOMFIELD, ROBERT CAMERON, federal judge; b. Detroit, June 18, 1933; s. David Campbell and Mabel Margaret (Van Deventer) B.; m. Cuma Lorena Cecil, Aug. 3, 1958; children: Robert Cameron Jr., Alyson Paige, Scott McKinley. BS, Pa. State U., 1955; LLB, U. Ariz., 1961. Bar: Ariz. 1961, U.S. Dist. Ct. Ariz. 1961. Assoc. Carson, Messinger, Elliot, Laughlin & Ragan, Phoenix, 1962-65, ptnr., 1966-71; judge Ariz. Superior Ct., Phoenix, 1971-85, presiding judge, 1974-85; judge U.S. Dist. Ct. Ariz., Phoenix, 1985—, chief judge, 1994-99. Faculty Nat. Jud. Coll., Reno, 1975-82. Contbr. articles to profl. jours. Adv. bd. Boy Scouts Am., Phoenix, 1968-75; tng. com. Ariz. Acad., Phoenix, 1980—; pres. Paradise Valley Sch. Bd., Phoenix, 1969-70; bd. dirs. Phoenix Together, 1982—, Crisis Nursery, Phoenix, 1976-81; chmn. 9th Cir. Task Force on Ct. Reporting, 1988—; space and facilities com. U.S. Jud. Conf., 1987-93, chmn., 1989-93, chmn. security, space and facilities com., 1993-95, budget com., 1997—. Recipient Faculty award Nat. Jud. Coll., 1979, Disting. Jurist award Miss. State U., 1986. Mem. ABA (chmn. Nat. Conf. State Trial Judges 1983-84, pres. Nat. Conf. Met. Cts. 1978-79, chmn. bd. dirs. 1980-82, Justice Tom Clark award 1980, bd. dirs. Nat. Ctr. for State Cts. 1980-85, Disting. Svc. award 1986), Ariz. Bar Assn., Maricopa County Bar Assn. (Disting. Pub. Svc. award 1980), Ariz. Judges Assn. (pres. 1981-82), Am. Judicature Soc. (spl. citation 1985), Maricopa County Med. Soc. (Disting. Svc. medal 1979). Lodge: Rotary. Office: US Dist Ct Sandra Day O'Connor Cthse 401 West Washington St #626 Phoenix AZ 85003-2158

BROPHY, DENNIS RICHARD, psychology and philosophy educator, administrator, clergyman; b. Milw., Aug. 6, 1945; s. Floyd Herbert and Phyllis Marie (Ingram) B. BA, Washington U., 1967, MA, 1968; MDiv, Pacific Sch. Religion, 1971; PhD in Indsl. & Orgnl. Psychology, Tex. A&M U., 1995. Cert. coll. tchr., Calif. Ednl. rschr. IBM Corp., White Plains, N.Y., 1968-71; edn. minister Cmty. Congl. Ch., Port Huron, Mich., 1971-72, Bethlehem United Ch. Christ, Ann Arbor, 1972-73, Cmty. Congl. Ch., Chula Vista, Calif., 1974; philosophy instr. Southwestern Coll., Chula Vista, 1975; assoc. prof. psychology & philosophy Northwest Coll., Powell, Wyo., 1975-96, prof., 1996—, assessment testing coord., 1999—. Chmn. social sci. divsn., 1992-95; religious edn. cons. Mont.-No. Wyo. Conf. United Ch. of Christ. Mem. APA (Daniel Berlyne award 1996), Wyo. Coun. Humanities, Soc. Indsl. Orgnl. Psychology, Soc. Tchg. of Psychology, Yellowstone Assn. United Ch. Christ, Phi Beta Kappa, Phi Kappa Phi, Sigma Xi, Omicron Delta Kappa, Theta Xi, Golden Key Nat. Honor Soc. Home: 533 Avenue C Powell WY 82435-2401 Office: Northwest Coll 231 W 6th St Powell WY 82435-1898 E-mail: brophyd@nwc.cc.wy.us

BRORBY, WADE, federal judge; b. 1934; BS, U. Wyo., 1956, JD with honor, 1958. Bar: Wyo. County and prosecuting atty. Campbell County, Wyo., 1963-70; ptnr. Morgan Brorby Price and Arp, Gillette, 1961-88; judge U.S. Ct. Appeals (10th cir.), Cheyenne, 1988-2001, sr. judge, 2001—. With USAF, 1958-61. Mem. ABA, Campbell County Bar Assn., Am. Judicature Soc., Def. Lawyers Wyo., Wyo Bar Assn. (commr. 1968-70). Office: US Ct Appeals 10th Cir O'Mahoney Fed Bldg Rm 2018 PO Box 1028 Cheyenne WY 82003-1028*

BROSE, CATHY, principal; Prin. Pomerado elem. sch.; co-prin. Highland Ranch Eler Sch., San Diego, 1997-98; prin. Sch. Creek Elem. Sch., San Diego, 1998—. Recipient Elem. Sch. Recognition award U.S. Dept. Edn., 1989-90. Office: Shoal Creek Elem Sch 11775 Shoal Creek Dr San Diego CA 92128-4753

BROSNAN, PETER LAWRENCE, documentary filmmaker; b. Bklyn., July 6, 1952; s. John Joseph and Audrey Barbara (Holran) B. BFA, NYU, N.Y.C., 1974; MA, U. So. Calif., 1979, Pepperdine U., 1995. Documentary filmmaker, writer, L.A., 1980—. Dir. DeMille Project, Hollywood Heritage, L.A., 1988—. Author: (screenplays) Heart of Darkness, 1992, The Ark, 1994, Perfect Target, 1996; co-author: (book) PML Report, 1989; writer: (documentary film) Ghosts of Cape Horn, 1980 (World Ship Trust award); prodr., dir.: (TV documentary) The Lost City, 1992; writer, segment prodr.: (PBS series) Faces of Culture, 1983-84 (Emmy award 1984), Writer Marketing, 1984 (Emmy award 1985); dir.: (documentary) Sand Castles, 1995. Democrat.

BROTHERS, CHERYL MARIANNE MORRIS, school superintendent; Supt. Happy Valley Elem. Sch., Santa Cruz, Calif. Recipient Leadership for Learning award, Amer. Assn. of Sch. Admin., 1994. Office: Happy Valley Elem Sch Dist 3125 Branciforte Dr Santa Cruz CA 95065-9661

BROTMAN, DAVID JOEL, retired architectural firm executive, consultant; b. Balt., Jan. 21, 1945; BS in Architecture, U. Cin., 1968. Registered architect, Ariz., Calif., Colo., D.C., Fla., Ga., Hawaii, La., Md., N.J., N.Y., Nev., Ohio, Oreg., Tex., Utah, Guam, No. Mariana Islands. Arch. Locke & Jackson, Balt., 1968, The Archtl. Affiliation, Towson, Md., 1968-75; joined RTKL, Balt., 1975-79, arch. Dallas, 1979-90, v.p., 1984-90, exec. v.p., mng. dir. L.A., 1990-2000, vice chmn., 1994-2000; prin. Sunset Cons., 2000—. Tchr. U. Tex. Sch. Architecture, Arlington, Catonsville (Md.) C.C.; arbitrator Am. Stock Exch., N.Y. Stock Exch., Nat. Assn. Security Dealers. Prin. works include Galleria at South Bay, Redondo Beach, Calif., Eton Sq. (Design Tex. Soc. Archs., 1986), Computer Sci. Corp., Fairfax County, Va., AT&T Customer Tech. Ctr., Dallas (Honor award Dallas chpt. AIA 1988), Tysons Corner Ctr., McLean Va. (Design award Monitor Ctrs. and Stores of Excellence 1989, Design award Internat. Shopping Ctrs. 1989, Exceptional Design award Fairfax County, Va. 1990, Modernization Excellence award Bldgs., 1990, Excellence award Urban Land Inst. 1992), St. Andrews (Scotland) Old Course Hotel, Tower City Ctr., Cleve., Eastland Shopping Ctr., Melbourne, Australia, Morley City Shopping Ctr., Perth, Australia, Dong An Market, Beijing, China, Desert Passage at Alladin, Las Vegas, Sci. and Tech. Mus., Shanghi, 825 Market St., San Francisco, many others; contbr. articles to profl. jours. Mem. AIA, Constrn. Specifications Inst., Internat. Coun. Shopping Ctrs., Internat. Assn. Corp. Real Estate Execs., Nat. Coun. Archtl. Registration Bds., World Trade Ctr. Inst., Urban Land Inst., World Affairs Coun. E-mail: sunset100@earthlink.net

BROTMAN, JEFFREY H. variety stores executive; b. 1942; JD, U. Wash., 1967. Ptnr. Lasher-Brotman & Sweet, 1967-74; with ENI Exploration Co., 1975-83; co-founder Costco Wholesale Corp., 1983, chmn. bd., chief exec. officer, 1983-88, chmn. bd., 1988—. Office: Costco Wholesale 999 Lake Dr Issaquah WA 98027

BROUSSARD, THOMAS ROLLINS, lawyer; b. Houston, May 30, 1943; s. Charles Hugh and Ethel (Rollins) B.; m. Mollie Brewster, Jan. 13, 1968. B.S. cum laude in Econs., U. Pa., 1964; J.D. cum laude, Harvard U., 1967. Bar: N.Y. 1968, Calif. 1973. Tax atty. Esso Standard Eastern, Inc., N.Y.C., 1967-70; gen. tax counsel Atlantic Richfield Co., N.Y.C., Los Angeles, 1970-74; v.p. corp. affairs, sec., gen. counsel Technicolor, Inc., Los Angeles, 1974-80; mem. firm Nelson & Broussard, Los Angeles, 1980-81; pres. Thomas R. Broussard, Ltd., P.C., Los Angeles, 1981—. Mem. ABA, Calif., Los Angeles County bar assns., Assn. of the Bar of the City of N.Y. Office: 5757 Wilshire Blvd Ste 648 Los Angeles CA 90036-3686

BROWDER, JOHN GLEN, former congressman, educator; b. Sumter, SC, Jan. 15, 1943; s. Archie Calvin and Ila (Frierson); m. Sara Rebecca Moore; 1 child, Jenny Rebecca. BA in History, Presbyn. Coll., 1965; MA in Polit. Sci., PhD in Polit. Sci., Emory U., 1971. Asst. in pub. relations Presbyn. Coll., Clinton, S.C., 1965; sportswriter The Atlanta Jour., 1966; investigator U.S. Civil Service Commn., Atlanta, 1966-68; prof. polit. sci. Jacksonville (Ala.) State U., 1971-87; mem. Ala. Ho. of Reps., Montgomery, 1982-86; sec. of state State of Ala., Montgomery, 1987-89; mem. 101st-104th Congresses from 3d Ala. dist., Washington, 1989-96; disting. vis. prof. nat. security affairs Naval Postgrad. Sch., Monterey, Calif., 1997—. Mem. Am. Polit. Sci. Assn., So. Polit. Sci. Assn. Democrat. Methodist.*

BROWN, ALAN J. electrical engineer; b. San Diego, Nov. 8, 1963; s. Vance E. and Doris C. B. BSEE, Calif. State U., Sacramento, 1987; MBA, U. San Diego, 1992. Registered profl. engr., Calif., Nev., Ariz. From engr. to pres. BSE Engring. (formerly Brown and Zammit Engring.), San Diego, 1987—. Mem. IEEE, Inst. Mgmt. Accts., Illuminating Engring. Soc. (pres. San Diego chpt. 1991-92), Soc. Mil. Engrs. (pres. San Diego post 1996-97), Internat. Assn. Electrical Inspectors. Office: BSE Engring 9620 Chesapeake Dr Ste 108 San Diego CA 92123-1324

BROWN, AMOS CLEOPHILUS, minister; b. Jackson, Miss., Feb. 20, 1941; s. Louetta Robinson Brown; m. Jane Evangeline Smith, June 25, 1966; children: Amos Cleophilus, David Josephus, Kizzie Maria. BA, Morehouse Coll., Atlanta, 1964; MDiv, Crozer Sem., Chester, Pa., 1968; DMin, United Sem., Dayton, Ohio, 1990; DDiv, Va. Sem., Lynchburg, 1984. Ordained to ministry, Am. Bapt. Chs. and Nat. Bapt. USA, Inc., 1965. Pastor St. Paul's Bapt. Ch., West Chester, Pa., 1966-70, Pilgrim Bapt. Ch., St. Paul, 1970-76, Third Bapt. Ch., San Francisco, 1976—; mem. City and County of San Francisco Bd. Suprs., 1996—. Instr. philosophy Cheyney (Pa.) State Coll., 1968-70; nat. chmn. Nat. Bapt. Commn. on Civil Rights and Human Svcs., 1982—; chmn. Bay Area Ecumenical Pastors Conf., 1980—. Vice pres. governing bd. San Francisco Community Coll., 1987-89. Recipient Martin Luther King Ministerial award, Colgate Rochester Div. Sch., 1984, Man of the Yr., San Francisco Bus. and Profl. Women's Clubs, 1985. Mem. NAACP, Rotary, Masons, Alpha Phi Alpha. Democrat. Office: Third Bapt Ch 13499 McAllister St San Francisco CA 94117 also: Board of Suprs City Hall 1 Dr Carlton B Goodlett Pl San Francisco CA 94102-4603

BROWN, ARTHUR CARL, JR. retired minister; b. Stockton, Calif., Dec. 16, 1915; s. Arthur Carl and Maud (Twitchings) B.; m. Inez Lundquist, May 10, 1940 (dec. Aug. 1982); 1 child, Arthur Carl III. BA, Coll. of the Pacific, 1937; MA, San Francisco Theol. Sem., 1939, BD with honors, 1940, postgrad., Stanford U., 1949 50. Ordained to ministry Presbyn. Ch., 1940. Pastor Presbyn. Ch., Sedro Woolley, Wash., 1940-44, Community Ch., Santa Clara, Calif., 1944-46; assoc. pastor First Presbyn. Ch., San Jose, 1946-49, minister edn. Palo Alto, 1949-51; organizing pastor Covenant Presbyn. Ch., Palo Alto, 1951-74; pastor Trinity Presbyn. Ch., Santa Cruz, Calif., 1974-78; outreach assoc. Los Gatos (Calif.) Presbyn. Ch., 1978-81. Commr. to gen. assembly United Presbyn. Ch., 1947, 52, 59; moderator San Jose Presbytery, 1950, chmn. various coms., 1950-78; mem. Synod Golden Gate and Synod of Pacific coms. Synod of Calif., 1947-82; pastor emeritus Covenant Presbyn. Ch. Treas., chmn. fin. com., bd. dirs. Internat. House, Davis, Calif., 1984 90, chmn. nominating com., 1990-96, mem. devel. com., 1991-97. Avocations: gardening, sports, study of Greek words in New Testament, writing, family history. Home: 4414 San Ramon Dr Davis CA 95616-5018

BROWN, BARBARA JUNE, hospital and nursing administrator; b. Milw., Aug. 17, 1933; d. Carl W. and Nora Anne (Damrow) Rydberg; children: Deborah, Robert, Andrea, Michael, Steven, Jeffrey. BSN, Marquette U., Milw., 1955, MSN, 1960, EdD, 1970. RN, Wash., Wis.; cert. nurse adminstr. advanced. Adminstr. patient care Family Hosp., Milw., 1973-78; assoc. clin. prof. U. Wash., Seattle, 1980-87; assoc. adminstr. nursing Virginia Mason Hosp., Seattle, 1980-87; assoc. exec. dir. King Faisal Specialist Hosp., Riyadh, Saudi Arabia, 1987-91. Project dir. NIH, Sexual Assault Treatment Ctr., Milw., 1975-78; lectr., cons., 1974—. Founder, editor Nursing Adminstrn. Quar., 1976—; editor-in-chief Nurseweek, MountainWest, 2000—. Vol. ski instr. for disabled, Winter Park, Colo. Fellow Am. Acad. Nursing (governing coun.), Nat. Acad. Practice; mem. ANA, Am. Orgn. Nurse Execs., Nat. League Nursing (bd. dirs.), Grand County Pub. Health and Emergency Svcs. (chmn. health adv. com. 1994-96), Sigma Theta Tau.

BROWN, BENJAMIN ANDREW, journalist; b. Red House, W.Va., Apr. 30, 1933; s. Albert Miller and Mary Agnes (Donegan) B.; m. Joanne Gretchen Harder, May 22, 1956; children: Benjamin Andrew, Gretchen, Mark, Betsy Brown Larson. BS in Journalism, Fla. State U., 1955. Sportswriter Charleston (W.Va.) Daily Mail, 1955-57; with AP, 1957-93, gen. exec., 1976-78, 82-93, chief bur. Los Angeles, 1978-82; assoc. Am. Newspapers Cons., Ltd., Milw., 1993-95. Bd. dirs. Last Chance Press Club, Helena, Mont., 1969; v.p. Minn. Press Club, 1975 Office: PO Box 3012 Paso Robles CA 93447-3012 E-mail: babrown@charter.net

BROWN, BIRCHEL S. steel products company executive; b. 1940; BS in Indsl. Mgmt., Purdue U.; MBA, U. Chgo. Sr. v.p. steel and wire ops. Northwestern Steel and Wire; sr. v.p. ops. Geneva Steel Holdings Corp., Vineyard, Utah, 1999—. Office: Geneva Steel Holdings Corp 10 S Geneva Rd Vineyard UT 84058 Office Fax: 801-227-9090

BROWN, BYRON WILLIAM, JR. biostatistician, educator; b. Chgo., Apr. 21, 1930; s. Byron William and Ruth (Munson) B.; m. Janet Louise Hyde, July 30, 1949; children: Byron William III, Eric Paul, Alan Thomas, Madeleine Magill, Mark Andrew, Lisa Anne. BA in Math., U. Minn., 1952, MS in Stats., 1955, PhD in Biostats., 1959. Asst. prof. biostats. Med. Sch. La. State U., New Orleans, 1956-57; from lectr. to prof. Sch. Pub. Health U. Minn., Mpls., 1957-65, prof., head biostats., 1965-68; prof., head divsn. Stanford (Calif.) U., 1968-98, chmn. dept. health rsch. and policy, 1988-96, prof. emeritus, 1998—. Cons. govt. and industry. Author, co-author books, book chpts., and articles in profl. jours. and encys. With USAF, 1949. Fellow AAAS, Am. Statis. Assn. (sect. pres., assoc. editor Jour.), Am. Heart Assn.; mem. Inst. Medicine (elected), Biometrics Soc. (pres. Western N.Am. region 1978), Inst. Math. Stats., Soc. for Clin. Trials (pres. 1988), Internat. Stats. Inst. (elected), Phi Beta Kappa, Sigma Xi. Home: 981 Cottrell Way Stanford CA 94305-1057

BROWN, CAROLYN SMITH, communications educator, consultant; b. Salt Lake City, Aug. 12, 1946; d. Andrew Delbert and Olive (Crane) Smith; m. David Scott Brown, Sept. 10, 1982. BA magna cum laude, U. Utah, 1968, MA, 1972, PhD, 1974. Instr. Salt Lake Ctr., Brigham Young U., Salt Lake City, 1976-78, vis. asst. prof. Provo, 1978; asst. prof. Am. Inst. Banking, Salt Lake City, 1977—; prof., chmn. English, communication and gen. edn. depts. Latter Day Saints Bus. Coll., Salt Lake City, 1973—, dean acad. affairs, 1986-96, v.p. for acad. affairs, 1996—, acting v.p. for student affairs, 1999-2000. Founder, pres. Career Devel. Tng., Salt Lake City, 1979—; cons. in-house seminars 1st Security Realty Svcs., USDA Natural Resource Conservation Svc., Utah Power & Light, Utah Soc. Svcs., Adminstrv. Office of Cts., HUD, Intermountain Health Care, Fidelity Investments, Am. Inst. Banking; mem. NW Assn. Schs. & Colls. Liaison, 1980—, Utah Bus. Coll. Dean's com., 1990—; acting v.p. student affairs Latter Day Saints Bus. Coll., Salt Lake City, 1999-2000. Author: (book) Writing Letters & Reports That Communicate, 8th edit., 1994, (poem) In Memory of the Baby Deers, 1996, Waiting (Editor's Choice award for Outstanding Achievement in Poetry), 1998. Demi-soloist Utah Civic Ballet (now Ballet West), Salt Lake City, 1964-68; active Mormon Ch.; C. of C. Bus. Edn. com., 1991-92. Named Tchr. of Month, Salt Lake City Kiwanis, 1981; NDEA fellow, U. Utah, 1972. Mem. Am. Bus. Communications Assn. (lectr. West/N.W. regional chpt. 1987), Delta Kappa Gamma (2d v.p. 1977-79), Lambda Delta Sigma (Outstanding Woman of Yr. 1983), Kappa Kappa Gamma (Outstanding Alumnus in Lit. 1974). Republican. Clubs: Alice Louise Reynolds Literary (Salt Lake City) (v.p. 1978-79, sec. 1985-86). Avocations: swimming, hiking, slide lectures on Israel and literary topics. Office: LDS Bus Coll 411 E South Temple Salt Lake City UT 84111-1302

BROWN, CATHIE, city official; b. Seattle, Mar. 23, 1944; d. G. Warren and Dorothy (Patterson) Cryer; m. Tom Brown, July 1, 1967; children: Amy, James W. BA in Criminology, U. Calif., Berkeley, 1966; MPA, Calif. State U., Hayward, 1985. Juvenile probation officer Santa Clara (Calif.) County, 1967-72; founder, dir. Tri-Valley Haven for Women, Livermore, Calif., 1976-79; planning commr. City of Livermore, 1980-82, city coun. mem., 1982-89, mayor, 1989—; exec. dir. Alameda County Project Intercept, Hayward, 1986-92. Dir. Svcs. for Families of Inmates, Pleasanton, Calif., 1981-82; active County Justice System Adv. Group, Oakland, Calif., 1990—; co-founder Tri-Valley Community Fund, Pleasanton. Active Alameda County Mayors' Conf., 1989—; del. Assn. Bay Area Govts., 1982-89; founder Youth For Action, Livermore, 1984-86, Youth Task Force, Livermore, 1989-90. Named Woman of Yr. Calif. State Legislature, 1990. Mem. League Calif. Cities (pres. East Bay div. 1982-89), MPA Alumni Assn. (pres. Calif. State U. chpt. 1989—). Democrat. Avocations: music, racquetball, reading. Home: 1098 Angelica Way Livermore CA 94550-5701

BROWN, CHADWICK EVERETT, professional football player; b. Pasadena, Calif., July 12, 1970; Degree in mktg., U. Colo., 1992. Linebacker Pitt. Steelers, 1993-97; owner Pro Exotics, Boulder, Colo.; linebacker Seattle Seahawks, 1997—. Named to Pro Bowl, 1996. Office: care Seattle Seahawks 11220 NE 53d St Kirkland WA 98033

BROWN, CHARLES R. lawyer; b. Twin Falls, Idaho, Aug. 25, 1945; Bar: Utah 1971, U.S. Tax Ct. 1972, U.S. Ct. Claims 1972, U.S. Ct. Appeals (D.C. cir.) 1972, U.S. Dist. Ct. Utah 1976, U.S. Ct. Appeals (10th cir.) 1976, U.S. supreme Ct. 1977. Trial atty. Office Chief Counsel IRS, 1971-76; ptnr. Hunter & Brown, Salt Lake City, 1976—. Mem. ABA (tax. sect., real property, probate and trust law), Utah State Bar Assn. (chmn. tax. sect. 1981-82, Tax Practitioner of Yr. 1995-96, bar commr. 1992-93 94—, chmn. standing com. on solo and small firm practice 1993-94), Salt Lake County Bar Assn. Office: Hunter & Brown One Utah Ctr 201 S Main St Ste 1300 Salt Lake City UT 84111-2216

BROWN, CRAIG L. state agency administrator; Dir. fin. dept. Calif. State Fin. Dept., Sacramento, until 1998. Office: Fin Dept State Capitol Rm 1145 Sacramento CA 95814-3700

BROWN, DARRELL, broadcast executive; BA in Comm., Brigham Young U. V.p., gen. mgr. Sta. KGTV-TV, San Diego, 1995—. Office: Sta KGTV-TV 4600 Air Way # San Diego CA 92102-2528

BROWN, DAVID R. former academic administrator; Pres., dir. Art Ctr. Coll. Design, Pasadena, Calif., 1985-99. Office: Art Ctr Coll of Design Office of Pres 1700 Lida St Pasadena CA 91103-1924

BROWN, DAVID RICHARD, school system administrator, minister; b. Manhattan, Kans., Oct. 22, 1929; s. Marion Arthur and Dorothy (Bailey) B.; m. Jeanette Christine Phoenix, July 28, 1962; children: David M., Mark, Thomas. BA, U. So. Calif., 1951; MDiv, U. Chgo., 1955; postgrad., U. So. Calif., 1956, 57. Ordained minister, Presbyn. Ch. Assoc. pastor Federated Community Ch., Flagstaff, Ariz., 1957-59; minister of edn. Lakeside Presbyn. Ch., San Francisco, 1959-62; pastor of edn. 1st Presbyn. Ch., Medford, Oreg., 1962-69, pastor Newark, 1969-75; founder, pastor Community Presbyn. Ch., Union City, 1975-89; founder, supt. Christian Heritage Acad., Fremont, 1984—; organizing pastor New Life Presbyn. Ch., Fremont, 1989—; asst. prof. Chabot Coll., Hayward, Calif., 1975-80. Moderator Presbytery of No. Ariz., 1959. Dir. various Shakespearian theatrical prodns., 1982-84 (Thesbian award 1984). Pres. Boys Christian League, L.A., 1953-54, Coconino Assn. for Mental Health, Flagstaff, 1958-59; chaplain Mozumdar YMCA Camp, Crestline, Calif., 1952-56; chmn. Tri-City Citizens Action Com., 1986-90. Recipient plaque KC, 1989. Mem. Rotary (chpt. pres. 1988-89, Paul Harris fellow 1989). Avocations: skiing, stamps, choir, drama. Office: Christian Heritage Acad PO Box 7688 Fremont CA 94537-7688

BROWN, DAVID W. lawyer; b. Seattle, Jan. 29, 1955; Student, Albion Coll.; BS, U. Oreg., 1977, JD, 1980. Bar: Oreg. 1980. Ptnr. Miller, Nash, Wiener, Hager & Carlsen, Portland, Oreg. Mem. Oreg. State Bar. Office: Miller Nash Wiener Hager & Carlsen 111 SW 5th Ave Ste 3500 Portland OR 97204-3699

BROWN, DON, museum director; Dir. Internat. Wildlife Mus., Tucson. Office: Internat Wildlife Mus 4800 W Gates Pass Rd Tucson AZ 85745-9600

BROWN, DONALD MALCOLM, plastic surgeon; b. Nelson, N.Z., May 28, 1945; came to U.S., 1947; s. Donald Roland and Edna M. (McPherson) B.; m. Susan E. Boeing, Sept. 3, 1989. MD, U. B.C., 1970. Diplomate Am. Bd. Otolaryngology and Plastic Surgery. Resident in otolarngology Manhattan Eye and Ear Hosp., N.Y.C., 1976; resident in plastic surgery Columbia U., N.Y.C., 1980; pvt. practice San Francisco, 1981—. Vis. prof. plastic surgery U. Liberia, Africa, 1980-81. Mem. AMA, Calif. Med. Assn., San Francisco Med. Assn., Am. Soc. Plastic and Reconstructive Surgery, Am. Soc. Aesthetic Surgery, Pacific Union Club, St. Francis Yacht Club. Avocations: flying helicoptors, skiing, wind surfing. Office: 2100 Webster St Ste 429 San Francisco CA 94115-2380

BROWN, DONALD WESLEY, lawyer; b. Cleve., Jan. 2, 1953; s. Lloyd Elton Brown and Nancy Jeanne Hudson. AB summa cum laude, Ohio U., 1975; JD, Yale U., 1978. Bar: Calif. 1978, U.S. Dist. Ct. (no. dist.) Calif. 1978, U.S. Dist. Ct. (cen. dist.) Calif. 1990. Assoc. Brobeck, Phleger & Harrison, San Francisco, 1978-85, ptnr., 1985—. Democrat. Home: 2419 Vallejo St San Francisco CA 94123-4638 Office: Brobeck Phleger & Harrison Spear St Tower 1 Market St San Francisco CA 94105-1420

BROWN, EDMUND GERALD See BROWN, JERRY

BROWN, ERIC JOEL, biomedical researcher, researcher; b. Ann Arbor, Mich., Sept. 27, 1950; s. Bernard and Shirley (Mark) B.; m. Marion Glynn Peters, Apr. 2, 1983; 1 child, Abigail. AB, Harvard Coll., 1971; MD, Harvard Med. Sch., 1975. Intern, then resident Beth Israel Hosp., Boston, 1975-77; clin. assoc. LCI/NIAID/NIH, Bethesda, Md., 1977-79, expert, 1979-81, sr. investigator, 1981-85; assoc. prof. Washington U., St. Louis, 1985-90, co-dir. divsn. infectious diseases, 1989-99, prof., 1990-99; prof. medicine and immunology U. Calif., San Francisco, 1999—. With USPHS, 1981-85. Fellow Infectious Diseases Soc.; mem. Soc. for Clin. Investigation, Am. Assn. Physicians. Office: U Calif San Francisco PO Box 0654 San Francisco CA 94143-0001 E-mail: ebrown@medicine.ucsf.edu

BROWN, GEOFFREY FRANCIS, public defender, lawyer; b. San Francisco, May 20, 1943; m. Wai Yung, 1973; children: Miranda, Simone, Olivia. BA in Polit. Sci., U. Calif., Berkeley, 1964; JD, San Francisco Law Sch., 1970. Bar: Calif. 1971, U.S. Dist. Ct. (no. dist.) Calif. 1971, U.S. Ct. of Appeals (9th cir.) 1971. Dep. pub. defender City of San Francisco, 1971-77, elected pub. defender, 1978—. Adj. prof. law New Coll. Calif. Sch. of Law; legal expert KRON-TV and Bay TV, 1995-97; cons. US AID in Italy, 1985, Bolivia, 1991, Argentina, 1995; bd. dirs. San Francisco Law Sch., 1998—; mem. human rsch. com. U. Calif., San Francisco, 1998—. Contbr. numerous articles to profl. jours. and newspapers, presented papers at legal symposia. Mem. Mayor's Task Force on Jail Overcrowding, 1979-95, Mayor's Coun. on Criminal Justice, 1979—; bd. dirs. San Francisco Neighborhood Legal Assistance Found., 1988-96. Mem. Calif Pub. Defenders Assn. (bd. dirs. 1979—, pres. 1984), Nat. Legal Aid and Defenders Assn. (defender com. 1981-82). Office: City & County San Francisco Pub Defender's Office 555 7th St San Francisco CA 94103-4732

BROWN, HANK, university administrator, former senator; b. Denver, Feb. 12, 1940; s. Harry W. and Anna M. (Hanks) B.; m. Nana Morrison, Aug. 27, 1967; children: Harry, Christy, Lori. BS, U. Colo., 1961, JD, 1969; LLM, M in Tax Law, George Washington U., 1986. Bar: Colo. 1969; CPA, 1988. Tax acct. Arthur Andersen, 1967-68; asst. pres. Monfort of Colo., Inc., Greeley, 1969-70, corp. counsel, 1970-71; v.p. Monfort Food Distbg., 1971-72, v.p. corp. devel., 1973-75, v.p. internat. ops., 1975-78, v.p. lamb div., 1978-80; mem. 97th-101st Congresses from Colo. 4th dist., 1981-90, Colo. State Senate, 1972-76, asst. majority leader, 1974-76; U.S senator from Colo. Washington, 1991-96; co-dir. Ctr. for Pub. Policy and Contemporary Policies, U. Denver, 1997-98; pres. U. No. Colo., Greeley, 1998—. Chmn. Fgn. Rel. subcom. Near Ea. and South Asian affairs, Judicorp subcom. on constl. law. With USN, 1962-66. Decorated Air medal, Vietnam Svc. medal, Nat. Defense medal, Naval Unit citation. Republican. Congregationalist. Office: Univ of Northern Colorado Office Of The Pres Greeley CO 80639-0001 E-mail: hbrown@mail.unco.edu

BROWN, HERMIONE KOPP, lawyer; b. Syracuse, N.Y., Sept. 29, 1915; d. Harold H. and Frances (Burger) Kopp; m. Louis M. Brown, May 30, 1937 (dec. Sept. 1996); children— Lawrence D., Marshall J., Harold A. BA, Wellesley Coll., 1934; LLB, U. So. Calif., 1947. Bar: Calif. 1947. Story analyst 20th Century-Fox Film Corp., 1935-42; assoc. Gang, Kopp & Tyre, Los Angeles, 1947-52; ptnr. to sr. ptnr. Gang, Tyre, Ramer & Brown, Inc., Los Angeles, 1952—. Lectr. copyright and entertainment law U. So. Calif. Law Sch., 1974-77. Contbr. to profl. publs. Fellow Am. Coll. Trust and Estate Coun.; mem. Calif. Bar Assn. (chair probate law cons. group nd. legal specialization 1977-82, trust and probate law sect., exec. com. 1983-86, advisor 1986-89), L.A. Copyright Soc. (pres. 1979-80), Order of Coif, Phi Beta Kappa. Avocations: literature, theatre, music. Office: Gang Tyre Ramer & Brown Inc 132 S Rodeo Dr Beverly Hills CA 90212-2415

BROWN, J. MARTIN, oncologist, educator; b. Doncaster, Eng., Oct. 15, 1941; married; 2 children. BSc, U. Birmingham, 1963; MSc, U. London, 1965; DPhil in Radiation Biology, Oxford U., 1968. NIH fellow radiation biology Stanford U. Med. Ctr., Calif., 1968-70, rsch. assoc., 1970-71, from asst. prof. to assoc. prof., 1971-84, prof., dir. divsn. radiation biology, 1984—, dir. Cancer Biology Rsch. Lab., 1985—. Sr. fellow Am. Cancer Soc. Dernham, 1971-74; mem. adv. com. biol. effects of ionizing radiations NAS, 1971—. Mem. AAAS, Am. Assn. Cancer Rsch., Am. Soc. Therapeutical Radiology & Oncology, Brit. Inst. Radiology, Brit. Assn. Cancer Rsch., Radiation Rsch. Soc. (9th Rsch. award 1980). Achievements include research in mammalian cellular radiobiology, tumor radiobiology, experimental chemotherapy, bioreductive cytotoxic agents, radiation carcinogenesis. Office: Stanford U Med Sch Cancer Biology Rsch Lab Dept of Radiation & Oncology GK103 Stanford CA 94305-5468

BROWN, JACK A. state legislator, rancher, real estate broker; b. St. Johns, Ariz., May 2, 1929; m. Beverly Butcher. Agr. and econs. degree, Brigham Young U., 1953. Mem. Ariz. Ho. Reps., 1963-74, 87-96, Dem. leader, 1969-72, asst. minority leader, 1989-92; mem. Ariz. Senate, Dist. 4, Phoenix, 1996—; mem. commerce, agr. and natural resources com. Ariz. Senate, fin. com., rules com., minority leader, 1997—. Former chair State Water Quality Control Coun. Mem. Apache City Bd. Realtors, Cattle Growers, Farm Bur., Ariz. Acad., State Cahmber, Kiwanis. Democrat. Office: State Senate 1700 W Washington St Ofc 213 Phoenix AZ 85007-2812 also: PO Box 220 Saint Johns AZ 85936-0220 Fax: 602-542-3429. E-mail: jbrown@azleg.state.az.us

BROWN, JACK H. supermarket company executive; b. L.A., June 14, 1939; Student, San Jose State U, UCLA. V.p. Sages Complete Marktes, San Bernardino, Calif., 1960-67, Marsh Supermarkets, Yorktown, Ind., 1971-77; pres. Pantry Supemarkets, Pasadena, Calif., 1977-79; pres. mid-west divsn. Cullum Cos., Dallas, 1979-81; pres., CEO Stater Bros. Markets, Colton, Calif., 1981—; also chmn. bd. dirs. Trustee U. Redlands, Calif.; bd. dirs. Goodwill Industries of inland Empire, San Bernardino; bd. councillors Calif. State U., San Bernardion. With USNR, 1956-62. Recipient Horation alger award Disting. Ams., 1992, Bus. Exec. of Yr. award U. so. Calif., 1993; Calif. State U., San Berardino Sch. Bus. named in his honor, 1992. Mem. Western Assn. Food Chains (v.p., bd. dirs., pres. 1987-88), Calif. Retailers Assn. (bd. dirs.), Food Mktg. Inst. (vice chmn.), So. Calif. Grocers Assn., Food Employers Coun. (bd. govs.), Life Savs. and Loan Assn. (dir.), Elks. Republican. Presbyterian. Office: Stater Bros Markets 21700 Barton Rd Colton CA 92324

BROWN, JAMES KEVIN, professional baseball player; b. McIntyre, Ga., Mar. 14, 1965; Student, Ga. Tech. Inst. With Tex. Rangers, 1986-94, Balt. Orioles, 1995, Fla. Marlins, Miami, 1996-97, San Diego Padres, 1997-98; pitcher L.A. Dodgers, 1998—. Named Sporting News Coll. All-Am. Team, 1986, Am. League All-Star Game, 1992, Nat. League All-Star Team, 1996. Ranked 2nd in Am. League in victories, 1992. Office: LA dodgers 1000 Elysian Park Ave Los Angeles CA 90012-1112

BROWN, JAMES W. gastroenterologist; b. Detroit, May 20, 1938; BS, U. Nebr., 1960; MD, Northwestern U., Chgo., 1964. Diplomate Am. Bd. [illegible] Internal Medicine in Gastroenterology. Gastroenterologist Wenatchee (Wash.) Valley Clinic, 1970—; chief gastroenterology U.S. Naval Hosp., San Diego. Vice-chmn., bd. dirs. Wenatchee [illegible] Bank, Wenatchee. Contbr. articles to profl. jours. Chmn. bd. dirs. Mustard Seed Neighbor Ctr., Wenatchee, 1990-92, bd. dirs. 1989-95. Lt. comdr. USN, 1968-70. Fellow Am. Coll. Gastroenterology; mem. Alpha Omega Alpha. Methodist. Avocations: cooking, hiking, reading, physical fitness, travel.

BROWN, J'AMY MARONEY, journalist, media relations consultant, investor; b. Oct. 30, 1945; d. Roland Francis and Jeanne (Wilbur) Maroney; m. James Raphael Brown, Jr., Nov. 5, 1967 (dec. July 1982); children: James Roland Francis, Jeanne Raphael. Student, U. So. Calif., 1963-67. Reporter L.A. Herald Examiner, 1966-67, Lewisville Leader, Dallas, 1980-81; editor First Person Mag., Dallas., 1981-82; journalism dir. Pacific Palisades Sch., L.A., 1983-84; freelance writer, media cons., 1984-88; media dir., chief media strategist Tellem Inc., 1990-92, comm. cons., issues mgr., 1992—. Press liaison U.S. papal visit, L.A., 1987; pres., CEO and owner PRformance Group Comm., 1995—; auction chmn. Assn. Pub. Broadcasting, Houston, 1974, 75; vice chmn. Dallas Arts Coun., 1976-80; vice chmn. Met. March of Dimes, Dallas, 1980-82; del. Dallas Coun. PTAs, 1976-80; bd. dirs. Santa Barbara City Coll. Bus. and Industry Coun., Montecito Assn., Women's Econ. Ventures; mem. core-coun. Santa Barbara Coun. on Self-Esteem; coord. specialist World Cup Soccer Organizing Com. Recipient UPI Editors award for investigative reporting, 1981. Mem. NAFE, Pub. Rels. Soc. Am. (accredited), Women Meeting Women, Women in Comm., Am. Bus. Women's Assn., Goleta Valley Art Assn., Santa Barbara C. of C. (media com.), Montecito Assn. (bd. dirs.). Republican. Roman Catholic. Home: 1143 High Rd Santa Barbara CA 93108-2430

BROWN, JAN WHITNEY, small business owner; b. Roundup, Mont., Mar. 16, 1942; d. John Estes and Janet Lillian (Snyder) Dahl; m. William A. Brown III; children: Erik Lane, Kimberly Elise. BA in Sociology, Social Work, Carroll Coll., 1976. Sec. 1st Nat. Bank, Bozeman, Mont., 1962, Office of Gov., Helena, 1963-69; pub. info. coord. Helena Model City Program, 1969-73; pub. relations and assn. mgmt. Mont. Bar Assn., Helena, 1973-76, Mont. Assn. Life Underwriters, Helena, 1973-76; legis. liaison Mont. Religious Legis. Coalition, Helena, 1975-81; exec. dir. Helena Food Share Inc., 1987; co-owner Jorud Photo and Gifts, Helena, 1971—; mem. state tax appeal bd., 1999—; legislator Mont. St. Legislature, Helena, 1983-92. Mem. legis. coun. Helena, 1989-92; bd. dirs. Helena Food Share, Inc., Bus. Improvement Dist.; chmn. state adminstrn. com. Mont. Ho. of Reps., 1989-92. Chmn. Mont. Medal of Valor Com., Helena, 1986-93; pres. United Way, Helena, 1982; bd. dirs. Mont. Area Health Edn. Ctr., Bozeman, 1988-93, Mont. Hunger Coalition, Helena, 1988-89, St. Peter's Hosp. Found. Bd., 1994-96, 97-2000, St. Peter's Hosp., 1994-2000, chair bd. dirs., 1997-99; Helena City Commr., 1993; vice chair Helena Citizens Coun., 1994-96; mem. cmty. adv. bd. U.S. Bank, 1994-99; sec.-treas. Mt. Soc. for Hosp. Governance, 1995-97; mem. visions com. United Way, 1997-98; mem. diocesan coun. Episcopal Diocese of Mont., 1997-99. Recipient Disting. Svc. award Mental Health Assn., 1976, Disting. Cmty. Svc. award Jaycees, 1982, Ann. Appreciation award Child Support Enforcement, 1985, United Way award, 1988, Cmty. Svc. award VFW, 1988. Mem. Nat. Assn. Hearing Officers, Nat. Assn. Adminstrv. Law Judges, Helena Unlimited. Democrat. Episcopalian. Avocations: symphony, choir. Office: State Tax Appeal Bd 1209 8th Ave Helena MT 59620

BROWN, JANICE ROGERS, state supreme court justice; State supreme ct. assoc. justice Calif. Supreme Ct., San Francisco. Office: Calif Supreme Ct 350 Mcallister St Rm 1295 San Francisco CA 94102-4712

BROWN, JERRY (EDMUND GERALD BROWN JR.), mayor, former governor; b. San Francisco, Apr. 7, 1938; s. Edmund Gerald and Bernice (Layne) B. B.A. in Latin/Greek, U. Calif., Berkeley, 1961; J.D., Yale U., 1964. Bar: Calif. 1965. Research atty. Calif. Supreme Ct., 1964-65; atty. Tuttle & Taylor, Los Angeles, 1966-69; sec. state State Calif., Sacramento, 1970-74, gov., 1975-83; chmn. Calif. Dem. Party, 1989-90; Dem. candidate for Pres. of United States, 1992; mayor Oakland, Calif., 1999—. Author: (book) Dialogues, 1988. Trustee Los Angeles Community Colls., 1969. Address: 1 Frank Ogawa Plz Oakland CA 94612-1997

BROWN, JOSEPH E. landscape architecture executive; b. 1947; BA, Cath. U., 1970; M in Landscape Architecture and Urban Design, Harvard U., 1972. With Edaw, Inc., San Francisco, 1973—, now pres. Office: Edaw Inc 753 Davis St San Francisco CA 94111-1414

BROWN, KATE, state legislator; b. Torrejon de Ardoth, Spain, 1960; BA, U. Colo.; JD, Lewis and Clark Northwestern. Mem. Oreg. Ho. of Reps., 1991-96, Oreg. Senate, 1996—; atty. Democrat. Office: State Capitol Bldg 900 Court St NE S-323 Salem OR 97301-4075 E-mail: brown.sen@state.or.us

BROWN, KATHLEEN, bank executive, lawyer; d. Edmund G. and Bernice Brown; m. George Rice (div. 1979); children: Hilary, Alexandra, Zebediah; m. Van Gordon Sauter, 1980; 2 stepsons. BA in History, Stanford U., 1969; JD, Fordham U. Sch. Law, 1985. Mem. L.A. Bd. Edn., 1975-80; with O'Melveny & Myers, N.Y.C., then L.A.; commr. L.A. Bd. Pub. Works, 1987-89; elected Treas. of Calif., 1990-94; exec. v.p. Bank of Am., L.A., 1994-99, pres. Pvt. Bank West, 1999—. Co-chmn. Capital Budget Commn., Washington, 1997—. Mem. Pacific Coun. on Internat. Policy, Stanford Inst. for Internat. Studies; dir. Children's Hosp. L.A., San Francisco Ballet. Democrat. Office: Bank of Am 555 S Flower St Fl 51 Los Angeles CA 90071-2300

BROWN, KEITH LAPHAM, retired ambassador; b. Sterling, Ill., June 18, 1925; s. Lloyd Heman and Marguerite (Briggs) B.; m. Carol Louise Liebmann, Oct. 1, 1949; children: Susan, Briggs (dec.), Linda, Benjamin. Student, U. Ill., 1943-44, Northwestern U., 1946-47; LLB, U. Tex., 1949. Bar: Tex., Okla., Colo. Assoc. Lang, Byrd, Cross & Ladon, San Antonio, 1949-55; v.p., gen. counsel Caulkins Oil Co., Oklahoma City, 1955-70, Denver, 1955-70; founder, developer Vail Assocs., Colo., 1962; pres. Brown Investment Corp., Denver, 1970-87; developer Colo. State Bank Bldg., Denver, 1971; amb. to Lesotho Dept. State, 1982-84, amb. to Denmark, 1988-92; ret., 1992; chmn. Brown Investment Corp., Denver, 1993—. Mem. adv. bd. Ctr. for Strategic and Internat. Studies. Chmn. Rep. Nat. Fin. Com., 1985-88; hon. trustee, past pres. bd. Colo. Acad. Served with USN, 1943-46. Mem. Coun. Am. Ambs. (pres.), Denver Country Club, San Antonio Country Club, Univ. Club, Bohemian Club. Presbyterian. Address: PO Box 1172 Edwards CO 81632-1172 also: 11 Auburn Pl San Antonio TX 78209-4739 Office: 1490 Colo State Bank Bldg 1600 Broadway Denver CO 80202-4927

BROWN, LILLIAN ERIKSEN, retired nursing administrator, consultant; b. Seattle, Feb. 7, 1921; d. Peter Louis and Lena (Lien) Eriksen; m. Jan. 21, 1942 (div. Nov. 1963); children: Patricia Lee, Michael Gregory, Kevin William. Student, U. Calif., Berkeley, 1939-40; diploma, St. Luke's Hosp. Sch. Nursing, San Francisco, 1943; AB, Calif. State U., San Francisco, 1952; MPA, U. So. Calif., 1975. RN, Calif. Pub. health nurse San Francisco Dept. Health, 1946-50; asst. dir. nursing San Francisco Gen. Hosp., 1950-56; dir. nursing Weimar (Calif.) Med. Ctr., 1956-62, Orange County Med. Ctr., Orange, Calif., 1962-76; assoc. dir. hosp. and clins., dir. nursing, lectr. U. Calif. Med. Ctr., Irvine, 1976-82; assoc. hosp. adminstr. King Khalid Eye Specialist Hosp., Riyadh, Saudi Arabia, 1982-86; cons. AMI-Saudi Arabia Ltd., Jeddah, 1986-90. Chmn. Western Teaching Hosp. Coun. Dirs. Nursing, 1972-75, 80-81; mem. planning project com. Calif. Dept. Rehab., 1967-69, mem. adv. com., 1970-73; mem. ad hoc president's com. on hosp. governance U. Calif., 1981-82; pres. dirs. nursing coun. Hosp. Coun. So. Calif., 1972-74, mem. pers. practices com., 1976-78, 80-83, area rep., 1975-82; mem. dept. nursing adv. com. to establish baccalaureate program U. So. Calif., 1980-82; mem. adv. bd. various coll. nursing programs. Contbr. articles to profl. jours. Sec. Olive (Calif.) Little League, 1967-72; mem. com. on emergency med. svcs. Orange County Health Planning Coun., 1977-78, mem. health promotion task force, 1978-79. 2d lt. Nurse Corps, U.S. Army, 1944-45. Recipient Lauds and

Laurels award U. Calif., Irvine, 1981 Fellow Am. Acad. Nurses; mem. ANA (cert. nurse adminstr. advanced), Nat. League for Nursing, APHA, Am. Orgn. Nurse Execs., Nat. Critical Care Inst. Edn., Calif. Nurses Assn. (Lillian E. Brown award named in her honor 1989), Calif. Orgn. for Nurse Execs. (hon.), Calif. Soc. for Nursing Svc. Adminstr., NOW. Republican. Avocations: travel, stamp collecting. Home: 1806 N Nordic Pl Orange CA 92865-4637

BROWN, LISA J. state legislator, educator; 1 child, Lucas. BA, U. Ill.; MA in Econs., PhD in Econs., U. Colo. Assoc. prof. econs. Eastern Wash. U., Cheney; mem. Wash. Senate, Dist. 3, Olympia, 1992—; chair energy, tech. and telecomms. com. Wash. Senate, Olympia, vice chair ways and means com., mem. edn. com. Recipient Woman of Distinction award Girls Scouts USA, Inland Empire Coun., Annual award for Saving Women's Lives Wash. State Pub. Health Assn., 1998, Achievement award Women's Club of Spokane, 1998, Child Care Champion award Child Care Workers Wash., 1998, Elected Ofcl. of Yr. Citizen's League of Greater Spokane, 1997, Random Acts Prevention award Greater Spokane Substance Abuse Coun.'s Prevention Ctr., 1997, Hunger Fighter award Anti-Hunger & Nutrition Coalition, 1997, Woman of Achievement Govt. award Spokane YWCA, 1997. Democrat. Avocations: reading, camping, bicycling. Office: 338 John Cherberg Bldg Olympia WA 98504-0001

BROWN, LOWELL SEVERT, physicist, educator; b. Visalia, Calif., Feb. 15, 1934; s. Volney Clifford and Anna Marie Evelyn (Jacobson) B.; m. Shirley Isabel Mitchell, June 23, 1956; 1 son, Stephen Clifford. AB, U. Calif., Berkeley, 1956; Ph.D. (NSF predoctoral fellow 1956-61), Harvard U., 1961; postgrad., U. Rome, 1961-62, Imperial Coll., London, 1962-63. From rsch. assoc. to assoc. prof. physics Yale U., 1963-68; mem. faculty U. Wash., Seattle, 1968—, prof. physics, 1970-2001, prof. emeritus, 2001—; mem. staff Los Alamos (N.Mex.) Sci. Lab., 2001—. Vis. prof. Imperial Coll., London, 1971-72, Columbia U., N.Y.C., 1990; vis. scientist Brookhaven Nat. Lab., summer, 1965-68, Lawrence Berkeley Lab., summer 1966, Stanford Accelerator Ctr., summer, 1967, CERN, Geneva, summer, 1979, Inst. for Theoretical Physics, U. Calif., Santa Barbara, winter 1999; mem. Inst. Advanced Study, Princeton, N.J., 1979-80; cons. Los Alamos Nat. Lab., spring 1999, vis. scientist, 1991; vis. physicist Deutches Elektronen-Synchrontron, Hamburg, 1986 Author: Quantum Field Theory, 1992; mem. editl. bd. Phys. Rev., 1978-81; editor Phys. Rev. D, 1987-95; contbr. articles to profl. publs. Trustee Seattle Youth Symphony Orch., 1986-95. Postdoctoral fellow NSF, 1961-63; sr. post-doctoral fellow, 1971-72; Guggenheim fellow, 1979-80 Mem. Ferrari Club of Am. (dir. Northwest region 1999—). Home: 1157 Federal Ave E Seattle WA 98102-4314 Office: U Wash Dept Physics Seattle WA 98195-0001 E-mail: lowellb@ferrariclub.com

BROWN, MICHAEL A. computer hardware company executive; b. 1958; BA in Econs., Harvard U.; MBA, Stanford U. Rsch. assoc. Braxton Assocs., strategic planning cons., 1982-84; various mktg. positions Quantum Corp., Milpitas, Calif., 1984-89, dir. product mktg., 1989-90, v.p. mktg., 1990-92, exec. v.p. responsible for hard drive bus., 1992-93, COO, 1993, pres. desktop and portable storage group, 1993-95, CEO, 1995—, also chmn.; acting pres. DLT & Storage. Office: Quantum Corp 500 Mccarthy Blvd Milpitas CA 95035-7909

BROWN, MICHAEL R. defense industry executive; b. Kans. BEd, Ottawa U. Mktg. mgr. Singer; mktg. mgr. Amecom divsn. Litton Industries, Inc., College Park, Md., 1968-77, v.p. bus. devel. electronic warfare comm. sys., 1977-87, v.p. bus. devel. electronic warfare sys. group, 1987-89, corp. v.p., group exec. electronic warfare sys., 1989-92, corp. sr. v.p., 1992-95, exec. commd., control, comm. sys. group, 1995, pres., 1995—, CEO, 1998—, chmn., 1999—. Mem. L.A. World Affairs Coun. Inducted into U. Ottawa Sports Hall of Fame. Mem. Navy League U.S., Assn. U.S. Army, Air Force Assn., Armed Forces Comm. Electronics Assn., Nat. Def. Indl. Assn., Aerospace Industries Assn., Assn. Old Crows. Office: Litton Industries Inc 21240 Burbank Blvd Woodland Hills CA 91367-6675

BROWN, PATRICK O. molecular biologist, educator; BA, U. Chgo., PhD, 1980, MD, 1982. Pediat. resident Children's Meml. Hosp., Chgo.; rschr. U. Calif., San Francisco; assoc. prof. biochemistry Stanford (Calif.) U. Sch. Medicine. Recipient award in molecular biology NAS, 2000. Office: Stanford Sch Medicine 300 Pasteur Dr Stanford CA 94305

BROWN, PAUL F, oil industry executive; CFO Flying J. Inc., Brigham City, Utah. Office: Flying J Inc PO Box 678 Brigham City UT 84302-0678

BROWN, PERRY JOE, university dean; Student, Foothill Coll., Los Altos, Calif., 1962-63; BS in Forestry, Utah State U., 1967, MS in Forest Recreation, 1968, PhD in Outdoor Recreation & Social Psych, 1971; postgrad., U. Mich., 1968, 69-70. Lectr. forest sci. Utah State U., Logan, 1968-71, asst. prof. forest sci., 1971-73; asst. prof. recreatin resources Colo. State U., 1973-74, assoc. prof. recreation resources, 1974-79, prof., dept. head forest recreation resources, 1979-88, asst. dean Coll. Forestry, 1982-84; assoc. dean instrn., continuing edn. and internat. programs Oreg. State U., 1988-94; dean Sch. Forestry, prof. forest resources U. Mont., Missoula, 1994—, dir. Mont. Forest and Conservation Expt. Sta., 1994—. Social sci. project leader Oreg. State U.-Nat. Park Svc. Coop. Park Studies Unit, 1990-93; interim dir. Oreg. Tourism Inst., Oreg. State Sys. Higher Edn., 1987-89; mem. adv. bd. Va. Poly. Inst. and State U. Coll. Forestry and Wildlife; mem. numerous panels and task forces NAS, regional planning commns., fed. and state agys. and domestic and internat. profl. orgns.; profl. cons. to numerous fed., state and internat. land mgmt. agys., univs., cos. and the Forest Ecosystem Mgmt. Assessment Team social sci. team; leader Rocky Mountain Coop. Ecosys. Studies Unit. Editor Utah Tourism and Recreation Rev., 1972-73; assoc. editor Jour. Leisure Rsch., 1977-79, Jour. Leisure Scis., 1982-85; mem. editl. bd. Jour. Forest and Landscape Rsch., 1993-99; author over 110 books, articles, papers and reports including 2 books and 16 book chpts. Recipient Cert. of Appreciation, USDA Forest Svc., 1988. Fellow Acad. Leisure Scis.; mem. Soc. Am. Foresters, Human Dimensions in Wildlife Study Group, Internat. Union Forestry Rsch. Orgns. (leader forest recreation, landscape planning and nature conservation sect. 1986-96, dep. coord. divsn. 6 1996—), Nat. Assn. Profl. Forestry Schs. and Colls. (western region chair, exec. bd. 1996-97, pres.-elect 1998-00, pres. 2000-02). Office: U Mont Sch Forestry Missoula MT 59812-0001

BROWN, ROBERT J. (BOB BROWN), secretary of state; b. Missoula, Mont., Dec. 11, 1947; s. Clifford Andrew and Jeanne M (Knox) Brown; m. Susan Kay Stoeckig, Sept. 20, 1975; children: Robin Sue, Kelly Charlynn. BS, Mont. State U, 1970, BS, 1974; MEd, U. Mont., 1988. Cert. secondary tchr. Tchr. govt., history Big Fork (Mont.) High Sch., 1970—86; tchr. history, econs. Flathead High Sch., Kalispell, 1986—; state rep. Mont. Ho. Reps., Helena, 1971—74; senator 2d dist. Mont. State Sen., Helena, 1974—96; sec. state State of Mont. With USN, 1972—73. Mem.: Phi Delta Kappa, Kiwanis, Am. Legion, Moose, Mont. Edn. Assn. Republican. Avocation: fishing. Home: 33 Cougar Trl Whitefish MT 59937 Office: Sec of State PO Box 202801 Helena MT 59620

BROWN, ROBERT MUNRO, museum director; b. Riverside, N.J., Mar. 4, 1952; s. James Wendell and Janet Elizabeth (Munro) B.; m. Mary Ann Noel, June, 1973 (div. 1977); m. Claudia Leslie Haskell, Jan. 14, 1978. BA in Polit. Sci. cum laude, Ursinus Coll., 1973; MA in Social Scis., Rivier Coll., 1978; PhD in Early Am. History, U. N.H., 1983. Grad. asst. dept. history U. N.H., Durham, 1979-83, instr., 1983-84; site curator T.C. Steele State Hist. Site Ind. State Mus. System, Nashville, 1984-91; exec. dir. Hist. Mus. at Ft. Missoula, Mont., 1991—. Hist. interpreter Strawberry Banke, Portsmouth, N.H., 1980-83; instr. Rivier Coll., Nashua, N.H., 1986-91, N.H. Coll., Nashua and Salem, 1986-91; supr. pub. programs Mus. Am. Textile History, North Andover, Mass., 1985-91; sec.-treas. Western Mont. Heritage Ctr./No. Rockies Heritage Ctr., 1992-93; mem. grad. com. U. Mont., 1993; mem. steering com. Ft. Missoula, 1993; reviewer Inst. Mus. Svcs., 1993, 94, 95, 97, 98, 99, 2000, 01; reviewer Am. Assn. Mus.-Mus. Asessment Programs, 1997—; mem. Mont. Com. of the Humanities Spkrs. Bur., 1995—; lectr., presenter, chair panels in field. Contbr. articles to profl. jours. Trustee Historic Harrisville, N.H., 1989-91; bd. dirs. United Peoples Found., 1991-93, v.p., 1993; mem. planning com. Western Mont. Heritage Ctr., 1991, U. Mont. Centennial Celebration, 1992, Leadership Missoula, 1992; active open space, parks and resource planning and mgmt. project team City of Missoula, 1993; mem. blue ribbon task force Five Valleys Luth. Retirement Community Planning Com., 1994. Scholar U. N.H., 1979-83, rsch. grantee, 1982; grantee Mass. Coun. on Arts and Humanities, 1986, 87, 88, Int. Mus. Svcs., 1988, 89, 90, 91, 93, 95, 97, 99, AT&T, 1988, Am. Wool Coun., 1988, BayBank, 1989, Am. Yarn Assn., 1989, North Andover Arts Lottery Coun., 1989, 90, Mass. Cultural Coun., 1990, Greater Lawrence Cmty. Found., 1991, Mass. Arts Lottery Coun., 1991, Gallery Assn. for Greater Art, 1991, 92, 94, 95, 96, 97, 98, Mont. Com. for Humanities, 1991, 92, 93, 94, 95, 96, 97, 98, 99, 2000, 01, Sinclair Oil Co., 1991, Mont. Rail Link, 1992, 98, 99, 01, U. Mont. Found., 1992, Pepsi-Cola Co., 1992, 93, 94, 95, 96, 97, Coca-Cola Bottling Co., 1998, Cmty. Med. Ctr., 1999, St. Patrick Hosp., 1999, U.S. WEST Found., 1992, 95, The Missoulian, 1992, 95, Champion Internat., 1992, Mont. Cultural Trust, 1993, 95, 97, Missoula Rotary, 1993, Tex. Mus. Assn., 1993, Inst. Mus. Svcs., 1993, 95, 97, 99, Zip Beverage Co., 1994, Bitterroot Motors, 1994, 95, 96, 97, 98, Grizzly Hackle, 1994, University Motors, 1995, 96, Earl's Distributing, 1996, Norwest Bank, 1996, 97, 98; Kellogg Found. fellow, 1987, Home Depot fellow 2000, Wells Fargo Bank fellow 2000. Mem. Am. Assn. Mus., Am. Assn. State and Local History (state membership rep. 1996-98), Am. Hist. Assn., Assn. Records Mgrs. and Adminstrs. (charter Big Sky chpt. 1992-94), Mont. Hist. Soc., Mus. Assn. Mont. (panelist 1994), Western Mont. Fundraisers Assn. (charter 1991, v.p. 1993-95, pres. 1995-97), Mtn. Plains Mus. Assn. (Mont. state rep. 1995-97, ann. meeting local arrangements chair 1997, chmn. scholarship com. 1998, 99, sec. 1998-2000, ann. meeting program co-chair 2000, treas. 2001—), Greater Boston Mus. Educator's Roundtable (steering com. 1988-90), Masons (Missoula chpt.), Kiwanis (Sentinel chpt.), Phi Alpha Theta (Psi Pi chpt.). Democrat. Avocations: canoeing, cross-country skiing, snowshoeing. Home: 216 Woodworth Ave Missoula MT 59801-6050 Office: Hist Mus at Ft Missoula Ft Missoula Bldg 322 Missoula MT 59801

BROWN, RONALD G. automotive company executive; b. 1937; Pres. North Star Plating Co., 1968; chmn. bd. dirs. Keystone Automotive Industries, Inc., Pomona, Calif., 1997—. Mem. Bumper Recycling Assn. N.Am. (bd. dirs., v.p.). Office: 700 E Bonita Ave Pomona CA 91767 Office Fax: 909-624-9136

BROWN, RONALD MALCOLM, engineering corporation executive; b. Hot Springs, S.D., Feb. 21, 1938; s. George Malcolm and Cleo Lavonne (Plumb) B.; m. Sharon Ida Brown, Nov. 14, 1964 (div. Apr. 1974); children: Michael, Troy, George, Curtis, Lisa, Brittney. AA, Southwestern Coll., 1970; BA, Chapman U., 1978. Commd. USN, 1956, advanced through grades to master chief, 1973, ret., 1978; engring. mgr. Beckman Inst., Fullerton, Calif., 1978-82; mfg. engring. br. mgr. Northrop Corp., Hawthorne, 1982-83; dir. of ops. Transco, Marina Del Rey, 1983-85; v.p. ops. Decor Concepts, Arcadia, 1985-87; design dir. Lockheed Aircraft Corp., Ontario, 1987-97; v.p. engring. and program mgmt. Ducommon Inc., Carson, 1997—. Mem. Soc. Mfg. Engrs., Inst. Indsl. Engrs., Nat. Trust for Hist. Preservation, Fleet Res. Assn., Am. Film Inst., Nat. Mgmt. Assn. Avocations: golf, running, racquetball.

BROWN, STEPHEN LAWRENCE, environmental consultant; b. San Francisco, Feb. 16, 1937; s. Bonnar and Martha (Clendenin) B.; m. Ann Goldsberry, Aug. 13, 1961; children: Lisa, Travis, Meredith. BS in Engring. Sci., Stanford U., 1958, MS in Physics, 1961; PhD in Physics, Purdue U., 1963. Ops. analyst Stanford Rsch. Inst., Menlo Park, Calif., 1963-74, program mgr., 1974-77, dir. Ctr. Resource and Environ. Systems Studies, 1977-80, dir. Ctr. Health and Environ. Rsch., 1980-83; assoc. dir. Commn. on Life Scis. NAS, Washington, 1983-86; prin. Environ Corp., Arlington, Va., 1986-91; mgr. risk assessment ENSR Cons. and Engring., Alameda, Calif., 1992-93; dir. Risks of Radiation and Chem. Compounds (R2C2), Oakland, 1993—. Mem. sci. adv. bd. EPA, Washington, 1991—; mem. coms. SAB, NAS, 1980-87. Contbr. over 20 articles to profl. jours., chpts. to books; author over 100 reports in field. Mem. Internat. Soc. Exposure Assessment, Soc. for Risk Analysis, Phi Beta Kappa, Sigma Xi, Sigma Pi Sigma, Tau Beta Pi. Office: R2C2 4700 Grass Valley Rd Oakland CA 94605-5622

BROWN, STUART I. ophthalmologist, educator; b. Chgo., Mar. 1, 1933; s. Leonard and Ann (Gladin) B.; m. Isabel Bodor; children: Sarah, Emily BMS, U. Ill., Chgo., 1955, MD, 1957. Intern Jackson Meml. Hosp., Miami, Fla., 1957-58; resident in opthalmology, Eye, Ear, Nose and Throat Hosp., Tulane Med.Sch., New Orleans, 1961; fellow in cornea Mass. Eye and Ear Infirmary, Boston, 1962-66; clin. asst. prof. dept. opthalmology N.Y. Hosp.-Cornell Med. Ctr., N.Y.C., 1966, dir. cornea svcs. cornea rsch. lab., 1966-69, clin. assoc. prof., 1970-73; chmn., prof. dept. opthalmology U. Pitts. Sch. Medicine, 1974-82, U. Calif. Sch. Medicine, San Diego, 1983—. Bd. dirs. nat. adv. commn. Nat. Eye Bank, Inc. Recipient Heed Ophthalmic Found. award, 1976 Mem. Am. Acad. Ophthalmology, AMA, Assn. Rsch. in Vision and Ophthalmology, Assn. U. Profs. Ophthalmology, Internat. Soc. Eye Rsch. Office: U Calif San Diego Shiley Eye Ctr - Ophthalmol 9415 Campus Dr La Jolla CA 92093-0946 E-mail: sbrown@eyecenter.ucsd.edu

BROWN, TIMOTHY DONELL, professional football player; b. Dallas, July 22, 1966; BA, U. Notre Dame, 1988. Wide receiver L.A. Raiders, 1988—. Recipient Heisman trophy, 1987; named Wide Reciever on The Sporting News Coll. All-Am. team, 1986, 87; Coll. Football Player of the Yr. The Sporting News, 1987, Kick Returner The Sporting News NFL All-Pro Team, 1988 Played in Pro Bowl, 1988, 91, 93-96. Office: Oakland Raiders 1220 Harbor Bay Pkwy Alameda CA 94502-6570

BROWN, TOD DAVID, bishop; b. San Francisco, Nov. 15, 1936; s. George Wilson and Edna Anne (Dunn) B. BA, St. John's Coll., 1958; STB, Gregorian U., Rome, 1960; MA in Theology, U. San Francisco, 1970, MAT in Edn., 1976. Dir. edn. Diocese of Monterey, Calif., 1970-80, vicar gen., clergy, 1980-82, chancellor, 1982-89, vicar gen., chancellor, 1983-89; pastor St. Francis Xavier, Seaside, 1977-82; bishop Roman Catholic Diocese of Boise, Idaho, 1989-98; appointed and installed bishop Roman Cath. Diocese of Orange, Calif., 1998. Mem. subcom. on laity U.S. Conf. Cath. Bishops, mem. 3d millenium com., chmn. com. on ecumenism and interreligious affairs, past mem. com. on mission, pastoral practices, past chair laity com.; mem. episcopal bd. govs. N.Am. Coll. Named Papal Chaplain Pope Paul VI, 1975. Mem. Cath. Theol. Soc. Am., Cath. Biblical Assn., Canon Law Soc. Am., Equestrian Order of the Holy Sepulchre in Jerusalem. Avocations: films, travel, reading, exercise. Office: Diocese of Orange Marywood Ctr 2811 E Villa Real Dr Orange CA 92867-1932

BROWN, WAYNE J. mayor; b. 1936; BS, Ariz. State U. Staff acct. Arthur Andersen & Co. CPA's, 1960-63; mng. ptnr. Wayne Brown & Co. CPA's, 1964-79; dir. acctg. Ariz. State Dept. Adminstrn., 1979-80; chmn. Brown Evans Distbg. Co., Mesa, Ariz., 1980—; mayor City of Mesa, 1996—. Office: Office of the Mayor PO Box 1466 Mesa AZ 85211-1466

BROWN, WILLIAM E. retail executive; With McCormick, Inc., McKesson Corp., 1972-77; sr. v.p. Vivitar Corp., 1977-80; CEO, chmn. Cen. Garden & Pet, Lafayette, Calif., 1980—. Office: Central Garden & Pet 3697 Mt Diablo Blvd Lafayette CA 94549

BROWN, WILLIE LEWIS, JR. mayor, former state legislator, lawyer; b. Mineola, Tex., Mar. 20, 1934; s. Willie Lewis and Minnie (Boyd) B.; children: Susan, Robin, Michael. B.A., San Francisco State Coll., 1955; LL.D., Hastings Coll. Law, 1958; postgrad. fellow, Crown Coll., 1970, U. Calif.-Santa Cruz, 1970. Bar: Calif. 1959. Mem. Calif. State Assembly, Sacramento, 1964-95, speaker, 1980-95, chmn. Ways and Means Com., 1971-74; chmn. revenue and taxation com., 1976-79; Democratic Whip Calif. State Assembly, 1969-70, majority floor leader, 1979-80, chmn. legis. black caucus, 1980, chmn. govtl. efficiency and economy com., 1968-84; mayor San Francisco, 1995—. Mem. U. Calif. bd. regents, 1972, Dem. Nat. Com., 1989-90; co-chmn. Calif. del. to Nat. Black Polit. Conv., 1972, Calif. del. to Nat. Dem. Conv., 1980; nat. campaign chmn. Jesse Jackson for Pres., 1988. Mem. State Legis. Leaders Found. (dir.), Nat. Conf. State Legislatures, NAACP, Black Am. Polit. Assn. Calif. (cofounder, past chmn.), Calif. Bar Assn., Alpha Phi Alpha, Phi Alpha Delta Democrat. Methodist. Office: Office of the Mayor City Hall Rm 200 1 Dr Carlton B Goodlett Pl San Francisco CA 94102-4603 also: US Conf Mayors Office of Exec Dir 1620 Eye St NW Washington DC 20006-4005

BROWNE, JOHN CHARLES, national research laboratory executive, physics researcher; b. Pottstown, Pa., July 29, 1942; s. Charles Ignatius and Mary Agnes (Titzer) B.; m. Susan Mary Mazzarella, Dec. 30, 1972 (div. Dec. 1984); children— Christopher Ryan, Adam Charles; m. Marti Moore, May 4, 1985; 1 child, Courtney Keese. B.S., Drexel U., 1965; Ph.D., Duke U., 1969; DSc (hon.), Drexel U., 1998. Instr. Duke U., Durham, N.C., 1969-70; staff scientist Lawrence Livermore Lab., Calif., 1970-79; group leader Los Alamos Nat. Lab., 1979-81, div. leader, 1981-84, assoc. dir., 1984-93; dir. Manuel J. Lujan, Jr. Neutron Scattering Ctr., Los Alamos, 1993-97, lab. dir., 1997—. Contbr. articles to profl. jours. NASA fellow, 1965-67 Fellow Am. Phys. Soc.; mem. AAAS. Roman Catholic Avocations: skiing, tennis. Office: Los Alamos Nat Lab MS A100 Los Alamos NM 87545-0001

BROWNE, SPENCER I. mortgage company executive, internet executive; b. 1949; married. BS, U. Pa., 1971; JD, Villanova U., 1974. Ptnr. Brownstein Hyatt Farber & Madden, Denver, 1983-84; pres., dir. MDC Holdings, Inc., 1984-96; pres., CEO, dir. Asset Investors Corp., 1988-96; pres., CEO & dir. Comml. Assets, Inc., 1994-96; with Strategic Asset Mgmt. LLC, Denver, 1996—. Bd. dirs. Annaly Mortgage Mgmt., Thermogenesis Corp., Micro Source, Inc., Nexus Resources Inc. Office: Strategic Asset Mgmt LLC 650 S Cherry St Ste 420 Denver CO 80246-1806 E-mail: sibsam@aol.com

BROWNING, JAMES ROBERT, federal judge; b. Great Falls, Mont., Oct. 1, 1918; s. Nicholas Henry and Minnie Sally (Foley) B.; m. Marie Rose Chapell. BA, Mont. State U., Missoula, 1938; LLB with honors, U. Mont., 1941, LLD (hon.), 1961, Santa Clara U., 1989. Bar: Mont. 1941, D.C. 1950, U.S. Supreme Ct. 1952. Spl. atty. antitrust div. Dept. Justice, 1941-43, spl. atty. gen. litigation sect. antitrust div., 1946-48, chief antitrust dept. N.W. regional office, 1948-49; asst. chief gen. litigation sect. antitrust div. Dept. Justice (N.W. regional office), 1949-51, 1st asst. civil div., 1951-52; exec. asst. to atty. gen. U.S., 1952-53; chief U.S. (Exec. Office for U.S. Attys.), 1953; pvt. practice Washington, 1953-58; lectr. N.Y.U. Sch. Law, 1953, Georgetown U. Law Center, 1957-58; clk. Supreme Ct. U.S., 1958-61; judge U.S. Ct. Appeals 9th Circuit, 1961-76, chief judge, 1976-88, judge, 1988—. Mem. Jud. Conf. of U.S., 1976-88, exec. com. of conf., 1978-87, com. on internat. conf. of appellate judges, 1987-90, com. on ct. adminstrn., 1969-71, chmn. subcom. on jud. stats., 1969-71, com. on the budget, 1971-77, adminstrn. office, subom. on budget, 1974-76, com. to study U.S. jud. conf., 1986-88, com. to study the illustrative rules of jud. misconduct, 1985-87, com. on formulation of standard of conduct of fed. judges, 1969, Reed justice com. on cont. edn., tng. and adminstrn., 1967-68; David T. Lewis Disting. Judge-in-residence, U. Utah, 1987; Blankenbaker lectr. U. Mont., 1987, Sibley lectr. U. Ga., 1987, lectr. Human Rights Inst. Santa Clara U. Sch. Law, Strasbourg. Editor-in-chief, Mont. Law Rev. Dir. Western Justice Found.; chmn. 9th Cir. Hist. Soc. 1st lt. U.S. Army, 1943-46. Decorated Bronze Star; named to Order of the Grizzly, U. Mont., 1973; scholar in residence Santa Clara U., 1989, U. Mont., 1991; recipient Devitt Disting. Svc. to Justice award, 1990. Fellow ABA (judge adv. com. to standing com. on Ethics and Profl. Responsibility 1973-75); mem. D.C. Bar Assn., Mont. Bar Assn., Am. Law Inst., Fed. Bar Assn. (bd. dirs 1945-61, Nat. council 1958-62), Inst. Jud. Adminstrn., Am. Judicature Soc. (chmn. com. on fed. judiciary 1973-74, bd. dirs. 1972-75), Herbert Harley award 1984), Am. Soc. Legal History (adv. bd. jour.), Nat Lawyers Club (bd. govs. 1959-63). Office: US Ct Appeals 9th Cir PO Box 193939 San Francisco CA 94119-3939

BROWNING, NORMA LEE (MRS. RUSSELL JOYNER OGG), journalist; b. Spickard, Mo., Nov. 24, 1914; d. Howard R. and Grace (Kennedy) B.; m. Russell Joyner Ogg, June 12, 1938. A.B., B.J., U. Mo., 1937; M.A. in English, Radcliffe Coll., 1938. Reporter Los Angeles Herald-Express, 1942-43; with Chgo. Tribune, from 1944, Hollywood columnist, 1966-75. Vis. lectr. creative writing, editorial cons., mem. nat. adv. bd. Interlochen Arts Acad., Northwood Inst. Author: City Girl in the Country, 1955, Joe Maddy of Interlochen, 1963, (with W. Clement Stone) The Other Side of the Mind, 1965, The Psychic World of Peter Hurkos, 1970, (with Louella Dirksen) The Honorable Mr. Marigold, 1972, (with Ann Miller) Miller's High Life, 1972, Peter Hurkos: I Have Many Lives, 1976, Omarr: Astrology and the Man, 1977, (with George Masters) The Masters Way to Beauty, 1977, (with Russell Ogg) He Saw A Hummingbird, 1978, (with Florence Lowell) Be A Guest At Your Own Party, 1980, Face-Lifts: Everything You Always Wanted to Know, 1981, Joe Maddy Of Interlochen: Portrait of A Legend, 1991; Contbr. articles to nat. mags. Recipient E.S. Beck award Chgo Tribune. Mem. Theta Sigma Phi, Kappa Tau Alpha. Address: 226 E Morongo Rd Palm Springs CA 92264-8402

BROWNING, RODERICK HANSON, banker; b. Salt Lake City, Oct. 9, 1925; s. Frank M. and Eugenia H. B.; m. Mary Wadsworth, Mar. 7, 1956; children— Patricia Ann, Jonathan Wadsworth, Frank Wadsworth, Anthony Stuart, Carolyn Rae. A.B., Stanford U., 1948. Vice pres. Bank of Utah, Ogden, 1954-59, chmn., 1959—; chmn. bd., pres. Bank of Brigham City, Utah, 1973—; chmn. bd. Bank No. Utah, Clearfield, 1971—; dir. Salt Lake City br. Fed. Res. Bank San Francisco, 1969-74. Bd. dirs., treas. Ogden Indsl. Devel. Corp., Weber County (Utah) Indsl. Devel. Bur.; adv. bd. St. Benedicts Hosp.; bd. dirs. Weber State Coll., Ogden; former pres. United Fund No. Utah. Served with U.S. Army, 1948-53. Mem. Am. Bankers Assn., Utah Bankers Assn. (former mem. exec. com.), Am. Legion. Clubs: Rotary (Ogden); Weber, Alta, Ogden Golf and Country. Office: Bank of Utah 2605 Washington Blvd Ogden UT 84401-3626

BROWNING, WILLIAM DOCKER, federal judge; b. Tucson, May 19, 1931; s. Horace Benjamin and Mary Louise (Docker) B.; children: Christopher, Logan, Courtenay; m. Zerilda Sinclair, Dec. 17, 1974; 1 child, Benjamin. BBA, U. Ariz., 1954, LLB, 1960. Bar: Ariz. 1960, U.S. Dist. Ct. Ariz. 1960, U.S. Ct. Appeals (9th cir.) 1965, U.S. Supreme Ct. 1967. Pvt. practice, Tucson, 1960-84; judge U.S. Dist. Ct., Tucson, 1984—. Mem. jud. nominating com. appellate ct. appointments, 1975-79; mem. Commn. on Structural Alternatives, Fed. Ct. Appeals, 1997-99. Del. 9th Cir. Jud. Conf., 1968-77, 79-82; trustee Inst. for Ct. Mgmt., 1978-84; mem. Ctr. for Pub. Resources Legal Program. 1st lt. USAF, 1954-57, capt. USNG, 1958-61. Recipient Disting. Citizen award U. Ariz., 1995. Fellow Am. Coll. Trial

Lawyers, Am. Bar Found.; mem. ABA (spl. com. housing and urban devel. law 1973-76, com. urban problems and human affairs 1978-80), Ariz. Bar Assn. (chmn. merit selection of judges com. 1973-76, bd. gove. 1968-74, pres. 1972-73, Outstanding Mem. 1980), Pima County Bar Assn. (exec. com. 1964-68, med. legal screening panel 1965-75, pres. 1967-68), Am. Bd. Trial Advocates, Am. Judicature Soc. (bd. dirs. 1975-77), Fed. Judges Assn. (bd. dirs.). Office: US Courthouse 405 W Congress St Ste 6160 Tucson AZ 85701-5061

BROWNLEE, DONALD EUGENE, II, astronomer, educator; b. Las Vegas, Nev., Dec. 21, 1943; s. Donald Eugene and Geraldine Florence (Stephen) B.; m. Paula Szkody. B.S. in Elec. Engring, U. Calif., Berkeley, 1965; Ph.D. in Astronomy, U. Wash., 1970. Research assoc. U. Wash., 1970-77, asso. prof. astronomy, 1977-89; asso. geochemistry Calif. Inst. Tech., Pasadena, 1977-82; prof. astronomy U. Wash., 1989—. Cons. NASA, 1976— Author papers in field, chpts. in books. Grantee NASA, 1975; recipient J. Lawrence Smith medal Nat. Acad. of Sciences, 1994. Mem. AAAS, Internat. Astron. Union, Am. Astron. Assn., Meteoritical Soc. (Leonard medal 1996), Com. Space Rsch. Dust, NAS (NASA PI stardust mission). Office: U Wash Dept Astronomy Seattle WA 98195-0001

BROWNLEE, WILSON ELLIOT, JR. history educator; b. Lacrosse, Wis., May 10, 1941; s. Wilson Elliot Sr. and Pearl (Woodings) B.; m. Mary Margaret Cochran, June 25, 1966; children: Charlotte Louise, Martin Elliot. BA, Harvard U., 1963; MA, U. Wis., 1965, PhD, 1969. Asst. prof. U. Calif., Santa Barbara, 1967-74, assoc. prof., 1974-80, prof. history, 1980—, spl. advisor to systemwide provost, 1995, assoc. systemwide provost, 1996. Vis. prof. Princeton (N.J.) U., 1980-81; chmn. dept. history U. Calif., Santa Barbara, 1984-87, acad. senate, 1983-84, 88-90, systemwide acad. senate, 1992-93; dir. U. Calif.-Santa Barbara Ctr., Washington, 1990-91; chmn. exec. com. dels. Am. Coun. Learned Socs., N.Y.C., 1988-90, bd. dirs.; bd. dirs. Nat. Coun. on Pub. History, Boston; bicentennial lectr. U.S. Dept. Treasury, 1989; faculty rep. U. Calif. Bd. Regents, 1991-93; adj. prof. history Calif. State U., Sacto., 1997-99; mem. bd. control, U. Calif. Press, 1996-99. Author: Dynamics of Ascent, 1974, 2nd edit., 1979, Progressivism and Economic Growth, 1974, Federal Taxation in America: A Short History, 1996; co-author: Essentials of American History, 1976, 4th edit., 1986, America's History, 1987, 3rd edit., 1997; editor: Women in the American Economy 1976, Funding the American State, 1996; contbr. numerous articles to profl. jours., chpts. to books. Chmn. schs. com. Harvard Club, Santa Barbara, 1971-80, 85, 86; pres. Assn. for Retarded Citizens, Santa Barbara, 1982-84; 1st v.p. Assn. for Retarded Citizens Calif., Sacramento, 1983-84; pres. Santa Barbara Trust for Hist. Preservation, 1986-87, 95-97; trustee Las Trampas Inc., 1994-97. Charles Warren fellow Harvard U., 1978-79, fellow Woodrow Wilson Ctr., Washington, 1987-88; recipient Spl. Commendation, Calif. Dept. Pks. and Recreation, 1988, Oliver Johnson award for Disting. Svc. U. Calif. Acad. Senate, 1998. Mem. Am. Hist. Assn., Orgn. Am. Historians, Econ. History Assn., Am. Tax Policy Inst. Office: U Calif Dept History Santa Barbara CA 93106 E-mail: brownlee@humanitas.ucsb.edu

BROWNSON, JACQUES CALMON, architect; b. Aurora, Ill., Aug. 3, 1923; s. Clyde Arthur and Iva Kline (Felter) B.; m. Doris L. Curry, 1946; children— Joel C., Lorre J., Daniel J. BS in Architecture, Ill. Inst. Tech., 1948, MS, 1954. Instr., asst. prof. architecture Ill. Inst. Tech., 1949-59; prof. architecture, chmn. dept. U. Mich., 1966-68; chief design C.F. Murphy Assocs., Chgo., 1959-6l; project architect, chief designer Chgo. Civic Ctr. Architects, l961-68; dir. state bldg. div. State of Colo., Denver, l986-88; pvt. practice Denver, 1988—. Former mng. architect Chgo. Pub. Bldg. Commn.; past dir. planning and devel. Auraria Ctr. for Higher Edn., Denver; bd. dirs. Capital Constrn., Denver; guest lectr. architecture in U.S. and Europe. Prin. works include Chgo. Civic Ctr., Lake Denver, Colo., 1985, Chgo. Tribune/Cabrini Green Housing, 1993; author: History of Chicago Architects, 1996, Oral History of Jacuqes Calmon Brownson, 1996. Recipient award for Geneva House Archtl. Record mag., 1956; Design award for steel framed factory Progressive Architecture mag., 1957 Home and Office: 659 Josephine St Denver CO 80206-3722

BROWNSTEIN, BARBARA LAVIN, geneticist, educator, university official; b. Phila., Sept. 8, 1931; d. Edward A. and Rose (Silverstein) Lavin; m. Melvin Brownstein, June 1949 (div. 1955); children: Judith Brownstein Kaufmann, Dena. Asst. editor Biol. Abstracts, Phila., 1957-58; research fellow dept. microbial genetics Karolinska Inst., Stockholm, 1962-64; assoc. Wistar Inst., Phila., 1964-68; assoc. prof. molecular biology, dept. biology Temple U., Phila., 1968-74, prof., 1974-96, prof. emeritus, 1996—, chmn. dept., 1978-81, provost, 1983-90; sr. assoc. Ctr. Ednl. Rsch. U. Wash., Seattle, 1994—. Vis. scientist dept. tumor cell biology Imperial Cancer Rsch. Fund Labs., London, 1973-74; bd. dirs. Univ. City Sci. Ctr., Greater Phila. Econ. Devel. Coun., Forum Exec. Women; program officer NSF, 1992-93; sr. assoc. Inst. Ednl. Inquiry, Seattle, 1994—. Recipient Liberal Arts Alumni award for excellence in teaching Temple U., 1980; recipient Outstanding Faculty Woman award Temple U., 1980 Fellow AAAS; mem. Am. Soc. Cell Biology, N.Y. Acad. Sci., Assn. Women in Sci., NSF (program officer 1992-93). Home: PO Box 835 Lopez Island WA 98261 Office: Inst Ednl Inquiry 124 E Edgar St Seattle WA 98102 E-mail: bbrownst@msn.com

BRUBAKER, CRAWFORD FRANCIS, JR. federal agency official, aerospace consultant; b. Fruitland, Idaho, Apr. 23, 1924; s. Crawford Francis and Cora Susan (Flora) B.; m. Lucile May Christensen, May 5, 1945; children: Eric Stephen, Alan Kenneth, Craig Martin, Paul David BA, Pomona Coll., 1946; MBA, U. Pa., 1948. Office mgr. Lockheed Calif. Co., Burbank, 1948-54, sales adminstr., 1954-57, with fighter contracts div., field office rep., 1959-65, asst. dir. fighter sales, 1965-69, dep. mgr. bid and proposals, 1969-74, mgr. govt. sales, 1974-76; dir. internat. mktg. devel. and policy Lockheed Corp., Burbank, 1976-83; dep. asst. sec. for aerospace U.S. Dept. Commerce, Washington, 1983-87; internat. aerospace cons., 1987—. Chair bd. trustees So. Calif. Presbyn. Homes; vice chmn. Industry Sector Adv. Com., Washington, 1979-83; mem. Aero. Policy Rev. Com., Washington, 1983-87. Vice chmn. So. Calif. Dist. Export Coun., L.A., 1980-83, 88-91, chmn., 1992-93. Lt. (j.g.) USN, 1943-45, PTO Mem. AIAA, Am. Defense Preparedness Assn., Kiwanis, Sigma Alpha Epsilon. Republican. Presbyterian. Avocations: numismatics, golf, fishing, photography. E-mail: dasbru@pacbell.net

BRUBAKER, WILLIAM ROGERS, sociology educator; b. Evanston, Ill., June 8, 1956; s. Charles William and Elizabeth (Rogers) B. BA summa cum laude, Harvard U., 1979; MA, Sussex U., Eng., 1980; PhD, Columbia U., 1990. Prof. UCLA, 1994—, assoc. prof. sociology, 1991-94. Author: The Limits of Rationality, 1984, Citizenship and Nationhood in France and Germany, 1992, Nationalism Reframed, 1996; editor: Immigration and Politics of Citizenship in Europe and North America, 1989. Jr. fellow Soc. Fellows Harvard U., 1988-91; MacArthur fellow, 1994-99; NSF Young Investigator awardee. Office: U Calif Dept Los Angeles Dept of Sociology 264 Haines Hall Los Angeles CA 90095

BRUCE, JAMES EDMUND, retired utility company executive; b. Boise, Idaho, June 23, 1920; s. James E. and Bessie (Barcus) B.; m. Lois I. Stevens, Aug. 24, 1946; children: James E. IV, Steven, Robert, David. Student, Coll. Idaho, 1937-39; BA, Portland U., 1941; postgrad., Georgetown U., 1941-42; LLB, U. Idaho, 1949. Bar: Idaho 1948. Asst. atty. gen. State of Idaho, 1948-49; dep. pros. atty. Ada County, Idaho, 1949-51; with Idaho Power Co., Boise, 1951-87, v.p., 1968-74, pres., chief operating officer, 1974-76, pres., chief exec. officer, 1976-85, chmn., 1985-87, ret., 1987. Dir. Albertson's Inc., First Security Corp., 1981-93; chmn. Blue Cross of Idaho, 1988-90, Bd. dirs. Mountain [illegible] 1977-89; mem. St. Alphonsus Found., Boise State U. Found., Bishop Kelly Found., Boise Park Bd., 1958-78; chmn. Idaho State Lottery; Idaho chmn. U.S. Savs. Bonds, 1976-85; chmn. bd. trustees St. Alphonsus, 1985-86; trustee Coll. Idaho, YMCA, Idaho Nature Conservancy; pres. Ada County Hwy. Dist. Commn. With U.S. Army, 1942-46. Mem. ABA, Boise Execs. Assn., Edison Electric Assn. (dir. 1978-85), N.W. Electric Light and Power Assn. (pres. 1982), Boise C. of C., Arid Club, Crane Creek Country Club, Rotary, Elks, K.C. Roman Catholic.

BRUCE, WILLIAM A. airport executive; BS in Polit. Sci., UCLA, 1967; MPA, Calif. State U., L.A., 1971. Budget analyst, chief negotiator employee rels. City of L.A., 1969-80, various other positions, 1980-99; dir. airports adminstrn. L.A. World Airports, 1999—. Office: Los Angeles Dept Airports 1 World Way Los Angeles CA 90045-5803

BRUCH, CAROL SOPHIE, lawyer, educator; b. Rockford, Ill., June 11, 1941; d. Ernest and Margarete (Willstätter) B.; m. Jack E. Myers, 1960 (div. 1973); children: Margarete Louise Myers Feinstein, Kurt Randall Myers A.B., Shimer Coll., 1960; J.D., U. Calif.-Berkeley, 1972; Dr. honoris causa, U. Basel, 2000. Bar: Calif. 1973, U.S. Supreme Ct. 1980. Law clk. to Justice William O. Douglas U.S. Supreme Ct., 1972-73; acting prof. law U. Calif.-Davis, 1973-78, prof., 1978-2001, rsch. prof., 2001—, chair doctoral program in human devel., 1996-2001. Acad. vis. law dept. U. Munich, 1978-79, 92, U. Cologne, 1990, U. Cambridge, 1990, London Sch. Econs. and Polit. Sci., 1991, Kings Coll., London, 1991; vis. prof. U. Calif., Berkeley, 1983, Columbia U., 1986, U. Basel, 1994, vis. Fulbright prof. Hebrew U., Jerusalem, 1996-97; vis. fellow Fitzwilliam Coll., Cambridge, Eng., 1990, U. Calif. Humanities Rsch. Inst., Irvine, 1999, vis. scholar, London Sch. Econs., King's Coll. (London) & Inst. for Advanced Legal Studies (Univ. London), 1991; cons. to Ctr. for Family in Transition, 1981, Calif. Law Revision Commn., 1979-82, NOW Legal Def. and Edn. Fund, 1980-81; lectr., legis. drafting and testimony, 1976—; mem. U.S. del. 4th Inter-Am. Specialized Conf. on Pvt. Internat. Law, OAS, 1989. Contbr. articles to legal jours. Editor Calif. Law Rev., 1971; editorial Bd. Family Law Quar., 1980-87; Representing Children, 1995—; lectr. in field. Mem. adv. com. child support and child custody Calif. Commn. on Status of Women, 1981-83, child support adv. com. Calif. Jud. Coun., 1991-94, adv. com. on private internat. law U.S. Dept. State, 1989—, internat. child abduction steering com. Internat. Ctr. for Missing and Exploited Children (London), 1999—; host parent Am. Field Service, Davis, 1977-78. Max Rheinstein sr. rsch. fellow Alexander von Humboldt Found., Fed. Republic Germany, 1978-79, 92, Fulbright fellow, Western Europe, 1990, Israel, 1997, rsch. fellow Univ. Calif. Humanities Rsch. Inst., 1999, Fulbright Sr. Scholar Awd., The Hebrew Univ. of Jersualem, 1997, Disting. Pub. Svc. award U. Calif. Davis Acad. Senate, 1990. Mem. ABA, Calif. State Bar Assn. (inactive), Am. Law Inst., Internat. Soc. Family Law (exec. coun. 1994-2000), Order of Coif. Democrat. Jewish. Office: U Calif Sch Law 400 Mrak Hall Dr Davis CA 95616-5201

BRUEN, JAMES A. lawyer; b. South Hampton, N.Y., Nov. 29, 1943; s. John Francis and Kathryn Jewell (Arthur) B.; m. Carol Lynn Heller, June 13, 1968; children: Jennifer Lynn, Garrett John. BA cum laude, Claremont Men's Coll., 1965; JD, Stanford U., 1968. Bar: Calif. 1968, U.S. Dist. Ct. (no., ea., so. and cen. dists.) Calif. 1970, U.S. Ct. Claims 1972, U.S. Tax Ct. 1972, U.S. Ct. Appeals (9th cir.) 1972, U.S. Supreme Ct. 1973, Ariz. 1993. Atty. FCC, Washington, 1968-70; asst. U.S. atty. criminal div. Office of US. Atty., San Francisco, 1970-73, asst. U.S. atty. civil div., 1973-75, chief of civil div., 1975-77; ptnr. Landels, Ripley & Diamond, San Francisco, 1977-2000, Farella Braun & Martel LLP, San Francisco, 2000—. Mem. faculty Nat. Jud. Coll. ABA; lectr. Am. Law Inst. Am. Bd. Trial Advocates, Practising Law Inst. Def. Rsch. Inst., others. Co-author: Pharmaceutical Products Liability, 1989; contbg. editor: Hazardous Waste and Toxic Torts Law and Strategy, 1987-92; contbr. numerous articles to profl. jours. Mem. ABA (vice chmn. environ. quality com. nat. resources sect. 1989-93, co-chmn. enforment litigation subcom. environ. litigation com. litigation sect. 1990-92), Am. Inn of Ct. (master-at-large), Internat. Soc. for Environ. Epidemiology. Avocations: scuba diving, travel. Office: Farella Brown & Martel Russ Bldg 30th Fl 235 Montgomery St San Francisco CA 94104 Fax: (415) 954-4480. E-mail: jbruen@fbm.com

BRUENING, GEORGE E. virologist; b. Chgo., Aug. 10, 1938; Diploma, Carroll Coll., 1960; MS, U. Wis., 1963, PhD in Biochemistry, 1965. Guggenheim Meml. Found. fellow, 1974-75; prof. plant pathology U. Calif., Davis. Vis. scientist plant path., Cornell U., Ithaca, N.Y., 1974-75, vis. scientist biochemistry, U. Adelaide, Australia, 1981; vis. sicentist plant indsl. CSIRO, Canberra, Australia, 1989. Fellow Am. Phytopath Soc.; mem. Nat. Acad. Sci., Am. Soc. Biochem. and Molecular Biology, Soc. Microbiol. UK, AAAS. Office: Dept Plant Pathology 5204 Storer Hall U Calif Davis Davis CA 95616

BRUFF, HAROLD HASTINGS, dean; b. 1944; BA in Am. History and Lit., Williams Coll.; JD magna cum laude, Harvard U. Law faculty Ariz. State U., Tempe, 1971-79; sr. atty.-advisor Office of Legal Counsel, U.S. Dept. Justice, 1979-81; cons. to chmn. Pres.'s Commn. on the Accident at Three Mile Island, 1981; law faculty U. Tex., Austin, 1983-85, John S. Redditt prof. law, 1985-92; Donald Rothschild rsch. prof. George Washington U. Law Sch., Washington, 1992-96; dean U. Colo. Sch. Law, Boulder, 1996—. Contbr. articles to profl. jours. Mem. ABA, Phi Beta Kappa. Office: U Colo Boulder Sch Law Boulder CO 80309-0001

BRUICE, THOMAS C. chemist, educator; PhD, U. So. Calif., 1954. Prof. chemistry U. Calif., Santa Barbara, 1964—. Contbr. articles to profl. jours. Recipient Career Devel. award NIH, 1979, Lifetime Investigator award, 1979, MERIT award, 1979, Richard C. Tolman medal, 1979, Arthur C. Scope Scholar award Am. Chem. Soc., 1987, Repligan medal, 1987, Alfred Bader medal, 1988, James Flack Norris award, 1996; Guggenheim fellow, 1979. Fellow AAAS, Royal Soc. Chemistry, Am. Acad. Arts and Scis.; mem. NAS. Office: U Calif Santa Barbara Dept Chemistry Santa Barbara CA 93106-9510

BRULTE, JAMES L. state legislator; b. Glen Cove, N.Y., Apr. 13, 1956; BA, Calif. State Poly. U. Mem. staff U.S. Senator S.I. Hayakawa, Rep. Nat. Com., 1981; asst. to asst. sec. for res. affairs Dept. Def., from 1984; later White House advance rep. for Vice Pres. of U.S.; mem. Calif. State Assembly, 1990-96, Calif. State Senate, 1996—, vice chair budget and fiscal rev. com., mem. fin., investment and internat. trade com., vice chair energy, utilities and comms. com. Served with Calif. Air N.G., 1974. Republican. Office: State Capitol Rm 5087 Sacramento CA 95814 also: 10861 Foothill Blvd Ste 325 Rancho Cucamonga CA 91730-3859

BRUMBAUGH, ROLAND JOHN, judge; b. Pueblo, Colo., Jan. 21, 1940; s. Leo Allen and Ethel Marie (Brummett) B.; m. Pamela Marie Hultman, Sept. 8, 1967; children: Kenneth Allen, Kimberly Marie. BS in Bus. with honors, U. Colo., 1968, JD, 1971. Bar: Colo. 1971, U.S. Dist. Ct. Colo. 1972, U.S. Ct. Appeals (10th cir.) 1973, U.S. Supreme Ct. 1980. Legal intern HUD, Denver, 1971-72; sole practice Denver, 1972-75; chief dep. city atty. City of Lakewood, Colo., 1975; dep. dir. Colo. Dept. of [illegible], Denver, 1975-78, asst. U.S. atty. Dist. of Colo., Denver, 1978-82; judge U.S. Bankruptcy Ct. Dist. of Colo., Denver, 1982—. Lectr. in field. Author: Colorado Liquor and Beer Licensing-Law and Practice, 1970; Handbook for Municipal Clerks, 1972. Contbr. articles to profl. jours. Served with USAF, 1962-65. Recipient numerous awards for excellence in law. Mem. Colo. Bar Assn., Alpha Kappa Psi, Beta Gamma Sigma, Rho Epsilon, Sigma Iota. Office: US Custom House 721 19th St Denver CO [illegible]

BRUMFIELD, JACK, communications executive; Grad., Alliane Coll. Pa. Various positions N.Y. Govs. Office, N.Y. Power Authority; with Winner/Wagner & Assocs., N.Y.C., L.A.; sr. exec. v.p. Stoorza Ziegaus & Metzer, San Diego, 1995-2000; gen. mgr. Stoorza Comm., L.A., 2000—. Mem. Ctrl. City Assn. L.A. (govt. rels. com., bd. dirs.). Office: Stoorza Comm 355 S Grand Ave Ste 2800 Los Angeles CA 90071-1565

BRUMMER, STEVEN E. protective services official; Chief of police, Bakersfield, Calif. Office: PO Box 59 1601 Truxtun Ave Bakersfield CA 93301-5109

BRUN, MARGARET ANN CHARLENE, semiconductor industry buyer, planner; b. Toledo, June 19, 1945; d. John Joseph and Maude Elizabeth (Harrell) Bartos; m. Paul Joseph Brun, June 17, 1967. Student, Phoenix Coll., 1964-67, Glendale C.C., 1991-93; Assocs., Mesa C.C., 1996. Cert. purchasing mgr. Contr. material inventory Digital Equipment Corp., Phoenix, 1975-76, contr. prodn. inventory, 1976-77, prodn. control planner, 1977-79, inventory control planner, 1979, buyer, 1979-91; buyer, planner ASM Am., Inc., 1991-95, sr. buyer, 1996—. Named Buyer of Yr., Purchasing World mag., 1987. Mem. Purchasing Mgmt. Assn. Ariz. affiliate of Nat. Assn. Purchasing Mgmt. Democrat. Methodist. Avocations: softball, golfing.

BRUNACINI, ALAN VINCENT, protective services official; b. Jamestown, N.Y., Apr. 18, 1937; s. John N. and Mary T. Brunacini; B.S., Ariz. State U., 1970, M.P.A., 1975; m. Rita McDaugh, Feb. 14, 1959; children— Robert Nicholas, John Nicholas, Mary Candice. Mem. Phoenix Fire Dept., 1959— , bn. chief, then asst. fire chief, 1971-78, fire chief, 1978— ; condr. nat. seminar on fire dept. mgmt., 1970— . Redford scholar, 1968. Mem. Am. Soc. Public Adminstrn. (Superior Service award 1980), Nat. Fire Protection Assn. (chmn. fire service sect. 1974-78, dir. 1978), Internat. Assn. Fire Chiefs, Soc. Fire Service Instrs. Author: Fireground Command; also articles in field. Office: Office of Fire Chief 150 S 12th St Phoenix AZ 85034-2301

BRUNELLO-MCCAY, ROSANNE, sales executive; b. Cleve., Aug. 26, 1960; d. Carl Carmello and Vivan Lucille (Caranna) B.; m. Walter B. McCay, Feb. 26, 1994 (div. 1998); 1 child, Angela Breanna. Student, U. Cin., 1978-81, Cleve. State U., 1981-82. Indsl. sales engr. Alta Machine Tool, Denver, 1982; mem. sales./purchases Ford Tool & Machine, Denver, 1982-84; sales/ptnr. Mountain Rep. Enterprises, Denver, 1984-86; pres., owner Mountain Rep. Ariz., Phoenix, 1986—; pres. Mountain Rep. Oreg., Portland, 1990—, Mountain Rep. Wash., 1991—, Mountain Rep. Calif., Sunnyvale, 1997—, San Clemente, 1998—, Port Clinton, Ohio, 1999—, Milford, 1999—. Sec. Computer & Automated Systems Assoc., 1987, vice chmn., 1988, chmn., 1989. Active mem. Rep. Party, 1985—; mem. Phoenix Art Mus., Grand Canyon Minority Coun., 1994; vol. Make-A-Wish Found. fund raiser, 1995—. Named Mrs. Chandler Internat., Mrs. Ariz. Internat. Orgn., 1996, Mrs. East Valley U.S., 1997; finalist Mrs. Ariz. Internat., 1996, Ms. Ariz. 2000, Ms. U.S. Continental Pageant. Mem. NAFE, Soc. Mfg. Engrs. (pres. award 1988), Computer Automated Assn. (sec. 1987, vice chmn. 1988 chmn. 1989), Nat. Hist. Soc., Italian Cultural Soc., Tempe C. of C., Vocat. Ednl. Club Am. (mem. exec. bd., pres. 1987—). Roman Catholic. Avocations: sports, aerobics, dancing, skiing, golfing, tennis. Office: Mountain Rep Ariz 410 S Jay St Chandler AZ 85225-6253 E-mail: rosanne@mtnrep.com

BRUNER, NANCY J. publishing executive; B, N.Mex. State U.; MFA, U. So. Calif. With US West Media Group, Denver; cons. dir. bus. devel. Spring Multimedia, Kansas City; dir. new media Seattle Times, now v.p. new media. Office: Seattle Times PO Box 70 Seattle WA 98111-0070

BRUNETT, ALEXANDER J. bishop; b. Detroit, Jan. 13, 1958; ordained priest July 13, 1958. Ordained bishop Diocese of Helena, 1994; archbishop Diocese of Seattle, 1997—. Office: Chancery Office 910 Marion St Seattle WA 98104-1274

BRUNETTI, MELVIN T. federal judge; b. 1933; m. Gail Dian Buchanan; children: Nancy, Bradley, Melvin Jr. BS, U. Nev., 1951-53, 1956-57, 1960; JD, U. Calif., San Francisco, 1964. Mem. firm Vargas, Bartlett & Dixon, 1964-69, Laxalt, Bell, Allison & Lebaron, 1970-78, Allison, Brunetti, MacKenzie, Hartman, Soumbeniotis & Russell, 1978-85; judge U.S. Ct. Appeals (9th cir.), Reno, 1985-99, sr. judge, 1999—. Mem. Council of Legal Advisors, Rep. Nat. Com., 1982-85. Served with U.S. Army N.G., 1954-56. Mem. ABA, State Bar of Nev. (pres. 1984-85, bd. govs. 1975-84). Office: US Ct Appeals US Courthouse 400 S Virginia St Ste 506 Reno NV 89501-2194*

BRÜNGER, AXEL THOMAS, biophysicist, researcher, educator; b. Leipzig, Germany, Nov. 25, 1956; came to U.S., 1982; s. Hans and Hildegard (Müller) B. Diploma, U. Hamburg (Germany), 1980; PhD, Tech. U. Munich, 1982. Postdoctoral fellow Max-Planck Inst., Martinsried, Germany, 1984; rsch. assoc. Harvard U., Cambridge, Mass., 1982-83, 85-87; asst. investigator Howard Hughes Med. Inst., New Haven, 1987-92, assoc. investigator, 1992-95, investigator, 1995—; asst. prof. Yale U., New Haven, 1987-91, assoc. prof., 1991-93, prof., 1993-2000, Stanford U., Calif., 2000—. Recipient Röntgen prize for bioscis. Würzburg U., 1995; NATO postdoctoral fellow Deutscher Akademischer Austauschdienst, Bonn, Germany, 1982-83. Mem. AAAS, Am. Crystallographic Assn., Am. Chem. Soc., Protein Soc. Achievements include studies of protein structure and function, developments in macromolecular x-ray crystallography and solution NMR spectroscopy. Office: Stanford U 1201 Welch Rd MSLS P210 Stanford CA 94305-5489

BRUNNER, HOWARD WILLIAM, professional land surveyor; b. Mobile, Ala., July 24, 1946; s. Joseph Edward and Beaulah (Howard) B.; m. Linda Marie Parker, Dec. 20, 1963 (div. June 1978); children: Leah Marie, Anne Marie; m. Catherine Cecilia Byrnes, June 27, 1981; 1 child, Jordan Thomas Howard. Grad. high sch., Santa Rosa, Calif. Lic. profl. land surveyor, Calif., Wash., Nev. Survey technician Roemer & Estes, Mill Valley, Calif., 1964-65, Ken Frost & Assocs., Mill Valley, 1965-66; engring. aide County of Marin, San Rafael, Calif., 1966-75; pres. Engring. Field Svcs., San Rafael, 1975-77, Brunner, Phelps & Assocs., Inc., Cotati, Calif., 1977-80; v.p. Ray Carlson & Assocs., Inc., Santa Rosa, 1980-92; ptnr. Bedford Brunner, Santa Rosa, 1993-96; prin. Howard W. Brunner, Profl. Land Surveyor, Santa Rosa, 1996—. Expert examiner, profl. land surveyor, cons., registrar, tech. adv. com. mem., expert witness, chmn. item writing com. Bd. Registration for Profl. Engrs. and Land Surveyors, Sacramento, 1985-96. Mem. Geysers Geothermal Assn. (bd. dirs. 1985-92), Calif. Land Surveyors Assn. (treas. 1987-88, sec. 1988-89, pres. 1990), Am. Consulting Engrs. Coun. (chmn. coun. profl. land surveyors 1995-96). Roman Catholic. Avocations: boating, skiing, skin diving, antique automobiles, Porsche's. Home: 420 Mcdonough Heights Rd Healdsburg CA 95448-4659 Office: 250 Healdsburg Ave Ste 201 Healdsburg CA 95448 E-mail: pls4206@ix.netcom.com

BRUNS, GEORGE H. electronics executive; Founder, pres. Systron-Donner Corp.; founder, dir. Giga-tronics Inc., San Ramon, Calif., 1980, chmn., 1980, CEO, 1995—. Gen. ptnr. The Bruns Co.; bd. dirs. Testronics, Inc., McKinney, Tex., Peninsula Wireless Comm., Inc., Sunnyvale, Calif., ASCOR, Inc., Fremont, Calif. Mem. exec. com. Calif. Found. for the Retarded; chmn. bd. Calif. Shakespeare Festival. Office: 4650 [illegible] Canyong Rd San Ramon CA 94583-1320 Fax: 925-328-4700

BRUNS, THOMAS DICKINSON, plant pathologist, educator; b. Blue Island, Ill., Apr. 13, 1953; s. Ralph Irving and Barbara Ann (Dickinson) B.; m. Barbara Jean Brown, Mar. 31, 1979; children: Emily Louise, Patricia Jeannine, Samuel Peter. Student, U. Ill., 1971-73; BS in Forest Sci., U. Minn., 1978, MS in Botany, 1982; PhD in Botany, U. Mich., 1987. Teaching asst. Coll. Forestry, U. Minn., St. Paul, 1977, Dept. Botany, U. Minn., St. Paul, 1979-82, Dept. Botany, U. Mich., Ann Arbor, 1982-85; Rackham predoctoral fellow U. Mich., Ann Arbor, 1985-86; rsch. asst. Dept. Botany, U. Mich., Ann Arbor, 1986-87; postdoctoral fellow Dept. Botany, U. Calif., Berkeley, 1987-89; asst. prof. Dept. Plant Pathology, U. Calif., Berkeley, 1989—. Lectr. in field. Contbr. articles to profl. jours. NSF grantee, 1987-90, 1990—; Mycol. Soc. Am. grad. fellow, 1984-85. Alexopoulos Prize, 1994; Mycological Society of America. Fellow AAAS; mem. Am. Phytopathol. Soc., Mycol. Soc. Am., Soc. for Study of Evolution. Office: Univ of Calif Plant Pathology Berkeley CA 94721

BRUSCA, RICHARD CHARLES, biologist, researcher, educator; b. L.A., Jan. 25, 1945; s. Finny John and Ellenora C. (McDonald) B.; m. Caren Irene Spencer, 1964 (div. 1971); m. Anna Mary Mackey, 1980 (div. 1987); children: Alec Matthew, Carlene Anne; m. Wendy Moore, 1998. BS, Calif. Poly. State U., 1967; MS, Calif. State U., L.A., 1969; PhD, U. Ariz., 1975. Curator, rschr. Aquatic Insects Lab., Calif. State U., L.A., 1969-70; resident dir. U. Ariz. and U. Sonora (Mex.) Coop. Marine Lab., Sonora, 1969-71; prof. biology U. So. Calif., L.A., 1975-86; head Invertebrate Zoology sect. Los Angeles County Mus. Natural Hist., 1984-87; Joshua L. Baily curator, chmn. dept. invertebrate zoology San Diego Natural History Mus., 1987-93; prof., dir. grad. program in marine biology U. Charleston, S.C., 1993-98, assoc. dir. Grice Marine Lab., 1993-98; vis. scholar dept. ecology and evolutionary biology U. Ariz., 1998-2001; dir. sci. and conservation Ariz.-Sonora Desert Mus., Tucson, 2001—. Dir. acad. program Catalina Marine Sci. Ctr., U. So. Calif.; field rschr. North, Ctrl. and South Ams., Polynesia, Australia, New Zealand, Antarctica, Sahran and Sub-Saharan Africa, Euorpe; bd. dirs. orng. for Tropical Studies, Slocum-Lunz Found., Intercultural Ctr. for the Study of Deserts and Oceans, Sonoran Sea Aquarium, Tucson; mem. panels NAS/NSF; chairperson adv. com. Smithsonian Instn., Systematics Agenda 2000, Internat. Union for Conservation of Nature Species Survival Commn.; adj. prof. U. Ariz., 1998—. Author: Common Intertidal Invertebrates of the Gulf of California, 1980; co-author: A Naturalist's Seashore Guide, 1978, Invertebrates, 1990; contbr. over 100 articles to sci. jours. Recipient U.S. Antarctic Svc. medal, 1965, numerous rsch. awards; grantee NSF, Nat. Geog. Soc., Charles Lindberg Found, NOAA, Am. Philos. Assn., others. Fellow Linnean Soc. London; mem. AAAs, Crustacean Soc. (pres.), Soc. for Systematic Biology, Willi Hennig Soc., U. Edinburgh Biogeography Study Group, S. Am. Exploreres Club, Assn. Sea of Cortez Rschrs. (hon. life), Sigma Xi. Avocations: photography, Mexican and Mesoamerican indigenous art and culture, Latin American politics. Office: Ariz-Sonora Desert Mus 2021 N Kinney Rd Tucson AZ 85743 E-mail: rbrusca@bio2.edu

BRYAN, A(LONZO) J(AY), retired service club official; b. Washington, Sept. 17, 1917; s. Alonzo J. and Anna Belle (Babcock) B.; m. Elizabeth Elfreida Koehler, June 25, 1941 (div. 1961); children: Donna Elizabeth, Alonzo Jay, Nadine; m. Janet Dorothy Onstad, Mar. 15, 1962 (div. 1977); children: Brenda Joyce, Marlowe Francis, Marilyn Janet. Student. Retail florist, Washington, 1941-64. Fund drive chmn. ARC, 1952; bd. dirs. Washington YMCA, 1945-55, N.J. Taxpayers Assn., 1947-52; mem. Washington Bd. Edn., 1948-55. Mem. Washington Grange, Sons and Daus. of Liberty, Soc. Am. Florists, Nat. Fedn. Ind. Businessmen, Florists Telegraph Delivery Assn., C. of C., Masons, Tall Cedars of Lebanon Club, Jr. Order United Am. Mechanics, Kiwanis (pres. Washington N.J. 1952, lt. gov. internat. 1953-54, gov. N.J. dist. 1955, sec. 1957-64, sec. S.E. area Chgo. 1965-74, editor The Jersey Kiwanian 1958-64, internat. staff 1964-85, sec.-treas. Rocky Mountain dist. 1989, pres. South Denver 1990-91, editor Rocky Mountain Kiwanian 1990-96), Breakfast Club (Chgo., pres. 1981-82). Methodist. Home: 8115 S Poplar Way B 203 Englewood CO 80112-3174

BRYAN, JAMES D. career officer; b. Birmingham, Ala. BS in Edn., Jacksonville State U.; grad., U.S. Army War Coll. Commd. 2d lt. U.S. Army, advanced through grades to brig. gen., 1997; early assignments include bn. signal officer 82d airborne divsn., 3d bn.; signal ops. officer, instr. U.S. Army JFK Spl. Warfare Ctr., 1971-72; bn. maintenance officer, S-3 122d signal bn., Korea, 1972-73; S-4, S-3 and commdg. officer support bn. 7th Spl. Forces Group, Ft. Bragg, N.C., 1973-77; bn. signal officer, 1st bn. 52d mechanized infantry 1st Armored Divsn., Bamberg, Germany, 1977-79; S-3 93d signal brigade, 1979-80; tng. and mgr. systems dir. U.S. Army Recruiting Command, 1980-83; asst. chief of staff comms.-electronics 1st Spl. Ops. Command, 1985-86; then comdr. 112th Spl. Ops. Signal Bn., 1986-88; mem. jt. staff for J-6, CINC C4 systems support officer USSOCOM, USCENTCOM, FORSCOM, 1988-91; chief J-6 architecture integration and interoperability divsn., 1991-93; comdr. 35th signal brigade XVIII Airborne Corps, 1993-95; exec. officer to dir. of info. systems for Command, Control Comm. and Computers, Hdqrs., U.S. Dept. Army, 1995-97. Dep. DISC4, Dept. of Army, Washington, 1997-99, dir. command, control, comm. and computer sys., U.S. Pacific Command, Camp H.M. Smith, Hawaii, 1999—.

BRYAN, RICHARD H. lawyer, educator, former senator; b. Washington, July 16, 1937; m. Bonnie Fairchild; 3 children. BA, U. Nev., 1959; LLB, U. Calif., San Francisco, 1963. Bar: Nev. 1963. Dep. dist. atty., Clark County, Nev., 1964-66; public defender Clark County, 1966-68; counsel Clark County Juvenile Ct., 1968-69; mem. Nev. Assembly, 1969-73, Nev. Senate, 1973-79; atty. gen. State Nev., 1979-83, gov., 1983-89; senator from Nevada U.S. Senate, 1989-2001; ptnr., mem. exec. com. Lionel, Sawyer & Collins, 2001—. Former mem. U.S. Senate coms. on commerce, sci. and transp.; former mem. Dem. Policy Com., Fin. Com., Banking, Housing and Urban Affairs Com., Sen. Nom. Steering and Coor. Com., select. Com. on Intelligence; adj. prof. polit. sci. U Nev., Las Vegas, 2001—. Bd. dirs. March of Dimes; former v.p. Nev. Easter Seal Soc.; former pres. Clark County Legal Aid Soc. Served with U.S. Army, 1959-60. Recipient Disting. Svc. award Vegas Valley Jaycees. Mem. ABA, Clark County Bar Assn., Am. Judicature Soc., Council of State Govts. (past pres.), Phi Alpha Delta, Phi Alpha Theta. Democrat. Clubs: Masons, Lions, Elks. Office: Lionel Sawyer & Collins 1700 Bank Am Plaza 300 S 4th St Las Vegas NV 89101*

BRYAN, ROBERT J. federal judge; b. Bremerton, Wash., Oct. 29, 1934; s. James W. and Vena Gladys (Jensen) B.; m. Cathy Ann Welander, June 14, 1958; children: Robert James, Ted Lorin, Ronald Terence. BA, U. Wash., 1956, JD, 1958. Bar: Wash. 1959, U.S. Dist. Ct. (we. dist.) Wash. 1959, U.S. Tax Ct. 1965, U.S. Ct. Appeals (9th cir.) 1985. Assoc., then ptnr. Bryan & Bryan, Bremerton, 1959-67; judge Superior Ct., Port Orchard, Wash., 1967-84; ptnr. Riddell, Williams, Bullitt & Walkinshaw, Seattle, 1984-86; judge U.S. Dist. Ct. (we. dist.) Wash., Tacoma, 1986—. Mem. State Jail Comm., Olympia, Wash., 1974-76, Criminal Justice Tng. Com., Olympia, 1978-81, State Bd. on Continuing Legal Edn., Seattle, 1984-86; mem., sec. Jud. Qualifications Commn., Olympia, 1982-83; chair Wash. Fed.-State Jud. Coun., 1997-98. Author: (with others) Washington Pattern Jury Instructions (civil and criminal vols. and supplements), 1970-85, Manual of Model Criminal Jury Instructions for the Ninth Circuit, 1992, Manual of Model Civil Jury Instruction for the Ninth Circuit, 1993. Chmn. 9th Ct. Jury Com., 1991-92; bd. dirs. Fed. Jud. Ctr., 2000—. Served to maj. USAR. Mem.: 9th Cir. Dist. Judges Assn. (sec.-treas. 1997—99, v.p. 1999—2001, pres. 2001—). Office: US Dist Ct 1717 Pacific Ave Rm 4427 Tacoma WA 98402-3234

BRYANT, ANDY D. computer company executive; BA in Econs., U. Mo.; MBA in Fin., U. Kans. With Chrysler Corp., Ford Motor Co.; contr. comml. memory sys. operation Intel Corp., Santa Clara, Calif., 1981-83, sys. group contr., 1983-87, dir. fin. for corp., 1987-90, v.p., dir. fin. Intel products group, 1990-94, CFO, corp. v.p., 1994—, exec. v.p. CA, 2001—. Office: Intel Corp 2200 Mission College Blvd Santa Clara CA 95052-8119

BRYANT, ARTHUR H. lawyer; b. Harrisburg, Pa., Aug. 11, 1954; s. Albert Irwin and Marjorie (Weinrib) B.; m. Nancy Kaye Johnson, Aug. 17, 1991; 1 stepchild, Vinnie Johnson; 1 child, Wallace Johnson Bryant. AB with hons., Swarthmore Coll., 1976; JD, Harvard U., 1979; D (hon.), Ripon Coll., 1998. Bar: Pa. 1981, U.S. Dist. Ct. (ea. dist.) Pa. 1981, U.S. Ct. Appeals (3d cir.) Pa. 1981, U.S. Ct. Appeals (11th cir.) Ga. 1985, U.S. Ct. Appeals (6th cir.) Ohio 1986, U.S. Ct. appeals (D.C. cir.) 1986, U.S. Ct. Appeals (9th cir.) Calif. 1987, U.S. Ct. Appeals (7th cir.) Ill. 1988, U.S. Ct. Appeals (5th cir.) Tex. 1988, D.C., 1989, U.S. Supreme Ct. 1989, U.S. Ct. Appeals (1st cir.) 1996. Intern Rosenman, Colin & Freund, N.Y.C., 1978, N.Y. Civil Liberties Union, N.Y.C., 1978, Cambridge & Somerville Legal Svcs., Cambridge, Pa., 1979; law clk. U.S. Dist. Ct. (so. dist.), Tex., 1979-80; atty. Kohn, Savett, Marion & Graf., Phila., 1980-84; staff atty. Trial Lawyers for Pub. Justice, Washington, 1984-87, exec. cir., 1987—. Named one of 20 young lawyers making a difference in the world ABA Barrister mag., 1991, one of 50 most influential people in coll. sports Coll. Sports Mag., 1994, one of 45 lawyers whose vision and commitment are changing lives The Am. Lawyer, 1997, one of 100 most influential lawyers in Am. Nat. Law Jour., 2000; recipient Wasserstein Pub. Interest law fellowship, 1996. Mem. ABA, Assn. Trial Lawyers Am. Office: Trial Lawyers Pub Justice Ste 275 One Kaiser Plaza Oakland CA 94612

BRYANT, KOBE, professional basketball player; b. Aug. 23, 1978; Student, Lower Merion (Pa.) High Sch. Player L.A. Lakers, 1996—. Named to NBA All-Rookie 2nd Team, 1996-97. Office: c/o LA Lakers 3900 W Manchester Blvd Inglewood CA 90305-2200

BRYANT, LELAND MARSHAL, business and nonprofit executive; b. Gainesville, Ga., Apr. 28, 1950; s. William Marcus and Pierre Lou (Milner) B.; children: Shauna, Natalie, Marcus, Jacob. Student, Vanderbilt U., 1968-70; BBA with hons., U. Tex., 1972; MBA, U. Pa., 1978. CPA, Tex. Acct. Arthur Andersen and Co., Dallas, 1978-81; exec. v.p. Walter Bennet Comms., Dallas, 1981-89; pres. Grand Canyon Railway, Flagstaff, Ariz., 1989-97; v.p., CFO, Grand Canyon (Ariz.) Assn., 1997—. Pres. Fray Marcos Hotel, Flagstaff, 1995-97. Bd. dirs. Grand Canyon Nat. Park Found., 1995—; nat. adv. bd. No. Ariz. U., Flagstaff, 1994-97. Mem. AICPA, Grand Canyon Assn. (bd. dirs. 1995-97), Nat. Parks Conservation Assn. (nat. adv. coun. 1995-98). Republican. Office: Grand Canyon Assn PO Box 399 Grand Canyon AZ 86023-0399

BRYANT, NEIL, state legislator, lawyer; b. Spokane, Wash., July 8, 1948; m. Mary Bryant. BA, Paficic Luth. U.; JD, Willamette U. Mem. Oreg. Legislature, Salem, 1992—, chair jud. com., mem. rules and elections com., mem. subcom. on human resources, mem. ways and means com., majority whip. Chair Bend Urban Renewal Dist., Deschutes County Children and Youth Svcs. Commn.; mem. Your Cmty. 2000. Republican. Home: PO Box 1151 Bend OR 97709-1151 Office: S-206 State Capitol Salem OR 97310-0001 E-mail: nmbryant@empnet.com

BRYANT, PETER JAMES, biologist, educator; b. Bristol, Eng., Mar. 2, 1944; came to U.S., 1967; s. Sydney Arthur and Marjorie Violet (Virgurs) B.; m. Toni Boettger, 1980; children: Katherine Emily, Sarah Grace. B.Sc. (Special) in Zoology with 1st class honors, Kings Coll., London, Eng., 1964; M.Sc. in Biochemistry, Univ. Coll., London, Eng., 1965; D.Phil. in Genetics, U. Sussex, Falmer, Eng., 1967. Postdoctoral research fellow Devel. Biology Ctr., Case Western Res. U., Cleve., 1967-70; postdoctoral research fellow Devel. Biology Lab., U. Calif.-Irvine, 1967-70, lectr. dept. devel. and cell biology, 1970-71, asst. prof., 1971-74, assoc. prof., 1974-77, prof. dept. devel. and cell biology, 1977—, vice chmn. dept. devel. and cell biology, 1978-79, dir. Devel. Biology Ctr., 1979—. Nat. and internat. lectr.; reviewer NSF, NIH. Contbr. numerous articles, book revs., abstracts to Cell, Proc. Nat. Acad. Sci., Jour. Cell Sci., Devel., Nature Sci., Jour. Insect Physiology, Developmental Biology, other profl. publs.; reviewer Cell, Devel. Biology, Genetics, Sci., Can. Jour. zoology, numerous other profl. jours.; assoc. editor: Developmental Biology, 1976-85, editor-in-chief, 1985-95. Bd. dirs. Orange County Natural History Mus., 1987-92. Recipient numerous grants NIH, NSF, 1974—, Am. Cetacean Soc. grantee, 1980-81, Nat. Marine Fisheries Svc. grantee, 1981; recipient Disneyland Community Svc. award (on behalf of Am. Cetacean Soc., Orange County chpt.), 1980. Mem. Soc. Devel. Biology, Genetics Soc. Am., Internat. Soc. Devel. Biologists, Soc. Exptl. Biology, Am. Cetacean Soc. (pres. 1982, founding pres. Orange County chpt. 1977-80). Avocations: insect photography, sailing, hiking, model building, conservation. Office: Univ California Devel Biology Ctr Irvine CA 92717

BRYANT, THOMAS LEE, magazine editor; b. Daytona Beach, Fla., June 15, 1943; s. Stanley Elson and G. Bernice (Burgess) B.; m. Patricia Jean Bryant, June 30, 1979. BA in Polit. Sci., U. Calif., Santa Barbara, 1965, MA in Polit. Sci., 1966. Fgn. svc. officer U.S. Dept. State, Washington, Buenos Aires, 1967-69; radio broadcaster KDB Sta., Santa Barbara, Calif., 1969-72; magazine editor, now editor-in-chief Road & Track, Newport Beach, 1972—. Mem. Internat. Motor Press Assn., Motor Press Guild, Sports Car Club of Am. Avocations: golf, trap and skeet shooting. Office: c/o Hachette Filipacchi Mags Inc 1499 Monrovia Ave Newport Beach CA 92663-2752

BRYANT, WOODROW WESLEY, architect; b. San Jose, Calif., June 5, 1949; s. Foy Eldean and Loraine (McKee) B.; m. Becky Ann Hoffmaster, June 27, 1981; 1 stepson: Jeremy Saul Martin. Student, Am. River Coll., Sacramento, Calif., 1968; BArch, Calif. State Polytechnic U., 1973. Registered architect, Calif., Nev., Utah, Idaho, Ariz. Designer, project mgr. Angello & Vitiello Assoc., Sacramento, 1971-75; draftsman Caywood, Nopp & Ward, Sacramento, 1975; architect W. Bryant Enterprises, Sacramento, 1975-76, Wright, Bryant & Johnson, Ketchum, Idaho, 1976—. Bd. dirs. Elkhorn Archtl. Design Commn., Uniform Bldg. Code Bd. Appeals, Ketchum, Uniform Fire Code Bd. Appeals, Ketchum, Blaine County, Idaho. Recipient Best Archtl. Interior Detailing award, Custom Builder mag., 1993. Mem. AIA. Avocations: photography, watercolors, computer graphics, snow skiing, sailing. Office: Wright Bryant & Johnson PO Box 21 Sun Valley ID 83353-0021

BRYCHEL, RUDOLPH MYRON, engineer, consultant; b. Milw., Dec. 4, 1934; s. Stanley Charles and Jean Ann (Weiland) B.; m. Rose Mary Simmons, Sept. 3, 1955; children: Denise, Rita, Rudolph Myron Jr., Patrick, Bradford, Matthew. Student, U. Wis., Stevens Point, 1953, U.S. Naval Acad., , 1954-55, U. Del., 1957, Colo. State U., 1969, North Park Coll., Chgo., 1973, Regis U., Denver, 1990-91. Lab. and quality tech. Thiokol Chem. Co., Elkton, Md., 1956; final test insp. Martin Aircraft Co., Middle River, 1956-57; system final insp. Delco Electronics Co., Oak Creek, Wis., 1957-58; test equipment design engr. Martin Marietta Co., Littleton, Colo., 1958-64; prodn. supr. Gates Rubber Co., Denver, 1964-65; freelance mfr., quality and project engr. Denver and Boulder, Colo., Raton, N.Mex., 1965-67; quality engr. IBM, Gaithersburg (Md.), Boulder (Colo.), 1967-73; sr. quality engr. Abbott Labs., North Chicago, Ill., 1973-74; instrumentation and control engr. Stearns Roger Co., Glendale, Colo., 1974-81; staff quality engr. Storage Tech., Louisville, 1981-83; sr. quality engr. Johnson & Johnson Co., Englewood, 1983-84; quality engr., cons. Staodynamics Co., Longmont, 1984-85; sr. engr. for configuration and data mgmt. Martin Marietta Astronautics Group, Denver, 1985-91; freelance cons. Littleton, Colo., 1991—. With USN, 1953-56. Mem. Am. Soc. Quality Control (cert. quality engr.), Regulatory Affairs Profl. Soc., Soc. for Tech. Communications (regional chpt. chmn. 1970), KC. Democrat. Roman Catholic. Avocations: berry and fruit gardening. Home and Office: 203 W Rafferty Gardens Ave Littleton CO 80120-1710

BRYDON, RUTH VICKERY, history educator; b. San Jose, Calif., June 2, 1930; d. Robert Kingston and Ruth (Bacon) Vickery; m. Harold Wesley Brydon, Mar. 28, 1951 (div.); children: Carol Ruth Brydon Koford, Marilyn Brydon Belove, Kenneth Wesley. BA, Stanford U., 1952; post-grad., San Jose State Coll., 1964-65; MA, Calif. State Coll., Chico, 1987. Cert. tchr., Calif.; cert. sch. adminstr. Tchr. Lincoln Sch., Kathmandu, Nepal, 1959-60, Am. Sch. Port-au-Prince, Haiti, 1962-63; tchr. social studies Norte Vista H.S., Riverside, Calif., 1965-67, chmn. social studies dept., 1966-67; tchr. home econs., social studies Westwood (Calif.) H.S., 1967-90, mentor tchr., 1984-85; media specialist Lake Havasu H.S., 1990-91; history instr. Mohave C.C., Lake Havasu Campus, 1990—. Instr. Elderhostel, 1992—; coord. extended day classes Lassen Coll., 1977-84. Author: Westwood, California: A Company Town in Comparative Perspective, 1990-1930, 1995. Co-chairperson Alamanor Art Show, 1980-84; curator Lake Havasu Mus. of History, 1999—; bd. dirs. Lake Havasu Mus. History. NDEA grantee, 1967. Mem. Archeol. Soc. Ariz. Episcopalian. Home: 2681 N Cisco Dr Lake Havasu City AZ 86403-5020 E-mail: rvbrydon@redrivernet.com

BRYNER, ALEXANDER O. state supreme court justice; b. Tientsin, China; m. Carol Crump; children: Paul, Mara. BA, Stanford U., 1966, JD, 1969. Law clk. to Chief Justice George Boney, Alaska Supreme Ct., 1969-71; legal editor Bancroft Whitney Co., San Francisco, 1971; with Pub. Defender Agy., Anchorage, 1972-74; ptnr. Bookman, Bryner & Shortell, 1974; Alaska dist. ct. judge Anchorage, 1975-77; U.S. atty. Alaska, 1977-80; chief judge Alaska Ct. Appeals, 1980-97; state supreme ct. justice Alaska Supreme Ct., Anchorage, 1997—. Office: Alaska Supreme Ct 303 K St Anchorage AK 99501-2013

BRYSON, ARTHUR EARL, JR. retired aerospace engineering educator; b. Evanston, Ill., Oct. 7, 1925; s. Arthur Earl and Helen Elizabeth (Decker) B.; m. Helen Marie Layton, Aug. 31, 1946; children: Thomas Layton, Stephen Decker, Janet Elizabeth, Susan Mary. Student, Haverford Coll., 1942-44; BS, Iowa State U., 1946; MS, Calif. Inst. Tech., 1949, PhD in Aeros, 1951; MA (hon.), Harvard., 1956. With Container Corp. Am., 1947-48, United Aircraft Corp., 1948; research asst. aero. Calif. Inst. Tech., 1949-50; mem. tech. staff Hughes Research & Devel. Labs., 1950-53; mem. faculty Harvard, 1953-68, Gordon McKay prof. mech. engring., 1961-68; mem. faculty Stanford, 1968-93, chmn. dept. applied mechanics, 1969-71, chmn. dept. aeros. and astronautics, 1971-79, Paul Pigott prof. engring., 1972-93; Hunsaker prof. Mass. Inst. Tech., 1965-66. Mem. nat. com. Fluid Mechanics Films, 1961-68 Author: (with Y.C. Ho) Applied Optimal Control, 1969, Control of Spacecraft and Aircraft, 1994, Dynamic Optimization, 1998. Served as ensign USNR, 1944-46. Recipient Rufus Oldenberger medal ASME, 1980, Control Systems Sci. and Engring. award IEEE, 1984, Bellman Heritage award Am. Auto Control Coun., 1990, von Karman lectureship Am. Inst. of Aeronautics and Astronautics, 1994 Fellow AIAA (hon., assoc. editor jour. 1963-65, bd. dirs. 1965-68, Pendray Award 1968, mechanics and control of flight award 1980, Dryden lectr. 1984, Von Karman lectr. 1994); mem. NAS, NAE (aero. and space engring. bd. 1970-79), Am. Acad. Arts and Scis., Am. Soc. Engring. Edn. (Westinghouse award 1969), Sigma Xi, Tau Beta Pi. Congregationalist Office: Stanford U Durand Building Stanford CA 94305 E-mail: brysonae@stanford.edu

BRYSON, GARY SPATH, cable television and telephone company executive; b. Longview, Wash., Nov. 8, 1943; s. Roy Griffin and Marguerite Elizabeth (Spath) B.; m. Bobbi Bryson; children: Kelly Suzanne, Lisa Christine. AB, Dartmouth Coll., 1966; MBA, Tuck Sch., 1967. With Bell & Howell Co., Chgo., 1967-79, pres. consumer and audio-visual group, 1977-79; chmn. bd., CEO Bell & Howell Mamiya Co., Chgo., 1979-81; exec. v.p. Am. TV & Communications Corp., subs. Time, Inc., Englewood, Colo., 1981-88; v.p. diversified group US West, Englewood, 1988-89, pres. cable communications div., 1989-92; pres., CEO TeleWest Internat., 1992-93; pres. SkyConnect, Boulder, 1994-96. Comm. cons., 1996—. Mem. Phi Beta Kappa, Sigma Alpha Epsilon. Republican. Lutheran. Home: 48 McCoy Oak Dr Edwards CO 81632-2097 E-mail: bobbibr@earthlink.net

BRYSON, JOHN E. utilities company executive; b. N.Y.C., July 24, 1943; m. Louise Henry B.A. with great distinction, Stanford U., 1965; student, Freie U. Berlin, Federal Republic Germany, 1965-66; J.D., Yale U., 1969. Bar: Calif., Oreg., D.C. Asst. in instrn. Law Sch., Yale U., New Haven, 1968-69; law clk. U.S. Dist. Ct., San Francisco, 1969-70; co-founder, atty. Natural Resources Def. Council, 1970-74; vice chmn. Oreg. Energy Facility Siting Council, 1975-76; assoc. Davies, Biggs, Strayer, Stoel & Boley, Portland, Oreg., 1975-76; chmn. Calif. State Water Resources Control Bd., 1976-79; vis. faculty Stanford U. Law Sch., Calif., 1977-79; pres. Calif. Pub. Utilities Commn., 1979-82; ptnr. Morrison & Foerster, San Francisco, 1983-84; sr. v.p. law and fin. So. Calif. Edison Co., Rosemead, 1984; exec. v.p., chief fin. officer Edison Internat. and So. Calif. Edison Co., 1985-90, chmn. of bd., CEO, 1990-99; chmn., pres., CEO Edison Internat., 2000—. Lectr. on pub. utility, energy, communications law.; former mem. exec. com. Nat. Assn. Regulatory Utility Commrs., Calif. Water Rights Law Rev. Commn., Calif. Pollution Control Financing Authority; former mem. adv. bd. Solar Energy Research Inst., Electric Power Research Inst., Stanford Law Sch.; bd. dirs. Pacific Am. Income Shares Inc., The Boeing Co., Walt Disney Co. Mem. bd. editors, assoc. editor: Yale U. Law Jour. Past bd. dirs. World Resources Inst., Washington, Calif. Environ. Trust, Claremont U. Ctr., Grad. Sch., Stanford U. Alumni Assn.; bd. dirs. The Keck Found.; former trustee Stanford U., 1991. Woodrow Wilson fellow Mem. Calif. Bar Assn., Oreg. Bar Assn., D.C. Bar Assn., Nat. Assn. Regulatory Utility Commrs. (exec. com. 1980-82), Stanford U. Alumni Assn. (bd. dirs. 1983-86), Phi Beta Kappa. Office: Edison Internat 2244 Walnut Grove Ave Rosemead CA 91770-3714

BRYSON, PEABO, vocalist, songwriter; b. Greenville, S.C., 1951; s. Marie Bryson; 1 child, Linda. Backup singer for Al Freeman and Upsetters, 1965-67, Mose Dillard and Textile Display, 1967-70; writer, prodr., arranger Bang Records, 1970-76. Albums include Peabo, 1976, Reaching for the Sky, 1977, Crosswinds, 1978, (with Natalie Cole) We're the Best of Friends, 1979, Paradise, 1980, (with Roberta Flack) Live and More, 1982, (with Flack) Born To Love, 1983, Straight from the Heart, 1984, Peabo Bryson Collection, reissued 1987, All My Love, 1989, Can You Stop the Rain, 1991,, Take No Prisoners; contbr. to Beauty and the Beast, 1992 (co-recipient Grammy award for best pop performance by duo or group 1992), The King and I, 1993, (with Flack) The Christmas Album, 1993. Office: care Windham Hill Records Sound Delivery PO Box 1862 Woodland CA 95776-1862

BUBAR, JOSEPH BEDELL, JR. pastor; b. Rochester, NH, June 7, 1947; BA in History, Gordon Coll., 1968; MDiv, Trinity Evang. Divinity Sch., 1972. Sr. pastor Bethany Evan. Free Ch., La Crosse, Wis., 1980-97, Grace Bible Ch., ArroyoGrande, Calif., 1997—. Bd. dirs. Bethany-St. Joe Care Ctr., La Crosse; vice chmn. Christian Svc. Brigade, Wheaton, Ill., 1980-89. Bd. dirs. Forest Lakes dist. Evan. Free Ch. of Am., 1989-91; bd. dirs., bd. chmn. Mission USA, 1989-91, vice-moderator, 1991-93, moderator, 1993-95.

BUBE, RICHARD HOWARD, materials scientist, educator; b. Providence, Aug. 10, 1927; s. Edward Neser and Ella Elvira (Baltteim) B.; m. Betty Jane Meeker, Oct. 9, 1948 (dec. Apr. 2, 1997); children: Mark Timothy, Kenneth Paul, Sharon Elizabeth, Meryl Lee; m. Mary Anne Harman, Sept. 9, 2000. Sc.B., Brown U., 1946; M.A., Princeton U., 1948, Ph.D., 1950. Mem. sr. research staff RCA Labs., Princeton, N.J., 1948-62; prof. materials sci. and elec. engring. Stanford U., 1962-92, prof. emeritus, 1992—, chmn. dept., 1975-86, assoc. chmn. dept., 1990-91. Cons. to industry and govt. Author: A Textbook of Christian Doctrine, 1955, Photoconductivity of Solids, 1960, The Encounter between Christianity and Science, 1968, The Human Quest: A New Look at Science and Christian Faith, 1971, Electronic Properties of Crystalline Solids, 1974, Electrons in Solids, 1981, 3d edit., 1992, Fundamentals of Solar Cells, 1983, Science and the Whole Person, 1985, Photoelectronic Properties of Semiconductors, 1992, Putting It All Together: Seven Patterns for Relating Science and Christian Faith, 1995, One Whole Life: Personal Memoirs of Richard H. Bube, 1995, Photoinduced Defects in Semiconductors, 1996, Photovoltaic Materials, 1998; also articles; editor Jour. Am. Sci. Affiliation, 1969-83; mem. editl. bd. Solid State Electronics, 1975-94, Christians in Sci.; assoc. editor Ann. Rev. Materials Sci., 1969-83. Fellow Am. Phys. Soc., AAAS, Am. Sci. Affiliation; mem. Am. Soc. Engring. Edn. (life), Internat. Solar Energy Soc., Sigma Xi. Evangelical. Home: 753 Mayfield Ave Stanford CA 94305-1043 Office: Dept Materials Sci/Engring Stanford Univ Stanford CA 94305-2205

BUCALO, LOUIS RANDALL, biotechnology executive; b. N.Y.C., Oct. 10, 1958; s. Louis and Anne (Aragona) B. Degree magna cum laude, Harvard Coll., 1980; degree, Stanford U. Med. Sch., 1980. Cons. Bain and Co., San Francisco, 1985-86; v.p. United Biomed. Inc., Lake Success, N.Y., 1987-88; assoc. dir. Titon Bioscis. Inc., Alameda, Calif., 1989—; CEO Titan Pharmaceuticals, Inc., S. San Francisco, CA. Mem. AMA, Assn. Clin. Pharmacology.

BUCCIERI, SHIRLEY H. lawyer; b. Terre Haute, Ind., Sept. 23, 1951; d. Mike and Dorothy Louise Hanna; m. Alexander C. Buccieri, Aug. 11, 1973; 1 child. BS in Maths., Purdue U., 1973; JD, U. Akron, 1982. Various positions GM Corp., Warren, Ohio, 1973-81, supt. indsl. engring., 1981-83; assoc. Gibson, Dunn & Crutcher, San Francisco, 1983-91, ptnr., 1991-95; sr. v.p., gen. counsel, sec. Transamerica Corp., San Francisco, 1995—. Mem. dean's adv. coun. Sch. Sci. Purdue U., 1999, West Lafayette, Ind., 1998—; mem. affil. leadership team Stanford U., Palo Alto, Calif., 1998—; old master Purdue U., 1999. Recipient Women in Leadership award San Francisco Bus. Times, 1997, 98, 99. Mem. Phi Beta Kappa. Roman Catholic. Office: Transamerica Corp 600 Montgomery St Ste 2300 San Francisco CA 94111-2770

BUCHANAN, JOHN E., JR. museum director; b. Nashville, July 24, 1953; BA in English Lit. with honors, U. of the South, 1975; MA in Art History, Vanderbilt U., 1979. Exec. dir. Lakeview Mus. of Arts and Scis., Peoria, Ill., 1982-86; dir. The Dixon Gallery and Gardens, Memphis, 1986; exec. dir. Portland Art Mus., Portland, Oreg. Contbr. articles to profl. jours. Former bd. dirs. Peoria City Beautiful, Peoria Mayor's Commn. on the Arts and Humanities, Ill. Valley Pub. Telecomms. Corp., Arts, Culture and Entertainment Com., Chgo. World's Fair, 1992, Number Art mag., Memphis Visitor and Conv. Bur.; mem. art competition com. Nat. Civil Rights Mus., Memphis; adv. bd. Moss Lecture Series, Rhodes Coll., Children's Mus. of Memphis, Pub. TV and Radio, WKNO; bd. dirs. Internat. Festival; chmn. 1994 Annual Meeting, Southeastern Mus. Conf. Recipient Thomas W. Briggs Cmty. Svc. award 1990. Mem. Assn. of Art Mus. Dirs., Am. Assn. of Mus. (state rep.), Southeastern Mus. Conf., Am. Ceramics Circle, The Dixon Gallery and Gardens (life), Midwest Mus. Conf. (former program com. mem.). Office: Portland Art Museum 1219 SW Park Ave Portland OR 97205-2486

BUCHI, MARK KEITH, lawyer; b. Salt Lake City; m. Denise Kimball, June 4, 1973; 7 children. BS, MBA, U. Utah, 1974, JD, 1978. Bar: Utah 1978. Divsn. chief tax and bus. Utah Atty. Gen. Office, Salt Lake City, 1980-83, asst. atty. gen., 1978-83; chmn. Utah Tax Commn., Salt Lake City, 1983-86; atty. Holme Roberts & Owen, Salt Lake City, 1986-88, ptnr., 1988-89, mng. ptnr., 1989-95, chmn. firmwide exec. com., 2000—, ptnr., 1999—. Mem. tax recodification commn. Utah State Tax Commn., Salt Lake City, 1984-91; mem. Utah Govs. Tax Rev. Commn., Salt Lake City, 1991—; mem. exec. com. Multistate Tax Commn., Boulder, Colo., 1985-86. Mem. tax platform com. Utah Rep. Party, 1986. Mem. ABA, Utah Taxpayers Assn. (chmn. 1992, bd. dirs. 1990—). Mormon. Avocations: golf, water skiing, fishing, gardening, carpentry. Office: Holme Roberts & Owen 111 E Broadway Ste 1100 Salt Lake City UT 84111-5233 E-mail: buchim@hro.com

BUCK, ANNE MARIE, library director, consultant; b. Birmingham, Ala., Apr. 12, 1939; d. Blaine Alexander and Marie Reynolds (McGeorge) Davis; m. Evan Buck, June 17, 1961 (div. Apr. 1977); children: Susan Elizabeth Buck Rentko, Stephen Edward. BA, Wellesley (Mass.) Coll., 1961; MLS, U. Ky., 1977. Bus. mgr. Charleston (W.Va.) Chamber Music Soc., 1972-74; dir. Dunbar (W.Va.) Pub. Libr., 1974-76; tech. reference libr. AT&T Bell Labs., Naperville, Ill., 1977-79, group supr. libr. Reading, Pa., 1979-83, group supr. support svcs. North Andover, Mass., 1983; dir. libr. network Bell Communications Rsch. (Bellcore), Morristown, N.J., 1983-89, dir. human resources planning Livingston, 1989-91; univ. libr. N.J. Inst. Tech., Newark, 1991-95, Calif. Inst. of Tech., Pasadena, 1995—. Adj. prof. Rutgers U., New Brunswick, N.J., 1989-90; instr. U. Wis., Madison, 1988-90; v.p. Engring. Info. Found., N.Y.C., 1994—; mem. Engring. Info. Inc. (bd. dirs.), Castle-Point-on-the-Hudson, Hoboken, N.J., 1988-98; spkr. profl. assn. confs., 1982—; libr. cons. North Port (Fla.) Area Libr., 1990-91; co-chair Caltech Conf. on Scholarly Comm., 1997. Mem. editorial adv. bd. Highsmith Press, 1991-97; contbr. articles to profl. jours. Sect. mgr. United Way of Morris County, Cedar Knolls, N.J., 1984-95; advisor Family Svc. Transitions Coun., Morristown, 1987-90; mem. local svcs. & programs com. San Gabriel Valley (Calif.) United Way, 1998-2000; libr. trustee Lisle (Ill.) Pub. Libr. Dist., 1978-80; bd. dirs. Kanawha County Bicentennial Commn., Charleston, W.Va., 1974-76; personnel com., denominational affairs com., Neighborhood Ch., Pasadena, Calif., 1996—; mem. Carnegie Mellon U. Librs. adv. bd., 1999—. Recipient Vol.'s Gold award United Way, 1991, Disting. Alumna award U. Ky. Sch. Libr. and Info. Sci., 1996. Mem. ALA (Grolier Nat. Libr. Week grantee 1975), Am. Soc. Info. Sci. and Tech. (chpt. chmn. 1987-89, Chpt. of Yr. award 1988, treas. 1992-95, chair Cretsos Leadership Award jury 1999—), Conf. Bd. Inc. (chmn. info. svcs. adv. coun. 1987-89), Spl. Libr. Assn., Am. Soc. Engring. Edn., Archons of Colophon, Indsl. Tech. Info. Mgrs. Group, Women in Engring. Programs and Advocates Network, Wellesley Coll. Alumni Assn. (class rep. 1986-91), N.J. Wellesley Club (regional chmn. 1986-89, corr. sec. 1994-95), Pasadena Wellesley Club (program chmn. 1999—), Rotary, Beta Phi Mu. Unitarian. Avocations: choral singing, travel, photography. Home: 2234 Loma Vista St Pasadena CA 91104-4906 Office: Calif Inst Tech Mail Stop 1-32 Pasadena CA 91125-0001 E-mail: buck@its.caltech.edu

BUCK, LINDA DEE, executive recruiting company executive; b. San Franciso, Nov. 8, 1946; d. Sol and Shirley D. (Setterberg) Press. Student, Coll. of San Mateo, Calif., 1969-70. Head hearing and appeals br. Dept. Navy Employee Rels. Svc., The Philippines, 1974-75; dir. human resources Homestead Savs. & Loan Assn., Burlingame, Calif., 1976-77; mgr. VIP Agy. Inc., Palo Alto, 1977-78; [illegible] Frequent Flyer Store, Inc., Mountain View, 1978-83; founder, pres. Buck & Co., San Mateo, 1983-91

Publicity mgr. for No. Calif., Osteogenesis Imperfecta Found. Inc., 1970-72; cons. Am. Brittle Bone Soc., 1979-88; mem. Florence (Oreg.) Area Humane Soc., 1994—, Friends of Libr., Florence, 1994—; bd. dirs. Florence Festival Arts, 1995; bd. dirs., dir. women Rhododendron Scholarship Program, Florence, 1995. Jewish.

BUCKINGHAM, MICHAEL JOHN, oceanography educator; b. Oxford, Eng., Oct. 9, 1943; s. Sidney George and Mary Agnes (Walsh) B.; m. Margaret Penelope Rose Barrowcliff, July 15, 1967. BSc with hons., U. Reading (Eng.), 1967, PhD, 1971. Postdoctoral rsch. fellow U. Reading, 1971-74; sr. sci. officer Royal Aircraft Establishment, Farnborough, Eng., 1974-76, prin. sci. officer, 1976-82; exchange scientist Naval Rsch. Lab., Washington, 1982-84; vis. prof. MIT, Cambridge, 1986-87; sr. prin. sci. officer Royal Aircraft Establishment, 1983-86, 1987-90; prof. oceanography Scripps Instn. of Oceanography, La Jolla, Calif., 1990—. Vis. prof. Inst. Sound and Vibration rsch., Southampton, Eng., 1990—; UK nat. rep. Commn. of European Communities, Brussels, Belgium, 1989-92; dir. Arctic rsch. Royal Aerospace Establishment, Farnborough, 1990-94; Lansdowne visitor U. Victoria, B.C., Can., 2000; chair Scripps Faculty, 2000-01. Author: Noise in Electronic Devices and Systems, 1983; editor: Sea Surface Sound '94, Proceedings of the III Internat. Mtg. on Natural Phys. Processes Related to Sea Surface Sound; editor-in-chief Jour. Computational Acoustics; editor Phys. Acoustics; contbr. articles to profl. jours.; patentee in field. Recipient Clerk Maxwell Premium, Inst. Electronic and Radio Engrs. London, 1972, A.B. Wood Medal, Inst. Acoustics, Bath, Eng., 1982, Alan Burman Pub. award, Naval Rsch. Lab., 1988, Commendation for Disting. Contbns. to ocean acoustics Naval Rsch. Lab., 1986. Fellow Inst. Acoustics (U.K.), Inst. Elec. Engrs. (U.K.), Acoustical Soc. Am. (chmn. acoustical oceanography tech. com. 1991-95, Sci. Writing award for profls. in acoustics 1997), Explorers Club; mem. Am. Geophys. Union, N.Y. Acad. Scis., Sigma Xi. Avocations: photography, squash, private pilot. Home: 7956 Caminito Del Cid La Jolla CA 92037-3404 Office: Scripps Inst Oceanography Marine Phys Lab La Jolla CA 92093-0238 E-mail: mjb@mpl.ucsd.edu

BUCKLAND, MICHAEL KEEBLE, librarian, educator; b. Wantage, Eng., Nov. 23, 1941; came to U.S., 1972; s. Walter Basil and Norah Elaine (Rudd) B.; m. Waltraud Leeb, July 11, 1964; children: Anne Margaret, Anthony Francis. B.A., Oxford U., 1963; postgrad. diploma in librarianship, Sheffield U., 1965, Ph.D., 1972. Grad. trainee Bodleian Library, Oxford, Eng., 1963-64; asst. librarian U. Lancaster (Eng.) Library, 1965-72; asst. dir. for tech. svcs. Purdue U. Libraries, West Lafayette, Ind., 1972-75; assoc. prof. Sch. of Info. Mgmt. and Sys. U. Calif., Berkeley, 1976-79, dean, 1976-84, prof., 1979—, asst. v.p. library plans and policies, 1983-87; v.p. Ind. Coop. Library Svcs. Auth., 1974-75. Co-dir. Electronic Cultural Atlas Initiative, 2000—; vis. scholar Western Mich. U., 1979; vis. prof. U. Klagenfurt, Austria, 1980, U. New South Wales, Australia, 1988. Author: Book Availability and the Library User, 1975, (with others) The Use of Gaming in Education for Library Management, 1976, Reader in Operations Research for Libraries, 1976, Library Services in Theory and Context, 1983, 2d edit., 1988, Information and Information Systems, 1991, Redesigning Library Services, 1992; editor: Historical Studies in Information Science, 1998, Robert Gitler and the Japan Library School, 1999. Fulbright Rsch. scholar U. Tech., Graz, Austria, 1989. Mem. ALA, Am. Soc. Info. Sci. (pres. 1998), Assn. Libr. and Info. Sci. Edn., Calif. Libr. Assn. Office: U Calif Sch Info Mgmt And Sys Berkeley CA 94720-0001

BUCKLEY, JAMES W. librarian; b. Los Angeles, Aug. 16, 1933; s. George W. and Alta L. (Hale) B.; m. Margaret Ann Wall, Aug. 7, 1965; children: Kathleen Ann, James William, John Whitney. AA, Los Angeles Harbor Coll., 1953; BA, Calif. State U., Long Beach, 1960; MLS, U. So. Calif., 1961, M in Pub. Adminstrn., 1974. Cert. tchr., Calif. Libr. West Gardena br. Los Angeles County Pub. Libr., 1961-62, librarian Carson br., 1962-63; libr. Montebello (Calif.) Regional Libr., 1963-68; regional librarian Orange County (Calif.) Pub. Libr., 1968, dir. pub. services, 1969-74; county librarian San Mateo County (Calif.) Libr., 1974-77, Marin County (Calif.) Libr., 1978; city librarian Torrance (Calif.) Pub. Libr., 1979—. Exec. dir. Calif. Nat. Libr. Week, 1970; tchr. pub. svc. Coll. San Mateo, 1975; chmn. Met. Coop. Libr. Sys., 1989-90, Calif. Libr. Assn. Assembly, 1993-95. Served with U.S. Army, 1955-57. Mem. ALA, Am. Soc. Pub. Adminstrn., Calif. Libr. Assn., Rotary. Office: Torrance Pub Libr 3301 Torrance Blvd Torrance CA 90503-5014 E-mail: jbuckley@torrnet.com

BUCKNER, JOHN KNOWLES, investor; b. Springfield, Mo., Sept. 8, 1936; s. Ernest Godfrey and Mary Helen (Knowles) B.; m. Lorraine Catherine Anderson, Sept. 22, 1962; children: John Knowles, Allison. B.A., Williams Coll., 1958; M.S., Mass. Inst. Tech., 1960; Ph.D., nuclear engring., Stanford U., 1965; grad., Advanced Mgmt. Program, Harvard, 1974. Mgr. analysis dept. EG&G Inc., Bedford, Mass., 1966-70; dir. electronic data processing, controller, v.p. financial ops. Eastern Gas & Fuel Assos., Boston, 1970-77; exec. v.p., chief operating officer, dir. Waters Assos., Inc., Milford, Mass., 1977-80; v.p., chief fin. officer Prime Computer, Inc., Natick, 1980-83; sr. v.p., chief fin. officer EG & G, Inc., Wellesley, 1983-86; vice chmn., chief fin. officer Control Data Corp., Mpls., 1986-89; chmn. Pensco Pension Svcs. Inc., San Francisco, 1989-98, Bohdan Automation, Inc., Mundelein, Ill., 1994-98. Contbr. articles on engring., data analysis and systems to profl. jours. AEC spl. fellow nuclear sci. and engring., 1959, 62-65 Mem. Phi Beta Kappa, Sigma Xi, Chi Psi. Home: 1824 Green St San Francisco CA 94123-4922 Office: Pensco Pension Svcs Inc 250 Montgomery St San Francisco CA 94104-3406

BUCKNER, PHILIP FRANKLIN, newspaper publisher; b. Worcester, Mass., Aug. 25, 1930; s. Orello Simmons and Emily Virginia (Siler) B.; m. Ann Haswell Smith, Dec. 21, 1956 (div. Nov. 1993); children: John C., Frederick S., Catherine A.; m. Mary Emily Aird, Dec. 15, 1995 (div. Sept. 1997). AB, Harvard U., 1952; MA, Columbia U., 1954. With Bay State Abrasive Products Co., 1954-59; Reporter Lowell (Mass.) Sun, 1959-60; pub. East Providence (R.I.) Post, 1960-62; asst. to treas. Scripps League Newspapers, Seattle, 1964-66, divsn. mgr., 1966-71; pres. Buckner News Alliance, Seattle, 1971—. Pub. daily newspaper group including Carlsbad (N.Mex.) Current-Argus, 1971-90, Pecos (Tex.) Enterprise, 1971—, Fontana (Calif.) Herald-News, 1971-89, Banning and Beaumont (Calif.) Gazette, 1971-74, Lewistown (Pa.) Sentinel, 1971-93, Tiffin (Ohio) Advertiser-Tribune, 1973-93, York (Pa.) Daily Record, 1978—, Winsted (Conn.) Citizen, 1978, Excelsior Springs (Mo.) Standard, 1978, Oroville (Calif.) Mercury-Register, 1983-89, Corona (Calif.) Independent, 1984-89, Minot (N.D.) News, 1989-93. Avocation: mountain climbing. Office: Buckner News Alliance 2101 4th Ave Ste 2300 Seattle WA 98121-2317

BUCKNER-DAVIS, ANNETT, professional volleyball player; b. Carson, Calif., Sept. 22, 1973; d. Cleveland Buckner; m. Byron Davis, 1996. Mem. Sydney Olympics Beach Volleyball Team, 2000. Named MVP and Offensive Player of the Yr., Bud Light Pro Beach Volleyball League, 1996, Rookie of Yr. and Sportsmanship awardee 1995; named to 1st Team NCAA All-American, 1993-94, others. Avocations: designing clothes, modeling. Office: USA Volleyball Bud Light Pro Volleyball 715 S Circle Dr Colorado Springs CO 80910-2368

BUCY, RICHARD SNOWDEN, aerospace engineering and mathematics educator, consultant; b. Washington, July 20, 1935; s. Edmond Howard and Marie (Glinke) B.; m. Ofelia Teresa Rivva, Aug. 25, 1961; children: Phillip Gustav, Richard Erwin. B.S. in Math., MIT, 1957; Ph.D. in Math. Stats., U. Calif.-Berkeley, 1963. Researcher in math. Rsch. Inst. Advanced Studies Towson, Md., 1960-61, 63-64; rsch. asst. U. Calif., Berkeley, 1961-63; asst. prof. [illegible] College Park, 1964-65, assoc. prof. aerospace engring.

U. Colo., Boulder, 1965-66; prof. aerospace engring. and math. U. So. Calif., Los Angeles, 1966—; professeur associe French Govt., Toulouse, 1973-74, Nice, 1983-84, 90-91. Vis. prof. Technische Universität Berlin, 1975-76; co-dir. NATO Advanced Study Inst. on Non-linear Scholastic Problems, Algarve, Portugal; cons. to industry Author: Filtering for Stochastic Processes, 1968, 2d edit., 1987, Nonlinear Stochastic Problems, 1984, Lectures on Discrete Filtering Theory, 1994; editor Jour. Info. Scis., Jour. Math. Modelling and Sci. Computing; founding editor (jour.) Stochastics, 1971-77; contbr. numerous articles to profl. publs. Recipient Humboldt prize Govt. W. Germany, Berlin, 1975-76; Air Force Office Sci. Sch. grantee, 1965-81, NATO Rsch. grantee, 1979—. Fellow IEEE (del. to Soviet Acad. of Scis. Info. Theory Workshop); mem. Am. Math. Soc. Republican. Home: 420 S Juanita Ave Redondo Beach CA 90277-3824 Office: U So Calif Dept Aerospace Engring Los Angeles CA 90089-0001

BUDINGER, THOMAS FRANCIS, radiologist, educator; b. Evanston, Ill., Oct. 25, 1932; married, 1965; 3 children. BS, Regis Coll., 1954; MS, U. Wash., 1957; MD, U. Calif. Berkeley, 1964, PhD, 1971. Asst. chemist Regis Coll., Colo., 1953-54; analytical chemist Indsl. Labs., 1954; sr. oceanographer U. Wash., 1961-66; physicist Lawrence Livermore Lab., U. Calif., 1966-67; resident physician Donner Lab. and Lawrence Berkeley Lab., 1967-76; H. Miller Prof. med. rsch. and group leader rsch. medicine Donner lab., prof. elec. engring. and computer sci. Donner Lab., U. Calif. Berkeley, 1976—. With Peter Bent Brigham Hosp., Boston, 1964; dir. med. svc. Lawrence Berkeley Lab., 1968-76, sr. staff scientist, 1980—; chmn. study sect. NIH, 1981-84; prof. radiology U. Calif. San Francisco, 1984—. Recipient Special award Am. Nuclear Soc., 1984. Mem. AAAS, Am. Geophysical Union, N.Y. Acad. Sci., Soc. Nuclear Medicine, Soc. Magnetic Rsch. Medicine (pres. 1984-85). Achievements include research in imaging body functions, electrical, magnetic, sound and photon radiation fields, electron microscopy, polar oceanography, nuclear magnetic resonance, reconstruction tomography and instrument development, cardiology. Office: Lawrence Berkeley Lab Ctr for Functional Imaging 1 Cyclotron Rd Mail Stop 55-121 Berkeley CA 94720-0001

BUDZINSKI, JAMES EDWARD, interior designer; b. Jan. 4, 1953; s. Edward Michael and Virginia (Caliman) B. Student, U. Cin., 1971-76. Mem. design staff Perkins & Wills Archs., Inc., Chgo., 1973-75, Med. Architectonics, Inc., Chgo., 1975-76; v.p. interior design Interior Environs., Inc., Chgo., 1976-78; pres. Jim Budzinski Design, Inc., Chgo., 1978-80; dir. interior design Robinson, Mills & Williams, San Francisco, 1980-87; dir. design, interior arch. Whisler Patri, San Francisco, 1987-90; v.p. design sales and mktg. Deepa Textiles, 1990-95; v.p. Workplace Studio One Workplace L. Ferrari, San Jose, Calif., 1997-2000, Strategic Envisioner, 2000—. Instr. design Harrington Inst. Design, Chgo.; cons. Chgo. Art Inst., Storwal Internat., Inc.; spkr. profl. confs. Designs include 1st Chgo. Corp. Pvt. Banking Ctr., 1st Nat. Bank Chgo. Monroe and Wabash Banking Ctr., 1978, IBM Corp., San Jose, Deutsche Bank, Frankfort, Crowley Maritime Corp., San Francisco, office for Brobeck, Phleger and Harrison, offices for chmn. bd. Fireman's Fund Ins. Cos., Nob Hill Club, Fairmont Hotel, San Francisco, offices for Cooley, Goodword, Castro, Huddleson, and Tatum, Palo Alto, Calif., offices for Pacific Bell Acctg. divsn., San Francisco, showroom for Knoll Internat., San Francisco, lobby, lounge TransAm. Corp. Hdqs., San Francisco, offices for EDAW, San Francisco, showroom for Steelcase, Inc., Bally of Switzerland, N.Am. Flagship store, San Francisco; corp. Hdqs. Next Inc., Redwood City, Calif., Schafer Furniture Design, Lobby Renovation 601 California, San Francisco, Bennedetti Furniture Inc. Furniture Design. Pres. No. Calif. chpt. Design Industries Found. for AIDS. E-mail: jbudzinski@oneworkplace.com

BUECHNER, JOHN C. academic administrator; Dir. govtl. rels., then dir. pub. affairs U. Colo. System Office, Denver, until 1989; chancellor U. Colo., Denver, 1988-96, pres., 1996—. Office: U Colo-Denver Office of Pres Campus Box 35 Boulder CO 80309-0035

BUEL, BOBBIE JO, editor; Mng. editor, Tucson, 1991—. Office: Arizona Daily Star PO Box 26807-85726-6807 4850 S Park Ave Tucson AZ 85714-3395

BUELL, BRUCE TEMPLE, lawyer; b. Pueblo, Colo., Mar. 18, 1932; s. Jewett C. and Eva Lorraine (Allen) B.; m. Joan Carol Souders, June 20, 1953; children: Alan D., Susan L. Buell, Bonnie L. Iten. AB, Princeton U., 1953; postgrad., Harvard Law Sch., 1953-54, George Washington U. Law Sch., 1955-57; LLB, U. Denver, 1958. Bar: Colo. Asst. trust dept. Cen. Bank & Trust Co., Denver, 1957-58; assoc. Holland & Hart, Denver, 1958-64, ptnr. Colorado Springs and Denver, Colo., 1964-96; atty. pvt. practice, Colorado Springs, 1996—. Bd. dirs., counsel Jefferson Bank & Trust, Lakewood, Colo., 1971-76; counsel, sec. Colo. Bus. Devel. Corp., Denver, 1965-83; gen. counsel Colo. Bankers Assn., Denver, 1961-85. Pres. Colo. Lawyer Trust Account Found., Denver, 1982-85, 88-89, Arvada (Colo.) Hist. Soc., 1974-75; chmn. adv. coun. Arvada Ctr. for Arts, 1978-79; dir. North Jeffco Recreation and Pk. Dist., Arvada, 1976-80; trustee, chmn. Presbytery of Denver Trust Fund, 1983-85; trustee, sec.-treas. Viola Vestal Coulter Found., 1964—, pres., 1998—; trustee Edmondson Found., 1996—, v.p., 2000—; trustee Pikes Peak Cmty. Found., 1998—; bd. dirs., v.p. Samaritan Counseling Ctr., Colorado Springs, 1991-96; mem. Colo. Forum, Denver, 1989-93. Served to capt. USNR, 1954-76. Recipient Vol. of Yr. award Denver Bar Assn., 1982, Man of Yr. award Arvada C. of C., 1983, Bruce T. Buell award Colo. Lawyer Trust Acct. Found., 1991, U. Denver Law Sch. Professionalism award, 1995. Fellow Colo. Bar Found.; mem. ABA, Colo. Bar Assn., El Paso County Bar Assn. (treas. 2000), Colorado Springs Estate Planning Coun., Broadmoor Golf Club, Winter Night Club (pres. 1996-97). Presbyterian. Avocations: tennis, music, prison ministry, church work. Home: 2512 Rigel Dr Colorado Springs CO 80906-1031 Office: Buell & Ezell LLP 118 S Wahsatch Ave Ste 210 Colorado Springs CO 80903-3679 E-mail: buell-law@msm.com

BUEN, JAN YAGI, state legislator; b. Dec. 30, 1942; m. Rick Buen; children: Althea, Kristi, Michael. BS in Human Resources, U. Hawaii. Dir. spl. projects Maui Electric Co.; mem. Hawaii Senate, Dist. 4, Honolulu, 1998—; vice chair econ. devel. com., mem. ways and means com. Hawaiian Senate, Honolulu, mem. transp. and intergovtl. affairs com. Bd. dirs. March of Dimes, Maui United Way, campaign chair, 1997; co-founder, bd. dirs. Friends of Maui Meml. Med. Ctr.; mem. Maui Okinawa Kenjin Kai. Mem. U. Hawaii Alumni Assn. Democrat. Office: State Capitol 415 S Beretania St Honolulu HI 96813-2407

BUFANO, RALPH A. museum director; Dir. Museum of Flight, Seattle. Office: Museum of Flight 904 E Marginal S Seattle WA 98108-4097

BUFFINGTON, JOHN DOUGLAS, ecologist; b. Jersey City, Nov. 26, 1941; s. John Franklin and Rosemary Eileen (Showay) B.; m. Mary Elizabeth Coughlin, Jan. 23, 1965; children: Jill Anne, John Matthew. BS cum laude, St. Peter's Coll., Jersey City, 1963; MS, U. Ill., 1965, PhD, 1967. Asst. prof. Ill. State U., Normal, 1969-72; scientist, asst. divsn. dir. Argonne (Ill.) Nat. Lab., 1972-77; sr. staff scientist Pres.'s Coun. Environ. Quality, Washington, 1977-80; chief office biol. svcs. U.S. Fish & Wildlife Svc., Washington, 1980-83, dep. reg. dir., 1983-89, regional dir., 1989-93; acting regional dir. Nat. Biol. Survey, Washington, 1993-95; dir. Alaska

Sci. Ctr., 1995-97; regional chief biologist U.S. Geol. Survey, Seattle, 1997-99, regional dir., 2000—. Mem. U.S. negotiating delegation Conv. Biol. Diversity, 1990-93. Capt. U.S. Army, 1967-69. Recipient Meritorious Svc. award U.S. Dept. Interior, 1994. Mem. Ecol. Soc. Am. (applied sect. chmn. 1981, Washington chpt. chmn. 1981). Office: US Geol Survey 900 1st Ave Ste 800 Seattle WA 98104

BUFFLER, PATRICIA ANN, epidemiology educator, retired dean; b. Doylestown, Pa., Aug. 1, 1938; d. Edward M. and Evelyn G. (Axenroth) Happ; m. Richard T. Buffler, Jan. 20, 1962; children: Martyn R., Monique L. BSN, Cath. U. Am., 1960; MPH, U. Calif., Berkeley, 1965, PhD in Epidemiology, 1973. Prof. epidemiology sch. pub. health U. Tex. Health Sci. Ctr., Houston, 1979-91; prof. U. Calif., Berkeley, 1991—, dean sch. pub. health, 1991-98, dean emerita, 1998—. Mem. expert adv. panel on occupl. health WHO, 1985—; mem. environment, safety and health adv. com. U.S. DOE, 1992-95; mem. bd. on water sci. and tech. Nat. Rsch. Coun., 1992-94; chair, bd. dirs. Mickey Leland Nat. Urban Air Toxics Rsch. Ctr., 1994-97, Societal Inst. of Math. Scis.; mem. Nat. Commn. on Superfund, Keystone Ctr., 1992-94; mem. adv. panel on mng. nuclear materials from warheads U.S. Congress Office Tech. Assessment, 1992-93; bd. scientific counselors Nat. Inst. for Occupl. Safety and Health, 1991-93; mem. sci. adv. bd. radiation adv. com. subcom. on cancer risks associated with electric and magnetic fields U.S. EPA, 1990-93; mem. sci. adv. bd. USEPA, 1996—; mem. Nat. Adv. Coun. on Environ. Health Scis., 1995-98; mem. NAS, Nat. Coun. Radiation Protection. Contbr. articles to profl. jours. Fellow AAS, Am. Coll. Epidemiology (pres.-elect 1990-91, pres. 1991-92), Inst. Medicine; mem. Soc. for Epidemiological Rsch. (pres.-elect, pres., past pres. 1984-88), Am. Pub. Health Assn. (epidemiology sect. 1964—), Am. Epidemiological Soc., Soc. for Occupl. and Environ. Health, Internat. Epidemiological Assn., Internat. Soc. for Environ. Epidemiology (pres.-elect 1989-91, pres. 1992-94), Internat. Soc. for Exposure Assessment (charter, bd. internat. councillors 1993—), Internat. Commn. on Occupl. Health, Collegium Ramazzini, Soc. of Toxicology. Office: U Calif Sch Pub Health 714-F University Hall 140 Earl Warren Hl Berkeley CA 94720-0001

BUFFMIRE, DONALD K. internist; b. Grand Rapids, Minn., Aug. 18, 1922; m. Jane Enkema, June 11, 1945; 3 children. BS, BM in Zoology, Northwestern U., 1944, MD, 1948. Diplomate Am. Bd. Internal Medicine. Intern Evanston (Ill.) Hosp., 1947-48; resident in internal medicine Mayo Found., Rochester, Minn., 1948-51, U. Minn., Mpls., 1950; founder, past chmn. Phoenix Med. Assocs.-Mayo Health Sys., 1954—; now ret. Elder Orangewood Presbyn. Ch.; Trustee, past chmn. Blood Sys., Inc., Scottsdale, Ariz.; former mem. coord. devel. adv. bd. U. Ariz. Coll. Medicine; trustee Flinn Found., Phoenix, 1965—, pres. bd. trustees 1982-98, chmn., 1984-98, chmn. emeritus, 1998—. Capt. Med. Corps U.S. Army, 1951-53. Recipient Dr. Joseph E. Ehrlich medal Maricopa County Med. Soc., 1992, Dr. Clarence Salsbury award Maricipa County Med. Soc., 1987, Disting. Svc. to Society award Northwestern U., 1998, The Spirit of Philanthropy award, Nat. Soc. Fund Raising Execs., 1999; Donald K. Buffmire Vis. Lectureship in medicine established at U. Ariz. by Flinn Found., 1998; named as one of 25 leaders who helped shape modern-day Phoenix, Phoenix mag., 1991; inducted into Grand Rapids, Minn. Sports Hall of Fame, 1990. Fellow ACP (Laureate award 1991), Am. Coll. Chest Physicians, Royal Soc. Medicine; mem. AMA, Am. Soc. Internal Medicine, Ariz. Med. Assn. (Pres.' Disting. Svc. award 1998), Ariz. Heart Assn. (pres. 1958-59), Sigma Chi (Significant Sig award 2001). Home: 3311 E Valley Vista Ln Paradise Valley AZ 85253-3739 Office: Phoenix Med Assocs Mayo Health Sys 3600 N 3rd Ave Phoenix AZ 85013-3904 E-mail: enkie@aol.com

BUFFORD, SAMUEL LAWRENCE, federal judge; b. Phoenix, Nov. 19, 1943; s. John Samuel and Evelyn Amelia (Rude) B.; m. Julia Marie Metzger, May 13, 1978. BA in Philosophy, Wheaton Coll., 1964; PhD, U. Tex., 1969; JD magna cum laude, U. Mich., 1973. Bar: Calif., N.Y., Ohio. Instr. philosophy La. State U., Baton Rouge, 1967-68; asst. prof. Ea. Mich. U., Ypsilanti, 1968-74; asst. prof. law Ohio State U., Columbus, 1975-77; assoc. Gendel, Raskoff, Shapiro & Quittner, L.A., 1982-85; atty. Paul, Weiss, Rifkind, Wharton & Garrison, N.Y.C., 1974-75, Sullivan Jones & Archer, San Francisco, 1977-79, Musick, Peeler & Garrett, L.A., 1979-81, Rifkind & Sterling, Beverly Hills, Calif., 1981-82, Gendel, Raskoff, Shapiro & Quittner, L.A., 1982-85; U.S. bankruptcy judge Ctrl. Dist. Calif., 1985—. Bd. dirs. Fin. Lawyers Conf., L.A., 1987-90, Bankruptcy Forum, L.A., 1986-88; lectr. U.S.-Romanian Jud. Delegation, 1991, Internat. Tng. Ctr. for Bankers, Budapest, 1993, Bankruptcy Technical Legal Assistance Workshop, Romania, 1994, Comml. Law Project for Ukraine, 1995-96, 99, Ea. Europe Enterprise Restructuring and Privitization Project, U.S. AID, 1995-96; cons. Calif. State Bar Bd. Examiners, 1989-90; bd. trustees Endowment for Edn.; bd. dirs. Nat. Conf. Bankruptcy Judges, 1994-2000; bd. dirs. San Pedro Enterprise Community, 1997—. Editor-in-chief Am. Bankruptcy Law Jour., 1990-94; contbr. articles to profl. jours. Younger Humanist fellowship NEH. Mem. ABA, L.A. County Bar Assn. (mem. profl. responsibility and ethics com. 1979—, chair profl. responsibility and ethics com. 1985-86, chair ethics 2000 liaison com. 1997—), Order of Coif. Office: US Bankruptcy Ct 255 E Temple St Ste 1582 Los Angeles CA 90012-3332

BUGBEE-JACKSON, JOAN, sculptor, educator; b. Oakland, Calif., Dec. 17, 1941; d. Henry Greenwood and Jeanie Lawler (Abbot) B.; m. John Michael Jackson, June 21, 1973; 1 child, Brook Bond. BA in Art, U. Calif., San Jose, 1964, MA in Art and Ceramics, 1966; student, Nat. Acad. Sch. Fine Arts, N.Y.C., 1968-72. Instr. pottery Greenwich House Pottery, N.Y.C., 1969-71, Craft Inst. Am., N.Y.C., 1970-72, Cordova Ext. Ctr., U. Alaska, 1972-79, Prince William Sound Cmty. Coll., 1979—. Represented by B Street Artworks, Cordova. One-woman exhbns. in Maine, N.Y.C., Alaska, Calif.; group exhbns. include Allied Artists Am., 1970-72, Nat. Acad. Design, 1971, 74, Nat. Sculpture Soc. Ann., 1971, 72, 73, Alaska Woman Art Show, 1987, 88, Cordova Visual Artists, 1991-96, Alaska Artists Guild Show, 1994, Am. Medallic Sculpture Nat. Travelling Exhbn., 1994-95, pres. Cordova Arts and Pageants Ltd., 1975-76; commns. include Merle K. Smith Commemorative plaque, 1973, Eyak Native Monument, 1978, Anchorage Pioneer's Home Ceramic Mural, 1979, Alaska Wildlife Series Bronze Medal, 1980, Armin F. Koernig Hatchery Plaque, 1985, Cordova Fishermen's Meml. Sculpture, 1985, Alaska's Five Govs., bronze relief, Anchorage, 1986, Reluctant Fishermen's Mermaid, bronze, 1987, Charles E. Bunnell, bronze portrait statue, Fairbanks, 1988, Alexander Baranof Monument, Sitka, Alaska, 1989, Wally Noerenberg Hatchery Plaque, Prince William Sound, Alaska, 1989, Russian-Alaskan Friendship Plaque (edit. of 4), Kayak Island, Cordova, Alaska and Vladivostok & Petropavlovsk-Kamchatskiy, Russia, 1991, Sophie-Last Among Eyak Native People, 1992, Alaska Airlines Medal Commn., 1993, Hosp. Aux. plaque, 1995, La Cirena, Mex., 1998, Alaska Vets. Monument lifesize bronze, Anchorage, 2001; also other portraits. Bd. dirs. Alaska State Coun. Arts, 1991-95. Scholar, Nat. Acad. Sch. Fine Arts, 1969-72; recipient J.A. Suydam Bronze medal, 1969, Dr. Ralph Weiler prize, 1971, Helen Foster Barnet award, 1971, Daniel Chester French award, 1972, Frishmuth award, 1971, Allied Artists Am. award, 1972, C. Percival Dietsch prize, 1973, citation Alaska Legislature, 1981, 82; named Alaskan Artist of Yr., 1991. Fellow Nat. Sculpture Soc. Address: PO Box 374 Cordova AK 99574-0374

BUGLI, DAVID, conductor, arranger, composer; b. N.Y.C., Apr. 2, 1950; BMus, Ithaca Coll., 1972; MMus, U. Mass., 1978. Founder, musical dir., condr. Carson City Symphony (formerly Carson City Chamber Orch.), Nev., 1984—. Pub. sch. music tchr., 1972-77; computer programmer/analyst, 1979—; 1st pres. Carson Access TV Found., 1991. Office: Carson City Symphony PO Box 2001 Carson City NV 89702-2001 E-mail: dbugli@aol.com

BUHLER, JILL LORIE, editor, writer; b. Seattle, Dec. 7, 1945; d. Oscar John and Marcella Jane (Hearing) Younce; 1 child, Lori Jill Moody; m. John Buhler, 1990; stepchildren: Christie Reynolds, Cathie Zatarian, Mike. AA in Gen. Edn., Am. River Coll., 1969; BA in Journalism with honors, Sacramento State U., 1973. Reporter Carmichael (Calif.) Courier, 1968-70; mng. editor Quarter Horse of the Pacific Coast, Sacramento, 1970-75, editor, 1975-84, Golden State Program Jour., 1978, Nat. Reined Cow Horse Assn. News, Sacramento, 1983-88, Pacific Coast Jour., Sacramento, 1984-88, Nat. Snaffle Bit Assn. News, Sacramento, 1988; pres., chief exec. officer Communications Plus, Port Townsend, Wash., 1988—; campaign mgr. N.W. Maritime Ctr., 2000-2001, bd. sec., 2001—. Mag. cons., 1975—. Interviewer Pres. Ronald Regan, Washington, 1983; mng. editor Wash. Thoroughbred, 1989-90. Mem. 1st profl. communicators mission to USSR, 1988; bd. dirs. Carmichael Winding Way, Pasadena Homeowners Assn., 1985-87; mem. scholarship com. Thoroughbred Horse Racing's United Scholarship Trust; mem. governing bd. Wash. State Hosp. Assn., 1996-2000, mem. legis. policy com., 1999—, hosp. commr. Jefferson Gen. Hosp., 1995—, chair bd. dirs. 1997-2000; mem. Jefferson County Bd. Health, 1997—, vice chmn., 1998, chmn. 2001. Recipient 1st pl. feature award, 1970, 1st pl. editorial award Jour. Assn. Jr. Colls., 1971, 1st pl. design award WCHB Yuba-Sutter Counties, Marysville, Calif., 1985, Photography awards, 1994, 95, 96. Mem. Am. River Jaycees (Speaking award 1982), Am. Horse Publs. (1st Pl. Editl. award 1983, 86), Port Townsend C. of C. (trustee, v.p. 1993, pres. 1994, officer 1996, 97, 98), Mensa (bd. dirs., asst. local sec., activities dir. 1987-88, membership chair 1988-90), Kiwanis Internat. (chair maj. emphasis program com., treas. 1992—), 5th Wheel Touring Soc. (v.p. 1970). Republican. Roman Catholic. Avocations: sailing, photography. Home: 440 Adelma Beach Rd Port Townsend WA 98368-9280 E-mail: commplus@wnypt.com

BUHNER, JAY CAMPBELL, professional baseball player; b. Louisville, Aug. 13, 1964; m. Leah Buhner; children: Brielle, Chase, Gunnar. Student, McClennan C.C., Waco, Tex. Outfielder New York Yankees, N.Y.C., 1987-88, Seattle Mariners, 1988—. Active Seattle chpt. Cystic Fibrosis Found., Juvenile Diabetes Assn. Named Houston Area Player of Yr. Houston chpt. Baseball Writers Assn. Am., 1993, 95; recipient Gold Glove award, 1996, Breath of Life award Cystic Fibrosis Found., 1997. Office: c/o Seattle Mariners PO Box 4100 1st Ave S and Atlantic Seattle WA 98104

BUIST, NEIL ROBERTSON MACKENZIE, medical educator, medical administrator; b. Karachi, India, July 11, 1932; m. Sonia Chapman; children: Catriona, Alison, Diana. Degree with commendation, U. St. Andrews, Scotland, MB, ChB, 1956; Diploma of Child Health, London U., England, 1960. Diplomate Am. Bd. Med. Genetics, Am. Bd. Clinical Genetics. House physician internal medicine Arbroath Infirmary, 1956-57; house physician externe cardiopulmonary dept. Hosp. Marie Lannelongue, Paris, 1957; house surgeon Royal Hosp. Sick Children, Edinburgh, Scotland, 1957; commd. far east med. officer Regimental Military Svc., 1957-60; house physician Royal Infirmary, Dundee, Scotland, 1960; registrar internal medicine Maryfield Hosp., Dundee, Scotland, 1960-62; lectr. child health U. St. Andrews, Dundee, Scotland, 1962-64; rsch. fellow pediatric micro-chemistry, Sch. Health Sci. U. Colo., Denver, 1964-66; asst. prof. pediatrics, Sch. Medicine U. Oreg., Portland, 1966-70; dir. Pediatrics Metabolic Lab, Oreg. Health Sci. U., Portland, 1966-93, Metabolic Birth Defects Ctr., Oreg. Health Sci. U., Portland, 1966-98; assoc. prof. pediatrics and med. genetics Health Sci Ctr., U. Oreg., Portland, 1970-76; prof. pediatrics and med. genetics Oreg. Health Scis. U., 1976-98, prof. emeritus. Med. cons. Northwest Regional Newborn Screening Program, Portland, 1970—; vis. prof. WHO, China, 1988, U. Colo., 1990, Wesley Med. Ctr., Kans., 1991, Phoenix Children's Hosp., Ariz., 1991, Tucson Med. Ctr., Ariz., 1991, U. Ill., Chgo., 1991, Kapioolani Med. Ctr., Hawaii, 1992, Shriners Hosp. for Crippled Children., Hawaii, 1992, Ark. Children's Hosp., 1993, Australasian Soc. for Human Genetics, New Zealand, 1994, LBJ Med. Ctr., Americas Samoa, 1994, Mahidol U., Bangkok, 1996, U. P.R., 1996, U. Auckland (New Zealand), 1997. Author: (with others) Textbook of Pediatrics, 1973, Inherited Disorders of Amino Acid Metabolism, 1974, 1985, Clinics in Endocrinolog and Metabolism: Aspects of Neonatal Metabolism, 1976, Textbook of Pediatrics, 1978, Practice of Pediatrics, 1980, Management of High-Risk Pregnancy, 1980, Current Occular Therapy, 1980, Practice of Pediatrics, 1981, Clinics in Endocrinology and Metabolism: Aspects of Neonatal Metabolism, 1981, Textbook of Pediatrics, 1984, Disorders of Fatty Acid Metabolism in the Pediatric Practice, 1990, Birth Defects Encyclopedia, 1990, 1991, Treatment of Genetic Disease, 1991, Pediatric Clinics of North America Medical Genetics II, 1992, Forfar & Arneil's Textbook of Paediatrics, 1992, 97, Galactosemia New Frontiers in Research, 1993, New Horizons in Neonatal Screening, 1994, New Trends in Neonatal Screening, 1994, Alpha-1-Antitrypsin Deficiency, 1994, Diseases of the Fetus and Newborn, 1995, Inborn Metabolic Diseases: Diagnosis and Treatment, 1995; cons. editor: Inborn Metabolic Disease Text, 1995; editorial bd. mem.: Jour. of Inherited Metabolic Diseases, 1977—, Kelley Practice of Pediatrics, 1980-87, Screening, 1991-96; jour. reviewer: Am. Jour. of Human Genetics, Jour. of Pediatrics, Pediatric Rsch., Screening. Adv. com. Tri County March of Dimes, Portland, 1977—; physician Diabetic Children's Camp, 1967—, Muscle Biopsy Clinic Shriners Hosp., 1989—; bd. dirs. Mize Info. Enterprises, Dallas, 1987—. Fellow Royal Coll. Physicians Edinburgh, Fogarty Internat. Vis. Scientist, Royal Coll. Physicians Edinburgh; mem. Brit. Med. Assn., Western Soc. Pediatric Rsch. (coun. mem. 1966—), Pacific North West Pediatric Soc., Am. Pediatric Soc., Soc. for the Study of Inborn Errors of Metabolism, Soc. for Inherited Metabolic Disorders (treas. 1977—), Oreg. Pediatric Soc., Oreg. Diabetes Assn., Portland Acad. Pediatrics, Internat. Newborn Screening Soc. Coun. (founding mem. 1988—). Avocations: fishing, gardening, travel. E-mail: buistn@ohsu.edu

BUITENHUIS, PETER MARTINUS, language professional, educator; b. London, Eng., Dec. 8, 1925; s. John A. and Irene (Cotton) B. B.A. with honors, Jesus Coll. Oxford (Eng.) U., 1949, M.A., 1954; Ph.D., Yale, 1955. Instr. U. Okla., Norman, 1949-51; instr. Am. studies Yale, 1954-59; assoc. prof. English Victoria Coll. U. Toronto, Ont., Can., 1959-66; vis. prof. U. Calif.-Berkeley, 1966-67; prof. McGill U., Montreal, Que., Can., 1967-75; prof., chmn. dept. English Simon Fraser U., Burnaby, B.C., Can., 1975-82; prof. emeritus English Simon Fraser U., Burnaby, Can., 1992. Author: Hugh MacLennan, 1968, The Grasping Imagination: the American Writings of Henry James, 1970, The Great War of Words: British, American and Canadian Propaganda and Fiction, 1914-1933, 1987, The House of the Seven Gables: Severing Family and Colonial Ties, 1991; editor: Selected Poems of E. J. Pratt, 1968, (with I. Nadel) George Orwell: A Reassessment, 1988, (with D. Staines) The Canadian Imagination; contbr. articles to profl. jours., popular press. Served to sub-lt. Royal Navy, 1943-46, Eng. Can. Coun. fellow, 1962-63; Am. Coun. Learned Socs. fellow, 1972-73; Social Scis. and Humanities Rsch. Coun. fellow, 1982-83, 91-94. Mem. Am. Studies Assn., Can. Assn. Am. Studies (pres. 1968-70), Can. Assn. Univ. Tchrs., Assn. Can. Studies. Home: 7019 Marine Dr West Vancouver BC Canada V7W 2T4 Office: Simon Fraser U Dept English Burnaby BC Canada V5A 1S6 E-mail: buitenhu@sfu.ca

BUKRY, JOHN DAVID, geologist; b. Balt., May 17, 1941; s. Howard Leroy and Irene Evelyn (Davis) Snyder Student, Colo. Sch. Mines, 1959-60; BA, Johns Hopkins U., 1963; MA, Princeton U., 1965, PhD, 1967; postgrad., U. Ill., 1965-66, De Anza Coll., 1995-96. Geologist U.S. Army Corp Engrs., Balt., 1963; research asst. Mobil Oil Co., Dallas, 1965; geologist U.S. Geol. Survey, La Jolla, Calif., 1967-84, U.S. Minerals Mgmt. Svc., La Jolla, 1984-86, U.S. Geol. Survey, Menlo Park, Calif., 1986-96, scientist emeritus La Jolla, 1996-98, Menlo Park, 1998—; rsch. assoc. Geol. Rsch. Divsn. Scripps Instn. Oceanography-U. Calif., San Diego, 1970—. Cons. Deep Sea Drilling Project, La Jolla, 1967-87; lectr. Vetlesen Symposium, Columbia U., N.Y.C., 1968, 3d Internat. Planktonic Conf., Kiel, Fed. Republic Germany, 1974, Brit. Petroleum Exploration Seminar on nannoplankton biostratigraphy, Houston, 1989; shipboard micropaleontologist on D/V Glomar Challenger, 5 Deep Sea Drilling Project cruises, 1968-78; mem. stratigraphic correlations bd. NSF/Joint Oceanographic Instns. for Deep Earth Sampling, 1976-79. Author: Leg I of the Cruises of the Drilling Vessel Glomar Challenger, 1969, Coccoliths from Texas and Europe, 1969, Leg LXIII of the Cruises of the Drilling Vessel Glomar Challenger, 1981; editor: Marine Micropaleontology, 1976-83, mem. edtl. bd. Micropaleontology, 1985-90. Mobil Oil, Princeton U. fellow, 1965-67; Am. Chem. Soc., Princeton U. fellow, 1966-67. Fellow AAAS, Geol. Soc. Am., Explorers Club; mem. NSTA, Hawaiian Malacological Soc., Paleontol. Rsch. Inst., Am. Assn. Petroleum Geologists, Soc. Econ. Paleontologists and Mineralogists, Internat. Nannoplankton Assn., Ecol. Soc. Am., European Union Geoscis., Oceanography Soc., U. Calif.-San Diego Ida and Cecil Green Faculty Club, San Diego Shell Club, Princeton Club No. Calif., Sigma Xi. Avocations: basketball, photography, shell and mineral collecting. Achievements include research in stratigraphy, paleoecology and taxonomy for 300 new species of marine nannoplankton used in ocean history studies. Office: US Geol Survey 910 345 Middlefield Rd Menlo Park CA 94025-3591 E-mail: dbukry@usgs.gov

BULL, BRIAN STANLEY, pathology educator, medical consultant, business executive; b. Watford, Hertfordshire, Eng., Sept. 14, 1937; came to U.S., 1954, naturalized, 1960; s. Stanley and Agnes Mary (Murdoch) B.; m. Maureen Hannah Huse, June 3, 1963; children: Beverly Velda, Beryl Heather. B.S. in Zoology, Walla Walla Coll., 1957; M.D., Loma Linda (Calif.) U., 1961. Diplomate: Am. Bd. Pathology. Intern Yale U., 1961-62, resident in anat. pathology, 1962-63; resident in clin. pathology NIH, Bethesda, Md., 1963-65, fellow in hematology and electron microscopy, 1965-66, staff hematologist, 1966-67; research asst. dept. anatomy Loma Linda U., 1958, dept. microbiology, 1959, asst. prof. pathology, 1968-71, assoc. prof., 1971-73, prof., 1973—, chmn. dept. pathology, 1973—, assoc. dean for acad. affairs sch. medicine, 1993-94, dean sch. medicine, 1994—. Cons. to mfrs. of med. testing devices; mem. panel on hematology FDA; mem. Nat. Com. on Clin. Lab. Standards; mem. Internat. Commn. for Standardization in Hematology, pres., 1997-99. Mem. bd. editors Blood Cells, Molecules and Diseases, 1995—; contbr. chpts. to books, articles to med. jours.; patentee in field; editor-in-chief Blood Cells N.Y. Heidelberg, 1985-94. Served with USPHS, 1963-67. Nat. Inst. Arthritis and Metabolic Diseases fellow, 1967-68; recipient Daniel D. Comstock Meml. award Loma Linda U., 1961, Merck Manual award, 1961, Mosby Scholarship Book award, 1961; Ernest B. Cotlove Meml. lectr. Acad. Clin. Lab. Physicians and Scientists, 1972; named Alumnus of Yr., Walla Walla Coll., 1984, Honored Alumnus, Loma Linda U. Sch. Medicine, 1987, Humanitarian award, 1991, Citizen of Yr., C. of C. of Loma Linda, 1997. Fellow Am. Soc. Clin. Pathologists, Am. Soc. Hematology, Coll. Am. Pathologists, FDA Panel on Hematology and Palhology Devices, Nat. Com. on Clin. Lab. Standards, Internat. Commn. for Standards in Hematology (pres.), N.Y. Acad. Scis.; mem. AMA, Calif. Soc. Pathologists, San Bernadino County Med. Soc. (William C. Cover Outstanding Contbn. to Medicine award 1994), Acad. Clin. Lab. Physicians and Scientists, Am. Assn. Pathologists, Sigma Xi, Alpha Omega Alpha. Seventh-day Adventist. Achievements include patents in field of blood analysis instrumentation; development of quality control algorithms for blood analyzer calibration; origination of techniques and instrumentation for the measurement of thrombosis risk and for regulation of anti-coagulation during cardiopulmonary bypass. Office: Loma Linda U Sch Medicine 11234 Anderson St Loma Linda CA 92354-2871 E-mail: bbull@som.llu.edu

BULL, HENRIK HELKAND, architect; b. N.Y.C., July 13, 1929; s. Johan and Sonja (Geelmuyden) B.; m. Barbara Alpaugh, June 9, 1956; children: Peter, Nina. B.Arch., Mass. Inst. Tech., 1952. With Mario Corbett, San Francisco, 1954-55; pvt. practice, 1956-68; ptnr. Bull, Field, Volkmann, Stockwell, Calif., 1968-82, Bull, Volkmann, Stockwell, Calif., 1982-90, Bull Stockwell and Allen, Calif., 1990-93, Bull, Stockwell, Allen & Ripley, San Francisco, 1993-96, BSA Architects, San Francisco, 1996—. Vis. lectr. Syracuse U., 1963; Mem. adv. com. San Francisco Urban Design Study, 1970-71 Works include Sunset mag. Discovery House, Tahoe Tavern Condominiums, Lake Tahoe, Calif., Snowmass Villas Condominiums, Aspen, Colo., Northstar Master Plan Village and Condominiums, Moraga Valley Presbyn. Ch., Calif., Spruce Saddle Restaurant and Poste-Montane Hotel, Beaver Creek, Colo., Bear Valley visitor ctr., Point Reyes, Calif., The Inn at Spanish Bay, Pebble Beach, Calif., Taluswood Cmty., Whistler, B.C., Jackson Gore Village, Okemo, Vt. Served as 1st lt. USAF, 1952-54. Fellow AIA (pres. N. Calif. chpt. 1968, Firm award Calif. chpt. 1989) Democrat. Office: BSA Architects 350 Pacific Ave San Francisco CA 94111-1708

BULL, JAMES ROBERT, publishing executive; b. Evanston, Ill., Jan. 9, 1956; s. David C. and Mary Louise (Stowers) B.; m. Erin M. Mulligan, Nov. 30, 1991. BA, Colby Coll., 1978. Sponsoring editor Mayfield Pub. Co., Mount View, Calif., 1984-96; pres., pub. Bull Pub. Co., Palo Alto, 1994—. Office: Bull Pub Co 110 Gilbert Ave Menlo Park CA 94025-2865

BULL, VIVIAN ANN, college president; b. Ironwood, Mich., Dec. 11, 1934; d. Edwin Russell and Lydia (West) Johnson; m. Robert J. Bull, Jan. 31, 1959; children: R. Camper, W. Carlson. BA, Albion (Mich.) Coll., 1956; postgrad., London Sch. Econs., 1957; PhD, NYU, 1974. Economist Nat. Bank Detroit, 1955-59; with Bell Telephone Labs., Murray Hill, N.J., 1960-62; dept. econs. Drew U., Madison, 1960-92, assoc. dean, 1978-86; pres. Linfield Coll., McMinnville, Oreg., 1992—. Bd. dirs. Chem. Bank N.J., Morristown; trustee Africa U., Zimbabwe; treas. Joint Expedition to Caesareu Maritima Archaeology, 1971—. Author: Economic Study The West Bank: Is It Viable?, 1975. Trustee, assoc. Am. Schs. Oriental Rsch., 1982-90; trustee Colonial Symphony Soc., 1984-92, The Albright Inst. of Archaeol. Record; commr. Downtown Devel. Commn., Madison, 1986-92; mem. Univ. Sen. United Meth. Ch., 1989-96, gen. bd. higher edn., 1988-92; mem. planning bd. Coll. Bus. Adminstrn., Africa U., Zimbabwe, 1990-91; exec. com. Nat. Assn. Commns. on Salaries, United Meth. Ch., 1986-92. Fulbright scholar, 1956, Paul Harris fellow Rotary Internat., 1988; named Disting. Alumna Albion Coll., 1979; recipient Salute to Policy Makers award Exec. Women in N.J., 1986, John Woolman Peacemaking award George Fox Coll., 1994, Equal Opportunity award Urban League of Portland, 1995. Mem. Nat. Assn. Bank Women, Phi Beta Kappa. Avocations: archaeology, traveling, music. Address: Linfield Coll Office of the Pres 900 S Baker St Mcminnville OR 97128-6808

BULLERDICK, KIM H. petroleum executive; b. 1953; BA, Wittenberg U.; JD, U. Va. Gen. coun. Giant Industries, Inc., Scottsdale, Ariz., v.p., sec., subs. officer. Office: Giant Industries Inc 23733 N Scottsdale Rd Scottsdale AZ 85255-3466 Fax: 480-585-8893

BULLOCK, THEODORE HOLMES, biologist, educator; b. Nanking, China, May 16, 1915; s. Amasa Archibald and Ruth (Beckwith) B.; m. Martha Runquist, May 30, 1937; children: Elsie Christine, Stephen Holmes. Student, Pasadena Jr. Coll., 1932-34; A.B., U. Calif. at Berkeley, 1936, Ph.D., 1940; Sterling fellow zoology, Yale U., 1940-41, Rockefeller fellow exptl. neurology, 1941-42. Research assoc. Yale U. Sch. Medicine, 1942-43, instr. neuroanatomy, 1943-44; instr. Marine Biol. Lab., Woods Hole, Mass., 1944-46, head invertebrate zoology, 1955-57, trustee, 1955-57; asst. prof. anatomy U. Mo., 1944-46; asst. prof. zoology U. Calif. at Los Angeles, 1946, assoc. prof., 1948, prof., 1955-66; Brain Research Inst., U. Calif. at Los Angeles, 1960-66; prof. neurosci. Med. Sch., U. Calif. at San Diego, 1966-82, prof. emeritus, 1982—. Mem. AEC 2d Resurvey of Bikini Expdn., 1948. Author: (with G.A. Horridge) Structure and Function in the Nervous Systems of Invertebrates, 2 vols., 1965; (with others) Introduction to Nervous Systems, 1977; (with W. Heiligenberg) Electroreception, 1986 (with E. Basar) Brain Dynamics, 1989, (with E. Basar) Induced Rhythms in the Brain, 1992, How Do Brains Work?, 1993. Fulbright scholar Stazione Zooologica, Naples, 1950-51; fellow Center Advanced Study in Behavioral Scis., Palo Alto, 1959-60 Fellow AAAS; mem. NAS, Am. Soc. Zoologists (chmn. comparative physiology div. 1961, pres. 1965), Soc. Neurosci. (pres. 1973-74), Internat. Soc. Neuroethology (pres. 1984-86), Am. Physiol. Soc., Soc. Gen. Physiologists, Am. Acad. Arts and Scis., Am. Philos. Soc., Internat. Brain Research Orgn., Phi Beta Kappa, Sigma Xi. E-mail: tbullock@ucsd.edu

BUNCH, KARL, information technology company executive; Pres., gen. mgr. Think Tank Sys., LLC, Cerritos, Calif. Office: Think Tank Sys 17871 Park Plaza Dr Ste 100 Cerritos CA 90703

BUNCHMAN, HERBERT HARRY, II, plastic surgeon; b. Washington, Feb. 23, 1942; s. Herbert H. and Mary (Halleran) B.; m. Marguerite Fransioli, Mar. 21, 1963 (div. Jan. 1987); children: Herbert H. III., Angela K., Christopher; m. Janet C. Quinlan, Oct. 4, 1998. BA, Vanderbilt U., 1964; MD, U. Tenn., 1967. Diplomate Am. Bd. Surgery, Am. bd. Plastic Surgery. Resident in surgery U. Tex., Galveston, 1967-72, resident in plastic surgery, 1972-75; practice medicine specializing in plastic surgery Mesa, Ariz., 1975—; chief surgery Desert Samaritan Hosp., 1978-80. Contbr. articles to profl. jours. Eaton Clin. fellow, 1975. Mem. AMA, Am. Soc. Plastic Surgery, Am. Soc. Aesthetic Plastic Surgery, Singleton Surgical Soc., Tex. Med. Assn., So. Med. Assn. (grantee 1974), Ariz. Med. Assn. Office: Plastic Surgery Cons PC 1520 S Dobson Rd Ste 314 Mesa AZ 85202-4727 Fax: 480-833-2967. E-mail: office@bunchman.com

BUNDA, ROBERT, state legislator; b. Waialua, Hawaii, Apr. 25, 1947; mm. Gail Bunda; children: Rachel, Ryan, Ashley, Robson, James Robert. BS, Tex. Weslayan Coll., 1974; postgrad., U. Tex., 1975. Ind. businessman; ins. broker, 1979—; banking exec., 1973-79; mem. Hawaii Ho. of Reps., Honolulu, 1983-94, Hawaii Senate, Dist. 22, Honolulu, 1994—; vice chair transp. and intergovtl. affairs com. Hawaii Senate, Honolulu, mem. commerce and consumer protection com., mem. edn. and tech. com. Creator Hawaii's first ocean mgmt. plan; co-creator Hawaii Hurricane Relief Fund. Mem. Wahiawa Cmty. and Bus. Assn.; dir. West Oahu YMCA; mem. Wahiawa Gen. Hosp.; pres. Eames Kumiai Assn. With USAF; with Tex. ANG, Hawaii NG. Mem. Lions (Wahiawa club). Democrat. Office: State Capitol 415 S Beretania St Honolulu HI 96813-2407

BUNDE, CON, state legislator, communication educator; b. Mankato, Minn., Aug. 4, 1938; s. Ralph Louis and Leona Dorothy (Lehman) B.; m. Angelene Hammer, Aug. 22, 1964; children: Joy, Kurt. BA, Ctrl. Wash. U., 1966, MS, 1970; AA, Anchorage C.C., 1970. Cert. speech pathologist. Speech therapist Gig Harbor (Wash.) Schs., 1967-68, Anchorage Sch. Dist., 1968-70; asst. prof. speech comm. Anchorage C.C., 1970-88; prof. U. Alaska, Anchorage, 1988-93; mem. Alaska Ho. of Reps., Juneau, Anchorage, 1993—. Pilot Ketchum Air Svc., Anchorage, 1975—; seminar leader in field. Mem. citizens adv. coun. Dept. Fish and Game, Anchorage, 1991-92, instr. bowhunter edn. program; active Anchorage Community Theater; mem. citizen's adv. bd. U. Alaska Anchorage Aviation Airframe and Power Plant degree program. With U.S. Army, 1956-59. Mem. Alaska Sled Dog Racing Assn. (pres. 1970-78), Alaska Airmen's Assn., Alaska Bowhunter Assn. (bd. dirs. 1991-92), Alaska Sportfishing Assn., Alaska Outdoor Coun. Republican. Avocations: flying, fishing, hunting, sled dog racing, community theater. Office: Alaska State Legislature Ho of Reps 716 W 4th Ave Ste 410 Anchorage AK 99501-2107

BUNDERSON, HAROLD R. state legislator; b. Stone, Idaho; m. Mary Bunderson; 3 children. B. CPA. Acct., ptnr. Arthur Andersen & Co.; ret.; residential real estate developer; mem. Idaho Senate, Dist. 14, Boise, 1992—. Vice-chair transp. com.; mem. judiciary and rules, health and welfare, fin., and local govt. and tax. coms. Author: Idaho Entrepreneurs, Profiles in Business. Bd. mem., past pres., Ore-Ida Coun.; sch. bond election co-chair, Meridian/Eagle Sch. Dist., 1990; bd. mem., past pres., Boy Scouts Am., we. region; past pres., past gen. campaign chair, United Way of Ada County, Inc. Republican. Office: State Capitol PO Box 83720 Boise ID 83720-3720

BUNDGAARD, SCOTT, state legislator; b. Oklahoma City, Jan. 11, 1968; BS in Bus. Adminstrn., Grand Canyon U., 1990; postgrad., Wharton Sch. Bus., 1992, Ariz. State U., 1992. Prodr. Y95 Morning Zoo, 1989; asst. mgr. GAP, Inc., 1990-91; dir. tng. svcs. IBM and Manpower, 1991-94; stock broker Dean Witter Reynolds Inc.; mem. Ariz. Ho. of Reps., 1994-96, Ariz. Senate, Dist. 19, Phoenix, 1996—; mem. banking and ins. com., vice-chmn. econ. devel. com.; chmn. fin. com., mem. fin. instns. and retirement com.; mem. commerce agr. and natural resources com. Basketball coach Peoria Boys and Girls Club, Glendale Pks. and Recreation, Ariz. Youth Sports; bd. mem. Leadership West; exec. mem. Maricopa County Sheriff's Posse; H.S. youth group leader Calvary Cmty. Ch.; founding dir. Rotaract, 1989. Named Coach of the Yr., Kids Basketball Assn., 1994. Mem. Am. Legis. Exch. Coun. (banking and labor task force, banking, ins. and real estate task force), Coun. State Govts. Western Legis. Conf. (econ. devel./NAFTA com.). Republican. Office: State Capitol Bldg 1700 W Washington St Ofc 303 Phoenix AZ 85007-2812 E-mail: sbundgaa@azleg.state.az.us

BUNDRANT, CHARLES H. food products executive; Pres., CEO Trident Seafoods Corp., Seattle, 1973—. Office: Trident Seafoods Corp 5303 Shilshole Ave NW Seattle WA 98107-4000

BUNDY, ROBERT CHARLES, prosecutor; b. Long Beach, Calif., June 26, 1946; s. James Kenneth and Kathleen Ilene (Klosterman) B.; m. Virginia Bonnie Lembo, Feb. 3, 1974; 2 children. BA cum laude, U. So. Calif., L.A., 1968; JD, U. Calif., Berkeley, 1971. Bar: Alaska 1972, Calif. 1972. Supervising atty. Alaska Legal Svcs. Corp., Nome, Alaska, 1972-75; dist. atty. Second Jud. Dist., Nome, 1975-78; asst. dist. atty. Alaska Dept. Law, 1978-80, asst. atty. gen. antitrust sect., 1980-82; chief asst. dist. atty. Alaskan Dept. Law, Anchorage, 1982-84; ptnr. Bogle & Gates, Anchorage, 1984-94; now U.S. atty. for Alaska dist. U.S. Dept. Justice, Anchorage, 1994—. Mem. Trout Unlimited, Alaska Flyfishers. Office: Office US Atty for Alaska Rm C-253 222 W 7th Ave Unit 9 Anchorage AK 99513-7504

BUNKER, JOHN BIRKBECK, cattle rancher, retired sugar company executive; b. Yonkers, N.Y., Mar. 28, 1926; s. Ellsworth and Harriet (Butler) B.; m. Emma Cadwalader, Feb. 27, 1954. BA, Yale U., 1950. With Nat. Sugar Refining Co., 1953-62; pres. Gt. Western Sugar Co., Denver, [illegible] chmn., CEO, 1971-81; pres., CEO Calif. and Hawaiian Sugar Co., San Francisco, 1981-88, vice chmn., 1988-89, ret., 1989; gen. ptnr. Bunker Ranch Co., 1989—; chmn. Wheatland Bankshares and First State Bank of Wheatland, 1992-99, dir. emeritus. Trustee Colo. Coll., 1973-94; trustee emeritus Asia Found., 1985-94. Mem. Wyo. Nature Conservancy, Wyo. Stockgrowers Assn., Wyo. Heritage Found. Home: 1451 Cottonwood Ave Wheatland WY 82201-3412

BUNN, PAUL A., JR. oncologist, educator; b. N.Y.C., Mar. 16, 1945; s. Paul A. Bunn; m. Camille Ruoff, Aug. 17, 1968; children: Rebecca, Kristen, Paul H. BA cum laude, Amherst Coll., 1967; MD, Cornell U., 1971. Diplomate Nat. Bd. Med. Examiners, Am. Bd. Internal Medicine, Am. Bd. Med. Oncology. Intern U. Calif., H.C. Moffitt Hosp., San Francisco, 1971-72, resident, 1972-73; clin. assoc. medicine br. Nat. Cancer Inst., NIH, Bethesda, Md., 1973-76; sr. investigator med. oncology br. Nat. Cancer Inst., Washington VA Hosp., 1976-81; asst. prof. medicine med. sch. Georgetown U., 1978-81; head cell kinetic sect., Navy med. oncology br. Nat. Cancer Inst., Bethesda, 1981-84; assoc. prof. medicine uniformed svcs. Univ. Health Scis., Bethesda, 1981-84; prof. medicine health scis. ctr. U. Colo., Denver, 1984—, head divsn. med. oncology, 1984-94, dir. cancer ctr., 1987—. Instl. rev. bd. NIH, Nat. Cancer Inst., 1982-84; intramural support contract rev. com. Nat. Cancer Inst., 1982-84; cancer com. U. Colo., 1984—, faculty senate health scis. ctr., 1985—, exec. com. sch. medicine, 1987—; med. bd. Univ. Hosp., 1987—; external sci. advisor cancer ctr. U. Miami, 1988-92, U. Ark., 1989-94, U. Va., 1991-94, others; oncology drug adv. com. FDA, 1992-96; sci. secretariat 7th World Conf. Lung Cancer, 1994; bd. dirs. Univ. Hosp. Resource Coun.; oncology drug adv. com. FDA, 1992-96. Author: Carboplatin (JM-8) Current Perspectives and Future Directions, 1990, Clinical Experiences With Platinum and Etoposide Therapy in Lung Cancer, 1992, (with M.E. Wood) Hematology/Oncology Secrets, 1994; assoc. editor Med. and Pediatric Oncology, 1984—, Jour. Clin. Oncology, 1991—, Cancer Rsch., 1992—, others; contbr. chpts. to books and articles to profl. jours. Bd. dirs. Colo. divsn. Am. Cancer Soc., 1989—, Leukemia Soc. Am., 1991—; bd. dirs. The Cancer Venture, 1993-94, Fair Share Colo., 1993-94; chmn. Solid Tumor Oncology Edn. Found., 1996—. With USPHS, 1973-84. Decorated Medal of Commendation; recipient Sci. of Yr. award Denver chpt. ARCS, 1992; named one of 400 Best Drs. in Am., Good Housekeeping Mag., 1991, 92; grantee Schering Plough, 1988-89, Burroughs Wellcome, 1991—, Bristol-Myers Squibb, 1993—, others. Fellow ACP; mem. AAAS, Am. Soc. Hematology (mem. sci. subcom. neoplasia 1989-92), Am. Assn. Cancer Rsch., Am. Soc. Clin. Oncology (chair program subcom. 1985-86, 90, pres.-elect 2001—), Am. Fedn. Clin. Rsch., Am. Assn. Cancer Insts. (bd. dirs. 1992—), Internat. Assn. Study Lung Cancer (bd. dirs. 1988—, pres. 1994-97), Western Assn. Physicians, S.W. Oncology Group, Lung Cancer Study Group, Alpha Omega Alpha. Office: U Colo Cancer Ctr Box B188 4200 E 9th Ave Denver CO 80220-3706

BUNNETT, JOSEPH FREDERICK, chemist, educator; b. Portland, Oreg., Nov. 26, 1921; s. Joseph and Louise Helen (Boulan) B.; m. Sara Anne Telfer, Aug. 22, 1942; children: Alfred Boulan, David Telfer, Peter Sylvester (dec. Sept. 1972). BA, Reed Coll., 1942; PhD, U. Rochester, 1945. Mem. faculty Reed Coll., 1946-52, U. N.C., 1952-58; mem. faculty Brown U., 1958-66, prof. chemistry, 1959-66, chmn. dept., 1961-64; prof. chemistry U. Calif., Santa Cruz, 1966-91, prof. emeritus, 1991—. Erskine vis. fellow U. Canterbury, N.Z., 1967; vis. prof. U. Wash., 1956, U. Wurzburg, Germany, 1974, U. Bologna, Italy, 1988; rsch. fellow Japan Soc. for Promotion of Sci., 1979; Lady Davis vis. prof. Hebrew U., Jerusalem, Israel, 1981; mem. adv. coun. dept. chemistry Princeton (N.J.) U., 1985-89; mem. NRC com. on alternative chem. demilitarization techs., 1992-93; mem. Dept. Def. panel on Gulf War Health Effects, 1993-94; co-chmn. peer rev. com. Russian-Am. Joint Evaluation Program, 1995-97; co-chmn. NATO Advanced Rsch. Workshop on Chem. Problems Associated with Old Arsenical and Mustard Munitions, Lodz, Poland, 1996; working group chem. weapons destruction, scientific adv. bd. Orgn. Prohibition Chem. Weapons, 1999—. Co-editor: Arsenic and Old Mustard: Chemical Problems in the Destruction of Old Arsenical and Mustard Munitions, 1998; contbr. articles to profl. jours. Trustee Reed Coll., 1970-97, trustee emeritus, 1997—. Fulbright scholar U. Coll., London, 1949-50, U. Munich, 1960-61; Guggenheim fellow U. Munich, 1960-61; recipient James Flack Norris award in phys. organic chemistry Am. Chem. Soc., 1992; named hon. mem. Societa Chimica Italiana. Fellow AAAS; mem. Am. Acad. Arts and Scis., Am. Chem. Soc. (editor jour. Accounts of Chem. Rsch. 1966-86), Royal Soc. Chemistry (London), Internat. Union Pure and Applied Chemistry (chmn. commn. phys. organic chemistry 1978-83, sec. organic chemistry divsn. 1981-83, v.p. 1983-85, pres. 1985-87, chmn. task force on sci. aspects of destruction of chem. warfare agts. 1991-95, chmn. com. on chem. weapon destruction 1995—), Pharm. Soc. Japan (hon.), Acad. Gioenia (U. Catania, hon.), Soc. Argentina de Investigaciones en Quimica Organica (hon.). Home: 608 Arroyo Seco Santa Cruz CA 95060-3148 Office: U Calif Dept Chemistry Santa Cruz CA 95064 Fax: 831-459-2935. E-mail: bunnett@chemistry.ucsc.edu

BUNTING, KENNETH FREEMAN, newspaper editor; b. Houston, Dec. 9, 1948; s. Willie Freeman and Sarah Lee (Peterson) B.; m. Juliana Amy Jafvert, July 13, 1989; 1 child, Maxwell Freeman. Student, U. Mo., 1966-67; AA in Journalism, Lee Coll., 1968; BA in Journalism and History, Tex. Christian U., 1970; advanced exec. program, Northwestern U., 1996. Mgmt. trainee, reporter Harte-Hanks Newspapers Inc., Corpus Christi, Tex., 1970-71; reporter, then copy editor San Antonio Express-News, 1971-73; exec. asst. to Hon. G.J. Sutton Tex. Ho. of Reps., San Antonio, 1973-74; reporter Cin. Post, 1974-78, Sacramento Bee, 1978; reporter, asst. city editor, state capitol corr. L.A. Times, 1978-87; capitol bur. chief, city editor, dep. mng. editor, sr. editor Ft. Worth Star-Telegram, 1987-93; mng. editor Seattle Post-Intelligencer, 1993-99; exec. editor Seattle Post-Intelligence, 2000—. Journalism instr. Orange Coast Coll., Costa Mesa, Calif., 1981-82; mem. adv. bd. Maynard Inst., Oakland, Calif., 1994—. Bd. dirs. Seattle Symphony, 1995-97; mem. commn. Woodland Park Zoo, Seattle, 1995-96, 98; mem. Leadership Ft. Worth; former mem. journalism adv. bd. Tex. Christian U.; former mem. minorities task force Assn. for Edn. in Journalism and Mass Comms.; past pres. Press Club, Orange County, Calif.; past bd. dirs. Covington (Ky.) Cmty. Ctr.; past 1st v.p. Young Dems. of Tex.; past treas., mem. exec. bd. Freedom of Info. Found. of Tex.; leadership coun. ARC; bd. dirs. Alfred Friendly Press Fellowships. Mem. Nat. Assn. Black Journalists, AP Mng. Editors Assn. (mem. ethics com. 1995-96, bd. dirs. 1996-99), Am. Soc. Newspaper Editors (mem. diversity, leadership coms., chair edn. com., bd. dirs. 1999—), Soc. Profl. Journalists (bd. dirs. western Wash. chpt. 1995-96), Seattle C. of C. (mem. cmty. devel. roundtable 1994—), Alliance for Edn. (bd. dirs.), Tex. Christian U. Alumni Assn. (bd. dirs.), Freedom of Info. Found. Tex., Rainier Club, Washington Athletic Club. Unitarian. Avocations: tennis, bridge, reading. Office: Seattle-Post Intelligencer PO Box 1909 101 Elliott Ave W Seattle WA 98111

BUNTING, ROBERT LOUIS, accounting firm executive, management consultant; b. Sacramento, Oct. 29, 1945; married; 3 children. BS in Acctg., U. Idaho, 1968. With Price Waterhouse & Co., 1968-72, Moss Adams, LLP, Seattle, 1972—, pres., 1981—. Named one of 100 Most Influential Businessmen in Seattle, Seattle Bus. Jour., one of 100 Most Influential Accts. in Am., Accts. Today. Office: Moss Adams LLP 1001 4th Ave Ste 2830 Seattle WA 98154-1161

BUNZEL, JOHN HARVEY, political science educator, researcher; b. N.Y.C., Apr. 15, 1924; s. Ernest Everett and Harriett (Harvey) B.; m. Barbara Bovyer, May 11, 1963; children— Cameron, Reed A.B., Princeton U., 1948; M.A., Columbia U., 1949; Ph.D., U. Calif.-Berkeley, 1954; [illegible] 1953-56, 63-70, vis. scholar Ctr. Advanced Study in Behavioral Scis., 1969-70; mem. faculty Mich. State U., East Lansing, 1956-57, Stanford U., Calif., 1957-63; pres. San Jose State U., 1970-78; sr. research fellow Hoover Inst. Stanford U., 1978—. Mem. U.S. Commn. on Civil Rights, 1983-86. Author: The American Small Businessman, 1962; Anti-Politics in America, 1967; Issues of American Public Policy, 1968; New Force on the Left, 1983, Challenge to American Schools: The Case For Standards and Values, 1985, Political Passages: Journeys of Change Through Two Decades 1968-1988, 1988, Race Relations on Campus: Stanford Students Speak, 1992; contbr. articles to profl. jours., popular mags., newspapers. Weekly columnist San Jose Mercury-News. Bd. dirs. No. Calif. Citizenship Clearing House, 1959-61; mem. Calif. Atty. Gen.'s Adv. Com., 1960-61; del. Calif. Democratic Conv., 1968; del. Dem. Nat. Conv., 1968 Recipient Presdl. award No. Calif. Polit. Sci. Assn., 1969, cert. of Honor San Francisco Bd. Suprs., 1974, Hubert Humprey Pub. Policy award Policy Studies Orgn., 1990; grantee Ford Found., Rockefeller Found., Rabinowitz Found. Mem. Am. Polit. Sci. Assn. Home: 1519 Escondido Way Belmont CA 94002-3634 Office: Stanford U Hoover Inst Stanford CA 94305

BURAS, NATHAN, hydrology and water resources educator; b. Barlad, Romania, Aug. 23, 1921; came to U.S., 1947; s. Boris and Ethel (Weiser) B.; m. Netty Stivel, Apr. 13, 1951; 1 child, Nir H. BS with highest honors, U. Calif., Berkeley, 1949; MS, Technion, Haifa, Israel, 1957; PhD, UCLA, 1962. Registered profl. engr., Israel. Prof. hydrology and water resources Technion, 1962-80, dean, 1966-68; vis. prof. Stanford (Calif.) U., 1976-81; prof., head of dept. hydrology and water resources U. Ariz., Tucson, 1981-89, prof. hydrology and water resources, 1989—. Vis. prof. Technical U. Valencia, Spain, 1998; cons. Tahal, Ltd., Tel Aviv, 1963-73, World Bank, Washington, 1972-76, 79-82, Regional Municipality of Waterloo, Ont., Can., 1991-93, U.S. AID, Washington, 1992-93, Great No. Paper Co., 1992—, Inner Mongolia Assn. for Sci. and Tech., China, 1993-99; apptd. mem. standing com. on terminology Internat. Glossary of Hydrology UNESCO, 1996. Author: Scientific Allocation of Water Resources, 1972; editor: Control of Water Resources Systems, 1976, Management of Water Resources in North America, 1995, Reflections on Hydrology, 1997. Mem. Israel-Mex. Mixed Commn. on Sci. Cooperation, 1976, So. Ariz. Water Resource Assn., 1982—; active Pugwash Workshops, 1991, 92, 93. Named Laureat du Congres, Internat. Assn. Agrl. Engrng., 1964; recipient Cert. of Appreciation, USDA., 1970, award for Edn. and Pub. Svc. in Water Resources U. Coun. on Water Resources, 1994, award for Excellence Gov. of Ariz., 1995. Fellow ASCE (life), Ariz.-Nev. Acad. Sci., Internat. Water Resources Assn.; mem. Am. Geophys. Union, Am. Water Resources Assn. (charter). Jewish. Avocations: music, hiking. Home: 5541 E Circulo Terra Tucson AZ 85750-1003 Office: U Ariz Dept Hydrology And Water Res Tucson AZ 85721-0001 E-mail: buras@hwr.arizona.edu

BURAS-ELSEN, BRENDA ALLYNN, retired public affairs executive; b. New Orleans, May 1, 1954; d. Allen Anthony and Gloria Violet (Short) B. BA in Commerce, Loyola U., New Orleans, 1976, MBA, 1984. Stenographer Texaco Inc., New Orleans, 1974-76, engr.'s asst., 1976-78, natural gas contracts analyst, 1978-80, pub. affairs asst., 1980-83, pub. and govt. affairs coord. S.E. region, 1983-89; banking officer, mgr. pub. rels. and mktg. promotion Alerion Bank, New Orleans, 1990, asst. v.p., cmty. reinvestment act officer, 1990; pub. affairs advisor Mobil Oil Corp., Chalmette, La., 1990-92; rep. western region Multi-Quest Internat., Inc., 1992. Cert. lectr. Silva Method Mind Devel. and Stress Control. Prodr. Bringing Out the Best Awards Show, 1988. Loaned exec. United Way Greater New Orleans, 1978, mem. speakers bur., 1979-83, vol. leadership devel. program, 1987; voting commr. St. Bernard Parish, 1976-80; chmn. subcom. United Way Corp. Recognition/Thank-You, 1988-89; vice chair yr.-round comm. com. United Way, 1989-90, external comm. com., 1990; mem. ctrl. svc. budget com., 1990; host media com. Rep. Conv., 1988; chair pub. rels. com., mem. grants and membership coms., bd. dirs. New Orleans Food Bank for Emergencies, 1989, bd. dirs., vice chair comm. com., mem. edn. svcs. com.; bd. dirs. Met. Area Com., 1991, Jefferson Performing Arts Soc., 1992, Friend of 4-H, St. Bernard Parish, 1992; mem. St. Bernard adv. coun. United Way Greater New Orleans, 1991-92, prodr. Saints Pre-game show, 1991; mem. adv. coun. Family Svc., 1991-92; mem. edn. com. Tacoma Art Mus. Named Outstanding Comm. Com. Vol., United Way, 1988. Mem. Assistance League. Republican. E-mail: nolalac@ez2.net

BURATTI, BONNIE J. aerospace scientist; b. Bethlehem, Pa., Mar. 24, 1953; d. Ralph J. and Hildegard M. (Singles) B.; children: Nathan, Reuben, Aaron. MS, MIT, 1976, Cornell U., 1980, PhD, 1983. Summer intern Maria Mitchell Observatory, Nantucket, Mass., 1973; assoc. scientist Am. Sci. and Engrng., Cambridge, 1974-76; rsch. asst. MIT, Cambridge, 1977-83; rsch. and teaching asst. Cornell U., Ithaca, N.Y., 1977-83; post-doctoral Jet Propulsion Lab. Calif. Inst. Tech., Pasadena, 1983-85, rsch. scientist Jet Propulsion Lab., 1985—. Cons. NASA, Washington, 1989—. Contbr. articles to profl. jours. Mem. MIT Ednl. Coun., Internat. Astro. Union, Am. Astro. Soc., Am. Women in Sci., Am. Geophys. Union. Office: Calif Inst Tech Jet Propulsion Lab 4800 Oak Grove Dr # 501 Pasadena CA 91109-8001

BURATTO, STEVEN K. chemistry educator; b. Clarkston, Wash., Dec. 3, 1964; s. Steven A. and Beth B. (Anderson) B.; m. Lauro Oliver, July 21, 1990; 1 child, William R. BS magna cum laude, U. Puget Sound, 1987; PhD, Calif. Inst. Tech., 1992. Mem. tech. staff AT&T Bell Labs., Murray Hill, N.J., 1992-94; asst. prof. chemistry U. Calif., Santa Barbara, 1994—. Contbr. articles to sci. jours. Recipient Henry and Camille Dreyfus New Faculty award Henry and Camille Dreyfus Found., 1994; trustee scholar U. Puget Sound, 1983-87, Wyatt meml. scholar, 1986-87; scholar AT&T Bell Labs., 1989-92. Mem. AAAS, Am. Phys. Soc., Phi Beta Kappa. Office: U Calif Dept Chemistry Santa Barbara CA 93106

BURBIDGE, E. MARGARET, astronomer, educator; b. Davenport, Eng. d. Stanley John and Marjorie (Stott) Peachey; m. Geoffrey Burbidge, Apr. 2, 1948; 1 child, Sarah. B.S., Ph.D., U. London; Sc.D. hon., Smith Coll., 1963, U. Sussex, 1970, U. Bristol, 1972, U. Leicester, 1972, City U., 1973, U. Mich., 1978, U. Mass., 1978, Williams Coll., 1979, SUNY, Stony Brook, 1985, Rensselaer Poly. Inst., , 1986, U. Notre Dame, 1986, U. Chgo., 1991. Mem. staff U. London Obs., 1948-51; rsch. fellow Yerkes Obs. U. Chgo., 1951-53, Shirley Farr fellow Yerkes obs., 1957-59, assoc. prof. Yerkes Obs., 1959-62; rsch. fellow Calif. Inst. Tech., Pasadena, 1955-57; mem. Enrico Fermi Inst. for Nuclear Studies, 1957-62; prof. astronomy dept. physics U. Calif. San Diego, 1964—; dir. Royal Greenwich Obs. (Herstmonceux Castle), Hailsham, Eng., 1971-73; univ. prof. U. Calif., San Diego, 1984-91, prof. emeritus, 1991—, rsch. prof. dept. physics, 1990—. Lindsay Meml. lectr. Goddard Space Flight Ctr., NASA, 1985; Abby Rockefeller Mauze prof. MIT, 1968; David Elder lectr. U. Strathclyde, 1972; V. Gildersleeve lectr. Barnard Coll., 1974; Jansky lectr. Nat. Radio Astronomy Observatory, 1977; Brode lectr. Whitman Coll., 1986. Author: (with G. Burbidge) Quasi-Stellar Objects, 1967; editor: Observatory mag., 1948-51; mem. editorial bd.: Astronomy and Astrophysics, 1969-85. Recipient (with husband) Warner prize in Astronomy, 1959, Bruce Gold medal Astronomy Soc. Pacific, 1982; hon. fellow Univ. Coll., London, Girton Coll., Lucy Cavendish Coll., Cambridge; U.S. Nat. medal [illegible] medal World Cultural Coun., 1988. Fellow Royal Soc., Nat. Acad. Scis. (chmn. sect. 12 astronomy 1986), Am. Acad. Arts and Scis., Royal Astron. Soc.; mem. Am. Astron. Soc. (v.p. 1972-74, pres. 1976-78; Henry Norris Russell lectr. 1984), Internat. Astron. Union (pres. commn. 28 1970-73), Grad. Women Sci. (nat. hon. mem.) Office: U Calif-San Diego Ctr Astrophysics Space Scis Mail Code # 0424 La Jolla CA 92093 E-mail: [illegible]

BURBIDGE, GEOFFREY, astrophysicist, educator; b. Chipping Norton, Oxon, Eng., Sept. 24, 1925; s. Leslie and Eveline Burbidge; m. Margaret Peachey, 1948; 1 dau. B.Sc. with spl. honors in Physics, Bristol U., 1946; Ph.D., U. Coll., London, 1951. Asst. lectr. U. Coll., London, 1950-51; Agassiz fellow Harvard, 1951-52; research fellow U. Chgo., 1952-53, Cavendish Lab., Cambridge, Eng., 1953-55; Carnegie fellow Mt. Wilson and Palomar Obs., Calif. Inst. Tech., 1955-57; asst. prof. dept. astronomy U. Chgo., 1957-58, assoc. prof., 1958-62, U. Calif. San Diego, La Jolla, 1962-63, prof. physics, 1963-83, 88—; dir. Kitt Peak Nat. Obs., Tucson, 1978-84. Phillips vis. prof. Harvard U., 1968; bd. dirs. Associated Univs. Research in Astronomy, 1971-74; trustee Associated Univs., Inc., 1973-82 Author: (with Margaret Burbidge) Quasi-Stellar Objects, 1967, (with F. Hoyle and J. Narlikar) A Different Approach to Cosmology, 2000; editor Ann. Rev. Astronomy and Astrophysics, 1973—; sci. editor Astrophys. Jour., 1996—; contbr. articles to sci. jours. Fellow Royal Soc. London, Am. Acad. Arts and Scis., Royal Astron. Soc., Am. Phys. Soc.; mem. Am. Astron. Soc., Internat. Astron. Union, Astron. Soc. of Pacific (pres. 1974-76) Office: U Calif-San Diego 0424 Ctr Astrophysics Space Scis La Jolla CA 92093

BURCH, ROBERT DALE, lawyer; b. Washington, Jan. 30, 1928; s. Dallas Stockwell and Hepsy (Berry) B.; m. Joann D. Hansen, Dec. 9, 1966; children: Berkeley, Robert Brett, Barrett Bradley. Student, Va. Mil. Inst., 1945-46; B.S., U. Calif. at Berkeley, 1950, J.D., 1953. Bar: Calif. bar 1954. Since practiced in, Los Angeles and Beverly Hills; ptnr. Gibson, Dunn & Crutcher, 1961—. Lectr. U. So. Calif. Inst. Fed. Taxation, 1960, 62, 65, 75; guest lectr. U. Calif.-L.A. Law Sch., 1959; lectr. C.E.B. seminars U. Calif.; founder Robert D. Burch Ctr. for Tax Policy and Pub. Fin., U. Calif., Berkeley. Author: Federal Tax Procedures for General Practitioners; Contbr. profl. jours., textbooks. Bd. dirs. charitable founds. With AUS, 1945-47. Mem. Beverly Hills Bar Assn. (bd. govs., chmn. probate and trust com.), Law Trust, Tax and Ins. Council (past czar), Los Angeles World Affairs Council. Home: 1301 Delresto Dr Beverly Hills CA 90210-2100 Office: Gibson Dunn & Crutcher 2029 Century Park E Ste 4000 Los Angeles CA 90067-3032 also: 333 S Grand Ave Los Angeles CA 90071-1504

BURCHARD, JOHN KENNETH, chemical engineer; b. St. Louis, May 12, 1936; s. Kenneth Reginald and Vernora Emma (Angell) B.; m. Elizabeth Lee Suesserott, Aug. 23, 1958; children— John Christopher, Gregory Charles. B.S., Carnegie Mellon U., 1957, M.S., 1959, Ph.D., 1962. Head systems analysis group United Tech. Ctr., Sunnyvale, Calif., 1961-68; chief scientist Combustion Power Co., Menlo Park, 1968-70; lab. dir. EPA, Research Triangle Park, N.C., 1970-80; dir. chem. engring. div. Research Triangle Inst., Research Triangle Park, 1980-83; pres. Search Assocs., Inc., Chapel Hill, N.C., 1983-85; dir. Office of Research Adminstrn. U. Cen. Ark., Conway, 1985-87; asst. dir. Office Research Devel. Ariz. State U., Tempe, 1987-90; mgr. spl. projects Ariz. Dept. Environ. Quality, Phoenix, 1990-98, sr. sci. advisor, 1998-2001. Mem. bd. sci. advisors N.C. Energy Inst. Contbr. articles to profl. jours. Served with AUS, 1963-64. Shell Oil fellow, 1958-59; NSF fellow, 1960-61 Mem. Am. Inst. Chem. Engrs., Soc. Rsch. Adminstrs., Sigma Xi, Tau Beta Pi. Office: Ariz Dept Environ Quality Phoenix AZ 85012

BURD, STEVE, food service executive; b. 1949; BS, Carroll Coll., 1971; MA in Econs., U. Wis., 1973. With fin. and mktg. So. Pacific Transp. Co., San Francisco; with Arthur D. Little, N.Y.C., 1982-87; mgmt. cons., 1986-91; cons. Stop & Shop Cos., Boston, 1988-89, Fred Meyer Inc., Portland, Oreg., 1989-90, Safeway Inc., Oakland, Calif., 1986-87, 91—, pres., CEO, 1992—, chmn. bd. dirs. Office: Safeway Inc 5918 Stoneridge Mall Rd Pleasanton CA 94588-3229

BURDGE, RABEL JAMES, sociology educator; b. Columbus, Ohio, Dec. 14, 1937; s. Alonzo Marshall and Mariam Francis (Prentice) B.; m. Sharon Sue Payne, June 30, 1962 (dec. June 1975); children— Stephanie, Amy, Jill; m. Joyce Loretta Piggush, Aug. 2, 1977. BS, Ohio State U., 1959, MS, 1961; PhD, Pa. State U., 1965. Asst. prof. sociology U.S. Air Force Acad., Colo., 1966-68; lectr. U. Colo., Colorado Springs, 1966-68; asst. prof. sociology U. Ky., Lexington, 1968-72, assoc. prof., 1972-76; assoc. prof. environ. sociology, rural sociology, urban and regional planning and leisure studies; dept. agrl. econs. and leisure studies U. Ill. Inst. Environ. Studies, Urbana, 1976-80, prof., 1980-95; prof. emeritus U. Ill., 1996—; prof. sociology and environ. studies Western Wash. U., Bellingham, 1996— Vis. scholar Sch. of Australian Environ. Studies, Griffith U., Brisbane, 1982, 86, hon. prof., 1991—. Author (books): (with N. Cheek and D. Field) Leisure and Recreation Places, 1976, (with Paul Opryszek) Coping with Change: An Interdisciplinary Assessment of the Lake Shelbyville Reservoir, 1981, (with F.M. Rogers) Social Change in Rural Societies, A Rural Sociology Textbook, 3d edit., 1988, A Community Guide to Social Impact Assessment, 1998, 2d edit., 1999, A Conceptual Approach to Social Impact Assessment, 1994, 2d edit., 1998; editor Jour. Leisure Rsch., 1971-74; co-editor, founder: Leisure Scis., an Interdisciplinary Jour., 1977-82, Society and Nat. Resources: An Internat. Jour., 1988-98; co-editor Longman-Cheshire Internat. Environ. Studies Series, 1990—; contbr. articles to profl. publs. Served to capt. arty. U.S. Army, 1965-68. Recipient George B. Hartzog Jr. award for environ. rsch. Clemson U., 1995. Mem. AAAS, Am. Sociol. Assn., Rural Sociol. Soc. (v.p. 1982-83, treas. 1994-2000, editor The Rural Sociologist, 1994-2000, named Disting. Rural Sociologist, 1996), Nat. Recreation and Park Assn. (Theodore/Franklin D. Roosevelt award for outstanding rsch. 1982), Internat. Assn. for Impact Assessment (pres. 1990-91, treas. 1993-96, Rose-Hulman Inst. Tech. award for contbns. to impact assessment), Acad. Leisure Scis., Sigma Xi, Phi Kappa Phi, Gamma Sigma Delta, Alpha Kappa Delta. Democrat. Methodist. Home: PO Box 4056 Bellingham WA 98227-4056 Office: Western Wash U Dept Sociology Bellingham WA 98225-9081 E-mail: burdge@cc.wwu.edu

BURDGE, RICHARD JAMES, JR. lawyer; b. Long Beach, Calif., Dec. 4, 1949; children: Kristin Alexis, Lindsay Michelle, Margaret Lynn, Kelly Anne. BS, Yale U., 1972; JD, UCLA, 1979. Bar: Calif. 1979, U.S. Dist. Ct. (cen. dist.) Calif. 1979, U.S. Ct. Appeals (9th cir.) 1980, U.S. Dist. Ct. (no. dist.) Calif. 1984, U.S. Supreme Ct. 1984, U.S. Dist. Ct. (ea. dist.) Calif. 1987, U.S. Dist. Ct. (so. dist.) Calif. 1990. Assoc., then ptnr. Lillick, McHose & Charles, L.A., 1979-86; ptnr. Dewey Ballantine and predecessor firms, L.A., 1986—. Del. L.A. County Bar Del. to Calif. State Bar Conf. of Dels., 1988—. Mng. editor UCLA Law Rev., 1978-79, mem. editl. staff, 1977-78. Chmn. UCLA Law Ann. Fund, 1989-91; co-chair UCLA Law Libr. Alumni Campaign, 1994-97. Lt. USN, 1972-76. Mem. Assn. Bus. Trial Lawyers (gov. 1989-91, 93-95, ann. seminar chair 1992, jud. coll. chair 1995, treas. 1995-96, sec. 1996-97, v.p. 1997-98, pres. 1998-99), L.A. County Bar Assn. (trustee 1999—), Chancery Club. Office: Dewey Ballantine LLP 333 S Hope St Ste 3000 Los Angeles CA 90071-3039

BURDICK, GINNY, state legislator; b. Portland, Oreg., Dec. 3, 1947; BA, U. Puget Sound; M in Journalism, Oreg. U. Mem. Oreg. Legislature, Salem, 1996—. Democrat. Home: 4641 SW Dosch Rd Portland OR 97201-1244 Office: S-309 State Capitol Salem OR 97310-0001 E-mail: burdick.sen@state.or.us

BURDICK, ROBERT W. newspaper editor; b. Feb. 11, 1948; m. Patty Burnett; 1 child, David. B in Polit. Sci., Fla. Atl. U., 1969. Reporter Miami Herald, Fla. Today; night city editor Palm Beach (Fla.) Post; mng. editor Palm Beach Daily News; asst. mng. editor Wichita (Kans.) Eagle; city editor/metro editor/asst. to exec. editor San Jose (Calif.) Mercury News, 1978-82; asst. mng. editor Denver Post, 1982-84; asst. mng. editor/mng. editor/editor L.A. Daily News, 1984-94; mng. editor, editor Rocky Mountain News, Denver, 1994-98, pres., 1998—. Mem. Am. Soc. Newspaper Editors, Soc. Profl. Journalists, AP News Execs. Coun. (past bd. mem., past pres. Calif., Nev. chpt., past editor AP Mng. Editors News), Metro Denver C. of C. (bd. dirs.), NCCJ (bd. dirs. Denver chpt.). Avocations: skiing, hiking. Office: Rocky Mountain News 400 W Colfax Ave Denver CO 80204-2694

BURFORD, ANNE MCGILL, lawyer; b. Casper, Wyo., Apr. 21, 1942; d. Joseph John and Dorothy Jean (O'Grady) McGill; m. David Gorsuch, June 4, 1964 (div. 1982); children: Neil, Stephanie, J.J.; m. Robert Fitzpatrick Burford, Feb. 20, 1983 (dec. 1993). Student, Nat. U. Mex., 1955-56, 58, Regis Coll., Denver, 1959; BA, U. Colo., 1961, LLB, 1964. Bar: Colo. 1964, D.C. 1985. Asst. trust adminstr. 1st Nat. Bank of Denver, 1966-67; instr. Metro State Coll., 1966-67; asst. dist. atty. Jefferson County, 1968-71; dep. dist. atty. Denver, 1971-73; hearing officer Real Estate Commn., State Bds. Cosmetology, 1974-75; corp. counsel Mountain Bell Telephone Co., Denver, 1975-81; mem. Colo. Ho. of Reps., 1977-81, chmn. state affairs com., 1979-80, chmn. legal svcs. com., 1980; pvt. practice Denver, 1993—. Author: Are You Tough Enough, 1986. Del. Nat. Conf. State Legislators; mem. Nat. Conf. Commrs. on Uniform State Law, 1979, 80; presdl. del. to Kenya's Independence, 1983; loaned exec. mgmt. and efficiency task force Colo. Dept. Regulatory Agys., 1976; adminstr. EPA, Washington, 1981-83; former bd. dirs. YMCA; environ. cons. Fulbright scholar, Jaipur, India, 1964-65. Mem. Mortar Bd., Phi Alpha Delta, Delta Delta Delta. Republican. Roman Catholic. Home and Office: 3853 S Hudson St Denver CO 80237-1050

BURG, JOHN PARKER, signal processing executive; b. Great Bend, Kans., Dec. 17, 1931; s. Kenneth Edwin and Viola Mae (Parker) B.; m. Ida Elizabeth Groome; children Ida Elizabeth, Clarence Oscar Edwin; m. Shirley Joan Steele, Apr. 10, 1976; children: Nathan Parker, Emily Diane, Paul Andrew. BS in Physics, BA in Math., U. Tex., 1953; MS in Physics, MIT, 1960; PhD in Geophysics, Stanford U., 1975. Asst. engr. Tex. Instruments, Inc., 1956-57, engr., 1960; sr. rsch. geophysicist Geophys. Svc., Inc., Dallas, 1960-73; chmn. bd. dirs. Time and Space Processing, Inc., Santa Clara, Calif., 1973-83; pres. Entropic Processing, Inc., Cupertino, 1983—, also chmn. bd. dirs. Cons. oil cos., ESL, Inc., Naval Undersea Ctr., 1969-75; cons. Digicon, Inc., Houston, 1982-83; chmn. bd. dirs. Entropic Rsch. Lab., Washington, 1984-98, Entropic Speech Inc., 1984—. Inventor patent predictive seismic deconvolution, multi-channel filtering. Recipient Rsch. Publication award Naval Rsch. Lab., 1984; named Life Master Am. Contract Bridge League. Fellow IEEE (contbr. to jour.). Avocation: bridge theory. Office: Entropic Processing Inc 20990 Valley Green Dr Apt 703 Cupertino CA 95014-1846 E-mail: john.parker.burg@att.net

BURG, WALTER A. airport terminal executive; Gen. manager, CEO Tucson Airport Authority, Ariz., 1966-79, pres., CEO, 1979—. Office: Tucson Internat Airport 7005 S Plumer Ave Tucson AZ 85706-6926

BURGE, WILLARD, JR. software company executive; b. Johnson City, N.Y., Oct. 2, 1938; s. Willard Sr. and Catherine Bernice (Matthews) B.; m. Carol Crockenberg, June 16, 1961; children: Willard III, Pennie Lynn. Registered profl. engr., Ohio. Indsl. engr. Harnischfeger Corp., Escanaba, Mich., 1966-67; sr. indsl. engr. Gen. Electric, Ladson, S.C., 1968-74, advanced mfg. engr. Mentor, Ohio, 1971-74; corp. staff engr. Eaton Corp., Willoughby Hills, 1974-79, supr. N/C programming, 1979-80, supr. mfg. engring., 1980-82, mgr. mfg. systems engring., 1982-87; bus. unit mgr. MSC Products, Eaton Corp., Costa Mesa, Calif., 1987-91; pres., CEO CAM Software, Inc., Provo, Utah, 1991-93; chief exec. officer Key Svcs., Cypress, Calif., 1993—. Bd. dirs. CAM Software, Inc.; presenter in field. With U.S. Army, 1957. Mem. Soc. Mfg. Engrs. Republican. Avocations: photography, computers, start-up businesses. Home and Office: 6150 Geanie Ct Chino Hills CA 91709-6364 E-mail: wburgejr@msn.com

BURGER, EDMUND GANES, architect; b. Yerington, Nev., Mar. 28, 1930; s. Edmund Ganes and Rose Catherine (Kobe) B.; m. Shirley May Pratini, Jan. 21, 1968; 1 dau., Jane Lee. B.M.E., U. Santa Clara, 1951; B.Arch., U. Pa., 1959. Engr. Gen. Electric Co., 1951-52; design engr. U. Calif. Radiation Lab., 1952-57; John Stewardson fellow in architecture, 1959; architect Wurster, Bernardi & Emmons, San Francisco, 1960-63; founder Burger & Coplans, Inc. (Architects), San Francisco, 1964, pres., 1964-79; owner Edmund Burger (Architect), 1979—. Guest lectr. U. Calif., Berkeley. Important works include Acorn Housing Project, Oakland, Calif., Crescent Village Housing Project, Suisun City, Calif., Coplans residence, San Francisco, Betel Housing Project, San Francisco, Grand View Housing Project, San Francisco, Albany (Calif.) Oaks Housing, Grow Homes, San Pablo, Calif., Mariposa Housing, Dunleavy Plaza Housing, Potrero Ct. Housing, San Francisco, Lee residence, Kentfield, Calif., Burger residences, Lafayette, Calif., Oceanside, Oreg., and El Cerrito, Calif., Yamhill Valley Vineyards Winery, McMinneville, Oreg., Portico De Mar, shop and restaurant complex, Barcelona, Spain, Hendrickson residence, Newport Beach, Calif., Hamilton residence, Winters, Calif., Sanders residence, Yuba City, Calif.; author: Geomorphic Architecture, 1986. Recipient citation for excellence in community architecture AIA, 1969, award of merit AIA, award of merit Homes for Better Living, 1970, 79, 1st Honor award, 1973, 81, Holiday award for a beautiful Am., 1970, Honor award 4th Biennial HUD awards for design excellence, 1970, Bay Area awards for design excellence, 1969, 74, 78, Apts. of Year award Archtl. Record, 1972, Houses of Year award, 1973, Calif. Affordable Housing Competition award, 1981, HUD Building Value into Housing award, 1981, Community Design award Calif. Council AIA, 1986; design grant Nat. Endowment for Arts, 1980, HUD, 1980; constrn. grant HUD, 1981. Office: PO Box 10193 Berkeley CA 94709-5193

BURGER, EUGENE J. property manager; Pres., CEO Eugene Burger Mgmt. Corp., Greenbrae, Calif., 1979—. Office: Eugene Burger Mgmt Corp 481 Via Hidago Greenbrae CA 94904

BURGESS, CHARLES ORVILLE, history educator; b. Portland, Oreg., Jan. 18, 1932; s. Rex Orville and Glendora Almanda (Sundrud) B.; m. Cora Cloepfil, June 22, 1952; children: Donna Claire Majer, Jo Dell Nicholls, Robert Charles; m. Patricia Stewart Anderson, Apr. 22, 1976; children: Marc Richard Anderson, Brian Stewart Anderson, Tricia Louise Crozier, Kristen Anne Klein. BA, U. Oreg., 1957; MS (Danforth fellow), U. Wis., 1958, PhD, 1962; Nat. Postdoctoral fellow, Harvard U., 1967-68. Asst. prof. U. Calif., Riverside, 1962-64; asst. prof. history edn. U. Wash., Seattle, 1964-66, assoc. prof., 1966-70, prof., 1970—, chmn. area ednl. policy studies, 1970-92; prof. emeritus, 1992. V.p. div. F Am. Ednl. Research Assn., 1977-79; fgn. expert Peoples Republic of China, 1984-85. Author: The Origins of American Thought (published in China as Meiguo Sixiang Yuanyuan); 1988, (with M.L. Borrowman) What Doctrines to Embrace, 1969, Profile of an American Philanthropist (Nettie Fowler McCormick), 1962; co-editor: (with Charles Strickland) G. Stanley Hall on Natural Education, 1965; co-author: (with Y. Yang and G. Zhu) Cultivating the World of Selfhood (published in China as Kaituo Zi Wode Shijie), 1997. Mem. Wash. com. civil rights ACLU, 1965-67; bd. dirs. Seattle Folklore Soc., 1966— . Served in USAF, 1950-54. Mem. Orgn. Am. Historians, Am. Hist. Assn., History Edn. Soc. (pres. 1971-72), Assocs. for Research on Pvt. Edn. (trustee 1982-83), Phi Beta Kappa Home: 2111 SW 174th St Seattle WA 98166-3259

BURGESS, FRANKLIN DOUGLAS, judge; b. Eudora, Ark., Mar. 9, 1935; m. Treava Annette Whitted. BS in Engring., Gonzaga U., 1961, JD, 1966. Asst. city atty. City of Tacoma (Wash.), 1967-69; judge pro tem Mcpl. Ct. and Pierce County Dist. Ct., 1971-80; ptnr. Tanner & Burgess, Tacoma, 1971-76, Tanner, McGavick, Felker, Fleming, Burgess & Lazares, Tacoma, 1976-79, McGavick, Burgess, Heller & Foister, Tacoma, 1979-80; regional counsel Dept. Housing and Urban Devel., Seattle, 1980-81; U.S. magistrate judge U.S. Dist. Ct. (we. dist.) Wash., Tacoma, 1981-93, 95—; dist. judge U.S. Ct. Appeals (9th cir.), Tacoma, 1994-95. Resource person annual Nat. Black History Mo., Shiloh Bapt. Ch.; mem. Tacoma Urban League. Named NCAA All Am., 1961, Gonzaga U. Hall of Fame Basketball, 1989. Mem. Wash. State Bar Assn., Pierce County Bar Assn., Loren Miller Bar Assn., Nat. Conf. U.S. Magistrate Judges, NAACP. Office: US Dist Ct Union Station Courthouse 1717 Pacific Ave Ste 3124 Tacoma WA 98402-3234

BURGESS, LARRY EUGENE, library director, history educator; b. Montrose, Colo., July 18, 1945; s. Eugene Floyd and Edyth Eleanor (Faussone) B.; m. Charlotte Reid Gaylord, Oct. 7, 1973. BA, U. Redlands, 1967; MA, Claremont Grad. U., 1969, PhD, 1972. Cert. Acad. Archivists. Archivist A.K. Smiley Pub. Libr., Redlands, Calif., 1972-85, libr. dir., 1986—. Adj. prof. history U. Redlands, 1972—, U. Calif., Riverside, 1979—; book reviewer Lincoln Herald, 1988—. Author: Mohonk: Its People and Spirit, 1980; (with others) A Day with Mr. Lincoln, 1994; co-author: The Hunt for Willie Boy, 1994. Vice-chmn. Calif. Heritage Preservattion Commn., 1977-84; dir. Hist. Soc. So. Calif., L.A., 1984—; bd. dirs. U. Redlands, 1987-2001. Recipient Archival award of excellence Calif. Heritage Preservation Commn., 1991, Preservation Merit award Calif. Hist. Soc., 1992, Cmty. Enrichment award Hist. Soc. So. Calif., 1994. Mem. Soc. Am. Archivists, So. Calif. Archivists (past pres.), Zamorano Club (bd. dirs. 1994—, pres. 2001), Rotary (bd. dirs. Redlands, pres. 1999-2000). Avocations: travel, book collecting, gardening. Home: 923 W Fern Ave Redlands CA 92373-5877 Office: AK Smiley Pub Libr 125 W Vine St Redlands CA 92373-4728 E-mail: admin@aksmiley.org

BURGESS, LEONARD RANDOLPH, business administration and economics educator, writer; b. Washington, Mar. 8, 1919; s. W. Randolph and May Ayres B.; m. Virginia Frost, May 26, 1946 (dec. Feb. 1978); m. Marga Minnick, Dec. 26, 1979 (div. 1983); m. Hyon Suk Kim, Dec. 30, 1983 BA, Brown U., 1947; MBA, Harvard U., 1947; PhD, Columbia U., 1961; grad. officer course, U.S. Army Cmd. and Gen. Staff, 1968. Chief statistician W.Va. Pulp and Paper Co., N.Y.C., 1947-52; sr. staff assoc. Nat. Indsl. Conf. Bd., N.Y.C., 1952-57; lectr., instr. CCNY, N.Y.C., 1958-59; asst. prof. N. Tex. State U., Denton, 1961-64; assoc. prof. Tex. A&M U., College Station, 1964-68, prof., 1968-73; vis. prof. Temple U., Phila., 1973-74; part-time prof. U. Del., Wilmington, 1974-75; from lectr. to assoc. prof. San Francisco State U., 1975-78; prof. Lincoln U., San Francisco, 1978-87, head dept. bus. adminstrn. and econs., 1981-87, trustee, 1991-2000, prof. Bus. Adminstrn., 1994—, Oakland. Mem. Lang. Rsch. Inc., Cambridge, Mass., 1961-76; substitute tchr. San Mateo County Sch. Dist., 1991-93. Author: Five Operations with a Tank Destroyer Platoon, 1945, Top Executive Pay Package, 1963, Wage and Salary Administration in a Dynamic Economy, 1968, Wage and Salary Administration: Pay and Benefits, 1984, Compensation Administration, 1989, An Open Letter to the President-Elect: Recommendations for a New U.S. Medical System, 1992; co-author: (with Malcolm C. Neuhoff) Managing Company Airplanes, 1954. Staff asst. Brazos County Cmty. Action Com., Tex., 1966-72, Brazos Valley Cmty. Action Program, 1972-73; chmn. Hastings-on-Hudson (N.Y.) Citizens for Eisenhower campaign, 1952. 1st lt., U.S. Army, 1941-45, ETO; ret. lt. col. USAR. Decorated 5 Battle Stars. Mem. AAUP, NOW, Acad. Mgmt., Acad. Polit. Sci., Harvard Bus. Sch. Assn., Nat. Writers Union/UAW, 893d Tank Destroyer Bn. Veterans Orgn., Am. Legion, Delta Upsilon. Home: 899 Crestview Dr San Carlos CA 94070-3458

BURGESS, MARY ALICE (MARY ALICE WICKIZER), publisher; b. San Bernardino, Calif., June 21, 1938; d. Russell Alger and Wilma Evelyn (Swisher) Wickizer; m. Michael Roy Burgess, Oct. 15, 1976; children from previous marriage: Richard Albert Rogers, Mary Louise Rogers Reynnells. AA, Valley Coll., San Bernardino, 1967; BA, Calif. State U., San Bernardino, 1975, postgrad., 1976-79, U. Calif., Riverside, 1976-79. Lic. real estate salesman, Calif.; real estate broker, Calif. Sec.-treas. Lynwyck Realty & Investment, San Bernardino, 1963-75; libr. asst. Calif. State U., San Bernardino, 1974-76, purchasing agt., 1976-81; co-pub. The Borgo Press, San Bernardino, 1975-99; owner MilleFleurs Info. Svcs., 2000—. Co-pub: (with Robert Reginald) Science Fiction and Fantasy Book Review, 1979-80; co-author (with M.R. Burgess) The Wickizer Annals: The Descendents of Conrad Wickizer of Luzerne County, Pennsylvania, 1983, (with Douglas Menville and Robert Reginald) Futurevisions: The New Golden Age of the Science Fiction Film, 1985, (with Jeffrey M. Elliot and Robert Reginald) The Arms Control, Disarmament and Military Science Dictionary, 1989, (with Michael Burgess) The House of the Burgesses, 2d edit., 1994; author: The Campbell Chronicles: A Genealogical History of the Descendants of Samuel Campbell of Chester County, Pennsylvania, 1989, (with Boden Clarke) The Work of Katherine Kurtz, 1992-93, (with Michael Burgess and Daryl F. Mallett) State and Province Vital Records Guide; editor: Cranberry Tea Room Cookbook, Still The Frame Holds, Defying the Holocaust, Risen from the Ashes: A Story of the Jewish Displaced Persons in the Aftermath of World War II, Being a Sequel to Survivors (Jacob Biber), 1989, Ray Bradbury: Dramatist (Ben P. Indick), 1989, Across the Wide Missouri: The Diary of a Journey from Virginia to Missouri in 1819 and Back Again in 1821, with a Description of the City of Cincinnati, (James Brown Campbell), Italian Theatre in San Francisco, Into the Flames: The Life Story of a Righteous Gentile, Jerzy Kosinski: The Literature of Violation, The Little Kitchen Cookbook, Victorian Criticism of American Writers, 1990, The Magic That Works: John W. Campbell and The American Response to Technology, 1993, Libido into Literature: The "Primĕra Época" of Benito Pérez Galdós, 1993, A Triumph of the Spirit: Stories of Holocaust Survivors, 1994, A Way Farer in a World in Upheaval, 1993, William Eastlake: High Desert Interlocutor, 1993, The Price of Paradise: The Magazine Career of F. Scott Fitgerald, 1993, The Little Kitchen Cookbook, rev. edit., 1994, An Irony of Fate: William March, 1994, Hard-Boiled Heretic: Ross Macdonald, 1994, We The People!, 1994, The Chinese Economy, 1995, Voices of the River Plate, 1995, Chaos Burning on My Brow, 1995; co-editor and pub. (with Robert Reginald) of all Borgo Press publs.; also reviewer, indexer, researcher and editor of scholarly manuscripts. Chmn. new citizens Rep. Women, San Bernardino, 1967; libr. San Bernardino Geneal. Soc., 1965-67; vol. Boy Scout Am., Girl Scouts U.S., Camp Fire Girls, 1960s. Recipient Real Estate Proficiency award Calif. Dept. Real Estate, San Bernardino, 1966. Mem. City of San Bernardino Hist. and Pioneer Soc., Calif. State U. Alumni Assn., Cecil County (Md.) Hist. Soc., Gallia County (Ohio) Hist. and Geneal. Soc., DAR (membership and geneal. records chmn. 1964-66, registrar and vice regent San Bernardino chpt. 1965-67). Avocations: genealogy, hist. research, films, travel. Office: MilleFleurs PO Box 2845 Box 2845 San Bernardino CA 92406-2845

BURGESS, MICHAEL, library science educator, publisher; b. Fukuoka, Kyushu, Japan, Feb. 11, 1948; came to U.S., 1949; s. Roy Walter and Betty Jane (Kapel) B.; m. Mary Alice Wickizer, Oct. 15, 1976; stepchildren: Richard Albert Rogers, Mary Louise Reynnells AB with honors, Gonzaga U., 1969; MLS, U. So. Calif., 1970. Periodicals librarian Calif. State U., San Bernardino, 1970-81, chief cataloger, 1981-94, prof., 1984—, head tech. svcs. and collection devel., 1994—. Editor Newcastle Pub. Co., North Hollywood, Calif., 1971-92; pub. Borgo Press, San Bernardino, 1991-99, Brownstone Books, San Bernardino, 1991-99, Sidewinder Press, San Bernardino, 1991-99, Unicorn & Son, San Bernardino, 1991-99, Burgess &

Wickizer, San Bernardino, 1991-99, Emeritus Enterprises, 1993-99, Starmont House, 1993-99; assoc. editor SFRA Rev., 1993-94, Millefleurs Info. Svcs., San Bernardino, 2000—. Author 92 books and short works under pen names Michael Burgess, R(obert) Reginald, Boden Clarke, and others, with occasional co-authors, including: Stella Nova, 1970, Cumulative Paperback Index, 1939-1959, 1973, Contemporary Science Fiction Authors, 1975, The Attempted Assassination of John F. Kennedy, 1976, Things to Come, 1977, Up Your Asteroid!, 1977, Science Fiction and Fantasy Literature, a Checklist, 1700-1974, 1979, The Paperback Price Guide, 1980, 2nd edit., 1983, Science Fiction & Fantasy Awards, 1981, If J.F.K. Had Lived, 1982, The House of Burgesses, 1983, 2nd edit., 1994, The Wickizer Annals, 1983, Tempest in a Teapot, 1983, A Guide to Science Fiction & Fantasy in the Library of Congress Classification Scheme, 1984, 2nd edit., 1988, The Work of Jeffrey M. Elliot, 1984, Futurevisions, 1985, Lords Temperal & Lords Spiritual, 1985, 2nd edit., 1995, The Work of Julian May, 1985, The Work of R. Reginald, 1985, The Work of George Zebrowski, 1986, 2nd edit., 1990, 3rd edit., 1996, Mystery and Detective Fiction in the Library of Congress Classification Scheme, 1988, The Work of William F. Nolan, 1988, 2nd edit., 1998, The Arms Control, Disarmament, and Military Security Dictionary, 1989, Hancer's Price Guide to Paperback Books, 3d edit., 1990, Reginald's Science Fiction and Fantasy Awards, 2nd edit., 1991, 3d edit., 1993, Reference Guide to Science Fiction, Fantasy, and Horror, 1992, Science Fiction and Fantasy Literature, 1975-1991, 1992, The Work of Robert Reginald, 2nd edit., 1992, The State and Province Vital Records Guide, 1993, The Work of Katherine Kurtz, 1993, St. James Guide to Science Fiction Writers, 1996, CSUSB Faculty Authors, Composers and Playwrights, 1996, rev. edit., 1996, BP 250, 1996, Xenograffiti, 1996, Codex Derynianus, 1998, Katydid and other Critters, 2001; editor: Ancestral Voices, 1975, Alistair MacLean, 1976, Ancient Hauntings, 1976, Phantasmagoria, 1976, R.I.P., 1976, The Spectre Bridegroom and Other Horrors, 1976, John D. MacDonald and the Colorful World of Travis McGee, 1977, Dreamers of Dreams, 1978, King Solomon's Children, 1978, They, 1978, Worlds of Never, 1978, Science Fiction & Fantasy Book Review, 1980, Candle for Poland, 1982, The Holy Grail Revealed, 1982, The Work of Bruce McAllister, 1985, rev. edit., 1986, George Orwell's Guide Through Hell, 1986, 2nd edit., 1994, The Work of Charles Beaumont, 1986, 2nd edit., 1990, California Ranchos, 1988, The Work of Chad Oliver, 1989, The Work of Colin Wilson, 1989, The Work of Ian Watson, The Work of Reginald Bretnor, 1989, The Work of Ross Rocklynne, 1989, To Kill or Not To Kill, 1990, The Work of Dean Ing, 1990, The Work of Jack Dann, 1990, The Work of Pamela Sargent, 1990, 2nd edit., 1996, The Trilemma of World Oil Politics, 1991, The Work of Louis L'Amour, 1991, The Work of Brian W. Aldiss, 1992, Geo. Alec Effinger, 1993, Polemical Pulps, 1993, Sermons in Science Fiction, 1994, The Work of Elizabeth Chater, 1994, The Work of Jack Vance, 1994, The Work of William Eastlake, 1994, The Work of William F. Temple, 1994, The Work of Gary Brandner, 1995, The Work of Stephen King, 1996, Running From The Hunter, 1996; author of 6000 essays, 16 short stories; editor of 650 books. Recipient MPPP award, 1987, Lifetime Collectors award for Contbn. to Bibliography, 1993, Pilgrim award, 1993; named title II fellow U. So. Calif., 1969-70. Mem. NEA, AAUP, ALA, ACLU, Sci. Fiction and Fantasy Writers Am., Mystery Writers Am., Calif. Tchrs. Assn., Calif. Faculty Assn. (statewide librs. task force 1986-89, 93—, editor newsletter 1987-89), Calif. Libr. Assn., San Bernardino Hist. and Pioneer Soc., Internat. Assn. for Fantastic in Arts, Internat. PEN, U.S.A. Ctr. West, Nat. Geneal. Soc., Sci. Fiction Rsch. Assn., Horror Writers Am. Office: Millefleurs PO Box 2845 San Bernardino CA 92406-2845 also: Calif State U Libr 5500 University Pkwy San Bernardino CA 92407-2318

BURGHDORF, ROGER, business executive; Exec. v.p. leasing & ctr. mgmt. West Corp, Inc., L.A., 1989—. Office: West Crop Inc 11601 Wilshire Blvd Ste 1200 Los Angeles CA 90025-1748

BURGIN, GEORGE HANS, computer scientist, educator; b. Liestal, Switzerland, Feb. 13, 1930; s. Jakob and Fanny B.; m. Ulrike Franziska, July 8, 1960; children: Bernard, Claudia, Paul. Diplom ingenieur, Swiss Fed. Inst. Tech., Zurich, 1953, PhD, 1961. Registered profl. engr., Calif. Design specialist Gen. Dynamics Corp., San Diego, 1962-64; sr. scientist Decision Sci., San Diego, 1964-82; chief scientist Titan Systems, San Diego, 1982-94; prin. staff engr. Titan Info. Systems, 1994-96, chief engr., 1996-98; staff engr. CommQuest Techs., 1998-99, IBM/Emcinitas, 1999-2000, Triton Newtork Systems, 2000—. Lectr. San Diego State U., 1979-89. Contbg. author: Simulation, 1968, 2d edit., 1989; author, inventor air combat simulation program Adaptive Maneuvering Logic; contbr. articles to profl. jours. Served to 1st lt. Swiss Army. Mem. IEEE. Achievements include invention of adaptive maneuvering logic air combat simulation program. Home: 6284 Avenida Cresta La Jolla CA 92037-6505 Office: Triton Network Systems 539 Encinitas Blvd Encinitas CA 92024-3731 E-mail: gburgin@triton-network.com, gburgin@incom.net

BURKE, ARTHUR THOMAS, engineering consultant; b. Nov. 26, 1919; s. Daniel Michael and Naomi Edith (Brashear) B.; m. Regina Ahlgren Malone, June 15, 1972 (dec. July 1996); children: Arthur Thomas, Craig Timothy. BS, U.S. Naval Acad., 1941; postgrad., UCLA. With USN Electronics Lab. Ctr., San Diego, 1947-72, sr. satellite comms. cons., 1964-72, satellite comms. engring. cons., 1974—. Patentee electronic bathythermograph. Judge San Diego Sci. Fair, 1960—. Served to comdr. USN, 1941-46, ret. Recipient Presdl. Unit citation, 1942, 9 WWII battle stars, Superior Performance award USN Electronics Lab. Ctr., 1967. Mem. IEEE (mem. San Diego membership com. 1958-68), AAAS, San Diego Astronomy Assn., San Diego Computer Assn., Am. Radio Relay League. Home and Office: 4011 College Ave San Diego CA 92115-6704 E-mail: usscv6a@home.com

BURKE, CAMERON S. legal administration; b. Nov. 23, 1953; m. Barbara; 3 children. BA in History, U. Oreg., 1976; MS in Judicial Adminstrn., U. Denver, 1980. Calendar & courtroom clk. U.S. Dist. Ct., Idaho, 1976-79; trial court adminstr. Lincoln County Cir. & Dist. Cts., 1981-85; chief deputy clk. U.S. Dist. Ct., Ariz., 1985-89; court exec. U.S. Dist. & Bankruptcy Cts., Idaho, 1989—. Contbr. articles to profl. jours. Recipient Bob Christ award Fed. Court Clk. Assn., 1996; Chi Psi Ednl. scholar. Chi Psi Ednl. scholar. Mem. Am. Judicature Soc., Nat. Ctr. State Cts., Nat. Assn. Ct. Mgmt., Oreg. Assn. Ct. Adminstrn. (past pres.), Fed. Ct. Clks. Assn. (past pres., Bob Christ award 1996, Angie award 2000), Ariz. Cts. Assn. (past pres.). Office: US Dist & Bankruptcy Cts Fed Bldg & US Courthouse 550 W Fort St # 39 Boise ID 83724-0101

BURKE, EDMOND WAYNE, retired judge, lawyer; b. Ukiah, Calif., Sept. 7, 1935; s. Wayne P. and Opal K. B.; children from previous marriage: Kathleen R., Jennifer E.; m. Anna M. Hubbard, Dec. 29, 1990. A.B., Humboldt State Coll., 1957, M.A., 1958, J.D., U. Calif., 1964. Bar: Calif., Alaska, Mont. Individual practice law, Calif. and Alaska, 1965-67; asst. atty. gen. State of Alaska, 1967; asst. dist. atty. Anchorage, 1968-69; judge Superior Ct., 1970-75; justice Supreme Ct. State of Alaska, Anchorage, 1975-93, chief justice, 1981-84; of coun. Bogle & Gates, 1994-95; mem. Burke Bauermeister, Anchorage, 1996—. Republican. Presbyterian.

BURKE, JOHN JAMES, utility executive; b. Butte, Mont., July 25, 1928; m. [illegible] M. Colvert, July 17, 1953; children: [illegible] Burke Orizotti, Kathleen Novak, John James, III, Elisabeth Orizotti. BS in Bus., BA in Law, U. Mont., 1950, JD, 1952. Bar: Mont. 1952, U.S. Supreme Ct. 1957. Ptnr. Weir, Gough, Booth and Burke, Helena, 1954-59; atty. Mont. Power Co., Butte, 1959-67, v.p., 1967-78, exec. v.p., 1979-84, vice chmn. bd. dirs., 1984-93. Dir. Lazard Funds Inc., Pacific Steel & Recycling, Sletten Constrn. Co. Trustee U. Mont. Found., Carroll Coll., [illegible] Mont. Renaissance Fund Bus. Coun.; past pres. City County Planning Bd., 1966-78; past dir. Vigilante coun. Boy Scouts Am., Shining Mountains coun. Girl Scouts U.S.A.; vice chmn. Gov. Task Force/Renew Mont. Govt. Capt. JAGC, USAF, 1952-54, with Res., 1954-61. Mem. ABA (mem. coun. pub. utility law sect.), State Bar Mont., Silver Bow County Bar Assn., Mountain States Legal Found. (past bd. dirs.), Nat. Assn. Mfrs. (past bd. dirs.), Edison Electric Inst. (exec. adv. com. on planning), Butte C. of C. (v.p. 1965-72), U. Mont. Alumni Assn. (past bd. dirs.), Montana Club, Butte Country Club, Elks, Rotary (sec. Helena 1955-58), 116 Club (Washington), Phi Delta Phi. Roman Catholic. Home and Office: 50 Burning Tree Ln Butte MT 59701-3904 E-mail: jjburke@in-tch.com

BURKE, KATHLEEN J. foundation administrator; Exec. v.p., pers. rels. officer BankAmerica Corp., San Francisco, now vice chmn., pers. rel. officer; exec. dir. Stupski Family Found., Tiburan, Calif., 2000—. Office: Stupiski Family Found 9 Via Paraiso E Tiburon CA 94920

BURKE, KENNETH JOHN, lawyer; b. Washington, Aug. 23, 1939; s. John Lawrence and Edna Catherine B.; m. Judith Ann Blass (div. July 1979); children: Jill Shannon, Corey Edmund, Erin Elisabeth; m. Gay Ann Crosier, June 4, 1983; 1 child, John Tynan. BS in Physics, Coll. Holy Cross, 1961; JD, U. Denver, 1969. Bar: Colo. 1969, U.S. Dist. Ct. Colo. 1969, U.S. Ct. Appeals (10th cir.) 1969, U.S. Supreme Ct. 1977. Assoc. Fuller & Evans, Denver, 1969-71; trial atty. U.S. Dept. Justice, Denver, 1971-74; ptnr. Bermingham, White, Burke & Ipsen, Denver, 1974-77, Holme, Roberts & Owen, Denver, 1977-86, Burke & Burke, 1986-88, Massey, Burke & Showalter, 1988-90, Baker & Hostetler, Denver, 1990-99, Bennington Johnson & Reeve, Denver, 1999—. Contbr. numerous articles to legal jours. 1st lt. USAF, 1962-66. Mem. ABA (vice chmn. water resources com. 1987-92, energy and natural resources litigation com. 1986-87), Colo. Bar Assn. Republican. Avocations: astronomy, fly fishing. Office: Bennington Johnson & Reeve 370 17th St Ste 2480 Denver CO 80202-1371

BURKE, MARIANNE KING, state agency administrator, financial executive, consultant; b. Douglasville, Ga., May 30, 1938; d. William Horace and Evora (Morris) King; divorced; 1 child, Kelly Page. Student, Ga. Inst. Tech., 1956-59, Anchorage C.C., 1964-66, Portland State U., 1968-69; BBA, U. Alaska, 1976. CPA, Alaska. Sr. audit mgr. Price Waterhouse, 1982-90; v.p. fin., asst. sec. NANA Regional Corp., Inc., Anchorage, 1990-95; v.p. fin. NANA Devel. Corp., Inc., Anchorage, 1990-95; sec.-treas. Vanguard Industries, J.V., Anchorage, 1990-95, Alaska United Drilling, Inc., Anchorage, 1990-95; treas. NANA/Marriott Joint Venture, Anchorage, 1990-95; v.p. fin. Arctic Utilities, Inc., Anchorage, 1990-95, Tour Arctic, Inc., Anchorage, 1990-95, Purcell Svcs., Ltd., Anchorage, 1990-95, Arctic Caribou Inn, Anchorage, 1990-95, NANA Oilfield Svcs., Inc., Anchorage, 1990-95, NANA Corp. Svcs., Inc., Anchorage, 1992-95; dir. divsn. ins. State of Alaska, 1995-99; pres. Marianne K. Burke Cons., 1999—. Mem. State of Alaska Medicaid Rate Commn., 1985-88, State of Alaska Bd. Accountancy, 1984-87; bd. dirs. Nat. Assn. Ins. Commrs. Edn. and Rsch. Found.; cons. internat. ins. domicle. Bd. dirs. Alaska Treatment Ctr., Anchorage, 1978, Alaska Hwy. Cruises; treas. Alaska Feminist Credit Union, Anchorage, 1979-80; mem. fund raising com. Anchorage Symphony, 1981. Mem. AICPA, Internat. Assn. Ins. Suprs. (funded mem.), Alaska Soc. CPAs, Govtl. Fin. Officers U.S. and Can., Fin. Execs. Inst. (bd. dirs.), Nat. Assn. Ins. Commrs. (bd. dirs.). Avocations: travel, reading. Home: 3818 Helvetia Dr Anchorage AK 99508-5016 E-mail: mkburke@gateway.net

BURKE, RICHARD T., SR. professional sports team executive; b. Raleigh, N.C. m. Jude; children: Taylor, Ryan, Brendan, Ian, Shannon. Grad., Ga. State U., U. Va. Founder, chmn., CEO United HealthCare Corp., 1974-95; owner Winnipeg Jets Hockey Team, 1995; owner, CEO, gov. Phoenix Coyotes Hockey Team. Office: c/o Phoenix Coyotes Cellular One Ice Den 9375 E Bell Rd Scottsdale AZ 85260-1500

BURKE, TIMOTHY JOHN, lawyer; b. Syracuse, N.Y., June 5, 1946; s. Francis Joseph and Alice Marie Burke; m. Denise Kay Blied, Mar. 18, 1978; 1 child, Aimee Noel; 1 child from a previous marriage, Ryan Alexander. BA with distinction, Ariz. State U., 1967, JD cum laude, 1970. Bar: Ariz. 1970, U.S. Dist. Ct. Ariz. 1970, U.S. Ct. Appeals (9th cir.) 1974. Trial atty. Antitrust divsn. U.S. Dept. Justice, Washington, 1970-72, asst. to dir. ops., 1972-74; assoc. Fennemore Craig, Phoenix, 1974—, dir., 1978—. Part-time instr. legal writing Ariz. State U., 1974-75, adj. faculty assoc. profl. responsibility Coll. of Law, 2001. Mem. panel rev. bd. Phoenix United Way, 1975-76; bd. dirs. Florence Crittenton Svcs., Phoenix, 1980-88, pres., 1985-87; bd. dirs. Law Soc. Ariz. State U. Coll. Law, 1991-97, 99—, pres., 2000—; bd. dirs. Valley of Sn Cmtys. in Schs., 1995—. Recipient spl. commendation U.s. Dept. Justice, 1973. Fellow Am. Bar Found., Ariz. Bar Found.; mem. ABA (antitrust and litigation sects., vice chmn. bus. torts and unfair competition com. 1996-98, chair 1998—, editor Bus. Torts and Unfair Competition Newsletter 1996-98), FBA, Assn. Profl. Responsibility Lawyers (bd. dirs. 1993-98, pres. 1996-97), State Bar Ariz. (coun. antitrust sect., chmn. 1985-88, chmn. advt. com. 1992-94, ethics com. 1994-2001, chmn. 1995-2001, mem. task force on future of profession 2000—), Maricopa County Bar Assn. Office: Fennemore Craig 3003 N Central Ave Ste 2600 Phoenix AZ 85012-2913

BURKE, WILLIAM THOMAS, law educator, lawyer; b. Brazil, Ind., Aug. 17, 1926; JD, U. Ind., 1953; JSD, Yale U., 1959. Bar: Ind. 1953. Rsch. assoc. and lectr. Yale U., 1956-62; assoc. prof. Ohio State U., 1962-64, prof., 1964-68, U. Wash. Sch. Law, Seattle, 1968-99, emeritus, 1999. Mem. adv. com. Law of Sea Task Force, Dept. State; mem. A217 Ocean Policy Com., Nat. Acad. Scis. Author: (with M. S. McDougal) The Public Order of the Oceans, 1962, Contemporary Legal Problems in Ocean Development, 1969, (with Legatski and Woodhead) National and International Law Enforcement in the Ocean, 1975, The New International Law of Fisheries, 1994, International Law of the Sea-Documents and Notes, 1997, 99. Office: U Wash Sch Law Condon Hall Seattle WA 98105 E-mail: sealaw1@home.com, burke@u.washington.edu

BURKEE, IRVIN, artist; b. Kenosha, Wis., Feb. 6, 1918; s. Omar Lars and Emily (Quardokas) B.; m. Bonnie May Ness, Apr. 12, 1945; children: Brynn, Jill, Peter (dec.), Ian (dec.). Diploma, Sch. Art Inst. Chgo., 1943, postgrad., 1944-45. Owner, silversmith, goldsmith Burkee Jewelry, Blackhawk, Colo., 1950-57; painter, sculptor, Aspen, 1957-78, Cottonwood, Ariz., 1978-92, Pietrasanta, Italy, 1978—. Instr. art U. Colo., 1946, 50-53, Stephens Coll., Columbia, Mo., 1947-49. Executed copper mural of human history of Colo, 1st Nat. Bank, Englewood, 1970, of wild birds of Kans., Ranchmart State Bank, Overland Park, 1974, copper, bronze and silver mural of Rocky Mountain wild birds for Aspen Ctr. Environ. Studies, 2000; exhibited in group shows Art Inst. Chgo., Smithsonian Instn. (award 1957), Milw. Art Inst., Krannert Mus., William Rockhill Nelson Coll., St. Louis Art Mus., Denver Art Mus.; represented in southwestern galleries, also pvt. collections throughout U.S.; work illustrated in books Design and Creation of Jewelry, Design through Discovery, Walls. John Quincy Adams Travel fellow Sch. Art Inst. Chgo., 1945; Rocky Mountain Coll. Sculpture grantee, 1972. Mem. Nat. Sculpture Soc., Sedona Chamber Music Soc. (painter yearly festival poster 1989—). Address: PO Box 5361 Lake Montezuma AZ 86342-5361

BURKET, JOHN MCVEY, dermatologist; b. Des Moines, Oct. 4, 1935; s. George Austin and Elma (McVey) B.; m. Janice Lee Feilmeyer, Dec. 29, 1956; children: Denise, Bradley, Brent, Diana, Dawn, Brian. BA, U. Iowa, 1957, MD, 1960. Diplomate Am. Bd. Dermatology, Am. Bd. Dermopathology. Resident in dermatology U. Iowa Hosp., Iowa City, 1964; chief dermatology USAF, March AFB, 1964-66; pvt. practice dermatology Medford, Oreg., 1966—. Contbr. articles to profl. jours., chpts. to books. Avocations: hunting, fishing. Office: 1000 E Main St Medford OR 97504-7460

BURKETT, MARVIN, personal computer manufacturing company executive; b. 1943; BS, MBA, U. Ariz. With semicondr. divsn. Raytheon Co., to 1972; v.p., contr., chief planning officer Advanced Micro Devices, Inc., 1972-88, sr. v.p., chief adminstrv. officer, CFO, 1989-98; exec. v.p. worldwide fin., CFO, Packard Bell NEC Inc., Sacramento, 1998—; CFO, chief adminstrv. officer Arcot Sys., Inc., Santa Clara, Calif., 2000—. Office: Arcot Sys Inc 3200 Patrick Henry Dr #200 Santa Clara CA 95054

BURKEY, MARCIA B. engineering executive; Degree, Macalester Coll.; M, Columbia U. Various sr. fin. positions SBC Warburg (now UBS Warburg); various exec. fin. positions including regional mgr. Bechtel Enterprises Holdings Inc., San Francisco, 1996-2000, mng. dir., CFO, 2000—. Office: Bechtel Group PO Box 193965 San Francisco CA 94119

BURKHART, WILLIAM HENRY, lawyer; b. Chgo., Jan. 3, 1931; s. Claude Albert and Mary Vern (Hall) B.; m. Rosemary Purcell, Apr. 28, 1973; 1 child, Aaron. BS Bus., Northwestern U., 1953; JD, U. Mich., 1958, MBA, 1959; LLM Taxation, NYU, 1963. Bar: Mich. 1958, N.Y. 1964, Washington 1975; CPA, Mich. Tax supr. Coopers & Lybrand, Detroit, 1960-62; assoc. atty. Cahill Gordon & Reindel, N.Y.C., 1963-72; tax ptnr. Preston, Gates & Ellis, Seattle, 1974—. Chmn. Seattle Tax Group, 1986, Seattle Internat. Tax Roundtable, 1983-85; bd. dirs. Atty. CPA Tax Clinic, Seattle. Lt. (j.g.) USN, 1953-55. Mem. Washington Athletic Club. Home: 10554 Riviera Pl NE Seattle WA 98125-6937 Office: Preston Gates & Ellis 701 5th Ave Ste 5000 Seattle WA 98104-7078 E-mail: billb@prestongates.com

BURKHOLDER, STEVE, mayor; Owner A&S Group; mayor City of Lakewood, Colo., 1999—. Office: City Hall 480 S Allison Pkwy Lakewood CO 80226-3123 E-mail: sburkholder@lakewood.org

BURKLE, RONALD W. former food service executive, business investor; b. 1953; Pvt. practice, 1975-88; pres. Jurgensen's, Pasadena, Calif., 1986-88; prin. Yucaipa Mgmt. Co., Claremont, 1986—; chmn. Food 4 Less Supermarkets, La Habra, 1989—, Dominick's Finer Foods, Northlake, Ill., until 1998; chmn., mem. exec. com. Kroger's Foods, Inc.; CEO Smith's Food & Drug Ctrs., Inc., Salt Lake City; chmn. Fred Meyer. Office: Yucaipa Co 5th Fl 10000 Santa Monica Blvd Fl 5 Los Angeles CA 90067-7007

BURLINGAME, ALMA LYMAN, chemist, educator; b. Cranston, R.I., Apr. 29, 1937; s. Herman Follett Jr. and Rose Irene (Kohler) B.; children: Mark, Walter; m. Marilyn F. Schwartz, Feb. 14, 1993; 1 stepchild, Corey Schwartz. BS, U. R.I., 1959; PhD, MIT, 1962. Asst. prof. U. Calif., Berkeley, 1963-68, assoc. chemist, 1968-72, rsch. chemist, 1972-78, prof. San Francisco, 1978—, Univ. Coll., London, 1996—. Vis. prof. Ludwig Inst. for Cancer Rsch., London, 1993-94. Editor: Topics in Organic Mass Spectrometry, 1970, Mass Spectrometry in Health and Life Science, 1985, Biological Mass Spectrometry, 1990, Mass Spectrometry in the Biological Sciences, 1995, Mass Spectrometry in Biology and Medicine, 2000; dep. editor: Molecular and Cellular Proteomics; dep. editor Molecular and Cellular Proteomics, 1999—; contbr. articles to profl. jours. With USAR, 1954-62. Guggenheim Found. fellow, 1970. Fellow AAAS. Office: U Calif Dept Pharm Chemistry San Francisco CA 94143-0001 E-mail: alb@itsa.ucsf.edu

BURNHAM, CLIFFORD WAYNE, educator; b. Murietta, Calif., Oct. 24, 1922; AB magna cum laude, Pomona Coll., 1951; MS in Geology, Calif. Inst. Tech., 1953, PhD in Geochem., 1955. Geologist Riverside Cement co., 1951; asst. prof. econ. geology Pa. State U., 1955-59, assoc. prof. geochem., 1959-65, prof. geochem., 1965-86, prof. emeritus, 1986—, head dept. geoscis., 1974-85. Adj. prof. U. Ind., 1987—. Ariz. State U., 1992—. Contbr. articles to profl. jours. Lt. USN, 1942-46. Fellow Am. Geophys. Union, Geol. Soc. Am. (Roebling medal 1998), Mineralogical Soc. Am.; mem. AAAS, Geochem. Soc. (pres. 1974), Soc. Econ. Geologists, Phi Beta Kappa, Sigma Xi. Office: Ariz State U Geology Dept PO Box 871404 Tempe AZ 85287-1404

BURNHAM, JOHN LUDWIG, agent; b. L.A., Mar. 1, 1953; s. Jerome Ludwig and Linda (Benjamin) B.; m. Andrea Buckland Feldstein, Aug. 12, 1989; 1 child, Daisy. BA, UCLA, 1976, JD, 1980. Agt. Kohnner Levy, L.A., 1979-81, ICM, L.A., 1981-84, William Morris Agy., Beverly Hills, Calif., 1984—, co-head, sr. v.p. movie dept., 1991—. Office: William Morris Agy Inc 151 S El Camino Dr Beverly Hills CA 90212-2775

BURNINGHAM, KIM RICHARD, former state legislator; b. Salt Lake City, Sept. 14, 1936; s. Rulon and Margie (Stringham) Burningham; m. Susan Ball Clarke, Dec. 19, 1968; children: Christian, Tyler David. BS, U. Utah, 1960; MA, U. Ariz., 1967; MFA, U. So. Calif., 1977. Cert. secondary tchr., Utah. Tchr. Bountiful (Utah) High Sch., 1960-88; mem. Utah Ho. of Reps., Salt Lake City, 1979-94; cons. Shipley Assocs., Bountiful, 1989-94, Franklin Covey, 1994—. Gubernatorial appointee as exec. dir. Utah Statehood Centennial Commn., 1994-96; mem. Utah State Bd. Edn., 1999-2000, vice chmn., 2000-01, chmn., 2001—; bd. dirs. Nat. Assn. Sch. Bds. Edn., 2000-2001. Author dramas for stage and film, also articles; columnist, Davis County Clipper, 2000—. Mem. state strategic planning com. Utah Tomorrow, 1989—. Mem. NEA, PTA (life), Utah Edn. Assn., Davis Edn. Assn., Nat. Forensic League. Mem. LDS Ch. Avocations: gardening, history. Home: 932 Canyon Crest Dr Bountiful UT 84010-2002 E-mail: krb54010@aol.com

BURNISON, BOYD EDWARD, lawyer; b. Arnolds Park, Iowa, Dec. 12, 1934; s. Boyd WIlliam and Lucile (Harnden) B.; m. Mari Amaral; children: Erica Lafore, Alison Katherine. BS, Iowa State U., 1957; JD, U. Calif., Berkeley, 1961. Bar: Calif. 1962, U.S. Supreme Ct. 1971, U.S. Dist. Ct. (no. dist.) Calif. 1962, U.S. Ct. Appeals (9th cir.) 1962, U.S. Dist. Ct. (ea. dist.) Calif. 1970, U.S. Dist. Ct. (ctrl. dist.) Calif. 1992. Dep. counsel Yolo County, Calif., 1962-65; assoc. Steel & Arostegui, Marysville, 1965-66, St. Sure, Moore & Hoyt, Oakland, 1966-70; ptnr. St. Sure, Moore, Hoyt & Sizoo, Oakland and San Francisco, 1970-75; v.p. Crosby, Heafey, Roach & May, P.C., Oakland, 1975-2000, also bd. dirs.; pres. Boyd E Burnison A Profl. Law Corp., Walnut Creek, Calif., 2001—. Advisor Berkeley YMCA, 1971—, Yolo County YMCA, 1962—65, bd. dirs., 1965; trustee, sec., legal counsel Easter Seal Found., Alameda County, 1974—79, hon. trustee, 1979—; trustee Alameda County Law Libr., 2001—; bd. dirs. Easter Seal Soc. Crippled Children and Adults of Alameda County Calif., 1972—75, Moot Ct. Bd., U. Calif., 1960—61, East Bay Conservation Corps, 1997—2000, treas., 2000. Named Vol. of Yr., Berkeley YMCA, 1999. Fellow: ABA Found. (life); mem.: ABA (labor rels. and employment law sect., equal employment law com. 1972—), Iowa State Alumni Assn., Order Knoll, Rotary, Round Hill Country Club, Pi Kappa Alpha, Phi Delta Phi, Nat. Conf. Bar Pres.'s, State Bar Calif. (spl. labor counsel 1981—84, labor and employment law sect. 1982—), Alameda County Bar Assn. (chmn. memberships and directory com. 1973—74, chmn. memberships and directory com. 1980, chmn. law office econs. com. 1975—77, assn. dir.

1981—85, pres. 1984, vice chmn. bench bar liaison com. 1983, chmn. 1984, Disting. Svc. award 1987), Alameda County Bar Found. (bd. dirs. 1993—95), Yolo County Bar Assn. (sec. 1965), Yuba Sutter Bar Assn., Bar Assn. San Francisco (labor law sect.), Contra Costa County Bar Assn. (labor law sect.), Indsl. Rels. Rsch. Assn., Sproul Assoc. Boalt Hall Law Sch. U. Calif. Berkeley. Democrat. Home: PO Box 743 2500 Caballo Ranchero Dr Diablo CA 94528 Office: Boyd E Burnison A Profl Law Corp 1600 South Main Plz Ste 130 Walnut Creek CA 94596 Fax: (925) 817-2411

BURNLEY, KENNETH STEPHEN, school system administrator; m. Eileen Burnley; children: Traci, Trevor. BS, MA, PhD, U. Mich. Tchr. various schs., Mich.; asst. track coach U. Mich.; tchr., coord., asst. prin., prin., dir. Ypsilanti Bd. Edn.; instr. Ea. Mich. U.; asst. supt. instrn. Waverly Bd. Edn.; supt./CEO Fairbanks (Alaska) North Star Borough Sch. Dist.; supt. schs. Colorado Springs (Colo.) Sch. Dist. 11, 1987—. Speaker in field. Bd. dirs. Colo. Nat. Bank Exch. Named Supt. of Year, Am. Assn. Sch. Adminstrs., 1993. Mem. Colo. Springs C. of C. (bd. dirs.). Avocations: exercising, weight training, boxing, reading, chess. Office: Colorado Springs Sch Dist #11 1115 N El Paso St Colorado Springs CO 80903-2519

BURNS, BRENDA, state legislator; b. LaGrange, Ga., Nov. 22, 1950; 3 children. Mem. Ariz. Senate, Dist. 17, Phoenix, 1994—; pres. Ariz. Senate, 2001—. Nat. chair Am. Leg. Exch. Coun., 1999; exec. bd. Am. Legis. Exch. Coun. Republican. Office: State Capitol Legis Dist 17 1700 W Washington St Phoenix AZ 85007-2812

BURNS, BRIAN PATRICK, lawyer, business executive; b. Cambridge, Mass., July 12, 1936; s. John Joseph and Alice (Blake) B.; m. Sheila Ann O'Connor, June 23, 1962; children: Sheila Ann, Brian Patrick, Sean Richard, Roderick O'Connor. BA, Holy Cross Coll., 1957; LLB, Harvard U., 1960. Bar: Mass. 1960, N.Y. 1961, Calif. 1965. Law clk., spl. asst. to regional adminstr. New York Regional Office, SEC, 1958-59; asso. Webster, Sheffield, Fleischmann, Hitchcock & Brookfield, N.Y.C., 1960-64; ptnr. Cullinan, Hancock, Rothert & Burns, San Francisco, 1965-74; sr. ptnr. Cullinan, Burns & Helmer, San Francisco, 1975-78; firm Burns & Whitehead, San Francisco, 1978-86; chmn., chief exec. officer, chmn. exec. com. Boothe Fin. Corp., San Francisco, 1981-87, also bd. dirs.; chmn. Robert Half Internat. Inc., 1987-88; chmn., CEO BF Enterprises Inc., 1987—. Dir. U.S. Banknote Corp., N.Y.C., from 1967, chmn. exec. and fin. coms., 1973-76; dir. Coca Cola Bottling Co., N.Y., 1974-86, chmn. exec. com., 1979-86; dir. Kellogg Co., 1979-89, chmn. fin. com. 1984-89; dir. Calif. Jockey, 1980-89; dir., chmn. audit com. Flexi-Van Corp., N.Y.C., 1984-85; dir., chmn. exec. com. Pinnacle Petroleum Corp., The Woodlands, Tex., 1983-85; dir., chmn. ops. review com. Brink's Inc., Chgo., 1976-78; dir., chmn. acquisition com. Pacific Holding Corp., Los Angeles, 1972-78; dir., mem. exec. com. Beverly Wilshire Hotel, Beverly Hills, Calif., Calif., 1967-86; dir., chmn. exec. com. USR Industries, The Woodlands, 1980-83; dir., chmn. audit com. ROCOR Internat., Palo Alto, Calif., 1976-82; underwriting mem. Lloyds of London, 1978-89; lectr. continuing edn. of bar U. Calif., 1969, 74, 76, advanced bus. seminar, 1971; seminar on investment opportunities in wine industry McGraw Hill Coll., N.Y., 1973, Legal Edn. Inst., 1976. Bd. dirs. Boys Club of San Francisco, 1971-80, Am. Irish Found., 1978-87, Am. Ireland Fund, 1987—; trustee Holy Cross Coll., 1978-89. Mem. ABA (mem. small bus. com. corp. bus. and banking sect. 1972-76), State Bar Cal. (vice chmn. com. on corps. 1971-75), Bar Assn. San Francisco (chmn. com. on corp. banking and bus. law 1968-69), Calif. Jockey Club (dir. San Mateo, Calif. 1988-89). Roman Catholic. Clubs: Royal Dublin Soc.; Bohemian, Burlingame Country, Family, Olympic, Sky, N.Y. Athletic, Les Ambassadeurs, Mil. and Hospitaller Order St. Lazarus of Jerusalem (comdr. companion). Office: BF Enterprises Inc 100 Bush St Ste 1250 San Francisco CA 94104-3914

BURNS, CONRAD RAY, senator; b. Gallatin, Mo., Jan. 25, 1935; s. Russell and Mary Frances (Knight) B.; m. Phyllis Jean Kuhlmann; children: Keely Lynn, Garrett Russell. Student, U. Mo., 1952-54. Field rep. Polled Hereford World Mag., Kansas City, Mo., 1963-69; pub. rels. Billings (Mont.) Livestock Com., 1969-73; farm dir. KULR TV, Billings, 1974; pres., founder No. Ag-Network, Billings, 1975-86; commissioner Yellowstone County, Billings, 1987-89; senator from Montana U.S. Senate, 1989—. Mem. Aging Com., Small Bus. Com., chmn. Appropriations Subcom. of Mil. Constrn., chmn. Com. Sci. and Transp. Subcom. of Comms., chmn. Energy and Nat. Resources With USMC, 1955-57. Mem. Nat. Assn. Farm Broadcasters, Am. Legion, Rotary, Masons, Shriners. Republican. Lutheran. Avocation: football officiating. Office: US Senate 187 Dirksen Senate Ofc Washington DC 20510-0001*

BURNS, DAN W. manufacturing company executive; b. Auburn, Calif., Sept. 10, 1925; s. William and Edith Lynn (Johnston) B.; 1 child, Dan Jr. Dir. materials Menasco Mfg. Co., 1951-56; v.p., gen. mgr. Hufford Corp., 1956-58; pres. Hufford div. Siegler Corp., 1958-61; v.p. Siegler Corp., 1961-62, Lear Siegler, Inc., 1962-64; pres., dir. Electrada Corp., Culver City, Calif., 1964; pres., chief exec. officer Sargent Industries, Inc., L.A., 1964-85, chmn. bd. dirs., 1985-88. Now chmn. bd. dirs., CEO Arlington Industries, Inc.; bd. dirs. Gen. Automotive Corp., Dover Tech. Internat., Inc., Kistler Aerospace Corp. Bd. dirs. San Diego Aerospace Mus., Smithsonian Inst., The Pres.'s Cir., Nat. Acad. Scis., Atlantic Coun. of U.S., George C. Marshall Found. Capt. U.S. Army, 1941-47; prisoner of war Japan; asst. mil. attache 1946, China; adc to Gen. George C. Marshall 1946-47. Mem. OAS Sports Com. (dir.), L.A. Country Club, St. Francis Yacht Club, Calif. Club, Conquistador del Cielo, Cosmos Club Washington. Home: 7400 Bryan Canyon Rd Carson City NV 89704-9588

BURNS, DENVER P. forestry research administrator; b. Bryan, Ohio, Oct. 27, 1940; married; 1 child. BS, Ohio State U., 1962, MS, 1964, PhD in Entomology, 1967; MPA, Harvard U., 1981. Asst. entomologist So. Forest Experiment Sta., 1962-68, rsch. entomologist, 1968-72, asst. dir., 1972-74; staff asst. to dep. chief for rsch. U.S. Forest Svc., 1974-76; dep. dir. North Ctrl. Experiment Sta., 1976-81; dir. Northeastern Forest Experiment Sta., Radnor, Pa., 1981-92, Rocky Mountain Sta., 1992—. Mem. AAAS. Office: US Forest Service Rocky Mountain Rsch Sta 2150 Centre Ave Bldg A Fort Collins CO 80526-1891

BURNS, JAMES S. judge; b. Honolulu, Apr. 19, 1937; m. Emme Tomimbang, July 25, 1987; 2 children from previouis marriage. BS, St. Benedicts Coll., 1959; JD, Villanova U., 1962. Bar: Hawaii 1962. Chief judge Hawaii Intermediate Ct. Appeals, Honolulu, 1982—. With U.S. Army, 1962-64, U.S. Army NG, 1964-77. Mem. Am. Inn Ct. (pres. Aloha chpt.), Am. Judicature Soc. (pres. Hawaii chpt.), Waialae Country Club. Avocations: golf, gardening. Office: Hawaii Intermediate Ct Appeals PO Box 2560 Honolulu HI 96804-2560

BURNS, LARRY ALAN, judge; b. Pasadena, Calif., June 29, 1954; m. Kristi Francis, 1980; 2 children. BA in English, Point Loma Coll., 1976; JD, U. San Diego, 1979. Bar: Calif. 1979. Deputy dist. atty., San Diego, 1979-85; asst. U.S. atty. San Diego, 1985-97; dir., corp. sec. Bank Commerce, San Diego, 1994-97; magistrate judge U.S. Dist. Ct., San Diego, 1997—. Adj. prof. Nat. U., 1981-86, Nat. U. Sch. Law, 1987-90, San Diego State U., 1988-96; lectr. Nat. Coll. Dist. Attys., 1983. Recipient Nat. Victim Assistance award, 1991, 92. Fellow Am. Coll. Trial Lawyers; mem. Calif. State Bar Assn. Avocation: gardening. Office: Edward J Schwartz US Courthouse 940 Front St Rm D San Diego CA 92101-8994

BURNS, MARCELLINE, psychologist, researcher; BA in Psychology, San Diego State U., 1955; MA, Calif. State U., L.A., 1969; PhD, U. Calif., Irvine, 1972. Co-founder So. Calif. Rsch. Inst., L.A., 1973—. Cons., expert witness alcohol and drug effects on performance, FSTs, HGN, and drug recognition; lectr. in field. Contbr. articles to profl. jours. Recipient Public Svc. award U.S. Dept. Trans., 1993. Achievements include research on alcohol and drug effects, field sobriety tests and drug recognition. Office: So Calif Rsch Inst 11914 W Washington Blvd Los Angeles CA 90066-5816

BURNS, MARVIN GERALD, lawyer; b. Los Angeles, July 3, 1930; s. Milton and Belle (Cytron) B.; m. Barbara Irene Fisher, Aug. 23, 1953; children: Scott Douglas, Jody Lynn, Bradley Frederick. BA, U. Ariz., 1951; JD, Harvard U., 1954. Bar: Calif. 1955. Bd. dirs. Inner City Arts for Inner City Children. With AUS, 1955-56. Clubs: Beverly Hills Tennis, Sycamore Park Tennis. Home: 10350 Wilshire Blvd Ph 4 Los Angeles CA 90024-4734 Office: 9107 Wilshire Blvd Ste 800 Beverly Hills CA 90210-5533 E-mail: mburns@rpab.com

BURNS, MICHAEL JOSEPH, operations and sales-marketing executive; b. Passaic, N.J., Feb. 18, 1943; s. Michael Joseph and Ellen Kathryn (Warman) B.; m. Emma Anne, Dec. 19, 1964; children: Michael, Jeffrey, Tricia, Stephen. B.A. in English, William Paterson Univ., Wayne, N.J., 1964; J.D., Seton Hall U., Newark, 1975. Bar: N.J. 1975. Purchasing analyst Am. Brands Co., 1972-75; div. purchasing mgr. Dutch Boy Paints, NL Industries, 1975-76; v.p. purchasing Dutch Boy, Inc., 1977-78; pres., gen. mgr. Dutch Boy, Inc. (Dutch Boy coatings div.), 1978-80; pres., CEO Kroehler Mfg. Co., Naperville, Ill., 1980-88; pres., COO Rymer Co., Rolling Meadows, 1983-88; pres. Emerald Group, Lake Forest, 1989-90; pres., CEO Designer Foods, Inc., Wilmington, Del., 1990-91; chmn., pres., CEO SeaWatch Internat., Ltd., Easton, Md., 1991-99; pres., CEO Pioneer Human Svcs., Seattle, 1999—. Served to capt. USMCR, 1964-67, Vietnam. N.J. State scholar; recipient Disting. Alumni award Wm. Paterson Univ. Mem. ABA, Am. Arbitration Assn. Presbyterian. Office: 7440 W Marginal Way S Seattle WA 98108-4141 E-mail: mike.burns@p-h-s.com

BURNS, RICHARD DEAN, history educator, publisher, writer; b. Des Moines, June 16, 1929; s. Richard B. and Luella (Everling) B.; m. Frances R. Sullivan, Jan. 14, 1950 (dec. July 1993); 1 son, Richard Dean; m. Glenda F. Burns, Sept. 21, 1996; stepchildren: Scott E. Burns, Kent C. Burns, Dana Burns Mayadag. B.S. with honors, U. Ill., 1957, M.A., 1958, Ph.D., 1960. Prof. emeritus Calif. State U., L.A., 1960-92, prof., 1970-92, chmn. dept., 1969-72, 86-92. Pubr./pres. Regina Books, 1980—; vis. lectr. L.A. City Coll., Whittier Coll., U. Minn., Mpls., 1964-65, UCLA, U. So. Calif.; program cons., lectr. Western Ctr., NEH, 1973-75. Author: (with W. Fisher) Armament and Disarmament, 1964, (with D. Urquidi) Disarmament in Historical Perspective, 4 vols, 1969, (with E. Bennett) Diplomats in Crisis, 1975; editor: An Arms Control and Disarmament Bibliography, 1977, Guide to American Foreign Relations Since 1770, 1982, (with M. Leitenberg) The Wars in Vietnam, Cambodia, and Laos, 1945-82, 1984, Harry S. Truman: A Bibliography of His Times and Presidency, 1984, Herbert Hoover: A Bibliography of His Times and Presidency, 1991, Encyclopedia of Arms Control and Disarmament, 3 vols., 1993; bibliographer, series editor: War/Peace Bibliographies, 1973—; pub. Regina Books, 1981—; contbr. articles to profl. jours. Served with USAF, 1947-56. Named Univ. Outstanding Prof., 1978-79; Social Sci. Rsch. Coun. fellow, 1959-60; grantee NEH, 1978-79, U.S. Inst. Peace, 1991-92. Mem. Conf. on Peace Rsch. (nat. coun. 1970-72), Soc. Historians Am. Fgn. Rels. (nat. coun. 1986-89), Phi Kappa Phi, Phi Alpha Theta. Office: Regina Books PO Box 280 Claremont CA 91711-0280

BURNSIDE, MARY BETH, biology educator, researcher; b. San Antonio, Apr. 23, 1943; d. Neil Delmont and Luella Nixon (Kenley) B. BA, U. Tex., 1965, MA, 1967, PhD in Zoology, 1968. Instr. med. sch. Harvard U., Boston, 1970-73; asst. prof. U. Pa., Phila., 1973-76, U. Calif., Berkeley, 1976-77, assoc. prof., 1977-82, prof., 1982—, dean biol. scis., 1984-90, chancellor prof., 1996-99, vice chancellor rsch., 2000—. Mem. nat. adv. eye coun. NIH, 1990-94; mem. sci. adv. bd. Lawrence Hall of Sci., Berkeley, 1983—, Whitney Labs., St. Augustine, Fla., 1993-97; mem. bd. sci. councillors Nat. Eye Inst., 1994—. Mem. editl. bd. Invest. Ophthalmol. Vis. Sci., 1992-94; contbr. numerous articles to profl. jours. Mem. sci. adv. bd. Mills Coll., Oakland, Calif., 1986-90; trustee Bermuda Biol. Sta., St. George's, 1978-83; dir. Miller Inst., Berkeley, Calif., 1995-98. Recipient Merit award NIH, 1989-99, Outstanding Alumna award U. Tex., 1999; rsch. grantee, NIH, 1972—, NSF. Fellow AAAS; mem. Am. Soc. Cell Biology (coun. 1980-84). Avocations: hiking, deserts, mountains, Great Danes. Office: U Calif MC # 3200 335 Life Scis Addn # 3200 Berkeley CA 94720-0001

BURR, EDWARD BENJAMIN, life insurance company executive, financial executive; b. Worcester, Mass., Dec. 19, 1923; s. Guy Weatherbee and Bertha Mary (Clark) B.; m. Mary Elizabeth Hayes, Sept. 2, 1944 (div. Sept. 1970); children: Susan Jean Burr Williams, Nancy Carol Burr Montanaro; m. Kay Frances Flanagan, Nov. 1, 1970 (div. 1992); children: Kristine Kay (dec.), Kelly Anne Carter. BA, Bowdoin Coll., 1945; MBA, U. Pa., 1948; grad., Am. Coll. Life Underwriters, 1951. CLU. Dir. Inst. Life Ins., N.Y.C., 1948-54; exec. dir. Investment Co. Inst., N.Y.C., 1954-58; exec. v.p., dir. One William Street Fund, N.Y.C., 1958-62; pres., dir. William Street Sales, Inc., N.Y.C., 1958-62; pres., vice chmn. Anchor Corp., Elizabeth, N.J., 1964-78; chmn. bd. Anchor Nat. Life, Phoenix, 1965-85, hon. chmn., 1985—; chmn. bd. Anchor Nat. Fin. Services, Phoenix, 1971-85, hon. chmn., 1986—; pres. United Planners Fin. Services Am., 1987-95. Trustee Scottsdale Meml. Hosp., Ariz., 1985-95, chmn., 1990-91; dir. Ariz. Cmty. Found., 1985-93. With U.S. Army, 1943-46, ETO. Decorated Bronze Star, Silver Star Mem. Am. Soc. CLUs, Nat. Assn. Life Underwriters, Phoenix Met. C. of C. (bd. dirs. 1982-88), Scottsdale Club at Gainey Ranch, Camelback Golf Club. Home: 7331 E Griswold Rd Scottsdale AZ 85258-2731 Office: United Planners Group 7333 E Doubletree Ranch Rd Scottsdale AZ 85258-2042 E-mail: benburr@aol.com

BURR, ROBERT LYNDON, information services specialist; b. Boonville, N.Y., May 9, 1944; s. James Isaac and Virginia Ellen (Davidson) B.; m. Angela Delores Tucci, June 26, 1965; 1 son, Robert Anthony. Student, U. Rochester, 1962-65; A.B., Canisius Coll., 1972; M.S. in L.S, Case-Western Res. U., 1973; Ed.D., Gonzaga U., 1981. Asst. prodn. mgr., purchasing mgr. Carleton Controls Corp., Buffalo, 1966-71; asst. to pres. Audn Corp., Buffalo, 1971-72; circulation services librarian Coll. William and Mary, Williamsburg, Va., 1973-77; dean libr. svcs. Gonzaga U., Spokane, 1977—, adj. asso. prof. edn., 1979—, assoc. acad. v.p., 1996—. Library cons. Contbr. articles to profl. jours. Trustee Mus. Native Am. Cultures, 1979— . Served with AUS, 1967-69. Mem. ALA (nat. research award 1974), Nat. Libraries Assn., Wash. Library Assn., Pacific N.W. Library Assn., AAUP, Mensa, Moses Lake Golf and Country Club. Office: Gonzaga U Foley Ctr 502 E Boone Ave Spokane WA 99258-0001

BURRELL, CALVIN ARCHIE, minister; b. Fairview, Okla., June 22, 1943; s. Lawrence Lester and Lottie Edna (Davison) B.; m. Barbara Ann Mann, May 29, 1966; children: Debra, Darla, Donna. BS, Northwestern State U., 1965; MA, So. Nazarene U., Bethany, Okla., 1978. Ordained to ministry Ch. of God, 1966. Tchr., prin., dean boys Spring Vale Acad., Owosso, Mich., 1964-76; pastor Ch. of God (Seventh Day), Ft. Smith, Ark., 1970-73, Shawnee, Okla., 1976-78, Denver, 1978-88, Ch. of God, Galena Park, Tex., 1996—, pres. gen. conf. Denver, 1987-97; editor Bible Advocate mag., Denver, 1997—. Instr. Summit Sch. Theology, Denver, 1978-95; officer Bible Sabath Assn., 1983-96. Editor: Bible Advocate, 1997—. Office: Ch of God 330 W 152d Ave PO Box 33677 Denver CO 80233-0677

BURRELL, GARLAND E., JR. federal judge; b. L.A., July 4, 1947; BA in Sociology, Calif. State U., 1972; MSW, Washington U., Mo., 1976; JD, Calif. Wes. Sch. Law, 1976. Bar: Calif. 1976, U.S. Dist. Ct. (ea. dist.) Calif. 1976, U.S. Ct. Appeals (9th cir.) 1981. Dep. dist. atty. Sacramento County, Calif., 1976-78; dep city atty. Sacramento, 1978-79; asst. U.S. atty., dep. chief civil divsn. Office of U.S. Atty. for Ea. Dist. Calif., 1979-85, asst. U.S. atty., chief civil divsn., 1990-92; litigation atty. Stockman Law Corp., Sacramento, 1985-86; sr. dep. city atty. Office of City Atty., Sacramento, 1986-90; judge U.S. Dist. Ct. (ea. dist.) Calif., Sacramento, 1992—. With USMC, 1966-68. Office: Dist Ct 501 I St Sacramento CA 95814-7300

BURROUGHS, GARY L. city official; b. Independence, Kans., Apr. 9, 1943; Auditor City of Long Beach, 1992—. Office: Office of City Auditor Civic Center Plz 333 W Ocean Blvd Fl 8 Long Beach CA 90802-4604

BURROWS, BENJAMIN, retired physician, educator; b. N.Y.C., Dec. 16, 1927; s. Samuel and Theresa Helen (Handelsman) B.; m. Nancy Kreiter, June 14, 1949; children— Jan C., Susan K., Lynn A., Steven M. MD, Johns Hopkins, 1949. Intern Johns Hopkins Hosp., 1949-50; resident King County Hosp., Seattle, 1950-51, U. Chgo., 1953-55, instr. to asso. prof. medicine, 1955-68; prof. internal medicine U. Ariz. Coll. Medicine, Tucson, 1968—, dir. Respiratory Sci. Ctr., 1987-96, Chalfant-Moore prof. of medicine, 1987-96, ret., emeritus prof. medicine, 1996. Cons. Tucson VA Hosp.; dir. Respiratory Scis. Ctr., Nat. Heart Lung and Blood Inst. Specialized Ctr. Research in Pulmonary Diseases, U. Ariz. Coll. Medicine, 1971-95. Mem. editl. bd. Am. Rev. Respiratory Diseases, 1967-71, 74-80, Chest, 1971-76, Annals Internal Medicine, 1973-76, Archives of Environ. Health, 1976-93, Jour. of allergy and clin. Immunology, 1992-95; contbr. articles to profl. jours., chpts. to books. Served to capt. USAF, 1951-53. Rsch. grantee USPHS, 1958-95. Fellow Am. Coll. Chest Physicians (regent dist. 11 1970-75), A.C.P.; mem. Assn. Am. Physicians, Am. Soc. Clin. Investigation (emeritus), Am. Physiol. Soc. Home: 6840 N Table Mountain Rd Tucson AZ 85718-1329

BURROWS, JAMES, television and motion picture director, producer; b. L.A., Dec. 30, 1940; s. Abe Burrows. BA, Oberlin Coll.; MFA, Yale U. Off-Broadway prodns.: dir. (motion picture) Partners, 1982, (TV film) More Than Friends, 1978, (TV series episodes) Mary Tyler Moore Show, Bob Newhart, Taxi, Lou Grant, Dear John, Night Court (pilot), Wings (pilot), Roc (pilot), Frasier (pilot), Friends (pilot), Newsradio (pilot), Third Rock from the Sun (pilot), Caroline in the City (pilot); co-creator, co-exec. producer, dir. (TV series) Cheers. Recipient Dirs. Guild Am. award for comedy direction, 1984, 91, 94, Emmy awards NATAS for dir. in comedy series Taxi, 1979-80, 81-82 seasons, Cheers, 1982-83, 90-91 seasons; Emmy award as co-producer Cheers, 1982-83, 83-84, 89-90, 90-91 seasons; Emmy award as director of a Comedy Series for Fraiser, 1994. Office: care Paramount TV Prodns 5555 Melrose Ave # Bung1 Los Angeles CA 90038-3112

BURT, CHRISTOPHER CLINTON, publishing company executive; b. N.Y.C., Oct. 12, 1954; s. Nathaniel and Margaret Brooks (Clinton) B.; m. Jeernen Songsaeng, Aug. 9, 1992. BA Econs., U. Wis., 1981. Pub., mng. dir. Pacific Rim Press, Inc., Bangkok, 1985—; pub. Compass Am. Guides, Inc., Oakland, Calif., 1990-92; exec. editor, creative dir. Compass Am. Guides, Inc./Random House, Inc., Oakland, 1992—. Bd. dirs. Jaquelin Found., Princeton, N.J., 1980—. Mem. Soc. of The Cincinatus. Office: Compass Am Guides 5332 College Ave Ste 201 Oakland CA 94618-2805

BURT, THOMAS WILLIAM, lawyer; b. Spokane, Wash., Jan. 24, 1955; s. Jack Wallace and Peggy (Windes) B.; m. Ann Darling, Apr. 2, 1989; children; Trevor D. Welling, Griffin D., Caroline D. AB in Human Biology, Stanford U., 1976; JD, U. Wash., 1979. Bar: Wash. 1979, U.S. Ct. Appeals (9th cir.) 1979, U.S. Dist. Ct. (we. dist.) Wash. 1980. Law clk. to judge Ozell Trask U.S. Ct. Appeals (9th cir.), Phoenix, 1979 80; ptnr., atty. Riddell, Williams, Bullitt & Walkinshaw, Seattle, 1980-95; from sr. corp. atty. litigation to gen. counsel litigation Microsoft Corp., Redmond, Wash., 1995—. Bd. dirs. Bainbridge Island (Wash.) Land Trust, 1990-91. Mem. ABA, Wash. Bar Assn., Seattle-King County Bar. Avocations: sports car racing, skiing, sailing. Office: Microsoft Corp One Microsoft Way Redmond WA 98052 E-mail: tburt@microsoft.com

BURTENSHAW, DON M. state senator; b. Shelton, Idaho, Aug. 14, 1933; m. Beverly Burtenshaw; children: Michel, Steven, Lynn, Van, Sharon, Annette, David, Lee. Diploma, Ucon (Idaho) H.S., 1951. Carpenter, 1953-63; farmer, rancher, 1955-98; agri-businessman, 1963-98; Rep. senator dist. 26 Idaho State Senate, 1996—. Mem. commerce and human resources, edn., resources and environ. coms. Idaho State Senate, vice chair agrl. affairs. Mem. sch. bd.; scout leader; dir. Owsley Canal Co.; pres. Cattle Coop. Named Farmer of Yr. Mem. LDS Ch. Office: 1603 N 1000 E Terreton ID 83450 also: Idaho State Senate State Capitol PO Box 83720 Boise ID 83720-0081 Fax: 208 663-4499. E-mail: infocntr@lso.state.id.us

BURTON, ANTHONY JOHN, bishop; b. Ottawa, Ont., Can., Aug. 11, 1959; s. Peter Michael and Rachel Harragin Wood (Greaves) B.; m. Anna Kristine Erickson, Apr. 8, 1989; children: Caroline Rachel Georgina, Peter Charles Hugh. BA with honors, Trinity Coll. U. Toronto, 1982, U. Oxford, 1987, MA, 1992; DD, U. King's Coll., 1994. Ordained priest, 1988; consecrated bishop, 1993. Curate St. John the Bapt. Ch., North Sydney, N.S., 1987-88; rector Trinity Ch., Sydney Mines, 1988-91; rector, canon residentiary Cath. Ch. St. Alban the Martyr, Prince Albert, Sask., 1991-93; dean Diocese of Saskatchewan, Prince Albert, 1991-94, bishop, 1993—. Contbg. author: Anglican Essentials: Reclaiming Faith Within the Anglican Church of Canada, 1995; contbr. articles and columns to profl. jours. Anglican. Avocation: walking. Office: Diocese of Sask Synod 1308 5th Ave E Prince Albert SK Canada S6V 2H7

BURTON, JOHN, state official; b. Ohio, Dec. 15, 1932; 1 child, Kimiko. Student, San Francisco State Coll., San Francisco Law Sch. Mem. Calif. Ho. of Reps., 1964-74, 88-96, U.S. Congress, 1974-82, Calif. Senate from 3rd dist., 1997—; Pres. pro tem Calif. Senate, 1998—. Founder Point Reyes Wilderness Area, Farallon Marine Sanctuary. Named Legislator of Yr. Calif. Abortion Rights Action League, Animal Rights Legislator of Yr.; recipient Community United Against Violence award, Sean Mcbride award, award Ancient Order of Hibernians. Office: State Capitol Rm 205 Sacramento CA 95814 also: 601 Van Ness Ave Ste 2030 San Francisco CA 94102-6310

BURTON, LAWRENCE DEVERE, agriculturist, educator; b. Afton, Wyo., May 27, 1943; s. Lawrence VanOrden and Maybell (Hoopes) B.; m. Arva Merrill, Nov. 20, 1967; children: LauraLee, Paul, Shawn, Renee, Kaylyn, Kelly, Brett. BS, Utah State U., 1968; MS, Brigham Young U., 1972; PhD, Iowa State U., 1987. Agr. tchr. Box Elder County Sch. Dist., Brigham City, Utah, 1967-68, Morgan County Sch. Dist., Morgan, 1968-70, Minidoka County Sch. Dist., Rupert, Idaho, 1972-79, Cassia County Sch. Dist., Declo, 1979-84; instr. Iowa State U., Ames, 1984-87; area vocat. edn. coord. Idaho State Div. Vocat. Edn., Pocatello, 1987-88, state supr. agrl. sci. and tech. Boise, 1988-97; dir. rsch. Idaho State Divsn. Vocat. Edn., Boise, 1997-99; mem. telecomm. coun. Idaho State Bd. Edn., 1997-98, mem. coun. acad. affairs and programs, 1997—; instrnl. dean Coll. So. Idaho, Twin Falls, 2000—. Biochem. cons. rep. Ctr. for Occupational Rsch. and Devel., Waco, Tex., 1989-94; chmn. Nat. Task Force, Agrl. Edn. Ind. Study Honors program, 1993; mem. Nat. Task Force, Environ. Edn., 1996. Author: Agriscience and Technology, 1991, 97, Ecology of Fish and Wildlife, 1995, Introduction to Forestry Science, 1998, Agriscience, Fundamentals and Applications, 2000; contbr. articles to profl.

jours. Vice-chmn. Minidoka County Fair Bd., Rupert, Idaho, 1977-80. Mem. Am. Vocat. Assn., Am. Vocat. Info. Assn., Nat. Vocat. Agrl. Tchrs. Assn., Idaho Vocat. Agrl. Tchrs. Assn. (pres. 1981-82, Adminstr. of Yr. 1989), Am. Vocat. Info. Assn., Nat. Assn. Suprs. Agrl. Edn. (western v.p. 1990-91, nat. pres. 1993-94), Gamma Sigma Delta, Alpha Zeta. Mem. LDS Ch. Home: 214 Carney St Twin Falls ID 83301-5010 Office: Coll So Idaho PO Box 1238 Twin Falls ID 83303-1238

BURTON, MICHAEL LADD, anthropology educator; b. Long Beach, Calif., June 6, 1942; s. Warren Nathan Burton and Dorothy Brent (Braden) Asquith; children: Melissa, Christopher; m. Ellen Greenberger, Aug. 26, 1979. BS in Econs., MIT, 1964; PhD in Anthropology, Stanford U., 1968. Rsch. fellow Harvard U., 1968-69; asst. prof. U. Calif., Irvine, 1969-76; rsch. fellow U. Nairobi, Kenya, 1973-74; assoc. prof. U. Calif., Irvine, 1976-83, prof., 1983—, chmn., dept. anthropology, 1986-91. Contbr. articles to profl. jours. NSF grantee, 1981-89, 91-93. Mem. Am. Anthropol. Assn., Soc. for Cross-Cultural Rsch., Soc. Econ. Anthropology, Soc. Applied Anthropology, Assn. Social Anthropology of Oceania. Home: 10 Morning Sun Irvine CA 92612-3715 Office: U Calif Dept Anthropology Irvine CA 92697-5100 E-mail: mlburton@uci.edu

BURTON, MIKE, county official; BA, Oreg. State U. Ret. lt. col. USAF; Mem. Oregon Ho. Reps., 1985, spkr. pro. tem., 1989; chmn. bus. mgmt. dept. Marylhurst Coll.; exec. officer Metro, Portland, Oreg., 1995—; exec dir. The Oregon Zoo, Portland. Mem. N.W. Coun. of Pres. Clinton's Coun. on Sustainable Devel., Transatlantic Policy Coun. for Clean Air and Transp., Oregon Gov.'s Growth Task Force, Gov.'s Salmon Strategy Group. Office: Metro 600 NE Grand Ave Portland OR 97232-2799

BURTON, PAUL FLOYD, social worker; b. Seattle, May 24, 1939; s. Floyd James and Mary Teresa (Chovanak) B.; m. Roxanne Maude Johnson, July 21, 1961; children: Russell Floyd, Joan Teresa. BA, U. Wash., 1961, MSW, 1967. Juvenile parole counselor Divsn. Juvenile Rehab. State of Wash., 1961-66; social worker VA, Seattle, 1967-72; social worker, cons. Work Release Program, King County, 1967-72; supr., chief psychiatry sect. Social Work Svc. VA, Topeka, 1972-73; pvt. practice Topeka and L.A., 1972—; chief social work svc. VA, Sepulveda, Calif., 1973-98; assoc. dir. Cmty. Care Svcs., VA Greater L.A. Healthcare System, 1998—2001, dir. cmty. residential care, 2001—. EEO coord. Med. ctr., 1974-77. Mem. NASW (newsletter edito Puget Sound chpt. 1970-71), Acad. Cert. Social Workers, Ctr. for Studies in Social Functioning, Am. Hosp. Assn., Soc. Social Work Adminstrs. in Health Care, Assn. VA Social Work Mgrs. (founder 1979, charter mem. and pres. 1980-81, newsletter editor 1982-83, 89-91, pres. elect 1993-95, pres. 1995-97, newsletter editor 2000-2002). Home: 14063 Remington St Arleta CA 91331-5359 Office: 16111 Plummer St Sepulveda CA 91343-2036

BURTON, R. JOHNNIE MEDINGER, state official, data processing executive, finance company executive; b. Birkadem, Algeria, Dec. 18, 1939; came to U.S., 1963; d. Georges Justin and Elise Rose (Pettinati) Medinger; m. Jean-Paul Gustin, June 4, 1959 (div. May 1965): M. Guy C. Burton Jr., Jan 21, 1966; children: Craig G., Valerie A. Licence-és-lettres, U. Sorbonne, 1962; MA, U. Wyo., 1974. Tchr. French Wantagh (N.Y.) Sch. Dist., 1963-65; lectr. Queens Coll., N.Y.C. U., 1965-66; tchr. Natrona County Sch. dist., Casper, Wyo., 1966-68; pres., chief exec. officer Hotline Energy Reports, Casper, 1978-84; mem. Wyo. Ho. of Reps., Cheyenne, 1982-88; corp. v.p. Dwight's Energy Data, Dallas, 1984-89; dir. dept. revenue State of Wyo., 1995—. Lectr. U. Ark., 1989-94. Mem. Natrona County Sch. Bd., Casper, 1976-82; adv. mem. Casper dist. Bur. Land Mgmt., 1986-88; bd. dirs. Wyo. Heritage Soc., 1986-88. Mem. Am. Assn. Tchrs. French, Société des Professeurs Francais en Amerique, Fgn. Relations Com. (Wyo. chpt.). Republican. Roman Catholic. Avocations: reading, needlepoint, folk arts and crafts. Office: Dept of Revenue Herschler Bldg Cheyenne WY 82002-0001 E-mail: johnnie.burton@state.wy.us

BURTON, RANDALL JAMES, lawyer; b. Sacramento, Feb. 4, 1950; s. Edward Jay and Bernice Mae (Overton) B.; children: Kelly Jacquelyn, Andrew Jameson; m. Kimberly D. Rogers, Apr. 29, 1989. BA, Rutgers U., 1972; JD, Southwestern U., 1975. Bar: Calif. 1976, U.S. Dist. Ct. (ea. dist.) Calif. 1976, U.S. Dist. Ct. (no. dist.) Calif., 1990, U.S. Supreme Ct, 1991. Assoc. Brekke & Mathews, Citrus Heights, Calif., 1976; pvt. practice, Sacramento, 1976-93; ptnr. Burton & White, Sacramento, 1993—; judge pro tem Sacramento Small Claims Ct., 1982—. Bd. dirs. North Highlands Recreation and Park Dist., 1978-86, Family Svc. Agy. of Sacramento, 1991-96; active Local Bd. 22, Selective Svc., 1982—, Active 20-30 Club of Sacramento, 1979-90, pres., 1987. Recipient Disting. Citizen award, Golden Empire Council, Boy Scouts Am. Mem. Sacramento Bar Assn., Sacramento Young Lawyers Assn. Presbyterian. Lodge: Rotary (pres. Foothill-Highlands club 1980-81). Office: 1540 River Park Dr Ste 224 Sacramento CA 95815-4609

BURTON, ROBERT LYLE, accounting firm executive; m. Lee Sanders; 2 children. Diploma, Kinman Bus. U. CPA. With LeMaster & Daniels, Spokane, Wash., 1963-86, mng. ptnr., 1986-97, sr. advisor, 1997—. Adv. bd. acctg. dept. U. Wash.; chmn. The Am. Group of CPA Firms. Trustee Econ. Devel. Coun.; past chmn. Samaritan Hosp. Found., Moses Lake, Wash. Mem. AICPA (agri-bus. com., adv. group B), Washington Soc. CPAs (former dir., v.p., com. chmn., legis. com.), Spokane Club, Inland Empire Fly Fishermen, Moses Lake Golf and Country Club, Rotary. Office: LeMaster & Daniels 8817 E Mission Ave Spokane WA 99212-2352

BUSCH, JOYCE IDA, small business owner; b. Madera, Calif., Jan. 24, 1934; d. Bruno Harry and Ella Fae (Absher) Toschi; m. Fred O. Busch, Dec. 14, 1956; children: Karen, Kathryn, Kurt. BA in Indsl. Arts & Interior Design, Calif. State U., Fresno, 1991. Cert. interior designer, Calif. Stewardess United Air Lines, San Francisco, 1955-57; prin. Art Coordinates, Fresno, 1982—, Busch Interior Design, Fresno, 1982—. Art cons. Fresno Community Hosp., 1981-83; docent Fresno Met. Mus., 1981-84. Treas. Valley Children's Hosp. Guidance Clinic, 1975-79, Lone Star PTA, 1965-84,; mem. Mothers Guild San Joaquin Mem. H.S., 1984-88. Mem. Am. Soc. Interior Designers. Republican. Roman Catholic. Club: Sunnyside Garden (pres. 1987-88). Avocations: gardening, art history.

BUSECK, PETER R. geochemistry educator; s. Paul M. and Edith G. (Stern) B.; m. Alice E. Bien, June 20, 1960; children: Lori, David, Susan, Paul. AB, Antioch Coll., 1957; MA, Columbia U., 1959, PhD, 1962. Fellow Geophys. Lab. Carnegie Inst., Washington, 1961-63; mem. faculty depts. chemistry and geology Ariz. State U., Tempe, 1963—, Regents' prof., 1989—. Vis. prof. geology Oxford (Eng.) U., 1970-71, Stanford (Calif.) U., 1979-80, U. Paris, 1986-87; spl. asst. to dir. NSF, 1994-95; mem. sci. staff Office of Sci. and Tech. Policy, White House, 1994-95. Contbr. articles to profl. jours. NSF fellow, 1970-71. Fellow AAAS, Geol. Soc. Am., Meteorite Soc., Mineral Soc. Am., Soc. Econ. Geologists; mem. Am. Geophys. Union, Geochem. Soc., Microbeam Soc., Can. Mineral Soc., Microscope Soc. Am., Am. Crystallographic Assn. Office: Ariz State U Dept Geology Tempe AZ 85287 E-mail: pbuseck@asu.edu

BUSH, SARAH LILLIAN, historian; b. Kansas City, Mo., Sept. 17, 1920; d. William Adam and Lettie Evelyn (Burrill) Lewis; m. Walter Nelson Bush, June 7, 1946 (dec.); children: William Read, Robert Nelson. AB, U. Kans., 1941; BS, U. Ill., 1943. Clk. circulation dept. Kansas City Pub. Library, 1941-42, asst. librarian Paseo br., 1943-44; librarian Kansas City Jr. Coll., 1944-46; substitute librarian San Mateo County Library, Woodside and Portola Valley, Calif., 1976-77; [illegible]

1979-87; owner Metriguide, Palo Alto, Calif., 1975-78. Author: Atherton Lands, 1979, rev. edition 1987. Editor. Atherton Recollections, 1973. Pres., v.p. Jr. Librarians, Kansas City, 1944-46; courtesy, yearbook & historian AAUW, Menlo- Atherton branch (Calif.) Br.; asst. Sunday sch. tchr., vol. Holy Trinity Ch., Menlo Park, 1955-78; v.p., membership com., libr. chairperson, English reading program, parent edn. chairperson Menlo Atherton High Sch. PTA, 1964-73; founder, bd. dirs. Friends of Atherton Community Library, 1967—, oral historian, 1968—, chair Bicentennial event, 1976; bd. dirs. Menlo Park Hist. Assn., 1979-82, oral historian, 1973—; bd. dirs. Civic Interest League, Atherton, 1978-81; mem. hist. county commn. Town of Atherton, 1980-87; vol. Allied Arts Palo Alto Aux. to Children's Hosp. at Stanford, 1967—, oral historian, 1978—, historian, 1980—; vol. United Crusade, Garfield Sch., Redwood City, 1957-61, 74-88, Encinal Sch., Menlo Park, Calif., 1961-73, program dir., chmn. summer recreation, historian, sec.; vol. Stanford Mothers Club, 1977-81, others; historian, awards chairperson Cub Scouts Boy Scouts Am.; founder Atherton Heritage Assn. 1989, bd. dirs., 1989—, dir., 1989-94; mem. Guild Gourmet, 1971—, Mid Peninsula History Consortium, 1993-95. Recipient Good Neighbor award Civic Interest League, 1992. Mem. PTA (life). Episcopalian. Avocations: gourmet cooking, entertaining, reading.

BUSH, SPENCER HARRISON, metallurgist, consultant; b. Flint, Mich., Apr. 4, 1920; s. Edward Charles and Rachel Beatrice (Roser) B.; m. Roberta Lee Warren, Aug. 28, 1948; children: David Spencer, Carl Edward. Student, Flint Jr. Coll., 1938-40, Ohio State U., 1943-44, U. Mich., 1946-53. Registered profl. engr., Calif. Asst. chemist Dow Chem. Co., 1940-42, 46; assoc. Engring. Rsch. Inst., U. Mich., 1947-53; research asst. Office Naval Rsch., 1950-53, instr. dental materials, 1951-53; metallurgist Hanford Atomic Products Operation, Gen. Electric Co., 1953-54, supr. phys. metallurgy, 1954-57, supr. fuels fabrication devel., 1957-60, metall. specialist, 1960-63, cons. metallurgist, 1963-65; cons. to dir. Battelle Pacific N.W. Labs., Richland, Wash., 1965-70, sr. staff cons., 1970-83, sr. staff scientist, 1985-2000; pres. Rev. & Synthesis Assocs., cons., 1983—. Lectr. metall. engring. Ctr. for Grad. Study U. Wash., 1953-67, affiliate prof., 1967-78; chmn., mem. com. study group on pressure vessel materials Electric Power Rsch. Inst., 1974-78; cons. U. Calif. Lawrence Livermore Labs., 1975-79, Integral Fast Reactor U. Chgo., 1984-94; chmn. com. on reactor safeguards U.S. AEC, 1971; mem. Wash. Bd. Boiler Rules, 1972-85; mem. spec. adv. com. for Argonne Nuc. Tech. Pgm., U Chgo. 1994—; chmn. piping design com. Joint NRC/Pressure Vessel Rsch. Coun., 1982-90, PVRC Peer Rev. on ASME Code Simplification, exec. com., 1982—, mem. steering com. on fatigue, 1992—, hon. emeritus mem., 1999; mem. nuclear safety rsch. rev. com. NRC, 1988-94; mem. high level waste structural integrity panel Dept. Energy Brookhaven Nat. Lab., 1992-97. Contbr. tech. articles to profl. jours. Served with U.S. Army, 1942-46. Recipient Silver Beaver award Boy Scouts Am.; Am. Foundrymens Soc. fellow, 1948-50; Regents prof. U. Calif., Berkeley, 1973-74 Fellow ASME (hon., bd. nuc. codes and stds. 1983-2000, chmn. sec. XI 1985-90, hon. mem. subcom. XI 1995, exec. bd. NDE divsn. 1984-90, chmn. 1987-88, nat. nominating com. 1988-90, Langer award 1983, Melvin R. Green Codes & Stds. medal 1997), ASM (life, chmn. program coun. 1966-67, trustee 1967-69, chmn. fellow com. 1968), Am. Nuc. Soc. (adv. editl. bd. nuc. applications 1965-77, bd. dirs. 1984-87, Thompson award 1987); mem. AIME (chmn. ann. seminar com. 1967-68), ASTM (Gillette lectr. 1975), Am. Soc. Nondestructive Testing (Mehl lectr.), Nat. Acad. Engring., Sigma Xi, Tau Beta Pi, Phi Kappa Phi. Home and Office: 630 Cedar Ave Richland WA 99352-3632 E-mail: snb2544@bossig.com

BUSH, STANLEY GILTNER, secondary school educator; b. Kansas City, Mo., Nov. 4, 1928; s. Dean Thomas and Sallie Giltner (Hoagland) B.; m. Barbara Snow Adams, May 23, 1975 (dec. Mar. 1994); stepchildren: Deborah Gayle Duclon, Douglas Bruce Adams. BA, U. Colo., 1949, MA, 1959, postgrad., 1971, U. Denver, 1980, 85, 90. Tchr. Gering (Nebr.) Pub. Schs., 1949-51, 54-57, Littleton (Colo.) Pub. Schs., 1957-91. Emergency plan dir. City of Littleton, 1961—; safety officer Littleton Pub. Schs., 1968—; founder, chief Arapahoe Rescue Patrol, Inc., Littleton, 1957-92, search mission coord., 1975—; pres. Arapahoe Rescue Patrol, Inc., 1957—, Expedition, Inc., Littleton, 1973—; owner Emergency Rsch. Cons., 1990—. Contbr. chpts. to Boy Scout Field Book, 1984; co-author: Managing Search Function, 1987; contbr. articles to profl. jours. Safety advisor South Suburban Parks Dist., Littleton, 1985—; advisor ARC, Littleton, 1987—, Emergency Planning Com., Arapahoe County, Colo., 1987—; coord. search and rescue Office of Gov., Colo., 1978-82; state judge Odyssey of the Mind, 1996-97. Sgt. U.S. Army, 1951-54. Shell Oil Co. fellow, 1964; recipient Silver Beaver award Boy Scouts Am., 1966, Vigil-Order of Arrow, 1966, Award of Excellence Masons, 1990, Service to Mankind award Arapahoe Sertoma, 1999. Mem. Nat. Assn. for Search and Rescue (life, Hall Foss award 1978), Colo. Search and Rescue Bd., NEA (life). Methodist. Avocations: mountaineering, wilderness emergency care, emergency services. Home: 2415 E Maplewood Ave Littleton CO 80121-2817 Office: Littleton Ctr 2255 W Berry Ave Littleton CO 80165-0001 E-mail: sbsbush@aol.com

BUSHEY, RICHARD KENNETH, utility executive; b. Alhambra, Calif., May 1, 1940; s. Kenneth H. and Dale E. (Wheeler) B.; m. Janeil Deane Anderson, Feb. 23, 1963; 1 child, Michael. BS, UCLA, 1963; postgrad., U. So. Calif., 1965; grad. Pub. Utility Execs. program, U. Mich., 1973; grad. fin. program, Stanford U., 1976. Acct., supr., mgr. So. Calif. Edison Co., Rosemead, 1963-74, asst. treas., 1974-75, asst. contr., 1975-84, v.p., contr., 1984—, Edison Internat., Rosemead, 1988—, supplemental employee. Lst lt. U.S. Air N.G., 1963-70. Mem. L.A. C. of C., UCLA Alumni Assn., Phi Kappa Psi. Office: So Calif Edison Co 2244 Walnut Grove Ave Rosemead CA 91770-3714

BUSHNELL, RODERICK PAUL, lawyer; b. Buffalo, Mar. 6, 1944; s. Paul Hazen and Martha Atlee Bushnell; m. Suzann Yvonne Kaiser, Aug. 27, 1966; 1 child, Arlo Phillip. BA, Rutgers U., 1966; JD, Georgetown U., 1969. Bar: Calif. 1970, U.S. Supreme Ct. 1980.; cert. Civil Trial Advocate, Nat. Bd. Trial Advocates. Atty. dept. water resources, Sacramento, 1969-71; ptnr. Bushnell, Caplan & Fielding, San Francisco, 1971—. Adv. bd. dirs. Bread & Roses, Inc., Mill Valley, Calif. Mem. ATLA, San Francisco Bar Assn. (labor and employment sects.; arbitrator), San Francisco Superior Ct. (arbitrator), Fed. Ct. Early Neutral Evaluator, Calif. Bar Assn. (labor and employement sects.), Consumer Attys. Calif., San Francisco Trial Lawyers Assn., No. Calif. Criminal Trial Lawyers Assn., Nat. Employment Lawyers Assn., Calif. Employment Lawyers Assn. Office: Bushnell Caplan & Fielding 221 Pine St Ste 600 San Francisco CA 94104-2705

BUSHRE, PETER ALVIN, retired investment company executive; b. Ketchikan, Alaska, Dec. 14, 1943; s. Robert Almon and Violet Orene (Neal) B. BS, U. Ariz., 1967, MA in Acctg., 1971. Staff auditor Peat Marwick Mitchell & Co., Honolulu, 1971-72; sr. auditor Touche Ross & Co., Anchorage, 1972-73; sr. legis. auditor State of Alaska, Juneau, 1973-76, comptroller, 1976-78, treas., 1978-83; comptroller Alaska Permanent Fund Corp., Juneau, 1983-93, CFO, 1993—; pres. Bushre & Co., Anchorage, 1980—. Republican. Baptist. Avocations: investing, art, history. Home: PO Box 240028 Douglas AK 99824-0028 Office: Alaska Permanent Fund Corp 801 W 10th St Ste 302 Juneau AK 99801-1878

BUSIG, RICK HAROLD, mining executive; b. Vancouver, Wash., June 21, 1952; s. Harold Wayne and Ramona (Riley) B. AA, Clark Coll., Vancouver, 1972; BA in Econs., U. Wash., 1974. CPA, Wash. Acct. Universal Svcs., Seattle, 1975-78; acct., acctg. mgr., controller Landura Corp., Woodburn, Oreg., 1978-80; asst. controller Pulte Home Corp., [illegible]

1981-82; controller Saga Exploration Co., Reno, 1982—. Acct. Sterling Mine Joint Venture, Beatty, Nev., 1982-95. Del. Nev. State Dem. Conv., Reno, 1984, 94, Las Vegas, 1988. Recipient Spaatz award CAP. Mem. AICPA, Wash. Soc. CPA's, Oreg. Soc. CPA's. Del. Nev. State Dem. Conv., Reno, 1984, 94, Las Vegas, 1988. Recipient Spaatz award CAP. Mem. AICPA, Wash. Soc. CPA's, Oreg. Soc. CPA's. Home: 2735 Lakeside Dr Apt A Reno NV 89509-4254 Office: Saga Exploration Co 2660 Tyner Way Reno NV 89503-4926 E-mail: rickb@sierra.net

BUSS, JERRY HATTEN, real estate executive, sports team owner; Children: John, Jim, Jeanie, Jane. BS in Chemistry, U. Wyo.; MS, PhD in Chemistry, U. So. Calif., 1957. Chemist Bur. Mines; past mem. faculty dept. chemistry U. So. Calif.; mem. missile div. McDonnell Douglas, Los Angeles; partner Mariani-Buss Assos.; former owner Los Angeles Strings; chmn. bd., owner Los Angeles Lakers (Nat. Basketball Assn.), 1979—; until 1988 owner Los Angeles Kings (Nat. Hockey League), 1979—. Office: care LA Lakers 555 N Nash St El Segundo CA 90245

BUSSARD, ROBERT WILLIAM, physicist; b. Washington, Aug. 11, 1928; s. Marcel Julian and Elsa Mathilda (Griesser) B.; m. Dolly H. Gray, 1981; children: Elise Marie Bussard Chisholm, William Julian, Robert Lee, Virginia Lesley Bussard Barausky. BS in Engring., UCLA, 1950, MS in Engring., 1952; MS in Physics, Princeton U., 1959, PhD in Physics, 1961. Design engr. Falcon program Hughes Aircraft Co., 1949-51; mech. engr. aircraft nuclear propulsion project Oak Ridge Nat. Lab., 1952-55; alt. group leader nuclear rocket program Los Alamos Sci. Lab., 1955-62, alt. leader laser div., 1971-73; dir. nuclear systems staff, asst. dir. mechanics div. Space Tech. Labs., TRW Inc., Redondo Beach, Calif., 1962-64; assoc. mgr. research and engring., corp. chief scientist Electro-Optical Systems div. Xerox Corp., Pasadena, 1964-69; with CSI Corp., Los Angeles, 1969-70; mgr. Cherokee Assocs., Pasadena, Calif., 1970-72; asst. dir. div. controlled thermonuclear research U.S. AEC, Washington, 1973-74; founder, pres., chmn. Energy Resources Group (ERG), Inc., Arlington, Va., 1974-86, Internat. Nuclear Energy Systems Co. (INESCO), Inc., La Jolla, Calif. and McLean, Va., 1976-84; sr. scientist PSR Corp., Arlington, Va., 1985-89; founder, tech. dir. Energy/Matter Conversion Corp. (EMC2), San Diego, 1984—. Cons. NATO, 1960-64, U.S. Dept. Energy, 1974-78, Los Alamos Sci. Lab., 1973-88, dir. ctrl. intelligence, 1971-78; lectr. UCLA, 1960-69, U. Fla., 1962-64 Author: (with R.D. DeLauer) Nuclear Rocket Propulsion, 1958, Fundamentals of Nuclear Flight, 1965; editor: Nuclear Thermal and Electric Rocket Propulsion, 1967; contbr. articles to profl. jours. Fellow AIAA; mem. Am. Phys. Soc., Internat. Acad. Astronautics. Clubs: Princeton (N.Y.C.); Cosmos (Washington), Capitol Hill (Washington). Achievements include patentee space nuclear propulsion, power generation, fusion and fission power, solar power systems. Office: Ste 103 9705 Carroll Center Rd San Diego CA 92126-6505 E-mail: emc2qed@compuserve.com

BUSTAMANTE, CRUZ M. state official; b. Dinuba, Calif., 1953; s. Cruz and Dominga Bustamante Jr.; m. Arcelia De La Pena; children: Leticia, Sonia, Marisa. Student, Fresno City Coll., Fresno State U. Past intern for Congressman B.F. Sisk, Washington; formerly with Fresno employment and tng. commn. City of Fresno, past program dir. summer youth employment tng. program; past dist. rep. Congressman Rick Lehman and Assemblyman Bruce Bronzan State of Calif.; mem. Calif. State Assembly, 1993, spkr. of assembly, 1996-98; lt. gov. State of Calif., 1998—. Mem. U.S. Census Monitoring Bd. Trustee Calif. State U. Named Legislator of Yr. Faculty Assn. Cmty. Colls., Assn. Mexican Am. Educators, U. Calif. Alumni Assn., True Am. Role Model Mexican Am. Polit. Assn.; recipient Lifetime award Golden State Mobilehome Owners League, Friend of Labor award Mexican Am. Polit. Assn. Office: State Capitol Rm 1114 Sacramento CA 95814 also: Ste 12702 300 S Spring St Los Angeles CA 90013 Office Fax: 916-323-4998; 213-897-7156

BUSTAMANTE, TOMMY A. protective services official; married; 3 children. B of Criminal Justice, N.Mex. State U., 1984. U.S. marshal U.S. Marshal Svc., Dept. of Justice, Brownsville, Tex., 1986-91, supervisory dep. U.S. marshal Albuquerque, 1991-98, chief dep. U.S. marshal for Dist. of N.Mex., 1998—.

BUTCHER, EDWARD B. state senator; b. Lewistown, Mont., July 20, 1943; m. Pamela Butcher; children: Trevis, Ross, Becky. BA, Ea. Mont. State, 1965; MA, U. Mont., 1967; postgrad., U. Colo., 1967, N.D. State U., 1969. Asst. prof. Valley City State U., 1968-71; owner Rolling Hills Ranch, 1972—; lectr. Am. studies U. Great Falls, 1974-79; nat. sales dir. Evans Bio Corp, 1987-88; sr. regional mgr. Attco Assocs., 1988—; Rep. senator dist. 47 Mont. State Senate, 2000—. Mem. exec. com. Gov.'s Agr. Adv. Bd., 1980-84; chair Montanans for Term Limits, 1992. Mem. Mont. Bd. Crime Control, 1976-80; chair Fergus County Review Commn., 1994-96. Lutheran. Office: PO Box 89 800 Butcher Rd Winifred MT 59489 E-mail: butcher@ttc-cmc.net

BUTENHOFF, SUSAN, public relations executive; b. N.Y.C., Jan. 13, 1960; BA in Internat. Rels. with hons., Sussex U., Eng.; MPhil, Wolfson Coll., Cambridge U., Eng. Account exec. Ellen Farmer Prodns., 1984-85, Ketchum Pub. Rels., N.Y.C., 1988-90, v.p., account supr., 1990-91; prin., CEO Access Pub. Rels., San Francisco, 1991—, pres., CEO. Mem. Pub. Rels. Soc. Am. Office: Access Comm 101 Howard St Fl 2D San Francisco CA 94105-1629

BUTLER, DASCHEL E. protective services official; Chief of police, Berkeley, Calif. Office: 2100 Martin Luther King Jr Way Berkeley CA 94704-1109

BUTLER, DAVID, lawyer; b. St. Paul, June 11, 1930; s. Francis David and Alida (Bigelow) B.; m. Diana Dodge Duffy, Aug. 29, 1952 (div. 1957); children: Anne, Lawrence David; m. Barbara Williams Clark, July 12, 1958; children: Molly Elizabeth, Peter, Katherine BA, Princeton U., 1952; LLB, Harvard U., 1957. Bar. Colo. 1958, U.S. Dist. Ct. Colo. 1958. Assoc. Holland & Hart, Denver, 1957-63, ptnr., 1963-95, chmn. mgmt. com., 1990-95; of counsel, 1996—. Gen. counsel 1st Interstate Bank Denver, 1984-86; bd. dirs. UMB Bank Colo., Denver. Mem. bd. editors Harvard Law Rev., 1955-57. Chmn. lawyers adv. com. United Way, Denver, 1989-94; bd. dirs. Met. Denver Legal Aid Soc., 1971-74, Colo. Lawyers Trust Found.; trustee Graland Country Day Sch., Denver, 1971-79, Legal Aid Found. Colo., 1991-97, chmn., 1993-97; chmn. Colo. Planning Group for Legal Svcs. to the Poor. 1st lt. U.S. Army, 1952-54. Mem. ABA, Colo. Bar Assn. (chmn. tax sect. 1970), Denver Bar Assn. Office: Holland & Hart 555 17th St Ste 2900 Denver CO 80202-3979

BUTLER, JACK FAIRCHILD, semiconductors company executive; b. El Centro, Calif., July 18, 1933; s. Jack Orval and Dorothy (Marsh) B.; m. Colette Alice Guerard, Sept. 6, 1959; children— Alice, Jack, Michael, Patricia. Student, San Jose State Coll., 1951-54; B.S., U. Calif., Berkeley, 1959, M.S., 1960, Ph.D., 1962. Research staff mem. Mass. Inst. Tech., Lincoln Lab., Lexington, Mass., 1962-68; staff scientist Gen. Dynamics Corp., Pomona, Calif., 1968-71; sr. staff mem. Arthur D. Little, Inc., Cambridge, Mass., 1971-74; co-founder, co-owner, dir., pres. Laser Analytics, Inc., Lexington, 1974-81; founder, owner, dir., pres. Butler Research and Engring., Inc., 1981-85; co-founder, co-owner, dir., pres. San Diego Semicondrs., Inc., 1985-91, Aurora Techs. Corp., 1991-95; co-founder, co-owner, pres. Digirad (formerly Aurora Techs. Corp.), 1995-98; ret., 1998. Contbr. articles to sci. jours. Served with USMC, 1954-57. Mem. [illegible]

BUTLER, JAMES ROBERTSON, JR. lawyer; b. Cleve., May 29, 1946; s. James Robertson and Iris Davis (Welborn) B. AB magna cum laude, U. Calif., Berkeley, 1966, JD, 1969. Bar: Calif. 1970, U.S. Tax Ct. 1977, U.S. Supreme Ct. 1980, Nev. 1997. Chmn. real estate dept. and Global Hospitality Group Jeffer, Mangels, Butler & Marmaro, LLP, L.A. and San Francisco, 1982—. Founder, chmn. JMBM Global Hospitality Group Briefing Series, 1991—, ULI Los Angeles Hospitality Product Coun., 2000—; expert panelist on hospitality industry topics NYU Hospitality Industry Investment Conf., UCLA Hospitality Investment Conf., Calif. Soc. CPAs ann. hospitality confs., 1992, 93, 94, 95; spkr., panelist Robert Morris Assocs. Nat. Conf., Chgo., 1989, nat. ann. conf. Ind. Bankers Assn. Am., 1992; frequent guest expert securities, real estate and banking various TV programs, 1985—; participant comml. real estate workouts workshop FDIC & RTC Nat. Tng. Conf., San Antonio, 1989, San Diego, 1990; adv. bd. Bur. Nat. Affairs, Washington. Author: Arbitration in Banking, A Robert Morris Associates State of the Art Book, 1988, Lender Liability: A Practical Guide, A BNA Special Report, 1987; editor Global Hospitality Advisor 1991—, Banking Law Report Capital Adequacy series, 1985, Global Hospitality Advisor, 1991—, Calif. Law Rev.; co-chmn. adv. council Money and Real Estate: The Jour. of Lending, Syndication, Joint Ventures, and the Third Market; contbr. chpt., Mapping the Minefield--Lender's Liability, The Workout Game, Solutions to Problem Real Estate Loans, 1987; contbr. more than 100 articles to profl. jours, chaps. to books. Mem. Am. Arbitration Assn., Comml. Arbitration Panel; founding dir. Liberty Nat. Bank; Charter Adv. bd. dirs., Adv. Council of the Banking Law Inst. Recipient Kraft Prize U. Calif., 1966; Bartley Cavenaugh Crum scholar U. Calif. Sch. Law, 1969. Mem. ABA (corp., banking and bus. law sect., taxation sect.), Urban Land Inst. (chmn. hospitality product coun., exec. com. L.A. Dist. coun. 2000—), Internat. Soc. Hospitality Cons., L.A. County Bar Assn., Century City Bar Assn. (chmn. fin. instn. sect. 1990-91), Beverly Hills Bar Assn., Calif. League of Savs. Instns. (chmn. arbitration com. 1987, 88), Young Pres.' Orgn. (internat. hospitality conference, Milan, 2001). Avocations: personal computers (beta reviewer for various software developers including, Microsoft). Office: Jeffer Mangels Butler & Marmaro LLP 2121 Avenue Of The Stars Los Angeles CA 90067-5010 E-mail: jbutler@jmbm.com

BUTLER, JON TERRY, computer engineering educator, researcher; b. Balt., Dec. 26, 1943; s. Herbert Harriss and Vera Esse (Buck) B.; m. Susan Beth Wood, Feb. 24, 1968 (d iv. Aug. 1996); 1 child, Anne Elizabeth; m. Fujiko Sakaguchi, Jan. 31, 1998. BEE, Rensselaer Poly. Inst., 1966, M in Engring., 1967; PhD, Ohio State U., 1973. Registered profl. engr., Ohio. NRC postdoctoral assoc. Air Force Avionics Lab., Wright-Patterson AFB, Ohio, 1973-74; sr. postdoctoral assoc. Naval Postgrad. Sch., Wright-Patterson AFB, 1980-81; assoc. prof. Northwestern U., Evanston, Ill., 1974-87; prof. Naval Postgrad. Sch., Monterey, Calif., 1987—, Navalex Chair prof., 1985-87. Editor: Multi-Valued Logic in VLSI, 1991; contbr. articles to profl. jours. Capt. USAF, 1967-70. Recipient Faculty Performance award Naval Postgrad. Sch., 1990-93. Fellow IEEE; mem. IEEE Computer Soc. (chmn. multiple-valued logic com. 1980-81, Disting. vis. 1982-86, press editor 1986-90, editor-in-chief Computer mag. 1991-92, editor-in-chief Computer Soc. Press 1993-97, chmn. Computer Soc. fellows evaluation com. 1999, chmn. Computer Soc. transactions ops. com. 1998-99, chmn. Computer Soc. Press ops. com. 2000—, Meritorious Svc. award 1988, 92, TAB Pioneer award 1989, cert. appreciation 1982, 89, 91, 95, 96, 99, 2000, Disting. Svc. award 1995, Third Centennial medal 2000, bd. govs. 1991-97). Presbyterian. Avocation: jogging. Office: Naval Postgrad Sch Dept Elec Computer Engring Code EC-BU Monterey CA 93943-5121

BUTMAN, HARRY RAYMOND, clergyman, writer; b. Beverly, Mass., Mar. 20, 1904; s. John Choate and Elsie Louise (Raymond) B.; m. Jennette Alice Stott, Jan. 5, 1929; children: Beverly, Raymond, Jack, Jennette. BD, Bangor Sem., 1928; postgrad., U. Vt., 1933; DD (hon.), Piedmont Coll., 1955. Ordained to ministry Congregational Ch., 1932. Minister Federated Ch., Edgartown, Mass., 1932-37, Congl. Ch., Randolph, 1937-45, Allin Congl. Ch., Dedham, 1945-53, Ch. of the Messiah, L.A., 1953-78; interim minister First Congl. Ch., L.A., 1978-81, cons., 1982—. Moderator Nat. Assn. Congl. Christian Chs., 1963, chmn. exec. com., 1958, 59, 74; editor, The Congregationalist, 1967-68; chmn. Internat. Congl. Fellowship, London, 1977-81. Author: History of Randolph, 1942, Far Islands, 1954, Preamble to Articles of Assn. for Nat. Assn. Congl. Christian Chs., 1956, The Measure of the Immeasurable, 1967, The Lord's Free People, 1968, Serve with Gladness, 1971, The Theology of Congregationalism, 1975, The Chislehurst Thanksgiving, 1976, The Argent Year, 1980, World Book Ency., Manuscript of Nat. Assn. Congl. Christian Chs., 1981, The Desert Face of God, 1985, Brown Boy, 1987, The Good Beasts, 1991, The Soul's Country, 1994, Symbols of Our Way, 1994, A Quiet and Durable Joy, 1996, A Long Green Flash, 2000, A Thinking Man's Faith, 2000; contbr. articles to profl. jours. Named for Best Patriotic Sermon Freedoms Found., 1972; honoree of the Harry R. Butman Endowed Chair of Religion and Philosphy Piedmont Coll., Demorest, Ga., 1994; prelate The Soc. of Descendants of Knights of the Most Noble Order of the Garter, 1972—. Republican. Avocations: boating, desert driving. Home: 2451 Soledad Canyon Rd Acton CA 93510-2416

BUTOW, ROBERT JOSEPH CHARLES, history educator; b. San Mateo, Calif., Mar. 19, 1924; s. Frederick W.C. and Louise Marie B.; m. Irene Elkeles; 1 child, Stephanie Cecile. BA magna cum laude, Stanford U., 1947, MA, 1948, PhD, 1953. Instr. history Princeton U., 1954-59, asst. prof., 1959-60, rsch. assoc. Ctr. of Internat. Studies, 1954-60; assoc. prof. East Asian history and internat. studies U. Wash., Seattle, 1960-66, prof., 1966-90, prof. emeritus, 1990—. Mem. Inst. for Advanced Study, 1962-63. Author: Japan's Decision to Surrender, 1954, 67, Tojo and the Coming of the War, 1961, 69, The John Doe Associates: Backdoor Diplomacy for Peace, 1941, 1974. 2d lt. U.S. Army, 1943-46. Grantee Social Sci. Rsch. Coun., 1956-57, Rockefeller Found., 1956-57, Eleanor Roosevelt Inst., 1977-78; Guggenheim fellow, 1965-66, 78-79, fellow Woodrow Wilson Ctr., 1987-88, Japan Found., 1987-88. Mem. Assn. of Mems. of Inst. for Advanced Study, Soc. Historians of Am. Fgn. Rels., World War Two Studies Assn. Office: U Wash Box 353650 Seattle WA 98195-3650

BUTTARS, D. CHRIS, state legislator; b. Logan, Utah, Apr. 1, 1942; m. Helen; children: Christie, David, Todd, Robin, Angie, Michelle. BS, Utah State U., 1967. Retail sales mgr. Amoco Oil Co., 1967-76; exec. dir. Petroleum/Retailers Orgn., 1976-86, Utah Boys Ranch, 1991—; mem. Utah State Senate, Salt Lake City, 2001—. Mem. West Jordan City Coun., 1979-83. Mem. LDS Ch. Office: 9241 S Lisa Ave West Jordan UT 84088*

BUTTARS, GERALD ANDERSON, librarian; b. Logan, Utah, Oct. 12, 1939; s. Thomas James and Mary (Anderson) B.; m. Jeannie Webb, June 3, 1966; children: Brian Gerald, Angela. BS, Utah State U., 1967; MLS, Brigham Young U., 1970. Dir. libr. for blind and phys. handicapped Utah State Libr., Salt Lake City, 1965—. Recipient Disting. Svc. awards Utah Coun. for Blind, 1979, Brigham Young U., 1986, Francis Joseph Campbell award and citation ALA, 1998. Mem. AIA, Utah Libr. Assn. (exec. sec. 1972-87), Nat. Fedn. Blind, Am. Coun. for Blind. Republican. Mem. LDS Ch. Home: 4749 W 3280 S Salt Lake City UT 84120-1566 Office: Utah State Libr Blind & Physically Handicapped Program 250 N 1950 W Ste A Salt Lake City UT 84116-7901 E-mail: gbuttars@library.state.ut.us

BUTTERFIELD, ALEXANDER PORTER, former business executive, government official; b. Pensacola, Fla., Apr. 6, 1926; s. Horace Bushnell and Susan A. (Alexander) B.; m. Charlotte Mary Maguire, Sept. 9, 1949 (div. Jan. 1985); children: Leslie Carter (dec.), Alexander Porter Jr., Susan Carter Holcomb, Elisabeth Gordon Buchholz. BS, U. Md., 1956; MS, George Washington U., 1967; PhD (hon.), Embry-Riddle U., 1973. Commd. 2d lt. USAF, 1949, advanced through grades to col., 1966, fighter pilot, fighter-gunnery instr., weapons officer, mem. Skyblazers (U.S. jet aerobatic team Europe), 1949-53; aide to comdr. 4th Allied Tactical Air Force NATO, 1954-55; ops. officer interceptor squadron, 1955-56; asst. prof. USAF Acad., 1957-59; sr. aide to comdr.-in-chief U.S. Pacific Air Forces, 1959-62; comdr. fighter squadron Okinawa, 1962-63; comdr. tactical reconnaissance task forces S.E. Asia, 1963-64; tactical air warfare policy planner USAF hdqrs., 1964-65; mil. asst. to spl. asst. sec. def., 1965-66; student Nat. War Coll., 1966-67; sr. U.S. mil. rep., comdr. in chief Pacific rep. Australia, 1967-69; retired, 1969; dep. asst. Pres. Richard M. Nixon, 1969-73; sec. to Cabinet, 1969-73; adminstr. FAA, 1973-75; lectr. Ethics in Govt. Am. Program Bur., 1975-76; exec. v.p., chief oper. officer, dir. Internat. Air Svc. Co. Ltd., 1977-79; pres., chief oper. officer, dir. Calif. Life Corp., 1979-80. Chmn. GMA Corp., Global Network Inc., 1981-82; chmn., chief exec. officer Armistead & Alexander, Inc., 1983-94; bd. dirs. Aloha Airlines Inc. Contbr. articles to profl. jours. and nat. mags.; mem. editorial bd. L.A. County Mus. Natural History mag. Terra, 1983-86. Presidentially apptd. mem. Nat. Armed Forces Mus. adv. bd. Smithsonian Instn., 1970-76; bd. dirs. Internat. Flight Safety Found., L.A. County Mus. Natural History, 1981-85; mem. mil. sci. expedition to South Pole, 1968; leader of U.S. govt. industry del. to Moscow for ministerial level talks on tech. and trade, 1973; key witness U.S. senate select com.'s hearings on Watergate, 1973, and before U.S. Ho. of Reps. Judiciary Com. during its deliberations of impeachment of Pres. Richard Nixon, 1974. Decorated Legion of Merit, DFC, Air medal with 3 bronze oak leaf clusters, Bronze Star. Mem. Am. Film Inst., Screen Actors Guild, Coun. for Excellence in Govt., Tailhook Assn., Air Force Assn., Bel-Air Country Club (L.A.), Univ. Club (San Diego).

BUTTERFIELD, DEBORAH KAY, sculptor; b. San Diego, May 7, 1949; BA, U. Calif., Davis, 1971, MFA, 1973. Asst. prof. sculpture U. Wis., Madison, 1975-76, Mont. State U., Bozeman, 1979-81, adj. prof., 1981-84. One-man shows include Lowe Mus. Art U. Miami, Coral Gables, Fla., 1992, San Diego Mus. Art, 1996; exhibited in groups shows U. Mus. Berkeley, Calif., 1974, Whitney Mus. Am. Art, N.Y., 1979, Albright-Knox Gallery, Buffalo, 1979, Israel Mus., Jerusalem, 1980, Arco Ctr. Visual Art, 1981, Walker Art Ctr., Mpls., 1982, Dallas Mus. Fine Arts, 1982, Oakland, 1983, Chgo., 1985, Contemporary Art Ctr., Honolulu, 1986, Whitney Mus., 1988, Contemporary Art Mus., Honolulu, 1993, Seattle Mus. Art, 1994, The White House, Washington, Yale U., New Haven, Conn., 1997; represented in permanent collections Whitney Mus. Am. Art, N.Y., San Francisco Mus. Contemporary Art, Israel Mus., Jerusalem, Walker Art Ctr., Mpls., Met. Mus. Art, N.Y., Hirshhorn Mus., Washington, Seattle Art Mus., UCLA Sculpture Garden; commd. Copley Square, Boston, Portland (Oreg.) Airport, Denver Art Mus., Kansas City (Mo.) Zoo, White House, Washington, 2000. Nat. Endowment Arts grantee, 1977, 80, Guggenheim grantee, 1980; Commission Portland Internat. Airport.

BUTTERFIELD, SAMUEL HALE, former government official, educator; b. Moscow, Nov. 8, 1924; s. Rolston Samuel and Leone (Hamilton) B.; m. Lois Herrington, Feb. 10, 1948; children: Charles Oliver, Stephen Crandall, Susan Hale (Mrs. Charles P. Waite, Jr.). Student, U. Idaho, 1942-43, 46-47; B.S. in Fgn. Service, Georgetown U., 1949, M.A. in Am. History, 1953. Retail salesman, 1949-50; labor economist Dept. Labor, 1950-53; examiner, fiscal economist, internat. div. Bur. Budget, 1953-58; with AID and predecessors, 1958-80; dir. Office East and So. Africa, 1960 62; dep. dir. Mission to Tanganyika, 1962-64, Mission to Sudan, 1964-65; dir. Mission to Tanzania, 1966-68; mem. sr. seminar in fgn. policy Dept. State, 1968-69; assoc. asst. adminstr. for tech. assistance AID, 1969-76; dir. Mission to Nepal, 1976-80; affiliate prof. U. Idaho, Moscow, 1981-89; sr. advisor on nat. conservation strategy Internat. Union Conservation Nature (IUCN), Govt. Botswana, 1985-87; environ. planning cons. Nepal, 1990. Contbr. articles profl. jours. Pres. Wash.-Idaho Symphony Assn., 1992-95. With USAAF, 1943-46. Recipient Superior Honor award U.S. AID, 1974, Outstanding Career Achievement award, 1981; named disting. vol. Wash.-Idaho Symphony, 1996; named to alumni Hall of Fame U. Idaho, 1999. Mem. ACLU, Soc. for Internat. Devel. (pres. Palouse chpt. 1982-83), Kalahari Conservation Soc., Wash. Idaho Symphony Assn., Nature Conservancy, Sr. Seminar Alumni Assn., Beta Theta Pi. Office: 328 N Polk St Moscow ID 83843-2747 E-mail: bfields5@gte.net

BUTTERWORTH, ROBERT ROMAN, psychologist, researcher, media therapist; b. Pittsfield, Mass., June 24, 1946; s. John Leon and Martha Helen (Roman) B. BA, SUNY, 1972; MA, Marist Coll., 1975; PhD in Clin. Psychology, Calif. Grad. Inst., 1983. Asst. clin. psychologist N.Y. State Dept. Mental Hygiene, Wassaic, 1972-75; pres. Internat. Trauma Assocs., L.A. and Downey, Calif., 1976—. Cons. L.a. County Dept. Health Svc.; staff clinician San Bernardino County Dept. Mental Health, 1983-85; staff psychologist State of Calif. Dept. Mental Health, 1985—; media interviews include PA, L.A. Times, N.Y. Times, USA Today, Wall St Jour., Washington Post, Redbook mag., London Daily Mail and many others; TV and radio interviews include Larry King Live, CBA, NBA and ABC networks, Oprah Winfrey Show, CNN Newsnight, Can. Radio Network, Mut. Radio Network and many others. Served with USAF, 1965-69. Mem. Am. Psychol. Assn. for Media Psychology, Calif. Psychol. Assn., Nat. Accreditation Assn. Psychoanalysis. Office: PO Box 76477 Los Angeles CA 90076-0477 E-mail: robert@drbutterworth.net

BUTZ, OTTO WILLIAM, political science educator; b. Floesti, Romania, May 2, 1923; came to U.S., 1949, naturalized, 1959; s. Otto E. and Charlotte (Engelmann) B.; m. Velia DeAngelis, Sept. 13, 1961. B.A., Victoria Coll., U. Toronto, 1947; Ph.D., Princeton, 1953. Asst. prof. polit. sci. Swarthmore Coll., 1954-55; asst. prof. politics Princeton U., 1955-60; asso. editor Random House, N.Y.C., 1960-61; prof. social sci. San Francisco State Coll., 1961-67; academic v.p. Sacramento State Coll., 1967-69, acting pres., 1969-70; pres. Golden Gate U., 1970-92; pres. emeritus, 1992—. Author: German Political Theory, 1955, The Unsilent Generation, 1958, Of Man and Politics, 1960, To Make a Difference— A Student Look at America, 1967. Recipient Calif. State Colls. Outstanding Tchr. award, 1966 Mem. Am. Polit. Sci. Assn. Home: Wolfback Rdg Sausalito CA 94965 Office: 536 Mission St San Francisco CA 94105-2921

BUURSMA, WILLIAM F. architect; BArch, U. Mich., 1964; MArch, U. Pa., 1965. Lic. arch. With various archtl. design firms; joined John Graham Assocs/DLR Group, Seattle, 1976—, prin. Tchg. fellow U. Tenn., also assoc. prof. France program. Prin. works include Madigan Army Med. Ctr., Ft. Lewis, Wash., Clackamas Town Ctr., Portland, Oreg., Kauai Hilton Resort and Condominium Complex, Hawaii, high-rise office bldgs., retail shopping malls, and numerous other complexes. Mem. AIA. Office: John Graham Assoc 900 4th Ave Ste 700 Seattle WA 98164-1003

BUXBAUM, RICHARD M. law educator, lawyer; b. 1930; AB, Cornell U., 1950, LLB, 1952; LLM, U. Calif., Berkeley, 1953; Dr. (hon.), U. Osnabrück, 1992, Eötvös Lorand U., Budapest, Hungary, 1993. Bar: Calif. 1953, N.Y. 1953. Practice law pvt. firm, Rochester, N.Y., 1957-61; prof. U. Calif., Berkeley, 1961—, dean internat. and area studies, 1993-99. Hon. prof. U. Peking, 1998. Editor-in-chief Am. Jour. Comparative Law. Recipient Humboldt prize, 1991, German Order of Merit, 1992, Officier Arts et Lettres, France, 1997, Order of Rio Branco, Brazil, 1998. Mem. German Soc. Comparative Law (corr.), Coun. on Fgn. Rels. Office: U Calif Sch Law 888 Simon Hall Berkeley CA 94720-0001 E-mail: bux@uclink.berkeley.edu

BUYERS, JOHN WILLIAM AMERMAN, agribusiness and specialty foods company executive; b. Coatesville, Pa., July 17, 1928; s. William Buchanan and Rebecca (Watson) B.; m. Elizabeth Lindsey; children: Elsie Buyers Viehman, Rebecca Watson Buyers-Basso, Jane Palmer Buyers-Russo. B.A. cum laude in History, Princeton U., 1952; M.S. in Indsl. Mgmt., MIT, 1963. Div. ops. mgr. Bell Telephone Co. Pa., 1953-66; dir. ops. and personnel Gen. Waterworks Corp., Phila., 1966-68, pres., chief exec. officer Phila, 1971-75; v.p. adminstrn. Internat. Utilities Corp., Phila., 1968-71; pres., chief exec. officer, dir. C. Brewer and Co., Ltd., Honolulu, 1975—, chmn. bd., 1982—. Chmn. Calif. and Hawaiian Sugar Co., 1982-84, 86-90; pres. Buyco, Inc., 1986—; mem. Hawaii Joint Coun. Econ. Edn., Japan-Hawaii Econ. Coun.; bd. dirs. BancWest, First Hawaiian Bank, John B. Sanfilippo & Sons, Inc., Outrigger Hotels and Resorts. Trustee U. Hawaii Found., Hawaii Prep. Acad., 1986—; chmn. bd. dirs. Hawaii Visitors Bur., 1990-91; mem. Gov.'s Blue Ribbon Panel on the Future of Healthcare in Hawaii; bd. dirs. Hawaii Sports Found., 1990-95; mem. adv. group to U.S. Dist. Ctr. With USMC, 1946-48. Sloan fellow MIT, 1962-63. Mem. Hawaiian Sugar Planters Assn. (chmn. bd. dirs. 1980-82, dir.), c. of C. Hawaii (chmn. bd. dirs. 1981-00), Nat. Alliance Bus. (chmn. Hawaii Pacific Metro chpt. 1978), Cap and Gown Club (Princeton), Hilo Yacht Club, Oahu County Club, Pacific Club, Waialae county Club, Prouts Neck (Maine) County Club, U.S. C. of C. (mem. food and gr. com. 1991—), Beretania Tennis Club. Presbyterian. Office: C Brewer & Co Ltd PO Box 1826 Papaikou HI 96781-1826 E-mail: jwabuyers@cbcl1826.com

BUZUNIS, CONSTANTINE DINO, lawyer; b. Winnipeg, Man., Can., Feb. 3, 1958; came to U.S., 1982; s. Peter and Anastasia (Ginakes) B. BA, U. Man., 1980; JD, Thomas M. Cooley Law Sch., 1985. Bar: Mich. 1986, U.S. Dist. Ct. (ea. and we. dists.) Mich. 1986, Calif. 1986, U.S. Dist. Ct. (so. dist.) Calif. 1987, U.S. Supreme Ct. 1993. Assoc. Church, Kritselis, Wyble & Robinson, Lansing, Mich., 1986, Neil, Dymott, Perkins, Brown & Frank, San Diego, 1987-94, ptnr., 1994—. Arbitrator San Diego County Mcpl. and Superior Cts.; judge pro tem San Diego Mcpl. Ct. Sec., treas. Sixty Plus Law Ctr., Lansing, 1985; active Vols. in Parole, San Diego, 1988—; bd. dirs. Hellenic Cultural Soc., 1993-98. Mem. Mich. Bar Assn., Calif. Bar Assn., San Diego County Bar Assn., Desert Bar Assn., So. Calif. Def. Coun., State Bar Calif. (gov. 9th dist. young lawyers divsn. 1991-94, 1st v.p. 1993-94, pres. 1994-95, bd. govs. 1995-96) San Diego Barristers Soc. (bd. dirs. 1991-92), San Diego Def. Lawyers Assn., Risk Ins. Mgmt. Soc. (assoc.), San Diego Ins. Adjusters Assn. (assoc.), Pan Arcadian Fedn., Order of Ahepa (chpt. bd. dirs., v.p. 1995-98, chpt. pres. 2001—), Hellenic Cultural Soc., Phi Alpha Delta. Home: 3419 Overpark Rd San Diego CA 92130-1865 Office: Neil Dymott Perkins Brown & Frank 1010 2nd Ave Ste 2500 San Diego CA 92101-4959 Fax: 619-238-1562. E-mail: cbuzunis@neil-dymott.com

BYBEE, JAY SCOTT, lawyer, educator; b. Oakland, Calif., Oct. 27, 1953; s. Rowan Scott and Joan (Hickman) B.; m. Dianna Jean Greer, Feb. 15, 1986; children: Scott, David, Alyssa, Ryan. BA, Brigham Young U., 1977, JD, 1980. Bar: D.C. 1981, U.S. Ct. Appeals (4th cir.) 1983, U.S. Supreme Ct. 1985, U.S. Ct. Appeals (5th cir.) 1986, U.S. Ct. Appeals (2d, 9th, 10th and D.C. cirs.) 1987. Law clk. to judge U.S. Ct. Appeals (4th cir.), 1980-81; assoc. Sidley & Austin, Washington, 1981-84; atty., advisor U.S. Dept. Justice, Washington, 1984-89; assoc. counsel to Pres. of U.S. The White House, 1989-91; prof. law La. State U., Baton Rouge, 1991-98, U. Nev., Las Vegas, 1999—. Contbr. articles to profl. jours. Missionary Mormon Ch., Santiago, Chile, 1973-75. Edwin S. Hinckley scholar, Brigham Young U., 1976-77. Mem. Phi Kappa Phi. Avocations: piano, all sports, reading. Home: 739 Sandy Hook Ter Henderson NV 89052-5207

BYBEE, RODGER WAYNE, science education administrator; b. San Francisco, Feb. 21, 1942; s. Wayne and Mary Genevieve (Mungon) B.; m. Patricia Ann Brovsky, May 28, 1966. BA, Colo. State Coll., 1966; MA, U. No. Colo., 1969; PhD, NYU, 1975. Tchr. sci. Greeley (Colo.) Pub. Schs., 1965-66; instr. sci. U. No. Colo., Greeley, 1966-70; teaching fellow NYU, N.Y.C., 1970-72; instr. edn. Carleton Coll., Northfield, Minn., 1972-75, asst. prof., 1975-81, assoc. prof., chmn. dept., 1981-85; assoc. dir. Biol. Scis. Curriculum Study, Colorado Springs, 1986-95, acting dir., 1992-93; exec. dir. Ctr. Sci., Math. and Engring. Edn. NRC, Washington, 1995-99; exec. dir. BSCS, Colorado Springs, Colo., 1999—. Mem. adv. bd. for sci. assessment Nat. Assessment Ednl. Progress, Princeton, N.J., 1987-89, 92-93, 95-96; mem. adv. bd. Social Sci. Edn. Consortium, Boulder, Colo., 1987-90; chairperson working group on curriculum NRC project on Nat. Sci. Ednl. Stds., 1993-95. Author: numerous books; contbr. numerous articles to profl. jours. NSF grantee, 1986—. Fellow AAAS (mem.-at-large 1987-90, chair sect. Q 1993-94, coun. del.), Nat. Assn. Rsch. Sci. Teaching (rsch. coord. 1986-89). Home: PO Box 563 Frisco CO 80443-0563 Office: BSCS 5415 Mark Dabling Blvd Colorado Springs CO 80918-3842 E-mail: rbybee@bscs.org

BYE, JAMES EDWARD, lawyer; b. Thief River Falls, Minn., May 2, 1930; s. Morris and Ida Mathilda (Dahl) B.; m. Patricia Ann Nadolski, Dec. 27, 1952; children: David Stanley, Anne Elizabeth. BBA with distinction, U. Minn., 1951; LLB cum laude, Harvard U., 1956. Bar: Colo. 1957, U.S. Tax Ct., U.S. Ct. Appeals (10th cir.), U.S. Supreme Ct. 1992. Assoc. Holme Roberts & Owen, Denver, 1957-61; ptnr. Holme, Roberts & Owen LLP, Denver, 1961—. Editor Harvard U. Law Rev. Chmn. continuing legal and jud. edn. Colo. Supreme Ct., Denver, 1977-78; chmn. Alexis de Tocqueville Soc. Met. Denver, 1986-89, Met. Denver GIVES, 1986-91; trustee Loretto Hts. Coll., Denver, 1977-88, Regis. Coll., 1988-92, U. Colo. Found., The Two Percent Club, 1991, Children's Hosp., 1993-95; chmn. urban emphasis program, Denver Area coun. Boy Scouts Am., 1992—, The Spot, 1996—; Tointon Inst. Adv. Bd., 2000—, Latin Am. Rsch. & Svc. Agy., 2000, Summer Scholars, 2000—, Hispanics in Philanthropy, 2000—; bd. dirs. Mex. Cultural Ctr. & Ctr. Affordable Housing. Recipient Silver Beaver award, 1996, Disting. Svc. to Humanity award Vols. of Am., 1996, Pub. Svc. award U. Colo. Grad. Sch. Pub. Affairs, 1996, Alex de Tocqueville Soc. award United Way, Reconocimiento Ohtli award Sec. of Fgn. Rels. of Mex., 1998, William Funk award Colo. Assn. Nonprofit Orgns., 1998, Ally award Women's Vision Found., 1999, Whitney M. Young Jr. Svc. award Boy Scouts Am., 1999, Maverick Thinker's award Urban Peak, 2001. Fellow Am. Bar Found. (life), Colo. Bar Found.; mem. ABA (natural resources com. tax sect.), Colo. Bar Assn., Denver Bar Assn., Am. Coll. Tax Counsel, Denver Estate Planning Coun., Greater Denver Tax Counsel Assn. Avocation: golfing. Office: Holme Roberts & Owen LLP 1700 Lincoln St Ste 4100 Denver CO 80203-4541 E-mail: byej@hro.com

BYEARS, LATASHA, professional basketball player; b. Aug. 12, 1973; Student, N.E. Okla. A&M Jr. Coll., 1992-94; grad., DePaul U., 1996. Basketball player Faenza, Italy, 1996-97, Beskijas, Turkey, 1996-97; basketball player Sacramento Monarchs Women's NBA, 1997—. Vol. Meals on Wheels. Office: Sacramento Monarchs One Sports Pky Sacramento CA 95834

BYER, ROBERT LOUIS, applied physics educator, university dean; b. Pasadena, Calif., May 9, 1942; s. Herbert Louis and Wilfrie (Schulz) B.; m. Eva Maria Guzsella, Aug. 15, 1964; children: Scott, Douglas, Mark, Evi-Lynn. BA in Physics, U. Calif., Berkeley, 1964; MS in Applied Physics, Stanford U., 1967, PhD in Applied Physics, 1969. Scientist Spectra Physics, Mountain View, Calif., 1964-65; asst. prof. Stanford (Calif.) U., 1969-74, assoc. prof., 1974-79, prof., 1979—, chair dept. applied physics, 1980-83, assoc. dean humanities and sci., 1984-86, dean rsch., 1987-92, chair dept. applies physics, 2000—. Bd. dirs. Lightwave Electronics Corp., Mountain View, Polystor, Gen. Lasertronics Corp. Contbr. 350 articles to profl. jours.; holder over 30 patents. Recipient Arthur L. Schawlow Awd. 1998, NAS award 2000. Fellow IEEE (millennium medal 2000), AAAS, Am. Phys. Soc., Optical Soc. Am. (Adolph Lomb medal 1972, bd. dirs. 1986-89, v.p. 1992, pres.-elect 1993, pres. 1994); mem. NAE, Lasers and Electro-Optic Soc. (pres. 1984), Calif. Coun. on Sci. and Tech. (vice chmn.). Office: Stanford University Dept of Applies Physics Stanford CA 94305 E-mail: Byer@Stanford.edu

BYERS, NINA, physics educator; b. Los Angeles, Jan. 19, 1930; d. Irving M. and Eva (Gertzoff) B.; m. Arthur A. Milhaupt, Jr., Sept. 8, 1974 (dec.). BA in Physics with highest honors, U. Calif., Berkeley, 1950; MS in Physics, U. Chgo., 1953, PhD, 1956; MA, U. Oxford, Eng., 1967. Research fellow dept. math. physics U. Birmingham, Eng., 1956-58; research assoc., asst. prof. Inst. Theoretical Physics and dept. physics Stanford, 1958-61; asst. then assoc. prof. physics UCLA, 1961-67, prof. physics, 1967—. Mem. Sch. Math., Inst. Advanced Studies, Princeton, N.J., 1964-65; ofcl. fellow Somerville Coll., Oxford, 1967-68, Janet Watson vis. fellow, 1968-74; faculty lectr., mem. dept. theoretical physics Oxford U., 1967-74, sr. vis. scientist, 1973-74; official fellow and tutor in physics, Somerville Coll. John Simon Guggenheim Meml. fellow, 1964-65, Sci. Rsch. Coun. fellow Oxford U., 1978, 85. Fellow AAAS (mem-at-large physics sect., com. on freedom and responsibility 1983-86), Am. Phys. Soc. (councillor-at-large 1977-81, panel pub. affairs 1980-83, vice-chmn. forum on physics and soc. 1981-82, chmn. 1982-83); mem. Fedn. Am. Scientists (nat. coun. 1972-76, 78-80, exec. com. 1974-76, 78-80). Achievements include research in theory of particle physics and superconductivity; history of physics; contributions of 20th century women to physics. Office: U Calif Dept Physics Los Angeles CA 90095-0001

BYERS, PETER H. geneticist; b. N.Y.C., May 31, 1943; MD, Case Western Reserve U., 1969. Diplomate Am. Bd. Internal Medicine, Am. Bd. Molecular Genetics, clin. geneticist. Intern U. Calif., San Francisco, 1969, resident, 1969-70; fellow U. Wash., Seattle, 1974-77, asst. prof. pathology and medicine, 1979-82, assoc. prof., 1982-86, prof., 1986—. Editor Am. Jour. Human Genetics, 1994-99. Fellow AAAS, Am. Soc. Human Genetics, Am. Soc. for Clin. Investigation; mem. Am. Bd. Med. Genetics (pres. 1997). Office: U Wash Dept Pathology PO Box 357470 Seattle WA 98195-7470

BYRD, CHRISTINE WATERMAN SWENT, lawyer; b. Oakland, Calif., Apr. 11, 1951; d. Langan Waterman and Eleanor (Herz) Swent; m. Gary Lee Byrd, June 20, 1981; children: Amy, George. BA, Stanford U., 1972; JD, U. Va., 1975. Bar: Calif. 1976, U.S. Dist. Ct. (ctrl., so. no., ea. dists.) Calif., U.S. Ct. Appeals (9th cir.). Law clk. to Hon. William P. Gray, U.S. Dist. Ct., L.A., 1975-76; assoc. Jones, Day, Reavis & Pogue, L.A., 1976-82, ptnr., 1987-96; asst. U.S. atty. criminal divsn. U.S. Atty.'s Office-Cen. Dist. Calif., L.A., 1982-87; ptnr. Irell & Manella, L.A., 1996—. Mem. Calif. Law Revision Commn., 1992-97. Author: The Future of the U.S. Multinational Corporation, 1975; contbr. articles to profl. jours. Mem. Calif. State Bar (com. fed. cts. 1985-88), Los Angeles County Bar Assn., Women Lawyers Assn. Los Angeles County, Am. Arbitration Assn. (large and complex case panel 1992—, nat. energy panel 1998—, bd. dirs. 1999—), Stanford Profl. Women Los Angeles County, Stanford U. Alumni Assn., 9th Jud. Cir. Hist. Soc. (bd. dirs. 1986—, pres. 1997—), Assn. Bus. Trial Lawyers (bd. govs. 1996-99). Republican. Office: Irell & Manella LLP 1800 Ave Of Stars Ste 900 Los Angeles CA 90067-4276

BYRD, MARC ROBERT, designer, florist; b. Flint, Mich., May 14, 1954; s. Robert Lee and Cynthia Ann (Poland) B.; m. Bonnie Jill Berlin, Nov. 25, 1975 (div. June 1977). Student, Ea. Mich. U., 1972-75; grad., Am. Floral Sch., Chgo., 1978; student, U. of Redlands, 2000—. Gen. mgr., dir. flowers shop; designer Olive Tree Florist, Palm Desert, Calif., 1978-79, Kayo's Flower Fashions, Palm Springs, 1979-80; owner, designer Village Florist, Inc., Palm Springs, 1980-85; pres. Mon Ami Florist, Inc., Beverly Hills, 1986-87; gen. mgr. Silverio's, Santa Monica, 1987; gen. mgr., hotel florist, creative dir. Four Seasons Hotel, Beverly Hills, 1988-90; pres. Marc Fredericks, Inc., Beverly Hills, 1990-97; event florist Marc Byrd of Floral Works, L.A., 1997—. Author: Celebrity Flowers, 1989. Del., Dem. County Conv., 1972, Dem. County Conv., 1972, Dem. State Conv., 1972, Dem. Nat. Conv., 1972. Mem. Soc. Am. Florists, So. Calif. Floral Assn., Desert Mus., Robinson's Gardens. Republican. Mem. Dutch Reformed Ch. Avocations: skiing, tennis, community service. Office: Floral Works 2415 Creston Dr Los Angeles CA 90068-2203 Fax: (323) 962-9275

BYRD, MILTON BRUCE, college president, former business executive; b. Boston, Jan. 29, 1922; s. Max Joseph and Rebecca (Malkiel) B.; m. Susanne J. Schwerin, Aug. 30, 1953; children: Deborah, Leslie, David. A.B. cum laude, Boston U., 1948, M.A., 1949; Ph.D., U. Wis., 1953; postgrad. (fellow), U. Mich., 1961-62. Teaching asst. English U. Wis., 1949-53; instr., asst. prof. English Ind. U., 1953-58; asst. prof., asso. prof. humanities So. Ill. U., 1958-62, head div. humanities, 1958-60, supr. acad. advisement, 1959-60, asso. dean, 1960- 62; v.p. acad. affairs No. Mich. U., 1962-66; pres. Chgo. State U., 1966-74; provost Fla. Internat. U., 1974-78; pres. Adams State Coll., Alamosa, Colo., 1978-81; v.p. corp. devel. Frontier Cos., Anchorage, 1981-85; pres. Charter Coll., 1985—. Bd. dirs Chgo. Council for Urban Edn., Union for Experimenting Colls. and Univs., Am. Assn. State Colls. and Univs., Resource Devel. Council Alaska, Alaska Commn. Econ. Edn.; v.p. Common Sense for Alaska, Inc.; former pres. Alaska Support Industry Alliance. Author: (with Arnold L. Goldsmith) Publication Guide for Literary and Linguistic Scholars, 1958; contbr. to profl. jours. Commr. Alaska Commn. on Postsecondary Edn. Served with USAAF, 1943-46. Mem. MLA, Nat. Council Tchrs. English, Coll. English Assn., Am. Studies Assn., AAUP, Fla. Assn. Univ. Adminstrs. (former pres.), Rocky Mountain Athletic Conf. (former pres.), Assn. for Higher Edn., Pub. Relations Soc. Am., NEA, Alaska Press Club, Mich. Edn. Assn., Phi Beta Kappa, Phi Delta Kappa. Club: Rotary. E-mial. Office: # 120 2221 E Northern Lights Blvd Anchorage AK 99508-4143 E-mail: mbyrd@chartercollege.edu

BYRNE, JEROME CAMILLUS, lawyer; b. Grand Rapids, Mich., Oct. 3, 1925; s. Camillus Abraham and Katherine Blanche (Kelly) B. BA, Aquinas Coll., 1948; JD magna cum laude, Harvard U., 1951. Bar: Calif. 1952. Assoc. Gibson Dunn & Crutcher, L.A., 1952-59, ptnr., 1960-93, adv. counsel, 1993—. Spl. counsel to regents U. Calif., 1965 Bd. dirs. Constl. Rights Found., 1967—, pres., 1971-72; bd. regents Mt. St. Mary's Coll., 1979—; trustee Aquinas Coll., 1983-95, trustee emeritus, 1995—; dir., sec. Kolb Found., 1984—. Office: Gibson Dunn & Crutcher 2029 Century Park E Ste 4000 Los Angeles CA 90067-3032

BYRNE, JOHN VINCENT, higher education consultant; b. Hempstead, N.Y., May 9, 1928; s. Frank E. and Kathleen (Barry) B.; m. Shirley O'Connor, Nov. 26, 1954; children: Donna, Lisa, Karen, Steven. AB, Hamilton Coll., 1951, JD (hon.), 1994; MA, Columbia U., 1953; PhD, U. So. Calif., 1957. Research geologist Humble Oil & Refinery Co., Houston, 1957-60; assoc. prof. Oreg. State U., Corvallis, 1960-66, prof. oceanography, 1966—, chmn. dept., 1968-72, dean Sch. Oceanography, 1972-76, acting dean research, 1976-77, dean research, 1977-80, v.p. for research and grad. studies, 1980-81, pres., 1984-95; adminstr. NOAA, Washington, 1981-84; pres. Oreg. State U., 1984-95; higher edn. cons. Corvallis, 1996—. Program dir. oceanography NSF, 1966-67; exec. dir. Kellogg Commn. on Future of State and Land Grant Univs., 1996-2000; dir. Oreg. Coast Aquarium, Harbor Br. Ocean Inst. Recipient Carter teaching award Oreg. State U., 1964. Fellow AAAS, Geol. Soc. Am., Am. Meteorol. Soc.; mem. Am. Assn. Petroleum Geologists, Am. Geophys. Union, Sigma Xi, Chi Psi. Home: 3190 NW Deer Run St Corvallis OR 97330-3107 Office: [illegible] Corvallis OR [illegible] E-mail: john.byrne@orst.edu

BYRNE, WILLIAM MATTHEW, JR. federal judge; b. L.A., Sept. 3, 1930; s. William Matthew Sr. and Julia Ann (Lamb) B. BS, U. So. Calif., 1953, LLB, 1956; LLD, Loyola U., 1971. Bar: Calif. 1956. Ptnr. Dryden, Harrington & Schwartz, 1960-67; asst. atty U.S. Dist. Ct. (so. dist.) Calif., 1958-60; atty. U.S. Dist. Ct. (cen. dist.) Calif., Los Angeles, 1967-70, judge, 1971—, now sr. judge; exec. dir. Pres. Nixon's Commn. Campus Unrest, 1970. Instr. Loyola Law Sch., Harvard U., Whittier Coll. Served with USAF, 1956-58. Mem. ABA, Fed. Bar Assn., Calif. Bar Assn., Los Angeles County Bar Assn. (vice chmn. human rights sect.), Am. Judicature Soc. Office: US Dist Ct 312 N Spring St Ste 110 Los Angeles CA 90012-4703

BYRNES, JAMES BERNARD, museum director, consultant; b. N.Y.C., Feb. 19, 1917; s. Patrick J.A. and Janet E. (Geiger) B.; m. Barbara A. Cecil, June 10, 1946; 1 son, Ronald L. Student, N.A.D., 1936-38, Am. Artist Sch., 1938-40, Art Students League, 1940-42, U. Perugia, Italy, 1951, Inst. Meschini, Rome, 1952. Art tchr. mus. activity program N.Y.C. Bd. Edn., 1936-40; indsl. designer Michael Saphier Assos., N.Y.C., 1940-42; docent L.A. County Mus., 1946-47, assoc. curator modern contemporary art, 1947-48, curator, asst. to dir., 1948-53; dir. Colorado Springs Fine Arts Center, 1954-55; from assoc. dir. to dir. N.C. Mus. Art, 1956-60; dir. New Orleans Mus. Art, 1961-71, dir. emeritus, 1989—; dir. Newport Harbor Art Mus., Newport Beach, Calif., 1972-75. Vis. lectr. U. Fla., 1961, Newcomb Coll., Tulane U., 1963; art cons. Author: Masterpieces of Art, W.R. Valentiner Memorial, 1959, Tobacco and Smoking in Art, 1960, Fetes de la Palette, 1963, Edgar Degas, His Family and Friends in New Orleans, 1965, Odyssey of an Art Collector, 1966, Art of Ancient and Modern Latin America, 1968, The Artist as Collector of Primitive Art, 1975, also numerous mus. catalogs. Decorated knight Order Leopold II (Belgium); recipient Isaac Delgado Meml. award New Orleans Mus. of Art, 1998. Mem. Am. Soc. Interior Design (hon. life), Am. Soc. Appraisers (sr.), Appraisers Assn. Am. Office: James B Byrnes and Assocs 7820 Mulholland Dr Los Angeles CA 90046-1223

BYRNES, LAWRENCE WILLIAM, dean; b. Windsor, Ont., Can., June 17, 1940; s. Carl Wilfred and Alice Hendrie (Thomson) B.; m. Margaret Amelia Snavely, June 26, 1965; children: Andrew Carl, Mary Margaret. BA in Social Sci., Mich. State U., 1963, MA in History, 1967, PhD in Edn., 1970. Tchr. social studies Grosse Pointe (mich.) Schs., 1963-66; prof. Calif. State U., Northridge, 1969-78; dean edn. Southeastern La. U., Hammond, 1978-83, Moorhead (Minn.) State U., 1983-88, Edinboro (Pa.) U., 1988-91; dir. Ctr. for Teaching and Learning U. So. Colo., 1991-95; dean Coll. Edn. and Tech. Eastern N.Mex. U., Portales, 1995—. Ptnr., cons. ML Byrnes and Assocs., Erie, Pa. Author: Religion and Republic Education, 1975; co-author: Total Quality Management in Higher Education, 1991, The Quality Teacher: Implementing TQM in the Classroom, 1992. Mem. Gov.'s Steering Com. on Strengthening Quality in Schs., N. Mex. Mem. Am. Assn. Colls. Tchr. Edn. (chmn. global and internat. tchrs. edn. com.), N. Mex. Assn. Colls. Tchr. Edn. (pres.), Phi Delta Kappa (pres. Moorhead chpt. 1987-88, historian Erie chpt. 1991—. hist. South Colo. chpt. 1994—) Democrat. Episcopalian. Avocations: running, drums, music. Home: 416 E 17th Ln Portales NM 88130-9266 Office: ENMU Coll Edn & Tech Portales NM 88130

BYYNY, RICHARD LEE, academic administrator, physician; b. South Gate, Calif., Jan. 6, 1939; s. Oswald and Essa Burnetta (McGinnis) B.; m. Jo Ellen Garverick, Aug. 25, 1962; children: Kristen, Jan, Richard. BA in History, U. So. Calif., 1960, MD, 1964. Intern and resident in internal medicine Columbia Presbyn. Med. Ctr., N.Y.C., 1964-66, chief resident, 1968-69; fellow in endocrinology Vanderbilt U., Nashville, 1969-71; asst. prof. medicine U. Chgo., 1971-74, head div. internal medicine, 1972-77, assoc. prof., 1975-77; prof. internal medicine U. Colo., Denver, 1977—, head div. internal medicine, 1977-94; vice-chmn. dept. medicine U. Colo. Health Scis. Ctr., Denver, 1977-85; exec. vice chancellor U. Colo., Denver, 1994-95, v.p. acad. affairs, 1995-97, chancellor Boulder, 1997—. Med. dir. ambulatory care, 1990-92; mem. Coun. on Econ. Devel., Boulder, Colo. Author: A Clinical Guide in the Care of Older Women, 1990, 95; contbr. numerous articles to profl. jours., chpts. to textbooks, monographs. Pres. Ill. Council Continuing Med. Edn., Ill., 1976-77; bd. dirs. Denver affiliate Am. Heart Assn., 1987-98 (pres. 1994-95), Boulder Com. Hosp., 1997—, Bank of Boulder, Boulder Econ. Coun., arm of Boulder C. of C., U.S. Coun. on Competitiveness Big 12 Conf. Served to capt. USAF, 1966-68. Recipient Merck award U. So. Calif., 1964; Am. Coun. Edn. fellow, 1992-93. Fellow ACP; mem. AAAS, Soc. for Gen. Internal Medicine (pres. 1979-80), Am. Soc. Hypertension, Western Soc. Clin. Investigation, Endocrine Soc., Am. Fedn. for Clin. Rsch., Am. Coun. Edn. (commn. leadership instl. effectiveness), Alpha Omega Alpha (bd. dirs. 1996—). Clubs: U. Club Denver; Arapahoe Tennis (Englewood, Colo.), Boulder Country Club. Avocations: tennis, skiing, running, surfing, sailing. Home: 2900 Park Lake Dr Boulder CO 80301-5139 Office: Office of Chancellor Regent Adminstrv Ctr Room 301 Campus Box 17 Boulder CO 80309-0017 Fax: 303-492-8866. E-mail: richard.byyny@colorado.edu

CABLE, JOHN FRANKLIN, lawyer; b. Hannibal, Mo., Dec. 22, 1941; s. John William and Dorothy (Stanley) C.; m. Leslie Gibbs, Apr. 5, 1965; child ren: Coventry, Tory, John. AB, Stanford U., 1964; LLB, Harvard U., 1967. Bar: Oreg. 1967. Assoc. Miller, Nash, Wiener, Hager & Carlsen, Portland, Oreg., 1967-73, ptnr., 1973—. Office: Miller Nash Wiener Hager & Carlsen 111 SW 5th Ave Fl 35 Portland OR 97204-3604 E-mail: cable@millernash.com

CABLE, WADE H. executive; CEO, pres. The Presley Cos., New Port Beach, Calif., 1979—. Office: PO Box 6110 19 Corp Plz 92660 Newport Beach CA 92658

CABRASER, ELIZABETH JOAN, lawyer; b. Oakland, Calif., June 23, 1952; AB, U. Calif., Berkeley, 1975; JD, U. Calif., 1978. Bar: Calif. 1978, U.S. Dist. Ct. (no., ea., cen. and so. dists.) Calif. 1979, U.S. Ct. Appeals (2d, 3rd, 5th, 6th, 9th, 10th, and 11th cirs.) 1979, U.S. Tax Ct. 1979, U.S. Dist. Ct. Hawaii 1986, U.S. Dist. Ct. Ariz. 1990, U.S. Supreme Ct. 1996. Ptnr. Lieff, Cabraser, Heimann & Bernstein LLP, San Francisco, 1978—. Contbr. articles to profl. jours. Named one of Top 50 Women Lawyers Nat. Law Jour., 1998, one of Top 100 U.S. Lawyers, 1997, 2000. Mem. ABA (tort and ins. practice sect., sect. litig. com. on class action and derivative skills, chair subcom. on mass torts), ATLA, Coun. Am. Law Inst., Calif. Constn. Rev. Commn., Nat. Ctr. for State Cts. (mass tort conf. planning com.), Women Trial Lawyer Caucus, Consumer Attys. Calif., Calif. Women Lawyers, Assn. Bus. Trial Lawyers, Nat. Assn. Securities and Comml. Attys., Bay Area Lawyers for Individual Freedom, Bar Assn. San Francisco (v.p. securities litig., bd. dirs.). Office: Lieff Cabraser Heimann & Bernstein LLP Embarcadero Ctr W 30th Fl 275 Battery St San Francisco CA 94111-3305 E-mail: ecabraser@lchb.com

CACCAMO, ALDO M. oil industry executive; BS in Civil Engring., N.J. Inst. Tech., 1960; MBA, Harvard U., 1964. With Chevron Corp., 1964—, fin. analyst, 1964; asst. area mgr. aviation sales Chevron International Oil Co., London, 1967, aviation fuels mgr. San Francisco, 1971, [illegible], 1993, mgr. pricing and evaluation Chevron U.S.A. Mktg., 1979, mktg. mgr. west ctrl. divsn., 1982; gen. mgr. eastern region supply and distbn. Chevron U.S.A. Products Co., 1986, gen. mgr. mktg. sales, 1988; v.p. pub. affairs Chevron Corp., 1996—. Dir. Caltex Petroleum Corp., 1996—. Bd. dirs. Global Climate Coalition, San Francisco Friends Urban Forest, San Francisco Acad. Mem. San Francisco C. of C. (bd. dirs.). Office: Chevron Corp [illegible] San Francisco CA [illegible]

CACHOLA, ROMY MUNOZ, state legislator; b. Vigan, Ilocos Sur, Philippines, Mar. 8, 1938; m. Erlinda M. Cachola; children: Lyla, Earl. LLB, M.L. Quezon U., The Philippines, 1961. Mem. State Ho. of Reps., 1984—. Chair com. on water and land use Ho. of Reps., past chair house tourism com., 1987-98. Bd. govs. Kalihi YMCA; bd. dirs. Susannah Wesley Cmty. Ctr.; hon. chmn. Statewide Sakada Com.; pres. St. Anthony's Sch. Bd. Recipient Pub. Servant of Yr. Community Advocate Mag., 1990, Disting. Legislator award Dem. State Legis. Leaders Assn., 1990. Mem. Filipino C. of C., Ilocos Surian Assn. of Hawaii, St. Anthony's Filipino Cath. Club, Waipahu Bus. Assn. (past. pres.), Kalakaua Lions Club, Kalihi Bus. Assn. (bd. dirs.). Office: House of Representatives State of Hawaii State Capitol Rm 402 Honolulu HI 96813

CAESAR, VANCE ROY, newspaper executive; b. New Kensington, Pa., Dec. 22, 1944; s. Jack Raymond and Norma Norine (Wiles) C.; m. Carol Ann Richards, Apr. 22, 1967; 1 son, Eric Roy BSBA, The Citadel, 1966; MBA, Fla. Atlantic U., 1969; grad., Stanford U. Exec. Program, 1982; PhD in Organizational Psychology Mgmt., Walden U., 1994. From asst. to gen. mgr. to consumer mktg. dir. Miami Herald, Fla., 1970-77; assoc. editor Detroit Free Press, 1977-78; sr. v.p., gen. mgr. Long Beach Press-Telegram, Calif., 1978-88; pres. P.C.H. Publs., 1989-93, Treasure Coast Newspapers Inc., 1992-93; chmn. The Vance Caesar Group, 1994—. Bd. dirs. Meml. Med. Ctr., Silverado Sr. Living Inc., Am. Women Econ. Devel., Rancho Los Alamitos; chmn. Sch. Bus. Adminstrn. Calif. State U., Long Beach; vice-chmn. adv. bd. Bus. Roundtable; exec. com. mem. Boy Scouts Am., Long Beach, Internat. Forum for Corp. Dirs.; chmn. Long Beach Bus. Devel. Group, So. Calif. Profl. Assocs.; pres., bd. dirs. Profl. Coaches & Mentors Assn.; bd. dirs. Orange County Venture Network, Accelerate Bus. Devel. Corp. Mem. Long Beach Area C. of C., Am. Newspaper Pubs. Assn., Stanford Bus. Sch. Alumni Assn., The Citadel Alumni Assn., World Trade Ctr. Assn., Assn. at Long Beach, Long Beach Yacht Club, Old Ranch Country Club, Rotary. Home: 110 Ocean Ave Seal Beach CA 90740-6027

CAHILL, RICHARD FREDERICK, lawyer; b. Columbus, Nebr., June 18, 1953; s. Donald Francis and Hazel Fredeline (Garbers) C.; m. Helen Marie Girard, Dec. 4, 1982; children: Jacqueline Michelle, Catherine Elizabeth, Marc Alexander. Student, Worcester Coll., Oxford, 1973; BA with highest honors, UCLA, 1975; JD, U. Notre Dame, 1978. Bar: Calif. 1978, U.S. Dist. Ct. (ea. dist.) Calif. 1978, U.S. Dist. Ct. (cen. dist.) Calif. 1983, U.S. Dist. Ct. (so. dist.) Calif. 1992, U.S. Ct. Appeals (9th cir.) 1992. Dep. dist. atty. Tulare County Dist. Atty., Visalia, Calif., 1978-81; staff atty. Supreme Ct. of Nev., Carson City, 1981-83; assoc. Acret & Perochet, Brentwood, Calif., 1983-84, Thelen, Marrin, Johnson & Bridges, L.A., 1984-89; ptnr. Hammond Zuetel & Cahill, Pasadena, Calif., 1989-98, Pivo, Halbreich, Cahill & Yim, Irvine, 1999—. Mem. Pasadena Bar Assn., Los Angeles County Bar Assn., Assn. So. Calif. Defense Counsel, Notre Dame Legal Aid and Defender Assn. (assoc. dir.), Phi Beta Kappa, Phi Alpha Delta (charter, v.p. 1977-78), Pi Gamma Mu, Phi Alpha Theta (charter pres. 1973-74), Phi Eta Sigma, Sigma Chi. Republican. Roman Catholic. Avocation: tennis. Home: 201 Windwood Ln Sierra Madre CA 91024-2677 Office: Pivo Halbreich Cahill & Yim 1920 Main St Ste 800 Irvine CA 92614-7227

CAHILL, THOMAS ANDREW, physicist, educator; b. Paterson, N.J., Mar. 4, 1937; s. Thomas Vincent and Margery (Groesbeck) C.; m. Virginia Ann Arnoldy, June 26, 1965; children: Catherine Frances, Thomas Michael. B.A., Holy Cross Coll., Worcester, Mass., 1959; Ph.D. in Physics; NDEA fellow, U. Calif., Los Angeles, 1965. Asst. prof. in residence U. Calif., Los Angeles, 1965-66; NATO fellow, research physicist Centre d'Etudes Nucleaires de Saclay, France, 1966-67; prof. physics U. Calif., Davis, 1967-94; acting dir. Crocker Nuclear Lab., 1972, dir., 1980-89. Dir. Inst. Ecology, 1972-75; cons. NRC of Can., Louvre Mus. UN Global Atmospheric Watch, 1990—; mem. Internat. Com. on PIXE and Its Application, Calif. Atty. Gen., Nat. Audubon Soc., Mono Lake Com. Author: (with J. McCray) Electronic Circuit Analysis for Scientists, 1973; editor Internat. Jour. Pixe, 1989—; contbr. articles to profl. jours. on physics, applied physics, hist. analyses and air pollution. Prin. investigator IMPROVE Nat. Air Pollution Network., 1987-97; co-dir. Crocker Hist. and Archeol. Projects.; mem. internat. com. Ion Beam Analysis. OAS fellow, 1968, Japanese Nat. Rsch. fellow, Kyoto, 1992. Mem. Am. Phys. Soc., Air Pollution Control Assn., Am. Assn. Aerosol Rsch., Sigma Xi Democrat. Roman Catholic. Home: 1813 Amador Ave Davis CA 95616-3104 Office: U Calif Dept Applied Sci One Shields Ave Davis CA 95616

CAHN, DAVID STEPHEN, cement company executive; b. Los Angeles, Jan. 12, 1940; s. Edward Lincoln and Monya (Schuchett) C.; m. Mary Constance Maschio, June 18, 1960 (div. 1972); children: Elizabeth Suzanne, Deborah Michelle; m. Sharon Ann Marting, Sept. 8, 1972; 1 child, Melissa Jacqueline. BS with honors, U. Calif.-Berkeley, 1962, MS, 1964, DEng, 1966. Engr. Bethlehem Steel Corp., 1966-68; research engr. Amcord, Inc., Riverside, Calif., 1968-71, dir. environ. matters Newport Beach, 1971-77, v.p., 1977-80; dir. environ. affairs Calif. Portland Cement Co., Los Angeles, 1980-82, v.p. regulatory matters, 1982-84, CalMat Co., 1984-90; sr. v.p. corp. svcs. Calif. Portland Cement Co., Glendora, 1990—. Recipient Rossiter W. Raymond award Soc. Mining Engrs., 1972 Mem. AIME, ASTM, AIChE, Air and Waste Mgmt. Assn., Calif. Mining Assn. (past pres.), Calif. Mfrs. and Tech. Assn. (chmn. bd.). Republican. Office: Calif Portland Cement Co 2025 E Financial Way Glendora CA 91741-4692

CAHN, ROBERT NATHAN, physicist; b. N.Y.C., Dec. 20, 1944; s. Alan L. and Beatrice (Geballe) C.; m. Frances C. Miller, Aug. 22, 1965; children: Deborah, Sarah. BA, Harvard U., 1966; PhD, U. Calif., Berkeley, 1972. Rsch. assoc. Stanford (Calif.) Linear Accelerator Ctr., 1972-73; rsch. asst. prof. U. Wash., Seattle, 1973-76; asst. prof. U. Mich., Ann Arbor, 1976-78; assoc. rsch. prof. U. Calif., Davis, 1978-79; sr. staff physicist Lawrence Berkeley Nat. Lab, 1979-91; div. dir. Lawrence Berkeley Lab., 1991-96, sr. scientist, 1996—, dep. dir. physics divsn. Author: Semi Simple Lie Algebras and Their Representations, 1984; co-author: Experimental Foundations of Particle Physics, 1989. Fellow Am. Phys. Soc. (sec.-treas. divsn. particles and fields 1992-94).

CAIN, DOUGLAS MYLCHREEST, lawyer; b. Chgo., Sept. 8, 1938; s. Douglas M. Jr. and Louise C. (Coleman) C.; m. Constance Alexis Adams Moffit, Apr. 18, 1970; children: Victoria Elizabeth Moffit, Alexandra Catherine Moffit. A.B., Harvard U., 1960; J.D. with distinction, U. Mich., 1966; LL.M., N.Y. U., 1970. Bar: Colo. 1966, U.S. Ct. Appeals (10th cir.) 1972, U.S. Supreme Ct. 1972. Assoc. Sherman & Howard, L.L.C., Denver, 1966-72, ptnr., 1972-93; equity mem., 1993—; chmn. policy council Sherman & Howard, Denver, 1984-87; adj. prof. law U. Denver, 1972-78. Mem. Rocky Mountain Estate Planning Council, pres., 1976-77 Assoc. editor: Mich. Law Rev, 1964-66; contbr. articles to profl. jours. Bd. dirs. Craig Hosp. Found., 1980-86, v.p., 1984-85, pres., 1986-87, 88-89; bd. dirs. Colo. Jud. Inst., 1990-96, chmn., 1992-93; bd. dirs. Colo. chpt. Am. Diabetes Assn., 1993, Breathe Better Found., 1993—, Colo. Coun. Econ. Edn., 1990-98, Fortune Found., 1998—; mem. Estate Planning Seminar Group. With USN, 1960-63. Fellow Am. Coll. Tax Coun., Am. Coll. Trust and Estate Counsel; mem. ABA, Colo. Bar Assn. (gov. 1980-82), Greater Denver Tax Coun. Assn. (v.p. 1987, pres. 1988), Assn. Harvard Alumni (regional dir. 1978-81), Rocky Mountain Harvard Club (pres. 1977-78, 92-93), Denver Country Club, Mile High Club, Rotary. Home: 1060 Hudson St Denver CO 80220-1459 Office: Sherman & Howard LLC 633 17th St Ste 3000 Denver CO 80202-3665

CAIN, RAYMOND FREDERICK, landscape architect, planning company executive; b. Harrisburg, Ill., Sept. 13, 1937; s. Raymond Ransome and Edna (Kirkham) C.; m. Galen S. Short, Sept. 13, 1965 (div. 1971); m. Lois A. Kiehl, Dec. 27, 1981. B.A., U. Ill., 1959, M.A., 1962. Cert. profl. landscape architect, Md., Hawaii. Landscape architect W.J. Spear & Assoc., Houston, 1962-66; landscape architect Belt, Collins & Assoc., Honolulu, 1966-76, dir. landscape architecture, 1976—, v.p., 1981—. Speaker Urban Devel. Seminar, Singapore, 1980, Fiji Hotel Assn., Nandi, Fiji, 1981; lectr. Tourist Mgmt. Sch., Honolulu, 1978 Mem. Hawaii Year 2000, Honolulu, 1971; advisor Outdoor Cir., Honolulu, 1976; mem. Waikiki Improvement Assn., Honolulu, 1973 Recipient Nat. Landscape award Mauna Kea Beach Hotel, Hawaii, 1976; Nat. Design award Kona Surf Hotel, Hawaii, 1980, Mauna Lani Golf course, 1982, Aga Khan award Tanjong Jara Hotel, Malaysia, 1983 Fellow Am. Soc. Landscape Architects (treas. 1975-76); mem. Am. Planning Assn. (assoc.) Clubs: Outrigger (ground chmn. 1976-77), Honolulu, Oahu Country (ground chmn. 1972-73) Office: Belt Collins & Assocs 680 Ala Moana Blvd Fl 1 Honolulu HI 96813-5406

CAIN, WILLIAM STANLEY, experimental psychologist, educator, researcher; b. N.Y.C., Sept. 7, 1941; s. William Henry and June Rose (Stanley) C.; m. Claire Murphy, Oct. 30, 1993; children: Justin, Alison; stepchildren: Michael, Jennifer, Courtney. BS, Fordham U., 1963; MSc, Brown U., 1966, PhD, 1968. From asst. fellow to fellow John B. Pierce Lab., New Haven, 1967-94; from instr. to assoc. prof. depts. Epidemiology, Pub. Health, and Psychology Yale U., New Haven, 1967-84, prof. dept. epidemiology, pub. health, psychology, 1984-94; prof. surgery (otolaryngology) U. Calif., San Diego, 1994—. Mem. sensory disorders study sect. NIH, Bethesda, Md., 1991-95; mem. sci. adv. bd. Ctr. Indoor Air Rsch., Linthicum, Md., 1991-99 Mem. editl. bd. Chem. Senses, 1985-94; editl. adv. bd. Indoor Air, 1990—, Physiology and Behavior, 1995-96; editor 5 books, 1971—; contbr. over 200 articles to profl. jours. Recipient Crosby Field award ASHRAE, 1984, Jacob Javits/Claude Pepper award NIH, 1984, Sense of Smell Rsch. award, Fragrance Rsch. Fund, 1986. Fellow APA, ASHRAE, Am. Psychol. Soc., Acad. Indoor Air Rsch.; mem. Assn. Chemoreception Scis. (exec. chmn. 1983-84), N.Y. Acad. Scis. (pres. 1986). Home: 4459 Nabal Dr La Mesa CA 91941-7168 Office: U Calif Dept Surgery 9500 Gilman Dr Rm Mc957 La Jolla CA 92093-0957

CAINE, STEPHEN HOWARD, data processing executive; b. Washington, Feb. 11, 1941; s. Walter E. and Jeanette (Wenborne) C. Student, Calif. Inst. Tech., 1958-62. Sr. programmer Calif. Inst. Tech., Pasadena, 1962-65, mgr. sys. programming, 1965-69, mgr. programming, 1969-70; pres. Caine, Farber & Gordon, Inc., Pasadena, 1970—; gen. mgr. Gatekeeper Systems, Pasadena, 1995—. Lectr. applied sci. Calif. Inst. Tech., Pasadena, 1965-71, vis. assoc. elec. engring., 1976, vis. assoc. computer sci., 1976-84; dir. San Gabriel Valley Learning Ctrs., 1992-95. Mem. Pasadena Tournament of Roses Assn., 1976—, vice chmn. com., 1996-2000, chmn. com., 2000—. Mem. AAAS, Nat. Assn. Corrosion Engrs., Am. Ordnance Assn., Assn. Computing Machinery, Athanaeum Club (Pasadena), Houston Club. Home: 77 Patrician Way Pasadena CA 91105-1039

CAIRNS, BRUCE EARLE, state senator; BA in History, Wheaton Coll. Rep. Senator dist. 28 Colo. State Senate, 2001; prin., owner bodyshop; realtor, 1991—. Lt. USAR, Vietnam. Republican. Office: Colo State Senate 200 E Colfax Denver CO 80203 E-mail: brucecairns@qwest.net

CAIRNS, ELTON JAMES, chemical engineering educator; b. Chgo., Nov. 7, 1932; s. James Edward and Claire Angele (Larzelere) C.; m. Miriam Esther Citron, Dec. 26, 1974; 1 dau., Valerie Helen; stepchildren: Benjamin David, Joshua Aaron. B.S. in Chemistry, Mich. Tech. U., Houghton, 1955; B.S. in Chem. Engring, 1955; Ph.D. in Chem. Engring. (Dow Chem. Co. fellow, univ. fellow, Standard Oil Co. Calif. grantee, NSF fellow), U. Calif., Berkeley, 1959. Phys. chemist GE Rsch. Lab., Schenectady, 1959-66; group leader, then sect. head chem. engring. div. Argonne (Ill.) Nat. Lab., 1966-73; asst. head electrochemistry dept. GM Rsch. Labs., 1973-78; assoc. lab. dir., dir. energy and environment divsn. Lawrence Berkeley Nat. Lab., Calif., 1978-96, C.D. Hollowell meml. lectr., 1996, head, Energy Conversion and Storage Program, 1982—; prof. chem. engring. U. Calif., Berkeley, 1978—. Cons. in field; mem. numerous govt. panels; Croft lectr. U. Mo., 1979. Author: (with H.A. Liebhafsky) Fuel Cells and Fuel Batteries, 1968; mem. editor bd. Advances in Electrochemistry and Electrochm. Engring., 1974—; div. editor Jour. Electrochem. Soc., 1968-91; regional editor Electrochimica Acta, 1984-99, editor, 2000—; contbr. articles to profl. jours.; patentee in field. Recipient IR-100 award, 1968, Centennial medal Case Western Res. U., 1980, R&D 100 award, 1992, Melvin Calvin medal of distinction Mich. Technol. U., 1998; named McCabe lectr. U. N.C., 1993; grantee DuPont Co., 1956. Fellow Am. Insts. Chemists, Electrochem. Soc. (chmn. phys. electrochem. divsn. 1981-84, v.p. 1986-89, pres. 1989-90, Francis Mills Turner award 1963); mem. AIChE (chmn. energy conversion com. 1970-94), AAAS, Am. Chem. Soc., Internat. Soc. Electrochemistry (chmn. electrochem. energy conversion divsn. 1977-85, U.S. nat. sec. 1983-89, v.p. 1984-88, pres. 1999-2000), Intersoc. Energy Conversion Engring. Conf. (steering com. 1970—, gen. chmn. 1976, 90, 97, program chmn. 1983). Home: 239 Langlie Ct Walnut Creek CA 94598-3615 Office: Lawrence Berkeley Nat Lab 1 Cyclotron Rd Berkeley CA 94720-0001 E-mail: ejcairns@lbl.gov, cairns@cchem.berkeley.edu

CALBORN, KEITH W. wholesale distribution executive; CEO Consolidated Elec. Distbrs., Thousand Oaks, Calif.; chmn. Office: Consolidated Elec Distbrs 31356 Via Colinas Ste 107 Thousand Oaks CA 91362

CALDWELL, COURTNEY LYNN, lawyer, real estate consultant; b. Washington, Mar. 5, 1948; d. Joseph Morton and Moselle (Smith) C. Student, Duke U., 1966-68, U. Calif., Berkeley, 1967, 1968-69; BA, U. Calif., Santa Barbara, 1970, MA, 1975; JD with highest honors, George Washington U., 1982. Bar: D.C. 1984, Wash. 1986, Calif. 1989. Jud. clk. U.S. Ct. Appeals for 9th Cir., Seattle, 1982-83; assoc. Arnold & Porter, Washington, 1983-85, Perkins Coie, Seattle, 1985-88; dir. western ops. Edn. Real Estate Svcs., Inc., Irvine, Calif., 1988-91, sr. v.p., 1991-98; ind. cons., Orange County, 1998—. Bd. dirs. Univ. Town Ctr. Assn., 1994; bd. dirs. Habitat for Humanity, Orange County, 1993-94, chair legal com., 1994. Named Nat. Law Ctr. Law Rev. Scholar, 1981-82. Mem. Calif. Bar Assn. Avocation: foreign languages. Home: 7204 West Esast Highway #46 Ona CA 72663 Office: 537 Newport Center Dr # 163 Newport Beach CA 92660-6937 E-mail: clcaldwell@earthlink.net

CALDWELL, KIM A. company executive; Exec. v.p. global tech. and new bus. devel. Avery Dennison Corp., Pasadena, Calif., 1998—. Office: Avery Dennison Corp 150 N Orange Grove Blvd Pasadena CA 91103-3534

CALDWELL, STRATTON FRANKLIN, kinesiology educator; b. Mpls., Aug. 25, 1926; s. Kenneth Simms and Margaret Mathilda (Peterson) C.; m. Mary Lynn Shaffer, Aug. 28, 1955 (div. May 1977); children: Scott Raymond, Karole Elizabeth; m. Sharee' Deanna Ockerman, Aug. 6, 1981; 1 stepchild, Shannon Sharee' Calder. Student, San Diego State Coll., 1946-48; BS in Edn. cum laude, U. So. Calif., 1951, PhD in Phys. Edn., 1966; MS in Phys. Edn., U. Oreg., 1953. Teaching asst. dept. phys. edn. UCLA, 1953-54, assoc. in phys. edn., 1957-65, vis. asst. prof. phys. edn., 1967; dir. phys. edn. Regina (Sask., Can.) Young Men's Christian Assn., 1954-56; tchr. sec. grades, dir. athletic Queen Elizabeth Jr.-Sr. High Sch., Calgary, Alta., Can., 1956-57; asst. prof. phys. edn. San Fernando Valley State Coll., Northridge, Calif., 1965-68, assoc. prof., 1968-71; prof. phys. edn. dept. kinesiology Calif. State U., Northridge, 1971-90, prof. kinesiology, 1990-92, prof. kinesiology emeritus, 1992. Vis. asst. prof. phys. edn. UCLA, 1967; vis. assoc. prof. phys. edn. U. Wash., Seattle, 1968, U. Calif., Santa Barbara, 1969. Author (with Cecil and Joan Martin Hollingsworth) Golf, 1959, (with Rosalind Cassidy) Humanizing Physical Education: Methods for the Secondary School Movement Program, 5th edit., 1975; also poetry, book chpts., articles in profl. jours., book revs. With USN, 1944-46. Recipient Meritorious Performance and Profl. Promise award Calif. state U., 1986, 87, 89, Disting. Teaching award, 1992; AAPHERD fellow, 1962, Am. Coll. Sports Medicine fellow, 1965, Can. Assn. for Health, Phys. Edn., and Recreation fellow, 1971. Fellow Am. Alliance for Health, Phys. Edn., Recreation and Dance (Centennial Commn. 1978-85, cert. appreciation 1985), Am. Coll. Sports Medicine; mem. Calif. Assn. for Health, Phys. Edn., Recreation and Dance (pres. L.A. coll. and univ. unit 1969-70, v.p. phys. edn. com. 1970-71, mem. editorial bd. CAHPER Jour. 1970-71, mem. forum 1970-71, Disting. Svc. award 1974, Honor award 1988, Verne Landreth award 1992), Nat. Assn. for Phys. Edn. in Higher Edn. (charter), Sport Art Acad., Nat. Assn. for Sport and Phys. Edn., N.Y. Acad. Scis., N.Am. Soc. for Sports History, Sport Lit. Assn., Acad. Am. Poets, Phi Epsilon Kappa (Svc. award 1980), Alpha Tau Omega (charter, Silver Circle award 1976, Golden Circle award 2001), Phi Delta Kappa, Phi Kappa Phi, others. Republican. Mem. Christian Ch. Avocations: reading, writing. Home: 80 Kanan Rd Oak Park CA 91377-1105

CALDWELL, WALTER EDWARD, editor, small business owner; b. L.A., Dec. 29, 1941; s. Harold Elmer and Esther Ann (Fuller) C.; m. Donna Edith Davis, June 27, 1964; 1 child, Arnie-Jo. AA, Riverside City Coll., 1968. Sales and stock profl. Sears Roebuck & Co., Riverside, Calif., 1963-65; dispatcher Rohr Corp., Riverside, 1965-67; trainee Aetna Fin., Riverside, 1967-68, mgr. San Bruno, Cal., 1968-70, Amfac Thrift & Loan, Oakland, Calif., 1970-74; free lance writer San Jose, 1974-76; news dir. Sta. KAVA Radio, Burney, Cal., 1977-79; editor-pub. Mountain Echo, Fall River Mills, Calif., 1979-81. Contbg. author Yearbook of Modern Poetry, 1976. Del. Farmers and Ranchers Congress, St. Louis, 1985; participant Am. Leadership Conf., San Diego, 1989; pres. United Way, Burney, 1979, co-chmn., 1977, chmn., 1979; disaster relief worker ARC, Redding, Calif., 1988-91, disaster action team leader, 1991-95; bd. dirs. Shasta County Women's Refuge, Redding, 1988-91, Shasta County Econ. Devel. Corp., 1986-90, Crossroads, 1985; bd. dirs. Shasta County Econ. Devel. Task Force, 1985-86, exec. bd. dirs., 1988; pres. Intermountain Devel. Corp., 1989; leader Girl Scouts U.S.A., San Jose, 1973-76; announcer various local parades; trustee Mosquito Abatement Dist., Burney, 1978-87, 89—, chmn., 1990—; commr. Burney Fire Protection Dist., 1987-91, v.p., 1990, pres., 1991; chmn. Burney Basin Days Com., 1984-95, Hay Days Com., 1995-96; candidate for Shasta County Bd. Suprs., 1992; alt. commr. Local Agy. Formation Commn. Shasta County, 1995—; mem. Intermountain Hospice, 1998—. With USMC, 1959-63. Mem. Burney Basin C. of C. (advt. chmn. 1982, Cmty. Action award 1990, 93), Fall River Valley C. of C. (bd. dirs. 1991, pres. 1995), Am. Legion (2d vice comdr. 2000—, post boys state chmn., 2001-, citation of recognition 1987, Cmty. Action award 1989, 93), Calif. Newspaper Pubs. Assn., Rotary (pres. 1977-78, chmn. bike race 1981-85), Lions (student spkr. chmn. Fall River 1983-97, 1st v.p. 1991, pres. 1992, co-chmn. disaster com., newsletter chmn. dist. 4-C1 1989-91), Moose, Masons (master 1995), Shriners (sec.-treas. 1992-94). Republican. Avocations: photography, painting, archeology. E-mail: mtechoWshasta.com. Office: Mountain Echo Main St Fall River Mills CA 96028 also: PO Box 224 Fall River Mills CA 96028-0224

CALE, CHARLES GRIFFIN, lawyer, private investor; b. St. Louis, Aug. 19, 1940; s. Julian Dutro and Judith Hadley (Griffin) C.; m. Jessie Leete Rawn, Dec. 30, 1978; children: Whitney Rawn, Walter Griffin, Elizabeth Judith. BA, Principia Coll., Elsah, Ill., 1961; LLB, Stanford U., 1964; LLM, U. So. Calif., 1966. Bar: Calif. 1965. Pvt. practice, L.A., 1965-90; ptnr. Adams, Duque & Hazeltine, L.A., 1970-81, Morgan, Lewis & Bockius, L.A., 1981-91. Bd. dirs., co-chmn., CEO World Cup USA 1994, Inc., L.A., 1991. Group v.p. sports L.A. Olympic Organizing Com., 1982-84; assoc. counselor U.S. Olympic Com., 1985, spl. asst. to pres., 1985-89, asst. to pres, dir. olympic del., 1989-92; bd. dirs. Century 21 Real Estate-Can. Ltd., 1995-97. Trustee St. Jhn's Hosp. and Med. Ctr., Santa Monica, Marymount H.S.; asst. chief de mission U.S. Olylmpic Team, 1988; bd. dirs. Hallum Prevention of Child Abuse Fund, 1976-96. Recipient Gold medal of Youth and Sports, France, 1984. Mem. State Bar Calif., Calif. Club, L.A. Country Club, The Beach Club, Ind. Order Foresters (bd. dirs.), Eagle Springs Golf Club, Country Club of the Rockies. Office: PO Box 688 Pacific Palisades CA 90272-0688

CALISE, NICHOLAS JAMES, lawyer; b. N.Y.C., Sept. 15, 1941; s. William J. and Adeline (Rota) C.; m. Mary G. Flannery, Nov. 10, 1965; children: James R., Lori K. AB, Middlebury Coll., 1962; MBA, LLB, Columbia U., 1965. Bar: N.Y. 1965, Conn., 1974, Ohio, 1986, Colo. 2000. Assoc., ptnr. Olvany, Eisner & Donnelly, N.Y.C., 1969-76; corp. staff atty. Richardson-Vicks Inc., Wilton, Conn., 1976-82, div. counsel, dir. planning and bus. devel. home care products div. Memphis, 1982-84; staff v.p., sec., asst. gen. counsel The B.F. Goodrich Co., Akron, Ohio, 1984-89, v.p., sec., assoc. gen. counsel, 1989-99. Mem. Flood and Erosion Control Bd., Darien, Conn., 1976, Rep. Town Meeting, Darien, 1977-78; chmn. Zoning Bd. Appeals, Darien, 1978-82; Justice of the Peace, Darien, 1982. Served to lt. USN, 1965-68, capt. JAGC, USNR, 1984-96, ret. Mem. ABA, Am. Soc. Corp. Secs. (bd. dirs. 1990-93, exec. steering com. 1992-93, chpt. treas. 1988-89, sec. 1989-90, v.p. 1990-91, pres. 1991-92, chmn. nat. conf. com. 1997, chmn. fin. com. 1998-2000, chmn. by-laws revision com. 1998-99), Am. Corp. Counsel Assn., N.Y. State Bar Assn., Colo. Bar Assn., Ohio Bar Assn., U.S. Naval Inst., Navy League (life), Judge Advs. Assn. (life), Naval Res. Assn. (life), Res. Officers Assn. (life), Am. Legion, Club Cordillera. Roman Catholic. Home: PO Box 1916 2035-4 Cordillera Way Edwards CO 81632 Office: PO Box 1964 Edwards CO 81632-1964 E-mail: caliselaw@yahoo.com

CALKINS, LOREN GENE, religious organization administrator, pastor; b. Walla Walla, Wash., Feb. 6, 1942; s. Albert T. and Verna M. (Smith) C.; m. Lorena L. Tittle, Apr. 19, 1962; children: Lance E., Lonny G., LaRae L. BS, George Fox Coll., Newburg, Oreg., 1967; MDiv, We. Evangel. Sem., Portland, Oreg., 1970; DMin, San Francisco Theol. Sem., 1980. Ordained to ministry Free Methodist Ch., 1970. Sr. pastor Free Meth. Ch., Carlton, Oreg., 1965-68, West Linn, 1968-69, Eugene, 1970-72, Christian and Missionary Alliance, Bainbridge Island, Wash., 1972-74, Memphis, 1975-79, Spokane, 1979-84, Dallas (Oreg.) Alliance Ch., 1995—; dist. dir. ext. Christian and Missionary Alliance, Canby, Oreg., 1984-89, dist. supt. Ft. Worth, 1989-95. Ch. growth cons. Christian and Missionary Alliance, 1984—, stewardship cons., 1985—. Trustee Crown Coll., St. Bonifacius, Minn., 1989—, LeTourneau U., Longview, Tex., 1991—. Mem. Nat. Assn. Evangelicals (local pres. 1970-72, 80-84), Kiwanis. Republican. Office: Dallas Alliance Ch 775 E Ellendale Ave Dallas OR 97338-3007

CALLAHAN, DARRY W. energy company executive; BSChemE, Oreg. State U., 1964. Various positions Chevron Corp., 1964-2000, exec. v.p., 2000—. Bd. dirs. Dynegy, Inc.; former pres. Warren Petroleum Co., Chevron Oil Bahamas, Ltd., Chevron Chem. Co. Office: Chevron Corp 575 Market St 39th Fl San Francisco CA 94105-2856

CALLAHAN, MARILYN JOY, social worker; b. Portland, Oreg., Oct. 11, 1934; d. Douglas Q. and Anona Helen Maynard; m. Lynn J. Callahan, Feb. 27, 1960 (dec.); children: Barbara Callahan Baer, Susan Callahan Sewell, Jeffrey Lynn. BA, Mills Coll., 1955; MSW, Portland State U., 1971, secondary teaching cert., 1963. Bd. cert. diplomate in clin. social work. Developer, adminstr. ednl. program Oreg. Women's Correctional Ctr., Oreg. State Prison, Salem, 1966-67; mental health counselor Benton County Mental Health, Corvallis, Oreg., 1970-71; inst. tchr. Hillcrest Sch., Salem, 1975-81; social worker protective svcs. Mid Willamette Valley Sr. Svcs. Agy., Salem, 1981-88; psychiat. social worker dept. forensics Oreg. State Hosp., 1988-93; pvt. practice treatment of adult male and female sexual offenders Salem, 1987—; pvt. practice in care/mgmt. of elderly, 1987—. Panel mem. Surgeon Gen.'s N.W. Regional Conf. on Interpersonal Violence, 1987; speaker in field; planner, organizer Seminar on Age Discrimination, 1985. Mem. NASW (past mem. bd. dirs. Oreg. chpt.), Nat. Org. Forensic Social Work, Am. Acad. Forensic Scis., Acad. Cert. Social Workers (lic. clin. social worker), Assn. for Treatment Sex Abusers, Oreg. Gerontol. Assn., Catalina 27 Nat. Sailing Assn., Mid Valley Alzheimers Assn. (bd. mem. 1998—). Office: 780 Commercial St SE Ste 304 Salem OR 97301-3455 E-mail: mjcsail@aol.com

CALLAN, JOSI IRENE, museum director; b. Yorkshire, Eng., Jan. 30, 1946; came to U.S., 1953; d. Roger Bradshaw and Irene (Newbury) Winstanley; children: James, Heather, Brett Jack; m. Patrick Marc Callan, June 26, 1984. BA in Art History summa cum laude, Calif. State U., Domingues Hills, 1978, MA in Behavioral Scis., 1981. Dir. community rels./alumni affairs Calif. State U., Dominguez Hills, adminstrv. fellow office chancellor Long Beach, assoc. dir. univ. svcs. office chancellor, 1979-85; dir. capital campaign, assoc. dir. devel. Sta. KVIE-TV, Sacramento, 1985-86; dir. project devel. Pacific Mountain Network, Denver, 1986-87; dir. mktg. and devel. Denver Symphony Orch., 1988-89; assoc. dir. San Jose (Calif.) Mus. Art, 1989-91, dir., 1991-99, Mus. of Glass, Tacoma, 1999—. Asst. prof. sch. social and behavioral scis. Calif. State U., Dominguez Hills, 1981—; mem. adv. com. Issues Facing Mus. in 1990s JKF U., 1990-91. Mem. com. arts policy Santa Clara Arts Coun., 1990-92; chair San Jose Arts Roundtable, 1992-93; active ArtTable, 1992—, Community Leadership San Jose, 1992-93, Am. Leadership Forum, 1994, bd. dirs., 2000—; mem. adv. bd. Bay Area Rsch. Project, 1992—; mem. Calif. Arts Coun., Visual Arts Panel, 1993-95, Santa Clara Arts Coun. Visual Arts Panel, 1993; bd. dirs. YWCA, 1993—. Recipient Leadership award Knight Found., 1995; Women of Vision honoree Career Action Ctr., 1998; fellow Calif. State U., 1982-83. Mem. AAUW, Am. Assn. Mus., Nat. Soc. Fund Raising Execs. (bd. dirs. 1991), Colo. Assn. Fund Raisers, Art Mus. Devel. Assn., Assn. Art Mus. Dirs., We. Mus. Assn., Calif. State U. Alumni Coun. (pres. 1981-83), Rotary Internat. E-mail: josi@museum ofglass.org. Office: Mus of Glass 934 Broadway Ste 204 Tacoma WA 98402-4413

CALLAWAY, ELY REEVES, JR. golf club manufacturer; b. LaGrange, Ga., June 3, 1919; s. Ely Reeves and Loula (Walker) C.; m. Jeanne Delaplaine Wiler, Oct. 7, 1942 (div. Jan. 1960); children: Ely Reeves III, Louise Wiler, Nicholas Delaplaine; m. Jane Dudley Atkins, Dec. 28, 1961; m. Lucinda Villa, 1983. A.B., Emory U., 1940; D. Textiles, Phila. Coll. Textiles and Sci., 1968. Sales exec. Deering, Milliken & Co., 1946-54; v.p., dir. Amerotron Corp. div. Textron, Inc., 1955-56; joined Burlington Industries, Inc., 1956, successively pres. various divs., then v.p. of corp., 1960, exec. v.p., 1961, pres., 1968-73; also dir., mem. exec. com., mgmt. com.; founder, owner-operator Callaway Vineyard and Winery, Inc., Temecula, Calif., 1973-81; founder, chmn., CEO Callaway Golf Co. (formerly Callaway Hickory Sticks), Carlsbad, CA, 1982—. Bd. dirs., chmn. corp. giving United Negro Coll. Fund, 1970-71; bd. Greater N.Y. council Boy Scouts America; board visitors Emory U.; trustee Hampshire Coll., Amherst, Mass., Menninger Found., Topeka, Kan. Served from 2d lt. to maj., Q.M.C. AUS, 1940-45; purchasing and contracting officer cotton clothing Phila. Q.M. Depot. Clubs: University (N.Y.), Blind Brook (N.Y.); Eldorado Country, Vintage (Indian Wells, Calif.); Pine Valley (N.J.) Golf. Office: Callaway Golf Co 2285 Rutherford Rd Carlsbad CA 92008-8815

CALLENDER, JONATHAN FERRIS, environmental geologist, resource planner; b. L.A., Nov. 7, 1944; s. Robert Ford and Ruth Merigold (Ferris) C.; m. Cynthia E. Bennett, Aug. 1967 (div. Apr. 1982); children: Katherine Callender Snowden, Elizabeth Alexa Eschallier, Jennifer, Sarah; m. Leila C. Hanson, 2001. BS, Calif. Inst. Tech., 1966; AM, Harvard U., 1968, PhD in Geology, 1975. Asst. prof. U. N.Mex., Albuquerque, 1972-77, assoc. prof., 1977-84, asst. chmn. geology dept., 1979-81, adj. prof. geology, 1985-90; chief sci. programs N.Mex. Mus. Natural History, Albuquerque, 1983-84, dir., 1984-90, also bd. dirs.; v.p., prin. Adrian Brown Cons., Denver, 1990-96; mgr. strategic resources Kennecott Utah Copper Corp., Magna, 1996-2001; v.p. resource devel. Kennecott Devel. Co., Salt Lake City, 2001—. Adj. prof. geology N.Mex. Inst. Mining and Tech., Socorro, 1985-90. Editor numerous books on N.Mex. geology; author numerous tech. papers in field. Active N.Mex. First, 1986-90, Hispanic Cultural Found., Albuquerque, 1986-90; bd. dirs. N.Mex. Mus. Found., 1984-90, Mining Life Cycle Ctr., MacKay Sch. Mines, 1999—. Nat. Sci. Found. fellow, 1971-72; recipient Presdl. Recognition award U. N.Mex., 1982. Fellow Geol. Soc. Am.; mem. Am. Assn. Petroleum Geologists, Am. Geophys. Union (chmn. transl. bd. 1985-96), N.Mex. Geol. Soc. (hon., pres. 1977). Avocations: photography, writing. Office: Kennecott Devel Co 5295 S 300 W Ste 323 Salt Lake City UT 84107 E-mail: JCalle2525@aol.com

CALLETON, THEODORE EDWARD, lawyer, educator; b. Newark, Dec. 13, 1934; s. Edward James and Dorothy (Dewey) C.; m. Elizabeth Bennett Brown, Feb. 4, 1961; children: Susan Bennett, Pamela Barritt, Christopher Dewey.; m. Kathy E'Beth Conkle, Feb. 22, 1983; 1 child, James Frederick. BA, Yale U., 1956; LLB, Columbia U., 1962. Bar: Calif. 1963, U.S. Dist. Ct. (so. dist.) Calif. 1963, U.S. Tax Ct. 1977. Assoc. O'Melveny & Myers, L.A., 1962-69, Agnew, Miller & Carlson, L.A., 1969, ptnr., 1970-79; pvt. practice L.A., 1979-83; ptnr. Kindel & Anderson, L.A., 1983-92, Calleton & Merritt, Pasadena, Calif., 1992-99, Calleton & Trytten, Pasadena, 1999—. Academician Internat. Acad. Estate and Trust Law, 1974—; lectr. Calif. Continuing Edn. Bar, 1970-96, U. So. Calif. Tax Inst., 1972, 76, 91, Calif. State U., L.A., 1974-93, Practicing Law Inst., 1976-86, Am. Law Inst., 1985; bd. dirs. UCLA/Continuing Edn. of Bar Estate Planning Inst., 1979—; adj. prof. Golden Gate U. Law Sch., 1997—, Layola U. Sch. Law, 2002—. Author: The Short Term Trust, 1977, A Life Insurance Primer, 1978, Calleton's Wills and Trusts, 1992-2002; co-author: California Will Drafting Practice, 1982, Tax Planning for Professionals, 1985; contbr. articles to legal jours. Chmn. Arroyo Seco Master Planning Commn., Pasadena, Calif., 1970-71; bd. dirs. Montessori Sch., Inc., 1964-68, chmn., 1966-68, Am. Montessori Soc., N.Y.C., 1967-72, chmn., 1969-72; trustee Walden Sch. of Calif., 1970-86, 90-94, chmn., 1980-86; trustee Episc. Children's Home of L.A., 1971-75; bd. dirs. L.A. Master Chorale Assn., 1989-94. Lt. USMC, 1956-59. Fellow Am. Coll. Trust and Estate Counsel; mem. L.A. County Bar Assn. (chmn. taxation sect. 1980-81, chmn. probate and trust law sect. 1981-82, Dana Latham Meml. award 1996), Aurelian Honor Soc., Elihu, Beta Theta Pi, Phi Delta Phi. Home: 301 Churchill Rd Sierra Madre CA 91024-1354 Office: Calleton & Trytten LLP 200 S Los Robles Ave Ste 678 Pasadena CA 91101-4600 E-mail: ted@calleton-trytten.com

CALLEY, JOHN, motion picture company executive, film producer; b. N.J., 1930; m. Olinka Schoberova, 1972 (div.) m. Meg Tilly, 1995; 4 stepchildren, Emily, David, Will, Sabrina. Dir. nighttime programming, dir. programming sales NBC, 1951-57; prodn. exec. and TV producer Henry Jaffe Enterprises, 1957; v.p. radio and TV Ted Bates Advt. Agy., 1958; exec. v.p., film producer Filmways, Inc., 1960-69; with Warner Bros., Inc., Burbank, Calif., 1969-87, exec. v.p. world-wide prodn., 1969-75, pres., 1975-80, vice chmn. bd., 1977-80, cons., 1980-87; film prodr., 1987—; pres., COO, United Artists Pictures, 1993-96; pres., CEO, Sony Pictures Entertainment, Inc., Culver City, Calif., 1996—, now chmn., CEO. Office: care Sony Pictures Entertainment Inc 10202 Washington Blvd Culver City CA 90232-3119

CALLIES, DAVID LEE, lawyer, educator; b. Chgo., Apr. 21, 1943; s. Gustav E. and Ann D. Callies; m. Laurie Breeden, Dec. 28, 1996; 1 child, Sarah Anne. AB, DePauw U., 1965; JD, U. Mich., 1968; LLM, U. Nottingham, England, 1969. Bar: Ill. 1969, Hawaii 1978, U.S. Supreme Ct. 1974. Spl. asst. states atty., McHenry County, Ill., 1969; assoc. firm Ross, Hardies, O'Keefe, Babcock & Parsons, Chgo., 1969-75, ptnr., 1975-78; prof. law Richardson Sch. Law, U. Hawaii, Honolulu, 1978—; Benjamin A. Kudo prof. law U. Hawaii, Honolulu, 1995—. Mem. adv. com. on planning and growth mgmt. City and County of Honolulu Coun., 1978-88, mem. citizens adv. com. on State Functional Plan for Conservation Lands, 1979-93. Author: (with Fred P. Bosselman) the Quiet Revolution in Land Use Control, 1971 (with Fred P. Bosselman and John S. Banta) The Taking Issue, 1973, Regulating Paradise: Land Use Controls in Hawaii, 1984, (with Robert Freilich and Tom Roberts) Cases and Materials on Land Use, 1986, 3d edit., 1999, Preserving Paradise: Why Regulation Won't Work, 1994 (in Japanese 1994, in Chinese 1999), Land Use Law in the United States, 1994; editor: After Lucas: Land Use Regulation and the Taking of Property Without Compensation, 1993, Takings! Land Development Conditions and Regulatory Takings: After Dolan and Lucas, 1995, (with Hylton, Mandelker and Franzese) Property Law and the Public Interest, 1998; co-editor Environ. and Land Use Law Rev., 2000—. Life Fell., Clare Hall, Cambridge Univ. Named Best Prof., U. Hawaii Law Sch., 1990-91, 91-92; Mich. Ford Found. fellow U. Nottingham (Eng.), 1969, life mem. Clare Hall, Cambridge U., 1999. Mem. ABA (chmn. com. on land use, planning and zoning 1980-82, coun. sect. on state and local govt. 1981-85, 95—, exec. com. 1986-90, sec. 1986-87, chmn. 1989-90), Am. Law Inst., Am. Inst. Cert. Planners, Am. Planning Assn., Hawaii State Bar Assn. (chair, real property and fin. svc. sect., 1997), Am. Bar Found., Ill. Bar Assn., Internat. Bar Assn. (coun. Asia Pacific Forum 1993-96, co-chair Acads. Forum 1994-96, chair 1996-98), Nat. Trust for Hist. Preservation, Royal Oak Soc., Lambda Alpha Internat. (pres. Aloha chpt. 1989-90, internat. v.p. Asia-Pacific region 2001—, Internat. Mem. of Yr. 1994). Home: 1532 Kamole St Honolulu HI 96821-1424 Office: U Hawaii Richardson Sch Law 2515 Dole St Honolulu HI 96822-2328 E-mail: dcallies@hawaii.edu

CALLISON, NANCY FOWLER, nurse administrator; b. Milw., July 16, 1931; d. George Fenwick and Irma Esther (Wenzel) Fowler; m. B.G. Callison, Sept. 25, 1954 (dec. Feb. 1964); children: Robert, Leslie, Linda. Diploma, Evanston Hosp. Sch. Nursing, 1952; BS, Northwestern U., 1954. RN, Calif.; cert. case mgr. Staff nurse, psychiat. dept. Downey VA Hosp., 1954-55; staff nurse Camp Lejeune Naval Hosp., 1955, 59-61; obstet. supr. Tri-City Hosp., Oceanside, Calif., 1961-62; pub. health nurse San Diego County, 1962-66; sch. nurse Rich-Mar Union Sch. Dist., San Marcos, Calif., 1966-68; head nurse San Diego County Community Mental Health, 1968-73; dir. patient care services Southwood Mental Health Ctr., Chula Vista, Calif., 1973-75; program cons. Comprehensive Care Corp., Newport Beach, 1975-79; dir. Manpower Health Care, Culver City, 1979-80; dir. nursing services Peninsula Rehab. Ctr., Lomita, 1980-81; clinic supr., coordinator utilization and authorizations, acting dir. provider relations Hawthorne (Calif.) Community Med. Group, 1981-86; mgr. Health Care Delivery Physicians of Greater Long Beach, Calif., 1986-87; cons. Quality Rev. Assocs., West L.A., 1988-93; case mgr. Mercy Physicians Med. Group, 1992-93; med. mgmt. specialist The Zenith Ins., 1993—. Mem. Rehab. Nurse Coord. Network, 1992-97, treas. 1997-98; clin. coord., translator Flying Samaritans, 1965—, mem. internat. bd. dirs., 1975-77, 79-86, 89—, dir. San Quentin project, 1991-93, dir. univ. program, 1996—, pres. South Bay chpt., 1975-81, v.p., 1982-85, bd. dirs. San Diego chpt., 1987-90, pres. San Diego chpt. 1991-92, adminstr. Clinica Esperanza de Infantil Rosarito Beach 1990-93. Mem. Rehab. Nurse Coord. Network (bd. dirs., treas. 1997-98), U.S.-Mex. Border Health Assn., Cruz Roja Mexicana (Delegacion Rosarito 1986-92). E-mail: CallisonCasemgt@Aol.com

CALLOWAY, DORIS HOWES, nutrition educator; b. Canton, Ohio, Feb. 14, 1923; d. Earl John and Lillian Ann (Roberts) Howes; m. Nathaniel O. Calloway, Feb. 14, 1946 (div. 1956); children: David Karl, Candace; m. Robert O. Nesheim, July 4, 1981. BS, Ohio State U., 1943; PhD, U. Chgo., 1947; DSc (Hon.), Tufts U., 1992. Head metabolism lab., nutritionist, chief div. QM Food and Container Inst., Chgo., 1951-61; chmn. dept. food sci. and nutrition Stanford Rsch. Inst., Menlo Park, Calif., 1961-63; prof. U. Calif., Berkeley, 1963-91, provost profl. schs. and colls., 1981-87, prof. and provost emeritus, 1991—. Mem. expert adv. panel on nutrition WHO, Geneva, 1972-92, tech. adv. com. Consultative Group on Internat. Agrl. Rsch., 1989-93, Internat. Commn. on Health Rsch. for Devel., 1987-90, adv. coun. Nat. Inst. Arthritis, Metabolic and Digestive Diseases, Nat. Inst. Aging, NIH, Bethesda, Md., 1974-77, 78-82; trustee Internat. Maize and Wheat Improvement Ctr., 1983-88; trustee, bd. dirs. Winrock Internat. Inst.; cons. FAO, UN, Rome, 1971, 74-75, 81-83; lectr. Cooper Meml., 1983, Roberts Meml., 1985. Author: Nutrition and Health, 1981, Nutrition and Physical Fitness 11th edit., 1984; mem. editorial bd. Am. Dietetic Assn. Jour., 1974-77, Environmental Biology and Medicine, 1969-79. Recipient Meritorious Civilian Svc. Dept. Army, 1959, Disting. Achievement in Nutrition Rsch. award Bristol-Myers Squibb, 1994, Edna and Robert Langholtz Internat. Nutrition award Am. Dietetic Assn., 1997; named Disting. Alumna Ohio State U., 1974, Wellcome vis. prof. Fedn. Am. Soc. Exptl. Biol., U. Mo., 1980. Fellow Internat. Union of Nutritional Scis., Am. Inst. Nutrition (pres. 1982-83, sec. 1969-72, editorial bd. 1967-72, Conrad A. Elvehjem award 1986); mem. Inst. Medicine NAS, Sigma Xi. Office: U Calif Morgan Hall Berkeley CA 94720

CALLOWAY, LARRY, columnist; b. Lovell, Wyo., Nov. 21, 1937; s. Joseph Charles and Frances (Linda) C.; children: Lara, Maia. BA, U. Colo., 1962. Staff writer United Press Internat., 1963-69; gov. and polit. writer The Associated Press, Santa Fe, 1969-79; bureau chief, zoned-edition editor The Albuquerque Jour., 1980-88, featured columnist, 1988—. Stanford U. fellow, 1979-80. Home: 12 Reno Rd Santa Fe NM 87505-2133 Office: Albuquerque Jour 328 Galisteo St Santa Fe NM 87501-2606

CALVERT, JACK GEORGE, atmospheric chemist, educator; b. Inglewood, Calif., May 9, 1923; s. John George and Emma (Eschstruth) C.; m. Doris Arlene Breimon, Nov. 8, 1946; children: Richard John, Mark Steven. BS in Chemistry, UCLA, 1944, PhD, 1949. Mem. faculty Ohio State U., 1950-81, prof. chemistry, 1960-81, Kimberly prof. chemistry, 1974-81, prof. emeritus, 1981—, chmn. dept., 1964-68; sr. scientist Nat. Ctr. Atmospheric Rsch., Boulder, Colo., 1982-94, sr. rsch. assoc., 1994—. Cons. air pollution tng. com. USPHS, 1964-66; mem. Nat. Air Pollution Control Manpower Devel. Com., 1966-69, chmn., 1968-69; bd. dirs. Gordon Rsch. Confs., 1969-71; mem. air pollution control rsch. grants com. EPA, 1970-72, chmn., 1971-72, mem. chemistry and physics adv. com., 1973-75; chmn. air pollution com. Conservation Found., 1968-70; mem. air conservation commn. Am. Lung Assn., 1973-75; chmn. EPA environ. chemistry/physics grants rev. panel, 1979-83; mem. State of Colo. Air Quality Control Commn., 1987-90, Disting. Acad. Adv. Group of Auto/Oil Air Quality Improvement Rsch. Program, 1989-96; mem. panel on atmospheric effects of aviation NRC/NAS, 1995-98, mem. com. on ozone potential of reformulated gasoline, 1997-99; atmospheric chemistry tech. implementation panel Am. Chem. Coun., 1998—. Author (with J. N. Pitts, Jr.) Photochemistry, 1966, Graduate School in the Sciences, 1972; also articles. Ensign USNR, 1944-46. Named Honor Prof. of Year Coll. Arts and Scis., Ohio State U., 1957; recipient Alumni award for disting. tchg., 1961, Disting. Rsch. award, 1981; fellow NRC Can., 1949; Guggenheim fellow, 1977-78 Fellow Ohio Acad. Sci., Am. Inst. Chemists, Am. [illegible] (award for creative rsch. in environ. sci. and tech. 1981, Columbus [illegible] 1991), [illegible] Control Assn. (Chambers award 1986), Phi Beta Kappa, Sigma Xi, Pi Mu Epsilon, Phi Lambda Upsilon, Alpha Chi Sigma. Achievements include research on photochemistry, reaction kinetics, atmospheric chemistry, mechanisms free radical reactions. Office: NCAR Atmospheric Chemistry Divsn PO Box 3000 Boulder CO 80307-3000 E-mail: calvert@ucar.edu

CALVERT, KEN, congressman; b. Corona, Calif., June 8, 1953; AA, Chaffey Coll., 1973; BA Econs., San Diego State U., 1975. Corona/ Norco youth chmn. for Nixon, 1968, 82; county youth chmn. rep. Vesey's Dist., 1970, 43d dist., 1972; congl. aide to Rep. Vesey, Calif., 1975-79; gen. mgr. Jolly Fox Restaurant, Corona, 1975-79, Marcus W. Meairs Co., Corona, 1979-81; pres., gen. mgr. Ken Calvert Real Properties, Corona, 1981—; Reagan-Bush campaign worker, 1980; co chmn. Wilson for Senate Campaign, 1982, George Deukmejian election, 1978, 82, 86, George Bush election, 1988, Pete Wilson senate elections, 1982, 88, Pete Wilson for Gov. election, 1990; mem. U.S. Congress from 43rd Calif. dist., 1993—; mem. armed svcs., resources, sci. com. Former v.p. Corona/ Norco Rep. Assembly; chmn. Riverside Rep. Party, 1984-88, County Riverside Asset Leasing; bd. realtors Corono/ Norco Exec. bd. Corona Community Hosp. Corp. 200 Club; mem. Corona Airport adv. commn.; adv. com. Temescal/ El Cerrito Community Plan. Mem. Riverside County Rep. Winners Circle (charter), Lincoln Club (co-chmn., charter, 1986-90), Corona Rotary Club (pres. 1991), Elks, Navy League Corona Norco, Corona C. of C. (pres. 1990), Noroco C. of C., Monday Morning Group, Corona Group (past chmn.), Econ. Devel. Ptnrship., Silver Eagles (March AFB support group, charter). Office: US Ho of Reps 2201 Rayburn Ho Office Bldg Washington DC 20515-0001*

CALVIN, ALLEN DAVID, psychologist, educator; b. St. Paul, Feb. 17, 1928; s. Carl and Zelda (Engelson) C.; m. Dorothy VerStrate, Oct. 5, 1953; children: Jamie, Kris, David, Scott. B.A. in Psychology cum laude, U. Minn., 1950; M.A. in Psychology, U. Tex., 1951, Ph.D. in Exptl. Psychology, 1953. Instr. Mich. State U., East Lansing, 1953-55; asst. prof. Hollins Coll., 1955-59, assoc. prof., 1959-61. Dir. Britannica Center for Studies in Learning and Motivation, Menlo Park, Calif., 1961; prin. investigator grant for automated teaching fgn. langs. Carnegie Found., 1960; USPHS grantee, 1960; pres. Behavioral Research Labs., 1962-74; prof., dean Sch. Edn., U. San Francisco, 1974-78; Henry Clay Hall prof. Orgn. and leadership, 1978—; pres. Pacific Grad. Sch. Psychology, 1984— Author textbooks. Served with USNR, 1946-47. Mem. Am. Psychol. Assn., AAAS, Sigma Xi, Psi Chi. Home: 1645 15th Ave San Francisco CA 94122-3523 Office: Pacific Grad Sch Psychology 935 E Meadow Dr Palo Alto CA 94303-4233 E-mail: a.calvin@pgsp.edu

CAMBRE, ATHLEO LOUIS, JR. plastic surgeon; b. L.A., Feb. 21, 1954; MD, Case Western Res. U., 1981. Intern U. Colo. Sch. Medicine, Denver, 1981-82, gen. surgeon, 1982-86; burn surgery fellow Cornell-N.Y. Hosp., N.Y.C., 1986-87; plastic surgeon UCLA, 1987-89, Cedars-Sinai Med. Ctr., L.A., 1989—. Asst. clin. prof. plastic surgery UCLA. Office: Plastic and Reconstructive Surg 120 S Spalding Dr Ste 205 Beverly Hills CA 90212-1840

CAMBRE, RONALD C. mining executive; m. Gail Cambre. BSCE, La. State U.; postgrad., Harvard U. Chmn. bd. Rio Tinto Minera SA; various positions, including pres., CEO Freeport-McMoRan Resource Ptnrs. subs. Freeport-McMoRan Inc., 1964-93; v.p., sr. technical adviser to chmn. Freeport-McMoRan Inc., 1988-93; vice chmn., CEO, bd. dirs. Newmont Mining Corp., Denver, 1993—, pres., 1994—, chmn. bd. dirs., 1995—. Vice chmn., CEO, chmn. bd. dirs. Newmont Gold Co. subs. Newmont Mining Corp. Office: Newmount Mining 1700 Lincoln St Denver CO 80203

CAMERON, ALEX BRIAN, accounting educator; b. Fresno, Calif., Nov. 20, 1943; s. Alexander Archer and Francette (Maize) C.; m. Judy Lea Helphrey, June 7, 1969; children: Michelle, Michael. BA, Eastern Wash. U., 1969, MBA, 1970; PhD, U. Utah, 1982. CPA, Wash.; cert. in mgmt. acctg. Mgr. prodn. planning Bunker Hill Mining Co., Kellog, Idaho, 1970-77; asst. prof. Wash. State U., Pullman, 1978-79; assoc. prof. Eastern Wash. U., Cheney, 1981-87, prof., 1987—, chmn. dept. acctg., 1988-89, assoc. dean, 1990-97, interimm v.p. bus. and fin., 1998-99, interim dean Coll. Bus. and Pub. Adminstrn., 1999-2001. Contbr. articles to profl. jours. Avocations: sailing, golf, volleyball. Home: 15212 Pinnacle Ln Veradale WA 99037-9163 Office: 668 N Riverpoint Blvd Spokane WA 99202-1677

CAMERON, CHARLES HENRY, petroleum engineer; b. Greeley, Colo., Oct. 21, 1947; s. Leo Leslie and Naomi Tryphena (Phillips) C.; m. Cheryl Christine Debelock, Aug. 30, 1969; 1 child, Ericka Dawn. AS, Mesa State Coll., 1968; BS in Geology, Mesa Coll., 1978; AS in Hazardous Materials Tech., Front Range C.C., Wesminister, Colo., 1990. Cert. info. resource mgmt. approving ofcl. (CIAO), 1998. Retardation technician Colo. State Home and Tng. Sch., Grand Junction, 1967-69; journeyman carpenter Brotherhood of Carpenters and Joiners, Grand Junction, 1969-76; hydrocompaction mgr. Colo. Dept. Hwys., Grand Junction, 1975-77; rsch. geologist Occidental Oil Shale, Inc., Grand Junction, 1977-78; geol. engr. Cleveland Cliffs Iron Co., Morgantown, W.Va., 1978-81; tech. advisor Ute Indian Tribe, Ft. Duchesne, Utah, 1981-86; ops. mgr. Charging Ute Corp., Golden, Colo., 1986-87; cons. Golden, 1987-90; petroleum engr. U.S. Dept. Interior/Bur. of Indian Affairs, Ft. Duchesne, 1990—, hazardous material mgr., freedom of info./privacy act coord., 1990-2000, minerals/realty officer, 1994, natural resources officer, 1996—, ADP com. chmn., LAN adminstr., PL 93-638 com. chmn. grants/loan mgr., 1999-2000, GIS committeeman, 1994, supervisory petroleum engr., realty officer, br. of realty, 2000—. Minerals specialist Phoenix area Bur. Indian Affairs, Y2K coord. U&O Agency computer systems upgrade project, 1998, acting realty officer, 1999. Contbr. articles to profl. jours. Mem. Colo. Oil Field Investigators Assn., Vernal (Utah) C. of C., Internat. Platform Assn. Avocations: motorcycle touring, antiques, photography, hunting, fishing, charles. Home: 255 East 200 North Vernal UT 84078-1713 Office: BIA Uintah Ouray Agy 988 S 7500 E PO Box 130 Fort Duchesne UT 84026-0130 E-mail: charlescameron@bia.gov, cameron@hotmail.com

CAMERON, DEAN L. state legislator; b. Burley, Idaho, Jan. 20, 1961; m. Linda Cameron; children: Carissa, Laci, Nathan. AA in Polit. Sci., Ricks Coll. Ind. ins. agt.; mem. Idaho Senate, Dist. 24, Boise, 1990—. Chair commerce and human resources com.; vice chair fin. com.; mem. resources and environment com. Mem. Nat. Assn. Life Underwriters, So. Idaho Life Underwriters Assn. (2-term past pres., area II v.p.), Minidoka County C. of C. (past bd. mem.), Rupert (Idaho) Rotary (past treas.). Republican. Office: State Capitol PO Box 83720 Boise ID 83720-3720

CAMERON, HEATHER ANNE, publishing executive; b. Montreal, Quebec, Can., Mar. 12, 1951; came to U.S., 1981; d. Douglas George and Jeanne Sutherland (Thompson) C.; m. Ward Eric Shaw, Dec. 20, 1980; 1 child, Geoffrey Cameron. BA, Queen's U., Kingston, Ont., Can., 1973; MLS, McGill U., Montreal, 1977. Head reference and bibliography sect. [illegible], 1977-81; head edit. dept. Libris. Unltd., Inc., Denver, 1981-86; v.p. acquisitions and editl. devel. ABC-CLIO, Inc., Santa Barbara, Calif., 1986-92, pres., pub. Santa Barbara, Denver and, Eng., 1992-97; v.p., gen. mgr. Westgroup, San Francisco, 1997—. Bd. dirs. Friends of Librs. U.S.A., v.p., 1996, pres., 1997—. Mem. ALA (com. chair 1993—), Friends of Librs. USA (dir. 1994—, pres. 1997—), Amnesty Internat., Phi Beta Mu. Office: West Group 50 California St Fl 19 San Francisco CA 94111-4024 E-mail: heather.cameron@westgroup.com

CAMERON, JAMES, film director, screenwriter, producer; b. Kapuskasing, Ont., Can., Aug. 16, 1954; m. Gale Ann Hurd (div.); m. Katheryn Bigelow (div.); 1 child with Linda Hamilton, Josephine Archer. Grad. in Physics, Calif. State U., Fullerton. Head Lightstorm Entertainment, Burbank, Calif., 1992—; CEO Digital Domain, 1993—. Film industry experience includes art dir.: Battle Beyond the Stars, 1980; prodn. designer: Galaxy of Terror, 1981; creator spl. effects: Escape from New York, 1981; film dir.: Piranha II: The Spawning, 1981; dir., screenwriter: The Terminator, 1984, Aliens, 1986, The Abyss, 1989; screenwriter: Rambo: First Blood Part II, 1985; dir., prodr., screenwriter: Terminator II: Judgement Day, 1991, True Lies, 1994; exec. prodr.: Point Break, 1991; dir., Terminator 2 3-D, 1996, Titanic, 1997; writer: Strange Days, 1995. Office: Lightstorm Entertainment 919 Santa Monica Blvd Santa Monica CA 90401-2704

CAMERON, PAUL DRUMMOND, research facility administrator; b. Pitts., Nov. 9, 1939; s. Nelson Drummond and Veronica (Witco) C.; m. Virginia May Rusthoi BA, L.A. Pacific Coll., 1961; MA, Calif. State U., L.A., 1962; PhD, U. Colo., 1966. Asst. prof. psychology Stout State U., Menomonie, Wis., 1966-67, Wayne State U., Detroit, 1967-69; assoc. prof. psychology U. Louisville, 1970-73, Fuller Grad. Sch. Psychology, Pasadena, Calif., 1976-79; assoc. prof. marriage and family U. Nebr., Lincoln, 1979-80; pvt. practice psychologist Lincoln, 1980-83; chmn. Family Rsch. Inst., Washington, 1982-95, Colo. Springs, 1995—. Reviewer Am. Psychologist, Jour. Gerontology, Psychol. Reports; presenter, witness, cons. in field. Author: Exposing the AIDS Scandal, 1988, The Gay 90's, 1993; contbr. articles to profl. jours. Mem. Ea. Psychol. Assn., Nat. Assn. for Rsch. and Treatment of Homosexuality. Republican. Lutheran. Achievements include investigation of health effects of second-hand tobacco smoke; investigation of first comprehensive national random sample of sexuality; documented abbreviated lifespan of homosexuals; documented poorer parenting by homosexuals. Office: Family Rsch Inst PO Box 62640 Colorado Springs CO 80962-2640

CAMMALLERI, JOSEPH ANTHONY, financial planner, retired air force officer; b. Bronx, N.Y., Feb. 2, 1935; s. Leo Anthony and Angela Marie (Mirandi) C.; children: Anthony R., Aaron L., Thomas K., Jeffrey A. BS, Manhattan Coll., 1956; MS, Okla. State U., 1966; postgrad., Golden Gate U., 1974. Cert. life ins. instr., Calif. Commd. 2d lt. USAF, 1956, advanced through grades to lt. col., 1973, trainee flight crew, 1956-58, crew mem. B-52, 1958-64; behavioral scientist Aerospace Med. Rsch. Labs., Wright-Patterson AFB, Ohio, 1966-68; EB-66 crew mem. Tahkli AFB, Thailand, 1968-69; faculty mem. dept. life and behavioral scis. USAF Acad., Colo., 1969-74, assoc. prof., dir. operational psychology div., 1972-74; B-1 hjman factors engrng. mgr. Air Force Flight Test Ctr., Edwards AFB, Calif., 1974-76, chief handbook devel., 1976-77; ret., 1977; account exec. Merrill Lynch, Pierce, Fenner & Smith, Sherman Oaks, Calif., 1977-80; acad. program rep. U. Redlands, 1980-84, regional dir. admissions, 1984-86; mem. faculty Whitehead Coll., 1979-99, assoc. dean admissions, 1986-89; mem. faculty Golden Gate U., 1975-80; account exec. Humanomics Ins., 1989-90; corp. dir. tng. and edn. Fin. West Group, 1990-92; prin. CEO Spectrum Securities Inc., Westlake Village, Calif., 1992-95; assoc. dean admission Alfred North Whitehead Coll. U. of Redlands, 1996; registered gen. securities prin. Thomas F. White & Co., Inc., 1996—; CFO, registered prin. PLC Securities Corp., Ventura, Calif., 1996-98; mem. adj. faculty Calif. Luth. U., 1990-91, Antioch U., 1992-93; regional mgr. So. Calif. Thomas F. White and Co., Inc., Ventura, Calif., 2001—. Sec. 7th Ann. Narrow Gauge Conv. Com., Pasadena, Calif., 1986. Contbr. articles to profl. jours. Sec. com. centennial celebration Rio Grande So. Ry., Dolores, Colo., 1991; USAF Acad. liaison officer, North Los Angeles County, 1992—. Decorated D.F.C., Air medal (5), Meritorious Service medal. Mem. NRA, KC, Nat. Ry. Hist. Soc., Ry. and Locomotive Hist. Soc., Rocky Mountain R.R. Club, L.A. Live Steamers, Colo. R.R. Hist. Found. (life), Alpine Tunnel Hist. Soc. (life), DAV (life), Santa Fe Ry. Hist. Soc., USAF Acad. Athletic Assn. (life), Katy Ry. Hist. Soc., Okla. Hist. Soc., Psi Chi. Home: 1177 Monte Sereno Dr Thousand Oaks CA 91360-2408 E-mail: Jcamma455@aol.com

CAMP, JOSEPH SHELTON, JR. film producer, director, writer; b. St. Louis, Apr. 20, 1939; s. Joseph Shelton and Ruth Wilhelmena (McLaulin) C.; m. Andrea Carolyn Hopkins, Aug. 7, 1960; children: Joseph Shelton III, Brandon Andrew. BBA, U. Miss., 1961. Jr. account exec. McCann-Erickson Advt., Houston, 1961-62; owner Joe Camp Real Estate, Houston, 1962-64; account exec. Norsworthy-Mercer, Dallas, 1964-69; dir. TV commls. Jamieson Film Co., Dallas, 1969-71; founder, pres., writer, producer, dir. feature films Mulberry Square Prodns., Inc., Dallas, 1971-90, Gulfport, Miss., 1991-94, Chapel Hill, N.C., 1994—. Producer, dir., writer films including Benji, 1974, Hawmps, 1976, For the Love of Benji, 1977, The Double McGuffin, 1979, Oh Heavenly Dog, 1980, Benji The Hunted, 1987; TV spls. The Phenomenon of Benji, 1978, Benji's Very Own Christmas Story, 1978, Benji at Work, 1980, Benji (Takes a Dive) at Marineland, 1981; TV series Benji, Zax and the Alien Prince, 1983; author: Underdog, 1993. Bd. trustees Piney Woods Country Life Sch., Warren Wilson Coll.; adv. bd. N.C. Sch. of Arts, Sch. of Film Making. Mem. Dir.'s Guild Am., Writer's Guild Am. Home: 31336 Cove Lantern Dana Point CA 92629

CAMPANA, MICHAEL EMERSON, hydrogeology and hydrology educator, researcher; b. May 13, 1948; BS in Geology, Coll. William and Mary, 1970; MS in Hydrology, U. Ariz., 1973, PhD in Hydrology, 1975. Cert. profl. geologist, Ind.; profl. hydrogeologist Am. Inst. Hydrology. Assoc. faculty Pima C.C., Tucson, 1973-75; asst. prof. hydrogeology dept. geol. scis. Mackay Sch. Mines U. Nev., Reno, 1976-79, assoc. prof., 1979-83, 84-89; asst. rsch. prof. Water Resources Ctr. Desert Rsch. Inst., Reno, 1976-79, assoc. rsch. prof. Water Resources Ctr., 1979-83, 84-89; assoc. prof. dept. geology Ga. State U., Atlanta, 1983-84; assoc. prof. dept. earth and planetary scis. U. N.Mex., Albuquerque, 1989-97, prof. dept. earth and planetary scis., 1997—, dir. water resources program, 1997—. Vis. assoc. prof. earth scis. bd. U. Calif., Santa Cruz, 1988-89; bd. dirs. Ground Water Pub. Co.; mem. nat. rsch. coun. com. U.S. Geol. Survey Water Resources Rsch. Assoc. editor: Environ. and Engrng. Geosci., 1995—, Ground Water, 1999—; guest co-editor: Hydrogeology Jour. E.S. Simpson meml. issue. Active Vols. in Tech. Assistance, 1984—, Vols. in Overseas Coop. Asstistance, 1995—, Lifewater Internat., 1997—. Fulbright scholar Univ. Coll. Belize, 1995-96. Mem. Am. Geophys. Union, Am. Inst. Hydrology, Internat. Assn. Hydrogeologist, Internat. Assn. Hydrol. Scis., Internat. Water Resources Assn., N.Am. Benthol. Soc., Geol. Soc. Am., European Geophys. Soc., Assn. Ground Water Scientists and Engrs. (bd. dirs. 1997—). Achievements include research to investigate and quantify the interactions between hydrologic systems and stream ecosystems in forested montane catchments; research in watershed hydrology, in regional subsurface flow system delineation and ground-water resource assessment; delineation of flow systems using hydraulic, environmental isotopic and geochemical data, environmental fluid mechanics. Home: PO Box 388 Sandia Park NM 87047-0388 Office: U NMex Dept Earth & Planetary Scis Albuquerque NM 87131-0001

CAMPBELL, ALLAN MCCULLOCH, bacteriology educator; b. Berkeley, Calif., Apr. 27, 1929; s. Lindsay and Virginia Margaret (Henning) C.; m. Alice Del Campillo, Sept. 5, 1958; children— Wendy, Joseph. B.S. in Chemistry, U. Calif. at Berkeley, 1950; M.S. in Bacteriology, U. Ill., 1951; Ph.D., 1953; Ph.D. hon. degree, U. Chgo., 1978, U. Rochester, 1981. Instr. bacteriology U. Mich., 1953-57; research asso. Carnegie Inst., Cold Spring Harbor, N.Y., 1957-58; asst. prof. [illegible], 1958-61, [illegible] prof., 1961-63, prof., 1963-68; prof. biol. sci. Stanford (Calif.) U., 1968—, Barbara Kimball Browning prof. humanities and scis., 1992—. Author:

Episomes, 1969; co-author: General Virology, 1978; editor Gene, 1980-90, mem. editl. bd., 1990—; assoc. editor Virology, 1963-69; assoc. editor Ann. Rev. Genetics, 1969-84, editor, 1984—; spl. editor Evolution, 1985-88; editl. bd. Jour. Bacteriology, 1966-72, Jour. Virology, 1967-75, New Biologist, 1989-92. Served with AUS, 1953-55. Recipient Research Career award USPHS, 1962-68 Mem. Nat. Acad. Scis., Am. Acad. Arts and Scis., Am. Soc. Microbiology, Soc. Am. Naturalists, Genetics Soc. Am., AAAS, Am. Acad. Microbiology. Democrat. Home: 947 Mears Ct Stanford CA 94305-1041 Office: Stanford U Dept Biol Scis Stanford CA 94305 E-mail: FA.AMC@Forsythe.stanford.edu

CAMPBELL, BEN NIGHTHORSE, senator; b. Auburn, Calif., Apr. 13, 1933; m. Linda Price; children: Colin, Shanan. BA, Calif. U., San Jose, 1957. Educator Sacramento Law Enforcement Agy.; mem. Colo. Gen. Assembly, 1983-86, U.S. Ho. Reps., 1987-93; senator from Colorado U.S. Senate, 1993—. Rancher, jewelry designer, Ignacio, Colo. Chief No. Cheyenne Tribe. Named Outstanding Legislator Colo. Bankers Assn., 1984, Man of Yr. LaPlata Farm Bur., Durango, Colo., 1984; named one of Ten Best Legislators Denver Post/Channel 4, 1986. Mem. Am. Quarter Horse Assn., Am. Brangus Assn., Am. Indian Edn. Assn. Republican. Office: US Senate 380 Russell Senate Office Bldg Washington DC 20510-0001

CAMPBELL, BRUCE ALAN, market research consultant; b. Washington, Jan. 19, 1944; s. Albert Angus and Jean Lorraine (Winter) C.; m. Jennifer Lee Drew, May 3, 1968 (div. Dec. 1986); children: Kirsten, Robert; m. Lorna Marion Wise Ekholm, Aug. 21, 1993. BA, Oberlin Coll., 1966; MA, U. Mich., 1968, PhD, 1971. Asst. prof. to assoc. prof. U. Ga., Athens, 1971-83, dir. survey rsch. ctr., 1981-83; v.p. Marktrend Mkt. Rsch., Vancouver, B.C., Can., 1983-84; pres., CEO Campbell Goodell Traynor Consul, Vancouver, Can., 1984—; sr. cons., CGT Rsch. Internat. CGT Rsch. Internat. (formerly named Campbell Goodell Traynor Consul), Vancouver, Can., 2000—; v.p. Corp. Insights, Inc., Vancouver, 1992-96. Dir. Downtown Vancouver Assn., 1989-96, pres., 1994-96, mem. adv. bd., 1996—; dir. Parking Corp. of Vancouver, 1992-2000, v.p., 1994-96, chmn. bd., 1996-98; bd. dir s. Downtown Vancouver Bus. Improvement Assn., 1994-96; mem. Vancouver Econ. Devel. Commn., 1996. Author: The American Electorate, 1979, profl. jours. Mem. Am. Assn. Pub. Opinion Rsch., Profl. Mktg. Rsch. Assn. Avocations: musical theatre, minor hockey officiating. Office: CAT Rsch 675 W Hastiup St Vancouver BC Canada V6B 1N2 E-mail: bcampbell@cgtnet.com

CAMPBELL, COLIN HERALD, former mayor; b. Winnipeg, Man., Can., Jan. 18, 1911; s. Colin Charles and Aimee Florence (Herald) C.; m. Virginia Paris, July 20, 1935; children: Susanna Herald, Corinna Buford, Virginia Wallace. BA, Reed Coll., 1933. Exec. sec. City Club of Portland, 1934-39; alumni sec., dir. endowment adminstrn. Reed Coll., 1939-42; exec. sec. N.W. Inst. Internat. Rels., 1940-42; supr. contract, engr. Kaiser Co., Inc., 1942-45; asst. pers. dir. Portland Gas & Coke Co., 1945-48; dir. indsl. rels. Pacific Power & Light Co., Portland, 1948-76. Mem. Oreg. Adv. Com. on Fair Employment Practices Act, 1949-55; trustee, chmn., pres. Portland Symphonic Choir, 1950-54; trustee Portland Civic Theater, 1941-54; bd. dirs. Portland Symphony Soc., 1957-60, Cmty. Child Guidance Clinic, 1966-68; active United Way, 1945-75; bd. drs. Contemporary Crafts Assn., 1972-76, treas., 1975-76; bd. dirs. Lake Oswego Corp., 1961-65, 71-73, 74-76, corp. sec., 1964, pres., 1973-74, treas., 1975-76; mem. Com. on Citizen Involvement, City of Lake Oswego, 1975-77; chmn. Bicentennial Com., Lake Oswego, 1975-76; sec.-treas. Met. Area Comms. Commn., 1980-85; treas. Clackamas County Cmty. Action Agy., 1980-82, chmn., 1982-85; mem. fin. adv. com. West Clackamas County LWV, 1974-76, 78-80; councilman City of Lake Oswego, 1977-78, mayor, 1979-85, chmn. libr. growth task force, 1987-89, chmn. hist. rev. bd., 1990-92; chmn. energy adv. com. League Oreg. Cities, 1982-84; mem. adv. bd., chmn. fin. com. Lake Oswego Adult Cmty. Ctr., 1985-88; pres Oswego Heritage coun., 1992-95, sec., 1995-96, treas., 1997-99, dir., 2000, dir. emeritus, 2001—; mem. County Blue Ribbon Com. on Law Enforcement, 1987-89; mem. fee arbitration panel Oreg. State Bar Assn., 1995—. Mem. Edison Electric Inst. (exec. com.), N.W. Electric Light and Power Assn., Lake Oswego C. of C. (v.p. 1986-87, chmn. land use com. 1990-91), Nat. Trust for Hist. Preservation, St. Andrew's Soc., Hist. Preservation League Oreg., Oreg. Hist. Soc., McLoughlin Meml. Assn., Oswego Heritage Coun., Clackamas County Hist. Assn., Rotary (treas. Lake Oswego chpt. 1990-93). Republican. Presbyterian. Home: Apt 306 17440 Holy Names Dr Lake Oswego OR 97034-5143

CAMPBELL, DEMAREST LINDSAY, artist, designer, writer; b. N.Y.C., June 4, 1951; d. Peter Stephen III and Mary Elizabeth (Edwards) C.; m. Dale Gordon Haugo, Apr. 7, 1978. BFA in Art History, MFA in Asian Art History, MFA in Theatre Design. Designer murals and residential interiors Campbell and Haugo Design Cons., San Francisco, 1975—; chargeman scenic artist Am. Conservatory Theatre, 1976—. Designed, painted and sculpted over 200 prodns. for Broadway, internat. opera, motion pictures. Mem. NOW, Asian Art Mus. Soc., San Francisco. Mem. NOW, United Scenic Artists, Scenic & Title Artists and Theatrical Stage Designers., Sherlock Holmes Soc. London, Amnesty Internat., Nat. Trust for Hist. Preservation (Gt. Britian and U.S.A. chpt.), Fine Arts Mus. Soc. San Francisco, Shavian Malthus Soc. (charter Gt. Britian chpt.), Humane Soc. of U.S. (millennium mem.). Avocations: medical history, pre-Twentieth Century military history.

CAMPBELL, EDWARD MICHAEL, research physicist, science administrator; b. Phila., Dec. 28, 1950; children: Heather, Chelsey, Nickolas. BS, U. Pa., 1972; MA, Princeton U., 1974, student, 1972-77. Staff physicist Lawrence Livermore Nat. Lab., Livermore, Calif., 1977-81, group leader, 1981-84, assoc. program leader, 1984-86, program leader, 1986-91, dep. inertial confinement fusion progam leader, 1989-91, dep. assoc. dir., 1993-94, assoc. dir. laser programs, 1994-99. Guggenheim fellow 1972-73; recipient Wiezman Rsch. Fellow award 1977, Edward Teller medal, 1995, E.O. Lawrence award, 1995, Fusion Power Assoc. Leadership award , 1995. Fellow Am. Physical Soc. (Excellence in Rsch. award 1985, Excellence in Plasma Physics award 1990, Teller award 1995). Achievements include research on physics of inertial confinement fusion and laboratory x-ray lasers; physics of intense laser-matter interaction; multiphoton, ionization and interaction of ultra short pulse lasers with matter; advanced diagnostics and technology for high energy density plasmas; high power solid state laser technology and physics. Office: Lawrence Livermore Nat Lab PO Box 5508 Livermore CA 94551-5508

CAMPBELL, FINLEY ALEXANDER, geologist, consultant; b. Kenora, Ont., Can., Jan. 5, 1927; s. Finley McLeod and Vivian (Delve) C.; m. Barbara Elizabeth Cromarty, Oct. 17, 1953; children— Robert Finley, Glen David, Cheryl Ann. B.Sc., Brandon Coll., U. Man., Can., 1950; M.A., Queen's U., Kingston, Ont., 1956; Ph.D., Princeton U., 1958. Exploration and mining geologist Prospectors Airways, Toronto, 1950-58; asst. and asso. prof. geology U. Alta., Can., Edmonton, 1958-65; prof., head dept. geology U. Calgary, Alta., 1965-69, v.p. capital resources, 1969-71, v.p. acad., 1971-76, prof. geology, 1976-84, v.p. priorities and planning, 1984-88, prof. emeritus, 1988—; geol. cons., 1988—. Bd. dirs., vice chmn. Can Energy Research Inst. Contbr. articles on geol. topics to profl. jours. Bd. dirs. Calgary Olympic Devel. Assn.; mem. minister's adv. bd. Tyrrell Mus. Palaeontology. Decorated Queen's Jubilee medal Can.; recipient Commemorative medal for 125th Anniversary of Can., Geology medal Brandon U. Honor Soc.; Sir James Dunne fellow, 1955-56; Princeton Alumni fellow, 1957-58. Fellow Royal Soc. Can.; mem. Assn. The Univ. of Calgary (pres. emeritus), Geol. Assn. Can., Mineral Assn. Can., Soc. Econ. Geologists, Assn. Profl. Geologists Alta., Am. Mineral Soc. Royal Soc. Can., Can. Inst. Mining and Metallurgy, Brandon Univ. Alumni Assn. (reg. dir., Disting. Svc. award Hockey Hall of Fame 1994), Glenmore Yacht Club, Silver Springs Golf and Country Club, Clearwater Bay Yacht Club. Home: 3408 Benton Dr NW Calgary AB Canada T2L 1W8 Office: U Calgary Dept Geology and Geophysics Calgary AB Canada T2N 1N4 E-mail: campbelf@ucalgary.ca

CAMPBELL, IAN DAVID, opera company director; b. Brisbane, Australia, Dec. 21, 1945; came to U.S., 1982; m. Ann Spira; children: Benjamin, David. BA, U. Sydney, Australia, 1967. Prin. tenor singer The Australian Opera, Sydney, 1967-74; sr. music officer The Australia Council, Sydney, 1974-76; gen. mgr., stage dir. The State Opera of South Australia, Adelaide, 1976-82; asst. artistic adminstr. Met. Opera, N.Y.C., 1982-83; gen. dir. San Diego Opera, 1983—. Guest lectr. U. Adelaide, 1978; guest prof. San Diego State U., 1986—; cons. Lyric Opera Queensland, Australia, 1980-81; bd. dirs. Opera Am., Washington, 1986-95, 1997-2001, chmn., 2001—; chmn. judges Met. Opera Auditions, Sydney, 1989, Masterclasses, Music Acad. of the West, 1993-96. Producer, host San Diego Opera Radio Program, 1984—, At the Opera with Ian Campbell, 1984-2001; stage director La Boheme, 1981, The Tales of Hoffmann, 1982 (both in South Australia), Falstaff (San Diego Opera), 1999, Cavalleria Rusticana/Pagliacci (Santa Barbara Grand Opera), 1999, Il Trovatore (San Diego Opera), 2000. Mem., bd. dirs. San Diego Conv. and Visitors Bur., 1997—. Recipient Peri award Opera Guild So. Calif., 1984; named Headliner of Yr., San Diego Press Club, 1991, Father of Yr., San Diego, 1997. Fellow Australian Inst. Mgmt.; mem. Kona Kai Club, Rotary, San Diego Pres Club (Headliner award 1991). Avocations: squash, golf, tennis. Office: San Diego Opera 1200 3rd Ave Fl 18 San Diego CA 92101-4112

CAMPBELL, JOHN D. religious organization administrator; Media contact, coord. ch. svc. mission Ch. God. Office: Ch God in Western Can 4717 56th St Camrose AB Canada T4V 2C4

CAMPBELL, JOHN RICHARD, pediatric surgeon; b. Pratt, Kans., Jan. 16, 1932; s. John Ross and Laura (Harkrader) C.; m. Susan Charlotte Baker, June 9, 1962; children: Kathryn, John Richard, George Ridgway. B.A., U. Kans., 1954, M.D., 1958. Diplomate Am. Bd. Surgery with cert. of spl. qualifications in pediatric surgery. Rotating intern Hosp. U. Pa., 1958-59; resident in gen. surgery U. Kans. Hosp., 1959-63; resident in pediatric surgery Children's Hosp. of Phila., 1965-67; asst. instr. U. Pa. Med. Sch., 1965-67; mem. faculty U. Oreg. Health Scis. Ctr., Portland, 1967—, prof. surgery emeritus, 2000, prof. surgery and pediatrics emeritus, 2000—, chief pediatric surgery, prof. emeritus surgery and pediats., 2000—; surgeon-in-chief Doernbecher Children's Hosp., Portland, 1967-99. Cons. VA, Shriners Crippled Children's hosps., Alaska Native Med. Ctr., Anchorage. Served to lt. comdr. M.C. USNR, 1963-65. Mem. A.C.S., Soc. Acad. Surgeons, Am. Acad. Pediatrics, Am. Pediatric Surg. Assn., Pacific Assn. Pediatric Surgeons, North Pacific Pediatric Soc., North Pacific Surg. Assn., Pacific Coast Surg. Assn., Portland Acad. Pediatrics, Portland Surg. Soc. Presbyterian. Office: Oreg Health Scis Univ 745 SW Gaines St # Cdw7 Portland OR 97201-2901 E-mail: campbell@ohsu.edu

CAMPBELL, JON R. financial services executive; Pres. Northwest Bank, Ill., Ind., 1977-93, pres., CEO, 1993-98; regional pres. Wells Fargo & Co., Phoenix, 1999—. Bd. dirs. Ariz. Cmty. Found.; campaign chmn. Valley of Sun United Way, 1997. Office: Wells Fargo & Co 100 W Washington St Fl 1 Phoenix AZ 85003-1869

CAMPBELL, KENNETH EUGENE, JR. vertebrate paleontologist, ornithologist; b. Jackson, Mich., Nov. 4, 1943; s. Kenneth Eugene and Betty Louise (Duffey) C. B.S., U. Mich., 1966, M.S., 1967, Ph.D., U. Fla., 1973. Research asso. Fla. State Mus., Gainesville, 1972-74; asst. prof. zoology U. Fla., Gainesville, 1974-77, asst. prof. geology, 1975-77; curator vertebrate paleontology/ornithology Natural History Mus. Los Angeles County, L.A., 1977—. Acting dir. George C. Page Mus., 1995-96. Contbr. articles to sci. publs. Mem. AAAS, Am. Ornithologists' Union, Assn. Tropical Biology, Cooper Ornithol. Soc., Soc. Vertebrate Paleontology, Wilson Ornithol. Soc., Sigma Xi. Office: Natural History Mus 900 Exposition Blvd Los Angeles CA 90007-4057 E-mail: kecampbe@bcf.usc.edu

CAMPBELL, LEONARD M. lawyer; b. Denver, Apr. 12, 1918; s. Bernard Francis and May (Moran) C.; m. Dot J. Baker, Sept. 23, 1944; children: Brian T., Teri Pat, Thomas P. AB, U. Colo., 1941, LLB, 1943. Bar: Colo. 1943. Of counsel Gorsuch, Kirgis, Campbell, Walker and Grove, 1948-88, sr. ptnr., 1951-88; city atty. Denver, 1951-53. Cons. pub. utility matters Colo. Mcpl. League. Mem. Denver Charter Com., 1947; mgr. Safety and Excise for Denver, 1947-48; chmn. Denver Com. Human Relations, 1954; mem. Denver Planning Bd., 1950-51; mem. Bd. Water Commrs., Denver, 1965-70, pres., 1968-69; mem. Gov.'s Com. on Jud. Compensation, 1972; chmn. U. Colo. Law Alumni Devel. Fund, 1962. Served with USAAF, 1943-46. Mem. ABA, Colo. Bar Assn. (pres. 1978-79, Award of Merit 1967), Denver Bar Assn. (pres. 1969), Am. Coll. Trial Lawyers, Cath. Lawyers Guild Denver (pres. 1962, St. Thomas More award 1978), Nat. Inst. Mcpl. Law Officers (v.p. 1952), Colo. Judicial Inst. (Chancellor Chester Alter award 1987). Democrat. Roman Catholic. Clubs: Denver Athletic (Denver) (sec. 1960-61, pres. 1962), Cherry Hills Country (Denver). Home: 3447 S Birch St Denver CO 80222-7212 Office: Gorsuch Kirgis LLC LLP 1515 Arapahoe St Ste 1000 Denver CO 80202-2120

CAMPBELL, MARY STINECIPHER, research chemist, educator; b. Chattanooga, Feb. 26, 1940; d. Jesse Franklin and Florence Gladys (Marshall) S.; m. John David Fowler Jr. (div. Mar. 1979); children: John Christopher, Jesse David; m. Billy M. Campbell, Jan. 1995. BA, Earlham Coll., 1962; PhD, U. N.C., 1967. Cert. organic fruit grower. Postdoctoral researcher Research Triangle Inst., Research Triangle Park, N.C., 1966-68, 74-76; mem. staff Los Alamos (N.Mex.) Nat. Lab., 1976—. Adj. prof. organic, inorganic and phys. chemistry U. N.Mex. Grad. Ctr., Los Alamos, 1989—; instr. chemistry lab., 1989; vis. scientist AFOSR (AFATL), Eglin AFB, Fla., 1980-81. Contbr. articles to profl. jours.; inventor ammonium nitrate explosive systems and other explosive salts. Commr. Acequia Sancochada Cmty. ditch; mem. Habitat for Humanity. Mem. Am. Chem. Soc., N.Mex. Network Women in Sci. and Engring. (v.p. 1985-86, pres. 1986-87, No. chpt. pres. 1999), Toastmasters Internat. (pres. 1988, 98, 696 Club), Bio-Integral Rsch. Ctr., N.Mex. Apple Coun. Democrat. Unitarian. Avocations: skiing, dog training, hiking, singing, gardening. Office: Los Alamos Nat Lab MS C920 Group DX-2 Los Alamos NM 87545-0001

CAMPBELL, RICHARD ALDEN, electronics company executive; b. Bend, Oreg., July 31, 1926; s. Corlis Eugene and Lydia Amney (Peck) C.; m. Edna Mary Seaman, June 12, 1948; children: Stephen Alden, Douglas Niall (dec.), Carolyn Joyce. B.S. in Elec. Engring., U. Ill., 1949, M.S. in Elec. Engring., 1950. With TRW Inc., Redondo Beach, Calif., 1954-87, exec. v.p., 1979-87; bus. cons., profl. co. dir. Rolling Hills Estates, 1987—. Patentee in radio communications. Bd. dirs. U. Ill. Found., Hugh O'Brian Youth Found. With USN, 1944-46. Recipient Alumni Honor award U. Ill. Coll. Engring. Mem. IEEE (life), Am. Electronics Assn. (pres. 1969, dir. 1970), Phi Kappa Phi, Tau Beta Pi, Eta Kappa Nu, Sigma Tau, Pi Mu Epsilon, Phi Eta Sigma, Rolling Hills Country Club, Rancheros Visitadores Club, Los Caballeros Club. Republican.

CAMPBELL, ROBERT CHARLES, minister, theology educator; b. Chandler, Ariz., Mar. 9, 1924; s. Alexander Joshua and Florence (Betzner) C.; m. Lotus Idamae Graham, July 12, 1945; children: Robin Carl, Cherry Colleen. AB, Westmont Coll., 1944; BD, Eastern Baptist Theol. Sem., 1947, ThM, 1949, ThD, 1951, DD (hon.), 1974; MA, U. So. Calif., 1959; postgrad., Dropsie U., 1949-51, U. Pa., 1951-52, NYU, 1960-62, U. Cambridge, Eng., 1969; DLitt (hon.), Am. Bapt. Sem. of West, 1972; HHD (hon.), Alderson-Broaddus Coll., 1979; LHD (hon.), Linfield Coll., 1982; LLD (hon.), Franklin Coll., 1986. Ordained to ministry Am. Bapt. Ch., 1947; pastor 34th St. Bapt. Ch., Phila., 1945-49; instr. Eastern Bapt. Theol. Sem., Phila., 1949-51; asst. prof. Eastern Coll., St. Davids, Pa., 1951-53; assoc. prof. N.T. Am. Bapt. Sem. of West, Covina, Cal., 1953-54, dean, prof., 1954-72; gen. sec. Am. Bapt. Chs. in U.S.A., Valley Forge, Pa., 1972-87; pres. Eastern Bapt. Theol. Sem., Phila., 1987-89, ret. Vis. lectr. Sch. Theology at Claremont, Calif., 1961-63, U. Redlands, Calif., 1959-60, 66-67, Fuller Theology Seminary, Calif., 1992-97; Bd. mgrs. Am. Bapt. Bd. of Edn. and Publ., 1956-59, 65-69; v.p. So. Calif. Bapt. Conv., 1967-68; pres. Am. Bapt. Chs. of Pacific S.W., 1970-71; Pres. N.Am. Bapt. Fellowship, 1974-76; mem. exec. com. Bapt. World Alliance, 1972-90, v.p., 1975-80; mem. exec. com., gov. bd. Nat. Council Chs. of Christ in U.S.A., 1972-87; del. to World Council of Chs., 1975, 83, mem. central com., 1975-80. Author: Great Words of the Faith, 1965, The Gospel of Paul, 1973, Evangelistic Emphases in Ephesians, Jesus Still Has Something To Say, 1987. Home: 125 Via Alicia Santa Barbara CA 93108-1769

CAMPBELL, ROBERT HEDGCOCK, investment banker, lawyer; b. Ann Arbor, Mich., Jan. 16, 1948; s. Robert Miller and Ruth Adele (Hedgcock) C.; m. Katherine Kettering, June 17, 1972; children: Mollie DuPlan, Katherine Elizabeth, Anne Kettering. BA, U. Wash., 1970, JD, 1973. Bar. Wash. 1973, Wash. State Supreme Ct. 1973, Fed. 1973, U.S. Dist. Ct. (we. dist.) Wash. 1973, Ct. Appeals (9th cir.) 1981. Assoc. Roberts & Shefelman, Seattle, 1973-78, ptnr., 1978-85; sr. v.p. Lehman Bros., Inc., Seattle, 1985-87, mng. dir., 1987—. Bd. dirs. Pogo Producing Co., 1999—; dir., treas. Nat. Assn. Bd. Lawyers, Hinsdale, Ill., 1982-85; pres., trustee Wash. State Soc. Hosp. Attys., Seattle, 1982-85; mem. econs. dept. vis. com. U. Wash., 1995-97; mem. Law Sch. dean's adv. bd. U. Wash., 1999—. Contbr. articles to profl. jours. Trustee Bellevue (Wash.) Schs. Found., 1988-91, pres., 1989-90; nation chief Bellevue Eastside YMCA Indian Princess Program, 1983-88; trustee Wash. Phikeia Found., 1983-91, Sandy Hook Yacht Club Estates, Inc., 1993-98; mem. Wash. Gov.'s Food Processing Coun., 1990-91. Mem. U. Wash. Varsity Swimming Alumni Bd. Republican. Avocations: skiing, wind surfing, bike riding, physical fitness, golf. Home: 8604 NE 10th St Medina WA 98039-3915 Office: Lehman Bros Columbia Seafirst Ctr 701 5th Ave Ste 7101 Seattle WA 98104-7016 E-mail: ibe2ski@aol.com, rhcampbe@lehman.com

CAMPBELL, SCOTT, newspaper publishing company executive; b. May 25, 1956; BS, U. Oreg., 1979. Pub. The Columbian, Vancouver, Wash., 1980-86, pres., COO, 1986-88, pub., 1988—. Chair adv. coun. Wash. State U.; chair S.W. Wash. Higher Edn. Consortium; mem. exec. bd. Columbia River Econ. Devel. Coun. Mem. Newspaper Assn. Am. (mem. bus. devel. com.), Pacific N.W. Newspaper Assn. (pres.), Allied Daily Newspapers Wash. Office: Columbian Pub Co PO Box 180 701 W 8th St Vancouver WA 98666

CAMPBELL, SCOTT ROBERT, lawyer, former food company executive; b. Burbank, Calif., June 7, 1946; s. Robert Clyde and Jenevieve Anne (Olsen) C.; m. Teresa Melanie Mack, Oct. 23, 1965; 1 son, Donald Steven. BA, Claremont Men's Coll., 1970; JD, Cornell U., 1973. Bar: Ohio 1973, U.S. Dist. Ct. (so. dist.) Ohio 1974, Minn. 1976, Calif. 1989, U.S. Dist. Ct. (no. dist.) Calif. 1989, U.S. Ct. Appeals (9th cir.) 1989, U.S. Dist. Ct. (cen. and so. dists.) Calif. 1990, U.S. Ct. Appeals (5th cir.) 1991, U.S. Tax Ct. 1991. Assoc. Taft, Stettinius & Hollister, Cin., 1973-76; atty. Mpls. Star & Tribune, 1976-77; sr. v.p., gen. counsel, sec. Kellogg Co., Battle Creek, Mich., 1977-89; ptnr. Furth Fahrner Mason, San Francisco, 1989-2000, Zelle, Hofmann, Voelbel, Mason & Gette, LLP, San Francisco, 2000—. U.S. del. ILO Food and Beverage Conf., Geneva, 1984; participant, presenter first U.S.-USSR Legal Seminar, Moscow, 1988; speaker other legal seminars. Mem. ABA, Ohio Bar Assn., Minn. Bar Assn., Calif. Bar. Assn. Office: Zelle Hofmann Voelbel Mason& Gette LLP 500 Sansome St Ste 400 San Francisco CA 94111-3219 E-mail: srclaw@ix.netcom.com, scampbel@zelle.com

CAMPBELL, TENA, judge; b. Twin Falls, Idaho, Dec. 11, 1944; BA, U. Idaho, 1967; MA in French Lit. with honors, Ariz. State U., 1970, JD, 1977. Bar: Utah 1977, U.S. Dist. Ct. Utah 1977, U.S. Ct. Appeals (10th cir.) 1982. Tchr. French Twin Falls (Idaho) Sch. Dist., 1967-69, Tempe (Ariz.) H.S., Phoenix Jr. Coll., 1972-73; assoc. atty. Johnson Durham and Moxley, Salt Lake City, 1977-79, Fabian and Clendenin, Salt Lake City, 1979-81; dep. county atty. Salt Lake County, Salt Lake City, 1981; asst. U.S. atty. criminal divsn. Office of U.S. Atty. Dist. Utah, 1981-95; judge U.S. Dist. Ct. Utah, 1995—. Mem. Utah Bar Assn., Ft. Douglas HIdden Valley Country Club. Office: US Dist Ct Utah Rm 235 US Ct House 350 S Main St Salt Lake City UT 84101-2106

CAMPBELL, THOMAS J. chiropractor, legislator; b. Bklyn., Oct. 27, 1954; s. Charles Marvin and Edna Mary (Sacer) C.; m. C. Lynn Hearn, July 2, 1983. AA in Social Scis., Fla. Tech. U., 1974; BA in Police Sci. and Adminstrn., Seattle U., 1977; DC, Life Chiropractic Coll., 1983; postgrad. in orthopedics, L.A. Chiropractic Coll., 1984-90. Diplomate Am. Acad. Pain Mgmt.; cert. chiropractic rehab. dr. Nat. Bd. Chiropractic Examiners-Physiotherapy; lic. chiropractor, Wash., Fla. Pvt. practice Chiropractic Spinal Care, Inc., 1984—. Mem. Wash. State Ho. of Reps., 1993-96, 99-2000. With inf. U.S. Army, 1977-79, capt. USAR/ARNG, 1979-85. Recipient Appreciation for Svc. award Chiropractic Disciplinary Bd., 1989-93, Gov. Appreciation Certificate Wash. State Disciplinary Bd., Legislator of Yr. award Wash. State Labor Coun., 1999, Legislator of Yr. award, Wash. State Trial Attys., 1999. Fellow Internat. Coll. of Chiropractors; mem. Am. Chiropractic Assn. (alt. del. House of Dels. 1988-92), Wash. State Chiropractic Assn. (chmn. mem. com. 1984-85, dist. 4A 1985-86, dir. exec. bd. 1985-88, v. chmn. disciplinary bd. 1990-93, pres. award outstanding achievement in the mem. com. 1985, legislative affairs com. 1986, Dist. of the Yr. award 1985-86, named Chiropractor of the Yr. 1987, 89, 90, 91, Appreciation award for outstanding svc to the profession, 1994, Exceptional Svc. award 1994), Fla. Chiropractic Assn., Pierce County Chiropractic Assn., Chiropractic Rehabilitation Assn. (bd. dirs.), Elks (Tacoma Lodge # 174), Am. Legion. Republican. Avocations: scuba diving, boating, fishing. Home: PO Box 443 Spanaway WA 98387-0443 E-mail: Campbell@aa.net

CAMPBELL, THOMAS J. former congressman; b. Chgo., Aug. 14, 1952; s. William J. and Marie Campbell; m. Susanne Martin. BA, MA in Econs. with highest honors, U. Chgo., 1973, PhD in Econs. with highest dept. fellowship, 1980; JD magna cum laude, Harvard U., 1976. Law clk. to presiding justice U.S. Ct. Appeals (D.C. cir.), 1976-77; law clk. to Justice Byron R. White U.S. Supreme Ct., Washington, 1977-78; assoc. Winston & Strawn, Chgo., 1978-80; White Ho. fellow Office Chief of Staff and White Ho. of Counsel, Washington, 1980-81; exec. asst. to dep. atty. gen. Dept. Justice, Washington, 1981; dir. Bur. Trade Competition FTC, Washington, 1981-83, head del. to OECD, Paris, com. experts on restictive bus. practices, 1982, 83; mem. 101st-105th Congresses from Calif. 12th Dist., 1989-92; mem. com. on sci., space and tech., com. on judiciary, banking, fin. and urban affairs 101st Congress from Calif. 12th Dist., 1989-92; mem. 104th-106th Congress from Calif. 15th Dist., 1995-2001,

Calif. State Senate, 1993-95. Prof. Stanford Law Sch., 1983-89; mem. Congressional Com. on Banking and Fin. Svcs., 1997—, Internat. Rels., 1997—. Referee Jour. Polit. Economy, Internat. Rev. Law and Econs. Mem. San Francisco Com. on Fgn. Relations. Mem. ABA (antitrust sect., coun. 1985-88, program chmn. 1983-84).*

CAMPBELL, WILLIAM STEEN, publishing executive, writer, speaker; b. New Cumberland, W.Va., June 27, 1919; s. Robert N. and Ethel (Steen) C.; m. Rosemary J. Bingham, Apr. 21, 1945 (dec. Dec. 1992); children: Diana J., Sarah A., Paul C., John W. Grad., Steubenville (Ohio) Bus. Coll., 1938. Cost acct. Hancock Mfg. Co., New Cumberland, 1938-39; cashier, statistician Weirton Steel Co., W.Va., 1939-42; travel exec. Am. Express Co., N.Y.C., 1946-47; adminstr., account exec. Good Housekeeping mag., 1947-55; pub. Cosmopolitan mag., 1955-57; asst. dir. circulation Hearst Mags., N.Y.C., 1957-61; gen. mgr. Motor Boating mag., 1961-62; v.p., dir. circulation Hearst Mags., 1962-85; pres. Internat. Circulation Distbrs., 1978-81, Mags., Meetings, Messages, Ltd., 1986—. With Periodical Pubs. Svc. Bur. subs. Hearst Corp., Sandusky, Ohio, 1964-85, v.p., chief exec., 1964-69, pres., chief exec., 1970-85; dir. Audit Bur. Circulations, 1974-86, Periodical Pubs. Svc. Bur., 1964-85, Nat. Mag. Co., Ltd., London, Randolph Jamaica Ltd., Omega Pub. Corp. Fla., Hearst Can. Ltd., 1964-85; former chmn. Ctrl. Registry, Mag. Pubs. Assn.; chmn. bd trustees Hearst Employees Retirement Plan, 1971-85; mem. pres.'s coun. Brandeis U., 1974-94; chmn. nat. corp. and found. com. U. Miami, 1979-85; dir. Broadway Assn., 1985-90, v.p., 1988-90; keynote spkr. Fifth Ann. Hospitality Industry Luncheon, Santa Barbara, Calif., 1996. Bd. dirs. Santa Barbara Rep. Club, 1993-94, Lobero Theatre Found., 1994-96, v.p., 1995-96. Lt. col. USAF, 1942-46, ETO. Recipient Lee C. Williams award Mag. Fulfillment Mgrs. Assn.; Torch of Liberty award Anti-Defamation League, 1979 Mem. Campbell Clan Soc., Mil. Order of World Wars (chaplain), Masons, Cosmopolitan Club (chaplain). Home and Office: 1150 Coast Village Rd Santa Barbara CA 93108-2722 E-mail: williamscampbell@yahoo.com

CAMPION, ROBERT THOMAS, manufacturing company executive; b. Mpls., June 23, 1921; s. Leo P. and Naomi (Revord) C.; m. Wilhelmina Knapp, June 8, 1946; 1 son, Michael. Student, Loyola U., Chgo., 1939-41, 46-48. C.P.A., Ill. With Alexander Grant & Co., Chgo., 1946-57, ptnr., 1954-57; with Lear Siegler, Inc., Santa Monica, Calif., 1957—, pres., 1971-85, chief exec. officer, dir., 1971-86, chmn., 1974-86; pvt. investor, 1987—. Served with AUS, 1942-46. Mem. AICPA, Ill. Soc. CPAs, Bel Air Country Club, Jonathan Club, La Quinta Country Club. Republican. Office: Blair House # 406 10490 Wilshire Blvd Los Angeles CA 90024-4646

CAMPOS, PETE, state legislator; b. Las Vegas, N.Mex., July 20, 1953; BA, U. N.Mex.; MA, N.Mex. Highlands U. Assoc. supt. for suypportive svcs. Sch. Dist.; mem. N. Mex. Senate, Dist. 8, 1988—; mem. fin. com., chair rules com. Democrat. Office: 500 Raynolds Ave Rm 302 Las Vegas NM 87701-4324 E-mail: pcampos@state.nm.us

CAMRON, ROXANNE, retired magazine editor, consultant; b. Los Angeles; d. Irving John and Roslyn (Weinberger) Spiro; m. Robert Camron; children: Ashley Jennifer, Erin Jessica. B.A. in Journalism, U. So. Calif. West Coast fashion and beauty editor, Teen mag., Los Angeles, 1969-70, sr. editor, 1972-75, editor, 1976-99, cons., 1999—; pub. relations rep. Max Factor Co., 1970; asst. to creative dir. Polly Bergen Co., 1970-71; ret., 1999. Lectr. teen groups; freelance writer. Active Homeowners Assn. Mem. Am. Soc. Exec. Women. Office: Teen Mag 6420 Wilshire Blvd Los Angeles CA 90048-5502

CANADA, WILLIAM H. plastic surgeon; b. Huntington, W.Va., Sept. 5, 1930; MD, W.Va. U., 1956. Intern Meml. Hosp., Charleston, W.Va., 1956-57, gen. surgeon, 1957-59; plastic surgeon Baylor U. Med. Ctr., Houston, 1959-61; chief plastic surgeon Las Vegas Surgery Ctr., 1987—. Attending surgeon Univ. Med. Ctr., Las Vegas; clin. instr. plastic surgery Baylor U., Houston. Fellow ACS. Office: 8068 W Sahara Ave Ste G Las Vegas NV 89117-1973

CANADAY, RICHARD A. lawyer; b. Alton, Ill., Aug. 26, 1947; AB, Stanford U., 1969; JD, U. Calif., 1973. Bar: Oreg. 1973, Wash. 1987. Ptnr. Miller Nash LLP, Portland, Oreg. Mem. ABA, Oreg. State Bar, Wash. State Bar Assn. Office: Miller Nash LLP 111 SW 5th Ave Ste 3500 Portland OR 97204-3638 E-mail: rcanaday@millernash.com

CANARELLI, LAWRENCE D. real estate developer; b. 1946; MBA in Fin., U. So. Calif., 1973. Mktg. dir. Continental Multi-Homes, Santa Monica, Calif., 1973-76; divsn. pres. Met. Devel., Inc., Las Vegas, 1976-84; pres. Am. West Devel., Las Vegas, 1981—; with Am. West Homes, Inc., Las Vegas, 1990—, now pres. With U.S. Army, 1967-71. Office: Am West Homes Inc 2700 E Sunset Rd Ste 5 Las Vegas NV 89120-3507

CANBY, WILLIAM CAMERON, JR. federal judge; b. St. Paul, May 22, 1931; s. William Cameron and Margaret Leah (Lewis) C.; m. Jane Adams, June 18, 1954; children— William Nathan, John Adams, Margaret Lewis. A.B., Yale U., 1953; LL.B., U. Minn., 1956. Bar: Minn. 1956, Ariz. 1972. Law clk. U.S. Supreme Ct. Justice Charles E. Whittaker, 1958-59; asso. firm Oppenheimer, Hodgson, Brown, Baer & Wolff, St. Paul, 1959-62; asso., then dep. dir. Peace Corps, Ethiopia, 1962-64, dir. Uganda, 1964-66; asst. to U.S. Senator Walter Mondale, 1966; asst. to pres. SUNY, 1967; prof. law Ariz. State U., 1967-80; judge U.S. Ct. Appeals (9th cir.), Phoenix, 1980-96, sr. judge, 1996—; chief justice High Ct. of the Trust Ter. of the Pacific Islands, 1993-94. Bd. dirs. Ariz. Center Law in Public Interest, 1974-80, Maricopa County Legal Aid Soc., 1972-78, D.N.A.-People's Legal Services, 1978-80; Fulbright prof. Makerere U. Faculty Law, Kampala, Uganda, 1970-71 Author: American Indian Law, 1998; also articles; note editor: Minn. Law Rev, 1955-56. Precinct and state committeeman Democratic Party Ariz., 1972-80; bd. dirs. Central Ariz. Coalition for Right to Choose, 1976-80. Served with USAF, 1956-58. Mem. State Bar Ariz., Minn. Bar Assn., Maricopa County Bar Assn., Phi Beta Kappa, Order of Coif. Office: Sandra Day O'Connor US Courthouse 401 W Washington St SPC 55 Phoenix AZ 85003-2156

CANFIELD, JAMES, artistic director; Art dir. Oreg. Ballet, Portland, 1988—. Office: Oregon Ballet 1120 SW 10th Ave Portland OR 97205-2400

CANIPAROLI, VAL WILLIAM, choreographer, dancer; b. Renton, Wash., Sept. 12, 1951; s. Francisco and Leonora (Marconi) C. Student, Wash. State U., 1969-71, San Francisco Ballet Sch., 1971-72. Dancer San Francisco Opera, 1973, San Francisco Ballet, 1974—, principal dancer, 1987—; co-dir. OMO, San Francisco, 1985; choreographer San Francisco Ballet, 1987, 1990—; res. choreographer Ballet West, 1994—. Choreographer (ballets) Street Song, 1980, Pacific Northwest Ballet, Seattle, 1980, 91, The Bridge, 1998, Love-lies-Bleeding, 1982, San Francisco Ballet, 1982— including Aria, 1998, Slow, 1998, Ciao Marcello, 1997; Hamlet and Ophelia, 1985, In Perpetuum, 1990, Oakland (Calif.) Ballet, 1983-87, Aubade, 1985 (Isadora Duncan award), Narcisse, 1987, Israel Ballet, Tel Aviv, 1985, Ballet West, Salt Lake City, 1987 [illegible] Dixie Woodbury Dance Co., 1988, Ritual, 1990, A Door is Ajar, 1990, Honk Kong Ballet, 1990, Richmond Ballet, 1989, Pitts. Ballet, Theatre, 1990, 1990, Jacob's Pillow Dance festival, 1990, Pulcinella, 1991, Concerto Grosso, 1992, Seeing Stars, 1993, Lady of the Camellias, Ballet Fla., 1993, Ballet West, 1994, Lambarena, 1995, Capriccio, Chgo. Lyric Opera, 1994, Bow Out, Richmond Ballet, 1995, San Francisco Symphony Pops, 1995, 96, Prawn Watching, [illegible] Richmond Ballet, [illegible], Open Veins, Atlanta Ballet, 1998, Book of Alleged Dances, Ballet West, 1998, Going for Baroque, Tulsa Ballet Theatre, 1999, Attention Please, Richmond Ballet, 1999, The Nutcracker, Cin. Ballet, 2001, Torque, Pacific N.W. Ballet, 2001, Jaybird Lounge, Pa. Ballet, 2001, Death of a Moth, San Francisco Ballet, 2001, numerous others. Recipient Isadora Duncan award, 1986, 97, Choo-San Goh and H. Robert Magee Found. award for Choreography, 1994, 97; Nat. Endowment Arts fellowship grantee, 1981-88. Fellow Calif. Arts Coun. Coreographers. Avocations: music, theatre, dance. Home: 81 Lansing St Apt 405 San Francisco CA 94105-2647 Office: San Francisco Ballet 455 Franklin St San Francisco CA 94102-4471

CANNELL, CYNDY MICHELLE, elementary school principal; b. Salt Lake City, July 27, 1948; d. Nick M. and Eugenie E. (Pfanmuller) Fasselin; m. Peter Anthony Cannell, Oct. 13, 1973; children: Peter John, David. BA, U. Utah, 1970, MA, 1973. Cert. adminstr., supr. severly handicapped, spl. edn., emotionally handicapped, gifted and talented. Tchr. Hab Ctr., 1973-74, Hill View Elem Sch., 1974-78; coord. spl. needs. Granite Sch. Dist., Salt Lake City, 1978-79, tchr. leader youth in custody, 1979-80, coord. spl. edn., 1980-84; asst. prin. Western Hills Elem. Sch., Salt Lake City, 1984-85; prin. Webster Elem. Sch., Salt Lake City, 1985-90, Plymouth Elem. Sch., Salt Lake City, 1990-95, Twin Peaks Elem. Sch., Salt Lake City, 1995—. Mem. state strategic planning com. for edn., 1990-91, elem. prin. adv. com., 1990-96, spl. edn. strategic planning com., 1990-91, exec. class size steering com., 1990, ptnrs. in edn. com., 1985—, sch. lunch com., 1989-91, emer. preparedness com., 1989-90; mem. Women's State Legis. Coun., Utah, 1991-92; co-coord. Corp. Games, 1988—. Contbr. articles to profl. mags. Prin. rep. to state PTA Community Involvement Commn., 1989-90, Oquirrh South PTA Coun., 1989; mem. Utah Youth Village Scholarship Com., 1996—. Named Outstanding Educator of Yr. Nat. PTA Phoebe Apperson Hearst, 1990, Outstanding Adminstr. Utah Congress of Parents and Tchrs., 1989-90, Region V PTA, 1988-90. Mem. Granite Assn. Elem. Sch. Prins. (sec. 1998—, Innovator of Yr. 1997-98), Granite Assn. Sch. Adminstrs. (sec., treas. 1990-91) Utah Assn. Sch. Adminstrs., Nat Assn. Elem. Adminstrs., Granite Assn. Sch. Adminstrs. Avocations: skiing, reading, tennis, golf, travel. Home: 10331 S 2375 E Sandy UT 84092-4422 Office: Twin Peaks Elem 5325 S 1045 E Salt Lake City UT 84117-7229

CANNON, CHRISTOPHER B. congressman; b. Salt Lake City, Oct. 20, 1950; m. Claudia Fox, 1978; 8 children. BS, Brigham Young U., 1974, JD, 1980; postgrad., Harvard U., 1974-75. Bar: Utah 1980. Atty., 1979-83; dep. assoc. solicitor U.S. Dept. Interior, 1983, assoc. solicitor, 1984-86; owner Cannon Industries, 1987—; mem. U.S. Ho. Reps. 105th Congress (now 106th Congress) from 3d Utah dist., 1996—. Mem. Resources, Judiciary, and Sci. coms. Republican. Office: US House of Reps 118 Cannon Bldg Washington DC 20515-4403 E-mail: cannon.uto3@mail.house.gov

CANNON, GRACE BERT, immunologist; b. Chambersburg, Pa., Jan. 29, 1937; d. Charles Wesley and Gladys (Raff) Bert; m. W. Dilworth Cannon, June 3, 1961 (div. 1972); children: Michael Quayle Cannon, Susan Radcliffe Cannon Antolin, Peter Bert Cannon. AB, Goucher Coll., 1958; PhD, Washington U., St. Louis, 1962. Fellow Columbia U., N.Y.C., 1962-64, Columbia U. Coll. Physicians and Surgeons, N.Y.C., 1964-65; staff fellow NIH Nat. Cancer Inst., Bethesda, Md., 1966-67; cell biologist Litton Bionetics, Inc., Kensington, 1972-80, head immunology sect., 1980-85; dir. sci. ImmuQuest Labs., Inc., Rockville, 1985-88; pres. Biomedical Analytics, Inc., Rockville, 1988-2001; mgr. ATLIS Fed. Svcs., Inc., Silver Spring, 1991-95, dir. Rockville, 1995-97; sr. assoc. United Info. Sys., Inc., Bethesda, 1998—. Mem. contract rev. coms. Nat. Cancer Inst., 1983-87. Contbr. articles to profl. jours. Mem. Pub. Svc. Health Club, Bethesda, Md., 1984—, sec., 1990-2000. Grantee USPHS, 1959-65, NSF, 1959. Mem. AAAS, Am. Assn. for Cancer Rsch., N.Y. Acad. Sci., Sigma Xi. Home and Office: 2708 Oak Rd # 36 Walnut Creek CA 94596

CANNON, JOSEPH A. steel products company executive; b. 1941; Asst. adminstr. EPA, 1981-85; assoc. Pillsbury, Madison & Sutro, Washington, 1985-87; dir. Geneva Steel Holdings Corp., Vineyard, Utah, 1987—, chmn. bd. dirs., 1987—, pres., 1987-91, CEO, 1991—. Mem. Am. Iron and Steel Inst. (dir., mem. policy and planning com.), N.Am. Steel Coun. Office: Geneva Steel Holdings Corp 10 S Geneva Rd Vineyard UT 84058

CANNON, M. ELIZABETH, geomatics engineer; Prof. dept. geomatics engring. U. Calgary, Alta., Can. Recipient Young Engr. Achievement award CCPE, 1995. Office: U Calgary Dept Geomatics 2500 University Dr NW Calgary AB Canada T2N 1N4

CANNON, MICHAEL R. manufacturing executive; b. 1953; V.p. S.E. Asia ops. Imprimis Tech.; sr. v.p. Syquest Tech. Inc.; various positions including v.p. mobile & desktop bus. unit IBM, v.p. product design, v.p. worldwide ops.; pres., CEO Maxtor, 1996—. Office: Maxtor 510 Cottonwood Dr Milpitas CA 95035

CANNON, ROBERT HAMILTON, JR. aerospace engineering educator; b. Cleve., Oct. 6, 1923; s. Robert Hamilton and Catharine (Putnam) C.; m. Dorothea Alta Collins, Jan. 4, 1945 (dec. Apr. 1988); children: Philip Gregory, Douglas Charles, Beverly Jo, Frederick Scott. David John, Joseph Collins, James Robert; m. Vera Berlin Crie, May 27, 1989. B.S., U. Rochester, 1944; Sc.D. (du Pont fellow), MIT, 1950. Rsch. engr. Baker Mfg. Co., Evansville, Wis., 1946-50; instr. MIT, 1949-50; research engr. Bendix Aviation Research Labs., Detroit, 1950-51; with Autonetics div. N.Am. Aviation Inc., Downey, Calif., 1951-57, supr. automatic flight control systems, 1951-54, systems engr. inertial nav. instruments and systems, 1954-57; assoc. prof. mech. engring. MIT, 1957-59; mem. faculty Stanford U., 1959-74, prof. aeros. and astronautics, 1962-74, dir. Guidance and Control Lab., 1960-69; chief scientist USAF, 1966-68; asst. sec. U.S. Dept. Transp. Washington, 1970-74; chmn. div. engring. and applied sci. Calif. Inst. Tech., Pasadena, 1974-79; Charles Lee Powell prof. aeronautics and astronautics Stanford U., 1979—, chmn. dept., 1979-90, dir. aerospace robotics lab., 1980-90, dir. emeritus, 1990—; chmn. sci. adv. com. to CEO GM, 1979-84. Bd. dirs. Key Tronic Corp; mem. Draper Corp., 1975—; bd. dirs. Parkin Hannifin Corp.; vice chmn. sci. adv. bd. USAF, 1968-70; chmn. assembly of engring. NRC, 1974-75, chmn. energy engring. bd., 1975-81, mem. aeros. and space engring. bd., 1975-79, 85-92, ocean studies bd., 1991-94, mem. governing bd., 1976-78; mem. Boeing Corp. Tech. Adv. Council, 1984-94, R.R. Donnelley Tech. Adv. Coun., 1984-89, Comsat Tech. Adv. Com., 1985-87; chmn. Gen. Electric Space Sta. Adv. Bd., 1985-87; chmn. Pres.'s Com. on Nat. Medal of Sci., 1984-88; chmn. NASA Flight Telerobotic Servicer Commn., 1987-91; mem. tech. adv. coun. United Techs. Corp., 1989-92; commn. underwater vehicles Marine Bd. Author: Dynamics of Physical Systems, 1967; also articles. Served to lt. (j.g.) USNR, 1944-46. Fellow AIAA (dir. 1968-70), Am. Acad. Arts and Scis., Internat. Acad. Astronautics; mem. Nat. Acad. Engring. (councillor 1975-81), Sigma Xi, Theta Chi (chpt. pres. 1943-44), Tau Beta Pi. Presbyterian. Achievements include participating in the devel. hydrofoil boats, automatic flight control, inertial guidance instruments and systems, space vehicle control, drag free satellite, gyro test of gen. relativity, tech. assessment of climatic impact of stratospheric flight, wave-actuated upwelling pump, flexible robot and space robot control systems, underwater free-flying robots, automonous task-commanded helicopter, nat. energy alternatives. Office: Stanford U Dept Aeronautics & Astronautics Durand Bldg Rm 250 Stanford CA 94305-8408

CANOVA-DAVIS, ELEANOR, biochemist, researcher; b. San Francisco, Jan. 18, 1938; d. Gaudenzio Enzio (dec. Apr. 2001) and Catherine (Bordisso) Canova; m. Kenneth Roy Davis, Feb. 10, 1957 (dec. Mar. 2000); children: Kenneth Roy Jr., Jeffrey Stephen. BA, San Francisco State U., 1968, MS, 1971; PhD, U. Calif., San Francisco, 1977. Lab. asst. Frederick Burk Found. for Edn., San Francisco, 1969-71; rsch., tchg. asst. U. Calif., San Francisco, 1972-77, asst. rsch. biochemist, 1980-84, NIH postdoctoral fellow Berkeley, 1977-80; sr. scientist Liposome Tech., Menlo Park, Calif., 1984-85, Genentech, Inc., South San Francisco, 1985—. Contbr. articles to profl. jours. Recipient Nat. Rsch. Svc. award NIH, 1977-80, Honors Convocation award San Francisco State U., 1966; grantee Chancellor's Patent Fund, U. Calif., San Francisco, 1976, Earl C. Anthony Trust; grad. div. fellow U. Calif., San Francisco, 1972-73. Mem. Am. Chem. Soc., Calif. Scholarship Fedn., Sequoia Woods Country Club, Protein Soc., Am. Soc. Mass Spectrometry. Roman Catholic. Avocations: reading, sewing, bridge. Home: 1203 Edgewood Rd Redwood City CA 94062-2728 Office: Genentech Inc 1 DNA Way South San Francisco CA 94080-4990 E-mail: ecd@gene.com

CANTOR, CHARLES ROBERT, biochemistry educator; b. Bklyn., Aug. 26, 1942; s. Louis and Ida Dianne (Banks) C. AB summa cum laude, Columbia U., 1963; PhD, U. Calif., Berkeley, 1966. Asst. prof. chemistry Columbia U., N.Y.C., 1966-69, assoc. prof. chemistry and biol. scis., 1969-72, prof., 1972-81, prof., chmn. genetics and devel., dep. dir. Comprehensive Cancer Ctr. Coll. Phys. and Surgs., 1981-89; dir. Human Genome Ctr. Lawrence Berkeley Lab, 1988-90; prof. molecular biology U. Calif., Berkeley, 1989-92; prof. biomed. engring. Boston U., 1992—, chmn., 1994-98, dir. Ctr. for Advanced Biotech, 1992—; prof. pharmacology, 1995—; prin. scientist human genome project Dept. Energy, 1990-92; chief sci. officer Sequenom, Inc., 1998—; also bd. dirs., 2000—. Sherman Fairchild vis. scholar Calif. Inst. Tech., 1975-76; mem. biophysics and biophys. chemistry study sect. NIH, 1971-75; mem. cell and molecular basis of disease rev. com. Nat. Inst. Gen. Med. Scis., 1977-81, coun. mem., 1986-89; mem. ozone update com. NRC, 1983, mem. rsch. opportunities in biology com., 1985-89, com. on the human genome, 1986-89, com. on bits of power, 1995-96; trustee Cold Spring Harbor Lab., 1977-83; mem. proposal rev. panel Stanford Sychrotron Radiation Lab., 1976-88; mem. U.S. Nat. Commn., Internat. Union Pure & Applied Biophysics, 1986-94, vice chmn., 1988-91, chmn., 1991-94; sci. adv. bd. Hereditary Disease Found., 1987-89; mem. coun. Human Genome Orgn., 1989-92, v.p. 1990-92, pres. America's, 1991-98; chmn. DOE Department of energy Human Genome Coordinating com., 1989-92; adv. com. Searle Scholars program, 1987-93, chair, 1993-94, mem. adv. com. program in parasite biology MacArthur Found., 1990-93; mem. sci. adv. coun. Roswell Park Cancer Inst. 1992-98; sci. adv. com. European Molecular Biology Lab., 1989-94; bd. sci. counselors Nat. Ctr. for Biotechnology Info., Nat. Libr. Medicine, 1990-95; cons. Incyte Pharm. Inc., 1992-98, Genelabs, Inc., 1988—, Samsung Advanced Inst. Tech., 2000—; mem. coun. Internat. Union Pure and Applied Biophysics, 1993-99; vis. com. biology Brookhaven Nat. Lab., 1986-89; bd. dirs. and chair sci. adv. com. Avitech Diagnostics, Inc. (formerly ATGC Inc.), 1992-1997; mem. nomenclature com. IUBMB, 1989—; chair adv. com. European Bioinformatics Inst., 1993-94; mem. USDA Genome Adv. Com., 1992—; co-chair biotech. adv. coun. Fisher Sci., 1994—; mem. biology adv. com. Lawrence Livermore Nat. Lab., 1995—, chair 2000—; chair sci. adv. com. Sequenom, Inc., Sequenom Instruments GmbH, 1995—, mem. sci. adv. com., Aclara, Inc., Caliper, Inc., 1996—, Carta, Inc. (formerly Thermaphore, Inc.), 1999—, bd. dirs. 2000—; Cistem, Inc., 1999—, Technoventures Mgmt., 1998—; mem. FASEB consensus conf. on fed. funding, 1995-2000; quest scholar Quest Diagnostics, Inc., 1997-99; mem. biotech. coun. DOE, 1996—; mem. unconventional pathogen countermeasures adv. com. DARPA (Defense Advanced Projects Research Agency , 1996-2000. Author: (with Paul R. Schimmel) Biophysical Chemistry, I, II, III, (with Cassandra L. Smith) Genomics; assoc. editor Ann. Rev. Biophysics, 1983-93. Trustee Assoc. Univs. Inc., 1999-2000; bd. dirs. Keystone Confs., 1999-2001. Recipient Fresenius award Phi Lambda Upsilon, 1972; Eli Lilly award in biol. chemistry Am. Chem. Soc., 1978; Alfred P. Sloan fellow, 1969-71; Guggenheim fellow, 1973-74; Nat. Cancer Inst. outstanding investigator grantee, 1985, Analytica prize, 1988; ISCO prize, 1989, Sober prize ASBMB, 1990. Fellow AAAS, Biophys. Soc. (mem. coun. 1977-81, Emily Gray prize 2000, fellow 2000); mem. Am. Acad. Arts and Scis., Nat. Acad. Sci., Am. Soc. Biol. Chemists, Am. Chem. Soc., Soc. Analytical Cytology, Harvey Soc., Am. Soc. Human Genetics, Biomed. Engring. Soc., Japanese Biochem. Soc. (hon.). Home: 526 Stratford Ct Apt E Del Mar CA 92014-2767 Office: Sequenom Inc 3595 John Hopkins Ct San Diego CA 92121 E-mail: ccantor@sequenom.com

CAPE, RONALD ELLIOT, retired biotechnology company executive; b. Montreal, Que., Can., Oct. 11, 1932; came to U.S., 1967, naturalized, 1972; s. Victor and Fan C.; m. Lillian Judith Pollock, Oct. 21, 1956; children: Jacqueline R., Julie A. AB in Chemistry, Princeton U., 1953; MBA, Harvard U., 1955; PhD in Biochemistry, McGill U., Montreal, 1967; postgrad., U. Calif., Berkeley, 1967-70. Customs, purchasing and advt. clk. Merck and Co., Ltd., Montreal, 1955-56; pres. Profl. Pharm. Corp., Montreal, 1960-67, chmn. bd., 1967-73; pres. Cetus Corp., Emeryville, Calif., 1972-78, chmn. bd., 1978-91. Founding chmn. Darwin Molecular Corp., 1992—; mem. adv. coun. dept. molecular biology Princeton U.; adj. prof. bus. adminstrn. U. Pitts.; vis. prof. biochemistry Queen Mary Coll., U. London; bd. dirs. Advanced Bioconcept Inc., Interactive Scis., Inc., Neutrogena Corp., The Found. Nat. Medals of Sci. & Tech., 1992—; founder, bd. dirs. Bay Area Biosci. Ctr., 1989—; mem. bus. adv. com. Neurobiol. Techs. Inc.; mem. sci. adv. bd. Can. Med. Discoveries Fund; mem. standing com. bus. devel. MEd. Rsch. Coun. (Can.); mem. bus. affairs com. Ann. Revs., Inc., 1975-80; mem. impacts of applied genetics adv. panel to Office Tech. Assessment; mem. adv. com. on life scis. Natural Scis. and Engring. Rsch. Coun. Can.; mem. bd. dirs. Whitehead Inst., Cambridge, Mass. Mem. Rockefeller U. Coun.; bd. dirs. U. Calif. Art Mus. Coun., Berkeley, 1974-76; trustee Head-Royce Schs., Oakland, Calif., 1975-80, Rockefeller U., 1986-90, San Francisco Conservatory Music, The Keystone Ctr., 1987-93; bd. dirs. San Francisco Opera Assn., mem. budget and fin. com., 1992—, U. Waterloo Inst. for Biotech. Rsch.; mem. bus. adv. com. U. Calif., Berkeley; mem. Berkeley Roundtable on Internat. Economy; mem. sci. adv. bd. Bio-Technology Mag., 1987—; trustee Princeton U., 1989-93; mem. bd. regents Nat. Libr. of Medicine, 1989-92; scientific adv. bd. Med. Rsch. Coun., Can., standing com. bus. devel. Fellow AAAS, Am. Acad. Arts and Scis., Am. Soc. Microbiology (Found. for Microbiology lectr. 1978-79); mem. Can. Biochem. Soc., Fedn. Am. Scientists, Royal Soc. Health, Soc. Indsl. Microbiology, Indsl. Biotech. Assn. (founding mem., pres. 1983-85, dir.), N.Y. Acad. Scis., Princeton Club of N.Y., Commonwealth Club of Calif., Sigma Xi. Jewish. Office: 220 Montgomery St Ste 1010 San Francisco CA 94104-3419

CAPECCHI, MARIO RENATO, geneticist, educator; b. Verona, Italy, Oct. 6, 1937; m. 1963. BS, Antioch Coll., 1961; PhD in Biophysics, Harvard U., 1967. Soc. fellows, jr. fellow biophysics Harvard U., 1966-69, from asst. prof. to assoc. prof. biochemistry med. sch., 1969-73; prof. Biology U. Utah, 1973-88; prof. human genetics U. Utah Sch. Medicine, Salt Lake City, 1989—; investigator Howard Hughes Inst./U. Utah, Salt Lake City, 1988—; disting. prof. human genetics Howard Hughes Inst./U.Utah, 1993—. Mem. bd. sci. counselors Nat. Cancer Inst. Recipient Biochemistry award Am. Chem. Soc., 1969, Bristol-Myers Squibb award, 1992, Gairdner Found. Internat. award Gairdner Found. (Can.), 1993, Gen. Motors Corp. Alfred P. Sloan Jr. Prize, 1994, Molecular Bioanalytics Prize, 1996, Kyoto Prize in Basic Scis., 1996, Franklin medal Franklin Inst., 1997, Baxter award AAMC, 1998, Horace Mann Disting. Alumni award Antioch Coll., 2000, Premio Phoenix-Anni Verdi award, 2000, 33rd

Jiménez-Diaz prize, 2001. Mem. NAS, Am. Biochem. Soc., Am. Soc. Biol. Chemistry, Am. Soc. Microbiology, Molecular Med. Soc., N.Y. Acad. Sci., Soc. Devel. Biology, Internat. Genome Soc., Genetics Soc. Am., Am. Acad. Microbiology. Achievements include research in gaining an understanding of how the information encoded in the gene is translated by the cell, elucidating the mechanism of genetic recombination in mouse embryo-derived stem (ES) cells, developing gene targeting in the mouse, gaining an understanding of embryonic and neuronal mammalian development through the use of gene targeting. Office: Howard Hughes Med Inst Univ Utah 15 N 2030 E Rm 5100 Salt Lake City UT 84112-5331 E-mail: mario.capecchi@genetics.utah.edu

CAPIZZI, MICHAEL ROBERT, prosecutor; b. Detroit, Oct. 19, 1939; s. I.A. and Adelaide E. (Jennelle) C.; m. Sandra Jo Jones, June 22, 1963; children: Cori Anne, Pamela Jo. BS in Bus. Adminstrn., Ea. Mich. U., 1961; JD, U. Mich., 1964. Bar: Calif. 1965, U.S. Dist. Ct. (so. dist.) Calif. 1965, U.S. Ct. Appeals (9th cir.) 1970, U.S. Supreme Ct. 1971. Dep. dist. atty., Orange County, Calif., 1965-68; head writs, appeals and spl. assignments sect., 1968-71; asst. dist. atty., dir. spl. ops., 1971-86; legal counsel, mem. exec. bd. Interstate Organized Crime Index, 1971-79, Law Enforcement Intelligence Unit, 1971-95, chief asst. dist. atty., 1986-90, dist. atty., 1990-99. Instr. criminal justice Santa Ana Coll., 1967-76, Calif. State U., 196-87. Commr. City Planning Commn., Fountain Valley, Calif., 1971-80, vice chmn. 1972-73, chmn. 1973-75, 79-80; candidate for Rep. nomination Calif. Atty. Gen., 1998. Fellow Am. Coll. Trial Lawyers; mem. Nat. Dist. Attys. Assn. (bd. dirs. 1995-96, v.p. 1996-99), Calif. Dist. Attys. Assn. (outstanding prosecutor award 1980, v.p. 1995, pres. 1996), Calif. Bar Assn., Orange County Bar Assn. (chmn. cts. com. 1977, chmn. coll. of trial advocacy com. 1978-81, bd. dirs. 1977-81, sec.-treas. 1982, pres. 1984). Office: PO Box 1938 Santa Ana CA 92702-1938 E-mail: mrclaw@socal.rr.com

CAPLAN, KAREN B. company executive; CEO, pres. Frieda's, Los Alamitos, Calif. Recipient awards in innovation and gen. excellence Working Woman mag. Office: Frieda's 4465 Corporate Center Dr Los Alamitos CA 90720-2561

CAPOZZI, ANGELO, surgeon; b. Solvay, N.Y., Apr. 20, 1933; s. Angelo and Daminana (Pirro) C.; m. Louise Armanetti, June 18, 1960; children: Angelo III, Leonard, Jeanne. BS, U. Notre Dame, 1956; MD, Loyola U., Chgo., 1960. Diplomate Am. Bd. Plastic Surgery. Intern St. Francis Hosp., Evanston, Ill., 1960-61, resident in gen. surgery, 1962-64; resident in plastic surgery U. Wis., Madison, 1964-66; chief plastic surgery USAF, Travis AFB, Calif., 1966-68; chief dept. plastic surgery St. Marys Hosp., San Francisco, 1974-77; assoc. clin. prof. dept. surgery U. Calif., San Francisco; chmn. dept. plastic and reconstructive surgery St. Francis Meml. Hosp., San Francisco, 1987-98, dir. plastic surgery residency program, 1987-98. Mem. tchg. staff St. Francis Meml. Hosp., Bothin Burn Ctr., San Francisco, 1968-98; chief plastic surgery Shriners Hosp., San Francisco, 1999—, pres. Calif. Soc. of Plastic Surgeons, 1998-99. Author: Change of Face, 1984; contbr. articles to profl. jours. Mem. parks and recreation com. City of Tiburon, Calif., 1973. Capt. USAF, 1966-68. Recipient Alumni citation Loyola U., 1983, Bru Brunnier fellow award San Francisco Rotary Found., 1996; named Man of Yr., U. Notre Dame Alumni, 1983. Mem. San Francisco Olympic Club, San Francisco Rotary (Outstanding Svc. award 1993, Svc. Above Self award 1995), Rotoplast, Inc. (founding mem.). Avocations: running, biking. Office: 1199 Bush St Ste 640 San Francisco CA 94109-5977

CAPP, MICHAEL PAUL, physician, educator; b. Yonkers, N.Y., July 1, 1930; s. Michael and Mary (Bybel) C.; children: Marianne, Michael, Steven, John; m. Constance Whitehead, Jan. 4, 1989. B.S., Roanoke Coll., Salem, Va., 1952; M.D., U. N.C., 1958. Diplomate: Am. Bd. Radiology (treas. 1982-85, v.p. 1985, pres. 1987-89, now exec. dir.). Lab. instr. physics Roanoke Coll., 1952; teaching asst. Grad. Sch. Physics, Duke, 1952-54; intern in pediatrics Duke Med. Center, 1958-59, resident in radiology, 1959-62, assoc. in radiology, 1962, asst. prof., 1963-66, assoc. prof., 1966-70, dir. diagnostic div., dept. radiology, 1967-70, asst. prof. pediatrics, 1968-70, radiologist in charge pediatric cardiology, 1962-70; dir. Duke Med. Center (Pediatric Radiology Program), 1965-70, Duke Med. Center (Med. Students Teaching Program Diagnostic Radiology), 1965-66; prof., chmn. dept. radiology U. Ariz. Coll. Medicine, Tucson, 1970-93; chief of staff Ariz. Med. Center, Univ. Hosp., 1971-73; exec. dir. Am. Bd. of Radiology, Tucson, 1993—. Mem. NRC com. on Radiology, James Picker Found., 1972; exec. dir. Am. Bd. Radiology, 1993—. Contbr. articles to profl. jours. Mem. AMA, Am. Coll. Radiology, Am. Roentgen Ray Soc. (pres. 1990), Am. Assn. U. Radiologists (exec. com. 1970, Gold medal 1988), Am. Heart Assn. (pres. coun. on cardiovascular radiology 1976-78), Am. Bd. Radiology (exec. dir. 1993—), Radiol. Soc. N. Am. (chmn. sci. exhibits com. 1976-79), N.Am. Soc. Cardiac Radiologists (pres. 1975), Nat. Acad. Scis., N. Y. Acad. Scis., Pima County Med. Soc., Ea. Radiol. Soc. (sci. program chmn. 1967, v.p. 1973—), Soc. for Pediatric Radiology, Soc. for Chmn. Acad. Radiology Depts. (pres. 1977), Inst. Medicine, Sigma Pi Sigma. Home: 5200 N Valley View Rd Tucson AZ 85718-6123 Office: 5255 E Williams Cir Ste 3200 Tucson AZ 85711-7473

CAPPS, LOIS RAGNHILD GRIMSRUD, congresswoman, former school nurse; b. Ladysmith, Wis., Jan. 10, 1938; d. Jurgen Milton and Solveig Magdalene (Gullixson) Grimsrud; m. Walter Holden Capps, Aug. 21, 1960 (dec.); children: Lisa Margaret, Todd Holden, Laura Karolina. BSN with honors, Pacific Luth. U., 1959; MA in Religion, Yale U., 1964; MA in Edn., U. Calif., Santa Barbara, 1990. RN, Calif.; cert. sch. nurse, Calif.; jr. coll. instr., Calif. Asst. instr. Emanuel Hosp. Sch. Nursing, Portland, Oreg., 1959-60; surgery flr. nurse Yale/New Haven Hosp., 1960-62, head nurse, out patient, 1962-63; staff nurse Vis. Nurse Assn., Hamden, Ct., 1963-64; sch. nurse Santa Barbara (Calif.) Sch. Dists., 1968-70, 77-98; dir. teenage pregnancy and parenting project Santa Barbara, 1985-86; mem. U.S. Congress from 22d Calif. dist., Washington, 1998—. Mem. commerce com., mem. sci. com., internat. rels. com. U.S. Congress, campaign finance reform task force, budget task force, Calif. ISTEA task force, congrl. caucus women's issues, congrl. task force tobacco and health, diabetes caucus, congrl. caucus on the arts; instr. Santa Barbara City Coll., 1990—. Bd. dirs. Am. Heart Assn., Santa Barbara, 1989—, The Adoption Ctr., Santa Barbara, 1986-90, Family Svc. Agy., Santa Barbara, 1994—, Stop AIDS Now, Santa Barbara, 1994—, Santa Barbara Women's Polit. Com., 1991—; instr. CPR, first aid, ARC, Santa Barbara, 1985—; bd. dirs. Pacific Luth. Theol. Sem. Democrat. Lutheran. Home: 1724 Santa Barbara St Santa Barbara CA 93101-1025 Office: US House of Reps 1118 Longworth Ho Office Bldg Washington DC 20515-0001 Fax: 202-225-5632. E-mail: lois.capps@mail.house.gov*

CAPRIOLI, JOSEPH, ophthalmologist; b. Deer Park, N.Y., May 15, 1954; m. Tracey Caprioli, June 1993; 1 child, Isabella; children from previous marriage: Peter, Joseph, Jessica, Marie. BS, SUNY, Stony Brook, 1975; MD, SUNY, Buffalo, 1979; MA Privatum, Yale U., 1993. Diplomate Nat. Bd. Med. Exmainers, Am. Bd. Ophthalmology; lic. physician, N.Y., Pa., Conn. Dir. Glaucoma Sect., 1984—; intern Yale U. Sch. Medicine, New Haven, 1979-80, resident ophthalmology, 1984-88, asst. prof. ophthalmology, dir. glaucoma svc., 1984-97, assoc. prof. ophthalmology, 1988-93, prof. ophthalmology, 1993-97; fellow glaucoma Wills Eye Hosp., Phila., 1983-84; acting chmn. Yale U. Sch. Medicine, New Haven, 1993-95; prof. ophthalmology, dir. glaucoma sect. UCLA/Jules Stein Eye Inst., L.A., 1997—. Lectr. Ill. Soc. for Preservation of Blindness, 1992; mem. basic sci. and clin. glaucoma panels, planning subcom. Nat. Adv. Eye Coun., NIH, 1990, visual scis. A study sect. NIH/Nat. Eye Inst., 1992-94, chmn., 1994—; steering com. Advanced Glaucoma Intervention Study, NIH, 1988-91; lectr. in field. Book rev. editor Ophthalmic Surgery, 1984-89; mem. editl. bd. Ophthalmic Surgery, 1989—, Am. Jour Ophthalmology, 1991—, Investigative Ophthalmology and Visual Sci., 1992—, Jour. Glaucoma, 1991-94; editor: Ophthalmology Clinics of North America: Contemporary Issues in Glaucoma, 1991; contbr. articles to profl. jours., chpts. to books. Recipient Jules Francois prize, 1989, Alcon Rsch. Inst. award, 1992, Rudin prize for glaucoma rsch., 1996; grantee Hoechst-Roussel Pharms., Inc., 1985-86, NIH/Nat. Eye Inst., 1987-89, 93—, New Haven Found., 1988-89, Merck Sharp & Dohme, 1989-90, 92-93, Alcon Pharms., 1989-90, Robert Leet and Clara Guthrie Patterson Trust, 1989-92, Alcon Rsch. Inst., 1992, Lewis Rudin Glaucoma prize, 1997. Fellow ACS, Am. Acad. Ophthalmology (mem. quality of care com. glaucoma panel 1988—, chmn. 1991—); mem. Am. Ophthalmological Soc., Assn. for Rsch. in Vision and Ophthalmology, Internat. Soc. Eye Rsch., Am. Glaucoma Soc., Soc. Neurosci., Glaucoma Soc. of Internat. Gongress Ophahtlmology, New Eng. Ophthalmol. Soc. Avocations: piano, cabinet-making, fitness. Office: Jules Stein Eye Inst Dept Opthalmology 100 Stein Plz # 2-118 Los Angeles CA 90095-7065

CAPRON, ALEXANDER MORGAN, lawyer, educator; b. Hartford, Conn., Aug. 16, 1944; s. William Mosher and Margaret (Morgan) C.; m. Barbara A. Brown, Nov. 9, 1969 (div. Dec. 1985); m. Kathleen West, Mar. 4, 1989; children: Jared Capron-Brown, Charles Spencer West Capron, Christopher Gordon West Capron, Andrew Morgan West Capron. BA, Swarthmore Coll., 1966; LLB, Yale U., 1969; MA (hon.), U. Pa., 1975. Bar: D.C. 1970, Pa. 1978. Law clk. to presiding judge U.S. Ct. Appeals, Washington, 1969-70; lectr., research assoc. Yale U., 1970-72; asst. prof. law U. Pa., 1972-75, vice dean, 1976, assoc. prof., 1975-78, prof. law and human genetics, 1978-82; exec. dir. Pres.'s Commn. for Study of Ethical Problems in Med. and Biomed. and Behavioral Rsch., Washington, 1980-83; prof. law, ethics and pub. policy Law Ctr. Georgetown U., Washington, 1983-84, inst. fellow Kennedy Inst. Ethics, 1983-84; Topping prof. law, medicine and pub. policy U. So. Calif., L.A., 1985-89, Univ. prof. law and medicine, 1989—, Henry W. Bruce prof. law, 1991—; co-dir. Pacific Ctr. for Health Policy and Ethics, L.A., 1990—. Mem. bd. advisors Am. Bd. Internal Medicine, 1985-95, chmn., 1991-95; cons. NIH, mem. recombinant DNA com., 1990-95, mem. subcom. on human gene therapy, 1984-92; chmn. Congrl. Biomed. Ethics Adv. Commn., 1987-91; mem. Joint Commn. on Accreditation of Healthcare Orgns., 1994—, mem. ethics adv. com., 1984-85; mem. Nat. Bioethics Adv. Commn., 1996—. Author: (with Katz) Catastrophic Diseases: Who Decides What?, 1976, (with others) Genetic Counseling: Facts, Values and Norms, 1979, Law, Science and Medicine, 1984, supplements, 1987, 89, 2d edit., 1996, (with others) Treatise on Health Care Law, 1991; contbr. articles to profl. jours. Bd. mgrs. Swarthmore Coll., 1982-85; bd. trustees The Century Found. Fellow AAAS, Am. Coll. Legal Medicine (hon.), Hastings Ctr. (Inst. Society, Ethics and Life Scis., bd. dirs. 1975-98); mem. Inst. Medicine NAS (bd. dirs. 1985-90), AAUP (exec. com. Pa. chpt.), Am. Soc. Law, Medicine and Ethics (pres. 1988-89), Swarthmore Coll. Alumni Soc. (v.p. 1974-77). Office: U So Calif Law Sch University Park Los Angeles CA 90089-0071 E-mail: acapron@law.usc.edu

CARATAN, ANTON G. food products executive; b. 1955; With Anton Caratan & Son, Delano, Calif., 1976—, ptnr., 1984—. Office: Anton Caratan & Son 1625 Road 160 Delano CA 93215-9436

CARATAN, GEORGE, food products executive; b. 1929; With Anton Caratan & Son, Delano, Calif., 1952—. Office: Anton Caratan & Son 1625 Road 160 Delano CA 93215-9436

CARD, DEBORAH FRANCES, orchestra administrator; b. Pottstown, Pa., Sept. 30, 1956; d. Marshall Anthony and Winifred (Hitz) R. BA, Stanford U., 1978; MBA, U. So. Calif., 1985. Orch. mgr. L.A. Philharm., 1978-86; exec. dir. L.A. Chamber Orch., 1986-92, Seattle Symphony, 1992—. Bd. dirs. AIDS project L.A., 1985-92; active Jr. League L.A., 1982-92. Mem. Am. Symphony Orch. League, Assn. Calif. Symphony Orchs. (pres. 1988-91), Assn. N.W. Symphony Orchs. (bd. dirs. 1993—), Chamber Music Soc. L.A. (bd. dirs. 1987-92), Ojai Festival (pres.'s coun.). Democrat. Episcopalian. Avocations: skiing, tennis, gardening, reading. Office: Seattle Symphony Ctr House PO Box 21906 Seattle WA 98111-3906

CARDIFF, ROBERT DARRELL, pathology educator; b. San Francisco, Dec. 5, 1935; s. George Darrell and Helen (Kohfield) C.; m. Sally Joan Bounds, June 23, 1962; children: Darrell, Todd, Shelley. BS, U. Calif., Berkeley, 1958, PhD, 1968; MD, U. Calif., San Francisco, 1962. Intern King's County Hosp., Bklyn., 1962-63; resident in pathology U. Oreg., Portland, 1963-66; NIH fellow U. Calif., Berkeley, 1966-68, mem. faculty med. sch. Davis, 1971—, prof. pathology med. sch., 1977—, chair dept. pathology, 1990-96; dir. Ctr. for Med. Informatics U. Calif. Davis Health-care System, Davis, 1996-98, faculty Ctr. for Comparative Medicine. Mem. sci. adv. bd. Contra Costa Cancer Fund, Walnut Creek, Calif., 1985-99; mem. Univ.-Wide AIDS Task Force, Berkeley, 1984-87; vis. prof. Sun-Yat Sen U. Med. Sci., Peoples Republic of China, 1985, 93, Harvard Med. Sch., 1990, U. Calif. San Diego, 1998-99. Mem. editorial bd. Human Pathology, 1992—, Tumor Markers, 1992—, Internat. Jour. Oncology, 1992—, Jour. Mamglnd Biol. and Neoplasia, 1998—; contbr. articles to profl. jours. Lt. col. U.S. Army, 1968-71. Recipient Triton Rsch. award Triton Bioscis., Inc., 1985, Kaiser Found. Teaching award U. Calif. Med. Sch., Davis, 1985, Disting. Teaching award U. Calif., Davis, Sadusk award Peralta Cancer Inst., 1986, Faculty Rsch. award U. Calif. Med. Sch., 1988, Affirmative Action award U. Calif. Davis Med. Ctr., 1991., others. Mem. AAUP (exec. com. 1983-85), Pluto Soc., Internat. Acad. Pathology, Internat. Assn. Breast Cancer (bd. dirs. 1984—), Sacramento Pathology Soc. (bd. dirs. 1985-96), No. Calif. Pathology Soc. (pres. 1990-96), Coll. Am. Pathology, Sigma Xi. Avocations: basketball, skiing, jogging. Office: U Calif-Davis Ctr for Comparative Medicine 98 County Rd & Hutchison Dr Davis CA 95616

CARDONE, BONNIE JEAN, freelance photojournalist; b. Chgo., Feb. 21, 1942; d. Frederick Paul and Beverly Jean Rittschof; m. David Frederick Cardone, June 9, 1963 (div. 1978); children: Pamela Susan, Michael David. BA, Mich. State U., 1963. Editorial asst. Mich. State Dental Assn. Jour., Lansing, 1963-64; asst. editor Nursing Home Adminstr. mag., Chgo., 1964-65, Skin Diver Mag., L.A., 1976-77, sr. editor, 1977-81, photographer, 1981—, exec. editor, 1981-97, editor, 1997-99; mystery novelist, 1999—. Author: Fireside Diver, 1993; co-author: Shipwrecks of Southern California, 1989. Named Woman Diver of Yr. Women's Scuba Assn., 1999; recipient Calif. Scuba Svc. award St. Brendan Corp., 1999; named to Women Diver's Hall of Fame, 2000, Women's Scuba Assn. Mem. Calif. Wreck Divers Club, Hist. Diving Soc. (bd. dirs. 1997-2001). E-mail: bjcardone@hotmail.com

CARDWELL, KENNETH HARVEY, architect, educator; b. Los Angeles, Feb. 15, 1920; s. Stephen William and Beatrice Viola (Duperrault) C.; m. Mary Elinor Sullivan, Dec. 30, 1946; children: Kenneth William, Mary Elizabeth, Ann Margaret, Catherine Buckley, Robert Stephen. A.A., Occidental Coll.; A.B., U. Calif.-Berkeley; postgrad., Stanford U. Lic. architect, Calif. Draftsman Thompsen & Wilson Architects, San Francisco, 1946-48, Michael Goodman, Architect, Berkeley, Calif., 1949; architect W.S. Wellington, Architect, Berkeley, 1950-59; prin. Kolbeck, Cardwell, Christopherson, Berkeley, 1960-66; prof. dept. arch. U. Calif.-Berkeley, 1950-82; prin. Kenneth H. Cardwell Architect, Berkeley, 1982—. Author: Bernard Maybeck, 1977. Pres. Civic Art Commn., Berkeley, 1963-65; mem. Bd. Adjustments, 1967-69, Alameda County Art Commn., 1969-72. Served to 1st lt. USAAF, 1941-45. Decorated D.F.C.; decorated Air medal with 3 oak leaf clusters; Rehman fellow, 1957; Graham fellow, 1961; recipient Berkeley citation U. Calif., 1982. Fellow AIA; mem. Alpha Rho Chi Home and Office: 1210 Shattuck Ave Berkeley CA 94709-1413

CARE, TERRY, state legislator, lawyer; b. Oklahoma City, Jan. 12, 1947; m. Jenny Lockhart; 1 child, Diana. Student, Clark Coll., Vancouver, Wash., Foothill Coll., Los Altos, Calif.; BA in History, JD, U. N.Mex. Mem. Nev. Senate, Dist. 7, 1998—; mem. govt. affairs com., judiciary com., transp. com. Nev. Senate. Mem. Nev. State Coun. Sr. Citizens. Served with inf. U.S. Army, 1966-69. Mem. Nev. Bar Assn., Clark County Bar Assn., DAV, Am. Legion. Democrat. Address: 4371 Woodcrest Rd Las Vegas NV 89121-4946 E-mail: tcare@sen.state.nv.us

CAREN, ROBERT POSTON, aerospace company executive; b. Columbus, Ohio, Dec. 25, 1932; s. Robert James and Charlene (Poston) C.; m. Linda Ann Davis, Mar. 27, 1963; children: Christopher Davis, Michael Poston. B.S., Ohio State U., 1953, M.S., 1954, Ph.D., 1961. Sr. physicist N.Am. Aviation, Columbus, 1959-60; assoc. research scientist research and devel. div. Lockheed Missiles and Space Co., Inc., Palo Alto, Calif., 1962-63, research scientist, 1963-66, sr. mem. research lab., 1966-69, mgr. def. systems space systems div., 1969-70, mgr. infared tech. R & D div., 1970-71, research dir., 1972-76, chief engr., 1976-86, v.p. gen. mgr. R & D div., 1986—, corp. v.p. sci. and engring., 1987-98; chmn. LITEX Inc., 1998—, Hawkeye Ventures, 1999—. Bd. dirs. LITEX Corp., Superconducting Tech. Inc.; mem. U.S./Israel Sci. and Tech. Commn., 1997—. Contbr. articles to profl. jours.; patentee in field. Mem. dean's adv. coun. Ohio State U., Calif. Poly. State U.-St. Louis Obispo, U. So. Calif., U. Calif., L.A., U. Calif., Davis. Fellow AIAA, AAAS, AAS, Soc. Automotive Engrs.; mem. NAE, IEEE (sr.), Am. Astron. Soc., Am. Def. Preparedness Assn. (past chmn. rsch. divsn.), Am. Phys. Soc., Aerospace Industries Assn. (past chmn. tech. and ops. coun.), Calif. Coun. on Sci. and Tech., Sigma Pi Sigma, Pi Mu Epsilon. Home: 6039 Gleneagles Cir San Jose CA 95138-2372 Office: 15260 Ventura Blvd Ste 2250 Sherman Oaks CA 91403-5338 E-mail: rcaren@sprynet.com

CARET, ROBERT LAURENT, university president; b. Biddeford, Maine, Oct. 7, 1947; s. Laurent J. and Anne (Santorsola) C.; m. Elizabeth Zoltan; children: Colin Ready, Katherine Ready, Katalyn Ford, Kellen Ford. BA, Suffolk U., 1969; PhD, U. N.H., 1974; DSc (hon.), Suffolk U., 1996; DHL (hon.), Nat. Hispanic U., 1997. Dean Coll. Natural and Math. Scis. Towson (Md.) State U., 1981-87, prof. chemistry, 1994—, assoc. v.p., 1985-86, exec. asst. to pres., 1986-87, provost, exec. v.p., 1987-95; pres. San Jose (Calif.) State U., 1995—. Author: (with A.S. Wingrove) Quimca Organica, 1984, Study Guide and Answer Book to Organic Chemistry, 1981, Organic Chemistry, 1981, (with P. Plante) Myths and Realities in Higher Education Administration, 1990, (with K. Denniston and J.J. Topping) Principles and Applications of Organic and Biological Chemistry, 1995, 2d edit., 1997, Principles and Applications of Inorganic, Organic and Biological Chemistry, 1992, 3d edit., 2000, Foundations of Inorganic, Organic and Biological Chemistry, 1995; contbr. articles to profl. jours. Chmn. Baltimore County Higher Edn. Adv. Bd., Towson, 1989—; co-chmn. Balt. Sci. Fair/Kiwanis, Towson, 1983-88; bd. dirs. San Jose Repertory Theater, San Jose Opera, Calif. State U. Inst. Recipient Employee Incentive award State of Md., 1987, Outstanding Chemistry Tchr. award Md. Inst. Chemists, 1971, Award for Excellence Suffolk U. Gen. Alumni Assn., 1986, Outstanding Pres. award AAFF, 2001; Lester A. Pratt fellow U. N.H., 1972, Albert W. Diniak fellow, U. N.H., 1972. Mem. AAUP (Towson State U. chpt., mem. exec. com. 1978-81, v.p. 1975-80, divsn. and dept. rep. 1975-80), Am. Assn. Higher Edn., Am. Assn. Univ. Adminstrs. (Md. membership rep. 1986—), Am. Coun. on Edn., EDUCOM (instl. rep. 1986-87), Am. Chem. Soc. (Chesapeake sect. alt. counselor 1979-87, mem. exec. com. 1978-87, mem.-at-large 1978-79, various coms. 1978-87), Am. Assn. State Colls. and Univs. (adv. bd. 1986—, Kellogg Leadership bd. 1989—, state rep. 1989—, joint venture Silicon Valley bd. dirs. 1997, co-chair econ. devel. team 1996—, co-chair econ. prosperity coun. 1998—), Silicon Valley Mfg. Group (bd. dirs.), San Jose C. of C. (bd. dirs.), Sigma Xi (Towson State U. chpt. pres. 1975-76), Sigma Zeta, Phi Beta Chi, Omicron Delta Kappa. Avocations: jogging, tae kwan do, cross country skiing, golf. Office: San Jose State U One Washington Sq San Jose CA 95192-0002 E-mail: sjsupres@sjsu.edu

CAREY, CHASE, broadcast executive; Chmn., CEO Fox TV, L.A. Office: Fox TV 10201 W Pico Blvd Los Angeles CA 90064-2606

CAREY, D. JOHN, electronics executive; b. 1936; came to U.S., 1959; Grad., U. Liverpool, England. Engr. Northern Electric Co., 1959-63, Fairchild Semiconductor, 1963-68; sr. v.p. Advanced Micro Devices, 1968-80; with Integrated Device Tech., Inc., 1980—, pres., 1982—, also bd. mem., now chmn. bd. Office: Integrated Device Tech Inc 2975 Stender Way Santa Clara CA 95054-3214

CAREY, JAMES C., JR. plastic surgeon; b. Chgo., 1932; MD, Northwestern U., 1957. Intern Cook County Hosp., Chgo., 1957-58, resident in gen. surgery, 1958-63; plastic surgeon U. Mo., Kansas City, 1980-82; now plastic surgeon Twin Cities Cmty. Hosp., Templeton, Calif. Office: 1101 Las Tablas Rd Ste K Templeton CA 93465-5604

CAREY, JOHN CLAYTON, pediatrician, medical geneticist; b. Balt., 1946; MD, Georgetown, 1972. Diplomate Am. Bd. Med. Genetics, Am. Bd. Pediatrics. Prof pediatrics U. Utah Med. Ctr., Salt Lake City. Co-author: Medical Genetics, 1998, (med. text) Care of the Child with Trisomy 18/13, 1996, rev. edit. 2000; editor-in-chief Am. Jour. Med. Genetics; contbr. over 180 articles to profl. jours. Med. advisor Support Orgn. Trisomy 18, 13 and Related Disorders, Utah Little People of Am., Utah Birth Defects Netowrk, Pregnancy Risk Line. Office: U Utah Med Ctr Pediatrics 2C412 SOM 50 N Medical Dr Salt Lake City UT 84132-0001 E-mail: john.carey@hsc.utah.edu

CAREY, KATHRYN ANN, advertising and public relations executive, editor, consultant; b. Los Angeles, Oct. 18, 1949; d. Frank Randall and Evelyn Mae (Walmsley) C.; m. Richard Kenneth Sundt, Dec. 28, 1980. BA in Am. Studies with honors, Calif. State U., L.A., 1971; postgrad., Georgetown U., Boston Coll. Cert. commercial pilot instrument rated, advanced cert. in corporate cmty. rels. Tutor Calif. Dept. Vocat. Rehab., L.A., 1970; teaching asst. U. So. Calif., 1974-75, UCLA, 1974-75; claims adjuster Auto Club So. Calif., San Gabriel, 1971-73; corp. pub. rels. cons. Carnation Co., L.A., 1973-78; cons., adminstr. Carnation Community Svc. Award Program, 1973-78; pub. rels. cons. Vivitar Corp., 1978; sr. advt. asst. Am. Honda Motor Co., Torrance, Calif., 1978-84; exec. dir. Am. Honda Found., 1984—, Honda Philanthropy, Office of the Ams., 1996—. Adminstr. Honda Matching Gift and Vol. Program, Honda Involvement Program; mgr. Honda Dealer Advt. Assns., 1978-84; cons. advt., pub. rels., promotions. Editor: Vivitar Voice, Santa Monica, Calif., 1978, Rod Machado's Instruments Pilots' Survival Manual, c. 1991; editor Honda Views, 1978-84, Found. Focus, 1984—; asst. editor Friskies Research Digest, 1973-78; contbg. editor Newsbriefs and Momentum, 1978—, Am. Honda Motor Co., Inc. employees publs. Calif. Life Scholarship Found. scholar, 1967; recipient Silver award, Wilmer Shields Rich award Coun. Founds. Excellence in Comm., 1995, Gold award, 1997, 2001, award of Excellence, Soc. Tech. Comm., 1995, Merit award, 1996, 97, 99, 2001, Apex award Excellence in Comms., 1997. Mem. Advt. Club L.A., Pub. Rels. Soc. Am., So. Calif. Assn. Philanthropy, Coun. on Founds., Affinity Group on Japanese Philanthropy (pres.), Ninety-Nines, Am. Quarter Horse

Assn., Aircraft Owners and Pilots Assn., Los Angeles Soc. for Cruelty to Animals, Greenpeace, Ocicats Internat., Am. Humane Assn., Humane Soc. U.S., Elsa Wild Animal Appeal, Calif. Advocates Nursing Home Reform (officer, sec./treas., treas. bd. dirs. 1997—). E-mail: kathryn. Office: Am Honda Found 1919 Torrance Blvd Torrance CA 90501-2722 E-mail: carey@ahm.honda.com

CAREY, PETER KEVIN, reporter; b. San Francisco, Apr. 2, 1940; s. Paul Twohig and Stanleigh M. (White) C.; m. Joanne Dayl Barker, Jan. 7, 1978; children: Brendan Patrick, Nadia Marguerite. BS in Econs., U. Calif., Berkeley, 1964. Reporter San Francisco Examiner, 1964, Livermore (Calif.) Ind., 1965-67, editor, 1967; aerospace writer, spl. projects and investigative reporter San Jose (Calif.) Mercury, 1967—. Recipient Pulitzer prize for internat. reporting Columbia U., 1986, George Polk award L.I. U., 1986, Investigative Reporters and Editors award, 1986, staff Pulitzer prize for gen. reporting, Columbia U., 1990, Thomas L. Stokes award Washington Journalism Ctr., 1991, Malcolm Forbes award Overseas Press Club of Am., 1993, Gerald Loeb award UCLA Grad. Sch. Mgmt., 1993, Best of the West, First Amendment Funding Inc., 1993, 95, Pub. Svc. award Calif. Newspapers Pub. Assn., 1996, Fairbanks award for pub. svc. AP, 1996; NEH profl. journalism fellow, Stanford U., 1983-84. Mem. Internat. Consortium of Investigative Journalists, Soc. Profl. Journalists, Investigative Reporters and Editors. Avocation: classical piano. Office: San Jose Mercury-News 750 Ridder Park Dr San Jose CA 95131-2432 E-mail: pcarey@sjmercury.com

CAREY, THERESA WILKINSON, small business owner, writer, editor; b. Santa Monica, Calif., July 9, 1955; d. Robert Raymond and Margaret Ann (Norris) Wilkinson; m. Kent W. Carey, June 25, 1977; children: Colleen Robin, Katharine Suzanne. BA in Econs., U. Calif., 1977; MS in Econometrics, U. Santa Clara, 1981. Sr. bus. analyst United Vintners, Heublein Wines, San Francisco, 1981-83; mgr. bus. analyst ISC Wines Calif., San Francisco, 1983-84; owner Alta Bus. Solutions, Palo Alto, Calif., 1984—. Spkr. in field. Author: Essential Finance Guide to Online Investing, 2000, Keep It Simple Series Guide to Online Investing, 2001, Guide to Online Investing, 2001, Essential Finance: Online Investing, 2001; contbg. editor Barron's mag., 1995—, Microsoft Interactive Developer (now MSDN mag.), 1996—; contbr. over 500 articles to computer and fin. mags. Mem. task force Palo Alto Child Care, 1987-89; mgr., coach Palo Alto Bobby Sox, 1995-97, v.p. 1996-97. Mem. Coll. Women's Assn. Japan (bd. dirs. 1999-2000), Calif. Band Alumni Assn. Avocations: piloting, softball and volleyball coaching, travel. Office: Alta Business Solutions PO Box 1630 Palo Alto CA 94302-1630

CAREY, W. DAVID P. hotel executive; m. Kathy Carey; 4 children. BSEE, Stanford U.; MBA with distinction, JD cum laude, Santa Clara U. Assoc. Carlsmith Tichman Case Mukai and Ichiki; exec. v.p., gen. counsel Outrigger Hotels, Inc., Honolulu, 1986-88, pres., 1988—, CEO, 1994—. Mem. Hawaii Tourism Authority. Mem. ABA, Hawaii Hotel Assn., Urban Land Inst., Hawaii State Bar Assn., Young Pres.' Orgn., Hawaii Bus. Roundtable, Beta Gamma Sigma. Avocations: soccer, golf. Office: Outrigger Hotels and Resorts 2375 Kuhio Ave Honolulu HI 96815-2992

CARGO, DAVID FRANCIS, lawyer; b. Dowagiac, Mich., Jan. 13, 1929; s. Francis Clair and Mary E. (Harton) C.; children: Veronica Ann, David Joseph, Patrick Michael, Maria Elena Christina, Eamon Francis. AB, U. Mich., 1951, M of Pub. Adminstrn., 1953, JD, 1957. Bar: Mich. 1957, N.Mex. 1957, Oreg. 1974. Practice in, Albuquerque, 1957; asst. dist. atty. Albuquerque, 1958-59; mem. N.Mex. Ho. of Reps., 1962; gov. N.Mex., 1967-71; practice law Santa Fe, 1970-73, Portland, Oreg., 1973-83. Chmn. Four Corners Regional Commn., 1967-71, Oil and Gas Conservation Commn.; chmn. N.Mex. Young Reps., 1959-61, Clackamas County Rep. Ctrl. Com.; mem. Israel Bond Com.; former mem. bd. govs. St. John Coll.; bd. dirs. Albuquerque Tech. Vocat. Sch.; chmn. governing bd. Albuquerque Tv.I. C.C.; mem. Albuquerque City Pers. Bd.; adv. bd. mem. N.Mex. State Fair; exec. bd. Found. for Open Govt. With AUS, 1953-55. Named Man of Yr. Albuquerque Jr. C. of C., 1964, Congregation Albert Man of Yr., 2001; recipient Outstanding Conservationist award N.Mex. Wildlife Assn., 1969, 70. Mem. Mich. Bar Assn., Oreg. Bar Assn., N.Mex. Bar Assn., Albuquerque Bar Assn., Isaac Walton League (past v.p. N.Mex.), World Affairs Coun. Oreg. (pres.), Interstate Oil and Gas Compact, Isaak Walton League Oreg., Hispano C. of C., Am. Leadership Conf. (bd. dirs.), Nat. Fedn. Blind. Home: 6422 Concordia Rd NE Albuquerque NM 87111-1228

CARLE, HARRY LLOYD, social worker; b. Chgo., Oct. 26, 1927; s. Lloyd Benjamin and Clara Bell (Lee) C.; m. Elva Diana Ulrich, Dec. 29, 1951 (div. 1966); adopted children: Joseph Francis, Catherine Marie; m. Karlen Elizabeth Howe, Oct. 14, 1967 (dec. Feb. 1991); children: Kristen Elizabeth and Sylvia Ann (twins), Eric Lloyd; m. Diane Wyland Gambs, May 23, 1993. BSS, Seattle U., 1952; postgrad., U. Wash., 1952-54, MSW, 1966. Pacific N.W. regional dir. Collegiate Coun. UN, 1952-53; rep. indsl. placement and employer rels. State of Wash., Seattle, 1955-57; parole and probation officer Seattle and Tacoma, 1957-61; parole employment splst., 1961-63; vocat. rehab. officer, 1963-66; clin. social worker Western State Hosp., Ft. Steilacoom, Wash., 1964-66, U.S. Penitentiary, McNeil Is., 1964-66; exec. dir. Shohomish County Cmty. Action Coun./Social Planning Coun., Everett, 1966-77; employment and edn. counselor Pierce County Jail Social Svcs., Tacoma, 1979-81; dir. employment devel. clinic coord. vocat. program North Rehab. Facility King County Divsn. Alcoholism and Substance Abuse, Seattle, 1981-90; staff devel. cons. Counseling for Ind. Living, Newport, R.I., 1992. Cmty. orgn. agy. mgmt. cons., 1968-92; cons. to pres. Geneal. Inst., Salt Lake City, 1974-78. Vol. Vis. Nurse Svc. Wash. Hospice and Home Care, Montlake Terrace, Wash., 1996-98; mem. social svc. project staff Pacific Luth. U., Tacoma, 1979-81. With USN, 1944-46. U.S. Office Vocat. Rehab scholar, 1965-66; named First Honoree Hall of Success Iowa Tng. Sch. for Boys, 1969. Mem. NASW, Seattle Geneal. Soc. (pres. 1974-76), Soc. advancement Mgmt. (chpt. exec. v.p. 1970-71), Acad. Cert. Social Workers (ret. 1998), Henckel Family Nat. Assn., Seattle Japanese Garden Soc. (v.p. 1993-96), various hist. and geneal socs. in Pa. and Ill. Roman Catholic. Home: Poem Rising Garden 258 Two Crane Ln NW Poulsbo WA 98370-9700 E-mail: ecopsych@silverlink.net

CARLESIMO, P. J. (PETER J. CARLESIMO), former professional basketball coach; b. Scranton, Pa., May 30, 1949; Grad., Fordham U., 1971. Asst. basketball coach Fordham U., Bronx, N.Y., N.H. Coll., Manchester; mem. staff Wagner Coll., Staten Island, N.Y.; head coach Seton Hall U., South Orange, N.J., 1982-94, Portland Trailblazers, 1994-97, Golden State Warriors, Oakland, Calif., 1997-99. Office: Golden State Warriors 1011 Broadway Oakland CA 94607-4027

CARLESON, ROBERT BAZIL, public policy consultant, corporation executive; b. Long Beach, Calif., Feb. 21, 1931; s. Bazil Upton and Grace Reynolds (Wilhite) C.; m. Betty Jane Nichols, Jan. 31, 1954 (div.); children: Eric Robert, Mark Andrew, Susan Lynn; m. Susan A. Dower, Feb. 11, 1984. Student, U. Utah, 1949-51; B.S., U. So. Calif., 1953, postgrad., 1956-58. Adminstrv. asst. City of Beverly Hills, Calif., 1956-57; asst. to city mgr. City of Claremont, 1957-58; sr. adminstrv. asst. to city mgr. City of Torrance, 1958-60; city mgr. City of San Dimas, 1960-64, Pico Rivera, 1964-68; chief dep. dir. Calif. Dept. Public Works, 1968-71; dir. Calif. Dept. Social Welfare, 1971-73; U.S. commr. welfare Washington, 1973-75; pres. Robert B. Carleson & Assocs., Sacramento, Calif. and Washington, 1975-81, chmn. Washington, 1987-93, 02—, San Diego, 1993-01; pres. Innovative Environ. Svcs. Ltd., Vancouver, B.C., Can., 1992; spl. asst. to with pres. for policy devel. Washington, 1981-84, prin., dir. govt. rels. KMG Main Hurdman, Washington, 1984-87; dir. transition team Dept. HHS, Office of Pres.-Elect, 1980-81; spl. adviser Office of Policy Coordination; sr. policy advisor, chmn. welfare task force Reagan Campaign, 1980. Bd. dirs. Fed. Home Loan Bank of Atlanta, 1987-90, I.E.S., Ltd., Can., Transenviro Co., USA, Churchill Co., USA; adv. com. Fed. Home Loan Mortgage Corp., 1985-87; mem. strengthening family policy coun. Nat. Policy Forum, Washington, 1994. Eagle Scout qtr. master sea scout, 1948; lt. gov. Calif. Boys' State, 1948; adv. coun. gen. govt. Rep. Nat. Com., Washington, 1980-81; sr. fellow Free Congress Found., 1994—; chmn. Am. Civil Rights Union, 1998—. Officer USN, 1953-56, USNR, 1956-63. Clubs: Masons, Rotary (pres. 1964), Army & Navy (Washington), Capitol Hill, Fairfax Hunt. Home and Office: 175 Cameron Station Blvd Alexandria VA 22304 E-mail: susancarleson@home.com

CARLIN, GEORGE DENIS, comedian; b. N.Y.C., May 12, 1937; m. Brenda Hosbrook, 1961; 1 child, Kelly Radio announcer Sta. KJOE, Shreveport, La., Sta. WEZE, Boston, Sta. KXOL, Ft. Worth, Sta. KDAY, L.A. Numerous TV appearances on Merv Griffin Show, Mike Douglas Show, Tonight Show (over 130), numerous other TV variety shows; regular on TV programs, Away We Go, 1967, John Davidson Show, 1966, Shining Time Station, 1992—, The George Carlin Show, sitcom on Fox TV, 1994-95; syndicated TV spl. The Real George Carlin, 1973; miniseries Streets of Laredo, 1995; movies include: With Six You Get Eggroll, 1968, Car Wash, 1976, Americathon, 1979, Outrageous Fortune, 1987, Justin Case, 1988, Bill & Ted's Excellent Adventure, 1989, Working Trash, 1990, Bill and Ted's Bogus Journey, 1990, Prince of Tides, 1991; albums include: At the Playboy Club Tonight, Burns and Carlin, 1960, Take-Offs & Put-Ons, 1967, FM/AM, 1972 (Grammy Award Best Comedy Record), Class Clown, 1972, Occupation: Foole, 1973; Toledo Window Box, 1974, An Evening with Wally Londo Featuring Bill Slaszo, 1975, The Original George Carlin, 1972, On The Road, 1977, Indecent Exposure, 1978, A Place for My Stuff, 1982, The Carlin Collection, 1984, Carlin On Campus, 1984, Playin' With Your Head, 1986, What Am I Doing In New Jersey, 1988, Parental Advisory—Explicit Lyrics, 1990, Jammin' in New York, 1992 (Grammy Award Best Spoken Comedy Album, 1994), Back in Town, 1996, You Are All Diseased, 1999; cable TV stand-up comedy specials include: On Location-USC Concert, 1977, On Location-Phoenix Concert, 1978, Carlin At Carnegie, 1982, Carlin On Campus, 1984, Playin' With Your Head, 1986, What Am I Doing In New Jersey, 1988, George Carlin—Doin' It Again, 1990 (Cable Ace award Best Stand Up Comedy Spl.), George Carlin: Jammin' in New York, 1992 (Cable Ace award Best Stand Up Comedy Spl.) Back In Town, 1996 (Cable Ace Awards: Best Stand-Up Comedy, Best Writing-Variety Spec.); 40 Years of Comedy, 1997, You Are All Diseased, 1999; author: Sometimes A Little Brain Damage Can Help, 1983, Brain Droppings, 1997. Office: Carlin Prodns 11911 San Vicente Blvd Los Angeles CA 90049-5086

CARLSMITH, JAMES MERRILL, psychologist, educator; b. New Orleans, Apr. 12, 1936; s. Leonard Eldon and Hope (Snedden) C.; m. Lyn Kuckenberg, July 27, 1963; children— Christopher, Kimberly, Kevin. A.B., Stanford U., 1958; Ph.D., Harvard U., 1963. Asst. prof. Yale U., 1962-64; from asst. prof. to prof. psychology Stanford U., 1964—, asso. dean grad. studies, 1972-75; fellow (Center for Advanced Study in Behavioral Scis.), 1975. Author: Social Psychology, 1970, Methods of Research In Social Psychology, 1976. Dir. Boys Town Center, 1980— . Office: Stanford U Dept Psychology Stanford CA 94305

CARLSON, ARTHUR W. lawyer; b. Chgo., Oct. 3, 1945; s. Arthur W. Sr. and Florence (Maul) C.; m. Jeri S. Waite, June 28, 1986; children: Mackenzie Waite Carlson, Sara Elizabeth Carlson. AB, Pomona Coll., 1967; JD, Duke U., 1971. Bar: Calif. 1972. Prin. Angle, Carlson & Goldrick, Santa Barbara, Calif., 1994—. Pres., bd. trustees Santa Barbara Mus. Natural History, 1990-93, 94-95. Office: Angle Carlson & Goldrick 200 E Carrillo St Ste 310 Santa Barbara CA 93101-7143

CARLSON, CURTIS R. electronics research industry executive; BS (Physics), Worchester Polytechnic Inst; MS, Rutgers U; PhD, Rutgers U. Mem. tech. staff Sarnoff Corp., Princeton, NJ, 1973-1981; founder, leader high definition TV program Sarnoff Corp. subs. SRI Internat., Princton, N.J., 1981-84; dir. Info. Systems Lab, 1984-90; vp, info. systems Sarnoff Corp., 1990-95; exec. v.p. Sarnoff Corp. subs. SRI Internat., Princton, N.J., 1995-98, past head ventures and licensing; pres., CEO SRI Internat., Menlo Park, Calif., 1998—. Co-founder, exec. dir. Nat. Info. Display Lab., 1990; past mem. adv. bd. USAF; past mem. rsch. lab. tech. assessment bd. U.S. Army; active Joint. Civilian Ops. Conf., 1996; served on several govt. task forces; cons. and presenter in field. Author 15 U.S. patents in the fields of image quality, image coding and computer vision. Mem. IEEE, Soc. Motion Picture and TV Engrs., Highlands Group (charter mem.), Sigma Xi, Tau Beta Pi. Address: 333 Ravenswood Ave Menlo Park CA 94025-3493 E-mail: inquiry.line@sri.com

CARLSON, DALE ARVID, university dean; b. Aberdeen, Wash., Jan. 10, 1925; s. Edwin C.G. and Anna A. (Anderson) C.; m. Jean M. Stanton, Nov. 11, 1948; children: Dale Ronald, Gail L. Carlson Manahan Joan M. Carlson Lee, Gwen D. Carlson Lundgren. AA, Grays Harbor Coll., 1947; BSCE, U. Wash., 1950, MS, 1951; PhD, U. Wis., 1960. Registered profl. engr., Wash. Water engr. City of Aberdeen, 1951-55; asst. prof., assoc. prof., prof., chmn. dept. civil engring. U. Wash., Seattle, 1955-76, dean (Coll Engring.), 1976-80, dean emeritus, 1980—, dir. Valle Scandinavian Exch., 1980—; chmn. dept. civil engring. Seattle U., 1983-88, acting dean sci. and engring., 1990, dean sci. and engring., 1990-92. Vis. prof. Tech. U. Denmark, Copenhagen, 1970, Royal Coll. Agr., Uppsala, Sweden, 1976, 78 Contbr. articles to profl. jours. Exec. bd. Pacific N.W. Synod Luth. Ch. in Am., chmn. fin. com., 1980-84, treas., 1986-87, bd. edn., fin. com. Evang. Luth. Ch. in Am., 1987-91; v.p. Nat. Luth. Campus Ministry, 1988-91; treas. N.W. Washington synod Evang. Luth. Ch. in Am., 1996-2000; exec. bd. Nordic Heritage Mus., 1981-86; bd. dirs. Hearthstone Retirement Ctrs., 1984-93, Evergreen Safety Coun., 1980-86. With AUS, 1943-45. Named Outstanding Grad. Weatherwax High Sch., Aberdeen, 1972, Outstanding Grad. Grays Harbor Coll., 1947; guest of honor Soppeldagene, Trondheim, 1978 Mem. ASCE, Internat. Water Acad., Am. Soc. Engring. Educators, Am. Acad. Environ. Engring., Water Pollution Control Fedn., Am. Water Works Assn., Am. Scandinavian Found., Swedish Am. C. of C. (bd. dirs. 1994-99), Norwegian Am. C. of C., Rainier Club, Chi Epsilon (hon.). Home: 9235 41st Ave NE Seattle WA 98115-3801 Office: U Wash 103 Wilson Box 352130 Seattle WA 98195-2130 E-mail: dcarlson@rio.engr.washington.edu

CARLSON, DON M. state senator; b. Wash. m. Jan Carlson; children: Rusty, Doug. BA, MA in Edn., Western Wash. U.; postgrad., U. Wash. Tchr., coach Hudson's Bay H.S., Columbia River H.S.; Rep. rep. dist. 49 Wash. Ho. of Reps., 1993-2000; Rep. senator dist. 49 Wash. State Senate, 2000—. Mem. edn., higher edn., human svcs. and corrections coms. Wash. State Senate, Rep. asst. floor leader; commr. Western Interstate Commn. on Higher Edn.; mem. Joint Com. on Pension Policy, Oral History Review Bd. Precinct committeeman Clark County Bd. Adjustment, 1970—; bd. dirs. Mainstream Reps. Wash.; coach baseball, softball; former coach volleyball Columbia River H.S., Clark Coll.; mem. First Christian Ch.; mem. adv. bd. Ft. Vancouver Seafirst Co. Recipient Medal of Honor award DAR, VIP award Coll. Women's Programs Coun., award Clark Coll. Hall of Fame, Cornerstone award Assn. Wash. Bus., Guardian of Small Bus. award Nat. Fedn. Ind. Bus., Legis. Excellence award Wash. State Ret. Tchr. Assn., Legis. Extraordinaire award Wash. Pub. Employees Assn., Outstanding Legislator award Wash. Paralyzed Vet. Am. Mem. Vancouver C. of C. Office: PO Box 40449 106B Irv Newhouse Bldg Olympia WA 98504-0449 Fax: 360 786-7819. E-mail: carlson_do@leg.wa.gov

CARLSON, GARY LEE, public relations executive, director, producer; b. Yakima, Wash., Oct. 15, 1954; s. Glenn Elmer and Helen Mary (McLean) Carlson. AA, Yakima Community Coll., 1975; BA in Communications, U. Wash., 1977. Dir. pub. affairs Sta. KCMU, Seattle, 1976-77; dir. programming and promotions Sta. KAPP-TV, Yakima, 1978-80; dir. promotions Sta. WBZ-TV, Boston, 1980-84; producer Sta. KCBS-TV, Los Angeles, 1985; dir. creative services Metromedia Producers, Los Angeles, 1985-86; dir. promotion publicity 20th Century Fox, Los Angeles, 1986—. Writer: (TV animation program) Bruno, the Kid, 1996; writer, co-prodr. (TV movie) Coaching a Murder, 1994; prodr., dir. M*A*S*H* 15th Ann. Campaign, 1987 (Internat. Film and TV Festival N.Y. award), The Fox Tradition, 1988 (Internat. Film and TV Festival N.Y. award, Clio finalist award 1988, Telly award 1988, B.P.M.E. award 1988); prodr., writer, dir. Consumer Reports, 1983 (Internat. Film and TV Festival N.Y. award, Houston Internat. Film and TV award). Mem. Broadcast Promotion and Mktg. Execs., Nat. Assn. TV Program Execs., Beta Theta Pi. Avocations: photography, scuba diving, history, traveling. Home: 1510 Rock Glen Ave Glendale CA 91205-2063 Office: 20th Century Fox Film Corp PO Box 900 Beverly Hills CA 90213-0900

CARLSON, GARY R. publishing executive; b. Ishpeming, Mich. s. James H. and Vivian M. (Maki) C.; m. Mardee G. Parkinson, Aug. 21, 1963 (div.Apr. 21, 1991); children: Bruce S., Robyn L.; m. Maryanne Koschier, June 25, 1994. BA Far Eastern Langs. and Lit., U. Mich., 1969. Sales rep. John Wiley and Sons, Ann Arbor, Mich., 1970-72, editor N.Y.C., 1972-80, pub., 1980-84; pres. SoftPress, Inc., Monroe, N.Y., 1984-86; v.p., dir. acquisitions W.H. Freeman and Co./Scientific Am. Books, N.Y.C., 1986-92; v.p., editor-in-chief Macmillan Coll. Pub., Inc., N.Y.C., 1992-94; v.p., editorial dir., publisher Wadsworth Pub. Co., Belmont, Calif., 1994-97; pub., exec. editor Brooks Cole Pub., 1990-2000; pub. cons., 2000—. Editor: (textbooks and trade books) General Chemistry by James B. Brady, 1975, Organic Chemistry by T.W.G. Solomons, 1976, Fundamentals of General, Organic and Biological Chemistry by John R. Holom, 1978, Basic Inorganic Chemistry by A. Cotton and G. Wilkinson, 1977; contbg. author: The Videodisc Book, 1984. With USAF, 1963-69, Taiwan. Mem. Am. Assn. Pubs. Office: Wadsworth Pub Co 10 Davis Dr Belmont CA 94002-3002

CARLSON, JAMES ROY, animal science educator; b. Windsor, Colo., Mar. 9, 1939; married; two children. BS, Colo. State U., 1961; MS, U. Wis., 1964, PhD in Biochemistry, 1966. From asst. prof. animal sci. Wash. State U., 1966-70, assoc. prof. animal sci., 1971-75, chmn. grad. program nutrition, 1973-83, prof. animal sci., 1976-96, assoc. dean of rsch., 1996-2000, assoc. dean emeritus. Chmn. dept. animal sci. Wash. State U., 1982-93, assoc. dir. agr. rsch. ctr., 1993-94, assoc. dean agr. rsch. ctr., 1994—. Mem. Am. Inst. Nutrition, Am. Soc. Animal Sci., Soc. Exptl. Biol. Medicine. Office: 325 SE Derby St Pullman WA 99163-2219

CARLSON, JOHN EARL, lawyer; b. Seattle, May 18, 1952; s. William Richard and H. Joan (Fitzpatrick) C.; m. Audrey Fucilla, Aug. 31, 1984; children: William Grant, Andrew Ivan. AA, Wenatchee Valley Coll., 1972; BA, U. Wash., 1975; JD, U. Puget Sound, 1978. Bar: Wash. 1975, Ill. 1980, Calif. 1980. Asst. to pres. ABA, Chgo., 1978-80; assoc. Lawler, Felix & Hall, L.A., 1980-84, Brobeck, Phleger & Harrison, San Francisco, 1984-86, ptnr., 1986—. Bd. visitors Sch. Law, U. Puget Sound, Tacoma, 1982—. Mem. ABA (nat. v.p. law student divsn. 1977-78), Wash. State Bar Assn., Bar Assn. of San Francisco (chmn. bridge the gap com. 1985-87), State Bar of Calif., Ill. State Bar Assn. Roman Catholic. Avocations: basketball, skiing, running, art. Office: Brobeck Phleger & Harrison Spear St Tower 1 Market Plz Fl 31 San Francisco CA 94105-1100

CARLSON, ROBERT CODNER, industrial engineering educator; b. Granite Falls, Minn., Jan. 17, 1939; s. Robert Ledin and Ada Louise (Codner) C.; children: Brian William, Andrew Robert, Christina Louise. BSME, Cornell U., 1962; MS, Johns Hopkins U., 1963, PhD, 1976. Mem. tech. staff Bell Tel. Labs., Holmdel, N.J., 1962-70; asst. prof. Stanford (Calif.) U., Stanford, 1970-77, assoc. prof., 1977-82, prof. indsl. engring., 1982-2000, prof. mgmt. sci. & engring., 2000—. Program dir., lectr., cons. various spl. programs U.S., Japan, France, 1971—; cons. Japan Mgmt. Assn., Tokyo, 1990—, Raychem, Menlo Park, Calif., 1989—, GKN Automotive, London, 1989—, Rockwell Internat., L.A., 1988—; vis. prof. U. Calif., Berkeley, 1987-88, Dartmouth Coll., Hanover, N.J., 1978-79; vis. faculty Internat. Mgmt. Inst., Geneva, 1984, 88. Contbr. articles to profl. jours. Recipient Maxwell Upson award in Mech. Engring. Cornell U., 1962; Bell Labs. Systems Engring. fellow, 1962-63, Bell Labs. Doctoral Support fellow, 1966-67. Mem. INFORMS (chmn. membership com. 1981-83), Inst. Indsl. Engrs., Am. Soc. Engring. Edn., Am. Prodn. and Inventory Control Soc. (bd. dirs. 1975-81), Tau Beta Pi, Phi Kappa Phi, Pi Tau Sigma, Soc. of Enophiles Club (Woodside, Calif.). Avocations: wine tasting, travelling. Office: Stanford Univ Dept Mgmt Sci & Engring Stanford CA 94305-4026 E-mail: r.c.carlson@stanford.edu

CARLSON, ROBERT EDWIN, lawyer; b. Bklyn., Oct. 11, 1930; s. Harry Victor and Lenore Marie (Hanrahan) C.; m. Maureen Eleanor Donnelly, Aug. 24, 1963; children: John T., Katherine L., Elizabeth A., Robert E. Jr. BS, U. Oreg., 1953; JD, U. Calif., San Francisco, 1958; LLM, Harvard U., 1963. Bar: Calif. 1959, U.S. Dist. Ct. (ctrl. dist.) Calif. 1959, U.S. Ct. Appeals (9th cir.) 1959. Assoc. Kindel & Anderson, L.A., 1958-63, ptnr., 1963-67, Agnew, Miller & Carlson, L.A., 1967-80, Hufstedler, Miller, Carlson & Beardsley, L.A., 1980-88, Paul, Hastings, Janofsky & Walker, L.A., 1988—. Pres. Constl. Rights Found., L.A., 1978-80, L.A. County Bar Found., 1988-89; mem. exec. com. bus. sect. L.A. Bar Assn., 1982-89; bd. dirs. Legal Aid Found., L.A. Bd. dirs. Westridge Sch. for Girls, Pasadena, Calif., 1985-91, Trust for Pub. Land, San Francisco, 1987—; chair bd. Skid Row Housing Trust, L.A., 1989—, Pasadena Cmty. Found.; bd. visitors Santa Clara Law Sch., 1986-92. With U.S. Army, 1953-55. Recipient Griffin Bell award Dispute Resolution Svcs., Inc., 1992, Katherine Krause award Inner City Law Ctr., 1996. Mem. ABA (mem. securities com., co-chair com. devel. investment svcs., mem. task force to prepare guidebook for dirs. mut. funds 1995, chairperson youth edn. for citizenship, Chgo. 1982-85), Calif. State Bar (mem. corp. com. 1990—), Valley Hunt Club, Chancery Club, Calif. Club. Democrat. Avocations: hiking, tennis, reading, skiing. Office: Paul Hastings Janofsky & Walker 555 S Flower St Fl 23 Los Angeles CA 90071-2300 E-mail: robertcarlson@paulhastings.com

CARLSON, ROBERT MICHAEL, artist; b. Bklyn., Nov. 19, 1952; s. Sidney Carlson and Vickey (Mihaloff) Woodward; m. Linda Schneider; m. Mary Elizabeth Fontaine, Feb. 24, 1984; 1 child, Nora. Student, CCNY, 1970-73; studied with Flora Mace and Joey Kirkpatrick, Pilchuck Glass Sch., 1981, studied with Dan Dailey, 1982. Teaching asst. Pilchuck Sch., Stanwood, Wash., 1986, 88, mem. faculty, 1989-90, 92, 95, Pratt Fine Arts Ctr., Seattle, 1988-90, Penland (N.C.) Sch. Crafts, 1994, Bild-Werk Sch., Germany, 1996-2000. Mem. artists adv. com. Pilchuck Sch., 1989, 90; vis. artist Calif. Coll. Arts and Crafts, Oakland, 1989, Calif. State U., Fullerton, 1991, blossom summer program Kent State U., Ohio, 1991, U. Ill., Urbana-Champaign, 1993, Toledo Mus. of Art Sch., 1994; visual-artist-in-residence Centrum Found., Port Townsend, Wash., 1992; prof. artist-in-residence Pilchuck Sch., Wash. One-man shows include Foster White Gallery, Seattle, 1987, 90, 92, The Glass Gallery, Bethesda, Md., 1988, Heller Gallery, N.Y.C., 1989, 95, Betsy Rosenfield Gallery, Chgo., 1991, 92, MIA Gallery, Seattle, 1994, Haratat Gall. Florida, 1998, William Traver Gall., Swattle, 2000, others; exhibited in group shows at Traver Gallery, Seattle, 1984, 89, Mindscape Gallery, Evanston, Ill., 1984, 86, T[illegible] Mus. Art., 1984 (Purchase award), 86 (Award of Merit), Hand and Spirit Gallery, Scottsdale, Ariz., 1985, 86, Craftsman Gallery, Scarsdale, N.Y.,

1985, Robert Kidd Gallery, Birmingham, Mich., 1985, 88, Gazebo Gallery, Gatlinburg, Tenn., 1985, The Glass Gallery, Bethesda, Md., 1986 (Jurors award), 91, 92, 94, Artists Soc. Internat., San Francisco, 1987 (Critics Choice award), William Traver Gallery, Seattle, 1987, 90, 91, 92, Japan Glass Artcrafts Assn., Tokyo, 1987, Heller Gallery, 1988, 89, 90, 91, 93, 94, 95, 96, 97, Washington Sq. Ptnrs., 1988, Foster White Gallery, 1988, 90, Bellvue Art Mus., Wash., 1988, 91, 94, Am. Arts and Crafts Inc., San Francisco, 1989, Mus. Craft and Folk Art, San Francisco, 1989, Great Am. Gallery, Atlanta, 1989, Dorothy Weiss Gallery, San Francisco, 1989, Habitat Gallery, Farmington Hills, Mich., 1990, 93, Philabaum Gallery, Tucson, 1990, Greg Kucera Gallery, Seattle, 1990, Connell Gallery, Atlanta, 1990, Net Contents Gallery, Bainbridge Island, Wash., 1991, Seattle Tacoma Internat. Airport Installation, 1991, 95, Pratt Fine Arts Ctr., Seattle, 1991, Crystalex, Novy Bor, Czechoslovakia, 1991, Whatcom County Mus., Bellingham, Wash., 1992, Art Gallery West Australia, 1992, 1004 Gallery, Port Townsend, 1992, Bainbridge Island Arts Coun., 1992, MIA Gallery, 1993, Betsy Rosenfield Gallery, Chgo., 1993, Blue Spiral Gallery, Asheville, N.C., 1995, Huntington Mus., 1996, Salem Art Assn., 1996, Judy Yovens Gallery, Houston, 1997, Internat. Glass Art Exchange, Tucson, 1997, Habatat Gallery, Boca Raton, Fla., 1998, Habatat Gallery, Farmington Hills, Mich., 1998, Tampa (Fla.) Mus. Art, 1998, Traver Gall., 2001, Glass Gall., 2201, Habatat Gall., 2000, Glasmus., 2000, Kentucky Art & Luak Gall., 2000; represented in permanent collections Corning (N.Y.) Mus. Glass, Tucson Mus. Art, Toledo Mus. Art, Glasmuseum Frauenau, Germany, Glasmuseum Ebeltoft, Denmark, Valley Nat. Bank, Phoenix, Fountain Assocs., Portland, Oreg., Iceland Air Co., Reykjavik, Iceland, Crocker Banks, L.A., Davis Wright Tremain, Seattle, Meiwa Trading Co., Tokyo, Safeco Ins. Corp., Seattle, Crystalex Corp., L.A. County Mus. Art. Bd. dirs. Am. Craft Counc., 1996-99. Fellow Tucson Pima Arts Coun., 1987, NEA, 1990; John Hauberg fellow, 2000. Mem. Glass Art Soc. (conf. lectr. 1991, bd. dirs. 1992-94, v.p. 1993-94, pres. 1995-96). Office: PO Box 11590 Bainbridge Island WA 98110 E-mail: bobwhan@earthlink.net

CARLSON, ROBERT WELLS, physician, educator; b. Concord, Calif., Apr. 14, 1952; s. Robert L. Carlson and Mae E. Fox. BS in Biol. Sci., Stanford U., 1974, MD, 1978. Diplomate Am. Bd. Internal Medicine, Am. Bd. Med. Oncology. Intern Barnes Hosp., St. Louis, 1978-79, resident, 1979-80, Stanford (Calif.) Univ. Hosp., 1980-81; fellow Stanford U., 1981-83, clin. asst. prof., 1983-85, asst. prof., 1985-92, assoc. prof., 1992-97, prof., 1997—; assoc. chief for clin. affairs div. oncology, 1994-96. Exec. officer No. Calif. Oncology Group, Palo Alto, Calif., 1984-87, group chmn., 1987-91. Bd. dirs. Theatreworks, Palo Alto, 1994-99. Recipient Career Devel. award Am. Cancer Soc., 1987-90. Fellow ACP; mem. Am. Soc. Clin. Oncology, Am. Assn. Cancer Rsch. Office: Stanford U Oncology Day Care Clinic Stanford Med Ctr H0274 Stanford CA 94305

CARLSON, THOMAS EDWARD, judge; b. 1947; m. Cynthia Hustad. BA, Beloit Coll., 1969; JD, Harvard U., 1975; LLM, NYU, 1985. Bar: Calif. 1976; U.S. Dist. Ct. (no. dist.) Calif. 1977, U.S. Dist. Ct. (cen. dist.) Calif. 1984, U.S. Ct. Appeals (9th cir.) 1978. Law clk. to Hon. Thomas Roberts Supreme Ct. R.I., 1975-76; law clk. to Hon. Donald Wright Supreme Ct. Calif., 1976-77; assoc. atty. Cooper, White & Cooper, San Francisco, 1977-78; dep. staff dir. Ninth Cir. Ct. Appeals, San Francisco, 1978-84; judge U.S. Bankruptcy Ct. No. Dist. Calif., San Francisco, 1985—. Mem. Nat. Conf. Bankruptcy Judges. Office: US Bankruptcy Ct Calif PO Box 7341 235 Pine St San Francisco CA 94120

CARLTON, MAGGIE, state legislator; b. St. Louis, July 24, 1957; m. Merritt Carlton; children: M. Grace, Lucy. Mem. Nev. Senate, 1998—, mem. commerce and labor com.; mem. legis. affairs and operation com. Nev. State Senate, mem. natural resources com. Democrat. Home: 5540 Cartwright Ave Las Vegas NV 89110-3802 E-mail: mcarlton@sen.state.nv.us

CARMACK, MILDRED JEAN, retired lawyer; b. Folsom, Calif., Sept. 3, 1938; d. Kermit Leroy Brown and Elsie Imogene (Johnston) Walker; m. Allan W. Carmack, 1957 (div. 1979); 1 child, Kerry Jean Carmack Garrett. Student, Linfield Coll., 1955-58; BA, U. Oreg., 1967, JD, 1969. Bar: Oreg. 1969, U.S. Dist. Ct. Oreg. 1980, U.S. Ct. Appeals (9th and fed. cirs.) 1980, U. S. Claims Ct. 1987. Law clk. to Hon. William McAllister Oreg. Supreme Ct., Salem, 1969-73, asst. to ct., 1976-80; asst. prof. U. Oreg. Law Sch., Eugene, 1973-76; assoc. Schwabe, Williamson & Wyatt, Portland, Oreg., 1980-83, ptnr., 1984-96, ret., 1996. Writer, lectr., legal educator, Oreg., 1969—; mem. exec. bd. Appellate sect. Oreg. State Bar, 1993-95. Contbr. articles to Oreg. Law Rev., 1967-70. Mem. citizen adv. com. State Coastal Planning Commn., Oreg., 1974 76, State Senate Judiciary Com., Oreg., 1984; mem. bd. visitors Law Sch. U. Oreg., 1992-95; mem. Oreg. Law Commn. Working Group on Conflict of Laws, 2000. Mem. Oreg. State Bar Assn., Order of Coif.

CARMAN, MICHAEL DENNIS, museum director; b. Monahans, Tex., Nov. 6, 1938; s. Herbert Charles and Marie Noelie (Watkins) C.; m. Malica Jean Brunet, Jan. 27, 1967 (div. June 1984); m. Sharon Ruth Morrisson, Nov. 29, 1985. BA in History, San Diego State U., 1970, MA in History, 1973. Commd. USN, 1956, advanced through grades to petty officer I, resigned, 1966; curator San Diego Hist. Soc., 1973-77, Pioneers Mus., Colorado Springs, Colo., 1978-82; chief curator Network Curatorial Services, Colorado Springs, 1982-84; dir. Ariz. State Capitol Mus., Phoenix, 1984—. Author: United States Customs and the Madero Revolution, 1975; contbr. articles to profl. jours. Mem. Am. Assn. Mus. (MAP evaluator 1980-86, curator com., sec. 1982-83), Am. Assn. State and Local History (rep. 1974-77, cons. 1975—), Mus. Assn. Ariz., Cen. Ariz. Mus. Assn. (v.p. 1987-89). Club: Phoenix City. Avocations: woodwork, hiking, photography. Office: Ariz State Capitol Mus 1700 W Washington St Phoenix AZ 85007-2812

CARMICHAEL, DAVID RICHARD, lawyer; BS, UCLA, 1964, JD, 1967. Bar: Calif. 1968. Assoc. Adams, Duque & Hazeltine, 1967-72; gen. counsel The Housing Group, Irvine, Calif., 1972-77; assoc. counsel Pacific Mut. Life Ins. Co., 1977-81, 2nd v.p., assoc. gen. counsel, 1981-89, v.p., investment counsel, 1989-92, sr. v.p., gen. counsel, 1992—. Office: Pacific Life Ins Co 700 Newport Center Dr Newport Beach CA 92660-6307

CARMICHAEL, IAN STUART EDWARD, geologist, educator; b. London, England, Mar. 29, 1930; came to U.S., 1964; s. Edward Arnold and Jeanette (Montgomerie) C.; children by previous marriages: Deborah, Graham, Alistair, Anthea. B.A., Cambridge U., Eng., 1954; Ph.D., Imperial Coll. Sci., London U., 1958. Lectr. geology Imperial Coll. Sci. and Tech., 1958-63; NSF sr. fgn. sci. fellow U. Chgo., 1964; mem. faculty U. Calif.-Berkeley, 1964—, prof. geology, 1967—, chmn. dept., 1972-76, 80-82, assoc. dean, 1976-78, 85-00, assoc. provost, 1986-2000, dir. Lawrence Hall of Sci., 1996—, acting dir. bot. garden, 1996-98. Author: Igneous Petrology, 1974; editor-in-chief Contbns. to Mineralogy and Petrology, 1973-90; contbr. numerous papers to profl. jours. Guggenheim fellow, 1992; recipient Arthur L. Day medal Geol. Soc. Am., 1991. Fellow Royal Soc. London, Mineral Soc. Am. (Roebling medal 1997), Mineral Soc. Gt. Britain (Schlumberger medal 1992), Am. Geophys. Union (Bowen award 1986), Geol. Soc. of London (Murchison medal 1995). Office: U Calif Berkeley Dept Earth/Planetary Sci Berkeley CA 94720-4767

CARNAHAN, ORVILLE DARRELL, retired state legislator, retired college president; b. Elba, Idaho, Dec. 25, 1929; s. Marion Carlos and Leola Pearl (Putnam) C.; m. Colleen Arrott, Dec. 14, 1951; children: Karen, Jeanie, Orville Darrell, Carla. B.S., Utah State U., 1958; M.Ed., U. Idaho, 1962, Ed.D., 1964. Vocat. dir., v.p. Yakima (Wash.) Valley Coll., Yakima, Wash., 1964-69; chancellor Eastern Iowa C.C. Dist., Davenport, 1969-71; pres. Highline Coll., Midway Wash., 1971-76; assoc. Utah Commr. for Higher Edn., Salt Lake City, 1976-78; pres. So. Utah U., Cedar City, 1978-81, Salt Lake C.C., Salt Lake City, 1981-90, pres. emeritus, 1990-98; mem. Utah Ho. of Reps., 1993-99; ret., 1999. Cons. in field. Active Boy Scouts Am. Served with U.S. Army, 1952-54, Korea. Mem. Am. Vocat. Assn., NEA, Idaho Hist. Soc., Utah Hist. Soc., Alpha Tau Alpha, Phi Delta Kappa, Rotary Internat. Mem. Ch. of Jesus Christ of Latter-Day Saints. Home: 1653 Cornerstone Dr South Jordan UT 84095-5501 Office: Salt Lake Community Coll 4600 S Redwood Rd Salt Lake City UT 84123-3197

CARNESALE, ALBERT, university chancellor; b. Bronx, N.Y., July 2, 1936; two children: Keith, Kimberly. BME, Cooper Union, 1957; MS, Drexel U., 1961, LLD (hon.), 1993; PhD, N.C. State U., 1966, LLD (hon.), 1997; AM (hon.), Harvard U., 1979; ScD (hon.), N.J. Inst. Technology, 1984. Prof. N.C. State U., Raleigh, 1962-69, 72-74; chief Def. Weapons Systems U.S. Arms Control and Disarmament Agy., Washington, 1969-72; prof. John F. Kennedy Sch. of Govt. Harvard U., Cambridge, Mass., 1974-97, acad. dean John F. Kennedy Sch. of Govt., 1981-91, dean John F. Kennedy Sch. of Govt., 1991-95, provost, Lucius N. Littauer Prof. Pub. Policy and Adminstrn., 1994-97; chancellor UCLA, 1997—. Author: New Nuclear Nations: Consequences for US Policy, 1993, Fateful Visions: Avoiding Nuclear Catastrophe, 1988, Superpower Arms Control: Setting the Record Straight, 1987, Hawks, Doves, and Owls: An Agenda for Avoiding Nuclear War, 1985, Living with Nuclear Weapons, 1983, Nuclear Power Issues and Choices: Report of the Nuclear Energy Policy Study Group, 1977. Gano Dunn award for Outstanding Profl. Achievement, Cooper Union, N.Y.C. Fellow Am. Acad. Arts and Scis.; mem. Coun. on Fgn. Rels., Internat. Inst. for Strategic Studies, L.A. World Affairs Coun. Office: U of Calif Office of the Chancellor 405 Hilgard Ave Los Angeles CA 90095-1405

CARNEY, JOHN MICHAEL, professional football player; b. Hartford, Conn., Apr. 20, 1964; Degree in mktg., U. Notre Dame, 1987. Place kicker Tampa Bay (Fla.) Buccaneers, 1988-89, San Diego Chargers, 1990—. Named to Sporting News NFL All-Pro Team, 1994, selected to Pro Bowl, 1994. Achievements include holding NFL record for most consecutive field goals (29), Nov. 1992-Sept. 1993; tied for NFL field goals (34), 1994. Office: Qualcomm Stadium Jack Murphy Field care San Diego Chargers PO Box 609609 San Diego CA 92160-9609

CARNOCHAN, WALTER BLISS, retired humanities educator; b. N.Y.C., Dec. 20, 1930; s. Gouverneur Morris and Sibyll Baldwin (Bliss) C.; m. Nancy Powers Carter, June 25, 1955 (div. 1978); children— Lisa Powers, Sarah Bliss, Gouverneur Morris, Sibyll Carter; m. Brigitte Hoy Fields, Sept. 16, 1979. A.B., Harvard, 1953, A.M., 1957, Ph.D., 1960. Asst. dean freshmen Harvard U., 1954-56; successively instr., asst. prof., assoc. prof., prof. English, Stanford (Calif.) U., 1960-94, prof. emeritus, 1994—, chmn. dept. English, 1971-73, dean grad. studies, 1975-80, vice provost, 1976-80, dir. Stanford Humanities Ctr., 1985-91, Anthony P. Meier Family prof. humanities, 1988-91, Richard W. Lyman prof. humanities, 1993-94, Richard W. Lyman prof. emeritus, 1994—, acting dir. Stanford Humanities Ctr., 1999. Mem. overseers com. to visit Harvard Coll, 1979-85, mem. bd. advisors Ehrenpreis Ctr. for Swift Studies, 1984—. Author: Lemuel Gulliver's Mirror for Man, 1968, Confinement and Flight: An Essay on English Literature of the 18th Century, 1977, Gibbon's Solitude: The Inward World of the Historian, 1987, The Battleground of the Curriculum: Liberal Education and American Experience, 1993, Momentary Bliss: An American Memoir, 1999. Trustee Mills Coll., 1978-85, Athenian Sch., 1975-88, Berkeley (Calif.) Art Mus., 1983-96, 98-2001. Home: 138 Cervantes Rd Portola Valley CA 94028-7725 Office: Stanford U Dept English Stanford CA 94305-2087 E-mail: carnochan@stanford.edu

CARON, ERNIE MATTHEW, airport executive; b. Morinville, Alta., Can., Sept. 15, 1938; m. Ellen Kinsella; 4 children. Grad., Banff Sch. Advanced Mgmt., 1977. V.p. eastern region Can. Airlines Internat., v.p. customer svc., v.p. properties and facilities, v.p. airports N.Am.; pres., CEO Calgary Airport Authority, 1992—. Vice-chmn. Calgary Econ. Devel. Authority Adv. Coun., 1996—, Can. Airports Coun., pres. com. of mgmt. Bd. dirs. Calgary Conv. and Visitors Bur., 1994—. Mem. Calgary Rotary Club. Avocations: racing horses, skiing, golfing. Office: Calgary Airport Authority 2000 Airport Rd NE Calgary AB Canada T2E 6W5

CAROOMPAS, CAROLE JEAN, artist, educator; b. Oregon City, Oreg., Nov. 14, 1946; d. John Thomas and Dorothy Lietta (Dirks) C. BA, Calif. State U., Fullerton, 1968; MFA in Painting, U. So. Calif., 1971. Instr. El Camino Coll., Torrance, Calif., 1971-72; vis. artist Calif. State U., Northridge, 1972-75; instr. Immaculate Heart Coll., L.A., 1973-76; vis. artist Calif. State U., Fullerton, 1976-78; instr. U. Calif., Irvine, 1976-80, Claremont (Calif.) Grad. Sch., 1976-79, Art Ctr. Coll. of Design, Pasadena, 1978-86, UCLA Extension, L.A., 1984-93; assoc. prof. fine arts Otis Coll. Art and Design, L.A., 1981—. Vis. artist Anderson Ranch Art Ctr., Aspen, Colo., 1996, 98. One-woman shows include Jan Baum Art Gallery, L.A., 1978-82, Karl Bornstein Gallery, L.A., 1985, L.A. Contemporary Exhbns., 1989, U. Calif., Irvine, 1990, Sue Spaid Fine Art, L.A., 1992, 94, P.P.O.W., N.Y.C., 1994, Otis Coll. of Art and Design Art Gallery, 1997-98, Mark Moore Gallery, Santa Monica, 1997, 99, Mark Moore Gallery, 2000; exhibited in group shows at Pasadena Mus. Art, 1972, Whitney Mus. of Art, 1978, Mus. Modern Art, N.Y.C., 1976, L.A. County Mus., 1982, Corcoran Gallery of Art, 43rd Biennial Exhbn. of Contemporary Am. Painting, Washington, 1993, Under Contstrn. Armory Ctr. for Arts, Pasadena, 1995, UCLA Hammer Mus. of Art, L.A., 1996, Art Gallery, L.A., 1997, L.A. County Mus. Art, 1996, Beaver Coll., 1996, L.A. Mcpl. Art Gallery, 1997, UCLA Hammer Mus. Art, 2000, Calif. State U., Fullerton, 2001; also a vocalist; recs. include 2 individual albums and inclusion in The Record: 13 Vocal Artists; contbr. articles to Paris Rev., Dreamworks, Whitewalls. NEA grantee, 1987, 93, faculty devel. grantee New Sch. of Social Rsch., 1989, support grantee Esther and Adolph Gottlieb Found., 1993; Guggenheim Meml. fellow, 1995. Office: Otis Coll Art and Design 9045 Lincoln Blvd Los Angeles CA 90045-3505

CARPENETI, WALTER L. state supreme court justice; b. San Francisco, 1945; m. Anne Dose, 1969; children: Christian, Marianna, Lia, Bianca. AB in History with distinction, Stanford U., 1967; JD, U. Calif., Berkeley, 1970. Law clk. Justice John H. Dimond Alaska Supreme Ct., 1970-71; pvt. practice San Francisco, 1972-74; pub. defender Juneau, Alaska, 1974-78; with William T. Council, 1978-81; judge Alaska Superior Ct., Juneau, 1981-98, state supreme ct. justice, 1998—. Office: Alaska Supreme Ct 123 4th St Juneau AK 99801-1141

CARPENTER, FRANK CHARLES, JR. retired electronics engineer; b. L.A., June 1, 1917; s. Frank Charles and Isobel (Crump) C.; A.A., Pasadena City Coll., 1961; B.S. in Elec. Engring. cum laude, Calif. State U.-Long Beach, 1975, M.S. in Elec. Engring., 1981; m. Beatrice Josephine Jolly, Nov. 3, 1951; children— Robert Douglas, Gail Susan, Carol Ann. Self-employed design and mfgr. aircraft test equipment, Los Angeles, 1946-51; engr. Hoffman Electronics Corp., Los Angeles, 1951-56, sr. engr., 1956-59, project mgr., 1959-63; engr.-scientist McDonnell-Douglas Astronautics Corp., Huntington Beach, Calif., 1963-69, spacecraft telemetry, 1963-67, biomed. electronics, 1967-69, flight test instrumentation, 1969-76; lab. test engr. Northrop Corp., Hawthorne, Calif., 1976-82, spl. engr., 1982-83; mgr. transducer calibration lab. Northrop Corp., Pico-Rivera, Calif., 1983-86. Served with USNR, 1941-47. Mem. IEEE (life), Amateur Radio Relay League. Contbr. articles to profl. jours. Patentee transistor squelch circuit; helicaland whip antenna. Home: 2037 Balearic Dr Costa Mesa CA 92626-3514

CARPENTER, KENNETH JOHN, nutrition educator; b. London, May 17, 1923; came to U.S., 1977; s. James Frederick and Dorothy (George) C.; m. Daphne Holmes, June 22, 1944 (dec. 1974); 1 child, Roger Hugh; m. Antonina Pecoraro, June 18, 1977. BA, U. Cambridge, Eng., 1944, PhD, 1948, ScD, 1974. Mem. sci. staff Rowett Inst., Aberdeen, Scotland, 1948-56; lectr., then reader in nutrition U. Cambridge, 1956-77; prof. nutrition U. Calif., Berkeley, 1977-91. Author: History of Scurvy and Vitamin C, 1986, Protein and Energy, 1994, Beriberi, WhiteRice and Vitamin B, 2000; editor: Pellagra, 1982. Kellogg fellow Harvard U., 1955-56, Commonwealth fellow Cen. Food Tech. Rsch. Inst., Mysore, India, 1961, fellow Sidney Sussex Coll., Cambridge, U.K., 1961-77. Fellow Am. Inst. Nutrition (Atwater medal 1993, Hatch medal 1993); mem. History of Sci. Soc. Avocations: art history, gardening. Home: 6201 Rockwell St Oakland CA 94618-1350 Office: U Calif Dept Nutritional Sci Berkeley CA 94720-3104 E-mail: kcarp@uclink.berkeley.edu

CARPENTER, RAY WARREN, materials scientist and engineer, educator; b. Berkeley, Calif., 1934; s. Fritz Josh and Ethel Thordis (Davisson) C.; m. Ann Louise Leavitt, July 10, 1955; children: Shannon R., Sheila A., Matthew L. BS in Engring., U. Calif., Berkeley, 1958, MS in Metallurgy, 1959, PhD in Metallurgy, 1966. Registered profl. engr., Calif. Sr. engr. Aerojet-Gen. Nucleonics, San Ramon, Calif., 1959-64; sr. metallurgist Stanford Rsch Inst., Menlo Park, 1966-67; mem. sr. rsch. staff Oak Ridge (Tenn.) Nat. Lab., 1967-80; prof. Solid State Sci. & Engring. Ariz. State U., Tempe, 1980—, dir. Facility for High Resolution Electron Microscopy, 1980-83, dir. Ctr. for Solid State Sci., 1985-91, also bd. dirs. Ctr. for Solid State Sci. Chmn. doctoral program on sci. and engring. of materials, 1987-90, 94-98; vis. prof. U. Tenn., 1976-78; adj. prof. Vanderbilt U., Nashville, 1979-81. Contbg. author books; contbr. articles to profl. rsch. jour. and symposia; editor Phys. and Material Scis., Jour. of the Microscopy Soc. of Am., 1994-97; editor Microscopy and Microanalysis, 1995-2000. Recipient awards, Internat. Metallographic Soc. and Am. Soc. for Metals competition, 1976, 77, 79; Faculty Disting. Achievement award Ariz. State U. Alumni Assn., 1990. Mem. Electron Microscopy Soc. Am. (pres. 1989, dir. phys. sci. 1980-83), Metall. Soc. of AIME, Materials Rsch. Soc., Am. Phys. Soc., Am. Ceramic Soc., Sigma Xi. Office: Ariz State U Ctr Solid State Sci Tempe AZ 85287-1704 E-mail: carpenter@asu.edu

CARR, GERALD FRANCIS, German educator; b. Pitts., Dec. 29, 1930; s. James Patrick and Hannah (Sweeney) C.; m. Irmengard Rauch, June 12, 1965; children: Christopher, Gregory. BEd, Duquesne U., 1958; MA, U. Wis., 1960, PhD, 1968. Instr. in German Duquesne U., Pitts., 1960-62, asst. prof. German, 1964-68; tchg. asst. U. Wis., Madison, 1962-64; asst. prof. German Ea. Ill. U., Charleston, 1968-70, assoc. prof. German, 1970-75, prof. German, 1975-87, Calif. State U., Sacramento, 1987—. Co-editor: Linguistic Method: Essays in Honor of Herbert Penzl, 1979, The Signifying Animal: The Grammar of Language and Experience, 1980, Language Change, 1983, The Semiotic Bridge, 1989, On Germanic Linguistics, 1992, Insights in Germanic Linguistics I, 1995, II, 1996, Semiotics Around the World, 1996, Interdigitations: Essays for Irmengard Rauch, 1998, New Insights in Germanic Linguistics I, 1999, II, 2000; series editor: Studies in Old Germanic Languages and Literatures; assoc. editor Interdisciplinary Jour. for Germanic Linguistics and Semiotic Analysis. Cpl. USMC, 1951-54. Dist. tchg. fellow U. Wis., 1966. Mem. MLA, Internat. Assn. for Semiotic Studies (co-dir. 5th congress 1994), Am. Coun. Tchrs. Fgn. Lang., Semiotic Soc. Am., Am. Assn. Tchrs. of German, Soc. German Philology, Calif. Fgn. Lang. Tchr. Assn., Semiotic Circle Calif., Kappa Phi Kappa, Delta Phi Alpha. Avocations: books, antiques. Office: Calif State U 6000 J St Sacramento CA 95819-2605

CARR, JAMES FRANCIS, lawyer; b. Buffalo, May 7, 1946; s. Maurice Kilner and Cecelia Francis (Harmon) C.; children: James Robert, Marguerite Louise. BS, USAF Acad., 1968; JD, George Washington U., 1971. Bar: D.C. 1972, Mich. 1972, Pa. 1972, U.S. Dist. Ct. D.C. 1972, U.S. Ct. Appeals (D.C. cir.) 1972, U.S. Supreme Ct. 1975, Colo. 1979, U.S. Dist. Ct. Colo. 1979, U.S. Ct. Appeals (10th cir.) 1979. Atty. Unity Ctr., Meadville, Pa., 1971-73; asst. pros. atty. Genesee County, Flint, Mich., 1973-79, sr. asst. atty. gen. State of Colo., Denver, 1979-82, 85—; assoc. Sumners, Miller & Clark, Denver, 1982-83, Miles & McManus, Denver, 1983-85. Mem. Colo. Bd. Law Examiners, 1992—. Contbr. articles to profl. jours. Mem. Mich. Pub. Consultation Panel of Internat. Joint Commn., 1976-78; treas. Denver South High Sch. PTSA, 1988-91, pres., 1991-93; athletic dir. Most Precious Blood Sch., 1988-90. bd. dirs. Pioneer Jr. Hockey Assn., 1988-90. Mem. ABA (house of dels. 1997—, chair commn. on mental & physical disability law, 1998—, commn. on mental and phys. disability law 1995—, chmn. 1998—, tort and ins. practice sect., chmn. environ. law com. 1978-81, liaison jud. adminstrn. divsn. 1987-90, chmn. govt. liability com. 1988-89, 92-93, chmn. emerging issues com. 1996-97, sect. sec. 1997-99, mem. TIPS coun. 1999—, mem. coun. govt. and pub. sector lawyers divsn. 1991-97, editor-in-chief The Brief 1981-87, spkr. ann. meeting 1991-94), ATLA, Denver Bar Assn. (chmn. pub. legal ednl. com. 1989-91, 99—, del. 1997—), Colo. Bar Assn. (spkr. ann. meetings 1991-95, chmn. health law sect. 1993-94, chmn. law edn. com. 1993-96, coun. licensure, enforcement and regulation, spkr. ann. meetings 1992-2001, chmn. profl. discipline com. 1992-93, 98-99, program chmn. ann. meeting 1993-94, chair publs. com. 1995-97). Democrat. Roman Catholic. Home: 10406 W Glasgow Ave Littleton CO 80127-3468 Office: Atty Gen Office 1525 Sherman St Fl 5 Denver CO 80203-1760 E-mail: jim.carr@state.co.us

CARR, MICHAEL HAROLD, geologist; b. Leeds, Eng., May 26, 1935; came to U.S., 1956, naturalized, 1965; s. Harry and Monica Mary (Burn) C.; m. Rachel F. Harvey, Apr. 14, 1961; son, Ian M. B.Sc., London U., 1956; M.S., Yale U., 1957, Ph.D., 1960. Rsch. assoc. U. Western Ont., 1960-62; with U.S. Geol. Survey, 1962—; chief astrogeologic studies br. U. Geol. Survey, Menlo Park, Calif., 1973-79; mem. Mariner Mars Imaging Team, 1969-73; leader Viking Mars Orbiter Imaging Team, 1969-80; mem. Voyager and Galileo Jupiter Imaging Teams, 1978—. Interdisciplinary scientist, Mars Global Surveyor. Author: The Surface of Mars, The Geology of the Terrestrial Planets, Water on Mars. Recipient Exceptional Sci. Achievement medal NASA, 1977, Disting. Svc. award Dept. of Interior, 1988, Lifetime Achievement award in space sci. and tech. Nat. Air and Space Mus., 1994. Fellow Geol. Soc. Am., Am. Geophys. Union. Home: 1389 Canada Rd Redwood City CA 94062-2452 Office: US Geol Survey 345 Middlefield Rd Menlo Park CA 94025-3591

CARR, RUTH MARGARET, plastic surgeon; b. Waco, Tex., July 2, 1951; MD, U. Okla., 1977. Intern U. Okla. Med. Sch., Oklahoma City, 1977-78; resident U. Okla. Health Sci. Ctr., Oklahoma City, 1978-81, UCLA, 1981-83; plastic surgeon St. John's Hosp., 1989—, Santa Monica (Calif.) Hosp., 1989—. Clin. asst. prof. UCLA, 1983—. Office: 1301 20th St Ste 470 Santa Monica CA 90404-2082 E-mail: rcarr@ucla.edu

CARR, WILLARD ZELLER, JR. lawyer; b. Richmond, Ind., Dec. 18, 1927; s. Willard Zeller and Susan (Brownell) C.; m. Margaret Paterson, Feb. 15, 1952; children: Clayton Paterson, Jeffrey Westcott. BS, Purdue U., 1948; JD, Ind. U., 1951. Bar: Calif. 1951, U.S. Supreme Ct. 1963. Ptnr. Gibson, Dunn & Crutcher, Los Angeles, 1952—. Mem. nat. panel arbitrators Am. Arbitration Assn.; former labor relations cons. State of

Alaska; lectr. bd. visitors Southwestern U. Law Sch.; mem. adv. council Southwestern Legal Found., Internat. and Comparative Law Ctr. Trustee Calif. Adminstrv. Law Coll.; bd. dirs. Employers' Group, Calif. State Pks. Found., Los Angeles coun. Boy Scouts Am.; mem. Mayor's Econ. Devel. Policies Com.; past chmn. Pacific Legal Found.; past chmn. men's adv. com. Los Angeles County-USC Med. Ctr. Aux. for Recruitment, Edn. and Service; past chmn. bd. Wilshire Republican Club; past mem. Rep. State Central Com.; past mem. pres.'s coun. Calif. Mus. Sci. and Industry; mem. Nat. Def. Exec. Res., Los Angeles World Affairs Coun.; bd. dirs., sec. Los Angeles Police Meml. Found.; past chmn. Los Angeles sect. United Way; mem. adv. com. Los Angeles County Human Rels. Commn., past commr., Calif. State World Trade Commn.; Los Angeles chpt. ARC. Fellow Am. Bar Found.; mem. Internat. Bar. Assn. (past chmn. labor law com. of bus. law sect.), chmn. Labor Employment Com., The Federalist Soc., Calif. Bar Assn., L.A. County Bar Assn., L.A. C. of C. (past chmn. 1991), Calif. C. of C. Home: 2185 Century Hl Los Angeles CA 90067-3516 Office: Gibson Dunn & Crutcher 333 S Grand Ave Ste 4400 Los Angeles CA 90071-3197 E-mail: wcarr@gdclaw.com

CARRARO, JOSEPH JOHN, state legislator, business owner, consultant; b. N.Y.C., Nov. 12, 1944; s. Joseph George and Katherine (Dankert) C. BA, U. N.Mex., 1968, M.Mgmt., 1981; Fin., N.Y. Inst. Fin., 1969; postgrad., Anderson Sch. Bus., 1983. Analyst Merrill, Lynch, Pierce, Fenner & Smith, N.Y.C., 1967-69; stock brocker Quinn & Co., Albuquerque, 1969-71; communications cons. N.Y. Tel. Co., N.Y.C., 1971-73; owner Carraro's Pizza & Italian Restaurants, Albuquerque, 1973-95; mem. N.Mex. Senate, Dist. 23, Santa Fe, 1984—; prof. Ethics and Human Behavior Pan Am. U., Albuquerque, 1996—. Lobbyist N.Mex. Restaurants, Santa Fe, 1979-80. Charter mem. Citizens Adv. Group, Albuquerque, 1975; participant Emergency Care Alliance, Albuquerque, 1980; founder Project Share-Homeless Feeding, Albuquerque, 1981—. Named Outstanding Legislator of Yr. Nat. Rep. Legis. Assn., 1987. Mem. Exec. Mgmt. Assn. N.Mex. (pres. 1981-84), Albuquerque C. of C. (Small Bus. of Yr. 1984), N.Mex. Restaurant Assn. Home: 10216 Carraro Pl NW Albuquerque NM 87114-4505

CARREKEA, JAMES, electronics company executive; CEO, chmn. Aspect Telecomm., San Jose, Calif. Office: Aspect Telecomm 1730 Fox Dr San Jose CA 95131-2311

CARREL, ANNETTE FELDER, writer; b. San Francisco, Dec. 11, 1929; m. Robert E. Carrel (dec. 1989); 3 children. AA, Notre Dame Coll.; BA, Lone Mountain Coll.; MA in Spl. Edn., U. Calif., San Francisco. Home: 2010 Garden St Santa Barbara CA 93105-3615

CARRELL, STEWART, computer company executive; b. Chgo., 1934; Grad., So. Meth. U., 1955, Stanford U., 1957. Chmn. bd. dirs. Evans & Sutherland Computer Corp., Salt Lake City. Office: Evans & Sutherland Computer Corp PO Box 58700 Salt Lake City UT 84158

CARRERAS, JOSÉ, tenor; b. Barcelona, Spain, Dec. 5, 1947; s. Jose and Antonio C.; (married); children: Alberto, Julia. Doctor honoris causa, U. Barcelona, Spain, U. Sheffield and Loughborough, U.K., U. Mendeleyev, Russia, u. Camerino, Italy. Mus. dir. opening ceremonies Barcelona Olympics, 1992. Author: Singing from the Soul, 1991; profl. opera debut as Gennaro in Lucrezia Borgia, Liceo Opera House, Barcelona, 1970-71 season; appeared in La Bohème, Un Ballo In Maschera and I Lombardi alla Prima Crociata in Teatro Regio, Parma, Italy, 1972 season; Am. debut as Pinkerton in Madame Butterfly with N.Y.C. Opera, 1972; Met. Opera debut as Cavaradossi, Vienna Staatsoper with rigoletto at London's Royal Opera House with Traviata and at the N.Y. Metropolitan Opera, Oper of Munich with Tosca, 1974, La Scala debut as Riccardo in Un Ballo In Maschera, 1975; appeared in film Don Carlos, 1980, TV Great Performances: West Side Story, 1985; other appearances throughout the world include Carnegie Hall, N.Y., Barbican and Royal Albert Hall, London, Salle Pleyel, Paris, Teatro Colón, Buenos Aires, Argentina, Covent Garden, London, Vienna Staatsoper, Easter Festival, Summer Festival, Salzburg, Aix en Provence, Edimburgh, Verona, Austria, Lyric Opera of Chgo., La Bohème San Francisco Opera, Musikverein and Konzerthaus, Vienna, Suntory Hall and NHK Hall Tokyo, others; recs. include Otello (Rossini), Un Ballo in Maschera, La Battaglia di Legnano, Il Corsaro, Un Giorno, I Due Fuscari, Simone Boccanegra, Macbeth, Don Carlo, Tosca, Thais, Aida, Cavalleria, Turandot, Pagliacci, Lucia di La mmermoor, Elisabetta d'Inghilterra, Amigos Para Siempre, Cabellé and Carreras in Paris, Hollywood Golden Classics, My Barcelona, With a Song in My Heart, Tenorissimi with Placido Domingo and Luciano Pavarotti, The Three Tenors, L.A. (also a PBS spl. and videotape); repertoire of over 60 operas include Andrea Chenier, La Bohème, Tosca, Werther, carmen, la Forza del Destino, I Pagliacci, L'Elisir d'Amore, Un Ballo in Maschera; leading role in operatic films for TV, Cinema, Video include La Bohème, I Lombardi, Andrea chnier, Turandot, Carmen, requiem (Verdi), Don Carlo, La Forza del Destino, Stiffelio, Fedora and jerusalem. Founder José Carreras Med. Rsch. Found.; pres. José Carreras Internat. Leukemia Found.; hon. mem. Leukemia Support Group; grand ofcl. Republic Italy; Goodwill Amb. UNESCO. Recipient Emmy Acad. TV, Grand Prix du Disque Acad. Paris, Luigi Illica prize, Grammy award, 1991, Sir Lawrence Olivier award, Gold medal N.Y. Spanish Inst., City Vienna, Fine Arts His Majesty the King of Spain, City of Barcelona, Autonomous Govt. Catalonia, Prince of Asturias award, 1991; honorary awardee Austrian Republic. Mem. Royal Acad. Music (hon.), European Soc. Medicine (hon.), Vienna Staatsoper (Kammersänger and lifetime hon. mem.) European Soc. Med.oncology (hon. patron); Commandeur des Arts et des Lettres and Chevalier dans l'Ordre de la Légion d'Honneur de la République Française, Gran Croce di Cavaliere, Albert Schweizer Music award ,1996, Internat. award St. Boniface Gen. Hosp. Rsch. Found., 1996. Office: William Morris Agency care Dick Allen 151 S El Camino Dr Beverly Hills CA 90212-2775 also: care Opera Caballe Via Augusta 59 Barcelona Spain also: Hoffamn Concerts Inc 1501 Broadway New York NY 10036-5601 also: Carreras Internat Leukemia Found Muntaner 383 2d 08021 Barcelona Spain Fax: 34 93 201 05 88. E-mail: fundacio@fcarreras.es

CARRICA, JEAN LEON, business educator; b. Albuquerque, June 1, 1931; s. Jean and Marie (Louissena) C.; m. Margaret Kiser, Jan. 24, 1938; children: Annette, Brigitte, Michelle, Loren, John. JD, Creighton U., 1961; MBA, Ind. U., 1963; PhD, U. Nebr., 1967. Asst. prof. Rockhurst Coll., Kansas City, Mo., 1965-67; assoc. prof. Creighton U., Omaha, 1967-73, dean Sch. Bus., 1973-82, Loyola Coll., Balt., 1982-84; prof. Gonzaga U., Spokane, Wash., 1984—. Pro bono cons. on small bus. Co-author: (book) Present Value Applications for Accountants, 1990; contbr. numerous articles to profl. jours. Mem. Greater Balt. Com., 1982-84; pres. Legion of Mary Curia, Spokane, 1988-94. Staff sgt. USAF, 1951-54. Mem. Beta Gamma Sigma (pres. 1993—). Home: 6012 S Martin St Spokane WA 99223-6838 Office: Gonzaga U Sch Bus 502 E Boone Ave Spokane WA 99258-0001

CARRICO, STEPHEN J. construction company executive; b. 1954; Grad., Ctrl. Mich. U., 1977. CPA. With Straka, Jarackas & Co., Detroit, 1977-84; various positions Hensel Phels Constrn. Co., Greeley, Colo., 1984—, now v.p. fin. Office: Hensel Phelps Construction Co 420 Sixth Ave [illegible]

CARRIGAN, JIM R. arbitrator, mediator, retired federal judge; b. Mobridge, S.D., Aug. 24, 1929; s. Leo Michael and Mildred Ione (Jaycox) C.; m. Beverly Jean Halpin, June 2, 1956. Ph.B., J.D., U. N.D., 1953; LL.M. in Taxation, NYU, 1956; LLD (hon.), U. Colo., 1989, Suffolk U., 1991, U. N.D., 1997. Bar: N.D. 1953, Colo. 1956. Asst. prof. law U. Denver, 1956-59; vis. assoc. prof. NYU Law Sch., 1958, U. Wash. Law Sch., 1959-60; Colo. jud. adminstr., 1960-61; prof. law U. Colo., 1961-67; partner firm Carrigan & Bragg (and predecessors), 1967-76; bd. regents U. Colo., 1975-76; justice Colo. Supreme Ct., 1976-79; judge U.S. Dist. Ct. Colo., 1979-95. Mem. Colo. Bd. Bar Examiners, 1969-71; lectr. Nat. Coll. State Judiciary, 1964-77, 95; bd. dirs. Nat. Inst. Trial Advocacy, 1971-73, 78—, chmn. bd. 1986-88, also mem. faculty, 1972—; adj. prof. law U. Colo, 1984, 1991—; bd. dirs. Denver Broncos Stadium Dist., 1996—. Editor-in-chief: N.D. Law Rev., 1952-53, Internat. Soc. Barristers Quar., 1972-79; editor: DICTA, 1957-59; contbr. articles to profl. jours. Bd. visitors U. N.D. Coll. Law, 1983-85. Recipient Disting. Svc. award Nat. Coll. State Judiciary, 1969, Outstanding Alumnus award U. N.D., 1973, Regent Emeritus award U. Colo., 1977, B'nai Brith Civil Rights award, 1986, Thomas More Outstanding Lawyer award Cath. Lawyers Guild, 1988, Oliphant Disting. Svc. award Nat. Inst. Trial Advocacy, 1993, Constl. Rights award Nat. Assn. Blacks in Criminal Justice (Colo. chpt.), 1992, Disting. Svc. award Colo. Bar Assn., 1994, Amicus Curiae award ATLA, 1995, Colo. Trial Lawyers Assn. Lifetime Achievement award, 2000. Fellow Colo. Bar Found., Boulder County Bar Found.; mem. ABA (action com. on tort system improvement 1985-87, TIPS sect. long range planning com., 1986-97; coun. 1987-91, task force on initiatives and referenda 1990-92, size of civil juries task force 1988-90, class actions task force 1995-97), Colo. Bar Assn., Boulder County Bar Assn., Denver Bar Assn., Cath. Lawyers Guild, Inns. of Ct., Internat. Soc. Barristers, Internat. Acad. Trial Lawyers (bd. dirs. 1995—), Fed. Judges Assn. (bd. dirs. 1985-89), Am. Judicature Soc. (bd. dirs. 1985-89), Tenth Circuit Dist. Judges Assn. (sec. 1991-92, v.p. 1992-93, pres. 1994-95), Order of Coif, Phi Beta Kappa. Roman Catholic. Office: Judicial Arbiter Group 1601 Blake St Ste 400 Denver CO 80202-1328 E-mail: carrigan2350@earthlink.net

CARRIKER, ROBERT CHARLES, history educator; b. St. Louis, Aug. 18, 1940; s. Thomas B. and Vivian Ida (Spaunhorst) C.; m. Eleanor R. Gualdoni, Aug. 24, 1963; children: Thomas A., Robert M., Andrew J. BS, St. Louis U., 1962, AM, 1963; PhD, U. Okla., 1967. Asst. prof. Gonzaga U., Spokane, Wash., 1967-71, assoc. prof., 1972-76, prof. history, 1976—. Author: Fort Supply, Indian Territory, 1970, 90, The Kalispel People, 1973, Father Peter De Smet, 1995; editor: (with Eleanor R. Carriker) Army Wife on the Frontier, 1975, (with William L. Lang) Great River of the West, 1999; book rev. editor Columbia mag., 1987—. Mem. Wash. Lewis and Clark Trail Com., 1978-99; commr. Wash. Maritime Bicentennial, Olympia, 1989-92; bd. dirs. Wash. Commn. for Humanities, Seattle, 1988-94. Burlington No. Found. scholar, 1985, 96; recipient Disting. Svc. award Lewis and Clark Trail Heritage Found., 1989. Mem. Wash. State Hist. Soc. (trustee 1981-90, v.p. 1993-2000), Western Hist. Assn., Phi Alpha Theta (councilor 1985-87). Roman Catholic. Avocations: travel, photography, cartography. Office: Gonzaga U 502 E Boone Ave Spokane WA 99258-0001 E-mail: CARRIKER@gonzaga.edu

CARRINGTON, JAMES C. botanist, educator; BS, U. Calif., Riverside, 1982; PhD, U. Calif., Berkeley, 1986. Prof., fellow Inst. Biol. Chemistry Wash. State U., Pullman. Recipient Ruth Allen award Am. Phytopathol. Soc., 2000. Office: Inst Biol Chemistry Wash State U PO Box 646340 Pullman WA 99164-6340

CARRISON, DALE MITCHELL, emergency medicine physician; b. Macomb, Ill., Sept. 24, 1939; married. AA in Police Sci., Santa Ana Coll., 1966; BS in Criminology, Calif. State U., Long Beach, 1968; MS in Biology, Calif. State U., San Bernardino, 1983; DO, Coll. Osteo. Medicine Pacific, 1987. Diplomate Am. Bd. Emergency Medicine; cert. ACLS instr./profider, ATLS provider. Dep. sheriff Orange County (Calif.) Sheriff's Dept., 1964-71; spl. agt. FBI, L.A. and Portland, Oreg., 1971-76; pres., gen. mgr. Carrison Enterprises, Inc., So. Calif., 1976-83; rotating intern Flint (Mich.) Osteo. Hosp., 1987-88; resident in emergency medicine Cook County Hosp., Chgo., 1988-91; asst. dir., attending physician dept. emergency medicine Univ. Med. Ctr., Las Vegas, 1991-92, Emergency Physicians' Med. Group, Univ. Med. Ctr., Las Vegas, Nev., 1992-94, dir., attending physician dept. emergency medicine, 1995—; asst. prof. emergency medicine dept. family medicine Coll. Osteo. Medicine of Pacific, 1993—; clin. prof. surgery U. Nev. Sch. Medicine, Las Vegas, 1994—. Med. dir. Sexual Assault Nurse Examiner, Univ. Med. Ctr., 1994—, vice chmn., staff physician dept. trauma medicine, 1994-96; bd. dirs. Emergency Physicians' Med. Group, San Francisco, 1994—, Nev. regional dir., 1996—; regional clin. coord. Coll. Osteo. Medicine of Pacific, Pomona, Calif., 1994—; med. dir. emergency med. svcs., Lake Mead Recreational Area, Henderson, Nev., 1993—; med. dir., tactical physician Las Vegas Met. Police Dept. SWAT Team, 1995—; instr. Heckler & Koch Internat. Tng. Divsn. for Tactical Emergency Medicine, Sterling, Va., 1995—; med. dir. Las Vegas Motor Speedway, 1995—; med. dir. Nev. region Sports Car Club Am., Las Vegas, 1993-98; mem. coun., reviewer Health Insight, Las Vegas, 1995—; med. dir. emergency med. svcs. Nat. Park Svc., Death Valley, Calif., 1992—; staff physician emergency dept. Gottlieb Meml. Hosp., Melrose Park, Ill., 1990-91, Lakeland Med. Ctr., Elkhorn, Wis., 1989-91, Westlake Cmty. Hosp., Melrose Park, 1989-91; presenter, rschr. in field. Contbr. articles to profl. publs. With USN, USNR, 1956-61, maj. Med. Corps USAR, 1987-95. Fellow Am. Coll. Emergency Physicians; mem. Am. Osteo. Assn. (Nev. del., bur. student affairs), Nev. Osteo. Med. Assn. (v.p., pres.), Coll. Osteo. Medicine of Pacific Alumni Assn. (past pres.), Wilderness Med. Assn., Internat. Coun. Motorsports Scis.

CARROLL, EARL HAMBLIN, federal judge; b. Tucson, Mar. 26, 1925; s. John Vernon and Ruby (Wood) C.; m. Louise Rowlands, Nov. 1, 1952; children— Katherine Carroll Pearson, Margaret Anne BSBA, U. Ariz., 1948, LLB, 1951. Bar: Ariz., U.S. Ct. Appeals (9th and 10th cirs.), U.S. Ct. of Claims, U.S. Supreme Ct. Law clk. Ariz. Supreme Ct., Phoenix, 1951-52; assoc. Evans, Kitchel & Jenckes, Phoenix, 1952-56, ptnr., 1956-80; judge U.S. Dist. Ct. Ariz., Phoenix, 1980—, sr. judge, 1994—. Spl. counsel City of Tombstone, Ariz., 1962-65, Maricopa County, Phoenix, 1968-75, City of Tucson, 1974, City of Phoenix, 1979; designated mem. U.S. Fgn. Intelligence Surveillance Court by Chief Justice U.S. Supreme Ct., 1993-99; chief judge Alien Terrorist Removal Ct., 1996-01, 2001—. Mem. City of Phoenix Bd. of Adjustment, 1955-58; trustee Phoenix Elem. Sch. Bd., 1961-72; mem. Gov.'s Council on Intergovtl. Relations, Phoenix, 1970-73; mem. Ariz. Bd. Regents, 1978-80. Served with USNR, 1943-46; PTO Recipient Nat. Service awards Campfire, 1973, 75, Alumni Service award U. Ariz., 1980, Disting. Citizen award No. Ariz. U., Flagstaff, 1983, Bicentenial award Georgetown U., 1988, Disting. Citizen award U. Ariz., 1990, Sidney S. Woods Alumni Svc. award, 2000. Fellow Am. Coll. Trial Lawyers, Am. Bar Found.; mem. ABA, Ariz. Bar Assn., U. Ariz. Law Coll. Assn. (pres. 1975), Sigma Chi (Significant Sig award 1991), Phi Delta Phi. Democrat. Office: US Dist Ct US Courthouse Ste 521 401 W Washington SPC 48 Phoenix AZ 85003-2151

CARROLL, ELLEN A. judge, lawyer; b. San Francisco, Feb. 6, 1947; BA, Mundelein Coll., 1970; JD with honors, U. San Francisco, 1980. Bar: Calif. 1980. Law clk. to Hon. Lloyd King No. Dist. Calif., 1981; partner Bronson, Bronson & McKinnon, San Francisco, 1988-93; counsel Murphy, Weir & Butler, San Francisco, 1993-98; judge U.S. Bankruptcy Ct., L.A., 1998-. Com. lawyer reps. of U.S. Bankruptcy Ct. No. Dist. Calif., 1988-90. [illegible] (bus. bankruptcy com., uniform comml. code com., bus. law sect. 1990—), State Bar Calif. (mem. uniform comml. code com. 1985-88), Bar Assn. San Francisco (bd. dirs. 1992—, chair 1989, comml. law and bankruptcy sect.), Bay Area Bankruptcy Forum (bd. dirs. 1991-92). Address: US Bankruptcy Ct Cent Calif 1634 Roybal Fed Bldg & US Ct House 255 E Temple St Los Angeles CA 90012-3332

CARROLL, JOHN SAWYER, newspaper editor; b. N.Y.C., Jan. 23, 1942; s. John Wallace and Margaret (Sawyer) C.; m. Kathleen Kirk, May 1, 1971 (div. Sept. 1982) children— Kathleen Louise, Margaret Adriane; m. Lee Huston Powell, Nov. 1985. B.A., Haverford Coll., 1963. Reporter Providence Jour. - Bull., 1963-64; reporter Balt. Sun., 1966-72, Vietnam, 1967-69, Middle East, 1969, Washington Bur., 1969-72; city editor, met. editor Phila. Inquirer, 1973-79; exec. v.p., editor Lexington Herald-Leader, Ky., 1979-91; editor, sr. v.p. Balt. Sun, 1991-98; v.p. Times Mirror Co., 1998—. Bd. dirs. Am. Soc. Newspaper Editors, Pulitzer prize juror, 1987, 89, 94, Pulitzer prize bd., 1994—. Served with U.S. Army, 1964-66 Named Nat. Press Found. Editor of the Yr., 1998; Nieman fellow Harvard U., 1971-72; vis. journalist fellow Queen Elizbeth House, U. Oxford, 1988. Office: Los Angeles Times The Times Mirror Co Times Mirror Sq Los Angeles CA 90053-0001

CARROLL, JON, newspaper columnist; Columnist San Francisco Chronicle. Office: Chronicle Pub Co 901 Mission St San Francisco CA 94103-2905

CARROLL, KAREN COLLEEN, physician, infectious disease educator, medical microbiologist; b. Balt., Nov. 7, 1953; d. Charles Edward and Ida May (Simms) C.; m. Bruce Cameron Marshall, Feb. 13, 1982; children: Kevin Charles Marshall, Brian Thomas Marshall. BA, Coll. Notre Dame of Md., 1975; MD, U. Md., 1979. Diplomate Am. Bd. Internal Medicine, Am. Bd. Infectious Diseases, Am. Bd. Pathology. Intern U. Md., 1979-80, U. Rochester, AHP, 1980-82, chief med. resident in internal medicine, 1982-83; fellow infectious diseases U. Mass., 1984-86; fellow med. microbiology Health Scis. Ctr. U. Utah, 1989-90; asst. prof. pathology U. Utah Med. Ctr., Salt Lake City, 1990-97, adj. asst. prof. infectious diseases, 1990-97, assoc. prof. pathology, adj. assoc. prof. infectious disease, 1997—; dir. microbiology lab. Associated Regional and Univ. Pathologists, Inc., Salt Lake City, 1990—. Contbr. articles to profl. jours. Fellow Am. Acad. Microbiology, Coll. Am. Pathologists; mem. Am. Soc. for Microbiology, Infectious Diseases Soc. Am. Avocations: skiing, hiking, reading. Office: U Utah Med Ctr Dept Pathology 50 N Medical Dr Salt Lake City UT 84132-0001 E-mail: carrolkc@aruplab.com

CARROLL, PHILIP JOSEPH, JR. engineering company executive; b. New Orleans, Sept. 24, 1937; s. Philip Joseph and Rosemary Agnes (McEntee) C.; m. Charlene Marie Phillips, Jan. 3, 1959; children: Philip III, Kenneth, Bruce. BS in Physics, Loyola U., New Orleans, 1958; MS in Physics, Tulane U., 1961. Petroleum engr. Shell Oil Co., New Orleans, L.A., N.Y.C. and Midland, Tex., 1961-73; dir. energy conservation div. U.S. Dept. Commerce, Washington, 1973-74; exec. dir. Nat. Ind. Energy Conservation Coun., Washington, 1974; regional engr., mgr. so. exploration and prodn. Shell Oil Co., New Orleans, 1974-75, div. mgr. prodn., western exploration and prodn. Houston, 1975-78, gen. mgr. prodn., western ops., 1978-79, gen. mgr. plans and integration, 1979, v.p. pub. affairs, 1979-85; mng. dir. Shell Internat. Gas, Shell Internat. Petroleum Co., London, 1985-86; sr. v.p. adminstrn. Shell Oil Co., Houston, 1986-88, exec. v.p. adminstrn., 1988-93, pres., 1993-98, mem. bd. dirs., 1990; chmn., CEO Fluor Corp, Irvine, CA, 1998—. Bd. dirs. Boise Cascade Corp. Bd. dirs. Am. Petroleum Inst., Cen. Houston, Tex. Med. Ctr., Am. Air Mus.; trustee Com. for Econ. Devel., 1991—, Baylor Coll. Medicine, Boys & Girls Clubs of Am.; mem. Gov.'s Bus. Coun. (Tex.), Nat. Petroleum Coun., Conf. Bd., 1991—, Nat. Action Coun. for Minorities in Engring., 1993—, bd. dirs.; adv. bd. mem. Salvation Army; bd. adminstrs. adv. bd. mem. Ctr. Bioenviron. Rsch., Tulane U. Mem. 25 Yr. Club Petroleum Industry, Tchefuncta Country Club (Covington, La.), River Oaks Country Club, Champions Golf Club. Avocation: golf.

CARROLL, WILLIAM, publishing company executive; Mgr., dir. Auto Book Press Coda Publs., San Marcos, Calif. Office: Auto Book Press Coda Publs Bin 711 San Marcos CA 92079-0711

CARROLL, WILLIAM JEROME, civil engineer; b. Los Angeles, Nov. 23, 1923; s. William Jerome and Adeline Marie (Verden) C.; m. Louise May Judson, June 6, 1944; children: Charisse Jean, Charles Gary, Christine Louise, Pamela Ann. B.S., Calif. Inst. Tech., 1948, M.S., 1949. Indsl. waste engr. Los Angeles County Engr., 1949-51; engr. James M. Montgomery (Cons. Engr., Inc.), Pasadena, Calif., 1951-56, v.p., 1956-69, pres., 1969-85, chmn. bd., 1985-90; vice chmn. bd. Montgomery Watson, 1991-98. Served with USAAF, 1943-46. Named So. Calif. Engr. of Yr., 1983; recipient Disting. Alumni award Calif. Inst. Tech., 1996. Mem. NAE, ASCE (nat. bd. dirs. 1976—, nat. v.p. 1986-87, pres. elect 1988, pres. 1988-89, Pres.'s medal 1997), Acad. Engrs. Russian Fedn., World Fedn. Engring. Orgns. (pres. 1991-95), Am. Acad. Environ. Engrs. (diplomate, pres. 1980—, Hoover medal 1994, Gordon Maskew Fair award 1992), Am. Water Works Assn., Water Pollution Control Fedn., Cons. Engrs. Assn. Calif. (pres. 1972), Alumni Assn. Calif. Inst. Tech. (pres. 1976), Pasadena C. of C., Am. Assn. Engring. Socs. (Kenneth Roe award 1992). Republican. Home: 2315 Rue des Chateaux Carlsbad CA 92008-2250 Office: Montgomery Watson Inc 300 N Lake Ave Ste 1200 Pasadena CA 91101-4184 E-mail: william.carroll@mw.com

CARRUTH, JAMES C. judge; b. Geneva, June 20, 1939; LLB, U. Ariz., 1964. Bar: Ariz. 1964. Assoc. Miller, Pitt & Feldman, 1964-73; ct. commr. Superior Ct. Ariz., Pima County, 1973; assoc. Lesher & Kimble, 1974-76; judge Ariz. Superior Ct., Pima County, 1976-97; magistrate judge U.S. Dist. Dt. for Dist. Ariz., Tucson, 1997—. Mem. State Bar Ariz., Ariz. Judges Assn. Office: US Dist Ct for Dist Ariz James A Walsh US Ct House 55 E Broadway Blvd Rm 312 Tucson AZ 85701-1719

CARSON, HAMPTON LAWRENCE, geneticist, educator; b. Phila., Nov. 5, 1914; s. Joseph and Edith (Bruen) C.; m. Meredith Shelton, Aug. 14, 1937; children: Joseph II, Edward Bruen. AB, U. Pa., 1936, PhD, 1943. Instr. U. Pa., 1938-42; faculty Washington U., St. Louis, 1943-70, prof. biology, 1956-70; prof. genetics U. Hawaii, 1971-85, emeritus, 1985—. Vis. prof. biology U. Sao Paulo, Brazil, 1951, 77. Author: Heredity and Human Life, 1963; Contbr. articles to profl. jours. Trustee B.P. Bishop Mus., Honolulu, 1982-88. Recipient medal for excellence in rsch. U. Hawaii, 1979, Leidy medal Acad. Natural Scis., Phila., 1985, Charles Reed Bishop medal Bishop Mus., Honolulu, 1992; Fulbright rsch. scholar zoology dept. U. Melbourne, Australia, 1961. Mem. Nat. Acad. Scis., Am. Acad. Arts and Scis., Genetics Soc. (pres. 1982), Soc. for Study Evolution (pres. 1971, George Gaylord Simpson award 1996), Am. Soc. Naturalists (pres. 1973), AAAS, Phi Beta Kappa, Sigma Xi. Office: Dept Cell & Molecular Biology U Hawaii at Manoa Honolulu HI 96822 E-mail: hampton@hawaii.edu

CARSON, JAY WILMER, pathologist, educator; b. Ki-Jang, Korea, Oct. [illegible] Jennifer C. White, June 28, 1968 (dec. Aug. 1990); m. Teresa M. Alberda, July 14, 1995. MD, Seoul Nat. U., 1958. Diplomate Am. Bd. Pathology. Intern Bellevue Hosp. Ctr., N.Y.C., 1961-62; resident in pathology Albert Einstein Coll. Medicine, N.Y.C., 1963-66; fellow U. Montreal, Que., Can., 1967-68; chief anatomic pathology VA Hosp., Martinez, Calif., 1969-91; dir. cytopathology VA Med. Ctr., San Francisco, 1992-96; assoc. prof. U. [illegible]

Oklahoma City, 1987-96; assoc. clin. prof. U. Calif., Davis, 1985—; hosp. comdr. 6253d Army Hosp., Santa Rosa, Calif., 1994-96. Patentee needle aspiration device. Mem. chmn.'s adv. bd. Nat. Rep. Com., Washington, 1995-96. Col. USAR, 1971-96. Fellow Coll. Am. Pathologists; mem. Internat. Acad. Pathology, Assn. Mil. Surgeons U.S. (life), Res. Officers Assn. (life), U.S. Army War Coll. Alumni Assn. (life), Soc. U.S. Army Flight Surgeons (life). Avocations: skiing, sailing, music. Home: 1550 Sorrel Ct Walnut Creek CA 94598-4800 E-mail: jntcarson@msn.com

CARSON, WALLACE PRESTON, JR. state supreme court chief justice; b. Salem, Oreg., June 10, 1934; s. Wallace Preston and Edith (Bragg) C.; m. Gloria Stolk, June 24, 1956; children: Scott, Carol, Steven (dec. 1981). BA in Politics, Stanford U., 1956; JD, Willamette U., 1962. Bar: Oreg. 1962, U.S. Dist. Ct. Oreg. 1963, U.S. Ct. Appeals (9th cir.) 1968, U.S. Supreme Ct. 1971, U.S. Ct. Mil. Appeals 1977; lic. comml. pilot FAA. Pvt. practice law, Salem, Oreg., 1962-77; judge Marion County Cir. Ct., Salem, 1977-82; assoc. justice Oreg. Supreme Ct., Salem, 1982-92, state supreme ct. chief justice, 1992—. Mem. Oreg. Ho. of Reps., 1967-71, maj. leader, 1969-71; mem. Oreg. State Senate, 1971-77, minority floor leader, 1971-77; dir. Salem Area Community Council, 1967-70, pres., 1969-70; mem. Salem Planning Commn., 1966-72, pres., 1970-71; co-chmn. Marion County Mental Health Planning Com., 1965-69; mem. Salem Community Goals Com., 1965; Republican precinct commiteeman, 1963-66; mem. Marion County Rep. Central Exec. Com., 1963-66; com. predinct edn. Oreg. Rep. Central Com., 1965; vestryman, acolyte, Sunday Sch. tchr., youth coach St. Paul's Episcopal Ch., 1935— ; task force on cts. Oreg. Council Crime and Delinquency, 1968-69; trustee Willamette U., 1970— ; adv. bd. Cath. Ctr. Community Services, 1976-77; mem. comporehensive planning com. Mid-Willamette Valley Council of Govts., 1970-71; adv. com. Oreg. Coll. Edn. Tchr. Edn., 1971-75; pres. Willamette regional Oreg. Lung Assn., 1974-75, state dir., exec. com., 1975-77; pub. relations com. Williamette council Campfire Girls, 1976-77; criminal justice adv. bd. Chemeketa Community Coll., 1977-79; mem. Oreg. Mental Health Com., 1979-80; mem. subcom. Gov's Task Force Mental Health, 1980; you and govt. adv. com. Oreg. YMCA, 1981— . Served to col. USAFR, 1956-59. Recipient Salem Disting. Svc. award, 1968; recipient Good Fellow award Marion County Fire Svc., 1974, Minuteman award Oreg. N.G. Assn., 1980; fellow Eagleton Inst. Politics, Rutgers U., 1971 Mem. Marion County Bar Assn. (sec.-treas. 1965-67, dir. 1968-70), Oreg. Bar Assn., ABA, Willamette U. Coll. Law Alumni Assn. (v.p. 1968-70), Salem Art Assn., Oreg. Hist. Soc., Marion County Hist. Soc., Stanford U. Club (pres. Salem chpt. 1963-64), Delta Theta Phi. Office: Oregon Supreme Ct Supreme Ct Bldg 1163 State St Salem OR 97310-1331

CARSTED, DOUGLAS J. geologist; b. Winnipeg, Man., Can. BS in Chemistry, U. Winnipeg, 1979; BS in Geology with honors, U. Man., 1982. Geologist Imperial Oil Ltd., Calgary, Can.; reservoir geologist Sproule Assocs. Ltd., 1994—, shareholder, 1995—. Mem. Assn. Profl. Engrs. (profl. geologist), Geologists and Geophysicists Alta. (profl. geologist), Am. Assn. Petroleum Geologists, Indonesian Petroleum Assn. (profl. divsn.), Can. Well Logging Soc., Can. Soc. Petroleum Geologists (Pres. award 1999), Can. Inst. Mining, Metallurgy and Petroleum (Petroleum Soc.). Office: Sproule Internat Ltd 140 4 Ave SW Ste 900 Calgary AB Canada T2P 3N3 E-mail: carstedd@sproule.com

CARSTEN, JACK CRAIG, venture capitalist; b. Cin., Aug. 24, 1941; s. John A. and Edith L. C.; m. Mary Ellis Jones, June 22, 1963; children: Scott, Elizabeth, Amy. BS in Physics, Duke U., 1963. Mktg. mgr. Tex. Instruments, Dallas, Houston, 1965-71, integrated circuits gen. mgr. Houston, 1971-75; v.p. sales and mktg. Intel Corp., Santa Clara, Calif., 1975-79, v.p., microcomputer gen. mgr., 1979-82, sr. v.p., components gen. mgr., 1982-87; gen. ptnr. U.S. Venture Ptnrs., Menlo Park, 1988-90; venture capitalist Tech. Investments, Los Altos, 1990-99, Horizon Ventures LLC, Los Altos, 2000—. Bd. dirs. Socket Comms., Inc., Comerica Bank-CA, and several privately held firms. Contbr. articles to profl.jours. Office: Horizon Ventures LLC 4 Main St Los Altos CA 94022-2998 E-mail: jack@carsten.com

CARTER, DALE LAVELLE, professional football player; b. Covington, Ga., Nov. 28, 1969; Student, Ellsworth C.C., U. Tenn. Cornerback, punt returner Kansas City (Mo.) Chiefs, 1992-98, Denver Broncos, 1998—. Named to Coll. All-Am. 1st Team, Sporting News, 1990, 91; named to NFL Pro Bowl Team, 1994, 95, 96. Office: c/o Denver Broncos 13655 Broncos Pkwy Englewood CO 80112-4150

CARTER, DAVID LAVERE, soil scientist, researcher, consultant; b. Tremonton, Utah, June 10, 1933; s. Gordon Ray and Mary Eldora (Hirschi) C.; m. Virginia Beutler, June 1, 1953; children: Allen David, Roger Gordon, Brent Ryan. BS, Utah State U., 1955, MS, 1957; PhD, Oreg. State U., 1961. Soil scientist USDA Agrl. Research Service, Corvallis, Oreg., 1956-60, research soil scientist, line project leader Weslaco, Tex., 1960-65; rsch. soil scientist USDA Agrl. Rsch. Svc., Kimberly, Idaho, 1965-68, supervisory soil scientist, rsch. leader, 1968-86, supervisory soil scientist, rsch. leader, dir., 1986-96; pvt. cons. Kimberly, 1996—. Cons., adviser to many projects and orgns. Contbr. articles to profl. jours.; author, co-author books. Recipient Emmett J. Culligan award World Water Soc. Fellow Am. Soc. Agronomy (cert.), Soil Sci. Soc. Am. (cert.); mem. Soil Conservation Soc. Am. (Soil Conservation award 1985), Internat. Soc. Soil Sci., Western Soc. Soil Sci., Internat. Soc. Soil Sci., OPEDA. Mormon.

CARTER, DAVID O. judge; b. Providence, Mar. 28, 1944; m. Mary Ellen Carter. BA cum laude, UCLA, 1967, JD, 1972. Bar: Calif. 1972, U.S. Dist. Ct. (ctrl. dist.) Calif. 1972. Asst. dist. atty. Dist. Atty.'s Office, Santa Ana, Calif., 1972-81; judge Orange County Mcpl. Ct., Westminster, 1981-82, Laguna Niguel, 1982, Orange County Superior Ct., Santa Ana, 1982-98, U.S. Dist. Ct. for Ctrl. Dist. Calif., Santa Ana, 1998—. Spkr. Supreme Ct. Rio de Janeiro and Brazilan Fed. Prosecutors, 1993; civilian participant Nat. Security Forum, Air War Coll., Montgomery, Ala., 1992; mem. faculty Calif. Judges Coll., 1983-89, 91-97, Jud. Criminal Law Inst., 1989, 90, 93, 97, Contributing Edn. Bar, 1994-95. Bd. dirs. Brandy's Friends, 1995—, Orange County on Track, 1996—, Children's Bur., 1996—, Kindercamarina, 1997—. Decorated Bronze Star, Purple Heart; recipient vol. award City of Santa Ana, 1990, Patriot of Yr. award Patriots Day Parade, Laguna Beach, 1991, Exceptional Support award Police Res. Officers, Santa Ana, 1995, Disting. Vis. Prof.'s award U. Calif., Irvine, 1996,, 97, 98, Exceptional Citizen's award Mayor of Santa Ana, 1998; Athletic scholar UCLA. Mem. Orange County Bar Assn. (bd. dirs. 1978), Orange County Bar Assn. (bd. dirs. 1994), Calif. Dist. Attys. Assn. (charter), DAV, VFW, Am. Legion, Mil. Order Purple Heart, 1st Bn. 9th Marine Network, Survivors of Khe Sanh. Office: US Dist Ct Ctrl Dist Calif Ronald Reagan Fed Bldg 411 W 4th St Santa Ana CA 92701-4500

CARTER, DENNIS LEE, marketing professional; b. Louisville, Oct. 23, 1951; s. Bernard Lee and Opal Delores (Jaggers) C.; m. Janice Lea Herbert, Dec. 31, 1976; children: Serra Kimberly, Scott Winston. BSEE, BS in Physics, Rose Hulman Inst., Terre Haute, Ind., 1973; MSEE, Purdue U., 1974, DSc (hon.), 1996; MBA, Harvard U., 1981. Instr. elec. engring. tech. Purdue U., West Lafayette, Ind., 1975; collateral engr. Rockwell-Collins, Cedar Rapids, Iowa, 1975-76, design engr., 1976-79; product mktg. engr. Intel Corp., Santa Clara, Calif., 1981-83, software products mktg. mgr., 1983-85, tech. asst. to pres., 1985-89, end-user mktg. mgr., 1989-90, gen. mgr. end-user components divsn., 1990-91, dir. corp. mktg., 1991-92, v.p., dir. corp. mktg., 1992-98, v.p., dir. strategic mktg., 1998—. Inventor radio reception path monitor for a diversity sys., 1985. Episcopalian. Avocation: baseball fan. Office: Intel Corp RN5-20 2200 Mission College Blvd Santa Clara CA 95054-1549

CARTER, EMILY ANN, physical chemist, researcher, educator; b. Los Gatos, Calif., Nov. 28, 1960; d. David and Rebecca (Blumberg) C.; m. Bruce E. Koel, 1994; 1 child, Adam. BS in Chemistry, U. Calif., Berkeley, 1982; PhD in Chemistry, Calif. Inst. Tech., 1987. Postdoctoral rsch. assoc. U. Colo., Boulder, 1987-88; asst. prof., physical chemistry UCLA, 1988-92, assoc. prof., 1992-94, prof., 1994—. Mem. Defense Sci. Study Group, 1996-97; vis. scholar in physics Harvard U., 1999; cons. Inst. for Def. Analysis, 1998—, Los Alamos Nat. Lab., 2000—, mem. theoretical divsn. rev. com., 2000—; vis. scholar in aeronautics, Cal. Inst. Tech., 2001; UCLA dir. of modeling and simulation, Calif. Nano Systems Inst. Mem. editl. bd. Jour. Phys. Chemistry, 1995-2000, Surface Sci., 1994-99, Encyclopedia Chemical Physics and Physical Chemistry 1996—, Chem. Phys. Letters, 1998—; mem. editl. bd. Phys. Chem. Comm., 1998—, Chem. Phys. Chem., 2000—, Jour. Chem. Phys., 2000—; Modeling and Simulation in Materials Science and Engineering; guest editor Jour. Phys. Chem., 2000; contbr. numerous articles to tech. jours; given over 180 invited lectures. Recipient rsch. innovation recognition awards Union Carbide Co., 1990, 91, New Faculty award Camille and Henry Dreyfus Found., 1988; NSF Presdl. Young Investigator award, 1988, Dreyfus Tchr. Scholar award, 1992, Alfred P. Sloan fellow, 1993, Internat. Acad. of Quantum Molecular Sci. medal, 1993, Exxon faculty fellow, 1993, Peter Mark Meml. award Am Vacuum Soc., 1995, Dr. Lee vis. rsch. fellow Oxford U., 1996. Fellow Am. Vacuum Soc., Am. Phys. Soc., AAAS; mem. Am. Chem. Soc., Material Rsch. Soc., Sigma Xi, Phi Beta Kappa. Democrat. Jewish. Avocations: theater, films, cooking, reading, tennis. Office: U California Dept Chem Box 951569 Los Angeles CA 90095-1569 E-mail: eac@chem.ucla.edu

CARTER, GEORGE KENT, oil company executive; b. Toledo, Nov. 5, 1935; s. Fred S. and Charlotte J. (Horen) C.; children from previous marriage: Caitlin, Seth; m. Kathleen Anne McKenna, July 22, 1990. AB, Stanford U., 1957, MBA, 1961. Various fin. positions Std. Oil of Calif., San Francisco, 1962-74, asst. treas., 1974, asst. comptr., 1974-81; comptr. Chevron U.S.A., Inc., San Francisco, 1981-83, v.p. fin., 1986-89; comptr. Chevron Corp. (formerly Std. Oil of Calif.), San Francisco, 1983-86, v.p. and treas., 1989—. Mem. Stanford Bus. Sch. Assn., Stanford U. Alumni Assn., Bankers Club. Office: Chevron Corp PO Box 6021 San Ramon CA 94583-0721 also: 6001 Bollinger Canyon Rd San Ramon CA 94583-2324

CARTER, HAROLD O. agricultural economics educator; b. Eaton Rapids, Mich., Dec. 13, 1932; s. Ola Gay and Lillian Darlene (Fox) C.; m. Janet M. Edger, June 21, 1952; children: Teresa, Lisa, Brian, Michael, Alison. BS, Mich. State U., 1954, MS, 1955; PhD, Iowa State U., 1958. From asst. prof. to assoc. prof. agrl. econs. U. Calif., Davis, 1958-66, prof. to prof. emeritus, 1966-93, 93—, chmn. dept., 1970-76, 87-89, dir. Agrl. Issues Ctr., 1985-96. Vis. prof. Agrl. Coll. Sweden, Uppsala, 1967, Ctr. Agrl. Econs. U. Naples, Italy, 1972, dept. agrl. econs U. Sydney, Australia, 1984; economist Giannini Found. Agrl. Econs. Fellow Am. Agrl. Econs. Assn. (Outstanding Rsch. awards 1963, 67, 71, 75, 89, Best Jour. Article award 1968), Western Agrl. Econs. Assn. (Outstanding Extension award 1975, Outstanding Rsch. award 1962, 69, 71). Republican. Home: 550 Oak Ave Woodland CA 95695-3945 Office: U Calif Dept Agrl Econs Davis CA 95616

CARTER, JAMES E. mining company executive; B in Mining Engring., Tech. U. Nova Scotia, 1973, DEng (hon), 1995; grad. advanced mgmt. program, Harvard U. Mine foreman Iron Ore Co. Can., 1973-74; gen. foreman McIntyre Mines Ltd., 1974-76, mine supt., 1976-77, mgr. surface mines, 1977-79; mgr. overburden ops. Syncrude, Fort McMurray, Alta., 1979-81, asst. gen. mgr. mining, 1981-86, gen. mgr. maintenance and ops., 1986-89, v.p. ops., 1989-97, pres., COO, 1997—. Founding chmn. industry adv. com. U. Atla. Sch. Mining and Petroleum; with faculty engring. adv. bd. U. Nova Scotia. Bd. dirs. No. Lights Regional Hosp. Found.; former gov. Keyano Coll. Mem. Can. Inst. Mining, Metallurgy and Petroleum (Past Pres. award, Fellowship award, founder Rocky Mt. br., chmn. 1978-79, speaker at confs.), Assn. Profl. Engrs., Geologists and Geophysicists Atla. (Centennial award 1999), Mining Assn. Can. (bd. dirs.), Alta. Chamber Resources (exec. com.), Vista-Ridge Ski Hill Assn. (bd. dirs.). Office: Syncrude PO Bag 4023 Fort McMurray AB Canada T9H 3H5

CARTER, JOHN CHARLTON See HESTON, CHARLTON

CARTER, JOHN DOUGLAS, lawyer; b. Pendleton, Oreg., Feb. 6, 1946; s. Douglas Toner and Carmen Lucile (Cecil) C.; m. Diane Louise Werthen, Aug. 15, 1970 (div. 1977); m. Linda Louise Levy, Aug. 5, 1977; children: Courtney, Douglas, Christopher. AB, Stanford U.; LLB, JD, Harvard U. Bar: Calif. Law clk to Hon. J.F. Kilkenny U.S. Ct. Appeals (9th cir.), San Francisco, 1971-72; from assoc. to ptnr. Thelen, Marrin, Johnson & Bridges, San Francisco, 1972-82; chief litigation counsel Bechtel Power Corp., San Francisco, 1982-86; from asst. gen. counsel to gen. counsel, sr. v.p. Bechtel Group, Inc., San Francisco, 1986-97, exec. v.p., 1997—, also bd. dirs. San Fransisco; pres. Bechtel Enterprises, San Fransisco, 1992-97; pres. N.Am. Bechtel Group Inc., San Francisco, 1997; pres. Europe, Africa, Mid. East, S.W. Asia Bechtel Group, Inc., San Fransisco, 1997-98. CFO, sr. officer pub. rels., internal audit Legis. Office, 1988-92; mem. chmn.'s leadership coun. Bechtel Group, Inc., 1996—; exec. sponsor Telecomms., Indsl., Water, Civil Inst., exec. sponsor corp. svcs., 2001—. Editor: Construction Litigation: Representing the Contractor, 1986, 2d edit., 1992, Dow Jones Handbook of Joint Venturing, 1988, Construction Litigation Formbook, 1990, Construction Disputes: Representing the Contractor, 3d edit., 2001. Mem. ABA, Calif. Bar Assn., San Francisco Bar Assn., Iternat. Bar Assn., San Francisco C. of C. (bd. dirs. 1988-92), Olympic Club, Bankers Club, Chmn.'s Club. Office: Bechtel Group Inc 50 Beale St San Francisco CA 94105-1813

CARTER, LARRY R. computer company executive; BS in Bus. Adminstrn. and Acctg., Ariz. State U. Various positions including v.p., contr. MOS group Motorola, Inc.; CFO, v.p. fin. and adminstrn. SGS Thompson Microelectronics, Inc.; v.p. fin., CFO VLSI Tech., Inc.; v.p., corp. contr. Advanced Micro Devices; v.p. fin. and adminstrn., CFO, sec. Cisco Sys., 1995—. Office: Cisco Systems Inc 170 W Tasman Dr San Jose CA 95134-1706

CARTER, MANDY, professional organization administrator; Nat. field dir. Nat. Black Gay and Lesbian Leadership Forum, Washington, also bd. dirs., liaison to human rights campaign. Pub. policy advocate Human Rights Campaign staff, 1992; active D.C. Coalition of Black Lesbians; founder N.C. Mobilization, 1996. Office: NBLGLF 1755 Broadway Fl 15 Oakland CA 94612-2155

CARTER, ROBERTA ECCLESTON, therapist, counselor; b. Pitts. d. Robert E. and Emily B. (Bucar) Carter; divorced; children: David Michael Kiewlich, Daniel Michael Kiewlich. Student, Edinboro State U., 1962-63; BS, California State U. Pa., 1966; MEd, U. Pitts., 1969; MA, Rosebridge Grad. Sch., 1987. Tchr. Bethel Park Sch. Dist., Pa., 1966-69; writer, media asst. Field Ednl. Pub., San Francisco, 1969-70; educator, counselor, specialist Alameda Unified Sch. Dist., Calif., 1970—. Master trainer Calif. State Dept. Edn., Sacramento, 1984—; personal growth cons., Alameda, 1983—. Author: People, Places and Products, 1970, Teaching/Learning Units, 1969; co-author: Teacher's Manual Let's Read, 1968. Mem. AAUW, NEA, Calif. Fedn. Bus. and Profl. Women (legis. chair Alameda br. 1984-85, membership chair 1985), Calif. Edn. Assn., Alameda Edn. Assn., Charter Planetary Soc., Oakland Mus., Exploratorium, Big Bros of East Bay, Alameda C. of C. (svc. awsard 1985). Avocations: aerobics, gardening, travel. Home: 1516 Eastshore Dr Alameda CA 94501-3118

CARTER, RONALD MARTIN, SR. pharmaceutical company executive; b. Chgo., Nov. 18, 1925; s. Jack Edward and Anna (Press) C.; m. Joy Wolf, Nov. 14, 1946; children: Ronald M. Jr., Craig Alan. Student, U. Ill., 1942-43, 45-46. Sales mgr. Preston Labs., Inc., Chgo., 1948-52; v.p. Myers-Carter Labs., Inc., Phoenix, 1952-69, pres., 1969-75, Carter-Glogau Labs., Inc., Glendale, Ariz., 1975-86, Steris Labs., Inc., Phoenix, 1987—, The Pharmikon Co., 1987—. Cons. Internat. Exec. Service Corp., Stamford, Conn., 1985—. Served as cpl. U.S. Army, 1943-45. Mem. Drug, Chem. Allied Trades, Generic Pharm. Industry Assn., Nat. Assn. Pharm. Mfrs., Nat. Pharm. Alliance (pres. 1983-84). Democrat. Jewish. Clubs: Arizona, Plaza (Phoenix). Avocations: hunting, fishing. Home: 5707 N 40th St Phoenix AZ 85018-1108 E-mail: roncar@home.com

CARTER, WILLIAM B. global development company official; Former pres., CEO AT&T Submarine Systems, Inc.; pres. Global Crossing Devel. Co., 1997—. Former mem. World Telecomms. Adv. Coun. to Internat. Telecomms. Union; sr. advisor to U.S. govt. on comms. and econ. devel. Office: Global Crossing 360 N Crescent Dr Beverly Hills CA 90210-4802

CARTER, WILLIAM GEORGE, III, career officer; b. Buffalo, June 18, 1944; s. William George Jr. and Elaine Ruth (Weber) C.; m. Linda Fay Yener, Oct. 2, 1965; children: Kris Ann, William George. BS, U. Tampa, 1972; MA, U. Shippensberg, 1982; MPE, U. Pitts., 1984. Commd. 2d. lt. U.S. Army, 1965, advanced through grades to lt. gen., 1995; various command and staff positions, 1964-77; exec. officer 3d Brigade, 1st Armored Div., Bamberg, Fed. Republic Germany, 1977-79; comdr. 1st Bn., 52d Inf., Bamberg, 1979-81, G3 1st Armored Div., VII U.S. Corps, Ansbach, Fed. Republic Germany, 1981-83; chief Plans and Integration Office, Hdqrs. U.S. Army, Washington, 1983-86; comdr. 1st Brigade, 4th Inf. Div., Ft. Carson, Colo., 1986-88; exec. asst. Office Chief of Staff Army, Washington, 1988-89; asst. div. comdr. 1st Inf. Div., Ft. Riley, Kans., 1989-91; comdr. Nat. Tng. Ctr., Ft. Irwin, Calif., 1991-93, 1st Armored Divsn., 1993-95; chief of staff Allied Forces So. Europe, 1995-97; exec. v.p. SY Technologies, Washington, 1993—. Decorated DDSM with oak leaf cluster, DSM with oak leaf cluster, Legion of Merit with six oak leaf clusters, Bronze Star with V device and two oak leaf clusters, Purple Heart with oak leaf cluster. Mem. Soc. of the Big Red One, Alpha Chi. Avocations: golf, hunting.

CARTMELL, NATHANIEL MADISON, III, lawyer; b. N.Y.C., Oct. 22, 1951; s. Nathaniel Madison Jr. and Ruth Kincer (Davies) C.; m. Suzanne Cameron Pettus, Jan. 3, 1981; children: Nathaniel Madison IV, Edmund Winston, Samuel Chapman Davies. BA, Yale U., 1973; JD, Vanderbilt U., 1978. Bar: Calif. State 1983, D.C. 1980, Va. State 1978. Mem. faculty Williston Northampton Sch., Easthampton, Mass., 1973-75; assoc. Hunton & Williams, Richmond, Va., 1978-80, Washington, 1980-81; atty. U.S. Synthetic Fuels Corp., Washington, 1981; assoc. Pillsbury Madison & Sutro LLP, Washington, 1982-83, San Francisco, 1983-86; ptnr. Pillsbury Winthrop LLP, San Francisco, 1987—, mgr. corp. and securities group, 1994-96, chair mergers and acquisitions specialty team, 1999—. Alumni bd. dirs. Vanderbilt Law Sch., 1998 ; alumni coun. Phillips Acad., 1997—. Mem. ABA (mem. fed. regulation of securities com., bus. law sect. 1990—), Calif. State Bar (mem. corps. com., bus. law sect. 1989-91). Episcopalian. Home: 24 Roble Ct Berkeley CA 94705-2836 Office: Pillsbury Madison & Sutro LLP 235 Montgomery St Fl 16 San Francisco CA 94104-3104 E-mail: ncartmell@pillsburywinthrop.com

CARTWRIGHT, BRIAN GRANT, lawyer; b. Seattle, May 29, 1947; s. John Brydonne and Helen Ruth (Engman) C.; m. Jean Claudia Libby, Jan. 5, 1975; children: Grant, Eliot, Bryce. BS, Yale U., 1967; PhD, U. Chgo., 1971; JD, Harvard U., 1980. Bar: D.C. 1981, U.S. Dist. Ct. D.C. 1981, U.S. Ct. Appeals (D.C. cir.) 1981, Calif. 1984. Law clk. U.S. Ct. Appeals (D.C. cir.), Washington, 1980-81, U.S. Supreme Ct., Washington, 1981-82; assoc. Latham & Watkins, L.A., 1982-88, ptnr., 1988—, mem. exec. com., 1994-98. Mem. Los Angeles County Bar Assn. (mem. exec. com., bus. and corps. law sect. 1992-99). Office: Latham & Watkins 633 W 5th St Ste 3800 Los Angeles CA 90071-2007

CARTWRIGHT, CHAS, national monument administrator; married. BA in Anthropology, Mich. State U., 1972. Seasonal fire fighter, fire lookout, river ranger U.S. Forestry Svc., Calif. and Idaho, 1972-75; seasonal archaeologist B.L.M., Idaho, Ariz. and Utah, 1979-87, archaeologist Utah, 1979-87; archaeololgist Arches and Canyonlands Nat. Parks, Natural Bridges Nat. Monument Nat. Pk. Svc., 1987-89, supt. Hovenweep Nat. Monument Utah and Colo., 1989-98, supt. Knife River Indian Villages Nat. Hist. Site N.D., 1989-98, supt., dir. Devils Tower (Wy.) Nat. Monument, 1998—. Office: care Devils Tower Monument PO Box 10 Devils Tower WY 82714-0010

CARTWRIGHT, PETER, electronics company executive; Pres., CEO Calpine, San Jose, Calif. Office: Calpine 50 W San Fernando St Ste 500 San Jose CA 95113-2433

CARVALHO, WAYNE G. protective services official; Chief of police, Hilo, Hawaii. Office: City of Hilo Police Dept 349 Kapiolani St Hilo HI 96720-3912

CARVER, CRAIG R. lawyer; b. Aug. 5, 1948; AB with distinction, Stanford U., 1970; JD, U. Mich., U. Denver, 1974. Bar: Colo. 1974. Ptnr. Gibson, Dunn & Crutcher, Denver, 1982-96; mem., mgr. Alfers & Carver, L.L.C., Denver, 1996—. Bd. trustees Rocky Mountain Mineral Law Found., 1982-84, 92-94, 99—. Mem. ABA, Colo. Bar Assn., Denver Bar Assn. Office: Alfers & Carver LLC 730 17th St Ste 340 Denver CO 80202-3513 E-mail: ccarver@alfers-carver.com

CARYL, NAOMI, artist; b. N.Y.C., June 27, 1931; d. Joseph Herman and Jennie (Berman) Hirshhorn. Student, Feagin Sch. Drama & Radio, 1951-52. Artist, composer, actor, producer, L.A., 1962—. One-woman shows include Ankrum Gallery, L.A., 1962, 69, 71, 72, 75, 83, 87, Zara Gallery, San Francisco, 1973, Lighthouse Gallery, Fla., 1989, Foster Harmon Gallery, Sarasota, Fla., 1991, Jerry Soloman Gallery, L.A., 1997; composer Spoon River Anthology, 1963 (Emmy nomination 1969), Mirror Image, 1995, others; author (plays) Nobody Safe Here, 1981 (new play award L.A. Weekly 1981, S.T.A.G.E. award 1997), The Start of The Blues, 1987, The Dressing Room, 1988, others. Co-chair, producer The S.T.A.G.E. Benefit, L.A., 1986—. Recipient L.A. Beautiful award Cactus Garden, 1989, Crystal Apple award AIDS Project, L.A., 1991, The Spirit of Hope award, 1999. Mem. ASCAP, SAG, Am. Fedn. TV and Radio Artists, Equity, Dramatists Guild, Theatre West. Avocations: gardening, reverand, personalized weddings. Home and Office: 2071 Castilian Dr Los Angeles CA 90068-2608

CASAMENTO, CHARLES JOSEPH, pharmaceutical industry executive; b. Hoboken, N.J., June 8, 1945; s. Charles Vincent and Mary (Brignola) C.; m. Evelyn Ann Kenez, June 8, 1968 (div. 1983); children: Christopher Charles, Suzanne Marie; m. Doris Ann Mason, May 25, 1985. BS in Pharmacy, Fordham U., 1968; MBA in Mktg., Iona Coll., 1971. Registered pharmacist, N.J., N.Y. Mgr. Sandoz Pharm. Div., East Hanover, N.J., 1970-71, fin. planner, 1972-73, product coordinator, 1973-74, mgr. new product planning, 1974-75, mgr. new product planning and licensing, 1975-77; mgr. product devel. Hoffmann-La Roche, Nutley, 1977-79; dir. new products and acquisitions Johnson & Johnson, New Brunswick, 1979-83; v.p. bus. devel. Am. Critical Care div. Am. Hosp. Supply, Waukegan, Ill., 1983-86; sr. v.p., gen. mgr. Genzyme Corp., Boston, 1986-89; pres. and CEO Interneuron Pharmaceuticals Inc., 1989-93;

chmn., pres and CEO RiboGene Inc., Hayward, CA, 1993—. Lectr. in field. Campaign mgr. Rep. Com., Veron, N.J., 1976; coach Little League, Upper Saddle River, 1978-79, Little League, Basking Ridge, 1980-82, local Soccer League, Upper SAddle River, 1978-79; pres. Ch. Parrish Council, 1979. Mem. Licensing Exec. Soc., Am. Pharm. Assn., Comml. Devel. Assn., Assn. Corp. Growth, Cambridge Racquet Club. Episcopalian. Avocations: photography, golf. Office: RiboGene Inc 26118 Research Pl Hayward CA 94545-3732

CASANOVA, ALDO JOHN, sculptor; b. San Francisco, Feb. 8, 1929; s. Felice and Teresa (Papini) C.; children: Aviva, Liana, Anabelle. BA, San Francisco State U., 1950, MA, 1951; PhD, Ohio State U., 1957. Asst. prof. art San Francisco State U., 1951-53; asst. prof. Antioch (Ohio) Coll., 1956-58; asst. prof. art Tyler Sch. Art, Temple U., Phila., 1961-64, Tyler Sch. Art, Temple U. (Italy campus), Rome, 1968-70; prof. art Scripps Coll., Claremont, Calif., 1966—, chmn. art dept., 1971-73; vis. prof. SUNY, 1981; faculty mem. Skowhegan Sch. Painting and Sculpture, Maine, summers 1973-74. One-man shows include Esther Robles Gallery, L.A., 1967, Santa Barbara (Calif.) Mus., 1967, Calif. Inst. Tech., 1972, Carl Schlosberg Fine Arts, L.A., 1977, SUNY, 1981; represented in permanent collections Whitney Mus., San Francisco Mus. Art, San Diego Mus. Sculpture Garden, Hirshhorn Collection, Cornell U., Columbus (Ohio) Mus., UCLA Sculpture Garden, Calif. Inst. Tech., Pasadena, Univ. Judaism, L.A., Air and Space Mus., Washington, Collection of Nat. Acad. of Design, N.Y.C., 1993, Robert Feldmuth Meml. Commn., W.M. Keck Sci. Ctr., Claremont, Calif., 1995, Newport Harbor Mus., Calif., 1996. Recipient Prix-de-Rome Am. Acad. in Rome, 1958-61; Louis Comfort Tiffany award, 1970 Fellow Am. Acad. in Rome; mem. NAD, NAS, Sculptors Guild, Nat. Sculpture Soc. Democrat. Roman Catholic. Office: Scripps Coll Art Dept Claremont CA 91711

CASE, CALE, state legislator, economist; b. Lander, Wyo., June 2, 1958; s. George Harold and Mayre Elizabeth (Tangemann) C.; m. Shirley Case. BA in Econs., U. Wyo., 1980, PhD in Econs., 1986. Staff economist City of Lander, 1981-82; ind. cons. Laramie, Wyo., 1982-84; econ. analyst Ill. Commerce Commn., Springfield, Ill., 1984, sr. economist, 1984-85, dir. telecommunications, 1985-86, mgr. policy analysis, 1986-87; mgr. econs. and fin. Palmer Bellevue Corp., Chgo., 1987-88, v.p., 1988—; sec. Tangemann Benedict Corp., 1988—; mem. Wyo. Ho. of Reps., 1992-98, Wyo. Senate, Dist. 25, Cheyenne, 1998—. Judiciary com., 1993-94, travel recreation and wildlife com., 1995—, corps. com. 1995—; instr. econs. U. Wyo., Laramie, 1982-83; instr. grad. econs. Sangamon State U., Springifeld, 1985; mem. comm. com. staff nat. Assn. Regulatory Utility Commns., 1985-87; mem. faculty Public Utility Rsch. and Tng. Inst., Laramie, 1989—; mem. corps., election and polit. coms., labor health and social svcs. com. Wyo. State Senate. Commr. Econ. Devel. Commn., Lander, 1987—. Recipient Disting. Alumni award U. Wyo. Coll. Commerce and Industry, 1989-90. Mem. Am. Econ. Assn., Internat. Assn. Energy Econs. Republican. Office: 787 S 4th St Lander WY 82520-3717 also: Wyo Senate State Capital Cheyenne WY 82002

CASE, CHARLES G., II, federal judge; b. Phoenix, Jan. 17, 1948; BA cum laude, Harvard U., 1969; JD magna cum laude, Ariz. State U., 1975. Bar: Ariz. 1975. With Lewis and Roca, Phoenix, 1975-88, Meyer, Hendricks, Victor, Osborn & Maledon P.C., Phoenix, 1988-93; judge U.S. Bankruptcy Ct., Phoenix, 1994—. Judge pro tempore Ariz. Ct. Appeals; adj. prof. law Ariz. State U., 1988-91, 97—. Contbg. author Comml. Law and Practice Guides, 1991. Mem. ABA. Home: PO Box 34151 Phoenix AZ 85067-4151 Office: 2929 N Central Ave Fl 9 Phoenix AZ 85012-2752

CASE, JAMES HEBARD, lawyer; b. Lihue, Hawaii, Apr. 10, 1920; s. Adrial Hebard and Elizabeth (McConnell) C.; m. Suzanne Catherine Espenett, Sept. 18, 1948; children: Edward E., John H., Suzanne D., Russell L., Elisabeth D. Marguleas, Bradford Case. AB, Williams Coll., 1941; JD, Harvard U., 1949. Bar: Hawaii 1949, U.S. Supreme Ct. 1985. Assoc. Pratt, Tavares & Cassidy, Honolulu, 1949-51, Carlsmith & Carlsmith, Hilo, Hawaii, 1951-59; ptnr. Carlsmith Ball, Honolulu, 1959—. Bd. dirs. ML Resources, Honolulu. Trustee Hanahauoli Sch., Honolulu, 1970-82, Cen. Union Ch., Honolulu, 1984-88, Arcadia Retirement Residence, Honolulu, 1985-91. Lt. comdr. USNR, 1943-46, PTO. Mem. ABA, Hawaii Bar Assn., Hawaii Yacht Racing Assn. (bd. dirs. 1994-2000). Republican. Congregationalist. Clubs: Pacific (bd. dirs. 1978-82); Kaneohe Yacht (Honolulu). Avocations: sailing, tennis. Home: 3757 Round Top Dr Honolulu HI 96822-5043 Office: Carlsmith Ball PO Box 656 Honolulu HI 96809-0656 E-mail: jhc@carlsmith.com

CASE, RICHARD W. sports association executive; m. Barbara Case; two children. Sec. gen. USA Baseball (formerly U.S. Baseball Fedn.), 1980—. Bd. dirs. U.S. Olympic Com.; cons., advisor and dir. in field; producer instrnl. videotapes, books and brochures with a concentration in the areas of player and coach tng., vol. enlistment, accident prevention, juv. delinquency, and youth tournament operation in all sports. Recipient USA Baseball Pres.'s award, Am. Baseball Coaches Assn. award of honor, Centenary medal Juan Antonio Samaranch, Internat. Olympic Com. Pres., others; inducted into Nat. Jr. Coll. Athletic Assn. Hall of Fame, Nat. Assn. Intercollegiate Athletics Hall of Fame, Nat. Police Assn. Hall of Honor; recipient numerous hon. citizenship and commendation awards. Mem. Internat. Baseball Assn. (sec. gen.). Office: USA Baseball c/o Paul Seiler 3400 E Camino Campestre Tucson AZ 85716-5800

CASE, THOMAS R. career officer; BS in Geography, U.S. Air Force Acad., 1969; Grad., Squadron Officer Sch., 1973; MS in Systems Mgmt., U. So. Calif., L.A., 1975; Diploma, U.S. Army Command/Gen. Staff, Coll., 1979, Nat. War Coll., , 1987. Commd. 2d lt. USAF, 1969, lt. gen., 1998; various assignments to dir. opers. U.S. Cen. Command, MacDill AFB, Fla., 1997, dep. comdr.-in-chief, chief of staff, 1997-98; comdr. Alaskan Command, 11th Air Force/N.Am. Aerospace Def. Command, Elmendorf AFB, Alaska, 1998—. Decorated Def. Disting. Svc. medal, Legion of Merit with oak leaf cluster, Disting. Flying Cross with oak leaf cluster, Def. Meritorious Svc. medal, Meritorious Svc. medal with two oak leaf clusters, Air medal with 10 oak leaf clusters. Office: 11 AF/CC 9480 Pease Ave Ste 101 Elmendorf AFB AK 99506-2100

CASELLI, VIRGIL P. real estate executive; b. San Francisco, May 29, 1940; s. Americo P. and Cressida N. C.; m. Mary T. McKeon, July 18, 1970; children— Monica, Megan, Virgil Paul. B.S., U. Calif., Berkeley, 1963; M.B.A., U. San Francisco, 1973. Security analyst Wells Fargo Bank, San Francisco, 1963-65; purchasing agt. Raychem Corp., Menlo Park, Calif., 1965-70; founding dir., v.p. 1st Montgomery Corp., San Francisco, 1970-72; div. mgr. Kaiser-Aetna Co., Oakland, Calif., 1972-75; chief exec. officer, exec. v.p., gen. mgr. Ghiradelli Sq., San Francisco, 1975-82; pres. Comml. Property Ventures, Inc., San Francisco, 1982—; CEO C.P. Ventures (named changed Comml. Property Ventures, Inc.), San Francisco, 1990—. Bd. dirs. San Francisco Conv. and Visitors Bur., 1975-83, Cable Car Friends, San Francisco, 1975—, The Guardsmen, Francisco, 1977-79; pres. Fisherman's Wharf Mchts. Assos., 1976-77, San Francisco Parking and Garage Owners Assocs., 1977. Founder, pres. C.O.B. Com. to Save Cable Cars, 1979-87; trustee U. Calif.-Berkeley Found., 1981-89; bd. dirs. Golden Gate Nat. Parks Assocs., 1983-95, chmn., 1983-87; mem. adv. com. U. San Francisco; mem. adv. coun. Bologna Ctr., Johns Hopkins U. Sch. Advanced Internat. Studies, 1985-92. Comdr. USCG Res., ret. Mem. Soc. Real Property Adminstrs., Bldg. Owners and Mgrs. Inst. Internat. Repub- [illegible] PO Box 1110 Belvedere Tiburon CA 94920-4116 E-mail: [illegible]

CASEY, BARBARA A. PEREA, state legislator, school superintendent; b. Las Vegas, N.Mex., Dec. 21, 1951; d. Joe D. and Julia A. (Armijo) Perea; m. Frank J. Casey, Aug. 5, 1978. BA, N.Mex. U., 1972; MA, Highland U., Las Vegas, N.Mex., 1973. Instr. N.Mex. Highlands U., Las Vegas, 1972-74; tchr. Roswell Ind. Schs., Roswell, N.Mex., 1974-96; supt. Hondo Valley Pub. Schs.; mem. N.Mex. Ho. of Reps., 1984—; supt. Hondo (N.Mex.) Valley Pub. Schs., 1996—. Instr. N.Mex. Mil. Inst., Roswell, 1977-82, Roswell Police Acad., 1984. N.Mex. advisor Nat. Trust for Hist. Preservation. Mem. NEA (Adv. of of Yr.), AAUW, Am. Bus. Women's Assn., N.Mex. Endowment for Humanities. Democrat. Roman Catholic. Avocations: hunting, reading, writing, poetry. Home: 1214 E 1st St Roswell NM 88203-7960

CASEY, MARY A. telecommunications company executive; Dir. operator svcs. Call Am., 1988-91; dir. customer svc. WCT, 1991-93; co-founder, sec. STAR Telcom., Inc., Santa Barbara, Calif., 1993—; pres. STAR Telecom., Inc., Santa Barbara, 1996—. Office: STAR Telecom Inc 223 E De La Guerra St Santa Barbara CA 93101-2206

CASEY, NANCY J. women's healthcare company executive; BA in English, San Diego State U. Owner, mgr. Nancy Casey Pub. Rels., 1985-97; dir. pub. rels. WestCom Group, 1987-90; sales asst. Dale Fitzmorris, 1990-92; co-founder, co-CEO, As We Change, LLC, 1995-98; v.p. catalog ops. Women First HealthCare, Inc., San Diego, 1998-99, v.p. pub. rels., 1999—. Office: Women First HealthCare Inc 23330 El Camino Real Ste 400 San Diego CA 92130 Fax: 619-509-1353

CASEY, SUE (SUZANNE MARGUERITE PHILIPS), actress, real estate broker; b. L.A., Apr. 8, 1926; d. Burke Dewey and Mildred Louise (Hansen) Philips; children: Colleen O'Shaughnessy, John Joseph Durant III, Christopher Kent Durant, Diane M. Kelly; m. Jack Hoffmann (div.); stepchildren: Joy Hoffmann Molloy, Kristen Hoffmann Blutman. Student, UCLA Extension, 1972-75. Lic. real estate broker and saleswoman, Calif. With Coldwell Banker/Jon Douglas Co., Beverly Hills, Calif. Appeared in numerous movies, including swimming in 5 Esther Williams films, singing and dancing in over 20 films, Goldwyn Girl, 1945-47; Star Is Born, Surf Terror, 1965, Catalina Caper, 1967, Happy Ending, Secrets of Monte Carlo, The Family Jewels, Marriage Young Stockbroker, The Big Circus, The Errand Boy, Two Weeks in Another Town, Paint Your Wagon, Camelot, Evil Speak, 1981, Swamp Country, Ladies Man, Lucky Lady, Annie Get Your Gun, Show Boat, Carpetbaggers, Rear Window, Breakfast at Tiffany's, The Scarf, Main Event, Brady Bunch Sequel, 1996, American Beauty, 1999; appeared in TV shows, including Hunter, Hotel, Hart to Hart, White Shadow, Sunny Valley, Lucy, Gunsmoke, Arnie, Marcus Welby, Sky Terror, Dallas, Days of Our Lives, Unsolved Mysteries, Rosie O'Neill, Haggerty, Emergency, California Fever, I Love Lucy, Farmer's Daughter, Beverly Hillbillies, Delta House, Bodies of Evidence, The Faculty, Divorce Court, Colgate Comedy Shows, Carol Burnett Shows, Red Skelton Show, Roy Bolger Show, All Star Revues, Bob Hope Specials, Ann Southern Show, Family Medical Center, Red Shoe Diaries, What Love Sees, Boy Meets World, 1997, Diagnosis Murder, 1999; has appeared in over 200 TV commls.; stage appearances include Picnic, Goodnight Ladies. Ball chmn. The Footlighters, Inc., 1971-73, 93-94, press chmn., 1972-73, pres., 1982-83, 98-99, parliamentarian, 1983-94, 99-00, hospitality chmn., 1992-93. Naemd Ms. Sr. Am. of L.A., 1993. Mem. AFTRA, SAG, Actors Equity Assn. Office: Coldwell Banker 301 N Canon Dr Beverly Hills CA 90210-4722 E-mail: caseysue@aol.com

CASEY, THOMAS J. communications company executive, lawyer; b. Frankfurt, Germany, Feb. 24, 1952; BA magna cum laude, Boston Coll., 1973; JD with honors, George Washington U., 1977. Bar: Va. 1977, D.C. 1979, Mass. 1984, U.S. Supreme Ct. 1985. With ITT, Washington, 1973-75, antitrust div. U.S. Dept. Justice, 1975-78, Fed. Communications Commn., 1978-81; assoc. and ptnr. Mintz, Levin, Cohn, Ferris, Glovsky & Popeo, P.C., 1981-89, ptnr., 1983-89; ptnr., co-head of telecoms. and media group Skadden, Arps, Slate, Meagher & Flom, 1990-95; mng. dir., co-head of global comms. investment banking group Merrill Lynch, 1995-98; pres., dir. Pacific Capital Group, Inc., 1998-2000; vice chmn. bd., mng. dir. Global Crossing Ltd., 1998-2000, vice chmn., CEO, 2000—. Co-author: Cable Television Law, 1983. Home and Office: Global Crossings Ltd 360 N Crescent Dr Beverly Hills CA 90210-4802 E-mail: tcasey@globalcrossing.com

CASH, R(OY) DON, gas and petroleum company executive; b. Shamrock, Tex., June 27, 1942; s. Bill R. and Billie Mae (Lisle) C.; m. Sondra Kay Burleson, Feb. 20, 1966; 1 child, Clay Collin. BS in Indsl. Engring., Tex. Tech U., 1966. Former engr. Amoco Prodn. Co.; v.p. Mountain Fuel Supply, Salt Lake City, 1976-79; pres. Wexpro Co., Salt Lake City, 1979-80; pres., CEO Mountain Fuel Supply Co., Salt Lake City, 1980-84, Questar Corp., Salt Lake City, 1984-85, pres., chmn., CEO, 1985—, also bd. dirs. Bd. dirs. Zions Bancorp., Zions First Nat. Bank, Salt Lake City br. Fed. Res. Bank, Aegis Ins. Svcs., Inc., Energen Corp., Interstate Natural Gas Assn. of Am.; trustee Inst. Gas Technology, Chgo., 1986—; chmn. 1992-94. Trustee Holy Cross Hosp., 1987-90, Salt Lake Organizing Com. of 2002 Olympic Winter Games, 1991—, So. Utah U., 1992-97; bd. dirs. Utah Symphony Orch., Salt Lake City, 1983-86, 93—; Gas Rsch. Inst., 1991-93. Mem. Soc. Petroleum Engrs., Rocky Mountain Oil and Gas Assn. (bd. dirs., pres. 1982-84), Utah Mfrs. Assn. (bd. dirs. 1983-89, chmn. 1986), Pacific Coast Gas Assn. (bd. dirs. 1981-85, 87-97, chmn. 1993-94), Am. Gas Assn. (bd. dirs. 1989-95), Am. Petroleum Inst. (bd. dirs. 1986-91), Nat. Petroleum Coun., Ind. Petroleum Assn. of Am., Salt Lake Area C. of C. (bd. dirs. 1981-84, 89-92, chmn. 1991-92), Alta Club, The Country Club. Avocations: boating, skiing, tennis, fishing, hunting. Office: Questar Corp PO Box 45433 Salt Lake City UT 84145-0433

CASHMAN, MICHAEL RICHARD, small business owner; b. Owatonna, Minn., Sept. 26, 1926; s. Michael Richard and Mary (Quinn) C.; m. Antje Katrin Paulus, Jan. 22, 1972 (div. 1983); children: Janice Katrin, Joshua Paulus, Nina Carolin. BS, U.S. Mcht. Marine Acad., 1947; BA, U. Minn., 1951; MBA, Harvard U., 1953. Regional mgr. Air Products & Chems., Inc., Allentown, Pa., 1959-64, then pres. so. div. Washington, 1964-68; mng. dir. Air Products & Chems., Inc. Europe, Brussels, 1968-72; internat. v.p. Airco Indsl. Gasses, Brussels, 1972-79; pres. Continental Elevator Co., Denver, 1979-81; assoc. Moore & Co., Denver, 1981-84; prin. Cashman & Co., Denver, 1984—. Committeeman Denver Rep. Com., 1986—, congl. candidate, 1988; chmn. "Two Forks or Dust" Ad Hoc Citizens Com.. Lt. (j.g.) USN, 1953-55. Mem. Bldg. Owners and Mgrs. Assn., Colo. Harvard Bus. Sch. Club, Am. Rights Union, Royal Golf de Belgique, Belgian Shooting Club, Rotary, Soc. St. George, Phi Beta Kappa. Avocations: skiing, golf, sailing, guitar, opera. Home: 2512 S University Blvd Apt 802 Denver CO 80210-6152

CASIDA, JOHN EDWARD, entomology educator; b. Phoenix, Dec. 22, 1929; s. Lester Earl and Ruth (Barnes) C.; m. Katherine Faustine Monson, June 16, 1956; children: Mark Earl, Eric Gerhard. B.S., U. Wis., 1951, M.S., 1952, Ph.D., 1954; D (hon.), U. Buenos Aires, 1997. Research asst. U. Wis., 1951-53, mem. faculty, 1954-63, prof. entomology, 1959-63, U. Calif.-Berkeley, 1964—; scholar-in-residence Bellagio Study and Conf. [illegible] Italy, 1978; Messenger lectr. Cornell U., 1985; Sterling B. Hendricks lectr. USDA and Am. Chem. Soc., 1992—; dir. Environ. Chemistry and Toxicology Lab., 1964—; William Muriece Hoskins chair in chem. and molecular entomology U. Calif., Berkeley, 1996—; faculty rsch. lectr. U. Calif., Berkeley, 1998; lectr. in sci. Third World Acad. Scis., U. Buenos Aires, 1997. Author research publs. Served with USAF, 1955. Recipient medal 7th Internat. Congress Plant Protection, Paris, 1970, Disting. Svc. award USDA, 1988, Wolf prize in agr., 1993; Haight traveling fellow, 1958-59, Guggenheim fellow, 1970-71, Founder's award Soc. Environ. Toxicology and Chemistry, 1994, Kôrô-sho prize Pesticide Sci. Soc. Japan, 1995; Jeffery lectr. U. NSW, Australia, 1983. Mem. NAS, Royal Soc. U.K. (fgn.), Am. Chem. Soc. (Internat. award rsch. pesticide chemistry 1970, Spencer award in agrl. and food chemistry 1978), Entomol. Soc. Am. (Bussart Meml. award 1989, fellow 1989), Soc. Environ. Toxicology and Chemistry (Founder's award 1994), Soc. Toxicology (hon.). Home: 1570 La Vereda Rd Berkeley CA 94708-2036

CASPER, GERHARD, academic administrator, law educator; b. Hamburg, Germany, Dec. 25, 1937; s. Heinrich and Hertha C.; m. Regina Koschel, Dec. 26, 1964; 1 child, Hanna. Legal state exam., U. Freiburg, U. Hamburg, 1961; LL.M., Yale U., 1962; Dr.iur., U. Freiburg, Germany, 1964; hon. degree, Yale U., 2000, Uppsala U., 2000. Asst. prof. polit. sci. U. Calif., Berkeley, 1964-66; assoc. prof. law and polit. sci. U. Chgo., 1966-69, prof., 1969-76, Max Pam prof. law, 1976-80, William B. Graham prof. law, 1980-87, William B. Graham Disting. Svc. prof. law, 1987-92, dean law sch., 1979-87, provost, 1989-92; prof. law Stanford (Calif.) U., 1992-2000, pres., 1992-2000; Peter and Helen Bing prof., 2000—. Vis. prof. law Cath. U., Louvain, Belgium, 1970, U. Munich, 1988, 91. Author: Realism and Political Theory in American Legal Thought, 1967, (with Richard A. Posner) The Workload of the Supreme Court, 1976; co-editor: The Supreme Ct. Rev., 1977-91, Separating Power, 1997. Successor, trustee Yale U., 2000—; bd. dirs. Am. Acad. in Berlin, 2000—. Fellow Am. Acad. Arts and Scis.; mem. Internat. Acad. Comparative Law, Am. Bar Found. (bd. dirs. 1979-87), Coun. Fgn. Rels., Am. Law Inst. (coun. 1980—), Oliver Wendell Holmes Devise (permanent com. 1985-93), Am. Philos. Soc., The Trilateral Commn., 1998—. E-mail: gcasper@stanford.edu

CASPER, WAYNE ARTHUR, city official, educator; b. Detroit, June 10, 1949; s. Arthur Eugene and Arlene (Burke) C.; m. Catherine Adelle Lyons, Jan. 22, 1972; children: Catherine, Jeff. BS, U. Ariz., 1971, MS, 1979. Buyer City of Tucson, 1971-74, adminstrv. asst., 1974-75, asst. purchasing agt., 1975-81; procurement dir. State or Ariz., Phoenix, 1981-90; dir. procurement City of Tucson, 1990—. Advisor, City of Mesa Risk Mgmt. Adv. Coun., 1983-88. Mem. Nat. Assn. State Purchasing Inst. (pres. 1991), Nat. Inst. Govtl. Purchasing (Ariz. chpt. treas. 1983, sec. 1984, v.p. 1985, pres. 1986). Roman Catholic. Office: City of Tucson PO Box 27210 Tucson AZ 85726-7210

CASS, GLEN ROWAN, environmental engineer; b. Pasadena, Calif., Apr. 18, 1947; s. Robert Mervin and Marie (Segner) C.; m. Jean Elizabeth Annis, Dec. 18, 1976; 1 child, Robert Covel. BSME, U. So. Calif., 1969; MSME, Stanford U., 1970; PhD, Calif. Inst. Tech., 1978. Officer USPHS, Atlanta, 1970-73; from instr. to prof. engring. Calif. Inst. Tech., Pasadena, 1978—. Clean air scientific adv. com. U.S. EPA, Washington, 1991-92; com. on haze in nat. parks and wilderness areas Nat. Rsch. Coun., Washington, 1990-93; rsch. adv. com. Health Effects Inst., Cambridge, Mass., 1993—; adv. com. ozone, fine particles, and regional haze EPA, 1996-98; cons. in field. Assoc. editor Aerosol Sci. and Tech., 1994-98; mem. editl. bd. Environ. Sci. Tech., 1998—. Environ. goals com. L.A. 2000, 1987-88; clean air com., Pasadena Lung Assn., 1977-85. Mem. Am. Chem. Soc., Am. Assn. Aerosol Rsch. (bd. dirs. 1996—). Office: Environ Engring Sci Dept Calif Inst Tech Pasadena CA 91125-0001

CASSARD, CHRISTOPHER D. lumber company executive; CFO and treas. North Pacific Group, Portland, Oreg. Office: North Pacific Group PO Box 3915 Portland OR 97208-3915 Office Fax: (503) 238-2646

CASSIDY, SAMUEL H. lawyer, lieutenant governor, state legislator, humanities educator; children: Rachael, Sarah, Samuel H. IV. BA, U. Okla., 1972; JD, U. Tulsa, 1975; postgrad., Harvard U., 1991. Bar: Okla., 1975, U.S. Supreme Ct. 1977, U.S. Ct. Appeals (10th cir.), 1977, Colo. 1982. Pvt. practice law, 1975—; mem. Colo. State Senate, 1991-94; lt. gov. State of Colo., 1994-95; pres. Jefferson Econ. Coun., 1995-97; pres., CEO Colo. Assn. Commerce and Industry, 1997-2000; prof. Daniels Sch. Bus. U. Denver, 2000—. Bd. dirs. Capital Reporter; instr. U. Tulsa, 1978-81, Tulsa Jr. Coll., 1979; owner High Country Title Co.; developer of residential and commercial real estate, pres. Sam Cassidy, Inc. oil and gas exploration and production co., mem. agriculture and natural resources com., 1991-92, state, mil. and vet. affairs com., 1991-92, local govt. com. 1991, legal svcs. com. 1991-92, hwy. legis. review com. 1991-93, nat. hazards mitigation coun., 1992-93, appropriations com., 1993, judiciary com., 1993; pres. Econ. Devel. Coun. of Colo., 1997-98; exec. com. legis coun., 1993-94, senate svcs. com. 1993; elected Senate Minority Leader, 1993-94, exec. com. Colo. Gen. Assembly; sr. fellow U. Denver, 1997—. Bd. dirs. Colo. DLC, 1993-95, Leadership Jefferson County, Rocky Flats Local Impacts Initiative, dir.; chmn. bd. Arts Comm., Inc. Named Outstanding Legislator for 1991 Colo. Bankers Assn., ACLU Outstanding Legis. 1994; recipient Outsatnding Legis. Efforts award Colo. Counties, Guardian of Small Bus. award, NFIB, 1992, 94; fellow Gates Found., 1991, U. Denver sr. fellow. Mem. Colo. Bar Assn. (bd. gov. 1993-94), S.W. Colo. Bar Assn., Nat. Conf. State Legis. (Colo. rep., task force on state-tribe rels.), Rotary (hon. mem., sustaining Paul Harris fellow), Club 20 (bd. dirs.), San Juan Forum (chmn., bd. dirs.). Avocations: fine art photography, skiing, fishing. Home: # 128 2800 S University Blvd Denver CO 80210 E-mail: scassidy@du.edu

CASTELLANO, MICHAEL ANGELO, research forester; b. Bklyn., June 26, 1956; s. Biagio and Mildred Anne (Cucco) C.; m. Elizabeth Marie Phillips, July 14, 1979; children: Nicholas Aaron, Daniel Robert Feller, Kelly Marie, Katlyn Morgan. AAS, Paul Smiths Coll., 1978; BS, Oreg. State U., 1982, MS, 1984, PhD, 1988. Forest technician Weyerhauser Co., Columbus, Miss., 1979; forester trainee USDA Forest Svc., Pacific N.W., Corvallis, Oreg., 1980-84, forester, 1984-87, rsch. forester, 1987—. Cons. CSIRO, Div. of Forestry, Australia, 1988-95, Spanish-Am. Binational Prog., Barcelona, 1987, 91. Author: Key to Hypogeous Fungi, 1989, (agr. handbook) Mycorrhizae, 1989, Handbook to Strategy I Fungal Species, 1999; contbr. articles to profl. jours. Bishop LSD Ch. Named one of Outstanding Young Men, Am. JayCees, 1984. Mem. Soc. Am. Foresters, N.Am. Truffling Soc. (advisor), Soil Ecology Soc., Mycol. Soc. of Am. (nomenclature 1986), Sigma Xi. Avocations: genealogy, baseball, computers, stamps, literature. Home: 1835 NW Garfield Ave Corvallis OR 97330-2535 Office: USDA Forest Svc 3200 SW Jefferson Way Corvallis OR 97331-4401 E-mail: michael.castellano@orst.edu

CASTELLINO, RONALD AUGUSTUS DIETRICH, radiologist, educator; b. N.Y.C., Feb. 18, 1938; s. Leonard Vincent and Henrietta Wilhelmina (Geffken) C.; m. Joyce Cuneo, Jan. 26, 1963; children: Jeffrey Charles, Robin Leonard, Anthony James. Student, Creighton U., Omaha, 1955-58, M.D., 1962. Diplomate: Am. Bd. Radiology. Rotating intern Highland Alameda County Hosp., Oakland, Calif., 1962-63; USPHS/Peace Corps physician Brazil, 1963-65; resident in diagnostic radiology Stanford U. Hosp., 1965-68, chief resident, 1967-68; asst. prof. radiology Stanford U. Med. Sch., 1968-74, assoc. prof., 1974-81, prof., 1981-93, chief diagnostic oncologic radiology, 1970-89, chief CT body scanning, 1979-85, dir. div. diagnostic radiology and assoc. chmn. dept. radiology, 1981-86, acting chmn. dept. diagnostic radiology and nuclear medicine, 1986-89, prof. emeritus, 1993—; chair dept. radiology, Carroll and Milton Petrie chair Meml. Sloan Kettering Cancer Ctr., N.Y.C., 1990-98; prof. radiology Cornell Med. Sch., 1994-98, chief med. officer R-2 tech., 1998—. Mem. U.S. Cancer del. People's Republic China, 1977 [illegible] Pediatric Oncologic Radiology, 1977; assoc. editor: Lymphology, 1973-97, Investigative Radiology, 1985-94, Academic Radiology, 1994-97, Radiology, 1986-94, Postgrad. Radiology, 1986-98; contbr. numerous rsch. papers to profl. jours., chpts. to books. Recipient T.F. Eckstrom Fund award, 1978; Guggenheim fellow, 1974-75 Mem. Internat. Soc. Lymphology (exec. com. 1975-85), Am. Coll. Radiology, Assn. Univ. Radiologists (exec. com. 1981-85), Radiol. Soc. N.Am., Soc. Cardiovascular and Interventional Radiology (charter), Am. Roentgen Ray Soc., Internat. Cantev Imaging Soc. (charter), Western Angiography Soc. (charter), Calif. Med. Assn. (adv. panel sect. radiology 1972-89), Calif. Radiol. Soc., Soc. Thoracic Radiology (charter), Soc. Cancer Imaging (charter), N.Am. Soc. Lymphology (charter, exec. com. 1982-86), Calif. Acad. Medicine, N.Y. Roentgen Soc., N.Y. Acad. Medicine, Am. Soc. Therapeutic Radiation Oncologists (hon.), Alpha Omega Alpha. Office: R-2 Tech 325 Distel Cir Los Altos CA 94022-1408 E-mail: rcastell@r2tech.com

CASTELLO, JOHN L. pharmaceutical executive; Chmn. bd., CEO, pres. Xoma Corp., Berkeley, Calif. Office: Xoma Corp 2910 7th St Ste 100 Berkeley CA 94710-2743

CASTILLO, SUSAN, state legislator; b. L.A., Aug. 14, 1951; m. Paul Machu. BA, Oreg. State U., 1981. Mem. staff Oreg. Pub. Broadcasting Radio, 1979-82; journalist, reporter legis. sessions Sta. KVAL-TV, Salem, 1991, 93, 95, journalist, reporter Eugene, 1982-97; mem. Oreg. Legislature, Salem, 1997—, vice chair edn. com., mem. health and human svcs. com., mem. transp. com. Leader Oreg. Women's Health & Wellness Alliance. Mem. Gov.'s Task Force on DUII, 1997, Gov.'s Task Force on Cmty. Right to Know; bd. dirs. Oreg. Commn. on Hispanic Affairs, 1997, Birth to Three, Oreg. Environ. Coun.; mem. adv. com. Oreg. Passenger Rail Adv. Coun.; mem. Labor Comm.'s Adv. Com. on Agrl. Labor; vice-chair Farm Worker Housing Task Force. Democrat. Achievements include being the first Hispanic woman to serve in Oregon legislature. Office: PO Box 5309 Eugene OR 97405-0309

CASTLE, EMERY NEAL, agricultural and resource economist, educator; b. Eureka, Kans., Apr. 13, 1923; s. Sidney James and Josie May (Tucker) C.; m. Merab Eunice Weber (dec.), Jan. 20, 1946; 1 child, Cheryl Diana Delozier; m. Betty Thompson, Mar. 18, 2000. BS, Kans. State U., 1948, MS, 1950; PhD, Iowa State U., 1952, LHD (hon.), 1997. Agrl. economist Fed. Res. Bank of Kansas City, 1952-54; from asst. prof. to prof. dept. agrl. econs. Oreg. State U., Corvallis, 1954-65, dean faculty, 1965-66, prof., head dept. agrl. econs., 1966-72, dean Grad. Sch., 1972-76, Alumni disting. prof., 1970, prof. univ. grad. faculty econs., 1986—; v.p., sr. fellow Resources for the Future, Washington, 1976-79, pres., 1979-86. Vice-chmn. Environ. Quality Commn. Oreg., 1988-95. Editor: The Changing American Countryside: Rural People and Places, 1995; mem. editl. bd. Land Econs., 1969—. Recipient Alumni Disting. Service award Kans. State U., 1976; Disting. Service award Oreg. State U., 1984 Fellow AAAS, Am. Assn. Agrl. Economists (pres. 1972-73), Am. Acad. Arts and Scis. Home: 1112 NW Solar Pl Corvallis OR 97330-3640 Office: Oreg State U 227 Ballard Extension Hall Corvallis OR 97331-8538

CASTLEBERRY, ARLINE ALRICK, architect; b. Mpls., Sept. 19, 1919; d. Bannona Gerhardt and Meta Emily (Veit) Alrick; m. Donald Montgomery Castleberry, Dec. 25, 1941; children: Karen, Marvin. B in Interior Architecture, U. Minn., 1941; postgrad., U. Tex., 1947-48. Designer, draftsman Elizabeth & Winston Close, Architects, Mpls., 1940-41, Northwest Airlines, Mpls., 1942-43, Cerny & Assocs., Mpls., 1944-46; archtl. draftsman Dominick and Van Benscotten, Washington, 1946-47; ptnr. Castleberry & Davis Bldg. Designers, Burlingame, Calif., 1960-65; prin. Burlingame, 1965-90. Recipient Smith Coll. scholarship. Mem. AIA, Am. Inst. Bldg. Designers (chpt. pres. 1971-72), Commaisini, Alpha Alpha Gamma, Chi Omega. Democrat. Lutheran. Home and Office: 1311 Parrott Dr San Mateo CA 94402-3630 E-mail: dcac6@juno.com

CASTLEBERRY, W. THOMAS, financial company executive; b. Tuscon, Ariz., Aug. 3, 1937; s. Wayne Texas and Dorothy (Roby) C.; m. Jean Ann Mrocek, Oct. 24, 1972; children: Melanie, Mark, Kelly, Cheryl, Nicole, Matthew. BS, U. Calif., Davis, 1960. Cons. Touche Ross, San Francisco, 1967-69; sr. v.p. Crocker Nat. Bank, 1969-72; sr. v.p. $D Ramada Inns, Phoenix, 1972-78; v.p. EDS, Phoenix, 1978-80; chmn. CEO Anasazi, Phoenix, 1980-83, 87-93; sr. v.p. VISA, Phoenix, 1983-87, FDC, Phoenix, 1993-95; vice chmn., CEO Rezsolutions, Phoenix, 1996—. Capt. U.S. Army, 1960-61, with USNG, 1961-72. Mem. Phoenix Boys and Girls Clubs. Office: Rezsolutions 7500 N Dreamy Draw Dr Phoenix AZ 85020-4660

CASTOR, JON STUART, electronics company executive; b. Lynchburg, Va., Dec. 15, 1951; s. William Stuart and Marilyn (Hughes) C.; m. Stephanie Lum, Jan. 7, 1989; 1 child, David Jon. BA, Northwestern U., 1973; MBA, Stanford U., 1975. Mgmt. cons., Menlo Park, Calif., 1981-96; pres. TeraLogic, Inc., 1996—. Dir. Midwest Consumer Adv. Bd. to FTC, 1971-73; v.p., bd. dirs. San Mateo coun. Boy Scouts Am., 1991-93; bd. dirs. Pacific Skyline Coun. Boy Scouts Am., 1994—; trustee Coyote Point Mus. Environ. Edn., San Mateo, 1992-95. Achievements include patents for in field. Office: TeraLogic Inc 1240 Villa St Mountain View CA 94041-1124

CASTOR, WILBUR WRIGHT, futurist, writer, consultant; b. Harrison Twp., Pa., Feb. 3, 1932; s. Wilbur Wright and Margaret (Grubbs) C.; m. Donna Ruth Schwartz, Feb. 9, 1963; children: Amy, Julia, Marnie. BA, St. Vincent Studies, 1959; PhD, Calif. U. Advanced Studies, 1990. Sales rep. IBM, Pitts. and Cleve., 1959-62; v.p. data processing ops. Honeywell, Waltham, Mass., 1962-80; pres., chief exec. officer Aviation Simulation Tech., Lexington, 1980-82; sr. v.p. Xerox Corp., El Segundo, Calif., 1982-89; freelance cons., 1989—. Author: (play) Un Certaine Soirire, 1958, (mus. comedy) Breaking Up, 1960, (stage play) This is Your Wife, 1997, (book) The Information Age and the New Productivity, 1990, (play) This is Your Wife, 1997; contbr. articles to profl. jours. Mem. Presdl. Rep. Task Force; pres., bd. dirs. Internat. Acad., Santa Barbara, North Theatre, Olendorf Found.; active Town Hall Calif.; chmn. bd. dirs. Marymount Coll., 1999—. Served to capt. USN, 1953-58, with USAFR, 1958-76. Recipient Disting. Alumnus of Yr. award St. Vincent Coll., 1990. Mem. World Bus. Acad., The Strategy Bd., U. Denver "Netthink", World Future Soc., Aircraft Owners and Pilots Assn., Caballeros Country Club, Rolling Hills (Calif.) Club, Tennis Club, U.S. Senator's Club. Avocations: flying, scuba diving, music, reading, writing. Home: 19 Georgeff Rd Rolling Hills CA 90274-5272

CASTRO, JOSEPH ARMAND, music director, pianist, composer, orchestrator; b. Miami, Ariz., Aug. 15, 1927; s. John Loya and Lucy (Sanchez) C.; m. Loretta Faith Haddad, Oct. 21, 1966; children: John Joseph, James Ernest. Student, San Jose State Coll., 1944-47. Mus. dir. Herb Jeffries, Hollywood, Calif., 1952, June Christy, Hollywood, 1959-63, Anita O'Day, Hollywood, 1963-65, Tony Martin, Hollywood, 1962-64, Tropicana Hotel, Las Vegas, Nev., 1980-97, Desert Inn, Las Vegas, 1992-93; orch. leader Mocambo Night Club, Hollywood, 1952-54; soloist Joe Castro Trio, L.A., N.Y.C., Honolulu, 1952-65, Sands Hotel, Desert Inn, Las Vegas, 1975-80; mus. dir. Folies Bergere, 1980-89; with Joe Castro Trio with Loretta Castro, 1995—. Recs. include Cool School with June Christy, 1960, Anita O'Day Sings Rodgers and Hart, 1961, Lush Life, 1966, Groove-Funk-Soul, Mood Jazz, Atlantic Records, Ballads for Night People with June Christy, Road Show with Stan Kenton Orch., Best of June Christy Jazz Series, Spotlight on June Christy, Anita O'Day, Verve Records, Billy May Swing Rodgers & Hart, also albums with Teddy EEdwards, Stan Kenton, Jimmy Borges with Joe Castro Trio, 1990, Loretta Castro with Joe Castro Trio, 1990, Honolulu Symphony concerts; command performance, Queen Elizabeth II, London Palladium, 1989, Concerts with Jimmy Borges and Honolulu Symphony Pops Concerts, 1991; jazz concert (with Nigel Kennedy) Honolulu Symphony, 1990; jazz-fest, Kailua-Kona, Hawaii, 1990; leader orch. Tropicana Hotel, 1989-97. With U.S. Army, 1946-47. Roman Catholic. Home: 2812 Colanthe Ave Las Vegas NV 89102-2026 Fax: 702-878-9588

CASTRO, JOSEPH RONALD, retired oncology researcher, educator, physician; b. Chgo., Apr. 9, 1934; m. Barbara Ann Kauth, Oct. 12, 1957. B.S. in Natural Sci., Loyola U., Chgo., 1956, M.D., 1958. Diplomate: Am. Bd. Radiology, 1964. Intern Rockford (Ill.) Meml. Hosp.; resident U.S. Naval Hosp., San Diego; assoc. radiotherapist and assoc. prof. U. Tex.-M.D. Anderson Hosp. and Tumor Inst., 1967-71; prof. radiology/radiation oncology U. Calif. Sch. Medicine, San Francisco, 1971-94, prof. emeritus radiation oncology, 1994-99, vice-chmn. dept. radiation oncology, 1980-94. Dir. particle radiotherapy Lawrence Berkeley Lab., 1975-99, faculty sr. scientist, 1991-94; mem. program project rev. com. NIH/Nat. Cancer Inst. Cancer Program, 1982-85. Author sci. articles. Past pres., chmn. bd. trustees No. Calif. Cancer Program, 1980-83. Served to lt. comdr., M.C. USN, 1956-66. Recipient Teaching award Mt. Zion Hosp. and Med. Center, San Francisco, 1972 Fellow Am. Coll. Radiology; mem. European Soc. Therapeutic Radiology and Oncology (hon.), Am. Soc. Therapeutic Radiology, Rocky Mountain Radiol. Soc. (hon.), Gilbert H. Fletcher Oncologic Soc. (past pres. 1988). Office: U Calif Radiation Oncology Dept L-75 San Francisco CA 94143-0001 E-mail: castro@radonc4.ucsf.edu

CASTRO, LEONARD EDWARD, lawyer; b. L.A., Mar. 18, 1934; s. Emil Galvez and Lily (Meyerholtz) C.; 1 son, Stephen Paul. A.B., UCLA, 1959, J.D., 1962. Bar: Calif. 1963, U.S. Supreme Ct. 1970. Assoc. Musick, Peeler & Garrett, Los Angeles, 1962-68, ptnr., 1968— . Mem. ABA, Los Angeles County Bar Assn.Bd. editors, note and comment editor: UCLA Law Review, 1961-62. Contbd. chpts. to books. Panelist, spkr., various legal edn. programs. Office: Musick Peeler & Garrett 1 Wilshire Blvd Ste 2000 Los Angeles CA 90017-3876

CASTRO, RAUL HECTOR, lawyer, former ambassador, former governor; b. Cananea, Mexico, June 12, 1916; came to U.S., 1926, naturalized, 1939; s. Francisco D. and Rosario (Acosta) C.; m. Patricia M. Norris, Nov. 13, 1954; children— Mary Pat, Beth. B.A., Ariz. State Coll., 1939; J.D., U. Ariz., 1949; LL.D. (hon.), No. Ariz. U., 1966, Ariz. State U., 1972, U. Autonoma de Guadalajara, Mex. Bar: Ariz. bar 1949. Fgn. service clk. Dept. State, Agua Prieta, Mexico, 1941-46; instr. Spanish U. Ariz., 1946-49; practiced in Tucson, 1949-51; dep. county atty. Pima County, Ariz., 1951-54; county atty., 1954-58; judge Superior Ct., Tucson, 1958-64, Juvenile Ct., Tucson, 1961-64; U.S. ambassador to El Salvador, San Salvador, 1964-68, to Bolivia, La Paz, 1968-69; practice internat. law Tucson, 1969-74, Phoenix, 1980—; gov. Ariz., 1975-77; U.S. ambassador to Argentina, 1977-80; operator Castro Pony Farm, 1954-64. Pres. Pima County Tb and Health Assn., Tucson Youth Bd., Ariz. Horseman's Assn.; Bd. dirs. Tucson chpt. A.R.C., Tucson council Boy Scouts Am., Tucson YMCA, Nat. Council Christians and Jews, YWCA Camp; Bd. Mem. Ariz. N.G., 1935-39. Recipient Outstanding Naturalized Citizen award Pima County Bar Assn., 1964, Outstanding Am. Citizen award D.A.R., 1964; Pub. Service award U. Ariz., 1966; John F. Kennedy medal Kennedy U., Buenos Aires. Mem. Am. Fgn. Service Assn., Am. Judicature Soc., Inter-Am. Bar Assn., Ariz. Bar Assn., Pima County Bar Assn., Nat. Council Crime and Deliquency (bd. dirs.), Assn. Trial Lawyers Am., Council Am. Ambassadors, Nat. Assn. Trial Judges, Nat. Council Juvenile Ct. Judges, Fed. Bar Assn., Nat. Lawyers Club, Phi Alpha Delta. Democrat. Roman Catholic. Club: Rotarian. Office: 404 W Crawford St Nogales AZ 85621-2594

CASTRUITA, RUDY, school system administrator; BA in Social Sci., Utah State U., 1966, MS in Sch. Adminstrn., 1967; EdD, U. So. Calif., 1983. Cert. adminstrv. svcs., std. secondary, pupil svcs. Dir. econ. opportunity program City of El Monte, Calif., 1966-67; secondary tchr., counselor, program coord. El Monte Union High Sch. Dist., 1967-75, asst. prin. Mountain View High Sch., 1975-80; prin. Los Alamitos (Calif.) High Sch. Los Alamitos Unified Sch. Dist., 1980-85; asst. supt. secondary divsn. Santa Ana (Calif.) Unified Sch. Dist., 1985-87, assoc. supt. secondary divsn., 1987-88, supt., 1988-94; supt. schs. San Diego County, 1994—. Adj. prof. Calif. State U., Long Beach, 1981-88, mem. adv. com. dept. ednl. adminstrn., 1983-86; adj. prof. U. San Francisco, 1984-88; mem. State Tchr. of Yr. Selection Com., 1988, Student Tchr. Edn. Project Coun., SB 620 Healthy Start Com., SB 1274 Restructuring Com., Joint Task Force Articulation, State High Sch. Task Force; mem. Latino eligibility study U. Calif., mem. ednl. leadership inst.; mem. state adv. coun. Supt. Pub. Instrn.; Delta Epsilon lectr. U. So. Calif.; rep. Edn. Summit; mem. selection com. Calif. Ednl. Initiatives Fund; co-chair subcom. at risk youth Calif. Edn. Com., 1989; mentor supt. Harvard Urban Supt.'s Program, 1993—. Chair Orange County Hist. Adv. Coun., South El Monte Coordinating Coun.; mem. exec. coun. Santa Ana 2000; mem. articulation coun. Rancho Santiago C.C. Dist.; active Hacienda Heights Recreation and Pks. Commn., Santa Ana City Coun. Stadium Blue Ribbon Com.; exec. dir. Orange County coun. Boy Scouts Am.; mem. adv. com. Bowers Mus.; mem. exec. bd. El Monte Boys Club; hon. lifetime mem. Calif. PTA; bd. dirs. Santa Ana Boys and Girls Club, Orange County Philharm. Soc., Santa Ana Pvt. Industry Coun., El Monte-South El Monte Consortium, Drug Use is Life Abuse, EDUCARE sch. edn. U. So. Calif. Named Supt. of Yr. League United Latin Am. Citizens, 1989; state finalist Nat. Supt. Yr. award, 1992. Mem. ASCD, Assn. Calif. Sch. Adminstrs. (rep. region XVII secondary prins. com. 1981-85, presenter region XVII 1984, Calif. Supt. of Year award 1991, Marcus Foster award 1991), Calif. Sch. Bds. Assn. (mem. policy and analysis com.), Assn. Calif. Urban Sch. Dists. (pres. 1992—), Orange County Supts. (pres.), Santa Ana C. of C. (bd. dirs.), Delta Epsilon (pres. 1990-91), Phi Delta Kappa. Office: San Diego County Supt Office 6401 Linda Vista Rd San Diego CA 92111-7319

CATCHPOLE, JUDY, state official; m. Glenn Catchpole; children: Glenda, Fred, Katie. BA in Edn., U. Wyo. CEO, state supt. pub. instrn. State Dept. Edn., Cheyenne, Wyo. Exec. dir. Wyoming Rep. Party; mem. Wyoming Land and Investment bd., CCSSO bd. dirs., U. Wyo. bd. trustees, Edn. Commn. of the States Commr., STARBASE bd. dirs. (pres.). Mem. Wyo. Sch. Bds. Assn. (past vice chmn.), Wyo. Early Childhood Assn. (past pres.). Office: Wyo Dept Edn 2300 Capitol Ave Fl 2 Cheyenne WY 82002-0050

CATE, RODNEY MICHAEL, academic administrator; b. Sudan, Tex., May 9, 1942; s. Tommy A. and Elsie P. (Cherry) C.; m. Patricia Cate, June 11, 1941; children: Brandi, Shani. BS in Pharmacy, U. Tex., 1965; MS in Family Studies, Tex. Tech. U., 1975; PhD in Human Devel. and Family Studies, Pa. State U., 1979. Asst. prof. Tex. Tech. U., Lubbock, 1978-79, Oreg. State U., Corvallis, 1979-83, assoc. prof., 1983-85; prof., dept. chmn. Washington State U., Pullman, 1985-90; assoc. dean Iowa State U., Ames, 1990-94; dir Sch. Family and Consumer Resources U. Ariz., Tucson, 1994-99, prof., 1999—. Co-author: Courtship, 1992; editor: Family and Cons. Rsch. Jour., 1992; contbr. articles to profl. jours. Lt. USN, 1966-69. Mem. Am. Assn. Family and Cons. Scis. Assn. (James D. Moran Meml. Rsch. award 1991), Am. Psychol. Assn., Nat. Coun. on Family Rels., Internat. Soc. for the Study Personal Relationships. Democrat. Office: U Ariz Sch Family and Consumer Resources Bldg 33 Tucson AZ 85721-0033

CATES, GILBERT, film, theater, television producer and director; b. N.Y.C., June 6, 1934; s. Nathan and Nina (Peltzman) Katz; m. Jane Betty Dubin, Feb. 9, 1957 (div.); children: Melissa Beth, Jonathan Michael, David Sawyer, Gilbert Lewis; m. Judith Reichman, Jan. 25, 1987; stepchildren: Ronit Reichman, Anat Reichman. BS, Syracuse U., 1955, MA, 1965. Prof. theatre, film and TV UCLA, 1990—, dean, 1990-99; with Cates-Doty Prodns., Inc.; artistic dir. Gefen Playhouse, L.A., 1995—. Com. mem. 1 drama dept. Syracuse U., 1969-73. TV prodr., dir. Haggis Baggis, 1959, Camouflage, 1961-62, Internat. Showtime, 1962-64, Hootenanny, 1962, To All My Friends on Shore, 1972, The Affair, 1974, After the Fall, 1974, Johnny, We Hardly Knew Ye, 1977, The Kid From Nowhere, 1982, Country Gold, 1982, Faerie Tale Theatre, 1982, Hobson's Choice, 1983, Consenting Adult, 1984, Child's Cry?, 1986, Fatal Judgement, 1988, One More Time, 1988, Muffin Man, 1989, Call Me Anna, 1990, Absolute Strangers, 1991, Overruled, 1992, Confessions-Two Faces of Evil, 1994, Innocent Victims, 1995, A Death in the Family - Masterpice Theatre, 2001; film prodr., dir.: The Painting, 1962, Rings Aroung the World, 1967, I Never Sang for My Father, 1970, Summer Wishes, Winter Dreams, 1973, Dragonfly, 1976, The Promise, 1978, The Last Married Couple in America, 1979, O God, Book II, 1980, Backfire, 1986; theatrical prodr.: You Know I Can't Hear You When the Water's Running, 1967, I Never Sang for My Father, 1968, The Chinese and Doctor Fish, 1970, Solitaire-Double Solitaire, 1971; dir.: Voices, 1972, Tricks of the Trade, 1980; prodr.: Ann. Acad. Awards, 1990-1995, 1997-99, 2001, To Life, America Celebrates Israel's 50th (CBS-TV), 1998, America Celebrates Ford's Theater (ABC-TV), 1999, 2000, 2001. Bd. dirs. Israeli Cancer Rsch. Fund, 1992-94. Recipient Best Short Film award Internat. Film Importers and Distbrs., 1962, Chancellor'smedal Syracuse U., 1974, Emmy award, 1991, Star on Hollywood Walk of Fame, 1994, Jimmy Doolittle award L.A. Theater, 1998, Best Prodn. Ovation award, 1999, Lifetime Dirs. Achievement award Caucus of Prodrs., Writers and Dirs., 1998. Mem. Dirs. Guild Am. (hon. life award 1990, v.p. Ea. region 1965, Western region 1980—, pres. 1983-87, Robert B. Aldrich award 1989, nat. sec.-tras. 1997—), Acad. Motion Picture Arts and Scis. (bd. govs., chmn. bd. dirs. 1985-94), Women in Film (bd. dirs. 1993-94), League N.Y. Theatres, Friars Club (gov. 1980—). Office: 10920 Wilshire Blvd Ste 820 Los Angeles CA 90024-6510

CATHCART, DAVID ARTHUR, lawyer; b. Pasadena, Calif., June 1, 1940; s. Arthur James and Martelle (Leeper) C.; m. Janet Eileen Farley, June 19, 1973; children: Sarah Emily, Rebecca Eileen. BA with gt. distinction, Stanford U., 1961; MA, Harvard U., 1966, LLB cum laude, 1967. Bar: Calif. 1968, U.S. Dist. Ct. (cen. dist.) Calif. 1969, U.S. Dist. Ct. (so., no. dists.) 1975, U.S. Dist. Ct. (ea. dist.) 1979, U.S. Ct. Appeals (9th cir.) 1975, U.S. Supreme Ct. 1979. Assoc. Gibson, Dunn & Crutcher LLP, L.A., 1968-70, 72-75, ptnr., 1975—. Legis. asst. U.S. Senate, Washington, 1971-72; mem. NLRB Adv. Com., 1994-98. Editor-in-chief: Employment Discrimination Law Five-Year Cumulative Supplement, 1989, Employment-At-Will: A 1989 State-By-State Survey, 1990; contbr. chpts. to legal texts, articles to profl. jours. Bd. dirs. Western Ctr. on Law and Poverty, L.A., 1985-88, U.S.-S. Africa Leadership Devel. Program, 1992—, The Employers Group, 2000—. Woodrow Wilson fellow, 1961-62, Danforth fellow, 1961-64. Fellow Coll. of Labor and Employment Lawyers; mem. ABA (mem. coun. 1997—, mgmt. co-chair equal employment opportunity law com., 1994-96, sect. of labor and employment law, co-chair employment and labor rels. law com., 1985-88, litigation sect.), L.A. County Bar Assn. (chair labor & employment law sect. 1991-92), Am. Employment Law Coun. (chair 1993—), Internat. Bar Assn. (vice-chmn. labor com., bus. law sect. 1987-90, U.S. country rep. 1989-93), Chancery Club, City Club on Bunker Hill, Harvard Club N.Y.C., Phi Beta Kappa. Office: Gibson Dunn & Crutcher LLP 333 S Grand Ave Los Angeles CA 90071-3197

CATHCART, RICHARD, state legislator; b. Cheyenne, Wyo., Apr. 23, 1946; married. AA, Casper Coll. Mem. Wyo. Senate, Cheyenne, 1992—, mem. agr., pub. lands, and water resources com., mem. labor, health and social svcs. com., mem. rev. com. Mem. Wyo. Consistory. With USN. Mem. Wyo. Steel Erectors Assn., Sr. Pro Rodeo Assn., Cheyenne Trap Club (past bd. dirs.), Masons. Democrat. Home: RR 1 Box 144 Carpenter WY 82054 Office: Wyo Senate State Capitol Cheyenne WY 82002-0001 Fax: 307-634-9263. E-mail: rich@cheyennehomes.com

CATHEY, WADE THOMAS, electrical engineering educator; b. Greer, S.C., Nov. 26, 1937; s. Wade Thomas Sr. and Ruby Evelyn (Waters) C.; children: Susan Elaine, Cheryl Ann. BS, U. S.C., 1959, MS, 1961; PhD, Yale U., 1963. Group scientist Rockwell Internat., Anaheim, Calif., 1962-68; from assoc. prof. to prof. elec. engring. U. Colo., Denver, 1968-85, chmn. dept. elec. engring. and computer sci., 1984-85, chmn. faculty senate, 1982-83, prof. Boulder, 1985-97, rsch. prof., 1997—. Pres. CDM Optics, 1996—; dir. NSF Ctr. Optoelectronic Computing Sys., Boulder, 1987-93; cons. in field, 1968—. Author: Optical Information Processing and Holography, 1978; contbr. articles to profl. jours.; inventor in field. Fellow Croft, U. Colo., 1982, Faculty, U. Colo., 1972-73. Fellow IEEE, Optical Soc. Am. (topical editor 1977-79, 87-90), Soc. Photo-Optic Instrumentation Engrs. Achievements include extend focal depth and passive ranging in imaging systems, rsch. on matching image acquisiton and signal processing systems. Home: 228 Alpine Way Boulder CO 80304-0406 Office: U Colo Dept Elec Engring Boulder CO 80309-0425 also: CDM Optics Inc 4001 Discovery Dr Ste 2110 Boulder CO 80303 E-mail: tomc@cdm-optics.com, cathey@colorado.edu

CATMULL, EDWIN E. computer graphics engineer; BS in Computer Sci. and Physics, PhD in Computer Sci., U. Utah. Co-founder, v.p., tech. officer Pixar Animation Studios, Emeryville, Calif., 1979—; v.p. divsn. computers Lucasfilm, Ltd. Recipient Coons award. Mem. NAE, Acad. Motion Picture Arts and Scis. (Sci. and Tech. engring. award, sci. and tech. awards com.). Achievements include research in computer graphics, video editing, video games, digital video, digital computer graphics and animation. Office: Pixar Animation Studios 1200 Park Ave Emeryville CA 94608

CATTERALL, WILLIAM A. pharmacology, neurobiology educator; b. Providence, Oct. 12, 1946; s. William V. and Alice (Aldred) C.; m. Nancy Sharples; children: W. Douglas, Elizabeth R. BA in Chemistry, Brown U., 1968; PhD in Physiol. Chemistry, Johns Hopkins U., 1972. Postdoctoral research fellow Lab. of Biochem. Genetics NIH, Bethesda, Md., 1972-76, staff scientist, 1976-77; assoc. prof. dept. pharmacology U. Wash., Seattle, 1977-82, prof., 1982—, chmn. dept. pharmacology, 1984—, chmn. interdisciplinary com. on neurobiology, 1986—. Editor Molecular Pharmacology, 1986-90; contbr. numerous articles to profl. jours. and textbooks. Recipient Young Scientist award Passano Found., 1981, Jacob Javits Neurosci award, NIH, 1984, 91, Basic Sci. Prize award Am. Heart Assn., 1992; numerous grants. Mem. Nat. Acad. Sci., Am. Soc. Pharmacology and Exptl. Therapeutics, Soc. for Neurosci., Am. Soc. Biol. Chemists, Neurosci. Research Program. Avocations: sailing, skiing. Office: Univ Wash Dept Pharmacology PO Box 357280 Seattle WA 98195-7280

CATTERTON, MARIANNE ROSE, occupational therapist; b. St. Paul, Feb. 3, 1922; d. Melvin Joseph and Katherine Marion (Bole) Maas; m. Elmer John Wood, Jan. 16, 1943 (dec.); m. Robert Lee Catterton, Nov. 20, 1951 (div. 1981); children: Jenifer Ann Dawson, Cynthia Lea Uthus. Student, Carleton Coll., 1939-41, U. Md., 1941-42; BA in English, U. Wis., 1944; MA in Counseling Psychology, Bowie State Coll., 1980; postgrad., No. Ariz. U., 1987-91. Registered occupational therapist, Occupational Therapy Cert. Bd. Occupational therapist VA, N.Y.C., 1946-50; cons. occupational therapist Fondo del Seguro del Estado, Puerto Rico, 1950-51; dir. rehab. therapies Spring Grove State Hosp., Catonsville, Md., 1953-56; occupational therapist Anne Arundel County Health Dept., Annapolis, 1967-78; dir. occupational therapy Eastern Shore Hosp. Ctr., Cambridge, 1979-85; cons. occupational therapist Kachina Point Health Ctr., Sedona, Ariz., 1986. Regional chmn. Conf. on revising Psychiat. Occupational Therapy Edn., 1958-59; instr. report writing Anne Arundel Community

Coll., Annapolis, 1974-78. Editor Am. Jour. Occupational Therapy, 1962-67. Active Md. Heart Assn., 1959-60; mem. task force on occupational therapy edn. Md. Dept. of Health, 1971-72; chmn. Anne Arundel Gov. Com. on Employment of Handicapped, 1959-63; gov.'s com. to study vocat. rehab., Md., 1960; com. mem. Annapolis Youth Ctr., 1976-78; ministerial search com. Unitarian Ch. Anne Arundel County, 1962; curator Dorchester County Heritage Mus., Cambridge, 1982-83; v.p., officer Unitarian-Universalist Fellowship Flagstaff, 1988-93, v.p., 1993-97; co-moderator, founder Unitarian-Universalist Fellowship Sedona, 1994—, pres., 1997-98, co-pres. 2001—; citizen interviewer Sedona Acad. Forum, 1993, 94; vol. Respite Care, 1994—, VerdeValley Caregivers, 1996—; mem. Sedona Arts Ctr. Mem. P.R. Occupl. Therapy Assn. (co-founder 1950), Am. Occupl. Therapy Assn. (chmn. history com. 1958-61), Md. Occupl. Therapy Assn. (del. 1953-59), Pathfinder Internat., Dorchester County Mental Health Assn. (pres. 1981-84), Internat. Platform Assn., Ret. Officers Assn., Air Force Assn. (Barry Goldwater chpt., sec. 1991-92, 94—), Severn Town Club (treas. 1965, sec. 1971-72, 94-95), Internat. Club (Annapolis, publicity chmn. 1966), Toastmasters, Newcomers (Sedona, pres. 1986), Pathfinder, Zero Population Growth, Nature Conservancy, Sedona Muses, Delta Delta Delta. Republican. Home: 415 Windsong Dr Sedona AZ 86336-3745

CAUBLE, ROBERT C. research scientist; BS in Physics, U. Ariz.; PhD in Nuc. Engring., U. Mich., 1980. Staff Berkeley Rsch. Assocs. Naval Rsch. Lab., Washington; rsch. scientist Lawrence Livermore (Calif.) Nat. Lab., 1985—. Recipient Am. Physical Soc. award for Excellence in Plasma Physics Rsch. 1998. Office: Lawrence Livermore Nat Lab PO Box 808 Livermore CA 94551-0808

CAUDILL, SAMUEL JEFFERSON, architect; b. Tulsa, June 5, 1922; s. Samuel Jefferson and Maymie Starling (Boulware) C.; m. Joy Maxwell, May 31, 1952; children: Jody Caudill Cardamone, Julie Hertzberg, Samuel Boone, Robert Maxwell, Anne Goertzen BArch, Cornell U., Ithaca, N.Y., 1946. Registered architect Colo., Calif., Idaho, Ariz. Prin. architect Samuel J. Caudill, Jr., Aspen, Colo., 1954-59, Caudill Assocs. Architects, Aspen, 1959-80; pres. Caudill Gustafson & Assocs. Architects, PC, Aspen, 1980-87, Caudill Gustafson Ross & Assocs., Architects, P.C., Aspen, 1987-92; pres., CEO Caudill Gustafson & Assocs., Architects, P.C., Aspen, 1992—. Mem. Pitkin County Planning and Zoning Commn., Colo., 1955-58; mem. outdoor edn. com. Colo. Dept. Edn., 1966-68; chmn. Pitkin County Bd. Appeals, 1970; mem. Colo. Water Quality Control Commn., 1977-80. Wildlife rep. adv. bd. Bur. Land Mgmt. Dept. Interior, Grand Junction, Colo., 1969-75, 80-85; chmn. citizens adv. com. Colo. Hwy. Dept. for I-70 through Glenwood Canyon, 1975-92; chmn. Colo. Wildlife Commn., 1978-79. Recipient Outstanding Pub. Service Bur. Land Mgmt., 1975; named to Aspen (Colo.) Hall of Fame, 1998. Fellow AIA (Community Svc. award 1976, Architect of Yr. award 1992); mem. Colo. Soc. Architects (pres. 1983), Colo. Coun. on Arts and Humanities, Aspen C. of C. (pres. 1956-57), Masons, Shriners (Denver). Home: 1055 Stage Rd Aspen CO 81611-1096 Office: Caudill Gustafson & Assocs Architects PC 234 E Hopkins Ave Aspen CO 81611-1938

CAULFIELD, W. HARRY, retired health care industry executive, physician; b. Waverly, N.Y., Aug. 22, 1936; m. Mary Sisk; children: Mary, Harry, James, Michael. AB, Harvard U., 1957, postgrad., 1976; MD, U. Pa., 1961. Diplomate Am. Bd. Internal. Medicine, Am. Bd. Cardiology. Rotating intern Hosp. U. Pa., 1961-62; resident Pa. Hosp., 1962-64; fellow in cardiology Georgetown U. Hosp., 1964-66; dir. ICU Kaiser Found. Hosp., San Francisco, 1969-75, asst. chief of staff, 1971-75, chief of staff, 1975-80; physician-in-chief, mem. exec. com. Permanente Med. Group, San Francisco, 1975-80, mem. internal medicine staff cardiology, 1968-90, from exec. dir.-elect to exec. dir., 1990-99. Assoc. clin. prof. medicine U. Calif., San Francisco, 1971-96. Capt. U.S. Army Med. Corps, 1966-68. Fellow Am. Coll. Cardiology, Am. Heart Assn.; mem. AMA (adv. com. on group practice physicians 1994—, fedn. study consortium 1994—), San Francisco Med. Soc. (alt. del. to Calif. Med. Assn. 1992, del. 1993-94, managed care task force, leadership devel. com.), Calif. Med. Assn., Calif. Hosp. Assn. (membership com. 1987), Am. Hosp. Assn., Calif. Acad. Medicine, Am. Med. Group Assn. (trustee 1994—, vice chmn. bylaws com. 994, fin. com. 1996—), Soc. Med. Adminstrs., Am. Assn. Health Plans (bd. dirs. 1994—). Office: Permanente Med Group Inc 1950 Franklin St Oakland CA 94612-5103

CAVANAGH, JOHN CHARLES, advertising agency executive; b. San Francisco, Dec. 19, 1932; s. John Timothy and Alicia Louise (McDowell) C.; m. Mary Ann Anding, Apr. 10, 1959; children: Karen, Brad. Student, U. Hawaii, 1950; BS, U. San Francisco, 1954. Pub. rels. rep. Kaiser Industries Corp., Oakland, Calif., 1956-58; pub. rels. mgr. Kaiser Cement & Gypsum Corp., Oakland, 1958-63; pub. relations dir. Fawcett-McDermott Assos. Inc., Honolulu, 1964-66, ops. v.p., 1966-69, exec. v.p., 1969-73, pres., dir., 1973-75, Fawcett McDermott Cavanagh Inc., Honolulu, 1975-87, Fawcett McDermott Cavanagh Calif., Inc., San Francisco, 1975-87; pres. The Cavanagh Group/Advt. Inc., Santa Rosa, Calif., 1987—. 1st. lt. 740th Guided Missile Bn. AUS, 1954-56. Named Advt. Man of Yr. Honolulu Advt. Fedn., 1985. Mem. Pub. Rels. Soc. Am. (accredited, v.p. 1970, pres. Hawaii chpt. 1971), Advt. Agy. Assn. Hawaii (pres. 1973), Am. Assn. Advt. Agys. (chmn. Hawaii coun. 1980-81), Affiliated Advt. Agys. Internat. (chmn. 1984-85), Outrigger Canoe Club, Commonwealth Club of Calif. Home: 3750 St Andrews Dr Santa Rosa CA 95403-0945 Office: The Cavanagh Group 3750 St Andrews Dr Santa Rosa CA 95403-0945

CAVANAUGH, KENNETH CLINTON, retired housing consultant; b. Fremont, Mich., Apr. 30, 1916; s. Frank Michael and Buryll Marie (Preston) C.; m. Barbara Blythe Boling, Feb. 24, 1979; children from previous marriage: Patricia Ann, James Lee, John Thomas. BS in Forestry, Mich. State U., 1939. County supr. Farm Security Adminstrn., USDA, Kalamazoo, 1939-43; community mgr. PHA, Willow Run, Mich., 1946-49, dir. fiscal mgmt. Washington, 1949-55, dir. elderly housing Housing & Home Fin. Agy., 1955-57, reg. dir. San Juan, P.R., 1957-58; dir. housing programs HUD, Washington, 1958-73; controller/dep. dir. San Francisco Housing Authority, 1973-78; pres. Ken C. Cavanaugh & Assocs., pvt. internat. housing and community devel. cons., Vista, Calif., 1978—; fin. finder Merrill Lynch-Huntoon Paige Co., San Francisco, 1979-81, Western Pacific Fin. Co., Newport Beach, Calif., 1981-83; gen. ptnr. The Knolls, Rogers, Ark., 1980-89. Exec. dir. Arlington (Va.) Youth Found., 1950-58; advisor Salvation Army adv. bd., Honolulu, 1985-88. Served to capt. USN, 1943-46, USNR, 1946-73. Recipient Superior Svc. award, Pub. Housing Adminstrn., 1956. Mem. Nat. Assn. Housing & Redevel. Ofcls., Ret. Officers Assn., Res. Officers Assn., Naval Res. Assn., Shadowridge Golf Club (Vista), Elks, Masons. Avocations: golf, travel. Home and Office: PO Box 749 Vista CA 92085-0749 E-mail: BlytheCav@aol.com

CAVANAUGH, MICHAEL EVERETT, lawyer, arbitrator, mediator; b. Seattle, Dec. 23, 1946; s. Wilbur R. Cavanaugh and Gladys E. (Herring) Barber; m. Susan P. Heckman, Sept. 7, 1968. AB, U. Calif., Berkeley, 1973; JD, U. Wash., 1976. Bar: Wash. 1976, U.S. Dist. Ct. (we. dist.) Wash. 1977, U.S. Ct. Appeals (9th cir.) 1977, U.S. Dist. Ct. (ea. dist.) Wash. 1978. Staff atty. U.S. Ct. of Appeals (9th crct.) Calif., San Francisco, 1976-77; from assoc. to ptnr. Preston & Thorgrimson, Seattle, 1981-85; ptnr. Bogle & Gates, Seattle, 1985-97, assoc., 1977-81, ptnr., 1985-97; propr. Michael E. Cavanaugh, J.D., Arbitration and Mediation, Seattle, 1997—. Contbg. author: Employment Discrimination Law, 3d edit., 1995. Avocations: sailing, creative writing, music. Office: 1420 5th Ave # 2200 Seattle WA [illegible]

CAVENEE, WEBSTER K. director; Dir., prof. Ludwig Inst. for Cancer Rsch. U. Calif., LaJolla, 1991—. Office: Ludwig Inst 9500 Gilman Dr La Jolla CA 92093-0660 E-mail: wcavenee@ucsd.edu

CAVOUKIAN, RAFFI See RAFFI

CAWLEY, LEO PATRICK, pathologist, immunologist; b. Oklahoma City, Aug. 11, 1922; s. Pat Bernard and Mary Elizabeth (Forbes) C.; m. Joan Mae Wood, June 20, 1948; children: Kevin Patrick, Karin Patricia, Kary Forbes. BS in Chemistry, Okla. State U., 1948; MD, Okla. Sch. Medicine, 1952. Diplomate Am. Bd. Pathology, Am. Bd. Nuclear Medicine, Am. Bd. Allergy and Immunology, Am. Bd. Med. Lab. Immunology, Am. Bd. Pathology in immunopathology. Intern Wesley Med. Ctr., Wichita, 1952-53, resident in pathology, 1953-54, Wayne County Gen. Hosp., Eloise, Mich., 1954-56, chief resident in pathology, 1956-57; clin. pathologist, asst. dir. lab. Wesley Med. Ctr., Wichita, Kans., 1957-69, dir. sci., 1965-86, dir. labs., 1969-77, dir. clin. immunology, 1979-86; med. dir. Roche Biomed. Lab., Wichita, 1979-86; dir. clin. labs. Vitizyme Corp., Tempe, Ariz., 1988—. Pres. Kilcawley Enterprises, 1986—. Author: Electrophoresis/Immunoelectric Phoresis, 1969; editor series Lab Med Little Brown, 1965-81; contbr. 210 articles to profl. jours. Pfc. USM, 1942-45. Fellow Am. Soc. Clin. pathologist (bd. dirs. 1968, Disting. Svc. award 1980, Dist. Pathology edn. award, 1998), Coll. Am. Pathologist; mem. AAAS, ACS, Am. Assn. Clin. Chemists, Alpha Pi Mu, Phi Lambda Upsilon, Alpha Omega Alpha. Avocations: reading, history. Office: Kil-Cawley Enterprises 7135 E Main St Scottsdale AZ 85251-4315

CAYETANO, BENJAMIN JEROME, governor, former state senator and representative; b. Honolulu, Nov. 14, 1939; s. Bonifacio Marcos and Eleanor (Infante) C.; m. Vicky Tiu, 1997; children: Brandon, Janeen, Samantha. BA, UCLA, 1968; JD, Loyola U., 1971; D in Pub. Svc. (hon.), Loyola Marymount U., 1998. Bar: Hawaii 1971. Practiced in, Honolulu, 1971-86; mem. Hawaii Ho. of Reps., 1975-78, Hawaii Senate, 1979-86; lt. gov. State of Hawaii, 1986-94, gov., 1994—. Bar examiner Hawaii Supreme Ct., 1976-78, disciplinary bd., 1982-86; arbitration panel 1st Cir. Ct. State of Hawaii, 1986; adv. U. Hawaii Law Rev., 1982-84 Mem. bd. regents Chaminade U., 1980-83; mem. adv. council U. Hawaii Coll. Bus. Adminstrn., 1982-83; chmn. Western Gov.'s Assn., 1999. Recipient Excellence in Leadership Medallion Asia-Pacific Acad. Consortium for Pub. Health, 1991, UCLA Alumni award for excellence in pub. svc., 1993, Leadership award Harvard Found., 1996, Edward A. Dickson Alumnus of Yr. award UCLA, 1998. Democrat. Office: Office of Gov State Capitol 415 S Beretania St Fl 5 Honolulu HI 96813-2407 E-mail: gov@gov.state.hi.us*

CAZIER, BARRY JAMES, electrical engineer, software developer; b. Phoenix, May 10, 1943; s. James Henry and Dorothy Marie (Lynton) C.; m. Susan Arline Shewey, June 13, 1964 (dec. July 1979); children: Suzanne, Bryan; m. Illene D. Miller, Dec. 19, 1994. Student, Colo. Sch. Mines, 1961-62; BSEE, U. Colo., 1965; student advanced bus. adminstrn., Ariz. State U., 1974-77. Mfg. mgmt. Gen. Electric, Richland, Wash., 1965-66, Warren, Ohio, 1966-67, system engr. Schenectady, N.Y., 1967-69; project mgr. Honeywell, Phoenix, 1970-80, dir. field ops., 1980-85, program mgr., 1985-99. Prin. Cazier Software Designs, Scottsdale, Ariz., 1985—. Adv. Jr. Achievement, Phoenix, 1972. Club: IBM PC Users (Phoenix). Avocations: music, jogging, camping, fishing, reading. Home: 8508 E Via Montoya Scottsdale AZ 85255-4936 E-mail: bjcazier@yahoo.com

CECI, JESSE ARTHUR, violinist; b. Phila., Feb. 2, 1924; s. Luigi Concezio and Catherine Marie (Marotta) C.; m. Catherine Annette Stevens, Aug. 5, 1979. BS, Juilliard Sch. Music, 1951; license de concert, L'Ecole Normale de Musique, Paris, 1954; MusM, Manhattan Sch. Music, 1971. Assoc. concertmaster New Orleans Philharm. Orch., 1953-54; violinist Boston Symphony Orch., 1954-59, N.Y. Philharm. Orch., N.Y., 1959-62, Esterhazy Orch., N.Y.C., 1962-68; concertmaster Denver Symphony Orch., 1974-89, Colo. Symphony Orch., 1989-95. Over 50 performances of 22 major works; mem. Zimbler Sinfonietta, Boston, 1957-59; participant Marlboro Festival Chamber Orch. Vt., summmers 1960-62, 65, Marlboro Festival Chamber Orch. European-Israeli tour, 1965, Grand Teton Festival, Wyo., 1972, with Denver Duo, 1975—, N.Mex. Festival, Taos, 1980, Carmel (Calif.) Bach Festival, 1987—, Whistler (B.C., Can.) Mozart Festival, 1989-90, Bear Valley (Calif.) Festival, 1995—, Mendocino (Calif.) Festival, 1996—; mem. faculty Congress of Strings, Dallas, 1985, N.Y. Coll. Music, 1961-71, NYU, 1971-74, U. Colo., 1975-79; guest mem. faculty Univ. Denver, 1986; mem., assoc. concertmaster Casals Festival Orch., San Juan, P.R., 1963-77; violinist Cleve. Orch. fgn. tours, 1967, 73, 78, Cin. Symphony Orch. world tour, 1966; 1st violinist N.Y. String Quartet in-residence at U. Maine, Orono, summer 1969; guest violinist Fla. West Coast Symphony, Sarasota, 1993-98; concertmaster Minn. Orch., summers 1970-71, Denver Chamber Orch., 1985-90; guest concertmaster Pitts. Symphony Orch., Pitts., L.A., 1988, mem. N.Y. Philharmonia Chamber Ensemble in-residence at Hopkins Ctr., Dartmouth U., summer 1973; recitalist, Paris, 1963, Amsterdam, 1963, recitalist Carnegie Recital Hall, N.Y.C., 1963, Town Hall, N.Y.C., 1968, 70, Alice Tully Hall, N.Y.C., 1972; fgn. tour Pitts. Symphony Orch., 1989; soloist Royal Chamber Orch. Japan, 1997-98, appointment to concert master position of the Royal Chamber Orchestra and the Royal Metropolitan Orchestra of Japan, 1999—. Cpl. U.S. Army, 1943-46, PTO. Fulbright fellow Paris, 1951-52 Democrat. Roman Catholic. Office: Colo Symphony Orch 1031 13th St Denver CO 80204-2156

CELLA, JOHN J. freight company executive; b. 1940; married. BBA, Temple U., 1965. Regional mgr. Japan ops. Airborne Freight Corp., Seattle, 1965-71, v.p. Far Ea. ops., 1971-72, sr. v.p. internat. div., from 1982, now exec. v.p. internat. div. Office: Airborne Freight Corp 3101 Western Ave Seattle WA 98121-1043

CELLIERS, PETER H. physicist; Physics rschr. Lawrence Livermore (Calif.) Nat. Lab. Recipient Plasma Physics Rsch. Excellence award, 1998. Mem. Am. Phys. Soc. Office: Lawrence Livermore Nat Lab U Calif 7000 East Ave Livermore CA 94550-9516

CENARRUSA, PETE T. state official; b. Carey, Idaho, Dec. 16, 1917; s. Joseph and Ramona (Gardoqui) C.; m. Freda B. Coates, Oct. 25, 1947; 1 son, Joe Earl (dec.). B.S. in Agr., U. Idaho, 1940. Tchr. high sch., Cambridge, Idaho, 1940-41, Carey and Glenns Ferry, 1946; tchr. vocat. agr. VA, Blaine County, 1946-51; farmer, woolgrower, nr. Carey, 1946-95; mem. Idaho Ho. of Reps., 1951-67, speaker, 1963-67; sec. state of Idaho, 1967-90, 91—. Mem. Idaho Bd. Land Commrs., Idaho Bd. Examiners; pres. Idaho Flying Legislators, 1953-63; chmn. Idaho Legis. Council, 1964— , Idaho Govt. Reorgn. Com.; Idaho del. Council State Govts., 1963— Elected ofcl., mem. BLM Adv. Coun., Boise Dist.; Rep. adminstr. Hall of Fame, 1978; sr. mem. State Bd. Land Commrs., 1967-96; dean Nations Secs. of State, 1967—. Maj. USMCR, 1942-46, 52-58. Named Hon. Farmer Future Farmers Am., 1955; inductee Agrl. Hall of Fame, 1973, Idaho Athletic Hall of Fame, 1976, Basque Hall of Fame, 1983, Idaho Hall of Fame, 1998; recipient Am. Century award for Idaho Washington Times Found. Mem. Blaine County Livestock Mktg. Assn., Idaho Wool Growers Assn. (chmn. 1954), Carey C. of C. (pres. 1952), U. Idaho Alumni Assn., Gamma Sigma Delta, Tau Kappa Epsilon. Republican. Achievements include serving longer than any constitutional official elected in Idaho concluding with 50 years on 12/1/00. Office: Office of Sec State PO Box 83720 Boise ID 83720-3720

CENTERWALL, WILLARD RAYMOND, pediatrician, educator; b. Missoula, Mont., Jan. 16, 1924; s. Willard Raymond Centerwall, Sr. and Charlotte Amanda (Brandon) Wood; m. Siegried Louise Achorn Centerwall, Sept. 2 , 1949 (dec. July 1992); children: Theodore, Brandon, Krista, Alison, Jennifer, Rebecca. BS in Zoology, Yale U., 1949, MD, 1952; MPH in Maternal & Child Health, U. Mich., 1967, MS in Human Genetics, 1968; D in Cultural Anthropology (hon.), World U., 1983. Diplomate Am. Bd. Pediatrics, Am. Bd. Preventive Medicine, Am. Bd. Med. Genetics. Rotating internship White Meml. Hosp., L.A., 1952-53; first yr. pediatric residency White Meml. Hosp., L.A. County Gen. Hosp., 1953-54; sr. yr. pediatric residency L.A. Children's Hosp., 1954-55; instr., asst. clin. prof., asst. prof. pediatrics Coll. Med. Evangelists Sch. of Medicine, L.A., 1955-61; lectr., reader, assoc. prof. pediatrics Christian Med. Coll., Vellore, South India, 1961-66; organizer, first head of dept. pediatrics Miraj Med. Sch., Maharashtra State, India, 1965; assoc. prof. pediatrics Loma Linda U. Sch. Medicine, 1968, prof. pediatrics, 1970-78; assoc. prof. pub. health Loma Linda U. Sch. Health, Calif., 1968, prof. maternal & child health, 1970-78, gen. cons., 1982—; prof. anthropology Loma Linda U. Grad. Sch., 1976-78; prof. emeritus of pediatrics and genetics Loma Linda U. Sch. Medicine, 1986; prof. pediatrics and genetics U. Calif. Sch. Medicine, Davis, 1978-85; prof. in residence dept. reproduction U. Calif. Sch. Veterinary Medicine, Davis, 1981-85; prof. emeritus of pediatrics and genetics U. Calif., Davis, 1986; clin. prof. depts. med. genetics & pediatrics Oreg. Health Scis. U. & Sch. Medicine, Portland, 1986—; ret. Dir. Satellite Genetic Diagnostic and Counseling Clinic, Reno, 1983-85, State Newborn Metabolic Screening Program at U. Calif., Davis, 1980-85, Chico-Oroville (Calif.) Satellite Genetic Diagnostic and Counseling Clinic, 1980-85, Satellite Genetic Diagnostic & Counseling Clinic, Redding, Calif., 1980-83, Genetic Disorders and Birth Defects Clinic Alta Regional Ctr., Sacramento, Calif., 1978-83; civilian med. specialist cons. in pediatrics David Grant USAF Med. Ctr., Travis AFB, 1982-85; organizer, 1st med. dir. Birth Defects and Genetics Clinic, Lakeport, Calif., 1978-84, Birth Defects and Genetics Diagnostic and Counseling Svc. Riverside County Health Dept., Calif., 1978, Birth Defects and Genetics Diagnostic and Counseling Svc. Loma Linda U. Med. Ctr., Calif., 1969-78, Birth Defects and Genetics Svc. Clarke County Dept. Pub. Health, Las Vegas, 1972, Birth Defects and Chromosome Lab. Svcs. Loma Linda U. Med. Ctr., Calif., 1969-78; organizer, 1st dir. Birth Defects and Genetics Clinic at Regional Ctr. for Devel. Disabilities, San Bernardino, Calif., 1976-78; spl. cons. to genetic disease section maternal & child health branch State Calif. Dept. Health, 1977-85, mem. adv. com. on inherited disorders, 1976; med. dir. Orthopedically Handicapped Clinic, Redlands, Calif., 1971-78; med. cons. Calif. Sch. for the Deaf, Riverside, Calif., 1969-78; pediatric cons. Pacific State Hosp. for Mentally Retarded, Pomona, Calif., 1955-60, 69-78, Sch. for Cerebral Palsied Children of Southern Calif., Altadena, 1956-60, and numerous others; vol. clin./acad. positions in Oreg., 1985—. Med. editor: Introduction series of booklets, 1958—; speaker in field. 1st lt. U.S. Army Corps of Engrs., 1943-47. Recipient of rsch. grants NIH, U.S. Pub. Health Svc., Meda Johnson & Co., Alumni Assn. of the Coll. of Med. Evangelists, Nat. Assn. for Retarded Children, Walter E. MacPherson Soc., The Nat. Found. March of Dimes, The Nat. Cancer Inst. and HEM Rsch., Inc., Calif. State Dept. Health; recipient Outstanding Svc. award for Excellence in the Provision of Med. Svcs. to Mentally Retarded Sacramento Assn. for the Retarded, Inc., 1982, 1st J.B.S. Haldane Oration medal Soc. Bionaturalists, 1985, Children's Bur. fellowship in Pub. Health and Human Genetics U. Mich., Ann Arbor, 1966-68. Avocations: travel, lecturing, birds and animals. Home: 101 Silverwood Ln Silverton OR 97381-9739

CEPEDA, ORLANDO, retired professional baseball player; b. Ponce, P.R., Sept. 17, 1937; m. Miriam Cepeda; children: Orlando Jr., Hector, Malcolm, Ali Manuel. 1st baseman San Francisco Giants, 1958-66, St. Louis Cardinals, 1966-69, Atlanta Braves, 1969-72, Oakland (Calif.) Athletics, 1972, Boston Red Sox, 1973, Kansas City Royals, 1974; cmty. rep. San Francisco Giants, 1990—. Lifetime .297 hitter with 379 home runs, 1,364 RBIs; appeared in 3 World Series; 11-time All-Star; hit over .300 9 times in career. Named Rookie of Yr. San Francisco Giants 1958, Comeback Player of Yr. St. Louis Cardinals 1966, Nat. League Most Valuable Player award 1967, Designated Hitter of Yr. award 1973; inductee P.R. Sports Hall of Fame, 1993, Baseball Hall of Fame, 1999. Office: c/o San Francisco Giants 3 Com Park San Francisco CA 94124-3904

CEPPOS, JEROME MERLE, newspaper editor; b. Washington, Oct. 14, 1946; s. Harry and Florence (Epstein) C.; m. Karen E. Feingold, Mar. 7, 1982; children: Matthew, Robin. B.S. in Journalism, U. Md., 1969; postgrad., Knight-Ridder Exec. Leadership Program, 1989-90. Reporter, asst. city editor, night city editor Rochester (N.Y.) Democrat & Chronicle, 1969-72; from asst. city editor, to nat. editor, to asst. mng. editor The Miami (Fla.) Herald, 1972-81; assoc. editor San Jose (Calif.) Mercury News, 1981, mng. editor, 1983-94, exec. editor, sr. v.p., 1995-99; v.p. news Knight Ridder, 1999—. Bd. visitors Coll. Journalism, U. Md.; pres. Accrediting Coun. on Edn. in Journalism and Mass Comm. Mem. AP Mng. Editors (immediate past pres.), Am. Soc. Newspaper Editors, Calif. Soc. Newspaper Editors (former mem. bd. dirs., past pres.), Soc. Profl. Journalists, Assn. for Edn. in Journalism and Mass Comm., No. Calif. Cancer Ctr. (bd. trustees), Silicon Valley Capital Club. Office: Knight Ridder 50 W San Fernando St San Jose CA 95113-2429 E-mail: jceppos@knightridder.com

CERNY, CHARLENE ANN, director; b. Jamaica, N.Y., Jan. 12, 1947; d. Albert Joseph and Charlotte Ann (Novy) Cerny; children: Elizabeth Brett Cerny-Chipman, Kathryn Rose Cerny-Chipman. BA, SUNY, Binghamton, 1969. Curator Latin-Am. folk art Mus. Internat. Folk Art, Santa Fe, 1972-84, mus. dir., 1984-99; dir. instnl. advancement Santa Fe Prep. Sch., 1999—. Adv. bd. C.G. Jung Inst., Santa Fe, 1990-98. Mem. Mayor's Commn. on Children and Youth, Santa Fe, 1990-93, adv. bd. Recipient Exemplary Performance award State of N.Mex., 1982, Internat. Ptnr. Among Mus. award, Mayor's Recognition award, 1999, Mus. N.Mex. Regents award, 1999; Smithsonian Instn. travel grantee, 1976; Florence Dibell Bartlett Meml. scholar, 1979, 91; Kellogg fellow, 1983. Mem. Am. Assn. Mus. Internat. Coun. Mus. (bd. dirs. 1991—, exec. bd. 1991-95), Am. Folklore Soc., Mountain-Plains Mus. Assn., N.Mex. Assn. Mus. (chair membership com. 1975-77). Office: Santa Fe Prep Sch 1301 Camino De Cruz Blanca Santa Fe NM 87501-4549

CERNY, JOSEPH, III, chemistry educator, scientific laboratory administrator, university dean and official; b. Montgomery, Ala., Apr. 24, 1936; s. Joseph and Olaette Genette (Jury) C.; m. Barbara Ann Nedelka, June 13, 1959 (div. Nov. 1982); children: Keith Joseph, Mark Evan; m. 2d Susan Dinkelspiel Stern, Nov. 12, 1983. BS in Chem. Engring., U. Miss.-Oxford, 1957; postgrad. Fulbright scholar, U. Manchester, Eng., 1957-58; PhD in Nuclear Chemistry, U. Calif.-Berkeley, 1961; PhD in Physics (hon.), U. Jyväskylä, Finland, 1990. Asst. prof. chemistry U. Calif., Berkeley, 1961-67, assoc. prof., 1967-71, prof., 1971—, chmn. dept. chemistry, 1975-79, head nuclear sci. div., 1979-84, assoc. dir. Lawrence Berkeley Lab., 1979-84, dean grad. div., 1985-2000, provost for research, 1986-94, vice chancellor for rsch., 1994-2000. Mem. Nat. Acad. Scis. Physics Commn., chair nuclear physics panel, 1983-86; mem. NASA Adv. Coun., Univ. Rels. Task Force, 1991-93, NRC Study of Rsch. Doctorates, 1992-95. Editor: Nuclear Reactions and Spectroscopy, 4 vols., 1974; contbr. numerous articles to field to profl. jours. Served with U.S. Army, 1962-63. Recipient E.O. Lawrence award AEC, 1974, A. von Humboldt sr. scientist award, 1985; named to U. Miss. Alumni Hall of Fame, 1988. Fellow AAAS, Am. Phys. Soc.; mem. Am. Chem. Soc. (Nuclear Chemistry award 1984), Assn. Grad. Schs. (v.p., pres. 1992-94). Democrat. Home: 860 Keeler Ave Berkeley CA 94708-1324 Office: Lawrence Berkeley Nat Lab Univ Calif Bldg 88 Berkeley CA 94720 E-mail: jcerny@uclink4.berkeley.edu

CERRELL, JOSEPH ROBERT, political scientist, public relations consultant; b. N.Y.C., June 19, 1935; BA, U. of So. Calif., 1957. Exec. dir. Dem. Party of Calif., 1959-66; disting. vis. prof. Pepperdine U., Malibu, Calif., 1994—; exec. v.p. Palumbo & Cerrell, Washington, 1989—; CEO Cerrell Assocs. Inc., pub. affairs cons. co., L.A. Adj. prof. U. So. Calif., 1978-94. Pres. Calif. Mus. Found.; bd. dirs. Long Beach (Calif.) Aquarium. Mem. PRSA, Am. Assn. of Polit. Cons., Internat. Assn. of Polit. Cons., Nat. Italian Am. Fedn. (chair). Office: Cerrell Assocs Inc 320 N Larchmont Blvd Fl 2D Los Angeles CA 90004-3012 E-mail: joe@cerrell.com

CERRITOS, RONALD, professional soccer player; b. San Salvador, El Salvador, Jan. 3, 1975; Forward San Jose Earthquakes (formerly San Jose Clash), 1997—; mem. All-Star West team, 1997. Named Honda's MVP, 1998. Office: c/o San Jose Earthquakes 3550 Stevens Creek Blvd Ste 100 San Jose CA 95117-1031

CESARIO, THOMAS CHARLES, dean; b. Kenosha, Wis., June 19, 1940; BS, U. Wis., 1961, MD, 1965. Resident internal medicine Harvard U., 1965-67; fellow Harvard and U. Calif., Irvine, 1969-72; dean med. sch. U. Calif., Irvine, 1995—. Office: U Calif Coll Medicine Irvine CA 92697-3950

CHACKO, GEORGE KUTTICKAL, systems science educator, consultant; b. Trivandrum, India, July 1, 1930; came to U.S., 1953. s. Geevarghese Kuttickal and Thankamma (Mathew) C.; m. Yo Yee, Aug. 10, 1957; children: Rajah Yee, Ashia Yo Chacko Lance. MA in Econs. and Polit. Philosophy, Madras U., India, 1950; postgrad., St. Xavier's Coll., Calcutta, India, 1950-52; B in Commerce, Calcutta U., 1952; cert. postgrad. tng., Indian Stat. Inst., Calcutta, 1951; postgrad., Princeton U., 1953-54; PhD in Econometrics, New Sch. for Social Rsch., N.Y.C., 1959; postdoctoral, UCLA, 1961. Asst. editor Indian Fin., Calcutta, 1951-53; comml. corr. Times of India, 1953; dir. mktg. and mgmt. rsch. Royal Metal Mfg. Co., N.Y.C., 1958-60; mgr. dept. ops. rsch. Hughes Semicondr. div., Newport Beach, Calif., 1960-61; cons., 1961-62; ops. research staff cons. Union Carbide Corp., N.Y.C., 1962-63; mem. tech. staff Research Analysis Corp., McLean, Va., 1963-65, MITRE Corp., Arlington, 1965-67; sr. staff scientist TRW Systems Group, Washington, 1967-70; cons. def. systems, computer, space, tech. systems and internat. devel. systems, assoc. in math. test devel. Ednl. Testing Service, Princeton, N.J., 1955-57; asst. prof. bus. adminstrn. UCLA, 1961-62; lectr. Dept. Agr. Grad. Sch., 1965-67; asst. professorial lectr. George Washington U., 1965-68; professorial lectr. Am. U., 1967-70, adj. prof., 1970; vis. prof. def. systems Mgmt. Coll., Ft. Belvoir, Va., 1972-73; vis. prof. U. So. Calif., 1970-71, prof. systems mgmt., 1971-83, prof. systems sci., 1983-94, prof. emeritus, 1994; prof. mgmt. U. Pertanian, Malaysia, 1996—, prin. investigator IRPA project, 1996-97; prof. U. Putra, Malaysia, 1997—; prof. tech. mgmt. Malaysian Grad. Sch. Mgmt., 1997—; founder, chmn. Joint MIT-MGSM Pan-Asian Program in Mgmt. of Tech., 1997—. Sr. Fulbright prof. Nat. Chengchi U., Taipei, 1983-84, sr. Fulbright rsch. prof., 1984-85; prin. investigator and program dir. Tech. Transfer Project, Taiwan Nat. Sci. Coun., 1984-85; disting. fgn. expert lectr. Taiwan Ministry Econ. Affairs, 1986; sr. vis. rsch. prof. Taiwan Nat. Sci. Coun. Nat. Chengchi U., Taipei, 1988-89; sr. vis. rsch. prof. Dah-Yeh Inst. Tech., Dah-Tsuen, Chang-Hwa, Taiwan, 1993-94; vis. prof. Nat. Chengchi U., Taipei, 1993-94; v.p. program devel. Systems and Telecom. Corp., Potomac, Md., 1987-90; chief sci. cons. RJO Enterprises, Lanham, Md., 1988-89; cons. Med. Svcs. Corp. Internat., vector biology and control project U.S. Agy. for Internat. Devel., 1991; guest lectr. Tech. Univs. Tokyo, Taipei, Singapore, Dubai, Cairo, Warsaw, Budapest, Prague, Bergen, Stockholm, Helsinki, Berlin, Madras, Bombay, London, 1992, Yokohoma, Taipei, Hong Kong, Kuala Lampur, Madras, Bombay, Alexandria, Jerusalem, Cairo, Paris, London, 1993-94, Madrid, Bologna, Milan, Monte Carlo, Amsterdam, Vienna, Austria, Kuala Lampur, Bangkok, 1994; Bogta, Quito, Lima, Santiago, Buenos Aires, Rio De Janeiro, Johannesburg, Kuala Lumpur, 1996; USIA sponsored U.S. sci. emissary to Egypt, Burma, India, Singapore, 1987; USIA sponsored U.S. expert on tech. transferand military conversion 1st Internat. Conf. on Reconstrn. of Soviet Republics, Hannover, Germany, 1992; keynote speaker 2d annual conf. on mgmt. edn. in China, Taipei, Taiwan, 1989, world conf. on transition to advanced market economies, Warsaw, Poland, 1992, annual conv. Indian Inst. Indsl. Engring., Hyderabad, India, 1993, First Sino-South Africa Bilateral Symposium on Tech. Devel., Taipei, 1994, First Asia-Pacific Convention on Bus. mgmt. Edn., Kuala Lompen, 1996, Annual Conf. of Malasian Soc. of Ops. Rsch. and Mgmt. Scis, 1997; mem. internat. adv. com. on restructuring strategies for electronics info. industry Asian Inst. Tech. Workshop, 1994, Technological Forecasting and Social Change, 1996—; mem. First Convention on Bus. and Mgmt. Edn., Kuala Lumpur, 1996, mem. Asian-Pacific Conf. on Mgmt. Sci., Malaysia, 1997. Author: 29 books in field including Applied Statistics in Decision Making, 1971, Computer Aided Decision Making, 1972, Systems Approach to Public and Private Sector Problems, 1976, Operations Research Approach to Problem Formation and Solution, 1976, Management Information systems, 1979, Trade Drain Interperative of Technology Transfer: U.S. Taiwan Concomitant Coalistions, 1985, Robotics/Artificial Intelligence/Productivity U.S.-Japan Concomitant Coalitions, 1986, Technology Management: Applications to Corporate Markets and Military Missions, 1988, The Systems Approach to Problem-Solving: From Corporate Markets to National Missions, 1989, Toward Expanding Exports Through Technology Transfer: IBM Taiwan Concomitant Coalitions, 1989, Dynamic Program Management: From Defense Experience to Commercial Application, 1989, Decision-Making Under Uncertainty: An Applied Statistics Approach, 1991, Operations Research/Management Science: Case Studies in Decision Making Under Structured Uncertainty, 1993, Invoking Intercessory Prayer Power: Mediating Modern-day Miracles, 1997, Targeting Strategies for Continuous Competitiveness: 33 Corporate, Country, and Cross-Country Applications for Information Technology (IT) Industry, 1988, Half-Indian, Half-Chinese, and All American, 1998, Synergizing Invention and Innovation for Missions and Markets: 31 Corporate, Country and Cross Country Applications in Integrating Technology and Territory within and Between Corporations and Countries, 1999, Survival Strategies of Hitech Corporations: Applicable Insights from 20th Century Eminent Executive Narratives, 1999; columnist: The Sunday Star, 1998—, Bus. Times, 1998—; contbr. articles to profl. pubs.; editor, contbr. 25 books including The Recognition of Systems in Health Services, 1969, Reducing the Cost of Space Transportation, 1969, Systems Approach to Environmental Pollution, 1972, National Organization of Health Services-U.S., USSR, China, Europe, 1979, Educational Innovation in Health Services-U.S., Europe, Middle East, Africa, 1979, Management Education in the Republic of China: Second Annual Conference, 1989, Expert Systems: 1st World Congress Proceedings, 1991, Transition to Advanced Market Economics: Internat. Conf. Proceedings, 1992, Industrial Engineering Interfaces: Inndian Nat. Conf. Proceedings, 1993, Technological Development: 1st Sino-South Africa Bilateral Symposium Proceedings, 1994, Lenten Daily Devotions, 1996, Asia Pacific Convention on Dynamism and Invention in Management Education Proceedings, 1996, Foundations of Game Theory, 1997; guest editor Jour. Rsch. Comm. Studies, 1978-79; assoc. editor Internat. Jour. Forecasting, 1982-85; mem. internat. editl. bd. Malaysian Jour. Mgmt. Scis., 1993—. Active Nat. Presbyn. Ch., Washington, 1967-84, mem. ch. coun., 1969-71, mem. chancel choir, 1967-84, co-dean ch. family camp, 1977, coord. life abundant discovery groups, 1979; chmn. worship com. Taipei Internat. Ch., 1984, founder, dir. Intercessory Prayer Power, 1984, mem. adult choir, 1983-85, 88-89, 93-96, chmn. membership com., 1985, chmn. stewardship and fin. com., 1985, chmn. com. Christian edn., 1988, Sunday Sch. supt., 1989, adult Sunday sch. leader, 1993; adult Sunday Sch. leader 4th Presbyn. Ch., Bethesda, Md., 1986-87, mem. sanctuary choir, 1985—; participant 9th Internat. Ch. Mus. Festival, Coventry Cathedral, 1992; mem. Men's Ensemble, 1986-93; mem. Ministry Com. Men of 4th Rep. to Session, 1990—; founder, dir. Prayer Power Partnership, 1990—; adult Sunday sch. leader Kuala Lumpur Internat. Ch., 1996—; mem. internat. adv. bd. Technol. Forecasting and Social Change, 1996—. Recipient Gold medal Inter-Collegiate Extempore Debate in Malayalam U. Travancore, Trivandrum, India, 1945, 1st pl. Yogic Exercises Competition U. Travancore, 1946, Jr. Lectureship prize Physics Soc. U. Coll., 1946, 1st prize Inter-Varsity Debating Team Madras, 1949, NSF internat. sci. lectures award, 1982, USIA citation for invaluable contbr. to America's pub. diplomacy, 1992, Commendation for 2 books on U.S. - Taiwan Technology Transfer by Presidential Palace, Taipei, 1993; Coll. scholar St. Xavier's Coll., 1950-52; Inst. fellow Indian Stat. Inst., 1951, S.E. Asia Club fellow Princeton U., 1953-54, Univ. fellow UCLA, 1961. Fellow AAAS (nat. coun. 1968-73, chmn. or co-chmn. symposia 1971, 72, 74, 76, 77, 78), Am. Astronautical Soc. (v.p. publs. 1969-71, editor Tech. Newsletter 1968-72, mng. editor Jour. Astronautical Scis. 1969-75); mem. Ops. Rsch. Soc. Am. (vice chmn. com. of representation on AAAS 1972-78, nat. coun. tech. sect. on health 1966-68, editor Tech. Newsletter on Health 1966-73), Washington Ops. Rsch. Coun. (trustee 1967-69, chmn. tech. colloquia 1967-68, editor Tech. Newsletter 1967-68, Banquet chmn. 1992-93), Inst. Mgmt. Scis. (rep. to Internat. Inst. for Applied Systems Analysis in Vienna, Austria 1976-77, session chmn. Athens, Greece 1977, Atlanta 1977), World Future Soc. (editl. bd. publs. 1970-71), N.Y. Acad. Scis., Soc. Scientific Mgmt. and Ops. Rsch. (Egypt, 1st hon. fgn. mem.), Inst. for Ops. Rsch. and the Mgmt. Scis. (founding, INFORMS 1994); Kiwanis (charter 1st v.p., Life-time Hickson fellow 1995), Costa Mesa North Club (charter 1st v.p., dir.), Friendship Heights Club (charter pres., dir., Outstanding Svc. award 1972-73, Life award), Bethesda Club (disting. divsn. one svc. award, 1968, 70, capital dist. chmn. 1967, 69-70, 71-72, inter divsn. chmn. Green Candle of Hope Dinner, 1965-82), Capital dist. Found. 1982, Taipei-Keystone Club (disting. dir., spl. rep. of internat. pres. and counselor to dist. of Republic of China 1983-86, Pioneer Premier Project award Asia-Pacific conf. 1986, Legion of Honor 1985), Bethesda Club (dir. 1967-69, 95, chmn. internat. rels. 1991—, chmn. hon. com. 1992—, numerous coms. 1966—). Democrat. Office: U So Calif Inst Safety And Sys Mgmt Los Angeles CA 90089-0001

CHACON, MICHAEL ERNEST, directory services and eBusiness specialist; b. L.A., Feb. 14, 1954; s. Ernest Richard and Teresa Marie (Venegas) C.; m. Virginia Marie; children: Mylan Graham, Aubrie Sarah, Christina Nabseth, Caitlyn Nabseth, Julia Anna. Student, Pierce Coll., 1972-74, Boise State U., 1980-82; BSBA, U. Phoenix, 1997. Sys. cons. MEC & Assocs., Riverside, Calif., 1986-91; regional mgr. Inacom Corp., Garden Grove, 1991-97; chief tech. officer Ascolta Tng. Co., Irvine, 1997-2000; prin. architect Netigy Corp., San Jose, 2000—. Cons. in field; lectr. Microsoft Corp., Bellvue, Wash., 1990-92; chief tng. officer Ascolta Tng. Co., Irvine, Calif.; instr. Irvine Valley Coll.; bd. dirs. Info. Tech. Tng. Assn. Author: Understanding Networks, 1991, Windows 2000 Acelerated Study Guide, 2000; columnist Microsoft Cert. Profl. Mag.; contbr. articles to profl. jours. Named to Dean's List, Pierce Coll., 1973, 74. Mem. Lake Elsinore Sportsman Assn., L.A. World Affairs Coun., 3Com Adv. Coun. (pres. tech. adv. bd. 1986-92). Avocations: songwriting/composing, rocketry, shooting, photography. E-mail: michael.chacon@netigy.com

CHAFE, WALLACE LESEUR, linguist, educator; b. Cambridge, Mass., Sept. 3, 1927; s. Albert J. and Nathalie (Amback) C.; m. Mary Elizabeth Butterworth, June 23, 1951 (div. 1980); children— Christopher, Douglas, Stephen; m. Marianne Mithun, Jan. 25, 1985 B.A., Yale U., 1950, M.A., 1956, Ph.D., 1958. Asst. prof. U. Buffalo, 1958-59; linguist Bur. Am. Ethnology, Smithsonian Instn., 1959-62; mem. faculty U. Calif. Berkeley, 1962-86, prof. linguistics, 1967-86, U. Calif., Santa Barbara, 1986-91, prof. emeritus, 1991—. Author: Seneca Thanksgiving Rituals, 1961, Seneca Morphology and Dictionary, 1967, Meaning and the Structure of Language, 1970, The Pear Stories, 1980, Evidentiality, 1986, Discourse, Consciousness, and Time, 1994. Served with USNR, 1945-46. Mem. Linguistic Soc. Am., Am. Psychol. Assn., Am. Anthrop. Assn. Office: Univ Calif Dept Linguistics Santa Barbara CA 93106

CHAFFEE, STEVEN, communication educator; b. South Gate, Calif., Aug. 21, 1935; s. Edwin W. and Nancy M. Chaffee; m. Sheila McGoldrick, 1966 (div. 1987); children: Laura, Adam, Amy; m. Debra Lieberman, 1989; 1 child, Eliot. s. Edwin W. and Nancy M. Chaffee; m. Sheila McGoldrick, 1959 (div. 1986); children: Laura, Adam, Amy; m. Debra Lieberman, 1989; 1 child, Eliot. BA in History, U. of Redlands, 1957; MS in Journalism, UCLA, 1962; PhD in Comm., Stanford U., 1965. News editor Angeles Mesa News-Advertiser, L.A., 1957; reporter Santa Monica (Calif.) Evening Outlook, 1962; from asst. prof. to full prof. U. Wis., Madison, 1965-81; prof. comm. Stanford (Calif.) U., 1981-99, U. Calif., Santa Barbara, 1999-2001. Author: Communication Concepts I: Explication, 1991; co-editor: Handbook of Communication Science, 1987; co-author: Television and Human Behavior, 1978; editor: Political Communication, 1975. Lt. (j.g.) USN, 1957-61. Fellow Internat. Comm. Assn. (pres. 1981); mem. Assn. for Edn. in Journalism and Mass Comm., Am. Polit. Sci. Assn. Democrat. Avocation: hiking.

CHAGALL, DAVID, journalist, writer; b. Phila., Nov. 22, 1930; s. Harry and Ida (Coopersmith) C.; m. Juneau Joan Alsin, Nov. 15, 1957. Student, Swarthmore Center Coll., 1948-49; B.A., Pa. State U., 1952; postgrad., Sorbonne, U. Paris, 1953-54. Social caseworker State of Pa., Phila., 1955-57; sci. editor Jour. I.E.E., 1959-61; pub. relations staff A.E.I.-Hotpoint Ltd., London, 1961-62; mktg. research assoc. Chilton Co., Phila., 1962-63; mktg. research project dir. Haug Assos., Inc. (Roper Orgn.), Los Angeles, 1964-74; research cons. Haug Assos., 1976-79; investigative reporter for nat. mags., 1975—. Host TV series The Last Hour, 1994—. Author: Diary of a Deaf Mute, 1960, The Century God Slept, 1963, The Spieler for the Holy Spirit, 1972, The New Kingmakers, 1981, The Sunshine Road, 1988, Surviving the Media Jungle, 1996, Target, 2000; contbr.: Television Today, 1981, The Media and Morality, 1999; pub.: Inside Campaigning, 1983; syndicated column, articles, revs., stories and poetry to mags., jours., newspapers; contbg. editor: TV Guide, L.A. Mag. Apptd. to Selective Svc. Bd., 1991, apptd. chmn., 1999; bd. dirs. Chosen Prophetic Ministries, 1991. Recipient U. Wis. Poetry prize, 1971; nominee Nat. Book award in fiction, 1972, Pulitzer prize in letters, 1973, Disting. Health Journalism award, 1978; Presdl. Achievement award, 1982; Carnegie Trust grantee, 1964 Home: PO Box 85 Agoura Hills CA 91376-0085 E-mail: Dchagall@aol.com

CHAHINE, MOUSTAFA TOUFIC, atmospheric scientist; b. Beirut, Lebanon, Jan. 1, 1935; s. Toufic M. and Hind S. (Tabbara) C.; m. Marina Bandak, Dec. 9, 1960; children: Tony T., Steve S. B.S., U. Wash., 1956, M.S., 1957; Ph.D., U. Calif., Berkeley, 1960. With Jet Propulsion Lab., Calif. Inst. Tech., Pasadena, 1960—, mgr. planetary atmospheres sect., 1975-78, sr. research scientist, mgr. earth and space scis. div., 1978-84, chief scientist, 1984—. Vis. scientist MIT, 1969-70; vis. prof. Am. U., Beirut, 1971-72; regent's lectr. UCLA, 1989-90; mem. NASA Space and Earth Sci. Adv. Com., 1982-85; mem. climate rsch. com. Nat. Acad. Scis., 1985-88, bd. dirs. atmospheric scis. and climate, 1988—; chmn. sci. steering group Global Energy and Water Cycle Experiment World Meteorol. Orgn., 1988-99; cons. U.S. Navy, 1972-76 Contbr. articles on atmospheric scis. to profl. jours. Recipient medal for exceptional sci. achievements NASA, 1969, NASA Outstanding Leadership medal, 1984, William T. Pecora award, 1989, Jule G. Charney award, 1991, Losey Atmospheric Scis. award AIAA, 1993, NASA Exceptional Achievement medal, 2000. Fellow AAAS, Am. Geophys. Union, Am. Phys. Soc., Royal Soc., Am. Meteorol. Soc.; mem. Internat. Acad. Astronautics, Sigma Xi. Office: 4800 Oak Grove Dr Pasadena CA 91109-8001

CHAI, WINBERG, political science educator; b. Shanghai, China, Oct. 16, 1932; came to U.S., 1951, naturalized, 1973; s. Ch'u and Mei-en (Tsao) C.; m. Carolyn Everett, Mar. 17, 1966 (dec. 1996); children: Maria May-lee, Jeffrey Tien-yu. Student, Hartwick Coll., 1951-53; BA, Wittenberg U., 1955, DHL, 1997; MA, New Sch. Social Rsch., 1958; PhD, NYU, 1968; DHL, Wittenberg U., 1987. Lectr. New Sch. Social Rsch., 1957-61; vis. asst. prof. Drew U., 1961-62; asst. prof. Fairleigh Dickinson U., 1962-65, U. Redlands, 1965-68, assoc. prof., 1969-73, chmn. dept., 1970-73; prof., chmn. Asian studies CCNY, 1973-79; disting. prof. polit. sci., v.p. acad. affairs, spl. asst. to pres. U. S.D., Vermillion, 1979-82; prof. polit. sci., dir. internat. programs U. Wyo., Laramie, 1988—. Hmn. Third World Conf. Found., Inc., Chgo., 1982—; pres. Wang Yu-fa Found., Taiwan, 1989—. Author: (with Ch'u Chai) The Story of Chinese Philosophy, 1961, The Changing Society of China, 1962, rev. edit., 1969, The New Politics of Communist China, 1972, The Search for a New China, 1975; editor: Essential Works of Chinese Communism, 1969, (with James C. Hsiung) Asia in the U.S. Foreign Policy, 1981, (with James C. Hsiung) U.S. Asian Relations: The National Security Paradox, 1983, (with Carolyn Chai) Beyond China's Crisis, 1989, In Search of Peace in the Middle East, 1991, (with Cal Clark) Political Stability and Economic Growth, 1994, China Mainland and Taiwan, 1994, revised edit. 1996, Hong Kong Under China, 1998; co-translator: (with Ch'u Chai) A Treasury of Chinese Literature, 1965; co-author (with May-Lee-Chai) The Girl from Purple Mountain, 2001. Haynes Found. fellow, 1967, 68; Ford Found. humanities grantee, 1968, 69, Pacific Cultural Found. grantee, 1978, 86, NSF grantee, 1970, Hubert Eaton Meml. Fund grantee, 1972-73, Field Found. grantee, 1973, 75, Henry Luce Found. grantee, 1978, 80, S.D. Humanities Com. grantee, 1980, Pacific Culture Fund grantee, 1987, 90-91. Mem. AAAS, AAUP, NAACP, Am. Polit. Sci. Assn., Am. Assn. Chinese Studies (pres.1978-80), N.Y. Acad. Scis., Internat. Studies Assn. Democrat. Home: 1071 Granito Dr Laramie WY 82072-5045 Office: PO Box 4098 Laramie WY 82071-4098 E-mail: WinbergChai@aol.com

CHAMBERLAIN, ADRIAN RAMOND, transportation engineer; b. Detroit, Nov. 11, 1929; s. Adrian and Leila (Swisher) C.; m. Melanie F. Stevens, May 19, 1979; children: Curtis (dec.), Tracy, Thomas (dec.). BS, Mich. State U., 1951, D Engring., 1971; MS, Wash. State U., 1952; PhD, Colo. State U., 1955; LittD, Denver U., 1974. Registered profl. engr., Colo. lic. real estate broker, Colo., 1981-91. Rsch. engr. Phillips Petroleum Co., 1955; rsch. coord., civil engr. Colo. State U., 1956-57, chief civil engr. sect., 1957-61, acting dean engring., 1959-61, v.p., 1960-66, exec. v.p., treas., governing bd., 1966-69, pres., 1969-80; chmn. bd. dirs. Univ. Nat. Bank, 1964-69, dir., 1964-74; pres., dir. Mitchell & Co., Inc., 1981-85; exec. v.p. Simons, Li & Assocs., Inc., 1985-87; pres., CEO, Chemagnetics, Inc., Ft. Collins, Colo., 1987-89; exec. dir. Colo. Dept. Hwys., Denver, 1987-91, Colo. Dept. Transp., 1991-94; v.p. Parsons Brinckerhoff, Denver, 1998—. Chmn. NSF Commn. Weather Modification, 1964-66; mem. Nat. Air Quality Criteria Adv. Com., 1967-70; vice chmn. rsch. and tech. coord. com. Fed. Hwy Adminstrn. of Transp. Rsch. Bd., NRC, 1991-94. Colo. commr. Western Interstate Commn. on Higher Edn., 1974-78; pres. State Bd. Agr. Sys., 1978-80; trustee Cystic Fibrosis Found., 1971-84, Univ. Corp. for Atmospheric Rsch., 1967-72, 74-81, chmn. bd. trustees, 1977-79; pres. Black Mountain Ranch, Inc., 1969-85; bd. dirs. Nat. Ctr. for Higher Edn. Mgmt. Sys., 1975-80, chmn. bd. dirs., 1977-78; bd. visitors Air U., USAF, 1973-76, chmn., 1975-76; exec. com. Nat. Assn. State Univs. and Land Grant Colls., 1976-80, pres.-elect, 1978-79, chmn., 1979-80; mem. adv. coun. to dir. NSF, 1978-81; chmn. Ft. Collins-Loveland Airport Authority, 1983-86; bd. dirs. Synergetics Internat. Inc., 1987-90; mem. exec. com. strategic hwy. rsch. commn. Transp. Rsch. Bd. NRC, 1989-93, chmn. strategic transp. rsch. study hwy. safety, 1989-90, exec. com., 1991-96, vice-chmn., 1992, chmn., 1993; mem. Gov.'s Cabinet, State of Colo., 1987-94; mem. Info. Mgmt. Commn., 1988-93. Fulbright student U. Grenoble, 1955-56 Mem. ASCE, Am. Assn. State Hwy. and Transp. Ofcls. (policy com. 1987-92, v.p. 1990-91, pres. 1991-92, bd. dirs. 1992-94, chmn. standing com. on adminstrn. 1993-94), Am. Trucking Assn. (v.p. for freight policy 1994-98, mng. dir. found. 1998), Order of Aztec Eagle, Mex., Sigma Xi, Tau Beta Pi, Phi Kappa Phi, Chi Epsilon. Home: 124 Idlewild Ln Winter Park CO 80482 Office: Parsons Brinckerhoff 1660 Lincoln St Ste 2100 Denver CO 80264-2001

CHAMBERLAIN, BOB, computer company executive; BS in Bus. Adminstrn., Calif. State U. Audit ptnr. KPMG Peat Marwick; v.p. fin. and ops. ElseWare Corp.; v.p., treas., CFO Midcom Comm., Inc.; co-pres. Photo Disc, Inc.; v.p. sales, bus. devel. Consilient, Inc., Berkeley, Calif. Office: Consilient Inc 1815 4th St Ste B Berkeley CA 94710

CHAMBERLAIN, OWEN, nuclear physicist; b. San Francisco, July 10, 1920; m. Babette Copper, 1943 (div. 1978; 4 children; m. June Steingart, 1980 (dec.); m. Senta Pugh, 1998. AB (Cramer fellow), Dartmouth Coll., 1941; PhD, U. Chgo., 1949. Instr. physics U. Calif., Berkeley, 1948-50, asst. prof., 1950-54, assoc. prof., 1954-58, prof., 1958-89, prof. emeritus, 1989—; civilian physicist Manhattan Dist., Berkeley, Los Alamos, 1942-46. Recipient Nobel prize (with Emilio Segré) for physics, for discovery anti-proton, 1959, The Berkeley citation U. Calif., 1989; Guggenheim fellow, 1957-58; Loeb lectr. at Harvard U., 1959. Fellow Am. Phys. Soc., Am. Acad. Arts and Scis.; mem. Nat. Acad. Scis., Berkeley Fellows. Office: U Calif Phys Dept Berkeley CA 94720-0001

CHAMBERLAIN, WILLIAM EDWIN, JR. management consultant; b. St. Louis, June 8, 1951; s. William Edwin Sr. and Grace (Salisbury) C. AA in Bus. Mgmt., Mesa (Ariz.) Community Coll., 1983; BBA, U. Phoenix, 1988. Tng. and human resources devel. specialist Motorola, Inc., Phoenix, 1979-87; pres., seminar speaker Chamberlain Cons. Svcs., Reno, 1987—. Curator, dir. ops. U.S. Wolf Refuge. Mem. Network for Profl. Devel. Avocations: wildlife preservation and management, hiking, backpacking, tennis, basketball, racquetball.

CHAMBERLIN, DONALD DEAN, computer engineer; b. San Jose, Calif., Dec. 21, 1944; BS, Harvey Mudd Coll., 1966; PhD in Elec. Engring., Stanford U., 1971. Rsch. staff mem. IBM, San Jose, Calif., 1971—. Adj. prof. Santa Clara U., 1992-95. Author: Using the New DB2: IBM's Object-Relational Database System, 1996, A Complete Guide to DB2 Universal Database, 1998; contbr. articles to profl. jours. Fellow Assn. Computing Machinery; mem. Nat. Acad. Engring., Inst. Elec. & Electronics Engrs. Office: Almaden Research Ctr IBM 650 Harry Rd San Jose CA 95120-6001 Fax: 408-927-3215. E-mail: chamberlin@almaden.ibm.com

CHAMBERLIN, ED, curator; b. Rochester, Mich., Nov. 11, 1958; BA, No. Mich. U., 1982. Mus. curator Grand Canyon Nat. Park, Ariz., 1981-89, Hubbell Trading Post Nat. Hist. Site, Ganado, 1989-92, 97—; pk. curator Carlsbad (N.Mex.) Caverns Nat. Pk., 1992-93; regional curator Bur. Reclamation, Boulder City, Nev., 1993-97. Office: Hubbell Trading Post National Historic Site PO Box 150 Ganado AZ 86505-0150

CHAMBERLIN, MICHAEL JOHN, biochemistry educator; b. Chgo., June 7, 1937; s. John Windsor and Marian (McMichael) C.; m. Caroline Marie Kane, Jan. 31, 1981. AB, Harvard U., 1959; PhD, Stanford U., 1963. Asst. prof. virology U. Calif., Berkeley, 1963-67, assoc. prof. molecular biology, 1967-71, assoc. prof. biochemistry, 1971-73, prof., 1973—, vice chmn. dept. biochemistry, 1983-88, prof. biochemistry and molecular biology, 1989—. Mem. physiol. chemistry study sect. NIH, 1970-74, molecular biology study sect., 1980-84; mem. study sect. Am. Heart Assn., 1983-86. Mem. editorial bd. Jour. Biol. Chemistry, 1975-78, Biochemistry,

1993—; contbr. articles to profl. jours. Recipient Charles Pfizer award Am. Chem. Soc., 1974. Mem. NAS, AAAS, Am. Acad. Arts and Scis., Am. Soc. Biochemistry and Molecular Biology, Am. Soc. Microbiology, Am. Acad. Microbiology, Phi Beta Kappa, Sigma Xi. Office: U Calif Dept Molecular/Cell Biology 401 Barker Hall Berkeley CA 94720-3208 E-mail: mar-lin@socrates.berkeley.edu

CHAMBERS, CAROLYN SILVA, communications company executive; b. Portland, Oreg., Sept. 15, 1931; d. Julio and Elizabeth (McDonnell) Silva; widowed; children: William, Scott, Elizabeth, Silva, Clark. BBA, U. Oreg. V.p., treas. Liberty Comm., Inc., Eugene, Oreg., 1960-83; pres. Chambers Comm. Corp., Eugene, 1983-95, chmn., 1996—; chmn., CEO, bd. dirs. Chambers Constrn. Co., 1986—. Bd. dirs., dep. chair bd. Fed. Res. Bank, San Francisco, 1982-92; bd. dirs. Portland Gen. Corp.; bd. dirs. U.S. Bancorp. Mem. Sacred Heart Med. Found., 1980—, Sacred Heart Gov. Bd., 1987-92, Sacred Heart Health Svcs. Bd., 1993-95, PeaceHealth Bd., 1995—; mem. U. Oreg. Found., 1980—, pres., 1992-93; chair U. Oreg. Found., The Campaign for Oreg., 1988-89; pres., bd. dirs. Eugene Arts Found.; bd. dirs., treas., dir. search com. Eugene Symphony; mem. adv. bd. Eugene Hearing and Speech Ctr., Alton Baker Park Commn., Pleasant Hill Sch. Bd.; chmn., pres., treas. Civic Theatre, Very Little Theatre; negotiator, treas., bd. dirs., mem. thrift shop Jr. League of Oreg. Recipient Webfoot award U. Oreg., 1986, U. Oreg. Pres.'s medal, 1991, Disting. Svc. award, 1992, Pioneer award, 1983, Woman Who Made a Difference award Internat. Women's Forum, 1989, U. Oreg. Found. Disting. Alumni award, 1995, Tom McCall awrd Oreg. Assn. Broadcasters, 1995, Disting. Alumni award U. Oreg., 1995, Outstanding Philanthropist award Oreg. chpt. Nat. Soc. Fund Raising Execs., 1994. Mem. Nat. Cable TV Assn. (mem. fin. com., chmn. election and by-laws com., chmn. awards com., bd. dirs. 1987-89, Vanguard award for Leadership 1982), Pacific Northwest Cable Comm. Assn. (conv. chmn., pres.), Oreg. Cable TV Assn. (v.p., pres., chmn. edn. com., conv. chmn., Pres.'s award 1986), Calif. Cable TV Assn. (bd. dirs., conv. chmn., conv. panelist), Women in Cable (charter mem., treas., v.p., pres., recipient star of cable recognition), Wash. State Cable Comm. Assn., Idaho Cable TV Assn., Community Antenna TV Assn., Cable TV Pioneers, Eugene C. of C. (first citizen award, 1985). Home: PO Box 640 Pleasant Hill OR 97455-0640 Office: Chambers Comm Corp PO Box 7009 Eugene OR 97401-0009

CHAMBERS, JOAN LOUISE, retired librarian, retired university educator and dean; b. Denver, Mar. 22, 1937; d. Joseph Harvey and Clara Elizabeth (Carleton) Baker; m. Donald Ray Chambers, Aug. 17, 1958 B.A. in English Lit., U. No. Colo., Greeley, 1958; M.S. in L.S., U. Calif.-Berkeley, 1970; M.S. in Systems Mgmt., U. So. Calif., 1985; cert., Coll. for Fin. Planning, 1989. Libr. U. Nev., Reno, 1970-79; asst. univ. libr. U. Calif., San Diego, 1979-81, univ. libr. Riverside, 1981-85; dean librs., prof. Colo. State U., Ft. Collins, 1985-97, emeritus dean and prof., 1997—. Mgmt. intern. Duke U. Libr., Durham, N.C., 1978-79; sr. fellow UCLA Summer, 1982; cons. tng. program Assn. of Rsch. Libraries, Washington, 1981; libr. cons. Calif. State U., Sacramento, 1982-83, U. Wyo., 1985-86, 94-95, U. Nebr., 1991-92, Calif. State U. System, 1993-94, Univ. No. Ariz., 1994-95. Contbr. articles to profl. jours., chpts. to books Bd. dirs. Consumers Union, 1996—; mem. adv. bd. Colo. Mountain Coll., 2000—. U. Calif. instl. improvement grantee, 1980-81; State of Nev. grantee, 1976, ARL grantee, 1983-84. Mem. Colo. Mountain Club, Chaine des Rotisseurs, Beta Phi Mu, Phi Lambda Theta, Kappa Delta Phi, Phi Kappa Phi. Avocations: hiking, snow shoeing, skiing, cycling, tennis. Home and Office: PO Box 1477 Edwards CO 81632-1477 E-mail: chamber@vail.net

CHAMBERS, JOHN T. computer company executive; m. Elaine Chambers; 2 children. BS, BA, JD, W.Va. U.; MBA, Ind. U. Sr. v.p. worldwide ops. Cisco Sys., Inc., San Jose, Calif., 1991-94, exec. v.p., 1994-95, pres., CEO, 1995—. Bd. dirs. Clarify, Inc., San Jose, Arbor Software, Sunnyvale, Calif. Office: Cisco Sys Inc 170 W Tasman Dr Bldg 10 San Jose CA 95134-1706 E-mail: jochambe@cisco.com

CHAMBERS, KENTON LEE, botany educator; b. Sept. 27, 1929; s. Maynard Macy and Edna Georgia (Miller) C.; m. Henrietta Laing, June 21, 1958; children: Elaine Patricia, David Macy. AB with highest honors, Whittier Coll., 1950; PhD (NSF fellow), Stanford U., 1955. Instr. biol. scis. Stanford (Calif.) U., 1954-55; instr. botany, asst. prof. Yale U., New Haven, 1956-60; assoc. prof., prof. botany Oreg. State U., Corvallis, 1960-90, prof. emeritus, 1991—. Curator Herbarium, 1960-90; program dir. systematic biology NSF, Washington, 1967-68. Contbr. articles in field to profl. jours. Fellow AAAS; mem. Bot. Soc. Am. (Merit award 1990), Am. Soc. Plant Taxonomists, Am. Inst. Biol. Scis., Calif. Bot. Soc. Home: 4761 SW Hollyhock Cir Corvallis OR 97333-1385 Office: Oreg State U Herbarium Botany Dept Corvallis OR 97331-2902 E-mail: chamberk@bcc.orst.edu

CHAMBERS, LOIS IRENE, insurance automation consultant; b. Omaha, Nov. 24, 1935; d. Edward J. and Evelyn B. (Davidson) Morrison; m. Peter A. Mscichowski, Aug. 16, 1952 (div. 1980); 1 child, Peter Edward; m. Frederick G. Chambers, Apr. 17, 1981. Clk. Gross-Wilson Ins. Agy., Portland, Oreg., 1955-57; sec., bookkeeper Reed-Paulsen Ins. Agy., Portland, 1957-58; office mgr., asst. sec., agt. Donn Biggs & Assocs., Vancouver, Wash., 1958-88, v.p. ops., 1988-89, automation mgr., 1989-91, mktg. mgr., 1991-94; automation cons. Antiques and Collectables, Chambers & Assocs., Tualatin, Oreg., 1985—; sys. mgr. Contractors Ins. Svcs., Inc., 1997-2000. Chmn. adv. com. Clark C.C., Vancouver, 1985-93, mem. adv. com., 1993-94. Mem. citizens com. task force City of Vancouver, 1976-78, mem. Block Grant rev. task force, 1978—. Mem. Ins. Women of S.W. Wash. (pres. 1978, Ins. Woman of Yr. 1979), Nat. Assn. Ins. Women, Nat. Users Agena Sys. (charter; pres. 1987-89), Soroptimist Internat. (Vancouver; pres. 1979-80). Democrat. Roman Catholic. Office: Chambers & Assocs 8770 SW Umatilla St Tualatin OR 97062-6340 E-mail: fchamb8026@aol.com

CHAMPAGNE, DUANE WILLARD, sociology educator; b. Belcourt, N.D., May 18, 1951; children: Talya, Gabe, Demelza. BA in Math., N.D. State U., 1973, MA in Sociology, 1975; PhD in Sociology, Harvard U., 1982. Teaching fellow Harvard U., Cambridge, Mass., 1981-82, rsch. fellow, 1982-83; asst. prof. U. Wis., Milw., 1983-84, UCLA, 1984-91, assoc. prof., 1991-97, prof., 1997—. Publs. dir. Am. Indian Studies Ctr., UCLA, 1986-87, assoc. dir., 1990, acting dir., 1991, dir., 1991—; adminstrv. co-head interdepartmental program for Am. Indian studies UCLA, 1992-93; mem. grad. rsch. fellowship panel NSF, 1990-92, minority fellowship com. ASA; cons. Energy Resources Co., 1982, No. Cheyenne Tribe, 1983, Realis Pictures, Inc., 1989-90, Sta. KCET-TV, L.A., 1990, 92, Salem Press, 1992, Book Prodns. Systems, 1993, Readers Digest, 1993, Rattlesnake Prodns., 1993. Author: American Indian Societies, 1989, Social Order and Political Change, 1992; editor: Native North American Almanac, 1994, Chronology of Native North American, 1994, Native America: Portrait of the Peoples, 1994; co-editor: A Second Century of Dishonor: Federal Inequities and California Tribes, 1996, Service Delivery for Native American Children in Los Angeles County, 1996; editor: Native Am. Studies Assn. Newsletter, 1991-92, Native American Almanac, 2d edit., 2001; co-editor: Native American Activism: Alcatraz to the Longest Walk, 1997, Contemporary Native American Cultural Issues, 1999; book [illegible] series editor: Contemporary American Indian Issues, 1998—; contbr. numerous articles to profl. jours. Mem. city of L.A. Cmty. Action Bd., 1993, L.A. County/City Am. Indian Commn., 1992-2000, chair, 1993, 95-97, 2000—, v. chair, 1997-2000; mem. subcom. for cultural and econ. devel. L.A. City/County Native Am. Commn., 1992-93; bd. dirs. Ctr. for Improvement of Child Caring, 1993—, Greater L.A. Am. Indian Culture [illegible] Nat. Mus. Am. Indian, 1998—; Master of Coll. of Humanities and Social Sci., N.D. State U., 1996. Recipient L.A. Sr. Health Peer Counseling Cmty. Vol. Cert. of Recognition, 1996; Writer of Yr. award Cir. Native Writers and Storytellers, 1999; honoree Nat. Ctr. Am. Indian Enterprise, 1999; named Wordcraft Circle of Writers & Storytellers Writer of Yr., 1999; grantee Rockefeller Found., 1982-83, U. Wis. Grad Sch. Rsch. Com., 1984-85, Wis. Dept. Edn., 1984-85, 87-88, 88-89, NSF, 1985-88, 88-89), Nat. Endowment for Arts, 1987-88, 91-92, NRC, 1988-89, Nat. Sci. Coun., 1989-90, John D. and Catherine T. MacArthur Found., 1990-91, Hayes Found., 1990-91, 92-93, Calif. Coun. for Humanities, 1991-92, Ford Found., 1990-92, Gale Rsch. Inc., 1991-93, 93-95, Rockwell Corp., 1991-93, GTE, 1992-93, Kellog Found., 1997-2000, Pequot Mus. and Rsch. Ctr., 1997-2000, So. Calif. Indian Ctr., 1998; Fund for the Improvement of Post Secondary Edn., 1998—; Am. Indian scholar, 1973-75, 80-82, Minority fellow Am. Sociol. Assn., 1975-78, RIAS Seminar fellow, 1976-77; Rockefeller Postdoctoral fellow, 1982-83, NSF fellow, 1985-88, Postdoctoral fellow Ford Found., 1988-89. Avocations: chess, basketball. Home: 2152 Balsam Ave Los Angeles CA 90025 Office: UCLA Am Indian Studies Ctr PO Box 951548 Los Angeles CA 90095-1548 E-mail: champagn@ucla.edu

CHAN, FRED S.L. electronics company executive; BSEE, MSC, U. Hawaii. Co-founder, pres., CEO CADCAM Tech., Inc.; founder, pres., CEO AC Design, Inc.; pres., dir. Niche Tech., Inc., 1991-93; pres. ESS Tech., Fremont, Calif., 1985—, dir., 1986—, CEO, 1994—. Chmn. bd. dirs. ESS Tech. Office: ESS Technology,Inc 48401 Fremont Blvd Fremont CA 94538

CHAN, PHILIP J. medical educator; b. Malaysia, May 11, 1956; m. Hilda, 1981; 3 children. BA cum laude in biology, Kalamazoo Coll., 1979; MS in Physiology, Mich. State U., 1981, PhD in Physiology, 1983. Diplomate Am. Bd. Bioanalysis. Dir. sperm processing & IVF and embryo transfer lab. Kennedy Meml. Hosps./U. Med. Ctr., Cherry Hill, N.J., 1983-87; dir. labs. Hillcrest Fertility Ctr., Tulsa, 1987-89; dir. andrology/male reproduction and molecular biology labs. Loma Linda (Calif.) U. Obstetrics Med. Group, 1989—. Mgr. info. sys. lab. computers and network Loma Linda U. Ob-Gyn. Med. Group, Inc., 1991—; from instr. to asst. prof. U. Medicine and Dentistry of N.J. Sch. Osteopathic Medicine, 1983-87; assoc. prof. Oral Roberts U. Sch. Medicine, 1987-89; from assoc. prof. to prof. Loma Linda U. Sch. Medicine, 1989—; mem. comparative medicine study sect. NIH, 1994-98, chmn. site visit Nat. Ctr. for Rsch. Resources, 1999; insp. Coll. Am. Pathologists, 1993—. Contbr. articles to profl. jours. Recipient Walter-MacPherson First Pl. Rsch. award The Walter E. Macpherson Soc., 1997. Mem. AAAS, Am. Soc. Reproductive Medicine, Internat. Soc. Andrology, Am. Soc. Primatologists, Am. Assn. Bioanalysts, European Soc. Human Reproduction and Embryology. Office: Loma Linda U Fac Med Office Dept Ob-Gyn Ste 3950 11370 Anderson St Loma Linda CA 92354-3450

CHAN, SHU-PARK, electrical engineering educator; b. Canton, China, Oct. 10, 1929; came to U.S., 1951, naturalized, 1965; s. Chi-Tong and Shui-Ying (Mok) C.; m. Stella Yok-Sing Lam, Dec. 28, 1956; children: Charlene Li-Hsiang, Yau-Gene. BEE, Va. Mil. Inst., 1955; MEE, U. Ill., 1957, PhD, 1963. Instr. elec. engring. and math. Va. Mil. Inst., 1957-59; instr. elec. engring. U. Ill., 1960-61, rsch. assoc., 1961-62, asst. prof. math., 1962-63; assoc. prof. elec. engring. U. Santa Clara, 1963-68, prof., 1968-92, chmn. elec. engring. and computer sci. dept., 1969-84; Nicholson Family Chair prof. Santa Clara U., 1987-92, prof. emeritus, 1992—, acting dean Sch. Engring., 1987-88; founder, pres. Internat. Technol. U., Santa Clara, 1994—; pres. Chu Hai Coll., Hong Kong, 1995-96. Prin. investigator NSF, NASA; Univ. fellow U. Ill., 1959-60; vis. spl. chair prof. elec. engring. dept. Nat. Taiwan U., 1973-74; spl. lectr. Acad. Sci., Peking, China, summer 1980; hon. prof. elec. engring. dept. U. Hong Kong, 1980-81; hon. prof. Anhuei U., China, 1982; spl. chair Tamkang U., Taipei, Taiwan, 1981; apptd. mem. J. William Fulbright Fgn. Scholarship Bd., 1991-93; founder, pres. Internat. Tech. U. Found., 1994—. Author: introductory Topological Analysis of Electrical Networks, 1969, (with others) Analysis of Linear Networks and Systems—A Matrix-Oriented Approach with Computer Applications, 1972, (with E. Moustakas) Introduction to the Applications of the Operational Amplifier, 1974; editor: Network Topology and Its Engineering Applications, 1975, Graph Theory and Applications, 1982. Chmn. bd., pres. Acad. Cultural Co., Santa Clara; founder, pres. China Exptl. U. Found., 1985—; chmn. Santa Clara County Bicentennial Chinese Festival Com.; pres. Chinese Arts and Culture Inst., 1976—; trustee Inst. Sino-Am. Studies, San Jose, Calif., 1971-76, West Valley-Mission C.C. Dist., Calif., 1988. Recipient Disting. Elec. Engring. Alumnus award U. Ill., 1983, 1991 Rschr. of Yr. award Sch. Engring., Santa Clara U., 1992, Courvoisier Leadership award in Edn., 1994; named Engr. of Yr. in Engring. Edn. San Francisco session AIAA, 1994, Chinese Am. Pioneer award Orgn. Chinese Ams., San Francisco, 1996; Hon. Prof. award S. China Normal U., Guangzhou, China, 1997—, Educator of Yr. award Chinese Consol. Benevolent Assn. and Chinese Consol. Women's Assn., 1999, Mayor's awrd City of San Francisco, 1999. Fellow IEEE (past chmn. circuit theory group San Francisco sect., chmn. asilomar conf. circuits and sys. 1970); mem. Am. Soc. Engring. Edn., Chineses Alumni Assn. U. Santa Clara (pres.), U. Santa Clara Faculty Club (pres. 1971-72), Sigma Xi, Tau Beta Pi, Eta Kappa Nu, Pi Mu Epsilon, Phi Kappa Phi. Home: 2085 Denise Dr Santa Clara CA 95050-4557 E-mail: spchan@itu.edu

CHAN, SUNNEY IGNATIUS, chemist, educator; b. San Francisco, Oct. 5, 1936; s. Sun and Hip-For (Lai) C.; m. Irene Yuk-Hing Tam, July 11, 1964; 1 son, Michael Kenneth. B.S. in Chem. Engring, U. Calif. at Berkeley, 1957, Ph.D. in Chemistry, 1960. Asst. prof. chemistry U. Calif. at Riverside, 1961-63; mem. faculty Calif. Inst. Tech., 1963—, prof. chem. physics, 1968-92, prof. biophys. chemistry, 1976-92, George Grant Hoag prof. biophys. chemistry, 1992—, exec. officer for chemistry, 1977-80, 89-94, master student houses, 1980-83, chmn. faculty, 1987-89; dir. Inst. of Chemistry, Academia Sinica, Taipei, Taiwan, 1997-99; v.p. Academia Sinica, Taipei, Taiwan, 1999—. R.T. Major lectr. U. Conn., 1998; Wilson T.S. Wang Disting. Internat. prof. Chinese U. Hong Kong, 1993; cons. in field. Author numerous articles in field. Guggenheim fellow, 1968-69; Sloan fellow, 1965-67; NSF Postdoctoral fellow, 1960-61; Reilly lectr. U. Notre Dame, 1973-74; Chan Meml. lectr. U. Calif., Berkeley, 1984; Fogarty fellow NIH, 1986 Mem. AAAS, Academia Sinica, Am. Chem. Soc., Chinese Am. Chem. Soc. (chmn. bd. 1988-97), Am. Phys. Soc., Am. Soc. Biochemistry and Molecular Biology, Biophys. Soc., Biophysical Soc. Taiwan (pres. 1998-2001), So. Calif. Chinese Engrs. and Scientists Assn. (Progress award 1971), Chinese Collegiate Colleagues So. Calif. (v.p. 1970-71, pres. 1971-72), Chinese Am. Faculty Assn. (pres. 1988, Achievement award 1991, Disting. Svc. award 2000), Phi Beta Kappa, Sigma Xi, Tau Beta Pi, Alpha Chi Sigma, Phi Tau Phi (pres. 1981-83). Home: 327 Camino Del Sol South Pasadena CA 91030-4107 Office: Calif Inst Tech Chem Dept Pasadena CA 91125-0001 E-mail: chans@its.caltech.edu, chans@chem.sinica.edu.tw

CHAN, WILMA, county official; b. Boston; married; 2 children. BA, [illegible] Stanford U. Mem. Oakland (Calif.) Bd. Edn., 1990-94, pres., 1991-93; supr. dist. 3, then v.p. Alameda County Bd. Suprs., Oakland, 1994—. Chair legis. com. and health com. Alameda County Bd. Suprs., chmn. budget tech. com., bd. rep. to Alameda Reuse and Redevel. Authority, San Francisco Bay Conservation Devel. Commn., Local Agy. Formation Commn.; past program coord. Effective Parenting Info. for Children. Office: Alameda County Bd Suprs 1221 Oak St Ste 536 Oakland CA 94612-4224

CHANCELLOR, WILLIAM JOSEPH, agricultural engineering educator; b. Alexandria, Va., Aug. 25, 1931; s. John Miller and Caroline (Sedlacek) C.; m. Nongkarn Bodhiprasart, Dec. 13, 1960; 1 child, Marisa Kuakul BS in Agr., BSME, U. Wis., 1954; MS in Agrl. Engring., Cornell U., 1956, PhD, 1957. Registered profl. agrl. engr., Calif. Prof. agrl. engring. U. California.-Davis, 1957-94; prof. emeritus. Vis. prof. agrl. engring. U. Malaya, Kuala Lumpur, Malaysia, 1962-63; UNESCO cons. Punjab Agrl. U., 1976 Contbr. articles to profl. jours.; patentee transmission, planters, dryer, 1961-73 East/West Ctr. sr. Fellow, Honolulu, 1976 Fellow Am. Soc. Agrl. Engrs. (Kishida Internat. award 1984); mem. Soc. Automotive Engrs., Sigma Xi. Office: Univ of California Dept Biol & Agrl Engineering Davis CA 95616 E-mail: wjchancellor@ucdavis.edu

CHANDLER, ALLEN, food products executive; b. 1942; With Northwest Wholesale, Wenatchee, Wash., 1964-68, No. Fruit Co., Wenatchee, 1968—, now v.p. Office: Northern Fruit Co PO Box 1986 Wenatchee WA 98807-1986

CHANDLER, BRUCE FREDERICK, internist; b. Bohemia, Pa., Mar. 26, 1926; s. Frederick Arthur and Minnie Flora (Burkhardt) C.; m. Janice Evelyn Piper, Aug. 14, 1954; children: Barbara, Betty, Karen, Paul, June. Student, Pa. State U., 1942-44; MD, Temple U., 1948. Diplomate Am. Bd. Internal Medicine, cert. internal medicine, subsplty. pulmonary disease. Commd. med. officer U.S. Army, 1948, advanced through grades to col., 1967; intern Temple U. Hosp., Phila., 1948-49; chief psychiatry 7th Field Hosp., Trieste, Italy, 1950; resident Walter Reed Gen. Hosp., Washington, 1949-53; battalion surgeon 2d Div. Artillery, Korea, 1953-54; chief renal dialysis unit 45th Evacuation Hosp. and Tokyo Army Hosp., Korea, Japan, 1954-55; various assignments Walter Reed Gen. Hosp., Fitzsimons Gen. Hosp., Letterman Gen. Hosp., 1955-70; comdg. officer 45th Field Hosp., Vicenza, Italy, 1958-62; pvt. practice internist Ridgecrest (Calif.) Med. Clinic, 1970-76; chief med. svc. and out-patients VA Hosps., Walla Walla, Spokane, Wash., 1976-82; med. cons. Social Security Adminstrn., Spokane, 1983-87; ret., 1987. Lectr. in field of pulmonary disease. Panel mem. TV shows, 1964-70; contbr. articles to profl. jours. Decorated Legion of Merit. Fellow ACP, Am. Coll. Chest Physicians; mem. AMA, Am. Thoracic Soc., N.Y. Acad. Scis., So. European Task Force U.S. Army Med. Dental Soc. (pres., founder 1958-62), Alpha Omega Alpha (alumnus). Republican. Methodist. Avocations: photography, travel, fishing, collecting books (especially by Jules Verne and Agatha Christie). Home: 6496 N Callisch Ave Fresno CA 93710-3902

CHANDLER, DAVID, scientist, educator; b. Bklyn., Oct. 15, 1944; SB, MIT, 1966; PhD, Harvard U., 1969. Research assoc. U. Calif., San Diego, 1969-70; from asst. prof. to prof. U. Ill., Urbana, 1970-83; prof. U.Pa., Phila., 1983-85, U. Calif., Berkeley, 1986—. Vis. prof. Columbia U., N.Y.C., 1977-78; vis. scientist IBM Corp., Yorktown Heights, N.Y., 1978, Oak Ridge Nat. Lab., 1979; cons. Los Alamos Nat. Labs., 1987-90; Miller rsch. prof., 1991; dir. de recherche Ecole Normale Superieure de Lyon, France, fall 1992; Christensen vis. fellow Oxford U., winter 1993, Hinshelwood lectr., 1993; Kolthoff lectr. U. Minn, 1994; faculty chemist Lawrence Berkeley Nat. Lab., 1996—, Miller rsch. prof., 1999-2000; Malliken lectr. U. Chgo. Editor Chem. Physics, 1985—; mem. editl. bd. Jour. Statis. Physics, 1976-78, 94-96, Jour. Chem. Physics, 1978-80, Chem. Physics Letters, 1980-82, 91—, Molecular Physics, 1980-87, Theoretica Chimica Acta, 1988-89, Jour. Phys. Chemistry, 1987-92, Phys. Rev. E, 1995—, Adv. Chem. Phys., 1995—; mem. editl. adv. bd. PhysChemComm, 1999—; author books in field; contbr. articles to profl. jours. Recipient Bourke medal Faraday divsn. Royal Chem. Soc., Eng., 1985, Hirschfelder Theoretical Chemistry prize U. Wis., 1998, Humboldt Rsch. award, 1999; fellow Alfred P. Sloan Found., 1972-74, Guggenheim Found., 1981-82; Flygare Meml. lectr., 1989, Mulliken lectr. U. Chgo., 2000; Lennard-Jones lectr. Royal Soc. Chemistry, 2001. Fellow AAAS, Am. Phys. Soc.; mem. NAS, Am. Acad. Arts and Scis., Am. Chem. Soc. (chmn. divsn. theoretical chemistry 1984, chmn. divsn. phys. chemistry 1990, Joel Henry Hildebrand award 1989, Theoretical Chemistry award 1996). Avocations: tennis; piano playing. Office: U Calif Dept Chemistry Berkeley CA 94720-0001 E-mail: chandler@gold.cchem.berkeley.edu

CHANDLER, E(DWIN) RUSSELL, clergyman, writer; b. L.A., Sept. 9, 1932; s. Edwin Russell Sr. and Mary Elizabeth (Smith) C.; m. Sandra Lynn Swisher, Aug. 24, 1957 (div. 1977); children— Heather, Holly, Timothy John; m. Marjorie Lee Moore, Dec. 21, 1978; 3 stepchildren Student, Stanford U., 1950-52; B.S. in Bus. Adminstrn., UCLA, 1952-55; postgrad., U. So. Calif. Grad. Sch. Religion, 1955, New Coll., Edinburgh, Scotland, 1955-56; M.Div., Princeton Theol. Sem., 1958; grad., Washington Journalism Ctr., 1967. Ordained to ministry Presbyterian Ch., 1958. Asst. pastor 1st Presbyn. Ch., Concord, Calif., 1958-61; pastor Escalon Presbyn. Ch., 1961-66; reporter Modesto Bee, 1966-67; religion editor Washington Star, 1968-69; news editor Christianity Today, Washington, 1969-72; reporter Sonora Daily Union Dem., Calif., 1972-73; religion writer L.A. Times, 1974-92; interim pastor 1st Presbyn. Ch., Columbia, Calif., 1995-96. Author: The Kennedy Explosion, 1972, Budgets, Bedrooms and Boredom, 1976; co-author: Your Family--Frenzy or Fun?, 1977, The Overcomers, 1978, Understanding the New Age, 1988 (Silver Angel award 1989, Wilbur award 1989), Racing Toward 2001, 1992, Doomsday, 1993, Feeding the Flock, 1998; contbr. articles to profl. jours. Recipient Arthur West award United Methodist Communications Council, 1978, Faith and Freedom award Religious Heritage of Am., 1993; co-recipient Silver Angel award, Religion in Media, 1985 Mem. Religion Newswriters Assn. (pres. 1982-84, James O. Supple Meml. award, 1976, 1984, 86, John M. Templeton Reporter of Yr. award 1984, 87, 89), Phi Delta Theta Republican Avocations: travel; beekeeping; birdwatching. Home and Office: 723 Rainier Ln Port Ludlow WA 98365-8711 also: 14304 Lake Vista Dr Sonora CA 95370-9692 E-mail: erchandler@aol.com

CHANDLER, MARSHA, academic administrator, professor; BA, CCNY, 1965; PhD, UNC Chapel Hill, 1972. Prof. political econ. Univ. Toronto, 1977-96, dean arts and sci., 1990-97; sr. vice chancellor U. Calif., San Diego, 1996—. Vis. scholar Harvard U., Boston, 1995-96. Co-author: Trade and Transmissions, 1990, The Political Economy of Business Bailouts, 2 vols., 1986, The Politics of Canadian Public Policy, 1983, Public Policy and Provincial Politics, 1979, Adjusting to Trade: A Comparative Perspective, 1988; contbr. articles to profl. jours. Fellow, Royal Soc. of Canada, mem., Dept. of Political Sci., Faculty of Law, bd. dirs. San Diego Opera, Mingei Mus. of Internatl. Folk Art, UCSD Found. Bd. and the Charter 100, adv. com. on Fed. Judicial Appts., bd. of Canadian Inst. for Adv. Rsch.; trustee, Art Gall. of Ontario, Mt. SInai Hosp., Huntsman Marine Sci. Ctr., Ontario Lightwave, Laser Rsch. Ctr. Office: U Calif 9500 Gilman Dr La Jolla CA 92093 5004

CHANDOR, STEBBINS BRYANT, pathologist; b. Boston, Dec. 18, 1933; s. Kendall Stebbins Bryant and Dorothy (Burrage) C.; m. Mary Carolyn White, May 30, 1959; children: Stebbins Bryant Jr., Charlotte White. B.A., Princeton U., 1955; M.D., Cornell U., 1960. Diplomate Am. Bd. Pathology. Intern Bellevue Hosp., N.Y.C., 1960-61, resident, 1965-66, Stanford U. Med. Ctr., Palo Alto, Calif., 1962-65; instr. Cornell U., Ithaca, N.Y., 1966; asst. prof. U. So. Calif. Med. Ctr., Los Angeles, 1969-73, assoc. prof., 1974-76, SUNY, Stony Brook, 1976-80; prof., chmn. dept. pathology Marshall U. Sch. Medicine, Huntington, W.Va., 1981-91, assoc. dean for clin. affairs, 1990-91; prof., vice chmn. Sch. Medicine U. So. Calif., L.A., 1991—; pathologist Tripler Army Med Ctr, Honolulu, 1966-69; dir. immunopathology U. So. Calif., Los Angeles County Med. Ctr., 1969-76; dir. clin. lab. Univ. Hosp., Stony Brook, N.Y., 1978-80; dir. JMMS Labs., Huntington, W.Va., 1981-91; dir labs. U. So Calif. U. Hosp., L.A., 1991—. Contbr. articles to profl. jours. Pres. San Marino Tennis Found., 1975;

governing bd. U. Pathol. Consortium, 1999—. Served to maj. USAR, 1966-69. Decorated Army Commendation medal; recipient Physicians Recognition award AMA, 1983, 86, 89, 93, 99. Fellow Am. Assn. Med. Coll. (exec. coun. 1998—), Am. Soc. Clin. Pathologists (deputy commn. 1993-98, continuing edn., bd. dirs. 1990-96, chair by-law com., 1993-96, chmn. pathology group, 1993-98, v.p. 1997-98, pres. 1999-2000), Coll. Am. Pathologists (state commr. I&A program 1987-91, dist. commr. 1991-99); mem. Calif. Soc. Pathologists (sec.-treas. 1974-75, pres. elect. 1975-76), Assn. Am. Pathologists, W.Va. Assn. Pathologists (pres. 1985-86), Assoc. Pathol. Chmn. Acad. Clin. Lab. Physicians and Scientists (rep. CAS 1991—, adminstrv. bd. 1997—), exec. coun. Am. Assn. Med. Colls. 1998-2000, L.A. Acad. Medicine, Princeton Club, Valley Club (v.p. 1975, bd. dirs. 1993), City Club (v.p. 1988-89, pres. 1989-90), San Gabriel Country Club, Valley Hunt Club, Valley Club of Montecito. Republican. Episcopalian. Home: Apt A 985 S Orange Grove Blvd Pasadena CA 91105-1727 Office: U So Calif Sch Medicine 2011 Zonal Ave Los Angeles CA 90033-1034 E-mail: sbcmcc@aol.com, chandor@usc.edu

CHANDRAMOULI, RAMAMURTI, electrical engineer; b. Oct. 2, 1947; s. Ramamurti and Rajalakshmi (Ramamurti) Krishnamurti; m. Ranjani, Dec. 4, 1980; children: Suhasini, Akila. BSc, Mysore U., 1965, BE, 1970; MEE, Pratt Inst., 1972; PhD, Oreg. State U., 1978. Instr. Oreg. State U., Corvallis, 1978; sr. engr. R & D group, tech. staff spacecraft datasys. sect. Jet Propulsion Lab., Pasadena, Calif., 1978-81; staff engr., design automotive group Am. Microsys. Inc., Santa Clara, 1982-83; staff software engr. corp. computer-aided design Intel, Santa Clara, 1983-86; project leader computer-aided design Sun Microsys., Mountain View, Calif., 1986-93; tech. mktg. engr. Mentor Graphics, San Jose, 1993-95; dir. Bist Products Logicvision, San Jose, 1995-98; product line mgr. test products Synopsys, Mountain View, 1998—. Adj. lectr. Calif. State U., Fullerton, 1987—. Sec. South India Cultural Assn., L.A., 1980-81; bd. dirs. Am. Assn. East Indians. Mem. IEEE, IEEE Computer Soc., Sigma Xi, Eta Kappa Nu. Home: 12167 Terrence Ave Saratoga CA 95070-3346 Office: Synopsys 700 E Middlefield Rd Mountain View CA 94043-4033

CHANDY, K. MANI, computer science educator; B Tech. in Elec. Engring., Indian Inst. Technology, Madras, 1965; MSEE, Polytechnic Inst. of Bklyn., 1966; PhD in Elec. Engring., MIT, 1969. Engr. Honeywell Electronic Data processing, Waltham, Mass., 1966-67; staff IBM Cambridge Scientific Ctr., 1969-70; asst. prof. computer scis. U. Tex., Austin, 1970-73, assoc. prof., 1973-78, prof., 1978-89; prof. computer scis. Calif. Inst. Technology, Pasadena, 1989—; Simon Ramo prof., exec. officer dept. computer scis Calif. Inst. Tech.; acting site dir. Ctr. for Rsch. in Parallel Computing, Caltech Site, 1994. Acting chmn. dep. computer scis., 1978-79, chmn. 1983-85, Regent's chair, 1988-89; scientific adv. panel Advanced Systems Inst., B.C., Can., 1986-89; mem. NSF panels; lectr. in field. Assoc. editor: Jour. of Capacity Mgmt., 1983-88, Info. Executive, 1983-88, Jour. of Info. Econs., 1983-88. Recipient John Sherman Fairchild scholarship John Sherman Fairchild Found., 1987-88, A.A. Michelson award, Computer Measurement Group, Dallas, 1985. Fellow IEEE (Koji Kobayashi Computers and Comms. award 1995, assoc. editor: IEEE Transactions on Software Engring. 1985-87); mem. NAE, Assn. Computing Machinery, Soc. for Computer Simulation Office: Calif Inst Technology Computer Sci 256 80 Pasadena CA 91125-0001

CHANG, BARBARA KAREN, medical educator; b. Milltown, Ind., Jan. 6, 1946; m. M.F. Joseph Chang-Wai-Ling, Oct. 6, 1967; children: Carla Marie Yvonnette, Nolanne Arlette. BA, Ind. U., 1968; MA, Brandeis U., 1970; MD, Albert Einstein Coll. Medicine, 1973. Diplomate Am. Bd. Internal Medicine, Am. Bd. Med. Oncology, Am. Bd. Hematology. Resident in internal medicine Montefiore Med. Ctr., Bronx, N.Y., 1973-75; fellow in hematology/oncology Duke U. Med. Ctr., Durham, N.C., 1975-78; staff physician VA Med. Ctr., Augusta, Ga., 1978-95, chief hematology/oncology, 1980-89, assoc. chief of staff edn., 1990-95; prof. medicine Med. Coll. Ga., Augusta, 1978-95; chief of staff, chief med. officer VA Med. Ctr., Albuquerque, 1995—; prof., assoc. dean U. N.Mex. Sch. Medicine, Albuquerque, 1995—. Mem. Sci. Adv. Bd., Washington, 1983-88; mem. expert panels computer applications Dept. Vets. Affairs, Washington, 1988—. Contbr. numerous articles on cancer rsch. to profl. jours. Youth coord. Am. Hemerocallis Soc., Augusta, 1993-95, pres. local chpt. 1997, garden judge 1997—, region 6 youth liaison, 2000—. Grantee Nat. Cancer Inst., Am. Cancer Soc., 1978-93. Fellow ACP, Am. Soc. Hematology, Am. Assn. Cancer Rsch., Am. Soc. Clin. Oncology, Bioelectromagnetic Soc. (bd. dirs. 1983-86). Office: Dept Vets Affairs Med Ctr 1501 San Pedro Dr SE Albuquerque NM 87108-5153

CHANG, DANIEL HAIMING, engineering executive; b. Guangzhou, Guang Dong, China, Apr. 16, 1953; came to U.S., 1981; s. Qizhong and Puqiong (Ye) C.; m. Caili Li; 1 child, Miao Miao. BE of Ceramic Engring., South China U. of Tech., Guangzhou, 1976, ME of Ceramic Engring., 1981; MS in Materials Sci., U. So. Calif., L.A., 1984. Foreman Guangzhou Cement Plant, 1970-72, asst. to chief engr., 1976-78; materials scientist Philips Components, L.A., 1984-85; mem. mgmt. team, sr. rsch. engr. Kyocera, San Diego, 1985-88; pres., CEO AEM, Inc., San Diego, 1988—. Holder 1 patent and 3 patents pending. Mem. IEEE (assoc.), Am. Ceramic Soc., U.S.-China Entrepreneur Assn. (pres. 1993-97), San Diego Chinese Assn. (v.p. 1993-97). Avocations: reading books and magazines, walking and running along the beach, competitive sports, driving fast cars. Office: AEM Holding Inc 11525 Sorrento Valley Rd San Diego CA 92121-1307 E-mail: dchang@aem-usa.com

CHANG, HENRY CHUNG-LIEN, library administrator; b. Canton, China, Sept. 15, 1941; came to U.S., 1964, naturalized, 1973; s. Ih-ming and Lily (Lin) C.; m. Marjorie Li, Oct. 29, 1966; 1 dau., Michelle. LL.B., Nat. Chengchi U., 1962; M.A., U. Mo., 1966; M.A. in L.S, U. Minn., 1968; Ph.D., 1974. Reader advisor Braille Inst. Am., Los Angeles, 1965-67; reference librarian U. Minn., Mpls., 1968-70, instr., librarian, 1970-72, asst. head govt. document div., 1972-74; library dir., lectr. in social scis. U. of the V.I., St. Croix, 1974-75; dir. div. libraries, museums and archeol. services, 1975-88; dir. V.I. Library Tng. Inst., 1975-76; coordinator, chmn. V.I. State Hist. Records Adv. Bd., 1976-88; pres., libr. cons., 1988-89; dir. libr. svcs. Braille Inst. Am., L.A., 1990—. Chmn. microfilm com. ACURIL, 1977-88; coordinator V.I. Gov.'s Library Adv. Council, 1975-87; mem. V.I. Bicentennial Commn., 1975-77, Ft. Frederik Commn., 1975-76; mem. adv. com. on research tng. Caribbean Research Inst., 1974-75; coordinator Library Conf., 1977-87; project dir. cultural heritage project Nat. Endowment for Humanities, 1979-83; chmn. nat. collection devel. com. nat. libr. svcs. Libr. of Congress, 1998, chmn. western conf. group, 2000-02. Author: A Bibliography of Presidential Commissions, Committees, Councils, Panels and Task Forces, 1961-72, 1973, Taiwan Democraphy, 1964-71: A Selected Annotated Bibliography of Government Documents, 1973, A Selected Annotated Bibliography of Caribbean Bibliographies in English, 1975, A Survey of the Use of Microfilms in the Caribbean, 1978, Long-Range Program for Library Development, 1978, Institute for Training in Library Management and Communications Skill, 1979; contbr. numerous articles and book revs. on libr. sci. to profl. jours. Chmn. bd. dirs. Eden Found. for People with Disabilities, 1995-98. 2d lt. Taiwan Army, 1962-63. Recipient Libr. Adminstrs. Devel. Program fellowship award, 1972, Cert. of Appreciation, Govt. V.I., 1985, L.A. Internat. Lions Club award, 1992, 95, Driver Safety award, 1993; named Mem. Staff of Yr., Coll. V.I., 1974-75; Nat. Commn. on Librs. and Info. Sci. grantee. Mem. ALA (counselor 1980-84), AAUP, Asian Pacific ALA (chmn. fin. com. 1993-96), Population Assn. Am., Am. Sociol. Assn., Chinese Am. Profl. Soc. Home: 3713 Lowry Rd Los Angeles CA 90027-1437 Office: Braille Inst Am 741 N Vermont Ave Los Angeles CA 90029-3594

CHANG, I-SHIH, aerospace engineer; b. Taipei, Taiwan, Dec. 2, 1945; came to U.S., 1968; s. I.H. and T.C. Chang; m. O.J. Chang, May 25, 1974; children: Anna, Brandon Degree in mech. engring., Taipei Inst. of Tech., 1965; MS, U. Kans., 1969; PhD, U. Ill., 1973. Scientist assoc.-rsch. Lockheed Missiles & Space, Huntsville, Ala., 1973-76; mem. tech. staff Rockwell Internat., Anaheim, Calif., 1976-77, The Aerospace Corp., El Segundo, 1977-80, engring. specialist, 1980-90, sr. engring. specialist, 1990-91, disting. engr., 1991—. Contbr. articles to profl. jours. Fellow AIAA (assoc.); mem. Phi Kappa phi. Democrat. Home: 890 S Calle Venado Anaheim CA 92807-5004 Office: The Aerospace Corp M4/967 2350 E El Segundo Blvd El Segundo CA 90245-4691 E-mail: i-shih.chang@aero.org

CHANG, WILLIAM SHEN CHIE, electrical engineering educator; b. Nantung, Kiangsu, China, Apr. 4, 1931; s. Tung Wu and Phoebe Y.S. (Chow) C.; m. Margaret Huachen Kwei, Nov. 26, 1955; children: Helen Nai-yee, Hugh Nai-hun, Hedy Nai-lin. BSE, U. Mich., 1952, MSE, 1953; PhD, Brown U., 1957. Lectr., rsch. assoc. in elec. engring. Stanford (Calif.) U., 1957-59; asst. prof. elec. engring. Ohio State U., 1959-62, asso. prof., 1962-65; prof. dept. elec. engring. Washington U., St. Louis, 1965-76, chmn. dept., 1965-71, dir. Applied Electronic Scis. Lab., 1971-79, Samuel Sachs prof. elec. engring., 1976-79; prof. dept. elec. and computer engring. U. Calif., San Diego, 1979—, chmn. dept., 1993-96. Author: Principles of Quantum Electronics, 1969; Contbr. articles to profl. jours. Fellow Am. Optical Soc., IEEE; mem. Am. Phys. Soc. Achievements include research on quantum electronics and guided wave optics. Home: 12676 Camanito Radiante San Diego CA 92130 Office: U Calif San Diego MS-0407 Dept Elec/Computer Engring La Jolla CA 92093-0407 E-mail: wchang@ucsd.edu

CHAO, CEDRIC C. lawyer; b. Cambridge, Mass., Apr. 9, 1950; BA, Stanford U., 1972; JD, Harvard U., 1977. Bar: Calif. 1977, U.S. Dist. Ct. (no. dist.) Calif. 1977, U.S. Ct. Appeals (9th cir.) 1979, U.S. Supreme Ct. 1988. Law clk.to Hon. William H. Orrick U.S. Dist. Ct. (no. dist.) Calif., San Francisco, 1977-78; asst. U.S. atty. U.S. Atty.'s Office, San Francisco, 1978-81; assoc. Morrison & Foerster, San Francisco, 1981-83, ptnr., 1983—. Lawyer del. 9th cir. judicial conf., 1990-92; chair magistrate judge selection com. No. Dist. Calif., 1996. Author: Creating Your Discovery Plan, 1999. Named One of Calif.'s Top 25 Lawyers Under Age 45, Calif. Law Bus., 1994. Fellow Am. Bar Found.; mem. ABA (standing com. fed. judiciary, 1991-94), State Bar Calif. (com. profl. responsibility and conduct 1980-84, exec. com. litigation sect. 1986-91, vice chair 1989-90, chair 1990-91), San Francisco Bar Assn. (bd. dirs. 1988-90), Am. Law Inst., Asian Am. Bar Assn. Greater Bay Area (bd. dirs. 1977-82, pres. 1982), 9th Judicial Cir. Hist. Soc. (trustee 2000—), San Francisco C. of C. (bd. dirs. 1996-99), Singapore Am. Bus. Assn. (bd. dirs. 1999—, pres. 2001), World Affairs Coun. No. Calif. (trustee 1994-99), Commonwealth Club Calif. (quar. chair 1989). Office: Morrison & Foerster 425 Market St San Francisco CA 94105-2482 E-mail: cchao@mofo.com

CHAPIN, CHARLES E. geologist, mineralogist; b. Porterville, Calif., Oct. 25, 1932; m. Carol R. Giles, 1958; children: Giles M., John E., Laura A. Geol. Engr., Colo. Sch. Mines, 1954, DSc in Geochemistry, 1965. Asst. prof. geology U. Tulsa, 1964-65; asst. prof. N.Mex. Inst. Mining and Tech., 1965-68, assoc. prof., head dept. geosci., 1968-70; geologist N.Mex. Bur. Mines and Mineral Resources, 1970-76, sr. geologist, 1976-91, dir., 1991-99, dir. emeritus. Recipient Van Diest Gold medal Colo. Sch. Mines, 1980. Mem. Geol. Soc. Am., Soc. Econ. Paleontologists and Mineralogists, Am. Geophys. Union, Am. Assn. Petroleum Geologists, Soc. Econ. Geologists, Sigma Xi. Office: NM Bur Mines & Mineral Resources Inst Mining and Mineral Tech Campus Station Socorro NM 87801

CHAPIN, DWIGHT ALLAN, columnist, writer; b. Lewiston, Idaho, June 16, 1938; s. Don Merle and Lucille Verna (Walker) C.; m. Susan Enid Fisk, Feb. 14, 1963 (div. 1973); children— Carla, Adam; m. Ellen Gonzalez, Aug. 10, 1983 B.A., U. Idaho, 1960; M.S. in Journalism, Columbia U., 1961. Reporter Lewiston Morning Tribune, Idaho, 1956-62; reporter, editor Vancouver Columbian, Wash., 1962-65; sportswriter Seattle Post-Intelligencer, 1965-67, Los Angeles Times, 1967-77; columnist San Francisco Examiner, 1977-2000, San Francisco Chronicle, 2000—. Co-author: Wizard of Westwood, 1973; contbr. numerous articles to popular mags. Served with USNG, 1962-68 Recipient Sports Writing award AP, Calif./Nev., 1968-69; Baseball Writing award Am. Assn. Coll. Baseball Coaches Mem. Sigma Delta Chi (sports writing award Wash. state 1964, 65, 66) Democrat Avocation: trading card and sports memorabilia collecting. Office: San Francisco Chronicle 901 Mission St San Francisco CA 94103-2988 E-mail: dchapin@sfchronicle.com

CHAPLIN, GEORGE, newspaper editor; b. Columbia, S.C., Apr. 28, 1914; s. Morris and Netty (Brown) C.; m. Esta Lillian Solomon, Jan. 26, 1937 (dec. Jan. 2001); children: Stephen Michael, Jerry Gay. BS, Clemson Coll., 1935; Nieman fellow, Harvard U., 1940-41; HHD (hon.), Clemson U., 1989; LHD (hon.), Hawaii Loa Coll., 1990. Reporter, later city editor Greenville (S.C.) Piedmont, 1935-42; mng. editor Camden (N.J.) Courier-Post, 1946-47, San Diego Jour., 1948-49; mng. editor, then editor New Orleans Item, 1949-58; asso. editor Honolulu Advertiser, 1958-59, editor in chief, 1959-86, editor at large, 1986—. Mem. selection com. Jefferson fellowships East-West Ctr.; chmn. Gov.'s Conf. on Year 2000, 1970; chmn. Hawaii Commn. on Year 2000, 1971-74; co-chmn. Conf. on Alt. Econ. Futures for Hawaii, 1973-75; charter mem. Goals for Hawaii, 1979-81; alt. U.S. rep. South Pacific Commn., 1978-81; chmn. search com. for pres. U. Hawaii, 1983; chmn. Hawaii Gov.'s Adv. Coun. on Fgn. Lang. and Internat. Studies, 1983-94; rep. of World Press Freedom Com. on missions to Sri Lanka, Hong Kong, Singapore, 1987. Editor, officer-in-charge: Mid-Pacific edit. Stars and Stripes World War II; editor: (with Glenn Paige) Hawaii 2000, 1973, Presstime in Paradise: The Life and Times of the Honolulu Advertiser 1856-1995, 1998. Bd. dirs. U. Hawaii Rsch. Corp., 1970-72, Inst. for Religion and Social Change, Hawaii Jewish Welfare Fund, Charleston Christian-Jewish Coun.; mem. bd. govs. East-West Ctr., Honolulu, 1980-89, chmn., 1983-89; mem. bd. govs. Pacific Health Rsch. Inst., 1984-90, 93-97, pres., 1995-96; bd. govs. Straub Med. Found., 1989-98, Hawaii Pub. Schs. Found., 1986-87; trustee Clarence T. C. Ching Found., 1986-95; mem. Temple K.K. Beth Elohim; Am. media chmn. U.S.-Japan Conf. on Cultural and Ednl. Interchange, 1978-86; co-founder, v.p. Coalition for Drug-Free Hawaii, 1987-90; panelist ABA Conf., 1989; mem. Civilian Adv. Group, U.S. Army, Hawaii, 1985-95; co-chair Hawaii State Commn. on Judicial Salaries, 1995-98. Capt. AUS, 1942-46. Decorated Star Solidarity (Italy), Order Rising Sun (Japan), Prime Minister's medal (Israel); recipient citations Overseas Press Club, 1961, 72, Headliners award, 1962, John Hancock award, 1972, 74, Distinguished Alumni award Clemson U., 1974, E.W. Scripps award Scripps-Howard Found., 1976, Champion Media award for Econ. Understanding, 1981, Judah Magnes Gold medal Hebrew U. Jerusalem, 1987, Herbert Harley award Am. Judicature Soc., 1991, Regents medal of distinction U. Hawaii, 1998; inductee Honolulu Press Club Hall of Fame, 1987. Mem. Honolulu Symphony Soc., Pacific and Asian Affairs Council (dir.), Internat. Press Inst., Am. Soc. Newspaper Editors (dir., treas. 1973, sec. 1974, v.p. 1975, pres. 1976), Friends of East-West Ctr., Harbour Club.

CHAPLIN, ROBERT C. naval officer; b. Fort Knox, Ky. BSc, U.S. Naval Acad., 1970; MSc in Computer Sys. Mgmt., Naval Postgrad. Sch., 1979. Enlisted USN, 1970, advanced through grades to rear adm.; naval aviator NAS, Bermuda, 1972-75; stationed at Helicopter Anti-Submarine Squadron Light 32, 1975; various assignments USS Richard L. Page, HSL-36, Mayport, Fla.; flag sec. Comdr. Seabased Anti-Submarine Warfare Wing Atlantic, 1982-84; various assignments HSL-42, 1984-86; ops. officer USS Iwo Jima, 1986-88; commanding officer HSL-41, San Diego, 1988-89; spl. asst. for flying hour program The Pentagon, Washington; comdr. USS Inchon, 1991-93, USS Wasp, 1993-94; dir. plans and policy U.S. Transp. Command, Scott AFB, Ill., 1994-96; supt. Naval Postgraduate Sch., Monterey, Calif., 1998—; comdr. Amphibious Forces Seventh Fleet, 1996-98. Decorated Legion of Merit with two gold stars, Meritorious Svc. medal with three gold stars.

CHAPMAN, BRUCE KERRY, institute executive; b. Evanston, Dec. 1, 1940; s. Landon Lincoln Chapman and Darroll Jesamine (Carlson Swanson) Shinn; m. Sarah Gilmore Williams, Aug. 22, 1976; children: Adam Winthrop, Andrew Howard. BA cum laude, Harvard U., 1962; Doctorate (hon.), Monmouth (Ill.) Coll., 1983. Pub. Advance Mag., Washington, Cambridge, Mass., 1960-64; editorial writer N.Y. Herald Tribune, N.Y.C., 1965-66; cons., speech writer Wash. State Commn. on Civil Disorders, Seattle, 1966-71; mem. city coun. City of Seattle, 1971-75; sec. of state State of Wash., Olympia, 1975-81; dir. U.S. Census Bur., Washington, 1981-83; dep. asst. to Pres. The White House, Washington, 1983-85; U.S. amb. State Dept. (UN Offices), Vienna, 1985-88; sr. fellow Hudson Inst., Indpls., 1988-91; pres. Discovery Inst., Seattle, 1991—. Author: The Wrong Man in Uniform, 1967, (with G. Gilder) The Party that Lost Its Head, 1966; author (documentary film) A Memory for the Future, 1975-76; author, dir. (documentary film) The Market, 1976. V.p. Harvard Young Reps., Cambridge, 1962; candidate for gov. State of Wash., 1980. Episcopalian. Avocations: travel, gardening, films. Office: Discovery Inst 1402 3d Ave Ste 400 Seattle WA 98101-3266

CHAPMAN, FAY L. lawyer; b. San Jose, Calif., Dec. 17, 1946; BA, UCLA, 1968; JD, NYU, 1972. Bar: N.Y. 1973, Wash. 1975. Atty. Foster Pepper & Shefelman, Seattle; sr. exec. v.p. & gen. counsel Washington Mutual Inc, Seattle. Mem. Wash. Bankers Assn., Wash. Mortgage Bankers Assn., Wash. Savs. League. Office: Washington Mutual Inc 1201 3rd Ave Ste 1501 Seattle WA 98101-3033

CHAPMAN, GARY T. aeronautics and astronautics scientist, educator; b. Elmwood, Wis., Apr. 28, 1934; married, 1954; 4 children. BA, U. Minn., 1957; MS, Stanford U, 1963, PhD in Aeronautics and Astronautics, 1970. Rsch. scientist fluid mechanics, 1957-71; rsch. scientist aerodynamics, 1971-73; chief Aerodynamics Rsch. Br., 1974-78; staff scientist fluid mechanics Ames Rsch. Ctr. NASA, 1978-89; vis. rsch. engr. U. Calif., Berkeley, 1989—, now adj. prof. Vis. prof. aerodynamics Iowa State U., 1973-74, U. Fla., 1981-82, project scientist, 1979-81 Recipient Ground Testing award AIAA, 1997. Mem. AAAS (assoc. fellow), Am. Soc. Engring. Edn., Soc. Indsl. and Applied Mechanics, Sigma Xi. Achievements include research in basic fluid mechanics; viscous flows including separation; vortices and turbulence; bodies and winged bodies at high angles of attack and flow modeling. Office: U Calif 6195 Etcheverry Hall Berkeley CA 94720-1741

CHAPMAN, MATTHEW WILLIAM, lawyer; b. Portland, Oreg., Aug. 7, 1950; s. James Don and Regan Mary (McCoy) C.; m. Lillian Louise Richards, Sept. 21, 1985; 1 child, Richard Scott. BA in Econs., U. Portland, 1971; JD, U. Oreg., 1974. Bar: U.S. Dist. Ct. Oreg. 1974, Wash. 1985. Assoc. Stoel, Rives, Boley, Fraser & Wyse, Portland, 1974-80; ptnr. Martin, Bischoff, Templeton, Biggs & Ericsson, Portland, 1980-81, Waggoner, Chapman, Farleigh, Wada & Bogrand, Portland, 1981-87; pres. CFI Bankers Service Group, Portland, 1987—; chmn. & CEO CFI Proservices, Inc., Portland, Oreg. Lectr. numerous bus. assn. seminars. Editor Oreg. Law Rev., 1973-74; contbr. articles to profl. jours. Paul Patterson fellow. Mem. ABA (subcom. credit unions, comml. fin. services com. sect. corp. banking and bus., consumer fin. services), Oreg. Bar Assn., Wash. State Bar Assn., Multnomah Bar Assn., Order of Coif, Oreg. Mortgage Bankers Assn. Republican. Roman Catholic. Clubs: Arlington, Multnomah Athletic. Lodge: Rotary. Home: 615 SW Burlingame Ter Portland OR 97201-2643 Office: CFI Prosservices Inc 400 SW Sixth Ave Ste 200 Portland OR 97204

CHAPMAN, MICHAEL WILLIAM, orthopedist, educator; b. Newberry, Mich., Nov. 29, 1937; m. Elizabeth Casady; adopted sons: Mark, Craig. AA, Am. River Coll., Sacramento, Calif., 1957; postgrad., U. Calif., Davis, 1957-58; BS, U. Calif., San Francisco, 1959, MD, 1962. Diplomate Am. Bd. Orthopaedic Surgery (ad hoc appeal com. 1986, site visitor 1986, certification renewal com. 1985-88, certification renewal com. chmn. 1986-88). Intern San Francisco Gen. Hosp., 1962-63, asst. chief orthopaedic surgery svc., 1971-79, acting chief orthopaedic surgery svc., 1972-73; resident in orthopaedic surgery U. Calif., San Francisco, 1963-67, asst. prof. dept. orthopaedic surgery, Sch. Medicine, 1971-76, assoc. prof. dept. orthopaedic surgery, Sch. Medicine, 1976-79; resident in orthopaedic surgery U. Calif. Hosps., San Francisco, 1963-64, Samuel Merritt Hosp., Oakland, Calif., 1964, Highland-Alameda County Hosp., Oakland, 1965, Children's Hosp. of the East Bay, Oakland, 1966, Shriners Hosp., Honolulu, 1966-67; fellow Nat. Orthopaedic Hosp., London, 1967-68; chmn. dept. orthopaedic surgery U. Calif., Davis, Sacramento, 1979-99, prof. dept. orthopaedic surgery, 1981-2000, David Linn chair orthopaedic surgery, 1998-2001, prof. emeritus, 2000—. Panelist Calif. Crippled Children Svcs. Panel in Orthopaedic Surgery; cons. VA Hospital, Martinez, Calif.; co-chmn. Zimmer Trauma Panel, 1983-84; vis. prof. Fresno Valley Med. Ctr., 1975, Dept. Orthopaedics, U. Calif., Davis, 1976, U. Hawaii, Honolulu, 1977; vis. prof., cons. to Surgeon Gen. U.S. Army, Europe, 1978; vis. prof. U. Basel, Switzerland, 1979, Phoenix Orthopaedic Residency Program, 1979, Stanford U., 1981, U. Hawaii, 1982, U. So. Calif., L.A., 1984, SUNY, Buffalo, 1985, U. Utah, 1985, U. Iowa Coll. Medicine, 1987, Duke U. Sch. Medicine, 1988, U. Calif. Irvine, Div. Orthopaedics, 1990, U. S.C., 1990, Mass. Gen. Hosp., Harvard U., 1990, Boston U., 1994, Stanford U., 1995, Med. Coll. Pa., 1996, numerous others; also guest lectr. numerous instns.; insp. for residency rev. com. ad hoc appeal com. Accreditation coun. for Grad. Med. Specialist Site, 1983-86. Editor: (with M. Madison) Operative Orthopaedics, 1988 (Best New Book in Clin. Medicine Assn. Am. Pubs.); contbr. numerous articles and numerous abstracts to profl. jours.; presenter exhibits, audiovisual programs, some 500 other presentations; cons. editor Skiing Mag., 1973-77; mem. bd. assoc. editors Clin. Orthopaedics and Related Rsch., 1982-85, Internat. Med. Soc. Paraplegia, 1972-80; reviewer Jour. Bone and Joint Surgery, 1980-85, trustee, 1995-03, sec. to bd. trustees, 1999, chmn. bd. trustees, 2000; past reviewer New Eng. Jour. Medicine; patentee in field. With U.S. Army, 1968-70. Decorated Army Commendation medal; recipient Outstanding Tchg. award U. Calif., San Francisco, 1972, Outstanding Tchr. award U. Calif., Davis, 1984, 93; named One of Best 100 Doctors Am., Good Housekeeping Mag.; Fogarty Sr. Internat. fellow NIH, 1978-79, 80-81; grantee Johnson & Johnson, 1983-84, Zimmer Inc., 1983-85, 85-86, 87-90, Interpore Internat., 1985-86, 89-90, Collagen Inc., 1985-86, 88-89, Upjohn Inc., 1985-86, Orthopaedic Rsch. and Edn. Found., 1988-89. Mem. AMA (Physicians Recognition award 1989-96), ACS, Am. Acad. Orthopaedic Surgeons (bd. dirs. 1982-83, numerous coms.), Am. Orthopaedic Assn. (bd. dirs. 1985-86, pres. 1990-91, various coms.), Internat. Orthopaedic Assn., Assn. for Study of Internal Fixation (N.Am. chpt.), Internat. Soc. Orthopaedic Surgery and Traumatology, Internat. Soc. for Fracture Repair, Brit. Orthopaedic Assn., South African Orthopaedic Assn. (hon.), Am. Acad. Orthopaedic Surgeons, Am. Assn. for Surgery of Trauma, Am. Bd. Med. Spltys., Assn. Am. Med. Colls., Leroy C. Abbott Orthopaedic Soc., Austrian Trauma Assn., Paul R. Lipscomb Soc., Northwestern Med. Assn., Orthopaedic Rsch. Soc., Orthopaedic Trauma Assn., Sierra Club, U. Calif. San Francisco Alumni Assn., Western Orthopaedic Assn., Houston Orthopaedic Assn. (hon.), Calif. Med. Assn., Calif. Orthopaedic Assn., Sacramento-El Dorado Med. Soc., Wilson Interurban Orthopaedic Soc., Alpha Omega Alpha. Avocations: skiing, mountaineering, backpacking, tennis, bicycling. Office: U Calif-Davis Sch Med Dept Orthopedics 4860 Y St Ste 3800 Sacramento CA 95817-2307

CHAPMAN, ORVILLE LAMAR, chemist, educator; b. New London, Conn., June 26, 1932; s. Orville Carmen and Mabel Elnora (Tyree) C.; m. Faye Newton Morrow, Aug. 20, 1955 (div. 1980); children: Kenneth, Kevin; m. Susan Elizabeth Parker, June 15, 1981. BS, Va. Poly. Inst., 1954; PhD, Cornell U., 1957. Instr. chemistry Iowa State U., 1957-59, asst. prof., 1959-62, assoc. prof., 1962-65, Prof. chemistry, 1965-74; prof. chemistry UCLA, 1974-2000. Cons. Mobil Chem. Co. Recipient NYAS award, 1974, Founders prize Tex. Instruments, George and Freda Halpern award in photochemistry N.Y. Acad. Scis., 1978, Outstanding Patent of Yr. award Mobil Corp., 1992, Best Use of Info. Tech. in Edn. and Academia award Computer World/Smithsonian Instn., 1995, Computer World-Smithsonian Instn. award in Edn., 1995. Mem. Am. Chem. Soc. (award in pure chemistry 1968, Arthur C. Cope award 1978, Midwest award 1978, Havinga medal 1982, McCoy award UCLA, 1985). Home: 1213 Roscomare Rd Los Angeles CA 90077-2202 Office: UCLA Dept Chemistry 405 Hilgard Ave Los Angeles CA 90095-9000 E-mail: chapman@chem.ucla.edu

CHAPMAN, REGINALD FREDERICK, entomologist; b. London, July 2, 1930; s. Reginald Alfred and Maria Martha (Seares) C.; m. Elizabeth Anna Bernays, June 1, 1983. BS, U. London, 1951, PhD, 1953, DS, 1965. Rsch. scientist Internat. Red Locust Orgn., N. Rhodesia (now Zambia), 1953-57, Biol. Rsch. Inst., Ghana, 1957-59; prof. U. London, 1959-70; asst. dir. Anti-Locust Rsch. Ctr., London, 1970-83; prof. U. Ariz., Tucson, 1989—. Vis. prof. U. Calif., Berkeley, 1983-89, U. Hull, U.K., 1975-83. Author: The Insects, Structure and Function, 1969, 4th edit., 1998; co-author: Host Finding by Phytophagous Insects, 1994; co-editor: Perspectives in Chemoreception and Behavior, 1987, Regulatory Mechanisms in Insect Feeding, 1995; editor Environ. Entomology, 1984-89; mem. editorial bd. CRC Plant-Insect Interactions, 1989-93; contbr. articles to profl. jours. Fellow Entomol. Soc. Am., Royal Entomol. Soc. (hon.), Inst. Biology; mem. Soc. Exptl. Biology, Internat. Soc. Chem. Ecology (silver medal 1999). Achievements include discovery of importance of plant surface waxes in plant recognition by insects; changes in chemosensory system in insect evolution. Office: Univ Ariz Div Neurobiology Tucson AZ 85721-0001

CHAPMAN, RICHARD GRADY, engineer; b. Greer, S.C., Oct. 25, 1937; s. Richard Grady Sr. and Mary Idell (Davis) C.; m. Eleanor Raye Kernells, Oct. 13, 1956 (div. Apr. 1978); children: Abby Leigh, Pamela Kathryn, Robert Pope; m. Georgia Ann Burke, Apr. 7, 1978. BS in Engring., U. Nebr., 1974; MS in Geoenviron. Engring., Shippensburg U., 1984. Registered profl. engr., Terr. of Guam. Commd. 2d lt. U.S. Army, 1959, advanced through grades to col., 1984, aviation officer U.S. and Vietnam, 1966-71, engr. officer U.S., Europe and Asia, 1971-89, ret., 1989; designer Coleman & Townes Architects and Engrs., Greenwood, S.C., 1960-66; rsch. engr. U. N.Mex., Albuquerque, 1990-97; cons. engr. Colorado Springs, Colo., 1997-99; gen. mgr. LB-B Assocs. O&M Contract, Ft. Carson, 1999—. Co-chair U.S.-Japan environ. com. U.S. Forces Japan, Tokyo, 1980-83; chief of facilities U.S. Army, Europe, Heidelberg, Germany, 1984-86; comdr. Kwajalein Missile Range, Marshall Islands, 1986-88; CINCPAC rep. to pres. Marshall Islands. Author: (tng. program) Hazardous Waste Management Course for BLM, 1990, (books) Energy Master Plan, 1994, NORAD's Cheyenne Mountain, 1996; co-author manual: Combat Air Base Planning Principles, 1991. Dir. Regional Water Dist., El Paso County, Colo., 1994-98, Regional Fire Dist., el Paso County, 1994-98; vice chmn. County-Wide Policy Plan, El Paso County, 1994-98; guide, v.p. Visually Impaired and Blind Skiers of Colorado Springs, 1998—. Recipient Resolution award Parliament, Republic of Marshall Islands, 1988, Bd. Commrs. El Paso County, 1998, plaque Visually Impaired and Blind Skiers of Colorado Springs, 1998. Fellow Am. Soc. Mil. Engrs. (pres. 1977-78, cert. 1985), Ret. Officers Assn. Baptist. Avocations: skiing, flying, scuba diving, art, travel. Home and Office: 4455 Spiceglen Dr Colorado Springs CO 80906-7691 E-mail: springsengr@aol.com

CHAPMAN, ROSALYN M. federal judge; b. Chgo., May 16, 1943; BA cum laude, U. Mich., 1964; JD, Boalt Hall, 1967. Adminstrv. law judge Office of Adminstrv. Hearings State of Calif., 1977-95; apptd. magistrate judge cen. dist. U.S. Dist. Ct. Calif., 1995. Arbitrator Fed. Mediation and Conciliation Svc. and Am. Arbitration Assn.; assoc. dir. Western Ctr. on Law and Poverty; lectr. UCLA Sch. Law. Office: US Courthouse 312 N Spring St Los Angeles CA 90012-4701 Fax: 213-894-4949

CHAPMAN, SAMUEL GREELEY, political science educator, criminologist; b. Atlanta, Sept. 29, 1929; s. Calvin C. and Jane (Greeley) C.; m. Patricia Hepfer, June 19, 1949 (dec. Dec. 1978); children: Lynn Randall, Deborah Jane; m. Carolyn Hughes, June 1, 1991. A.B., U. Calif.-Berkeley, 1951, M.A., 1959. Officer Police Dept., Berkeley, 1951-56; police cons. Pub. Adminstrn. Service, Chgo., 1956-59; asst. prof. Sch. Police Adminstrn., Mich. State U., East Lansing, 1959-63; police chief Multnomah County, Portland, Oreg., 1963-66; asst. dir. Pres.'s Commn. on Law Enforcement and Adminstrn. of Justice, Nat. Crime Commn., Washington, 1966-67; prof. dept. polit. sci. U. Okla., Norman, 1967-91; prof. emeritus, 1991—; chmn. athletic council U. Okla., 1971-72, 79-80. Adj. prof. criminal justice U. Nev., Reno, 1995—; assoc.'s disting. lectr., 1985-86. Author: Dogs in Police Work, 1960, The Police Heritage in England and America, 1962, Police Patrol Readings, 1964, rev. edit., 1970, Perspectives on Police Assaults in the South Central United States, 1974, Short of Merger, 1976, Police Murders and Effective Countermeasures, 1976, Police Dogs in North America, 1979, 2d. edit., 1990, Cops, Killers and Staying Alive: The Murder of Police Officers in America, 1986; Murdered On Duty: The Killing of Police Officers in America, 1998; contbr. chpts. to books, articles to profl. jours. Mem. Norman City Council, 1972-83, mayor pro-tem, 1975-76, 79-80, 81-83. Recipient Amoco Found. award, 1986. Mem. Alpha Delta Phi. Republican. Home and Office: 680 Kane Ct Reno NV 89512-1354 E-mail: sgchapman@renonevada.net

CHAPPELL, CHARLES FRANKLIN, meteorologist, consultant; b. St. Louis, Dec. 7, 1927; s. Hubert Guy and Wilma Halle (Lindsey) C.; m. Doris Mae Kennedy, Aug. 4, 1951; children— Christa Ann, Susan Lynne, Deborah Louise B.S., Washington U., St. Louis, 1949; postgrad., St. Louis U., 1952-54; M.S., Colo. State U., 1967, Ph.D., 1971. Flight data engr. McDonnell Aircraft Co., St. Louis, 1950-55; weather forecaster U.S. Weather Bur., Kansas City, Mo., 1956-67; research assoc. Colo. State U., Ft. Collins, 1967-70; assoc. prof. Utah State U., Logan, 1970-72; research meteorologist NOAA, Boulder, Colo., 1972-79, research dir., 1979-87; head applied sci. group Nat. Ctr. for Atmospheric Research, Boulder, 1988-89, sr. scientist coop. program for operational meteorology edn. and tng., 1989-94; meteolologist cons., Boulder, 1995—. Cons. meteorologist Midwest Weather Service, Kansas City, Mo., 1958-60 Assoc. editor Jour. Atmospheric Sci., 1984-87; contbr. articles to prof. jours. (Best Sci. Paper award in NOAA-Environ. Research Labs. 1981). Served as seaman 1st class USN, 1945-46 Recipient silver medal Dept. Commerce, 1957 Fellow Am. Meteorol. Soc.; mem. Nat. Weather Assn., Weather Modification Assn., Am. Geophys. Union, Phi Kappa Phi. Avocations: hiking, painting, gardening, piano. Home and Office: 3110 Heidelberg Dr Boulder CO 80305-7010

CHAPPELL, WILLARD RAY, physics educator, environmental scientist; b. Boulder, Colo., Feb. 27, 1938; s. Willard Bruce and Mildred Mary (Weaver) C.; m. Juanita June Benetin, Mar. 5, 1981; children: Ginger Ferguson, Robert Ferguson. B.A. in Math., U. Colo., 1962, Ph.D. in Physics, 1965; A.M. in Physics, Harvard U., 1963. Postdoctoral research assoc. Smithsonian Astrophys. Obs., Cambridge, Mass., 1965-66; postdoc- [illegible] physics U. Colo., Boulder, 1967-70, assoc. prof., 1970-73, prof., 1973-76, prof. physics, dir. Ctr. for Environ. Scis. Denver, 1976—. Chmn. Dept. Energy Oil Shale Task Force, 1978-83; mem. adv. com. to dir. on health scis. Los Alamos Nat. Lab.; mem. Colo. Gov.'s Sci. Adv. Com., 1974-76, chmn., 1975-76 Author: Transport and Biological Effects of Molybdenum in the Environment, 1975 Served with U.S. Army, 1956-58 NSF fellow, 1962-65; grantee Fleishman Found., 1969-71, NSF, 1971-76, EPA, 1975-79, Dept. Energy, 1976-83, U.S. Bur. Mines, 1979-81 Mem. Am. Phys. Soc., AAAS, Soc. Environ. Geochemistry and Health (exec. com. 1981-83, 86-88, sec./treas. 1988—), Phi Beta Kappa Democrat Office: U Colo Environ Scis PO Box 173364 Denver CO 80217-3364

CHAR, PATRICIA HELEN, lawyer; b. Honolulu, Mar. 23, 1952; d. Lincoln S. and Daisy Char; m. Thomas W. Bingham, Mar. 20, 1982; children: Matthew Thomas Bingham, James Nathan Bingham. BA, Northwestern U., 1974; JD, Georgetown U., 1977. Bar: Wash. 1977, U.S. Dist. Ct. (we. dist.) Wash. 1977, U.S. Dist. Ct. (ea. dist.) Wash. 1982, U.S. Ct. Appeals (9th cir.) 1981, U.S. Supreme Ct. 1984. Assoc. Bogle & Gates, Seattle, 1977-84; ptnr., mem. Bogle & Gates PLLC, Seattle, 1984-99; of counsel Garvey, Schubert & Barer, Seattle, 1999-2000; ptnr. Preston Gates & Ellis LLP, Seattle, 2000—. Author: Ownership By a Fiduciary, 1997. Trustee YWCA, Seattle-King County-Snohomish County; vol. King County Big Sisters, United Way of King County, Seattle, 1987-90, Guardian Ad Litem Program, Seattle, 1987-93. Mem. ABA, Wash. State Bar Assn. (co-author chpts. 3 and 4 Wash. Civil Procedure Deskbook 1992). Office: Preston Gates & Ellis LLP 701 5th Ave Ste 5000 Seattle WA 98104-7078 E-mail: pchar@prestongates.com

CHAR, VERNON FOOK LEONG, lawyer; b. Honolulu, Dec. 15, 1934; s. Charles A. and Annie (Ching) C.; m. Evelyn Lau, June 14, 1958; children: Richard, Daniel, Douglas, Charles, Elizabeth. BA, U. Hawaii, 1956; LLB, Harvard U., 1959. Bar: Hawaii 1959. Dep. atty. gen. Office of Atty. Gen., Honolulu, 1959-60, 62-65; ptnr. Damon Key Char & Bocken, Honolulu, 1965-89, Char, Sakamoto, Ishii, Lum & Ching, Honolulu, 1989—. Chmn. Hawaii Ethics Commn., Honolulu, 1968-75, Hawaii Bicentennial Com., 1986-91, 1st Hawaii Jud. Conf., 1985. Mem. ABA (bd. govs. 1991-94), Hawaii Bar Assn. (pres. 1985), U. Hawaii Alumni Assn. (pres. 1989-90). Home: 351 Anonia St Honolulu HI 96821-2052 Office: Char Sakamoto Ishii Lum & Ching Davies Pacific Ctr 841 Bishop St Ste 850 Honolulu HI 96813-3957 E-mail: vflchar@lawcsilc.com

CHARLES, BLANCHE, retired elementary education educator; b. Spartanburg, S.C., Aug. 7, 1912; d. Franklin Grady and Alice Floride (Hatchette) C. BA, Humboldt State U., 1934; adminstrv. cert., U. So. Calif., 1940. Tchr. Calexico (Calif) Unified Sch. Dist., 1958-94; ret., 1994. Libr. Calexico Pub. Libr., El Centro Pub. Libr. Elem. sch. named in her honor, 1987. Mem. NEA, ACT, Calif. Tchrs. Assn., DAR, Nat. Soc. Daus. of Confederacy, Delta Kappa Gamma. Avocations: gardening, reading. Home: 37133 Hwy 94 Space 3 Boulevard CA 91905-9524

CHARLES, RAY, musician, composer, lyricist, arranger, conductor; b. Chgo., Sept. 13, 1918; s. Isador and Gertrude (Gendon) Offenberg; m. Bernice Rosengarden, Oct. 16, 1940; children: Michael, Jonathan, Wendy. Grad. high sch., Chgo. Mem., choral arranger radio choirs, Chgo.; choral dir., vocal arranger Perry Como; dir. Ray Charles Singers; choral arranger, dir. Your Hit Parade. Cons. Muppet Show. Recorded albums (6 Grammy nominees); composer, lyricist TV spls. including The 1st Nine Months are the Hardest, 1971 (Emmy award 1971), The Funny Side of Marriage, 1971 (Emmy award 1972); TV spls. with John Denver, Frank Sinatra, Bing Crosby, Julie Andrews, Mac Davis, The Carpenters, Acad. Awards, Kennedy Ctr. Honors, Salute to Billy Wilder; co-dir. music (TV series) Sha-Na-Na; conductor Broadway play Finian's Rainbow; choral work (films) Funny Lady, Racing With Moon; singer (TV series theme song) Three's Company. With USN, 1944-46. Mem. AFTRA, NARAS, SAG, Am. Fedn. Musicians, Acad. TV Arts and Scis. Office: Ray Charles Enterprises Inc 2107 W Washington Blvd Ste 200 Los Angeles CA 90018-1597

CHARLSON, ROBERT JAY, atmospheric sciences educator, scientist; b. San Jose, Calif., Sept. 30, 1936; s. Rolland Walter and Harriet Adele (Stucky) C.; m. Patricia Elaine Allison, Mar. 16, 1964; children: Daniel Owen, Amanda Marcella. B.S. in Chemistry, Stanford U., 1958, M.S. in Chemistry, 1959; Ph.D. in Atmospheric Scis., U. Wash., 1964; postgrad. (Fulbright scholar), London U., 1964-65; PhD (hon.), Stockholm U., 1993. Rsch. engr. Boeing Co., Seattle, 1959-62; rsch. asst. prof. dept. civil engring. U. Wash., Seattle, 1965-69, assoc. prof. atmospheric chemistry, 1969-71, assoc. prof. civil engring. and geophysics, 1971-74, prof. atmospheric chemistry in civil engring. geophysics and environ. studies, 1974-94, prof. atmospheric scis., 1985-98, adj. prof. chemistry, 1985-96, prof., 1996-98, prof. emeritus, 1998—; King Carl XVI Gustaf prof. environ. sci. Sweden, 1999-2000. Author: (with S.S. Butcher) An Introduction to Air Chemistry, 1972; assoc. editor: Jour. Applied Meteorology, 1971-73; co-editor: Global Biogeochemical Cycles, 1992; Earth System Science: From Biogeochemical Cycles to Global Change, 2000; mem. editorial bd. Jour. Boundary Layer Meteorology, 1971-86, Water, Air and Soil Pollution, 1971-85; contbr. articles on atmosphere chemistry to profl. jours.; patentee in field. Co-recipient Gerbier/Mumm award World Meteorol. Orgn., 1988; grantee USPHS, EPA, NSF, NASA, NOAA. Fellow Am. Meteorol. Soc., Am. Geophys. Union; mem. AAAS, Am. Chem. Soc., Sigma Xi, Phi Lambda Upson (hon.). Office: U Wash Dept Atmospheric Scis PO Box 351640 Seattle WA 98195-0001

CHARTIER, VERNON LEE, electrical engineer; b. Feb. 14, 1939; s. Raymond Earl and Margaret Clara (Winegar) C.; m. Lois Marie Schwartz, May 20, 1967; 1 child, Neal Raymond. BSEE, BS in Bus., U. Colo., 1963. Registered profl. engr., Pa.; cert. electromagnetic compatibility engr. Rsch. engr., cons. Westinghouse Electric Co., East Pitts., Pa., 1963-75; prin. engr. high voltage phenomena Bonneville Power Adminstrn., Vancouver, Wash., 1975-95; power sys. EMC cons. Portland, 1995—. Contbr. articles to profl. jours. Treas. First Bapt. Ch., Portland; budget and fin. officer Am. Bapt. Chs. of Oreg. Fellow IEEE (past fellow com. 1993-96, Herman Halperin Transmission and Distbn. award 1995, 3d Millennium medal 2000); mem. Power Engring. Soc. of IEEE (chmn. transmission and distbn. com. 1987-88, chmn. fellows com. 1990-92), Internat. Conf. Large High Voltage Electric Sys. (W.G. 36.01 EMC Aspects of Corona and Magnetic Fields, Attwood Assoc. award 1999), Internat. Electrotech. Commn. (U.S. rep. to subcom. on High Voltage Lines & Traction Sys.), Chartier Family Assn. Baptist. Home and Office: 13095 SW Glenn Ct Beaverton OR 97008-5664 E-mail: vichartier@ieee.org

CHARWAT, ANDREW FRANCISZEK, engineering educator; b. Poland, Feb. 10, 1925; came to U.S., 1945; s. Franciszek and Wanda (Niec) C.; m. Halina M. Stieglitz, Aug. 18, 1948; 1 child, Danuta K. Charwat McCall. M Engring., Stevens Inst. Tech., 1948; PhD, U. Calif., Berkeley 1952. Aerodynamicist Propulsion Research Corp., Los Angeles, 1952-53; designer Northrup Aircraft Corp., Los Angeles, 1953-55; prof., dept. mech. and aerospace engring. UCLA, 1955-92, prof. emeritus, 1992—. Cons. to numerous industry and govt. agys., 1955—; expert witness various legal cases; dir. Univ. Study Ctr., Lyon and Grenoble, France, 1986-88. Contbr. over 80 articles and research papers. Guggenheim fellow, 1962. E-mail: [illegible]

CHASE, ROBERT ARTHUR, surgeon, educator; b. Keene, N.H., Jan. 6, 1923; s. Albert Henry and Georgia Beulah (Bump) C., m. Ann Crosby Parker, Feb. 3, 1946; children: Deborah Lee, Nancy Jo, Robert N. B.S. cum laude, U. N.H., 1945, DSC (hon.), 1993; M.D., Yale, 1947. Diplomate: Am. Bd. Surgery, Am. Bd. Plastic Surgery. Intern New Haven Hosp., 1947-48, asst. resident, 1949-50, sr. resident surgery, 1952-53, chief resident surgeon, 1953-54; mem. faculty Yale Sch. Medicine, 1948-54, 59-62, asst. prof. surgery, 1959-62; mem. faculty U. Pitts., 1957-59, resident plastic surgeon, also teaching fellow, 1957-59; attending surgeon VA Hosp., W. Haven, Conn., 1959-62, Grace New Haven Community Hosp., 1959-63; prof., chmn. dept. surgery Stanford Sch. Medicine, 1963-74, Emile Holman prof. surgery, 1972—; prof. surgery U. Pa., 1974-77; attending surgeon Pa. Hosp., Hosp. U. Pa., Grad. Hosp., Phila., 1974-77; pres., dir. Nat. Bd. Med. Examiners, Phila., 1974-77; prof. anatomy Stanford (Calif.) U., 1977—. Cons. plastic surgery Christian Med. Coll. and Hosp., Vellore, S. India, 1962; cons. to surgeon gen. USAF, 1970— ; Benjamin K. Rank prof. Australasian Coll. Surgeons, 1974 Author: Atlas of Hand Surgery; Editor: Videosurgery, 1974— ; editorial bd.: Med. Alert Communication; Contbr. articles to profl. jours. Served to maj. M.C. AUS, 1949-57. Recipient Francis Gilman Blake award Yale Sch. Medicine, 1962, Henry J. Kaiser award Stanford U. Sch. Medicine, 1978, 79, 84, 86, 90, 93, Calif. Golden Apple award 1991, Albion William Hewlett award, 1992, Pettee award U. N.H., 1998. Fellow ACS, Australasian Coll. Surgeons (hon.); mem. NAS, Am. Assn. Plastic Surgeons (hon.), Calif. Acad. Medicine (pres.), San Francisco Surg. Soc., Am. Surg. Assn., Santa Clara County Med. Soc., Conn. Med. Soc., Am. Soc. Surgery Hand (pres.), Am. Assn. Clin. Anatomists (hon., pres.), Am. Soc. Cleft Palate Rehab., Am. Assn. Surgery Trauma, Plastic Surgery Rsch. Coun., AMA, Soc. Clin. Surgery, Western Surg. Assn., Pacific Coast Surg. Soc., Am. Assn. Plastic Surgery (hon.), James IV Assn. Surgeons, Am. Cancer Soc. (clin. fellowship com.), Found. Am. Soc. Plastic and Reconstructive Surgery (dir.), Soc. Univ. Surgeons, Inst. Medicine (exec. com. 1976, coun. 1986—), Am. Soc. Most Venerable Order Hosp., St. John of Jerusalem, Halsted Soc., South African Soc. Surgery Hand (hon.), South African Soc. Plastic and Reconstructive Surgery (hon.), Am. Soc. Clin. Anatomists (hon., pres.)Phi Beta Kappa, Sigma Xi. Home: 69 Pearce Mitchell Pl Stanford CA 94305 Office: Stanford U Div Anatomy 269 Campus Dr Stanford CA 94305-5102 E-mail: rchase6880@aol.com

CHASSMAN, LEONARD FREDRIC, labor union administrator, retired; b. Detroit, Sept. 30, 1935; s. Joachim and Lillian (Abrams) C.; m. Phyllis Perlman, Aug. 25, 1957; children: Mark, Cheryl, Gregory. B.A., UCLA, 1957. Rep. AFTRA, Los Angeles, 1959-63, Screen Actors Guild, Los Angeles, 1963-65; staff exec. Writers Guild Am., West, Inc., Los Angeles, 1965-77, exec. dir., 1978-82; nat. exec. sec. Screen Extras Guild Inc., 1982-84; Hollywood exec. dir. Screen Actors Guild Inc., 1984-01, trustee Screen Actors Guild producers pension and health funds; bd. dirs. Entertainment Industry Found. Pres. Hollywood Entertainment Labor Coun. Bd. dirs. L.A. Pvt. Industry Coun. E-mail: lchassman@aol.com

CHASTAIN, BRANDI DENISE, professional soccer player; b. San Jose, Calif., July 21, 1968; Mem. U.S. Women's Soccer Team; asst. coach women's soccer team Santa Clara U. Mem. U.S. Women's Nat. Team, 1996, Shiroke Serena, Japan, 1993. Recipient Gold medal Olympic Games, 1996; mem. championship team U.S. Olympic Festival, 1991, CONCACAF Championship, N.Y., 1993. Office: c/o Santa Clara U Athletics Dept 500 El Camino Real Santa Clara CA 95050-4345 also: US Soccer Fedn 1801 S Prairie Ave # 1811 Chicago IL 60616-1319

CHATARD, PETER RALPH NOEL, JR. aesthetic plastic surgeon; b. New Orleans, June 25, 1936; s. Peter Ralph Sr. and Alberta Chatard; m. Patricia Myrl White, Jan. 31, 1963; children: Andrea Michelle, Faedra Noelle, Tahra Deonne. BS in Biology, Morehouse Coll., 1956; MD, U. Rochester, 1960. Diplomate Am. Bd. Plastic Surgery, Am. Bd. Otolaryngology. Intern Colo. Gen. Hosp., 1960-61; asst. resident in gen. surgery Highland Gen. Hosp., Rochester, N.Y., 1963-64; resident in otolaryngology Strong Meml. Hosp., Rochester, 1964-67; resident in plastic and reconstructive surgery U. Fla., 1980-82; staff otolaryngologist Group Health Corp. of Puget Sound, Seattle, 1967-68; practice medicine specializing in otolaryngology Seattle, 1968-80; practice medicine specializing in plastic surgery Seattle, 1982—; clin. asst. prof. otolaryngology, head and neck surgery U. Wash., Seattle, 1975—. Plastic surgery cons. western sec. Maxillofacial Rev. Bd. State of Wash., 1982-90, cons. Conservation of Hearing Program, 1968-80; trustee Physicians and Dentist Credit Bur., 1974-80, 84-87, pres. 1976-77, 84-85; active staff mem. Northwest Hosp., Seattle; courtesy staff Swedish Hosp., Children's Hosp. Med. Ctr., Seattle, Providence Hosp., Seattle, Stevens Meml. Hosp., Edmond, Wash., Seattle, others. Capt. USAF, 1961-63. Fellow ACS, Am. Rhinologic Soc., Seattle Surg. Soc., Am. Acad. Facial Plastic and Reconstructive Surgery, Am. Acad. Otolaryngology-Head and Neck Surgery, Northwest Acad. Otolaryngology and Head and Neck Surgery, Soc. for Ear, Nose and Throat Advances in Children, Pacific Oto-Ophthalmological Soc.; mem. Am. Soc. Plastic Surgery, Am. Soc. for Aesthetic Plastic Surgery, Inc., Lipoplasty Soc. N. Am., Wash. Soc. Plastic Surgeons, Nat. Med. Assn., King County Med. Soc., Wash. Med. Assn., N.W. Soc. of Plastic Surgeons. Avocations: photography, cynology, microcomputing, architecture and design. Home: 13211 Frazier Pl NW Seattle WA 98177-4132 Office: AEsteem Aesthetic Plastic Surgery Inc 1200 N Northgate Way Seattle WA 98133-8916 E-mail: chatard@aol.com

CHATER, SHIRLEY SEARS, health educator; d. Raymond and Edna Sears; m. Norman Chater, Dec. 5, 1959 (dec. Dec. 1993); children: Cris, Geoffrey. BS, U. Pa., 1956; MS, U. Calif., San Francisco, 1960; PhD, U. Calif., Berkeley, 1964. Asst., assoc., prof. dept. social and behavioral scis. Sch. Nursing U. Calif.-San Francisco, Sch. Edn.-Berkeley, 1964-86; asst. vice chancellor acad. affairs U. Calif., San Francisco, 1974-77, vice chancellor acad. affairs, 1977-82; council assoc. Am. Council Edn., Washington, 1982-84; sr. assoc. Presdl. Search Consultation Svc. Assn. Governing Bds., Washington, 1984-86; pres. Tex. Woman's U., Denton, 1986-93; chair Gov's health policy task force State of Texas, 1992; commr. Social Security Adminstrn., Washington, 1993-97; Regent's prof. Inst. for Health and Aging U. Calif., San Francisco, 1997-98. Vis. prof. Inst. Health & Aging U. Calif., San Francisco, 1998—. Bd. dirs. Carnegie Found. for Advancement of Teaching, United Educators Ins. Risk Retention Group, Denton United Way, 1986-93; mem. commn. on women Am. Coun. on Edn. Mem. Inst. Medicine, NAS, San Francisco Women's Forum West, Internat. Alliance, Nat. Acad. Pub. Adminstrn., Nat. Acad. Social Ins., Nat. Acad. Nursing. Office: Inst Health and Aging 3333 California St Ste 340 San Francisco CA 94118-1944

CHATHAM, RUSSELL, artist; b. San Francisco, Oct. 27, 1939; m. Mary Fanning (div.); m. Doris Meyer (div.); m. Suzanne Porter; children: Georgina, Lea, Rebecca, Paul. Ed., San Francisco. Painter, writer, Calif.; landscape artist, lithographer, Mont., 1972—. Address: PO Box 659 Livingston MT 59047-0659 Also: c/o Angler Art & Gifts Cherry Creek North 201 Fillmore St Unit D Denver CO 80206-5015

[illegible] Albert Blas and Yolanda (Garcia) C.; m. Irma Laura Cavazos, Dec. 21, 1996. BA, U. Tex., El Paso, 1979; MBA, Stanford U., 1985. CPA, Calif. Mem. profl. staff Deloitte Haskins and Sells, L.A., 1980-83; planning analyst corp. fin. planning Boise (Idaho) Cascade Co., 1984; treasury analyst corp. treasury RCA Corp., N.Y.C., 1985; asst. contr. RCA/Ariola Records, Mexico City, 1986; fin. analyst corp. exec. office GE Co., [illegible]

Litigation Support Svcs., L.A., 1990-91; co-founder, sr. v.p., CFO El Dorado Comm., Inc., L.A., 1991-98; fin. cons. entertainment and tech. industries, 1999—. Bd. dirs., treas. L.A. Conservation Corps, 1990—; bd. dirs. Wave Cmty. Newspapers, 1999-2000. Mem. AICPA, Calif. Soc. CPAs. Democrat. Home: 18744 Strathern St Reseda CA 91335-1221

CHAVEZ, EDWARD, protective services official; b. Stockton, Calif., Mar. 22, 1943; m. Nancy Ruhr; children: Eric, Jill. AA, San Joaquin Delta Coll., 1971; BA, Calif. State U., 1972; MS, Calif. Polytechnic Pomona, 1990; grad., POST Command Coll., Delinquency Control Inst., Leadership Stockton Program, FBI Nat. Acad. With USAF, 1962-70; officer Stockton Police Dept., 1973, sgt., 1980, lt., 1986, capt., 1990, dep. chief of police, 1990, acting chief of police, 1993, chief of police, 1993—. Bd. dirs. St. Joseph's Med. Ctr., San Joaquin United Way, Lilliput Childrens Svcs., Greater Stockton C. of C.; active Hispanics for Polit. Action; adv. com. Leadership, Stockton. With USAF, 1962-70. Mem. Calif. Peace Officers Assn., Hispanic Am. Police Command Officer's Assn., Mexican Am. C. of C., Stockton E. Rotary, Coun. for Spanish Speaking (past bd. dirs.), Leadership Stockton Alumni Assn. Office: Stockton Police Dept 22 E Market St Stockton CA 95202-2802

CHAVEZ, GILBERT ESPINOZA, bishop; b. Ontario, Calif., May 9, 1932; Student, St. Francis Sem., El Cajon, Calif., Immaculate Heart Sem., San Diego, U. Calif. Ordained priest Roman Cath. Ch., 1960. Titular bishop of Magarmel and aux. bishop Diocese of San Diego, 1974—. Bishop; b. Ontario, Calif., Mar. 19, 1932; ed. St. Francis Sem., El Cajon, Calif., Immaculate Heart Sem., San Diego, U. Calif., San Diego. Ordained priest Roman Cath. Ch., 1960; titular bishop of Magarmel and aux. bishop Diocese of San Diego, 1974—. Office: St Joseph Cathedral 1535 3rd Ave San Diego CA 92101-3101

CHAVEZ, LLOYD G. automotive executive; CEO Burt on Broadway. Office: Burt Automotive Network 5200 S Broadway Englewood CO 80110-6708

CHAVEZ, MARTIN JOSEPH, lawyer, former mayor; b. Albuquerque, Mar. 2, 1952; s. Lorenzo Armijo and Sara (Baca) C.; m. Margaret Chavez de Aragon, July 28, 1988; children: Martinique, Ezequiel Lorenzo. BS, U. N.Mex., 1975; JD, Georgetown U., 1978. Staff asst. U.S. Senate, Washington, 1976-77; dep. dir. LULAC Nat. Scholarship Fund, Washington, 1977-78; law clk. N.Mex. Atty. Gen., 1978-79; pvt. practice, 1979-86, 87-93, 98—; first and founding dir. N.Mex. Workers Compensation Adminstrn., 1986-87; mem. N.Mex. Senate, 1988-93; mayor City of Albuquerque, 1993-97. Mem. Med. Rev. Commn., 1990—; bd. dirs. Senior Arts Project, 1987—, Tree New Mex., 1991-92. Mem. Citizens Rev. Bd., 1988—; bd. dirs. N.Mex. First, Sr. Arts; founding mem., bd. dirs. Tree N.Mex.; mem. Citizens Adv. Bd., N.Mex. Med. Rev. Commn.; Dem. candidate for Gov., 1998. Recipient Outstanding Young Men of Am. award, 1984, Appreciation award Friends of Albuquerque Petroglyphs, 1989, Cert. Appreciation, Am. Merchant Marines, 1989, Disting. Svc. award N.Mex. Dietetic Assn., 1989, Appreciation award West Mesa Little League, 1989, Excellence in Edn. award Friend of Edn., 1990, Appreciation award FHP N.Mex., Inc., 1990, Devoted and Invaluable Svc. award Indian Pueblo Cultural Ctr., 1990, Recognition award Ind. Ins. Agts. N.Mex., 1991, Accomplishment, Dedication and Performance award West Mesa High Sch., 1991, N.Mex. State Meml. award, 1991, Exemplary Dedication and Svc. award Sec. of State, 1991, Cert. Spl. Appreciation, MADD, 1991, Disting. Svc. award Hispanic Bar Assn., 1992, Legis. Recognition award Dem. Party N.Mex., 1992, Commitment to Edn. award Alamosa Elem. Sch., 1992, Recognition and Appreciation award N.Mex. First, 1992, Dedication award Albuquerque Hispano C. of C., 1993, Pride of N.Mex. award Hispanic Round Table, 1993; named Outstanding Youth Advocate, Youth Devel., Inc., 1993. Mem. N.Mex. State Bar Assn. (Pub. Svc. Recognition award 1989). Avocation: fly fishing. Home: 3313 La Mancha Dr NW Albuquerque NM 87104-3029

CHÁVEZ, THOMAS ESTEBAN, curator; b. Las Vegas, Jan. 19, 1948; AA, Pasadena (Calif.) City Coll., 1968; BA, Calif. State Coll., 1970, U. N.Mex., 1974, MA, 1976, PhD, 1980. Instr. Coll. Santa Fe, 1979-82; from mus. coord. edn. bur. to dir. Palace of the Govs. Mus. of N.Mex., Santa Fe, 1978—. Instr. U. N.Mex. No. Consortium, 1978. Author: Manuel Alvarez, 1974-1856: A Southwestern Biography, 1990, Illustrated History of New Mexico, 1992, In Quest for Quivera: Spanish Exploration on the Plains from 1540 to 1821, 1992, editor: Conflict and Acculturation. Manuel Alvarez' 1942 Memorial, 1989; contbr. articles to profl. jours. Served in U.S. Army, 1970-72. Mem. Hist. Soc. N.Mex. (bd. dirs., past chmn. membership com., past chmn. conf. com.), N.Mex. Assn. Mus. (pres. 1979-81), Western History Assn., Am. Assn. State and Local History, Conf. for Latin Am. History, The Old Santa Fe Assn. (bd. dirs. 1979-81, pres. 1981-84), The Westerners, N.Mex. Endowment for the Humanities (vice chmn. bd. dirs. 1990-91, chmn. 1991—), Hispanic Culture Found. (bd. dirs. 1989—). Office: Muse New Mex Palace of Govs PO Box 2087 Santa Fe NM 87504-2087

CHAVEZ, VICTOR EDWIN, judge; b. L.A., Aug. 28, 1930; s. Raymond C. and Sarah (Baca) C.; children: Victoria, Catherine, Stephanie, Christopher, Robert, Elizabeth. BS, Loyola U., L.A., 1953, JD, 1959. Bar: Calif. 1960. Mem. firm Early, Maslach, Foran and Williams, L.A., 1960-69, Pomerantz and Chavez, L.A., 1969-90; judge L.A. Superior Ct., 1990—, mem. exec. com., 1991, 92, 96, asst. presiding judge, 1997, 98, presiding judge, 1999—. Mem. com. State Bar Examiners, 1972-76; del. to State Bar, 1971-75; bd. regents Loyola Marymount U., 1973-78. 1st lt. USAF, 1953-55. Mem. ABA (standing com. on fed. judiciary 1979-86), L.A. County Bar Assn., Mex.-Am. Bar Assn. (pres. 1971), Am. Bd. Trial Advocates (pres. L.A. chpt. 1979), Law Soc. Office: Dept I 111 N Hill St Los Angeles CA 90012-3117

CHAYKIN, ROBERT LEROY, manufacturing and marketing executive; b. Miami, Fla., May 2, 1944; s. Allan Leroy and Ruth (Levine) C.; m. Patty Jean Patton, Feb. 1971 (div. May 1975); m. Evalyn Marcy Slodzina, Sept. 3, 1989; children: Stephanie Lee, Michelle Alee, Catrina Celia, Ally Sue. BA in Polit. Sci., U. Miami, Fla., 1965, LLB, 1969. Owner, operator Serrating Svcs. Miami, 1969-71, Serrating Svcs. Las Vegas, Nev., 1971-84; pres. Ser-Sharp Mfg., Inc., Las Vegas, 1984—; nat. mktg. dir. Coserco Corp., Las Vegas, 1987—. Patentee in mfg. field. With U.S. Army, 1962. Recipient 2d degree black belt Tae Kwon Do, Profl. Karate Assn., 1954-61. Avocations: travel, camping.

CHAZEN, STEPHEN I. oil company executive; b. Buffalo, Aug. 26, 1946; s. Michael M. and Marcia Chazen; m. Patricia L. Orr, Nov. 20, 1971. AB, Rutgers Coll., 1968; PhD, Mich. State U., 1973; MS, U. Houston, 1977. Lab. mgr. Northrop Svcs., Inc., Houston, 1973-77; dir. project evaluation Columbia Gas Devel. Corp., Houston, 1977-81; v.p. Merrill Lynch, Houston, 1982-86, mng. dir. N.Y.C., 1987-93; exec. v.p. Occidental Petroleum Corp., L.A., 1994—, CFO, exec. v.p. corp. devel. Dir. Premcor Inc., St. Louis, 1996—. Mem. L.A. C. of C. (dir. 1996—). Home: PO Box 427 Pacific Palisades CA 90272-0427 Office: Occidental Petroleum Group 10889 Wilshire Blvd Los Angeles CA 90024-4201

CHEATHAM, ROBERT WILLIAM, lawyer; b. St. Paul, June 4, 1938; s. Robert William and Hildegard Frances Cheatam; m. Kay C. Sarnecki, Mar. 20, 1964; children: Ann Marie, Lynn Marie, Paul William BCE, U. Minn., 1961, JD, 1966. Bar: Calif. 1967, U.S. Dist. Ct. (no. dist.) Calif. 1967. Assoc. Brobeck, Phleger & Harrison, San Francisco, 1967-74, ptnr., 1974-88, Cheatham & Skovronski, San Francisco, 1988-96, Cheatham & Tomlinson, San Francisco, 1996-97, Cassidy, Cheatham, Shimko & Dawson, San Francisco, 1997-2000, Foley & Lardner, 2000—. Speaker on continuing legal edn., San Francisco. Co-author: Calif. Attorneys Guide to Real Estate Syndicates, 1970, Cheatham and Merritt California Real Estate Forms and Commentaries, 1984-90. Mem. ABA, Calif. Bar Assn. Office: Foley & Lardner 1 Maritime Plz Fl 6 San Francisco CA 94111-3416 E-mail: rcheatham@foleylaw.com

CHEDID, JOHN G. bishop; b. Eddid, Lebanon, July 4, 1923; Educated, Sems. in Lebanon and Pontifical Urban Coll., Rome. Ordained priest Roman Cath. Ch., 1951. Titular bishop of Callinico and aux bishop St. Maron of Bklyn., 1981. Office: Our Lady of Lebanon Ch 333 S San Vicente Blvd Los Angeles CA 90048-3313

CHEESEMAN, DOUGLAS TAYLOR, JR. wildlife tour executive, photographer, educator; b. Honolulu, July 16, 1937; s. Douglas Taylor Cheeseman and Myra Bettencourt; m. Gail Macomber, Apr. 7, 1963; children: Rosie M., Ted F. BA, San Jose (Calif.) State U., 1959, MA, 1964. Cert. secondary tchr., Calif. Naturalist Crater Lake (Oreg.) Nat. Park, summers 1959-60; tchr. biology Woodside High Sch., Redwood City, Calif., 1961-65; teaching asst. U. Colo., Boulder, 1966-67; prof. biology De Anza Coll., Cupertino, Calif., 1967—, dir. environ. study area, 1970—, dir. Student Ecology Rsch. Lab., 1990—; pres. Cheeseman's Ecology Safaris, Saratoga, 1981-98; expedition leader Ioffe, Antarctic, 1998—. Instr. wildlife and natural history photography, Saratoga, 1984—; rsch. cooperator Fish and Wilflife Svc., 1972—, guest lectr. numerous conservation groups, No. Calif., 1978—; spkr. on rainforest destruction, zone depletion, global warming; participant, spkr. to save planet; spkr. Calif. Acad. Antarctic Ecology, Am. Acad. African Birds, 1996; expdn. leader Sengey Vavilov, Antarctic, 1994; active in saving flora and fauna in third world; expdn. leader, Antarctica, 1996, ship Alla Tarasova, 1996; expdn. leader in Antarctic, 1998, 2000. Photographs represented in books and on calendars. Recipient Outstanding Svc. and Tchr. award, Pres.'s award De Anza Coll., 1988, Nat. Leadership award U. Tex., Austin, 1989; NSF fellow, 1969, 71; NEDA Title III grantee, 1970. Mem. Ecol. Soc. Am., Am. Ornithologists Union, Am. Soc. Mammalogists, Brit. Trust Ornitology, Brit. Ornithologists Union, AfricanWildlife Soc., Marine Mammal Soc. (founding), Calif. Native Plants Soc., Bay Area Bird Photographers (co-founder), Santa Clara Valley Audubon Soc. (bd. dirs., v.p., program chmn. 1983—), Cooper Soc. Avocations: wildlife rsch. and photography, lecturing on rainforest conservation, studying natural ecosystems, birding. Home: 20800 Kittridge Rd Saratoga CA 95070-6322 Office: De Anza Coll Dept Biology Cupertino CA 95014

CHEIFETZ, LORNA GALE, psychologist; b. Phoenix, Mar. 22, 1953; d. Walter and Ruth Cheifetz. BS, Chapman Coll., Orange, Calif., 1975; D of Psychology, Ill. Sch. Profl. Psychology, 1981. Psychology intern Cook County Hosp., Chgo., 1979-80; clin. psychologist City of Chgo., 1980-84, Phoenix Inst. for Psychotherapy, 1984-87; pvt. practice Phoenix, 1987—. Cons. to judges, attys., cts., 1984—; adj. faculty Met. U., Phoenix, 1984-88, Ill. Sch. Profl. Psychology, 1982-86. Contbr. chpt. to book Listening and Interpreting, 1984; contbg. editor Internat. Jour. Communicative Psychoanalysis and Psychotherapy, 1991-93. Cons., vol. Ariz. Bar Assn. Vol. Lawyer Program, 1985—; co-coord. Psychology Info. Referral Svc., Maricopa County, Ariz., 1984-96. Named Psychologist of Yr. Ariz. Bar Assn., 1987, 95, 99. Mem. APA (activist 1989—), Nat. Register Health Svc. Providers in Psychology. Avocations: parenting. Office: 3930 E Camelback Rd Ste 207 Phoenix AZ 85018-2634

CHEIT, EARL FRANK, economist, educator; b. Mpls., Aug. 5, 1926; s. Morris and Etta (Warshausky) C.; m. June Doris Andrews, Aug. 28, 1950; children: Wendy, David, Ross, Julie. BS, U. Minn., 1947, LLB, 1949, PhD, 1954. Research economist, prof. Sch. Bus. Adminstrn. U. Calif., Berkeley, 1960—, exec. vice chancellor, 1965-69, dean Sch. Bus. Adminstrn., 1976-82, 90-91, dean emeritus Sch. Bus. Adminstrn., 1991—; dir. Inst. Indsl. Rels. Program officer in charge higher edn. and rsch. Ford Found., 1972-73; assoc. dir., sr. rsch. fellow Carnegie Coun. on Policy Studies in Higher Edn., 1973-75; sr. adv. con. Asian-Pacific econ. affairs Asia Found.; dir. CNF Transp., Inc., Shaklee Corp., 1976-99, Simpson Mfg. Corp. Author: The Useful Arts and the Liberal Tradition, 1975, The New Depression in Higher Education, 1971, Foundations and Higher Education, 1979; Editor: The Business Establishment, 1964. Trustee Richmond (Calif.) Unified Sch. Dist., 1961-65, Russell Sage Found., N.Y.C., 1979-89; chmn. State of Calif. Wage Bd. for Agrl. Occupations, 1980-81. Office: U Calif Haas Sch Bus Berkeley CA 94720-0001

CHEITLIN, MELVIN DONALD, physician, educator; b. Wilmington, Del., Mar. 25, 1929; s. James Cheitlin and Mollie Budman; m. Hella Hochschild, July 4, 1952; children: Roger, Kenneth, Julie. AB, Temple U., 1950, MD, 1954. Intern, resident internal medicine Walter Reed Army Med. Ctr., Washington, 1954-59, cardiology fellow, 1959-60, chief cardiology, 1971-74, Madigan Army Med. Ctr., Tacoma, 1960-64, Tripler Army Med. Ctr., Honolulu, 1964-68, Letterman Army Med. Ctr., San Francisco, 1968-71; assoc. chief cardiology San Francisco Gen. Hosp., 1974-91, chief cardiology, 1991-97. Prof. medicine U. Calif., San Francisco, 1974-97, prof. medicine emeritus, 1997—. Author: Clinical Cardiology, 1994; assoc. editor: Cardiology, 1988, rev. edit., 1993. Master ACP; fellow Am. Coll. Cardiology. Democrat. Jewish. Home: 224 Castenada Ave San Francisco CA 94116-1445 Office: San Francisco Gen Hosp 1001 Potrero Ave San Francisco CA 94110-3594 E-mail: mellac@earthlink.net

CHEMLA, DANIEL S. physics educator; Grad., l'Ecole Nat. Super Telecomms., Paris; DSc, U. Paris, 1972. Mem. tech. staff, group leader, dept. head Ctr. Nat. d'Etudes des Telecomms., Berkeley; with AT&T Bell Labs., Holmdel, N.J., 1981-83, head of quantum physics and electonic rsch. dept., 1983-91; prof. physics, dir. materials scis. divsn. Lawrence Berkeley Nat. Lab., U. Calif., Berkeley, 1991—; dir. Advanced Light Source U. Calif., Berkeley, 1998—. Contbr. articles to profl. jours. Fellow IEEE (Quantum Electronics award 1995, Humboldt Rsch. award 1995), Optical Soc. Am. (R. W. Wood prize 1988), Am. Phys. Soc.; mem. NAS. Achievements include research in manybody interactions and quantum size effects in semiconductor nanostructures and detection and spectroscopy of single molecules and single molecular paris. Fax: 510-486-7769. E-mail: dschemla@lbl.gov

CHEN, FRANCIS F. physics and engineering educator; b. Canton, Kwangtung, Republic of China, Nov. 18, 1929; came to U.S., 1936; s. M. Conrad and Evelyn (Chu) C.; m. Edna Lau Chen, Mar. 31, 1956; children: Sheryl F., Patricia A., Robert F. AB, Harvard U., 1950, MA, 1951, PhD, 1954. Research staff mem. Princeton (N.J.) Plasma Physics Lab., 1954-69; prof. elec. engring. UCLA, 1969-94, prof. emeritus, 1994—. Chmn. plasma physics div. Am. Phys. Soc., N.Y.C., 1983. Author: Introduction to Plasma Physics and Controlled Fusion, 1974, 2d edit., 1984; contbr. over 200 articles to sci. jours. Fellow IEEE (Plasma Sci. and Application award 1994), Am. Phys. Soc. (James Clerk Maxwell Prize, 1995); mem. IEEE, Fusion Power Assocs., Am. Vacuum Soc. Avocations: tennis, marathons, photography, backpacking, woodworking. Office: Univ Calif 56-125B Engr Iv Los Angeles CA 90095-0001 E-mail: ffchen@ee.ucla.edu

CHEN, IRVIN SHAO YU, microbiologist, educator; b. Toms River, N.J., Sept. 29, 1955; s. Tseh-An and Cheh-Chen (Chang) C.; m. Diven Sun, June 21, 1981; children: Katrina Nai Ching, Kevin Nai Hong. BA, Cornell U., 1977; PhD, U. Wis., 1981. Asst. prof. UCLA Sch. Medicine, 1984-86, assoc. prof., 1986-90, prof., 1990—. Dir. AIDS Inst. UCLA, 1991—, Core BSL3 SCID-hu Mouse Lab., 1989—, Core Human REtrovirus Lab., 1989—, AIDS Ctr. Virology Lab., 1986, UCLA Sch. of Medicine Core Human Retrovirus Facility, 1989; Wellcome vis. prof. microbiology East Carolina U., 1993; bd. dirs. Arthur Ashe Found. for the Defeat of AIDS. Mem. editl. adv. bd. Oncogene, 1986, Cancer Cells, 1989; mem. editl. bd. AIDS Rsch. and Human Retrovirus, 1990, Jour. of Virology, 1991; contbr. articles to Sci., Nature, Cell; contbr. chpt.: HTLV-1 and HTLV-II in Virology, 1990. Grantee NIH, 1982—, U. Calif. U. Task Force on AIDS, 1986—; recipient Jr. Faculty award Am. Cancer Soc., 1984, Scholar award Leukemia Soc. Am., 1989, Stohlman Scholar award, 1992, Jr. Faculty award Am. Cancer Soc., 1984, Richard F. Dwyer-Eleanor W. Dwyer Award for Exellence Jonsson Comprehensive Cancer Ctr., 1984, Merit award Nat. Cancer Inst. Mem. AAAS, Am. Soc. Microbiology, Jonsson Comprehensive Cancer Ctr. Achievements include patent for retroviral polypeptides associated with human transformation; first to achieve molecular cloning of human T-cell leukemia virus type II, discovery of trans-activation gene as essential gene for HTLV-II, molecular basis for HIV-1 tropism for macrophages. Office: UCLA Sch Medicine Dept Medicine and Immunology 11-934 Factor Los Angeles CA 90024-1678

CHEN, JOSEPH TAO, historian, educator; b. Shanghai, China, Jan. 30, 1925; came to U.S., 1951, naturalized, 1964; s. Hung Chun and Wei Tseng (Sze) C.; m. Lucy Zhu; children: Barbara Joanne, Cynthia Anne. B.A., Coll. Emporia, Kans., 1953; M.A., U. Calif., Berkeley, 1958, Ph.D., 1964. Head librarian Center for Chinese Studies U. Calif., Berkeley, 1963-64; asst. prof. history Calif. State U., Northridge, 1964-68, asso. prof., 1968-71, prof., 1971—; guest lectr. history U. Calif., Santa Barbara, 1970-73, Immaculate Heart Coll., Los Angeles, 1965-79. Author: The May Fourth Movement in Shanghai, 1971, (transl. into Chinese), 1981; contbr. articles to profl. jours. Served with Chinese Navy, 1944-45. Grantee Social Sci. Research Council; Grantee Am. Philos. Soc.; Grantee Calif. State U. Found., Northridge; asso. Danforth Found. Mem. Assn. Asian Studies. Office: Calif State U Dept History Northridge CA 91330-0001

CHEN, STEPHEN SHI-HUA, pathologist, biochemist; b. Taipei, Taiwan, Republic of China, Dec. 25, 1939; came to U.S., 1965; s. Ah-wen and Shun (Pan) C.; m. Hsin-Hsin Yii, July 5, 1969; children: Peter T., Margaret T. MD, Nat. Taiwan U., 1964; PhD, U. Pitts, 1972. Diplomate Am. Bd. of Pathology. Asst. prof. pathology U. Pitts., 1972-76; staff pathologist Presbyn. Hosp., Pitts., 1973-76; asst. prof. pathology dept. Stanford U., Palo Alto, Calif., 1976-80, clin. assoc. prof. pathology dept., 1980-96, clin. prof., 1996—; staff pathologist Veterans Affairs Med. Ctr., Palo Alto, 1976—. Contbr. articles to Jour. Cellular Physiology, Jour. Chromatography, Clinica Chimca Acta. Fellow Coll. Am. Pathologists; mem. Am. Soc. Investigative Pathology, U.S. and Can. Acad. Pathology Inc., Am. Soc. Clin. Pathologists, Am. Soc. Cytopathology. Achievements include chromatography of phospholipids. Office: Vets Affairs Med Ctr 113 3801 Miranda Ave Palo Alto CA 94304-1207

CHEN, TU, computer executive; b. I-Lan, Taiwan, Republic of China, Mar. 19, 1935; s. Wen-Fang and Ye-Wo (Chu) C.; m. Pi-Fang Chen, Sept. 10, 1961; children: Glenn K., John K. BS, Cheng Kung U., Tainan, Taiwan, 1958; MS, U. Minn., 1964, PhD, 1967. Staff engr. IBM Corp., Endicott, N.Y., 1967-68; prin. scientist Northrop Corp., Hawthorn, Calif., 1968-71, Xerox Corp., Palo Alto, 1971-83; founder Komag, Inc., Milpitas, 1983—, also chmn. bd. dirs. Chmn. program session 3M Corp., Dallas, 1979, 80, Intermag., 1983. Contbr. articles to profl. jours. Bd. dirs. Taiwan Tribune, N.Y., 1982—. Mem. IEEE, Am. Chem. Soc., Materials Research Soc., Am. Crystal Growth Soc. (exec. com. No. Calif. chpt. 1975-76), World Fedn. Taiwanese Assocs. (pres. 1983—), Taiwanese Assn. Am., No. Calif. Taiwanese Assn. Democrat. Avocations: IEEE, Am. Chem. Soc., Materials Research Soc., Am. Crystal Growth Soc. (exec. com. No. Calif. chpt. 1975-76). Home: 18225 Gregory Pl Monte Sereno CA 95030-2137 Office: Komag Inc 1710 Automation Pkwy San Jose CA 95131-1873

CHEN, WAI-FAH, civil engineering educator; b. Chekiang, China, Dec. 23, 1936; m. Lily; children: Eric, Arnold, Brian. BS, Cheng-Kung U., 1959; MS, Lehigh U., 1963; PhD, Brown U., 1966. From asst. prof. to prof. civil engring. Lehigh U., 1966-76; prof. civil engring. Purdue U., Lafayette, Ind., 1976-92, head structural engring., 1980-99, George E. Goodwin disting. prof., 1992-99; dean Coll. Engring. U. Hawaii, Honolulu, 1999—. Cons. Exxon Products, 1979—, Karagozian & Case Structural Engrs., 1985—, Ga. Tech., 1987—, Skidmore, Owings & Merrill, 1987, World Bank, 1988—. Editor-in-chief: The Civil Engineering Handbook, 1995, The Handbook of Structural Engineering, 1997, Bridge Engineering Handbook, 1999, Earthquake Engineering Handbook, 2001. Mem. ASCE (hon.), Internat. Assn. Bridge & Structural Engring., Strucural Stability Rsch. Coun., Am. Acad. Mech., Am. Concrete Inst., Am. Inst. Steel Constrn., Nat. Acad. Engring., Academia Sinica. Office: U Hawaii Coll Engring 2540 Dole St Honolulu HI 96822-2303

CHEN, WAI-KAI, electrical engineering and computer science educator, consultant; b. Nanking, China, Dec. 23, 1936; came to U.S., 1959; s. You-Chao and Shui-Tan (Shen) C.; m. Shirley Shiao-Ling, Jan. 13, 1939; children— Jerome, Melissa BS in Elec. Engring., Ohio U., 1960, MS in Elec. Engring., 1961; PhD in Elec. Engring., U. Ill., Urbana, 1964. Asst. prof. Ohio U., 1964-67, assoc. prof., 1967-71, prof., 1971-78, disting. prof., 1978-81; prof., head dept. elec. engring. and computer sci. U. Ill., Chgo., 1981-2001; vis. assoc. prof. Purdue U., 1970-71; v.p. for acad. affairs Internat. Technol. U., 2000—. Hon. prof. Tianjing U., Peoples Republic of China, 1990, Beijin U. of Posts and Telecomms., Beijing U. of Aeronautics and Astronautics, 1992. Author: Applied Graph Theory, 1970, Theory and Design of Broadband Matching Networks, 1976, Applied Graph Theory: Graphs and Electrical Networks, 1976, Active Network and Feedback Amplifier Theory, 1980, Linear Networks and Systems, 1983, Passive and Active Filters: Theory and Implementations, 1986, The Collected Papers of Professor Wai-Kai Chen, 1987, Broadband Matching: Theory and Implementations, 1988, Theory of Nets, 1990, Linear Networks and Systems: Computer-Aided Solutions and Implementations, 1990, Active Network Analysis, 1991, Modern Network Analysis, 1992, Computer-Aided Design of Comm. Networks World Scientific, 2000; editor: Brooks/Cole Series in Electrical Engineering, 1982-84; editor in chief Advanced Series in Elec. and Computer Engring., World Sci. Pub. Co., Singapore, 1986—, Jour. Circuits, Systems and Computers, 1989—, The Circuits and Filters Handbook, 1995, The VLSI Handbook, 2000, The Electrical Engineering Handbook, 1998—, Imperial Coll. Press, 1998—, others; editor The VLSI Series, 2000—; assoc. editor: Jour. Circuits, Systems and Signal Processing, 1981—; editor in charge Advanced Series in Circuits and Systems, World Scientific Publ. Co., 1991—; sect. editor Encyclopedia of Physical Science & Technology, 1998—. Recipient Lester R. Ford award Math. Assn. Am., 1967, Baker Fund award Ohio U., 1974, 78, Disting. Accomplishment award Chinese Acad. & Profl. Assn. in Mid-Am., 1985, disting. Guest Prof. award Chuo U., Tokyo, 1987, Outstanding Service award Chinese Acad. & Profl. assn. in Mid-Am., 1988, Outstanding Achievement award Mid-Am. Chinese Sci. & Tech. Assn, 1988, disting. alumnus award Electrical and Computer Engring. Dept. Alumni Assn. U. Ill. Urbana-Champaign, 1988, Alexander von Humboldt award Alexander von Humboldt Stiftung, Fed. Republic of Germany, 1985, Rsch. award U. Ill. Chgo. Coll. Engring., 2000, hon. prof. award Nanjing Inst. of Technology and Zhejing U., Peoples Republic of China, 1985, The Northeast U. Tech., East China Inst. Tech., Nanjing Inst. of Posts & Telecommunications, AnHui U., Chengdu Inst. Radio Engring., Wuhan Univ.; Research Inst. fellow Ohio U., 1972, Japan Soc. for Promotion of Sci., 1986, Sr. U. Scholar award U. Ill., 1986, Ohio U. Alumni Medal Merit for Disting. Achievement in Engring. Edn., 1987, hon. prof. award Hangzhu U. of Electronic Tech., Peoples Republic of China, 1990, Disting. Prof. award Internat. Technol. U., 1995. Fellow IEEE (Circuits and Sys. Soc. Meritorious Svc. award

1997, Edn. award 1998, Golden Jubilee medal 2000, Third Millennium medal 2000), AAAS; mem. NSPE, IEEE Cirs. and Sys. Soc. (adminstrv. com. 1985-87, exec. v.p. 1987, assoc. editor Trans. on Cirs. and Sys. 1977-79, editor 1991-93, pres.-elect 1993, pres. 1994), Md.-Am. Chinese Sci. and Tech. Assn. (bd. dirs. 1984-86, 89-93, pres. 1991-92), Chinese Acad. and Profl. Assn. Mid-Am. (advisor to bd. dirs. 1984-89, pres. 1986-87), Soc. Indsl. and Applied Math., Assn. Computing Machinery, Tensor Soc. Gt. Britain, Sigma Xi (sec.-treas. Ohio U. chpt. 1981), Phi Kappa Phi, Eta Kappa Nu. Office: Internat Technol U 1650 Warburton Ave Santa Clara CA 95050-3714

CHENEY, JAMES ADDISON, civil engineering educator; b. Los Angeles, Feb. 2, 1927; s. Burton Howard and Esther Jesse (Dumaresq) C.; m. Frankyee Jane Jackson, June, 23, 1951 (dec. Oct. 1966); children: John Addison, Linanne Dando, Matthew Jackson, Sarah Allan, Sharla Ryan, Jennifer Dumaresq; m. Barbara Louise Chadwick, June 1967 (div. Feb. 1987); children: Michael Chadwick, David Grant; m. Elaine Disbrow Barratt, Apr. 1988. BS, UCLA, 1951, MS, 1953; PhD, Stanford U., 1963. Registered profl. civil engr., Calif. Assoc. engr. L.T. Evans, Foundation Engrs., Los Angeles, 1953-55; staff engr. Lockheed Missile and Space Co., Sunnyvale, Calif., 1955-65; prof. civil engring. U. Calif., Davis, 1962-91, prof. emeritus civil engring., 1991—. Contbr. over 50 articles to scientific jours. Served with USN, 1944-45. Fellow ASCE; mem. Alpha Sigma Phi. Republican. Episcopalian. Home: 418 Anza Ave Davis CA 95616-0404 Office: U Calif Dept Civil Engring Davis CA 95616 E-mail: jacheney@ucdavis.edu

CHENG, TSEN-CHUNG, electrical engineering educator; b. Shanghai, Peoples Republic of China, Dec. 24, 1944; s. Yik Yu and Shun Lan (Tsui) C.; m. Doris Tin Gen Lee, Aug. 25, 1974; 1 child, Jason. BS, MIT, 1969, MSEE, 1970, ScD, 1974. Asst. prof. U. So. Calif., Los Angeles, 1974-80, assoc. prof., 1980-84, Lloyd F. Hunt prof., dir. electric power program, 1984—. Pres. T.C. Cheng ScD Inc., San Marino, Calif., 1981—; cons. Los Angeles Dept. Water and Power, 1984—, So. Calif. Edison Co., 1982—, Pacific Gas & Electric Co., San Francisco, 1982—, and numerous other pub. utilities and elec. and electronic mfrs. worldwide. Patentee in field; author over 120 publs. Recipient Outstanding Elec. Engring. faculty award U. So. Calif., 1976, Engring. Service award U. So. Calif., 1981. Fellow IEEE (relay com. award 1986, Best Paper award 1988), Sigma Xi, Eta Kappa Nu, Tau Beta Pi. Office: Univ of So Calif Phe 634 Dept Ee Ep # 634 Los Angeles CA 90089-0001 E-mail: tccheng@socal.rr.com

CHENG, WAN-LEE, mechanical engineer, industrial technology educator; b. Yi-Hsin, Chaing-Su, Republic of China, Dec. 28, 1945; came to U.S., 1971; s. Teh-Chih and Mei-Nung (Shih) C.; m. Viki Shu-Whei Lu, Dec. 16, 1972; children: Julie Wheichung, Paul Yichung, Lisa Yenchung. BS, Chung Yuan U., Taiwan, 1969; MEd, Sul Ross State U., 1972; PhD, Iowa State U., 1976. Mech. engr. Taiwan Power Co., Taipei, 1970-71; instr. Iowa State U., Ames, 1974-76; asst. prof., then prof. U. N.D., Grand Forks, 1976-85; prof., chmn. dept. design and industry San Francisco State U., 1985-2000, assoc. dean Coll. Creative Arts, 2000—. Cons. High-Tech Mobile Lab., N.D. Vocat. Edn. Dept., Bismarck, 1984-85; vis. prof. Nat. Sci. Coun. and Chung Yuan U., Taiwan, Republic of China, 1990-91; chief adminstrv. cons. Coll. of Design, Chung Yuan Christian U., Taiwan, 1994-95, dean. Author computer software; contbr. articles to profl. jours.; mem. rev. bd. Jour. Indsl. Tech., 1986— Session elder 1st Presbyn. Ch., Grand Forks, 1984-85; session elder Lakeside Presbyn. Ch., 1989-91. Recipient Indsl. Arts Profl. Devel. award N.D. Indsl. Arts Assn., Bismarck, 1985, Outstanding Teaching and Faculty Devel. award Burlington No. Found., Grand Forks, 1985, Outstanging Prof. Indsl. Tech. award Nat. Assn. Indsl. Tech., 1992; 10 grants U. N.D., 1979-85. Mem. Soc. Mfg. Engrs. (sr.), Chinese Inst. Engrs. (v.p. 1993), Chung Yuan Alumni Assn. No. Calif. (pres. San Francisco 1987-88), Chinese Am. Econ. and Tech. Devel. Assn. (pres. 1997-99), Joint Alumni Assn. Chinese Univs. and Colls. No. Calif. (pres. San Francisco, 1988-89), Phi Kappa Phi, Epsilon Pi Tau (trustee Gamma Gamma chpt. Grand Forks 1984-85, Laureate award Beta Beta chpt. San Francisco 1991, Disting. Svc. award 2000). Office: San Francisco State Univ Coll Creative Arts 1600 Holloway Ave San Francisco CA 94132-1722 E-mail: wlcheng@sfsu.edu

CHENOWETH-HAGE, HELEN P. former congresswoman; b. Topeka, Jan. 27, 1938; 2 children. Attended, Whitworth Coll., 1975-79; cert. in law office mgmt., U. Minn., 1974; student, Rep. Nat. Com. Mgmt. Coll., 1977. Bus. mgr. Northside Med. Ctr., 1964-75; state exec. dir. Idaho Rep. Party, 1975-77; chief of staff Congressman Steve Symms, 1977-78; campaign mgr. Symms for Congress Campaign, 1978, Leroy for Gov., 1985-86; v.p. Consulting Assocs., Inc., 1978—; mem. U.S. Congress from Idaho, Washington, 1995-2001. Mem. agriculture, resources, vets. affairs coms.; bd. dirs. Ctr. Study of Market Alternatives. Deacon Capitol Christian Ctr., Boise.*

CHER, (CHERILYN SARKISIAN), singer, actress; b. El Centro, Calif., May 20, 1946; d. Gilbert and Georgia LaPiere; m. Sonny Bono, Oct. 27, 1964 (div.); 1 child, Chastity; m. Gregg Allman, June 1975 (div.); 1 child, Elijah Blue. Student drama coach, Jeff Corey. Singer with husband as team, Sonny and Cher, 1964-74; star TV shows: Cher, 1975-76, The Sonny and Cher Show, 1976-77; concert appearances with husband, 1977, numerous recs., TV, concert and benefit appearances with Sonny Bono; TV appearances, ABC-TV, 1978, appearance with Sonny Bono in motion pictures, Good Times, 1966, Chastity, 1969; film appearances include Silkwood, 1983, Mask, 1985 (Best Actress, Cannes Internat. Film Festival), The Witches of Eastwick, 1987, Suspect, 1987, Moonstruck (Golden Globe award 1988, Acad. award for best actress 1988), 1987, Mermaids, 1990, The Player, 1992, Pret-a-Porter, 1994, Faithful, 1996, Tea With Mussolini, 1999; TV movies; If These Walls Could Talk, 1996, Happy Birthday Elizabeth: A Celebration of Life, 1997, AFI's 100 Years...100 Movies, 1998; helped form rock band, Black Rose, 1979; recorded albums Black Rose, 1980, Cher, 1987, Heart of Stone, 1989 (Double Platinum and 3 Gold Singles), Love Hurts, 1991, It's A Man's World, 1996, The Casablanca Years, 1996, Believe, 1998 (Grammy award best dance recording 1999). Office: c/o ICM 8942 Wilshire Blvd Beverly Hills CA 90211-1934 also: Reprise Records 3000 Warner Blvd Burbank CA 19010-4694

CHERN, SHIING-SHEN, mathematics educator; b. Kashing, Chekiang, China, Oct. 26, 1911; s. Lien Ching and Mei (Han) C.; m. Shih-ning Chern, July 28, 1939; children: Paul, May B.S., Nankai U., Tientsin, China, 1930; hon. dr., Nankai U., 1985; M.S., Tsing Hua U., Peiping, 1934; D.Sc., U. Hamburg, Germany, 1936, D.Sc. (hon.), 1972, U. Chgo., , 1969, SUNY-Stony Brook, 1985; LL.D. honoris causa, Chinese U., Hong Kong, 1969; Dr. Math (hon.), Eidgenossische Technische Hochschule, Zurich, Switzerland, 1982; DSc (hon.), U. Notre Dame, 1994. Prof. math. Nat. Tsing Hua U., China, 1937-43; mem. Inst. Advanced Study, Princeton, N.J., 1943-45; acting dir. Inst. Mathematics, Academia Sinica, China, 1946-48; prof. math. U. Chgo., 1949-60, U. Calif., Berkeley, 1960-79, prof. emeritus, 1979—; dir. Math. Scis. Rsch. Inst., 1981-84, dir. emeritus, 1984—; dir. Inst. Mathematics, Tianjin, P.R., China. Hon. prof. various fgn. univs.; Recipient Chauvenet prize Math. Assn. Am., 1970, Nat. Medal of Sci., 1975, Wolf prize Israel, 1983-84 Fellow Third World Acad. Sci. (founding mem. 1985); mem. NAS, Am. Math. Soc. (Steele prize 1983), Am. Acad. Arts and Scis., N.Y. Acad. Scis. (hon. life), Am. Philos. Soc., Indian Math. Soc. (hon.), Brazilian Acad. Scis. (corr.), Academia Sinica, Royal Soc. London (fgn.), Academia Peloritana (corr. mem. 1986), London Math. Soc. (hon.)., Acad. des sciences Paris (fgn. mem.), Acad. der Lincei Rome (stranieri), Russian Acad. Scis. (fgn.). Home: 8336 Kent Ct El Cerrito CA 94530-2548 Office: Univ Calif Berkeley Dept Of Mathematics Berkeley CA 94720-0001

CHERNESKY, JOHN JOSEPH, JR. retired career officer, healthcare executive; b. Hartford, Conn., July 6, 1944; s. John Joseph and Mary (Milewski) C.; m. Patricia Ann Wolf, Oct. 9, 1967 (div. June, 1988); m. Melinda Anne Brown, Aug. 31, 1991; children: Karen Elizabeth, John David. BS, Miami U., 1967. Commd. ensign USN, 1967, advanced through grades to capt., 1985; flag lt., aide Commander Submarines Pacific, Pearl Harbor, Hawaii, 1971-73; engr. officer USS Blueback, Pearl Harbor, 1973-75; exec. officer USS Bonefish, Pearl Harbor, 1975-77; head officer retention Bur. Naval Personnel, Washington, 1977-79; exec. officer USS Dale, commanding officer USS Patterson Mayport, Fla., 1979-83; exec. officer USS Iowa, Norfolk, Va., 1983-85; dir. navy programs Office of Legisl. Affairs, Washington, 1985-88; commanding officer USS Missouri, Long Beach, Calif., 1988-90; ret., 1990; exec. dir. Cedars-Sinai Comprehensive Cancer Ctr., L.A., 1994-97; sr. v.p., chief info. officer Salick Health Care, Inc., L.A., 1997-99, exec. v.p. N.Y. ops., 1998-99, exec. v.p. ops., 1999-2000, COO, 2000—. Decorated Legion of Merit. Mem. Am. Legion, Delta Tau Delta. Republican. Roman Catholic. Avocation: sailing, golfing. Office: 8201 Beverly Blvd Los Angeles CA 90048-4505 E-mail: jcher@salick.com

CHERNIN, PETER, motion picture company executive; Pres. entertainment group Fox Broadcasting Co., L.A.; former chmn. Twentieth Century Fox Film Corp., Beverly Hills, Calif.; now chmn., CEO The Fox Group, Beverly Hills; pres., COO News Corp., 1996—. Office: Fox Inc Rm 5080 10201 W Pico Blvd Bldg 100 Los Angeles CA 90064-2606

CHERNY, ROBERT WALLACE, history educator; b. Marysville, Kans., Apr. 4, 1943; s. Clarence L. and Lena M. (Hobbs) C.; m. Rebecca Ellen Marshall, June 11, 1967; 1 child, Sarah Catherine. BA with distinction, U. Nebr., 1965; MA, Columbia U., 1967, PhD, 1972. Instr. history San Francisco State U., 1971-72, asst. prof., 1972-77, assoc. prof., 1977-81, prof., 1981—, assoc. dean behavioral and social scis., 1984, acting dean behavioral and social scis., 1985, chair history dept., 1987-92. Disting. Fulbright lectr. Moscow State U., 1996; vis. rsch. scholar U. Melbourne, 1997; cons. in field. Author: A Righteous Cause: The Life of William Jennings Bryan, 1985, rev. edit., 1994, Populism, Progressivism and the Transformation of Nebraska Politics, 1981, American Politics in the Gilded Age, 1869-1868, 1997; co-author: (with William Issel) San Francisco, 1865-1932, 1986, San Francisco: Presidio, Port and Pacific Metropolis, 1981, (with Carol Berkin, Christopher L. Miller, James L. Gormly) Making America: A History of the United States, 1995, 2d edit., 1999. Woodrow Wilson fellow, 1965-66, Woodrow Wilson dissertation fellow, 1969, NEH fellow, 1992-93. Mem. Am. Hist. Assn., Orgn. Am. Historians, S.W. Labor Studies Assn. (pres. 1982-86), Calif. Hist. Soc., Soc. Historians of Gilded Age and Progressive Era (pres. 1995), Nebr. State Hist. Soc. Democrat. Office: San Francisco State U Dept of History 1600 Holloway Ave San Francisco CA 94132-1722

CHEROUTES, MICHAEL LOUIS, lawyer; b. Chgo., Apr. 27, 1940; s. Louis Samuel Cheroutes and Maria Jane (Zimmerman) Dodd; m. Trisha Flynn, Oct. 30, 1965; children: Michael Louis Jr., Trisha Francesca, Matthew Dodd. BA, Harvard U., 1962; LLB, Stanford U., 1965. Bar: Colo. 1965. Assoc., then ptnr. Sherman & Howard, Denver, 1965-85; chief of staff to Rep. Patricia A. Shroeder U.S. Ho. of Reps., Washington, 1972-74; ptnr. Davis, Graham & Stubbs, Denver, 1985-93, Hogan & Hartson, Denver, 1993—. Contbr. articles to profl. jours. Mem. Colo. Commn. on Higher Edn., 1988-91, chmn., 1989-91; mem. state bd. Gt. Outdoors Colo. Trust Fund, 1996-97. Mem. ABA, Colo. Bar Assn., Nat. Assn. Bond Lawyers. Avocation: sailing. Home: 2625 E Cedar Ave Denver CO 80209-3205 Office: Hogan & Hartson 1200 17th St Ste 1500 Denver CO 80202-5840

CHERRY, JAMES DONALD, pediatrician; b. Summit, N.J., June 10, 1930; s. Robert Newton and Beatrice (Wheeler) C.; m. Jeanne M. Fischer, June 19, 1954; children— James S., Jeffrey D., Susan J., Kenneth C. BS, Springfield (Mass.) Coll., 1953; MD, U. Vt., 1957; MSc in Epidemiology, London Sch. Hygiene and Tropical Medicine, 1983. Diplomate Am. Bd. Pediat., Am. Bd. Pediat. Infectious Diseases. Intern, then resident in pediat. Boston City Hosp., 1957-59; resident in pediat. Kings County Hosp., Bklyn., 1959-60; rsch. fellow in medicine Harvard U. Med. Sch.-Thorndike Meml. Lab., Boston City Hosp., 1961-62; instr. pediatrics U. Vt. Coll. Medicine, also asst. attending physician Mary Fletcher DeGoesbriand Meml. hosps., Burlington, Vt., 1960-61; asst. prof., then assoc. prof. pediat. U. Wis. Med. Sch., Madison, 1963-66; assoc. attending physician Madison Gen., U. Wis. hosps., 1963-66; dir. John A. Hartford Rsch. Lab., Madison Gen. Hosp., 1963-66. Mem. faculty St. Louis U. Med. Sch., 1966-73, prof. pediatrics, 1969-73, vice chmn. dept., 1970-73; mem. staff Cardinal Glennon Meml. Hosp. Children, St. Louis U. Hosp., 1966-73; prof. pediatrics, chief divsn. infectious diseases UCLA Med. Ctr. UCLA Sch. Medicine, 1973—; acting chmn. dept. pediatrics UCLA Med. Ctr., 1977-79; attending physician, chmn. infection control com. UCLA Med. Ctr., 1975-93; cons. Project Head Start; vis. worker dept. cmty. medicine Middlesex Hosp. and Med. Sch., London, 1982-83; vis. worker Common Cold Rsch. Unit, 1969-70; mem. immunization adv. com. Los Angeles County Dept. Health Svcs., 1978—. Co-editor Textbook of: Pediatric Infectious Diseases, 1981, 2nd edit., 1987, 4th edit., 1998; assoc. editor: Clin. Infectious Diseases, 1990-99; Am. regional editor: Vaccine, 1991-2000; author numerous papers in field; editl. reviewer profl. jours. Bd. govs. Alexander Graham Bell Internat. Parents Orgn., 1967-69. With USAR, 1958-64. John and Mary R. Markle scholar acad. medicine, 1964 Mem. AAAS, APHA, Am. Acad. Pediat. (mem. exec. com. Calif. chpt. 2 1975-77, mem. com. infectious diseases 1977-83, assoc. editor 19th Red Book 1982), Am. Soc. Microbiology, Am. Fedn. Clin. Rsch., Soc. Pediat. Rsch., Infectious Diseases Soc. Am., Am. Epidemiol. Soc., Am. Pediat. Soc., L.A. Pediat. Soc., Internat. Orgn. Mycoplasmologists, Am. Soc. Virology, Soc. Hosp. Epidemiologists Am., Pediat. Infectious Diseases Soc. (pres. 1989-91), Alpha Omega Alpha. Office: UCLA Sch Medicine Dept Pediatrics Rm 22-442 10833 Le Conte Ave Los Angeles CA 90095-3075 E-mail: jcherry@mednet.ncln.edu

CHESBRO, WESLEY, state senator; b. 1952; m. Cindy Chesbro; children: Collin, Alan. Student, Humboldt State U.; BA in Orgnl. Behavior, U. San Francisco. Mem. Calif. State Senate, chair standing com. on revenue and taxation, chair select com. on Calif.'s wine industry, chair select com. on devel. disabilities and mental health, mem. budget and fiscal rev. com., edn. com., mem. environ. quality com., govtl. orgn. com., VA com. Founding mem. Calif. INtegrated Waste Mgmt. Bd., 1990-98; mem. Humboldt County Bd. Suprs., 1980-90; mem. Arcata City Coun., 1974-80. Democrat. Office: 50 D St Ste 120A Santa Rosa CA 95404-6535 also: State Capitol Rm 3070 Sacramento CA 95814

CHESNE, EDWARD LEONARD, physician; b. Chgo., June 11, 1931; m. Carol Chesne; children: Lauren, Christopher, Greig. BA, U. Chgo., 1950; MD, Northwestern U. Med. Sch., Chgo., 1955. Lic. phys., Ill., Calif., Hawaii, Guam, Saipan. Capt. U.S. Army, 1957. Fellow Am. Coll. Physicians, Am. Coll. Cardiology, Coun. Clin. Cardiology, Am. Heart Assn. Office: 1380 Lusitana St Ste 1002 Honolulu HI 96813-2461

CHESNEY, MAXINE M. judge; b. 1942; BA, U. Calif., Berkeley, 1964, JD, 1967. Trial atty. Office Dist. Atty., San Francisco, 1968-69, sr. trial atty., 1969-71, prin. trial atty., 1971-76, head atty., 1976, asst. chief dep., 1976-79; judge San Francisco Mcpl. Ct., 1979-83, San Francisco Superior Ct., 1983-95, U.S. Dist. Ct. (no. dist.) Calif., San Francisco, 1995—. Bd. dirs. San Francisco Child Abuse Coun., 1976-79, Hosp. Audiences, 1978-81. Mem. Fed. Judges Assn., Nat. Assn. Women Judges, Edward J. McFetridge Am. Inn of Ct., U.S. Assn. Constl. Law, Queen's Bench, Ninth Jud. Cir. Hist. Soc. Office: US Dist Ct No Dist Calif PO Box 36060 450 Golden Gate Ave San Francisco CA 94102-3661

CHESSER, AL H. union official; b. Pettis County, Mo., Feb. 26, 1914; s. James A. and Mary Pearl (Dirck) C.; m. Rose Burns. Grad. high sch. Brakeman-condr. Santa Fe Ry., Amarillo, Tex., 1941; sec.-treas., legis. rep. Brotherhood R.R. Trainmen, Local 608, 1945-56; sec. Tex. Legis. Bd., 1952-56, legis. dir., 1956-61; nat. legis. rep. Washington, 1961-71, United Transp. Union, 1969-71, pres., 1971-79, pres. emeritus, 1979—; v.p., mem. exec. council AFL-CIO; chmn. Congress of Ry. Unions, 1972—. Chmn. Amarillo Civil Svc. Commn., 1950-56, Amarillo Labor Polit. Council, 1954-56; mem. Gov.'s Indsl. Commn., 1957-61, Fed. Task Force on R.R. Safety, 1964-69, Pres.'s Consumers Adv. Council, 1964-68, Greater Cleve. Growth Bd. and Transp. Study Group of Domestic Affairs Task Force, 1973— ; mem. adv. panel U.S. Congress Office of Tech. Assessment, 1976; hon. co-chmn. Internat. Guiding Eyes, Inc., 1976 Author: Transportation and Energy, 1975, Economic Advantages of Transporting Coal by Rail, 1976. Bd. dirs. Dem. Nat. Com., 1973; mem. transp. adv. com. FEA, 1975; co-chmn. R.R. Safety Rsch. Bd., 1975; chmn. bd. CSC; bd. dirs. Amarillo Community Chest, Maverick Boys Club; hon. staff mem. U.S. Army Transp. Sch. Named to Smith-Cotton H.S. Hall of Fame, Sedalia, Mo.; United Transp. Union bldg. named Al H. Chesser Bldg. in his honor; recipient Eugene V. Debs award, 2001. Mem. Nat. Def. Execs. Res., Masons, Shriners. Office: United Transp Union Sundance Hills 10437 E Dorado Pl Greenwood Village CO 80111-3711

CHESTER, MARVIN, physics educator; b. N.Y.C., Dec. 29, 1930; s. Herman and Sadye C.; m. Ruth Chester (div. 1960); 1 child, Karen; m. Sandra Chester (div. 1963); 1 child, Lisa; m. Elfi Bollert, July 30, 1977; children: Chaim Peter, Sadye Vera. BS, CCNY, 1952; PhD, Calif. Inst. Tech., 1961. Prof. physics U. Calif., L.A., 1961-92, prof. emeritus, 1992—. Sr. rsch. fellow U. Sussex, Eng., 1973. Author: Primer of Quantum Mechanics, 1987; contbr. articles to profl. jours. Recipient Alexander von Humboldt award, Von Humboldt Stifftung, 1974-75. Mem. Am. Phys. Soc. Office: UCLA Dept Physics Los Angeles CA 90024

CHESTON, MICHAEL GALLOWAY, airport executive; m. Laurie; children: Kenny, Geoffrey. AA in Gen. Edn., Catonsville (Md.) C.C., 1975; BA in English, St. Mary's Coll. of Md., 1977; MBA in Real Estate Devel., George Washington U., 1994. Cert. air traffic control specialist. Corporate recruiting supr., computer resource acquisition specialist Electronic Data Sys., Inc., Bethesda, Md., 1984-86; dir. European ops. Corporate Devel. Sys., Inc., Wellesley, Mass., 1986-87; acting mgr., ops. officer, bus. analyst Met. Washington Airports Authority, Alexandria, Va., 1987-93; airport mgr. Portland (Oreg.) Internat. Airport, 1993—, gen. mgr. ops., maintenance and aviation. Comdr. USMC, 1977-84; maj., USMCR. Mem. Am. Assn. Airports Execs., Airports Coun. Internat., Portland Highland Games Assn. (pub. safety mgr.), Marine Corps Assn., Marine Corps Res. Officers Assn. (chpt. pres.). Office: Portland Internat Airport PO Box 3529 Portland OR 97208-3529

CHEUNG, JOHN B. research and development executive; b. 1943; COO Quest Integrated, Inc., Kent, Wash.; pres. Flow Dril Corp., Kent. Office: Flow Dril Corp 21411 72nd Ave S Kent WA 98032-2416

CHEVALIER, PAUL EDWARD, retired retail executive, lawyer; b. N.Y.C., Jan. 30, 1939; s. Arthur and Grace (Eaton) C.; m. Maggie Helfer, Dec. 29, 1996; 1 child, Marc. BA, Columbia U., 1960, LLB, MBA, Columbia U., 1966; AMP, Harvard U., 1979. Bar: Ill. 1968, U.S. Supreme Ct. 1974. Dir. labor rels. Carter Hawley Hale Stores, Inc., L.A., 1972-74, v.p. employee rels., 1974-86, sr. v.p. employee rels., 1986-93; pres. Chevalier Cons. Group, 1993-98. Vice chmn. Western Fed. Credit Union, 1989-93; bd. dirs. Sedona Cultural Park. Past pres., bd. dirs. Calif. Employment Law Coun., Sedona Cultural Park; chmn. Art and Culture Commn., City of Sedona, 1999—. Lt. USN, 1960. Mem. Nat. Retail Fedn. (chmn. employee rels. com. 1979-82), Calif. Retail Assn., Harvard Bus. Sch. Assn. (bd. dirs. 1980-90, pres. 1984-85), Harvard Bus. Sch. Alumni Coun., Jonathan Art Found. (chmn. emeritus).

CHEVERS, WILDA ANITA YARDE, former state official and educator; b. N.Y.C. d. Wilsey Ivan and Herbert Lee (Perry) Yarde; m. Kenneth Chevers, May 14, 1950; 1 child, Pamela Anita. BA, CUNY, 1947; MSW, Columbia U., 1959, PhD, 1981. Probation officer, Office Probation for Cts., N.Y.C., 1947-55, supr. probation officer, 1955-65, br. chief, 1965-72, asst. dir. probation, 1972-77, dept. commr. dept. probation, 1978-86; prof. pub. adminstrn. John Jay Coll. Criminal Justice, CUNY, 1986-91. Conf. faculty mem. Nat. Council Juvenile and Family Ct. Judges; mem. faculty N.Y.C. Tech. Coll., Nat. Coll. Juvenile Justice; mem. adv. com. Family Ct., First Dept. Ec. Susan E. Wagner Adv. Bd., 1966-70; sec., bd. dirs. Allen Cmty. Dar Care Ctr., 1971-75; bd. dirs. Allen Sr. Citizens Housing, Queensboro Soc. for Prevention Cruelty to Children; chmn., bd. dirs. Allen Christian Sch., 1987-91; mem. Las Vegas EMA Ryan White Title I Planning Coun., 1998-2000. Named to Hall of Fame, Hunter Coll., 1983. Mem. ABA (assoc.), ASPA (coun.), NASW, N.Y. Acad. Pub. Edn., Nat. Coun. on Crime and Delinquency, Acad. Cert. Soc. Workers, Mid. Atlantic States Conf. on Correcton, Alumni Assn. Colmbia U. Sch. Social Work, NYU Alumni Assn., NAACP, Counselors, Hansel and Gretel Club (pres. Queens, N.Y. 1967-69), Delta Sigma Thera. Home: 9012 Covered Wagon Ave Las Vegas NV 89117-7010

CHEW, GEOFFREY FOUCAR, physicist; b. Washington, June 5, 1924; s. Arthur Percy and Pauline Lisette (Foucar) C.; m. Ruth Wright, June 10, 1945 (dec. Apr. 1971); children— Berkeley, Beverly; m. Denyse Odette Mettel, Dec. 30, 1971; children— Pierre-Yves, Jean-Francois, Pauline BS in Physics, George Washington U., 1944; PhD in Physics, U. Chgo., 1948. Research physicist Los Alamos Sci. Lab., N.Mex., 1944-46; research physicist Lawrence Berkeley Lab., Calif., 1948-49; asst. prof. physics U. Calif., Berkeley, 1949-50; asst. prof., assoc. prof. physics U. Ill., Urbana, 1950-56; prof. physics U. Calif., Berkeley, 1957—, chmn. dept. physics, 1974-78, Miller prof., 1981-82, dean physical scis., 1986-92. Group leader theoretical physics Lawrence Berkeley Lab., Calif., 1964-83; vis. prof. Princeton U., N.J., 1970-71; sci. assoc. CERN, Geneva, 1978-79; vis. prof. U. Paris, 1983. Author: S-Matrix Theory of Strong Interactions, 1961; Analytic S Matrix, 1966; contbr. articles to profl. jours. Chmn. passport com. Fedn. Am. Scientists, Washington, 1951-56 Recipient E.O. Lawrence award AEC, 1969, Disting. Alumni award George Washington U., 1974, Berkeley citation U. Calif., 1991; Churchill Coll. overseas fellow, 1962 Fellow Am. Phys. Soc. (Hughes prize 1962); mem. Nat. Acad. Scis., Am. Acad. Arts and Scis. Home: 10 Maybeck Twin Dr Berkeley CA 94708-2037 Office: Lawrence Berkeley Lab Berkeley CA 94720 E-mail: gfchew@lbl.gov

CHEW, RON ALPHA, museum director; b. Seattle, May 17, 1953; s. Soo Hong and Gam Har (Wee) C.; m. Loan Thi Nguyen. Student, U. Wash., 1972-76. Editor Internat. Examiner, Seattle, 1977-80, 81-88; asst. dir. McKenzie River Gathering Found., Seattle, 1980-81; multicultural program coord. Seattle Cen. C.C., 1988-89; confidential sec. Commn. in Asian Am. Affairs, Seattle, 1989-91; dir. Wing Luke Asian Mus., Seattle, 1991—. Coord. Chinese Oral History Project, Seattle, 1990—. Bd. dirs. Chinese Info. and Svc. Ctr., Seattle, 1991—, Inter-Im Cmty. Devel. Assn., Seattle, 1979—; adv. bd. Northwest Nikkei Newspaper, 1989—; pub. com. Kin On [illegible] media adv. coun. Amerasia Jour., 1988-89; publ. adv. com. Neighborhood House, Seattle, 1988. David Douglas fellow Wash. Hist. Soc., 1993. Mem. Internat. Dist. Econ. Assn. (cmty. svc. award 1988), Western Mus. Assn., Wash. Mus. Assn. (instnl. excellence award 1993), Assn. King County Hist. Orgns. (outstanding exhibit award 1993), Asian Am. Journalist Assn. (co-founder Seattle chpt., treas. 1985-89), Northwest Minority Publishers Assn. (co-founder, sec. 1987-88). Avocations: research of Chinese American history, Seattle's Chinatown. Office: Wing Luke Asian Mus 407 7th Ave S Seattle WA 98104-2948

CHIASSON, WILLIAM B. apparel executive; BA in Antrhopology and Polit. Sci., U. Ariz., 1974; MBA, U. So. Calif., 1976. Sr. v.p. fin. and info. sys. Kraft Foods; sr. v.p., CFO Levi Strauss & Co., San Francisco, 1998—. Mem. AICPA. Office: Levi Strauss & Co 1155 Battery St San Francisco CA 94111

CHIATE, KENNETH REED, lawyer; b. Phoenix, June 24, 1941; s. Mac Arthur and Lillian (Lavin) C.; m. Jeannette Jensen, Aug. 21, 1965; children: Gregory Jensen, Carley MkKay. BA with honors, Claremont Men's Coll., 1963; JD, Columbia U., 1966; postgrad., U. So. Calif. Law Sch., 1967. Bar: Calif. 1967, U.S. Dist. Ct. (cen. dist.) Calif. 1967, Ariz. 1971, U.S. Dist. Ct. Ariz. 1971, U.S. Dist. Ct. (no. Dist.) Calif. 1982. Law clk. presiding justice U.S. Dist. Ariz., 1971; ptnr. Lillick McHose & Charles, L.A., 1971-91, Pillsbury Winthrop, LLP (formerly Pillsbury Madison), L.A., 1991—. Arbitrator Los Angeles Superior Ct. Arbitration Panel, 1979-82; mcpl. ct. judge protem Los Angeles, 1979-81; vice chmn. Los Angeles Open Com., 1969-71. Named among Calif. Lawyers of Yr. 2000, Calif. Mag. Mem. ABA, L.A. County Bar Assn., Calif. State Bar Assn., Ariz. State Bar Assn., Maricopa County Bar Assn., Am. Trial Lawyers Assn., L.A. Bus. Trial Lawyers Assn. Office: Pillsbury Winthrop LLP 725 S Figueroa St Ste 2800 Los Angeles CA 90017-5443 E-mail: kchiate@pillsburywinthrop.com

CHIAVERINI, JOHN EDWARD, construction company executive; b. Providence, Feb. 6, 1924; s. John and Sadie (Ginsberg) C.; m. Cecile Corey, Mar. 31, 1951; children: Caryl Marie, John Michael. Cert. advanced san. engring., U. Ill., 1945; BS in Civil Engring., U. R.I., 1947. Registered profl. engr., Mass., R.I. Project engr. Perini Corp., Hartford, Conn., 1950-51, project mgr., 1951-55, asst. project mgr. Pitts. and Que., 1955-61, v.p. Framingham, Mass., 1965-84, sr. v.p. San Francisco, 1984—; pres., dir. Compania Perini S.A., Colombia, 1961—; v.p., exec. mgr. Perini Yuba Assocs., Marysville, Calif., 1966-70, v.p. Western ops., 1970-78, 79-84, group v.p., 1978-79; sr. v.p. spl. projects Perini Corp., 1984-90, dir., asst. to chmn., 1991—. Mem. U.S. com. Internat. Commn. on Large Dams; bd.dirs. Building Futures Coun., 1990—, vice chmn., 1993, chmn., 1994—; active Civil Engring. Rsch. Found., 1990—, mem. corp. adv. bd., 1992—. Served to 2d lt. USAAF, 1944-46. Recipient Golden Beaver award Supervision, San Francisco Bay Area Coun. Boy Scouts Am., 1989, Good Scout award, 1989; named to R.I. Engring. Hall of Fame, 1997. Fellow ASCE (mem. exec. com. constrn. divsn., vice chmn. 1994-95, chmn. 1995—), Soc. Am. Mil. Engrs. (Acad. of Fellows 1997, pres. San Francisco post 1991-92, bd. dirs.); mem. NSPE (life), Am. Arbitrators Assn., Calif. Soc. Profl. Engrs., Beavers (bd. dirs.), Moles, Commonwealth Club of Calif., KC, Rotary. Democrat. Roman Catholic. Home: 37 Dutch Valley Ln San Anselmo CA 94960-1045 Office: Perini Corp 101 Spear St Ste 222 San Francisco CA 94105-1554 E-mail: ceejayiii3@home.com, ceejayIII@aol.com

CHICAGO, JUDY, artist; b. Chgo., July 20, 1939; d. Arthur M. and May (Levenson) Cohen. BA, UCLA, 1962, MA, 1964; hon. doctorate, Russell Sage Coll., 1992, Lehigh U., 2000, Smith Coll., 2000. Co-founder Feminist Studio Workshop, L.A., 1973, Through the Flower Corp., 1977; vis. artist Ind. U., fall 1999, Duke U. fall 2000, U. N.C., fall 2000. Author: Through the Flower: My Struggle as a Woman Artist, 1975, The Dinner Party: A Symbol of Our Heritage, 1979, Embroidering Our Heritage: The Dinner Party Needlework, 1980, The Birth Project, 1985, Holocaust Project: From Darkness Into Light, 1993, Beyong the Flower: The Autobiography of a Feminist Artist, 1996, The Dinner Party, 1996, Women and Art: Contested Territory, 1999; one-woman shows include, Pasadena (Calif.) Mus. Art, 1969, Jack Glenn Gallery, Corona del Mar, Calif., 1972, JPL Fine Arts, London, 1975, Quay Ceramics, San Francisco, 1976, San Francisco Mus. Modern Art, 1979, Bklyn. Mus., 1980, Parco Galleries, Japan, 1980, Fine Arts Gallery, Irvine, Calif., 1981, Musee d'Art Contemporain, Montreal, 1982, ACA Galleries, N.Y.C., 1984, 85, 86; group exhbns. include Jewish Mus., N.Y.C., 1966, 67, Whitney Mus., 1972, Winnipeg Art Gallery, 1975; represented in permanent collections Bklyn. Mus., San Francisco Mus. Modern Art, Oakland Mus. Art, Pa. Acad. Fine Arts, L.A. County Mus. Art, also numerous pvt. collections. Office: 101 N 2d St Belen NM 87002 E-mail: throughtheflower@compuserve.com

CHICK, LAURA, councilwoman; BA, UCLA; MSW, U. So. Calif. Chief field dept. 3rd dist., L.A.; city councilwoman City of L.A., 1993—, chair govtl. efficiency com., vice chair info. tech. and gen. svcs. com., former chair pub. safety com. Vice chair Pub. Works Commn. Office: LA City Coun 200 N Main St Ste 415 Los Angeles CA 90012-4117 E-mail: lchick@council.lacity.org

CHICOREL, MARIETTA EVA, publishing company executive, consultant; b. Vienna, Austria; came to U.S., 1939, naturalized, 1945; d. Paul and Margaret (Gross) Selby. AB, Wayne State U., 1951; MALS, U. Mich., 1961. Asst. chief libr. acquisitions divsn. U. Wash., Seattle, 1962-66; project dir. Macmillan Info. Scis., Inc., N.Y.C., 1968-69; pres. Chicorel Library Pub. Corp., N.Y.C., 1969-79, Am. Libr. Pub. Co., Inc., 1979—; pub. cons. Creative Solutions Co., 1986—. Asst. prof. dept. libr. sci. CUNY (Queens Coll.), 1986—; mem. edn. com. Gov.'s Commn. on Status of Women, Wash., 1963-65; instr. libr. scis. No. Ariz. U., Flagstaff, 1990; bd. dirs. Skills Devel. Tng. counseling; pub. cons. creative solutios. Chief editor: Ulrich's International Periodicals Directory, 1966-68; editor, pub.: Chicorel Indexes, 1969—; founding editor: Jour. Reading, Writing and Learning Disabilities International, 1985-90; contbr. chpt. on univs. to Library Statistics: A Handbook of Concepts, Definitions and Terminology, 1966. Mem. ALA (exec. bd. tech. svcs. divsn. 1965-68, chmn. libr. materials price index com. 1968-69, councillor 1969-73), Am. Assn. Profl. Cons., Am. Book Prodrs. Assn., Book League N.Y. (bd. govs. 1975-79), Am. Soc. for Info. Sci., Can. Libr. Assn., Pacific N.W. Libr. Assn., N.Y. Libr. Club, N.Y. Tech. Svcs. Librarians. Home and Office: PO Box 4272 Sedona AZ 86340-4272

CHIEN, SHU, physiology and bioengineering educator; b. Beijing, June 23, 1931; came to U.S., 1954; s. Shih-liang and Wan-tu (Chang) C.; m. Kuang-Chung Hu, Apr. 7, 1957; children: May Chien Busch, Ann Chien Guidera. MB, Nat. Taiwan U., Taipei, Republic of China, 1953; PhD, Columbia U., 1957. Instr. physiology Columbia U. Coll. Physicians & Surgeons, N.Y.C., 1956-58, asst. prof. physiology, 1958-64, assoc. prof. physiology, 1964-69, prof. physiology, 1969-88, dir. div. circulatory physiology and biophysics, 1974-88; dir. Inst. Biomed. Scis. Academia Sinica, Taipei, 1987-88; prof. bioengring and medicine U. Calif.-San Diego, La Jolla, 1988—, bioengring. group coord., 1989-94, dir. Whitaker Inst. Biomed. Engring., 1991—, chmn. dept. bioengring., 1994-99. Chmn. adv. com. Am. Bur. for Med. Advancement in China, N.Y.C., 1991—, Inst. Biomed. Scis., Academia Sinica, Taipei, 1991—, Nat. Health Rsch. Inst., Taipei, 1991—. Editor: Vascular Endothelium in Health and Disease, 1988, Molecular Biology in Physiology, 1989, Molecular Biology of Cardiovascular System, 1990; co-editor: Nuclear Magnetic Resonance in Biology and Medicine, 1986, Handbook of Bioengineering, 1986, Clinical Hemorheology, Applications in Cardiovascular and Hematological Disease, Diabetes, Surgery and Gynecology, 1987, Fibrinogen, Thrombosis, Coagulation and Fibrinolysis, 1990, Biochemical and Structural Dynamics of the Cell Nucleus, 1990, others; contbr. more than 300 sci. articles on physiology, bioengring. and related biomed. rsch. to profl. jours. Recipient Fahraeus award European Soc. for Clin. Haemorheology, London, 1981, Melville award ASME, 1990, 96, Zweifach award World Congress of Microcirculation, Louisville, 1991, Spl. Creativity Grant award NSF, 1985-88, Merit Grant award NIH, 1989-99, Nat. Health medal, Taiwan, 1998. Mem. NAE, Academia Sinica (Taipei), Am. Physiol. Soc. (pres. 1990-91, Daggs award 1999), Biomed. Engring. Soc. (sr., ALZA award 1993), Internat. Soc. Biorheology (v.p. 1983-89), Microcirculatory Soc. (pres. 1980-81, Landis award 1983), N.Am. Soc. Biorheology (chmn. steering com. 1985-86), Fedn. Am. Socs. for Exptl. Biology (pres. 1992-93), Am. Inst. for Med. and Biol. Engring. (pres. 2000-01), Inst. Medicine of NAS. Achievements include elucidation of the mechanism of red cell aggregation in terms of energy balance at cell surface; demonstration of the role of endothelial cell turnover in the transport of protein molecules into the artery wall; research on the molecular basis and physiological implications of blood cell deformability; studies on the effects of mechanicsl forces on endothelial cell gene expression and signal transduction. Office: U Calif San Diego Inst Biomed Engring La Jolla CA 92093-0427

CHIHULY, DALE PATRICK, artist; b. Tacoma, Sept. 20, 1941; s. George and Viola C. BA, U. Wash., 1965; MS, U. Wis., 1967; MFA, R.I. Sch. Design, 1968. Apprentice Venini Glass Factory, Murano, Venice, Italy, 1968; instr. R.I. Sch. Design, also Haystack Mtn. Sch., Me.; founder, Pilchuk Sch., 1971. Mem. various juries and panels Nat. Endowment for Arts One-man exhbns. include U. Minn., 1976, Handler Galleries, Houston, 1977, Crocker Art Mus., Sacamento, Calif., 1984, Bellevue (Wash.) Art Mus., 1984-87, Israel Museum, Jerusalem 1990, Hudson River Museum, Yonkers 1990, Contemporary Museum Honolulu 1990, Azabu Museum, Tokyo Japan 1990, Museum of Arts and Crafts, Hamburg 1992; Group shows include Charles Cowles Gallery, N.Y. 1981-83, "World glass Now" Hokkaido Museum of Modern Art, Sapporo, Japan, 1982, Columbus Coll. Art and Design, Ohio, 1983; represented in permanent collections including Seattle Art Mus., Met. Mus. Art, N.Y.C., Wadsworth Atheneum, Hartford, Conn., Phila. Mus. Art, Corning Mus. Glass, N.Y., Lannan Found., Palm Beach, Fla., Mus. Art of RISD, Providence, Victoria and Albert Mus., London, Mus. Contemporary Crafts of Am., Crafts Council, N.Y.C.; head glass program RISD; dir. Pilchuk Glass Ctr., Stanwood, Wash.; author: Chihuly: Glass, 1982, Chihuly: Color Glass and Form, 1986. Recipient Louis F. Tiffany Found. award, 1967; Nat. Endowment for Arts grantee, 1975, 77, Governor's Art Award (Washington State) 1984, 85; Fulbright fellow, Murano, Italy, 1968 Club: Providence Art Address: Foster/White Gallery 311 1/2 Occidental Ave S Seattle WA 98104-2839

CHIKALLA, THOMAS DAVID, retired science facility administrator; b. Milw., Sept. 9, 1935; s. Paul Joseph and Margaret Ann (Dittrich) C.; m. Ruth Janet Laun, June 20, 1960; children: Paul, Mark, Karyn. BS in Metallurgy, U. Wis., 1957, PhD in Metallurgy, 1966; MS in Metallurgy, U. Idaho, 1960. Research scientist Gen. Electric Co., Richland, Wash., 1957-62; sr. research scientist Battelle Pacific N.W. Labs., Richland, 1964-72, sect. mgr., 1972-80, programs mgr., 1980-83, dept. mgr., 1983-86, assoc. dir., 1986 95; ret., 1995. Tchr. U. Wis., Madison, 1962-64. Contbr. articles to profl. jours. Fellow AEC. Fellow Am. Ceramic Soc. (counselor 1974-80); mem. AAAS, Am. Nuclear Soc., Sigma Xi. Republican. Roman Catholic. Clubs: Desert Ski (pres. 1958-59), Alpine. Avocations: skiing, golfing, woodworking, mountain climbing. Home: 2108 Harris Ave Richland WA 99352-2021 E-mail: healey1828@aol.com

CHILDEARS, LINDA, banker; b. Council Bluffs, Iowa, Jan. 25, 1950; d. Nolan Glen and Mary Lucile (Dunken) Jackson. Grad., U. Wis., Am. Inst. Banking; student, U. Colo., U. Denver. Various positions First Nat. Bank Bear Valley (formerly Norwest Bank Bear Valley), Colo., 1969-79; v.p. adminstrn. First Nat. Bancorp., 1979-83; pres., CEO, Equitable Bank of Littleton, 1983—; founder The Fin. Consortium; pres., CEO, Young Ams. Bank, Denver, 1987—, also vice-chmn. bd. dirs. Pres., CEO, vice chmn. Young Ams. Edn. Found. Contbr. articles to Time and Newsweek. Bd. dirs. Cherry Creek Art Festival, Denver, 1989-96, Jr. Achievement, Mile High United Way, Cherry Creek Bus. Improvement Dist., U. Denver Bridge Project; mem. adv. bd., nat. past pres. Camp Fire Coun. Colo. Named hon. life mem. Nat. CampFire, past chmn., numerous other awards Camp Fire Inc. Mem. Am. Bankers Assn. (past chmn. Edn. Found.), Found. Tchg. Econs. (trustee), Colo. Bankers Assn., Metro C. of C. Republican. Office: Young Ams Bank 311 Steele St Denver CO 80206-4414

CHILDERS, CHARLES EUGENE, mining company executive; b. West Frankfort, Ill., Oct. 29, 1932; s. Joel Marion and Cora E. (Choate) C.; m. Norma A. Casper, June 8, 1952; children: Joel M., Katrina K. BS, U. Ill., 1955; LLD (hon.), U. Saskatchewan, 1994. With Duval Corp., Carlsbad, N.Mex., 1955-62, Internat. Minerals Corp. (IMC), 1963-77; v.p. Esterhazy oper. IMC, 1977-79; pres. IMC Coal, Lexington, 1979-81; v.p. potash oper. IMC, 1981-82, v.p. expansion and devel., 1982-87; pres., chief exec. officer Potash Corp. of Sask., Inc., Saskatoon, Can., 1987-90, chmn., pres., chief exec. officer Can., 1990-98, chmn., chief exec. officer Can., 1998-99, chmn. Can., 1999—. Bd. dirs., past chmn. bd. Canpotex Ltd., Sask., Found. for Agronomic Rsch.; past chmn. bd. The Fertilizer Inst.; bd. dirs. Conf. Bd. Can., Battle Mountain Gold Corp.; past chmn. Potash and Phosphate Inst.; mem. fertilizer industry adv. com. to FAO. Dir. at large Jr. Achievement of Can. 1st lt. U.S. Army, 1955-57. Mem. AIME, Can. Inst. Mining and Metallurgy, Sask. Potash Producers Assn. (past. chmn.), Internat. Fertilizer Industry Assn. (past pres.). Republican Baptist.

CHILDS, DONALD RICHARD, pediatric endocrinologist; b. Chgo., Sept. 14, 1945; s. Robert Henry Edward and Dorothy Jane (Mills) C.; m. Diane E. Martin, Apr. 26, 1972 (div. 1981); 1 child, Elena M.; m. Jacquelynne Celeste Bostrom, Aug. 26, 1989; stepchildren: Brandon R. Alexander, Eric T. Alexander. MD, U. Mich., 1970. Diplomate Am. Bd. Pediatrics. Intern Children's Hosp., L.A., 1970-71; resident William Beaumont Hosp., Royal Oak, Mich., 1973-75; fellow U. Calif., Davis, 1975-77; pvt. practice Riverside, Calif., 1977—. Capt. U.S. Army, 1971-73. Fellow Am. Acad. Pediatrics; mem. Am. Diabetes Assn., Calif. Perinatal Assn., Calif. Med. Assn., Endocrine Soc., Juvenile Diabetes Found. Avocations: music, water skiing. Office: Riverside Med Clinic 9041 Magnolia Ave Riverside CA 92503-3900

CHILLIDA, EDUARDO, sculptor; b. Donostia, Basque Country, 10 Jan. s. Pedro Chillida and Carmen Juantegui Eguren; m. Pilar Belzunce, 1950. Student arch., U. Madrid, 1943-46; degree in arch. (hon.), High Coun. Arch.'s Assn., Spain, 1989; Dr. Honoris Causa, U. Alicante, Spain, 1996. Vis. prof. Harvard U., 1971. One-man shows include Clan Gallery, Madrid, 1954, Galerie Maeght, Paris, 1956, 64, McRoberts and Tunnard Gallery, London, 1965, Galeria Iolas Velasco, madrid, 1977, Carpenter Ctr. Visual Arts, Harvard U., Boston, 1977, Nat. Gallery, Washington, Mus. Art, Carnegie Inst., Pitts., 1979, Min. Culture Palacio Cristal, Parque Retiro, Madrid, 1980, Mus. Fine Art, Bilbao, Basque Country, 1981, Hayward Gallery, London, 1990, Tasende Gallery, L.A., 1997; group shows include Mus. Fine Arts, Houston, 1961, Galerie Art Moderne, Basel, Switzerland, 1974, Hastings Gallery Spanish Inst., N.Y.C., 1974, Solomon R. Guggenheim Mus., N.Y.C., 1980, Galerie Beyeler, Basel, 1982, Galerie Herbert MeyerEllinger, Frankfurt, Germany, 1983, Mary-Anne Martin/Fine Art, N.Y.C., 1984, Tasende Gallery, La Jolla, Calif., 1985; represented in permanent collections Kuntmuseaum, Basel, Nationalgalerie, Berlin, Museo Bellas Artes, Bilbao, Art Inst. Chgo., Museo Art, Cuenca, Spain, Mus. Fine Art, Houston, La Jolla Mus. Contemporary Art, Tate Gallery, London, Museo Espanol Arte Contemporaneo, Madrid, Museo Rufino Tamayo, Mexico City, Solomon R. Guggenheim Mus., N.Y.C., Mus. Art, Carnegie Inst., Pitts., Collezione Arte Contemporanea, Musei Vaticani, Rome, Galleria Nazionale Arte Moderna, Rome, Hirshorn Mus., Washington; illustrator Le Chernin des Devins, 1965, Meditation in Kastilien, 1968, Die Kunst und der Raum, 1969, Más Allá, 1973, Voz Acorde: Homenaje a Jorge Guillén, 1982, Ce Maudit Moi, 1983. Recipient Graham Found. prize, 1958, Kandinsky prize, 1960, Wilhelm-Lehmbruck prize, 1966, Nordrhein-Westfalen prize, 1966, Wellington prize, 1970, Critica Arte prize, 1971, Encomienda Ciudad, 1971, Engraving prize Internat. Exhbn. Rijeka, Yugoslavia, 1972, Internat. Biennale Ljubljana, Yugoslavia, 1973, La Taula award Josep Lluis Sert, 1973, Premio Internat. Diano Marino award, 1974, Rembrandt prize, Goethe Found., 1975, First prize Japanese Ministry Fgn. Affairs, 1976, Peace and Truce prize Victor Seix Inst. Polemics, 1978, Gold Merit medal Mus. Fine Art Madrid, 1981, European Fine Arts prize City of Strasbourg, 1983, Gold medal U. Basque Country, 1984, Grand Nat. prize Arts for Sculpture, French Govt., 1984, Internat. Wolf Found. prize, 1985, Imperial Ring, City of Goslar, 1985, Revista Euzkadi prize, 1986, Prince Asturias award, 1987, Lorenzo-il Magnifico prize, 1987, Order Sci. and Art, Fed. German Govt., 1988, Imperial prize Japan Art Assn., 1991, Fundacion Sabino Arana prize, 1992, Gold medal City of Donostia, 1992, Assn. Española Critica Arte, 1995, Cross, Portuguese Order Merit Mario Soares, 1995, Freedom prize, 1995; co-recipient Andrew W. Mellon prize, 1978, Ildefonso Cerda medal Engrs. Coll. Cataluna, 1990. Fellow Hispanic Soc. Am. (hon.); mem. AAAS, Royal Acad. Arts London, Hispanic Soc. N.Y. (hon.), REal Academia Bellas Arts (hon.). Office: Tasende Gallery 8808 Melrose Ave West Hollywood CA 90069-5604

CHILTON, KEVIN P. career officer; BSc in Engring. Sci., USAF Acad., Colo. Springs, Colo., 1976; MME, Columbia U., 1977. Commdr. 2d. lt. USAF, 1976, advanced through grades to brigadier gen., 1999; student various, 1976-78; various assignments Kadena Air Base, Japan, 1978-82; pilot, instr. pilot Holloman AFB, N. Mex., 1982-83; test pilot, ops. officer Eglin AFB, Fla., 1985-87; astronaut candidate NASA, Houston, 1987-88, astronaut, 1988-96, dep. program mgr., 1996-98; dep. dir. ops. Peterson AFB, Colo., 1998-99; comdr. 9th Reconnaissance Wing, Beale AFB, Calif., 1999—. Decorated Legion of Merit, Distinguished Flying Cross, Meritorious Svc. medal with oak leaf cluster, NASA Space Flight medal with two oak leaf clusters, NASA Outstanding Leadership medal; recipient Leadership award Sec. of the Air Force, 1982, Liethen-Tittle award 1984; Guggenheim fellow Columbia U., 1977.

CHILVERS, ROBERT MERRITT, lawyer; b. Long Beach, Calif., Oct. 23, 1942; s. James Merritt and Elizabeth Louise (Blackburn) C.; m. Sandra Lee Rigg, Sept. 5, 1969; children: Jeremy Merritt, Jessica Rigg. AB, U. Calif., Berkeley, 1972; JD, Harvard U., 1975. Bar: Calif. 1975, U.S. Dist. Ct. (no. dist.) Calif. 1975, U.S. Ct. Appeals (9th cir.) 1980, U.S. Supreme Ct. 1980, U.S. Dist. Ct. (ctrl. dist.) Calif. 1981, U.S. Ct. Fed. Claims, 1984, U.S. Dist. Ct. (ea. dist.) Calif. 1987, U.S. Ct. Appeals (fed. cir.) 1987. Assoc. Brobeck, Phleger & Harrison, San Francisco, 1975-82, ptnr., 1982-93; spl. master U.S. Dist. Ct. (no. dist.) Calif., 1994-99; shareholder Chilvers & Taylor, PC, San Rafael, Calif., 1996—. Faculty U. Calif., Hastings Sch. Law, San Francisco, 1983-89, Emory U., Atlanta, 1984-90, fed. practice program U.S. Dist. Ct. (no. dist.) Calif., 1984-86, Nat. Inst. for Trial Advocacy, 1986—, Cardozo Law Sch., Yeshiva U., N.Y.C., 1993—, Stanford U. Law Sch., 1994—, Widener U. Sch. Law, Wilmington, 1994-96, U. San Francisco Sch. Law, 1994—. Mem. Calif. Sch. Bds. Assn, 1985-89; trustee Mill Valley Sch. Dist., Calif., 1985-89, chmn., 1987-89; bd. dirs. Marin County Sch. Bds. Assn., Calif., 1985-86, Artisans, Mill Valley, Calif., 1999—. With USMC, 1964-71. Mem. Calif. Bar Assn. (commendation for Outstanding Contbns. to the delivery of vol. legal svcs. 1984), Marin County Bar Assn., Tau Beta Pi, Sigma Tau. Office: Chilvers & Taylor PC 83 Vista Marin Dr San Rafael CA 94903-5228 E-mail: chilvers-taylor@home.com

CHIN, MING, state supreme court justice; b. Klamath Falls, Oreg., Aug. 31, 1942; m. Carol Lynn Joe, Dec. 19, 1971; children: Jennifer, Jason. BA in Polit. Sci., U. San Francisco, 1964, JD, 1967. Bar: Calif., 1970, U.S. Fed. Ct., U.S. Tax Ct. Assoc., head trial dept. Aiken, Kramer & Cummings, Oakland, Calif., 1973-76, prin., 1976-88; dep. dist. atty. Alameda County, 1970-72; judge Alameda County Superior Ct., 1988-90; assoc. justice divsn. 3 Ct. Appeal 1st Dist., 1990-94; presiding justice 1st Dist. Ct. Appeal Divsn. 3, San Francisco, 1994-96; state supreme ct. assoc. justice Calif. Supreme Ct., San Francisco, 1996—. Capt. U.S. Army, 1967-69, Vietnam, USAR, 1969-71. Mem. ABA, Calif. Judges Assn., State Bar Calif., Alameda County Bar Assn., San Francisco Dist. Atty.'s Commn. Hate Crimes, Commonwealth Club of Calif. (pres. 1998), Asian Am. Bar Assn., Alpha Sigma Nu. Office: Supreme Court Calif 350 Mcallister St Fl 1 San Francisco CA 94102-4783

CHIN, SUE SOONE MARIAN (SUCHIN CHIN), conceptual artist, portraitist, photographer, community affairs activist; b. San Francisco; d. William W. and Soo-Up (Swebe) C. Grad., Calif. Coll. Art, Mpls. Arts Inst.; scholar, Schaeffer Design Ctr.; student, Yasuo Kuniyoshi, Louis Hamon, Rico LeBrun. Photojournalist All Together Now Show, 1973, East-West News, Third World Newscasting, 1975-78, Sta. KNBC Sunday Show, L.A., 1975, 76, Live on 4, 1981, Bay Area Scene, 1981. Chmn. Full Moon Products; pres., bd. dirs. Aumni Oracle Inc. Graphics printer, exhbns. include: Kaiser Ctr., Zellerbach Pla., Chinese Culture Ctr. Galleries, Capricorn Asunder Art Commn. Gallery (all San Francisco), Newspace Galleries, New Coll. of Calif., L.A. County Mus. Art, Peace Pla. Japan Ctr., Congress Arts Comm., Washington, 1989; SFWA Galleries, Inner Focus Show, 1989—, Calif. Mus. Sci. and Industry, Lucien Labaudt Gallery, Salon de Medici, Madrid, Salon Renacimento, Madrid, 1995, Life is a Circus, SFWA Gallery, 1991, 94, UN/50 Exhibit, Bayfront Galleries, 1995, Somar Galleries, 1997, Sacramento State Fair, 2000, Star Child, Women thru the Ages - Somarts Gallery, 2000, AFL-CIO Labor Studies Ctr., Washington, Asian Women Artists (1st prize for conceptual painting, 1st prize photography), 1978, Yerba Buena Arts Ctr. for the Arts Festival, 1994; represented in permanent collections L.A. County Fedn. Labor, Calif. Mus. Sci. and Industry, AFL-CIO Labor Studies Ctr., Australian Trades Coun., Hazeland and Co., also pvt. collections; author: (poetry) Yuri and Malcolm, The Desert Sun, 1994 (Editors Choice award 1993-94). Del. nat., state convs. Nat. Women's Polit. Caucus, 1977-83, San Francisco chpt. affirmative action chairperson, 1978-82, nat. conv. del., 1978-81, Calif. del., 1976-81. Recipient Honorarium AFL-CIO Labor Studies Ctr., Washington, 1975-76, Bicentennial award 1976; award Centro Studi Ricerche delle Nazioni, Italy, 1985; bd. advisors Psycho Neurology Found. Bicentennial award L.A. County Mus. Art, 1976, 77, 78. Mem. Asian Women Artists (founding v.p., award 1978-79, 1st award in photography of Orient 1978-79), Calif. Chinese Artists (sec.-treas. 1978-81), Japanese Am. Art Coun. (chairperson 1978-84, dir.), San Francisco Women Artists, San Francisco Graphics Guild, Pacific/Asian Women Coalition Bay Area, Chinatown Coun. Performing and Visual Arts. Address: PO Box 421415 San Francisco CA 94142-1415

CHINCHINIAN, HARRY, pathologist, educator; b. Troy, N.Y., Mar. 7, 1926; s. Ohaness and Armen (Der Arakelian) C.; m. Mary Corcoran, Aug. 22, 1952; children: Armen, Marjorie, Matthew. BA, U. Colo., 1952; MS, Marquette U., 1956, MD, 1959. Cert. anatomic and clin. pathologist. Co-dir. Pathologists Regional Labs., Lewiston, Idaho, 1964-96; chief of staff Tri-State Hosp., Clarkston, Wash., 1967, St. Joseph's Hosp., Lewiston, 1971; assoc. prof. pathology Wash. State U., Pullman, 1972—. Author: Antigens to Melanoma, 1957, Parasitism and Natural Resistance, 1958, Pathologist in Peril, 1996, Immigrant Son, 1996, Immigrant Son II, 1997, Murder in the Mountains, 1997, Princess and the Beggar, 1998, Holly and the Dragon Dingle, 1998, Beware of the Drifters, 1998; co-author: Malakoplakia, 1957, Pneumocystis, 1965, Immigrant Son Book Two, 1997. Pres. Am. Cancer Soc., Asotin County, Wash., 1968, Lewiston Roundup, 1972-73, N.W. Soc. Blood Banks, 1973-74. Sgt. U.S. Army, 1944-46. Fellow Am. Coll. Pathologists (cert., lab. inspector 1970-2000), Am. Soc. Clin. Pathologists; mem. Idaho Soc. Pathologists (pres. 1970). Avocations: writing, drawing, horses. Home: 531 Silcott Rd Clarkston WA 99403-9784

CHING, CHAUNCEY TAI KIN, agricultural economics educator; b. Honolulu, July 25, 1940; m. Theodora Lam, July 7, 1962; children: Donna, Cory. AB in Econs., U. Calif., Berkeley, 1962; MS in Agrl. Econs., U. Calif., Davis, 1965, PhD in Agrl. Econ., 1967. Asst. prof. U. N.H., Durham, 1968-72; assoc. prof. U. Nev., Reno, 1972-77, prof., head div. agrl. and resource econs., 1977-80; prof., chmn. dept. agrl. and resource econs. U. Hawaii, Honolulu, 1980-84, prof. agrl. econs., 1992—, dir. Hawaii Inst. Tropical Agr. and Human Resources, 1984-92. Recipient Charles H. Seurferle award U. Nev., Reno, 1977. Office: Hawaii Inst Tropical Agr 3050 Maile Way # 202 Honolulu HI 96822-2231 E-mail: cching@erols.com

CHING, DAVID T. food products executive; BSEE magna cum laude, U. Wis.; MS in Computer Scis., U. Calif., Berkeley; MS in Mgmt. Sci., Stanford U. Formerly with Bell Canada and Control Data Canada, Ltd., Toronto; sr. v.p. info. systems Lucky Stores, Inc., 1989-93; gen. mgr. in N. Am. Brit.-Am. Cons. Group, 1993-94; chief info. officer, sr. v.p. Safeway, Inc., Pleasanton, Calif., 1994—. Office: Safeway Inc PO Box 99 Pleasanton CA 94566-0009

CHIPMAN, JACK, artist; b. L.A., Oct. 31, 1943; s. George Geotz and June Naomi (Hanson) C. BFA, Calif. Inst. Arts, 1966. Dealer Calif. pottery Calif. Spectrum, Redondo Beach, 1980-90. Cons. Schroeder Pub., Paducah, Ky., 1982-99. Author: Complete Collectors Guide Bauer Pottery, 1982, Collector's Encyclopedia California Pottery, 1992, 2d edit., 1998, Collector's Encyclopedia Bauer Pottery, 1997, (periodicals) Antique Trader Weekly, 1981-83, Am. Clay Exch., 1982-88, Making Heirlooms: Barbara Willis Pottery, 2001; one-person shows include Oakland Mus. Calif., Long Beach Mus. Art, U. Santa Clara Art Mus.; represented in permanent collections at Oakland (Calif.) Art Mus., Long Beach (Calif.) Mus. Art, U. Santa Clara (Calif.) Art Mus. Bd. dirs. Angels Gate Cultural Ctr., San Pedro, Calif., jour. editor, 1990-93. Avocation: collecting Calif. pottery. Office: PO Box 1079 Venice CA 90294-1079

CHIPPERFIELD, JOHN, geologist; b. Toowoomba, Queensland, Australia, 1947; arrived in Can., 1967; BS in Geology, U. Alta., Can., 1972. With ERCB and Energy and Natural Resources; joined Sproule Assocs., Calgary, Can., 1990, v.p. geology, shareholder. Contbr. articles to profl. jours. Mem. Can. Soc. Petroleum Geologists (Pres. award 1999), Can. Well Logging Soc., Am. Assn. Petroleum Geologists, Assn. Profl. Engrs. (profl. geologist). Office: Sproule Internat Ltd 140 4 Ave SW Ste 900 Calgary AB Canada T2P 3N3

CHIROT, DANIEL, sociology and international studies educator; b. Bélâbre, Indre, France, Nov. 27, 1942; came to U.S., 1949; s. Michel and Hélène C.; m. Cynthia Kenyon, July 19, 1974; children: Claire, Laura. BA in Social Studies, Harvard U., 1964; PhD in Sociology, Columbia U., 1973. Prof. internat. studies and sociology Henry M. Jackson sch. U. Wash., Seattle, 1975—, chair internat. studies program. Author: Social Change in a Peripheral Society, 1976, Social Change in the Twentieth Century, 1977, Social Change in the Modern Era, 1986, Modern Tyrants: The Power and Prevalence of Evil in Our Age, 1994, rev. edit., 1996, How Societies Change, 1994; translator: (with Holley Coulter Chirot) Traditional Romanian Villages (Henri H. Stahl), 1980; editor: The Origins of Backwardness in Eastern Europe, 1989, The Crisis of Leninism and the Decline of the Left, 1991, (with Anthony Reid) Essential Outsiders, 1997, (with Martin Seligman) Ethnopolitical Warfare, 2001. John Simon Guggenheim fellow 1991-92. Avocations: skiing, hiking. Office: U Washington Jackson Sch Intl Studies PO Box 353650 Seattle WA 98195-3650

CHISUM, EMMETT DEWAIN, historian, archeologist, researcher; b. Monroe, La., Mar. 19, 1922; BA in Social Sci., Northwestern State U., 1942; MA in Social Sci., La. State U., 1946; MA in History, U. Wyo., 1952, MA in Polit. Sci. an dAnthropology, 1961. Tchr. sci. Cameron (La.) Parish Sch. System, 1947-51; tchr. English Welsh (La.) High Sch., 1946-47; social sci. librarian U. Wyo., Laramie, 1954-77, prof. rsch. history, archeology, 1977—. Mem. faculty senate U. Wyo., 1986—. Author: (books) Guide to Library Research, 1969, Guide to Research in Political Science, 1970, Guide to Research in Education, 1974, Memories: University of Wyoming 1886-1986, 1987; contbr. articles to Ency. of Lir. and Info. Sci. (45 vols.), 1986—, profl. jours. Mem. AAAS, ALA, Am. Archeol. Soc., Western Pol. Sci. Assn., Am. Assn. for State and Local History for Wyo. Publs. (Agnes Milstead award for Outstanding Librarianship 1995). Home: 2032 Holliday Dr Laramie WY 82070-4803

CHIU, ARTHUR NANG LICK, engineering educator, consultant; b. Singapore, Mar. 9, 1929; came to U.S., 1948; s. S.J. and Y.N. (Wong) C.; m. Katherine N. Chang, June 12, 1952; children: Vicky, Gregory. BSCE, BA, Oreg. State U., 1952; MSCE, MIT, 1953; PhD in Structural Engring., U. Fla., 1961. Lic. profl. engr., Hawaii. Instr. U. Hawaii, Honolulu, 1953-54, asst. prof., 1954-59, assoc. prof., 1959-64, chmn. dept. civil engring., 1963-66; prof. structural engring. Colo. State U. (on assignment to Asian Inst. Tech., Bangkok, Thailand), 1966-68; acting assoc. dean research, tng. and fellowships grad. div. U. Hawaii, Monoa, 1968, assoc. dean rsch., tng. and fellowships grad. div. Manoa, 1972-76, prof. civil engring., 1964-95, emeritus prof. civil engring., 1995—. Rsch. specialist Space and Info. Sys. divsn. N.Am. Aviation, Inc. (now Rockwell Internat.), Downey, Calif., 1962; vis. scholar UCLA and vis. assoc. Calif. Inst. Tech., Pasadena, 1970; vis. rsch. scientist Naval Civil Engring. Lab., Port Hueneme, Calif., 1976-77; mem. several univ. coms., U. Hawaii; co-chmn. Indo-US Workshop on Wind Disaster Mitigation, 1985, U.S.-Asia Conf. on Engring. for Mitigating Natural Hazards Damage, 1987, 92, U.S.-Japan seminar Wind Effects on Structures, 1970, 74; spkr. in field. Contbr. articles, papers to profl. jours. Recipient Lifetime Achievement award Hawaii Coun. Engring. Socs., 1998, Engr. of Yr. award Hawaii Soc. of Profl. Engrs., 1989, Harold T. Larsen award Chi Epsilon, 1982; NSF sci. faculty fellow, 1959, 60, Phi Kappa Phi fellow, 1952; NSF research grantee 1970—. Hon. mem. ASCE (chmn. wind effects com. 1994-00, Kaoiki earthquake damage assessment team 1983, past pres. Hawaii sect., vice-chmn. coun. disaster reduction 1997—, control mem. 1994-97, mem. aerodynamics com. 1996-00), NSPE, NRC (past chmn., leader Hurricane Iwa damage assessment team, 1982, com. on natural disasters 1985-93, co-chmn. wind engring. panel), Am. Concrete Inst., Structural Engrs. Assn. Hawaii (past. pres., leader Hurricane Iniki damage assessment team 1992), Applied Technology Coun. (bd. dirs. 1996—, v.p. 1999, pres. 2000), Am. Soc. Engring. Edn., Earthquake Engring. Rsch. Inst., Pan-Pacific Tall Bldgs. Conf. (chmn.), Blue Key, Sigma Xi, Chi Epsilon (nat. pres. 1986-88, 88-90, Pacific Dist. councillor 1982-2000, councillor emeritus 2000—, trustee emeritus U. Hawaii chap. 1999—), Pi Mu Epsilon, Phi Eta Sigma, Tau Beta Pi, Phi Beta Delta, Phi Kappa Phi. Home: 1654 Paula Dr Honolulu HI 96816-4316 Office: U Hawaii Manoa Dept Civil Engring 2540 Dole St Honolulu HI 96822-2303 Fax: 808-956-5014. E-mail: [illegible]

CHIU, DOROTHY, retired pediatrician; b. Hong Kong, Aug. 8, 1917; came to U.S., 1946; d. Yan Tse Chiu and Connie Kwai-Ching Wan; m. Kitman Au; children: Katherine, Margo, Doris, James, Richard. BS, Lingnan U., 1939; MD, Nat. Shanghai Med. Coll., 1945. Diplomate Am. Bd. Pediats. Sch. physician L.A. Sch. Dist., 1954-55; pvt. practice Burbank, Calif., 1954-55, San Fernando, 1955-2000. Staff pediatrician Holy Cross Med. Ctr., Mission Hills, Calif., 1961-2000. Bd. dirs. Burbank Cmty. Concert, 1970-80. Fellow Am. Acad. Pediats.; mem. Calif. Med. Assn., L.A. County Med. Assn. Republican. Avocations: handicrafts, music, travel, reading, photography.

CHIU, JOHN TANG, physician; b. Macao, Jan. 8, 1938; s. Lan Cheong and Yau Hoon C.; m. Bonnie Doolan, Aug. 28, 1965 (div. Apr. 1986); children: Lisa, Mark, Heather; m. Karin Adams, Jan. 3, 2001. Student, U. Vt., 1959, BA, 1960, MD, 1964. Diplomate Am. Bd. Allergy & Immunology. Pres. Allergy Med. Group, Inc., Newport Beach, Calif., 1969-72, Newport Beach, 1972—. Clin. prof. medicine U. Calif., Irvine, 1975—. Contbr. articles to profl. jours. Active Santa Ana Heights Adv. Commn., 1982-83; life mem. Orange County Sheriff's Adv. council, 1987—. Recipient Freshman Chem. Achievement award, Am. Chem. Soc., 1958. Fellow Am. Acad. Allergy Asthma and Immunology, Am. Coll. Allergy and Immunology, Am. Coll. Chest Physicians (sec. steering com. allergy 1977-81), Orange County Med. Assn. (chmn. communications com. 1985-88, communications com., mem. bulletin edit. bd. 1995-01). Avocations: snow skiing, golf, aerobics, travels. Office: Allergy Med Group Inc 400 Newport Center Dr Newport Beach CA 92660-7601

CHIU, PETER YEE-CHEW, physician; b. China, May 12, 1948; came to U.S., 1965; naturalized, 1973; s. Man Chee and Yiu Ying Chiu. BS, U. Calif., Berkeley, 1969, MPH, 1970, DrPH, 1975; MD, Stanford U., 1983. Diplomate Am. Bd. Family Practice, Am. Bd. Preventive Medicine; registered profl. engr., Calif.; registered environ. health specialist, Calif. Asst. civil engr. City of Oakland, Calif., 1970-72; assoc. water quality engr. Bay Area Sewage Services Agy., Berkeley, 1974-76; prin. environ. engr. Assn. Bay Area Govts., Berkeley, 1976-79; intern San Jose (Calif.) Hosp., 1983-84, resident physician, 1984-86; ptnr. Chiu and Crawford, San Jose, 1986-89, Good Samaritan Med. Group, San Jose, 1989-90, The Permanente Med. Group, 1991—. Adj. prof. U. San Francisco, 1979-83; clin. assoc. prof. Stanford U. Med. Sch., 1987—. Contbr. articles to profl. publs.; co-authored one of the first comprehensive regional environ. mgmt. plans in U.S.; composer, pub. various popular songs Southeast Asia, U.S. Mem. Chinese for Affirmative Action, San Francisco, 1975—; bd. dirs. Calif. Regional Water Quality Control Bd.,Oakland, 1979-84, Bay Area Comprehensive Health Planning Coun., San Francisco, 1972-76; mem. Santa Clara County Ctrl. Dem. Com., 1987—; mem. exec. bd. Calif. State Dem. Ctrl. Com.; commr. U.S. Presdl. Commn. on Risk Assessment and Risk Mgmt., Washington, 1993-97, U.S. Presdl. Rank Rev. Bd., Washington, 2000. Recipient Resident Tchr. award Soc. Tchrs. Family Medicine, 1986, Resolution of Appreciation award Calif. Regional Water Quality Control Bd., 1985. Fellow Am. Acad. Family Physicians; mem. Am. Pub. Health Assn., Chi Epsilon, Tau Beta Pi. Democrat. Avocations: songwriting, recording. Office: The Permanente Med Group 770 E Calaveras Blvd Milpitas CA 95035-5491

CHLOUBER, KEN, state legislator; b. Shawnee, Okla., Jan. 24, 1939; m. Pat Chlouber. BS, Okla. Bapt. U. Miner; auctioneer; shift boss Climax Molybdenum; former employee Liberty Mutual Ins. Co.; staff Okla. Dept. Wildlife; mem. Colo. Ho. Reps., 1987-96, Colo. Senate, Dist. 4, Denver, 1996; vice-chair agr., natural resources and energy com.; mem. bus. affairs and labor com.; mem. joint legis. coun. Active Colo. Tourism Bd., Western Legislators Conf. Water Policy Com., High Altitude Sports Fitness Coun., Lake County Civic Ctr. Assn.; organizer, pres. Leadville Improvement Group; founder, chair Leadville Trail 100; charter v.p. Colo. Pack Burro Racing Assn. With U.S. Army. Republican. Home: 220 W 8th St Leadville CO 80461-3530 Office: State Capitol 200 E Colfax Ave Ste 263 Denver CO 80203-1716

CHMELKA, BRADLEY FLOYD, chemical engineering educator; b. Phoenix, Feb. 23, 1960; BSChemE, Ariz. State U., 1982; PhD in Chem. Engring., U. Calif., Berkeley, 1990. Retort startup engr. Unocal Oil Shale Ops., Parachute, Colo., 1982-84; NSF-chemistry postdoctoral fellow dept. chemistry U. Calif., 1990; NSF-NATO postdoctoral fellow Max-Planck-Institut für Polymerforschung, Mainz, Germany, 1991; asst. prof. dept. chem. engring. U. Calif., Santa Barbara, 1992-95, assoc. prof., 1995-99, prof., 1999—. Recipient Young Investigator award NSF, 1992, Tchr.-Scholar award Camille & Henry Dreyfus Found., 1992; Sci. and Engring. Packard fellow David & Lucile Packard Found., 1993, Rsch. fellow Alfred P. Sloan Found., 1996. Mem. AIChE, Am. Chem. Soc., Am. Phys. Soc., Materials Rsch. Soc. Achievements include devel. and application of nuclear magnetic resonance spectroscopy methods to the characterization of optical, mechanical, absorption and transport properties of new solid-state materials; correlation of macroscopic material properties and function with molecular structure and dynamics, particularly in heterogeneous macromolecular solids. Office: U Calif Dept Chem Engring Santa Barbara CA 93106

CHO, HYUN JU, veterinary research scientist; b. Chinju, Korea, June 12, 1939; s. Gil Rae and Sun Gae (Park) C.; m. Kim Bok Mee, June 13, 1967; children— Jae Shin, Elisa, Jane. D.V.M., Gyeongsang Nat. U., 1963; M.Sc., Seoul Nat. U., 1966; Ph.D., U. Guelph, 1973. Vet. rsch. scientist Inst. Vet. Rsch., Anyang, Korea, 1965-70; vis. scientist Wallaceville Animal Rsch. Ctr., New Zealand, 1968; rsch. scientist Animal Diseases Research Inst. Can. Food Inspection Agy., Lethbridge, Alta., Can., 1973—. Contbr. articles to profl. jours. Achievements include discovering virus of Aleutian disease of mink and developed practical diagnostic test for it. Home: 14 Coachwood Rd W Lethbridge AB Canada T1K 6B6 E-mail: chojdvm@home.com

CHO, LEE-JAY, social scientist, demographer; b. Kyoto, Japan, July 5, 1936; came to U.S., 1959; s. Sam-Soo and Kyung-Doo (Park) C.; m. Eun-Ja Chun, May 20, 1973; children: Yun-Kyong Nuy, Sang-Mun Ray, Han-Jae Jeremy. BA, Kookmin Coll., Seoul, Korea, 1959; MA in Govt., George Washington U., 1962; MA in Sociology (Population Council fellow), U. Chgo., 1964, PhD in Sociology, 1965; D in Econs. (hon.), Dong-A U., 1982; DSc in Demography, Tokyo U., 1983; D in Econs., Keio U., Tokyo, 1989; D in Econs. (hon.), Russian Acad. Scis., 2000. Statistician Korean Census Council, 1958-61; research assoc., asst. prof. sociology Population Research and Tng. Center, U. Chgo., 1965-66; asso. dir. Community and Family Study Center, 1969-70; sr. demographic adv. to Malaysian Govt., 1967-69; assoc. prof. U. Hawaii, 1969-73, prof., 1973-78; asst. dir. East-West Population Inst., East-West Center, Honolulu, 1971-74, dir., 1974-92; pres. pro tem East-West Center, 1980-81, v.p., 1987-98, sr. advisor, 1998—. Cons. in field; mem. Nat. Acad. Scis. Com. on Population and Demography; mem. U.S. 1980 Census Adv. Com., Dept. Commerce. Author: (with others) Differential Current Fertility in the United States, 1970; editor: (with others) Introduction to Censuses of Asia and the Pacific: 1970-74, 1976, (with Kazumasa Kobayashi) Fertility Transition in East Asian Populations, 1979, (with Suharto, McNicoll and Mamas) Population Growth of Indonesia, 1980, The OWN Children of Fertility Estimation, 1986, (with Y.H. Kim) Economic Development of Republic of Korea: A Policy Perspective, 1989, (with Kim) Korea's Political Economy: An Institutional Perspective, 1994, (with Yada) Tradition and Change in the Asian Family, 1994, (with Y.H. Kim) Hedging Bets on Growth in a Globalizing Industrial Order, 1997, (with Y.H. Kim) Korea's Choices in Emerging Global Competition and Cooperation, 1998, (with Kim) Ten Paradigms of Market Economies and Land Systems, 1998, (with Kim) The Multi-Lateral Trading System in a Globalizing World, 2000; contbr. numerous articles on population and econ. devel. to profl. jours. Bd. dirs. Planned Parenthood Assn., Hawaii, 1976-77. Ford Found. grantee, 1977-79; Population Council grantee, 1973-75; Dept. Commerce grantee, 1974-78; recipient Award of Mugunghwa-Jang, govt. Republic of Korea, 1992, 4th N.E. Asia Niigata prize, 1996. Mem. Internat. Statis. Inst. (tech. adv. com. World Fertility Survey), Internat. Union Sci. Study Population, Population Assn. Am., Am. Statis. Assn., Am. Sociol. Assn., N.E. Asia Econ. Forum (founding chmn.). Home: 1718 Halekoa Dr Honolulu HI 96821-1027 Office: 1601 E West Rd Honolulu HI 96848-1601

CHO, MARGARET, comedian, actress; b. San Francisco, Dec. 5, 1968; d. Sueng-Hoon Cho and Young-Hie. Comedian, 1991—. TV appearances include All-American Girl, 1994—. Named Best Female Comedian Am. Comedy Awards, 1993. Office: Abrams Artist Agy 9200 W Sunset Blvd Ste 1130 Los Angeles CA 90069-3606

CHO, ZANG HEE, physics educator; b. Seoul, Korea, July 15, 1936; came to U.S., 1972; m. Jung Sook. BSc, Seoul Nat. U., 1960, MSc, 1962; PhD, Uppsala (Sweden) U., 1966. Assoc. prof. Stockholm U., 1971-76, UCLA, 1972-78; prof. Columbia U., N.Y.C., 1979-85, U. Calif., Irvine, 1985—; hon. chair prof. Korea Acad. Indsl. Tech., 1990—. Assoc. dir. Imaging Rsch. Ctr., Columbia U., 1979-84; dir. Nuclear Magnetic Resonance rsch. U. Calif., Irvine, 1985—; organizer tech. programs, symposia and workshops. Author: Foundations of Medical Imaging, 1993; editor-in-chief Internat. Jour. Imaging Sys. and Tech., 1994—; guest editor IEEE Nuclear Sci., 1974, Computers Medicine and Biology, 1976, Image Sci. and Tech., 1989; mem. editorial bd. Physics in Medicine and Biology, Inst. Physics, U.K., 1993, Magnetic Resonance in Medicine, 1984, Computerized Med. Imaging and Graphics, 1989; author/co-author more than 200 original sci. papers in internat. tech. and sci. jours. Named Disting. Scientist, Asilomar, 1982; recipient Grand Sci. prize Seoul, 1984, Jacob Javits Neurosci. award, NIH, 1984, Sylvia Sorkin Greenfield award Am. Assn. Med. Physicists, 1989, Nat. Applied Sci. prize (presdl. award) Korea Sci. Found., 1995, Nat. Acad. Sci. prize Nat. Acad. Scis., Republic of Korea, 1997. Fellow IEEE, Instn. Elec. Engrs. (U.K.), Third World Acad. Sci., Korea Acad. Sci. and Tech. (life); mem. Inst. Medicine of NAS, Nat. Acad. Scis. Republic of Korea. Home: 29 Harbor Pointe Dr Corona Del Mar CA 92625-1333 Office: Univ Calif Dept Radiological Sci Irvine CA 92697-0001

CHOCK, CLIFFORD YET-CHONG, family practice physician; b. Chgo., Oct. 15, 1951; s. Wah Tim and Leatrice (Wong) C. BS in Biology, Purdue U., 1973; MD, U. Hawaii, 1978. Intern in internal medicine Loma Linda (Calif.) Med. Ctr., 1978-79, resident in internal medicine, 1979, U. So. Calif.-L.A. County Med. Ctr., L.A., 1980; physician Pettis VA Clinic, Loma Linda, Calif., 1980; pvt. practice Honolulu, 1981—. Chmn. Dept. of Family Practice, 1990-98, chmn. utilization rev. com. 1991, 95; physician reviewer St. Francis Med. Ctr., Liliha, Hawaii,, 1985—, chmn. Quality Care for Family Practice, 1990-93, 95-98; chmn. credentials Family Practice, 1990-93, 95-96, acting chmn. credentials com., 1992; physician reviewer Peer Rev. Orgn. Hawaii, Honolulu, 1987-93. Fellow Am. Acad. Family Physicians, Internat. Platform Assn. Avocations: model/toy collector, SLCC audiovisual ministry, Christian ministry, King James Bible study. Office: 321 N Kuakini St Ste 513 Honolulu HI 96817-2361

CHODOROW, NANCY JULIA, sociology educator; b. N.Y.C., Jan. 20, 1944; d. Marvin and Leah (Turitz) C.; children: Rachel Esther Chodorow-Reich, Gabriel Issac Chodorow-Reich. BA, Radcliffe Coll., 1966; PhD, Brandeis U., 1975; grad., San Francisco Psychoanalytic, 1993, cert. in adult psychoanalysis, 2000. From lectr. to assoc. prof. U. Calif., Santa Cruz, 1974-86, from assoc. prof. sociology to prof. Berkeley, 1986—, clin. prof. dept. psychology, 1999—. Faculty San Francisco Psychoanalytic Inst., 1994—. Author: The Reproduction of Mothering, 1978 (Jessie Bernard award Sociologists for Women in Soc. 1979, named one of Ten Most Influential Books of Past 25 Years, Contemporary Sociology 1996), 2nd edit., 1999, Feminism and Psychoanalytic Theory, 1989, Femininities, Masculinities, Sexualities, 1994, The Power of Feelings: Personal Meaning in Psychoanalysis, Gender, and Culture, 1999 (L. Bryce Boyer prize Soc. for Psychol. Anthropology 2000; contbr. articles to profl. jours. Fellow Russell Sage Found., NEH, Ctr. Advanced Study Behavioral Scis., ACLS, Guggenheim Found., Radcliffe Inst. for Advanced Study; recipient Contbn. to Women and Psychoanalysis award APA, L. Bryce Bryer prize Soc. for Psychol. Anthropology, 2000. Mem. Internat. Psychoanalytic Assn., Am. Psychoanalytic Assn., San Francisco Psychoanalytic Soc. Office: U Calif Dept Sociology 5305 College Ave Oakland CA 94618

CHONG, ALBERT VALENTINE, artist, educator; b. Kingston, Jamaica, W.I., Nov. 20, 1958; came to U.S., 1977; s. Albert George and Gloria Agnes (Chin) C.; m. Frances Irene Ann Charteris, Nov. 23, 1982; children: Ayinde Jordan, Chinwe Amelia. BFA, Sch. of Visual Arts, N.Y.C., 1981; MFA, U. Calif., San Diego, 1991. Instr. Sch. of Visual Arts, N.Y.C., 1986-88; adjunct faculty Mira Costa Coll., Oceanside, Calif., 1989-90, vis. scholar, 1990-91; asst. prof. art U. Colo., Boulder, 1991—. Program auditor, cons. N.Y. State Coun. on the Arts, N.Y.C., 1984-88. Author: (book) Ancestral Dialogues, 1993; one-man shows include Allen Meml. Art Mus., Oberlin (Ohio) Coll., 1998, William Benton Mus. Art, U. Conn., Storrs, 1998, William King Regional Arts Ctr., Abingdon, Va., 1999, Kiang Gallery, Atlanta, 1999, U. Art Gallery Atrium, U. Mass., Dartmouth, 1999, Carl Keller Gallery, Denver, 1999, Waterloo (Iowa) Mus. Art, 2000, Robert B. Menschel Photography Gallery, Schine Student Ctr., Syracuse (N.Y.) U., 2000; group exhbns. include MEIAC, Spain, 1998, XXIV Biennial, São Paulo, Brazil, 1998, Emmanuel Gallery, Denver, 1999, CUNY, Harlem, 1999, City Gallery East, Atlanta, 1999, Yale U. Art Gallery, New Haven, 2000, Anacostia Mus. and Ctr. for African Am. History and Culture, Washington, 2000. Recipient Regional fellowship NEA, Santa Fe, N. Mex., 1991, Artist's fellowship , Washington, 1992. Home: 5155 Santa Clara Pl Apt 1 Boulder CO 80303-4117 Office: Univ Colo Boulder PO Box 318 Boulder CO 80309-0318

CHONG, RACHELLE B. lawyer, federal communications commissioner; b. Stockton, Calif., June 22, 1959; m. Kirk E. Del Prete. BA in Journalism with high honors, U. Calif., Berkeley, 1981; JD, Hastings Coll. of Law, San Francisco, 1984. Bar: Calif. 1984, D.C. 1985. Assoc. Kadison, Pfaelzer, Woodard & Rossi, Washington and Palo Alto, Calif., 1984-87, Graham & James, San Francisco, 1987-92, ptnr., 1992-94; commr. FCC, Washington, 1994-97; ptnr. Coudert Bros., San Francisco, 1998-2000; gen. counsel, v.p. govt. affairs BroadBand Office Inc., San Mateo, Calif., 2000—. Commr. Legal Svc. Trust Fund Commn. of Calif. State Bar, San Francisco, 1992-94. Editor-in-chief Comm/Ent Law Jour., 1983-85. Finalist for 1994 Woman of Yr., Marketplace Channel 7 KGO-TV, San Francisco, 1994. Mem. ABA (mem. forum fed. comm. bar assn.), Women in Telecomm. (co-chair), Fed. Comm. Bar Assn. Republican. Methodist. Office: BroadBand Office Inc 951 Mariners Island Blvd San Mateo CA 94404-1561

CHONG, RICHARD DAVID, architect; b. Los Angeles, June 1, 1946; s. George and Mabel Dorothy (Chan) C.; m. Roze Gutierrez, July 5, 1969; children: David Gregory, Michelle Elizabeth. BArch, U. So. Calif., 1969; MArch, UCLA, 1974. Registered architect, Utah, Calif., Wyo., Wash. Assoc. Pulliam, Matthews & Assocs., Los Angeles, 1969-76; dir. Asst. Community Design Ctr., Salt Lake City, 1976-77; prin. Richard D. Chong & Assocs., Salt Lake City, L.A., 1977—, Santa Ana, 1977—. Planning cons. Los Angeles Harbor Dept., 1974-76; asst. instr. So. Calif. Inst. Architecture, Santa Monica, 1973-74; vis. design critic Calif. State Poly U., Pamona, 1975, U. Utah, Salt Lake City, 1976-78; design instr. Calif.

State Poly. U., 1975-76; adj. asst. prof. urban design, U. Utah, 1980-84; bd. dirs. Utah Housing Coalition, Salt Lake City; Salt Lake City Housing Adv. and Appeals Bd., 1976-80; presenter Rail-Volution Conf., Washington, 1996. Author: Design of Flexible Housing, 1974; prin. works include Airmen's Dining Hall, 1985 (1st Pl. Mil. Facility Air Force Logistics Command, 1986), Oddfellows Hall, 1984 (Heritage Found. award, 1986), Light Rail Sys. for Salt Lake City. Mem. Task Force for the Aged Housing Com. Salt Lake County, Salt Lake City, 1976-77; Salt Lake City Mortgage Loan Instns. Rev. Com., 1978; bd. dirs. Neighborhood Housing Svcs. of Fed. Home Loan Bank Bd., Salt Lake City, 1979-81, devel. com.; vice-chmn. Water Quality Adv. Coun., Salt Lake City, 1981-83; vice-chmn. Salt Lake City Pub. Utilities Bd., 1985-87; mem. adv. bd. Pub. Utilities Commn., Salt Lake City, 1985—; bd. dirs. Kier Mgmt. Corp.; bd. mem. Camp Kostopulos, Altro Nat. Risk Mgmt. Adv. Bd., 1996—, Ft. Douglas Social Adv. Bd., 1996—, Altro Nat. Safety Bd., 1996—. Mem. AIA (jury mem. Am. Soc. Interior Designs Ann. awards 1981-82, treas. Salt Lake chpt. 1988-89, treas. Utah Soc. 1991, sec. 1992, pres.-elect AIA Utah 1993, pres. 1994-95), Am. Inst. Planning (juror Ann. Planning award 1984-85), Am. Planning Assn., Am. Arbitration Assn., Nat. Panel Arbitrators, Ft. Douglas Country Club. Democrat. Avocations: tennis, sailing, fgn. travel. Office: Richard D Chong & Assocs 244 Edison St Salt Lake City UT 84111-2307 also: 714 W Olympic Blvd Ste 732 Los Angeles CA 90015-1439 also: 106 W 4th St Santa Ana CA 92701-4646

CHOOK, EDWARD KONGYEN, university administrator, disaster medicine educator; b. Shanghai, Apr. 15, 1937; s. Shiu-heng and Shuiking (Shek) C.; m. Ping Ping Chew, Oct. 30, 1973; children by previous marriage: Miranda, Bradman. MD, Nat. Def. Med. Ctr., Taiwan, 1959; MPH, U. Calif., Berkeley, 1964, PhD, 1969; ScD, Phila. Coll. Pharmacy & Sci., 1971; JD, La Salle U., 1994. Assoc. prof. U. Calif., Berkeley, 1966-68; dir. higher edn. Bay Area Bilingual Edn. League, Berkeley, 1970-75; prof., chancellor United U. Am., Oakland and Berkeley, Calif., 1975-84; regional adminstr. U. So. Calif., L.A., 1984-90; pres. Pacific Internat. U., Berkeley and Pomona, Calif., and Guam, 1996—, Shanghai Internat. Coll., 1997—; chancellor Bi-Lingual Coll. Zhuhai (China)-Pacific Internat. Joint U., Hong Kong, 1998—; pres. Main Coin Investment Mgmt., LTD., Oakland, Calif., 1999—; mem. staff Pacific Internat. U., Guangdong, 2000—; internat. dir. Silver State Air Corp., Las Vegas, Nev. Vis. prof. Nat. Def. Med. Ctr., Taiwan Armed Forces U., 1982—, Tongji U., Shanghai, 1992, Foshan U., China, 1992—; cons. specialist Beijing Hosp., 1988—; founder, pres. United Svc. Coun., Inc., 1971—; pres. Pan Internat. Acad., Changchun, China and San Francisco, 1979—, China Gen. Devel. Corp., U.S., 1992—; pub. Unity Jour./Power News, San Francisco, 1979—; Goodwill Amb. of Asia, Federated States of Micronesia, 1997—, mem. NAS-NRC, Washington, 1968-71; spl. cons. cultural sensitivity seminars; spl. lectr. KPMG/Peat Warwick Accts., 1996; advisor Ka Wa Bank, Hong Kong, 1986-96. Assoc. editor U.S.-Chinese Times, 1996-98; pub. US-China Times, 1996—, Unity Jour., N.Am. edit., 1996—; contbr. articles to profl. jours. Trustee Rep. Presdl. Task Force, Washington, 1978—; advisor on mainland China affairs Ctrl. Com. Chinese Nationalist party, Taiwan, 1994-97; pres. Oakland Chinese Nationalist Party, 1998—; deacon Am. Bapt. Ch.; sr. advisor U.S. Congl. Adv. Bd.; mem. Presdl. Adv. Commn., 1991—; hon. dep. sec. of state State of Calif., 1990-93; spl. advisor to sec. of state, 1991—; pres. Yuen Kong Found. for Internat. Understanding (aka March Fong EU Found.), 1994-96, 96—; mem. Capital Hill Club, Washington, 1992—; senatorial commn. Rep. Senatorial Inner Cir., 1996; pres. Pacific Environ. Svc. Corp., 2001—; chartered mem. Presdl. Roundtable Chamber, 2001. August 9, 1997 proclaimed Ed Chook Day by City of Oakland. Mem. World Affairs Coun. San Francisco, Rotary (com. chmn. 1971). Achievements include rsch. on hearing conservation program in U.S. Army, criteria for return to work, principles and practices of nuclear, biol. and chem. weapons. Address: Main Coin Investment Mgmt 1212 Broadway Ste 610 Oakland CA 94706-1810 E-mail: pacuniversity@webtv.net

CHOPER, JESSE HERBERT, law educator, university dean; b. Wilkes-Barre, Pa., Sept. 19, 1935; s. Edward and Dorothy (Resnick) C.; m. Mari Smith; children: Marc Steven, Edward Nathaniel. BS, Wilkes U., 1957, DHL, 1967; LLB, U. Pa., 1960. Bar: D.C. 1961. Instr. Wharton Sch. U. Pa., 1957-60; law clk. to Chief Justice Earl Warren U.S. Supreme Ct., 1960-61; asst. prof. U. Minn. Law Sch., 1961-62, assoc. prof., 1962-65; prof. Law Sch. U. Calif., Berkeley, 1965—, dean, 1982-92, Earl Warren prof. Pub. Law, 1991—. Vis. prof. Harvard U., 1970-71, Fordham U., 1999. Author: Constitutional Law: Cases-Comments-Questions, 9th edit., 2001, The American Constitution, Cases and Materials, 9th edit., 2001, Constitutional Rights and Liberties, Cases and Materials, 9th edit., 2001, Corporations, Cases and Materials, 5th edit., 2000, Judicial Review and the National Political Process, 1980, Securing Religious Liberty, 1995; contbr. articles to profl. jours. Mem. AAUP, Am. Law Inst., Am. Acad. Arts and Scis., Order of Coif. Jewish. Office: U Calif Sch Law Berkeley CA 94720-0001

CHOPP, FRANK, state official; m. Nancy Long; 2 children. BA magna cum laude, U. Wash., 1975. Exec. dir. Fremont Pub. Assn., 1983—; part-time lectr. U. Wash. Grad. Sch. Pub. Affairs, 1992-95; co-speaker of house State of Wash. 43d Dist., Olympia. Dir. Cascade Cmty. Ctr., 1975-76; mgr. No. Cmty. Svc. Ctr. Seattle Dept. Human Resources, 1976-79, 81-83; adminstrv. dir. Pike Market Senior Ctr., 1980-81. Office: 3D Fl Legislative Bldg Olympia WA 98504-0001 also: 4209 Sunnyside Ave N Seattle WA 98103-7658

CHOPRA, ANIL KUMAR, civil engineering educator; b. Peshawar, India, Feb. 18, 1941; came to U.S., 1961, naturalized, 1977; s. Kasturi Lal and Sushila (Malhotra) C.; m. Hamida Banu, Dec. 7, 1976. B.Sc. in Engring, Banaras Hindu U., Varanasi, India, 1960; M.S., U. Calif., Berkeley, 1963, Ph.D., 1966. Design engr. Standard Vacuum Oil Co., New Delhi, India, 1960-61, Kaiser Engrs. Overseas Corps, India, 1961; asst. prof. civil engr. U. Minn., Mpls., 1966-67; mem. faculty U. Calif., Berkeley, 1967—, prof. civil engring., 1976-92, Johnson prof. engring., 1992—. Dir. Applied Tech. Council, Palo Alto, 1972-74; mem. com. natural disasters NRC, 1980-85, chmn., 1982-83; cons. earthquake engring. to govt. and industry. Author: Dynamics of Structures, A Primer, 1981, Dynamics of Structures: Theory and Applications to Earthquake Engineering, 1995, 2001; author more than 230 publs. in structural dynamics and earthquake engring.; mem. adv. bd. MIT Press Series in Structural Mechanics. Recipient Gold medal Banaras Hindu U., 1960, Disting. Alumnus award, 1980, certificate of merit for paper Indian Soc. Earthquake Tech., 1974, honor award Assn. Indians in Am., 1985, AT&T Found. award Am. Soc. Engring. Edn., 1987, Disting. Tchg. award Berkeley Campus, 1999. Mem. ASCE (EMD exec. com. 1981-87, chmn. 1985-86, mem. STD exec. com. 1988-92, chmn. 1990-91, Walter L. Huber prize 1975, Norman medal 1979, 91, Reese rsch. prize 1989, Newmark medal 1993, Howard award 1998), Nat. Acad. Engring., Seismol. Soc. Am. (bd. dirs. 1982-83), Structural Engrs. Assn. No. Calif. (bd. dirs. 1987-89), Earthquake Engring. Rsch. Inst. (bd. dirs. 1990-93), U.S. Com. on Large Dams. Home: 635 Cross Ter Orinda CA 94563 Office: Univ Calif Dept Civil Engring Berkeley CA 94720-0001

CHOPRA, DEEPAK, writer; Author: Return of the Rishi, 1989, Quantum Healing, 1990, Perfect Health, 1990, Unconditional Life, 1991, Creating Health, 1991, Creating Affluence, 1993, Ageless Body, Timeless Mind, 1993, Restful Sleep, 1994, Perfect Weight, 1994, Journey Into Healing, 1994, The Seven Spiritual Laws of Success, 1995, Return of Merlin, 1995, Como Crear Abundancia/How to Create Wealth, 1999, How to Know God: The Soul's Journey into the Mystery of Mysteries, 2000, Everyday Immorality: A Concise Course in Spiritual Transformation, 1999. Office: Chopra Ctr for Well Being 7630 Fay Ave La Jolla CA 92037-4841

CHORIN, ALEXANDRE JOEL, mathematician, educator; b. Warsaw, Poland, June 25, 1938; came to U.S., 1962, naturalized, 1971; s. Joseph and Hannah (Judowicz) C.; m. Alice Louise Jones, Aug. 11, 1965; 1 son, Ethan Daniel. Diploma in engring., Swiss Fed. Inst. Tech., Lausanne, 1961; MSc, NYU, 1964, PhD, 1966. Rsch. scientist NYU, 1966-69, asst. prof. math., 1969-71; assoc. prof. U. Calif., Berkeley, 1972-73, prof., 1973—, Miller rsch. prof., 1971-72, 82-83, dir. Ctr. Pure and Applied Math., 1980-82, 95—, Chancellor's prof., 1997-2000; sr. staff scientist Lawrence Berkeley Lab., 1980—. Disting. vis. prof. Inst. for Advanced Study, Princeton, N.J., 1991-92; faculty rsch. lectr. U. Calif., Berkeley, 1999-00; vis. prof. Coll. France, 1992. Author: (with J. Marsden) A Mathematical Introduction to Fluid Dynamics, 1979, Computational Fluid Mechanics, selected papers, 1989, Vorticity and Turbulence, 1994; contbr. articles to profl. jours. Recipient Nat. Acad. Scis. award in applied math. and numerical analysis, 1989, Norbert Wiener prize Am. Math. Soc. and Soc. for Indsl. and Applied Math., 2000; fellow Sloan Found., 1972-74, Guggenheim Found., 1987-88. Fellow Am. Acad. Arts and Scis.; mem. NAS. Home: 2501 Hawthorne Ter Berkeley CA 94708-1908 Office: U Calif Dept Math Berkeley CA 94720-0001 E-mail: chorin@math.berkeley.edu

CHORY, JOANNE, plant biologist; Rsch. scientist Salk Inst. for Biological Studies, San Diego, now assoc. prof. Recipient Initiatives in Rsch. NAS, 1994, Charles Albert Shull award Am. Soc. Plant Physiologists. Office: Salk Inst Biol Studies PO Box 85800 San Diego CA 92186-5800

CHOW, ANTHONY WEI-CHIK, physician; b. Hong Kong, May 9, 1941; s. Bernard Shao-Ta and Julia Chen (Fan) C.; m. Katherine Cue, May 20, 1967; children: Calvin Anthony, Byron Calbert. Student, Brandon (Man., Can.) Coll., 1961-63; MD, U. Man., 1967. Intern Calgary (Atla., Can.) Gen. Hosp., 1967-68; resident in internal medicine Winnipeg (Man.) Gen. Hosp., 1968-70; fellow in infectious disease UCLA Harbor Gen. Hosp., 1970-72, from asst. prof. to assoc. prof., assoc. head div. infectious disease, 1972-78; practice medicine specializing in infectious disease; prof. medicine, head div. infectious disease U. B.C., Vancouver Gen. Hosp., 1979-94; prof. medicine, dir. MD/PhD Program U. B.C., Vancouver, 1995—. Mem. Can. Bacterial Disease Network, 1989—, MRC, NIH, FDA coms.; councilor Can. Soc. Clin. Invest., Western Soc. Clin. Invest.; apptd. Can. Inst. Acad. Medicine, 1993. Contbr. articles to profl. jours. Med. Research Council Can. grantee, 1979—. Mem. Am. Soc. Microbiology, Am. Fedn. Clin. Rsch., Western Assn. Physicians, Infectious Disease Soc. Am., Western Soc. Clin. Investigation, Can. Soc. Clin. Investigation, Can. Infectious Disease Soc., Can. Inst. of Acad. Medicine, Can. Bacterial Diseases Network, Nat. Ctr. of Excellence. Roman Catholic. Achievements include rsch. in microbial pathogenesis, cellular and molecular immunology, staphylococcal toxins. Home: 1119 Gilston Rd West Vancouver BC Canada V7S 2E7 Office: Vancouver Gen Hosp/Div Infect Dis 2733 Heather St Vancouver BC Canada V5Z 1M9

CHOW, WINSTON, engineering research executive; b. San Francisco, Dec. 21, 1946; s. Raymond and Pearl C.; m. Lilly Fah, Aug. 15, 1971; children: Stephen, Kathryn. BSChemE, U. Calif. Berkeley, 1968; MSChemE, Calif. State U., San Jose, 1972; MBA cum laude, Calif. State U., San Francisco, 1985. Registered profl. chem. and mech. engr.; instr.'s credential Calif. Community Coll. Chem. engr. Sondell Sci. Instruments, Inc., Mountain View, Calif., 1971; mem. R & D staff Raychem Corp., Menlo Park, 1971-72; supervising engr. Bechtel Power Corp., San Francisco, 1972-79; sr. project mgr. water quality and toxic substances control program Electric Power Rsch. Inst., Palo Alto, Calif., 1979-89, program mgr., 1990-97, product line mgr. environ. market sector, 1997-99, indsl. and agrl. energy techs. and svcs. bus. area mgr., 1999-2000, exec. dir. ctrs. network, 1999-2001, dept. mgr. energy utilization rsch. and devel., 2001—. Mem. steering com. Indsl. Energy Tech. Conf., 1999—. Editor: Hazardous Air Pollutants: State-of-the-Art, 1993; co-editor: Clean Water: Factors that Influence Its Availability, Quality and Its Use, 1996; co-author: Water Chlorination, vols. 4, 6; co-editor 1997 Internat. Clean Water Conf.-Today's Sci. for Tomorrows Policies, The Environ. Profl., 1997; contbr. articles to profl. jours. Pres., CEO Directions, Inc., San Francisco, 1985-86, bd. dirs., 1984-87, chmn. strategic planning com., 1984-85; industry com. Am. Power Conf., 1988—; with strategic long-range planning and restructuring com. Sequoia Union H.S. Dist., 1990-93, chmn. dist. ctrl. com., 1992-94. Recipient Grad. Disting. Achievement award, 1985; Calif. Gov.'s Exec. fellow, 1982-83. Mem. ASME, AIChE (profl. devel. recognition award), NSPE, Calif. Soc. Profl. Engrs. (pres. Golden Gate chpt. 1983-84, v.p. 1982-83, state dir.), Water Environ. Fedn., Air and Waste Mgmt. Assn. (mem. electric utility com. 1990-2000), Calif. State U. Alumni Assn. (bd. dirs., treas. 1989-91), U. Calif. Alumni Assn., Beta Gamma Sigma. Democrat. Presbyterian. Office: Electric Power Rsch Inst 3412 Hillview Ave Palo Alto CA 94304-1344

CHOY, HERBERT YOUNG CHO, federal judge; b. Makaweli, Hawaii, Jan. 6, 1916; s. Doo Wook and Helen (Nahm) C.; m. Dorothy Helen Shular, June 16, 1945. BA, U. Hawaii, 1938; JD, Harvard U., 1941. Bar: Hawaii 1941. Law clk. City and County of Honolulu, 1941; assoc. Fong & Miho, 1947-48; ptnr. Fong, Miho and Choy, 1948-57; atty. gen. Territory of Hawaii, 1957-58; ptnr. Fong, Miho, Choy & Robinson, Honolulu, 1958-71; sr. judge U.S. Ct. Appeals (9th cir.), Honolulu, 1971—. Adv. com. on constrn. judiciary bldgs. Chief Justice Hawaii, 1970-71; compilation commn. to compile Revised Laws of Hawaii, 1955, 1953-57; com. to draft Hawaii rules of criminal procedure Supreme Ct., 1958-59; com. on pacific ocean territories Jud. Conf. the U.S., 1976-79. Dir. Legal Aid Soc. Hawaii, 1959-61; trustee Hawaii Loa Coll., 1963-79. Capt. U.S. Army, 1941-46, lt. col. Res. Recipient Order of Civil Merit award Republic of Korea, 1973. Fellow Am. Bar Found.; mem. ABA, Hawaii Bar Assn. (exec. com. 1953, 57, 61, legal ethics and unauthorized practices com. 1953, com. on legis. 1959). Office: US Ct Appeals 300 Ala Moana Blvd Rm C305 Honolulu HI 96850-0305

CHRISPEELS, MAARTEN JAN, biology educator; b. Kortenberg, Belgium, Feb. 10, 1938; married, 1966; 2 children. PhD in Agronomy, U. Ill., 1964. Rsch. asst. agronomy U. Ill., La Jolla, 1963-64; rsch. assoc. plant biochemistry Rsch. Inst. Advanced Studies, 1964-65, AEC, 1965-67; rsch. assoc. microbiology Perdue U., 1967, from asst. prof. to assoc. prof., 1967-79; prof. biology U. Calif., San Diego, 1979—. Program mgr. competitive rsch. grant office USDA, 1979. John. S. Guggenheim Found. fellow, 1973-74. Mem. AAAS, NAS, Am. Soc. Plant Physiologists (Stephen Hales prize 1996), Am. Soc. Cell Biologists. Office: U Calif at San Diego Dept Biology 9500 Gilman Dr La Jolla CA 92093-5004*

CHRIST, CAROL TECLA, English educator, former academic administrator; b. N.Y.C., May 21, 1944; d. John George and Tecla (Bobrick) Christ; m. Larry Sklute, Aug. 15, 1975 (div. Dec. 1983); children—Jonathan, Elizabeth B.A., Douglas Coll., 1966; M.Ph., Yale U., 1969, Ph.D., 1970. Asst. prof. English U. Calif., Berkeley, 1970-76, assoc. prof. English, 1976-83, prof. English, 1983—, dean dept. English, 1985-88, dean dept. humanities, 1988, acting provost, dean, 1989-90, provost, dean Coll. Letters and Sci., 1990-94, vice chancellor, provost, 1994-2000. Former dir. summer seminars for secondary and coll. tchrs. NEH; former tchr. Bread Loaf Sch. of English; invited lectr. Am. Assn. Univs., Am. Coun. Edn. Author: The Finer Optic: The Aesthetic of Particularity in Victorian Poetry, 1975, Victorian and Modern Poetics, 1984; mem. editl. bd. Victorian Literature, The Victorian Visual Imagination, The Norton Anthology of English Literature; contbr. articles to profl. jours. Mem. MLA Office: Univ Calif Dept English 324 Wheeler Berkeley CA 94720-0001

CHRISTENSEN, BRUCE LEROY, former academic administrator, commercial broadcasting executive; b. Ogden, Utah, Apr. 26, 1943; s. LeRoy and Wilma (Olsen) C.; m. Barbara Lucelle Decker, June 17, 1965; children— Jennifer, Heather, Holly, Jesse BA cum laude, U. Utah, 1968; MS, Northwestern U., 1969. Radio and TV news reporter KSL, Inc., Salt Lake City, 1965-68, state house corr., 1969-70; weekend sports writer WGN Radio and TV News, 1968-69; instr. U. Utah, 1969-70, adj. assoc. prof. broadcast regulation, 1980-81, gen. mgr. Sta. KUED-TV and KUER-FM, 1979-82, dir. media svcs., 1981-82; asst. to dir. univ. rels. Brigham Young U., 1970-72, asst. prof., 1971-79, dir. dept. broadcast svcs., 1972-79; pres. Nat. Assn. Pub. TV Stas., Washington, 1982-84; pres., chief exec. officer PBS, Washington, 1984-93; dean Coll. Fine Arts and Comm., prof. comm. Brigham Young Univ., Provo, 1993-2000; sr. v.p. New Media Bonneville Internat., Salt Lake City, 2000—. Bd. govs. Pacific Mt. Network, 1979-82, chmn., 1978-80; vice chmn. (USA) Internat. Coun. Nat. Acad. Arts and Scis., 1990-91, pres. Internat. Coun. NATAS, 1992-93; pres. Prix Italia, 1993; producer, writer Channel 5 Eye-Witness News, 1967-68; bd. dirs. Bonneville Internat. Corp., Fund for Ancient and Mormon Studies, Lance Armstrong Found. for Cancer Rsch. Exec. producer numerous TV documentaries including The Great Dinosaur Discovery, 1973, A Time to Dance, 1976, Navajo, 1976, Christmas Snows, Christmas Winds, 1978 (Emmy award 1978). Bd. dirs. Utah Lung Assn., 1976-82, pres., 1978-80 Recipient Disting. Alumnus award U. Utah, 1989; Allen-Heath fellow Medill Sch. Journalism Northwestern U., 1969; recipient Ralph Lowell medal Corp. for Pub. Broadcasting, 1994. Fellow Internat. Coun. NATAS; mem. Rocky Mountain Corp. for Pub. Broadcasting (bd. dirs.), Sigma Delta Chi (pres. U. Utah chpt. 1967-68), Kappa Tau, Phi Kappa Phi. Avocation: photography. Office: Bonnieville Internat PO Box 1160 Salt Lake City UT 84110-1160

CHRISTENSEN, RAY RICHARDS, lawyer; b. Salt Lake City, July 7, 1922; s. E.R. and Carrie (Richards) C.; m. Carolyn Crawford, July 9, 1954 (dec. 1986); children: Carlie, Paul Ray, Joan, Eric.; m. Jeanne F. Pyke, June 24, 1989. LL.B., U. Utah, 1944. Bar: Utah 1944. Enforcement atty. OPA, 1946; law clk. to Utah Supreme Ct. Justice Wolfe, 1947-48; practice in Salt Lake City, 1949—; ptnr. Christensen & Jensen, P.C. (and predecessors), 1949—. Mem. Utah Bar Commn., 1963-66. Bd. dirs. Salt Lake City Jr. C. of C., 1949-53, v.p., 1950-52. Served with AUS, 1943-46. Fellow Internat. Acad. Trial Lawyers (bd. dirs. 1982-88), Am. Coll. Trial Lawyers (state chmn. 1984-85); mem. ABA (mem. council jr. bar conf. 1952-56, ho. of dels. 1966-68, 73-79, mem. council bar activities sect. 1967-70), Utah State Bar (pres. 1965-66, Utah Lawyer of Yr. 1981, Utah Trial Lawyer of Yr. 1993), Salt Lake County Bar Assn., Western States Bar Conf. (pres. 1969-70), Internat. Assn. Def. Counsel, Fedn. Ins. Counsel, Phi Eta Sigma, Phi Kappa Phi. E-mail: ray. Home: 992 Oak Hills Way Salt Lake City UT 84108-2022 Office: Christensen & Jensen PC 50 S Main St Ste 1500 Salt Lake City UT 84144-2044 E-mail: christensen@chrisjen.com

CHRISTENSEN, RICHARD MONSON, mechanical engineer, materials engineer; b. Idaho Falls, Idaho, July 3, 1932; married, 1958; 2 children. BSc, U. Utah, 1955; ME, Yale U., 1956, DEng, 1961. Structural engr. Convair Divsn., Gen. Dynamics, 1956-58; with technical staff TRW Systems, 1961-64; asst. prof. mech. engring. U. Calif. Berkeley, 1964-67; staff rsch. engr. Shell Devel. Co., 1967-74; prof. mech. engring. Washington U., 1974-76; sr. scientist technical staff Lawrence Livermore (Calif.) Nat. Lab., 1976—. Lectr. U. So. Calif., 1962-64, U. Calif. Berkeley, 1969-70, 78, 80, U. Houston, 1973; mem. U.S. Nat. Com. Theoretical and Applied Mechanics, 1980-82, 85-94; mem. Dept. Energy Panel, 1985-87; cons. prof. Stanford U., 1994—, rsch. prof., 1996—; Sir Geoffrey Taylor Meml. lectr. U. Fla., 1991. Assoc. editor Jour. Applied Mechanics, 1984-90. Fellow ASME (chmn. applied mechanics divsn. 1980-81, hon. mem. 1992, William Prager medal); mem. Nat. Acad. Engring. (Worcester Reed Warner Gold medal), Am. Chem. Soc., Soc. Rheology. Achievements include research in properties of polymers, in wave propagation, in failure theories, in crack kinetics, in composite materials. Office: Lawrence Livermore Nat Lab PO Box 808 Livermore CA 94551-0808

CHRISTIAENS, CHRIS (BERNARD FRANCIS CHRISTIAENS), financial analyst, state legislator; b. Conrad, Mont., Mar. 7, 1940; s. Marcel Jules and Virgie Jeanette (Van Spyk) C. BA in Chemistry, Coll. Gt. Falls, 1962, M in human svcs., 1994. Fin. and ins. mgr. Rice Motors, Gt. Falls, Mont., 1978-84; mem. Mont. Senate, Dist. 23, Helena, 1983-87, 1991—; majority whip 49th legis., 1985-86; fin. planner Jack Stevens CPA, Gt. Falls, 1984-85; adminstr., fin. analyst Gt. Falls Pre-Release, 1986-92; mem. Reforming States Group Health Care Reform, 1994—. Owner Oak Oak Inn-Bed and Breakfast, 1989-95; mem. faculty U. Gt. Falls, part-time 1995—; bd. dirs. World Wide Press Inc., svc. rep., 1994—; gen. mgr. Gt. Falls Transit Dist. Chmn. Balance of State Pvt. Industry Coun., Mont., 1984—; mem. Mont. Human Rights Commn., 1981 84; bd. dirs. St. Thomas Child and Family Ctr., Gt. Falls, 1983—, Coll. of Gt. Falls, 1984—, Cascade County Mental Health Assn., 1986—, Salvation Army, Habitat for Humanity, 1992-95; mem. adv. bd. State Drug and Alcohol Coun., State Mental Health Coun.; bd. dirs. treas. Gt. Falls Cmty. Food Bank, 1984-86; Dem. committeeman Cascade County, 1976-82; Mont. del. to Nat. Rules Conv., 1980; pub. chmn. Cascade County chpt. ARC, 1986; mem. adv. bd. Cambridge Court Sr. Citizen Apt. Complex, 1986; treas. Cascade County Mental Health Ctr.; vice chmn. Gov.'s Task Force on Prison Overcrowding, mem. regional jail com.; mem. Re-Leaf Gt. Falls Com., 1989—, mem. steering com.; mem. Gt. Falls and Cascade County Housing Task Force, 1995—. Recipient Outstanding Young Alumni award Coll. of Gt. Falls, 1979, Hon. Alumni Achievement award, 1994; Disting. Svc. award Rocky Mountain Coun. Mental Health Ctrs., 1995. Mem. Gt. Falls Ski Club, Toastmasters, Optimists, Big Sky Cum Christo. Roman Catholic. Avocations: skiing, tennis, fishing, reading, hiking. Address: 600 36th St S Great Falls MT 59405-3508

CHRISTIAN, GARY DALE, chemistry educator; b. Eugene, Oreg., Nov. 25, 1937; s. Roy C. and Edna Alberta (Trout) Gonier; m. Suanne Byrd Coulbourne, June 17, 1961; children: Dale Brian, Carol Jean, Tanya Daniele, Tabitha Star. BS, U. Oreg., 1959; MS, U. Md., 1962, PhD, 1964. Rsch. analytical chemist Walter Reed Army Inst. Rsch., Washington, 1961-67; asst. prof. U. Md., College Park, 1965-66, U. Ky., Lexington, 1967-70, assoc. prof., 1970-72; prof. chemistry U. Wash., Seattle, 1972—, acting chmn. dept., 1990, assoc. chmn., 1991-92, divisional dean Arts and Scis., 1993-2001. Vis. prof. Free U. Brussels, 1978-79; invited prof. U. Geneva, 1979; cons. Ames Co., 1968-72, Beckman Instruments, Inc., 1972-84, 88, Westinghouse Hanford Co., 1977-83, Tech. Dynamics, 1983-85, Porton Diagnostics, 1990-91, Bend Rsch., 1992-93, E.I. DuPont de Nemours, Inc., 1993; examiner Grad. Record Exam., 1985-90. Author: Analytical Chemistry, 5th edit., 1994, Instrumental Analysis, 1978, 2d edit., 1986, Atomic Absorption Spectroscopy, 1970, Trace Analysis, 1986, Problem Solving in Analytical Chemistry, 1988, Calculations in Pharmaceutical Sciences, 1993; editl. bd. Analytical Letters, 1971—, Can. Jour. Spectroscopy, 1974-96, Analytical Instrumentation, 1974-93, Talanta, 1980-88 (spl. editor USA honor issue, 1989), Analytical Chemistry, 1985-89, Critical Revs. in Analytical Chemistry, 1985—, The Analyst, 1986-90, Jour. Saudi Chem. Soc., 1995—; editor in chief Talanta, 1989—, Electroanalysis, 1988—, Jour. Pharm. and Biochem. Analysis, 1990-97, Fresenius' Z. Analytical Chem., 1991-93, Laborator Automation, 1992—, Quimica Analitica, 1993—; contbr. articles to profl. jours. Recipient Talanta medal Elsevier Sci., 1995, Charles U. Commemorative medal, 1999; Fulbright Hays scholar, 1978-79. Mem. Am. Chem. Soc. (sect. chmn. 1982-83, chmn. elect divsn. Analytic chemistry 1988-89, chmn. 1989-90, divsn. Analytical Chemistry award for Excellence in Tchg. 1988, Fisher award in analytical chemistry 1996), Soc. Applied Spectroscopy (sect. chmn. 1982), Spectroscopy Soc. Can., Am. Inst. Chemists (cert.), Soc. Electroanalytical Chemistry (bd. dirs. 1993-98). Republican. Home: PO Box 26 Medina WA 98039-0026 Office: U Wash Dept Chemistry Box 351700 Seattle WA 98195-1700 E-mail: christian@chem.washington.edu

CHRISTIAN, RALPH GORDON, agricultural research administrator; b. Lethbridge, Alta., Can., Apr. 17, 1942; s. Wesley Peel and Mary (Patterson) C.; m. Brenda Esther Kheong, 1976. DVM, U. Guelph, Ont., Can., 1966; vet. pathology diploma, U. Sask., Saskatoon, 1970. Cert. in vet. pathology Am. Coll. Vet. Pathologists. Instr. Vet. Sch. U. Melbourne, Australia, 1977; dir. animal health divsn. Alta. Dept. Agr., Edmonton, 1982-87; acting asst. dep. min. Alta. Agrl. Prodn. Sector, Edmonton, 1987; exec. dir. Alta. Agrl. Rsch. Inst., Edmonton, 1987—; exec. dir. rsch. divsn. Alta. Dept. Agr., Food and Rural Devel., Edmonton, 1987-2000; pres. Ralph Christian Constrn., Inc., 2001—. Br. head pathology br. Alta. Agr. Vet. Lab., Edmonton, 1972-79, 79-82; lab. head Vet. Lab., Fairview, Alta., 1970-72; instr., resident pathology dept. Western Coll. Vet. Medicine, Saskatoon, 1969-70. Mem. Am. Coll. Vet. Pathologists, Can. Vet. Med. Assn. (chmn. specialization com. 1986-88), Alta. Vet. Med. Assn. (pres. 1981-82). Avocations: skiing, equine driving. Home: RR 1 Edmonton AB Canada T6H 5T6 Office: Alta Agrl Food and Rural De 7000 113 St Edmonton AB Canada T6H-5T6 E-mail: rchristi@msn.com

CHRISTIANSEN, DAVID K. hospital administrator; b. Logan, Utah, Sept. 10, 1952; s. John R. and Lucele (Kartchner) C.; m. Cynthia Ann Kutsko, July 28, 1982. BS, Brigham Young U., 1977; M in Health Care Adminstrn., U. Ala., 1979. Purchasing asst. McDonald Health Clinic, Provo, Utah, 1975-77; adminstrv. resident Bapt.-Montclair Hosp., Birmingham, Ala., 1978-79, adminstrv. asst., 1979-80; asst. adminstr. Lakeview Cmty. Hosp., Bountiful, Utah, 1980-83; adminstr. Shasta Gen. Hosp., Redding, Calif., 1983-84; CEO Knoxville (Iowa) Cmty. Hosp., 1984-89; COO Med. Ctr. Independence, Kansas City, Mo., 1989-92; CEO Newman Regional Hosp., Emporia, Kans., 1992-96; exec. v.p. MED/MAX Health Mgmt., San Diego, 1996—. Exec. dir. Salt Lake Sr. Clinic, 1999-2001; v.p. Vector Healthcare Mgmt., 2001—; cons. Ctr. Health Studies, Nashville, 1981-83; mem. faculty Ctr. for Health Studies/Hosp. Corp. Am., Nashville, 1980-82. Explorer advisor Boy Scouts Am., Birmingham, 1977-80; campaign coord. United Way, Bountiful, 1983; exec. bd. dirs. Boy Scouts Am., Topeka, Kans., 1994-96. Named Outstanding Young Man of Am., U.S. Jaycees, 1982. Fellow Am. Coll. Healthcare Execs.; mem. Knoxville C. of C. (chmn. commerce com. 1986-87), Emporia Kans. C. of C. (bd. dirs. 1994-96), Rotary (membership chmn. REdding 1984, Knoxville bd. dirs. 1987-89).

CHRISTIANSEN, LARRY K. college president; AA, North Iowa Area C.C.; BA in Bus. Edn., U. Northern Iowa; MS in Ednl. Adminstrn., Drake U.; DEd, U. N.D. Distributive edn. coord., chmn. bus. dept. Perry (Iowa) Cmty. H.S., 1967-74; assoc. prof., chmn. bus. divsn. U. Minn. Tech. Coll., Crookston, 1974-82; dean adminstrv. svc., acting dean of instrn., assoc. dean Glendale C.C.; pres. Mesa C.C. Chair acad. internat. exec. adv. bd. Nat. C.C.; mem. Megacorp Bd.; adv. bd. Nat. Campus Compact Cmty.; spkr. in field. Author: (with others) A Case Approach, 1980; co-author: To the Future and Counselor's Guide to..the Future. Pres. East Valley Partnership Bd.; cabinet chair Mesa United Way, 1996; campaign chair Maricopa C.C. Dist. Mem. Mesa C. of C. (nat. campus compact cmty. adv. bd.), Mesa Baseline Rotary, Nat. Assn. of Distributive Edn. Tchrs. Office: 1833 W Southern Ave Mesa AZ 85202-4822

CHRISTIANSEN, PEGGY, principal; Prin. Sequoia Elem. Sch., Santa Rosa, Calif., Blinkley Elem. Sch., Santa Rosa, 1995—. Recipient Elem. Sch. Recognition award U.S. Dept. Edn., 1989-90. Office: Blinkley Elem Sch 4965 Canyon Dr Santa Rosa CA 95409-3204

CHRISTIANSEN, WALTER HENRY, aeronautics educator; b. McKees Rocks, Pa., Dec. 14, 1934; s. Walter Henry and Elizabeth (Miller) C.; m. Joan Marilyn Swisler, Aug. 5, 1960; children: Walter, Audrey. BS in Mech. Engring., Carnegie Inst. Tech., 1956; MS in Aero. Engring., Calif. Inst. Tech., 1957, PhD, 1961. Sr. scientist Jet Propulsion Lab., Pasadena, Calif., 1961-62, Pasadena, 1963-67; rsch. assoc. prof. aero. and aeronautics U. Wash., Seattle, 1967-70, assoc. prof., 1970-74, prof., 1974—, dept. chmn., 1992-98. Cons. Boeing Sci. Rsch. Lab., 1967-69, Math. Scis. N.W., 1970-85, Spectra Tech., 1985-88, 91. Contbr. articles to profl. jours.; patentee in field. Com. mem. Directions for 70's Bellevue (Wash.) Sch. Dist., 1970. Served to capt. U.S. Army, 1961-63. Dept. Def. grantee, 1970-91, NSF grantee, 1977, 80, NASA grantee, 1980-89; Mesa Machine fellow, 1952-56, Convair fellow, 1958, Boeing fellow, 1960. Fellow AIAA (Pacific N.W. chpt. Sect. award 1972); mem. Am. Phys. Soc., Sigma Xi, Tau Beta Pi, Pi Tau Sigma, Theta Xi. Home: 9633 NE 28th St Bellevue WA 98004-1846 Office: Dept Aero & Astro Box 352400 Univ Wash Seattle WA 98195-0001 E-mail: walt@aa.washington.edu

CHRISTIE, HANS FREDERICK, retired utility company subsidiaries executive, consultant; b. Alhambra, Calif., July 10, 1933; s. Andreas B. and Sigrid (Falk-Jorgensen) C.; m. Susan Earley, June 14, 1957; children: Brenda Lynn, Laura Jean BS in Fin., U. So. Calif., 1957, MBA, 1964. Treas. So. Calif. Edison Co., Rosemead, 1970-75, v.p., 1975-76, sr. v.p., 1976-80, exec. v.p., 1980-84, pres., dir., 1984-87; pres., chief exec. officer The Mission Group (non-utility subs. SCE Corp.)., Seal Beach, Calif., 1987-89, ret., 1989, cons., 1989—. Bd. dirs. L.A. Ducommun Inc., L.A., UntramarDiamond Shamrock Corp., C.T., Am. Mut. Fund, Inc., AMCAP, Am. Variable Ins., I.H.O.P. Corp., AECom Tech., L.A., Internat. House of Pancakes, Inc., Southwest Water Co., L.A., Smallcap World Fund, L.A., Bond Fund Am., Inc., L.A., Tax-Exempt Bond Fund Am., L.A., Ltd. Term Tax-Exempt Bond Fund Am., Am. High Income Mcpl. Bond Fund, Capital Income Builder, L.A., Capital World Bond Fund, L.A., Capital World Growth Fund, Capital World Growth and Income Fund, Intermediate Bond Fund Am., L.A., Intermediate Tax-Exempt Bond Fund Am., Capital World Growth 2d Income Fund, L.A.; trustee Cash Mgmt. Trust Am., New Economy Fund, L.A., Am. Funds Income Series, L.A., The Am. Funds Tax-Exempt Series II, Am. High Income Trust, L.A., Am. High-Inc Mun. Board Fund, Am. Variable Ins. Trust, U.S. Treasury Fund Am., L.A. Bd. councillor sch. policy, planning and devel. U. So. Calif.; trustee Occidental Coll., 1984-96, Idllwild Sch. Arts, Chadwick Sch., Nat. History Mus. L.A. County. With U.S. Army, 1953-55. Named Outstanding mem. Arthritis Found., L.A., 1975, Outstanding Trustee, Multiple Sclerosis Soc. So. Calif., 1979 Mem. Pacific Coast Elec. Assn. (bd. dirs. 1981-87, treas. 1975-87), L.A. C. of C. (bd. dirs. 1983-87), Calif. Club. Republican. Avocations: swimming; horseback riding; jogging. Home: 548 Paseo Del Mar Pls Vrds Est CA 90274-1260 Office: PO Box 144 Palos Verdes Peninsula CA 90274-0144

CHRISTMAN, ALBERT BERNARD, historian; b. Colorado Springs, Colo., May 18, 1923; s. James S. and Olga Emelia (Nelson) C.; m. Kate Gresham, July 1945 (div. July 1952); 1 child, Lloyd James; m. Jean Stewart, Apr. 4, 1954 (dec. Sept. 1984); children: Neil Stewart, Laura Elizabeth. BA, U. Mo., 1949, BJ, 1950; MA, Calif. State U., Dominguez Hills, 1982. Reporter Comml. Leader, North Little Rock, 1950-51; tech. [illegible] head presentation divsn., 1956-63; historian, info. specialist Naval Weapons Ctr., China Lake, 1963-72, head pubs., 1973-79; historian Navy Labs., San Diego, 1979-82; freelance historian, writer San Marcos, Calif., 1982—. Author: Sailors, Scientists and Rockets, 1971, Naval Innovators, 1776-1900, 1989, Target Hiroshima, Deak Parsons and the Creation of the Atomic Bomb, 1998; co-author: Grand Experiment at Inyokern, 1979; contbr. articles to profl. jours. Founding mem. Red Rock Canyon State Park Adv. Com., Tehachapi, Calif., 1969-74. Pvt. U.S. Army, 1942-45; maj. USAFR, ret. Recipient Robert H. Goddard Meml. award Nat. Space, 1972, Superior Civilian Svc. award Dept. of The Navy, 1982, Helen Hawkins Meml. Rsch. grants, 1994, 2000. Mem. Maturango Mus. (trustee-sec. 1973-76), Naval Hist. Found., USN Inst., OX-5 Aviation Pioneers, Smithsonian Inst. (assoc.), Libr. of Congress Assn. (founding mem.), San Diego Aerospace Mus., Authors Guild. Democrat. Unitarian. Avocations: photography, golfing, tennis, hiking. Home and Office: 1711 Birchwood Dr San Marcos CA 92069-9609

CHRISTMAN, ARTHUR CASTNER, JR. scientific advisor; b. North Wales, Pa., May 11, 1922; s. Arthur Castner and Hazel Ivy (Schirmer) C.; m. Marina Ilia Diterichs, Apr. 17, 1945; children: Candace Lee Christman Canto, Tatiana Marina Christman Harvey, Deborah Ann Christman Clark, Arthur C. III, Keith Ilia, Cynthia Ellen Christman Buckwalter. BS in Physics, Pa. State U., 1944, MS, 1950. Teaching asst. dept. physics Pa. State U., State College, 1943-44, grad. asst., 1946-48; instr. dept. physics George Washington U., Washington, 1948-51; cons. U.S. Navy, 1950-51; physicist ops. research office Johns Hopkins U., Chevy Chase, Md., 1951-58; sr. physicist SRI Internat., Menlo Park, Calif., 1958-62, head ops. research group, 1962-64, dept. mgr., 1965-67, dir. dept., 1968-71, dir. tactical weapons systems, 1971-75; sci. advisor to comdg. gen. and dep. chief staff combat devel. U.S. Army tng. and doctrine command Ft. Monroe, Va., 1975-87; cons. in field, 1988—. Author numerous publs. Pres. Valle Verde Continuing Care Retirement Cmty. Coun., 1991-93, 94-95, Am. Bapt. Homes of West Assn. of CCRC Resident Presidents, 1991-92; mem. bd. mgrs. fin. com. Valle Verde, 1988—; mem. Valle Verde Adv. Bd., 1997—, mem. fin. com., 1988—, chair environ. svcs. com., 1999—; bd. dirs. Am. Bapt. Homes of the West, 1997—, mem. fin. and investment com., 1998—, Ctrl. Coast Commn. for Sr. Citizens Ara Agy. on Aging, 1993; mem. continuing care contract statutes rev. task force State of Calif., 1999-2000; umpire Palo Alto Little League, Calif., 1962-72. Lt. USNR, 1944-46, PTO. Decorated Meritorious Civilian Service award Dept. Army, 1983, Exceptional Civilian Service award Dept. Army, 1987; recipient Presdl. Rank, 1985. Fellow AAAS; mem. Am. Phys. Soc., Inst. for Ops. Rsch. and the Mgmt. Scis. (U.S. del. internat. confs. Operational Rsch., France 1960, Norway 1963, U.S. 1966, Ireland 1972), Santa Barbara Lawn Bowls Club (bd. dirs. 1990-93), MacKenzie Park Lawn Bowls Club, Sigma Xi, Sigma Pi Sigma, Delta Chi (chpt. pres.). Republican. Baptist (deacon, trustee). Avocations: golf, swimming, tennis, bowling, photography. Home and Office: 900 Calle De Los Amigos Apt W8 Santa Barbara CA 93105-4407 E-mail: achristman@abhow.com

CHRISTOFFERSEN, RALPH EARL, chemist, researcher; b. Elgin, Ill., Dec. 4, 1937; s. Arthur Henry and Mary C.; m. Barbara Hibbard, June 10, 1961; children: Kirk Alan, Rachel Anne. BS, Cornell Coll., 1959, LLD (hon.), 1983; PhD, Ind. U., 1963. Asst. prof. chemistry U. Kans., Lawrence, 1966-69, assoc. prof., 1967-72, prof., 1972-81, asst. vice chancellor for acad. affairs, 1974-75, assoc. vice chancellor for acad. affairs, 1976-79, vice chancellor for acad. affairs, 1979-81; pres. Colo. State U., Ft. Collins, 1981-83; exec. dir. Upjohn Co., 1983-85, v.p. biotech. and basic research support, 1985-87, v.p. discovery research, 1987-89; v.p. rsch. SmithKline Beecham, King of Prussia, Pa., 1989-90, sr. v.p. rsch., 1990-92; CEO, pres. Ribozyme Pharms., Inc., Boulder, Colo., 1992-2001, chmn. bd., 2001—. Bd. dirs. Genomica Corp., Biotech. Industry Orgn. Contbr. articles to profl. jours. NIH fellow, 1962-63, 64-66 Fellow Am. Inst. Chemists; mem. Am. Chem. Soc., Am. Phys. Soc. (v.p. theoretical div. 1981), Internat. Soc. Quantum Biology (pres. 1977-79), Pharm. Mfrs. Assn. (chmn. biotech. adv. com. 1983-86, chmn. R&D steering com. 1989-90), Sigma Xi, Phi Lambda Upsilon.

CHRISTOL, CARL Q(UIMBY), lawyer, political science educator; b. Gallup, S.D., June 28, 1913; s. Carl and Winifred (Quimby) C.; m. Jeannette Stearns, Dec. 18, 1949 (dec.); children: Susan Quimby Christol-Deacon, Richard Stearns (dec.). AB, U. S.D., 1934, LLD (hon.), 1977; AM, Fletcher Sch. Law and Diplomacy, 1936; postgrad., Institut Universitaire des Hautes Etudes Internationales, Geneva, 1937-38, U. Geneva, , 1937-38; PhD, U. Chgo., 1941; LLB, Yale U., 1947; postgrad., Acad. Internat. Law, The Hague, 1950. Bar: Calif. 1949, S.D. 1948. Assoc. firm Guthrie, Darling and Shattuck, Los Angeles, 1948-49; of counsel Fizzolio, Fizzolio & McLeod, Sherman Oaks, Calif., 1949-94; assoc. prof. polit. sci. U. So. Calif., 1949-59, prof., 1959-87, prof. emeritus, 1987—, chmn. dept. polit. sci., 1960-64, 75-77. Stockton chair internat. law U.S. Naval War Coll., 1962-63, cons., 1963-70 ; cons. World Law Fund; mem. L.A. Mayor's Adv. Com. Human Rels., Commn. to Study Orgn. of Peace; mem. adv. panel on internat. law Dept. State, 1970-76; v.p. Ct. of Man Found., 1971-77; scholar-in-residence Rockefeller Found. Bellagio Conf. and Study Ctr., Italy, 1980. Author: Transit by Air in International Law, 1941, Introduction to Political Science, 1957, 4th edit., 1982, Readings in International Law, 1959, The International Law of Outer Space, 1966, The International Legal and Institutional Aspects of the Stratosphere Ozone Problem, 1975, The Modern International Law of Outer Space, 1982, Space Law: Past, Present and Future, 1991; bd. editors: Western Polit. Quar, 1970-75, Internat. Lawyer, 1975-84, Space Policy, 1985— , Internat. Legal Materials, 1985—, Australian Internat. Law Jour., 1998—; contbr. articles on legal, polit. and mil. subjects to profl. jours. Bd. dirs. Los Angeles County Heart Assn., 1956-61. Served to lt. col. AUS, 1941-46; col. Res. ret. Decorated Bronze Star medal; recipient Dart award U. So. Calif., 1970, Assos. award for excellence in teaching, 1977, Raubenheimer award, 1982, Disting. Emeritus award, 1990, Rockefeller Found. fellow, 1958-59 Mem. Am., Los Angeles bar assns., Am. Soc. Internat. Law (exec. council 1973-76), Internat. Studies Assn. (chmn. internat. law sect. 1977-78), Internat. Acad. Astronautics, State Bar Calif., UN Assn. Los Angeles (pres. 1961-63), Am. Polit. Sci. Assn., Internat. Inst. Space Law (pres. Am. br. 1973-75, Lifetime Achievement award 1998), Town Hall, AIAA, Internat. Law Assn., UN Assn. U.S. (dir. 1967-69), Masons, Blue Key, Skull and Dagger, Rotary, Phi Beta Kappa, Phi Kappa Phi (award 1987), Alpha Tau Omega. Republican. Presbyterian. Home: 1041 Anoka Pl Pacific Palisades CA 90272-2414 Office: U So Calif Polit Sci Dept Los Angeles CA 90089-0044

CHRISTOPHER, JAMES WALKER, architect, educator; b. Phila., Nov. 5, 1930; s. Arthur Bailey and Cornelia (Slater) C.; m. Carolyn Kennard, July 9, 1955; children: William W., Kathryn A., Kimberley, James S., Pamela W. B.A., B.S. in Architecture, Rice U., 1953; M.Arch., MIT, 1956. Registered architect, Utah, Colo., Nev., Idaho, Wyo. Asst. prof. architecture U. Utah, Salt Lake City, 1956-60, adj. prof. architecture, 1983; archtl. designer various firms, Salt Lake City, 1960-63; founding prin. Brixen & Christopher Architects, Salt Lake City, 1963—. Architect, Phase I, Snowbird, Alta Canyon, Utah (AIA Western Mountain Region award 1971), Numemaker Place Chapel, Salt Lake City (AIA Western Mountain Region award 1977), Congregation Kol Ami, Salt Lake City (AIA Western Mountain Region award 1977), Block 53 Master Plan, Salt Lake City (Utah chpt. AIA award 1979). Mem. Utah Environ. Transp. Council, Salt Lake City, 1970-77, vice chmn., 1970-75; mem. Big Cottonwood Citizens Planning Com., Salt Lake County, Utah, 1975, Salt Lake City Downtown Planning Com., 1981, Utah Transit Authority Transplan, Salt Lake City, [illegible] to lt. (j.g.) USNR, 1953-55. Fellow AIA (pres. Utah Soc. 1970 12 Utah Soc. Design awards, 12 Western Mountain Region Design awards 1968-83, 8 nat. Design awards 1975-83, Presdl. citation 1982, nat. design and planning com. 1976—, chmn. R/UDAT task group 1987-91, western mountain region Firm of the Yr. award 1987, Silver medal 1991, Utah Soc. Bronze medal 1999). Episcopalian. Club: Alta Home: 2954 Millcreek Rd Salt Lake City UT 84109-3108 Office: Brixen & Christopher Architects 252 S 2nd E Salt Lake City UT 84111-2487

CHRISTOPHER, WARREN, lawyer, former government official; b. Scranton, N.D., Oct. 27, 1925; s. Ernest W. and Catharine Anna (Lemen) C.; m. Marie Josephine Wyllis, Dec. 21, 1956; children— Lynn, Scott, Thomas, Kristen. Student, U. Redlands, 1942-43; B.S. magna cum laude, U. So. Calif., 1945; LL.B., Stanford, 1949; LL.D. (hon.), Occidental U., 1977, Bates Coll., 1981, Brown U., 1981, Claremont Coll., 1981. Bar: Calif. 1949, N.Y., U.S. Supreme Ct. 1949. Law clk. U.S. Supreme Ct. Justice William O. Douglas, Washington, 1949-50; practice in Los Angeles, 1950-67, 69-76, 81-93, 97—; mem. firm O'Melveny & Myers, LLP, 1950-67, 69, ptnr., 1958-67, 69-76, 81-93, sr. ptnr., 1997—; dep. atty. gen. U.S., Washington, 1967-69; dep. sec. of state Dept. State, Washington, 1977-81; sec. U.S. Dept. of State, Washington, 1993-97. Spl. counsel to Gov. Calif., 1959; cons. Office Under Sec. State, 1961-65; mem. bd. bar examiners State Bar Calif., 1966-67; dir. So. Calif. Edison Co., First Interstate Bancorp, Lockheed Corp.; chmn., trustee Carnegie Corp. N.Y.; mem. Calif. Coordinating Coun. for Higher Edn., 1960-67, pres., 1963-65; vice chmn. Gov.'s Commn. on L.A. Riots, 1965-66; chmn. U.S. delegations to U.S.-Japan Cotton Textile Negotiations, 1961, Geneva Conf. on Cotton Textiles, 1961; spl. rep. sec. state for Wool Textile Meetings, London, Rome, Tokyo, 1964-65; mem. Trilateral Commn., 1975-77, 81-88; mem. internat. adv. coun. Inst. Internat. Studies; chmn. Ind. Commn. on L.A. Police Dept., 1991. Author: In the Stream of History, 1998, Chances of a Lifetime, 2000; co-author: American Hostages in Iran: The Conduct of a Crisis, 1985. Trustee Stanford U., 1971-77, 81-93, pres. bd. trustees, 1985-88; bd. dirs., vice chmn. Coun. on Fgn. Rels., 1982-91; bd. dirs. L.A. World Affairs Coun.; mem. exec. com. Am. Agenda, 1988; mem. U.S.-Korea Wisemen Coun., 1991-93. Lt. (j.g.) USNR, 1943-46. Decorated Medal of Freedom 1981; recipient Harold Weill award NYU, 1981, Louis Stein award Fordham U., 1981, Jefferson award Am. Inst. for Pub. Svc., UCLA medal, Thomas Jefferson award in law U. Va. Fellow Am. Bar Found., Am. Coll. Trial Lawyers, AAAS; mem. ABA (ho. dels. 1975-77, chmn. standing com. fed. judiciary 1975-77), Calif. Bar Assn. (gov. 1975-77), L.A. County Bar Assn. (pres. 1974-75), Am. Law Inst., Order of Coif, Calif. Club, Chancery Club, Phi Kappa Phi. Office: O'Melveny & Meyers LLP 1999 Ave Of Stars Fl 7 Los Angeles CA 90067-6022

CHRITTON, GEORGE A. theater producer; b. Chgo. s. George A. and Dorothea G. Chritton; m. Martha Gilman, Aug. 26, 1956; children: Stewart, Andrew, Douglas, Laura, Neil, Lyle. BA, Occidental Coll., 1955; postgrad., Princeton U., 1955-57. With CIA & various U.S. govt. agys., 1960-89; gen. ptnr. Margeo Investment Co., L.A., 1963-76; pres. Wildacre Prodns., Inc., L.A., 1990—. Pres., CEO Fin. Svcs. Bancorp, Reno, 1990—; pres. Sycamore Prodns. Ltd., Nev. and Calif., 1994—. Prodr. theater prodns. Thornton Wilder's Youth, In Shakespeare and The Bible, A Ringing of Doorbells, The Rivers under the Earth, 1999. Mem. Am. Fgn. Svc. Assn., Washington, 1960—; chmn. bd. Neighborhood Learning Ctr., Capitol Hill, Washington, 1985-87; vol. Options House, Hollywood, Calif.; vol. coord. Rebuild L.A.; spl. advocate L.A. County Juvenile Ct., 2000—. Maj. USAF, 1957-60. Named Princeton Nat. Fellow, 1955-56, Vis. Fellow & Lectr. U. Calif., 1987-88. Mem. AFTRA, Am. Film Inst., Nat. Assn. Ind. Film & T.V. Prodrs., L.A. World Affairs Coun., Phi Beta Kappa, Phi Gamma Delta, Alpha Mu Gamma, Alpha Phi Gamma, Princeton Club (So. Calif.). Office: Wildacre Prodns Inc PO Box 719 Beverly Hills CA 90213-0719

CHRONLEY, JAMES ANDREW, real estate executive; b. Springfield, Mass., July 31, 1930; s. Robert Emmett and Eleanor Agnes (Sullivan) C.; m. Monique Mary Delpech, July 29, 1955; children: Mary Elizabeth, James Michael, Jean Louise, Patricia, Joseph Patrick, John Peter, Robert Emmett. A.B., Brown U., 1952; diploma in real estate, U. R.I., 1963; MBA, Peppderdine U., 1991. With Arco Co., 1954-74, Eastern area mgr., until 1972; nat. real estate dir. Atlantic Richfield Co., Los Angeles, 1972-74; v.p. restaurant real estate Marriott Corp., Washington, 1974-78; exec. v.p. Burger Chef Systems, Inc., Indpls., 1978-82, pres., 1982; sr. v.p. devel. Taco Bell, Irvine, Calif., 1983-94. Served with AUS, 1952-54. Mem. Nat. Assn. Corp. Real Estate Execs. (chpt. pres. 1979, chmn. bd. 1985-87, elected trustee 1987-92), Am. Arbitration Assn., Internat. Exec. Svc. Corps, Orange County Assn. Investment Mgrs. Roman Catholic. Office: Taco Bell 19800 Macarthur Blvd Ste 1450 Irvine CA 92612-2421

CHRYSTAL, WILLIAM GEORGE, minister; b. Seattle, May 22, 1947; s. Francis Homer and Marjorie Isabell (Daubert) C.; m. Mary Frances King, Aug. 24, 1970; children: Shelley, Sarah, John, Philip. BA, U. Wash., 1969, MEd, 1970; MDiv, Eden Theol. Sem., 1978; MA, Johns Hopkins U., 1984. Ordained to ministry, United Ch. of Christ, 1977. Learning resources specialist Seattle C.C. Dist., 1970-71; dir. learning resources ctr. Whatcom C.C., Ferndale, Wash., 1971-73; minister St. Peter's United Ch. of Christ, Granite City, Ill., 1978-79; sr. minister 1st Congl. Ch., Stockton, Calif., 1979-83; minister Trinity United Ch. of Christ, Adamstown, Md., 1983-85; sr. minister Edwards Congl. Ch., Northampton, Mass., 1985-86, 1st Congl. Ch., Reno, 1991—. Hosp. chaplain Washoe Med. Ctr., Reno, 1993-99; host Thomas Jefferson Hour, on Nat. pub. radio stas. Author: Young Reinhold Niebuhr: His Early Writings, 1911-1931, 1977, 2d edit., 1982, A Father's Mantle: The Legacy of Gustav Niebuhr, 1982, The Fellowship of Prayer, 1987; author monographs; contbr. articles to profl. jours. V.p. Reno-Sparks Met. Ministry, Reno, 1994-97; Chautauqua scholar Great Basin Chautauqua, Reno, 1993, 94, 98, 99. Lt. comdr. USN, 1986-91, maj. Nev. Army N.G., 1992-96. Decorated (2) Meritorious Svc. medal. Mem. Am. Soc. Ch. History, Nev. Soc. Mayflower Descs. (past gov.), Am. Legion, Disabled Vets. (life), VFW (life), Rotary Club (Paul Harris fellow 1997). Home: 3820 Bluebird Cir Reno NV 89509-5601 Office: 1st Congl Ch 627 Sunnyside Dr Reno NV 89503-3515 E-mail: chrystal@intercomm.com

CHU, JAMES, computer display equipment manufacturing executive; b. Taiwan; m. Lily Chu; children: Tina, Kevin. Various sales positions, Taiwan; pres. Taiwanese keyboard mfg. co., U.S., 1986; founder Keypoint Tech. Corp., 1987-90; reorganized Keypoint Tech. Corp. (now ViewSonic Corp.), 1990; CEO ViewSonic Corp., Walnut, Calif. Avocations: reading, tennis, exploring Internet.

CHU, MORGAN, lawyer; b. N.Y.C., Dec. 27, 1950; m. Helen M. Wong, Dec. 29, 1970. BA, UCLA, 1971, MA, 1972, PhD, 1973; MSL, Yale U., 1974; JD magna cum laude, Harvard U., 1976. Bar: Calif. 1976, U.S. Dist. Ct. (ctrl. dist.) Calif. 1977, U.S. Dist. Ct. (no. dist.) Calif. 1980, U.S. Ct. Appeals (9th cir.) 1980, U.S. Dist. Ct. (so. dist.) Calif. 1984, U.S. Dist. Ct. (ea. dist.) Calif. 1986, U.S. Ct. Appeals (fed. cir.) 1989, U.S. Supreme Ct. 1991. Law clk. to judge U.S. Ct. Appeals (9th cir.), San Francisco, 1976-77; assoc. Irell & Manella, LLP, L.A., 1977-82; ptnr. Irell & Manella, L.A., 1982—, co-mng. ptnr., 1997—, exec. com., 1984—. Adj. prof. UCLA Sch. Law, 1979-82; judge pro tem L.A. Mcpl. Ct., 1980—. Mem. editl. bd. Litigation News, 1981-84. Recipient Significant Achievement award for excellence and innovation in alternative dispute resolution Ctr. for Pub. Resources, 1987; Postdoctoral fellow Yale U., 1974; named one of 10 New Superstars of 1st ammendment law Legal Times of Washington, 1986, one of 100 Most Influential Lawyers in Am., Nat. Law Jour., 1994, 97, 2000, one of Top Ten Trial Lawyers in U.S., 1995, one of top 45 Lawyers in U.S. Under 45 Years Old by Am. Lawyer, 1995; Exec. of Yr. in Law, L.A. Bus. Jour., 1994, one of top 20 lawyers in L.A., Calif. Law and Bus., one of top 100 Most Influential Lawyers in Calif., Calif. Law Bus., 1998, 99, 2000. Mem. ABA (chmn. high tech. intellectual property and patent trials subcom. 1986-90, trial practice com., litigation sect.), Calif. Bar Assn., L.A. County Bar Assn. (judiciary com. 1983—), L.A. Intellectual Property Law Assn. (bd. dirs. 1991-93, bd. dirs. pub. counsel 1993—, exec. com. bd. dirs. pub. counsel 1995—). Office: Irell & Manella LLP 1800 Avenue Of The Stars Los Angeles CA 90067-4276 E-mail: mchu@irell.com

CHU, STEVEN, physics educator; b. St. Louis, Feb. 28, 1948; s. Ju Chin and Ching Chen (Li) C.; children: Geoffrey, Michael. BS in Physics, AB in Math., U. Rochester, 1970; PhD in Physics, U. Calif., Berkeley, 1976. Post doctoral fellow U. Calif., Berkeley, 1976-78; mem. tech. staff Bell Labs., Murray Hill, N.J., 1978-83; head quantum electronics rsch. dept. AT&T Bell Labs., Holmdel, 1983-87; prof. physics and applied physics Stanford (Calif.) U., 1987—, Frances and Theodore Geballe prof. physics and applied physics, 1990—, chmn. physics dept., 1990-93. Morris Loeb lectr. Harvard U., Cambridge, Mass., 1987-88; vis. prof. Coll. de France, fall 1990; Richtmeyer Meml. lectr., 1990. Contbr. papers in laser spectroscopy and atomic physics, especially laser cooling and trapping, and precision spectroscopy of leptonic atoms, polymer and biophysics. Recipient Humboldt sr. scientist award, Sci. for Art prize, 1995; co-recipient King Faisal prize for sci., 1993, Nobel prize for physics, 1997; Woodrow Wilson fellow 1970, doctoral fellow NSF, 1970-74, postdoctoral fellow 1977-78, Guggenheim fellow, 1996. Fellow Am. Phys. Soc. (Herbert P. Broida prize for laser spectroscopy 1987, chair laser sci. topical group 1989, A.L. Schawlow prize 1994), Optical Soc. Am. (William F. Meggars award 1994), Am. Acad. Arts and Scis.; mem. NAS, Academica Sinica, Am. Philos. Soc., Chinese Acad. Sci. (fgn.), Korean Acad. Sci. and Tech. (fgn.). Office: Stanford Univ Varian Bldg Rm 230 Stanford CA 94305-4060

CHUANG, KEVIN, electronics manufacturing executive; CFO Synnex, Fremont, Calif. Office: Synnex 3797 Spinnaker Ct Fremont CA 94538 Office Fax: (510) 668-3777

CHUCK, WALTER G(OONSUN), lawyer, director; b. Wailuku, Maui, Hawaii, Sept. 10, 1920; s. Hong Yee and Aoe (Ting) C.; m. Marian Chun, Sept. 11, 1943; children: Jamie Allison, Walter Gregory, Meredith Jayne. Ed.B., U. Hawaii, 1941; J.D., Harvard U., 1948. Bar: Hawaii 1948. Navy auditor, Pearl Harbor, 1941; field agt. Social Security Bd., 1942; labor law insp. Terr. Dept. Labor, 1943; law clk. firm Ropes, Gray, Best, Coolidge & Rugg, 1948; asst. pub. prosecutor City and County of Honolulu, 1949; with Fong, Miho & Choy, 1950-53; ptnr. Fong, Miho, Choy & Chuck, 1953-58; pvt. practice law Honolulu, 1958-65, 78-80; ptnr. Chuck & Fujiyama, Honolulu, 1965-74; ptnr. firm Chuck, Wong & Tonaki, Honolulu, 1974-76, Chuck & Pai, Honolulu, 1976-78; pres. Walter G. Chuck Law Corp., Honolulu, 1980-94; pvt. practice Honolulu, 1994—. Dist. magistrate Dist. Ct. Honolulu, 1956-63; gen. ptnr. M & W Assocs., Kapalama Investment Co.; bd. dirs. Aloha Airlines, Inc., Honolulu Painting Co., Ltd. Chmn. Hawaii Employment Rels. Bd., 1955-59; bd. dirs. Nat. Assn. State Labor Rels. Bds., 1957-58, Honolulu Theatre for Youth, 1977-80; chief clk. Hawaii Ho. of Reps., 1951, 53, Hawaii Senate, 1959-61; govt. appeal agt. SSS, 1953-72; former mem. jud. coun. State of Hawaii; former mem. exec. com. Hawaiian Open; former dir. Friends of Judiciary History Ctr. Inc., 1983-94; former mem. bd. dirs. YMCA. Capt. inf. Hawaii Terr. Guard. Recipient Ha'Aheo award for cmty. svc. Hawaii chpt. Am. Bd. Trial Advocates, 1995. Fellow Internat. Acad. Trial Lawyers (founder, dean, bd. dirs., state rep.), Am. Coll. Trial Lawyers; mem. ABA (former chmn. Hawaii sr. lawyers divsn., former mem. ho. of dels.), Hawaii Bar Assn. (pres. 1963), ATLA (former editor), U. Hawaii Alumni Assn. (Disting. Svc. award 1967, former dir., bd. govs.), Law Sci. Inst., Assoc. Students U. Hawaii (pres.), Am. Judicature Soc., Internat. Soc. Barristers, Am. Inst. Banking, Chinese C. of C., U. Hawaii Founders Alumni Assn. (v.p., bd. dirs., Lifetime Achievement award 1994), Harvard Club of Hawaii, Waialae Country Club (pres. 1975), Oahu Country Club. Republican. Home: 2691 Aaliamanu Pl Honolulu HI 96813-1216 Office: Pacific Tower 1001 Bishop St Ste 2450 Honolulu HI 96813-3430

CHUI, CHARLES K. mathematics educator; b. Macau, May 7, 1940; m. Margaret K. Lee, Aug. 22, 1964; children: Herman, Carie. BS, U. Wis., 1962, MS, 1963, PhD, 1967. Asts. prof. math. SUNY, Buffalo, 1967-70; assoc. prof. math. Tex. A&M U., College Station, 1970-74, prof. math., 1974-89, disting. prof. math., 1989—, dir. Ctr. for Approximation Theory, 1988-99, joint appointment in stats., computer sci. and electrical engring.; cons. prof. statistics Stanford U., 1997—; chief tech. officer TeraLogic, Inc., Mountain View, Calif., 1996-2000. Author: Multivariate Splines, 1988 (translated into Japanese and Chinese), An Introduction to Wavelets, 1992 (translated into Japanese and Chinese), Wavelets, A Mathematical Tool for Signal Analysis, 1997 (translated into Japanese); co-author: Elements of Calculus, 1983, 2nd edit., 1988, Kalman Filtering with Real-Time Applications, 1987, 2nd edit., 1991, 3d edit., 1997, Linear Systems and Optimal Control, 1988, Signal Processing and Systems Theory, Selected Topics, 1992, Hx Control, 1998; editor: Approximation Theory and Functional Analysis, 1991, Wavelets: A Tutorial in Theory and Applications, 1992 (translated into Japanese), (series) Wavelet Analysis and Its Applications, Approximations and Decompositions; co-editor: Approximation Theory II, 1976, Approximation Theory IV, 1983, Approxiamtion Theory V, 1986, Topics in Multivariate Approximation, 1987, Approximation Theory VI, vols. 1 and II, 1989, Multivariate Approximation Theory IV, 1989, Approximation Theory VII, 1992, Approximation Theory VIII, 1995; editor-in-chief Applied and Computational Harmonic Analysis: Wavelets, Signal Processing and Applications; editor: Wavelets: Theory, Algorithms, and Applications, Approximation Theory and Its Applications, Jour. Approximation Theory, Advances in Computational Math., Annals Numerical Math., Electronic Jour. Differential Equations, Advances in Computational Math., Neurocomputing; assoc. editor Jour. Math. Rsch. and Exposition, Revista de Matemáticas Aplicadas; patentee spline-wavelet signal analyses and methods for processing signals; patent pending method and apparatus for video image compression and decompression using boundary-spline-wavelets. Named. Hon. Prof., Ningxia U., China, 1987; Erskine fellow U. Canterbury, New Zealand, 1987; fellow Houston Advanced Rsch. Ctr., 1994. Fellow IEEE; mem. Am. Math. Soc., Math. Assn. Am., Soc. for Indsl. and Applied Math., Assn. Former Students Tex. A&M U. (Disting. Rsch. Achievement award 1981, 94). Roman Catholic. Avocations: music, fishing. Home: 340 Olive St Menlo Park CA 94025-5855

CHUMBLEY, AVERY B. state legislator; b. Champaign, Ill., Mar. 19, 1955; m. Mary Jay Chumbley. Student, Parkland C.C., Champaign, Ill.; grad., Ford Mktg. Inst., Dearborn, Mich. Pres. Wailuku Agribus. Co., Inc.; gen. mgr. Maui Tropical Plantation; mem. Hawaii Ho. of Reps., Honolulu, 1992-94, Hawaii Senate, Honolulu, 1994—, co-chair jud. com., mem. edn. and tech. com., mem. labor and environ. com. Apptd. Maui rep. Hawaii State Bd. Agr.; Maui Hist. Commn.; mem. steering com. Edn. Comn. of the States; dir. pub. policies World Sustainable Agr. Assn.; bd. dirs. Fmaily Lit. Adv. Bd., Maui Vis. Bur., Maui Econ. Devel. Bd., Maui Cmty. Arts and Cultural Ctr.; mem. Am. Cancer Assn.; pres. Maui County Fair Assn. Named Ofcl. of Yr. Maui Cmty. Choice, 1993, Cert. Appreciation and Recognition award Hawaii State Adult and Cmty. Edn. Adv. Coun., 1995, Mahalo award Friends of the Libr. of Hawaii, 1996, Ohana award Jr. League of Honolulu, 1997, Cert. of Appreciation Keiki Injury Prevention Coalition, 1998. Mem. Nat. Congress Parents and Tchrs. (hon. life mem.). Democrat. Office: State Capitol 415 S Capitol Rm 230 Honolulu HI 96813

CHUN, JONATHAN J. state legislator; b. Hilo, Hawaii, Jan. 26, 1957; m. Sandra Chun; children: Lauren, Jason. BA, U. Hawaii; JD cum laude, Gonzaga U. Assoc. White & Thom; dep. corp. counsel City of County of Honolulu; 1st dep. county atty. Office of the County Atty., County of Kauai; of counsel Belles, Graham, Proudfoot & Wilson, Honolulu; mem. Hawaii Senate, Dist. 7, Honolulu, 1998—; mem. ways and means com. Hawaii Senate, Honolulu, mem. water, land, and Hawaiian affairs com., mem. govt. ops. and housing com. Mem. Gonzaga Law Rev., 1980, tech. editor, 1981. Asst. coach Lihue T-Ball League; mem. King Kaumuali'i Elem. Sch. PTA; bd. dirs. 'Ae Kamali'i Presch. Bd., Lihue Christian Ch., Ho'ike Pub. Access TV; bd. dirs., bd. elders, youth ministry team Lihue Missionary Ch. Mem. Kauai Bar Assn. Democrat. Office: State Capitol 415 S Beretania St Honolulu HI 96813-2407 E-mail: senchun@capitol.hawaii.gov

CHUNG, KYUNG CHO, Korean specialist, educator, writer; b. Seoul, Korea, Nov. 13, 1921; s. Yang Sun and Kyung Ok (Peng) C.; m. Yosi S. Chung, Oct. 10, 1958; children: In Kyung, In Ja. Student, Waseda U., Tokyo, 1941-43; B.A., Seoul Nat. U., 1947; postgrad., Columbia U., 1948-49; M.A., N.Y. U., 1951; LL.D., Pusan Nat. U., 1965; Litt.D., Sungkyunkwan U., 1968; M.A., Monterey Inst. Fgn. Studies, 1974. Mem. faculty U.S. Def. Lang. Inst., Monterey, Calif., 1951-92, Monterey Inst. Fgn. Studies, 1973-74, Hartnell Coll., Salinas, Calif., 1974-93. Pres. Korean Rsch. Coun.; adviser Korean Assn., Monterey, 1974—, Am.-Korean Found., Crossroads, Inc., 1992, Asia Devel. Inc.; treas. Korean Rsch. Bull.; hon. prof. Kunkuk U.; pres. South Carmel Hills Assn., 1962-99; hon. chmn. Inst. Far Eastern Studies Joint Rsch. Program U.S.-Russia-Korea-Japan-China, 1993—; chmn. Korea-Am. Assn. Author: Korea Tomorrow, 1957, New Korea, 1962, Seoul (Ency. Americana), 1965, Naeil Hankuk, 1965, Sae Hankuk, 1968, Korea: The Third Republic, 1972, Korean Unification, 1973, Korea Reunion and Reunification, 1974, Kankuk Gaido, 1988, The Korea Guidebook: North and South Korea, 6th edit., 1999, Korea edit., 2000, Hankuk-chongran, 1999, East and West 1000 Munsun, 1995, Japanese Kangoku Gaizobuk, 2000. Recipient Superior Performance award U.s. Govt., 1964, Korean Prime Min. citation, 1965, cert. of achievement U.S. Def. Lang. Inst., 1976, Outstanding Performance award U.S. Def. Lang. Inst., 1980, Olympic-svc. Gold medal Korean Pres., 1989, Spl. Commendation award Korean Pres., 1990, Commendation award U.S. Def. Lang. Inst., 1991, Recognition award of 40 Yrs. Svc., U.S. Govt., 1991, Excellency medal U.S. Govt., 1992, Nobel Peace prize candidate, 2001. Mem. AAUP, Am. Assn. Asian Studies, Am. Assn. Modern Langs., Am.-Korean Polit. Assn., Carmel Found. Democrat. Mem. Korean Ch. Home and Office: 25845 S Carmel Hills Dr Carmel CA 93923-8310

CHUN OAKLAND, SUZANNE NYUK JUN, state legislator; b. Honolulu, June 27, 1961; d. Philip Sing and Mei-Chih (Chung) Chun; m. Michael Sands Chun Oakland, June 11, 1994; children: Mailene Nohea Pua Oakland, Christopher Michael Sing Kamakaku Oakland, Lauren Suzanne LeRong Kemelenohea Oakland. BAs in Psychology and Comms., U. Hawaii, 1983. Adminstrv. asst. Au's Plumbing and Metal Works, Hawaii, 1979-90; community svc. specialist Senator Anthony Chang, 1984; adminstrv. asst. Smolenski and Woodell, 1984-86; rsch. asst., office mgr. City Coun. Mem. Gary Gill, 1987-90; mem. Hawaii Ho. of Reps., 1990-96, Hawaii Senate, Dist. 14, Honolulu, 1996—; chair com. health and human svcs. Hawaii Senate, 1999—, co-chair com. human resources, 1997—; mem. coms. health and environ., consumer protection; commerce and info. tech., 1997—. Past chair, mem. several coms. Hawaii State Senate; mem. Sterile Needle Exch. Oversight Com., 1992—; apptd. pres. Kalihi-Palama Svc. Area Bd on Mental Health and Substance Abuse, gov. Hawaii, 1985-89. Mem. adv. bd. Lanakila Multi-Purpose Sr. Ctr., 1991—, Sex Abuse Treatment Ctr., 1993—, Teen Line, 1993, Hawaii Cmty. Found. Children's Trust Fund, 1995—, Habitat for Humanity, 1998—; mem. Grow For It Program, 1996—, Hawaii Early Childhood Alliance, 1995-96, Families Together Initiative Core Team, 1993-95; coun. mem. Hawaii Even Start Family Literact Program, 1993-94; mem. coord. coun. Hawaii Early Intervention, 1993—, Early Childhood Edn. and Care, 1992-96; mem. adv. coun. Children's Trust Fund, 1993—; mem. adv. com. West Honolulu Pub. Health Nursing Sect., 1992—, Honolulu divsn. Casey Family Program, 1994—, Early Childhood Sys. Cost/Implementation, 1992-94; chair Liliha/Kalapama Neighborhood Bd., 1984-90; mem. project steering com. Hawaii Summit 2011, 1996—; mem. Healthy Mothers, Healthy Babies Coalition, 1992; convenor Elder Abuse and Neglect Task Force, 1995—; mem. task force Blueprint for Change, Child Protective Svcs., 1994-96, Hawaii Assistive Tech. Tng. and Svcs. Project Cmty., 1995—; mem. coun. Hawaii Kids Count, 1994—; bd. dirs. Honolulu Neighborhood Housing Svcs., 1986-88, 89—, pres., 1987-88, 92-93, 93-94; bd. dirs. McKinley H.S. Found, 1989—; Catholic Immigration Ctr., 1991-97, Hawaii Dem. Movement, 1991-97, Hawaii Cmty. Svcs. Coun., 1993-97, Hawaii Cmty. Edn. Assn., 1984-98, Hawaii Lawyers Care, 1994—, Susannah Wesley Cmty. Ctr., 1994—, Hawaii Housing Devel. Corp., 1993—, YWCA, 1994—, ARC, 1998—, Breakthroughs for Youth at Risk, 1998—, Providing Awareness Referrals Edn. Nurturing Therapy Support, 1999—; precinct pres. Hawaii Dem. Party, 1990. Named Legis. of Yr. Hawaii Long Term Care Assn., 1993, 98, Healthcare Assn. Hawaii, 1993, 95, Hawaii Psychiat. Med. Assn., 1994, Autism Soc. Hawaii, 1994, Mental Health Assn. Hawaii, 1996, Aloha State Assn. of Deaf, 1999; recipient cert. of appreciation YMCA, 1985, Hawaii Assn. for Edn. of Young Children, 1992, Winners at Work, 1993, Am. Box Car Racing Internat., 1996, Congress of Visayan Orgn., 1996, Pack 201 Boys Scouts Am., 1997, Partners in Policymaking Hawaii, 1998, Excellence award Honolulu Neighborhood Housing Svcs. Inc., 1988, mini internship program cert. Honolulu County Med. Soc., 1993, Friend of Social Workers award NASW, 1995, Outstanding Govt. Svc. award Hawaii Pacific Gerontol. Soc., 1996, Outstanding Legislator award Hawaii Med. Assn., 1996, Na Lima Kokua Ma Waema O Makua award Pacific Gerontol. Soc., 1996, Friend of the Family award Hawaii Assn. for Marriage and Family Therapy, 1998. Mem. Liliha/Palama Bus. Assn. (bd. dirs. 1994—), Hawaii Women's Legal Found., Good Beginnings Alliance, Kalihi-Palama Culture and Arts Soc., Chung Wah Chung Kung Hui, Hawaii Chinese Civic Assn., Hawaii State Youth Vol. Bd. (past pres.), Ma'ema'e Sch. SCBM, Legis. Women's Caucus, Small Bus. Caucus, Keiki Caucus (co-chair 1991—), Chinese C. of C., McKinley Alumni Assn. (bd. dirs. 1989—). Democrat. Episcopalian. Avocations: raising animals, gardening, swimming. Office: State Senate 415 S Beretania St Rm 228 Honolulu HI 96813-2407

CHURCH-GAULTIER, LORENE KEMMERER, retired government official; b. Jordan, Mont., Oct. 18, 1929; d. Harry F. and Laura (Stoller) Kemmerer; m. Scott Johnston, Sept. 8, 1948 (div. 1953); children: Linda M., Theodore O.; m. Fred C. Church, May 9, 1956 (dec. 1967); children: Ned B., Nia J.; m. Charles F. Gaultier, Oct. 1996 (dec. Jan. 2000). Student, Portland Community Coll., 1973-76, Portland State U., 1978-79. Sec. intelligence div. IRS, Portland, Oreg., 1973-75; trade asst. Internat. Trade Adminstrn., U.S. Dept. Commerce, Portland, 1975-84, internat. trade specialist, 1984-94; ret., 1995. Mem. NAFE, World Affairs Coun., N.W. China Coun., Portland C. of C. (Europe 1992 com. 1988-89, internat. trade adv. bd. 1988-89, treas. dist. export coun. 1996—), Western Internat. Trade Coun. Democrat. Roman Catholic. Avocations: music, growing roses. Home: 19725 SW Pike St Beaverton OR 97007-1446 Office: US Dept Commerce US&FCS 121 SW Salmon St Portland OR 97204-2901

CHURCHILL, JAMES ALLEN, lawyer, director; b. Kingsport, Tenn., Sept. 13, 1935; s. Robert Lang and Jamie Louise (Hill) C.; m. Jackeen Kelleher, Aug. 9, 1958; children: James Allen Jr., Courtney Bartlett. AB, Princeton U., 1957; LLB, Harvard U., 1960; M in Civil Law, Tulane U., 1963. Bar: La. 1961, U.S. Dist. Ct. (ea. dist.) La. 1962, U.S. Ct. Appeals (5th cir.) 1965; admitted as Gaikokuho Jimu Bengoshi, Japan, 1992. Ptnr. Lemle, Kelleher, Kohlmeyer & Matthews, New Orleans, 1960-79; dir. Barham & Churchill, New Orleans, 1979-88; ptnr. Pillsbury Madison & Sutro, L.A. and Tokyo, 1988-95; sr. v.p., gen. counsel., corp. sec. Ventura Foods, LLC, City of Industry, Calif., 1995—. Mem. ABA, Am. Law Inst., Calif. Bar Assn., La. Bar Assn., Calif. Club (L.A.), Boston Club (New Orleans), Annandale Golf Club. Democrat. Office: Ventura Foods LLC 14840 Don Julian Rd City Industry CA 91746-3109

CHURCHILL, MAIR ELISA ANNABELLE, medical educator; b. Liverpool, Eng., Nov. 28, 1959; BA in Chemistry, Swarthmore (Pa.) Coll., 1981; PhD in Chemistry, Johns Hopkins U., 1987. Lab. asst. Swarthmore Coll., 1979-81; teaching asst. Johns Hopkins U., Balt., 1981-83; non-clin. sci. staff grade I MRC Lab. Molecular Biology, Cambridge, Eng., 1987-93; asst. prof. biophysics U. Ill., Urbana, 1993-98; assoc. prof. biophysics U. Colo., Denver, 1998—. Contbr. numerous articles to profl. jours. Am. Cancer Soc. fellow, 1987-89, Cambridge U. fellow, 1988-91. Mem. Am. Chem. Soc., Sigma Xi (assoc.). Office: U Colo Health Scis Dept Pharm Campus Box C236 4200 E 9th Ave Denver CO 80220-3706

CHURCHILL, WILLIAM DELEE, retired education educator, psychologist; b. Buffalo, Nov. 4, 1919; s. Glenn Luman and Ethel (Smith) C. AB, Colgate U., 1941; MEd, Alfred U., 1951; EdD, U. Rochester, 1969. m. Beulah Coleman, Apr. 5, 1943; children: Cherylee, Christie. Tchr. secondary sci., Canaseraga, N.Y., 1947-56; dir. guidance Alfred-Almond Sch., Almond, 1956-63; grad. asst. U. Rochester, 1963-65; asst. prof. psychology Alfred (N.Y.) U., 1965-66; assoc. prof. edn. Ariz. State U., Tempe, 1966-86. Author: Career Survey of Graduates, 1973. Served with U.S. Army Air Corps 1942-46, USAF Res. 1946-79, ret. lt. col. Mem. Ariz. Psychol. Assn. Home: 11454 N 85th St Scottsdale AZ 85260-5727

CHURGIN, AMY, publishing executive; Pub. K III Mag. Corp. (now Primedia Corp.--N.Y. Mag.), N.Y.C., 1993—, Archtl. Digest, Condé Nast, L.A., 1999—. Office: Architectural Digest Condé Nast 6300 Wilshire Blvd Ste 1100 Los Angeles CA 90048-9083

CICCONE, AMY NAVRATIL, art librarian; b. Detroit, Sept. 19, 1950; d. Gerald R. and Ruth C. (Kauer) Navratil. BA, Wayne State U., 1972; AM in Library Sci., U. Mich., 1973. Rsch. libr. Norton Simon Mus., Pasadena, Calif., 1974-81; chief libr. Chrysler Mus., Norfolk, Va., 1981-88; head libr. Architecture and Fine Arts Libr. U. So. Calif., L.A., 1988-97, acting asst. univ. libr. pub. svcs., 1993-95, ref. libr., 1997—. Contbr. articles to profl. jours.; cons. editor Art Reference Svcs., 1990-98. Mem. Art Libraries Soc. N.Am. (moderator Decorative Arts Roundtable, 1991-93, facilities standards com. 1986-91, chmn. strategic planning task force 1994-96, vice-chmn. So. Calif. chpt. 1989, chmn. 1990, chmn. 2001 conf.), Rsch. Librs. Group, Art & Architecture Group (steering com. 1992-94). Office: U So Calif Libr Los Angeles CA 90089-0001

CICCONE, MADONNA LOUISE VERONICA See MADONNA

CICERONE, RALPH JOHN, academic administrator, geophysicist; b. New Castle, Pa., May 2, 1943; married; 1 child. SB, MIT, 1965; MS, U. Ill., 1967, PhD in Elec. Engring. and Physics, 1970. Physicist U.S. Dept. Commerce, 1967; rsch. asst. aeronomy U. Ill., 1967-70; assoc. rsch. scientist aeronomy space physics rsch. lab. U. Mich., Ann Arbor, 1970-78; assoc. rsch. chemist ocean rsch. divsn. U. Calif., San Diego, 1978-80, rsch. chemist Scripps inst. oceanography, 1980-81, Daniel G. Aldrich prof., chair geosci. dept. Irvine, 1989-94, dean Sch. Phys. Scis., 1994-98, chancellor, 1998—; sr. scientist, dir. atmospheric chemistry divsn. Nat. Ctr. Atmospheric Rsch., Boulder, Colo., 1980-89. Lectr., asst. prof. elec. engring. U. Mich., Ann Arbor, 1973-75; mem. Bd. Sustainable Devel., 1995-99, Coun. of NAS, 1996-99. Assoc. editor Jour. Geophysics Rsch., 1977-79, editor, 1979-83. Recipient Bower award for Achievement in Sci., Franklin Inst., 1999. Fellow AAAS, Am. Chem. Soc., Am. Meteorol. Soc., Am. Geophysical Union (Macelwane award 1979); mem. NAS (elected 1990, mem. com. atmospheric sci. 1980-82, mem. bd. atmospheric sci. and climate 1987-89, mem. commn. geosci., environment and resources), Am. Acad. Arts and Scis., Am. Philos. Soc. Office: U Calif Irvine Chancellors Office 501 Administration Bldg Ofc Irvine CA 92697-1900

CIENFUEGOS, MAURICIO, professional soccer player; b. San Salvador, El Salvador, Feb. 12, 1968; Profl. soccer player El Salvador's First Divsn., 1988-91, 93-95, Mex. Nat. Team, 1991-93; midfielder L.A. Galaxy, 1996—. Three time MLS All-Star; named Galaxy's Most Valuable Player, 1997; one of six Galaxy players selected to 1996 All-Star game. Office: Los Angeles Galaxy 1010 Rose Bowl Dr Pasadena CA 91103-2864

CIESLAK, WILLIAM, academic administrator; b. East Chgo., Sept. 12, 1946; s. Walter Bernard and Irene Joan (Koziol) C. BA in Philosopy, BA in Theology, St. Joseph Coll., 1969; MDiv., Franciscan Sch. Theology, Berkeley, Calif., 1973; PhD, Grad. Theol. Union, Berkeley, Calif., 1979. Prof. Franciscan Sch. Theology, Berkeley, 1980—, pres., 1993—. Mem. Soc. Liturgica, N. Am. Acad. Liturgy, Cath. Theol. Soc. Am. Democrat. Office: Franciscan Sch Theology 1712 Euclid Ave Berkeley CA 94709-1294

CIFFONE, DONALD, electronics company executive; Pres., CEO EXAR, Freemont, Calif. Office: EXAR 48720 Kato Rd Fremont CA 94538-7312

CIMINO, JAY, automotive company executive; BA, U of Denver, Denver. CEO Phil Long Dealerships, Colorado Springs, Colo. Office: Phil Long Ford 1212 Motor City Dr Colorado Springs CO 80906-1392

CINQUE, THOMAS JOSEPH, dean; Dean Creighton U. Sch. Medicine, Omaha, 1992-97; med. dir. edn. Sierra Health Svcs., Inc., Las Vegas, Nev., 1997-99; prof. medicine U. Nev. Sch. Medicine; med. dir. case mgmt. Valley Hosp., Las Vegas.

CIRILLO, EDWARD J. state legislator, retired financial manager; b. Troy, N.Y., Feb. 2, 1934; m. Regina Cirillo; three children. BBA in Acctg., Siena Coll.; MA in Bus. Enterprise, SUNY, Binghamton. Mem. fin. mgmt. staff IBM Corp.; ret.; mem. Ariz. Senate, Dist. 15, Phoenix, 1996—; vice chmn. appropriations subcom.; mem. fin., transp. and rules com.; chmn. fin. instns. and retirement com.; vice-chmn. appropriations com. Village trustee Tarrytown, N.Y.; chair Tarrytown GOP; pres. Property Owners and Residents Assn.; trustee Sun City Mus. Art; v.p. Rep. Club. Mem. Rotary Club (pres.), Elks Lodge (exalted ruler). Office: State Capitol Bldg 1700 W Washington St Ofc 306 Phoenix AZ 85007-2812 E-mail: ecirillo@azleg.state.az.us

CISNEROS, CARLOS R. state legislator; b. Questa, N.Mex, 1951; BS, N. Mex. Highlands U.; MA, U. Montana-Missoula. Mem. N. Mex. Senate, Dist. 6, Sante Fe, 1985—; vice chmn. revenue stabilization and tax policy com.; mem. Indian and cultural affairs com., ways and means com., coms. com. Home: PO Box 1129 Questa NM 87556-1129

CISNEROS, EVELYN, dancer; b. Long Beach, Calif., 1955; Mem. San Francisco Ballet Co., 1977—. Performances include Scherzo, Mozart's C Minor Mass, Romeo and Juliet, Medea, The Tempest, 1980, Stars and Stripes, In the Night, A Midsummer Nights Dream, Cinderella, A Song for Dead Warriors, 1984, Confidences, 1986, Sleeping Beauty, 1992, Swan Lake, 1993. Office: San Francisco Ballet 455 Franklin St San Francisco CA 94102-4471

CIURCZAK, ALEXIS, librarian; b. Long Island, N.Y., Feb. 13, 1950; d. Alexander Daniel and Catherine Ann (Frangipane) C. BA Art History magna cum laude, U. Calif., L.A., 1971; MA Libr. Sci., San Jose State U., 1975; cert. tchr. ESL, U. Calif., Irvine, 1985. Intern IBM Rsch. Libr., San Jose, Calif., 1974-75; tech. asst. San Bernardino Valley Coll. Libr., 1975; tech. svcs. librarian Palomar Coll., San Marcos, 1975-78, pub. svcs. librarian, 1978-81, libr. dir., 1981-86, pub. svcs. librarian, 1987—, instr.

Libr. Technology Cert. Program, 1975—; exchange librarian Fulham Pub. Libr., London, 1986-87; coord. San Diego C.C. Consortium Semester-in-London Am. Inst. Fgn. Study, 1988-89. Mem. ALA, San Diego Libr. Svcs. com., Calif. Libr. Media Educators Assn., Patronato por Niños, Kosciuszko Found., So. Calif. Tech. Processes Group, Pacific Coast Coun. Latin Am. Studies, Libros, Reforma, Libr. Assn. (British), Calif. Libr. Assn., Calif. Tchrs. Assn., Phi Beta Kappa, Beta Phi Mu. Office: Palomar CC 1140 W Mission Rd San Marcos CA 92069-1415

CLABAUGH, ELMER EUGENE, JR. retired lawyer; b. Anaheim, Calif., Sept. 18, 1927; s. Elmer Eugene and Eleanor Margaret (Heitshusen) C.; m. Donna Marie Organ, Dec. 19, 1960 (div.); children: Christopher C., Matthew M. BBA cum laude, Woodbury U.; BA summa cum laude, Claremont McKenna Coll., 1958; JD, Stanford U., 1961. Bar: Calif. 1961, U.S. Dist. Ct. (cen. dist.) Calif., U.S. Ct. Appeals (9th cir.) 1961, U.S. Supreme Ct. 1971. With fgn. svc. U.S. Dept. State, Jerusalem, Tel Aviv, 1951-53, Pub. Adminstrn. Svcs., El Salvador, Ethiopia, U.S., 1953-57; dep. dist. atty. Ventura County, Calif., 1961-62; pvt. practice Ventura County, 1962-97; mem. Hathaway, Clabaugh, Perrett and Webster and predecessors, 1962-79, Clabaugh & Perfloff, Ventura, 1979-97; state inheritance tax referee, 1968-78; ret. Bd. dirs. San Antonio Water Conservation Dist., Ventura Cmty. Meml. Hosp., 1964-80; trustee Ojai Unified Sch. Dist., 1974-79; bd. dirs. Ventura County Found. for Parks and Harbors, 1982-96, Ventura County Maritime Mus., 1982-94. With USCGR, 1944-46, USMCR, 1946-48. Mem. NRA, Calif. Bar Assn., Safari Club Internat., Mason, Shriners, Phi Alpha Delta. Republican.

CLAES, DANIEL JOHN, physician; b. Glendale, Calif., Dec. 3, 1931; s. John Vernon and Claribel (Fleming) C.; m. Gayla Christine Blasdel, Jan. 19, 1974. AB magna cum laude, Harvard U., 1953, MD cum laude, 1957. Intern UCLA, 1957-58; Bowyer Found. fellow for rsch. in medicine L.A., 1958-61; pvt. practice specializing in diabetes L.A., 1962—. Biotech. cons. SIRA Techs., 1995—; v.p. Am. Eye Bank Found., 1978-83, pres., 1983—, dir. rsch., 1980—, chmn., CEO 1995—; pres. Heuristic Corp., 1981—. Contbr. papers on diabetes mellitus, computers in medicine to profl. lit. Mem. L.A. Mus. Art, 1960—. Mem. AMA, AAAS, Calif. Med. Assn., L.A. County Med. Assn., Am. Diabetes Assn. (profl. coun. on immunology, immunogenetics and transplantation), Internat. Diabetes Fedn., Internat. Pancreas & Islet Transplant Assn., Math. Assn. Am., Harvard and Harvard Med. Sch. of So. Calif. Club, Royal Commonwealth Club (London). Office: Am Eyebank Found 15237 W Sunset Blvd Ste 108 Pacific Palisades CA 90272-3690

CLAFLIN, ARTHUR CARY, lawyer; b. Bowling Green, Ohio, July 7, 1950; s. Edward Scott and Mona Sophia (Cretney) C.; m. Gretchen Elaine Anders, May 31, 1975; children: Rachel Anders, Emily Anders. BA magna cum laude, Wesleyan U., 1972; JD, Yale U., 1975. Bar: Wash. 1975, U.S. Dist. Ct. (we. dist.) Wash. 1975, U.S. Dist. Ct. (ea. dist.) Wash. 1981, U.S. Ct. Appeals (9th cir.) 1979, U.S. Ct. Appeals (5th cir.) 1982. Assoc. Bogle & Gates, Seattle, 1975-81, ptnr., 1981-99, Claflin & Christensen, Seattle, 1999-2000; mem. Hall Zanzig Widell, Seattle, 2000—. Mem. Phi Beta Kappa. Presbyterian. Office: Hall Zanzig Widell 1200 5th Ave Ste 1414 Seattle WA 98101-3106

CLAFLIN, BRUCE, communications company executive; BA in Polit. Sci., Pa. State U. Formerly with IBM Corp.; gen. mgr. IBM PC Co., 1989-93; pres. PC Co. Americas, 1993-94, gen. mgr. products and brand mgmt., 1994-97; former sr. v.p. and gen. mgr. sales and mktg. Digital Equipment Corp., 1997-98; pres., CEO 3Com Corp., Santa Clara, Calif., 1998—. Alumni fellow Pa. State U., 1998. Office: 3Com Corp 5400 Bayfront Plz Santa Clara CA 95054-3601

CLAGUE, DAVID A. geologist; b. Phila., Aug. 3, 1948; married; 1 child. PhD in Earth Sci., Scripps Inst. Oceanography, 1974. With nat. rsch. coun. U.S. Geol. Survey, 1974-75, rsch. geologist, 1979-96; asst. prof. geology Middleberry Coll., 1975-79; scientist-in-charge Hawaiian Volcano Obs., 1991-96; dir. rsch. an devel. Monetary Bay Aquarium Rsch. Inst., 1996-99, sr. scientist, 1999—. Fellow Geol. Soc. Am., Am. Geophys. Union, Calif. Acad. Sci. Office: Monterey Bay Aquarium Rsch Inst 7700 Sandholdt Rd Moss Landing CA 95039-9644 E-mail: clague@zmbari.org

CLAIR, THEODORE NAT, educational psychologist; b. Stockton, Calif., Apr. 19, 1929; s. Peter David and Sara Renee (Silverman) C.; m. Laura Gold, June 19, 1961; children: Shari, Judith. AA, U. Calif., Berkeley, 1949, AB, 1950; MS, U. So. Calif., 1953, MEd, 1963, EdD, 1969. Tchr., counselor L.A. City Schs., 1957-63; psychologist Alamitos Sch. Dist., Garden Grove, Calif., 1963-64, Arcadia (Calif.) Unified Sch. Dist., 1964-65; head psychologist Wiseburn Sch. Dist., Hawthorne, Calif., 1966-69; asst. prof. spl. edn., coord. sch. psychology program U. Iowa, Iowa City, 1969-72; dir. pupil pers. svcs. Orcutt (Calif.) Union Sch. Dist., 1972-73; adminstr. Mt. Diablo Unified Sch. Dist., 1973-77; program dir., psychologist San Mateo County Office Edn., Redwood City, 1977-91; assoc. prof. John F. Kennedy U. Sch. Mgmt., 1975-77; pvt. practice as ednl. psychologist specializing in Attention Defecit Disorders Menlo Park, 1978—; pvt. practice marriage and family counselor specializing in Attention Defecit Disorders Menlo Park, 1978—. Dir. Peninsula Vocat. Rehab. Inst., 1978—; psychologist Coll. Counseling Svc., Menlo Pk., 1992—, Calif. Pacific Hosp., San Francisco, 1993—. Author: Phenylketonuria and Some Other Inborn Errors of Amino Acid Metabolism, 1971; editor Jour. Calif. Ednl. Psychologists, 1992-94; contbr. articles to profl. jours. Served with USNR, 1952-54. Mem. APA, Nat. Assn. Sch. Psychologists, Calif. Assn. Marriage and Family Counselors, Nat. Rehab. Assn., Palo Alto B'nai B'rith Club (pres.), Stanford Club Palo Alto. Home and Office: 56 Willow Rd Menlo Park CA 94025-3654

CLAREY, PATRICIA, association executive; BS, Union Coll.; M Pub. Adminstrn., Harvard U. John F. Kennedy Sch. of Govt. With Nat. Park Svc., Washington, Dept. of Interior, Washington; govt. affairs rep. Chevron Corp., San Francisco; dep. chief of staff Calif. Gov. Pete Wilson; v.p. public affairs Transamerica, San Francisco, 1999—. Pres. Transamerica Found., 1998—. Office: Transamerica Found 600 Montgomery St San Francisco CA 94111-2702

CLARK, ALAN FRED, physicist; b. Milwaukee, June 29, 1936; B.S. in Physics, U. Wis., Madison, 1958, M.S. in Nuclear Engrin., 1959; Ph.D. in Nuclear Sci., U. Mich., Ann Arbor, 1964. NAS-NRC postdoctoral assoc. Nat. Bur. Standards, Boulder, Colo., 1964-66, physicist, 1966-78, chief cryogenic properties of solids, 1978-80, group leader supercondr. and magnetic measurements, 1981-87; liaison scientist Office Naval Rsch., London and Europe, 1987-89; group leader fundamental elec. measurements Nat. Inst. Stds., Gaithersburg, Md., 1989-92, 95-98, sr. scientist electricity divsn., 1992-94, dep. chief optoelectronics divsn. Boulder, Colo., 1998-2001, chief magnetic tech. divsn., 2001—. Chmn., founder Internat. Cryogenic Materials Conf. Bd., Boulder, Colo., 1975—; mem. [illegible] to profl. jours.; editor Cryogenics Jour., 1982-94, IEEE Trans. Applied Superconductivity, 1994-98, 8 conf. proceedings, 4 books. Recipient Superior Rsch. Nat. Bur. Standards, 1967, 74, 82, 83, 84, 85, 86, 93-97. Fellow IEEE, Am. Phys. Soc.; mem. ASTM (chmn. superconductor com. 1980-89), IEEE Superconductivity Com. (chmn. 1989-94), Internat. Acad. Electrotech. Scis. Office: Nat Inst Standards & Tech MS 816 00 325 [illegible]

CLARK, BRIAN THOMAS, mathematical statistician, operations research analyst; b. Rockford, Ill., Apr. 7, 1951; s. Paul Herbert and Martha Lou (Schiensker) C.; m. Suzanne Drake, Nov. 21, 1992; 1 child, Branden Ward. BS cum laude, No. Ariz. U., 1973; postgrad., Ariz. State U., 1980-82; MBA, Heriot-Watt U., Edinburgh, Scotland, 1999. Math. aide Ctr. for Disease Control, Phoenix, 1973-74, math. statistician, 1979-83, Ctrs. for Disease Control, Atlanta, 1983-84; ops rsch. analyst U.S. Army Info. Systems Command, Ft. Huachuca, Ariz., 1984—. Math. statistician U.S. Navy Meteorology Engring. Ctr., Pomona, Calif., 1974-79. Republican. Mormon. Office: US Army Signal Command Dep Chief Staff Resource Mgmt G8 Managerial Acctg Pricing Fort Huachuca AZ 85613

CLARK, BRUCE ROBERT, geology consultant; b. Pitts., June 17, 1941; s. Harold Thomas and Florence (Miller) C.; m. Karen Pelton Heath, Dec. 30, 1967; children: Adam, Andrea. BS, Yale U., 1963; PhD, Stanford U., 1967. Asst. prof. U. Mich., Ann Arbor, 1968-73, assoc. prof., 1973-77; v.p. Leighton and Assocs., Inc., Irvine, Calif., 1977-85, pres., 1986—, chief exec. officer, 1988—. Contbr. articles to profl. jours. Chmn. bd. YMCA Orange County, Calif., 1999—; commr. Calif. Seisic Safety Commn., 2000—. Fellow Geological Soc. Am.; mem. Earthquake Engring. Rsch. Inst., Am. Geophysical Union, Assn. Engring. Geologists, Seismological Soc. Am., Sigma Xi. Office: Leighton & Assocs Inc 17781 Cowan Irvine CA 92614-6009

CLARK, BURTON ROBERT, sociologist, educator; b. Pleasantville, N.J., Sept. 6, 1921; s, Burton H. and Cornelia (Amole) C.; m. Adele Halitsky, Aug. 31, 1949; children: Philip Neil (dec.), Adrienne. BA, UCLA, 1949, PhD, 1954; PhD (hon.), U. Strathclyde, 1998, U. Turku, Finland, 2000. Asst. prof. sociology Stanford U., 1953-56; research asso., asst. prof. edn. Harvard U., 1956-58; asso. prof., then prof. edn. and asso. research sociologist, then research sociologist U. Calif. at Berkeley, 1958-66; prof. sociology Yale U., 1966-80, chmn. dept., 1969-72, chmn. higher edn. rsch. group, 1973-80; Allan M. Cartter prof. higher edn. UCLA, 1980-91, prof. emeritus, 1991—. Author: Adult Education in Transition, 1956, The Open Door College, 1960, Educating the Expert Society, 1962, The Distinctive College, 1970, The Problems of American Education, 1975, Academic Power in Italy, 1977, The Higher Education System, 1983, The Academic Life, 1987, Places of Inquiry, 1995, Creating Entrepreneurial Universities, 1998; co-author: Students and Colleges, 1972, Youth: Transition to Adulthood, 1973, Academic Power in the United States, 1976, Academic Power: Patterns of Authority in Seven National Systems of Higher Education, 1978; editor: Perspectives on Higher Education, 1984, The School and The University, 1985, The Academic Profession, 1987, The Research Foundations of Graduate education, 1993; co-senior editor: Encyclopedia of Higher Education, 1992. Served with AUS, 1942-46. Recipient Comenius medal UNESCO, 1998. Fellow Brit. Soc. for Rsch. in Higher Edn.; mem. Am. Sociol. Assn., Am. Ednl. Rsch. Assn. (Am. Coll. Testing award 1979, Divsn. J. Disting. Rsch. award 1988, Outstanding Book award 1989), Assn. Study Higher Edn. (pres. 1979-80, Rsch. Achievement award 1985, Howard Bowen Distinguished Svc. award 1997), Am. Assn. Higher Edn., Nat. Acad. Edn. (v.p. 1989-93), Consortium Higher Edn. Rschrs., European Assn. for Instnl. Rsch. (disting. mem.) Home: 201 Ocean Ave 1710B Santa Monica CA 90402 Office: UCLA Dept Edn Los Angeles CA 90095-1521 E-mail: clark@qseis.ucla.edu

CLARK, CHAPIN DEWITT, law educator; b. Lawrence, Kans., Dec. 27, 1930; s. Carroll DeWitt and Pearl (Holl) C.; m. Dorothy L. Becker, May 25, 1952; children— Julia Kay, Jeffrey Becker. A.B., U. Kans., 1952, LL.B., 1954; LL.M., Columbia U., 1959. Bar: Kans. 1954, Oreg. 1965. Asst. prof. law U. S.D., 1959-62; assoc. prof. law U. Oreg., 1962-67, prof., 1967-91, prof. emeritus, 1991—, dean Sch. Law, 1974-80. Vice chmn. Oreg. Water Policy Rev. Bd., 1975-77, chmn., 1977-79; vis. prof. U.S. Mil. Acad., West Point, N.Y., 1980-81, 86-87; pres. Pacific 10 Athletic Conf., 1984-85; vis. prof. Wash. U. Law Sch., 1992. Contbr. articles to profl. jours. Pres. Planned Parenthood Lane County, 1975-76; mem. Gov.'s Commn. on Oceanography, 1967-68. Served with JAGC U.S. Army, 1954-58; col. USAR. Mem. Am. Bar Assn., AAUP (pres. U. Oreg. chpt. 1970-71, pres. Oreg. State conf. 1985-86), Am. Alpine Club. Home: 3565 Knob Hill Ln Eugene OR 97405-4738 Office: U Oreg Sch of Law Eugene OR 97403

CLARK, CHARLES SUTTER, interior designer; b. Venice, Calif., Dec. 21, 1927; s. William Sutter and Lodema Ersell (Fleeman) C. Student Chouinard Art Inst., Los Angeles, 1950-51. Interior designer LM.H. Co., Gt. Falls, Mont., 1956-62, Andreason's Interiors, Oakland, Calif., 1962-66, Western Contact Furnishers Internat., Oakland, 1966-70, Design Five Assocs., Lafayette, Calif., 1972-73; owner, interior designer Charles Sutter Clark Interiors, Greenbrae, Calif., 1973-91, San Rafael, Calif., 1991—. Served with USAF, 1951-55. Recipient prizes Mont. State Fair, 1953-55. Mem. Am. Soc. Interior Designers. Home: 429 El Faisan Dr San Rafael CA 94903-4517

CLARK, COLIN WHITCOMB, mathematics educator; b. Vancouver, B.C., Can., June 18, 1931; s. George Savage and Irene (Stewart) C.; m. Janet Arlene Davidson, Sept. 17, 1955; children: Jennifer Kathleen, Karen Elizabeth, Graeme David. BA, U. B.C., 1953; PhD, U. Wash., 1958; DSc (hon.), U. Victoria, 2000. Instr. math. U. Calif., Berkeley, 1958-60; asst. prof. math. U. B.C., 1960-65, assoc. prof., 1965-68, prof., 1968-94, acting dir. Inst. Applied Math., 1983-86, prof. emeritus, 1994—. Vis. prof. math. N.Mex. State U., 1970-71; vis. scientist Fisheries and Oceanography div. C.S.I.R.O., Cronulla, Australia, 1975-76, Ecology and Evolutionary Biology, U. Ariz., 1992; Regents lectr. U. Calif., Davis, 1986; vis. prof. Biol. Scis. Cornell U., 1987; vis. prof. Princeton U., 1997. Author: The Theoretical Side of Calculus, 1972, Mathematical Bioeconomics, 1976, 2d edit., 1990, Elementary Mathematical Analysis, 1982, Bioeconomic Modelling and Fisheries Management, 1985, (with J. Conrad) Resource Economics: Notes and Problems, 1987, (with M. Mangel) Dynamic Modeling in Behavorial Ecology, 1988, (with J. Yoshimura, eds.) Adaption in Stochastic Environments, 1993, (with M. Mangel) Dynamic State Variable Models in Ecology, 2000; contbr. articles to profl. jours. Fellow Royal Soc. Can., Royal Soc. (U.K.); mem. Can. Applied Math. Soc. (pres. 1981-83), Soc. Indsl. and Applied Math., Resource Modeling Assn. (pres. 1988-90), Internat. Soc. for Ecol. Econ. Office: Univ BC Dept Math Vancouver BC Canada V6T 1Z2

CLARK, DICK, performer, producer; b. Mt. Vernon, N.Y., Nov. 30, 1929; m. Kari Wigton; children— Richard, Duane, Cindy. Grad., Syracuse U., 1951. Founder Dick Clark Corp. Prodns., Dick Clark Film Group, Dick Clark's Am. Bandstand Grills. Announcer, Sta. WRUN, summer 1950; then staff announcer, Sta. WOLF; rejoined, Sta. WRUN, then joined, Sta. WKTV, announcer, Sta. WFIL, Phila., 1952; host Am. Bandstand, 1956-89 (Outstanding Popular Music Program, Popular Music Mag. 1958, Daytime Emmy award 1981-82, 82-83), 32d Ann. Emmy Awards, 1981, Daytime Emmy Awards; formed, Dick Clark Prodns., 1956. Leading ind. T.V. producer with over 8500 hours of programming to credit, including The Savage Seven, 1968, Psych-Out, 1968, Killers Three, 1968, The Man in the Santa Claus Suit, 1979, The Birth of the Beatles, 1979, Elvis, 1979, The Dark, 1979, Murder in Texas, 1981, Demon Murder Case, 1983, Woman Who Willed a Miracle, 1983 (5 Emmmy awards, Peabody award), Remo [illegible] 1988, Town Bully, 1988, Promised a Miracle, 1988, Death Dreams, 1991, Elvis and the Colonel: The Untold Story, 1993, Secret Sins of the Father, 1994, The Good Doctor: The Paul Fleiss Story, 1996, Deep Family Secrets, 1997; producer/host TV series: American Bandstand, The Dick Clark Show, Where the Action Is, The Rock'n Roll Years, others; host Dick Clark's Rock 'n Roll Revue, $ 20,000 Pyramid (Emmy award 1978-79), [illegible] USA, Miss Teen USA, Miss Universe; host/ exec. producer Super Bloopers and New Practical Jokes, New Years Rockin' Eve, 40th Anniversary of American Bandstand; exec. producer Acad. of Country Music Awards, Am. Music awards, Golden Globe Awards, Soap Opera Awards, Daytime Emmy Awards, Cable Ace Awards; author: Your Happiest Years, 1959, To Goof or Not To Goof, 1963, Rock, Roll and Remember, 1976, Dick Clark & Richard Robinson, Looking Great, Staying Young, 1981, Dick Clark's The First 25 Years of Rock 'N Roll, 1981, The History of American Bandstand, 1985, Dick Clark's Guide to Good Grooming, 1985; producer VH1's Best fo American Bandstand, 1996, 97, Primetime Country, 1996, 97, Beyond Belief: Factor Fiction, 1997, The Weird Al Show, 1997, Dick Clarks's American Bandstand Collectors Edition, 1997; Donny & Marie, 1998-2000, Your Big Break, 1999, 2000, Greed, 1999, 2000; founder Dick Clark Media Archives. Recipient 6 Emmy awards as both prodr. and host, Grammy Nat. Trustees award, 1990, Am. Classic award ASCAP, 1990, Billboard Radio award Countdown Am., 1991, Disting. Svc. award Nat. Assn. Broadcasting, 1993, Daytime Emmys Lifetime Achievement award, 1994, Lifetime Achievement award Am. D.J. Assn., 1994, Lifetime Achievement award Syracuse U., 1994; named to Emerson Radio Hall of Fame, 1990, Broadcasting Mag. Hall of Fame, 1992, Rock 'N' Roll Hall of Fame, 1993, Internat. Person of Yr., NAPTE, 1990, Person of Yr., Phila. Advt. Club, 1995; inducted TV Hall of Fame, 1993. Address: Dick Clark Productions Inc 3003 W Olive Ave Burbank CA 91505-7811

CLARK, EARNEST HUBERT, JR. tool company executive; b. Birmingham, Ala., Sept. 8, 1926; s. Earnest Hubert and Grace May (Smith) C.; m. Patricia Margaret Hamilton, June 22, 1947; children: Stephen D., Kenneth A., Timothy R., Daniel S., Scott H., Rebecca G. BS in Mech. Engring, Calif. Inst. Tech., 1946, MS, 1947. Chmn., chief exec. officer Friendship Group, Baker Hughes, Inc. (formerly Baker Oil Tools, Inc.), L.A., 1947-89, v.p., asst. gen. mgr., 1958-62, pres., chief exec. officer, 1962-69, 75-79, chmn. bd., 1969-75, 79-87, 87-89, ret., 1989; chmn. The Friendship Group, Newport Beach, Calif., 1989—. Bd. dirs. Regenesis Inc. Past chmn., bd. dirs. YMCA of U.S.A.; past chmn. bd. YMCA for Met. L.A.; mem. nat. coun. YMCA; trustee Harvey Mudd Coll. With USNR, 1944-46, 51-52. Mem. AIME, Am. Petroleum Inst., Petroleum Equipment Suppliers Assn. (bd. dirs.), Tau Beta Pi. Office: Friendship Group 3822 Calle Ariana San Clemente CA 92672-4502 E-mail: ehclarkjr@home.com

CLARK, GLEN EDWARD, judge; b. Cedar Rapids, Iowa, Nov. 23, 1943; s. Robert M. and Georgia L. (Welch) C.; m. Deanna D. Thomas, July 16, 1966; children: Andrew Curtis, Carissa Jane. BA, U. Iowa, 1966; JD, U. Utah, 1971. Bar: Utah 1971, U.S. Dist. Ct. Utah 1971, U.S. Ct. Appeals (10th cir.) 1972. Assoc. Fabian & Clendenin, 1971-74, ptnr., 1975-81, dir., chmn. banking and comml. law sect., 1981-82; judge U.S. Bankruptcy Ct. Dist. Utah, Salt Lake City, 1982-86, chief judge, 1986—. Bd. govs. nat. Conf. Bankruptcy Judges, 1988-94; mem. com. on bankruptcy edn. Fed. Jud. Ctr., 1989-92; vis. prof. U. Utah, Salt Lake City, 1977-79, 83; pres. Nat. Conf. Bankruptcy Judges, 1992-93; chair bd. trustees Nat. Conf. Bankruptcy Judges Endowment for Edn., 1990-92; vis. assoc. prof. law Univ. Utah; instr. adv. bus. law Univ. Utah. Articles editor: Utah Law Review. With U.S. Army, 1966-68. Finkbine fellow U. Iowa. Fellow Am. Coll. Bnakruptcy (charter, mem. bd. regents 1995-2000); mem. Jud. Conf. U.S. (mem. com. jud. br. 1992-99, 10th cir. bankruptcy appellate panel 1996—), Utah Bar Assn., Order of Coif. Presbyterian. Office: 365 US Courthouse 350 S Main St Salt Lake City UT 84101-2106

CLARK, JAMES HENRY, publishing company executive; b. Chgo., Aug. 30, 1931; s. James Henry and Mildred Beth (Rutledge) C.; children: Garrette Elizabeth, James Henry. A.B., U. Calif.-Berkeley, 1959. With personnel dept. Fireman's Fund, San Francisco, 1959-60; coll. textbook salesman Prentice-Hall Inc., Berkeley, 1960-63, regional editor, 1963-64, editor N.J., 1964-67; dir. Western editorial office, Belmont, Calif., 1967-68; assoc. pub. Aldine Pub. Co., Chgo., 1969; editor-in-chief coll. div. Harper & Row Pubs., Inc., N.Y.C., 1969-70, pub., v.p., 1970-77; dir. Univ. Press U. Calif., Berkeley, 1977—. Served with USAF, 1949-53. Mem. Am. Assn. Univ. Presses (pres. 1986.) Office: U Calif Univ Press 2120 Berkeley Way Berkeley CA 94720-5804

CLARK, JEFFREY RAPHIEL, research and development company executive; b. Provo, Utah, Sept. 29, 1953; s. Bruce Budge and Ouida (Raphiel) C.; m. Anne Margaret Eberhardt, Mar. 15, 1985; children: Jeffrey Raphiel, Mary Anne Elizabeth, Edward William Eberhardt. BS, Brigham Young U., 1977, MBA, 1979. CPA, Tex. Fin. analyst Exxon Coal USA, Inc., Houston, 1979-83; constrn. mgr. Gen. Homes, Inc., Houston, 1983-84; controller Liberty Data Products, Houston, 1984-86; v.p. Tech. Rsch. Assocs., Inc., Salt Lake City, 1987—, also dir. Scoutmaster Boy Scouts Am., Salt Lake City, 1989-91. Mem. AICPA, Utah Inst. CPAs, Salt Lake C. of C. (legis. action com.), Salt Lake Country Club. Republican. Mormon. Avocations: snow skiing, golf, mountain climbing. Home: 1428 Michigan Ave Salt Lake City UT 84105-1609 Office: Technical Rsch Assocs 2257 S 1100 E Salt Lake City UT 84106-2379

CLARK, JOHN DESMOND, anthropology educator; b. London, Apr. 10, 1916; came to U.S., 1961, naturalized 1993; s. Thomas John Chown and Catherine (Wynne) C.; m. Betty Cable Baume, Apr. 30, 1938; children: Elizabeth Ann (Mrs. David Miall Winterbottom), John Wynne Desmond. BA with honors, Cambridge U., 1937, MA, 1942, PhD, 1950, ScD, 1974; ScD (hon.), U. Witwatersrand, Johannesburg, 1985, U. Cape Town, , 1985. Dir. Rhodes-Livingstone Mus., No. Rhodesia, 1938-61; prof. anthropology U. Calif., Berkeley, 1961-86, prof. emeritus, 1986—. Faculty rsch. lectr. U. Calif., 1979; Raymond Dart lectr. Inst. for Study of Man, Africa, 1979; Sir Mortimer Wheeler lectr. Brit. Acad., 1981; J.D. Mulvaney lectr. Australian Nat. U., 1990. Author: The Stone Age Cultures of Northern Rhodesia, 1950, The Prehistoric Cultures of the Horn of Africa, 1954, The Prehistory of Southern Africa, 1959, Prehistoric Cultures of Northeast Angola, 1963, Distribution of Prehistoric Culture in Angola, 1966, The Atlas of African Prehistory, 1967, Kalambo Falls Prehistoric Site, Vol. I, 1969, Vol. II, 1974, The Prehistory of Africa, 1970; editor: Cambridge History of Africa, Vol. I, 1982; (with G.R. Sharma) Palaeo environment and Prehistory in the Middle Son Valley Madhya Pradesh, North Central India, 1983; (with S.A. Brandt) The Causes and Consequences of Food Production in Africa, 1984, Cultural Beginnings: Approaches to Understanding Early Hominid Lifeways in the African Savanna, 1991; contbr. articles to profl. jours. Served with Brit. Army, 1941-46. Decorated comdr. Order Brit. Empire; comdr. Nat. Order Senegal; recipient Huxley medal Royal Anthrop. Inst., London, 1974, Ad personam internat. Gold Mercury award Addis Ababa, 1982, Berkeley citation U. Calif., 1986, Fellows medal Calif. Acad. Scis., 1987, Gold medal Am. Archaeol. Inst., 1989. Fellow AAAS, Brit. Acad. (Grahame Clark medal for prehistory 1997), Royal Soc. South Africa, Soc. Antiquaries London (Gold medal 1985); mem. NAS, Am. Anthropol. Assn. (disting. lectr. 1992, emeritus prof. of yr. 1996, L.S.B. Leakey Found. prize, 1996), Pan-African Congress Prehistory, Geog. Soc. Lisbon, Instituto Italiano di Preistoria e Protostoria, Body Corporate Livingstone Mus., Deuschen Archaologischen Instituts (corr. mem.). Office: U Calif Dept Anthropology Berkeley CA 94720-0001 E-mail: jdclark@uclink4.berkeley.edu

[illegible] Wesley Pelton and Lois (Ellenberger) Heath; m. Bruce Robert Clark,Dec. 30, 1967; children: Adam Heath, Andrea Pelton. Student, Pomona Coll., Claremont, Calif., 1962-64; BA, Stanford U., 1964-66; MA in History, U. Wash., 1968; JD, U. Mich., 1977. Bar: Calif. 1978. Instr. Henry Ford Community Coll., Dearborn, Mich., 1968-72; assoc. Gibson, Dunn & Crutcher LLP, Irvine, Calif., 1977-86, ptnr., 1986—. Bd. dirs. Dem. Found. [illegible]

Ana, Calif., 1979-82, New Directions for Women, Newport Beach, 1986-91, Women in Leadership, chair, 1995-99; deans adv. coun. Sch. Humanities, U. Calif., Irvine. Recipient 1996 Choice award Planned Parenthood of Orange & San Bernardino Counties. Mem. Women in Leadership (founder 1993), Comml. Real Estate Women, Bldg. Industries Assn. So. Calif., Internat. Coun. Shopping Ctrs., Calif. Mortgage Bankers Assn. Office: Gibson Dunn & Crutcher LLP 4 Park Plz Ste 1400 Irvine CA 92614-8557 E-mail: kclark@gibsondunn.com

CLARK, LOYAL FRANCES, public affairs specialist; b. Salt Lake City, July 16, 1958; d. Lloyd Grant and Zina (Okelberry) C. Student, Utah State U., 1976-78. Human resource coord. U.S. Forest Svc., Provo, Utah, 1984—, fire info. officer, 1987—, pub. affairs officer, interpretive svcs. coord., edn. coord., 1988—. Mem. Take Pride in Utah Task Force, Salt Lake City, 1989—; chairperson Utah Wildlife Ethics Com., Provo, 1989—. Instr. Emergency Svcs., Orem, Utah, 1990—. Recipient Presdl. award for outstanding leadership in youth conservation programs Pres. Ronald Reagan, 1985, Superior Svc. award USDA, 1987, Exemplary Svc. award U.S. Forest Svc., 1992, Nat. Eyes on Wildlife Achievement award USDA Forest Svc., 1993, Employee of the Nineties award USDA Forest Svc., 1999. Mem. Nat. Wildlife Fedn., Nat. Assn. Interpretation, Utah Soc. Environ. Educators, Utah Wildlife Fedn. (bd. dirs. 1981-85, v.p. 1985-87, Achievement award 1983, 85, 87), Utah Wilderness Assn., Am. Forestry Assn., Nature Conservancy, Women in Mgmt. Coun., Nat. Assn. Female Execs. Avocations: hiking, photography, gardening, antiques. Office: Uinta Nat Forest 88 W 100 N Provo UT 84601-4452

CLARK, MARCIA RACHEL, former prosecutor; b. Berkeley, Calif., 1954; d. Abraham I. Kleks; m. Gabriel Horowitz, 1976 (div. 1980); m. Gordon Clark (div. 1994); 2 children. BA in Polit. Sci., UCLA, 1974; JD, Southwestern U., 1979. Atty. Brodey and Price, L.A., 1979-81, L.A. County Dist. Attys. Office, 1981-97. Author (with Teresa Carpenter) Without a Doubt, 1997. Office: LA County Dist Attys Office 210 W Temple St Los Angeles CA 90012-3210

CLARK, MELVIN EUGENE, chemical company executive; b. Ord, Nebr., Oct. 2, 1916; s. Ansel B. and Ruth Joy (Bullock) C.; m. Virginia May Hiller, Sept. 16, 1938; children— John Robert, Walter Clayton, Dale Eugene, Merry Sue. BSChemE cum laude, U. Colo., 1937; grad. exec. program, Columbia U., 1952; grad. advanced mgmt. program, Harvard U., 1961. Asst. editor Chem. Engring., McGraw-Hill, N.Y.C., 1937-41; mktg. staff Wyandotte Chem. Corp., Mich., 1941-53; chief program br. War Prodn. Bd., Washington, 1942-44; v.p. mktg. Frontier Chem. Co., Wichita, 1953-69; exec. v.p. chems. div. Vulcan Materials Co., Birmingham, Ala., 1969-81, v.p. planning, chems. and metals group, 1981-82; cons., 1982—. Pres. Chlorine Inst., 1977-80 Contbr. numerous articles to profl. jours. Recipient U. Colo. Alumni Recognition award, 1972; named Chem. Market Rsch. Assn. Man of Year, 1963, Disting. Engring. Alumnus, U. Colo., 1985, Centennial medalist Coll. of Engring., U. Colo., 1994. Mem. AIChE, Comml. Devel. and Mktg. Assn., Am. Chem. Soc., Boulder Country Club, Tau Beta Pi, Pi Mu Epsilon. Republican. Mem. Christian Ch. Home and Office: 7145 Cedarwood Cir Boulder CO 80301-3716 E-mail: meclark1@aol.com

CLARK, MICHAEL PHILLIP, English educator; b. Marlin, Tex., May 27, 1950; s. Burton Francis and Nelda (Blount) C.; m. Kathleen Mack, 1971 (div. 1973); m. Katherine Weber, May 26, 1977. BA magna cum laude, Rice U., 1972; MA, U. Calif., Irvine, 1973, PhD, 1977. Asst. prof. U. Mich., Ann Arbor, 1977-83; prof. in English and comparative lit. U. Calif., Irvine, 1983—. Author: Michael Foucault, 1983, Jacques Lacan, 1989; contbr. articles to profl. publs. Mem. MLA, Soc. Early Americanists. Office: U Calif Dept English Irvine CA 92697-0001

CLARK, PATRICIA ANN, federal judge; b. Buffalo, July 26, 1936; d. Andrew A. and Mary (Gardner) Zacher; m. James A. Clark, Mar. 25, 1960; B.A., Goucher Coll., Towson, Md., 1958; postgrad. Duke U., 1958-60; LL.B., U. Colo., 1961. Bar: Colo. 1961, U.S. Dist. Ct. D.C. 1961. With Transamerica Title Ins. Co., 1962-65; assoc. Holme, Roberts and Owen, 1965-70, ptnr., 1970-74; judge U.S. Bankruptcy Ct., Denver, 1974— . Commr., Colo. Civil Rights Commn., 1969-72; trustee Waterman Fund, 1978— ; mem. transition adv. com. U.S. Cts., 1980-84, com. jud. resources, 1987-91. Recipient Disting. Alumni award U. Colo. Sch. Law, 1984. Mem. Colo. Bar Assn., Denver Bar Assn. Office: US Bankruptcy Ct US Custom House 721 19th St Denver CO 80202-2500

CLARK, PETER BRUCE, newspaper executive; b. Detroit, Oct. 23, 1928; s. Rex Scripps and Marian (Peters) C.; m. Lianne Schroeder, Dec. 21, 1952 (dec. Jan. 1996); children: Ellen Clark Brown, James. B.A., Pomona Coll., 1952, LL.D. (hon.), 1972; M.P.A., Syracuse U., 1953; Ph.D., U. Chgo., 1959; H.H.D., Mich. State U., 1973, Lawrence Inst. Tech., 1982; LL.D. (hon.), U. Mich., 1977. Research assoc., then instr. polit. sci. U. Chgo., 1957-59; asst. prof. polit. sci. Yale U., 1959-61; with Evening News Assn., Detroit, 1960-86, corp. sec., 1960-61, v.p., 1961-63, pres., 1963-86, chmn. bd., chief exec. officer, dir., 1969-86; pub. Detroit News, 1963-81, also dir.; dir. Gannett Co., Inc., 1986-99. Regent's prof. UCLA Grad. Sch. Mgmt., 1987; chmn. Fed. Res. Bank Chgo., 1975-77, former chmn. br. Fed. Res. Bank Detroit. Served with AUS, 1953-55. Mem. Am. Newspaper Pubs. Assn. (dir. 1966-74), Am. Soc. Newspaper Editors, Detroit Club, Ironwood Country Club.

CLARK, RAYMOND OAKES, banker; b. Ft. Bragg, N.C., Nov. 9, 1944; s. Raymond Shelton and Nancy Lee (McCormick) C.; m. Patricia Taylor; children: Matthew Patrick, Geoffry Charles. BBA, U. Ariz., 1966; postgrad., U. Wash., 1984-86. Mgnt. trainee First Interstate Bank, Phoenix, 1966, credit analyst, 1968-69, asst. br. mgr. Scottsdale, Ariz., 1969-72, asst. v.p., br. mgr. Tempe, 1972-90, v.p. br. mgr. Scottsdale, 1990-92, v.p. mgr. main office Phoenix, 1992—.

CLARK, RICHARD WARD, trust company executive, consultant; b. N.Y.C., Oct. 23, 1938; s. Richard Leal and Dorothy Jane (Whittaker) C. BA with distinction, U. Rochester, N.Y., 1960; MBA in Fin., U. Pa., 1962. Corp. planning analyst Campbell Soup Co., Camden, N.J., 1965-67; asst. product mgr. Gen. Mills, Inc., Mpls., 1967-70; sr. fin. analyst McKesson Corp., San Francisco, 1970-71, asst. div. controller, 1971-72, div. controller, 1972-78, gen. mgr. grocery products devel., 1978-79; v.p., controller McKesson Foods Group/McKesson Corp., 1979-85, dir. strategic planning, 1985-87; v.p. fin., CFO, Provigo Corp., San Rafael, Calif., 1987-90; cons. on hotel devel., Napa Valley Assocs., S.A., San Francisco, 1990-92, health care cons., 1993-97; exec. trust dir. Comml. Bank Korea, San Francisco, 1998—. Bd. dirs. Taylor Cuisine, Inc., San Francisco. Author: Some Factors Affecting Dividend Payout Ratios, 1962; musician (albums) Dick Clark at the Keyboard, I Love a Piano, 1990, I Play the Songs, 1993, On My Way to You, 1997, Christmas Piano with Violin, 1999. Mem. adv. bd. Salvation Army, San Francisco, 1984—, chmn., 1993-2000; bd. dirs. Svcs. for Srs., San Francisco, 1990-93. Lt. (j.g.) USNR, 1962-64, PTO. Sherman fellow U. Rochester, 1960. Mem. Bohemian Club, Beta Gamma Sigma. Republican. Presbyterian. Avocations: piano, skiing, tennis, singing, jogging. Home: 2201 Sacramento St Apt 401 San Francisco CA 94115-2314

CLARK, ROBERT NEWHALL, electrical and aeronautical engineering educator; b. Ann Arbor, Mich., Apr. 17, 1925; s. Ellef S. and Esther (Baker) C.; m. Mary Quiatt, Aug. 20, 1949; children: Charles W., John R., Timothy J., Franklin T. BSEE, U. Mich., 1950, MSEE, 1951; PhD, Stanford U., 1969. Registered profl. engr., Wash., Minn. Rsch. engr. Honeywell, Inc., Mpls., 1951-57; lectr. Stanford U., 1968; prof. elec. engring. U. Wash., Seattle, 1957—, prof. aeronautics and astronautics, 1986-94; prof. emeritus, 1994—. Vis. scientist Fraunhofer Gesellschaft, Karlsruhe, W.Ger., 1976-77; guest prof. U. Duisburg, W.Ger., 1983-84; cons. analyst Boeing Aerospace Co., Seattle, 1971-92. Author: Introduction to Automatic Control Systems, 1962, Fault Diagnosis in Dynamic Systems, 1989, Control System Dynamics, 1996, Issues of Fault Diagnosis for Dynamic Systems, 2000. With USMC, 1943-46. NSF fellow, 1966-68. Fellow IEEE (life), AIAA (assoc.). Home: 3900 50th Ave NE Seattle WA 98105-5238 Office: U Wash PO Box 352500 Seattle WA 98195-2500

CLARK, SCOTT H. lawyer; b. Logan, Utah, Jan. 7, 1946; BA with honors, U. Utah, 1970; JD, U. Chgo., 1973. Bar: Utah 1973. Ptnr. Ray, Quinney & Nebeker P.C., Salt Lake City, 1980—. Mem. ABA, Utah State Bar, Salt Lake County Bar Assn., Phi Beta Kappa, Phi Kappa Phi, Pi Sigma Alpha. Office: Ray Quinney & Nebek PC PO Box 45385 Salt Lake City UT 84145-0385 E-mail: SClark@RQN.com

CLARK, STANFORD E. accountant; b. Farmington, Utah, Sept. 21, 1917; m. Merrial Jane Knight Mackay, Nov. 16, 1942 (dec. July 1993); m. Evelyn Harrow, Nov. 3, 1995. Student, LDS Bus. Coll., Salt Lake City, 1935. With Utah Constrn. Co., Riverton, Wyo., 1955-57; rancher Riverton, 1948-55; office mgr. Superior Bit Svc., Riverton, 1958-68; v.p., sec., treas. Allied Nuclear Corp., Riverton, 1957-69, Western Std. Corp., Riverton, 1957-83, pres., treas., dir., 1989—; also bd. dirs. Treas., v.p., sec., bd. dirs. Snow King Resort Mgmt. Inc., Jackson, 1992-99, Jackson Hole Springs Water Co., 1995—; treas. S.K. Land Ltd. Liability Co., 1992—; v.p., treas., bd. dirs. Snow King Resort Ctr., Inc., 1999—, Snow King Resort, Inc., 1999—; sec., treas., bd. dirs., 1991-99; pres. Western Recreation Corp., 1957—. With USCG, 1942-45. Republican. Office: Western Standard Corp 205 S Broadway Ave Riverton WY 82501-4331

CLARK, THOMAS P., JR. lawyer; b. N.Y.C., Sept. 16, 1943; AB, U. Notre Dame, 1965; JD, U. Mo., Kansas City, 1973. Bar: Calif. 1973. Shareholder Stradling, Yocca, Carlson & Rauth P.C., Newport Beach, Calif., 1978—. Editor-in-chief The Urban Lawyer, 1972-73; contbr. articles to profl. jours. Capt. USMC, 1966-70. Mem. State Bar Calif., Orange County Bar Assn., Phi Kappa Phi. Office: Stradling Yocca Carlson & Rauth PC 660 Newport Center Dr Ste 1600 Newport Beach CA 92660-6458 E-mail: tclark@sycr

CLARK, TRENT L. government public affairs manager; b. Jackson Hole, Wyo., July 12, 1961; s. Richard L. and Carolyn T. Clark; m. Rebecca L. Lee, May 23, 1986; children: Brittany, Kathleen, Christin, Alexander. AS, Ricks Coll., 1980; BA, Brigham Young U., 1984; cert. pub. health, Harvard U., 1995. Legis. staff U.S. Senate, Washington, 1983-90; chief environ. economist Joint Econ. Com. Congress, Washington, 1990-91; state dir. Idaho Farm Svcs. Adminstrn., Boise, 1991-93; sr. comms. specialist Monsanto Co., Soda Springs, Idaho, 1993-98; fed. affairs mgr. Solutia, Inc., Soda Springs, 1998-99; dir. govt. and pub. affairs Monsanto Co., Soda Springs, 1999—. Dir. Get the Waste Out, Soda Springs, 1996; vice chmn. Idaho Rep. Orgn., Region 6, Pocatello, 1998; chmn. Idaho Rural Devel. Coun., Boise, 1997; chmn. Idaho Rep. Party, 1999. Recipient Merit award USDA, 1992, Gov.'s Safety Conf. award Gov. Idaho, 1998. Mem. Idaho Assn. Commerce and Industry (vice chmn., dir. 1993—), Idaho Coun. on Industry and the Environment (dir. 1998—), Soda Springs C. of C. (pres. 1998-99). Mem. LDS Ch. Avocations: fencing, backcountry horsepacking. Office: Monsanto 1853 Highway 34 Soda Springs ID 83276-5227 E-mail: Trent.L.Clark@monsanto.com

CLARKE, DAVID R. materials engineer; BSc with First Class Honors, U. Sussex, Eng.; PhD in Physics, Cambridge U., Eng. With U. Calif., Berkeley, 1974-77; with structural ceramics group Rockwell Internat. Sci. Ctr., 1977; assoc. prof. MIT, Cambridge, Mass.; from mgr. ceramic scis. group to sr. mgr. dept. materials IBM Rsch. Divsn., Yorktown Heights, N.Y.; with faculty U. Calif., Santa Barbara, 1990—. Chair ceramic scis. Gordon Rsch. Conf., 1982; Morrison lectr. McMaster U., 1998; Van Horn lectr. Case We. Reserve U., 1999. Mem. editl. bd. Cambridge Solid State Sci. Series, 1993-97; editorial adv. bd. Philosophical Mag., Materials Sci. and Tech., Interface Sci.; assoc. editor Jour. Am. Ceramic Soc. Recipient Sr. Scientist award Alexander von Humboldt Found., 1992. Fellow Am. Ceramic Soc. (Ross Coffin Purdy award 1982, Sosman Meml. award 1999, Edward C. Henry award 1999), Am. Phys. Soc.; mem. NAE, Internat. Acad. Ceramics (academician). Office: U Calif Santa Barbara Dept Materials Santa Barbara CA 93106-5050 E-mail: clarke@engineering.ucsb.edu

CLARKE, JAMES WESTON, political science educator, writer; b. Elizabeth, Pa., Feb. 16, 1937; s. Alonzo Peterson and Beatrice (Weston) C.; m. Jeanne Nienaber; children— Julianne, Michael BA, Washington and Jefferson Coll., 1962; MA, Pa. State U., 1964, PhD, 1968. Asst. prof. Fla. State U., 1967-71; assoc. prof. U. Ariz., Tucson, 1971-76, prof. polit. sci., 1976—, chmn. dept., 1973-78, univ. disting. prof., 2000. Author: American Assassins: The Darker Side of Politics, 1982, Last Rampage: The Escape of Gary Tison, 1988, On Being Mad or Merely Angry: John W. Hinckley Jr. and Other Dangerous People, 1990,l The Lineaments of Wrath: Race, Violent Crime, and American Culture, 1998. Served with USMC, 1955-58 Recipient James Gillespie Blaine prize Washington and Jefferson Coll., 1962, Matthew Brown Ringland prize, 1962, Burlington Northern Found. award for excellence in tchg., 1987, Golden Key Nat. Honor Soc. award for tchg., 1989, Social and Behavioral Scis. award for outstanding tchg., 1991, 96; Udall fellow, 1993; Fulbright scholar, Ireland, 1999. Mem. Am. Polit. Sci. Assn. (Outstanding Tchg. in Polit. Sci. 2000), Authors Guild Am. Home: 855 E Placita Leslie Tucson AZ 85718-1960 Office: U Ariz 315 Social Sci Bldg Tucson AZ 85721-0001 E-mail: jclarke@u.arizona.edu

CLARKE, JOHN, physics educator; b. Cambridge, Eng., Feb. 10, 1942; came to U.S., 1968; s. Victor Patrick and Ethel May (Blowers) C.; m. Grethe Fog Pedersen, Sept. 15, 1979; 1 child, Elizabeth Jane. BA, Cambridge U., 1964, MA, PhD, Cambridge U., 1968. Postdoctoral scholar U. Calif.-Berkeley, 1968-69, asst. prof. physics, 1969-71, assoc. prof., 1971-73, prof., 1973—; chair exptl. physics Luis W. Alvarez Meml., 1994—. Contbr. numerous articles to profl. jours. Recipient Charles Vernon Boys prize Brit. Inst. Physics, 1977, award Soc. Exploration Geophysics, 1979, Outstanding Teaching award U. Calif., 1983, Fritz London award for low temperature physics, 1987, Fed. Lab. Consortium award for excellence in technology transfer, 1992, div. materials scis. award in solid state physics Dept. Energy, 1986, 92, IEEE U.S. Activities Bd. Electrotechnology Transfer award, 1995, Comstock prize Physics NAS, 1999; fellow Sloan Found., 1970-72, Miller Inst. for Basic Rsch., 1975-76, 94-95; Guggenheim fellow, 1977-78; named Calif. Scientist of Yr., 1987. Fellow AAAS, Royal Soc. London, Am. Phys. Soc. (Joseph F. Keithley Advances in Measurement Sci. award 1998), Brit. Inst. Physics. Office: U Calif Dept Physics Berkeley CA 94720-7300

CLARKE, JUDY, lawyer; b. Asheville, N.C., 1953; B in Psychology, Furman U., 1974; JD, U. S.C., 1977. Trial atty. Fed. Defenders San Diego, Inc., exec. dir.; pvt. practice, 1991-92; pub. defender Fed. Pub. Defender's Office, Spokane, Wash., 1992—. Mem. faculty Nat. Criminal Def. Coll., Macon, Ga., bd. regents, 1985—. Author: Federal Sentencing Manual; contbr. articles to profl. jours. Mem. NADCL (pres. 1996-97). Office: Fed Pub Defenders Office 10 N Post St Ste 700 Spokane WA 99201-0705

CLARKE, PETER, communications and health educator; b. Evanston, Ill., Sept. 19, 1936; s. Clarence Leon and Dorothy (Whitcomb) C.; m. Karen Storey, June 4, 1962 (div. 1984); 1 child, Christopher Michael BA, U. Wash., 1959; MA, U. Minn., 1961, PhD, 1963. Dir., asst. prof. Comm. Rsch. Ctr. U. Wash., Seattle, 1965-68, assoc. prof. sch. comm., 1967-72, dir. sch. comm., 1971-72; prof. dept. journalism U. Mich., Ann Arbor, 1973-74, chmn., prof. dept. journalism, 1975-78, chmn., prof. dept. comm., 1979-80; dean, prof. Annenberg Sch. Comm., U. So. Calif., L.A., 1981-92, prof., 1993—; prof. preventive medicine U. So. Calif. Sch. Medicine, L.A., 1985—. Co-dir. From the Wholesaler to the Hungry, 1991—; dir. Ctr. for Health and Med. Comm., 1997—; cons. for various fed. and state govt. commns. on mass media and social problems Co-author: (with Susan H. Evans) Covering Campaigns: Journalism in Congressional Elections, 1983, Surviving Modern Medicine: How to Get the Best from Doctors, Family and Friends, 1998; editor: New Models for Communication Research, 1973; co-editor: (with Susan H. Evans) The Computer Culture, 1985; contbr. articles to profl. jours. Numerous Fed., corp., pvt. founds. grants. Office: U So Calif Annenberg Sch Comm 3502 Watt Way Los Angeles CA 90089-0054 E-mail: chmc@usc.edu

CLARKE, PETER J. physicist, technology executive; b. N.Y.C. m. Carole; 5 children. BS in Physics, Iona Coll., 1959; postgrad., Union Coll. With Rsch. Lab. GE, Schenectady, N.Y., with Vacuum Products divsn.; with product devel. labs. Veeco Instruments, Plainview, N.Y.; founder, pres. Sputtered Films, Inc., Santa Barbara, Calif. Contbr. articles to profl. jours. With USAF. Scholarship established in honor of Peter J. and Carole Clarke. Mem. Am. Vacuum Soc. (Albert Nerken award 1998), Soc. Vacuum Coaters (Nathaniel Sugerman Meml. award 1998). Achievements include patents for S-Gun, the first magnetron sputtering device, C-to-C Coater Cassette to Cassette wafer metallizer, the first automated system for vacuum coating wafers using physical vapor deposition (PVD), Endeavor, a PVD cluster tool used in semiconductor industry to manufacture system interconnects and in under-bump metallization, Shamrock tm MR/GMR orbital planetary PVD system with produces magneto-resistive and gian magneto-resistive thin films for the magnetic storage industry, numerous other patents. Office: Sputtered Films Inc 320 N Nopal St Santa Barbara CA 93103-3225 E-mail: pjclarke@sputtered-films.com

CLARKE, RICHARD ALAN, electric and gas utility company executive, lawyer; b. San Francisco, May 18, 1930; s. Chauncey Frederick and Carolyn (Shannon) C.; m. Mary Dell Fisher, Feb. 5, 1955; children: Suzanne, Nancy C. Stephen, Douglas Alan. AB Polit. Sci. cum laude, U. Calif., Berkeley, 1952, JD, 1955. Bar: Calif. 1955. Pres. Pacific Gas and Electric Co., San Francisco, 1985-86, chmn. bd., CEO, 1986-94, chmn. bd., 1994-95; ptnr. Rockwell, Fulkerson and Clarke, San Rafael, Calif., 1960-69. Mem. Bus. Coun.; bd. dirs. Potlatch Corp., CNF TransInc. Bd. dirs., past chmn. Bay Area Coun.; trustee Berkeley Found.; mem. adv. bd. Walter A. Haas Sch. Bus., U. Calif., Berkeley; chmn. adv. bd. Ctr. for Orgnl. and Human Resource Effectiveness, U. Calif., Berkeley; bd. dirs. Nature Conservancy of Calif.; co-chair U. Calif. Regents Outreach Adv. Bd.; former mem. Pres.'s Coun. on Environ. Quality; former chair Bay Area Econ. Coun. Mem. San Francisco C. of C. (past dir., v.p. econ. devel.), Edison Elect. Inst. Office: Pacific Gas & Electric Co 123 Mission St # H17F San Francisco CA 94105-1551

CLARKE, ROBERT F. utilities company executive; b. Oakland, Calif. BA, U. Calif., Berkeley, 1965, MBA, 1966. Pres., CEO, chmn. Hawaiian Electric, Honolulu, 1991—. Office: Hawaiian Electric Industries Inc 900 Richards St Honolulu HI 96813-2919

CLARKE, STEVEN GERARD, chemistry educator; b. L.A., Nov. 19, 1949; BA in Chemistry/Zoology magna cum laude, Pomona Coll., 1970; PhD in Biochemistry & Molecular Biology, Harvard U., 1976. NIH undergrad. fellow Glynn Rsch. Labs., Bodmin, Eng., summer 1969; NSF predoctoral fellow Harvard U., 1970-73, biochemistry and molecular biology instr., 1973-74; Miller Inst. fellow U. Calif., Berkeley, 1976-78; asst. prof. chemistry and molecular biology UCLA, 1978-83, assoc. prof. chemistry and biochemistry, 1983-87, prof. chemistry and biochemistry, 1987—. Vis. fellow molecular biology Princeton (N.J.) U., 1986-87; mem. sci. com. 1st Internat. Symposium on Post-Translational Modifications of Proteins and Aging, Lacco Ameno d'Ischia, Naples, Italy, 1987; chair, symposium organizer ann. meeting Am. Soc. for Biochemistry and Molecular Biology, Atlanta, 1991; mem. adv. bd. nutrition and metabolism sect. biol. aging Nat. Inst. Aging, NIH, 1993; co-chair Fedn. Am. Socs. for Exptl. Biology summer rsch. conf., Vt., 1995. Assoc. editor Protein Sci., 1995-98, mem. editl. adv. bd., 1994-95; mem. editl. bd. Jour. Biol. Chemistry, 1994-98; contbr. more than 170 articles to profl. jours. Woodrow Wilson fellow, 1970; grantee Am. Heart Assn., 1984-85, 85-86, 87-88, 89, NSF, 1989, 90, 91, NIH, 1995. Mem. Am. Chem. Soc. (Ralph F. Hirschmann award 1996), Am. Soc. Biochemistry and Molecular Biology, The Protein Soc., Assn. Med. and Grad. Depts. Biochemistry, Phi Beta Kappa, Alpha Chi Sigma. Office: UCLA Dept Chemistry & Biochem 607 Charles E Young Dr East Los Angeles CA 90095-1569 E-mail: clarke@mbi.ucla.edu

CLARKE, THOMAS E. apparel executive; b. Binghamton, N.Y., Aug. 8, 1951; married. MS, U. Fla., 1977; D in Biomechanics, Penn State, 1980. Rschr. Sports and Rsch. Lab NIKE, Inc., Exeter, N.H., various to dir. product devel., corp. v.p. of mktg., 1983-94, pres. Beaverton, Oreg., 1994-2000, co-CFO, pres. new bus. ventures, 2000—. Avocation: running (competitive marathon runner). Office: Nike Inc One Bowerman Dr Beaverton OR 97005-6453

CLARK-JOHNSON, SUSAN, publishing executive; Pres., pub. Reno Gazette-Jour., 1985—; sr. group pres. Pacific Newspaper Group, Gannett, 1985—. Bd. dirs. Harrah's Entertainment, Inc.; bd. visitors John S. Knight Fellowships for Profl. Journalists, Stanford U. Office: Gannett Co Inc Box 22000 955 Kuenzli St Reno NV 89520-1160

CLARK-LANGAGER, SARAH ANN, curator, director, university official; b. Lynchburg, Va., May 14, 1943; d. James Thomas and Mary Whitworth (Cooper) Clark; m. Craig T. Langager, 1979. BA in Art History, Randolph-Macon Woman's Coll., 1965; postgrad., U. Md., 1968; MA in Art History, U. Wash., 1970; PhD in Art History, CUNY, 1988. Assoc. edn. dept., lectr. Yale U. Art Gallery, New Haven, 1965-67, Albright-Knox Art Gallery, Buffalo, 1967-68; asst. to dir. Richard White Gallery, Seattle, 1969-70; curatorial asst. to curators painting and sculpture San Francisco Mus. Modern Art, 1970; assoc. edn. dept., lectr. Seattle Art Mus., 1971-73, 74-75; asst. curator, and then assoc. curator modern art, lectr. Seatle Art Mus., 1975-79; curator 20th century art, lectr. Munson-Williams-Proctor Inst., Utica, N.Y., 1981-86; asst. prof. art history, dir. Univ. Art Gallery, U. North Tex., Denton, 1986-88; dir. Western Gallery, curator outdoor sculpture collection Western Wash. U., Bellingham, 1988—, mem. adj. faculty, 1988—. Lectr., cons. in edn. N.Y. Cultural Ctr., N.Y.C., 1973-74; editl. asst. October, MIT Press, N.Y.C., 1980; lectr. art history South Seattle C.C., 1975; lectr. 20th century art Cornish Inst. Fine Arts, Seattle, 1977-78; sole rep. for N.Y. State, Art Mus. Assn. Am., 1984-86; mem. Wash. Art Consortium, 1988—, v.p., 1989-90, pres., 1990-93, acting pres., 1996; mem. ad hoc del. concerning issues confronting Nat. Endowment for Arts, Bellingham, 1990; cons. State of Wash. SOS (Save Outdoor Sculpture), 1994—; also others. Contbr. articles to profl. jours.; curator exhbns., 1970—, including Rodney Ripps traveling exhbn., 1983, Sculpture Space: Recent Trends, 1984, Order and Enigma: American Art Between the Two Ward, 1984, Stars over Texas: Top of the Triangle, 1988, Master Works of American Art from the Munson-Williams-Proctor Institute, 1989, Public Art/Private Visions, 1989, Drawing Power, 1990, Audiophone Tour for

Sculpture Collection-20 Interviews, 1991, Focus on Figure, 1992, Chairs: Embodied Objects, 1993, Northwest Native American and First Nations People's Art, 1993, New Acquisitions, 1995, Stars and Stripes: American Prints and Drawings, 1995, Photographs from America, 1996, (catalog introduction) Metalcrafts, 1998. Juror Arts in Pub. Places, Seattle Arts Commn., 1975, 78-79, Wash. State Arts Commn., 1976, 91, 92-93, King County Arts Commn., Seattle, 1979, Ctrl. N.Y. regional art exhbns., Syracuse, Utica, Rome, Potsdam, 1981-86, East Tex. State U., Commerce, 1987, Brookhaven C.C., Farmers Branch, Tex., 1988, Bellingham Mcpl. Arts Commn., 1989, 90; mem. adv. com. Steuben Park Fountain, Utica, 1985-86. Recipient Woman of Merit in Arts award Mohawk Valley C.C. and YWCA, Utica, 1985; Kress Found. fellow U. Wash., 1970; Helena Rubenstein Found. scholar CUNY Grad. Ctr., 1980. Office: Western Wash U Western Gallery Fine Arts Complex Bellingham WA 98225-9068

CLARKSON, LAWRENCE WILLIAM, airplane company executive; b. Grove City, Pa., Apr. 29, 1938; s. Harold William and Jean Henrietta (Jaxtheimer) C.; m. Barbara Louise Stevenson, Aug. 20, 1960; children: Michael, Elizabeth, Jennifer. BA, DePauw U., 1960; JD, U. Fla., 1962. Counsel Pratt & Whitney, West Palm Beach, Fla., 1967-72, program dep. dir., 1972-75, program mgr., 1974-75, v.p., mng. dir. Brussels, Belgium, 1975-78, v.p. mktg. West Palm Beach, 1978-80, v.p. contracts Hartford, Conn., 1980-82, pres. comml. products div., 1982-87; sr. v.p. Boeing Comml. Airplanes Group, Seattle, 1988-91; corp. v.p. planning and internat. devel. Boeing Co., Seattle, 1992-93, sr. v.p., 1994-99; pres. Boeing Enterprises, Seattle, 1997-99; sr. v.p. Project Internat., Seattle, 2000—. Bd. dirs. Partnership for Improved Air Travel, Washington, 1988-91; bd. dirs. Atlas Air, Avnet Inc., Interturbine NV, chmn., 2000—. Trustee DePauw U., Greencastle, Ind., 1987—, vice chmn., 1996—; overseer Tuck Sch. Dartmouth, Hanover, N.H., 1993-99; corp. coun. Interlochen (Mich.) Ctr. for Arts, 1987, trustee, 1988—, chmn., 1996—; trustee Seattle Opera, 1990—, chmn., 1991—; pres. Japan-Am. Soc., Wash., 1993, pres. Wash. State China Rels. com., 1992-93; chmn. Nat. Bur. of Asia Rsch., Coun. Fgn. Rels.; chmn. U.S. Pacific Econ. Corp. Coun., 1993-2000. Mem. Nat. Assn. Mfrs. (bd. dirs. 1993-99), N.Y. Yacht Club, Seattle Yacht Club, Met. Opera Club, Wings Club (bd. govs. 1987-91, Order of St. John (comdr.), Met. Club D.C., Am. Inst. Contemporary German Studies (bd. dirs. 1997-99). Episcopalian. Home: 10127 NE 66th Ln Kirkland WA 98033-6870 E-mail: lckarlsonpii@cs.com, LARRYWCLARKSON@compuserve.com

CLARNO, BEVERLY ANN, state legislator, farmer; b. Langlois, Oreg., Mar. 29, 1936; d. Howard William and Evelyn June (Young) Boice; m. Ray Clarno, July 15, 1983; children: Dan, Don, Randy, Cindi. Student, Marylhurst Coll., 1985, Lewis & Clark Law Sch., 1985-87. Real estate broker Lake Realty and Hatfield & Skopil, Lake Oswego, Oreg., 1984-85; pres. T & H Hog Farms, Wasco, 1973-76; securities examiner State of Oreg., Salem, 1981-83; circuit ct. clerk Deschutes County, Bend, Oreg., 1987-88; mem. Oreg. Ho. of Reps., Salem, 1988-2000, Oreg. Senate from 27th dist., Salem, 2001—. Spkr. Oreg. House, 1995—. Recipient Cost Cutting award, Citizens for Cost Effective Govt., Portland, 1991. Mem. Boys & Girls Aid Soc., Kiwanis Club, Lions Club, High Desert Mus., Eastern Star. Republican. Methodist. Avocations: flying, trap shooting, cattle drives. Home: PO Box 7970 Bend OR 97708-7970

CLARREN, STERLING KEITH, pediatrician; b. Mpls., Mar. 12, 1947; s. David Bernard and Lila (Reifel) C.; m. Sandra Gayle Bernstein, June 8, 1970; children: Rebecca Pia, Jonathan Seth. BA, Yale U., 1969; MD, U. Minn., 1973. Pediatric intern U. Wash. Sch. Medicine, Seattle, 1973-74, resident in pediatrics, 1974-77, asst. prof. dept. pediatrics, 1979-83, assoc. prof., 1983-88, prof., 1988, Robert A. Aldrich chair in pediatrics, 1989—. Head divsn. congenital defects U. Wash. Sch. Medicine, 1987-95; dir. dept. congenital defects Children's Hosp. and Med. Ctr., Seattle, 1987-96, dir. fetal alcohol syndrome clinic Child Devel. and Mental Retardation Ctr. U. Wash., 1992—, dir. Fetal Alcohol Syndrome Network, 1995—; dir. inpatient svcs. Children's Hosp. & Med. Ctr., Seattle, 1996—. Contbr. articles to profl. jours.; patentee for orthosis to alter cranial shape. Cons. pediatrician Maxillofacial Rev. Bd., State of Wash., Seattle, 1984—, chmn. Health-Birth Defects Adv. Com., Olympia, 1980—; mem. gov.'s task force on FAS State of Wash., 1994-95; mem. fetal alcohol adv. com. Children's Trust Found., Seattle, 1988—; mem. adv. bd. Nat. Orgn. on Fetal Alcohol Syndrome; mem. fetal alcohol com. Inst. Medicine, NAS, 1994-95. Rsch. grantee Nat. Inst. Alcohol Abuse & Alcoholism, 1982—, Ctrs. for Disease Control, 1992—. Fellow AAAS; mem. Am. Acad. Pediatrics, Soc. for Pediatric Rsch., Teratology Soc., Rsch. Soc. on Alcoholism (pres. fetal alcohol study group 1993), Am. Cleft Palate Assn., N.Y. Acad. Scis. Avocations: cross-country skiing, fishing, hiking, sailing. Home: 8515 Paisley Dr NE Seattle WA 98115-3944 Office: Children's Hosp and Med Ctr Divsn Genetics and Devel PO Box C-5371 Seattle WA 98105

CLAYTON, MACK LOUIS, surgeon, educator; b. Round Mountain, Ala., Nov. 25, 1921; s. James Euclid and Alma (Longshore) C.; m. Sara Elizabeth Lee, June 3, 1948; children: James Lee, Lee Alison. BS, U. Ariz., 1942; MD, Columbia U., 1945. Diplomate Am. Bd. Orthopedic Surgery. Founder Denver Orthopedic Clinic, 1952-90; physician Denver Broncos, 1969-73, U.S. Ski Team, 1971; clin. prof. orthopedic surgery U. Colo., 1985-95, disting. clin. prof., 2000—. Author, editor: Surgery for Rheumatoid Arthritis, 1992; contbr. numerous articles to profl. jours. Elder Presbyn. Ch., Denver, 1958; with armed forces, 1946-48. Recipient Best Clinical Rsch. award U. Colo Med. Sch., 1958, 25 yrs. svc. award Arthritis Found., 1982. Mem. Am. Orthop. Assn., Am. Soc. for Surg. of Hand, Clin. Orthop. Soc. (pres. 1978). Avocations: skiing, golf, fishing, hunting. Home: 2552 E Alameda Ave Unit 18 Denver CO 80209-3324

CLAYTON, PAUL DOUGLAS, health care administrator; b. Salt Lake City, Mar. 9, 1943; PhD in Physics, U. Ariz. Dir. Ctr. for Advanced Tech., Columbia Presbyn. Med. Ctr., 1994-98, dir. clin. info. svcs., 1992-98; chmn., prof. med. info. Columbia U., 1987-98; info. sys. dir., dir. clin. info. sys. Intermountain Health Care, 1998—; prof. med. info. U. Utah, 2001—. Mem. Inst. Medicine of Nat. Acad. Sci., Am. Med. Info. Assn. (pres. 1998-99).

CLAYTON, RAYMOND EDWARD, government official; b. Saskatoon, Sask., Can., Nov. 6, 1942; m. Joan Ann Snodgrass, Sept. 21, 1963; children: Grant, Sheila, Matthew, Daniel. B. of Commerce, U. Sask., 1964; MA in Econs., 1965. Dir. rsch. Dept. Mcpl. Affars, Govt. Sask., Regina, 1965-67, Dept. Edn., Govt. Sask., Regina, 1967-69, dir. ednl. adminstrn., 1969-77, dep. minister, 1979-84; dir. taxation and fiscal policy Dept. Fin., Govt. Sask., Regina, 1977-78; dep. minister Dept. Urban Affairs, Govt. Sask., Regina, 1978-79; chmn. Govt. Fin. Commn., Regina, 1984-86; asst. dep. minister Dept. Energy & Mines, Govt. Sask., Regina, 1986-94, dep. minister, 1994—. Office: Dept Energy and Mines 2101 Scarth St Regina SK Canada S4P 3V7 E-mail: rclayton@sem.gov.sk.ca

CLAYTON, WAYNE CHARLES, protective services official, educator; b. Topeka, Dec. 16, 1932; s. Alford Henry and Anna Ellen (Lynch) C.; m. Donna Marie Corrigan, March 3, 1962; Mark Wayne, Leslie Marie. AA in Liberal Arts, Mt. San Antonio Coll., 1959; BS, Calif. State U., L.A., 1968. [illegible] Calif. From reserve police officer to dept. chief El Monte Police Dept., 1957-1978, chief, 1978—. Mem. session FBINA, 1980. With U.S. Navy, 1952-56. Recipient Golden Apple award West San Gabriel Valley Adminstrs. Assn., 1982, Spl. Medallion award Boys Club Am., 1982, Disting. Svc. award Dept. Youth Authority, 1983, Outstanding Svc. award C. of C., 1983, Spl. Appreciation award El Monte Police Officers Assn., 1985, Calif. Police Chief Officer of the Yr. award Internat. Union Police [illegible] E. Thompson Disting. Scouter award El Monte Explorer Post # 522, 1988, Appreciation award, 1992, Outstanding Svc. award Internat. Footprint Assn., 1991, award for continuing concern and dedication to the well being of Officers of El Monte Police Dept. Calif. Orgn. of Police and Sheriffs, 1991, Police Chief of the Yr. Perpetual award First Annual Shriners Club, 1994, C. of C. Citizen of Yr., 1994, Coord. Coun. Lifetime Achievement award, 1995. Mem. FBI Nat. Acad. Assocs., L.A. County Police Chiefs Assn., San Gabriel Valley Police Chiefs Assn., San Gabriel Valley Peace Officers Assn. (past pres.), Boys and Girls Club of San Gabriel Valley (v.p.), Civitan of El Monte (internat., charter pres. 1973). Democrat. Roman Catholic. Avocations: fishing, water skiing, reading. Office: Police Dept Box 6008 11333 Valley Blvd El Monte CA 91731-3210

CLEARWATER, YVONNE A. psychologist; BA in Psychology summa cum laude, Calif. State U., Long Beach; PhD in Psychology, U. Calif., Davis. Sr. prin. investigator, rsch. psychologist NASA Ames Rsch. Ctr., Moffett Field, Calif., testbed devel. mgr., govt. industry liaison, info. designer, project mgr. Human Exploration Demonstration Project, design rsch. psychologist. Mem. panels Internat. Conf. Environ. Sys.; mem. sci. adv. com. Nat. Space Soc.; NASA rep. to Broad Alliance for Multimedia Tech. and Applications; lectr. Stanford U., U. Calif.; lectr. in field. Exec. prodr. SAE Human Modeling Tech. Standards Com.; contbr. articles to profl. jours. Recipient Nat. Human Environ. award Am. Soc. Interior Designers, 1989. Mem. Nat. Acad. TV Arts and Scis. (bd. govs. No. Calif. chpt.). Avocations: painting. Office: NASA Ames Rsch Ctr Moffett Field CA 94035

CLEARY, THOMAS CHARLES, technology company executive; b. Chgo., Nov. 15, 1921; s. Thomas Harold and Mary Margaret (Russell) C.; m. Barbara Winnifred Johnson, Dec. 18, 1948; children: Thomas Robert, Margaret Mary Cleary Nurmia, Mary Ann Cleary Robitaille. BS in Mech. Engring., UCLA, 1949. Pres., gen. mgr. Whittaker Corp., Denver, 1950-63; dir. program mgmt. Litton Industries, Woodland Hills, Calif., 1963-65; asst. gen. mgr. Teledyne Sys., Inc., 1965-66; v.p., CEO Viking Industries, Chatsworth, Calif., 1966-67; v.p. Power Conversion, Inc., Long Beach, 1967-68; chmn. bd. dirs., mng. dir. TRW Electronic Comp. Co., Taiwan, Republic of China, 1968-69; pres., CEO Deutsch Relays, Inc., East Northport, N.Y., 1969-89, Struthers Dunn-Hi G, Pitman, N.J., 1989-91; chmn., CEO G&H Tech., Inc., Camarillo, Calif., 1992—. Author: Dynamic Management System, 1990, Management By Intent, 1991. Fundraiser Meml. Sloan-Kettering Cancer Ctr., N.Y., 1989—; mem. chancellor's assocs. UCLA, 1992—, mem. exec. com., dean's coun., sch. engring., 1992—; mem. bd. councillors UCLA Found., 1997. Capt. inf. U.S. Army, 1942-50, PTO. Named Entrepreneur of Yr. in mfg. Greater L.A. Area, 1997. Republican. Roman Catholic. Achievements include patents in the gyroscope and relay areas. Office: G&H Tech Inc 750 W Ventura Blvd Camarillo CA 93010-8382

CLEARY, WILLIAM JOSEPH, JR. lawyer; b. Wilmington, N.C., Aug. 14, 1942; s. William Joseph and Eileen Ada (Gannon) C. AB in History, St. Joseph's U., 1964; JD, Villanova U., 1967. Bar: N.J., 1967, Calif. 1982, U.S. Ct. Appeals (3d cir.) 1969, U.S. Ct. Appeals (9th cir.) 1983, U.S. Dist. Ct. (ctrl. dist.) Calif. 1983, U.S. Supreme Ct. 1992. Law sec. to judge N.J. Superior Ct., Jersey City, 1967-68; assoc. Lamb, Blake, H&D, Jersey City, 1968-72; dep. pub. defender State of N.J., Newark, 1972-73; 1st asst. city corp. counsel Jersey City, 1973-76; assoc. Robert Wasserwald, Inc., Hollywood, Calif., 1984-86, Gould & Burke, Century City, 1986-87; pvt. practice Hollywood, 1989—. Mem. ABA, FBA, N.J. State Bar Assn., Calif. Bar Assn., L.A. County Bar Assn., Nat. Jesuit Hon. Soc., Alpha Sigma Nu. Democrat. Roman Catholic. Office: 1853 1/2 Canyon Dr Los Angeles CA 90028-5607 E-mail: wjclaw42@aol.com

CLEAVER, JAMES EDWARD, radiologist, educator; b. Portsmouth, England, May 17, 1938; came to the U.S., 1964; s. Edward Alfred and Kathleen Florence (Cleveley) C.; m. Christine J. Cleaver, Aug. 8, 1964; children: Jonathan, Alison. BA, St. Catharine's Coll., 1961; PhD, U. Cambridge, 1964. Rsch. fellow Mass. Gen. Hosp., Boston, 1964-66; asst. rsch. biophysicist lab. radiobiology environ. health U. Calif., San Francisco, 1966-68, asst. prof. radiology, 1968-70, assoc. prof. radiology, 1970-74, prof. radiology, 1974—; vis. prof. Imperial Cancer Rsch. Fund, London, 1973-74, prof. radiology, 1975-96, prof. dermatology, 1996—. Contbr. over 300 articles to profl. jours. Recipient Lila Gruber award Am. Acad. Dermatology, 1976, Sr. Investigator award Am. Soc. Photobiology, 1995, Luigi Provasoli Awd., 1992, Phycol. Soc. Am. Mem. NAS, Nat. Coun. on Radiation Protection, Radiation Rsch. Soc. (councillor 1982-84, rsch. award 1973).

CLEGG, JAMES STANDISH, physiologist, biochemist, educator; b. Aspinwall, Pa., July 27, 1933; divorced; 3 children; m. Eileen Clegg; 1 stepchild. BS, Pa. State U., 1958; PhD in Biology, Johns Hopkins U., 1961. Rsch. assoc. biologist Johns Hopkins U., 1961-62; asst. prof. zoology U. Miami, 1962-64, from assoc. prof. biology to prof., 1964-70; prof. sect. molecular and cellular biology U. Calif., Davis, 1986—, dir. Bodega Marine Lab., 1986-98. With CNRS Thias France, 1983; pres. Nat. Assn. Marine Labs., 1992-94. Recipient Fulbright Sr. Rsch. award U. London, 1978, U. Ghent, 1999; Wilson fellow, 1958-59. Fellow AAAS; mem. Am. Soc. Zoologists, Am. Soc. Cell Biology, Biophys. Soc., Soc. Cryobiology, Sigma Xi. Achievements include research in comparative biochemistry and biophysics; mechanisms of cryptobiosis; properties and role of water in cellular metabolism; cytoplasmic organization. Office: U Calif Bodega Marine Lab PO Box 247 Bodega Bay CA 94923-0247 E-mail: jsclegg@ucdavis.edu

CLEGG, MICHAEL TRAN, genetics educator, researcher; b. Pasadena, Calif., Aug. 1, 1941; AA, Sacramento City Coll., 1967; BS, U. Calif., Davis, 1969, PhD, 1972. chmn. biology bd., NRC, mem. commn. on life scis., NRC, 1990-96. Asst. prof. Brown U., Providence, 1972-76; assoc. prof. U. Ga., Athens, 1976-82, prof., 1982-84, U. Calif., Riverside, 1984—, acting dean Coll. Natural and Agrl. Scis., 1994-97, dean Coll. Natural and Agrl. Scis., 1997-2000. Chmn. biology bd. NRC, mem. commn. on life scis., NRC, 1990-96, chmn., 1998-2000. Co-author: Principles of Genetics, 1988; co-editor: Plant Population Genetics, 1989, Molecular Evolution, 1990. Sgt. U.S. Army, 1960-63. Guggenheim Found. fellow, 1981-82. Fellow Am. Acad. Arts and Scis.; mem. NAS, Am. Soc. Naturalists (v.p. 1986), Am. Genetics Assn. (pres. 1987), Soc. for the Study of Evolution (v.p. 1986), Genetics Soc. Am., MOlecular Biology and Evolution Soc. (pres.-elect 2001). Avocations: skiing, flying. Office: U Calif Dept Botany And Plant Sci Riverside CA 92521-0001

CLEMENT, DOUGLAS BRUCE, medical educator; b. Montreal, Que., Can., July 15, 1933; BSc, U. Oreg., 1955; MD, U. B.C., Vancouver, Can., 1959. Intern St. Mary's Hosp., San Francisco, 1960; adj. assoc. prof. Simon Fraser U., 1976-79; from asst. to assoc. prof. U. B.C., Vancouver, 1979-90, prof., 1990-99, prof. emeritus, 1999—. Vis. assoc. prof. Simon Fraser U., 1979-88; coach track and field team U. B.C., 1981-87, mem. family practice promotion and tenure com., 1987-98, mem. search com. dept. family practice, 1988-89, co-founder clin. fellowship sports medicine Allan McGavin Sports Medicine Ctr.; cons. in sports medicine; radio, TV presenter, speaker in field. Regional editor Sports Tng., Medicine and Rehab., 1987-88; mem. editorial bd. Clin. Sports Medicine, 1989-90, Clin. Jour. Sports Medicine, 1991-2000, The Physician and Sports Medicine, 1999-2000; sect. editor Can. Jour. Sport Scis., 1990-93; contbr. articles to profl. jours. and chpts. to books. Recipient Vanier award, 1965, Centennial medal, 1967, Op. Lifestyle medal, 1980, Longines/Wittnauer Coaching Excellence award, 1989, Order of Can. medal, 1991, Can. 125 medal, [illegible] Wallace Wilson award, 1995, R.T. McKenzie medallion, 1999; named to U. B.C. Sports Hall of Fame, 1995, B.C. Sports Hall of Fame, 2000; named Coach of Yr., Sport B.C., 1988; grantee Sport Can., 1984, 86, Beecham Labs., 1984, Ciba Geigy, 1985, Sport Medicine Coun. Can., 1985-86, CFLRI, 1990; Town Club scholar U. Oreg., 1954. Fellow Am. Coll. Sports Med., Can. Acad. Sport Medicine (travelling, past pres., mem. accreditation com. 1987-97); mem. Can. Med. Assn., Can. Assn. Sport Sci. (past sec.), Can. Ctr. Drug Free Sport (mem. sci. adv. com. 1992), Can. Olympic Assn. (gen. mgr. Can. team Pan Am. Games 1975, mem. com. doping control, com. accreditation sports sci. facilities, bd. dirs. 1985-93), Athletics Can. (chmn. med. com. 1981-87, mem. sports sci. com. 1983-87, nat. coach various games), B.C. Athletics (master coach 1988—, Coach of Yr. 1987-92), B.C. Med. Assn. (mem. com. athletics and recreation health planning coun. 1971-96, bd. dirs. 1999-2000), Sports Medicine Coun. B.C. (chmn. high performance sports sci. unit 1985-89, com. anti-doping 1989-92), Achilles Internat. Athletics Soc. (chmn. 1964-72, 86—), Kajak Track and Field Club (co-founder, coach 1962-99). Achievements include research on effect of exercise on the human body, stressor effects of running on local tissue as well as central effects. Fax: 604-264-0749. E-mail: dclementoo@home.com

CLEMENT, RICHARD WILLIAM, plastic and reconstructive surgeon; b. Pontiac, Mich., Nov. 10, 1953; s. William Henry and Jean Elizabeth (Girst) C.; m. Phyllis Jean Hobson, Aug. 15, 1981; children: Nicholas William, Kimberly Ashley, Christopher Richard. BS, Alma Coll., 1975; MD, U. Va., 1979. Diplomate Am. Bd. Plastic Surgery; fellow Am. Coll. Surgeons. Asst. prof. surgery Washington U., St. Louis, 1984-88; dir. Southwest Plastic Surgeons, Paradise Valley, Ariz., 1988—. Contbr. articles to profl. jours.; co-author: Essentials of Plastic Surgery, 1987. Fellow Am. Coll. Surgeons; mem. AMA, Am. Soc. Plastic and Reconstructive Surgeons., Bellerive Country Club. Republican. Presbyterian. Office: 9220 E Mountain View Rd Ste 214 Scottsdale AZ 85258-5136

CLEMENTE, CARMINE DOMENIC, anatomist, educator; b. Penns Grove, N.J., Apr. 29, 1928; s. Ermanno and Caroline (Friozzi) C.; m. Juliette Vance, Sept. 19, 1968. AB, U. Pa., 1948, MS, 1950, PhD, 1952; postdoctoral fellow, U. London, 1953-54. Asst. instr. anatomy U. Pa., 1950-52; mem. faculty UCLA, 1952—, prof., 1963-95, chmn. dept. anatomy, 1963-73, dir. brain rsch. inst., 1976-87; prof. surg. anatomy Charles R. Drew U. Medicine and Sci., L.A., 1974—; prof. neurobiology and anatomy UCLA, 1995—. Hon. rsch. assoc. Univ. Coll., U. London, 1953-54; vis. scientist Nat. Inst. Med. Rsch., Mill Hill, London, 1988-89, 91; cons. VA Hosp., Sepulveda, Calif., NIH; mem. med. adv. panel Bank Am.-Giannini Found.; chmn. sci. adv. com., bd. dirs. Nat. Paraplegia Found.; bd. dirs. Charles R. Drew U., 1985-94. Author: Aggression and Defense: Neurol Mechanisms and Social Patterns, 1967, Physiological Correlates of Dreaming, 1967, Sleep and the Maturing Nervous System, 1972, Anatomy: An Atlas of the Human Body, 1975, 4th edit., 1997, Clemente's Anatomy Dissector, 2001; editor: Gray's Anatomy, 1973, 30th Am. edit., 1985, also Exptl. Neurology; assoc. editor Neurol. Rsch., Jour. Clin. Anatomy; contbr. articles to sci. jours Recipient award for merit in sci. Nat. Paraplegia Found., 1973; 23d Ann. Rehfuss Lectr. and recipient Rehfuss medal Jefferson Med. Coll., 1986, award for excellence in med. edn., UCLA, 1996, Award of Extraordinary merit UCLA Med. Alumni Assn., 1997; John Simon Guggenheim Meml. Found. fellow, 1988-89. Mem. NAS (mem. com. on neuropathology, mem. BEAR coms.), Inst. Medicine of NAS (mem. sci. adv. bd.), Pavlovian Soc. N.Am. (Ann. award 1968, pres. 1972), Brain Rsch. Inst. (dir. 1976-87), Am. Physiol. Soc., Am. Assn. Anatomists (v.p. 1970-72, pres. 1976-77, Henry Gray award 1993), Am. Acad. Neurology, Am. Assn. Clin. Anatomists (Honored Mem. of Yr. 1993), Am. Acad. Cerebral Palsy (hon.), Am. Neurol. Assn., Assn. Am. Med. Colls. (mem. exec. com. 1978-81, disting. svc. mem. 1982), Coun. Acad. Socs. (mem. adminstrv. bd. 1973-81, chmn. 1979-80), Nat. Bd. Med. Examiners (bd. dirs. 1978-84, mem. anatomy test com. 1980-84), Assn. Anatomy Chairmen (pres. 1972), Biol. Stain Commn., Internat. Brain Rsch. Orgn., AMA-Assn. Am. Med. Colls. (mem. liaison com. on med. edn. 1981-87), Med. Rsch. Assn. Calif. (bd. dirs. 1976—), N.Y. Acad. Scis., Japan Soc. Promotion of Sci. (Rsch. award 1978), Soc. for Neurosci., Penn Club (N.Y.C.), Sigma Xi, Alpha Omega Alpha. (hon.). Democrat. Home: 11737 Bellagio Rd Los Angeles CA 90049-2158 Office: UCLA Sch Medicine Dept Neurobiology Los Angeles CA 90095-0001 E-mail: cdclem@ucla.edu

CLEMENTS, JOHN ALLEN, physiologist; b. Auburn, N.Y., Mar. 16, 1923; s. Harry Vernon and May (Porter) C.; m. Margot Sloan Power, Nov. 19, 1949; children: Christine, Carolyn. MD, Cornell U., 1947; MD (honoris causa), U. Berne, Switzerland, 1990, Philipps U., Marburg, Germany, 1992; ScD (honoris causa), U. Manitoba, 1993. Rsch. asst. dept. physiology Med. Coll. N.Y., Cornell U., Ithaca, 1947-49; commd. 1st lt. U.S. Army, 1949, advanced through grades to capt., 1951; asst. chief clin. investigation br. Army Chem. Ctr., 1951-61; assoc. rsch. physiologist U. Calif., San Francisco, 1961-64, prof. pediat., 1964—, Julius H. Comroe Jr. prof. pulmonary biology, 1987—; mem. staff Cardiovascular Research Inst. Cardiovasc. Rsch. Inst., San Francisco, 1961—, mem. grad. group in biophysics, 1987—. Career investigator Am. Heart Assn., 1964-93; mem. group in biophysics and med. physics U. Calif., Berkeley, 1969-87; cons. Surgeon Gen. USPHS, 1964-68, Surgeon Gen. U.S. Army, 1972-79; sci. counselor Nat. Heart and Lung Inst., 1972-75, Bowditch lectr. Am. Physiol. Soc., 1961; 2d ann. lectr. Neonatal Soc., London, 1965; Distinguished lectr. Can. Soc. Clin. Investigation, 1973; mem. Nat. Heart Lung and Blood Adv. Coun., 1990-93; Ulf von Euler Meml. lectr. Karolinska Inst., 1996. Mem. editorial bd.: Jour. Applied Physiology, 1961-65, Am. Jour. Physiology, 1965-72, Physiol. Reviews, 1965-72, Jour. Developmental Physiology, 1979-85; assoc. editor: Am. Rev. Respiratory Diseases, 1973-79; chmn. publs. policy com.: Am. Thoracic Soc., 1982-86; assoc. editor: Ann. Rev. Physiology, 1988-93, Am. Jour. Physiology: Lung Cellular and Molecular Physiology, 1988-94. Recipient Dept. Army R & D Achievement award, 1961, Modern Medicine Disting. Achievement award, 1973, Howard Taylor Ricketts medal and award U. Chgo., 1975, Mellon award U. Pitts., 1976, Calif. medal Am. Lung Assn. Calif., 1981, Trudeau medal Am. Lung Assn., 1982, Internat. award Gairdner Found., 1983, J. Burns Amberson lecture award Am. Thoracic Soc. and Am. Lung Assn., 1991, Christopher Columbus Discovery award NIH, 1992, Albert Lasker Clin. Med. award, 1994, Virginia Apgar award Am. Acad. Pediat., 1994, Warren Alpert Found. award, 1995, Discover award Pharm. Rsch. and Mfrs. of Am.; named Mayo Clinic Disting. Lectr. in Med. Sci., 1993, APA Julius H. Conroe Disting. Lectr., 2000. Fellow AAAS, Am. Coll. Chest Physicians (hon.), Royal Coll. Physicians (London); mem. NAS, Western Assn. Physicians, Western Soc. Clin. Rsch., Perinatal Rsch. Soc. (councillor 1973-75), Am. Lung Assn. (hon., life) Office: U Calif Sch Medicine Cardiovascular Rsch Inst 3rd And Parnassus Ave San Francisco CA 94143-0001

CLEMINS, ARCHIE RAY, career officer; b. Mt. Vernon, Ill., Nov. 18, 1943; s. Archie Cornell and Earline (Pepple) C.; m. Marilyn Paddick, June 30, 1967; children: Becky, Travis. BSEE, U. Ill., 1966, MSEE, 1972. Commd. ensign USN, 1966, advanced through grades to rear adm., 1991; engr. officer USS Tunny, Charleston, S.C., 1972-75; staff engr. Comdr. in Chief, U.S. Pacific Fleet, Pearl Harbor, Hawaii, 1973-78, exec. officer USS Parche, Mare Islands, Calif., 1978-81; comdg. officer USS Pogy, Mare Islands, 1982-85; exec. asst. Dep. Chief of Naval Ops., Washington, 1985-86; comdr. Submarine Group 7, Yokosuka, Japan, 1986-88; chief of staff, comdr. U.S. Seventh Fleet, Yokosuka, 1988-90; comdr. Tng. Command, U.S. Pacific Fleet, San Diego, 1990-2000; pres. Caribou Technologies, Boise, Idaho, 2000—. Republican. Office: 2041 White Pine Ln Boise [illegible]

CLEMMENSON, LARRY P. investment company executive; CEO Capital Group Cos., L.A. Office: Capital Group Companies 333 S Hope St Los Angeles CA 90071 Office Fax: (213) 486-9217

CLEVELAND, CHARLES SIDNEY, secondary education educator; b. Portland, Oreg., Apr. 8, 1951; s. Sidney Charles and Virginia May (Seitzinger) C.; m. Joyce Kristine Nofziger, Nov. 5, 1972; children: Justin Charles, Christpher Joseph Sidney. BS, Portland State U., 1974; MAT, Lewis and Clark Coll., 1980. Geography tchr. Hillsboro (Oreg.) Union High Dist., 1976-98, Hillsborough (Oreg.) H.S., 1998—. Pres. Hillsboro (Oreg.) Active 20-30 Club, 1989, Oreg. Soccer Coaches Assn., 1983-84; asst. scoutmaster Boy Scouts Am., Hillsboro, 1991—; bd. dirs. Oreg. Geog. Alliance, 1987-93, Hillsboro Edn. Assn., 1983-86, 92—. Recipient Instructional Leadership Inst. award Nat. Geog. Soc., 1989; named Oreg. and Region IV Soccer Coach of Yr. by Nat. High Sch. Athletic Coaches Assn., 1984, Outstanding Young Man by Hillsboro C. of C., 1976. Mem. Assn. Am. Geographers, Nat. Coun. Geog. Edn. (Disting. Teaching Achievement award 1992), Nat. Coun. Social Studies, Oreg. Coun. Social Studies (bd. dirs.), Active 20-30 Internat. (life), Elks. Avocations: photography, coaching soccer, scout leader. Office: Hillsborough HS 3285 SE Roodridge Rd Hillsboro OR 97123

CLEVENGER, JEFFREY GRISWOLD, mining company executive; b. Boston, Sept. 1, 1949; s. Galen William and Cynthia (Jones) C. BS in Mining Engring., N.Mex. Inst. Mining and Tech., Socorro, 1973; grad. advanced mgmt. program, Harvard U., 1996. Engr. Phelps Dodge, Tyrone, N.Mex., 1973-78, gen. mine foreman, 1979-81, mine supt., 1981-86, Morenci, Ariz., 1986, gen. supt., 1987; asst. gen. mgr. Chino Mines Co., Hurley, N.Mex., 1987-88, Phelps Dodge, Morenci, 1988-89, gen. mgr., 1989-92; pres. Phelps Dodge Morenci, Inc., 1989-92, Morenci Water & Electric Co., 1989-92; sr. v.p. Cyprus Copper Co., Tempe, 1992-93; pres. Cyprus Climax Metals Co., Tempe, 1993—; sr. v.p. Cyprus Amax Minerals Co., Littleton, Colo., 1993-97, exec. v.p., 1998—. Contbr. articles to profl. jours. Bd. dirs. Valley of the Sun YMCA, Mining Hall of Fame; chmn. Copper Devel. Assn. Recipient Disting. Achievement award N.Mex. Inst. Mining & Tech., 1988. Mem. AIME (chmn. S.W. N.Mex. chpt. 1982), Soc. Mining Engrs. (Robert Peele award 1984), Mining and Metall. Soc. Am., Coppr Devel. Assn. (chmn.), Elks. Home: 4575 N Launfal Ave Phoenix AZ 85018-2961 Office: Cyprus Climax Metals Co PO Box 22015 1501 W Fountainhead Pkwy Tempe AZ 85282-1868

CLEVER, LINDA HAWES, physician; b. Seattle; d. Nathan Harrison and Evelyn Lorraine (Johnson) Hawes; m. James Alexander Clever, Aug. 20, 1960; 1 child, Sarah Lou. AB with distinction, Stanford U., 1962, MD, 1965. Diplomate Am. Bd. Internal Medicine, Am. Bd. Preventive Medicine in Occupational Medicine. Intern Stanford U. Hosp., Palo Alto, Calif., 1965-66, resident, 1966-67, fellow in infectious disease, 1967-68; fellow in cmty. medicine U. Calif., San Francisco, 1968-69, resident, 1969-70; med. dir. Sister Mary Philippa Diagonostic and Treatment Ctr. St. Mary's Hosp., San Francisco, 1970-77; chmn. dept. occupl. health Calif. Pacific Med. Ctr., San Francisco, 1977—. Clin. prof. medicine Med. Sch., U. Calif., San Francisco; NIH rsch. fellow Sch. Medicine, Stanford U., 1967-68, mem. nat. adv. panel Inst. Rsch. on Women and Gender, 1990—, chair panel, 1998—; mem. San Francisco Comprehensive Health Planning Coun., 1971-76, bd. dirs.; mem. Calif.-OSHA Adv. Com. on Hazard Evaluation System and Info. Svc., 1979-85, Calif. Statewide Profl. Stds. Rev. Coun., 1977-81, San Francisco Regional Commn. on White House Fellows, 1979-81, 83-89, 92, 95, chmn., 1979-81, bd. sci. counselors Nat, Inst. of Occupl. Safety and Health, 1995-2001. Editor Western Jour. Medicine, 1990-98; contbr. articles to profl. jours. Trustee Stanford U., 1972-76, 81-91, v.p. 1985-91; trustee Marin Country Day Sch., 1978-85; bd. dirs. Sta. KQED, 1976-83, chmn., 1979-81; bd. dirs. Ind. Sector, 1980-86, vice chmn. 1985-86; bd. dirs. San Francisco U. H.S., 1983-90, chmn. 1987-88; active Womens Forum West, 1980—, bd. dirs. 1992, 93; mem. Lucile Packard Children's Hosp. Bd., 1993-97, Lucile Packard Found. Children, 1997-99; mem. policy adv. com. U. Calif. Berkeley Sch. of Pub. Health, 1995—, chair, 1995-2000; bd. dirs. The Redwoods Retirement Cmty., 1996-2001, Buck Inst. for Rsch. in Aging, 2000; bd. govs. Stanford Med. Alumni Assn., 1997—. Master ACP (gov. No. Calif. region 1984-89, chmn. bd. govs. 1989-90, regent 1990-96, vice-chair bd. regents 1994-95); Fellow Am. Coll. Occupl. and Environ. Medicine; mem. Inst. Medicine NAS, Calif. Med. Assn., Calif. Acad. Medicine, Am. Pub. Health Assn., Western Occupl. Medicine Assn., Western Assn. Physicians, Stanford U. Women's Club (bd. dirs. 1971-80), Chi Omega. Office: 2351 Clay St San Francisco CA 94115-1931

CLICK, JAMES H. automotive executive; Co-CEO Tuttle-Click Automotive Group. Office: 14 Auto Center Dr Irvine CA 92618-2802

CLIFFORD, STEVEN FRANCIS, science research director; b. Boston, Jan. 4, 1943; s. Joseph Nelson and Margaret Dorothy (Savage) C.; children from previous marriage: Cheryl Ann, Michelle Lynn, David Arthur; m. Theresa Kavanagh, Aug. 1996. BSEE, Northeastern U., Boston, 1965; PhD, Dartmouth Coll., 1969. Postdoctoral fellow NRC, Boulder, Colo., 1969-70; physicist Wave Propagation Lab., NOAA, Boulder, 1970-82, program chief, 1982-87, dir. environ. tech. lab., 1987—. Mem. electromagnetic propagation panel, NATO, 1989-93; vis. sci. closed acad. city Tomsk, Siberia, USSR; apptd. mem. NAS Bd. on Atmospheric Sci. and Climate, 1999—. Author: (with others) Remote Sensing of the Troposphere, 1978; contbr. 125 articles to profl. jours.; patentee in acoustic scintillation liquid flow measurement, single-ended optical spatial filter, acoustic sensor of surface ocean current and waves, high resolution GPS scatterometer. Recipient 5 Outstanding publs. awards Dept. Commerce, 1972, 75, 89, 96, Outstanding Career Performance, U.S. Presidental award, 1998; inducted NAE, 1997. Fellow Optical Soc. Am. (editor atmospheric optics 1978-84, advisor atmospheric optics 1982-84), Acoustical Soc. Am.; mem. IEEE (sr.), NAE, NAS (bd. atmospheric sci. and climate), Internat. Radio Sci. Union, Am. Geophys. Union. Avocations: running, cross country skiing. Office: NOAA Environ Tech Lab 325 Broadway St Boulder CO 80305-3337

CLIFT, WILLIAM BROOKS, III, photographer; b. Boston, Jan. 5, 1944; s. William Brooks C. and Anne (Pearmain) Thomson; m. Vida Regina Chesnulis, Aug. 8, 1970; children: Charis, Carola, William. Free lance comml. photographer in partnership with Steve Gersh under name Helios, 1963-71; pres. William Clift Ltd., Santa Fe, 1980-85. Cons. Polaroid Corp., 1965-67 Photographer one-man shows, Carl Siembab Gallery, Boston, 1969, Mus. Art, U. Oreg., Eugene, 1969, New Boston City Hall Gallery, 1970, U. Mass., Berkshire Mus., Pittsfield, Mass., William Coll., Addison Gallery of Am. Art, Wheaton Coll., Mass., Worcester Art Mus., 1971, Creative Photography Gallery, MIT, 1972, St. John's Coll. Art Gallery, Santa Fe, 1973, Wiggin Gallery, Boston Pub. Library, 1974, Australian Ctr. for Photography, Sydney, 1978, Susan Spiritus Gallery, Newport Beach, Calif., 1979, MIT Creative Photography Gallery, 1980, William Lyons Gallery, Coconut Grove, Fla., 1980, Eclipse Gallery, Boulder, Colo., 1980, Atlanta Gallery of Photography, 1980, Phoenix Art Mus., 1981, Jeb Gallery, Providence, 1981, Portfolio Gallery, 1981, Images Gallery, Cin., 1982, Boston Atheneum, 1983, Bank of Santa Fe, 1984, Susan Harder Gallery, N.Y.C., 1984, Cleve. Art Mus., 1985, Art Inst. Chgo., 1987, Amon Carter Mus., Ft. Worth, 1987, Clarence Kennedy Gallery, Cambridge, Mass., 1988, Equitable Gallery, N.Y.C., 1993, Vassar Coll. Art Mus., N.Y., 1994, Vassar Coll. Art Gallery, N.Y., 1995; exhibited in group shows Gallery 216, N.Y., N.Y. Grover Cronin Gallery, Waltham, Mass., 1964, Carl Seimbab Gallery, Boston, 1966, Lassall Jr. Coll., 1967, Hill's Gallery, Santa Fe, Tyler Mus. Art, Austin, Tex., Dupree Gallery, Dallas, 1974, Quindacqua Gallery, Washington, 1978, Zabriskie Gallery, Paris, 1978, Am. Cultural Ctr., Paris, 1978; photographer AT&T Project-Am. Images, 1978, Seagram's Bicentennial Project, Courthouse, 1975-77, Readers Digest Assn. Project, 1984, Hudson River Project, 1985-92; author: Photography Portfolios, Old Boston City Hall, 1971, Photography Portfolios, Courthouse, 1979, Photography Portfolios, New Mexico, 1975, Certain Places, Photographs, 1987, A Hudson Landscape, Photographs, 1993. Nat. Endowment for Arts photography fellow, 1972, 79; Guggenheim fellow, 1974, 80, N.Mex. Gov.'s Excellence in The Arts award, 1987 Home and Office: PO Box 6035 Santa Fe NM 87502-6035

CLIFTON, MICHAEL EDWARD, English language educator; b. Reedley, Calif., Jan. 6, 1949; s. Edward Eugene and Helen May (Peters) C.; m. Anita May Bernardi, June 22, 1973. BA, Calif. State U., Fresno, 1971, MA with distinction, 1977; PhD, Ind. U., 1984. Tchr. English Hoover High Sch., Fresno, 1971-74; assoc. instr. Ind. U., Bloomington, 1978-80; lectr. Calif. State U., Fresno, 1982—. Reader, presenter Internat. Assn. Fantastic in Arts, Ft. Lauderdale, Fla., 1988, 93, Houston, Tex., 1987, Am. Imagery Assn., San Francisco, 1986, Eaton Conf., U. Calif. Riverside, 1985. Contbr. articles to popular mags. and profl. jours. Chair Tower Dist. Design Rev. Com. Mem. MLA, AAUP. Democrat. Avocations: reading, birding, computers, historical preservation. Home: 921 N San Pablo Ave Fresno CA 93728-3627 Office: Calif State U Dept English Peters Bldg Fresno CA 93740-0001

CLIMAN, RICHARD ELLIOT, lawyer; b. N.Y.C., July 19, 1953; s. David Arthur and Mary (Vitale) C. AB cum laude, Harvard U., 1974, JD cum laude, 1977. Bar: Calif. 1977. Assoc. Pettit & Martin, San Francisco, 1977-83, ptnr., 1984-94; ptnr., head mergers and acquisitions group Cooley Godward LLP, Palo Alto, San Francisco, Calif., 1994—. Adv. bd. BNA Mergers & Acquisitions Law Report; lectr. and panelist in field; co chair Doing Deals Practising Law Inst., Mergers & Acquisitions Inst. Glasser Legal Works. Contbr. articles to profl. jours. Mem. ABA (sect. bus. law, vice chair com. on negotiated acquisitions). Home: 1 Tulip Ln San Carlos CA 94070-1551 Office: Cooley Godward LLP 5 Palo Alto Sq 3000 El Camino Real Palo Alto CA 94306-2120 E-mail: climanre@cooley.com

CLINE, CAROLYN JOAN, plastic and reconstructive surgeon; b. Boston, May 15, 1941; d. Paul S. and Elizabeth (Flom) Cline. BA, Wellesley Coll., 1962; MA, U. Cin., 1966; PhD, Washington U., 1970; diploma, Washington Sch. Psychiatry, 1972; MD, U. Miami, 1975. Diplomate Am. Bd. Plastic and Reconstructive Surgery. Rsch. asst. Harvard U. Dental Sch., Boston, 1962-64; rsch. asst. physiology Laser Lab., Children's Hosp. Rsch. Found., Cin., 1964, psychology dept. U. Cin., 1964-65; intern in clin. psychology St. Elizabeth's Hosp., Washington, 1966-67; psychologist Alexandria (Va.) Cmty. Mental Health Ctr., 1967-68; rsch. fellow NIH, Washington, 1968-69; chief psychologist Kingsbury Ctr. for Children, Washington, 1969-73; sole practice clin. psychology Washington, 1970-73; intern internal medicine U. Wis. Hosp. Ctr. for Health Sci., Madison, 1975-76; resident in surgery Stanford U. Med. Ctr., 1976-78; fellow microvasc. surgery dept. surgery U. Calif., San Francisco, 1978-79; resident in plastic surgery St. Francis Hosp., San Francisco, 1979-82; practice medicine specializing in plastic and reconstructive surgery, San Francisco, 1982-95; free-lance writer profl. and popular publs., 1995—. Contbr. chpts. to plastic surgery textbooks, articles to profl. jours. Mem. Am. Soc. Plastic and Reconstructive Surgeons, Royal Soc. Medicine, Calif. Medicine Assn., Calif. Soc. Plastic and Reconstructive Surgeons, San Francisco Med. Soc.

CLINE, FRED ALBERT, JR. retired librarian, conservationist; b. Santa Barbara, Calif., Oct. 23, 1929; s. Fred Albert and Anna Cecelia (Haberl) C. AB in Asian Studies, U. Calif., Berkeley, 1952, MLS, 1962. Resident Internat. House, Berkeley, 1950-51; trainee, officer Bank of Am., San Francisco, Düsseldorf, Fed. Republic Germany, Kuala Lumpur, 1954-60; adminstrv. reference libr. Calif. State Libr., Sacramento, 1962-67, head libr. Asian Art Mus. San Francisco, 1967-93; ret., 1993. Contbg. author: Chinese, Korean and Japanese Sculpture in the Avery Brundage Collection, 1974; author, editor: Ruth Hill Cooke, 1985; contbr. articles and book revs. on AIDS to various publs. Bd. dirs. Tamalpais Conservation Club, 1990-94, 98-99; dissident AIDS activist. Sgt. M.C., U.S. Army, 1952-54. Mem. Metaphys. Alliance (sec., bd. dirs. San Francisco chpt. 1988-91), Sierra Club. Democrat. Avocations: hiking, music, reading. Home: 825 Lincoln Way San Francisco CA 94122-2369

CLINE, ROBERT STANLEY, air freight company executive; b. Urbana, Ill., July 17, 1937; s. Lyle Stanley and Mary Elizabeth (Prettyman) C.; m. Judith Lee Stucker, July 7, 1979; children: Lisa Andre, Nicole Lesley, Christina Elaine, Leslie Jane. BA, Dartmouth Coll., 1959. Asst. treas. Chase Manhattan Bank, N.Y.C., 1960-65; v.p. fin. Pacific Air Freight Co., Seattle, 1965-68; exec. v.p. fin. Airborne Express (formerly Airborne Freight Corp.), Seattle, 1968-78, vice chmn., CFO, dir., 1978-84, chmn., CEO, dir., 1984—. Bd. dirs. Safeco Corp., Esterline Techs. Corp. Trustee Seattle Repertory Theatre, 1974-90, chmn. bd., 1979-83; trustee Children's Hosp. Found., 1983-91, 96—, Corp. Coun. of Arts, 1983—; bd. dirs. Washington Roundtable, 1985—, chmn. 1995-96; chmn. bd. dirs. Children's Hosp. Found., 1987-89; trustee United Way of King County, 1991-93. With U.S. Army, 1959-60. Home: 1209 39th Ave E Seattle WA 98112-4403 Office: Airborne Express PO Box 662 Seattle WA 98111-0662

CLINE, THOMAS WARREN, molecular biologist, educator; b. Oakland, Calif., May 6, 1946; married, 1986. AB, U. Calif. Berkeley, 1968; PhD in Biochemistry, Harvard U., 1973. Fellow devel. genetics Helen Hay Whitney Found., U. Calif. Irvine, 1973-76; from asst. to prof. biology Princeton U., 1976-90; prof. genetics and devel. U. Calif. Berkeley, 1990—. Recipient Molecular Biology award NAS, 1992. Fellow Am. Acad. Arts and Scis.; mem. AAAS, Genetics Soc. Am., Soc. Devel. Biology. Achievements include research in development regulation of gene expression and pattern formation in Drosophila melanogaster with emphasis on oogenesis, sex determination, and X-chromosome dosage compensation. Office: U Calif 401 Barker Hall Spc 3204 Berkeley CA 94720-3204

CLINTON, RICHARD M. lawyer; b. Milw., June 25, 1941; s. William J. and Idella (Loftis) C.; m. Barbara Lynch, June 14, 1969; children: Amanda, Camille, Rebecca. BS, U. Wis., 1963, JD, 1967; LLM, George Washington U., 1971. Bar: Wis. 1967, Wash. 1971, U.S. Dist. Ct. (ea. dist.) Wash. 1975, U.S. Ct. Appeals (9th cir.) 1972. Instr. legal writing U. Wis. Law Sch., Madison, 1966-67; trial atty. antitrust div. U.S. Dept. Justice, Washington, 1967-71; assoc. Bogle & Gates, Seattle, 1971-75, mem., 1975-99; ptnr. Dorsey & Whitney LLP, 1999—. Fellow Am. Coll. Trial Lawyers; mem. ABA, Wash. Bar Assn. (pres. antitrust sect. 1982-83), Fed. Bar Assn. (pres. 1986-87), Wash. Athletic Club, Columbia Tower Club. Roman Catholic. Avocations: sailing, skiing, fishing, hiking, travel. Home: 3863 50th Ave NE Seattle WA 98105-5235 Office: Dorsey & Whitney LLP US Bank Centre 1420 5th Ave Seattle WA 98101-4087

CLIVER, DEAN OTIS, microbiologist, educator; b. Oak Park, Ill., Mar. 2, 1935; s. Milton Clarence and Ivy Ada (Erb) C.; m. Carolyn Elaine Parker, Aug. 13, 1960; children— Blanche Irena, Frederick Lajos, Carl Milan, Marguerite Estelle. B.S., Purdue U., 1956, M.S., 1957; Ph.D., Ohio State U., 1960. Postdoctoral rsch. assoc. Ohio State U., 1960; resident rsch. assoc. NAS-NRC, U.S. Army Biol. Labs., Ft. Detrick, Md., 1961-62; rsch. assoc., instr. Food Rsch. Inst., U. Chgo., 1962-66; asst. prof. dept. food microbiology and toxicology, dept. bacteriology Food Rsch. Inst., U. Wis., Madison, 1966—, assoc. prof., 1967-76; prof. Food Rsch. Inst. U. Wis., 1976-95, Dept. Animal Health and Biomed. Scis. U. Wis, 1992-95; prof. dept. population health and reprodn. Sch. Vet. Medicine, U. Calif., Davis, 1995—. Prin. investigator, head WHO Collaborating Centre for Food Virology, Davis. Contbr. articles to profl. jours. and chpts. to books; editor 4 books in field. Served as 2d lt. U.S. Army Res., 1957. Recipient Borden undergrad. award Purdue U., 1956; Ralston-Purina grad. fellow, 1956-57 Mem. Am. Soc. Microbiology, Inst. Food Technologists (food sci. communicator 1991—), Internat. Assn. Food Protection, Internat. Assn. Water Quality, Sigma Xi. Home: 920 Villanova Dr Davis CA 95616-1749 Office: U Calif Sch Vet Medicine Dept Population Health/Rep Davis CA 95616-8743 E-mail: docliver@ucdavis.edu

CLOPTON, KAREN VALENTIA, lawyer, president civil services commission; BA with hons., Vassar Coll., 1980; JD, Antioch U., 1983. Bar: Calif. Maguire fellow internat. and comparative labor studies, London, 1984; trial atty NLRB, Washington, San Francisco; counsel Leland, Parachini, Steinberg, Matzger & Melnick LLP, San Francisco, 1998—. Lectr. mgmt. tng. programs emphasizing preventive labor rels.; mem. faculty San Francisco State U. Coll. Extended Learning. Past mem. L.A. Dist. Atty.'s Office Youth Adv. Bd; pres. San Francisco City and County Civil Service Commn. Mem. Lawyers Club of San Francisco (bd. govs.), Calif. Young Lawyers Assn. (Jack Berman Individual award of achievement 1994). Office: Leland Parachini et al 333 Market St Ste 2700 San Francisco CA 94105-2128

CLOSE, SANDY, journalist; b. N.Y.C., Jan. 25, 1943; BA, U. Calif., Berkeley, 1964. Exec. dir., editor Pacific News Svc., San Francisco. MacArthur fellow, 1995. Office: Pacific News Service 660 Market St Ste 210 San Francisco CA 94104-5011

CLOSE, TIMOTHY, art museum administrator; Exec. dir. Albany (Ga.) Mus. Art, Boise Art Museum, Boise, Idaho. Office: Boise Art Museum 670 S Julia Davis Dr Boise ID 83702-4168

CLOW, LEE, advertising agency executive; Formerly exec. v.p., creative dir. Chiat/Day, L.A., now pres., chief creative officer, chmn, cco, 1995, chief creative officer worldwide. Office: TBWA Chiat/Day 5353 Grosvenor Blvd Los Angeles CA 90066

CLOWES, ALEXANDER WHITEHILL, surgeon, educator; b. Boston, Oct. 9, 1946; s. George H.A. Jr. and Margaret Gracey (Jackson) C.; m. Monika Meyer (dec.); m. Susan E. Detweiler, Aug., 2000. AB, Harvard U., 1968, MD, 1972. Resident in surgery Case Western Reserve, Cleve., 1972-74, 76-79; rsch. fellow in pathology Harvard Med. Sch., Boston, 1974-76; fellow in vascular surgery Brigham and Womens Hosp. Harvard Med. Sch., 1979-80; asst. prof. surgery U. Wash., Seattle, 1980-85, assoc. prof., 1985-90, prof., 1990—, assoc. chmn. dept., 1989-91, acting chmn. dept., 1992-93, adj. prof. pathology, 1992, chief divsn. vascular surgery, 1995—, dept. vice chmn., 1995—. Contbr. chpts. to books; author numerous sci. papers. Trustee Marine Biol. Labs., Woods Hole, Mass., 1989-2000, Seattle Symphony, 1994, v.p., 1998-2000; bd. dirs. Seattle Chamber Music Festival, 1990. Recipient NIH Rsch. Career Devel. award, 1982-87; NIH Tng. fellow, 1974-77; Loyal Davis Traveling Surg. scholar ACS, 1987. Mem. Am. Surg. Assn., Am. Assn. Pathologists, Am. Heart Assn. (coun. on arteriosclerosis), Am. Soc. Cell Biology, Internat. Soc. Applied Cardiovasc. Biology, Seattle Surg. Soc., Soc. Vascular Surgery, Cruising Club Am., Quisset Yacht Club, Sigma Xi. Episcopalian. Home: 3425 Perkins Ln W Seattle WA 98199-1858 Office: U Wash Dept Surgery PO Box 356410 Seattle WA 98195-6410

CLUFF, LLOYD STERLING, earthquake geologist; b. Provo, Utah, Sept. 29, 1933; s. Colvin Sterling and Melba (Walker) C.; m. Anne Provstgard, Aug. 28, 1958 (div. June 1974); m. Janet L. Peterson, Dec. 21, 1976; children: Tanya, Sasha, Branden. BS in Geology, U. Utah, 1960. Registered profl. geologist, Calif.; cert. engring. geologist, Calif. Jr. geologist El Paso Natural Gas Co., Salt Lake City, 1957-59; teaching asst. dept. geology U. Utah, Salt Lake City, 1958-60; geologist Lottridge Thomas & Assocs., Salt Lake City, 1960; v.p., prin. geologist Woodward-Clyde Cons., San Francisco, 1960-85; assoc. prof. U. Nev., Reno, 1967-73; mgr. dept. geoscis. Pacific Gas and Electric Co., San Francisco, 1985—. Cons. Trans-Alaska Pipeline Siting Study, 1972-74, Aswan High Dam, Govt. of Egypt, 1982-86; mem. com. Nat. Earthquake Hazards Reduction Program, Washington, 1987, Decade for Natural Disaster Reduction, Washington, 1989; advisor Venezuela Pres.'s Earthquake Safety Com., 1967-72; advisor Joint Legis. Com. on Seismic Safety, State of Calif., 1970-74; chmn. seismic rev. panel Calif. Pub. Utilities Commn., San Francisco, 1980-81; mem. Calif. Seismic Safety Commn., 1985-99, chmn., 1988-90, 95-97; adv. bd. So. Calif. Earthquake Ctr., 1996—; chmn. Tech. Adv. Bd. on Earthquake Risk, Israel, 1996—; organizing com. for Pub. Policy Partnership 2000-White House Confs. on Natural Disaster Loss Reduction, 1997-98; com. on assessing costs of natural disasters NAS, 1998-99, natural disaster roundtable, 2000—; nat. pre-disaster mitigation program adv. panel FEMA, 1998-99; exterl adv. panel for Pacific Earthquake Engring. Rsch. Ctr., 1998-99, implementation adv. bd., 1999—; natural disaster panel Heinz Ctr. Inst. for Natural Disasters, 2000—. Recipient Hogentagler award ASTM, 1968, Alfred E. Alquist medal, 1998, John Wesley Powell award, 2000; named Woodward lectr., San Francisco, 1979. Fellow Calif. Acad. Scis.; mem. NAE, NSF (adv. panel on earth scis. 1992-95), NAS (chmn. com. Practical Lessons from the Loma Prieta Earthquake 1994), Seismol. Soc. Am. (pres. 1982-83), Assn. Engring. Geologists (pres. 1968-69), Earthquake Engring. Rsch. Inst. (hon., pres. 1993-95, chmn. Internat. Conf. on Seismic Zonation, Nice, France 1995), Geol. Soc. Am., Structural Engrs. Assn. No. Calif. (H.J. Degenkolb award 1992). Republican. Avocations: photography, skiing, mountain climbing, hiking, bicycling. Office: Pacific Gas & Elec Co 245 Market St San Francisco CA 94105-1797 E-mail: lsc2@pge.com

CLYDE, LARRY FORBES, banker; b. Heber, Utah, Nov. 19, 1941; s. Don and Kathryn (Forbes) C.; m. Barbara Eliason, Dec. 23, 1963 (div. Jan. 1985); children: Lynne, Karen Lee; m. Katharyn L. Decker, July 3, 1986. BA, Utah State U., 1963, MS, 1965. With Pitts. Nat. Bank, 1965-68; with Crocker Nat. Bank, San Francisco, 1968-86, mgr. investment banking, 1973-75, mgr. capital markets divsn., 1975-86, sr. v.p., 1976-78, exec. v.p., mem. policy com., 1978-86; mng. dir., chief exec. U.S. capital markets activities Midland Bank Group, N.Y.C., 1986-87; CEO Midland Montagu Govt. Securities, Midland Montagu Mcpl. Securities, and Midland Montagu Trust Co., 1986-87; exec. v.p., mgr. global fin. institutions mktg. Am. Express Bank, 1987-88; exec. v.p., mgr. global securities lending, mem. sr. mgmt. com. Mellon Bank N.A., Pitts., 1988-2000. Bd. dirs. Pub. Securities Assn., 1976-83, mem. govt. borrowing com., 1981-87, vice chmn., 1981, chmn., 1982; treas., dir. No. Calif. chpt. Invest-In-Am., 1975-87; dir. ABA Securities Assn., 1995—; bd. dirs. Fed. Farm Credit Funding Corp. Mem. Am. Bankers Assn. (vice chmn. bank investment and funds mgmt. divsn. exec. com. 1982, chmn. exec. com. 1983), Dealer Bank Assn. (bd. dirs. 1986-87), San Francisco Bond Club, Duquesne Club, Allegheny Country Club. Office: 12 Mustang Mesa Santa Fe NM 87501-7702

COALE, KENNETH HAMILTON, biogeochemist, educator; b. N.Y.C., Jan. 24, 1955; s. Franklin Steele Coale and Mary Louise (Price) Moses; m. Susan Elizabeth Lange, June 23, 1979; children: Megan Elizabeth Coale, Tyler Hamilton Coale. BA in biology, U. Calif., 1977, PhD in biology, 1988. Marine tech. Moss Landing (Calif.) Marine Labs., 1976-77; asst. specialist U. Calif., Santa Cruz, 1978-83, assoc. specialist, 1983, rsch. asst., 1983-88; postdoctoral researcher Moss Landing (Calif.) Labs., 1988, sr. rsch. assoc., 1991-92, adj. prof., 1992—; acting dir. Moss Landing Marine Labs., 1998—. Vis. scientist KFA Juelich Germany, NIOZ, The Netherlands, 1982; guest editor Deep Sea Rsch., Oxford, Sidney, London,

1994—. Co-author: Dynamic Processing in the Chemistry of the Upper Oceans, 1986; contbr. articles to profl. jours. Sec., bd. dirs. Land Trust of Santa Cruz Co., 1991-2000 Recipient rsch. grants in field. Mem. AAAS, Am. Geophysical Union, Am. Soc. Limnology & Oceanography, Oceanography Soc., Am. Chemical Soc. Achievements include development of 234th; 238 U disequilibria as a tracer for chemical biological removal process; development of DPASV to determine copper complexation in the North Pacific Ocean, COPi and chief scientist of the Iron Ex experiments. Avocations: woodworking, welding, camping, music. Office: Moss Landing Marine Labs 8272 Moss Landing Rd Moss Landing CA 95039-9647 E-mail: coale@mlml.calstate.edu

COAN, PATRICIA A. magistrate judge; b. N.Y.C., July 21, 1945; 2 children. BSN, Georgetown U., 1967; JD, U. Denver, 1981. Bar: Colo. 1982; RN, N.Y., Conn., Mont., Colo. Pvt. practice, Denver, 1982-96; magistrate judge U.S. Dist. Ct. for Dist. Colo., Denver, 1996—. Bd. dirs. Colo. Lawyers Health Program. Mem. FBA, Women's Bar Assn., Am. Soc. Law and Medicine, Colo. Bar Assn., Denver Bar Assn., Sigma Theta Tau, Gamma Pi Epsilon. Office: US Dist Ct 1929 Stout St Rm C-160 Denver CO 80236

COATS, NATHAN B. judge; m. Mary Ricketson; 1 child, Johanna. BA in Econs., U. Colo., 1971, JD, 1975. Assoc. Hough, Grant, McCarren and Bernard, 1977-78; asst. atty. gen. Appellate Sect., Colo., 1978-83, dep. atty. gen., 1983-86; adj. prof. U. Colo., 1990; chief appellate dep. dist. atty. 2d Jud. Dist., Denver, 1986-2000; apptd. state supreme ct. judge Colo. Supreme Ct., 2000—. Chief reporter Erickson Commn. on Officer-Involved Shootings, 1996-97; lectr. Denver Police Acad., 1986-97; reporter Govs. Columbine Commn., 1999-2000; mem. Colo. Supreme Ct. Criminal Rules Com., 1983-2000, chmn., 1997-2000, Colo. Supreme Ct. Appellate Rules Com., 1985-2000, Colo. Supreme Ct. Civil Rules Com., Colo. Supreme Ct. Criminal Pattern Jury Instructions Com., 1987-2000, Colo. Supreme Ct. Jury Reform Pilot Project Com., 1998-2000, Colo. Dist. Attys. Coun. Legis. Com., 1990-2000. Office: Colo State Supreme Ct Judicial Bldg 2 E 14th Ave Denver CO 80203-2115

COBB, JEWEL PLUMMER, former college president, educator; b. Chgo., Jan. 17, 1924; divorced; 1 child. AB, Talladega Coll., 1944; MS, NYU, 1947, PhD in Biology, 1950. Fellow Nat. Cancer Inst., 1950-52; instr. anatomy U. Ill. Coll. Medicine, 1952-54; rsch. surgery staff NYU Postgrad. Med. Coll., 1955, asst. prof., 1955-60; Cancer Rsch. Found. prof. biology Sarah Lawrence Coll., 1960-69; prof. zoology, dean Conn. Coll., 1969-76; prof. biology, dean Douglass Coll., Rutgers U., 1976-81; pres. Calif. State U., Fullerton, 1981-90, pres. emerita, prof. emerita, 1990—, trustee prof. L.A., 1990—. Prin. investigator, dir. Access Ctr.; mem. Nat. Inst. Medicine; bd. dirs. 21st Century Found. Trustee Drew U. Medicine and Sci., Calif. Inst. Tech.; bd. fellows Calif. Grad. U. Claremont. Recipient Alumnae Woman of Yr. award N.Y. U., 1979 Fellow N.Y. Acad. Scis., Tissue Culture Assn.; mem. AAUW, Sigma Xi. Achievements include research on tissue culture studies human neoplasms, on changes produced by promising chemotherapeutic agents, on mechanisms of normal and abnormal pigment cell metabolism.

COBB, JOHN CANDLER, medical educator; b. Boston, July 8, 1919; s. Stanley and Elizabeth Mason (Almy) C.; m. Helen Imlay-Franchot, July 27, 1946; children: Loren, Nathaniel, Bethany, Julianne. BS in Astronomy cum laude, Harvard U., 1941, MD, 1948; MPH, Johns Hopkins U., 1954. Diplomate Nat. Bd. Med. Examiners, Am. Bd. Preventive Medicine and Pub. Health; lic. physician, Conn., Md., N.Mex. Intern Yale New Haven Hosp., 1948-49, fellow in pediatrics, 1949-50; jr. asst. resident Yale Psychiatric Clinic, 1950-51; instr. pediatrics Johns Hopkins U., 1951-56, asst. prof. hygiene, 1954-56; cons. Indian Health divsn. USPHS, Albuquerque, 1956-60; prof. preventive medicine U. Colo., Denver, 1965-85, emeritus prof., 1985—, chmn. dept., 1966-73; emeritus prof., 1985—. Dir. med. social rsch. project on population Govt. of Pakistan, 1960-64; cons. Am. Friends Svc. Commn., Algeria, 1964; short term cons. WHO, Indonesia and Western Pacific Region, 1969, 70-73, USAID, Togo and Niger, 1979; exch. prof. Guangxi Med. Coll., Nanning, China, 1985-86; coord. ethics seminars U. Health Scis. Ctr., 1980-85; cons. in field. Contbr. numerous articles to profl. jours. Bd. mem., pres. Am. Assn. Planned Parenthood Physicians, 1966-67; chmn. Task Force for Preparing 314(b) Agy. Grant Applicaiton, 1969; mem. Gov.'s Task Force on Health Effects of Air Pollution, 1978-79; commr. Air Pollution Control Commn. of Colo., 1976-79; mem. air quality policy com. Denver Regional Coun. of Govts., 1978-80, environ. council, U. Colo., 1970-75, Gov.'s Scientific adv. council, Colo., 1973-80, Gov.'s Blue Ribbon Task Force on Transportation, Colo., 1977; bd. dirs. ROMCOE Ctr. for Environ. Problem Solving, 1978-81, Colo. Coalition for Full Employment, 1978-80; mem. Am. Friends Svc. Com. Adv. Group on Rocky Flats/Nuclear Weapons Project, 1979-85. Recipient Florence Sabin award Colo. Pub. Health Assn., 1979, Jack Gore Meml. Peace award Am. Friends Svc. Com., 1980; U.S. EPA grantee, 1975-82. Mem. AAAS, WHO, Internat. Solar Energy Soc., Am. Solar Energy Soc., Internat. Physicians for Prevention of Nuclear War (del. to Congresses in Moscow and Montreal), Appropriate Rural Tech. Assn. (bd. dirs. 1987—, v.p. 1991-92), Nat. Resources Def. Coun. (bd. advisors 1991-92), N.Mex. Solar Energy Assn. (bd. dirs.), Physicians for Human Rights, Physicians for Social Reponsibility. Home and Office: # 4320 10501 Lagrima De Oro NE Albuquerque NM 87111

COBB, JOHN RICHARDSON, state senator; b. Great Falls, Mont., Jan. 22, 1954; m. Cheryl Lux; 2 children. BBA, Mont. State U., 1975, BA in Econs., 1976; JD, U. Mont., 1979. Atty.; rancher; Rep. rep. dist. 50 Mont. Ho. of Reps., 1984-2000; Rep. senator dir. 25 Mont. State Senate, 2000—. Mem. appropriations com. Mont. Ho. of Reps. Office: PO Box 388 Augusta MT 59410-0388 also: Mont State Senate Capitol Station Helena MT 59620 E-mail: cobbchar@3rivers.net

COBB, MILES ALAN, retired lawyer; b. Salt Lake City, May 8, 1930; s. Miles Cobb and June (Ray) Cobb Wilson; children: Jennifer, Melissa, Mary. B.S., U. Calif.-Berkeley, 1953, LL.B., 1958. Bar: Calif. 1958. Assoc. Bronson, Bronson & McKinnon, San Francisco, 1958-65, ptnr., 1965-76, 78-84; gen. counsel FDIC, Washington, 1976-78; pres. Bell Savs & Loan Assn., San Mateo, Calif., 1984-85. Author: Federal Regulation of Depository Institutions, 1984. Served to 1st lt. U.S. Army, 1953-55; Korea Democrat Avocations: photography; golf; gardening. E-mail: cobb7@earthlink.net

COBB, ROY LAMPKIN, JR. retired computer sciences corporation executive; b. Oklahoma City, Sept. 23, 1934; s. Roy Lampkin and Alice Maxine Cobb; m. Shirley Ann Dodson, June 21, 1958; children: Kendra Leigh, Cary William, Paul Alan. BA, U. Okla., 1972; postgrad., U. Calif., Northridge, 1976-77. Naval aviation cadet USN, 1955, advanced through grades to comdr., 1970, ret., 1978; mktg./project staff engr. Gen. Dynamics, Pomona, Calif., 1978-80; mgr. dept. support svcs. Computer Scis. Corp., Point Mugu, 1980-97; ret. Decorated Navy Commendation medal, Air medal (13). Mem. Assn. Naval Aviators, Soc. Logistic Engrs. (editor Launchings 1990-98), Navy League, Las Posas Country Club, Spanish Hills Country Club. Republican. Home: 2481 Brookhill Dr Camarillo CA 93010-2112 E-mail: cobbweb@aol.com

COBBAN, WILLIAM AUBREY, paleontologist; b. Anaconda, Mont., Dec. 31, 1916; s. Ray Aubrey and Anastacia (McNulty) C.; m. Ruth Georgina Loucks, Apr. 15, 1942; children: Georgina, William, Robert. BA, U. Mont., 1940; PhD, Johns Hopkins U., 1949. Geologist Carter Oil Co., [illegible] paleontologist U.S. Geol. Survey, Washington, [illegible] emeritus scientist, 1992—. Contbr. numerous articles to profl. jours. Recipient Meritorious Svc. award Dept. Interior, 1974, Paleontol. medal Paleontol. Soc. Am., 1985, Disting. Svc. award U.S. Dept. Interior, 1986. Fellow AAAS, Geol. Soc. Am.; mem. Soc. Econ. Paleontologists and Mineralogists (hon.; Disting. Pioneer Geologist award 1985, Raymond C. Moore Paleontology medal 1990), Rocky Mountain Assn. Geologists (hon.), Mont. Geol. Soc. (hon.), Wyo. Geol Assn. (hon.), Paleontol. Soc., Am. Assn. Petroleum Geologists, Paleontol. Rsch. Inst. (Gilbert Harris award 1996), Phi Beta Kappa, Sigma Xi. Republican. Mem. United Ch. of Christ. Office: US Geol Survey Federal Ctr PO Box 25046 # 913 Denver CO 80225

COBBLE, JAMES WIKLE, chemistry educator; b. Kansas City, Mo., Mar. 15, 1926; s. Ray and Crystal Edith (Wikle) C.; m. Margaret Ann Zumwalt, June 9, 1949 (dec.); children— Catherine Ann, Richard James. Student, San Diego State Coll., 1942-44; BA, No. Ariz. U., 1946; MS, U. So. Calif., 1949; PhD, U. Tenn., 1952. Chemist Oak Ridge Nat. Lab., 1949-52; postdoctoral research asso. U. Calif., Berkeley, 1952-55, instr. dept. chemistry, 1954; asst. prof. dept. chemistry Purdue U., Lafayette, Ind., 1955-58, asso. prof., 1958-61, prof., 1961-73; prof., dean Grad. div. San Diego State U., 1973—; v.p. rsch., dean Grad. divsn. San Diego State U., 1997—. Cons. in field. Contbr. articles to sci. publs. Mem. bd. visitors USAF Air Univ. , 1984—92, chmn., 1988—90; vpres. San Diego State Univ. Found., 1975—; trustee Calif. Western Law Sch. , 1987—93; mem. Joint Grad. Bd., 1973—78; Lt. (j.g.) USNR, 1945—46. Recipient E.O. Lawrence award U.S. AEC, 1970, Disting. Svc. award USAF, 1992; Guggenheim fellow, 1966; Robert A. Welch Found. lectr., 1971. Fellow Am. Inst. Chemists, Am. Phys. Soc.; mem. Am. Chem. Soc., Sigma Xi, Phi Kappa Phi, Alpha Chi Sigma, Phi Lambda Upsilon. Home: 1380 Park Row La Jolla CA 92037-3709 Office: San Diego State Univ Grad & Rsch Affairs San Diego CA 92182-8020

COBLE, HUGH KENNETH, engineering and construction company executive; b. Rochester, Pa., 26 Sept. s. John L. and Victoria (Neilson) C.; m. Constance Stratton, June 2, 1956; children: Keith Allen, Kimberly Ann, Jon Arthur, Scott Arnold, Neal Stewart. BSChemE, Carnegie Mellon U., 1956; postgrad., UCLA, 1966, U. Houston, 1963-65, Stanford U., 1981. Engr. Standard Oil Calif., El Segundo, 1956-61; sales mgr. Turco Products, Houston, 1961-63; sales dir. W.R. Grace, Houston, 1963-65; vice chmn. emeritus Fluor Corp., Irvine, Calif., 1966-97, Irvine, 1997—. Bd. dirs. Beckman Instruments, Inc., Flowserve Corp., ICO Global Comm. Bd. dirs. John Henry Found., Orange, Calif., 1992-96, Sedona Cultural Park, Sedona Med. Ctr.; trustee Scripps U., Claremont, Calif., 1991-93, Fluor Found.; mem. adv. bd. Thunderbird U., Phoenix, 1992—; exec. engrng. adv. com. U. Calif.-Irvine. Mem. Am. Petroleum Inst., Am. Inst. Chem. Engrs. (bd. dirs. 1983-88). Presbyterian. Avocation: golf, piano, organ.

COBURN, MARJORIE FOSTER, psychologist, educator; b. Salt Lake City, Feb. 28, 1939; d. Harlan A. and Alma (Ballinger) Polk; m. Robert Byron Coburn, July 2, 1977; children: Polly Klea Foster, Matthew Ryan Foster, Robert Scott Coburn, Kelly Anne Coburn. B.A. in Sociology, UCLA, 1960; Montessori Internat. Diploma honor grad. Washington Montessori Inst., 1968; M.A. in Psychology, U. No. Colo., 1979; Ph.D. in Counseling Psychology, U. Denver, 1983. Licensed clin. psychologist. Probation officer Alameda County (Calif.), Oakland, 1960-62, Contra Costa County (Calif.), El Cerrito, 1966, Fairfax County (Va.), Fairfax, 1967; dir. Friendship Club, Orlando, Fla., 1963-65; tchr. Va. Montessori Sch., Fairfax, 1968-70; spl. edn. tchr. Leary Sch., Falls Church, Va., 1970-72, sch. administr., 1973-76; tchr. Aseltine Sch., San Diego, 1976-77, Coburn Montessori Sch., Colorado Springs, Colo., 1977-79; pvt. practice psychotherapy, Colorado Springs, 1979-82, San Diego, 1982— ; cons. spl. edn., agoraphobia, women in transition. Mem. Am. Psychol. Assn., Am. Orthopsychiat. Assn., Phobia Soc., Council Exceptional Children, Calif. Psychol. Assn., San Diego Psychological Assn., The Charter 100, Mensa. Episcopalian. Lodge: Rotary. Contbr. articles to profl. jours.; author: (with R.C. Orem) Montessori: Prescription for Children with Learning Disabilities, 1977. Office: 826 Prospect St Ste 101 La Jolla CA 92037-4206

COBURN, ROBERT CRAIG, philosopher, educator; b. Mpls., Jan. 25, 1930; s. William Carl and Esther Therice (Rudd) C.; m. Martha Louise Means, July 12, 1974. B.A., Yale U., 1951; B.D., U. Chgo., 1954; M.A., Ph.D., Harvard U., 1958. Asst. prof. philosophy U. Chgo., 1960-65, assoc. prof., 1965-68, prof., 1968-71; prof. philosophy U. Wash., Seattle, 1971—. Vis. assoc. prof. philosophy Cornell U., 1966, U. Bergen, Norway, spring 1986; condr. NEH summer seminar, 1983; cons. ERDA. Author: The Strangeness of the Ordinary: Issues and Problems in Contemporary Metaphysics, 1989; contbr. articles to philos. jours., chpts. to books. Ordained elder Rocky Mountain Conf. United Methodist Ch. Andrew Mellon postdoctoral fellow in philosophy U. Pitts., 1961-62; NSF grantee, 1968-69 Mem. Am. Philos. Assn. (exec. com. Pacific div. 1973-74), AAUP, Soc. Values in Higher Edn., Phi Beta Kappa. Home: 6852 28th Ave NE Seattle WA 98115-7145 Office: Univ Wash Dept Philosophy Seattle WA 98195-3350

COCCHIARELLA, VICKI MARSHALL, state legislator; b. Livingston, Mont., Dec. 19, 1949; d. James and Ruth E. (Officer) Marshall; m. Larry Ray Cocchiarella, 1973; children: Cara Jo, Michael James. BA, U. Mont., 1978, MA, 1985. Property mgr., 1975 ; teaching asst. U. Mont., 1979-80, adminstrv. clk., 1981-89; mem. Mont. Ho. of Reps., 1989-98, mem. interim com. state employee compensation; mem. Environ. Qual. Council, 1993-, Mont. Senate, Dist. 32, Helena, 1998—. Bd. dirs. Child & Family Resource Coun. Mem. Mont. Pub. Employees Assn. (former bd. dirs., former 1st v.p., pres. 1987—). Democrat. Office: Mont State Senate State Capitol Helena MT 59620

COCHRAN, JAMES ALAN, mathematics educator; b. San Francisco, May 12, 1936; s. Commodore Shelton and Gwendolyn Audrey (Rosenau) C.; m. Katherine Koehler Kern, Sept. 6, 1958; children: Cynthia Royal, Sarah Lynn. BS in Physics, Stanford U., 1956, MS in Physics, 1957; PhD in Math., Stanford U., 1962. Mem. tech. staff, supr. applied math. Bell Telephone Labs. Inc, Whippany, N.J., 1962-72; prof. math. Va. Poly. Inst. and State U., Blacksburg, 1972-78; prof., chmn. dept. math. Wash. State U., Pullman, 1978-84, prof., 1978-89, campus exec. officer and founding dean tri-cities Richland, Wash., 1989-98, prof. math., 1999—. Vis. prof. math. Stanford U., 1968-69, Wash. State U., 1977, U. NSW, Sydney, Australia, 1985, Southeast U., Nanjing, China, 1994; fgn. scholar math. and mechanics Nanjing Inst. Tech., 1984; vis. fellow Deakin U., Victoria, Australia, 1985, 87. Author: Analysis of Linear Integral Equations, 1972, Applied Mathematics: Principles, Techniques, and Applications, 1982, Advanced Engineering Mathematics, 1987; also articles. Mem. nat. coun. Boy Scout Am., 1973-76, 99—, mem. local coun., 1974-77, 82-84, 93—, coun. pres., 1999-2001, mem. western region, 1996—; chmn. bd. commrs. Morris County (N.J.) Area Libr. Sys., 1971-72; mem. bd. dirs. Tri-Cities Sci. and Tech. Park Assn., 1990—, chmn., 1990-93; bd. dirs. Wash. Environ. Industry Assn., 1990-95, TRIDEC, 1996—; dir. state bd. Math. Engring. Sci. Achievement, 1992—; mem. Am. Pub. TV Stas. Bd., 1992-96; exec. com. Tri-Cities Commercialization Partnership, 1993-97; mem. Hanford Adv. Bd., 1994—; sr. advisor Tri-Cities Corp. Coun. for the Arts, 1991-2000. Recipient Silver Beaver award Boy Scouts Am., 1997, disting. Eagle Scout award, 1997; Gordon vis. fellow, Deakin U., Victoria, Australia, 1985. Mem. Am. Math. Soc., Math. Assn. Am., Soc. Indsl. Applied Math., Nat. Eagle Scout Assn. (young man pres. 1957-58, adviser 1958-71, Disting. Service award 1976), Phi Beta Kappa, Sigma Xi, Golden Key, Alpha Phi Omega. Republican. Presbyterian. Home: 1927 Cypress Pl Richland WA 99352-2414 Office: Wash State U Tri-Cities 2710 University Dr Richland WA [illegible] E-mail: cochranj@tricity.wsu.edu

COCHRAN, JOHN HOWARD, plastic and reconstructive surgeon; b. Muncie, Ind., Sept. 6, 1946; s. John H. and Lois M. (Woolridge) C.; m. Elizabeth M. Cochran; 1 child, Ryan K. BS cum laude, Colo. State U., 1968; MD, U. Colo. Sch. Medicine, 1973. Intern surgery U. Calif., San Diego, 1973-74; resident head and neck surgery Stanford U., Palo Alto, Calif., 1974-77; resident plastic surgery U. Wis., Madison, 1979-81; pvt. practice plastic surgery Denver, 1981-90; chief plastic surgery St. Joseph Hosp., Denver, 1987-93, Colo. Med. Group, Denver, 1990-95; chmn. dept. surgery St. Joseph Hosp., 1993-99; exec. med. dir. Med. Group, Denver. Pres. bd. trustees Kilimanjaro Children's Hosp., Tanzania, E. Africa, 1989—. Fellow Am. Soc. Plastic and Reconstructive Surgery, Am. Coll. SUrgeons, Acad. Otolaryngology, Head and Neck Surgery; mem. Am. Assn. Plastic Surgeons. Avocations: fly fishing, skiing. Office: 10350 E Dakota Ave Denver CO 80231-1314

COCHRAN, JOHNNIE L., JR. lawyer; b. Shreveport, La., Oct. 2, 1937; BS, UCLA, 1959; JD, Loyola U., 1962; postgrad., U. So. Calif. Bar: Calif. 1963, U.S. Dist. Ct. (we. dist.) Tex. 1966, U.S. Supreme Ct. 1968. Dep. city atty. criminal divsn. City of L.A., 1963-65; asst. dist. atty. L.A. County, 1978-82; now pvt. practice atty. L.A. Former adj. prof. law UCLA Sch. Law, Loyola U. Sch. Law; lawyer rep. U.S. Dist .Ct. (ctrl. dist.) Calif., 1990, U.S. Ct. Appeals (9th cir.) Judicial Conf., 1990; bd. dirs. L.A. Family Housing Corp., Lawyers Mut. Ins. Co. Spl. counsel, chmn. rules com. Dem. Nat. Convention, 1984; spl. counsel com. on standard ofcl. conduct, ethics com. 99th congress U.S. Ho. Reps.; bd. dirs. L.A. Urban League, Oscar Joel Bryant Found., 28th St. YMCA, ACLU Found. So. Calif. Fellow Am. Bar Found.; mem. Am. Coll. Trial Lawyers, State Bar Calif. (co-chair bd. legal svc. corps 1993), L.A. African Am. C. of C. (bd. dirs.), Airport Commrs. City of L.A., Black Bus. Assn. L.A. (pres. 1989). Office: 4929 Wilshire Blvd Ste 1010 Los Angeles CA 90010-3825

COCHRAN, SUSAN MILLS, librarian; b. Grinnell, Iowa, Nov. 21, 1949; d. Lawrence Omen and Louise Jane (Morgan) Mills; m. Stephen E. Cochran, July 1, 1972; children: Bryan, Jeremy. Libr. Iowa Geneal. Soc., Des Moines, 1987-96; asst. to dir. Local History Ctr., Canon City (Colo.) Pub. Libr., 1997—. Editor: Mingo, Iowa 1884-1984, 1984; contbr. articles to profl. jours. Past bd. dirs. Jasper County Libr., Newton, Iowa; past mem. Jasper County Cemetery Commn., Newton; mem. Jasper County His. Soc. Mem. Iowa Geneal. Soc., Jasper County Geneal. Soc., State Assn. for the Preservation of Iowa Cemeteries (charter), Fremont County Geneal. Group (coord.), Colo. Coun. Geneal. Socs. Avocations: genealogy, history, birding. Office: Canon City Pub Libr 516 Macon Ave Canon City CO 81212-3310

COCHRAN, WENDELL ALBERT, science editor; b. Carthage, Mo., Nov. 29, 1929; s. Wendell Albert and Lillian Gladys (Largent) C.; m. Agnes Elizabeth Groves, Nov. 9, 1963; remarried Corinne Des Jardins, Aug. 25, 1980. A.B., U. Mo., Columbia, 1953, A.M. in Geology, 1956, B.J., 1960. Geologist ground-water br. U.S. Geol. Survey, 1956-58; reporter, copyeditor Kansas City (Mo.) Star, 1960-63; editor Geotimes and Earth Sci. mags., Geospectrum newsletter, Alexandria, Va., 1963-84; v.p. Geol. Survey Inc., Bethesda, Md., 1984-86. Co-author: Into Print: A Practical Guide to Writing, Illustrating, and Publishing, 1977; sr. editor: Geowriting: A Guide to Writing, Editing and Printing in Earth Science, 1973; contbr. articles to profl. jours. and encys. Mem. geol. socs. Washington, London, Assn. Earth Sci. Editors (award Outstanding Contbns. 1982), Dog in the Night-time. Home: 4351 SW Willow St Seattle WA 98136-1769 E-mail: atrypa@eskimo.com

COCHRAN, WILLIAM MICHAEL, librarian; b. Nevada, Iowa, May 6, 1952; s. Joseph Charles and Inez (Larson) C.; m. Diane Marie Ohm, July 24, 1971. BLS, U. Iowa, 1979, MA with distinction in Libr. Sci., 1983; MA in Pub. Adminstrn., Drake U., 1989. Dir. Red Oak (Iowa) Pub. Libr., 1984; patron svcs. libr. Pub. Libr. of Des Moines, 1984-87; LSCA program coord. State Libr. of Iowa, Des Moines, 1987-88, dir. libr. devel., 1988-89, asst. state libr., 1989-90; dir. Parmly Billings Libr., 1990—. Contbr. articles to profl. jours. Bd. dirs. Billings Cmty. Cable Corp., 1994-97. Mem. ALA, Mont. Libr. Assn. (pub. libr. divsn., chair 1991-92, legis. com. chair 1992-93, pres. 1998-99; named Libr. of Yr., 1998), Mont. Gov.'s Blue Ribbon Telecommunications Task Force, White House Conf. on Libr. and Info. Svcs., Libr. Adminstrn. and Mgmt. Assn., Pub. Libr. Assn., U. Iowa Alumni Assn. (life), Beta Phi Mu. Office: Parmly Billings Libr 510 N Broadway Billings MT 59101-1156

COCKRUM, WILLIAM MONROE, III, investment banker, consultant, educator; b. Indpls., July 18, 1937; s. William Monroe C. II and Katherine J. (Jaqua) Moore; m. Andrea Lee Deering, Mar. 8, 1975; children: Catherine Anne, William Monroe IV. AB with distinction, DePauw U., 1959; MBA with distinction, Harvard U., 1961. With A.G. Becker Paribas Inc., L.A., 1961-84, mgr. nat. corp. fin. div., 1968-71, mgr. pvt. investments, 1971-74, fin. and adminstrv. officer, 1974-80, sr. v.p., 1975-78, vice chmn., 1978-84, also bd. dirs.; prin. William M. Cockrum & Assocs., L.A., 1984—; mem. faculty Northwestern U., 1961-63. Vis. lectr. grad. sch. mgmt. UCLA, 1984-88, adj. prof., 1988—. Mem. Monterey Club (Palm Desert, Calif.), Deke Club (N.Y.C.), UCLA Faculty Club, Alisal Golf Club (Solvang, Calif.), Bel-Air Country Club (L.A.), Delta Kappa Epsilon. E-mail: bcockrum@anderson.ucla.edu

CODON, DENNIS P. lawyer; V.p., gen. counsel, corp. sec. Unocal Corp., L.A., 1999—. Office: Unocal Corp 2141 Rosecrans Ave Ste 4000 El Segundo CA 90245-4746

COE, HENRY H. R. state legislator; b. Cody, Wyo., Apr. 29, 1946; married. Student, U. Wyo. Mem. Wyo. Senate, Dist. 18, Cheyenne, 1988—; mem. travel, recreation, wildlife, and cultural com. Wyo. Senate, Cheyenne, chair resources com., mem. rules and procedure com. Mem. Wyo. Heritage Soc., Yellowstone Regulatory Authority Bd.; commr. Park County, 1978-86; trustee Buffalo Bill Hist. Soc.; pres. Cody Med. Found.; mem. Cody Fire Dept. Republican. Home: PO Box 1088 Cody WY 82414-1088 Office: 1234 Sheridan Ave Cody WY 82414-3630 also: Wyo Senate State Capitol Cheyenne WY 82002-0001 Fax: 307-527-6853

COE, MARGARET LOUISE SHAW, community service volunteer; b. Cody, Wyo., Dec. 25, 1917; d. Ernest Francis and Effie Victoria (Abrahamson) Shaw; m. Henry Huttleston Rogers Coe, Oct. 8, 1943 (dec. Aug. 1966); children: Anne Rogers Hayes, Henry H.R., Jr., Robert Douglas II. AA, Stephens Coll., 1937; BA, U. Wyo., 1939. Asst. to editor The Cody Enterprise, 1939-42, editor, 1968-71. Bd. trustees Buffalo Bill Historical Ctr., 1966—, chmn., 1974-98, chmn. emeritus, 1998—; trustee emeritus Ctrl. City Opera House Assn., Millicent Rogers Found.; commr. Wyo. Centenniel Commn., Cheyenne, 1986-91. Recipient The Westerner award Old West Trails Found., 1980, Gold Medallion award Nat. Assn. Sec. of State, 1982, disting alumni award U. Wyo., 1984, exemplary alumni award, 1994, Gov.'s award for arts, 1988; inducted Nat. Cowgirl Hall of Fame, 1983. Mem. P.E.O., Delta Delta Delta. Republican. Episcopalian. Avocation: duplicate bridge. Home: 1400 11th St Cody WY 82414-4206

COE, ROBERT CAMPBELL, retired surgeon; b. Seattle, Nov. 14, 1918, s. Herbert Everett and Lucy Jane (Campbell) C.; m. Josephine Austin Weiner, Mar. 24, 1942; children: Bruce Everett, Virginia Austin, Matthew Daniel. BS, U. Wash., 1940; MD, Harvard U., 1950. Diplomate: Am. Bd. Thoracic Surgery, Am. Bd. Surgery. Intern Mass. Gen. Hosp., Boston, 1950-51, asst. resident, 1951-54, chief surg. resident, 1955, chief surg. clinics, 1956; instr. surgery Med. Sch. Harvard U., 1956; pvt. practice medicine specializing in thoracic and vascular surgery Seattle, 1957-84.

Hon. mem. staff Children's Hosp.; attending surgeon Swedish Hosp.; cons. thoracic surgeon Firland Sanitarium, Seattle, 1957-68, Children's Hosp. Tumor Clinic, 1968-84; mng. ptnr. Invex & Inpark med. offices, Seattle, 1970-88; clin. prof. U. Wash., 1973—; mem. Wash. State Med. Disciplinary Bd., 1981-86; chmn. med. adv. bd. Physio-control. div. Eli Lilly, 1979-85; pres. 1st Mercer (Wash.) Corp., 1969-73, 80-91, treas., 1973-80; owner, operator Hidden Valley Guest Ranch Cle Elum, Wash., 1969-93; developer Kula Estate, Maui, Hawaii; treas. 13th Internat. Cancer Congress. Editor: King County Med. Soc. Bull, 1964-70; mem. adv. bd. Pacific N.W. Mag. 1968-85; contbr. articles to profl. jours. Mem. Mayor's Harbor Adv. Com., 1958-61; chmn. bd. N.W. Seaport, Inc., hist. mus. Seattle, 1974-75; mem. Mercer Island City Coun., 1988-92. With USNR, 1941-46. Decorated Bronze Star, Presdl. Unit citation. Fellow ACS; mem. North Pacific Surg. Assn. (sr. mem.), Pacific Coast Surg. Assn. (sr. mem.), King County Med. Soc. (jud. coun. 1972-78, chmn. 1976-78), Seattle Surg. Soc. (pres. 1969), Psi Upsilon, Seattle Yacht Club, Cruising of Am. Club (bd. govs. 1992-95). Episcopalian. Home and Office: 7260 N Mercer Way Mercer Island WA 98040-2132

COFFIN, CHRIS, managing editor; b. Portland, Oreg., Sept. 19, 1960; BA, Univ. Oreg., 1983. Mng. editor Grapevine Publs. Inc., Corvallis, Oreg., 1983—. Office: Grapevine Publ Inc PO Box 2449 Corvallis OR 97339-2449

COFFIN, JAMES ROBERT, state legislator, small business owner; b. Anaheim, Calif., Oct. 7, 1942; m. Mary Hausch; children: James, Walter, Anna Maria. BS in Acctg. and Bus. Adminstrn., U. Nev., Las Vegas, 1969. Owner Bob Coffin Ins., Las Vegas, 1969—, Bob Coffin Books, Las Vegas, 1989—; mem. Nev. Assembly, 1983-86, Nev. Senate, Dist. 3 Clark County, 1986—; mem. fin. com., taxation com., natural resources com. Nev. State Senate. Chair Western Legis. Conf. Annual Meeting, 1993. With USAR, 1962. Named Man of Yr. Nev. Women's Polit. Caucus, 1995. Mem. Nat. Fedn. Ind. Bus., Nat. Conf. State Legislatures (invitational com. Am. Leadership Conf.), U. Nev. Las Vegas Alumni Assn., Latin C. of C. Nev. (bd. dirs.), Las Vegas C. of C., Sigma Alpha Epsilon. Democrat. Home: 1139 5th Pl Las Vegas NV 89104-1413 Office: Nev State Legis Bldg 401 S Carson St Rm 203 Las Vegas NV 89104-1413 Fax: 702-384-9501/702-384-9629. E-mail: bcoffin@sen.state.nv.us

COFFIN, JUDY SUE, lawyer; b. Beaumont, Tex., Aug. 17, 1953; d. Richard Wilson and Genie (Mouton) C.; m. Gary P. Scholick, Nov. 10, 1983; children: Jennie Sue, Kate Frances. BA, U. Tex., 1974; JD, So. Meth. U., 1976. Bar: Tex. 1977, Calif. 1982. Atty. NLRB, Tex., 1977-80; shareholder Littler Mendelson, San Francisco, 1980-99, also bd. dirs.; sr. counsel, employment and labor law Cath. Healthcare West, San Francisco, 2000—. Office: Catholic Healthcare West Legal Dept 1700 Montgomery St Ste 300 San Francisco CA 94111-1024 E-mail: jcoffin@chw.edu

COFFIN, THOMAS M. federal magistrate judge; b. St. Louis, May 30, 1945; s. Kenneth C. and Agnes M. (Ryan) C.; m. Penelope Teaff, Aug. 25, 1973; children: Kimberly, Laura, Colleen, Corey, Mary, Brendan, T.J. BA, St. Benedict's Coll., 1967; JD, Harvard, 1970. Bar: Mo. 1970, Calif. 1972, Oreg. 1982, U.S. Dist. Ct. (so. dist.) Calif. 1971, U.S. Dist. Ct. Oreg. 1980, U.S. Ct. Appeals (9th cir.) 1971. Asst. U.S. atty., chief criminal divsn. U.S. Attys. Office, San Diego, 1971-80, asst. U.S. atty., supr. asst. U.S. atty. Eugene, Oreg., 1980-92; U.S. Magistrate judge U.S. Dist. Ct., Eugene, 1992—. Sr. litigation counsel U.S. Dept. Justice, 1984. Mem. Oreg. Bar Assn. Avocations: soccer, jogging. Office: US Dist Ct 211 E 7th Ave Eugene OR 97401-2774

COFFINGER, MARALIN KATHARYNE, retired career officer, consultant; b. Ogden, Iowa, July 5, 1935; d. Cleo Russell and Katharyne Frances (McGovern) Morse. BA, Ariz. State U., 1957, MA, 1961; diploma, Armed Forces Staff Coll., 1972, Nat. War Coll., 1977; postgrad., Inst. for Higher Def. Studies, 1985. Commd. 2nd lt. USAF, 1963, advanced through grades to brig. gen., 1985; base comdr., dep. base comdr. Elmendorf AFB, Anchorage, 1977-79; base comdr. Norton AFB, San Bernardino, Calif., 1979-82; chmn. spl. and incentive pays Office of Sec. Def., Pentagon, Washington, 1982-83; dep. dir. pers. programs USAF Hdqrs., Pentagon, Washington, 1983-85; command dir. NORAD, Combat Ops., Cheyenne Mountain Complex, Colo., 1985-86; dir. pers. plans USAF Hdqrs., Pentagon, Washington, 1986-89; ret. USAF, 1989; dir. software products ops. Walsh America, 1992 94. Keynote speaker, mem. dedication ceremonies Vietnam Meml. Com., Phoenix, 1990; mem. Phoenix Symphony Orch., 1954-63; prin. flutist Scottsdale Cmty. Orch., Scottsdale Concert Band, Sonoran Wind Quintet, Ambiance Woodwind Quintet. Decorated Air Force D.S.M., Def. Superior Svc. medal, Legion of Merit, Bronze Star; recipient Nat. Medal of Merit. Mem. NAFE, Air Force Assn. (vet./retiree coun., pres. Sky Harbor chpt. 1990), Nat. Officers Assn., Ret. Officers Assn., Maricopa County Sheriff's Exec. Posse, Ariz. State U. Alumni Assn. (Profl. Excellence award 1981), Nat. Assn. Uniformed Svcs. Roman Catholic. Home: 8059 E Maria Dr Scottsdale AZ 85255-5418 E-mail: mcoffinger@att.net

COGHLAN, PAUL, electronics executive; b. N.Y.C., June 12, 1945; s. Patrick J. and Nellie (McCormack) C.; m. Angela Sowa, Sept. 15, 1973; children: Nicole, Monica. BA, Boston Coll., 1966; MBA, Babson Coll., 1968. CPA, Mass. Mgr. Price Waterhouse, Paris, 1973-76, sr. mgr. Boston, 1976-81; corp. controller GenRad, Inc., Waltham, Mass., 1981-83, v.p., 1984-86, v.p., gen. mgr. Milpitas, Calif., 1985-86; v.p., chief fin. officer Linear Tech. Corp., Milipitas, 1986—. Mem. Am. Electronics Assn., Am. Inst. CPA's. Home: 686 Bicknell Rd Los Gatos CA 95030-2145 Office: Linear Tech Corp 1630 Mccarthy Blvd Milpitas CA 95035-7417

COHAN, CHRISTOPHER, professional sports team executive; b. Salinas, Calif., 1951; s. Helen C.; m. Angela; three children. BA, Ariz. State U., 1973. With Feather River Cable TV Corp., Orinda, Calif., 1973-77; owner Sonic Comms., Alaska, 1977; owner, CEO Golden State Warriors, Calif. Bd. dirs. Calif. TV Assn. Office: c/o Golden State Warriers 1011 Broadway Oakland CA 94607-4019 also: Golden State Warriors 1221 Broadway Fl 20 Oakland CA 94612-1837

COHAN, JOHN ROBERT, retired lawyer; b. Arnhem, Netherlands, Feb. 10, 1931; came to U.S., 1940, naturalized, 1945; s. Max and Ann (deWinter) C.; m. Joan B. Gollob, Sept. 6, 1954; children: Deborah Joyce, Steven Mark, Judson Seth; m. Patricia S. Cohan, Nov. 8, 1970; m. Roberta Cohan, Nov. 23, 1980; 1 child, Alexis Marissa Muffin. B.S. in Bus. Adminstrn, U. Ariz., 1952; LL.B., Stanford U., 1955. Bar: Calif. 1956; cert. specialist in taxation. Assoc. firm Irell & Manella, Los Angeles, 1955-61, ptnr., 1961-95; ret., 1995. Adj. prof. U. Miami Sch. Law, 1975-85, Ventura/Santa Barbara Coll. Law, 1996—; lectr. fed. income taxation U. So. Calif. Sch. Law, 1961-63; lectr., writer Calif. Continuing Edn. Bar Program, 1959, Practicing Law Inst., 1968—, also various tax and probate insts. Editor: Drafting California Revocable Trusts, 1972, 2d edit., 1984, Drafting California Irrevocable Trusts, 1973, 3d edit., 1997, Inter Vivos Trusts, Shephard's Citations, 1975; mem. supervisory bd. Thesaurus of World Tax Data, 1987—; contbr. articles on tax, estate planning, probate law to profl. jours. Pres. Portals House, Inc., 1966-69; chmn. Jewish Big Bros., Los Angeles, 1963-65; trustee Hope for Hearing Research Found., 1979-81, pres., 1972-75; chmn. charitable founds. com. Big Bros. Big Sisters Am., 1965-67, chmn. internat. expansion, 1967—, pres. western region, 1977-78, also bd. dirs.; bd. dirs. Jewish Community Found., 1979—, v.p., chmn. legal com., 1978—; mem. planning com. U. So. Calif. Tax Inst., 1969—, chmn., 1983—; mem. planning com. U. Miami Estate Planning Inst., 1971-86; bd. dirs. Los Angeles Campus Hebrew Union Coll., 1974-77; mem. Mayor's Commn. on Ethics in Charitable Giving, L.A., 1991-93. Fellow Am. Coll. Probate Counsel (mem. planning com. 1986—); mem. ABA (chmn. com. on estate planning for closely held bus. 1979-80, vice chmn. estate and gift tax com. of sect. on taxation), Los Angeles Bar Assn. (com. on fed. and Calif. death and gift taxation 1965-67, co-chmn. com. on bioethics 1979-80, Outstanding Tax Lawyers of the Year Dana Latham award 1987), Beverly Hills Bar Assn. (past chmn., lawyer placement com. and probate com.), Calif. State Bar (probate and trust com. 1971-74), Internat. Acad. Probate and Trust Law (exec. com.), Town Hall of Los Angeles (exec. com., past pres. Western div.), Beta Gamma Sigma, Alpha Kappa Psi, Phi Alpha Delta. Home: 79 Daily Dr # 199 Camarillo CA 93010-5807 Office: Irell & Manella 1800 Avenue Of The Stars Los Angeles CA 90067-4276

COHEN, ALBERT, musician, educator; b. N.Y.C., Nov. 16, 1929; s. Sol A. and Dora C.; m. Betty Joan Berg, Aug. 28, 1952; children— Eva Denise, Stefan Berg. B.S., Juilliard Sch. Music, 1951; M.A., NYU, 1953, Ph.D. (Fulbright fellow), 1959; postgrad., U. Paris, 1956-57. Mem. faculty U. Mich., Ann Arbor, 1960-70, assoc. prof. music, 1964-67, prof., 1967-70; prof. music, chmn. dept. SUNY-Buffalo, 1970-73, Stanford U., Calif., 1973-87, William H. Bonsall prof. music, 1974—, prof. emeritus, 2000—. Editor Broude Bros. Ltd., N.Y.C., Info. Coordinators, Detroit. Author: Treatise on the Composition of Music, 1962, Elements or Principles of Music, 1965; (with J.D. White) Anthology of Music for Analysis, 1965; (with L.E. Miller) Music in the Paris Academy of Sciences, 1666-1793, An Index, 1979, Music in the French Royal Academy of Sciences, 1981, Music in the Royal Society of London 1660-1806, 1987; contbr. articles to profl. jours. Guggenheim fellow, 1968-69; NEH fellow, 1975-76, 82-83, 85-89 Mem. Internat., Am., French musicol. socs., Galpin Soc. (Eng.), Music Library Assn. Office: Stanford U Dept Music Stanford CA 94305

COHEN, ARNOLD NORMAN, gastroenterologist; b. N.Y.C., Nov. 5, 1949; s. Norman and Edna Clara (Arnold) C.; m. Colleen Ruth Carey; children: Eric Arnold, Leslie Carey. BA summa cum laude, Hobart Coll., 1971; MD, Harvard U., 1975. Diplomate Am. Bd. Internal Medicine, Am. Bd. Gastroenterology. Resident internal medicine U. Pa., Phila., 1975-78, asst. instr. medicine, 1977-78; fellow gastroenterology, instr. medicine Northwestern U., Chgo., 1978-80; asst. clin. prof. medicine U. Wash. Med. Sch., Seattle, 1980—; mem. faculty Spokane (Wash.) Family Medicine Residency, 1980—; pvt. practice gastroenterology Spokane, 1980—. Mem. various coms. St. Lukes-Deaconess Hosp., Spokane, 1980—; pres. med. staff St. Lukes Hosp., 1985-86. Contbr. articles to profl. jours. and textbooks. Fellow ACP, Am. Coll. Gastroenterology; mem. Am. Soc. Gastrointestinal Endoscopy, Am. Gastroent. Soc., Wash. Med. Soc., Spokane Internal Med. Soc., Phi Beta Kappa, Alpha Omega Alpha. Avocations: shooting sports, martial arts, swimming. Home: 3514 S Jefferson St Spokane WA 99203-1441 Office: Spokane Digestive Disease Ctr 801 W 5th Ave Spokane WA 99204-2823

COHEN, CYNTHIA MARYLYN, lawyer; b. Bklyn., Sept. 5, 1945; AB, Cornell U., 1967; JD cum laude, NYU, 1970. Bar: N.Y. 1971, U.S. Ct. Appeals (2nd cir.) 1972, U.S. Dist. Ct. (so. and ea. dists.) N.Y. 1972, U.S. Supreme Ct. 1975, U.S. Dist. Ct. (ctrl. and no. dists.) Calif. 1980, U.S. Ct. Appeals (9th cir.) 1980, U.S. Dist. Ct. (so. dist.) Calif. 1981, U.S. Dist. Ct. (ea. dist.) Calif. 1986. With Paul, Hastings, Janofsky & Walker, LLP, L.A., N.Y.C. Bd. dirs. N.Y. chpt. Am. Cancer Soc., 1977-80; active Pres.'s Coun. Cornell Women. Recipient Am. Jurisprudence award for evidence, torts and legal instns., 1968-69; John Norton Pomeroy scholar NYU, 1968-70, Founders Day Cert., 1969. Mem. ABA, Assn. Bar City N.Y. (trade regulation com. 1976-79), Assn. Bus. Trial Lawyers, Fin. Lawyers Conf., N.Y. State Bar Assn. (chmn. class-action com. 1979), State Bar Calif., Los Angeles County Bar Assn., Order of Coif, Delta Gamma. Avocations: tennis, bridge, rare books, wines. Home: 4531 Dundee Dr Los Angeles CA 90027-1213 Office: Paul Hastings Janofsky & Walker LLP 555 S Flower St 23d Fl Los Angeles CA 90071 E-mail: cynthiacohen@paulhastings.com

COHEN, DANIEL MORRIS, museum administrator, marine biology researcher; b. Chgo., July 6, 1930; s. Leonard U. and Myrtle (Gertz) C.; m. Anne Carolyn Constant, Nov. 4, 1955; children— Carolyn A., Cynthia S. BA, Stanford U., 1952, MA, 1953, PhD, 1958. Asst. prof., curator fishes U. Fla., Gainesville, 1957-58; systematic zoologist Bur. Comml. Fisheries, Washington, 1958-60; dir. systematics lab. Nat. Marine Fisheries Service, Washington, 1960-81, sr. scientist Seattle, 1981-82; chief curator life scis. Los Angeles County Mus. of Natural History, 1982-93, dep. dir. rsch. and collections, 1993-95; emeritus, 1995—. Adj. prof. biology U. So. Calif., 1982-98. Contbr. numerous articles to profl. jours. Bd. advisors All Species Found., 2000—. Fellow AAAS, Calif. Acad. Sci. (rsch. assoc.); mem. Am. Soc. Ichthyologists and Herpetologists (v.p. 1969, 70, pres. 1985, Gibbs award 1997), Biol. Soc. Washington (pres. 1971-72), Soc. Systematic Biology (mem. coun. 1976-78). Avocation: gardening, cooking, reading, hiking. Home: PO Box 192 Bodega Bay CA 94923-0192 E-mail: dmco@monitor.net

COHEN, ELAINE HELENA, pediatrician, pediatric cardiologist, educator; b. Boston, Oct. 14, 1941; d. Samuel Clive and Lillian (Stocklan) C.; m. Marvin Leon Gale, May 7, 1972; 1 child, Pamela Beth Gale. AB, Conn. Coll., 1963; postgrad., Tufts U., 1963-64; MD, Woman's Med. Coll. Pa., 1969. Diplomate Am. Bd. Pediats. Intern in pediats. Children's Hosp. of L.A., 1969-70, resident in pediats., 1970-71; fellow in pediat. cardiology UCLA Ctr. Health Scis., 1971-72, L.A. County/U. So. Calif. Med. Ctr., L.A., 1972-74; pediatrician Children's Med. Group of South Bay, Chula Vista, Calif., 1974—. Clin. instr. dept. pediats. UCLA Sch. Medicine, 1971-72, U. So. Calif., L.A., 1972-74; asst. clin. prof. dept. pediats. U. Calif., Calif. Sch. Medicine, San Diego, 1974-98, preceptor dept. pediats., 1992—, assoc. clin. prof. dept. pediats., 1998—. Fellow Am. Acad. Pediats.; mem. Calif. Med. Assn., San Diego County Med. Soc. Avocations: sketching, design. Office: Children's Med Group South Bay 280 E St Chula Vista CA 91910-2945

COHEN, HARVEY JOEL, pediatric hematology and oncology educator; b. N.Y.C., July 4, 1943; s. Phillip and Ida (Teitel) C.; m. Ilene Verne Bookseger, Aug. 15, 1965; children: Philip Jason, Jonathan Todd. BS, CUNY, 1964; MD, PhD, Duke U., 1970. Intern Children's Hosp., Boston, 1970-71, resident, 1973-74; instr. pediatrics Harvard U. Med. Sch., Boston, 1974-76, asst. prof., 1976-79, assoc. prof., 1979-81; assoc. prof. pediatrics U. Rochester (N.Y.) Med. Ctr., 1981-84, prof., 1984-93, assoc. chmn. dept., 1987-93, chief pediatric hematology and oncology, 1981-93; prof., chmn. dept. pediatrics Stanford (Calif.) U. Sch. Medicine, 1993—; chief staff Lucile Salter Packard Children's Hosp. at Stanford, 1993-98. Med. advisor Montgomery Med. Ventures, San Francisco, 1984-97; sci. advisor St. Jude Children's Rsch. Hosp., Memphis, 1985-90; chmn. hematology study sect. NIH, Washington, 1986-88. Editor: Hematology: Basic Principles and Practice, 1991, 94, 99. Med. dir. Camp Good Days and Spl. Times, Rochester, 1981-93, Monroe County chpt. Am. Cancer Soc., Rochester, 1983-93, Rochester br. Cooley's Anemia Found., 1984-93; bd. dirs. Lucile Packard Children's Hosp., 1993-97, Ronald McDonald House of Palo Alto, Calif., 1995—, Children's Health Coun., 1996—, Lucile Packard Found. for Children's Health, 1997—. Tng. grantee Nat. Inst. Gen. Med. Scis., 1983-90, Nat. Inst. Child Health and Human Devel., 1990-94. Mem. Soc. for Pediatric Rsch. (pres. 1988-89), Am. Soc. for Clin. Investigation, Am. Pediatric Soc. Democrat. Jewish. Achievements include research on continuous assay for superoxide production, effect of selenium on synthesis of glutatnione peroxidase, relationship of in vitro and in vivo killing of leukemic cells by asparaganse. Office: Stanford U Sch Medicine Dept Pediatrics Rm H-310 Stanford CA 94305

COHEN, JON STEPHAN, lawyer; b. Omaha, Nov. 9, 1943; s. Louis H. and Bertha N. (Goldstein) C.; children: Carolyn, Sherri, Barbara, Shayna, Jordan; m. Cheryl A. Jiroux, Oct. 7, 1994. Student, London Sch. Econs., 1963-64; BA, Claremont Men's Coll. (now Claremont McKenna Coll.), 1965; JD, Harvard U., 1968. Bar: Ariz. 1968. Assoc. Snell & Wilmer, Phoenix, 1968-73, ptnr., 1973—. Bd. dirs. Vika Corp., Phoenix, Enterprise Network, Phoenix, Ariz. Software Assn., Phoenix, Ariz. Sci. Ctr., Phoenix. Bd. dirs. Kronos Found., Phoenix, Aurora Found., Phoenix. Fellow Ariz. Bar Found.; mem. ABA, Ariz. Bar Assn., Maricopa County Bar Assn., Village Athletic Club, City Sq. Athletic Club. Avocations: record collecting, skiing, racquetball. Home: 6528 N 27th St Phoenix AZ 85016 Office: Snell & Wilmer One Arizona Ctr Phoenix AZ 85004-0001 E-mail: jcohen@swlaw.com

COHEN, KARL PALEY, nuclear energy consultant; b. N.Y.C., Feb. 5, 1913; s. Joseph M. and Ray (Paley) C.; m. Marthe H. Malartre, Sept. 20, 1938; children: Martine-Claude Lebouc, Elisabeth M. Brown, Beatrix Josephine Cashmore. A.B., Columbia U., 1933, M.A., 1934, PhD in Phys. Chemistry, 1937; postgrad., U. Paris, 1936-37. Research asst. to Prof. H. C. Urey Columbia U., 1937-40; dir. theoretical div., SAM Manhattan project, 1940-44; physicist Standard Oil Devel. Co., 1944-48; tech. dir. H.K. Ferguson Co., 1948-52; v.p. Walter Kidde Nuclear Lab., 1952-55; cons. AEC, sr. sci. Columbia U., 1955; mgr. advance engrng. atomic power equipment dept. Gen. Electric Co., 1955-65, gen. mgr. breeder reactor devel. dept., 1965-71, mgr. strategic planning, nuclear energy div., 1971-73, chief scientist, nuclear energy group, 1973-78; cons. prof. Stanford U., 1978-81. Author: The Theory of Isotope Separation as Applied to Large Scale Production of U-235, 1951; contbr. articles to profl. jours. Recipient Energy Research prize Alfried Krupp Found., 1977; Chem. Pioneer award Am. Inst. Chemists, 1979 Fellow AAAS, Am. Nuclear Soc. (pres. 1968-69, bd. dirs.), Am. Inst. Chemists; mem. NAE, IEEE, Am. Phys. Soc., Cactus and Succulent Soc., Phi Beta Kappa, Sigma Xi, Phi Lambda Upsilon. Home and Office: 928 N California Ave Palo Alto CA 94303-3405 E-mail: karlpc@earthlink.net

COHEN, LAWRENCE EDWARD, sociology educator, criminologist; b. L.A., July 20, 1945; s. Louis and Florence (White) C. BA, U. Calif., Berkeley, 1969; MA, Calif. State U., 1971; PhD, U. Wash., 1974; postdoctorate study, SUNY, Albany, 1973-75. Rsch. assoc. Sch. of Criminal Justice, SUNY, Albany, 1973-76; asst. prof. U. Ill., Urbana, 1976-80; assoc. prof. U. Tex., Austin, 1980-85; prof. Ind. U., Bloomington, 1985-88, U. Calif., Davis, 1988—. Cons. editor Social Forces, 1981-84, Jour. Criminal Law and Criminology, 1982-2000, Am. Sociol. Rev., 1982-84, Am. Jour. Sociology, 1990-98, Criminology, 1996-98; contbr. numerous articles to profl. jours. Sgt. USMC, 1963-66, Vietnam. Grantee NIMH, 1978-80, NSF, 1983-89. Mem. Am. Sociol. Assn., Am. Soc. Criminology, Acad. Criminal Justice Scis., Soc. for Study Social Problems. Office: U Calif Dept Sociology Davis CA 95616

COHEN, LEONARD (NORMAN COHEN), poet, novelist, musician, songwriter; b. Montreal, Que., Can., Sept. 21, 1934; s. Nathan B. and Marsha (Klinitsky) C. B.A., McGill U., 1955; postgrad., Columbia.; LLB (hon.), Dalhousie U., 1971; LLD (hon.), McGill U., 1992. Author: (poetry) Let Us Compare Mythologies, 1956, The Spice Box of Earth, 1961, Flowers for Hitler, 1964, Parasites of Heaven, 1966, Selected Poems, 1956-68, 1968, The Energy of Slaves, 1972, Death of a Lady's Man, 1979, Book of Mercy, 1984, Stranger Music: Selected Music and Songs, 1993, Dance Me to the End of Love, 1995, (novels) The Favorite Game, 1963, Beautiful Losers, 1966, also articles, songs including music for McCabe and Mrs. Miller, 1971, Natural Born Killers, 1994; rec. artist for Sony Music; albums include I'm Your Man, 1988, The Future, 1992, Cohen Live, 1993, More Best Of, 1997, Field Commander Cohen: Tour of 1979, 2001, Ten New Songs, 2001. Decorated Order of Can., 1992; recipient McGill Lit. award, 1956, Que. Lit. award, 1964, Gov. Gen.'s Performing Arts award, Can., 1993; Can. Coun. grantee, 1960-61. Office: c/o Kelley Lynch Stranger Mgmt Inc 419 N Larchmont Blvd Ste 88 Los Angeles CA 90004-3013

COHEN, MALCOLM MARTIN, psychologist, researcher; b. New Brunswick, N.J., May 13, 1937; s. Nathan and Esther (Greenhaus) C.; m. Marilyn Jerrow, Jan. 2, 1959 (dec. 1967); m. Eleanor Johnson, June 30, 1969 (div. 1988); m. Suzana Gal, Feb. 14, 1988. BA, Brandeis U., 1959; MA, U. Pa., 1961, PhD, 1965. Lic. psychologist, Pa. Asst. instr. U. Pa., Phila., 1961-63; rsch. psychologist Naval Air Engrng. Ctr., Phila., 1963-67; supervisory rsch. psychologist Naval Air Devel. Ctr., Warminster, Pa., 1967-82; asst. chief biomed. rsch. divsn. NASA-Ames Rsch Ctr., Moffett Field, Calif., 1982-85, chief neurosci. br., 1985-88, rsch. scientist, 1988—, chief human info. processing rsch., 2000—. Lectr. dept. aeros. and astronautics Stanford (Calif.) U., 1982-92, lectr. human biology program, 1994-95, consulting assoc. prof. human biology program, 1995-98, cons. prof. human biology program, 1998—; aerospace med. adv. panel Am. Inst. Biol. Scis., Washington, 1984-92; v.p. Nat. Hand Rehab. Fund, Washington, 1975—. Contbr. articles to profl. jours. Patentee light bar to monitor human acceleration tolerance. Founding mem. Common Cause of Phila., 1973 Recipient Exceptional Sci. Achievement medal NASA, 1994. Fellow Aerospace Med. Assn. (editorial bd. Aviation Space and Environ. Medicine 1985-93, Environ. Sci. award 1985, William F. Longacre award 1989), Aerospace Human Factors Assn. (pres. 1992); mem. AAAS, AIAA, N.Y. Acad. Scis., Psychonomics Soc., Sigma Xi. Jewish. Avocation: scuba diving. Office: NASA Ames Rsch Ctr Mail Stop 262-2 Moffett Field CA 94035 E-mail: mmcohen@mail.arc.nasa.gov

COHEN, MARSHALL HARRIS, astronomer, educator; b. Manchester, N.H., July 5, 1926; s. Solomon and Mollie Lee (Epstein) C.; m. Shirley Kekst, Sept. 19, 1948; children: Thelma, Linda, Sara. BEE, Ohio State U., 1948, MS, 1949, PhD, 1952. Rsch. assoc. Ohio State U., Columbus, 1950-54; asst. prof. elec. engring. Cornell U., Ithaca, N.Y., 1954-58, assoc. prof., 1958-63, assoc. prof. astronomy, 1963-66; prof. applied electrophysics U. Calif., San Diego, 1966-68; prof. radio astronomy Calif. Inst. Tech., Pasadena, 1968-90, prof. astronomy, 1990-96, exec. officer for astronomy, 1981-84, prof. emeritus, 1996. Prof. associé U. Paris VI, 1989; mem. numerous coms. NSF, NRC, vis. coms. various obs. in U.S., Fed. Republic Germany. Contbr. articles, book revs. to profl. jours.; patentee radio astronomy. With U.S. Army, 1943-46. Co-recipient Rumford medal Am. Acad. Arts and Scis., 1971; Guggenheim Found. fellow Paris Obs., 1960-61, MIT/Inst. Astronomy, Cambridge, Eng., 1980-81; Morrison fellow Lick Obs., 1988. Fellow AAAS; mem. NAS (chmn. sect. astronomy 1989-92), Am. Astron. Soc. (publ. bd. 1980-83), Astron. Soc. Pacific (bd. dirs. 1969-72), Am. Acad. Arts and Scis., Internat. Union for Sci. Radio (chmn. commn. V of U.S. nat. com. 1970-73), Internat. Astron. Union (U.S. nat. com. 1989-92). Avocation: mountain hiking. Office: Calif Inst Tech Dept Astronomy Pasadena CA 91125-0001

COHEN, MARVIN LOU, physics educator; b. Montreal, Que., Can., Mar. 3, 1935; came to U.S., 1947, naturalized, 1953; s. Elmo and Molly (Zaritsky) C.; m. Merrill L. Gardner, Aug. 31, 1958 (dec. Apr. 1994); children: Mark, Susan; m. Suzy R. Locke, Sept. 8, 1996. AB, U. Calif., 1957; MS, U. Chgo., 1958, PhD, 1964. Mem. tech. staff Bell Telephone Labs., Murray Hill, N.J., 1963-64; asst. prof. physics U. Calif., Berkeley, 1964-66, assoc. prof., 1966-69, prof. physics, 1969-95, univ. prof., 1995—, prof. Miller Inst. Basic Resch. in Sci., 1969-70, 76-77, 88, chmn., 1977-81, U. Calif. Faculty Rsch. lectr., 1997—. Chmn. Gordon Rsch. Conf. Chemistry and Physics of Solids, 1972; U.S. rep. to Semicondr. Commn., Internat. Union Pure and Applied Physics, 1975-81; Alfred P. Sloan fellow Cambridge U., Eng., 1965-67; vis. prof. Cambridge U., Eng., 1966, U. Paris, France, 1972-73, summers 68, 75, 87, 88, U. Hawaii, Honolulu,

1978-79, Technion, Haifa, Israel, 1987-88; chmn. planning com. Pure and Applied Sci. Inst. U. Hawaii, 1980—; mem. selection com. Presdl. Young Investigator Awards, 1983; mem. Com. on Nat. Synchrotron Radiation Facilities, 1983-84; chmn. 17th Internat. Conf. on Physics of Semicondrs., 1984; mem. exec. com. Govt.-Univ.-Industry Research Roundtable, 1984—; vice chmn. Govt.-U. Industry Research Roundtable Working Group on Sci. and Engring. Talent, 1984—; mem. rev. bd. for Ctr. for Advanced Materials Lawrence Berkeley Lab., 1986-87; mem. panel on Implications for Mechanisms of Support and Panel on High Temperature Superconductivity, NAS, NSF, 1987; mem. adv. bd. Tex. Ctr. for Superconductivity, 1988-90, vice chair, 1991—; mem. U.S. del. to Bilateral Dialog R&D in the U.S. and Japan, NRC, 1989; mem. sci. policy bd. Stanford Synchrotron Rad. Lab., 1990-92. Editorial bd. Perspectives in Condensed Matter Physics, 1987—; adv. bd. Internat. Jour. Modern Physics B., 1987—, Modern Physics Letters B, 1987—; assoc. editor Materials Sci. and Engring., 1987—; contbr. more than 600 articles to tech. jours. Mem. vis. com. Ginzton Lab., Stanford U., 1991; mem. sci. policy com. Stanford Linear Accelerator, 1993-95. Recipient Outstanding Accomplishment in Solid State Physics award U.S. Dept. Energy, 1981, Sustained Outstanding Rsch. in Solid State Physics award U.S. Dept. Energy, 1990, Cert.of Merit, Lawrence Berkeley Lab., 1991; A.P. Sloan fellow, 1965-67, Guggenheim fellow, 1978-79, 90-91. Fellow AAAS, Am. Phys. Soc. (exec. coun. divsn. solid state physics 1975-79, chmn. 1977-78, Oliver E. Buckley prize for solid state physics 1979, Buckley prize com. 1980-81, chmn. 1981, Julius Edgar Lilienfeld prize 1994, Lilienfeld prize com. 1994—, Isakson Prize com. 1995-98, chmn. 1999); mem. NAS (chmn. condensed matter physics search/screening com. 1981-82, 1988—, chmn. Comstock prize com. 1988, nominating com. for selection of pres., v.p., councilors 1992-93), Am. Acad. Arts and Scis., Nat. Acad. Scis. Home: 201 Estates Dr Piedmont CA 94611-3315 Office: U Calif Dept Physics Berkeley CA 94720-0001

COHEN, PAUL JOSEPH, mathematician; b. Long Branch, N.J., Apr. 2, 1934; Student, Bklyn. Coll., 1950-53; M, U. Chgo., 1954, PhD, 1958. Instr. U. Rochester, 1947-58, MIT, 1958-59; fellow Inst. Advanced Study, Princeton U., 1959-61; faculty Stanford (Calif.) U., 1961—, prof. math., 1964—. Recipient Bôcher Meml. Prize Am. Math. Soc., 1964, Fields medal Internat. Congress Math., Moscow, 1966, Nat. Medal Sci., 1967. Mem. Nat. Acad. Scis. Achievements include a technique called forcing to prove the independence in set theory of the axiom of choice and of the generalised continuum hypothesis. Office: Stanford U Dept Math Bldg 380 MC 2125 Stanford CA 94305

COHEN, ROBERT STEPHEN, drama educator; b. Washington, July 14, 1938; s. Lester Ellis and Lydia Rita (Goldblatt) C.; m. Lorna Lee Buck, Nov. 13, 1972; children: Michael Geoffrey, Whitney. Student, Dartmouth Coll., 1956-58; BA, U. Calif., Berkeley, 1961; DFA, Yale U., 1965. Prof. drama U. Calif., Irvine, 1965—, chmn. drama dept., 1970-91; acting dean fine arts, 1994-95. Stage dir. Colo. Shakespeare Festival, Boulder, 1982—, Utah Shakespearean Festival, Cedar City, 1985—, FRP in Medieval Drama, Irvine, 1985—. Author: Giraudoux, 1968, Acting Professionally, 1972, 97, Creative Play Direction, 1974, Acting Power, 1978, Theater, 1981, 99, Acting One, 1984, 97, 2001, Acting in Shakespeare, 1990, (play) The Prince, 1998, Enjoy the Play, 2000, Advanced Acting, 2001. Recipient Career Achievement award Assn. for Theatre in Higher Edn., 1999; NEH grantee, 1989. Mem. Actors Equity Assn., Am. Theatre Critics Assn., Phi Beta Kappa. Office: U Calif Irvine Dept Drama Irvine CA 92697-0001 E-mail: cohen@uci.edu

COHEN, STANLEY NORMAN, geneticist, educator; b. Perth Amboy, N.J., Feb. 17, 1935; s. Bernard and Ida (Stolz) C.; m. Joanna Lucy Wolter, June 27, 1961; children: Anne, Geoffrey. B.A., Rutgers U., 1956; M.D., U. Pa., 1960, ScD (hon.), 1995, Rutgers U., 1994. Intern Mt. Sinai Hosp., N.Y.C., 1960-61; resident Univ. Hosp., Ann Arbor, Mich., 1961-62; clin. assoc. arthritis and rheumatism br. Nat. Inst. Arthritis and Metabolic Diseases, Bethesda, Md., 1962-64; sr. resident in medicine Duke U. Hosp., Durham, N.C., 1964-65; Am. Cancer Soc. postdoctoral rsch. fellow Albert Einstein Coll. Medicine, Bronx, 1965-67, asst. prof. devel. biology and cancer, 1967-68; mem. faculty Stanford (Calif.) U., 1968—, prof. medicine, 1975—, prof. genetics, 1977—, chmn. dept. genetics, 1978-86, K.-T Li Prof., 1993—. Mem. com. recombinant DNA molecules NAS-NRC, 1974; mem. com. on genetic experimentation Internat. Council Sci. Unions, 1977-96 Mem. editl. bd. Jour. Bacteriology, 1973-79, Molecular Microbiology, 1986—, Procs. Nat. Acad. Sci., 1996—, Current Opinion in Microbiology, 1997—; assoc. editor Plasmid, 1977-86. Trustee U. Pa., 1997—. With USPHS, 1962-64. Recipient Burroughs Wellcome Scholar award, 1970, Mattia award Roche Inst. Molecular Biology, 1977, Albert Lasker basic med. rsch. award, 1980, Wolf prize, 1981, Marvin J. Johnson award, 1981, Disting. Grad. award U. Pa. Sch. Medicine, 1986, Disting. Svc. award Miami Winter Symposium, 1986, Nat. Biotech. award, 1989, LVMH Inst. de la Vie prize, 1988, Nat. Medal Sci., 1988, City of Medicine award, 1988, Nat. Medal of Tech., 1989, Am. Chem. Soc. Spl. award 1992, Helmut Horten Rsch. award, 1993, Jerome H. Lemelson MIT prize for excellence in invention and innovation, 1996; Guggenheim fellow, 1975; Josiah Macy Jr. Found. faculty scholar, 1975-76; named to Nat. Inventors Hall of Fame, 2001. Fellow AAAS; mem. NAS (chmn. genetics sect. 1988-91), Am. Acad. Microbiology, Am. Soc. Biol. Chemists, Genetics Soc. Am., Am. Soc. Microbiology (Cetus award 1988), Am. Soc. Pharmacology and Exptl. Therapeutics, Am. Soc. Clin. Investigation, Assn. Am. Physicians, Inst. Medicine, Sigma Xi, Phi Beta Kappa, Alpha Omega Alpha. Office: Stanford U Sch Med Dept Genetics Rm M-322 Stanford CA 94305

COHEN, S(TEPHEN) MARSHALL, philosophy educator; b. N.Y.C., Sept. 27, 1929; s. Harry and Fanny (Marshall) C.; m. Margaret Dennes, Feb. 15, 1964; children: Matthew, Megan. B.A., Dartmouth Coll., Hanover, N.H., 1951; postgrad., Harvard U., 1953; M.A., Oxford U., Eng., 1977; MA, Oxford U., 1977. Jr. fellow, Soc. of Fellows Harvard U., Cambridge, Mass., 1955-58, asst. prof. philosophy and gen. edn., 1958-62; asst. prof. U. Chgo., 1962-64, assoc. prof., 1964-67, acting chair Coll. Philosophy, 1965-66; assoc. prof. Rockefeller U., N.Y.C., 1967-70; prof. philosophy Richmond Coll. (now Coll. of S.I.), 1970-83, CUNY, 1970-83, exec. officer program in philosophy Grad. Ctr., 1975-83; prof. philosophy and law U. So. Calif., L.A., 1983-97, dean div. humanities, 1983-94, interim dean Coll. Letters, Arts and Sci., 1993-94; univ. prof. emeritus Coll. Letters, Arts and Sci., U. So. Calif., L.A., 1998—. Lectr. Lowell Inst., Boston, 1957-58; vis. fellow All Souls Coll., Oxford, Eng., 1976-77; mem. Inst. for Advanced Study, Princeton, N.J., 1981-82. Editor: The Philosophy of John Stuart Mill, 1961, Philosophy and Public Affairs, 1970-99, Philosophy and Society series, 1977-83, Ethical, Legal and Political Philosophy series, 1983-99; co-editor: Film Theory and Criticism, 1974, 79, 85, 92, 98, War and Moral Responsibility, 1974, The Rights and Wrongs of Abortion, 1974, Equality and Preferential Treatment, 1977, Marx, Justice and History, 1980, Medicine and Moral Philosophy, 1982, What Is Dance?, 1983, International Ethics, 1985, Punishment, 1995. Rockefeller Found. humanities fellow, 1977, Guggenheim fellow, 1976-77. Mem. Am. Philos. Assn., Am. Coun. Learned Socs. (bd. dirs. 1987-91, 93—), Coun. on Internat. Ednl. Exch. (bd. dirs. 1991-94). Democrat. Jewish. Office: U So Calif Law Sch Los Angeles CA 90089-0071 E-mail: mcohen@law.usc.edu

COHEN, VALERIE A. entertainment company executive; Sr. v.p. bus. devel. Walt Disney Co., Burbank, Calif. Office: Walt Disney Co 500 S Buena Vista St Burbank CA 91521-0006

COHEN, WILLIAM, law educator; b. Scranton, Pa., June 1, 1933; s. Maurice M. and Nellie (Rubin) C.; m. Betty C. Stein, Sept. 13, 1952 (div. 1976, dec. 2000); children: Barbara Jean, David Alan (dec. 1995), Rebecca Anne; m. Nancy M. Mahoney, Aug. 8, 1976; 1 dau., Margaret Emily. BA, UCLA, 1953, LLB, 1956. Bar: Calif. 1961. Law clk. to U.S. Supreme Ct. Justice William O. Douglas, 1956-57; from asst. prof. to assoc. prof. U. Minn. Law Sch., 1957-60; vis. asso. prof. UCLA Law Sch., 1959-60, mem. faculty, 1960-70, prof., 1962-70, Stanford (Calif.) Law Sch., 1970—, C. Wendell and Edith M. Carlsmith prof. law, 1983-99, Carlsmith prof. emeritus, 1999—. Vis. prof. law European U. Inst., Florence, Italy, fall 1977; Merriam vis. prof. Ariz. State U. Law Sch., Spring 1981 Co-author: The Bill of Rights, a Source Book, 1968, Comparative Constitutional Law, 1978, Constitutional Law Cases and Materials, 1981, 6th edit., 2001, Constitutional Law: The Structure of Government, 1981, Constitutional Law: Civil Liberty and Individual Rights, 1982, 2d edit., 1994, 3rd edit., 1997. Home: 698 Maybell Ave Palo Alto CA 94306-3819 Office: Stanford Law Sch Nathan Abbott Way Stanford CA 94305

COHEN, WILLIAM, construction executive; b. 1962; Graduate, Loyola U., 1974. Assoc. Monteleone & McCrory, L.A., 1974-80; v.p. Valley Crest Landscape, Inc., Calabasas, Calif., 1980—. Office: Valley Crest Landscape Inc 24121 Ventura Blvd Calabasas CA 91302-1449

COHEN, WILLIAM ALAN, marketing educator, author, consultant; b. Balt., June 25, 1937; s. Sidney Oliver and Theresa (Bachman) C.; m. Janice Dawn Stults, Jan. 3, 1963 (div. Jan. 1966); 1 child, William Alan II; m. Nurit Kovnator, May 28, 1967; children— Barak, Nimrod. BS, U.S. Mil. Acad., 1959; MBA, U. Chgo., 1967; MA, Claremont Grad. Sch., 1978; PhD, Indsl. Coll. of the Armed Forces, 1989. Registered profl. engr., Israel. Project mgr. Israel Aircraft Industries, 1970-73; mgr. rsch. and devel. Sierra Engring. Co., Sierra Madre, Calif., 1973-76; pres. Global Assocs., 1973—; mgr. advanced tech. mktg. McDonnell-Douglas Co., Huntington Beach, Calif., 1976-78; prof. mktg. Calif. State U., L.A., 1979—, dir. bur. bus. and econ. rsch., 1979-83, chmn. mktg. dept., 1986—. Bd. dir. Inst. Bus. Devel.; cons. Fortune 500 cos. Author: The Executives Guide to Finding a Superior Job, 1978, 83, Principles of Technical Management, 1980, Successful Marketing for Small Business, 1981, How to Sell to Government, 1981, The Entrepreneur and Small Business Problem Solver, 1983, 89, Direct Response Marketing, 1984, Building a Mail Order Business, 1982, 85, 91, 96, Making It Big as a Consultant, 1985, 90, 2001, Winning on the Marketing Front, 1986, High Tech Management, 1986, Developing a Winning Marketing Plan, 1987, The Students Guide to Finding a Superior Job, 1987, 93, The Practice of Marketing Management, 1988, 91, The Entrepreneur and Small Business Financial Problem Solver, 1989, The Art of Leader, 1990, The Entrepreneur and Small Business Marketing Problem Solver, 1991, Get a Great Job Fast, 1993, The Paranoid Corporation and Eight Other Ways Your Company Can Be Crazy, 1993, The Marketing Plan, 1994, 98, 2001, Making It!, 1994, Model Business Plans for Service Businesses, 1995, Model Business Plans for Product Businesses, 1995, The Stuff of Heroes: The 8 Universal Laws of Leadership, 1998, The New Art of the Leader, 2000, Marketing Your Small Business Made E-Z, 2000, The Wisdom of the Generals, 2001, Break the Rules, 2001; contbr. numerous articles to profl. jours. Maj. USAF, 1959-70, maj.-gen. USAFR, ret. Decorated Disting. Svc. Medal, Legion of Merit, D.F.C. with 3 oak leaf clusters, Meritorious Svc. medal with 2 oak leaf clusters, Air medal with 11 oak leaf clusters, numerous other U.S. and fgn. awards; named Disting. Grad. Indsl. Coll. Armed Forces, 1989; recipient Ministry Def. award State of Israel, 1976, Outstanding Svc. award Nat. Mgmt. Assn., 1979, Pres.'s award West Point Soc., 1982, Outstanding Prof. award, 1983, Chgo. Tribune Gold medal, George Washington medal Freedoms Found. at Valley Forge, 1986, CSULA Statewide Outstanding Prof., 1996, Great Tchr. in Mktg. award Acad. of Mktg. Sci., 1999. Fellow Acad. Mktg. Sci.; mem. Direct Mktg. Assn. (fellow 1980, 83), World Mktg. Congress (del. N.S. 1983), Direct Mktg. Club So. Calif. (bd. dirs., grantee 1981), Am. Mktg. Assn. (award 1982), West Point Soc. (pres., bd. dirs. 1981-82), Beta Gamma Sigma, Phi Sigma Phi. Republican. Jewish Office: Calif State U Sch Bus & Econs Los Angeles CA 90032

COHEN-VADER, CHERYL DENISE, municipal official; b. Ft. Bragg, N.C., Mar. 23, 1955; BA, Princeton U., 1977; MBA, Columbia U., 1983. Treas. internat. divsn. commodity import-export financing Bank of N.Y., N.Y.C., 1977-81; v.p. Citicorp Securities Markets, Inc. Citicorp, N.Y.C., 1983-90; v.p. Weldon, Sullivan, Carmichael & Co., 1990-92; asst. v.p. Kirkpatrick Pattis, 1993-95; mgr. revenue dept. City of Denver, 1996—. Mem. Mcpl. Securities Rulemaking Bd., 1998-2001. Bd. dirs. Mile High chpt. ARC, Colo. Episcopal Found., Mcpl. Securities Rulemaking, 1998-2001. Recipient Consortium of Grad. Mgmt. Edn. fellowship, 1981-83, Recognition of Achievement award Five Points Bus. Assn., Inc., 1995, Leadership Denver award Denver C. of C., 1994; honored in Living Portraits of African-Am. Women Nat. Coun. Negro Women, 1997. Mem. Govt. Finance Officers Assn. Office: City Denver Revenue Dept McNichols Bldg Rm 300 144 W Colfax Ave Denver CO 80202-5391

COHN, BRUCE, film and television company executive; b. San Francisco, Apr. 8, 1931; s. Theodore and Rosebud Enid (Schmulian) C.; 1 child, Mitchell Barry. M of Journalism, U. Calif., Berkeley, 1954. Writer, producer Clete Roberts News Sta. KTLA-TV, Hollywood, Calif., 1957-62; west coast producer Huntley Brinkley and Today Show NBC, Burbank, 1962-63; news dir. Sta. KNBC-TV, Burbank, 1963-66; Washington producer ABC Evening News, 1966-68; west coast producer Los Angeles, 1968-71; exec. producer Nat. Pub. Affairs Ctr. for TV Pub. Broadcasting System, Washington, 1971-73; ind. producer, writer various film studios, Burbank, 1973-75, Burbank, 1973—; pres. Bruce Cohn Prodns., Inc., Mill Valley, Calif., 1975—. Screenwriter ((film) Good Guys Wear Black, 1979; writer, producer (TV documentary) 1968-A Crack in Time, 1978, Secret Files of J. Edgar Hoover, 1990; producer (documentary series) Time Was, 1980; producer, dir. (documentary series) Rember When, 1981; writer, producer, dir. (documentary) Kisses with Lauren Bacall, 1991; writer, producer (documentary) Tom Clancy Presents John Ehrlichman In the Eye of the Storm, 1998, Couples, 2000. Recipient Cable Ace award, 1979, 81, 2 Gold medals N.Y. Internat. Film Festival, 1981, Gold plaque Chgo. Internat. Film Festival, 1982, Emmy award NATAS, 1984, 97. Mem. Writers Guild Am., Am. Film Inst. Home and Office: 1 Weatherly Dr Ste 101 Mill Valley CA 94941-3231 E-mail: bcp333@aol.com

COHN, DANIEL HOWARD, laboratory director; b. Santa Monica, Calif., Aug. 24, 1955; s. Sidney Lorber and Mynda Ellen (Zimmerman) C.; m. Ludmila Bojman, May 16, 1982; children: Zachary, Marissa, Rachel. BA, U. Calif., Santa Barbara, 1977; PhD, Scripps Inst. Oceanography, 1983. Postdoctoral fellow U. Wash., Seattle, 1983-88; 0sch. scientist, asst. prof. Cedars-Sinai Med. Ctr./UCLA, 1988-93, assoc. prof., 1993-97, prof., 1997—. Mem. genetics tng. program UCLA, 1988—; reviewer various jours. and granting agys. Editorial bd. various jours.; contbr. articles to profl. jours. and books. Grants com. chair, bd. dirs. Concern Found. for Cancer Rsch., L.A., 1988—. Recipient Martin Kamen award U. Calif., San Diego, 1983, Eckhart prize Scripps Inst. Oceanography, 1983; postdoctoral award NIH, 1985-88, grantee, 1988—. Mem. AAAS, Phi Beta Kappa. Democrat. Jewish. Avocations: gardening, golf, volleyball, waterskiing, [illegible] CA 90048-1865

COHN, THEODORE ELLIOT, optometry educator, vision scientist; b. Highland Park, Ill., Sept. 5, 1941; s. Nathan and Marjorie (Kurtzon) C.; m. Barbara Adler, Nov. 29, 1975; children: Avery Simon, Adrienne Leah, Harris Samuel. SB in Elec. Engring., MIT, 1963; MS in Bioengring., U. Mich., 1965, MA in Math., 1966, PhD in Bioengring., 1969. Asst. prof. U. Calif., Berkeley, 1970-76, assoc. prof., 1976-84, prof., 1985—. Vis. fellow John Curtin Med. Sch., Australian Nat. U., Canberra, 1977; vis. scholar U. Calif., San Diego, 1981-90; chair grad. group in bioengring. U. Calif., Berkeley/U. Calif., San Francisco, 2000—; vice chair grad. affairs, dept. bioengring., U. Calif. Berkeley, 1999—. Author, editor: Visual Detection, 1993. Bd. dirs. Berkeley-Richmond Jewish Cmty. Ctr., 1995—. Fellow Optical Soc. Am. (chairvision tech. group 1984-86); mem. IEEE (sr. mem.), Assn. Rsch. Vision & Ophthalmology, Vision Scis. Soc., Human Factors and Ergonomics Soc., Sigma Xi. Office: U Calif Sch Optometry 360 Minor Hall Berkeley CA 94720-2020 E-mail: tecohn@spectacle.berkeley.edu

COHRS, DAN, fiber optics company executive; BS in Engring., Mich. State U.; PhD in Econs., Fin. & Pub. Policy, Cornell U. V.p. project fin., v.p. fin. planning & acquisitions Marriott Corp., 1986-90; v.p. capital markets, v.p. internat. fin. Northwest Airlines, 1990-93; asst. treas. capital markets, v.p.-treas. GTE, 1993-98; sr. v.p., chief fin. officer Global Crossings, Ltd., Beverly Hills, Calif., 1998—. Office: Global Crossings Ltd 360 N Crescent Dr Beverly Hills CA 90210-4802

COIT, R. KEN, financial planner; b. Aug. 26, 1943; s. Roger L. and Thelma D. C.; m. Donna M. Schemanske, Oct. 8, 1977; children: Kristin M., Shannon, Darren, Lauryn. BS, U. Ariz., 1967; MBA, Pepperdine U., 1981. Mem. adj. faculty Coll. Fin. Planning, Denver, 1978-79; pres. Walnut Creek adv. bd. Summit Bank, 1987-95, Sequoia Equities Securities Corp., Walnut Creek, Calif. Bd. dirs. R.H. Phillips Winery; mem. adv. bd. Mt. Diablo Nat. Bank, 1996—. Mem. dean's adv. bd. Pepperdine U., 1988-91; nat. bd. adv. Coll. Pharmacy U. Ariz., 1991-93; bd. dirs., chmn. investment com. East Cmty. Found., 1994-97, mem. investment and fin. com., 1997—; asst. scoutmaster Boy Scouts Am., 1994-2000; bd. dirs. Mont. Diablo Ctr. for the Arts, 2000. Recipient Outstanding Alumnus award Pepperdine U. Sch. Bus. and Mgmt., 1986. Mem. Internat. Assn. Fin. Planners (chpt. pres. 1978-79), Inst. Cert. Fin. Planners, East Bay Gourmet Club, Blackhawk Country Club. Office: 1655 N Main St Ste 270 Walnut Creek CA 94596-4642

COKELET, GILES ROY, biomedical engineering educator; b. N.Y.C., Jan. 7, 1932; s. Roy S. and Anna M. (Trippel) C.; m. Sarah Drew, June 15, 1963; children— Becky, Bradford BS, Calif. Inst. Tech., 1957, MS, 1958; ScD, MIT, 1963. Rsch. engr. Dow Chem. Co., Williamsburg, Va., 1958-60; asst. prof. Calif. Inst. Tech., Pasadena, 1964-68; assoc. prof. Mont. State U., Bozeman, 1969-76, prof., 1976-78, U. Rochester, N.Y., 1978-98; rsch. prof. Mont. State U., Bozeman, 1998—. Contbr. articles to profl. jours. With U.S. Army, 1954-55, Japan Recipient Sr. U.S. Scientist award Humboldt-Stiftung, Bonn, Fed. Republic Germany, 1981-82, 88. Fellow AAAS; mem. Biomed. Engring. Soc., Microcirculatory Soc., Soc. Rheology, No. Am. Soc. Biorheology, Internat. Soc. Biorheology (past pres., Poiseuille medal 1999), European Microcirculation Soc. Avocations: stamp collecting, hiking. Office: Mont State U Dept Chem Engring Bozeman MT 59717-0001

COLANGELO, BRYAN, professional sports team executive; BS in Bus. Mgmt. and Applied Econ., Cornell U., 1987. Scout Phoenix Suns, 1990-92, asst. dir. player personnel, 1992-95, v.p. adminstrn., gen. mgr., 1995-97, exec. v.p., gen. mgr., 1997—. Alt. gov. bd. govs. NBA; tournament dir. NIKE Desert Classic; pres. Phoenix Arena Sports; bd. dirs. Ariz. Sports Coun., Phoenix Suns Charities, Home Base Youth Svcs. Bd. dirs. Phoenix C. of C., vice chmn. econ. devel., mem. exec com. Named one of top 25 Valley Bus. Leaders, Ariz. Bus. Jour., 1995. Office: Phoenix Suns 201 E Jefferson St Phoenix AZ 85004-2412

COLANGELO, JERRY JOHN, professional sports team executive; b. Chicago Heights, Ill., Nov. 20, 1939; s. Larry and Sue (Drancek) C.; m. Joan E. Helmich, Jan. 20, 1961; children: Kathy, Kristen, Bryan. B.A., U. Ill., 1962. Partner House of Charles, Inc., 1962-63; assoc. D.O. Klein & Assocs., 1964-65; dir. merchandising Chgo. Bulls, 1966-68; gen. mgr. Phoenix Suns, 1968-87, now also exec. v.p., until 1987, pres., chief exec. officer, 1987—; mng. gen. ptnr. Arizona Diamondbacks, Phoenix, 1998—. Mem. Basketball Congress Am. (exec. v.p., dir.), Phi Kappa Psi. Republican. Baptist. Clubs: University, Phoenix Execs. Office: Phoenix Suns 201 E Jefferson St Phoenix AZ 85004-2412 also: Arizona Diamondbacks 401 E Jefferson St Phoenix AZ 85004-2438

COLBERT, EDWIN HARRIS, paleontologist, museum curator; b. Clarinda, Iowa, Sept. 28, 1905; s. George Harris and Mary (Adamson) C.; m. Margaret Mary Matthew, July 8, 1933; children: George Matthew, David William, Philip Valentine, Daniel Lee, Charles Diller. Student, N.W. Mo. State Tchrs. Coll., 1923-26; BA, U. Nebr., 1928, ScD, 1973; AM, Columbia U., 1930, PhD, 1935; ScD, U. Ariz., 1976, Wilmington Coll., 1984. Student asst. Univ. Mus. U. Nebr., 1926-29; univ. fellow Columbia U., 1929-30, lectr. dept. zoology, 1938-39, prof. vertebrate paleontology, 1945-69, prof. emeritus, 1969—. Research asst. Am. Museum Natural History, 1930-32, asst. curator, 1933-42, acting curator, 1942, curator, 1943, chmn. dept. amphibians and reptiles, 1943-44, curator of fossil reptiles and amphibians, 1945-70, chmn. dept. geology and paleontology, 1958-60, chmn. dept. vertebrate paleontology, 1960-66, curator emeritus, 1970—; hon. curator vertebrate paleontology Mus. No. Ariz., Flagstaff, 1970—. Author: Evolution of Vertebrates, 1955, 60, 80, 91, (with M. Morales) Millions of Years Ago, 1958, Dinosaurs, 1961, (with M. Kay) Stratigraphy and Life History, 1965, The Age of Reptiles, 1965, 97, Men and Dinosaurs, 1968, Wandering Lands and Animals, 1973, The Year of the Dinosaur, 1977, A Fossil Hunter's Notebook, 1980, Dinosaurs: An Illustrated History, 1983, Digging into the Past, 1989, William Diller Matthew, Paleontologist, 1992, The Little Dinosaurs of Ghost Ranch, 1995; also sci. papers and monographs. Recipient John Strong Newberry prize Columbia U., 1931, Am. Mus. Natural History medal, 1970, Nat. Ghost Ranch Found. Spl. award, 1986, Disting. Alumni award Dept. Geology, U. Nebr., 1986, George W. Clinton award The Buffalo Soc. Natural Scis., 1987, Hayden medal Geol. award Acad. Nat. Scis. Phila., 1996. Fellow AAAS, Geol. Soc. Am., Paleontol. Soc. (v.p. 1963), N.Y. Zool. Soc.; mem. Soc. Vertebrate Paleontology (sec.-treas. 1944-46, pres. 1946-47, Romer-Simpson medal 1989), Soc. Mammalogy, Soc. Ichthyology and Herpetology, Soc. for Study Evolution (editor 1950-52, v.p. 1957, pres. 1958), Nat. Acad. Sci. (Daniel Giraud Elliot medal 1935), Sigma Xi. Office: Mus of No Ariz 3101 N Fort Valley Rd Flagstaff AZ 86001-8348

COLBERT, MARGARET MATTHEW, artist; b. N.Y.C., Apr. 18, 1911; d. William Diller and Kate (Lee) Matthew; m. Edwin Harris Colbert, July 8, 1933; children: George, David, Philip, Daniel, Charles. BFA, Calif. Coll. Arts and Crafts, 1931. Sci. illustrator Am. Mus. Natural History, N.Y.C., 1931-33. Contbr. numerous illustrations to books; executed murals of extinct life for Mus. No. Ariz., Big Bend Nat. Pk., Petrified Forest Nat. Pk., Albuquerque Natural History Mus.; one-person show Mus. No. Ariz., 1984; exhibited in group shows in N.Y., N.J., Calif. and Ariz. Recipient engraved crystal award Soc. Vertebrate Paleontology, plaque Dinosaur Soc. Avocations: watercolor and oil portraits, ceramics, various crafts.

COLBURN, DONALD D. lawyer; b. Seward, Nebr., May 20, 1948; BA, U. Nebr., Lincoln, 1970, JD with distinction, 1974. Bar: Ariz. 1974, Tex. 1994. Law clk. for Chief Justice Nebr. Supreme Ct., 1973-74; sr. ptnr. Snell & Wilmer, Phoenix, 1974-99; ptnr. Colburn Law Offices, Phoenix, 1999—. Office: Colburn Law Offices 7501 N 16th St Ste 200 Phoenix AZ 85020-4677

COLBURN, KEITH W. electronics executive; Chmn. bd., CEO Consolidated Electrical Distrs, Thousand Oaks, Calif., -1999. Office: Consolidated Electrical Distrs PO Box 5041 Thousand Oaks CA 91359-5041

COLBURN, RICHARD DUNTON, business executive; b. Carpentersville, Ill., June 24, 1911; s. Cary R. and Daisy (Dunton) C.; children: Richard Whiting, Carol Dunton, Keith Whiting, Christine Isabel, David Dunton, McKee Dunton, Daisy Dunton, Franklin Anthony. Student, Antioch Coll., 1929-33. Pres. Consol. Foundries Mfg. Corp. (and predecessors), 1944-64. Underwriting mem. Lloyds of London. Home and Office: 1120 La Collina Dr Beverly Hills CA 90210-2616 also: 30 Chester Sq London SW1W 9HT England

COLDEWEY, JOHN CHRISTOPHER, English literature educator; b. Beloit, Wis., June 13, 1944; s. George Henry and Frances Mary (McLoughlin) C.; m. Carolyn Culver (div.); children: Christopher, Devin; m. Christine May Rose, Sept. 9, 1989. BA, Lewis U., 1966; student, U. London, Eng., 1966; MA, No. Ill. U., 1967; PhD, U. Colo., 1972. Acting asst. prof. English U. Wash., Seattle, 1972-73, asst. prof. English, 1973-79, assoc. prof. English, 1979-91, prof. English, 1991—, dir. grad. studies, 1995-99; postdoctoral rsch. fellow Nottingham (Eng.) U., 1979-80; Fulbright exchange prof. U. East Anglia, Norwich, Eng., 1986-87. Lectr., speaker and reader in field. Author: Pseudomagia: A 17th Century Neo-Latin Tragicomedy by William Mewe, 1979, Renaissance Latin Drama in England, Vol. IV, 1987, Vol. 14, 1991, Contexts for Early English Drama, 1989, Early English Drama: An Anthology, 1993, Drama: Classical Through Contemporary, 1998; editor: Modern Lang. Quar., 1983-93; contbr. chpts. to books, articles to profl. jours. Bd. dirs. Friends U. Wash. Libr., 1991-99 (pres. 1995-97); hon. advisor Brit. Univs. Summers Schs. Program, 1977-94. Fellow Medieval Acad. Am., 1974-75; grantee Am. Coun. Learned Socs., 1974-75, 1976-77, 86-87, 89-90, grantee NEH, 1979-80, 82-83, 92-93, fellow, 1999-2000. Mem. Coun. Editors Learned Jours. (pres. 1992-94, v.p. 1990-92, sec.-treas. 1989-90), Medieval and Renaissance Drama Soc. (exec. coun. 1997-98, v.p. 1998-00), Medieval European Drama Coun. (Am. rep. 1997-99). Avocations: skiing, mountain travel, running, biking. Home: 333 35th Ave E Seattle WA 98112-4923 Office: U Wash Dept English Box 354330 Seattle WA 98195-0001 E-mail: jcjc@u.washington.edu

COLDREN, LARRY ALLEN, engineering educator, consultant; b. Lewistown, Pa., Jan. 1, 1946; s. Roscoe Calvin and Mary (Hutchinson) C.; m. Donna Kauffman, Sept. 4, 1966; children: Christopher William, Bret Allen. BS and AB, Bucknell U., 1968; MS, Stanford U., 1969, PhD, 1972. Registered profl. engr., N.J. Mem. tech. staff Bell Labs., N.J., 1968-84, supr., 1984; prof. U. Calif., Santa Barbara, 1984—. Contbr. 400 papers to tech. jours.; patentee in field. Fellow IEEE (mem. ad com. 1988—), Optical Soc. Am.; mem. Phi Beta Kappa, Tau Beta Pi, Pi Mu Epsilon, Sigma Pi Sigma. Presbyterian. Avocation: flying. Home: 4665 Via Vistosa Santa Barbara CA 93110-2333

COLE, CHARLES EDWARD, lawyer, former state attorney general; b. Yakima, Wash., Oct. 10, 1927; married; 3 children. BA, Stanford U., 1950, LLB, 1953. Law clk. Vets. Affairs Commn. Territory of Alaska, Juneau, 1954, Territorial Atty. Gen.'s Office, Fairbanks, Alaska, 1955-56, U.S. Dist. Ct. Alaska, Fairbanks, 1955-56; city magistrate City of Fairbanks, 1957-58; pvt. practice law, 1957-90; atty. gen. State of Alaska, 1990-94; pvt. law comml. litigation, 1995—. Profl. baseball player, Stockton, Calif. and Twin Falls, Idaho, summers of 1950, 51, 53. With U.S. Army, 1946-47. Mem. Calif. State Bar, Washington State Bar Assn., Alaska Bar Assn. Office: Law Dept State of AK Office of Atty Gen PO Box 110300 Juneau AK 99811-0300 also: Law Offices of Charles E Cole 406 Cushman St Fairbanks AK 99701-4632

COLE, CRAIG W. grocery chain executive; b. 1950; s. Jack Cole; m. Sue Cole. Saxophonist, singer rock band; mgr. human rels. dept. Foss Launch and Tug; asst. to exec. dir. Wash. Human Rights Commn.; legis. aide; pres., CEO Brown & Cole Stores Inc., Bellingham, Wash., 1986—. Chmn. bd. Assoc. Grocers. Former councilman Whatcom County, Wash.; former mem. Wash. Gov.'s Com. on Employment of Handicapped, Gov.'s Com. on Affirmative Action; former trustee Western Wash. U.; mem. Wash. Gov.'s Commn. on Early Learning. Mem. Food Mktg. Inst. (bd. dirs.). Office: Brown & Cole Stores Inc PO Box 9797 Bellingham WA 98227-9797

COLE, DAVID MACAULAY, journalist, consultant; b. Richmond, Calif., Feb. 17, 1954; s. Frederick George and Norma Ann C. Student, San Francisco State U., 1972-77. Mng. editor Feed/Back Mag., San Francisco, 1974-78, exec. editor, 1978-83; asst. music editor Rolling Stone Mag., San Francisco, 1976-77; from copy editor to asst. mng. editor The San Francisco Examiner, 1979-87, asst. mng. editor, 1987-89; prin., owner The Cole Group, Pacifica, Calif., 1989—. Editor, publisher The Cole Papers, 1989—, NewsInc., 1997—; author: Cole's Notes--Profiles in Pagination, 1996, Cole's Guide to Publishing Systems, 1994, 95, 96, 97; contbg. editor Presstime Magazine, 1994—, TechNews Mag., 1994—. Trustee Jr. Statesman Found, San Mateo, Calif., 1997—, exec. com., 2001—. Mem. Nat. Press Photographers Assn., Soc. News Design, Soc. Profl. Journalists (v.p. local chpt. 1979). Avocations: steam train preservation. Office: The Cole Group PO Box 719 Pacifica CA 94044-0719 Fax: 650-557-9696. E-mail: dmc@colegroup.com

COLE, GEORGE THOMAS, lawyer; b. Orlando, Fla., Mar. 14, 1946; s. Robert Bates and Frances (Arnold) C.; m. Peggy Ellen Stimson, May 23, 1981; children: Leslie Elizabeth, Ashley Ellen, Robert Warren. AB, Yale U., 1968; JD, U. Mich., 1975. Bar: Ariz. 1975, U.S. Dist. Ct. Ariz. 1975, U.S. Ct. Appeals (9th cir.) 1978; cert. real estate specialist Ariz. Bar. With Fennemore, Craig, von Ammon, Udall & Powers, Phoenix, 1975-81; ptnr. Fennemore Craig, P.C., Phoenix, 1981—. Mem. Ariz. State U. Coun. for Design Excellence. Served to lt. (j.g.) USN, 1968-71. Fellow Ariz. Bar Found. (founding); mem. Nat. and Ariz. Assns. Home Builders, Urban Land Inst. (cmty. devel. coun.), Community Assns. Inst., Nat. Golf Found (assoc.), Ariz. Bar Assn. (council Real Property sect. 1985-88, chmn. 1987-88), Maricopa Bar Assn., Yale Club (pres. 1984), Paradise Valley Country Club (Phoenix), White Mountain Country Club (Pinetop, Ariz.). Republican. Methodist. Home: 5102 E Desert Park Ln Paradise Valley AZ 85253-3054 Office: Fennemore Craig 3003 N Central Ave Ste 2600 Phoenix AZ 85012-2913 E-mail: gcole@fclaw.com

COLE, GLEN DAVID, minister; b. Tacoma, Dec. 21, 1933; s. Ray Milton and Ruth Evelyn (Ranton) C.; m. Mary Ann Von Moos, June 6, 1953; children: Randall Ray, Ricky Jay. BA in Theology, Cen. Bible Coll., 1956; DD, Pacific Coast Bible Coll., 1983. Pastor Assembly of God, Marion, Ohio, 1957-60, Maple Valley, Wash., 1960-65; assoc. pastor Calvary Temple, Seattle, 1965-67; sr. pastor Evergreen Christian Ctr., Olympia, Wash., 1967-78, Capital Christian Ctr., Sacramento, 1978-95, pastor emeritus, 1995—; dist. supr. Assemblies of God, Sacramento, 1997—. Exec. presbyter Assemblies of God, Springfield, 1985—; trustee Bethany Bible Coll., Santa Cruz, Calif., 1979—; bd. dirs. Cen. Bible Coll., Springfield, Mo., 1988—; bd. dirs. Calif. Theol. Sem., Fresno, 1985-90. Mem. Rotary (pres. Olympia chpt. 1977-78). Republican. Office: Assemblies of God 6051 S Watt Ave Sacramento CA 95829-1304 Address: 11277 Crocker Grove Ln Gold River CA 95670-4524

COLE, MACK, state legislator, rancher; b. Forsyth, Mont., June 4, 1936; m. Judy Cole; 3 children. BS, Mont. State U., 1958; MS, Thunderbird Grad Sch. Mgmt., 1962. Rancher; with Bur. Indian Affairs; mem. Mont. Senate, Dist. 4, Helena, 1995—; chair state adminstrn. com. Mont. State Senate, mem. hwys./transp. com., conf. com., natural resources com. With Bur. Indian Affairs. Republican. Roman Catholic. Office: PO Box 286 Hysham MT 59038-0286

COLE, NATALIE MARIA, singer; b. L.A., Feb. 6, 1950; d. Nathaniel Adam and Maria (Hawkins) C.; m. Marvin J. Yancy, July 30, 1976 (div.); m. Andre Fisher (div.). B.A. in Psychology, U. Mass., 1972. Rec. singles and albums, 1975—; albums include Dangerous, 1985, Everlasting, 1987, The Natalie Cole Collection, 1987, Inseparable, Thankful, Good To Be Back, 1989, Unforgettable, 1991 (4 grammys, 3 grammys 1992), Too Much Weekend, 1992, I'm Ready, 1992, I've Got Love On My Mind, 1992, Take A Look, 1993 (Grammy award nominee best jazz vocal 1994), Holly and Ivy, 1994, Stardust (2 Grammy awards), Magic of Christmas, 1999; television appearances include Lily in Winter, USA, 1994. Recipient Grammy award for best new artist, best Rhythm and Blues female vocalist 1975, 76; recipient 1 gold single, 3 gold albums; recipient 2 Image awards NAACP 1976, 77; Am. Music award 1978, other awards. Mem. AFTRA, Nat. Assn. Rec. Arts and Scis., Delta Sigma Delta. Baptist. Office: PMK c/o Jennifer Allen 955 Carrillo Dr Ste 200 Los Angeles CA 90048-5400

COLE, PAULA, pop singer, songwriter; b. Rockport, Mass. Student, Berklee Sch. Music, Boston. Back-up singer Melissa Etheridge, Sarah McLachlan, Peter Gabriel; rec. artist Imago Records, 1992; rec. artist Harbinger, 1992, This Fire, 1996, Amen, 2000. Office: Warner Bros Records Inc 3300 Warner Blvd Burbank CA 91505-4694

COLE, RICHARD GEORGE, public administrator; b. Irvington, N.J., Mar. 11, 1948; s. Warner W. and Laurel M. (Wilson) C. AS in Computer Sci., Control Data Inst., Anaheim, Calif., 1972; BA in Sociology with high honor, Calif. State U., Los Angeles, 1974; MA in Social Ecology, U. Calif., Irvine, 1976; postgrad., So. Oreg. State Coll., 1979. Computer operator Zee Internat., Gardena, Calif., 1971; teaching asst. U. Calif., Irvine, 1974-75; planner Herman Kimmel & Assocs., Newport Beach, Calif., 1976-78; program analyst The Job Council, Medford, Oreg., 1980-81, compliance officer, 1981-82, bus. mgr., 1982—. Instr. credential Calif. C.C.; chmn. bd. trustees Job Coun. Pension Trust, Medford, 1982-97; mem. curriculum adv. com. Rogue C.C., Grants Pass, Oreg., 1986; mgr. computer project State of Oreg., Salem, 1983-84; mem. Oreg. Occupational Info. Coordinating Com., Salem, 1982-84. Pres. bd. trustees Vector Control Dist., Jackson County, Oreg., 1985, treas., 1986, bd. dirs., 1984-87, mem. budget com., 1988-99, sec., 1988-89; cand. bd. dirs. Area Edn. Dist., Jackson County, 1981; treas. Job Svc. Employer Com., Jackson County, 1987-99 (Spl. Svc. award 1991), Oreg. Employers Coun., 1997-99; dir. fin. joint pub. venture System Devel. Project, Salem, Oreg., 1986-89; mem. adv. bd. New Jobs Planning, Medford, Oreg., 1987-88, Fin. Audit and Risk Mgmt. Task Force, 1987-91, chm., 1989-90. Fellow LaVerne Noyes, U. Calif., Irvine, 1974; Dr. Paul Doehring Found. scholar, Glendale, Calif., 1973; Computer Demonstration grantee State of Oreg., Salem, 1983; recipient Award of Fin. Reporting Achievement Govt. Fin. Officers Assn. of U.S. and Can., 1989-90, Fin. Ops. recognition Vector Control Dist., Jackson County, Oreg., 1990, Nat. 2d Pl. Chpt. award Jackson County Job Svc. Employer Com., 1989, Oreg. Job Svc. Employer Com. Stat award, 1991, Oreg. Individual Citation award Internat. Assn. Profls. in Employment Security, 1993. Mem. Soc. for Human Resources Mgmt., Assn. So. Oreg. Pub. Adminstrs., Oreg. Employment and Tng. Assn., Pacific N.W. Personnel Mgmt. Assn. (chpt. treas. 1985-87, orgnl. liaison dir. 1988-89, Appreciation award 1985), Govt. Fin. Officers Assn., Oreg. Mcpl. Fin. Officers assn., The Nature Conservancy. Home: 575 Morey Rd Talent OR 97540-9725 Office: The Job Council 673 Market St Medford OR 97504-6125

COLE, STEPHEN E. magistrate judge; b. Powell, Wyo., Apr. 18, 1947; BA, U. Wyo., 1969, JD, 1974. Pvt. law practice, Worland, Wyo.; judge Worland Mcpl. Ct., 1975-81, Ten Sleep Mcpl. Ct., 1977-81; justice of the peace Washakie County Justice Ct., 1977-81; magistrate judge U.S. Dist. Ct. Wyo., 1975—. Office: PO Box 387 Yellowstone National Park WY 82190-0387 E-mail: stephen_cole@wyd.uscourts.gov

COLE, TERRI LYNN, organization administrator; b. Tucson, Dec. 28, 1951; m. James R. Cole II. Student, U. N.Mex., 1975-80; cert., Inst. Orgn. Mgmt., 1985. Cert. chamber exec. With SunWest Bank, Albuquerque, 1971-74, employment adminstr., 1974-76, communications dir., 1976-78; pub. info. dir. Albuquerque C. of C., 1978-81, gen. mgr., 1981-83, pres., 1983—. Pres. N.Mex. C. of C. Execs. Assn., 1986-87, bd. dirs., 1980—; bd. regents Inst. for Orgn. Mgmt., Stanford U., 1988—, vice chmn., 1990-91, chmn., 1991; bd. dirs. Hosp. Home Health, Inc. Recipient Bus. Devel. award Expn. Mgmt. Inc., 1985, Women on Move award YWCA, 1986; named one of Outstanding Women of Am., 1984. Mem. Am. C. of C. Execs. Assn. (chmn. elect bd. 1992—). Republican. Avocations: skiing, cycling, gardening. Office: Greater Albuquerque C of C PO Box 25100 Albuquerque NM 87125-0100

COLE, WILLIAM L. lawyer; b. L.A., May 13, 1952; AB magna cum laude, U. Calif., Irvine, 1974; JD, Stanford U., 1977. Bar: Calif. 1977. Atty. Mitchell, Silberberg & Knupp, L.A., mng. ptnr., 1991—. Mem. ABA, State Bar Calif., Los Angeles County Bar Assn. (mem. exec. com. labor law sect. 1989-90), Phi Beta Kappa, Order of Coif. Office: Mitchell Silberberg & Knupp 11377 W Olympic Blvd Los Angeles CA 90064-1625

COLEMAN, ARLENE FLORENCE, retired nurse practitioner; b. Braham, Minn., Apr. 8, 1926; d. William and Christine (Judin) C.; m. John Dunkerken, May 30, 1987. Diploma in nursing, U. Minn., 1947, BS, 1953; MPH, Loma Linda U., 1974. RN, Calif. Operating room scrub nurse Calif. Luth. Hosp., L.A., 1947-48; indsl. staff nurse Good Samaritan Hosp., L.A., 1948-49; staff nurse Passavant Hosp., Chgo., 1950-51; student health nurse Moody Bible Inst., Chgo., 1950-51; staff nurse St. Andrews Hosp., Mpls., 1951-53; pub. health nurse Bapt. Gen. Conf. Bd. of World Missions, Ethiopia, Africa, 1954-66; staff pub. health nurse County of San Bernadino, Calif., 1966-68, sr. pub. health nurse, 1968-73, pediatric nurse practitioner, 1973—. Contbr. articles to profl. jours. Mem. bd. dist. missions Bapt. Gen. Conf., Calif., 1978-84; mem. adv. coun. Kaiser Hosp., Fontana, Calif., 1969-85, Bethel Sem. West, San Diego, 1987—; bd. dirs. Casa Verdugo Retirement Home, Hemet, Calif., 1985—; active Calvary Bapt. Ch., Redlands, Calif., 1974—; mem. S.W. Bapt. Conf. Social Ministries, 1993—. With Cadet Nurse Corps USPHS, 1944-47. Calif. State Dept. Health grantee, 1973. Fellow Nat. Assn. Pediatric Nurse Assocs. and Practitioners; mem. Calif. Nurses Assn. (state nursing coun. 1974-76). Democrat. Avocations: gardening, travel, reading. Home: 622 Esther Way Redlands CA 92373-5822

COLEMAN, CHARLES CLYDE, physicist, educator; b. York, Eng., July 31, 1937; came to U.S., 1941; s. Jesse C. and Geraldine (Doherty) C.; m. Sharon R. Slutsky, Aug. 12, 1976; children: Jeffrey Andrew, Matthew Casey. BA, UCLA, 1959, MA, 1961, PhD, 1968. Asst. prof. physics Calif. State U., Los Angeles, 1968-71, assoc. prof, 1971-76, prof., 1976—. Cons. Gen. Dynamics Corp., 1975-77, China Lake Naval Rsch. Labs., 1981; dir. Csula Accelerator Facility; exec. dir. Csula Applied Physics Inst., 1978-83; sr. rsch. fellow Darwin Coll., Cambridge (Eng.) U., 1975-76; project specialist Chinese Provincial Univs. Devel. Project of World Bank, 1987-90; vis. prof. physics U. Istanbul, Turkey, 1969, 72, U. Sydney, Australia, 1977, Arya Mar U., Iran, 1976, U. Natal, South Africa, 1977, UCLA, 1990-91, U. Leicester, U.K., 1995—; mem. NASA review panel, 1992. Contbr. articles to sci. publs.; referee Solid State Electronics, Phys. Rev., Phys. Rev. Letters, Jour. Phys. Chem. Solids, Jour. Solid State Chem. Trustee Calif. State U. L.A. Found., 1981-85 Grantee NSF, 1976—, Rsch. Corp., 1987-91; NATO Collaborative Rsch. grantee, 1991—; NATO Sr. Rsch. fellow Cavendish Lab. (U.K.), 1983-84, Am. Chem. Soc. Rsch. Faculty fellow, 1990. Fellow Brit. Interplanetary Soc., Royal Philatelic Soc. (London); mem. Am. Phys. Soc., Am. Radio Relay League, Sigma Xi, Phi Kappa Phi, Phi Beta Delta, Sigma Pi Sigma. Office: Calif State U Dept Physics Los Angeles CA 90032 E-mail: ccolema@calstatela.edu

COLEMAN, COURTNEY STAFFORD, mathematician, educator; b. Ventura, Calif., July 19, 1930; s. Courtney Clemon and Una (Stafford) C.; m. Julia Wellnitz, June 26, 1954; children: David, Margaret, Diane. BA, U. Calif., Berkeley, 1951; PhD, Princeton U., 1955. Asst. prof. Wesleyan U., Middletown, Conn., 1955-58; from asst. prof. to full prof. Harvey Mudd Coll., Claremont, Calif., 1959-98. Lectr. Princeton (N.J.) U., 1954-55; rsch. in field. Author, editor: Differential Equations Models, 1983; editor, translator: Local Methods in Nonlinear Differential Equations, 1988; author: (with others) Differential Equations, 1987, Differential Equations Laboratory Workbook, 1992 (EDUCOM award for best math./computer course materials), Ordinary Differential Equations: A Modeling Perspective, 1998 , ODE Architect, 1999 (award of excellence and Gold medal for best CD-ROM in edn.); mem. editl. bd. Jour. of Differential Equations, 1964—, UMAP Jour., 1980—. Mem. Am. Math. Soc., Math. Assn. Am., Soc. Indsl. Applied Math. Office: Harvey Mudd Coll Math Dept 1250 N Dartmouth Ave Claremont CA 91711 E-mail: coleman@hmc.edu

COLEMAN, DEBORAH ANN, electronics company executive; b. Central Falls, R.I., Jan. 22, 1953; d. John Austin and Joan Mary Coleman. BA, Brown U., 1974; MBA, Stanford U., 1978; PhD in Engring. (hon.), Worcester (Mass.) Poly., 1987. Mfg. supr. Tex. Instruments, Attleboro, Mass., 1974; with fin. mgmt. tng. program Gen. Electric, Providence, 1975-76; with fin. mgmt. Hewlett-Packard, Cupertino, Calif., 1978-81; contr. Macintosh/Apple 32 group Apple Computer, Cupertino, 1981-84, dir. ops., 1984-85, v.p. worldwide mfg., 1985-87, CFO, 1987-89, CIO, 1990-92; v.p. materials ops. Tektronix Inc., Wilsonville, OR, 1992-94; chmn., CEO Merix Corp., Forest Grove, 1994—; CIO Apple Computer, Cupertino, 1990-92; v.p. materials ops. Tektronix Inc., Wilsonville, Oreg., 1992-94; chmn., CEO, pres. Merix Corp., Forest Grove, 1994—. Mem. U.S. Dept. Def. Mfg. Sci. Tech. Bd., 1988-91; bd. dirs. VMX, Inc., Software Pub Corp., Octel. Mem. adv. coun. Stanford Inst. Mfg. Automation, 1985-87; mem. Harvard U. Bus. Sch. Vis. Com., 1987—, Com. of 200, 1987—; trustee San Jose/Cleve. Ballet, 1989-92, Brown U., 1994—. Mem. Internat. Women's Forum. Democrat. Roman Catholic. Office: Merix Corp 1521 Poplar Ln Forest Grove OR 97116-0300

COLEMAN, LEWIS WALDO, bank executive; b. San Francisco, Jan. 2, 1942; s. Lewis V. and Virginia Coleman; m. Susan G.; children: Michelle, Gregory, Nancy, Peter BA, Stanford U., 1965. With Bank Calif., San Francisco, 1965-73, Wells Fargo Bank, San Francisco, 1973-86, exec. v.p., chmn. credit policy com., until 1986; vice chmn., CFO, treas. Bank Am., San Francisco, 1986-95; sr. mng. dir. Montgomery Securities, San Francisco, 1995-98; CEO Nations Bank Mongomery Securities, San Francisco, 1998—.

COLEMAN, PAUL JEROME, JR. physicist, educator; b. Evanston, Ill., Mar. 7, 1932; s. Paul Jerome and Eunice Cecile (Weissenberg) C.; m. Doris Ann Fields, Oct. 3, 1964, children: Derrick, Craig. BS in Engring. Math., BS in Engring. Physics, U. Mich., 1954, MS in Physics, 1958; PhD in Space Physics, UCLA, 1966. Rsch. scientist Ramo-Wooldridge Corp. (name now TRW Systems), El Segundo, Calif., 1958-61; instr. math. U. So. Calif., L.A., 1958-61; mgr. interplanetary scis. program NASA, Washington, 1961-62; rsch. scientist UCLA, 1962-66, prof. geophysics, space physics, 1966—; asst. lab. dir., mgr. Earth and Space Scis. divsn., chmn. Inst. Geophysics and Planetary Physics Nat. Lab., Los Alamos, N.Mex., 1981-86; dir. Inst. Geophysics and Planetary Physics UCLA, 1989-92; dir. Nat. Inst. for Global Environ. Change, 1994-96; pres. Univs. Space Rsch. Assn., Columbia, Md., 1981-2000. Bd. dirs. Axcess Inc., Dallas, Biocentrie Solutions, Inc., Madison, Wis., others; mem. adv. bd. San Diego Supercomputer Ctr., 1986-90, chmn., 1987-88, others; trustee Univs. Space Rsch. Assn., Columbia, Md., 1981-2000, Am. Tech. Alliances, 1990—, Internat. Small Satellite Orgn., 1992-96; vis. scholar U. Paris, 1975-76; vis. scientist Lab. for Aeronomy Ctr. Nat. Rsch. Sci., Verrieres le Buisson, France, 1975-76; com. mem. numerous sci. and ednl. orgns., cons. numerous fin. and indsl. cos. Co-editor: Solar Wind, 1972; co-author: Pioneering the Space Frontier, 1986; mem. editorial bd. Geophysics and Astrophysics Monographs, 1970—; assoc. editor Cosmic Electrodynamics, 1968-72; contbr. revs. to numerous profl. jours. Apptd. to Nat. Commn. on Space, Pres. of U.S., 1985, apptd. to Space Policy Adv. Bd., Nat. Space Coun., v.p. of U.S., 1991; bd. dirs. St. Matthew's Sch., Pacific Palisades, Calif., 1979-82, v.p., 1981-82. 1st lt. USAF, 1954-56, Korea. Recipient Exceptional Sci. Achievement Medal NASA, 1970, 1972, spl. recognition for contributions to the Apollo Program, 1979; Guggenheim fellow 1975-76, Fulbright scholar, 1975-76, Rsch. grantee NASA, NSF, Office Naval Research, Calif. Space Inst., Air Force Office Sci. Research, U.S. Geol. Survey. Mem. AIAA, Am. Geophys. Union, Internat. Acad. Astronautics, Bel Air Bay Club (L.A.), Birnam Wood Golf Club (Monteceito, Calif.), Cosmos Club (Washington), Valley Club (Montecito, Calif.), Eldorado Country Club (Indian Wells, Calif.), Tau Beta Pi, Phi Eta Sigma. Avocations: flying, skiing, racquetball, tennis, golf. Home: 1323 Monaco Dr Pacific Palisades CA 90272-4007 Office: UCLA Inst Geophysics & Planetary Physics 405 Hilgard Ave Los Angeles CA 90095-9000

COLEMAN, ROBERT GRIFFIN, geology educator; b. Twin Falls, Idaho, Jan. 5, 1923; s. Lloyd Wilbur and Frances (Brown) C.; m. Cathryn J. Hirschberger, Aug. 7, 1948; children: Robert Griffin Jr., Derrick Job, Mark Dana. BS, Oreg. State U., 1948, MS, 1950; PhD, Stanford U., 1957. Mineralogist AEC, N.Y.C., 1952-54; geologist U.S. Geol. Survey, Washington, 1954-57, Menlo Park, Calif., 1958-80; prof. geology Stanford U., 1981-93, prof. emeritus, 1993—. Vis. petrographer New Zealand Geol. Survey, 1962-63; br. chief isotope geology U.S. Geol. Survey, Menlo Park, 1964-68, regional geologist, Saudi Arabia, 1970-71, br. chief field geochemistry and petrology, Menlo Park, 1977-79; vis. scholar Woods Hole Oceanographic Inst., Mass., 1975; vis. prof. geology Sultan Qaboos U., Oman, 1987, 89; cons. geologist, 1993—; instr. geobotany field sch. Siskiyou Inst., Oreg., 1998-99. Author: Ophiolites, 1977, Geologic Evolution of the Red Sea, 1993, Ultrahigh Pressure Metamorphism, 1995; contbr. articles to profl. jours. Named Outstanding Scientist, Oreg. Acad. Sci., 1977; Fairchild scholar Calif. Inst. Tech., Pasadena, 1980; recipient Meritorious award U.S. Dept. Interior, 1981 Fellow AAAS, Geol. Soc. Am. (coun.), Am. Mineral Soc. (coun., editor), Am. Geophys. Union; mem. Nat. Acad. Scis., Russian Acad. Sci. (fgn. assoc.). Republican Avocations: wood carving, art. Home: 2025 Camino Al Lago Atherton CA 94027-5938 E-mail: coleman@pangea.stanford.edu

COLEMAN, ROGER DIXON, bacteriologist; b. Rockwell, Iowa, Jan. 18, 1915; s. Major C. and Hazel Ruth Coleman; m. Lee Aden Skov, Jan. 1, 1978. AB, UCLA, 1937; postgrad., Balliol Coll., Oxford, Eng., 1944; MS, U. So. Calif., 1952, PhD, 1957. Diplomate Am. Bd. Bioanalysts. Sr. laboratorian Napa (Calif.) State Hosp., 1937-42; dir. Long Beach (Calif) Clin. Lab., 1946-86, pres., 1980-86. Mem. Calif. State Clin. Lab. Commn., 1953-57. Author papers to profl. publs. Officer AUS, 1942-46. Mem. Am.

Assn. Bioanalysts, Am. Assn. Clin. Chemists, Am. Soc. Microbiologists, Am. Chem. Soc., Am. Venereal Disease Assn., Calif. Assn. Bioanalysts (past officer), Med. Rsch. Assn. Calif., Bacteriology Club So. Calif., Sigma Xi, Phi Sigma (past chpt. pres.). Home and Office: 31086 Montesa Laguna Niguel CA 92677-2721 Office: PO Box 7073 Laguna Niguel CA 92607-7073

COLEMAN, THOMAS YOUNG, lawyer; b. Richmond, Va., Jan. 6, 1949; s. Emmet Macadium and Mary Katherine (Gay) C.; m. Janet Clare Norris, Aug. 30, 1980; children: Dana Alicia, Amanda Gay, Blair Norris. BA, U. Va., 1971, JD, 1975. Bar: Va. 1975, U.S. Dist. Ct. (we. dist.) Va. 1975, U.S. Ct. Appeals (4th cir.) 1976, Calif. 1977, U.S. Dist Ct. (no. dist.) Calif. 1977. Law clk. chief judge U.S. Dist. Ct. (we. dist.) Va., Charlottesville, 1975-76; assoc. Morrison & Foerster, San Francisco, 1976-79; v.p., counsel Calif. 1st Bank (now Union Bank of Calif.), San Francisco, 1979-85; of counsel Orrick, Herrington & Sutcliffe, San Francisco, 1985-86, ptnr., 1987—. Speaker in field; vis. atty. Clifford-Turner Solicitors (now Clifford Chance), London, 1984. Mem. bus. gifts com. San Francisco Symphony. Mem. Internat. Bankers Assn. in Calif. (co-counsel). Office: Orrick Herrington & Sutcliffe 400 Sansome St San Francisco CA 94111-3143

COLES, H. BRENT, mayor; m. Julie Allred; 5 children. B in Polit. Sci., Brigham Young U., 1977; MPA, Calif. State U., Long Beach, 1980. Asst. city mgr. City of Boise, city planner, mem. city coun., mayor, 1993—. Mem. adv. bd. U.S. Conf. Mayors. Bd. dirs. Assn. Idaho Cities, Boise Future Found., Ada Planning Assn.; co-chair Drug Control Task Force. Address: PO Box 500 Boise ID 83701-0500

COLGATE, STIRLING AUCHINCLOSS, physicist; b. N.Y.C., Nov. 14, 1925; s. Henry A. and Jeannette (Pruyn) C.; m. Rosemary B. Williamson, July 12, 1947; children; Henry A., Sarah, Arthur S. BA, Cornell U., 1948, PhD in Physics, 1952. Physicist Radiation Lab., Univ. Calif., Berkeley, 1951-52, Lawrence Livermore (Calif.) Lab., 1952-64; pres. N.Mex. Inst. Mining and Tech., Socorro, 1964-74; physicist Los Alamos (N.Mex.) Nat. Lab., 1976—. Contbr. over 200 articles to profl. jours. Served with Merchant Marines, 1943-46. Recipient Rossi prize, 1990, Wetherill prize, 1994. Fellow Am. Phys. Soc.; mem. NAS, Am. Astron. Soc. Home: 422 Estante Way Los Alamos NM 87544-3812 Office: Los Alamos Nat Lab MS B288 Los Alamos NM 87545-0001 E-mail: colgate@lanl.gov

COLLANTON, GREG, manufacturing executive, controller; Controller Power Lift Corp., Pico Rivera, Calif. Office: Power Lift Corp 8314 Slauson Ave Pico Rivera CA 90660-4323

COLLAS, JUAN GARDUÑO, JR. lawyer; b. Manila, Apr. 25, 1932; s. Juan D. and Soledad (Garduño) C.; m. Maria L. Moreira, Aug. 1, 1959; children: Juan Jose, Elias Lopes, Cristina Maria, Daniel Benjamin. LLB, U. of Philippines, Quezon City, 1955; LLM, Yale U., 1958, JSD, 1959. Bar: Philippines 1956, Ill. 1960, Calif. 1971, U.S. Supreme Ct. 1967. Assoc., Sy Cip, Salazar & Assocs., Manila, 1956-57; atty. N.Y., N.H. & H. R.R., New Haven, 1959-60; assoc. Baker & McKenzie, Chgo., 1960-63, ptnr., Manila, 1963-70, San Francisco, 1970-95, Manila, 1995—. Contbr. articles to profl. jours. Trustee, sec. Friends of U. of Philippines Found. in Am., San Francisco, 1982—; co-chmn. San Francisco Lawyers for Better Govt., 1982—; chmn. San Francisco-Manila Sister City Com., 1986-92. Recipient Outstanding Filipino Overseas in Law award, Philippine Ministry Tourism Philippines Jaycees, 1979. Mem. ABA, Am. Arbitration Assn. (panelist), Ill. State Bar Assn., State Bar Calif., Integrated Bar of Philippines, Filipino-Am. C. of C. (bd. dirs. 1974-91, 94-96, pres. 1985-87, chmn. bd. dirs. 1987-89, 95-96). Republican. Roman Catholic. Clubs: World Trade, Villa Taverna (San Francisco). Office: Baker & McKenzie 2 Embarcadero Ctr Ste 2400 San Francisco CA 94111-3909

COLLEN, MORRIS FRANK, medical association administrator, physician; b. St. Paul, Nov. 12, 1913; s. Frank Morris and Rose (Finkelstein) C.; m. Frances B. Diner, Sept. 24, 1937; children: Arnold Roy, Barry Joel, Roberta Joy, Randal Harry. BEE, U. Minn., 1934, MB with distinction, 1938, MD, 1939. Diplomate Am. Bd. Internal Medicine. Intern Michael Reese Hosp., Chgo., 1939-40; resident Los Angeles County Hosp., 1940-42; chief med. service Kaiser Found. Hosp., Oakland, Calif., 1942-52, chief of staff, 1952-53; med. dir. Permanente Med. Group, West Bay Div., 1953-79, dir. med. methods research, 1962-79, dir. tech. assessment, 1979-83, cons. div. research, 1983—. Chmn. exec. com. Permanente Med. Group, Oakland, 1953-73; dir. Permanente Services, Inc., Oakland, 1958-73; lectr. Sch. Pub. Health, U. Calif., Berkeley, 1966-78; lectr. info. sci. U. Calif., San Francisco, 1970-85; lectr. U. London, 1972, Stanford U. Med. Ctr., 1973, 75, 84-86, Harvard U., 1974, Johns Hopkins U., 1976, also others; adj. asst. prof. biomed. informatics Uniformed Svcs. U. Health Scis., 2000—; cons. Bur. Health Services, USPHS, 1965-68, chmn. health care systems study sect., 1968-72, mem. adv. com. demonstration grants, 1967; advisor VA, 1968; cons. European region WHO, 1968-72; cons. med. fitness program U.S. Air Force, 1968; cons. Pres.'s Biomed. Research Panel, 1975; mem. adv. com. automated Multiphasic Health Testing, 1971; discussant Nat. Conf. Preventive Medicine, Bethesda, Md., 1975; mem. com. on tech. in health care NAS, 1976; mem. adv. group Nat. Commn. on Digestive Diseases, U.S. Congress, 1978; mem. adv. panel to U.S. Congress Office of Tech. Assessment, 1980-85; mem. peer rev. adv. group TRIMIS program Dept. Def., 1978-90; program chmn. 3d Internat. Conf. Med. Informatics, Tokyo, 1980; chmn. bd. sci. counselors Nat. Libr. Medicine, 1985-87, mem. lit. selection tech. rev. com., 1997—, chmn., 2000; cons. Nat. Libr. Med., 1985-88, Nat. Cancer Inst., 1999-00. Author: Treatment of Pneumococcic Pneumonia, 1948, Hospital Computer Systems, 1974, Multiphasic Health Testing Services, 1978, Medical Informatics: A Historical Review, 1995; editor: Permanente Med. Bull., 1943-53; mem. editl. bd. Preventive Medicine, 1970-80, Jour. Med. Sys., Methods Info. Medicine, 1980-97, Diagnostic Medicine, 1980-84, Computers in Biomed. Rsch., 1987-94; contbr. articles to med. jours., chpts. to books. Recipient Computers in Health Care Pioneer award, 1992, Japan Hirohara award for preventive medicine, 2001, David E. Morgan award for achievement in health care info., 1998, Cummings Psyche award, 2001; fellow fellow Ctr. Advanced Studies in Behavioral Scis., Stanford U., 1985—86; scholar Johns Hopkins Centennial scholar, 1976, scholar-in-residence, Nat. Libr. Medicine, 1987—. Fellow: ACP, Am. Coll. Cardiology, Am. Coll. Chest Physicians, Am. Inst. Med. and Biol. Engring.; mem.: Internat. Med. Informatics Assn. Sr. Officers Club, Alpha Omega Alpha, Tau Beta Pi, AMA, Salutis Unitas (v.p. 1972), Inst. Medicine of NAS (chmn. tech. subcom. for improving patient records 1990, chmn. workshop on informatics in clin. preventive medicine 1991), Am. Fedn. Clin. Rsch., Am. Coll. Med. Informatics (pres. 1987—88, Morris F. Collen medal named in his honor 1993), Soc. Adv. Med. Sys. (pres. 1973), Nat. Acad. Practice in Medicine (chmn. 1982—88, co-chmn. 1989—91), Am. Med. Informatics Assn. (bd. dirs. 1985—96), Internat. Health Evaluation Assn. (pres. 1995—96). Home: 4155 Walnut Blvd Walnut Creek CA 94596-5834 Office: 3505 Broadway Oakland CA 94611-5714 E-mail: mfcollen@aol.com

COLLEN, TOM, women's basketball coach; b. 1953; B in Health and Phys. Edn., Bowling Green U., 1977; M in Health Edn., Miami U. of Ohio, 1982, M in Recreational Programming, 1983. Asst. coach Miami of Ohio, 1982-84, U. Utah, 1984-86, Purdue U., 1987-93; asst. coach, asst. head coach U. Ark., 1994-97; head coach women's basketball Colo. State U., Ft. Collins, 1997—. Office: Colo State U Dept Athletics 215 D Moby Arena Fort Collins CO 80523-0001

COLLETT, JENNIE, principal; Prin. OB Whaley Sch., San Jose, Calif., 1995—. Recipient Elem. Sch. Recognition award U.S. Dept. Edn., 1989-90. Office: O B Whaley Sch 2655 Alvin Ave San Jose CA 95121-1609

COLLETT, ROBERT LEE, financial company executive; b. Ardmore, Okla., July 1, 1940; s. Pat (Dowell) Conway; m. Sue Walker Healy; 1 child, Catherine April. BA in Math., Rice U., 1962; MA in Econs., Duke U., 1963. Chief actuarial asst. Am. Nat. Ins. Co., Galveston, Tex., 1963-66; actuary Milliman & Robertson, Inc., Phila., 1966-70, prin. Houston, 1970-89, pres., 1990, pres., CEO Houston and Seattle, 1991-92, Seattle, 1992—. Bd. dirs. Seattle Symphony, 1992—. Fellow Soc. Actuaries (chmn. internat. sect. 1992—); mem. Rainier Club. Episcopalian. Avocations: tennis, traveling, music, reading. Office: Milliman & Robertson Inc 1301 5th Ave Ste 3800 Seattle WA 98101-2646

COLLIER, CHARLES ARTHUR, JR. lawyer; b. Columbus, Ohio, Apr. 18, 1930; s. Charles Arthur and Gertrude Clara (Roe) C.; m. Linda Louise Biggs, Aug. 5, 1961; children: Sheila Collier Rogers, Laura Collier Prescott. AB magna cum laude, Harvard U., 1952, LLB, 1955. Law clk. U.S. Dist. Ct. (cen. dist.) Calif., L.A., 1959-60; assoc. Freston & Files, L.A., 1960-66; assoc., ptnr. Mitchell, Silberberg & Knupp, L.A., 1967-82; ptnr. Irell & Manella, L.A., 1982-95, of counsel, 1995—. Lectr. Calif. Continuing Edn. of Bar, 1976-89; advisor Restatement of Property, Donative Transfers, 1990—; speaker numerous local bar assns. Contbr. articles to profl. jours. Recipient Arthur K. Marshall award Probate and Trust sect. L.A. County Bar Assn. Fellow Am. Coll. Trust and Estate Counsel (chmn. state laws com. 1986-89, regent 1989-98, joint editl. bd. uniform trust and estate acts, 1988—, chmn. expanded practice com. 1989-92, chmn. nominating com. 1998-99, spkr. 1988, exec. com. 1989-98, treas. 1992-93, sec. 1993-94, v.p. 1994-95, pres.-elect 1995-96, pres. 1996-97, immediate past pres. 1997-98), ABA Found.; mem. ABA (mem. real property, trust and probate law sect. spkr. 1985, 89, moderator teleconf. 1998, coun. 1989-93, chmn. com. trust adminstrn. 1982-85, chmn. task force on fiduciary litigation 1986-89, sr. lawyers divsn., vice chair wills, probate and trusts com. 1999-2000, chair 2000—, vice chair book pub. com. 2000—, others), Estate Planning, Trust and Probate Law Sect. of State Bar Calif. (chmn. 1980-81, vice chmn. 1979-80, mem. exec. com. 1977-82, advisor 1982-85, chmn. probate com. 1977-78, mem. legislation com. 1977-80, sect. liaison to Calif. Law Revision Commn. 1982-88), Internat. Acad. Estate and Trust Law, Harvard Alumni Assn. (dir. 1975-77, v.p. 1979-82), Harvard Club So. Calif. (pres. 1970-72). Republican. Methodist. Office: Irell & Manella LLP 1800 Ave Of Stars Ste 900 Los Angeles CA 90067-4276 E-mail: ccollier@irell.com

COLLIER, LUCILLE ANN See MILLER, ANN

COLLIGAN, JOHN C. (BUD COLLIGAN), multimedia company executive; married; 3 children. BS in Internat. Econs., Georgetown U., 1976; MBA, Stanford U., 1983. With Macintosh divsn. Apple Computer Corp., 1983-85, head higher edn. mktg. and sales, 1985-89; pres., CEO Authorware, Inc., 1989-92; chmn. Macromedia, Inc., San Francisco, 1992-98; ptnr. Accel Ptnrs., Palo Alto, Calif., 1998—. Bd. dirs. S3 Corp., c/net Inc. Mem. Interactive Multimedia Assn. (bd. dirs.). Office: Accel Ptnrs 428 University Ave Palo Alto CA 94301-1812

COLLING, KENNETH FRANK, retired hospital administrator; b. Watertown, N.Y., Apr. 17, 1945; BA, Cornell U., 1967, M Hosp. Adminstrn., 1969. Adminstrv. res. New Britain (Conn.) Gen. Hosp., 1968; asst. prof. Baylor Army program Healthcare Adminstrn., San Antonio, 1971-73; asst. adminstr. Kaiser Found. Hosp., Fontana, Calif., 1973-75, assoc. adminstr., 1979-81, asst. adminstr. Panorama City, 1975-79, adminstr. San Diego, 1981-99, sr. v.p., area mgr., 1995-99. Contbr. articles to profl. jours. Mem. Calif. Hosp. Assn. (exec. com., trustee). Home: 3024 Cadencia St Carlsbad CA 92009-8307 Office: Kaiser Found Hosp 4647 Zion Ave San Diego CA 92120-2507

COLLINS, AUDREY B. judge; b. 1945; BA, Howard U., 1967; MA, Am. U., 1969; JD, UCLA, 1977. Asst. atty. Legal Aid Found. L.A., 1977-78; with Office L.A. County Dist. Atty., 1978-94, dept. dist. atty., 1978-94, head dep. Torrance br. office, 1987-88, asst. dir. burs. ctrl. ops. and spl. ops., 1988-92, asst. dir. atty., 1992-94; judge. U.S. Dist. Ct. (Ctrl. Dist.) Calif., 1994—. Dep. gen. counsel Office Spl. Acad. scholar Howard U.; named Lawyer of Yr., Langston Bar Assn., 1988; honoree Howard U. Alumni Club So. Calif., 1989; recipient Profl. Achievement award UCLA Alumni Assn., 1997, Ernestine Stahlhut award, Women Lawyers Assn., 1999. Mem. FBA, Nat. Assn. Women Judges, Nat. Bar Assn. (life), State Bar Calif. (com. bar examiners, chmn. subcom. on moral character 1992-93, co-chmn. 1993-94), Los Angeles County Bar Assn. (exec. com. litigation sect.), Assn. Los Angeles County Dist. Attys. (pres. 1983), Black Women Lawyers Los Angeles County, Women Lawyers L.A. (life, Ernestine Stahlhut award 1999), Calif. Women Lawyers (life), Order of Coif, Phi Beta Kappa. Office: US Dist Ct Edward R Roybal Fed Bldg 255 E Temple St Ste 670 Los Angeles CA 90012-3334

COLLINS, CURTIS ALLAN, oceanographer; b. Sept. 16, 1940; s. Ralph Charlie and Noma Lovella (Buckley) C.; m. Judith Ann Petersen, Dec. 22, 1962; children: Nathaniel Christopher and Hillary Victoria. BS, U.S. Mcht. Marine Acad., 1962; MS, Oreg. State U., 1964, PhD, 1967. Instr. Chapman Coll. (Calif.) in Barcelona, Spain, 1964; 3d mate on ship Reynolds Metals, Corpus Christi, Tex., 1967-68; rsch. scientist Govt. of Can., Nanaimo, B.C., 1968-70; ocean engr. Cities Svc. Oil, Tulsa, 1970-72; program dir. NSF, Washington, 1972-87; prof. oceanography Naval Postgrad. Sch., Monterey, 1987—, chmn., 1987-94, chmn. faculty coun., 2002. Guest investigator Woods Hole Oceanographic Instn. (Mass.), 1983; commr. Moss Landing Harbor Dist., 1993-94, pres. 1994. vis. prof. U. Calif., Santa Cruz, 1998. Oceanography editor Geophys. Rsch. Letters, 1996-98. Capt. USNR, ret. Decorated Nat. Def. medal; recipient Admiral E.S. Land award Dept. Commerce, 1962, Meritorious Svc. award NSF, 1987, grad. fellow NSF, 1963-64, Fulbright fellow Instituto Investigaciones Oceanológicas U. Autonomia de Baja, Calif., 1994-95. Mem. Am. Geophys. Union (Oceans Scis. award 1985, pres. ocean scis. sect. 1993-94), Ocean Soc. Japan. Home: 24010 Ranchito Del Rio Ct Salinas CA 93908-9652 Office: Naval Postgrad Sch Code Occo-833 Dyer Rd Rm 331 Monterey CA 93943 E-mail: collins@nps.navy.mil

COLLINS, DENNIS ARTHUR, foundation executive; b. Yakima, Wash., June 9, 1940; s. Martin Douglas and Louise Constance (Caccia) C.; m. Mary Veronica Paul, June 11, 1966; children: Jenifer Ann, Lindsey Kathleen. BA, Stanford U., 1962, MA, 1963; LHD, Mills Coll., 1994. Assoc. dean admissions Occidental Coll., Los Angeles, 1964-66, dean admissions, 1966-68, dean of students, 1968-70; headmaster Emma Willard Sch., Troy, N.Y., 1970-74; founding headmaster San Francisco U. High Sch., 1974-86; pres. James Irvine Found., San Francisco, 1986—. Trustee Coll. Bd., N.Y.C., 1981-86, Ind. Ednl. Svcs., Princeton, N.J., 1981-85, Calif. Assn. Ind. Schs., L.A., 1982-86, Branson Sch., 1987-89, Aspen Inst. Nonprofit Sector rsch. Fund, 1992—; chmn. bd. So. Calif. Assn. Philanthropy, L.A., 1989-91, No. Calif. Grantmakers, 1987-90; dir. Rebuild L.A., 1992-93. Trustee Cathedral Sch. for Boys, San Francisco, 1976-82, Marin Country Day Sch., Corte Madera, Calif., 1978-84, San Francisco Exploratorium, 1984-86, Ind. Sector, Washington, 1987-95, Am. Farmland Trust, Washington, 1992—, bd. dirs., vice chmn. Children's Hosp. Found., San Francisco, 1984-86; chmn. bd. dirs. Coun. for Cmty. Based Devel., Washington, 1989-92. Mem. Council on Founds. Democrat. Episcopalian. Clubs: World Trade, University; California (L.A.). Home: 432 Golden Gate Ave Belvedere Tiburon CA 94920-2447 Office: The James Irvine Found 1 Market St Ste 2500 San Francisco CA 94105-1416

COLLINS, GILBERT WILSON, physicist; b. Livermore, Calif., Sept. 13, 1961; s. Gilbert Wilson and Betty Jean (Buchagen) C.; m. Rebecca Marie Carrozza, June 18, 1983; children: Gilbert Wilson, Natasha Marie, Alexander Brian. BSBA, U. Cin., 1983; MS, Ohio State U., 1986, PhD in Physics, 1989. Physicist Lawrence Livermore (Calif.) Nat. Lab., 1989—. Contbr. articles to profl. jours. including Phys. Rev. B., Phys. Rev. Letters. Mem. Am. Phys. Soc., Sigma Pi Sigma. Achievements include research on determination and characterization of storage and disposal mechanisms for energetic impurities in solid molecular hydrogen, of solid hydrogen containing energetic impurities and how may be used as the next generation of rocket propellents, of solid heavy hydrogen with no rotationally excited molecules and possibility of fuel with 50 percent higher cross section for nuclear fusion than unpolarized heavy hydrogen; determination of effect of unpaired atoms and electrons on molecular rotations and thermal transport in solid hydrogen. Home: 10655 Morgan Territory Rd Livermore CA 94550-9448 Office: Lawrence Livermore Lab PO Box 808 Mail Code L-482 7000 East Ave Livermore CA 94550-9516

COLLINS, JAMES FRANCIS, toxicologist; b. Balt., Jan. 26, 1942; s. James Murphy and Mary M. (Dolan) C.; m. Barbara Joan Betka, June 21, 1969; children: Chris, Cavan. BS, Loyola Coll., Balt., 1963; PhD, U.N.C., 1968. Diplomate Am. Bd. Toxicology. Fellow NIH, Bethesda, Md., 1968-75; faculty mem., rsch. chemist U. Tex. Health Sci. Ctr. and VA Med. Ctr., San Antonio, 1975-86; staff toxicologist Calif. EPA and Dept. Health Svcs., Oakland, Calif., 1986—. Instr. U. Calif. Berkeley/Extension, 1987-95; instr. U. San Francisco, 1995—. Contbr. numerous articles to profl. jours., publs. Mem. Am. Soc. Biochemistry and Molecular Biology. Democrat. Roman Catholic. Avocations: reading. Home: 822 Rogers Way Pinole CA 94564-2409 Office: Calif EPA 1515 Clay St Fl 16 Oakland CA 94612-1499 E-mail: jcollins@oehha.ca.gov, collins113@juno.com

COLLINS, JULIE, healthcare organization executive; Chief adminstrv. officer Sun Healthcare Group, Inc., Albuquerque, 1998—. Office: Sun Healthcare Group Inc 101 Sun Ave NE Albuquerque NM 87109-4373

COLLINS, MARIBETH WILSON, foundation president; b. Portland, Oreg., Oct. 27, 1918; d. Clarence True and Maude (Akin) Wilson; m. Truman Wesley Collins, Mar. 12, 1943; children: Timothy Wilson and Terry Stanton (twins), Cherida Smith, Truman Wesley Jr. BA, U. Oreg., 1940. Pres. Collins Found., Portland, Oreg., 1964—. Dir. Collins Pine Co., Collins Holding Co., Ostrander Resource Co. Bd. trustees Willamette U., Salem, Oreg., also mem. campus religious life. Mem. Univ. Club, Gamma Phi Beta. Republican. Methodist. Home: 2275 SW Mayfield Ave Portland OR 97225-4400 Office: Collins Found 1618 SW 1st Ave Ste 505 Portland OR 97201-5708

COLLINS, MARY, management consultant, former Canadian legislator; b. Vancouver, B.C., Can., Sept. 26, 1940; d. Fredrick Claude and Isabel Margaret (Copp) Wilkins; children: David, Robert, Sarah. Student, U. B.C., Queen's U., Kingston, Ont., Can.; LLD (hon.), Royal Rds. Mil. Coll., 1994. Mem. Can. Ho. of Commons, 1984-93; pres., CEO B.C. Health Assn., 1994-97; pres. Amarok Holdings, Ltd. Mem. fed. cabinet Can., assoc. min. nat. def., 1989-92, min. Western econ. diversification, 1993, min. state environ., 1993, min. responsible for status of women, 1990-93, min. of health, 1993; dir. Can. Blood Svcs. Trustee Queen's U.; bd. dirs. Vancouver Libr., Vancouver Bd. Trade, A.C. Global Corp. Mem. Internat. Womens Forum. Mem. Progressive Conservative Party. Office: Amarok Holdings Ltd 1185 W 7th Ave Vancouver BC Canada V6H 1B5 E-mail: amarok@telus.net

COLLINS, MICHAEL K. lawyer; b. Sikeston, Mo., Feb. 13, 1943; AB, Washington U., St. Louis, 1965, JD, 1969. Bar: Calif. 1970, U.S. Dist. Ct. (cen., so. and no. dists.) Calif. 1970, U.S. Ct. Appeals (9th cir.) 1970. With Greenberg, Glusker, Fields, Claman & Machtinger, L.A., 1969—. Editor-in-Chief Washington U. Law Quar., 1968-69. Mem. Assn. Bus. Trial Lawyers, State Bar Calif., L.A. County Bar Assn. (exec. com. real property sect. 1981-83), Century City Bar Assn., Order of Coif, Wilshire Hunting Club. Office: Greenberg Glusker Fields Claman & Machtinger Ste 2100 1900 Avenue Of The Stars Los Angeles CA 90067-4502

COLLINS, PATRICIA A. lawyer, judge; b. Camp Lejeune, N.C., Mar. 12, 1954; d. Thomas and Margaret (Parrish) C. BA, U. Va., 1976; JD, Gonzaga U., 1982. Bar: Alaska 1982, U.S. Dist. Ct. Alaska, U.S. Ct. Appeals (9th cir.) 1982. Assoc. Guess & Rudd, Anchorage and Juneau, 1982-84, 85-87; asst. pub. defender Alaska Pub. Defender's Office, Ketchikan, 1984-85; prin. Collins Law Office, Juneau, 1987-95; judge Alaska Dist. Ct., Ketchikan, 1995-1999, Juno Superior Ct., Alaska, 1999—. Part time fed. magistrate judge U.S. Cts., Juneau, 1988-95, Kitchikan, 1996—; adj. prof. U. Alaska, Juneau, 1991-95. Mem. Alaska Bar Assn., Ketchikan Sailing Club. Office: Alaska Superior Ct 114100 Juneau AK 99811-4100

COLLINS, RANER CHRISTERCUNEAN, judge; b. Malvern, Ark., July 8, 1952; m. Theresa Ann Ollison. BA in Sociology with honors, Ark. Poly. Coll., 1973; JD, U. Ariz., 1975. Bar: Ariz. 1976, U.S. Dist. Ct. Ariz. 1981. Laborer Reynolds Metals Co., Jones Mills, Ark., 1974; law clk. Pima County Atty.'s Office, Tucson, 1975-76, trial atty., 1976-81, atty. civic divsn., 1983-85; judge pro tem Pima County Superior Ct., Tucson, 1985-88, judge divsn. 22, 1988-98; presiding judge Juvenile Ct. divsn. 22 Pima County Juvenile Ct., Tucson, 1991-94; judge U.S. Dist. Ct. for Dist. Ariz., Tucson, 1998—; city magistrate City of Tucson, 1981-83. Bd. dirs. Ariz. Jud. Coll., 1995—, assoc. dean, 1998; chmn. Ariz. Jud. Conf., 1996.; mem. Jud. Performance Rev. Com., 1994—, Suprerior Ct. Com., 1995—. Bd. dirs. Info. and Referral Svc., sec., 1984-85; bd. dirs. The Haven, Inc., ptreas., 1984-85; bd. dirs. ARC, chmn. pers. com., 1988-91; trustee Gideon Missionary Bapt. Ch., 1993-96; bd. dirs. YMCA Triangle Ranch, 1994-95; mem. Black Student Support Group; mem. steering com. Tucson Police Dept., 1997—. Honor scholar United Steelworkers, Chester H. Smith Meml. scholar. Mem. NAACP, Ariz. Bar Assn., Ariz. Minority Bar Assn., Alpha Phi Alpha. Baptist. Office: US Dist Ct 55 E Broadway Blvd Rm 302 Tucson AZ 85701-1719

COLLINS, RICHARD FRANCIS, microbiologist, educator; b. St. Paul, Jan. 22, 1938; s. Francis Bernard and Maude Roegene (Night) C.; m. Deanne Margaret Scafati, Dec. 28, 1960 (div. 1970); children: Lisa, Mark, Michael; m. Judy A. Wright, Feb. 15, 1978; children: Kristyn, Todd. AB, Shepherd Coll., 1962; MA, Wake Forest U., 1968; PhD, U. Okla., 1973. Tchr. Alexandria (Va.) Schs., 1962-66; instr. U. Okla., Oklahoma City, 1972-73; lab. dir. Infectious Disease Svc. U. Ill./Rockford Sch. of Medicine, 1974-80; asst. prof. U. Ill., Rockford, 1973-80; assoc. prof. U. Osteo. Medicine and Health Scis., Des Moines, 1980-85, faculty pres., 1990-91, pres.-elect, 1997-98, prof., dept. head, 1985-95; prof., divsn. head Midwestern U., Glendale, 1997—. Cons. U.S. EPA, Washington, 1975-81; mem. Nat. Bd. Podiatry Examiners, Princeton, N.J., 1983-96, Nat. Bd. Osteo. Med. Examiners, Des Plaines, Ill., 1994-97; participant mission project Christian Med. Soc., Dominican Republic, 1977. Mem. editorial bd. African Jour. Clin. Exptl. Immunology, 1979-83; contbr. articles to profl. jours. Vol. Blank Guild Iowa Meth. Hosp., Des Moines, 1988-91. Recipient awards NSF, 1962-67, fellowship NIH, 1969-70, Gov.'s Vol.

awards State of Iowa, 1988, 89. Mem. Am. Soc. for Microbiology, Am. Soc. Tropical Medicine and Hygiene, Sigma Xi (pres. 1987-90, 96-97, treas. 1990-91). Avocations: photography, auto restoration. Home: 4131 W Tierra Buena Ln Phoenix AZ 85053-3717 Office: Midwestern U Ariz Coll Osteo Medicine 19555 N 59th Ave Glendale AZ 85308-6813 E-mail: rcolli@arizona.midwestern.edu

COLLINS, ROBERT OAKLEY, history educator; b. Waukegan, Ill., Apr. 1, 1933; s. William George and Louise Van Horsen (Jack) C.; m. Janyce Hutchins Monroe, Oct. 6, 1974; children by previous marriage: Catharine Louise, Randolph Ware, Robert William. BA, Dartmouth Coll., 1954; AB (Marshall scholar 1954-55), Balliol Coll., Oxford U., 1956, MA, 1960; MA (Ford fellow), Yale U., 1958, PhD, 1959. Instr. history Williams Coll., Williamstown, Mass., 1959-61; lectr. U. Mass. Extension, Pittsfield, 1960-61; vis. asst. prof. history Columbia U., N.Y.C., 1962-63; asst. prof. history Williams Coll., 1963-65; mem. faculty U. Calif., Santa Barbara, 1965—, prof. history, 1969-94, dir. Ctr. for Study Developing Nations, 1967-69, acting vice chancellor for research and grad. affairs, 1970-71, dean grad. div., 1971-80; prof. emeritus, 1994—; vis. sr. assoc. fellow St. Antony's Coll., Oxford U., Eng., 1980-81; Trevelyan fellow Durham U., 1986—. Dir. Washington Ctr. U. Calif., Santa Barbara, 1992-94; mem. Internat. Adv. Group for the Nile Basin, World Bank, 1997. Author: The Southern Sudan, 1883-1898, 1962, King Leopold, England and the Upper Nile, 1968, Problems in African History, 1968, The Partition of Africa, 1979, Land Beyond the Rivers: The Southern Sudan, 1898-1918, 1971, Europeans in Africa, 1971, An Arabian Diary, 1969, The Southern Sudan in Historical Perspective, 1975, Shadows in the Grass: Britain in the Southern Sudan, 1983, The British in the Sudan, 1898-56, 84, The Waters of the Nile: Hydropolitics and the Jonglei Canal, 1900-1988, 1990, Western African History, Eastern African History, Central and Southern African History, 1990, The Nile Waters: An Annotated Bibliography, 1991, Problems In African History, The Pre-Colonial Centuries, 1993, Requiem for the Sudan, 1994, Historical Problems of Imperial Africa, 1994, Problems in the History of Modern Africa, 1996, Africa's Thirty Years' War: Chad, Libya and the Sudan, 1963-1993, 1999, Historical Dictionary of Pre-Colonial Africa, 2001, Documents from the African Past, 2001. Recipient Gold class award Order Scis. and Arts Dem. Republic of Sudan, 1980; John Ben Snow Found. prize, 1984; NDEA lang. fellow, 1960-61, Social Sci. Rsch. Coun. fellow, 1962-63; Rockefeller Found. scholar-in-residence Bellagio, Italy, 1979, 87; Ford Found. fellow, 1979-81; Fulbright sr. rsch. fellow, 1982, 90; Woodrow Wilson fellow, 1983; vis. fellow Trevelyan Coll. mem. Soc. Fellows Durham U., 1986, fellow Balliol Coll., Oxford U., 1986-87; fellow Am. Coun. Learned Soc. 1990. Fellow Am. Philos. Soc.; mem. Am. Hist. Assn., African Studies Assn., Western River Guides Assn., Sudan Studies Assn., Explorers Club, Phi Beta Kappa. Home: 735 Calle De Los Amigos Santa Barbara CA 93105-4438 Office: U Calif Dept History Santa Barbara CA 93106

COLLINS, RUSSELL AMBROSE, retired advertising executive, creative director; BA, U. Calif., Berkeley, 1976; postgrad., U. Calif., Irvine, 1978-80. Project dir. Douglas Boyd Design & Mktg., L.A., 1980-82; pres., exec. creative dir. Fattal & Collins, Santa Monica, Calif., 1982-87; pres., exec. creative dir., vice chmn. GEM/Fattal & Collins, Santa Monica, 1987-99; ret., 1999. Recipient Clio award Art Dirs. Club N.Y.; Belding award Art Dirs. Club L.A., Lulu award, Key Art award.

COLLINS, TERRY, professional baseball manager; b. Midland, Mich., May 27, 1949; Mgr. Houston Astros, 1994-96, Anaheim Angels, 1996-99. Office: Anaheim Angels 2000 Gene Autry Way Anaheim CA 92806-6100

COLLINS, THEODORE JOHN, lawyer; b. Walla Walla, Wash., Oct. 2, 1936; s. Robert Bonfield and Catherine Roselle (Snyder) C.; m. Patricia Spengler Pasieka, May 11, 1968; children: Jonathan, Caitlin, Matthew, Patrick, Flannary. BA, U. Notre Dame, 1958; postgrad., U. Bonn, Fed. Republic Germany, 1959; LLB, Harvard U., 1962. Bar: Wash. 1962, U.S. Supreme Ct. 1982, U.S. Ct. Appeals (fed. cir.) 1982, U.S. Dist. Ct. (ea. dist.) Wash. 1965, U.S. Dist. Ct. (we. dist.) Wash. 1962. Ptnr. Perkins Coie Law Firm, Seattle, 1962-86; v.p., gen. counsel The Boeing Co., Seattle, 1986-98, sr. v.p., gen. counsel, 1998-2000; of counsel Perkins Coie Law Firm, 2001—. Adj. prof. Seattle U. Law Sch. Mem. ABA, Boeing Mgmt. Assn., Wash. State Bar Assn., King County Bar Assn., Wash. Athletic Club. E-mail: tcoll10236@aol.com, collt@perkinscoie.com

COLLINS, WILLIAM LEROY, telecommunications engineer; b. Laurel, Miss., June 17, 1942; s. Henry L. and Christene E. (Finnegan) C. Student, La Salle U., 1969; BS in Computer Sci., U. Beverly Hills, 1984. Sr. computer operator Dept. Pub. Safety, Phoenix, 1975-78, data communications specialist, 1978 79, supr. computer ops., 1981-82; mgr. network control Valley Nat. Bank, Phoenix, 1979-81; mgr. data communications Ariz. Lottery, Phoenix, 1982-85; mgr. telecommunications Calif. Lottery, Sacramento, 1985—. Mem. Telecomm. Study Mission to Russia, Oct. 1991. Contbr. to profl. publs. Served as sgt. USAF, 1964-68. Mem. IEEE, Nat. Sys. Programmers Assn., Centrex Users Group, DMS Centrex User Group, Accunet Digital Svcs. User Group, Telecomms. Assn. (v.p. edn. Sacramento Valley chpt. 1990-94, pres. 1995, chpt. assn. dir. 1996-97, chpt. past pres. 1996, Prestigious Svc. award 1997), Telecom. Assn. (chmn. corp. edn. com. 1994-95, conf. com. 1994-95, co-chair conf. program com. 1996, program dir. edn. 1996, corp. dir. edn. 1996-97, pres.-elect 1998, pres. and ceo, 1999), SynOptics User Group, Timeplex User Group, Assn. Data Comm. Users, Soc. Mfg. Engrs., Data Processing Mgmt. Assn., Am. Mgmt. Assn., Assn. Computing Machinery, Am. Soc. for Quality Control, Bldg. Industry Cons. Svc. Internat., Assn. for Quality and Participation, KC, Calif. Integrated Svcs. Digital Network User Group, Computer Security Inst., Assn. Pub. Comms. Officials, Armed Forces Comms. and Electronics Assn., Assn. Info. Tech. Profls., H.P. Open View Forum. Roman Catholic. Home: 116 Valley Oak Dr Roseville CA 95678-4378 Office: Calif State Lottery 600 N 10th St Sacramento CA 95814-0393

COLLINSON, JEFFREY JOSEPH, venture capitalist; b. Springfield, Ohio, Nov. 26, 1941; s. Joseph Bruard and Jean Brock (Crayton) C.; m. Sharon Jewils, July 2, 1966; children: Robin, Christy, Andrew. BA, Yale U., 1963; MBA, Harvard Bus. Sch., 1966. Pres. Schroder Venture Mgrs., N.Y.C., 1981-90, Collinson Howe Venture Ptnrs., Stamford, Conn., 1990—. Bd. dirs. Incyte Pharms., Palo Alto, Calif., Neurogen Corp., Branford, Conn., Intensiva Healthcare Corp., Clayton, Mo. Office: Incyte Pharmaceuticals Inc 3174 Porter Dr Palo Alto CA 94304

COLLMAN, JAMES PADDOCK, chemistry educator; b. Beatrice, Nebr., Oct. 31, 1932; married. B.Sc., U. Nebr., 1954, M.S., 1956; Ph.D. (NSF fellow), U. Ill., 1958; Docteur Honoris Causa, U. Dijon, France, 1988, U. Borgogne, 1988; D (hon.), U. Nebr., 1988. Instr. chemistry U. N.C., Chapel Hill, 1958-59, asst. prof., 1959-62, asso. prof., 1962-67; prof. chemistry Stanford U., 1967—; George A. and Hilda M. Daubert prof. chemistry Stanford U., 1980—. Frontiers in Chemistry lectr., 1964, Nebr. lectureship, 1968; Venable lectr. U. N.C., 1971; Edward Clark Lee lectr. U. Chgo., 1972; vis. Erskine fellow U. Canterbury, 1972; Plenary lectr. French Chem. Soc., 1974; Dreyfus lectr. U. Kans., 1974; Disting. inorganic lectr. U. Rochester, 1974; Reilley lectr. U. Notre Dame, 1975; William Pyle Philips lectr. Haverford Coll., 1975; Merck lectr. Rutgers U., 1976; FMC lectr. Princeton, 1977; Julius Steiglitz lectr. Chgo. sect. Am. Chem. Soc., 1977; Pres.'s Seminar Series lectr. U. Ariz., 1980; Frank C. Whitmore lectr. Pa. State U., 1980; Plenary lectr. 3d IUPAC Symposium on Organic Synthesis, 1980, 2d Internat. Kyoto Conf. on New Aspects Inorganic Chemistry, 1982, Internat. Symposium on Models of Enzyme Action, Brighton, Eng., 1983, Internat. Symposium, Italy, 1984; Brockman lectr. U. Ga., 1981; Samuel C. Lind lectr. U. Tenn., 1981, Syntex Disting. lectr. Colo. State U., 1983; Disting. vis. lectr. U. Fla., 1983; vis. prof. U. Auckland, New Zealand, 1985; Nelson J. Leonard lectr. U. Ill., 1987; plenary lectr. Internat. Symposium on Activation of Dioxygen and Homogeneous Catalytic Oxygenations, Tsukuba, Japan, 1987; plenary lectr. 12th Internat. Symposium on Macrocyclic Chem., Hiroshima, Japan, 1987; lectr. Texas A&M, 1988; J. Clarence Karcher lectr. U. Okla., 1989; Musselman lectr. Gettysburg Coll., 1990; Davis lectr. U. New Orleans, 1991; PLU lectr. Okla. State U., 1991; lectr. 5th Internat. Fischer Symposium, Karlsruhe, Ger., 1991; lectr. Euchem Conf., 1991; Pratt lectr. U. Va., 1992, others; lectr. series Harvard/MIT, 1992, Yale U., 1993; invited speaker symposia, univs., confs. Recipient Disting. Teaching award Stanford U., 1981, Calif. Scientist of Year award, 1983, Allan V. Cox medal for excellence in fostering undergrad. rsch., 1988, LAS Alumni Achievement award Coll. Liberal Arts and Scis. U. Ill., 1994, John C. Bailar Jr. medal, 1995, Joseph Chatt medal Royal Soc., 1998; named George A. and Hilda M. Daubert Prof. Chemistry (endowed chair, Stanford U.), 1980; Guggenheim fellow, 1977-78, 85-86, Churchill fellow, Cambridge, 1977—, Bing fellow, 1996. Fellow Calif. Acad. Sci. (hon.); mem. Am. Chem. Soc. (Calif. sect. award 1972, soc. award in inorganic chemistry 1975, Arthur C. Cope scholar 1986, Pauling award Puget Sound and Oreg. sect. 1990, Disting. Svc. award in inorganic chemistry 1991, Alfred Bader award in bioinorganic or bioorganic chemistry 1997, Joseph Chatt lectr. 1998, Marker lectr. medal 1999), N.Y. Acad. Sci. (Basolo medal 2000), Chem. Soc. (London), Nat. Acad. Sci., Am. Acad. Arts and Scis., Phi Beta Kappa, Sigma Xi, Phi Lambda Upsilon, Alpha Chi Epsilon. Office: Stanford U Dept Chemistry Stanford CA 94305

COLSON, ELIZABETH FLORENCE, anthropologist; b. Hewitt, Minn., June 15, 1917; d. Louis H. and Metta (Damon) C. BA, U. Minn., 1938, MA, 1940, Radcliffe Coll., 1941, PhD, 1945; PhD (hon.), Brown U., 1978, D of Sociology, 1979; D.Sc., U. Rochester, 1985, U. Zambia, 1992. Asst. social sci. analyst War Relocation Authority, 1942-43; research asst. Harvard, 1944-45; research officer Rhodes-Livingstone Inst., 1946-47, dir., 1948-51; sr. lectr. Manchester U., 1951-53; assoc. prof. Goucher Coll., 1954-55; research assoc., assoc. prof. African Research Program, Boston U., 1955-59, part-time, 1959-63; prof. anthropology Brandeis U., 1959-63, U. Calif.-Berkeley, 1964-84, prof. emeritus, 1984—; vis. prof. U. Zambia, 1987. Lewis Henry Morgan lectr. U. Rochester, 1973; vis. rsch. assoc. Refugee Studies Program Queen Elizabeth House, Oxford, 1988-89. Author: The Makah, 1953, Marriage and the Family Among The Plateau Tonga, 1958, Social Organization of the Gwembe Tonga, 1960, The Plateau Tonga, 1962, The Social Consequences of Resettlement, 1971, Tradition and Contract, 1974, A History of Nampeyo, 1992; jr. author Secondary Education and the Formation of an Elite, 1980, Voluntary Efforts in Decentralized Management, 1983, sr. author For Prayer and Profit, 1988; sr. editor: Seven Tribes of British Central Africa, 1951; jr. editor People in Upheaval, 1987. AAUW travelling fellow, 1941-42, fellow Ctr. Advanced Study Behavioral Scis., 1967-68, Fairchild fellow Calif. Inst. Tech., 1975-76. Fellow Am. Anthrop. Assn., Assn. Social Anthropologists of the Commonwealth, Royal Anthrop. Inst. (hon.); mem. Nat. Acad. Sci., Am. Acad. Arts and Scis., Am. Assn. African Studies (Disting. Africanist award 1988), Soc. Applied Anthropology, Soc. Woman Geographers, Phi Beta Kappa. Avocations: walking, opera, reading. Office: U Calif Dept Anthropology Berkeley CA 94720-0001

COLSON, WILLIAM E. management company executive; Founder Holiday Mgmt. Co. (Holiday Retirement Corp.), 1970—; pres., mng. gen. ptnr. Colson & Colson Construction Co.; pres. Colson & Colson Gen. Contractor, Inc. Bd. dirs. mem Emeritus Corp.; exec. bd. mem. Am. Srs. Housing Assn. Office: Holiday Retirement Corp PO Box 1411 Salem OR 97309

COLTEN, HARVEY RADIN, pediatrician, educator; b. Houston, Jan. 11, 1939; s. Oscar Aaron and Zina Mae (Radin) C.; m. Susan J. Kaplowitz, July 29, 1959; children: Jennifer J., Lora, Charles Thomas. BA, Cornell U., 1959; MD, Western Res. U., 1963; MA (hon.), Harvard U., 1978. Diplomate Am. Bd. Allergy and Clin. Immunology, Am. Bd. Pediats. Intern Univ. Hosps., Cleve., 1963-64, resident in pediat., 1964-65, Children's Hosp. of D.C., Washington, 1968-69; rsch. assoc. Nat. Inst. Child and Human Devel., NIH, Bethesda, Md., 1965-67; asst. prof. pediat. George Washington U., 1969-70; from asst. prof. pediat. to prof. Harvard U., 1970-86; chief divsn. cell biology, dir. cystic fibrosis program Children's Hosp. Med. Ctr., Boston, 1976-86; pediatrician-in-chief Jewish Hosp., 1986-89; Harriet B. Spoehrer prof. pediat. Washington U. Med. Sch., St. Louis, 1986-97, chmn. dept. pediat., 1986-95; pediatrician-in-chief Children's and Barnes Hosps., 1986-95; dean, v.p. med. affairs Northwestern U. Sch. Medicine, Chgo., 1997-99; pres. iMetrikus, Inc., Carlsbad, Calif., 2000—. Prof. pediat. and microbiology/immunology Northwestern U. Sch. Medicine, 1999-2000; clin. prof. pediatrics U. Calif., San Francisco, 2001—; past chmn. pediat. allergy Nat. Inst. Allergy and Infectious Disease Task Force on Asthma and Allergy; past mem. Nat. Inst. Child and Human Devel. Task Force on Cystic Fibrosis; past rsch. rev. com. Nat. Cystic Fibrosis Found.; past mem. pulmonary diseases adv. com. NIH. Assoc. editor Jour. Immunology, 1971-74, Immunochemistry, 1972-75, Jour. Allergy and Clin. Immunology, 1977-80, New Eng. Jour. Medicine, 1978-81, Jour. Clin. Investigation, 1982-85, Am. Jour. Respiratory Cell and Molecular Biology, 1988-91, New Insights into CF, 1993-94; mem. editl. bd. Molecular and Cellular Biochemistry, 1983-87, Jour. Pediat., 1981-88, Jour. Clin. Immunology, 1985-89, Ann. Rev. Immunology, 1986-90, Clin. Immunology and Immunopathology, 1987-91, Blood, 1987-92, New Eng. Jour. Medicine, 1990-98, Jour. Biomed. Sci., 1992—, Proc. Assn. Am. Physicians, 1995-99, Encyclopedia of Life Scis., 1997—; contbr. articles to profl. jours. Vice-chmn. bd. dirs. Parents As Tchrs. Nat. Ctr.; bd. dirs. The Oasis Inst., Immtech Internat. Inc.; past mem. pediat. scientist program selection com. AMSPDC; sci. adv. coun. March of Dimes; mem. Nat. Heart, Lung, Blood Adv. Coun., NIH; past bd. mgrs. Ctrl. Inst. for Deaf. Recipient Spl. Faculty Rsch. award Western Res. U., 1963, E. Mead Johnson award, 1979. Fellow AAAS, Am. Acad. Allergy and Immunology, Am. Acad. Pediat.; mem. NAS (vice-chmn. coun. Inst. Medicine 1997—), Fedn. Am. Socs. for Exptl. Biology, E. Mead Johnson Award Program Com. (past chmn.), Am. Assn. Immunologists (past sec.-treas., Disting. Svc. award), Am. Soc. Clin. Investigation, Assn. Am. Physicians, Soc. Pediat. Rsch., Am. Pediat. Soc., Am. Thoracic Soc., Am. Soc. Biochem. & Molecular Biol., Hungarian Soc. Immunology (hon.). Office: iMetrikus 5950 LaPlace Ct Carlsbad CA 92008

COLTMAN, KYLE, diversified financial services company executive; BA in Econs., U. Calif., San Diego; MBA in Fin., U. Calif., Berkeley. With Menke & Assocs., San Francisco, 1979—, CEO. Office: Menke & Assocs 690 Market St 12th Fl San Francisco CA 94104-5113

COLTON, DAVID S. lawyer, company executive; b. 1955; BA in Econs., JD, Brigham Young U. Ptnr. VanCott, Bagley, Cornwall & McCarthy, Salt Lake City; exploration counsel Phelps Dodge, Phoenix, 1988-95; v.p. Phelps Dodge Exploration Corp., 1995-98; v.p., gen. counsel Phelps Dodge, 1998-99, sr. v.p., gen. counsel, 1999—, mem. sr. mgmt. team, 1999—. Mem. ABA, Utah Bar Assn. Office: 2600 N Central Ave Phoenix AZ 85004-3050

COLTON, ROY CHARLES, management consultant; b. Phila., Feb. 26, 1941; s. Nathan Hale and Ruth Janis (Baylinson) C. BA, Knox Coll., 1962; MEd, Temple U., 1963. With Sch. Dist. of Phila., 1963-64; sys. analyst Wilmington Trust Co., 1967-69; exec. recruiter Atwood Consultants Inc., Phila., 1969-71; pres. Colton Bernard Inc., San Francisco, 1971—. Occasional lectr. Fashion Inst. Tech., Phila. Coll. Textiles and Scis. Served with AUS, 1964-66. Mem. San Francisco Fashion Industries, San Francisco C. of C., Calif. Exec. Recruiter Assn., Nat. Assn. Exec. Recruiters, Am. Apparel Mfrs. Assn., Am. Arbitration Assn. (panel arbitrators). Office: Colton Bernard Inc 870 Market St Ste 822 San Francisco CA 94102-2921 Fax: 415-399-0750. E-mail: rcolton@coltonbernard.com

COLUMBUS, CHRIS, film director, screenwriter; b. Spangler, Pa., Sept. 10, 1958; s. Alex Michael and Mary Irene (Puskar) C. BFA, NYU, 1980. Writer: (films) Reckless, 1983, Gremlins, 1984, Goonies, 1985, Young Sherlock Holmes, 1985, Little Nemo, 1992; dir.: (films) Adventures in Babysitting, 1987, Home Alone, 1990, Home Alone 2: Lost in New York, 1992, Mrs. Doubtfire, 1993; dir., writer: (films) Heartbreak Hotel, 1988, Only the Lonely, 1991; dir., writer, prodr.: Nine Months, 1995; dir., prodr.: Stepmom, 1998, Bicentennial Man, 1999; prodr.: Jingle All the Way, 1996, Monkey Bone, 1999. Democrat. Office: CAA c/o Beth Swofford 9830 Wilshire Blvd Beverly Hills CA 90212-1804

COLVIN, HARRY WALTER, JR. physiology educator; b. Schellsburg, Pa., Dec. 5, 1921; s. Harry Walter and Maude Elizabeth (Girven) C.; m. Marie Catherine McNinch, Apr. 8, 1950; children: Sarah Lee, William McNinch. BS, Pa. State U., 1950; PhD, U. Calif., Davis, 1957. Instr. Okla. State U., Stillwater, 1955-57; assoc. prof. physiology U. Ark., Fayetteville, 1957-65; prof. U. Calif., Davis, 1965—. Cons. Pel-Freez Biologicals, Inc., Rogers, Ark., 1960-65. Assoc. editor Hilgardia, 1981-92; contbr. articles to profl. jours. Served with U.S. Army, 1942-45, ETO. Recipient Fulbright award CIES, Washington, 1972, 86. Mem. Am. Dairy Sci. Assn., Am. Soc. Animal Sci., Sigma Xi, Phi Kappa Phi, Alpha Zeta, Gamma Sigma Delta, Phi Sigma , Phi Eta Sigma. Republican. Club: El Macero (Calif.) Country. Avocations: golf, flying. Home: 1515 Shasta Dr Apt 3326 Davis CA 95616 Office: U Calif Davis Dept Neurobiology Physiol & Behavior Davis CA 95616

COLWELL, KENT LEIGH, real estate counselor, investor; b. Pasadena, Calif., Feb. 21, 1931; s. Max F. and Ruth (Chamberlain) C.; m. Margaret Hayes, Nov. 9, 1963; children: David, Hilary, Stacy. BA, Stanford U., 1951; MBA, Harvard U., 1957. Asst. to pres. Transam. Corp., San Francisco, 1962-64, v.p. real estate svcs., 1977-96; fin. v.p. Bankers Mortgage Co., San Francisco, 1965-68, pres., 1968-84; trustee, sec. Mortgage Trust Am. (name later Transam. Realty Investors), San Francisco, 1969-72, trustee, pres., 1973-86; pres. Transam Realty Svcs., San Francisco, 1972-96, Ventana Inn, Inc., Big Sur, Calif., 1980-97; ltd. ptnr. Montreux Equity Ptnrs., 1997-98; prin. Parthenon Assocs., San Francisco, 1998—. Dir. Custom Diversification and Fund Mgmt., Inc.; bd. dirs. Bridge Housing Corp., San Francisco. Lt. USN, 1952-55. Baker scholar Harvard U. Bus. Sch., 1957. Mem. Am. Soc. Real Estate Counselors (cert.), Urban Land Inst., Nat. Assn. Real Estate Investment Trusts (nat. pres. 1984), Bankers Club, Lagunitas Club (Ross, Calif.), Phi Beta Kappa, Lambda Alpha. Office: Parthenon Assocs Penthouse 10 220 Montgomery St San Francisco CA 94104-3402

COMANOR, WILLIAM S. economist, educator; b. Phila., May 11, 1937; s. Leroy and Sylvia (Bershad) C.; m. Joan Thall; children: Christine, Katherine, Lauren, Gregory. Student, Williams Coll., 1955-57; BA, Haverford Coll., 1959; MA, PhD, Harvard U., 1963; postgrad., London Sch. Econs., 1963-64. Spl. econ. asst. to asst. atty. gen. Antitrust div. U.S. Dept. Justice, Washington, 1965-66; asst. prof. econs. Harvard U., Cambridge, Mass., 1966-68; assoc. prof. Stanford (Calif.) U., 1968-73; dir. bur. econs. FTC, Washington, 1978-80; prof. econs. U. Calif., Santa Barbara, 1975—, dept. chmn., 1984 87, prof. Sch. Pub. Health L.A., 1990—. Author: National Health Insurance in Ontario, 1980, Advertising and Market Power, 1974, Competition Policy in Europe and North America, 1990, Competition Policy in the Global Economy, 1997; contbr. articles to profl. jours. Mem. Am. Econ. Assn. Home: 519 S Arden Blvd Los Angeles CA 90020-4737 Office: U Calif Dept Econs Santa Barbara CA 93106 E-mail: comanor@ucla.edu

COMES, ROBERT GEORGE, research scientist; b. Bangor, Pa., July 7, 1931; s. Victor Francis and Mabel Elizabeth (Mack) C.; student U. Detroit, 1957-58, Oreg. State Coll., 1959-60, U. Nev., 1960, Regis Coll., 1961-62; m. Carol Lee Turinetti, Nov. 28, 1952; children: Pamela Jo, Robert G. II, Shawni Lee, Sheryl Lynn, Michelle Ann. Tech. liaison engr. Burroughs Corp., Detroit, 1955-60, mgr. reliability and maintainability engring., Paoli, Pa., 1962-63, Colorado Springs, Colo., 1963-67; sr. engr. Martin Marietta Corp., Denver, 1960-62; program mgr., rsch. scientist Kaman Scis. Corp., Colorado Springs, 1967-75; dir. engring. Sci. Applications, Inc., Colorado Springs, 1975-80; mgr. space def. programs Burroughs Corp., Colorado Springs, 1980-82; tech. staff Mitre Corp., Colorado Springs, 1982-85; dir. Colorado Springs opn. Beers Assoc., Inc., 1985; dir. space programs Electro Magnetic Applications, Inc., Colorado Springs, 1985-87; dir. Space Systems, Profl. Mgmt. Assocs., Inc., 1987-88; mgr. Computer Svcs., Inc., Colorado Springs, 1989—; dir. mktg. Proactive Techs., Inc., Colorado Springs, 1990—; chmn. Reliability and Maintainability Data Bank Improvement Program, Govt.-Industry Data Exch. Program, 1978-80—; cons. in field. Youth dir. Indian Guides program YMCA, 1963-64; scoutmaster Boy Scouts Am., 1972-73; chmn. bd. dirs. Pikes Peak Regional Sci. Fair, 1972-84. Served with USAF, 1951-55. Mem. AAAS, IEEE, Inst. Environ. Scis., Soc. Logistics Engrs., Am. Soc. Quality Control. Lutheran. Club: Colorado Springs Racquet. Author: Maintainability Engineering Principles and Standards, 1962. Inventor Phase Shifting aircraft power supply, 1957. Home and Office: Proactive Tech Inc 4309 Tipton Ct Colorado Springs CO 80915-1034

COMFORT, ROBERT DENNIS, lawyer; b. Camden, N.J., Nov. 22, 1950; s. Joseph Albert Sr. and Elizabeth (Rogers) C.; m. Loretta Masullo, Aug. 24, 1974; 1 child, Adam. AB summa cum laude, Princeton U., 1973; JD magna cum laude, Harvard U., 1976. Bar: Pa. 1976, N.J. 1977, U.S. Dist. Ct. N.J. 1977, U.S. Dist. Ct. (ea. dist.) Pa. 1977, U.S. Ct. Appeals (3d cir.) 1977, U.S. Tax Ct. 1978, U.S. Claims Ct. 1983. Law clk. to Hon. James Hunter III U.S. Ct. Appeals 3d Cir., Phila., 1976-77; law clk. to Lewis F. Powell Jr. U.S. Supreme Ct., Washington, 1977-78; assoc. Morgan, Lewis & Bockius, Phila., 1978-82, ptnr., 1982-2000; v.p. tax and tax policy Amazon.com, Seattle, 2000—. Adj. prof. U. Pa. Law Sch., Rutgers-Camden Law Sch. Mem. ABA, Phila. Bar Assn. (vice chair tax sect. 1990-92, chair 1993-94). Avocations: golf, camping, music, history, fishing. Office: Amazon.com PO Box 81226 Seattle WA 98108-1300

COMINGS, DAVID EDWARD, physician, medical genetics scientist; b. Beacon, N.Y., Mar. 8, 1935; s. Edward Walter and Jean (Rice) C.; m. Shirley Nelson, Aug. 9, 1958; children: Mark David, Scott Edward, Karen Jean.; m. Brenda Gursey, Mar. 20, 1982. Student, U. Ill., 1951-54; BS, Northwestern U., 1955, MD, 1958. Intern Cook County Hosp., Chgo., 1958-59, resident in internal medicine, 1959-62; fellow in med. genetics U. Wash., Seattle, 1964-66; dir. dept. med. genetics City of Hope Med. Ctr., Duarte, Calif., 1966—. Mem. genetics study sect. NIH, 1974-78; mem. sci. adv. bd. Hereditary Disease Found., 1975— , Nat. Found. March of Dimes, 1978-92. Author: Tourette Syndrome and Human Behavior, 1990, Search for the Tourette Syndrome and Human Behavior Genes, 1996, The Gene Bomb, 1996; editor: (with others) Molecular Human Cytogenetics, 1977; mem. editorial bd.: (with others) Cytogenetics and Cell genetics, 1979—; editor in chief Am. Jour. Human Genetics, 1978-86. Served with U.S. Army, 1962-64. NIH grantee, 1967— Mem. Assn. Am. Physicians, Am. Soc. Clin. Investigation, AAAS, Am. Soc. Human Genetics (dir. 1974-78, pres. 1988), Am. Soc. Cell Biology, Am. Fedn. Clin. Research, Western Soc. Clin. Research, Council Biology Editors. Office: City Hope Med Ctr 1500 Duarte Rd Duarte CA 91010-3000

COMISAROW, MELVIN B. chemist, educator; Prof. dept. chemistry U. B.C., Vancouver, Canada. Recipient Barringer award Spectroscopy Soc. Can., 1989, award in chem. analysis and instrumentation Royal Soc. Chemistry, 1993, Frank H. Field and Joe L. Franklin award Am. Chem. Soc., 1995, Fisher Sci. award Can. Soc. Chemistry, 1996, Killam Rsch. award U. B.C., 1996, Disting. Contbn. award Am. Soc. Mass Spectrometry, 1999. Fellow Royal Soc. Can. Office: U British Columbia Dept Chemistry Vancouver BC Canada V6T 1Z1

COMMANDER, EUGENE R. lawyer; b. Sioux City, Iowa, Jan. 10, 1953; BA in Architecture, Iowa State U., 1975; JD with distinction, U. Iowa, 1977. Bar: Iowa 1977, Colo. 1981. Mem. Hall & Evans, LLC, Denver, 1981—. Mem. ABA (forum com. on constrn. industry, subcoms. on bonds, liens, ins. and contract documents, tort and ins. practice sect. coms. on fidelity, surety law, property ins.), AIA (profl. affiliate, Colo. chpt.), Am. Arbitration Assn. (panel constrn. industry arbitrators 1983—), Am. Law Firm Assn. (constrn. industry practice group), Def. Rsch. Inst. (constrn. law and fidelity and surety law coms.), Profl. Liability Underwriting Soc. Office: Hall & Evans LLC 1200 17th St Ste 1700 Denver CO 80202-5817

COMPTON, ALLEN T. retired state supreme court justice; b. Kansas City, Mo., Feb. 25, 1938; 3 children. B.A., U. Kans., 1960; LL.B., U. Colo., 1963. Pvt. practice, Colorado Springs, 1963-68; staff atty. Legal Svcs. Office, Colorado Springs, 1968-69, dir., 1969-71; supervising atty. Alaska Legal Svcs., Juneau, Alaska, 1971-73; pvt. practice Juneau, 1973-76; judge Superior Ct., Alaska, 1976-80; justice Alaska Supreme Ct., Anchorage, 1980-98, state supreme ct. chief justice, 1995-97, ret., 1998. Part-time judge Alaska Supreme Ct. Mem. 4 bar assns. including Juneau Bar Assn. (past pres.) Office: Alaska Supreme Ct 303 K St Anchorage AK 99501-2013

COMRIE, SANDRA MELTON, human resource executive; b. Plant City, Fla., Sept. 15, 1940; d. Finis and Estelle (Black) Melton; m. Allan Crecelius; children: Shannon Melissa, Colleen Megan. BA, UCLA, 1962, grad. exec. program, 1984. Div. mgr. City of L.A., 1973-77, asst. pers. dir., 1977-84; v.p. Transam. Life Cos., L.A., 1984-89; chief operating officer Treacy & Rhodes Consultants, Solana Beach, Calif., 1989-92; exec. dir. Reward Strategy Group, Inc., Del Mar, 1992-98. Bd. dirs. Found. for Employment and Disability, Sacramento, Clif.; mem. Asian Pacific Employment Task Force, Los Angeles, 1986-89. Bd. dirs. L.A. Urban League, 1985-92, Vols. of Am.-L.A., 1985-89; active United Way Downtown Bus. Consortium, Child Care Task Force, L.A., 1985-86; mem. adv. bd. L.A. City Child Care, 1987-89. Recipient Young Woman of Achievement award Soroptimists of Los Angeles, 1979. Mem. Internat. Pers. Mgmt. Assn. (mem. assessment coun., co-chair program com. for 1982 nat. conf., chair human rights com. 1983, pres. 1985), So. Calif. Pers. Mgmt. Assn., Planning Forum, Human Resource Planning Soc., Soc. for Human Resource Mgmt., Am. Compensation Assn., Am. Mgmt. Assn., L.A. C. of C. (human resources com. 1986-89). Democrat. Avocation: travel. Office: Reward Strategy Group Inc 2775 Via De La Valle Ste 200 Del Mar CA 92014-1920

COMSTOCK, DALE ROBERT, mathematics educator; b. Frederic, Wis., Jan. 18, 1934; s. Walter and Frances (Lindroth) C.; m. Mary Jo Lien, Aug. 18, 1956; children— Mitchell Scott, Bryan Paul. BA, Ctrl. Wash. State Coll., 1955; MS, Oreg. State U., 1962, PhD, 1966. Tchr. math. Kennewick (Wash.) High Sch., 1955-57, 59-60; instr. Columbia Basin Coll., Pasco, Wash., 1956-57, 59-60; programmer analyst Gen. Electric Co., Hanford Atomic Works, Richland, 1963; prof. math. Cen. Wash. U., Ellensburg, 1964—, dean Grad. Sch. and Research, 1970-90; on leave as sr. program mgr. U.S. ERDA, also Presdl. interchange exec., 1976-77; mem. Pres.'s Commn. on Exec. Devel., 1976-77; bd. dirs. Council Grad. Schs. in U.S., 1981-84, dean in residence, 1984-85. Cons. Indian program NSF, 1968, 69, USIA, India, 1985, NSF, Saudi Arabia, 1986; mem. grant proposal rev. panels NSF, 1970, 71, 76, 77, 89, 90; pres. Western Assn. Grad. Schs., 1979-80, sec.-treas. 1984-90; pres. N.W. Assn. Colls. and Univs. for Sci., 1988-89; Russian exch. prof., St. Petersburg, 1993; vis. prof. U. Wash., 1990-91. With U.S. Army, 1957-59. NSF fellow, 1960-61; grantee, summer 1964 Mem. Am. Math Soc., Math. Assn. Am., Assn. Computing Machinery (exec. com.), Soc. Indsl. and Applied Math., Northwest Coll. and Univ. Assn. for Sci. (pres. 1980-83) Methodist. Office: Cen Wash U Dept Math Ellensburg WA 98926

COMUS, LOUIS FRANCIS, JR. lawyer; b. St. Marys, Ohio, Feb. 26, 1942; BA, Antioch Coll., 1965; JD, Vanderbilt U., 1968. Bar: N.Y. 1969, Ariz. 1973. Dir. Fennemore Craig P.C., Phoenix, 1975—. Notes editor Vanderbilt Law Rev., 1967-68. Fellow Am. Coll. Trust and Estate Counsel; mem. ABA, State Bar Ariz., Maricopa County Bar Assn., Order of Coif. Office: Fennemore Craig PC 3003 N Central Ave Ste 2600 Phoenix AZ 85012-2913 E-mail: lcomus@fclaw.com

CONDIE, CAROL JOY, anthropologist, research facility administrator; b. Provo, Utah, Dec. 28, 1931; d. LeRoy and Thelma (Graff) C.; m. M. Kent Stout, June 18, 1954; children: Carla Ann, Erik Roy, Paula Jane. BA in Anthropology, U. Utah, 1953; MEd in Elem. Edn., Cornell U., 1954; PhD in Anthropology, U. N.Mex., 1973, Quivira Rsch. Ctr. Edn. coordinator Maxwell Mus. Anthropology, U. N.Mex., Albuquerque, 1973, interpretation dir., 1974-77; asst. prof. anthropology U. N.Mex., 1975-77; cons. anthropologist, 1977-78; pres. Quivira Research Ctr., Albuquerque, 1978—. Cons. anthropologist U.S. Congl. Office Tech. Assessment, chair Archeol. Resources Planning Adv. Com., Albuquerque, 1985-86; leader field seminars Crow Canyon Archeol. Ctr., 1986—; appointee Albuquerque dist. adv. coun., bur. land mgmt. U.S. Dept. Interior, 1989; study leader Smithsonian Instn. Tours, 1991; mem. Albuquerque Heritage Conservation Adv. Com., 1992. Author: The Nighthawk Site: A Pithouse Site on Sandia Pueblo Land, Bernalillo County, New Mexico, 1982, Five Sites on the Pecos River Road, 1985, Data Recovery at Eight Archeological Sites on the Rio Nutritas, 1992, Data Recovery at Eight Archeological Sites on Cabresto Road Near Questa, 1992, Archeological Survey in the Rough and Ready Hills/Picacho Mountain Area, Dona Ana County, New Mexico, 1993, Archeological Survey on the Canadian River, Quay County, New Mexico, 1994, Archeological Testing at LA 103387, Nizhoni Extension, Gallup, McKinley County, New Mexico, 1995, Two Archeological Sites on San Felipe Pueblo Land, New Mexico, 1996, Four Archeological Sites at La Cienega, Santa Fe County, New Mexico, 1996, A Brief History of Berino, Berino Siding, and Early Mesilla Valley Agriculture, Dona Ana County, New Mexico, 1997; (with M. Kent Stout) Historical and Architectural Study of the Old Peralta Elementary School, Valencia County, New Mexico, 1997, Archeological Survey of 720 Acres on Ball Ranch, Sandoval County, New Mexico, 1998; (with H. H. Franklin and P. J. McKenna) Results of Testing at Three Sites on Tesuque Pueblo Land, Santa Fe County, New Mexico, 1999, Cultural Resources Investigations at the Old Roswell Airport for the Proposed Cielo Grande Recreation Area, Chaves County, New Mexico, 2000; co-editor: Anthropology in the Desert West, 1986. Mem. Downtown Core Area Schs. Com., Albuquerque, 1982. Ford Found. fellow, 1953-54; recipient Am. Planning Assn. award, 1985-86, [illegible] 1998. Fellow Am. Anthrop. Assn.; mem. Soc. Am. Archeology (chmn. native Am. rels. com. 1983-85), N.Mex. Archeol. Coun. (pres. 1982-83, hist. preservation award 1988), Albuquerque Archeol. Soc. (pres. 1992), Maxwell Mus. Assn. (bd. dirs. 1980-83), Las Arañas Spinners and Weavers Guild (pres. 1972), N.Mex. Heritage Preservation Alliance. Democrat. Avocations: spinning, weaving, gardening. Home and Office: Quivira [illegible]

CONDIT, GARY ADRIAN, congressman; b. Salina, Okla., Apr. 21, 1948; AA, Modesto Jr. Coll., 1970; BA, Calif. State Coll., 1972. Councilman City of Ceres, Calif., 1972-74, mayor, 1974-76; supr. Stanislaus County, 1976-82; assemblyman State of Calif., 1982-89; mem. U.S. Congress from 18th Calif. dist., 1989—; mem. agr. com. Democrat. Office: US Ho Reps 2234 Rayburn Ho Office Bldg Washington DC 20515*

CONDIT, PHILIP MURRAY, aerospace executive, engineer; b. Berkeley, Calif., Aug. 2, 1941; s. Daniel Harrison and Bernice (Kemp) C.; m. Madeleine K. Bryant, Jan. 25, 1963 (div. June 1982); children: Nicole Lynn, Megan Anne; m. Janice Condit, Apr. 6, 1991. BS MechE, U. Calif., Berkeley, 1963; MS in Aero. Engring., Princeton U., 1965; MS in Mgmt., MIT, 1975. Engr. The Boeing Co., Seattle, 1965-72, mgr. engring., 1973-83, v.p., gen. mgr., 1983-84, v.p. sales and mktg., 1984-86, exec. v.p., 1986-89, exec. v.p., gen. mgr. 777 divsn., 1989-92, pres., 1992-96, chmn., CEO, 1996—. Adv. coun. Dept. Mech. and Aerospace Engring., Princeton (N.J.) U., 1984—; chmn. aero. adv. com. NASA Adv. Coun., 1988-92; bd. dirs. The Fluke Corp., Nordstom, Inc. Co-inventor design of a flexible wing. Active Mercer Island (Wash.) Utilities Bd., 1975-78; bd. dirs. Camp Fire, Inc., 1987-92; exec bd. chief Seattle coun. Boy Scouts Am., 1988-90; trustee Mus. of Flight, Seattle, 1990—. Co-recipient Laurels award Aviation Week & Space Tech. magazine, 1990; Sloan fellow MIT, Boston, 1974. Fellow AIAA (Aircraft Design award 1984, Edward C. Wells tech. mgmt. award 1982, Wright Brothers Lectureship Aeronautics 1996), Royal Aero. Soc.; mem. NAE, Soc. Sloan Fellows (bd. govs. 1985-89), Soc. Automotive Engrs., Rainer Club, Columbia Tower Club (Seattle). Clubs: Rainier, Columbia Tower (Seattle). Office: The Boeing Co 7755 E Marginal Way S Seattle WA 98108-4000

CONDON, ROBERT EDWARD, surgeon, educator, consultant; b. Albany, N.Y., Aug. 13, 1929; s. Edward A. and Catherine (Kilmartin) C.; m. Marcia Jane Pagano, June 16, 1951; children: Sean Edward, Brian Robert. AB, U. Rochester, 1951, MD, 1957; MS, U. Wash., 1965. Diplomate Am. Bd. Surgery, Nat. Bd. Med. Examiners. N.Y. Bd. Regents scholar U. Rochester, 1957; intern King County Hosp., Seattle, 1957-58; resident dept. surgery U. Wash. Sch. Medicine (and affiliated hosps.), 1958-65; postdoctoral rsch. fellow Nat. Heart Inst., 1961-63; asst. prof. surgery Baylor Coll. Medicine, Houston, 1965-67; assoc. prof. surgery U. Ill. Coll. Medicine, Chgo., 1967-69, prof., 1969-70; prof., head dept. surgery U. Iowa Coll. Medicine, Iowa City, 1971-72; prof. surgery Med. Coll. Wis., Milw., 1972—, chmn. dept. surgery, 1979-95; chief surg. svcs. Wood VA Hosp., Milw., 1972-81. Attending surgeon Froedtert Meml. Luth. Hosp., 1982-98; cons. Columbia Hosp., Milw., St. Joseph Hosp., Milw.; clin. prof. surgery U. Wash., 2000—. Author: (with others) Abdominal Pain: A Guide to Rapid Diagnosis, 2d edit., 1995, Manual of Surgical Therapeutics, 9th edit., 1996, Hernia, 4th edit., 1995, Surgical Care, 1980. Recipient sr. class award as Outstanding Faculty Member Baylor U. Coll. Medicine, 1966, Excellence in Teaching award Phi Chi, 1967, Cert. Appreciation U. Iowa Coll. Medicine, 1971, Tchr. of Yr. award U. Iowa Coll. Medicine, 1972, Tchr. of Yr. award Med. Coll. Wis., 1983, 95, Disting. Svc. award Med. Coll. Wis., 1993, Disting. Alumnus award U. Wash., 1998; rsch. fellow Guggenheim Found., 1963-64. Mem. ACS, Am. Surg. Assn. (v.p.) , Surg. Infection Soc. (pres.), Am. Assn. Surgery of Trauma, Internat. Soc. Surgery, Collegium Internationale Chirurgiae Digestivae (pres.), Assn. for Acad. Surgery, Cen. Surg. Assn. (pres.), So. Surg. Assn., Western Surg. Assn., Wis. Surg. Soc. (pres.), Milw. Surg. Soc. (pres.), Chgo. Surg. Soc., Soc. U. Surgeons, Soc. Clin. Surgery, Milw. Acad. Medicine, Soc. Surgery Alimentary Tract (v.p.), Milw. Acad. Surgery (pres.). Home and Office: 2722 86th Ave NE Clyde Hill WA 98004-1653 E-mail: rec@wolfenet.com

CONDON, STANLEY CHARLES, gastroenterologist; b. Glendale, Calif., Feb. 1, 1931; s. Charles Max and Alma Mae (Chinn) C.; m. Vaneta Marilyn Mabley, May 19, 1963; children: Lori, Brian, David. BA, La Sierra Coll., 1952; MD, Loma Linda U., 1956. Diplomate Nat. Bd. Med. Examiners, Am. Bd. Internal Medicine, Am. Bd. Gastroenterology; cert. nutrition support physician. Intern L.A. County Gen. Hosp., 1956-57, resident gen. pathology, 1959-61; resident internal medicine White Meml. Med. Ctr., L.A., 1961-63, attending staff out-patient clinic, 1963-64; active jr. attending staff L.A. County Gen. Hosp., 1964-65; dir. intern-resident tng. program Manila Sanitarium and Hosp., 1966-71, med. dir., 1971-72; chief resident internal medicine out-patient clinic Loma Linda U. Med. Ctr., 1972-74; fellow in gastroenterology Barnes Hosp./Wash. U., 1974-76; attending staff, asst. prof. medicine Loma Linda U. Med. Ctr., 1976-91, assoc. prof. medicine, 1991—, med. dir. nutritional support team, 1984—. Contbr. articles to profl. jours. Capt. U.S. Army, 1957-59. Fellow ACP; mem. AMA, Am. Soc. for Parenteral and Enteral Nutrition, Am. Gastroent. Assn., Calif. Med. Assn., So. Calif. Soc. Gastroenterology, Inland Soc. Internal Medicine, San Bernardino County Med. Soc. Republican. Seventh-day Adventist. Avocations: trombone, choral singing, camping, hiking, gardening. Home: 11524 Ray Ct Loma Linda CA 92354-3630 Office: Loma Linda U Med Ctr 11370 Anderson St Loma Linda CA 92354-3450

CONDRY, ROBERT STEWART, retired hospital administrator; b. Charleston, W.Va., Aug. 16, 1941; s. John Charles and Mary Louise (Jester) C.; m. Mary Purcell Heinzer, May 21, 1966; children: Mary-Lynch, John Stewart. BA, U. Charleston, 1963; MBA, George Washington U., 1970. Asst. hosp. dir. Med. Coll. of Va., Richmond, 1970-73, assoc. adminstr., 1973-75; assoc. hosp. dir. McGaw Hosp., Loyola U., Maywood, Ill., 1975-84, hosp. dir., 1984-93, ret., 1993. Pres. Inter-Hosp. Planning Assn. of Western Suburbs, Maywood, 1983-93; bd. dirs. PentaMed, Inc., San Antonio. Bd. dirs. Met. Chgo. Healthcare Coun., 1985-93, mem. exec. com., 1989-93; bd. dirs. Cath. Hosp. Alliance, 1992, chmn. bd. dirs., 1992, mem. exec. com. 1988-94; mem. Ill. Gov.'s Adv. Bd. on Infant Mortality Reduction, 1988-93, Rev. Bd. on Emergency Medicine Svcs., 1989-93. With U.S. Army, 1964-66. Recipient preceptorship George Washington U., 1985, U. Chgo., 1984, St. Louis U., 1984, Tulane U., 1984, Yale U., 1991. Fellow Am. Coll. Healthcare Execs., Am. Acad. Med. Adminstrs.; mem. Am. Hosp. Assn., Cath. Hosp. Assn., Am. Mgmt. Assn. Republican. Roman Catholic Avocations: golf, tennis, camping, travel. E-mail: bobandmarycondry@montereybay.com

CONE, LAWRENCE ARTHUR, medical educator; b. N.Y.C., Mar. 23, 1928; s. Max N. and Ruth (Weber) C.; m. Julia Haldy, June 6, 1947 (dec. 1956); m. Mary Elisabeth Osborne, Aug. 20, 1960; children: Lionel Alfred. AB, NYU, 1948; MD, U. Berne, Switzerland, 1954; DSc (hon.), Rocky Mountain Coll., 1993. Diplomate Am. Bd. Internal Medicine, Am. Bd. Infectious Diseases, Am. Bd. Allergy and Immunology, Am. Bd. Med. Oncology. Intern Dallas Meth. Hosp., 1954-55, resident internal medicine, 1955; resident Flower 5th Hosp., N.Y.C., 1957-59, Met. Hosp., N.Y.C., 1959-60; rsch. fellow infectious diseases and immunology NYU Med. Sch., N.Y.C., 1960-62; from asst. prof. to assoc. prof. N.Y. Med. Coll., N.Y.C., 1962-72, chief sect immunology and infectious diseases, 1962-72; assoc. clin. prof. medicine Harbor UCLA Med. Sch., 1984—; clin. prof. internal medicine U. Calif., Riverside, 1997-98. Career scientist Health Rsch. Coun. N.Y.C., 1962-68; chief sect. immunology and infectious diseases Eisenhower Med. Ctr., Rancho Mirage, Calif., 1973—, chmn. dept. medicine, 1976-78, pres. elect, pres., past pres. med. staff, 1984-90; [illegible] basic sci. U. Calif., Riverside Biomed. Scis.; mem. mycosis study group NIAID, 1993—, co-cardiodonycocis study group, 1993—, eastern coop. oncology group affil. Stanford U., 1994. Contbr. articles to profl. jours. Bd. dirs. Desert Bighorn Rsch. Inst., Palm Desert, Calif., pres., bd. dirs., 1995-99; nat. adv. coun., mem., bd. trustees Rocky Mountain Coll., Billings, Mont.; mem. med. adv. staff Coll. of Desert, Palm Desert; Pres. Ctr. Desert Mus., Palm Springs, Calif., Idaho Conservation League, Gilcrease Mus., Tulsa, Sun Valley Ctr. for Arts and Humanities. L.A. County Mus., Smithsonian Inst., Buffalo Bill Historic Mus., Cody, Wyo.; mem. Nat. Mus. Wildlife Art; life mem. The Living Desert, Palm Desert, L.A. County Mus.; mem. cmty. adv. coun. Jr. League. Recipient Outstanding Contbn. to Medicine award Riverside County Med. Assn., 1998, Disting. Achievement award AMC Cancer Rsch. Ctr., 1998. Fellow ACP, Royal Soc. Medicine, Interam. Soc. Chemotherapy, Am. Coll. Allergy, Am. Acad. Allergy and Immunology, Am. Soc. Infectious Diseases, Am. Geriatric Soc. (founding fellow we. divsn.); mem. AAAS, Internat. AIDS Soc., Am. Soc. Microbiology, Reticulocudothelial Soc., Am. Fedn. for Clin. Rsch., Faculty Soc. UCLA, Surg. Soc. N.Y. Med. Coll. (hon.), Woodstock Artists Assn., Harvey Soc., N.Y. Acad. Scis., NYU Alumni Assn., Berne Alumni Assn., Lotos Club, Tamarisk Country Club, Coachella Valley Gun and Wildlife Club, Faculty Soc. UCLA Harbor Med. Ctr., O'Donnell Golf Club, Sigma Xi. Republican. Avocations: golfing, fishing, hunting, skiing. Home: 765 Via Vadera Palm Springs CA 92262-4170 Office: Probst Profl Bldg #308 39000 Bob Hope Dr Rancho Mirage CA 92270-3221 also: Larkspur Condominiums PO Box 1503 Sun Valley ID 83353-1503

CONGDON, ROGER DOUGLASS, theology educator, minister; b. Ft. Collins, Colo., Apr. 6, 1918; s. John Solon and Ellen Avery (Kellogg) C.; m. Rhoda Gwendolyn Britt, Jan. 2, 1948; children: Rachel Congdon Lidbeck, James R., R. Steven, Jon B., Philip F., Robert N., Bradford B., Ruth A. Mahner, Rebecca York Skones, Rhoda J. Miller, Marianne C. Potter, Mark Alexander. BA, Wheaton Coll., 1940; postgrad, Eastern Bapt. Sem., 1940-41; ThM, Dallas Theol. Sem., 1945; ThD, Dallas Theology Sem., 1949. Ordained to ministry Bapt. Ch., 1945. Exec. sec., dean Altanta Bible Inst., 1945-49; prof. theology Carver Bible Inst., Atlanta, 1945-49; prof. Multnomah Bible Coll., Portland, Oreg., 1950-87; pastor Emmanuel Bapt. Ch., Vancouver, Wash., 1985—. Past dean of faculty, dean of edn., v.p., chmn. libr. com., chmn. achievement-award com., chmn. lectureship com., advisor grad. div. and mem. pres.'s cabinet Multnomah Bible Co.; chmn. Chil Evang. Fellowship of Greater Portland, 1978—; founder, pres. Preaching Print Inc., Portland, 1953—. Founder, speaker semi-weekly radio broadcast Bible Truth Forum, KPDQ, Portland, Oreg., 1989-98, KPAM 1999—, DZAM, Manila, Philippines, 1996—, Radio Africa 2, 1998—; author: The Doctrine of Conscience, 1945. Chmn. Citizen's Com. Info. on Communism, Portland, 1968-75. Recipient Outstanding Educators of Am. award, 1972, Loraine Chafer award in Systematic Theology, Dallas Theol. Sem. Mem. Am. Assn. Bible Colls. (chmn. testing com. 1953-78), N.Am. Assn. Bible Colls. (N.W. rep. 1960-63), Near East Archaeol. Soc., Evang. Theol. Soc. Republican. Home: 16539 NE Halsey St Portland OR 97230-5607 Office: Emmanuel Bapt Ch 14810 NE 28th St Vancouver WA 98682-8357

CONGER, HARRY MILTON, mining company executive; b. Seattle, July 22, 1930; s. Harry Milton Jr. and Caroline (Gunnell) C.; m. Phyllis Nadine Shepherd, Aug. 14, 1949 (dec.); children: Harry Milton IV, Preston George; m. Rosemary L. Scholz, Feb. 22, 1991. D in Bus. Adminstrn. (hon.), S.D. Sch. Mines and Tech., 1983; D. in Engring. (hon.), Colo. Sch. Mines, 1988, hon. degrees. Registered profl. engr., Ariz., Colo. Shift foreman Asarco, Inc., Silver Bell, Ariz., 1955-64; mgr. Kaiser Steel Corp. Eagle Mountain Mine, 1964-70; v.p., gen. mgr. Kaiser Resources, Ltd., Fernie, B.C., Can., 1970-73, Consolidation Coal Co. (Midwestern div.), Carbondale, Ill., 1973-75; v.p. Homestake Mining Co., San Francisco, 1975-77, pres., 1977-78, pres., chief exec. officer, 1978-82, chmn., pres., chief exec. officer, 1982-86, chmn., chief exec. officer, 1986-96, chmn., 1996-98, chmn., CEO emeritus, also bd. dirs., 1998, ret., 1998. Bd. dirs. ASA Ltd., Apex Silver Mines, PG&E Corp.; chmn. Am. Mining Congress, 1986-89, World Gold Coun., 1995-97. Chmn. World Gold Coun.; trustee Calif. Inst. Tech. With C.E., U.S. Army, 1956. Recipient Disting. Achievement medal Colo. Sch. Mines, 1978, Am. Mining Hall of Fame, 1990, Disting. Svc. award Am. Mining Congress, 1995. Mem. NAE, Nat. Mining Assn. (hon. bd. dirs.), Am. Inst. Mining Engrs. (disting., Charles F. Rand gold medal 1990), Mining and Metallurgy Soc. Am., Mining Club, Bohemian Club, Commonwealth Club, Pacific Union Club, World Trade Club. Republican. Episcopalian.

CONGROVE, JIM, state legislator; m. Judy Congrove. AA, BA, MA. Mem. Colo. House of Reps., 1994-96, Colo. State Senate, 1996—, chair local govt., vice-chair state, vets. and mil. affairs. Active Civil Air Patrol. With U.S. Army. Republican. Office: State Capitol 200 E Colfax Ave Ste 346 Denver CO 80203-1716

CONLISK, RAIMON L. high technology management consulting executive; Pres. Conlisk Assocs., Fremont, Calif.; chmn. Exar Corp. Chmn. bd. dirs. SBE, Inc., San Ramon, Calif.; bd. dirs. Xetel, Inc. Office: 48720 Kato Rd Fremont CA 94538

CONLY, JOHN FRANKLIN, engineering educator, researcher; b. Ridley Park, Pa., Sept. 11, 1933; s. Harlan and Mary Jane (Roberts) C.; m. Jeannine Therese McDonough, Apr. 14, 1967; children: J. Paul, Mary Ann. B.S., U. Pa., 1956, M.S., 1958; Ph.D., Columbia U., 1962. Instr. U. Pa., Phila., 1956-58; research asst. Columbia U., N.Y.C., 1959-62; asst. prof. engring. San Diego State U., 1962-65, assoc. prof., 1965-69, prof., 1969—, chmn. dept., 1971-74, 77-85, wind tunnel dir., 1978—. D. and F. Guggenheim fellow, 1958 Assoc. fellow AIAA (sect. chmn. 1970 best U.S. sect.) Republican. Episcopalian. Office: San Diego State U Dept Aerospace Engring San Diego CA 92182

CONN, ERIC EDWARD, plant biochemist; b. Berthoud, Colo., Jan. 6, 1923; s. William Elmer and Mary Anna (Smith) C.; m. Louise Carolyn Kachel, Oct. 17, 1959; children: Michael E., Kevin E. BA in Chemistry, U. Colo., 1944; PhD in Biochemistry, U. Chgo., 1950. Instr. biochemistry U. Chgo., 1950-52; instr. U. Calif., Berkeley, 1952-53, asst. prof., 1953-58, assoc. prof. Davis, 1958-63, prof., 1964—. Author: (with P.K. Stumpf) Outlines of Biochemistry, 1963, 5th edit., 1987; editor: (with P.K. Stumpf) (book series) Biochemistry of Plants, 1980-90. With U.S. Army, 1944-46. Fellow USPHS, 1960; Fulbright Rsch. grantee, 1965; recipient Pergamon Phytochemistry prize and cert., 1994. Mem. NAS, Phytochem. Soc. N.Am. (hon. life mem., pres. 1971-72, editor in chief 1984-89), Am. Soc. Plant Physiologists (pres. 1986-87, Charles Reid Barnes life mem.), Am. Soc. Biol. Chemistry, Phytochemistry Soc. Europe, Am. Soc. Pharmacognasy. Democrat. Avocations: gardening, philately. Office: U Calif Sect Molecular & Cellular Biol Davis CA 95616

CONN, ROBERT WILLIAM, engineering science educator; b. N.Y.C., Dec. 1, 1942; s. William Conrad and Rose Marie (Albanese) C.; children: Carole, William. BChemE, Pratt Inst., 1964; MS in Mech. Engring., Calif. Inst. Tech., 1965, Ph.D. in Engring. Sci., 1968. NSF postdoctoral fellow Euratom Cmty. Rsch. Center, Ispra, Italy, 1968-69; rsch. assoc. Brookhaven Nat. Lab., Upton, N.Y., 1969-70; vis. assoc. prof. U. Wis., Madison, 1970-72, assoc. prof., 1972-75, prof., 1975-80, dir. fusion tech. program, 1974-79, Romnes faculty prof., 1977-80; prof. engring. and applied sci. UCLA, 1980-93, dir. Inst. Plasma and Fusion Rsch., 1987-93, dean Sch. Engring., Zable prof. engring. U. Calif., San Diego, 1994—; founder, chmn. bd. Trikon, Inc. (formerly Plasma & Materials Techs., Inc., L.A., 1986-93. Chair, sec. Energy's Fusion Energy Adv. Com., 1991-96; cons. to govt. and industry. Author papers, chpts. in books. Recipient Curtis McGraw Rsch. award Am. Assn. Engring. Edn., 1982, Outstanding Svc. cert. U.S. Dept. Energy, E.O. Lawrence Meml. award, 1984, Fusion Power Assocs. Leadership award, 1992, Disting. Assoc.'s award Sec. of Energy,

Dept. of Energy, 1996, Calif. Inst. Tech. Disting. Alumni Yr. award, 1998; named San Diego Outstanding Educator of Yr., 1997. Fellow Am. Nuclear Soc. (Outstanding Achievement award for excellence in research fusion div. 1979), Am. Phys. Soc.; mem. NAE. Office: U Calif San Diego Jacobs Sch Engring 9500 Gilman Dr La Jolla CA 92093-5004

CONNELL, EVAN SHELBY, JR. writer; b. Kansas City, Mo., Aug. 17, 1924; s. Evan Shelby and Elton (Williamson) C. Student, Dartmouth, 1941-43; AB, U. Kans., 1946-47; grad. study, Stanford U., 1947-48, Columbia U., 1948-49. Editor Contact mag., Sausalito, Calif., 1960-65. Author: The Anatomy Lesson and Other Stories, 1957, Mrs. Bridge, 1959, The Patriot, 1960, Notes From a Bottle Found on the Beach at Carmel, 1963, At the Crossroads: Stories, 1965, The Diary of a Rapist, 1966, Mr. Bridge, 1969, Points for a Compass Rose, 1973, The Connoisseur, 1974 (Calif. Literature Silver medal 1974), Double Honeymoon, 1976, A Long Desire, 1979, The White Lantern, 1980, St. Augustine's Pigeon, 1980, Son of the Morning Star: Custer and the Little Bighorn, 1984 (Nat. Book Critics Circle award nomination 1984, L.A. Times Book award 1985), The Alchymist's Journal, 1991, Mesa Verde, 1992, Collected Stories, 1996, Deus Lo Volt!: Chronicle of the Crusades, 2000; editor: Jerry Stoll's I Am A Lover, 1961, Women by Three, 1969. Served as naval aviator 1943-45. Eugene Saxton fellow, 1953, Guggenheim fellow, 1963; Rockefeller Found. grantee, 1967; recipient Am. Acad. Inst. Arts and Letters award, 1987. Mem. AAAL

CONNELL, KATHLEEN, state official; PhD, UCLA. Holder 6 lics. SEC. Instr. UCLA Bus. Sch., U. Calif. Bus. Sch., Berkeley; owner, mgr. investment banking firm, until 1994; contr. State of Calif., Sacramento, 1994—. Chmn. Franchise Tax Bd. Named One of 10 Rising Stars of Dem. Party, Time mag., 1996. Office: State Calif Office Contr 300 Capitol Mall Ste 1850 Sacramento CA 95814-4341

CONNELLY, JAMES P. prosecutor; b. Hartford, Conn., Apr. 15, 1947; BA, Marquette U., 1969; JD, Georgetown U., 1972. Bar: Wis. 1972. Spl. asst. to Sec. of Treasury, 1975-76; ptnr. Foley & Lardner, Milw.; U.S. atty. U.S. Dist. Ct. (ea. dist.) Wash., Spokane, 1994—. Editor-in-chief Georgetown Law Jour., 1971-72. Mem. State Bar Wis., Phi Alpha Delta. Office: US Atty Office US Courthouse PO Box 1494 920 W Riverside Ave Spokane WA 99210-1494

CONNELLY, THOMAS, construction executive; CFO Western Pacific Housing, El Segundo, Calif., 1997—. Office: Western Pacific Housing 300 Continental Blvd Ste 390 El Segundo CA 90245-5023

CONNER, LINDSAY ANDREW, screenwriter, producer; b. N.Y.C., Feb. 19, 1956; s. Michael and Miriam (Mintzer) C. BA summa cum laude, UCLA, 1976; MA, Occidental Coll., 1977; JD magna cum laude, Harvard U., 1980. Bar: Calif. 1980, U.S. Dist. Ct. (cen. dist.) Calif. 1983. Assoc. Kaplan, Livingston, Goodwin, Berkowitz & Selvin, Beverly Hills, Calif., 1980-81, Fulop & Hardee, Beverly Hills, 1982-83, Wyman, Bautzer, Kuchel & Silbert, L.A., 1983-86; ptnr., entertainment dept. head Hill Wynne Troop & Meisinger, L.A., 1986-93. Author: (with others) The Courts and Education, 1977; editor: Harvard Law Rev., 1978-80. Trustee L.A. Community Coll., 1981-97, bd. pres., 1989-90; pres. Calif. Community Coll. Trustees, 1992-93. Mem. ABA, UCLA Alumni Assn. (life), Harvard-Radcliffe Club, Phi Beta Kappa. Office: 54th St Prodns 10880 Wilshire Bld Ste 1840 Los Angeles CA 90024-4101

CONNICK, CHARLES MILO, retired religious studies educator, clergyman; b. Conneaut Lake Park, Pa., Mar. 23, 1917; s. Walter and Iola Belle (Wintermute) C.; m. Genevieve Shaul, June 7, 1941 (dec. June 1992); children: Joy (Mrs. J. Bruce Parker), Christopher Milo, Nancy (Mrs. David F. Jankowski); m. Sonia J. Banisch, July 24, 1994. Student, Edinboro State U., 1935-36; AB, Allegheny Coll., 1939, DD, 1960; DMin, Boston U., 1942, PhD, 1944; Roswell R. Robinson fellow, Harvard U., 1942-43; postgrad., Episcopal Div. Sch., 1942-44. Ordained deacon United Meth. Ch., 1941, elder, 1942; assoc. minister St. Paul's Methodist Ch., Lowell, Mass., 1940-41, Copley Meth. Ch., Boston, 1941-42; dir. Wesley Found., Harvard U.; also minister to students Harvard Epworth Meth. Ch., Cambridge, Mass., summers 1943-44; sr. instr. pub. speaking Curry Coll., Boston, 1942-44; head Bible dept. Northfield Sch., East Northfield, Mass., 1944-46; prof. religion, chmn. dept. philosophy, religion Whittier (Calif.) Coll., 1946-82, prof. religion emeritus, 1982—. Chmn. social sci. div., 1950, 60, pres. faculty senate, 1970-71, dir. coll. study tour to Europe, Middle East, around the world, summers 1955-69; pres. I-TAC, 1976-87; Danforth assoc., 1959—, Danforth sr. assoc., 1964-82; spl. lectr. Bibl. lit. Sch. Religion, First Congl. Ch., Los Angeles, 1948 61; mem. Western Pa. Conf., United Meth. Ch., 1942—; exec. sec. Presdl. Selection Com., 1969-70; cons. for colls. and univs. seeking new presidents, 1971-82; adv. council Calif. Christian Com. for Israel, 1974-82. Author: Build on the Rock, You and the Sermon on the Mount, 1960, Jesus, the Man, the Mission, and the Message, 1963, 2d edit., 1974, The Message and Meaning of the Bible, 1965, The New Testament: An Introduction to its History, Literature and Thought, 1972, 2d edit., 1978; editorial adviser to maj. pubs., 1964-88; contbr. articles to religious jours. and mags. Trustee Whittier Coll., 1982-2001. Recipient Distinguished Alumnus award Boston U., 1971, Gold award Allegheny Coll., 1989; C. Milo Connick chair in religion established Whittier Coll., 1982 Mem. Consumers Coop. Whittier Inc. (pres. 1949-53), AAUP (Whittier pres. 1970-72), Pacific Coast Assn. for Religious Studies (exec. com. 1947-60), Am. Acad. Religion (pres. Western Region 1953-54), Soc. Bibl. Lit., Am. Oriental Soc., Am. Christian Assn. for Israel (mem. nat. adv. com. 1964-69), Phi Sigma Tau, Kappa Phi Kappa, Chi Delta Sigma, Omicron Delta Kappa. Home: 6249 Roundhill Dr Whittier CA 90601-3836 Office: Whittier Coll 13421 Philadelphia St Whittier CA 90601

CONNIFF, RAY, popular musician, conductor, composer, arranger; b. Attleboro, Mass., Nov. 6, 1916; s. John Lawrence and Maude (Angela) C.; m. Emily Jo Ann Imhof, Feb. 14, 1938; children: James Lawrence, Jo Ann Patricia; m. Ann Marie Engberg, Aug. 23, 1947, 1 foster son, Richard J. Bibo.; m. Vera Schmidheiny, Aug. 24, 1968; 1 dau., Tamara Allegra. Student, Juilliard Sch. Music; studied with Tom Timothy, Sol Kaplan, Hugo Friedhofer. Trombone Player, arranger, Bunny Berigan, Bob Crosby, Artie Shaw, Harry James orchestras, arranger, composer, conductor, rec. artist, Columbia Records; recordings include Here We Come A-Caroling, 1986, Concert in Rhythm, Vol. 1, 1987, Broadway in Rhythm, 1988, Hollywood in Rhythm, 1988, Rhapsody in Rhythm, 1989, Invisible Tears, 1994, Speak To Me Of Love, 1994, Friendly Persuasion, 1994. Office: PO Box 46395 Los Angeles CA 90046-0395 also: Sony Music Entertainment 550 Madison Ave New York NY 10022-3211

CONNOLLY, JOHN EARLE, surgeon, educator; b. Omaha, May 21, 1923; s. Earl A. and Gertrude (Eckerman) C.; m. Virginia Hartman, Aug. 12, 1967; children: Peter Hart. John Earle, Sarah. AB, Harvard U., 1945, MD, 1948. Diplomate: Am. Bd. Surgery (bd. dirs. 1976-82), Am. Bd. Thoracic and Cardiovascular Surgery, Am. Bd. Vascular Surgery. Intern. in surgery Stanford U. Hosps., San Francisco, 1948-49, surg. research fellow, 1949-50, asst. resident surgeon, 1950-52, chief resident surgeon, 1953-54, surg. pathology fellow, 1954-55, San Francisco, 1957-60, John and Mary Markle Scholar in med. scis., 1957-62; surg. registrar professional unit St. Bartholomew's Hosp., London, 1952-53; resident in thoracic surgery Bellevue Hosp., N.Y.C., 1955; resident in thoracic and cardiovascular surgery Columbia-Presbyn. Med. Ctr., N.Y.C., 1956; from instr. to assoc. prof. surgery Stanford U., 1957-65; prof. U. Calif., Irvine, 1965—, chmn. dept. surgery, 1965-78; attending surgeon Stanford Med. Ctr., Palo Alto, Calif., 1959-65; chmn. cardiovascular and thoracic surgery Irvine Med. Ctr. U. Calif., 1968—; attending surgeon Children's Hosp., Orange, Calif., 1968—, Anaheim (Calif.) Meml. Hosp., 1970—. Vis. prof. Beijing Heart, Lung, Blood Vessel Inst., 1990, A.H. Duncan vis. prof. U. Edinburgh, 1984; Hunterian prof. Royal Coll. Surgeons Eng., 1985-86; Kinmonth lectr. Royal Coll. Surgeons, Eng., 1987, Hume Lectr. Soc. for Clin. Vascular Surgery, 1998, Dist. Prof. Lectr. Uniformed Svcs. U. Health Scis., Bethesda, 1998; mem. adv. coun. Nat. Heart, Lung, and Blood Inst.-NIH, 1981-85; cons. Long Beach VA Hosp., Calif., 1965—. Contbr. articles to profl. jours.; editorial bd.: Jour. Cardiovascular Surgery, 1974—, chief editor, 1985—; editorial bd. Western Jour. Medicine, 1975—, Jour. Stroke, 1979—, Jour. Vascular Surgery, 1983—. Bd. dirs. Audio-Digest Found., 1974—; bd. dirs. Franklin Martin Found., 1975-80; regent Uniformed Svcs. U. of Health Scis., Bethesda, 1992—. Served with AUS, 1943-44. Recipient Cert. of Merit, Japanese Surg. Soc., 1979, 90. Fellow ACS (gov. 1964-70, regent 1973-82, vice chmn. bd. regents 1980-82, v.p. 1984-85), Royal Coll. Surgeons Eng., 1982 (hon.), Royal Coll. Surgeons Ireland, 1988 (hon.), Royal Coll. Surgeons Edinburgh, 1983 (hon.); mem. Japanese Surg. Soc. (hon.), Am. Surg. Assn., Soc. U. Surgeons, Am. Assn. Thoracic Surgery (coun. 1974-78), Pacific Coast Surg. Assn. (pres. 1985-86), San Francisco Surg. Soc., L.A. Surg. Soc., Soc. Vascular Surgery, Western Surg. Assn., Internat. Cardiovascular Soc. (pres. 1977), Soc. Internat. Chirurgie, Soc. Thoracic Surgeons, Western Thoracic Surg. Soc. (pres. 1978), Orange County Surg. Soc. (pres. 1984-85), James IV Assn. Surgeons (councillor 1983—), San Francisco Golf Club, Pacific Union Club, Bohemian Club (San Francisco), Harvard Club (N.Y.C.), Big Canyon Club (Newport Beach, Calif.), Cypress Point Club (Pebble Beach). Home: 7 Deerwood Ln Newport Beach CA 92660-5108 Office: U Calif Dept Surgery Irvine CA 92717

CONNOLLY, THOMAS JOSEPH, retired bishop; b. Tonopah, Nev., July 18, 1922; s. John and Katherine (Hammel) C. Student, St. Joseph Coll. and St. Patrick Sem., Menlo Park, Calif., 1936-47, Catholic U. Am., , 1949-51; JCD, Lateran Pontifical U., Rome, 1952; DHL (hon.), U. Portland, 1972. Ordained priest Roman Cath. Ch., 1947. Asst. St. Thomas Cathedral, Reno, 1947, asst., rector, 1953-55; asst. Little Flower Parish, Reno, 1947-48; sec. to bishop, 1949; asst. St. Albert the Gt., Reno, 1952-53, pastor, 1960-68, St. Joseph Ch., Elko, 1955-60, St. Theresa's Ch., Carson City, Nev., 1968-71; bishop of Baker, Bend, Oreg., 1971-2000; bishop emeritus Bend, 2000—. Tchr. Manogue High Sch., Reno, 1948-49; chaplain Serra Club, 1948-49; officialis Diocese of Reno; chmn. bldg. com., dir. Cursillo Movement; moderator Italian Cath. Fedn.; dean, mem. personnel bd. Senate of Priests; mem. Nat. Bishops Liturgy Com., 1973-76; region XII rep. to adminstrv. bd. Nat. Conf. Cath. Bishops, 1973-76, 86-89, mem. adv. com., 1974-76; bd. dirs. Cath. Communications Northwest, 1977-82. Club: K.C. (state chaplain Nev. 1970-71). Office: Bishop of Baker PO Box 5999 911 SE Armour Dr Bend OR 97702-1489

CONNOR, ROBERT W., JR. federal judge; b. 1942; Magistrate judge U.S. Dist. Ct. Wyo., Sheridan, 1977—; ptnr. Conner and Smith, Sheridan. Office: PO Box 607 Sheridan WY 82801-0607

CONNOR, WILLIAM ELLIOTT, physician, educator; b. Pitts., Sept. 14, 1921; s. Frank E. and Edna S. (Felt) C.; m. Sonja Lee Newcomer, Sept. 19, 1969; children: Rodney William, Catherine Susan, James Elliott, Christopher French, Peter Malcolm. B.A., U. Iowa, 1942, M.D., 1950. Diplomate Am. Bd. Internal Medicine, Am. Bd. Nutrition. Intern USPHS Hosp., San Francisco, 1950-51; resident in internal medicine San Joaquin Gen. Hosp., Stockton, Calif., 1951-52; practice medicine specializing in internal medicine Chico, 1952-54, resident in internal medicine VA Hosp., Iowa City, 1954-56; cons., 1967-75; mem. faculty U. Iowa Coll. Medicine, 1956-75, prof. internal medicine, 1967-75; acting dir., then dir. Clin. Research Center, 1967-75, dir. lipid-atherosclerosis sect., cardiovascular div., 1974-75. Vis. prof. Basic Sci. Med. Inst., Karachi, Pakistan, Ind. U., 1961-62, Baker Med. Rsch. Inst., Melbourne, Australia, 1982; vis. fellow clin. sci. Australian Nat. U., Canberra, 1970; prof. cardiology and metabolism-nutrition, dept. medicine, 1975-79, head sect. clin. nutrition, 1979-90, acting head, head div. endocrinology, metabolism and nutrition, 1984-90, prof. sect. clin. nutrition, 1990—, dir. lipid-atherosclerosis lab., assoc. dir. Clin. Rsch. Ctr., Oreg. Health Scis. U. Portland, 1975-94; chmn. heart and lung program project com. Contbr. numerous articles to med. jours.; editor Jour. Lab. and Clin. Medicine, 1970-73; mem. editorial bds., reviewer profl. jours. Mem. Johnson County (Iowa) Cen. Dem. Com., 1965-69; mem. nat. council Fellowship Reconciliation; nat., North Central and Pacific Northwest bds. Am. Friends Service Com. Served with AUS, 1943-46. Research fellow Am. Heart Assn., 1956-58; ACP traveling fellow Sir William Dunn Sch. Pathology, Oxford, Eng., 1960; recipient Career Devel. Research award Nat. Heart Inst., 1962-73, Discovery award Med. Research Found. Oreg. Mem. AAAS, ACP, AMA, AAUP (pres. U. Iowa chpt. 1968-69, pres. Oreg. Health Sci. U. chpt. 1978-79), Am. Diabetes Assn. (vice chmn. food and nutrition com. 1972-74), Am. Dietitic Assn. (hon.), Am. Fedn. Clin. Rsch., Am. Heart Assn. (chmn. coun. arteriosclerosis 1975-78, exec. com. coun. epidemiology 1967-70, exec. com. coun. cerebral vascular disease 1966-68, C. Lyman Duff meml. lectrue 1989), Am. Soc. Clin. Nutrition (pres. 1978), Nat. Acad. Sci. (food and nutrition bd. 1986-89), Am. Inst. Nutrition, Am. Oil Chemists Soc., Am. Physiol. Soc., Am. Soc. Clin. Investigation, Am. Soc. Study Arteriosclerosis, Assn. Am. Physicians, Ctrl. Soc. Clin. Rsch., Nutrition Soc., Soc. Exptl. Biology and Medicine (coun. 1971-72, pres. Iowa sect. 1971-72), Western Assn. Physicians, Western Soc. Clin. Rsch., Phi Beta Kappa, Sigma Xi, Alpha Omega Alpha. Achievements include research in nutrition, lipid metabolism, blood vessel diseases. Home: 2600 SW Sherwood Pl Portland OR 97201-2285 Office: Oreg Health Scis U L465 Portland OR 97201 E-mail: connorw@ohsu.edu

CONNORS, JOHN G. computer company executive; cert. CPA. Mgmt. Microsoft, 1989, gen. mgr. worldwide fin. ops., corp. controller, 1994-96, v.p. worldwide enterprise group, sr. v.p. fin., CFO. Office: Microsoft Corp 1 Microsoft Way Redmond WA 98052

CONOVER, FREDERIC KING, lawyer; b. Portchester, N.Y., June 4, 1933; s. Julian D. and Josephine T. Conover; m. Kathryn B. Conover, Dec. 21, 1955; children: Frederic, Elizabeth, Pamela, Margaret; m. 2d, Jacquelyn Wonder, Aug. 24, 1979. B.A., Amherst Coll., 1955; J.D., U. Mich., 1961. Bar: Colo. 1962, U.S. Dist. Ct. Colo. 1962, U.S. Ct. Appeals (10th cir.) 1962. Ptnr. Conover, McClearn & Heppenstall, P.C., Denver, 1972-88, Faegre & Benson, Devner, 1988—, ptnr. in charge dispute resolution svcs. The Faegre Group, 1993—. Trustee Mt. Airy Psychiat. Ctr.; dir. Legal Aid Soc.; chmn. citizens adv. com. Denver Regional Council Govts., bd. govs., trustee, Nat. Ctr. for Preventive Law, pannel of disting. neutrals, Ctr. for Pub. Resources; bd. dirs., Lawyers Alliance for World Security. Served to lt. USN, 1955-59. Fellow Am. Coll. Trial Lawyers, Am. Bar Found., Colo. Bar Found.; mem. ABA, Denver Bar Assn. (pres. 1983-84), Colo. Bar Assn. (pres. 1990-91), Law Club (v.p.), City Club of Denver (dir.), Denver Tennis Club. Democrat. Office: The Faegre Group 2500 Republic Plz 370 17th St Denver CO 80202-1370

CONQUEST, (GEORGE)ROBERT (ACWORTH), writer, historian, poet, critic, journalist; b. Malvern, Worcestershire, Eng., July 15, 1917; s. Robert Folger Westcott and Rosamund Alys (Acworth) C.; m. Joan Watkins, 1942 (div. 1948); children: John, Richard; m. Elizabeth Neece, Dec. 1, 1979. Student, Winchester Coll., Eng., 1931-35, U. Grenoble, France, 1935-36, U. Oxford, , 1936-39; MA, U. Oxford, Eng., 1972; DLitt, U. Oxford, 1975. First sec. H.M. Fgn. Svc., Sofia, Bulgaria, U.N., London, 1946-56; rsch. fellow London Sch. Econs., 1956-58; vis. poet U. Buffalo, N.Y., 1959-60; lit. editor The Spectator, London, 1962-63; sr. fellow Russian Inst. Columbia U., N.Y.C., 1964-65; fellow Woodrow Wilson Internat. Ctr., Washington, 1976-77; sr. rsch. fellow Hoover Inst., Stanford (Calif.) U., 1977-79, 81—. Disting. vis. scholar Heritage Found., Washington, 1980-81; adv. bd. Freedom House, N.Y.C., 1980—; rsch. assoc. Ukrainian Rsch. Inst. Harvard U., Cambridge, Mass., 1983—; adj. fellow Washington Ctr. Strategic Studies., 1984—. Author: Poems, 1955, A World of Difference, 1955, Common Sense About Russia, 1960, Power and Policy in the USSR, 1961, The Pasternak Affair, 1962, Between Mars and Venus, 1962, (with Kingsley Amis) The Egyptologists, 1965, Russia after Khrushchev, 1965, The Great Terror, 1968, Arias from a Love Opera, 1969, The Nation Killers, 1970, Where Marx Went Wrong, 1970, V I Lenin, 1972, Kolyma: The Arctic Death Camps, 1978, Coming Across, 1978, The Abomination of Moab, 1979, Forays, 1979, Present Danger: Towards a Foreign Policy, 1979, We and They: Civic and Despotic Cultures, 1980, (with Jon. M. White) What to do When the Russians Come, 1984, Inside Stalin's Secret Police: NKVD Politics 1936-39, 1985, The Harvest of Sorrow: Soviet Collectivization and the Terror-Famine, 1986, New and Collected Poems, 1988, Stalin and the Kirov Murder, 1988, Tyrants and Typewriters, 1989, The Great Terror: A Reassessment, 1990, Stalin: Breaker of Nations, 1991, Demons Don't, 1999, Reflections on a Ravaged Century, 1999. Capt. inf. Brit. Army, 1939-46, ETO. Decorated Officer Order of the Brit. Empire, London, 1955, Companion Order St. Michael and St. George, London, 1996; recipient Alexis de Tocqueville award, 1992, Light Verse award Acad. Arts and Letters, 1997; Jefferson lectr. humanities, Washington, 1993, Richard M. Weaver prize for scholarly letters, 1999; Royal Soc. Lit. fellow, 1972. Fellow Brit. Acad., Brit. Interplanetary Soc.; mem. Soc. for Promotion of Roman Studies. Club: Travellers (London). Home: 52 Peter Coutts Cir Stanford CA 94305-2506 Office: Stanford U Hoover Inst Stanford CA 94305-6010

CONRAD, PAUL FRANCIS, editorial cartoonist; b. Cedar Rapids, Iowa, June 27, 1924; s. Robert H. and Florence G. (Lawler) C.; m. Barbara Kay King, Feb. 27, 1954; children: James, David, Carol, Elizabeth. B.A., U. Iowa, 1950. Editorial cartoonist Denver Post, 1950-64, L.A. Times, 1964-93; cartoonist L.A. Times Syndicate, 1973-2000, Tribune Media Svcs., 2000—. Richard M. Nixon chair Whittier Coll., 1977-78 Exhibited sculpture and cartoons, Los Angeles County Mus. Art, 1979, Libr. of Congress, 1999; author: The King and Us, 1974, Pro and Conrad, 1979, Drawn and Quartered, 1985, CONArtist: Thirty Years With The Los Angeles Times, 1993, Drawing The Line, 1999. Served with C.E. AUS, 1942-46, PTO. Recipient Editl. Cartoon award Sigma Delta Chi, 1963, 69, 71, 81-82, 88, 97, Pulitzer prize editl. cartooning, 1964, 71, 84, Overseas Press Club award, 1970, 81, Journalism award U. So. Calif., 1972, Robert F. Kennedy Journalism award, 1st Prize, 1985, 90, 92, 93, Hugh M. Hefner 1st Amendment award, 1990, Lifetime Achievement award Am. Assn. Editl. Cartoonists, 1998, Lifetime Pub. Svc. award Edmund G. Brown Inst. Pub. Affairs, 2000; sr. fellow Sch. Pub. Policy and Social Rsch., UCLA, 1990—. Fellow Soc. Profl. Journalists; mem. Phi Delta Theta. Democrat. Roman Catholic. Office: LA Times Syndicate 2121 Rosecrans Ave Ste 2370 El Segundo CA 90245-4745

CONRAN, JAMES MICHAEL, consumer advocate, public policy consultant; b. N.Y.C., Mar. 15, 1952; s. James Adrian and Mary Ellen (McGarry) C.; m. Phyllis Jean Thompson, Aug. 1, 1984; children: Michael O., Thomas O. BA, Calif. State U., Northridge, 1975; M in Urban Studies, Occidental Coll., 1978. Mgr. regulatory rels. Pacific Bell, San Francisco, 1985-88, mgr. pub. affairs & pub. issues, 1988-91; dir. State of Calif. Dept. Consumer Affairs, Sacramento, 1991-94; founder, pres. Consumers First, 1994—. Bd. dirs. Consumer Fedn. Calif., Consumer Action, World Instn. Disabilities, Calif. Small Bus. Assoc., Calif. Small Bus. Roundtable, Consumer Interest Rsch. Inst., Nat. Consumers League, Elec. Consumers Alliance, TRW Consumer Adv. Coun., Great Western Fin. Corp., Consumer Adv. Panel, Electric Inst. Consumer Adv. Panel; mem. Coun. Licensing Enforcement and Regulation; nat. bd. certification occupl. therapy World Inst. on Disabilities. Contbr. articles to profl. jours. Bd. dirs. Fight Back! Found., L.A., 1991—, Disabled Children's Computer Group, Orinda, Calif., Telecomm. Edn. Trust Fund-Calif. Pub. Utilities Commn., San Francisco, 1990-91; chair adminstrv. sect. United Calif. State Employees Campaign, Sacramento; mem. Stream Preservation Commn., Orinda, 1988-91, Calif. Rep. Party Cen. Com., Orinda, 1992; del. Rep. Nat. Conv., Houston, 1992; regional chair Bush-Quayle campaign, Orinda, 1992. Fellow Coro Found., 1977, Levere Meml. Found., 1976. Mem. Coro Assocs., Calif. Agenda for Consumer Edn., Sigma Alpha Epsilon. Roman Catholic. Avocations: politics, golf, camping, skiing, wine collecting.

CONROY, THOMAS FRANCIS, insurance company consultant; b. Chgo., Sept. 26, 1938; s. Thomas Francis and Eleanor Althea (Heatherly) C.; m. Mary Elizabeth Schaeffer, June 19, 1965; children: Alexandra B., Margaret E. BSc, De Paul U., 1959; MBA, U. Chgo., 1969. CPA, CDP. Mgr. Ernst & Whinney, Chgo., 1959-74; exec. v.p. fin., treas., contr. Security Life of Denver, 1974-93; prin. Ea. Hemisphere Trading Corp., Denver, 1990—; pres. Security Life Reins., 1993-99, ING Re Internat., 2000-01; mng. prin. Strategic Reins. Cons. Internat., Englewood, Colo., 2001—. Bd. dirs. Buffalo Mountain Met. Dist. Bd. trustees Denver Chamber Orch., 1988-93. Capt. U.S. Army, 1960-62. Fellow Life Mgmt. Inst. Roman Catholic. Office: 3825 S Colorado Blvd Englewood CO 80110-4202 E-mail: tom-conroy@strategicre.com

CONROY, WILLIAM B. retired university administrator; b. Malone, N.Y. m. Patricia Conroy; children: Kathryn, William Michael, David, Carol, Kevin. B in History magna cum laude, U. Notre Dame, 1953; MEd, Syracuse U., 1959, D in Social Sci., 1963. Tchr. U. Tex., U. Wash., Tex. Tech. U.; exec. v.p. N.Mex. State U., Las Cruces, 1985-97, interim pres., 1994-95, pres., 1997—, now pres. emeritus. Mem. Nat. Coun. Geog. Edn., Assn. Am. Geographers, Southwestern Social Sci. Assn. (past pres.), N.Mex. Coun. Univ. Presidents, Las Cruces C. of C. (bd. trustees town-gown com.). Office: NMex State U MSC 388 PO Box 30001 Las Cruces NM 88003-8001 Fax: 505-646-6344. E-mail: wconroy@nmsu.edu

CONSTANTINO, BECKY, political organization administrator; State chmn. Wyo. Rep. State Ctrl. Com., 1999—. Mem. Rep. Nat. Com. Western State Chmn. Assn., 1999—. Office: 400 E 1st St Ste 314 Casper WY 82601-2561

CONSTATINE, DOW, state senator; b. Seattle, Nov. 15, 1061; BA, U. Wash., 1985, JD, 1989, MA, 1992. Atty., 1990-97; legis. aide King County Coun., 1994-96; Dem. rep. dist. 34 Wash. Ho. of Reps., 1997-2000; Dem. senator dist. 34 Wash. State Senate, 2000—. Asst. majority floor leader Wash. State Senate, mem. rules, natural resources, pks. and shorelines coms., vice chair judiciary, ways and means coms. Past pres. West Seattle H.S. Alumni Assn.; founder, v.p. West Seattle H.S. Found.; bd. dirs. Delridge Neighborhoods Devel. Assn., West Seattle Help Line; bd. trustees Allied Arts Seattle; mem. Seattle Design Review Bd., Seattle Open Space Oversight Com. Office: PO Box 40434 Olympia WA 98504-0434 Fax: 360 786-7524. E-mail: constant_do@leg.wa.gov

CONTE, MARIO G., JR. lawyer; BA in English, St. Michael's Coll., Vt., 1965; MS in Pharmacology and Physiology, N.Y. Med. Coll., 1968; JD cum laude, U. Conn., 1978. Bar: Conn. 1978, U.S. Dist. Ct. Conn., Calif. 1979, U.S. Dist. Ct. (so. dist.) Calif., U.S. Ct. Appeals (9th cir.), U.S. Supreme Ct. Law clk. to sr. judge Robert C. Zampano U.S. Dist. Ct. for Dist. Ct., 1978-79; ptnr. Jamison, Conte and McFadden, 1983; trial atty. Fed. Defenders San Diego, Inc., 1979-82, chief trial atty., 1984-91, exec. dir., 1991—, also mem. Fed. Defender's Newsletter. Adj. prof. law U. San Diego Sch. Law, Calif. Western Sch. Law; mem. faculty Nat. Criminal Def. Coll. Contbg. author: Defending a Federal Criminal Case. Bd. dirs. Nat.

Clearinghouse for Battered Women, San Diego, San Diego chpt. Arthritis Found. Recipient President's Accommodation award. Mem. Inst. for Criminal Def. Advocacy (bd. dirs.), San Diego Criminal Def. Bar Assn. (bd. dirs.). Office: Fed Defenders San Diego Inc 225 Broadway Ste 900 San Diego CA 92101-5030

CONTI, ISABELLA, psychologist, consultant; b. Torino, Italy, Jan. 1, 1942; came to U.S., 1964; d. Giuseppe and Zaira (Melis) Ferro; m. ugo Conti, Sept. 5, 1964; 1 child, Maurice. JD, U. Rome, 1966; PhD in psychology, U. Calif., Berkeley, 1975. Lic. psychologist. Sr. analyst Rsch. Inst. for Study of Man, Berkeley, Calif., 1967-68; postgrad. rsch. psychologist Personality Assessment and Rsch. Inst./U. Calif., Berkeley, 1968-71; intern U. Calif. - Berkeley and VA Hosp., San Francisco, 1969-75; asst. prof. St. Mary's Coll., Moraga, Calif., 1978-84. Cons. psychologist Conti Resources, Berkeley, Calif., 1977-85; v.p. Barnes & Conti Assocs., Inc., Berkeley, 1985-90; pres. Lisardco, El Cerrito, Calif., 1989—; bd. dirs. ElectroMagnetic Instruments, Inc., El Cerrito, Calif., 1985—. Author: (with Alfonso Montuori) From Power to Partnership, 1993; contbr. articles on creativity and mgmt. cons. to profl. jours. Trustee Monterey Inst. Internat. Studies, 1996-98. Regents fellow U. Calif.-Berkeley, 1972; NIMH predoctoral rsch. fellow, 1972-73. Mem. APA. Office: Lisardco 1318 Brewster Dr El Cerrito CA 94530-2526

CONTI, PETER SELBY, astronomy educator; b. N.Y.C., Sept. 5, 1934; s. Attilio Carlo and Marie (Selby) C.; m. Carolyn Safford, Aug. 26, 1961; children: Michael, Karen, Kathe BS, Rensselaer Poly. Inst., 1956; PhD, U. Calif-Berkeley, 1963; Honoris Causa degree, U. Utrecht, 1993. Rsch. fellow Calif. Inst. Tech., Pasadena, 1963-66; asst. prof. astronomy U. Calif./Santa Cruz, 1966-71; astronomer Lick Obs., Santa Cruz, 1966-71; prof., fellow Joint Inst. Lab. Astrophysics U. Colo., Boulder, 1971-99, chmn., 1989-90, chmn. dept. astrophys., planetary scis., 1980-86, prof. emeritus, 1999—. Chmn. bd. dirs. Assoc. Univs. for Rsch. in Astronomy Inc., Tuscon, 1983-86; vis. prof. U. Utrecht, The Netherlands, 1969-70, minnaert prof. U. Utrecht, 1995. Editor: Mass Loss and Evolution of O-type Stars, 1979, O Stars and Wolf Rayet Stars, 1988; contbr. over 200 articles to profl. jours. Served to lt. (j.g.) USNR, 1956-59 Recipient Gold medal U. Liege, Belgium, 1975; Fulbright fellow, 1969-70 Fellow AAAS (chmn. sect. D in astronomy 1980); mem. Am. Astron. Soc. (councillor 1983-86), Astron. Soc. of Pacific, Internat. Astron. Union (organizing com. 1983-85, v.p. 1985-88, pres. 1988-91, commn. 29 stellar spectra). Democrat. Home: 817 Racquet Ln Boulder CO 80303-2972 Office: U Colo-Boulder Joint Inst Lab Astrophysics Campus Box 440 Boulder CO 80309-0440

CONTI, SAMUEL, federal judge; b. L.A., July 16, 1922; s. Fred and Katie C.; m. Dolores Crosby, July 12, 1952; children: Richard, Robert, Cynthia. BS, U. Santa Clara, 1945; LLB, Stanford U., 1948, JD. Bar: Calif. 1948. Pvt. practice, San Francisco and Contra Costa County, 1948-60; city atty. City of Concord, Calif., 1960-69; judge Superior Ct. Contra Costa County, 1968-70, U.S. Dist. Ct. (no. dist.) Calif., San Francisco, 1970-88, sr. judge, 1988—. Mem. Ctrl. Contra Costa Bar Assn. (pres.), Concord C. of C. (pres.), Alpha Sigma Nu. Office: US Dist Ct 450 Golden Gate Ave Ste 36052 San Francisco CA 94102-3482

CONTINETTI, ROBERT E. chemistry educator; Prof. dept. chemistry U. Calif. San Diego, La Jolla, Calif., 1992—. Recipient Packard Found. fellow, 1994. Office: U Calif San Diego Dept Chem & Biochem Dept 332 MC-0340 9500 Gilman Dr La Jolla CA 92093-0340 E-mail: icontinetti@ucsd.edu

CONTOS, PAUL ANTHONY, engineer, investment consultant; b. Chgo., Mar. 18, 1926; s. Anthony Dimitrios and Panagiota (Kostopoulos) C.; m. Lilian Katie Kalkines, June 19, 1955 (dec. Apr. 1985); children: Leslie, Claudia, Paula, Anthony. Student, Am. TV Inst., Chgo., 1946-48, U. Ill., , 1949-52, 53-56, Ill. Inst. Tech., 1952-53, U. So. Calif., 1956-57. Engr. J.C. Deagan Co., Inc., Chgo., 1951-53, Lockheed Missile and Space Co., Inc., Sunnyvale, Calif., 1956-62, engring. supr., 1962-65, staff engr., 1965-88; genealogy rsch. San Jose, Calif., 1970—; pres. PAC Investments, Saratoga, 1984-88, San Jose, 1988—, also advisor, cons., 1984—. Mem. Pres. Coun. U. Ill., 1994—. With U.S. Army, 1944-46, ETO. Decorated Purple Heart. Mem. DAV (life, commdr. Chgo. unit 1948-51), VFW (life), Pi Sigma Phi (pres. 1951-53). Republican. Greek Orthodox. Avocation: genealogy research. Home and Office: Paseo Villas No 407 130 E San Fernando Street San Jose CA 95112-7414 E-mail: paulacontos@illinoisalumni.org

CONTRERAS, THOMAS J., JR. career officer; b. Morenci, Ariz. m. Gloria Rachel Gutierrez, Sept. 4, 1965; children: Naomi, Thomas. BS in Chemistry and Secondary Edn., No. Ariz. U., 1967; MS in Phys. Organic Chemistry, U. Utah, 1969; PhD in Physiology, Uniformed Svcs. U. Health Sci., 1983. Commd. lt. (j.g.) USN, 1971, advanced through grades to capt.; prin. investigator Naval Blood Rsch. Lab., Boston, 1972-76, Armed Forces Radiobiology Rsch. Inst., Bethesda, Md., 1976-79, Naval Med. Rsch. Inst., Bethesda, 1982-85; rsch. area mgr. combat casualty care Naval Med. R&D Command, Bethesda, 1985-87; tech. area mgr. biomed. and chem./biol. warfare def. program Office of Naval Tech., Office of Chief of Naval Rsch., Arlington, Va., 1987-91, dep. dir. support technologies directorate, 1989-91; exec. officer Naval Health Rsch. Ctr., San Diego, 1991-95; comdg. officer Naval Med. Rsch. Inst., Bethesda, 1995-98, Naval Med. Rsch. Ctr., Forest Glen, Md., 1998-99, Naval Health Rsch. Ctr., San Diego, 1999-2001. Contbr. articles to profl. jours. Decorated Joint Svc. Commendation medal, Meritorious Svc. medal with 2 gold stars, Legion of Merit with gold star; recipient Hispanic Engring. Nat. Achievement award for profl. achievement in govt., 1991, Hispanic Mag. Role Model of the Yr. award, 1992, Nat. Image Inc. Meritorious Svc. award, 1993, No. Ariz. U. Disting. Citizen award, 1995, Outstanding Alumnus award of Dept. Chemistry, 1995. Mem. Soc. Armed Forces Med. Lab. Scientists, Soc. for Advancement of Chicanos and Native Americans in Sci., Assn. Naval Svc. Officers. Office: Commanding Officer Naval Health Rsch Ctr PO Box 85122 San Diego CA 92186-5122 E-mail: co@nhrc.navy.mil

CONWAY, CRAIG, computer software executive; Exec. v.p. mktg., sales & ops. Oracle Corp.; pres., chief exec. TGV Software, Inc., OneTouch Syss.; pres., COO, CEO PeopleSoft, Pleasanton, Calif., 1999—. Bd. dirs. PeopleSoft, Aspect Telecomm. Corp., SalesLogix Corp. Office: PeopleSoft 4460 Hacienda Dr Pleasanton CA 94588

CONWAY, JOHN E. federal judge; b. 1934; BS, U.S. Naval Acad., 1956; LLB magna cum laude, Washburn U., 1963. Assoc. Matias A Zamora, Santa Fe, 1963-64; ptnr. Wilkinson, Durrett & Conway, Alamogordo, N.Mex., 1964-67, Durrett, Conway & Jordon, Alamogordo, 1967-80, Montgomery & Andrews, P.A., Albuquerque, 1980-86; city atty. Alamogordo, 1966-72; mem. N.Mex. State Senate, 1970-80, minority leader, 1972-80; chief fed. judge U.S. Dist. Ct. N.Mex., Albuquerque, 1986-2000, sr. fed. judge, 2000—. Mem. Jud. Resources Com., 1995-98. 1st lt. USAF, 1956-60. Mem. 10th Cir. Dist. Judges Assn. (pres. 1995-98), Fed. Judges Assn. (bd. dirs. 1996—), Nat. Commrs. on Uniform State Laws, N.Mex. Bar Assn., N.Mex. Jud. Coun. (vice chmn. 1973, chmn. 1973-75, disciplinary bd. of Supreme Ct. of N.Mex. vice chmn. 1980, chmn. 1981-84). Office: US Dist Ct Chambers #740 333 Lomas Blvd NW Albuquerque NM [illegible]

CONWAY, JOHN S. history educator; b. London, Dec. 31, 1929; s. Geoffrey S. and Elsie (Philips) C.; m. Ann P. Jefferies, Aug. 10, 1957; children— David, Jane, Alison BA, Cambridge U., Eng., 1952; MA, Cambridge U., 1955, PhD, 1956. Asst. prof. U. Man., Can., 1955-57; asst. prof., assoc. prof., then prof. history U. B.C., Vancouver, 1957-94, prof. emeritus, 1995—. Mem. editl. bd. dirs. Holocaust and Genocide Studies, Kirchliche Zeitgeschichte; Smallman Disting. vis. prof. history U. Western On., 1998. Author: The Nazi Persecution of the Churches, 1968, 2d edit., 1997. Contbr. numerous articles on churches and the holocaust to topical publs. Pres. Tibetan Refugee Aid Soc., Can., 1971-81; chmn. Vancouver Coalition with World Refugees, 1982-84. Recipient Queen's Silver Jubilee medal, 1977. Mem. Can. Inst. Internat. Affairs, German Studies Assn., Can. Hist. Assn. Anglican. Home: 4345 Locarno Crescent Vancouver BC Canada V6R 1G2 Office: U BC Dept History Wesbrook Mall Vancouver BC Canada V6T 1Z1

CONWAY, NANCY ANN, newspaper editor; b. Foxboro, Mass., Oct. 15, 1941; d. Leo T. and Alma (Goodwin) C.; children: Ana Lucia DaSilva, Kara Ann Martin. Cert. in med. tech., Carnegie Inst., 1962; BA in English, U. Mass., 1976, cert. in secondary edn., 1978. Tchr. Brazil-Am. Inst., Rio de Janeiro, 1963-68; freelance writer, editor Amherst, Mass., 1972-76; staff writer Daily Hampshire Gazette, North Hampton, 1976-77; editor Amherst Bull., 1977-80, Amherst Record, 1980-83; features editor Holyoke (Mass.) Transcript/Telegram, 1983-84; gen. mgr. Monday-Thursday Newspapers, Boca Raton, Fla., 1984-87; dir. editorial South Fla. Newspaper Network, Deerfield Beach, 1987-90; pub., editor York (Pa.) Newspapers, Inc., 1990-95; metro editor Denver Post, 1995-96; exec. editor, v.p. Alameda Newspaper Group, Pleasanton, Calif., 1996—. Bd. dirs. Math.: Opportunities in Engring., Sci. and Tech.-Pa. State, York, 1991-95. Recipient writing awards, state newspaper assns. Mem. Am. Soc. Newspaper Editors, Soc. Profl. Journalists. Avocations: literature, photography, communication gardening. Office: The Tribune Tower 401 13th St Oakland CA 94612 E-mail: nconway@angnewspapers.com

CONWAY, TIM, comedian; b. Willoughby, Ohio, Dec. 15, 1933; m. Mary Anne Dalton, 1961; children: Kelly Ann, Timothy, Patrick, Jaimie, Corey, Seann. Student, Bowling Green (Ohio) State U. Writer, dir., occasional performer, Sta. KYW-TV, Cleve.; regular TV series The Steve Allen Show, 1961, McHale's Navy, 1962-66, The John Gary Show, 1966, Rango, 1967, (host) Turn-On, 1965, The Tim Conway Show, 1970, The Carol Burnett Show, 1975-79, The Tim Conway Comedy Hour, 1980-81, Tim Conway's Funny America, 1990, (voice) Disney's Hercules, 1998; other TV appearances include: Hollywood Palace, Steve Allen Show, Garry Moore Show, That's Life; film appearances include McHale's Navy, 1964, McHale's Navy Joins the Air Force, 1965, The World's Greatest Athlete, 1973, The Apple Dumpling Gang, 1975, Gus, 1976, The Shaggy D.A., 1976, Cannonball Run II, 1984, Cyclone, 1987, Dear God, 1996, Speed 2: Cruise Control, 1997, Air Bud 2, 1998; actor, writer Billion Dollar Hobo, 1978, They Went That-a-Way and That-a-Way, 1978, The Prizefighter, 1979, The Private Eyes, 1981, The Longshot, 1986; also numerous nightclub appearances, TV commls.; TV movie Roll, Freddy, Roll, 1974; appeared on episodes TV series Married...with Children, The Larry Sanders Show, Coach, Diagnosis Murder, (voice) The Simpsons, Touched by an Angel, Suddenly Susan, The Drew Carey Show, (voice) The Wild Thornberrys, Ellen, The Roseanne Show, Clueless, Mad About You; videos include Dorf's Golf Bible, 1987, Dorf on Golf, 1987, Dorf and the First Games of Mount Olympus, 1988, Dorf Goes Auto Racing, 1990, Dorf Goes Fishing, 1993, Dorf on the Diamond, 1996, Tim and Harvey in the Great Outdoors, 1998. Served in U.S. Army. Recipient Emmy awards, 1973, 77, 78. Mem. AFTRA. Office: Conway Enterprises PO Box 17047 Encino CA 91416-7047

COOK, ALBERT THOMAS THORNTON, JR. financial advisor; b. Cleve., Apr. 24, 1940; s. Albert Thomas Thornton and Tyra Esther (Morehouse) C.; m. Mary Jane Blackburn, June 1, 1963; children: Lara Keller, Thomas, Timothy. BA, Dartmouth Coll., 1962; MA, U. Chgo., 1966. Asst. sec. Dartmouth Coll., Hanover, N.H., 1972-77; exec. dir. Big Brothers, Inc., N.Y.C., 1977-78; underwriter Boettcher & Co., Denver, 1978-81; asst. v.p. Dain Bosworth Inc., Denver, 1981-82, Colo. Nat. Bank, Denver, 1982-84; pres. The Albert T.T. Cook Co., Denver, 1984—. Arbitrator Nat. Assn. Securities Dealers, N.Y.C., 1985—, Mcpl. Securities Rulemaking Bd., Washington, 1987-98. Pres. Etna-Hanover Ctr. Community Assn., Hanover, N.H., 1974-76; mem. Mayor's Task Force, Denver, 1984; bd. dirs. Rude Park Community Nursery, Denver, 1985-87, Willows Water Dist., Colo., 1990—, pres., 1998-99; trustee The Iliff Sch. Theol., Denver, 1986-92; mem. Dartmouth Coll. Com. on Trustees, 1990-93. Mem. Dartmouth Alumni Coun. (exec. com., chmn. nominating and trustee search coms. 1987-89), University Club (chmn. admissions com. 1997-98), Cactus Club (Denver), Dartmouth Club of N.Y.C., Yale Club, Lions (bd. dirs. Denver chpt. 1983-85, treas. 1986-87, pres. Denver Found. 1987-88, 2d v.p. 2001—), Delta Upsilon. Congregationalist. Avocations: fly fishing, furniture making, running, skiing, backpacking. Home: 7099 E Hinsdale Pl Centennial CO 80112-1610 Office: One Tabor Ctr 1200 17th St Ste 960 Denver CO 80202-5835

COOK, BRIAN R. corporate professional; BA in Acctg., We. Wash. U. CPA. Various fin. and managerial positions Sea Galley Stores, Inc.; chmn. bd., pres. & CEO Direct Focus, Inc., Vancouver, Wash., 1986—. Office: Direct Focus Inc 2220 NE 65th Ave Vancouver WA 98661

COOK, DAVID ALASTAIR, pharmacology educator; b. Haslemere, Surrey, Eng., May 19, 1942; emigrated to Can., 1967; s. James W. and Monica (Reekes) C. M.A., D.Phil, Oriel Coll., Oxford U. Postdoctoral fellow U. Alta., Edmonton, 1967-70, asst. prof., 1970-74, assoc. prof., 1974-79, prof., 1979—, chmn. dept. pharmacology, 1981-91, dir. div. study med. edn., 1990—. Contbr. articles to profl jours. Named Tchr. of Yr., Med. Students Assn., 1974, 79, 81, 83, 94, Hon. Graduating Class Pres., 1987; recipient Pharm. Soc. Jour. award, 1977; 3M Tchg. fellow, 1996, Rutherford Tchg. award, 2000. Mem. Pharm. Soc. Can., Can. Soc. Clin. Pharmacology, Can. Assn. Med. Edn., Western Pharm. Soc., Soc. Toxicology of Can., Brit. Pharm. Soc., Soc. Dirs. Rsch. in Med. Edn. (pres.) Office: U Alta Divsn Studies Med Edn Edmonton AB Canada T6G 2R7

COOK, DONALD E. pediatrician, educator; b. Pitts., Mar. 24, 1928; s. Merriam E. and Bertha (Gwin) C.; m. Elsie Walden, Sept. 2, 1951; children: Catherine, Christopher, Brian, Jeffrey. BS, Colo. Coll., 1951; MD, U. Colo., 1955. Diplomate Am. Bd. Pediatrics, 1961. Intern Fresno County Gen. Hosp., Calif., 1955-56; resident in gen. practice Tulare (Calif.) County Gen. Hosp., 1956-57; resident in pediatrics U. Colo., 1957-59; practice medicine specializing in pediatrics Aurora, Colo., 1959-64, Greeley (Colo). Med. Clin., Greeley Sports Medicine Clin., 1964-93; med. adv. Centennial Develop. Svcs., Inc., 1993-95; clin. faculty U. Colo., clin. prof., 1977—; pres. Am. Acad. Pediatrics, Elk Grove Village, Il., 1999-2000. Organizer, dir. Sports Medicine Px Exam Clinic for indigent Weld Co. athletes, 1990-96; mem. adv. bd. Nat. Center Health Edn., San Francisco, 1978-80; mem. adv. com. on maternal and child health programs Colo. State Health Dept., 1981-84, chmn., 1981-84; preceptor Sch. Nurse Practitioner Program U. Colo., 1978-88; affiliate prof. nursing U. No. Colo., 1990; vol. physician Monfort Children's Clinic, 2000-01. Mem. Weld County Dist. 6 Sch. Bd., 1973-83, pres. 1973-74, 76-77, chmn. dist. 6 accountability com., 1972-73; mem. adv. com. dist. 6 teen pregnancy program, 1983-85; mem. Weld County Task Force on teen-aged pregnancy, 1986-89, Dream Team Weld County Task Force on sch. dropouts, 1986-92, Weld County Interagy. Screening Bd., Weld County Cmty. Ctr. Found. 1984-89, Weld County Task Force Spkrs. Bur. on AIDS, 1987-94; mem. Weld County Task Force Adolescent Health Clinic; mem. Task Force Child Abuse, C. of C.; bd. dirs. No. Colo. Med. Ctr., 1993-98, No. Colo. Med. Ctr. Found., 1994—; med. advisor Weld County Sch. Dist. VI-Nurses, 1987—; mem. Sch. Dist. 6 Health Coalition, Task Force on access to health care; group leader neonatal group Colo. Action for Healthy People Colo. Dept. Pub. Health, 1885-86; co-founder Colorodoans for seatbelts on sch. buses, 1985-90; co-founderm v,p. Coalition of primary care physicians, Colo., 1986; mem. adv. com. Greeley Cen. Drug and Alcohol Abuse, 1984-86, Rocky Mtn. Ctr. for Health Promotion and Edn., bd. dirs., 1984—, v.p., 1992-93, pres., 1994-95; rep. coun. on med. specialty soc., AAP, 1988-89, mem. coun. pediatric rsch., communications, rep. to nat. PTA, 1990-94, mem. coun. on govt. affairs, 1989-90, rep. to coun. sects. mgmt. com., mem. search com. for new exec. dir.; med. cons. Sch. Dist. 6, 1989—; adv. com. bd. comm., adv. com. bd. membership comm., adv. com. bd. fin., adv. com. bd. dirs. AAP, 1990-95, AAP com. govt. affairs, 1990; United Way Weld County, 1993-98; founder, med. dir. Montfort Children's Clinic, 1994-98. With USN, 1946-48. Recipient Disting. Svc. award Jr. C. of C., 1962, Disting. Citizenship award Elks, 1975-76, Svc. to Mankind award Sertoma Club, 1972, Spark Plug award U. No. Colo., 1981, Eta Sigma Gamma Svc. award, 1996; Mildred Doster award Colo. Sch. Health Coun. for sch. health contbns., 1992, Citizen of Yr. award No. Colo. Med. Ctr. Found., 1996, Humanitarian of Yr. award Weld County United Way, 1996, Alfred Winchester Humanitarian award Greeley/Weld Sr. Found., Inc., 1996, Silver and Gold award U. Colo. Med. Alumni Assn., 1997, Franklin Geggenbach award Denver Children's Hosp. Pediatric Alumni award, 1997, Benezet award Colo. Coll., 2000, Svc. to Mankind award Elks Club, 2000-01. Mem. Colo. Med. Soc. Sch. Health Com. (chmn. 1967-78), Am. Acad. Pediatrics (pres. 1999-2000, alt. dist. chmn. 1987-93, dist. chmn. dist. VIII 1993-98, chmn. alt. dist. chmn. com. 1991-93, chmn. sch. health com. 1975-80, chmn. Colo. chpt. 1982-87, mem. task force on new age of pediatrics 1982-85, Ross edn. and award com. 1985-86, media spokesperson Speak Up for Children 1983—, mem. coun. sects. mgmt. 1991-92, mem. search com., exec. dir., candidate for pres. 1998, pres. elect 1998-99, v.p., AAP, 1998-99, pres. 1999—), AMA (chmn. sch. and coll. health com. 1980-82, James E. Strain Community Svc. award 1987, 94, coun. pediatric practice), Adams Aurora Med. Soc. (pres. 1964-65), Weld County Med. Soc. (pres. 1968-69), Colo. Med. Soc. (com. on sports medicine 1980-90, com. chmn. 1986-90, chmn. com. sch. health 1988-91, A.H. Robbins Community Svc. award 1974), Centennial Pediatric Soc. (pres. 1982-86), Rotary (bd. dirs. Greely chpt. 1988-91, mem. immunization com. 1994—, chmn. immunization campaign Weld county 1994). Republican. Methodist. Office: Monfort Children's Clinic 100 N 11th Ave Greeley CO 80631 Address: Amer Acad Pediatrics 141 NW Point Blvd Elk Grove Village IL 60007-1019 E-mail: dcook@aap.org

COOK, DOUGLAS NEILSON, theater educator, producer, artistic director; b. Phoenix, Sept. 22, 1929; s. Neil Estes and Louise Y. (Wood) C.; m. Joan Stafford Buechner, Aug. 11, 1956; children: John Richard, Peter Neilson, Stephen Barton. Student, Phoenix Coll., 1948-49, U. Chgo., 1949-50, UCLA, 1950-51, Los Angeles Art Inst., 1948; B.F.A., U. Ariz., 1953; M.A., Stanford U., 1955; postgrad., Lester Polakov Studio Stage Design, 1966-67. Instr. San Mateo (Calif.) Coll., 1955-57, Nat. Music Camp, Interlochen, Mich., 1961; asst. prof. drama U. Calif., Riverside, 1957-66, assoc. prof., chair theatre dept., 1967-70; head dept. Pa. State U., University Park, 1970-88, sr. prof. theatre arts, 1988-92, prof. emeritus, 1992—; prodr., artistic dir. Utah Shakespearean Festival, Cedar City. Actor Corral Theatre, Tucson, 1952-53, Orleans (Mass.) Arena Theatre, 1953; dir., designer Palo Alto (Calif.) Community Theatre, 1954, Peninsula Children's Theatre, 1956-57; assoc. producer Utah Shakespearean Festival, Cedar City, 1964-90, producing artistic dir., 1990—; producer Pa. State Festival Theatre, State College, 1970-85, The Nat. Wagon Train Show, 1975-76. Instl. rep. Juniata Valley council Boy Scouts Am., 1973-77; bd. dirs. Central Pa. Festival Arts, 1970-75, 84-87, v.p., 1984-86; bd. dirs. Nat. theatre Conf., 1980-90, v.p. 1983-85, pres. 1987-88. Recipient disting. alumni award U. Ariz., 1990; named to Coll. of Fellows of the Am. Theatre, 1994. Mem. AAUP, Shakespeare Theatre Assn. Am. (v.p. 1990-92, pres. 1993-94), Nat. Assn. Schs. Theatre, Am. Theatre Assn. (bd. dirs. 1977-86, exec. com. 1979-80, pres. 1984-85), U.S. Inst. Theatre Tech., Am. Soc. Theatre Rsch., Univ. Resident Theatre Assn. (bd. dirs. 1970-88, v.p. 1975-79, pres. 1979-83), Theatre Assn. Pa. (bd. dirs. 1972-76). Home: PO Box 10194 Phoenix AZ 85064-0194 Office: Utah Shakespearean Festival 351 W Center St Cedar City UT 84720-2470

COOK, MELANIE, lawyer; Ptnr. Bloom Hergott Cook Diemer & Klein, Beverly Hills, Calif. Office: Bloom Hergott Diemer & Cook 150 S Rodeo Dr Fl 3 Beverly Hills CA 90212-2410

COOK, MERRILL A. former congressman, explosives industry executive; b. Phila., May 6, 1946; s. Melvin A. and Wanda (Garfield) C.; m. Camille Sanders, Oct. 24, 1969; children: Brian, Alison, Barbara Ann, David, Michelle. BA magna cum laude, U. Utah, 1969; MBA, Harvard U., 1971. Profl. staff cons. Arthur D. Little, Inc., Cambridge, Mass., 1971-73; mng. dir. Cook Assocs., Inc., Salt Lake City, 1973-78; pres. Cook Slurry Co., Salt Lake City, 1978—; mem. U.S. Congress from 2d Utah dist., 1997-2001. Patentee in field. Del. Rep. Nat. Conv., Kansas City, Mo., 1976, San Diego, 1996, Phila., 2000. Mem. Salt Lake City C. of C., Phi Kappa Phi. Mormon. Home: 631 16th Ave Salt Lake City UT 84103-3704*

COOK, PAUL MAXWELL, technology company executive; b. Ridgewood, N.J. BSChemE, MIT, 1947. With Stanford Rsch. Inst., Menlo Park, Calif., 1948-53, Sequoia Process Corp., 1953-56, Raychem Corp., Menlo Park, Calif., 1957-95, founder, former pres., CEO, until 1990, chmn., bd. dirs., until 1995; chmn., CEO CellNet Data Sys., San Carlos, 1990-94; chmn., bd. dirs. SRI Internat., 1993-98; chmn. DIVA Sys. Corp., Menlo Park, Calif., 1995—, CEO, 1995-99; founder, CEO, Agile TV Corp., 2000—. Mem. exec. com. San Francisco Bay Area Coun., 1988-94, chmn., 1990-91. Recipient Nat. Medal Tech., 1988; named to San Francisco Bay Area Bus. Hall of Fame, 1999. Mem. NAE, Am. Acad. Sci., Environ. Careers Orgn. (past chmn., bd. trustees), MIT Corp. (life, emeritus). Office: Diva Sys Corp 800 Saginaw Dr Bldg 205 Redwood City CA 94063-4740 E-mail: pcook@agile.tv

COOK, RICHARD A. aerospace engineer; BS in Engring. Physics, U. Colo.; MS in Aerospace U., U. Tex., 1989. With Jet Propulsion Lab., Pasadena, Calif., 1989—, flight ops. mgr. Mars Pathfinder project. Office: Jet Propulsion Lab 4600 Oak Grove Dr Pasadena CA 91109

COOK, RICHARD W. motion picture company executive; b. Bakersfield, Calif., Aug. 20, 1950; Ed., U. So. Calif. Saels rep. Disneyland, 1971-74, sales mgr., 1974-77; mgr. pay TV and non-theatrical releases Disney Studios, 1977-80; asst. domestic sales mgr. Buena Vista, 1980-81, v.p., asst. gen. sales mgr., 1981-84, v.p., gen. sales mgr., 1985-88, sr. v.p. domestic distbn., 1988-94; pres. Buena Vista Pictures Distbn., 1994; pres. worldwide mktg. Buena Vista Pictures Mktg., 1994-97; chmn. Walt Disney Motion Pictures Group, Burbank, Calif., 1997—. Office: Walt Disney Studios 500 S Buena Vista St Burbank CA 91521-0006

COOK, ROBERT CROSSLAND, research chemist; b. New Haven, June 5, 1947; s. Russell C. and Tensia (Veazey) C. BS in Chemistry, Lafayette Coll., 1969; MPh in Phys. Chemistry, Yale U., 1971, PhD in Theoretical Chemistry, 1973. Mem. faculty Lafayette Coll., Easton, Pa., 1973-81; staff scientist Lawrence Livermore (Calif.) Nat. Lab., 1981—. Instr. Calif. State

U., Hayward, 1985-86, 94, Chabot Coll., 1986-90, Las Positas Coll., 1990-92; mem. vis. faculty Dartmouth Coll., Hanover, N.H., 1977, 78, 79, Colo. State U., Ft. Collins, 1980. Contbr. articles to profl. jours. Grantee in field. Mem. Am. Chem. Soc., Am. Phys. Soc., Sigma Xi. Office: Lawrence Livermore Nat Lab L-481 PO Box 808 Livermore CA 94551-0808 E-mail: bobcook@llnl.gov

COOK, STEPHEN CHAMPLIN, retired shipping company executive; b. Portland, Oreg., Sept. 20, 1915; s. Frederick Stephen and Mary Louise (Boardman) C.; m. Dorothy White, Oct. 27, 1945 (dec. Sept. 1998); children: Mary H. Cook Goodson, John B., Samuel D., Robert B. (dec.). Student, U. Oreg., 1935-36. Surveyor U.S. Engrs. Corp., Portland, Oreg., 1934-35; dispatcher Pacific Motor Trucking Co., Oakland, Calif., 1937-38; manifest clk. Pacific Truck Express, Portland, 1939; exec. asst. Coastwise Line, San Francisco, 1940-41, mgr. K-Line svc., 1945-56; chartering mgr. Ocean Svc. Inc. subs. Marcona Corp., San Francisco, 1956-75, ret., 1975. Cons., San Francisco, 1976-78. Author 1 charter party, 1957. Mem. steering com. Dogwood Festival, Lewiston, Idaho, 1985-92; sec. Asotin County Reps., Clarkston, Wash., 1986-88; adv. bd. Clarkston Pt. Commrs., 1989-92. Lt. USN, 1941-45, PTO; grand marshall Asotin Christmas Parade, 2000. Recipient Pres.'s award Marin (Calif.) coun. Boy Scouts Am., 1977, Order of Merit, 1971, 84, Skillern award Lewis Clark coun., 1982, Silver Beaver award 1987; Lewis-Clark Valley Vol. award, 1987, Youth Corps award Nat. Assn. Svc. and Conservation Corps, 1990, Pres.'s Spl. award Clarkston C. of C., 1983, Asotin Citizen of Yr. award, 1999. Mem. VFW, Asotin County Hist. Soc. (hon. life pres. 1982-83, bd. dirs.), Asotin C. of C. (v.p. 1994-95). Republican. Mem. Stand for United Ch. of Christ. Avocations: hiking, camping, stamp collecting.

COOK, TIMOTHY D. computer company executive; BS in Indsl. Engring., Auburn U.; MBA, Duke U. Dir. N.Am. fulfillment IBM; COO reseller divsn. Intelligent Electronics; v.p. corp. materials Compaq; sr. v.p. worldwide ops. Apple Computer, Inc., Cupertino, Calif. Fuqua scholar Duke U. Office: 1 Infinite Loop Cupertino CA 95014-2083

COOK, TONY MICHAEL, legislative staff member; m. Joy Cook; children: Michael, Libby. BA, Wash. State U., 1970; JD, Stanford U., 1973. Bar: Wash. 1973. With Senate Rsch. Ctr., 1973, U. Wash.; mem. staff Utilities and Transp. Commn., 1977; counsel Wash. State Senate, 1991, sec., 1999—; counsel Legis. Ethics Bd., 1997. Office: Wash State Senate PO Box 40482 Olympia WA 98504-0482 Fax: 360-786-7520. E-mail: cook_to@leg.wa.gov

COOK, WILLIAM HOWARD, architect; b. Evanston, Ill., Dec. 19, 1924; s. Clare Cyril and Matilda Hermine (Schuldt) C.; m. Nancy Ann Dean, Feb. 1, 1949; children: Robert, Cynthia, James. BA, UCLA, 1947; BArch, U. Mich., 1952. Chief designer Fabrica de Muebles Camacho-Roldan, Bogota, Colombia, S.Am., 1949-52; assoc. architect Orus Eash, Traverse City, Mich., Ft. Wayne, Ind., 1952-60; ptnr. Cook & Swaim (architects), Tucson, 1961-68; project specialist in urban devel. Banco Interamericano de Desarrollo, Buenos Aires, Argentina, 1968-69; pres. Cain, Nelson, Wares, Cook and Assocs., architects, Tucson, 1969-82. Vis. lectr. architecture U. Ariz., 1980-89; coord. archtl. exch. with U. LaSalle, Mexico City, 1983, 85, 87, 89, 93. Lt. (j.g.) USNR, 1943-46. Served to lt. (j.g.) USNR, 1943-46. Fellow AIA (pres. So. Ariz. 1967); mem. Ariz. Soc. Architects (pres. 1970), Ariz. Soc. of AIA (Architect's medal 1981) Presbyterian. Home and Office: PO Box 347 Sonoita AZ 85637-0347 E-mail: fincadesonoita@theriver.com

COOKE, CHRISTOPHER ROBERT, former state judge, lawyer; b. Springfield, Ohio, Dec. 23, 1943; s. Warren and Margaret Louise (Martin) C.; m. Margaret (Nick), July 1, 1970; children— Karen, Anastasia, Nicholas. B.A., Yale U., 1965; J.D., U. Mich., 1968. Bar: Ohio 1968, Alaska 1970, U.S. Dist. Ct. Alaska 1970. Atty., Alaska Legal Services Corp., Anchorage, 1968-71, supervising atty., Bethel, 1971-73; mem. firm Rice, Hoppner & Hedland, Bethel, 1973-76; superior ct. judge State of Alaska, Bethel, 1976-86; ptnr. Hedland, Fleischer, Friedman, Brennan & Cooke, Bethel and Anchorage, 1986—. Composer, singer Chris Cooke's Tundra Music, 1981. Bd. regents U. Alaska-Fairbanks, 1975-77; mem. com. Alaska Humanities Forum, Anchorage, 1979-86; adv. bd. Bethel Sch. Bd., 1982-83. Mem. ABA, Alaska Bar Assn. Home and Office: PO Box 555 Bethel AK 99559-0555

COOKE, JOHN F. entertainment company executive; Exec. v.p. corp. affairs Walt Disney Co., Burbank, Calif.; exec. v.p. external affairs J. Paul Getty Trust, L.A., 2000 . Office: J Paul Getty Trust 1200 Getty Center Dr Ste 400 Los Angeles CA 90049-1681

COOKE, JOHN P. cardiologist, medical educator, medical researcher; BA in Biology, Cornell U., 1976; MD, Wayne State U., 1980; PhD in Physiology, Mayo Grad. Sch. of Medicine, 1985. Diplomate Am. Bd. Internal Medicine, Am. Bd. Cardiovascular Disease; cert. instr. advanced cardiac life support Am. Heart Assn. Assoc. physician Brigham and Women's Hosp., Boston, 1987-90; asst. prof. medicine Harvard Med. Sch., Boston, 1987-90, Stanford (Calif.) U. Sch. of Medicine, 1990-95, dir. sect. vascular medicine, 1991—, assoc. prof. medicine, 1995—, dir. sect. cardiovascular medicine, 1995—. Mem. editl. bd. Jour. Vascular Medicine and Biology, 1990—; contbr. articles to profl. jours. Rsch. fellow Mayo Grad. Sch. of Medicine, 1980-87; Merck fellow Am. Coll. Cardiology, 1985-86; recipient Henry Christian award Am. Fedn. Clin. Rsch., 1990, Vascular Acad. award NIH, 1991. Mem. Soc. Vascular Medicine and Biology (fouder). Office: Stanford U Divsn Cardiovascular Medicine 300 Pasteur Dr Palo Alto CA 94304-2203

COOKE, ROGER ANTHONY, retired lawyer; b. Bklyn., June 11, 1948; s. John J. and Virginia (Humphreys) C.; m. Joan J. Cirillo, June 19, 1976; children: Julia Cirillo, Elizabeth Cirillo. AB, Georgetown U., 1970, JD, 1973. Bar: N.Y. 1974. Assoc. Simpson, Thacher and Bartlett, 1973-80; dep. gen. counsel, sec. Pan Am. World Airways, N.Y.C., 1981-90; v.p., gen. counsel Fred Meyer Inc., 1990-2000. Mem. Assn. of Bar of City of N.Y. (aeros. com.). Office: Fred Meyer Incorporated 3800 SE 22nd Ave PO Box 42121 Portland OR 97242-0121

COOLEDGE, RICHARD CALVIN, lawyer; b. Charleston, S.C., Apr. 20, 1943; s. Russell Clarence and Lorena Ann (Weymuth) C.; m. Nancy Jean Western, June 15, 1965 (div. Dec. 1986); children: Dean Richard, Mark Alan, Jocelyn Joy; m. Jeanine Diana Smith, Apr. 12, 1989 (div. Nov. 1993). BA in Econs. with honors, U. Mo., Columbia, 1965; JD, U. Mich., 1968. Bar: Ariz. 1969, U.S. Dist. Ct. Ariz. 1969, U.S. Ct. Appeals (9th cir.) 1973, U.S. Supreme Ct. 1973. Mem. Brown & Bain P.A., Phoenix, 1968—. Contbg. editor: Banking and Lending Institutions Forms, Business Workouts Manual; contbr. articles to profl. jours. Fellow Ariz. Bar Found.; mem. Phoenix Rolls Royce Owners (pres. 1980), Harley Owners Group, Motorcycle Safety Found. (instr.), Bentley Drivers Club Ltd. Avocations: motorcycling, golf, music, aviculture. Office: Brown & Bain PA 2901 N Central Ave Fl 20 Phoenix AZ 85012-2700 E-mail: colledge@browngain.com

COOLEY, WES, former congressman; b. L.A., Calif., Mar. 28, 1932; married; 4 children. AA, El Camino C. C.; BS in Bus., U. So. Calif., 1958. Asst. to pres. Hyland Labs. divsn. Baxter Labs. Allergan Pharmaceuticals; asst. to chmn. bd. ICN, divsn. mgr., dir. drug regulatory affairs; v.p. Virateck divsn.; founder, co-owner Rose Labs., Inc., 1981—; mem. Oregon State Senate, 1992-94; congressman 104 Congress from 2nd Oreg. dist., 1994-96. Mem. House Com. Agriculture, House Com. Resources, House Com. Veteran Affairs, Subcommittee Gen. Farm Commodities, Subcommittee on Livestock, Dairy and Poultry, Subcommittee on Nat. Pks., Forests and Lands, Subcom. Water and Power Resources. With U.S. Army Spl. Forces, 1952-54. Address: 25550 Walker Rd Bend OR 97701-9323 E-mail: honwescooley@cs.com

COOMBE, GEORGE WILLIAM, JR. lawyer, retired banker; b. Kearny, N.J., Oct. 1, 1925; s. George William and Laura (Montgomery) C.; A.B., Rutgers U., 1946; LL.B., Harvard, 1949; m. Marilyn V. Ross, June 4, 1949; children— Susan, Donald William, Nancy. Bar: N.Y. 1950, Mich. 1953, Calif. 1976, U.S. Supr. Ct. Practice in N.Y.C., 1949-53, Detroit, 1953-69; atty., mem. legal-staff Gen. Motors Corp., Detroit, 1953-69, asst. gen. counsel, sec., 1969-75; exec. v.p., gen. counsel Bank of Am., San Francisco, 1975-90; ptnr. Graham and James, San Francisco, 1991-95; sr. fellow Stanford Law Sch., 1995—. Served to lt. USNR, 1942-46. Mem. Am., Mich., Calif., San Francisco, Los Angeles, N.Y.C. bar assns., Phi Beta Kappa, Phi Gamma Delta. Presbyterian. Home: 2190 Broadway St Apt 2E San Francisco CA 94115-1312 Office: Am Arbitration Assn Asia Pacific Ctr 225 Bush St San Francisco CA 94104-4207

COOMBS, ROBERT HOLMAN, behavioral scientist, medical educator, therapist, writer; b. Salt Lake City, Sept. 16, 1934; s. Morgan Scott and Vivian (Holman) C.; m. Carol Jean Cook, May 29, 1958; children: Robert Scott, Kathryn, Lorraine, Karen Youn Jung, Holly Ann, Krista Ho Jung, David Jeremy. BS, U. Utah, 1958, MS, 1959; PhD, Wash. State U., 1964. Asst. prof. sociology Iowa State U., 1963-66; fellow Behavioral Sci. Ctr.-Bowman Gray Sch. Medicine/Wake Forest U, 1966, asst. prof., 1966-68; assoc. prof. Behavioral Sci. Center, Bowman Gray Sch. Medicine, Wake Forest U., 1968-70; career rsch. specialist Calif. Dept. Mental Hygiene, Camarillo, 1970-73; assoc. rsch. sociologist UCLA, 1970-77, assoc. prof. biobehavioral scis. Sch. Medicine, 1977-78, prof., 1978—; chief Camarillo Neuropsychiat. Inst., 1970-78; asst. dir. rsch. UCLA Neuropsychiat. Inst., Center for Health Scis., 1978-81; dir. Office Edn. of Neuropsychiat. Inst., 1980-90, UCLA Family Learning Center, Oxnard, Calif., 1977-84. Cons. World Fedn. for Med. Edn., 1990-92; dir. grief and bereavement program UCLA, 1993-98. Author: Psychosocial Aspects of Medical Training, 1971, Junkies and Straights: The Camarillo Experience, 1975, Socialization in Drug Abuse, 1976, Mastering Medicine: Professional Socialization in Medical School, 1978, Making It in Medical School, 1979, Inside Doctoring: Stages and Outcomes in the Professional Socialization of Physicians, 1986, The Family Context of Adolescent Drug Use, 1988, Drug Testing: Issues and Options, 1991, Handbook on Drug Abuse Prevention, 1995, Drug-Impaired Professionals, 1997, Surviving Medical School, 1998, Cool Parents, Drug-free Kids: A Family Survival Guide, 2001, Addiction Recovery Tools: A Practical Handbook, 2001; assoc. editor Family Rels.: Jour. Applied Family and Child Studies, 1970-80, Clin. Sociology Rev., Jour. Clin. Sociology, Jour. Marriage and the Family, 1982-96, Qualitative Health Rsch., 1990-94, Family Dynamics and Addiction Quar., 1990-94; corr. editor Med. Edn. (U.K.); contbg. editor Jour. Drug Issues, 1977; series editor Sage Book Series on Medical Student Survival, 1997-2000; contbr. articles to profl. jours., chpts. to books. Bishop Winston Salem (N.C.) Ward, Ch. Jesus Christ of Latter-day Saints, 1969-70, Camarillo (Calif.) Ward, 1972-77; mem. Calif. Atty.-Gen.'s Commn. on Prevention of Drug and Alcohol Abuse, 1985-86; high risk youth prevention grant rev. com. USPHS, 1990—; com. to combat drug abuse World Fedn. Mental Health, 1989—. With U.S. Army, 1958-64. Grantee NIMH, 1968-73, Nat. Fund Med. Edn., 1969-71, Law Enforcement Assistance Adminstrn., 1971-76, Nat. Inst. Drug Abuse, 1977-80, Calif. Dept. Alcohol and Drug Programs, 1977-78, Father Flanagan's Boys Home, 1977-79, CETA, Ventura County, Calif., 1978 Fellow AAAS, APS, Am. Assn. Applied and Preventive Psychology; mem. Internat. Sociol. Assn., Internat. Family Therapy Assn., World Fedn. Menal Health (mem. com. to combat drug abuse), Assn. Am. Med. Colls., Am. Psychotherapy Assn. (cert.), Sigma Xi, Phi Kappa Phi. Democrat. Office: UCLA Sch Medicine Dept Psychiatry Biobehavioral Scis 760 Westwood Plz Los Angeles CA 90095-8353 E-mail: rcoombs@mednet.ucla.edu

COONEY, JOHN P. judge; b. Sedalia, Mo., Jan. 21, 1932; Student, Westminster Coll., 1949-51, So. Oreg. Coll., 1957-59; JD, Willamette U., 1962. Bar: Oreg. 1962. Pvt. practice, Oreg., 1962-94; part-time U.S. magistrate judge Medford, 1990-94; full-time U.S. magistrate judge Medford, 1994—. Mem. Oreg. Bar Assn. Office: US Dist Ct James Redden US Courthouse 310 W 6th St Rm 302 Medford OR 97501-2766

COONEY, MIKE, state official; b. Washington, Sept. 3, 1954; s. Gage Rodman and Ruth (Brodie) C.; m. Dee Ann Marie Gribble; children: Ryan Patrick, Adan Cecelia, Colin Thomas. BA in Polit. Sci., U. Mont., 1979. State rep. Mont. Legislature, Helena, 1976-80; exec. asst. U.S. Sen. Max Baucus, Butte, Mont., 1979-82, Washington, 1982-85, Helena, Mont., 1985-89; sec. of state State of Mont., Helena, 1988—. Bd. dirs. YMCA; mem. adv. panel Fed. Clearinghouse. Mem. Nat. Secs. of State (pres.), Nat. Assns. Secs. of State (pres. 1997) Home: PO Box 754 Helena MT 59624-0754 Office: Office Mont Sec State PO Box 202801 Helena MT 59620

COONING, CRAIG R. career officer; BSc in Engring., Auburn U., 1973; MBA, U. Ala., 1977. Commd. 2d. lt. USAF, 1973, advanced through grades to brig. gen., 1998; procurement contracting officer San Antonio (Tex.) Air Logistics Ctr., Kelly AFB, 1973-76; stationed at Wright-Patterson AFB, Ohio, 1977-82, Randolph AFB, Tex., 1982-86; dep. comdr. Hughes Missile Sys. Group, Tuscon, Ariz., 1986-88; comdr. Morton Thiokol Inc., Brigham City, Utah, 1988-90; various assignments Hill AFB, 1990-93; various assignments, program dir. reconnaissance office Wright-Patterson AFB, 1994-98; program dir., milsatcom joint program office Space and Missile Sys. Ctr., L.A., 1998—. Decorated Legion of Merit, Meritorious Svc. medal with five oak leaf clusters.

COONTS, STEPHEN PAUL, novelist; b. Morgantown, W.Va., July 19, 1946; s. Gilbert Gray and Violet (Gadd) C.; m. Nancy Quereau, Feb. 19, 1971 (div. 1985); children: Rachael Diane Quereau, Lara Danielle Quereau, David Paul; m. Deborah Buell, Apr. 12, 1995. AB in Polit. Sci., W.Va. U., 1968; JD, U. Colo., 1979. Commd. ensign USN, 1968, with attack squadron 196 Wash., flight instr., asst. catapult-arresting gear officer USS Nimitz; pvt. practice Hymes & Coonts Attys., Buckhannon, W.Va., 1980-81; in-house counsel Petro-Lewis Corp., Denver, 1981-86; freelance novelist, 1986—. Author: Flight of the Intruder, 1986 (Author of Yr. award U.S. Naval Inst. 1986), Final Flight, 1988, The Minotaur, 1989, Under Siege, 1990, The Cannibal Queen: An Aerial Odyssey Across America, 1992, The Red Horseman, 1993, The Intruders, 1994, War In the Air, 1996, Fortunes of War, 1998, Cuba, 1999. Trustee W.Va. Wesleyan Coll., 1990-98. Inductee Acad. of Dist. Alumni W.Va. U., 1992.

COOP, FREDERICK ROBERT, retired city manager; b. San Diego, Mar. 1, 1914; s. Ernest Frederick and Hazel (Angier) C.; m. Jean Haven, Feb. 11, 1939; children— Susan, Robert, Thomas, Elizabeth. A.B., U. Calif. at Berkeley, 1935; M.S. in Pub. Adminstrn, U. So. Calif., 1937. Pers. technician Calif. Personnel Bd., 1937-41; pers. dir. Pasadena, Calif., 1941-49; pers. cons. UN, 1947; city mgr. Inglewood, Calif., 1949-56, Fremont, 1956-58; chief pub. svcs. div. U.S. Ops. Mission to Yugoslavia, 1958-61; city mgr. Newport Beach, Calif., 1961-64, Phoenix, 1964-69; regional dir. HEW, San Francisco, 1969-71; dir. pub. adminstrn. svcs. Arthur D. Little, Inc., San Francisco, 1972-78; pres. Robert Coop Assocs., Moraga, Calif., 1978-81, Coop Mgmt. Svcs. Inc., 1981-91. Pres., bd. dirs. Pub. Svc. Skills Inc. Served to lt. comdr. USNR, World War II. Named Young Man of Year, 1947, Young Man of Year Pasadena Jr. C. of C. Mem. Internat. City Mgmt. Assn. (regional v.p. 1965-67, Disting. Svc. award 2000), Am. Soc. Pub. Adminstrn. (bd. dirs.), Nat. Acad. Pub. Adminstrn., League Calif. Cities (hon. life. city mgrs. dept.).

COOPER, ALLEN DAVID, medical researcher, educator; b. N.Y.C., Sept. 18, 1942; s. Samuel and Fay (Sussman) C.; m. Kristina Speer, 1997; children: Ian, Todd. BA, NYU, 1963; MD, SUNY Downstate Med. Ctr., N.Y.C., 1967. Intern then resident Boston City Hosp., 1967-69; resident fellow in gastroenterology U. Calif., San Francisco, 1969-72; clin. asst. prof. medicine U. Tex. Med. Sch., San Antonio, 1972-74; asst. prof. medicine Stanford (Calif.) U., 1974-80, assoc. prof. medicine, 1980-89, courtesy assoc. prof. physiology, 1987-90, prof. medicine, 1990—; dir. Palo Alto (Calif.) Med. Found. Rsch. Inst., 1986—. Sci. adv. bd. ChemTrak. Recipient Scholastic Achievement award Am Inst. Chem., 1963; Univ. fellow Stanford U., 1981-83, Andrew W. Mellon Found. fellow, 1977-79. Fellow ACP, Molecular Medicine Soc.; mem. Am. Soc. Clin. Investigation, Am. Soc. Biochemistry and Molecular Biology, Western Soc. Clin. Investigation (sec.-treas. 1988, pres. 1992), Am. Fedn. Clin. Rsch. (pres. 1974), South Beach Yacht Club, Single Handed Sailing Soc., Pi Lambda Xi, Alpha Omega Alpha. Avocation: sailing. E-mail: adc@stanford.edu

COOPER, EDWIN LOWELL, anatomy educator; b. Oakland, Tex., Dec. 23, 1936; s. Edwin Ellis and Ruthesther (Porché) C.; m. Helene Marie Antoinette Tournaire, Sept. 13, 1969; children— Astrid Madeleine, Amaury Tournaire. B.S., Tex. So. U., 1957; M.S., Atlanta, 1959; Ph.D., Brown U., 1963. UHPHS postdoctoral fellow UCLA, 1962-64, asst. prof. anatomy, 1964-69, assoc. prof., 1969-73, prof., 1973—. Vis. prof. Instituto Politecnico Nacional, Mexico City, 1966; Mem. adv. com. Office Sci. Personnel, NRC, 1972-73; mem. bd. sci. counselors Nat. Inst. Dental Research, 1973— Author: Comparative Immunology; Editor: Phylogeny of Transplantation Reactions, 1970, Invertebrate Immunology, 1974; founding editor: Internat. Jour. Developmental and Comparative Immunology, 1977— . Guggenheim fellow, 1970; Fulbright scholar, 1970; Eleanor Roosevelt fellow Internat. Union Against Cancer, 1977-78 Fellow AAAS (council 1971, chmn. sect. 1976); mem. Soc. Invertebrate Pathology (founding), Pan Am. Congress Anatomy (founding), Am. Assn. Anatomy, Transplantation Soc., Am. Assn. Immunologists, Am. Soc. Zoologists (program officer 1974— , founder div. comparative immunology 1975, pres.), Brit. Soc. Immunology, Societe d'Immunologie Francaise, Sigma Xi. Office: UCLA Sch Medicine Dept Neurobiology 10833 Le Conte Ave Los Angeles CA 90095-3075

COOPER, GINNIE, library director; b. Worthington, Minn., 1945; d. Lawrence D. and Ione C.; m. Richard Bauman, Dec. 1995; 1 child, Daniel Jay. Student, Coll. St. Thomas, U. Wis., Parkside; BA, S.D. State U.; MA in Libr. Sci., U. Minn. Tchr. Flandreau (S.D.) Indian Sch., 1967-68, St. Paul Pub. Schs., 1968-69; br. libr. Wash. County Libr., Lake Elmo, Minn., 1970-71, asst. dir., 1971-75; assoc. adminstr., libr. U. Minn. Med. Sch., Mpls., 1975-77; dir. Kenosha (Wis.) Pub. Libr., 1977-81; county libr. Alameda County (Calif.) Libr., 1981-90; dir. librs. Multnomah County Libr., Portland, Oreg., 1990—. Chair County Mgr. Assn.; county adminstr. Mayor's Exec. Roundtable. Mem. ALA (mem. LAMA, PLA and RASD coms., elected to coun. 1987, 91, mem. legislation com. 1986-90, mem. orgn. com. 1990—), Calif. Libr. Assn. (pres. CIL, 1985, elected to coun. 1986, pres. Calif. County Librs. 1986), Oreg. Libr. Assn., Pub. Libr. Assn. (pres. 1997-98). Office: Multnomah County Libr 205 NE Russell St Portland OR 97212-3708

COOPER, GREGORY M. protective services official; Chief of police, Provo, Utah. Office: 48 S 300 W Provo UT 84601-4362

COOPER, MARTIN, electronics company executive; b. Chgo., Dec. 26, 1928; s. Arthur and Mary C.; children from previous marriage: Scott David, Lisa Ellen; m. Arlene Harris, Jan. 26, 1991. BSEE, Ill. Inst. Tech., 1950, MSEE, 1957. Rsch. engr. Teletype Corp., Chgo., 1953-54; with Motorola, Inc., Schaumburg, Ill., 1954-83, ops. dir., 1967-76, divsn. mgr., 1977-78, v.p., corp. dir. R & D, 1978-83; chmn., CEO Cellular Bus. Systems, Inc., 1983-86, Cellular Pay Phone Inc., Chgo. and Del Mar, Calif., 1986-92, Arraycomm, Inc., San Jose, 1992—. Mem. computer-telecommunications bd. NRC, 1979-83; mem. indsl. adv. bd. U. Ill.-Chgo., 1980-90. Patentee in field. Trustee, mem. pres.'s counsel Ill. Inst. Tech. Served with USNR, 1950-54. Fellow IEEE (pres. vehicular tech. soc. 1973-74, telecomms. policy bd. 1976— , award for contbns. to radiotelephony, Centennial medal awardee), Internat. Electronics Consortium (disting. lectr., adv. bd.), Radio Club of Am. (Fred Link award). Home and Office: Arraycomm Inc 100 Via De La Valle Del Mar CA 92014-2031 E-mail: marty@arraycomm.com

COOPER, MILTON E. computer science company professional; V.p. program devel. Computer Scis. Corp., El Segundo, Calif., 1984-92, v.p., pres. federal sector, 1992—. Chmn. bd. dirs. AFCEA Internat. Recipient 21st Century Commerce Leadership award for Industry, Assn. for Enterprise Integration, 1999, Leadership award AFCEA, 1997. Office: Computer Scis Corp 2100 E Grand Ave El Segundo CA 90245-5024

COOPER, PAUL DOUGLAS, lawyer; b. Kansas City, Mo., July 22, 1941; s. W.W. and Emma Marie (Ringo) C.; m. Elsa B. Shaw, June 15, 1963 (div. 1991); children: Richard, Dean; m. Kay J. Rice, Aug. 30, 1992; 1 child, Natanya. BA in English, U. Mich., 1963; LLB, U. Calif., 1966. Bar: Colo. 1966, U.S. Dist. Ct. Colo. 1966, U.S. Ct. Appeals (10th cir.) 1967, U.S. Supreme Ct. 1979. Dep. dist. atty., Denver, 1969-71; asst. U.S. atty. Dist. of Colo., 1971-73; ptnr. Yegge, Hall & Evans, Denver, 1973-80; pres., dir. Cooper & Kelley PC, Denver, 1980-94, Cooper & Clough PC, Denver, 1994—. Faculty trial practice seminar Denver U. Law Sch., 1982; spl. asst. U.S. atty. Dist. of Colo., 1973-75; spl. prosecutor Mar. 1977 term, Garfield County Grand Jury; pres. Bow Mar Owners, Inc., 1976-77; English adv. bd. U. Mich., 2000—. Recipient Spl. Commendation award for outstanding svc., 1972. Mem. ABA, Am. Bd. Trial Advocates, Colo. Bar Assn. (interprofl. com., bd. govs.), Denver Bar Assn. (trustee, 1st v.p. 1982-83), Colo. Med. Soc. (chmn. interprofl. com., Denver bar liaison com), Internat. Assn. Def. Counsel (exec. com. 1989-92), Denver Athletic Club. Republican. Home: 1890 Bellaire St Denver CO 80220-1051 Office: 1512 Larimer St Ste 600 Denver CO 80202-1610 E-mail: pcooper@cooper-clough.com

COOPER, ROBERTA, mayor; b. Mar. 18, 1937; m. Jerrel Cooper. BA, MA. Ret. secondary sch. tchr.; mem. Hayward (Calif.) City Coun., 1988-92; mayor City of Hayward, 1994—. Former mem. Gen. Plan Revision Task Force, dir. League of Calif. Cities. Active Eden (Calif.) Youth Ctr., Literacy Plus, Hayward Edn. Assn. Democrat. Avocations: reading mysteries, gardening. Office: Mayors Office 777 B St Hayward CA 94541-5007

COOPER, WILLIAM SECORD, information science educator; b. Winnipeg, Man., Can., Nov. 7, 1935; m. Helen Clare Dunlap, July 22, 1964. BA, Principia Coll., 1956; MSc, MIT, 1959; PhD, U. Calif.-Berkeley, 1964. Alexander von Humboldt scholar U. Erlangen, Germany, 1964-65; asst. prof. info. sci. U. Chgo., 1966-70; assoc. prof. info. sci. U. Calif., Berkeley, 1971-76, prof., 1976-94, prof. grad. sch., 1994-96, prof. emeritus, 1996—. Miller prof. Miller Inst., Berkeley, 1975-76. Hon. rsch. fellow Univ. Coll., London, 1977-78; ACM/SIGIR Triennial Rsch. award, 1994. Office: Univ Calif Sch Info Mgmt & Sys Berkeley CA 94720-0001 E-mail: wcooper@socrates.berkeley.edu

COOPERMAN, DANIEL, lawyer; b. Perth Amboy, N.J., Nov. 27, 1950; s. Eli Louis and Dorothy (Salinger) C.; m. Linda Louise Schmidt, June 10, 1979; children: Jeffrey Eli, Justin Andrew. AB, Dartmouth Coll., 1972; JD, MBA, Stanford U., 1976. Bar: Calif. 1976. Cons. McKinsey & Co., San Francisco, 1976-77; atty. McCutchen Doyle Brown & Enersen, San Francisco, 1977-83, ptnr., 1983-97; sr. v.p., gen. counsel Oracle Corp., Redwood Shores, Calif., 1997—. Sec., bd. dirs. Children's Discovery Mus., San Jose, Calif., 1993—; bd. advisors Cmty. Found. Santa Clara County, San Jose, 1994—. Mem. Santa Clara County Bar Assn. (chair bus. law sect. 1992-93). Avocation: squash. Office: Oracle Corp M/S 5op7 500 Oracle Pkwy Redwood City CA 94065-1675

COOPER-SMITH, JEFFREY PAUL, botanic garden administrator; b. New Haven, July 12, 1951; s. Robert Ernest and Marilyn (Blake) C.-S.; m. Maria de los Angeles Gonzalez Alvarado, 1981 (div. 1995); 1 child, Brandon Andrés. BA in Botany and Biology summa cum laude, Pomona Coll., 1974; MA in Botany, Duke U., 1978; postgrad., Duke U./Cornell U., 1974-78; MBA in Fin. and Mktg., U. Chgo., 1985. Sci. instr. Costa Rica Acad., San Antonio de Belén, 1978-80; prof. Sch. Biol. Scis. Universidad Nacional, Heredia, Costa Rica, 1980-82; analyzer promotional programs Citibank, U.S.A., Chgo., 1984; bus. devel. assoc. ICI Ams., Inc., Wilmington, Del., 1985-87; mgr. capital planning S.E. Bank, N.A., Miami, Fla., 1987-89; comml. svcs. mgr. Nat. Starch & Chem. (Unilever), Bridgewater, N.J., 1990-91; exec. dir. U.S. Botanic Garden, Washington, 1992, Coyote Point Museum for Environmental Education, San Mateo, Calif. Cons. reforestation project Ministry Environ., Maracaibo, Venezuela, 1979. Vol. Red Cross, Costa Rica, 1978-82. Mem. Internat. Coun. of Mus., Am. Assn. Mus., Bat Conservation Internat., Orgn. Tropical Studies, Nature Conservancy. Avocations: music, gardening, swimming, natural history, foreign cultures. Address: Coyote Point Museum for Environmental Education 1651 Coyote Point Dr San Mateo CA 94401

COOR, LATTIE FINCH, university president; b. Phoenix, Sept. 26, 1936; s. Lattie F. and Elnora (Witten) C.; m. Ina Fitzhenry, Jan. 18, 1964 (div. 1988); children: William Kendall, Colin Fitzhenry, Farryl MacKenna Witten; m. Elva Wingfield, Dec. 27, 1994. AB with high honors (Phelps Dodge scholar), No. Ariz. U., 1958; MA with honors (Univ. scholar, Universal Match Found. fellow, Carnegie Corp. fellow), Washington U., St. Louis, 1960, PhD, 1964; LLD (hon.), Marlboro Coll., 1977, Am. Coll. Greece, 1982, U. Vt., 1991. Adminstrv. asst. to Gov. Mich., 1961-62; asst. to chancellor Washington U., St. Louis, 1963-67, asst. dean Grad. Sch. Arts and Scis., 1967-69, dir. internat. studies, 1967-69, asst. prof. polit. sci., 1967-76, vice chancellor, 1969-74, univ. vice chancellor, 1974-76; pres. U. Vt., Burlington, 1976-89; prof. public affairs, and pres. Ariz. State U., Tempe, 1990—. Cons. HEW; spl. cons. to commr. U.S. Commn. on Edn., 1971-74; chmn. Commn. on Govtl. Rels., Am. Coun. on Edn., 1976-80; dir. New Eng. Bd. Higher Edn., 1976-89; co-chmn. joint com. on health policy Assn. Am. Univs. and Nat. Assn. State Univs. and Land Grant Colls., 1976-89; mem. pres. commn. NCAA, 1984-90, chmn. div. I, 1989; mem. Ariz. State Bd. Edn., 1993-98; chmn. Pacific 10 Conf., 1995-96. Trustee emeritus Am. Coll. Greece. Mem. Nat. Assn. Stae Univs. and Land Grant Colls. (chmn. bd. dirs. 1991-92), New Eng. Assn. Schs. and Colls. (pres. 1981-82), Am. Coun. on Edn. (bd. dirs. 1991-93, 2000—), Kellogg Commn. on Future of State and Land-Grant Univs. Office: Ariz State U Pres Office Tempe AZ 85287 E-mail: Lattie.Coor@asu.edu

COORS, JEFFREY H. technology manufacturing executive; b. Denver, Feb. 10, 1945; s. Joseph Coors B.Chem. Engring., Cornell U., 1967, M.Chem. Engring., 1968. With Coors Porcelain Co., 1968-70; with Adolph Coors Co., Golden, Colo., 1970-92, pres., 1985-89; chmn., chief exec. officer Coors Techs. Cos., Golden, 1989-92; pres. ACX Techs., Golden, 1992—. Office: ACX Techs Inc 16000 Table Mountain Pkwy Golden CO 80403-1663

COORS, WILLIAM K. brewery executive; b. Golden, Colo., Aug. 11, 1916; BSChemE, Princeton U., 1938, grad. degree in chem. engring., 1939. Pres. Adolph Coors Co., Golden, Colo., 1956-2000, chmn. bd., 1970—. Chmn. ACX Technologies, Inc. Office: Adolph Coors Co PO Box 4030 Golden CO 80401

COOTS, LAURIE, advertising executive; Chief mktg. officer TBWA Chiat/ Day L.A., Venice, Calif., now COO Playa Del Rey. Office: TBWA Chiat/Day LA 5353 Grosvenor Blvd Playa Del Rey CA 90296

COPE, THOMAS FIELD, lawyer; b. Oak Park, Ill., Feb. 29, 1948; s. Benjamin Thomas and Myra Norma (Lees) C.; m. Ann Wattis, Mar. 21, 1970; children: Elizabeth Ann, Philip Thomas. BA, U. Denver, 1970, MA, 1976, JD, 1974; PhD, U. Chgo., 2001. Bar: Colo. 1974, Ill. 1978, Wyo. 1996, D.C. 2001, U.S. Dist. Ct. Colo. 1974, U.S. Ct. Appeals (10th cir.) 1989, U.S. Dist. Ct. D.C. 2001. Assoc. Holme Roberts & Owen, Denver, 1974-78, 81-83, ptnr., 1984—. Instr. IIT/Chgo.-Kent Coll. Law, 1980, Loyola U. Sch. Law, Chgo., 1980-81. Co-editor: Colorado Environmental Law Handbook, 1989, 4th rev. edit., 1996, Colorado Environmental Compliance Update, 1993-96; contbg. editor Oil & Gas Law and Taxation Rev., Oxford, Eng., 1987-93; mng. editor Shepard's Environ. Liability in Comml. Transactions Reporter, 1990-92; mem. bd. editors Denver Law Jour., 1972-74; contbr. articles to profl. jours. Bd. dirs. Colo. Fourteeners Initiative, 1996—. Mem. Am. Law Inst., Am. Soc. Legal History, Irish Legal History Soc., Selden Soc. (state corr. Colo. 1997—), Rocky Mountain Mineral Law Found. (mem. grants com. 1983-95, chmn. 1995—), Order St. Ives, Am. Alpine Club, Colo. Mountain Club (chair high altitude mountaineering sect. 2001). Democrat. Mem. Orthodox Ch. in Am. Avocations: mountaineering, history. Home: 2800 S University Blvd Unit 108 Denver CO 80210-6072 Office: Holme Roberts & Owen LLP 1700 Lincoln St Ste 4100 Denver CO 80203-4541 E-mail: copet@hro.com

COPELAND, LAWRENCE R. construction company executive; b. 1947; Graduate, U. Notre Dame. With Fluor Corp., Irvine, Calif., 1969-93; now pres. Fluor Constructors Internat., Irvine, 1993—. Office: Fluor Constructors Intl 3353 Michelson Dr Irvine CA 92612-0650

COPELAND, PHILLIPS JEROME, former academic administrator, former air force officer; b. Oxnard, Calif., Mar. 22, 1921; s. John Charles and Marion (Moffatt) C.; m. Alice Janette Lusby, Apr. 26, 1942 (dec. April 1998); children: Janette Ann Copeland Bosserman (dec. Aug. 2000), Nancy Jo Copeland Briner; m. Joanne Barra Lankenau, July 9, 1999. Student, U. So. Calif., 1947-49; BA, U. Denver, 1956, MA, 1958; grad., Air Command and Staff Coll., 1959, Indsl. Coll. Armed Forces, 1964. Commd. 2d lt. USAF, 1943, advanced through grades to col., 1964; pilot 8th Air Force, Eng., 1944-45; various flying and staff assignments, 1945-51; chief joint tng. sect. Hdqrs. Airsouth (NATO), Italy, 1952-54; asst. dir. plans and programs USAF Acad., 1955-58; assigned to joint intelligence Washington, 1959-61; plans officer Cincpac Joint Staff, Hawaii, 1961-63; staff officer, ops. directorate, then team chief Nat. Mil. [illegible] Staff, Washington, 1964-67; dir. plans and programs USAF Adv. Group, 1967-68; prof. aerospace studies U. So. Calif., L.A., 1968-72, exec. asst. to pres., 1972-73, assoc. dir. office internat. programs, 1973-75, dir. adminstrv. svcs. Coll. Continuing Edn., 1975-82, dir. employee rels., 1982-84. Advisor Vietnamese Air Force, Vietnam, 1967-68. Decorated D.F.C., Bronze Star, Air medal with 3 clusters, Medal of Honor (Vietnam). Mem. Air Force Assn., Order of Daedalians.

COPELAND, ROBERT GLENN, lawyer; b. San Diego, Mar. 15, 1941; s. Glenn Howard and Luella Louise (Schmid) C.; m. Harriet S. Smith, June 27, 1964 (div. Jan. 1977); children: Katherine Louise, Matthew Robert; m. Marcia Diane Cummings, Jan. 8, 1977 (div. June 1990); m. Lynne Newman, Oct. 10, 1993; 1 child, Zachary Newman. AB, Occidental Coll., 1963; JD, U. So. Calif., 1966. Bar: Calif. 1966, U.S. Dist. Ct. Calif. (so. dist.), 1967. Ptnr. Gray, Cary, Ware & Freidenrich, San Diego, 1966-95, Luce, Forward Hamilton & Scripps LLP, 1995—. Mem. ABA, Calif. Bar Assn. Republican. Avocations: shooting, fishing, hiking, racquetball. Office: Luce Forward Hamilton & Scripps LLP 600 W Broadway Ste 2600 San Diego CA 92101-3311 E-mail: rcopeland@luce.com

COPES, PARZIVAL, economist, researcher; b. Nakusp, B.C., Can., Jan. 22, 1924; s. Jan Coops and Elisabeth Catharina Coops-van Olst; m. Dina Gussekloo, May 1, 1946; children: Raymond Alden, Michael Ian, Terence Franklin. BA, U. B.C., 1949, MA, 1950; PhD, London Sch. Econs., 1956; D of Mil. Sci. (hon.), Royal Roads Mil. Coll., Victoria, B.C., Can., 1991; Dr. Philos. (hon.), U. Tromsö, Norway, 1993. Economist, statistician Dominion Bur. of Stats., Ottawa, Can., 1953-57; from assoc. prof. to prof., head econs. dept. Meml. U. Nfld., St. John's, Can., 1957-64; founding dir. econ. rsch. Inst. Social and Econ. Rsch. Meml. U. Nfld., St. John's, 1961-64; prof. Simon Fraser U., Burnaby, B.C., Can., 1964-91, head dept. econs. and commerce Can., 1964-69, chmn. dept. econs. and commerce Can., 1972-75, dir. Ctr. for Can. Studies Can., 1978-85, founding dir. Inst. of Fisheries Analysis Can., 1980-94, prof. emeritus Can., 1991—. Governor Inst. Can. Bankers, Montreal, Que., 1967-71; dir. "Can.-Fgn. Arrangements Project," Can. Govt. Dept. Environment, 1976; pres., chmn. Pacific Regional Sci. Conf. Orgn., 1977-85; spl. advisor to Minister of Fisheries, B.C., 1998. Author: St. John's and Newfoundland: An Economic Survey, 1961, The Backward-Bending Supply Curve of the Fishing Industry, 1970, The Resettlement of Fishing Communities in Newfoundland, 1972, Factor Rents, Sole Ownership and the Optimum Level of Fisheries Exploitation, 1972, A Critical Review of the Individual Quota as a Device in Fisheries Management, 1986. Active Netherlands Resistance Army, 1942-45; Lt. Can. Army, 1945-46, 50-51. Fgn. fellow Acad. Natural Scis. of Russia, Moscow, 1992. Mem. Internat. Inst. Fisheries Econs. and Trade (exec. com. 1982-86, Disting. Svc. award 1996), Internat. Assn. for Study of Common Property, Can. Regional Sci. Assn. (pres. 1983-85), Can. Econs. Assn. (v.p. 1972-73), Assn. for Can. Studies, Western Regional Sci. Assn. (pres. 1977-78), Social Sci. Fedn. Can. (dir., v.p. 1979-83), Can. Assn. Univ. Tchrs., Internat. Arctic Sci. Com. Achievements include some of earliest research contributions to establish sub-discipline of fisheries economics; writing, speaking, research and international consulting in fisheries policy and resource management. Home: 2341 Lawson Ave West Vancouver BC Canada V7V 2E5 Office: Simon Fraser U Dept Economics Burnaby BC Canada V5A 1S6 E-mail: copes@sfu.ca

COPLEY, DAVID C. newspaper publishing company executive; s. Mrs. James S. Copley. BSBA, Menlo Coll. Formerly pres. Copley Press, Inc., La Jolla, Calif., pres., CEO, 1988—, also mem. exec. com., chmn. sr. mgmt. bd. and bd. dirs. Chair, pres. Copley N.W., Inc., Puller Paper Co.; pes. Copley News Svc.; pub. Borrego Sun.. Mem. editl. bd. San Diego Union-Tribune. Pres., trustee James S. Copley Found.; trustee Canterbury Sch., San Diego Crew Classic Found.; trustee emeritus La Jolla Playhouse, Am. Craft Coun., Mus. Photog. Arts; bd. dirs. San Diego Mus. Art, St. Vincent de Paul Soc.; pres. assocs., pres. adv. com., exhibits com. Zool. Soc. San Diego; adv. bd. San Diego Automotive Mus.; pres. coun. Scripps Clinic and Rsch. Found., San Diego Kind Corp.; active Pres. Club U. San Diego, San Diego Aerospace Mus., San Diego Hall Sci., San Diego Maritime Mus., San Diego Coun. on Literacy. Mem. Nat. Newspaper Assn., U.S. Humane Soc., F.O.C.A.S., San Diego Hist. Soc., San Diego Humane Soc., Bachelor Club San Diego. Office: Copley Press PO Box 1530 La Jolla CA 92038-1530

COPLEY, HELEN KINNEY, newspaper publisher; b. Cedar Rapids, Iowa, Nov. 28, 1922; d. Fred Everett and Margaret (Casey) Kinney; m. James S. Copley, Aug. 16, 1965 (dec.); 1 child, David Casey. Attended, Hunter Coll., N.Y.C., 1945. Assoc. The Copley Press, Inc., 1952—, chmn. exec. com., chmn. corp., dir., 1973—, CEO, sr. mgmt. bd., 1974—; chmn. bd. Copley News Svc., San Diego, 1973—; chmn. editl. bd. Union-Tribune Pub. Co., 1976—; pub. The San Diego Union-Tribune, 1973—; chmn. bd. Copley Newspapers. Bd. dirs. Fox Valley Press., Inc. Chmn. bd., trustee James S. Copley Found., 1973—; life mem. Friends of Internat. Ctr., La Jolla, Mus. Contemporary Art, San Diego, San Diego Hall of Sci., Scripps Meml. Hosp. Aux., San Diego Opera Assn., Star of India Aux., Zool. Soc. San Diego; mem. La Jolla Town Coun. Inc., San Diego Soc. Natural History, YWCA, San Diego Symphony Assn.; life patroness Makua Aux.; hon. chmn., bd. dirs. Washington Crossing Found.; hon. chmn. San Diego Coun. Literacy. Mem. Inter-Am. Press Assn., Newspaper Assn. Am., Calif. Press Assn., Am. Press Inst., Calif. Newspaper Pubs. Assn., Calif. Press Inst., San Francisco Press Club, L.A. Press Club. Republican. Roman Catholic. Clubs: Aurora (Ill.) Country, Army and Navy (D.C.), Univ. Club San Diego, La Jolla Beach and Tennis, La Jolla Country. Office: Copley Newspapers 7776 Ivanhoe Ave La Jolla CA 92037-4520

COPMAN, LOUIS, radiologist; b. Phila., Jan. 17, 1934; s. Jacob and Eve (Snyder) C.; m. Avera Schuster, June 8, 1958; children: Mark, Linda. BA, U. Pa., 1955, MD, 1959. Diplomate Am. Bd. Radiology; Nat. Bd. Med. Examiners. Commd. ensign Med. Corps USN, 1958; advanced through grades to capt. M.C. USN, 1975; ret.; asst. chief radiology dept. Naval Hosp., Pensacola, Fla., 1966-69; chief radiology dept. Doctors Hosp., Phila., 1969-73; radiologist Mercer Hosp. Ctr., Trenton, N.J., 1973-75; chmn. radiology dept. Naval Hosp., Phila., 1975-84; chief. radiology dept. Naval Med. Clinic, Pearl Harbor, Hawaii, 1984-89; pvt. practice radiologist Honolulu, 1989-92. Cons. Radiology Services, Wilmington, Del., 1978-84, Yardley (Pa.) Radiology, 1979-84. Author: The Cuckold, 1974. Recipient Albert Einstein award in Medicine, U. Pa., 1959. Mem. AMA, Assn. Mil. Surgeons of the U.S., Royal Soc. Medicine, Radiol. Soc. N.Am., Am. Coll. Radiology, Photographic Soc. Am., Sherlock Holmes Soc., Phi Beta Kappa, Alpha Omega Alpha. Avocations: photography, hang-gliding, scuba diving. Home: PO Box 384767 Waikoloa HI 96738-4767 Office: 68-1771 Makanahele Pl Waikoloa HI 96738-5128 E-mail: loucopman@earthlink.net

COPPERSMITH, SAM, lawyer; b. Johnstown, Pa., May 22, 1955; m. Beth Schermer, Aug. 28, 1983; children: Sarah, Benjamin, Louis. AB in Econs. magna cum laude, Harvard U., 1976; JD, Yale Law Sch., 1982. Fgn. svc. officer U.S. Dept. State, Port of Spain, Trinidad, 1977-79; law clk. to Judge William C. Canby Jr. U.S. Ct. Appeals (9th cir.), Phoenix, 1982-83; atty. Sacks, Tierney & Kasen, P.A., Phoenix, 1983-86; asst. to Mayor Terry Goddard City of Phoenix, 1984; atty. Jones, Jury, Short & Mast P.C., Phoenix, 1986-88, Bonnett, Fairbourn & Friedman P.C., Phoenix, 1988-92; mem. 103d Congress from 1st Ariz. Dist., 1993-95; atty. Coppersmith [illegible] Former dir., pres. Planned Parenthood Ctrl. and No. Ariz.; former chair City of Phoenix Bd. of Adjustment; former dir. Ariz. Cmty. Svc. Legal Assistance Found., 1986-89; chair Ariz. Dem. Party, 1995-97; trustee Devereux Found., 1997—. Mem. ABA, State Bar of Ariz., State Bar of Calif., Maricopa County Bar Assn. Democrat. Office: Coppersmith Gordon Schermer Owens & Nelson PLC 2633 E Indian School Rd Ste 300 Phoenix AZ 85016-6759 E-mail: sam@cgson.com

COPPLE, WILLIAM PERRY, federal judge; b. Holtville, Calif., Oct. 3, 1916; s. Perry and Euphie (Williams) C.; m. Nancy Matson, May 30, 1981; children by previous marriage— Virginia (Mrs. Richard Schilke), Leonard W., Steven D. A.B., U. Calif. at Berkeley, 1949, LL.B., 1951. Bar: Ariz. 1952. Various positions with U.S. Govt., also pvt. employers, 1936-48; practice in Yuma, Ariz., 1952-65; U.S. dist. atty. Dist. Ariz., Phoenix, 1965-66; judge U.S. Dist. Ct. Dist. Ariz., 1966—, now sr. judge. Mem. Ariz. Hwy. Commn., 1955-58, Gov. Ariz. Com Fourteen for Colo. River, 1963-65; chmn. Yuma County Democratic Central Com., 1953-54, 59-60 Mem. Am. Bar Assn. Office: US Dist Ct US Courthouse & Fed Bldg 230 N 1st Ave Ste 3007 Phoenix AZ 85025-0230

COPPOLA, ARTHUR M. real estate company executive, lawyer; CPA, Calif. With Macerich Group, 1970—; pres., CEO Macerich Co., Santa Monica, Calif., also bd. dirs. Bd. dirs. Macerich Mgmt. Cos. Mem. NAREIT (bd. govs.), Real Estate Round Table (exec. com.). Office: Macerich Co 233 Wilshire Blvd Ste 700 Santa Monica CA 90401-1207

COPPOLILLO, HENRY PETER, psychiatrist; b. Cervicati, Cosenza, Italy, July 27, 1926; s. Vincent Louis and Maria Giovanna (Chidichimo) C.; m. Ruthann Butler, June 6, 1962 (dec. Apr. 1993); children: Catherine, Peter, Robert. Student, U. Ill., 1943-44; MD, U. Rome, 1955. Lic. physician, Ill., Mich., Tenn., Colo.; diplomate Am. Bd. Psychiatry and Neurology. Intern Cook County Hosp., Chgo., 1955-56; resident U. Chgo. Clinics, Chgo., 1956-59; assoc. attending physician Michael Reese Hosp., Chgo., 1959-66; asst. prof. to prof. U. Mich., Ann Arbor, 1966-70; prof. psychiatry Vanderbilt U., Nashville, 1970-76, U. Colo. Med. Sch., Denver, 1976-85; pvt. practice specializing in psychiatry Englewood, Colo., 1985—; clin. prof. psychiatry U. Colo. Sch. Medicine, 1997—. Clin. instr. dept. psychology U. Colo., Boulder, 1985—, Denver U., 1985—. Author: Psychodynamic Psychotherapy of Children, 1987; contbr. articles to profl. jours. Mem. Nat. Assn. Christians & Jews. Named Tchr. of the Yr., Residents & Fellows Psychiatry U. Mich., 1971, Disting. Tchr., Child. Psychiatriy Fellows, U. Colo., 1985. Fellow Am. Psychiatric Assn., Am. Acad. Child and Adolescent Psychiatry. Avocations: fishing, skiing, woodworking. E-mail: papacop@qwest.net

CORAM, DAVID JAMES, gaming industry professional; b. San Diego, Oct. 17, 1962; s. Thomas Harry and Joan Catherine (Reuter) C.; m. Irma Elizabeth Aquino, Jan. 14, 1989 (dec. July 1991); children: Catherine May, Corinna Briann, Carston James, Caitlin Kay; m. Corinna Kay Ward, May 6, 1995. AS with honors, Miramar Coll., 1989; honor grad. sheriff acad. basic tng., Southwestern Coll., 1986. Computer oper. Cubic Data Systems, San Diego, 1981-83, Electronic Data Systems, San Diego, 1983-84; ct. svc. officer San Diego County Marshal, 1985-86, dep. marshal, 1986-2000, San Diego County sheriff, 2000-01; regulatory compliance adminstr. Harrah's Rincon Casino, 2001—. Pres. Coram Cons. Group, 1994—; owner franchise Fantastic Sams Hair Salon, 1998—. Mediator San Diego Community Mediation Ctr., 1990-2000; soccer coach Temecula Valley Soccer Assn., dir. planning & devel., 1999-2000; mem. nominating com. Outstanding Young Women Am. Awarded Gold medal soccer Ariz. Police Olympics, 1990, 91, Silver medal, 1993, Marksmanship award San Diego Marshal, Outstanding Young Men Am. award, 1989; 2d pl. Mid. Weight San Diego Gold's Gym Classic, 1993, Bronze medal Bodybuilding Calif. Police Olympics, 1994. Mem. Calif. State Marshal's Assn. (dir. on state bd. 1994), San Diego County Marshal's Assn. (parliamentarian 1988, dir. 1989-91, 93-94), San Diego County Marshal's Athletic Fedn. (dir. 1993-95), Nat. Physique Com. (contest judge). Republican. Avocations: golf, baseball, camping, computers, weight lifting. Office: Coram Cons Group 45620 Corte Montril Temecula CA 92592-1206

CORBETT, LUKE ROBINSON, lawyer; b. Pinehurst, N.C., May 21, 1930; s. Paschal Butler and Delia Jane (McKenzie) C.; m. Joan Cole (div.); children: Steven, Rebecca, Laurie, Charles, Carolyn; m. Maria Angelica Golden. AB in Polit. Sci., U. N.C., 1956, JD, 1959. Bar: Calif. 1959, U.S. Dist. Ct. (so. dist.) Calif. 1960. Assoc. Lindley, Scales & Patton, San Diego; ptnr. Scales, Patton, Ellsworth & Corbett, San Diego; shareholder, dir., pres. Lindley, Lazar & Scales, San Diego. 1st lt. USAF, 1951-55. Mem. ABA, San Diego County Bar Assn. (bd. dirs., treas., v.p. 1971-74), Am. Bar Found., San Diego County Bar Found. (bd. dirs.), State Bar Calif. (del., chmn. exec. com. conf. of dels. 1975-78), Am. Inns. of Ct. (master Louis F. Welch chpt. 1984), Assn. of Bus. Trial Lawyers (bd. dirs.). Office: Lindley Scales & Corbett 550 W C St Ste 1800 San Diego CA 92101-3545 E-mail: lsc@adnc.com

CORBIN, ROSEMARY MACGOWAN, mayor; b. Santa Cruz, Calif., Apr. 3, 1940; d. Frederick Patrick and Lorena Maude (Parr) MacGowan; m. Douglas Tenny Corbin, Apr. 6, 1968; children: Jeffrey, Diana. BA, San Francisco State U., 1961; MLS, U. Calif., Berkeley, 1966. Libr. Stanford (Calif.) U., 1966-68, Richmond (Calif.) Pub. Libr., 1968-69, Kaiser Found. Health Plan, Oakland, Calif., 1976-81, San Francisco Pub. Libr., 1981-82, U. Calif., Berkeley, 1982-83; mem. coun. City of Richmond, 1985-93, vice mayor, 1986-87, mayor, 1993—. Mem. Solid Waste Mgmt. Authority, 1985—, Contra Costa Hazardous Materials Commn., Martinez, Calif., 1987—, San Francisco Bay Conservation and Devel. Commn., 1987—; mem. League of Calif. Cities Environ. Affairs Com., 1994—; mem. energy and environ. com. U.S. Conf. Mayors and Nat. League of Cities, 1993—. Contbr. articles to profl. publs. Mem. East Bay Pub. Safety Corricor Project. Mem. LWV, NOW, Nat. Women's Polit. Caucus, Inst. for Local Self Govt., Calif. Libr. Assn., Local Govt. Commn., League Calif. Cities, Sierra Club. Democrat. Avocations: reading, hiking, golf, quilting. Home: 114 Crest Ave Richmond CA 94801-4031 Office: Richmond City Hall 2600 Barrett Ave Richmond CA 94804-1654

CORBIN, WILLIAM R. wood products executive; BS in Forest Products, U. Wash., 1964; MS in Forestry, Yale U., 1956. Cons. forest products, Seattle, 1970's; v.p. ops. Vancouver Plywood Co., Inc.; v.p. So. timber and wood products Zellerbach Corp., 1974; sr. v.p. timber and wood products, group pres.; exec. v.p. wood products Weyerhaeuser Co., 1992-95, 98—, exec. v.p. timberlands and distbn., 1995-98. Bd. dirs. Weyerhaeuser Can. Ltd.; mem. mgmt. bd. World TimerFund. Trustee, mem. exec. com. Weyerhaeuser Co. Found., mem. policy com.; mem. adv. bd. U. Wash. Sch. Bus. Adminstrn. and Coll. Forest Resources, charter mem. internat. adv. bd. Inst. Environment and Natural Resource Rsch. and Policy; v.p., mem. exec. com. The Mountains to Sound Greenway Trust. Office: Weyerhaeuser Co Corporate Headquarters Tacoma WA 98477-0001

CORBOY, JAMES MCNALLY, investment banker; b. Erie, Pa., Nov. 3, 1940; s. James Thomas and Dorothy Jane (Schluraff) C. ; m. Suzanne Shaver, July 23, 1965; children: Shannon, James McNally. BA, Allegheny Coll., 1962; MBA, U. Colo., 1986. Mem. sales staff Boettcher & Co., Denver, 1964-70, Blyth Eastman Dillon, Denver and Chgo., 1970-74, William Blair & Co., Chgo., 1974-77; mgr. corp. bond dept. Boettcher & Co., Denver, 1977-79; ptnr. in charge William Blair & Co., [illegible] 1979-86; first v.p. Stifel, Nicolaus & Co., Denver, 1986-88; pres., CEO SKB Corboy Inc., Denver, 1988-97, Century Capital Group Inc., 1997-98; ptnr. Corboy and Jerde, LLC, Englewood, Colo., 1999—. Chmn. Colo. Capital Alliance. With USMC, 1962-67. Mem. Nat. Assn. Securities Dealers, Country Club at Castle Pines, Met. Club. Republican. Presbyterian. Home: Castle Pines Village 870 Homestake Ct Castle Rock CO 80104-0081 Office: [illegible] 5817 E-mail: corboy@corboyjerde.com

CORBRIDGE, JAMES NOEL, JR. law educator, educator; b. Mineola, N.Y., May 27, 1934; s. James Noel Sr. and Edna (Springer) C.; children: Loren, Stuart. AB, Brown U., 1955; LLB, Yale U., 1963. Assoc. Lord, Day & Lord, N.Y.C., 1963-65; asst. prof. law U. Colo., Boulder, 1965-67, assoc. prof., 1967-73, prof., 1973—, v.p. student affairs, 1970-72, v.p. student and minority affairs, 1972-74, vice chancellor acad. affairs, 1974-77, interim vice chancellor acad. services, 1979-81, acting vice chancellor acad. affairs, 1986, chancellor, 1986—. Vis. scholar Inst. for Advanced Legal Studies U. London, 1977, 85, Univ. Linkoping, Sweden, 1985, 1997. Contbr. articles to profl. jours. Served to lt. (j.g.) USNR, 1957-60. Mem. Colo. Bar Assn., Boulder County Bar Assn., Internat. Assn. Water Lawyers, Internat. Water Resources Assn. Episcopalian. Club: Boulder Country. Avocations: golf, bird carving, birding. Home: 1635 Dilar Dr Grove OK 74344-5500 Office: U Colo PO Box 401 Boulder CO 80309-0401

CORCORAN, ANTHONY AUSTIN, union organizer, state senator; b. Bessboro, County Cork, Ireland, May 17, 1949; came to U.S., 1952; s. Patrick Joseph and Thelma Elizabeth (Gonda) C.; m. Jeannie Marie Merrick, Mar. 14, 1976; 1 child, Simon. Student, Goddard Coll., 1975-76, U. San Francisco, 1967-70. Mental health counselor State of Vt., Waterbury, 1973-76; dep. sheriff Lane County, Eugene, Oreg., 1980-84; welfare worker State of Oreg., Eugene, 1984-88; union organizer Oreg. Pub. Employees Union, Eugene, 1988—; mem. Oreg. Ho. of Reps., Salem, 1995-98, Oreg. Senate, Salem, 1998-. Bd. dirs. Coast Fork Learning Ctr., Cottage Grove, Oreg., 1985-87, Lane County Corrections Adv. Com., Eugene, 1983-94; coach, referee Kidsports and Cottage Grove Recreation, 1984-86; chair Lane Co. Dem. Platform Conv., 1991-93. Avocations: tennis, golf. Home: 34475 Kizer Creek Rd Cottage Grove OR 97424-9411 Office: Oreg Senate S-314 State Capitol Salem OR 97310-0001

CORCORAN, MAUREEN ELIZABETH, lawyer; b. Iowa City, Feb. 4, 1944; d. Joseph and Velma (Tobin) C. BA in English with honors, U. Iowa, 1966, MA in English, 1967; JD, Hastings Coll. of Law, San Francisco, 1979. Bar: Calif. 1979, D.C. 1988, U.S. Ct. Appeals (9th cir.), 1979, U.S. Dist. Ct. (no. dist.) Calif., 1979, U.S. Dist. Ct. (cen. dist.) Calif., 1979, US. Ct. Appeals (D.C. cir.) 1983. Assoc. Hassard Bonnington Rogers & Huber, San Francisco, 1979-81; spl. asst. to gen. counsel HHS, Washington, 1981-83; assoc. Weissburg & Aronson, San Francisco, 1983-84; gen. counsel U.S. Dept. Edn., Washington, 1984-86; of counsel Pillsbury Winthrop LLP (and predecessor firms), San Francisco, 1987-; bd. dirs. Hastings Coll. Law U. Calif., San Francisco, 1993—, chmn., 1998-2000. Chmn. Managed Health Care Conf., 1989; mem. AIDS adv. com. Ctrs. for Disease Control, 1989-91; spkr. health law mtgs. Author: (book) Managed Care Contracting: Advising the Managed Care Organization, 1996; contbr. articles on health law to profl. jours. Mem. U.S. delegation to 1985 World Conf. to Review and Appraise Achievements of UN Decade for Women, Nairobi, Kenya, 1985; mem. Adminstrv. Conf. U.S., Washington, 1985. Mem. ABA (sect. health law), Calif. State Bar Assn., Am. Health Lawyers Assn. Office: Pillsbury Winthrop LLP Ste 1022 50 Fremont St San Francisco CA 94105-2230

CORDNER, TOM, advertising executive; Co-chmn. bd., creative dir. Team One Advertising, El Segundo, Calif. Office: Team One Advertising 1960 E Grand Ave Ste 700 El Segundo CA 90245-5059

CORDOVA, DONALD E. judge; b. Trinidad, Colo., Jan. 26, 1938; AB, Regis Coll., 1961; JD, U. Colo., 1964. Bar: Colo. 1964. Asst. U.S. atty. Colo., 1964-68; ptnr. Zarlengo, Mott & Carlin; mem. Denver County Ct. Judicial Selection Commn., 1968-71; ptnr. Cordova, DeMoulin, Harris & Mellon, P.C., Denver; judge U.S. Bankruptcy Ct., Denver, 1990-. Mem. Judicial Conf. Adv. Com. Bankruptcy Rules, 1994-2000; mem. Nat. Conf. of Bankruptcy Judges, bd. dirs. 1996-99. Mem. ABA (mem. ho. of dels. 1996-98), Denver Bar Assn. (v.p. 1981-82, pres. 1987-88, adminstr. Waterman Fund 1997—) Colo. Bar Assn. (v.p. 1978-79, mem. bd. govs 1970-72, 80-82, 86-89, Supreme Ct. com. on pattern jury instructions 1987-90), Nat. Conf. Bankruptcy Judges (bd. govs. 1996-99), Hispanic Bar Assn. (pres. 1984), Denver Law Club (pres. 1977-78). Office: US Bankruptcy Ct US Custom House 721 19th St Denver CO 80202-2500

CORK, LINDA KATHERINE, veterinary pathologist, educator; b. Texarkana, Tex., Dec. 14, 1936; d. Albert James and Martine Sessions (Buntyn) Collins; m. P.S. Cork Jr., Mar. 1955 (div. 1965); children: Robin E., Jerald W. BS, Tex. A&M U., 1969, DVM, 1970; PhD, Wash. State U., 1974. Diplomate Am. Coll. Vet. Pathologists. Fellow Wash. State U., Pullman, 1970-74; asst. prof. U. Ga., Athens, 1974-76, Johns Hopkins U., Balt., 1976-82, assoc. prof., 1982-88, assoc. dir. rsch. Alzheimer's Disease Rsch. Ctr., 1985-93, prof., 1988-93; prof., chmn. Dept. Comparative Medicine Stanford U., 1994—. Coun. mem. NIH div. Rsch. Resources, Bethesda, Md., 1985-89; adv. bd. Registry Comparative Pathology, Bethesda. Grantee Nat. Inst. on Aging, 1985-89, Nat. Inst. Health, 1986-91, 86-93, 87-92. Mem. Inst. Medicine, Am. Assn. Neuropathologists (chmn. June 1988), Am. Assn. Pathology, U.S.-Can. Acad. Pathology. Methodist. Avocation: music. Office: Stanford Univ Dept Comparative Medicine MSOB Bldg Stanford CA 94305-5415

CORMAN, MARVIN LEONARD, surgeon, educator; b. Phila., Dec. 17, 1939; s. Joseph Mayer and Dorothy Frances (Stern) C.; children: John Mayer, Alexander Stern. BA, U. Pa., 1961, MD, 1965. Diplomate Nat. Bd. Med. Examiners, Am. Bd. Surgery, Am. Bd. Colon and Rectal Surgery; lic. surgeon, Mass., N.J., Fla., Calif. Sr. registrar, vis. lectr. gen. infirmary, profl. surg. unit U. Leeds, Eng., 1968-69; surg. intern Boston City Hosp.-Fifth (Harvard) Surg. Svc., 1965, surg. resident, 1966-68, surg. resident, chief surg. resident, 1969-71; staff surgeon divsn. colon and rectal surgery, dept. surgery Lahey Clinic Med. Ctr., Boston, 1971-81, Sansum Med. Clinic, Santa Barbara, Calif., 1981-95; surgeon divsn. colon and rectal surgery UCLA, 1996-98; prof. surgery U. So. Calif. Sch. Medicine, 1998—. Instr. surgery Sch. Medicine Harvard U., Boston, 1972-77, clin. asst. prof. surgery, 1977-82, prof. surgery UCLA, 1996—; co-dir. tng. program colon and rectal surgery Sansum Med. clinic, 1981-95, chmn. divsn. edn., 1983-90; credentials com. Santa Barbara Cottage Hosp., 1984-95, mem. libr. com., 1985-95, mem. com. on grad. med. edn., 1989-94, vice-chmn. dept. surgery, 1994-95; pres. alumni assn. Harvard Surg. Svc., Boston City Hosp., 1983-84; vis. prof. U. Tex. Health Sci. Ctr., San Antonio, 1982, Throckmorton Surg. Soc., Des Moines, 1985, Ogden (Utah) Surg. Soc., 1985, 20th ann. Surg. Congress Orange County Surg. Soc., Newport Beach, Calif., 1988, Royal Australasian Coll. Surgeons, Adelaide, Australia, 1989, Northwest Permanente Dept. Surgery, Portland, Oreg., 1991, Hahnemann U., Phila., 1991, El Colegio de Cirujanos Gererales de Mexicali, Mexico, 1991, Cleve. Clinic Fla., Ft. Lauderdale, Fla., 1992, Univ. Hosp. de Clinicas do Parana, Curitiba, Brazil, 1993; Ralph Coffey vis. prof. Sch. Medicine, U. Mo., Kansas City, 1988; Ralph B. Samson Meml. lectr. Grant Med. Ctr., Columbus, Ohio, 1991; Louis A. Buie vis. lectr. Mayo Med. Sch., Rochester, Minn., 1992; ann. vis. surgeon Queen Elizabeth Hosp. Ctr. of Montreal, Que., 1993; vis. prof. U. So. Calif. Sch. Medicine, L.A., 1995; Neil Swinton vis. prof. Lahey Clinic, Burlington, Mass., 1997; del. leader Citizen Amb. Program Colon and Rectal Surgery Del. to Russia, Hungary and Czechoslovakia, 1992. Author: (textbook) Colon and Rectal Surgery, 1984, 89, 93, 99; assoc. editor: Diseases of the Colon and Rectum, 1977-92, Lahey Clinic Bull., 1972-81; contbr. numerous articles to profl. jours. Recipient Hoffman-LaRoche award, 1965, Piedmont Proctologic Soc. award, 1973, 1st prize of Med. Book award, 1985. Fellow ACP; mem. ACS (So. Calif. chpt.), AMA (chmn. residency rev. com. for colon and rectal surgery 1985-86), Internat. Soc. Univ. Colon and Rectal Surgeons, Am. Soc. Colon and Rectal Surgeons (v.p. 1995-96), Am. Surg. Assn., Am. Med. Writers Assn. (hon.), Am. Coll. Gastroenterology, Assn. for Program Dirs. in Colon and Rectal Surgery, We. Surg. Assn., Pan Am. Med. Assn. (coun. sect. on colon and rectal surgery 1989—), Royal Australasian Coll. Surgeons (hon., sect. colon and rectal surgery 1989), New Eng. Surg. Soc., Calif. Med. Soc., New Eng. Soc. Colon and Rectal Surgeons (sec.-treas. 1977-81), Boston Surg. Soc., Northeastern Soc. Colon and Rectal Surgeons, Soc. Surgery Alimentary Tract, Santa Barbara County Med. Soc., So. Calif. Soc. Colon and Rectal Surgeons, Piedmont Proctologic Soc. (hon.). Office: USC Sch Medicine Divsn Colon & Rectal Surgery 1450 San Pablo St Ste 5400 Los Angeles CA 90033-1042

CORMIER, JEAN G. communications company executive; b. Campbellton, N.B., Can., May 3, 1941; s. Simon and Leona (Arsenault) C.; m. Helen Morrison, Sept. 9, 1965; children: Paul, Michel. BA in Philosophy, Bathurst Coll., N.B., 1963; postgrad., McMaster U., Hamilton, Ont., Can., 1963-64. Dir. pub. affairs Dofasco, Hamilton, 1970-75; v.p. pub. rels. Can. Nat., Montreal, Que., Can., 1975-79; pres. CN Hotels and Tower, Montreal, 1979-81; sr. v.p. corp. affairs B.C. Resources Investment Corp., Vancouver, Can., 1981-86; pres. Cormier Communicators, Inc., Vancouver, 1986—. Contbr. articles to profl. jours. Fellow Internat. Assn. Bus. Communicators (bd. dirs. 1983-89, past chmn. 1987-88); mem. Can. Pub. Rels. Soc. (accredited), Vancouver Club, Marine Dr. Golf Club (pres. 1999, 2000). Roman Catholic. Avocation: photography. Office: Cormier Communicators Inc 1050 W Pender St Ste 910 Vancouver BC Canada V6E 2N7

CORNABY, KAY STERLING, lawyer, former state senator; b. Spanish Fork, Utah, Jan. 14, 1936; s. Sterling A. and Hilda G. Cornaby; m. Linda Rasmussen, July 23, 1965; children: Alyse, Derek, Tara, Heather, Brandon. AB, Brigham Young U., 1960; postgrad. law, Heidelberg, Germany, 1961-63; JD, Harvard U., 1966. Bar: N.Y. 1967, Utah 1969, U.S. Patent and Trademark Office 1967. Assoc. Brumbaugh, Graves, Donahue & Raymond, N.Y.C., 1966-69; ptnr. Mallinckrodt & Cornaby, Salt Lake City, 1969-72; sole practice Salt Lake City, 1972-85; mem. Utah State Senate, 1977-91, majority leader, 1983-84; shareholder Jones, Waldo, Holbrook & McDonough, Salt Lake City, 1985—. Mem. Nat. Commn. on Uniform State Laws, 1988-93; mem. adv. bd. U. Mich. Ctr. for Study of Youth Policy,1990-93; mem. Utah State Jud. Conduct Commn., 1983-91, chmn., 1984-85; bd. dirs. KUED-KUER Pub. TV and Radio, 1982-88; bd. dirs. Salt Lake Conv. and Visitors Bur., 1985—. Mem. N.Y. Bar Assn., Utah Bar Assn., Utah Harvard Alumni Assn. (pres. 1977-79), Harvard U. Law Sch. Alumni Assn. (pres. 1995—). Office: Jones Waldo Holbrook & McDonough 1500 Wells Fargo Bank Plz 170 S Main St Salt Lake City UT 84101-1605

CORNELL, ERIC ALLIN, physics educator; s. Allin and Elizabeth (Greenberg) C.; m. Celeste Landry; 1 child, Eliza. BS in Physics with honors, Stanford U., 1985; PhD in Physics, MIT, 1990. Tchr. English as Fgn. Lang. Taichung YMCA, Taiwan, 1982; rsch. asst. Stanford (Calif.) U., 1982-85; tchg. fellow Harvard Ext. Sch., 1989; postdoctoral Rowland Inst., Cambridge, Mass., summer 1990; postdoctorate Joint Inst. Lab. Astrophysics, Boulder, Colo., 1990-92; asst. prof. adj. dept. physics U. Colo., Boulder, 1992-95; staff scientist Nat. Inst. Stds. and Tech., Boulder, 1992—; fellow JILA U. Colo and Nat. Inst. Stds. and Tech., Boulder, 1994—. Contbr. over 30 articles to profl. jours.; patentee in field. Recipient Grad. fellowship NSF, 1985-88, Undergrad. Rsch. award for excellence Firestone, 1985, Samuel Wesley Stratton award, 1995, Newcomb-Cleveland prize, 1995-96, Carl Zeiss award, 1996, Fritz London prize in low temperature physics, 1996, Gold medal Dept. Commerce, 1996, Presdl. Early Career award in sci. and engring., 1996, I.I. Rabi prize in atomic, molecular and optical physics Am. Phys. Soc., 1997, King Faisal Internat. prize in sci., 1997, Alan T. Waterman award NSF, 1997. Achievements include being the first of Bose-Einstein condensation, 1995. Office: Univ Colo JILA Campus Box 440 Boulder CO 80309-0440

CORNWALL, JOHN MICHAEL, physics educator, consultant, researcher; b. Denver, Aug. 19, 1934; s. Paul Bakewell and Dorothy (Zitkowski) C.; m. Ingrid Linderos, Oct. 16, 1965. AB, Harvard U., 1956; MS, U. Denver, 1959; PhD, U. Calif., 1962. NSF postdoctoral fellow Calif. Inst. Tech., Pasadena, 1962-63; mem. Inst. Advanced Study, Princeton, N.J., 1963-65; prof. physics UCLA, 1965—. Vis. prof. Niels Bohr Inst., Copenhagen, 1968-69, Inst. de Physique Nucléaire, Paris, 1973-74, MIT, 1974, 87, Rockefeller U., N.Y.C., 1988; faculty RAND Grad. Sch., 1999; cons. Inst. Theoretical Physics, Santa Barbara, Calif., 1979-80, 82, bd. dirs., 1979-83; assoc. Ctr. Internat./Strategic Affairs, UCLA, 1987—; cons. MITRE Corp., Aerospace Corp., Los Alamos Nat. Labs., RAND Corp., Inst. Def. Analysis; mem. dir.'s adv. com. Lawrence Livermore Labs., 1991—; mem. Def. Sci. Bd., 1992-93, mem. task force, 1996; chmn. external rev. com. accelerator oper. and technol. divsn., Los Alamos Nat. Labs., 1995-97, mem. Los Alamos Neutron Scattering Ctr. adv. bd., 2000—; chmn. external rev. com. Ctr. for Internat. Security and Arms Control, Stanford U., 1996; adv. commn. Accelerator Prodn. Tritium Project, 1997-2000; cons. John D. and Catherine T. MacArthur Found.; prof. sci. and policy analysis RAND Grad Sch., 1998-2000; mem. sci. and tech. panel Def. Threat Reduction Agy., 2000; mem. rev. com. Advanced Accelerator Applications, 2001—; mem. adv. bd. Los Alamos Neutron Scattering Ctr., 2000. Author: (with others) Academic Press Ency. of Science and Technology, Union of Concerned Scientists Report on Nat. Missile Def., other encys. and books; contbr. numerous articles to profl. jours. With U.S. Army, 1956-58. Grantee Dept. Energy, NSF, NASA, Dept. Edn.; pre and postdoctoral fellow NSF, 1960-63, A.P. Sloan fellow, 1967-71. Fellow AAAS; mem. Am. Phys. Soc., Am. Geophys. Union, N.Y. Acad. Sci. Avocations: jogging, bicycling, golf, bridge. Office: UCLA Dept Physics Los Angeles CA 90095-0001 E-mail: cornwall@physics.ucla.edu

CORONITI, FERDINAND VINCENT, physics educator, consultant; b. Boston, June 14, 1943; s. Samuel Charles and Ethel Marie (Havlik) C.; m. Patricia Ann Smith, Aug. 30, 1969; children: Evelyn Marie, Samuel Thomas. AB, Harvard U., 1965; PhD, U. Calif.-Berkeley, 1969. Rsch. physicist UCLA, 1967-70, asst. prof. physics, 1970-74, assoc. prof., 1974-78, prof. physics and astronomy, 1978—. Cons. TRW Systems Contbr. articles to sci. jours. NASA grantee, 1974, NSF grantee, 1974—. Fellow Am. Geophys. Union, Am. Phys. Soc.; mem. Am. Astron. Soc., Internat. Union Radiol. Sci. Home: 10475 Almayo Ave Los Angeles CA 90064-2301 Office: UCLA Dept Physics & Astronomy 405 Hilgard Ave Los Angeles CA 90095-1547 E-mail: coroniti@physics.ucla.edu

COROTIS, ROSS BARRY, civil engineering educator, academic administrator; b. Woodbury, N.J., Jan. 15, 1945; s. A. Charles and Hazel Laura (McCloskey) C.; m. Stephanie Michal Fuchs, Mar. 19, 1972; children: Benjamin Randall, Lindsay Sarah. SB, MIT, Cambridge, 1967, SM, 1968, PhD, 1971. Lic. profl. engr., Ill., Md., Colo., structural engr., Ill. Asst. prof. dept. civil engring. Northwestern U., Evanston, Ill., 1971-74, assoc. prof. dept. civil engring., 1975-79, prof. dept. civil engring., 1979-81, Johns Hopkins U., Balt., 1981-82, Hackerman prof., 1982-83, Hackerman prof., chmn. dept. civil engring., 1983-90, Hackerman prof., assoc. dean engring., 1990-94; dean Coll. Engring. and Applied Sci. U. Colo., Boulder, 1994-2001, Denver Bus. Challenge prof., 2001—. Mem. bldg. rsch. bd. Nat. Rsch. Coun., Washington, 1985-88; lectr. profl. confs. Editor in chief Internat. Jour. Structural Safety, 1991-2000; contbr. articles to profl. jours. Mem. Mayor's task force City of Balt. Constrn. Mgmt., 1985. Recipient Engring. Tchg. award Northwestern U., 1977, Disting. Engring. Alumnus award U. Colo. Coll. Engring. and Applied Scis., 2000; named Md. Engr. of Yr., Balt. Engrs. Week Coun., 1989; rsch. grantee NSF, Nat. Bur. Stds., U.S. Dept. Energy, 1973-96. Fellow ASCE (chmn. safety bldgs. com. 1985-89, chmn. tech. adminstrv. com. structural safety and reliability 1988-92, chmn. probabilistic methods com. 1996-98, v.p. Md. chpt. 1987-88, pres. 1988-89, Walter L. Huber rsch. prize 1984, Civil Engr. of Yr. award Md. chpt. 1987, Outstanding Educator award Md. chpt. 1992); mem. Internat. Assn. for Structural Safety and Reliability (chair exec. bd. 1998-2001), Am. Soc. for Engring. Edn. (mem. pub. policy com. 1998-2001, mem. deans exec. bd. 1998-2001), Am. Concrete Inst. (chmn. structural safety com. 1986-88), Am. Nat. Stds. Inst. (chmn. live loads com. 1978-84), Nat. Inst. Stds. and Tech. (panel on assessment 1999—). Office: U Colo Coll Engring & Applied Sci PO Box 428 Boulder CO 80309-0428

CORRADINI, DEEDEE, mayor; Student, Drew U., 1961-63; BS, U. Utah, 1965, MS, 1967. Adminstrv. asst. for public info. Utah State Office Rehab. Svcs., 1967-69; cons. Utah State Dept. Cmty. Affairs, 1971-72; media dir., press sec. Wayne Owens for Congress Campaign, 1972; press sec. Rep. Wayne Owens, 1973-74; spl. asst. to N.Y. Congl. Rep. Richard Ottinger, 1975; asst. to pres., dir. cmty. rels. Snowbird Corp., 1975-77; exec. v.p. Bonneville Assocs., Inc., Salt Lake City, 1977-80, pres., 1980-89, chmn., CEO, 1989-91; mayor Salt Lake City, 1992—. Pres. U.S. Conf. of Mayors, 1998—, mem. unfunded fed. mandates task force, mem. crime and violence task force; chair Mayor's Gang Task Force; mem. interngovtl. policy adv. com. U.S. Trade Rep., 1993-94, 99—; mem. transp. and comm. com. Nat. League of Cities, 1993-94. Bd. trustees Intermountain Health Care, 1980-92; bd. dirs., exec. com. Utah Symphony, 1983-92, vice chmn., 1985-88, chmn., 1988-92; dir. Utah chpt. Nat. Conf. Christians and Jews, Inc., 1988; bd. dirs. Salt Lake Olympic Bid Com., 1989—; chmn. image com. Utah Partnership for Edn. and Econ. Devel., 1989-92; co-chair United Way Success by 6 Program; pres. Shelter of the Homeless Com.; active Sundance Inst. Utah Com., 1990-92; disting. bd. fellow So. Utah U., 1991; active numerous other civic orgns. and coms. Mem. Salt Lake Area C. of C. (bd. govs. 1979-81, chmn. City/County/Govt. com. 1976-86). Office: Mayors Office City Hall 451 S State St Rm 306 Salt Lake City UT 84111-3104

CORRIGAN, ROBERT ANTHONY, academic administrator; b. New London, Conn., Apr. 21, 1935; s. Anthony John and Rose Mary (Jengo) C.; m. Joyce D. Mobley, Jan. 12, 1975; children by previous marriage: Kathleen Marie, Anthony John, Robert Anthony; 1 stepdau., Erika Mobley. AB, Brown U., 1957; MA, U. Pa., 1959, PhD, 1967; LHD (hon.), 1995. Researcher Phila. Hist. Commn., 1957-59; lectr. Am. civilization U. Gothenburg, Sweden, 1959-62, Bryn Mawr Coll., 1962-63, U. Pa., 1963-64; prof. U. Iowa, 1964-73; dean U. Mo., Kansas City, 1973-74; provost U. Md., 1974-79; chancellor U. Mass., Boston, 1979-88; pres. San Francisco State U., 1988—. Author: American Fiction and Verse, 1962, 2d edit., 1970, also articles, revs.; editor: Uncle Tom's Cabin, 1968. Vice chmn. Iowa City Human Rels. Commn., 1970-72, Gov.'s Commn. on Water Quality, 1983-84; mem. Iowa City Charter Commn., 1972-73; chmn. Md. Com. Humanities, 1976-78, Assn. Urban Univs., 1988-92; mem. Howard County Commn. Arts, Md., 1976-79; bd. dirs. John F. Kennedy Libr.; trustee San Francisco Econ. Devel. Corp., 1989-92, Modern Greek Studies Found., Found. of Spain and U.S., Adv. Coun. of Calif. Acad. Scis., Bishop Desmond Tutu South African Refugee Scholarship Fund, Calif. Hist. Soc., 1989-92; co-chmn., bd. dirs. Calif. Compact, 1990-93; mem. exec. com. Campus Compact, 1991—, chmn., 1995—; Mayor's Blue Ribbon Commn. on Fiscal Stability, 1994-95; chmn. Pres. Clinton's Steering Com. of Coll. Pres. for Am. Reads and Am. Counts, 1996—. Smith-Mundt prof., 1959-60; Fulbright lectr., 1960-62; grantee Std. Oil Co. Found., 1968, NEH, 1969-74, Ford Found., 1969, Rockefeller Found., 72-75, Dept. State, 1977; recipient Clarkson Able Collins Jr. Maritime History award, 1956, Pa. Colonial Soc. Essay award, 1958, 59, William Lloyd Garrison award Mass. Ednl. Opportunity Assn., 1987; Disting. Urban Fellow Assn. Urban U., 1992. Mem. San Francisco C. of C. (bd. dirs.), San Francisco World Affairs Coun. (bd. dirs.), Pvt. Industry Coun. (bd. dirs.), Boston World Affairs Coun. (1983-88), Greater Boston C. of C. (v.p. 1987-89), Fulbright Alumni Assn. (bd. dirs. 1978-80), Univ. Club, City Club, World Trade Club, Commonwealth Club (bd. dirs. 1995-99), Phi Beta Kappa. Democrat. Office: San Francisco State U 1600 Holloway Ave San Francisco CA 94132-1722

CORRIGAN, WILFRED J. data processing and computer company executive; b. 1938; Divsn. dir. Motorola, Phoenix, 1962-68; pres. Fairchild Camera & Instrument, Sunnyvale, Calif., 1968-80; chmn. bd., CEO LSI Logic Corp., Milpitas, 1980—, also dir. Office: LSI Logic Corp 1551 Mccarthy Blvd Milpitas CA 95035-7451

CORRY, CHARLES ELMO, geophysicist, consultant; b. Salt Lake City, May 15, 1938; s. Elmo Leigh Corry and Sylvia Birch; children: Christopher Charles, Matthew Lee. BS in Geology, Utah State U., 1970; MS in Geophysics, U. Utah, 1972; PhD in Geophysics, Tex. A&M U., 1976. Electronic missile checkout GD Convair-Astronautics, San Diego, 1960-64; rsch. assoc. Scripps Inst. Oceanography, La Jolla, Calif., 1965-68, Woods Hole (Mass.) Oceanographic Inst., 1968; mgr. geophys. rsch. AMAX, Golden, Colo., 1977-82; v.p. Nonlinear Analysis, Inc., Bryan, Tex., 1982-84; vis., adj., assoc. prof. geophysics Tex. A&M U., College Station, 1983-87; assoc. prof. geophysics U. Mo., Rolla, 1984-89; coord. world ocean circulation experiment Woods Hole Oceanographic Inst., 1990-95; cons. Golden, Denver, Colorado Springs, 1995—. Author: Laccoliths, Mechanics of Emplacement and Growth, 1988, Geology of the Solitario, Trans-Pecos Texas, 1990, Domestic Violence Against Men, 1999, (award); contbr. articles to profl. jours. and conf. procs., including Trans. Am. Geophys. Union, Jour. Applied Geophysics, others. Cpl., USMC, 1956-59, Calif.; pres. Equal Justice Found., 2001—. Fellow Geol. Soc. Am.; mem. ACLU, Am. Geophys. Union, Soc. Exploration Geophysicists, Am. Coalition for Fathers and Children (bd. advisors). Buddhist. Achievements include overturning of paradigm that had existed for over 150 years, regarding galvanic current flow in ore bodies; discovery that ore minerals are commonly ferroelectrics and that ore bodies behave as a polarized dielectric medium, or solid plasma, in electrical surveys; development of the controlled source audiomagnetotelluric method for electrical exploration; field and theoretical studies of magmatic intrusions; terrestrial heat flow studies in the North Pacific; coordination of hydrographic program of World Ocean Circulation Experiment; relational database design and data modeling; civil liberties. Home: 455 Bear Creek Rd Colorado Springs CO 80906-5820 E-mail: ccorry@pcisys.net

CORRY, DALILA BOUDJELLAL, internist; b. El-Arrouch, Algeria, July 7, 1943; came to U.S., 1981; MD, U. Algiers, 1974; Specialty in Nephrology Diploma, Faculty of Medicine Paris V, 1979. Diplomate Am. Bd. Internal Medicine. Intern Hosp. Mustapha Algiers, 1972-73; resident Hosp. Tenon, Paris, 1975-79; fellow in nephrology UCLA, 1981-83; chief renal divsn. Olive View-UCLA Med. Ctr., Sylmar, Calif., 1983—; asst. prof. medicine UCLA Sch. Medicine, 1993—. Assoc. prof. clin. medicine UCLA. Recipient Clinician-Scientist award Am. Heart Assn., 1995-96. Fellow Am. Heart Assn. (coun. for high blood pressure rsch. 2000); mem. Am. Hosp. Assn., Am. Soc. Nephrology, Am. Soc. Hypertension (spls. in clin. hypertension), Women in Nephrology. Office: Olive View-UCLA Med Ctr Dept Medicine 2B182 14445 Olive View Dr Sylmar CA 91342-1437

CORTESE, CHARLES FRANKLIN, sociologist, educator, planning consultant; b. Pueblo, Colo., Aug. 31, 1940; s. Charles and Frances (Sichile) C.; m. Marian Jane Archer, Aug. 10, 1963 (div. Mar. 1981); children: Jennifer Cortese Hallam, Elisabeth Archer Cortese; m. Judith Baxter, Oct. 12, 1985. BA, U. Denver, 1962, MA, 1966; PhD, Brown U., 1974. Asst. in sociology Brown U., Providence, 1968-70; instr. U. Denver, 1971-73, asst. prof., 1973-77, assoc. prof., internship dir., 1977—, dean coll., 1984-89, chmn. dept. sociology, 1993-96, dean emeritus, 2000—. Cons. NAS, Washington, 1976, mem. subcom., 1978-79; sr. sociologist Louis Berger and Assocs., Anchorage, 1979-82; mem. def. sci. bd. U.S. Dept. Def., Washington, 1980-81; rsch. sociologist Nat. Park Svc., Washington, 1981-92. Editor: Social Impacts of Energy Development in the West, 1981; assoc. editor Soc. & Nat. Resources, 1992-95; contbr. articles to profl. jours. Founder, officer Washington Park Neighborhood Assn., Denver, 1973-78; cons., vol. Found. Urban & Neighborhood Devel., Denver, 1977-80, So. Ute Indian Tribe, Ignacio, Colo., 1981; mem. natural resources com. Rocky Mt. Arsenal Wildlife Refuge, Denver, 1989-92. Recipient Nat. Inst. Advising/ADA/ Ass. for Coll. Tchg. award, 1989. Fellow Am. Sociol. Assn., Western Social Sci. Assn. (v.p. 1977-78, 82-83), Am. Assn. for Advancement of Core Curriculum (nat. dir. 1990-93); mem. Am. Water Resources Assn., Internat. Assn. Impact Assn., Front Range Fly Fishers (pres. 1990-92). Democrat. Avocations: fly fishing, hiking, woodcarving. Home: 3234 S Gregg Ct Denver CO 80210-6943 Fax: 303-871-2020. E-mail: ccortese@du.edu

CORTEZ, EDWARD S. mayor; Mayor City of Pomono, Calif. Office: City of Pomona 505 S Garey Ave Pomona CA 91766-3320

CORTNER, HANNA JOAN, research scientist, educator; b. Tacoma, May 9, 1945; d. Val and E. Irene Otteson; m. Richard Carroll Cortner, Nov. 14, 1970. BA in Polit. Sci. magna cum laude with distinction, U. Wash., 1967; MA in Govt., U. Ariz., 1969, PhD in Govt., 1973. Grad. tchg. and rsch. asst. dept. govt. U. Ariz., Tucson, 1967-70, rsch. assoc. Inst. Govt. Rsch., 1974-76, rsch. assoc. forest-watershed and landscape resources divsns. Sch. Renewable Natural Resources, 1975-82, adj. assoc. prof. Sch. Renewable Natural Resources, 1983-89; exec. asst. Pima County Bd. Suprs., 1985-86; adj. assoc. prof. renewable natural resources, assoc. rsch. scientist Water Resources Rsch. Ctr. U. Ariz., Tucson, 1988-89, prof., rsch. scientist Water Resources Rsch. Ctr., 1989-90, prof., rsch. scientist, dir. Water Resources Rsch. Ctr., 1990-96, prof., rsch. scientist Sch. Renewable Resources, 1997-2000; rsch. prof. Ecological Restoration Inst. No. Ariz. U., Flagstaff, 2001—. Program analyst USDA Forest Svc., Washington, 1979-80; vis. scholar Inst. Water Resources, Corps of Engrs., Ft. Belvoir, Va., 1986-87; com. arid lands AAAS, 1986-89; com. natural disasters NAS/NRC, 1988-91, com. on planning and remediation of irrigation-induced water quality impacts, 1994-95; rev. com. nat. forest planning Conservation Found., Washington, 1987-90; chair adv. com. renewable resources planning techs. for pub. lands Office of Tech. Assessment U.S. Congress, 1989-91; mem. policy coun. Pinchot Inst. Conservation Studies, 1991-93; co-chair working party on evaluation of forest policies Internat. Union Forestry Rsch. Orgns., 1990-95, chair working party on forest instns. and forestry adminstrn., 1996; vice chair Man and the Biosphere Program, Temperate Directorate, U.S. Dept. State, 1991-96; bd. dirs. 7th Am. Forest Congress, 1994-96, mem. comtys. com. steering com. and rsch. com., 1996—; mem. sci. adv. com. Consortium for Environ. Risk Evaluation, 1996-97; cons. Greeley and Hansen, Cons. Engrs., U.S. Army Corps Engrs., Ft. Belvoir, U.S. Forest Svc., Washington, Portland, Oreg., Ogden, Utah. Assoc. editor Society and Natural Resources, 1992-94; book reviewer Western Polit. Sci. Quar., Am. Polit. Quar., Perspectives, Natural Resources Jour., Climatic Change, Society and Natural Resources, Jour. of Forestry, Environment; mem. editl. bd. Jour. Forest Planning, 1995—, Forest Policy and Econs., 1999—; co-author: The Politics of Ecosystem Management, 1999; co-editor: The State and Nature, 2002; contbr. articles to profl. jours. Bd. dirs. Planned Parenthood So. Ariz., 1992-94, mem. planning com., 1992, mem. bd. devel. and evaluation com., 1994; bd. dirs. N.W. Homeowners Assn., 1982-83, v.p., 1983-84, pres., 1984; vice chmn., chmn. Pima County Bd. Adjustment Dist. 3, 1984; active Tucson Tomorrow, 1984-88; mem. water quality subcom. Pima Assn. Govts., 1983-84, mem. environ. planning adv. com., 1989-90, chmn., 1984, mem. Avra Valley task force, 1988-90; bd. dirs. So. Ariz. Water Resources Assn., 1984-86, 87-95, sec., 1987-89, mem. com. alignment and terminal storage, 1990-94, mem. CAP com., 1988-92, chairperson, 1989-90, mem. basin-wide mgmt. com., 1983-86, chairperson, 1992-93; active Ariz. Interagy. Task Force on Fire and the Urban/Wildland Interface, 1990-92; mem. wastewater mgmt. adv. com. Pima County, 1988-92, mem. subcom. on effluent reuse Joint CWAC-WWAC, 1989-91, mem. citizens water adv. com. Water Resources Plan Update Subcom., 1990-91; bd. dirs. Ctrl. Ariz. Water Conservation Dist., 1985-90, mem. fin. com., 1987-88, mem. spl. studies com., 1987-88, mem. nominating com., 1987; mem. Colo. River Salinity Control, 1989-90; chairperson adv. com. Tucson Long Range Master Water Plan, 1988-89; active water adv. com. City of Tucson, 1984. Travel grantee NSF/Soc. Am. Foresters; Rsch. grantee US Geol. Survey, US Army Corps of Engrs., USDA Forest Svc., Soil Conservation Svc., Utah State U., Four Corners Regional Commn., Office of Water Rsch. & Tech.; Sci. & Engring. fellow AAAS, 1986-87; recipient Copper Letter Appreciation cert. City of Tucson, 1985, 89, SAWARA award, 1989. Mem. Am. Water Resources Assn. (mem. nat. award com. 1987-90, mem. statues and bylaws com. 1989-90, tech. co-chairperson ann. meeting 1993), Am. Forests Assn. (mem. forest policy ctr. adv. coun. 1991-95), Soc. Am. Foresters (mem. task force on sustaining long-term forest health and productivity 1991-92, mem. com. on forest policy 1994-96), Am. Polit. Sci. Assn., Western Polit. Sci. Assn. (mem. com. on constrn. and bylaws 1976-80, chairperson 1977-79, mem. exec. coun. 1980-83, mem. com. on profl. devel. 1984-85, mem. com. on status of women 1984-85), Nat. Fire Protection Assn. (mem. tech. com. on forest and rural fire protection 1990-94), Phi Beta Kappa. Democrat. Achievements include research in political and socioeconomic aspects of natural resources policy, administration, and planning, water resources management, ecosystem management, wildland fire policy and management. Home: 4445 Savannah Cir Flagstaff AZ 86004 Office: Ecological Restoration Inst Northern Arizona U Flagstaff AZ 86011 E-mail: hjcortner@aol.com, hanna.cortner@nau.edu

CORTRIGHT, INGA ANN, accountant; b. Silver City, N.Mex., Sept. 30, 1949; d. Lester Richard and Claudia Marcella (Huckaby) Lee; m. Russell Joseph Cortright, June 25, 1986 (dec. Jan. 2000). BS in Acctg., Ariz. State U., 1976, MBA, 1978; postgrad., Walden U., 1995. CPA, Ariz., Tex. Sole practice cert. pub. acctg., Ariz., 1981—. Cons. in field. Mem. AICPA. Republican. Episcopalian. Avocation: travel. Office: 12630 N 103d Ave Ste 141 Sun City AZ 85351-3423 E-mail: icortright@aol.com

CORWIN, AMBER, figure skater; b. Harbor City, Calif., Dec. 21, 1978; Placed 6th in World Jr. U.S. Team Selections, 1997, 5th place Nat. Sr., 1997, 10th place NHK Trophy, 1996, 3rd place Vienna Cup, 1996, 7th place World Jr. Selections Competition, 1997, 6th place Nat. Sr., 1996, 3rd place Pacific Coast Sr., 1996, 2d place Southwest Pacific Sr., 1996, 2nd place ISU Jr. Grand Prix Finals, 1998, 6th place U.S. Championships, 1998, 6th place World Jr. Selection Competition, 1998, 1st place Pacific Coast Sr., 1998, 8th place Cup of Russia, 1998, 2nd place Vienna Cup, 1998, 5th place Skate Canada, 1998, 2nd place Four Continents Championships, 1999, 6th place U.S. Championships, 1999, 4th place Skate Canada, 1999, 4th place Nebelhorn Trophy, 1999, 7th place NHK Trophy, 1999, 13th place U.S. Championships, 2000. Avocations: rollerblading, boogie boarding, movies, friends. Office: USFSA 20 1st St Colorado Springs CO 80906-3624

CORWIN, STANLEY JOEL, book publisher; b. N.Y.C., Nov. 6, 1938; s. Seymour and Faye (Agress) C.; m. Donna Gelgur; children: Alexandra, Donna, Ellen. AB, Syracuse U., 1960. Dir. subsidiary rights, v.p. mktg. Prentice-Hall, Inc., Englewood Cliffs, N.J., 1960-68; v.p. internat. Grosset & Dunlap, Inc., N.Y.C., 1968-75, founder, pres. Corwin Books, N.Y.C., 1975; pres., pub. Pinnacle Books, Inc., L.A., 1976-79; pres. Stan Corwin Prodns. Ltd., 1980—; pres., CEO Tudor Pub. Co., N.Y.C. and L.A., 1987-90. Lectr. Conf. World Affairs, U. Colo., 1976, U. Denver, 1978, Calif. State U., Northridge, 1980, The Learning Annex; participant Pubmart Seminar, N.Y.C., 1977, UCLA, 1985, 93, 98; guest lectr. U. So. Calif., 1987—, iVillage Internet Chat Room, 1999-2001; expert witness nat. media trials. Author: Where Words Were Born, 1977, How to Become a Best Selling Author, 1984, 3d edit., 1999, The Creative Writer's Companion, 2000; contbr. articles to L.A. Times, N.Y. Times, short stories to Signature Mag.; prodr. motion picture Remo Williams-The Adventure Begins, 1986, (golf video) How to Golf with Jan Stephenson, 1987; exec. prodr. The Elvis Files TV Show, 1991, The Marilyn Files, 1993; pub. The Movie Script Libr., 1994; columnist Buddhascape Internet Network. Mem. Pres. Carter's U.S. Com. on the UN, 1977. Served with AUS, 1960. Nat. prize winner short story contest Writers' Digest, 1966 Mem. Assn. Am. Pubs., PEN. Home and Office: 470 S El Camino Dr Beverly Hills CA 90212-4222

CORY, WALLACE NEWELL, retired civil engineer; b. Olympia, Wash., Mar. 10, 1937; s. Henry Newell and Gladys Evelyn (Nixon) C.; m. Roberta Ruth Matthews, July 4, 1959; children: Steven Newell, Susan Evelyn Cory Carbon. BS in Forestry, Oreg. State U., 1958, BSCE, 1964; MSCE, Stanford U., 1965. Registered profl. engr., Idaho, Oreg. Asst. projects mgr. CH2 M/Hill, Boise, Idaho, 1965-70; environ. mgr. Boise Cascade Corp., 1970-78, dir. state govt. affairs, 1978-82; dir. indsl. group JUB Engrs., Boise, 1982-84; chief engr. Anchorage Water & Wastewater, 1984-90; dir. pub. works City of Caldwell, Idaho, 1990-92; prin. engr. Montgomery Watson, Pasadena, Calif., 1992-95; adminstr. Idaho Divsn. Environ. Quality, Boise, 1995-98; planning and assessment leader Alexandria Wastewater Project Chemonics Interna., 1998-99. Precinct committeeman Idaho Rep. Com., Boise, 1968-72, region chmn., 1973-77. Capt. USAF, 1958-62. Fellow ASCE; mem. NSPE, Idaho Soc. Profl. Engrs. (pres. 1976-77, Young Engr. of Yr. award 1971), Air Pollution Control Assn. (chmn. Pacific N.W. sect. 1977-78), Idaho Assn. Commerce and Industry (chmn. environ. com. 1974-75). Avocations: hunting, fishing, shooting. Home: 7247 Cascade Dr Boise ID 83704-8635

COSMEZ, MARK H., II, electronics executive; BA in Chemistry, Calif. State U., Hayward, 1973, MB in Acctg., 1976. CPA Calif. Corp. contr. ShareBase Corp., 1988-94, The Software Toolworks, 1994-95; v.p. fin., CFO Internat. Microcomputer Software, Inc.; CFO Pacific Bell Pub. Comm.; v.p. fin., CFO Giga-tronics, 1997—. Office: Giga-tronics Inc 4650 Norris Canyon Rd San Ramon CA 94583-1320 Fax: 925-328-4700

COSSINS, EDWIN ALBERT, biology educator, academic administrator; b. Havering, Eng., Feb. 28, 1937; came to Can., 1962; s. Albert Joseph and Elizabeth H. (Brown) C.; m. Lucille Jeannette Salt, Sept. 1, 1962; children: Diane Elizabeth (dec. 1995), Carolyn Jane. BSc, U. London, 1958, PhD, 1961, DSc, 1981. Rsch. assoc. Purdue U., Lafayette, Ind., 1961-62; from asst. prof. to prof. U. Alta., Edmonton, Can., 1962-96, acting head dept. botany Can., 1965-66, assoc. dean of sci. Can., 1983-88, prof. biol. scis. emeritus Can., 1996—. Mem. grant selection panel Natural Scis. and Engring. Research Council, Ottawa, Ont., Can., 1974-77, 78-81 Author: (with others) Plant Biochemistry; 1980, 1988, Folates and Pterins, 1984. Assoc. editor Can. Jour. Botany, 1969-78. Contbr. numerous articles to profl. jours. Recipient Centennial medal Govt. of Can., 1967 Fellow Royal Soc. Can. (life); mem. Can. Soc. Plant Physiologists (western dir. 1968-70, pres. 1976-77, gold medal 1998), Faculty Club (U. Alta.), Derrick Golf and Winter Club. Clubs: Faculty (U. Alta.), Derrick Golf and Winter Avocations: gardening, golf, curling, cross-country skiing. Home: 99 Fairway Dr Edmonton AB Canada T6J 2C2 E-mail: ecossins@ualberta.ca

COSTA, GUSTAVO, Italian studies educator; b. Rome, Mar. 21, 1930; came to U.S., 1961; s. Paolo and Ida (Antonangelo) C.; m. Natalia Zalessow, June 8, 1963; 1 child, Dora L. Maturità Classica, Liceo Virgilio, Rome, 1948; PhD cum laude, U. Rome, 1954. Asst. Istituto di Filosofia, Rome, 1957-60; instr. Italian Univ. de Lyon, Lyons, France, 1960-61, U. Calif., Berkeley, 1961-63, asst. prof., 1963-68, assoc. prof., 1968-72, prof., 1972-91, prof. emeritus, 1991—, chmn. dept. Italian, 1973-76, 88-91. Vis. prof. Scuola di Studi Superiori, Naples, 1984, Inst. Philosophy, U. Rome La Sapienza, 1992; reviewer RAI Corp., Rome, 1982-89. Author: La critica Omerica di Thomas Blackwell (1701-1757), 1959, La leggenda dei secoli d'oro nella lett. ital., 1972, Le antichità germaniche nella cultura italiana, 1977, Il sublime e la magia da Dante a Tasso, 1994, Vico e l'Europa: Contro la boria delle nazioni, 1996, Malebranche y Vico, 1998, Vico e l' Inquisizione, 1999; mem. editl. bd. Romance Philology, Nouvelles de la République des Lettres, New Vico Studies, L'anello che non tiene, Cuadernos sobre Vico. Istituto Italiano Studi Storici fellow, Naples, Italy, 1954-57, Guggenheim Meml. Found. fellow, N.Y.C., 1977; grantee French Govt., Paris, 1956, Belgian Govt., Brussels, 1956, Targa d'oro Apulia, Italy, 1990. Mem. Am. Assn. Tchrs. Italian, Am. Soc. for Eighteenth-Century Studies, Renaissance Soc. Am., Am. Soc. for Aesthetics, Dante Soc. Am., Faculty Club (Berkeley). Avocations: gardening, stamp collecting. Office: U Calif MC 2620 Dept Italian Studies Berkeley CA 94720-0001

COSTA, JERALITA, state legislator; b. San Diego, Sept. 18, 1959; Student, Everett C.C., Highline C.C. Cons., nat. trainer on criminal justice and victim svcs.; mem. customer svc. staffg Alaska Airlines, 1984-94; exec. dir. Families and Friends of Missing Persons and Violent Crimes, 1989-93; asst. dir. edn. and tng. Nat. Victim Ctr., 1993-94; mem. Wash. Senate, Dist. 38, Olympia, 1994—; mem. health and long-term care com. Wash. Legislature, Olympia, vice chair human svcs. and corrections com., mem. jud. com., mem. rules com., mem. transp. com., mem. sentencing guidelines commn. Mem. Crime Victims Compensation Bd.; exec. bd. dirs. Possession Sound Dem. Soc., Jail Industries Bd. State Wash.; mem. election adminstrn. and cert. bd. Wash. State Office Sec. State; mem. Everett C.C. Coll. Found. Bd. Recipient Outstanding Programs award Nat. Orgn. Victim Assistance, 1990, Cert. Merit for Exemplary Programs to Families and Friends of Mission Persons and Violent Crime Victims Nat. Victim's Ctr., 1992, Golden Hand award Deaconess Children Svcs., 1995, 99. Mem. Wash. Coalition Crime Victim Advocates, Learning Disabilities Assn. Wash., Marysville Bus. and Profl. Women, Mothers Against Violence in Am., Lions. Democrat. Office: 405 John Cherberg Bldg Olympia WA 98504-0001

COSTA, JIM, state senator; b. 1954; B of Polit. Sci., Calif. State U., Fresno. Spl. asst. to Congressman John Krebs, 1975-76; adminstrv. asst. Assembly Mem. Richard Lehman, 1976-78; mem. Calif. Assembly, 1978-94, Calif. State Senate, 1994—, chmn. agr. and water resources com., housing and land use com., mem. fin., investment and internat. trade com., transp. com. Senate rep. Calif. World Trade Commn., 1995—; pres. Nat. Conf. State Legislatures, 2000-01. Mem. Fresno County Farm Bur., I.D.E.S. Men's Lodge, Fresno Cabrillo Club. Democrat. Office: Calif State Senate State Capitol Rm 5100 Sacramento CA 95814 also: 2550 Mariposa Mall Ste 2016 Fresno CA 93721-2219

COSTA, MAURICE, health care company executive; With Indsl. Indemnity Co., 1971-87; founder Bus. Ins. Co. (later sold to Found. Health Corp.), 1987-93; pres. bus. ins. group Found. Health Sys., pres. employer & occupl. svcs. divsn. Calif., 1999—. Office: FHS Inc 21600 Oxnard St Woodland Hills CA 91367-4976

COSTA, WALTER HENRY, architect; b. Oakland, Calif., July 2, 1924; s. Walter H.F. and Mamie R. (Dunkle) C.; m. Jane Elisabeth Ledwich, Aug. 28, 1948; 1 dau., Laura. B.A., U. Calif., Berkeley, 1948, M.A., 1949. Designer Mario Corbett (architect), San Francisco, 1947-48, Ernst Born (architect), San Francisco, 1949; draftsman Milton Pflueger, San Francisco, 1950-51; designer Skidmore, Owings & Merrill, San Francisco, 1951-57, participating assoc., then assoc. prtnr., 1957-69, gen. prtnr., 1969-89, ret. 1990. Bd. dirs. East Bay Regional Park Dist., 1977-87, pres., 1984-85; mem. city council, Lafayette, Calif., 1972-76, mayor, 1973. Served with USSNR, 1943-46. Fellow AIA. Clubs: Olympic (San Francisco), Univ. (San Francisco), Lakeview (Oakland, Calif.). Home: 1264 Redwood Ln Lafayette CA 94549-2416 Office: Skidmore Owings & Merrill 333 Bush St Ste 2020 San Francisco CA 94104-2894

COSTANZO, PATRICK M. construction executive; Sr. v.p. for heavy constrn. Granite Constrn. Inc., Watsonville, Calif. Office: Granite Construction Inc PO Box 50024 Watsonville CA 95077-5024

COSTEA, NICOLAS VINCENT, physician, researcher; b. Bucharest, Romania, Nov. 10, 1927; came to U.S., 1957; s. Nicolas and Florica (Ionescu) C.; m. Ileana Paunescu, Apr. 20, 1973 BA, Nat. Coll. Bucharest, 1946; MS, U. Paris, 1949, MD, 1956. Intern St. Francis Hosp., N.Y.C., 1956-57; resident L.I. Jewish Hosp., 1957-59; fellow in hematology Tufts U., 1959-62; dir. clinic Pratt Clinic, Boston, 1962-63; clin. investigator Va. West Side Med. Ctr., Chgo., 1963-68; chief hematology U. Ill., Chgo., 1968-70, prof. medicine, 1970-72; chief hematology-oncology UCLA-VA Hosp., Sepulveda, 1972-87; prof. UCLA, 1972-96; vis. prof. Nat. Acad. Scis., 1972. Contbr. numerous chpts., articles to profl. publs. Recipient Lederle award Lederle Industries, 1966 Mem. Am. Soc. Hematology, Am. Soc. Immunology, N.Y. Acad. Scis., Western Soc. Clin. Research Home and Office: 3651 Terrace View Dr Encino CA 91436-4019

COSTELLO, FRANCIS WILLIAM, lawyer; b. Cambridge, Mass., Apr. 16, 1946; s. Frank George and Anna M. (Sinnott) C. BA, Columbia U., 1968, JD, 1973. Bar: N.Y. 1974, Calif. 1977. Assoc. Whitman & Ransom, N.Y.C., 1973-74, L.A., 1976-82, ptnr., 1982-93, Whitman, Breed, Abbott & Morgan, L.A., 1993-2000, Holland & Knight, LLP, L.A., 2000—, mem. dirs. com., 2001—. Bd. dirs. Sunritz Corp., L.A., Japan Travel Bur. Internat., L.A. Served with U.S. Army, 1968-70, Vietnam. Mem. State Bar Calif., State Bar N.Y., L.A. County Bar Assn., Pumpkin Ridge Golf Club (Oreg.), Wilshire Country Club (L.A.), Calif. Club (L.A.). E-mial. Home: 415 Knight Way La Canada Flintridge CA 91011-2725 E-mail: fcostell@hklaw.com

COSTELLO, RICHARD NEUMANN, advertising agency executive; b. Phila., Sept. 2, 1943; s. Joseph Neumann and Katherine Cash (Birkhead) C.; m. Ann M. Dodds, Oct. 24, 1970; children: Brian Stuart, Gregory Scott. BA in English, U. Pa., 1965, MBA in Mktg., 1967. Account mgr. Ogilvy & Mather, Inc., N.Y.C., 1967-71; v.p. Rosenfeld, Sirowitz & Lawson, Inc., N.Y.C., 1971-73; pres. Baron, Costello & Fine, Inc., N.Y.C., 1973-77, TBWA Advt., Inc., N.Y.C., 1977-95, internat. bd. dirs., 1984-96, COO, 1987-94; pres., CEO TBWA Chiat/Day-East, 1995-96; pres. universal strategic mktg. group Universal Studios Inc., Universal City, Calif., 1996-98; pres. New Bus. Initiatives Univ. Studios, Inc., 1998—. Mem. Young Pres.'s Orgn. Office: Universal Studios Inc 100 Universal City Plz Universal Cty CA 91608-1002

COSTERTON, JOHN WILLIAM FISHER, microbiologist; b. Vernon, B.C., Can., July 21, 1934; married, 1955; 4 children. BA, U. B.C., 1955, MA, 1956; PhD in Microbiology, U. Western Ont., Can., 1960. Prof. biology Baring Union Christian Coll., Punjab, India, 1960-62, dean sci. India, 1963-64; fellow bot. Cambridge (Eng.) U., 1965; prof. assoc. microbiology McGill U., 1966-67, asst. prof., 1968-70; assoc. prof. U. Calgary, Alta., Can., 1970-75, prof. microbiology Can., 1975-93, indsl. rsch. chair biofilm microbiology Can., 1985-93; dir. Ctr. Biofilm Engring. Mont. State U., Bozeman, 1993—. Author 2 books on biofilms; contbr. more than 750 articles to profl. jours. Recipient Sir Frederick Haultain prize, 1985, Isaac Walton Killam prize, 1990. Mem. Can. Soc. Microbiology, Am. Soc. Microbiology. Achievements include research in architecture of bacterial cell walls and including extracellular carbohydrate coats; originator of universal biofilm theory in microbiology; thought of as leader in the biofilm concept in engring., medicine, dentistry, and environ. sci. Office: Montana State Univ Ctr Biofilm Engineering 366 Ets Bldg Bozeman MT 59717-0001

COTCHETT, JOSEPH WINTERS, lawyer, author; b. Chgo., Jan. 6, 1939; s. Joseph Winters and Jean (Renaud) C.; children— Leslie F., Charles P., Rachael E., Quinn Carlyle, Camilla E. BS in Engring., Calif. Poly. Coll., 1960; LLB, U. Calif. Hastings Coll. Law, 1964. Bar: Calif. 1965, D.C. 1980. Ptnr. Cotchett, Pitre & Simon, Burlingame, Calif., 1965—. Mem. Calif. Jud. Coun., 1975-77, Calif. Commn. on Jud. Performance, 1985-89, Commn. 2020 Jud. Coun., 1991-94; select com. on jud. retirement, 1992—. Author: (with R. Cartwright) California Products Liability Actions, 1970, (with F. Haight) California Courtroom Evidence, 1972, (with A. Elkind) Federal Courtroom Evidence, 1976, (with Frank Rothman) Persuasive Opening Statements and Closing Arguments, 1988, (with Stephen Pizzo) The Ethics Gap, 1991, (with Gerald Uelmen) California Courtroom Evidence Foundations, 1993; contbr. articles to profl. jours. Chmn. San Mateo County Heart Assn., 1967; pres. San Mateo Boys and Girls Club, 1971; bd. dirs. U. Calif. Hastings Law Sch., 1981-93. With Intelligence Corps, U.S. Army, 1960-61; col. JAGC, USAR, ret. Fellow Am. Bar Found., Am. Bd. Trial Advs., Am. Coll. Trial Lawyers, Internat. Acad. Trial Lawyers, Internat. Soc. of Barristers, Nat. Bd. Trial Advs. (diplomate civil trial adv.), State Bar Calif. (gov. 1972-75). Clubs: Commonwealth, Press (San Francisco) Office: 840 Malcolm Rd Burlingame CA 94010-1401 also: 12100 Wilshire Blvd Ste 1100 Los Angeles CA 90025-7124

COTSAKOS, CHRISTOS MICHAEL, internet financial services company executive; b. Paterson, N.J., July 29, 1948; s. Michael John and Lillian (Scoulikas) C.; m. Hannah Batami Fogel, July 1, 1973; 1 child, Suzanne Renee. BA in Communications and Polit. Sci., William Paterson Coll., 1972; MBA, Pepperdine U., 1984. Tour guide Universal Studios, Burbank, Calif., 1973; courier Fed. Express Corp., Burbank, 1973-74, sales rep. Long Beach, Calif., 1974, sta. mgr. San Jose, 1974, we. dist. mgr., 1974, region engring. mgr., 1975, mng. dir. Chgo., 1975-80, v.p. Sacramento, 1980-92; pres., COO Nielsen, Europe, Middle East, Africa, 1992-93; pres., CEO Nielsen Internat., 1993-95; pres., co-CEO, COO, dir. A.C. Nielsen, Inc., 1995-96; CEO, chmn. E*TRADE Group, Inc., Palo Alto, Calif., 1996—. Instr. Consumers River Coll., Placerville, Calif., 1985-86; bd. dirs. Airlifeline, Sacramento, Nat. Processing, Inc., Louisville, Forté Software, Inc., Oakland, 4th Comms. Network, San Jose, Datacard, Mpls. Served as sgt. U.S. Army, 1967-70, Vietnam. Decorated Bronze Star, 1967, Purple Heart, 1967. Mem. World Econ Forum (Davos, Switzerland), Sutter Club, Comstock Club. Office: E Trade Group Inc 4500 Bohannon Dr Menlo Park CA 94025

COTTAM, KEITH M. librarian, educator, administrator; b. St. George, Utah, Feb. 13, 1941; s. Von Bunker and Adrene (McArthur) C.; m. Laurel Springer, June 16, 1961 (div. 2000); children: Mark Patrick, Lisa Diane, Andrea Jill, Brian Lowell, Heather Dawn. BS, Utah State U., 1963; MLS, Pratt Inst., 1965. Trainee Bklyn. Pub. Libr., 1963-65, asst. instr. reading improvement program, 1964-65, adult services libr., 1965; asst. social scis. libr., instr. So. Ill. U., Edwardsville, 1965-67; head, social sci. libr., instr. asst. prof. Social Scis. Libr., Brigham Young U., Provo, Utah, 1967-72; supr., inst. Libr. Technician Program Brigham Young U., Provo, 1969-72; head undergrad. libr., assoc. prof. U. Tenn., Knoxville, 1972-75, asst. dir. librs., assoc. prof., 1975-77; asst. dir. for pub. svcs. and employee rels. Vanderbilt U. Libr. (formerly Joint Univ. Librs.), Nashville, 1977-80, assoc. dir., 1980-82, acting dir., 1982-83; dir. libraries, prof. U. Wyo., Laramie, 1983-2000, dean univ. librs., 2001, assoc. dean outreach sch., dir. Casper Coll. Ctr., Casper. Vis. lectr. U. Tenn., 1972-77; vis. asst. prof. Vanderbilt U., 1979-80; adj. prof. journalism U. Wyo., 1987-89; vis. lectr.

comm. and mass media, 1990, 94; cons., adv. to various orgns. in Tenn., Ill., Wyo.; advisor Nat. Inst. Adminstrn., Saigon, Vietnam, 1971; pres. Tenn. Libr. Assn., 1979-80; cons. tng. program office of mgmt. studies Assn. of Rsch. Librs., 1979-80. Author: Writer's Research handbook, 1977, 2d edit., 1978; editor Utah Libraries jour., 1971-72; mem. editl. bd. RQ jour., 1980-84; contbr. articles to profl. jours. Fellow Coun. Libr. Resources, 1975-76; sr. fellow UCLA Grad. Sch. Libr. Info. Sci., 1985-86. Mem. ALA, Assn. Coll. Rsch. Librs., Wyo. Libr. Assn. (pres. 1998-99), Beta Phi Mu, Phi Kappa Phi. Republican. Mem. Ch. of Jesus Christ of Latter-day Saints. Avocations: bicycling, racing and touring; free-lance writer; gardening. Home: 1035 S David Casper WY 82601-3779 Office: 125 College Dr Casper WY 82601 E-mail: kcottam@uwyo.edu

COTTLE, GAIL ANN, retail executive; b. Yakima, Wash. Student, U. Wash. With Nordstrom, Inc., 1969—, corp. mdse. mgr. Brass Plum Jr. Women's Apparel, 1982-92, v.p., officer Jr. Women's Apparel divsn., 1985-92, exec. v.p. product devel., 1992-2000; pres. Nordstrom Product Group, Seattle, 2000—. Trustee P.N. Ballet. Ford Found. grantee. Mem. Columbia Tower Club, Fashion Group Internat., Broadmoor Golf Club, Thunderbird Golf Club. Office: Nordstrom Inc 1617 6th Ave Seattle WA 98101-1742

COTTRELL-ADKINS, LEONE, opera company director; Artistic dir., founder Kitsap Peninsula Opera, Bremerton, Wash., 1992—. Founder Kitsap Peninsula Opera, 1992. Office: Kitsap Peninsula Opera PO Box 1071 Bremerton WA 98337-0223

COUCH, JOHN CHARLES, retired diversified company executive; b. Bremerton, Wash., May 10, 1939; s. Richard Bailey and Frances Harriet (Gilmore) C. BS in Engring., U. Mich., 1963, MS, 1964; MBA, Stanford U., 1976. With Ingalls Shipbldg. div. Litton Industries, 1967-74; asst. to sr. v.p. engring. and marine ops. Matson Navigation Co. subs. Alexander and Baldwin., San Francisco, 1976-78, v.p., 1978-84, exec. v.p., COO, 1984, pres., COO, 1985, Alexander and Baldwin Inc., Honolulu, 1991-98; pres., CEO Alexander and Baldwin, Inc., Honolulu, 1992-95, chmn., pres., CEO, 1995-98; ret., 1999. Bd. dirs. A&B Devel. Co., Calif., A&B Properties, Inc., McBryde Sugar Co., Ltd., Kauai Coffee Co., Inc., WDCI Inc., Calif. and Hawaiian Sugar Co., First Hawaiian Bank, First Hawaiian Inc., Hawaiian Sugar Transp. Co., Inc., A&B Hawaii, Inc., Alexander & Baldwin, Inc., Kukuiula Devel. Co., Inc., Matson Navigation Co., Inc. Mem. Maui Econ. Devel. Bd., 1986—; mem. exec. bd. Aloha coun. Boy Scouts Am., 1986—; bd. dirs. Aloha United Way, 1988, campaign chmn., 1988, chmn. bd. dirs.; bd. dirs. Alexander & Baldwin Found., The Std. Steamship Owners' Protection and Indemnity Assn. (Bermuda) Ltd.; chmn. bd. trustees Bishop Mus., 1997—. Mem. Hawaii Maritime Ctr. (vice-chmn. 1988-89, 97—, chmn. 1990-97), Honolulu Club, Oahu Country Club, Plaza Club, Pacific Club, The Pacific-Union Club. Office: Alexander & Baldwin Inc PO Box 3440 822 Bishop St Honolulu HI 96813-3925

COUDER, ALAIN, personal computer manufacturing company executive; Various sr. positions IBM, Hewlett Packard; COO in charge ops. and corp. strategy Groupe Bull France, until 1998; pres., CEO, chmn. exec. com. of bd. dirs. Packard Bell NEC, Inc., Sacramento, 1998-2000; exec. v.p., COO Agilent Technologies Inc., Palo Alto, Calif., 2000—. Office: Agilent Technologies Inc 395 Page Mill Rd Palo Alto CA 94306

COUGHENOUR, JOHN CLARE, federal judge; b. Pittsburg, Kans., July 27, 1941; s. Owren M. and Margaret E. (Widner) C.; m. Gwendolyn A. Kieffaber, June 1, 1963; children: Jeffrey, Douglas, Marta. BS, Kans. State Coll., 1963; JD, U. Iowa, 1966. Bar: Iowa 1963, D.C. 1963, U.S. Dist. Ct. (we. dist.) Wash. 1966. Ptnr. Bogle & Gates, Seattle, 1966-81; vis. asst. prof. law U. Washington, Seattle, 1970-73; judge U.S. Dist. Ct. (we. dist.) Wash., Seattle, 1981-97, chief judge, 1997—. Mem. Iowa State Bar Assn., Wash. State Bar Assn. Office: US Dist Ct US Courthouse 1010 5th Ave Ste 609 Seattle WA 98104-1130

COUGHLAN, JOHN P. investment company executive; Vice-chmn., enterprise pres., retirement plan svcs. The Charles Schwab Corp., San Francisco, 1999—. Office: The Charles Schwab Corp 101 Montgomery St Ste 200 San Francisco CA 94104-4175

COUILLAUD, BERNARD J. executive; M in Physics & PhD, U. Bordeaux, France, 1968. Asst. prof. U. Bordeaux, France, 1968-72, assoc. prof. France, 1972-74, 80-82, prof. France, 1982-83; pres., CEO Coherent, Inc., Santa Clara, Calif., 1983—. Vis. prof. Stanford (Calif.) U., 1982-83. CNRS fellow, 1975-76, 79-80, vis. scholar Stanford U., 1980-82. Office: Coherent Inc PO Box 54980 Santa Clara CA 95056-0980 also: MS P41 PO Box 54980 Santa Clara CA 95056-0980

COUNTS, STANLEY THOMAS, aerospace consultant, retired naval officer, retired electronics company executive; b. Okfuskee County, Okla., July 3, 1926; s. Claud Curtley and Thelma (Thomas) C.; m. Bettejan Heft, Nov. 18, 1949; 1 child, Ashlie Heft. B.S., U.S. Naval Acad., 1949; B.S. in Elec. Engring, U.S. Naval Postgrad. Sch., 1954, M.S. in Elec. Engring, 1955. Commd. ensign U.S. Navy, 1949, advanced through grades to rear adm., 1972; comdg. officer USS Bronstein, 1963-64; comdg. officer USS Towers, 1966-68; project mgr. NATO Seasparrow Surface Missile System, 1968-70; comdg. officer USS Chgo., 1970-71; dir. ships, weapons, electronics and asso. systems Office Asst. Sec. Def. for Installations and Logistics Washington, 1971-73; dep. comdr. Naval Ordnance Systems Command, 1973-74; comdr. (Naval Ordnance Systems Command), 1974; vice comdr. Naval Sea Systems Command, 1974-76; comdr. Cruiser-Destroyer Group 5 San Diego, 1976-78; ret., 1978; exec. Hughes Aircraft Co., Fullerton, Calif., 1979-89; ret., 1989; aerospace cons., chief exec. officer Bjan Enterprises, La Jolla, Calif., 1989-99. Chmn. Seasparrow steering com. NATO, 1973-76. Bd. dirs. San Diego chpt. Freedoms Found. at Valley Forge, 1992-94, 97-98; bd. dirs. Greater La Jolla Meals on Wheels, Inc., 1998—, pres., 2000—. Decorated Legion of Merit with three oak leaf clusters, Bronze Star with combat distinguishing device. Mem. VFW, Surface Navy Assn. (life, bd. dirs. 1985-93), U.S. Naval Inst. (life), DAV (life), Ret. Officers Assn. (life), Navy League, Am. Legion, Rest and Aspiration Club San Diego. Home: 856 La Jolla Rancho Rd La Jolla CA 92037-7408 E-mail: okkid1926@yahoo.com

COURTNEY, PETER C. state legislator; b. Phila., June 18, 1943; m. Margie Courtney; 3 children. BA, U. R.I., 1965, MPA, 1966; JD, Boston U., 1969. Legal aid atty., 1974-75; hearings officer, 1975-80; pvt. practice, 1981-83; asst. to pres. Western Oreg. State Coll.; mem. Oreg. Legislature, Salem, 1998—, mem. edn. com., mem. info. mgmt. and tech. com., vice chair, vice chair jud. com. Bd. dirs. YMCA, Salem United Soccer; coach Boys and Girls Club. Democrat. Democrat. Roman Catholic. Home: 2925 Island View Dr NE Salem OR 97303-6522 Office: State Capitol S-310 Salem OR 97310

COUSAR, RONNY, city official; b. Newark, Sept. 20, 1957; BS in Natural Resource Mgmt., Rutgers U., 1980. Natural resource pk. ranger Gateway Nat. Recreation Area Nat. Pk. Svc., Sandy Hook, N.J., 1980-81; city forester, landscape arch. engring. dept. City of Newark, 1981-83; city forester dept. pks. and recreation forestry divsn. City of Balt., 1983-91, City of Colorado Springs, Colo., 1991-97, dir. neighborhood svcs., 1997—. Grad. Pikes Peak Leadership program; mem. Senate Bill 94 Juvenile Svcs. Com., Gov.'s Environ. Task Force, Md.; bd. dirs. Colo. Tree Coalition. Recipient cert. of recognition Nat. Pk. Svc. Mem. Alpha Phi Alpha. Office: Neighborhood Svcs City Adminstrn Bldg 30 S Nevada Ave Ste 302 Colorado Springs CO 80903-1802

COUSER, WILLIAM GRIFFITH, medical educator, academic administrator, nephrologist; b. Lebanon, N.H., July 11, 1939; s. Thomas Clifford and Winifred Priscilla (Ham) C. B.A., Harvard U., 1961, M.D., 1965; B.M.S., Dartmouth Med. Sch., 1963. Diplomate Am. Bd. Internal Medicine. Intern Moffitt Hosp./U. Calif. Med. Ctr., San Francisco, 1965-66, 66-67; resident Boston City Hosp., 1969-70; asst. prof. medicine U. Chgo., 1972-73; asst. prof. Boston U., 1972-77, assoc. prof., 1977-82; prof., head div. nephrology U. Wash., Seattle, 1982—, Belding Scribner prof.medicine, 1995—. Mem. sci. adv. bd. Kidney Found. Mass., Boston, 1974-82; mem. research grant com. Nat. Kidney Found., N.Y.C., 1981-86; mem. rev. bd. for nephrology VA, Washington, 1981-84; mem. exec. com. Coun. on Kidney in Cardiovascular Disease, Am. Heart Assn., Dallas, 1982-85; mem. pathology A study sect. NIH (chmn. 1988-89), subspecialty bd. in nephrology Am. Bd. Internal Medicine, 1988-92; dir. George M. O'Briend Kidney Rsch. Ctr., U. Wash., 1993—. Co-editor: Immunologic Renal Diseases, 1997, 2d edit. 2001; contbr. numerous articles, chpts., abstracts to profl. publs.; mem. editl. bd. Kidney Internat., 1982-96, Am. Jour. Kidney Diseases, Am. Jour. Nephrology, Jour. Am. Soc. Nephrology, editor-in-chief, 2001—. Served to capt. U.S. Army, 1967-69, Vietnam. Recipient Rsch. Career Devel. award NIH, 1975-80, Method to Extend Rsch. in Time award, 1991-97; fellow Nat. Kidney Found., 1971, NIH, 1973; grantee, 1974—. Fellow AAAS, ACP, Am. Soc. Clin. Investigation (v.p. 1983-84), Am. Assn. Physicians, Am. Soc. Nephrology (coun. 1991-94, pres. 1996), Internat. Soc. Nephrology (coun. 1999), Am. Assn. Exptl. Pathology, Western Assn. Physicians (coun.). Avocation: boating. Office: U Wash Box 356521 1959 NE Pacific St Seattle WA 98195-0001

COVELL, RUTH MARIE, medical educator, medical school administrator; b. San Francisco, Aug. 12, 1936; d. John Joseph and Mary Carolyn (Coles) Collins; m. James Wachob Covell, 1963 (div. 1972); 1 child, Stephen; m. Harold Joachim Simon, Jan. 4, 1973; 1 child, David. Student, U. Vienna, Austria, 1955-56; BA, Stanford U., 1958; MD, U. Chgo., 1962. Clin. prof. and assoc. dean sch. medicine U. Calif. San Diego, La Jolla, 1969—; dir. Acad. Geriatric Resource Ctr. Bd. dirs. Calif. Coun. Geriatrics and Gerontology, Beverly Found., Pasadena, Alzheimer's Family Ctr., San Diego, San Diego Epilepsy Soc., Devel. Svcs. Inc., San Ysidro Health Ctr., NIH SBIR Stude Sect. Geriatrics; cons. Agy. Health Care Po licy and Rsch.; chair Calif. Ctr. Access to Care Adv. Bd. Contbr. articles on health planning and quality of med. care to profl. jours. Mem. AMA (sect. on med. schs. governing coun.), Am. Health Svcs. Rsch., Assn. Tchrs. Preventive Medicine, Am. Pub. Health Assn., Assn. Am. Med. Colls. Group on Instl. Planning (chair 1973-74, sec. 1983-84), Phi Beta Kappa, Alpha Omega Alpha. Home: 1604 El Camino Del Teatro La Jolla CA 92037-6338 Office: U Calif San Diego Sch Medicine M-002 La Jolla CA 92093

COVER, THOMAS M. statistician, electrical engineer, educator; b. San Bernardino, Calif., Aug. 7, 1938; s. William Llewellyn and Carolyn (Merrill) C.; 1 child, William. BS in Physics, MIT, 1960; MS in EE, Stanford U., 1961, PhD in EE, 1964. Asst. prof. elec. engring. Stanford (Calif.) U., 1964-67, assoc. prof., 1967-71, assoc. prof. elec. engring. and statistics, 1972-73, prof., 1973—, lab. dir. info. systems elec. engring., 1989-96, Kwoh-Ting Li Prof. Engring., 1994. Vis. assoc. prof. elec. engring. MIT, Cambridge, 1971-72. Author: Elements of Information Theory, 1991; editor: Open Problems in Communication and Computation, 1987; contbr. over 100 articles to profl. jours. Vinton Hayes fellow Harvard U., 1971-72. Fellow AAAS, IEEE (pres. info. theory soc. 1972, Claude E. Shannon award 1990, Outstanding Paper prize 1972, Jubilee Paper award 1998, Richard W. Hamming medal 1997), Inst. Math. Stats.; mem. Soc. for Indsl. and Applied Math., Nat. Acad. Engring. Office: Stanford U Dept Elec Engring & Stats Durand # 121 Stanford CA 94305

COVEY, JOY D. finance and administration executive; BSBA summa cum laude, Calif. State U., Fresno; MBA, JD magna cum laude, Harvard U. CPA, Calif. CPA Arthur Young & Co. (now Ernst & Young); mergers and acquisitions assoc. Wasserstein Perella & Co.; CFO Digidesign, 1991-95; v.p. bus. devel., v.p. ops. broadcast divsn. Avid Tech.; CFO, v.p. fin. and adminstrn. Amazon.com, Seattle, 1996—. Office: Amazon.Com Po Box 81226 Seattle WA 98108-1300

COVINGTON, GERMAINE WARD, municipal agency administrator; BS in Social Work, Ind. State U., 1966; MA in Urban Studies, Occidental Coll., 1972; postgrad., Harvard U., 1998. Budget analyst City of Seattle, Office Mgmt. and Budget, 1978-87; cmty. affairs mgr. City of Seattle, Engring. Dept., 1987-90, property and ct. svcs. mgr., 1990-91, dir. exec. mgmt., 1993-94, acting dir. drainage and wastewater utility, 1993-94; dep. chief staff City of Seattle, Mayor's Office, 1991-93; dir. City for Seattle, Office for Civil Rights, 1994—. Office: Seattle Office for Civil Rights 700 3rd Ave Ste 250 Seattle WA 98104-1827 E-mail: germaine.covington@ci.seattle.wa.us

COVITZ, CARL D. state official, real estate and investment executive; b. Boston, Mar. 31, 1939; s. Edward E. and Barbara (Matthews) C.; m. Aviva Habert, May 15, 1970; children: Philip, Marc. BS, Wharton Sch., U. Pa., 1960; MBA, Columbia U., 1962. Product mgr. Bristol-Myers Co., N.Y.C., 1962-66; dir. mktg. Rheingold Breweries, N.Y.C., 1966-68; nat. mktg. mgr. Can. Dry Corp., N.Y.C., 1968-70; v.p. mktg., dir. corp. devel. ITT/Levitt & Sons, Lake Success, N.Y., 1970-73; owner, pres. Landmark Communities, Inc., Beverly Hills, Calif., 1973-87, pres., 1989-91; undersec. HUD, Washington, 1987-89; sec. bus., transp. and housing State of Calif., Sacramento, 1991-93; pres. Landmark Capital, Inc. (formerly Landmark Communities, Inc.), 1993—; chmn. bd. Century Housing Corp., 1995-2000. Bd. dirs. Arden Realty Group, chmn. acquisition com.; chmn. bd. Fed. Home Loan Bank, San Francisco, 1989-91, Century Housing Corp., 1995—; trustee SunAmerica Annuities Funds, 2000—, Kane Andersobn Mut. Funds, 2000—. Exec. com. Presl. Commn. Cost Control and Efficiency (Grace Commn.); co-chmn. Dept. Def. Task Force; past chmn. ops. com. Mus. Contemporary Art Los Angeles; chmn. L.A. County Delinquency and Crime Commn.; dir. Columbia U. Grad. Bus. Sch. Alumni Assn. Mem. Young Pres. Orgn.; chmn. L.A. Housing Authority Commn., 1989-91. Home: 818 Malcolm Ave Los Angeles CA 90024-3104 Office: 9595 Wilshire Blvd Beverly Hills CA 90212-2512 E-mail: cdcovitz@aol.com

COWAN, GEORGE ARTHUR, chemist, bank executive, director; b. Worcester, Mass., Feb. 15, 1920; s. Louis Abraham and Anna (Listic) C.; m. Helen Dunham, Sept. 9, 1946. BS, Worcester Poly. Inst., 1941; DSc, Carnegie-Mellon U., 1950. Rsch. asst. Princeton U., 1941-42, U. Chgo., 1942-45; mem. staff Columbia U., N.Y.C., 1945; mem. staff, dir. rsch., sr. fellow Los Alamos (N.Mex.) Sci. Lab., 1945-46, 49-88, sr. fellow emeritus, 1988—; tchg. fellow Carnegie Mellon U., Pitts., 1946-49. Chmn. bd. dirs. Trinity Capital Corp., Los Alamos, 1974-95; pres. Santa Fe Inst., 1984-91; mem. The White House Sci. Coun., Washington, 1982-85, cons., 1985-90, Air Force Tech. Applications Ctr., 1952-88; chmn. Los Alamos Nat. Bank, 1965-94; bd. dirs. Universal Properties, inc. Contbr. sci. articles to profl. jours. Bd. dirs. Santa Fe Opera, 1964-79; treas. N.Mex. Opera Found., Santa Fe, 1970-79; regent N.Mex. Inst. Tech. Socorro, 1972-75; bd. dirs. N.Am. Inst., Santa Fe Inst., Nat. Found. for Brain Imaging, Los Alamos Nat. Lab. Found., Adv. Bd. Ctr. for Neural Basis of Cognition, Carnegie-Mellon U. Recipient E.O. Lawrence award, 1965, Disting. Scientist award N.Mex. Acad. Sci., 1975, Robert H. Goddard award Worcester Poly. Inst., 1984, Enrico Fermi award, Presdl. Citation, Dept. Energy, 1990; disting. fellow Santa Fe Inst. Fellow AAAS, Am. Phys. Soc.; mem. Am. Chem. Soc., Am. Acad. Arts and Scis., N.Mex. Acad. Sci., Sigma Xi. Avocations: skiing, fly-fishing. Home: 721 42nd St Los Alamos NM 87544-1804 Office: Santa Fe Inst 1399 Hyde Park Rd Santa Fe NM 87501-8943 E-mail: gac@santafe.edu

COWAN, MARIE JEANETTE, nurse, pathology and cardiology educator; b. Albuquerque, July 20, 1938; d. Adrian Joseph and Leila Bernice (Finley) Johnson; m. Samuel Joseph Cowan, Aug. 14, 1961; children: Samuel Joseph, Kathryn Anne, Michelle Dionne. Diploma, Mary's Help Coll., 1961; BS, U. Wash., 1964, MS, 1972, PhD, 1979. Charge nurse Herrick Meml. Hosp., Berkeley, Calif., 1961-62; staff nurse ICU Univ. Hosp., Seattle, 1966-68; asst. prof. Seattle U., 1972-75; from asst. prof. to prof. nursing U. Wash., Seattle, 1979-97, assoc. dean rsch., 1985-96; dean UCLA Sch. Nursing, 1997—. Rsch. grant reviewer Am. Heart Assn. Wash., Seattle, 1977-82, divsn. rsch. grants reviewer nursing study sect., 1987-90; chair CVN AHA, 1989-91. Mem. editl. bd. Ann. Rev. Nursing Rsch., Rsch. in Nursing and Health, Nursing Rsch.; contbr. articles to profl. jours. NIH grantee, 1977, 81, 84, 85, 91, 96, 2000. Fellow Am. Acad. Nursing; mem. ANA, AACN, Wash. State Nurses Assn., Calif. State Nurses Assn. Roman Catholic. Office: UCLA Sch Nursing PO Box 951702 Los Angeles CA 90095-1702

COWAN, RICHARD, manufacturing executive; CEO Power Lift Corp., Pico Rivera, Calif. Office: Power Lift Corp 8314 Slauson Ave Pico Rivera CA 90660-4323

COWDERY, JOHN J. state senator; b. Mo., 1930; m. Juanita Chowdery; 3 children. Contr.; Rep. rep. dist. I Alaska Ho. of Rep., 1982-84, 96-2000; Rep. senator dist. I Alaska State Senate, 2000—. Mem. transp., labor and commerce oil and gas, internat. trade and tourism coms. Alaska Ho. of Reps., chmn. rules com., co-chmn. commn. on privatization; mem. numerous coms. Alaska State Senate; founder Anchorage Caucus; spl. projects mgr. Municipality of Anchorage. Avocations: family, music, boating, photography. Office: Alaska State Senate State Capitol Rm 101 Juneau AK 99801-1182 also: 716 W 4th Ste 530 Anchorage AK 99501-2133 Fax: 907 465-2069; 907 258-0223. E-mail: Senator_John_Cowdery@legis.state.ak.us

COWELL, FULLER A. newspaper publisher; m. Christmas Cowell; 1 child, Alexis. BBA, U. Alaska Fairbanks. With McClatchy Newspapers, 1981-93; pub. Gavilan Newspapers, Calif., 1987-91, Anchorage Daily News, 1993—. Former pub. Cordova Times. Office: Anchorage Daily News PO Box 149001 Anchorage AK 99514-9001

COWENS, DAVID WILLIAM (DAVE COWENS), professional basketball coach, insurance executive, retired professional basketball player; b. Newport, Ky., Oct. 25, 1948; m. Deborah Cmaylo; children: Meghan, Samantha. BS, Fla. State U., 1970. Basketball player Boston Celtics, 1970-80, head coach (68 games), 1978-79; player Milw. Bucks, 1983; owner, pres., dir. David W. Cowens Basketball Sch., Inc., Needham, Mass., 1972—; pres. Survivors Income Option, Inc. (life ins.), 1987—; head coach Charlotte Hornets, 1996-98; assist. coach Denver Nuggets, 1998-99, head coach, 1999-2000, Golden State Warriors, 2000—. Athletic dir. Regis Coll., Weston, Mass., 1981-82; coach Bay State, Continental Basketball Assn., 1984-85; chmn. bd. New Eng. Sport Mus. Named Rookie of Yr. 1970-71, NBA Most Valuable Player, 1972-73; mem. NBA All Star teams, yearly 1971-77, NBA Championship team, 1974, 76; honored by having his number retired; inducted into Naismith Meml. Basketball Hall of Fame, 1990. Office: David W Cowens Basketball Sch 3430 Gray Moss Rd Charlotte NC 28270-0486 also: Golden State Warriors 1011 Broadway Oakland CA 94607-4027

COWGILL, URSULA MOSER, biologist, educator, environmental consultant; b. Bern, Switzerland, Nov. 9, 1927; came to U.S., 1943, naturalized, 1945; d. John W. and Mara (Siegrist) Moser. A.B., Hunter Coll., 1948; M.S., Kans. State U., 1952; Ph.D., Iowa State U., 1956. Staff MIT, Lincoln Lab., Lexington, Mass., 1957-58; field work Doherty Found., Guatemala, 1958-60; research assoc. dept. biology Yale U., New Haven, 1960-68; prof. biology and anthropology U. Pitts., 1968-81; environ. scientist Dow Chem. Co., Midland, Mich., 1981-84, assoc. environ. cons., 1984-91; environ. cons., 1991—. Mem. environ. measurements adv. com. Sci. Adv. Bd. EPA, 1976-80; Internat. Joint Commn., 1984-89. Contbr. numerous articles on ecology, biology and minerology to sci. publs. Trustee Carnegie Mus., Pitts., 1971-75. Grantee NSF 1960-78, Wenner Gren Found., 1965-66, Penrose fund Am. Philos. Soc., 1978; Sigma Xi grant-in-aid, 1965-66 Mem. AAAS, Am. Soc. Limnology and Oceanography, Internat. Soc. Theoretical and Applied Limnology. Home and Office: PO Box 1329 Carbondale CO 81623-1329

COWLES, WILLIAM STACEY, newspaper publisher; b. Spokane, Wash., Aug. 31, 1960; s. William Hutchinson 3rd and Allison Stacey C.; m. Anne Cannon, June 24, 1989. BA in Econs., Yale Coll., 1982; MBA in Fin., Columbia U., 1986. Pres., pub. The Spokesman Rev., Spokane, Wash. Office: Cowles Publishing Co PO Box 2160 Spokane WA 99210-2160

COWLEY, JOHN MAXWELL, physics educator; b. Peterborough, South Australia, Feb. 18, 1923; came to U.S., 1970; s. Alfred Ernest and Doris (Milway) C.; m. Roberta Joan Beckett, Dec. 15, 1951; children: Deborah Suzanne, Jillian Patricia. BS, U. Adelaide, Australia, 1942, MS, 1945, DSc, 1957; PhD, Mass. Inst. Tech., 1949. Research officer Commonwealth Sci. and Indsl. Research Orgn., Melbourne, Australia, 1945-62, chief research officer, head crystallography sect., 1960-62; prof. physics U. Melbourne, Australia, 1962-70; Galvin prof. physics Ariz. State U., Tempe, 1970-94, Regents' prof., 1988-94, regents prof. emeritus, 1994—. Mem. U.S. Nat. Com. for Crystallography, 1973-78, 84-86. Author: Diffraction Physics, 1975; editor: (with others) Acta Crystallographica, 1971-80; contbr. (with others) articles to profl. jours. Fellow Australian Acad. Sci., Inst. Physics (London), Australian Inst. Physics, Royal Soc. (London), Am. Phys. Soc.; mem. Internat. Union Crystallography (mem. exec. com. 1963-69, chair commn. on electron diffraction 1987-93, Ewald Prize 1987), Am. Inst. Physics, Am. Crystallographic Assn., Electron Microscope Soc. Am. (dir. 1971-75). Home: 2625 E Southern Ave Unit C90 Tempe AZ 85282 Office: Ariz State U Dept Physics & Astronomy Tempe AZ 85287 E-mail: cowleyj@asu.edu

COX, CHARLES SHIPLEY, oceanography researcher, educator; b. Paia, Hawaii, Sept. 11, 1922; s. Joel Bean and Helen Clifford (Horton) C.; m. Maryruth Louise Melander, Dec. 23, 1951; children: Susan (dec.), Caroline, Valerie, Ginger, Joel. BS, Calif. Inst. Tech., 1944; PhD, U. Calif., San Diego, 1955. From asst. rschr. to prof. U. Calif., San Diego, 1955—. Researcher in field. Fellow AAAS, NAS (Alexander Agassiz medal 2001), Am. Geophys. Union (Maurice Ewing medal 1992), Royal Astron. Soc. Democrat. Office: U Calif San Diego Scripps Inst Oceanography Scripps Inst Oceanography La Jolla CA 92093-0213 E-mail: cscox@ucsd.edu

COX, CHRISTOPHER (CHARLES COX), congressman; b. St. Paul, Oct. 16, 1952; s. Charles C. and Marilyn A. (Miller) C.; m. Rebecca Gernhardt; children: Charles, Kathryn, Kevin. BA, U. So. Calif., 1973; MBA, JD, Harvard U., 1977. Bar: Calif. 1978, D.C. 1980. Law clk. to judge U.S. Ct. Appeals (9th cir.), 1977-78; assoc. Latham & Watkins, Newport Beach, Calif., 1978-82; lectr. bus. adminstrn. Harvard U., 1982-83; ptnr. Latham & Watkins, Newport Beach, Calif., 1984-86; sr. assoc. counsel to the Pres. The White House, Washington, 1986-88; mem. U.S. Congresses from 47th dist. Calif., Washington, 1989—; mem. energy and commerce com., steering com.; mem. fin. svcs. com.; chmn. house policy com.; mem. Bipartisan Commn. on Entitlement and Tax Reform, Washington, 1994—. Prin., founder Context Corp., St. Paul, 1984-88. Editor Harvard Law Rev., 1975-77. Republican. Roman Catholic. Office: US Ho Reps 2402 Rayburn Ho Office Bldg Washington DC 20515 also: 1 Newport Place Dr Ste 420 Newport Beach CA 92660-2412*

COX, DAVID R. geneticist, educator; Prof. genetics, pediatrics sch. of medicine Stanford U.; co-dir. Stanford Human Genome Project. Office: Stanford U Sch Medicine Dept Genetics M-344 300 Pasteur Dr Stanford CA 94305-5120

COX, DONALD CLYDE, electrical engineering educator; b. Lincoln, Nebr., Nov. 22, 1937; s. Elvin Clyde and C. Gertrude (Thomas) C.; m. Mary Dale Alexander, Aug. 27, 1961; children: Bruce Dale, Earl Clyde. BS, U. Nebr., 1959, MS, 1960, DSc (hon.), 1983; PhD, Stanford U., 1968. Registered profl. engr., Ohio, Nebr. With Bell Tel. Labs., Holmdel, N.J., 1968-84, head radio and satellite systems rsch. dept., 1983-84; mgr. radio and satellite systems rsch. divsn. Bell Comm. Rsch., Red Bank, 1984-91, exec. dir. radio rsch. dept., 1991-93; prof. elec. engring. Stanford (Calif.) U., 1993—, Harald Trap Friis Prof. Engring., 1994—, dir. telecomms., 1993-99. Em. commns. U.S. nat. com. Internat. Union of Radio Sci.; participant enbanc hearing on Personal Comm. Sys., FCC, 1991. Contbr. articles to profl. jours.; patentee in field. 1st lt. USAF, 1960-63. Johnson fellow, 1959-60; recipient Guglielmo Marconi prize in Electromagnetic Waves Propagation, Inst. Internat. Comm., 1983. Fellow IEEE (Morris E. Leeds award 1985, Alexander Graham Bell medal 1993, Millenium medal 2000), AAAS, Bellcore 1991, Radio Club Am.; mem. NAE, Comm. Soc. of IEEE (Leonard G. Abraham Prize Paper award 1992, Comms. Mag. Prize Paper award 1990), Vehicular Tech. Soc. of IEEE (Paper of Yr. award 1983), Antennas and Propagation Soc. of IEEE (elected mem. adminstrn. com. 1986-88), Sigma Xi. Achievements include rsch. in wireless communication systems, cellular radio systems, radio propagation. Home: 924 Mears Ct Stanford CA 94305-1029 Office: Stanford U Dept Elec Engring Packard 361 Stanford CA 94305-9515 E-mail: dcox@spark.stanford.edu

COX, FRED B. software company executive; b. 1934; Founder Emulex, pres., CEO, 1988-90, chmn. bd. Founder, mgr. various cos. including Microdata (acquired by McDonnell Douglas Corp.); mktg. exec. IBM Corp. Office: 3535 Harbor Blvd Costa Mesa CA 92626

COX, JOSEPH WILLIAM, academic administrator; b. Hagerstown, Md., May 26, 1937; s. Joseph F. and Ruth E. C.; m. Regina M. Bollinger, Aug. 17, 1963; children: Andrew, Matthew, Abigail. B.A., U. Md., 1959, Ph.D., 1967; Doctor (hon.), Towson State U., 1990. Successively instr., asst. prof., assoc. prof., prof. history Towson (Md.) State U., 1964-81, dean evening and summer programs, 1972-75, acting pres., 1978-79, v.p. acad. affairs and dean of univ., 1979-81; prof. history, v.p. acad. affairs. No. Ariz. U., Flagstaff, 1981-87; pres. So. Oregon U., Ashland, 1987-94; chancellor Oreg. Univ. Sys., Eugene, 1994—. Author: Champion of Southern Federalism: Robert Goodloe Harper of South Carolina, 1972, The Early National Experience: The Army Corps of Engineers, 1783-1812, 1979; mem. bd. editors Md. Hist. Mag., 1979-89; columnist So. Oreg. Hist. Mag., 1989-94; contbr. articles to profl. jours. Bd. dirs. Oreg. Hist. Soc., Oreg. Shakespearean Festival, 1989-95, So. Oreg. Econ. Devel. Bd., 1988-94, Jackson/Josephine Co., Western Bank, 1993-97, Portland Ctr. Stage, 1999. Mem. AAUP, Am. Assn. Higher Edn., Am. Assn. State Colls. and Univs., Phi Kappa Phi, Omicron Delta Kappa. Episcopalian. Home: 2237 Spring Blvd Eugene OR 97403-1897 Office: Oreg Univ Sys Chancellors Office PO Box 3175 Eugene OR 97403-0175

COX, MARK BAKER, financial executive; b. Mexico, Mo., Dec. 6, 1958; s. Gerald Lampton and Connie (Baker) C.; m. Lisa Marie Chance, June 8, 1985; children: Chance Martin, Joshua Baker. BSBA, U. Mo., Columbia, 1981, MBA, 1982. Treasury analyst Conoco Inc., Houston, 1982-85, fin. coordinator, 1985-88; asst. treas. Vista Chem. Co., Houston, 1988—. V.p. Conoco Credit Union, Kansas City, Mo., 1983-85. Mem. Houston Pension Mgrs. Club. Republican. Baptist. Avocations: woodworking, sports. Office: Giant Industries Inc 23733 N Scottsdale Rd Scottsdale AZ 85255

COX, PAT, artist; b. Pasadena, Calif., Mar. 6, 1921; d. Walter Melville and Mary Elizabeth (Frost) Boadway; m. Dale William Cox Jr., Feb. 19, 1946; children: Brian Philip, Dale William III, Gary Walter. BA, Mills Coll., 1943, MA, 1944. Graphic artist Pacific Manifolding Book Co., Emeryville, Calif., 1944-45; tchr. art to adults China Lake, 1957-63; tchr. art to children Peninsula Enrichment Program, Rancho Palos Verdes, 1965-67; graphic artist Western Magnum Corp., Hermosa Beach, 1970-80; tchr. art workshop Art at Your Fingertips, Rancho Palos Verdes, 1994-95. One-woman shows include Palos Verdes Art Ctr., Rancho Palos Verdes, Calif., 1977, 79, 83, 92, Thinking Eye Gallery, L.A., 1988, Ventura (Calif.) Coll. Art Galleries, 1994, Mendenhall Gallery, Whittier (Calif.) Coll., 1995, The Gallery at Stevenson Union, So. Oreg. Coll., Ashland, 1996, Fresno Art Museum, Fresno, Calif., 1999; two person exhibits Laguna Art Mus., Laguna Beach, Calif., 1971, Creative Arts Gallery, Burbank, Calif., 1993; group exhibits include Long Beach Mus. Art, Art Rental Gallery, 1979, L.A. County Mus. Art, Art Rental Gallery, 1979, Palm Springs Mus. Art, 1980, Laguna Art Mus., 1981, N.Mex. Fine Arts Gallery, 1981, Pacific Grove Art Ctr., 1983, Phoenix Art Mus., 1983, Riverside Art Mus., 1985, Laguna Art Mus., 1986, Zanesville Art Ctr., Ohio, 1987, The Thinking Eye Gallery, L.A., 1987, 89, Hippodrome Gallery, Long Beach, 1988, N.Mex. State Fine Arts Gallery, 1988, Newport Harbor Art Mus., 1988, Downey Mus. Art, 1990, 92, Internat. Contemporary Art Fair L.A., 1986, 87, 88, 92, U. Tex. Health Sci. Ctr., 1992, Long Beach Arts, 1991, 92, 93, Young Aggressive Art Mus., Santa Ana, 1993, U. Ark. Fine Arts Gallery, Fayetteville, 1994, Laura Knott Art Gallery, Bradford Coll., Mass., 1994, Bridge Street Gallery, Big Fork, Mont., 1994, St. John's Coll. Art Gallery, Santa Fe, 1995, L.A. Harbor Coll., Calif., 1995, Walker Art Collection, Garnett, Kans., 1995, San Francisco State U., 1996, Coleman Gallery, Albuquerque, 1996, Loyola Law Sch., L.A., 1996, San Bernardino County Mus., 1996, Prieto Gallery, Mills Coll., Oakland, Calif., 1996, U. So. Calif. Hillel Gallery, L.A., 1997, The Stage Gall. Merrick, NY, 1999, Nabisco Gall., E. hanover, NJ, 2000, California State U., Los Angeles, 2001. Trustee L.A. Art Assn., 1972-79; bd. dirs. Palos Verdes Art Ctr., 1966-70, 87-89, chair exhbn. com., 1982-85, co-chair Art for Fun(d)s Sake, 1966; judge Tournament of Roses Assn., Pasadena, 1975; mem. strategic planning Palos Verdes Art Ctr., 1988; mem. Pacific Pl. Planning Commn. Percent for Art, San Pedro, Calif., 1989; juror Pasadena Soc. Artists, 1973, 81, Women Painters West, 1984-85. Recipient Silver Pin award Palos Verdes Art Ctr., 1988, Calif. Gold Discovery award V.I.P. Jury Panel, L.A., 1994. Mem. Nat. Watercolor Soc. (juror 1981, 1st v.p. 1980, 4th v.p. 1984), Nat. Mus. Women in the Arts, Oakland Mus. Art, Mus. Contemporary Art, L.A. County Mus. Art, Palos Verdes Cmty. Art Assn. (cert. appreciation 1981). Avocations: gardening, reading.

COX, PAUL ALAN, ethnobotanist, educator; b. Salt Lake City, Oct. 10, 1953; s. Leo A. and Rae (Gabbitas) C.; m. Barbara Ann Wilson, May 21, 1975; children: Emily Ann, Paul Matthew, Mary Elisabeth, Hillary Christine, Jane Margaret. BS, Brigham Young U., 1976; MSc, U. Wales, 1978; AM, Harvard U., 1978, PhD, 1981; DSc (hon.), U. Guelph, Can., 2000. Teaching fellow Harvard U., Cambridge, Mass., 1977-81; Miller research fellow Miller Inst. Basic Research in Sci., Berkeley, Calif., 1981-83; asst. prof. Brigham Young U., Provo, Utah, 1983-86, assoc. prof., 1986-91, prof., 1991—, dean gen. edn. and honors, 1993-97; King Gustav XVI prof. environ. sci. Swedish Biodiversity Ctr., 1997—; dir. Nat. Tropical Botanical Garden, Kalaheo, Hawaii, 1998—. Disting. prof. Brigham Young U., Hawaii, 2000—; ecologist Utah Environ. Coun., Salt Lake City, 1976; project ecologist Utah MX Coordination Office, Salt Lake City, 1981. Mem. editorial bd. Pacific Studies. Recipient Bowdoin prize, The Goldman Environ. prize, 1997; Danforth Found. fellow, 1976-81, Fulbright fellow, 1976-77, NSF fellow, 1977-81, Linnaen Soc. fellow, Melbourne Univ. fellow, 1985-86; named NSF Presdl. Young Investigator, 1985-90, Hero of Medicine, Time Mag., 1997. Mem. AAAS, Brit. Ecol. Soc., Internat. Soc. Ethnopharmacology (pres.), Am. Soc. Naturalists, Assn. Tropical Biology, Soc. Econ. Botany (pres.), New Eng. Bot. Club. Mem. LDS Ch. Office: Dir Nat Tropical Botanical Gardens 3530 Papalina Rd Kalaheo HI 96741-9599

COX, RICHARD HORTON, civil engineering executive; b. Paia, Hawaii, Oct. 10, 1920; s. Joel B. and Helen Cliford (Horton) C.; m. Hester Virginia Smith, Dec. 12, 1942 (dec. Aug. 12, 1995); children: Millicent, Janet, Lydia, Evelyn, David, Samuel (dec.). BS, Calif. Inst. Tech., 1942, MS, 1946. Registered profl. engr., surveyor, Hawaii. Supr. rocket range Calif. Inst. Tech., Pasadena, 1942-46; civil engr. McBryde Sugar Co., Eleele, Hawaii, 1946-56; land mgr. Alexander & Baldwin, Honolulu, 1956-71, v.p., 1971-86; engring. cons. Honolulu, 1986—. Mem. State Commn. on Water Resource Mgmt., 1987-94, 95-99. Fellow ASCE; mem. AAAS, NSPE, Am. Geophys. Union. Mem. Soc. of Friends. Home and Office: 1951 Kakela Dr Honolulu HI 96822-2156

COX, ROBERT GENE, management consultant; b. Liberal, Kans., June 3, 1929; s. Clarice Eldon and Margaret Verene (Jones) C.; m. Eileen Frances Hinshaw, July 10, 1953; children: Ann Rebecca Cox Taylor, Allan Robert. B.A. with honors, U. N.Mex., 1951, J.D., 1955; grad., Fgn. Service Inst., 1956, Harvard Bus. Sch., 1978, 79. Joined Fgn. Svc., 1956; 3d to 2d sec. Am. Embassy, Panama, 1956-58; Am. Consul, Caracas, Venezuela, 1959-61; Korea desk officer Dept. State, Washington, 1961-62, chief of staff mgmt. planning, 1963-65, officer in charge Mission to Israel, 1965; staff asst. to President U.S. The White House, 1966-68; ptnr. William H. Clark Assos., N.Y.C. and Chgo., 1968-71; sr. staff officer UN Secretariat, Vienna and N.Y.C., 1971-72; pres. Hennes & Cox, Inc., N.Y.C., Washington and Los Angeles, 1972-75; prin., nat. dir. human resource systems Ernst & Ernst, Cleve., 1975-78; ptnr., mng. dir. Arthur Young & Co., N.Y.C., 1979-83; pres. PA Exec. Search Group, N.Y.C., 1983-86; chmn. PA Computers and Telecommunications NA, N.Y.C., 1985-86; mng. dir. A.T. Kearney, Inc., 1987-90, 93-96; exec. v.p. Oxford Analytica, Inc., N.Y.C., 1990-92; exec. dir. Oxford Analytica Ltd., Eng., 1990-92; pres. Nelson O'Connor & Cox, Tucson, 1996—. Mem. history faculty Fla. State U., 1958; cons. Commn. U.S.-Latin-Am. Rels., 1974; sr. advisor Commn. Orgn. of Govt. for Conduct of Fgn. Policy, 1974-75; expert witness on mil. value of Panama Canal U.S. Ho. of Reps., 1977; ITT lectr. Georgetown U., 1981. Author: Defense Department Diplomacy in Latin America, 1964, Choices for Partnership or Bloodshed in Panama, 1975, The Canal Zone: New Focal Point in U.S.-Latin American Relations, 1977, The Chief Executive, 1980, Planning for Immigration: A Business Perspective, 1981, Selection of the Chief Executive Officer, 1982. Mem. Pacific Coun. Internat. Policy; bd. dirs. cmty. drug control program, Glen Ridge, N.J., 1971-72, Unitarian-Universalist Christian Fellowship, 1987-90; dep. to county chmn. Albuquerque Dem. Party, 1954; advisor on exec. selection to transition staff of Pres.-elect Carter, 1976-77; mem. bd. advisors Georgetown U. Program in Bus. Diplomacy, 1985-95; bd. dirs. Coun. on Econ. Priorities, 1982-86, LeRoy Industries, Inc., 1984-87, 89-91, Alden Owners, Inc., 1986-88; trustee Meadville Theol. Sch. U. Chgo., 1986-92; gov. Manchester Coll. Oxford U., 1991-96, councillor, 1992-96, hon. gov. 1996—; trustee Unitarian Ch. of All Souls, N.Y.C., 1980-84, sec., 1979-80, pres., 1983-84, deacon, 1985-92; lay preacher Manchester Coll. Chapel, Oxford U., 1990-96; mem. vestry St. Philip's Episc. Ch., Tucson, 1996—, sr. warden, 1997—. Mem. Jonesville (Mich.) Heritage Assn., Coun. Fgn. Rels. (chmn. study group on immigration and U.S. fgn. policy 1978), Royal Econ. Soc. (Eng.), Am. Soc. Internat. Law, Unitarian Hist. Soc. Eng., Martineau Soc. Eng., Internat. Assn. Religious Freedom, SAR. Episcopalian. Office: PO Box 1495 Silver City NM 88062-1495

COYE, MOLLY JOEL, state agency administrator; b. Bennington, Vt., May 11, 1947; d. Robert Dudley Coye and Janet (Loper) Coye Nelson; m. Daniel Noah Lindheim, Sept. 22, 1974 (div. 1980); m. Mark Douglas Smith, Feb. 22, 1980; 1 child, Langston Matthew Coye. BA, U. Calif., Berkeley, 1968; MA, Stanford U., 1972; MPH, MD, Johns Hopkins U., 1977. Chief of occupational health clinic U. San Francisco, 1979-84; med. officer Nat. Inst. for Occupational Safety & Health, 1980-85; advisor health and environment Gov.'s Office of Policy & Planning, Trenton, N.J., 1985-86; dep. commr. N.J. Dept. Health, Trenton, 1986-87; v.p. strategic devel. Health Desk Corp., Berkely, Calif., 1988-98; sr. v.p. The Lewin Group, San Francisco, 1998—. Chair adv. com. graduate program in pub. health U. Medicine and Dentistry of N.J., Newark, 1986—; mem. tech. bd. Milbank Meml. Fund, N.Y.C., 1986-88; mem. com. role of primary care physician in occupational/environ. medicine Nat. Acad. Scis, Inst. Medicine, Washington, 1986-88; mem. adv. com. AIDS U.S. Pub. Health Svc., Washington, 1989; mem. adv. coun. Nat. Inst. for Environ. Health Scis., Betheseda, Md., 1989. Co-author, editor: China: Inside the People's Republic, 1972, co-editor: China Yesterday and Today. Contbr. peer review articles to profl. jours. Recipient Virginia Apgar award March of Dimes, Plainsboro, N.J., 1988, Woman of the Yr. award Jersey Woman mag., 1989. Mem. AMA, Am. Coll. Preventive Medicine, Am. Pub. Health Assn. (chair exec. bd. 1988), Assn. for Health Svcs. Rsch., Assn. State and Territorial Health Officers (chair exec. bd. 1988—, mem. AIDS com. 1988—), Soc. for Occupational and Environ. Health (mem. governing coun. 1988—). Avocations: murder mysteries, cooking. Office: The Lewin Group 455 Market St Ste 14 San Francisco CA 94105-2450

COYLE, MARIE BRIDGET, retired microbiology educator, laboratory director; b. Chgo., May 13, 1935; d. John and Bridget Veronica (Fitzpatrick) C.; m. Zheng Chen, Oct. 30, 1995 (div. Aug. 2000). BA, Mundelein Coll., 1957; MS, St. Louis U., 1963; PhD, Kans. State U., 1965. Diplomate Am. Bd. Med. Microbiology. Sci. instr. Sch. Nursing Columbus Hosp., Chgo., 1957-59; research assoc. U. Chgo., 1967-70; instr. U. Ill., Chgo., 1970-71; asst. prof. microbiology U. Wash., Seattle, 1973-80, assoc. prof., 1980-94, prof., 1994-2000; ret., 2000. Assoc. dir. microbiology labs Univ. Hosp., Seattle, 1973-76; dir. microbiology labs Harborview Med. Ctr., Univ. Wash., 1976—; co-dir. Postdoc Training Clinic Microbiology, Univ. Wash., 1978-96; dir. postdoctoral tng. clin. microbiology, 1996-2000. Contbr. articles to profl. jours. Recipient Pasteur award Ill. Soc. Microbiology, 1997, Profl. Recognition awards Am. Bd. Med. and Molecular Microbiology, Am. Bd. Med. Lab. Immunology, 2000. Fellow Am. Acad. Microbiology; mem. Acd. Clin. Lab. Physicians and Scientists (sec.-treas. 1980-83, exec. com. 1985-90), Am. Soc. Microbiology (chmn. clin. microbiology divsn. 1984-85, coun. policy com. 1996-99, bd. govs. 2000—, recipient bioMerieux Vitek Sonnenwirth Meml. award 1994), Kappa Gamma Pi. Avocations: hiking, skiing, cycling.

COYLE, ROBERT EVERETT, federal judge; b. Fresno, Calif., May 6, 1930; s. Everett LaJoya and Virginia Chandler C.; m. Faye Turnbaugh, June 11, 1953; children— Robert Allen, Richard Lee, Barbara Jean BA, Fresno State Coll., 1953; JD, U. Calif., 1956. Bar: Calif. Ptnr. McCormick, Barstow, Sheppard, Coyle & Wayte, 1958-82; chief judge U.S. Dist. Ct. (ea. dist.) Calif., 1990-96, sr. judge, 1996—. Former chair 9th Cir. Conf. of Chief Dist. Judges, chair 9th Cir. space and security com., mem. com. on state and fed. cts. Mem. Calif. Bar Assn. (exec. com. 1974-79, bd. govs. 1979-82, v.p. 1981), Fresno County Bar Assn. (pres. 1972). Office: US Dist Ct 5116 US Courthouse 1130 O St Fresno CA 93721-2201

COZEN, LEWIS, orthopedic surgeon; b. Montreal, Aug. 14, 1911; came to U.S. 1922; AB, U. Calif., San Francisco, 1929, MD, 1934. Diplomate Am. Bd. Orthopedic Surgery. Intern San Francisco Hosp., 1933-34; resident orthopedic surgeon U. Iowa, 1934-35; resident and fellow orthopedic surgery San Francisco County Hosp., 1935-36, Children's Hosp. and Mass. Gen. Hosp., Boston, 1936-39; pvt. practice orthopedic surgery L.A., 1939-40, 45—. Clin. prof. orthopedic surgery UCLA, 1965-93; assoc. clin. prof. emeritus Loma Linda Med. Sch., 1963—; attending orthopedic surgeon, emeritus Cedars Sinai Med. Ctr., 1939—, Orthopaedic Hosp., 1939—; chief orthopedic surgery City of Hope, 1948-67; sr. attending orthopedic surgeons, emeritus Unit One L.A. County Hosp., 1950-63; vis. lectr. U. Santo Tomas, Manila, U. Madrid, Spain; Far East Sch. of Medicine, Manila, 1994, Hadassah Med. Ctr., Jerusalem, 1994, U. Brussels; lectr. in field; vis. lectr. Brussels, U. London, Stammore, Eng., U. Guadalajara, Mexico, others. Author: Office Orthopedics, 1955, 4th edit. 1973, Operative Orthopedic Clinics (with Dr. Avia Brockway), 1960, Atlas of Orthopedic Surgery, 1966, Difficult Orthopedic Diagnosis, 1972, Plannings and Pitfalls in Orthopedic Surgery, Natural History of Orthopedic Disease, 1993, Supplement Book, 1996; mem. editl. bd. Resident & Staff Physician; contbr. numerous articles to profl. jours. Vol. physician Internat. Children's Program, Orthopedic Hosp., Mexicali, Mexico. Lt. col. U.S. Army, 1940-45. Fellow ACS, Internat. Coll. Surgeons, Am. Coll. Rheumatology, Royal Soc. Medicine; mem. Am. Rheumatism Assn., Internat. Orthopedic Assn., Am. Orthopaedic Assn. (sr.), Am. Acad. Orthopaedic Surgeons, So. Calif. Rheumatism Assn. (pres. 1979), Western Orthopaedic Assn., Phi Beta Kappa, Alpha Omega Alpha. Avocations: swimming, golf, dancing, travel.

CRAFT, CHERYL MAE, neurobiologist, anatomist, researcher; b. Lynch, Ky., Apr. 15, 1947; d. Cecil Berton and Lillian Lovelle (Ellington) C.; m. Laney K. Cormney, Oct. 14, 1967 (div. Sept. 1980); children: Tyler Craft Cormney, Ryan Berton Cormney; m. Richard N. Lolley (dec. Apr. 2000). BS in Biology, Chemistry and Math., Valdosta State Coll., 1969; cert. in tchg. biol. and math., Ea. Ky. U., 1971; PhD in Human Anatomy and Neurosci., U. Tex., San Antonio, 1984. Undergrad. rsch. asst. Ea. Ky. U., Richmond, 1965-67; tchg. asst. dept. cell-structural biology U. Tex. Health Sci. Ctr., San Antonio, 1979-84; postdoctoral fellowship lab. devel. neurobiology NICHD and LMDB/NEI, Bethesda, Md., 1984-86; instr. dept. psychiatry U. Tex. Southwestern Med. Ctr., Dallas, 1986-87, asst. prof., 1987-91; dir. lab. Molecular Neurogenetics, Schizophrenia Rsch. Ctr., VA Med. Ctr., Dallas, 1988-94; dir. Lab. Molecular Neurogenetics Mental Health Clinic Rsch. Ctr., U. Tex. Southwestern Med. Ctr., 1990-94; assoc. prof. U. Tex. Southwestern Med. Ctr., 1991-94; Mary D. Allen prof. Doheney Eye Inst. U. So. Calif. Keck Sch. Medicine, L.A., 1994—, chmn. dept. cell and neurobiology, 1994—. Ad hoc reviewer NEI/NIH, Bethesda, 1993—; reviewer Molecular Biology, NSPB Fight for Sight Grants, 1991-94; STAR-sci. adv. bd. U. So. Calif./Bravo Magnet H.S., L.A., 1995—. Contbr. author: Melatonin: Biosynthesis, Physiological Effects, 1993; exec. editor Exptl. Eye Rsch. jour., 1993—; editor Molecular Vision. Recipient Merit award for rsch. VA Med. Ctr., 1992, 93, 94, nomination for Women in Sci. and Engring. award Dallas VA, 1992, 93; NEI fellow, 1986, NICHD/NIH fellow, 1986. Mem. AAAS, AAUW, Assn. for Rsch. in Vision and Ophthalmology (chair program planning com. 1991-94), Am. Soc. for Neurochemistry (Jordi Folch Pi Outstanding Young Investigator 1992), Sigma Xi (sec./treas. 1986-93, pres. 1993-94). Avocations: reading, travel. Home: 1191 Brookmere Rd Pasadena CA 91105-3301 Office: Univ So Calif Keck Sch Medicine 1333 San Pablo St Rm 401 Los Angeles CA 90033-1026 E-mail: ccraft@hsc.usc.edu

CRAIB, KENNETH BRYDEN, resource development executive, physicist, economist; b. Milford, Mass., Oct. 13, 1938; s. William Pirie and Virginia Louise (Bryden) C.; m. Gloria Faye Lisano, June 25, 1960; children: Kenneth Bryden, Judith Diane, Lori Elaine, Melissa Suzanne. BS in Physics, U. Houston, 1967; MA in Econs., Calif. State U., 1982; postgrad., Harvard U., 1989. Aerospace technologist NASA, Houston, 1962-68; staff physicist Mark Sys., Inc., Cupertino, Calif., 1968-69; v.p. World Resources Corp., Cupertino, 1969-71; dir. resources devel. divsn. Aero Svc. Corp., Phila., 1971-72; dir. ops. Resources Devel. Assocs., Los Altos, Calif., 1972-80, pres., CEO Diamond Springs, 1980-85; owner Sand Ridge Arabians, 1980-98; chmn., dir. Resources Devel. Assocs., Inc., 1982-86, Devel. Support Internat. Inc., Placerville, Calif., 1981-86; pres., chn., dir. RDA Internat., Inc., 1985-96, chmn., CEO, dir., 1995—. Bd. dirs. Sierra Gen. Investments, 1985—, Transatlantic Fisheries, Inc., 1995—; adj. prof. Sacramento City Coll., 1996—, U. Phoenix, Sacramento, 1997—. Contbr. articles to profl. jours. Served with USAF, 1957-61. Recipient Sustained Superior Performance award NASA, 1966; NASA grantee, 1968. Mem. Am. Soc. Photogrammetry, Soc. Internat. Devel., Agrl. Rsch. Inst., Calif. Select Com. Remote Sensing, Internat. Assn. Natural Resources Pilots, Remote Sensing Soc. (coun.), Am. Soc. Oceanography (charter), Aircraft Owenrs and Pilots Assn., Gulf and Cribbean Fisheries Inst., Placerville C. of C., Harvard Alumni Assn., Exptl. Aircraft Assn., Asian Fisheries Soc. Office: RDA Internat Inc 801 Morey Dr Placerville CA 95667-4411

CRAIG, CAROL MILLS, marriage, family and child counselor; b. Berkeley, Calif. BA in Psychology (hon.), U. Calif., Santa Cruz, 1974; MA in Counseling Psychology, John F. Kennedy U., 1980; doctoral student, Calif. Sch. Profl. Psychology, Berkeley, 1980-87, Columbia Pacific U., San Rafael, Calif., 1987—. Psychology intern Fed. Correction Inst., Pleasanton, Calif., 1979-81, Letterman Army Med. Ctr., San Francisco, 1980-82, VA Mental Hygiene Clinic, Oakland, Calif., 1981-82; instr. Martinez Adult Sch., 1983, Piedmont Adult Edn., Oakland, 1986; biofeedback and stress mgmt. cons. Oakland, 1986—; child counselor Buddies-A Nonprofit, Counseling Svc. for Persons in the Arts, Lafayette, Calif., 1993—; founder Chesley Sch., 1994, Healing with Music for People and All Animals, 1996, Music Therapy for animals, 1998—. Rsch. asst. Irvington Pubs., N.Y.C., 1979, Little, Brown and Co., Boston, 1983; music therapist for people and animals, 1998—. Mem. Calif. Scholarship Fedn. (life). Avocations: music-guitar, violin, folk and opera singing, song writing, art.

CRAIG, JENNY, weight management executive; From mgr. to nat. dir. ops. Body Contour, Inc.; pres., co-founder, vice chmn. Jenny Craig Weight Loss Prog., 1982—. Achievements include providing a comprehensive weight mgmt. prog. designed by registered dietitians, psychologists and a med. adv. bd. to grow into one of the largest weight mgmt. cos. in the world; only weight mgmt. co. listed on N.Y. Stock Exch. Office: Jenny Craig Inc 11355 N Torrey Pines Rd La Jolla CA 92037-1013

CRAIG, LARRY EDWIN, senator; b. Council, Idaho, July 20, 1945; s. Elvin and Dorothy Craig. B.A., U. Idaho; postgrad, George Washington U. Farmer, rancher, Midvale area, Idaho; mem. Idaho Senate, 1974-80, 97th-101st Congresses from 1st Dist. Idaho, 1981-90; senator from Idaho U.S. Senate 102nd Congress, 1990-97; mem. com. agr., nutrition and forestry, com. energy and natural resources, spl. com. on aging, chmn. com. Rep. policy, vets. affairs, appropriations U.S. Senate 102nd Congress from Idaho, chmn. subcom. on forests and pub. land mgmt., chmn. subcom. energy rsch., devel., prodn. and regulation, subcom. water and power; senator from Idaho U.S. Senate 105th Congress (now 106th Congress), 1996—. Chmn. Idaho Rep. State Senate Races, 1976-78, chmn. senate steering com., mem. joint econ. com., com. veterans' affairs, subcom. energy R & D. Pres. Young Rep. League Idaho, 1976-77; mem. Idaho Rep. Exec. Com., 1976-78; chmn. Rep. Ctrl. Com. Washington County, 1971-72; advisor vocat. edn. in pub. schs. HEW, 1971-73; mem. Idaho Farm Bur., 1965-79. Served with U.S. Army N.G., 1970-74. Mem. NRA (bd. dirs. 1983—), Future Farmers of Am. (v.p. 1965). Methodist. Office: US Senate 520 Hart Senate Office Bldg Washington DC 20510-0001*

CRAIG, SIDNEY RICHARD, theatrical agent; b. Cleve. s. Norman Benjiman and Rose Craig. BA in Bus. and Social Psychology, U. So. Calif., 1967. Adv. bd. D.E.F. Found., L.A., 1991—. Judge Tops and Blue USAF World Talent Competition, 1973—. With USN, 1966-68. Mem. Acad. Motion Picture Arts and Scis., Assn. Talent Agts. (v.p., bd. dirs. 1982—), D.E.F. Found. Office: Craig Agy 8485 Melrose Pl # E Los Angeles CA 90069-5311

CRAIGHEAD, FRANK COOPER, JR. ecologist; b. Washington, Aug. 14, 1916; s. Frank Cooper and Carolyn (Johnson) C.; m. Esther Melvin Stevens, Nov. 9, 1943 (dec. 1980); children: Frank Lance, Charles Stevens, Jana Catherine; m. Shirley Ann Cocker, July, 1987. AB, Pa. State U., 1939; MS, U. Mich., 1940, PhD, 1950. Sr. rsch. assoc. Atmospheric Scis. Rsch. Ctr., N.Y., 1967-77; wildlife biologist, cons. U.S. Dept. Interior, Washington, 1959-66; wildlife biologist U.S. Forest Svc., Washington, 1957-59; mgr. desert game range U.S. Dept. Interior, Las Vegas, 1955-57; cons. survival tng. Dept. Def., Washington, 1950-55; pres. Craighead Environ. Rsch. Inst., Moose, Wyo., 1955—; rsch. assoc. U. Mont., Missoula, 1959—, Nat. Geog. Soc., Washington, 1959—. Lectr. in field. Author: Hawks in the Hand, 1937, How to Survive on Land and Sea, 1943, Hawks, Owls and Wildlife, 1956, A Field Guide to Rocky Mountain Wildflowers, 1963, Track of the Grizzly, 1979, For Everything There is a Season, 1994. Mem. Pryor Mountain Wild Horse Adv. Com., Dept. Interior, 1968; mem. Horizons adv. group Am. Revolution Bicentennial Commn., 1972. Recipient citation Sec. of Navy, 1947; recipient letter of commendation U.S. Dept. Interior, 1963, Disting. Alumnus award Pa. State U., 1970; alumni fellow Pa. State U., 1973; recipient John Oliver LaGorce Gold medal Nat. Geog. Soc., 1979, U. Mich. Sch. Natural Resources Alumni Soc. award for Disting. Service, 1984, Centennial award Nat. Geog. Soc., 1988. Mem. AAAS, Wilderness Soc., Wildlife Soc., Explorers Club, Phi Beta Kappa, Sigma Xi, Phi Sigma, Phi Kappa Phi. Office: Craighead Environ Rsch Inst PO Box 156 Moose WY 83012-0156

CRAIGHEAD, JOHN JOHNSON, wildlife biologist; b. Washington, Aug. 14, 1916; married; 3 children. BA, Pa. State U., 1939; MS, U. Mich., 1940, PhD, 1950. Biologist N.Y. Zool. Soc., 1947-49; dir. survival tng. for armed forces U.S. Dept. Def., 1950-52; wildlife biologist, leader Mont. coop. rsch. unit Bur. Sport Fisheries and Wildlife, 1952-77; prof. zoology and forestry U. Mont., 1952-77; bd. dirs., founder Craighead Wildlife-Wildlands Inst., Missoula, Mont., 1978—. Recipient Conservation award Am. Motors, 1978, John Oliver LaGorce Gold medal Nat. Geog. Soc., 1979, Centennial award, 1988, Lud Browman award Scientific and Tech. Writing, U. Mont., 1990; grantee NSF, AEC, NASA, U.S. Forest Svc., Mont. Fish and Game Dept. Mem. AAAS, Wildlife Soc., Wilderness Alliance. Office: Craighead Wildlife-Wildlands Inst 5200 Miller Creek Rd Missoula MT 59803-1904

CRAINE, THOMAS KNOWLTON, non-profit administrator; b. Utica, N.Y., Apr. 19, 1942; s. Donald Holmes and Marjorie (Knowlton) C.; m. Susan Lynda Moseley, Dec. 21, 1966; children: Matthew Moseley, Tish Marjorie. BA, U. Rochester, 1964; MEd, SUNY, Buffalo, 1966, EdD, 1972. Dir. architecture and planning SUNY, Buffalo, 1968-72, asst. to pres., 1972-76, clin. assoc. prof., 1975-83, asst. v.p. acad. affairs, 1976-79; exec. v.p., assoc. prof. D'Youville Coll., Buffalo, 1979-83; pres. Loretto Heights Coll., Denver, 1983-88; v.p. instl. advancement and planning Iliff Sch. Theology, Denver, 1988-98; pres./CEO YMCA Met. Denver, 1998—. Evaluator North Cen. Assn. Instns. Higher Edn., 1984—, Assn. Theol. Schs., 1993—; cons. in strategic planning, bd. devel., fund raising. Mem. editl. bd. Jour. for Higher Edn. Mgmt. Mem. Newcomen Soc., Univ. Club, Theta Chi, Rotary. Office: YMCA Met Denver 25 E 16th Ave Denver CO 80202-5195 E-mail: tcraine@denverymca.org

CRAM, BRIAN MANNING, school system administrator; AA, Dixie Jr. Coll., 1959; BA (hon.), U. Utah, 1961; MA, Ariz. State U., 1962, EdS, 1964, EdD (hon.), 1967. Asst. prin. Clark (Nev.) H.S., 1965-69, prin., 1969-73; asst. supt. Clark County (Nev.) Sch. Dist., 1973-78; supt. schs. Clark County (Nev,) Sch. Dist., 1989—; prin. Western H.S., 1978-89. Cons. Glendale Unified Sch. Dist., Whittier Sch. Dist., South Bay Union H.S. Dist., Elk Grove Unified Sch. Dist., No. Ill. U., State of Hawaii; co-chmn. Supt.'s Coun. Ednl. Tech., Coll. Prep Feasibility sub-com.; mem. Spkrs. Bur. Pay as You Go Bond Plan, Disting. Scholar's com., Extended Day com., In-Svc. com., State Attendence Audit, Spl. Assistance Team, Computer Mgmt. Project, Prin. Attendance adv. com., Prin.'s Math Curriculum com; spkr. in field. Contbr. articles to profl. jours. Bd. dirs. Boulder Dam Area Coun. Boy Scouts Am., Las Vegas Coun. PTA, United Way, Clark County Sch. Dist. Articulation Com., Nev. Assn. Handicapped, Nev. Devel. Authority, Nev. Inst. Contemporary Art, Animal Found., Las Vegas Mus. Nat. History, Southwest Regional Ednl. Lab., Nat. Coun. Christians and Jews; adv. bd. U. Nev. Las Vegas Spl. Svcs., U. Nev. Sch. Medicine, Clark County C.C. Mem. Nev. Assn. Secondary Sch. Prins. (past sec.), Nev. Educator Awards Selection Com., Clark County Assn. Sch. Administrs. (chmn. negotiations, past exec. coun., past sec., past pres.), Ariz. State U. Alumni Assn. (past pres. So. Nev. chpt.), Greater Las Vegas C. of C., Latin C. of C., Nev. Black C. of C., Rotary, Phi Delta Kappa. Home: 10700 Elk Lake Ave Las Vegas NV 89144-4439 Office: Clark County School District 2832 E Flamingo Rd Las Vegas NV 89121-5295

CRAMER, CHUCKIE, legislative staff member; b. Havre, Mont., Nov. 7, 1941; Sgt.-at-arms Mont. Ho. of Reps., Helena, 1985-88, Mont. State Senate, Helena, 1995—. Office: Mont State Senate Sgt at Arms Mont State Capitol RM 375 Helena MT 59620

CRAMER, EUGENE NORMAN, nuclear power engineer, computer educator; b. Arkansas City, Kans., Apr. 26, 1932; s. Norman Charles and Hulda Margaret (Maier) C.; m. Donna Marie Gagliardi, May 18, 1957 (dec 1984); children: Lorene, Kristine, Eileen, Carla; m. Marlene McLean, Dec. 29, 1985. BS in Physics, BS in Math., Kans. State Coll., 1955; grad., Oak Ridge Sch. Reactor Tech., 1959; MA in Mgmt., Claremont Grad. Sch., 1976, MBA, 1985. Registered profl. engr., Calif. Jr. engr. Westinghouse Bettis, Pitts., 1955-57; devel. engr. Oak Ridge Nat. Lab., 1959-69; cons. examiner AEC, 1961-73; engr. advanced energy system So. Calif. Edison, Los Angeles, 1969-88, mgr. nuclear comm., 1988-95, pres., asst. to edn., 1995—. Sec. task force on nuc. safety rsch. Electric Rsch. Coun., 1969-74; chmn. Pub. Edn. Utility Nuc. Waste Mgmt. Group, 1978-81, Pub. Edn. Calif. Radioactive Waste Mgmt. Forum, 1982-97. Sect. editor Nuclear Safety jour., 1964-69; contbr. articles to profl. jours. Mem. Capistrano Unified Sch. Dist. Edn. Found., 1994-96. Served as 1st lt. Signal Corps, U.S. Army, 1957-59. Fellow Inst. for Advancement Engring.; mem. Am. Nuclear Soc. (bd. dirs. 1978-81, Meritorious Service award 1981, pub. info. com. 1983-2000), Health Physics Soc., Soc. for Risk Analysis. Republican. Roman Catholic. Club: Sierra. Home and Office: 2176 Via Teca San Clemente CA 92673-5648

CRAMER, JAMES DALE, physicist, scientific company executive; b. Canton, Ohio, Aug. 4, 1937; s. Dale and Vera Arlene (Lindower) C.; m. Geraldine M. Bendoski, July 20, 1957; children: Karen Lynn, Eric James. BS, Calif. State U., Fresno, 1960; MS, U. Oreg., 1962; PhD, U. N.Mex., 1969. Mem. tech. staff U. Calif., Los Alamos, 1962-70; v.p. Davis-Smith Corp., San Diego, 1970-73; mem. tech. staff Sci. Applications, Inc., LaJolla, Calif., 1970-73, group v.p. Albuquerque, 1973-80, dir., 1974-80; pres. Sci. & Enging. Assocs., Inc., Albuquerque, 1980—. Cons. in field; pres. Albuquerque Mus. Found., 1981-83. Contbr. articles to profl. publs. Mem. Am. Phys. Soc., IEEE. Home: PO Box 30691 Albuquerque NM 87190-0691 Office: 6100 Uptown Blvd NE Ste 700 Albuquerque NM 87110-4174

CRAMER, JOHN GLEASON, JR. physics educator, experimental physicist; b. Houston, Oct. 24, 1934; s. John Gleason and Frances Ann (Sakwitz) C.; m. Pauline Ruth Bond, June 2, 1961; children: Kathryn Elizabeth, John Gleason III, Karen Melissa. B.A., Rice U., 1957, M.A., 1959, Ph.D. in Physics, 1961. Postdoctoral fellow Ind. U., Bloomington, 1961-63, asst. prof., 1963-64; asst. prof. physics U. Wash., Seattle, 1964-68, assoc. prof., 1968-74, prof., 1974—, dir. nuclear physics lab., 1983-90. Guest prof. W. Ger. Bundesministerium and U. Munich, 1971-72; mem. program adv. com. Los Alamos Meson Physics Facility, Los Alamos Nat. Lab., 1976-78, Nat. Superconducting Cyclotron Lab., 1983-87, TRIUMF (U. B.C.), 1985-88; program adviser-cons. Lawrence Berkeley Lab., Calif., 1979-82; mem. exec. coun. STAR Collaboration, 1991—, CERN Experiments NA 35 and NA 49, 1991—; guest prof. Hahn-Meitner Inst., West Berlin, 1982-83, Max-Planck-Inst. für Physik, Munich, Germany, 1994-95. Author: Twistor, 1989, Einstein's Bridge, 1997; columnist Analog Mag., 1983—; contbr. articles to physics and popular publs. Fellow AAAS, Am. Phys. Soc. (mem. panel on pub. affairs 1998—). Home: 7002 51st Ave NE Seattle WA 98115-6132 Office: U Wash Dept Physics PO Box 351560 Seattle WA 98195-1560

CRAMER, OWEN CARVER, classics educator; b. Tampa, Fla., Dec. 1, 1941; s. Maurice Browning and Alice (Carver) C.; m. Rebecca Jane Lowrey, June 23, 1962; children: Alfred, Thomas, Ethan, Benjamin AB, Oberlin Coll., 1962; PhD, U. Tex., 1973. Spl. instr. U. Tex., Austin, 1964-65; instr. in classics Colo. Coll., Colorado Springs, 1965-69, asst. prof. classics, 1969-75, assoc. prof. classics, 1975-84, M.C. Gile prof. classics, 1984—, dir. comparative lit., 1993—. Cons. humanist Colo. Humanities Program, Denver, 1982-83; vis. prof. U. Chgo., 1987-88; reader Advanced Placement Latin Exam., 1995-99. Editorial asst. Arion, 1964-65; contbr. papers, articles on Greek lang. and lit. to profl. publs., 1974— ; contbr. classical music revs. to Colorado Springs Sun, 1984-86. Chorus tenor Colo. Opera Festival, Colorado Springs, 1976-82; mem. El Paso County Dem. Ctrl. Com., Colo., 1968-88; ordained elder Presbyn. Ch., 1992. Hon. Woodrow Wilson fellow, 1962; univ. fellow U. Tex., Austin, 1962-64 Mem. Am. Philol. Assn. (campus adv. svc. 1989—, chmn. com. on smaller depts. 1979-80), Am. Comparative Lit. Assn., Classical Assn. Middle West and South, Modern Greek Studies Assn., Colo. Classics Assn., Round Table (Colorado Springs) Club,. Phi Beta Kappa. Home: 747 E Uintah St Colorado Springs CO 80903-2546 Office: Colo Coll Dept Classics Colorado Springs CO 80903 E-mail: ocramer@coloradocollege.edu

CRANDALL, IRA CARLTON, consulting electrical engineer; b. South Amboy, N.J., Oct. 30, 1931; s. Carlton Francis and Claire Elizabeth (Harned) C.; m. Jane Leigh Ford, Jan. 29, 1954; children— Elizabeth Anne, Amy Leigh, Matthew Garrett BS in Radio Engring., Ind. Inst. Tech., 1954, BS in Elec. Engring., 1958; BS in Electronics Engring., U.S. Naval Postgrad. Sch., 1962; PhD, U. Sussex, 1964; MA, Piedmont U., 1967, DSc (hon.), 1968; LLB, Blackstone Sch. Law, 1970; DLitt, St. Matthew U., 1970; EdD, Mt. Sinai U., 1972; Assoc. Bus., LaSalle U., 1975, B in Computer Sci., 1986; D. Internat. Rels., Australian Inst. for Coordinated Rsch., 1991. Tchr. Madison Twp. Pub. Schs., N.J., 1954-55; commd. ensign U.S. Navy, 1955, advanced through grades to lt. comdr., 1965, released to inactive duty, 1972; engring. cons. Concord, Calif., 1972—. Pres. 7C's Enterprises, Concord, 1972-96; v.p. Dickinson Enterprises, Concord, 1972-77, Williamson Engring., Inc., Walnut Creek, Calif., 1974-82; pres., chmn. bd. I.C. Crandall and Assocs., Inc., Concord and Westminster, Calif., Tigard, Oreg., 1976-82; pres. Internat. Rsch. Assocs., Concord, 1982-98; v.p. Gayner Engring. Inc., San Francisco, 1982-92; sr. engr. Ajmani Assoc., San Francisco, 1992-99, Syska and Hennesy, L.A., 1999—. Vice pres. PTA, Concord, 1969; tribal organizer Mt. Diablo YMCA Indian Guide Program, 1971-74; pres. Mt. Diablo Unified Schs. Interested Citizens. Decorated Vietnamese Cross of Valor Fellow Am. Coll. Engrs.; mem. IEEE, U.S. Naval Inst. Am. Naval Assn., Assn. Elec. Engrs., Am. Inst. Tech. Mgmt. (sr.), Soc. Am. Mil. Engrs., Nat. Model Ry. Assn., Assn. Old Crows, Concord Homeowners Assn., Concord Chamber Singers, Concord Blue Devils, Scottish-Am. Military Soc., Am. Legion, Order of the Knights (knight), Templar of Jerusalem, Lofsensic Ursinius Order (knight commdr. 1991—), Pi Upsilon Eta, Gamma Chi Epsilon, Alpha Gamma Upsilon Republican. Methodist (adminstrv. bd. ch. 1971-76). Clubs: Navy League, Century. Lodge: Optimists (pres.) Home and Office: 5754 Pepperridge Pl Concord CA 94521-4821 E-mail: ccrandall@syska.net

CRANDALL, KEITH C. dean; Assoc. dean U. Calif., Berkeley. Recipient Peurifoy Constrn. Rsch. award, 1998. Mem. ASCE. Office: U Calif Civil Environ Engring Dept 215 Mclaughlin Hall Berkeley CA 94720-1712

CRANE, HEWITT DAVID, science advisor; b. Jersey City, Apr. 27, 1927; m. Suzanne Gorlin, June 20, 1954; children: Russell Philip, Douglas Mitchell, Daniel Bruce. BSEE, Columbia U., 1947; PhD, Stanford U., 1960. With IBM, N.Y.C., 1949-51, Inst. for Advanced Study, Princeton, N.J., 1952-55, RCA Labs., Princeton, 1955-56; sr. sci. advisor SRI Internat., Menlo Park, Calif., 1956—. A founder Ridge Winery, Cupertino, Calif., 1959-86, Comm. Intelligence Corp., 1981. Author: (with D. Bennion and D. Nitzan) Digital Magnetic Logic, 1969, The New Social Marketplace: Notes on Effecting Social Change in America's Third Century, 1980; contbr. over 70 articles to profl. jours.; patentee in various fields. With USN, 1945-46. Recipient award NASA, 1970, numerous others. Fellow IEEE, Optical Soc. Am. Home: 25 Cordova Ct Menlo Park CA 94028-7908 Office: SRI Internat Sensory Scis & Tech Ctr 333 Ravenswood Ave Menlo Park CA 94025-3453

CRANE, KAREN R. library director; BA, Ind. U., 1970, MLS, 1971. Dir. Alaska State Librs., Archives and Mus., Juneau, 1986—. Office: Alaska State Libr PO Box 110571 Juneau AK 99811-0571 also: 333 Willoughby Ave Juneau AK 99801-1770

CRANE, ROBERT MEREDITH, health care executive; b. Phila., Apr. 5, 1947; s. Frederick Barnard and Roberta Futhey (Philips) C.; m. Susan Gail Dewald, May 5, 1973; 1 child, Alexis Meredith. BA, Coll. of Wooster, 1969; M Pub. Adminstrn., Cornell U., Ithaca, N.Y., 1971. Health planning specialist U.S. Dept. Health, Edn. and Welfare, Rockville, Md., 1971-73, tech. assistance bur. chief, 1973-76, regulatory methods bur. chief, 1976-77; sr. staff assoc. U.S. Ho. of Reps., Washington, 1977-79; dep. commr. N.Y. State Health Dept., Albany, 1979-82; dir. N.Y. State Office Health Sys. Mgmt., Albany, 1982-83; v.p. govt. rels. Kaiser Found. Health Plan, Oakland, calif., 1983-88, sr. v.p. nat. accts. and pub. rels., 1988-92, sr. v.p. quality mgmt. Calif., 1992-94, sr. v.p., chief adminstrv. officer, 1994-99; sr. v.p., dir. Inst. for Health Policy, Oakland, 1999—. Bd. dirs. Acad. Health Svcs. Rsch. and Health Policy, 2000—; mem. Nat. Acad. Social Ins., 2000—. Campaign cabinet United Way Bay area, 1989-90; steering com. Bay Area Econ. Forum, 1988-94, Bay Area Coun., 1991—; selection judge, preceptor Coro Found., San Francisco, 1985-86; chmn. bd. Alpha Ctr., 1992-98; co-chair conf. bd. Coun. of Shared Bus. Svcs. Execs., 1996—; trustee Employee Benefits Rsch. Inst. Sr. exec. fellow Harvard U., 1981. Mem. APHA (chmn. cmty. health planning sect. 1983-84, bd. govs. 1979-81), Am. Health Planning Assn. (bd. dirs. 1986-92). Presbyterian. Avocations: tennis, golf. Office: Kaiser Found Health Plan 1 Kaiser Plz Oakland CA 94612-3610

CRAPO, MICHAEL DEAN, senator, former congressman, lawyer; b. Idaho Falls, Idaho, May 20, 1951; s. George Lavelle and Melba (Olsen) C.; m. Susan Diane Hasleton, June 22, 1974; children: Michelle, Brian, Stephanie, Lara, Paul. BA Polit. Sci. summa cum laude, Brigham Young U., 1973; postgrad., U. Utah, 1973-74; JD cum laude, Harvard U., 1977. Bar: Calif. 1977, Idaho 1979. Law clk. to Hon. James M. Carter U.S. Ct. Appeals (9th cir.), San Diego, 1977-78; assoc. atty. Gibson, Dunn & Crutcher, L.A., 1978-79; atty. Holden, Kidwell, Hahn & Crapo, Idaho Falls, 1979-92, ptnr., 1983-92; mem. Idaho State Senate from 32A Dist., 1984-93, asst. majority leader, 1987-88; pres. Pro Tempore, 1989-92; congressman U.S. House of Reps., 2d Idaho dist., Washington, 1992-98; mem. commerce com., new mem. leader 103rd Congress, sophomore class leader 104th Congress, co-chair Congl. Beef Caucus, dep. whip western region U.S. House of Reps., Washington, vice chair energy and power subcom., strategic planning leader House Leadership 105th Congress, mem. house resources com., mem. commerce com., mem. resources com.; senator from Idaho U.S. Senate, 1998—. Precinct committeeman Dist. 29, 1980-85; vice chmn. Legislative Dist. 29, 1984-85; Mem. Health and Welfare Com., 1985-89, Resources and Environ. Com., 1985-90, State Affairs Com., 1987-92; Rep. Pres. Task Force, 1989. Leader Boy Scouts Am., Calif., Idaho, 1977-92; mem. Bar Exam Preparation, Bar Exam Grading; chmn. Law Day.; Bonneville County chmn. Phil Batt gubernatorial campaign, 1982. Named one of Outstanding Young Men of Am., 1985; recipient Cert. of Merit Rep. Nat. Com., 1990, Guardian of Small Bus. award Nat. Fedn. of Ind. Bus., 1990, 94, Cert. of Recognition Am. Cancer Soc., 1990, Idaho Housing Agy., 1990, Idaho Lung Assn., 1985, 86, 89, Friend of Agr. award Idaho Farm Bur., 1989-90, medal of merit Rep. Presdl. Task Force, 1989, Nat. Legislator of Yr. award Nat. Rep. Legislators Assn., 1991, Golden Bulldog award Watchdogs of the Treas., 1996, Thomas Jefferson award Nat. Am. Wholesale Grocers Assn.-Ind. Food Distbrs. Assn., 1996, Spirit of Enterprise award U.S. C. of C., 1993, 94, 95, 96. Mem. ABA (antitrust law sect.), Idaho Bar Assn., Rotary. Mormon. Avocations: sports, backpacking, hunting, skiing. Office: US Senate 111 Russell Senate Ofc Bldg Washington DC 20510-0001*

CRASEMANN, BERND, physicist, educator; b. Hamburg, Germany, Jan. 23, 1922; came to U.S., 1946, naturalized, 1955; s. Pablo Joaquin and Hildegard Carlota (Vorwerk) C. AB, UCLA, 1948; PhD, U. Calif.-Berkeley, 1953. With Lavadora de Lanas S.A., Viña del Mar, Chile, 1941-46; asst. prof. physics U. Oreg., Eugene, 1953-58, assoc. prof., 1958-63, prof., 1963-89, prof. emeritus, 1989—, chmn. dept., 1976-84, dir. Chem. Physics Inst., 1984-87. Guest assoc. physicist Brookhaven Nat. Lab., Upton, N.Y., 1961-62; vis. prof. U. Calif., Berkeley, 1968-69, Université Pierre et Marie Curie, Paris, 1977; vis. scholar Stanford U., 1983; cons. Lawrence Radiation Lab., 1954-68, physicist, 1968-69; mem. com. on atomic and molecular sci. NRC/Nat. Acad. Scis., 1976-82; vis. scientist NASA Ames Rsch. Ctr., 1975-76; mem. panel on radiation rsch. NRC, 1985-87, chair bd. on assessment of NIST programs panel on atomic molecular and optical physics, 1989-90; chair exec. com. Advanced Light Source Users, 1984-88, sci. policy bd., 1989-92; chair adv. bd. Basic Energy Scis. Synchrotron Radiation Ctr. Argonne Nat. Lab, 1991-93; mem. U. Chgo. Review Com. for Argonne Nat. Lab. Physics Divsn., 1993-98; U.S. advisor in physics U.S.-Mex. Found. for Sci., 1994-97. Author: (with J.L. Powell) Quantum Mechanics, 1961; editor: Atomic Inner Shell Processes, 1975, Atomic Inner-Shell Physics, 1985; editor Phys. Rev. A., 1992—; mem. editorial bd. Phys. Rev. C, 1978, Atomic Data and Nuclear Data Tables, 1982—; mem. publs. bd. Am. Inst. Physics, 1992—; contbr. articles to sci. jours. Mem. region XIV selection com. Woodrow Wilson Nat. Fellowship Found., 1959-61, 62-68. Recipient Ersted award for distinguished teaching U. Oreg., 1959; NSF research grantee, 1954-64; U.S. AEC grantee, 1964-72; NASA grantee, 1972-79; AFOSR grantee, 1979-86; NSF grantee, 1986-95. Fellow AAAS, Am. Phys. Soc. (chmn. div. electron and atomic physics 1981-82, councillor 1983-86, mem. com. on internat. sci. affairs 1997-2000, chmn. 2000); mem. ACLU, Am. Assn. Physics Tchrs. (pres. Oreg. sect. 1956-57), Croatian Acad. Scis. and Arts (corr. mem.), Sierra Club, Phi Beta Kappa. Office: U Oreg Dept Physics Eugene OR 97403-1274 E-mail: berndc@oregon.uoregon.edu

CRAVENS, KENT L. state senator; Owner small bus.; Rep. senator N.Mex. State Senate. Mem. conservation and edn. coms. N.Mex. State Senate. Home: 10717 Richfield Ave NE Albuquerque NM 87122 Office: NMex State Senate State Capitol Mail Rm Dept Santa Fe NM 87503 E-mail: senate@state.nm.us

CRAVER, THEODORE F., SR. utilites/energy executive; CEO Edison Internat., Rosemead, Calif., 2000—. Office: Edison Internat 2244 Walnut Grove Ave Rosemead CA 91770

CRAW, NICHOLAS WESSON, motor sports association executive; b. Governor's Island, N.Y., Nov. 14, 1936; s. Demas Thurlow Craw and Mary Victoria Wesson. BA cum laude, Princeton U., 1959; MBA, Harvard U., 1982. Dir. ops. Project Hope, Washington, 1960-68; pres., CEO Scorpio Racing, Washington, 1968-80, Sports Car Club Am., Englewood, Colo., 1983—. Pres. Sports Car Club Am. Found, Englewood, 1986—; chmn. Nat. Motorsports Coun., 1992—; bd. dirs. SCCA Pro Racing Ltd., SCCA Enterprises, Inc., USRRC, Rsch. Sys., Inc. Dir. Manpower divsn. VISTA, Washington, 1970-72; assoc. dir. ACTION, Washington, 1972-73; dir. U.S. Peace Corps, Washington, 1973-74. Office: Sports Car Club Am 9033 E Easter Pl Englewood CO 80112-2122

CRAWFORD, CINDY, model, actress; b. Dekalb, Ill., Feb. 20, 1966; d. Dan and Jennifer C.; m. Richard Gere, Dec. 12, 1991 (div.); m. Rande Gerber; 1 child. Student, Northwestern U. Model for Victor Skrebneski, 1984-86; signed with Elite Modeling Agy., 1986; spokesperson Revlon, 1989—, JH Collectibles, Pepsi Cola, Kay Jewelers; host MTV's House of Style, 1989-95. First featured on cover Vogue, 1986; exercise videos: Cindy Crawford's Shape Your Body Workout, 1992, The Next Challenge Workout, 1993; film appearances include: Fair Game, 1995; host TV special, 1995, also Sex with Cindy Crawford; feature corr. MTV. Supporter breast cancer rsch.; active Leukemia Soc. of Am. Office: Wolf-Kasteler 132 S Rodeo Dr Ste 300 Beverly Hills CA 90212-2414

CRAWFORD, CURTIS J. computer and electronics company executive; CEO Zilog, Campbell, Calif. Office: Zilog 910 E Hamilton Ave Ste 110 Campbell CA 95008-0612

CRAWFORD, DAVID L. astronomer; b. Tarenton, Pa., Mar. 2, 1931; s. William Letham and A. Blanche (Livingstone) C.; m. Mary Louise Meuller, Aug. 16, 1940; children: Christine, Deborah, Lisa. PhD, U. Chgo., 1958. Rsch. asst. Yerkes Obs., Chgo., 1953-57; asst. prof. Vanderbilt U., Nashville, 1957-59; staff astronomer Kitt Peak Nat. Obs., Tucson, 1960-96, emeritus astronomer, 1997—. Rsch. asst. McDonald Obs., 1955-57; project mgr. Kitt Peak Nat. Obs., 1963-73, assoc. dir. rsch., 1970-73, head office univ. rels., 1984-85, head office of tech. transfer, 1993-95; exec. dir. Internat. Dark-Sky Assn., 1987—, pres. bd. dirs. GNAT, Inc., 1993—. Recipient outstanding svc. award Astron. League, 1992. Fellow AAAS (coun. 1986-89, com. on coun. affairs 1986-88), Illuminating Engring. Soc. N.Am. (roadway lighting com., outdoor environ. lighting impact com., sports lighting com.); mem. Am. Astron. Soc. (coun. 1972-75, Van Briesbrock award 1997), Astron. Soc. Pacific (bd. dirs. 1970-76, nominating com., publs. com.), Internat. Astron. Union (active numerous commns., exec. coms., past chmn. working group on amateur/profl. rels.). Avocations: travel, reading, teaching, trout fishing, photography. Office: 1DA 3225 N First Ave Tucson AZ 85719 E-mail: crawford@darksky.org

CRAWFORD, DEBRA P. women's healthcare company executive; BSBA in Acctg., San Diego State U. CPA, Calif. Dir. fin., mfg. contr. Advanced Cardiovasc. Sys., Inc., 1992-94; v.p. fin. and adminstrn., treas., asst. sec. IVAC Corp., 1994; CFO, v.p., CFO, treas., sec. IVAC Med. Sys., Inc., 1995-96; CFO, treas. IVAC Holdings, Inc., 1996; ind. fin. cons., acting CFO or corp. devel. fin. cons., 1997-98; v.p., CFO, treas. Women First HealthCare, Inc., San Diego, 1998—, asst. sec., 1998-99, sec., 1999—. Office: Women First HealthCare Inc 12220 El Camino Real Ste 400 San Diego CA 92130-2091 Fax: 619-509-1353

CRAWFORD, DONALD WESLEY, philosophy educator, university official; b. Berkeley, Calif., July 30, 1938; s. Arthur Loyd and Josephine (Gareffa) C.; m. Sharon Dee Messenger, Nov. 5, 1960; children: Kathryn, Alison. BA, U. Calif., Berkeley, 1960; PhD, U. Wis., 1965. Teaching asst. U. Wis., Madison, 1962-64, instr., 1965, asst. prof., 1968-70, assoc. prof., 1970-74, prof., 1974-79, chair dept. philosophy, 1973-76, 79-81, dean Coll. Letters and Sci., 1989-92; asst. prof. U. Sask., Saskatchewan, Can., 1965-68; vice chancellor acad. affairs U. Calif., Santa Barbara, 1992-93, exec. vice chancellor, 1993-98, dir. London Ctr. for Edn. Abroad program, 1998-2000. Author: Kant's Aesthetic Theory, 1974; editor Jour. Aesthetics and Art Criticism, 1989-93. Bd. dirs. Meriter Hosp., Madison, 1989-92, Santa Barbara Bot. Garden, 1993-98, U. Calif. Santa Barbara Found., 1992-98. NEH fellow, 1974. Mem. Am. Philos. Assn., Am. Soc. for Aesthetic, Brit. Soc. for Aesthetic. Office: U Calif Dept Philosophy South Hall Santa Barbara CA 93106 E-mail: crawford@humanities.ucsb.edu

CRAWFORD, JAMES DEE, chemical distribution executive; b. Boise, Idaho, June 23, 1950; s. Glen E. and Beverly J. (Thomas) C.; m. Diane E. Crawford (Ball), July 8, 1994. BBA, Boise State U., 1972. CPA, Idaho. Staff acct. J.R. Simplot Co., Boise, 1972-75, corp. acctg. mgr., 1975-79, asst. controller Caldwell, Idaho, 1979-80; treas. Simcal Chem. Co., Fresno, Calif., 1980-83; dir. fin services J.R. Simplot Co., Boise, 1983-85, treas., 1985—; CFO Wilbur-Ellis, CA, 2000—. Bd. dirs. Micron Tech., Inc., Boise, formerly, dir. Investors Financial Corp., Bosie. Com. chmn. St. Alphonsus Found., Boise, 1985. Named one of Outstanding Young Men Am., Jaycees, 1974. Mem. Am. Inst. CPA's, Idaho Soc. CPA's, Nat. Assn. Corp. Treas. Republican. Episcopalian. Club: Crane Creek Country (Boise), City Club of San Francisco. Avocations: golf, skiing.

CRAWFORD, JOHN EDWARD, geologist, scientist; b. Richmond, Va., June 6, 1924; s. James Henry and Loretta Ellen (Bankerd) C.; m. Mary Elizabeth Ayres, May 15, 1948; children: Michelle Lorraine, Caprice Lizette. BA, Johns Hopkins, 1947. Reg. geologist, Calif. Geologist uranium exploration program U.S. Geol. Survey, 1948-51; nat. stockpile materials specialist Munitions Bd., Office Sec. Def., 1951-53; prodn. engr. AEC, 1953-54; specialist on source, feed, fissionable materials Bur. Mines, 1954-57, nuclear tech. adviser to dir., 1957-60, chief nuc. engr. for atomic rsch. programs, 1960-63; dir. Marine Mineral Tech. Ctr., Tiburon, Calif., 1963-66; pres., founder Crawford Marine Specialists, Inc., San Francisco, also Suva, Fiji, 1966-76; pres. Earth Tech. Corp., San Rafael, 1973-77; mgr. geothermal rsch. programs and Salton Sea sci. drilling project U.S. Dept. Energy Ops. Office, Oakland, Calif., 1977-89; mgr. ops. and prin. geologist Western Geologic Resources, Inc., San Rafael, 1989-90; cons. geothermal and environ. affairs, 1990—; assoc., regional mgr. Western Ops. Earth Resources Internat., L.C., Carson City, Nev., 1994-2000. Author: Facts Concerning Uranium Exploration and Production, 1956; contbr. articles to govt. and profl. jours., Leaders in Am. Sci. Vol. VIII, 1968-69. Mem. Calif. Gov.'s Commn. Ocean Resources, 1966-67, Calif. Gov.'s Small Hydro Task Force, 1981-82. Served with AUS, 1943-46. Mem. Internat. Marine Minerals Soc. (Moore medal for excellence in devel. of marine minerals 1998), Geol. Soc. Am., Geysers Geothermal Assn., Marine Tech. Soc. (past chmn. marine mineral resources com., past chmn. marine resources div.), Delta Upsilon. Home and Office: 1510 Valencia Ct Carson City NV 89703-2333

CRAWFORD, MARC, professional hockey coach; Head coach Quebec Nordiques, 1994-95, Colo. Avalanche, 1995-97, Vancouver Canucks, Vancouver, 1998-. Recipient Louis A.R. Pieri Meml. award, 1992-93, Jack Adams award, 1994-95; named NHL Coach of Yr. The Sporting News, 1994-95.

CRAWFORD, MICHAEL, city council; married. BS in Computer Sci., Wright State U., 1988; law degree, U. Ariz., 1991. Clk. Ariz. Ct. Appeals; computer software cons.; vice chmn. Ariz. Common Cause; criminal def. atty. Pima County Pub. Defenders Office, 1994-98; with O'Connor, Cavanaugh, Malloy, Jones, Tucson, 1998—. Office: O'Connor Cavanaugh Malloy Jones 32 N Stone Ave Ste 2100 Tucson AZ 85701-1403

CRAWFORD, MICHAEL HOWARD, cardiologist, educator, researcher; b. Madison, Wis., July 10, 1943; s. William Henry and A. Kay (Keller) C.; m. Janis Raye Kirschner, June 23, 1968; children: Chelsea Susan, Dinah Jaye, Stuart Michael. AB, U. Calif., Berkeley, 1965; MD, U. Calif., San Francisco, 1969. Diplomate Am. Bd. Internal Medicine and sub-bd. Cardiovascular Disease. Med. resident U. Calif. Hosps., San Francisco, 1969-71; sr. med. resident Beth Israel Hosp., Boston, 1971-72; teaching fellow Harvard Med. Sch., Boston, 1971-72; cardiology fellow U. Calif. Hosps., San Diego, 1972-74; asst. prof. medicine U. Calif. Sch. Medicine, San Diego, 1974-76, U. Tex. Health Sci. Ctr., San Antonio, 1976-78, assoc. prof. medicine, 1978-82, prof. medicine, 1982-89; Robert S. Flinn prof. cardiology U. N.Mex. Sch. Medicine, Albuquerque, 1989—. Asst. dir. Ischemic Heart Disease Specialized Ctr. of Rsch., San Diego, 1975-76; adj. scientist S.W. Found. for Biomed Rsch., San Antonio, 1980-89; co-dir. div. cardiology U. Tex. Health Sci. Ctr., San Antonio, 1983-89; chief div. cardiology U. N.Mex. Sch. Medicine, Albuquerque, 1989—. Editor: Current Diagnosis and Treatment in Cardiology, 1995; editor Clin. Cardiology Alert newsletter, 1990—; cons. editor (periodical) Cardiology Clinics, 1989—; mem. editl. bd. Circulation jour., 1990-99, Jour. Am. Coll. Cardiology, 1992-95. Pres. Am. Heart Assn., San Antonio, 1981, Austin, Tex., 1987, chmn. coun. clin. cardiology, Dallas, 1989, pres., Albuquerque, 1995-96. Recipient Paul Dudley White award Assn. Mil. Surgeons of U.S., 1981, Merit Review grant Dept. VA, 1985; Rsch. Tng. grantee Nat. Heart Lung and Blood Inst., 1993—. Fellow Am. Coll. Cardiology, Am. Coll. Physicians, Am. Soc. Nuclear Cardiology; mem. Am. Soc. Echocardiography (bd. dirs. 1980-83), Am. Soc. Physician Execs., So. Soc. Clin. Investigation, Assn. Univ. Cardiologists, Western Assn. Physicians, Assn. Profs. Cardiology. Avocation: skiing. Office: Univ NMex Hosp 2211 Lomas Blvd NE Albuquerque NM 87106-2745

CRAWFORD, RANDI, women's healthcare company executive; d. Edward F. Calesa. BA in Liberal Arts, Villanova U. Cons. on creation and prodn. children's programming Fox TV, Lifetime TV, DIC Entertainment, Saban Entertainment, 1991-95; rsch. analyst Calesa Assocs., 1995-97; co-founder, v.p. mktg. rsch., sec. Women First HealthCare, Inc., San Diego, 1997-98, v.p. edn. program devel., 1998—. Office: Women First Health-Care Inc 12220 El Camino Real Ste 400 San Diego CA 92130-2091 Fax: 619-509-1353

CRAWFORD, RONALD MERRITT, history and geography educator; b. San Diego, Apr. 21, 1949; s. Leslie Merritt and Annie Louise (Briden) C. BA in History and Geography, UCLA, 1971, MA in History, 1972. Cert. standard secondary tchr. Tchr. social scis. divsn. Anchorage C.C., 1972-87; prof. Coll. Arts and Scis. U. Alaska Anchorage, 1987—, chmn. history/geography dept., 1988—. V.p. Anchorage C.C. Campus Assembly, 1985-87; 1st v.p. Faculty Senate U. Alaska Anchorage, 1987-89, 2d v.p., 1990-91; mem. Univ. Assembly, 1988-89; mem. Bartlett lectr. com. U. Alaska Anchorage, 1987-90, audio-visual adv. bd., 1989—, promotion and tenure appeals com., 1989-90; mem. exec. bd. Alaska C.Cs. Fedn. Tchrs., 1984—, Harry S. Truman scholarship com. Anchorage C.C., 1978-82; advisor Golden Key Honor Soc., 1993—, Campus Cinema Film Series, 1972—, Anchorage C.C. Student Assn., 1983-85; coord. history/geography discipline Anchorage C.C., 1979-87; columnist Anchorage Daily News, 1984-87; host Alaska Home and Gardens Program Sta. KAKM-TV, 1990. Host fund drives Sta. KAKM-TV, 1983—; guest speaker Anchorage Sch. Dist. Community Resource Ctr., 1972—, McLaughlin Youth Ctr., 1975—; advisor Friends of Libr. Film Program Loussac Libr., 1985—; presenter geography awareness programs Alaska Staff Devel. Network Summer Acad., 1990, 91, Alaska Geog. Alliance Inst., 1992, 93. Recipient Disting. Teaching Achievement award Alaska State Legislature, 1992, Disting. Teaching Achievement award Nat. Coun. Geog. Edn., 1992. Mem. Am. Fedn. Tchrs., Am. Film Inst., Nat. Coun. Geographic Edn., Alaska Geography Alliance, Assn. Pacific Coast Geographers, Univ. Film and Video Assn., Phi Alpha Theta. Avocations: travel, movie history, hiking, photography, videography. Home: PO Box 670572 Chugiak AK 99567-0572 Office: U Alaska Dept History & Geography 3211 Providence Dr Anchorage AK 99508-4614

CRAWFORD, ROY EDGINGTON, III, lawyer; b. Topeka, Dec. 23, 1938; s. Roy E. and Ethel Trula (Senne) C.; children: Michael, Jennifer. B.S., U. Pa., 1960; LL.B., Stanford U., 1963. Bar: Calif. 1964, U.S. Ct. Mil. Appeals 1964, U.S. Tax Ct. 1969, U.S. Dist. Ct. (no. dist.) Calif. 1971, U.S. Ct. Claims 1974, U.S. Supreme Ct. 1979. Assoc. Brobeck Phleger & Harison, San Francisco, 1967-73, ptnr., 1973—. Bd. dirs. Sqauw Valley Ski Corp. Contbr. chpts. to books; bd. editors: Stanford U. Law Rev., 1962-63. Served to capt. AUS, 1964-67. Recipient award of merit U.S. Ski Assn., 1980 Mem. ABA (chmn. com. on state and local taxes 1979-81), Calif. State Bar Assn., San Francisco Bar Assn., Calif. Trout (bd. dirs. 1970—, v.p. 1975-94, sec.-treas. 1994-2001), The Nature Conservancy of Idaho (bd. dirs. 1994—), Yosemite Inst. (bd. dirs. 1997—), Beta Gamma Sigma. Office: Brobeck Phleger & Harrison Spear St Tower 1 Market Plz Ste 341 San Francisco CA 94105-1420

CREAGER, JOE SCOTT, geology and oceanography educator; b. Vernon, Tex., Aug. 30, 1929; s. Earl Litton and Irene Eugenia (Keller) C.; m. Barbara Clark, Aug. 30, 1951 (dec.); children: Kenneth Clark, Vanessa Irene; m. B. J. Wren, Sept. 5, 1987 (dec.); m. Eva R. Milligan, Mar. 18, 2001. BS, Colo. Coll., 1951; postgrad., Columbia, 1952-53; MS, Tex. A&M U., 1953, PhD, 1958. Asst. prof. dept. oceanography U. Wash., Seattle, 1958-61, assoc. prof., 1962-66, prof. oceanography, 1966-91, prof. geol. scis., 1981-91, prof. emeritus, 1991—, asst. chmn. dept. oceanography, 1964-65, assoc. dean arts and scis. for earth and planetary scis., 1966-95, assoc. dean for rsch., 1966-91, divisional dean emeritus, 1995—; program dir. for oceanography NSF, 1965-66; chief scientist numerous oceanographic expdns. to Arctic and Sub-arctic including Leg XIX of Deep Sea Drilling project, 1959-91. Vis. geol. scientist Am. Geol. Inst., 1962, 63, 65; U.S. Nat. coord. Internat. Indian Ocean Expedition, 1965-66; vis. scientist program lectr. Am. Geophys. Union, 1965-72; Battelle cons., advanced waste mgmt., 1974; cons. to U.S. Army C.E., 1976, U.S. Depts. Interior and Commerce, 1975; exec. sec., exec. com., chmn. planning com. Joint Oceanographic Insts. Deep Earth Sampling, 1970-72, 76-78; mem. evaluation com. Northwest Assn. Schs. and Colls., 1989-99. Mem. editorial bd. Internat. Jour. Marine Geology, 1964-91; assoc. editor Jour. Sedimentary Petrology, 1963-76; asst. editor Quaternary Research, 1970-79; contbr. articles to profl. jours. Skipper Sea Scout Ship, Boy Scouts Am., Bryan, Tex., 1957; coach Little League Baseball, Seattle, 1964-71, sec., 1971; cons. sci. curriculum Northshore Sch. Dist., 1970; mem. Seattle Citizens Shoreline Com., 1973-74, King County Shoreline Com., 1980. Served with U.S. Army, 1953-55. Colo. Coll. scholar, 1949-51; NSF grantee, 1962-82; ERDA grantee, 1962-64; U.S. Army C.E. grantee, 1975-82; Office of Naval Research grantee; U.S. Dept. Commerce grantee; U.S. Geol. Survey grantee. Fellow Geol. Soc. Am., AAAS; mem. Internat. Assn. Quaternary Research, Am. Geophys. Union, Internat. Assn. Sedimentology, Internat. Assn. Math. Geologists, Soc. Econ. Paleontologists and Mineralists, Marine Tech. Soc. (sec.-treas. 1972-75), Sigma Xi, Beta Theta Pi, Delta Epsilon. Home: 13432 NE 36th Pl Bellevue WA 98005 Office: U Wash PO Box 353765 Seattle WA 98195-3765 E-mail: bjajoe@worldart.att.net

CREAN, JOHN C. retired housing and recreational vehicles manufacturing company executive; b. Bowden, N.D., 1925; married Founder Fleetwood Enterprises, Inc., Riverside, Calif., 1950, pres., 1952-70, chmn., chief exec. officer, 1950-98, also dir. Served with USN, 1942; with U.S. Mcht. Marines, 1944-45 Office: PO Box 8449 Newport Beach CA 92658-8449

CREECH, WILBUR LYMAN, retired career officer; b. Argyle, Mo., Mar. 30, 1927; s. Paul and Marie (Maloney) C.; m. Carol Ann DiDomenico, Nov. 20, 1969; 1 son, William L. Student, U. Mo., 1946-48; B.S., U. Md., 1960; M.S., George Washington U., 1966; postgrad., Nat. War Coll., 1966. Commd. 2d lt. U.S. Air Force, 1949; advanced through grades to gen.; fighter pilot 103 combat missions USAF, North Korea, 1950-51; pilot USAF Thunderbirds, 1953-56; comdr., leader Skyblazers, Europe aerial demo team USAF, 1956-60; dir. Fighter Weapons Sch., Nellis AFB, Nev., 1960-61; advisor to comdr. Argentine Air Force, 1962; exec., aide to comdr. Tactical Air Command, 1962-65; dep. comdr. fighter wing, 177 combat missions in F-100 fighters and asst. dep. chief staff for ops. 7th Air Force, Vietnam, 1968-69; comdr. fighter wings USAF in Europe, Spain and W.Ger., 1969-71; dep. for ops. and intelligence Air Forces Europe, 1971-74; comdr. Electronic Systems Div., Hanscom AFB, Mass., 1974-77; asst. vice chief of staff HQS Air Force, Washington, 1977-78; comdr. Tactical Air Command, Langley AFB, Va., 1978-85. Lectr., internat. mgmt. expert; cons. in field. Author: The Five Pillars of TQM, 1994. Decorated D.S.M. with three oak leaf clusters, Silver Star medal, Legion of Merit with two oak leaf clusters, D.F.C. with three oak leaf clusters, Air medal with 14 oak leaf clusters, Air Force Commendation medal with two oak leaf clusters, Army Commendation medal; Spanish Grand Cross. Home and Office: 20 Quail Run Rd Henderson NV 89014-2147

CREGG, HUGH ANTHONY See LEWIS, HUEY

CREIGHTON, JOHN WALLIS, JR. novelist, publisher, former management educator, consultant; b. Yeung Kong, China, Apr. 7, 1916; s. John Wallis and Lois (Jameson) C.; m. Harriet Harrington, June 30, 1940; childrn: Carol (Mrs. Brian LeNeve), Joan (Mrs. Robert Nielsen). Student, Wooster Coll., 1933-36; BS in Forestry, U. Mich., 1938; AB, Hastings Coll., 1939; PhD in Wood Tech. and Indsl. Engring., U. Mich., 1954. Operator, sawmill, Cayahoga Falls, Ohio, 1939-41; mem. staff U.S. Bd. Econ. Warfare, Ecuador, 1941-44; asst. gen. mgr. R.S. Bacon Veneer Co., Chgo., 1944-45; gen. mgr., v.p. Bacon Lumber Co., Sunman, Ind., 1944-45; mem. faculty Mich. State U., Lansing, 1945-54, prof. wood tech., 1945-54; asst. to gen. mgr., v.p. Baker Furniture Inc., Grand Rapids, Mich., 1954-58; pres. Creighton Bldg. Co., Santa Barbara, Calif., 1958-65; prof. mgmt. Colo. State U., Fort Collins, 1965-67, U.S. Naval Postgrad. Sch., Monterey, Calif., 1967-86, emeritus prof., 1986—, chmn. dept., 1967-71, dir. fed. exec. mgmt. program, 1974-82. Cons. to govt. Assoc editor and co-founder Jour. Tech. Transfer, 1975-88; contbr. papers to field. Former mem. Forestry Commn., Carmel, Calif., 1986-95. Recipient various research grants in lumber mfg., research and orgn. studies for U.S. Navy and U.S. Forest Service. Mem. Tech. Transfer Soc., Writer's Internat. Network, Calif. Writer's Club. Presbyterian. Home: 8065 Lake Pl Carmel CA 93923-9514

CREIGHTON, NORMAN P. bank executive; B in Banking and Fin. with honors, U. Mont. With Ariz. Bank, Gt. Western Bank and Trust; pres., CEO Imperial Bank, Inglewood, Calif., 1985-97, CEO, vice chmn., 1997—. Bd. dirs. Imperial Bancorp. Bd. dirs. Ind. Colls. So. Calif., U. Mont. Found. Mem. Assn. Res. City Bankers, Def. Orientation Conf. Assn. Office: Imperial Bankcorp 9920 S La Cienega Blvd Fl 14 Inglewood CA 90301-4417

CREMIN, ROBERT W. manufacturing executive; b. 1940; BS in Metallurgical Engring., Polytech. Inst. Brooklyn; MBA, Harvard U. Grad. Sch. Bus. Mktg. mgmt. Omark Inds., Portland, Oreg.; exec. mgmt. Esterlin Techs., Bellevue, Wash., 1989-97, pres., COO, 1997-01, pres., COO, chmn. bd. dirs., 2001—. Office: Esterline Techs Corp 10800 NE 8th St Ste 600 Bellevue WA 98004

CRERAND, RAYMOND F. hospital administrator; MA in Healthcare Adminstrn., Washington U., St. Louis. Assoc. adminstr. Providence Portland (Oreg.) Med. Ctr.; sr. assoc. adminstr. St. Joseph Med. Ctr., Burbank, Calif.; with Good Samaritan Hosp. and Med. Ctr., Portland, Providence Health Sys., Portland, 1979—, CEO. Fellow Am. Coll. Healthcare Execs. (mem. bd. govs. dist. 7, regent, 1991-95); mem. Am. Hosp. Assn. (mem. policy bd. region 9), Wash. State Hosp. Assn. (chair). Office: Providence Health Sys NW Wash PO Box 1147 1321 Colby Everett WA 98206-1147 Fax: 425-261-4051. E-mail: rcrerand@providence.org

CREWS, FREDERICK CAMPBELL, humanities educator, writer; b. Phila., Feb. 20, 1933; s. Maurice Augustus and Robina (Gaudet) C.; m. Betty Claire Peterson, Sept. 9, 1959; children: Gretchen Elizabeth, Ingrid Anna Crews Márquez. AB, Yale U., 1955; PhD, Princeton U., 1958. Faculty U. Calif., Berkeley, 1958—, instr. in English, 1958-60, asst. prof., 1960-62, assoc. prof., 1962-66, prof., 1986-94, vice-chair for grad. studies, 1988-92, chair dept., 1992-94; prof. emeritus, 1994—. Mem. study fellowship selection com. Am. Coun. Learned Socs., 1971-73; mem. selection com. summer seminars Nat. Endowment for Humanities, 1976-77; Ward-Phillips lectr. U. Notre Dame, 1974-75, Dorothy T. Burstein lectr. UCLA, 1984; Frederick Ives Carpenter vis. prof. U. Chgo., 1985; Lansdowne visitor U. Victoria, 1987-88; John Dewey lectr., 1988, Nina Mae Kellogg lectr. Portland (Oreg.) State U., 1989; mem. exec. com. bd. dirs. Mark Twain Project, 1984-94; faculty rsch. lectr. U. Calif., Berkeley, 1991-92; David L. Kubal Meml. lectr. Calif. State U., L.A., 1994; mem. sci. and profl. adv. bd. False Memory Syndrome Found., 1994—; mem. exec. coun. Com. for Sci. Investigation of Claims of the Paranormal, 2000—. Author: The Tragedy of Manners, 1957, E.M. Forster: The Perils of Humanism, 1962, The Pooh Perplex, 1963, The Sins of the Fathers, 1966, The Patch Commission, 1968, The Random House Handbook, 1974, 6th edit., 1992, Out of My System, 1975, Skeptical Engagements, 1986, 2000, The Critics Bear it Away, 1992, Postmodern Pooh, 2001; co-author: The Borzoi Handbook for Writers, 1985, 3d edit., 1993; prin. author: The Memory Wars, 1995; editor: The Red Badge of Courage (Crane), 1964, Great Short Works of Nathaniel Hawthorne, 1967, Starting Over, 1970, Psychoanalysis and Literary Process, 1970, The Random House Reader, 1981, Unauthorized Freud, 1998; mem. contbg. bd. editors The Common Review, 2000—. Recipient Essay prize Nat. Endowment Arts, 1968, Disting. Tchg. award U. Calif., Berkeley, 1985, Spielvogel Diamonstein PEN prize, 1992; named Fulbright lectr. Turin, Italy, 1961-62; fellow Am. Coun. Learned Socs., 1965-66, Ctr. for Advanced Study in Behavioral Scis., 1965-66, Guggenheim Found., 1970-71, Am. Acad. Arts and Scis., 1992. Home: 636 Vincente Ave Berkeley CA 94707-1524 E-mail: fredc@socrates.berkeley.edu

CREWS, JAMES CECIL, hospital administrator; b. Marshalltown, Iowa, July 29, 1937; married. BA, U. Wis., 1959; MA, U. Iowa, 1964. Asst. adminstr. Meth. Asbury Hosps., Mpls., 1964, adminstrv. resident, 1963-64, adminstr., 1964-66, Illini Hosp., Silvis, Ill., 1966-69, Charleston Gen. Hosp., W.Va., 1969-72; exec. v.p. Charleston Area Med. Ctr., Charleston, 1972-81, pres., 1981-88; exec. v.p., COO VHA Enterprises Inc., Irving, Tex., 1988-89, acting pres., CEO, 1989-90; pres., CEO Samaritan Health Svcs., Phoenix, 1990, Samaritan Health System, Phoenix, 1991—. Mem. W.Va. Hosp. Assn. (bd. dirs., pres 1979—). Office: Samaritan Health System 1441 N 12th St Phoenix AZ 85006-2837

CREWS, WILLIAM ODELL, JR. religious organization administrator; b. Houston, Feb. 8, 1936; s. William O. Sr. and Juanita (Pearson) C.; m. Wanda Jo Ann Cunningham; 1 child, Ronald Wayne. BA, Hardin Simmons U., 1957, HHD, 1987; BDiv, Southwestern Bapt. Theol. Sem., 1964; DD, Calif. Bapt. Coll., 1987; DMin, Golden Gate Bapt. Theol. Sem., 2000. Ordained to ministry Bapt. Ch., 1953. Pastor Grape Creek Bapt. Ch., San Angelo, Tex., 1952-54, Plainview Bapt. Ch., Stamford, 1955-57, 1st Bapt. Ch., Sterling City, 1957-60, 7th St. Bapt. Ch., Ballinger, 1960-65, Woodland Heights Bapt. Ch., Brownwood, 1965-67, Victory Bapt. Ch., Seattle, 1967-72, Met. Bapt. Ch., Portland, Oreg., 1972-77; dir. comm. N.W. Bapt. Conv., Portland, 1977-78; pastor Magnolia Ave Bapt. Ch., Riverside, Calif., 1978-86; pres. Golden Gate Bapt. Theol. Sem., Mill Valley, 1986—. Pres. N.W. Bapt. Conv., Portland, 1974-76, So. Bapt. Gen. Conv. Calif., Fresno, 1982-84. Trustee Fgn. Mission Bd., Richmond, Va., 1973-78, Golden Gate Bapt. Theol. Sem., 1980-85, Marin Cmty. Hosp. Found., 1992-95; bd. dirs. Midway Seatac Boys Club, Des Moines, 1969-72, Marin Gen. Hosp., 1998—, Norm Bay Coun., 1998—. Mem. Marin County C. of C. (bd. dirs. 1987-95), Midway C. of C. (bd. dirs. 1968-72), Rotary (bd. dirs. San Rafael chpt. 1992—, pres. Portland club 1975-76, pres.-elect Riverside club 1984-85). Home: 157 Chapel Dr Mill Valley CA 94941-3168 Office: Golden Gate Bapt Theol Sem 201 Seminary Dr Mill Valley CA 94941-3197

CRICK, FRANCIS HARRY COMPTON, science educator, researcher; b. June 8, 1916; s. Harry and Anne Elizabeth (Wilkins) C.; m. Ruth Doreen Dodd, 1940 (div. 1947); 1 son; m. Odile Speed, 1949; 2 daus. B.Sc., Univ. Coll., London; PhD, Cambridge U., Eng. Scientist Brit. Admiralty, 1940-47, Strangeways Lab., Cambridge, Eng., 1947-49; with Med. Rsch. Coun. Lab. of Molecular Biology, Cambridge, 1949-77; Kieckhefer Disting. prof. Salk Inst. Biol. Studies, San Diego, 1977—, non-resident fellow, 1962-73, pres., 1994-95. Adj. prof. psychology U. Calif., San Diego; vis. lectr. Rockefeller Inst., N.Y.C., 1959; vis. prof. chemistry dept. Harvard U., 1959, vis. prof. biophysics, 1962; fellow Churchill Coll., Cambridge, 1960-61; Korkes Meml. lectr. Duke U., 1960; Henry Sidgewick Meml. lectr. Cambridge U., 1963; Graham Young lectr., Glasgow, 1963; Robert Boyle lectr. Oxford U., 1963; Vanuxem lectr. Princeton U., 1964; William T. Sedgwick Meml. lectr. MIT, 1965; Cherwell-Simon Meml. lectr. Oxford U., 1966; Shell lectr. Stanford U., 1969; Paul Lund lectr. Northwestern U., 1977; Dupont lectr. Harvard U., 1979, numerous other invited meml. lectrs. Author: Of Molecules and Men, 1966, Life Itself, 1981, What Mad Pursuit, 1988, The Astonishing Hypothesis: The Scientific Search for the Soul, 1994; contbr. papers and articles on molecular, cell biology and neurobiology to sci. jours. Recipient Prix Charles Leopold Mayer French Academies des Scis., 1961; (with J.D. Watson) Rsch. Corp. award, 1961, Warren Triennial prize, 1959, (with J.D. Watson & Maurice Wilkins) Lasker award, 1960, Nobel Prize for medicine, 1962; Gairdner Found. award, 1962, Royal Medal Royal Soc., 1972, Copley medal, 1975, Michelson-Morley award, 1981, Benjamin P. Cheney medal, 1986, Golden Plate award, 1987, Albert medal Royal Soc. Arts, London, 1987, Wright Prize VIII Harvey Mudd Coll., 1988, Joseph Priestly award Dickinson Coll., 1988, Order of Merit, 1991, Disting. Achievement award Oreg State U. Friends of Libr., 1995, Liberty medal, 2000, Benjamin Franklin award Disting. Achievement in Scis., 2001; hon. fellow Harris Manchester Coll., Oxford. Fellow AAAS, Univ. Coll. London, Royal Soc., Indian Nat. Sci. Acad., Rochester Mus., Indian Acad. Scis. (hon.), Churchill Coll. Cambridge (hon.), Royal Soc.

Edinburgh (hon.), Caius Coll. Cambridge (hon.), John Muir Coll. U. Calif., San Diego (hon.), Tata Inst. Fundamental Rsch., Bombay (hon.), Inst. Biology London (hon.); mem. Acad. Arts Scis. (fgn. hon.), Am. Soc. Biol. Chemists (hon.), U.S. Nat. Acad. Scis. (fgn. assoc.), German Acad. Sci., Am. Philos. Soc. (fgn. mem.), French Acad. Scis. (assoc. fgn. mem.), Royal Irish Acad. (hon.), Hellenic Biochemical and Biophysical Soc. (hon.), Academia Europaea. Office: Salk Inst Biol Studies PO Box 85800 San Diego CA 92186-5800

CRILLY, EUGENE RICHARD, engineering consultant; b. Phila., Oct. 30, 1923; s. Eugene John and Mary Virginia (Harvey) C.; m. Alice Royal Roth, Feb. 16, 1952. ME, Stevens Inst. Tech., 1944, MS, 1949, U. Penn., 1951; postgrad., UCLA, 1955-58. Sr. rsch. engr. N.Am. Aviation, L.A., 1954-57, Canoga Park and Downey, Calif., 1962-66; process engr. Northrop Aircraft Corp., Hawthorne, 1957-59; project engr., quality assurance mgr. HITCO, Gardena, 1959-62; sr. rsch. splist. Lockheed-Calif. Co., Burbank, 1966-74; engrng. splist. N.Am. aircraft ops. Rockwell Internat., El Segundo, 1974-89. Author tech. papers. Mem. nat. com. 125th Anniversary Founding of Stevens Inst. Tech. in 1870. Served with USNR, 1943-46; comdr. Res. ret. Mem. Soc. for Advancement Material and Process Engrng. (chmn. L.A. chpt. 1978-79, gen. chmn. 1981 symposium exhbn., nat. dir. 1979-86, treas. 1982-85, Award of Merit 1986), Naval Inst., Naval Res. Assn., VFW, Mil. Order World Wars (adj. San Fernando Valley chpt. 1985, 2d vice comdr. 1986, comdr. 1987-89, vice comdr. West, Dept. Cen. Calif., 1988-89, comdr. Cajon Valley San Diego chpt. 1990-92, adj./ROTC chmn. region XIV 1990-91, comdr. Dept. So. Calif. 1991-93, vice comdr. region XIV, 1992-93, dept. comdr. Gen. Staff Officer region XIV 1993-94, comdr. region XIV, 1994-95, Disting. Chpt. Comdr. Region XIV 1990-91, treas. region XIV 1998-99, treas. San Diego chpt. 1999-2000), Former Intelligence Officers Assn. (treas. San Diego chpt. one 1990-94), Ret. Officers Assn. (treas. Silver Strand chpt. 1992-2000, asst. treas. San Diego natl. conv., 2000), Navy League U.S. (treas. Coronado coun. 1997-2001), Naval Order U.S., Naval Intelligence Profls. Assn., Brit. United Svc. Club L.A., Marines Meml. Club (San Francisco), Coronado Round Tab le, Hammer Club of San Diego, Sigma Xi, Sigma Nu. Republican. Roman Catholic. Home and Office: 276 J Ave Coronado CA 92118-1138 E-mail: genecrilly@aol.com

CRIMINALE, WILLIAM OLIVER, JR. applied mathematics educator; b. Mobile, Ala., Nov. 29, 1933; s. William Oliver and Vivian Gertrude (Sketoe) C.; m. Ulrike Irmgard Wegner, June 7, 1962; children: Martin Oliver, Lucca. B.S., U. Ala., 1955; Ph.D., Johns Hopkins U., 1960. Asst. prof. Princeton (N.J.) U., 1962-68; asso. prof. U. Wash., Seattle, 1968-73, prof. oceanography, geophysics, applied math., 1973—, chmn. dept. applied math., 1976-84. Cons. Aerospace Corp., 1963-65, Boeing Corp., 1968-72, AGARD, 1967-68, Lenox Hill Hosp., 1967-68, ICASE, NASA Langley, 1990—; guest prof., Can., 1965, 2001, France, 1967-68, Germany, 1973-74, Sweden, 1973-74, Scotland, 1985, 89, 91, Eng., 1990, 91, Stanford, 1990, Brazil, 1992, 2001, Italy, 1999; Nat. Acad. exch. scientist USSR, 1969, 72. Author: Stability of Parallel Flows, 1967; Contbr. articles to profl. jours. Served with U.S. Army, 1961-62. Boris A. Bakmeteff Meml. fellow, 1957-58, NATO postdoctoral fellow, 1960-61, Alexander von Humboldt Sr. fellow, 1973-74, Royal Soc. fellow, 1990-91. Fellow Am. Phys. Soc.; mem. Am. Acad. Mechanics, Am. Geophys. Union, Fedn. Am. Scientists. Home: 1635 Peach Ct E Seattle WA 98112-3428 Office: U Wash Dept Applied Math Box 352420 Seattle WA 98195-2420 E-mail: lascala@amath.washington.edu

CRIPPIN, BRUCE D. state legislator, real estate manager; b. Billings, Mont., June 13, 1932; m. Mary Crippen; 4 children. BS, U. Mont., 1956, grad. Sch. Law, NYU. Mem. Mont. Ho. of Reps., Billings, 1981-99, minority whip, 1985-86, minority leader, 1991-92, 93-94; pres. pro tempore Mont. Senate, Billings, 1997-98, pres., 1999—, mem. ethics com., jud. com., legis. adminstrn. com., rules com. Served USN, 1952-54. Lutheran. Office: PO Box 80747 Billings MT 59108-0747 also: Capitol Station Helena MT 59620-1702

CRISCI, MATHEW G. marketing executive, writer; b. N.Y.C. s. Mathew Anthony and Frances (Coscia) C.; m. Mary Ann, Nov. 14, 1968; children: Mathew Joseph, Mark David, Mitchell Justin. BS, Iona Coll. Sr. v.p. Young & Rubicam, Inc., N.Y.C. and Sydney, Australia, 1968-82; exec. v.p., COO, bd. dirs. Integrated Barter Internat., N.Y.C., 1982-85; sr. v.p., gen. mgr., bd. dirs. Chiat/Day Advt. Inc., San Francisco, 1986-90; exec. v.p., mng. dir. Lowe Lintas Worldwide, N.Y.C., 1991-97; exec. v.p., chief mktg. officer Alton Entertainment Co., L.A., 1997—, also bd. dirs. Author: Observations of a Kind, 1998, This Little Piggy, 2001. Advisor bolt.com, ADZ Corp., Nat. Assn. H.S. Newspapers. Mem. Nat. Assn. H.S. Newspapers (mng. dir. 1996—, bd. dirs.). Office: Alton Entertainment Co 11340 W Olympic Blvd Los Angeles CA 90064-1608 E-mail: mcrisci-orcapub@msn.com, mattcrisci@home.com

CRISMAN, MARY FRANCES BORDEN, librarian; b. Tacoma, Nov. 23, 1919; d. Lindon A. and Mary Cecelia (Donnelly) Borden; m. Fredric Lee Crisman, Apr. 12, 1975 (dec. Dec. 1975). BA in History, U. Wash., 1943, BA in Librarianship, 1944. Asst. br. libr. in charge work with children Mottet br. Tacoma Pub. Libr., 1944-45, br. libr., 1945-49, br. libr. Moore br., 1950-55, asst. dir., 1955-70, dir., 1970-74, dir. emeritus, 1975—; mgr. corp. libr. Frank Russell Co., 1985-96, ret., 1997. Chmn. Wash. Cmty. Libr. Coun., 1970-72. Hostess program Your Libr. and You, Sta. KTPS-TV, 1969-71. Mem. Highland Homeowners League, Tacoma, 1980—, incorporating dir. 1980, sec. and registered agt., 1980-82; mem. Denham West Condominium Assn., Sun City, Ariz., 1995—, chairperson by laws com., 1999. Mem. ALA (chmn. mem. com. Wash. 1957-60, mem. nat. libr. week com. 1965, chmn. libr. adminstrn. divsn. nominating com. 1971, mem. ins. for librs. com. 1970-74, vice chmn. libr. adminstrn. divsn. personnel adminstrn. sect. 1972-73, chmn. 1973-74, mem. com. policy implementation 1973-74, mem. libr. orgn. and mgmt. sect. budgeting acctg. and costs com. 1974-75), Am. Libr. Trustee Assn. (legis. com. 1975-78, conf. program com. 1978-80, action devel. com. 1978-80), Pacific N.W. (trustee divsn. nominating com 1976-77), Wash. Libr. Assn. (exec. bd. 1957-59, state exec., dir. Nat. Libr. Week 1965, treas., exec. bd. 1969-71, 71-73), Urban Librs. Coun. (editl. sec. Newsletter 1972-73, exec. com. 1974-75), Ladies Aux. to United Transp. Union (past pres. Tacoma), Friends Tacoma Pub. Libr. (registered agt. 1975-83, sec. 1975-78, pres. 1978-80, bd. dirs. 1980-83), Smithsonian Assocs., Nat. Railway Hist. Soc., U. Wash. Alumni Assn., U. Wash. Sch. Librarianship Alumni Assn. Roman Catholic. Club: Quota Internat. (sec. 1957-58, 1st v.p. 1960-61, pres. 1961-62, treas. 1975-76, pres. 1979-80) (Tacoma). Home: 6501 N Burning Tree Ln Tacoma WA 98406-2108 also: 9054 N 109th Ave Sun City AZ 85351-4676

CRISMORE, WILLIAM, state legislator; b. Hot Springs, Mont., May 9, 1933; m. Carol Crismore. Grad., Hot Springs H.S. Owenr Crismore Logging and Road Maintenance Co.; mem. Mont. Senate, Dist. 41, Helena, 1994—; chair natural resources com.; mem. fish and game com., fin. and claims com. Mem. Mont. State Land. Bd. Adv. Coun., 1995—. Republican. Home: 237 Airfield Rd Libby MT 59923-8600 E-mail: crismore@libby.org

CRISP, DAVID, atmospheric physicist, research scientist; b. Las Vegas, May 10, 1956; s. Carroll and Louise (Martin) C.; m. Joy Anne Miller, June 13, 1981. BS in Edn. Curriculum and Instrn., Tex. A&M U., 1977; MA in Geophys. Fluid Dynamics, Princeton U., 1981, PhD in Geophys. Fluid Dynamics, 1983. Cert. secondary sch. tchr., Tex. Rsch. asst. Geophys. Fluid Dynamics Program, Princeton, N.J., 1979-83; postdoctoral fellow planetary sci. dept. Calif. Inst. Tech., Pasadena, 1984-86, rsch. scientist Jet Propulsion Lab., 1986—. Mem. planetary sci. data steering group NASA, Washington, 1975—. Contbr. articles to profl. publs. Grad. student fellow NASA, 1981-83; recipient Group Achievement award NASA, 1986, 94, Cert. of Appreciation NASA, 1991, 93, 94. Mem. Am. Astron. Soc., Am. Geophys. Union, Am. Meteorol. Soc. Achievements include patent for high performance miniature hygrometer and method thereof. Office: Calif Inst Tech Jet Propulsion Lab 241-105 4800 Oak Grove Dr Pasadena CA 91109

CRISP, MICHAEL GRAVES, publishing executive; b. Heath, Ky., July 4, 1937; s. Dwight Dean and Marie (Graves) C.; m. Jean Leslie Millspaugh, June 12, 1965; children: Michael Dwight, Jennifer Leslie, Meredith Brooke. AB, Colgate U., 1959; SEP, Stanford U., 1973. Editor-in-chief McGraw-Hill, N.Y.C., 1962-70; v.p., pub. Sci. Rsch. Assn., Chgo., 1970-85; chmn., CEO Crisp Publs. Inc., Menlo Park, Calif., 1985—. Bd. dirs. Mayfield Pub., Mountain View, Calif., Journeyware Multimedia, San Francisco, No. Calif. Employers Group, San Francisco, Crisp Publs., Inc., Menlo Park; adj. faculty U. Calif. Extension, Berkeley, 1990-94. Author: The Book Publishing Industry, 1984; editor: Rate Your Skills as a Manager, 1991, Twelve Steps to Self-Improvement, 1991, Achieving Job Satisfaction, 1994. Bd. dirs. Ladera (Calif.) Community Assn., 1972-74. Lt. j.g. USCG, 1959-62. Named Top Ten Bay Area Employers, Career Community Edn. Ctr., San Mateo, Calif., 1993, 100 Fastest Growing Bay Area Cos., San Francisco Business Times, 1993. Mem. Instrnl. Systems Assn., Tng. Media Assn., Am. Soc. Assn. Execs., U.S. C. of C., Internat. Soc. Retirement Planners, Nat. Soc. for Performance and Instruction. Republican. Avocations: winemaking, golf, travel, cooking. Office: Crisp Publs Inc 1200 Hamilton Ct Menlo Park CA 94025-1427

CRISTIANO, MARILYN JEAN, speech communication educator; b. New Haven, Jan. 10, 1954; d. Michael William and Mary Rose (Porto) C. BA, Marquette U., 1975, MA, 1977; postgrad., Ariz. State U., 1977; EdD, Nova Southeastern U., 1991. Speech comm. instr. Phoenix Coll., 1977-87, Paradise Valley C.C., Phoenix, 1987—. Presenter at profl. confs., workshops and seminars. Author tng. manual on pub. speaking, 1991, 92, 95, 97, 99. Named Technology Tchr. of Yr. for Ariz. Cmty. Colls., CCS Presentation Systems and Proxima Corp., 2000. Mem. Speech Comm. Assn., Western Speech Comm. Assn., Ariz. Comm. Assn. Avocation: tennis. Office: Paradise Valley CC 18401 N 32nd St Phoenix AZ 85032-1210

CRISTOL, STANLEY JEROME, chemistry educator; b. Chgo., June 14, 1916; s. Myer J. and Lillian (Young) C.; m. Barbara Wright Swingle, June 1957; children: Marjorie Jo, Jeffrey Tod. BS, Northwestern U., 1937; MA, UCLA, 1939, PhD, 1943. Rsch. chemist Std. Oil Co., Calif., 1938-41; rsch. fellow U. Ill., 1943-44; rsch. chemist U.S. Dept. Agr., 1944-46; asst. prof., then assoc. prof. U. Colo., 1946-55, prof., 1955—, Joseph Sewall Disting. prof., 1979—, chmn. dept. chemistry, 1960-62, grad. dean, 1980-81. Vis. prof. Stanford U., summer 1961, U. Geneva, 1975, U. Lausanne, Switzerland, 1981; with OSRD, 1944-46; adv. panels NSF, 1957-63, 69-73, NIH, 1969-72 Author: (with L.O. Smith, Jr.) Organic Chemistry, 1966; editorial bd., Chem. Revs., 1957-59, Jour. Organic Chemistry, 1964-68; contbr. rsch. articles to sci. jours. Guggenheim fellow, 1955-56, 81, 82; recipient James Flack Norris award in phys.-organic chemistry, 1972, Alumni Merit award Northwestern U., 1987. Fellow AAAS (councilor 1986-92); mem. NAS, AAUP, Am. Chem. Soc. (chmn. organic chemistry div. 1961-62, adv. bd. petroleum rsch. fund 1963-66, coun. policy com. 1968-73), Colo.-Wyo. Acad. Sci., Phi Beta Kappa, Sigma Xi, Phi Lambda Upsilon. Home: 2918 3d St Boulder CO 80304-3041 Office: U Colo Dept Chemistry-Biochemistry Cb 215 Boulder CO 80309-0215 E-mail: stanley.cristol@colorado.edu

CRISWELL, STEPHEN, astronomer; Program mgr. Fred Lawrence Whipple Obs., Amada, Ariz. Office: Fred Lawrence Whipple Obs PO Box 97 Amado AZ 85645-0097

CROCKER, MYRON DONOVAN, federal judge; b. Pasadena, Calif., Sept. 4, 1915; s. Myron William and Ethel (Shoemaker) C.; m. Elaine Jensen, Apr. 26, 1941; children— Glenn, Holly. A.B., Fresno State Coll., 1937; LL.B., U. Calif. at Berkeley, 1940. Bar: Calif. bar 1940. Spl. agt. FBI, 1940-46; practiced law Chowchilla, Calif., 1946-58; asst. dist. atty. Madera County, 1946-51; judge Chowchilla Justice Ct., 1952-58, Superior Ct. Madera County, 1958-59; U.S. judge Ea. Dist. Calif., Sacramento, 1959—; now sr. judge Eastern Dist. Calif., Sacramento. Mem. Madera County Rep. Ctrl. Com., 1950—. Named Outstanding Citizen Chowchilla, 1960 Mem. Chowchilla C. of C. (sec.) Lutheran. Club: Lion. Office: US Dist Courthouse 1130 O St Rm 5007 Fresno CA 93721-2201

CROCKER, THOMAS DUNSTAN, economics educator; b. Bangor, Maine, July 22, 1936; s. Floyd M. and Gloria F. (Thomas) C.; m. Sylvia Fleming, Dec. 31, 1961 (div. Sept. 1986); children: Sarah Lydia, Trena Elizabeth; m. Judith Powell, Sept. 9, 1989. AB, Bowdoin Coll., 1959; PhD, U. Mo., 1967. Asst. prof. econs. U. Wis., Milw., 1963-70; assoc. prof. U. Calif., Riverside, 1970-75; prof. U. Wyo., Laramie, 1975-2001, chairperson dept. econs. and fin., 1991-93, dir. Sch. Environment and Natural Resources, 1993-98, J.E. Warren distng. prof of Energy and Environment, 1997—, disting. prof. emeritus, 2001—. Rsch. assoc. U. Calif., Berkeley, 1973, Pa. State U., 1974; cons. Asarco, Inc., 1985-89, Mathtech, Inc., Princeton, N.J., 1987-88, Indsl. Econs., Inc., Cambridge, Mass., 1998-99, Shea and Gardner, Washington, 1989, Arco, Inc., 1992, A. Coors Co., 1992, Eastern Rsch. Group, 1997; mem. sci. adv. bd. EPA, Washington, 1973-76; mem. panel on long range transport issues U.S. Congress, Washington, 1981; mem. Gov.'s Competition Rev. Com., State of Wyo. Co-author: Environmental Economics, 1971; author, editor: Economic Perspectives on Acid Deposition Control, 1984; editorial coun. Jour. Environ. Econs. and Mgmt., 1973-88, 95-99; contbr. articles to profl. jours. Mem. com. impacts pollution on agriculture Orgn. for Econ. Cooperation and Devel., Paris, 1987-88. Grantee NSF, 1968, 73, 81, EPA, 1971, 76-85, 97-2001. Mem. Am. Econ. Assn., Assn. Environ. Resource Econs. (mem. awards structure com. 1981-83, contributed papers com. 1989), European Assn. Environ. Resource Econs., The Nature Conservancy. Republican. Avocations: skiing, bicycling, travel, trekking, rafting. Office: Univ Wyo Dept Econs Laramie WY 82071-3985 E-mail: tcrocker@uwyo.edu

CROCKETT, CLYLL WEBB, lawyer; b. Preston, Idaho, Feb. 16, 1934; s. Frank Lee and Alta (Webb) C.; m. Nan Marie Mattice, June 27, 1958; children— Jeffrey Webb, Nicole, Karen, Cynthia. B.S., Brigham Young U., 1958; M.B.A. Northwestern U, 1959; LL.B., U. Ariz., 1962. Bar: Ariz. 1962, U.S. Supreme Ct. 1970. Clk. Ariz. Supreme Ct., 1962-63; ptnr. Fennemore Craig, Phoenix, 1968—. Instr. eve. div. Mesa (Ariz.) C.C.; bd. dirs. S.W. Airlines Co. Mem. editorial bd. Ariz. Law Rev, 1961. Mem. charter rev. com., Scottsdale, Ariz., 1966-67; mem. bd. adjustment, Scottsdale, 1968-73, chmn., 1971-73; bd. dirs. Maricopa Mental Health Assn., 1976-78, Phoenix Cmty. Alliance, Valley Forward Assn.; mem. Mesa Crime Commn., 1980-82; mem. social scis. adv. bd. LDS Ch.; mem. State of Ariz. Gov.'s Regulatory Rev. Coun; mem. bd. of adjustment City of Mesa, 1996—. Mem. ABA, State Bar Ariz., Maricopa County Bar Assn., Am. Judicature Soc., Phoenix C. of C., Ariz. Acad. Republican. Home: 1510 N Gentry Cir Mesa AZ 85213-4001 Office: Fennemore Craig Ste 2600 3003 North Central Ave Phoenix AZ 85012-2913

CROCKETT, DONALD HAROLD, composer, university educator; b. Pasadena, Calif., Feb. 18, 1951; s. Harold Brown and Martha Amy C.; m. Karen Anne Gallagher Crockett, Nov. 11, 1972 (div. 1986); 1 child: Katherine Jane Crockett; m. Vicki Lyn Ray, June 6, 1988. MusB, U. So. Calif., 1974, MusM, 1976; PhD, U. Calif., Santa Barbara, 1981. Composer-in-residence Pasadena Chamber Orch., 1984-86, L.A. Chamber Orch., 1991-97. Asst. prof. U. So. Calif., L.A. 1981-84, assoc. prof., 1984-94,prof. 1994—; music dir., condr. U. So. Calif. Contemporary Music Ensemble, L.A., 1984—. Composer: Celestial Mechanics oboe and string quartet, 1990, Array string quartet number 1, 1987, Roethke Preludes for Orchestra, 1994, Concerto for Piano and Wind Ensemble, 1988, Scree for cello, piano and percussion, 1997, Island for concert band, 1998, The Falcon's Eye for solo guitar, 2000. Recipient Friedheim award Kennedy Ctr., Washington, 1991, Aaron Copland award Copland Heritage Assn., 1998; Goddard Lieberson Fellowship Am. Acad. of Arts and Letters, N.Y.C., 1994; Nat. Endowment for the Arts grantee, Washington, 1993; artists' fellow Calif. Arts Coun., 1999. Mem. BMI, Am. Music Ctr., Am. Composers Forum, Phi Kappa Phi. Avocations: reading, backpacking, skiing. Office: Univ Southern Calif School Of Music Los Angeles CA 90089-0851 E-mail: dcrocket@usc.edu

CROFTS, RICHARD A. academic administrator; PhD in Reformation History, Duke U. Mem. faculty U. Toledo; assoc. v.p. rsch., dean Grad. Sch. E. Tenn. State U.; dep. commr. acad. affairs Mo. Univ. Sys., Helena, 1994-96, commr. higher edn. Mont., 1996—. Office: Mont Univ Sys PO Box 203101 2500 E Broadway St Helena MT 59620-3101

CROMBIE, DOUGLASS DARNILL, aerospace communications system engineer; b. Alexandra, N.Z., Sept. 14, 1924; came to U.S., 1962, naturalized, 1967. s. Colin Lindsay and Ruth (Darnill) C.; m. Pauline L.A. Morrison, Mar. 2, 1951. B.Sc., Otago U., Dunedin, N.Z., 1947, M.Sc., 1949. N.Z. nat. rsch. fellow Cavendish Lab., Cambridge, Eng., 1958-59; head radio physics divsn. N.Z. Dept. Sci. and Indsl. Rsch., 1961-62; chief spectrum utilization divsn., chief low frequency group Inst. Telecommunications Scis., Dept. Commerce, Boulder, Colo., 1962-71, dir. inst., 1971-76; dir. Inst. Telecommunication Scis., Nat. Telecommunications and Info. Adminstrn., Boulder, 1976-80; chief scientist Nat. Telecommunication and Info. Agy., 1980-85; sr. engrng. specialist Aerospace Corp., Los Angeles, 1985—. Served with N.Z. Air Force, 1943-44. Recipient Gold medal Dept. Commerce, 1970, citation, 1972 Fellow IEEE; mem. NAE, Union Radio Sci. Internat. Home: 524 Standard St El Segundo CA 90245-3039 Office: The Aerospace Corp PO Box 92957 Los Angeles CA 90009-2957

CROMLEY, BRENT REED, lawyer; b. Great Falls, Mont., June 12, 1941; s. Arthur and Louise Lilian (Hiebert) C.; m. Dorothea Mae Zamborini, Sept. 9, 1967; children: Brent Reed Jr., Giano Lorenzo, Taya Rose. AB in Math., Dartmouth Coll., 1963; JD with honors, U. Mont., 1968. Bar: Mont. 1968, U.S. Dist. Ct. Mont. 1968, U.S. Ct. Appeals (9th cir.) 1968, U.S. Supreme Ct. 1978, U.S. Ct. Claims 1988, U.S. Ct. Appeals (D.C. cir.) 1988. Law clk. to presiding justice U.S. Dist. Ct. Mont., Billings, 1968-69; assoc. Hutton & Sheehy and predecessor firms, Billings, 1969-77, ptnr., 1977-78, Moulton, Bellingham, Longo & Mather, P.C., Billings, 1979—, also bd. dirs.; mem. Montana Ho. Reps., 1991-92; pres. State Bar Mont., 1998-99. Contbr. articles to profl. jours. Mem. Yellowstone Bd. Health, Billings, 1972—; chmn. Mont. Bd. Pers. Appeals, 1974-80. Mem. ABA (appellate practice com.), ACLU, Internat. Assn. Def. Counsel, State Bar Mont. (chmn. bd. trustees 1995-97, trustee 1991—, pres. 1998-99), Yellowstone County Bar Assn. (various offices), Internat. Assn. Def. Counsel, Christian Legal Soc., Internat. Brotherhood of Magicians, Kiwanis. Avocations: running, magic, pub. speaking. Home: 235 Parkhill Dr Billings MT 59101-0660 Office: Moulton Bellingham Longo & Mather PC 27 N 27th St Ste 1900 Billings MT 59101-2399 E-mail: Cromley@moultonlawfirm.com

CRONIN, THOMAS EDWARD, academic administrator; b. Milton, Mass., Mar. 18, 1940; s. Joseph M. and Mary Jane Cronin; m. Tania Zaroodny, Nov. 26, 1966; 1 child, Alexander. AB, Holy Cross Coll., 1961; MA, Stanford U., 1964, PhD, 1968; LLD (hon.), Marietta Coll., 1987, Franklin Coll., 1993. Tchg. fellow Stanford (Calif.) U., 1962-64; staff mem. The White House, Washington, 1966-67; faculty mem. U. N.C., 1967-70; staff fellow Brookings Instn., 1970-72; faculty mem. Brandeis U., Waltham, Mass., 1975-77, U. Del., Newark, 1977-79; McHugh prof. of Am. instns. The Colo. Coll., Colorado Springs, 1985-93, acting pres., 1991; pres. Whitman Coll., Walla Walla, Wash., 1993—. Bd. dirs. Cascade Natural Gas Co.; moderator Aspen Inst. Exec. Seminars, 1975—; pres. CRC, Inc., 1980—, Presidency Rsch. Group, 1981-82; cons. in field; guest polit. analyst various tv programs; mem. Wash. Commn. on Humanities, Marcus Whitman Found. Author: The State of the Presidency, 1980, Direct Democracy, 1989, Colorado Politics and Government, 1993, The Paradoxes of the American Presidency, 1998; co-author: Government By the People, 2001. Dir. Nat. Civic League, Denver, Inst. for Ednl. Leadership, Washington; bd. dirs. Inst. Am. Am. Univs. Mem. Am. Polit. Sci. Assn. (exec. com. 1990-92), Western Polit. Sci. Assn. (pres. 1993-94), Inst. Edn. Internat. Students, C. of C., Pi Sigma Alpha. Avocations: tennis, skiing, basketball, squash. Office: Whitman Coll Pres Ofc Memorial 303 345 Boyer Ave Walla Walla WA 99362-2067

CRONK, WILLIAM F., III, food products executive; b. 1943; m. Janet Cronk; 3 children. Pres., dir. Dreyer's Grand Ice Cream, Inc., Oakland, Calif., 1977—. Mem. adv. bd. Haas Bus. Sch. U. Calif., Berkeley. Nat. commr. Boy Scouts Am.; mem. Nat. Recreation Lakes Study Commn. Office: Dreyer's Grand Ice Cream Inc 5929 College Ave Oakland CA 94618

CROOK, SEAN PAUL, aerospace systems division director; b. Pawtucket, R.I., July 6, 1953; s. Ralph Frederick and Rosemary Rita (Dolan) C.; m. Mary Wickman, June 10, 1978; children: Kimberly Anne, Kelly Dolan, Erin Webster, Mary Katherine. BSME, U.S. Naval Acad., 1975; MBA, U. So. Calif., 1991. Commd. ensign USN, 1975, advanced through grades to lt., 1979, resigned, 1981; sr. systems engr. space divsn. GE, Springfield, Va., 1982-84; sr. aerospace systems engr. Martin Marietta Aero. Def. Systems, Long Beach, Calif., 1984-87; sr. aerospace system engrng. mgr. Martin Marietta Aero Def. Systems, Long Beach, 1987-93; chief engr. GDE Sys. Inc., A Tracer Co., San Diego, 1993-96, program mgr., 1996-99; program dir. BAE Sys., San Diego, 1999-2001; divsn. dir. BAE Sys.-Integrated Sys., Reston, Va., 2001—. Sec., bd. dirs. Guardian Minerals Inc. Comdr. USNR, 1992-97. Mem. Am. Mgmt. Assn., U. So. Calif. Exec. MBA Alumni Assn. (bd. dirs.), U.S. Naval Acad. Alumni Assn. Avocation: financial planning. Home: 23565 Via Calzada Mission Viejo CA 92691-3625 Office: BAE Sys PO Box 509008 San Diego CA 92150-9008 E-mail: scrook9344@aol.com, sean.crook@baesystems.com

CROOKE, STANLEY THOMAS, pharmaceutical company executive; b. Indpls., Mar. 28, 1945; m. Nancy Alder (dec.); 1 child, Evan; m. Rosanne M. Snyder. BS in Pharmacy, Butler U., 1966; PhD, Baylor Coll., 1971, MD, 1974. Asst. dir. med. rsch. Bristol Labs., N.Y.C., 1975-76, assoc. dir. med. rsch., 1976-77, assoc. dir. R&D, 1977-79, v.p. R&D, 1979-80, Smith Kline & French Labs., Phila., 1980-82; pres. R&D Smith Kline French, Phila., 1982-88; chmn. bd., CEO ISIS Pharms., Inc., Carlsbad, Calif., 1989. Chmn. bd. dirs. GES Pharms., Inc., Houston, 1989-91; adj. prof. Baylor Coll. Medicine, Houston, 1982, U. Pa., Phila., 1982-98; chmn. bd. dirs. GeneMedicine, Houston, 1996-98; bd. dirs. Calif. Healthcare Inst., Indsl. Biotech. Assn., Washington, Idun Pharms., San Diego 1997—, Epix Med., Cambridge, Mass., 1996—, BIO, Washington; mem. sci. adv. bd. SIBIA, La Jolla, Calif. 1992-99; adj. prof. pharmacology UCLA, 1991, U. Calif. San Diego, 1994; bd. dirs. Synsorb Biotech Inc., Calgary, Can., 1999—; bd. dirs. Axon Instruments, Inc., Foster City, Calif. 1999—, Valentis, Inc., Burlingame, Calif., 1999—. Mem. editl. adv. bd. Molecular Pharmacology, 1986-91, Jour. Drug Targeting, 1992; editl. bd. Antisense Rsch. and Devel., 1994; sect. editl. bd. for biologicals and immunologicals Expert Opinion on Investigational Drugs, 1995. Trustee Franklin Inst., Phila., 1987-89; bd. dirs. Mann Music Ctr., Phila., 1987-89; children's com. Children's Svcs., Inc., Phila., 1983-84; adv. com. World Affairs Coun., Phila. Recipient

Disting. Prof. award U. Ky., 1986, Julius Stermer award Phila. Coll. Pharmacy and Sci., 1981, Outstanding Lectr. award Baylor Coll. Medicine, 1984. Mem. AAAS, Am. Assn. for Cancer Rsch. (state legis. com.), Am. Soc. for Microbiology, Am. Soc. Pharmacology and Exptl. Therapeutics, Am. Soc. Clin. Pharmacology and Therapeutics, Am. Soc. Clin. Oncology, Indsl. Biotech. Assn. (bd. dirs. 1992-93). Achievements include numerous patents in field. Office: ISIS Pharms Inc 2292 Faraday Ave Carlsbad CA 92008-7208 E-mail: scrooke@isiph.com

CROSBY, GLENN ARTHUR, chemistry educator; b. nr. Youngwood, Pa., July 30, 1928; s. Edwin Glenn and Bertha May (Ritchey) C.; m. Jane Lichtenfels, May 29, 1950; children: Brian, Alan, Karen B.S., Waynesburg Coll., 1950; Ph.D., U. Wash., 1954. Rsch. assoc. Fla. State U., Tallahassee, 1955-57, vis. asst. prof. physics, 1957; asst. prof. chemistry U. N. Mex., Albuquerque, 1957-62, assoc. prof. chemistry, 1962-67; prof. chemistry and chem. physics Wash. State U., Pullman, 1967—, chmn. chem. physics program, 1977-84. Mem. adv. com. Rsch. Corp., Tucson, 1981-88, 90-92; vis. prof. phys. chemistry U. Tübingen, Fed. Republic Germany, 1964; vis. prof. physics U. Canterbury, Christchurch, N.Z., 1974; Humboldt sr. scientist, vis. prof. phys. chemistry U. Hohenheim, Fed. Republic Germany, 1978-79; mem. commn. on life scis. NRC, 1991-96, com. on programs for advanced study math. & sci. in U.S. h.s., 1999—. Author: Chemistry: Matter and Chemical change, 1962; also numerous sci. and sci.-related articles Recipient U.S. Sr. Scientist award Humboldt Found., Fed. Republic Germany, 1978-79, Catalyst award Chem. Mfrs. Assn., 1979, Disting. Alumnus award Waynesburg Coll., 1982, Wash. State U.Faculty Excellence award in instrn., 1984, Wash. State U. Faculty Excellence award for pub. svc., 1989, Disting. Prof. award Wash. State U. Mortar Bd., 1990, Pres.'s medallion Waynesburg Coll. for disting. lifetime sci. and ednl. achievement, 1998; named Prof. of Yr., U. N.Mex., 1967; NSF fellow U. Wash., Seattle, 1953-54; Rsch. Corp. Venture grantee, 1960; Fulbright fellow, 1964. Fellow AAAS, Inter-Am. Photochem. Soc.; mem. Am. Chem. Soc. (numerous activities including chmn. div. chem. edn. 1982, chmn. com. on edn. 1990-91, We. Conn. sect. Vis. Scientist award 1981, nat. award in chem. edn. 1985, bd. dirs. 1994—, Harry and Carol Mosher award Santa Clara Valley sect. 1998), Am. Phys. Soc., Nat. Sci. Tchrs. Assn., Wash. Sci. Tchrs. Assn. (Outstanding Coll. Sci. Tchr. award 1975), Sigma Xi, Phi Kappa Phi, Sigma Pi Sigma. Home: 1208 E Excelsior Rd Spokane WA 99224-9257 Office: Wash State U Dept Chemistry Pullman WA 99164-0001

CROSBY, JOHN O'HEA, opera general director; b. N.Y.C., July 12, 1926; s. Laurence Alden and Aileen Mary (O'Hea) C. Grad., Hotchkiss Sch., 1944; BA, Yale U., 1950, DFA (hon.), 1991; LittD (hon.), U. N.Mex., 1967; MusD (hon.), Coll. of Santa Fe, 1968, Cleve. Inst. Music, 1974; LHD (hon.), U. Denver, 1977. Pres. Manhattan Sch. Music, 1976-86 Accompanist, opera coach, condr., N.Y.C., 1951-56, founder, gen. dir., mem. conducting staff Santa Fe Opera, 1957-2000; guest condr. various opera cos. in U.S. and Can. and Europe, 1967—; condr. U.S. stage premiere Daphne, 1964; U.S. profl. premier Friedenstag, 1988; world premiere Wuthering Heights, 1958. With inf. AUS, 1944-46, ETO. Recipient Nat. Medal of Arts, 1991, Verdienstkreuz 1st klasse Bundesrepublik, Deutschland, 1992. Roman Catholic. Office: PO Box 2408 Santa Fe NM 87504-2408

CROSBY, NORMAN LAWRENCE, comedian; b. Boston, Sept. 15, 1927; s. John and Ann (Lansky) C.; m. Joan Crane Foley, Nov. 1, 1966; children: Daniel Joseph, Andrew Crane. Student, Mass. Sch. Art, Boston. Ind. comedian, entertainer, 1947—. Nat. spokesman Anheuser-Busch Natural Light Beer. Began work as comedian in New England clubs, fraternity and polit. dinners, numerous civic and charity functions; N.Y.C. debut Latin Quarter; several appearances London Palladium, regular appearances at all major hotels in Las Vegas, numerous other night clubs, concert halls, theaters, TV variety and panel shows; host: (syndicated TV series) Norm Crosby's Comedy Shop; nat. co-host on Jerry Lewis Muscular Dystrophy Assn. Telethon. Nat. hon. chmn. better Hearing Inst., Washington; trustee Hope for Hearing Found., UCLA; sponsor Norm Crosby Ann. Celebrity Golf Tournament benefitting City of Hope. With USCG, 1945-46. Recipient Jack Benny Comedy award Authors and Celebrities, 1981, Star on Hollywood (Calif.) Walk of Fame, Hollywood C. of C., 1982, Lifetime Achievement award in Entertainment, Touchdown Club, Washington, 1988, Victory award, Kennedy Ctr. PRes. George Bush, 1991; named Internat. Variety Clubs Man of Yr., 1986. Mem. Friars Club (N.Y.C., L.A.; 17th term Internat. Amb. of Good Will for City of Hope), Masons, Shriners. Jewish.

CROSBY, PETER ALAN, management consultant; b. Santa Barbara, Calif., Oct. 20, 1945; s. Harold Bartley and Margaret Maida (Peterson) C.; m. Stephanie Jay Ellis, Dec. 20, 1969; children: Kelly Michelle, Michael Ellis. BS in Engring., U. Calif., Berkeley, 1967; MS in Ops. Rsch., Stanford U., 1969; ED, Stanford Bus. Sch., 1971. Cert. mgmt. cons. Logistics inventory analyst Ford Motor Co., Palo Alto, Calif., 1967-71; corp. ops. planning analyst FMC Corp., San Jose, 1972; assoc. mgmt. cons. A.T. Kearney, Inc., San Francisco, 1972-75; mgr. materials mgmt. cons. svcs. Coopers & Lybrand, Los Angeles, 1976-78; ptnr. gen. cons. unit (Case & Co.) Towers Perrin Forster & Crosby, L.A., 1978-81; prin. Crosby, Gustin, Rice & Co. (CGR Mgmt. Cons.), 1981—. Dir. Carbide Products Internat. Co.; bd. dirs. Impact Cons. Group, Inc.; pres. Inst. of Mgmt. Cons. Mem. adv. bd. dirs. Stanton Chase. Mem. Coun. Logistic Mgmt., Inst. Mgmt. Cons., Phi Gamma Delta. Office: CGR Mgmt Consultants Ste 1900 1901 Avenue Of The Stars Los Angeles CA 90067-6020

CROSBY, THOMAS F. judge; b. Long Beach, Calif., June 4, 1940; m. Patty Wichite, Nov. 20, 1982; 2 children. AB with great distinction, Stanford U., 1962; LLB, U. Calif., Berkeley, 1965; LLM, U. Va., 1988. Bar: Calif. 1966, U.S. Dist. Ct. (no. dist.) Calif. 1966, U.S. Ct. Appeals (9th cir.) 1966, U.S. Dist. Ct. (ctrl. dist.) Calif. 1977, U.S. Dist. Ct. (so. dist.) Calif. 1979; cert. in criminal law. With NLRB, 1965-66, Peace Corps, 1966-68, Orange County (Calif.) Dist. Atty.'s Office, 1968-73; ptnr. Crosby & Luesebrink, then Crosby, Garey & Bonner, Calif., 1973-81; judge Superior Ct., 1981-82; assoc. justice Calif. Ct. Appeals, Santa Ana, 1982—. Contbr. articles to law jours. Mem. Delta Upsilon, Phi Alpha Sigma. Office: Calif Ct Appeals 925 N Spurgeon St Santa Ana CA 92701-3700

CROSS, BRUCE MICHAEL, lawyer; b. Washington, Jan. 30, 1942; AB magna cum laude, Dartmouth Coll., 1964; JD magna cum laude, Harvard U., 1967. Bar: Wash. 1967. Law clk. to Hon. Frank P. Weaver Supreme Ct. Wash., 1967-68; mem. Perkins Coie, Seattle. Office: Perkins Coie 1201 3rd Ave Fl 40 Seattle WA 98101-3099 E-mail: crosb@perkinscoie.com

CROSS, ELIZABETH, apparel manufacturing company executive; b. 1959; married; 3 children. Grad., U. Colo.; MBA, Stanford U., 1988. Cons. Bain and Co.; co-founder, co-pres. Ariat Internat., Inc., San Carlos, Calif., 1990—. Office: Ariat Internat Inc 940 Commercial St San Carlos CA 94070-4017

CROSS, HARRY MAYBURY, retired law educator, consultant; b. Ritz- [illegible] C.; m. Mylinn A. Gould, Dec. 25, 1935 (dec. May 1999); children: Harry Maybury, Bruce Michael, Kim Judson. B.A., Wash. State U., 1936; J.D., U. Wash., 1940; Bar: Wash. 1941. Reporter Yakima (Wash.) Morning Herald, 1937; abstracter, title examiner Wash. Title Ins. Co., Seattle, 1937-40; Sterling fellow in law Yale U., 1940-41; atty. U.S. Treasury Dept., Washington, 1941-42, TVA, Chattanooga, 1942-43; asst. prof. law U. Wash., Seattle, [illegible], assoc. prof., [illegible], prof., 1949-84, prof. emeritus, 1984—; assoc. dean U. Wash. (Sch. of Law), 1975-78, acting dean, 1978, 79. Vis. prof. Columbia U., 1956-57, NYU, 1964, U. Mich., 1972 Contbg. editor: Community Property Deskbook, 2d edit., 1989. Recipient Law medal Gonzaga U., 1994, Don Palmer award U. Wash. Alumni, 1997, named one of 10 Outstanding Profs. of 20th Century, Student Bar Assn., 2000; honoree recognition banquet U. Wash. Law Sch., 1979. Mem. Wash. State Bar Assn. (Honor and Merit award 1984), ABA, Nat. Collegiate Athletic Assn. (pres. 1969, 70), U. Wash. Retirement Assn. (pres. 1987-88), Order of Coif, Crimson Circle, Oval Club, Phi Beta Kappa, Phi Kappa Phi, Sigma Delta Chi, Phi Alpha Delta, Kappa Sigma. Home: 10125 NE 126th St Kirkland WA 98034-2855 Office: U Wash Law Sch JB 20 Seattle WA 98105 E-mail: hmcrosssr@aol.com

CROSS, KATHRYN PATRICIA, education educator; b. Normal, Ill., Mar. 17, 1926; d. Clarence L. and Katherine (Dague) C. BS, Ill. State U., 1948; MA, U. Ill., 1951, PhD, 1958; LLD (hon.), SUNY, 1988; DS (hon.), Loyola U., 1980, Northeastern U., 1975; DHL (hon.), De Paul U., 1986, Open U., The Netherlands, 1989. Math. tchr. Harvard (Ill.) Community High Sch., 1948-49; rsch. asst. dept. psychology U. Ill., Urbana, 1949-53, asst. dean of women, 1953-59; dean of women then dean of students Cornell U., Ithaca, N.Y., 1959-63; dir. coll. and univ. programs Ednl. Testing Svc., Princeton, N.J., 1963-66; rsch. educator Ctr. R&D in Higher Edn. U. Calif., Berkeley, 1966-77; rsch. scientist, sr. rsch. psychologist, dir. univ. programs Ednl. Testing Svc., Berkeley, 1966-80; prof. edn., chair dept. adminstrn., planning & social policy Harvard U., Cambridge, Mass., 1980-88; Elizabeth and Edward Conner prof. edn. U. Calif., Berkeley, 1988-94, David Pierpont Gardner prof. higher edn., 1994-96. Mem. sec. adv. com. on automated personal data sys. Dept. HEW, 1972-73; del. to Soviet Union, Seminar on Problems in Higher Edn., 1975; vis. prof. U. Nebr., 1975-76; vis. scholar Miami-Dade C.C., 1987; trustee Carnegie Found., 1999—, Berkeley Pub. Libr., 1998—; spkr., cons. in field; bd. dirs. Elderhostel. Author: Beyond the Open Door: New Students to Higher Education, 1971, (with S. B. Gould) Explorations in Non-Traditional Study, 1972, (with J. R. Valley and Assocs.) Planning Non-Traditional Programs: An Analysis of the Issues for Postsecondary Education, 1974, Accent on Learning, 1976, Adults as Learners, 1981, (with Thomas A. Angelo) Classroom Assessment Techniques, 1993, (with Mimi Harris Steadman) Classroom Research, 1996; contbr. articles, monographs to profl. publs., chpts. to books; mem. editl. bd. to several ednl. jours.; cons. editor ednl. mag. Change, 1980—. Active Nat. Acad. Edn., 1975—, Coun. for Advancement of Exptl. Learning, 1982-85; trustee Bradford Coll., Mass., 1986-88, Antioch Coll., Yellow Springs, Ohio, 1976-78; mem. nat. adv. bd. Nat. Ctr. of Study of Adult Learning, Empire State Coll.; mem. nat. adv. bd. Okla. Bd. Regents; mem. higher edn. rsch. program Pew Charitable Trusts; mem. vis. com. Harvard Grad. Sch. Edn., 1998—; bd. dirs. Elderhostel, 1999—; trustee Berkeley Pub. Libr., 1999—, Carnegie Found., 1999—. Mem. Am. Assn. Higher Edn. (bd. dirs. 1987—, pres. 1975, chair 1989-90), Am. Assn. Comty. and Jr. Colls. (vice chair commn. of future comty. colls.), Carnegie Found. Advancement of Tchg. (adv. com. on classification of colls. and univs.), Nat. Ctr. for Devel. Edn. (adv. bd.), New Eng. Assn. Schs. and Colls. (commn. on instns. higher edn. 1982-86), Am. Coun. Edn. (commn. on higher edn. and adult learner 1986-88). E-mail: patcross@socrates.berkeley.edu

CROSS, SUE, newspaper editor; Bur. chief AP, L.A., 1993—. Office: 221 S Figueroa St Los Angeles CA 90012-2552

CROSSON, JOHN ALBERT, advertising executive; b. L.A., Oct. 5, 1961; s. Albert J. and Virginia (Kienzle) C.; m. Carolyn Stevens, Oct. 3, 1992. BA, Loyola Marymount U., 1983; MBA, U. So. Calif., 1984. Exec. v.p. Dailey & Assocs. Advt., L.A., 1984-98; exec. v.p., mng. dir. L.A., Grey Advt., 1998—. Lectr. Loyola Marymount U., L.A., 1986-89. Avocations: tennis, golf.

CROUCH, PAUL FRANKLIN, minister, religious organization administrator; b. St. Joseph, Mo., Mar. 30, 1934; s. Andrew Franklin and Sarah Matilda (Swingle) C.; m. Janice Wendell Bethany, Aug. 25, 1957; children: Paul F., Matthew W. B.Th., Central Bible Coll. and Sem., Springfield, Mo., 1955. Ordained to ministry, 1955; dir. fgn. missions film and audio visual dept. Assemblies of God, 1955-58; assoc. pastor 1st Assembly of God, Rapid City, S.D., 1958-60, Central Assembly of God, Muskegon, Mich., 1960-62; gen. mgr. TV and film prodn. center Assemblies of God, Burbank, Calif., 1962-65; gen. mgr. Sta. KREL, Cornona, 1965-71, Sta. KHOF, KHOF-TV, Glendale, 1971-73; founder, pres. Sta. KTBN-TV, Trinity Broadcasting Network, Los Angeles, 1973—. Recipient Best Religious film award Winona Lake Film Festival, 1956 Mem. Nat. Assn. Religious Broadcasters, Western Religious Broadcasters Assn., Assn. Christian TV Stas. (founder) Office: Trinity Broadcasting Network 2442 Michelle Dr Tustin CA 92780-7015

CROW, EDWIN LOUIS, mathematical statistician, consultant; b. Browntown, Wis., Sept. 15, 1916; s. Frederick Marion and Alice Blanche (Cox) C.; m. Eleanor Gish, June 13, 1942; children: Nancy Rebecca, Dorothy Carol Crow-Willard. B.S. summa cum laude, Beloit Coll., 1937; Ph.M., U. Wis., 1938, Ph.D., 1941; postgrad., Brown U., 1941, 42, U. Calif.-Berkeley, 1947, 48, Univ. Coll., London, 1961-62. Instr. math. Case Sch. Applied Sci., Cleve., 1941-42; mathematician Bur. Ordnance Dept. Navy, Washington, 1942-46, U.S. Naval Ordnance Test Sta., China Lake, Calif., 1946-54; cons. statistics Boulder Labs., U.S. Dept. Commerce, Boulder, Colo., 1954-73, Nat. Telecommunications and Info. Adminstrn., Boulder, 1974—; statistician Nat. Ctr. Atmospheric Research, Boulder, 1975-82. Instr. math. extension div. UCLA, China Lake, 1947-54; adj. prof. math. U. Colo., Boulder, 1963-81; lectr. stats. Met. State Coll., Denver, 1974. Co-author: Statistics Manual, 1960; co-editor: Lognormal Distributions, 1988; assoc. editor: Communications in Statistics, 1972-98, Jour. Am. Statis. Assn., 1967-75, Current Index to Stats., 1981—; contbr. articles to profl. jours. Survey statistician Boulder Valley Sch. Dist., 1971-72; founder, pres. Boulder Tennis Assn., 1967-69, pres., 1982. Recipient Outstanding Publ. award Nat. Telecommunications and Info. Adminstrn., 1980, 82; Bronze medal U.S. Dept. Commerce, 1970, Editor's award Am. Meteorol. Soc., 1987. Fellow Royal Statis. Soc., Am. Statis Assn. (coun. mem. 1959-60, 68-69, Outstanding Chpt. mem. 1989), AAAS; mem. Am. Math. Soc., Math. Assn. Am., Inst. Math. Stats., Bernoulli Soc. for Math. Stats. and Probability, Soc. Indsl. and Applied Math., U.S. Tennis Assn., Sigma Xi, Phi Beta Kappa. Democrat. Unitarian. Clubs: Colo. Mountain, Harvest House Sporting Assn. (Boulder). Achievements include theory and applications of mathematical statistics in ordnance, radio standards, radio propagation, communication systems, weather modification, and ranking data. Home: 605 20th St Boulder CO 80302-7714 Office: Nat Telecomms & Info Adminstrn ITS N3 325 Broadway Boulder CO 80303-3337

CROW, GORDON F. state legislator; b. L.A., Dec. 15, 1950; m. Sandy Crow; 1 child, Andrew. Media cons.; owner, pub. rels. agy.; senator, dist. 3 Idaho State Senate, Boise, 1994—. Chair commerce and human resources [illegible] health and welfare, and resources and environment coms. With U.S. Army. Mem. Coeur d'Alene (Idaho) C. of C., Rotary. Republican. Office: State Capitol PO Box 83720 Boise ID 83720-3720

CROWE, CLAYTON T. engineering educator; Prof. Sch. Mech. and Materials Engring. Wash. State U., Pullman. Recipient Fluids Engring. award ASME, 1995. Office: Wash State U Sch Mech & Materials Engring Pullman WA 99164-0001

CROWELL, JOHN B., JR. lawyer, former government official; b. Elizabeth, N.J., Mar. 18, 1930; s. John B. and Anna B. (Trull) C.; m. Rebecca Margaret McCue, Feb. 13, 1954; children— John P., Patrick E., Ann M. A.B., Dartmouth Coll., 1952; LL.B., Harvard U., 1957. Bar: N.J. bar 1958, Oreg. bar 1959. Law clk. to Judge Gerald McLaughlin U.S. Ct. Appeals, Newark, 1957-59; atty. Ga.-Pacific Corp., Portland, Oreg., 1959-72; gen. counsel La.-Pacific Corp., Portland, 1972-81; asst. sec. for natural resources and environment Dept. Agr., Washington, 1981-85; ptnr. Lane Powell Spears Lubersky, Portland, 1986-98, of counsel, 1998—. Served with USN, 1952-54. Mem. ABA, Am. Ornithologists Union, Wilson Ornithol. Soc., Cooper Ornithol. Soc., Soc. Am. Foresters, Soil Conservation Soc. Am. Republican. Presbyterian. Club: Univ. (Portland). Home: 1185 Hallinan Cir Lake Oswego OR 97034-4970 Office: Lane Powell Spears Lubersky 601 SW 2nd Ave # Ste #2100 Portland OR 97204-3154

CROWELL, JOHN C(HAMBERS), geology educator, researcher; b. State College, Pa., May 12, 1917; s. James White and Helen Hunt (Chambers) C.; m. Betty Marie Bruner, Nov. 22, 1946; 1 child, Martha Lynn Crowell Bobroskie. BS in Geology, U. Tex., 1939; MA in Oceanographic meteorology, Scripps Inst. Oceanography UCLA, 1946; PhD in Geology, UCLA, 1947; DSc (hon.), U. Louvain, Belgium, 1966. Geologist Shell Oil Co., Inc., Ventura, Calif., 1941-42; from instr. to prof. geology UCLA, 1947-67, chmn. dept., 1957-60, 63-66; prof. geology U. Calif., Santa Barbara, 1967-87, prof. emeritus, 1987, rsch. geologist Inst. for Crustal Studies, 1987—. Chmn. Office of Earth Scis., NRC, Nat. Acad. Scis., 1979-82. Served to capt. U.S. Army USAAF, 1942-46. Fellow Geol. Soc. Am. (Penrose medal 1995), Am. Acad. Arts and Scis.; mem. Am. Assn. Petroleum Geologists, Am. Geophys. Union, AAAS, Am. Inst. Profl. Geologists, Nat. Acad. Scis. Achievements include special research in structural geology, tectonics, interpretation sedimentary rocks, studies Andreas fault system, tectonics California ancient glaciation, continental drift. Home: 300 Hot Springs Rd Apt 99 Santa Barbara CA 93108 Office: U Calif Inst Crustal Studies Santa Barbara CA 93106 E-mail: crowell@geol.ucsb.edu

CROWLEY, JEROME JOSEPH, JR. investment company executive; b. South Bend, Ind., Sept. 18, 1939; s. Jerome J. and Rosaleen C.; m. Carol Ann Ellithorn, June 23, 1962; children: Michael, Karen, Brian, Colleen. BS, U. Notre Dame, 1961; MBA, U. Chgo., 1967. With O'Brien Corp., Mountain View, Calif., 1965—, pres., 1975—. With USMC, 1961-65. Roman Catholic. Office: O'Brien Corp 2483 Old Middlefield Way Mountain View CA 94043-2359

CROWLEY, JOHN CRANE, real estate developer; b. Detroit, June 29, 1919; s. Edward John and Leah Helen (Crane) C.; m. Barbara Wenzel Gilfillan, Jan. 12, 1945; children: F. Alexander, Leonard, Philip, Eliot, Louise, Sylvia. BA, Swarthmore Coll., 1941; MS, U. Denver, 1943. Asst. dir. Mcpl. Fin. Officers Assn., Chgo., 1946-48; So. Calif. mgr. League Calif. Cities, Los Angeles, 1948-53; mgr. City of Monterey Park, Calif., 1953-56. Founder, exec. v.p. Nat. Med. Enterprises, L.A., 1968; pres. Ventura Towne House (Calif.), 1963-96; mem. faculty U. So. Calif. Sch. Pub. Adminstrn., 1950-53; bd. dirs. Regional Inst. of So. Calif., The L.A. Partnership 2000, Burbank-Glendale-Pasadena Airport Authority. Trustee Pacific Oaks Friends Sch. and Coll., Pasadena, 1954-57, 92-98, Swarthmore Coll., 1987—; bd. dirs. Pasadena Area Liberal Arts Ctr., 1962-72, pres., 1965-68; bd. dirs. Pacificulture Found. and Asia Mus., 1971-76, pres., 1972-74; bd. dirs. Nat. Mcpl. League, 1986-92, AAF Rose Bowl Aquatics Ctr., 1997—; chmn. Pasadena Cultural Heritage Commn., 1975-78; city dir. Pasadena, 1979-91; mayor City of Pasadena, 1986-88; bd. dirs. Western Justice Ctr., 1992—, v.p., 1995—, LA County Commn. on Efficiency and Economy, 1994—; mem. L.A. County Commn. on Local Govt., 2000—. Sloan Found. fellow, 1941-43; recipient Arthur Nobel award City of Pasadena. Mem. Am. Soc. Pub. Adminstrn. (local chpt., Winston Crouch award 1990), Internat. City Mgmt. Assn., Nat. Mcpl. League (nat. bd. 1980-92, Disting. Citizen award, 1984), Inst. Pub. Adminstrn. (sr. assoc.), Phi Delta Theta. Democrat. Unitarian. Home: 615 Linda Vista Ave Pasadena CA 91105-1122

CROWLEY, JOSEPH MICHAEL, electrical engineer, educator; b. Phila., Sept. 9, 1940; s. Joseph Edward and Mary Veronica (McCall) C.; m. Barbara Ann Sauerwald, June 22, 1963; children: Joseph W., Kevin, James, Michael, Daniel. B.S., MIT, 1962, M.S., 1963, Ph.D., 1965. Vis. scientist Max Planck Inst., Goettingen, W.Ger, 1965-66; asst. prof. elec. engring. U. Ill., Urbana, 1966-69, assoc. prof., 1969-78, prof., dir. applied electrostats. research lab., 1978-88; pres. JMC Inc., 1981-91, Electrostatic Applications, 1986—; Piercey Disting. prof. chem. engring. U. Minn., 1993. Adj. prof. U. Ill., 1988-94; cons. to several corps. Contbr. articles to profl. jours.; patentee ink jet printers. Pres. Champaign-Urbana Bd. Cath. Edn., 1978-80. Recipient Gen. Motors scholarship, 1958-62; AEC fellow, 1962-65; NATO fellow, 1965-66 Fellow IEEE, Electrostats. Soc. Am. (pres. 1992-95), Am. Phys. Soc., Soc. Inf. Display, Mensa. Roman Catholic.

CROWLEY, JOSEPH NEIL, university president, political science educator; b. Oelwein, Iowa, July 9, 1933; . James Bernard and Nina Mary (Neil) C.; m. Johanna Lois Reitz, Sept. 9, 1961; children: Theresa, Neil, Margaret, Timothy. BA, U. Iowa, 1959; MA, Calif. State U., Fresno, 1963; PhD (Univ. fellow), U. Wash., 1967. Reporter Fresno Bee, 1961-62; asst. prof. polit. sci. U. Nev., Reno, 1966-71, asso. prof., 1971-79, prof., 1979—, chmn. dept. polit. sci., 1976-78, pres., 1978-2000. Bd. dirs. Citibank Nev.; policy formulation officer EPA, Washington, 1973-74; dir. instl. studies Nat. Commn. on Water Quality, Washington, 1974-75. Author: Democrats, Delegates and Politics in Nevada: A Grassroots Chronicle of 1972, 1976, Notes From the President's Chair, 1988, No Equal in the World; An Interpretation of the Academic Presidency, 1994, The Constant Conversation: A Chronicle of Campus Life, 2000; editor: (with R. Roelofs and D. Hardesty) Environment and Society, 1973. Mem. Commn. on Colls., 1980-87; mem. adv. comn. on mining and minerals rsch. U.S. Dept. Interior, 1985-91; mem. coun. NCAA, 1987-92, mem. pres.' commn., 1991-92, pres., 1993-95; bd. dirs. Nat. Consortium for Acads. and Sports, 1992—; mem. Honda Awards Program Adv. Bd., 1994—; bd. dirs., campaign chmn. No. Nev. United Way, 1985, 97—. Recipient Thornton Peace Prize U. Nev., 1971, Humanitarian of Yr. award NCCJ, 1986, Alumnus of Yr. award Calif. State U., 1989, ADL Champion of Liberty award, 1993, Disting. Alumni award U. Iowa, 1994, Giant Step award Ctr. for Study of Sport in Soc., 1994, William Anderson award AAHPERD, 1998, Lifetime Achievement award Nat. Consortium for Acads. and Sports, 2001; Nat. Assn. Schs. Pub. Affairs and Adminstrn. fellow, 1973-74. Mem. Nat. Assn. State Univs. and Land Grant Colls. (bd. dirs. 1999-2000). Roman Catholic. Home: 1265 Muir Dr Reno NV 89503-2629 Office: U Nev Pres Office Reno NV 89557-0001 E-mail: crowley@admin.unr.edu

CROWLEY, THOMAS B., JR. water transportation executive; b. 1966; BS in Fin., U. Wash. With Crowley Maritime Corp., Oakland, Calif., [illegible] Oakland CA 94612-3758

CROWN, TIMOTHY A. computer technology company executive; BS in Bus. and Computer Sci., U. Kans., 1986. Adminstrv. analyst NCR Corp., 1986-87; various positions to pres. Insight Enterprises, Tempe, Ariz., 1988-89, co-CEO, co-chmn., 1994—. Ind. computer bus. cons., 1987-88. Office: Insight Enterprises 6820 S Harl Ave Tempe AZ 85283

CROWTHER, RICHARD LAYTON, architect, consultant, researcher, author, lecturer; b. Newark, Dec. 16, 1910; s. William George and Grace (Layton) C.; m. Emma Jane Hubbard, 1935 (div. 1949); children: Bethe Crowther Allison, Warren Winfield, Vivian Layton; m. 2d Pearl Marie Tesch, Sept. 16, 1950. Student, Newark Sch. Fine and Indsl. Arts, 1928-31, San Diego State Coll., 1933, U. Colo., 1956. Registered architect, Colo. Prin. Crowther & Marshall, San Diego, 1946-50, Richard L. Crowther, Denver, 1951-66, Crowther, Kruse, Landin, Denver, 1966-70, Crowther, Kruse, McWilliams, Denver, 1970-75, Crowther Solar Group, Denver, 1975-82, Richard L. Crowther FAIA, Denver, 1982—. Vis. critic, lectr. U. Nebr., 1981; holistic energy design process methodology energy cons. Holistic Health Ctr., 1982-83; adv. cons. interior and archtl. design class U. Colo., 1982-83, Cherry Creek, Denver redevel., 1984-88, Colo. smoking control legislation, 1985, interior solar concepts Colo. Inst. Art, 1986, Bio-Electro-Magnetics Inst., 1987-88; mentor U. Colo. Sch. Architecture, 1987-88. Author Sun/Earth, 1975 (Progressive Architecture award, 1975), rev. edit., 1983, reprint, 1995, Affordable Passive Solar Homes, 1983, reprint, 1996, Paradox of Smoking, 1983, Women/Nature/Destiny: Female/Male Equity for Global Survival, 1987, (monographs) Context in Art and Design, 1985, Existence, Design and Risk, 1986, Indoor Air: Risks and Remedies, 1986, Human Migration in Solar Homes for Seasonal Comfort and Energy Conservation, 1986, 88, Ecologic Architecture, 1992, Ecologic Digest, 1993, Ecologic Connections, 1996, Colorado Architect Monographs on Environmental Themes, 1998, Environmental Sustainability, 1999. NSF grantee, 1974-75 Fellow AIA (commr. research, edn. and environ. Colo. Central chpt. 1972-75, bd. dirs. chpt. 1973-74 AIA Research Corp. Solar Monitoring Program contract award, spkr. and pub. Colo. Ecologic Connections open forum 1996). Achievements include ecologic bio-toxic and bio-electromagnetic research.

CRUMB, ROBERT, cartoonist; b. Phila., Aug. 30, 1943; s. Charles Sr. C.; m. Dana Morgan (div. 1977); m. Aline Kominski, 1978. Colorist Am. Greetings Corp., 1963-67; cartoonist Fantagraphics Books, Seattle, 1967—. Creator: (comic book) Zap, 1968; founder, cartoonist: (mag.) Wierdo, 1981-89; author: The Complete Crumb Comics, (with Aline Kominski) My Troubles with Women, 1991, Wierdo Art of R. Crumb: His Early Period 1981-85, 1992, Crumb's Complete Dirty Laundry Comics, 1993; illustrator: The Monkey Wrench Gang by Edward Abbey, 1985; frequent contbr. to comic mags.; subject of documentary film: Crumb, 1994; creator cartoon character Fritz the Cat. Office: Fantagraphics Books 7563 Lake City Way NE Seattle WA 98115-4218

CRUMLEY, ROGER LEE, surgeon, educator; b. Perry, Iowa, Oct. 8, 1941; s. Dwight Moody and Helen Ethelwyn (Anderson) C.; m. Janet Lynn Conant, Nov. 13, 1987; children: Erin Kelly Helen, Danielle Nicole. BA, Simpson Coll., 1964; MS, U. Iowa, 1975, MD, 1967; MBA, U. Phoenix, 1999. Diplomate Am. Bd. Otolaryngology (dir. 1992—). Intern L.A. County Gen. Hosp., 1967-68; resident in surgery Highland-Alameda Hosp., Oakland, Calif., 1968-69; bn. surgeon 1st Marine Div., Vietnam, 1968-69; resident in otolaryngology U. Iowa, Iowa City, 1971-75; chief otolaryngology San Francisco Gen. Hosp., 1975-81; assoc. prof., then prof. U. Calif., San Francisco, 1981-87, prof., chief otolaryngology-head and neck surgery Irvine, 1987—. Guest prof. Humboldt U., East Berlin, 1982, M.S. McLeod vis. prof. S. Australian Postgrad. Edn. Ctr., Adelaide, 1988; treas., pres. Am. Acad. Facial Plastic Surgeons, 1994-95; McBride lectr. U. Edinburgh, 1998. Contbr. articles and book chpts. to profl. publs. With USN, 1969-71, Vietnam. Recipient Alumni Achievement award Simpson Coll., 1984. Fellow ACS, Am. Acad. Otolaryngology (bd. dirs. 1988—, award 1989); mem. Soc. Univ. Otolaryngologists, Bohemian Club (San Francisco), Center Club (Costa Mesa, Calif.). Republican. Methodist. Avocations: music, piano, jazz flügelhorn, running, skiing. Office: U Calif-Irvine Med Ctr Dept Otolaryngology Head & Neck 101 The City Dr S Orange CA 92868-3201

CRUMLEY, THEODORE, paper lumber company executive; CFO, sr. v.p. Boise (Idaho) Cascade. Office: Boise Cascade 1111 W Jefferson St Boise ID 83728-0071

CRUMP, SPENCER, publishing company executive; b. San Jose, Calif., 25 Nov. s. Spencer M. and Jessie (Person) C.; m. Cynthia Fink, 1992 (div. 1999); children by previous marriage: John Spencer, Victoria Elizabeth Margaret. B.A., U. So. Calif., 1960, M.S. in Edn, 1962, M.A. in Journalism, 1969. Reporter Long Beach (Calif.) Ind., 1945-49; freelance writer Long Beach, 1950-51; travel columnist, picture editor Long Beach Ind.-Press-Telegram, 1952-56; pres. Crest Industries Corp., Long Beach, 1957-58, editor suburban sects. L.A. Times, 1959-62; editl. dir. Trans-Anglo Books, L.A., 1962-73, pub., 1973-81, Zeta Pubs. Co., Corona Del Mar, Calif., 1981—. Mng. dir. Person-Crump Ranch and Investment Co. (formerly Person Properties Co.), Justiceburg, Tex., 1951—; chmn. dept. journalism Orange Coast Coll., 1966-84; chmn. bd. Zeta Internat., 1976—; cons. Queen Beach Press, 1974-87, Flying Spur Press, 1976—, So. Pacific Transp. Co., 1979-80, Interurban Press/Trans-Anglo Books, 1981-87; bd. dirs. Zeta Britain, Zeta Internat.; chmn. bd. T & S Publs. Group, Inc., Canyon Lake, Calif., 1988-89. Author: Ride the Big Red Cars, 1962, Redwoods, Iron Horses and the Pacific, 1963, Western Pacific-The Railroad That was Built Too Late, 1963, California's Spanish Missions Yesterday and Today, 1964, Black Riot in Los Angeles, 1966, Henry Huntington and the Pacific Electric, 1970, Fundamentals of Journalism, 1974, California's Spanish Missions—An Album, 1975, Suggestions for Teaching the Fundamentals of Journalism in College, 1976, The Stylebook for Newswriting, 1979, Newsgathering and Newswriting for the 1980s and Beyond, 1981, Riding the California Western Skunk R.R., 1988, Durango to Silverton by Narrow Gauge Rail, 1990, Riding the Cumbres & Toltec Railroad, 1992, Rails to the Grand Canyon, 1993, Route 66: America's First Main Street, 1994. Mem. Los Angeles County Democratic Central Com., 1961-62. Mem. Book Pubs. Assn. So. Calif., Fellowship Reconciliation, Soc. Profl. Journalists. Unitarian-Universalist. Office: Zeta Pubs Co PO Box 38 Corona Del Mar CA 92625-0038

CRUSE, ALLAN BAIRD, mathematician, computer scientist, educator; b. Aug. 28, 1941; s. J. Clyde and Irma R. Cruse. Postgrad. (Woodrow Wilson fellow), U. Calif., Berkeley, 1962-63; MA, 1965. Fellow Dartmouth Coll., 1963-64; instr. U. San Francisco, 1966-73; asst. prof. math., 1973-76; assoc. prof., 1976-79; prof., 1979—. Chmn. math. dept. 1988-91; vis. instr. Stilman Coll., summer 1967; vis. assoc. prof. Emory U., spring 1978; prof. computer sci. Sonoma State U., 1983-85; cons. math edn. NSF fellow, 1972-73. Author: (with Millianne Granberg) Lectures on Freshman Calculus, 1971; rsch. publs. in field. Mem. Am. Math. Soc., Math. Am. Math. Soc., Math. Assn. Am. (chmn. No. Calif. sedt. 1995-96), Assn. Computing Machinery, U. San Francisco Faculty Assn., Sigma Xi (dissertation award 1974). Office: U San Francisco Harney Sci Ctr San Francisco CA 94117

CRUZ, B. ROBERT, academic administrator; m. Guadalupe Rojas; children: Roberto, Marco Antonio, Fernando Rey. BA in Edn., Wichita State U., 1964; MA in Edn., U. Calif., Berkeley, 1968, PhD in Policy, Planning and Administrn., 1971. Asst. prof. Sch. Edn. St. Mary's Coll., 1972-74; lectr. Sch. Edn. Stanford (Calif.) U., 1978-79; pres. Nat. Hispanic U., San Jose, Calif., 1981—. Apptd. nat. adv. coun. dealing with edn. lang. minority students; exec. dir. non-profit ednl. orgn. 5 sch. dist. consortium. Contbr. articles to profl. jours. Recipient numerous awards and honors including Legis. Recognition award in Bilingual Edn., 1974, Cmty. Appreciation award Bakersfield Parent Bd., 1975, Appreciation award Asian Edn. Assn. San Francisco, 1977, Outstanding Leadership award in Edn. U. Calif. Berkeley Chpt. Phi Delta Kappa, 1977, Meritorious award Edn. Limited and Non-English Speaking Students, 1977, Edn. Excellence award Operation Push, 1983; inducted Hispanic Hall of Fame, 1987. Mem. Nat. Assn. Bilingual Edn. (past pres.), Calif. Assn. Bilingual Edn. (past pres., Leadership award 1978). Office: The Nat Hispanic U Pres Office 14271 Story Rd San Jose CA 95127-3889

CSENDES, ERNEST, chemist, corporate and financial executive; b. Satu-Mare, Szatmár-Németi, Romania, Mar. 2, 1926; came to U.S., 1951, naturalized, 1955; s. Edward O. and Sidonia (Littman) C. m. Catharine Vera Tolnai, Feb. 7, 1953; children: Audrey Carol, Robert Alexander Edward. BA, Protestant Coll., Hungary, 1944; BS, U. Heidelberg (Ger.), 1948, MSc, 1950, PhD summa cum laude, 1951. Rsch. asst. chemistry U. Heidelberg, 1950-51; rsch. assoc. biochemistry Tulane U., New Orleans, 1952; rsch. fellow chemistry Harvard U., 1952-53; rsch. chemist organic chems. dept. E. I. Du Pont de Nemours and Co., Wilmington, Del., 1953-56, elastomer chems. dept., 1956-61; dir. rsch. and devel. agrl. chems. div. Armour & Co., Atlanta, 1961-63; v.p. corp. devel. Occidental Petroleum Corp., L.A., 1963-64, exec. v.p. rsch., engring. and devel., mem. exec. com., 1964-68; COO, exec. v.p., dir. Occidental Rsch. and Engring. Corp., L.A., London, Moscow, 1963-68. Mng. dir. Occidental Rsch. and Engring. (U.K.) Ltd., London, 1964-68; pres., CEO TRI Group, London, Amsterdam, Rome and Bermuda, 1968-84; chmn., CEO Micronic Techs., Inc., L.A., 1981-85; mng. ptnr. Inter-Consult Ltd., Pacific Palisades, Calif.; internat. cons. on tech., econ. feasibility and mgmt., 1984—; pres., CEO, chief tech. officer Gen. Grinding Corp., L.A., 1991—; chmn., CEO Eden Mgmt. Ltd., L.A. and London, 1993—. Contbr. 250 articles to profl. and trade jours., studies and books. Recipient Pro Mundi Beneficio gold medal Brazilian Acad. Humanities, 1975; Harvard U. fellow, 1953. Fellow AAAS, Am. Inst. Chemists, Royal Soc. Chemistry (London); mem. AIAA, IEEE, SMME, AIChE, Am. Chem. Soc., German Chem. Soc., N.Y. Acad. Sci., Am. Concrete Inst., Am. Water Works Assn., AMS Internat., Acad. Polit. Sci., Nat. Def. and Indsl. Assn., Sigma Xi. Achievements include 53 patents; rsch. in area of elastomers, rubber chemicals, adhesives, dyes and intermediates, organometallics, organic and biochemistry, high polymers, antioxidants, superphosphoric acid and ammonium polyphosphates, plant nutrients, pesticides, process engineering, design of fertilizer plants, sulfur, potash, phosphate and iron ore mining and metallurgy, coal combustion and cleanup of acid gases and air toxics, self-cleaning micronized coal fuels, municipal water clean-up, methods for aerodynamic grinding of solids, particles technology, advanced building materials, petrochemicals, biomed. engring., consumer products; also acquisitions, mergers, internat. fin. related to leasing investments and loans, trusts and ins., new Eurodollar instruments; regional indsl. devel. related to agr. and energy resources; projects in western Europe, no. Africa, Russia, Japan, Saudi Arabia, India, China, Australia and the Philippines. Home: 514 N Marquette St Pacific Palisades CA 90272-3314

CUADRA, CARLOS ALBERT, information scientist, management executive; b. San Francisco, Dec. 21, 1925; s. Gregorio and Amanda (Mendoza) C.; m. Gloria Nathalie Adams, May 3, 1947; children: Mary Susan Cuadra Nielsen, Neil Gregory, Dean Arthur. AB with highest honors in Psychology, U. Calif., Berkeley, 1949, PhD in Psychology, 1953. Staff psychologist VA, Downey, Ill., 1953-56; with Sys. Devel. Corp., Los Angeles, Calif., 1957-78, mgr. libr. and documentation sys. dept., 1968-70, mgr. edn. and libr. sys. dept., 1971-74; gen. mgr. SDC Search Svc., 1974-78; founder Cuadra Assocs., L.A., 1978—. Contbr. articles to profl. jours.; Editor: Ann. Rev. of Info. Sci. and Tech., 1964-75. Mem. Nat. Commn. Librs. and Info. Sci., 1971-84. Served with USN, 1944-46. Recipient Merit award Am. Soc. Info. Sci., 1968, Best Info. Sci. Book award, 1969; named Disting. Lectr. of Year, 1970; received Miles Conrad award Nat. Fedn. Abstracting and Info. Svcs., 1980, hon. fellow, 1997. Mem. Info. Industry Assn. (bd. dirs., Hall of Fame award 1980), Chem. Abstracts Soc. (governing bd. 1991-96), Am. Chem. Soc. (governing bd. pub. 1997-2000). Home: 13213 Warren Ave Los Angeles CA 90066-1750 Office: Cuadra Associates 11835 W Olympic Blvd Ste 855 Los Angeles CA 90064-5033

CUBBISON, CHRISTOPHER ALLEN, newspaper editor; b. Honolulu, Dec. 22, 1948; s. Donald Cameron and Mary (Pritchett) C.; m. Linda Cicero, Jan. 3, 1976; children: Genevieve, Cameron. BJ, U. Mo., 1971. Reporter N.Y. Daily News, N.Y.C., 1971-72, St. Petersburg (Fla.) Times, 1972-76, asst. city editor, 1976-78; editor various locations including The Miami Herald, 1978-89; asst. mng. editor Rocky Mountain News, Denver, 1989-90, mng. editor projects, 1990—. Avocations: golf, skiing. Home: 11 Sycamore Ln Littleton CO 80127-3525 Office: Rocky Mountain News 400 W Colfax Ave Denver CO 80204-2694

CUBIN, BARBARA LYNN, congresswoman, former state legislator; b. Salinas, Calif., 30 Nov. d. Russell G. and Barbara Lee (Howard) Sage; m. Frederick William Cubin, Aug. 1; children: William Russell, Frederick William III. BS in Chemistry, Creighton U., 1969. Chemist Wyo. Machinery Co., Casper, Wyo., 1973-75; social worker State of Wyo.; office mgr. Casper, Wyo.; mem. Wyo. Ho. Reps., 1987-92, Wyo. Senate, 1993-94; pres. Spectrum Promotions and Mgmt., Casper, 1993-94; mem. U.S. Congress from Wyo., Washington, 1995—; mem. resources com., energy and commerce com. Mem. steering com. Exptl. Program to Stimulate Competitive Rsch. (EPSCOR); mem. Coun. of State Govts.; active Gov.'s Com. on Preventive Medicine, 1992; vice chmn. Cleer Bd. Energy Coun., Irving, Tex., 1993—; chmn. Wyo. Senate Rep. Conf., Casper, 1993—; mem. Wyo. Rep. Party Exec. Com., 1993; pres. Southridge Elem. Sch. PTO, Casper, Wyo. Toll fellow Coun. State Govts., 1990, Wyo. Legislator of Yr. award for energy and environ. issues Edison Electric Inst., 1994. Mem. Am. Legis. Exch. Coun., Rep. Women. Avocations: duplicate bridge, golfing, singing, reading, hunting. Office: US Ho Reps 1114 Longworth Ho Office Bldg Washington DC 20515-0001*

CUDDY, DANIEL HON, bank executive; b. Valdez, Alaska, Feb. 8, 1921; s. Warren N. and Lucy C.; m. Betty Puckett, Oct. 6, 1947; children: Roxanna, David, Gretchen, Jane, Lucy, Laurel. BA, Stanford U., 1946. Bar: Alaska 1948. Pvt. practice, Anchorage, 1948-53; pres. First Nat. Bank Anchorage, 1951—, chmn. bd. With U.S. Army, World War II, ETO. Office: First Nat Bank 101 W 36th Ave Anchorage AK 99503-5904

CULBERT, PETER V. lawyer; b. San Antonio, July 27, 1944; s. Robert William and Dorothy Fairfax (Kift) C.; m. Elizabeth Tamara Spagnola, July 12, 1980; children: Michael, Daniel, Robert, David, William. BA, Cornell U., 1966; MA, SUNY, Buffalo, 1969; JD, U. N.Mex., 1977. Bar: N.Mex. 1977, U.S. Dist. Ct. N.Mex. 1977, U.S. Ct. Appeals (10th cir.) 1977. Law clk. to Hon. Mack Easley N.Mex. Supreme Ct., Santa Fe, 1977-78; sr. ptnr. Jones, Snead, Wertheim, Wentworth & Jaramillo, Santa Fe, 1978-98; pvt. practice Santa Fe, 1998—. Mem. adv. bd., legal counsel Desert Chorale, Santa Fe, 1991—, bd. dirs., 1986-91. Recipient hon. cert. Strathmore Registry Bus. Leaders, 1995-97. Mem. ABA, ATLA, N.Mex. Trial Lawyers Assn., Canyon Assn., Alpha Delta Phi (life). Avocations: flamenco guitarist, bicycling, horticulture, camping. Office: 911 Old Pecos Trl Santa Fe NM 87501-4566 E-mail: pvculbert@law-sf.com

CULICK, FRED ELLSWORTH CLOW, physics and engineering educator; b. Wolfeboro, N.H., Oct. 25, 1933; s. Joseph Frank and Mildred Beliss (Clow) C.; m. Frederica Mills, June 11, 1960; children: Liza Hall, Alexander Joseph, Mariette Huxham. Student, U. Glasgow, Scotland, 1957-58; SB, MIT, 1957, PhD, 1961. Rsch. fellow Calif. Inst. Tech., Pasadena, 1961-63, asst. prof., 1963-66, assoc. prof., 1966-70, prof. mech. engring. and jet propulsion, 1970-97, Richard L. and Dorothy M. Hayman prof. mech. engring., 1997—, prof. jet propulsion, 1997—. Cons. to govt. agys. and indsl. orgns. Fellow AIAA; mem. Internat. Acad. Astronautics, Internat. Fedn. Astronautics, Am. Phys. Soc. Home: 1375 Hull Ln Altadena CA 91001-2620 Office: Calif Inst Tech Caltech 205-45 207 Guggenheim Pasadena CA 91125

CULLEN, BRUCE F. anesthesiologist; b. Iowa City, May 6, 1940; MD, UCLA, 1966. Intern Blodgett Meml. Hosp., Grand Rapids, Mich., 1966-67; resident in anesthesiology U. Calif., San Francisco, 1967-70; chief anesthesiologist Harborview Med. Ctr., Seattle. Prof. U. Wash. Office: U Wash HMC Anesthesiology 325 9th Ave Seattle WA 98104-2420

CULLEN, JACK JOSEPH, lawyer; b. Sept. 20, 1951; s. Ray Brandes (stepfather) and Helen Cullen; m. Deborah L. Vick, Oct. 28, 1978; children: Cameron, Katherine. BA, Western Wash. State Coll., 1973; JD, U. Puget Sound, 1976. Bar: Wash. 1977, U.S. Dist. Ct. (we. dist.) Wash. 1977, U.S. Dist. Ct. (ea. dist.) Wash. 1977, U.S. Tax Ct. 1984, U.S. Ct. Appeals (9th cir.) 1980. Staff atty. Wash. State Bar Assn., Seattle, 1977-79; assoc. Hatch & Leslie, Seattle, 1979-85, mng. ptnr., 1985-91; ptnr. Foster Pepper & Shefelman, Seattle, 1991-96, mng. ptnr., 1996—, mng. chair, 1991—. Spkr. in field. Co-author: Prejudgment Attachment, 1986. Active Frank Lloyd Wright Bldg. Conservancy, 1989—; trustee Seattle Repertory Theater, 1999—. Mem. ABA (bus. law sect.), Am. Bankruptcy Inst., Wash. State Bar Assn. (creditor-debtor sect., chair exec. 1982-90, spl. dist. counsel 1988—, hearing officer 1990), Seattle-King County Bar Assn. (bankruptcy rules subcom. 1988-90), Vancouver-Seattle Involvency Group (charter mem. 1990—), U.S. Sport Parachuting Team (nat. and world champions 1976, instrument rated pilot). Office: Foster Pepper & Shefelman PLLC 1111 3rd Ave Ste 3400 Seattle WA 98101-3299 E-mail: jc@foster.com

CULLER, FLOYD LEROY, JR. chemical engineer; b. Washington, Jan. 5, 1923; m. Della Hopper, 1946 (dec. 1995); 1 son, Floyd Leroy III. B. Chem. Engring. cum laude, Johns Hopkins, 1943. With Eastman Kodak and Tenn. Eastman at Y-12, Oak Ridge, 1943-47; design engr. Oak Ridge Nat. Lab., 1947-53, dir. chem. tech. div., 1953-64, asst. lab. dir., 1965-70, dep. dir., 1970-77; pres. Electric Power Research Inst., Palo Alto, Calif., 1978-88, pres. emeritus, 1988—. Research design chem. engring. applied to atomic energy program, chem. processing, radiation waste disposal, nuclear reactor plants, energy research. Mem. sci. adv. com. Internat. Atomic Energy Agy., 1974-87; mem. energy research adv. bd. Dept. Energy, 1981-86. Recipient Ernest Orlando Lawrence award, 1964; Atoms for Peace award, 1969, Robert E. Wilson award in nuclear chem. engring., 1972, Engring. Achievement award East Tenn. Engrs. Joint Council, 1974, Outstanding Scientist award State of Tenn., 1988. Fellow AAAS, Am. Nuclear Soc. (dir. 1973-80, spl. award 1977, Walter Zinn award 1988), Am. Inst. Chemists, Inst. Chem. Engrs.; mem. Am. Chem. Soc., Nat. Acad. Engring. Office: Electric Power Rsch Inst Inc 3412 Hillview Ave Palo Alto CA 94304-1344

CULP, GORDON LOUIS, consulting engineer; b. Topeka, Dec. 30, 1939; s. Russell Louis and Dorothy Marion (Wilson) C.; m. Rosemary Anne Smith, Apr. 7, 1990. BS in Civil Engring., U. Kans., 1961, MS in Environ. Health Engring., 1962; MA in Applied Psychology, U. Santa Monica, 1991. Registered profl. engr., 41 states. San. engr. USPHS, Cin., 1962-64, CH2M/Hill Engrs., Corvallis, Oreg., 1964-66; rsch. engr. Neptune Microfloc, Corvallis, 1966-70; rsch. mgr. Battelle N.W., Richland, Wash., 1970-71; regional mgr. CH2M/Hill Engrs., Reston, Va., 1971-73; pres. Culp, Wesner Culp (acquired by HDR Engring. 1986), Cameron Park, Calif., 1973-93, Smith Culp Consulting, Las Vegas, 1993—. Author: New Concepts in Water Purification, 1974, Handbook of Advanced Wastewater Treatment, 1978, 2d edit., 2001, Managing People (including Yourself) for Project Success, 1991, others; assoc. editor Jour. Engring. Mgmt. Mem. ASCE (chmn. urban wastewater com.), Am. Water Works Assn., Water Pollution Control Fedn., Am. Acad. Environ. Engrs., Rotary (pres. 1977-78). Office: Smith Culp Consulting 653 Ravel Ct Las Vegas NV 89145-8628 E-mail: gordon@smithculp.com

CULP, MILDRED LOUISE, corporate executive; b. Ft. Monroe, Va., Jan. 13, 1949; d. William W. and Winifred (Stilwell) C. BA in English, Knox Coll., 1971; AM in Religion and Literature, U. Chgo., 1974, PhD The Com. on History of Culture, 1976. Faculty, adminstr. Coll., 1976-81; dir. Exec. Résumés, Seattle, 1981—; pres. Exec. Directions Internat., Inc., Seattle, 1985—. MBA mgmt. skills adv. com. U. Wash. Sch. Bus. Adminstrn., 1993; spkr. in field; contract rschr. U.S. Army Recruiting Command, 1997. Author: Be WorkWise: Retooling Your Work for the 21st Century, 1994; columnist Seattle Daily Jour. Commerce, 1982-88; writer Singer Media Corp., 1991-95, WorkWise syndicated column, 1994—, Universal Press Syndicate, 1997-2001, syndicated in U.S., in print and online svcs., WorkWise Registered, 1992 (radio), 96 (print), 2000 (Internet audio); WorkWise syndicated Internet audio program, 2000—; featured on TV and radio; contbr. articles and book revs. to profl. jours.; presenter WorkWise Report, Sta. KIRO, 1991-96. Admissions counselor U. Chgo., 1981—; mem. Nat. Alliance Mentally Ill, 1984—, bd. dirs., 1987, mem. adv. bd., 1988; mem. A.M.I. Hamilton County, 1984—; founding mem. People Against Telephone Terrorism and Harassment, 1990; co-sponsor WorkWise award, 1999—. Recipient Alumni Achievement award Knox Coll., 1990, 8 other awards; named Hon. Army Recruiter. Mem. Knox Coll. Alumni Network, U. Chgo. Puget Sound Alumni Club (bd. dirs. 1982-86).

CULPEPPER, DAVID CHARLES, lawyer; b. Quantico, Va., Mar. 15, 1946; s. Carlton Milburn and Eleanor Louise (Hart) C.; m. Marie T. Francher, June 21, 1969; children: Larissa, Danielle. BA, Santa Clara (Calif.) U., 1968; JD, U. Oreg., 1974. Bar: Oreg. 1974, U.S. Dist. Ct. Oreg. 1974, U.S. Tax Ct. 1974, U.S. Ct. Appeals (9th cir.) 1974. Ptnr. Miller, Nash, Wiener, Hager & Carlsen, Portland, Oreg., 1974—. Contbg. author: Advising Oregon Businesses, 1986, 89; contbr. articles to profl. jours. Mem. ABA (partnership com. taxation sect. 1983), Oreg. Bar Assn. (chair exec. com. tax sect. 1992-93), Portland Tax Forum (bd. dirs., co-chair tax force on ltd. liability co. legis.). Office: Miller Nash Wiener Hager & Carlsen 111 SW 5th Ave Ste 3500 Portland OR 97204-3699

CULTON, PAUL MELVIN, retired counselor, educator, interpreter; b. Council Bluffs, Iowa, Feb. 12, 1932; s. Paul Roland and Hallie Ethel Emma (Paschal) C. AB, Minn. Bible Coll., 1955; BS, U. Nebr., Omaha, 1965; MA, Calif. State U., Northridge, 1970; EdD, Brigham Young U., 1981. Cert. tchr., Iowa. Tchr. Iowa Sch. for Deaf, Council Bluffs, 1956-70; ednl. specialist Golden West Coll., Huntington Beach, Calif., 1970-71, dir. disabled students, 1971-82, instr., 1982-88; counselor El Camino Coll., Via Torrance, 1990-93, acting assoc. dean, 1993-94, counselor Calif., 1994-97. Interpreter various state and fed. cts., Iowa, Calif., 1960-90; asst. prof. Calif. State U., Northridge, Fresno, Dominguez Hills, 1973, 76, 80, 87-91, L.A., 1999—; vis. prof. U. Guam, Agana, 1977; mem. allocations task force, task force on deafness, trainer handicapped students Calif. C.C.s, 1971-81. Editor: Region IX Conf. for Coordinating Rehab. and Edn. Svcs. for Deaf proceedings, 1970, Toward Rehab. Involvement by Parents of Deaf conf. proceedings, 1971; composer Carry the Light, 1986. Bd. dirs. Iowa NAACP, 1966-68, Gay and Lesbian Cmty. Svcs. Ctr., Orange County, Calif., 1975-77; founding sec. Dayle McIntosh Ctr. for Disabled, Anaheim and Garden Grove, Calif., 1974-80; active Dem. Cent. Com. Pottawattamie County, Council Bluffs, 1960-70; del. People to People N.Am. Educators

Deaf Vis. Russian Schs. & Programs for Deaf, 1993. League for Innovation in Community Coll. fellow, 1974. Mem. Registry of Interpreters for Deaf, Am. Fedn. Tchrs., Am. Sign Lang. Tchrs. Assn., Nat. Assn. Deaf. Mem. Am. Humanist Assn. Avocations: vocal music, languages, community activism, travel, politics. Home: 3939 N Virginia Rd 110 Long Beach CA 90807

CUMMING, GEORGE ANDERSON, JR. lawyer; b. Washington, Apr. 16, 1942; s. George Anderson and Gene (Chapman) C.; m. Linda Lucille Harder, Aug. 25, 1963; children: Mary Elizabeth, Andrew Gordon. AA, Coll. San Mateo, 1962; AB magna cum laude, San Francisco State U., 1963; JD, U. Calif., Berkeley, 1967. Bar: Calif. 1967, U.S. Dist. Ct. (no. dist.) Calif. 1967, U.S. Ct. Appeals (9th cir.) 1967, U.S. Supreme Ct. 1974. Assoc. Brobeck, Phleger & Harrison, San Francisco, 1967-75, ptnr., 1975-98; spl. trial counsel antitrust divsn. U.S. Dept. Justice, Washington, 1996-97; with Brobeck Phleger & Harrison, San Francisco, 1998—. Fellow Am. Coll. Trial Lawyers; mem. ABA, San Francisco Bar Assn., Order of Coif. Avocation: model railroading. Office: Brobeck Phleger & Harrison Antitrust Divsn One Market Spear St Tower San Francisco CA 94105

CUMMING, THOMAS ALEXANDER, stock exchange executive; b. Toronto, Ont., Can., Oct. 14, 1937; s. Alison A. and Anne B. (Berry) C.; m. E. Mary Stevens, Mar. 12, 1965; children: Jennifer, Allison, Katy. BAS, U. Toronto, 1960. Registered profl. engr., Can. With Bank of Nova Scotia, 1965-88; spl. rep. Toronto, 1965-68; br. mgr. Dublin, Ireland, 1969-71, London, 1971-75; v.p. Calgary, Alta., Can., 1975-80; sr. v.p. Calgery, Can., 1980-85, Toronto, 1986-88; pres., CEO Alta. Stock Exchange, Calgary, 1988-99. Mem. coun. Power Pool of Alta; bd. dirs. Calgary Techs Inc., Pengrowth Corp., E-Tronics Inc. Bd. dirs. YMCA of Calgary Found. Mem. Assn. Profl. Engrs., Calgary C. of C. (pres. 1991), Calgary Golf and Country Club, Calgary Petroleum Club. Home and Office: 2906 10th St SW Calgary AB Canada T2T 3H2

CUMMINGS, BARTON, musician; b. Newport, N.H., July 10, 1946; s. C. Barton and Ruth (Ricard) C.; m. Florecita L. Lim, July 23, 1983 BS in Music Edn., U. N.H., 1968; MusM, Ball State U., Muncie, Ind., 1973. Dir. music Alton (N.H.) Pub. Sch., 1971-72; lectr. San Diego State U., 1974-79; instr. music Point Loma Coll., San Diego, 1976-79; instr. San Diego Community Coll. Dist., 1977-79, Delta State U., Cleveland, Miss., 1979-82; supr. Clarksdale Separate Sch. Dist., 1982-84; dir. music Walnut (Calif.) Creek Concert Band, 1985--, Richmond Unified Sch. Dist., 1988—, Golden Hills Concert Band, 1990—; condr. Devil Mountain Symphony, 1991—. Tuba player Vallejo Symphony Orch., 1988—, Concord Pavilion Pops Orch., 1985—, Brassworks of San Francisco, 1985—, Solano Dixie Jubilee. Author: The Contemporary Tuba, 1984, The Tuba Guide, 1989, Teaching Techniques for Brass Instruments, 1989; composer over 6 dozen pub. compositions; recorded on Capra, Coronet and Crystal, Channel Classics, Mark labels. Mem. ASCAP, NACUSA, T.U.B.A., Am. Fedn. of Musicians, Conductor's Guild, Phi Mu Alpha Sinfonia. Avocations: travel, cooking, writing, composing, reading. Home: 550 Cambridge Dr Benicia CA 94510-1316 E-mail: cbc_21@yahoo.com

CUMMINGS, NICHOLAS ANDREW, psychologist; b. Salinas, Calif., July 25, 1924; s. Andrew and Urania (Sims) C.; m. Dorothy Mills, Feb. 5, 1948; children: Janet Lynn, Andrew Mark. AB, U. Calif., Berkeley, 1948; MA, Claremont Grad. Sch., 1954; PhD, Adelphi U., 1958. Chief psychologist Kaiser Permanente No. Calif., San Francisco, 1959-76; pres. Found Behavioral Health, San Francisco, 1976—; chmn., CEO Am. Biodyne, Inc., San Francisco, 1985-93, Kendron Internat., Ltd., Reno, 1992-95; chmn. Nicholas & Dorothy Cummings Found., Reno, 1994—; chmn., pres. U.K. Behavioural Health, Ltd., London, 1996-98; Disting. prof. U. Nev., 1997—; chmn., CEO DynaMed Integrated Care, Inc., 1998—. Co-dir. South San Francisco Health Ctr., 1959-75; pres. Calif. Sch. Profl. Psychology, L.A., San Francisco, San Diego, Fresno campuses, 1969-76; chmn. bd. Calif. Cmty. Mental Health Ctrs., Inc., L.A., San Diego, San Francisco, 1975-77; pres. Blue Psi, Inc., San Francisco, 1972-80, Inst. for Psychosocial Interaction, 1980-84; mem. mental health adv. bd. City and County San Francisco, 1968-75; bd. dirs. San Francisco Assn. Mental Health, 1965-75; pres., chmn. bd. Psycho-Social Inst., 1972-80; dir. Mental Rsch. Inst., Palo Alto, Calif., 1979-80; pres. Nat. Acads. of Practice, 1981-93. Served with U.S. Army, 1944-46. Fellow APA (dir. 1975-81, pres. 1979); mem. Calif. Psychol. Assn. (pres. 1968). Office: Nicholas & Dorothy Cummings Found 561 Keystone Ave PMB 212 Reno NV 89503-4331

CUMMINS, JOHN STEPHEN, bishop; b. Oakland, Calif., Mar. 3, 1928; s. Michael and Mary (Connolly) C. A.B., St. Patrick's Coll., 1949. Ordained priest Roman Catholic Ch., 1953; asst. pastor Mission Dolores Ch., San Francisco, 1953-57; mem. faculty Bishop O'Dowd H.S., Oakland, 1957-62; chancellor Diocese of Oakland, 1962-71; rev. monsignor, 1962; domestic prelate, 1967; exec. dir. Calif. Cath. Conf., Sacramento, 1971-77; consecrated bishop, 1974; aux. bishop of Sacramento, 1974-77; bishop of Oakland, 1977—. Campus min. San Francisco State Coll., 1953-57, Mills Coll., Oakland, 1957-71; trustee St. Mary's Coll., 1968-79 Home: 634 21st St Oakland CA 94612-1608 Office: Oakland Diocese 2900 Lakeshore Ave Oakland CA 94610-3614

CUMMISKEY, CHRIS, state legislator; b. Point Pleasant, N.J., Aug. 15, 1964; Student, Brophy Coll., 1983; BA in Comm., Ariz. State U., 1987. Mem. Ariz. Ho. Reps., 1990-94, Ariz. Senate, Dist. 25, Phoenix, 1994—; asst. minority leader Ariz. State Senate, mem. banking com., mem. ins. and elections com., mem. commerce and econ. devel. com., mem. fin. com., others, asst. floor leader. Active Dem. Leadership Coun. Nat. Adv., Valley Citizen League, Fiesta Bowl, Boys Club Phoenix and Scottsdale; bd. dirs. Valley Leadership; sponsor Ariz. Town Hall, Ariz. Acad.; precinct committeeman. Mem. Nat. Conf. State Legislatures, Ariz. Policy Forum, Nucleus Club, Ariz. State U. Alumni Assn. Democrat. Office: State Capitol Bldg 1700 W Washington St Ofc 213 Phoenix AZ 85007-2812 E-mail: ccummisk@azleg.state.az.us

CUNNANE, PATRICIA S. medical facility administrator; b. Clinton, Iowa, Sept. 7, 1946; d. Cyril J. and Corinne Spain; m. Edward J. Cunnane, June 19, 1971. AA, Mt. St. Clare Coll., Clinton, Iowa, 1966. Mgr. Eye Med. Clinic of Santa Clara Valley, San Jose, Calif. Mem. Med. Adminstrs. Calif. Polit. Action Com., San Francisco, 1987. Mem. Med. Group Mgmt. Assn., Am. Coll. Med. Group Adminstrs. (nominee), Nat. Notary Assn., NAFE, Exec. Women Internat. (v.p. 1986-87, pres. 1987—), Profl. Secs. Internat. (sec. 1979-80), Am. Soc. Ophthalmic Adminstrs., Women Health Care Execs., Healthcare Human Resource Mgmt. Assn. Calif. Roman Catholic. Avocations: calligraphy, golf. Home: 232 Tolin Ct San Jose CA 95139-1445 Office: Eye Med Clinic Santa Clara Valley 220 Meridian Ave San Jose CA 95126-2903 E-mail: patricia.cunnane@gte.net

CUNNING, TONIA, newspaper managing editor; BS in Journalism, U. Nev. Soc. editor/feature writer-editor/asst. mng. editor Reno (Nev.) Gazette Journ., 1971-[illegible] 1000. Office: Reno Gazette Journal PO Box 22000 Reno NV 89520-2000

CUNNINGHAM, ANDREA LEE, public relations executive; b. Oak Park, Ill., Dec. 15, 1956; d. Ralph Edward and Barbara Ann C.; m. Rand Wyatt Siegfried, Sept. 24, 1983. BA, Northwestern U., 1979. Feature writer Irving-Cloud Pub. Co., Lincolnwood, Ill., 1979-81; account exec. Burson-Marsteller Inc., Chgo., 1981-83, group account mgr. Regis McKenna Inc., Palo Alto, Calif., 1983-85; founder, owner, pres. Cunningham Communication Inc., Santa Clara, 1985—. Mem. Am. Electronics Assn., U.S. C. of C., Young Pres.' Orgn., Software Pubs. Assn., Boston Computer Soc., Leadership Calif., U.S. Cambridge C. of C. Republican. Avocations: running, roller skating, aerobics, racquetball.

CUNNINGHAM, BRUCE ARTHUR, biochemist, educator; b. Winnebago, Ill., Jan. 18, 1940; s. Wallace Calvin and Margaret Wright (Clinite) C.; m. Katrina Sue Susdorf, Feb. 27, 1965; children— Jennifer Ruth, Douglas James. B.S., U. Dubuque, 1962; Ph.D., Yale U., 1966. NSF postdoctoral fellow Rockefeller U., N.Y.C., 1966-68, asst. prof. biochemistry, 1968-71, assoc. prof., 1971-77, prof. molecular and devel. biology, 1978-92; prof. dept. neurobiology The Scripps Rsch. Inst., San Diego, 1992—. Editl. bd.: Jour. Biol. Chemistry, 1978-82, Jour. Cell Biology, 1992-96. Camille and Henry Dreyfus Found. grantee, 1970-75; recipient Career Scientist award Irma T. Hirschl Trust, 1975-80. Mem. AAAS, Am. Soc. Biol. Chemists, Am. Soc. Cell Biology, Protein Soc., Am. Chem. Soc., Harvey Soc., Am. Gynecol. Obstet. Soc. (hon.), Sigma Xi. Achievements include research on structure and function of molecules on cell surfaces. Office: Scripps Rsch Inst 10550 N Torrey Pines Rd La Jolla CA 92037-1000

CUNNINGHAM, GEORGE, state senator; m. Marjorie Fisher; children: Paul, Eve, Molly. B of Pub. Adminstrn., M of Pub. Adminstrn., U. Ariz. Spl. asst. to pres. Ariz. State Senate, Tucson, 1956; v.p. adminstrv. svcs. U. Ariz., Tucson, 1985-88; chief of staff Gov. Rose Mofford, 1988-90; with U. Ariz., Tucson, 1990-93; rep. State of Ariz., 1993-96; Dem. Senator dist. 13 Arizona State Senate , 1996—. Co-chmn. Pima County Com. on Property Tax and State Revenue Reform, 1996.

CUNNINGHAM, JOEL DEAN, lawyer; b. Seattle, Feb. 19, 1948; s. Edgar Norwood and Florence (Burgunder) C.; m. Amy Jean Radewan, Oct. 1, 1970; children: Erin Jane, Rad Norwood. BA in Econs., U. Wash., 1971, JD with high honors, 1974. Lawyer, ptnr. Williams, Kastner & Gibbs, Seattle, 1974-95; ptnr. Luvera, Barnett, Brindley, Beninger & Cunningham, Seattle, 1995—. Fellow Am. Coll. Trial Lawyers, Internat. Soc. Barristers; mem. Am. Bd. Trial Attys. (pres. Washington chpt. 1994), Damage Attys. Round Table, Order of Coif. Avocations: fishing, cycling, boating. Office: Luvera Barnett Brindley Beninger & Cunningham 6700 Columbia Ctr 701 5th Ave Seattle WA 98104-7097

CUNNINGHAM, RANDY, congressman; b. L.A., Dec. 8, 1941; m. Nancy Jones; 3 children. BA, MA, U. Mo.; MBA, Nat. U. Mem. U.S. Congress from 51st (formerly 44th) Calif. dist., 1991—; mem. intelligence com.; mem. appropriations com. Republican. Office: US Ho Reps 2350 Rayburn Ho Office Bldg Washington DC 20515-0551*

CUNNINGHAM, ROBERT D. lawyer; BA, Occidental Coll., Calif., 1971; JD, UCLA, 1975. Bar: Calif. 1975. Assoc. Lawler, Felix & Hall, L.A., 1975-78; atty. Buena Vista Pictures Distbn., Inc., Burbank, Calif., 1978-84, v.p., sec., gen. counsel, 1984-96; sr. v.p., sec., gen. counsel Buena Vista Pictures Distbn., Inc. (now Walt Disney Pictures & TV), Burbank, 1996—. Office: Walt Disney Pictures & TV 500 S Buena Vista St Burbank CA 91521-0006

CUNNINGHAM, RON, choreographer, artistic director; b. Chgo., Sept. 15, 1939; m. Carrine Binda, June 12, 1982; children: Christopher, Alexandra. Student, Allegro Ballet, 1961-65, Am. Ballet Theatre, 1968-70; studies with Merce Cunningham, N.Y.C., 1968-70; BS in Mktg., Roosevelt U., 1966. Dancer Allegro Am. Ballet Co., Chgo., 1962-66; artistic dir. Ron Cunningham Contemporary Dance Co., Chgo., 1966-68; dancer Lucas Hoving Dance Co., 1968-72, Lotte Goslar Pantomime Circus, 1968-72, Daniel Nagrin Dance Co., 1968-72; prin. dancer, resident choreographer Boston Ballet, 1972-85; artistic dir. Balt. Ballet, 1985-86; artistic assoc. Washington Ballet, 1986-87; ind. choreographer, 1987-88; artistic dir. Sacramento Ballet, 1988—. Panelist various regional and state art councils, 1979—; dir. Craft of Choreography, 1985; adjudicator, master tchr. Nat. Assn. Regional Ballet, 1985—, Am. Coll. Dance Assn., 1986. Dancer, choreographer 40 original internat. ballets, 1972—, 4 ballets Nat. Choreography Plan, 1978—, Cinderella, Peoples Republic of China, 1980. Nat. Endowment Arts fellow, 1977, 86, Mass. Art Coun. fellow, 1984, Md. Arts Coun. fellow, 1988. Mem. Nat. Assn. Regional Ballet, Dance/U.S.A. Avocation: archeology--bronze age cultures.

CURB, JESS DAVID, medical educator; b. Raton, N.Mex., Dec. 29, 1945; s. Leslie Calvin and Evelyn Lula (Lindley) C.; m. Beatriz Lorenza Rodriquez; children: Jess Calvin, William Noa, Maria Lorenza, Isabel Alani. BA, U. Colo., 1967; MD, U. N.Mex., 1971; MPH, U. Tex., Houston, 1974. Diplomate, cert. geriatric medicine Am. Bd. Internal Medicine. Intern Harlem Hosp., Columbia U., N.Y.C., 1971-72; rsch. assoc. U. Tex. Sch. Pub. Health and Medicine, Houston, 1973-76, asst. prof., 1978-80; resident internal medicine Northwestern U. Sch. Medicine, Chgo., 1976-78; asst. prof. Baylor Coll. Medicine, Houston, 1980-83; assoc. prof. U. Hawaii, Honolulu, 1983-85, prof., 1985-87; assoc. dir. Nat. Inst. on Aging, Bethesda, Md., 1986-89; prof. geriatric medicine, chief divns. clin. epidemiology U. Hawaii, Sch. Medicine, Honolulu, 1989—; CEO, med. dir. Pacific Health Rsch. Inst., 1995—. Contbr. articles to profl. jours. Grantee Honolulu Heart Program, Nat. Heart, Lung and Blood Inst., Honolulu, 1989—, Hawaii Asia Aging Study, Nat. Inst. on Aging, Honolulu, 1994—, Women's Health Initiative, NIH, Honolulu, 1994—, Family Blood Pressure Program, 1995—. Fellow ACP, Am. Heart Assn. (coun. on epidemiology); mem. Am. Geriatric Soc. Office: Univ Hawaii Sch Medicine 347 N Kuakini St Honolulu HI 96817-2306 E-mail: curb@phn.hawaii-health.com

CURCIO, CHRISTOPHER FRANK, city official; b. Oakland, Calif., Feb. 3, 1950; s. Frank William and Virginie Theresa (Le Gris) C. BA in Speech/Drama, Calif. State U., Hayward, 1971; MBA in Arts Adminstrn., UCLA, 1974; MPA in Pub. Policy, Ariz. State U., 1982. Intern John F. Kennedy Ctr. for Arts, Washington, 1973; gen. mgr. Old Eagle Theatre, Sacramento, 1974-75; cultural arts supr. Fresno (Calif.) Parks and Recreation Dept., 1975-79; supr. cultural and spl. events Phoenix Parks, Recreation and Libr. Dept., 1979-87, budget analyst, 1987, mgmt. svcs. adminstr., 1987-97, dep. dir., 1997—. Mgmt. and budget analyst City of Phoenix, 1985; grants panelist Phoenix Arts Commn., 1987, Ariz. Commn. on Arts, 1987-88; voter Zony Theatre Awards, 1991-92; freelance theater critic, 1987-89; theater critic Ariz. Republic, 1990-98, PHX Downtown, 1997-98, CityAZ, 1997-98, Ariz. Foothills Mag., 1998—, Sunday Showtunes Broadway's Biggest Hits, 1998-2000, In Theater Mag., 1999—, Variety, 1995—, KBAQ-FM Radio, 1999—, Broadway's Biggest Hits, 2000—. Active Valley Leadership Program, Phoenix, 1987—, Valley Big Bros./Big Sisters, 1980-94; chair allocation panel United Way, 1990-92; sec. Los Olivos Townhome Assn., Phoenix, 1986-92. Mem. Am. Soc. Pub. Adminstrn., Nat. Recreation and Park Assn., Am. Theatre Critics Assn., Internat. Theater Critics Assn., Ariz. Park and Recreation Assn. Republican. Avocations: theater history, writing, reading, cooking, gardening. Office: Phoenix Parks Recreation Libr Dept 200 W Washington St Fl 16 Phoenix AZ [illegible]

CURD, JOHN GARY, physician, scientist; b. Grand Junction, Colo., July 2, 1945; s. H. Ronald and Edna (Hegested) C.; m. Karen Wendel, June 12, 1971; children: Alison, Jonathan, Edward, Bethany. BA, Princeton U., 1967; MD, Harvard U., 1971. Diplomate Am. Bd. Internal Medicine, Am. Bd. Rheumatology, Am. Bd. Allergy and Immunology. Rsch. assoc. NIH, Bethesda, Md., 1973-75; fellow in rheumatology U. Calif., San Diego, 1975-77; fellow in allergy-immunology Scripps Clinic, La Jolla, Calif., 1977-78, asst. mem. rsch. inst., 1978-81, mem. div. rheumatology, 1981-91, head div. rheumatology, vice chmn. dept. medicine, 1989-91; pres. med. staff Green Hosp., La Jolla, 1988-90; clin. dir. Genentech Inc., South San Francisco, Calif., 1991-96, sr. dir., head clin. sci., 1996-97, v.p. clin. devel., 1997—. Author numerous. sci. papers in field. Med. dir. San Diego Scleroderma Found., 1983-91; sec. San Diego Arthritis Found., 1986-87. Lt. comdr. USPHS, 1973-75. Mem. Princeton Club No. Calif. Republican. Home: 128 Reservoir Rd Hillsborough CA 94010-6957 Office: Genentech Inc Dir Clinical Rsch 460 Point San Bruno Blvd South San Francisco CA 94080-4918

CURLEY, ELMER FRANK, librarian; b. Florence, Pa., Jan. 13, 1929; s. Augustus Wolfe and Bessie (Andrews) C. BA, U. Pitts., 1961; MLS, Carnegie Mellon U., Pitts., 1962; Adv. Cert., U. Pitts., 1964. Ref. libr. U. Pitts., 1962-64; head ref. dept. SUNY-Stony Brook, 1964-67; head pub. svcs. U. Nev.-Las Vegas, 1967-76, asst. dir. libr. svcs., 1976-81, ref. bibliographer, 1981-94, ret., 1994.

CURRAN, DARRYL JOSEPH, photographer, educator; b. Santa Barbara, Calif., Oct. 19, 1935; s. Joseph Harold and Irma Marie (Schlagel) C.; m. Doris Jean Smith, July 12, 1968. A.A., Ventura Coll., 1958; B.A., UCLA, 1960, M.A., 1964. Designer, installer UCLA Art Galleries, 1963-65; mem. faculty Los Angeles Harbor Coll., 1968-69, UCLA Ext., 1972-79, Sch. Art Inst. Chgo., 1975; prof. art Calif. State U., Fullerton, 1967-2001, chmn. art dept., 1989-99; curator various shows, 1971—. Bd. dirs. Los Angeles Center Photog. Studies, 1973-77, pres., 1980-83; juror Los Angeles Olympics Photog. Commns. Project, 1983 One-man shows include U. Chgo., 1975, U. R.I., 1975, Art Space, L.A., 1978, Photoworks Gallery, Richmond, Va., 1979, Alan Hancock Coll., Santa Maria, Calif., 1979, G. Ray Howkins Gallery, L.A., 1981, Portland (Maine) Sch. Art, 1983, Grossmont Coll., San Diego, 1982, (retrospective) Chaffey Coll., Alta Loma, Calif., L. A. Ctr. for Photographic Studies, 1984, U. Calif. Ext. Ctr., San Francisco, 1986, Cuesta Coll., San Luis Obispo, Calif., 1992, Cypress Coll., 1993, Tex. Woman's U., Denton, 1997, Irvine Valley Coll., 1997, Ellen Kim Murphy Gallery, Santa Monica, 2000, William Marten Gallery, Rochester, N.Y., 2001; two-person show No. Ky. U., 1995; group exhbns. include Laguna Mus. Art, San Francisco, 1992, Friends of Photography, San Francisco, 1993, U.S. Info. Agy. Empowered Images, 1994—, USIA, Jan Abrams Gallery, L.A., 1995; group exhbns. include Mt. St. Mary's Coll., 1997, Ranch Santiago Coll., 1997; represented in permanent collections Mus. Modern Art, Royal Photog. Soc., London, Nat. Gallery Can., Ottawa, Mpls. Inst. Art, Oakland Mus., U. N.Mex., UCLA, Seagram's Collection, N.Y.C., Mus. Photog. Arts, San Diego, Phila. Mus. Art, J. Paul Getty Mus., Phila. Mus. Art, San Francisco Mus. Art. Bd. dirs. Cheviot Hills Home Owners Assn., 1973. Served with U.S. Army, 1954-56. Recipient Career Achievement award Calif. Mus. Photography, 1986; NEA Photographers fellow, 1980; Honored Educatior award Soc. Photographic Edn., 1996. Mem. Soc. Photog. Edn. (dir. 1975-79, honored educator 1996). Home: 10537 Dunleer Dr Los Angeles CA 90064-4317 E-mail: localdj@mindspring.com

CURRAN, WILLIAM P. lawyer; b. Mpls., Feb. 27, 1946; s. William P. and Margaret L. (Killoren) C.; m. Jean L. Stabenow, Jan. 1, 1978; children: Patrick, Lisa, John. BA, U. Minn., 1969; JD, U. Calif., Berkeley, 1972. Law clk. Nev. Supreme Ct., Carson City, 1973-74, state ct. adminstr., 1973-74; assoc. Wiener, Goldwater & Galatz, Las Vegas, Nev., 1974-75; chief dept. dist. atty. Clark County Dist. Atty.'s Office, Las Vegas, 1975-79; county counsel Clark County, Las Vegas, 1979-89; pvt. practice Las Vegas, 1989-94; ptnr. Curran & Parry, Las Vegas, 1994—. Co-author: Nevada Judicial Orientation Manual, 1974. Mem. Nev. Gaming Commn., Carson City, 1989-99, chmn., 1991-99. Recipient Educator Yr. award UNLV Internat. Gaming Inst., 1998. Mem. ABA (state del. 1994—), Internat. Assn. Gaming Regulators (chmn. 1992-94), Nat. Assn. County Civil Attys. (pres. 1984-85), State Bar Nev. (pres. 1988-89), Nev. Gaming Commn. (chmn. 1989-99). Democrat. Roman Catholic. Office: Curran & Parry 601 S Rancho Dr Ste C-23 Las Vegas NV 89106-4825 E-mail: curran_parry@msn.com

CURRIE, PHILIP JOHN, research paleontologist, museum curator; b. Toronto, Ont., Can., Mar. 13, 1949; children: Tarl, Devin, Brett. BSc, U. Toronto, 1972; MSc, McGill U., 1975, PhD in Biology, 1981. Curator paleontology Provincial Mus. Alta., Edmonton, 1976-81; mus. curator Palaeontology Mus. and Rsch. Inst., Drumheller, Alb., Can., 1981-82; asst. dir. rsch. Tyrrell Mus. Paleontology, Drumheller, Alta., 1982-89, head dinosaur rsch., 1989—. Sec. Alta. Paleontology Adv. Com., 1977-89; treas. Palaeont Can., 1981-84. Author: Flying Dinosaurs, 1991, Dinosaur Renaissance, 1994; co-author: The Great Dinosaurs, 1994, 101 Questions About Dinosaurs, 1996, Troodon, 1997, Albertosaurus, 1998, Centrosaurus, 1998, Sinosauropteryx, 1999; co-editor: Dinosaur Systematics, 1990, Dinosaur Encyclopedia, 1997, Newest and Coolest Dinosaurs, 1998; contbr. articles to profl. publs.; featured in numerous articles and programs. Recipient Commendation medal 125th Anniversary of Govt. of Can., 1993, Sir Frederick Haultain award Govt. of Alta., 1988, Michel Halbouty award Am. Assn. Petroleum Geologists, 1999. Fellow Royal Soc. Can.; mem. Soc. Vertebrate Paleontology (program officer 1985-87, conf. chmn. 1988, conf. chmn. Mesozoic Terrestrial Ecosystems 1987), Paleontol. Soc., Can. Soc. Petroleum Geologists, Am. Soc. Zoologists, Sigma Xi. Achievements include research in fossil reptiles including Permian Sphenacodonts from Europe and United States; Permian eosuchians from Africa and Madagascar; Jurassic and Cretaceous dinosaurs from Canada, Argentina and Asia and their footprints. Office: Royal Tyrrell Mus Palaeontology Box 7500 Drumheller AB Canada T0J 0Y0

CURRIE, ROBERT EMIL, lawyer; b. Jackson, Tenn., Oct. 10, 1937; s. Forrest Edward Currie and Mary Elizabeth (Nuckolls) Empson; m. Brenda Ray Eddings, July 2, 1960; children: Cheryl Lynn, Forrest Clayton, Kristin Emil. BS with distinction, U.S. Naval Acad., 1959; LLB cum laude, Harvard U., 1967. Bar: Calif. 1967, U.S. Ct. Appeals (9th cir.) 1970, U.S. Supreme Ct. 1979. Assoc. Latham & Watkins, L.A., 1967-75, ptnr. Costa Mesa, Calif., 1975—, mng. ptnr., 1993-97. Dir. Constl. Rights Found., Orange County, Calif., 1986-91; lawyer rep. 9th Cir. Jud. Conf., 1991-93. Mem. exec. com. Orange County coun. Boy Scouts Am., Costa Mesa, 1982-95. Capt. USNR, 1955-83. Recipient Silver Beaver award Boy Scouts Am., Orange County coun., 1991. Fellow Am. Coll. Trial Lawyers; mem. Orange County Bar Assn. (dir. 1984-91), U.S. Supreme Ct. Hist. Soc. (chmn. So. Calif. 1992-93), Orange County Bar Found. (dir. 1999—). Home: 24 Pinehurst Ln Newport Beach CA 92660 Office: Latham & Watkins 650 Town Center Dr Ste 2000 Costa Mesa CA 92626-1925 E-mail: robert.currie@lw.com

CURRY, CYNTHIA J. R. geneticist; b. Cleve., July 20, 1941; MD, Yale U., 1957. Diplomate Am. Bd. Med. Genetics; Am. Bd. Pediatrics. Intern U. Wash., Seattle, 1967-68, resident, 1968-69, U. Minn., Mpls., 1969-70; fellow med. genetics U. Calif., San Francisco, 1975-76; med. faculty UCSF, Fresno, Calif.; med. dir. genetics Valley Children's Hosp., Madera, 1976—. Contbr. 15 chpt. to books, numerous articles to profl. jours. Office: Valley Childrens Hosp Genetic Med FC21 9300 Valley Childrens Pl Madera CA 93638-8762

CURRY, DANIEL ARTHUR, judge; b. Phoenix, Mar. 28, 1937; s. John Joseph and Eva May (Wills) C.; m. Joy M. Shallenberger, Sept. 5, 1959; children: Elizabeth, Catherine, Peter, Jennifer, Julia , David. B.S., Loyola U., Los Angeles, 1957, LL.B., 1960; postgrad. exec. program, Grad. Sch. Bus., Stanford U., 1980. Bar: Calif. 1961, Hawaii 1972, N.Y. 1988, U.S. Dist. Ct. (cen. dist.) Calif. 1961, U.S. Ct. Appeals (9th cir.) 1961, U.S. Ct.

Mil. Appeals 1963, U.S. Customs Ct. 1968, U.S. Dist. Ct. Hawaii 1972, U.S. Dist. Ct. (no. dist.) Calif. 1983 . Assoc. Wolford, Johnson, Pike & Covell, El Monte, Calif., 1964-65, Demetriou & Del Guercio, L.A., 1965-67; counsel, corporate staff divisional asst. Technicolor, Inc., Hollywood, Calif., 1967-70; v.p., sec., gen. counsel Amfac, Inc., Honolulu, 1970-78, sr. v.p., gen. counsel Honolulu and San Francisco, 1978-87; v.p., gen. counsel Times Mirror, L.A., 1987-92; judge Superior Ct. of State of Calif., 1992-98; assoc. justice Calif. Ct. Appeal 2d dist., L.A., 1998—. Served to capt. USAF, 1961-64. Mem. L.A. Country Club, Phi Delta Phi. Office: Calif Ct Appeal 2d Dist 4th Fl North Tower 300 S Spring St Los Angeles CA 90013-1230

CURRY, WILLIAM SIMS, county official; b. Mt. Vernon, Washington, Feb. 6, 1938; s. Eli Herbert Curry and Winona Geraldine (Davis) Mickelson; m. Kirsten Ingeborg Arms, May 20, 1971; children: William II, Kevin, Randal, Kim Cannova, Derek. BS in Bus. Mgmt., Fla. State U., 1967; MBA, Ohio State U., 1968. Cert. profl. contracts mgr. Asst. purchasing officer Stanford (Calif.) Linear Accelerator Ctr., 1977-80; subcontract adminstr. Lockheed Missiles & Space Co., Sunnyvale, Calif., 1980-81; materials mgr. Altus Corp., San Jose, 1981-86; purchasing mgr. Litton Electron Devices, San Carlos, 1986-95, Comms. & Power Industries, Palo Alto, 1995-97; contracts mgr. Landacorp, Chico, 1998; purchasing svcs. mgr. Butte County, Oroville, 1998-01, dep. adminstrv. officer, 2001—. Bd. dirs. Industry Coun. for Small Bus. Devel., Sunnyvale, 1992-97, v.p. programs, 1992-93, exec. v.p., 1994-95, pres., 1995-97. Contbr. articles to profl. jours. Capt. USAF, 1955-77. Decorated Meritorious Svc. medal with one oak leaf cluster, USAF, 1977. Fellow Nat. Contract Mgmt. Assn.; mem. Calif. Assn. Pub. Purchasing Officers, Am. Mensa, Beta Gamma Sigma. Republican. Avocations: chess, writing, cycling. Home: 17 Northwood Commons Pl Chico CA 95973-7213 Office: Butte County 25 County Center Dr Oroville CA 95965-3380 E-mail: bill_curry@earthlink.net

CURTIN, DANIEL JOSEPH, JR. lawyer; b. San Francisco, Jan. 7, 1933; s. Daniel Joseph and Nell Helen (Lenihan) C.; m. Myrtle Rose Wanke, Feb. 7, 1959; children: Kathleen, Mary, Patricia, Thomas, Carol. AB in Polit. Sci., U. San Francisco, 1954, JD, 1957. Bar: Calif. 1958. Asst. sec. State Senate Calif., Sacramento, 1959; cons., counsel Assembly Com. on Local Govt., Sacramento, 1959-60; dep. city atty. Richmond, Calif., 1961-65; city atty. Walnut Creek, 1965-82; with Williams, Caploe, Robbins & Curtin, Benicia, 1983-84; ptnr. McCutchen, Doyle, Brown & Enersen, Walnut Creek, 1984—. Mem. bd. advisors environ. affairs Boston Coll. Sch. of Law, 1987—; mem. State Sen. Housing Adv. Task Force, 1983-84, State Sen. Subcom. on the Redevel. of Antiquated Subdivs., 1986; instr. continuing edn. of the bar, 1975, 82, 88, U. San Francisco Sch. of Law, 1988-92, Golden Gate U. Sch. of Law, 1979-82, U. Calif. Extension, 1973—, John F. Kennedy U. Sch. of Law, Walnut Creek, 1983-90; mem. adv. com. Alcohol and Drug Abuse Coun., Pleasant Hill, Calif. Contbr. articles to profl. jours. Lt. U.S. Army, 1958, 56-64. Recipient Disting. Leadership award, Nat. Planning award Am. Planning Assn., 1988; named City Atty. of Yr., 1971 and others. Mem. ABA (sect. on state and local govt. law, coun. chair 2001-02, chmn. land use, planning and zoning com. 1976-78, vice-chair 1999), Calif. State Bar Assn. (mem. exec. com., real property law sect. 1988-91, mem. com. on environ. 1977-80), Nat. Inst. Mcpl. Law Officer (chmn. zoning and planning com. 1969-79, regional v.p. 1979-82, Lifetime Achievement in Mcpl. Law Charles S. Rhyne award), Calif. Pk. and Recreation Soc., League of Calif. Cities (pres. city atty.'s dept. 1973-74), Lambda Alpha, others. Democrat. Roman Catholic. Avocations: pub. speaking, gardening. Office: McCutchen Doyle Brown & Enersen 1333 N Calif Blvd Ste 210 PO Box V Walnut Creek CA 94596-4534 Office Fax: 925-975-5390. E-mail: dcurtin@mdbe.com

CURTIN, DAVID STEPHEN, newswriter; b. Kansas City, Mo., Dec. 18, 1955; s. Gerald and Nadine (Pemberton) C. BS in Journalism, U. Colo., 1978. Newswriter Littleton (Colo.) Independent, 1976-77, Boulder (Colo.) Daily Camera, 1978-79, Greeley (Colo.) Daily Tribune, 1979-84, Durango (Colo.) Herald, 1984-87, Colorado Springs (Colo.) Gazette Telegraph, 1987-97, Denver Post, 1997—. Pulitzer Prize juror, 1991-92. Recipient Pulitzer Prize for feature writing, 1990. Democrat. Methodist. Avocations: skiing, hiking, mountain climbing.

CURTIN, THOMAS LEE, ophthalmologist; b. Columbus, Ohio, Sept. 9, 1932; s. Leo Anthony and Mary Elizabeth (Burns) C.; m. Constance L. Sallman; children: Michael, Gregory, Thomas, Christopher. BS, Loyola U., L.A., 1954; MD, U. So. Calif., 1957; cert. navy flight surgeon, U.S. Naval Sch. Aerospace Med., 1959. Diplomate Am. Bd. Ophthalmology. Intern Ohio State U. Hosp., 1957-58; resident in ophthalmology U.S. Naval Hosp, San Diego, 1961-64; practice medicine specializing in ophthalmology Oceanside, Calif., 1967—. Mem. staff Tri City, Scripps Meml. hosps.; sci. adv. bd. So. Calif. Soc. Prevention Blindness, 1973-76; bd. dirs. North Coast Surgery Ctr., Oceanside, 1987-96; cons. in field. Trustee Carlsbad (Calif.) Unified Sch. Dist., 1975-83, pres., 1979, 82, 83; trustee Carlsbad Libr., 1990-99, pres., 1993, 98. Officer, MC, USN, 1958-67. Mem. AMA, Calif. Med. Assn., San Diego County Med. Soc., Am. Acad. Ophthalmology, Aerospace Med. Assn., San Diego Acad. Ophthalmology (pres. 1979), Calif. Assn. Ophthalmology (bd. dirs.), Carlsbad Rotary, El Camino Country Club. Repubican. Roman Catholic. Office: 3231 Waring Ct Ste S Oceanside CA 92056-4510

CURTIS, JOHN JOSEPH, lawyer; b. Fairmont, W.Va., Nov. 23, 1942; s. John Joseph and Marie Francis (Christopher) C.; m. Shirley Ann Slater, Oct. 15, 1971 (div. June 1993); children: Christopher, Kevin. AB, U. W.Va., 1964, JD, 1967. Bar: W.Va. 1967, Ill. 1972, Calif. 1979. Pvt. practice law, South Charleston, W.Va., 1967-68; chief counsel, asst. dir. W.Va. Tax Dept., Charleston, 1968-71; tax atty. Sears, Roebuck & Co., Chgo., 1971-73; chief tax counsel, dir. taxes Pacific Lighting, L.A., 1973-87; ptnr. Baker & Hostetler, L.A., 1987-93, Law Offices of John Curtis, L.A., 1994—. Com. mem. Pasadena Tournament Roses, 1978-93. Lt. comdr. USNR, 1968-80. Mem. ABA, L.A. County Bar Assn. (chmn. com. 1989), Calif. Bar Assn., Inst. Property Tax, So. Calif.Tax Found. (pres. 1990-96), L.A. Taxpayers Assn. (pres. 1990-95), Calif. Taxpayers Assn. (pres. 1987-88). Avocations: skiing, scuba, fishing. Office: 2 Arado Rancho Santa Margarita CA 92688-2749 E-mail: jcurtislaw@dol.com

CURTIS, LEGRAND R., JR. lawyer; b. Ogden, Utah, Aug. 1, 1952; BA summa cum laude, Brigham Young U., 1975; JD cum laude, U. Mich., 1978. Bar: Utah 1978, U.S. Ct. Appeals (10th cir.) 1985, U.S. Ct. Claims 1986, U.S. Supreme Ct. 1987. Ptnr. Manning, Curtis Bradshaw & Bednar, LLC, Salt Lake City, 1997—. Mem. Utah State Bar, Salt Lake County Bar Assn. Office: Manning Curtis Bradshaw & Bednar LLC 10 Exchange Pl Ste 300 Salt Lake City UT 84111-5104

CURZON, SUSAN CAROL, university administrator; b. Poole, Eng., Dec. 11, 1947; came to U.S., 1952. d. Kenneth Nigel and Terry Marguerite (Morris) C. AB, U. Calif., Riverside, 1970; MLS, U. Wash., 1972; PhD, U. So. Calif., 1983. Spl. libr. Kennecott Exploration, San Diego, 1972-73; various positions L.A. County Pub. Libr., 1973-89; dir. libr. Glendale (Calif.) Pub. Libr., 1989-92; dean univ. libr. Calif. State U., Northridge, 1992—, Northridge, 1992—. Cons. Grantsmanship Ctr., L.A., 1981-83; vis. lectr. Grad. Sch. Libr. and Info. Sci. UCLA, 1986-92. Author: Managing Change, Managing the Interview. Libr. of the Year, Libr. Jour., 1994. Mem. ALA, Calif. Libr. Assn. Democrat. Avocations: history, horseback riding. Office: Calif State U Libr Office Dean 18111 Nordhoff St Northridge CA 91330-0001

CUSAMANO, GARY M. real estate executive; BS Agrl. Econ., U. Calif., Davis. COO, Newhall Land & Farming Co., Valencia, Calif., 1987—, pres., 1989—, also bd. dirs. Bd. dirs. Watkins-Johnson. Chmn. bd. dirs. Calif. C. of C.; bd. dirs. Henry Mayo Newhall Meml. Hosp. Office: The Newhall Land & Farming Co 23823 Valencia Blvd Valencia CA 91355-2103

CUSHING, MATTHEW, internist; b. Salem, Mass., Apr. 29, 1932; s. Matthew and Marita Jane (Teague) C.; m. Mary Genevieve Connors, June 22, 1957; children: Hugh Austin, Evan Albert. AB, Harvard U., 1953; MD, Tufts U., 1957. Diplomate Am. Bd. Internal Medicine. Intern Colo. Gen. Hosp., Denver, 1957-58; resident U. Calif., San Francisco, 1958-59, San Francisco Gen. Hosp., 1959-61; practice medicine specializing in internal medicine, Andover, Mass., 1963-94; pres. Andover Internal Medicine P.C., 1963—. Mem. staff Lawrence General, Bon Secours, 1963-94, chief internal medicine, 1982-84; med. dir. Suburban Healthcare Ctr., Andover, 1986-94; mem. staff Mill Valley (Calif.) Med. Group, 1994-98; active staff Marin Gen. Hosp., 1994—, Ross Hosp., Kentfield, Calif., 1995-99. Contbg. editor MD Computing, 1983—. Served to lt. comdr. USNR, 1960-62. Mem. Alpha Omega Alpha. Democrat. Unitarian. E-mial. Home: 7 Elizabeth Cir Greenbrae CA 94904-3033 Office: 1300 S Eliseo Dr # 200 Greenbrae CA 94904-2003 E-mail: cushing14@home.com, mcushing@ipninet.com

CUSUMANO, JAMES ANTHONY, filmmaker, retired pharmaceutical company executive; b. Elizabeth, N.J., Apr. 14, 1942; s. Charles Anthony and Carmella Madeline (Catalano) C.; m. Jane LaVerne Melvin, June 15, 1985; children: Doreen Ann, Polly Jean. BA, Rutgers U., 1964, PhD, 1967; grad. Exec. Mktg. Program, Stanford U., 1981, Harvard U., 1988. Mgr. catalyst rsch. Exxon Rsch. and Engring. Co., Linden, N.J., 1967-74; pres., chief exec. officer, founder Catalytica Inc., Mountain View, Calif., 1974-85, chmn., 1985-2000, also bd. dirs.; pres., CEO, bd. dirs. Catalytica Fine Chems., Inc., Mountain View, 1993-97; chmn., CEO, bd. dirs. Catalytica Pharms., Inc., 1997-99, chmn., chief strategic officer, 1999-2000; pres., CEO, founder Chateau Wally Films LLC, Ojai, Calif., 2000—. Lectr. chem. engring. Stanford U., 1978, Rutgers U., 1966-67, Charles D. Hurd lectr. Northwestern U., 1989-90, Jean Day hon. lectr. Rutgers U.; advisor Fulbright scholar progam Inst. Internat. Edn.; mem. dean's adv. bd. Rutgers U., 1997—; speaker in field; mem. com. on catalysts and environ. NSF; exec. briefings with Pres. George Bush and Cabinet mems., 1990, 92, plenary lectr. in field; bd. dirs. Catalytica Advanced Techs., Inc. Author: Catalysis in Coal Conversion, 1978, (with others) Critical Materials Problems in Energy Production, 1976, Advanced Materials in Catalysis, 1977, Liquid Fuels from Coal, 1977, Kirk-Othmer Encyclopedia of Chemical Technology, 1979, Chemistry for the 21st Century, Perspectives in Catalysis, 1992, Science and Technology in Catalysis 1994, 1995; contbr. articles to profl. jours., chpts. to books; founding editor Jour. of Applied Catalysis, 1980; exec. prodr. feature film: What Matters Most, 2000; rec. artist with Royal Teens and Dino Take Five for ABC Paramount, Capitol and Jubilee Records, 1957-67; single records include Short Shorts, Short Shorts Twist, My Way, Hey Jude, Rosemarie, Please Say You Want Me, Lovers Never Say Goodbye; albums include The Best of the Royal Teens, Newies But Oldies; appeared in PBS TV prodn. on molecular engring., Little by Little, 1989. Recipient Surface Chemistry award Continental Oil Co., 1964; Henry Rutgers scholar, 1963, Lever Bros. fellow, 1965, Churchill Coll. fellow Cambridge Univ., 1992. Mem. AIChE, Am. Chem. Soc. (plenary lectr. to chem. educators nat. meeting 1994), Am. Phys. Soc., N.Y. Acad. Scis., Soc. Organic Chems. Mfrs. (bd. dirs. 1996), Am. Mus. Natural History, Pres.'s Assn., Smithsonian Assocs., World Future Soc., Sigma Psi, Phi Lambda Upsilon. Republican. Roman Catholic. Achievements include 20 patents in catalysis and surface science; avocations: mountain climbing, skiing, hiking, sailing, swimming, travel. Home: 620 McNell Rd Ojai CA 93023-9315 Office: Chateau Wally Films LLC 323 E Matilija St #110 Ojai CA 93023 E-mail: jacusumano@earthlink.net

CUTLER, DAVID N. software engineer; BS, Olivet Coll., Mich., 1965. Programmer E.I. duPont Nemours and Co.; software engr. Digital Equipment Corp., Microsoft Corp., Redmond, Wash., 1988—, disting. engr., 2000—. Mem. NAE. Office: Microsoft Corp 1 Microsoft Way Redmond WA 98052-6399

CUTLER, LEONARD SAMUEL, physicist; b. Los Angeles, Jan. 10, 1928; s. Morris and Ethel (Kalech) C.; m. Dorothy Alice Pett, Feb. 13, 1954; children: Jeffrey Alan, Gregory Michael, Steven Russell, Scott Darren. BS in Physics, Stanford U., 1958, MS, 1960, PhD, 1966. Chief engr. Gertsch Products Co., Los Angeles, 1948-56, v.p. R&D, 1956-57; with Hewlett-Packard Co., Palo Alto, Calif., 1957-99, dir. physics rsch., 1969-85, dir. instruments and photonics lab., 1985-87, dir. superconductivity lab., 1987-89, disting. contbr., 1989-99; disting. contbr. tech. staff Agilent Techs., 2000—. Mem. adv. panels Nat. Bur. Standards; cons. Kernco, Inc., Danvers, Mass., 1982—, others. Patentee in field. Served with USNR, 1945-46. Recipient Achievement award Indsl. Rsch. Inst., 1990, Industrial Applications prize Am. Inst. of Physics, 1993 Fellow IEEE (Morris Leeds award 1984, Rabi award 1989), Am. Phys. Soc.; mem. AAAS, NAE, Sigma Xi. Home: 26944 Almaden Ct Los Altos CA 94022-4349 Office: Agilent Techs PO Box 10350 Palo Alto CA 94303-0867 E-mail: len_cutler@agilent.com

CUTONE, KATHALEEN KELLY, figure skater, former skating judge, athletic representative; Athletic rep. U.S. Figure Skating Assn., Colo. Springs, Colo., 1998—. Placed 16th Nat. Sr. competition, 1997, 2nd place Ea. Sr., 1997, New England Sr., 1997, 12th place Nat. Sr., 1996, 4th place Ea. Sr., 1996, 1st place New England Sr., 1996, 6th place World Univ. Games, 1995, 11th place Nat. Sr. competition, 1995, tie for 5th place Nat. Sr., 1995, 2d place Ea. Sr., 1995, 3rd place Ea. Sr., 1995, 1st place Nat. Collegiates, 1994, 12th place U.S. Olympic Festival, 1990, others. Mem. U.S. Figure Skating Assn. Office: USFSA 20 1st St Colorado Springs CO 80906-3624

CUTTER, DAVID LEE, pharmaceutical company executive; b. Oakland, Calif., Jan. 3, 1929; s. Robert Kennedy and Virginia (White) C.; m. Nancy Lee Baugh, Sept. 14, 1950; children: David Lee, Jr., Thomas White, William Baugh, Steven Kennedy, Michael Lee. Student, U. Calif.-Berkeley, 1947; A.B., Stanford U., 1950, M.B.A., 1952. C.P.A., Calif. Staff accountant Webb & Webb, C.P.A.'s, San Francisco, 1952-54; with Cutter Labs., Inc., 1954-84, pres., 1967-74, chmn., 1974-80, vice-chmn., 1980-82; sr. cons., 1982-84. Dir. Chad Therapeutics, Inc., Chatsworth, Calif., 1983—, Civic Bancorp, Civic Bank of Commerce, Oakland, 1984—. Active various community drives; mem. Citizens Com. to Study Discrimination in Housing, Berkeley, 1961-62; troop committeeman Boy Scouts Am., 1964-74; v.p. Mt. Diablo Coun., 1975-77, pres., 1978-80, bd. dirs., 1975—; bd. dirs. Golden Gate Scouting, 1978-90, pres. 1980-84; bd. dirs. Park Hills Homes Assn., 1961-63, HEALS, Emeryville, Calif., 1980-87, Alameda County (Calif.) Taxpayers Assn., 1967-69, Insts. Med. Scis., San Francisco, 1974-76, San Francisco Bay Area Coun., 1968-84, pres. Cutter Found., 1967-86; trustee United Way of Bay Area, 1981-86, Miles Found., 1986-92; mem. adv. bd. Herrick Hosp., 1968-76, trustee, 1976-84, pres. bd. trustees, 1978-84; mem. Accrediting Commn. on Edn. in Health Svcs. Adminstrn., 1982-88, adv. coun. Sch. Bus., San Francisco State Coll., 1966-70; bd. dirs. Alta Bates Health Sys., 1984-95, Alta Bates Med. Ctr., 1988-95, chmn., 1991-95, East Bay Community Found., 1984-89, Hosp. Coun. No. Calif., 1983-89, Pathology Inst., 1986-90; bd. dirs. Acute Care Affiliates, 1987-89, chmn. 1988-89, Calif. Healthcare System, 1992-95; bd. govs. Vol. Trustees Not-for-Profit Hosps., 1989-95, vice chmn. 1990-92, treas. 1993-95; dir. Rossmoor Med. Ctr., 2000—, chmn., 2000—. Recipient Silver Beaver award Boy Scouts Am., 1982. Mem. AICPA, Stanford Alumni Assn., Berkeley C. of C. (dir. 1977-83, v.p. 1978-83), Rotary (Paul Harris fellow 1990), Delta Upsilon. E-mail: Davcutter@aol.com

CUTTER, GARY RAYMOND, biostatistician; b. St. Louis, Feb. 18, 1948; s. Daniel and Mildred (Mandel) C.; m. Sharon R. Gornek, Aug. 24, 1969; children: Corey N., Scott J., Todd J. BA in Math., U. Mo., 1970; MS in Biometry, U. Tex., Houston, 1971, PhD in Biometry, 1974. Asst. prof. biometry U. Tex. Sch. Pub. Health, Houston, 1974-78; expert, cons. Nat. Cancer Inst., Bethesda, Md., 1978-79; assoc. prof. biostats. U. Ala., Birmingham, 1979-89; prof. pub. health St. Jude Children's Rsch. Hosp., Memphis, 1979-89, chair biostats and info. sys., 1989-91; pres. Pythagoras, Inc., Birmingham, 1991—; chmn. Ctr. for Rsch. Methodology and Biometrics AMC Cancer Rsch. Ctr., Denver, 1994—. Adj. prof. U. Colo. Health Sci. Ctr., Denver, 1994—, U. Denver, 1996—, U. Nev., Reno, 1999—. Author: A Module of Math., 1972, (with others) Evaluation of Health Education and Promotion Programs: Principles, Guidelines and Methods for the Practitioner, 1984, 2d edit., 1994; contbr. numerous articles to profl. jours. Bd. dirs. Legal Environ. Assistance Found., Birmingham, 1986-89, Temple Emanu El, Birmingham, 1987-89, Jewish Cmty. Ctr., Birmingham, 1984-88, Fair Share for Health, Denver, 1994-96. Grantee NIH, NHLBI, NIDDK, NCI, Multiple Sclerosis Soc., others. Mem. APHA, Am. Statis. Assn., Am. Biometric Soc., Soc. Clin. Trials, Am. Optometric Assn., Mountain Brook Soccer Club (bd. dirs. 1983-94), Mountain Brook Athletic Assn. (bd. dirs. 1986-88). Office: AMC Cancer Rsch Ctr 1600 Pierce St Denver CO 80214-1897

CYNADER, MAX SIGMUND, psychology, physiology, brain research educator, researcher; b. Berlin, Feb. 24, 1947; arrived in Can., 1951; s. Samuel and Maria (Kraushar) C.; m. Moira Elizabeth Langton, May 30, 1985; children: Madeleine Maria, Rebecca Kay, Alexandra Josephine. BSc, Mc Gill U., Montreal, Que., Can., 1967; PhD, MIT, 1972. Fellow neuroanatomy Max-Planck Inst. Psychiatry, Munich, 1972-73; asst. prof. psychology Dalhousie U., 1973-77, assoc. prof., 1977-81, assoc. prof. physiology, 1979-84, prof. psychology, 1981-84, Killam rsch. prof., 1984-88, prof. physiology, 1984-88; prof. psychology U. B.C., 1988—, prof. physiology, 1988—, prof. dept. ophthalmology, 1988—, dir., 1988-99; dir. Brain Rsch. Ctr., U. B.C. and Vancouver Hosp. and Health Scis. Ctr., 1997. Mem. pres.'s workshop on five yr. plan strengthening sci. support in Can. Natural Scis. and Engring. Rsch. Coun. Can., 1984, workshop for Steacie fellows, 1988; mem. task force on curriculum devel. in Can. neurosci., 1984; mem. spl. adv. panel on rsch. preparedness USAF, 1985; rep. Internat. Human Frontiers Sci. program Med. Rsch. Coun. Can., 1988; mem. grants com. behavioural scis. Med. Rsch. Coun. Can., program grants com. 1989—; referee senate rev. grad. program in neurosci. U. Western Ont., 1989; mem. math., computational and theoretical spl. rev. com. NIMH, 1989—; external reviewer Med. Rsch. Coun. Can., Alta. Heritage Fund Med. Rsch., NIH, NSF, USAF Office Sci. Rsch., Multiple Sclerosis Soc. Can., Vancouver Found., March of Dimes, Fight for Sight. Mem. editorial bd. jours. Behavioral Brain Rsch., Clin. Vision Scis., Concepts in Neurosci., Devel. Brain Rsch., Exptl. Brain Rsch., Neural Networks, Visual Neurosci.; mem. adv. bd. series Rsch. Notes in Neural Computing; contbr. articles to profl. jours. Recipient Killam Rsch. prize U. B.C., 1989—; E.W.R. Steacie fellow Natural Sci. and Engring. Rsch. Coun. Can., 1979, Can. Inst. Advanced Rsch. fellow, 1986—, Bank of Montreal fellow Can. Inst. for Advanced Rsch., 1998; grantee Med. Rsch. Coun. Can., 1973—, Natural Sci. and Engring. Rsch. Coun. Can., 1975—, NIH, 1978-81. Fellow Can. Inst. Advanced Rsch., Royal Soc. Can.; mem. Soc. Neurosci. (Halifax chpt., pres. 1985, edn. com. 1986-89), Can. Assn. Neurosci. (pres. 1986), Assn. Rsch. Otolaryngology, Assn. Rsch. in Vision and Opthalmology, Can. Physiol. Soc., Internat. Brain Rsch. Orgn., Internat. Soc. Devel. Neurosci., Internat. Strabismol. Assn., World Fedn. Neuroscientists. Achievements include being named semifinalist Can. Astronaut program, 1983. Office: U BC Vancouver Hosp Brain Rsch Ctr 2211 Wesbrook Mall Vancouver BC Canada V6T 2B5 E-mail: cynader@brain.ubc.ca

D'ACCONE, FRANK ANTHONY, music educator; b. Somerville, Mass., June 13, 1931; s. Salvatore and Maria (DiChiappari) D'A. Mus. B., Boston U., 1952, Mus.M., 1953; A.M., Harvard U., 1955, Ph.D., 1960. Asst. prof. music SUNY at Buffalo, 1960-63, assoc. prof., 1964-68; prof. music UCLA, 1968-94, chmn. dept., 1973-76; chmn. faculty UCLA (Coll. Fine Arts), 1976-79; chmn. dept. musicology UCLA, 1989-93. Vis. prof. music Yale U., 1972-73 Author: The History of a Baroque Opera, 1985, The Civic Muse, 1997; editor: Music of the Florentine Renaissance, vols. 1-12, 1967-94; gen. editor Corpus Mensurabilis Musicae, 1986—; co-editor Musica Disciplina, 1990—; contbr. articles to profl. jours. Fellow Am. Acad. Rome, 1963-64, Fulbright Found., 1963-64, NEH, 1975; recipient G.K. Delmas Venetian Studies award, 1977, J.S. Guggenheim Found. award, 1980, Internat. Galilei prize, Pisa, 1997. Fellow Am. Acad. of Arts and Scis.; mem. Am. Musicol. Soc. (dir. 1973-74), Internat. Musicol. Soc. Home: 725 Fontana Way Laguna Beach CA 92651-4010 Office: U Calif Dept Music Los Angeles CA 90024

DACHS, ALAN MARK, investment company executive; b. N.Y.C., Dec. 7, 1947; s. Sidney and Martha (Selz) D.; m. Lauren B. Dachs, June 23, 1973. BA, Wesleyan U., Middletown, Conn., 1970; MBA, NYU, 1978. Account officer Chem. Bank, N.Y.C., 1971-74; various positions Bechtel Group, Inc., San Francisco, 1974-81; v.p., CFO Dual Drilling Co., Wichita Falls, Tex., 1981-82; sr. v.p., mng. dir. Bechtel Investments, Inc., San Francisco, 1982-89; pres., dir., mem. exec. com. and CEO Fremont Group, L.L.C., San Francisco, 1989—. Bd. dirs. Bechtel Group, Bechtel Enterprises, Inc., ESCO Corp., Portland, Oreg., Sequoia Ventures Inc., San Francisco. Charter trustee, chair bd. trustees Wesleyan U.; trustee The Brooking Instn. Mem. Young Pres. Orgn. Office: Fremont Group LLC 199 Fremont St Ste 3700 San Francisco CA 94105-2230

DACKAWICH, S. JOHN, sociology educator; b. Loch Gelley, W.Va., Jan. 31, 1926; s. Samuel and Estelle (Jablonski) D.; m. Shirley Jean McVay, May 20, 1950; children: Robert John, Nancy Joan. B.A., U. Md., 1955; Ph.D., U. Colo., 1958. Instr. U. Colo., 1955-57; instr. Colo. State U., 1957-59; prof., chmn. sociology Calif. State U., Long Beach, 1959-70, prof. sociology Fresno, 1970-94, chmn. dept., 1970-75, prof. sociology emeritus, 1994—. Pvt. practice survey rsch., 1962— Author: Sociology, 1970, The Fiery Furnace Effect, 2000; contbr. articles and rsch. papers to profl. publs. Mem. Calif. Dem. Ctrl. Com., 1960-62; co-dir. Long Beach Ctrl. Area Study, 1962-64, Citizen Participation Study, Fresno. With USMCR, 1943-46, U.S. Army, 1950-53. Mem. Am., Pacific sociol. assns. Home: 5841 W Judy Ct Visalia CA 93277-8601 Office: Calif State U Dept Sociology 5340 N Campus Dr Fresno CA 93740-8019

DACKOW, OREST TARAS, insurance company executive; b. Wynyard, Sask., Can., Sept. 17, 1936; s. Luke Dackow and Irene Stacheruk; m. Florence Dorothy Waples, Sept. 20, 1958; children: Trevor Wade, Heather Lynn, Donna Louise B in Commerce with honors, U. Man., Winnipeg, Can., 1958; grad. advanced mgmt. program, Harvard U., 1976. Enrolled actuary. V.p. individual ops. Great-West Life Ins. Co., Winnipeg, Man., Can., 1976-78, sr. v.p. individual ops. Can., 1978-79, sr. v.p. U.S. Can., 1979-83; exec. v.p., COO U.S. Great-West Life Assurance Co., Denver, 1983-88, exec. v.p. corp. fin. and control Winnipeg, 1988-90, pres., 1990-94, dir., 1992—; pres., CEO, dir. Great-West Lifeco Inc., Inglewood, Colo., 1992—. Bd. dirs. London Life. Bd. dirs. Met. YMCA, Winnipeg,

1971-80, pres., 1979-80; bd. dirs. Met. YMCA, Denver, 1981-84, Colo. Alliance of Bus., 1986-87, Nat. Jewish Ctr. for Immunology and Respiratory Medicine, 1985—, Health Scis. Centre Rsch. Found., 1990-94, Instrumental Diagnostics Devel. Office, 1992-94. Fellow Soc. Actuaries, Can. Inst. Actuaries; mem. Am. Acad. Actuaries. Avocation: sailing.

DAFFORN, GEOFFREY ALAN, biochemist; b. Cunningham, Kans., Feb. 4, 1944; s. Francis Elston and Anna Elizabeth Dafforn; m. Gail McLaughlin, July 14, 1973; 1 child, Christine Elizabeth. BA cum laude, Harvard U., 1966; PhD, U. Calif., Berkeley, 1970. Postdoctoral fellow U. Calif., Berkeley, 1973; asst. prof. U. Tex., Austin, 1974; from asst. prof. to assoc. prof. Bowling Green (Ohio) State U., 1974-81; sr. chemist Syva Co., Palo Alto, Calif., 1982-87, rsch. fellow, 1987—, group mgr., 1999—. Author articles and abstracts; patentee in field. Grantee Army Rsch. Office, 1979-82, Am. Chem. Soc., 1975-80. Mem. AAAS, Am. Chem. Soc., Sierra Club. Office: Dade Behring 3403 Yerba Buena Rd San Jose CA 95135-1500 E-mail: alandafform@aol.com

DAFOE, DONALD CAMERON, surgeon, educator; b. Appleton, Wis., Nov. 22, 1949; BS in Zoology, U. Wis., 1971, MD, 1975. Diplomate Am. Bd. Surgery. Intern Hosp. of U. of Pa., Phila., 1975-76, resident, 1976-80, Measey rsch. fellow, 1978-80, chief resident, 1980-81, clin. fellow, Culpeper Found. fellow, 1981-82; asst. prof. surgery U. Mich., Ann Arbor, 1982-87; dir. clin. pancreas transplantation program u. Mich., Ann. Arbor, 1984-87; assoc. prof. surgery U. Mich., Ann Arbor, 1987; assoc. prof. surgery, chief divsn. transplantation Hosp. of U. of Pa., Phila., 1987-91, Stanford (Calif.) U. Med. Ctr., 1991-99, dir. kidney/kidney pancreas program, 1999-2000; Chief ofSurgery Thomas Jefferson Sch. of Med., 2000-. Reviewer various publs.; mem. editorial bd. Transplantation Sci., 1992, The Chimera, 1993; contbr. over 100 articles to profl. jours; also numerous book chpts. Mem. ACS, Am. Surg. Assn., Am. Diabetes Assn., Am. Soc. Transplant Surgeons, Assn. for Acad. Surgery, Soc. Internat. de Chirurgie, The Transplantation Soc., Pacific Coast Surg. Assn., Ctrl. Surg. Assn., Frederick A. Coller Surg. Soc., Soc. Univ. Surgeons, Surg. Biology Club II, Ravdin-Rhoads Surg. Soc., United Network for Organ Sharing, Calif. Transplant Donor Network, Western Assn. Transplant Surgeons. Office: 750 Welch Rd Ste 200 Palo Alto CA 94304-1509

DAGNON, JAMES BERNARD, human resources executive; b. St. Paul, Jan. 31, 1940; s. James Lavern and Margaret Elizabeth (Coughlin) D.; m. Sandra Ann McGinley, June 4, 1960; children: Sheri T. Dagnon Tice, Terry J., Laurie M., Diana L. BS in Bus. with distinction, U. Minn., St. Paul, 1979, cert. in indsl. rels., 1978. Various clerical positions No. Pacific Ry. Co., St. Paul, 1957-70; supr., then mgr. pers. rsch. and stats. Burlington No. R.R. Co., St. Paul, 1970, mgr. manpower planning, 1970-78, dir. compensation and orgnl. planning, 1978-81; asst. v.p. compensation and benefits Burlington No. Inc., Seattle, 1981-84, from v.p. labor rels. to exec. v.p. employee rels. Ft. Worth, 1984-95; sr. v.p. employee rels. Burlington No. Santa Fe Ry Co., Ft. Worth, 1995-97; sr. v.p. people The Boeing Co., Seattle, 1997—. Bd. trustees Bellvue Cmty. Coll., 2000—; bd. dirs. Inroads Inc., Seattle Inroads, Inc., Washington Early Learning Found. Pres. Cath. Evang. Outreach, Seattle, 1981-84; chmn. Corp. Champions, Ft. Worth, 1994-96; bd. trustees Cook-Ft. Worth Children's Med. Ctr., 1995-97; bd. dirs. United Way Met. Tarrant County, 1995-97, Wash. State Gov.'s Commn. on Higher Edn. in 2020; trustee Bellvue C.C., 1999, Washington Early Learning Found., 1999. Capt. USAR, 1957-70. Mem. Beta Gamma Sigma. Republican. Avocations: flying, scuba diving, photography. Home: 1237 Evergreen Point Rd Medina WA 98039-3136 Office: The Boeing Co 7755 E Marginal Way S Seattle WA 98108-4000

DAHL, RICHARD J. financial company executive, banking executive; b. Idaho; BS in Acctg., U. Idaho. From staff auditor to mgr. audit dept. Ernst & Young; CFO Pacific Century Fin. Corp./Bank of Hawaii, Honolulu, 1987-94, pres., COO, 1994—. Bd. dirs. Oceanic Inst., Le Jardin Windward Oahu Acad., Punahou Sch., Pacific Health Rsch. Inst.; mem. exec. adv. com. Brigham Young H., Hawaii campus; mem. adv. coun. Boy Scouts Am., Girl Scouts U.S. Mem. Hawaii Med. Svc. Assn. (bd. dirs.), C. of C. Hawaii (bd. dirs.). Office: Pacific Century Fin Corp 130 Merchant St Honolulu HI 96813

DAHLGREN, DOROTHY, museum director; b. Coeur d'Alene, Idaho; m. Robert Eagan, 1985; 1 child, Ivan. BS in Museology and History, U. Idaho, 1982; M in Orgnl. Leadership, Gonzaga U., 1998. Dir. Mus. N. Idaho, Coeur d'Alene, 1982—. Grant reviewer gen. operating support grants Inst. Mus. and Libr. Svcs., 1993—; mem. Kootenai County Hist. Preservation Commn. Author: (with Simone Carbonneau Kincaid) In All the West No Place Like This; A Pictorial HIstory of the Coeur d'Alene Region, 1996. Mem. Idaho Heritage Trust com. N. region. Office: Mus N Idaho PO Box 812 Coeur D Alene ID 83816 E-mail: museumni@nidlink.com

DAHLSTEN, DONALD LEE, entomology educator, university dean; b. Clay Center, Nebr., Dec. 8, 1933; s. Leonard Harold and Shirley B. (Courtright) D.; m. Reva D. Wilson, Sept. 19, 1959 (div.); children: Dia Lee, Andrea; m. Janet Clair Winner, Aug. 7, 1965; stepchildren: Karen Rae, Michael Allen. BS, U. Calif., Davis, 1956; MS, U. Calif., Berkeley, 1960, PhD, 1963. Asst. prof. Los Angeles State Coll., 1962-63; asst. entomologist U. Calif., Berkeley, 1963-65, lectr., 1965-68, asst. prof., 1968-69, assoc. prof., 1969-74, prof. entomology, 1974—, chmn. divsn. Biol. Control, 1980-88;, 1990-91; chmn. dept. cons. and resource studies U. Calif., Berkeley, 1989-91, dir. lab. biol. control, 1992-94; assoc. dean instrn. and student affairs Coll. Natural Resources, U. Calif., Berkeley, 1996—. Vis. prof. Yale Sch. Forestry and Environ. Studies, 1980-81, Integrated Pest Mgmt. Team People's Republic China, 1980, 81.. Mem. AAAS, Am. Inst. Biol. Scis. (vis. prof., lectr. 1970-71), Entomol. Soc. Am., Entomol. Soc. Can., Soc. Am. Foresters. Office: U Calif Ctr Biol Control 201 Wellman Hall Berkeley CA 94720-3112 E-mail: donaldd@nature.berkeley.edu

DAICHENDT, GARY J. executive sales professional; BA in Math., Youngstown State U.; MS in Math., Ohio State U. Formerly with IBM, Wang Labs.; former sr. v.p. worldwide ops., v.p. intercontinental ops. Cisco Systems, Inc., San Jose, Calif., exec. v.p. worldwide ops., 1996—. Office: Cisco Systems Inc 170 W Tasman Dr San Jose CA 95134-1706

DAILEY, DAWN ELAINE, public health service official; b. Berkeley, Calif., Feb. 2, 1965; d. Stanley Wilfred Sr. and Mercedes Anderson; m. Kenneth Lamar Dailey, Apr. 19, 1986; 1 child, Mariana. BSN, U. San Francisco, 1988; MSN, Samuel Merritt Coll., 1997. RN, CNS, Calif.; bd. cert. Clin. Nurse Specialist, Calif., Cert. Specialist in Cmty. Health Nursing; ANCC. Nurse Alta Bates Hosp., Berkeley, 1988-91; home health nurse Kaiser Permanente, Martinez, Calif., 1992-94; coord. Contra Costa SIDS Program, Martinez, 1995—, Fetal Infant Mortality Review Program, Martinez, 1998—. Pub. health nurse Contra Costa County, Martinez, 1989—; instr. univ. extension U. Calif., Davis; mem. SIDS/OID adv. com. Nat. Ctr. on Cultural Competence, Georgetown U., 1999—; cons. Calif. SIDS Program, Fair Oaks, 1994-98; mem. Calif. SIDS Adv. Coun., Sacramento, 1996—, pres. No. Calif. Regional SIDS Adv. Coun., Berkeley, 1993-98; mem. Contra Costa Immunization Coalition, Martinez, 1996-97, Childhood Injury Prevention Coalition, Contra Costa County, 1993—; bd. mem. No. Calif. SIDS Alliance, Berkeley; v.p. Assn. of SIDS and Infant Mortality Program. Bd. dirs. Child Abuse Prevention Coun. Contra Costa County; mem. profl. edn. com. Bay Area chpt. March of Dimes, 1999—. Recipient Excellence award, Contra Costa County, 1998, Outstanding Grad. award, Samuel Merritt Coll., 1997; fellow Eugene Cota-Robles, Univ. Calif. San Francisco, 2001; scholar Shirley C. Titus, Calif. Nurses Assn., 1995, Nursing Edn., 1996. Mem. Assn. SIDS and Infant Mortality Programs (v.p.), Sigma Theta Tau, Chi Eta Phi (Basileus 1997, Omicron Phi chpt.). Avocations: boating, quilting. Home: 980 Cashel Cir Vacaville CA 95688-8572

DAILEY, DIANNE K. lawyer; b. Great Falls, Mont., Oct. 10, 1950; d. Gilmore and Patricia Marie (Linnane) Halverson. BS, Portland State U., 1977; JD, Lewis & Clark Coll., 1982. Assoc. Bullivant, Houser, Bailey, et. al., Portland, Oreg., 1982-88, ptnr., 1988—. Contbr. articles to profl. jours. Mem.: ABA (vice chair tort and ins. practice sect. 1995—96, chair-elect tort and ins. practice sect. 1996—97, chair tort and ins. practice sect. 1997—98, governing coun. 1992—99, property ins. law com., ins. coverage litigation com., comm. com., chair task force on involvement of women 1990—93, liaison to commn. on women 1993—97, chair task force CERCLA reauthorization, litigation sect., standing com. environ. law 1996—99, chair sect. officers conf. 1998—2001), Wash. Bar Assn., Oreg. State Bar, Multnomah Bar Assn. (bd. dirs. 1994—95), Internat. Assn. Def. Counsel, Def. Rsch. Inst., Fedn. Ins. and Corp. Counsel. Office: Bullivant Houser Bailey 300 Pioneer Tower 888 SW 5th Ave Ste 300 Portland OR 97204-2089

DALE, DAVID C. physician, medical educator; b. Knoxville, Tenn., Sept. 19, 1940; s. John Irvin and Cecil (Chandler) D.; m. Rose Marie Wilson, June 22, 1963 BS magna cum laude, Carson-Newman Coll., 1962; MD cum laude, Harvard U., 1966. Intern and resident Mass. Gen. Hosp., 1966-68; resident U. Wash. Hosp., Seattle, 1971-72; clin. assoc. NIH, 1968-71; prof., assoc. chmn. dept. medicine U. Wash., Seattle, 1976-82, dean Sch. of Medicine, 1982-86. Contbr. numerous articles to profl. jours. Served to comdr. USPHS, 1968-70, 72-74 Mem. Am. Soc. Hematology, Assn. Am. Physicians, Am. Soc. for Clin. Investigation, ACP Avocations: woodworking, gardening, backpacking, sports. Office: U Wash Sch Medicine RG-22 PO Box 356422 Seattle WA 98195-6422 E-mail: dcdale@u.washington.edu

DALE, MARCIA LYN, nursing educator; b. Ft. Dodge, Iowa, Mar. 4, 1938; d. William R. and Erma (Umland) Bradley; m. William G. Dale, Jr., June 30, 1967; children: Dori Lyn, Devin Glenn. BS, U. Wyo., 1960; M. Nursing, U. Wash., 1961; EdD, U. No. Colo., 1981. Prof. U. Wyo., Laramie, 1971—, dean sch. nursing, assoc. dean coll. health scis., 1991—. Recipient Disting. Alumni award Sch. Nursing U. Wyo., 1985. Fellow Am. Acad. Nursing; mem. Wyo. Nurses Assn. (Wyo.'s Search for Excellence Leadership award 1989), Wyo. League for Nursing, Sigma Theta Tau. Home: 827 Evergreen St Cheyenne WY 82009-3218

DALEN, JAMES EUGENE, cardiologist, educator; b. Seattle, Apr. 1, 1932; s. Charles A. and Muriel E. (Joanise) Robinson. BS, Wash. State U., 1955; MA, U. Mich., 1956; MD, U. Wash., 1961; MPH, Harvard U., 1972. Intern and asst. med. resident Boston City Hosp., 1961-63; sr. resident New Eng. Med. Ctr., Boston, 1963-64; rsch. fellow in cardiology Peter Bent Brigham Hosp., Boston, 1964-67, assoc. dir. cardiovascular lab., 1967-75; instr., asst. prof., asso. prof. medicine Harvard Med. Sch., 1967-75; chmn. dept. cardiovascular medicine U. Mass. Med. Sch., 1975-77, prof., chmn. dept. medicine, 1977-88; physician-in-chief U. Mass. Hosp., 1977-88; acting chancellor U. Mass. at Worcester, 1986-87; dean, vice provost med. affairs U. Ariz. Coll. of Medicine, Tucson, 1988-95; dean, v.p. health scis. U. Ariz. Coll. Medicine, Tucson, 1995—. Contbr. articles to med. jours.; editor: Archives of Internal Medicine, 1987—. Served with USN, 1951-53. Mem. A.C.P., Assn. Univ. Cardiologists, Am. Coll. Cardiology, Am. Coll. Chest Physicians (pres. 1985-86), Am. Fedn. Clin. Research Home: 5305 N Via Velazquez Tucson AZ 85750-5989 Office: U Ariz Deans Office Coll Medicine Tucson AZ 85724-0001 E-mail: JDalen@u.arizona.edu

DALESIO, WESLEY CHARLES, former aerospace educator; b. Paterson, N.J., Mar. 26, 1930; s. William James and Sarah (Sheets) Delison; m. Dorothy May Zellers, Nov. 17, 1951; children: Michael Kerry, Debra Kaye Dalesio Weber. Student, Tex. Christian U., 1950, U. Tex., Arlington, 1957. Enlisted USAF, 1948, advanced through grades to sr. master sgt., 1968, aircraft engine mech., mgmt. analyst worldwide, 1948-70; ins. agt. John Hancock Ins., Denver, 1970-71; office mgr. Comml. Builder, Denver, 1972-73; aerospace educator Sch. Dist. 50, Westminster, Colo., 1973-93. Dir. aerospace edn. CAP, Denver, 1982-86, 94—. Mem. Crimestoppers, Westminster, 1988-91, Police and Citizens Teamed Against Crime, Westminster, 1992-93. Lt. col. CAP, 1981—. Mem. Nat. Assn. Ret. Mil. Instrs. (charter mem.), Westminster Edn. Assn., 7th Bomb Wing B-36 Assn., Internat. Platform Assn., Nat. Aeronautic Assn., Acad. Model Aeronautics, Arvada Associated Modelers (life). Episcopalian. Avocations: antique collecting, leatherwork, flying miniature aircraft, model car collecting. Home: 2537 W 104th Cir Westminster CO 80234-3507

DALESSIO, DONALD JOHN, physician, neurologist, educator; b. Jersey City, Mar. 2, 1931; s. John Andrea and Susan Dorothy (Minotta) D.; m. Jane Catherine Schneider, Sept. 4, 1954 (dec. Mar. 1998); children: Catherine Leah, James John, Susan Jane. BA, Wesleyan U., 1952; MD, Yale U., 1956. Diplomate Am. Bd. Internal Medicine. Intern N.Y.C. Hosp., 1956-57, asst. resident in medicine and neurology, 1959-61; resident in medicine Yale Med. Ctr., 1961-62; pres. med. staff Scripps Clinic, La Jolla, Calif., 1974-78; chmn. dept. medicine Scripps Clin., La Jolla, 1974-89, chmn. emeritus, 1989—, cons., 1982—, pres. med. group, 1980-81; clin. prof. neurology U. Calif., San Diego, 1973—. Physician in chief Green Hosp., La Jolla, 1974-89; Musser-Burch lectr. Tulane U., 1979, Kash lectr. U. Ky., 1979; pres. Am. Assn. Study Headache, Chgo., 1974-76, Nat. Migraine Found., Chgo., 1977-79; chmn. Fedn. Western Soc. Neurology, Santa Barbara, Calif., 1976-77. Author: Wolff's Headache, 7th edit., 2001, Approach to Headache, 1973, 6th edit., 1999; editor: Headache jour., 1965-75, 79-84, Scripps Clinic Personal Health Letter; mem. editl. bd. Jour. AMA, 1977-87; columnist San Diego Tribune. Capt. U.S. Army, 1957-59. Recipient Disting. Alumnus award Wesleyan U., Middletown, Conn., 1982. Fellow ACP; mem. Am. Acad. Neurology (assoc.), World Fedn. Neurology (Am. sec. 1980-90, rsch. group on migraine), La Jolla Country Club, La Jolla Beach/Tennis Club. Republican. Roman Catholic. Avocations: tennis, squash, piano. Home: 8891 Nottingham Pl La Jolla CA 92037-2131 Office: Scripps Clinic & Rsch Found 10666 N Torrey Pines Rd La Jolla CA 92037-1092

DALEY, RICHARD HALBERT, museum director; b. Centralia, Ill., Oct. 8, 1948; s. Richard Glen D.; m. Lucy W. Costen, Nov. 27, 1976. Student, Lake Forest (Ill.) Coll., 1966-67; BS, Colo. State U., 1970, MS, 1972. Instr. Colo. State U., Ft. Collins, 1972; from dir. biol. svcs. to dir. programs Mo. Bot. Garden, St. Louis, 1973-84; exec. dir. Mass. Hort. Soc., Boston, 1984-91, Denver Botanic Gardens, 1991-94; instr. Environ. Ethics Denver U., 1992-94; exec. dir. Sonara Desert Museum, Tucson, 1994—. Mem. editorial com. Am. Mus. Natural History, N.Y.C., 1983-92. Bd. trustees Ctr. for Plant Conservation, 1994—. Mem. Am. Assn. Bot. Gardens (bd. trustees), Hort. Club Boston, Rotary Club Denver. Office: Ariz Sonara Desert Museum 2021 N Kinney Rd Tucson AZ 85743-9719

DALIS, IRENE, mezzo-soprano, opera company administrator, music educator; b. San Jose, Calif., Oct. 8, 1925; d. Peter Nicholas and Mamie Rose (Boitano) D.; m. George Loinaz, July 16, 1957; 1 child, Alida Mercedes. AB, San Jose State Coll., 1946; MA in Teaching, Columbia U., 1947; MMus (hon.), San Jose State U., 1957; studied voice with, Edyth Walker, N.Y.C., 1947-50, Paul Althouse, , 1950-51, Dr. Otto Mueller, Milan, Italy, 1952-72, MusD (hon.), Santa Clara U., 1987, DFA (hon.), Calif. State U., 1999. Prin. artist Berlin Opera, 1955-65, Met. Opera, N.Y.C., 1957-77, San Francisco Opera, 1958-73, Hamburg (Fed. Republic Germany) Staatsoper, 1966-71; prof. music San Jose State U., Calif., 1977—; founder, gen. dir. Opera San Jose, 1984—. Dir. Met. Opera Nat. Auditions, San Jose dist., 1980-88. Operatic debut as dramatic mezzo-soprano Oldenburgisches Staatstheater, 1953, Berlin Staedtische Opera, 1955; debut Met. Opera, N.Y.C., 1957, 1st Am.-born singer, Kundry Bayreuth Festival, 1961, opened, Bayreuth Festival, Parsifal, 1963; commemorative Wagner 150th Birth Anniversary; opened 1963 Met. Opera Season in Aida; premiered: Dello Joio's Blood Moon, 1961, Henderson's Medea, 1972; rec. artist Parsifal, 1964 (Grand Prix du Disque award); contbg. editor Opera Quar., 1983. Recipient Fulbright award for study in Italy, 1951, Woman of Achievement award Commn. on Status of Women, 1983, Pres.'s award Nat. Italian Am. Found., 1985, award of merit People of San Francisco, 1985, San Jose Renaissance award for sustained and outstanding artistic contbn., 1987, Medal of Achievement Acad. Vocal Arts, 1988; named Honored Citizen City of San Jose, 1986; inducted into Calif. Pub. Edn. Hall of Fame, 1985, others. Mem. Beethoven Soc. (mem. adv. bd. 1985—), San Jose Arts Round Table, San Jose Opera Guild, Am. Soc. Univ. Women, Arts Edn. Week Consortium, Phi Kappa Phi, Mu Phi Epsilon. Office: Opera San Jose 2049 Paragon Dr San Jose CA 95131 E-mail: dalis@operasj.org

DALIS, PETER T. athletic director; BS in Phys. Edn., UCLA, 1959, MS in Edn., 1963. Dir. Cultural & Recreational Affairs Dept. UCLA, 1963-83, athletic dir., 1983—. Capital project cons. U. Conn., U. New South Wales, Australia; spl. events com. Pacific-10 Conf., chair TV com. Mem. L.A.-Athens Sister City Com., L.A. Sports Coun., Rose Bowl Mgmt. Com.; bd. dirs. So. Calif. Com. Olympic Games. Named Axios Sportsman of Yr., 1987-88. Office: UCLA Dept Athletics PO Box 24044 Los Angeles CA 90024-0044

DALLAGER, JOHN R. career officer; BS in Mech. Engring., USAF Acad., 1969; disting. grad. pilot tng., Craig AFB, Ala., 1970; student F-4 replacement tng., Davis-Monthan AFB, Ariz., 1970-71; MBA, Troy State U., 1978; student, Air Command and Staff Coll., 1983, Nat. Def. U., 1983, U.S. Army War Coll., 1988. Commd. 2d lt. USAF, 1969, lt. gen., 2000, various pilot assignments, 1971-74; air staff tng. officer, legis. liaison Pentagon, Washington, 1974-75; flight comdr., chief wing aircrew tng. 347th Tactical Fighter Wing, Moody AFB, Ga., 1975-76; air liaison officer 601st Tactical Air Support Group, Gelnhausen, W. Germany, 1976-77; instr. Air and Ground Ops. Sch. USAF Europe, Sembach Air Base, W. Germany, 1977-79; A-10 weapons and tactics instr. then exec. officer 355th Tactical Tng. Squadron/Wing, Davis-Monthan AFB, 1979-82; mgr. tactical flying hour programs, other positions Hdqs. USAF, Pentagon, Washington, 1983-85; stationed at Davis-Monthan AFB, 1985-87; various comdr. positions USAF, 1988-92, 94-98; dep. dir. logistics and security asst. then dep. chief staff Hdqs. U.S. Ctrl. Command, MacDill AFB, Fla., 1992-94; asst. chief staff ops. and logistics Supreme Hdqs. Allied Powers Europe, 1998-2000; dir. ops. Joint Guard Bosnia, Joint Guarantor Bosnia, Mons, Belgium, 1998-2000; commd. lt. gen., supt. USAF Acad., 2000—. Decorated D.S.M., Legion of Merit with oak leaf cluster, D.F.C. with two oak leaf clusters, Air medal with 15 oak leaf clusters, Rep. Vietnam Gallantry Cross with Palm, Rep. Vietnam Campaign Medal. Office: Lt Gen Supt Ste 342 2304 Cadet Dr U S A F Academy CO 80840 E-mail: john.dallager@usafa.af.mil

DALLAS, SANDRA, writer; b. Washington, June 11, 1939; d. Forrest Everett and Harriett (Mavity) Dallas; m. Robert Thomas Atchison, Apr. 20, 1963; chidlren: Dana Dallas, Povy Kendal Dallas. BA, U. Denver, 1960. Asst. editor U. Denver Mag., 1965-66; editl. asst. Bus. Week, Denver, 1961-63, 67-69, bur. chief, 1969-85, 90-91, sr. corr., 1985-90; freelance editor, 1990—. Book reviewer Denver Post, 1961—, regional book columnist, 1980—. Author: Gaslights and Gingerbread, 1965, rev. edit., 1984, Gold and Gothic, 1967, No More Than 5 in a Bed, 1967, Vail, 1969, Cherry Creek Gothic, 1971, Yesterday's Denver, 1974, Sacred Paint, 1980, Colorado Ghost Towns and Mining Camps, 1985, Colorado Homes, 1986, Buster Midnight's Cafe, 1990, reissued 1998, The Persian Pickle Club, 1995, The Diary of Mattie Spenser, 1997; editor: The Colorado Book, 1993; contbr. articles to various mags. Bd. dirs. Vis. Nurse Assn., Denver, 1983-85, Hist. Denver, Inc., 1979-82, 84-87, Rocky Mountain Quilt Mus., 2001—. Recipient Wrangler award Nat. Cowboy Hall of Fame, 1980, Lifetime Achievement award Denver Posse of Westerners, 1996, disting. svc. award U. Colo., 1997; named Colo. Exceptional Chronicler of Western History by Women's Library Assn. and Denver Pub. Library Friends Found., 1986; finalist Spur award We. Writers of Am., 1998. Mem. Women's Forum Colo., Denver Woman's Press Club, Western Writers Am., Women Writing the West. Democrat. Presbyterian. Home and Office: 750 Marion St Denver CO 80218-3434

DALLAS, SATERIOS (SAM), aerospace engineer, researcher, consultant; b. Detroit, May 9, 1938; s. Peter and Pauline (Alex) D.; m. Athena Ethel Spartos, July 12, 1964; children: Gregory Dean, Paula Marie. BS in Aero. Engring., U. Mich., 1959, BS in Engring. Math., 1960; MS in Astrodynamics, UCLA, 1963, PhD in Engring., 1968. Rsch. engr. astrodynamics dept. Jet Propulsion Lab., Pasadena, Calif., 1965-78, supr. tech. group mission design, 1978-82, flight engring. office mgr. Voyager Project, 1982-84, sci. and mission design mgr. Magellan Project, 1984-89, tech. mgr. spacecraft analysis, 1989-90, mission mgr. Mars Observer Project, 1990-93, mission mgr. Mars Global Surveyor Project, 1994-97, mission mgr. space interferometry mission, 1997-99, flight project mentor, 2000—. Instr. Pepperdine U., Malibu, Calif., 1973-75; lectr. on space missions Kennedy Space Ctr., Cape Canaveral, Fla., 1988, Australian Dept. Industry, Tech. and Commerce, Canberra, 1988, USAF-CAP-PLR Ctr. Aerospace Edn., Las Vegas, Neb., 1991. Author: Progress in Astronautics and Aeronautics, 1964, Natural and Artificial Satellite Motion, 1979; contbr. articles to sci. jours. Coach Glendale (Calif.) Little League, 1979-82; com. mem. troop 125 Boy Scouts Am., Glendale, 1980. Recipient Apollo achievement award NASA, 1969, cert. of recognition, 1974, Laurels award Aviation Week, 1989, 94. Mem. AIAA, Am. Astron. Soc. (astrodynamics tech. com. 1970-80). Republican. Greek Orthodox. Avocations: snow skiing, hiking, woodworking, tennis, computer applications development. Home: 3860 Karen Lynn Dr Glendale CA 91206-1218 Office: Jet Propulsion Lab 4800 Oak Grove Dr Pasadena CA 91109-8001 E-mail: ssd1938@hotmail.com

DALLMAN, MARY F. physiology educator; BA in Chemistry, Smith Coll., 1956; PhD in Physiology, Stanford U., 1967; postgrad., Swedish Royal Vet. Sch., 1968, U. Calif., San Francisco, 1969-70. Lectr. U. Calif. Dept. Physiology, San Francisco, 1970-72, aast., 1972-76, assoc. prof., 1976-81, prof., 1981—, vice-chair, 1987—. Assoc. editor: Am. Jour. Physiol.: Endocrinology and Metabolism, 1979-85, Steroids, 1985-87, Am. Jour. Physiol.: Regulatory, Integrative and Comparative Physiology, 1990-92; contbr. articles to profl. jours. Recipient Am. Diabetes Rsch. award, 1996. Mem. NIH (mem. endocrine study sect. 1977-81, mem. diabetes, digestive, kidney grants rev. subcom. 1988-92, chair 1992-93), Women in Endocrinology (pres. 1993-95), Internat. Soc. Neuroendocrinology (pres. 1996). Office: U Calif Dept Physiology Box 0444 HSW 747 513 Parnassus Ave San Francisco CA 94143

DALRYMPLE, CHERYL, former online information company executive; CFO LEXIS-NEXIS, Dayton, Ohio, 1997-98, CFO, sr. v.p., 1998-99; CFO Oblix, Inc., Cupertino, Calif., 1999—. Office: Oblix Inc 18922 Forge Dr Cupertino CA 95014

DALRYMPLE, GARY BRENT, research geologist; b. Alhambra, Calif., May 9, 1937; s. Donald Inlow and Wynona Edith (Pierce) D.; m. Sharon Ann Tramel, June 28, 1959; children: Stacie Ann, Robynne Ann Sisco, Melinda Ann Dalrymple McGurer. AB in Geology, Occidental Coll., 1959; PhD in Geology, U. Calif., Berkeley, 1963; DSc (hon.), Occidental Coll., Los Angeles, 1993. Rsch. geologist U.S. Geol. Survey, Menlo Park, Calif., 1963-81, 84-94, asst. chief geologist we. region, 1981-84; dean, prof. Coll. Oceanic and Atmospheric Sci., Oregon State U., Corvallis, 1994-2001; ret. Vis. prof. sch. earth scis. Stanford U., 1969-72, cons. prof., 1983-85, 90-94; disting. alumni centennial spkr. Occidental Coll., 1986-87. Author: Potassium-Argon Dating, 1969, Age of Earth, 1991; contbr. chpts. to books and articles to profl. jours. Fellow NSF, 1961-63; recipient Meritorius Svc. award U.S. Dept. Interior, 1984. Fellow Am. Geophys. Union (pres.-elect 1988-90, pres. 1990-92), Am. Acad. Arts and Scis., Geol. Soc. Am.; mem. AAAS, NAS (chair geology sect. 1997-2000), Am. Inst. Physics (bd. govs. 1991-97), Consortium for Oceanographic Rsch. & Edn. (bd. govs. 1994-2001), Joint Oceanographic Inst. (bd. govs. 1994-2001, chair 1996-98). Achievements include discovery that the earth's magnetic field reverses polarity and determination of time scale of these reversals for the past 3.5 million years; development of ultra-fast high-sensitivity thermoluminescence analyzer for studying lunar surface processes; development and refinement of K-Ar and 40 Ar/39 Ar dating methods and instrumentation, continuous laser probe for determining ages of microgram-sized mineral samples; research on volcanoes in the Hawaiian-Emperor volcanic chain, chronology of lunar basin formation, development and improvement of isotopic dating techniques and instrumentation, geomagnetic field behavior, plate tectonics of the Pacific Ocean basin, evolution of volcanoes, various aspects of Pleistocene history of the western U.S. Home: 1847 NW Hillcrest Dr Corvallis OR 97330-1859 E-mail: bdalrymple@attglobal.net

DALTON, BONNIE, life science administrator; MBA in mgmt. Dep. chief life sci. divsn. Ames Rsch. Ctr., Moffett Field, Calif. Recipient NIH Pub. Health fellowship. Avocations: flying, gardening, playing piano. Office: NASA Ames Rsch Ctr Life Sciences Divsn Moffett Field CA 94035

DALTON, LARRY RAYMOND, chemistry educator, researcher, consultant; b. Belpre, Ohio, Apr. 25, 1945; s. Leonard William Henry and Virginia (Maylee) D.; m. Nicole A. Boand. BS with honors, Mich. State U., 1965, MS, 1966; AM, PhD, Harvard U., 1971. Asst. prof. chemistry Vanderbilt U., Nashville, 1971-73, assoc. prof., 1973-77, research prof. biochemistry, 1977-98; assoc. prof. SUNY-Stony Brook, 1976-81, prof., 1981-82, U. So. Calif., Los Angeles, 1982-94, Harold Moulton prof. chemistry, 1994-98, sci. co-dir. Loker hydrocarbon rsch. inst., 1994-98, prof. materials sci. and engring., 1994-98; prof. chemistry U. Wash., 1998—. Cons., IBM Corp., Yorktown, N.Y., IBM Instruments Co., Danbury, Conn., 1977-85, Celanese Rsch. Corp., 1987-90, Lockheed Missiles and Space Co., 1988-90, Maxdem Inc., 1990; cons. rev. of NIH sickle cell ctrs. USPHS, 1981-82; mem. parent com. for rev. of comprehensive sickle cell ctrs. Nat. Heart, Lung, Blood Inst.-NIH, 1987, 92; panelist for presdl. young investigator awards NSF, Washington, 1983, 89, panelist for presdl. faculty fellow awards, 1986, mem. materials rsch. adv. com., 1984-90, mem. high magnetic field panel, 1987, info. tech. rsch. panel, 2000; bd. dirs. Key Mgmt., Inc., Bomans, Inc.; mem. NAS-NRC panel for selection of NSF predoctoral fellows, 1989—; mem. panel for selection DOD predoctoral fellows. Editor-author: EPR and Advanced EPR Studies of Biological Systems, 1985 Recipient Burlington No. Found. Faculty Achievement award, 1986, U. So. Calif. Assocs. award, 1990, Profl. Achievement award Spring Arbor Coll., 1993, Disting. Alumni award Mich. State U., 2000; Camille and Henry Dreyfus tchr./scholar, 1975-77; rsch. career devel. grantee NIH, 1976-81; Alfred P. Sloan Found. fellow, 1974-77. Mem. Am. Chem. Soc. (Richard C. Tolman medal 1996), Sigma Xi Avocations: skiing, hiking. Office: U Wash Dept Chemistry PO Box 351700 Seattle WA 98195-1700 E-mail: dalton@chem.washington.edu

DALTON, MATT, retired foundry executive; b. Chgo., June 27, 1922; s. Donald J. and Jessie (Shrimplim) D.; children: D. J., J. B., Katherine A.; m. Frances Walter, Jan. 1, 1994. Student, Pomona Coll., Claremont, Calif., Butler U.; grad. advanced mgmt. program, Harvard U., 1956. Pres. Dalton Foundries, Inc., Warsaw, 1959-68, chmn. bd., 1968-91, chmn. emeritus, 1992-94. Founder Warsaw Jr. Achievement, 1953; charter mem. bd. dirs. Warsaw Devel. Corp., 1973; mem. Warsaw Cmty. Sch. Bd., 1962-68, Kosciusko County Coun., 1981-84—; trustee Ind. Vocat. Tech. Coll., 1964-70; chmn. Gov. of Ind. Com. on Youth Employment, 1979-82; pres. Lake Tippecanoe Property Owners Assn., 1979-82; founder, chmn. Kosciusko Econ. Devel. Corp., 1984, Kosciusko Leadership Acad., 1981; mem. Ind. Econ. Devel. Coun., 1984-88, Ind. Commn. on Vocat. and Tech. Edn., 1988-89; del. Ind. Gov.'s Far East Tour, 1987. With AUS, 1943-45. Mem. Ind. State C. of C. (chmn. 1982-84), Warsaw C. of C. (chmn., found. Indsl. Div. 1959). Office: PO Box 181099 Coronado CA 92178-1099

DALTON, PHYLLIS IRENE, library consultant; b. Marietta, KS, Sept. 25, 1909; d. Benjamin Reuben and Pearl (Travelute) Bull; m. Jack Mason Dalton, Feb. 13, 1950. BS, U. Nebr., 1931, MA, 1941, U. Denver, 1942. Tchr. City Schs., Marysville, Kans., 1931-40; reference libr. Lincoln (Nebr.) Pub. Libr., 1941-48; libr., asst. state libr. Calif. State Libr., Sacramento, 1948-72; pvt. libr. cons. Scottsdale, Ariz., 1972—. Libr. U. Nebr., Lincoln, 1941-48. Author: Library Services to the Deaf and Hearing Impaired Individuals, 1985, 91 (Pres.' Com. Employment of Handicapped award 1985), also poems; contbr. chpt., articles, reports in books and publs. in field. Mem. exec. bd. So. Nev. Hist. Soc., Las Vegas, 1983-84; mem. So. Nev. Com. on Employment of Handicapped, 1980-89, chairperson, 1988-89; mem. adv. com. Nat. Orgn. on Disability, 1982-94; mem., sec. resident coun. Forum Pueblo Norte Retirement Village, 1990-91, pres. resident coun., 1991-94; bd. dirs. Friends of So. Nev. Libraries; trustee Univ. Libr. Soc., U. Nev.-Las Vegas; mem. Allied Arts Coun., Pres.' Com. on Employment of People with Disabilities, emeritus, 1989—, Ariz. Gov.'s Com. on Employment of People with Disabilities, 1990—, Scottsdale Mayor's Com. on Employment of People with Disabilities, 1990—, chmn., 1996—; mem. Scottsdale Publ Libr. Ams. With Disabilities Com., 1994—. Recipient Libraria Sodalitas, U. So. Calif., 1972, Alumni Achievement award U. Denver, 1977, U. Nebr., Lincoln, 1983, Outstanding Sr. Citizen Vol. award City of Scottsdale, 1997, citation for svc. to people with disabilities Mayor of Scottsdale, 1999; named Mover and Shaker Scottsdale Mag., 1994. Mem. LWV, ALA (councilor 1963-64, Exceptional Svc. award 1981, award com. O.C.L.C. Humphreys Forest Press award 1994), AAUW, Assn. State Librs. (pres. 1964-65), Calif. Libr. Assn. (pres. 1969), Nev. Libr. Assn. (hon.), Internat. Fedn. Libr. Assns. and Instns. (chair working group on libr. svc. to prisons, standing com. Sect. Librs. Serving Disadvantaged Persons 1981-95), Nat. League Am. Pen Women (Las Vegas chpt. 1988-94, com. on qualifications for Letters membership 1994—, parlimentarian Scottsdale chpt. 1989-94, v.p. 1992-94, 96-98, v.p. state chpt. 1996-98, sec. 1998-2001), Am. Correctional Assn. (libr. svcs. instns. com. 1994—), Internat. Soc. Poets (disting.), Pilot Internat. (at-large). Home: 7090 E Mescal St Apt 261 Scottsdale AZ 85254-6125

DALY, DONALD F. retired engineering company executive; b. Morristown, N.J., Jan. 10, 1933; s. John F. and Sophie E. (Podeski) D.; m. Bennie L. London, Nov. 2, 1963; children: Stephen, David, Eric. ME, Stevens Inst. Tech., 1955. Equipment engr. Corning (N.Y.) Glass Works, 1955-56; sales engr. Mundet Cork, 1958-60; process engr. Thiokol Chem. Corp., 1961-65; dir. engring. Syntex Corp., 1966-78; v.p., project mgr. Indsl. Design Corp., 1978-2000; dir. Tech. Design & Constrn. Co., Portland, Oreg., 1992-94; ret., 2000. Republican. Avocations: golf, skiing, horse ranching. E-mail: bddaly@att.net

DALY, PAUL SYLVESTER, mayor, retired academic administrator, management consultant; b. Belmont, Mass., Jan. 8, 1934; s. Matthew Joseph and Alice Mary (Hall) D.; m. Maureen Teresa Kenny, May 25, 1957; children: Judith Mary, Paul S. Jr., Susan Marie, John Joseph, Maureen Hall. BS in Engring. Sci., Naval Postgrad. Sch., 1968; MBA, U. W. Fla., 1971. Commd. ensign USN, 1955; advanced through grades to capt., 1979; coll. dean Embry-Riddle Aero. U., Daytona Beach, Fla., 1979-81, chancellor Ariz., 1981-95; mayor City of Prescott, 1996-99; mgmt. cons., 1999—. Lectr. seminars, 1979-85; cons. British Aerospace, 1979-84, McDonnell Douglas, 1979-84, IBM, 1983-84; sr. faculty U. Phoenix, 1983-86. Bd. dirs. Yavapai Regional Med. Ctr., Prescott, Ariz., 1983-86, Prescott C. of C., 1982-84; chmn. Ariz. State Bd. Pvt. Postsecondary Edn.; pres. Ind. Coll. and Univs. of Ariz., Phoenix, 1982—; pres., founder West Yavapai County Am. Heart Assn. Chpt., chmn. affiliate of Am. Heart Assn./Ariz. Decorated Legion of Merit. Mem. Ret. Officers Assn. Republican. Roman Catholic. Avocation: sports. E-mail: dalyps@yahoo.com

DALY, ROBERT ANTHONY, professional baseball team executive, former film executive; b. Bklyn., Dec. 8, 1936; s. James and Eleanor D.; children: Linda Marie, Robert Anthony, Brian James. Student, Bklyn. Coll. From dir. bus. affairs to v.p. bus. affairs, to exec. v.p. CBS TV Network, 1955-80; pres. CBS Entertainment Co., 1977—; chmn., CEO Warner Bros., Burbank, Calif., 1982-94; chmn., co-CEO Warner Music Group, 1995-99; chmn., CEO, mng. ptnr. L.A. Dodgers, 1999—. Bd. dirs. Am. Film Inst. Trustee Am. Film Inst. Mem. NATAS, Acad. Motion Picture Arts and Scis., Motion Picture Pioneers, Hollywood Radio and TV Soc. Roman Catholic. Club: Bel Air Country. Office: LA Dodgers 1000 Elysian Park Ave Los Angeles CA 90012-1112 also: Warner Bros & Warner Music Group 75 Rockefeller Plz New York NY 10019-6908

DALY, TOM, mayor; m. Debra Daly; children: Anna, Ryan. BA, Harvard U., 1976. Elected mem. City Coun. of Anaheim, 1988, elected mayor, 1992-94, 94—. Mem. bd. trustees Anaheim Union Hish Sch. Dist., 1985—; active Anaheim Library Bd., 1985—; mem. adv. bd. Anaheim Boys and Girls Club; mem. bd. dirs. cmty. support group Anaheim Meml. Hosp.; mem. bd. dirs. Orange County Transp. Authority, Urban Water Inst.; mem. El Toro Citizens Adv. Commn.; chair regional adv. planning coun. Orange County, 1992—. Office: Office of the Mayor/City Council City Hall 7th Fl 200 S Anaheim Blvd Anaheim CA 92805-3820

D'AMICO, MICHAEL, architect, urban planner; b. Bklyn., Sept. 11, 1936; s. Michael and Rosalie (Vinciguerra) D.; BArch, U. Okla., 1961; postgrad. So. Meth. U. Sch. Law, 1962-63, Coll. Marin, 1988-89;, San Francisco Law Sch., 1994—; m. Joan Hand, Nov. 26, 1955; children: Michael III, Dion Charles. Supr. advanced planning sect. Dallas Dept. City Planning, 1961-63; designer, planner in charge Leo A. Daly Co., San Francisco, 1963-66; project planner Whisler, Patri Assos., San Francisco, 1966-67; architect, urban planner D'Amico & Assocs., San Francisco, N.Y., Guam, 1967-73, pres. D'Amico & Assocs., Inc., Mill Valley and San Francisco, Calif., and Guam, 1973—; pres. Jericho Alpha Inc., 1979-82, pres. Alpha Internet Syss., Inc., 1996—; cons. arch., planner City of Seaside (Calif.), 1967-72, 79-81, 89—; cons. urban redevel. Eureka (Calif.), 1967-82; cons. planner, Lakewood, Calif.; redevel. cons. to Daly City (Calif.), 1975-77; redevel. adviser to Tamalpais Valley Bus. Assn., 1975-77; archtl. and hist. analyst to Calif. Dept. Transp., 1975-77; agt. for Eureka, Calif. Coastal Commn., 1977-79; devel. cons. City of Scotts Valley, 1988-95, City of Suisun, 1988-89, City of Union City, 1989-91. Mem. steering com. San Francisco Joint Com. Urban Design, 1967-72. Recipient Cmty. Design award AIA, 1970; First prize award Port Aransas (Tex.) Master Plan Competition, 1964; Design award Karachi Mcpl. Authority, 1987, Merit award St. Vincent's/Silveira. Mem. AIA (inactive), Am. Inst. Cons. Planners, Am. Planning Assn., Calif. Assn. Planning Cons. (sec., treas. 1970-72), World Future Soc., Solar Energy Soc. Am. Office: 525 Midvale Way Mill Valley CA 94941-3705

DAMON, WILLIAM VAN BUREN, developmental psychologist, educator, writer; b. Brockton, Mass., Nov. 10, 1944; s. Philip Arthur and Helen (Meyers) D.; m. Wendy Obernauer (div. 1982); children: Jesse Louis, Maria; m. Anne Colby, Sept. 24, 1983, 1 child, Caroline. BA, Harvard U., 1967; PhD, U. Calif., Berkeley, 1973. Social worker N.Y.C. Dept. Social Svcs., 1968-70; prof. psychology Clark U., Worcester, Mass., 1973-89, dean Grad Sch., 1983-87, chmn. dept. edn., 1988-89; Disting. vis. prof. U. P.R., 1988; prof., chair edn. dept. Brown U., Providence, 1989-92, prof., Mittlemann Family dir. Ctr. for Study of Human Devel., 1993-98; univ. prof., 1997-98; fellow Ctr. for Advanced Study in the Behavioral Scis., 1994-95; prof., dir. Ctr. on Adolescence Stanford (Calif.) U., 1997—. Sr. fellow Hoover Instn., 1999—; mem. study sect. NIMH, Bethesda, Md., 1981-84; cons. State of Mass., 1976, State of Calif., 1978, Allegheny County, Pa., 1979, Pinellas County, Fla., 1990, Com. of Va., 1993, Hawaii, 1995, Children's TV Workshop, 1991-09, Annenberg Adv. Coun. on Excellence in Children's TV, 1996-99; mem. nat. adv. bd. Fox Family TV Network, 1998—. Author: Social World of the Child, 1977, Social and Personality Development, 1983, Self-Understanding in Childhood and Adolescence, 1988, The Moral Child, 1988, Child Development Today and Tomorrow, 1989, Some Do Care, 1992, Greater Expectations, 1995 (Parent's Choice Book award 1995), The Youth Charter, 1997; editor: New Directions for Child Devel., 1978—, Handbook of Child Psychology, 1998. Trustee Bancroft Sch., Worcester, Mass., 1982-84; mem. adv. bd. Ednl. Alliance, 1991—. Grantee Carnegie Corp., N.Y.C., 1975-79, 97—, Spencer Found., 1980, 92-96, 98—, N.Y. comty. Trust, 1984-88, Inst. Noetic Scis., 1988-90, MacArthur Found., 1990-95, Pew Charitable Trusts, 1990-95, 98—, Ross Inst., 1996—, Hewlett Found., 1997—, The Templeton Found., 1998—. Mem. APA, Jean Piaget Soc. (bd. dirs. 1983-87), Am. Ednl. Rsch. Assn., Soc. for Rsch. in Child Devel., Nat. Acad. Edn. Republican. Office: Stanford U Ctr on Adolescence Cypress Bldg C Stanford CA 94305-4145 E-mail: wdamon@stanford.edu

DAMOOSE, GEORGE LYNN, lawyer; b. Grand Rapids, Mich., Feb. 2, 1938; s. George G. and Geneva J. (Joseph) D.; m. Carol Sweeney, Dec. 7, 1968; children: Alison Dana, George Christopher. AB cum laude, Harvard U., 1959, JD cum laude, 1965. Bar: Calif. 1966, U.S. Tax Ct., 1973. Assoc. O'Melveny and Myers, L.A., 1965-72; ptnr. Jennings, Engstrand, Henrikson, P.C., San Diego, 1972-76, Procopio, Cory, Hargreaves, and Savitch, San Diego, 1976—. Bd. dirs. San Diego Civic Light Opera Assn., 1984-90, 92; trustee The Bishops Sch., LaJolla, 1987-90, La Jolla Chamber Music Soc., 1988-89; commr. San Diego Crime Commn., 1987-90. Served to lt. (j.g.) USN, 1959-62. Mem. Am. Bar Found., San Diego County Bar Assn. (chmn. tax sect. 1974-75, 86-87), Calif. Bar Assn. (ind. inquiry and rev. panel, program for certifying legal specialists 1986-87), State Bar Calif. (exec. com., taxation sect. 1990-95, chair 1994-95, chair CEB joint adv. com. taxation 1996-98), San Diego C. of C. (bd. dirs. 1994-96), La Jolla Country Club, La Jolla Beach and Tennis Club. Republican. Episcopalian. Avocations: tennis, bicycling, music, golf. Home: 208 Avenida Cortez La Jolla CA 92037-6502 Office: Procopio Cory et al 530 B St Ste 2100 San Diego CA 92101-4496

DAMPHOUSSE, VINCENT, professional hockey player; b. Montreal, Ont., Can., Dec. 17, 1967; Left wing/center Edmonton (Can.) Oilers, 1991-93; left wing Montreal Canadiens, 1993-99, San Jose (Calif.) Sharks, 1999—. Mem. Stanley Cup championship team, 1993. Shares NHL All-Star single-game record for most goals (4), 1991. Office: San Jose Sharks San Jose Arena 525 W Santa Clara St San Jose CA 95113-1500

DAMRELL, FRANK C., JR. judge; BA, U. Calif., Berkeley, 1961; JD, Yale U., 1964. Judge U.S. Dist. Ct. (ea. dist.) Calif., 1997—. Office: 501 I St Sacramento CA 95814-7300

DANCE, FRANCIS ESBURN XAVIER, communication educator; b. Bklyn., Nov. 9, 1929; s. Clifton Louis and Catherine (Tester) D.; m. Nora Alice Rush, May 1, 1954 (div. 1974); children: Clifton Louis III, Charles Daniel, Alison Catherine, Andrea Frances, Frances Sue, Brendan Rush; m. Carol Camille Zak, July 4, 1974; children: Zachary Esburn, Gabriel Joseph, Caleb Michael, Catherine Emily BS, Fordham U., 1951; MS, Northwestern U., 1953, PhD, 1959. Instr. speech Bklyn. Adult Labor Schs., 1951; instr. humanities, coord. radio and TV U. Ill. at Chgo., 1953-54; instr. Univ. Coll., U. Chgo., 1958; asst. prof. St. Joseph's (Ind.) Coll., 1958-60; asst. prof., then assoc. prof. U. Kans., 1960-63; mem. faculty U. Wis., Milw., 1963-71, prof. communication, 1965-71, dir. Speech Comm. Ctr., 1963-70; prof. U. Denver, 1971—, John Evans prof., 1995—. Content expert and mem. faculty adv. bd. to Internat. U. on Knowledge Channel, 1993-95; cons. in field. Author: The Citizen Speaks, 1962, (with Harold P. Zelko) Business and Professional Speech Communication, 1965, 2d edit., 1978, Human Communication Theory, 1967, (with Carl E. Larson) Perspectives on Communication, 1970, Speech Communication: Concepts and Behavior, 1972, The Functions of Speech Communication: A Theoretical Approach, 1976, Human Communication Theory, 1982, (with Carol C. Zak-Dance) Public Speaking, 1986, Speaking Your Mind, 1994, 2d edit., 1996; editor Jour. Comm., 1962-64, Speech Tchr., 1970-72; adv. bd. Jour. Black Studies; editl. bd. Jour. Psycholinguistic Rsch; contbr. articles to profl. jours. Bd. dirs. Milw. Mental Health Assn., 1966-67. 2d lt. AUS, 1954-56. Knapp Univ. scholar in communication, 1967-68; recipient Outstanding Prof. award Standard Oil Found., 1967; Master Tchr. award U. Denver, 1985, University Lectr. award U. Denver, 1986. Fellow Internat. Communication Assn. (pres. 1967); mem. Nat. Communication Assn. (pres. 1982), Psi Upsilon. Office: U Denver Dept Human Comm Studies Denver CO 80208-0001 E-mail: fdance@du.edu

DANCIK, JO MARIE, accountant, accounting company executive; m. George Dancik. CPA, Colo. With Ernst & Young, Cleve., until 1985, ptnr. Denver, 1985-91, mng. ptnr., 1991—. Mem. bd. Fed. Res. Bank Kansas City, 1996—, dep. chmn., 1998, chmn., 1998—. Trustee Boy Scouts Am., Denver; chmn. fund raising campaign Metro-Denver United Way, 1995; bd. dirs. Mile High United Way; mem. bus. adv. coun. U. Colo.; mem. Colo. Women's Forum, Wise Women's Coun., Colo. Concern, Colo. Forum; mem. Colo. Gov.'s Tech. Learning Com. Named Banking and Fin. Exec. of Yr., Denver Bus. Jour., 1996; chosen to carry Olympic torch through Denver, 1996. Mem. Colo. Soc. CPAs (state steering com.), Econ. Club Colo. (bd. dirs.). Avocation: mountain climbing. Office: Ernst & Young LLP 370 17th St Ste 4300 Denver CO 80202-5663

DANDO, PAT, city official; City coun., San Jose, Calif. Office: 801 N 1st St Rm 600 San Jose CA 95110-1704

D'ANGELO, ROBERT WILLIAM, lawyer; b. Buffalo, Nov. 10, 1932; s. Samuel and Margaret Theresa Guercio D'A.; m. Ellen Frances Neary, Sept. 17, 1959; children: Christopher Robert, Gregory Andrew. B.B.A., Loyola U. Los Angeles, 1954; J.D., UCLA, 1960. Bar: Calif. 1960; cert. specialist taxation law. Practiced in L.A., 1960-89; mem. firm. Myers & D'Angelo, Pasadena, Calif., 1967—. Adj. prof. law, taxation Whittier Coll. Sch. of Law., 1981 Served to capt. USAF, 1954-57. Mem. ABA, AICPA, State Bar Calif., L.A. County Bar Assn., Wilshire Bar Assn., Pasadena Bar Assn., Calif. Soc. CPAs, Am. Assn. Atty. CPAs, Calif. Assn. Atty. CPAs (pres. 1980), Phi Delta Phi, Alpha Sigma Nu. Home: 1706 Highland Ave Glendale CA 91202-1265 Office: 301 N Lake Ave Ste 800 Pasadena CA 91101-4108 E-mail: m-dlaw@pacbell.net

DANGERMOND, JACK, geographer; Grad., Calif. Polytech. Coll., Pomona, U. Minn., Harvard U. Founder, pres. Environ. Sys. Rsch. Inst., Redlands, Calif., 1969—. Adv. com. NASA, EPA, NAS, NCGIA. Recipient Horward award Urban and Regional Info. Sys. Assn., Anderson medal Assn. Am. Geographers, John Wesley Powell award U.S. Geol. Survey, Cullum Geog. Medal Am. Geographical Soc., 1999. Mem. Eurasian Acad. Soc., numerous orgns. Office: Environ Sys Rsch Inst 380 New York St Redlands CA 92373 E-mail: jdangermond@esri.com

DANIEL, JAMES RICHARD, accountant, computer company financial executive; b. Chgo., June 26, 1947; s. Elmer Alexander and June B. (Bush) D.; m. Marsha Ruth Stone, Nov. 8, 1969; children: Jennifer Rae, Michael James. BS in Acctg., U. Ill., 1970; MBA, Loyola U., 1974. CPA, Ill., La. Dir. fin. Baxter Travenol Labs., Chgo., 1974-79; corp. contr. Bio-Rad Labs. Inc., Richmond, Calif., 1979 81; v.p., treas., contr. Lykes Bros. Steamship Co. Inc., New Orleans, 1981-84; CFO SCI Systems Inc., Huntsville, Ala., 1984-91; sr. v.p., CFO Dell Computer Corp., Austin, Tex., 1991-93; exec. v.p., CFO, pres. hdqrs. support, treas. MicroAge, Inc., Tempe, 1993-2000; cons., 2000-01; sr. v.p., CFO PetsMart Inc., Phoenix, 2001—. Mem. issuer affairs com. NASDAQ, 1996-97. With U.S. Army, 1970-73. Recipient Outstanding Alumnus award Loyola U. Grad. Sch. Bus., 1995. Mem. AICPA. Republican. Home: 3858 E Cholla Ln Phoenix AZ 85028-5023

DANIEL, THOMAS L. zoology educator; b. N.Y.C., Aug. 21, 1954; BS in Anthropology and Engring., U. Wis., 1976, MS in Zoology and Engring., 1978; PhD in Zoology, Duke U., 1982; postgrad., Calif. Inst. Tech. Myron A. Bantrell postdoctoral fellow in sci. and engring. Calif. Inst. Tech., 1982-84; asst. prof. dept. zoology U. Wash., Seattle, 1984-88, assoc. prof. dept. zoology, 1988-92, prof. dept. zoology, 1992—. External grad. faculty Oreg. State U., 1987—; mem. various coms. at U. Wash. including chair grad. admissions dept. zoology, 1989-91, chair grad. program dept. zoology, 1991-94, dir. math. biology tng. program, 1993—; panel mem. physiol. processes NSF, 1991—; presenter in field. Mem. editl. bd. Jour. Exptl. Biology, Cambridge U., 1988-90, 93—; contbr. articles to profl. jours. Grantee NSF, 1984-87, 88-91, 91-93, 93, U. Wash., 1987-88, J. Fluke Co., 1988, Reticon, Inc., 1988, Am. Soc. Zoologists Symposium on Efficiency in Organisms, 1988-89, Whitaker Found. for Biomed. Rsch., 1988-91, Howard Hughes Found., 1989-94, M.J. Murdock Meml. Trust, 1989-94, Apple Computer, 1991; MacArthur fellow, 1996. Office: U Wash Dept Zoology PO Box 351800 Seattle WA 98195-1800*

DANIEL, WILEY Y. lawyer; b. Louisville, Sept. 10, 1946; m. Ida S. Daniel; children: Jennifer, Stephanie, Nicole. BA in History, JD, Howard U. Ptnr. Gorsuch, Kirgis, Campbell, Walker & Grover, Denver, 1977-88; shareholder Popham, Haik, Schnobrich & Kaufman Ltd., Denver, 1988-95, mng. ptnr., 1993-95; judge U.S. Dist. Ct. Colo., Denver, 1995—. Trustee Am. Inns of Ct. Found.; chair bd. trustees Iliff Sch. Theology; bd. dirs., mentor Bridge Project; mem. Just Beginning Found. Mem. ABA, Nat. Bar Assn., Colo. Bar Assn. (pres. 1992-93), Denver Bar Assn., Sam Cary Bar Assn., State Bd. Architecture. Democrat. Office: US District Court of Colorado Byron White US Courthouse 1929 Stout St # C218 Denver CO 80294-1929

DANIELS, CAROLINE, publishing company executive; b. San Francisco, Dec. 11, 1948; d. William L. and Gladys Daniels; m. Jack Wernick, Nov. 30, 1985 (div.); children: Martin, Katherine. Student, U. Dijon, France, 1965; BA in Psychology, U. Colo., 1970; postgrad. mgmt. program, Harvard U., 1983-85. Export agt. Air Oceanic Shippers, San Francisco, 1972-73; library supr. Aircraft Tech. Pubs., San Francisco, 1973-75, ops. mgr., 1975-80, v.p., 1980-82, exec. v.p. Brisbane, Calif.,

1982-84, pres., CEO, chmn. bd. dirs., 1984—. Pres. adv. bd. Embry Riddle Aero. U.; bd. dirs. Acad. Art Coll., San Francisco. Bd. dirs. Jr. Achievement of The Bay Area. Mem. Gen. Aviation Mfg. Assn. (bd. dirs., mem. exec. com., former chmn. pub. affairs com., chmn. safety affairs com.). Office: Aircraft Tech Pubs 101 S Hill Dr Brisbane CA 94005-1251

DANIELS, JAMES WALTER, lawyer; b. Chgo., Oct. 13, 1945; s. Ben George and Delores L. (Wolanin) D.; m. Gail Anne Rihacek, June 14, 1969; children: Morgan, Abigail, Rachel. AB, Brown U., 1967; JD, U. Chgo., 1970. Bar: Calif. 1970, U.S. Dist. Ct. (ctrl. dist.) Calif. 1970, U.S. Tax Ct., 1972, U.S. Supreme Ct. 1979. Assoc. firm Latham & Watkins, L.A. and Newport Beach, Calif., 1970-77, ptnr., 1977-2000. Arbitrator Orange County Superior Ct., Santa Ana, Calif., 1978-88, judge pro tem, 1979-87. Fin. dir. St. Elizabeth Ann Seton Parish, Irvine, Calif., 1975-82; sec. Turtlerock Tennis Com., Irvine, 1981-83, 86—, pres., 1985-86; bd. dirs. Turtlerock Terr. Homeowners Assn., 1983-85, 87-89. Mem. ABA, Internat. Coun. Shopping Ctrs., Center club, Irvine Racquet Club, Palm Valley Country Club. Democrat. Roman Catholic. Home: 19241 Beckwith Ter Irvine CA 92612-3503 Office: Latham & Watkins 650 Town Center Dr Ste 2000 Costa Mesa CA 92626-7135

DANIELS, JOHN PETER, lawyer; b. N.Y.C., Feb. 5, 1937; s. Jack Brainard and Isabelle (McConachie) D.; m. Lynn Eldridge, Aug. 28, 1978 (div. Jan. 1980); m. Susan Gurley, Apr. 1, 1983. AB, Dartmouth Coll., 1959; JD, U. So. Calif., 1963. Bar: Calif. 1964; diplomate Am. Bd. Trial Advocates. Assoc. Bolton, Groff and Dunne, L.A., 1964-67, Jones and Daniels, L.A., 1967-70, Acret and Perrochet, L.A., 1971-81; ptnr. Daniels, Baratta and Fine, L.A.Angeles, 1982-99, Daniels, Fine, Israel & Schonbuch, L.A.Angeles, 1999—. Mem. Assn. So. Calif. Def. Counsel (bd. dirs. 1975-80), Fedn. Ins and Corp. Counsel. Club: Wilshire Country (Los Angeles). Avocations: scuba diving, golf, hunting. Office: Daniels Fine Israel & Schonbuch 1801 Century Park E Fl 9 Los Angeles CA 90067-2302

DANIELS, JOHN R. oncologist, educator; b. Detroit, May 9, 1938; BA, Stanford U., 1959, MD, 1964. Diplomate Am. Bd. Internal Medicine. Postdoctoral fellow dept. cell biology Albert Einstein Coll. Medicine, 1964; intern in medicine Stanford U. Sch. Medicine, 1964-65; rsch. assoc. Nat. Inst. Dental Rsch., NIH, 1966-69; sr. resident in medicine Stanford U. Sch. Medicine, 1969-70, instr. div. oncology, 1970-71, asst. prof. div. oncology, 1971-78, clin. assoc. prof. div. oncology, 1978-79; v.p. for sci. and tech. affairs Collagen Corp., 1978-79; CEO, dir. Target Therapeutics, 1985-89; assoc. prof. medicine div. oncology U. So. Calif. Sch. Medicine, L.A., 1979—, assoc. prof. radiology, 1990—. Bd. dirs. Collagen Corp. Contbr. over 85 articles to profl. jours.; 9 patents in field. Mem. Am. Assn. for Cancer Rsch., Am. Soc. Clin. Oncology. Home: 842 N Las Casas Ave Pacific Palisades CA 90272-2340 Office: Cohesion Technologies Inc 2500 Faber Pl Palo Alto CA 94303

DANIELS, LORI S. state legislator, insurance agent; b. Burlingame, Calif., Nov. 5, 1955; d. Robert William and Sue Ann (McCowen) McCroskey; m. Stephen L. Daniels, June 19, 1976 (div. June 1980). Student, Ariz. State U., 1973-76; BA in Mgmt., U. Phoenix, 1994. CLU. Trainer Campus Crusade for Christ, San Bernadino, Calif., 1977-79; with instalment loans dept. Ariz. Bank, Mesu, 1979-80; ins. agt. State Farm Ins., Chandler, Ariz., 1980—; mem. Ariz. Ho. Reps., 1992-00; majority leader Ariz. Ho. Reps., Dist. 6, 1997-00; mem. Ariz. Senate, Dist. 6, Phoenix, 2001—. Bus. cons. Jr. Achievement, Mesu, 1987-92; mem. various com. including ways and means, rules, 1997—. V.p. Valley of Sun United Way, Phoenix, 1991-93, chmn. Chandler Area Reg. Coun., 1991-92. Recipient Small Bus. Person of Yr. award Gilbert C. of C., 1989. Mem. Chandler C. of C. (v.p. cmty. devel. 1991-92, v.p. membership svc., 1992-93, Pres.'s award 1990, Chamber cup 1992). Republican. Home: 700 N Dobson Rd Unit 7 Chandler AZ 85224-6939 Office: 1700 W Washington St Ste 110 Phoenix AZ 85007-2812

DANIELS, RICHARD MARTIN, public relations executive; b. Delano, Calif., Feb. 24, 1942; s. Edward Martin and Philida Rose (Peterson) D.; m. Kathryn Ellen Knight, Feb. 28, 1976; children: Robert Martin, Michael Edward. AA, Foothill Coll., 1965; BA, San Jose State U., 1967; MA, U. Mo., 1971. News reporter Imperial Valley Press, El Centro, Calif., summers 1963-66, San Diego Evening Tribune, 1967-68, Columbia (Mo.) Daily Tribune, 1969-70; nat. news copy editor Los Angeles Times, 1966-67; staff writer San Diego Union, 1971-74, real estate editor, 1974-77; v.p. pub. rels. Hubbert Advt. & Pub. Rels., Costa Mesa, Calif., 1977-78; ptnr. Berkman & Daniels, San Diego, 1979-91; prin. Nuffer, Smith, Tucker, Inc., 1991-94, RMD Comms., 1994-97, 99—; exec. dir. comms. San Diego City Schs., 1997-99; prin. RMD Comms., 1999—. Lectr. various bus. groups and colls. Chmn. bd. dirs. March of Dimes San Diego County, 1984-87; bd. dirs. Nat. Coun. Vols., 1983-91. Served with USN, 1959-62. Mem. Pub. Rels. Soc. Am. (accredited), Counselors Acad. Republican. Office: 2261 Ritter Pl Escondido CA 92029-5608 E-mail: dick@rmdcomm.com

DANIELS, RONALD DALE, conductor; b. San Mateo, Calif., Aug. 19, 1943; s. Worth W. and Margurite Pearl (Chandler) D.; 1 child, Ryan Stark. BMus, San Francisco Conservatory, 1968. Condr., music dir. Musical Arts of Contra Costa (Calif.) County, 1968-75, U. Calif., Berkeley, 1973-75, Contra Costa Symphony, 1976-79, Reno (Nev.) Philharm., 1979-98, conductor Laureate, 1998—. Guest conductor various orchs.; grants rev. cons. in field. With USMC, 1966. Recipient Lucien Wulsin award Baldwin Piano Co., Tanglewood Festival, 1968, Gov.'s Art award State of Nev., 1981. Avocations: ice skating, skiing, sailing, hiking. Office: Reno Philharm Assn Ste 3 925 Riverside Dr Reno NV 89503

DANIELSON, JUDITH A. state legislator; b. Boise, Dec. 30, 1951; m. John Danielson; children: Jason, Jaymee. Student, Boise State U., U. Idaho, Long Beach City Coll. Nurse/LPN, 1971-81; dep. sheriff for juvenile offenders; mem. Idaho Ho. of Reps., Boise, 1989-94, Idaho Senate, Dist. 8, 1994—. Past Boise County Commr.; past City Coun. pres.; vice chair resources and environment com.; mem. fin., health and welfare, and transp. coms. Active bicycle safety program for Boy Scouts. Mem. Ida-Ore Planning Devel. Assn. (v.p.), PTA, Idaho Assn. Pvt. Industry Couns. (past chair), Adams County Devel. Corp. Republican. Office: State Capitol PO Box 83720 Boise ID 83720-3720

DANIHER, JOHN M. retired engineer; b. LaJunta, Colo., Aug. 2, 1926; s. Gerald and Mary Isabelle (Manly) D.; m. Edna Erle Hoshall, Sept. 4, 1948; children: Lyn Mari, Suzanne Laurie, Patricia Gail, Jerome Matthew, Michael Kevin. AB, Western State Coll., Gunnison, Colo., 1948; postgrad. Idaho State U., 1957-74, U. Idaho, 1974-76. H.S. tchr., Grand Junction, Colo., 1948-52; salesman Century Metalcraft, Denver, 1952-53; chem. plant supr. U.S. Chem. Corps., Denver, 1953-56; sr. engr. instrument and controls Phillips Petroleum Co., Idaho Falls, 1956-76, project engr. E G & G Idaho, Idaho Falls, 1976-85, engring. specialist, 1985-91; adv. Eastern Idaho Vocat. Tech. Sch., 1975-80. Cubmaster, Boy Scouts Am., 1970-75, asst. scoutmaster, 1975-80; v.p. Bonneville Unit Am. Cancer Soc., 1994, pres., v.p., 1995—. Recipient Cub Man of Yr., Boy Scouts Am., 1973. Mem. Am. Nuc. Soc. Roman Catholic. Club: K.C. (state dep. 1979-81, Supreme council 1979-84, 94) Home: 250 12th St Idaho Falls ID 83404-3370

DANILOV, VICTOR JOSEPH, museum management program director, consultant, writer, educator; b. Farrell, Pa., Dec. 30, 1924; s. Joseph M. and Ella (Tominovich) D.; m. Toni Dewey, Sept. 6, 1980; children: Thomas J., Duane P., Denise S. BA in Journalism, Pa. State U., 1945; MS in Journalism, Northwestern U., 1946; EdD in Higher Edn., U. Colo., 1964. With Sharon Herald, Pa., 1942, Youngstown Vindicator, 1945, Pitts. Sun-Telegraph, 1946-47, Chgo. Daily News, 1947-50; instr. journalism U. Colo., 1950-51; asst. prof. journalism U. Kans., 1951-53; with Kansas City Star, 1953; mgr. pub. rels. Ill. Inst. Tech. and IIT Rsch. Inst., 1953-57; dir. univ. rels. and pub. info. U. Colo., 1957-60; pres. Profile Co., Boulder, Colo., 1960-62; exec. editor, exec. v.p. Indsl. Rsch. Inc., Beverly Shores, Ind., 1962-69, pub., exec. v.p., 1969-71; dir., v.p. Mus. Sci. and Industry, Chgo., 1971-77, pres., dir., 1978-87, pres. emeritus, 1987—; dir. mus. mgmt. program, adj. prof. U. Colo., 1987—. Mem. rural industrialization adv. group Dept. Agr., 1967; mem. panel internat. transfer tech. Dept. Commerce, 1968; mem. sci. info. coun. NSF, 1969-72; chmn. Conf. on Implications Metric Change, 1972, Nat. Conf. Indsl. Rsch., 1966-70; chmn. observance Nat. Indsl. Rsch. Week, 1967-70; chmn. Midwest White House Conf. on Indsl. World Ahead, 1972, Internat. Conf. Sci. and Tech. Museums, 1976, 82; mem. task force on fin. acctg. and reporting by non bus. orgns., others. Author: Public Affairs Reporting, 1955, Starting a Science Center, 1977, Science and Technology Centers, 1982, Science Center Planning Guide, 1985, Chicago's Museums, 1987, rev. edit., 1991, America's Science Museums, 1990, Corporate Museums, Galleries, and Visitor Centers: A Directory, 1991, A Planning Guide for Corporate Museums, Galleries, and Visitors Centers, 1992, Museum Careers and Training: A Professional Guide, 1994, University and College Museums, Galleries, and Related Facilities, 1996, Hall of Fame Museums: A Reference Guide, 1997, Colorado Museums and Historical Sites, 2000; also articles; editor: Crucial Issues in Public Relations, 1960, Corporate Research and Profitability, 1966, Innovation and Profitability, 1967, Research Decision-Making in New Product Development, 1968, New Products--and Profits, 1969, Applying Emerging Technologies, 1970, Nuclear Power in the South, 1970, The Future of Science and Technology, 1975, Museum Accounting Guidelines, 1976, Traveling Exhibitions, 1978, Towards the Year 2000, 1981; editor profl. procs. Trustee Women of the West Mus., 1991-99, v.p., 1991-99; trustee La Rabida Childrens Hosp. and Rsch. Ctr., 1973-83; mem. U. Chgo. Citizens Bd., 1978-87. Mem. Am. Assn. Mus. (exec. com. 1976-77, bd. dirs. 1985-88, chmn. mus. studies task force 1988-89), AAAS, Assn. Sci.-Tech. Ctrs. (bd. dirs. 1973-84, sec.-treas. 1973-74, pres. 1975-76), Internat. Coun. Mus. (com. on sci. and tech. mus. 1972—, vice chmn. 1977-87, chmn. 1982-83, bd. dirs. 1985-88), Chgo. Coun. on Fine Arts (chmn. 1976-84), Ill. Arts Alliance (bd. dirs. 1983-86), Sci. Mus. Exhibit Collaborative (pres. 1983-86), Mus. Film Network (pres. 1984-86). Home: 250 Bristlecone Way Boulder CO 80304-0413 Office: Univ Colo Mus Mus Mgmt Program Campus Box 218 Boulder CO 80309-0218

DANN, FRANCIS JOSEPH, dermatologist, educator; b. N.Y.C., Aug. 26, 1946; s. Richard William and Helen (Brennan) D. BA, Columbia U., 1968, MD, 1972. Bd. cert. dermatologist Am. Bd. Dermatology. Pvt. practice specializing in dermatology, 1976-99; asst. clin. prof. dermatology UCLA, 1993—. Recognized expert med. reviewer State of Calif., 1995; specialized tng. in leprosy USPHS Hosp., Carville, La., 1972, 95. Contbr. articles to profl. and med. jours. Recipient Cert. of Appreciation for charitable med. missions to The Philippines, 1986, 88, 92. Mem. AMA, Am. Acad. Dermatology, Philippine Med. Assn. Hawaii, L.A.-Metro Dermatology Soc., Pacific Dermatology Soc., L.A. Acad. Medicine (bd. dirs. 1995-99), Aloha Med. Mission. Roman Catholic. Avocations: sports, photography. Office: 100 Ucla Medical Plz Ste 545 Los Angeles CA 90024-6992

DANNER, BRYANT CRAIG, lawyer; b. Boston, Nov. 18, 1937; s. Nevin Earle and Marjorie (Harms) D.; m. Judith I. Baker, Aug. 23, 1958; 1 child Debra Irene. BA, Harvard U., 1960, LLB, 1963. Bar: Calif. 1963, U.S. Dist. Ct. (cen. dist.) Calif. 1963. Assoc. Latham & Watkins, L.A., 1963-70, ptnr., 1970-92; sr. v.p., gen. counsel So. Calif. Edison Co., Rosemead, Calif., 1992-95, exec. v.p., gen. counsel, 1995-2000, Edison Internat., Rosemead, 2000—. Mem. L.A. County Bar Assn. (chmn. environ. sect. 1988-89). Avocations: fly fishing, photography. Office: Edison International 2244 Walnut Grove Ave Rosemead CA 91770-3714

DANOFF, DUDLEY SETH, surgeon, urologist; b. N.Y.C., June 10, 1937; s. Alfred and Ruth (Kauffman) D.; m. Hevda Amrani, July 1, 1971; children: Aurele, Doran. BA summa cum laude, Princeton U., 1959; MD, Yale U., 1963. Diplomate Am. Bd. Urology. Surg. intern Columbia-Presbyn. Med. Ctr., N.Y.C., 1963-64; resident in surgery Yale New Haven Med. Ctr., 1964-65; resident in urologic surgery Squier Urologic Clinic, Columbia-Presbyn. Med. Ctr., 1965-69; NIH trainee Francis Delafield Hosp., N.Y.C., 1969; asst. in urology Columbia U..Columbia-Presbyn. Hosp., N.Y.C., 1969; cons., surgeon New Orleans VA Hosp., 1970; asst. surgeon Tulane U., New Orleans, 1970; pvt. practice urologic surgery L.A., 1971—. Attending urologic surgeon Cedars-Sinai Med. Ctr., L.A., Midway Hosp., L.A., Century City Hosp., L.A. VA Hosp., L.A.; attending urologic surgeon, clin. faculty UCLA. Author: Superpotency, 1993, Research: Laparoscopic Urologic Procedures; contbr. articles to profl. jours. Bd. dirs. Tel-Hashomer Hosp., Israel, Christian Children's Fund, Beverly Hills Edn. Found.; trustee Anti-Defamation League; mem. prof. adv. bd. The Wellness Comty.; mem. nat. exec. bd. Gesher Found.; mem. adv. com., past pres. Med. divsn. L.A. Jewish Fedn. Coun.; mem. nat. leadership cabinet United Jewish Appeal; chmn. Am. Friends of Assaf Harofeh Med. Ctr., Israel; pres. western states region and internat. bd. govs. Am. Friends Hebrew U. Jerusalem; pres. western region Am. Commn. for Shaare Zedek Med. Ctr. Jerusalem. Recipient Excellence in Medicine award Israel Cancer Rsch. Found., 1998. Fellow ACS; mem. AMA, Internat. Coll. Surgeons, Israeli Med. Assn., Am. Fertility Soc., Soc. Air Force Clin. Surgeons, Am. Urologic Assn., Societe International d'Urologie, Transplant Soc. So. Calif., Los Angeles County Med. Assn., Soc. for Laparoendoscopic Surgeons, Am. Technion Soc., Profl. Men's Club of L.A. (past pres.), Princeton Club So. Calif., Yale Club So. Calif., Hillcrest Country Club, Phi Beta Kappa, Sigma Xi, Alpha Omega Alpha, Phi Delta Epsilon (past pres., exec. com.). Jewish. Avocations: golf, swimming, reading, writing. Office: Cedars-Sinai Med Ctr Towers 8631 W 3d St Ste 915E Los Angeles CA 90048-5912 Fax: (310) 854-0267. E-mail: danoff@aol.com

DANOFF, ERIC MICHAEL, lawyer; b. Waukegan, Ill., June 30, 1949; m. Barbara Madsen, May 27, 1979; children: Nicholas Madsen Danoff, Alexander Madsen Danoff. AB, Dartmouth Coll., 1971; JD, U. Calif., Berkeley, 1974. Bar: Calif. 1974, U.S. Dist. Ct. (no., cen., ea. and so. dists.) Calif., U.S. Ct. Appeals (9th cir.), U.S. Supreme Ct. Assoc. Graham & James, San Francisco, 1974-80, ptnr., 1981-97, Kaye, Rose & Ptnrs., San Francisco, 1998-2001, Emard, Danoff, Port & Tamulski, LLP, San Francisco, 2001—. Contbr. articles to profl. publs. Mem. Maritime Law Assn. Office: Emard Danoff Port & Tamulski LLP Ste 400 49 Stevenson St San Francisco CA 94105

DANTON, JOSEPH PERIAM, librarian, educator; b. Palo Alto, Calif., July 5, 1908; s. George Henry and Annina (Periam) D. Ph.D., U. Chgo., 1935. Libr., assoc. prof. bibliography Temple U., Phila., 1936-46; dean Sch. Librarianship, U. Calif.-Berkeley, 1946-61, assoc. prof., 1946-47, prof., 1947-76, prof. emeritus, 1976—, J. Periam Danton dean, prof., 1946-76. Vis. prof. Grad. Libr. Sch., U. Chgo., 1942, Columbia, 1946; vis. lectr. U. Toronto, 1963, Univs. of Belgrade, Ljubljana, Novi Sad, Zagreb, 1965, U. B.C., 1968, 79, McGill U., 1969, U. P.R., 1970, U. Md., 1977, U. N.C., 1977, U. Tex., 1979, Hebrew U., Jerusalem, 1965, 85; Fulbright rsch. scholar Germany, 1960-61, Austria, 1964-65; surveyor and cons. numerous libraries; UNESCO Libr. Cons., Jamaica, 1968; del. Internat. Fedn. Libr. Assns. meeting, 1939-1972; Ford Found. cons. on libraries in SE Asia (with R. C. Swank), 1963; hon. research fellow U. London, 1974-75. Author various works, 1946-99. Served as lt. USNR, 1942-45, PTO. Recipient Berkeley citation, 1976, Beta Phi Mu award, 1983; Carnegie fellow, 1933-35, Guggenheim fellow, 1971. Mem. Assn. Am. Libr. Schs. (pres. 1949-50), Internat. Fedn. Libr. Assns. (chmn. com. libr. edn. 1967-72). Democrat. Home: 500 Vernon St Apt 402 Oakland CA 94610-5303 Office: U Calif Sch Info Mgmt & Sys Berkeley CA 94720-0001

D'ANTONI, MIKE, former professional basketball coach; b. Mullens, W.Va., May 8, 1951; m. Laurel D'Antoni; 1 child, Michael. Basketball player Kings NBA, 1973-1975, basketball player San Antonio Spurs, 1975-76; past basketball player Milan Italian League, winner 2 European Cups, 2 InterContinental Cups Milan, coach Milan, 1990-93, head coach Milan, 1996-97, winner Italian Cup, 1997; dir. player pers. Denver Nuggets NBA, 1997-98, profl. basketball coach Denver Nuggets, 1998-99. Named to Marshall U. Hall of Fame, 1997. Office: care Denver Nuggets 1635 Clay St Denver CO 80204-1743

DANTZIG, GEORGE BERNARD, applied mathematics educator; b. Portland, Oreg., Nov. 8, 1914; s. Tobias and Anja (Ourisson) D.; m. Anne Shmuner, Aug. 23, 1936; children: David Franklin, Jessica Rose, Paul Michael A.B. in Math. and Physics, U. Md., 1936; M.A. in Math., U. Mich., 1937; Ph.D. in Math., U. Calif.-Berkeley, 1946; hon. degree, Technion, Israel, Linkoping U., Sweden, U. Md., Yale U., Louvain U., Belgium, Columbia U., U. Zurich, Switzerland, Carnegie-Mellon U., U. Mich. Chief combat analysis br. Statis. Control Hdqrs. USAF, 1941-46, math. advisor, 1946-52; rsch. mathematician Rand Corp., Santa Monica, Calif., 1952-60; prof., chmn. Ops. Research Ctr., U. Calif.-Berkeley, 1960-66; prof. ops. rsch. and computer sci. Stanford (Calif.) U., Calif., 1966-97, prof. emeritus, 1997—. Chief methodology Internat. Inst. Applied System Analysis, Austria, 1973-74; cons. to industry. Author: Linear Programming and Extensions, 1963; co-author: Compact City, 1973; co-author: Linear Programming I Introduction, 1997; contbr. articles to profl. jours.; assoc. editor Math. Programming, Math. of Ops. Research, others Recipient Exceptional Civilian Svc. medal War Dept, 1944, NAS award, 1971, in applied math. and numerical analysis, 1977, Nat medal of sci. for inventing linear programming and simplex algorithm, 1975, Von Neumann theory prize in ops. rsch., 1975, Harvey prize Technion, 1985, Silver medal Operational Rsch. Soc. Gt. Britain, 1986, Coors Am. Ingenuity award, 1989, Pender award U. Pa., 1995. Fellow Am. Acad. Arts and Scis., Econometric Soc., Inst. Math. Stats.; mem. AAAS, IEEE, Assn. Computing Machinery, Nat. Acad. Scis., Nat. Acad. Engring., Ops. Research Soc., Am. Math. Soc., Math. Programming Soc. (chmn. 1973-74), Inst. Mgmt. Sci. (pres. 1966), Phi Beta Kappa, Sigma Xi, Phi Kappa Phi, Pi Mu Epsilon, Omega Rho Soc. Home: 821 Tolman Dr Stanford CA 94305-1025 Office: Stanford Univ Dept Mgmt Sci and Engring Stanford CA 94305-4023 E-mail: goerge-dantzig@worldnet.att.net

DANZIGER, BRUCE EDWARD, structural engineer; b. N.Y.C., Feb. 14, 1964; s. Frederick Benjamin Danziger and Elise Lee (Saranow) Gold. BS in Archtl. Engring., Calif. Poly. U., 1988. Project engr. Ove Arup & Ptnrs., London, 1988-90, Sevilla, Spain, 1990-92, L.A., 1992-93, N.Y.C., 1993-97, San Francisco, 1997—. Recipient 1st prize MakMax Membrane Design Competition, 1993, Hon. Mention award, 1995, Hon. Mention award, 1996. Office: Ove Arup & Ptnrs 901 Market St Ste 260 San Francisco CA 94103-1735

DANZIGER, JAMES NORRIS, political science educator; b. L.A., May 28, 1945; s. Edward and Beverly Jane Danziger; m. Lesley Robson, June 12, 1971; children: Nicholas James, Vanessa Margaret. BA, Occidental Coll., L.A., 1966; MA, Sussex U., Brighton, Eng., 1968; MA, PhD, Stanford U., 1974. Prof. polit. sci. U. Calif., Irvine, 1972—, chmn. dept. polit. sci., 1974-76, 81-83, 88-92, assoc. dean Sch. Social Scis., 1978-81, chmn. acad. senate, 1994-95, dean of undergrad. edn., 1995-99; rsch. assoc. Ctr. Rsch. Info. Tech. and Orgns., Irvine, 1974—, dir., 2000-01; scholar-in-residence LaVerne (Calif.) U., 1983-84. Vis. prof. Univ. Pitts., 1996; vis. prof. Aarhus (Denmark) U., 1985. Author: Making Budgets, 1978, Understanding the Political World, 1991, 5th edit., 2001; co-author: Computers and Politics, 1982, People and Computers, 1986; mem. editl. bd. local govt. studies, 1981—; assoc. editor Social Sci. Computer Rev. Bd. dirs. South Laguna Civic Assn., 1983-86, chair South Laguna Annexation Task Force, 1986, bd. dirs. Irvine Campus Housing Authority, 1996—. Recipient Disting. Teaching award U. Calif., 1979, Daniel Aldrich disting. svc. award, 1997; Marshall scholar Govt. of U.K., 1966-68; named Disting. Faculty Lectr. U. Calif. Acad. Senate, 1987; NSF grantee, 1973-79, 80-83, 1996-98, 99—. Mem. Am. Polit. Sci. Assn. (Leonard White award 1974), ASPA (Marshall Dimock award 1977), Phi Beta Kappa (pres. local chpt. 1988-89, sec.-treas. local chpt. 1996-99, Pi Sigma Alpha (pres. local chpt. 1987—). Avocations: travel, basketball, cycling, literature. Office: U Calif Sch Social Scis Irvine CA 92697-5100 E-mail: danziger@uci.edu

DANZIGER, JERRY, broadcasting executive; b. N.Y.C., Jan. 23, 1924; s. Harry and Lillie (Lacher) D.; m. Zelda Bloom, Dec. 26, 1948; children: Sydney, Alan, Lee. Grad. high sch. With Sta. WTTV, Bloomington, Ind., 1950-53, ops. mgr. Indpls., 1953-57; program mgr. Sta. WTSK-TV, Knoxville, Tenn., 1953; pres. Sta. KOB-TV, Albuquerque, 1957-88, v.p., 1983-88, pres., 1988-93, vice-chmn., 1993—. Mem. Gov. N.Mex. Commn. for Film Entertainment, 1970-71 Bd. dirs. KIPC All Indian Pueblo Coun., 1975-88, Albuquerque Little Theatre, Albuquerque Pub. Broadcast, Albuquerque Jewish Welfare Fund, Albuquerque Econ. Devel. 1989-97, Albuquerque Conv. and Visitors Bur., 1990-93, Great Southwest Coun. Boy Scouts Am., 1994—; v.p. for TV AP Broadcasting, 1980-88, Goodwill Industries N.Mex., 1980, bd. dirs., 1991—; mem. Albuquerque Econ. Forum, 1997; adv. bd. AAA, 1995—. Recipient Compadre award Am. Women in Radio and TV, 1978, 80, Silver Medal award N.Mex. Advt. Fedn., 1990; named to N.Mex. Broadcasters Hall of Fame, 2001. Mem. N.Mex. Broadcasters Assn. (pres. 1972-73, Broadcaster of Yr. award , 1976, 78), Press Club, Advt. Club, Albuquerque Country Club. Office: Sta KOB-TV PO Box 1351 Albuquerque NM 87103-1351 E-mail: jdanziger@kobtv.com

DANZIGER, LOUIS, graphic designer, educator; b. N.Y.C., 1923; m. Dorothy Patricia Smith, 1954. Student, Art Ctr. Sch., Los Angeles, 1946-47, New Sch., N.Y.C., 1947-48. Asst. art dir. War Assets Adminstrn., Los Angeles, 1946-47; designer Esquire mag., N.Y.C., 1948; freelance designer, cons. Los Angeles, 1949—; instr. graphic design Art Ctr. Coll. Design, Los Angeles, 1952-60, 86—, Chouinard Art Inst., Los Angeles, 1960-72; instr. Calif. Inst. Arts, 1972-88, head graphic design program, 1972-82; vis. prof. Harvard U., Cambridge, Mass., summers 1978-80, 83, 84, 86-88; instr. Art Ctr. Coll. Design. Mem. graphic evaluation panel Fed. Design Program, Nat. Endowment Arts, 1975— ; design cons. Los Angeles County Mus. Art, 1957— Served with cav. U.S. Army, 1943-45; PTO Recipient Disting. Achievement award Contemporary Art Coun., L.A. County Mus. Art, 1982, Disting. Designer award NEA, 1985, "Stars of Design" Lifetime Achievement award Pacific Design Ctr., 1997, numerous awards and medals in art design. Mem. Alliance Graphique Internationale, Am. Inst. Graphic Arts (medal 1998), Am. Ctr. for Design (hon.). Home: PO Box 660189 Arcadia CA 91066-0189

DARABONT, FRANK, screenwriter, director; Screenwriter: (films) (with Wes Craven, Chuck Russell, and Bruce Wagner) A Nightmare on Elm Street 3: Dream Warriors, 1987, (with Russell) The Blob, 1988, (with Mick Garris, Jim Wheat, and Ken Wheat) The Fly II, 1989, (with Steph Lady) Mary Shelley's Frankenstein, 1994; dir.: (TV movies) Till Death Do Us Part, 1990, Buried Alive, 1990; screenwriter, dir.: (films) The Shawshank Redemption, 1994 (Academy award nomination best adapted screenplay 1994), The Green Mile, 1999. Office: William Morris Agency care Robert Stein 151 S El Camino Dr Beverly Hills CA 90212-2775

DARBEE, PETER A. electric power company executive; BA in Econ., MBA, Darmouth Coll. Mgmt. Salomon Brothers, AT&T; investment banker, v.p. Goldman Sachs; v.p., CFO, controller Pacific Bell; v.p., CFO Advance Fibre Commns., Inc.; sr. v.p., CFO, treas. PG&E Corp. Office: PG&E 1 Market Spear Tower San Francisco CA 94105

DARBY, G(EORGE) HARRISON, lawyer; b. N.Y.C., Jan. 24, 1942; s. Stephen John and Madge B. (Leh) D. BA, Muhlenberg Coll., 1963; LLB, Bklyn. Law Sch., 1967. Bar: N.Y. 1967. Ptnr. Jackson Lewis Schnitzler & Krupman, L.A. and other offices, 1967—. Mem. child adv. group Internat. Inst. of L.A., 1989-96. Office: Jackson Lewis et al 1888 Century Park E Los Angeles CA 90067-1702

DARBY, MICHAEL RUCKER, economist, educator; b. Dallas, Nov. 24, 1945; s. Joseph Jasper and Frances Adah (Rucker) D.; children: Margaret Loutrel, David Michael; Lynne Ann Zucker-Darby, 1992; stepchildren: Joshua R. Zucker, Danielle T. Zucker. AB summa cum laude, Dartmouth Coll., 1967; MA, U. Chgo., 1968, PhD, 1970. Asst. prof. econ. Ohio State U., 1970-73; vis. asst. prof. econ. UCLA, 1972-73, assoc. prof., 1973-78, prof., 1978-87, 96—, prof. Anderson Grad. Sch. Mgmt., 1987-94, Warren C. Cordner prof. money and fin. mkts., 1995—, vice-chmn., 1992-93; dir. John M. Olin Ctr. for Policy, 1993—; assoc. dir. orgnl. rsch. program UCLA Inst. for Social Sci. Rsch., 1995—; assoc. dir. Ctr. for Internat. Sci., Tech., Cultural Policy Sch. Pub. Policy and Social Rsch., UCLA, 1996—; rsch. assoc. Nat. Bur. Econ. Rsch., 1976-86, 92—; asst. sec. for econ. policy U.S. Dept. Treasury, Washington, 1986-89; mem. Nat. Commn. on Superconductivity, 1988-89; under sec. for econ. affairs U.S. Dept. Commerce, Washington, 1989-92; adminstr. Econs. and Stats. Adminstrn., 1990-92. V.p., dir. Paragon Industries, Inc., Dallas, 1964—83; mem. exec. com. Western Econ. Assn., 1987—90, v.p., 1998—99, pres.-elect, 1999—2000, pres., 2000—01; chmn. The Dumbarton Group, 1992—; adj. scholar Am. Ent. Inst. for Pub. Policy Rsch., 1992—; economist stats. income divsn. IRS, 1992—94; mem. regulatory coord. adv. com. Commodity Futures Trading Commn., 1992—96. Author: Macroeconomics, 1976, Have Controls Ever Worked: The Post-War Record, 1976, Intermediate Macroeconomics, 1979, 2d edit., 1986, The Effects of Social Security on Income and the Capital Stock, 1979, The International Transmission of Inflation, 1981, Labor Force, Employment, and Productivity in Historical Perspective, 1984, Reducing Poverty in America: Views and Approaches, 1996; editor Jour. Internat. Money and Fin., 1981-86, mem. editl. bd., 1986—; mem. editl. bd. Am. Econ. Rev., 1983-86, Contemporary Policy Issues, 1990-93, Contemporary Econ. Policy, 1994—, Internat. Reports, 1992—. Bd. dirs. The Opera Assoc., 1992—; mem. acad. adv. bd. Ctr. Regulation and Econ. Growth of the Alexis de Tocqueville Instn., 1993-96. Recipient Alexander Hamilton award U.S. Treasury Dept., 1989; sr. fellow Dartmouth Coll., 1966-67, Woodrow Wilson fellow, 1967-68, NSF grad. fellow, 1967-69, FDIC grad. fellow, 1969-70, Harry Scherman rsch. fellow Nat. Bur. Econ. Rsch., 1974-75, vis. fellow Hoover Instn., Stanford U., 1977-78. Mem. AAAS, Am. Econ. Assn., Am. Fin. Assn., Am. Statis. Assn., Am. Law & Econs. Assn., Nat. Assn. Bus. Economists, Royal Econ. Soc., So. Econ. Assn., Western Econ. Assn., N.Y. Acad. Scis., Capitol Hill Club (D.C.), Nat. Econ. Club. Episcopalian. Home: 18108 Meandering Way Dallas TX 75252-2763 Office: UCLA Anderson Grad Sch Mgmt Los Angeles CA 90095-0001

DARDEN, CHRISTOPHER A. lawyer, actor, writer; BA in Criminal Justice, Calif. State U., San Jose; JD, U. Calif., San Francisco, 1980. Bar: Calif. 1980. Former atty. Nat. Labor Rels. Bd.; former asst. head dep. in spl. investigations divsn. L.A. County Dist. Attys. Office, former dep. dist. atty. in maj. crimes divsn.; actor, writer, 1996—; assoc. prof. law Sch. Law Southwestern U., L.A., 1996—. Author: (with Jeff Walter) In Contempt, 1996. Office: Southwestern U Sch Law 675 S Westmoreland Ave Los Angeles CA 90005-3905

DARDEN, EDWIN SPEIGHT, SR. architect; b. Stantonsburg, N.C., Oct. 14, 1920; s. Edwin Speight and Sallie (Jordan) D.; m. s. Pauline K. Bartlett, Feb. 26, 1944; children: Edwin Speight III, Judith Ann, Diane Russell. BS in Archtl. Engring., Kans. State U., 1947. Registered architect, Calif. Assoc., Fred L. Swartz and William G. Hyberg, Fresno, Calif., 1949-59; ptnr. Nargis and Darden (Architects), Fresno, 1959-69; pres. Edwin S. Darden Assocs., Inc., Fresno, 1969-85, cons., 1985—. Bd. dirs. Murphy Bank; mem. state adv. bd. Office of Architecture and Constrn., 1970-78; cons. ednl. facilities, 1975—. Prin. works include Clovis (Calif.) High Sch., 1969, Clovis W. High Sch., 1976, Ahwahnee Jr. High Sch., Fresno, 1966, Tehipite Jr. High Sch., Fresno, 1973, Fresno County Dept. Health, 1978, Floyd B. Buchanan Edn. Ctr., Clovis, 1990. Served to 1st lt. C.E., AUS, 1942-46. Fellow AIA; mem. Sigma Phi Epsilon, Alpha Kappa Psi. Presbyterian. Club: Fresno Rotary. Office: Edwin S Darden Assocs Inc 1177 W Shaw Ave Fresno CA 93711-3704 E-mail: esda@pacbell.net

DARLING, JUANITA MARIE, correspondent; b. Columbus, Ohio, Apr. 7, 1954; d. Robert Lewis and Joanne Mae (Oiler) D. BA in L.Am. Studies, BA in Comms., Calif. State U., Fullerton, 1976; MA in Internat. Journalism, U. So. Calif., L.A., 1989; bur. chief, L.A. Times, Ctrl. America. Reporter Daily News Tribune, Fullerton; bus. editor The News, Mexico City; reporter Orange County Register, Santa Ana, Calif.; corr. L.A. Times, Mexico City, El Salvador, Cen. Am. bur. chief. Office: LA Times Times Mirror Sq Los Angeles CA 90053

DARLING, SCOTT EDWARD, lawyer; b. Los Angeles, Dec. 31, 1949; s. Dick R. and Marjorie Helen (Otto) D.; m. Cynthia Diane Harrah, June 1970 (div.); 1 child, Smokie; m. Deborah Lee Cochran, Aug. 22, 1981; children: Ryan, Jacob, Guinevere. BA, U. Redlands, 1972; JD, U.S.C., 1975. Bar: Calif. 1976, U.S. Dist. Ct. (cen. dist.) Calif. 1976. Assoc. atty. Elver, Falsetti, Boone & Crafts, Riverside, 1976-78; ptnr. Falsetti, Crafts, Pritchard & Darling, Riverside, 1978-84; pres. Scott Edward Darling, A Profl. Corp., Riverside, 1984—. Grant reviewer HHS, Washington, 1982-88; judge pro tem Riverside County Mcpl. Ct., 1980, Riverside County Superior Ct., 1987-88; bd. dirs. Tel Law Nat. Legal Pub. Info. System, Riverside, 1978-80. Author, editor: Small Law Office Computer Legal System, 1984. Bd. dirs. Youth Adv. Com. to Selective Svc., 1968-70, Am. Heart Assn. Riverside County, 1978-82, Survival Ministries, 1986-89; atty. panel Calif. Assn. Realtors, L.A., 1980—; pres. Calif. Young Reps., 1978-80; mem. GI Forum, Riverside, 1970-88; presdl. del. Nat. Rep. Party, 1980-84; asst. treas. Calif. Rep. Party, 1981-83; Rep. Congl. candidate, Riverside, 1982; treas. Riverside Sickle Cell Found., 1980-82, recipient Eddie D. Smith award; pres. Calif. Rep. Youth Caucus, 1980-82; v.p. Riverside County Red Cross, 1982-84; mem. Citizen's Univ. Com., Riverside, 1978-84, World Affairs Council, 1978-82, Urban League, Riverside, 1980-82. Calif. Scholarship Fedn. (life). Named one of Outstanding Young Men in Am., U.S. Jaycees, 1979-86. Mem. ABA, Riverside County Bar Assn., Speaker's Bur. Riverside County Bar Assn., Riverside Jaycees, Riverside C. of C. Lodge: Native Sons of Golden West. Avocations: skiing, swimming, reading. Office: 3697 Arlington Ave Riverside CA 92506-3938

DARMSTANDLER, HARRY MAX, real estate executive, retired air force officer; b. Indpls., Aug. 9, 1922; s. Max M. and Nonna (Holden) D.; m. Donna L. Bender, Mar. 10, 1957; children: Paul William, Thomas Alan. B.S., U. Omaha, 1964; M.S., George Washington U., 1965; grad., Nat. War Coll., 1965. Commd. 2d lt. USAAF, 1943; advanced through grades to maj. gen. USAF, 1973; served with (15th Air Force), Europe, 1943, (5th Air Force), Korea, 1952; comdr.-in-chief Pacific, 1960-63; served with joint chiefs of staff, 1965-68; supreme comdr. (Allied Powers Europe), 1969-71; comdr. 12th Air Div. SAC, 1972, dep. chief of staff for plans, 1973; spl. asst. to chief of staff USAF, 1974-75; chmn. bd. and chief exec. officer Rancho Bernardo Savs. Bank, San Diego, 1983-90; ptnr. Allied Assocs., Colorado Springs, Colo., 1968—, D & H Inc., Woodland Park, 1979—; founding ptnr. Assocs. Group, San Diego, 1995—. Cons. Mid East matters and bd. dirs. Palomar Pomerado Health Found, San Diego; bd. dirs. Clean Found., San Diego. Author numerous articles on nat. def. requirements. Elder, Rancho Bernardo Community Presbyn. Ch., San Diego. Decorated D.S.M. with oak leaf cluster, Legion of Merit with oak leaf cluster, D.F.C., Air medal with 3 oak leaf clusters; research fellow UCLA, 1969. Mem. AIAA, Order Daedalians, Soc. Strategic Air Command, Eagle Scout Alumni Assn., Bernardo Heights Country Club (San Diego, past pres.), Phi Tau Alpha. Home: La Jolla Village Towers 8515 Costa Verde Blvd #1707 San Diego CA 92122

DARNELL, RAY D. city official; Dir. Rio Grande Zool. Park, Albuquerque; dir. cultural svcs. dept. City of Albuquerque, 2000—; dir. Albuquerque Biological Park, Albuquerque. Office: City of Albuquerque PO Box 1293 Albuquerque NM 87103-1293

DA ROSA, ALISON, travel editor; Travel editor San Diego Union-Tribune. Office: San Diego Union-Tribune 350 Camino De La Reina San Diego CA 92108-3003

DA ROZA, VICTORIA CECILIA, human resources administrator; b. East Orange, N.J., Aug. 30, 1945; d. Victor and Cynthia Helen (Krupa) Hawkins; m. Thomas Howard Kaminski, Aug. 28, 1971 (div. 1977); 1 child, Sarah Hawkins; m. Robert Anthony da Roza, Nov. 25, 1983. BA, U. Mich., 1967; MA, U. Mo., 1968. Contract compliance mgr. City of San Diego, 1972-75; v.p. personnel Bank of Calif., San Francisco, 1975-77; with human resources Lawrence Livermore (Calif.) Nat. Lab., 1978-86; pvt. cons. Victoria Kaminski-da Roza & Assocs., 1986—. Lectr. in field; videotape workshop program on mid-career planning used by IEEE. Contbr. numerous articles to profl. jours. Mem. ASTD, Gerontol. Soc. Am., San Ramon Valley Gnealogy Soc. (pres. 1999-01), P.E.O. (officer chpt. RV 1989-01). Home and Office: 1835 Monte Sereno Dr Alamo CA 94507-2734 E-mail: daRozal@go.com

DARRINGTON, DENTON C. state legislator; b. Burley, Idaho, Apr. 30, 1940; m. Virgene, five children, Lyn, Dee, Kimel, Kae, Matthew. BS in Agr., Utah State U., 1963. Mem. Farm Bur., Cassia County Hist. Soc., Delco Sch. Alumni Assn., Nat. Republican Legislators Assn. Office: State Capitol PO Box 83720 Boise ID 83720-3720

DASHIELL, G. RONALD, protective services official; U.S. marshal U.S. Dist. Ct. (ea. dist.) Wash., Spokane. Office: US Courthouse 920 W Riverside Ave Ste 888 Spokane WA 99201-1008

DA SILVA, LUIS B. scientist; BS in Engring. Physics, U. British Columbia, 1982, PhD in Plasma Physics, 1988. Scientist U. Calif., Lawrence Livermore Nat. Lab., Berkeley, 1988; staff scientist Lawrence Livermore (Calif.) Nat. Lab., 1992—. Recipient Early Achievement award IEEE, award for Excellence in Plasma Physics Rsch. 1998. Fellow Optical Soc. Am.; mem. Am. Physical Soc., Internat. Soc. Optical Engrs., IEEE. Office: Lawrence Livermore Nat Lab PO Box 808 Livermore CA 94551-0808

DASMANN, RAYMOND FREDRIC, ecologist; b. San Francisco, May 27, 1919; s. William H. and Mary (McDonnell) D.; m. Elizabeth Sheldon, May 30, 1944; children— Sandra, Marlene, Lauren. A.B., U. Calif., Berkeley, 1948, M.A., 1951, Ph.D., 1954. Mem. faculty Humboldt State Coll., 1954-59, 62-66; research biologist Nat. Museums Rhodesia, 1959-61; lectr. zoology U. Calif., Berkeley, 1961-62; ecologist Conservation Found., Washington, 1966-70; sr. ecologist Internat. Union Conservation Nature, Morges, Switzerland, 1970-77; prof. U. Calif., Santa Cruz, 1977—. Author: Pacific Coastal Wildlife, 1957, Environmental Conservation, 1959, 84, African Game Ranching, 1963, Last Horizon, 1963, Wildlife Biology, 1964, 81, Destruction of California, 1965, A Different Kind of Country, 1968, No Further Retreat, 1971, Planet in Peril, 1972, Ecological Principles for Economic Development, 1973, The Conservation Alternative, 1975, California's Changing Environment, 1981; contbr. articles to profl. jours. Fellow AAAS (hon.), Calif. Acad. Scis. (hon.), World Conservation Union (hon.); mem. Am. Soc. Mammalogists, Wildlife Soc. (pres.), Soc. for Conservation Biology, Golden Gate Biosphere Res. Assn. (pres.). Home: 116 Meadow Rd Santa Cruz CA 95060-2014 Office: U Calif Dept Environ Studies Santa Cruz CA 95064 E-mail: dasmann@cruzio.com

DASSANOWSKY, ROBERT VON, educator, producer, writer, editor; b. N.Y., Jan. 28, 1960; s. Elfi von Dassanowsky. Grad., Am. Acad. Dramatic Arts; BA with honors, UCLA, 1985, MA, 1988, PhD, 1992. Actor, 1975—; asst. prof. German, UCLA, 1992-93; asst. prof. German U. Colo., Colorado Springs, 1993-99, head German studies, 1993—, assoc. prof. German and film, dir. film studies, 1999—, interim chair dept. visual and performing arts, 2000-01, chair dept. langs. and cultures, 2001—. Councillor ProEuropa League Journalists and Scholars, 1998—. Author: (plays) The Brithday of Margot Beck, 1980, Briefly Noted, 1981, Vespers, 1982 (Beverly Hills Theatre Guild award 1984), Tristan in Winter, 1986, Songs of a Wayfarer, 1986, Coda, 1991, (criticism) Phantom Empires: The Novels of A. Lernet-Holenia and the Question of Postimperial Austrian Identity, 1996, Verses of a Marriage, Translation of Poetry Collection by Hans Raimund, 1996, Telegrams from the Metropole: Selected Poetry, 1999, Gale Encyclopedia of Multicultural America, 2nd edit., 2000; contbg. editl. advisor: International Dictionary of Films and Filmmakers, 4th edit., 2001; founding editor Rohwedder: Internat. Jour. Lit. and Art, 1986-93; editor Pen Center mag., 1992-98; contbg. editor Osiris; exec. prodr. The Nightmare Stumbles Past, 2001, Semmelweis, 2001, Wilson Chance, 2001; co-prodr. Epicure, 2001. Mem. Accademia Culturale d'Europa, Italy; bd. dir. L.A. Flickapalooza Film Festival. City of L.A. cultural grantee, 1990, 91, 92, U. Colo. Pres. Fund for Humanities grantee, 1996, 2001; recipient Residency award Karolyi Found., France, 1979, Accademico Honoris Causa Diploma, Accademia Culturale d'Europa, Italy, 1989, Outstanding Letters Arts and Scis. Faculty award U. Colo., Colorado Springs, 1998, Outstangind Tchr. award, 2001. Mem. PEN (West bd. dirs. L.A. 1992-99, founder and pres. Colo. chpt. 1994-99), PEN Austria, Internat. Lernet-Holenia Soc. (v.p. 1998—), Austrian Am. Film Assn. (v.p. 1997—), Soc. Cinema Studies, Poets and Writers, Modern Lang. Assn., Nat. Adv. Bd., Los Angeles Poetry Festival, SAG, ProEuropa League Journalists and Scholars (charter mem.), Concordia Assn. Journalists and Writers (Austria), Am. Coll. Heraldry (bd. govs. 2000—), Am. Fedn. Film Prodrs. Office: U Colo Dept Langs and Cultures Colorado Springs CO 80933 E-mail: belvederefilm@yahoo.com

DATE, ELAINE SATOMI, physiatrist, educator; b. San Jose, Calif., Feb. 19, 1957; BS, Stanford U., 1978; MD, Med. Coll. Pa., 1982. Diplomate of Nat. Bd. Med. Examiners. Diplomate Am. Bd. Phys. Medicine and Rehab. Dir. phys. medicine and rehab. Stanford (Calif.) U. Sch. Medicine, 1985—, rehab. medicine sect. chief, 1988-90, head phys. medicine and rehab. div., 1990—, assoc. prof. dept. functional rehab., 1995—; rehab. medicine chief Palo Alto (Calif.) VA Med. Ctr., 1988—. Fellow Am. Acad. Phys. Medicine and Rehab., Am. Assn. Electromyography and Electrodiagnosis. Avocations: reading, jogging.

DATYE, ABHAYA KRISHNA, chemical and nuclear engineer, educator; B in Tech., Indian Inst. Tech., 1975; MS, U. Cin., 1980; PhD, U. Mich., 1984. Asst. prof., assoc. prof. engring. U. N.Mex., Albuquerque, 1984-93, prof. chem. and nuclear engring., 1993—. Dir. Ctr. for Microengineered Ceramics, U. N.Mex., 1994—; tchg. asst. U. Cin., 1978-80; rsch. asst. U. Mich., Ann Arbor, 1980-84; presenter in field; cons. Integrated Circuit Engring. Corp., Scottsdale, Ariz., 1986-88, PDA Engring., Albuquerque, 1986-89, Allied-Signal, Des Plaines, Ill., 1990—, W.R. Grace & Co., Columbia, Md., 1992—, Chevron Rsch., Richmond, Calif., 1992—. Contbr. numerous articles to profl. jours.; reviewer jours. in field. Grantee Sandia Nat. Labs., 1985-87, 87-88, 88-89, 89-91, 91-92, 92-93, 93-94, Engring. Found., 1985-86, NSF, 1987-89, 89-90, 90-93, 92-95, 93-97, Am. Chem. Soc., 1989-90, 91-92, 93-95, Allied Signal, Mobil R&D, Waste Edn. Rsch. Consortium, 1993-94, 94-95. Mem. AIChE, Am. Chem. Soc., Am. Vacuum Soc. (N.Mex. chpt. chair 1995, Symposium organizer 1994), N.Am. Catalysis Soc. (Symposium organizer Albuquerque 1992, program com. co-chair Snowbird, Utah, 1995), Electron Microscopy Soc. Am. (session co-chmn. 1986, 88). Office: Univ NM NSF Ctr Micro-Engineered Ceramic Farris 203 Albuquerque NM 87131-0001 E-mail: datye@unm.edu

DAUER, DONALD DEAN, investment executive; b. Fresno, Calif., June 1, 1936; s. Andrew and Erma Mae (Zigenman) D.; m. LaVerne DiBuduo, Jan. 23, 1971; children: Gina, Sarah. BS in Bus. Adminstrn., Calif. State U. Fresno; postgrad., U. Wash., 1964. Loan officer First Savs. and Loan, Fresno, 1961-66, v.p., 1966-71, sr. v.p., 1971-81, exec. v.p., 1978-81; pres. Uniservice Corp., Fresno, 1976-81, Don Dauer Investments, Fresno, 1981—; pres., chief oper. officer Riverbend Internat. Corp., Sanger, Calif., 1985-89. Chmn. bd. dirs. Univ. Savs. and Loan, 1991-92, acting pres., CEO, 1992; loan officer Norwest Mortgage, 1993-95; mgr. CMB Fin., 1995-96. Chmn. bd. dirs. City of Fresno Gen. Svcs. Retirement Bd., 1973-83, West Fresno Econ. and Bus. Devel. Program Bd., 1980-83; pres. bd. dirs. Cen. Calif. United Cerebral Palsy Assn., 1979-82; bd. dirs. Valley Children's Hosp. Found., Fresno, 1984-93; trustee, chmn. Valley Children's Hosp., 1987-93; bd. dirs. Youth for Christ USA, 1988-94, Twilight Haven Inc., 2000—; vice chmn. Riverbend Internat., 1985-91. Mem. Soc. Real Estate Appraisers (past pres.). Office: 2733 W Palo Alto Ave Fresno CA 93711-1110

DAUER, EDWARD ARNOLD, law educator; b. Providence, Sept. 28, 1944; s. Marshall and Shirly (Moverman) D.; m. Carol Jean Egglestone, June 18, 1966; children: E. Craig, Rachel P. AB, Brown U., 1966; LLB cum laude, Yale U., 1969; MPH, Harvard U., 2001. Bar: Conn. 1978, Colo. 1986. Asst. prof. law sch. U. Toledo, 1969-72; assoc. prof. law U. So. Calif., L.A., 1972-74, Yale U., New Haven, 1975-85, assoc. dean, 1978-83, dep. dean law sch., 1983-85; dean, prof. law U. Denver, 1985-90, dean emeritus, prof. law, 1991—. Vis. scholar Harvard U. Sch. Pub. Health, 1996-97; of counsel Popham, Haik, Schnobrich and Kaufman, 1990-97; pres. CEJAD Aviation Corp.; sr. assn. Health Care Negotiation Assocs., Inc. Author: Materials on a Nonadversarial Legal Process, 1978, Conflict Resolution Strategies in Health Care, 1993, Manual of Dispute Resolution: ADR Law and Practice, 1994 (CPr Book award 1994), Health Care Dispute Resolution, 2000; contbr. articles to profl. jours. Bd. dirs. New Haven Cmty. Action Agy., 1978-81, Cerebral Palsy Found. Denver, 1989—, pres., 1992-95; founder, pres. Nat. Ctr. Preventive Law; mem. Colo. Commn. Higher Edn., 1987-91; commr. Colo. Advanced Tech. Inst., 1989-91. Recipient W. Quinn Jordan award Nat. Blood Found., 1994, Paella award Harvard Sch. Pub. Health, 1996, Sanbar award Am. Coll. Legal Medicine, 1999. Mem. Am. Law Inst., Order of Coif, Met. Club, Greenwood Athletic Club. Republican. Jewish. Home: 127 S Garfield St Denver CO 80209 Office: U Denver Coll Law 1900 Olive St Denver CO 80220 E-mail: edauer@du.edu, edauer@hcna.net

DAUGHENBAUGH, RANDALL JAY, retired chemical company executive, consultant; b. Rapid City, S.D., Feb. 10, 1948; s. Horace Allan and Helen Imogene (Reder) D.; m. Mary R. Wynja, Aug. 25, 1973; children: Jason Allan, Jill Christen. BS, S.D. Tech., 1970; PhD, U. Colo., 1975. Rsch. chemist Air Prod. and Chem., Allentown, Pa., 1975-80; rsch. dir. Chem. Exch. Industries, Boulder, Colo., 1980-83; pres. Hauser Chem. Rsch., Inc., Boulder, 1983-93, chief tech. officer, exec. v.p., 1993-99. Contbr. articles to profl. jours.; patentee in field. Recipient R&D Mag. IR-100 award, 1993; named Inc. Mag. Entrepreneur of Yr., 1992. Mem. Am. Chem. Soc. Home: 10755 Sheridan Lake Rd Rapid City SD 57702-6506 Office: Hauser Chem Rsch Inc 5555 Airport Blvd Boulder CO 80301-2339 E-mail: rjdaugh@rapidnet.com

DAUGHERTY, ROBERT MELVIN, JR. university dean, medical educator; b. Kansas City, Mo., May 2, 1934; s. Robert Melvin and Mildred Josephine (Johnson) D.; m. Sandra Allison Keller, Aug. 10, 1957; children— Robert Melvin III, Allison, Christopher. BS, Kans. U., 1956; MD, U. Kans., 1960; MS, U. Okla. Med. Ctr., 1964; PhD, U. Okla., 1965. Intern Jefferson Davis Hosp., Houston, 1960-61; resident U. Okla. Med. Ctr., Oklahoma City, 1961-63, asst. prof. physiology and medicine, 1965-66; assoc. prof. physiology and medicine Mich. State U. Coll. Human Medicine, East Lansing, 1969-71; prof., dir. Office Curriculum Implementation, 1969-76; prof. physiology and medicine U. Wyo. Coll. Human Medicine, Laramie, 1976-78, dean, 1976-78; prof. physiology and medicine Ind. U. Sch. Medicine, Indpls., 1978-81, assoc. dean, 1978-81, dir. continuing med. edn., 1978-81; dean Sch. Medicine, U. Nev., 1981-99, dean emeritus, 1999—; dir. health cre polity R&D, U. Nev. Sch. Medicine, Reno, 1999—. Tchg. scholar Am. Heart Assn., 1970-75. Mem. AMA (coun. med. edn. 1991—), LCME (chair 1999—), Am. Physiol. Soc., Am. Heart Assn., Ctrl. Soc. for Clin. Investigation. Presbyterian. Home: 820 Marsh Ave Reno NV 89509-1945 Office: U Nev Sch Med Dir Hlth Care Policy R&D 411 W Second St Reno NV 89503-5308

DAUGHTON, DONALD, lawyer; b. Grand River, Iowa, Mar. 11, 1932; s. F.J. and Ethel (Edwards) D.; m. Sally Daughton; children by previous marriage: Erin, Thomas, Andrew, J.P. BSc, U. Iowa, 1953, JD, 1956. Bar: Iowa, 1956, Ariz., 1958. Asst. county atty. Polk County, Des Moines, 1956, 1958-59; atty. Snell & Wilmer, Phoenix, 1959-64, Browder and Daughton, Phoenix, 1964-65; judge Superior Ct. of Ariz., Phoenix, 1965-67, 97—; atty. Browder Gillenwater and Daughton, Phoenix, 1967-72, Daughton Feinstein and Wilson, Phoenix, 1972-86, Daughton Hawkins and Bacon, Phoenix, 1986-88; resident mng. ptnr. Brian Cave, Phoenix, 1988-92; atty. Daughton Hawkins Brockelman Guinnan and Patterson, Phoenix, 1992-97. Asst. county atty. Polk County, 1958-59 chmn. Phoenix Employees Relations Bd., 1976. Pres. Maricopa County Legal Aid Soc., 1971-73. 1st lt. JAG, USAF, 1956-58. Fellow Am. Bar Found., Ariz. Bar Found. (founder); mem. ABA (bd. govs. 1989-92, exec. com. 1991-92), State Bar Ariz. (chmn. pub. rels. com. 1980-84, jud. evaluation poll com. 1984-94), Iowa State Bar, Maricopa County Bar Assn. (bd. dirs. 1962-64), 9th Cir. Jud. Conf. (lawyer rep. 1981-84, 88), Nat. Acad. Arbitrators, Chartered Inst. Arbitrators, Univ. Club. Home: 6021 N 51st Pl Paradise Valley AZ 85253-5143 Office: Superior Ct of Ariz 201 W Jefferson St Phoenix AZ 85003-2205

DAVENPORT, JANET LEE, real estate agent, small business owner; b. Napa, Calif., Dec. 10, 1938; d. George Perry and Stella Dolores (Ramalho) Gomez; m. Bingo George Wesner, Aug. 4, 1957 (July 1978); children: Bing George, Diane Estelle; m. Marvin Eugene Davenport, Jan. 13, 1979. Student, U. Calif., Davis, 1956-57, Nat. Jud. Coll., , 1975-79. Co-owner, operator Bar JB Ranch, Benicia, Calif., 1960-71, Lovelock, Nev., 1971-78; owner, mgr. Wesner Bookkeeping Svc., Lovelock, 1973-78; chief tribal judge Ct. Indian Offenses, Lovelock, 1975-79; justice of peace, coroner County of Pershing, Lovelock, 1975-79; paralegal, legal sec. Samuel S. Wardle, Carson City, Nev., 1979; dep. ct. adminstr. Reno Mcpl. Ct., Reno, 1979-81; co-owner horse farm Reno, 1979—; freelance real estate investor Reno, 1979—; real estate saleswoman Merrill Lynch Realtors, Sparks, Nev., 1981-82; realtor, farm and ranch div. mgr. Copple and Assocs., Realtors, Sparks, 1982-91; real estate saleswoman Vail and Assocs. Realty, Reno, 1991—. Co-owner, operator Lovelock (Nev.) Merc. Co., 1988—; sec. Nev. Judges Assn., 1977-78. Dir. Pershing County Drug and Alcohol Abuse Council, Lovelock, 1976-78. Mem. Reno/Sparks Bd. Realtors, Nat. Assn. Realtors, Nev. Assn. Realtors, Am. Quarter Horse Assn. Republican. Roman Catholic. Home: 4805 Sinelio Dr Reno NV 89502-9510 Office: Vail and Assocs Realty 2470 Wrondel Way # 105 Reno NV 89502-3701

DAVENPORT, ROGER LEE, research engineer; b. Sacramento, Oct. 27, 1955; s. Lee Edwin and Ada Fern (Henderson) D.; m. Cynthia Ann Carle, June 20, 1998. AB Physics, U. Calif., Berkeley, 1977; MSME, U. Ariz., 1979. Assoc. engr. Solar Energy Rsch. Inst., Golden, Colo., 1979-82; cons. Darmstadt, Fed. Republic Germany, 1982-84; missionary Eastern European Sem., Vienna, Austria, 1984-87; staff researcher Sci. Applications Internat. Corp., San Diego, 1987—. Mem. Am. Solar Energy Soc., Denver Electric Vehicle Coun., Sierra Club, Phi Beta Kappa. Home: 19076 W 59th Dr Golden CO 80403-1057 Office: SAIC 15874 W 6th Ave Golden CO 80401-5020 E-mail: roger.l.davenport@saic.com

DAVID, CLIVE, event planning executive; b. Manchester, Eng., June 6, 1934; came to U.S., 1957, naturalized, 1962; s. Marcus Wiener and Claire Rose (Levy) Wiener Kattenburg. Student, Blackpool Tech. Coll., 1951-52, Royal Coll. Art, 1955-57. Designer Chippendale's, London, 1955-57; asst. to pres. pub. relations Maybruck Assocs., N.Y.C., 1959; Ea. regional dir. City of Hope, Phila., 1960-62; pres. Clive David Assocs., N.Y.C., Clive David Enterprises div. Party Enterprises Ltd., Beverly Hills, Calif., Party Enterprises, Ltd., Beverly Hills, 1962—. Lectr. Party Planning par excellence, 1966—. Arranger major parties including Miss Universe Coronation Ball, Miami Beach, 1965, State visit of Queen Elizabeth and Prince Philip, Duke of Edinburgh, Bahamas, 1966, An Evening at the Ritz-Carlton, Boston, 1967, 69, Un Ballo in Maschera, Venice, 1967, An Evening over Boston, 1968, M.G.M. Cavalcade of Style, L.A., 1970, Symposium on Fund Raising through Parties, L.A., 1970, Great Midwest Limestone Cave Party, Kansas City, 1972, Une Soiree de Gala, Phila., 1972, 11th Anniv. of the Mike Douglas Show, Phila., 1972, The Mayor's Salute to Volunteers, Los Angeles, 1972, Twenty Fifth Anniv. Salute to Israel, Jerusalem, 1973, The Bicentenary, 1976, The World Affairs Council Silver Ball, Boston, 1977, The Ohio Theatre Jubilee, Columbus, 1978, Mayor's Salute to Vols., 1978, Dedication and Gala Performance, Northwestern U. Performing Arts Ctr., 1980, Metromedia Gala, Los Angeles Bicentennial, 1981, The Albemarle Weekend, Charlottesville, 1985, The La Costa Weekend, Carlsbad, 1987, The Embassy Ball, N.Y.C., 1987, The Lagoon Cycle Premiere, Los Angeles, 1987, State Visit Gala for Her Majesty Queen Elizabeth, Miami, 1991, The Grand Brazilian Clambake, Southampton, 1995, The Democratic Senatorial Campaign Committee Gala, Charlottesville, 1996, DSCC reception for Hillary Rodham Clinton, 1996, Rep. Nat. Conv. Team 100 Reception, San Diego, 1996; mem. Pres.' Summit for Am.'s Future Leadership Roundtable, Phila., 1997, Rep. Govs. Conf. Opening Banquet, 1999; contbr. articles to profl. jours. Served with Royal Arty. Brit. Army, 1953-55. Recipient Freedom Found. award Valley Forge, Pa., 1961, City of Hope award Phila., 1962, Mayor's medal for vol. services Los Angeles, 1972, Shalom award State of Israel, 1974, Mayor's medal City of Columbus; named hon. citizen City of Columbus. Mem. AFTRA Jewish Office: 282 S Reeves Dr Beverly Hills CA 90212-4005

DAVIDSON, DAVID SCOTT, architect; b. Great Falls, Mont., Dec. 17, 1925; s. David Adams and Florence Mae (Scott) D.; m. Marjorie Luella Huffman, Sept. 10, 1949; children: Carol M., Marilyn S., Scott L., Bruce F., Craig S. Student, U. Utah, 1943, Pasadena City Coll., 1944; B.S. in Architecture, Mont. State U., 1950. Registered architect, Mont. Architect in tng. Shanley & Shanley Architects, Great Falls, 1950-52; architect van Teylingen, Knight, van Teylingen, Great Falls, 1952-54; prin. David S. Davidson, Architect, Great Falls, 1954-56; ptnr. Davidson & Kuhr Architects, Great Falls, 1956-75; pres. Davidson & Kuhr Architects, P.C., Great Falls, 1975—. Dir., pres. Great Falls Arts Assn., 1980-83; dir., pres. Mont. Inst. Arts, 1981—; mem. state constrn. adv. council State of Mont., 1983-84; dir., v.p. Paris Gibson Square, Great Falls, 1982—. Mem. Great Falls Zoning Bd., 1972-75; mem. rehab. com. Great Falls Housing Task Force, 1975-78; chmn. architecture div. United Way, 1975-78; dir. Great Falls Symphony Assn., 1992-93. Served with U.S. Army, 1943-46. Recipient 1st honor Mont. chpt. AIA, 1973, 75; recipient honor award in architecture Mont. chpt. AIA, 1973, 74, 78, 83, merit in architecture Mont. chpt. AIA, 1965, 2 awards U.S. Dept. Energy, 1986, Interior Design award Arch. Record, 1976, Internat. Union Bricklayers and Allied Crafts award, 1986, 87, 92. Fellow AIA (chpt. pres. 1965-66, dir. 1962 66), Great Falls Soc. Architects (pres. 1958-59), Jr. C. of C. (dir. 1956-60) Home: 1212 Buena Dr Great Falls MT 59404-3750 Office: Davidson and Kuhr Archs PC 401 Division Rd Great Falls MT 59404-1409

DAVIDSON, DONALD HERBERT, philosophy educator; b. Springfield, Mass., Mar. 6, 1917; s. Clarence Herbert and Grace (Anthony) D.; m. Nancy Hirschberg, Apr. 4, 1975 (dec. 1979); 1 child, by previous marriage, Elizabeth Ann; m. Marcia Cavell, July 3, 1984. BA, Harvard U., 1939, MA, 1941, PhD, 1949; DDL (hon.), LittD (hon.), Oxford U., 1995; PhD (hon.), Stockholm U., 1999. Instr. philosophy Queen's (N.Y.) Coll., 1947-50; from asst. prof. to prof. Stanford (Calif.) U., 1951-67; prof. Princeton (N.J.) U., 1967-70, chmn. dept. philosophy, 1968-70, prof., 1970-76, Rockefeller U., N.Y.C., 1970-76, U. Chgo., 1976-81, U. Calif., Berkeley, 1981—. Apptd. Willis S. and Marion Slusser prof., vis. prof. Tokyo U., 1955; Gavin David Young lectr. U. Adelaide, 1968; John Locke lectr. Oxford (Eng.) U., 1970; vis. prof. U. Sydney, 1968, U. Pitts., 1972, U. Capetown, 1980, U. Venice, 1991, U. Rome, 1993, law & philosophy NYU, 1993; John Dewey lectr. U. Minn., 1975; Matchette Found. lectr. U. Wis., 1976; Carus lectr., 1980; Hägerstrom lectr., 1980; Josè Gaos vis. lectr. U. Mex., 1980; George Eastman vis. prof. Balliol Coll., Oxford, 1984-85; Kant lectr. Stanford U., 1986; S.J. Keeling Meml. lectr. Greek philosophy Univ. Coll., U. London, 1986; Fulbright Disting. lectr., India, 1985-86; Selfridge lectr. Lehigh U., 1986; Thalheimer lectr. Johns Hopkins U., Balt., 1987, David Ross Boyd lectr. U. Okla., 1988, John Dewey lectr. Columbia U., 1989, Alfred North Whitehead lectr. Harvard U., 1990, Heisenberg lectr., Munich, 1981; Kant lectr. U. Munich, 1993, Spinoza lectr. Jerusalem U., 1993, Grambieh and Orr lectr. Dartmouth Coll., 1993, Alan Donagan meml. lectr. Notre Dame, 1994, Josep Ferrater Mora lectr., Girona Spain, 1994; Franquini chair lectr. U. Leuven, Belgium, 1994; Jean Nicod lectr. Caen & Paris, 1995; Shearman Meml. lectr. Univ. Coll., London, 1995; Hill vis. prof. U. Minn., [illegible] 2001. Co-Author: (with Patrick Suppes) Decision Making: An Experimental Approach, 1957; author: Essays on Actions and Events, 1980, Inquiries into Truth and Interpretation, 1983; co-editor: (with J. Hintikka) Words and Objections, 1969, (with Gilbert Harman) Semantics for Natural Language, 1970, The Logic of Grammar, 1975, Subjective, Intersubjective, Objective, 2001, mem. edit. bd. Philosophia, 1970—, Theoretical Linguistics, [illegible]

Commentary in the Behavioral and Brain Sciences, 1976—. Lt. (s.g.) USNR, 1942-45, MTO. Recipient Hegel prize City of Stuttgart, Fed. Republic Germany, 1991; Teschemacher fellow in classics and philosophy, 1939-41; Rockefeller fellow in humanities, 1945-46; Rockefeller fellow for research, 1948; Ford Faculty fellow, 1953-54; Am. Council Learned Socs. fellow, 1958-59, Center Advanced Study Behavioral Scis. fellow, 1969-70, Guggenheim fellow, 1973-74, All Souls Coll. Oxford U. fellow, 1973-74, Vis. fellow Rsch. Sch. Social Scis., Australian Nat. U., 1977, Hon. Rsch. fellow Univ. Coll., London, 1978; Sherman Fairchild Disting. scholar Calif. Inst. Tech., 1989; Rsch. grant NSF, 1964-65, 68. Fellow Am. Acad. Arts and Scis., AAAS, Brit. Acad. (corr.); mem. Am. Philos Assn. (sec. Pacific Coast div. 1956-59, v.p. 1961, pres. Eastern div. 1973-74, pres. Pacific div. 1985-86), Am. Philos Soc., Institute Internacional de Philosophie, Norwegian Acad. Sci. and Letters, AAUP. Office: U Calif Philosophy Dept Berkeley CA 94720-0001

DAVIDSON, DONETTA, state official; County clk. and recorder Bent County, Colo., 1978-86; dir. of elections State of Colo., 1986-94; county clerk and recorder Arapahoe County, Colo., 1994-99; sec. of state State of Colo., 1999—. Office: Office of Sec of State Denver Post Bldg 1560 Broadway Ste 200 Denver CO 80202-5169 E-mail: sos.admin1@state.co.us

DAVIDSON, ERIC HARRIS, molecular and developmental biologist, educator; b. N.Y.C., Apr. 13, 1937; s. Morris and Anne D. B.A., U. Pa., 1958; Ph.D., Rockefeller U., 1963. Research asso. Rockefeller U., 1963-65, asst. prof., 1965-71; asso. prof. devel. molecular biology Calif. Inst. Tech., Pasadena, 1971-74, prof., 1974—, Norman Chandler prof. cell biology, 1981—. Author: Gene Activity in Early Development, 3d edit, 1986, Genomic Regulatory Systems, 2001. NIH grantee, 1965— ; NSF grantee, 1972— Mem. Nat. Acad. Scis. Achievements include research, numerous publs. on DNA sequence orgn., gene expression during embryonic devel., gene regulation, evolutionary mechanisms, gene networks. Office: Calif Inst Tech Div Biology Mail Code 156 29 Pasadena CA 91125-0001

DAVIDSON, EZRA C., JR. physician, educator; b. Water Valley, Miss., Oct. 21, 1933; s. Ezra Cap and Theresa Hattie (Woods) D.; children: Pamela, Gwendolyn, Marc, Ezra K. BS cum laude, Morehouse Coll., 1954; MD, Meharry Med. Coll., 1958. Diplomate: Am. Bd. Ob-Gyn. (examiner 1973—). Intern San Diego County Gen. Hosp., 1958-59; resident in ob-gyn. Harlem Hosp., N.Y.C., 1963-66, asst. attending ob-gyn, obstet. coordinator maternal and infant care clinics, 1967-68; dir. departmental research, assoc. attending, acting chmn. ob-gyn, co-dir. coagulation research lab. Roosevelt Hosp., N.Y.C., 1968-70; fellow blood coagulation, asst. ob-gyn Columbia U. Coll. Physicians and Surgeons, N.Y.C., 1966-67, instr. dept. ob-gyn, 1967-69, asst. clin. prof., 1970; cons. ob-gyn Office Health Affairs, OEO, Washington, 1970-72; prof. Charles R. Drew U. of Medicine and Sci., L.A., 1971—, acad. v.p., 1982-87, chmn. dept. ob.-gyn., 1971-96, assoc. dean primary care, 1997—; prof. U. So. Calif., Los Angeles, 1971-80, UCLA, 1980—. Chief svc. dept. ob-gyn. King/Drew Med. Ctr., L.A., 1971-96; attending physician dept. ob-gyn. L.A. County-U. So. Calif. Med. Ctr., 1971-80; mem. nat. med. adv. com. Nat. Found. March of Dimes, 1972-76; bd. cons. Internat. Childbirth Edn. Assn., 1973-81; mem. sec.'s adv. com. population affairs HEW, 1974-77, chmn. svcs. task force, 1975-77; chmn. bd. dirs. L.A. Regional Family Planning Coun., 1975-77; bd. dirs. Nat. Alliance Sch. Age parents, 1975-79; mem. corp. bd. Blue Shield, Calif., 1989—; chmn. fertility and maternal health drugs adv. com. FDA, 1992-96, active, 1990-96; mem. adv. com. to the dir. NIH, 1995-98, mem. dirs. adv. panel on clin. rsch., 1995-98; mem. roundtable on health care quality Inst. of Medicine, 1995-98; mem. coun. grad. med. edn. HHS, 1997-2000; bd. dirs., chair med. policy com. Blue Shield of Calif., 1998—; chair DHHS Sec.'s Adv. Com. on Infant Mortality, 1990-93. Bd. dirs. The Calif. Wellness Found., 1995—, chmn., 1996-98; bd. dirs. Children's Bur. So. Calif., 1999—, v.p., 1995-99, pres. 1999—; bd. dirs. Jacobs Inst. of Womens Health, 1999—. Served with USAF, 1959-63. Johnson Found. Health Policy fellow Inst. Medicine, Nat. Acad. Scis., 1979-80 Fellow ACS, Am. Coll. Ob-Gyn. (nat. sec. 1983-89, pres.-elect 1989-90, pres. 1990-91), Royal Coll. Ob-Gyn., L.A. Ob-Gyn. Soc. (pres. 1982-83); mem. Am. Gyn.-Ob Soc., N.Am. Soc. Pediatric and Adolescent Gynecology (pres.-elect 1993-94, pres. 1994-95), Pacific Coast Ob-Gyn. Soc., Ob-Gyn. Assembly So. Calif. (chmn. 1989-90), Nat. Med. Assn. (chmn. nat. sect. ob-gyn. 1975-77, mem. sci. coun. 1979-88, trustee 1989-95, chmn. bd. trustees 1992-95), Golden State Med. Assn. (pres. 1989-90), Assn. Profs. Ob-Gyn. (pres. 1989-90). Office: 12021 Wilmington Ave Los Angeles CA 90059-3019

DAVIDSON, GORDON, theatrical producer, director; b. Bklyn., May 7, 1933; s. Joseph H. and Alice (Gordon) D.; m. Judith Swiller, Sept. 21, 1958; children: Adam, Rachel. B.A., Cornell U.; M.A., Case Western Res. U.; L.H.D. (hon.), Bklyn. Coll.; D. Performing Arts (hon.), Calif. Inst. Arts; D.F.A. (hon.), Claremont U. Ctr. Stage mgr. Phoenix Theatre Co., 1958-60, Am. Shakespeare Festival Theatre, 1958-60, Dallas Civic Opera, 1960-61, Martha Graham Dance Co., 1962; mng. dir. Theatre Group at UCLA, 1965-67; artistic dir., producer Center Theatre Group Mark Taper Forum, 1967—; co-founder New Theatre For Now, Mark Taper Forum, 1970. Past mem. theatre panel Nat. Endowment for Arts; past pres. Theatre Communications Group; mem. adv. council Internat. Theatre Inst.; mem. adv. com. Cornell Ctr. for Performing Arts; cons. Denver Center for the Performing Arts; bd. dirs. several arts orgns. including Am. Arts Alliance. Producer, dir. over 150 major theatrical prodns. including The Deputy, 1965, Candide, 1966, The Devils, 1967, Who's Happy Now, 1967, In the Matter of J. Robert Oppenheimer, 1968 (N.Y. Drama Desk award), Sew, Murderous Angels, 1970, Rosebloom, 1970, The Trial of the Catonsville Nine, 1971 (Obie award, Tony award nomination), Henry IV, Part I, 1972, Mass, 1973, Hamlet, 1974, Savages, 1974 (Obie award), Too Much Johnson, 1975, The Shadow Box, 1975 (Tony award, Outer Critics Circle Best Dir. award), And Where She Stops Nobody Knows, 1976, Getting Out, 1977, Black Angel, 1978, Terra Nova, 1979, Children of a Lesser God, 1979, The Lady and the Clarinet, 1980, Chekhov in Yalta, 1981, Tales from Hollywood, 1982, The American Clock, 1984, The Hands of Its Enemy, 1984, Traveler in the Dark, 1985, The Real Thing, 1986, Ghetto, 1986, A Lie of the Mind, 1988; dir. operas including Cosi Fan Tutte, Otello, Beatrice and Benedick, Carmen, La Boheme, Il Trovatore, Harriet, A Woman Called Moses, A Midsummer Night's Dream, 1988; TV film The Trial of the Catonsville Nine, 1971; exec. producer Zoot Suit, 1981; producer for TV It's the Willingness, PBS Visions Series, 1979, Who's Happy Now?, NET Theatre in Am. Series; dir. A Little Night Music, 1990. Trustee Ctr. for Music, Drama and Art; past pres. League Resident Theatres; past v.p. Am. Nat. Theatre Acad; advisor Fund for New Am. Plays. Recipient N.Y. Drama Desk award for direction, 1969; recipient Los Angeles Drama Critics Circle awards for direction, 1971, 74, 75, Margo Jones award New Theatre for Now, 1970, 76, Obie award, 1971, 77, Outer Critics Circle award, 1977, Tony award for direction, 1977, award John Harvard, award Nat. Acad. TV Arts and Scis., award Nosotros Golden Eagle, award N.Y. League for Hard of Hearing, award N.Y. Speech and Hearing Assn., award Am. Theatre Assn., award Los Angeles Human Relations Commn.; Guggenheim fellow, 1983 Mem. League Resident Theatres (past pres.), ANTA (v.p. 1975) Office: [illegible] Angeles CA 90012-3013

DAVIDSON, HERBERT ALAN, Near Eastern languages and cultures educator; b. Boston, May 25, 1932; s. Louis Nathan and Ettabelle (Baker) D.; m. Kinneret Bernstein; children: Rachel and Jessica. BA, Harvard U., 1953, MA, 1955, PhD, 1959. Lectr. Harvard U., Cambridge, Mass., [illegible], asst. prof. UCLA, [illegible], assoc. prof., [illegible]-72, prof., 1972-94, prof. emeritus, 1994—, chmn. dept. near eastern langs. and cultures, 1984-91. Author: The Philosophy of Abraham Shalom, 1964, medieval Hebrew transls. of Averroes' Middle Commentary on the Isagoge and Categories, 1969, English transl., 1969, Proofs for Eternity, Creation, and the Existence of God in Medieval Islamic and Jewish Philosophy, 1987, Alfarabi, Avicenna, and Averroes on Intellect, 1992; contbr. articles and book revs. to profl. jours. Office: UCLA Dept Near Ea Langs and Cultures 405 Hilgard Ave Los Angeles CA 90095-9000

DAVIDSON, MARK, writer, educator; b. N.Y.C., Sept. 25, 1928; BA in Polit. Sci., UCLA, 1948; MS in Journalism, Columbia U., 1950. Sci. writer U. So. Calif., L.A., 1980-90; prof. comm. Calif. State U., Dominguez Hills, Carson, 1985-99; freelance writer. Faculty adviser Soc. Profl. Journalists, 1993-96; lectr. in field; writer for Steve Allen Show, 1964, Dinah Shore Show, 1978, CBS Mag. Show with Connie Chung, 1980. Author: Uncommon Sense (About Systems Science), 1984, Japanese transl., 2000, Invisible Chains of Thought Control, 1999, Watchwords: A Dictionary of American English Usage, 2001. Sackett scholar Columbia U.; recipient Nat. Emmy for writing Dinah Shore Show NATAS, 1978. Mem. PEN, Am. Soc. Journalists and Authors, Nat. Assn. Sci. Writers, Am. Med. Writers Assn., Authors Guild, Writers Guild Am., Calif. Faculty Assn. (v.p. Dominguez Hills chpt. 1992-96), Soc. Advancement Edn. (assoc. mass media editor 1997—). E-mail: wordwatcher@earthlink.net

DAVIDSON, MAYER B. medical educator, researcher; b. Balt., Apr. 11, 1935; s. David and Esther (Crockin) D.; m. Naomi Berger, Nov. 25, 1961 (div. 1977); children: Elke W., Seth J.; m. Roseann Herman, Aug. 31, 1980. AB, Swarthmore Coll., 1957; MD, Harvard U., 1961. Diplomate Am. Bd. Internal Medicine, Am. Bd. Endocrinology and Metabolism. Intern Bellevue Hosp., N.Y.C., 1961-62, jr. asst. resident, 1962-63; sr. asst. resident U. Wash. Affiliated Hosps., Seattle, 1963-64; rsch. fellow dept. endocrinology and metabolism King County Hosp., U. Wash., Seattle, 1964-66; asst. prof. medicine UCLA Sch. Medicine, 1969-74, from assoc. prof. to prof., 1974-95, clin. prof., 1996—, acting chief div. endocrinology and metabolism, 1973-74. Dir. diabetes program Cedars-Sinai Med. Ctr., L.A., 1979-95; assoc. dir. clin. diabetes City of Hope Nat. Med. Ctr., 1995-98; dir. clin. trials unit Charles R. Drew U.; nat. advisor Diabetes Ctr. Humana Hosp., Phoenix, 1985-91; attending physician diabetic clinic Boston City Hosp., 1966-68; clin. asst. Harvard Med. Sch., 1968-69; cons. AMA Dept. Drugs. Author: Diabetus Mellitus: Diagnosis and Treatment, 4th edit., 1998; contbr. 28 chpts. to books, numerous revs., editls., articles and abstracts; presenter 140 sci. papers; mem. editl. bd. Jour. Clin. Endocrinology and Metabolism, 1981-84, 93-95, Jour. Diabetes Care, 1984-87, Geriatrics, 1986—, Diabetes Reports, 1987-89, Today in Medicine,1987-88, Clin. Diabetes, 1989-92, Diabetes Spectrum, 1989-92, Diabetes Rsch. & Clin. Practice, 1992—; founding editor Current Diabetes Reports, 2001—; editor-in-chief Diabetes Care, 2002—. Co-founder, bd. dirs. free med. facility Venice (Calif.) Family Clinic, 1970. Maj. Med. Svc. Corps U.S . Army, 1966-69. USPHS rsch. fellow Nat. Inst. Arthritis and Metabolic Diseases, 1965-66; recipient Upjohn award for Outstanding Diabetes Educator, 1990, Robert H. Williams/Rachmiel Levine award for sci. contbns. and humanism in tng. young rschrs., 1995, Banting medal for Disting. Svc., 1998; named to Best Doctors in Am., 1992-93, 95-96, 96-97. Fellow ACP; mem. AAAS, Am. Diabetes Assn. (rsch. prizes 1965, 66, R&D award 1974-75, rsch. 1978-81, bd. dirs. 1986-89, 93-99, v.p. 1995-96, pres.-elect 1996-97, pres. 1997-98), Am. Fedn. Clin. Rsch., Western Soc. Clin. Rsch., Endocrine Soc., Am. Soc. Clin. Investigation, Western Assn. Physicians, Am. Assn. Diabetes Educators (editl. bd. jour. 1980-83), Boylston Med. Soc., Am. Diabetes Assn. (pres. 1997-98), Sigma Xi. Democrat. Jewish. E-mail: madavids@cdrewu.edu

DAVIDSON, NORMAN RALPH, biochemistry educator; b. Chgo., Apr. 5, 1916; s. Bernard Ralph and Rose (Lefstein) D.; m. Annemarie Behrendt, July 11, 1942; children: Terence Mark, Laureen Davidson Reitman Agee, Jeffrey Norman, Brian Lee. BS, U. Chgo., 1937, PhD in Chemistry, 1941; BS, Oxford (Eng.) U., 1939; DSc (hon.), U. Chgo., 1992, Scripps Rsch. Inst., 1999. Research scientist Manhattan Project U. Chgo., 1942-46; instr. chemistry Calif. Inst. Tech., Pasadena, 1946-49, asst. prof., 1949-52, assoc. prof., 1952-57, prof., 1957-82, Chandler prof. chem. biology, 1982-86, prof. emeritus, 1986—, acting chair div. biology, 1989, exec. officer div. biology, 1990. Sr. cons. Am Gen., Thousand Oaks, Calif., 1992—; mem., chmn. biophysics and biophys. chemistry study sect. NIH, Bethesda, Md., 1964-88, mem. nat. adv. coun. human genome rsch., 1989-93. Author: Statistical Mechanics, 1962. Rhodes scholar, 1938-39; recipient Calif. sect. award Am. Chem. Soc., 1954, Peter Debye award in phys. chemistry, 1971; named Calif. Scientist of Yr., Calif. Mus. Sci. and History, 1980, Nat. Medal of Sci., 1996. Mem. NAS (Dickson prize sci. 1985, Robert A. Welch award in chemistry 1989). Office: Calif Inst Tech Div Biology 156 29 Pasadena CA 91125-0001 E-mail: normand@cco.caltech.edu

DAVIDSON, ROBERT C., JR. manufacturing executive; b. Memphis, Oct. 3, 1945; s. Robert C. Sr. and Thelma (Culp) D.; m. Alice Faye Berkley, Jan. 5, 1978; children: Robert III, John Roderick, Julian. BA, Morehouse Coll., 1967; MBA, U. Chgo., 1969. V.p. Urban Nat. Corp., Boston, 1972-74, Avant Garde Enterprises, Los Angeles, 1974-76; pres. Surface Protection, Industries, Los Angeles, 1976—, now CEO. Bd. dirs. Pasadena Art Workshop, 1986—; planning commr. City of Pasadena, 1986—. Mem. Young Pres. Orgn. Club: 100 Black Men (Los Angeles). Avocations: tennis, skiing. Office: Surface Protection Industries Inc 3411 E 15th St Los Angeles CA 90023-3822

DAVIDSON, ROBERT WILLIAM, merchant banker; b. Colfax, Wash., Sept. 18, 1949; s. William Martin and Lena (Soli) D.; m. Molly Evoy, Apr. 16, 1977; children: Ford Patrick, Matthew Harpur, Marshall Andrew. AB, Harvard U., 1971; MBA, U. Wash., 2000. Exec. dir. Sabre Found., Cambridge, Mass., 1971-72; adminstrv. asst. Congressman Joel Pritchard, Washington, 1973-79; asst. sec. state State of Wash., Olympia, 1979-80; pres. Frayn Fin. Printing, Seattle, 1982-87, Frayn Printing Co., Seattle, 1985-87; exec. dir. Woodland Park Zool. Soc., Seattle, 1987-93, pres., 1993-94; prin. Alistar Capital Group, Bellevue, Wash., 1994—. Mem. adv. com. Wash. State Software Ind. Devel. Bd., 1984-85. Chmn. pub. funding com. Mayor's Zoo Commn., Seattle, 1984-85; dir. Discovery Inst., 1992—, Internat. Snow Leopard Trust, 1994-96; mem. sch. bd. Cath. Archdiocese of Seattle, 1995-98; mem. Seattle U. Exec. Masters in Not-for-Profit Mgmt. vis. com., 1995-96; mem. King County Bond Oversight Com., 1986-93. Mem. N.W. Devel. Officers Assn. (pres. 1994), Downtown Rotary Club (v.p. found. 1997-98), Wash. Athletic Club. Republican. Roman Catholic. Avocations: tennis, photography. Office: Alistar Capital Group 600 108th Ave NE Ste 1014 Bellevue WA 98004-5129 E-mail: rwdavidson@hotmail.com

DAVIDSON, ROGER H(ARRY), political scientist, educator; b. Washington, July 31, 1936; s. Ross Wallace and Mildred (Younger) D.; m. Nancy Elizabeth Dixon, Sept. 29, 1961; children: Douglas Ross, Christopher Reed. AB magna cum laude, U. Colo., 1958; PhD, Columbia U., 1963. Asst. prof. govt. Dartmouth Coll., Hanover, N.H., 1962-68; assoc. prof. polit. sci. U. Calif., Santa Barbara, 1968-71, prof., 1971-83, assoc. dean letters and sci., 1978-80, vis. prof., 1999—; sr. specialist Congl. Rsch. Svc., [illegible], prof. govt., politics U. Md., College Pk., 1981-99. Profl. staff mem. U.S. Ho. of Reps., Washington, 1973-74; rsch. dir. U.S. Senate, Washington, 1976-77; cons. White House, 1970-71, U.S. Com. on Violence, Washington, 1968-69; vis. prof. U. Calif., Santa Barbara, 1994, 99—; Leon Sachs vis. scholar Johns Hopkins U., 1997. Author: The Role of the Congressman, 1969; co-author: A More Perfect Union, 4th edit., 1989, Congress and Its Members, 8th edit., 2001; editor: The Postreform Congress, 1992, Remaking Congress, 1995, Understanding the Presidency,

3rd edit., 2002; co-editor: Ency. of the U.S. Congress, 1995, Remaking Congress, 1995, Masters of the House, 1998; contbr. articles to profl. jours. Co-chmn. Upper Valley Human Rights Coun., Hanover, N.H., 1966-68; chmn. Goleta Valley Citizens Planning Group, Santa Barbara, 1974-76; bd. dirs. Dirksen Congl. Ctr., Governance Inst.; rsch. com. of legis. specialists Internat. Polit. Sci. Assn.; mem. adv. commn. on records of Congress Nat. Archives and Records Adminstrn., 1995-99. Woodrow Wilson Nat. Found. fellow, 1958, Gilder fellow Columbia U., 1960, Faculty fellow Dartmouth Coll., 1965-66. Fellow Nat. Acad. Pub. Adminstrn.; mem. Nat. Capital Area Polit. Sci. Assn. (pres. 1985-86), Legis. Studies Group (charter, nat. chmn. 1980-81), Am. Polit. Sci. Assn. (joint com. mem. Project 87-Am. Hist. Assn./Am. Polit. Sci. Assn., chmn. congl. fellowship com. 1990, 93, endowed programs com. 1994-95, chmn. 1995-96, co-chmn. exec. com. Centennial Campaign 1997—), Western Polit. Sci. Assn. (bd. editors 1977-78). Baptist. Avocations: music, history. Home: 400 E Pedregosa St Apt L Santa Barbara CA 93103-1970 Office: Dept Polit Sci U Calif Santa Barbara CA 93106

DAVIDSON, SUZANNE MOURON, lawyer; b. Oxford, Miss., Aug. 5, 1963; d. Bertrand D. Jr. and Barbara Jean (Baca) Mouron; m. Garrison H. Davidson III, Dec. 12, 1987; children: Jane Harrington, Catherine Stender. AB in English Lit., U. Calif., 1985, JD, 1988. Assoc. Peterson, Ross, L.A., 1988-89; asst. litigation counsel Ticor Title Ins., Rosemead, Calif., 1989-91; corp. counsel Forest Lawn, Glendale, 1991—. Deacon San Marino Cmty. Ch., 1995-98; bd. dirs. San Marino Cmty. Ch. Nursery Sch., 1995—; mem. Jr. League, Pasadena, Calif., 1989—. Mem. Calif. State Bar Assn., L.A. County Bar Assn. (com. professionalism), Pasadena Athletic Club, Salt Air Club, Chi Omega (chmn. nat. area rush info. 1988-95). Presbyn. Office: Forest Lawn Co Legal Dept 1712 S Glendale Ave Glendale CA 91205-3320

DAVIE, EARL WARREN, biochemistry educator; b. Tacoma, Oct. 25, 1927; s. Charles William and Teckla E. Davie; m. Anita Thalia Roe, July 15, 1952; children: James, John, Karen, Marilyn. BS in Chemistry, U. Wash., 1950, PhD in Biochemistry, 1954; MD (hon.), Lund (Sweden) U., 1995. Asst. prof. biochemistry Western Res. U., Cleve., 1956-62, assoc. prof. Biochemistry, 1962, U. Wash., Seattle, 1962-66, chmn. biochemistry dept., 1975-84, prof. biochemistry, 1966—. Mem. Nat. Heart, Lung, Blood Adv. Coun., NIH, Bethesda, Md., 1985-90. Mem. editorial bd. Jour. Biol. Chemistry, 1968-73, 75-80; assoc. editor Biochemistry, 1980—, Fibrinolysis, 1986-93; contbr. over 180 articles on basic rsch. in hematology to profl. jours. Sec. Am. Soc. Biol. Chemistry, Bethesda, 1975-78; mem. exec. com. coun. on thrombosis Am. Heart Assn., Dallas, 1972-74; bd. trustees Wash. State Heart Assn., 19743-76. Recipient Internat. prize French Assn. for Hemophilia, Paris, 1983, Waterford Bio-Med. Rsch. prize Scripps Clinic & Rsch. Found., 1985, Robert P. Grant medal Internat. Soc. on Thrombosis & Hemostasis, Tokyo, 1989, Stratton medal Am. Soc. Hematology, 1993, Disting. Achievement award Am. Heart Assn., 1995, Bristol-Myers Squibb award for cardiovasc./metabolic rsch., 1999; fellow Nat. Found. for Infantile Paralysis, Mass. Gen. Hosp., 1954, Commonwealth Fund, U. Geneva, 1966. Mem. NAS, Am. Acad. Arts and Scis., Royal Danish Acad. Scis. and Letters (fgn.), Japanese Biochem. Soc. (fgn.). Achievements include establishment of mechanisms for blood coagulation, isolation and characterization of various proteins involved; determination of the structure of their genes. Office: U Wash Dept Biochemistry Sj 70 Seattle WA 98195-0001

DAVIES, CAROL B. computer programmer, researcher; married, 1968; 2 children. Contractor NASA Ames Rsch. Ctr., Moffett Field, Calif., 1968, with Pioneer Space Project, contractor with Sterling Software, 1980, rsch. specialist; tchr. statistics, cons. to computer sci. dept. U. Singapore, 1976-80. Vol. Stanford Health Libr.; tutor for local mid. sch. Office: NASA Ames Rsch Ctr Moffett Field CA 94035

DAVIES, DAVID GEORGE, lawyer, educator; b. Waukesha, Wis., July 19, 1928; s. David Evan and Ella Hilda (Degler) D.; m. Elaine Kowalchik, May 12, 1962; children: Thea Kay, Bryn Ann, Degler Evan. B.S., U. Wis., 1950, J.D., 1953. Bar: Wis. 1953, Ariz. 1959. Trust rep. First Nat. Bank of Ariz., Phoenix, 1957-58, asst. trust officer, 1958-62, trust officer, head bus. devel. in trust dept., 1962-66, v.p., trust officer, 1966; practice in Phoenix, 1967—; assoc. Wales & Collins, 1967-68; ptnr. Wales, Collins & Davies, 1968-75, Collins, Davies & Cronkhite, Ltd., 1975-85, David G. Davies, Ltd., 1986—. Instr. bus. law local chpt. C.L.U.s, 1965; instr. estate and gift taxation, 1973— ; instr. estate planning Phoenix Coll., 1968— ; past instr. Maricopa County Jr. Coll. Pres. Central Ariz. Estate Planning Council; pres., bd. dirs. Vis. Nurse Service, United Fund Agy.; chmn. bd. Beatitudes Campus of Care; bd. dirs. Phoenix chpt. Nat. Hemophilia Found.; bd. dirs., treas. trusteeship St. Luke's Hosp. Med. Ctr., Phoenix, 1982—; mem. adv. bd. planned giving com. Salvation Army, 1997—. Served to capt. JAGC, AUS, 1953-57. Mem. Central Assn. Life Underwriters (assoc.), ABA, Wis. Bar Assn., State Bar Ariz., Am. Assn. Homes for Aged (legal affairs com., future com.) Congregationalist (chmn. bd. trustees, moderator). Office: 5110 N 40th St Ste 236 Phoenix AZ 85018-2151

DAVIES, HUGH MARLAIS, museum director; b. Grahamstown, South Africa, Feb. 12, 1948; came to U.S., 1956; s. Horton Marlais and Brenda M. (Deakin) D.; children: Alexandra, Dorian; m. Lynda Forsha; 1 stepdaughter, Mackenzie Forsha Fuller. AB summa cum laude, Princeton U., 1970, MFA, 1972, PhD, 1976. Dir. Univ. Gallery, U. Mass., Amherst, 1975-83; dir. Mus. of Contemporary Art (formerly La Jolla Mus. Contemporary Art), San Diego, 1983—. Vis. prof. fine arts Amherst Coll., 1980-83; mem. adv. coun. dept. art and archeology Princeton U., 1989—, panel mem. fed. adv. com. internat. exhbns., 1990-94; co-curator Whitney Mus. Am. Art Biennial, 2000. Author: Francis Bacon: The Early and Middle Years: 1928-58; co-author: Sacred Art in a Secular Century: 20th Century Religious Art, 1978, Francis Bacon (Abbeville), 1986. Nat. Endowment Arts fellow, 1982, 95. Mem. Am. Assn. Mus., Coll. Art Assn., Assn. Art Mus. Dirs. (trustee 1994-2001, pres. 1997-98), Am. Fedn. Arts. Office: Mus Contemporary Art San Diego 700 Prospect St La Jolla CA 92037-4228

DAVIES, ROGER, geoscience educator; b. London, Aug. 29, 1948; came to U.S., 1972, naturalized, 1985; s. Trevor Rhys and Gracie Rhys (Beaton) D.; m. Corinne Marie Scofield, Oct. 29, 1977 (div. 1999); children: Colin, Gavin. BS with honors, Victoria U., Wellington, N.Z., 1970; PhD, U. Wis., 1976. Meteorologist New Zealand Meteorol. Svc., Wellington, 1971-77; scientist U. Wis., Madison, 1977-80; from asst. prof. to assoc. prof. atmospheric sci. Purdue U., West Lafayette, Ind., 1980-87; assoc. prof. McGill U., Montreal, Que., Can., 1987-95; from assoc. prof. to prof. U. Ariz., Tucson, 1995—. Mem. Earth Radiation Budget Expt. Sci. Team, 1980-92, First Internat. Satellite Cloud Climatology Project, Regional Exptl. Sci. Team, 1984-87, Internat. Radiation Commn., 1993-99. Assoc. editor: Jour. Geophys. Rsch., 1987-92; contbr. articles and book revs. to profl. publs. Rsch. grantee NASA. Mem. Am. Geophys. Union, Hungarian Meteorol. Soc. (hon. fgn. mem.). Avocations: sailing, tennis. Office: U Ariz Inst Atmospheric Physics Pas Bldg 81 Tucson AZ 85721-0001 E-mail: davies@atmo.arizona.edu

DAVIES, WILLIAM RALPH, service executive; b. Santa Barbara, Calif., Aug. 17, 1955; s. Ralph Emmett and Georgann Marie (Cordingly) D.; m. Karen L. Blake, May 12, 1984 (div. 1999). AA in Real Estate, Am. River Coll., 1978; BS in Fin., Ins. and Real Estate, Calif. State U., Sacramento, 1980; postgrad. in Internat. Bus., Golden Gate U., 1982-84. Real estate assoc. Kiernan Realtors, Sacramento, 1975-77; co-owner real estate firm Sacramento, 1977; pvt. practice real estate cons., property mgr. Sacramento, 1978-80; broker assoc. MBA Bus. Brokers, Sacramento, 1980-85, pres., 1985—, WRD Cons. Group, El Dorado Hills, 1984—. Bd. dirs. WRD, Inc., El Dorado Hills, Vista Sr. Living, Inc., El Dorado Hills; v.p., bd. dirs. Vista Sr. Living, Inc., 1999. Mem. Assisted Living Fedn., Calif. Assisted Living Facilities Assn. (bd. dirs.). Republican. Avocations: history, bridge, golf. Office: 895 Embarcadero Dr Ste 203 El Dorado Hills CA 95762 E-mail: wmdavies@worldnet.att.net

DAVIS, ALLEN, professional football team executive; b. Brockton, Mass., July 4, 1929; s. Louis and Rose (Kirschenbaum) D.; m. Carol Segall, July 11, 1954; 1 son, Mark. Student, Wittenberg Coll., 1947; A.B., Syracuse U., 1950. Asst. football coach Adelphi Coll., 1950-51; head football coach Ft. Belvoir, Va., 1952-53; player-personnel scout Baltimore Colts, 1954; line coach The Citadel, 1955-56, U. So. Calif., 1957-59; asst. coach San Diego Chargers, 1960-62; gen. mgr., head coach Oakland Raiders (now Los Angeles Raiders), 1963-66, owner, mng. gen. ptnr., 1966—, now pres., gen. ptnr. Former mem. mgmt. council and competition com. Nat. Football League. Served with AUS, 1952-53. Named Profl. Coach of Year A.P., Profl. Coach of Year U.P.I., Profl. Coach of Year Sporting News, Profl. Coach of Year Pro-Football Illustrated, 1963; Young Man of Yr. Oakland, 1963; only individual in history to be an asst. coach, head coach, gen. mgr., league commr. and owner. Mem. Am. Football Coaches Assn. Office: Oakland Raiders 1220 Harbor Bay Pkwy Alameda CA 94502-6570

DAVIS, ANTHONY, composer, pianist, educator; b. Paterson, N.J., Feb. 20, 1951; m. Cynthia Aaronson-Davis; 1 child: Jonah. BA in Music, Yale U., 1975; student, Wesleyan U. Lectr., music and Afro-Am. studies Yale U., New Haven, 1981-82; resident fellow Berkeley Coll. of Mus., Yale U., 1981-82; sr. fellow, Soc. of the Humanities Cornell U., Ithaca, N.Y., 1987; prof. Yale U Sch. Music, 1990-98; prof. music U. Calif., San Diego, 1998—. Vis. composer Yale Sch. Music, 1990, 93, 96; vis. lectr. Afro-Am. studies Harvard U., 1992-96; composer-in-residence Detroit Symphony Orch., Miss. Symphony Orch., 1995. Composer: film scores for A Man around the House, Steve Hannock, 1981, Miraj, 1983; compositions include Middle Passage, Hemispheres, (operas) X: The Life and Times of Malcolm X, 1986, Wayang No. 5, 1984, Wayang No. 6, 1985, song was sweeter even so, 1987, violin concerto 1988, Notes from the Underground, 1988, Under the Double Moon, 1989, Tania, 1992, X: The Life and Times of Malcolm X, 1986, Under the Double Moon, 1989, Tania, 1992, Amistad, 1997 (incidental music) Angels in Ameria: Millennium Approaches-Part One, 1993, Part Two-Perestroika, 1993, Esu Variations, 1995, Jacob's Ladder, 1997, Amistad, 1997, Acict Ctace'l of a Signifying Donkey, 1998; violin sonata, 1991; performer: Wayang No. 5, 1984, 87, Still Waters, 1984; solo performer Carnegie Hall, 1983, Berklee Theater, 1984, Joyce Theater (N.Y.C.), 1984, Exploratorium (San Francisco), 1984, Nippon Theater (Seattle), 1984, Portland Ctr. for Visual Arts, 1984, Erie Art Museum, 1987; recs. include Of Blues and Dreams, 1978, Lady of the Mirrors, 1979, Variations in Dreamtime, 1981, Episteme, 1981, I've Known Rivers, 1982, Hemispheres, 1983, Middle Passage, 1984, Undine, 1987; mem. ensemble, Episteme. Recipient Bessie award, 1984, Esquire Registry award. 1984, award AAAL, 1996, Nat. Endowment of the Arts, N.Y. Found. of Arts, Mass. Arts Coun., Chamber Music Am., Lila Wallace Fund/Meet the Composer Fund for Jazz and Opera Am.; Grammy nominee 1992. Bd. dirs. Parabola Arts Found. Inc.; mem. NYSCA (panelist 1983-85), ASCAP. Office: UCSD Dept of Music Mandeville Center La Jolla CA 92093

DAVIS, ARTHUR DAVID, psychology educator, musician; m. Gladys Lesley Joyce, Dec. 29, 1965; children: Kimaili, Mureithi, Taisha. Student, Manhattan Sch. Music, 1953-56, Juilliard Sch. Music, 1953-56; BA suma cum laude, CUNY, 1973; MA, City Coll., N.Y.C., 1976, NYU, , 1976, PhD with distinction, 1982. Lic. sch. psychologist. Musician various worldwide tours, 1962—, NBC-TV Staff Orch., N.Y.C., 1962-63, Westinghouse TV Staff Orch., N.Y.C., 1964-68, CBS-TV Staff Orch., N.Y.C., 1969-71; prof. Manhattan Community Coll., N.Y.C., 1971-86, U. Bridgeport, Conn., 1978 82; psychologist Lincoln Med. and Mental Health Ctr., Bronx, 1982-85; sch. psychologist, cons. Lakeside Union Free Sch. Dist., Spring Valley, N.Y., 1985-86; psychologist, tchr. N.Y. Med. Coll., Valhalla, 1982-87; prof. Orange Coast Coll., Costa Mesa, Calif., 1987—, Calif. State U., Fullerton, 1988-90, U. Calif.-Irvine, 1993-94; psychologist Cross Cultural Ctr., San Diego, 1986-91; mem. faculty U. Calif., Irvine, 1999—. Cons. Head Start, Bklyn., 1981-82, Orange County Minority AIDS, Santa Ana, Calif., 1987-88, Orange County Fair Housing, Costa Mesa, 1988, Sickle Cell Anemia Assn., Santa Ana, Calif., 1987-88, Human Rels. Orange County City, Costa Mesa, 1988-89, William Grant Still Mus., L.A., 1988—; musician various symphonies Radio City Music Hall Orch. Nat. Symphony, Symphony of the Air N.Y. Philharmonic, Met. Opera Orch., L.A. Philharmonic, 1995; John Coltrane, others, 1960—. Author: The Arthur Davis System for Double Bass, 1976, A Brief History of Jazz, 1995; record composer Interplay, 1980, Art Davis Reemeryance, ARKIMU, 1985, Dr. Art Davis, Live, Soulnote, 1987, Art Davis, Live, A Time Remembered, 1995. Composer, condr., mem. coun. Diaglogue, Costa Mesa, 1988; mgr. Little League of Cortlandt, N.Y., 1979-82; pack master Cub Scouts Am., Cortlandt and Croton, N.Y., 1979-80, dist. chmn., 1980-81; bd. dirs. Local 47 Musicians' Union, Hollywood, Calif., 1993—, Orange County Urban League, Inc., 1992-95; chmn. Better Advantages for Students and Soc., Corona del Mar, Calif., 1993; adv. bd. dirs. John W. Cultrane Cultural Soc., Inc. NIMH grantee, 1976-77; named World's Foremost Double Bassist IBA, 1969—; recipient Lion award Black MBA Assn., 1985, Chancellor's Disting. Lectr.'s award U. Calif., Irvine, 1991-92, Exemplary Standards in Music Edn. award Orange County Urban League, 1993; Ann. Dr. Art Davis Scholarships established in his honor Dr. Art Davis Fan Club. Mem. APA, ASCAP, Am. Soc. Music Arrangers & Composers, Chamber Music Am., N.Y. Acad. Scis., Astron. Soc. of the Pacific (charter), Orange County Psychol. Assn., Assn. of Black Psychologists, Planetary Soc. (charter), Am. Hort. Soc., Nat Trust for Hist. Preservation Soc., Rec. Musicians Assn., Stanford U. Alumni Assn., NYU Alumni Assn., CCNY Alumni Assn., Sierra Club. Avocations: astronomy, gourmet cooking, gardening, photography, DXing. Office: ARKIMU 3535 E Coast Hwy # 50 Corona Del Mar CA 92625-2404

DAVIS, BART MCKAY, state legislator, lawyer; b. Rapid City, S.D., Mar. 7, 1955; s. Harold William and Enid (Lee) D.; m. Marion Woffinden, Aug. 18, 1976; children: Christopher, Weston, Cameron, Jill, Rebecca, Annie. BA, Brigham Young U., 1978; JD, U. Idaho, 1980. Bar: Idaho 1981, U.S. Dist. Ct. Idaho 1981, U.S. Ct. Appeals (9th cir.) 1987, U.S. Supreme Ct. 1989, Ariz. 1994. Assoc. Law Office of Marc J. Weinpel, Idaho Falls, Idaho, 1981-84; ptnr. Weinpel, Woolf, Just, Combo & Davis, Idaho Falls, 1984-90; CFO Electrical Wholesale Supple Co., Inc., Idaho Falls, 1990-93; pvt. practice Idaho Falls, 1990—; senator Idaho State Legislature, Boise, 1998-2000, vice chmn. commerce and human resources com., 1998-2000, vice chmn. change in employment compensation com., 1998-2000, mem. edn. com., mem. judiciary and rules com., 1998-2000, mem. ad hoc joint adv. com. on tech., 1999-2000. Mgr. ops., bd. dirs. Electrical Wholesale Supply Co., Inc., Idaho Falls, 1990-93; bd. dirs., chmn. Idaho Bankruptcy and Comml. Law, Boise, 1982-88; mem. rules com. U.S. Bankruptcy Ct., 1990—, recorder rules rewrite, 1997-2000, recorder, 1998—; mem. long range planning com. U.S. Dist. Ct. Idaho, 1993-94; lawyer rep. State Idaho to Ninth Cir., 1993-95; exec. com. mem. 9th Cir. Jud. Conf., 1995-98; mem. Ea. Idaho divsn. facilities com. U.S. Ct., 1997-99; chmn. small bus. chpt. 11 rules subcom. Bankruptcy Ct. Rules Com., 1997-98; legis. mem. exec. com. Coun. on State Govts. West, 1999-2000, mem. innovations selection com., 1999; mem. Idaho Govs. Exec. Com. on Safety in Schs., 1999; co-chair legis. tech. com. Idaho State Legislature, 2000; spkr. in field. Contbr. articles to profl. publs. Mem. Bonneville County Rep. County Ctrl. Com., 1982-84; chmn. Bonneville County Young Rep., 1982-84; chair Young Reps. Idaho, 1983-84; fundraising com. State Idaho Rep. Party, 1994; co-chair Idaho Legislators for George W. Bush for Pres., 2000 Idaho del.-at-large Rep. Nat. Conv., Phila., 2000; organ fund com. mem. Idaho Falls Civic Auditorium, 1989-90; mem. Idaho Falls Edn. Adv. Coun., 1998-2000; bd. mem. Ea. Idaho Spl. Svcs. Agy., 2000; active Boy Scouts Am. Toll fellow Coun. State Govts., 1999. Mem. Idaho State Bar (founding bd. mem. comml. and bankruptcy law sect. 1983-88, chmn. comml. and bankruptcy law sect. 1986-87, com. on jud. independence and jud. integrity 2000, Professionalism award comml. law and bankruptcy sect. 1999), Rotary (Paul Harris fellow). Avocations: skiing, golf, music, computers. Office: PO Box 50660 Idaho Falls ID 83405-0660

DAVIS, BETTYE, state senator; b. La., May 17, 1938; m. Troy Davis; children: Tony, Sonia. Cert. of Nursing, St. Anthony Sch. Nursing, 1961; BSW, Grambling U., 1971; postgrad., U. Alaska, 1976-77. Dem. rep. Alaska Ho. of Reps., 1990-96; Dem. Senator dist. K Alaska State Senate. Chair State Bd. Edn., 1998—; chair Children's Caucus, Alaska Black Caucus; pres. Nat. Caucus of Black Sch. Bd. Mems. Mem. LWV, Ch. Woman United, Alaska Black Leadership Conf., Anchorage Zonta Club; mem. Anchorage Sch. Bd., 1981—, pres., 1986-87, 81-90. Mem. NAACP, Alaska Fedn. Bus. and Profl. Women (pres. 1999—), Young Women's Christian Assn., Alaska Women's Polit. Caucus, Delta Sigma Theta. Avocations: grandchildren, cooking, charitable fundraising. Office: Alaska State Senate State Capitol Rm 504 Juneau AK 99801-1182 Fax: 907 465-3756. E-mail: Senator-Bettye_Davis@legis.state.ak.us

DAVIS, BRUCE, cultural organization administrator; Exec. dir. Acad. Motion Picture Arts Sci., Beverly Hills, Calif. Office: Acad Motion Picture Arts Assn 8949 Wilshire Blvd Beverly Hills CA 90211-1972

DAVIS, CATHY, publishing executive; Sr. v.p. mktg. and devel., Ariz. Republic, Phoenix; pres. and CEO Tucson Newspapers, Tucson, 2000—. Office: Tucson Newspapers 6781 N Thornydale Rd Tucson AZ 85741-2771

DAVIS, CRAIG ALPHIN, lawyer, manufacturing company executive; b. Oakland, Calif., July 28, 1940; s. Alphin Craig and Joyce Ida (Nevers) D.; m. Betty Rankin, July 13, 1963; children: Chelsea Alyson, Channing MacLaren. A.B. in Polit. Sci, U. Calif., Berkeley, 1964, J.D., 1967. Bar: Calif. 1968. Assoc. Heller, Ehrman, White & McAuliffe, San Francisco, 1968-71; counsel Aluminum div. AMAX Inc., San Mateo, Calif., 1971-74; dir. law Alumax Inc., San Mateo, 1974, gen. counsel, sec., 1974-84, v.p., 1978-82, group v.p., gen. counsel, 1982-84, sr. v.p., 1984-86, exec. v.p., 1986-89; internat. bus. transaction advisor, of counsel Hughes, Hubbard & Reed, N.Y.C., 1990—; chmn. Ravenswood Aluminum Corp., N.Y.C., 1992—; chmn. & CEO Century Aluminum Co., Monteray, Calif. Mem. editorial bd., research editor: Hastings Law Jour, 1966-67. Mem. ABA, State Bar Calif. Office: Century Aluminum Co 2511 Garden Rd Monterey CA 93940

DAVIS, DONALD ALAN, news correspondent, writer, lecturer; b. Savannah, Ga., Oct. 5, 1939; s. Oden Harry and Irma Artice (Gay) D.; m. Robin Murphy, Mar. 17, 1983; children by previous marriage— Russell Glenn, Randall Scott. B.A. in Journalism, U. Ga., 1962. Reporter Athens (Ga.) Banner-Herald, 1961-62, Savannah Morning News, 1962; with UPI, 1963-65; reporter, editor St. Petersburg (Fla.) Times, 1965-66; with UPI, 1967-83, Vietnam corr., 1971-73, New Eng. editor, 1977-80, White House corr., 1981-83; polit. reporter, columnist San Diego Union, 1983-91; pub. Pacific Rim Report newsletter, 1985-88. Instr. journalism Boston U., 1979; instr. writing U. Colo., 1998-99; lectr. U.S. Naval War Coll., 1983, Queen Elizabeth 2, 1991; bd. dirs. Fgn. Corr. Club, Hong Kong, 1974 Author: The Milwaukee Murders, 1991, The Nanny Murder Trial, 1992, Bad Blood, 1994, Death of An Angel, 1994, Fallen Hero, 1994, Appointment with the Squire, 1995, Death Cruise, 1996, A Father's Rage, 1996, The Gris-Gris Man, 1997, Hush, Little Babies, 1997, The Last Man on the Moon, 1999, JonBenét, 2000. Fellow Keizai Koho Ctr., Tokyo, 1985. Overseas Press Club, 2000. Mem. Overseas Press Club. Presbyterian. Office: 6350 Modena Ln Longmont CO 80503-8770 E-mail: tedsalad@msn.com

DAVIS, EARL JAMES, chemical engineering educator; b. St. Paul, July 22, 1934; s. Leo Ernest and Mary (Steiner) D.; children: Molly Kathleen, David Leo. BS cum laude, Gonzaga U., 1956; PhD, U. Wash., 1960. Design engr. Union Carbide Chems. Co., South Charleston, W.Va., 1956; from asst. prof. chem. engring. to assoc. prof. Gonzaga U., Spokane, Wash., 1960-68, dir. computing ctr., 1967-68; rsch. fellow Imperial Coll., London U., 1964-65; assoc. prof. chem. engring. Clarkson U., 1968-73, head socio-environ. program, 1972-74, prof., 1973-78, chmn. chem. engring. dept., 1973-74, assoc. dir. Inst. Colloid and Surface Sci., 1974-78; prof., chmn. chem. and nuclear engring. dept. U. N.Mex., 1978-80; dir. engring. divsn., prof. Inst. Paper Chemistry, Appleton, Wis., 1980-83; rsch. fellow in chem. engring. U. Wash., Seattle, 1957-60, prof. chem. engring., 1983—, assoc. vice provost for rsch., 2001—. Guest prof. Tech. U. of Vienna, Austria, 2000; sr. scientist, cons. Unilever Rsch. Lab., Port Sunlight, Eng., 1974-75; vis. scholar NAS/Chinese Acad. Scis., China, 1989; adj. prof. Sichuan U., Chengdu, China, 2001—. Assoc. editor Aerosol Sci. and Tech., 1993-97; mem. editl. bd. Jour. Colloid and Interface Sci., 1984-86; mem. editl. bd. Jour. Aerosol Sci., 1992-98, editor-in-chief, 1999—; mem. adv. bd. Surface and Colloid Sci., 2000—; regional editor (N.Am. and S.Am.) Colloid and Polymer Sci., 1994-99; contbr. articles to sci. publs. NSF fellow, 1964-65, grantee, 1963-89, 92—; recipient Burlington No. award for rsch., 1988; Leeds and Northrup fellow U. Wash., 1960. Fellow AAAS, mem. AIChE (adminstr. Design Inst. Multiphase Processing 1979-87), Am. Chem. Soc., Am. Assn. Aerosol Rsch. (treas. 1990-92, David Sinclair award 1991, v.p. 1996-97, pres. 1997-98), Soc. Applied Spectroscopy, Gesellschaft für Aerosolforschung, Sigma Xi, Phi Lambda Upsilon. Achievements include research on air pollution control, aerosol physical chemistry ane colloid science. Office: U Wash Dept Chem Enging PO Box 351750 Seattle WA 98195-1750 E-mail: davis@cheme.washington.edu

DAVIS, EDMOND RAY, lawyer; b. Glendale, Calif., Sept. 4, 1928; s. Archie Allen and Eve Mae (Hoover) D.; m. Ruby Evelyn Davis, Oct. 17, 1954; children: Phillip A., Sandra A. Ed., Pepperdine Coll.; JD, U. Calif., San Francisco, 1952. Bar: Calif. 1952, U.S. Dist. Ct. (cen. dist.) Calif. 1952. Assoc. Bailie, Turner & Sprague, 1955-60; trust counsel Security Pacific Nat. Bank, 1960-67; ptnr. Overton, Lyman & Prince, L.A., 1967-87, Brobeck, Phleger & Harrison, L.A., 1987-99, Davis & Whalen, Pasadena, Calif., 1999—. Chmn. legal adv. com. San Marino Unified Sch. Dist., 1981—; mem. legal com. Music Ctr. Found., Performing Arts Council, Los Angeles County, 1980—; trustee WM Group of Funds. Chmn., pub. adminstr. Pub. Guardian Adv. Commns., Los County Bd. Suprs., 1974-76; bd. dirs. Braille Inst. Am., Inc., 1974—, Children's Bur. So. Calif., Children's Bur. Found.; pres. Calif. Jaycees, 1962. With U.S. Army, 1952-54. Recipient Alumni award Pepperdine Coll., 1962. Fellow Am. Coll. Trust and Estate Counsel (chmn. Calif. chpt. 1981-86); mem. Internat. Acad. Estate and Trust Law (academician), State Bar of Calif. (chmn. estate planning, trust and probate law sect. 1977-78), L.A. County Bar Assn. (exec. com., probate and trust law sect. 1986-89, Arthur K. Marshall award Probate and Trust Law sect. 1991), Order of Coif, Calif. Club, Chancery Club, Breakfast Club. Office: Davis & Whalen LLP 553 S Marengo Ave Pasadena CA 91101-3114 E-mail: edavis@daviswhalen.com

DAVIS, GENE, public relations professional, state legislator; b. Salt Lake City, July 2, 1945; s. John Albert and Glenna Rachel (Cameron) D.; m. Penny Lou Hansen, Mar. 9, 1971; children: James, Pamela. Cert. electronic engring., Radio Operational Engring., Burbank, Calif., 1963; LLB, LaSalle Ext. U., Chgo., 1974. Announcer KNAK Radio, Salt Lake City, 1965-75; prodn. continuity dir. KALL Radio AM/FM, Salt Lake City, 1976-86;

owner G. Davis Advt., Pub. Rels., Salt Lake City, 1986-91; pub. rels. profl. Valley Mental Health, Salt Lake City, 1990—; mem. Utah Senate, Dist. 3, Salt Lake City, 1998—. Treas. Comm. Fed. Credit Union, Salt Lake City, 1981-86. Vice chair East County Recreation Bd., Salt Lake City, 1991—2000; rep. Utah State House of Reps., Salt Lake City, 1986—98; mem. Utah State Senate, Salt Lake City, 1998—, mem. bus., labor & human svcs. com., exec. appropriations com., coun. of state govt.-health capacity task force. Mem. Sugar House Rotary Club, Sugar House Cmty. Coun. (chmn. 1984-85). Democrat. Mem. LDS Ch. Avocations: golf, gardening, politics. Home: 865 Parkway Ave Salt Lake City UT 84106-1704 Office: Valley Mental Health 5965 S 900 E Salt Lake City UT 84121-1794 E-mail: gened@vmh.com

DAVIS, GEORGE DONALD, executive land use policy consultant; b. Oneida, N.Y., Nov. 19, 1942; s. Pearl Floyd and Kathrine Virginia (Connolly) D.; m. Anita Face Riner, June 26, 1976; children: Maria Lisa, Brett Hollis, Sarah Bessie, Lara Emily; stepchildren: Andrea G. Riner, Joel S. Riner. BS in Forestry, SUNY, 1964; postgrad., Cornell U., 1968, 70. Forester, pub. land adminstr. U.S. Forest Svc. Dept. Agr., Colo., 1964-68; ecologist Gov. N.Y. State Temp. Study Commn. on Future of Adirondacks, 1969-71; pvt. land use and natural resources cons. Ithaca, N.Y., 1971; dir. planning Adirondack Park Agy., Ray Brook, 1971-76; exec. dir. Wilderness Soc., Washington, 1976-77; spl. asst. U.S. Forest Svc., Washington, 1977-79; dep. forest supr. Idaho Panhandle Nat. Forests, Coeur d'Alene, 1979-82; land use, natural resource cons. Wadhams, N.Y., 1982-94; program dir. Adirondack Coun., 1983-88; exec. dir. Adirondack Land Trust, 1984-88; prin. Davis Assocs., 1988—. Pres. Ecol. Sustainable Devel., Inc., 1994-97; coord. Global Assocs. in Sustainable Develop., 1997—; project dir. Land Use Policy and Allocation Program for Lake Baikal Watershed in Russia, 1991-93, Lake Hovsgol/Selenge River Watershed in Mongolia, 1992-94, Ussuri River Watershed in Russian Far East and China, 1993-97, Altai Rep. Russia, 1994-97, exec. dir. Gov. Commn. on Adirondacks in the 21st Century, 1989-90; mem. environ. task force Rockefeller Bros. Fund; mem. Hudson Basin project task force Rockefeller Found. Co-author: The Unfinished Agenda, 1977, Developing a Land Conservation Strategy, 1987; author: Ecosystem Representative as a Criterion for World Wilderness Designation, 1987, 2020 Vision: Fulfilling the Promise of the Adirondack Park, 1988, Completing the Adirondack Wilderness System, 1990, The Lake Baikal Region in the Twenty-First Century: A Model of Sustainable Development or Continued Degradation?, 1993, A Comprehensive National Program of Sustainable Land Use Policies for the Lake Hovsgol-Selenge River Watershed, 1994, A Sustainable Land Use and Allocation Program for the Ussuri/Wusuli River Watershed and Adjacent Territories, 1996; contbr. to profl. pubs. Active Gov. N.Y. State Forest Industry Task Force, 1987-89, N.Y.-New Eng. Gov. Task Force on No. Forest Lands, 1988-90. MacArthur fellow, 1989-94. Roman Catholic. Home and Office: 2482 N 32d St Springfield OR 97477-7900 E-mail: davisassoc1@aol.com

DAVIS, GRAY (JOSEPH GRAHAM DAVIS), governor; b. N.Y.C., Dec. 26, 1942; m. Sharon Ryer, Feb. 20, 1983. BA cum laude, Stanford U., 1964; JD, Columbia U., 1967. Chief of staff to Gov. Jerry Brown State of Calif., Sacramento, 1974-81, mem. Calif. State Assembly, 1982-86, state contr., 1986-94, lt. gov., 1995-99, gov., 1999—. Chmn. Housing and Community Devel. Com., Calif. Coun. on Criminal Justice, Franchise Tax Bd., State Lands Commn.; mem. Bd. Equalization, State Tchrs. Retirement System, Pub. Employees Retirement System, Nat. Coun. Institutional Investors; U. Calif. Regent, Calif. State U. trustee; mem. intergovtl. policy adv. com. on trade Office of U.S. Trade Rep. Founder Calif. Found. for the Protection of Children. Office: Office of Governor State Capitol Sacramento CA 95814-4906*

DAVIS, HARLEY CLEO, retired career officer; b. Van Buren, Ark., May 7, 1941; s. Aleta (Johnson) D.; m. Patricia Ann White, Mar. 9, 1985. BS, Ark. Tech. U., 1963; MA, Ea. Ky. U., 1972; exec. devel. program, U. N.H., 1987. Commd. 2d lt. U.S. Army, 1963, advanced through grades to maj. gen., 1993; platoon leader 1st Bn., 50th inf., 2d Armored Div., 1963; various assignments, 1963-80; comdr. 3d Bn., 5th Spl. Forces Group, Ft. Bragg, N.C., 1980-82; chief leadership br. Hdqrs. Dept. of the Army, Washington, 1982-84; chief of staff JFK Spl. Warfare Ctr. and Sch., Ft. Bragg, 1985-86; comdr. 5th Spl. Forces Group, Ft. Campbell, Ky., 1987-89; asst. comdt. JFK Spl. Warfare Ctr. and Sch., Ft. Bragg, 1989-91; dep. commdg. gen. U.S. Army Sp. Ops. Command, Ft. Bragg, 1991-92; comdg. gen. U.S. Army Spl. Forces Command (Airborne), Ft. Bragg, 1992-95; dep. commdg. gen. Fifth U.S. Army (west), Ft. Lewis, Wash., 1995-97. Decorated DSM with oak leaf cluster, Legion of Merit, Soldier's Medal, Bronze Star with two oak leaf clusters, Air medal with with oak leaf cluster. Office: Internatl Charter Inc of Oregon 1860 Hawthorne Ave NE Ste 390 Salem OR 97303-2495

DAVIS, J. ALAN, lawyer, writer; b. N.Y.C., Nov. 7, 1961; Student, Marlborough Coll., Eng., 1979; BA with distinction, So. Meth. U., 1983; JD with honors, U. Tex., 1987. Bar: Calif. 1988. Assoc. O'Melveny & Myers, L.A., 1987-89, Rosenfeld, Meyer & Susman, Beverly Hills, Calif., 1989-90; pvt. practice L.A., 1990-94; ptnr. Davis & Benjamin, L.A., 1995-98, Garvin, Davis & Benjamin, LLP, L.A., 1998-99; pvt. practice L.A., 1999-2000; head legal and bus. affairs Warner Bros. Internat. TV Prodn., Burbank, Calif., 2000—. Mem. Calif. Bar Assn., Beverly Hills Bar Assn. (entertainment law sect. exec. com.), Brit. Acad. Film and TV Arts, L.A. (mng. dir. 1998, bd. dirs.). Avocations: skiing, scuba diving, tennis. Office: Bldg 170 Rm 3046 4000 Warner Blvd Burbank CA 91522-0001

DAVIS, J. STEVE, advertising agency executive; b. Alliance, Nebr., Feb. 26, 1945; s. John P. and Ruth M. (Annen) D.; m. Courtney Boyd Crowder, June 28, 1973 (div. Oct. 2000); children: Cullen Boyd, J. Scott, Robert Charles. BA, U. Nebr., 1967. Asst. account exec. Benton & Bowles Inc., N.Y.C., 1972-73, account exec., 1973-76, v.p., account supr., 1976-79, sr. v.p., mgmt. supr., 1978-79, 81-85, sr. v.p., account dir. Brussels, 1979-81, N.Y.C., 1985-90; pres. Altschiller Reitzfeld Davis Tracy-Locke, Inc., N.Y.C.; exec. v.p., gen. mgr. J. Walter Thompson, Chgo., 1990-96, dir. worldwide bd., 1991; pres., CEO, dir. Young & Rubicam, N.Y.C., 1996-97; chmn., CEO Wells BDDP, New York, NY, 1998; pres., COO Qorvis Media Group, Inc., San Francisco, 1997-98; pres. Qorvis Media Group, San Francisco, 1998-99. Bd. dirs. Qorvis Media Group, San Francisco; pres., CEO Giraffe Inc., San Carlos. Founders Coun. Our Lady of Missippi Valley; bd. dirs. Steppenwolf Theatre Co., Chgo., 1993, Off The Street Club, 1993, pres., 1995. Named Exec. of Yr. Midwest Advt. Agy., 1992. Mem. Chgo. Econs. Club (chmn. advt. & mass media membership com. 1995), Westmoreland Club, Sigma Chi (publs. bd. 1998—, Significant Sig 1996). E-mail: giraffa@mindspring.com

DAVIS, JAMES ALLAN, gerontologist, educator; b. Portland, Oreg., May 20, 1953; s. Alfred Jack and Anne (Dickson) D.; m. Lois Carol Lindsay, Dec. 17, 1978; children: Sarah Elizabeth, Matthew Simon. BS, U. Oreg., 1975, MS, 1976, EdD, 1980. State mental health gerontologist Oreg. Mental Health Div., Salem, 1978-80; project dir. Oreg. Long Term Care Tng. Project, Salem, 1979-80; tng. specialist Nat. Assn. Area Agys. on Aging., Washington, 1981; asst. dir. for internships and vol. svc. exptl. learning programs U. Md., 1981-86, mem. rsch. and instructional faculty, 1982-86; com. adminstr. Oreg. State Human Resources Com., Salem, 1987; exec. dir. Oreg. State Coun. Sr. Citizens, Salem, 1987-90; program coord. for sr. mental health care Oreg. Sr. and Disabled Svcs. Div., Salem, 1989—; pres. James A. Davis and Assocs. Inc., Portland, 1991—; state project dir. Oreg. Assn. RSVPs, 1995—. Vis. asst. prof. Ctr. for Gerontology U. Oreg., 1990-92; co-chair Audio-Visual Program Internat. Congress Gerontology, 1985; nat. gerontology acad. adv. panel, Nat. Hosp. Satellite Network, 1983-85; presenter nat. confs. on aging, health care, exptl. edn., age stereotyping; lobbyist United Srs. Oreg., Oreg. State Coun. Sr. Citizens, Oreg. State Denturist Assn., Oreg. State Pharmacist Assn., Oreg. Soc. Physician Assts., Oreg. Legal Techs. Assn., Oreg. Dental Lab. Assn., Wash. Denturist Assn., Nat. Denturist Assn. Co-author: TV's Image of the Elderly, 1985; contbg. editor Retirement Life News, 1988-92; sr. issues editor Sr. News, 1989-96; contbr. articles to profl. jours.; producer, host approximately 400 TV and radio programs. Founding pres. Oreg. Alliance for Progressive Policy, 1988-89; co-chair mental health com., vice chair legis. com., Gov.'s Commn. on Sr. Svcs., 1988-89; exec. coun., media chair Human Svcs. Coalition Oreg., 1988-89; bd. dirs. Oreg. Health Action Campaign, 1988-92; 2d v.p., bd. dirs. Oreg. State Coun. for Sr. Citizens, 1977-80, 90-92, Oreg. Medicaid Com., 1996—; co-chair Oreg. Medicare/Medicaid Coalition, 1995—, Oreg. Long Term Care Campaign, 1996-98; mem. Gov's. Task Force for Volunteerism, State of Md., 1983-84, State Legis. Income Tax Task Force, 1990; vice chair Oreg. State Bd. Denture Technology, 1991-96; mem. com. for assessment on needs for volunteerism, Gov.'s Vol. Coun., State of Md., 1984-86; project dir. Oreg. Assn. Ret. and Sr. Vol. Programs, 1995—; mem. exec. bd. dirs. Oreg. Advocacy Coalition of Srs. and People with Disabilities, 1997—; chmn., bd. dirs. Oreg. Campaign for Patient Rights, 1997—. Recipient Disting. Svc. award City of Salem, 1980, Spl. Human Rights award, 1981, Svc. award U. Md., 1984, Hometown U.S.A. award Community Cable TV Producers, 1988, Disting. Svc. award Oreg. State Coun. Sr. Citizens, 1991. Mem. Nat. Assn. State Mental Health Dirs. (nat. exec. com. 1978-80, vice chmn. 1979-80, mem. aging div., spl. cons. 1981-82), Gerontol. Soc. Am. (mental health task force 1982-84, co-chmn. 1983-84), Nat. Gray Panthers (nat. bd. dirs. 1984-92, nat. exec. com. 1984-87, co-chmn. nat. program com. 1984-87, nat. media chair 1985-92, program co-chmn. nat. biennial conv. 1986, nat. health task force 1981—, co-chmn. 1983-84, chmn. mental health subcom. 1981-86, editor Health Watch, 1982-84, state program developer Oreg. chpt. 1979-80, 89, lobbyist 1987—), Nat. Denturist Assn. (exec. dir. 1992-98). Democrat. Office: James A Davis and Assocs Inc 1020 SW Taylor St Ste 610 Portland OR 97205-2506 E-mail: davisjasr@aol.com

DAVIS, JOHN MACDOUGALL, lawyer; b. Seattle, Feb. 20, 1914; s. David Lyle and Georgina (MacDougall) D.; m. Ruth Anne Van Arsdale, July 1, 1939; children: Jean, John, Bruce, Ann, Margaret, Elizabeth. B.A., U. Wash., 1936, LLB, JD, 1940. Bar: Wash. 1940. Assoc. Poe, Falknor, Emory & Howe, Seattle, 1940-45; pvt. practice Seattle, 1945-46; ptnr. Davis & Riese, Seattle, 1946-48, Emory, Howe, Davis & Riese, Seattle, 1948-50, Howe, Davis & Riese, Seattle, 1951-53, Howe, Davis, Riese & Aiken, Seattle, 1953-58, Howe, Davis, Riese & Jones, Seattle, 1958-68, Davis, Wright, Todd, Riese & Jones, Seattle, 1969-85; of counsel Davis, Wright & Jones, Seattle, 1985-89, Davis Wright Tremaine, Seattle, 1990—. Lectr. U. Wash. Law Sch., 1947-52. Bd. dirs. Virginia Mason Hosp., Seattle, 1952-79, pres., 1970-72; bd. dirs. Pacific Sci. Ctr., 1971-90, dir. emeritus, 1991—, past pres., past chmn.; trustee Whitman Coll., 1971-86, chmn., 1983-86; bd. dirs. Blue Cross Wash. and Alaska, 1982-89, Diabetic Trust Fund, 1954—, Wash. Student Loan Guaranty Assn., 1978-83; mem. adv. bd. Chief Seattle council Boy Scouts Am.; mem. Mercer Island Sch. Bd., 1956-66. Served with USNG, 1931-34. Recipient Disting. Eagle Scout award, 1982 Mem. ABA, Wash. State Bar Assn. (merit award 1965), Seattle-King County Bar Assn. (pres. 1960-61), Order of Coif, Rainier Club (Seattle), The Mountaineers Club, Phi Delta Phi, Alpha Delta Phi. Presbyterian. Clubs: Rainier (Seattle). Avocation: mountain climbing. Home: 9104 Fortuna Dr #3305 Mercer Island WA 98040-3166 Office: Davis Wright Tremaine 2600 Century Sq 1501 4th Ave Ste 2600 Seattle WA 98101-1688

DAVIS, JOHN ROWLAND, university administrator; b. Mpls., Dec. 19, 1927; s. Roland Owen and Dorothy (Norman) D.; m. Lois Marie Falk, Sept. 4, 1947; children— Joel C., Jacque L., Michele M., Robin E. BS, U. Minn., 1949, MS, 1951; postgrad., Purdue U., 1955-57; PhD, Mich. State U., 1959. Hydraulic engr. U.S. Geol. Survey, Lincoln, Nebr., 1950-51; instr. Mich. State U., 1951-55; asst. prof. Purdue U., 1955-57; lectr. U. Calif., Davis, 1957-62; hydraulic engr. Stanford Rsch. Inst., South Pasadena, Calif., 1962-64; prof. U. Nebr., Lincoln, 1964-65, dean coll. engring. and architecture, 1965-71, faculty rep. intercollegiate athletics; prof., head dept. agrl. engring. Oreg. State U., Corvallis, 1971-75, instl. athletic rep., 1972-87, dir. Agrl. Expt. Sta., assoc. dean Sch. Agr., 1975-85, dir. spl. programs Office of Academic Affairs, assoc. dir. athletics, 1987-89, prof. emeritus, assoc. dir. athletics, 1989—. Governing bd. Water Resources Research Inst., 1975-85; dir. Western Rural Devel. Center, 1975-85, Agrl. Research Found., Jackman Inst.; cons. Stanford Research Inst., Dept. Agr., Consortium for Internat. Devel.; dir. Engrs. Council Profl. Devel., 1966-72; pres. Pacific-10 Conf., 1978-79. Contbr. articles to profl. jours. With USNR, 1945-46. Fellow Am. Soc. Agrl. Engrs. (dir. 1971-73, agrl. engr. of year award Pacific N.W. region 1974), NCAA (v.p. 1979-83, sec.-treas. 1983-85, pres. 1985-87). Home: 2940 NW Aspen St Corvallis OR 97330-3307 Office: Oreg State U Gill Coliseum Corvallis OR 97331 E-mail: john.r.davis@orst.edu

DAVIS, LANCE EDWIN, economics educator; b. Seattle, Nov. 3, 1928; s. Maurice L. and Marjorie Dee (Seibert) D.; m. Susan Elizabeth Gray, Dec. 2, 1977; 1 child, Maili. BA, U. Wash., Seattle, 1950; PhD (Ford Found. dissertation fellow summer 1956), Johns Hopkins U., 1956. Teaching asst. U. Wash., 1950-51, 52-53; teaching asst., then instr. Johns Hopkins U., 1953-55; from instr. to prof. econs. Purdue U., 1955-62; mem. faculty Calif. Inst. Tech., Pasadena, prof. econs., 1968—, Mary Stillman Harkness prof., 1980—; rsch. assoc. Nat. Bur. Econ. Rsch., 1979—. Author: The Growth of Industrial Enterprise, 1964; co-author: The Savings Bank of Baltimore, 1956, American Economic History: The Development of a National Economy, 2d rev. edit, 1968, Institutional Change and American Economic Growth, 1971, Mammon and the Pursuit of Empire: The Political Economy of British Imperialism, 1860-1912, 1987, Internat. Capital Markets and Economic Growth 1820-1914, 1994, In Pursuit of Leviathan: Technology, Institutions, Productivity and Profits in American Whaling, 1816-1906, 1997, Evolving Financial Markets and Foreign Capital Flows: Britain, the Americas, and Australia, 1870-1914, 1999; co-editor: American Economic Growth: An Economist's History of the United States, 1971; mem. bd. editors Jour. Econ. History, 1965-73, Explorations in Economic History, 1984-88, THESIS, Theory, and History of Econ. and Social Instns. and Structures, with Soviet and Western Scholars, 1991—. With USNR, 1945-48, 51-52. Recipient Arthur Cole prize Econ. History Assn., 1966, Alice Hanson Jones prize, 1998, Sanwa Monograph prize Ctr. for Japan-U.S. Bus. and Econ. Studies, 1995, Libr. Co. Phila. program in early Am. economy and society prize, 2000; Ford Found. Faculty fellow, 1959-60; Guggenheim fellow, 1964-65; fellow Ctr. for Advanced Study in Behavioral Scis., 1985-86. Fellow Am. Acad. Arts and Scis.; mem. Coun. 1 Rsch. Econ. History (chmn. 1973-74, 75-76), Econ. History Assn. (pres. 1978-79, trustee 1980-82, Alice Hanson Jones prize 1998), Anglo-Am. Hist. Assn. (gov. 1978-80), Econs. Inst. (policy and adv. bd. 1984-87), Cliometric Soc. (trustee 1993-97). Home: 1746 Grevelia St South Pasadena CA 91030-2733 Office: Calif Inst Tech Humanities And Social Scis Dv Pasadena CA 91125-0001 E-mail: led@hss.caltech.edu

DAVIS, LARRY, park director; b. Price, Utah, Sept. 24, 1937; BA, Brigham Young U., 1968, M in Anthropology, 1975. Asst. Anasazi State Park, Boulder, park mgr., 1970—. Mem. Am. Assn. Mus. Office: Anasazi State Park PO Box 1429 Boulder UT 84716-1429

DAVIS, LORI, foundation executive; m. Scott; children: Jacob, Josh, Caitlin, Michael, Eric, Travis. Grad. in acctg., Fresno State C.C., Fresno, Calif. Acctg. position with a cons. co.; acctg. position with a bank; engring. asst. for an ind. oil prodr.; asst. dir. Trend Lightly!, Ogden, Utah, interim exec. dir., exec. dir. Office: Trend Lightly 298 24th St Ste 325 Ogden UT 84401-1482

DAVIS, MARK E. chemical engineering educator; Prof. dept. chemistry Calif. Inst. Tech., prof. chem. engring. Recipient Alan T. Waterman award Nat. Sci. Found., 1990, Ipatieff prize Am. Chemical Soc., 1992, Profl. Progress award for outstanding Progress in chem. engring., Am. Inst. of Chem. Engrs, 1999. Office: Calif Inst Tech Dept Chemistry 210-41 1200 E California Blvd Pasadena CA 91125-0001

DAVIS, MARK M. microbiologist, educator; b. Paris, Nov. 27, 1952; BA in Molecular Biology, Johns Hopkins U., 1974; PhD in Molecular Biology, Calif. Inst. Tech., 1981. Fellow lab. of immunology NIH, Bethesda, Md., 1980-82, staff fellow lab. of immunology, 1982-83; asst. prof. med. microbiology Stanford (Calif.) U. Sch. Medicine, 1983-86, assoc. prof. microbiology and immunology, 1986-91, prof. microbiology and immunology, 1991—, dir. predoctoral program in immunology, 1994—; assoc. investigator Howard Hughes Med. Inst., Stanford U., 1987-91, faculty coord., 1989—, investigator, 1991—. Instr. Cold Spring Harbor (N.Y.) Lab., 1983; mem. sci. adv. bd. Damon Runyon-Walter Cancer Found., 1985-88; co-organizer UCLA Symposium, 1987; mem. allergy and immunology study sect. divsn. rsch. grants NIH, 1988-92. Recipient Intra-Sci. Rsch. Found. award 1980, Youth Scientist award Passano Found., 1985, Eli Lilly award 1986, Kayden award N.Y. Acad. Scis., 1986, Howard Taylor Ricketts award U. Chgo., 1988, Gairdner Found. award, 1989, King Faisal Internat. prize 1995, Sloan prize Gen. Motors Rsch. Found., 1996; scholar PEW Found. 1985-89. Mem. Nat. Acad. Scis. Office: Stanford U Sch Medicine Fairchild Bldg Rm # D-300 Stanford CA 94305-5124

DAVIS, MARVIN, petroleum company executive, entrepreneur; b. Newark, Aug. 28, 1925; s. Jack Davis; m. Barbara Davis; 5 children. BSCE, NYU, 1947. Gen. ptnr., owner Davis Oil Co., Denver; co-owner 20th Century-Fox, 1981-85; owner Davis Cos. Office: Davis Cos 2121 Ave Of Stars Ste 2800 Los Angeles CA 90067-5052

DAVIS, MURDOCH, editor-in-chief journal; b. New Waterford, Can., Feb. 19, 1954; married; 3 children. BAA in Jounralism, Ryerson Polytech. Inst., 1975. Reporter, feature writer Toronto Star, Can., 1976-78; reporter, then asst. city editor, news editor, city editor Ottawa Citizen, Can., 1979-89; mng. editor Edmonton Jour., Can., 1989-92, editor Can., 1992—. Office: 10006 101 St PO Box 2421 Edmonton AB Canada T5J 2S6

DAVIS, NATHANIEL, humanities educator; b. Boston, Apr. 12, 1925; s. Harvey Nathaniel and Alice Marion (Rohde) D.; m. Elizabeth Kirkbride Creese, Nov. 24, 1956; children: Margaret Morton Davis Mainardi, Helen Miller Davis Presley, James Creese, Thomas Rohde. Grad., Phillips Exeter Acad., 1942; AB, Brown U., 1944, LLD, 1970; MA, Fletcher Sch. Law and Diplomacy, 1947, PhD, 1960; postgrad. Russian lang. and area, Columbia, Cornell U., Middlebury Coll., 1953-54, U. Central de Venezuela, 1961-62, Norwich U., 1989. Asst. history Tufts Coll., 1947; joined U.S. Fgn. Service, 1947; 3d sec. Prague, Czechoslovakia, 1947-49; vice consul Florence, Italy, 1949-52; 2d sec. Rome, Italy, 1952-53, Moscow, USSR, 1954-56; Soviet desk officer State Dept., 1956-60; 1st sec. Caracas, Venezuela, 1960-62; acting Peace Corps dir. Chile, 1962; spl. asst. to dir. Peace Corps, 1962-63, dept. asso. dir., 1963-65; U.S. minister to Bulgaria, 1965-66; sr. staff Nat. Security Council (White House), 1966-68; U.S. ambassador to Guatemala, 1968-71; to Chile, 1971-73; dir. gen. Fgn. Service, 1973-75, asst. sec. of state for African affairs, 1975; U.S. ambassador to Switzerland, 1975-77; State Dept advisor and Chester Nimitz prof. Naval War Coll., 1977-83, lectr., 1991—; Alexander and Adelaide Hixon prof. humanities Harvey Mudd Coll., Claremont, Calif., 1983—, faculty exec. com., 1986-89, acting dean of faculty, 1990. Mem. Mellon Found. Grant Inter-coll. Steering Com. for the Six Claremont Colls., establishing a Summer Lang. Inst. and coordinated lang. program; mem. Consortiumn, Task Force on the Future of the Clairmont Colleges, 1996, Fulbright scholarship, Moscow, Russia, 1996-97; lectr. U.S. history Centro Venezolano-Americano, 1961; lectr. Russian and Soviet history Howard U., 1962-65, 66-68; lectr. constnl. law and social problems Salve Regina Coll., 1981-83; vis. prof. Russian State U. Humanities, 1996-97; mem. governing bd. European Union Ctr. Calif., 1998—. Author: The Last Two Years of Salvador Allende, 1985, Equality and Equal Security in Soviet Foreign Policy, 1986, A Long Walk to Church: A Contemporary History of Russian Orthodoxy, 1995. Mem. ctrl. com. Calif. Dem. Party, 1987-90, 91—, mem. exec. bd., 1993—, mem. exec. com., bus. and profl. caucus, 1992-96; mem. L.A. County Dem. Ctrl. Com., 1988-90, 92—, regional vice chmn., 1994-96; del. Dem. Nat. Conv., 1988, 92, 96, 2000; del. So. Calif. conf. United Ch. of Christ, 1986-87. Lt. (j.g.) USNR, 1944-46. Recipient Cinco Aguilas Blancas Alpinism award Venezuelan Andean Club, 1962, Disting. Pub. Svc. award U.S. Navy, 1983, Elvira Roberti award for outstanding leadership Los Angeles County Dem. Com., 1995, Prism award for nat., state, county and local svcs. Jerry Voorhis Claremont Dem. Club, 1999, spl. merit award, 1998 (as author) So. Calif. Motion Picture Coun., 1998. Mem. AAUP (pres. Claremont Coll. chpt. 1992-96, 98, rep. so. Calif. pvt. colls., Calif. coun.), Am. Fgn. Svc. Assn. (bd. dirs., vice chmn. 1964), Coun. on Fgn. Rels., Am. Acad. Diplomacy, Nat. Book Critics Cir., Cosmos Club, Phi Beta Kappa. Home: 1783 Longwood Ave Claremont CA 91711-3129 Office: Harvey Mudd Coll 301 E 12th St Claremont CA 91711-5901

DAVIS, NICHOLAS HOMANS CLARK, finance company executive; b. N.Y.C., Dec. 1, 1938; s. Feltz Cleveland and Loraine Vanderpool (Homans) D.; children from previous marriage: Loraine, Helen, Alexandra, Eleanor; m. Brenda Jean Molen, Dec. 18, 1982; children: Nicholas, Elizabeth. BA in Geology with honors, Princeton U., 1961; MBA in Fin., Stanford U., 1963. Chartered fin. analyst; cert. NYSE supervisory analyst. Research analyst Fahnestock & Co., N.Y.C., 1963-67; mgr. research Andresen & Co., N.Y.C., 1967-71; dir. research Boettcher & Co., Denver, 1971-75; v.p. corp. fin. White Weld & Co., Denver, 1975-78; v.p. asset mgmt. Paine Webber Co., Denver, 1978-92; pres. Mont. Investment Advisors, Inc., Bozeman, 1991—. Trustee, investment officer Thenen Found., Montclair, N.J., 1966—. Chmn. Jr. Achievement Gallatin County. Mem. Denver Soc. Security Analysts (chmn., pres. 1972—), Riverside Country Club, Rotary. Avocations: skiing, flyfishing, deepwater voyaging, writing, backpacking. Home: 2302 Springcreek Dr Bozeman MT 59715-6035 Office: Mont Investment Advisors Inc 104 E Main St # 416 PO Box 7090 Bozeman MT 59771-7090 E-mail: mintnd@aol.com

DAVIS, RICHARD CALHOUN, dentist; b. Manhattan, Kans., Jan. 4, 1945; s. William Calhoun and Alison Rae (Wyland) D.; Danna Ruth Ritchel, June 13, 1968; 1 child, Darin Calhoun. Student, Ariz. State U., 1963-65, BA, 1978, U. Ariz., 1966; DDS, U. of Pacific, 1981. Retail dept. head Walgreens, Tucson, 1965-66, mgmt. trainee Tucson, San Antonio, 1967-70, asst. store mgr. Baton Rouge, 1970-72; field rep. Am. Cancer Soc., Phoenix, 1972-74; dept. head Lucky Stores, Inc., Tempe, Ariz., 1976-78; practice dentistry specializing in gen. dentistry Tucson, 1981—. Bd. dirs. Home Again, Inc. Chmn. bd. Capilla Del Sol Christian Ch., Tucson, 1984. Fellow Internat. Congress Oral Implantologists, Am. Coll. Oral Implantology, Am. Soc. Osseointegration; mem. ADA, Acad. Gen. Dentists, Am. Straight Wire Orthodontic Assn., Am. Assn. Functional

Orthodontics, Sleep Disorders Dental Soc., So. Ariz. Bus. Assn. (treas. 1998), N.W. Dental Study Club, Tucson Advanced Cosmetic Study Club, Optimists (past pres. N.W. club, preceptorship in dental implantology), Elks. Republican. Mem. Disciples of Christ Ch. Avocation: golf, skiing, watersports, fishing, camping. Office: 2777 N Campbell Ave Tucson AZ 85719-3101

DAVIS, RICHARD MALONE, economics educator; b. Hamilton, N.Y., June 2, 1918; s. Malone Crowell and Grace Edith (McQuade) D. AB, Colgate U., 1939; MA, Cornell U., 1941, PhD, 1949. From instr. to assoc. prof. econs. Lehigh U., Bethlehem, Pa., 1941-54; assoc. prof. econs. U. Oreg., Eugene, 1954-62, prof., 1962-83, prof. emeritus, 1983—. Contbr. articles to profl. jours. Served with U.S. Army, 1942-45, CBI. Mem. Phi Beta Kappa. Republican Home: 1040 Ferry St Apt 503 Eugene OR 97401-3332 Office: Univ Oreg Dept Econs Eugene OR 97403

DAVIS, ROGER LEWIS, lawyer; b. New Orleans, Jan. 27, 1946; s. Leon and Anada A. (Russ) D.; m. Annette Vucinich; 1 child, Alexandra. BA, Tulane U., 1967; MA, UCLA, 1969; PhD, UCLA, 1971; JD, Harvard U., 1974. Bar: Calif. 1974. Assoc. Orrick, Herrington & Sutcliffe, L.L.P., San Francisco, 1974-79, ptnr., 1980—, chmn. pub. fin. dept., 1981—. Mem. Bay Area Coun., San Francisco, 1988-90; mem. mcpl. fiscal adv. com. Mayor of San Francisco; tech. adv. com. Calif. Debt & Investment Adv. Commn. Fellow Am. Coll. of Bond Counsel; mem. ABA (tax sect., mem. com. tax exempt financing), Nat. Assn. Bond Lawyers (mem. com. profl. responsibility and securities law and disclosure), Calif. Pub. Securities Assn. (dir. 1998—). Office: Orrick Herrington & Sutcliffe LLP 400 Sansome St San Francisco CA 94111-3143 E-mail: rogerdavis@orrick.com

DAVIS, RONALD WAYNE, genetics researcher, biochemistry educator; b. Moroa, Ill., July 17, 1941; s. Lester and Gerzella Mary (Brown) D.; m. Janet L. Dafoe, May 2, 1949; children: Whitney Allen, Ashley Halcyon. BS, Ea. Ill. U., 1964; PhD, Calif. Inst. Tech., 1970. Postdoctoral fellow Harvard U., Cambridge, Mass., 1970-71; asst. prof. biochemistry Stanford (Calif.) U., 1972-77, assoc. prof., 1977-80, prof., 1980—. Mem. sci. adv. bd. Collaborative Rsch., Bedford, Mass., 1978—. Author: Manual for Genetic Engineering, 1980. Recipient Eli Lilly award in microbiology, 1976, U.S. Steel award in molecular biology, 1981, Louis S. Rosenstiel award Brandeis U., 1992. Mem. NAS. Avocation: backpacking. Office: Stanford U Dept Biochemistry 855 California Ave Stanford CA 94305*

DAVIS, ROY KIM, otolaryngologist, health facility administrator; b. Logan, Utah, Jan. 20, 1947; m. JoNell Davis; children: Kimberly, Roy Neal, Tamralyn, Cynthia Joy, Mindy Anne, Ricks Eric. BS magna cum laude, Utah State U., 1972; MD, U. Utah, 1975. Diplomate Am. Bd. Otolaryngolgoy. Resident in prespecialty surgery Madigan Army Med. Ctr., 1975-76, resident in otolaryngology, 1976-79; fellow Boston U., 1979-80; instr. surgery Uniformed Svcs. U. Health Scis., Bethesda, Md., 1980-81, asst. prof. surgery, 1981-83; asst. chief otolaryngology svc. Walter Reed Army Med. Ctr., 1980-83; from asst prof. to assoc. prof. U. Utah, Salt Lake City, 1983-85; chief otolaryngology head and neck surgery S.L. VA Med. Ctr., Salt Lake City, 1986-93, 99—; dir. John A. Dixon Laser Inst. U. Utah, 1993-98. Adj. prof. comm. disorders U. Utah, 1993—, prof. surgery, 1993; course instr. Am. Acad. Otolaryngology; scientific dir. Rocky Mountain Cancer Data System, 1985-96; mem. head and neck com. S.W. Oncology Group, 1985—; vis. prof. Madigan Army Medical Ctr., 1980, Brooke Army Medical Ctr., 1981, Tripler Army Medical Ctr., 1982, U. N.C., 1986, U. Tex., 1988, Szent-Gyorgyi Albert Univ., Szeged, Hungary, 1989, First Pavlov Medical Inst., Leningrad, USSR, 1990, Univ. Keil, Germany, 1990, Georg-August U., Gottingen, Germany, 1990, 96, Wilhelm-Pieck Univ. Rostock, Germany, 1990, U. Indonesia, Jakarta, 1995, Bowman-Gray Med. Sch.-Wake Forest U., 1996; guest examiner Am. Bd. Otolaryngology, 1994-95, 99. Co-author numerous books and book chpts.; contbr. articles to profl. jours. Mem. Jon A. Huntsman Cancer Inst. Fellow Am. Acad. Otolaryngology, Am. Laryngological Assn., Am. Soc. Laser Medicine and Surgery, Am. Coll. Surgeons, Am. Soc. Head and Neck Surgery; Soc. Univ. Otolaryngolgoists, Utah Soc. Otolaryngology, Am. Laryngo., Rhinol. & Otol. Soc., Am. Bronchoesophagol. Soc., Soc. Univ. Otolaryngologists, Alpha Epsilon Delta, Am. Laryngo. Assn. Office: Otolaryngology Head & Neck Surgery 3c134A U Utah Hlth Scis Ctr Salt Lake City UT 84132-0001 E-mail: r.kim.davis@hsc.utah.edu

DAVIS, SHELBY MOORE CULLOM, investment executive, consultant; b. Phila., Mar. 20, 1937; s. Shelby Cullom and Kathryn (Wasserman) D.; m. Wendy Ann Adams, June 20, 1959 (div. 1975); children: Andrew, Christopher, Victoria; m. Gale Abbie Lansing, Apr. 17, 1976; children: Lansing, Alida, Edith. AB with honors, Princeton U., 1958. V.p. in charge equity rsch. Bank of N.Y., N.Y.C., 1958-66; founding ptnr. Davis, Palmer & Biggs, N.Y.C., 1966-78; sr. v.p. Fiduciary Trust Co., N.Y.C., 1978-83, cons., 1983-98; pres. various mut. funds Davis Selected Advisers, Santa Fe, 1983-98, also dir. all mut. funds, 1969-78, 83-98. Contbr. articles to Fin. Analysts Jour. Bd. dirs., trustee Beekman Downtown Hosp., N.Y.C., early 1960s; bd. dirs. Am. Cancer Soc., N.Y.C., early 1970s; trustee United World Coll., 1988—, Teton Sci. Sch., 2001—; mem. adv. bd. Coll. of the Atlantic, 1999—. Mem. N.Y. Soc. Security Analysts (bd. dirs. 1965), Univ. Club, River Club (N.Y.C.), Harbor Club (Seal Harbor, Maine), Tuxedo Club (Tuxedo Park, N.Y.), Jupiter Island Club, Jackson Hole Golf and Tennis Club. Republican. Avocations: skiing, hiking, travel, swimming, tennis. Home: PMB 25185 PO Box 20000 Jackson WY 83001-7000 Office: Davis Selected Advisers PO Box 1688 Santa Fe NM 87504-1688 E-mail: shelby@dsaco.com

DAVIS, STANLEY NELSON, hydrologist, educator; b. Rio de Janeiro, Brazil, Aug. 6, 1924; s. Nelson Caryl and Mary Faye (Caulkins) D.; m. Barbara Jean Wickham, Apr. 14, 1949 (div.); children: Gerald Nelson, Ruth Ann, Darlene Grace, Randall Wayne, Betty Jean, Nancy Faye.; m. Augusta G. Felty, Feb. 12, 1982; children— Tara Devi, Locana Kamala B.S. in Geology, U. Nev., 1949; M.S., U. Kans., 1951; Ph.D., Yale, 1955. Geologist U.S. Bur. Reclamation, 1949, Mo. Geol. Survey, 1952, 53, 55; instr. U. Rochester, 1953-54; mem. faculty Stanford, 1954-67, prof. geology, 1965-67, U. Mo., 1967-73, chmn. dept., 1969-72; asso. dean Coll. Arts and Scis., 1972-73; prof. geology Ind. U., Bloomington, 1973-75; prof. hydrology U. Ariz., Tucson, 1975—, head dept. hydrology and water resources, 1975-79. Vis. prof. U. Chile, Santiago, 1960-61; tchr. Bowling Green U., summer 1963, Princeton, summer 1965, U. Hawaii, fall 1966; instr. U. Oriente in Venezuela, summer 1967-68, 72; lectr. Am. Geol. Inst.; mem. East Greenland Expdn., Arctic Inst. N. Am., summer 1959; cons. to govt. and industry, 1955— Author: Hidrogeología, 1961, (with R.M. DeWiest) Hydrogeology, 1966, (with P. Reitan and R. Pestrong) Geology, Our Physical Environment, 1976, (with D.J. Campbell, H.W. Bentley, T.J. Flynn) Ground Water Tracers, 1984; also articles. Served with AUS, 1943-46, PTO. Fellow AAAS, Geol. Soc. Am. (O.E. Meinzer award 1989), Am. Geophys. Union; mem. Assn. Ground Water Scientists and Engrs., Soc. Econ. Paleontologists and Mineralogists, Sigma Xi. Home: 6540 W Box Canyon Dr Tucson AZ 85745-9681 Office: U Ariz Dept Hydrology & Water Resou Tucson AZ 85721-0001 E-mail: sndavis@u.arizona.edu

DAVIS, SUSAN A. congresswoman; b. Cambridge, Mass., 1944; m. Steve, 1970; children: Jeffrey, Benjamin. Degree in Sociology, U. Calif., Berkeley; MA in Social Work, U. N.C. Social worker; exec. dir. Aaron Price Fellowship Program, 1990-93; served Calif. State Assembly, 1994-2000; congresswoman Calif. 49th Dist., 2000—. Mem. Congressional com. House Armed Svcs., Edn. and Workforce; chaired Women's Caucus for Senate and Assembly, Consumer Protection, Govt. Efficiency, Econ. Devel. com.; created and co-chaired Select com. on Adolescence. Mem. San Diego City Sch. Bd., 1983-1992, pres. and v.p.; pres. League of Women Voters San Diego., Office: 1517 Longworth House Office bldg Washington DC 20515*

DAVIS, TERRELL, professional football player; b. San Diego, Oct. 28, 1972; Student, Long Beach State U., U. Ga. Running back Denver Broncos, 1995—; player AFC Championshig Game, 1997, Super Bowl, 1997, Pro Bowl, 1996, 97. Achievements include being named Sporting News NFL-Pro Team Running Back, 1996, 97. Office: Denver Broncos 13655 Broncos Pkwy Englewood CO 80112-4150

DAVIS, WAYNE ALTON, computer science educator; b. Ft. Macleod, Alta., Can., Nov. 16, 1931; s. Frederick and Anna Mary (Barr) D.; m. Audrey M. Zorolow, July 17, 1959 (div. 1989); children: Fredrick M., Peter W., Timothy M.; m. Patricia Ruth Syme, Mar. 24, 1990. BSE, George Washington U., 1960; MSc, U. Ottawa, 1963, PhD, 1967. Sci. officer Def. Resch. Bd., Ottawa, Ont., 1960-68; research scientist Dept. Comms., Ottawa, 1968-69; vis. scientist NRC, Ottawa, 1975-76; assoc. prof. U. Alta., Edmonton, 1969-77, prof. computing sci., 1977-91, prof. emeritus, 1991—, acting chmn. computing sci., 1982-83; acting dir. Alta. Centre for Machine Intelligence and Robotics, 1988-89. Lectr. U. Ottawa, 1965-69; sessional lectr. Carleton U., 1967; cons. Editor: The Barrs of Ardenville, 1978; editor Procs. Graphics Interface, 1994, 95, 96, 97, 98. Grantee NRC, 1970-78; rsch. grantee Natural Scis. and Engring. Rsch. Coun., 1978-92; strategic grantee Natural Scis. and Engring. Rsch. Coun., 1981-83; grantee Def. Rsch. Bd., 1974-76; hon. prof. Harbin Shipbldg. Engring. Inst., China, 1985. Mem. IEEE, Can. Info. Processing Soc. (pres. 1978-79), Can. Human Computer Comms. Soc. (pres. 1981-96), Can. Soc. Computational Study of Intelligence (treas. 1976-86), Assn. Computing Machinery, Faculty Club. Anglican. Home: Box 817 605-21st St Fort Macleod AB Canada T0L 0Z0 Office: U Alta Dept Computing Sci Edmonton AB Canada T6G 2E8 E-mail: davis@cs.ualberta.ca

DAVIS, WILLIAM F. state legislator; b. 1949; BS, U.S. Air Force Acad., 1970; MBA, U. N.Mex., JD, 1984. Bar: N.Mex. Practice of law; mem. N.Mex. State Senate, 1996—, mem. Indian and cultural affairs com., mem. judiciary com. Republican. Office: PO Box 6 Albuquerque NM 87103-0006 E-mail: wdavis@state.nm.us

DAWSON, CHANDLER ROBERT, ophthalmologist, educator; b. Denver, Aug. 24, 1930; married; 3 children. AB, Princeton U., 1952; MD, Yale U., 1956. USPHS epidemiologist Communicable Disease Ctr., 1957-60; resident dept. ophthalmology Sch. Medicine U. Calif., San Francisco, 1960-63; asst. clin. prof. U. Calif., San Francisco, 1963-66, asst. prof. in residence, 1966-69, assoc. prof. ophthalmology, 1969-75, prof. ophthalmology, 1975-97, prof. emeritus, assoc. dir. Francis I. Proctor Found., 1970-84, dir., 1984-95. Fellow Middlesex Hosp. Med. Sch., London, 1963-64; co-dir. WHO Collaborating Ctr. for Reference and Rsch. on Trachoma and other Chlamydial Infections, 1970-79, dir. Collaborating Ctr. for Prevention of Blindness and Trachoma, 1979—. Recipient Knapp award AMA, 1967, 69, Medaille Trachome, 1978. Mem. Am. Soc. Microbiology, Am. Acad. Ophthalmology, Assn. Rsch. Vision & Ophthalmology. Achievements include rsch. in epidemiology of infectious eye diseases and cataracts; prevention of blindness; pathogenesis of virus diseases of the eyes; electron microscopy of eye diseases; clinical trials of treatment for trachoma and for herpes simplex eye infections. Office: U Calif San Francisco Francis I Proctor Found Rsch Ophthalmology San Francisco CA 94143-0001

DAWSON, DEREK, investment company executive; b. 1942; With Hendale Group, London, 1965-82; officer Southbrook and City Holdings, London, 1982-87; chmn. Southbrook Corp., Beverley Hills, Calif., 1987—. Office: Southbrook Corp 150 S El Camino Dr Ste 106 Beverly Hills CA 90212-2736 also: Southbrook Group 21 Upperbrook St London WIK 7PY United Kingdom

DAWSON, FRANCES EMILY, poet, nurse; b. Augsburg, Germany, Dec. 7, 1952; d. Emmett C. Jr. and B. Louise (Boddie) D. BS in Nursing, Pa. State U., 1974. RN, D.C. Staff nurse Howard U. Med. Ctr., Washington, 1974 75, charge nurse, 1975-77. Author: Live for Today, 1986, With You in Mind, 1987, Reflections, 1988, (poetry cassette rec.) Soul Connection, 1992. Active Disabled Resource Ctr., Lupus Found. Am., Calif. Assn. Physically Handicapped; model Operation Confidence Program for the Disabled, 1985 86, head cheerleader drill team, 1985-86; mem. Long Beach Task Force for the Ams. with Disabilities Act, 1994—; active Christ 2d Baptist Ch., 1985—. Recipient Golden Poetry award, 1985-92, excellence in lit. award Pinewood Poetry, 1987-89. Mem. BMI, Walt Whitman Guild, Internat. Soc. Poets (hon. charter), Pa. State U. Alumni Assn., Detroit Black Poets Guild. Democrat. Baptist. Avocations: needlepoint, sewing. Home: 250 Pacific Ave Long Beach CA 90802-3000

DAWSON, JOHN JOSEPH, lawyer; b. Binghamton, N.Y., Mar. 9, 1947; s. Joseph John and Cecilia (O'Neill) D. BA, Siena Coll., 1968; JD, U. Notre Dame, 1971. Bar: Ariz. 1971, Nev. 1991, Calif. 1993, D.C. 1994, N.Y. 1996. Nat. practice group chair, bankruptcy and creditors rights practice group Quarles & Brady Streich Lang LLP, Phoenix. Reporter local rules ct. U.S. Bankruptcy Ct. for Dist. Ariz.; atty. rep. U.S. Ct. Appeals (9th cir.), 1992-95 Co-author: Advanced Chapter 11 Bankruptcy, 1991. Cpl. U.S. Army, USAR, 1964-70. Fellow Ariz. Bar Found.; mem. State Bar Ariz. (chmn. bankruptcy sect. 1976-77, 80-81), Am. Bankruptcy Inst., Comml. Law League Am. Republican. Roman Catholic. Avocations: sports, reading, movies, travel, writing. Office: Quarles & Brady Streich Lang LLP Renaissance One Two North Central Ave Phoenix AZ 85004-2391 E-mail: jdawson@quarles.com

DAWSON, JOHN MYRICK, physics educator; b. Champaign, Ill., Sept. 30, 1930; s. Walker Myrick and Wilhelmina Emily (Stephan) D.; m. Nancy Louise Wildes, Dec. 28, 1957 (dec. May 1994); children: Arthur Walker, Margaret Louise. B.S., U. Md., 1952, M.S., 1954, Ph.D., 1957. Fulbright scholar Inst. Plasma Physics, Nagoya, Japan, 1964-65; research physicist Plasma Physics Lab. Princeton U., 1956-73, head theoretical group, 1965-73; prof. plasma physics UCLA, 1973—, assoc. head Inst. for Plasma Physics & Fusion Engring., 1976-88. Cons. in field; John Danz lectr. U. Wash., 1974; guest Russian Acad. Scis., 1971; invited lectr. Inst. Plasma Physics, Nagoya, Japan, 1972; Kerst lectr. U. Wis., 1994. Contbr. articles in field to profl. jours. Recipient Exceptional Sci. Achievement award TRW Sys., 1977, James Clerk Maxwell prize in plasma physics, 1977; named Calif. Scientist of Yr., 1978. Aneesur Rahman Prize, Am. Physical Soc., 1994. Fellow AAAS, Am. Phys. Soc. (chmn. plasma div. 1970-71, Aneesun Rahmah prize 1994); mem. NAS, Am. Acad. Arts and Scis., N.Y. Acad. Scis., N.J. Acad. Scis., Sigma Xi, Sigma Pi Sigma, Phi Kappa Phi. Unitarian. Achievements include patents in field. Home: 359 Arno Way Pacific Palisades CA 90272-3348 Office: Univ Calif 405 Hilgard Ave Los Angeles CA 90095-9000

DAWSON, PATRICIA LUCILLE, surgeon; b. Kingston, Jamaica, W.I., Sept. 30, 1949; came to U.S. 1950. d. Percival Gordon and Edna Claire (Overton) D.; m. Stanley James Hiserman, Sept. 6, 1980; children: Alexandria Zoe, Wesley Gordon. BA in Sociology, Allegheny Coll., 1971; MD, N.J. Med. Sch., Newark, 1977; MA in Human and Orgn. Devel., The Fielding Inst., 1996, PhD in Human and Orgnl. Sys., 1998. Membership dir. N.J. ACLU, Newark, 1972; resident in surgery U. Medicine and Dentistry N.J. N.J. Med Sch., 1977-79; Virginia Mason Med. Ctr., Seattle, 1979-82; pvt. practice specializing in surgery Arlington, Wash., 1982-83; dir. med. staff diversity Group Health Coop., Seattle, 1993-98, staff surgeon, 1983-98; pvt. practice Seattle, 1998—. Author: Forged by the Knife—The Experience of Surgical Residency from the Perspective of a Woman of Color. Fellow ACS, Seattle Surg. Soc.; mem. Am. Med. Women's Assn., Physicians for Social Responsibility, Assn. Women Surgeons, Wash. Black Profls. in Health Care, NOW. Avocations: fiction, walking, cooking. Office: Providence Comp Breast Ctr Jefferson Twr 1600 E Jefferson St Ste 300 Seattle WA 98122-5645

DAY, ANN, state legislator; b. EL Paso, Tex. BAEducation, Ariz. St. U.; M.Ed, U. Ariz. Former tchr., counselor; mem. Ariz. Senate, Phoenix, 1990-. Republican. Home: PO Box 65417 Tucson AZ 85728-5417 Office: Arizona State Senate 1700 W Washington St Ste S Phoenix AZ 85007-2890

DAY, ANTHONY, book critic; b. Miami, Fla., May 12, 1933; s. Price and Alice (Alexander) D.; m. Lynn Ward, June 25, 1960; children— John, Julia (dec.). A.B. cum laude, Harvard U., 1955, postgrad. (Nieman fellow), 1966-67; L.H.D. (hon.), Pepperdine U., 1974. Reporter Phila. Bull., 1957-60, Washington, 1960-69, chief Washington bur., 1969; chief editorial writer L.A. Times, 1969-71, editor editorial pages, 1971-89, sr. corr., 1989-95; contbg. writer L.A. Times Book Review, 1995—. Mem. Signet Soc. Harvard, Asia Soc., Santa Fe Coun. Internat. Rels.

DAY, GERALD W. wholesale grocery company executive; With Albertson's, Heber City, Utah, 1945-72; CEO Days Markets; chmn., bd. dirs. Associated Food Stores Inc. Office: Day's Market 890 S Main St Heber City UT 84032-2463

DAY, HOWARD WILMAN, geology educator; b. Burlington, Vt., Nov. 17, 1942; s. Wilman Forrest and Virginia Louise (Morton) D.; children: Kristina, Sarah, Susan. AB, Dartmouth Coll., 1964; MS, Brown U., 1968, PhD, 1971. From asst. prof. to assoc. prof. geology U. Okla., Norman, 1970-76; from asst. prof. to prof. geology U. Calif., Davis, 1976—, chmn. dept., 1990-96. Co-editor Jour. Metamorphic Geology, 1985-92; contbr. articles to profl. jours. Fulbright fellow, Norway, 1964, Alexander von Humboldt fellow, Fed. Republic Germany, 1977. Fellow Geol. Soc. Am., Mineral Soc. Am.; mem. Am. Geophys. Union. Office: U Calif Dept Geology Davis CA 95616 E-mail: hwday@ucdavis.edu

DAY, JAMES MCADAM, JR. lawyer; b. Detroit, Aug. 18, 1948; s. James McAdam and Mary Elizabeth (McGibbon) D.; m. Sally Marie Sterud; children: Cara McAdam, Brenna Marie, Michael James. AB, UCLA, 1970; JD magna cum laude, U. Pacific, 1973. Bar: Calif. 1973, U.S. Dist. Ct. (no. dist.) Calif. 1973, U.S. Ct. Appeals (9th cir.) 1975. Assoc. Downey, Brand, Seymour & Rohwer, Sacramento, 1973-78, ptnr., 1978—, chmn. natural resources dept., 1985-90; mng. ptnr. Downey, Brand, Seymour & Rohmer, Sacramento, 1990-94, 97—. Contbr. articles to profl. jours. Pres., bd. dirs. Sacramento Soc. for Prevention of Cruelty to Animals, 1976-79, Children's Home Soc. of Calif., Sacramento, 1979-85; bd. dirs. Sta. KXPR/KXJZ, Inc. Pub. Radio, Sacramento, 1984-94, chmn., 1990-93; bd. dirs. Calif. State Libr. Found., 1995—, chmn., 1995-2000. Mem. ABA (natural resources sect. 1998), Calif. Bar Assn. (exec. com. 1985-89, chmn. real property law sect. 1988), Rocky Mountain Mineral Law Found., Sacramento Petroleum Assn., Calif. Mining Assn., U. Pacific McGeorge Law Sch. Alumni Assn. (bd. dirs. 1980-83). Avocations: yacht racing and cruising, fishing. Office: Downey Brand Seymour & Rohwer 555 Capitol Mall Fl 10 Sacramento CA 95814-4504

DAY, JOHN DENTON, retired company executive, cattle and horse rancher, breeder, trainer, wrangler, actor, educator; b. Salt Lake City, Jan. 20, 1942; s. George W. and Grace (Denton) Jenkins; m. Susan Hansen, June 20, 1971; children: Tammy Denton Wadsworth, Jeanett B, Barber. Student, U. Utah, 1964-65; BA in Econs. and Bus. Adminstrn. with high honors, Westminster Coll., 1971. Riding instr., wrangler Uinta wilderness area U-Ranch, Neola, Utah, 1955-58; stock handler, driver, ruffstock rider Earl Hutchinson Rodeo Contractor, Idaho, 1959; wrangler, riding instr. YMCA Camp Rodger, Kamas, Utah, 1957; with Mil. Data Cons., Inc., L.A., 1961-62, Carlseon Credit Corp., Salt Lake City, 1962-65; sales mgr. sporting goods Western Enterprises, Salt Lake City, 1965-69; founder Rockin d Ranch, Millcreek, Utah, 1969; ski instr. Brighton (Utah) Ski Sch., 1969-71; Western rep. PBR Co., Cleve., 1969-71; dist. sales rep. Crown Zellerbach Corp., Seattle and L.A., 1971-73; pres., founder Dapco paper, chem., instl. food and janitorial supplies, Salt Lake City, 1973-79, John D Day Greeting Cards, 1990—; owner, founder, pres. John D. Day, mfrs. reps., 1972—; dist. sales mgr. Surfonics Engrs., Inc., Woods Cross, Utah, 1976-78, Garland Co., Cleve., 1978-81; rancher Heber, Utah, 1976-90, horse tng. facility, horsemanship sch. and ranch, Temecula, Calif., 1984-90, St. George, Utah, 1989-99; horse training Horsemanship Sch., Quarter Horse Breeding Facility, Yerington, Nev., 1999—. Sec. bd. Acquadyne, 1974, 75. Actor, dir., prodr. (movies) The Big Sky, 1952, Rebel Without a Cause, 1955, Devils Brigade, 1967, Coyote Summer, 1995, (videos) Someday Soon, 1993, A Tour of Snows Canyon, 1993, All For the Love of Horse, 1982-83, Stallion Management, 1985, others; tv commls., Chev., Palmer, others; contbr. articles to jours., including Western Artist. Group chmn. Tele-Dex fund raising project Westminster Coll.; founder, supr. vol. group Day's Rangers, 1990-99; vol. Dixie Nat. Forest, 1989-94, USDA Forest Svc.; 1st U.S. wilderness ranger USDA, US Forest Svc., Dixie Nat. Forest, Pine Valley Ranger Dist., Pine Valley Mountain Wilderness, So. Utah, 1994-99. With AUS, 1963-64. Recipient grand nat. award Internat. Custom Car Show, San Diego, 1962, Award of Excellence Winternationals Nat. Hot Rod Assn., 1962-63, Key to City, Louisville, 1964, Champion Bareback Riding award, 1957, Vol. award USDA Forest Svc., 1991, 92, 93, nominated U.S. Vol. award, Safety award Dixie Nat. Forest, P.V.R.D., 1992-99; recipient Outstanding Performance award USDA, 1995, 98, Cert. Appreciation, 1997, DNF Outstanding Svc. award, 1997, Pine Valley Mountain Wilderness; Dally team roping heading and heeling champion, 1982. Mem. Internat. Show Car Assn. (co-chmn. 1978-79), Am. Quarter Horse Assn. (life), Profl. Horseman Assn. (high point reigning champion 1981, awarded Nat. Reining Horse Assn. Bronze, qualified for world championship, Dodge, Toyota Fall Futurite Circuit Champion Working Cowhorse 1994-95, World Championship Show qualifier and participant Oklahoma City Sr. Cutting 1994), Intermountain Quarter Horse Assn. (sr. reining champion 1981, champion AMAT reining 1979-81), Utah Quarter Horse Assn. (state champion AMAT reining 1979, 80, AMAT barrel racing 1980, working cowhorse champion 1982, trained working cowhorse and rider champion 1992, 98, trained amateur reining horse and rider champion 1996, open cutting res. champion 1993-95, 97, open cutting champion 1994, Menlove Dodge Toyota Fall Futurity circuit champion working cowhorse, 1994-95, open working cowhorse champion & broadmare halter champion 1995, Rose cir. working cowhorse champion 1995, 98, Rose Cir. Open working cowhorse champion, showed cir. champion Brodmare at Halter Rose cir. open cutting champion 1996, 97, bd. dirs. 1992-94, trained amateur barrel racing and amateur pole bending horse and rider 1998, State Reserve Champion amateur cutting horse and rider), Profl. Horseman's Assn., Nat. Cutting Horse Assn. (affiliate), Profl. Cowhorseman's Assn. (world champion team roping, heeling 1986, 88, high point rider 1985, world champion stock horse rider 1985-86, 88, world champion working cowhorse 1985, PCA finals open cutting champion, 1985-88, PCA finals 1500 novice champion 1987, PCA finals all-around champion 1985-88, inducted into Hall of Fame 1988, first on record registered Tex. longhorn cutting contest, open champion, PCA founder, editor newsletter 1985-89, pres. 1984-88), World Rodeo Assn. Profls. (v.p. Western territory 1989-98, judge nat. high sch. rodeo, cutting horse and rodeo queen contest, 1990—, hon. v.p. Western Terr. U.S. 1998—, Nevada Quarter House Assn. (mem. com., Am. Quarter House Assn., Ride 2000, "Let Freedom Ride", Fall Circuit 2000 Open Cutting Champion), Nev. Quarter Horse Assn.

DAY, KEVIN THOMAS, banker, community services director; b. London, Aug. 24, 1937; came to U.S., 1957; s. William Stanley and Mary Ann (Hook) D.; m. Mary Violet Scheuber, Aug., 1960. BA, Brisbane Tech. Coll., Queensland, Australia, 1957. Pres. Americana Investments, San Francisco, 1960-63; stockbroker Sutro and Co., San Francisco, 1963-66; regional v.p. Am. Express Investment Co., San Francisco, 1966-70; dir. mktg. ITT Fin. Svcs., N.Y.C., 1970-78; pres. Exec. Assocs., Reno, 1978-83, First Interstate Bank Found., Reno, 1983-1991; exec. dir. Cath. Community Svcs., Reno, 1991—. Chmn. Nev. Fgn. Trade Zone, Reno, 1986-91, Desert Rsch. Inst., Reno. Pres. Econ. Devel. Authority, Reno, 1985, Nev. Mus. Art, 1989-91; mem. exec. com. Western Indsl. Nev., Reno, 1985-90; commr. Nev. Commn. on Econ. Devel., Carson City, 1987-90. Named Man of Yr., Reno mag., 1988, Torch of Liberty award, 1989; named to Nev. Order of Silver Spur, 1990. Republican. Roman Catholic. Avocations: sailing, wilderness camping, art collecting. Home: 4835 Pinesprings Dr Reno NV 89509-6504 Office: Cath Community Svcs 500 E 4th St Reno NV 89512-3316

DAY, LUCILLE LANG, health facility administrator, educator, writer; b. Oakland, Calif., Dec. 5, 1947; d. Richard Allen and Evelyn Marietta (Hazard) Lang; m. Frank Lawrence Day, Nov. 6, 1965 (div. 1970); 1 child, Liana Sherrine; m. Theodore Herman Fleischman, June 23, 1974 (div. 1985); 1 child, Tamarind Channah. AB, U. Calif., Berkeley, 1971, MA, 1973, PhD, 1979; MA, San Francisco State U., 1999. Tchg. asst. U. Calif., Berkeley, 1971-72, 75-76, rsch. asst., 1975, 77-78; tchr. sci. Magic Mountain Sch., Berkeley, 1977; specialist math. and sci. Novato (Calif.) Unified Sch. Dist., 1979-81; instr. sci. Project Bridge Laney Coll., Oakland, Calif., 1984-86; sci. writer and mgr. precoll. edn. programs Lawrence Berkeley (Calif.) Nat. Lab., 1986-90, life scis. staff coord., 1990-92, mgr. Hall of Health, 1992—. Lectr. St. Mary's Coll. of Calif., Moraga, Calif., 1997—2000. Author numerous poems, articles and book reviews; author: (with Joan Skolnick and Carol Langbort) How to Encourage Girls in Math and Science: Strategies for Parents and Educators, 1982; (poetry collections) Self-Portrait with Hand Microscope, 1982, Fire in the Garden, 1997, Wild One, 2000, Lucille Lang Day, Greatest Hits, 1975-2000, 2001. NSF Grad. fellow, 1972-75; recipient Joseph Henry Jackson award in lit. San Francisco Found., 1982. Mem. No. Calif. Sci. Writers Assn., Nat. Assn. Sci. Writers, Math./Sci. Network, Soc. for Pub. Health Edn. (No. Calif. chpt.), Phi Beta Kappa, Iota Sigma Pi. Home: 1057 Walker Ave Oakland CA 94610-1511 Office: Hall of Health 2230 Shattuck Ave Berkeley CA 94704-1416 E-mail: lucyday@hallofhealth.org, lucyday@earthlink.net

DAY, ROBERT WINSOR, preventive medicine physician, researcher; b. Framingham, Mass., Oct. 22, 1930; s. Raymond Albert and Mildred (Doty) D.; m. Jane Alice Boynton, Sept. 6, 1957 (div. Sept. 1977); m. Cynthia Taylor, Dec. 16, 1977; children: Christopher, Nathalia, Natalia, Julia. Student, Harvard U., 1949-51; MD, U. Chgo., 1956; MPH, U. Calif., Berkeley, 1958, PhD, 1962. With USPHS, 1956-57; resident U. Calif., Berkeley, 1958-60; research specialist Calif. Dept. Mental Hygiene, 1960-64; asst. prof. Sch. Pub. Health and Sch. Medicine UCLA, 1962-64; dep. dir. Calif. Dept. Pub. Health, Berkeley, 1965-67; prof., chmn. dept. health services Sch. Pub. Health and Community Medicine, U. Wash., Seattle, 1968-72, dean, 1972-82, prof., 1982—; pres., dir. Fred Hutchinson Cancer Rsch. Ctr., Seattle, 1981-97, pres., dir. emeritus, 1997—, mem. pub. health scis., 1997—. Mem. Nat. Cancer Adv. Bd., 1992-98, Nat. Cancer Policy Bd., 1996-2000; chief med. officer Epigenomics, Inc.; scientific dir. Internat. Consortium Rsch. Health Effects Radiation; cons. in field. Fellow AAAS, Am. Pub. Health Assn., Am. Coll. Preventive Medicine; mem. Am. Soc. Clin. Oncology, Soc. Preventive Oncology, Am. Assn. Cancer Rsch., Assn. Schs. Pub. Health (pres. 1981-82), Am. Assn. Cancer Insts. (bd. dirs. 1983-87, v.p. 1984-85, pres., chmn. bd. dirs.). E-mail: dlcllc@home.com

DAY, STOCKWELL BURT, government official; b. Barrie, Ont., Can., Aug. 16, 1950; s. Stockwell and Gwendolyn (Gilbert) D.; m. Valorie Martin Day, Oct. 2, 1971; children: Logan, Luke, Ben. Auctioneer, Alta., Can., 1972-74; dir. Teen Challenge Outreach Ministries, Edmonton, 1974-75; contractor Comml. Interiors, 1976-78; sch. adminstr./asst. pastor Bentley (Alta) Christian Centre, 1978-85; mem. Legis. Assembly Alta. Legis., Edmonton, 1986—, govt. caucus whip, 1989-92, govt. house leader, 1994-97, min. of labor, 1992-96, min. of family and social svcs., 1996-97, provincial treas., acting premier, 1997-2000; leader The Canadian Alliance, Calgary, 2000—. Chmn. Alta. Tourism Edn. Coun., Edmonton, 1987-89, Premier's Coun. on Family, Edmonton, 1990-92. Mem. Red Deer Rotary, Red Deer Legion (assoc.). Avocations: tennis, roller blading, backpacking, reading. Office: Government of Alberta The Canadian Alliance Ste 600 833 4 Ave SW Calgary AB Canada T2P 3T5

DAYTON, SKY, communications company executive; Grad., Delphi Acad., 1988. Mgr. computer graphics dept. Mednick & Assocs., 1988-90; founder Cafe Mocha, L.A., 1990-92; co-founder Dayton Walker Design, 1992 94; founder Earthlink Network, Pasadena, Calif., 1994—, chmn., 1994-99, also bd. dirs. Mem. Assn. Online Profls. (bd. dirs.), Internet Access Coalition. Office: Earthlink Network 3100 New York Dr Pasadena CA 91107-1500

DEADMARSH, ADAM, professional hockey player; b. Trail, B.C., Can., May 10, 1975; Right wing Colo. Avalanche, Denver. Office: Colo Avalanche 1000 Chopper Cir Denver CO 80204-5809

DEAKTOR, DARRYL BARNETT, lawyer; b. Pitts., Feb. 2, 1942; s. Harry and Edith (Barnett) D.; children: Rachael Alexandra, Hallie Sarah. BA, Brandeis U., 1963; LLB, U. Pa., 1966; MBA, Columbia U., 1968. Bar: Pa. 1966, Fla. 1980, N.Y. 1980. Assoc. firm Goodis, Greenfield & Mann, Phila., 1968-70, ptnr., 1971; gen. counsel Life of Pa. Fin. Corp., Phila., 1972; asst. prof. U. Fla. Coll. Law, Gainesville, 1972-74, assoc. prof., 1974-80; with Mershon, Sawyer, Johnston, Dunwody & Cole, Miami, Fla., 1980-81, ptnr., 1981-84, Walker Ellis Gragg & Deaktor, Miami, 1984-86, White & Case LLP, Miami, 1987-95, White & Case LLC, Johannesburg, South Africa, 1995-2000, Palo Alto, Calif., 2000—. Mem. Dist. III (Fla.) Human Rights Advocacy Com. for Mentally Retarded Citizens, 1974-78, chmn., 1978-80; mem. adv. bd. Childbirth Edn. Assn. Alachua County, Fla., 1974-80; mem. resource devel. bd. Mailman Ctr. for Child Devel., 1981-88. Mem. Fla. Bar. Office: White & Case LLP 3000 El Camino Real Five Palo Alto Sq 10th Fl Palo Alto CA 94306 E-mail: ddeaktor@whitecase.com

DE ALESSI, ROSS ALAN, lighting designer; b. San Francisco, Apr. 16, 1955; s. August Eugene De Alessi and Angela Maria (Caredio) Leonard; m. Susan Tracey Stearns, Aug. 11, 1990; 1 child, Chase Arthur. BFA, Stephens Coll., 1978. In-house lighting designer GUMP'S, San Francisco, 1981-84; prin. Ross De Alessi & Assoc., San Francisco, 1984-87, Luminae Lighting Design, San Francisco, 1987-93, prin., co-founder Ross De Alessi Lighting Design, Seattle, 1993—. Works include GUMP'S Christmas Windows, San Francisco (Award of Distinction Gen. Electric, 1986, Spl. Citation 1989, Edwin F. Guth Award of Merit Illuminating Engring. Soc. 1989, 90), TAB Products Showroom, L.A. (Award of Distinction Gen. Electric 1987), St. Augustine's Ch., Pleasanton, Calif. (Sect. award Illuminating Engring. Soc. 1988), L.A. Quinta (Calif.) Resort Plz. Fountains (Award of Excellence Gen. Electric 1988, Paul Waterbury Award of Excellence Illuminating Engring. Soc. 1989), McKesson Bldg. Lobby, San Francisco (Award of Excellence Gen. Electric 1988, Edwin F. Guth Award of Merit Illuminating Engring. Soc. 1989), Brown & Bain, Phoenix (Award of Merit Gen. Electric 1989), Saxe Gallery, San Francisco (Edwin F. Guth Award of Merit Illuminating Engring. Soc. 1989), Plz. Pk., San Jose, Calif. (Paul Waterbury Spl. Citation Illuminating Engring. Soc. 1990), The Palace of Fine Arts, San Francisco (Edison Award Gen. Electric 1990, Paul Waterbury Award of Excellence Illuminating Engring. Soc. 1991, Award of Excellence Internat. Assn. Lighting Designers 1991), Le Touessrok, Island of Mauritius (Award of Merit Gen. Electric 1993, Sect. Award Illuminating Engring. Soc. 1994, Paul Waterbury Award of Excellence 1994), St. Patrick's Sem., Menlo Park, Calif. (Edison award Gen. Electric 1993, Edwin F. Guth award of Excellence Illuminating Engring. Soc. 1994, Citation Internat. Assn. Lighting Designers 1994), Palace of the Lost City, Republic of Boputhatswana (Award of Merit Gen. Electric 1992, Paul Waterbury Award of Excellence 1993, Award of Excellence Internat. Assn. Lighting Designers 1993), Wells Fargo Bank-Flagship Bank, San Francisco (Award of Excellence Gen. Electric 1992, Award of Merit Illuminating Engring. Soc. 1993, Citation Internat. Assn. Lighting Designers 1993), Santa Barbara County Courthouse, Santa Barbara (Paul Waterbury Award of Merit Illuminating Engring. Soc. 1995, Award of Excellence Internat. Assn. Lighting Designers 1995), City of Bridges, Cleve. (Edison award 1995, Paul Waterbry award Illuminating Engring. Soc. 1997), MGM Grand Gateway of Entertainment, Las Vegas (Award of Excellence Gen. Elec. 1998, Edwin F. Guth Award of Excellence Illuminating Engring. Soc. 1999, Award of Merit Internat. Assn. Lighting Designers 1999), Helsinki Master Plan-Esplanade (Edison award 1999, Award of Distinction, Illuminating Engring. Soc. 2000, Award of Merit, Internat. Assn. Lighting Designers), Space Needle (award of excellence GE 2000, Illuminating Engring. Soc. 2001, award of merit Internat. Assn. Lighting Designers 2001). Mem. Internat. Assn. Lighting Designers (lighting cert.), Nat. Coun. on the Certification Lighting Profls., Illuminating Engring. Soc., Washington Athletic Club. Avocations: scuba diving, traveling. Office: Ross De Alessi Lighting Design 2815 2nd Ave Ste 280 Seattle WA 98121-3217

DEAN, JAMES BENWELL, lawyer; b. Dodge City, Kans., May 23, 1941; s. James Harvey and Bess (Benwell) D.; m. Sharon Ann Carver, Sept. 1, 1962 (div. 1991); m. Patricia A. Bostick, Aug. 23, 1993 (div. 1999); children: Cynthia G. Dean Vosburgh, James M. Student, Southwestern Coll., 1959-60, U. Colo., 1961; BA, Kans. State U., 1962; JD, Harvard U., 1965. Bar: Colo. 1965, U.S. Dist. Ct. Colo. 1965, U.S. Tax Ct. 1966, Nebr. 1971, U.S. Ct. Appeals (10th cir.) 1971. From assoc. to ptnr. Tweedy & Mosley, Denver, 1965-71, Kutak Rock Cohen Campbell Garfinkle & Woodward, Omaha, 1971-73; ptnr. Mosley, Wells & Dean, Denver, 1973-77, Kutak Rock & Huie, Denver, 1977-81, James B. Dean, P.C., Denver, 1981-91, Dean, McClure, Eggleston & Husney, Denver, 1991-95, James B. Dean, PC, Denver, 1995-2000, Dean & Stern, PC, Denver, 2001—; spl. asst. atty. gen. State of Colo., Denver, 1989—. Lectr. U. Ark. Law Sch., Fayetteville, 1982-86, C.C. Aurora, Colo., 1996-97. Co-editor Agricultural Law Jour., 1979-84; contbr. articles to profl. jours. Mem. ABA (advisor bd. forum com. on rural lawyers and agrl. bus. 1983-89), Nebr. Bar Assn., Colo. Bar Assn. (sec. agrl. law sect. 1991-94, bd. dirs. 1989—), Denver Bar Assn., Am. Agrl. Law Assn. (pres. elect 1985-86, pres. 1986-87, bd. dirs. 1981-83, strategic planning com. 2000-01, Disting. Svc. award 1989). Republican. Avocations: photography, woodworking, hiking, piano. Office: 4155 E Jewell Ave Ste 703 Denver CO 80222-4511 E-mail: jim@deanandstern.com

DEAN, LEE, protective services executive; b. Ardmore, Okla., 1950; BA, Calif. State U., Sacramento, 1976; JD, Lincoln U., Sacramento, 1984. Pastrolman L.A. Police Dept., 1972-73; patrolman to chief dep. Sacramento Sheriff's Dept., 1974-91; chief of police Vacaville (Calif.) Police Dept., 1991-95, San Bernardino (Calif.) Police Dept., 1996—. Author: Target: Excellence, 1990. Office: San Bernardino Police Dept PO Box 1559 San Bernardino CA 92402-1559

DEAN, PAUL JOHN, magazine editor; b. Pitts., May 11, 1941; s. John Aloysius and Perle Elizabeth (Thompson) D.; m. Jo-ann Tillman, Aug. 19, 1972 (div. Mar. 1981); children: Jennifer Ann, Michael Paul. Student engring., Pa. State U., 1959-60. Gen. mgr. Civic Ctr. Honda Co., Pitts., 1965-68, Washington-Pitts. Cycle Co., Canonsburg, Pa., 1968-70; nat. svc. mgr. Yankee Motor Co., Schenectady, 1970-73. Competition congressman Am. Motorcyclist Assn., 1971, 72, trustee, sec. bd., 1988-91, chmn., 1991-97; bd. dirs. AMA ProRacing, 1997—; adv. bd., guest speaker L.A. Trade Tech. Coll., 1974-90; trustee Am. Motorcyclist Heritage Found., 1990-91. Engring. editor Cycle Guide mag., Compton, Calif., 1973-74, editor-in-chief, 1974-80, editorial dir., 1980-84; editor-in-chief Cycle World mag., Newport Beach, Calif., 1984-88, editorial dir. Cycle and Cycle World mags., 1988-92; v.p., editorial dir. Cycle World Mag. Group, 1992—; author manuals. Served with AUS, 1964-65. Home: 5915 Arabella St Lakewood CA 90713-1203 Office: Hachette Filipacchi Mags 1499 Monrovia Ave Newport Beach CA 92663-2752 E-mail: CW1Dean@aol.com

DEAN, RICHARD ANTHONY, mechanical engineer, engineering executive; b. Bklyn., Dec. 22, 1935; s. Anthony David and Anne Mylod Dean; m. Sheila Elizabeth Grady, Oct. 5, 1957; children: Carolyn Anne, Julie Marie, Richard Drews. BSME, Ga. Inst. Tech., 1957; MSME, U. Pitts., 1963, PhDME, 1970. Registered profl. engr., Calif. From jr. engr. to mgr. thermal and hydraulic engring. Westinghouse Nuclear Energy Sys., 1959-70; v.p., tech. dir. water reactor fuels General Atomics, San Diego, 1970-74, v.p. uranium and light water reactor fuel, 1974-80, sr. v.p., 1980-92; pres. Leading Edge Engring., San Diego, 1993—; pres., CEO Cutting Edge Products, Inc., San Diego, 1997—. Cons. U.S. Congress Office Tech. Assessment. 1st lt. U.S. Army, 1957-59. Mem. AAAS, ASME (former chmn. nuclear fuels tech. com.), Am. Nuclear Soc. (gen. chmn. annual meeting 1993), Global Found. (bd. advisors), Internat. Thermonuclear Experimental Reactor (adv. bd.). Achievements include the develpoment of commercial nuclear power stations; advanced the understanding of boiling heat transfer phenomena; invention of advanced nuclear fuel assembly. Home: 6699 Via Estrada La Jolla CA 92037-6432 Office: Leading Edge Engring 13100 Kirkham Way Ste 210 Poway CA 92064-7128 E-mail: leeinc@cts.com

DEAN, WILLIAM EVANS, aerospace industry executive; b. Greenville, Miss., July 6, 1930; s. George Thomas Dean and Martha Myrtle (Evans) Carlton; m. Dorothy Sue Hamilton, Oct. 14, 1953; children: Janet Lea, Jody Anne, Justin H. B in Aero. Engring., Ga. Inst. Tech., 1952; MBA, Pepperdine U., 1970; PhD in Aero Engring., Columbia State U., 1997. FAA cert. airplane and instrument flight instr. Commd. officer USAF, 1952, advanced through grades to maj., 1962; divsn. mgr., dir. Rockwell Internat. Corp., L.A., 1962-67, v.p., divsn. gen. mgr., 1967-80; exec. v.p. Acurex Corp., Mountain View, Calif., 1981-82, pres., COO, 1982-83, pres., CEO, 1983-90, vice chmn., 1990-91; assoc. dir. Ames Rsch. Ctr. NASA, Moffett Field, Calif., 1991-93, dep. ctr. dir., 1994-97; v.p., dir. Univs. Space Rsch. Assn., Columbia, Md., 1997—. Lectr. Calif. State U., Chico, 1988, Santa Clara U., 1993-98. Contbr. articles on gen. mgmt. and aero. engring. to profl. jours. Bd. dirs. NCCI, San Jose, Calif., 1984-97, co-chmn., 1988-91; bd. dirs. Santa Clara County Mfg. Group, San Jose, 1984-91, vice-chmn., 1988-91; bd. dirs. Saddleback Community Coll., Mission Viejo, Calif., 1976-77, United Fund, Orange County, Calif., 1971; United Way, Santa Clara County, San Jose, 1985-91; vice-chmn., bd. advisors Leavey Sch. Bus., Santa Clara U., 1987-97, vice chmn., 1989-91; tech. com. Orange County Bus. Coun., 1998-2000. Maj. USAF, 1952-62. Decorated Air Force Commendation medal with oak leaf cluster; named Disting. Engring. alumnus Ga. Inst. Tech., 1995; recipient Spl. Svc. award United Way, 1986, Astronaut Personal Achievement award NASA Astronaut Corps, 1972, 84, Outstanding Contbn. to Manned Exploration of the Moon award NASA, 1972, Medal for Outstanding Leadership, 1995, Group Achievement awards, 1995, Disting. Svc. medal, 1997, Silver Knight of Mgmt. award Nat. Mgmt. Assn., 1978, Commendation Cert. Calif. State Assembly, 1986, Pres.' award Santa Clara U., 1993; named Disting. Alumnus award Woodward Acad., 1999; inducted to Engring. Hall of Fame, Ga. Inst. Tech., 1997. Fellow AIAA (bd. dirs. 1979-86, 91-95, Space Shuttle award 1984), Internat. Acad. Astronautics (Paris), Am. Astron. Soc.; mem. Am. Electronics Assn. (edn. found. 1982-88), Aircraft Owners and Pilots Assn., Air Force Assn., Armed Forces Comm. and Electronics Assn. Republican. Baptist. Office: Universities Space Rsch Assn Orange county Site 13422 Laurinda Way Santa Ana CA 92705-1926 E-mail: dean@usra.edu

DEANGELIS, DAN, transportation executive; b. Stockton, Calif., July 23, 1947; m. Shari Thornton, 1973; children: Ryan, Jamie. BA in Adminstrn. Justice, Delta Coll., 1967. Lic. comml. pilot; cert. airline transport pilot. Chief pilot, flight instr. Werner's Aero Svc. Stockton Metropolitan Airport; with City of Manteca, 1974-76; airport ops. dep. Dept. Aviation County of San Joaquin, 1976-85, asst. airport ops. mgr., 1985-87, dep. airport mgr. ops., 1987-90; airport mgr. Stockton Metropolitan Airport, 1990—. Office: Stockton Met Airport 5000 S Airport Way Ste 202 Stockton CA 95206-3911

DE ANTONI, EDWARD PAUL, cancer control research scientist; b. San Francisco, Mar. 7, 1941; s. Attilio Mario and Zita Elizabeth (Lolich) DeA.; m. Karen Dolores Thode, Jan. 22, 1966; children: Marc Edward, Christopher Earl. A.B., U. San Francisco, 1962; Ph.D., Cornell U., 1971. Vol. Peace Corps, Turkey, 1964-66; sr. analyst Planning Bur. State of S.D., Pierre, 1973-76; dir. health planning Dept. Health, 1976-81; asst. dir. Assoc. Sch. Bds. S.D., 1981-84; dir. cancer control program Colo. Dept. Health, 1986-90; rsch. dir. Cancer Ctr., Porter Meml. Hosp., Denver, 1991-92; chair genitourinary cancer control Southwest Oncology Group, 1991-97; rsch. dir. Prostate Cancer Edn. Coun., 1991-97; asst. prof. urology Health Sci. Ctr., U. Colo., Denver, 1992-99, sr. instr., 2000—, sr. instr pathology/urology, 2001—. Woodrow Wilson fellow, 1962-63; ESEA fellow, 1966-69 E-mail: ed.deantoni@uchsc.edu

DEASY, CORNELIUS MICHAEL, architect; b. Mineral Wells, Tex., July 19, 1918; s. Cornelius and Monetta (Palmo) D.; m. Lucille Laney, Sept. 14, 1941; children— Diana, Carol, Ann. B. Arch., U. So. Calif., 1941. Practice architecture, Los Angeles, 1946-76, partner, Robert D. Bolling, 1960-76; Prin. works include prin. offices student union, Calif. State U., Los Angeles.; Author: Design for Human Affairs, 1974, Designing Places for People, 1985. Vice pres. Los Angeles Beautiful; dir. Regional Plan Assn. Commr., Los Angeles Bd. Zoning Appeals, 1973— . Recipient numerous design awards, Nat. Endowment Arts award, 1983. Fellow AIA (past pres., dir. So. Calif. chpt., chmn. com. research) Home and Office: Davenport Creek Farm 4979 Davenport Creek Rd San Luis Obispo CA 93401-8109

DEAVER, PHILLIP LESTER, lawyer; b. Long Beach, Calif., July 21, 1952; s. Albert Lester and Eva Lucille (Welton) D. Student, USCG Acad., 1970-72; BA, UCLA, 1974; JD, U. So. Calif., 1977. Bar: Hawaii 1977, U.S. Dist. Ct. Hawaii 1977, U.S. Ct. Appeals (9th cir.) 1978, U.S. Supreme Ct. 1981. Assoc. Carlsmith, Wichman, Case, Mukai & Ichiki, Honolulu, 1977-83, ptnr., 1983-86, Bays, Deaver, Lung, Rose & Baba, Honolulu, 1986, mng. ptnr., 1986-95. Contbr. articles to profl. jours. Bd. dirs. Parents and Children Together, v.p. Mem. ABA (forum com. on the Constrn. Industry), AIA (affiliate Hawaii chpt.), Am. Arbitration Assn. (arbitrator). Home: 2471 Pacific Heights Rd Honolulu HI 96813-1029 Office: Bays Deaver Lung Rose and Baba PO Box 1760 Honolulu HI 96806-1760 E-mail: pdeaver@legalhawaii.com

DEBARTOLO, JACK, JR. architect; b. Youngstown, Ohio, May 6, 1938; s. Jack and Virginia (Sassinelli) DeB.; m. Patsy McLamore, Aug. 15, 1958; children: Ava, Gina, Jack III. B.Arch., U. Houston, 1962; M.Arch., Columbia U., 1964. Sr. v.p., dir. design Caudill Rowell Scott, 1964-73; sr. v.p. William Wilde & Assocs., Tucson, 1973-75; pres. Anderson DeBartolo Pan Inc., Phoenix, 1975-85, dir. design, founding prin. Tucson, 1973-95; prin. DeBartolo Archs. Ltd., Phoenix, 1995—. Fellow Am. Inst. of Archs., bd. dirs., U. of Ariz. Found., mem. of exec. comm. of AIA Col. of Fellows, chancellor, 1997. Notable works include: (award winning project), CRS Office Bldg., Houston, Joilet Jr. Coll., Ill., Pima Cmty. Coll., Tucson, West Campus & Life Sci. Bldg of Ariz. State U. Deacon Phoenix First Assembly Ch. Fellow AIA (past pres. Ariz., So. Ariz. chpt., chmn. jury of fellows 1987-90, chancellor Coll. of Fellows 1997); mem. Tuscon Tomorrow, City of Tuscon Pres.'s Club, U. Ariz. Found. Bd., Ariz. State U. Coll. Architecture Coun. of Design Excellence. Republican. Club: Tucson Breakfast. Office: DeBartolo Archs Ltd 4450 N 12th St Ste 268 Phoenix AZ 85014-6032

DEBARTOLO-YORK, DENISE, sports team executive; m. John C. York II; 4 children. Grad., Notre Dame U. Team pres. Pitts. Penguins; exec. v.p. personnel and corp. mktg./comm. The Edward J. Bartolo Corp., vice chmn., 1994; chmn. The Edward J. DeBartolo Corp. Supporter DeBartolo Family Found. Mem. fin. adv. bd. Ursuline Sisters; mem. MADD; recognized for contbn. to St. Charles Elem. Sch., Boardman, Ohio. Office: care San Francisco 49ers 4949 Centennial Blvd Santa Clara CA 95054-1229

DEBAS, HAILE T. gastrointestinal surgeon, physiologist, educator; b. Asmara, Eritrea, Feb. 25, 1937; came to U.S., 1981; s. Tesfaye and Keddes (Gabre) D.; m. Ignacia Kim Assing, May 23, 1969. BS in Biology, U. Coll., Addis Ababa, Ethiopia, 1958; MD, CM, McGill U., Montreal, Que., Can., 1963. Intern Ottawa (Ont.) Civic Hosp., Can., 1963-64; resident in surgery U. B.C., Vancouver, 1964-69, asst. prof. surgery, 1971-75, assoc. prof., 1976-80; fellow in gastrointestinal physiology UCLA, 1972-74, prof. of surgery, 1981-85; chief gastrointestinal surgery U. Wash., Seattle, 1985-87; prof., chmn. dept. surgery U. Calif., San Francisco, 1987-93; dean U. Calif. Sch. Medicine, San Francisco, 1993—, chancellor, 1997-98, vice chancellor med. affairs, 1998—. Key investigator Ctr. for Ulcer Rsch. and Edn., UCLA, 1980-90; cons. Bd. Med. Quality Assurance, Calif., 1981—. Mem. editorial bd. Am. Jour. Physiology, Am. Jour. Surgery, Jour. Surg. Rsch., Western Jour. Medicine, Gastroenterology; contbr. articles to profl. jours. and chpts. to books. Fellow Med. Rsch. Coun. of Can., 1972-74; rsch. grantee NIH, 1976—. Fellow ACS, Royal Coll. Physicians and Surgeons Can.; mem. Am. Surg. Assn. (pres. 2001—), Am. Gastroent. Assn. (bd. govs. 1995—), Am. Assn. Endocrine Surgeons, Collequium Internat. Chirugiae Digestivae, Soc. Univ. Surgeons, Soc. Surgeons Alimentary Tract (trustee 1984-89), Soc. Black Acad. Surgeons (pres. 1998-99), Inst. Medicine, AAMC (chair elect coun. deans), Am. Acad. Arts and Scis., Internat. Hepato-Biliary Pancreatic Assn. (pres. 1991-92), Assn. Minority Acad. Physicians (pres. 1992-93). Office: U Calif Sch Medicine Office of the Dean 513 Parnassus Ave # S224 San Francisco CA 94143-0001 E-mail: hdebas@medsch.ucsf.edu

DE BENEDICTIS, DARIO, arbitrator, mediator; b. Providence, Aug. 22, 1918; s. Anthony and Efra (Bassani) DeB.; m. Leanna May Carlson, July 22, 1950; children: Marc, Don, Gail. AB, U. Calif., Berkeley, 1946; JD, Harvard U., 1949. Bar: Calif., 1949, U.S. Supreme Ct., 1962. Draftsman, title examiner Calif. Pacific Title Co., Redwood City, 1936-38, 39-46; law sec. to Judge Clifton Mathews U.S. Circuit Ct., San Francisco, 1949-50; ptnr. Thelen, Marrin, Johnson and Bridges, San Francisco, 1950-88, of counsel, 1989-93. Instr. San Francisco Law Sch., 1949-53, lectr. U. Calif. Bus. Sch.

Extension, 1965-72, Golden Gate U., San Francisco, 1973-75; lectr., author Fed. Publs., Washington, 1978-89; judge pro tem Mcpl. Ct., San Francisco, 1980-97; chmn. 22 dispute review bds. Caltrans, 1996—; mem. Dispute Rev. Bd. Found. Contbg. author to handbooks on constrn. practices. Bd. dirs. Legal Aid Soc., San Francisco, 1952-88, Camron-Stanford House Preservation Assn., 1992-94; mem. Calif. Pub. Works Contract Arbitration Com., panel of arbitrators. Capt. U.S. Army, 1942-46, PTO, lt. col. USAR, 1946-62; ret. Mem. ABA, FBA, Calif. Bar Assn., San Francisco Bar Assn., Coutra Costa County Bar Assn., Am. Arbitration Assn. (nat. panel arbitrators, nat. panel mediators, panel Large Complex Case Program-Constrn., Disting. Svc. award for outstanding contbn. in area of comml. disputes 1990), Soc. Profls. in Dispute Resolution, Calif. Dispute Resolution Coun., Assoc. Gen. Contractors Calif. (Assocs. Achievement award 1992, legal adv. com. lifetime achievement award 1999). Home and Office: 1200 Rockledge Ln Apt 3 Walnut Creek CA 94595-2877 Fax: 925-280-0601

DEBERRY, FISHER, college football coach; b. Cheraw, S.C., June 9, 1938; m. LuAnn DeBerry; children: Joe, Michelle BA, Wofford Coll., 1960. Coach, tchr. high schs., S.C., 6 yrs.; asst. football coach Wofford Coll., Spartanburg, 2 yrs., Appalachian State Coll., Boone, N.C., 9 yrs.; quarterbacks coach Air Force Acad., USAF Acad., Colo., 1980-81, offensive coord., 1981-83, head football coach, 1984—. Led teams in Ind. Bowl, 1984, Blue Bonnnet Bowl, 1985, Freedom Bowl, 1987, Liberty Bowl, 1989-92, Copper Bowl, 1995, Las Vegas Bowl, 1997. Motivational spkr. to religious and corp. groups; fund raiser Easter Seals, March of Dimes, Salvation Army; chmn. Am. Heart Assn. Named Western Athletic Conf. Coach of Yr., 1985, 95, Nat. Coach of Yr., 1985. Mem. Fellowship Christian Athletes. Office: Hdqs USAF Acad 2304 Cadet Dr Ste 200 U S A F Academy CO 80840-5099

DE BOER, JEFFREY B. auto dealership executive; Degree cum laude, Pomona Coll., 1988; MBA in Fin. and Investment Mgmt., London Bus. Sch., 1994. Internat. credit officer Fuki Bank Ltd., Tokyo, 1988-92; equity analyst, sector fund mgr. Fidelity Investments Japan, 1994-97; v.p. fin. and investor rels. Lithia Motors, Inc., Medford, Oreg., 1997-2000, sr. v.p., CFO, 2000—. Office: Lithia Motors Inc 360 E Jackson St Medford OR 97501

DE BOER, SYDNEY B. auto dealership executive; Student, Stanford U. Chmn., CEO Lithia Motors Inc., Medford, Oreg., 1968—. Office: Lithia Motors Inc 360 E Jackson St Medford OR 97501

DEBREU, GERARD, economics and mathematics educator; b. Calais, France, July 4, 1921; came to U.S., 1950, naturalized, 1975; s. Camille and Fernande (Decharne) D.; m. Françoise Bled, June 14, 1945; children: Chantal, Florence. Student, Ecole Normale Supérieure, Paris, 1941-44, Agrégé de l'Université, France, 1946; DSc, U. Paris, 1956; Dr. Rerum Politicarum honoris causa, U. Bonn, 1977; D. Scis. Economiques (hon.), U. Lausanne, 1980; DSc (hon.), Northwestern U., 1981; Dr. honoris causa, U. des Scis. Sociales de Toulouse, 1983, Yale U., 1987, U. Bordeaux I, 1988. Rsch. assoc. Centre Nat. De La Recherche Sci., Paris, 1946-48; Rockefeller fellow U.S., Sweden and Norway, 1948-50; rsch. assoc. Cowles Commn., U. Chgo., 1950-55; assoc. prof. econs. Cowles Found., Yale, 1955-61; fellow Ctr. Advanced Study Behavioral Scis., Stanford U., 1960-61; vis. prof. econs. Yale U., fall 1961; prof. emeritus U. Calif., Berkeley, 1962—, prof. Miller Inst. Basic Rsch. in Sci., 1973-74, prof. math., 1975—, prof. emeritus, 1985—. Guggenheim fellow, vis. prof. Ctr. Ops. Rsch. and Econometrics, U. Louvain, 1968-69, vis. prof., 1971, 72, 88; Erskine fellow U. Canterbury, Christchurch, New Zealand, 1969, 87, vis. prof., 1973, Overseas fellow Churchill Coll., Cambridge, Eng., 1972; Plenary address Internat. Congress Mathematicians, Vancouver, 1974; vis. prof. Cowles Found. for Rsch. in Econs., Yale U., 1976; vis. prof. U. Bonn, 1977; rsch. assoc. Cepremap, Paris, 1980; faculty rsch. lectr. U. Calif., Berkeley, 1984-85, univ. prof., 1985—, Class of 1958 Chair, 1986—; vis. prof. U. Sydney, Australia, 1987; lectr. in field. Author: Theory of Value, 1959, Mathematical Economics: Twenty Papers of Gerard Debreu, 1983; assoc. editor Internat. Econ. Rev., 1959-69; mem. editorial bd. Jours. Econ. Theory, 1972—, SIAM Jours. on Applied Math., 1976-79, Jours. of Complexity, 1985—, Games and Econ. Behavior, 1989—, Econ. Theory, 1991; mem. adv. bd. Jours. Math. Econs., 1974—; correspondent Math. Intelligencer, 1983-84. Served with French Army, 1944-45. Decorated Chevalier de la Légion d'Honneur, Commandeur de l'Ordre National du Mérite, Officier Le Légion d'Honneur; recipient Nobel Prize in Econ. Scis., 1983, Berkeley Citation, 1991; sr. U.S. Sci. awardee Alexander von Humboldt Found., 1977. Fellow AAAS, Econometric Soc. (mem. coun. 1964-72, 78-85, Fisher-Schultz lectr. 1969, exec. com. 1969-72, 80-82, pres. 1971), Am. Econ. Assn. (disting. fellow 1982, pres.-elect 1989, pres. 1990); mem. NAS (chmn. sect. econ. scis. 1982-85, com. human rights 1984-90, chair class V behavioral and social scis. 1989-92, mem. Coun. of NAS of USA 1993—), Am. Philos. Soc., French Acad. Scis. (fgn. assoc.), Berkeley Fellows.

DE BRIER, DONALD PAUL, lawyer; b. Atlantic City, Mar. 20, 1940; s. Daniel and Ethel de B.; m. Nancy Lee McElroy, Aug. 1, 1964; children: Lesley Anne, Rachel Wynne, Danielle Verne. B.A. in History, Princeton U., 1962; LL.B. with honors, U. Pa., 1967. Bar: N.Y. 1967, Tex. 1977, Utah 1983, Ohio 1987. Assoc. firm Sullivan & Cromwell, N.Y.C., 1967-70, Patterson, Belknap, Webb & Tyler, N.Y.C., 1970-76; v.p., gen. counsel, dir. Gulf Resources & Chem. Corp., Houston, 1976-82; v.p. law Kennecott Corp. (former subs. BP America Inc.), Salt Lake City, 1983-89; assoc. gen. counsel BP America Inc., Cleve., 1987-89; gen. counsel BP Exploration Co. Ltd., London, 1989-93; exec. v.p., gen. counsel Occidental Petroleum Corp., L.A., 1993—. Bd. dirs. L.A. Philharm., 1995—. Served to lt. USNR, 1962-64. Mem. Calif. Club, Riviera Tennis Club. Home: 699 Amalfi Dr Pacific Palisades CA 90272-4507 Office: Occidental Petroleum Corp 10889 Wilshire Blvd Los Angeles CA 90024-4201

DEBRO, JULIUS, university dean, sociology educator; b. Jackson, Miss., Sept. 25, 1931; s. Joseph and Seleana (Gaylor) D.; m. Darlene Conley. B.A. in Polit. Sci., U. San Francisco, 1953; M.A. in Sociology, San Jose State U., 1967; Ph.D., U. Calif.-Berkeley, 1975. Research asst. U. Calif. Sch. Criminology, Berkeley, 1964-68; instr. dept. sociology Laney Coll., Alameda, Calif., 1968-69, Alameda Coll., Oakland, 1971, U. Md., College Park, 1971-72, asst. prof. Inst. for Criminal Justice and Criminology, 1972-79; mem. faculty Atlanta U., 1979-91, prof. criminal justice, 1979-91, chmn. dept. pub. adminstrn., 1979-80, chmn. dept. Criminal Justice Inst., 1979-89, chmn. dept. sociology, 1985-86; assoc. dean Grad. Sch., acting asst. provost U. Wash., Seattle, 1991—, affiliate prof. society and justice program, 1991—. Mem. adv. bd. dirs. Criminal Justice Rev., 1977-87; prin. investigator Joint Commn. on Criminology and Criminal Justice Edn. and Standards, 1978-79; v.p. Atlanta Met. Crime Commn., 1986, pres., 1987; mem. investigative bd. Ga. Bar Assn., 1987; editor Blacks in Criminal Justice quar. news mag., 1987—. Assoc. editor Criminal Justice Quar., 1989—. Chmn. program evaluation com. Boys and Girls Home, Montgomery County, Md., 1979; bd. dirs. YMCA, Bethesda, Md., 1979, Totem Coun. Girl Scouts. Served to col. USAR, 1953-84. NIMH fellow, 1969-70; Ford fellow, 1971; grantee NIMH, 1974, Law Enforcement Assistance Adminstrn., 1979-81; postdoctoral rsch. assoc. Narcotic and Drug Rsch. Inc., N.Y.C., 1989-90; Inter-Univ. Seminar on Armed Forces and Soc. fellow, 1989; Western Soc. Criminology fellow, 1989; recipient Herbert Bloch award for Outstanding Svcs. to Criminal Justice Criminology, svc. to Am. Soc. Criminology. Fellow Narcotic Drug Rsch.; mem. NAACP, Nat. Assn. Blacks in Criminal Justice (editor quar. news mag. 1987—), Nat. Assn. Black Sociologists, Am. Sociol. Assn., Acad. Criminal Justice Sci., Urban League, Rotary, Alpha Phi Alpha, Sigma Pi Phi (boule Alpha Omicron chpt.). Democrat Office: U Wash 107 Gowen Box 353530 Seattle WA 98195-0001 E-mail: jdebro@u.washington.edu

DE BRUYCKER, LLOYD HENRY, rancher, feedlot operator; b. Great Falls, Mont., Dec. 1, 1933; s. Achiel Henry and Rose Presperine (Emperor) De B.; m. Jane Crystal, July 2, 1954; 7 children. Grad. high sch., Dutton, Mont. Grain elevator laborer, 1954-59; rancher, 1959—. Avocation: thoroughbred horses. Home: Box 7700 Dutton MT 59433 Office: North Mt Feeders Inc PO Box 218 Choteau MT 59422-0218

DEBUS, ELEANOR VIOLA, retired business management company executive; b. Buffalo, May 19, 1920; d. Arthur Adam and Viola Charlotte (Pohl) D. Student, Chown Bus. Sch., 1939. Sec. Buffalo Wire Works, 1939-45; home talent prodr. Empire Producing Co., Kansas City, Mo.; sec. Owens Corning Fiberglass Buffalo; pub. rels. and publicity Niagara Falls Theatre, Ont., Can.; pub. rels. dir. Woman's Internat. Bowling Congress, Columbus, Ohio, 1957-59; publicist, sec. Ice Capades, Hollywood, Calif., 1961-63; sec. to contr. Rexall Drug Co., L.A., 1963-67; bus. mgmt. acct. Samuel Berke & Co., Beverly Hills, Calif., 1967-75, Gadbois Mgmt. Co., Beverly Hills, 1975-76; sec., treas. Sasha Corp., L.A., 1976-92; former bus. mgr. Dean Martin, Eleanor Powell, Debbie Reynolds, Shirly MacLaine. Contbr. articles to various mags. Mem. Am. Film Inst. Republican.

DECARIA, KEN, state legislator, educator; b. Ogden, Utah, Nov. 5, 1953; married. BS in Biology, U. Utah. Mem. Wyo. Ho. Reps., Cheyenne, 1996-98, Wyo. Senate, Dist. 15, Cheyenne, 1998—; mem. edn. com. Wyo. Senate, Cheyenne; mem. transp. and hwys. com. Wyo. State Senate, Cheyenne. Democrat. Home: 202 Broken Circle Dr Evanston WY 82930-4746 Office: Wyo Senate State Capitol Cheyenne WY 82002-0001 E-mail: kDecaria@senate.wyoming.com

DE CASTRO, HUGO DANIEL, lawyer; b. Panama City, Panama, Sept. 12, 1935; came to U.S., 1947; s. Mauricio Fidanque and Armida Rebecca (Salas) de C.; m. Isabel Shapiro, July 25, 1958; children: Susan M., Teresa A., Andrea L., Michele L. BSBA in Econs. cum laude, UCLA, 1957, JD summa cum laude, 1960. Bar: Calif. 1961; CPA, Calif. Prin. de Castro, West, Chodorow, Glickfeld & Nass Inc., L.A., 1961—. Lectr. UCLA, 1962-67, 68, counsel to dean Law Sch., 1963—; commr. tax adv. com. State Bar Calif. Editor UCLA Law Rev., 1959-60, Taxation for Lawyers, 1971-88; contbr. articles to profl. jours. Trustee Stephen S. Wise Temple, Jewish Fedn. Cmty. Found.; trustee, bd. dirs., chmn. fin. com. UCLA Found.; bd. dirs. Western L.A. Found., Hebrew Union Coll.; bd. govs. Trustee Endowment Trusts. Mem. ABA 9chmn. taxation subcom.), ACLU, L.A. County Bar Assn., Beverly Hills Bar Assn. (bd. dirs. Law Found.), L.A. C. of C. (former chmn., dir.), L.A. World Affairs coun., Am. Jewish Com., Del Rey Yacht Club (Calif., former dir., officer), Founders of Music Ctr., Las Hadas Country Club (Mex.), Pi Lambda Phi. Office: de Castro West Chodorow et al 10960 Wilshire Blvd Ste 1400 Los Angeles CA 90024-3702

DECATUR, RAYLENE, museum administrator; Pres., CEO Denver Mus. of Nature & Sci. (formerly Denver Mus. of Natural History), 1995—. Office: Denver Mus of Nature & Sci 2001 Colorado Blvd Denver CO 80205-5732

DECCIO, ALEXANDER A. state legislator; b. Walla Walla, Oct. 28, 1921; m. Lucille Deccio; 7 children. Mem. Wash. Senate, Dist. 14, Olympia, 1974—; Rep. whip Wash. Senate; mem. health and long-term care com. Wash. Legislature, Olympia, mem. legis. oversight com. on Seahawks Stadium, mem. Gov.'s Commn. on Early Childhood Edn. com. Bd. dirs. Providence Med. Ctr., Yakima Neighborhood Health Svcs., Yakima Vis. and Conv. Bur. Recipient 100 Percent Voting Record award Wash. State Farm Bur. Republican. Office: 407 Legislative Bldg Olympia WA 98504-0001

DE CHERNEY, ALAN HERSH, obstetrics and gynecology educator; b. Phila., Feb. 13, 1942; s. William Aaron and Ruth (Hersh) DeC.; m. Deanna Faith Saver, June 26, 1966; children: Peter, Alexander, Nicholas. BS in Natural Scis., Muhlenberg Coll., 1963; MD, Temple U., 1967; MA (hon.), Yale U., 1985. Diplomate Am. Bd. Ob.-Gyn. (examiner 1984—, bd. dirs. 1995—), Am.Bd. Reproductive Endocrinology (bd. dirs. 1988-94), Nat. Bd. Med. Examiners (examiner 1987-90). Intern in gen. medicine U. Pitts., 1967-68; resident in ob-gyn. U. Pa., Phila., 1968-72, instr. dept. ob-gyn, 1970-72; asst. prof. ob-gyn. Yale U. Sch. Medicine, New Haven, 1974-78, assoc. prof., 1979-84, prof., 1984-91, John Slade Ely prof. ob-gyn, 1987-92, dir. div. reproductive endocrinology, dept. ob-gyn, 1982-92, lectr. dept. biology, 1985-92; Louis E. Phaneuf prof., chmn. dept. ob-gyn. Tufts U. Sch. Medicine, 1992-96; prof., chmn. dept. ob-gyn. UCLA, 1996—. Maj. U.S. Army, 1972-74. Recipient Disting. Alumni award Temple U., 1989, Muhlenberg Coll., 1994. Fellow ACOG, Am. Fertility Soc. (pres. 1994-95), Am. Assn. History of Medicine, Soc. for Assisted Reproductive Tech. (pres. 1987-88), Soc. Reproductive Endocrinologists (pres. 1988), Soc. Reproductive Surgeons (charter, pres. 1991), Endocrine Soc., European Soc. Human Reproductions and Embryology, Soc. Gynecologic Surgeons, Soc. for Study of Reproduction, Soc. Gynecologic Investigation (pres. 1994-95). Office: UCLA Sch Medicine Dept Ob/Gyn 27-117 CHS Mail Code 174017 10833 Le Conte Ave Los Angeles CA 90095-3075

DECIL, STELLA WALTERS (DEL DECIL), artist; b. Indpls., Apr. 26, 1921; d. William Calvin and Hazel Jean (Konkle) Smith; m. John W. Walters, June 19, 1940 (div. Sept. 1945); m. Casimir R. Decil, Feb. 6, 1965. Grad., Indpls. Acad. Comml. Art, 1939, John Heron Art Inst., Indpls., 1941. Staff artist William H. Block Co., Indpls., 1945-50, art dir., 1952-62, Frank R. Jelleff Co., Washington, 1950-51, Diamonds Dept. Stores, Phoenix, 1962-67; freelance artist Phoenix, Chgo., others, 1967-70. Curator Mature Eye bi-ann. Prescott (Ariz.) Fine Arts Assn., 1996-2000; instr., lectr. Mountain Artists Guild, Prescott, 1995-97; mem. visual arts bd. Prescott Fine Arts Assn., 1990-2000; painting instr. Art Groups in Ariz.-N.Mex., 1970—, Phoenix Art Mus., 1975-77. Exhibited work in galleries in Phoenix, Scottsdale, Ariz., Las Cruces, N.Mex., Hoosier Salon, Folger Gallery, Indpls., Mammen II Gallery and Garelick Gallery, Scottsdale, Ariz.; 1-woman exhibits include Cave Creek, Carefree, Scottsdale, Ariz., N.Mex.; represented in pvt. collections in more than 20 states; in corp. collections including Continental Bank, Humana Hosp., Pueblo Grande Mus., VA Med. Ctr., Prescott, Mayo Ctr. for Women's Health, Scottsdale, Proctor Bank Vt., Bank of Rio Grande, Las Cruces, N.Mex. Past pres. Scottsdale Art League. Recipient Maxine Cherrington Meml. award Hoosier Salon, 1973; named Ad Woman of Yr., Indpls. Ad Club, 1958. Mem. No. Ariz. Watercolor Soc., Royal Scorpion Status, Ariz. Artists Guild, Ariz. Watercolor Assn. (past pres.). Home: 9460 E Towago Dr Prescott Valley AZ 86314-7140

DECIUTIIS, ALFRED CHARLES MARIA, medical oncologist, television producer; b. N.Y.C., Oct. 16, 1945; s. Alfred Ralph and Theresa Elizabeth (Manko) de C.; m. Catherine L. Gohn. B.S. summa cum laude, Fordham U., 1967; M.D., Columbia U., 1971. Diplomate Am. Bd. Internal Medicine, Am. Bd. Med. Oncology. Intern N.Y. Hosp.-Cornell Med. Ctr., N.Y.C., 1971-72, resident, 1972-74; fellow in clin. immunology Meml. Hosp.-Sloan Kettering Cancer Ctr., N.Y.C., 1974-75, fellow in clin. oncology, 1975-76, spl. fellow in immunology, 1974-76; guest investigator, asst. physician exptl. hematology Rockefeller U., N.Y.C., 1975-76; practice medicine, specializing in med. oncology Los Angeles, 1977—. Host cable TV shows, 1981—; med. editor Cable Health Network, 1983—, Lifetime Network, 1984—; mem. med. adv. com. 1984 Olympics; co-founder Meditrina Med. Ctr., free out-patient surg. ctr., Torrance, Calif., physician asst. supr., 1984; mem. fgn. policy leadership project Ctr. for Internat. Affairs, Harvard, Ill. Syndicated columnist Coast Media News, 1980's; producer numerous med. TV shows; contbr. articles to profl. jours.; author first comprehensive clin. description of chronic fatique syndrome as a neuro-immunologic acquired disorder. Founder Italian-Am. Med. Assn., 1982; co-founder Italian-Am. Legal Alliance, L.A., 1982—; mem. gov. bd. med. coun. Italian-Am. Found.; mem. Italian-Am. Civic Com., L.A., 1983, UCLA Chancellor's Assocs., Cath. League for Civil and Rel. Liberty, World Affairs Coun., L.A., Boston Mus. Fine Arts, Met. Mus. Served to capt. M.C., U.S. Army, 1972-74. Leukemia Soc. Am. fellow, 1974-76. Fellow ACP, Internat. Coll. Physicians and Surgeons; mem. AMA (Physician's Recognition award 1978-80, 82-85, 86-89, 89-91, 91-94, 94-96, 96—), Am. Soc. Clin. Oncology, N.Y. Acad. Sci. (life), Calif. Med. Assn., Los Angeles County Med. Assn., AAAS, Am. Union Physicians and Dentists, Internat. Health Soc., Am. Pub. Health Assn., Am. Geriatrics Soc., Chinese Med. Assn., Drug Info. Assn., Nat. Geographic Soc. (life), Internat. Platform Assn., Am. Soc. Hematology (emeritus), N.Y. Acad. Scis. (life), Fondazione Giovanni Agnelli, Smithsonian Instn., Nature Conservancy, Nat. Wildlife Fedn., Mensa, Phi Beta Kappa, Alpha Omega Alpha, Sigma Xi. Office: PO Box 384 Agoura Hills CA 91376-0384

DECKER, PETER RANDOLPH, rancher, former state official; b. N.Y.C., Oct. 1, 1934; s. Frank Randolph and Marjorie (Marony) D.; m. Dorothy Morss, Sept. 24, 1972; children: Karen, Christopher, Hilary. BA, Middlebury Coll., Vt., 1957; MA, Syracuse U., 1961; PhD, Columbia U., 1974. Tchr. Cate Sch., Carpinteria, Calif., 1961-63; sr. writer Congl. Quar., Washington, 1963-64; asst. to pres. Middlebury (Vt.) Coll., 1964-67; staff asst. Sen. Robert Kennedy, Washington, 1967-68; corr. AP, Laos, Vietnam, 1970; instr./lectr. Columbia U., N.Y.C., 1972-74; asst. prof. Duke U., Durham, N.C., 1974-80; owner, operator Double D Ranches, Ridgway, Colo., 1980—; commr. agr. State of Colo., Denver, 1987-89; pres. Decker & Assocs., Denver, 1989—. Dir. Inst. Am. West, Nat. Western Stock Show, Denver; bd. dirs. Fed. Res. Bd. Kansas City, Denver, 1992-98; bd. dirs. Western Colo. Bank, Montrose; pres. Telluride Bancorp, Inc., 1990-97. Author: Fortunes and Failures, 1978, Old Fences, New Neighbors, 1998; contbr. articles to profl. jours. and mags. Overseer Middlebury Coll., 1988—, Colo. Commn. on Higher Edn., 1985-93; chmn. Ouray County Dem. Party, 1982-85; chmn. Ouray County Planning Commn., 1981-85; chmn. Colo. Endowment Humanities, 1982-85. Lt. U.S. Army, 1957-60, capt. Res., 1960-67. English Speaking Union scholar, 1952-53; Nat. Endowment for Humanities fellow Yale U., 1977-78, Rockefeller Found. fellow, 1979-80. Mem. Nat. Cattlemen's Assn., Colo. Livestock Assn., Denver Athletic Club, Elks, Colo. Author's League, Angler's Club (Key Largo, Fla.), Columbia U. Club (N.Y.C). Democrat. Home: Double D Ranch 395 Race St Denver CO 80206-4118

DECKER, RICHARD JEFFREY, lawyer; b. Manhasset, N.Y., Aug. 26, 1959; s. Alan B. and Shelley T. (Belkin) D.; m. Carrie Ann Gordon, Aug. 13, 1989. BA, Union Coll., Schenectady, N.Y., 1981; JD, Boston U., 1984. Bar: N.Y. 1985, Calif. 1985, Mass. 1985, U.S. Dist. Ct. (cen. dist.) Calif. 1985. Assoc. Turner, Gesterfeld, Wilk & Tigerman, Beverly Hills, Calif., 1985-86, Shapiro, Posell & Close, L.A., 1986-90, Katten, Muchin, Zavis & Weitzman, L.A., 1990-93; of counsel Ginsburg, Stephan, Oringher & Richman, L.A., 1993—. Mem. Los Angeles County Bar Assn., Beverly Hills Bar Assn., Century City Bar Assn. Avocations: sports, guitar playing, travel, reading. Office: 2029 Century Park E Ste 600 Los Angeles CA 90067-2907

DECKERT, RYAN P. state senator; b. Corpus Christi, Tex., Mar. 17, 1971; m. Inga Deckert. BA, U. Oreg., 1993. Legis. aide State Senator Bob Shoemaker, 1992-93; congl. aide Congressman Les AuCoin, 1993; Washington County coord. Gov. John Kitzhaber, 1994; employment counselor, 1995-96; devel. dir. Assn. Retarded Citizens, 1997-98, Hewlett Packard, Innovators in Edn., 1999-2000; Dem. rep. dist. 8 Oreg. Ho. of Reps., 1996-2000; Dem. senator dist. 4 Oreg. State Senate, 2000—. Mem. edn., gen. govt. and rules and elections coms. Oreg. Ho. of Reps., bus. labor and econ. develop., natural resources, agr., salmon, and water coms. Youth dir. Living Enrichment Ctr.; mem. bd. dirs. Portland Habitat for Humanity; mem. Garden Home Citizen Participation Orgn., Oreg. Disabilities Commn., Washington County Dem. Party; vol. SMART; mem. adv. bd. Portland Art Mus. Mem. Beaverton C. of C., Friars Honor Soc. Office: PO Box 2247 Beaverton OR 97075 also: Oreg State Senate S-314 State Capitol Salem OR 97301 E-mail: deckert.sen@state.or.us

DE CONCINI, DENNIS, lawyer, former senator, consultant; b. Tucson, May 8, 1937; s. Evo and Ora (Webster) DeC.; children: Denise, Christina, Patrick Evo. BA, U. Ariz., 1959, LLB, 1963. Bar: Ariz. 1963, D.C. 1963. Mem. firm Evo DeConcini; ptnr. DeConcini & McDonald, Tucson, 1968-73; dep. Pima County atty. Sch. Dist. 1, 1971-72, county atty., 1972-76; U.S. Senator from Ariz., 1977-95; atty. Perry-Romani Assocs., Washington, 1995—; ptnr. De Concini, McDonald, Yetwin & Lacy, Tuscon, 1995—, now ptnr. Washington. Mem. appropriations com., U.S. Senate, chmn. subcom. on Treasury, Postal Svc. and Gen. Govt.; mem. subcom. on Def., subcom. on Energy and Water Devel., subcom. on Fgn. Ops., subcom. on Interior Related Agys.; mem. Jud. com.; chmn. subcom. on Patents, Copyrights and Trademarks; mem. subcom. on Antitrust, Monopolies and Bus. Rights, subcom. on the Constitution, com. on Rules and Adminstrn., com. on Vets. Affairs; chmn. select com. on Intelligence; chmn. Commn. on Security and Cooperation in Europe; select com. Indian Affairs; mem. Internat. Narcotics Control Caucus, West Coalition of Senators; former pres., bd. dirs. Shopping Ctrs., Inc.; bd. dirs. Fed. Home Mortgage Corp., Schuff Steel. Chmn. legis. com. Tucson Dem. Cmty. Coun., 1966-67; mem. major gifts com., devel. fund drive St. Joseph's Hosp., 1970, mem. devel. coun., 1971-73; bd. dirs. Nat. Ctr. for Missing and Exploited Children, 1995—; mem. major gifts com. Tucson Mus. and Art Ctr. Bldg. Fund, 1971; adminstr. Ariz. Drug Control Dist., 1975-76; precinct committeeman Ariz. Dem. Ctrl. Com., 1958—; mem. Pima County Dem. Ctrl. Com., 1958-67, Dem. State Exec. Com., 1958-68; state vice chmn. Ariz. Dem. Com., 1964-66, 70-72; vice chmn. Pima County Dem. Com., 1970-73. Served to 2d lt. JAG U.S. Army, 1959-60. Named Outstanding Ariz. County Atty., 1975 Mem. ABA, NAACP, Nat. Dist. Attys. Assn., Am. Judicature Soc., Ariz. Bar Assn., D.C. Bar Assn., Ariz. Sheriffs and County Attys. Assn., Ariz. Pioneer Hist. Soc., Pima County Bar Assn., U. Ariz. Alumni Assn., Pres.'s Club, Tucson Fraternal Order Police, Phi Delta Theta, Delta Sigma Rho, Phi Alpha Delta. Roman Catholic. Office: 233 Constitution Ave NE Washington DC 20002-7307 also: 2025 N 3rd St Ste 230 Phoenix AZ 85004-1472

DE CORDOVA, FREDERICK TIMMINS, television producer, director; b. N.Y.C., Oct. 27, 1910; s. George and Margaret (Timmins) de C.; m. Janet Thomas, Nov. 27, 1963. B.S., Northwestern U., 1931. Author: (autobiography) Johnny Came Lately, 1988; prodr.-dir. Warner Bros. Pictures, 1943-48, Universal Internat. Pictures, 1948-53, CBS and NBC, 1953; prodns. include Tonight Show, 1970-97 (Emmy award NATAS 1963, 68, 76, 79, 92), prodr.-dir. Burns and Allen Show, Jack Benny Program, My Three Sons. Mem. Bel Air Country Club (L.A.) Home: 1875 Carla Rdg Beverly Hills CA 90210-1936 Office: Nbc Burbank CA 91523-0001

DEDEAUX, PAUL J. orthodontist; b. Pass Christian, Miss., Feb. 22, 1937; s. Mack and Harriet D.; m. Janet Louise Harter, June 29, 1971; children: Michele, Kristen, Kelly. BA, Dillard U., 1959; DDS, Howard U., 1963; MS, Fairleigh Dickinson U., 1975. Pvt. practice, Washington, 1976-93, Santa Ana, Calif., 1976-93; instr. Howard U., Washington,

1967-69; dental dir. Dr. Martin Luther King Health Ctr., Bronx, N.Y., 1969-70, dentist, 1970-76; chief dentist Calipatria State Prison, Calif., 1993-96, Calif. Med. Facility, Vacaville, 1996—. Instr. Howard U., Washington, 1967-69; cons. Hostos C.C., Bronx, 1971-76; mem. adv. panel Dental Econs. mag., 1976; adj. assoc. prof. Columbia U., N.Y.C., 1970-72. Contbr. articles to profl. jours. Capt. U.S. Army, 1963-67, USAR, 1975—, col., 1985—, comdr., 1994-97, ret. 1997. Mem. Am. Assn. Orthodontists, Pacific Coast Soc. Orthodontists, ADA, Calif. Dental Assn., Assn. Mil. Surgeons of U.S. Democrat. Methodist. Avocations: photography, fishing. Home: 940 Celestine Cir Vacaville CA 95687-7853 Office: Calif Med Facility PO Box 2000 1600 California Dr Vacaville CA 95687

DEDERER, MICHAEL EUGENE, public relations company executive; b. Seattle, Apr. 30, 1932; s. Michael and Clare (Collon) D.; separated; children— David M., Claire M. B.A. in Journalism, U. Wash., 1953. Account exec. Hugh A. Smith Mktg. & Pub. Relations Co., Seattle, 1956-59; account exec. Kraft, Smith & Ehrig, Inc., Seattle, 1959-63, Jay Rockey Pub. Relations and The Rockey Co., Inc., Seattle, 1963, v.p., 1970-78, exec. v.p., 1978-86, pres., 1986-94; vice chmn. The Rockey Co., Inc., Seattle, 1994-98, sr. cons., 1998—. Served to 1st lt. U.S. Army, 1953-55. Mem. Pub. Rels. Soc. Am. (pres. Wash. chpt. 1970). Roman Catholic. Avocations: Alpine skiing; fly fishing. Office: Rockey Co Inc 2121 5th Ave Seattle WA 98121-2596

DEENY, ROBERT JOSEPH, lawyer; b. Cedar Rapids, Iowa, Jan. 8, 1941; s. Myles C. and Betty S. (Schissel) D. BA, Ariz. State U., 1963; JD, Cath. U., Washington, 1970. Bar: Ariz. 1971, U.S. Dist. Ct. (D.C. cir.) 1971, D.C. 1978, U.S. Supreme Ct. 1978, U.S. Ct. Appeals (9th cir) 1980. Field examiner NLRB, Phoenix, 1964-67, exec. asst. to chief adminstrv. judge Washington, 1967-70, field atty. Phoenix, 1970-72; with Shimmel Hill, Phoenix, 1972-79, Snell & Wilmer, Phoenix, 1979-99, Gallagher & Kennedy, Phoenix, 1999—. With USMCR, 1960-63. Mem. ABA, Ariz. State Bar, S.C. Bar Assn., Maricopa County Bar, Phoenix Country Club. Office: Gallagher & Kennedy 2575 E Camelback Rd Phoenix AZ 85016-4240

DEERING, THOMAS PHILLIPS, lawyer; b. Winfield, Kans., Feb. 15, 1929; s. Frederick Arthur and Lucile (Phillips) D.; m. Marilyn Marie Anderson, Sept. 6, 1952; children: Thomas P. Jr., Robert E., Paul A. BS, U. Colo., 1951, LLB, 1956. Bar: Oreg. 1956, Colo. 1956, U.S. Dist. Ct. Oreg. 1956. Assoc. Hart Spencer McCulloch Rockwood & Davies (now Stoel Rives), Portland, Oreg., 1956-62; ptnr. Stoel Rives LLP, Portland, 1962—. Active Western Pension & Benefits Conf., 1989—; mem. faculty Am. Law Inst.-ABA, 1985-96. Co-author: Tax Reform Act of 1986, 1987. Bd. dirs. Girl Scouts Columbia River Coun., Portland, 1961-70; trustee, moderator First Unitarian Ch., Portland, 1967-70; trustee, pres. Catlin Gabel Sch., Portland, 1970-76; bd. dirs., v.p. ACLU, Portland, 1966-71, 73-80; chmn. Multnomah County Task Force on Edgefield Manor, Portland, 1972-75; bd. dirs., treas. Portland Art Mus., Contemporary Arts Coun., 1986-88; mem. City County Task Fore on Svc. Evaluation, Portland, 1982-85, Citizen's Adv. Com. West Side Corridor Project, Portland, 1988-93; bd. govs. Pacific N.W. Coll. Art, 1991-2000, chair, 1996-2000; mem. collections com. Portland Art Mus., 1992-96; trustee Oreg. Coll. Art and Craft Endowment, Portland, 1991-97. With U.S. Army, 1952-54. Recipient Disting. Mem. award Western Pension & Benefits Conf., 1999. Fellow Am. Coll. Tax Coun., Am Coll. Benefits Counsel (emeritus); mem. ABA (tax sect., EB com. 1989-2000), City Club Portland (bd. govs. 2000—). Democrat. Avocations: hiking, skiing, sailing, reading. Home: 5235 SW Burton Dr Portland OR 97221-2517 Office: Stoel Rives LLP 900 SW 5th Ave Ste 2600 Portland OR 97204-1268 E-mail: tpdeering@stoel.com, tomdeering@home.com

DEERNOSE, KITTY, curator; b. Crow Agency, Mont., Apr. 14, 1956; AA in Mus. Studies, Inst. Am. Indian Arts, Santa Fe, 1985. Mus. intern Heard Mus. Anthropology and Primitive Art, Phoenix, 1984; interpreter Little Bighorn Battlefield Nat. Monument, Crow Agency, Mont., 1985-90, mus. curator, 1990—. Mus. intern in Crow studies Smithsonian Instn., Washington, 1988. Recipient White Glove award Nat. Park Svc., 1995. Mem. Am. Assn. Muss., Am. Assn. State and Local History, Mountain Plains Mus. Assn., Smithsonian Nat. Mus. Am. Indian, Internal Coun. Museums. Office: Little Bighorn Battlefield Nat Monument PO Box 39 Crow Agency MT 59022-0039 E-mail: Kitty-Deernose@nps.gov

DEETS, DWAIN AARON, retired aerospace technology executive; b. Bell, Calif., Apr. 16, 1939; s. Kenneth Robert and Mildred Evelyn (Bergman) D.; m. Catherine Elizabeth Meister, June 18, 1961; children: Dennis Allen, Danelle Alaine. AB, Occidental Coll., 1961; MS in Physics, San Diego State U., 1964; ME, UCLA, 1978. Rsch. engr. Dryden Flight Rsch. Ctr. NASA, Edwards, Calif., 62-78, 79-85, hdqrs. liaison engr. Washington, 1978-79, mgr. Edwards, 1979-85; dir. rsch. engring. Dryden Flight Rsch. Ctr., Edwards, 1990-96, dir. aerospace projects, 1996-97, dir. flight rsch. R&T, 1997-99; hdqrs. mgr. flight rsch. NASA, Washington, 1988-89; ret., 1999. Chmn. Reusable Launch Vehicles Non-Advocate Rev., 1995-96. Contbr. articles to profl. jours. Recipient Exceptional Svc. medal NASA, 1988, Pres. Rank award SES, 1998. Fellow AIAA (assoc., Wright Bros. lectr. aeros. 1987); mem. Soc. Automotive Engrs. (chmn. aerospace control and guidance systems com. 1988 90), Toastmasters. Democrat. E-mail: dad2wrk@hughes.net

DEFAZIO, LYNETTE STEVENS, dancer, choreographer, educator, chiropractor, author, actress, musician; b. Berkeley, Calif., Sept. 29, 1930; d. Honore and Mabel J. (Estavan) Stevens; children: J.H. Panganiban, Joanna Pang. Student, U. Calif., Berkeley, 1950-55, San Francisco State Coll., , 1950-51; studied classical dance teaching techniques and vocabulary with Gisella Caccialanza and Harold and Lew Christensen, San Francisco Ballet, 1952-56; D in Chiropractic, Life-West Chiropractic Coll., San Lorenzo, Calif., 1983; cert. techniques of tchg., U. Calif., 1985; BA in Humanities, New Coll. Calif., 1986. Lic. chiropracter, Mich.; diplomate Nat. sci. Bd.; eminence in dance edn., Calif. C.C. dance specialist, std. svcs., childrens ctrs. credentials Calif. Dept. Edn., 1986. Contract child dancer Monogram Movie Studio, Hollywood, Calif., 1938-40; dance instr. San Francisco Ballet, 1953-65; performer San Francisco Opera Ring, 1960-67; performer, choreographer Oakland (Calif.) Civic Light Opera, 1963-70; dir. Ballet Arts Studio, Oakland, 1960; tchg. specialist Oakland Unified Sch. Dist., 1965-80; fgn. exch. dance dir. Academie de Danses-Salle Pleyel, Paris, 1966; instr. Peralta C.C. Dist., Oakland, 1971—, chmn. dance dept., 1985—. Cons., instr. ext. courses UCLA, Dirs. and Suprs. Assn., Pitts. Unified Sch. Dist., 1971-73, Tulare (Calif.) Sch. Dist., 1971-73; rschr. Ednl. Testing Svcs., HEW, Berkeley, 1974; resident choreographer San Francisco Childrens Opera, 1970—, Oakland Civic Theater; ballet mistress Dimensions Dance Theater, Oakland, 1977-80; cons. Gianchetta Sch. Dance, San Francisco, Robicheau Boston Ballet, TV series Patchwork Family, CBS, N.Y.C.; choreographer Ravel's Valses Nobles et Sentimentales, 1976. Author: Basic Music Outlines for Dance Classes, 1960, rev., 1968, Teaching Techniques and Choreography for Advanced Dancers, 1965, Basic Music Outlines for Dance Classes, 1965, Goals and Objectives in Improving Physical Capabilities, 1970, A Teacher's Guide for Ballet Techniques, 1970, Principle Procedures in Basic Curriculum, 1974, Objectives and Standards of Performance for Physical Development, 1975, Techniques of the Ballet School, 1970, rev., 1974, The Opera Ballets: A Choreographic Manual Vols. I-V, 1986; assoc. music arranger Le Ballet du Cirque, 1964; assoc. composer, lyricist The Ballet of Mother Goose, 1968; choreographer: Valses Nobles Et Sentimentales (Ravel), Transitions (Kashevaroff), 1991, The New Wizard of Oz, 1991, San Francisco Children's Opera (Gingold), Canon in D for Strings and Continuo (Pachelbel), 1979, Oakland Cmty. Orch. excerpts from Swan Lake, Faust, Sleeping Beauty, 1998, Rodeo, Alameda Coll. Cultural Affairs Program, 2000; solo dancer Three Stravinsky Etudes, Alameda Coll. Cultural Affairs Program, 1999; appeared in Flower Drum Song, 1993, Gigi, 1994, Fiddler on the Roof, 1996, The Music man, 1996, Sayonara, 1997, Bye, Bye Birdie, 2000, Barnum, the circus musical, 2001; violinst Oakland Cmty. Concert Orch., 1995—; condr. Gil Gleason. Bd. dirs. Prodrs. Assocs., Inc., Oakland, 1999—. Recipient Foremost Women of 20th Century, 1985, Merit award San Francisco Children's Opera, 1985, 90. Mem. Calif. State Tchrs. Assn., Bay Area Chiropractic Rsch. Soc., Profl. Dance Tchrs. Assn. Home and Office: 4923 Harbord Dr Oakland CA 94618-2506 E-mail: balletarts@bigplanet.com

DEFAZIO, PETER A. congressman; b. Needham, Mass., May 27, 1947; m. Myrnie Daut. BA in Econs. and Polit. Sci., Tufts U., 1969; postgrad., U. Oreg., 1969-71, MS in Pub. Adminstrn./Gerontology, 1977. Aide to U.S. Rep. Jim Weaver, 1977-82; sr. issues specialist, caseworker, dist. field office U.S. rep. Jim Weaver, 1977-78, legis. asst. Washington office, 1978-80, dir. constituent services, 1980-82; mem. commn. representing Springfield Lane County (Oreg.) Commn., 1982-86; mem. U.S. Congress from 4th Oreg. dist., Washington, 1987—; mem. resources com., water and power subcom.; mem. transp. and infrastructure com., ranking mem. water resources and environ. subcom. Mem. Lane County Econ. Devel. com., Intergovtl. Relations com.; bd. dirs. Eugene-Springfield Met. Partnership; Lane County Dem. precinct person, 1982—. Served with USAFR. Mem. Assn. of Oreg. Counties (legis. com.), Nat. Assn. of Counties (tax and fin. com.). Office: US Ho of Reps 2134 Rayburn Ho Office Bldg Washington DC 20515-0001*

DE FONVILLE, PAUL BLISS, monument and library administrator; b. Oakland, Calif., Mar. 3, 1923; s. Marion Yancey and Charlotte (Bliss) de F.; m. Virginia Harpell, June 17, 1967. Student, Calif. Poly. U., 1942-44, Michael Chekhov Group, 1947-52. Founder, pres. Cowboy Meml. and Libr., Caliente, Calif., 1969—; tchr. outdoor edn. Calif. State U., Bakersfield, 1980. Life mem. Presdl. Task Force, Washington, 1984—, Rep. Senatorial inner circle, Washington, 1989—, Nat. Rep. Congl. Com., Washington, 1990—, Rep. Nat. Com., 1987—, U.S. Senatorial Club, 1988—, Rep. Senatorial Commn., 1991, Presdl. Election Registry, 1992; del. Presdl. Trust, 1992; mem. Presdl. Commn. Am. Agenda; affiliate Lake Isabella Bd. Realtors, 1993; hon. marshall Lake Isabella, Kern County Christmas Parade, 1993. Recipient Slim Pickens award Calif. State Horsemen, 1980, Marshall-Working Western award Rose Parade, Pasadena, 1980, recognition Kern County, 1984, proclamations Mayor of Bakersfield, 1984, 85, Govt. of Calif., 1984, resolution Calif. Senate, 1988, Calif. Assembly, 1990, Presdl. Order of Merit, 1991, Congl. Cert. of Merit, 1992, Rep. Presdl. Legion of Merit award, 1992, Rep. Presdl. Legion of Merit award, 1992, document Gov. of Calif., 1993, Rep. Nat. Com. Cert. Recognition, 1992, Rep. Presdl. adv. Commn. Cert. award, 1993, Congl. Cert. Appreciation, 1993, Cert. Commendation Washington Legal Found., 1993, Rep. Presdl. award, 1994, Rep. Congl. Order of Liberty, 1993, Internat. Order of Merit medal, 1993, 20th Century award for achievement, 1993, Rep. Senatorial Medal of Freedom, 1994, Ronald Reagan Eternal Flame of Freedom medal and cert., 1995, Cmty. Svc. and Profl. Achievement medal, 1995, World Lifetime achievement award ABI-USA, 1996, Millennium medal of Freedom, 1999. Mem. SAG, NRA, Calif. State Horsemen (life), Equestrian Trails (life), Forty Niners (life), Calif. Rep. Assembly, Heritage Found., Cowboy Turtles Assn. (life), Rodeo Cowboys Assn. (life), Pro Rodeo Cowboys Assn. (life), Internat. Platform Assn., Lake Isabella C. of C., Kern County C. of C. Baptist. Avocations: heritage, horses, cowboys, mountain men, Indians. Home: 40371 Cowboy Ln Caliente CA 93518-1405

DE FRIES, JOHN CLARENCE, behavioral genetics educator, researcher; b. Delrey, Ill., Nov. 26, 1934; s. Walter C. and Irene Mary (Lyon) De F.; m. Marjorie Jacobs, Aug. 18, 1956; children: Craig Brian, Catherine Ann. BS, U. Ill., 1956, MS, 1958, PhD, 1961. Asst. prof. U. Ill., Urbana, 1961-66, assoc. prof., 1966-67; rsch. fellow U. Calif., Berkeley, 1963-64; assoc. prof. behavioral genetics and psychology U. Colo., Boulder, 1967-70, prof., 1970—, dir. Inst. for Behavioral Genetics, 1981-2001. Author: (with G.E. McClearn) Introduction to Behavioral Genetics, 1973, (with Plomin and McClearn) Behavioral Genetics: A Primer, 1980, 4th edit., 2001, (with R. Plomin) Origins of Individual Differences in Infancy, 1985; (with R. Plomin and D.W. Fulker) Nature and Nurture During Infancy and Early Childhood, 1988, Nature and Nurture During Middle Childhood, 1994; co-founder Behavior Genetics jour., 1970, mem. editl. adv. bd. 1st lt. U.S. Army, 1957-65. Grantee in field. Fellow AAAS (sect. J), Internat. Acad. for Rsch. in Learning Disabilities; mem. Am. Psychol. Soc., Am. Soc. Human Genetics, Behavior Genetics Assn. (sec. 1974-77, pres. 1982-83, Th. Dobzhansky award for outstanding rsch. in field 1992), Internat. Soc. for Study of Ind. Differences, Internat. Dyslexia Assn., Rodin Remediation Acad. and Found. Office: U Colo Inst Behavioral Genetics 447 UCB Boulder CO 80309-0447

DE GARCIA, LUCIA, marketing professional; b. Medellin, Colombia, June 26, 1942; came to the U.S., 1962; d. Enrique Giraldo Botero and Carolina (Vega) Estrada; m. Alvaro Garcia Osorio, July 30, 1962; children: Carolina Alexandra, Claudia Maria. BS, Nat. U., 1962. Engring. arch. designer VTN, Newport Beach, Calif., 1974-78; pres., CEO Elan Internat., Newport Beach, 1984—. Speaker, lectr. on success, protocol in bus. with Latin Am., free trade agreement between U.S. and Mexico. Editor: Elan mag., 1988-90. Trustee Nat. U., Calif., 1989-93; area campaign mgr. Bush for Pres., Orange County, Calif., 1988, Christopher Cox for Congress, 1988, Pete Wilson for Gov., 1990, People to Watch, 1994; bd. dirs. ARC, 1985-90, Am. Cancer Rsch. Ctr., 1986—; active South Coast Repertory Theater, 1982—. Named Dama de Distincion U.S./Mexico Found., 1991, Hispanic Woman of Yr. LULAC, 1986, One on the 10 Most Influential Women in Orange County, Orange County Metropolitan, 1994, One of the Hispanic 100 Most Influential in the U.S., Hispanics Bus. Mag., 1994; recipient Internat. award U.S. Hispanic C. of C., 1992, Mgr. of Yr. 2000 award Soc. Advancement of Mgmt. Mem. U.S./Mexico Found. (trustee 1990—), Latin Bus. Assn. (bd. dirs. 1992-93), World Trade Ctr. Assn. Republican. Roman Catholic. Avocations: travel, arts, hiking, walking on the beach. Home: 17532 Wayne Ave Irvine CA 92614-6658 Office: Elan Internat 620 Newport Center Dr Fl 11 Newport Beach CA 92660-6420

DEGENERES, ELLEN, actress, comedian; b. New Orleans, Jan. 26, 1958; TV appearances include: Duet, 1988-89, Open House, 1989, Laurie Hill, 1992, Ellen, 1994-98; films include Coneheads, 1993.

DE GETTE, DIANA LOUISE, congresswoman, lawyer; b. Tachikawa, Japan, July 29, 1957; came to U.S., 1957; d. Richard Louis and Patricia Anne (Rose) De G.; m. Lino Sigismondo Lipinsky de Orlov, Sept. 15, 1984; children: Raphaela Anne, Francesca Louise. BA magna cum laude, The Colo. Coll., 1979; JD, NYU, 1982. Bar: Colo. 1982, U.S. Dist. Ct. Colo. 1982, U.S. Ct. Appeals (10th cir.) 1984, U.S. Supreme Ct. 1989. Dep. state pub. defender Colo. State Pub. Defender, Denver, 1982-84; assoc. Coghill & Goodspeed, P.C., Denver, 1984-86; sole practice Denver, 1986-93; of counsel McDermott & Hansen, Denver, 1993-96; mem. Colo. Ho. of Reps., 1992-96, asst. minority leader, 1995-96; mem. U.S. Congress from 1st Colo. dist., 1997—; mem. commerce com. Editor: (mag.) Trial Talk, 1989-92. Mem. Mayor's Mgmt. Rev. Com., Denver, 1983-84; resolutions chair Denver Dem. Party, 1986; bd. dirs. Root-Tilden Program, NYU Sch. Law, N.Y.C., 1986-92; bd. trustees, alumni trustee Colo. Coll., Colorado Springs, 1988-94. Recipient Root-Tilden scholar NYU Sch. Law, N.Y.C., 1979, Vanderbilt medal, 1982. Mem. Colo. Bar Assn. (bd. govs. 1989-91), Colo. Trial Lawyers Assn. (bd. dirs., exec. com. 1986-92), Colo. Women's Bar Assn., Denver Bar Assn., Phi Beta Kappa, Pi Gamma Mu. Avocations: reading, backpacking, gardening.*

DE GEUS, AART J. computer software company executive; MSEE, Swiss Fedn. Polytech Inst.; PhD, So. Meth. U. Chmn., CEO Synopsys, Mountain View, Calif. Office: Synopsys 700 E Middlefield Rd Mountain View CA 94043-4033

DEGIACOMO, ROBERT J. federal judge; Former judge and chief judge, 1st jud. dist. N.Mex. dist. Ct.; magistrate judge U.S. Dist. Ct. N.Mex., Albuquerque. Office: US Magistrate 333 Lomas Blvd NW Ste 670 Albuquerque NM 87102-2276

DE GRASSI, LEONARD, art historian, educator; b. East Orange, N.J., Mar. 2, 1928; s. Romulus-William and Anna Sophia (Sannicolo) DeG.; m. Dolores Marie Welgoss, June 24, 1961; children: Maria Christina, Paul. BA, U. So. Calif., 1950, BFA, 1951, MA, 1956; postgrad., Harvard U., 1953, Istituto Centrale del Restauro di Roma, 1959-60, U. Rome, 1959-60, UCLA, 1970-73. Tchr. art Redlands (Calif.) Jr. High Sch., 1951-53, Toll Jr. High Sch., Glendale, Calif., 1953-61, Wilson Jr. High Sch., Glendale, 1961; mem. faculty Glendale Coll., 1962—, prof. art history, 1974-92, chmn. dept., 1972, 89, prof. emeritus, 1992—. Prin. works include: (paintings) high altar at Ch. St. Mary, Cook, Minn., altar screen at Ch. St. Andrew, El Segundo, Calif., 1965-71, 14 Stas. of the Cross Ch. St. Mary, Cook, Minn., altar screen at Ch. of the Descent of the Holy Spirit, Glendale, 14 Stas. of the Cross at Ch. of St. Benedict, Duluth, Minn; also research, artwork and dramatic work for Spaceship Earth exhbn. at Disney World, Orlando, Fla., 1980. Decorated Knight Grand Cross Holy Sepluchre, 1974, knight St. John of Jerusalem, 1976, knight Order of Merit of Republic of Italy, 1973 Cross of Merit, 1984, 89; recipient J. Walter Smith Svc. award, 2001, numerous commendations; named First Disting. Faculty, 1987, Outstanding Educator of Am., 1971. Mem. Art Educators Assn., Am. Rsch. Ct. Egypt, Tau Kappa Alpha, Kappa Pi, Delta Sigma Rho. Office: 1500 N Verdugo Rd Glendale CA 91208-2809

DE HAAS, DAVID DANA, emergency physician; b. Hollywood, Calif., May 31, 1956; S. Martin and Norma (Deutsch) De H.; m. Mary Danuta Przybylowski, June 27, 1982; children: Lindsay Alexandra, Heather Brittany, Lance Austin. BS in Biochemistry, UCLA, Westwood, Calif., 1979; MD, Chgo. Med. Sch., 1983. Diplomate Am. Bd. Internal Medicine, Am. Bd. Emergency Medicine, Nat. Bd. Med. Examiners; cert. provider advanced trauma life support, ACLS, Pediatric Advanced Life Support, BCLS, Med. Disaster Response, instr. ACLS, Pediatric Advanced Life Support, Med. Disaster Response. Resident emergency medicine/internal medicine Kern Med. Ctr., Bakersfield, Calif., 1983-87; assoc. med. dir. Family Care Med. Assocs., Huntington Beach, 1987—; emergency physician Anaheim (Calif.) Meml. Hosp., 1988—; asst. clin. prof. medicine dept. internal medicine U. Calif.-Irvine Med. Ctr., Orange, 1989—; emergency physician St. Bernardine Med. Ctr., San Bernardino, Calif., 1991—; ptnr. Calif. Emergency Physicians Med. Group, San Bernardino, 1991—. Expert reviewer Med. Bd. Calif.; affiliate faculty ACLS, Pediatric Advanced Life Support, Am. Heart Assn.; vice chmn. dept. emergency medicine St. Bernardine Med. Ctr., ACLS dir., dir. quality assurance/continuous quality improvement dept. emergency medicine; mem. edn. com. Med. Disaster Response; ptnr.Calif. Emergency Physician Med. Group. Fellow ACP, Am. Coll. Emergency Physicians; mem. AMA, Calif. Med. Assn., Orange County Med. Soc., Soc. Orange County Emergency Physicians (bd. dirs.), Assn. Clin. Faculty U. Calif., Irvine Coll. Medicine. Avocations: pin collecting, gardening, reading, 1st edit. book collecting, western Americana. Home: 26882 Via La Mirada San Juan Capistrano CA 92675-4935 Office: St Bernardine Med Ctr 2101 N Waterman Ave San Bernardino CA 92404-4836

DEHAAS, JOHN NEFF, JR. retired architecture educator; b. Phila., July 4, 1926; s. John Neff and Sadie Lavinia (Hagel) DeH.; m. C. Bernice Wallace, Dec. 27, 1950; children: Kenneth Eric, Jocelyn Hilda. BArch, Tex. A&M U., 1948, MEd, 1950. Registered architect, Mont. Instr. Tex. A&M U., College Station, 1948-50, U. Tex., Austin, 1950-51; successively instr. to prof. Mont. State U., Bozeman, 1951-80. Supervisory architect Historic Am. Bldgs. Survey, summers San Francisco, 1962, Bozeman, 1963, 65, Milw., 1969; cons. Mont. Historic Preservation Office, Helena, 1977-78, mem. rev. bd., 1968-79. Author: Montana's Historic Structures, Vol. 1, 1864, Vol. 2, 1969, Historic Uptown Butte, 1977; editor quar. newsletter Mont. Ghost Town Preservation Soc., 1972— Bd. dirs. Mont. Assn. for Blind, Butte, 1984-95. Recipient Centennial Preservation award Mont. Historic Preservation Office, 1989, Dorothy Bridgman award for Outstanding Svc. to the Blind Montana Assn. for the Blind, 1990. Fellow AIA (com. on historic resources 1974—); mem. Mont. Hist. Soc. (trustee's award 1989). Republican. Methodist. Home: 1021 S Tracy Ave Bozeman MT 59715-5329

DE HERRERA, JUAN ABRAN (AGE), federal judicial security official; b. Costilla, N.Mex., Jan. 2, 1942; s. Gilbert and Maria (Arellano) De H.; m. Roberta Jo Vogel, June 22, 1959; 5 children. Grad., Nat. Crime Prevention Inst. Acad., 1975, Nat. FBI Acad., 1976; grad. in adminstrn. of jail facilities, U. Colo., 1977; BA in Edn., U. Wyo., 1993. Patrol officer Rawlins (Wyo.) Police Force, 1965-67, sgt. patrol divsn., 1968-71, lt. patrol divsn., 1972-76, chief of police, 1977-82, ret., 1986; U.S. marshal dist. of Wyo. apptd. by Pres. Clinton Dept. Justice, Cheyenne, 1996. Boxing coach Amateur Athletic Union, 1963-82. Mem. city counsel, 1987-92, Wyo. State Libr. Bd., 1988-91. Hearst Minority scholar U. Wyo., 1988, 89, 90, 91, Sundin scholar, 1988, 89, 90, 91, SEO scholar, 1990, Nat. Hispanic scholar, 1990, 91, 92; state and regional nat. Golden Gloves champion. Mem. Nat. FBI Acad. Assocs., Wyo. Peace Officers Assn., Rawlins Police Protective Assn., Pershing Elem. Sch. Parent Tchr. Assn. (life), K of C., Latin Am. Assn. Cheyenne. Roman Catholic. Avocations: family camping, cross country skiing, boating, hunting, walking. E-mail: juandeherrera@usdoj.gov

DEHMELT, HANS GEORG, physicist, educator; b. Germany, Sept. 9, 1922; came to U.S., 1952, naturalized, 1962; s. Georg Karl and Asta Ella (Klemmt) D.; 1 child from previous marriage, Gerd; m. Diana Elaine Dundore, Nov. 18, 1989. Grad., Graues Kloster, Berlin, Abitur, 1940; D Rerum Naturalium, U. Goettingen, 1950; D Rerum Naturalium (hon.), Ruprecht Karl-Universitat, Heidelberg, 1986; DSc (hon.), U. Chgo., 1987. Postdoctoral fellow U. Goettingen, Germany, 1950-52, Duke U., Durham, N.C., 1952-55; vis. asst. prof. U. Wash., Seattle, 1955, asst. prof. physics, 1956, asso. prof., 1957-61, prof., rsch. physicist, 1961—. Cons. Varian Assocs., Palo Alto, Calif., 1956-76. Contbr. articles to profl. jours. Recipient Humboldt prize, 1974, award in basic research Internat. Soc. Magnetic Resonance, 1980, Rumford prize Am. Acad. Arts and Scis., 1985, Nobel prize in Physics, 1989, Nat. Medal of Science, 1995; NSF grantee, 1958—. Fellow Am. Phys. Soc. (Davisson-Germer prize 1970); mem. Am. Acad. Arts and Scis., Am. Optical Soc., Nat. Acad. Scis., Sigma Xi. Achievements include co-discoverer (with Hubert Krüger) nuclear quadrupole resonance, 1949; inventor schemes using single trapped atomic particles as million-fold quantum amplifier, employed them as a leader of groups in for the first time permanently isolating and identifying at rest in vacuum an individual electron, a subatomic particle, a charged atom, ion

Astrid, an antimatter particle, positron Priscilla, and in demonstrating spontaneous quantum jumps and measuring magnetism and size on single electron and positron with precisions 1,000 times higher than previously attained on millions of them. Home: 1600 43rd Ave E Seattle WA 98112-3205 Office: U Wash PO Box 35-1560 Seattle WA 98195-1560

DEIDE, DARREL A. state legislator; b. Sioux City, Iowa, Mar. 25, 1936; m. LaDonna Deide; children: Lori, Gina, David. BS in Biology, Albertson Coll. Idaho, 1960, MEd in Sch. Adminstrn. and Counseling, 1966. Sch. tchr., counselor, 1960-66; bldg. sch. adminstr., 1967-71; ctrl. office asst. supt., 1972-95; mem. Idaho Senate, Dist. 10, Boise, 1996—. Mem. agrl. affairs, commerce and human resources, edn., judiciary and rules, and transp. coms. Bd. dirs. Caldwell Edn. Found.; mem. Idaho Sch. Reform com.; mem. Caldwell Parks and Recreation Commn.; mem. Canyon County Rep. Ctrl. Com.; adv. bd. Salvation Army, mem. Caldwell Econ. Devel. Project; active Canyon Area United Way. With Idaho N.G., 1954-64. Recipient Disting. Citizen award, Idaho Statesman, Disting. Alumni award Caldwell H.S. Mem. Idaho Sch. Adminstrs. Assn., Idaho Profl. Stds. Assn., Caldwell (Idaho) Kiwanis (Kiwanian of Yr. 1986-87), Caldwell C. of C., Albertson Coll. Alumni Assn. Republican. Office: State Capitol PO Box 83720 Boise ID 83720-3720

DEILY, LINNET FRAZIER, banker; b. Dallas, June 20, 1945; d. William Harold and Ruth (White) Frazier; m. Myron Bonham Deily, Apr. 18, 1981. B.A., U. Tex.-Austin, 1967; M.A., U. Tex-Dallas, 1976. Banking officer, asst. v.p., then v.p. Republic Bank Dallas, N.A., 1975-80, sr. v.p., 1980-81; v.p. First Interstate Bancorp, Los Angeles, 1981-83; sr. v.p., div. mgr. First Interstate Bank Calif., 1983-84; past sr. v.p., chief fin. officer, now pres. First Interstate Bank Ltd.; vice chmn., pres. Charles Schwab Corp., San Francisco; bd. dirs. First Interstate Inst., Los Angeles. Club: Univ. (mem. fin. com.) (Los Angeles). Office: Charles Schwab Corp 101 Montgomery St Ste 200 San Francisco CA 94104-4175

DEISENROTH, CLINTON WILBUR, electrical engineer; b. Louisville, Aug. 9, 1941; s. Clifton Earl and Nell (Pierce) D.; m. Lisbeth D. Isaacs, May 10, 1974; 1 dau., Susan Michelle. BEE, Ga. Inst. Tech., 1965. With Raytheon Co., 1966-81, div. mgr. Addington Labs., Inc., solid state products div., Santa Clara, Calif., 1975-77, program mgr. electromagnetic systems div., Goleta, Calif., 1977-79, dir. surface navy electronic warfare systems, 1979-81; sr. v.p. systems div. Teledyne-MEC, 1981-84; pres. Teledyne CME, 1984-90; exec. v.p., gen. mgr. Aerospace Products div. G&H Tech., Inc., 1990-92; v.p. bus. devel. Whittaker Electronic Systems, 1992-94, v.p., gen. mgr., 1994-96, pres., 1996; pres. CWD and Assocs. Mem. IEEE. Home: 2052 Hartwick Circle Thousand Oaks CA 91360-1905

DEITCHLE, GERALD WAYNE, restaurant company executive; b. Lockbourne AFB, Ohio, Sept. 19, 1951; BBA, Tex. A&M U., 1973; MBA, U. Tex., San Antonio, 1975. CPA, Tex. Div. controller Church's Fried Chicken Inc., San Antonio, 1978-80; asst. controller W. R. Grace and Co., San Antonio, 1980-84; v.p., controller Jerrico Inc., Lexington, Ky., 1984-87, sr. v.p. fin., 1987—; v.p. & CFO Cheesecake Factory Inc., Calabasas Hills, Calif. With USAF, 1974-78. Mem. AICPA, Tex. Soc. CPA's, Fin. Execs. Inst., Nat. Assn. Accts., Inst. Mgmt. Acctg., Nat. Assn. Securities Dealers Automated Quotations. Office: Cheesecake Factory Inc 26950 Agoura Rd Agoura Hills CA 91301 Address: Long John Silvers PO Box 11988 Lexington KY 40579-1988

DEITRICH, RICHARD ADAM, pharmacology educator; b. Monte Vista, Colo., Apr. 22, 1931; s. Robert Adam and Freda Leona (Scott) D.; m. Mary Margaret Burkholder, Jan. 29, 1954; children: Vivian Gay, Leslie Lynn, Lori Christine. BS, U. Colo., 1953, MS, 1954, PhD, 1959. Postdoctoral fellow, then instr. Johns Hopkins U., Balt., 1959-63; asst. prof., then assoc. prof. U. Colo., Denver, 1963-76, prof. pharmacology, 1976—, sci. dir. Alcohol Rsch. Ctr., 1977—. Vis. prof. U. Berne, Switzerland, 1973-74. Editor: Development of Animal Models, 1981, Initial Sensitivity to Alcohol, 1990; contbr. over 100 articles to sci. publs. Pres. Mile High Coun. on Alcoholism, Denver, 1972-73; moderator 1st Universalist Ch., Denver, 1979. With U.S. Army, 1954-56. Grantee Nat. Inst. Alcoholism, 1977—, Nat. Inst. Communicative Disease and Stroke, 1963, numerous others. Mem. Rsch. Soc. on Alcoholism (pres. 1981-83), Internat. Soc. Biomed. Rsch. on Alcoholism (treas. 1986-94), Am. Soc. Pharmacology, Am. Soc. Biol. Chemistry. Avocations: photography, fishing, camping. Office: Univ Colo 4200 E 9th Ave Denver CO 80220-3700

DEKKER, GEORGE GILBERT, literature educator, literary scholar, writer; b. Long Beach, Calif., Sept. 8, 1934; s. Gilbert J. and Laura (Barnes) D.; m. Linda Jo Bartholomew, Aug. 31, 1973; children by previous marriage: Anna Allegra, Clara Joy, Ruth Siobhan, Laura Daye. B.A. in English, U. Calif.-Santa Barbara, 1955; M.A. in English, 1958; M.Litt., Cambridge U. (Eng.), 1961; Ph.D. in English, U. Essex (Eng.), 1967. Lectr. U. Wales, Swansea, 1962-64; lectr. in lit. U. Essex, 1964-69, reader in lit., 1969-72, dean Sch. Comparative Studies, 1969-71; assoc. prof. English Stanford (Calif.) U., 1972-74, prof., 1974—, chmn. dept., 1978-81, 84-85, Joseph S. Atha prof. humanities, 1988—, dir. program in Am. Studies, 1988-91, assoc. dean grad. policy, 1993-96. Author: Sailing After Knowledge, 1963, James Fenimore Cooper the Novelist, 1967; Coleridge and the Literature of Sensibility, 1978, The American Historical Romance, 1987; editor: Donald Davie: The Responsibilities of Literature, 1983. Nat. Endowment Humanities fellow, 1977; Inst. Advanced Studies in Humanities fellow U. Edinburgh (Scotland), 1982; hon. fellow, Clare Hall Cambridge, 1997, Stanford Humanities Ctr., 1997. Mem. Am. Lit. Assn. Democrat. Office: Stanford U Dept English Stanford CA 94305

DEKMEJIAN, RICHARD HRAIR, political science educator; b. Aleppo, Syria, Aug. 3, 1933; came to U.S., 1950, naturalized, 1955; s. Hrant H. and Vahede V. (Matossian) D.; m. Anoush Hagopian, Sept. 19, 1954; children: Gregory, Armen, Haig. BA, U. Conn., 1959; MA, Boston U., 1960; Middle East Inst. cert., Columbia U., 1964, PhD, 1966. Mem. faculty SUNY, Binghamton, 1964-86; prof., chmn. dept. polit. sci. U. So. Calif., Los Angeles, 1986-90, prof. internat. bus. Marshall Sch. Bus.; also master Hinman Coll., 1971-72. Lectr. Fgn. Svc. Inst., Dep. State, 1976-87; vis. prof. Columbia U., U. Pa., 1977-78; cons. Dept. State, AID, USIA, UN Def. Author; Egypt Under Nasir, 1971, Patterns of Political Leadership, 1975; Islam in Revolution, 1985, 2nd edit., 1995, Ethnic Lobbies in U.S. Foreign Policy, 1997, Troubled Waters: The Geopolitics of the Caspian Region, 2001; contbr. articles to profl. jours. Pres. So. Tier Civic Ballet Co., 1973-76. Served with AUS, 1955-57. Mem. Am. Polit. Sci. Assn., Middle East Inst., Middle East Studies Assn., Internat. Inst. Strategic Studies, Skull and Dagger, Pi Sigma Alpha, Phi Alpha Theta. Office: U So Calif Dept Polit Sci Los Angeles CA 90089-0001 E-mail: dekmejia@usc.edu

DEKOK, ROGER GREGORY, career officer; b. Kenosha, Wis., Jan. 10, 1947; s. Roger Gerritt Dekok and Hazel Deloris (Wilkinson) Busche; m. Carolyn Susan Flinkow, June 15, 1968; children: Kristen Laura, Ryan Matthew. BA in Math., U. Wis., 1968; MS in Sys. Mgmt., Air Force Inst. Tech., 1979, postgrad., 1978-79; attended, Air War Coll., 1983-84. Commd. 2d lt. USAF, 1968, advanced through grades to lt. gen., 1995, space sys. staff officer HQ, 1979-83, dir. space plans HQ Air Force Space Command Maxwell AFB, Ala., 1983-84, dir. space programs Nat. Security Coun., White House Washington, 1987-88, spl. asst. to Pres., Nat. Security Coun., White House, 1988, comdr. 1st Space Wing Peterson AFB, 1989-90, comdr. 50th Space Wing Falcon AFB, Colo., 1990-93; dir. plans HQ Air Force Space Command USAF, Peterson AFB, 1993-95; dir. ops. U.S. Space Command, Peterson AFB, 1995-96; comdr. Space and Missle Systems Ctr., L.A., 1996-98; dep. chief of staff for plans and programs USAF-Pentagon, Washington, 98—; vice comdr. U.S. Space Commd, Peterson AFB, 2000—. Recipient Nat. Space Achievement award Nat. Rotary Club, 1987, James V. Hartinger award for career space achievement NSIA, 1995. Mem. Air Force Assn., Nat. Space Club (bd. govs. 1988-89, 96—). Lutheran. Avocations: golf, skiing, tennis, personal computing. Office: USAF/VC 150 Vandenberg St Ste 1104 Peterson AFB CO 80914-4020

DELACOTE, GOERY, museum director; Exec. dir. The Exploratorium, San Francisco. Office: The Exploratorium 3601 Lyon St San Francisco CA 94123-1099

DELA CRUZ, JOSE SANTOS, retired state supreme court justice; b. Saipan, Commonwealth No. Mariana Islands, July 18, 1948; s. Thomas Castro and Remedio Sablan (Santos) Dela C.; m. Rita Tenorio Sablan, Nov. 12, 1977; children: Roxanne, Renee, Rica Ann. BA, U. Guam, 1971; JD, U. Calif., Berkeley, 1974; cert., Nat. Jud. Coll., Reno, 1985. Bar: No. Mariana Islands, 1974, U.S. Dist. Ct. No. Mariana Islands 1978. Staff atty. Micro. Legal Svcs. Corp., Saipan, 1974-79; gen. counsel Marianas Pub. Land Corp., Saipan, 1979-81; liaison atty. CNMI Fed. Laws Commn., Saipan, 1981-83; ptnr. Borja & Dela Cruz, Saipan, 1983-85; assoc. judge Commonwealth Trial Ct., Saipan, 1985-89; state supreme ct. chief justice Supreme Ct. No. Mariana Islands, 1989-95; retired, 1995. Mem. Conf. of Chief Justices, 1989-95, Adv. Commn. on Judiciary, Saipan, 1980-82; chmn. Criminal Justice Planning Agy., Saipan, 1985-95. Mem. Coun. for Arts, Saipan, 1982-83; chmn. Bd. of Elections, Saipan, 1977-82; pres. Cath. Social Svcs., Saipan, 1982-85. Mem. No. Marianas Bar Assn. (pres. 1984-85). Roman Catholic. Avocations: golf, reading, walking.

DE LA CUEVA, JULIO JOSE IGLESIAS **See IGLESIAS, JULIO**

DE LA FUENTE, LAWRENCE EDWARD, artist; b. Chgo., Sept. 29, 1947; Student, Kansas City Art Inst., 1966-68. Exhbns. include San Francisco Art Commn., 1971, 72, Berkeley (Calif.) Art Ctr., 1973, San Jose (Calif.) State U., 1973, Gallery West, Mendocino, Calif., 1973, San Francisco Mus. Art, 1973, 74, 75, 76, 78, Mendocino Art Ctr., 1977, 80, 83, 93, Wilkinson-Cobb Gallery, Mendocino, 1977, Tucson (Ariz.) Mus. Art, 1977, Nat. Coll. Fine Art, Smithsonian, Washington, 1977, 80, mus. Mill Valley, Calif., 1978, Albuquerque Mus. Art, 1978, El Paso (Tex.) Mus.. Art, 1978, Blaffer Gallery, U. Houston, 1978, Taylor Mus. Art, Colorado Springs, 1978, Everson Mus., Syracuse, N.Y., 1979, Witte Mus., San Antonio, 1979, Contemporary Arts Mus., Chgo., 1979, U. Ga., Athens, 1979, Tyler U., Phila., 1979, Palacio de Mineria, Mexico City, 1980, Internat. Sculpture Conf., Washington, 1980, Western States Fair, Pomona, Calif., 1980, Macintosh-Drysdale Gallery, Washington, 1981, Fondo del Sol Gallery, Wahsington, 1981, Alternative Mus., N.Y.C., 1982, P.S.1 Clocktower, N.Y.C., 1982, Ronald Feldman Gallery, N.Y.C., 1982, Knot Art Gallery, Mendocino, 1983, U. Houston, 1984, Cultural Arts Ctr. Santa Barbara, 1985, Pulsations, Phila., 1986, Retreti Art Ctr., Helsinki, 1987, Living Art Show, Mendocino, 1987, Philbrook Mus. Art, Tulsa, Okla., 1987, Chgo. Pub. Libr., 1988, Kohler Mus. Art, Sheboygan, Wis., 1989, Va. Mus. Fine Art, Richmond, 1989, Orlando (Fla.) Mus. Art, 1989, Tokyo Mus. Modern Art, 1990, Kyoto (Japan) Mus. Modern Art, 1990, Smithsonian Instn. Renwick Gallery, 1990, Calif. State U. Chico, 1993, Natural History Mus., L.A., 1994, Smithsonian Traveling Exhbn., 1994, others. NEA fellow 1980, 88, 95; recipient 1st prize Houston ArtCarr Parade, 2000. Home: PO Box 954 Mendocino CA 95460-0954 also: 41401 Comptche Ukiah Rd Mendocino CA 95460-9786

DELANEY, MARION PATRICIA, bank executive; b. Hartford, Conn., May 20, 1952; d. William Pride Delaney Jr. and Marian Patricia (Utley) Murphy. BA, Union Coll., Schenectady, N.Y., 1973. Adminstrv. asst. N.Y. State Assembly, Albany, 1973-74; account exec. Foote, Cone & Belding, N.Y.C., 1974-78, sr. account exec. Dailey & Assocs., L.A., 1978-81, pub. rels. cons. NOW, Washington, 1981-83; account supr. BBDO/West, L.A., 1983-85; v.p. Grey Advt., L.A., 1985-87, San Francisco, 1987-89; sr. v.p. McCann-Erickson, San Francisco, 1989-95; sr. v.p., dir. advt./mktg. comms. Bank of Am., San Francisco, 1995-99; owner children's arts tore doodlebug, San Anselmo, Calif., 2001—. Del. Dem. Nat. Conv., San Francisco, 1984; bd. dirs. JED Found., Hartford, Conn., 1989—, Easter Seals Soc., Bay Area, 1995-97. Mem. NOW (v.p. L.A. chpt. 1980-83, pres. 1984, advisor 1985-87). Congregationalist. Home: 11 Gary Way Fairfax CA 94930-1002

DELANEY, MATTHEW SYLVESTER, mathematics educator, academic administrator; b. Ireland, Nov. 26, 1927; s. Joseph C. and Elizabeth M. (Bergin) D.; came to U.S., 1947, naturalized, 1952; student St. John's Coll., 1947-51; BA, Immaculate Heart Coll., L.A., 1958; MS, Notre Dame U., 1960; PhD, Ohio State U., 1971. Ordained priest Roman Cath. Ch., 1951; assoc. pastor L.A. Cath. Diocese, 1951-55; instr. math., physics Pius X High Sch., Downey, Calif., 1955-58, vice prin., 1960-62; instr. math. Immaculate Heart Coll., L.A., 1962-65, asst. prof., 1965-72, assoc. prof., 1972-76, prof., 1976— ; asst. acad. dean, 1973-78; dean acad. devel. Mt. St. Mary's Coll., L.A., 1978-82, acad. dean, 1978-91; prof. math., 1991—, prof. emeritus, 1996—. NSF grantee, 1959-60, 61. Achievements include: Formal recognition of the eponyms, "Delaney Sets" and "The Delaney Symbol" in the disciplines of discrete geometry and math. crystallography, 1985. Mem. Internat. Union Crystallography, Am. Math. Soc., Math. Assn. Am., N.Y. Acad. Scis.. Democrat. Contbr. articles to math. publs., profl. jours. Home: Apt 32C 13700 El Dorado Dr Seal Beach CA 90740-3843 Office: Mount Saint Mary's Coll 12001 Chalon Rd Los Angeles CA 90049-1526

DELANEY, WILLIAM FRANCIS, JR. reinsurance broker; s. William F. and Viola (Kelly) D.; m. Virginia Beers; children: Marcia, Gayle. Student, Ecole Albert de Mun, Nogent sur Marne, France, Douai Sch., Eng.; Oxford and Cambridge Sch. Cert.; AB, Princeton U.; LLB, Harvard U.; student, NYU, Practising Law Inst., Ins. Soc. N.Y.; Studied law, Paris. Bar: N.Y., U.S. Supreme Ct. Atty. Irving Trust Co., N.Y.C.; gen. counsel Am. Internat. Underwriters Group; N.Y. reins. mgr. Fairfield & Ellis; pres. Delaney Offices, Inc., N.Y., 1954—. Founding mem., broker, N.Y. Ins. Exchange; reins. intermediary and cons. for U.S. and world wide; reins. lectr. Ins. Soc. N.Y. Author: Reinsurance Laws of South America and Mexico; contbr. articles to ins. publs. Mem. Ins. Soc. N.Y. Roman Catholic. Clubs: Princeton, Deal Golf. Office: 4365 Bridle Way Reno NV 89509-2904

DELAPP, TINA DAVIS, nursing educator; b. L.A., Dec. 18, 1946; d. John George and Margaret Mary (Clark) Davis; m. John Robert DeLapp, May 31, 1969; children: Julia Ann, Scott Michael. Diploma, Good Samaritan Hosp., Phoenix, 1967; BSN, Ariz. State U., 1969; MS, U. Colo., Denver, 1972; EdD, U. So. Calif., 1986. Cert. med.-surg. nurse. Health aide instr. Yukon-Kuskokwim Health Corp., Bethel, Alaska, 1970-71; asst. prof. nursing Bacone Coll., Muskogee, Okla., 1972-74; instr. nursing Alaska Meth. U., Anchorage, 1975-76; prof., assoc. dean for nursing U. Alaska, Anchorage, 1976-96, dir. sch. nursing, 1996—. Mem. Alaska Bd. Nursing, 1989-92. Contbr. articles to profl. jours. Fellow Western Acad. Nursing; mem. Western Inst. Nursing (chair program com. 1994-95, sec.-treas. 1995—), Sigma Theta Tau (pres. chpt. 1986-88, v.p. 1988-93, counselor 1995-2000).

DELAWIE, HOMER TORRENCE, architect; b. Santa Barbara, Calif., Sept. 24, 1927; s. Fred Ely and Gertrude (Torrence) D.; m. Billie Carol Sparlin (div. 1969); m. Ethel Ann Mallinger, Sept. 3, 1973; children: Gregory, Claire, Shandell, Tracy, Stephanie, Scott. BS in Archtl. Engring., Calif. Poly. State U., San Luis Obispo, 1951. Registered architect, Calif. Pvt. practice architecture, San Diego, 1958-61; founder, CEO Delawie Wilkes Rodrigues Barker & Bretton Assocs., San Diego, 1961—, ptnr. emeritus, 1998—. Mem. Planning Commn., City of San Diego, 1969-82; adv. bd. KPBS Pub. TV. Recipient Award of Merit Calif. chpt. Am. Inst. Planners, Lay Citizens award Phi Delta Kappa, 1975, award Calif chpt. Am. Planning Assn., 1982; named Disting. Alumnus, Calif. Poly. State U., 1972. Fellow AIA (over 60 design awards 1973—, Architects Svc. award Calif. coun. 1973, spl. award San Diego chpt. 1978, Pub. Svc. award Calif. coun. 1981, Outstanding Firm award San Diego chpt. 1986, Calif. Coun. Lifetime Achievement award 1998). Democrat. Home: 2749 Azalea Dr San Diego CA 92106-1132 Office: Delawie Wilkes Rodrigues Barker & Bretton Assocs 2827 Presidio Dr San Diego CA 92110-2722

DEL CAMPO, MARTIN BERNARDELLI, architect; b. Guadalajara, Mex., Nov. 27, 1922; came to U.S., 1949; s. Salvador and Margarita (Bernardelli) Del C.; m. Laura Zaikowska, May 25, 1945; children: Felicia (dec.), Margarita, Mario. BA, Colegio Frances Morelos, Mexico City, 1941; archtl. degree, Escuale Nacionale de Arquitect, Mexico City, 1948. Ptnr. Del Campo & Fruiht, architects, Santa Rosa, Calif., 1955-56, Del Campo & Clark, San Francisco, 1957-63; mgr. Hotel Victoria, Oaxaca, Mex., 1964-67; pres. Gulli-Del Campo, architects, San Francisco, 1968-70; ptnr. Del Campo Assocs., San Francisco, 1977-81. Lectr. archtl. design Coll. Environmental Design, U. Calif., Berkeley, 1973-74. Archtl. works include: Calif. Med. Facility South, Vacaville, Phillip Burton Fed. Bldg. remodeling, San Francisco, Hall of Justice, San Francisco, San Francisco Airport Internat. Terminal, Mex. Heritage Gardens, San Jose, Four Seasons Tower, San Francisco. Mem. AIA. Address: Del Campo & Maru Architects Inc 45 Lansing St San Francisco CA 94105-2611

DELISI, DONALD PAUL, geophysicist, fluid mechanic; b. Pitts., Nov. 15, 1944; s. Samuel P. and Jennie (Moffie) D.; m. Adele Pedicord Orr, Aug. 7, 1971; 1 child, Bergen Orr Delisi. B.S.E. magna cum laude, Princeton U., 1966; MS, U. Calif., Berkeley, 1967, PhD, 1972. Resident rsch. assoc. Geophys. Fluid Dynamics Lab./NOAA, Princeton, N.J., 1972-74; sr. rsch. scientist Flow Rsch., Inc., Kent, Wash., 1974-77; staff scientist Phys. Dynamics Inc., Bellevue, 1977-86; v.p., treas., sr. rsch. scientist N.W. Rsch. Assocs., Inc., Bellevue, 1986—. Contbr. articles to Jour. Geophys. Rsch., Jour. of the Atmospheric Scis., Pure and Applied Geophysics, AIAA Jour., Jour. of Aircraft. Mem. Am. Meteorol. Soc., Am. Geophys. Union, AIAA, Am. Inst. Physics. Achievements include research on stratified shear and vortex flows; on observational studies of atmospheric dynamics. Office: NW Rsch Assocs Inc 14508 NE 20th St Bellevue WA 98007-3713

DE LISIO, STEPHEN SCOTT, lawyer, director; b. San Diego, Dec. 30, 1937; s. Anthony J. and Emma Irving (Cheney) DeL.; m. Margaret Irene Winter, June 26, 1964; children: Anthony W., Stephen Scott, Heather E. Student, Am. U., 1958-59; BA, Emory U., 1959; LLB, Albany Law Sch., 1962; LLM, Georgetown U., 1963. Bar: N.Y. 1963, D.C. 1963, Alaska 1964. Practice law, Fairbanks, 1963-71, Anchorage, 1972-96; asst. dist. atty. Fairbanks, 1963-65; assoc. McNealy & Merdes, 1965-66; lectr. U. Alaska, 1965-67; ptnr. Staley, DeLisio & Cook, 1966-93, DeLisio, Moran, Geraghty & Zobel, Inc., 1994—. Bd. dirs. Woodstock Property Co., Inc., Pasit Inc., Challenger Films Inc.; vice chmn. Crosstown CBMC, 1986-87, chmn., 1987-88, 90-91, area coord., 1987-92; city atty., Fairbanks, 1967-70, Barrow, 1969-72, Ft. Yukon and North Pole, 1970-72; past sec. U. Alaska Heating Corp., Inc.; past sec.-treas. Trans-Alaska Electronics, Inc., Baker Aviation, Inc.; arbitrator, mem. Alaska regional coun. Am. Arbitration Assn. Author: (with others) Law and Tactics in Federal Criminal Cases, 1964. Rep. precinct committeeman, 1970-76; chmn. Alaska Rep. Rules Com., Anchorage Rep. Com., 1973; v.p. We The People, 1977-79; vice-chmn. Alaska Libertarian party, 1983-84; mem. nat. com. Libertarian party, 1982 85; past pres. Tanana Valley State Fair Assn.; past v.p. Fairbanks Mental Health Assn., Fairbanks United Good Neighbors Fund; deacon Anchorage Bible Fellowship, 1986-90, elder, 1990—; bd. dirs. Anchorage Community Chorus, 1975-77, Commonsense for Alaska, 1987-94, Alaska chpt. Lupus Found., 1989-96; chmn. bd. Alaska Voluntary Health Assn., 1993-96; former bd. dirs. Greater Fairbanks Community Hosp. Found.; met. dir. Christian Businessmen's Outreach, 1993-94, bd. dirs. Anchorage, 1985-92; Alaska coord. Crown Ministries, 1991-93; met. dir. Anchorage Christian Businessmen's Com. U.S.A., 1994-2000. Recipient Jaycee Disting. Service award, 1968 Mem. Am. Trial Lawyers Assn., Am. Judicature Soc., Alaska Bar Assn., D.C. Bar Assn., Anchorage Bar Assn., Spenard Bar Assn. (pres. 1975-77), U.S. Jaycees (past dir.), Alaska Jaycees (past pres.), Fairbanks Jaycees (past pres.), Chi Phi, Pi Sigma Phi, Woodstock Golf Inc. Club (pres. 1984—). Home: 5102 Shorecrest Dr Anchorage AK 99502-1029 Office: CBMC 943 W 6th Ave Ste 120 Anchorage AK 99501-2033 E-mail: cbmcak@alaska.net

DELL, ROBERT MICHAEL, lawyer; b. Chgo., Oct. 4, 1952; s. Michael A. and Bertha Dell; m. Ruth Celia Schiffman, May 29, 1976; children: David, Michael, Jessica. BGS, U. Mich., 1974; JD, U. Ill., 1977. Bar: U.S. Dist. Ct. (no. dist.) Ill. 1977, U.S. Ct. Appeals (7th cir.) 1977, U.S. Dist. Ct. (no. dist.) Calif. 1990. Law clk. to justice U.S. Ct. Appeals (7th cir.), Chgo., 1977-79; assoc. Latham & Watkins, Chgo., 1982-85, ptnr., 1985—, mng. ptnr. San Francisco office, 1990-94, firm chmn. and mng. ptnr., 1995—. Home: 19 Tamal Vista Ln Kentfield CA 94904-1005 Office: Latham & Watkins 505 Montgomery St Ste 1900 San Francisco CA 94111-2552

DELLAS, ROBERT DENNIS, investment banker; b. Detroit, July 4, 1944; s. Eugene D. and Maxine (Rudell) D.; m. Shila L. Clement, Mar. 27, 1976; children: Emily Allison, Lindsay Michelle B.A. in Econs., U. Mich., Ann Arbor, 1966; M.B.A., Harvard U., Cambridge, 1970. Analyst Burroughs Corp., Detroit, 1966-67, Pasadena, Calif., 1967-68; mgr. U.S. Leasing, San Francisco, 1970-76; pres., dir. Energetics Mktg. & Mgmt. Assn., San Francisco, 1978-80; sr. v.p. E.F. Hutton & Co., San Francisco, 1981-85; prin. founder Capital Exchange Internat., San Francisco, 1976—. Gen. ptnr. Kanland Assocs., Tex., 1982, Claremont Assocs., Calif., 1983, Lakeland Assocs., Ga., 1983, American Assocs., Calif., 1983, Chatsworth Assocs., Calif., 1983, Walnut Grove Assocs., Calif., 1983, Somerset Assocs., N.J., 1983, One San Diego Assocs., Calif., 1984, Big Top Prodns., L.P., Calif., 1994. Bd. dirs., treas. Found. San Francisco's Archtl. Heritage. Mem. U.S. Trotting Assn., Calif. Harness Horse Breeders Assn. (Breeders award for Filly of Yr. 1986, Aged Pacing Mare, 1987, 88, Colt of Yr. 1990), Calif. Golf Club San Francisco. Office: Capital Exch Internat 1911 Sacramento St San Francisco CA 94109-3419 E-mail: bobdellas@earthlink.net

DEL OLMO, FRANK, newspaper editor; b. L.A., May 18, 1948; s. Francisco and Margaret Rosalie (Mosqueda) D.; m. Karen Margaret King, Feb. 6, 1970 (div. Sept. 1982); 1 child, Valentina Marisol; m. Magdalena Beltran-Hernandez, Nov. 10, 1991; 1 child, Francisco Manuel. Student, UCLA, 1966-68; BS magna cum laude in Journalism, Calif. State U., Northridge, 1970. Reporter-intern L.A. Times, 1970-71, gen. assignment reporter, 1971-80, columnist, editorial bd., 1980-90, deputy editor, 1990-98, assoc. editor, 1998—. Instr. Chicano Studies, Calif. State U., 1970-71; contbg. editor Race Relations Reporter, Nashville, 1973-75; on-air host, writer "Ahora" Sta. KCET-TV, L.A., 1974; chief writer, rschr. KNBC, 1975; bd. contbrs., freelance reporter Nuestro Mag., 1976-81; program co-dir. Summer Program Minority Journalists, 1990, faculty mem. 1979, vis. faculty mem. 1978, 80-83, 85, 89; vis. profl. Dow-Jones Newspaper Fund U. So. Calif. Sch. Journalism, 1975, bd. dirs. Numerous lectrs., presentations at colls., univs. Named Senior Faculty of Summer Program Minority Journalists Inst. Journalism Edn.; recipient Emmy award, 1976, Sigma Delta Chi Achievement award, 1982, Profl. Achievement award UCLA Alumni, 1990, Pulitzer Prize, 1984; Neiman fellowship Harvard U., 1987-88. Office: Los Angeles Times 202 W 1st St Los Angeles CA 90012-4105

DELORENZO, DAVID A. food products executive; b. 1947; , Colgate U.; MBA, U. Pa. With Dole Food Co., Inc., Thousand Oaks, Calif., 1970—, exec. v.p., 1990-91, 93—, pres., 1991-93, Dole Food Co., Internat., 1993—. Office: Dole Food Co Inc 1 Dole Dr Westlake Vlg CA 91362-7300

DEL PAPA, FRANKIE SUE, state attorney general; b. 1949; BA, U. Nev.; JD, George Washington U., 1974. Bar: Nev. 1974. Staff asst. U.S. Senator Alan Bible, Washington, 1971-74; assoc. Law Office of Leslie B. Grey, Reno, 1975-78; legis. asst. to U.S. Senator Howard Cannon, Washington, 1978-79; ptnr. Thornton & Del Papa, 1979-84; pvt. practice Reno, 1984-87; sec. of state State of Nev., Carson City, 1987-91, atty. gen., 1991—. Mem. Sierra Arts Found. (bd. dirs.), Trust for Pub. Land (adv. com.), Nev. Women's Fund. Democrat.

DEL PRADO, SERGIO, professional soccer team executive; b. Havana, Cuba; came to U.S., 1962; m. Leslie; children: Monica, Eric. BS in Bus. Adminstrn., Calif. State U., Long Beach. Formerly with L.A. Kings/Nat. Hockey League, dir. mktg., corp. acct. mgr., 1997-92, Hispanic broadcast mgr., 1992-94, corp. account mgr., dir. mktg.; gen. mgr. L.A. Galaxy, 1999—. Office: care LA Galaxy 1010 Rose Bowl Dr Pasadena CA 91103-2864

DELUCA, DOMINICK, medical educator, researcher; BA in Bacteriology, UCLA, 1969, PhD in Microbiology, 1974. Predoctoral fellow NIH dept. bacteriology UCLA, 1970-74, rsch. asst. dept. bacteriology, 1974; postdoctoral fellow Leukemia Soc. Am., Walter and Eliza Hall Inst., Parkville, Australia, 1974-77; scientist cancer biology program Frederick (Md.) Cancer Rsch. Ctr., 1977-80; asst. prof. biochemistry Med. U. S.C., Charleston, 1980-85, assoc. prof. biochemistry, 1985-90; assoc. prof. microbiology and immunology U. Ariz., 1990—. Mem. pub. policy com. Ariz. Diabetes Control Coun., 1997—, chmn., 1999—; mem. AIDS rsch. program basic scis. rev. panel U. Calif., 1996-99; mem. brain disorders and clin. neurosci. study sect. NIH, 1999—. Mem. editl. adv. bd. Devel. and Comparative Immunology, 1995—; contbr. articles to profl. jours., chpt. to books. Recipient Developing Scholar award Health Scis. Found. Med. U. S.C., 1987, Rsch. award NIH, 1983, 86, 89, NASA, 1999, Rsch. award Juvenile Diabetes Found., 1988, 98, 2001, Ariz. Disease Control Rsch. Commn., 1992, 96, 98, 2000, Am. Diabetes Assn., 1995. Mem. Southeastern Immunology Conf. (pres. elect 1982-83, pres. 1983-84, bd. dirs. 1985), Ariz. Cancer Ctr. Office: U Ariz Dept Micro Immuno PO Box 245049 Tucson AZ 85724-5049 E-mail: deluca@u.arizona.edu

DELUCA, MICHAEL, film company executive; Pres. prodn. and devel. New Line Cinema, L.A., now pres., COO of prodn. Office: New Line Cinema 116 N Robertson Blvd Fl 2D Los Angeles CA 90048-3103 also: 888 7th Ave Fl 20 New York NY 10106-0001

DELUCE, RICHARD DAVID, lawyer; b. Nanaimo, B.C., Can., Oct. 3, 1928; came to U.S., 1929; s. Robert and Myrtle (Hickey) DeL.; m. Joanne Strang, Sept. 10, 1955; children: David S., Amy Jane Eigner, Daniel R. AB, UCLA, 1950; JD, Stanford U., Palo Alto, Calif., 1955. Bar: Calif., 1955, U.S. Dist. Ct. (no. dist.) Calif. 1955, U.S. Ct. Appeals (9th cir.) 1955, U.S. Dist. Ct. (cen. dist.) Calif. 1956, U.S. Supreme Ct. 1963, U.S. Dist. Ct. (so. dist.) Calif. 1972. Rsch. atty. Calif. Supreme Ct., San Francisco, 1955-56; assoc. Lawler, Felix & Hall, L.A., 1956-62, ptnr., 1962-90, Arter, Hadden, Lawler, Felix & Hall, L.A., 1990—. Co-author: California Civil Writ Practice, 2d edit., 1987. Capt. U.S. Army, 1951-53, Korea. Fellow Am. Coll. Trial Lawyers, Am. Bar Found.; mem. Calif. Club. Home: 3617 Paseo Del Campo Palos Verdes Peninsula CA 90274-1161 Office: Arter & Hadden LLP 725 S Figueroa St Ste 3400 Los Angeles CA 90017-5434

DELUGACH, ALBERT LAWRENCE, journalist; b. Memphis, Oct. 27, 1925; s. Gilbert and Edna (Short) D.; m. Bernice Goldstein, June 11, 1950; children: Joy, David, Daniel, Sharon. B.J., U. Mo., 1951. Reporter Kansas City (Mo.) Star, 1951-60, St. Louis Globe Democrat, 1960-69, St. Louis Post Dispatch, 1969-70; investigative reporter Los Angeles Times, 1970-89. Served with USNR, 1943-46. Recipient Pultizer prize for spl. local reporting, 1969, Gerald Loeb award for disting. bus. and fin. journalism, 1984 Home: 4313 Price St Los Angeles CA 90027-2815

DELUSTRO, FRANK ANTHONY, biomedical company executive, research immunologist; b. N.Y.C., May 8, 1948; s. Frank and Yolanda (Lombardi) DeL.; m. Barbara Mary Cervini, May 4, 1974; 1 child, Laura Marie. BS, Fordham U., 1970; PhD, SUNY, Syracuse, 1976. Rsch. assoc. dept. immunology Med. U. S.C., Charleston, 1976-78, instr. dept. medicine, 1978-80, asst. prof. dept. medicine, 1980-83; mgr. immunology R & D Collagen Corp., Palo Alto, Calif., 1983-85, mgr. clin. sci., 1985-86, dir. med. affairs, 1986-88, program dir., 1988-90, v.p., 1990-91, sr. v.p., 1991-96; pres., CEO Cohesion Corp., Palo Alto, 1996-98; pres. Cohesion Technologies, Inc., Palo Alto, 1998—. Contbr. articles to profl. jours. Mem. Am. Assn. Immunology, Am. Urol. Assn., Soc. Biomaterials, Soc. Investigative Dermatology. Office: Cohesion Technologies Inc 2500 Faber Pl Palo Alto CA 94303-3329

DE LUTIS, DONALD CONSE, investment adviser, consultant; b. Rome, Apr. 25, 1934; s. Conse R. and Mary D.; m. Ruth L.; 1 child, Dante. BS in Econs., Niagara U., 1956; MBA, Boston Coll., 1962. V.p. John Nuveen & Co., Inc., San Francisco, 1968-74; acct. exec. Dean Witter & Co., London, 1975-77; sr. investment officer Buffalo Savs. Bank, N.Y., 1978-80; exec. v.p. Robert Brown & Co., Inc., San Francisco, 1980-89, Capitol Corp. Asset mgmt., 1989-91; exec. v.p., dir. Pacific Securities, Inc., San Francisco, 1980-91; chmn. Orrell & Co., Inc., 1991-98; mng. dir. Coast Ptnrs. Securities, Inc., 1998-99; chmn. Orrell & Co. Inc., 2000—. Commr. San Francisco Bay Conservation and Devel. Commn., 1983-93, State of Calif. Commn. Housing and Community Devel., 1974-77. Served with USAF, 1957-58. Mem. Nat. Assn. Bus. Economists, San Francisco Bond Club. Republican. Roman Catholic.

DEMARCHI, ERNEST NICHOLAS, aerospace engineering administrator; b. Lafferty, Ohio, May 31, 1939; s. Ernest Constante and Lena Marie (Cireddu) D.; m. Sharon Titherley, 1996; children: Daniel Ernest, John David, Deborah Marie. BME, Ohio State U., 1962; MS in Engring., UCLA, 1969. Registered profl. engr., Ohio; registered profl. cert. mgr. With Boeing, 1962—. Mem. Apollo, Skylab and Apollo-Soyuz missions design team in electronic and elec. systems, mem. mission support team for all Apollo and Skylab manned missions, 1962-74, mem. Space Shuttle design team charge elec. systems equipment, 1974-77, in charge Orbiter Data Processing System, 1977-81, in charge Orbiter Ku Band Communication and Radar System, 1981-85, in charge orbitor elec. power distbr., displays, controls, data processing, 1984-87, in charge space based interceptor flt. exper., 1987-88, kinetic energy systems, 1988-90, ground based interceptor program, 1990-97, dep. program mgr. Nat. Missile Def. Program, 1997-2000, assoc. dep. program mgr. Space Shuttle Program, 2000—. Recipient Apollo Achievement award NASA, 1969, Apollo 13 Sustained Excellent [illegible]

Internat., 1972, Outstanding Contbn. award, 1976, NASA ALT award, 1979, Shuttle Astronaut Snoopy award, 1982, Pub. Svc. Group Achievement award NASA, 1982, Rockwell Pres.'s award, 1983, 87. Mem. AIAA, ASME, Nat. Mgmt. Assn., Varsity O Alumni Assn. Home: 8227 E Hillsdale Dr Orange CA 92869-2440 Office: 3370 E Miraloma Ave Anaheim CA 92806-1911

DEMARCO, RALPH JOHN, real estate developer; b. N.Y.C., Mar. 22, 1924; s. Frank and Mary (Castriota) DeM.; m. Arlene Gilbert, July 1, 1945; children: Sheryl DeMarco Grahn, Stephen, Laura DeMarco Wilson. BA, Claremont Men's Coll., 1956. Assoc. John B. Kilroy Co., Riverside, Calif., 1960-64, also mgr. ops. Riverside and San Bernardino counties, 1960-64; v.p. Marcus W. Meairs Co., 1964-67; pres. Diversified Properties, Inc., Riverside, 1967-72; v.p. Downey (Calif.) Savs. and Loan Assn., 1972-75; exec. v.p. DSL Svc. Co., 1972-75; pres. Interstate Shopping Ctrs., Inc., Santa Ana, Calif., 1975-87; exec. dir. comml. devel. Lewis Homes Mgmt. Corp., Upland, 1987-89; pvt. practice San Diego, 1989—. Mem. City of Riverside Planning Commn., 1955-59; mem. Airport Commn., 1960-70; mem. Urban Land Inst. 1st lt. USAF, 1942-45. Mem. Internat. Coun. Shopping Ctrs. Home: 44-489 Town Center Way # D 273 Palm Desert CA 92260-2723 Office: 1125 Linda Vista Dr Ste 107 San Marcos CA 92069-3819

DEMAREST, DAVID FRANKLIN, JR. banker, former government official; b. Glen Ridge, N.J., Oct. 8, 1951; s. David Franklin Demarest and Alison (Clark) Fahrer; m. Leigh Ann Wisniewski, Feb. 5, 1977 (div. 1981); m. Sarah Tinsley, July 16, 1983; 2 children. BA, Upsala Coll., 1973. Dep. dir. local elections Republican Nat. Com., Washington, 1977-80; dir. pub. and intergovtl. affairs U.S. Trade Rep., Washington, 1981-84; asst. U.S. Trade Rep. Exec. Office of Pres., Washington, 1984; dep. undersec. U.S. Labor Dept., Washington, 1985-87, asst. sec. labor, 1987-88; dir. comm. George Bush for Pres. Com., 1988; dir. pub. affairs Presdl. Transition Office, 1988-89; asst. to pres. for comm. White House, Washington, 1989-92; sr. cons. Internat. Mgmt. and Devel. Group, Ltd., Alexandria, Va., 1993; dir. corp. comms., exec. v.p. Bank of Am., San Francisco, 1993-99; exec. v.p. global corp. rels. Visa Internat., San Francisco, 1999—. Presbyterian Home: 28 Cypress Pl Sausalito CA 94965-1523 Office: Visa Internat PO Box 8999 San Francisco CA 94128-8999

DEMARIA, ANTHONY NICHOLAS, cardiologist, educator; b. Elizabeth, N.J., Jan. 12, 1943; s. Anthony and Charlotte DeMaria; m. Delores Horn; children: Christine, Anthony, Jonathon. BA, Coll. Holy Cross, 1964; MD, N.J. Coll. Medicine, 1968. Diplomate Am. Bd. Internal Medicine, Am. Bd. Cardiovascular Disease, Am. Bd. Cardiovascular Medicine. Intern St. Vincent Hosp., Worcester, Mass., 1968-69; resident USPHS Hosp., Staten Island, N.Y., 1969-71; fellow cardiology U. Calif., Davis, 1969-73, asst. prof. medicine, 1972-77, assoc. prof. medicine, 1977-81, prof. medicine, 1977-81; prof. medicine, chief cardiology div. U. Ky., Lexington, 1981-92; dir. Ky. Heart Inst., Lexington, 1989—; prof. medicine, chief cardiology U. Calif. Sch. Medicine, San Diego, 1992—, vice chmn. internal medicine, 1998—, med. dir. cardiovascular ctr., Judith and Jack White chair cardiovascular medicine. Mem. rev. bds. Vets. Adminstrn. Med. Research Merit in Cardiovascular Studies, Nat. Inst. Health, NSF, NIH, NHLBI, U. Calif., U.S. FDA; chmn. Diagnostic Radiology Study Sect. NIH; vice-chmn. dept. medicine U. Calif., San Diego, 1998—. Mem. editl. bd. Am. Heart Jour., Am. Jour. Cardiac Imaging, Circulation, Am. Jour. Cardiology, Jour. Am. Coll. Cardiology, Health News from New Eng. Jour. Medicine; editor-in-chief Jour. Am. Coll. Cardiology, 2001—; assoc. editor Jour. Club, Cardiology, Jour. Am. Coll. Cardiology; editl. cons. Am. Jour. Physiology, Annals Internal Medicine, Archives Phys. Medicine and Rehab., Catheterization and Cardiovascular Diagnosis, Jour. Clin. Investigation, New Eng. Jour. Medicine; contbr. numerous articles to profl. jours. ; host Cardiology Update, Lifetime Med. TV. Recipient Humanitarian award Theodore and Susan Cummings, 1978, Disting. Alumnus award Coll. Medicine and Dentistry of N.J., 1988, Echocardiography award Tufts U., 1988, award of excellence Am. Acad. Med. Adminstrs., 1994, William Hawry award Am. Med. Writers Assn., 1996; named one of Best Doctors in Am., Best Heart Specialist in U.S. Good Housekeeping mag., 1996; Golden Empire Heart Assn. grantee, Am. Heart Assn. grantee, Ky. Heart Assn. grantee, Vet. Adminstrn. grantee, Nat. Heart, Lung and Blood Inst. grantee; teaching scholar Am. Heart Assn. Fellow ACP, Am. Coll. Cardiology (chmn. 27th ann. scientific session 1978, cardiovascular procedures com., govt. rels. com., v.p. elect 1986, pres. elect 1987-88, pres. 1988—, active various coms., Young Investigator award 1976), Am. Coll. Chest Physicians; mem. Am. Heart Assn. (bd. dirs. work evaluation unit Yolo Sierra chpt., Ky. chapter, active various coms., Teaching scholar 1979-82), Am. Fedn. Clin. Rsch., Yolo County Med. Socs., Am. Inst. Ultrasound in Medicine (bd. dirs.), Am. Soc. Echocardiography (bd. dirs. 1975-87, v.p. 1983-85, pres. 1985-87, assoc. editor), N.Am. Soc. for Cardiac Radiology, Assn. U. Cardiologists. Roman Catholic. Office: U Calif Med Ctr 225 Dickinson St Ste 360 San Diego CA 92103-1910

DE MASSA, JESSIE G. media specialist; BJ, Temple U.; MLS, San Jose State U., 1967; postgrad., U. Okla., U. So. Calif. Tchr. Palo Alto (Calif.) Unified Sch. Dist., 1966; librarian Antelope Valley Joint Union High Sch. Dist., Lancaster, Calif., 1966-68, ABC Unified Sch. Dist., Artesia, 1968-72; dist. librarian Tehachapi (Calif.) Unified Sch. Dist., 1972-81; media specialist, free lance writer, 1981—; assoc. Chris DeMassa & Assocs., 1988—. Contbr. articles to profl. jours. Mem. Statue of Liberty Ellis Island Found., Inc.; charter supporter U.S. Holocaust Meml. Mus., Washington; supporting mem. U.S. Holocaust Meml. Coun., Washington; mem. Nat. Trust for Hist. Preservation. Named to Nat. Women's Hall of Fame, 1995. Fellow Internat. Biog. Assn.; mem. Calif. Media and Libr. Educators Assn., Calif. Assn. Sch. Librs. (exec. coun.), AAUW (bull. editor chpt., assoc. editor state bull., chmn. publicity, 1955-68), Nat. Mus. Women in Arts (charter), Hon Fellows John F. Kennedy Libr. (founding mem.), Women's Roundtable of Orange County, Nat. Writer's Assn. (so. Calif. chpt.), Calif. Retired Tchrs. Assn. (Harbor Beach divsn. 77), The Heritage Found., Claremont Inst., Libr. of Congress (nat. charter mem.), Cato Inst. Home: 9951 Garrett Cir Huntington Beach CA 92646-3604 E-mail: jdwriter10@aol.com

DEMENT, IRIS, vocalist, songwriter; b. Paragould, Ark., Jan. 5, 1961; d. Patric Shaw and Flora Mae DeM. Represented by Rounder/Philo, 1991-92, Warner Bros., 1993—. Songwriter, 1986—; performer open mic. nights, Kansas City. Albums include Infamous Angel, 1992, rereleased 1993, My Life, 1994, The Way I Should, 1996. Home: PO Box 28856 Kansas City MO 64188-8856 Office: Warner Bros 3300 Warner Blvd Burbank CA 91505-4694

DEMENT, WILLIAM CHARLES, medical researcher, medical educator; b. Wenatchee, Wash., July 29, 1928; s. Charles Frederick and Kathryn (Severyns) D.; m. Eleanor Weber, Mar. 23, 1956; children: Catherine Lynn, Elizabeth Anne, John Nicholas. B.S., U. Wash., 1951; M.D., U. Chgo., 1955, Ph.D., 1957. Bd. cert. in clin. polysomography. Intern Mt. Sinai Hosp., N.Y.C., 1957-58, research fellow dept. psychiatry, 1958-63; assoc. prof. dept. psychiatry and behavioral scis. Stanford U., 1963-67, prof., 1967—; dir. Stanford Sleep Disorders Clinic and Lab., 1970—, Sleep Research Lab., Stanford, Calif., 1963—. Chmn. U.S. Surgeon Gen.'s Joint Coord. Coun., Project Sleep, 1979—, Nat. Commn. on Sleep Disorders Rsch., 1990-92. Author: Some Must Watch While Some Must Sleep, 1972, The Sleep Watchers, 1992; editor-in-chief: Sleep, 1977—; mem. editorial bd. Neurobiology of Aging, 1982—. Recipient medal Intra-Sci. Research [illegible]

Assn., 1978 Mem. Sleep Research Soc. (founder), Assn. Sleep Disorders Ctrs. (pres. 1982 Nathaniel Kleitman prize), Inst. Medicine of Nat. Acad. Scis., Psychiat. Research Found., Soc. Neurosci., Western EEG Soc., Am. EEG Soc., Am. Physiol. Soc. Office: Stanford Sleep Disorders Ctr 701 Welch Rd Ste 2226 Palo Alto CA 94304-1711

DEMERY, DOROTHY JEAN, secondary school educator; b. Houston, Sept. 5, 1941; d. Floyd Hicks and Irene Elaine Burns Clay; m. Leroy W. Demery, Jan. 16, 1979; children: Steven Bradley, Rodney Bradley, Craig Bradley, Kimberly Bradley. AA, West L.A. Coll., Culver City, Calif., 1976; AS, Harbor Coll., Wilmington, Calif., 1983; BS in Pub. Adminstrn., Calif. State U., Carson, 1985; MS in Instructional Leadership, Nat. U., San Diego, 1991. Cert. real estate broker, tchr. math. and bus. edn., bilingual tchr., crosscultural lang. and acad. devel.; lang. devel. specialist. Eligibility social worker Dept. Pub. Social Svcs., L.A., 1967-74; real estate broker Dee Bradley & Assocs., Riverside, Calif., 1976—; tchr. math L.A. Unified Sch. Dist., 1985-91; math/computer sci. tchr. Pomona (Calif.) Unified Sch. Dist., 1991—. Adj. lectr. Riverside C.C., 1992-93; mem. Dist. Curriculum Coun./Report Card Task Force, Pomona, 1994—; del. rep. assembly NEA, 1991—. Chairperson Human Rights Com., Pomona, 1992—, sec. steering com., 1993—, adv. bd., 1993—; mem. polit. action com. Assoc. Pomona Tchrs., 1993-94. Recipient Outstanding Svc. award Baldwin Hills Little League Assn., L.A., 1972. Mem. Nat. Bus. Assn., Nat. Coun. Tchrs. Math., Aux. Nat. Med. Assn., Associated Pomona Tchrs. (bd. dirs.), Calif. Tchrs. Assn. (mem. state coun., 2000, chair site base, chair dept. math.) Avocations: hiking, tennis, walking. Home: PO Box 2796 Riverside CA 92516-2796 Office: Simons Middle School 900 E Franklin Ave Pomona CA 91766-5362

DE MICHELE, O. MARK, utility company executive; b. Syracuse, N.Y., Mar. 23, 1934; s. Aldo and Dora (Carno) De M.; m. Faye Ann Venturin, Nov. 8, 1957; children: Mark A., Christopher C., Michele M., Julianne; m. Barbara Joan Stanley, May 22, 1982; 1 child, Angela Marie. BS, Syracuse U., 1955; hon. doctorate, No. Ariz. U., 1997. Mgr. Seal Right Co., Inc., Fulton, N.Y., 1955-58; v.p., gen. mgr. L.M. Harvey Co. Inc., Syracuse, 1958-62; v.p. Niagara Mohawk Power, Syracuse, 1962-78, Ariz. Pub. Svc., Phoenix, 1978-81, exec. v.p., 1981-82, pres., CEO, 1982-97, also bd. dirs.; pres., CEO Greater Phoenix Econ. Coun., 1997-98; chmn., CEO Urban Realty Ptnrs. LLC, 1998—. Bd. dirs. Ont. Power Generation. Pres. Jr. Achievement, Syracuse, 1974-75, Phoenix, 1982-83, United Way Ctrl. N.Y., Syracuse, 1978, Ariz. Opera Co., Phoenix, 1981-83, Phoenix Symphony, 1984-86, United Way Phoenix, 1985-86, Ariz. Mus. Sci. and Tech., 1988-90; pres. Childrens Action Alliance, 1989-92; chmn. Valley Sun United Way, 1984-86, Phoenix Econ. Coun., 1991-94; chmn. Morrison Inst. Pub. Policy at Ariz. State U.; chmn. Ariz. Cities in Schs., 1994-97, Nat. Environ. Edn. Found., 1997—. Named Outstanding Young Man of Yr., Syracuse Jaycees, 1968, Phoenix Man of Yr., Phoenix Ad Club, 1992; recipient Humanitarian award Nat. Conf., 1995. Mem. Phoenix C. of C. (chmn. bd. 1986-87). Republican. Clubs: Phoenix Country, Ariz. (Phoenix). Home: 840 Glorietta Blvd Coronado CA 92118-2306 Office: Urban Realty Ptnrs LLC 2415 E Camelback Rd Ste 700 Phoenix AZ 85016-4245 E-mail: mdemichele@aol.com

DEMIERI, JOSEPH L. bank executive; b. N.Y.C., Aug. 31, 1940; s. Leo A. and Frances (Garone) DeM.; m. Anne Patricia McCue, May 15, 1965. B.B.A., Tex. A&M U., 1962. C.P.A., N.Y. With Peat, Marwick, Mitchell & Co., N.Y.C., 1962-68; v.p., controller City Investing Co., N.Y.C. and Beverly Hills, Calif., 1968-82; exec. v.p. Motown Industries, Los Angeles, 1982-84; chmn., CEO Calif. Millworks Corp., Valencia, 1985-95; sr. v.p., CFO Western Security Bank, Burbank, Calif., 1995—. Home: 6259 Ebbtide Way Malibu CA 90265-3608 Office: 4100 W Alameda Ave Burbank CA 91505-4195

DEMMEL, JAMES W. computer science educator; b. Pitts., Oct. 19, 1955; BS, Calif. Inst. Tech., 1975; PhD in Computer Sci., U. Calif., Berkeley, 1983. Prof. computer sci. NYU, 1983-90; prof. computer sci. divsn. U. Calif., Berkeley, 1990—. Recipient Presdl. Young Investigator award. Mem. NAE, IEEE, Am. Math. Soc., Math. Assn. Am., Soc. Indsl. and Applied Math. (J.H. Wilkinson prize). Office: U Calif Dept Math Berkeley CA 94710-1625

DEMOFF, MARVIN ALAN, lawyer; b. L.A., Oct. 28, 1942; s. Max and Mildred (Tweer) D.; m. Patricia Caryn Abelov, June 16, 1968; children: Allison Leigh, Kevin Andrew. BA, UCLA, 1964; JD, Loyola U., L.A., 1967. Bar: Calif. 1969. Asst. pub. defender Los Angeles County, 1968-72; ptnr. Steinberg & Demoff, L.A., 1973-83, Craighill, Fentress & Demoff, L.A. and Washington, 1983-86; of counsel Mitchell, Silberberg & Knupp, L.A., 1987—. Mem. citizens adv. bd. Olympic Organizing Com., L.A., 1982-84; bd. trustees Curtis Sch., L.A., 1985-94, chmn. bd. trustees, 1988-93; sports adv. bd. Constitution Rights Found., L.A., 1986—. Mem. ABA (mem. forum com. on entertainment and sports), Calif. Bar Assn., UCLA Alumni Assn., Phi Delta Phi. Avocations: sports, music, art. Office: Mitchell Silberberg Knupp 11377 W Olympic Blvd Los Angeles CA 90064-1625

DEMOUTH, ROBIN MADISON, lawyer, corporate executive; b. Warwick, N.Y., Apr. 2, 1939; s. Claude Cornelius and Mary Louise (Shaw) D.; m. Mary Eileen Burns, April 25, 1992. BA, U. Va., 1961; postgrad., U. Ill., 1962; JD, John Marshall Law Sch., 1965; LLM, Lawyer's Inst., 1970; MBA, U. Chgo., 1976. Bar: Ill. 1966, U.S. Supreme Ct. 1970. Assoc. Madsen & Friese, Chgo., 1965-67; atty. Stewart-Warner Corp., Chgo., 1965-70, sr. atty., 1970-78, sec., chief legal officer, 1978-81, sec., gen. counsel, 1981-83, v.p., sec., gen. counsel, 1983-88; sec., gen. counsel Sandoz Corp., Des Plaines, Ill., 1989-98; v.p., gen. counsel, sec. Valent U.S.A. Corp., Walnut Creek, Calif., 1998—. Mem. Gt. Lakes Commn., 1975-78; mem. internat. trade and port promotional adv. com. State of Ill., 1975-78. Bd. dirs., v.p., counsel Easter Seal Soc. of Met. Chgo. Inc., 1983-87. Mem. ABA, Am. Soc. Corp. Secs., Am. Assn. Corp. Counsel, Chgo. Bar Assn., Nat. Agrl. Chem. Assn. (vice chmn. law com. 1993, chmn. law com. 1995-96), Chgo. Yacht Club (bd. dirs. 1987, vice commodore 1992, commodore 1995-96, bd. dirs. 1995—), Mackinaw Island Yacht Club, Judd Gold Adaptive Sailing Found. (dir., 1990—), Econ. Club Chgo. Republican. Episcopalian. Avocation: sailing.

DEMPSEY, PAUL STEPHEN, law educator; b. Aug. 27, 1950; BA in Journalism, U. Ga., 1972, JD, 1975; LLM in Internat. Law summa cum laude, George Washington U., 1978; DCL cum laude, McGill U., Montreal, Canada, 1986. Bar: Colo., Ga., D.C. Atty., advisor Office Proceedings Interstate Commerce Comm., Wash., D.C., 1975-77, legal advisor to chmn., 1981-82; atty., advisor Office Gen. Counsel Civil Aeronautics Bd., 1977-79; asst., assoc. prof. Coll. Law U. Denver, 1979-85, prof. Coll. Law, 1986—, Hughes Rsch. prof. Coll. Law, 1985-86, 89-91; prof. law distinguished vis. DePaul U., Chgo., 1989-90; Hughes prof. law, dir. transp. law program U. Denver, 1993—. Dir. U. Denver Transp. Law Program, 1979—; vice chmn. Frontier Airlines, Inc., 1994—; appeared on ABC Evening News with Peter Jennings, MacNeil-Lehrer News Hour, ABC World Bus. Report, NBC Today, CNN Crossfire, Nat. Pub. Radio, CBS Radio, NBC Mutual Radio and other news broadcasting programs; host Your Right to Say It, KWGN-TV, 1986—. Author: Law and Foreign Policy in International Aviation, 1987, The Social and Economic Consequences of Deregulation, 1989, Flying Blind: The Failure of Airline Deregulation, 1990, Airline Deregulation & Laissez Faire Mythology, 1992, Aviation Law and Regulation, 2 vols., 1993, Denver International Airport: Lessons Learned, 1997, Airline Management: Strategies for the 21st Century, 1997, Air Transportation: Foundations for the 21st Century, 1997; (with William [illegible] others) The Law of Transnational Business Transactions; editor: Transp. Law Jour.; mem. editl. bd. Aviation Law Quarterly, 1996—, Denver Bus. Jour., 1996—; contbr. articles to profl. jours. Fulbright fellow, 1986-87; Canadian Institutional Rsch. grantee, 1989-90, Econ. Policy Inst. grantee, 1989, Hughes Foun. Rsch. grantee, 1987-88, 82, Rocky Mountain Minearl Law Inst. Rsch. grantee, 1987; U. Denver Burlington No. Foun. Outstanding scholar, 1987; recipient Transp. Lawyers Assn. Distinguished Svc. award 1986, Cert. Claims Profl. Accreditation Coun. Outstanding Svc. award 1983. Mem. ABA (vice chmn. transp. com. of adminstrv. law sect. 1988-91), Assn. Am. Law Schs. (chmn. air and space law 1989-90), Cert. Claims Profl. Accreditation Coun. (chmn. bd. dirs. 1981-83), Am. Arbitration Assn. (bd. arbitrators 1987—), Citizens Responsible Transp. (pres. bd. dirs. 1984-86), Internat. Aerospace Inst. (bd. dirs. 1982-86). Office: U Denver Coll Law 1900 Olive St Denver CO 80220-1857 also: FRONTIER AIRLINES INC P O bOX 39177 DENVER CO 80239

DEMSETZ, HAROLD, economist, educator; b. Chgo., 1930; BA, U. Ill., 1953; MBA, Northwestern U., 1954, PhD in Econs., 1959. Prof. econs. U. Chgo., 1963-71; sr. rsch. fellow Hoover Instn., Stanford, Calif., 1971-77; prof. econs. UCLA, 1971—, Arthur Anderson Alumni prof. bus. econs, 1988-95, emeritus, 1995—. Author: Economic, Legal, and Political Dimensions of Competition, 1982, The Organization of Economic Activity, Vol. I, 1988, Vol. II, 1989, The Economics of the Firm, 1995; contbr. numerous articles, book chpts. Fellow AAAS; mem. Mont Pelerin Soc., Am. Econs. Assn., WEA Internat. (pres. 1996). Office: UCLA Dept Econs 405 Hilgard Ave Los Angeles CA 90095-9000 E-mail: hdemsetz@ucla.edu

DEMURO, PAUL ROBERT, lawyer; b. Aberdeen, Md., Mar. 21, 1954; s. Paul Robert and Amelia C. DeMuro; m. Susan Taylor, May 26, 1990; children: Melissa Taylor, Natalie Lauren, Alanna Leigh. BA summa cum laude, U. Md., 1976; JD, Washington U., 1979; MBA, U. Calif., Berkeley, 1986. Bar: Md. 1979, U.S. Dist. Ct. Md. 1979, D.C. 1980, U.S. Dist. Ct. D.C. 1980, U.S. Dist. Ct. (ea. dist.) Calif. 1986, U.S. Ct. Appeals (4th cir.) 1981, U.S. Tax Ct. 1981, Calif. 1982, U.S. Dist. Ct. (no. dist.) Calif. 1982; CPA, Md. Assoc. Ober, Grimes & Shriver, Balt., 1979-82; ptnr. Carpenter et al, San Francisco, 1982-89, McCutchen, Doyle, Brown & Enerson, San Francisco, 1989-93, Latham & Watkins, San Francisco, 1993—. Bd. dirs. HFMA Learning Solutions Inc. Author: The Financial Managers Guide to Managed Care and Integrated Delivery Systems, 1995, The Fundamentals of Managed Care and Network Development, 1999; co-author: Health Care Mergers and Acquisitions: The Transactional Perspective, 1996, Health Care Executives' Guide to Fraud and Abuse, 1998; editor, contbg. author Integrated Delivery Systems, 1994; article and book rev. editor Washington U. Law Qrtly., St. Louis, 1975-76. Mem. San Francisco Mus. Modern Art, 1985—. Fellow Healthcare Fin. Mgmt. Assn. (bd. dirs. No. Calif. chpt. 1990-93, 99—, sec. 1999-2001, pres.-elect 2001—, nat. principles and practices bd. 1992-95, vice chair 1993-95, nat. bd. dirs. 1995-97, exec. com. 1996-97, chair compliance officers forum adv. coun. 1998-2000); mem. ABA (health law sect., chair transactional and bus. health care interest group 1998-2000, chair programs com. 2000—, governing coun. 2000—),AICPA. L.A. County Bar Assn. (health law sect.), Calif. Bar Assn., San Francisco Bar Assn., Am. Health Lawyers Assn. (fraud and abuse and self-referral substantive law com. 1998—, task force on best practices in advising clients 1998-99), The IPA Assn. Am. (mem. legal adv. coun. 1996—), Med. Group Mgmt. Assn. Republican. Office: Latham & Watkins 505 Montgomery St Ste 1900 San Francisco CA 94111-2552 E-mail: paul.demuro@lw.com

DEMUTH, LAURENCE WHEELER, JR. lawyer, utility company executive; b. Boulder, Colo., 22 Nov. s. Laurence Wheeler and Eugenia Augusta (Roach) DeM.; m. Paula Phipps, Mar. 7, 1987; children: Debra Lynn, Laurence Wheeler III, Brant Hill. AB, U. Colo., 1951, LLB, 1953. Gen. atty. Mountain State Telephone and Telegraph Co., Denver, 1968, v.p., gen. counsel, 1968-84, sec., 1974-84; exec. v.p., gen. counsel, sec. U.S. West, Inc., Englewood, Colo., 1984-92, ret., 1992. Dist. capt. Rep. Precinct Com., 1957-70' trustee Lakewood (Colo.) Presbyn. Ch., 1965-68; bd. dirs. Colo. Epilepsy Assn., 1973-79; bd. litigation Mountain States Legal Found., 1980-89; Colo. Commr. on Uniform State of Laws, 1997—. Mem. ABA, Colo. Bar Assn. (chmn. ethics com. 1973-74, bd. govs., fellow found.), Denver Bar Assn., Am. Judicature Soc., Colo. Assn. Corp. Counsel (pres.), Order of Coif, Phi Beta Kappa, Pi Gamma Mu. Clubs: University, Metropolitan. Office: US West Inc 9785 S Maroon Cir Ste 210 Englewood CO 80112-5918

DEN BESTEN, PAMELA KAY, biomedical researcher, dentist; b. Iowa City, Sept. 20, 1954; d. Lawrence and Shirley Ann (Langeland) Den B.; m. Brian John Awbrey, Aug. 22, 1981; children: Matthew, Nathan. BS in Chemistry, St. Olaf Coll., 1976; DDS, U. Iowa, 1980. Pedodontic resident N.C. Meml. Hosp., Chapel Hill, N.C., 1980-82; clin. asst. prof. U. N.C., Chapel Hill, 1982-85; instr. pediatric dentistry Harvard Sch. Dental Medicine, Boston, 1985—; staff assoc. Forsyth Dental Ctr., Boston, 1985-88, asst. mem. staff, 1988—; asst. in pediatric dentistry Children's Hosp., Boston, 1986—. Ad hoc mem. study sect. NIH, Bethesda, Md., 1990. Editorial rev. bd. Jour. Dental Rsch., 1988—; contbr. articles to profl. jours. Deacon Park Ave. Congl. Ch., Arlington, Mass., 1990—. Mem. AAAS, Am. Acad. Pediatric Dentistry, Am. Soc. Dentistry for Children, Internat. Assn. Dental Rsch. Democrat. Mem. United Ch. of Christ. Achievements include advances made in understanding the mechanisms by which fluoride affects tooth enamel development. Office: UCSF Dept Growth & Develop PO Box 640 San Francisco CA 94143-0001

DENDAHL, JOHN, political organization administrator; Chmn. Rep. Party N.Mex., Albuquerque. Office: Rep Party NMex 2901 Juan Tabo Blvd NE Ste 116 Albuquerque NM 87112-1885 Fax: 505-292-0755

DENHAM, ROBERT EDWIN, lawyer, investment company executive; b. Dallas, Aug. 27, 1945; s. Wilburn H. and Anna Marie (Hughes) D; m. Carolyn Hunter, June 3, 1966; children: Jeffrey Hunter, Laura Maria. BA, U. Tex., 1966; MA, Harvard U., 1968, JD, 1971. Bar: Calif. 1972. Assoc. Munger Tolles and Olson, L.A., 1971-73; ptnr. Munger Tolles Olson, L.A., 1973-85, 92-93; mng. ptnr. Munger Tolles and Olson, L.A., 1985-91; chmn., chief exec. officer Salomon Inc, N.Y.C., 1992-97; ptnr. Munger Tolles and Olson, L.A., 1998—. Pres. Pasadena (Calif.) Ednl. Found., 1977-79; bd. dirs. Pub. Counsel, L.A., 1981-84, United Way, N.Y.C., 1994-97; trustee Cathedral Corp. Diocese of L.A., 1986-92, Poly. Sch. Pasadena, 1989-93, v.p. bd. trustees, 1991-93; bd. trustees New Sch. Social Rsch., 1995—, Natural Resources Def. Coun., 1992—; adv. bd. of the pres. Calif. State U., Sonoma, 1993—; bd. trustees The Conference Bd., 1994—, Russell Sage Found., 1997—; pub. mem. Independence Stds. Bd., 1997—; former co-chmn. Subcoun. on Capital Allocation of the Competitiveness Policy Coun.; former mem. Bipartisan Commn. on Entitlement and Tax Reform; former U.S. rep. to the Asia Pacific Econ. Coun. Bus. Adv. Coun.; mem. bus. sector adv. group on corp. governance OECD; bd. dirs. U.S. Trust Co., AMKOR Tech., Inc. Mem. ABA, State Bar Calif., L.A. County Bar (bus. and corps. exec. com. 1985—). Democrat. Episcopalian. Avocations: soccer, cooking. Office: Munger Tolles and Olson 355 S Grand Ave # 3500 Los Angeles CA 90071-1560

DENHART, GUN, direct mail order company executive; b. Lund, Sweden, July 14, 1945; came to U.S., 1975; d. Gunnar Arnold and Elsa (Bjôrklund) Brime; m. Thomas E. Denhart, Aug. 29, 1975; children: Philip, Christian. MBA, Lund U., Sweden, 1967. Tchr. Swedish Pub. Sch., Landskrona, Sweden, 1972-73; asst. to sec. gen., bus. and industry adv. com. OECD, Paris, 1973-75; fin. mgr. EF Colls. Ltd., Greenwich, Conn., 1978-84; chief exec. officer Hanna Andersson Corp., Portland, Oreg., 1984—. Trustee Ednl. Fund for Fgn. Colls., Greenwich, Conn. Mem. Young Pres. Orgn. Office: Hanna Andersson Corp 1010 NW Flanders St Portland OR 97209-3119

DENIOUS, SHARON MARIE, retired publisher periodical; b. Rulo, Nebr., Jan. 27, 1941; d. Thomas Wayne and Alma (Murphy) Fee; m. Jon Parks Denious, June 17, 1963; children: Timothy Scot, Elizabeth Denious Cessna. Grad. high sch. Operator N.W. Pipeline co., Ignacio, Colo., 1975-90; pub. The Silverton Standard & The Miner, 1990-99. Avocations: reading, hiking. E-mail: denious@frontier.net

DENISH, DIANE D. political organization administrator; Assoc. pub., bus. devel. and advt. sales Starlight Pub. Ltd., Albuquerque Living and NMex. Monthly, Albuquerque; state chmn. N.Mex Dem. Party. Office: 5317 Menaul Blvd NE Albuquerque NM 87110-3113

DENMARK, BERNHARDT, manufacturing executive; b. Bklyn., June 6, 1917; s. William M. and Kate (Lazarus) D.; m. Muriel Schechter, Sept. 22, 1943; children: Richard J., Karen. A.B., NYU, 1941; postgrad., Am. U., 1941-42, Nat. Inst. Pub. Affairs, 1941-42. Vice pres. sales Telecoin Corp., N.Y.C., 1946-49; v.p. sales Internat. Latex Corp., N.Y.C., 1949-55; mgr. mktg. Playtex Co., N.Y.C., 1955-59, v.p., gen. mgr. family products div., 1959-63, v.p. mktg., 1963-65; pres. Playtex Co. Playtex div., 1965-67, Internat. Playtex Corp., N.Y.C., 1968-69, chmn. bd., 1969; exec. v.p., dir., mem. exec. com. Glen Alden Corp., N.Y.C., 1969-72; pres. Bevis Industries, Inc., White Plains, N.Y., 1972-76, Bus. Mktg. Corp. for N.Y.C., 1977-78; chmn. Denmark, Donovan & Oppel Inc., N.Y.C., 1978-85; chmn. bd. dirs. Advanced Photonix, Inc., Camarillo, Calif., 1992—, Xsirius, Inc., Camarillo, 1992—. Bd. dirs. Stanley Warner Corp., Schenley Industries, BVD Corp., Kleinerts Inc., Advanced Photonics Inc. Served to capt. AUS, 1942-46. Clubs: Fairview Country (Greenwich, Conn.); City Athletic (N.Y.C.). Home: 870 United Nations Plz Apt 34B New York NY 10017-1820 Office: 1240 Avenida Acaso Camarillo CA 93012-8754

DENNIS, DAVID L. healthcare executive; B Econs., San Diego State U.; MBA in Fin. and Corp. Strategy, UCLA. With def. attache office Am. Embassy, Lisbon, Portugal; with investment banking divsn. Merrill Lynch Capital Markets; mng. dir., co-head L.A. office Donaldson, Lufkin and Jenrette; vice chmn., chief corp. officer, CFO Tenet Healthcare Corp., Santa Barbara, Calif., 2000—. With USAF, Vietnam. Office: Tenet Healthcare Corp 3820 State St Santa Barbara CA 93105

DENNIS, GINETTE E. (GIGI), state legislator; b. Kansas City, Mo., Nov. 28, 1961; m. Dean Dennis. Student, Adams State Coll., U. So. Colo., Harvard U. With Band of Monte Vista, 1982-87; customer svc. rep. Pub. Svc. Co. Colo., Alamosa, 1987-91, Pueblo, 1991-94; mem. Colo. Senate, Dist. 5, Denver, 1994—. Bd. mem. El Pueblo Boys and Girls Ranch; active Sangre de Cristo Arts Ctr., Rosemount Mus.; sec., past sec. Rio Grande County Reps.; past chair Ho. Dist. 60; mem. Local, State and Nat. Campaign Com., 1984—. Mem. Pueblo Zool. Soc., Bel Nor Rep. Women, Monte Vista C. of C., Pueblo West Rotary, Colo. Cattle Assn. Republican. Roman Catholic. Office: State Capitol 200 E Colfax Ave Ste 263 Denver CO 80203-1716 also: PO Box 7416 Pueblo West CO 81007-0416 Fax: 719-547-9330

DENNIS, KAREN MARIE, plastic surgeon; b. Cleve., Dec. 23, 1948; d. Chester and Adele (Wesley) D.; m. Miles Auslander, June 21, 1974; 1 child, Kristin. BS, Ohio State U., 1971, MD, 1974. Diplomate Am. Bd. Plastic Surgery, Am. Bd. Otolaryngology. Intern Kaiser Permanente, L.A., 1974-75; resident in otolaryngology Roosevelt Hosp., N.Y.C., 1976-79; resident in plastic surgery Ohio State Univ. Hosps., Columbus, 1979-81; pvt. practice Beverly Hills, Calif., 1981—. Mem. Am. Soc. Reconstructive and Plastic Surgeons, Calif. County Med. Assn., L.A. County med. Assn., L.A. Soc. Plastic Surgeons (sec. 1993-94), Phi Beta Kappa. Avocations: tennis, golfing, traveling, reading. Office: 433 N Camden Dr Beverly Hills CA 90210-4426

DENNISH, GEORGE WILLIAM, III, cardiologist; b. Trenton, N.J., Feb. 14, 1945; s. George William and Mary Ann (Bodnar) D.; div. 1993; children: Andrew Stuart, Brian George, Michael John; m. Cheryl A. Henry, Aug. 6, 1993; 1 stepson, Joshua J. Morris. AB magna cum laude, Seton Hall U., 1967; MD, Jefferson Med. Coll., 1971. Diplomate Nat. Bd. Med. Examiners, Am. Bd. Internal Medicine (subspecialty cert. in cardiovascular diseases). Intern Naval Hosp., Phila., 1971-72, jr. asst. resident, 1972-73, sr. asst. resident, 1973-74; fellow cardiovascular diseases Naval Regional Med. Ctr., San Diego, 1974-76, dir. coronary care unit, 1977-78; pvt. practice cardiology San Diego, 1978—. V.p. Splty. Med. Clinic, La Jolla and San Diego, 1982—; staff cardiologist Naval Regional Med. Ctr., Faculty Medicine, San Diego, 1976—; dir. spl. care units Scripps Meml. Hosp., La Jolla, 1981-88, chmn. cardiology div., 1987—; chief medicine Scripps-Encinitas Hosp., 1983-87; co-editor Cardiac CATV, 1987—; adj. asst. prof. medicine Baylor Coll., Houston; assoc. clin. prof. medicine U. Calif., San Diego, 1976—. Contbr. articles to med. jours. Bd. dirs. San Diego County Heart Assn.; pres. San Diety County divsn. Am. Heart Assn., 1999-2000; founder, pres. Cardiovascular Inst., La Jolla. Lt. comdr. USNR, 1971—. Decorated Knight of Holy Sepulcre; recipient Physician's Recognition award AMA, 1974-77. Fellow ACP, Am. Coll. Cardiology, Am. Heart Assn. (clin. coun.), Am. Coll. Chest physicians, Am. Coll. Angrology; mem. Am. Soc. Internal Medicine, AAAS, Am. Coll. Clin. Pharmacology, N.Y. Acad. Scis., Am. Fedn. Clin. Rsch., N.Am. Soc. Pacing and Electrophysiology, Soc. for Cardiac Angiography, Soc. for Cardiac Antiography and Intervention, Old Mission Players Club, K.C. Home: 13063 Caminito Pointe Del Ma Del Mar CA 92014-3854 Address: 9850 Genesee Ave Ste 940 La Jolla CA 92037-1220 E-mail: gdennish@ucsc.edu

DENNISON, GEORGE MARSHEL, academic administrator; b. Buffalo, Aug. 11, 1935; s. Earl Fredrick and Irene Gladys (McWhorter) D.; m. Jane Irene Schroeder, Dec. 26, 1954; children: Robert Gene, Rick Steven. AA, Custer County (Mont.) Jr. Coll., 1960; BA, U. Mont., 1962, MA, 1963; PhD, U. Wash., 1967. Asst. prof. U. Ark., Fayetteville, 1967-68; vis. asst. prof. U. Wash., Seattle, 1968-69; asst. prof. Colo. State U., Fort Collins, 1969-73, assoc. prof., 1973-77, assoc. dean Coll. Arts, Humanities and Social Sci., 1976-80, prof., 1977-87, acting acad. v.p., 1980-82, acting assoc. acad. v.p., 1982-86, assoc. acad. v.p., 1987; provost, v.p. acad. affairs Western Mich. U., Kalamazoo, 1987-90; pres. U. Mont., Missoula, 1990—. Cons. U.S. Dept. Justice, 1976-84; bd. Community Med. Ctr, Missoula, 1st Bank, Missoula, Inst. Medicine and Humanities, Missoula. Author: The Dorr War, 1976; contbr. articles to jours. in field. Bd. dirs. Kalamazoo Ctr. for Med. Studies, 1989-90. With USN, 1953-57. ABA grantee, 1969-70; Colo. State U. grantee, 1970-75, Nat. Trust for Hist. Preservation grantee, 1976-78; U.S. Agy. for Internat. Devel. grantee, 1979—; Colo. Commn. on Higher Edn. devel. grantee, 1985. Mem. Am. Hist. Assn., Orgn. Am. Historians, Am. Assn. Higher Edn., Am. Soc. for Legal History. Avocations: handball, cross-country skiing. Office: U Montana Office of The Pres Univ UH 109 Missoula MT 59812-0001

DENNISON, RONALD WALTON, engineer; b. San Francisco, Oct. 23, 1944; s. S. Mason and Elizabeth Louise (Hatcher) D.; m. Deborah Ann Rutter, Aug. 10, 1991; children: Ronald, Frederick. BS in Physics and Math., San Jose State U., 1970, MS in Physics, 1972. Physicist, Memorex, Santa Clara, Calif., 1970-71; sr. engr. AVCO, San Jose, Calif., 1972-73; advanced devel. engr. Perkin Elmer, Palo Alto, Calif., 1973-75; staff engr. Hewlett-Packard, Santa Rosa, Calif., 1975-79; program gen. mgr. Burroughs, Westlake Village, Calif., 1979-82; dir. engring., founder EIKON, Simi Valley, Calif., 1982-85; sr. staff technologist Maxtor Corp., San Jose, 1987-90; dir. engring. Toshiba Am. Info. Systems, 1990-93, cons. engr., 1994—; materials. Author tech. publs. Served to sgt. USAF, 1963-67. Mem. IEEE, Am. Vacuum Soc., Internat. Soc. Hybrid Microelectronics, Internat. Disk Drive Equipment and Materials Assn. Republican. Methodist. Mem. Aircraft Owners and Pilots Assn., Internat. Comanche Soc. Home: 4050 Soelro Ct San Jose CA 95127-2711

DENNY, MATTHEW, political organization administrator; Acct. Denny & Co., CPAs, Missoula, Mont.; mem. Mont. State Ho. Reps. Dist. 63, chmn. state adminstrn. com., mem. local govt. and edn com., mem. select joint ethics com.; state chmn. Mont. Rep. Party, 1999—. Mem. Missoula County Ctrl. Com., State Ctrl. Com.; bd. dirs. Rep. Legis. Campaign Com. Mem. Five Valleys Pachyderm Club (bd. dirs.). Office: 1419B Helena Ave Helena MT 59601-3024

DENSLEY, COLLEEN T. elementary educator, curriculum specialist; b. Provo, Utah, Apr. 12, 1950; d. Floyd and Mary Lou (Dixon) Taylor; m. Steven T. Densley, July 23, 1968; children: Steven, Tiffany, Landon, Marianne, Wendy, Logan. BS in Elem. Edn., Brigham Young U., 1986, MEd in Tchg. and Learning, 1998. Cert. in elem. edn., K-12 adminstrn., Utah. Substitute tchr. Provo Sch. Dist., 1972-85; tchr. 6th grade, mainstreaming program Canyon Crest Elem. Sch., Provo, 1985-99; curriculum specialist Provo Sch. Dist., 1999-2001; prin. Wasatch Elem. Sch., Provo, Utah, 2001—. Tchr. asst., math tutor Brigham Young U., 1968-69; attendee World Gifted and Talented Conf., Salt Lake City, 1987, Tchr. Expectations and Student Achievement, 1988-89, Space Acad. for Educators, Huntsville, Ala., 1992; supr. coop. tchr. for practicum tchrs., 1987-90; co-chmn. accelerated learning and devel. com.; trainee for working with handicapped students in mainstreamed classroom, 1989; mem. elem. sch. lang. arts curriculum devel. com., 1990; mem. task force Thinking Strategies Curriculum, 1990-91; extensions specialist gifted and talented, 1990-91, math, 1991—; master tchr. Nat. Teacher Tng. Inst., 1993. Co-author (curricula) Provo Sch. Dist.'s Microorganism Sci. Kit, 1988, Arthropod Sci. Kit, 1988, Teaching for Thinking, 1990—, PAWS Presents the Internet and the World Wide Web, 1997. Recipient Honor Young Mother of Yr. award State of Utah, 1981; named Utah state Tchr. of Yr., 1992. Mem. NEA, Nat. Coun. Tchrs. Math., Utah Edn. Assn. Utah Coun. Tchrs. of Math, Internat. Space Edn. Initiative (adv. bd.), Prove Edn. Assn. (Tchr. of Yr. 1991-92). Republican. Mem. LDS Ch. Office: Wasatch Elem Sch 1080 N 900 E Provo UT 84604 E-mail: colleend@provo.k12.ut.us

DENT, ERNEST DUBOSE, JR. pathologist; b. Columbia, S.C., May 3, 1927; s. E. Dubose and Grace (Lee) D.; m. Dorothy McCalman, June 16, 1949; children: Christopher, Pamela; m. 2d, Karin Frehse, Sept. 6, 1970. Student, Presbyn. Coll., 1944-45; M.D., Med. Coll. S.C., 1949. Diplomate clin. pathology and pathology anatomy Am. Bd. Pathology. Intern U.S. Naval Hosp., Phila., 1949-50; resident pathology USPHS Hosp., Balt., 1950-54, chief pathology Norfolk, Va., 1954-56; assoc. pathology Columbia (S.C.) Hosp., 1956-59; pathologist, dir. labs. Columbia Hosp., S.C. Baptist Hosp., 1958-69; with Straus Clin. Labs., L.A., 1969-72; staff pathologist Hollywood (Calif.) Community Hosp., St. Joseph Hosp., Burbank, Calif., 1969-72; dir. labs. Glendale Meml. Hosp. and Health Ctr., 1972-94; ret. Bd. dirs. Glendale Meml. Hosp. and Health Ctr. Author papers nat. med. jours. Mem. Am. Cancer Soc., AMA, L.A. County Med. Assn. (pres. Glendale dist. 1980-81), Calif. Med. Assn. (councillor 1984-90), Am. Soc. Clin. Pathology, Coll. Am. Pathologists (assemblyman S.C. 1965-67; mem. publs. com. bull. 1968-70), L.A. Soc. Pathologists (trustee 1984-87), L.A. Acad. Medicine, S.C. Soc. Pathologists (pres. 1967-69). Lutheran. Home: 1605 La Plaza Dr San Marcos CA 92069-4841 Office: 1420 S Central Ave Glendale CA 91204-2508

DENTON, CHARLES MANDAVILLE, corporate consultant; b. Glendale, Calif., June 22, 1924; s. Horace Bruce and Marguerite (Mandaville) D.; m. Jean Margaret Brady, Dec. 3, 1955; children— Charles Mandaville II, Margot Elizabeth. Student, U. Calif., 1942, Okla. A. and M. Coll., 1943; B.A. in Journalism, U. So. Calif., 1949. Reporter San Fernando Valley Times, N. Hollywood, Calif., 1949-50, U.P., Los Angeles, 1950-52; reporter, sportswriter, columnist I.N.S., Los Angeles, 1952-59; reporter, feature writer, TV editor-columnist Los Angeles Examiner, 1959-62; free-lance TV and mag. writer, 1962-63; reporter Los Angeles Times, 1963; columnist San Francisco Examiner, 1963-68; communications dir. Leslie Salt Co., San Francisco, 1968-73. Comm. dir. Crown Zellerbach Corp., San Francisco, 1973-83; v.p. Hilland Knowlton Inc., 1983-90. Author: (with Dr. W. Coda Martin) A Matter of Life, 1964. Pres. Greater Los Angeles Press Club Welfare Found., 1961. Served with USNR, 1943-46. Mem. Phi Beta Kappa, Phi Kappa Phi, Sigma Delta Chi, Blue Key. Clubs: Greater Los Angeles Press (pres. 1955-57), Tiburon Peninsula, Bohemian. Home and Office: 40 Seafirth Rd Belvedere Tiburon CA 94920-1125 Fax: (415) 435-0454. E-mail: chzdenton@aol.com

D'ENTREMONT, AMY, professional figure skater; b. Stoneham, Mass., May 2, 1977; Placed 17th Nat. Sr. Competition, 1997, 4th Ea. Sr., 1997, 5th New Eng. Sr., 1997, 3rd U.S. Olympic Festival, 1995, 4th nat. Jr., 1995, 1st, New England Jr., 1995, 6th U.S. Olympic Festival, 1994, 6th Nat. Jr., 1994, 2nd Ea. Jr., 1994, 1st New England Jr., 1994, others. Mem. U.S. Figure Skating Assn. Avocations: white water rafting, rollerblading, dancing, friends. Office: 20 1st St Colorado Springs CO 80906-3624

DEPALMA, RALPH GEORGE, surgeon, educator; b. N.Y.C., Oct. 29, 1931; s. Frank and Maria (Sibilio) deP.; m. Maleva Tankard, Sept. 17, 1955; children: Ralph L., Edward F., Maleva B., Malinda G. AB, Columbia U, 1953; MD, NYU, 1956. Diplomate Am. Bd. Surgery, Am. Bd. Vascular Surgery. Resident in surgery Univ. Hosps., Cleve., 1962-64; from instr. to prof. surgery Case Western Res. U., Cleve., 1964-80; prof., chmn. surgery U. Nev., Reno, 1980-82, George Washington U. Sch. Medicine, Washington, 1982-92; Lewis B. Saltz prof. of surgery George Washington U. Med. Ctr., Washington, 1992-94; prof. surgery, vice-chmn. dept. surgery, assoc. dean U. Nev., Reno, 1994-2000, nat. dir. surgery, dept. vets. affairs, 2000—. Editor: (with J.M. Giordano) Reoperative Vascular Surgery, 1987, Basic Science of Vascular Surgery, 1988; assoc. editor: Haimovici Vascular Surgery: Principles and Techniques, 1989; co-editor: Basic Science in Vascular Disease, 1997; assoc. editor Internat. Vascular Surgery, Internat. Jour. Impotence Rsch.; contbr. articles to profl. jours. Stroke liaison nat. chpt. Am. Heart Assn., 1992-94; bd. dirs. Reno Chamber Orch., 1999-2000. Capt. USAF, 1958-61. Grantee USPHS, 1974-82. Fellow ACS; mem. Cleve. Vascular Soc. (pres. 1977-78), Rocky Mt. Vascular Soc. (pres. 1981-82), Am. Surg. Assn., Soc. Vascular Surgery, Washington Acad. Surgery (sec. 1991-92, v.p. 1992-93, pres. 1993-94), Am. Venous Forum (sec. 1991-94, bd. dirs. found. 1992-95), Am. Coll. Healthcare Execs. (assoc.), 1996, Cosmos Club (admissions com. 1992-94, awards com. 2001—), Reno Rotary, Western Vascular Soc., Prospectors Club Reno. E-mail: rgdepalma@mail.va.gov

DEPATIE, DAVID HUDSON, motion picture company executive; b. Los Angeles, Dec. 24, 1930; s. Edmond LaVoie and Dorothy (Hudson) DeP.; m. Marcia Lee MacPherson, June 1972; children: David Hudson, Steven Linn, Michael Linn. Student, U. of South, 1947-48; A.B., U. Calif.-Berkeley,

1951. With Warner Bros. Pictures, Inc., 1951-63, v.p., gen. mgr. comml. and cartoon films div., 1963; pres. DePatie-Freleng Enterprises, Inc., Van Nuys, Calif., 1963—; founder, proprietor The DePatie Vineyards, 1983-90. Producer: Pink Panther and Inspector theatrical cartoon series; TV series The New Mr. Magoo; TV live-action and animation spl. The Hoober Bloob Highway; TV spl. Clerow Wilson Great Escape; TV series The Houndcats and the Barkleys; Christmas TV spls. The Tiny Tree; ABC aftersch. spl. My Mom's Having a Baby (recipient Emmy award); Dr. Seuss spl. Halloween Is Grinch Night (recipient Emmy award), Fantastic Four, Spider-Woman, The Pink Panther Christmas Special, The Bugs Bunny Christmas Special, Spider-Man & his Amazing Friends, The Pink Panther in Pink at First Sight, Pink Panther & Sons, 1985; Dr. Seuss Spls. The Grinch Grinchesthe Cat-In-The-Hat (Emmy award 1982); others.; nominated for Emmy award 1974-75; exec. producer: The Incredible Hulk, Pandamonium, Meatballs and Spaghetti, Dungeons and Dragons. Recipient First award for the Lorax Zagreb Internat. Film Festival, 1972; recipient Emmy Award for Dr. Seus special The Grinch Grinches The Cat-in-the Hat, 1982; Calif. State Fair Double Gold award for Best Zinfandel Wine of 1983, 1985, Wine & Spirits Mag. Am. Champion Zinfandel wine of 1984, 1986. Mem. Acad. Motion Picture Arts and Scis. (Oscar award for Pink Panther 1964), Soc. Motion Picture Editors, Phi Gamma Delta. Republican. Episcopalian. Office: DePatie-Freleng Enterprises Inc 3425 Stiles Ave Camarillo CA 93010-3900

DEPINTO, DAVID J. public relations executive; BA in Polit. Sci., Brown U.; MBA, U. So. Calif. Dir. mktg., pub. rels., pub. affairs Coca-Cola Bottling Co., L.A.; exec. v.p. Pacific/West Comm. Group, L.A.; pres., CEO Stoorza Comm., Inc., San Diego. Mem. bd. dirs. L.A. Ednl. Partnership, Adopt-A-School-Coun. L.A. Unified Sch. Dist., Crescenta Youth Sports Assn. Office: Stoorza Ziegaus Metzger 225 Broadway Fl 18 San Diego CA 92101-5005

DEPRATU, ROBERT L. state legislator; b. Eureka, Mont., July 21, 1939; m. Beatrice DePratu. AA, Kinman Bus. Coll. Owner DePartu Ford, VW and Audi; mem. Mont. Senate, Dist. 40, Helena, 1996—; chair joint select com. on jobs and income; vice chair taxation com., mem. hwys. and transp. com.; mem. pub. health, welfare and safety com. Republican. Office: PO Box 1217 6331 Hwy 93 S Whitefish MT 59937-8236 E-mail: bobbe@digisys.net

DEPREIST, JAMES ANDERSON, conductor; b. Phila., Nov. 21, 1936; s. James Henry and Ethel (Anderson) De P.; m. Betty Louise Childress, Aug. 10, 1963; children: Tracy Elisabeth, Jennifer Anne; m. Ginette Grenier, July 19, 1980. Student, Phila. Conservatory Music, 1959-61; BS, U. Pa., 1958, MA, 1961, LHD (hon.), 1976, Reed Coll., 1990, Portland State U., 1993; MusD (hon.), Laval U., Quebec City, Can., 1980, Linfield Coll., , 1986, Juilliard, 1993; DFA (hon.), U. Portland, 1983, Pacific U., 1985, Willamette U., 1987, Drexel U., 1989, Oreg. State U., 1990; Doctor of Arts and Letters (hon.), St. Mary's Coll., Moraga, Calif., 1985; HHD (hon.), Lewis and Clark U., 1986. Am. specialist music for State Dept., 1962-63; condr.-in-residence Bangkok, 1963-64; condr. various symphonies and orchs., 1964—; conductor, music dir. Oreg. Symphony, Portland, 1980—. Condr.: Am. debut with N.Y. Philharm., 1964, asst. condr. to Leonard Bernstein, N.Y. Philharm. Orch., 1965-66, prin. guest condr. Symphony of New World, 1968-70, European debut with Rotterdam Philharm., 1969; Helsinki Philharm., 1993; assoc. condr. Nat. Symphony Orch., Washington, 1971-75, prin. guest condr. Nat. Symphony Orch., 1975-76; music dir. L'Orchestre Symphonique de Que., 1976-83, Oreg. Symphony, 1980—, prin. guest condr. Helsinki Philharmonic, 1993, Mus. Dir. Monte Carlo Philharm., 1994; appeared with Phila. Orch., 1972, 76, 84, 85, 87, 90, 92, 93, 94, Chgo. Symphony, 1973, 90, 92, 94, Boston Symphony, 1973, 97, 98, 99, Cleve. Orch., 1974; condr.: Am. premiere of Dvorak's First Symphony, N.Y. Philharm., 1972; chief condr. Malmö Symphony, 1991-94; author: (poems) This Precipice Garden, 1987, The Distant Siren, 1989. Trustee Lewis and Clark Coll., 1983—. Recipient 1st prize gold medal Dimitri Mitropoulos Internat. Music Competition for Condrs., 1964, Merit citation City of Phila., 1969, medal of City of Que., 1983; grantee Martha Baird Rockefeller Fund for Music, 1969, Insignia of Comdr. of Order of Lion of Finland, 1992. Fellow Am. Acad. Arts and Scis.; mem. Royal Swedish Acad. Music. Office: Oreg Symphony 921 SW Washington St Ste 200 Portland OR 97205-2800

DERBES, DANIEL WILLIAM, manufacturing executive; b. Cin., Mar. 30, 1930; s. Earl Milton and Ruth Irene (Grauten) D.; m. Patricia Maloney, June 4, 1952; children: Donna Ann, Nancy Lynn (dec.), Stephen Paul. BS, U.S. Mil. Acad., 1952; MBA, Xavier U., Cin., 1963. Devel. engr. AiResearch Mfg. Co., Phoenix, 1956-58; with Garrett Corp., L.A., 1958-80, v.p., gen. mgr., then exec. v.p., 1975-80, dir., 1976-87; pres. Signal Cos., Inc., 1980-82, La Jolla, Calif., 1982-83, Signal Advanced Tech Group, 1983-85, Allied-Signal Internat. Inc., 1985-88; exec. v.p. Allied-Signal, Inc., Morristown, N.J., 1985-88; pres. Signal Ventures, Solana Beach, Calif., 1990—. Bd. dirs. WD-40 Co., So. Calif. Gas Co., Pacific Enterprises, Enova Corp.; chmn. bd. dirs. Sempra Energy, 2000—. Exec. bd. nat. coun. Boy Scouts Am., 1981-95; trustee U. San Diego, 1981—, vice-chmn., bd. trustees, 1990-93, chmn., 1993-96. With AUS, 1952-56. Republican. Roman Catholic. Office: Signal Ventures 777 S Pacific Coast Hwy Ste 107 Solana Beach CA 92075-2623

DERFLER, EUGENE L. state legislator, real estate broker; b. Portland, Oreg., May 24, 1924; s. Leo and Jessie E. (Tatom) D.; m. Thelma M. Brekke, Aug. 14, 1944; children: Judith Lynne, Dennis Gene, Richard Henry. Grad., Pensacola Naval Aviator Sch.; student, W. Wash. Coll. Mgr. Firestone Tire & Rubber Co., Tillamook, Oreg., 1946-52; owner Nico Furniture & Appliance Co., Salem, 1952-81; broker Coldwell Banker, Salem, 1982—; mem. Oreg. Ho. of Reps., Salem, 1989-94, Oreg. Senate, Salem, 1995-. Pres. Transit System fpr Salem, 1981-84; chmn. Marion County Juvenile Service Commn., Salem, 1983-87; bd. dirs. YMCA, Salem, 1984-85. Lt. USN, 1943-46. Republican. Avocations: photography, jogging, hiking. Office: Coldwell Banker Mountain West 1011 Commercial St NE Salem OR 97301-1049 Address: Oreg Senate 900 Court St S-223 Salem OR 97301

DERICCO, LAWRENCE ALBERT, college president emeritus; b. Stockton, Calif., Jan. 28, 1923; s. Giulio and Agnes (Giovacchini) DeR.; m. Alma Mezzetta, June 19, 1949; 1 child, Lawrence Paul. BA, U. Pacific, 1949, MA, 1971, LLD (hon.), 1987. Bank clk. Bank of Am., Stockton, 1942-43; prin. Castle Sch. Dist., San Joaquin County, Calif., 1950-53; dist. supt., prin. Waverly Sch. Dist., Stockton, 1953-63; bus. mgr. San Joaquin Delta Jr. Coll. Dist., Stockton, 1963-65, asst. supt., bus. mgr., 1965-77, v.p. mgmt. services, 1977-81; pres., supt. San Joaquin Delta Coll., 1981-87, pres. emeritus, 1988—. Mem. Workforce Investment Bd. With AUS, 1943-46, PTO. Mem. NEA, Calif. Tchrs. Assn., Native Sons of Golden West (past pres.), Phi Delta Kappa Office: 6847 N Pershing Ave Stockton CA 95207-2524 E-mail: ldericco@softcom.net

DERKSEN, CHARLOTTE RUTH MEYNINK, librarian; b. Newberg, Oreg., Mar. 15, 1944; BS in Geology, Wheaton (Ill.) Coll., 1966; MA in Geology, U. Oreg., 1968, MLS, 1973. Faculty and libr. Moeding Coll., Ootse, Botswana, 1968-70, head history dept. Botswana, 1970-71; tchr. Jackson (Minn.) Pub. High Sch., 1975-77; sci. libr. U. Wis., Oshkosh, 1977-80; libr. and bibliographer Stanford (Calif.) U., 1980—. Acting chief scis. 1985-86, head Sci. and Engring. Librs. 1992-97. Contbg. author: Union List of Geologic Field Trip Guidebooks of North America; contbr. articles to profl. publs. Mem. ALA, Western Assn. Map Librs., Geosci. Info. Soc. (v.p. 1997-98, pres. 1998-99), Cartographic Users Adv. Coun. (chair 1988-90), GeoRef Adv. Bd. (chair 1998—). Republican. Lutheran. Home: 128 Mission Dr Palo Alto CA 94303-2753 Office: Stanford U Branner Earth Scis Library Stanford CA 94305 E-mail: cderksen@stanford.edu

DERMANIS, PAUL RAYMOND, architect; b. Jelgava, Latvia, Aug. 2, 1932; came to U.S., 1949; s. Pauls and Milda (Argals) D. BArch, U. Wash., 1955; MArch, MIT, 1959. Registered architect, Wash. Architect John Morse & Assocs., Seattle, 1961-62; assoc. Fred Bassetti & Co., Seattle, 1963-70; arch. Ibsen Nelsen & Assocs., Seattle, 1970-71; ptnr. Streeter/Dermanis & Assocs., Seattle, 1973-97; owner Paul Dermanis Archs., 1997—. Designs include Sunset house (citation 1984), treatment plant, 1992. Mem. Phinney Ridge Neighborhood Assn., Seattle, 1985—. With USN, 1955-57. Mem. AIA, Apt. Assn. Seattle and King County, U. Wash. Alumni Assn., MIT Club of Puget Sound, Phi Beta Kappa, Tau Sigma Delta. Democrat. Lutheran. Avocations: skiing, painting, photography.

DE ROO, REMI JOSEPH, retired bishop; b. Swan Lake, Man., Can., Feb. 24, 1924; s. Raymond and Josephine (De Pape) De R. Student, St. Boniface (Man.) Coll.; STD, Angelicum U., Rome, Italy.; LLD (hon.), U. Antigonish, N.S., 1983, U. Brandon, Man., 1987; DD (hon.), U. Winnipeg, Man., 1990; LLD (hon.), U. Victoria, B.C., 1991. Ordained priest Roman Cath. Ch., 1950. Curate Holy Cross Parish, St. Boniface, 1952-53; sec. to archbishop of St. Boniface, 1954-56; diocesan dir. Cath. action Archdiocese St. Boniface, 1953-54; exec. sec. Man. Cath. Con., 1958; pastor Holy Cross Parish, 1960-62; bishop of Victoria, B.C., Can., 1962—. Can. Episcopal rep. Internat. Secretariat Apostleship See, 1964-78, Pontifical Commn. Culture, 1984-87; chairperson Human Rights Commn. B.C., 1974-77; mem. social affairs commn. Can. Conf. Cath. Bishops, 1973-87, 91-95, mem. theology commn., 1987-91; pres. Western Cath. Conf. Bishops, 1984-88; hon. pres. World Conf. for Religion and Peace for Can., 1994—. Hon. fellow Ryerson Poly. Inst., 1987. Address: 4044 Nelthorpe St # 1 Victoria BC Canada V8X 2A1

DEROSA, FRANCIS DOMINIC, chemical company executive; b. Seneca Falls, N.Y., Feb. 26, 1936; s. Frank and Frances (Bruno) DeR.; m. Vivian DeRosa, Oct. 24, 1959; children: Kevin, Marc, Terri. Student, Rochester Inst. Tech., 1959-61; BS, MBA, Chadwick U.; PhD, City U. L.A. Cert. med. photographer. CEO Advance Paper & Equipment Supply Inc., Mesa, Ariz., 1974—, Pottery Plus Ltd., Mesa, 1984—, Advance Tool Supply Inc., Mesa, 1989-94. Vice chmn. bd. adjustments City of Mesa, 1983-89, bd. dirs. dept. parks and recreation, 1983-86; pres. Christ the King Mens Club, 1983-84; bd. dirs. Mesa C. of C., 1983-88. Mem. Ariz. Sanitary Supply Assn. (pres. 1983-84), Internat. Sanitary Supply Assn. (coord. Ariz. chpt. 1994-96, sec. bd. 1994-96), Gilbert, Ariz. C. of C. (bd. dirs., v.p. 1992-96, pres. 1996-97, sec. internat. bd. 1994-96), Gilbert Heights Owners Assn. (pres. 1992-93), Mesa Country Club, Calif. Yacht Club, Santa Monica (Calif.) Yacht Club, Rotary (pres. Mesa Sunrise chpt. 1987-88, Paul Harris fellow 1988), Masons (32 degree, pres. 1973), Sons of Italy (pres. 1983-84), Shriners. Avocations: music, physical fitness, sailing, golf. Home: 513 E Horseshoe Ave Gilbert AZ 85296-1705 Office: Advance Paper & Maintenance Supply Inc 33 W Broadway Mesa AZ 85210-1505 E-mail: frank26phd@aol.com

DEROSIER, ARTHUR HENRY, JR. college president; b. Norwich, Conn., Feb. 18, 1931; s. Arthur Henry and Rose (Raymond) DeR.; m. Linda Preston Scott, Dec. 26, 1979; children: Deborah Ann, Marsha Carol, Brett Preston Scott, Melissa Estelle. BS, U. So. Miss., 1953; MA, U. S.C., 1955, PhD, 1959. Asst. prof. history The Citadel, 1956-57, Converse Coll., Spartanburg, S.C., 1957-59; asst. prof. U. So. Miss., 1959-60, assoc. prof., 1960-64, prof., 1964-65; assoc. prof. history U. Okla., 1965-67, asst. dean, Grad. Coll., 1966-67; dean Grad. Sch., prof. history East Tenn. State U., Johnson City, 1967-72, v.p. for adminstrn., 1972-74; vice chancellor for acad. affairs, prof. history U. Miss., 1974-76, vice chancellor, 1976-77; pres. East Tenn. State U., 1977-80, Coll. of Idaho, Caldwell, 1980-87, Rocky Mountain Coll., Billings, Mont., 1987—. Pres. Ind. Colls. of Mont., 1992—; vis. prof. history U. Mass., summer 1964; ednl. TV series on Am. history, 1966-72; bd. dirs. Rocky Mountain Bank. Author: Through the South with a Union Soldier, 1969, The Removal of the Choctaw Indians, 1970, (with others) Four Centuries of Southern Indians, 1975, Forked Tongues and Broken Treaties, 1975, Appalachia: Family Traditions in Transition, 1975, Pioneer Trails West, 1985, Institutional Revival: Case Histories, 1986; contbr. articles to hist. jours. Active numerous Indian philanthropies; mem. Idaho Commn. on Pardons and Parole, 1985-87; commr., U.S. Senate Commn. Online Child Proection, 1999—; bd. dirs. Deaconess Med. Ctr., 1988-92. With USAF, 1948-52. So. fellow, 1958; Am. Philos. Soc. grantee, 1964 Mem. Am. Hist. Assn., Orgn. Am. Historians, So. Hist. Assn., Western Hist. Assn., Nat. Assn. Ind. Colls. and Univs. (fin. com. higher edn. 1990-97), Coun. Ind. Colls., Western Ind. Colls. Fund, Nat. Assn. Sch. and Coll. of United Meth. Ch. (chmn. com. on internat. edn. 1993-96, bd. dirs. 1994-97), Rotary, Phi Beta Kappa. Home: 1809 Mulberry Dr Billings MT 59102-0601 Office: Rocky Mountain Coll Office of President 1511 Poly Dr Billings MT 59102-1739 E-mail: derosier@rocky.edu

DEROUIN, JAMES GILBERT, lawyer; b. Eau Claire, Wis., July 11, 1944; BA cum laude, U. Wis., 1967, JD, 1968. Bar: Wis. 1968, Ariz. 1986. Ptnr. Steptoe & Johnson LLC, Phoenix; atty. Meyer, Hendricks, Victor, Osbonn & Maledon, Phoenix; ptnr. Dewitt, Ross & Stevens, Madison, Wis. Polychlorinatedbyphenol chair Wis. Dept. Natural Resources, 1976-78; mem. spl. com. on solid waste mgmt. Wis. Legis. Coun., 1976-79, ad hoc com. on hazardous waste mgmt., 1980-82, spl. com. on groundwater mgmt.; mem. Wis. Dept. Nat. Resources Metallic Mining Coun., 1978-85; chair Phoenix Environ. Quality Commn., 1986, Phoenix Environ. Quality Com., 1989-92; mem. Ariz. Govs. Regulatory Review Coun. 1986—; co-chair Ariz. Dept. Environ. Quality/Ariz. Dept. Water Resources Groundwater Task Force, 1996-97. Chair. State Bar Ariz. (environ. and nat. resources law sect. 1989-90). Office: 2 Renaissance Sq 40 N Central Ave Ste 240024th Phoenix AZ 85004-4424

DERR, KENNETH T. retired oil company executive; b. 1936; m. Donna Mettler, Sept. 12, 1959; 3 children BME, Cornell U., 1959, MBA, 1960. With Chevron Corp. (formerly Standard Oil Co. of Calif.), San Francisco, 1960—, v.p., 1972-85; pres. Chevron U.S.A., Inc. subs. Chevron Corp., San Francisco, 1978-84; head merger program Chevron Corp. and Gulf Oil Corp., San Francisco, 1984-85; vice-chmn. Chevron Corp., San Francisco, 1985-88, chmn., CEO, 1989-99; ret., 1999. Bd. dirs. AT&T, Am. Productivity & Quality Ctr., Citigroup, Potlatch Corp. Trustee emeritus Cornell U. Mem. The Bus. Coun., San Francisco Golf Club, Orinda Country Clb, Pacific Union Club. Office: Chevron Corp PO Box 7643 575 Market St San Francisco CA 94105-2856

D'ERRICO, DIDI, public relations executive; BA in Mass Comm., MA in Pub. Rels., Ball State U. Mgr. employee comm. Ball Corp.; v.p. Blanc & Otus, San Francisco. Office: 4 Embarcadero Ctr Lbby 8 San Francisco CA 94111-4112

DER TOROSSIAN, PAPKEN, engineering executive; B of Mech. engring., MIT; M, Stanford U. Pres., CEO EVS Microsystems, Inc.; pres. Santa Cruz divsn., v.p. telephone products group Plantronics; pres. Silicon Valley Group, San Jose, Calif., 1984—, CEO, 1986—, chmn. bd. dirs., 1991—. Spkr. in field. Office: 101 Metro Dr Ste 400 San Jose CA 95110-1343

DERVAN, PETER BRENDAN, chemistry educator; b. Boston, July 28, 1945; s. Peter Brendan and Ellen (Comer) D.; m. Jackqueline K. Barton; children: Andrew, Elizabeth. BS, Boston Coll., 1967; PhD, Yale U., 1972. Asst. prof. Calif. Inst. Tech., Pasadena, 1973-79, assoc. prof., 1979-82, prof. chemistry, 1982-88, Bren prof. chemistry, 1988—; chmn. div. chemistry & chem. engring., 1994—. Adv. bd. ACS Monographs, Washington, 1979-81 Mem. adv. bd. Jour. Organic Chemistry, Washington, 1981—; mem. editorial bd. Bioorganic Chemistry, 1983—, Chem. Rev. Jour., 1984—, Nucleic Acids Res., 1986—, Jour. Am. Chem. Soc., 1986—, Acct. Chem. Res., 1988—, Bioorganic Chem. Rev., 1988—, Bioconjugate Chemistry, 1989—, Jour. Med. Chemistry, 1991—, Tetrahedron, 1992—, Bioorganic and Med. Chemistry, 1993—, Chemical and Engineering News, 1992—; contbr. articles to profl. jours. A.P. Sloan Rsch. fellow, 1977; Camille and Henry Dreyfus scholar, 1978; Guggenheim fellow, 1983; recipient Arthur C. Cope Scholar award 1986, Maison de la Chimie Found. prize, 1996. Fellow Am. Acad. Scis.; mem. NAS, Am. Chem. Soc. (Nobel Laureate Signature award 1985, Harrison Howe award 1988, Arthur C. Cope award, 1993, Willard Gibbs medal, 1993, Rolf Sammet prize, 1993, William H. Nichols medal 1994, Kirkwood medal 1998, Alfred Bader award 1999), Inst. Medicine (Remsen award 1998, Linus Pauling medal 1999, Richard Tolman medal 1999), French Acad. Scis. (fgn., Tetrahedron prize 2000). Office: Calif Inst Tech 1201 E California Blvd Pasadena CA 91125-0001

DE SÁ E SILVA, ELIZABETH ANNE, secondary school educator; b. Edmonds, Wash., Mar. 17, 1931; d. Sven Yngve and Anna Laura Elizabeth (Dahlin) Erlandson; m. Claudio de Sá e Silva, Sept. 12, 1955 (div. July 1977); children: Lydia, Marco, Nelson. BA, U. Oreg., 1953; postgrad., Columbia U., 1954-56, Calif. State U., Fresno, 1990, U. No. Iowa, , 1993; MEd, Mont. State U., 1978. Cert. tchr., Oreg., Mont. Med. sec., 1947-49; sec. Merced (Calif.) Sch. Dist., 1950-51; sec., asst. Simon and Schuster, Inc., N.Y.C., 1954-56; tchr. Casa Roosevelt-União Cultural, São Paulo, Brazil, 1957-59, Coquille (Oreg.) Sch. Dist., 1978-96; music tchr. Cartwheels Presch., North Bend, Oreg., 1997-99, 2001—. Tchr. piano, 1967-78; instr. Spanish, Southwestern Oreg. C.C., Coos Bay, 1991-94; pianist/organist Faith Luth. Ch., North Bend, Oreg., 1995—, vocal soloist, 1996—, voice tchr., 1997-99. Chmn. publicity Music in Our Schs. Month, Oreg. Dist. VII, 1980-85; sec. Newcomer's Club, Bozeman, Mont., 1971. Quincentennial fellow U. Minn. and Found. José Ortega y Gasset, Madrid, 1991. Mem. AAUW (sec., scholarship chmn., co-pres., pres., treas., editor newsletter), Nat. Trust Hist. Preservation, Am. Coun. on Tchg. Fgn. Langs., Am. Assn. Tchrs. Spanish and Portuguese, Nat. Coun. Tchrs. English, Music Educators Nat. Conf., Oreg. Music Educators Assn., Oreg. Coun. Tchrs. English, Confedn. Oreg. Fgn. Lang. Tchrs., VoiceCare Network. Republican. Avocations: swimming, walking, travel, drama. Home: 3486 Spruce St North Bend OR 97459-1130

DESAI, KAVIN HIRENDRA, pediatrician; b. Bombay, Oct. 8, 1963; MD, Wayne State U., 1988. Resident in pediatrics Stanford U., Palo Alto, Calif., 1989-91, fellow in pediatric cardiology, 1991—, staff pediat. cardiologist, 1994—. Recipient Clinician-Scientist award Am. Heart Assn., 1995-98. Office: Stanford U Pediat Cardio Divsn 750 Welch Rd Ste 305 Palo Alto CA 94304-1510

DESHAZER, JAMES ARTHUR, biological engineer, educator, administrator; b. Washington, July 18, 1938; s. Grant Arthur and Velma DeShazer; m. Alice Marie Burton, Apr. 5, 1969; children: Jean Marie, David James. BS in Agriculture, U. Md., 1960, BSME, 1961; MS, Rutgers U., 1963; PhD, N.C. State U., 1967. Profl. engr., Idaho, Nebr. Assoc. prof. U. Nebr., Lincoln, 1967-75, prof., 1975-91, asst. dean, 1988-89; head agrl. engring. dept. U. Idaho, Moscow, 1991-95, head biol. and agrl. engring. dept., 1995—. Chair animal care & use com. U. Nebr., 1989-90; program coord. North Cen. Sustainable Agrl., Washington, 1988-89; nat. chair Modeling Responses of Swine-CSRS, Washington, 1989-90, Systems Approach to Poultry Prodn.-CSRS, Washington, 1990-91; dir. Idaho Rsch. Found. Editor procs. Optics in Agr., 1990, Optics in Agr. & Forestry, 1992, Optics in Agr., Forestry & Biol. Processing, 1994, Optics in Agr., Forestry & Biol. Processing II, 1996, Precision Agriculture and Biological Quality, 1998, vol. II, 2000; contbr. chpt. in book. Trustee ASAE Found., 1996—. Recipient Livestock Svc. award Walnut Grove, Iowa, 1988. Fellow Am. Soc. Agrl. Engrs. (chair 1984-94, nat. medal 1979); mem. NSPE (chpt. chair 1986-87, 93-94, bd. dirs. 1994—, state pres. 1998-99, Young Engr. award 1974), Am. Soc. for Engring. Edn. (chair 1993-94), Internat. Soc. Biometeorology, Lions (chpt dir. 1995-97), Alpha Gamma Rho (alumni bd. dirs. 1993-99). Home: 819 Nylarol St Moscow ID 83843-9313 Office: Biol & Agr Engring Dept Univ Idaho Moscow ID 83844-0001 E-mail: Jades@uidaho.edu

DESJARDIN, DENNIS E. plant pathologist, educator; b. Crescent City, Calif., May 18, 1950; 1 child, Spenser L. BS in Biology and Botany, San Francisco State U., 1983, MA in Ecology and Systematic Biology, 1985; PhD in Botany and Mycology, U. Tenn., 1989. Asst. prob. Oberlin (Ohio) Coll., 1989-90; asst. prof. San Francisco State U., 1990-93, assoc. prof., 1993-97, prof., 1997—, dir. H.D. Thiers Herbarium, 1991—. Bd. dirs. Sierra Nev. Field Campus; sci. adv. bd. Golden Gate Nat. Recreation Area; chief mycologist N.Am. Mycological Assn. Foray, 1998, Colo. Mycological Soc. Foray, 1998; cons. in field; presenter in field. Grantee NSF, 1986, 93, 96, 97, U. Tenn. Dept. Botany, 1991, San Fransisco State U., 1991, 94, U.S. Forest Svc., 1995, 97, others. Mem. Internat. Assn. for Plant Taxonomy, Mycological Soc. Am. (liaison with amateur socs. 1992-95, awards com. 1993-96, chair awards com. 1996, councilor for systematics and evolution nomenclature com. 1996-98, grad. fellow 1986, Alexopoulos prize 1998, William H. Weston award 1998), Am. Bryological and Lichenological Soc., Am. Inst. Biol. Scis., Biosystematists, Brit. Mycological Soc., Calif. Bot. Soc. (v.p. 1993-94), Mycological Soc. San Francisco (sci. advisor 1990—), Sigma Xi, Phi Kappa Phi. Office: San Francisco State U Dept Biology 1600 Holloway Ave San Francisco CA 94132 E-mail: ded@sfsu.edu

DESMOND, MARK LAWRENCE, financial executive; b. Normal, Ill., July 25, 1958; s. Lawrence John and May Catherine Desmond; m. Kathryn Hanson, July 29, 1989; children: Erin Ruby, William Mark. BA in Econs. cum laude, U. Calif., Irvine, 1980; MBA, U. So. Calif., 1982. Sr. acct. Arthur Andersen & Co., L.A., 1982-86; acctg. mgr. Beverly Enterprises, Pasadena, Calif., 1986-88; contr. Nationwide Health Properties, Pasadena, 1988-90, v.p., treas. Newport Beach, Calif., 1990-96, sr. v.p., CFO, 1996—. Mem. AICPA. Office: Nationwide Health Properties 610 Newport Center Dr Ste 1150 Newport Beach CA 92660-6493

DESOER, CHARLES AUGUSTE, electrical engineer; b. Ixelles, Belgium, Jan. 11, 1926; came to U.S., 1949, naturalized, 1958; s. Jean Charles and Yvonne Louise (Peltzer) D.; m. Jacqueline K. Johnson, July 21, 1966; children: Marc J., Michele M., Craig M. Ingenieur Radio-Electricien, U. Liege, Belgium, 1949, DSc (hon.), 1976; ScD in Elec. Engring, MIT, 1953. Rsch. asst. M.I.T., 1951-53; mem. tech. staff Bell Telephone Labs., Murray Hill, N.J., 1953-58; assoc. prof. elec. engring. and computer scis. U. Calif., Berkeley, 1958-62, prof., 1962-91, prof. emeritus, 1991—, Miller research prof., 1970-71. Author: (with L. A. Zadeh) Linear System Theory, 1963, (with E. S. Kuh) Basic Circuit Theory, 1969, (with M. Vidyasagar)

Feedback Systems: Input Output Properties, 1973, Notes for a Second Course on Linear Systems, 1970, (with F. M. Callier) Multivariable Feedback Systems, 1982, (with L.O. Chua and E.S. Kuh) Linear and Nonlinear Circuits, 1987, (with A.N. Gündes) Alegebraic Theory of Linear Feedback Systems with Full and Decentralized Compensation, 1990, (with F.M. Callier) Linear System Theory, 1991; contbr. numerous articles on systems and circuits to profl. jours. Served with Belgian Arty., 1944-45. Decorated Vol.'s medal; recipient Best Paper prize 2d Joint Automatic Control Conf., 1962, Univ. medal U. Liège, 1976, Disting. Teaching award U. Calif., Berkeley, 1971, Prix Montefiore Inst. Montefiore, 1975; award for outstanding paper IEEE, 1979, Field award in control sci. and engring., 1986, Am. Automatic Control Council Edn. award, 1983, Berkeley Citation, 1992; Guggenheim fellow, 1970-71. Fellow IEEE (Edn. medal 1975), AAAS.; mem. IEEE Control Sys. Soc., IEEE Circuits and Systems Soc. (Mac Van Valkenburg award 1996), Nat. Acad. Engring., Am. Math. Soc. Office: U Calif Dept Elec Engring And Comput Berkeley CA 94720-1770

DESOTO, LEWIS DAMIEN, art educator; b. San Bernardino, Calif., Jan. 3, 1954; s. Lewis Dan and Albertina (Quiroz) DeS. BA, U. Calif., Riverside, 1978; MFA, Claremont Grad. Sch., 1981. Tchr. Otis Parsons, L.A., 1982-85; chmn. art dept. Cornish Coll. of Arts, Seattle, 1985-88; prof. art San Francisco State U., 1988-93, 95—; dir. grad. studies Calif. Coll. Arts and Crafts, Oakland, 1993-95. Exhibited at New Mus., N.Y.C., 1992, Centro Cultural De La Raza, San Diego, 1993, Moderna Museet, Stockholm, Sweden, 1993, Christopher Grimes Gallery, Santa Monica, Calif., 1994, Denver Art Mus., 1994, Columbus Mus. Art, 1994, Des Moines Art Ctr., 1995, Fundacao Serralves, 1995, Oporto, Portugal, 1995, MetronÓm, Barcelona, Spain, 1997, Public Art Commn., San Francisco Courthouse, 1998, San Francisco Internat. Airport, 2000, U. Tex., San Antonio, 2001, Public Art Commn., List Visual Art Ctr., MIT, Cambridge, 1998, Bill Maynes Gallery, N.Y.C., 1999, 2000, Museum of Contemporary Religious Art, St. Louis, 2000. Mem. photo coun. Seattle Art Mus., 1987-88, Eureka Fellowship, vis. arts, 1999. Recipient New Genres award Calif. Arts Coun., 1992, NEA fellow, 1996. Mem. L.A. Ctr. for Photographic Studies (bd. dirs. 1983-85), CameraWork (exec. bd. dirs. 1991-93), Ctr. for Arts (adv. bd. 1993-95), Friends of Photography (peer award bd. 1991-96). Office: San Francisco State U Art Dept 1600 Holloway Ave San Francisco CA 94132-1722 E-mail: Sotolux@aol.com

DESSLER, ALEXANDER JACK, astrophysicist, educator; b. San Francisco, Oct. 21, 1928; s. David Alexander and Julia (Shapiro) D.; m. Lorraine Hudek, Apr. 18, 1952; children: Pauline Karen, David Alexander, Valerie Jan, Andrew Emory. B.S., Calif. Inst. Tech., 1952; Ph.D., Duke, 1956. Sect. head Lockheed Missiles & Space Co., 1956-62; prof. Grad. Research Center, Dallas, 1962-63, prof. space physics and astronomy, 1963-82, 86-93; chmn. dept. Rice U., Houston, 1963-69, 79-82, 87-92, campus bus. mgr., 1974-76; dir. space sci. lab. MSFC NASA, Huntsville, Ala., 1982-86; sr. rsch. scientist Lunar and Planetary Lab. U. Ariz., Tucson, 1993—. Sci. adviser Nat Aeros. and Space Council, 1969-70; pres. Univs. Space Research Assn., 1975-81 Editor Jour. Geophys. Research, 1965-69, Revs. of Geophysics, 1969-74, The John Wiley Space Science Text Series, 1968-76, Geophys. Research Letters, 1986-89, Atmospheric and Space Science Series, 1986—; adv. bd.: Planetary and Space Sci., 1963-92; assoc. editor Space Solar Power Rev., 1980-85. Served with USN, 1946-48. Recipient Outstanding Young Scientist award Tex. Wing Air Force Assn., 1964, medal for contbns. to internat. geophysics Soviet Geophys. Com., 1984, Stellar award for acad. devel., Rotary Nat., 1988. Fellow AAAS, Am. Geophys. Union (Macelwane award 1963, John Adam Fleming medal 1993); mem. Am. Astron. Soc., Internat. Assn. Geomagnetism and Aeronomy (v.p. 1979-83), Royal Swedish Acad. Scis. (fgn. mem.), Cosmos Club (Washington). Home: 1434 E Seneca St Tucson AZ 85719-3645 Office: U Ariz Lunar Planetary Lab 901 Gould-Simpson Bldg Tucson AZ 85721-0001 E-mail: dessler@arizona.edu

DETELS, ROGER, epidemiologist, physician, former university dean; b. Bklyn., Oct. 14, 1936; s. Martin P. and Mary J. (Crooker) D.; m. Mary M. Doud, Sept. 14, 1963; children: Martin, Edward. BA, Harvard U., 1958; MD, NYU, 1962; MS in Preventive Medicine, U. Wash., 1966. Diplomate Am. Bd. Preventive Medicine. Intern U. Calif. Gen. Hosp., San Francisco, 1962-63; resident U. Wash., Seattle, 1963-66; med. officer, epidemiologist Nat. Inst. Neurol. Diseases, Bethesda, Md., 1969-71; assoc. prof. epidemiology Sch. Pub. Health UCLA, 1971-73, prof. Sch. Pub. Health, 1973—, dean, 1980-85, head div. epidemiology Sch. Pub. Health, 1972-80. Guest lectr. various univs., profl. confs. and med. orgns., 1969—; sci. adv. com. Am. Found AIDS Rsch.; dir. UCLA/Fogarty AIDS Internat. Tng. & Rsch. Program, 1988—, Tng. Program in Epidemiology of HIV/AIDS, 1995—; cons. Ministries of Health, Thailand, Myanmar, The Philippines, 1989, Global Program on AIDS, 1995, Singapore, 1996, WHO, 1999, U.S. Agy. Internat. Devel., 1998, 99, 2000, 01, Cambodia, 1998, 99, 2000, 01, St. Thomas Med. Sch., London, 1993-94, Myanmar, 1997; mem. Nat. Adv. Environ. Health Scis. Coun., 1990-94; com. to study transmission of HIV through blood products Inst. Medicine, 1994-95. Editor: Oxford Textbook of Public Health, 1985, 2d edit. 1991, 4th edit., 2001; contbr. articles to profl. jours. Lt. comdr. M.C. USN, 1966-69. Grantee in field. Fellow AAAS, Am. Coll. Preventive Medicine, Am. Coll. Epidemiology (coun. 1987-89), Faculty Pub. Health Medicine Royal Coll. Physicians of U.K. (hon.); mem. Am. Epidemiol. Soc., Soc. Epidemiologic Rsch. (pres. 1977-78), Assn. Tchrs. Preventive Medicine (chmn. essay com. 1969-75), Am. Pub. Health Assn., Am. Assn. Cancer Edn. (membership com. 1978-85), Internat. Epidemiol. Assn. (exec. com. 1984-99, treas. 1984-90, pres. 1990-93), Assn. Schs. Pub. Health (sec.-treas. 1980-85), Sigma Xi, Delta Omega. Office: UCLA Dept Epidemiology Ctr for Health Scis Box 951772 Los Angeles CA 90095-1772 Fax: 310-206-6039. E-mail: detels@ucla.edu

DETERMAN, JOHN DAVID, lawyer; b. Mitchell, S.D., Feb. 18, 1933; s. Alred John and Olive Gertrude (Lovinger) D.; m. Gloria Esther Rivas, Nov. 15, 1980; children by previous marriage: James Taylor, Mark Sterling. B.Engring. in Elec. Engring. cum laude, U. So. Calif., 1955; LL.D. magna cum laude, UCLA, 1961. Electronics engr. Hughes Aircraft Co., L.A., 1955-60; sr. ptnr. Tuttle & Taylor, Inc., L.A., 1961-86; gen. counsel Provena Foods Inc., Chino, Calif., 1986-92, CEO, 1992-98, chmn. bd., 1992—, also bd. dirs. Founder Carl D. Spaeth Scholarship Fund, Stanford U. Law Sch., 1972; mem. nat. panel arbitrators Am. Arbitration Assn., L.A., 1962—, mem. adv. coun., 1982—, mem. nat. panel of mediators, 1986—, mem. large complex case panel of arbitrators, 1993—. Mem. Am. Coll. Constrn. Arbitrators (charter 1982—), Order of Coif, Eta Kappa Nu, Tau Beta Pi. Home: 25 S El Molino St Alhambra CA 91801-4102 Office: Provena Foods Inc 5010 Eucalyptus Ave Chino CA 91710-9216

DETHERO, J. HAMBRIGHT, banker; b. Chattanooga, Jan. 2, 1932; s. Jacob Hambright and Rosalie Frances (Gasser) D.; m. Charlotte Nixon Lee, Sept. 19, 1959; children: Dinah Lee, Charles Drew. BS in Bus. Adminstrn., U. Fla., 1953; BFT, Am. Grad. Sch. Internat. Mgmt., Phoenix, 1958. With Citibank, N.Y.C., P.R., Caracas, Venezuela, San Francisco, 1958-69; mgr. First Nat. City Bank (Internat.), San Francisco, until 1969; v.p. internat. div. Crocker Nat. Bank, San Francisco, 1969-75; sr. v.p. London, 1976-80, San Francisco, 1980-84, Bank America World Trade Corp., San Francisco, 1984-85; 1st v.p. Security Pacific Nat. Bank, Los Angeles, 1986-87; regional mgr. Calif. Export Fin. Office, Calif. State World Trade Commn., San Francisco, 1988-93; sr. v.p. Comml. Bank of San Francisco, 1994-98. Internat. bus. cons., instr., 1998—; adj. prof. Grad. Sch. Bus., St. Mary's Coll., Moraga, Calif., 1988—, John F. Kennedy U., Walnut Creek, Calif., 1997—. Author: Exporting Guide for California, 1993, 2d edit., 1999.. Bd. dirs. Calif. Coun. Internat. Trade, 1972-77, 82-98, pres., 1974-76; trustee World Affairs Coun. No. Calif., 1971-77, 88-93; chmn. dist. Export Coun. No. Calif., 1983-93; dir. Internat. Diplomacy Coun., San Francisco, 1995—, treas., 1997-2000, pres., 2000—; mem. San Francisco Host Com., 2000—. Recipient Export Citizen of the Year award No. Calif. Export Coun./San Francisco Bus. Times, 1996. Home and Office: 694 Old Jonas Hill Rd Lafayette CA 94549-5214 E-mail: hamdethero@aol.com

DETLEFSEN, WILLIAM DAVID, JR. chemicals executive; b. Scottsbluff, Nebr., Nov. 14, 1946; s. William David Sr. and Janette Fern (Tuttle) D.; m. Melba Kay Cunningham, Nov. 12, 1982; children: Michael David, Erika Lee, Whitney Anne. BS in Forestry, U. Idaho, 1970; PhD in Chemistry, U. Oreg., 1993. Chemist, applications technologist Borden, Adhesives and Resins, Springfield, Oreg., 1972-76, coord. tech. svc., 1976-78, supr. phenolic resins devel., 1983-87, mgr. R & D, 1987-94; dir. R & D, resins, adhesives specialties, 1994—; sr. devel. chemist Ga.-Pacific Resins, Crossett, Ark., 1978-83. Contbr. articles to profl. jours. 1st. lt. U.S. Army, 1970-72, Germany. Mem. AAAS, Am. Chem. Soc., Forest Products Rsch. Soc. Republican. Achievements include patents in field; codiscoverer first commercially feasible resins for gluing high moisture veneers into phenolic-bonded plywood. Office: Borden Chem Inc Adhesives & Resins Divsn 610 S 2nd St Springfield OR 97477-5398

DETTER, GERALD L. transportation company executive; b. York, Pa. m. Iris Detter; 3 children. Student exec. mgmt. program, Columbia U. Dockman Consol. Freightways subs. CNF Transp. Svcs., York, 1964, line-haul dispatcher, various other positions, 1965, mgr. terminal Richfield, Ohio, 1971-76, divsn. mgr. Detroit, 1976-82, pres., CEO Con-Way Express, 1982, pres. CEO Con-Way Transp. Svcs., sr. v.p. Calif. Active Mission of Hope Cancer Fund, Jackson, Mich., Boy Scouts of Am., Girl Scouts of Am., United Way. Office: CNF Transp Inc 3240 Hillview Ave Palo Alto CA 94304-1201

DETTERMAN, ROBERT LINWOOD, financial planner; b. Norfolk, Va., May 1, 1931; s. George William and Jeanneille (Watson) D.; m. Virginia Armstrong; children: Janine, Patricia, William Arthur. BS in Engring., Va. Poly. Inst., 1953; PhD in Nuclear Engring., postgrad., Oak Ridge Sch. Reactor Tech., 1954; cert. in fin. planning, Coll. Fin. Planning, Denver, 1986. Registered investment advisor, Calif. Engring. test dir. Foster Wheeler Co., N.Y.C., 1954-59; sr. research engr. Atomics Internat. Co., Canoga Park, Calif., 1959-62; chief project engr. Rockwell Internat. Co., Canoga Park, 1962-68, dir. bus. devel., 1968-84, mgr. internat. program, 1984-87; pres. Bo-Gin Fin., Inc., Thousand Oaks, 1987—; owner Bo-Gin Arabians, Thousand Oaks, 1963—. Nuclear cons. Danish Govt., 1960, Lawrence Livermore Lab., Calif., 1959. Trustee, mem. exec. com. Morris Animal Found., Denver, 1984—, chmn., 1984-88, now trustee emeritus; mem. pres.' adv. com. Kellog Arabian Ranch, U. Calif. Poly., Pomona; treas., trustee Arabian Horse Trust, Denver, 1979-94, now trustee emeritus; chmn. Cal Bred Futurity. Named to Arabian Tent of Honor, Arabian Horse Trust, 1997. Mem. Nat. Assn. Personal Fin. Advisers, Fin. Planning Assn., Acad. Magical Arts, Am. Horse Shows Assn., Am. Horse Coun., Magic Castle Club, Internat. Arabian Horse Assn. Club, Tau Beta Phi, Eta Kappa Nu, Phi Kappa Phi. Republican. Avocations: collecting stamps, growing orchids. Office: Bo-Gin Fin Inc Ste 220 3609 E Thousand Oaks Blvd Westlake Village CA 91359 E-mail: boginfin@aol.com

DETTON, DAVID K. lawyer; b. Rupert, Idaho, Sept. 20, 1949; BA cum laude, Brigham Young U., 1973, JD magna cum laude, 1976. Bar: Utah, 1976. Law clk. to Hon. David T. Lewis U.S. Ct. Appeals (10th cir.), 1976-77; ptnr. Dorsey & Whitney, Salt Lake City, 1997 . Part time faculty Oil and Gas Law Brigham Young U., 1979—. Comment and Case Note editor Brigham Young U. Law Review, 1975-76. J. Clark Reuben scholar. Mem. Utah State Bar, Phi Kappa Phi. Office: Dorsey & Whitney LLP 170 S Main St Ste 925 Salt Lake City UT 84101-1666

DEUBLE, JOHN L., JR. environmental science and engineering services consultant; b. N.Y.C., Oct. 2, 1932; s. John Lewis and Lucille (Klotzbach) D.; m. Thelma C. Honeychurch, Aug. 28, 1955; children: Deborah, Steven. AA, AS in Phys. Sci., Stockton Coll., 1957; BA, BS in Chemistry, U. Pacific, 1959. Cert. profl. chemist, profl. engr., environ. inspector; registered environ. profl., registered environ. assessor. Sr. chemist Aero-Gen Corp., Sacramento, 1959-67; asst. dir. rsch. Lockheed Propulsion Co., Redlands, 1968-73; asst. div. mgr. Systems, Sci. and Software, La Jolla, 1974-79; gen. mgr. Wright Energy Nev. Corp., Reno, 1980-81; v.p. Energy Resources Co., La Jolla, 1982-83; dir. hazardous waste Aerovironment Inc., Monrovia, Calif., 1984-85; sr. program mgr. Ogden Environ. and Energy Svcs., San Diego, 1989-96; environ. cons. Encinitas, Calif., 1986-88, 97—. Contbr. articles profl. jours. With USAF, 1951-54. Recipient Tech. award Am. Ordnance Assn., 1969, Cert. of Achievement Am. Men and Women of Sci., 1986, Envrion. Registry, 1992. Fellow Am. Inst. Chemists; mem. ASTM, NSPE, Am. Chem. Soc., Am. Inst. Chem. Engrs., Am. Meteorol. Soc., Am. Def. Inds. Assn., Air and Waste Mgmt. Assn., Calif. Inst. Chemists, Hazardous Materials Control Rsch. Inst., N.Y. Acad. Scis., Environ. Assessors Assn. Republican. Lutheran. Achievements include development and pioneering use of chemical (non-radioactive) tracers--gaseous, aqueous, and particulate in environmental and energy applications. Home and Office: Planning Asssocs 369 Cerro St Encinitas CA 92024-4805

DEUKMEJIAN, GEORGE, lawyer, former governor; b. Albany, N.Y., June 6, 1928; s. C. George and Alice (Gairdan) D.; m. Gloria M. Saatjian, 1957; children: Leslie Ann, George Krikor, Andrea Diane. BA, Siena Coll., 1949; JD, St. John's U., 1952. Bar: N.Y. 1952, Calif. 1956, U.S. Supreme Ct. 1970. Mem. Calif. Assembly, 1963-67, Calif. Senate, 1967-79, minority leader; atty. gen. State of Calif., 1979-82, gov., 1983-91; former dep. county counsel Los Angeles County.; former ptnr. Sidley & Austin, 1991-2000. Served with U.S. Army, 1953-55. Republican. Episcopalian. Office: 5366 E Broadway Long Beach CA 90803-3549

DEUTSCH, BARRY JOSEPH, consulting and management development company executive; b. Gary, Ind., Aug. 10, 1941; s. Jack Elias and Helen Louise (La Rue) D. BS, U. So. Calif., 1969, MBA magna cum laude, 1970. Lectr. mgmt. U. So. Calif., L.A., 1967-70; pres., founder The Deutsch Group, Inc., L.A., 1970—; founder, CEO, chmn. bd. Investment Planning Network, Inc., 1988—. Author: Leadership Techniques, 1969, Recruiting Techniques, 1970, The Art of Selling, 1973, Professional Real Estate Management, 1975, Strategic Planning, 1976, Employer/Employee: Making the Transition, 1979, Managing by Objectives, 1980, Conducting Effective Performance Appraisal, 1982, Advanced Supervisory Development, 1984, Managing a Successful Financial Planning Business, 1988, How to Franchise Your Business, 1991. Chmn. bd. govs. Am. Hist. Ctr., 1980—; mentor U. S.C. Career Advancement Program, 1999—. Mem. ASTD, Am. Mgmt. Assn., Am. Soc. Bus. and Mgmt. Cons., Internat. Mgmt. by Objectives Inst., Internat. Soc. for Performance Improvement, Organization Devel. Network, Planning Execs. Inst. Office: 1140 Highland Ave Ste 200 Manhattan Beach CA 90266-5335

DEVAN, DAVID, opera company director; Gen. mgr. Pacific Opera of Victoria, B.C., Can. Office: Pacific Opera Victoria 1316 B Government St Victoria BC Canada V8W 1Y8

DEVENS, PAUL, lawyer; b. Gary, Ind., June 8, 1931; s. Zenove and Anna (Brilla) Dewenetz; m. Setsuko Sugihara, Aug. 14, 1955; children: Paula, Vladimir, Mignon. BA in Econs. cum laude, Ind. U., 1954; LLB, Columbia U., 1957. Bar: N.Y. 1958, U.S. Dist. Ct. Hawaii 1960, Hawaii 1961, U.S. Ct. Appeals (9th cir.) 1962, U.S. Ct. Internat. Trade 1963, U.S. Supreme Ct. 1970. Pvt. practice law, N.Y.C., 1958-60; ptnr. Lewis, Saunders & Key, Honolulu, 1960-69; corp. counsel City and County of Honolulu, 1969-72, mng. dir., 1973-75; ptnr. Devens, Nakano, Saito, Lee, Wong & Ching, Honolulu, 1975-94, of counsel, 1994—. Bd. dirs. Ctrl. Pacific Bank, Honolulu, CPB, Inc., Honolulu; judge Nuclear Claims Tribunal, Majuro, Republic of the Marshall Islands, 1988-90. Mem. Japan-Hawaii Econ. Coun., 1975-95, Honolulu Charter Reorgn. Com., 1979-80, Pacific and Asian Affairs Coun., 1983; trustee Japan-Am. Soc. Honolulu, 1981—, pres., 1987-89; chmn. bd. dirs. Nat. Assn. Japan-Am. Socs., 1989-91; mem. bd. govs. Japanese Cultural Ctr., Hawaii, 1989-94, mem. bd. dirs., v.p., 1994-96, chmn. bd. dirs., 1996-97. Decorated Imperial Order of the Sacred Treasure, Gold Rays with Neck ribbon Govt. of Japan, 1993. Democrat. Eastern Orthodox. Office: Devens Nakano Saito Lee Wong & Ching 220 S King St Ste 1600 Honolulu HI 96813-4597

DEVIN, IRENE K. state legislator, nurse; b. Sumter, S.C., Jan. 24, 1943; m. Jerry Devin. BSN, U. Iowa, 1965. RN. Mem. Wyo. Ho. Rep., Cheyenne, 1992-96, Wyo. Senate, Dist. 10, Cheyenne, 1996—; mem. edn. com. Wyo. Senate, Cheyenne, mem. labor, health, and social svcs. com. Trustee Dist. Hosp., 1986-92, past pres.; mem. Laramie Econ. Devel. Corp., Friends of 4-H; pres. Ivinson Meml. Hosp. Found.; mem. state adv. bd. Medicaid, Rural Health TB Program; mem. adv. bd. Cmty. Pub. Health. Mem. Laramie C. of C., Soroptomists Internat. Republican. Home: 3601 Grays Gable Rd Laramie WY 82072-5032 Office: Wyo Senate State Capitol Cheyenne WY 82002-0001

DEVINCINTIS, LANI, adult education educator; Dean Glendale (Calif.) C.C., dean credit & continuing edn. Recipient Regional Person of Yr. award, 1993, State Cmty. Educator of Yr. award, 1996. Office: Glendale Community Coll 1500 N Verdugo Rd Glendale CA 91208-2809

DEVINE, BRIAN KIERNAN, pet food and supplies company executive; b. Washington, Mar. 1, 1942; s. William John and Rita Marie (Kiernan) D.; m. Silvija Viktorija Kutlets, June 13, 1964; children— Brian Jr., Brooke BA, Georgetown U., 1963; postgrad., Am. U., 1964-65, Yale U., 1965. Statis. adv. USPHS, Washington, 1963-70; with Toys "R" Us, 1970-88; gen. mgr. San Jose, Calif., 1970-75; regional gen. mgr. Chgo., 1975-77; v.p. Saddle Brook, N.J., 1977-82; sr. v.p. Rochelle Park, 1982-88; pres. of furniture mfr./retailer Krause's Sofa Factory, Fountain Valley, Calif., 1988-89; pres., CEO Petco, San Diego, 1990—, chmn., pres., CEO pet food and supplies, 1994—. Bd. dirs. Nat. Retail Fedn., Students in Free Enterprise, Wild Oats Markets, Inc.; mem. coll. bd. advisers Georgetown U. Contbr. articles to profl. publs. Mem. Internat. Mass Retail Assn. (bd. dirs.). Republican. Roman Catholic. Home: 6608 La Valle Plateada PO Box 1305 Rancho Santa Fe CA 92067-1305 Office: 9125 Rehco Rd San Diego CA 92121-2270

DEVINE, D. GRANT, agriculturalist; Recipient fellow Agrl. Inst. of Can., 1994. Office: Grant Devine Mgmt 1777 Victoria Ave Ste 1000 Regina SK Canada S4P 4K5

DEVINE, PERCY, III, human services administrator; b. Jan. 8, 1952; m. Sharon Floore; four children. BS with honors, Weber State U., 1975; MSW with honors, U. Utah, 1978. Cert. social worker and gerontologist. Long term care ombudsman State of Utah, 1978-82, legal svc. supr., 1982-83, mgr. of older Am. activity program, 1984-88, state dir. of aging, 1988-92; regional adminstr. Dept. of Health and Human Svcs., Denver, 1992—. Bd. dirs. Oasis Denver Program, Red Cross, Utah United Way, Utah RSVP Program, Utah Domestic Violence Bd., Adult Protective Svc. Bd., Resident Care Bd. Mem. Oasis Program, Mile-Hi Sand Bagger's Golf Club, Rocky Mountain Gerontology Soc. (v.p.). Baptist. Avocations: golfing, reading, writing, inventions, walking.

DEVINE, SHARON JEAN, lawyer; b. Milw., Feb. 27, 1948; d. George John Devine and Ethel May (Langworthy) Devine Chase; children: Devin Curtiss, Katharine Langworthy. BS in Linguistics magna cum laude, Georgetown U., 1970; JD, Boston U., 1975. Bar: Ohio, Colo. Staff atty. FTC, Cleve., 1975-79, asst. regional dir. Denver, 1982-84; atty. Mountain Bell, Denver, 1982-84, U.S. West Direct, 1984-85, assoc. gen. counsel, 1985-87, Landmark Pub. Co., Denver, 1987-88; antitrust counsel U.S. West, Denver, 1988-91, corp. counsel, 1991-99, assoc. gen. counsel, 1999-2000, 2 West Commns. Internat. Inc., 2000—. Dir. Denver Consortium, 1982-83, Ctr. for Applied Prevention, Boulder, Colo., 1982-90; dir. Legal Aid Found. of Colo., 1990-96, Suzuki Assn. of Colo., 1990-94. Active mem. Jr. League, Denver, 1980-87. Mem. Am. Corp. Counsel Assn. (dir. Colo. chpt. 1994-2000, pres. 1999-2000), Colo. Bar Assn., Denver Assn., Colo. Women's Bar Assn.- Home: 118 Pika Rd Boulder CO 80302-9517 Office: 2West 1801 California St Ste 4900 Denver CO 80202-2610 E-mail: sjdevine@qwest.com

DEVLIN, DEAN, producer, writer, actor; b. Aug. 27, 1962; Prodr., writer Godzilla, 1998, Independence Day, 1996, Stargate, 1994 (Sci-Fi Universe Mag. Reader's Choice award); prodr. The Patriot, 2000; writer Universal Soldier, 1992; creator, exec. prodr. (TV series) The Visitor, 1997; actor (film) Total Exposure, 1991, Moon 44, 1990, Martians Go Home, 1990, City Limits, 1985, Real Genius, 1985, The Wild Life, 1984, My Bodyguard, 1980, (TV) Generations, 1989, Hard Copy, 1987, North Beach and Rawhide, 1985; guest appearances on L.A. Law, Happy Days, Misfits of Science. Recipient George Pal Meml. Award, 1998. Office: Astaire East 3rd Fl 10202 Washington Blvd Culver City CA 90232-3119

DEVLIN, GERRY, state legislator, farmer, rancher; b. Miles City, Mont., Sept. 11, 1932; m. Isabelle Devlin. Grad., Terry H.S. Farmer, rancher; mem. Mont. Ho. of Reps., 1981-88; chair taxation com., vice chair fish and game com.; mem. Mont. State Senate, 1988—, chair com. on taxes, chair taxation com., mem. agr., livestock and irrigation com. Served with U.S. Army, 1951-53. Republican. Home: 517 Mississippi Ave Miles City MT 59301-4137

DEVLIN, MIKE, software company executive; Pres. Rational Software, Cupertino, Calif. Office: Rational Software 18880 Homestead Rd Cupertino CA 95014-0721

DEVLIN, PATRICIA, lawyer; b. Vallejo, Calif., July 25, 1945; BA magna cum laude, U. Wash., 1968; JD, U. Calif., 1977. Bar: Calif. 1977, Hawaii 1978, U.S. Dist. Ct. Hawaii 1978. With Carlsmith Ball LLP, Honolulu. Mem. ABA, State Bar Calif., Hawaii Soc. Corp. Planners (pres. 1992-93), Phi Beta Kappa. Office: Carlsmith Ball LLP Pacific Tower # 2200 1001 Bishop St Honolulu HI 96813-3429 E-mail: pdevlin@carlsmith.com

DEVORE, PAUL CAMERON, lawyer; b. Great Falls, Mont., Apr. 25, 1932; s. Paul Theodore and Maxine (Cameron) DeV.; m. Roberta Humphrey, Feb. 3, 1962; children: Jennifer Ross, Andrew Cameron, Christopher Humphrey. BA, Yale U., 1954; MA, Cambridge U., 1956; JD, Harvard U., 1961. Bar: Wash. 1961. Assoc. Wright, Innis, Simon & Todd, Seattle, 1961-66; ptnr. Davis Wright Tremaine, Seattle, 1967—, chmn. exec. com., 1983-95. Mem. adv. bd. BNA Media Law Reporter, 1978—. Chmn. Seattle C.C., 1967-68, Bush Sch., Seattle, 1976-79, Virginia Mason Med. Found., 1984-85, Virginia Mason Rsch. Ctr., 1983-84, Seattle Found., 1985-87, Children's Hosp. Found., 1993-95; trustee Lakeside Sch., 1995—; chmn. bd. visitors U. Wash. Sch. Comm., 1989-98; pres. A Contemporary Theatre, Seattle, 1972-74; sec. Seattle Art Mus., 1973-2000. Mem. ABA (chmn. forum on comm. law 1981-84), Wash. State Bar Assn. (chmn. sect. corp.

bus. and banking law 1981-82, bench, bar, press com. 1984-90), Seattle-King County Bar Assn. (trustee 1975-76), Seattle Tennis Club, Phi Beta Kappa, Beta Theta Phi. Home: 5740 27th Ave NE Seattle WA 98105-5512 Office: Davis Wright Tremaine 2600 Century Sq 1501 4th Ave Ste 2600 Seattle WA 98101-1688 E-mail: camdevore@dwt.com

DE VRIES, KENNETH LAWRENCE, mechanical engineer, educator; b. Ogden, Utah, Oct. 27, 1933; s. Sam and Fern (Slater) DeV.; m. Kay M. McGee, Mar. 1, 1959; children: Kenneth, Susan. AS in Civil Engring., Weber State Coll., 1953; BSME, U. Utah, 1959, PhD in Physics, Mech. Engring., 1962. Registered profl. engr., Utah. Rsch. engr. hydraulic group Convair Aircraft Corp., Fort Worth, 1957-58; prof. dept. mech. engring. U. Utah, Salt Lake City, 1969-75, Salt Lake City, 1976-91, disting. prof., 1991—, chmn. dept., 1970-81; sr. assoc. dean U. Utah Coll. Engring., Salt Lake City, 1983-97, acting dean, 1997-98. Program dir. div. materials rsch. NSF, Washington, 1975-76; materials cons. Browning, Morgan, Utah, 1972—; cons. 3M Co., Mpls., 1985—; tech. adv. bd. Emerson Electric, St. Louis, 1978—; mem. Utah Coun. Sci. and Tech., 1973-77; trustee Gordon Rsch. Conf., 1989-97, chair, 1992-93. Co-author: Analysis and Testing of Adhesive Bonds, 1978; contbr. chpts. to numerous books, articles and abstracts to profl. publs. Fellow ASME, Am. Phys. Soc.; mem. Am. Chem. Soc. (polymer div.), Soc. Engring. Scis. (nat. officer), Adhesion Soc. (nat. officer). Mem. LDS Ch. Office: U Utah Coll Engring 50 S Central Campus Dr Salt Lake City UT 84112-9249

DEW, WILLIAM WALDO, JR. bishop; b. Newport, Ky., Dec. 14, 1935; s. William Waldo and Thelma (Dittus) D.; m. Mae Marie Eggers, Jan. 5, 1958; children: Linda Dew-Hiersoux, William, Marilyn. BA, Union Coll., Barbourville, Ky., 1957; MDiv, Drew Theol. Sch., 1961; PhD (hon.), Rust Coll., 1991, Union Coll., 1992. Ordained to ministry United Meth. Ch. as deacon, 1958, as elder, 1963. Pastor Springville (Calif.) United Meth. Ch., 1961-64, Lindsay (Calif.) United Meth. Ch., 1964-67, Meml. United Meth. Ch., Clovis, Calif., 1967-72, Epworth United Meth. Ch., Berkeley, 1972-79; dist. supt. Cen. Dist. Calif.-Nev. Annual Conf., Modesto, 1979-84; pastor San Ramon Valley United Meth. Ch., Alamo, 1984-88; bishop United Meth. Ch., Portland, Oreg., 1988-96, United Meth. Ch. Desert S.W. Conf., Phoenix, 1996—. Lectr. Pacific Sch. Religion, Berkeley, 1976-79. Trustee Willamette U., Salem, Oreg., 1988-96, Alaska Pacific U., Anchorage, 1988-96, Claremont Sch. Theology, 1996—. Paul Harris fellow Rotary Internat., 1988. Democrat. Avocations: fishing, golf, reading, travel. Office: United Meth Desert Southwest Conf 1550 E Meadowbrook Ave # 200 Phoenix AZ 85014-4040

DEWEY, DONALD ODELL, dean, academic administrator; b. Portland, Oreg., July 9, 1930; s. Leslie Hamilton and Helen (Odell) D.; m. Charlotte Marion Neuber, Sept. 21, 1952; children: Leslie Helen, Catherine Dawn, Scott Hamilton. Student, Lewis and Clark Coll., 1948-49; BA, U. Oreg., 1952; MS, U. Utah, 1956; PhD, U. Chgo., 1960. Mng. editor Condon (Oreg.) Globe-Times, 1952-53; city editor Ashland (Oreg.) Daily Tidings, 1953-54; asst. editor, assoc. editor The Papers of James Madison, Chgo., 1957-62; instr. U. Chgo., 1960-62; from asst. prof. to prof. Calif. State U., L.A., 1962-96, dean Sch. Letters and Sci., 1970-84, dean Sch. Natural and Social Sci., 1984-96, dean emeritus, prof. emeritus, 1996—; v.p. acad. affairs Trinity Coll. Grad. Studies, Anaheim, Calif., 2000—. Author: The Continuing Dialogue, 2 vols., 1964, Union and Liberty: Documents in American Constitutionalism, 1969, Marshall versus Jefferson: The Political Background of Marbury v. Madison, 1970, Becoming Informed Citizens: Lessons on the Constitution for Junior High School Students, 1988, revised edit., 1995, Invitation to the Dance: An Introduction to Social Dance, 1991, Becoming Informed Citizens: The Bill of Rights and Limited Government, 1995, That's a Good One: Cal State L.A. at 50, 1997, The Federalist and Antifederalist Papers, 1998, Controversial Elections, 2001; contbr. chpts. to books. Recipient Outstanding Prof. award Calif. State U., 1976 Mem. Am. Hist. Assn. (exec. coun. Pacific Coast br. 1971-74), Orgn. Am. Historians, Am. Soc. Legal History (adv. bd. Pacific Coast br. 1972-75), Gold Key, Phi Alpha Theta, Pi Sigma Alpha, Phi Kappa Phi, Sigma Delta Chi. Office: Calif State U Dept History 5151 State University Dr Los Angeles CA 90032-4226 E-mail: ddewey@calstatela.edu

DEWILDE, DAVID MICHAEL, executive search consultant, financial services executive, lawyer; b. Bridgeton, N.J., Aug. 11, 1940; s. Louis and Dorothea (Donnelly) deW.; m. Katherine August, Dec. 30, 1984; children: Holland Stockdale, Christian DuCroix, Nicholas Alexander, Lucas Barrymore. AB, Dartmouth Coll., 1962; LLB, U. Va., 1967; MS in Mgmt., Stanford U., 1984. Bar: N.Y. 1968, D.C. 1972. Assoc. Curtis, Mallet-Prevost, Colt & Mosle, N.Y.C., 1967-69; assoc. gen. counsel HUD, Washington, 1969-72; investment banker Lehman Bros., Washington, 1972-74; dep. commr. FHA, Washington, 1974-76; pres. Govt. Nat. Mortgage Assn., Washington, 1976-77; mng. dir. Lepercq DeNeuflize & Co., N.Y.C., 1977-81; exec. v.p. policy and planning Fed. Nat. Mortgage Assn., Washington, 1981-82; pres. deWilde & Assocs., Washington, 1982-84; mng. dir., dir. fin. svcs. Boyden Internat., San Francisco, 1984-88; CEO Chartwell Ptnrs. Internat., San Francisco, 1989-97; mng. dir. LAI Worldwide, San Francisco, 1998-99; mng. ptnr. TMP Worldwide, San Francisco, 1999-2001. Bd. dirs. Berkshire Realty Investment Trust, Fritzi of Calif., Silicon Valley Bankshares; bd. dirs. St. Luke's School, San Francisco, chair, 2001—. Editor-in-chief Va. Jour. Internat. Law, 1966-67. Lt. USN, 1962-64. Mem. Pacific Union Club (San Francisco), Met. Club (Washington), Belvedere Tennis Club. Republican. E-mail: ddewilde@pacbell.net

DEWITT, BARBARA JANE, journalist; b. Glendale, Calif., Aug. 5, 1947; d. Clarence James and Irene Brezina; m. Don DeWitt, Apr. 21, 1974; children: Lisa, Scarlett. BA in Journalism, Calif. State U., Northridge, 1971. Features editor The Daily Ind. Newspaper, Ridgecrest, Calif., 1971-84; fashion editor The Daily Breeze, Torrance, 1984-89; freelance fashion reporter The Seattle Times, 1990; fashion editor, columnist The Los Angeles Daily News, L.A., 1990—. Instr. fashion writing UCLA, 1988, Am. InterContinental U., L.A., 1996—. Dir. Miss Indian Wells Valley Scholarship Pageant, 1980-84. Recipient 1st Pl. Best Youth Page, Calif. Newspaper Pubs. Assn., 1980, 1st Pl. Best Fashion, Wash. Press Assn., 1989, The Internat. Aldo award for fashion journalism, 1995, 96. Republican. Lutheran. Avocations: antiques, reading, swimming. Office: The Daily News 21221 Oxnard St Woodland Hills CA 91367-5081

DE YOUNG, DAVID SPENCER, astrophysicist, educator; b. Colorado Springs, Colo., Nov. 29, 1940; s. Henry C. and Zona L. (Church) DeY.; m. Mary Ellen Haney. BA, U. Colo., 1962; PhD, Cornell U., 1967. Rsch. physicist Los Alamos Nat. Labs., Los Alamos, N. Mex., 1967-69; astronomer Nat. Radio Astronomy Obs., Charlottesville, Va., 1969-80, Kitt Peak Nat. Obs., Tucson, 1980—, assoc. dir., 1983-88, dir., 1988-94. Organizer numerous sci. confs.; mem. adv. bd. Aspen (Colo.) Ctr. Physics, 1977—, trustee, 1992—, pres., 2001—; mem. exec. com. steering com. San Diego Supercomputer Ctr., 1985-98, chmn., 1989-91; mem. steering com. Nat. Virtual Obs., 2000—; bd. dirs. WIYN Telescope Consortium, Tucson. Contbr. articles to profl. jours. NASA grantee. Mem. Am. Phys. Soc., Am. Astron. Soc., Astron. Soc. Pacific, Internat. Astron. Union, Internat. Union Radio Soc., Phi Beta Kappa. Office: Kitt Peak Nat Obs 950 N Cherry Ave Tucson AZ 85719-4933

DHIR, VIJAY K. mechanical engineering educator; b. Giddarbaha, Panjab, India, Apr. 14, 1943; came to U.S., 1969; s. Harnand Lal and Parsinni Devi (Sofat) D.; m. Komal Lata Khanna, Aug. 31, 1973; children: Vinita, Vashita. BScME, Punjab Engring. Coll., India, 1965; MTechME, Indian Inst. Tech., 1969; PhD in Mech. Engring., U. Ky., 1972. Asst. devel. engr. Jyoti Pumps, Ltd., Baroda, India, 1968-69; postgrad. engr. Engring. Rsch. Ctr. Tata Engring. & Locomotive Co., Poona, India, 1969; rsch. asst. U. Ky., Lexington, 1969-72, rsch. assoc., 1972-74; asst. prof. chem., nuclear & thermal engring. dept. UCLA, 1974-78, assoc. prof., 1978-82, prof. mech., aerospace & nuclear engring. dept., 1982—, vice chmn. mech., aerospace & nuclear engring. dept., 1988-91, chmn. dept., 1994-2000. Cons. Nuclear Regulatory Commn., Seabulk Corp., Ft. Lauderdale, Fla., Argonne (Ill.) Nat. Lab., Pickard, Lowe & Garrick, Inc., Irvine, Calif., Rockwell Internat., Canoga Park, Calif., GE Corp., San Jose, Calif., Battelle N.W. Lab., Richland, Wash., Phys. Rsch., Inc., Torrance, Calif., Nat. Bur. Stds., Gaithersburg, Md., Los Alamos (N.Mex.) Nat. Lab., Sci. Applications Inc., El Segundo, Calif., Brookhaven Nat. Lab., Upton, N.Y.; chmn. numerous conf. sessions. Contbr. over 100 articles to profl. jours., over 100 papers to procs./conf. & symposia records; assoc. editor Applied Mechs. Rev., 1985-88, Jour. Heat Transfer, Transactions ASME, 1993-96, editor, 2000—; assoc. editor ASME Symposium Vol., 1978; referee numerous jours. Recipient Donald O. Kera award AIChE, 1999. Fellow ASME (Heat Transfer Meml. Award Sci. Category 1992, sr. tech. editor Jour. Heat Transfer 2000-05), ASChE (Donald Q. Kern award 1999), Am. Nuc. Soc. Office: Sch of Engring & Applied Sc U Calif 46-147 K Engineering IV Los Angeles CA 90024

DIAMA, BENJAMIN, retired educator, artist, composer, writer; b. Hilo, Hawaii, Sept. 23, 1933; s. Agapito and Catalina (Buscas) D. BFA, Sch. Art Inst. Chgo., 1956. Cert. tchr., Hawaii. Tchr. art, basketball coach Waimea (Kauai, Hawaii) High Sch., 1963-67; tchr. music and art Campbell High Sch., Honolulu, 1967-68; tchr. math. and art Waipahu High Sch., Honolulu, 1968-69; tchr. art and music Palisades Elem. Sch., Honolulu, 1969-70; tchr. typing, history, art and music Honokaa (Hawaii) High Sch., 1970-73; tchr. music Kealakehe Sch., Kailua, 1973-74; ret., 1974. Author, writer, composer: Hawaii, 1983; author: Poems of Faith, 1983-88, School One vs. School Two On The Same School Campus, 1983, The Calendar-Clock Theory of the Universe with Faith -- Above and Beyond, 1984-90, Phonetic Sound-Musical Theory, 1990; contbr. author to book: Benjamin Diama -- The Calendar Clock Theory of the Universe, 1991, 92, (poetry) Celebration of Poets, 1998, Poets Elite, Internat. Soc. of Poets, 2000; producer, composer (Cassette) Hawaii I Love You, 1986; inventor universal clock, 1984, double floater boat, 1985, Gardener's Water Box, 2001. Recipient Achievement award Waimea Dept. Edn., 1964-67, Purchase award State Found. Arts on Culture and the Arts, 1984, State Found. Arts and Culture Acquisition Painting Art award State of Hawaii Govt. Art Collection. Mem. NEA, Hawaii Tchrs. Assn., Hawaii Edn. Assn., AAAS, Nat. Geog. Soc., Smithsonian Assocs., ASCAP, N.Y. Acad. Scis., Nat. Libr. Poetry (assoc.), Internat. Soc. Poets, Am. Geophysical Union. Mem. Salvation Army. Avocations: singing, writing science, coaching basketball. Home: PO Box 2997 Kailua Kona HI 96745-2997

DIAMOND, JARED MASON, biologist; b. Boston, Sept. 10, 1937; s. Louis K. and Flora K. D. B.A., Harvard U., 1958; Ph.D., Cambridge (Eng.) U., 1961. Jr. fellow Soc. Fellows Harvard U., 1962-65; assoc. in biophysics, 1965-66; asso. prof. physiology U. Calif. Med. Center, Los Angeles, 1966-68, prof., 1968—. Cons. in conservation and nat. park planning govts., Papua New Guinea, Solomon Islands, Indonesia. Author: Avifauna of the Eastern Highlands of New Guinea, 1972, Ecology and Evolution of Communities, 1975, Guns, Germs, and Steel (Pulitzer prize 1998, Cosmos prize 1998); research and articles in membrane physiology and ecology Recipient Burr medal Nat. Geog. Soc., 1979, Bowditch prize Am. Physiol. Soc., 1976, Disting. Achievement award Am. Gastroent. Assn., 1975, Nat. Medal Science, 1999. Fellow Am. Acad. Arts and Scis., MacArthur Found.; mem. Nat. Acad. Scis. Office: UCLA Med Ctr Dept of Physiology 10833 Le Conte Ave Los Angeles CA 90095-3075*

DIAMOND, MARIAN CLEEVES, anatomy educator; b. Glendale, Calif., Nov. 11, 1926; d. Montague and Rosa Marian (Wamphler) Cleeves; m. Richard M. Diamond, Dec. 20, 1950 (div.); m. Arnold B. Scheibel, Sept. 14, 1982; children: Catherine, Richard, Jeffrey, Ann. AB, U. Calif., Berkeley, 1948, MA, 1949, PhD, 1953. With Harvard U., Cambridge, 1952-54, Cornell U., Ithaca, N.Y., 1954-58, U. Calif., San Francisco, 1954-58, prof. anatomy Berkeley, 1962—. Asst. dean U. Calif., Berkeley, 1967-70, assoc. dean, 1970-73, dir. The Lawrence Hall of Sci., 1990-95, dir. emeritus, 1995—; vis. scholar Australian Nat. U., 1978, Fudan U., Shanghai, China, 1985, U. Nairobi, Kenya, 1988. Author: (with J. Hopson) Magic Trees of the Mind, 1998; author: Enriching Heredity, 1989; co-author: The Human Brain Coloring, 1985; editor: Contraceptive Hormones Estrogen and Human Welfare, 1978; contbr. over 155 articles to profl. jours. V.p. County Women Dems., Ithaca, 1957; bd. dirs. Unitarian Ch., Berkeley, 1969. Recipient Calif. Gifted award, 1989, C.A.S.E. Calif. Prof. of Yr. award, Nat. Gold medalist, 1990, Woman of Yr. award Zonta Internat., 1991, U. medal La. Universidad Del Zulia, Maricaibo, Venezuela, 1992, Alumna of the Yr. award U. Calif., Berkeley, 1995; Calif. Acad. Scis. fellow, 1991, Calif. Soc. Biomedical Rsch. Dist. Svc. award, 1998, Alumnae Resources-Women of Achievement Vision and Excellence award, 1999, Benjamin Ide Wheeler award 1999, Achievement award Calif. Child Devel. Adminstrs. Assn., 2001; named to Internat. Educators Hall of Fame, 1999. Fellow AAAS, AAUW (sr.; fellowship chair 1970-85, 1st Sr. Scholar award 1997); mem. Am. Assn. Anatomists, Soc. Neurosci., Philos. Soc. Washington, The Faculty Club (Berkeley, v.p. 1979-85, 90-95). Avocations: hiking, sports, painting. E-mail: diamond. Home: 2583 Virginia St Berkeley CA 94709-1108 Office: U Calif Dept Integrative Biology 3060 Valley Life Sciences Bldg Berkeley CA 94720-3116 E-mail: socrates@berkeley.edu

DIAMOND, NEIL LESLIE, singer, composer; b. Bklyn., Jan. 24, 1941; m. Marcia Murphey, 1975; children: Jesse, Micah; children by previous marriage: Marjorie, Elyn. Student, NYU. Formerly with Bang Records, Uni, MCA Records, Los Angeles, now rec. artist, singer, composer, Columbia Records; songs include Solitary Man, Cherry, Cherry, Kentucky Woman, I'm a Believer, September Morn, Sweet Caroline, Holly Holy, A Little Bit Me, A Little Bit You, Longfellow Serenade, Song Sung Blue, America, I Am, I Said; albums include: The Feel of Neil Diamond, 1966, Just for You, 1967, Neil Diamond's Greatest Hits, 1968, Velvet Gloves and Spit, 1968, Touching You, Touching Me, 1969, Brother Love's Travelling Salvation Show, 1969, Gold, 1970, Tap Root Manuscript, 1970, Shilo, 1970, Stones, 1971, Do It!, 1971, Hot August Nights, 1972, Moods, 1972, Rainbow, 1973, Jonathan Livingston Seagull, 1973, Greatest Hits, 1974, Serenade, 1974, Gold 1, 1974, Gold 2, 1974, Diamonds, 1975, Focus On, 1975, Beautiful Noise, 1976, And the Singer Sings His Song, 1976, Live at the Greek, 1977, I'm Glad You're Here With Me Tonight, 1977, You Don't Bring Me Flowers, 1978, 20 Golden Greats, 1978, Neil Diamonds, 1979, September Morn, 1980, Jazz Singer, 1980, Best Of, 1981, Solitary, 1981, Love Songs, 1981, On the Way to the Sky, 1981, Live Diamond, 1982, Heart Light, 1982, Song Sung Blue, 1982, Primitive, 1984, Headed For the Future, 1986, Hot August Night II, 1987, The Best Years of Our Lives, 1989, Lovescape, 1991, Neil Diamond The Greatest Hits, 1966-92, 1992, The Christmas Album, 1992, Neil Diamond Glory Road 1968-72, 1992, Live in America, 1994, His 12 Greatest Hits, 1996, As Time Goes By-Movie Album, 1998, Best of Neil Diamond, 1999, Best of The Movie Album, 1999, (videos) Neil Diamond: Greatest Hits Live, 1988, Neil Diamond: Under a Tennessee Moon, 1996 (with others) Tennessee Moon, 1996; composer film scores Jonathan Livingston Seagull (Grammy award 1973), Every Which Way but Loose, 1978, The Jazz Singer (also actor), 1980; guest artist network TV shows. Recipient 19 platinum albums, 28 gold albums. Office: care Columbia Records 2100 Colorado Ave Santa Monica CA 90404-3504

DIAMOND, PHILIP ERNEST, lawyer; b. L.A., Feb. 11, 1925; s. William and Elizabeth (Weizenhaus) D.; m. Dorae Seymour (dec.); children: William, Wendy, Nancy; m. 2d, Jenny White Carson. B.A., UCLA, 1949, M.A., 1950; J.D., U. Calif., Berkeley, 1953. Bar: Calif. 1953, U.S. Dist. Ct. (no., ea. and cen. dists.) Calif. 1953, U.S. Ct. Appeals (9th cir.) 1953. Law clk. to presiding justice Calif. Dist. Ct. Appeals, 1953-54; assoc. Landels & Weigel, San Francisco, 1954-60; ptnr. Landels Weigel & Ripley, San Francisco, 1960-62; sr. ptnr. Landels, Ripley & Diamond, San Francisco, 1962-93—; pres. Diamond Wine Mchts., San Francisco, 1976—; bd. dirs. Yasutomo & Co. Pres. Contra Costa Sch. Bd. Assn., 1966-68. With USN, 1943-46. Mem. ABA, Am. Arbitration Assn., Calif. State Bar Assn., San Francisco Bar Assn., Phi Beta Kappa. Democrat. Clubs: Commonwealth, Mchts. & Exch. Office: 350 The Embarcadero San Francisco CA 94105-1204

DIAMOND, RICHARD MARTIN, nuclear chemist; b. L.A., Jan. 7, 1924; divorced; 4 children. BS, UCLA, 1947; PhD in Nuclear Chemistry, U. Calif. Berkeley, 1951. Instr. chemistry Harvard U., 1951-54; asst. prof. Cornell U., 1954-58; mem. sr. staff Lawrence Berkeley Lab., U. Calif., 1958—, sr. scientist emeritus, 1995—. Mem. U.S. Physics del. to Russia, 1966, rev. com. physics divsn. Oak Ridge Lab., 1972-74, Dept. of Energy rev. com. Brookhaven (n, gamma) Facility and Isotope Separator, 1983, 8pi Gamma Spect. Com., Chalk River, Canada, 1983, adv. com. Ind. Cyclotron Facility, 1980-83, Tandem-Linac Facility Argonne Nat. Lab., 1983-86, Holifield Rsch. Facility, 1988-90, Holifield Radioactive Ion Beam Facility, 1994-97; chmn. Gordon Conf. on Nuclear Chemistry, 1965, Gordon Conf. on Ion Exch., 1969, rev. com. UNISOR, Oak Ridge Nat. Lab., 1974-75, subcom. high spin and nuclei far from stability Dept. Energy-NSF, 1983; vis. fellow Japan Soc. for Promotion of Sci., 1981; co-organizer Int. Conf. Nuclear Physics, 1980, workshop on nuclear str., 1986, workshop Nat. Gamma-Ray Facility, 1987. Guggenheim fellow, 1966-67, Fullbright fellow, 1977. Fellow AAAS, Am. Phys. Soc. (shared Tom W. Bonner award 1980); mem. Am. Chem. Soc. (award in nuclear chemistry 1993). Achievements include research in nuclear spectroscopy, coulomb excitation, high-spin nuclear structure. Home: 574 Santa Clara Ave Berkeley CA 94707-1647 Office: Lawrence Berkeley Nat Lab Nuclear Science Divsn Bldg 88 Berkeley CA 94720-0001 E-mail: rmdiamond@lbl.gov

DIAMOND, STANLEY JAY, lawyer; b. Los Angeles, Nov. 27, 1927; s. Philip Alfred and Florence (Fadem) D.; m. Lois Jane Broida, June 22, 1969; children: Caryn Elaine, Diana Beth. B.A., UCLA, 1949; J.D., U. So. Calif., 1952. Bar: Calif. 1953. Practiced law, Los Angeles, 1953—; dep. Office of Calif. Atty. Gen., Los Angeles, 1953; ptnr. Diamond & Tilem, Los Angeles, 1957-60, Diamond, Tilem & Colden, Los Angeles, 1960-79, Diamond & Wilson, Los Angeles, 1979—. Lectr. music and entertainment law UCLA; Mem. nat. panel arbitrators Am. Arbitration Assn. Bd. dirs. Los Angeles Suicide Prevention Center, 1971-76. Served with 349th Engr. Constrn. Bn. AUS, 1945-47. Mem. ABA, Calif. Bar Assn., Los Angeles County Bar Assn., Beverly Hills Bar Assn., Am. Judicature Soc., Calif. Copyright Conf., Nat. Acad. Rec. Arts and Scis., Zeta Beta Tau, Nu Beta Epsilon. Office: 12304 Santa Monica Blvd Fl 3D Los Angeles CA 90025-2551

DIAZ, CONSUELO, health facility administrator; BA, U. So. Calif., 1966, MPA, 1989. CEO Rancho Los Amigos Nat. Rehab. Ctr., 1993—. Office: 7601 E Imperial Hwy Downey CA 90242-3456

DIAZ, DAVID, illustrator; married; 3 children. Degree, Ft. Lauderdale (Fla.) Art Inst. Illustrator of children's books including Neighborhood Odes (Gary Soto), 1992, Smoky Night (Eve Bunting), 1994 (Caldecott medal 1995), Anansi's Narrow Waist (Len Cabral), 1994, Wilma Unlimited: How Wilma Rudolph Became the World's Fastest Woman (Kathleen Krull), 1996, Passing Strange: True Tales of New England Hauntings and Horrors (Joseph Citro), 1996, Just One Flick of the Finger (Marybeth Lorbiecki), 1996, The Inner City Mother Goose (Eve Merriam), 1996, Going Home (Eve Bunting), 1996, December (Eve Bunting), 1997, The Disappearing Alphabet (Richard Wilbur), 1999, The Little Scarecrow Boy (Margaret Wise Brown); one-man shows include Thurber Ctr. Gallery. Recipient awards Parents' Choice, Am. Illustrations, Comm. Arts, Am. Inst. Graphic Arts, N.Y. Art Dirs. Club. Office: care Harcourt Brace & Co 1697 Robin Pl Carlsbad CA 92009-5037

DIAZ, SHARON, education administrator; b. Bakersfield, Calif., July 29, 1946; d. Karl C. and Mildred (Lunn) Clark; m. Luis F. Diaz, Oct. 19, 1968; children: Daniel, David. BS, San Jose State U., 1969; MS, U. Calif., San Francisco, 1973; PhD (hon.), St. Mary's Coll. Calif., 1999. Nurse Kaiser Found. Hosp., Redwood City, Calif., 1969-73; lectr. San Jose (Calif.) State Coll., 1969-70; nurse San Mateo (Calif.) County, 1970-71; instr. St. Francis Meml. Hosp. Sch. Nursing, San Francisco, 1973-76, asst. dir., 1976-78; dir. Samuel Merritt Hosp. Sch. Nursing, Oakland, Calif., 1978-84; founding pres. Samuel Merritt Coll., Oakland, 1984—. V.p. East Bay Area Health Edn. Ctr., Oakland, 1980-87; mem. adv. com. Calif. Acad. Partnership Program, 1990; mem. nat. adv. com. Nursing Outcomes Project. Bd. dirs. Head Royce Sch., 1990-98, vice chair, 1993-95, chair, 1995-97; bd. dirs. Ladies Home Soc., 1992—, sec. 1994-95, treas., CFO 1995-97, 2nd v.p. 1997-99; adv. bd. Ethnic Health Inst., 1997—; mem. com. minorities higher edn. Am. Coun. Edn., 1998—. Named Woman of Yr., Oakland YWCA, 1996. Mem. Am. Assn. of Pres. Ind. Colls. and Univs., Sigma Theta Tau (Leadership award Nu Xi chpt. 2001). Office: Samuel Merritt Coll 450 30th St Oakland CA 94609-3302 E-mail: sdiaz@samuelmerritt.edu

DIAZ-ZUBIETA, AGUSTIN, nuclear engineer, engingeering executive; b. Madrid, Spain, Mar. 24, 1936; came to U.S., 1953; s. Emilio Diaz Cabeza and Maria Teresa Zubieta Atucha; m. Beth Lee Fortune, Sept. 6, 1958; children: Walter Agustin, Michael Joel, Anthony John. B, U. Madrid, 1953; BSc in Physics, U. Tenn., 1958; MSc in Mech. Engring., Duke U., 1960; PhD in Nuclear Engring., U. Md., 1981. Nuclear engr. Combustion Engring., Tenn., 1954-58; instr. engring. Duke U., Durham, N.C., 1958-60; nuclear physicist Allis Chalmers Co., Washington, 1960-64, country mgr. South Africa, 1964-66; mgr. internat. power generation projects GE, N.Y.C., 1966-69, mgr. Europe and Middle East strategic planning, 1969-71, dir. internat. constrn. planning Westport, Conn., 1971-75, dir. constrn., 1975-83; CEO GE Affiliate, Westport, 1983-87; v.p. internat. sales, devel. Internat. Tech. Corp., L.A., 1987-94. Mng. dir. IT Italia S.P.A., IT Spain, S.A. Author: Measurement of Subcriticality of Nuclear Reactors by Stocastic Processes, 1981. Pres. Fairfield (Conn.) Assn. Condo Owners, 1983-87. Named Astronomer of Yr. Barnard Astronomical Soc., Chattanooga, 1957; fgn. exchange scholar U.S. Govt., 1953-58; grantee, NSF, 1958-60, U.S. Office of Ordinance Rsch. U.S. Army, 1958-60. Mem. Am. Nuclear Soc., Am. Soc. Mech. Engrs., Am. Soc. Profl. Engrs., Sigma Xi. Republican. Roman Catholic. Avocations: golf, tennis, swimming, sailing, music. Home: 47 Country Meadow Rd Rolling Hills Estates CA 90274

DICICCIO, SAL, city official; b. Youngstown, Ohio; Grad., Ariz. State U. City coun., Phoenix, 1994—. Chair internal policy subcom. Phoenix City Coun., chmn. arts and culture subcom., environment and natural resources subcom., economy subcom., downtown and sports subcoms.; real estate agt.; mem. Gov's Alternative Transp. Sys. Task Force, gov. appointee Growing Smarter Working Adv. Com., 1998—. Past bd. dirs. Ariz. Ctr. for Blind; mem. Ariz. Mcpl. Tax Code Commn., mem. State Land Conservation Task Force. Mem. Fiscal Accountability and Reform Effort, Republican Caucus, Kiwanis, Roman Catholic. Office: 200 W Washington St Fl 11 Phoenix AZ 85003-1611

DICK, BERTRAM GALE, JR. physics educator; b. Portland, Oreg., June 12, 1926; s. Bertram Gale and Helen (Meengs) D.; m. Ann Bradford Volkmann, June 23, 1956; children— Timothy Howe, Robin Louise, Stephen Gale. B.A., Reed Coll., 1950; B.A. (Rhodes scholar), Wadham Coll., Oxford (Eng.) U., 1953, M.A., 1958; Ph.D., Cornell U., 1958. Rsch. assoc. U. Ill., 1957-59; mem. faculty U. Utah, 1959-98, prof. physics, 1965-98, prof. emeritus, 1998—, Univ. prof., 1979-80, chmn. dept., 1964-67, dean grad. sch., 1987-93. Cons. Minn. Mining and Mfg. Co., 1960-67; vis. prof. Technische Hochschule, Munich, 1967-68; vis. scientist Max Planck Institut für Festkörperforschung, Stuttgart, Fed. Republic Germany, 1976-77; faculty Semester at Sea, fall 1983, 86. Mem. Alta Planning and Zoning Commn., 1972-76; pres. Chamber Music Salt Lake City, 1974-76; bd. trustees Citizen's Com. to Save Our Canyons, 1972—, Coalition for Utah's Future Project 2000, 1989-96. Served in USNR, 1944-46. Fellow Am. Phys. Soc.; mem. Am. Alpine Club, Phi Beta Kappa, Sigma Xi. Achievements include research in solid state theory. Home: 1377 Butler Ave Salt Lake City UT 84102-1803 Office: U Utah Dept Physics 115 S 1400 E Rm 201 Salt Lake City UT 84112-0830 E-mail: gdick@xmission.com

DICK, HENRY HENRY, minister; b. Russia, June 1, 1922; s. Henry Henry and Mary (Unger) D.; m. Erica Penner, May 25, 1946; children— Janet (Mrs. Arthur Enns), Judith (Mrs. Ron Brown), James, Henry. Th.B., Mennonite Brethren Bible Coll., 1950. Ordained to ministry Mennonite Brethren Ch., 1950; pastor in Orillia, Ont., Can., 1950-54, Lodi, Calif., 1954-57, Shafter, 1958-69; faculty Tabor Coll., 1954-55; gen. sec. Mennonite Brethren Conf. of U.S.A., 1969-72; pres. Mennonite Brethren Bibl. Sem., Fresno, Calif., 1972-76; vice moderator Gen Conf. Mennonite Brethren Ch., 1975-78, moderator, 1979-84; pastor Reedley Mennonite Brethren Ch., 1976-88; ret., 1989; dir. ch. and constituency relations Mennonite Brethren Biblical Sem., 1987-89. Moderator Pacific Dist. Conf., 1959-60, 61-63, 75-77; mem. exec. com. Mennonite Central Com. Internat., 1967-75, mem. bd. reference and counsel, 1966-69, 72-75, mem. bd. missions and services, 1969-72; exec. sec. Bd. Edn. Mennonite Brethren, 1969-72; chmn. Bd. Missions and Services, 1985-91; pastor emeritus Reedley Mennonite Brethren Ch., 1987. Columnist bi-weekly publ. Christian Leader, 1969-75. Bd. dirs. Bob Wilson Meml. Hosp., Ulysses, Kans., 1969-72; dist. minister Pacific Dist. Conf. Mennonite Brethren, 1989—. Recipient Humanitarian award Shafter C. of C., 1969, Citation bd. dirs. Bibl. Sem. Clubs: Kiwanis, Reedley Rotary. Home: 783 W Carpenter Ave Reedley CA 93654-3903 Office: 1632 L St Reedley CA 93654-3340

DICKERSON, COLLEEN BERNICE PATTON, artist, educator; b. Cleburne, Tex., Sept. 17, 1922; d. Jennings Bryan and Alma Bernice (Clark) Patton; m. Arthur F. Dickerson; children: Sherry M., Chrystal Charmine. BA, Calif. State U., Northridge, 1980; studied with John Pike. Presenter demonstrations Cayucos Art Assn., Morro Bay Art Assn., El Camino Real Art Assn. One-woman shows include Morro Bay Cmty. Bldg., Amandas Interiors, Arroyo Grande, Calif., 1996, Gt. Western Savs., San Luis Obispo, Calif.; exhibited in group shows; represented in permanent collections, including Polk Ins. Co., San Luis Obispo, Med. Ctr. MDM Ins. Co., L.A. Mem. Ctrl. Coast Watercolor Soc. (pres. 1986-87, Svc. award 1998), Art Ctr., Oil Acrylic Pastel Group (chmn., co-chmn. 1989-98, prize Brush Strokes show 1999), Morro Bay Art Assn. (scholarship judge 1998), San Luis Obispo Art Ctr., Valley Watercolor Soc. (co-founder). Avocations: Egyptology, Chinese painting, art history. Home: 245 Hacienda Ave San Luis Obispo CA 93401-7967

DICKERSON, GARY E. electronics executive; b. 1957; BS in Engrng. Mgmt., U. Mo., Rolla; MBA, U. Mo., Kansas City. Head photo engrng. sect. AT&T Techs.; various KLA-Tencor Corp., San Jose, Calif., 1986-99, COO, 1999—. Office: KLA Tencor Corp 160 Rio Robles San Jose CA 95134 Fax: 408-468-4200

DICKEY, BOH A. investment company executive; m. Marilyn. BS, U. Mont., 1966; LLD (hon.), Seattle U., 1999. With Deloitte Haskins & Sells, 1966-78, ptnr., 1978-82; v.p., controller SAFECO, Seattle, 1982-89, CFO, 1989-92, exec. v.p., 1992—; also bd. dirs., chmn. Chair bds. Pacific Sci. Ctr., Acctg. Career Awareness Program, Jr. Achievement Greater Seattle, United Way, 2000—; vice chair bd. U. Wash. Med. Ctr.; bd. trustees Seattle U. Recipient Nat. Gold Leadership award Jr. Achievement, 1997, Leadership award Seattle U., 1999, Spirit of Life award City of Hope Nat. Med. Ctr., 1999; named Humanitarian of Yr. Wash. Soc. CPA's, 1994, Alumnus of Yr. Deloitte & Touche. Office: SAFECO Safeco Plz Seattle WA 98185-0001

DICKEY, GLENN ERNEST, JR. sports columnist; b. Virginia, Minn., Feb. 16, 1936; s. Glenn Ernest and Madlyn Marie (Emmert) D.; m. Nancy Jo McDaniel, Feb. 25, 1967; 1 son, Kevin Scott. B.A., U. Calif., Berkeley, 1958. Sports editor Watsonville (Calif.) Register-Pajoronian, 1958-63; sports writer San Francisco Chronicle, 1963-71, sports columnist, 1971—. Author: The Jock Empire, 1974, The Great No-Hitters, 1976, Champs and Chumps, 1976, The History of National League Baseball, 1979, The History of American League Baseball, 1980, (with Dick Berg) Eavesdropping America, 1980, America Has a Better Team, 1982, The History of Professional Basketball, 1982, The History of the World Series, 1984, (with Jim Tunney) Impartial Judgment: The Dean of NFL Referees Calls Football As He Sees It, 1988, San Francisco Forty-Niners: The Super Year, 1989; (with Bill Walsh) Building a Champion, 1990; Just Win, Baby, Al Davis and His Raiders, 1991; Sports Hero Kevin Mitchell (juvenile), 1993, Sports Hero Jerry Rice (juvenile), 1993, San Francisco 49ers: 50 Years, 1995, San Francisco Giants: 40 Seasons, 1997, Glenn Dickey's 49ers, 2000; contbr. stories to Best Sports Stories, 1962, 68, 71, 75, 76. Home: 120 Florence Ave Oakland CA 94618-2249 Office: Chronicle Pub Co 901 Mission St San Francisco CA 94103-2905

DICKEY, ROBERT MARVIN (RICK DICKEY), property manager; b. Charleston, S.C., Dec. 3, 1950; s. John Lincoln II and Ruth (Marvin) D.; m. Teresa Ann Curry, Dec. 19, 1969 (div. 1979); 1 child, Gena Lynette; m. Martha Suzanne Coup, July 21, 1999; 1 child, Dylan Thomas. A of Computer Sci., USMC Degree Program, Washington, 1975. Cert. apt. property supr. Nat. Apt. Assn., Wash., occupancy specialist Nat. Ctr.for Housing Mgmt., Wash. Enlisted USMC, 1968, advanced through grades to staff sgt., 1968-78; shop mgr., bookkeeper Amalgamated Plant Co., Las Vegas, Nev., 1978-79; supr. constrn. Joseph Yousem Co., Las Vegas, 1979-80; apt. mgr. Robert A. McNeil Corp., Las Vegas, 1980, comml. bldg. mgr., leasing agt., 1980-82; asst. v.p., regional property mgr. Westminster Co., Las Vegas, 1982-87, Weyerhaeuser Mortgage Co., Las Vegas, 1988-89; pres., ptnr. Equinox Devel., Inc., Las Vegas, 1989-91; dir. residental properties R.W. Robideaux & Co., Spokane, Wash., 1992-97; mgr. residential divsn. G&B Real Estate Svcs., Spokane, 1997—. Contbr. articles to profl. jours. Mem. Nat. Assn. Realtors, Wash. Assn. Realtors, Spokane Assn. Realtors, Inst. Real Estate Mgmt. (accredited residential mgr., legis. chmn. 1987-88, Accredited Residential Mgr. award 1985, 86, 90), Nev. Apt. Assn. (v.p. 1985, pres. 1988—, bd. dirs.), So. Nev. Homebuilders Assn., Las Vegas Bd. Realtors (mgmt. legis. com. 1988).

DICKEY, ROBERT PRESTON, writer, educator, poet; b. Flat River, Mo., Sept. 24, 1936; s. Delno Miren D. and Naomi Valentine (Jackson) D.; children: Georgia Rae, Shannon Ezra, Rain Dancer. BA, U. Mo., 1968, MA, 1969; PhD, Walden U., 1975. Instr. U. Mo., 1967-69; asst. prof. English and creative writing U. So. Colo., 1969-73; assoc. mem. faculty Pima Coll., Tucson, 1975-78. Author: (with Donald Justice, Thomas McAfee, Donald Drummond) poetry Four Poets, 1967, Running Lucky, 1969, Acting Immortal, 1970; Concise Dictionary of Lead River, Mo., 1972, The Basic Stuff of Poetry, 1972, Life Cycle of Seven Songs, 1972, McCabe Wants Chimes, 1973, Admitting Complicity, 1973; opera librettos Minnequa, 1976, The Witch of Tucson, 1976; Jimmie Cotton!, 1979, Way Out West, 1979, The Poetica Erotica of R.P. Dickey, 1989, The Little Book on Racism and Politics, 1990, The Way of Eternal Recurrence, 1994, Ode on Liberty, 1996, The Lee Poems, 1998, Self-Liberation, 1998, Exercise Anytime, 1998, Collected Poems, 1999, (with Lee Foster) Taos and Other Works of Art, 2002; contbr. poetry to popular mags., Poetry, Saturday Rev., Commonwealth, Prairie Schooner; founder, editor: The Poetry Bag quar., 1966-71; poetry editor: So. Colo. Std., 1973-74. With USAF, 1955-57. Recipient Mahan award for poetry U. Mo., 1965-66 Home: PO Box 87 Ranchos De Taos NM 87557-0087

DICKINSON, ELEANOR CREEKMORE, artist, educator; b. Knoxville, Tenn., Feb. 7, 1931; d. Robert Elmond and Evelyn Louise (Van Gilder) C.; m. Ben Wade Oakes Dickinson, June 12, 1952; children: Mark Wade, Katherine Van Gilder, Peter Somers. BA, U. Tenn., 1952; postgrad., San Francisco Art Inst., 1961-63, Academié de la Grande Chaumière, Paris, 1971; M.F.A., Calif. Coll. Arts and Crafts, 1982, Golden Gate U., 1984. Escrow officer Security Nat. Bank, Santa Monica, Calif., 1953-54; mem. faculty Calif. Coll. Arts and Crafts, Oakland, 1971-2001, assoc. prof. art, 1974-84, prof., 1984-2001, prof. emeritus, 2001—, dir. galleries Calif., 1975-85. Artist-in-residence U. Tenn., 1969, Ark. State U., 1993, Fine Arts Mus. of San Francisco, 2000; mem. faculty U. Calif. Ext., 1967-70; lectr. in field. Co-author, illustrator: Revival, 1974, That Old Time Religion, 1975; also mus. catalogs; illustrator: The Complete Fruit Cookbook, 1972, Human Sexuality: A Search for Understanding, 1984, Days Journey, 1985; commissions: University of San Francisco, 1990-2001; one-person exhbns. include Corcoran Gallery Art, Washington, 1970, 74, San Francisco Mus. Modern Art, 1965, 68, Fine Arts Mus. San Francisco, 1969, 75, U. Tenn., 1976, Michael Himovitz Gallery, Sacramento, Calif., 1988, 89, 91, 93, 97, 98; touring exhbns. include Smithsonian Inst., 1975-81, Oakland Mus., 1979, Interart Ctr., N.Y., 1980, Tenn. State Mus., 1981-82, Galeria de Arte y Libros, Monterrey, Mex., 1978, Hatley Martin Gallery, San Francisco, 1986, 89, Gallery 10, Washington, 1989, Diverse Works, Houston, 1990, Ewing Gallery, U. Tenn., 1991, G.T.U. Gallery, U. Calif., Berkeley, 1991, Mus. Contemporary Religious Art, St. Louis, 1995, Thacher Gallery, U. San Francisco, 2000; represented in permanent collections Nat. Collection Fine Arts, Corcoran Gallery Art, Libr. of Congress, Smithsonian Instn., San Francisco Mus. Modern Art, Butler Inst. Art, Oakland Mus., Santa Barbara Mus., Nat. Mus. Women in Arts, Washington; prodr. (TV program) The Art of the Matter-Professional Practices in Fine Arts, 1986—. Bd. dirs. Calif. Confedn. of the Arts, 1983-88; bd. dirs., v.p. Calif. Lawyers for the Arts, 1986—; mem. coun. bd. San Francisco Art Inst., 1966-91, trustee, 1964-67; sec., bd. dirs. YWCA, 1955-62; treas., bd. Westminster Ctr., 1955-59; bd. dirs. Children's Theater Assn., 1958-60, 93-94, Internat. Child Art Ctr., 1958-68. Recipient Disting. Alumni award San Francisco Art Inst., 1983, Master Drawing award Nat. Soc. Arts and Letters, 1983, Cert. of Recognition, El Consejo Mundial de Artistas Plasticos 2d Internat. Conf., 1993, Pres.'s award Nat. Womens Caucus for Art, 1995; grantee Zellerbach Family Fund, 1975, Calif. Coll. Arts and Crafts, 1994, NEH, 1978, 80, 82-85, Thomas F. Stanley Found., 1985, Bay Area Video Coalition, 1988-92, PAS Graphics, 1988, San Francisco Cmty. TV Corp., 1990, Skaggs Found., 1991. Mem. Coalition of Women's Art Orgns. (dir., v.p. 1978-80, 2000—), Coll. Art Assn., AAUP, Calif. Confederation of Arts (bd. dirs. 1983-89), Calif. Lawyers for Arts (v.p. 1986—), San Francisco Art Assn. (sec., dir. 1964-67), NOW, Artists Equity Assn. (nat. v.p., dir. 1978-92), Arts Advocates, Women's Caucus for Art (nat. Affirmative Action officer 1978-80, nat. bd. 2000—). Democrat. Episcopalian. Office: Calif Coll Arts and Crafts 1111 8th St San Francisco CA 94107-2247 E-mail: eleanordickinson@bigfoot.net

DICKINSON, JANET MAE WEBSTER, relocation consulting executive; b. Cleve., Oct. 2, 1929; d. Richard and Gizella (Keplinger) Fisher; m. Rodney Earl Dickinson, June 18, 1965 (div. 1976); 1 child, Kimberly Cae. Grad., Larson Coll. for Women, New Haven; student, Portland State Coll. Lic. broker, Oreg. Pub. rels./promotion dir. KPTV-Channel 27, Portland, Oreg., 1951-54; exec. dir. Exposition-Recreation Commn., Portland, 1954-58; v.p. Art Lutz & Co., Realtors, Portland, 1975-79, Lutz Relocation Mgmt., Portland, 1977-79; corp. relocation mgr. Ga. Pacific Corp., Portland, 1979-82; pres., broker Ga. Pacific Fin. Co., Portland, 1980-82; pres., chief exec. officer The Dickinson Cons. Group, Portland, 1982—; pres. Wheatherstone Press, Lake Oswego, Oreg., 1983—, The Relocation Ctr., Portland, 1984—. Cons. in field; lectr. in field; conductor workshops/seminars in field. Author: The Complete Guide to Family Relocation, The International Move, Building Your Dream House, Obtaining the Highest Price for Your Home, Have a Successful Garage Sale, Moving with Children, My Moving Coloring Book, The Group Move, Counseling the Transferee, Games to Play in the Car, Portland (Oreg.) Facts Book, Welcome to the United States, many others; contbr. articles to profl. jours. Mem. Pres.'s Com. to Employ Physically Handicapped, Oreg. Prison Assn.; established Women's Aux. for Waverly Baby Home; bd. dirs. Columbia River coun. Girl Scouts U.S.A., Salvation Army; active various polit. orgns.; chmn. ways and means com. Oreg. Symphony Soc., Portland Art Mus., Assistance League, Portland Jr. Symphony, March of Dimes, others. Mem. Employee Relocation Coun., City Club, Multnomah Athletic Club, Tualatin Valley Econ. Devel. Assn. (dir. 1988—). Republican. Episcopalian. Home: 6903 SE Riverside Dr # 16 Vancouver WA 98664-1672 Office: The Dickinson Cons Group Lincoln Ctr 10250 SW Greenburg Rd Ste 125 Portland OR 97223-5470 E-mail: jandickinson@home.com, relocntr@europa.com

DICKINSON, WADE, physicist, oil and gas company executive, educator; b. Sharon, Pa., Oct. 29, 1926; s. Ben Wade Orr and Gladys Grace (Oakes) D.; m. Eleanor Creekmore, June 12, 1952; children: Mark, Katherine, Peter. Student, Carnegie Inst. Tech., 1944-45; BS, U.S. Mil. Acad., 1949; postgrad., Oak Ridge Sch. Reactor Tech., 1950-51. Commd. 2d lt. USAF, 1949, advanced through grades to capt., 1954, resigned, 1954; cons. physicist Rand Corp., Santa Monica, Calif., 1952-54; engrng. cons. Bechtel Group, Inc., San Francisco, 1954-87; tech. advisor U.S. Congress, Washington, 1957-58; pres. Agrophysics, Inc., San Francisco, 1968—, Petrolphysics Inc., San Francisco, 1975—; ptnr. Radialphysics Ltd., San Francisco, 1980—, Robotphysics Ltd., San Francisco, 1983—; mng. mem. The Spark Group, 00—. Lectr. engrng., bus. U. Calif., Berkeley, 1984—; cardiology cons. Mt. Zion Med. Ctr., U. Calif., San Francisco, 1970-95; chmn. bd. Calif. Med. Clin. Psychotherapy. Contbr. articles to profl. jours; patentee in field. Trustee World Affair Coun., 1958-62; mem. San Francisco Com. Fgn. Rels., Young Republicans, Calif. Mem. Am. Phys. Soc., Am. Soc. Petroleum Engrs. Episcopalian. Club: Bohemian (San Francisco). Lodges: Masons, Guardsmen. Home: 2125 Broderick St San Francisco CA 94115-1627 Office: Petrolphysics Inc 1388 Sutter St Ste 603 San Francisco CA 94109-5452 E-mail: petrojet@ix.netcom.com

DICKMAN, FRANCOIS MOUSSIEGT, former foreign service officer, educator; b. Iowa City, Dec. 23, 1924; s. Adolphe Jacques and Henriette Louise (Moussiegt) D.; m. Margaret Hoy, June 3, 1947; children: Christine, Paul. BA, U. Wyo., 1947; MA, Fletcher Sch. Law & Diplomacy, 1948. Rsch. asst. Brookings Instn., Washington, 1950; with U.S. Fgn. Svc., 1951-84; consular/comml. officer Barranquilla, Colombia, 1952-54; Arabic lang. trainee Beirut, Lebanon, 1955-57; econ./comml./consular officer Khartoum, Sudan, 1957-60; Egyptian-Syrian affairs desk officer Dept. State, 1961-65; econ. officer Tunis, Tunisia, 1965-68; student U.S. Army War Coll., Carlisle, Pa., 1968-69; econ. counselor Jidda, Saudi Arabia, 1969-72; dir. Arabian Peninsula affairs Dept. State, 1972-76; ambassador to United Arab Emirates, 1976-79, to Kuwait, 1979-83; diplomat in residence Marquette U., 1984; adj. prof. polit. sci. U. Wyo., Laramie, 1985—. Served with AUS, 1943-46, 50-51. Recipient Dept. State Meritorious Honor award, 1965, Disting. Alumni award U. Wyo., 1980, Exemplary Alumnus, 1993. Mem. VFW, U.S. Army War Coll. Alumni Assn., U. Wyo. Alumni Assn., Phi Beta Kappa, Phi Kappa Phi. Office: U Wyo Polit Sci Dept Laramie WY 82071-3197

DICKS, NORMAN DE VALOIS, congressman; b. Bremerton, Wash., Dec. 16, 1940; s. Horace D. and Eileen Cora D.; m. Suzanne Callison, Aug. 25, 1967; children: David, Ryan. BA, U. Wash., 1963, JD, 1968; LLD (hon.), Gonzaga U., 1987. Bars: Wash. 1968, D.C., 1978. Salesman, Boise Cascade Corp., Seattle, 1963; labor negotiator Kaiser Gypsum Co., Seattle, 1964; legis. asst. to Senator Warren Magnuson of Wash., 1968-73, adminstrv. asst., 1973-76; mem. U.S. Congress from 6th Wash. Dist., Washington, 1977—; mem. appropriations com. Mem. U. Wash. Alumni Assn., Sigma Nu. Democrat. Lutheran. Office: US Ho Reps 2467 Rayburn Ho Office Bldg Washington DC 20515-0001*

DICKS, PATRICIA K. legislative staff member; b. Detroit, Nov. 22, 1951; BS, U. Colo., 1973. Sec. Colo. Senate, Denver, 1998—. Office: State Capitol 200 E Colfax Ave Ste 250 Denver CO 80203-1716

DICKSON, KATHRYN, science educator; PhD in Comparative Animal Physiology, U. Calif., San Diego, 1988. Assoc. prof. biology Calif. State U., Fullerton, 1988—. Recipient award Women in Sci. and Tech., 1999. Achievements include research in development and evolution of endothermy in marine fishes and energetics and morphology associated with locomotion in fishes. Office: U Calif Dept Biology 800 N State College Blvd Fullerton CA 92831-3547

DICKSON, ROBERT LEE, lawyer; b. Hot Springs, Ark., Sept. 3, 1932; s. Constantine John and Georgia Marie (Allen) D.; m. Christina Farrar, Oct. 29, 1978; children— Robert Lee, Geoffrey, Alexandra, Christopher, George, John. BBA, U. Tex., 1959, LLB, 1960. Bar: Tex. 1960, Calif. 1965, U.S. Dist. Ct. (no. dist.) Tex. 1960, U.S. Dist. Ct. (ea. dist.) Wis. 1979, U.S. Supreme Ct. 1980, U.S. Dist. Ct. (ea. dist.) Calif. 1983, U.S. Ct. Appeals (7th cir.) 1983, U.S. Dist. Ct. (no. and so. dists.) Calif. 1984, U.S. Ct. Appeals (9th cir.) 1987, U.S. Ct. Appeals (1st and 10th cirs.) 1989. Assoc. to ptnr. Eplen, Daniel & Dickson, Abilene, Tex., 1960-65; assoc. to sr. ptnr. Haight, Dickson, Brown & Bonesteel, Santa Monica, Calif., 1965-88; sr. ptnr. Dickson, Carlson & Campillo, Santa Monica, 1988-98; ptnr. Arter & Hadden, L.A., 1998—. Bd. advisors UCLA Sch Nursing. Contbr. articles to profl. jours. Fellow Am. Coll. Trial Lawyers; mem. Ind. Bar Com., Def. Rsch. Inst. (steering com. of drug and device litigation com.), Fedn. Ins. and Corp. Counsel (chmn. pharm. liability litigation sect. 1984-87, v.p. 1986-89, bd. dirs. 1989-95, sec.-treas. 1991-92, pres.-elect 1992-93, pres. 1993-94, chmn. 1994-95), Am. Bd. Trial Advocates, Assn. So. Calif. Def. Counsel (pres. 1976), Bel Air Country Club, Bel Air Bay Club (Pacific Palisades). Republican. Roman Catholic. Home: 14952 Alva Dr Pacific Palisades CA 90272-4401 Office: Arter & Hadden 725 S Figueroa St Ste 3400 Los Angeles CA 90017-5434 E-mail: rdickson@arterhadden.com

DIDION, JAMES J. real estate company executive; b. Sacramento; s. Frank R. D. and Eduene J. Didion. AB in Polit. Sci., U. Calif., Berkeley, 1962. With Coldwell Banker Co., 1962—, v.p., resident mgr., 1969-71, sr. v.p., regional mgr. Houston, from 1971; chmn., CEO, Coldwell Banker Comml. Group, L.A.; now chmn. Coldwell Banker, Carmel, Calif. Office: Coldwell Banker PO Box 1150 Carmel CA 93921-1150

DIEDERICH, J(OHN) WILLIAM, internet publisher; b. Ladysmith, Wis., Aug. 30, 1929; s. Joseph Charles and Alice Florence (Yost) D.; m. Mary Theresa Klein, Nov. 25, 1950; children: Mary Theresa Diederich Evans, Robert Douglas, Charles Stuart, Michael Mark, Patricia Anne Diederich Irelan, Donna Maureen (dec.), Denise Brendan, Carol Lynn Diederich Weaver, Barbara Gail, Brian Donald, Tracy Maureen Diederich Jorgensen, Theodora Bernadette Diederich Davidson, Tamara Alice Diederich Williams, Lorraine Angela. PhB, Marquette U., Milw., 1951; MBA with high distinction, Harvard U., 1955. With Landmark Comm., Inc., Norfolk, Va., 1955-90, v.p., treas., 1965-73, exec. v.p. fin., 1973-78, exec. v.p. community newspapers, 1978-82, exec. v.p., CFO, 1982-90, fin. cons., 1990—; internet pub. Wide World Web Internat., Incline Village, 1996—. Chmn. bd. dirs. Landmark Cmty. Newspapers, Inc., 1977-88; pres. Exec. Productivity Sys., Inc., 1982-88, LCI Credit Corp., 1991-93, Landmark TV Inc., 1991—, LTM Investments, Inc., 1991—; v.p., treas., KLAS, Inc., 1994-95; v.p. Internet Express, Inc., 1994-2000; pres., bd. dirs. Wide World Web Internat., 1995—, TWC Holdings, Inc., 1996—; instr. Boston U., 1954, Old Dominion U., 1955-59. Lt. col. USMC, 1951-53, USMCR, 1953-71. Baker scholar Harvard U., 1955. Mem. SAR, Nat. Assn. Accts., Am. Numismatic Assn., Nat. Geneal. Soc., Wis. Geneal. Soc., Pa. Geneal. Soc., Sigma Delta Chi. Roman Catholic. Home and Office: PO Box 7677 925 Jupiter Dr Incline Village NV 89451

DIEKMANN, GILMORE FREDERICK, JR. lawyer; b. Evansville, Ind., Jan. 14, 1946; s. Gilmore Frederick Sr. and Mabel Pauline (Daniel) K.; children: Anne Westlake, Andrew Gilmore, Matthew Frederick. BSBA, Northwestern U., 1968, JD, 1971. Bar: Calif. 1972, U.S. Dist. Ct. Calif. (no., ea., cen. and so. dists.) Calif. 1972, U.S. Ct. Appeals (9th cir.) 1972, U.S. Supreme Ct. 1978. Assoc. Bronson, Bronson & McKinnon, San Francisco, 1971-78, ptnr. labor and employment law, 1979-99, chmn., mng. ptnr., 1991-93, chmn. labor, employment dept., 1993-99; ptnr. Seyfarth, Shaw, Fairweather & Geraldson, San Francisco, 1999—. Author and speaker in field. Mem. ABA, American Bar Assn., Def. Rsch. Inst., Am. Emp. Law Coun., Order of Coif. Republican. Lutheran. Home: 901 Powell St # 6 San Francisco CA 94111 Office: Seyfarth Shaw Fairweather & Geraldson 101 California St Ste 2900 San Francisco CA 94111-5858 E-mail: gdiekmann@sf.seyfarth.com

DIERCKMAN, THOMAS E. land use planner; Grad., U. Ill.; postgrad, U. Ca. Construction, facilities mgmt. U.S. Navy Civil Engr. Corps, 1971-82; The Newhall Land & Farming Co, Valencia, Ca., 1982, sr. v.p., Valencia Co., 1990—, pres., Valencia Co., 1994—. Bd dirs. L.A. Econ. Devel. Corp., Valencia Bank and Trust, Valencia Water Co., Boys and Girls Club Santa Clarita; chmn. Santa Clarita Valley United Way Campaign, 1997-98; mem. Urban Land Inst. Capt., Naval Reserve. Office: The Newhall Land & Farming Co 23823 Valencia Blvd Valencia CA 91355-2103

DIERKS, RICHARD ERNEST, veterinarian, educational administrator; b. Flandreau, S.D., Mar. 11, 1934; s. Martin and Lillian Ester (Benedict) D.; m. Eveline Carol Amundson, July 20, 1956; children— Jeffrey Scott, Steven Eric, Joel Richard. Student, S.D. State U., 1952-55; BS, U. Minn., 1957, DVM, 1959, MPH, PhD, U. Minn., 1964; MBA, U. Ill., 1985. Diplomate Am. Coll. Vet. Microbiologists, Am. Coll. Vet. Preventive Medicine. Supervisory microbiologist Communicable Disease Ctr., Atlanta, 1964-68; prof. coll. veterinary medicine Iowa State U., Ames, 1968-74; head dept. veterinary sci. Mont. State U., Bozeman, 1974-76; dean Coll. Veterinary Medicine U. Ill., Urbana, 1976-89, dean emeritus, 1989—; dean Coll. Veterinary Medicine U. Fla., Gainesville, 1989-97, prof., dean emeritus, 1997—. Mem. tng. grant rev. com. Nat. Inst. Allergy and Infectious Diseases, 1973-74 Contbr. articles on virology, immunology and epidemiology to profl. jours. Served with USPHS, 1964-67. Career Devel. awardee Nat. Inst. Allergy and Infectious Diseases, 1969-74, Nat. Acad. Practitioners, 1995. Mem. Am. Vet. Medicine Assn., Am. Soc.

Virology, Am. Soc. Microbiologists, Am. Assn. Immunologists, Am. Assn. Vet. Lab. Diagnosis, Colo. Vet. Medicine Assn., Soc. Exptl. Biology and Medicine, Gamma Sigma Delta, Phi Kappa Phi, Phi Zeta. Republican. Lutheran. Club: Rotary. Office: 13651 N 115th St Longmont CO 80504-8017 Fax: 303-678-1399. E-mail: redierks@worldnet.att.net

DIERS, JAMES ALAN, municipal official; b. Burnaby, B.C., Can., Dec. 13, 1952; m. Sarah Driggs, 1975. BA in Third World Devel., Grinnell Coll., 1975, Doctorate (hon.), 2001. Organizer South End Seattle Comty. Orgn., 1976-82; asst. dir. for coop. affairs Group Health Coop. of Puget Sound, Wash., 1982-88; dir. Dept. of Neighborhoods, Seattle, 1988—. Founder Sr. Caucus and Nuclear Awareness Group, Ptnrs. for Health; dir. Seattle Little City Halls program, mgr. 57 cmty. gardens, and the Historic Preservation Program overseeing adminstrn. of 200 bldgs., seven hist. dists. Neighborhood Matching Fund under his adminstrn. named one of most innovative local govt. programs in nation, Ford Found. and Kennedy Sch. of Govt. Office: Dept Neighborhoods City of Seattle 700 3rd Ave Ste 400 Seattle WA 98104-1848

DIETERICH, JAMES H. geologist; b. Elgin, Ill., June 7, 1942; BS, U. Wash., 1964; MPh, Yale U., 1967, PhD in Geology and Geophysics, 1968. Dep. dir. US-USSR Coop. Exchange Agreement, 1982-94; with Nat. Earthquake Protection Coun., 1982-96, 96—; sr. scientist we. earthquake hazard team U.S. Geol. Survey, Menlo Park, Calif. Cons. Dept. State, U.S., Costa Rica, 1983, UN, Turkey, 1991; with Internat. Commn. Lithosphere, 1983-86; adv. coun. So. Calif. Earthquake Ctr., 1991— vis. prof., adj. prof. Tex. A&M Univ., 1987; with earthquake hazards reduction program. U.S. Geol. Survey, 1996—. Recipient Basic Rsch. award U.S. Nat. Com. Rock Med., 1985. Fellow Am. Geophys. Union (Walter H. Bucher medal 2000); mem. Internat. Assn. Seismology and Physics Earth's Interior (subcom. 1992—). Office: US Geol Survey 345 Middleford Rd MS 977 Menlo Park CA 94025-3591

DIETLER, CORTLANDT S. oil company executive; Founder, CEO Associated Natural Gas Corp.; chmn., CEO TransMontaigne Oil Co.; chmn. TransMontaigne, Inc., Denver, 1999—. Office: TransMontaigne Inc 2750 Republic Plz 370 17th St Denver CO 80202

DIETRICH, WILLIAM ALAN, writer, journalist; b. Tacoma, Sept. 29, 1951; s. William Richard and Janice Lenore (Pooler) D.; m. Holly Susan Roberts, Dec. 19, 1970; children: Lisa, Heidi. BA, Western Wash. U., 1973. Reporter Bellingham (Wash.) Herald, 1973-76, Gannett News Svc., Washington, 1976-78, Vancouver (Wash.) Columbian, 1978-82, Seattle Times, 1982-97; freelance writer, 1998—. Author: The Final Forest, 1992, Northwest Passage, 1995, Ice Reich, 1998, Getting Back, 2000, Dark Winter, 2001. Recipient Paul Tobenkin award Columbia U., 1986, Pulitzer prize for nat. reporting, 1990; Nieman fellow Harvard U., 1987-88.

DIFFIE, WHITFIELD, computer and communications engineer; b. June 5, 1944; m. Mary L. Fischer. BS in Maths., MIT, 1965; postgrad. in elec. engring., Stanford U., 1975-78; D in Tech. Scis. honoris causa, Swiss Fed. Inst. Tech., Zurich, 1992. Rsch. asst. The Mitre Corp., Bedford, Mass., 1965-69; rsch. programmer artificial intelligence lab. Stanford U., Palo Alto, Calif., 1969-73, rsch. asst., 1975-78, rsch. programmer, 1975; self-supported researcher in cryptography, 1973-74; mgr. secure syss. rsch. No. Telecom, Mountain View, Calif., 1978-91; disting. engr., adv. computer and comm. security Sun Microsyss., Palo Alto, 1991—. Organizer conf. Crypto '81, '83; mem. program com. Crypto 89; mem. program com. Status and Prospects of Rsch. in Cryptography '93, First ACM Conf. on Comms. and Computer Security, 1993; mem. adv. bd. Electronic Privacy Info. Ctr.; presenter in field. Contbr. numerous articles to scientific jours.; featured in Scientific Am., Sience, Time, Omni, Newsweek, N.Y. Times Mag., others. G.C. Steward fellow Gonville and Caius Coll., 1996; recipient award for Disting. Contbn. to Consumer Protection Calif. State Psychol. Assn., 1978, Nat. Computer Syss. Security award Nat. Inst. Stds. and Tech. and Nat. Security Agy., 1996, Louis E. Levy medal Franklin Inst., 1997, First Paris Kanellakis award ACM, 1997. Mem. IEEE (Info. Theory Soc. Paper award 1979, Donald G. Fink award 1981, conf. organizer 1983). Achievements include discovery of the concept fo public key cryptography, 1975; development of Mathlab symbolic manipulation system, of Lisp 1.6 systme; research on interactive debugging and extensible compiling, proof of correctnes of programs, proof checking and extensible compilers, on cryptography and its applications; patents (with Martin E. Hellman and Ralph Merkle) for cryptographic apparatus and method, 1980, (with Ashar Aziz) on security of mobile communications, 1993. Home: 288 Eleanor Dr Woodside CA 94062-1116 Office: Sun Microsystems MAK 15-214 901 San Antonio Rd Palo Alto CA 94303-4900

DIGGS, BRADLEY C. lawyer; b. Missoula, Mont., Sept. 18, 1948; BA magna cum laude, Amherst Coll., 1970; JD cum laude, Harvard U., 1973. Bar: Wash. 1973. Mng. ptnr. Davis Wright Tremaine, Seattle. Mem. ABA, Phi Beta Kappa. Office: Davis Wright Tremaine 1501 4th Ave Ste 2600 Seattle WA 98101-1688

DIGNAM, WILLIAM JOSEPH, obstetrician, gynecologist, educator; b. Manchester, N.H., Aug. 11, 1920; s. Walter Joseph and Margaret Veronica (Lowe) D.; m. Winifred Kennedy, June 7, 1947; children— Mary Brett, Kevan Jean, Erin Margaret, Meighan Ann A.B., Dartmouth Coll., 1941; M.D., Harvard U., 1943. Intern Boston City Hosp., 1944; resident in ob-gyn U. Kans. Med. Ctr., Kansas City, 1947-50; from asst. prof. to prof. ob-gyn UCLA, 1951—. Affiliated with UCLA Med. Ctr., Cedars-Sinai Med. Ctr., Harbor-UCLA Med. Ctr. Roman Catholic Home: 820 Alma Real Dr Pacific Palisades CA 90272-3704 Office: UCLA Sch Medicine Dept Ob-Gyn 10833 Le Conte Ave Los Angeles CA 90095-3075 E-mail: wdignam@mednet.ucla.edu

DILBECK, CHARLES STEVENS, JR. real estate company executive; b. Dallas, Dec. 2, 1944; s. Charles Stevens Sr. and Betty Doris (Owens) D.; 1 child, Stephen Douglas; m. Carolyn Jane DeBoer, Sept. 4, 1994. BS, Wichita State U., 1968; MS, Stanford U., 1969, postgrad., 1970-71. Engr. United Tech. Ctr., Sunnyvale, Calif., 1971-72; cons. Diversicom, Inc., Santa Clara, 1972-73; engr. Anamet Labs., San Carlos, 1973-75; cons. real estate investment Cert. Capital Corp., San Jose, 1975-82; pvt. practice in real estate, San Jose, 1981—; prin. Am. Equity Investments, San Jose, 1982—. Mem. Los Gatos (Calif.) Rent Adv. Com., 1988. Mem. Nat. Apt. Assn., San Jose Real Estate Bd., Tri-County Apt. Assn., Gold Key Club, Tau Beta Pi (pres. 1968), Sigma Gamma Tau. Republican. Avocation: ocean yacht racing. Office: Am Equity Investments 301 Alta Loma Ln Santa Cruz CA 95062-4620

DILL, LADDIE JOHN, artist; b. Long Beach, Calif., Sept. 14, 1943; s. James Melvin and Virginia (Crane) D.; children: Ariel, Jackson Caldwell. [illegible] Santa Monica, Calif. Lectr. painting and drawing UCLA, 1975-88. Exhbns. include: San Francisco Mus. Modern Art, 1977-78, Albright Knox Mus., Buffalo, 1978-79, Charles Cowles Gallery, N.Y.C., 1983-85, The First Show, Los Angeles; represented in permanent collections: Mus. Modern Art, N.Y.C., Laguna Mus. Art, Los Angeles County Mus., Mus. Contemporary Art, Los Angeles, Santa Barbara Mus., San Francisco Mus. Modern [illegible] Instn. IBM Nat. Mus. Seoul Republic of Korea, San Diego Mus. Art, La,

Mus., Denmark, Am. Embassy, Helsinki, Finland, Corcoran Gallery Art, Washington, Chgo Art Inst., Greenville County (S.C.) Mus., Palm Springs Desert Mus., Phoenix Art Mus., William Rockhill Nelsen Mus., Kansas City, Phillips Collection. Nat. Endowment Arts grantee, 1975, 82; Guggenheim Found. fellow, 1979-80; Calif. Arts Council Commn. grantee, 1983-84

DILLARD, MICHAEL L. food products company executive; b. 1942; BS in Acctg., Miss. Coll., 1964. Various acctg. positions Chrysler Corp., Cape Canaveral, Fla., 1964-66; divsn. acct. Blue Goose Growers, Vero Beach, 1966-76; CFO Pure Gold, Redlands, Calif., 1976-85, Saticoy Lemon Assocs., Inc., Santa Paula, 1985—. Office: Saticoy Lemon Assoc Inc 103 N Pack Rd Santa Paula CA 93060

DILLENBERG, JACK, public health officer; b. N.Y.C., Nov. 22, 1945; m. Marianna Dillenberg. BA in Psychology, Tulane U., 1967; DDS, NYU, 1971; MPH, Harvard Sch. Pub. Health, 1978. Dentist Southbury (Conn.) Tng. Sch., 1973-75; mgr. Rural Dental Health Clinic, Jamaica, 1975-77; vis. lectr. Cape Cod C.C., 1978-84; tutor dept. population scis. Harvard Sch. Pub. Health, 1978-81; cons. Mass. Dept. Mental Health, 1978-84; pvt. practice Beacon St. Dental Assocs., Brookline, Mass., 1980-84; instr. Harvard Sch. Dental Medicine, 1980-84; cons. Pan Am. Health Orgn., 1993-97; dir. Ariz. Dept. Health Svcs., 1998-99; area health officer L.A. County Dept. Health Svcs., Santa Monica, Calif., 1997-99. Cons. Dillenberg & Friends, Inc., 1979-84; pres. Dentanomics, Inc., 1984-86; pub. health cons. World Bank, 1978-99; clin. instr. Harvard Sch. Dental Medicine, 1988—; mem. faculty U. Phoenix, 1989—. Recipient Presdl. Citation ADA, 1992, Nat. Fluoridation award CDC, 1991, Alunmi award of Merit, Harvard Sch. Pub. Health, 1997; named Marketer of the Yr., Am. Mktg. Assn., 1997, CEO of Yr., Am. Pub. Adminstrn. Assn., 1997. Mem. ADA, Assn. State and Territorial Dental Dirs., Ariz. Pub. Health Assn., Pres. Assoc. State and Ter. Health Officials, 1997. Office: 2313 5th St # 5 Santa Monica CA 90405-2403 also: LA County Dept Health Svcs Burke Health Ctr 2509 Pico Blvd Rm 325 Santa Monica CA 90405-1828 E-mail: jdillenberg@dhs.co.la.ca.us

DILLEY, BARBARA JEAN, college administrator, choreographer, educator; b. Chgo., Mar. 13, 1938; d. Robert Vernon and Jean Phyllis (Fairweather) D.; m. Lewis Lloyd, May 1961 (div.); 1 child, Benjamin Lloyd; m. Brent Bondurant, Mar. 1977 (div.); 1 child, Owen Bondurant. BA, Mt. Holyoke Coll., 1960. Dancer Merce Cunningham Dance Co., N.Y.C., 1963-68; ind. dancer, choreographer N.Y.C. and Boulder, Colo., 1966-82; dancer Yvonne Rainer Co., N.Y.C., 1967-70; dancer, choreographer The Grand Union, N.Y.C., 1970-76; mem. faculty dance program Naropa Inst., Boulder, 1974—, dir. dance program, 1974-84. Condr. pvt. workshops Toronto, Ont., Can., Montreal, Que., Can., Halifax, N.S., Can., The Netherlands, Eng., Switzerland, Germany, 1978—; vis. faculty European Dance Devel. Ctr., Arnheim, The Netherlands, 1993-94; artistic dir. Crystal Dance, Boulder, 1978-81; mem. vis. faculty NYU, Radcliffe Coll., Cornell U., U. Colo., George Washington U., others; dir. dance symposium, 1981; adjudicator S.W. divsn. Am. Coll. Dance Festival, Loretto Heights, Colo., 1986. Mem. grants selection panel Colo. Coun. of Arts and Humanities, 1981, mem. panel on policy devel. for individual grants, 1983. NEA Choreographic fellow, 1974, 76, 81; Boulder City Arts Coun. grantee, 1981. Democrat. Buddhist. Office: Naropa Inst 2130 Arapahoe Ave Boulder CO 80302-6697

DILLMAN, DONALD ANDREW, sociologist, educator, survey methodologist; b. Chariton, Iowa, Oct. 24, 1941; BS, Iowa State U., 1964, MS, 1966, PhD, 1969. Rsch. assoc. Iowa State U., Ames, 1967-69; asst. prof. Wash. State U., Pullman, 1969-73, assoc. prof., dept. chair, 1973-81, prof., 1978—, dir. social and econ. scis. rsch. ctr., 1986-96, dep. dir. R&D Social Econ. Scis. Rsch. Ctr., 1996—, Thomas S. Foley disting. prof. govt. and pub. policy, 2000—. Guest prof. German Ctr. for Survey Methods Rsch., Mannheim, Fed. Republic of Germany, 1985, 87, 2000; sr. survey methodologist Office of Dir. U.S. Bur. Census, 1991-95; sr. scientist Gallup Orgn., 1995—; cons. and lectr. in field. Author: Mail and Telephone Surveys, 1978, Mail and Internet Surveys, 2000; co-author 5 books; contbr. articles to profl. jours. Kellogg fellow, 1981-83; grantee in field. Fellow AAAS, Am. Statis. Assn. (Roger Herriot award 2000); mem. Am. Sociol. Assn., Rural Sociol. Soc. Am. (pres. 1983-84, Outstanding Svc. award 1983, Excellence in Rsch. award 1998), Am. Assn. Pub. Opinion Rsch. (sec.-treas. 1995-97, councillor-at-large 1999, pres. 2001). Home: 705 SW Mies St Pullman WA 99163-2056 Office: Wash State U Wilson Hall 133 Pullman WA 99164-0001 E-mail: dillman@wsu.edu

DILLON, FRANCIS PATRICK, human resources executive, financial, insurance and tax consultant; b. Long Beach, Calif., Mar. 15, 1937; s. Wallace Myron and Mary Elizabeth (Land) D.; m. Vicki Lee Dillon, Oct. 1980; children: Cary Randolph, Francis Patrick Jr., Randee, Rick. BA, U. Va., 1959; MS, Def. Fgn. Affairs Sch., 1962; MBA, Pepperdine U., 1976. Traffic mgr., mgr. pers. svcs. Pacific Telephone Co., Sacramento and Lakeport, Calif., 1966-69; asst. mgr. manpower planning and devel. Pan-Am. World Airways, N.Y.C., 1969-71; mgr. pers. and orgn. devel. Continental Airlines, L.A., 1971-74; dir. human resources Bourns, Inc., Riverside, Calif., 1974-80; v.p. employee and cmty. rels. MSI Data Corp., 1980-83; pres. Pavi Enterprises, 1983—. Cons. mgmt. Pers. Outplacement Counseling/Sales/Mgmt., fin. svcs., ins., tax oriented strategies, retirement planning for srs., and estate planning, 1983—; pres., CEO Pers. Products & Svcs., Inc., 1984-91; v.p. Exec. Horizons, Inc., 1988-94; sr. profl. svcs. cons. Right Assocs., 1994-97; pres. Meditrans Inc., 1977-80. Bd. dirs. Health Svcs. Maintenance Orgn., Inc., Youth Svcs. Ctr., Inc.; vol. precinct worker. Lt. comdr. USN, 1959-66; asst. naval attaché, Brazil, 1963-65. Recipient Disting. Svc. award Jaycees, 1969, Jack Cates Meml. Vol. of Year award Youth Svc. Ctr., 1977. Mem. ASTD, Assn. Internal Mgmt. Cons., Am. Soc. Pers. Adminstrn., Pers. Indsl. Rels. Assn., Am. Electronics Assn. (human resources com., chmn. human resources symposium), Lake Mission Viejo Assn. (sec., bd. dirs. 1990-94), Mission Viejo Sailing Club, YMCA Bike Club, Mission Viejo Ski Club, Caving Club, Toastmasters (pres. 1966-67), Have Dirt Will Travel, Capo Valley 4 Wheelers. Republican. Episcopalian. Office: Pavi Enterprises 27331 Via Amistoso Mission Viejo CA 92692-2410

DILLON, MICHAEL EARL, engineering executive, mechanical engineer, educator; b. Lynwood, Calif., Mar. 4, 1946; s. Earl Edward and Sally Ann (Wallace) D.; m. Bernardine Jeanette Staples, June 10, 1967; children: Bryan Douglas, Nicole Marie, Brendon McMichael. BA in Math., Calif. State U., Long Beach, 1978, postgrad. Registered profl. engr., Calif., Colo., Tex. Nev., Utah, Ariz., Wyo., Pa., Hawaii, N.Y., Wash., Oreg., Idaho, Alaska, La., N.Mex., Mont., Nebr., Mich., Ind., Okla., Tenn., N.J., Ga., Fla., Ohio, Va., Wis., Ill., Arks., Iowa, Okla., others; chartered engr., U.K. Journeyman plumber Roy E. Dillon & Sons, Long Beach, 1967-69, ptnr., 1969-73; field supr. Dennis Mech., San Marino, 1973-74; chief mech. official City of Long Beach, 1974-79; mgr. engr. Southland Industries, Long Beach, 1979-83; v.p. Syska & Hennessy, L.A. and N.Y., 1983-87; prin. Robert M. Young & Assoc., Pasadena, Calif., 1987-89; pres. Dillon Cons. Engrs., Long Beach, 1989—. Mech. cons. in field; instr. U. Calif., [illegible] Beach, U. Tex., Arlington; lectr. in field. Contbr. over 160 poems to various publs., co articles to profl. jours. Vice chair Mechanical, Plumbing, Elec. and Energy Code Adv. Commn. of Calif., Bldg. Stds. Commn.; bd. examiners Appeals and Condemnations, Long Beach; mem. State Fire Marshals Adv. Bd., Sacramento, Calif.; mem. adv. bd. City of L.A.; mem. bus. adv. bd. City of Long Beach. Recipient Environ. Ozone Protection [illegible] Fellow ASHRAE (Disting. Svc. award 1991), Chartered Inst. Bldg. Svc. Engrs. Gt. Britain and Ireland, Inst. Refrigeration, Heating, Air Conditioning Engrs. of New Zealand, Inst. Advancement Engring.; mem. ASCE, NSPE, ASTM, ASME, Am. Cons. Engrs. Coun., Internat. Soc. Fire Safety Sci., Nat. Inst. for Engring. Ethics, Nat. Fire Protection Assn., Internat. Conf. Bldg. Ofcls. (John Fies award 1995), Internat. Fire Code Inst., So. Bldg. Code Congress Internat., Bldg. Ofcls. and Code Adminstrn. Internat., Cons. Engrs. and Land Surveyors Calif., Soc. Fire Protection Engrs., Tau Beta Pi, Pi Tau Sigma, Chi Epsilon, others. Avocation: poetry. Home: 669 Quincy Ave Long Beach CA 90814-1818 Office: Dillon Cons Engrs 671 Quincy Ave Long Beach CA 90814-1818 E-mail: medillon@dillon-consulting.com

DILORENZO, FRANCIS X. bishop; b. Philadelphia, PA, Apr. 15, 1942; ordained priest May 18, 1968. Titular bishop of Tigia, 1988; aux. bishop Diocese of Scranton, 1988; Most Rev. Bishop Diocese of Honolulu, 1993-94, bishop, 1994—. Office: Bishop of Honolulu 1184 Bishop St Honolulu HI 96813-2838

DIMATTIO, TERRY, historic site administrator; Park supt. Cabrillo National Monument, San Diego. Office: Cabrillo Nat Monument 1800 Cabrillo Monument Dr San Diego CA 92106

DIMICK, NEIL FRANCIS, medical products wholesale executive; married; four children. BS in Acctg. summa cum laude, Brigham Young U. Corp. auditor Deloitte and Touche, 1973-77, mgr. tech. rsch. dept., 1977-80, ptnr., nat. dir. real estate industry divsn.; CFO Bergen Brunswig Corp., 1991, exec. v.p., CFO, also bd. dirs.; pres. Bergen Brunswig Specialty Corp. subsidiary Bergen Brunswig. Co-author: Real Estate Accounting and Reporting Manual. Bd. mem., past chair Orange County chpt. Nat. Multiple Sclerosis Soc.; adv. bd. mem. Am. Cancer Soc.; trustee Mardan Ctr. Ednl. Therapy, Irvine, Calif. Office: Bergen Brunswig Corp 4000 Metropolitan Dr Orange CA 92868-3510

DIMITRIADIS, ANDRE C. health care executive; b. Istanbul, Turkey, Sept. 29, 1940; s. Constantine N. and Terry D. BS, Robert Coll., Istanbul, 1964; MS, Princeton U., 1965; MBA, NYU, 1967, PhD, 1970. Analyst Mobil Oil Internat., N.Y.C., 1965-67; mgr. TWA, N.Y.C., 1967-73; dir. Pan Am. Airways, N.Y.C., 1973-76, asst. treas., 1976-79; v.p., chief fin. officer Air Calif., Newport Beach, 1979-82; exec. v.p. fin. and adminstrn., chief fin. officer Western Airlines, Los Angeles, 1982-85, dir.; sr. v.p. (fin) Am. Med. Internat., from 1985, chief fin. officer, 1985-89, exec. v.p., 1988-89; dir., exec. v.p. fin., chief fin. officer Beverly Enterprises Inc., Ft. Smith, Ark., 1989-92; chmn., CEO LTC Properties, Inc., 1992—. Bd. dirs. Magellan Health Svc. Democrat. Greek Orthodox. Home: 4470 Vista Del Preseas Malibu CA 90265-2540 Office: Ltc Properties Inc 300 E Esplanade Dr Ste 1860 Oxnard CA 93030-1286

DIMMICK, CAROLYN REABER, federal judge; b. Seattle, Oct. 24, 1929; d. Maurice C. and Margaret T. (Taylor) Reaber; m. Cyrus Allen Dimmick, Sept. 10, 1955; children: Taylor, Dana. BA, U. Wash., 1951, JD, 1963, LLD, Gonzaga U., 1982, CUNY, 1987. Bar: Wash. 1953. Asst. atty. gen. State of Wash., Seattle, 1953-55; pros. atty. King County, Wash., 1955-59, 60-62; sole practice Seattle, 1959-60, 62-65; judge N.E. Dist. Ct. Wash., 1965-75, King County Superior Ct., 1976-80; justice Wash. Supreme Ct., 1981-85; judge U.S. Dist. Ct. (we. dist.) Wash., Seattle, 1985-94, chief judge, 1994-97, sr. judge, 1997—. Chmn. Jud. Resources Com., 1991-94, active, 1987-94. Recipient Matrix Table award, 1981, World Plan Execs. Council award, 1981, Vanguard Honor award King County of Washington Women Lawyers, 1996, Honorable mention U. Wash. Law Rev., 1997, Disting. Alumni award U. Wash. Law Sch., 1997. Mem. ABA, Am. Judges Assn. (gov.), Nat. Assn. Women Judges, World Assn. Judges, Wash. Bar Assn., Am. Judicature Soc., Order of Coif (Wash. chpt.). E-mail: carolyn. Office: US Dist Ct 407 US Courthouse 1010 5th Ave Seattle WA 98104-1189 E-mail: dimmick@wawd.uscourts.gov

DINEL, RICHARD HENRY, lawyer; b. L.A., Sept. 16, 1942; s. Edward Price and Edith Elizabeth (Rheinstein) D.; m. Joyce Ann Korsmeyer, Dec. 26, 1970; children: Edward, Alison. BA, Pomona Coll., 1964; JD, Stanford U., 1967. Bar: Calif. Owner Richard H. Dinel, Profl. Law Corp., L.A., 1971-79; ptnr. Richards, Watson & Gershon, L.A., 1979-92, of counsel, 1992-93; pres. R.H. Dinel Investment Counsel, Inc., L.A., 1992—. Chmn. bd. Pomona Coll. Assocs., 1987-89; ex-officio trustee Pomona Coll., 1987-89; arbitrator Chgo. Bd. Options Exch., 1978—, Pacific Stock Exch., 1979—; bd. govs. Western Los Angeles County coun. Boys Scouts Am., 1993—. Mem. Securities Ind. Assn. (speaker compliance and legal div. 1978-92), Pomona Coll. Alumni Assn. (chmn. alumni fund and continuing edn. com. 1972-73), Nat. Assn. Securities Dealers (mem. nat. bd. arbitrators 1978-90), City Club on Bunker Hill, Bond Club L.A. Office: 11661 San Vicente Blvd Ste 400 Los Angeles CA 90049-5112

DINI, JOSEPH EDWARD, JR. state legislator; b. Yerington, Nev., Mar. 28, 1929; s. Giuseppe and Elvira (Castellani) D.; m. Mouryne Landing; children: Joseph, George, David, Michael. BSBA, U. Nev., Reno, 1951. Mem. Nev. State Assembly, Carson City, 1967—, majority leader, 1975, speaker, 1977, 87, 89, 91, 93, 97, 99, minority leader, 1985, interim fin. com. mem., 1985-01, speaker pro tem, 1973, co-spkr., 1995, chmn. water policy com. Western Legis. Conf., 1993-94, 96-00, speaker emeritus, 2001; pres. Dini's Lucky Club Casino, Yerington, Nev., 1972—. Mem. legis. com. Nev. State Assembly, 1971-77, 91, 93, 95, 97, vice chmn., 1981-82, 96-97, chmn., 1982-83, 93-94. Mem. Yerington Vol. Fire Dept.; mem. Lyon County Dem. Ctrl. Com., Nev. Am. Revolution Bicentennial Commn.; past dist. gov., active mem. 20-30 Club. Recipient Outstanding Citizen award Nev. Edn. Assn., 1973, Friend of Edn. award Nev. State Edn. Assn., 1986, Citizen of Yr. award Nev. Judges Assn., 1987, Dedicated and Valued Leadership award Nat. Conf. State Legislatures, 1989, Excellence in Pub. Svc. award Nev. Trial Lawyers Assn., 1990, Silver Plow award Nev. Farm Bur., 1991, Skill, Integrith, Responsibility award Assoc. Gen. Contractors, 1994, Guardian of Small Bus. award Nat. Fedn. Ind. Bus., 1996, Spl. Recognition award Nev. State Firefighters Assn., 1998, Appreciation award Nev. Emergency Preparedness Assn., 1998; named Conservation Legislator of Yr. Nev. Wildlife Fedn., 1991, Alumni of Yr., U. Nev. Alumni Assn., 1997, Legislator of Yr.; named legislator of yr. Nev. Rural Water Assn., 1999; recipient Friendship Medal of Diplomacy, Taiwan, 2000. Mem. Mason Valley C. of C. (pres.), Rotary (pres. Yerington 1989), Lions (pres. Yerington chpt. 1975), Masons, Shriners, York Rite, Scottish Rite, Order Ea. Star, Gamma Sigma Delta, Phi Sigma Kappa (Disting. Alumna award 1993). Home: 104 N Mountain View St Yerington NV 89447-2239 Office: Dini's Lucky Club Inc 45 N Main St Yerington NV 89447-2230

DINKEL, JOHN GEORGE, internet publisher; b. Bklyn., Aug. 1, 1944; s. Charles Ernest and Loretta Gertrude D.; m. Leslie Hawkins, Oct. 25, 1969; children: Meredith Anne, Kevin Carter. BS in Mech. Engring, U. Mich., 1967, MS in Mech. Engring, 1969. Staff engr. Chrysler Corp., Highland Park, Mich., 1967-69; engring. editor Car Life Mag., Newport Beach, Calif., 1969-70, Road & Track Mag., Newport Beach, 1972-79, editor, 1979-88, editor in chief, 1988-91, editor at large, 1991-92; dir. product communications Hill Holliday, 1991-92; pres. John Dinkel & Assocs., 1991—; editor-at-large Sports Car Internat., 1992—; v.p. editl. ops. Calcar, 1995-97; group mgr. member info. and comm. svcs. Automobile Club So. Calif., Costa Mesa, 1998-2000; pub. Westways, 1998-2000; v.p. pub. Driving Media, Inc./Driving.com, 2000—. Commencement spkr. U. Mich., Dearborn, 1987; hon. judge Meadow Brook Hall Concourse D'Elegance, 1985-86, Hillsborough Concourse D'Elegance, 1989, Palo [illegible] SCCA competition driving instr., 2000—. Author: Road & Track Auto

Dictionary, 1977, Road & Track Illustrated Auto Dictionary, 2000; co-author: RX-7: Mazda's Legendary Sports Car, 1991, Mazda MX-5 Miata, 1998; co-host daily radio show Auto Report, 1986-88; host weekly radio show Drive Time, 1996—; contbr. articles to profl. jours.; patentee method and sys. for adjusting settings of vehicle functions, 2000. Nat. chmn. U. Mich. Ann. Fund, 1988—; commr. Irvine (Calif.) Baseball Assn.; sec. Irvine Pony Baseball-Softball, 1995—; organizer clothing drive victims of Armenia earthquake, 1988; soccer coach AYSO, 1984-90, Irvine Soccer Club, 1991—; baseball coach Northwood Little League, 1994—; basketball coach Irvine Boys and Girls Club, 1993—. Honored by Colden Ctr. for the Performing Arts, Queens Coll., N.Y.C., 1990. Mem. SAE (panelist conf. on impacts of intelligent vehicle hwy. systems 1990, organizer, chmn. sessions on fuel economy and small cars 1978-79, chmn. pub. affairs Future Transp. Conf. 1997), Am. Racing Press Assn., Internat. Motor Press Assn., Sports Car Club Am., Internat. Motor Sports Assn., Motor Press Guild (pres. 1991), Pi Tau Sigma. Achievements include being the Four-time winner of SCCA Nelson Ledges 24-hour endurance auto race. Office: 1391 Warner Ave Ste B Tustin CA 92780-6456

DINNERSTEIN, LEONARD, historian, educator; b. N.Y.C., May 5, 1934; s. Abraham and Lillian (Kubrik) D.; m. Myra Anne Rosenberg, Aug. 20, 1961; children: Andrew, Julie. B of Social Scis., CCNY, 1955; MA, Columbia U., 1960, PhD, 1966. Instr. N.Y. Inst. Tech., N.Y.C., 1960-65; asst. prof. Fairleigh Dickinson U., Teaneck, N.J., 1967-70; prof. Am. history U. Ariz., Tucson, 1970—, dir. Judaic studies, 1993-2000. Adj. prof. Columbia U., summers 1969, 72, 74, 81, 87, 89, NYU, summers 1969-70, 82, 86. Author: The Leo Frank Case, 1968 (Anisfield-Wolf award 1969), America and the Survivors of the Holocaust, 1982, Uneasy at Home, 1987; (with David M. Reimers) Ethnic Americans: A History of Immigration and Assimilation, 1987; (with R.L. Nichols, D.M. Reimers) Natives and Strangers, 1996, Antisemitism in America, 1994 (Nat. Jewish Book prize 1994); contbr. articles to profl. jours.; editor: (with Fred Jaher) The Aliens, 1970; (with Kenneth T. Jackson) American Vistas, 1971, 7th edit., 1995; (with Mary Dale Palsson) Jews in the South, 1973; (with Jean Christie) Decisions and Revisions: Interpretations of 20th Century American History, 1975, America Since World War II, 1976. Mem. Orgn. Am. Historians, Am. Hist. Assn., Am. Jewish Hist. Assn. Democrat. Jewish. Home: 1981 E Miraval Cuarto Tucson AZ 85718-3032 Office: U Ariz Dept History Tucson AZ 85721-0027 E-mail: dinnerst@u.arizona.edu

DINSMORE, CRAIG, zoo director; Exec. dir. Utah's Hogle Zoo, Salt Lake City. Office: Utah's Hoyte Zoo 2600 Sunnyside Ave Salt Lake City UT 84108-1454

DION, PHILIP JOSEPH, consumer products and services executive, real estate and construction company executive; b. Chgo., Nov. 30, 1944; s. Philip J. and Loretta (Loftus) D.; m. Patricia Ann Reichert, June 24, 1967; children: Philip Joseph, David, Jaime. BA, St. Ambrose Coll., 1966; MBA, Loyola :U., Chgo., 1968. Cons. Booz, Allen & Hamilton, Chgo., 1966-68; pres., gen. mgr. Cocrema Inc., Lorenzo DeMexico, Chgo., 1968-70; with Armour-Dial Inc., Phoenix, 1970-82, pres. subs., 1970-82; sr. v.p. fin. Del Webb Corp., Phoenix, 1982-83, exec.v.p., 1983-87, pres., 1987, chmn. bd., CEO, 1987-99, chmn., 1999—. Pres. coun. St. Ambrose U.; mem. Allendale Adv. Bd.; chmn. bd. dirs., dir. nat. bd. Boy's Hope; bd. dirs. United for Ariz., Scottsdale Meml. Found.; mem. Govs. Leadership Coun. Mem. Assn. Corp. Growth, Paradise Valley Country Club.

DI PALMA, JOSEPH ALPHONSE, investment company executive, lawyer; b. N.Y.C., Jan. 17, 1931; s. Gaetano and Michela May (Ambrosio) Di P.; m. Joycelyn Ann Engle, Apr. 18, 1970; children: Joycelyn Joan, Julianne Michelle. BA, Columbia U., 1952; JD, Fordham U., 1958; LLM in Taxation, NYU, 1959. Bar: N.Y. 1959. Tax atty. CBS, N.Y.C., 1960-64; v.p. tax dept. TWA, N.Y.C., 1964-74; pvt. practice law N.Y.C., 1974-87; investor, exec. dir. Di Palma Family Holdings, Las Vegas and N.Y.C., 1987—. Cons. in field; head study group Comprehensive Gaming Study, N.Y.C. and Washington, 1990—; think tank exec. dir. Di Palma Position Papers; founder Di Palma Forum, U. Nev., Las Vegas; established The Di Palma Ctr. for Study of Jewelry and Precious Metals at Cooper-Hewitt, Nat. Design Mus., Smithsonian Instn., N.Y.C. Contbr. articles to profl. jours.; author: Di Palma Postion Papers. Bd. dirs. Friends of the Henry St. Settlement, N.Y.C., 1961-63, Outdoor Cleanliness Assn., N.Y.C., 1961-65; chmn. Air Transport Assn. Taxation Com., 1974. With U.S. Army, 1953-54. Recipient Disting. Svc. and Valuable Counsel commendation award, Air Transport Assn., 1974, spl. commendation, NYC mayor Rudolph Giuliani, 1997, U. Nev., Las Vegas, 1999, Tiffany Smithsonian Benefactors Circle award, 2001. Mem. Internat. Platform Assn., N.Y. State Bar Assn., N.Y. Athletic Club. Roman Catholic. Home: 3111 Bel Air Dr Apt 21B Las Vegas NV 89109-1506 Office: PO Box 72158 Las Vegas NV 89170-2158 also: 930 5th Ave # 4 J&H New York NY 10021-2651

DIPOTO, JERRY, professional baseball player; b. Jersey City, May 24, 1968; m. Tammie; children: Taylor Elizabeth, Jordan Taire, Jonah Seaver. Grad., Va. Commonwealth U. Pitcher Cleve. Indians, 1993-94, N.Y., 1995-96, Colo. Rockies, Denver, 1997—. Office: Colo Rockies 2001 Blake St Denver CO 80205-2008

DIRKS, LEE EDWARD, newspaper executive; b. Indpls., Aug. 4, 1935; s. Raymond Louis and Virginia Belle (Wagner) D.; m. Barbara Dee Nutt, June 16, 1956 (div. Jan. 1985); children: Stephen Merle, Deborah Virginia, David Louis. B.A., DePauw U., 1956; M.A., Fletcher Sch. Law and Diplomacy, 1957. Reporter Boston Globe, 1957, Nat. Observer, Washington, 1962-65, news editor, 1966-68; securities analyst specializing in newspaper stocks Dirks Bros., Ltd., Washington, 1969-71, Delafield, Childs, Inc., Washington, 1971-75, C.S. McKee & Co., Washington, 1975-76; asst. to pres. Detroit Free Press, 1976-77, v.p., gen. mgr., 1977-80; chmn. Dirks, Van Essen & Murray, Santa Fe, 1980—. Author: Religion in Action, 1965; pub.: Newspaper Newsletter, 1970-76. Bd. dirs. Nat. Ghost Ranch Found., Santa Fe, 1973-97, Santa Fe Opera, 1998—; pres. Georgia O'Keeffe Mus., Santa Fe, 2000—. Capt. USAF, 1957-61. Named Religion Writer of Yr. Religious Newswriters Assn., 1964 Fellow Religious Pub. Relations Council; mem. Phi Beta Kappa, Lambda Chi Alpha. Presbyterian. Clubs: Nat. Press (Washington); Oakland Hills (Detroit); Las Campanas (Santa Fe). Home: 11 E Arrowhead Cir Santa Fe NM 87506-8248 Office: 119 E Marcy St Ste 100 Santa Fe NM 87501-2046 E-mail: info@dirksvanessen.com

DISAIA, PHILIP JOHN, gynecologist, obstetrician, radiology educator; b. Providence, Aug. 14, 1937; s. George and Antoinette (Vastano) DiS.; divorced; children: John P., Steven D.; m. Patricia June; children: Dominic J., Vincent J. BS cum laude, Brown U., 1959; MD cum laude, Tufts U., 1963; MD (hon.), U. Genoa, Italy, 1999. Diplomate Am. Bd. Ob-Gyn. (examiner 1975—, bd. dirs. 1994, v.p. bd. dirs. 1997—), Am. Bd. Gynecologic Oncology (bd. dirs. 1987—). Intern Yale U. Sch. Medicine, New Haven Hosp., 1963-64, resident in ob-gyn., 1964-67, instr. ob-gyn., 1966-67; fellow in gynecologic oncology U. Tex. M.D. Anderson Hosp. and Tumor Inst., Houston, 1969-70, NIH sr. fellow, 1969-70, instr. ob-gyn., 1969-71; asst. prof. ob-gyn. and radiology U. So. Calif. Sch. Medicine, L.A., 1971-74, assoc. prof., 1974-77; prof., chmn. dept. ob-gyn. U. Calif., Irvine Med. Ctr. Calif. Coll. Medicine, 1977-88, prof., 1977—, prof. radiology, radiation therapy div., 1978—, assoc. vice chancellor for health scis. Irvine Coll. Medicine, 1987-89, Dorothy Marsh chair of reproductive biology, 1989—, dep. dir. cancer ctr., 1989—, pres. med. staff, 1993-97; pres. UCI Clin. Practice Group, 1994—. Dir. div. gynecol. oncology Am. Bd. Obstetrics & Gynecology, 1995—, bd. dirs., 1994—; bd. dirs. U. Calif. Irvine Med. Ctr., 1995, chair health sys. steering com., 1995, chair health sys. capital planning group, 1995, health sys. bd. dirs., 1995; clin. enterprise adv. coun. to pres. U. Calif., 1995; academic planning task force U. Calif. Irvine, 1994, continuing med. edn. com., 1991-94; cancer liaison commn. on cancer Am. Coll. Surgeons, 1981-94; bd. dirs., dir. at large Am. Cancer Soc., 1985—; clin. prof. dept. ob-gyn. U. Nev. Sch. Medicine, Reno, 1985—; chmn. site visit team for surgery br. Nat. Cancer Inst. NIH, 1983, subcom. surg. oncology rsch. devel., 1982-83, mem. sci. counselors div. cancer treatment, 1979-83; mem. gov.'s adv. coun. on cancer State of Calif., 1980-85; vis. prof., lectr., speaker various sci. meetings, confs., courses. Author: (with E.J. Quilligan) Ovarian Tumors, Current Diagnosis, 1974, (with others) Synopsis of Gynecologic Oncology, 1975, (with W.T. Creasman) Clinical Gynecologic Oncology, 1980, 4th edit. 1993, 5th edit. 1997; contbr. numerous articles to profl. jours., book chpts.; assoc. editor Gynecologic Oncology, Endocurietherapy/Hyperthermia Oncology, Danforth's Textbook of Obstetrics & Gynecology; mem. editorial adv. bd. Am. Jour. Reproductive Immunology, Cancer Clinical Trials, The Female Patient, New Trends in Gynecology and Obstetrics (Italian publ.); reviewer Am. Jour. Ob-Gyn., Med. and Pediatric Oncology, New Eng. Jour. Medicine, Ob-Gyn. jour., Cancer; physician cons. Patient Care Standards jour.; sci. adv. bd. The Clin. Cancer Letter. Recipient Disting. Alumnus award M.D. Anderson Hosp. and Tumor Inst. U. Tex., 1980, Silver Apple award U. Calif. Med. Students, 1983, Lauds and Laurels Profl. Achievement award U. Calif. Alumni Assn., 1983, Hubert Haussel's award Long Beach Meml. Hosp., 1983, Dist. Faculty Lectureship award for Teaching, U. Calif. Irvine Acad. Senate, 1993-94, also various rsch. awards. Fellow Am. Coll. Obstetricians and Gynecologists (com. on human rsch. for cancer 1979—, chmn. 1984—, chmn. subcom. on gynecologic oncology 1984-85, prolog editorial and adv. com. 1986—, v.p. 1997-99, various others), ACS (bd. govs. 1998—), Commn. on Cancer Liaison, Western Assn. Gynecologic Oncologists (founder 1971, pres. 1978-79), Am. Gynecol. and Obstet. Soc. (exec. coun. 1986—), Am. Gynecologic Soc., Pacific Coast Ob/Gyn Soc., South Atlantic Assn. Obstetricians and Gynecologists (hon.); mem. AMA, Am. Cancer Soc. (bd. dirs. L.A. County unit 1975-77, Orange County 1979, unit pres. 1993—; bd. dirs. Calif. div. 1985—, chmn. med. scientific com. 1993-94), Nat. Am. Cancer Soc. (dir.-at-large, bd. dirs. 1985—, chmn. program com. for nat. conf. 1986, vice-chmn. detection and treatment adv. group gynecol. cancer 1993-94, active in others), Am. Coll. Radiology (commn. on cancer 1984-85), Am. Soc. Clin. Oncologists, Soc. Gynecologic Oncologists (exec. coun. 1975-80, pres. 1982-83), Internat. Gynecologic Oncology Cancer Soc., Italian Soc. Ob-Gyn. (Camillo Golgi prof. U. Brescia 1991), Calif. Med. Assn., other profl. orgns., Alpha Omega Alpha. Office: U Calif Irvine Med Ctr 101 The City Dr S Rm 403 Orange CA 92868-3201

DISARCINA, GARY THOMAS, professional baseball player; b. Malden, Mass., Nov. 19, 1967; BS, U. Mass. Shortstop Calif. Angels (now Anaheim Angels), 1989—. Named to Am. League All-Star Team, 1995. Office: Anaheim Angels 2000 Gene Autry Way Anaheim CA 92806-6100

DISHMAN, ROSE MARIE RICE, academic administrator, researcher; BS in Physics with honors, U. Mo., 1966; MS in Physics, U. Calif., Riverside, 1968, PhD, 1971; MBA, San Diego State U., 1979. Physics instr., elem. particle rsch. assoc. U. Tenn., Knoxville, Oak Ridge, 1968-71; computer programmer, analyst Signal Processing Divsn. Sys. Ctrl., Inc., Palo Alto, Calif., 1971-72; instr. physics San Diego State U., 1974-75; instr. algebra, calculus, physics San Diego C.C., Navy Tng. Ctr., Marine Corps Recruit Depot, 1975-78; instr. Grossmont Coll., San Diego, 1976-77; prof., dept. head Sch. Engring. and Applied Sci. U.S. Internat. U., San Diego, 1977-92, dean Sch. Engring. and Applied Sci., 1989-92, acting provost, v.p. acad. affairs, 1991-92; dean acad. affairs DeVry Inst. Tech., Pomona, Calif., 1992-94, pres. Pomona, Long Beach, 1994—. Supr. world-wide acad. progs. including campuses in Mex., Eng., Kenya, U.S. Internat. U., primary supr. deans Schs. of Edn., Bus., Visual and Performing Arts, Human Behavior, Hotel and Restaurant Mgmt., Libr., Learning Resource Ctr., developer civil engring., engring. mgmt., electronics tech., elec. engring. progs. resulting in Engring. Accreditation Commn. of the Accreditation Bd. for Engring. and Tech. accreditation for civil engring. prog. for San Diego, London campuses, mem. curriculum coun. for all univ. progs., advisor U.S. Internat. U. Engring. Club; elected mem. Calif. Engring. Liaison Com., pres. pvt. univ. segment. Named outstanting engring. educator Am. Soc. Engring. Edn., 1989; rsch. grantee Fulbright-Hayes, 1972-73, grantee Am. Soc. Engring. Edn., NASA, 1979, Am. Soc. Engring. Edn., Dept. Energy, 1981, 82, 1984-85, Fed. Emergency Mgmt. Agy., 1983, 86. Office: DeVry Inst Tech Univ Ctr 901 Corp Ctr Dr Pomona CA 91768-2642 Fax: 909-623-5666

DISNEY, ROY EDWARD, broadcasting company executive; b. Los Angeles, Jan. 10, 1930; s. Roy Oliver and Edna (Francis) D.; m. Patricia Ann Dailey, Sept. 17, 1955; children: Roy Patrick, Susan Margaret, Abigail Edna, Timothy John. B.A., Pomona Coll., 1951. Guest relations exec. NBC, Hollywood, Calif., 1952; apprentice film editor Mark VII Prodns., Hollywood, 1942; asst. film editor, cameraman prodn. asst., writer, producer Walt Disney Prodns., Burbank, Calif., 1954-77, dir., 1967—; pres. Roy E. Disney Prodns. Inc., Burbank, 1978—; chmn. bd. dir. Shamrock Broadcasting Co., Hollywood, 1979—; chmn. bd. dir., founder Shamrock Holdings Inc., Burbank, 1980—; trustee Calif. Inst. Arts, Valencia, 1967—; vice chmn. Walt Disney Co., Burbank. Author: novelized adaptation of Perri; producer (film) Pacific High, Mysteries of the Deep (TV show) Walt Disney's Wonderful World of Color, others; exec. producer Cheetah; writer, dir., producer numerous TV prodns. Bd. dirs. Big Bros. of Greater Los Angeles; mem. adv. bd. dirs. St. Joseph Med. Ctr., Burbank; mem. U.S. Naval Acad. Sailing Squadron, Annapolis, Md.; fellow U. Ky. Recipient Acad. award nomination for Mysteries of the Deep Mem. Dirs. Guild Am. West, Writers Guild Am. Republican. Clubs: 100, Confrerie des Chevaliers du Tastevin, St. Francis Yacht, Calif. Yacht, San Diego Yacht, Transpacific Yacht, Los Angeles Yacht. Office: Walt Disney Co 500 S Buena Vista St Burbank CA 91521

DISTECHE, CHRISTINE M. geneticist; b. Liege, Belgium, July 22, 1949; PhD, U. Liege, Belgium, 1976. Genetics fellow Harvard U., Boston, 1977-80; now med. geneticist U. Wash. Hosp., Seattle. Prof. pathology U. Wash., Seattle. Office: U Wash Hosp Dept Pathology PO Box 357470 Seattle WA 98195-7470

DISTEFANO, TONY E. communications executive; BS in Elec. Power Engring., MS in Elec. Power Engring., Rensselaer Poly. Inst.; MBA, Stanford U. V.p. corp. devel Pacific Telesis Corp.; pres. PacTel Cable U.K. Ltd.; head unregulated subs. PG&E Enterprises, 1994, sr. v.p. corp. devel.; sr. v.p. PG&E Corp.; CFO PG&E Energy Svcs., 1997—; CEO Arrival Comm., San Francisco. Bd. dirs. Pacific Exch., World Affairs Coun. of No. Calif. Office: Arrival Comm Sears Tower 32400 601 Montgomery St Ste 675 San Francisco CA 94111

DIVELY, DWIGHT DOUGLAS, finance director; b. Spokane, Wash., Sept. 24, 1958; s. Richard Lorraine and Marie Eleanor (Barnes) D.; m. Susan Lorraine Soderstrom, June 13, 1987; children: Nathan Douglas, Natalie Lorraine. BSChemE, Rose-Hulman Inst. Tech., 1980; MPA of Pub. Affairs, Princeton U., 1982; PhC in Civil Engring., U. Wash., 1986. Rsch. scientist Battelle, Seattle, 1982-84; policy analyst, staff dir. Wash. High Tech. Coord. Bd., Seattle, 1984-86; cons. Bellevue, Wash., 1986-87; legis. analyst Seattle City Coun., 1987-90, supervising analyst, 1990-92, staff dir., 1992-94; dir. Seattle Fin. Dept., 1994-96, Seattle Exec. Svcs. Dept., 1997—; CFO city of Seattle, 1999—. Cons. We. Interstate Commn. on Higher Edn., Boulder, Colo., 1986-91; affiliate prof. U. Wash., 1989—; instr. South Seattle C.C., 1992—; mem. faculty Cascade Ctr., Seattle, 1992—. Co-author: Benefit-Cost Analysis in Theory and Practice, 1994. Chmn. interview panel Truman Scholarship Found., Washington, 1989—. Recipient Elmer B. Staats award Truman Scholarship Found., 1994. Mem. Govt. Fin. Officers Assn. Lutheran. Avocations: cooking, rose gardening. Office: Exec Svcs Dept 600 4th Ave Ste 103 Seattle WA 98104-1874

DIXIT, VISHVA M. pathology educator; MD, U. Nairobi, Kenya, 1980; postgrad., Washington U., St. Louis, 1982-86. Intern dept. medicine Kenyatta Nat. Hosp., 1980-81; resident pathology and medicine Barnes Hosp., St. Louis, 1981-86; asst. prof. pathology Med. Sch. U. Mich., Ann Arbor, 1986-91, assoc. prof., 1991—, prof. pathology, 1995-97; dir. molecular oncology Genentech, San Francisco, 1997—. Contbr. articles to profl. jours. Recipient Best Pathology Student award Kenya Med. Assn., 1980, Best Overall Med. Student Kamala Meml. award, 1980, Warner-Lambert/Parke-Davis Exptl. Pathology award Am. Soc. Investigative Pathology, 1996; Josiah Macy Found. fellow, 1989. Office: Genentech 1 Dna Way South San Francisco CA 94080-4990

DIXON, FRANK JAMES, medical scientist, educator; b. St. Paul, Mar. 9, 1920; s. Frank James and Rose Augusta (Kuhfeld) D.; m. Marion Edwards, Mar. 14, 1946; children: Janet Wynne, Frank, Michael. BS, U. Minn., 1941, MB, 1943, MD, 1944; DS (hon.), Med. Coll. Ohio, 1983; DSc (hon.), Washington U., 1992. Diplomate: Am. Bd. Pathology. Intern U.S. Naval Hosp., Great Lakes, Ill., 1943-44; research asst. dept. pathology Harvard, 1946-48; instr. dept. pathology Washington U., 1948-50, asst. prof., 1950-51; prof., chmn. dept. pathology U. Pitts. Med. Sch., 1951-60; chmn. dept. exptl. pathology Scripps Clinic and Research Found., La Jolla, Calif., 1961-74, chmn. biomed. research depts., 1970-74, dir. research inst., 1974-86, dir. emeritus, 1987—. Rsch. assoc. dept. biology U. Calif., San Diego, 1961-64, prof. in residence dept. biology, 1965-68, adj. prof. dept. pathology, 1968-96; sci. advisor NIH, Nat. Found., Helen Hay Whitney Found., St. Jude's Med. Ctr., Christ Hosp. Inst., Cin.; mem. expert adv. panel on immunology WHO; sci. adv. bd. Nat. Kidney Found.; Pahlavi lectr. Ministry of Sci. and Higher Tech., Iran, 1976: mem. adv. com. Lupus Rsch. Inst., Nat. Multiple Sclerosis Soc., Harold C. Simmons Arthritis Rsch. Ctr., Irvington House Inst., Mass. Gen. Hosp. Editor: Advances in Immunology; mem. editorial bd. Excerpta Medica, Jour. Exptl. Medicine, Am. Jour. Pathology, Cellular Immunology, Kidney Hosp. Practice, Perspectives in Biology and Medicine, Jour. Exptl. Clin. Cancer Rsch., Springer Seminars in Immunopathology, Immunological Revs.; contbr. articles to profl. jours. Served with M.C. USNR, 1943-46. Recipient Theobald Smith award, 1952, Parke-Davis award in exptl. pathology, 1957, Disting. Achievement award Modern Medicine, 1961, Martin E. Rehfuss award in internal medicine, 1966, Von Pirquet medal Ann. Forum on Allergy, 1967, Bunim medal Am. Rheumatism Assn., 1968, Internat. award Gairdner Found., 1969, Mayo Soley award Western Soc. Clin. Research, 1969, Albert Lasker Basic Med. Research award, 1975, Dickson prize U. Pitts., 1975, Homer Smith award N.Y. Heart Assn., 1976, Rous-Whipple award Am. Assn. Pathologists, 1979, So. Calif. Permanente Med. Group Immunology award, 1979, Regents award U. Minn., 1985, H.P. Smith award Am. Soc. Clin. Pathologists, 1985, Gold-Headed Cane award, 1987, Distinguished Service award Lupus Found. Am., 1987, 88; Flame of Hope award Terri Gotthelf Rsch. Inst., 1987, Paul Klemperer award N.Y. Acad. Medicine, 1989, Jean Hamburger award Internat. Soc. Nephrology, 1990. Fellow Am. Coll. Allergists, Am. Acad. Allergy, Royal Coll. Pathologists (hon.); mem. NAS, N.Y. Acad. Scis. Western Assn. Physicians, Western Soc. Clin. Research, Soc. Exptl. Biology and Medicine, Transplantation Soc., AAAS, Am. Soc. Clin. Investigation, Am. Acad. Allergists, Interurban Path. Soc., Harvey Soc. (lectr. 1962), Am. Soc. Exptl. Pathology (pres. 1966), Am. Assn. Immunologists (pres. 1972), Am. Assn. for Cancer Research, Assn. Am. Physicians, Am. Acad. Arts and Scis., Am. Heart Assn., Coun. on the Kidney in Cardiovascular Disease, Fedn. Am. Scientists, Internat. Acad. Pathology, U.S. Acad. Pathologists, Can. Acad. Pathologists, Scandinavian Soc. for Immunology (hon.), Japanese Nephrology Soc. (hon.), Sigma Xi, Nu Sigma Nu, Alpha Omega Alpha. Office: Scripps Rsch Inst 10550 N Torrey Pines Rd La Jolla CA 92037-1000

DIXON, GORDON HENRY, biochemist, educator; b. Durban, South Africa, Mar. 25, 1930; Can. citizen; s. Walter James and Ruth (Nightingale) D.; m. Sylvia W. Gillen, Nov. 20, 1954; children: Frances Anne, Walter Timothy, Christopher James, Robin Jonathan. M.A. with honors, U. Cambridge, Eng., 1951; Ph.D., U. Toronto, 1956. Rsch. assoc. U. Wash., 1954-58, U. Oxford, Eng., 1958-59; asst. prof. biochemistry U. Toronto, 1959-61, assoc. prof., 1961-63; prof. U. B.C., 1963-72; prof., chmn. dept. biochemistry U. Sussex, Eng., 1972-74; prof. med. biochemistry U. Calgary, Alta., Can., 1974-94; emeritus, 1994—; chmn. U. Calgary, Alta., Can., 1983-88. Contbr. articles to profl. jours. Recipient Steacie prize Steacie Found., 1966, Killam Meml. prize Can. Coun., 1991; named Officer of the Order of Canada, 1993. Fellow Royal Soc. London, Royal Soc. Can. (Flavelle medal 1980); mem. Am. Soc. Biol. Chemists, Am. Soc. Cell Biology, Can. Biochem. Soc. (pres. 1982-83, Ayerst award 1966), Pan-Am. Assn. Biochem. Socs. (v.p. 1984-87, pres. 1987-90), Internat. Union Biochemistry (exec. coun. 1988-94). E-mail: gordon.dixon@home.com

DIXON, TAMECKA, professional basketball player; b. Dec. 14, 1975; Grad., Kans. State U., 1997. Basketball player Los Angeles Sparks Women's NBA, Inglewood, Calif., 1997—. Mem. Olympic Festival Team South, 1995. Avocations: dancing, shopping. Office: Los Angeles Sparks Gt Western Forum 3900 W Manchester Blvd Inglewood CA 90305-2200

DIXON, TERRY, automotive executive; CEO Courtesy Auto Group, Littleton, Colo. Office: Courtesy Auto Group 7590 S Broadway Littleton CO 80122-2607

DJERASSI, CARL, chemist, educator, writer; b. Vienna, Austria, Oct. 29, 1923; s. Samuel and Alice (Friedmann) D.; m. Virginia Jeremiah (div. 1950); m. Norma Lundholm (div. 1976); children: Dale, Pamela (dec.); m. Diane W. Middlebrook, 1985. AB summa cum laude, Kenyon Coll., 1942, DSc (hon.), 1958; PhD, U. Wis., 1945; DSc (hon.), Nat. U. Mex., 1953, Fed. U., Rio de Janeiro, 1969, Worcester Poly. Inst., , 1972, Wayne State U., 1974, Columbia U., 1975, Uppsala U., 1977, Coe Coll., 1978, U. Geneva, 1978, U. Ghent, 1985, U. Man., 1985, Adelphi U., 1993, U. Wis., 1995, U. S.C., 1995, Swiss Fed. Inst. Tech., 1995, U. Md.- Balt. County, 1997, Bulgarian Acad. Scis., 1998, U. Aberdeen, 2000, Polytechnic U., 2001. Rsch. chemist Ciba Pharm. Products, Inc., Summit, N.J., 1942-43, 45-49; assoc. dir. rsch. Syntex, Mexico City, 1949-52, rsch. v.p., 1957-60; v.p. Syntex Labs., Palo Alto, Calif., 1960-62, Syntex Rsch., 1962-68, pres., 1968-72, Zoecon Corp., 1968-83, chmn. bd. dirs., 1968-86; prof. chemistry Wayne State U., 1952-59, Stanford (Calif.) U., 1959—. Founder Djerassi Resident Artists Program, Woodside, Calif. Author: The Futurist and Other Stories, 1988, (novels) Cantor's Dilemma, 1989, The Bourbaki Gambit, 1994, Marx Deceased, 1996, Menachem's Seed, 1997, NO, 1998; (poetry) The Clock Runs Backward, 1991, (drama) An Immaculate Misconception, 1998, BBC World Svc. "Play of Week", 2000, (with Roald Hoffmann) Oxygen, 2001, BBC World Svc. "Play of Week", 2001, (autobiography) The Pill, Pygmy Chimps and Degas' Horse, 1992 (memoir), This Man's Pill, 2001, also 9 others; mem. editl. bd. Jour. Organic Chemistry, 1955-59, Tetrahedron, 1958-92, Steroids, 1963—, Proc. of NAS, 1964-70, Jour. Am. Chem. Soc., 1966-75, Organic Mass Spectrometry, 1968-91; contbr. numerous articles to profl. jours., poems, memoirs and short stories to lit. publs. Recipient Intrasci. Rsch. Found. award, 1969, Freedman Patent award Am. Inst. Chemists, 1970, Chem. Pioneer award, 1973, Nat. Medal Sci. for first synthesis of oral contraceptive, 1973, Perkin medal, 1975, Wolf prize in chemistry, 1978, John and Samuel Bard award in sci. and medicine, 1983, Roussel prize, Paris, 1988, Discovers award Pharm. Mfg.

Assn., 1988, Nat. Medal Tech. for new approaches to insect control, 1991, Nev. medal, 1992, Thomson medal Internat. Soc. Mass Spectroscopy, 1994, Prince Mahidol award, Thailand, 1995, Sovereign Fund award, 1996, Austrian Cross of Honor First Class, 1999, Othmer Gold medal Chem. Heritage Found., 2000, Author's prize German Chem. Soc., 2001; named to Nat. Inventors Hall of Fame. Mem. NAS (Indsl. Application of Sci. award 1990), NAS Inst. Medicine, Am. Chem. Soc. (award pure chemistry 1958, Baekeland medal 1959, Fritzsche award 1960, award for creative invention 1973, award in chemistry of contemporary tech. problems 1983, Esselen award 1989, Priestley medal 1992, Gibbs medal 1997), Royal Soc. Chemistry (hon. fellow, Centenary lectr. 1964), Am. Acad. Arts and Scis., German Acad. (Leopoldina), Royal Swedish Acad. Scis. (fgn.), Royal Swedish Acad. Engring. Scis. (fgn.), Am. Acad. Pharm. Scis. (hon.), Brazilian Acad. Scis. (fgn.), Mexican Acad. Scis., Bulgarian Acad. Scis. (fgn.), Phi Beta Kappa, Sigma Xi (Proctor prize for sci. achievement 1998), Phi Lambda Upsilon (hon.). Office: Stanford U Dept Chemistry Stanford CA 94305-5080 E-mail: djerassi@stanford.edu

DJORDJEVICH, MIROSLAV-MICHAEL, bank executive; b. Belgrade, Yugoslavia, 1936; came to the U.S., 1956; s. Dragoslav and Ruzica Georgevich; m. Marie Louise Hohman, 1963; children: Marie, Alexander, Michelle. BS, U. Calif., Berkeley, 1960; MBA, San Francisco State U., 1963; cert. advanced fin., U. Stanford. Fin. analyst Fireman's Fund Ins. Co., San Francisco, 1962-68, asst. v.p. investments, 1972-76, v.p. investments, 1976-78, v.p., treas., 1978-84; pres., CEO U.S. Fidelity and Guaranty Fin. Co., San Francisco, 1985-86; chmn., pres., CEO Capital Guaranty Ins. Co., San Francisco, 1986-94; pres., CEO Monad Fin., San Rafael, Calif., 1994-97, Bank S.E. Europe Internat., San Juan, P.R., 1997—. Author: About Happy Living, 1985. State pres. Calif. Young Reps., 1965-66; commr. Statue of Liberty Ellis Island Centennial Commn., 1986; pres. Serbian Unity Congress, 1990-93, Coun. for Dem. Changes, 1998-01. Pvt. U.S. Army, 1961-63. Recipient Excellence award Am. Security Coun., 1967, Americanism medal Nat. Soc. DAR, 1969. Mem. First Serbian Benevolent Soc. (treas. 1978-82, pres. Studenica Found. 1995—). Avocations: reading, tennis, politics. Office: Bank SE Europe Internat 535 4th St Ste 203 San Rafael CA 94901-3314 E-mail: monadf@ix.netcom.com

DMITRICH, MIKE, state legislator; b. Murray, Utah, Oct. 23, 1936; m. Bo Dmitrich; 3 children. Student, Coll. Eastern Utah, Utah State U. Formerly with Cyprus AMAX Minerals Corp.; mem. Utah Ho. of Reps., 1968-92, asst. minority whip, minority leader; mem. Utah Senate, Dist. 27, Salt Lake City, 1992—; mem. judiciary com., revenue and taxation com.; mem. exec. appropriations com.; senate minority whip, 1993-94. Democrat. Home: 566 N Dover Cir Price UT 84501-2206

DMYTRYSHYN, BASIL, historian, educator; b. Poland, Jan. 14, 1925; came to U.S., 1947, naturalized, 1951; s. Frank and Euphrosinia (Senchak) Dmytryshyn; m. Virginia Roehl, July 16, 1949; children: Sonia, Tania. BA, U. Ark., 1950; MA, U. Ark, 1951; PhD, U. Calif.-Berkeley, 1955; hon. diploma, U. Kiev-Mohyla Acad., 1993. Asst. prof. history Portland State U., Oreg., 1956-59, assoc. prof., 1959-64, prof., 1964-89, prof. emeritus, 1989—, assoc. dir. Internat. Trade and Commerce Inst., 1984-89. Vis. prof. U. Ill., 1964-65, Harvard U., 1971, U. Hawaii, 1976, Hokkaido U., Sapporo, Japan, 1978-79; adviser U. Kiev-Mohyla Acad., 1993. Author books including: Moscow and the Ukraine, 1918-1953, 1956, Medieval Russia, 900-1700, 3d edit., 1990, Imperial Russia, 1700-1917, 3d edit., 1990, Modernization of Russia Under Peter I and Catherine II, 1974, Colonial Russian America 1817-1832, 1976, A History of Russia, 1977, U.S.S.R.: A Concise History, 4th edit., 1984, The End of Russian America, 1979, Civil and Savage Encounters, 1983, Russian Statecraft, 1985, Russian Conquest of Siberia 1558-1700, 1985, Russian Penetration of the North Pacific Archipelago, 1700-1799, 1987, The Soviet Union and the Middle East, 1917-1985, 1987, Russia's Colonies in North America, 1799-1867, 1988, The Soviet Union and the Arab World of the Fertile Crescent, 1918-1985, 1994, Imperial Russia, 1700-1917, 1999, Medieval Russia, 850-1700, 2000; contbr. articles to profl. jours. U.S., Can., Yugoslavia, Italy, South Korea, Fed. Republic Germany, France, Eng., Japan, Russia, Ukraine. State bd. dirs. PTA, Oreg., 1963-64; mem. World Affairs Council, 1965-92. Named Hon. Rsch. Prof. Emeritus, Kyungnam U., 1989—; Fulbright-Hays fellow W. Germany, 1967-68; fellow Kennan Inst. Advanced Russian Studies, Washington, 1978; recipient John Mosser award Oreg. State Bd. Higher Edn., 1966, 67; Branford P. Millar award for faculty excellence Portland State U., 1985, Outstanding Retired Faculty award, 1994; Hillard scholar in the humanities U. Nev., Reno, 1992. Mem. Am. Assn. Advancement Slavic Studies (dir. 1972-75), Am. Hist. Assn., Western Slavic Assn. (pres. 1990-92), Can. Assn. Slavists, Oreg. Hist. Soc., Nat. Geog. Soc., Conf. Slavic and East European History (nat. sec. 1972-75), Am. Assn. for Ukrainian Studies (pres. 1991-93), Ctr. Study of Russian Am. (hon.), Assn. Study Nationalities (bd. mem.-at-large USSR & Ea. Europe 1993—), Czechoslovak Soc. Arts and Scis., Soc. Jewish-Ukraine Contacts, Assn. Home: 2745 S Via Del Bac Green Valley AZ 85614-1071

DOAN, MARY FRANCES, advertising executive; b. Vallejo, Calif., Apr. 16, 1954; d. Larry E. and Dudley (Harbison) D.; m. Timothy Warren Hesselgren, Mar. 19, 1988; children: Edward Latimer, Clinton Robert. BA in Linguistics, U. Calif., Berkeley, 1976; M in Internat. Mgmt., Am. Grad. Sch. Internat. Mgmt., 1980. Trading asst. The Capital Group, L.A., 1980-81; fin. analyst Litton Industries, Beverly Hills, Calif., 1981-82; account exec. Grey Advt., San Francisco, L.A., 1982-84, J. Walter Thompson, San Francisco, 1984-85, Lowe Marshalk, San Francisco, 1985-86; account supr. Young & Rubicam, San Francisco, 1986-89; CEO, pres. Saatchi & Saatchi, San Francisco, 1989-96, worldwide dir. client svc. applications, 1996-98; cons., 1999; v.p. mktg. Roundl, San Francisco, 1999-2000; cons., 2000—. E-mail: mfdoan@hotmail.com

DOBAY, SUSAN VILMA, artist; b. Budapest, Hungary, May 12, 1937; came to U.S., 1957; d. Otto and Lenke Stiasny Heltai; m. Endre Imre Dobay, Oct. 16, 1954; children: Vivian, Andrew. Diploma, Famous Artists Sch., Westport, Conn., 1963. Featured artist in exhbns. at Vasarely Mus., Budapest, 1993, Joslyn Arts Ctr., Torrance, Calif., 1994, Allied Arts Ctr., Richland, Wash., 1995, Deri Mus., Hungary, 1999, BGH the Loft Gallery, Santa Monica, Calif., 2001; exhibited in group shows at Calif. Mus. Sci. and Industry, L.A., 1967, 75, UN Woman Conf., Nairobi, Kenya, 1985, Jillian Coldirow Fine Art, South Pasadena, Calif., 1993—, Hungarian Consulate, N.Y.C., 1996, Kortars Galleria, Budapest, 1996, Mus. Downtown L.A., 1998; illustrator Lloyd's Advt., L.A., 1963-64; fashion illustrator Pasadena Star News, 1965. Mem. World Fedn. Hungarian Artists, N.Y. Artists Equity, L.A. Artists Equity. Avocations: reading, travel, theater, movies, classical music. Home: 125 W Scenic Dr Monrovia CA 91016-1610 E-mail: endred@earthlink.net

DOBBEL, RODGER FRANCIS, interior designer; b. Hayward, Calif., Mar. 11, 1934; s. John Leo and Edna Frances (Young) D.; m. Joyce Elaine Schnoor, Aug. 1, 1959; 1 child, Carrie Lynn. Student, San Jose State U., 1952-55, Chouinard Art Inst., L.A., 1955-57. Asst. designer Monroe Interiors, Oakland, Calif., 1957-66, owner, designer Rodger Dobbel Interiors, Piedmont, 1966—. Pub. in Showcase of Interior Design, Pacific edit., 1992, 100 Designers' Favorite Rooms, 1993, 2d edit., 1994; contbr. articles to mags. and newspapers. Decorations chmn. Trans Pacific Ctr. Bldg. Opening, benefit Oakland Ballet, various other benefits and openings, 1982—; chmn. Symphonic Magic, Lake Marritt Plaza, Opening of Oakland Symphony Orch. Season and various others, 1985—; cons. An Evening of Magic, Oakland Hilton Hotel, benefit Providence Hosp. Found., bd. dirs. 1991; auction chair County Meals on Wheels 1994-95; prodn. chmn. Nutcracker Ball, benefit Oakland Ballet, 1995; mem. bd. regents Holy Names Coll., 1997—. Recipient Cert. of Svc., Nat. Soc. Interior Designers, 1972, 74; recipient Outstanding Contbn. award, Oakland Symphony, 1986, Nat. Philanthropy Day Disting. Vol. award, 1991. Mem. Nat. Soc. Interior Designers (profl. mem. 1960-75, v.p. Calif. chpt. 1965, edn. found. mem. 1966—, nat. conf. chmn. 1966), Am. Soc. Interior Designers , Claremont Country, Diabetic Youth Found. Democrat. Roman Catholic. Avocations: travel, gardening.

DOBBS, DAN BYRON, lawyer, educator; b. Ft. Smith, Ark., Nov. 8, 1932; s. George Byron and Gladys Pauline (Stone) D.; m. Betty Jo Teeter, May 31, 1953 (div. 1978); children: Katherine, George, Rebecca, Jean. B.A., LL.B., U. Ark., 1956; LL.M., U. Ill., 1961, J.S.D., 1966. Bar: Ark. 1956. Partner firm Dobbs, Pryor & Dobbs, Ft. Smith, 1956-60; asst. prof. law U. N.C., Chapel Hill, 1961-63, assoc. prof., 1963-66, prof., 1967, Aubrey L. Brooks prof. law, 1975-77; Rosenstiel prof. law U. Ariz., 1978—, Regents prof., 1992—. Vis. asst. prof. U. Tex., summer 1961; vis. prof. U. Minn., 1966-67, Cornell Law Sch., 1968-69, U. Va. Law Sch., 1974, U. Ariz. Law Sch., 1977-78 Author: Handbook on the Law of Remedies, Damages, Equity, Restitution, 1973, Problems in Remedies, 1974, The Law of Remedies, 3 vols., 2d edit., 1993, The Law of Torts, 2000; co-author: Prosser and Keeton on Torts, 5th edit., 1984, Torts and Compensation, 1985, 2d edit., 1993, 3d edit. (with Paul Hayden), 1997; contbr. articles to legal jours. Office: U Ariz Law Coll Tucson AZ 85721-0001

DOBBS, GREGORY ALLAN, journalist; b. San Francisco, Oct. 9, 1946; s. Harold Stanley and Annette Rae (Lehrer) D.; m. Carol Lynn Walker, Nov. 25, 1973; children: Jason Walker, Alexander Adair. BA, U. Calif., Berkeley, 1968; MSJ, Northwestern U., 1969. Assignment editor, reporter Sta. KGO-TV, San Francisco, 1966-68; news dir. San Francisco Tourist Info. Program Service, 1968; editor ABC Radio, Chgo., 1969-71; producer ABC News, Chgo., 1971-73, corr., 1973-77, London, 1977-82, Paris, 1982-86, Denver, 1986-92; host The Greg Dobbs Show/Sta. KOA Radio, 1992—. Lectr. Northwestern U. Sch. Journalism, 1975, 76; prof. U. Colo. Sch. Journalism, 1996—. Columnist The Denver Post, 1996—. Recipient Sigma Delta Chi Disting. Svc. award for TV reporting Soc. Profl. Journalists, 1980, Emmy award for outstanding documentary, 1989, award of excellence Colo. Broadcasters Assn., 1993, 94, award for best talk show Colo. Soc. Profl. Journalists, 1994; Lippmann fellow Ford Found., 1975. Office: 1153 Bergen Pkwy Ste M150 Evergreen CO 80439-9501

DOBEY, JAMES KENNETH, banker; b. Vallejo, Calif., June 20, 1919; s. Austin E. and Margaret (Hansen) D.; m. Jean Smith, Apr. 18, 1942; children: James A., Peter M. AB, U. Calif., Berkeley, 1940; postgrad., Rutgers U., 1956. With Shell Oil Co., Comml. Credit Corp., 1940-42, Wells Fargo Bank, San Francisco, 1946-72, exec. v.p., 1965-72, vice chmn. bd., 1973, chmn. bd., 1977-80, ret. Capt. airborne inf. AUS, 1942-46. Mem. Delta Chi. Office: PO Box 1419 Aptos CA 95001-1419

DOBLER, DONALD WILLIAM, retired college dean, consultant, corporate executive; b. Rocky Ford, Colo., Apr. 18, 1927; s. William L. and Anna (Nelson) D.; m. Elaine Carlson, Dec. 27, 1951; children: Kathleen, David, Daniel. BS in Engring., Colo State U., 1946-50; MBA, Stanford U., 1958, PhD, 1960. Application and sales engr. Westinghouse Elec. Corp., Pitts. and Phila., 1950-53; mgr. purchasing and materials FMC Corp., Green River, Wyo., 1953-57; guest lectr. Stanford Sch. Bus., 1960; asst. prof. mgmt. State U. Utah, Logan, 1960-63, assoc. prof., 1964-66, head dept. bus. adminstrn., 1964-66; vis. prof. mgmt. Dartmouth Coll., 1963-64; dean Coll. Bus., Colo. State U., Ft. Collins, 1966-86; ind. mgmt. cons. Ft. Collins, 1986-91; corp. v.p. for cert. and program devel. Nat. Assn. Purchasing Mgmt., Tempe, Ariz., 1990-94. Past bd. dirs. U. Nat. Bank, Home Fed. Savs. Bank; pres. Parklane Arms, Inc., 1967-77; part-time mgmt. cons., 1960-86; cons. European Logistics Mgmt. Program, 1970, 72, 77, European Fedn. Purchasing, 1970; faculty Mgmt. Center Netherlands, 1972; dean's adv. coun. logistics mgmt. program Ariz. State U., 1991-94; mem. adv. bd. Mgmt. Inst. U. Wis., 1992-97. Sr. author: Purchasing and Supply Management, 1965, 6th edit., 1996; co-author: The Purchasing Handbook, 1993; mem. editl. bd. European Jour. Purchasing and Supply Mgmt., 1993—; contbr. articles on mgmt. to profl. jours., chpts. to books. Mem. Colo. Gov.'s Adv. Com., 1968-77, Ft. Collins Mayor's Budget Com., 1968-71; dist. chmn. Boy Scouts Am., 1974-77; mem. adv. council Colo. Region, SBA, 1973-79, No. Region, Colo. Div. Employment, 1975-77; bd. dirs., div. chmn. Ft. Collins United Way, 1973-80, pres., 1977; bd. dirs. Ft. Collins Jr. Achievement, 1973-87; bd. dirs. Colo. Assn. Commerce and Industry Ednl. Found., 1988-91. Served with USNR, 1945-46. Mem. Acad. Mgmt., Nat. Assn. Purchasing Mgmt. (Shipman Medalist 1987, chmn. nat. acad. plan com. 1976-81, mem. profl. cert. bd. 1981-86, chmn. 1985-86, assoc. editor Internat. Jour. Purchasing and Materials Mgmt. 1975-80, editor 1980-97), Denver Purchasing Mgmt. Assn. (dir. 1975-83, v.p. 1977, pres. 1979), Am. Prodn. and Inventory Control Soc., Green River Jr. C. of C. (pres. 1955), Am. Assn. Collegiate Schs. Bus. (nat. com. continuing accreditation 1972-78, nat. standards commn. 1978-81, dir. 1980-83, chmn. fin. and audit com. 1983), Sigma Tau, Phi Kappa Phi (editorial cons. Nat. Forum, 1988-94), Rotary, Beta Gamma Sigma (nat. gov. 1975-78) Methodist.

DOBROTKA, DAVID ALLEN, protective services official; m.; 2 children. BS, MPA. With Minn. Police Dept., Mpls., 1976-94; chief Glendale (Ariz.) Police Dept., 1994—. Office: Glendale Police Dept 6835 N 57th Dr Glendale AZ 85301-3218

DOBROWOLSKI, JAMES PHILLIP, agriculturist, educator; b. Los Angeles, June 2, 1955; s. Joseph Adolph and Lois Ann (Hibbs) D.; m. Janet Ann Brown, Mar. 10, 1984; children: Jessica, Jonathan. BS, U. Calif., Davis, 1977; MS, Wash. State U., 1979; PhD, Tex. A&M U., 1985. Systems analyst The Norac Co., Inc., Azusa, Calif., 1980-81; W.G. Mills fellow in hydrology Tex. Water Resources Inst., College Station, 1981-83; Tom Slick fellow in Agr. Tex. A&M U., College Station, 1983-84; research asst. prof. Utah State U., Logan, 1984-85, asst. prof., 1985-91, assoc. prof., 1992—. Cons. Dern & Polk Cons., Belton, Tex., 1981; co-dir. Inst. Land Rehab., Logan, 1985—. Contbr. articles to profl. jours. Recipient Advisor of Yr. award Utah State U., 1989, Prof. of Yr. award, 1991. Mem. Soc. Range Mgmt., Am. Water Resources Assn., Am. Soc. Agrl. Engrs. (affiliate), Soc. Ecol. Restoration, Sigma Xi, Phi Kappa Phi. Avocations: cross-country skiing, fishing, camping. Office: Utah State U Dept Range Sci Logan UT 84322-0001

DOCKSTADER, JACK LEE, retired electronics executive; b. L.A., Dec. 14, 1936; s. George Earl and Grace Orine (Travers) D.; m. Kerry Jo King, Oct. 24, 1987; children: Travis Adam Mayer, Bridget Olivia Mayer. Student, UCLA, 1960-70. Rate analyst Rate Bur. So. Pacific Co., L.A., 1954-57; traffic analyst traffic dept. Hughes Aircraft Co., Fullerton, Calif., 1957-58, Culver City, 1958-59; traffic mgr. Hughes Rsch. Labs., Malibu, 1959-70, material mgr., 1970-75, Hughes Aircraft Co., Culver City, 1975-80; prodn. material mgr. Electro-Optical and Data Sys. Group, El Segundo, Calif., 1980-84, mgr. material total quality, 1984-85, mgr. cen. material ops. and property mgmt., 1987-88, mgr. group property mgmt., 1988-93, mgr. electro optical sys., property mgmt., aerospace/def., 1993, ret., 1993. Mem. adv. council transp. mgmt. profl. designation program UCLA, 1966-80, mem. Design for Sharing Com., 1977-82; adv. com. transp. program L.A. Trade Tech. Coll., 1970-80; vol. USN Ret. Activities Office, Seal Beach, Calif., 1995—; mem. Friends of Phineas Banning Mus., Wilmington, Calif., 1996—; apptd. sec. Navy's Retiree Coun., 2000—. With USNR, 1954-96, ret., 1996. Mem. Nat. Property Mgmt. Assn. (pres. L.A. chpt. 1992-93), UCLA Alumni Assn., Nat. Contracts Mgmt. Assn., Naval Enlisted Res. Assn., Hughes Aircraft Co. Mgmt. Club, Hughes Aircraft Retirees Assn., Sec. of the Navy's Retiree Coun., Delta Nu Alpha (pres. San Fernando Valley chpt. 1965-66, v.p. Pacific S.W. region 1969-71, regiona man of yr. 1971). Presbyterian. Home: PO Box 3156 Redondo Beach CA 90277-1156 E-mail: jkdocks@gte.net

DOCTOR, KENNETH JAY, publishing executive; b. L.A., Jan. 5, 1950; s. Joseph and Ruth (Kazdoy) D.; m. Katherine Conant Francis, June 14, 1971; children: Jenika, Joseph, Katy. BA in Sociology, U. Calif., Santa Cruz, 1971; MS in Journalism, U. Oreg., 1979. Editor, pub. Willamette Valley Observer, Eugene, Oreg., 1975-82; mng. editor Oreg. Mag., Portland, 1982-84; mng. editor, features Boulder (Colo.) Daily Camera, 1984-86; assoc. editor, features St. Paul Pioneer Press, 1986-90, mng. editor, features, 1990-94, mng. editor, 1994-97; v.p. editl. Knight Ridder New Media, San Jose, Calif., 1997-99; v.p. strategy Knight-Ridder.com., 1999-2001; v.p. content svcs. Knight-Ridder Digital, 2001—. Chair Knight-Ridder Task Force on Family Readers, Miami, Fla., 1991, Knight-Ridder mgmt. devel. program, Harvard U., 1993. Recipient Achievement award Oreg. Civil Liberties Union, Eugene, 1982. Mem. Soc. Newspaper Design, Am. Soc. Newspaper Editors. Avocations: baseball, travel. Office: Knight Ridder com 35 S Market St San Jose CA 95113 E-mail: kdoctor@pacbell.net

DODD, CHARLES GARDNER, physical chemist; b. St. Louis, Jan. 26, 1915; s. Harry Gardner and Ruth Esther (Hauskins) D.; m. Edel Marie Bovbjerg, June 10, 1943; children— Sally Little, Karen Elise, Mary Bartlett, Frederick Porter. B.S., Rice U., 1940; M.S., U. Mich., 1945, Ph.D., 1948. In academic work and indsl. rsch. with Fed. Bur. Mines, Bartlesville, Okla., 1953-74; with Warner Lambert Co., Milford, Conn., 1974-80; pres. CTC Technologies, Inc., 1999—. Importer, distbr. sci. instruments. Contbr. articles to sci. and tech. publs. Fellow AAAS; mem. Am. Vacuum Soc., Am. Chem. Soc., Clay Minerals Soc., Chemists Club. Office: CTC Technolgies Inc 12995 N Oracle Rd Ste 141 Tucson AZ 85739-9524

DODDS, ROBERT JAMES, III, lawyer; b. San Antonio, Sept. 19, 1943; s. Robert James Jr. and Kathryn (Bechman) D.; m. Deborah N. Detchon, June 25, 1966 (div. Mar. 1989); children: Zachary Bechman, Seth Detchon; m. D.J. Knowles, Dec. 27, 1990. BA, Yale U., 1965; LLB, U. Pa., 1969. Assoc. Reed Smith Shaw & McClay, Pitts., 1969-77, ptnr., 1978-91; ptrn. Davenport & Dodds, LLP, Santa Fe, 1992—; of counsel Strassburger, McKenna, Gutnick & Potter, Pitts., 1991—. Bd. dirs. ATP Inc., Davison Sand & Gravel Co., Pitts.; pres. Homewood Cemetery, Pitts., 1980-91, bd. dirs. Trustee Mus. Art, Carnegie Inst, 1974-84, Westmoreland Mus. Art, Greensburg, Pa., YMCA of Pitts., Carnegie-Mellon U.; dir., pres. Pitts. Plan for Art, 1981-85; dir., chmn. West Pa. Hosp. Found., Carnegie Mellon Art Gallery; bd. dirs. Western Pa. Hosp., Western Pa. Healthcare Systems Inc., Pitts. Athletic Assn., Inst. Am. Indian Arts Found., Santa Fe. Democrat. Episcopalian. Home: 3101 Old Pecos Trl Unit 687 Santa Fe NM 87505-9547 Office: Davenport & Dodds LLP 721 Don Diego Ave Santa Fe NM 87501-4222

DODGE, PETER HAMPTON, architect; b. Pasadena, Calif., July 1, 1929; s. Irving C. and Edna D. (Allison) D.; m. Janice Coor-Pender, Aug. 30, 1952; children: Susan Julia, Sarah Caroline. Student, Art Center Sch., Calif., 1947-49; A.B. with honors in Architecture, U. Calif., Berkeley, 1956. Cert. architect, Calif., Hawaii, Nev., Idaho, Colo., The Nat. Coun. of Archtl. Registration Bds., (NCARB). Apprentice Alvin Lustig (designer), Los Angeles, 1949-50; draftsman Joseph Esherick (AIA), 1956, architect, 1959-63; asso. architect Joseph Esherick and Assos. (architects), San Francisco, 1963-72; prin. Esherick, Homsey, Dodge and Davis (architects and planners, P.C.), San Francisco, 1972—, pres., 1979-85. Lectr. dept. architecture U. Calif., Berkeley, 1961-64, 71; vis. lectr. dept. design San Francisco Art Inst., 1965 Prin. archtl. works include grad. residence facility U. Calif.-Davis, 1970, Shortstop Inc. markets, office and warehouse, Benicia, Calif., 1976, Ekahi Village (297 condominium units) Wailea, Hawaii, 1976, TWA and Western Airlines at San Francisco Internat. Airport, 1977, Citizens Utility Ctr., Susanville, Calif., 1983, various projects Golden Gate U., San Francisco, 1984—, additions and renovation Forest Hill Mcpl. R.R. Sta., San Francisco, 1985, Life Sci. Bldg. Mills Coll., Oakland, Calif., 1986, showroom R.A.B. Motors Mercedes-Benz , San Rafael, Calif., 1986, U.S. Embassy, La Paz, Bolivia, 1979-87, boarding area "B" expansion San Francisco Internat. Airport, 1987, additions and renovations Mills. Coll. Art Ctr., Oakland, 1987, F.W. Olin Libr. Mills Coll., Oakland, 1989, Calif. State U. at Bakersfield Walter Stiern Libr., 1993, Mills Hall restoration, Olney Hall rehab. Mills Coll., 1994 ; mem. editorial bd. Architecture Calif. mag., 1984-88, chmn. bd., 1985-88, Landscape mag., 1986—. Mem. Rockridge Community Planning Council, Oakland, Calif., 1971. Served with C.E., U.S. Army, 1957-58. Firm recipient of highest nat. honor for archtl. firm. AIA, 1986. Fellow AIA (dir. Calif. council 1979-81, dir. San Francisco chpt. 1977-78, sec. 1979, v.p. 1980, pres. San Francisco chpt. 1981, Honor award 1970, Bartlett award 1970); mem. U. Calif. at Berkeley Coll. Environ. Design Alumni Assn. (mem. founding steering com., pres. 1990-91). Office: Esherick Homsey Dodge & Davis 500 Treat Ave Ste 201 San Francisco CA 94110-2014

DODS, WALTER ARTHUR, JR. bank executive; b. Honolulu, May 26, 1941; s. Walter Arthur Sr. and Mildred (Phillips) D.; m. Diane Lauren Nosse, Sept. 18, 1971; children: Walter A. III, Christopher L., Peter D., Lauren S. BBA, U. Hawaii, 1967. Mktg. officer 1st Hawaiian Bank, Honolulu, 1969, asst. v.p. mktg. div., 1969-71, v.p., chmn. mktg. and rsch. group, 1971-73, sr. v.p. mktg. and rsch. group, 1973-76, exec. v.p. retail banking group, 1976-78, exec. v.p. gen. banking group, 1978-84, pres., 1984-89, chmn., ceo, 1989—; chmn., pres., CEO First Hawaiian, Inc., 1989-90; chmn., CEO BancWest Corp, 1989—, First Hawaiian Creditcorp., 1989-92. Bd. dirs. First Hawaiian Inc., 1st Hawaiian Bank, First Hawaiian Creditcorp Inc., First Hawaiian Leading, Inc., Alexander & Baldwin Inc., A&B-Hawaii Inc., Duty Free Shoppers Adv. Bd., Matson Navigation Co. Inc., 1st Ins. Co. Hawaii Ltd., GTE Calif., GTE Hawaiian Telephone Co., GTE Northwest, Grace Pacific Corp., Oceanic Cablevision Inc., Pacific Guardian Life Ins. Co., Princeville Adv. Group, RHP, Inc., Restaurant Suntory USA, Inc., Suntory Resorts, Inc. Bd. dirs. Ahahui Koa Anuenue, East-West Ctr. Found.; past sec., treas. The Rehab. Hosp. of the Pacific; exec. bd. mem. Aloha Coun., Boy Scouts Am.; trustee, past chmn., trustee Blood Bank Hawaii; past chmn. bd. Aloha United Way; past chmn. Bd. Water Supply; bd. govs., v.p. fin. Ctr. for Internat. Comml. Dispute Resolution; bd. dirs., treas. Coalition for Drug-Free Hawaii; trustee Contemporary Mus. co-chmn. corp. campaign com.; mem. Duty Free Shoppers Adv. Bd.; past chmn. Gubernatorial Inauguration, 1974, 82; bd. govs. Hawaii Employers Coun.; trustee Hawaii Maritime Ctr; mem. Gov.'s Adv. Bd. Geothermal/Inter-Island Cable Project, Gov.'s Blue Ribbon Panel on the Future of Healthcare in Hawaii; dir., past chmn. Hawaii Visitors Bur.; exec. com. Hawaiian Open; past spl. dir. Homeless Kokua Week; bd. gov. Honolulu Country Club, Japanese Cultural Ctr. Hawaii, Pacific Peace Found.; trustee Japan-Am. Inst. Mgmt. Sci., The Nature Conservancy Hawaii, Punahou Sch.; Hawaii chmn. Japan-Hawaii Econ. Coun.; chmn., dir. Pacific Internat. Ctr. for High Tech. Rsch.; past co-chmn., chmn. bldg. fund St. Louis High Sch., treas. The 200 Club; dir. World Cup Honolulu 1994. Named Outstanding Jaycee in Nation, 1963, Outstanding Young Man Am. from Hawaii, 1972, Marketer of Yr., Am. Mktg. Assn., 1987; recipient Riley Allen Individual Devel. award, 1964, Hawaii State Jaycees 3 Outstanding Young Men award, 1971, Am. Advt. Fedn. Silver medal, 1977, St. Louis High Sch.'s Outstanding Alumnus award, 1980. Mem. Am. Bankers Assn., Bank Mktg. Assn., Hawaii Bankers Assn., Hawaii Bus. Roundtable, C. of C. of Hawaii, Honolulu Press Club. Office: BancWest Corp PO Box 3200 Honolulu HI 96847-0001

DOEBLER, PAUL DICKERSON, publishing management executive; b. Milw., July 3, 1930; s. Paul Henry and Grace Elizabeth (Whittaker) D.; m. Aileen Mary Hunt, May 15, 1958 (dec. 1966); m. Terry Gerda Moss, Dec. 15, 1967 B.S. in Journalism, Northwestern U., 1953; B.S. in Printing Mgmt., Carnegie-Mellon U., 1956. Editor-in-chief Book Prodn. Industry mag. Penton Pub. Co., N.Y.C., 1965-71; pub. mgmt. cons. N.Y.C., 1972-80; mgr. bus. devel. R.R. Bowker subs. Xerox, N.Y.C., 1980-82, editor-in-chief profl. books, 1983-84; pub. cons. Xerox Systems Group, El Segundo, Calif., 1984-85, mgr. documentation cons. services, 1985-86, mgr. documentation systems mktg., 1986-89; pres. Paul Doebler Enterprises, Camarillo, 1990—. Instr. Assn. Am. Pubs., 1985, CCNY, 1980-85; guest lectr. The Writing Program MIT, 1988-90; instr. learning Tree U., 1997—. Contbr. articles to mags. Mem. Carnegie Printers Alumni Assn. (pres. 1972) Home: 6343 Gitana Ave Camarillo CA 93012-8135

DOERPER, JOHN ERWIN, journal editor, publishing executive; b. Wuerzburg, Germany, Sept. 17, 1943; came to U.S., 1963, naturalized resident, 1973; s. Werner and Theresia (Wolf) D.; m. Victoria McCulloch, Dec. 2, 1970. BA, Calif. State U., Fullerton, 1968; MA/ABD, U. Calif., Davis, 1972. Writer/author, Seattle, 1984—; food columnist Washington, Seattle, 1985-88, Seattle Times, 1985-88; food editor Wash.-The Evergreen State Mag., Seattle, 1989-94, Pacific Northwest mag., 1989-94, Seattle Home and Garden, 1989-91; pub., editor, founder Pacific Epicure, Quarterly Jour. Gastronomy, Bellingham, Wash., 1988—. Dir. Annual N.W. Invitational Chef's Symposium. Author: Eating Well: A Guide to Foods of the Pacific Northwest, 1984, The Eating Well Cookbook, 1984, Shellfish Cookery: Absolutely Delicious Recipes from the West Coast, 1985; author, illustrator: The Blue Carp, 1994, Wine Country: California's Napa and Sonoma Valleys, 1996, Pacific Northwest, 1997, Coastal California, 1998 (Lowell Thomas Travel Journalism Competition Gold medal 1999); contbr. articles to profl. jours., intro. and chpts. to books; co-author: Washington: A Compass Guide, 1995, Fodor's Pacific Northwest, 2000, Fodor's Seattle, 2000. Recipient Silver medal, White award for city and regional mags. William Allen White Sch. Journalism, U. Kans., Lowell Thomas award Gold medal for best guide book, 1999. Mem. Oxford Symposium Food and Cookery (speaker 26th Ann. Pacific N.W. Writer's Conf. 1982, 92). Avocations: food, wine, travel, painting, printmaking. Home: 610 Donovan Ave Bellingham WA 98225-7315 E-mail: pacificepicure@att.net

DOERR, STEPHEN, lawyer; b. Misawa AFB, Japan, Jan. 30, 1953; BS, Eastern N.Mex. U., 1977; JD, U. N.Mex., 1980. Bar: N.Mex. 1980, U.S. Dist. Ct. N.Mex. 1984, U.S. Dist. Ct. (ea. dist.) Okla. Ptnr. Doerr & Knudson, Clovis, N.Mex. Bus. law and real property instr. Eastern N.Mex. U., 1982-84; bar commr. Fifth Bar Dist. Curry, Roosevelt, and Quay Counties. With USMC, 1972. Mem. ABA, ATLA, State Bar N.Mex. (pres.), N.Mex. Trial Lawyers Assn., Roosevelt County Bar Assn. (pres. 1984-85), Curry County Bar Assn. (pres. 1983, v.p. 1982), Curry-Roosevelt County Bar Assn. (pres. 1986), Phi Kappa Phi, Delta Theta Pi. Office: Doerr & Knudson PA 600 Mitchell St Clovis NM 88101-7358

DOHERTY, STEVE, lawyer, state legislator; b. Great Falls, Mont., May 5, 1952; s. Arthur Frederick and Myra M. (Sheldon) D. BA, U. Pa., 1975; JD, Lewis & Clark Law Sch., 1984. Assoc. Spears, Lubersky, Campbell, Bledsoe, Anderson & Young, Portland, 1984-86; from assoc. to ptnr. Graybill, Ostrem, Warner & Crotty, Great Falls, Mont., 1986-92; assoc. Smith & Guenther, Great Falls, 1992-97; mem. Mont. Senate, Dist. 24, Helena, 1991—; majority whip, chmn. jud. com. Mont. Senate, Great Falls, Mont., 1993-94, mem. taxation and nat. resources com., 1991-94, mem. environ. quality coun. com., 1991-94, mem. edn. com., 1995, mem. fish and game and ethics com., 1997, minority leader, 1999-2001, mem. rules com., 1999—; ptnr. Smith & Doherty, Great Falls, 1998—. Bd. dirs. Rural Employment Opportunities, Helena, 1990-92. Recipient Conservation Eagle award N.W. Energy Coalition, 1999; Flemming fellow Ctr. for Policy Alts., 1998. Mem. Great Falls Pub. Radio Assn. (bd. dirs. 1986-91). Democrat. Avocations: hunting, fishing, hiking, skiing, Western history. Office: Smith & Doherty 410 Central Ave Ste 522 Great Falls MT 59401-3128 Fax: (406) 452-9787

DOHRING, DOUG, marketing executive; Chmn. Dohring Co., Calif. Office: Dohring Co 412 W Broadway Ste 300 Glendale CA 91204-1297

DOHRING, LAURIE, marketing executive; CEO Dohring Co., Glendale, Calif. Office: Dohring Co 412 W Broadway Ste 300 Glendale CA 91204-1297

DOI, LOIS, psychiatric social worker; b. Honolulu, Oct. 24, 1951; d. James Masato and Thelma Kimiko Miyamoto; m. Brian Doi, May 26, 1972; children: Michael, Lorian. BS, U. Hawaii, 1974, MSW, 1978. Lic. clin. social worker, Calif. Psychiat. social worker, child specialist Desert Community Mental Health Ctr., Indio, Calif., 1979-92, coordinator children's day treatment program, 1982-91; pvt. practice psychiat. social worker 1-2-1 Counseling, Palm Springs, 1992—, owner, ptnr. Rancho Mirage; psychiat. social worker, adult case mgr. Desert Community Mental Health Ctr., Palm Springs, 1992-93; clin. dir. Barbara Sinatra Children's Ctr., Rancho Mirage, 1998-2000; with Desert Cmty. Mental Health Ctr., Cathedral City, 2000—. Expert examiner, Bd. of Behavioral Sci. Examiners, 1987—. Vol. advisor Community Recreation Ctr. Youth Group, Hawaii, 1967-69; vol. interviewer ARC Food Stamp Program, Hawaii, 1973; vol. asst. YWCA Programs Young Mothers and Teens, Hawaii, 1973; vol. group leader YWCA Juvenile Delinquent Program, Hawaii, 1973; placement counselor Vols. In Service to Am., L.A., 1975; VISTA counselor L.A. Urban League, 1975-76. Mem. Nat. Assn. Social Workers. Avocations: needlework, reading.

DOLAN, ANDREW KEVIN, lawyer; b. Chgo., Dec. 7, 1945; s. Andrew O. and Elsie (Grafner) D.; children: Andrew, Francesca, Melinda. BA, U. Ill., Chgo., 1967; JD, Columbia U., 1970, MPH, 1976, DPH, 1980. Bar: Wash. 1980. Asst. prof. law Rutgers-Camden Law Sch., N.J., 1970-72; assoc. prof. law U. So. Calif., L.A., 1972-75; assoc. prof. pub. health U. Wash., Seattle, 1977-81; ptnr. Bogle & Gates, Seattle, 1988-93; pvt. practice law, 1993—. Commr. Civil Svc. Commn., Lake Forest Park, Wash., 1981; mcpl. judge City of Lake Forest Park, 1982-98. Russell Sage fellow, 1975. Mem. Order of Coif, Washington Athletic Club. Avocation: book collecting. Office: 5800 Columbia Ctr 701 5th Ave Seattle WA 98104-7097

DOLAN, JAMES MICHAEL, JR. zoological park administrator; b. N.Y.C., Feb. 27, 1937; s. James Michael and Emily Catherine (Wackerbauer) D. BS, Mt. St. Mary's Coll., Emmitsburg, Md., 1959; PhD, Inst. fur Haustierkunde, U. Kiel, Fed. Republic Germany, 1963. Asst. curator birds Zoological Soc. San Diego, The San Diego Zoo, 1963-64, assoc. curator birds, 1964-73, dir. animal sci., 1973-74; gen. curator Zoological Soc. San Diego, The San Diego Wild Animal Pk., 1974-81; gen. curator mammals Zoological Soc. San Diego, 1982-85, dir. collections, 1986—. Advisor Econ. Rsch. Assocs.; adj. prof. zoology San Diego State U.; tech. asst. UN in Malaysia, 1970, Indian Zool. Gardens, 1976, Kuwait Zool. Garden, 1978, Seoul (Korea) Zool. Garden; mem. Survival Svc. Commn., Faro, Portugal, 1978; zoo advisory for U.S. Fish & Wildlife Svc. to India, 1980; del. internat. confs. including Conv. on Internat. Trade in Endangered Species Wild Fauna and Flora, Buenos Aires, 1985, Internat. Conf. Rupricaprines, Japan, 1987. Collecting expdns. to Cen. Am. countries, 1965, Australia, 1966, Papua-New Guinea, 1966, Java and Borneo, 1969, Fiji, 1970, Costa Rica, 1976; participant giant eland capture expdn. Senegal and Mali, 1979; mem. adv. bd. Internat. Zoo Yearbook, London. Fellow Am. Assn. Zool. Pks. and Aquariums (coordinator Arabian oryx group species survival plan); mem. Internat. Union Dirs. Zool. Gardens, Internat. Union for Conservation of Nature & Natural Resources (active several species survival commn. specialist groups, del. meetings and confs. Eng., Australia, Czechoslovakia, Hong Kong 1980-84, Fed. Republic Germany, 1987, reintroduction program Przewalski's horse Republic of China and Tibet, 1987, conf. Arabian oryx Saudi Arabia, 1987, com. to review new Taipei Zoo 1987), Am. Pheasant and Waterfowl Assn., African Lovebird Soc., Avicultural Soc., Explorer's Club, Fauna Preservation Soc., Found. Protection and Preservation of Przewalski Horse, Internat. Crane Found., World Pheasant Assn., Zooculturists, German Soc. Mammalogists. Avocations: book collecting, aviculture. Home: 18836 Paradise Mountain Rd Valley Center CA 92082-7430 Office: San Diegi Zool Soc San Diego Zoo PO Box 120551 San Diego CA 92112-0551

DOLAN, MARY ANNE, journalist, columnist; b. Washington, May 1, 1947; d. William David and Christine (Shea) D.. BA, Marymount Coll., Tarrytown, N.Y., 1968; HHD (hon.) , Marymount Coll., %, 1984; student, Queen Mary, Royal Holloway colls., U. London, London Sch. Econs., Kings Coll., Cambridge U., 1966-68. Reporter, editor Washington Star, 1969-77; asst. mng. editor, 1976-77; mng. editor L.A. Herald Examiner, 1978-81, editor, 1981—, now commentator. Mem. Pulitzer Prize Journalism Jury, 1981—82; bd. selectors for Neiman Fellows Harvard U. Recipient Golden Flame award, Calif. Press Women, 1980, Woman Achiever award, Calif. Fed. Bus. and Profl. Women's Clubs, 1981. Mem.: NOW, Am. Soc. Newspaper Editors. Office: MAD Inc 1033 Gayley Ave Ste 205 Los Angeles CA 90024-3417

DOLAN, PETER BROWN, lawyer; b. Bklyn., Mar. 25, 1939; s. Daniel Arthur and Eileen Margaret (Brown) D.; m. Jacqueline Elizabeth Gruning, Sept. 9, 1961; children: Kerry Anne, Peter Brown Jr. BS, U.S. Naval Acad., 1960; JD, U. So. Calif., 1967. Bar: Calif. 1967, U.S. Ct. Appeals (9th cir.) 1968, U.S. Dist. Ct. (no. and ctrl. dists.) Calif. 1967, U.S. Dist. Ct. (ea. dist.) Calif. 1972, U.S. Dist. Ct. (so. dist.) Calif. 1973, U.S. Claims Ct. 1982, U.S. Supreme Ct. 1986. Dep. L.A. County counsel, 1967-69; assoc. Macdonald, Halsted & Laybourne, L.A., 1969-71, ptnr., 1972-77, Overton, Lyman & Prince, L.A., 1977-87, Morrison & Foerster, L.A., 1987-93, Morgan, Lewis & Bockius LLP, L.A., 1993-99; prin. ptnr. The Dolan Law Firm, L.A., 1999—. Active Pasadena (Calif.) Tournament of Roses Assn., 1973—; pres. West Pasadena Residents Assn., 1979-81. Served to lt. USN, 1960-64, comdr. USNR, 1964-86. Mem. ABA, Fed. Bar Assn., State Bar Calif., Assn. Bus. Trial Lawyers, L.A. County Bar Assn., Bel-Air Bay Club, Chancery (L.A.), City Club on Bunker Hill, Phi Delta Phi. Democrat. Roman Catholic. Fax: 213-680-9889. E-mail: dolanlaw@earthlink.net, jacquiedol@aol.com

DOLBY, RAY MILTON, engineering company executive, electrical engineer; b. Portland, Oreg., Jan. 18, 1933; s. Earl Milton and Esther Eufemia (Strand) D.; m. Dagmar Baumert, Aug. 19, 1966; children—Thomas Eric, David Earl. Student, San Jose State Coll., 1951-52, 55, Washington U., St. Louis, 1953-54; BSEE, Stanford U., 1957; Ph.D. in Physics (Marshall scholar 1957-60, Draper's studentship 1959-61, NSF fellow 1960-61), Cambridge (Eng.) U., 1961, ScD (hon.), 1997; Doctor of the U. (hon.), U. York. Comml. pilot instrument rating FAA. Electronic technician/jr. engr. Ampex Corp., Redwood City, Calif., 1949-53, engr., 1955-57, sr. engr., 1957; PhD research student in physics Cavendish Lab., Cambridge U., 1957-61, research in long wavelength x-rays, 1957-63; fellow Pembroke Coll., 1961-63; cons. U.K. Atomic Energy Authority, 1962-63; UNESCO adviser Central Sci. Instruments Orgn., Chandigarh, Punjab, India, 1963-65; owner, chmn., CEO Dolby Labs. Inc., San Francisco and Wootton Bassett, U.K., 1965—. Trustee Univ. High Sch., San Francisco, 1978-84; bd. dirs. San Francisco Opera; bd. govs. San Francisco Symphony; mem. Marshall Scholarship selection com., 1979-85. Served with U.S. Army, 1953-54. Decorated officer Most Excellent Order of Brit. Empire; recipient Beech-Thompson award Stanford U., 1956, Emmy award, 1957, 89, Trendsetter award Billboard, 1971, Top 200 Execs. Bi-Centennial award, 1976, Lyre award Inst. High Fidelity, 1972, Emile Berliner Maker of the Microphone award Emile Berliner Assn., 1972, Sci. and Engring. award Acad. Motion Picture Arts and Scis., 1979, Oscar award, 1989, Pioneer award Internat. Teleprodn. Soc., 1988, Edward Rhein Ring award Edward Rhein Found., 1988, Life Achievement award Cinema Audio Soc., 1989, Grammy award NARAS, 1995, Nat. Medal Tech., U.S. Dept. Commerce, 1997, Medal of Achievement, Am. Electronics Assn., 1997; named Man of Yr. Internat. Tape Assn., 1987; hon. fellow Pembroke Coll., Cambridge U., 1983. Fellow Audio Engring. Soc. (bd. govs. 1972-74, 79-84 Silver Medal award 1971, Gold medal award 1992, pres. 1980-81), Brit. Kinematograph, Sound and TV Soc. (outstanding tech. and sci. award 1995), Soc. Motion Picture and TV Engrs. (Samuel L. Warner award 1979, Alexander M. Poniatoff Gold Medal 1982, Progress award 1983, hon. mem. 1992), Inst. Broadcast Sound; mem. IEEE (Ibuka award 1997), St. Francis Yacht Club, Pacific Union Club, Tau Beta Pi. Achievements include inventions, research, publs. in video tape recording, x-ray microanalysis, noise reduction and quality improvements in audio and video systems; holder 50 U.S. patents. Office: Dolby Labs 100 Potrero Ave San Francisco CA 94103-4886*

DOLCOURT, JOHN (JACK) LAWRENCE, pediatrician; b. Denver, May 13, 1949; s. Benjamin and Nessie (Badion) D.; m. Joyce Linda Papper, Sept. 3, 1972; children: Bram, Cameron. BA, U. Colo., 1971, MD, 1975. Diplomate Am. Bd. Pediatrics, Am. Bd. Neonatal, Perinatal Medicine. Asst. prof. pediatrics U. Utah Sch. of Medicine, Salt Lake City, 1990-86, assoc. prof., 1986—. Med. dir. Ctr. for Pediatric Continuing Edn., Primary Childen's Med. Ctr., Salt Lake City, Utah, 1986—. Contbr. articles to profl. jours.; inventor percutaneously placed catheter. Bd. dirs. Jewish Reconstructionist Fedn., Phila., 1990-93, v.p., 1993—. Fellow Am. Acad. Pediatrics. Home: 509 Northmont Way Salt Lake City UT 84103-3324 Office: U Utah Sch Medicine Divsn Neonatology 50 N Medical Dr Ste 2a111 Salt Lake City UT 84132-0001

DOLENZ, MICKEY (GEORGE MICHAEL DOLENZ), singer, actor, television producer; b. Los Angeles, Mar. 8, 1945; s. George and Janelle Dolenz; m. Trina Dow, 1977-91 (div.), m. Samantha Just, 1967-1975 (div.). Student, Valley Coll., Los Angeles Tech. Inst. Star TV series Circus Boy, 1956-58; ind. actor, musician, 1958-66; mem. The Monkees, 1966-70, 85—, star TV series, 1966-68; cartoon voice-over artist, actor, musician, 1970-77; TV dir., producer Eng., 1977-85. Rec. artist: (The Monkees: Dolenz, Mike Nesmith, Davey Jones, Peter Tork) The Monkees, 1966, More of the Monkees, 1967, Headquarters, Pisces, Aquarius, Capircorn & Jones Ltd., 1967, The Birds, the Bees & the Monkees, 1968, (film soundtrack) Head, 1968, Instant Replay, 1969, The Monkees Present, 1969, Changes, 1969, The Monkees Greatest Hits, 1969, The Monkees Golden Hits, (The Monkees: Dolenz, Jones, Tork) Then and Now, 1986, Missing Links, 1987, vol. 2, 1990, Listen To The Bard, 1991; hit singles include Last Train to Clarksville, Daydream Believer, Valerie, Peter Percival and his Pet Pig Porky, I'm a Believer, Steppin' Stone, Pleasant Valley Sunday; other TV series appearances include My Three Sons, Adam 12, Pacific Blues, 1995; (cartoon series) Scooby Doo, Devlin, The Funky Phantom, 1971, The Tick, 1995; (TV movies) 33 1/3 Revolutions per Monkee, 1969, Hey, Hey, It's the Monkees, 1997, The Love Bug, 1997; (films) Head, 1968, Keep off my Grass!, 1971, Night of the Strangler, 1972, Keep Off! Keep Off!, 1975, Linda Lovelace for President, 1976, Deadfall, 1993, The Brady Bunch Movie, 1995, Mom, Can I keep Her?, 1998; stage appearances include Tom Sawyer, Sacramento, 1976, The Point by Harry Nilsson, London. Office: 8369-A Sausalito Ave Box Canyon CA 91304

DOLICH, ANDREW BRUCE, sports marketing executive; b. Bklyn., Feb. 18, 1947; s. Mac and Yetta (Weiselter) D.; m. Ellen Andrea Fass, June 11, 1972; children: Lindsey, Caryn, Cory. BA, Am. U., 1969; MEd, Ohio U., 1971. Adminstrv. asst. to gen. mgr. Phila. 76ers, NBA, 1971-74; v.p. Md. Arrows Lacrosse, Landover, 1974-76; mktg. dir. Washington Capitals, NHL, Landover, 1976-78; exec. v.p., gen. mgr. Washington Diplomats Soccer, 1978-80; v.p. bus. ops. Oakland A's Baseball, Calif., 1980-92, exec. v.p., 1993-95; pres., COO Golden State Warriors NBA, Oakland, 1995-98; pres. Dolich & Assoc. Sports Mktg., Alameda, 1996—; exec. v.p. Tickets.com, 1998—; pres. Memphis Grizzlies, 2000—. Nat. fundraising chmn. sports adminstrs. program Ohio U., Athens, dir., 1978-82; lectr. sports mktg. U. Calif. Ext. Bd. dirs. Bay Area Sports Hall of Fame, 1982—, Internat. Sports Mktg. Coun., Oakland Zoo Adv. Coun.; bd. dirs. Grizzlies Found. Recipient Alumni of Yr. award Ohio U. Sports Adminstrs. Program, Athens, 1982; recipient Clio award Am. Advt. Fedn., 1982 E-mail: adolich@tickets.com

DOLL, LYNNE MARIE, public relations agency executive; b. Glendale, Calif., Aug. 27, 1961; d. George William and Carol Ann (Kennedy) D.; m. David Jay Lans, Oct. 11, 1986. BA in Journalism, Calif. State U., Northridge, 1983. Freelance writer Austin Pub. Rels. Systems, Glendale, 1978-82; asst. account exec. Berkhemer & Kline, L.A., 1982-83; pres. Rogers & Assocs., L.A., 1983—. Exec. dir. Suzuki Automotive Found. for Life, Brea, Calif., 1986-91; mem. strategic planning com. Gateway to Indian Am. Corp. for Am. Indian Devel., San Francisco, 1988-90. Pub. rels. cons., Rape Treatment Ctr., L.A., 1986—. Mem. Ad Club L.A. (bd. dirs., pres. 1994-95), Pub. Rels. Soc. Am. (L.A. chpt. Outstanding Profl. 1999), So. Calif. Assn. Philanthropy, Coun. on Founds., Internat. Motor Press Assn., Nat. Conf. for Cmty. and Justice (bd. dirs. 1996—). Democrat. Office: Rogers & Assocs 1875 Century Park E Ste 300 Los Angeles CA 90067-2504

DOLLIVER, JAMES MORGAN, retired state supreme court justice; b. Ft. Dodge, Iowa, Oct. 13, 1924; s. James Isaac and Margaret Elizabeth (Morgan) D.; m. Barbara Babcock, Dec. 18, 1948; children: Elizabeth, James, Peter, Keith, Jennifer, Nancy. BA in Polit. Sci. with high honors, Swarthmore Coll., 1949; LLB, U. Wash., 1952; D in Liberal Arts (hon.), U. Puget Sound, 1981. Bar: Wash. 1952. Clk. to presiding justice Wash. Supreme Ct., 1952-53; pvt. practice Port Angeles, Wash., 1953-54, Everett, 1961-64; adminstrv. asst. to Congressman Jack Westland, 1955-61, Gov. Daniel J. Evans, 1965-76; state supreme ct. justice Supreme Ct. State of Wash., 1976-99, state supreme ct. chief justice, 1985-87. Adj. prof. U. Puget Sound Sch. Law, 1988-92. Chmn. United Way Campaign Thurston County, 1975; chmn. Wash. chpt. Nature Conservancy, 1981-83; pres. exec. bd. Tumwater Area coun. Boy Scouts Am., 1972-73, Wash. State Capital Hist. Assn., 1976-80, 85—, also trustee, 1983-84; trustee Deaconess Children's Home, Everett, 1963-65, U. Puget Sound, 1969—, chair exec. com., 1990-93, Wash. 4-H Found., 1977-93, Claremont (Calif.) Theol. Sem., assoc. mem., Community Mental Health Ctr., 1977-84; bd. mgrs. Swarthmore Coll., 1980-84; bd. dirs. Thurston Mason Community Health Ctr., 1977-84, Thurston Youth Svcs. Soc., 1969-84, also pres., 1983, mem. exec com. 1970-84, Wash. Women's Employment and Edn., 1982-84; mem. jud. coun. United Meth. Ch., 1984-92, gen. cong., 1970-72, 80—, gen. bd. ch. and soc., 1976-84; adv. coun. Ret. Sr. Vol. program, 1979-83; pres. Wash. Ctr. Law-related Edn., 1987-89, bd. dirs. 1987-95; bd. dirs. World Assn. for Children and Parents, 1987-93; trustee U. Wash. Law Sch. Found., 1982-90, Olympic Park Inst., 1988-94; mem. bd. visitors U. Wash. Sch. Social Work, 1987-93; chair bd. visitors U. Puget Sound Sch. Law, 1988-90, bd. visitors, 1988-93; chmn. bd. dirs. Pub. Lands Employee Recognition Fund, 1994—; mem. bd. dirs. St. Peter Hosp. Med. Rehab. Community Adv. Bd., 1993—. With USN, 1943-45; ensign USCG, 1945-46. Recipient award Nat. Council Japanese Am. Citizens League, 1976; Silver Beaver award, 1971; Silver Antelope award, 1976 Mem. ABA, Wash. Bar Assn., Am. Judges Assn., Am. Judicature Soc., Pub. Broadcast Found. (bd. dirs. 1982-95), Masons, Rotary, Phi Delta Theta, Delta Theta Phi.

DOMENICI, PETE V. (VICHI DOMENICI), senator; b. Albuquerque, May 7, 1932; s. Cherubino and Alda (Vichi) D.; m. Nancy Burk, Jan. 15, 1958; children: Lisa, Peter, Nella, Clare, David, Nanette, Helen, Paula. Student, U. Albuquerque, 1950-52; BS, U. N.Mex., 1954, LLD (hon.); LLB, Denver U., 1958; LLD (hon.), Georgetown U. Sch. Medicine; HHD (hon.), N.Mex. State U. Bar: N.Mex. 1958. Tchr. math. pub. schs., Albuquerque, 1954-55; ptnr. firm Domenici & Bonham, Albuquerque, 1958-72; chmn., ex-officio mayor Albuquerque, 1967; city commr. Albuquerque, 1966-68; senator from N.Mex. U.S. Senate, N.Mex., 1972—. Mem. appropriations com., energy and natural resources com., chmn. subcom. on energy rsch. and devel.; mem. com. on environ. and pub. works, mem. govtl. affairs com.; chmn. budget com., com. on Indian affairs; mem. Presl. Adv. Com. on Federalism; senate Rep. policy com. Mem. Gov.'s Policy Bd. for Law Enforcement, 1967-68; chmn. Model Cities Joint Adv. Com., 1967-68. Recipient Nat. League of Cities award Outstanding Performance in Congress; Disting. Svc. award Tax Found., 1986, Legislator of Yr. award Nat. Mental Health Assn., 1987, public sector leadership award, 1996. Mem. Nat. League Cities, Middle Rio Grande Council Govts. Office: US Senate 328 Hart Senate Office Bldg Washington DC 20510-0001*

DOMEÑO, EUGENE TIMOTHY, elementary education educator, principal; b. L.A., Oct. 22, 1938; s. Digno and Aurora Mary (Roldan) D. AA, Santa Monica (Calif.) City Coll., 1958; BA, Calif. State U., 1960, MA, 1966. Cert. elem. tchr., gen. sch svcs, special secondary tchr. Elem. tchr. L.A. Unified Sch. Dist., 1960-70; asst. prin. Pomona (Calif.) Unified Sch. Dist., 1970-71, prin., 1971—. Cons. testing and evaluation Pomona Unified Sch. Dist., 1990—. With USNR, 1958-65. Recipient PTA Hon. Svc. award Granada Elem. PTA, Granada Hills, Calif., 1960, Armstrong Sch. PTA, Diamond Bar, Calif., 1990, Calif. Disting. Sch. Calif. Dept. Edn., 1989, Nat. Blue Ribbon Sch. U.S. Dept. Edn., Washington, 1990, Prin. and Leadership award, 1990. Mem. ASCD, Nat. Assn. Elem. Sch. Prins. (Prin. of Leadership award with Nat. Safety Com., 1991), Nat. Assn. Year Round Sch., Assn. Calif. Sch. Administrs., Diamond Bar C. of C. (edn. com.). Avocations: golf, dancing, church, playing the flute. Office: Neil Armstrong Elem Sch 22750 Beaverhead Dr Diamond Bar CA 91765-1566 E-mail: auroratlc@aol.com

DOMINGUEZ, EDDIE, artist; b. Tucumcari, N.Mex., Oct. 17, 1957; BFA, Cleve. Inst. Art, 1981; MFA, Alfred U., 1983. Grad. asst., ceramics and visual design courses Alfred (N.Y.) U., 1981-83; artist-in-residence, lectr. Ohio State U., Columbus, 1984; artist-in-edn. N.Mex. Arts Divsn., Santa Fe, 1985-86; artist-in-residence Cleve. Inst. Art, 1986; artist-in-residence, lectr. U. Mont., Missoula, 1988; asst. prof. art U. Nebr., Lincoln, 1998—. Lectr., presenter workshops, mem. panels Ill. Arts Coun., Chgo., 1994, NEA, Washington, 1994, Ariz. Commn. on the Arts, 1994, Concordia U., Montreal, Que., Can., 1994, Mass. Coll. Art, Boston, 1994, Bennington (Vt.) Coll., 1994, 95, 96, Peters Valley, Layton, N.J., 1994, Firehouse Art Ctr., Norman, Okla., 1994, Haystack Mountain Sch. Arts & Crafts, Deer Isle, Maine, 1994, Ghost Ranch, Abiquiu, N.Mex., 1995, We. States Arts Fedn., Santa Fe, 1995, Colo. Coun. on the Arts, Boulder, 1995, Durango (Colo.) Art Ctr., 1995, Tamarind Inst., Albuquerque, 1995, 96, Kansas City (Mo.) Ar Inst., 1995, Hallmark Cards, Kansas City, 1996, Wichita (Kans.) Ctr. Arts, 1996, La. State U., Baton Rouge, 1996, Idaho State Arts Coun. Grants, Boise, 1996, Mattie Rhodes Counseling and Art Ctr., Kansas City, 1996, Southwest Ctr. Crafts, San Antonio, 1997, Very Spl. Arts, Albuquerque, 197, Topeka (Kans.) and Shawnee County Pub. Libr., 1997, U. Alaska, Anchorage, 2000, Craft Guild of Tex., Dallas, RISD, 2001, numerous others; mem. fellowship panelist Colo. Coun. on the Arts, Denver, Penland

Sch. of Crafts, N.C., 2001. Solo exhbns. include Pro Art Gallery, St. Louis, 1990, Mobilia Gallery, Cambridge, Mass., 1990, Munson Gallery, Santa Fe, 1990, 92, 94, 95, 97, 99, Mariposa Gallery, Albuquerque, 1990, Joanne Rapp Gallery, Scottsdale, Ariz., 1991, 93, 95, Felicita Found., Escondido, Calif., 1991, Tucumcari (N.Mex.) Area Vocat. Sch., 1992, Manchester Art Ctr., Pitts., 1993, Wetsman Collection, Detroit, 1993, Clovis (N.Mex.) C.C., 1993, Firehouse Art Ctr., 1994, Kavesh Gallery, Sun Valley, Idaho, 1995, Jan Weiner Gallery, Kansas City, 1995, 96, 2000, numerous others; group exhbns. include Fred Jones Mus. Art, U. Okla., Norman, 1995, Roswell (N.Mex.) Mus. & Art Ctr., 1995, Nancy Margolis Gallery, N.Y.C., 1995, Sharadin Art Gallery, Kutztown (Pa.) U., 1995, Richard Kavesh Gallery, 1995, Jan Weiner Gallery, 1995, Ariz. State U. Art Mus., Tempe, 1995, Islip (N.Y.) Mus., 1995, Bruce Kapson Gallery, Santa Monica, Calif., 1996, Site Sante Fe Gallery, 1996, Johnston County C.C., Overland Parks, Kans., 1996, Jane Haslem Gallery, Washington, 1996, Karen Ruhlen Gallery, Santa Fe, 1996, Margo Jacobson Gallery, Portland, Oreg., 1996, Very Spl. Arts Gallery, Albuquerque, 1997, Joanne Rapp Gallery, 1997, Munson Gallery, 1999, Jan Weiner Gallery, 2000, Gallerymateria, Scottsdale, Ariz., 2001, Munson Gallery, Santa Fe, 2001, Univ. Tulsa, Okla., 2001, numerous others; pub. art project include, among others, murals at Great Brook Valley Health Ctr., Worcester, Mass., 1994, Mass. Gen. Hosp., 1996, (mural) Island Nursing Home, Deer Isle, 2000, (mural) Big Red, Lincoln, Nebr., 2000; represented in many permanent collections, including Cooper-Hewitt, N.Y.C., Mus. Fine Arts, Santa Fe, Cleve. Inst. Art, Fed. Reserve Bank, Dallas, Roswell Mus. and Art Ctr., Albuquerque Mus. Fine Arts, City of Tucson (Ariz.), Phoenix Airport, Renwick Gallery Nat. Mus. Am. Art Smithsonian Inst., Washington, Detroit Inst. Art, Hallmark Cards Corp., Kansas City, State Capitol Art Collection, Santa Fe, pvt. collections. Recipient numerous grants, including NEA fellowships, 1986, 88, Kohler Arts-in-Industry grant, Sheboygan, Wis., 1988, 2000, Percent for Art Project grant, Phoenix Arts Coun., 1990, 1992, artist-in-residence grantee Roswell (N.Mex.) Mus. and Art Found., 1986, 2001.

DOMINICK, PETER HOYT, JR. architect; b. N.Y.C., June 9, 1941; s. Peter Hoyt and Nancy Parks D.; m. Philae M. Carver, Dec. 9, 1978; children: Philae M., James W. BA, Yale U., 1963; MArch, U. Pa., 1967. Registered architect, Colo. Project designer John R. Wild, Pty., Ltd., Papau, New Guinea, 1968-69, Spence Robinson, Hong Kong, 1969-71, W.C. Muchow & Ptnrs., Denver, 1971-74; pres. Wazee Design/Devel., Denver, 1973-75; prin. Dominick Architects, Denver, 1975-88; sr. prin. Urban Design Group, Inc., Denver, 1988—. Architect; b. N.Y.C., June 9, 1941; s. Peter Hoyt and Nancy Parks D.; m. Philae M. Carver, Dec. 9, 1978; children— Philae M., James W. B.A., Yale U., 1963; M.Arch., U. Pa., 1967. Registered architect, Colo. Project designer John R. Wild, Pty., Ltd., Papau, New Guinea, 1968-69, Spence Robinson, Hong Kong, 1969-71, W.C. Muchow & Ptnrs., Denver, 1971-74; pres. Wazee Design/Devel., Denver, 1973-75; prin. Dominick Architects, Denver, 1975-88; sr. prin. Urban Design Group, Inc., 1988—. Trustee Downtown Denver, Inc., Civic Ventures, 1984-94 , Met. Denver Arts Alliance, 1983-84; mem. Mayor's Commn. on the Arts, 1983; juror Gov.'s awards, Denver, 1982. Fellow AIA (nat. com. on design, bd. dirs.); mem. Colo. Soc. Architects. Republican. Episcopalian. Club: Cactus, Arapahoe Tennis. Trustee Downtown Denver, Inc., Civic Ventures, 1984-94, Met. Denver Arts Alliance, 1983-84; active Mayor's Commn. on the Arts, 1983; juror Gov.'s awards, Denver, 1982. Fellow AIA (nat. com. on design, bd. dirs.); mem. Colo. Soc. Architects, Cactus Club, Arapahoe Tennis Club. Republican. Episcopalian. Office: Urban Design Group Inc 1621 18th St Ste 200 Denver CO 80202-1267 E-mail: pdominick@urbandesigngroup.com

DONAHUE, RICHARD KING, athletic apparel executive, lawyer; b. Lowell, Mass., July 20, 1927; s. Joseph P. and Dorothy F. (Riordan) D.; m. Nancy Lawson, Sept. 19, 1953; children: Gail M., Timothy J., Michael R., Nancy C., Richard K., Daniel J., Alicia A., Stephen J., Christopher P., Tara E., Philip A. AB, Dartmouth Coll., 1948; JD, Boston U., 1951. Bar: Mass. 1951. Ptnr. Donahue & Donahue, Attys., P.C., Lowell, Mass., 1951-60, 63-90; v.p., chmn. bd. dirs. Nike, Inc., 1990—. Asst. to Pres. Kennedy, Washington, 1960-63. Served with USNR. Recipient Herbert Harley award Am. Judicature Soc., 1981. Mem. Am. Bd. Trial Advs., ABA (gov., ho. of dels. 1972—), Am. Coll. Trial Lawyers, Mass. Bar Assn. (past pres., Gold medal 1979), New Eng. Bar Assn. (past pres.), Union League Club (Boston), Vesper Country Club (Tyngsboro, Mass.), Fed. City Club (Washington), Yorick Club (Lowell). Office: Nike Inc 1 Bowerman Dr Beaverton OR 97005-6453

DONALD, JACK C. oil company executive; b. Edmonton, Alta., Can., Nov. 29, 1934; s. Archibald Scott and Margaret Catherine (Cameron) D.; m. Joan M. Schultz, Oct. 29, 1955. Student, Southern Alberta Inst. Tech., 1959. Owner, operator Parkdale Auto Svc., Edmonton, 1957-60; sales mgr. Sanford Oil Ltd., Edmonton, 1960-63, Pacific Petroleums, Edmonton, 1963-64; pres., gen. mgr. Parkland Oil Products, Red Deer, Alta., 1964-71; v.p. mktg. Turbo Resources, Calgary, 1971-76; pres., chief exec. officer Parkland Industries Ltd., Red Deer, 1977—. Chmn., bd. dirs. Can. Western Bank, Edmonton, Can. Western Trust; v.p., bd. dirs. Brandt Industries Ltd., Regina, 1984—; bd. dirs. TransAlta Utilities Corp., Ensign Resources Svc. Group Inc., Can. Petroleum Products Inst.; pub. mem. coun. Inst. Chartered Accts. Alta. Alderman City of Red Deer, 1971-77. Mem. Rotary. Office: Parkland Industries Ltd 4919 59th St # 236 Red Deer AB Canada T4N 6C9 E-mail: jack.donald@parklandindustries.com

DONALD, JAMES E. career officer; b. Jackson, Miss., Apr. 20, 1949; m. August S. Green; children: Jeff, Cheryl. BA in Polit. Sci. and History, U. Miss., 1970; MPA, U. Mo., 1983; grad., Command Gen. Staff Coll., Nat. War Coll. Commd. 2d lt. U.S. Army Inf., 1970, advanced through grades to maj. gen., bn. adj./comdr. C Co. 1st Bn., 87th Inf. Regiment Germany, inf. advisor Readiness Group Stewart N.Y., inspector gen., inspection team chief 101st Airborne Divsn. Ky., bn. exec. officer 2d Bn., 502d Inf. Regiment, bn. comdr. 1st Bn., 502d Inf. Regiment, chief forces team War Plans divsn., Office Dep. Chief Staff, comdr. 1st Brigade, 101st Airborne divsn., chief mil. support divsn., dep. dir. ops./JE U.S. Pacific Command Hawaii, asst. divsn. comdr. ops. 25th Inf. Divsn. Schofield Barracks, Hawaii-; dep. commdg. gen. U.S. Army Pacific, Ft. Shafter, 1998—. Decorated Def. Superior Svc. medal, Legion of Merit with oak leaf cluster, Bronze Star, Meritorious Svc. medal with four oak leaf clusters, Army Commendation medal with oak leaf cluster, Nat. Def. Svc. medal with svc. star, Armed Forces Expeditionary medal, Kuwait Liberation medal, S.W. Asia Svc. ribbon.

DONALDSON, EDWARD MOSSOP, research scientist, aquaculture consultant; b. Whitehaven, Cumbria, England, June 25, 1939; arrived in Can., 1961; s. Edward and Margaret Elizabeth (Mossop) D.; m. Judith Denise Selwood, Aug. 8, 1964; 1 child, Heather Jean. BSc with honors, Sheffield (Eng.) U., 1961, DSc, 1975; PhD, U. B.C., Vancouver, Can., 1964. Rsch. scientist Dept. Fisheries and Oceans, West Vancouver, B.C., 1965-97, sect. head fish culture rsch., 1981-89, sect. head biotech., genetics and nutrition, 1989-97, head Ctr. of Disciplinary Excellence for Biotech. and Genetics in Aquaculture, 1987-97, scientist emeritus, 1997—; cons. in aquaculture and the environment, 1997—. Hon. rsch. assoc. U. B.C., 1979-88, adj. prof., 1988—; cons. finfish aquaculture FAO, UN Devel. Program, Can. Internat. Devel. Agy., Internat. Devel. Rsch. Ctrs., U.S. AID, Office of Tech. assessment of the U.S. Congress, Can. Exec. Svc. Overseas, Sci. Com. on Problems of Environment, WHO, U.S. Seagrant, others; mem. Nat. Scis. and Engring. Rsch. Coun. Can., mem. strategic grant selection com. for food agriculture and aquaculture, 1988-93; mem., active in strategic planning for applied rsch. and knowledge com. biotech. B.C. Sci. Coun. Mem. editl. bd. [illegible] and Comparative Endocrinology, 1971-78, Can. Jour. Fisheries and Aquatic Sci., 1985-88, Aquaculture, 1983—, sect. editor, 1999—; mem. editl. bd. Can. Jour. Zoology, 1986-91, Revista Italiana de Acquacoltura, 1991-96; contbr. over 400 articles to sci. jours. and conf. procs.; contbr. to books on endocrinology, biotech. and aquaculture; patentee in field. Recipient award for best publs. in Transactions of Am. Fisheries Soc., 1977, Ministerial Merit award Min. of Fisheries and Oceans, 1989, B.C. Sci. Coun. Gold medal, 1992, Ministries Commendation award, 1997; B.C. Sugar Co. scholar, 1961; NIH fellow, 1964-65; recipient Thomas W. Eadie medal Royal Soc. Can., 1995 Fellow Acad. Sci. of Royal Soc. Can. (mem. Rowmanoswky medal com. 1994, Thomas W. Eadie medal com. 1995-96); mem. Can. Soc. Zoologists (councilor 1980-83), World Aquaculture Soc., Aquaculture Assn. Can. Office: Dept Fisheries & Oceans 4160 Marine Dr West Vancouver BC Canada V7V 1N6 E-mail: donaldso@direct.ca

DONALDSON, SARAH SUSAN, radiologist; b. Portland, Oreg., Apr. 20, 1939; BS, RN, U. Oreg., 1961; MD, Harvard U., 1968. Intern U. Wash., 1968-69; resident in radiol. therapy Stanford (Calif.) Med. Ctr., 1969-72; fellow in pediatric oncology Inst. Gustave-Roussy, 1972-73; prof. radiol. oncology Stanford U. Sch. Medicine., 1973—. Office: Stanford U Med Ctr Dept Radio/Oncology 300 Pasteur Dr Palo Alto CA 94304-2203

DONALDSON, SCOTT, English language educator, writer; b. Mpls., Nov. 11, 1928; s. Frank Arthur and Ruth Evelyn (Chase) D.; m. Janet Kay Mikelson, Apr. 12, 1957 (div.); children— Matthew Chase, Stephen Scott, Andrew Wilson; m. Vivian Lee Baker, Mar. 5, 1982; stepchildren— Janet Breckenridge, Britton Donaldson. BA in English, Yale U., 1951; MA in English, U. Minn., 1952, PhD in Am. Studies, 1966. Reporter Mpls. Star, 1956-58; editor, pub. Bloomington Sun, Minn., 1958-61; exec. editor Sun Newspapers, Twin City suburbs, 1961-64; asst. prof. English Coll. William and Mary, Williamsburg, Va., 1966-69, assoc. prof., 1969-74, prof., 1974—, Louise G.T. Cooley prof. English, 1984-92. Author: The Suburban Myth, 1969, Poet in America: Winfield Townley Scott, 1972, By Force of Will: The Life and Art of Ernest Hemingway, 1977, (with Ann Massa) American Literature: Nineteenth and Early Twentieth Centuries, 1978, Fool for Love, F. Scott Fitzgerald, 1983, John Cheever: A Biography, 1988, Archibald MacLeish: An American Life, 1992 (Ambassador Book award), Hemingway vs. Fitzgerald, 1999; editor: On the Road, 1979, Critical Essays on F. Scott Fitzgerald's The Great Gatsby, 1984, Conversations with John Cheever, 1987, New Essays on a Farewell to Arms, 1990, Cambridge Companion to Hemingway, 1996; also numerous revs. and articles on Am. lit. and Am. culture. Served with U.S. Army, 1953-56 Recipient Mid Am. award Soc. for Study of Midwestern Lit., 1996, Monroe K. Spears award, 1999; Fulbright Sr. lectureship, 1970-71, 79-80; fellow Bruern Found., 1972-73, MacDowell Colony, 1980-81, Rockefeller Found., 1982, NEH, 1984-85, 90—. Mem. MLA, Am. Studies Assn., Fulbright Alumni Assn. (bd. dirs. 1977-80), Authors Guild, Hemingway Soc. (treas. 1999—, pres. 2000—), PEN, Nat. Book Critics Cir., Mpls. Club, Minikahda Club (Mpls.), Cosmos Club (Washington), Phi Beta Kappa. Avocations: tennis, golf, duplicate bridge. Home and Office: Desert Highlands 303 10040 E Happy Valley Rd Scottsdale AZ 85255-2395 E-mail: scottd10@mac.com

DONE, ROBERT STACY, educator, consultant; b. Tucson, Apr. 7, 1965; s. Richard Avon Done and Nancy Jane (Meeks) Burks; m. Michele Renae Barwick, May 17, 1987 (div. Mar. 1990); m. Elizabeth Evans Robinson, Feb. 20, 1993; children: Rachel Evans, Ethan James. AS in Law Enforcement, BS in Criminal Justice Adminstrn., Mo. So. State Coll., 1987; MPA, U. Ariz., 1992, MS in Mgmt., 1998; PhD in Mgmt., U. Az., 2000. Criminal investigator Pima County, Tucson, 1988-99; asst. rsch. prof. U. Ariz., Tucson, 2000—. Pres. Data Methods Corp., Tucson, 1984—. Contbr. articles to profl. jours. Mem. APA, Soc. for Indsl. and Orgnl. Psychology, Acad. Mgmt., Soc. for Human Resource Mgmt. Home: 805 N Camino Miramonte Tucson AZ 85716-4623

DONLEY, DAVE, state legislator; b. Anchorage, Aug. 29, 1954; BS in Polit. Sci., U. Oreg., 1976; JD, U. Wash., 1979. Mem. Alaska Ho. of Reps., 1986-92, Alaska Senate, Dist. J, Juneau, 1992—. Former vol. fireman; active Anchorage Waterways Coun., Anchorage Sch. Dist. Curriculum Com., Alaska Juvenile Justice Com. Recipient Victims for Justice Svc. award, Legis. award MADD, 1991, 92, Svc. award Alaska Pub. Radio, Neighborhood Support award Anchorage Neighborhood Housing; named Sportsman Legislator of Yr., Alaska Outdoors Coun., 1989. Mem. NRA (life, Defender of Freedom award 1994), MENSA, Alaska Bar Assn., Constrn. Laborers 341, Phi Beta Kappa. Republican. Avocations: hunting, fishing, softball, bicycling. Office: State Capitol 120 4th St Rm 508 Juneau AK 99801-1142 also: 716 W 4th Ave Ste 430 Anchorage AK 99501-2107 Fax: 907-269-0238. E-mail: donley@legis.state.ak.us

DONLEY, DENNIS LEE, school librarian; b. Port Hueneme, Calif., July 19, 1950; s. Mickey Holt and Joan Elizabeth (Smith) D.; m. Ruth Ann Shank, June 10, 1972; children: Eric Holt, Evan Scott. AA, Ventura Coll., 1970; BA with honors, U. Calif., Santa Barbara, 1973; MLS, San Jose State U., 1976. Cert. secondary tchr., Calif. Libr. media tchr. San Diego Unified Sch. Dist., 1975—. Lectr. Calif. State U., L.A., 1987-89; libr. cons. San Diego C.C. Dist., 1990, chmn. sch. adv. com. Point Loma H.S., San Diego, 1986-87; coop. book rev. bd. San Diego County, 1984-86; creator adult sch. curriculum, 1984-86; contbr. Deadbase X, Deadbase 94, The Deadhead's Taping Compendium, Vols. 1-3. Mem. ALA, Calif. Libr. Media Educators Assn. Avocations: reading, music, fitness. Office: Hoover HS 4474 El Cajon Blvd San Diego CA 92115-4312 E-mail: ddonley@mail.sandi.net

DONLEY, RUSSELL LEE, III, former state legislator; b. Salt Lake City, Feb. 3, 1939; s. R. Lee and Leona (Sherwood) D.; m. Karen Kocherhans, June 4, 1960; children: Tammera Sue, Tonya Kay, Christina Lynn. BSCE with honors, U. Wyo., 1961; MS in Engring., U. Fla., 1962. From mem. to spkr. of house Wyo. Ho. of Reps., 1969-84; chmn. bd. Nat. Ctr. Constl. Studies, Wyo. region, 1983-87; CEO Constitution Schs. Inc., Casper, 1987—; owner Russell L. Donley & Assocs., 1988—; v.p. Nat. Bus. Solutions, LLC, 1997-99. Chmn. appropriations com. Wyo Ho. of Reps., 1975-78, chmn. legis. mgmt. coun., 1983-84. Chmn. Western Region Coun. State Govts., 1982-83; Rep. candidate for gov. Wyo, 1986; precinct committeeman Rep. Cen. Com., 1987-96; chmn. Wyo. Young Reps., 1968; fin. chmn. Natrona County Rep. Cen. Com., 1970; pres. bd. dirs. YMCA, Casper, 1976-77; state chmn. Initiative # 3 dr. Invest in Wyo. not Wall St., 1994. Recipient award for engring. excellence Am. Cons. Engrs. Council; recipient Legislator of Yr. award Nat. Republican Legislators Assn., 1981; named Wyo. Outstanding Young Engr. Sigma Tau, 1974, Disting. Wyo. Engr. Tau Beta Pi., 1976 Former mem. Am. Water Works Assn., Nat. Soc. Profl. Engrs., Wyo. Soc. Profl. Engrs., Wyo. Engring. Soc., Wyo. Assn. Cons. Engrs. and Surveyors Mem. LDS Ch. Home: 1140 Ivy Ln Casper WY 82609-2702 Office: 240 S Wolcott St Ste 234 Casper WY 82601-2552 E-mail: russ@nbsweb.com

DONLON, TIMOTHY A., cytogeneticist; b. Pasadena, Calif., Apr. 16, 1952; PhD, U. Oreg., 1984. Med. genetics fellow Children's Hosp., Boston, 1984-86; chief molecular clin. cytogenetics Kapiolani Med. Ctr., Honolulu, 1992-98, dir., 1995; assoc. prof., rschr. Cancer Rsch. Ctr. of Hawaii, 1998—; dir., lab. molecular and cytogenetics Ohana Genetics, Honolulu, 1998-2000; dir. lab molecular genetics Queens Med. Ctr., Honolulu, 2000—. Assoc. prof. U. Hawaii Burns Sch. Medicine, Honolulu, [illegible] Office: Queens Med Ctr [illegible] Honolulu HI 96814-1701

DONNALLY, PATRICIA BRODERICK, writer; b. Cheverly, Md., Mar. 11, 1955; d. James Duane and Olga Frances (Duenas) Broderick; m. Robert Andrew Donnally, Dec. 30, 1977; 1 child, Danielle Christine. BS, U. Md., 1977. Fashion editor The Washington Times, 1983-85, The San Francisco Chronicle, 1985-2000; sr. fashion and beauty editor eLuxury.com, 2000. Recipient Atrium award U. Ga., 1984, 87-89, 90, 94-98, 99, Lulu award U. Ga., 1985, 87, award Am. Cancer soc., 1991, Aldo award, 1994, George A. Hough III award, 1999. Avocation: travel. E-mail: donnallyt@hotmail.com

DONNALLY, ROBERT ANDREW, lawyer, real estate broker; b. Washington, July 10, 1953; s. Reaumur Stearnes and Katherine Ann (Sutliff) D.; m. Patricia Kane Broderick, Dec. 30, 1977; 1 child, Danielle Christine. BA in Psychology, U. Md., 1976; JD, U. Balt., 1980; cert. in bus., Stanford U., 1996. Bar: Md. 1980, Calif. 1986. Pvt. practice, Oxen Hill, Md., 1980-81; rsch. contract staff officer Dept. Def., Ft. Meade, 1981-85; with legal and contractual ops. ARGOSystems, Inc., Sunnyvale, Calif., 1985-90; asst. dir. Inst. Def. Analyses, San Diego, 1990-91; dep. chief counsel ARGOSystems, Inc., 1991-93, chief counsel, corp. sec., 1993-98; chief counsel comms. and infomanagement divsn. Boeing Co., 1997-98; gen. counsel, mng. ptnr. BT Comml. Real Estate, Palo Alto, Calif., 1998-99; assoc. gen. counsel Inhale Therapeutic Sys. Inc., San Carlos, 1999—. Editor-in-chief The Forum, 1979-80. Active The Pillars Soc./United Way, 1991-98. Waxter Legal scholar U. Baltimore, 1978. Mem. Am. Corp. Counsel, Nat. Contract Mgmt. Assn., Md. Bar Assn., Calif. Bar Assn., Assn. of Silicon Valley Brokers, Tae Kwon Do Assn. (Black Belt), Black Belt, Kukkiwon World Tae Kwon Do Assn. Avocations: martial arts, marathons, hiking, travel, reading. E-mail: rdonnally@inhale.com

DONNELLY, RUSSELL JAMES, physicist, educator; b. Hamilton, Ont., Can., Apr. 16, 1930; naturalized 2000; s. Clifford Ernest and Bessie (Harrison) D.; m. Marian Card, Jan. 21, 1956; 1 son, James. BSc, McMaster U., 1951, MSc, 1952, LLD, 1999; MS, Yale U., 1953, PhD, 1956. Faculty U. Chgo., 1956-66, prof. physics, 1965-66, U. Oreg., Eugene, 1966—, chmn. dept., 1966-72, 82-83; vis. prof. Niels Bohr Inst., Copenhagen, Denmark, 1972; co-founder Pine Mountain Obs., 1967. Cons. GM Co. Rsch. Labs., 1958-68, NSF, 1968-76, 79-84, mem. adv. panel for physics, 1970-73, chmn., 1971-72; mem. adv. coms. on matls. rsch., 1979-84; mem. Task Force on Fundamental Physics and Chemistry in Space, Space Sci. Bd., NRC; cons. Jet Propulsion Lab., Calif. Inst. Tech., Pasadena, 1973-82; chmn. Sci. Adv. Com. for Low Temp. Facilities in Space, 1990-91; mem. fluid dynamics discipline working group, NASA, 1992-95; gen. chmn. 20th Internat. Conf. on Low Temp. Physics, 1993. Author: (with Parks, Glaberson) Experimental Superfluidity, 1967, (with Francis) Cryogenic Science and Technology: Contributions of Leo Dana, 1985, Quantized Vortices in Helium II, 1991; editor: (with Herman, Prigogine) Non-Equilibrium Thermodynamics Variational Techniques and Stability, 1966, High Reynolds Number Flows Using Liquid and Gaseous Helium, 1991, Procs. 20th Internat. Conf. Low Temperature Physics, Physica B, 1994; editor: (with Sreenivasan) Flow at Ultra-High Reynolds and Rayleigh Numbers; mem. editorial bd. Physics of Fluids, 1966-68, Phys. Rev. E, 1978-84, assoc. editor, 1987-93; mem. editorial bd. Jour. Phys. and Chem. Ref. Data, 1989-92, Handbook of Chemistry and Physics, 1989-98; contbr. articles to profl. jours. Bd. dirs. U. Oreg. Found., 1970-72, 88-91, investment com., 1990-91; bd. dirs. Oreg. Mus. Park Commn., 1975-87, chmn., 1975-82; bd. dirs. Oreg. Bach Festival, 1975-87, Oreg. Mozart Players, 1990-93. Alfred P. Sloan fellow, 1959-63; sr. vis. fellow Sci. Rsch. Coun., U.K., 1978; recipient Disting. Alumnus award McMaster U., 1992, Lars Onsager medal Norwegian U. Sci. and Tech., 1996; 1995 Chia-Shun Yih lectr. U. Mich., 1996 Fritz London Meml. lectr. Duke U, Howard Vollum award Reed Coll., 1997. Fellow AAAS, Am. Phys. Soc. (exec. com. div. fluid dynamics 1966-72, 80-84, 88-91, sec.-treas. 1967-70, 88-91, chmn. 1971-72, 82-83, APS Otto Laporte award 1974), Inst. of Physics (London); mem. Nat. Trust for Scotland, Soc. Archtl. Historians, Cosmos Club. Episcopalian. Achievements include research on physics fluids, especially hydrodynamic stability, turbulence and superfluidity. Home: 2175 Olive St Eugene OR 97405-2837 Office: Univ Oreg Dept Physics Eugene OR 97403-1274 E-mail: russ@vortex.uoregon.edu

DONOGHUE, JOHN, communications executive; Sr. v.p. mktg. MCI Comm. Corp., Washington, 1993-99. Bd. dirs. Firstworld Comm., Inc., 2000—. Office: Firstworld Comm 8390 E Crescent Pkwy Ste 300 Greenwood Vlg CO 80111-2813

DONOGHUE, MILDRED RANSDORF, education educator; b. Cleve. d. James and Caroline (Sychra) Ransdorf; m. Charles K. Donoghue (dec. 1982); children: Kathleen, James. EdD, UCLA, 1962; JD, Western State U., 1979. Asst. prof. edn. and reading Calif. State U., Fullerton, 1962-66, assoc. prof., 1966-71, prof., 1971—. Author: Foreign Languages and the Schools, 1967, Foreign Languages and the Elementary School Child, 1968, The Child and the English Language Arts, 1971, 75, 79, 85, 90, Using Literature Activities to Teach Content Areas to Emergent Readers, 2001; co-author: Second Languages in Primary Education, 1979; contbr. articles to profl. jours. and Ednl. Resources Info. Ctr. U.S. Dept. Edn. Mem. AAUP, AAUW, TESOL, Nat. Network for Early Lang. Learning, Nat. Coun. Tchrs. English, Nat. Coun. Tchrs. Math., Am. Dialect Soc., Am. Ednl. Rsch. Assn., Nat. Soc. for Study of Edn., Am. Assn. Tchrs. Spanish and Portuguese, Internat. Reading Assn., Nat. Assn. Edn. Young Children, Orange County Med. Assn. Women's Aux., Assn. for Childhood Edn. Internat., Phi Beta Kappa, Phi Kappa Phi, Pi Lambda Theta, Alpha Upsilon Alpha. Address: Dept Elem and Bilingual Edn 800 State College Blvd Fullerton CA 92834

DONOVAN, DENNIS MICHAEL, psychologist, researcher; b. Oregon City, Oreg., June 7, 1948; s. Dennis Joseph Donovan and Josephine R. (Spees) Middleton; m. Anne Mary Waldock, Jan. 27, 1973; 1 child, Collin Thomas. BS, Seattle U., 1970; MA, Western Wash. U., 1972; PhD, U. Wash., 1980. Lic. psychologist, Wash. Asst. chief alcohol dependence treatment program VA Med. Ctr., Seattle, 1980-86, chief in-patient sect. addictions treatment ctr., 1986—, asst. chief addictions treatment ctr., 1987—. Assoc. prof. dept. psychiatry and behavioral scis. U. Wash. Sch. of Medicine, 1984—; cons., reviewer Nat. Inst. on Alcohol Abuse & Alcoholism, Rockville, Md., 1986—; assoc. editor Psychology of Addictive Behaviors, Chgo., 1990—. Editor: Assessment of Addictive Behaviors, 1988; field editor: Jour. of Studies on Alcohol, 1987—; contbr. numerous articles to profl. jours. Named one of Outstanding Young Man of Am., U.S. Jaycees, 1977. Mem. Am. Psychol. Assn., Assn. for the Advancement of Behavior Therapy, Rsch. Soc. on Alcoholism, Soc. Psychologists in Addictive Behavior (sec., treas. 1988—), Wash. State Psychol. Assn. Office: VA Med Ctr 1660 S Columbian Way Seattle WA 98108-1532

DONOVAN, JOHN ARTHUR, lawyer; b. N.Y.C., Apr. 11, 1942; children: Lara, Alex. AB, Harvard U., 1965; JD, Fordham Law Sch., 1967. Bar: N.Y. 1967, U.S. Tax. Ct. 1968, U.S. Ct. Appeals (2nd cir), 1968, U.S. Dist. Ct. (so., no. dists.) N.Y. 1969, U.S. Supreme Ct. 1971, U.S. Ct. Appeals (10th cir.) 1972, U.S. Ct. Appeals (9th cir.) 1976, Calif. 1982, U.S. Dist. Ct. (so., no. dists.) Calif. 1982, U.S. Ct. Appeals (5th cir.) 1983, Alaska 1993. Assoc. Hughes, Hubbard & Reed, N.Y.C., 1967-74, ptnr. N.Y.C., L.A., 1974-85, Skadden, Arps, Slate, Meagher & Flom, L.A., 1985—. Mem. adj. faculty law sch. U. So. Calif., L.A., 1986-87. Office: Skadden Arps Slate Meagher & Flom 300 S Grand Ave Ste 3400 Los Angeles CA 90071-3109

DONOVAN, WILLARD PATRICK, retired elementary education educator; b. Grand Rapids, Mich., Sept. 1, 1930; s. Willard Andrew and Thelma Alfreda (Davis) D.; m. Dorothy Jane Nester, Nov. 27, 1954 (dec. [illegible] MA, 1969. Cert. grades K-8, Mich. Enlisted U.S. Army, 1947, advanced through grades to master sgt., 1953; platoon sgt. U.S. Army of Occupation, Korea, 1947-48, Japan, 1948-50, U.S. Army Korean War Svc., 1950-51; ret. U.S. Army, 1964; pharm. sales Nat. Drug Co., Detroit, 1964-66; tchr. Cromie Elem. Sch. Warren (Mich.) Consol. Schs., 1966—, ret., 1995. Reading textbook and curriculum devel. com. Warren (Mich.) Consol. Schs., 1969-73, sci. com., 1970-95; curriculum and textbook com. Macomb County Christian Schs., Warren, 1982-95. Decorated Combat Infantry badge U.S. Army, Korea, 1947-50, Purple heart with three clusters, Korea-Japan Svc. medal, 1951, Presdl. citation, 1951, Korean medal with three campaign clusters, 1951, Nat. Def. Svc. medal, 1951, Bronze star, Silver star; Chosin few Army and Marines Assn. 31st Inf. Assn. Mem. NRA, Am. Quarterhouse Assn., Assn. U.S. Army, Detroit Area Coun. Tchrs. Math., Met. Detroit Sci. Tchrs. Assn., The Chosin Few (U.S. Army), Nat. Edn. Assn., Mich. Edn. Assn., Warren (Mich.) Edn. Assn., U.S. Army Assn. Avocations: theatre, arts, horsemanship, traveling, pistol shooting. Home: PO Box 563 8440 Mission Hills Arizona City AZ 85223

DONZE, JERRY LYNN, electrical engineer; b. Wauneta, Nebr., June 12, 1943; s. John Henry and Virgina May (Francis) D.; m. Marilyn Grace Bascue, Feb. 22, 1964 (div. May. 1980); children: Scott L., Michele A.; m. Sandra Kay Morris, July 25, 1981. Cert. technician, Denver Inst. Tech., 1964; BSEE, U. Colo., 1972; postgrad., Advanced Metaphysics Inst. Religios Sci., 1986. Electronic technician A.B.M. Co., Lakewwod, Colo., 1964-71; computer programmer Nat. Bur. Standards, Boulder, 1971-72; electronic engr. Autometrics Co., Boulder, 1972-76, Gates Research and Devel., Denver, 1976-77; devel. engr. Emerson Electric Co., Lakewood, 1977; engring. mgr. Storage Tech., Louisville, 1977—. Cons. Sun Co., Arvada, Colo., 1974-75. Patentee in field. Mem. IEEE Student Soc. (treas. 1971-72), Eta Kappa Nu. Republican. Religious Scientist. Avocation: giving workshops and presentations. Home: 12021 W 54th Ave Arvada CO 80002-1907 Office: Storage Tech 2270 S 88th St Louisville CO 80028-0002

DONZI, ALEC See SCHERF, DIETMAR

DOOLEY, CALVIN MILLARD, congressman; b. Visalia, Calif., Jan. 11, 1954; BS, U. Calif., Davis, 1977; MA, Stanford U., 1987. Mem. U.S. Congresses from 17th Calif. dist., 1991-93, U.S. Congresses from 20th Calif. dist., 1993—; mem. agriculture com.; mem. natural resources com. Democrat. Methodist. Office: Ho of Reps 1201 Longworth Bldg Washington DC 20515-0520*

DOOLEY, GEORGE JOSEPH, III, metallurgist; b. Greenwich, Conn., Aug. 8, 1941; s. George Joseph and Susan Marilyn (Robustelli) D.; children: Deborah Susan, Jennifer Ann, Daniel Paul; m. Marye Khrys Von Tellrop, Oct. 27, 1984; children: Samantha Joel, Charles Douglas, Anastacia Halley, James Huston, Cynthia Maureen, Sandra Robin, Karen Linn, Kimberly Marie. BS, U. Notre Dame, 1963; MS, Iowa State U., 1966; PhD, Oreg. State U., 1969. Research asst. Ames (Iowa) Lab. AEC, 1963-66; research metallurgist U.S. Bur. Mines, Albany, Oreg., 1966-68, dir. Albany Research Ctr., 1984—; research scientist Aerospace Research Labs. USAF, Wright Patterson AFB, Ohio, 1968-72; dir. research and devel. Oreg. Metall. Corp., Albany, 1974-83, dir. metall. and quality assurance, 1983-84. Mem. metallurgy adv. bd. Linn Benton Community Coll., Albany, 1976—. Contbr. articles to profl. jours. Served to capt. USAF, 1968-72. Democrat. Roman Catholic. Home: 8804 NW Arboretum Rd Corvallis OR 97330-9571 Office: US Dept Energy Albany Rsch Ctr 1450 Queen Ave SW Albany OR 97321-2152

DOOLEY, JAMES H. product company executive; BS in Agrl. Engring., Calif. Poly., San Luis Obispo, 1971; M in Engring., U. Calif., Davis, 1972; PhD in Forest Resources/Forest Engring., U. Wash., 2000. Registered profl. engr., Hawaii, Wash. Dir. control and devel. Puna Papaya Inc., Keaau, Hawaii, 1973-77; mgr. nursery, seed orchard and greenhouse sys. unit-silvicultural engring. dept. Weyerhaeuser Co., Tacoma, 1977-82, mgr., biomech. engring unit, diversified r & d, 1982-85, dir. rsch. and engring., nursery products div., 1986-89, product engring. mgr., sensor and simulation products div., 1989-90, program mgr., corp. r & d div., 1991-94, interim mgr. strategic biol. scis. program, 1994-95; pres., CEO Silverbrook Ltd., Federal Way, Wash., 1995—. Mem. Nursery and Greenhouse Plant Prodn. Sys. com. ASAE, 1977, Environ. Plant Structures com., 1979—, expt. sta. com. on orgn. and policy Nat. Assn. State U. and Land Grant Colls., 1986, plant biol. engring., strategic planning com., 1989-94; task force on univ., industry and govt. coop. ASAE, 1989; emerging technologies devel. com. ASAE, 1994-95; emerging technologies adv. com. chair ASAE, 1995-96; adv. com. past chmn. biol. engring ASAE, 1992-93; engring and tech. accreditation com. ASAE, 1984—; comprehensive review team U.S. Dept. Agr., Coop. State Rsch. Svc., Auburn U., 1989, Pa. State U., 1991, U. Ga., 1993; adv. com. forest biology project Inst. Paper Sci. Tech., 1994; adv. group biol. engring. program indsl. adv. group Wash. State U., 1994—, agrl. engring. dept. Calif.Poly, 1992—; engring. accreditation commn. ABET, 1990-95. Presenter in field; contbr. articles to profl. jours., newspapers and periodicals. Recipient Am. Soc. Agrl. Engrs. fellow award, 1996. Fellow Am. Soc. Agrl. Engrs. (Pres. Citation, 1994, Dirs. award, 1994, Dir. Citation, 1996, Fellow award 1996); mem. Coun. Forest Engring., Inst. Biol. Engring. (pres. 2000), Licensing Execs. Soc., Soc. Am. Foresters. Achievements include patents for a Seed Planter a double-row vacuum precision sower for foresty and other densely planted seeds, Seed Supply Sytem for Multiple Row Sower a method of ensuring all rows of a sower run out of seed at the same time, engineered wood structure for watershed restoration. Address: 1911 SW Campus Dr # 545 Federal Way WA 98023-6473

DOOLEY, JAMES T. electronic manfacturing executive; BBA in Acctg., Hofstra U. Sr. mgmt. IRT Corp., Eli Lilly Co., INTERMEDICS Inc., Johnson and Johnson, Inc.; controller elec. component sys. ESI, 1992-94, corp. controller, 1994, dir. manfacturing, 1994-00, CFP, v.p., 2000—. Office: Electro Scientific Ind Inc 13900 NW Science Park Dr Portland OR 97229-5497

DOOLITTLE, JOHN TAYLOR, congressman; b. Glendale, Calif., Oct. 30, 1950; s. Merrill T. and Dorothy Doolittle; B.A. in History with honors, U. Calif., Santa Cruz, 1972; J.D., McGeorge Sch. Law, U. Pacific, 1978; m. Julia Harlow, Feb. 17, 1979; children: John Taylor Jr., Courtney A. Bar: Calif. 1978. Mem. Calif. State Senate, 1980-90; mem. U.S. Congress from 4th Calif. dist., 1991—; mem. agriculture com., mem. resource com., chair water and power resources subcom. Republican. Mem. LDS Ch. *

DOOLITTLE, RUSSELL FRANCIS, biochemist, educator; b. New Haven, Jan. 10, 1931; s. Russell A. and Mary Catherine (Bohan) D.; m. Frances Ann Tynan, June 6, 1931; children: Lawrence Russell, William Edward. BA, Wesleyan U., 1952; MA, Trinity Coll., 1957; PhD, Harvard U., 1962. Instr. biochemistry Amherst (Mass.) Coll., 1961-62; asst. research biologist U. Calif.-San Diego, La Jolla, 1964-65, asst. prof. biochemistry, 1965-67, assoc. prof., 1967-72, prof., 1972—, chmn. dept. chemistry, 1981-84, rsch. prof. biology and chemistry, 1994—. Advisor Can. Inst. for Advanced Rsch. Author: of Urfs and Orfs, 1987; contbr. articles to profl. jours. Served as sgt. U.S. Army, 1952-54. Guggenheim fellow, 1984-85, Non-Resident fellow Salk Inst., 1990-98. Fellow AAAS; mem. NAS, Am. Soc. Biol. Chemistry, Am. Acad. Arts and Scis., Am. Philos. Soc. (Paul Ehrlich prize 1989, Stein and Moore award 1991). Office: Univ Calif San Diego Ctr Molecular Genetics La Jolla CA 92093

DOR, YORAM, accountant, firm executive; b. Tel Aviv, Apr. 17, 1945; came to U.S., 1974; s. Simon and Shulamit (Remple) D.; m. Ofra Lipshitz, Apr. 9, 1967; children: Gil, Ron. Diploma in Acctg., Hebrew U. Jerusalem, 1969; BA in Econs., Tel Aviv U., 1971; MBA, UCLA, 1977. CPA, Calif. Sr. auditor Somekh Chaikin, CPA, Tel Aviv, 1969-72; CFO East African Hotels, Dar-es-Salaam, Tanzania, 1972-74; staff acct. Hyatt Med. Enterprises, Inc. (name now Nu Med, Inc.), Encino, Calif., 1974-75, asst. contr., 1975-77, corp. contr., 1977-79, v.p. fin., 1979-82, sr. v.p. fin., CFO, 1982-87, exec. v.p. fin., CFO, 1987-95; ptnr. Sloman and Dor, Encino, 1995—; also bd. dirs. Mem. AICPA, Calif. Soc. CPA's. Office: Sloman & Dor 16633 Ventura Blvd Ste 913 Encino CA 91436-1849

DORAN, TIMOTHY PATRICK, educational administrator; b. N.Y.C., July 1, 1949; s. Joseph Anthony and Claire (Griffin) D.; m. Kathleen Matava, Aug. 1, 1981; children: Claire Marie, Bridget Anne. BA in Econs., Le Moyne Coll., 1971; MA in Teaching, U. Alaska, 1984, Education Specialist, 1990. Cert. type A secondary, econs., type B K-12 prin., supt. Svc. rep. Emigrant Savings Bank, N.Y.C., 1971-72; exec., dir. Project Equality Northwest, Seattle, 1972-73, Jesuit Vol. Corps., Portland, Oreg., 1973-75, adminstv. advisor Kaltag City (Alaska) coun., 1975-77; program developer Diocese Fairbanks, Alaska, 1978-81, adminstr., supt. St. Mary's Cath. High Sch., 1981-83; prin. intern U. Alaska, Fairbanks, 1984, vis. instr., 1990-94; tchr. Anthony A. Andrews Sch., St. Michael, Alaska, 1984-86; prin., tchr. James C. Isabell Sch, Teller, 1986-88; prin. Unalakleet (Alaska) Schs., 1988-90, Denali Elem. Sch., Fairbanks, 1992—. Acad. coord. U. Alaska, summers 1984-86, Elderhostel instr., 1991—, sch. edn. curr. adv. bd., 1998—; docent U. Alaska Mus., 1991. Active nat. com. Campaign for Human Devel., 1980-83; mem. manpower planning coun. Tanana Chiefs Conf., 1976-77, parish coun. Sacred Heart Cathedral, 1979-81; Sunday Sch. tchr. St. Mark's Univ. Parish, 1990-97, adv. coun., 1998-2001; mem. com. chair Fairbanks Arts and Culture in Edn., 1995—; bd. dirs., v.p., pres. Literacy Coun. Alaska, 1997—. Recipient Merit awards Alaska Dept. Edn., 1986-90; named Alaska Disting. Prin., 1998. Mem. ASCD, Nat. Assn. Elem. Sch. Prins., Alaska Assn. Elem. Sch. Prins. (v.p., pres.-elect, pres. 2000—), Fairbanks Prins. Assn. (v.p., pres. 1999-2000), Alaska Math. Consortium (bd. dirs. 1992-99). Home: 512 Windsor Dr Fairbanks AK 99709-3439 Office: Denali Elem Sch 1042 Lathrop St Fairbanks AK 99701-4124 E-mail: tdoran@northstar.k12,ak.us

DORATO, PETER, electrical and computer engineering educator; b. N.Y.C., Dec. 17, 1932; s. Fioretto and Rosina (Lachello) D.; m. Marie Madeleine Turlan, June 2, 1956; children: Christopher, Alexander, Sylvia, Veronica. BEE, CCNY, 1955; MSEE, Columbia U., 1956; DEE, Poly. Inst. N.Y., 1961. Registered profl. engr., Colo. Lectr. elec. engring. dept. CCNY, 1956-57; instr. elec. engring. Poly. Inst. N.Y., Bklyn., 1957-61, prof., 1961-72; prof. elec. engring., dir. Resource System Analysis U. Colo., Colorado Springs, 1972-76; Gardner-Zemke prof. elec. and computer engring. U. N.Mex., Albuquerque, 1984—, chmn. dept., 1976-84. Hon. chaired prof. Nanjing Aero. Inst., 1989; vis. prof. Politecnico di Torino, Italy, 1991-92l dir. Ctr. for Intelligent Systems Engring. U. N.Mex., 2001. Author: Analytic Feedback Systems Design, 2000; co-author Linear Quadratic Control, 1995, Robust Control for Unstructured Perturbations, 1992, Robust Control-System Design, 1996, Italian Culture—A View from America, 2001; editor: Robust Control, Recent Results in Robust Control and Advances in Adaptive Control, reprint vols., 1987, 90, 91, IEEE Press Reprint Vol. Series, 1989-90; assoc. editor Automatica Jour., 1969-83, 89-92, editor rapid publs., 1994-98; assoc. editor IEEE Trans on Edn., 1989-91; contbr. articles on control systems theory to profl. jours. Recipient John R. Ragazzini edn. award Am. Automatic Control Coun., 1998 Fellow IEEE (3rd Millenium medal); mem. IEEE Control Systems Soc. (Disting. Mem. award). Democrat. Home: 1514 Roma Ave NE Albuquerque NM 87106-4513 Office: U NMex Dept Elec Computer Eng Albuquerque NM 87131-1356 E-mail: peter@eece.unm.edu

DORER, FRED HAROLD, retired chemistry educator; b. Auburn, Calif., May 3, 1936; s. Fred H. and Mary E. (Fisher) D.; m. Marilyn Pearl Young, Sept. 6, 1958; children: Garrett Michael, Russell Kenneth. B.S., Calif. State U.-Long Beach, 1961; Ph.D., U. Wash., 1965; postgrad., U. Freiburg, (Germany), 1965-66. Rsch. chemist Shell Devel. Co., Emeryville, Calif., 1966-67; prof. chemistry Calif. State U., Fullerton, 1967-75; assoc. program dir. chem. dynamics NSF, Washington, 1974-75; chmn., prof. chemistry San Francisco State U., 1975-81; dean natural sci. Sonoma State U., Rohnert Park, Calif., 1981-82, provost, v.p., 1982-84; acad. v.p. Calif. State U., Bakersfield, 1984-99, provost v.p., 1996-99, ret., 1999, emeritus provost, v.p. acad. affairs, 2000—. Contbr. articles to profl. jours. Served with USMC, 1954-57. Grantee Research Corp., 1968; grantee NSF, 1969-75, Petroleum Research Fund, 1978, 80; fellow NSF, 1965 Mem. AAAS, Am. Chem. Soc. Home: 5704 Muirfield Dr Bakersfield CA 93306-9518 Office: Calif State U 9001 Stockdale Hwy Bakersfield CA 93311-1022

DOREY, WILLIAM G. construction company executive; BS in Constrn. Mgmt., Ariz. State U. Br. mgr. Granite Constrn., Inc., Santa Barbara, Calif., 1973-83, asst. divsn. mgr., br. divsn. mgr., sr. v.p., mgr. br. divsn.; exec. v.p., COO Granite Constrn. Inc., Watsonville, Calif., 1998—. Office: Granite Constrn Inc 585 W Beach St Watsonville CA 95076 also: PO Box 50085 Watsonville CA 95077-5085

DORF, RICHARD CARL, electrical engineering and management educator; b. N.Y.C., Dec. 27, 1933; s. William Carl and Marion (Fraser) D.; m. Joy H. MacDonald, June 15, 1957; children: Christine, Renée. BS, Clarkson U., 1955; MS, U. Colo., 1957; PhD, U.S. Naval Postgrad. Sch., 1961. Registered profl. engr., Calif. Instr. Clarkson U., Potsdam, N.Y., 1956-58; instr., asst. prof. U.S. Naval Postgrad. Sch., Monterey, Calif., 1958-63; prof., chmn. U. Santa Clara, 1963-69; v.p. Ohio U., Athens, 1969-72; dean of extended learning U. Calif., Davis, 1972-81, prof. in mgmt. and elec. engring., 1972—. Lectr. U. Edinburgh, Scotland, 1961-62; cons. Lawrence Livermore (Calif.) Nat. Lab., 1981—; chmn. Sacramento Valley Venture Capital Forum, 1985-90. Author: The Mutual Fund Portfolio Planner, 1988, The New Mutual Fund Advisor, 1988, Electric Circuits, 5d edit., 2000, Modern Control Systems, 9th edit., 2000; editor: Ency. of Robotics, 1987, Circuits, Devices and Systems, 1991, Handbook of Electrical Engineering, 2d edit., 1997, Handbook of Manufacturing and Automation, 1994, Handbook of Technology Management, 1999, Technology, Humans and Society, 2001. Bd. dirs. Sta. KVIE, PBS, Sacramento, 1976-79; ruling elder Davis Cmty. Ch., 1973-76, 1999—; chmn. Sonoma Valley Econ. Devel. Assn., 1993—; mem. City Coun., City of Sonoma, 1994-98; vice mayor City of Sonoma, 1994, 98, mayor, 1996. With U.S. Army, 1956. Recipient Alumni award Clarkson U., 1979, Disting. Alumni award Colo. U., 1998. Fellow IEEE; mem. Am. Soc. Engring. Edn. (sr., chmn. div. 1980—), University Club (bd. dirs. 1988-91), Rotary (bd. dirs. 1978-80). Presbyterian. Office: U Calif Elec Engring Dept Davis CA 95616 E-mail: rcdorf@ucdavis.edu

DORFAN, JONATHAN MANNIE, physicist, educator; b. Cape Town, South Africa, Oct. 10, 1947; came to U.S., 1969; s. Charles Archie and Esther (Levine) D.; m. Renee Bing, Dec. 15, 1969; children: Nicole Michelle, Rachel Lauren. Rsch. assoc. Stanford (Calif.) Linear Accelerator Ctr., 1976-78, staff physicist, 1978-83, assoc. prof., 1984-88, prof. physics, 1989—, assoc. dir., 1994-99, dir., 1999—. Office: Stanford Linear Accelerator Ctr MS17 Stanford CA 94305

DORIAN, BRETT J. federal judge; b. 1934; BA, San Francisco State U., 1959; JD, Boalt Hall, 1962. Apptd. bankruptcy judge ea. dist. U.S. Dist. Ct. Calif., 1988—. With U.S. Army, 1952-54. Office: 2656 US Courthouse 1130 O St Fresno CA 93721-2201 Fax: 209-498-7344

DORMAN, ALBERT A. consulting engineer executive, architect; b. Phila., Apr. 30, 1926; s. William and Edith (Kleiman) D.; m. Joan Bettie Heiten, July 29, 1950; children: Laura Jane, Kenneth Joseph, Richard Coleman. BS, Newark Coll. Engring., 1945; MS, U. So. Calif., 1962; ScD (hon.), N.J. Inst. Tech., 1999. Registered profl. engr., Calif., N.Y., Ill., Oreg., Ariz., Pa., Nev., registered architect, Calif., Oreg. Owner firm Albert A. Dorman, Hanford, Calif., 1954-66; v.p. Daniel, Mann, Johnson & Mendenhall, Los Angeles, 1967-73, pres., chief oper. officer, 1974-77, pres., chief exec. officer, 1977-84, chmn., chief exec. officer, 1984-91, chmn., 1991-99; chmn., chief exec. officer AECOM Tech. Corp., L.A., 1984-91, chmn., 1991-92; founding chmn. AECOM Tech Corp., L.A., 1992—; chmn. Holmes & Narver, Inc., Orange, Calif., 1991-97, Frederic R. Harris, Inc., N.Y.C., 1988-91, Consoer, Townsend and Assocs., Inc., Chgo., 1988-91. Pres., chmn. bd. dirs. Hanford Savs. & Loan Assn., 1963-72. Contbr. articles to profl. jours. Pres. Cmty. Concerts Assn., 1962-64; past mem. bd. councilors Sch. Urban and Regional Planning, U. So. Calif.; trustee Harvey Mudd Coll., J. David Gladstone Found., 1988—, Nat. Found. Advancement in Arts, 1988-99; bd. overseers N.J. Inst. Tech., 1989—; vice chmn. Los Angeles County Earthquake Fact-Finding Commn., 1980. With U.S. Army, 1945-47. Recipient Civil Engring. Alumnus award U. So. Calif., 1976, Edward F. Weston medal N.J. Inst. Tech., 1986, Golden Beaver Engring. award, 1991, Eponym, Albert Dorman Honors Coll., N.J. Inst. Tech., 1993, Disting. Award of Merit, ACEC, 1996, Medal, U. Calif., San Francisco, 1996. Fellow AIA, Am. Cons. Engrs. Coun. (life); mem. ASCE (hon. mem., Harland Bartholomew award 1976, Opal Outstanding Lifetime Achievement award 2000), NAE (elected mem.), Parcel-Sverdrup Civil Engring. Mgmt. award 1987, pres. L.A. sect. 1984-85), Real Estate Constrn. Industries (Humanitarian award 1986), Am. Pub. Works Assn. (life), Cons. Engrs. Assn. Calif. (bd. dirs. 1982-88, pres. 1985-86), Am. Water Works Assn. (life), Water Pollution Control Fedn. (life), Calif. C. of C. (bd. dirs. 1986-94), L.A. Area C. of C. (bd. dirs. 1983-88, exec. com. 1985-87), Calif. Club, Met. Club, Kiwanis (pres. 1962), Tau Beta Pi, Chi Epsilon. Office: AECOM Tech Corp 3250 Wilshire Blvd Los Angeles CA 90010-1577

DORNAN, ROBERT KENNETH, former congressman; b. N.Y.C., Apr. 3, 1933; s. Harry Joseph and Gertrude Consuelo (McFadden) D.; m. Sallie Hansen, Apr. 16, 1955; children: Robin Marie, Robert Kenneth II, Theresa Ann, Mark Douglas, Kathleen Regina. Student, Loyola U., Westchester, Calif., 1950-53. Nat. spokesman Citizens for Decency Through Law, 1973-76; mem. 95th-97th Congresses from 27th Calif. dist., 1977-83, 99th-103rd Congresses from 38th Calif. dist., 1985-93, 103rd Congress and 104th Congress from 46th Calif. dist., 1993-96. Chmn. Nat. Sec. Subcom. on Military Personnel, chmn. Tech. and Tactical Intelligence. Host TV polit. talk shows in Los Angeles, 1965-73; host, producer: Robert K. Dornan Show, Los Angeles, 1970-73; combat photographer/broadcast journalist assigned 8 times to Laos-Cambodia-Vietnam, 1965-74; originator POW/MIA bracelet. Served to capt., fighter pilot USAF, 1953-58, fighter pilot, amphibian rescue pilot and intelligence officer USAFR, 1958-75. Mem. Am. Legion, Navy League, Air Force Assn., Res. Officers Assn., AMVET, Assn. Former Intelligence Officers, Am. Helicopter Soc. Special Forces Assn., AFTRA. Republican. Roman Catholic. Lodge: K.C. also: Dornan For Congress PO Box 3260 Garden Grove CA 92842-3260*

DORNE, DAVID J. lawyer; b. Chgo., Dec. 9, 1946; BS magna cum laude, U. Ill., 1969; MSc, London Sch. Econs., 1970; JD cum laude, Boston U., 1973. Bar: N.Y. 1973, U.S. Ct. Appeals (2d cir.) 1973, U.S. Tax Ct. 1973, U.S. Dist. Ct. (so. dist.) N.Y. 1975, Calif. 1978. Mem. Seltzer Caplan McMahon Vitek P.C., San Diego. Mem. City of San Diego Charter Rev. Commn., 1989—. Mem. ABA (taxation sect., corp., banking and bus. law sect.), State Bar Calif. (taxation sect., real property law sect., chmn. personal income tax subcom. 1982-84), San Diego County Bar Assn., Assn. of Bar of City of N.Y. (taxation sect.), Beta Gamma Sigma. Office: Seltzer Caplan McMahon Vitek PC 2100 Symphony Tower 750 B St San Diego CA 92101-8114

DORNETTE, RALPH MEREDITH, religious organization administrator, educator, minister; b. Cin., Aug. 31, 1927; s. Paul A. and Lillian (Bauer) D.; m. Betty Jean Pierce, May 11, 1948; 1 child, Cynthia Anne Dornette Orndorff. AB, Cin. Bible Coll., 1948; DD (hon.), Pacific Christian Coll., 1994. Ordained to ministry Christian Ch., 1947. Min. Indian Creek Christian Ch., Cynthiana, Ky., 1946-51; assoc. prof. Cin. Bible Coll., 1948-51; sr. min. First Christian Ch., Muskogee, Okla., 1951-57; founding min. Bellaire Christian Ch., Tulsa, 1957-59; exec. dir. So. Calif. Evangelistic Assn., Torrance, Calif., 1959-62, 68-77; sr. min. Eastside Christian Ch., Fullerton, 1962-68; dir. devel., prof. ministries Cin. Bible Coll. & Sem., 1977-79; exec. dir. Ch. Devel. Fund, Inc., Fullerton, 1968-77, CEO, 1979-94; sr. preaching minister 1st Christian Ch., Downey, Calif., 1971, 91; preaching minister Hemet (Calif.) Valley Christian Ch., 1992-98; ret., 1998. Pres. So. Calif. Christian Mins. Assn., Fullerton, 1975. Author: Bible Answers to Popular Questions, 1954, Walking With Our Wonderful Lord, 1955, Bible Answers to Popular Questions II, 1964. Pres. Homeowners Assn., Anaheim, Calif., 1980-81. Named Churchman of Yr. Pacific Christian Coll., Fullerton, 1973; recipient Disting. Alumni award Cin. Bible Coll. and Seminary, 1994. Mem. N.Am. Christian Conv. (conv. com. Cin. chpt. 1963, chair nat. registration 1963, v.p. 1972, exec. com. 1963, 70-72, 80-82). E-mail: rmdorn27@earthlink.net

DORNFELD, DAVID ALAN, engineering educator; b. Horicon, Wis., Aug. 3, 1949; s. Harlan Edgar and Cleopatra D.; Barbara Ruth Dornfeld, Sept. 18, 1976. BS in Mech. Engring. with honors, U. Wis., 1972, MS in Mech. Engring., 1973, PhD in Mech. Engring., 1976. Asst. prof. dept. sys. design U. Wis., Milw., 1976-77; asst. prof. mfg. engring. U. Calif., Berkeley, 1977-83, assoc. prof. mfg. engring., 1983-89, vice-chmn. instrn. dept. mech. engring., 1987-88, dir. Engring. Sys. Rsch. Ctr., 1989-98, prof. mfg. engring., 1989—, Will C. Hall Family prof. engring., 1999—, assoc. dean interdisciplinary studies Coll. Engring., 2001—; assoc. dir. rsch. Ecole Nationale Superieure des Mines de Paris, Berkeley, 1983-84; assoc. dean of interdisciplinary studies Coll. Engring. U. Calif., Berkeley, 2001—. Invited prof. Ecole Nationale Superieure D'Arts et Metiers, Paris, 1992-93; cons., expert witness for intellectual property issues, sensor systems, mfg. automation. Contbr. articles to profl. jours., chpts. in books; presenter numerous seminars, confs.; patentee in field. Recipient Dist. Svc. citation U. Wis. Coll. Engring, Madison, 2000. Fellow ASME (past editor, mem. editl. bd. Mfg. Rev. Jour., pres advisory com., Blackall Machine Tool and Gage Award 1990), Soc. Mfg. Engrs. (fellow editl. bd. Jour. Mfg. Systems, Outstanding Young Engr. award 1982); mem. Am. Soc. Precision Engring., Acoustic Emission Working Group, N.Am. Mfg. Rsch. Inst. (past pres., scientific com.), Japan Soc. Precision Engring., Coll. Internat. pour l'Etude Scientifique des Techniques de Production Mechanique (CIRP). Avocations: hiking, travelling, reading. Office: U Calif Dept Mech Engring Berkeley CA 94720-1740 E-mail: dornfeld@me.berkeley.edu

DORPAT, THEODORE LORENZ, psychoanalyst; b. Miles City, Mont., Mar. 25, 1925; s. Theodore Ertman and Eda (Christiansen) D.; married; 1 child, Joanne Katherine. B.S., Whitworth Coll., 1948; M.D., U. Wash., 1952; grad., Seattle Psychoanalytic Inst., 1964. Resident in psychiatry Seattle VA Hosp., 1953-55, Cin. Gen. Hosp., 1955-56; instr. in psychiatry U. Wash., 1956-58, asst. prof. psychiatry, 1958-59, asso. prof., 1969-75, prof., 1976—; practice medicine specializing in psychiatry Seattle, 1958-64; practice psychoanalysis, 1964; instr. Seattle Psychoanalytic Inst., 1966-71, tng. psychoanalyt, 1971—, dir., 1984. Chmn. Wash. Gov.'s Task Force for Commitment Law Reform; trustee Seattle Community Psychiat. Clinic; pres., trustee Seattle Psychoanalytic Inst. Contbr. numerous articles, revs. to profl. books and jours. Served to ensign USNR, 1943-46. Fellow Am. Psychiat. Assn.; mem. Am. Psychoanalytic Assn., AMA, Seattle Psychoanalytic Soc. (sec.-treas. 1965-67, pres. 1972-73), AAAS, Alpha Omega Alpha, Sigma Xi. Home: 7700 E Green Lake Dr N Seattle WA 98103-4971 Office: Blakely Bldg 2271 NE 51st St Seattle WA 98105-5713

DORSEY, DOLORES FLORENCE, corporate treasurer, business executive; b. Buffalo, May 26, 1928; d. William G. and Florence R. D. B.S., Coll. St. Elizabeth, 1950. With Aerojet-Gen. Corp., 1953—, asst. to treas. Calif., 1972-74, asst. treas., 1974-79, treas., 1979—. Mem. Cash Mgmt. Group San Diego (past pres.), Nat. Assn. Corp. Treas., Fin. Execs. Inst. (v.p.). Republican. Roman Catholic. Office: 10300 N Torrey Pines Rd La Jolla CA 92037-1020

DOSCHER, RICHARD JOHN, protective services official; b. Livermore, Calif., Aug. 31, 1952; s. Henry John and Violet Mary (Sutton) D.; m. Kathryn Laura Vierria, May 5, 1979; children: Cameron, Shannon. AS in Adminstrn. Justice, Yuba C.C., Maryville, Calif., 1987; BPA, U. San Francisco, 1991, MPA, 1993. From police officer to sgt. Yuba City (Calif.) Police Dept., 1977-85, sgt., watch commander, 1985-86, lt., divsn. commdr., 1986-89, lt., divsn. cmmdr. tech. svcs. and support, 1989-91, capt., divsn. cmmdr. field ops, 2d in commd agy., 1991-93, capt., divsn. cmmdr. investigation, 2d in commd. agy., chief of police, 1995—. Adj. prof. ethics Yuba C.C., 1997—. Bd. dirs. Yuba/Sutter Easter Seal Soc., 1988—; vol. Calif. Prune Festival, 1988—, Spl. Olympics, 1987—, Bok Kai Chinese Cultural Festival, 1993—, Yuba City Cmty. Theater, 1992—; adv. com. Adminstrn. of Justice Yuba Coll., 1993—; eucharistic min. St. Isidore's Cath. Ch., 1984—. With USAF, 1972-76. Mem. Am. Soc. for Pub. Adminstrn., Calif. Assn. Police Tng. Officers, Calif. Police Chiefs Assn. (bd. dirs. 1998—), , Calif. Peace Officers Assn., Peace Officers' Rsch. Assn. Calif., Yuba City Police Officers Assn. (past officer 1978-80), Kiwanis Club (bd. dirs., 2d v.p. Yuba City), Yuba City Health and Racquet Club. Avocation: astronomy. Office: Yuba City Police Dept 1545 Poole Blvd Yuba City CA 95993-2615

DOTI, JAMES L. academic administrator; Dean Chapman U., 1991—, pres., 1991—. Office: Chapman U Office of President 1 University Dr Orange CA 92866-1005

DOTO, IRENE LOUISE, statistician; b. Wilmington, Del., May 7, 1922; d. Antonio and Teresa (Tabasso) D. BA, U. Pa., 1943; MA, Temple U., 1948, Columbia U., 1954; MQS, Ariz. State U., 1986. Engring. asst. RCA-Victor, 1943-44; rsch. asst. U. Pa., 1944; actuarial clk. Penn Mut. Life Ins. Co., 1944-46; instr. math. Temple U., 1946-53; commd. lt. health svcs. officer USPHS, 1954, advanced through grades to capt., 1963; statistician Communicable Disease Ctr., Atlanta, 1954-55, Kansas City, Kans., 1955-67; chief statis. and publ. svcs., ecol. investigations program Ctr. for Disease Control, Kansas City, 1967-73, chieef statis. svcs., divsn. hepatitis and viral enteritis Phoenix, 1973-83; statis. cons., 1984—. Mem. adj. faculty Phoenix Ctr., Ottawa U., 1982-98. Mem. APHA, Am. Statis. Assn., Ariz. Pub. Health Assn., Ariz. Coun. Engring. and Sci. Assn. (officer 1982-90, pres. 1988-89), Primate Found. Ariz. (mem. animal care and use com. 1986—), Bus. and Profl. Women's Club Phoenix, The Ret. Officers Assn. (state sec.-treas. 1995-96), Ariz. SPCA (bd. dirs. 2000-), Sigma Xi, Pi Mu Epsilon. Office: PO Box 22197 Phoenix AZ 85028-0197

DOTSON, GERALD RICHARD, retired biology educator; b. Brownsville, Tex., Sept. 8, 1937; s. Jasper William and Mary Agnes (Courtney) D.; m. Rose Dolores Gonzales; children: Roberta Ann, Deborah Irene, Matthew Charles. BS, Coll. Santa Fe (N.Mex.), 1960; MS, U. Miss., 1966; PhD, U. Colo., 1974; postgrad., U. Tex., El Paso, 1960-61, Loyola U., New Orleans, 1962-63. Sci. tchr. Cathedral High Sch., El Paso, Tex., 1959-61; sci./math./music tchr. St. Paul's High Sch., Covington, La., 1961-62; sci./math./Spanish tchr. Christian Bros. Sch., New Orleans, 1962-63; sci. tchr., chmn. Hanson High Sch., Franklin, La., 1963-67; biology instr. Coll. Santa Fe (N.Mex.), 1967-69, U. Colo., Boulder, 1969-70, C.C. Denver, 1970-77; prof. biology, chmn. dept. sci. Front Range C.C., Westminster, Colo., 1977-98, prof. emeritus, 1998—. Reviewer biology textbooks, media software, 1970-98; contbr. articles to profl. jours. Mem. recreation dept. City of Westminster, 1971-98. Mem. NSTA (regional sec. 1965), , Am. Microscopical Soc., Am. Soc. Limnology and Oceanography, Nat. Assn. Biology Tchrs., Human Anatomy and Physiology Soc., Eagles, KC (3rd and 4th deg.), Elks, Sigma Xi, Phi Sigma. Roman Catholic. Avocations: fishing, hunting, camping, golf, bowling. Home: 8469 Otis Dr Arvada CO 80003-1241

DOTTEN, MICHAEL CHESTER, lawyer; b. Marathon, Ont., Can., Feb. 23, 1952; came to U.S., 1957; s. William James and Ona Adelaide (Sheppard) D.; m. Kathleen Curtis, Aug. 17, 1974 (div. July 1991); children: Matthew Curtis, Tyler Ryan; m. Cheryl Calvin, Apr. 16, 1994. BS in Polit. Sci., U. Oreg., 1974, JD, 1977. Bar: Idaho 1977, Oreg. 1978, U.S. Dist. Ct. Idaho 1977, U.S. Dist. Ct. Oreg. 1978, U.S. Ct. Appeals (9th cir.), U.S. Ct. Appeals (D.C. cir.) 1987, U.S. Ct. Claims 1986, U.S. Supreme Ct. 1996. Staff asst. to Senator Bob Packwood, U.S. Senate, Washington, 1973-74; asst. atty. gen. State of Idaho, Boise, Idaho, 1977-78; chief rate counsel Bonneville Power Adminstrn., Portland, Oreg., 1978-83; spl. counsel Heller, Ehrman, White & McAuliffe, Portland, 1983-84, ptnr., 1985-98, 99—; gen. counsel PG&E Gas Transmission, N.W. Corp., Portland, 1998-99. Utility com. mem. Ctr. for Pub. Resources, N.Y.C., 1992—. Coun. Emanual Hosp. Assocs., Portland, 1988-92; bd. dirs. William Temple House, 1995-99, chmn. devel. com., 1996-98, v.p., 1997-98, pres., 1998-99; active Portland Interneighborhood Trans. Rev. Commn., 1986-88; vestryman Christ Episcopal Ch., Lake Oswego, Oreg., 1999—, sr. warden, 2001—. Hunter Leadership scholar U. Oreg., 1973, Oreg. scholar, 1970. Mem. ABA (chmn. electric power com. sect. natural resources 1985-88, coun. liaison energy com. 1990-93, coordinating group on energy law 1992-96), Fed. Bar Assn. (pres. Oreg. chpt. 1989-90, Chpt. Activity award 1990, Pres. award 1988-89), Oreg. State Bar (chmn. dispute resolution com. 1986-87), U. Oreg. Law Sch. Alumni Assn. (pres. 1989-92), Multnomah Athletic Club. Democrat. Episcopalian. Avocations: snow skiing, golf, hiking, travel, racquetball. Office: Heller Ehrman White & McAuliffe 200 SW Market St Ste 1750 Portland OR 97201-5722

DOTY, MICHAEL JOHN, financial executive; b. Mankato, Minn., Feb. 14, 1947; s. Lewis L. and Maisie C. (Roberts) D.; m. Diane M. Skluzacek, June 24, 1972; children: Jacob B., Benjamin J., Joseph M. BS in Chemistry, U. Minn., 1970, BS in Acctg., 1972; MBA, U. St. Thomas, 1977. CPA. Lead auditor Kraft Foods, Chgo., 1972-74; audit mgr. Pub. Acctg., Mpls., 1974-76; mgr. internat. treasury 3M, St. Paul, 1976-80; mgr. internat. planning Honeywell Inc., Mpls., 1980-83; mgr. planning, analysis planning Copeland Corp., Sidney, Ohio, 1983-84; group controller, dir. internal audit Amcast Industrial Corp., Dayton, 1984-86; chief fin. officer Reckitt & Colman Inc., Wayne, N.J., 1986—. Chmn. of bd. Environ. for Learning, St. Paul, 1983. Avocations: running, skiing, sailing. Home: 4412 Dunham Dr Edina MN 55435-4140 Office: Inamed Corp 5540 Ekwill St Ste D Santa Barbara CA 93111

DOUGHERTY, BETSEY OLENICK, architect; b. Guantanamo Bay, Cuba, Oct. 25, 1950; (parents Am. citizens); d. Everett and Charlotte (Kristal) Olenick; m. Brian Paul Dougherty, Aug. 25, 1974; children: Gray Brenner, Megan Victoria. AB in Architecture, U. Calif., Berkeley, 1972, MArch, 1975. Registered architect, Calif.; cert. Nat. Coun. Archtl. Registration Bds. Designer, drafter Maxwell Starkman, L.A., 1972-73, HO & K, San Francisco, 1975-76; job capt. Wm. Blurock & Ptnrs., Newport Beach, Calif., 1976-78; assoc. architect U. Calif., Irvine, 1978-79; arch. Dougherty & Dougherty Archs. LLP, Costa Mesa, 1979—. Author: Green Architecture, 1995; contbr. articles to profl. jours. Mem. Newport Beach Specific Area Plan Com., 1985, Career Edn. Adv. Com., Newport Beach, 1986; leader Orange County bd. Girl Scouts U.S.A., 1995-2001. Recipient Gold Nugget grand award Pacific Coast Builders Conf., 1998, Coalition for Adequate Sch. Housing award of excellence, 1992, 94, 96, Calif. Masonry award, 1992, So. Calif. Edison award of excellence, 1994, Disting. Svc. citation AIACC, 1994. Fellow AIA (pres. Orange County chpt. 1984, Calif. chpt. 1988, nat. bd. dirs. 1989-91, nat. sec. 1992-94, design awards Orange County chpt. 1981-86, 89-90, 98, Nathaniel Owings award Calif. Coun. 1997), Calif. Archtl. Found. (pres. 1995-97). Avocations: family, sailing, camping. Email: www.ddaia.com. Office: Dougherty & Dougherty Archs LLP 3194 Airport Loop Dr Ste D Costa Mesa CA 92626-3405

DOUGHERTY, DENNIS A. chemistry educator; b. Harrisburg, Pa., Dec. 4, 1952; s. John E. and Colleen (Canning) D.; m. Ellen M. Donnelly, June 3, 1973; children: Meghan, Kayla. BS, MS, Bucknell U., 1974; PhD, Princeton U., 1978. Postdoctoral fellow Yale U., New Haven, 1978-79; asst. prof. Calif. Inst. Tech., Pasadena, 1979-85, assoc. prof. chemistry, 1985-89, prof., 1989—. Contbr. articles to sci. jours. Recipient ICI Pharms. award for excellence in chemistry, 1991, Arthur C. Cope Scholar award, 1992; Alfred P. Sloan Found. fellow, 1983; Camille and Henry Dreyfus Tchr. scholar, 1984. Fellow AAAS, Am. Acad. Arts and Scis.; mem. Am. Chem. Soc., Biophys. Soc., Phi Beta Kappa. Home: 1817 Bushnell Ave South Pasadena CA 91030-4905 Office: Calif Inst Tech Div Chemistry & Chem Engring # 164-30 Pasadena CA 91125-0001

DOUGHERTY, ELMER LLOYD, JR. retired chemical engineering educator, consultant; b. Dorrance, Kans., Feb. 7, 1930; s. Elmer Lloyd and Nettie Linda (Anspaugh) D.; m. Joan Victoria Benton, Nov. 25, 1952 (div. June 1963); children: Sharon, Victoria, Timothy, Michael (dec.); m. Ann Marie Da Silva Student, Ft. Hays State Coll., 1946-48; B.S. in Chem. Engring., U. Kans., 1950; M.S. in Chem. Engring., U. Ill., 1952, Ph.D. in Chem. Engring., 1955. Chem. engr. Esso Standard Oil Co., Baton Rouge, 1951-52; chem. engr. Dow Chem. Co., Freeport, Tex., 1955-58; research engr. Standard Oil of Calif., San Francisco, 1958-65; mgr. mgmt. sci. Union Carbide Corp., N.Y.C., 1965-68; cons. chem. engring. Stamford, Conn. and Denver, 1968-71; founder and owner Maraco, Inc., Monarch Beach, Calif., 1980—; prof. chem. engring. U. So. Calif., L.A., 1971-95, prof. emeritus, 1995—. Cons. OPEC, Vienna Austria, 1978-82, SANTOS, Ltd., Adelaide, Australia, 1980—, Kuwait Oil Co., 1995—. Contbr. numerous articles to profl. jours. Mem. Soc. Petroleum Engrs. (Disting. mem., chmn. Los Angeles Basin sect. 1984-85, Ferguson medal 1964, J.J. Arps award 1989), Am. Inst. Chem. Engrs., Internat. Assn. Energy Economists, Inst. Mgmt. Sci. Republican. Clubs: El Niguel Country (bd. dirs. 1976-78) (Laguna Niguel, Calif.). Avocation: golf. Home and Office: Maraco Inc 33531 Marlinspike Dr Monarch Beach CA 92629-4426 E-mail: eld@maraco.com

DOUGHERTY, PATRICK, editor; Mng. editor Anchorage Daily News. Recipient Pulitzer prize, 1989; Neiman fellow Harvard U., 1988-89. Office: Anchorage Daily News 1001 Northway Dr Anchorage AK 99508-2098 E-mail: pdougherty@adn.com

DOUGHERTY, RALEIGH GORDON, manufacturer representative; b. Saginaw, Mich., Aug. 19, 1928; s. Raleigh Gordon and Helen Jean (McCrum) D.; 1 child, Karen Kealani. Salesman H.D. Hudson Mfg. Co., Chgo., 1946-48; field sales rep. Jensen Mfg. Co., Chgo., 1948-50; field sales mgr. Regency Idea, Indpls., 1950-54; mgr. Brenna & Browne, Honolulu, 1954-56; owner, pres. Dougherty Enterprises, Honolulu, 1956—. With U.S. Army, 1950-52. Mem. Internat. Exec. Housekeepers Assn., Hawaii Hotel Assn., Internat. Home Furnishings Reps. Assn., Air Force Assn., DAV (life), Navy League U.S., Am. Legion, Korean Vet., Elks (past trustee Hawaii). Republican. Methodist. Home and Office: 1326 Lunalilo Home Rd Honolulu HI 96825-3216

DOUGHERTY, WILLIAM G. microbiologist, educator; Prof. dept. microbiology Oreg. State U., Corvallis. Recipient Ruth Allen award Am. Phytopathol. Soc., 2000. Office: Oreg State Univ Dept Microbiology 220 Nash Hall Corvallis OR 97331-3804

DOUGLAS, DIANE MIRIAM, museum director; b. Harrisburg, Pa., Mar. 25, 1957; d. David C. and Anna (Barron) D.; m. Steve I. Perlmutter, Jan. 23, 1983; 1 child, David Simon. BA, Brown U., 1979; MA, U. Del., 1982. Oral history editor Former Members of Congress, Washington, 1979-80; assoc. curator exhibitions John Michael Kohler Arts Ctr., Sheboygan, Wis., 1982-83; dir. arts ctr. Lill Street Gallery, Chgo., 1984-88; exec. dir. David Adler Cultural Ctr., Libertyville, Ill., 1988-91; dir. Bellevue (Wash.) Art Mus., 1992—. Program chair, exec. bd. nat. coun. for Edn. in Ceramic Arts, Bandon, Oreg., 1990-93; nat. adv. bd. Friends of Fiber Art, 1992; artists adv. com. Pilchuck Glass Sch., 1993—; mem. bd. dirs. Archie Bray Found., Helena, Mont., 1995—. Office: Bellevue Art Mus 510 Bellevue Way NE Bellevue WA 98004-5014

DOUGLAS, JOEL BRUCE, lawyer; b. L.A., Jan. 25, 1948; BA magna cum laude, Calif. State U., Northridge, 1970; postgrad., East L.A. Coll.; JD, Loyola U., L.A., 1973. Bar: Calif. 1973, U.S. Dist. Ct. (ctrl. dist.) Calif. 1974, U.S. Ct. Appeals (9th cir.) 1978, U.S. Supreme Ct. 1979. Ptnr. Bonne, Bridges, Mueller, O'Keefe & Nichols P.C., L.A. Adj. prof. sch. law Pepperdine U., Malibu, Calif., 1981-84; judge pro tempore L.A. Mcpl. Ct., 1980—, L.A. Superior Ct., 1988—. Assoc. editor Loyola U. L.A. Law Rev., 1972-73. Mem. ABA (litigation sect., tort and ins. practice sect.), State Bar Calif., L.A. County Bar Assn. (mem. legal-med. com. 1979-83, staff atty. med.-legal hot line 1979-82), Am. Bd. Trial Advocates, St. Thomas Moore Law Honor Soc., Phi Alpha Delta. Office: Bonne Bridges Mueller O'Keefe & Nichols PC 3699 Wilshire Blvd Fl 10 Los Angeles CA 90010-2719

DOUGLASS, DONALD ROBERT, banker; b. Evanston, Ill., Oct. 7, 1934; s. Robert William and Dorothy (Gibson) D.; m. Susan Douglass. BBA, U. N.Mex., 1959, MBA, 1966. With Security Pacific Nat. Bank, L.A., 1961—, mgmt. trainee, 1962-63, asst. mgr. Vernon, Calif., 1963-64, Whittier, 1964, asst. v.p., 1965, asst. v.p., credit officer regional adminstrn. L.A., 1966-69, v.p. San Francisco, 1969-74; mgr. corp. accts. credit adminstrn. No. Calif. Corp. Banking, 1974-77; group v.p. Annco Properties, Burlingame, Calif., 1977-79; v.p., sr. loan officer Borel Bank and Trust Co., San Mateo, 1979-83, sr. v.p., 1983-84, exec. v.p. mortgage banking divsn. comml. property sales Los Altos, 1984-87. Ptnr. Key Equities, Inc., San Mateo, 1987—; ptnr., broker Centre Fin. Group, Inc., San Mateo, 1987-96, Centre Fin. Group South Inc., Menlo Park, 1987-96; pres. ServiCtr. Mortgage, Inc., 1996—, Sage Fin., Inc., 1999—; instr. Am. Inst. Banking, 1963, Coll. San Mateo, 1982—; nat. adv. bd. Anderson Schs. Mgmt. U. N.Mex. With AUS, 1954-56. Mem. U. N.Mex. Alumni Assn., Sigma Alpha Epsilon, Delta Sigma Phi. Republican. Presbyterian. Home: 745 Celestial Ln San Mateo CA 94404-2771 E-mail: ddouglass@aol.com

DOUGLASS, ENID HART, educational program director; b. L.A., Oct. 23, 1926; d. Frank Roland and Enid Yandell (Lewis) Hall; m. Malcolm P. Douglass, Aug. 28, 1948; children: Malcolm Paul Jr., John Aubrey, Susan Enid. BA, Pomona Coll., 1948; MA, Claremont (Calif.) Grad. Sch., 1959. Research asst. World Book Ency., Palo Alto, Calif., 1953-54; exec. sec., asst. dir. oral history program Claremont Grad. U., 1963-71, dir. oral history program, 1971—, lectr. history, 1977—. Mem. Calif. Heritage Preservation Commn., 1977-85, chmn. 1983-85. Contbr. articles to hist. jours. Mayor pro tem City of Claremont, 1980-82, mayor, 1982-86; mem. planning and rsch. adv. coun. State of Calif.; mem. city coun. City of Claremont, 1978-86; founder Claremont Heritage, Inc., 1977-80; bd. dirs., 1986-95; bd. dirs. Pilgrim Pla., Claremont; founder, steering com., founding bd. Claremont Cmty. Found., 1989-95, pres., 1990-94. Mem. Oral History Assn. (pres. 1979-80), Southwest Oral History Assn. (founding steering com. 1981, J.V. Mink award 1984), Nat. Coun. Pub. History (founding com. 1980), LWV (bd. dirs. 1957-59, Outstanding Svc. to Cmty. award 1986). Democrat. Home: 1195 N Berkeley Ave Claremont CA 91711-3842 Office: Claremont Grad U Oral History Program 710 N College Ave Claremont CA 91711-3921 E-mail: enid.douglass@cgu.edu

DOVE, DONALD AUGUSTINE, city planner, educator; b. Waco, Tex., Aug. 7, 1930; s. Sebert Constantine and Amy Delmena (Stern) D.; m. Cecelia Mae White, Feb. 9, 1957; children: Angela Dove Gaddy, Donald, Monica Gilstrap, Celine, Austin, Cathlyn, Dianna, Jennifer. BA, Calif. State U., L.A., 1951; MA in Pub. Adminstrn., U. So. Calif., 1966. Planning & devel. cons. D. Dove Assocs., L.A., 1959-60; supr. demographic rsch. Calif. Dept. Pub. Works, L.A., 1960-66, environ. coord. Sacramento, 1971-75; dir. transp. employment project State of Calif., L.A., 1966-71, chief L.A. Region transp. study, 1975-84; chief environ. planning Calif. Dept. Transp., L.A., 1972-75; dir. U. So. Calif., L.A., 1984-87; panelist, advisor PRes. Conf. Aging, Washington, 1970—, Internat. Conf. Energy Use Mgmt., 1981. Guest lectr. univs. western U.S., 1969—. Author: Preserving Urban Environment, 1976, Small Area Population Forecasts, 1966. Chmn. Lynwood City Planning Commn., Calif., 1982—; pres. Area Pastoral Coun., L.A., 1982-83; mem., del. Archdiocesan Pastoral Coun., L.A., 1979-86, Compton Cmty. Devel. Bd., Calif., 1967-71; pres. Neighborhood Esteem/Enrichment Techniques Inst., 1992-93. With U.S. Army, 1952-54. Mem. Am. Planning Assn., Am. Inst. Planners (transp. chmn. 1972-73), Calif. Assn. Mgmt. (pres. 1987-88), Am. Inst. Cert. Planners, Assn. Environ. Profls. (co-founder 1973), Optimists (sec. 1978-79). Democrat. Roman Catholic. Home and Office: 11356 Ernestine Ave Lynwood CA 90262-3711 E-mail: dondve@aol.com

DOWDLE, PATRICK DENNIS, lawyer; b. Denver, Dec. 8, 1948; s. William Robert and Helen (Schraeder) D.; m. Eleanor Pryor, Mar. 8, 1975; children: Jeffery William, Andrew Peter. BA, Cornell Coll., Mt. Vernon, Iowa, 1971; JD, Boston U., 1975. Bar: Colo. 1975, U.S. Dist. Ct. Colo. 1975, U.S. Ct. Appeals (10th cir.) 1976, U.S. Supreme Ct. 1978. Acad. dir. in Japan Sch. Internat. Tng., Putney, Vt., 1974; assoc. Decker & Miller, Denver, 1975-77; ptnr. Miller, Makkai & Dowdle, Denver, 1977—. Designated counsel criminal appeals Colo. Atty. Gens. Office, Denver, 1980-81; guardian ad litem Adams County Dist. Ct., Brighton, Colo., 1980-83; affiliated counsel ACLU, Denver, 1980—. Mem. Colo. Bar Assn., Denver Bar Assn. (various coms.), Porsche Club of Am. Avocations: scuba diving, photography, wine making, travel, skiing. Home: 3254 Tabor Ct Wheat Ridge CO 80033-5367 Office: Miller Makkai & Dowdle 2325 W 72nd Ave Denver CO 80221-3101 E-mail: pdowdle@rmi.net

DOWER, WILLIAM J. research company executive; Sr. dir. Affymax Rsch. Inst., Palo Alto, Calif. Recipient Newcomb-Cleve. prize, 1996-97. Office: Affymax Rsch Inst 4001 Miranda Ave Palo Alto CA 94304-1218

DOWIE, IAN JAMES, management consultant; b. London, Mar. 3, 1938; came to U.S., 1980; s. James George and Ethel (Watker) D.; m. Barbara Eva Page, Jan. 9, 1960 (div. 1991); children: Paul James, David Ian; m. Nancy M. Pollard, 1993. BSEE, A.City & Guilds Inst., U. London, 1958. Registered profl. engr., Ont., Can. Seismic engr. Seismograph Svcs. Ltd., Eng., 1958-61; design engr. GE, Toronto, Ont., 1961-62; v.p., div. dir. IBM Can., Toronto, 1962-80; v.p. field ops. Exxon Office Systems, Stamford, Conn., 1980-82; pres. Aregon Internat. Inc., Stamford, 1983-84, Benchmark East, Westport, Conn., 1985-96, Park City, Utah, 1993-97, Benchmark Pub. Inc., Park City; developer Goshawk Ranch, Park City, 1997—, The Overlook, Park City, 1997—. Pres. Benchmark-Goshawk, Inc., Park City, Utah. Pub. Once A Londoner, 1989, What's Love Got To Do With It?, 1993, From Womb to Tomb, 1994, Remuda Dust, 1994. Chmn. Credit Valley Assn. for Handicapped Children, Toronto, 1972-79. Mem. Shore and Country Club (Norwalk, Conn.), Jeremy Ranch Golf Club (Park City, Utah). Avocations: tennis, travel, skiing, golf. E-mail: ian@benchmarkventures.com

DOWNES, WILLIAM F. judge; b. 1946; BA, U. North Tex., 1968; JD, U. Houston, 1974. Ptnr. Clark and Downes, Green River, Wyo., 1976-78; mem. Brown & Drew, Casper, 1978-94; dist. judge U.S. Dist. Ct. Wyo., Casper, 1994—; chief judge. Capt. USMC, 1968-71. Mem. Wyo. State Bar, Natrona County Bar Assn., Casper Petroleum Club, Wyo. Athletic Club. Office: US Dist Ct 111 S Wolcott St Rm 210 Casper WY 82601-2534

DOWNEY, ARTHUR HAROLD, JR. lawyer, mediator; b. N.Y.C., Nov. 21, 1938; s. Arthur Harold Sr. and Charlotte (Bailey) D.; m. Gwen Vanden Berg, May 28, 1960; children: Anne Leigh, Neal Arthur, Drew Thomas. BA, Cen. Coll., Pella, Iowa, 1960; LLB, Cornell U., 1963. Bar: Colo. 1963, Wyo. 1991, U.S. Dist. Ct. Colo. 1963, U.S. Dist. Ct. Wyo. 1993, U.S. Ct. Appeals (10th cir.) 1963; diplomate Am. Bd. Forensic Examiners. From assoc. to ptnr. Weller, Friedrich, Ward & Andrew, Denver, 1963-82; ptnr., chief exec. officer Downey Law Firm P.C., Denver, 1982—. Trustee panel Colo. Hosp. Assn., 1988-93; del. Nat. Congress Hosp. Trustees, Am. Hosp. Assn., 1988-93. Contbr. articles to profl. jours. Vice moderator Presbytery of Denver, 1972; past pres. Columbine Village Homeowners Assn., Trails End Homeowners Assn., Upper Village Homeowners Assn., Powderhorn Condominium Homeowners Assn., Breckenridge, Colo.; chmn bd. trustees Bethesda Psychealth Sys., Inc., 1990-93. Fellow Internat. Soc. Barristers; mem. ABA, Colo. Bar Assn., Denver Bar Assn., Wyo. Bar Assn., Def. Rsch. Inst. (disting. svc. award), Nat. Inst. Trial Advocacy (teaching faculty, team leader 1973—), Colo. Def. Lawyers Assn. (pres. 1977-78), Am. Coll. Legal Medicine (assoc. in law), Nat. Bd. Trial Advocacy (cert.), Am. Arbitration Assn. Republican. Mem. Reformed Ch. Am. Avocations: photography, woodworking, skiing. Office: Downey Law Firm PC 6655 W Jewell Ave Ste 106 Lakewood CO 80232-7108 E-mail: artandgwen@home.com, downeypc@netone.com

DOWNING, DAVID CHARLES, minister; b. South Gate, Calif., June 24, 1938; s. Kenneth Oliver and Edna Yesobel (Casaday) D.; m. Tommye Catherine Tew, July 11, 1959 (dec. Dec. 11, 1985); children: Sheri Lynn, Teresa Kay, Carla Jeane, Michael David. BA, N.W. Christian Coll., 1961; B in Divinity, Tex. Christian U., 1966, M in Theology, 1973; DMin, San Francisco Theol. Sem., 1987. Ordained to ministry Christian Ch., 1961. Min. Marcola (Oreg.) Ch. of Christ, 1958-59; assoc. min. First Christian Ch., Lebanon, Oreg., 1960-63, min. Ranger, Tex., 1963-65, Knox City, 1966-68, Fredonia, Kans., 1968-74, Ctrl. Christian Ch., Huntington, Ind., 1974-77; regional min., pres. Christian Ch. Greater Kansas City, Mo., 1978-94; sr. minister Univ. Christian Ch., Disciples of Christ, San Diego, 1994—. Trustee Phillips Grad. Sem., Enid, Okla., 1988-94; bd. dirs. Ch. Fin. Coun., Indpls., Midwest Career Devel. Svc., Chgo.; v.p. bd. dirs. Midwest Christian Counseling Ctr., Kansas City. Author: A Contrast and Comparison of Pastoral Counseling in Rural and Urban Situation Churches, 1972, A Design for Enabling Urban Congregations to Cope with Their Fear of Displacement When Faced with Communities in Transition, 1987. Pres. Kansas City Interfaith Peace Alliance, 1980-82. Democrat. Avocations: swimming, camping, fishing, water skiing, collecting chalices. Home: 4325 Caminito De La Escena San Diego CA 92108-4201 Office: Univ Christian Ch 3900 Cleveland Ave San Diego CA 92103-3403 E-mail: davidd624@aol.com, drdowning@univchristianchurch.com

DOWNING, KATHRYN M. newspaper publishing executive, lawyer; b. Portland, Oregon, Mar. 24, 1953; BA in Econs., Lewis and Clark Coll., 1973; JD, Stanford U., 1979. Various positions Mead Data Ctrl., 1981-90, sr. dir. legal info. pub., 1988; pres., COO Electronic Pub. divsn. Thomson Profl. Pub., 1990-93; pres., CEO Lawyers Coop. Pub. divsn. Thomson Legal Pub., 1993-95, Mathew Bender, 1995-97; pres., CEO Mosby Matthew Bender unit, sr. v.p. Times Mirror, N.Y.C., 1997-98, vice pres., 1996-97, sr. v.p., 1997-98, exec. v.p., 1998-99; pres., ceo. L.A. Times, 1998-99, pres., CEO, publisher, 1999. Mem. bd. visitors Sch. Law Stanford U., trustee Friends of Law Libr. Mem. Am. Assn. Pubs. (bd. dirs.), Am. Inns of Ct. (past pub. trustee), Stanford Law Sch. Bd. of Visitors (mem.), Friends of the Law Lib. of Congress (bd. mem.), Los Angeles Chamber of Commerce, Newspaper Assoc. of Amer., UCLA Anderson Sch. of Bus. (bd of visitors), Times Mirror Found., Jim Murray Mem. Found., Los Angeles Times Fund (pres.). Fax: 908-771-8736

DOWS, DAVID ALAN, chemistry educator; b. San Francisco, July 25, 1928; s. Samuel Randall and Rita M. (Bowers) D.; m. Wena Hunt Waldner, July 29, 1950; children— Janet Louise, Carol Marie, Joyce Ellen. B.S., U. Calif. at Berkeley, 1952, Ph.D., 1954. Instr. chemistry Cornell U., 1954-56; instr. U. So. Calif., Los Angeles, 1956-57, asst. prof., 1957-59, assoc. prof., 1959-63, prof. chemistry, 1963—, chmn. dept., 1966-72; NATO prof., 1970. Contbr. articles profl. jours. NSF fellow, 1962-63 Mem. Am. Chem. Soc., Am. Phys. Soc., Phi Beta Kappa. Office: U So Calif Dept Chemistry University Park Los Angeles CA 90089-0482 E-mail: dows@usc.edu

DOYLE, PATRICK JOHN, otolaryngologist, department chairman; b. Moose Jaw, Sask., Can., Nov. 17, 1926; s. William E. and Bertha L. (Fisher) D.; m. Irene Strilchuk, May 21, 1949; children: Sharon, Patrick, Robert, Barbara, Joseph, Kathleen. BSc, U. Alta., 1947, MD, 1949. Diplomate Am. Bd. Otolaryngology (bd. dirs., v.p. 1986-88, pres. 1988-90). Intern U. B.C. Hosp., 1949-50; resident in medicine and pediatrics, 1950-51; resident in otolaryngology U. Oreg. Hosp., 1958-61; asst. prof., then asso. prof. U. Oreg. Med. Sch., 1965-70; mem. faculty U. B.C. Med. Sch., 1963—, prof. otolaryngology, 1972-91, prof. otolaryngology emeritus, 1992—, head dept., 1972-91, program dir. residency tng. program, 1972-91. Head div. otolaryngology St. Paul's Hosp., mem. numerous nat. med. coms. Author numerous articles in field; mem. editorial bds. profl. jours. Fellow Royal Coll. Surgeons Can., Am. Laryngol., Rhinol. and Otol. Soc. (v.p. western sect. 1988, pres. 1994), Am. Laryngol. Soc., Am. Acad. Otolaryngology-Head and Neck Surgery (v.p. 1984, bd. dirs. 1985-87), Am. Otol. Soc.; mem. Can. Soc. Otolaryngology-Head and Neck Surgery (pres. 1987), Pacific Coast Oto-Ophthal. Soc. (pres. 1977), Soc. Univ. Otolaryngologists, U. Oreg. Otolaryngology Alumni Assn. (pres. 1968-70), Am. Otological Soc., Centurion Club, Tinnitus Rsch. Found. Roman Catholic. Office: # 301-5704 Balsam St Vancouver BC Canada V6M 4B9

DOYLE, WILFRED EMMETT, retired bishop; b. Calgary, Alta., Can., Feb. 18, 1913; s. John Joseph and Mary (O'Neill) D. B.A., U. Alta. 1935; D.C.L., U. Ottawa, Ont., Can., 1949. Ordained priest Roman Cath. Ch., 1938; chancellor Archdiocese Edmonton, Alta., Can., 1949-58; bishop Nelson, B.C., Can., 1958-89; bishop emeritus Nelson, Can., 1989—. Chmn. bd. govs. Notre Dame U., Nelson, 1963-74 Address: 635 Tranquil Rd Kamloops BC Canada V2B 3H5

DOYLE, WILLIAM THOMAS, retired newspaper editor; b. Oakland, Calif., May 22, 1925; s. Albert Norman and Catherine (Stein) D.; m. Claire Louise Wogan, Sept. 1, 1946 (dec. Nov. 10, 1984); children: Patrick, Lawrence, Brian, Carrie; m. Mary M. Doren, May 3, 1986. B.Journalism, U. Nev., 1950. Reporter Richmond (Calif.) Independent, 1950-53; reporter Oakland Tribune, 1953-62, asst. state editor, 1962-64, telegraph editor, 1964-67, fin. editor, 1967-79; editor San Francisco Bus. Jour., 1979-81, news dir. Fireman's Fund Ins. Cos., Novato, Calif., 1981-84; mng. editor West County Times, Pinole, 1984-88. Mem. editorial adv. bd.: Catholic Voice. Pres. Richmond Jr. C. of C., 1957-58; bd. dirs. Cath. Social Svc. Contra Costa County, Calif., 1959-62, Bay Area Coop. Edn. Clearing House, 1977-88, Contra Costa Coll. Found., 1984-88, Richmond Unified Edn. Fund, 1984, Am. Cancer Soc.—West Contra Costa, 1986-96; mem. Richmond Schs. Citizens Adv. Com., 1969; pastoral coun. St. David's Cath. Ch., Richmond, 1994—. With USAAF, 1943-45. Recipient award for best financial sect. daily newspaper Calif., Calif. Newspaper Pubs. Assn., 1968, 70, 72, 74, Knowland award for outstanding performance, 1972, Gen. Excellence award Nat. Newspaper Assn., 1987, Outstanding Editorial Writing award Suburban Newspapers Assn., 1989, 90, 1st Place award for editorial writing Nat. Newspaper Assn., 1992; Hughes fellow Rutgers U., 1969. Mem. Soc. Am. Bus. Writers, Marine Exchange San Francisco Bay Area, Sigma Delta Chi, Elks. Clubs: Contra Costa (Calif.); Press (Best News Story award 1965) (pres. 1956), Serra of West Contra Costa. Home: 2727 Del Monte Ave El Cerrito CA 94530-1507 E-mail: marbilldoyle@aol.com

DRACUP, KATHLEEN ANNE, nursing educator; b. Santa Monica, Calif., Sept. 28, 1942; d. Paul Joseph and Lucy Elizabeth (Milligan) Molloy; children: Jeffrey, Jonathan, Joy, Jan, Brian. BS in Nursing, St. Xavier's Coll., Chgo., 1967; M of Nursing, U. Calif., L.A., 1974; D of Nursing Sci., U. Calif., San Francisco, 1982. Clin. nurse Little Co. of Mary Hosp., Chgo., 1967-70, UCLA Med. Ctr., 1970-74; asst. clin. prof. U. Calif., L.A., 1974-78, rsch. fellow dept. medicine, 1979-81, asst. prof. to prof., 1982-99; clin. nurse U. Calif. San Francisco Med. Ctr., 1979; pvt. practice psychotherapist, 1980—; dean, sch. nursing U. Washington, Seattle, 2000-. Editor Heart and Lung Jour., 1981-91, Am. Jour. Critical Care, 1991—; editor Critical Care Nursing Series; contbr. chpts. to books, articles to profl. jours. Disting. Practitioner Nat. Acad., Washington, 1987; Fulbright Sr. scholar, 1995. Fellow Coun. Cardiovascular Nursing, Am. Heart Assn., Am. Assn. Cardiopulmonary Rehab.; mem. Am. Nurses' Assn., Am. Assn. Critical Care Nurses (life), Sigma Theta Tau. Office: UCLA Sch Nursing PO Box 951702 Los Angeles CA 90095-1702

DRAIN, ALBERT STERLING, business management consultant; b. Decatur, Tex., July 5, 1925; s. Albert S. and Bessie (Burk) D.; m. Mauvaline Joyce Beam, Apr. 18, 1946; children: Ronald Dale, Deborah Kay Drain Crawford. Student, Bellville (Ill.) Jr. Coll., Tex. Christian U., Iowa U., Milsaps Coll., Pittsburg (Kans.) Coll. With Armour & Co., 1945-79, regional mgr., 1966-67, mgr. pork div. Chgo., 1967-68, fresh meats div. mgr., 1968-69, corporate v.p., 1968-75, exec. v.p., 1971-73, group v.p. food marketing div., 1973-75; pres. Armour Foods, 1975-79; also dir.; exec. v.p. for Iowa Beef Processors Inc., Dakota City, Nebr., 1979-80; group v.p. Greyhound Corp., Phoenix, 1977—; pres. Sterling Mktg. Inc. (ind. bus. cons. to meat industry), Phoenix, 1980-91; pvt. practice mgmt. cons. meat packing Phoenix, 1991-94; pvt. practice Al Drain Mgmt. Cons., Phoenix, 1994—. Served with USNR, 1943-45. Mem. Am. Soc. Agrl. Cons., Masons, Shriners. Baptist. Home and Office: 24 E San Miguel Ave Phoenix AZ 85012-1337 Fax: 602-266-4797. E-mail: AlDrainl@aol.com

DRAKE, CHARLES WHITNEY, physicist; b. South Portland, Maine, Mar. 8, 1926; s. Charles Whitney and Katharine Gabrielle (O'Neill) D.; m. Ellen Tan, June 15, 1952; children— Judith Ellen, Robert Charles, Linda Ann. B.S., U. Maine, 1950; M.A., Conn. Wesleyan U., 1952; Ph.D., Yale U., 1958. Scientist Westinghouse Atomic Power Div., 1952-53; instr. Yale U., New Haven, 1957-60, asst. prof., 1960-66, rsch. assoc., 1966-69; assoc. prof. Oreg. State U., 1966-74; prof., 1974-93; prof. emeritus, 1993—; chmn. dept. physics, 1976-84. Vis. prof. Oxford U. Clarendon Lab. and St. Peter's Coll., 1972-73, U. Tuebingen (W.Ger.), 1982 Contbr. articles to profl. jours. Served with USNR, 1944-46. Recipient various fellowships and grants. Mem. Am. Phys. Soc., Am. Assn. Physics Tchrs., Sigma Xi, Tau Beta Pi, Sigma Pi Sigma. Office: Oreg State U Dept Physics Corvallis OR 97331

DRAKE, E. MAYLON, academic administrator; b. Nampa, Idaho, Feb. 8, 1920; s. Austin Henry and Daisy Naomi (Smith) D.; m. Lois Elloise Noble, Oct. 12, 1940; children: E. Christopher, Cameron Lee. BS, U. So. Calif., Los Angeles, 1951, MS, 1954, EdD, 1963. Mgr. Frederick Post Co., San Francisco, 1943-47; asst. supt. Baldwin Park (Calif.) Schs., 1947-51; supt. Duarte (Calif.) Schs., 1951-64, Alhambra (Calif.) City Schs., 1964-70; dep. supt. Los Angeles County Schs., 1970-78; dir. Acad. Ednl. Mgmt., Los Angeles, 1978-80; pres. L.A. Coll. Chiropractic, Whittier, 1980-90, chancellor, 1990-93, chancellor emeritus, 1993—. Adj. prof. U. So. Calif., 1964-90, bd. councilors, 1991—. Author Attaining Accountability in Schools, 1972; contbr. articles to profl. jours. Pres. Industry-Ednl. Council So. Calif., 1978; dir. United Way 1970; dir. Greater Los Angeles Zoo Bd., 1970; dir. Planned Parenthood of Pasadena, Calif., 1996; trustee L.A. Coll. Chiropractic Whittier, Calif., 1996. Recipient Am. Educator's medal Freedom Found.; named Educator of Yr. Los Angeles Chiropratic Soc., 1981. Mem. Coun. on Chiropractic Edn. (pres. 1988-90), Rotary (pres. Duarte 1954-56, bd. dirs. Alhambra 1964-70). Republican. Presbyterian. Avocation: performing arts. Home: Pasadena Highlands 323 1575 E Washington Blvd Pasadena CA 91104 Office: LA Coll Chiropractic PO Box 1166 Whittier CA 90609-1166 E-mail: Maylon@webtv.net

DRAKE, FRANK DONALD, radio astronomer, educator; b. Chgo., May 28, 1930; s. Richard Carvel and Winifred (Thompson) D.; m. Elizabeth Bell, Mar. 7, 1953 (div. 1977); children: Stephen, Richard, Paul; m. Amahl Zekin Shakhashiri, Mar. 4, 1978; children: Nadia, Leila. B in Engring. Physics, Cornell U., 1952; MA in Astronomy, Harvard U., 1956, PhD in Astronomy, 1958. Astronomer Nat. Radio Astron. Obs., Green Bank, W.Va., 1958-63; sect. chief Jet Propulsion Lab., Pasadena, Calif., 1963-64; prof. Cornell U., Ithaca, N.Y., 1964-84; dir. Nat. Astron. and Ionospace Ctr., Ithaca, 1971-81; dean natural sci. dept. U. Calif., Santa Cruz, 1984-88, prof. astronomy, 1984-95, prof. emeritus, 1995—; pres. SETI Inst., Mountain View, Calif., 1984-2000, chmn. bd. trustees, 2000—. Author: Intelligent Life in Space, 1962, Murmurs of Earth, 1978, Is Anyone Out There, The Scientific Search for Extraterrestrial Intelligence, 1992. Lt. USN, 1947-55. Fellow AAAS, Am. Acad. Arts and Scis.; mem. NAS, Internat. Astron. Union (chmn. U.S. nat. com.), Astron. Soc. Pacific (pres. 1988-90), Explorers Club. Avocation: jewelry making. Home: SETI Inst 2035 Landings Dr Mountain View CA 94043 E-mail: drake@seti.org

DRAKE, HUDSON BILLINGS, aerospace and electronics company executive; b. L.A., Mar. 3, 1935; s. Hudson C. and Blossom (Billings) D.; m. Joan M. Johnson, Feb. 9, 1957 (dec. 1997); children: Howard Billings, Paul Marvin; m. Mary H. Vaugier, Nov. 1, 2000. BA in Econs., UCLA, 1957, postgrad., 1990; MBA, Pepperdine U., 1976. Mgr. Autonetics div. Rockwell Inc., Anaheim, Calif., 1958-68; exec. dir. Pres.'s Commn. White House Fellows, Washington, 1969-70; dep. under sec. U.S. Dept. Commerce, Washington, 1970-72; v.p., gen. mgr. Teledyne Ryan Electronics, San Diego, 1972-80, pres., 1980-84; pres., group exec. Teledyne Ryan Aero., San Diego, 1984-88; v.p., group exec. Teledyne Inc., L.A., 1987-88, sr. v.p., group exec., 1988-89, sr. v.p., pres. aerospace and electronics segment, 1989-96; v.p., pres. aerospace and electronics segment Allegheny Teledyne Inc., L.A., 1996-97; ltd. ptnr. Carlisle Enterprises, La Jolla, Calif., 1997—; dir. Parex Inc., Washington, 1997—. Mem. Def. Procurement Adv. Com. on Trade, Washington, 1988-93. Contbr. articles to profl. jours. Trustee Children's Hosp., San Diego, 1981-86, chmn. rsch. corp., 1983-86; mem. Pres.'s Coun. San Diego (Calif.) State U., 1984-90; mem. bd. overseers U. Calif., San Diego, 1985-88; mem. vestry, St. James by the Sea, LaJolla, Calif. With USNR, 1953-61; bd. dirs. Jonsson Cancer Ctr. Found., UCLA, 1998—. Recipient Exec. of Yr. award Nat. Mgmt. Assn., 1995; named silver knight of mgmt. Nat. Mgmt. Assn., 1975, gold knight of mgmt., 1986; San Diego Bd. Suprs resolution, 1988; White House fellow, 1968. Mem. IEEE, AIAA, Navy League (life), Inst. Navigation, San Diego C. of C. (bd. dirs.), La Jolla Country Club. Republican. Episcopalian. Avocation: golf, sports cars. Home: 1205 Coast Blvd Unit E La Jolla CA 92037-3636 Office: Carlisle Enterprises 7777 Fay Ave Ste 200 La Jolla CA 92037-4390 E-mail: hdrake1@san.rr.com

DRAKE, MICHAEL J. meteoriticist, planetary scientist, educator; b. Bristol, Eng., July 8, 1946; Am. citizen; married; 2 children. BSc, U. Manchester, 1967; PhD in Geology, U. Oreg., 1972. Rsch. assoc. lunar sci. Smithsonian Astrophys. Obs., 1972-73; from asst. prof. to assoc. prof. planetary sci. U. Ariz., Tucson, 1973-83, assoc. dir. Lunar and Planetary Lab., 1978-80, assoc. dean sci., 1986-87, prof. planetary sci., 1983—, prof. geosci., 1988—, head dept. planetary scis., dir. Lunar and Planetary Lab., 1994—. Mem. numerous coms. and working groups NASA. Assoc. editor Jour. Geophys. Rsch., 1982. Fellow Meteoritical Soc. (v.p. 1996), Am. Geophys. Union; mem. Am. Astron. Soc., European Union Geosci., others. Office: Univ Ariz Lunar & Planetary Lab Tucson AZ 85721-0001

DRAKE, MICHAEL V. ophthalmologist, educator, dean; MD, U. Calif., San Francisco. Resident U. Calif., San Francisco, fellow ophthalmology, prof. ophthalmology, vice chmn. dept. ophthalmology, dir. vision care and clin. rsch. unit, assoc. dean admissions and student programs; fellow glaucoma Harvard Med. Sch. Author: (with D.O. Harrington) The Visual Fields: Text and Atlas of Clinical Perimetry, 1990.

DRAKE, SYLVIE (JURRAS DRAKE), theater critic; b. Alexandria, Egypt, Dec. 18, 1930; came to U.S., 1949, naturalized, 1952; d. Robert and Simonette (Barda) Franco; m. Kenneth K. Drake, Apr. 29, 1952 (div. Dec. 1972); children— Jessica, Robert I.; m. Ty Jurras, June 16, 1973. M. Theater Arts, Pasadena Playhouse, 1969. Free-lance TV writer, 1962-68; theater critic Canyon Crier, L.A., 1968-72; theater critic, columnist L.A. Times, 1971-91, theater critic, 1991-93, theatre critc emeritus, 1993—; lit. dir. Denver Ctr. Theatre Co., 1985; free lance travel writer, book reviewer, pres., translator L.A. Drama Critics Circle, 1979-81. Mem. Pulitzer Prize Drama Jury, 1994; adv. bd. Nat. Arts Journalism Program, 1994-97. Dir. media rels. and publs. Denver Ctr. for the Performing Arts, 1994—; artistic assoc. for spl. projects Denver Ctr. Theatre Co., 1994—. Mem. Am. Theater Critics Assn. Office: Denver Ctr Performing Arts 1245 Champa St Denver CO 80204-2100

DRAPER, WILLIAM HENRY, III, business executive; b. White Plains, N.Y., Jan. 1, 1928; s. William Henry and Katherine (Baum) D.; m. Phyllis Culbertson, June 13, 1953; children: Rebecca, Polly, Timothy. BA, Yale U., 1950; MBA, Harvard U., 1954; LLD (hon.), Southeastern U., 1985; MA (hon.), Yale U., 1991. With Inland Steel Co., Chgo., 1954-59, Draper, Gaither & Anderson, Palo Alto, Calif., 1959-62; pres. Draper & Johnson Investment Co., Palo Alto, 1962-65; founder, gen. ptnr. Sutter Hill Ventures, Palo Alto, 1965-81; pres., chmn. U.S. Export-Import Bank, Washington, 1981-86; adminstr., CEO, UN Devel. Programme, 1986-93; mng. dir. Draper Richards, San Francisco, 1994—. Bd. dirs. numerous cos. Chmn. bd. Am. Conservatory Theatre, 1980-81, 1977-81; bd. dirs. Population Crisis Com., 1976-81, Atlantic Coun., 1989—, World Rehab. Fund, 1988-92, Ctr. for Econ. Policy Rsch., Stanford U., 1988; chmn. Internat. Inst. Edn. West, 1989-2000; vice chmn. Population Action Internat., 1993—; mem. adv. bd. Stanford Grad. Sch. Bus. Adminstrn., 1980-86; nat. co-chmn. fin. com. George Bush for Pres., 1980; bd. dirs., former chmn. Rep. Alliance.; trustee Yale U., 1991-98, George Bush Libr. Found., 1993—; bd. dirs. Inst. Internat. Studies Stanford U., 1997-99, World Affairs Coun. No. Calif., 2000—. With U.S. Army, 1946-48, 51-52. Recipient Alumni Achievement award Harvard Bus. Sch., 1982, Medal of Honor Ellis Island, 1992; named one of the U.S.'s 50 New Corp. Elite, Bus. Week mag., 1985. Mem. Coun. on Fgn. Rels., Overseas Devel. Coun., Pacific Union Club, Bohemian Club, Met. Club, Chevy Chase Club, River Club. Home: 91 Tallwood Ct Atherton CA 94027-6431 Office: Draper Richards 50 California St Ste 2925 San Francisco CA 94111-4726

DRECHSEL, EDWIN JARED, retired magazine editor; b. Bremen, Germany, Apr. 17, 1914; came to U.S., 1924, naturalized, 1935; s. William A. and Estelle Laura D.; m. Ilona Bolya, Aug. 12, 1972; children: John M., Barbara A. Grad., Dartmouth Coll., Amos Tuck Sch. Bus. Adminstrn., 1936. With Standard Oil Co., N.J., 1936-43; with U.S. News and World Report, 1943-79, regional editor, editorial ombudsman, 1976-79. Author shipping company histories and fleet lists, catalogs of ship mail postal markings, including A Century of German Ship Posts, 1886-1986, 1987, Norddeutscher Lloyd, Bremen 1857-1970, vol. 1, 1994, vol. 2, 1995. Former chmn. Reed Sch. Bd., Marin County, Calif.; lay reader, former vestryman St. Stephen's Episcopal Ch., Belvedere, Calif., former mayor, City of Belvedere. Club: San Francisco Press. Home: 170 Hillcrest Rd Berkeley CA 94705-2846

DREHER, NICHOLAS C. lawyer; b. Michigan City, Ind., Nov. 15, 1948; AB magna cum laude, Harvard U., 1970; JD, Stanford U., 1973. Bar: Hawaii 1973. Ptnr. Cades Schutte Fleming & Wright, Honolulu, 1980—, chmn. of fin. and real estate dept., 1991—. Vice-chmn. local rules com. U.S. Bankruptcy Ct. Mem. ABA (mem. com. foreclosure and related remedies sect. real property, probate and trust law 1991—), Am. Bankruptcy Inst. (chmn. Hawaii membership com. 1989—, mem. adv. com. bankruptcy rules 1990—), Hawaii State Bar Assn. (v.p. bankruptcy law sect. 1990-91, pres. 1991—, bd. dirs. 1990—). Office: Cades Schutte Fleming & Wright PO Box 939 Honolulu HI 96808-0939 E-mail: ndreher@cades.com

DREIER, DAVID TIMOTHY, congressman; b. Kansas City, Mo., July 5, 1952; s. H. Edward and Joyce (Yeomans) D. BA cum laude, Claremont McKenna Coll., 1975; MA in Am. Govt., Claremont Grad. Sch., 1976. Dir. corp. rels. Claremont McKenna Coll., 1975-78; dir. mktg. and govt. rels. Indsl. Hydro, San Dimas, Calif., 1978-80; mem. U.S. Congress from 28th (formerly 33rd) Calif. dist., 1981—; v.p. Dreier Devel. Co., Kansas City, Mo., 1985—. Vice chmn. rules of the house com., 1995-99, chmn. rules com., 1999—; bd. dirs. Internat. Rep. Inst.; mem. spkrs. steering com. Recipient Golden Bulldog award Watchdogs of the Treasury, 1981-99, Taxpayers Friends award Nat. Taxpayers Union, 1981-99, Clean Air Champion award Sierra Club, 1988. Office: US Ho Reps 237 Cannon Ho Office Bldg Washington DC 20515-0001*

DREIER, R. CHAD, construction and mortgage company executive; BSBA. Loyola Marymount U., 1969. Exec. v.p. Golden West Holding Corp., L.A., 1979-80; v.p., dir. devel. Daon Corp., 1980-85; exec. v.p., CFO Kaufman and Broad Home Corp., 1986; chmn. Kaufman & Broad Mortgage Corp.; pres., CEO The Ryland Group, Inc., Woodland Hills, Calif., 1993—; also bd. dirs. 1st lt. USAF. Office: Ryland Group 6300 Canoga Ave Woodland Hills CA 91367

DREILINGER, CHARLES LEWIS (CHIPS DREILINGER), dean; b. Bklyn., Feb. 19, 1945; s. Samuel Leonard and Harriet Karen (Kaplan) D.; m. Anna Douglas, Mar. 21, 1966; children: Sean Eric, Daniel Ethan, Seth Aaron. BA, Antioch Coll., 1967; MA, Claremont Grad. Sch., 1968. Assoc. for program devel. Union Experimenting Colls. and Univs., Yellow Springs, Ohio, 1968-70; asst. dean, assoc. dean Antioch Coll., Yellow Springs, 1970-73, assoc. dean, acting dean Hobart Coll., Geneva, 1973-79; dean John Muir Coll. U. Calif.-San Diego, La Jolla, 1979—. Democrat. Avocation: horticulture. Office: U Calif San Diego J Muir Coll Deans Office La Jolla CA 92093

DREISBACH, JOHN GUSTAVE, investment banker; b. Paterson, N.J., Apr. 24, 1939; s. Gustave John and Rose Catherine (Koehler) D.; m. Janice Lynn Petitjean; children: John Gustave Jr., Christopher Erik. BA, NYU, 1963. With Dreyfus & Co., 1959-62, Shields & Co., Inc., 1965-68, Model, Roland & Co., Inc., N.Y.C., 1968-72, F. Eberstadt & Co., Inc., N.Y.C., 1972-74; v.p. Bessemer Trust Co., 1974-78; pres. Cmty. Housing Capital, Inc., 1978-80; chmn., pres. John G. Dreisbach, Inc., Santa Fe, 1980—, JDG Housing Corp., 1982—, JGD Mgmt. Corp., 1996—. Gen. ptnr. numerous real estate ltd. partnerships; bd. dirs., pres. The Santa Fe Investment Conf., 1986—; assoc. Sta. KNME-TV. Mem. Santa Fe Cmty. Devel. Commn.; bd. dirs. Friends of Berry Pomeroy Ch. With USAFR, 1964. Mem. Internat. Assn. for Fin. Planning, Nat. Assn. Securities Dealers, Inc., NYU Alumni Assn., N.Mex. First, Friends of Vieilles Maisons Francaises Inc., Mensa, Santa Fe C. of C., Augustan Soc., St. Bartholomew's Cmty. Club, Essex Club, Hartford Club, Amigos del Alcalde Club. Republican. Mem. Ch. of Eng. Avocations: travel, art, arch-design appreciation, classical music, Shotokan karate (1st Dan). Home: 11 Castle Ct Totnes Devon TQ9 5PD England Office: 369 Montezuma Ave Santa Fe NM 87501-2626 Fax: 505-989-7381

DRELL, SIDNEY DAVID, physicist, educator; b. Atlantic City, Sept. 13, 1926; s. Tulla and Rose (White) D.; m. Harriet Stainback, Mar. 22, 1952; children: Daniel White, Persis Sydney, Joanna Harriet. AB, Princeton U., 1946; MA, U. Ill., 1947, PhD, 1949, DSc (hon.), 1981. Rsch. assoc. U. Ill., 1949-50; instr. physics Stanford U., 1950-52, assoc. prof., 1956-60, prof., 1960-63, Lewis M. Terman prof. and fellow, 1979-84; co-dir. Stanford U. Ctr. for Internat. Security and Arms Control, 1983-89; prof. Stanford Linear Accelerator Ctr., 1963-98, dep. dir., 1969-98, exec. head theoretical physics, 1969-86, prof. emeritus, 1998—. Rsch. assoc. MIT, 1952-53, asst. prof., 1953-56, adv. bd. Lincoln Lab., 1985-90; vis. scientist Guggenheim fellow CERN Lab., Switzerland, 1961, U. Rome, 1972; vis. prof., Loeb lectr. Harvard U., 1962, 70; vis. Schrodinger prof. theoretical physics U. Vienna, 1975; vis. fellow All Souls Coll., Oxford, 1979; I.I. Rabi vis. prof. Columbia U., 1984; adj. prof. engring., pub. policy Carnegie Mellon U., 1989-96; cons. Office Sci. and Tech., 1960-73, Office Sci. and Tech. Policy, 1977-82, ACDA, 1969-81; adviser NSC, 1973-81, Office Tech. Assessment U.S. Congress, 1975-90, House Armed Svcs. Com., 1990-93, Senate Select Com. on Intelligence, 1990-93; mem. Jason, 1960—; mem. high energy physics adv. panel Dept. Energy, 1973-86, chmn., 1974-82, energy rsch. adv. bd., 1978-80; mem. Carnegie Commn. on Sci., Tech. and Govt., 1988-93, Pres.'s Fgn. Intelligence Adv. Bd., 1993—; Richtmyer lectr. to Am. Assn. Physics Tchrs., San Francisco, 1978; Danz lectr. U. Wash., 1983; Hans Bethe lectr. Cornell U., 1988; chmn. U.C. pres. coun. on nat. labs., 1992—; chmn. internat. adv. bd. Inst. Global Conflict and Cooperation, U. Calif., 1990-93; mem. bd. dirs. Internat. Sci. Found., 1993-96. Author 8 books; contbr. articles to profl. jours. Trustee Inst. Advanced Study, Princeton, 1974-83; bd. govs. Weizmann Inst. Sci., Rehovoth, Israel, 1970—; bd. dirs. Ann. Revs., Inc., 1976-97; mem. Pres. Sci. Adv. Com., 1966-70. Recipient Ernest Orlando Lawrence Meml. award and medal for rsch. in theoreticl physics AEC, 1972, Alumni award for disting. svc. in engring. U. Ill., 1973, Alumni Achievement award, 1988, Hilliard Roderick prize in sci., arms. control and internat. security AAAS, 1993, Woodrow Wilson award Princeton U., 1994, Ettore Majorana-Erice Sci. for Peace prize, 1994, Gian Carlo Wick medal, 1996, Disting Assoc. award U.S. Dept. Environ., 1997, I. Pomeranchuk prize, 1998, Linus Pauling medal, Stanford U., 1999-2000; MacArthur fellow, 1984-89, Sr. fellow Hoover Inst., 1998—. Fellow Am. Phys. Soc. (pres. 1986, Leo Szilard award for physics in the pub. interest 1980); mem. AAAS, NAS, Am. Acad. Arts and Scis., Am. Philos. Soc., Arms Control Assn. (bd. dirs. 1978-93), Coun. on Fgn. Rels., Aspen Strategy Group (emeritus 1991), Academia Europaea. Home: 570 Alvarado Row Stanford CA 94305-8501 Office: Stanford Linear Accelerator Ctr 2575 Sand Hill Rd Menlo Park CA 94025-7015

DRENNAN, JERRY M. career officer; BS in Engring. Mgmt., USAF Acad., 1972; MBA, U. Mo., 1976; grad., Squadron Officer Sch., 1976, Armed Forces Staff Coll., 1984, Air War Coll., 1989; program for execs., Carnegie-Mellon U., 1995. Commd. 2d lt. USAF, 1972, advanced through grades to brigadier gen., 1997; missile ops. staff officer Air Staff tng. program Dep. Chief Staff for Ops., Hdqs. USAF, Washington, 1977-78, ground-launched cruise missile plans officer, 1980-82, asst. exec. officer, 1982-84; ops. officer 564th Strategic Missile Squadron, Malmstrom AFB, Mont., 1984-85; comdr. 12th Strategic Missile Squadron, Malmstrom AFB, 1985-86; dep. base comdr. 341st Combat Support Group, Malmstrom AFB, 1986-87; dep. comdr. for ops., vice comdr. 487th Tactical Missile Wing, Comiso Air Sta., Italy, 1989-91; comdr. 842d Combat Support Group, Grand Forks AFB, N.D., 1991-92, 321st Missile Wing, Grand Forks AFB, 1992-93; asst. dir. nuclear ops. Hdqs. Def. Nuclear Agy., Alexandria, Va., 1993-95; dep. dir. plans, dir. logistics Hdqs. Air Force Space command, Peterson AFB, Colo., 1995-96; commandant Air Command and Staff Coll., Maxwell AFB, Ala., 1996-98; comdr. 21st Space Wing, Peterson AFB, 1998—. Decorated Def. Superior Svc. medal, Legion of Merit, Meritorious Svc. medal with 5 oak leaf clusters. Office: 21 SWICC 775 Loring Ave Ste 205 Peterson AFB CO 80914-1290

DRESHER, PAUL JOSEPH, composer, music educator, performer; b. L.A., Jan. 8, 1951; s. Melvin J. and Martha (Whitaker) D.; m. Robin Naomi Kirck, Mar. 8, 1986 (dec. 1999); 1 child, Cole Kirck Dresher. MusB, U. Calif., Berkeley, 1977; MA in Composition, U. Calif., La Jolla, 1979. Prof. music Cornish Inst. Arts, Seattle, 1980-83; artistic dir. Paul Dresher Ensemble, Berkeley, 1984—. Cons. Nat. Endowment for the Arts, Calif. Arts Coun., 1982-94, Rockefeller Found. Composer: (opera) Slow Fire, 1987, Power Failure, 1989, (music theater) Pioneer, 1989, (orchestral work) Reaction, 1984; (chamber orch.) Cornucopia, 1990; (dances) Shelf Life, 1987, Age of Unrest, 1991, The Gates, 1993, Outawak, 1997, Kalasam, 2000; (trio) Double Ikat, 1989; (chamber) Din of Iniquity, 1994; (solo piano) Blue Diamonds, 1995, Violin Concerto (chamber), 1996-97, Elapsed Time (for violin and piano), 1998, (music theater) Sound Stage, 2001, (chamber) Cello Concerto, 2001, (dance) In the Name, 2001; works presented by numerous symphonic and other orchs. including N.Y. Philharm. Munich State Opera, London Internat. Festival of Theatre; recordings on New Albion, Lovely, Starkland and New World labels. Bd. dirs. New Langton Arts Orgn., San Francisco, 1984-2001, Am. Music Ctr., 1994-2000. Recipient numerous grants NEA, 1979-2000; Fulbright grantee, 1984; Goddard Lieberson fellow, 1982. Mem. Broadcast Music, Inc., Am. Music Ctr., Opera America, Chamber Music America. Home and Office: 51 Avenida Dr Berkeley CA 94708-2145 E-mail: pauldresher@compuserve.com

DRESSLER, ALAN MICHAEL, astronomer; b. Cin., Mar. 23, 1948; s. Charles and Gay (Stein) Dressler. BA in Physics, U. Calif., Berkeley, 1970; PhD in Astronomy, U. Calif., Santa Cruz, 1976. Carnegie Instn. of Washington fellow Hale Obs., Pasadena, Calif., 1976-78, Las Campanas fellow, 1978-81; sci. staff Carnegie Obs. (formerly Mt. Wilson and Las Campanas Obs., formerly Hale Obs.), Pasadena, 1981—, acting assoc. dir., 1988-89. Contbr. to sci. jours. Recipient Pub. Svcs. medal NASA 1999. Fellow Am. Acad. Arts and Scis.; mem. NAS, Am. Astron. Soc. (councilor 1989-91, Pierce prize 1983), Internat. Astron. Union. Office: Carnegie Obs 813 Santa Barbara St Pasadena CA 91101-1232

DREVER, MARK, food products executive; b. 1956; BA, U. the Pacific; JD, Loyola U. Atty. Fresh Express Inc., Salinas, Calif., 1988—, pres. Office: Fresh Express Inc PO Box 80599 1020 Merrill St Salinas CA 93912

DREW, CLIFFORD JAMES, university administrator, special education and educational psychology educator; b. Eugene, Oreg., Mar. 9, 1943; s. Albert C. and Violet M. (Caskey) D. B.S. magna cum laude, Eastern Oreg. Coll., 1965; M.Ed., U.Ill., 1966; Ph.D. with honors, U. Oreg., 1968. Asst. prof. edn. Kent (Ohio) State U., 1968-69; asst. prof. dir. research and spl. edn. U. Tex., Austin, 1969-71; assoc. prof. spl. edn. U. Utah, Salt Lake City, 1971-76, prof., 1977—; asst. dean Grad. Sch. Edn., 1974-77, assoc. dean, 1977-79, 89-95, prof. spl. edn. and ednl. psychology, 1979—, coord. instrnl. tech., acad. v.p.'s office, 1995-97, assoc. acad. v.p., 1997—. Cons. HEW, 1969-80; Bd. dirs. Far West Lab. Ednl. Research and Devel., San Francisco, 1974-80; mem. exec. bd. Salt Lake County Assn. Retarded Children, 1971-72; mem. adv. com. Mental Retardation Counseling Service, Tex. Dept. Mental Health Mental Retardation, 1969-70 Author: (with P. Chinn and D. Logan) Mental Retardation: A Life Cycle Approach, 2d edit., 1979, Introduction to Designing Research and Evaluation, 2d edit., 1980, (with M. Hardman and H. Bluhm) Mental Retardation: Social and Educational Perspectives, 1977, (with D. Gelfand and W. Jenson) Understanding Children's Behavior Disorders, 1982, 3d edit., 1997, (with M. HArdman and D. Logan) Mental Retardation: A Life Cycle Approach, 4th edit., 1988, 5th edit., 1992, 6th edit., 1996, (with M. Hardman) Mental Retardation: A Life Cycle Approach, 7th edit., 2000, Designing and Conducting Behavioral Research, 1985, (with M. Hardman and W. Egan) Human Exceptionality: Society, School and Family, 1984, 7th edit., 2002, (with B. Wampold) Theory and Application of Statistics, 1990, (with M. Hardman and A. Hart) Designing and Conducting Research: Inquiry in Education and Social Science, 1996; numerous articles in field. NDEA fellow, 1965-66; U.S. Office Edn. fellow, 1966-68 Fellow Am. Assn. Mental Retardation; mem. Am. Psychol. Assn., Am. Ednl. Rsch. Assn. Office: U Utah Acad VPs Office 201 Presidents Cir Rm 205 Salt Lake City UT 84112-9007

DREW, PAUL S. entrepreneur; b. Detroit, Mar. 10, 1935; s. Harry and Elizabeth (Schneider) Schlachman; m. Dove Ann Austin, Sept. 9, 1961. BA, Wayne State U., Detroit, 1957. Disc jockey, Port Huron, Mich. and Atlanta, 1955-67; program dir. Sta. WQXI, Atlanta, 1966-67, Sta. CKLW, Detroit, 1967-68; program cons. Storer Broadcasting Co., Phila., 1968-69; program dir. RKO Radio stas. in, Detroit, San Francisco, Washington and L.A., 1970-73; v.p. programming RKO Radio stas., 1973-77; pres. Paul Drew Enterprises, L.A., 1977—; dir. USIA-Radio Marti, 1984-85; pres. USA Japan Co., 1985—, The Mobotron Corp., Hollywood, Calif., 1988—, Fuzzmug Corp., 1991—, 2151 Corp., 1991—. Personal mgr. Pink Lady, outside Japan, 1978; ptnr. Teacup-Teaspoon Music Pub. Co., 1978; chmn. Billboard Internat. Programming Conf., 1976; commr. Calif. Motion Picture Coun., 1979-85. Del. Dem. Nat. Conv., 1976; mem. Dem. Nat. Com., Calif. Dem. Com., Dem. Nat. Fin. Council. Named DeeJay of Year Sixteen Mag., 1965; Program Dir. of Year Bill Gavin Report, 1967; recipient Superior Achievement award RKO Radio, 1973; also numerous gold records for contbs. toward million selling records. Mem. NARAS, Am. Advt. Fedn., Am. Film Inst., Hollywood Radio and TV Soc., L.A. World Affairs Coun., Town Hall Calif., Japan Am. Soc., Variety, Friars, Frat. of Friends, Music Ctr. Home: PO Box 2667 Cumming GA 30028-6508 Office: Sunset-Gower Studios 1565 N Harmony Cir Anaheim CA 92807-6003

DREXLER, FRED, insurance executive; b. Oakland, Calif., Nov. 17, 1915; s. Frederic I. and Jessie (Day) D.; m. Martha Jane Cunningham, Dec. 26, 1936 (dec. June 1987); children: Kenneth, Roger Cunningham, Martha Drexler Lynn. A.B., U. Redlands, 1936; J.D., Golden Gate U., 1947, LL.D., 1971. Bar: Calif. 1947. Editor Mill Valley (Calif.) Record, 1936-42; employee relations Marinship Corp., 1942-45; office mgr. Bechtel Corp., 1945-46; asst. to pres. Indsl. Indemnity Co., San Francisco, 1946-48, asst. sec., 1948-51, sec., 1951-56, sr. v.p., sec., 1956-67, exec. v.p., sec., 1967-68, pres., 1968-70, chmn. bd., chief exec. officer, 1970-76, chmn. exec. com., 1976-78, dir., 1957-86. Dir. Crum & Forster, 1970-83, Montgomery St. Income Securities, Inc. (dir. 1977, chmn. bd. 1988-91); mem. Calif. Workmen's Compensation Study Commn., 1963-65; founder Calif. Workers Compensation Inst., 1964, pres., 1971-74, honoree testimonial dinner, 1985; pres. Pacific Ins. and Surety Conf., 1967-68 Pres. Marin (Calif.) United Fund, 1956; exec. bd. Marin coun. Boy Scouts Am., 1948-69, adv. bd., 1970—, mem. nat. exec. bd., 1973-87; trustee Marin Country Day Sch., 1960-62, United Bay Area Crusade, 1955-73; trustee Golden Gate U., 1957—, chmn. bd., 1968-70; bd. dirs. San Francisco Bay Area Coun., 1972-76, Buck Inst. for Age Rsch., 1989—; trustee Pacific Presbyn. Med. Ctr., 1974-91; chmn. bd. Inst. Philos. Rsch., 1978-95, trustee, 1973-95; trustee World Affairs Coun. No. Calif., 1973-79, Calif. Pacific Med. Ctr., 1991—. Recipient Silver Beaver, Silver Antelope awards Boy Scouts Am. Mem. Calif. Bar Assn. Baptist. Clubs: Bankers (San Francisco) (pres. 1976-78), Bohemian (San Francisco), Pacific Union (San Francisco). Home: 1 Myrtle Ave Mill Valley CA 94941-1023 Office: 275 Battery St San Francisco CA 94111-3305

DREXLER, JEROME, technology company executive; Chmn. bd., CEO Drexler Tech. Corp., Mountain View, Calif. Office: 1077 Independence Ave Mountain View CA 94043-1601

DREXLER, KIM ERIC, researcher, writer; b. Oakland, Calif., Apr. 25, 1955; s. Allan Barry and Hazel Edna (Gassmann) D.; m. Christine Louise Peterson, June 18, 1981. BS in Interdisciplinary Sci., MIT, 1977, MS in Engring., 1979, PhD in Molecular Nanotech., 1991. Researcher, author, lectr., inventor, Cambridge, Mass., 1980-85; researcher, author, lectr., cons. Palo Alto, Calif., 1985—; rsch. affiliate MIT Space Lab, Cambridge, 1980-86, MIT Artificial Intelligence Lab, Cambridge, 1986-87; sr. rsch. fellow Inst. for Molecular Mfg., 1991—. Vis. scholar Stanford (Calif.) U. Computer Sci. Dept., 1986-92; bd. dirs., chmn. The Foresight Inst., Palo Alto, 1986—. Author: Engines of Creation, 1986, Nanosystems, 1992 (Assn. Am. Pubs. Best Computer Science Book, 1992); co-author: Unbounding the Future, 1991; contbr. articles to profl. jours.; inventor high performance solar sail, method for processing and fabricating metals in space. Sec. bd. dirs. L5 Soc., Tucson, 1981, bd. dirs., 1979-86, advisor, 1979-86, co-editor jour., 1983-84; bd. dirs. Nat. Space Soc., 1986-96. Grad. fellow NSF, MIT, 1977; recipient Space Pioneer award for Scientist/Engr., Nat. Space Soc., 1991, Kilby Young Innovator award Kilby Found., Dallas, 1993. Mem. AAAS, Am. Vacuum Soc., Am. Chemistry Soc. Office: The Foresight Inst PO Box 61058 Palo Alto CA 94306-6058

DREXLER, MILLARD S. retail executive; b. 1944; married. Exec. v.p. merchandising, pres. Gap Stores div. Gap Inc., San Bruno, Calif., from 1983; now pres., bd. dirs. The Gap Inc., San Bruno; pres., CEO Ann Taylor Co., The Gap Inc., San Francisco, 1995—. Office: Gap Inc 1 Harrison St San Francisco CA 94105-1602

DREYFUSS, JOHN ALAN, retired health facility administrator; b. N.Y.C., Dec. 1, 1933; s. Henry and Doris (Marks) D.; m. Katharine Elizabeth Rich, June 28, 1958; children: Karen Elizabeth, James Henry, Kimberly Anne, Katharine Marks. BS in Biology, Boston U., 1959. Tchr. schs. in, Montclair, Pebble Beach and Los Olivos, Calif., 1959-63; reporter, editor San Luis Obispo (Calif.) Telegram Tribune, 1963-64; advt. salesman Ventura County (Calif.) Star-Free Press, 1964-66; gen. assignment writer L.A. Times, 1966-69, 73-75, higher edn. writer, 1969-72, environment writer, 1972-73, architecture and design critic, 1975-84, feature writer View sect., 1984-87, graphics editor View sect., 1987-89, asst. to assoc. editor, 1989-93; v.p., CFO, sec. J. Dreyfuss & Assocs., Santa Monica, Calif., 1993-94; newswriter Sta. KTLA-TV, L.A., 1994-95; pub. info. officer Jonsson Comprehensive Cancer Ctr./UCLA, 1995-96, dir. for comm., 1996-98, dir. for planning and comm., 1998-2000. Ret., 2000. With U.S. Army, 1953-55. E-mail: dreyfuss@ucla.edu

DRINKWARD, CECIL W. construction company executive; CE, Calif Tech. CEO Hoffman Corp., Portland, Oreg. Office: Hoffman Corp PO Box 1300 Portland OR 97207-1300

DRINKWATER, PETER LOFTUS, airport executive; m. Joanne Loftus Drinkwater; children: Adam, Nathan. AA, U. N.H., 1975, BA, 1977; MPA, Golden Gate U., 1981. Enlisted USAF, 1971-75, advanced through grades to lt. col., 1977-98, ret., 1998; airport mgr. Ontario Internat. Airport, 1998—. Active Boy Scouts Am. With USAF. Mem. Exptl. Aircraft Assn. Avocation: licensed pilot. Office: Ontario Internat Airport Terminal Bldg Rm 200 Ontario CA 91761 E-mail: peterdrink@cs.com, peterdrink@la.org

DRINNON, RICHARD, retired history educator; b. Portland, Oreg., Jan. 4, 1925; s. John Henry and Emma (Tweed) D.; m. Anna Maria Faulise, Oct. 20, 1945; children: Donna Elizabeth, Jon Tweed. B.A. summa cum laude, Willamette U., 1950; M.A., U. Minn., 1951, Ph.D., 1957. Instr. humanities U. Minn., 1952-53, social sci., 1955-57; instr. Am. history U. Calif., 1957-58, asst. prof., 1958-61; Bruern fellow in Am. studies U. Leeds, 1961-63; faculty research fellow Social Sci. Research Council, 1963-64; asso. prof. history Hobart and William Smith Colls., 1964-66; chmn. dept. history Bucknell U., 1966-74, prof. history, 1974-87, prof. emeritus, 1987—. Vis. prof. U. Paris, 1975 Author: Rebel in Paradise: a Biography of Emma Goldman, 1961, White Savage: The Case of John Dunn Hunter, 1972, Facing West: The Metaphysics of Indian-Hating and Empire-Building, 1980, 90, 97, Keeper of Concentration Camps: Dillon S. Myer and American Racism, 1987; co-editor: Nowhere at Home: Letters from Exile of Emma Goldman and Alexander Berkman, 1974; contbr. articles and revs. to profl. jours. and mags. Served with USNR, 1942-46. NEH sr. fellow, 1980-81 Office: PO Box 1001 Port Orford OR 97465-1001

DRISCOLL, CHARLES FREDERICK, physics educator; b. Tucson, Feb. 28, 1950; s. John Raymond Gozzi and Barbara Jean (Hamilton) Driscoll; m. Suzan C. Bain, Dec. 30, 1972; children: Thomas A., Robert A. BA in Physics summa cum laude, Cornell U., 1969; MS, U. Calif. San Diego, La Jolla, 1972, PhD, 1976. Staff scientist Gen. Atomics, San Diego, 1969; rsch. asst. U. Calif. San Diego, La Jolla, 1971-76, rsch. physicist, sr. lectr., 1976-96, prof. physics, 1996—, assoc. dir. Inst. for Pure and Applied Scis., 1998—. Cons. Sci. Applications, Inc., 1980-81; staff physicist, cons. Molecular Biosystems, Inc., 1981-82. Editor: Non-Neutral Plasma Physics, 1988; contbr. numerous articles to sci. jours. Fellow NSF, 1969-71. Fellow Am. Phys. Soc. (Excellence in Plasma Physics Rsch. award 1991); mem. AAAS, Math. Assn. Am., Phi Beta Kappa. Achievements include development of quantitative analysis of magnetic targeting of microspheres in capillaries, experiments and theory on magnetized electron plasmas, new camera-diagnosed electron plasma apparatus, new laser-diagnosed ion plasma apparatus for in-situ transport measurements; establishment of magnetic containment characteristics of unneutralized plasmas; measurement of collisional transport of heat and particles to thermal equilibrium; observation of new 2D fluid instability and relaxation of 2D turbulence to vortex crystal states. Office: U Calif San Diego Dept Physics 0319 9500 Gilman Dr Dept 0319 La Jolla CA 92093-5004 E-mail: fdriscoll@ucsd.edu

DRISCOLL, MICHAEL P. bishop; b. Long Beach, Calif., Aug. 8, 1939; Student, St. John's Sem., Camarillo, Calif.; MSW, U. So. Calif., 1975. Ordained priest Roman Cath. Ch., 1965, titular bishop of Massita. Aux. bishop, Orange, Calif., 1990-99; bishop Boise, Idaho 1999— Office: Boise Diocese 303 Federal Way Boise ID 83705-5925

DRISKILL, JAMES LAWRENCE, minister; b. Rustburg, Va., Aug. 18, 1920; s. Elijah Hudnall and Annie Pharr (Carwile) D.; m. Ethel Lillian Cassel, May 28, 1949; children: Edward Lawrence, Mary Lillian. BA, Pa. State U., 1946; BD, San Francisco Theol. Sem., 1949; ThM, Princeton Sem., 1957; S.T.D., San Francisco Theol. Sem., 1969. Ordained minister in Presbyn. Ch., 1949. Missionary Presbyn. Ch. USA, Japan, 1949-72; stated supply pastor Madison Square Presbyn. Ch., San Antonio, 1973; minister Highland Presbyn. Ch., Maryville, Tenn., 1973-82; supply pastor of Japanese-Am. chs. Presbyn. Ch. USA, Long Beach, Calif., Hollywood, Calif., Altadena, Calif., 1984-99. Vis. prof. religion dept. Trinity U., 1972-73. Author: Adventures in Senior Living, 1997, Christmas Stories from Around the World, 1997, Worldwide Mission Stories for Young People, 1996, Cross-Cultural Marriages and the Church, 1995, Mission Stories from Around the World, 1994, Japan Diary, 1993, Mission Adventures in Many Lands, 1992; contbr. articles to profl. jours. Mem. Sierra Club, Calif., 1988—; trustee Osaka (Japan) Girls Sch., 1952-65, Seikyo Gakuen Christian Sch., Japan, 1953-92. With USN, 1943-46. Mem. Am. Acad. Religion, Presbyn. Writers Guild. Democrat. Home and Office: 1420 Santo Domingo Ave Duarte CA 91010-2698

DRUEHL, LOUIS DIX, biology educator; b. San Francisco, Oct. 9, 1936; naturalized Can. citizen, 1974; s. Louis Dix and Charlotte (Primrose) D.; m. Jo Ann Reeve, Aug. 17, 1967 (div. 1974); m. Rae Kristanne Randolph, Aug. 11, 1983. BSc, Wash. State U., 1958; MSc, U. Wash., 1962; PhD, U. B.C., Vancouver, B.C., 1966. Rsch. advisor Brazil Navy, Cabo Frio, 1975-77; cons. biomass program GE, Catalina, Calif., 1981-83; from asst. prof. to assoc. prof. Simon Fraser U., Burnaby, B.C., 1966-88, prof. biology, 1988—, dir. Inst. Aquaculture Rsch., 1988-90; assoc. dir. Bamfield (B.C.) Marine Sta., 1992-96. Rsch. assoc. Inst. Algae Rsch. U. Hokkaido, 1972-73; pres. Can. Kelp Resources Ltd., Bamfield, 1982—. Mem. editorial bd. European Jour. Phycology, 1993-96; contbr. over 50 articles to profl. jours. Recipient Provasoli best paper award Jour. Phycology, 1988, Luigi Provasoli award, 1990, Phycological Soc. Am. Mem. Western Soc. Naturalists (pres. 1988). Avocation: writing poetry. Home: 4 Port Desire Bamfield BC Canada V0R 1B0 Office: Bamfield Marine Sta Bamfield BC Canada V0R 1B0 E-mail: druehl@sfu.ca

DRUMMOND, MARSHALL EDWARD, business educator, university administrator; b. Stanford, Calif., Sept. 14, 1941; s. Kirk Isaac and Fern Venice (McDeritt) D. BS, San Jose State U., 1964, MBA, 1969; EdD, U. San Francisco, 1979. Adj. prof. bus. and edn. U. San Francisco, 1975-81; adj. prof. bus. and info. systems San Francisco State U., 1981-82; prof. MIS, Ea. Wash. U., Cheney, 1985—, exec. dir. info. resources, 1988, assoc. v.p. adminstrv. svcs., chief info. officer, 1988-89, v.p. adminstrv. svcs., 1989-90, exec. v.p., 1990, pres., 1990-98; chancellor L.A. C.C. Dist., 1999—. Cons. Sch. Bus., Harvard Coll., U. Ariz. Contbg. editor Diebold Series; contbr. articles to profl. jours. Democrat. Avocations: running, water sports. Office: LA C C Dist 770 Wilshire Blvd Los Angeles CA 90017-3856

DRYER, MURRAY, physicist, educator; b. Bridgeport, Conn., Nov. 4, 1925; s. Sol and Sarah (Shapiro) D.; m. Geraldine Gray Goodsell, May 12, 1955; children: Steven Michael, Lisa Dryer Travis. Student, U. Conn., 1943-44; B.S., Stanford U., 1949, M.S., 1950; Ph.D., Tel-Aviv U., 1971. Research asst. NACA-NASA Ames Research Ctr., Calif., 1949; aero. research scientist NACA-NASA Lewis Research Ctr., Cleve., 1950-59; assoc. research scientist Martin Marietta Corp., Denver, 1959-65; chief interplanetary physics Space Environ. Lab., NOAA Environ. Research Labs., Boulder, Colo., 1965-94, guest worker emeritus, 1994—; sr. scientist Coop. Inst. for Rsch. in Environ. Scis., U. Colo., Boulder, 1994-96; cons. Exploration Physics Internat., Inc., 1996—. Lectr. dept. aerospace engring. scis. U. Colo., 1963-76, dept. astrogeophysics, 1978; vis. assoc. prof. dept. mech. engring. Colo. State U., 1966-67; mem. com. solar terrestrial rsch. NAS, 1976-80, 84-91, com. geophys. data NAS, 1987-93. Author: (with others) Solar-Terrestrial Physics in the 1980's, 1981; editor: (with others) Solar Observations and Predictions of Solar Activity, 1972, Exploration of the Outer Solar System, 1976, Solar and Interplanetary Dynamics, 1980, Advances in Solar Connection wirh Interplanetary Phenomena, 1998; spl. issue editor Space Sci. Revs., 1976; contbr. articles to profl. jours. With U.S. Navy, 1944-46. Mem. Am. Phys. Soc., Am. Geophys. Union, AAAS, Sci. Com. Solar-Terrestrial Physics, Internat. Astron. Union, Com. Space Research, AIAA (Space Sci. award 1975), Sigma Xi Office: Space Environment Ctr NOAA-ERL Mail Code R-E-SE Boulder CO 80305-3328 E-mail: murraydryer@msn.com

DU BAIN, MYRON, financial services executive; b. Cleve., June 3, 1923; s. Edward D. and Elaine (Byrne) Du B.; m. Alice Elaine Hilliker, Sept. 30, 1944; children— Cynthia Lynn, Donald Aldous. BA, U. Calif., Berkeley, 1946; grad. exec. program, Stanford U., 1967. Pres., chief exec. officer Fireman's Fund Ins. Cos., 1974-75, chmn., pres., chief exec. officer, 1975-81, Fireman's Fund Corp., 1981-82; vice chmn. bd. Am. Express Corp., 1977-82; pres., chief exec. officer, dir. Amfac, Inc., San Francisco, 1983-85; chmn. bd. dirs. SRI Internat., Menlo Park, Calif., 1985-89, also bd. dirs., 1989-98. Bd. dirs. SRI Internat., Menlo Park, Calif., Transamerica Corp., Wells Fargo Bank, SCIOS, Inc. Contbg. author: Property and Casualty Handbook, 1960, The Practical Lawyer, 1962. Bd. dirs. San Francisco Opera; past bd. dirs., past chmn. Invest-In-Am., Inc.; chmn. bd. dirs. James Irvine Found., 1989-96; sr. mem. Conf. Bd. With USNR, 1943-46, 50-52; bd. advisors U. Calif., Berkeley. Mem. Bohemian Club, Pacific Union Club, Calif. Tennis Club, Lagunitas Country Club, Villa Taverna Club. Republican. Episcopalian. Office: 160 Sansome St Ste 1700 San Francisco CA 94104-3723

DUBÉ, SUSAN E. women's healthcare company executive; BA, Simmons Coll., 1969; MBA, Harvard U., 1981. V.p. ventures Brigham and Women's Hosp., Boston, 1985-91; exec. v.p., COO, v.p. bus. devel. Adeza Biomed., Inc., Sunnyvale, Calif., 1991-93; ind. cons. to numerous health cos., 1993-94; pres., CEO, BioIntervensions, Inc., Saratoga, Calif., 1994-95; cons. LifeSci. Econs., Inc., Menlo Park, 1995; v.p. mktg. and bus. devel., v.p. bus. devel. Imagyn Med., Inc., Laguna Niguel, 1996-97; sr. v.p. strategy and corp. devel. Imagyn Med. Techs., Inc., Newport Beach, 1997-98; jr. v.p., v.p. strategic planning and acquisitions Women First HealthCare, Inc., San Diego, 1998—. Office: Women First HealthCare Inc 12220 El Camino Real Ste 400 San Diego CA 92130-2091 Fax: 619-509-1353

DUBIN, MARK WILLIAM, educator, neuroscientist; b. N.Y.C., Aug. 30, 1942; s. Sidney Stanley and Dorothy (Cirinsky) D.; m. Alma Hermine Heller, June 27, 1964; children: Lila Rachel, Miriam Rebecca AB in Biophysics, Amherst Coll., 1964; PhD in Biophysics, Johns Hopkins U., 1969. Research fellow Australian Nat. U., Canberra, 1969-71; asst. prof. dept. molecular, cellular and devel. biology U. Colo., Boulder, 1971-77, assoc. prof., 1977-82, prof., 1982—, chmn. dept., 1983-87, assoc. vice chancellor for acad. affairs, 1988-97, chief info. officer, 1996-97, faculty fellow info. tech. svcs., 1997-98. Sci. cons. Wills Found., 1981-91; cons., mem. bd. sci. advisors Columbine Venture Fund, Denver, 1984-94, Photometrics, Tucson, 1987-89; owner MWm Crafts, 1996—; mem. acad. adv. bd. higher edn. Apple Computing, 1997-98. Contbr. articles to profl. jours. Bd. dirs. Congregation Har Ha-Shem, Boulder, 1976-80, pres., 1978, 79, Cmty. Access TV of Boulder, 1996-97. Grantee NIH-Nat. Eye Inst., 1972-90, NSF, 1976-83, March of Dimes Found., 1982-83; Fight for Sight fellow Australian Nat. U., 1969-71 Mem. AAAS, AAHE, AAUP, Assn. Rsch. in Vision and Ophthalmology (sec. chmn. 1981), Soc. Neurosci., Sigma Xi. Democrat. Jewish Avocation: woodworking. Home: 1010 Grape Ave Boulder CO 80304-2129 Office: Univ Colo Dept Molecular Cellular Biology PO Box 347 Boulder CO 80309-0347

DUBOFSKY, JEAN EBERHART, lawyer, retired state supreme court justice; b. 1942; m. Frank Dubofsky; children: Joshua, Matthew. BA, Stanford U., 1964; LLB, Harvard U., 1967. Admitted to Colo. bar, 1967. Legis. asst. to U.S. Senator Walter F. Mondale, 1967-69; atty. Colo. Rural Legal Services, Boulder, 1969-72, Legal Aid Soc. Met. Denver, 1972-73; ptnr. Kelley, Dubofsky, Haglund & Harnsey, Denver, 1973-75; dep. atty. gen. Colo., 1975-77; counsel Kelly, Haglund, Garnsey & Kahn, 1977-79, 88-90, Jean E. Dubofsky, P.C., Boulder, 1991—. Justice Colo. Supreme Ct., Denver, 1979-87; vis. prof. U. Colo. Law Sch., Boulder, 1987-88. Office: 1000 Rosehill Dr Boulder CO 80302-7148

DUBOIS, PHILIP LEON, university administrator, political science educator; b. Oakland, Calif., Oct. 17, 1950; s. Fernand Edmond and Germaine (Goodrich) D.; m. Lisa Lewis, Aug. 28, 1976; 3 children. AB with highest honors in Polit. Sci., U. Calif., Davis, 1972; MA in Polit. Sci., U. Wis., Madison, 1974, PhD in Polit. Sci., 1978. Asst. prof. polit. sci. U. Calif., Davis, 1976—82, assoc. prof., faculty asst. to vice chancellors, 1983—91, prof., asst. vice chancellor acad. programs, 1983—88, assoc. vice chancellor, 1988—91; vice chancellor for acad. affairs, provost U. N.C., Charlotte, 1991—97; pres. U. Wyo., 1997—. Cons. (profl. jours., comml. book pubs.);contbr. articles numerous articles, book revs. to law revs. and jours.; author ((with Floyd Feeney)): (novels) Lawmaking by Initiative, 1998; author: From Ballot to Bench: Judicial Elections and the Quest for Accountability, 1980; editor The Analysis of Judicial Reform, 1982 (Philip L. Dubois), The Politics of Judicial Reform, 1982 (Philip L. Dubois). Fellow, Ford Found., Jud. fellow, U.S. Supreme Ct., 1979—80; scholar, U. Wis. Madison. Mem.: Phi Beta Kappa, Pi Sigma Alpha, Am. Polit. Sci. Assn., Am. Judicature Soc. Democrat. Office: Univ Wyoming Box 3434 University Sta Laramie WY 82071-3434 E-mail: pdubois@uwyo.edu

DUBON, OSCAR D., JR. engineering educator; BS in Materials Engrng., UCLA, 1989; MS in Materials Sci. & Mineral Engrng., U. Calif., Berkeley, 1992, PhD in Materials Sci. & Mineral Engrng., 1996. Grad. student rsch. asst. U. Calif./Lawrence Berkeley Nat. Lab., 1989-96, vis. postdoctoral rsch. engr., 1996-97; postdoctoral fellow Harvard U., 1997-2000; asst. prof. dept. materials sci. and mineral engrng. U. Calif., Berkeley, 2000—. Presenter in field. Contbr. articles to profl. jours. Recipient Robert Lansing Hardy gold medal Minerals, Metals and Materials Soc., 2000; ASM scholar, 1987; Nat. Phys. Sci. Consortium fellow, 1989-95, Japanese Soc. for the Promotion Sci. postdoctoral fellow, 1996. Mem. Am. Phys. Soc., Materials Rsch. Soc. Achievements include research on electronic materials processing, low-temperature molecular beam epitaxy, growth and properties of group IV alloys, synthesis of semiconductor nanostructures. Office: U Calif Berkeley Dept Materials Sci 587 Evans Hall #1760 Berkeley CA 94720-1760 E-mail: oddubon@socrates.berkeley.edn

DUBOSE, FRANCIS MARQUIS, clergyman; b. Elba, Ala., Feb. 27, 1922; s. Hansford Arthur and Mayde Frances (Owen) DuB.; BA cum laude, Baylor U., 1947; MA, U. Houston, 1958; BD, Southwestern Bapt. Sem., 1957, ThD, 1961; postgrad. Oxford (Eng.) U., 1972; m. Dorothy Anne Sessums, Aug. 28, 1940; children: Elizabeth Anne Parnell, Frances Jeannine Huffman, Jonathan Michael, Celia Danielle. Pastor Bapt. chs., Tex., Ark., 1939-61; supt. missions. So. Bapt. Conv., Detroit, 1961-66; prof. missions Golden Gate Bapt. Sem., 1966—, dir. World Mission Ctr., 1979—, sr. prof., 1992; lectr., cons. in 115 cities outside U.S., 1969-82; v.p. Conf. City Mission Supts., So. Bapt. Conv., 1964-66; trustee Mich. Bapt. Inst., 1963-66; mem. San Francisco Inter-Faith Task Force on Homelessness. Mem. Internat. Assn. Mission Study, Am. Soc. Missiology, Assn. Mission Profs. Co-editor: The Mission of the Church in the Racially Changing Community, 1969; author: How Churches Grow in an Urban World, 1978, Classics of Christian Missions, 1979, God Who Sends: A Fresh Quest for Biblical Mission, 1983, Home Cell Groups and House Churches, 1987, Mystic on Main Street, 1994; contbr. to Toward Creative Urban Strategy; Vol. III Ency. of So. Baptists, also articles to profl. jours. E-mail: fddubose@aol.com. Home: 2 Carpenter Ct San Francisco CA 94124-4429

DUBROFF, HENRY ALLEN, newspaper editor, publisher; b. Neptune, N.J., Nov. 28, 1950; s. Sol and Gilda (Burdman) D.; married, 1980 (div. 1986). AB in History and Lit., Lafayette Coll., 1972; MS in Journalism, Columbia U., 1982. Staff writer Dept. Health and Human Svcs., Washington, 1972-73; tchr. English Holyoke (Mass.) St. Sch., 1974-78; employment & tng. program mgr. Knoxville (Tenn.)-Knox CY Community Action, 1978-81; bus. writer, columnist Springfield (Mass.) Newspapers, 1982-85, The Denver Post, 1985-88, bus. editor, 1988-95; editor Denver Bus. Jour., 1995-99; editor, pub. Pacific Coast Bus. Times, 1999—. Contbg. writer CFO Mag., Boston, 1985-90. Contbr. articles to N.Y. Times, 1982-89. Vol. Russian Resettlement Program Jewish Family & Children's Svcs., Denver, 1989-90. Recipient N.Y. Fin. Writers Assn. scholarship, 1982, Morton Margolin prize U. Denver, 1988, Bus. Story of Yr. award AP, 1989, Gen. Excellence award Am. City Bus. Jour., 1996, 97, Human Svc. award Am. Jewish Com., 1999. Mem. Soc. Am. Bus. Editors and Writers (past pres., Best in Bus. award 1995, 96, 98, 2000). Avocations: photography, writing, golf. Office: 675B Cold Springs Rd Santa Barbara CA 93108-1005

DUCKER, BRUCE, novelist, lawyer; b. N.Y.C., Aug. 10, 1938; s. Allen and Lillian Ducker; m. Jaren Jones, Sept. 1, 1962; children: Foster, Penelope, John. AB, Dartmouth Coll., 1960; MA, Columbia U., 1963, LLB, 1964. Bar: Colo. 1964, U.S. Dist. Ct. Colo. 1964, U.S. Ct. Appeals (10th cir.) 1964. Gen. counsel Great Western United Corp., Denver, 1972-73; pres., chmn. bd. dirs. Great Western Cities Inc., Denver, 1974-75; pres. Ducker, Montgomery Lewis & Aronstein P.C., Denver, 1979-97. Author: (novels) Rule by Proxy, 1976, Failure at the Mission Trust, 1986, Bankroll, 1989, Marital Assets, 1993, Lead Us Not Into Penn Station, 1994, Bloodlines, 2000; contbr. articles, poetry and short stories to lit. jours. Former trustee Legal Aid Found. of Colo., Denver Symphony Assn., Kent Denver Country Day Sch. Mem. ABA, P.E.N., Colo. Bar Assn., Denver Bar Assn., Authors' Guild, Poetry Soc. Am., Denver Club, Cactus Club. Office: Ducker Montgomery et al 1560 Broadway Ste 1400 Denver CO 80202-5151

DUCKWORTH, GUY, musician, pianist, educator; b. L.A., Dec. 19, 1923; s. Glenn M. and Laura (Lysle) D.; m. Ballerina Maria Farra, May 23, 1948. BA, UCLA, 1951; MusM, Columbia U., 1953, PhD, 1969. Piano soloist Metro Goldwyn Mayer Studios, 1936-41, Warner Bros. Studios, 1936-41, Sta. KFI, L.A., 1938, Sta. KNX, L.A., 1939, Sta. KHJ, L.A., 1940; artist Columbia Artists, 1942-49; asst. prof. music. U. Minn., Mpls., 1955-60, assoc. prof., 1960-62; prof. piano, fellow Northwestern U., Evanston, Ill., 1962-70, chmn. dept. preparatory piano, 1962-70; prof. music U. Colo., Boulder, 1970-88, prof. emeritus, 1988, originator, coordinator masters and doctoral programs in mus. arts. Piano concert tours in U.S., Can., Mexico, 1947-49; condr. various music festivals, U.S., 1956—; dir. Walker Art Children's Concerts, Mpls., 1957-62; nat. piano chmn. Music Educators Nat. Conf., 1965-71; vis. lectr., scholar 96 univs., colls. and conservatories, U.S. and Can., 1964—; cons. to Ill. State Dept. Program Devel. for Gifted Children, 1968-69; vis. prof. U. Colo., 1988-90. Television series "A New Dimension in Piano Instruction", 1959, rec. Natl. award from Natl. Edn. Television, creator/performer. Author: Keyboard Explorer, 1963, Keyboard Discoverer, 1963, Keyboard Builder, 1964, Keyboard Musician, 1964, Keyboard Performer, 1966, Keyboard Musicianship, 1970, Guy Duckworth Piano Library, 1974, Guy Duckworth Musicianship Series, 1975, Keyboard Musician: The Symmetrical Keyboard, 2 vols., 1987-88, Keyboard Musician: The Symmetrical Keyboard, 1988, rev. edit., 1990; contbr. to over 6 books, 23 articles on pedagogy of music to various jours.; producer, performer video tapes on piano teaching; producer, writer (film) The Person First: A Different Kind of Teaching, 1984 Nominator Irving S. Gilmore Internat. Keyboard Festival, Gilmore Artist and Young Artist Awards. With U.S. Army, 1943-46. Recipient All-Univ. Teaching award for excellence, U. Colo., 1981, Pedagogy Honors award Nat. Conf. Piano Pedagogy, Chgo., 1994; named Pioneer Pedagogue Nat. Corp. Piano Pedagogy, Princeton U. Retrospective, 1992. Mem. Music Tchrs. Nat. Assn., Colo. State Music Tchrs. Assn., Coll. Music Soc., Music Educators Nat. Conf., Music Teachers Assn. Calif., Phi Mu Alpha, Pi Kappa Lambda. Office: U Colo Coll of Music Boulder CO 80302

DUCKWORTH, WALTER DONALD, museum executive, entomologist; b. Athens, Tenn., July 19, 1935; s. James Clifford and Vesta Katherine (Walker) D.; m. Sandra Lee Smith, June 17, 1955; children: Clifford Monroe, Laura Lee, Brent Cullen. Student, U. Tenn., 1953-55; BS, Middle Tenn. State U., 1955-57; MS, N.C. State U., 1957-60, PhD, 1962. Entomology intern Nat. Mus. Nat. History, Washington, 1960-62, asst. curator, 1962-64, assoc. curator, 1964-75, entomology curator, 1975-78, spl.asst. to dir., 1975-78; spl. asst. to asst. sec. Smithsonian Inst., Washington, 1978-84; dir. Bishop Mus., Honolulu, 1984-86, pres., dir., 1986—; pres., CEO Hawaii Maritime Ctr. subs. Bishop Mus. Trustee Sci. Mus. Va., Richmond, 1982-86, bd. dirs., 1982-84, Hawaii Maritime Mus., Honolulu, 1984-95; mem. Sci. Manpower Commn., Washington, 1982-84. Co-editor: Amazonian Ecosystems, 1973; Am. editor: Dictionary of Butterflies and Moths, 1976; author, co-author numerous monographs and jour. articles in systematic biology. Pres. Social Ctr. for Psychosocial Rehab., Fairfax, Va., 1975. N.C. State U. research fellow, 1957-62; recipient numerous grants NSF, Am. Philos. Soc., Smithsonian Research Found. Assn., Exceptional Service awards Smithsonian Inst., 1973, 77, 80, 82, 84, Disting. Alumnus award Middle Tenn. State U., 1984. Mem. Am. Inst. Biol. Scis (pres. 1985-86, sec.-treas. 1978-84), Entomol. Soc. Am. (pres. 1982-83, governing bd. 1976-85, Disting. Svc. award 1981), Assn. Tropical Biology (exec. dir. 1971-84, sec.-treas. 1976-81), Hawaii Acad. Sci. (coun. 1985—), Arts Coun. Hawaii (legis. com. 1986-87), Assn. Sci. Mus. Dirs., Social Sci. Assn., Assn. Systematic Collections (v.p. 1988-89, pres. 1990-91, Disting. Svc. award 1992), Pacific Sci. Assn. (pres. 1987-91, pres. Pacific Sci. Congress, Honolulu 1991). Democrat. Presbyterian. Lodges: Rotary, Masons, Order Eastern Star. Office: Bishop Mus 1525 Bernice St Honolulu HI 96817-2704

DUDDLES, CHARLES WELLER, food company executive; b. Cadillac, Mich., Mar. 31, 1940; s. Dwight Irving and Bertha (Taylor) D.; m. Judith Marie Robinson, June 23, 1962; children: Paul, Steven, Lisa. B.S., Ferris State U., 1961. C.P.A. Mich., Mo. Audit mgr. Price Waterhouse & Co., Battle Creek, Mich., 1961-72; mgr. gen. acctg. Ralston Purina Co., St. Louis, 1973-77, dir. spl. acctg. svcs., 1977-79; v.p., contr. Jack in the Box, Inc., San Diego, 1979-81; sr. v.p. fin. and adminstrn., CFO Foodmaker, Inc., San Diego, 1981-87, sr. v.p., CFO, 1988, exec. v.p., CFO, chief adminstrv. officer, dir., 1988—. Chmn. ARC, San Diego; bd. dirs. Imperial County. Mem. Fin. Execs. Inst., Nat. Assn. Accts., Am. Inst. C.P.A.s Republican. Presbyterian. Lodge: Rotary (San Diego). Office: Jack in the Box Inc 9330 Balboa Ave San Diego CA 92123-1516

DUDZIAK, MARY LOUISE, law educator, lecturer; b. Oakland, Calif., June 15, 1956; d. Walter F. Dudziak and Barbara Ann Campbell; 1 child, Alicia. AB in Sociology with highest honors, U. Calif., Berkeley, 1978; JD, Yale Law Sch., 1984; MA, MPhil in Am. Studies, Yale U., 1986, PhD in Am. Studies, 1992. Adminstrv. asst. to dep. dir. Ctr. Ind. Living, Berkeley, 1978-80; law clk., nat. legal staff ACLU, N.Y.C., 1983; law clk. Judge Sam J. Ervin, III Fourth Cir. Ct. Appeals, Morganton, N.C., 1984-85; assoc. prof. coll. law U. Iowa, Iowa City, 1986-90, prof. coll. law, 1990-98. Vis. prof. U. So. Calif., 1997-98, prof. U. So. Calif., 1998—; mem. faculty senate task force on faculty devel. U. Iowa, 1989-90, mem. faculty welfare com., 1990-92, mem. faculty senate task force on faculty spouses and ptnrs., 1991-92, mem. presdl. lecture com., 1992-95; v.p. rsch. adv. com. in social scis., 1992-94; presenter in field. Author: Cold War Civil Rights: Race and the Image of American Democracy, 2000; contbr. articles to profl. jours. Bd. dirs. Iowa Civil Liberties Union, 1987-88; chairperson office svcs. for persons with disabilities program rev. com., U. Iowa, 1987-88, law sch. ombudsperson, 1991. Charlotte W. Newcombe Doctoral Dissertation fellow Woodrow Wilson Fellowship Found., 1985-86; Old Gold fellow U. Iowa, 1987, 88, 89, Moody Grant Lyndon Baines Johnson Fdn., 1998, Theodore C. Sorenson Fell., JFK Libr. Fdn., 1997, Orgn. Am. Historians-Japanese Assn. for Am. Studies fellow 2000; travel grantee Eisenhower World Affairs Inst., 1993; recipient Scholars Devel. award Harry S. Truman Libr. Inst., 1990. Mem. Am. Soc. Legal History (mem. com. on documentary preservation 1988—, mem. program com. for 1988 conf., mem. exec. com., bd. dirs. 1990-92, 95-97, chairperson program com. 1993, mem. nominating com. 1999—), Am. Hist. Assn. (Littleton-Griswold rsch. grantee 1987), Am. Studies Assn. (mem. nominating com. 1999—), Assn. Am. Law Schs. (sec.-treas. legal history sect. 1987, vice chairperson 1988, chairperson 1989), Law and Soc. Assn. (mem. Hurst prize com. 1992), Orgn. Am. Historians, Soc. Am. Law Tchrs., Soc. for Historians Am. Fgn. Rels. Democrat. Office: U So Calif Law Sch Los Angeles CA 90089-0001 E-mail: mdudziak@law.usc.edu

DUDZIAK, WALTER FRANCIS, physicist; b. Adams, Mass., Jan. 7, 1923; s. Michael Casimer and Mary (Piekielniak) D.; m. Barbara Ann Campbell, June 25, 1954; children: Diane, Mary, Daniel, Suzanne. BS, Rensselaer Poly. Inst., 1946, MS in Physics, 1947; PhD in Physics, U. Calif., Berkeley, 1954. Instr. physics Rensselaer Poly. Inst., Troy, 1946-48; aero scientist NASA, Cleve., 1948-49; rsch. assoc. U. Calif., Berkeley, 1949-54, lectr. physics Santa Barbara, 1954-60; mgr. computer sci. Gen. Electric Co., Santa Barbara, 1958-64; exec. v.p. Pan Fax Corp., Santa Barbara, 1964-68; pres. Info. Sci., Inc., Santa Barbara, 1968—. Rsch. analsyt Manhattan Dist. Project, Oak Ridge, Tenn., 1942-44, Carbon Carbide Corp., Oak Ridge, 1944-46. With U.S. Army, 1942-44. Recipient Livetime Achievement award Dept. of Def., 1998; dams scholar City of Adams. Mem. KC (grand knight 1974—), Elks. Roman Catholic. Home: 1390 Camino Manadero Santa Barbara CA 93111-1048 Office: 123 W Padre St Santa Barbara CA 93105-3960

DUFF, WILLIAM LEROY, JR. university dean emeritus, business educator; b. Oakland, Calif., Sept. 14, 1938; s. William Leroy and Edna Francis (Gunderson) D.; m. Arline M. Wight, Sept. 1, 1962; children—Susan M., William Leroy III. B.A., Calif. State U.-, San Francisco, 1963, postgrad., 1963-64; M.S.Sc., Nat. Econs. Inst., U. Stockholm, 1965; Ph.D., UCLA, 1969. Research assoc. C.F. Kettering Found., 1967-69; asst. JOBS program Nat. Alliance Businessmen, 1969-70; prof. U. No. Colo., Greeley, 1970—, dir. Sch Bus., Bur Bus. and Pub. Research, 1972-75, dean Coll. Bus. Adminstrn., 1984—, interim v.p. acad. affairs, 1987, chmn. faculty senate, 1981-82. On leave as UN adviser to Govt. of Swaziland, 1975-77; cons. in field. Contbr. articles to profl. jours. Mem. Greeley Planning Commn., 1972-75, chmn., 1974-75; trustee U. No. Colo., 1983; mem. Greeley Water and Sewer Bd., 1994-98, Greeley City Coun., 2000. With U.S. Army, 1958-60. Mem. Greeley Rotary Club (bd. dirs.), Greeley Area C. of C. (bd. dirs.). Home: 1614 Lakeside Dr Greeley CO 80631-5343 Office: U No Colo Coll Bus Adminstrn Kepner Greeley CO 80639-0001

DUFFIELD, THOMAS ANDREW, art director, production designer; b. Grosse Pointe, Mich., Sept. 8, 1951; s. Thomas A. Sr. and Grace A. (Schaefer) D. BArch, Calif. State Poly. U., San Luis Obispo, 1976. Set designer Universal Studios, L.A., 1976-79; freelance designer L.A., 1979-84, 87—; asst. art dir. Michael Landon Prodns., Culver City, Calif., 1984-86; art dir. Warner Bros., Burbank, 1986-87; prodn. designer Touchstone Pictures, L.A., 1993—. Prodn. designer: (films) Ed Wood, 1994; art dir.: (films) The Lost Boys, 1987, The Accidental Tourist, 1988, Beetlejuice, 1988, Ghostbusters II, 1989, Joe Versus the Volcano, 1990, Edward Scissorhands, 1990, Batman Returns, 1992, Grand Canyon, 1991, Wolf, 1994, A Little Princess, 1995, The Bird Cage, 1996, Men In Black, 1996, Primary Colors, 1997, Wild, Wild West, 1998, What Planet are you From, 2000. Mem. SAG, Acad. Motion Picture Arts and Scis., Internat. Alliance Theatrical Stage Employees. Avocations: art, sports, photography, sports car racing, investments, computer technology. Home: 17031 Lisette St Granada Hills CA 91344-1435 Office: c/o Soc Motion Picture Art Dirs 11365 Ventura Blvd Studio City CA 91604-3148

DUFFY, IRENE KAREN, artist; b. Chgo., Mar. 10, 1942; d. Andrew Earl and Irene Margaret Kane (Barthley) James; m. James Ora Duffy, Jan. 24, 1963 (div. Oct. 20, 1993); children: Dawn Ann, James Sean, Maureen Marie. BA, Wash. State U., 1985, MFA, 1989. Juried invitational exhbns. include Gallery X "Out of the Box", Art Inst. Chgo., 1995, Wash. State U./U. Ill., 1994, Virginia Inn, Seattle, 1993, Chase Gallery, Spokane, 1992, Union Gallery, Pullman, 1991, Acad. Arts, Riga, Latvia, 1990, Galeria 5, Caracas, Venezuela, 1989; collections include Johanna Bur. for the Handicapped, Chgo., Gordon Gilkey Collection, Portland Art Mus., Modern Art Gallery, Leningrad, Russia, Neill Pub. Libr., Vetreria 2001, S.R.L., Murano, Italy. Bd. dirs. Pullman/Moscow Regional Airport, 1981-84; mem. Global Vols. Project, Ostuni, Italy, 1998, Passport in Time Forest Svc., 2000. Recipient Civic Appreciation award City of Pullman (Mayor Pete Butkus), 1984. Mem. Palouse Folklore Soc., Lions Club Internat. Avocations: folk dancing, flying, travel, gardening. Home: PO Box 215 Palouse WA 99161-0215 Studio: Artspace 114 E 525 Church PO Box 247 Palouse WA 99161-0247 E-mail: ireneduffy@hotmail.com

DUFFY, LAWRENCE KEVIN, biochemist, educator; b. Bklyn., Feb. 1, 1948; s. Michael and Anne (Browne) D.; m. Geraldine Antoinette Sheridan, Nov. 10, 1972; children: Anne Marie, Kevin Michael, Ryan Sheridan. BS, Fordham U., 1969; MS, U. Alaska, 1972, PhD, 1977. Tchg. asst. dept. chemistry U. Alaska, 1969-71, rsch. asst. Inst. Arctic Biology, 1974-77; postdoctoral fellow Boston U., 1977-78, Roche Inst. Molecular Biology, 1978-80; rsch. asst. prof. U. Tex. Med. Br., Galveston, 1980-82; asst. prof. neurology (biol. chemistry) Med. Sch. Harvard U., Boston, 1982-87, adv. biochemistry instr. Med. Sch., 1983-87; instr. gen. and organic chemistry Roxbury C.C., Boston, 1984-87; prof. chemistry and biochemistry U. Alaska, Fairbanks, 1992—, head dept. chemistry and biochemistry, 1994-99; assoc. dean for grad. studies and outreach Coll. Sci. Engrng. and Math., U. Alaska, Fairbanks, 2000—. Coord. program biochemistry and molecular biology for summer undergrad. rsch., 1987-96; pres. U. Alaska Fairbanks Faculty Senate, 2000-01. Mem. editl. bd. Sci. of Total Environment. Pres., bd. dirs. Alzheimer Disease Assn. of Alaska, 1994-95; mem. instnl. rev. bd. Fairbanks Meml. Hosp., 1990; sci. adv. bd. Am. Fedn. Aging Rsch, 1994-95. Lt. USNR, 1971-73. NSF trainee, 1971; J.W. McLaughlin fellow, 1981; W.F. Milton scholar, 1983; recipient Alzheimers Disease and Related Disorders Assoc. Faculty Scholar award, 1987; Carol Fiest Outstanding Advisor award, 1994, 97, Nat. Inst. Deafness & Commn. Disorders, NIH Cert. of Merit for mentoring, 1996, North Star Bough Sch. Dist. Svc. award, 1998, Alumni Achievement award for profl. activity U. Alaska-Fairbanks, 1999. Fellow Am. Inst. Chemists (cert. profl. chemist, mem. editl. bd. Sci. of Total Environment 1999, assoc. editor Jour. Alzheimer's Disease, 2000); mem. Am. Soc. Neurochemists, Am. Soc. Biol. Chemists, N.Y. Acad. Scis., Am. Chem. Soc. (Analytical Chemistry award 1969), Internat. Soc. Toxinologists, Am. Soc. Circumpolar Health (bd. dirs. 1999-01), Soc. Environ. Toxicologists and Chemists, Sigma Xi (pres. 1991 Alaska club, regional nominating com., assoc. reg. dir. 2000-02), Phi Lambda Upsilon. Roman Catholic. Office: U Alaska Fairbanks Inst Arctic Biology Fairbanks AK 99775

DUFFY, PATRICK, broadcast executive; V.p., gen. mgr. Sta. KRTH-FM, L.A. Office: Sta KRTH-FM 5901 Venice Blvd Los Angeles CA 90034-1708

DUFRESNE, ARMAND FREDERICK, management and engineering consultant; b. Manila, Aug. 10, 1917; s. Ernest Faustine and Maude (McClellan) DuF.; m. Theo Rutledge Schaefer, Aug. 24, 1940 (dec. Oct. 1986); children: Lorna DuFresne Turnier, Peter; m. Lois Burrell Klosterman, Feb. 21, 1987. BS, Calif. Inst. Tech., 1938. Dir. quality control, chief product engr. Consol. Electrodynamics Corp., Pasadena, Calif., 1945-61; pres., dir. DUPACO, Inc., Arcadia, 1961-68; v.p., dir. ORMCO Corp., Glendora, 1966-68; mgmt., engrng. cons. Duarte and Cambria, 1968—. Dir., v.p., sec. Tavis Corp., Mariposa, Calif., 1968-79; dir. Denram Corp., Monrovia, Calif., 1968-70, interim pres., 1970; dir., chmn. bd. RCV Corp., El Monte, Calif., 1968-70; owner DUFCO, Cambria, 1971-82; pres. DUFCO Electronics, Inc., Cambria, Calif., 1982-86, chmn. bd. 1982-92; pres. Freedom Designs, Inc., Simi Valley, Calif., 1982-86, chmn. bd. dirs., 1982-97; owner DuFresne Consulting, 1992—; chmn. bd., pres. DUMED-CO,Inc., 1993-95. Patentee in field. Bd. dirs. Arcadia Bus. Assn., 1965-69; bd. dirs. Cambria Community Services Dist., 1976, pres., 1977-80; mem., chmn. San Luis Obispo County Airport Land Use Commn., 1972-75. Served to capt. Signal Corps, AUS, 1942-45. Decorated Bronze Star. Mem. Instrument Soc. Am. (life), Arcadia (dir. 1965-69), Cambria (dir. 1974-75), C. of C., Tau Beta Pi. Home: 61 Broad St Apt 211 San Luis Obispo CA 93405-1772

DUGAN, MICHAEL, communications company professional; BSEE, Rochester Inst. Technology. Former v.p. engrng., dir. product mktg., engrng. Tandon Corp.; former pres. Echostar Technologies; pres., chief opers. officer Echostar Comms., Littleton, Colo.; formerly with Xeros Corp. Office: Echostar Comms 5701 S Santa Fe Littleton CO 80120

DUGAN, MICHAEL JOSEPH, former career officer, health agency executive; b. Albany, N.Y., Feb. 22, 1937; s. D. Joseph and Dorothy M. (Krebs) D.; m. Grace A. Robinson, Aug. 9, 1958; children: Colleen, Erin, Mike, Sean, Kathleen, Kevin. BS, U.S. Mil. Acad., 1958; MBA, U.Colo., 1972. Commd. officer USAF, 1958, advanced through grades to gen.; comdr.-in-chief U.S. Air Forces Europe, 1989-90; comdr. Allied Air Forces Cen. Europe, 1989-90; chief of staff USAF, 1990, ret., 1991; lectr. in strategic studies Johns Hopkins U., Washington, 1991-92; pres., CEO Nat. Multiple Sclerosis Soc., N.Y.C., 1992—. Decorated D.S.M., Silver Star, Legion of Merit, D.F.C., Purple Heart; Knight's Cross (Germany). Home: 36 James Ct Dillon CO 80435 Office: NMSS 700 S Broadway Ste 810 Denver CO 80203-3442 E-mail: mike.dugan@nmss.org

DUGONI, ARTHUR A. orthodontics educator, university dean; b. San Francisco, June 29, 1925; s. Arthur B. and Lina Marie (Bianco) D.; m. Katherine Agnes Groo, Feb. 5, 1949; children: Steven, Michael, Russell, Mary, Diane, Arthur, James. DDS, Coll. Physicians and Surgeons, San Francisco, 1948; MSD, U. Wash., 1963; BS, Gonzaga U., 1986; DHL honoris causa, U. Detroit, 1997. Diplomate Am. Bd. Orthodontics (bd. dirs., pres. 1979-86). Clin. instr. operative dentistry Coll. Physicians and Surgeons, San Francisco, 1951-55, asst. clin. prof. operative dentistry, 1955-60, asst. clin. prof. orthodontics, 1963-64, chair dept. orthodontics, 1963-67; assoc. prof. orthodontics U. Pacific, San Francisco, 1966-77, prof., 1977—, dean sch. dentistry, 1978—. Chair coun. deans Am. Assn. Dental Schs., Washington, 1985; active Pew Commn. for the Health Professions, 1993-96. Recipient award San Mateo County Dental Soc., 1971, Disting. Svc. award Pacific Coast Soc. Orthodontists, 1976, Disting. Practitioner award Nat. Acads. Practice Press Club, 1987, Hinman medallion, 1989, medallion of distinction U. Pacific, 1989, Orthodontic Edn. and Rsch. Found. disting. merit award, 1993, Albert H. Ketcham award Am. Bd. Orthodontics, 1994, Chmn.'s award Am. Dental Trade Assn., 1994, Dr. Irving E. Gruber award, 1997, List of Honor of FDI World Dental Fedn., 1998, award of merit Pacific Coast Soc. Orthodontists, 2001; named Person of Yr., South San Francisco, 1960, Alumnus of Yr., U. Pacific Sch.

Dentistry, 1983, U. Wash., 1984, U. San Francisco, 1988, Gonzaga U., 1992, Gold medal Pierre Fauchard Acad., 1996, Callahan Internat. award Ohio Dental Assn., 1999. Fellow Am. Coll. Dentists (William John Gies award 2001), Internat. Coll. Dentists, Pierre Fauchard Acad., Acad. Dentistry Internat., Acad. Gen. Dentistry (hon. fellow 1992); mem. ADA (trustee 1984-87, treas. 1987-88, pres. 1988-89, Pres.'s citation 1994, 99, Disting. Svc. award 1995), Fedn. Dentaire Internat. (councilor 1989-92, treas. 1992-98, List of Honour 1999), Am. Assn. Dental Schs. (pres. 1995, Disting. Svc. award 2000), Calif. Dental Assn. (pres. 1982-83), Concordia-Argonaut Club, Peninsula Golf and Country Club, Phi Kappa Phi, Omicron Kappa Upsilon, Tau Kappa Omega, Xi Psi Phi. Republican. Roman Catholic. Avocation: golf. Office: U Pacific 2155 Webster St San Francisco CA 94115-2333 E-mail: adugoni@sf.uop.edu

DUHL, LEONARD, psychiatrist, educator; b. N.Y.C., May 24, 1926; s. Louis and Rose (Josefsberg) D.; m. Lisa Shippee; children: Pamela, Nina, David, Susan, Aurora. BA, Columbia U., 1945; MD, Albany Med. Coll., 1948, postgrad., 1956-64. Diplomate Am. Bd. Psychiatry and Neurology (examiner 1977, 85). With USPHS, 1951-53, 54-72, med. dir., 1954-72; fellow Menninger Sch. Psychiatry Menninger Sch. Psychiatry, Winter VA Hosp., Topeka, 1949-51, resident psychiatry, 1953-54; asst. health officer Contra Costa County (Calif.) Health Dept., 1951-53; with USPHS, 1949-51, 53-54; psychiatrist profl. svcs. br., chief office planning NIMH, 1954-66; spl. asst. to sec. HUD, 1966-68; cons. Peace Corps, 1961-68; assoc. psychiatry George Washington Med. Sch., 1961-63, asst. clin. prof., 1963-68, assoc. prof., 1966-68; prof. public health Sch. Pub. Health U. Calif., Berkeley, 1968—; prof. city planning Coll. Environ. Design U. Calif., Berkeley, 1968-92; dir. dual degree program in health and med. scis. U. Calif., Berkeley, 1971-77, clin. prof. psychiatry San Francisco, 1969—; pvt. practice psychiatry Berkeley; sr. assoc. Youth Policy Inst., Washington. Mem. sci. adv. coun. Calif. Legis., 1970-73, sr. cons. Assembly Office of Rsch., 1981-85; cons. Health Cities Program, Environ. Health, WHO, UNICEF, ICDC, Florence, Global Forum of Parliamentarians and Spitiual Leaders, 1989—, Ctr. for Fgn. Journalists, 1987-90, Am. Hosp. Assn. Health Rsch. and Edn. Trust, 1995—. Author: Approaches to Research in Mental Retardation, 1959, The Urban Condition, 1963, (with R.L. Leopold) Mental Health and Urban Social Policy, 1969, Health Planning and Social Change, 1986, Social Entrepreneurship of Change, 1990, 1995, Health and the City, 1993; bd. editors Jour. Community Psychology, 1974, Jour. Cmty. Mental Health, 1974—, Jour. Mental Health Consultation and Edn., 1978—, Jour. Prevention, 1978—, Nat. Civic Rev., 1991—; contbr. articles to tech. lit. Trustee Robert F. Kennedy Found., 1971-83; bd. dirs. Citizens Policy Ctr., San Francisco, 1975-85, New World Alliance, 1980-84, Calif. Inst. for Integral Studies, 1991-95, Ptnrs. for Dem. Change, 1990—; chair First Internat. Healthy Cities Conf., San Francisco, 1993; exec. trustee Nat. Inst. for Citizen Participation and Negotiation, 1988-90; trustee Menninger Found., Topeka, 1994—, bd. dirs., 1995—; bd. dirs. Louis August Jonas Found. (Camp Rising Sun), 1990—, Ctr. for Transcultural Studies, 1996—; exec. dir. Internat. Healthy Cities Found., 1993—. Recipient World Health Day award for Healthy Cities, WHO, 1996, Health Cities award for Coalition of Healthier Cities and Cmtys., 1999. Fellow Am. Psychiat. Assn. (life), Am. Coll. Psychiatry (life), No. Calif. Psychiat. Soc. (life), Group for Advancement in Psychiatry (chmn. com. preventive psychiatry 1962-66), APHA. Home: 639 Cragmont Ave Berkeley CA 94708-1329 Office: U Calif Sch Pub Health 410 Warren Hl Berkeley CA 94720-0001 E-mail: len-duhl@socrates.berkeley.edu

DUKE, DONALD NORMAN, publisher; b. L.A., Apr. 1, 1929; s. Roger V. and Mabel (Weineger) D. BA in Ednl. Psychology, Colo. Coll., 1951. Comml. photographer, Colorado Springs, Colo., 1951-53; pub. rels. Gen. Petroleum, L.A., 1954-55; agt. Gen. S.S. Corp., Ltd., 1956-57; asst. mgr. retail advt., sales promotion Mobil Oil Co., 1958-63; pub. Golden West Books, Alhambra, Calif., 1964—. Dir. Pacific R.R. Publs., Inc., Athletic Press; pub. relations cons. Santa Fe Ry., 1960-70. Author: The Pacific Electric: A History of Southern California Railroading, 1958, Southern Pacific Steam Locomotives, 1962, Santa Fe...Steel Rails to California, 1963, Night Train, 1961, American Narrow Gauge, 1978, RDC: the Budd Rail Diesel Car, 1989, The Brown Derby, 1990, Camp Cajon, 1991, Fred Harvey: Civilizer of the American West, 1994, editor: Water Trails West, 1977, Branding Iron, 1988-91, Santa Fe...The Railroad Gateway to the American West, Vol. 1, 1995, Vol. 2, 1997, Incline Railways of Los Angeles and Southern California, 1998, Electric Railroads of San Francisco Bay, Vols. 1 and 2, 1999, Pacific Electric Railway (The Northern Division), vol. 1. Recipient Spur award for Trails of the Iron Horse Western Writers Am., 1975 Mem. Ry. and Locomotive Hist. Soc. (dir. 1944-98), Western History Assn., Newcomen Soc., Lexington Group of Transp. History, Western Writers Am., P.E.N. Internat. (v.p. 1975-77), Authors Guild Am., Book Pubs. Assn. So. Calif. (dir. 1968-77), Cal. Writers Guild (dir. 1976-77), Calif. Book Pubs. Assn. (dir. 1976-77), Westerners Internat. (hon., editor Branding Iron 1971-80, 88-91), Hist. Soc. So. Calif. (dir. 1972-75), Henry E./Arabella Huntington Soc., Kappa Sigma (lit. editor Caduceus 1968-80). Home: PO Box 80250 San Marino CA 91118-8250 Office: Golden West Books 525 N Electric Ave Alhambra CA 91801-2032 E-mail: trainbook@earthlink.net

DUKE, WILLIAM EDWARD, public affairs executive; b. Bklyn., July 18, 1932; m. Leilani Kamp Lattin. BS, Fordham U., 1954. City editor Middletown (N.Y.) Record, 1956-60; asst. state editor Washington Star, 1961-63; exec. asst. to U.S. Senator from N.Y. State, Jacob K. Javits, Washington, 1963-69; dir. pub. affairs Corp. Pub. Broadcasting, Washington, 1969-72; dir. fed. govt. rels. Atlantic Richfield Co., Washington, 1973-78, mgr. pub. affairs, L.A., 1978-91; mgr. external affairs We. States Petroleum Assn., 1993-95; pres. W.E. Duke and Co., 1996—; lectr. U. So. Calif. Grad. Sch. Journalism, 1988—; cons. in field. Fellow Pub. Rels. Soc. Am., Nat. Press Club, Capitol Hill Club, L.A. Athletic Club.

DUKE DE LEONEDES OF SPAIN SICILY GREECE, HIS ROYAL HIGHNESS See SANCHEZ, LEONEDES MONARRIZE WORTHINGTON

DUKES, JOAN, state legislator; b. Tacoma, Oct. 1, 1947; 3 children. BA, Evergreen State Coll. Commissioner Clatsop County, 1983-87; mem. Oreg. Senate, Dist. 1, Salem, 1986-; senate dem. whip. Democrat. Office: Oreg State Senate 210 State St # S-318 Salem OR 97310-0001 Address: RR 2 Box 503 Astoria OR 97103-9617

DULBECCO, RENATO, biologist, educator; b. Catanzaro, Italy, Feb. 22, 1914; came to U.S., 1947, naturalized, 1953; s. Leonardo and Maria (Virdia) D.; m. Gulseppina Salvo, June 1, 1940 (div. 1963); children: Peter Leonard (dec.), Maria Vittoria; m. Maureen Rutherford Muir; 1 child, Fiona Linsey. M.D., U. Torino, Italy, 1936; D.Sc. (hon.), Yale U., 1968, Vrije Universiteit, Brussels, 1978; LL.D., U. Glasgow, Scotland, 1970. Asst. U. Torino, 1940-47; research asso. Ind. U., 1947-49; sr. research fellow Calif. Inst. Tech., 1949-52, asso. prof., then prof. biology, 1952-63; sr. fellow Salk Inst. Biol. Studies, San Diego, 1963-71; asst. dir. research Imperial Cancer Research Fund, London, 1971-74, dep. dir. research, 1974-77; disting. research prof. Salk Inst., La Jolla, Calif., 1977—, pres., 1989-92, pres. emeritus, 1993—, prof. pathology and medicine U. Calif. at San Diego Med. Sch., La Jolla, 1977-81, mem. Cancer Ctr.; with Nat. Rsch. Coun. Milan. Vis. prof. Royal Soc. G.B., 1963-64, Leeuwenhoek lectr., 1974; Clowes Meml. lectr. Atlantic City, 1961; Harvey lectr. Harvey Soc., 1967; Dunham lectr. Harvard U., 1972; 11th Marjory Stephenson Meml. lectr., London, 1973, Harden lectr., Wye, Eng., 1973, Am. Soc. for Microbiology lectr., L.A., 1979; mem. Calif. Cancr Adv. Coun., 1963-67; mem. vis. com. Case Western Res. Sch. Medicine, adv. bd. Roche Inst., 1968-71, Inst. Immunology, Basel, Switzerland, others; esperto Italian Nat. Rsch. Coun.; trustee Am.-Italian Fedn. for Cancer Rsch.; mem. bd. dirs. Scientific Counselors Dept. Etiology NCI; cons. Nat. Rsch. Coun. ESPERTO, 1994—. Trustee La Jolla Country Day Sch., Am.-Italian Fedn. for Cancer Rsch.; bd. mem. sci. counselors dept. etiology Nat. Cancer Inst. Recipient John Scott award City Phila., 1958, Kimball award Conf. Pub. Health Lab. Dirs., 1959, Albert and Mary Lasker Basic Med. Rsch. award, 1964, Howard Taylor Ricketts award, 1965, Paul Ehrlich-Ludwig Darmstaedter prize, 1967, Horwitz prize Columbia U., 1973, (with David Baltimore and Howard Martin Temin) Nobel prize in medicine, 1975, Targa d'oro Villa San Giovanni, 1978, Mandel Gold medal Czechoslovak Acad. Scis., 1982, Via de Condotti prize, 1990, Cavaliere di Gran Croce Italian Rep., 1991, Natale Di Roma prize, 1993, Columbus prize, 1993, Spl. Oscar of Italian TV, 1999; named Man of Yr., London, 1975, Italian Am. of Yr., San Diego County, 1978; hon. citizen City of Imperia (Italy), 1983, City of Arezzo, City of Sommariva Perno, City of Catanzaro, City of Torino; Guggenheim and Fulbright fellow, 1957-58; decorated grand ufficiale Italian Republic, 1981; hon. founder Hebrew U., 1981. Mem. NAS (Selman A. Waksman award 1974, com. on human rights), Am. Assn. Cancer Rsch., Internat. Physicians for Prevention Nuclear War, Am. Philos. Assn., Academia Nazionale del Lincel (fgn.), Academia Ligure di Scienze e Lettre (hon.), Royal Soc. (fgn.), Fedn. Am. Scientists, Am. Acad. Arts and Scis., Comitato di Collaborazione Culturale (hon. mem.), Alpha Omega Alpha. Office e-mail: dulbeccomd.cs.com. Home: 7525 Hillside Dr La Jolla CA 92037-3941 Office: Telethon Ufficio di Milano Via Nino Bixio 30 20129 Milan Italy also: Salk Inst PO Box 85800 San Diego CA 92186-5800

DULLEA, CHARLES W. university chancellor emeritus, priest; Joined S.J., ordained priest Roman Catholic Ch. Chancellor emeritus U. San Francisco. Office: U San Francisco Xavier Hall 650 Parker Ave San Francisco CA 94118-4267

DUMAINE, R. PIERRE, bishop; b. Aug. 2, 1931; Student, St. Joseph Coll., Mountain View, Calif., 1945-51, St. Patrick Sem., Menlo Park, Calif., 1951-57; PhD, Cath. U. Am., 1962. Ordained priest Roman Cath. Ch., 1957. Asst. pastor Immaculate Heart Ch., Belmont, Calif., 1957-58; mem. faculty dept. edn. Cath. U. Am., Belmont, 1961-63; tchr. Serra High Sch., San Mateo, 1963-65; asst. supt. Cath. schs. Archdiocese of San Francisco, 1965-74, supt., 1974-78; ordained bishop, 1978; bishop of San Jose Santa Clara, Calif., 1981—. Dir. Archdiocesan Ednl. TV Ctr., Menlo Park, Calif., 1968-81. Mem. Pres.'s Nat. Adv. Council on Edn. of Disadvantaged Children, 1970-72. Bd. dirs. Cath. TV Network, 1968-81, pres. 1975-77; bd. dirs. Pub. Svc. Satellite Consortium, 1975-81. Mem. Nat. Cath. Edn. Assn., Assn. Cath. Broadcasters and Allied Communicators, Internat. Inst. Communications, Assn. Calif. Sch. Adminstrs. Office: San Jose Diocese 900 Lafayette St Ste 301 Santa Clara CA 95050-4966

DUMITRESCU, DOMNITA, Spanish language educator, researcher; b. Bucharest, Romania; came to U.S., 1984; d. Ion and Angela (Barzotescu) D. Diploma, U. Bucharest, 1966; MA, U. So. Calif., 1987, PhD, 1990. Asst. prof. U. Bucharest, 1966-74, assoc. prof., 1974-84; asst. prof. Spanish Calif. State U., L.A., 1987-90, assoc. prof., 1990-94, prof., 1995—. Author: Gramatica Limbii Spaniole, 1976, Indreptar Pentru Traducerea Din Limba Romana in Limba Spaniola, 1980; translator from Spanish lit. to Romanian; assoc. editor: Hispania, 1996—; contbr. articles to profl. jours. Fulbright scholar, 1993—. Mem. MLA, Linguistic Soc. Am., Internat. Assn. Hispanists, Linguistic Assn. S.W., Am. Assn. Tchrs. Spanish and Portuguese (past pres. So. Calif. chpt., Tchr. of Yr. award 2000), Sigma Delta Pi (v.p. West 1996—). Office: Calif State U 5151 State University Dr Los Angeles CA 90032-4226 E-mail: ddumitr@calstatela.edu

DUMMETT, CLIFTON ORRIN, dentist, educator; b. Georgetown, British Guiana, May 20, 1919; came to U.S., 1936; s. Alexander Adolphus and Eglantine Annabella (Johnson) D.; m. Lois Maxine Doyle, Mar. 6, 1943; 1 child, Clifton Orrin Jr. BS in Psychology, Roosevelt U., Chgo., 1941; DDS, Northwestern U., 1941, MScD, 1942, DSc (hon.), 1976; MPH, U. Mich., 1947; ScD (hon.), U. Pa., 1978. Diplomate Am. Bd. Periodontology, Am. Bd. Oral Medicine. Dean, prof. periodontology Meharry Med. Coll., Nashville, 1945-49; chief dental service VA Hosp., Tuskegee, Ala., 1949-65, assoc. chief staff for rsch. and edn., 1958-65, chief dental service Chgo., 1965-66; dental dir., dir. ctr. Watts Health Ctr., L.A., 1966-69; assoc. dean, chmn. dept. cmty. dentistry U. So. Calif. Sch. Dentistry, L.A., 1969-75, prof., 1969-89, prof. emeritus, 1989-96, disting. emeritus prof., 1997—. Adj. prof. Northwestern U. Dental Sch., 1989; vis. prof., cons. Sch. Vet. Medicine, Tuskegee Inst., 1962-65; vis. prof. Meharry Med. Coll., 1989—; trustee Am. Fund Dental Health, Chgo., 1968-78; chmn. devel. component rev. panel Calif. Regional Med. Programs, L.A., 1975-77; mem. Pres.'s Com. on Nat. Health Ins., 1977; sr. reviewer U.S. Surgeon Gen. Report on Oral Health, 2000. Author: Community Dentistry, 1974, Afro-Americans in Dentistry: Sequence and Consequence of Events, 1977, Charles Edwin Bentley, 1982, Dental Education at Meharry Medical College: Origin and Odyssey, 1992, Culture and Education in Dentistry at Northwestern University, 1993, NDA.II. The Story of America's Second National Dental Association, 2000; (edtl.) Nor Yet the Last, 1962 (W.J. Gies award 1963), The Hillenbrand Era, 1986; editor Nat. Dental Assn., 1953-75; contbr. over 300 articles to profl. jours., chpts. to books. Chmn. adv. bd. Econ. and Youth Opportunity Agy. Project Head Start, Tuskegee, Ala, 1964-65; mem. spl. health adv. com. Calif. Bd. Edn., L.A., 1972-74; mem. L.A. regional hearing planning council, President's Com. on Health Edn., L.A., 1973-74. Lt. col. USAF, 1955-58 Recipient Alumni award of Merit Northwestern U., 1971, Fones Gold medal Conn. Dental Assn., 1976, Pierre Fauchard Gold medal Pierre Fauchard Acad., 1980; named to U. So. Calif. Dental Hall of Fame, 1997. Fellow Internat. Coll. Dentists, Am. Coll. Dentists (Wm. J. Gies award 1992), Am . Pub. Health Assn. (John W. Knutson Disting. Svc. award 1992), Am. Pub. Health Assn. (v.p. for U.S., 1995-96), AAAS (chmn. dental sect. 1975-76, 87-88), Am. Acad. History of Dentistry (pres. 1982-83, Hayden and Harris award 1987); mem. ADA (hon.), Internat. Assn. Dental Rsch. (pres. 1969-70), Assn. Mil. Surgeons U.S. (life), Am. Assn. Dental Editors (editor 1963-72, pres. 1974-75, Disting. Svc. medal 1976), Nat. Acads. Practice (Disting. Practitioner 1987), Inst. Medicine Nat. Acad. Sci. (sr. mem.), Sigma Xi. Sigma Pi Phi, Alpha Phi Alpha, Omicron Kappa Upsilon (pres., founder Nashville chpt. 1947-49), Delta Omega. Democrat. Episcopalian Avocations: music, politics, track. Home: 5344 Highlight Pl Los Angeles CA 90016-5119 Office: U So Calif Sch Dentistry PO Box 77006 Los Angeles CA 90007-0006

DUMONT, JAMES KELTON, JR. actor, producer; b. Chgo., Aug. 12, 1965; s. James Kelton and Judith Katherine (Johnson) DuM.; m. Wendell Faith Hall, Dec. 14, 1968; 1 child, Sinclair Marie. Student, Boston U., 1983-85. Field recruiter Nat. Rsch. Group, Hollywood, 1993-2000; pres., CEO DuMont Entertainment Group, Hollywood, Calif., 1994—; sr. acct. mgr. The Snowballeffect Co., Hollywood, 2000—. Mem. Ensemble Studio Theatre, N.Y.C., 1989—; co-artistic dir. Ensemble Studio Theatre-The L.A. Project, 1994-96; producer Winterfests 1994-96—, First Look L.A., 1996. Appeared in Broadway play Six Degrees of Separation, 1990-93, (off-Broadway play) Tony & Tina's Wedding, 1989-90; films Speed, 1993, Combination Platter, 1993, Bombshell, 1996, The Peacemaker, 1996, Primary Colors, 1996, Erasable You, 1997, In Quiet Night, 1997, Bellyfruit, 1998, Love & Basketball, 1999; television series NYPD Blue, 1995, Lois & Clark, 1996, Chgo. Sons, 1996, Track Takes on 1995, Fallen Angels, 1995, The Client, 1995, Sweet Justice, 1995, Can't Hurry Love, 1995, Arliss, 1998, Then Came You, 1999, (TV) The West Wing, 2000, Becker, 2000, Titus, 2001, (TV films) Pentagon Wars, 1998, Winchell, 1999, Gotta Kick It Up, 2001; producer, actor: (film) The Confession, 1996. Democrat. Buddhist. Avocations: writing prose and short stories, plays and screenplays. Office: Ensemble Studio Theatre 137 N Larchmont Blvd # 134 Los Angeles CA 90004-3704 E-mail: dumontentgrp@earthlink.net, jdumont@snowballeffect.com

DUNBAR, MAURICE VICTOR, English language educator; b. Banner, Okla., May 24, 1928; s. Moyer Haywood and Louise Edna (Curry) D.; m. Carol Ann Cline, July 28, 1948 (div. 1963); children: Kurt, Karl, Karla, Karen, Kristen. AA, Compton Jr. Coll., 1948; BA, U. Calif., Berkeley, 1952; MA, Calif. State U., Sacramento, 1965. Elem. tchr. Lone Tree Sch., Beale AFB, Calif., 1962-64; tchr. Anna McKenney Jr. H.S., Marysville, 1964-66, Yuba City (Calif.) H.S., 1966-67; instr. Foothill Coll. Jr. Coll., Los Altos Hills, Calif., 1967-82; prof. English, De Anza Coll., Cupertino, 1982-98; ret., 1998. Author: Fundamentals of Book Collecting, 1976, Books and Collectors, 1980, Collecting Steinbeck, 1983, Hooked on Books, 1997; contbr. articles to profl. jours. With U.S. Army, 1948-58, PTO. Mem. Masons, Shriners (orator, libr. 1982—), B'nai B'rith. Avocations: book collecting, reading, travel, visiting university campuses. E-mail: mvdkcch@home.com

DUNCAN, GRIFF, music theater company executive; b. Morrilton, Ark., Mar. 25, 1933; BA, Chico State Coll., 1957. Co-founder Contra Costa Music Theatre, Walnut Creek, Calif., 1961—; co-founder, gen. mgr. Fullerton (Calif.) Civic Light Opera Co., 1971—. Producer more than 100 Broadway musicals. Recipient Best Prodn. award Critic's Choice, 1995, Bus. of Yr. award Fullerton C. of C., 1993, Founder's award, 1997. Mem. Nat. Alliance Music Theatre Producers. Office: Fullerton Civic Light Opera Co 218 W Commonwealth Ave Fullerton CA 92832-1880

DUNCAN, JAMES DANIEL, paper distribution company executive; b. LaSalle, Ill., June 12, 1941; s. Lawrence James and Margaret Mary (Brehm) D.; m. Sandra Ruth Crowe, Nov. 10, 1963; children: Lawrence, Brian, Stephen. BA in Journalism, U. Notre Dame, Ind., 1963; MBA in Mgmt., Xavier U., Cin., 1978. With sales dept. Campbell Soup Co., Chgo. and Mich., 1963-66; with sales and sales mgmt. depts. Weyerhaeuser Co., Chgo. and Houston, 1966-70; with sales mgmt. dept. Boise Cascade, Chgo. and Marion, Ind., 1970-71; with sales mgmt. and mgmt. depts. Internat. Paper Co., Pitts., N.Y.C. and Cin., 1971-82; exec. v.p., chief operating officer WWF Paper Corp., Phila., 1982-87, also bd. dirs.; pres. Grant Paper Co., Pennsauken, N.J., 1988-89; pres., chief exec. officer Sequoia Pacific Systems, Inc. (subs. Jefferson Smurfit Group), Exeter, Calif., 1989—. Mem. exec. com. Paper Distbn. Coun., N.Y., 1987—. Editor sales tng. manual, 1976. Mem. Nat. Paper Trade Assn. (printing paper com. 1986—). Republican. Roman Catholic. Avocations: golf, tennis, bridge. Home: 19255 Pinnacle St Visalia CA 93277 Office: Sequoia Pacific Sys Inc 1030 N Anderson Rd Exeter CA 93221-9341

DUNCAN, MARK, government official; BME, Royal Mil. Coll., 1968; Diploma of Pub. Adminstrn., Dalhousie U., 1975; MA in Pub. Adminstrn., Carleton U., 1981. Comml. pilot, 1974; registered profl. engr., Ont. Supt. airport sys. Transport Can., Ottawa, Ont., 1975-78, dep. airport gen. mgr., mgr. ops. Lester B.Pearson Airport Toronto, 1978-87, regional dir. gen. Airports Group Vancouver, B.C., 1987-96, regional dir. gen. Pacific Region, 1996—. Chmn. Pacific Coun. of Sr. Fed. Ofcls., 1994-95. Account exec. United Way; mem. Vancouver Bd. of Trade. Recipient Achievement award Internat. N.W. Aviation Coun., 1995. Home: 3116 Duchess Ave North Vancouver BC Canada V7K 3B6 Office: Dept Transport Pacific Reg 800 Burrard St PO Box 620 Vancouver BC Canada V6Z 2J8

DUNCAN, RONALD A. telecommunications company executive; b. 1953; B in Econs., Johns Hopkins U.; MBA, Harvard U. Founder, pres. Alaskavision; ptnr. Lyall Assocs.; with Gen. Comm. Inc., Anchorage, exec. v.p., founder, pres., CEO, 1989—. Bd. dirs., past chmn. Anchorage Econ. Devel. Corp.; chmn. Alaska Sci. and Tech. Found.; asst. dir. Johns Hopkins U. Ctr. for Met. Planning andRsch.; spl. asst. to Congressman John Dow. Office: Gen Comm Inc 2550 Denali St Ste 1000 Anchorage AK 99503-2781

DUNCAN, VERNE ALLEN, state legislator, university dean; b. McMinnville, Oreg., Apr. 6, 1934; s. Charles Kenneth and S. La Verne (Robbins) D.; m. Donna Rose Nichols, July 11, 1964; children: Annette Marie Kirk, Christine Lauree Didway. B.A., Idaho State U., 1960; M.Ed., Univ. Idaho, 1964; Ph.D., U. Oreg., 1968; M.B.A., U. Portland, 1976. Tchr. Butte County (Idaho) Pub. Schs., 1954-56, prin., 1958-63, supt. schs., 1963-66; rsch. asst. U. Oreg., 1966-68, asst. prof. ednl. adminstrn., 1968-70; supt. Clackamas County (Oreg.) Intermediate Edn. Dist., 1970-75; elected supt. pub. instrn. State of Oreg., 1975-89, re-elected, 1978, 82, 86; dean Sch. Edn. U. Portland, 1989-96, prof. emeritis, 1996-; mem. Idaho Ho. of Reps., Boise, 1963-65, Oreg. Senate, Salem, 1997—, asst. majority leader, 2001—. Chmn. commn. on ednl. credits and credentials Am. Coun. on Edn.; commr. Gov's Commn. on Futures Rsch.; mem. Edn. Commn. of States Author numerous articles on ednl. adminstrn. Trustee Marylhurst Coll.; mem. gov. bd. Fund for Improvement & Reform of Schs. & Teaching U.S. Dept. Edn., 1989-92; mem. Idaho Ho. of Reps., 1962-65, chmn. econ. affairs com.; mem. interim com. Oreg. Legis. Assembly Improvements Com.; mem. Nat. Coun. Chief State Sch. Officers, 1975-89, pres., 1987-89; bd. dirs. Nat. Conf. State Legislators. Served to col. U.S. Army, 1956-58. Mem. Am. Assn. Sch. Officers (pres. 1987-89), Res. Officers Assn., Nat. Forum Edn. Leaders, Sons and Daus. of Oreg. Pioneers (state pres. 1993—), Oreg. Assn. Colls. Tchr. Edn. (pres. 1994—), Phi Delta Kappa (educator-statesman of yr. award 1977). Presbyterian. Office: Oreg Senate S-317 State Capitol Salem OR 97310-0001

DUNDAS, DENNIS FRANKLIN, plastic surgeon; b. L.A., Oct. 12, 1942; s. John Arthur and Wanda (Yoakum) D.; m. Zoe Lynn Anderson, Feb. 9, 1969; children: Gregory, Denise. BA, Johns Hopkins U., 1964; MD, U. So. Calif., 1968. Diplomate Am. Bd Plastic Surgery. Pvt. practice, Kirkland, Wash., 1978—. Lt. comdr. USN, 1978—. Fellow ACS; mem. Am. Soc. Plastic Surgeons. Office: 13114 120th Ave NE Kirkland WA 98034-3014

DUNDES, ALAN, writer, folklorist, educator; b. N.Y.C., Sept. 8, 1934; s. Maurice and Helen (Rothschild) D.; m. Carolyn M. Browne, Sept. 8, 1958; children: Alison, Lauren, David. BA, Yale U., 1955, M.A.T., 1958; PhD, Ind. U., 1962. Instr. English U. Kans., 1962-63; asst. prof. anthropology U. Calif., Berkeley, 1963-65, assoc. prof., 1965-68, prof. anthropology and folklore, 1968—. Author: The Morphology of North American Indian Folktales, 1964, Analytic Essays in Folklore, 1975, Essays in Folkloristics, 1978, Interpreting Folklore, 1980, Life is Like a Chicken Coop Ladder: A Portrait of German Culture Through Folklore, 1984, Cracking Jokes: Studies of Sick Humor Cycles and Stereotypes, 1987, Parsing Through Customs: Essays by a Freudian Folklorist, 1987, Folklore Matters, 1989 From Game to War and Other Psychoanalytic Essays on Folklore, 1997, Two Tales of Crow and Sparrow: A Freudian Folkloristic Essay on Caste and Untouchability, 1997, Holy Writ as Oral Lit: The Bible as Folklore, 1999; co-author: La Terra in Piazza: An Interpretation of the Palio of Siena, 1975, Urban Folklore from the Paperwork Empire, 1975, The Art of Mixing Metaphors: A Folkloristic Interpretation of the Netherlandish Proverbs of Pieter Bruegel the Elder, 1981, First Prize: Fifteen Years! An Annotated Collection of Romanian Political Jokes, 1985, When You're Up to Your Ass in Alligators: More Urban Folklore from the Paperwork Empire, 1987, Never Try to Teach a Pig to Sing: Still More Urban Folklore from the Paperwork Empire, 1991, Sometimes The Dragon Wins: Yet More Urban Folklore from the Paperwork Empire, 1996, Why Don't Sheep Shrink When It Rains: A Further Collection of Photocopier Folklore, 2000;

editor: The Study of Folklore, 1965, Every Man His Way: Readings in Cultural Anthropology, 1968, Mother Wit from the Laughing Barrel: Readings in the Interpretation of Afro-American Folklore, 1972, Varia Folklorica, 1978, The Evil Eye: A Folklore Casebook, 1981, Cinderella: A Folklore Casebook, 1982, Sacred Narrative: Readings in the Theory of Myth, 1984, The Flood Myth, 1988, Little Red Riding Hood: A Casebook, 1989, The Blood Libel Legend: A Casebook in Anti-Semitic Folklore, 1991, The Cockfight: A Casebook, 1994, The Walled-Up Wife: A Casebook, 1996, The Vampire: A Casebook, 1998, International Folkloristics: Classic Contributions by the Founders of Folklore, 1999; co-editor: The Wisdom of Many: Essays on the Proverb, 1981, Oedipus: A Folklore Casebook, 1983, The Wandering Jew: Essays in The Interpretation of a Christian Legend, 1986, Folk Law: Essays in the Theory and Practice of Lex Non Scripta, 1994; compiler: Folklore Theses and Dissertations in the United States, 1976; contbr. articles to Ency. Britannica, Worldbook Ency., The Book of Knowledge, various profl. jours. With USNR, 1955-57. Recipient Chgo. Folklore 2d prize 1962, 1st prize 1976, Pitrè Prize, Sigillo d'oro, 1993; Guggenheim fellow, 1966-67, NEH sr. fellow, 1972-74. Mem. AAAS, Am. Folklore Soc. (pres. 1980), Fellows of the Am. Folklore Soc. (pres.) Calif. Folklore Soc., Internat. Soc. Folk Narrative Rsch. Home: 1590 La Vereda Rd Berkeley CA 94708-2036 Office: U Calif Dept Anthropology 201 Kroeber Hall Berkeley CA 94720-3711

DUNFORD, DAVID JOSEPH, foreign service officer, ambassador; b. Glen Ridge, N.J., Feb. 24, 1943; s. Thomas Joseph and Katherine Celeste (Jahn) D.; m. Sandra Corbett Mitchell, Dec. 18, 1965; children: Gregory, Kristina. BS in Engring., MIT, 1964; MA in Polit. Sci., Stanford U., 1965, MA in Econs., 1976. Jr. officer Am. Embassy, Quito, Ecuador, 1967-68, econ.-commercial officer Helsinki, Finland, 1969-72; dir. planning and econ. analysis staff Dept. State, Washington, 1977-79, dir. Office of Devel. Fin., 1979-80; dep. asst. U.S. trade rep. Office of U.S. Trade Rep., Washington, 1980-81; minister-counselor for econ. affairs Am. Embassy, Cairo, 1981-84; dir. Egyptian affairs Dept. State, Washington, 1984-87; dep. chief of mission Am. Embassy, Riyadh, Saudi Arabia, 1988-92, amb. to Oman, Muscat, 1992-95; ret. from fgn. svc., 1995; adj. prof. dept. polit. sci. U. Ariz., 1995—; coord. transition team Menabank, Cairo, 1997-98; adj. prof. Am. Grad. Sch. Internat. Mgmt., 1998-00. Bd. mem. Assn. for Internat. Practical Tng. Recipient Presdl. Meritorious Svc. awards, 1991, 92, Disting. Citizen award U. Ariz. Alumni Assn., 1994. Mem. Am. Fgn. Svc. Assn. (Christian A. Herter award 1991). Avocations: skiing, biking, hiking, writing fiction, photography.

DUNHAM, ANNE, educational institute director; Exec. dir. Youth Sci. Inst., L.A., 1995—. Office: Youth Sci Inst 296 Garden Hill Dr Los Gatos CA 95032-7669

DUNHAM, STEPHEN SAMPSON, lawyer; b. Bloomington, Ind., Oct. 19, 1945; s. Allison and Anne Campbell (Toll) D.; m. Victoria Baldwin Cass, May 24, 1969; children: Sarah W., Isaac P. BA, Princeton U., 1966; JD, Yale U., 1969. Bar: Calif. 1970, U.S. Dist. Ct. (no. dist.) Calif. 1972, U.S. Ct. Appeals (9th cir.) 1972, U.S. Dist. Ct. (cen. dist.) Calif. 1973, U.S. Supreme Ct. 1978, Minn. 1979, U.S. Dist. Ct. Minn. 1982, U.S. Ct. Appeals (8th cir.) 1983, Colo. 1988, U.S. Ct. Appeals (10th cir.) 1990. Law clk to Judge Stanley A. Weigel U.S. Dist. Ct. Calif., San Francisco, 1969-70; acting prof. law U. Calif., Davis, 1970-71; vis. assoc. prof. law Nat. Chengchi U., Taipei, 1971-72; assoc. Morrison & Foerster, San Francisco, 1972-76, ptnr., 1976-79, Denver, 1988—; assoc. prof. law U. Minn., Mpls., 1979-82, gen. counsel, 1982-85, v.p., gen. counsel, 1985-88. Instr. Nat. Inst. Trial Advocacy, Boulder, Colo., 1980, 83, Harvard U. Law Sch., Cambridge, Mass., 1985. Mem. Calif. State Bar (chair com. on legal svcs. 1978), Nat. Assn. Coll. and Univ. Attys. (bd. dirs. 1986-88), Colo. Lawyers Com. (bd. dirs. 1989—). Home: 650 Emerson St Denver CO 80218-3217 Office: Morrison & Foerster 5200 Republic Plaza 370 17th St Denver CO 80202-1370

DUNKLIN, BETSY D. state legislator; b. Goshen, Va., Oct. 9, 1949; m. Charles F. Cole; 1 child, Kate. BA in English, Newberry Coll., 1971; postgrad., U. S.C., 1972-73; MSW, U. Md., Balt., 1981. Svcs. coord. Families Forward, Boise, 1986, dir., 1986-87, Women's and Children's Crisis Ctr., Boise, 1987-89; bd. pres. Idaho Women's Network, Inc., Boise, 1989-90, exec. dir., 1990-94, pub. affairs coord. Planned Parenthood of Idaho, Boise, 1995-96; mem. Idaho Senate, Dist. 19, Boise, 1996—. Mem. edn. and judiciary and rules com.; adj. faculty, Boise State U., 1988-89. Mem. Idaho Coun. Tech. and Learning, Hispanic Commn. Idaho, Baltimore City Tenants' Assn., United Farm Workers. Mem. Idaho Women's Network (founding mem.; Opal Brooten award), Idaho Rivers United, WCA of Boise (pres. we. states ctr.). Democrat. Unitarian-Universalist. Office: State Capitol PO Box 83720 Boise ID 83720-3720

DUNLAP, F. THOMAS, JR. lawyer, electronics company executive; b. Pitts., Feb. 7, 1951; s. Francis Thomas and Margaret (Hubert) D.; m. Kathy Dunlap; children: Bridgette, Katie. B.S.E.E., U. Cin., 1974; J.D., U. Santa Clara, Calif., 1979. Bar: Calif., 1979, U.S. Dist. Ct. (no. dist.) Calif. 1979. Mgr. engring. Intel Corp, Santa Clara, Calif., 1974-78, adminstr. tech. exchange, 1978-80, European counsel, 1980-81, sr. atty., 1981-83, gen. counsel, sec., 1983-87, v.p., gen. counsel, sec., 1987—. Drafter, lobbyist Semiconductor Chip Protection Act, 1984 Republican. Roman Catholic. Avocation: jogging. Office: Intel Corp 2200 Mission College Blvd Ste 4 Santa Clara CA 95054-1549

DUNLEAVY, MICHAEL JOSEPH, professional basketball coach; b. Brooklyn, NY, Mar. 21, 1954; m. Emily Dunleavy; children: Michael, William Baker, James. Ed., Univ. S.C. Player Phila. 76ers, NBA, 1976-77; former player-coach Carolina Lightning, All-Am. Basketball Alliance; player Houston Rockets, NBA, 1978-83, San Antonio Spurs, NBA, 1982, Milw. Bucks, 1984, asst. coach, to 1990; head coach L.A. Lakers, 1990-92, Milw. Bucks, 1992-93, gen. mgr., v.p. basketball ops., 1993-96; head coach Portland (Oreg.) Trailblazers, 1997—. Office: Portland Trailblazers One Center Ct Ste 200 Portland OR 97227

DUNLOP, JOHN BARRETT, foreign language educator, research institution scholar; b. Boston, Sept. 10, 1942; s. John Thomas and Dorothy Emily (Webb) D.; m. Olga Verhovskoy, Sept. 12, 1965; children: Maria, John, Olga, Catherine BA, Harvard Coll., 1964; MA, Yale U., 1965, PhD, 1973. Prof. Russian Oberlin Coll., Ohio, 1970-83, chmn. dept. German and Russian, 1976-82; sr. fellow Hoover Instn., Stanford U., Calif., 1983—, assoc. dir., 1983-87. Mem. Soviet Union in the Eighties Project, CSIS, Georgetown U., 1982-83; mem. Eastern Great Lakes regional selection com. Mellon Fellowships in Humanities, 1982-83, applicant evaluations com. Woodrow Wilson Internat. Ctr. for Scholars, 1989-93; exec. coun. Midwest Slavic Conf., 1977-79; mem. editl. bd. Russian Archives Preservation Project, 1992—; mem. rsch. coun. Internat. Forum Democratic Studies Nat. Endowment for Democracy, 1994—; mem. exec. com. Assn. Study of Nationalities, 1994-97, mem. adv. com., 1997—; mem. steering com. Ctr. Russian and East European Studies Stanford U., 1995-97, 2000—; mem. overseers' com. Vis. to Kathryn W. and Shelby Cullom Davis Ctr. for Russian Studies, Harvard U., 1997—; disting. vis. U. Alta., 1995. Author: Staretz Amvrosy, 1972, 2d edit. 1975; The New Russian Revolutionaries, 1976; The Faces of Contemporary Russian Nationalism, 1983, The New Russian Nationalism, 1985, The Rise of Russia and the Fall of the Soviet Empire, 1993, 2d edit. 1995, Russia Confronts Chechnya, 1998; co-editor: Aleksandr Solzhenitsyn, 1973, 2d edit, 1975; Solzhenitsyn in Exile, 1985 Recipient Edward Chandler Cumming prize Harvard Coll., 1964; Woodrow Wilson fellow, 1965, Younger Humanist fellow, 1974-75, Hoover Instn. nat. fellow, 1978-79, Olin vis. sr. Fellow Radio Liberty, Munich, 1991-92; rsch. scholar Kennan Inst., 1987. Mem. Am. Assn. for Advancement of Slavic Studies, Western Slavic Assn. Eastern Orthodox Office: Stanford U Hoover Instn Stanford CA 94305

DUNN, ARNOLD SAMUEL, biochemistry educator; b. Rochester, N.Y., Jan. 31, 1929; s. Alexander and Dora (Cohen) D.; m. Doris Ruth Frankel, Sept. 14, 1952; children: Jonathan Alexander, David Hillel. B.S., George Washington U., 1950; Ph.D., U. Pa., 1955; LHD (hon.), Hebrew Union Coll., 1995. Research assoc. Michael Reese Hosp. Research Inst., Chgo., 1955-56; asst. prof. NYU Sch. Medicine, N.Y.C., 1956-62; vis. prof. Weizmann Inst. Sci., Rehovot, Israel, 1972-73, 83-84, Hebrew U., Jerusalem, 1972-73; prof. molecular biology U. So. Calif., Los Angeles, 1962—, dir. molecular biology L.A., 1982-90, assoc. dean, 1990-92; vis. fellow history sci. Princeton U., 1993. Contbr. articles to profl. jours.; mem. editorial bd.: Am. Jour. Physiology, 1979— , Analytical Biochemistry, 1980— . Recipient award for Teaching Excellence U. So. Calif., 1969; recipient award for Research Excellence U. So. Calif., 1972, Raubenheimer award U. So. Calif., 1981; UPSHS fellow, 1972, 83; Meyerhoff fellow Weizmann Inst. Sci., 1983 MEm. Am. Physiol. Soc., Am. Soc. Biol. Chemists, Endocrine Soc., Phi Beta Kappa, Sigma Xi, Phi Kappa Phi, Golden Key. Office: U So Calif University Park Los Angeles CA 90089-0001

DUNN, BRUCE SIDNEY, materials science educator; b. Chgo., Apr. 22, 1948; s. George Bernard and Goldye Rosalyn (Opper) D.; m. Wendy Joan Rader, June 7, 1970; 1 child, Julianne. BS in Ceramic Engring., Rutgers U., 1970; MS in Materials Sci., UCLA, 1972, PhD in Materials Sci., 1974. Staff scientist GE, Schenectady, N.Y., 1976-80; assoc. prof. materials sci. UCLA, 1981-85, prof., 1985—. Cons. to numerous corps.; invited prof. U. Paris, 1986, 91, 92, 93, 98, U. Bordeaux, 2000. Contbr. articles to profl. jours. Fulbright fellow, 1985-86. Fellow Am. Ceramic Soc.; mem. Electrochem. Soc., Materials Rsch. Soc. Achievements include patents in field. Office: UCLA Dept Materials Scis & Engring 6532 Boelter Hl Los Angeles CA 90095-0001

DUNN, DAVID JOSEPH, financial executive; b. Bklyn., July 30, 1930; s. David Joseph and Rose Marie (McLaughlon) D.; n. Marilyn Percaccia, June 1955 (div.); children: Susan, Steven, Linda; m. Marilyn Bell, Apr. 1994. BS, U.S. Naval Acad., 1955; MBA, Harvard U., 1961. Investment banker G.H. Walker & Co., N.Y.C., 1961-62; ptnr. J.H. Whitney & Co., N.Y.C., 1962-70; mng. ptnr. Idanta Ptnrs., San Diego, 1971—. Chmn. bd. Iomega Corp., Ogden, Utah, Munchkin Bottling, Inc., Van Nuys, Calif.; bd. dirs. Boxer/Cross, Menlo Park, Calif. With USMC, 1950-51, 55-59. Mem. Univ. Club (N.Y.C.), San Diego Yacht Club, LaJolla Country Club, Vintage Club, DelMar Country Club. Office: Idanta Ptnrs Ste #850 4660 La Jolla Village Dr San Diego CA 92122-4601

DUNN, GORDON HAROLD, physicist, researcher; b. Montpelier, Idaho, Oct. 11, 1932; s. Jesse Harold and Winifred Roma (Williams) D.; m. Donetta Dayton, Sept. 25, 1952; children: Jesse Lamont, Randall Dayton, Michael Scott, Brian Eugene, David Edward, Susan, Harold Paul, Richard Elzo. BS in Physics, U. Wash., 1954, PhD in Physics, 1961. NRC postdoctoral rsch. assoc. Nat. Bur. Standards, Washington, 1961-62; physicist Nat. Bur. Standards/Join Inst. for Lab. Astrophysics, Boulder, Colo., 1962-77, chief quantum physics divsn., 1977-85; sr. scientist and fellow Nat. Inst. Standards/Joint Inst. for Lab. Astrophysics, Boulder, 1985—. Lectr. dept. physics U. Colo., Boulder, 1964-74, adj. prof., 1974—; commerce sci. fellow Commn. on Sci. & Tech., U.S. Ho. of Reps., Washington, 1975-76; chmn. com. on atomic molecular & optical sci. NRC, Washington, 1990—, vice-chair, 1989-90, mem. com., 1983-86; mem. NRC Panel on Instruments and Facilities, Washington, 1983-84, NRC Panel on Ion Storage Rings for Atomic Physics, 1985-88; mem. gen. com. Internat. Conf. on Physics of Electron & Atomic Collisions, 1995-97, vicei chair, 1993-95, exec. com., 1991-93, gen. com., 1969-73, program com., 1974-75; chmn. Gaseous Electronics Conf., 1968-69, com. mem., 1966-70, sec., 1967-68; chmn. Atomic Processes in High Temperature Plasmas, 1980-81, com. mem., 1977-81, co-sec., 1978-79; co-organizer NATO Advanced Study Inst., 1984-85, U.S.-Japan Workshop, 1985-86; bd. editors Jour. Phys. & Chem. Reference Data, 1990—. Editor, author. Electron-Impact Ionization, 1985; contbr. more than 160 articles to profl. jours. Scoutmaster Boy Scouts Am., Boulder, 1967-72, 87-88; coach, league pres. Little League, Boulder, 1966-71, 76-77; pres. Parent-Tchr. Orgns., Boulder, 1973, 75; bishop LDS Ch., Boulder, 1977-82; trainer family history missionaries Family History Libr., Salt Lake City, 1999-2000. Recipient Gold medal U.S. Dept. Commerce, 1970. Fellow Am. Phys. Soc. (chmn. div. atomic & molecular physics 1989-90, vice-chair 1988-89, exec. com. 1969, 85-88, 91, counsilor 1995-99, audit com. 1996-97, com. constitution & by-laws 1997-99, task force governance 1998-99, panel pub. affairs, Davisson-Germer prize 1984), Joint Inst. for Lab. Astrophysics. Avocations: jogging, skiing, dancing, hunting, camping. Office: U Colo Joint Inst Lab Astrophysics Chmn PO Box 440 Boulder CO 80309-0440 E-mail: gdunn28@home.com, gdunn@jila.colorado.edu

DUNN, JENNIFER BLACKBURN, congresswoman; b. Seattle, July 29, 1941; d. John Charles and Helen (Gorton) Blackburn; div.; children: Bryant, Reagan. Student, U. Wash., 1960-62; BA in English Lit., Stanford U., 1963. Sys. engr. IBM, 1964-69; with King County Dept. of Assessments, 1979-80; former chmn. Rep. Party State of Wash., 1981-92; mem. U.S. Congress from 8th Wash. dist., Washington, 1993—. Bd. dirs. Nat. Endowment Democracy; mem. ways and means com.; mem. adv. bd. Internat. Rep. Inst.; participant Preparatory Commn. World Conf. Status of Women, Nairobi, 1985, World Econ. Forum, Davos, Switzerland, 2000. Del. Rep. Nat. Conv., 1980, 84, 88; presdl. apptd. adv. coun. Historic Preservation, adv. coun. volunteerism SBA; apptd. presdl. commn. on debates; N.W. Regional Dir. Met. Operal Regional Auditions; mem. Jr. League of Seattle Named one of 25 Smartest Women in Am., Mirabella mag., one of 10 Most Powerful Women in Wash., Washington Law and Politics mag. Mem. Internat. Women's Forum (Wash. chpt.), Gamma Phi Beta. Office: US Ho Reps 1501 Longworth Ho Office Bldg Washington DC 20515-4708*

DUNN, JOSEPH, state legislator; b. 1958; m. Diane Dunn; 2 children. BA, Coll. St. Thomas, 1980; JD, U. Minn., 1983. Atty. in pvt. practice; mem. Calif. State Senate, 1998—, mem. edn., budget, govtl. orgn. and vets. affairs coms., vice chmn. transp. com. Named Outstanding State Senator, Calif. chpt. VFW. Democrat. Avocations: racquetball, long distance bicycling. Office: Calif State Senate State Capitol Rm 2068 Sacramento CA 95814 also: 12397 Lewis St Ste 203 Garden Grove CA 92840-4679

DUNN, LIN, professional basketball coach; b. Nashville, May 10, 1947; BS in Health and Phys. Edn., U. Tenn., Martin, 1969; MS in Phys. Edn., U. Tenn., 1970. Women's basketball coach Austin Peay State, 1970-76, U. Miss., Oxford, 1977-78, U. Miami, 1979-87, Perdue U., W. Lafayette, Ind., 1987-96; head coach Portland Power, Oreg., 1996-98; draft consultant & assist. coach Houston Comets, 1998-99; head coach & gen. mgr. Seattle Storm, 1999—. Asst. coach silver-medal winning Select Team, 1986, gold-medal winning Pam Am. Games, 1987, Select Team, 1989, gold-medal winning Goodwill Games, gold-medal winning World Championship teams, 1990, Olympic bronze-medal winning team, Barcelona, Spain, 1992; head coach bronze-medal winning R. Williams Jones Cup team, Taipei, Taiwan, 1995; mem. Player Selection Com. that overseas the selection of players for all U.S.A. basketball teams. Achievements include being the first Big Ten coach to serve on an Olympic staff. Office: Seattle Storm 351 Elliott Ave W Seattle WA 98119-4101 E-mail: info@portlandpower.com

DUNN, PATRICIA C. investment company executive; AB in Journalism and Econ., U. Calif., Berkeley. With Barclays Global Investors, N.A., San Francisco, 1976—, chmn. Bd. dirs. Hewlett-Packard Co. Contbr. articles to profl. jours. Mem. new media bd., U. Calif. Sch. Journalism, Berkeley. Office: Barclays Global Investors 45 Fremont St San Francisco CA 94105-2204

DUNN, RANDALL L. federal judge; Apptd. bankruptcy judge U.S. Dist. Ct. Oreg., 1998. Office: 1001 SW 5th Ave Ste 700 Portland OR 97204-1141

DUNN, RICHARD BRADNER, retired solar astronomer; b. Balt., Dec. 14, 1927; s. Halbert Louis and Katherine (Brandner) D.; m. Alice Jane Biggam, July 21, 1951. B.M.E., U. Minn., 1949; M.S., 1950; Ph.D., Harvard U., 1961. Solar astronomer Nat. Solar Obs., Sunspot, N.Mex., 1953-98, acting dir., 1975-76. Served with U.S. Army, 1945-46. Mem. Am. Astron. Soc. (George Ellery Hale award 1997). Achievements include designer of the vacuum solar telescope, 1969. Home: 4015 Cholla Rd Las Cruces NM 88011-7604 Office: Nat Solar Observatory PO Box 62 Sunspot NM 88349-0062

DUNN, RICHARD JOSEPH, retired investment counselor; b. Chgo., Apr. 5, 1924; s. Richard Joseph and Margaret Mary (Jennett) D. m. Marygrace Calhoun, Oct. 13, 1951 (dec. May 2000); children: Richard, Marianne, Anythony, Gregory, Noelle. AB, Yale U., 1948; LLB, Harvard U., 1951; MBA, Stanford U., 1956. Bar: Tex. 1952. Mem. Carrington, Gowan, Johnson & Walker, Dallas, 1951-54; investment counselor Scudder, Stevens & Clark, San Francisco, 1956-84, v.p., 1965-77, sr. v.p., 1977-84, gen. ptnr., 1974-84, ret. Served with AUS, 1943-46. Decorated Combat Infantry Badge, Bronze Star, Purple Heart, Knight of the Sovereign Mil. Hospitalier Order of St. John of Jerusalem of Rhodes and of Malta, Western Assn., 1978, chancellor, 1987-93, pres. 1993-99, sovereign coun., 1999, knight of obedience, 1990, Grand Cross of Merit, 1999, Grand Cross The Sacred Mil. Constantinian Order of St. George, 1995, Grand Cross of Grace and Devotion in Obedience, 2000, Knight of St. Gregory, 2000; recipient Assumpta award Archdiocese of San Francisco, 1996. Roman Catholic. Home: 530 Junipero Serra Blvd San Francisco CA 94127-2727

DUNNE, KEVIN JOSEPH, lawyer; b. Pitts., Sept. 22, 1941; s. Matthew S. and Marjorie (Whelan) D.; m. Heather Wright Dunne, Sept. 27, 1963; children: Erin, Kevin Jr., Patrick, Sean. BA, U. Conn., 1963; JD, Georgetown U., 1966. Bar: Calif. 1967, U.S. Dist. Ct. (no. dist.) Calif., 1967, U.S. Dist. Ct. (ea. dist.) Calif. 1969, U.S. Dist. Ct. (ctrl. dist.) Calif. 1971, U.S. Ct. Appeals (9th cir.) 1971. Assoc. Sedgwick, Detert, Moran & Arnold, San Francisco, 1968-75, ptnr., 1975—. Adj. prof. U. San Francisco Sch. Law, 1980-86; bd. editorial advisors Bender's Drug Product Liability Reporter, 1988-92. Author: Dunne on Depositions, 1995; editor Defense Counsel Training Manual, 1989; contbr. articles to profl. jours. Capt. U.S. Army, 1966-68, Vietnam. Recipient Bronze Star, Army Commendation medal; recipient Exceptional Performance award Def. Rsch. Inst., 1988. Fellow Internat. Acad. Trial Lawyers, Am. Coll. Trial Lawyers; mem. No. Calif. Assn. Def. Counsel (pres. 1987-88), Internat. Assn. Def. Counsel (pres. elect 1994-95), Am. Bd. Trial Advocates. Roman Catholic. Avocation: golf. Office: Sedgwick Detert Moran & Arnold 1 Embarcadero Ctr Ste 1600 San Francisco CA 94111-3716

DUNNE, THOMAS, geology educator; b. Prestbury, U.K., Apr. 21, 1943; came to U.S., 1964; s. Thomas and Monica Mary (Whitter) D. BA with honors, Cambridge (Eng.) U., 1964; PhD, Johns Hopkins U., 1969. Research assoc. USDA-Agrl. Research Service, Danville, Vt., 1966-68; research hydrologist U.S. Geol. Survey, Washington, 1969; asst. prof. McGill U., Montreal, Que., Can., 1969-73; from asst. prof. to prof. U. Wash., Seattle, 1973-95, chmn. dept., 1984-89; prof. sch. environ. scis. & mgmt. U. Calif., Santa Barbara, 1995—. Vis. prof. U. Nairobi, Kenya, 1969-71; cons. in field, 1970—. Author (with L.B. Leopold) Water in Environmental Planning; (with L.M. Reid) Rapid Evaluation of Sediment Budgets, 1996. Fulbright scholar 1984; grantee NSF, NASA, Rockefeller Found., 1969—; named to NAS. 1988, Guggenheim fellow, 1989-90. Fellow AAAS, Am. Acad. Arts and Scis., Am. Geophys. Union (Robert E. Horton award 1987), Calif. Acad. Scis.; mem. NAS (G.K. Warren prize in Fluviatile Geology 1998), Geol. Soc. Am., Sigma Xi. Office: U Calif Donald Bren Sch Environ Scis & Mgmt 4670 Physical Sciences N Santa Barbara CA 93106

DUNNER, DAVID LOUIS, medical educator; b. Bklyn., May 27, 1940; s. Edward and Reichel (Connor) D.; m. Peggy Jane Zolbert, Dec. 27, 1964; children: Laura Louise, Jonathan Michael. AA, George Washington U., 1960; MD, Washington U., St. Louis, 1965. Diplomate Am. Bd. Psychiatry and Neurology. Intern Phila. Gen. Hosp., 1965-66; resident in psychiatry Barnes Renard Hosp. of Washington U., St. Louis, 1966-69; research psychiatrist N.Y. State Psychiat. Inst., N.Y.C., 1971-79; from asst. prof. to assoc. prof. clin. psychiatry Columbia U., N.Y.C., 1972-79; chief psychiatry Harborview Med. Ctr., Seattle, 1979-89, dir. outpatient psychiatry, 1989-97; prof. psychiatry and behavioral scis. U. Wash., Seattle, 1979—, vice chmn. clin. svcs., 1989-97; dir. Ctr. for Anxiety & Depression, 1997—. Cons. Found. for Depression and Manic Depression, N.Y.C., 1974—. Editor-in-chief Comprehensive Psychiatry, 1997—; contbr. articles to profl. jours. Served to lt. comdr. USPHS, 1969-71. Fellow Am. Psychiat. Assn., Am. Psychopathol. Assn. (pres. 1986), Am. Coll. Neuropsychopharmacology, West Coast Coll. Biol. Psychiatry (charter, pres. 1987); mem. Psychiat. Research Soc. (pres. 1984). Office: Ctr for Anxiety & Depression 4225 Roosevelt Way NE Ste 306C Seattle WA 98105-6099 E-mail: ddunner@u.washington.edu, dldunner@hotmail.com

DUNNING, KENNETH LAVERNE, research physicist; b. Yale, Iowa, Sept. 24, 1914; s. Howard Grant and Gertrude Estelle (Dygert) D.; m. Ruth Ellen Pyle, Sept. 2, 1941; children: David M., Jane B., John K., Marion Leigh. BEE, U. Minn., 1938; MS in Physics, U. Md., 1950; PhD in Physics, Cath. U. Am., 1968. Engr. Western Union, N.Y.C., 1938-41; physicist U.S. Naval Research Lab., Washington, 1945-80; cons. Port Ludlow, Wash., 1981—. Contbr. articles to profl. jours. Pres. Highland Greens Condominium Assn., Port Ludlow, 1983-84, v.p. 1984-85. Served to maj. U.S. Army, 1941-45. Recipient Research Pub. award Naval Research Lab., 1971. Mem. IEEE, Am. Phys. Soc., Sigma Xi, Tau Beta Pi, Eta Kappa Nu. Home and Office: 10 Foster Ln Port Ludlow WA 98365-9611

DUNNING, THOM H., JR. environmental molecular science executive; BS in Chemistry, U. Mo., Rolla, 1965; PhD in Chem. Physics, Calif. Inst. Tech., 1970. Rsch. fellow, instr. Calif. Inst. Tech.; staff mem. Los Alamos Nat. Lab., 1973-78; sr. scientist Argonne Nat. Lab., 1978-89, group leader theoretical and computational chemistry group, 1978-89, head chem. dynamics program, 1978-89; assoc. dir. for theory, modeling and stimulation Pacific Northwest Nat. Lab., 1989-94, dir. Environ. Molecular Scis. Lab., 1994-97, Battelle fellow, sr. staff mem. environ. health scis. divsn., 1997—, mgr. fundamental sci. products, 1997—. Mem. chemistry adv. com. NSF; mem. exec. com. Energy Rsch. Supercomputer Users Group; mem. policy bd. Concurrent Supercomputing Consortium; mem. CRF adv.

com. Sandia Nat. Lab., DOE's Coun. on Chem. Scis., NRC's Chem. Scis. Roundtable; affiliate prof. U. Wash., 1990—; adj. prof. Wash. State U., 1990—; mem. adv. com. Sandia Nat. Labs., Livermore, 1995—; mem. sci. and tech. adv. com. Brookhaven Nat. Lab., 1997—; mem. rsch. mgmt. team U.S. Army Rsch. Lab., 1998—. Series editor Advances in Molecular Electronic Structure, 1987—; topical editor Computer Physics Comm.; mem. editl. bd. Jour. Chem. Physics, 1998—; contbr. articles to profl. jours. Mem. coun. for chem. scis. Chem. Scis. Divsn. U.S. Dept. Energy, 1996—; vice-chmn. chem. scis. roudtable, bd. mem. Nat. Rsch. Coun., 1997—. Recipient E.O. Lawrence award DOE, 1996, Ernest Orlando Lawrence Meml. award, 1996; Woodrow Wilson fellow, 1965-66, NSF fellow, 1966-69, postdoctoral fellow Battelle Meml. Inst., 1970. Fellow AAAS, Am. Phys. Soc. (sec.-treas. 1998—); mem. Am. Chem. Soc. (councilor 1998—). Office: Battelle Pacific NW Labs PO Box 999 Richland WA 99352-0999

DUNSTAN, LARRY KENNETH, insurance company executive; b. Payson, Utah, May 26, 1948; s. Kenneth Leroy Dunstan and Verna Matilda (Carter) Taylor; m. Betty K. Limb, Sept. 23, 1966 (div. June 1975); children: Tamara, Thane; m. Jacqueline Lee Darron, Oct. 7, 1975; children: Tessa, Matthew, Bennett, Spencer, Adam. CLU, CPCU, chartered fin. cons., registered health underwriter, life underwriter tng. council fellow. Mgr. Diamond Bar Inn Ranch, Jackson, Mont., 1972-73; agt. Prudential Ins. Co., Missoula, 1973-77, devel. mgr. Billings, 1977-78, div. mgr. Gt. Falls, 1978-83; pres. Multi-Tech Ins. Services, Inc., West Linn, Oreg., 1983—; agy. mgr. Beneficial Life Ins. Co., Portland, 1983-88. Mem. planning commn. City of West Linn, Oreg., 1985-87; mem. bishopric Ch. Jesus Christ of Latter Day Sts., West Linn, 1984-86, exec. sec. Lake Oswego Oreg. Stake, 1987-89; scouting coord. Boy Scouts Am., West Linn, 1984-86, scoutmaster various troops; pres. West Linn Youth Basketball Assn., 1991-97, West Linn/Wilsonville Youth Track Club, 1993-96. Named Eagle Scout Boy Scouts Am., 1965, recipient Heroism award 1965. Fellow Life Underwriter Tng. Coun. (bd. dirs. local chpt. 1980-81); mem. Gen. Agts. and Mgrs. Assn. (bd. dirs. local chpt. 1981-82), Am. Soc. CLU (pres. local chpt. 1982-83). Republican. Avocations: sports, stamp collecting, hunting, gardening, photography. Home: 19443 Wilderness Dr West Linn OR 97068-2005 Office: Multi-Tech Ins Svcs 19125 Willamette Dr West Linn OR 97068-2019

DUNYE, CHERYL, artist, film maker; b. Phila. BA, Temple U.; MFA, Rutgers U. Part-time instr. dept. media studies Pitzer Coll., Calif. Film maker (short film) Greetings from Africa, 1994, (video) The Potluck and the Passion; dir., creator (film) The Watermelon Woman; contbr. articles to profl. jours. Recipient MARMAF Pa. Major Artists award, 1993; grantee Astrea Found., 1992, Frameline, 1992, Nat. Endowment of the Arts, 1995; fellow Rugers U., 1990, 91, Art Matters, Inc., 1992. Office: c/o Media Studies Pitzer Coll Scott Hall Basement 1050 N Mills Ave Claremont CA 91711-3908

DU PEN, EVERETT GEORGE, sculptor, educator; b. San Francisco, June 12, 1912; s. George E. and Novelle (Freeman) DuP.; m. Charlotte Canada Nicks, July 1, 1939; children: Stuart, Destia, Novelle, William, Ninia, Marguerite. Student, U. So. Calif., 1931-33, Chouinard Art Sch., Los Angeles, summer 1932, Harvard Sch. Architecture, , summer 1933; B.F.A. (scholar), Yale, 1937; B.F.A. European traveling fellow, 1937-38. Teaching fellow Carnegie Inst. Tech. Sch. Art, 1939-39; teaching asst. sculpture Washington U. Sch. Art, St. Louis, 1939-42; marine draftsman and loftsman Sausalito Shipbldg. Corp., Calif., 1942-45; instr. sculpture U. Wash. Sch. Art, Seattle, 1945-47, asst. prof., 1947-54, asso. prof. sculpture, 1954-60, prof. art, 1960-82, prof. emeritus, 1982—, chmn. sculpture div. One-man shows include Seattle Art Mus., 1950, Bon Marche Nat. Gallery, Seattle, 1970, Fred Cole Gallery, Seattle, 1973, Pacific Luth. U., Tacoma, 1975, Wash. Mut. Savs. Bank, Seattle, 1979-80, Frye Art Mus., Seattle, Martin and Zambito Gallery, Seattle; exhibited Prix de Rome Exhbn., Grand Central Gallery, N.Y.C., 1935-37, 39, St. Louis Mus. Ann., 1939-42, Nat. Acad. Design, N.Y.C., 1943, 49, 53-55, 57-58, Seattle Art Mus. Ann., 1945-59, Pa. Acad. Art, Phila., 1950-52, 55-58, Ecclesiastical Sculpture competition, 1950, Sculpture Ctr., N.Y.C., 1951, 53, 54, Pa. Acad. Fine Arts, 1954-58, Detroit Mus. Art, 1958, N.W. Inst. Sculpture, San Francisco Art Assn., 1959, Mainstreams, 1972, Marietta Coll., 1972, Holt Galleries, Olympia, Wash., 1980, Martin & Zambotti Gallery, Seattle, 1991-92, Freemont Art Gallery, Seattle, 1991-92, Ellensburg, Wash. Community Art Gallery, 1988, Bellevue, Wash. Invitational, Bellevue Art Mus., 1988, NAD, 1989, Wash. State Art Centennial Exhbn., Tacoma Art Mus., 1990; retrospective exhibits at Martin & Zambet Gallery, Seattle, 1994, Firye Art Mus., Seattle, 1994; represented in permanent collections Wash. Mut. Savs. Bank, Seattle, Bell Telephone Co., Seattle, Nat. Acad. Design, N.Y.C. (Saltus medal 1954), Seattle Art Mus., Safeco Ins. Co., U. Wash., also sculptures in pvt. collections; creator garden figures and portrait heads, small bronze, terra cotta, hardwood sculptures, archtl. medallions, sculpture panels for comml. bldgs. and theatres, figures and wood carvings various chs., relief panels U. Wash. campus, 1946, 83, bronze fountain Wash. State Library, Olympia, 1959, Du Pen Fountain, bronze fountain Coliseum Century 21, Seattle World's Fair, 2 walnut screens Mcpl. Bldg., Seattle, 8 large sculpture commns. Seattle chs., 1957-64, wood carving Risen Christ, St. Pius X Cath. Ch., Montlake Terrace, Wash., 1983, 3-foot wood carving St. Joseph and Mary, 1985, 6-foot wood carving Ascension, St. Elizabeth Seton Ch., Bothell, Wash., 1986, Elizabeth and Mary, 5-foot mahogany for Visitation Ctr., Fed. Way, Wash., 1990, 2-figure group for Dallas, 1982, bronze figure Edmonds, Wash., 1983-84, bronze sculpture of Charles Odegaard, pres. U. Wash., 1973, pvt. commns. Mem. U. Wash. Senate, 1952-55, exec. com., 1954-55; v.p. Allied Arts Movement for Seattle; mem. Seattle Municipal Art Commn., 1958-63. Recipient Saltus gold medal NAD, 1954, 1st prize for sculpture Bellevue (Washington) Arts and Crafts Fair, 1957; U. Wash. research grantee for creative sculpture, 1953-54 Fellow Nat. Sculpture Soc. (hon. mention Henry Herring competition); mem. Artists Equity Assn. (bd. Seattle chpt.), Nat. Acad. Design, Puget Sound N.W. Painters Group (bd.), N.W. Inst. Sculpture (pres. 1957), Allied Artists Am., U. Wash. Research Soc., Northwest Stone Sculptors, Seattle (bd. dirs. 1989—). Home: 4400 Stone Way N Apt 240 Seattle WA 98103-7486

DUPREE, STANLEY M. lawyer; b. Thomaston, Ga., Sept. 7, 1946; BA, Stanford U., 1971; JD, U. Calif., 1974. Bar: CAlif. 1974. Instr. U. Calif., 1976-82; law clerk, acting ct. commr. San Francisco Superior Ct., 1974-76; ptnr. Schultz & Dupree, San Francisco, Dupree & Colvin. Mem. ABA, State Bar Calif., Bar Assn. San Francisco. Office: Dupree & Colvin Ste 200 777 E Tahquitz Canyon Way Palm Springs CA 92262-6797

DUQUETTE, DIANE RHEA, library director; b. Springfield, Mass., Dec. 15, 1951; d. Gerard Lawrence and Helen Yvette (St. Marie) Morneau; m. Thomas Frederick Duquette Jr., Mar. 17, 1973. BS in Sociology, Springfield Coll., 1975; MLS, Simmons Coll., 1978. Libr. asst. Springfield City Libr., 1975-78; reference libr. U. Mass., Amherst, 1978-81; head libr. Hopkins Acad., Hadley, Mass., 1980; instr. Colo. Mountain Coll., Steamboat Springs, 1981-83; libr. dir. East Routt Libr. Dist., Steamboat Springs, 1981-84; agy. head Solano County Libr., Vallejo, Calif., 1984; dir. libr. svcs. Shasta County Libr., Redding, 1984-87; dir. librs. Kern County Libr., Bakersfield, 1987—. Chmn. San Joaquin Valley Libr. System, 1988. Contbr. articles to profl. jours. Recipient John Cotton Dana Spl. Pub. Rels. award, H.W. Wilson and ALA, 1989. Mem. ALA, Calif. Libr. Assn. (mem. coun. 1987—), Calif. County Librs. Assn. (pres. 1990). Democrat. Roman Catholic. Avocations: golf, skiing, bicycling, reading, gardening. Home: Pine Mountain Club PO Box 6505 Frazier Park CA 93222-6505 Office: Kern County Libr 701 Truxtun Ave Bakersfield CA 93301-4800

DURAN, DIANNA J. state legislator; b. Tularosa, 1956; Dep. chief clk. County; mem. N.Mex. Senate, Dist. 40, Sante Fe, 1992—; mem. edn. com., mem. ways and means com. N.Mex. Senate. Republican. Office: 909 8th St Rm 423 Tularosa NM 88352-2221 E-mail: dduran@state.nm.us

DURAN, MICHAEL CARL, bank executive; b. Colorado Springs, Colo., Aug. 27, 1953; s. Lawrence Herman and Jacqueline Carol (Ward) D. BS magna cum laude, Ariz. State U., 1980. With Valley Nat. Bank (name now Bank One, Ariz., N.A.), Phoenix, 1976—; corp. credit trainee Bank One Ariz. (formerly Valley Nat. Bank Ariz.), Phoenix, 1984-85; comml. loan officer Valley Nat. Bank Ariz. (name now Bank One Ariz.), Phoenix, 1985-86; br. mgr., asst. v.p. Valley Nat. Bank Ariz. (name now Bankone, Ariz.), Phoenix, 1986-90, comml. banking officer, asst. v.p., 1990-93, credit mgr., v.p., 1993-99, relationship mgr., v.p., 1999—. Cons. various schs. and orgns., 1986—; incorporator Avondale Neighborhood Housing Svcs., 1988. Mem. Cen. Bus. Dist. Revitalization Com., Avondale, Ariz., 1987-88, Ad-Hoc Econ. Devel. Com., 1988; coord. Avondale Litter Lifters, 1987-88; vol. United Way, Phoenix, 1984; bd. dirs. Jr. Achievement, Yuma, Ariz., 1989-91, vol., Phoenix, 1993—; yokefellow 1st So. Bapt. Ch. of Yuma, 1990-91; treas. Desert View Bapt. Ch., Gilbert, Ariz., 1998—. Recipient Outstanding Community Svc. award City of Avondale, 1988. Mem. Robert Morris Assocs., Ariz. State U. Alumni Assn. (life), Toastmasters, Kiwanis (local bd. dirs. 1986-88), Beta Gamma Sigma, Phi Kappa Phi, Phi Theta Kappa, Sigma Iota Epsilon. Democrat. Baptist. Avocations: art, photography, hiking, jogging. Home: 925 N Quartz St Gilbert AZ 85234-3661

DURAND, BARBARA, dean, nursing educator; Dean Coll. Nursing, prof. Ariz. State U., Tempe. Office: Ariz State U PO Box 872602 458 Nursing Bldg Tempe AZ 85287-2602

DURCAN, MARK D. engineering executive; BS, M in Chem. Engring., Rice U. Diffusion engr. Micron Tech. Inc., 1984, various positions, process integration mgr., process R&D devel. mgr., v.p. process R&D, chief tech. officer, 1996—. Office: Micron Tech Inc PO Box 6 8000 S Federal Way Boise ID 83707-0006

DURDEN, ROME L. aircraft manufacturing company executive; b. L.A., Apr. 5, 1935; s. Rome and Hortense (Anderson) D.; m. Priscilla Louise Bibby, Oct. 27, 1962; children: Suzette, Steven. B in Laws, La Salle Extension U., 1971; DD (hon.), Universal Life, Modesto, Calif., 1980. Tech. writer Hughes Aircraft Co., Culver City, Calif., 1962-72, sr. tech. editor, 1972-79, sr. mgmt. systems specialist, 1979-89. Author: (Manuals) Guide for Drafting Procedure, 1981, Simplified Drawing Substitutions, 1984. Treas. Marysville United Meth. Ch., 1997-99; mem. Lake Stevens Governance Coun., 1999, 2000. Recipient Presentation gavel Ramona Park Adv. Coun., Long Beach, Calif., 1971. Mem. Harmony Woods Homeowners Assn. (bd. dirs., treas. 1996-99, v.p. 2000—). Home: PO Box 1322 Lake Stevens WA 98258-1322

DURHAM, BARBARA, retired state supreme court justice; b. 1942; BSBA, Georgetown U.; JD, Stanford U. Bar: Wash. 1968. Former judge Wash. Superior Ct., King County; judge Wash. Ct. Appeals; justice Wash. Supreme Ct., 1985-99, chief justice, 1995-99. Office: Wash Supreme Ct Temple of Justice PO Box 40929 Olympia WA 98504-0929

DURHAM, CHRISTINE MEADERS, state supreme court justice; b. L.A., Aug. 3, 1945; d. William Anderson and Louise (Christensen) Meaders; m. George Homer Durham II, Dec. 29, 1966; children: Jennifer, Meghan, Troy, Melinda, Isaac. A.B., Wellesley Coll., 1967; J.D., Duke U., 1971. Bar: N.C. 1971, Utah 1974. Sole practice law, Durham, N.C., 1971-73; instr. legal medicine Duke U., Durham, 1971-73; adj. prof. law Brigham Young U., Provo, Utah, 1973-78; ptnr. Johnson, Durham & Moxley, Salt Lake City, 1974-78; judge Utah Dist. Ct., 1978-82; state supreme ct. assoc. justice Utah Supreme Ct., 1982—. Pres. Women Judges Fund for Justice, 1987-88. Fellow Am. Bar Found.; mem. ABA (edn. com. appellate judges' conf.), Nat. Assn. Women Judges (pres. 1986-87), Utah Bar Assn., Am. Law Inst. (coun. mem.), Nat. Ctr. State Courts (bd. dirs.), Am. Inns of Ct. Found. (trustee). Office: Utah Supreme Ct PO Box 140210 Salt Lake City UT 84114-0210

DURHAM, ROBERT DONALD, JR. state supreme court justice; b. Lynwood, Calif., May 10, 1947; s. Robert Donald Durham and Rosemary Constance (Brennan) McKelvey; m. Linda Jo Rollins, Aug. 29, 1970; children: Melissa Brennan, Amy Elizabeth. BA, Whittier Coll., 1969; JD, U. Santa Clara, 1972; LLM in the Judicial Process, U. Va., 1998. Bar: Oreg. 1972, Calif. 1973, U.S. Dist. Ct. Oreg. 1974, U.S. Ct. Appeals (9th cir.) 1980, U.S. Supreme Ct. 1987. Law clk. Oreg. Supreme Ct., Salem, 1972-74; ptnr. Bennett & Durham, Portland, Oreg., 1974-91; assoc. judge Oreg. Ct. Appeals, Salem, 1991-94; state supreme ct. assoc. justice Oreg. Supreme Ct., Salem, 1994—. Mem. adv. com. to Joint Interim Judiciary Com., 1984-86; chair Oreg. Commn. on Adminstrv. Hearings, 1988-89; faculty Nat. Jud. Coll., Reno, Nev., 1992; mem. Case Disposition Benchmarks Com., 1992-93, Coun. on Ct. Procedures, 1992-93, 95—; mem. Oreg. Rules of Appellate Procedure Com., 1998—; bd. dirs. Oreg. Law Inst., 2001—. Mem. ACLU Lawyer's Com., Eugene and Portland, Oreg., 1978-91. Recipient award for civil rights litigation ACLU of Oreg., 1988, Ed Elliott Human Rights award Oreg. Edn. Assn., Portland, 1990. Mem. Am. Acad. Appellate Lawyers (ninth cir. screening com. 1991—, rules com. 1994, co-chair appellate cts. liaison com. 1994), Oreg. Appellate Judges Assn. (pres. 1996-97), Oreg. State Bar (chair labor law sect. 1983-84, adminstrv. law com. govt. law sect. 1986), Willamette Valley Inns of Ct. (master of bench, team leader 1994—). Office: Oreg Supreme Ct 1163 State St Salem OR 97310-1331

DURRANT, MATTHEW B. state judge; JD, Harvard U., 1984. Adj. prof. Brigham Young U., Salt Lake City; law clerk U.S. Supreme Ct. Appeals (10th cir.), Salt Lake City; shareholder Parr, Waddoups, Brown & Gee, Salt Lake City; judge Third Dist. Ct., Salt Lake City, 1997-2000, Utah Supreme Ct., 2000—. Office: Utah Supreme Ct PO Box 140210 Salt Lake City UT 84114-0210

DURYEE, DAVID ANTHONY, management consultant; b. Tacoma, July 29, 1938; s. Schuyler L. and Edna R. (Muzzy) D.; m. Anne Getchell Peterson, Nov. 26, 1966; children: Tracy Anne, Tricia Marie. BA in Bus., U. Wash., 1961, MBA, 1969; diploma, Pacific Coast Banking Schs., Seattle, 1973. Cert. fin. planner. Lending officer Seattle 1st Nat. Bank, 1964-68, v.p., trust officer, 1970-80; cons., chmn. Mgmt. Adv. Svcs., Inc., Seattle, 1980-93; mng. prin. Moss Adams Adv. Svcs., Moss Adams LLP, 1994—. Bd. dirs. Lafromboise Newspapers, Inc., Seattle; lectr. in field; expert witness Wash., N.Y., Md., Calif., Mass., Ind., Fla. Author: The Business Owners Guide to Achieving Financial Success, 1994; contbr. articles to profl. jours. Capt. U.S. Army, 1962-64. Mem. Am. Soc. Appraisers, Internat. Assn. Fin. Planners, Inst. for Cert. Planners, Inst. Bus. Appraisers (speaker), Am. Bankers Assn., Nat. Retail Jewelers, Nat. Moving and Storage Assn., Pacific N.W. Bankers Assn., Internat. Assn. for Fin. Planning, Estate Planning Coun. Seattle, Washington Bar Assn., Wash. State Trial Lawyers Assn., Wash. State Automobile Dealers Assn., Ky./Mo. Auto Dealers Assn., Motor Dealers Assn. B.C., Nat. Office Products Assn., Mayflower Warehousemen's Assn., Can. Movers Assn., Fedn. of Automobile Dealer Assns. of Can., Seattle Tennis Club, Seattle Yacht Club, Rotary. Avocations: tennis, boating, skiing. Home: 3305 E John St Seattle WA 98112-4030 Office: [illegible] 1001 [illegible] 2700 Seattle WA 98154-1101

DUSCHA, JULIUS CARL, journalist; b. St. Paul, Nov. 4, 1924; s. Julius William and Anna (Perlowski) D.; m. Priscilla Ann McBride, Aug. 17, 1946 (dec. Sept. 1992); children: Fred C., Steve D., Suzanne, Sally Jean; m. Suzanne Van Den Heurk, June 21, 1997. Student, U. Minn., 1943-47; AB, Am. U., 1951; postgrad., Harvard Coll., 1955-56. Reporter St. Paul Pioneer Press, 1943-47; publicist Dem. Nat. Com., 1948, 52; writer Labor's League for Polit. Edn., AFL, 1949-52, Internat. Assn. Machinist, 1952-53; editorial writer Lindsay-Schaub Newspapers, Ill., 1954-58; nat. affairs reporter Washington Post, 1958-66; assoc. dir. profl. journalism fellowships program Stanford (Calif.) U., 1966-68; dir. Washington Journalism Ctr., 1968-90; columnist, freelance journalist, West Coast corr. Presstime mag., San Francisco, 1990-99; sr. corr. News Inc., San Francisco, 1998—. Author: Taxpayer's Hayride: The Farm Problem from the New Deal to the Billie Sol Estes Case, 1964, Arms, Money and Politics, 1965, The Campus Press, 1973; editor: Defense Conversion Advisory; contbr. articles to mags., including Washingtonian, N.Y. Times Mag., Changing Times. Recipient award for distinguished Washington corr. Sigma Delta Chi, 1961 Mem. Cosmos Club (Washington), Kappa Sigma. Home: 2200 Pacific Ave Apt 7D San Francisco CA 94115-1412 E-mail: juliusduscha@aol.com

DUTSON, THAYNE R. university dean; b. Idaho Falls, Oct. 3, 1942; s. Rollo and Thelma (Fugal) D.; m. Joyce Cook, Dec. 19, 1962 (div. 1980); 1 child, Bradley; m. Margaret McCallum, June 23, 1989; children: Taylor, Alexandra. BS, Utah State U., 1966; MS, Mich. State U., 1969, PhD, 1971. Postdoctoral fellow U. Nottingham, Sutton Bonnington, Eng., 1971-72; prof. Tex. A&M U., College Station, 1972-83; dept. head Mich. State U., East Lansing, Mich., 1983-87; dir. agrl. exptl. sta. Oreg. State U., Corvallis, 1987-93, dean, dir. Coll. Agrl. Sci., 1993—. Editor: Advances in Meat Research (11 vols.) 1985-97; contbr. articles to profl. jours. Scoutmaster Boy Scouts Am., Mich., 1966-71. Fellow Inst. Food Technologists; mem. Am. Meat Sci. Assn. (bd. dirs. 1979-81, Disting. Rsch. award 1985), Am. Soc. Animal Sci. (Meat Rsch. award 1981), Coun. for Agr. Sci. and Tech. (pres. 1988), Phi Kappa Phi, Sigma Xi. Avocations: skiing, running, exercise, golf.

DUTT, BIRENDRA, research specialist; b. 1950; Cons., L.A.; with R & DLabs., Culver City, Calif., 1983—, now pres. Office: Rsch & Devel Labs 5800 Uplander Way Culver City CA 90230-6608

DUTT, RONALD F. transportation executive; MBA in Fin., U. Wash., 1976. With contr.'s office Ford Truck Ops. Ford Motor Co., internat. fin. mgr. office corp. treas; various sr. fin. positions USL Capital subs. Ford Motor Co., v.p. corp. analysis, v.p. fin., corp. dir. pricing; sr. v.p. fin. planning and analysis worldwide ops. Visa Internat.; exec. v.p., CFO, mem. exec. com. Fritz Cos., 1999—. Office: Fritz Cos Inc 706 Mission St Fl 6 San Francisco CA 94103

DUUS, PETER, history educator; b. Wilmington, Del., Dec. 27, 1933; s. Hans Christian and Mary Anita (Pennypacker) D.; m. Masayo Umezawa, Nov. 25, 1964; 1 child, Erik. AB magna cum laude, Harvard U., 1955, PhD, 1965; MA, U. Mich., 1959. Asst. prof. history Washington U., St. Louis, 1964-66, Harvard U., Cambridge, Mass., 1966-70; assoc. prof. history Claremont (Calif.) Grad. Sch., 1970-73, Stanford (Calif.) U., 1973-78, prof., 1978—. Author: Party Rivalry and Political Change in Taishó Japan, 1968, Feudalism in Japan, 1969, The Rise of Modern Japan, 1976, The Cambridge History of Japan, Vol. 6: The Twentieth Century, 1989, The Japanese Informal Empire in China, 1989, The Abacus and the Sword: The Japanese Penetration of Korea, 1995, The Japanese Discovery of America, 1996, Modern Japan, 1997. Exec. sec. Inter-Univ. for Japanese Lang. Studies, Tokyo, 1974-90; bd. dirs. Com. for Internat. Exchange of Scholars, Washington, 1987-91. Served with U.S. Army, 1955-57. NEH sr. fellow, 1972-73, Japan Found. postdoctoral fellow, 1976-77, Fulbright rsch. fellow, 1981-82, 94-95, Japan Found. rsch. fellow, 1986-87. Fellow AAAS, mem. Assn. for Asian Studies (bd. dirs. 1972-75, nominating com. 1983, v.p. 1999-2000, pres. 2000—), Am. Hist. Assn. (bd. editors 1984-87). Home: 818 Esplanada Way Palo Alto CA 94305-1015 Office: Stanford U History Dept Stanford CA 94305 E-mail: pduus@leland.stanford.edu

DUVAL, JULIAN J. arboretum administrator; b. Oak Park, Ill., Feb. 15, 1947; s. Julian Adrian Duval and Isabel (Klawczyk) Luther; m. Becky Kotsarelis, Jan. 10, 1975 (div. Oct. 1980); m. Leslie Ann Berling, Feb. 5, 1990. AA, Coll. of Dupage, 1972; BS in Wildlife Mgmt., N.Mex. State U., 1974. Marine mammal trainer Brookfield Zoo, Chgo., 1965-71; curator, mammal and reptiles Parque Zool. Nat., Dominican Rep., 1975-78; adminstr. gen. Auto Safari Chapin, Guatemala, 1978-80; gen. curator Indpls. Zoo, 1980-87, v.p. zool. and botanical collections, 1987-94, v.p. scientific and program devel., 1994-95; exec. dir., CEO Quail Botanical Gardens, Encinitas, Calif., 1995—. Mem. IUCN Species Survival Commn., Conservation Breeding, Specialist Group. Co-host: (TV program) At the Zoo, WRTV/ABC Indpls. Channel 6, 1989-95. Dir. Encinitas C. of C. Mem. Encinitas Rotary. Avocations: horticulture, wildlife study, photography, herpetology. Office: Quail Botanical Gardens 230 Quail Gardens Dr PO Box 230005 Encinitas CA 92023-0005

DUVAL, MICHAEL RAOUL, investment banker; b. San Francisco, July 18, 1938; s. Richard and Sylvia Raoul-Duval. A.B., Georgetown U., 1961; J.D., U. Calif., San Francisco, 1967. Bar: Calif. 1967, U.S. Supreme Ct. 1971. Atty. U.S. Dept. Transp., Washington, 1967-70; staff asst. to Pres., asso. dir. Domestic Council, spl. counsel to Pres., Washington, 1970-77; various exec. positions Mead Corp., Dayton, Ohio, 1977-84; mng. dir. First Boston Corp., N.Y.C., 1984-90; ltd. ptnr. Anthem Ptnrs., L.P., N.Y.C., 1990-92; chmn. Michael Duval & Assocs., Ltd., Santa Fe, 1994—. Bd. dirs. British Aerospace Holdings, Inc. Mem. Def. Policy Bd., 1989-94, SEC's Emerging Markets Adv. Com., 1989, Nat. Commn. on Fin. Instn. Reform, Recovery and Enforcement, Washington. Capt. USMC, 1960-64. Mem. N.Y. Council Fgn. Relations. Republican. Roman Catholic.

DUXBURY, THOMAS CARL, planetary scientist; b. Fort Wayne, Ind., Dec. 8, 1941; s. John Lawrence and Justine Agnus (Jaron) D.; m. Natalia Duxbury, Nov. 8, 1990; children: Brett Harding, Katerina Seregina. BSEE, Purdue U., 1965, MSEE, 1966. Planetary scientist Jet Propulsion Lab., Pasadena, Calif., 1966—. Co-author: Television Investigations of Phobos, 1994. Recipient Sci. Achievement medal NASA, Washington, 1972, Space Mission Svc. medal Russian Lavochkin Assn., The Hague, The Netherlands, 1991, Burka award Inst. of Navigation, 1973, Achievement awards NASA, 1980, 82. Mem. Am. Geophysical Union, 1978—, Am. Astronomical Soc., 1980—, Russian Assn. for Space Sci. & Tech., 1993—. Achievements include prodn. of first map of another planet's moon, 1972; discovery of the Groove Network on Phobos (Mars moon), 1978; co-discovery of the Rings of Jupiter, 1979, of the Jupiter Lightning, 1979; selection by NASA/Soviet Union to participate in the Soviet PHOBOS Mission to Mars, 1988-89, Dept. Def. (DOD) Clementing Sci. Team for Lunar Exploration, 1992-94, Russian Mars 1994-96 Mission Sci. Team, 1992-97, project dir. NASA STARDUST Mission, 1996—, participating scientist Mars Global Surveyor Mission, 1996—, USAF/NASA Sci. Definition Team Deputy Leader, 1997-98, interdisciplinary scientist on European Space Agy. Mars Express Mission, 1999—. Office: Jet Propul-[illegible] Pasadena CA 91109-8001 E-mail: tduxbury@jpl.nasa.gov

DUYCK, KATHLEEN MARIE, poet, musician, retired social worker; b. Portland, Oreg., July 21, 1933; d. Anthony Joseph Dwyer and Edna Elisabeth Hayes; m. Robert Duyck, Feb. 3, 1962; children: Mary Kay Boeyen, Robert Patrick, Anthony Joseph. BS, Oreg. State U., 1954; MSW, U. Wash., 1956. Cert. NASW, Oreg. Adoption worker Cath. Svcs., Portland, 1956-61, Cath. Welfare, San Antonio, 1962; musician Tucson Symphony, 1963-65; prin. cellist Phoenix (Ariz.) Coll. Orch., 1968-78, Scottsdale (Ariz.) Symphony, 1974-80; poet, 1993—. Author: (poetry cassettes) Visions, 1993 (Contemporary Series Poet 1993), Visions II, 1996 (Contemporary Series Poet 1996); contbr. to 13 Nat. Libr. of Poetry Anthologies. Rep. worker Maricopa County Reps., Phoenix, 1974; mem. Scottsdale Cultural Coun.; NASW bd. Cath. Charities Rep., Portland, 1959-61. Recipient Golden Poet award World of Poetry, 1991, 92, Editor's Choice awards Nat. Libr. Poetry, 1993-2001, Sec. gift Phoenix Exec. Bd., 1976. Recognition award Archbishop Howard, 1961, 5-Yr. Kathleen Duyck award Cello Congress V, 1996. Mem. Internat. Poetry Hall Fame, Ariz. Cello Soc., Nat. Libr. Poetry, Internat. Soc. Poets, Phoenix Symphony Guild (exec. bd. 1970-80). Republican. Roman Catholic. Avocations: pianist, photography, poetry, artistic collections, concerts. Home: 4545 E Palomino Rd Phoenix AZ 85018-1719

DVORA, SUSAN (SUSAN BERNSTEIN), non-profit organization professional; b. Chgo., May 17, 1938; d. Herman and Frances Dobkin Powell; m. Phillip Bernstein, Sept. 4, 1957 (div. July 1995); children: Kenneth, Robert, Michael. BA in Human Svcs., Northeastern Ill. U., 1978, postgrad., 1978-80. Real estate salesperson Martin-Marbry, Skokie, Ill., 1971—; exec. dir. Land of Lakes region B'nai Brith Women Internat., Chgo., 1978-83; founder, pres. Nat. Forum of Women, Woodstock, Ill., 1980-83; dir. resource devel. Travelers & Immigrants Aid, Chgo., 1983-86; dir. Ctr. Ch.-State Studies, DePaul U. Sch. of Law, Chgo., 1986-90; cons. to non-profit orgns., Chgo., Md., Israel, and South Africa, 1986—. Owner, mgr. Siza Gallery, Evanston, Ill., 1989-92. Dir., prodr. (documentary) Legacy of Charlotte Perkins Gilman, 1996. Dir. alumni rels. Agrl. Edn. Found., Templeton, Calif., 1995-97; active Ill. Women's Agenda, Chgo., 1978-82; mem. Gov.'s Commn. on Status of Women, Ill., 1981; asst. to sculptor Andries Botha human rights work, South Africa, 1999—; sec., treas. Create Africa South. Named Citizen of Yr., Lerner-Life Newspapers, Skokie, 1979-80. Democrat. Jewish. Avocations: swimming, reading, travel. Address: PO Box 2311 Avila Beach CA 93424 E-mail: svedvora@aol.com

DWAN, DENNIS EDWIN, broadcast executive, photographer; b. St. Joseph, Mich., Oct. 6, 1958; s. Edwin O. and Elizabeth L. (Miller) D.; m. Tami L. Nixon, Oct. 13, 1984; children: Megan, Kaitlyn. BA, Mich. State U., 1981. Photographer Sta. WJIM-TV, Lansing, Mich., 1981-83, Sta. KAYU, Spokane, Wash., 1984-86, Sta. KREM-TV, Spokane, 1984-87; ops. mgr. Sta. KOMO-TV, Seattle, 1987—. Mem. Nat. Press Photographers Assn. E-mail: DennisD@Komotv.com

DWORKIN, SAMUEL FRANKLIN, dentist, psychologist; b. Freedom, Ohio, Sept. 26, 1933; s. Louis and Minnie (Katz) D.; m. Mona Mae Moskowitz, Dec. 23, 1956; children: Adam, Ted. B.S., CCNY, 1954; D.D.S., NYU, 1958, Ph.D., 1969. Practice dentistry, N.Y.C., 1959-65; Nat. Inst. Dental Research spl. fellow, 1965-69; asst. prof. dept. preventive dentistry and community health NYU Coll. Dentistry, 1969-70; assoc. prof. div. preventive dentistry, dir. office of edn. and behavioral research Columbia U. Sch. Dental and Oral Surgery, 1970-74; prof. oral surgery, assoc. dean acad. affairs U. Wash. Sch. Dentistry, Seattle, 1974-77; prof. psychiatry and behavioral sci. U. Wash. Sch. Medicine, 1977—; prof. oral medicine, 1977—; dir. psychophysiologic liaison clinic dept. psychiatry and behavioral sci. U. Wash. Sch. Medicine, 1978-89, Washington dental svc. disting. prof. dentistry, 1999—. Clin. dir. Regional Clin. Dental Rsch. Ctr., U. Wash., 1992-99; cons. NIH, mem. behavioral medicine study sect., 1985-90, mem. rsch. adv. coun. 1999—; cons. ADA, Am. Dental Hygiene Assn. Cons. editor Jour. Dental Edn., 1976—, Jour. Dental Rsch., 1976—, Pain, 1984—, Clin. Jour. Pain, 1989—, Psychosomatic Medicine, 1989—; guest editor Jour. Preventive Dentistry, 1977, Jour. ADA, Pain; contbr. articles to profl. jours. Co-founder, pres. League of Parents of Hearing Impaired Infants, N.Y.C., 1966-70; v.p. N.Y. State Parents of Hearing Impaired Children, 1970-74; adv. coun. Lexington Sch. of Deaf, N.Y.C., 1970-74; bd. dirs. Seattle Pro-Musica, 1977, v.p., 1978-81, treas., 1991-98, pres. 1995-98, pres. emeritus, 1999. Grantee NIH, 1979-99. Fellow Internat. Assn. for Study of Pain, Am. Pain Soc.; mem. ADA (coun. dental health edn., coun. nat. bd. exams. 1974-79), AAAS, APA, Am. Assn. Dental Schs., Behavioral Scientists in Dental Rsch. (pres. 1975, 90), Internat. Assn. for Dental Rsch. (Disting. Scientist award behavior and health svcs. rsch.), Internat. Soc. Clin. and Exptl. Hypnosis, Behavioral Scis. Group (Disting. Rschr. award), Behavioral and Health Svcs. Rsch. Group (pres. 1990-91). Office: U Wash Dept Psychiatry Seattle WA 98195-0001 E-mail: dworkin@u.washington.edu

DWORSKY, DANIEL LEONARD, architect, educator; b. Mpls., Oct. 4, 1927; s. Lewis and Ida (Fineberg) D.; m. Sylvia Ann Taylor, Aug. 10, 1957; children: Douglas, Laurie, Nancy. B.Arch., U. Mich., 1950. Practice architecture as Dworsky Assocs., L.A., 1953-2000, Cannon Dworsky, L.A., 2000—; design critic, lectr. arch. U. So. Calif., U. Mich., UCLA, 1983-84. Chmn. archtl. rev. panel Fed. Res. Bank. Recipient Design citation Progressive Arch. mag. 1967, Gov. Calif. award 1966, 3 Los Angeles Grand Prix awards So. Calif. AIA and City of Los Angeles 1967; prin. works include Angelus Plaza Elderly Housing, Los Angeles, 1981, Ontario (Calif.) City Hall, 1980, CBS Exec. Office Bldg, North Hollywood, Calif., 1970, U. Calif. at Los Angeles Stadium, 1969, Fed. Res. Bank Bldg., Los Angeles, 1987, U. Mich. Crisler Arena at Ann Arbor, 1966, Dominguez Hills State U. Theatre, 1977, Ventura County Govt. Center, 1979, Northrop Electronics Hdqrs., Los Angeles, 1983, Hewlett-Packard Region Office, North Hollywood, 1984, Los Angeles County Mcpl. Cts. Bldg., 1985, Tom Bradley Internat. Terminal L.A. Airport, 1984, City Tower, City Orange Calif., 1988, The Met. Apt. L.A., 1989, Fed. Office Bldg., Long Beach, Calif., 1992. Fellow AIA (more than 100 awards including 24 awards Calif. chpts., Nat. Honor award 1974, 68-69, Firm award Calif. chpt. 1985, L.A. Gold Medal award 1994). Home: 9225 Nightingale Dr Los Angeles CA 90069-1117 Office: Cannon Dworsky 1901 Ave of States Ste 175 Los Angeles CA 90067 E-mail: dan@cannondworsky.com

DWYER, JOHN CHARLES, lawyer; b. San Francisco, Mar. 26, 1962; s. Richard Thomas and Dorothy (Blake) D. BS, U. Calif., Berkeley, 1984; JD, Harvard U., 1988. Bar: Calif. 1988, U.S. Dist. Ct. (no. dist.) Calif. 1988, U.S. Ct. Appeals (9th cir.) 1988, U.S. Supreme Ct. 1996. Assoc. Jackson, Tufts, Cole & Black, San Francisco, 1989-93; dep. assoc. atty. gen. U.S. Dept. Justice, Washington, 1993-96, acting assoc. atty. gen., 1997; ptnr. Cooley Godward LLP, Palo Alto, Calif., 1998—. Democrat. Roman Catholic. Office: Cooley Godward LLP 3000 El Camino Real Palo Alto CA 94306

DWYER, WILLIAM L. federal judge; b. Olympia, Wash., Mar. 26, 1929; s. William E. and Ila (Williams) D.; m. Vasiliki Asimakopulos, Oct. 5, 1952; chidren: Joanna, Anthony, Charles. BS in Law, U. Wash., 1951; JD, NYU, 1953; LLD (hon.), Gonzaga U., 1994. Bar: Wash. 1953, U.S. Ct. Appeals (9th cir.) 1959, U.S. Supreme Ct. 1968. Law clk. Supreme Ct. Wash., Olympia, 1957; ptnr. Culp, Dwyer, Guterson & Grader, Seattle, 1957-87; judge U.S. Dist. Ct. (we. dist.) Wash., Seattle, 1987—, now sr. judge. Author: The Goldmark Case, 1984 (Gavel award ABA 1985, Gov.'s award Wash. 1985). 1st lt. U.S. Army, 1953-56. Recipient Outstanding Svc. award U. Wash. Law Rev., 1985, Helen Geisness disting. Svc. award Seattle-King County Bar Assn., 1985, Disting. Alumnus award U. Wash. Sch. of Law, 1994, W.G. Magnuson award King County Mcpl. League, 1994, Judge of Yr. Wash. State Trial Lawyers, 1994, Outstanding Jurist award Am. Bd. Trial Advocates, Washington, 1998, William L. Dwyer Lifetime Achievement award, King County Bar Assn., 1998, Civil Rights award Anti-Defamation League, 1999, Ahepa Periclean award, 2000, William L. Dwyer award U. Wash. Sch .Law, 2001. Fellow Am. Coll. Trial Lawyers, Am. Bar Found., Hon. Order of Coif; mem. ABA, Inter-Am. Bar Assn., Am. Judicature Soc., Supreme Ct. Hist. Soc., 9th Cir. Hist. Assn. Office: US Dist Ct 713 US Courthouse Seattle WA 98104-1189

DWYRE, WILLIAM PATRICK, journalist, public speaker; b. Sheboygan, Wis., Apr. 7, 1944; s. George Leo and Mary Veronica (O'Brien) D.; m. Jill Ethlyn Jarvis, July 30, 1966; children— Amy, Patrick B.A., U. Notre Dame, Ind. Sports copy editor Des Moines Register, 1966-68; sports writer, asst. sports editor, sports editor Milw. Jour., 1968-81; asst. sports editor, sports editor Los Angeles Times, 1981—. Speaker Mark Reede's Sportstars, Los Angeles, 1986; columnist Referee Mag., 1977—; voting mem., bd. dirs. Amateur Athletic Found. Nat. Sports Hall of Fame, 1981—. Bd. dirs. Honda-Brockerick Cup Women's Collegiate Athlete of Yr.; bd. dirs. Casa Colina Hosp. Rehab., Pomona. Named Sportswriter of Yr., Wis. Nat. Sportscasters and Sportswriters Assn., 1980; Nat. Editor of Yr., Nat. Press Found., 1985; recipient award for Sustained Excellence by Individual, L.A. Times, 1985, Red Smith award AP sports Editors, 1996. Mem. Nat. Sportscasters and Sportswriters Assn. (pres. 2000, Powerade Sport Story of Yr. award 1999), Assoc. Press Sports Editors (pres. 1989), Nat. Baseball, Pro Basketball and Football Writers Assn. Club: Milw. Pen and Mike. Avocation: tennis. Office: Los Angeles Times Times Mirror Sq Los Angeles CA 90012 E-mail: Bill.Dwyre@latimes.com

DYCK, ANDREW ROY, philologist, educator; b. Chgo., May 24, 1947; s. Roy H. and Elizabeth (Beck) D.; m. Janis Mieko Fukuhara, Aug. 20, 1978. BA, U. Wisc., 1969; PhD, U. Chgo., 1975. Sessional lectr. U. Alta., Edmonton, Can., 1975-76; asst. prof. U. Minn., Mpls., 1977-78; vis. asst. prof. Classics UCLA, 1976-77, asst. prof., 1978-82, assoc. prof., 1982-87, prof., 1987—, chmn. dept. classics, 1988-91. Mem. Inst. for Advanced Study, Princeton, 1991-92; vis. fellow All Souls Coll., Oxford, 1998, Clare Hall, Cambridge, 1999. Author: A Commentary on Cicero, De Officiis, 1996; editor: Epimerismi Homerici, 2 vols., 1983, 95, Essays on Euripides and George of Pisidia and on Helidorus and Achilles Tatius (Michael Psellus), 1986. Alexander von Humboldt-Stiftung fellow, Bonn, Fed. Republic of Germany, 1980-89; NEH fellow, 1991-92. Mem. Am. Philol. Assn., Calif. Classical Assn., U.S. Nat. Com. on Byzantine Studies. Office: UCLA Classics Dept 405 Hilgard Ave Los Angeles CA 90095-9000

DYDEK, MALGORZATA, professional basketball player; b. Poland, Apr. 28, 1974; Center Poznan Olympia, 1992-94, France, 1994-96, Spain, 1996-98, Utah Starzz, Salt Lake City, 1998—. Mem. Polish Nat. Team. Avocations: billiards, reading, videos, movies. Office: Utah Starzz 301 W South Temple Salt Lake City UT 84101-1216

DYEN, ISIDORE, linguistic scientist, educator; b. Phila., Aug. 16, 1913; s. Jacob and Dena (Bryzell) D.; m. Edith Brenner, June 11, 1939 (dec. 1976); children— Doris Jane, Mark Ross. B.A., U. Pa., 1933, M.A., 1934, Ph.D. in Indo-European Linguistics, 1939; postgrad. Slavic, Columbia, 1938-39, Yale, 1939-40. Faculty Yale U., 1942-84, prof. Malayan langs., 1957-58, prof. Malayopolynesian and comparative linguistics, 1958-73, prof. comparative linguistics and Austronesian langs., 1973-84, prof. emeritus, 1984—, dir. grad. studies Indic and Far Eastern langs. and lit., 1960-62, Indic and Southeast Asia, 1960-66, dir. grad. studies linguistics, 1966-68; adj. prof. linguistics U. Hawaii, 1985-89; linguist Coordinated Investigation Micronesian Anthropology, Truk, 1947, Sci. Investigation Micronesia, Yap, 1949. Vis. prof. U. Padjadjaran, Bandung, 1960-61, U. Auckland, summer 1969, Australian Nat. U., fall 1971, U. Philippines, spring 1972, Inst. Study of Langs. and Cultures of Asia and Africa, Tokyo U. for Fgn. Langs., 1982-83; coordinator linguistics sect. 10th Pacific Sci. Congress, Honolulu, 1961; asso. prof. U. Chgo. and Linguistic Soc. Am. Summer Inst., 1955; prof. U. Mich. and Linguistic Soc. Am. Summer Inst., 1957; dir. SE Asia Linguistics Program, 28th Internat. Congress Orientalists, Canberra, 1971; organizing com. Conf. Genetic Lexicostatistics, New Haven, 1971; organizer 1st Eastern Conf. Austronesian Linguistics, New Haven, 1973; adv. com. 1st Internat. Conf. Comparative Austronesian Linguistics, Honolulu, 1974; mem. adv. bd. Oceanic Linguistics. Author: Spoken Malay, 2 vols., 1945, The Proto-Malayo-Polynesian Laryngeals, 1953, A Lexicostatistical Classification of the Austronesian Languages, 1965, A Sketch of Trukese Grammar, 1965, A Descriptive Indonesian Grammar, 1967, Beginning Indonesian, 4 vols., 1967, Lexicostatistics in Genetic Linguistics: Proc. of Yale Conf., 1973, (with David Aberle) Lexical Reconstruction: The Case of the Athapaskan Kinship System, 1974, Linguistic Subgrouping and Lexicostatistics, 1975, (with Guy Jucquois) Lexicostatistics in Genetic Linguistics II, 1976, (with Joseph B. Kruskal and Paul Black) An Indoeuropean Classification: A Lexicostatistical Experiment, 1992. Research fellow Slavic Am. Council Learned Socs., 1938-40; Guggenheim fellow, 1949, 64; Tri-Instl. Pacific Program grantee, 1956-57; NSF grantee, 1960-77 Mem. Linguistic Soc. Am., Am. Oriental Soc. (v.p. 1965-66), Am. Anthrop. Assn., Current Anthropology, Société de Linguistique de Paris, Koninklijk Instituut voor Taal-, Land-, en Volkenkunde, New Haven Oriental Club (pres. 1963-64, 74-76) Office: Univ Hawaii Manoa Dept Linguistics Honolulu HI 96822 also: Yale U Dept Linguistics Hall Grad Studies New Haven CT 06520

DYER, CHARLES RICHARD, law librarian, law educator; b. Richmond Heights, Mo., Aug. 20, 1947; s. Helmuth Kinner and Sue Anne (Stone) D.; m. Cecelia Ann Duncan, Dec. 20, 1969 (div. June 1982); m. Roberta Sharlyn Monroe, June 2, 1984; 1 child, Christina L. Floyd. BA, U. Tex., 1969; MA, Northwestern U., 1971; JD, U. Tex., 1974, MLS, 1975. Bar: Tex. 1974. Assoc. law libr., asst. prof. law St. Louis U., 1975-77; law libr., assoc. prof. U. Mo., Kansas City, 1977-87; dir. librs. San Diego County Pub. Law Libr., 1987—. Cons. in field. Editor Law Libr. Jour., 1972-74. Mem. Am. Assn. Law Librs., Mid-Am. Assn. Law Librs (sec.-treas. 1976-78), Southwestern Assn. Law Librs. (v.p. 1981-82, pres. 1982-83), So. Calif. Assn. Law Librs. (mem. exec. bd. 1991-93), Coun. Calif. County Law Librs. (pres. 1998-2000). Democrat. Unitarian. Home: 2323 Montclair St San Diego CA 92104-5344 Office: San Diego County Pub Law Library 1105 Front St San Diego CA 92101-3904 E-mail: cdyer@sdcll.org

DYER, JIM, state senator; b. St. Joseph, Mo., Dec. 9, 1937; m. Sharon Dyer; three children. BA, Benedictine Coll., 1959, Ft. Lewis Coll., 1986. With USMC, 1959-79; mem. Colo. Ho. of Reps., Dist. 59, 1986-98; Rep. Senator dist. K Colo. State Senate, 1998—; mem. agr., natural resources and energy com.; mem. state, vets. and mil. affairs com.; mem. transp. com. Mem. NRA, VFW, Marine Corp. Assn., Durango Hist. Soc., Am. Legion. Democrat. Roman Catholic. Home: PO Box 5225 Durango CO 81301-6814 Office: State Capitol 200 E Colfax Ave Ste 274 Denver CO 80203-1716 E-mail: jimdyer@frontier.net

DYER, PHILIP E. insurance company executive; b. Salem, Oreg., Feb. 10, 1953; s. William Connell Jr. and Clara Belle (Burnside) D.; m. Carolyn J. Pierce, Mar. 11, 1978; children: Pierce, Peyton. BS, Oreg. State U., 1976; grad., U.S. Army Command and Gen. Coll., Leavenworth, Kans., 1983. Cert. ins. counselor. Commd. 2d lt. U.S. Army Nat. Guard, 1971, advanced through grades to maj.; account exec. Marsh and McLennan, Inc., Seattle, 1977-80, 85-86; comml. mktg. rep. Indsl. Indemnity, Seattle, 1980-81; regional v.p. Ins. Corp. Am., Houston, 1981-85; pres. Doctor's Agy. Wash., Inc., Seattle, 1987-94; sr. v.p. Wash. Casualty Co., 1994-96; v.p. The Doctors' Co., Seattle, 1996—. Cons. Group Health Coop., Seattle, 1987. Pres. Eagle Ridge Homeowners Assn.; rep. 5th Legis. Dist. Wash. Ho. of Reps., Issaquah, chmn. health care com., 1994—; tech. advisor Wash. State Health Care Commn., Olympia, 1990-92; ranking minority mem. Ho. Reps. Health Care Com.; asst. ranking mem. Fin. Inst. Ins. Commn.; mem. legis. com. Liability Reform Coalition, Seattle, 1988—; precinct officer Rep. Com., Issaquah, 1991—; cons., mem. ins. com. Issaquah Sch. Dist., 1992; mem. youth div. staff Re-elect Pres. Ford Commn., Washington; staff researcher Oreg. Legislature; chmn. Health Care Com. Wash. Ho. of Reps.; mem. Wash. Health Policy Bd. Mem. Wash. Health Care Risk Mgmt. Soc. (com. chair 1989-90), Soc. Am. Mil. Engrs., Aircraft Owners and Pilot Assn., Profl. Liability Underwriting Soc. (bd. dirs. 1988-89), Issquah Valley Kiwanis. Republican. Episcopalian. Avocations: snow and water skiing, reading, private piloting. Office: Doctors Company 6100 219th St Sw Ste 580 Mountlake Terrace WA 98043

DYESS, KIRBY A. computer company executive; BS in Physics, U. Idaho, 1968. Human resource staffing mgr. Intel Corp., Oreg., 1979-81, with computer info. svc. orgn., 1981-87, mktg. mgr. Pers. Computer Enhancement Divsn., 1987-89, bus. unit mgr., 1989-92, v.p., dir. human resources, 1992, mem. exec. staff, 1993-96, corp. v.p., 1996, v.p., dir. With ICN Med. Labs., Inc., Portland. Office: Intel Corp 2111 NE 25th Ave Hillsboro OR 97124-5961 E-mail: kirby.dyess@intel.com

DYLEWSKI, GARY R. retired career officer; b. Erie, Pa., Nov. 22, 1952; m. Lynne Rousey; 2 children: Christopher, Matthew. BA in Biology, Kent State U., 1974; M in Mgmt., Troy State U., 1980; grad., Squadron Officer Sch., 1985, Air Command and Staff Coll., 1993, Air War Coll., 1993. Commd. 2d lt. USAF, 1975, advanced through grades to col., 1993; squadron weapons officer, flight examiner, instr. 425th Tactical Fighter Tng. Squadron, Williams AFB, Ariz., 1980-85; assignments officer, rated force mgr. for dep. chief staff Pers., Hdqs., Tactical Air Command, Langley AFB, Va., 1985-88; Air Force aide to Pres. Reagan The Pentagon, Washington, 1988-89; dir. tng. 21st Tactical Fighter Wing, Elmendorf AFB, Alaska, 1989-90; ops. officer 43d Tactical Fighter Squadron, Elmendorf AFB, 1990-91; comdr. 90th Tactical Fighter Squadron, Elmendorf AFB, 1991-92; joint dir. for ops. Alaskan Air Command, Elmendorf AFB, 1993-95; comdr. 33d Fighter Wing, Eglin AFB, Fla., 1996-97, 1st Fighter Wing, Langley AFB, 1997—, Space Warfare Ctr, Schriever AFB, CO, 1999—. Decorated Def. Superior Svc. medal, Meritorious Svc. medal with 3 oak leaf clusters. Office: SWC/USAF 730 Irwin Ave Ste 83 Schriever AFB CO 80912-7398

DYM, CLIVE LIONEL, engineering educator; b. Leeds, Eng., July 15, 1942; came to U.S., 1949, naturalized, 1954; s. Isaac and Anna (Hochmann) D.; children: Jordana, Miriam; m. Joan Dym, June 28, 1998. BCE, Cooper Union, 1962; MS, Poly. Inst. Bklyn., 1964; PhD, Stanford U., 1967. Asst. prof. SUNY, Buffalo, 1966-69; assoc. professorial lectr. George Washington U., Washington, 1969; research staff Inst. Def. Analyses, Arlington, Va., 1969-70; assoc. prof. Carnegie-Mellon U., Pitts., 1970-74; vis. assoc. prof. TECHNION, Israel, 1971; sr. scientist Bolt Beranek and Newman, Inc., Cambridge, Mass., 1974-77; prof. U. Mass., Amherst, 1977-91, head dept. civil engring., 1977-85; Fletcher Jones prof. engring. design Harvey Mudd Coll., Claremont, Calif., 1991—, dir. Ctr. Design Edn., 1995—, chair dept. engring., 1999—. Vis. sr. rsch. fellow Inst. Sound and Vibration Rsch., U. Southampton, Eng., 1973; vis. scientist Xerox PARC, 1983-84; vis. prof. civil engring. Stanford U., 1983-84, Carnegie Mellon U., 1990; Eshbach vis. prof. Northwestern U., 1997-98; cons. Bell Aerospace Co., 1967-69, Dravo Corp., 1970-71, Salem Corp., 1972, Gen. Analytics Inc., 1972, ORI, Inc., 1979, BBN Inc., 1979, Avco, 1981-83, 85-86, TASC, 1985-86, D.H. Brown Assocs., 1991, Johnson Controls, 1996; vice chmn. adv. bd. Amerinex Artificial Intelligence, 1986-88. Author: (with I.H. Shames) Solid Mechanics: A Variational Approach, 1973, Introduction to the Theory of Shells, rev. edit. 1990, Stability Theory and Its Applications to Structural Mechanics, 1974, (with E.S. Ivey) Principles of Mathematical Modeling, 1980, (with I.H. Shames) Energy and Finite Element Methods in Structural Mechanics, 1985, (with R.E. Levitt) Knowledge-Based Systems in Engineering, 1990, Engineering Design: A Synthesis of Views, 1994, Structural Modeling and Analysis, 1997, (with P. Little) Engineering Design: A Project-Based Introduction, 1999, (with P.D. Cha and Jo Jo Rosenberg) Fundamentals of Modeling and Analyzing Engineering Systems, 2000; editor: (with A. Kalnins) Vibration: Beams, Plates, and Shells, 1977, Applications of Knowledge-Based Systems to Engineering Analysis and Design, 1985, Computing Futures in Engineering Design, 1997, Designing Design Education for the 21st Century, 1999, (with L. Winner) Social Dimensions of Engineering Design, 2001, Artificial Intelligence for Engring. Design Analysis and Mfg., 1986-96; contbr. articles and tech. reports to profl. publs. NATO sr. fellow in sci., 1973 Fellow Acoustical Soc. Am., ASME, ASCE (Walter L. Huber research prize 1980); mem. Am. Assn. for Artificial Intelligence, Computer Soc. of IEEE, ASEE (Western Electric Fund award 1983). Jewish. Office: Harvey Mudd Coll Engring Dept 301 E 12th St Claremont CA 91711-5901

DYMALLY, MERVYN MALCOLM, retired congressman, international business executive; b. Cedros, Trinidad, W.I., May 12, 1926; s. Hamid A. and Andreid S. (Richardson) D.; m. Alice M. Gueno; children: Mark, Lynn. BA in Edn., Calif. State U., 1954; MA in Govt., Calif. State U., Sacramento, 1970; PhD in Human Behavior, U.S. Internat. U., 1978; JD (hon.), Lincoln U., Sacramento, 1975; LLD (hon., U. W. L.A., 1970, Calif. Coll. Law, L.A., City U., L.A., 1976, Fla. Meml. Coll., 1987, Lincoln U., San Francisco, 1984; HLD (hon.), Shaw U., N.C., 1981; PHD (hon.), Calif. Western. U., 1982. Cert. elem., secondary and exceptional children tchr. Tchr. L.A. City Schs., 1955-61; coord. Calif. Disaster Office, 1961-62; mem. Calif. Assembly, 1962-66, Calif. Senate, 1967-74; lt. gov. Calif., 1975-79; mem. 97th-102nd Congresses from 31st Calif. dist., 1981-92; pres. Dymally Internat. Group Inc., Inglewood, Calif., 1992—. Mem. Com. on Fgn. Affairs and its subcoms. on Internat. Ops., chmn. subcom. on Africa, 1989-92; mem. Com. on D.C. and chmn. subcom. on judiciary and edn., 1981-92; chmn. Congl. Task Force on Minority Set Asides, 1987-92; chmn. Senate Majority Caucus, Senate Select Com. on Children and Youth; chmn. Senate coms. on mil. and vets. affairs, social welfare, elections and reapportionment, subcom. on med. edn. and health needs; chmn. joint coms. on legal equality for women, on revision of election code; chmn. assembly com. on indsl. rels.; current mem. Congl. Hispanic Caucus, Congl. Caucus Women's Issues, Congl. Human Rights Caucus, Congl. Black Caucus and chmn. of its task force on Caribbean; chmn. Caribbean Action Lobby, Caribbean Am. Rsch. Inst.; founder Congl. Inst. for Space, Sci. and Tech., chmn. adv. bd.; past chmn. Calif. Commn. Econ. Devel., Commn. of Califs. (U.S., Baja Calif., Calif. Sur, Mex.); past vice chmn., Nat. Conf. Lt. Govs.; former Gov.'s designee U.S. Border States Commn.; past mem. State Lands Commn., others; lectr. Claremont (Calif.) Grad. Sch., Golden Gate U., Sacramento, Pepperdine U., L.A., Pomona (Calif.) Coll., U. Calif., Davis, Irvine, Whittier (Calif.) Coll., Shaw U., Raleigh, N.C.; Disting. prof. Ctrl. State U.; mem. faculty Drew U. Medicine and Sci.; adj. prof. Compton Coll.; cons. to chancellor L.A. C.C. Author: The Black Politician-His Struggle for Power, 1971; co-auhtor: (with Dr. Jeffrey Elliot) Fidel Castro: Nothing Can Stop the Course of History, 1986, also articles; former editor:The Black Politician (quar.) Mem. L.A. County Water Appeals Bd.; advisor to Calif. Assembly Spkr. for Cmty. Congress; chmn. Calif. Black Leadership Roundtable, Caribbean Am. Coalition. Recipient numerous awards including Chaconia Gold medal Govt. Trinidad and Tobago, Adam Clayton Powell award Congl. Black Caucus, Dr. Solomon P. Fuller award Black Psychiatrists of Am., others from Golden State Med. Assn., United Tchrs. L.A., Bd. Suprs. L.A., L.A. City Coun., various univs., colls., orgns. Mem. AAUP, NAACP, Am. Acad. Polit. Sci., Am. Polit. Sci. Assn., Am. Acad. Polit. and Social Sci., ACLU, Urban League, Phi Kappa Phi, Kappa Alpha Psi Office: Dymally Internat Group Inc 222 W Florence Ave Inglewood CA 90301-1213 E-mail: dymally@interlink.net

DYMOND, LEWIS WANDELL, lawyer, mediator, educator; b. Lansing, Mich., June 28, 1920; s. Lewis Wandell and Irene (Parker) D.; m. Betty Louise Blood, Sept. 6, 1942; children: Lewis W., Jean Ann; m. Joann Surrey, Sept. 3, 1966; 1 son, Steven Henry. J.D. cum laude, U. Miami, 1956. Bar: Fla. 1957; cert. ct. mediator, Fla. With Nat. Airlines, Inc., Miami, Fla., 1938-62, mechanic, agt., sta. mgr., flight dispatcher, ops. mgr., pilot, v.p. ops., maintenance and engring., 1955-62; pres., chief exec. officer, dir. Frontier Airlines, 1962-79. Adj. prof. Sch. Bus. U. Miami, Coral Gables, Fla. Mem. U. Miami Alumni Club, Union League, Surf Club, Masons, Shriners, Phi Kappa Phi, Phi Alpha Delta. Home and Office: 6 E Belleview Way Greenwood Village CO 80121-1408

DYNES, ROBERT C. academic administrator; b. London, Can. B of Math. & Physics, U. Western Ont.; M of Physics, D of Phys., McMaster U. Rsch. scientist, dept. head, dir. chem. phys. rsch. AT&T Bell Labs., 1968-90; prof. U. Calif., San Diego, 1991-95, sr. vice chancellor, 1995—, Chancellor. Recipient Fritz London award Low Temp. Physics, 1990. Fellow Am. Phys. Soc., Can. Inst. Advanced Rsch.; mem. Nat. Acad. Scis., Am. Acad. Arts & Scis. Office: U Calif Chancellor Office 9500 Gilman Dr La Jolla CA 92093-0005

DYSON, ALLAN JUDGE, librarian; b. Lawrence, Mass., Mar. 28, 1942; s. Raymond Magan and Hilda D.; m. Susan Cooper, 1987; 1 child, Brenna Ruth. BA in Govt., Harvard U., 1964; MSLS, Simmons Coll., 1968. Asst. to dir. Columbia U. Librs., N.Y.C., 1968-71; head Moffitt Undergrad. Libr. U. Calif., Berkeley, 1971-79, univ. libr. Santa Cruz, 1979—. Editor Coll. and Rsch. Librs. News, 1973-74; chmn. editl. bd. Choice mag., 1978-80, Am. Librs., 1986-89. CFO Cabrillo (Calif.) Music Festival, 1985-86; chmn. No. Calif. Regional Libr. Bd., 1986-88, 94-98, U. Calif. Librs. Group, 1998-2001. Lt. U.S. Army, 1964-66. Decorated Army Commendation medal; Coun. on Libr. Resources fellow, 1973-74. Mem. ALA, ACLU, Assn. Coll. and Rsch. Librs., Librs. Assn. U. Calif. (pres. 1976), Sierra Club. Home: 110 Rollingwoods Dr Santa Cruz CA 95060-1030 Office: U Calif McHenry Libr Santa Cruz CA 95064

DZIEWANOWSKA, ZOFIA ELIZABETH, neuropsychiatrist, pharmaceutical executive, researcher, educator; b. Warsaw, Poland, Nov. 17, 1939; came to U.S., 1972; d. Stanislaw Kazimierz Dziewanowski and Zofia Danuta (Mieczkowska) Rudowska; m. Krzysztof A. Kunert, Sept. 1, 1961 (div. 1971); 1 child, Martin. MD, U. Warsaw, 1963; PhD, Polish Acad. Sci., 1970. MD recert. U.K., 1972, U.S., 1973. Asst. prof. of psychiatry U. Warsaw Med. Sch., 1969-71; sr. house officer St. George's Hosp., U. London, 1971-72; assoc. dir. Merck Sharp & Dohme, Rahway, N.J., 1972-76; vis. assoc. physician Rockefeller U. Hosp., N.Y.C., 1975-76; adj. asst. prof. of psychiatry Cornell U. Med. Ctr., N.Y.C., 1978—; v.p., global med. dir. Hoffmann-La Roche, Inc., Nutley, N.J., 1976-94; sr. v.p. and dir. global med. affairs Genta Inc., San Diego, 1994-97; sr. v.p. drug devel. and regulatory Cypros Pharms. Corp., Carlsbad, Calif., 1997-99; pres., med. dir. New Drug Assocs., La Jolla, 1999—. Lectr. in field U.S. and internat. confs. Contbr. articles to profl. pubs. Bd. dirs Royal Soc. Medicine Found.; mem. alumni coun. Cornell U. Med. Ctr. Recipient TWIN Honoree award for Outstanding Women in Mgmt., Ridgewood (N.J.) YWCA, 1984. Mem. AMA, AAAS, Am. Soc. Pharmacology and Therapeutics, Am. Coll. Neuropsychopharmacology, N.Y. Acad. Scis., PhRMA. (vice chmn. steering com. med. sect., chmn. internat. med. affairs com., head biotech. working group), Royal Soc. Medicine (U.K.), Drug Info. Assn. (Woman of Yr. award 1994), Am. Assn. Pharm. Physicians. Roman Catholic. Achievements include original research on the role of the nervous system in the regulation of respiratory functions, research and development and therapeutic uses of many new drugs, pharmaceutical medicine and biotechnology; molecular biology derived as well as conventional products including antisense, interferon efficacy in cancer, virology and AIDS and drugs useful in cardiovascular, immunological, neuropsychiatric, infectious diseases, and others; impact of different cultures on medical practices and clinical research; drug evaluation and development management strategies of pharmaceutical industries; treatments against cardiac and brain ischemia, cytoprotection; speaker in field.

EARHART, DONALD MARION, management consultant, health care company executive; b. Hastings, Nebr., May 22, 1944; s. Donald Glen and Mary Elizabeth (Alber) E.; m. June 3, 1977 (div. July 1988); children: Timothy, Daniel, Cynthia; m. Chelu Travieso, Nov. 22, 1988. BS Indsl. Engring., Ohio State U., 1967; MBA, Roosevelt U., 1979. Engr. Eastman Kodak Co., Rochester, N.Y., 1967-70; mgmt. cons. Peat, Marwick, Mitchell, Cleve., 1970-71; div. dir. Abbott Labs., North Chicago, I, 1971-78; corp. officer , v.p. Abbott Metals, Chgo., 1978-79; div. pres., corp. officer Bausch & Lomb, Rochester, 1979-86, Allergan Inc., Irvine, Calif., 1986-90; chmn., pres., CEO I-Flow Corp., Irvine, 1990—. Bd. dirs. AnPing, Ltd., Alamar Bioscis., Inc. Republican. Avocation: photography. Home and Office: 10 Delphinus Irvine CA 92612-5705 Office: I-Flow Corp 20202 Windrow Dr Lake Forest CA 92630

EARLE, SYLVIA ALICE, research biologist, oceanographer; b. Gibbstown, N.J., Aug. 30, 1935; d. Lewis Reade and Alice Freas (Richie) E. BS, Fla. State U., 1955; MA, Duke U., 1956, PhD, 1966, PhD (hon.), 1993, Monterey Inst. Internat. Studies, 1990, Ball State U., 1991, George Washington U., 1992, U. R.I., 1996, Plymouth State Coll., 1996; DSc (hon.), Ripon Coll., 1994, U. Conn., 1994. Resident dir. Cape Haze Marine Lab., Sarasota, Fla., 1966-67; research scholar Radcliffe Inst., 1967-69; research fellow Farlow Herbarium, Harvard U., 1967-75, researcher, 1975—; research assoc. in botany Natural History Mus. Los Angeles County, 1970-75; research biologist, curator Calif. Acad. Scis., San Francisco, from 1976; research assoc. U. Calif., Berkeley, 1969-75; fellow in botany Natural History Mus., 1989—; chief scientist U.S. NOAA, Washington, 1990-92, advisor to the adminstr., 1992-93; founder, pres., CEO, bd. dirs. Deep Ocean Engrs., Inc., Oakland, Calif., 1981-90; founder, chmn., CEO Deep Ocean Exploration and Rsch., Oakland, 1992—, bd. dirs., 1992—; advisor SeaWeb, 1996—. Bd. dirs. Dresser Industries, Oryx Energy, Inc.; explorer-in-residence Nat. Geog., 1998; dir., Natl. Geographic Suatainable Seas Expedition, 1998—. Author: Exploring the Deep Frontier, 1980, Sea Change, 1995; editor: Scientific Results of the Tektite II Project, 1972-75; contbr. 100 articles to profl. jours. Trustee World Wildlife Fund U.S., 1976-82, mem. coun., 1984—; trustee World Wildlife Fund Internat., 1979-81, mem. coun., 1981-95; trustee Charles A. Lindbergh Fund, pres., 1990-95; trustee Ctr. Marine Conservation, 1992—, Perry Found., chmn., 1993-95; mem. coun. Internat. Union for Conservation of Nature, 1979-81; corp. mem. Woods Hole Oceanographic Inst., trustee, 1996—; mem. Nat. Adv. Com. on Oceans and Atmosphere, 1980-94. Recipient Conservation Svc. award U.S. Dept. Interior, 1970, Boston Sea Rovers award, 1972, 79, Nogi award Underwater Soc. Am., 1976, Conservation Svc. award Calif. Acad. Sci., 1979, Order of Golden Ark Prince Netherlands, 1980, David B. Stone medal New Eng. Aquarium, 1989, Gold medal Soc. Women Geographers, medal Radcliffe Coll., 1990, Pacon Internat. award, 1992, Dir. award Natural Resources Coun. Am., 1992, Washburn award Boston Mus. Sci., 1995, Charles A. and Ann Morrow Lindbergh award, 1996, Julius Stratton Leadership award, 1997, Kilby award, 1997, Bal de la Mar Found. Sea Keeper award, 1997, Sea Space Environment award, 1997; Environmental Global Zoo Awd., 1998; U.S. Environmental Hew Awd., 1998; named Woman of Yr. L.A. Times, 1970, Scientist of Yr., Calif. Mus. Sci. and Industry, 1981, National Women's Hall of Fame, 2000. Fellow AAAS, Marine Tech. Soc. (Compass award 1997), Calif. Acad. Scis., Calif. Acad. Sci., Explorers Club (hon., bd. dirs. 1989-94, Lowell Thomas award 1980, Explorers medal 1996); mem. Internat. Phycological Soc. (sec. 1974-80), Phycological Soc. Am., Am. Soc. Ichthyologists and Herpetologists, Am. Inst. Biol. Scis., Brit. Phycological Soc., Ecol. Soc. Am., Internat. Soc. Plant Taxonomists. Home and Office: 12812 Skyline Blvd Oakland CA 94619-3125

EARLY, DELOREESE PATRICIA See REESE, DELLA

EARLY, JAMES MICHAEL, electronics research consultant; b. Syracuse, N.Y., July 25, 1922; s. Frank J. and Rhoda Gray Early; m. Mary Agnes Valentine, Dec. 28, 1948; children: Mary Beth Early Dehler, Kathleen, Joan Early Farrell, Rhoda Early Alexander, Maureen Early Mathews, Rosemary Early North, James, Margot Early Staton. B.S., N.Y. Coll. Forestry, Syracuse, N.Y., 1943; M.S., Ohio State U., 1948, Ph.D., 1951. Instr., research assoc. Ohio State U., Columbus, 1946-51; dir. lab. Bell Telephone Labs., Murray Hill, N.J., 1951-64, Allentown, Pa., 1964-69; dir. research and devel. Fairchild Semicondr. Corp., Palo Alto, Calif., 1969-83, sci. advisor, 1983-86; research cons., 1987—. Contbr. over 20 papers to profl. jours. Served with U.S. Army, 1943-45. Fellow AAAS, IEEE (numerous coms., John Fritz Medal bd. of award); mem. IEEE Electron Device Soc. (J.J. Ebers award 1979), Am. Phys. Soc. Roman Catholic. Achievements include 14 patents; discovery of Space Charge Layer Widening effect (now called Early effect); invention of the high frequency bipolar transistor and intrinsic barrier transistor; developer of Telstar solar cells and transistors, of sealed junction beam lead integrated circuits; design theory of bipolar transistors; definition of fundamental speed-power limits in junction devices; first commercial use of ion implanter in semiconductor devices; first use of buried channel charge coupled devices, of traveling wave charge-coupled detectors, of high speed ECL and advanced CMOS; procurement of first practical commercial electron beam machine for maskmaking; proposing fastest bipolar circuit. Home and Office: 708 Holly Oak Dr Palo Alto CA 94303-4142

EARLY, ROBERT JOSEPH, magazine editor; b. Indpls., Sept. 22, 1936; s. Robert Paul and Helen Theresa (Schluttenhofer) E.; m. Gail Louise Horvath, Sept. 6, 1958; children: Mary Jane, Joseph Robert, Jill Ann. BA, U. Notre Dame, 1958. Reporter Indpls. Star, 1958-61, The Ariz. Republic, Phoenix, 1961-66, asst. city editor, 1966-69, city editor, 1969-77, asst. mng. editor, 1977-78, mng. editor, 1978-82; pres. Telesource Communication Svcs. Inc., Phoenix, 1982-90; editor Phoenix Mag., 1985-89, Ariz. Hwys., Phoenix, 1990—. Lectr. Ariz. State U., 1992, 94; editor in residence No. Ariz. U., 1992, 93, 94.. Chmn. Victims Bill of Rights Task Force, Phoenix, 1989. Recipient Virg Hill Newsman of Yr. award Ariz. Press Club, 1976. Mem. Soc. Profl. Journalists. Republican. Roman Catholic. Office: Ariz Hwys 2039 W Lewis Ave Phoenix AZ 85009-2819

EARNHARDT, HAL J., III, automotive executive; b. Mar. 20, 1956; CEO, pres. Earnhardt's Motor Cos., Gilbert, Ariz., 1986. Office: Earnhardts Motor Cos 1301 N Arizona Ave Gilbert AZ 85233-1600

EAST, JOHN, computer company executive; Pres., CEO Actel Corp., Sunnyvale, Calif. Office: Actel 955 E Arques Ave Sunnyvale CA 94085-4533

EASTAUGH, ROBERT L. state supreme court justice; b. Seattle, Nov. 12, 1943; BA, Yale U., 1965; JD, U. Mich., 1968. Bar: Alaska 1968. Asst. atty. gen. State of Alaska, 1968-69, asst. dist. atty., 1969-72; lawyer Delaney, Wiles, Hayes, Reitman & Brubaker, Inc., 1972-94; state supreme ct. assoc. justice Alaska Supreme Ct., 1994—. Office: Alaska Supreme Ct 303 K St Anchorage AK 99501-2013

EASTHAM, JOHN D. business executive; Profl. Degree, Burnley Sch., Seattle, 1967. Mng. ptnr. EMB Ptnrs., Seattle, 1994—. Recipient Clio awards, 1986, Effie, Am. Mktg. Assn., 1991, Totem awards Pub. Rels. Soc. Am., 1982. Office: EMB Ptnrs 1520 4th Ave Ste 600 Seattle WA 98101-3608

EASTHAM, THOMAS, foundation administrator; b. Attelboro, Mass., Aug. 21, 1923; s. John M. and Margaret (Marsden) E.; m. Berenice J. Hirsch, Oct. 12, 1946; children: Scott Thomas, Todd Robert. Student English, Northwestern U., 1946-52. With Chgo. American, 1945-56, asst. Sunday editor, 1953-54, feature writer, 1954-56; news editor San Francisco Call Bull., 1956-62, exec. editor, 1962-65; exec. editor, then D.C. bur. chief San Francisco Examiner, 1965-82; dir. pub. info,press sec. to mayor of San Francisco, 1982-88; v.p., western dir. William Randolph Hearst Founds., 1988—. Active Nat. Trust Historic Preservation; mem. Pres.'s Roundtable, U. San Francisco. Pulitzer prize finalist, 1955, Disting Acheivement in Journalism award, Assn. Schs. of Journalism & Mass Comm., 1994. Mem. Am. Soc. Newspaper Editors, Inter-Am. Press Assn., Am., Internat. press insts., White House Corrs. Assn., Nat. Press Club, Ind. Sector, Coun. on Foundations, Commonwealth Club, Marine Meml. Club, San Francisco Planning and Urban Rsch. Assn., Sigma Delta Chi. Home: 1473 Bernal Ave Burlingame CA 94010-5559 Office: Hearst Found 90 New Montgomery St Ste 1212 San Francisco CA 94105-4596

EASTIN, DELAINE ANDREE, state agency administrator; b. San Diego, Aug. 20, 1947; d. Daniel Howard and Dorothy Barbara (Robert) Eastin; m. John Stuart Saunders, Sept. 17, 1972. BA in Polit. Sci., U. Calif., Davis, 1969; MA in Polit. Sci., U. Calif., Santa Barbara, 1971. Instr. Calif. Community Colls., various locations, 1971-79; acctg. mgr. Pacific Bell, San Francisco, 1979-84; corp. planner Pacific Telesis Group, San Francisco, 1984-86; assemblywoman Calif. State Legis., Sacramento, 1986-95; supt. of public instruction Calif. Edn. Dept., Sacramento, 1995—. Bd. dirs. CEWAER, Sacramento, 1988—; commr. Commn. on Status of Women, Sacramento, 1990—; mem. coun. City of Union City, Calif., 1980-86; chair Alameda County Libr. Commn., Hayward, Calif., 1981-86; planning commr. City of Union City, 1976-80; mem., pres. Alameda County Solid Waste Mgmt. Authority, Oakland, Calif., 1980-86. Named Outstanding Pub. Ofcl. Calif. Tchrs. Assn., 1988, Cert. of Appreciation Calif. Assn. for Edn. of Young Children, 1988-92, Legislator of the Yr. Calif. Media Libr. Educators, 1991, Calif. Sch. Bd. Assn., 1991, Ednl. Excellence award Calif. Assn. Counseling and Devel., 1992. Mem. Am. Bus. Women's Assn. (Outstanding Bus. Woman 1988), The Internat. Alliance (21st Century award 1990), World Affairs Coun., Commonwealth Club. Democrat. Avocations: photography, hiking, reading, theater. Home: 4228 Dogwood Pl Davis CA 95616-6066

EASTMAN, DAN R. state legislator; Mem. Utah State Senate, Salt Lake City, 2001—. Office: 968 Canyon Crest Dr Bountiful UT 84010 E-mail: deast1964@aol.com*

EASTMAN, DONALD, religious organization administrator; b. Sheboygan, Wis., Feb. 1, [illegible] minister Assemblies of God. Pastor Assemblies of God, Wis., 1966-72; ofcl. Am. Lung Assn., Iowa, 1972-75; pastor MCC congregations UFMCC, Des Moines and Dallas, 1978-86, 2d vice moderator, treas. Activist civil and human rights of gays and lesbians; lobbyist repeal of state sodomy laws, Iowa; speaker Tex. State Bd. of Health; bd. dirs. AIDS Nat. Interfaith Network, 1988-90, founding mem., first chairperson. Office: UFMCC 8704 [illegible] DonEastman@aol.com

EASTWOOD, CLINT, actor, film director, former mayor; b. San Francisco, May 31, 1930; m. Dina Ruiz. Student, Oakland Tech. High Sch.; attended, Los Angeles City Coll. Worked as lumberjack in Oreg. before being drafted into the Army; formed Malpaso Prodns., 1969. Chmn. AT&T/Pebble Beach Pro Am. Golf Tournament; owner, pres. Malpaso Records Co., Mission Ranch Resort, Carmel, Calif.; owner, co-ptnr. Prime Golf/Tenama Clothing Co., owner/pres. Malpaso Records Co., owner Mission Ranch Resort, Carmel, Calif., owner/co-partner Prime Gold/Tenama Clothing Co. Starred in TV series Rawhide, 1959-1966. Motion pictures include: (actor) Revenge of the Creature, 1955, Francis in the Navy, 1955, Lady Godiva, 1955, Tarantula, 1955, Never Say Goodbye, 1956, The First Travelling Saleslady, 1956, Star in the Dust, 1956, Away All Boats, 1956, Escapade in Japan, 1957, Ambush at the Cimmaron Pass, 1958, Lafayette Escadrille, 1958, A Fistful of Dollars, 1964, For a Few Dollars More, 1965, The Good The Bad and The Ugly, 1966, The Witches, 1967, Hang 'Em High, 1968, Coogan's Bluff, 1968, Where Eagles Dare, 1969, Paint Your Wagon, 1969, Two Mules for Sister Sara, 1970, Kelly's Heroes, 1970, The Beguiled, 1971, Dirty Harry, 1972, Joe Kidd, 1972, Magnum Force, 1973, Thunderbolt and Lightfoot, 1974, The Enforcer, 1976, Every Which Way But Loose, 1978, Escape from Alcatraz, 1979, Any Which Way You Can, 1980, City Heat, 1984, (dir. Amazing Stories TV) Vanessa in the Garden, 1985, Pink Cadillac, 1989, In the Line of Fire, 1993; (dir.) Breezy, 1973, (dir., actor) Play Misty For Me, 1971, High Plains Drifter, 1973, The Eiger Sanction, 1975, The Outlaw Josey Wales, 1976, The Gauntlet, 1977, Bronco Billy, 1980, The Rookie, 1990, A Perfect World, 1994, Absolute Power, 1996; (actor, prod.) Tightrope, 1984, The Dead Pool, 1988; (dir., prod.) Bird, 1988, Midnight in the Garden of Good and Evil, 1997; (dir., actor, producer) Firefox, 1982, Honky Tonk Man, 1982, Sudden Impact, 1983, Pale Rider, 1985, Heartbreak Ridge, 1986, White Hunter, Black Heart, 1990, Unforgiven, 1992 (Academy Award Best Director, Best Picture), The Bridges of Madison County, 1995, Absolute Power, 1997, True Crime, 1998, Space Cowboys (dir./actor/prodr.), 2000; (exec. producer) Thelonious Monk-Straight, No Chaser, 1989, The Stars Fell on Henrietta, 1995; (cameo) Casper; singer (Midnight soundtrack album) Ac.cent.uate the Positive, 1997, (with Randy Travis) Smokin' the Hive; documentaries include Don't Pave Main St., 1994, Eastwood After Hours: A Night of Jazz. Mem. Nat. Coun. Arts, 1973; chmn. (Monterey) AT&T/Pebble Beach Pro-Am Golf Tournament. Office: c/o Leonard Hirshan Wm Morris Agy Inc 151 S El Camino Dr Beverly Hills CA 90212-2704

EATON, CURTIS HOWARTH, banker, lawyer; b. Twin Falls, Idaho, Sept. 3, 1945; s. Curtis Turner and Wilma (Howarth)E.; m. Mardo Ohisson, Aug. 2, 1969; 1 child, Dylan Alexander. BA, Stanford U., 1969; MPA, Johns Hopkins U., 1971; JD, U. Idaho, 1974. Bar: Idaho 1974. Atty. Idaho Atty. Gen.'s Office, Boise, 1974-76; ptnr. Stephan, Slavin, Eaton, Twin Falls, 1975-82; exec. v.p. Twin Falls Bank & Trust, 1982-84, area pres., from 1984, also bd. dirs., from 1984; former v.p., bd. dirs. 1st Security Bank at Idaho, Twin Falls, pres., 1992—. Bd. dirs. San Francisco Fed. Res. Bank, Salt Lake City. Bd. dirs. United Way Magic Falley, 1978—, Sr. Citizens, 1978-82; mem. Idaho Bd. Edn., 1993—, now pres.; trustee YFCA, 1981—; pres. Coll. So. Idaho Found., 1986-88. Mem. ATLA, Idaho Bar Assn.

EATON, GARETH RICHARD, chemistry educator, university dean; b. Lockport, N.Y., Nov. 3, 1940; s. Mark Dutcher and Ruth Emma (Ruston) E.; m. Sandra Shaw, Mar. 29, 1969. BA, Harvard U., 1962; PhD, MIT, 1972. Asst. prof. chemistry U. Denver, 1972-76, assoc. prof., 1976-80, prof., 1980-97, dean natural scis., 1984-88, vice provost for rsch., 1988-89, John Evans prof., 1997—. Organizer Internat. Electron-Paramagnetic Resonance Symposium. Author, editor 4 books; mem. editorial bd. 4 jours.; contbr. articles to profl. jours. Lt. USN, 1962-67. Mem. AAAS, Am. Chem. Soc., Royal Soc. Chemistry (London), Internat. Soc. Magnetic Resonance, Soc. Applied Spectroscopy, Am. Phys. Soc., Internat. Electron Paramagnetic Resonance Soc. Office: U Denver Dept Chem/Biochem Denver CO 80208 E-mail: geaton@du.edu

EATON, GEORGE WESLEY, JR. petroleum engineer, oil company executive; b. Searcy, Ark., Aug. 3, 1924; s. George Wesley and Inez (Roberson) E.; m. Adriana Amin, Oct. 28, 1971; 1 child, Andrew. BS in Petroleum Engring., U. Okla., 1948. Registered profl. engr. Tex., N.Mex. Petroleum engr. Amoco, Longview, Ft. Worth, Tex., 1948-54, engring. supr. Roswell, N.Mex., 1954-59, dist. engr. Farmington, 1959-70; constrn. mgr. Amoco Egypt Oil Co., Cairo, 1970-81; ops. mgr. Amoco Norway Oil Co., Stavanger, 1981-84; petroleum cons. G.W. Eaton Cons., Albuquerque, 1984-94. Adj. prof. San Juan Coll., Farmington, 1968-70. Bd. dirs. Paradise Hills Civic Assn., Albuquerque, 1986-89; elder Rio Grande Presbyn. Ch., Albuquerque, 1987-90; mem. Rep. Nat. Com., Washington, 1986-92. Mem. N.Mex. Soc. Profl. Engrs. (bd. dirs. 1967-70), Soc. Petroleum Engrs. (Legion of Honor), Egyptian Soc. Petroleum Engrs. (chmn. 1980-81). Home: 5116 Russell Dr NW Albuquerque NM 87114-4325

EATON, GORDON PRYOR, geologist, consultant; b. Dayton, Ohio, Mar. 9, 1929; s. Colman and Dorothy (Pryor) E.; m. Virginia Anne Gregory, June 12, 1951; children: Gretchen Maria, Gregory Mathieu. BA, Wesleyan U., 1951, Doctorate (hon.), 1995; MS, Calif. Inst. Tech., 1953, PhD, 1957; Doctorate (hon.), Colo. Sch. Mines, 2001. From instr. geology to asst. prof. Wesleyan U., Middletown, Conn., 1955-59; from asst. prof. to assoc. prof. U. Calif., Riverside, 1959-67, chmn. dept. geol. sci., 1965-67; with U.S. Geol. Survey, 1963-65, 67-81, 94-97; dep. chief Office Geochemistry and Geophysics, Washington, 1972-74; project chief geothermal geophysics Office Geochemistry Geophysics, Denver, 1974-76; scientist-in-charge Hawaiian Volcano Obs., 1976-78; assoc. chief geologist Reston, Va., 1978-81; dean Tex. A&M U. Coll. Geoscis., 1981-83; provost, v.p. acad. affairs Tex. A&M U., 1983-86; pres. Iowa State U., Ames, 1986-90; dir. Lamont-Doherty Earth Obs. Columbia U., Palisades, N.Y., 1990-94, U.S. Geol. Survey, Reston, Va., 1994-97; prin. Pac NW, Sea-Mountain Country, Colo., Tex., Wash., W.Va., 1997—. Former mem. Com. on Internat. Edn., Am. Coun. Edn.; mem. bd. earth scis. and resources; ocean studies bd., and com. on formation of nat. biol. survey NRC, also mem. geophysics study com.; bd. dirs. Midwest Resources, Inc., Bankers Trust; mem., chair adv. com. U.S. Army Command and Gen. Staff Coll.; adv. bd. Sandia Nat. Lab. Geoscis. & Environ. Ctr.; adv. bd. Ohio State U. Ctr. Mapping. Mem. editl. bd. Jour. Volcanology and Geothermal Rsch., 1976-78; contbr. articles to profl. jours. Trustee Wesleyan U., 1995-98; pres., bd. dirs. Iowa 4-H Found., 1986-90; mem. adv. bd. Sch. Earth Sci. Stanford (Calif.) U., 1995-2000; mem. U.S. del. sci. & tech. com. Gore-Chernomyrdin Commn., 1996-97; mem. vis. com. Colo. Sch. Mines; mem. water res. adv. com. Island Co., 2001—. Standard Oil fellow Calif. Inst. Tech., 1953; NSF grantee, 1955-59. Fellow Geol. Soc. Am., AAAS. Office: SeaMountain Country 705 N Snowberry Ln Ste O Coupeville WA 98239-3110 E-mail: geaton@whidbey.net

EATON, JERRY, television executive; b. L.A., June 13, 1945; BS in Biology, Trinity Coll. V.p., gen. mgr. KYW, Phila., KPIX-TV, San Francisco, 1997—. Office: KPIX-TV 855 Battery St San Francisco CA 94111-1597

EATON, PAULINE, artist; b. Neptune, N.J., Mar. 20, 1935; d. Paul A. and Florence Elizabeth (Rogers) Freidrich; m. Charles Adams Eaton, June 15, 1957; children: Grogory, Eric, Paul, Joy. BA, Dickonson Coll., 1957; MA, Northwestern U., 1958. Lic. instr., Calif. Instr. Mira Costa Coll., Oceanside, Calif., 1980-82, Idyllwild Sch. Music and Arts, 1983—; instr. dept. continuing edn. U. N.Mex. Juror, demonstrator numerous art socs. One-woman shows include Nat. Arts Club, N.Y.C., 1977, Designs Recycled Gallery, Fullerton, Calif., 1978, 80, 84, San Diego Art Inst., 1980,

Spectrum Gallery, San Diego, 1981, San Diego Jung Ctr., 983, Marin Civic Ctr. Gallery, 1984, R. Mondayi Winery, 1987; group shows include Am. Watercolor Soc., 1975, 77, Butler Inst. Am. Art, Youngstown, Ohio, 1977, 78, 79, 81, NAD, 1978, N.Mex. Arts and Cragts Fair (Best in Show award), 1994, Corrales Bosque Gallery; represented in permanent collections at Butler Inst. Am. Art, St. Mary's Coll., Md., Mercy Hosp., San Diego, Sharp Hosp., San Diego, Redlands Hosp., Riverside; work featured in books: Watercolor, The Creative Experience, 1978, Creative Seascape Painting, 1980, Painting the Spirit in Nature, 1984, Exploring Painting (Gerald Brommer); author: Crawling to the Light, An Artist in Transition, 1987, (with Mary Ann Beckwith) Best of Watercolor Texture, 1997; contbr. chot., artwork Bridging Time and Space, Essays in Layered Art, 1998. Trustee San Diego Art Inst., 1977-78, San Diego Mus. Art, 1982-83. Recipient award Haywood (Calif.) are Forum for the Arts, 1986, Best of Show award N.Mex. Arts and Crafts Fair, 1994, Grumbacker award Conf. 96 Hill Country Art Ctr., 2d award Tex. Friends and Neighbors, Irving, 2000. Mem. Nat. Watercolor Soc. (exhibited traveling shows 1978, 79, 83, 85), Rocky Mountain Watermedia Soc. (Golden award 1979, Mustard Seed award 1983), Nat. Soc. Painters in Acrylic and Casein (hon.), Watercolor West (strathmore award 1979, Purchase award 1986), Watercolor USA Soc. (hon., Veloy Vigil Meml. award 1998), Internat. Soc. Exptl. Artists (Nautilus Merit award 1992, 98,), Marin Arts Guild (instr. 1984-87), San Diego Watercolor Soc. (pres. 1976-77, workshop dir. 1977-80), Artists Equity (v.p. San Diego 1979-81), San Diego Artists Guild (pres. 1982-83), N.Mex. Watercolor Soc. (Grumbacker award, Wingspread award 1999), Western Fedn. Watercolor Socs. (chmn. 1983, 3d prize 1982, Grumbacher Gold medal 1983), West Coast Watercolor Soc. (exhbns. chmn. 1983-86, pres. 1989-92), Eastbay Watercolor Soc. (v.p. 1988-90), Soc. Layerists in multi-Media (bd. dirs. 1992—), Corrales Basque Gallery (charter mem., pres. 1996-98), Watercolor USA Honor Soc. (Veloy Vejil Meml. award 1998). Democrat. Home: 68 Hop Tree Trl Corrales NM 87048-9613 E-mail: pfeaton@earthlink.net

EAVES, ALLEN CHARLES EDWARD, hematologist, medical agency administrator; b. Ottawa, Ont., Can., Feb. 19, 1941; s. Charles Albert and Margaret Vernon (Smith) E.; m. Connie Jean Halperin, July 1, 1975; children: Neil, Rene, David, Sara BSc, Acadia U., Wolfville, N.S., Can., 1962; MSc, Dalhousie U., Halifax, N.S., 1964, MD, 1969; PhD, U. Toronto, Ont., Can., 1974. Intern Dalhousie U., Halifax, N.S., Can., 1968-69; resident in internal medicine Sunnybrook Hosp., Toronto, 1974-75, Vancouver Gen. Hosp., 1975-79; dir. Terry Fox Lab., Cancer Control Agy. B.C., Vancouver, Can., 1980—; asst. prof. medicine U. B.C., 1979-83, assoc. prof., 1983-88, head div. hematology, 1985—, prof., 1988—; pres. StemCell Technologies, Inc., Vancouver, 1993—, Malachite Mgmt., Inc., 1996—, StemSoft Software Inc., 2000—. Treas. Found. for Accreditation of Hematopoetic Cell Therapy, 1995—. Fellow Royal Coll. Physicians (Can.), ACP; mem. Internat. Soc. Hematotherapy and Graft Engrng. (pres. 1995-97), Am. Soc. Blood and Marrow Transplantation (pres. elect 1998-99, pres. 1999-2000). Home: 2705 W 31st Ave Vancouver BC Canada V6L 1Z9 Office: Terry Fox Lab Cancer Rsch 601 W 10th Ave Vancouver BC Canada V5Z 1L3 E-mail: aeaves@bccancer.bc.ca

EBBELING, WILLIAM LEONARD, physician; b. Whitinsville, Mass., June 29, 1947; s. Titus Jr. and Agnes Ebbeling; m. Dianne Wilder, Apr. 10, 1976; children: Jennifer Lynn, Daniel Wilder. BS, Wheaton Coll., 1969; MD, Wake Forest U. Sch. Medicine, 1974. Commd. ensign USN, 1974, advanced through grades to capt., 1988; resident Naval Med. Ctr., Portsmouth, Va., 1974-77, pediatrician Naples, Italy, 1977-80; fellow in allergy Duke U. Med. Ctr., Durham, N.C., 1985-88; head ambulatory pediatrics, staff pediatrician Nat. Naval Med. Ctr., Bethesda, Md., 1981-85, head allery, immunology and clin. investigation dept., 1988-93; dep. chief med. corps for career planning Navy Bur. Medicine and Surgery, Washington, 1993-95; head direct med. care divsn. Naval Healthcare Support Office, San Diego, 1995-97; staff allergist Naval Tng. Ctr., Allergy Clinic, San Diego, 1997—. Fellow Am. Acad. Allergy, Asthma and Immunology, Am. Acad. Pediat.; mem. Am. Coll. Physician Execs., Assn. Mil. Allergists (chmn. 1996-97). Avocations: tennis, computers, fishing. Home: 10870 Autillo Way San Diego CA 92127-1366 Office: Naval Med Ctr Allergy Clinic at NTC 2650 Stockton Rd Bldg 624 San Diego CA 92106-6000

EBEL, DAVID M. federal judge; b. 1940; BA, Northwestern U., 1962; JD, U. Mich., 1965. Law clk. assoc. justice Byron White U.S. Supreme Ct., 1965-66; pvt. practice Davis, Graham & Stubbs, Denver, 1966-88; judge U.S. Ct. Appeals (10th cir.), Denver, 1988—. Adj. prof. law U. Denver Law Sch., 1987-89; sr. lectr. fellow Duke U. Sch. Law, 1992-94. Mem. Am. Coll. Trial Lawyers, Colo. Bar Assn. (v.p. 1982), Jud. Conf. U.S. (com. on codes of conduct 1991-98, co-chair 10th cir. gender bias task force 1994-99). Office: US Ct Appeals 1823 Stout St Rm 109L Denver CO 80257-1823 E-mail: david_m._ebel@ca10.uscourts.gov

EBERHARDT, MARTY LAMPERT, botanical garden administrator; b. Albuquerque, Aug. 6, 1952; d. Charles Lampert and Mary Elizabeth (Marty) E.; m. Thomas George Schramski, Mar. 19, 1977 (div. May 1986); children: Paul, Sam; m. Philip Alan Hastings, Dec. 12, 1987. BA, Prescott Coll., 1974; MEd, U. Ariz., 1978. Program dir. Tumamoc Hill Environ. Edn. Ctr., Tucson, 1978-79; tchr. Cmty. Psychology and Edn. Svcs., Tucson, 1985-87; asst. dir./edn. coord. Tucson Bot. Gardens, 1986-88, exec. dir., 1988—. Reviewer grants Inst. Mus. and Libr. Svcs., Washington, 1994—; mem. adv. bd. Registree, 1993—. Mem. steering com. Nat. and Cultural Heritage Alliance of Pima County, 1996—; mem. exec. com. Intercultural Ctr. for Study of Deserts and Oceans, Puerto Peñasco, Mex., 1998—, Tucson Cmty. Found., 1997-99, Tucson Origins Project, 1999—. Recipient Women on the Move award YWCA, Tucscon, 1993, various grants from corps. and founds., 1988—. Mem. Exec. Women's Coun., Strategic Leadership in Changing Environ., Am. Assn. Bot. Gardens and Arboreta (regional coord.), Am. Assn. Museums (reviewer grants 1994-98), Native Seeds/SEARCH. Avocations: hiking, backpacking, reading, gardening. Office: Tucson Bot Gardens 2150 N Alvernon Way Tucson AZ 85712-3153

EBERHART, GREGORY E. pharmacist, registrar, administrator; Registrar, treas. Alberta Pharm. Assn., 1990—, pres., 1989—.

EBERHART, RALPH E. career officer; b. Nevada, MO, Dec. 26, 1946; m. Karen Sue Gies. BS in Polit. Sci., USAF Acad., 1968; grad., Squadron Officer Sch., 1973, Air Command and Staff Coll., 1974; MS in Polit. Sci., Troy State U., 1977; postgrad. studies, Nat. War Coll., Ft. Lesley J. McNair, Washington, 1987. Commd. 2d lt. USAF, 1968, advanced through grades to gen., 1997; forward air controller Tactical Air Support Squadron USAF, Plieka Air Base, S. Viet Nam, 1970; from instr. pilot to squadron hdqrs. comdr. 71st Flying Tng. Wing Air Tng. Command USAF, Vance AFB, Okla., 1970-74; flight commdr., instr. pilot 525th Tactical Fighter Squadron USAFs in Europe, Bitburg Air Base, Germany, 1975-77; instr. pilot. flight examiner, asst. chief evaluation 50th Tactical Fighter Wing, Hahn Air Base, Germany, 1977-78; action officer, chief exec. com. Air Force Budget team Hdqs. USAF, Washington, 1979-80; aide to comdr.-in-chief, comdr. Air Forces Ctrl. Europe USAF, Ramstein AFB, Germany, 1980-82; comdr. 10th tactical fighter squadron, asst. dep. comdr. ops. 50th tactical fighter wing USAF in Europe, Hahn Air Base, Germany; exec. officer to Air Force chief of staff Hdqs. USAF, Washington, 1984-86; vice comdr. to comdr. 363d tactical fighter wing Tactical Air Command USAF, Shaw AFB, S.C., 1987-90; dep. chief of staff, plans and ops. Hdqs. USAF, Washington, 1995-96; cmdr. U.S. Forces Japan, cmdr. 5th Air Force USAF, Yokota Air Base, Japan, 1996-97; vice chief of staff Hdqs. USAF, Washington, 1997—. Numerous decorations include: Legion of Merit with Oak Leaf cluster, Disting. Flying Cross, Air medal with 11 Oak Leaf clusters, Vietnam Svc. medal with 3 svc. stars, Humanitarian Svc. medal with svc. star, Republic of Vietnam Gallantry Cross with Palm, Republic of Vietnam Campaign medal, The Grand Cordon of the Order of the Sacred Treasure, Japan. and many others. Mem. Coun. of Fgn. Rels. Office: CC/NAADC Dept Def 150 S Peterson Blvd Ste 1105 Colorado Springs CO 80914-3086

EBERSOLE, BRIAN, mayor; b. Tenn. BA, U. Tenn.; M in Ednl. Psychology, U. Conn. Tchr., counselor, adminstr. Tacoma Pub. Schs.; adminstr. Tacoma C.C., 1989-91; spkr. Wash. State Ho. of Reps.; state house majority leader; mayor Tacoma, 1995—. Chair House Edn. Com., 1985-87; prime sponsor Omnibus Sch. Fin. Reform Act, 1987, Omnibus Drug Bill, 1989. Named Legislator of Yr. (6 consecutive yrs.), Assn. for Vocat. Edn., Legislator of Yr., Wash. State Firefighters Assn. and Wash. State Coun. of Policy Officers. Office: 747 Market St Ste 1200 Tacoma WA 98402-3701

EBIE, WILLIAM D. museum director; b. Akron, Ohio, Feb. 7, 1942; s. William P. and Mary Louise (Karam) E.; m. Gwyn Anne Schumacher, Apr. 11, 1968 (div. Jan. 1988); children: Jason William, Alexandra Anne; m. Mary Teresa Hayes, June 10, 1989. BFA, Akron Art Inst., 1964; MFA, Calif. Coll. of Arts and Crafts, 1968. Graphic artist Alameda County Health Dept., Oakland, Calif., 1967-68; instr. painting Fla. A&M U., Tallahassee, 1968-69; instr. photography Lawrence (Kans.) Adult Edn. Program, 1969-70; asst. dir. Roswell (N.Mex.) Mus. & Art Ctr., 1971-87, dir., 1987-98, Millicent Rogers Mus., Taos, N.Mex., 1998—. Juror various art exhbns., 1971—; panelist N.Mex. Arts Divsn., Santa Fe, 1983-87; field reviewer Inst. for Mus. Svcs., 1988-90; mem. State Capitol Renovation Art Selection Com., Santa Fe, 1991-92; bd. dirs. State Capitol Found., Santa Fe, 1992—. Bd. dirs. Helene Wurlitzer Found., Taos, N.Mex., 1999—. Mem. Am. Assn. of Mus., Mountain Plains Mus. Assn., N.Mex. Assn. of Mus. Democrat. Avocations: photography, carpentry. Office: Millicent Rogers Museum PO Box A Taos NM 87571-0546 E-mail: mrm@newmex.com

ECCLES, MATTHEW ALAN, landscape and golf course architect; b. Ft. Dodge, Iowa, Apr. 19, 1956; s. Guy Eldon Jr. and Mary Ellen (Baldwin) E.; m. Debra Kay Sorenson, Mar. 19, 1983; children: Stephanie Ann, Jason Alan. BS in Landscape Architecture, Iowa State U., 1978. Registered landscape architect, Kans., Minn. From project mgr. to dir. golf course design THK Assocs., Inc., Greenwood Village, Colo., 1980-94; pres. Eccles Design Inc., Englewood, 1994—. Mem. Am. Soc. Landscape Architects, U.S. Golf Assn., Golf Course Supts. Assn. Am., Nat. Golf Found., Nat. Ski Patrol, Tau Sigma Delta. Avocations: golf, skiing, fishing, photography. Office: Eccles Design Inc 8120 S Monaco Cir Englewood CO 80112-3022

ECCLES, SPENCER FOX, banker; b. Ogden, Utah, Aug. 24, 1934; s. Spencer Stoddard and Hope (Fox) E.; m. Cleone Emily Peterson, July 21, 1958; children: Clista Hope, Lisa Ellen, Katherine Ann, Spencer Peterson. BS, U. Utah, 1956; MA, Columbia U., 1959; degree in bus. (hon.), So. Utah State Coll., 1982; LLB (hon.), Westminster Coll., Salt Lake City, 1986. Trainee First Nat. City Bank, N.Y.C., 1959-60; with First Security Bank of Utah, Salt Lake City, 1960-61, First Security Bank of Idaho, Boise, 1961-70; exec. v.p. First Security Corp., Salt Lake City, 1970-75, pres., 1975-86, COO, 1980-82, chmn. bd. dirs., CEO, 1982—. Dir. Union Pacific Corp., Anderson Lumber Co., Zions Corp., Merc. Instn.; mem. adv. council U. Utah Bus. Coll. 1st lt. U.S. Army. Recipient Pres.'s Circle award Presdl. Commn., 1984, Minuteman award Utah N.G., 1988; Named Disting. Alumni U. Utah, 1988. Mem. Am. Bankers Assn., Bankers Roundtable, Salt Lake Country Club, Alta Club. Office: 1st Security Corp PO Box 30006 79 S Main St Salt Lake City UT 84111-1901

ECHOHAWK, JOHN ERNEST, lawyer; b. Albuquerque, Aug. 11, 1945; s. Ernest V. and Emma Jane (Conrad) E.; m. Kathryn Suzanne Martin, Oct. 23, 1965; children: Christopher, Sarah. BA, U. N.M., 1967, JD, 1970. Bar: Colo. 1972, U.S. Dist. Ct. Colo. 1972, U.S. Appeals (8th cir.) 1976, U.S. Ct. Appeals (9th cir.) 1980. Research assoc. Calif. Indian Legal Services, Escondido, 1970, Native Am. Rights Fund, Berkeley Calif. and Boulder, Colo., 1970-72, dep. dir. Boulder, 1972-73, 1975-77, exec. dir., 1973-75, 1977—. Mem. task force Am. Indian Policy Rev. Commn., U.S. Senate, Washington, 1976-77; bd. dirs. Am. Indian Lawyer Tng. Program, Oakland, Calif., 1975—; bd. dirs. Assn. Am. Indian Affairs, 1980—, Nat. Com. Responsive Philanthropy, Washington, 1981—; mem. Clinton Adminstrn. Transition Team for Interior Dept., 1992-93. Presdl. appointee Western Water Policy Rev. Adv. Commn., 1995-97; Ind. Sector, Washington, 1986-92; mem. Natural Resources Def. Coun., N.Y.C., 1988—; bd. dirs. Nat. Ctr. Enterprise Devel., 1988—, Keystone Ctr., 1993—, Environ. and Energy Study Inst., 1994—. Recipient Disting. Service award Ams. For Indian Opportunity, 1982, Pres. Indian Service award Nat. Congress Am. Indians, 1984, Annual Indian Achievement award Indian Council Fire, 1987; named one of most influential attys. Nat. Law Jour., 1988, 91, 94. Mem. Native Am. Bar Assn., Colo. Indian Bar Assn. Democrat. Avocations: fishing, skiing. Home: 4660 Quail Creek Ln Boulder CO 80301-3871 Office: Native Am Rights Fund 1506 Broadway St Boulder CO 80302-6217

ECK, DOROTHY FRITZ, state legislator; b. Sequim, Wash., Jan. 23, 1924; d. Ira Edward and Ida (Hokanson) Fritz; m. Hugo Eck, Dec. 16, 1942 (dec. Feb. 1988); children: Laurence, Diana. BS in Secondary Edn., Mont. State U., 1961, MS in Applied Sci., 1966. Mgr. property mgmt. bus., 1955—; conf. coord. Am. Argl. Econs. Assn., 1967-68; state-local coord. Office of Gov. Mont., Helena, 1972-77; mem. Mont. State Senate, 1981—, Mont. Environ. Quality Coun., 1981-87. Bd. dirs. Meth. Youth Fellowship, 1960-64, Mont. Coun. for Effective Legislature, 1977-78, Rocky Mountain Environ. Coun., 1982—; del. Western v.p. Mont. Constl. Conv., 1971-72; chmn. Gov.'s Task Force on Citizen Participation, 1976-77; mem. adv. com. No. Rockies Resource and Tng. Ctr. (now No. Lights Inst.), 1979-81. Recipient Outstanding Alumna award Mont. State U., 1981, Centennial Faculty award, 1989. Mem. LWV (state pres. 1967-70), Common Cause, Nat. Women's Polit. Caucus. Democrat. Home: 10 W Garfield St Bozeman MT 59715-5602 Office: State Senate State Capitol Helena MT 59620

ECK, ROBERT EDWIN, physicist; b. Ames, Iowa, Nov. 28, 1938; s. John Clifford and Helen (Behrendt) E.; m. Carolyn Jennie Vodicka, May 11, 1974; children: David Michael, Elizabeth Claire. BA in Physics, Rutgers U., 1960; MS in Physics, U. Pa., 1962, PhD in Physics, 1966; MA in Econs., U. Calif., Santa Barbara, 1973. Sr. rsch. scientist Ford Motor Co., Newport Beach, Calif., 1966-69; project engr. Santa Barbara Rsch. Ctr., Goleta, 1969-73, asst. mgr. infrared components, 1974-81, mgr. major program, 1982-84, dir. tech., 1985-88, dir./mgr. engring., 1989-95; new bus. devel. mgr. R.G. Hansen & Assocs., Santa Barbara, 1995-96; program mgr. Optoelectronics-Textron, Petaluma, 1996-2000. Bd. dirs. Goleta Edn. Found. Mem. Goleta Noontime Rotary Club (pres. 1989-90). Achievements include patents on superconductors, infrared detector testing and magnetoresistor sensors.

ECKERSLEY, NORMAN CHADWICK, bank executive; b. Glasgow, Scotland, June 18, 1924; came to U.S., 1969; s. James Norman and Beatrice (Chadwick) E.; m. Rosemary J. Peters, May 23, 1986; 1 child, Anne. D Laws, Strathclyde U., Scotland. With Chartered Bank, London and Manchester, 1947-48; acct. Bombay, 1948-52, Singapore, 1952-54, Sarawak, 1954-56, Pakistan, 1956-58, Calcutta, 1958-59, Hong Kong, 1959-60; asst. mgr. Hamburg, 1960-62; mgr. Calcutta and Thailand, 1962-67; pres. Chartered Bank London, San Francisco, 1964-74, chmn., CEO, 1974-79; chmn. Std. Chartered Bancorp, 1978-82; dep. chmn. Union Bank, L.A., 1979-82; chmn., CEO The Pacific Bank, San Francisco, 1982-93; chmn. emeritus, 1993. Chmn. Diners Club (Asia), 1967-69, Devel. Bank Thailand, 1967-69, Scottish Am. Investment Com., U. Strathclyde Found.; chmn. Balmoral Fin. Corp., 1995-99; exec. Bank of the Orient, San Francisco, 1999—. With RAF, 1940-46. Decorated D.F.C., comdr. Order Brit. Empire. Mem. Overseas Banks Assn. Calif. (chmn. 1972-74), Calif. Coun. Internat. Trade, San Francisco C. of C., World Trade Assn., Hong Kong Assn. (San Francisco) (bd. dirs.), Royal and Ancient Club, St. Andrews (Scotland), Royal Troon Golf Club (Scotland), World Trade Club, San Francisco Golf Club, Pacific Union Club (San Francisco). Mem. Ch. of Scotland. Home: 11718 Saddle Rd Monterey CA 93940-6653 Office: Bank of the Orient 233 Sansome St Fl 12 San Francisco CA 94104-2305

ECKERT, ROBERT A. manufacturing company executive; BSBA, U. Ariz., 1976; MBA in Mktg. and Fin., Northwestern U., 1977. Various mktg. positions Kraft Foods, 1977-87, v.p. strategy and devel. grocery products divsn., 1987-89, v.p. mktg. refrigerated products, 1989-90, v.p., gen. mgr. cheese divsn., 1990-97, pres., CEO, 1997-2000; chmn. bd., CEO Mattel, Inc., 2000—. Active adv. bd. J.L. Kellogg Grad. Sch. Mgmt., Northwestern U.; bd. dirs., mem. exec. com. Met. Family Svcs.; bd. dirs., chmn. govt. affairs coun. Grocery Mfrs. Am.; trustee Ravinia Festival Assn., Art Inst. Chgo.; nat. trustee Lake Forest Coll. Office: Mattel Inc 333 Continental Blvd El Segundo CA 90245-5012 Fax: 310-252-2179

ECKHART, WALTER, molecular biologist, educator; b. Yonkers, N.Y., May 22, 1938; s. Walter and Jean (Fairnington) E. BS, Yale U., 1960; postgrad., Cambridge U., Eng., 1960-61; PhD, U. Calif.-Berkeley, 1965. Postdoctoral fellow Salk Inst., San Diego, 1965-69, mem., 1970-73, assoc. prof. molecular biology, 1973-79, prof., 1979—, dir., 1976—. Adj. prof. U. Calif.-San Diego, 1973— Contbr. articles on molecular biology and virology to profl. jours. NIH research grantee, 1967—. Mem. AAAS, Am. Assn. Cancer Rsch., Am. Soc. Microbiology, Am. Soc. Virology Home: 951 Skylark Dr La Jolla CA 92037-7731 Office: Salk Inst PO Box 85800 San Diego CA 92186-5800

ECKSTUT, MICHAEL KAUDER, management consultant; b. Prague, Czechoslovakia, Mar. 13, 1952; came to U.S., 1960; s. Robert and Erika Kauder (Neumann) E.; m. Mary Jane Haymond, May 21, 1978; children: Martina, Robert. BS in Chem. Engring., Rensselaer Poly., 1973, MS in Chem. Engring., 1974; MBA, Harvard U., 1978. Chem. engr. E.I. DuPont de Nemours, Wilmington, Del., 1974-76; assoc. Idanta Ptnrs., La Jolla, Calif., 1978-79; v.p. Booz, Allen & Hamilton, Inc., N.Y.C., 1979-93, A.T. Kearney Inc., N.Y.C., 1993-99; sr. v.p. bus. devel. Chemconnect, San Francisco, 1999—. Home: 1878 Greenwich St San Francisco CA 94123-3508 Office: 44 Montgomery St Ste 250 San Francisco CA 94104-4604

ECTON, DONNA R. business executive; b. Kansas City, Mo., May 10, 1947; d. Allen Howard and Marguerite (Page) E.; m. Victor H. Maragni, June 16, 1986; children: Mark, Gregory. BA (Durant Scholar), Wellesley Coll., 1969; MBA, Harvard U., 1971. V.p. Chem. Bank, N.Y.C., 1972-79, Citibank, N.A., N.Y.C., 1979-81; pres. MBA Resources, Inc., N.Y.C., 1981-83; v.p. adminstrn., officer Campbell Soup Co., Camden, N.J., 1983-89; chmn. Triangle Mfg. Corp. subs. Campbell Soup Co., Raleigh, N.C., 1984-87; sr. v.p., officer Nutri/System, Inc., Willow Grove, Pa., 1989-91; pres., CEO Van Houten N.Am., Delavan, Wis., 1991-94, Andes Candies Inc., Delavan, 1991-94; chmn., pres., CEO Bus. Mail Express, Inc., Malvern, Penn., 1995-96; COO PETsMART, Inc., Phoenix, 1996-98; chmn., pres., CEO EEI Inc., Phoenix, 1998—. Bd. dirs. H&R Block, Kansas City, Mo., commencement spkr. Pa. State U., 1987. Bd. Overseers Harvard U., 1984-90; mem. Coun. Fgn. Rels., N.Y.C., 1987—; trustee Inst. for Advancement of Health, 1988-92. Named One of 80 Women to Watch in the 80's, Ms. mag., 1980, One of All Time Top 10 of Last Decade, Glamour mag., 1984, One of 50 Women to Watch, Bus. Week mag., 1987, One of 100 Women to Watch, Bus. Month mag., 1989; recipient Wellesley Alumnae Achievement award, 1987; Fred Sheldon Fund fellow, 1971-72. Mem. Harvard Bus. Sch. Assn. (pres. exec. council 1983-84), N.Y.C. Harvard Bus. Sch. Club (pres. 1979-80), Wellesley Coll. Nat. Alumnae Assn. (bd. dirs., 1st v.p.). Avocations: pub. speaking, art, gardening, skiing, reading.

EDDY, DAVID MAXON, health policy and management administrator; BA, Stanford (Calif.) U., 1964, PhD with great distinction, 1978; MD, U. Va., 1968. Intern in gen. surgery Stanford U. Med. Ctr., 1968-69, resident, postdoct. fellow cardiovascular surgery, 1969-71, acting asst. prof., 1976-78; assoc. prof. Dept. Engring.-Econ. Systems, Stanford U., 1978-80, prof., 1980-81; J. Alexander McMahon prof. health policy and mgmt. Duke U., 1986-90, prof. health policy and mgmt., 1990-95; dir. WHO Collaborating Ctr. for Rsch. in Cancer Policy, 1984-95. Sr. advisor health policy, mgmt. Kaiser Permanente So. Calif. Region, 1991—; columnist Jour. of the AMA, 1990—; spl. govt. employee Hillary Rodham Clinton's Health Care Task Force, 1993; expert adv. panel on cancer WHO, 1981-96; cons. numerous cos., orgns. and assns. Author: A Manual for Assessing Health Practices and Designing Practice Policies, 1992, FAST*PRO: Software for Meta-Analysis by the Confidence Profile Method, 1992, The Synthesis of Statistical Evidence: meta-Analysis by the Confidence Profile Method, 1992, Common Screening Tests, 1991, Screening for Cancer: Theory, Analysis and Design, 1980, (Lanchester Prize, 1981), Clinical Decision Making: From Theory to Practice, 1996; contbr. articles to profl. jours. Recipient Sci. and Technol. Achievement award EPA, 1993, FHP Prize Internat. Soc. of Tech. Assessment in Health Care, 1991, USQA Quality Algorithm award, 1995, Novartis Outcomes Leadership award, 1997, Founders award Am. Coll. Med. Quality, 1998. Mem. Inst. of Medicine, Nat. Acad. Scis.

EDELBROCK, O. VICTOR, automotive part manfacturing executive; m. Nancy E.; 1 child, Cathleen. Chmn., CEO Edelbrock Corp., Torrance, Calif., 1962—. Office: Edelbrock Corp 2700 California St Torrance CA 90503

EDELMAN, GERALD MAURICE, biochemist, neuroscientist, educator; b. N.Y.C., N.Y., July 1, 1929; s. Edward and Anna (Freedman) E.; m. Maxine Morrison, June 11, 1950; children: Eric, David, Judith. B.S., Ursinus Coll., 1950, Sc.D., 1974; M.D., U. Pa., 1954, D.Sc., 1973; Ph.D., Rockefeller U., 1960; M.D. (hon.), U. Siena, Italy, 1974; DSc (hon.), Gustavus Adolphus Coll., 1975, Williams Coll., 1976; DSc Honoris Causa, U. Paris, 1989; LSc Honoris Causa, U. Cagliari, 1989; DSc, Georgetown U., 1989; DSc Honoris Causa, U. degli Studi di Napoli, 1990, Tulane U., 1991, U. Miami, 1995, Adelphi U., 1995, U. Bologna, 1998, U. Minn., 2000. Med. house officer Mass. Gen. Hosp., 1954-55; asst. physician hosp. of Rockefeller U., 1957-60, mem. faculty, 1960-92, assoc. dean grad. studies, 1963-66, prof., 1966-74, Vincent Astor disting. prof., 1974-92; mem. faculty and chmn. dept. neurobiology Scripps Rsch. Inst., La Jolla, Calif., 1992—. Mem. biophysics and biophys. chemistry study sect. NIH, 1964-67; mem. Sci. Council, Ctr. for Theoretical Studies, 1970-72; assoc., sci. chmn. Neurosciences Research Program, 1980—, dir. Neuroscis. Inst., 1981—; mem. adv. bd. Basel Inst. Immunology, 1970-77, chmn., 1975-77; non-resident fellow, trustee Salk Inst., 1973-85; bd. overseers Faculty Arts and Scis., U. Pa., 1976-83; trustee, mem. adv. com. Carnegie Inst., Washington, 1980-87; bd. govs. Weizman Inst. Sci., 1971-87, mem. emeritus; researcher structure of antibodies, molecular and devel. biology. Author: Neural Darwinism, 1987, Topobiology, 1988, The Remembered Present, 1989, Bright Air, Brilliant Fire, 1992, A Universe of Consciousness: How Matter Becomes Imagination, 2000. Trustee Rockefeller Bros. Fund., 1972-82. Served to capt. M.C. AUS, 1955-57. Recipient Spencer Morris award U. Pa., 1954, Ann. Alumni award Ursinus Coll., 1969, Nobel prize for physiology or medicine, 1972, Albert Einstein Commemorative award Yeshiva U., 1974, Buchman Meml. award Calif. Inst. Tech., 1975, Rabbi Shai Shacknai meml. prize Hebrew U.-Hadassah Med. Sch., Jerusalem, 1977, Regents medal Excellence, N.Y. State, 1984, Hans Neurath prize, U. Washington, 1986, Sesquicentennial Commemorative award Nat. Libr. Medicine, 1986, Cécile and Oskar Vogt award U. Dusseldorf, 1988, Disting. Grad. award U. Pa., 1990, Personnalité de l'année, Paris, 1990, Warren Triennial Prize award Mass. Gen. Hosp., 1992m C.V. Ariens-Kappers medal, 1999, medal of the Presidency of the Italian Republic, 1999. Fellow AAAS, N.Y. Acad. Scis., N.Y. Acad. Medicine; mem. Am. Philos. Soc., Am. Soc. Biol. Chemists, Am. Assn. Immunologists, Genetics Soc. Am., Harvey Soc. (pres. 1975-76, Am. Chem. Soc., Eli Lilly award biol. chemistry 1965), Am. Acad. Arts and Scis., Nat. Acad. Sci., Am. Soc. Cell Biology, Acad. Scis. of Inst. France (fgn.), Japanese Biochem. Soc. (hon.), Pharm. Soc. Japan (hon.), Soc. Developmental Biology, Coun. Fgn. Rels., Century Assn., Cosmos Club, Phi Beta Kappa, Sigma Xi, Alpha Omega Alpha. Office: Scripps Rsch Inst Dept Neurobiol SBR-14 10550 N Torrey Pines Rd La Jolla CA 92037-1000

EDELSTEIN, MARK GERSON, college president; BA in English, Colby Coll., 1968; MA in English, U. N.H., 1971; PhD in English, SUNY, Stony Brook, 1982. English faculty Palomar C.C., 1976-85; exec. dir. intersegmental coordinating coun. Coll. of Redwoods, 1987-91, v.p. acad. affairs, 1991-96; pres. Diablo Valley Coll., 1996—. Pres. acad. senate Calif. C.C.; spkr. in field. Co-author: Inside Writing. Office: Diablo Valley Coll 321 Golf Club Rd Pleasant Hill CA 94523-1529

EDENS, GARY DENTON, broadcasting executive; b. Asheville, N.C., Jan. 6, 1942; s. James Edwin and Pauline Amanda (New) E.; m. Hannah Suellen Walter, Aug. 21, 1965; children: Ashley Elizabeth, Emily Blair. BS, U. N.C., 1964. Account exec. PAMS Prodns., Dallas, 1965-67, Sta. WKIX, Raleigh, N.C., 1967-69; gen. mgr. Sta. KOY, Phoenix, 1970-81; sr. v.p. Harte-Hanks Raido, Inc., Phoenix, 1978-81, pres., CEO, 1981-84; chmn., CEO Edens Broadcasting, Inc., 1984-95. Dir. Citibank Ariz., 1986—, Inter-Tel, Inc., 1994—; chmn. The Hanover Cos., Inc., 1995—; chair fin. seminar Chief Execs. Orgn./World Pres. Orgn., N.Y.C., 1998. Bd. dirs. Valley Big Bros., 1972-80, Ariz. State U. Found., 1979—, COMPAS, 1979—, Men's Arts Coun., 1975-78. Named one of Three Outstanding Young Men, Phoenix Jaycees, 1973; entrepreneurial fellow U. Ariz., 1989; inducted into Ariz. Broadcasters Assn. Hall of Fame, 2000. Mem. Phoenix Execs. Club (pres. 1976), Nat. Radio Broadcasters Assn. (dir. 1981-86), Radio Advt. Bur. (dir. 1981—), Young Pres. Orgn. (chmn. Ariz. chpt. 1989-90), Chief Execs. Orgn., Ariz. Pres. Orgn. Republican. Methodist. Office: 5112 N 40th St Ste 102 Phoenix AZ 85018-2142 E-mail: edens@hanover.com

EDGERTON, BRADFORD WHEATLY, plastic surgeon; b. Phila., May 8, 1947; s. Milton Thomas and Patricia Jane (Jones) E.; children: Bradford Wheatly Jr., Lauren Harrington; m. Louise Dungan Edgerton; stepchildren: Catherine Kelleher, Robert Kelleher. BA in Chemistry, Vanderbilt U., 1969, MD, 1973. Diplomate Am. Bd. Plastic Surgery, Am. Bd. Hand Surgery. Intern U. Calif., San Francisco, 1973-74; resident U. Va., Charlottesville, 1974-78; resident in plastic surgery Columbia-Presbyn., N.Y., 1979-81; fellow in hand surgery NYU, 1981-82, clin. instr. plastic surgery, 1981-89; ptnr. So. Calif. Permanente Med. Group, L.A., 1989—; assoc. prof. clin. plastic surgery U. So. Calif., L.A., 1989—. Chmn. bd. trustees W. Alton Jones Found., Charlottesville, Va., 1978—; trustee Harvard-Westlake Sch., L.A., 2001—. Mem. Am. Assn. Hand Surgery, Am. Soc. Plastic and Reconstructive Surgery, Am. Soc. Surgery of Hand, L.A. Tennis Club. Episcopal. Home: 494 S Spalding Dr Beverly Hills CA 90212-4104 Office: 6041 Cadillac Ave Los Angeles CA 90034-1702

EDGINGTON, THOMAS S. pathologist, educator, molecular biologist, vascular biologist; b. L.A., Feb. 10, 1932; BA in Biol. Scis., Stanford U., 1953, MD, 1957. Diplomate Am. Bd. Pathology, spl. cert. immunopathology. Intern Hosp. Univ. Pa., Phila., 1957-58; resident Ctr. Health Scis. UCLA, 1958-60; sr. postdoctoral fellow immunology Scripps Clinic & Rsch. Found., La Jolla, Calif., 1965-68, assoc. mem. dept. exptl. pathology, 1968-71; founder, head dept. anatomic pathology and lab. medicine Scripps Clinic and Rsch. Found., La Jolla, 1968-74, prof. depts. immunology and vascular biology, 1971—; asst. prof., surg. pathologist dept. pathology UCLA Sch. Medicine, 1962-65; assoc. adj. prof. pathology U. Calif., San Diego, La Jolla, 1968-75, adj. prof., 1975—. Cons. Centocor, 1993-95, Eli Lilly, 1982-85, Becton-Dickinson, 1977-80; founder, bd. dirs. Corvas Internat., NuVas. Contbr. numerous articles to profl. jours. Recipient Coll. de France medal, 1981, John A. Lynch Molecular Biology award U. Notre Dame, 1992, Rous-Whipple prize Am. Soc. Investigative Pathology, 1995, Disting. Career award Internat. Soc. Thrombosis and Hemostatis, 1995. Fellow AAAS; mem. Fedn. Am. Socs. Exptl. Biology (pres., chmn. bd. 1990-91), Internat. Soc. Thrombosis and Haemostatis, Thrombosis Inst. (bd. sci. govs. 1995—), Inst. of Medicine of NAS. Office: The Scripps Rsch Inst C-204 10550 N Torrey Pines Rd # C204 La Jolla CA 92037-1000 E-mail: tsedgington@hotmail.com

EDGINTON, JOHN ARTHUR, lawyer; b. Kingsburg, Calif., July 23, 1935; s. Arthur George and Pochantas Clementina (Ball) E.; m. Jane Ann Simmons, June 25, 1960. AA, U. Calif., Berkeley, 1955, AB in Econs., 1957, JD, 1963. Bar: Calif. 1964, No. Marianas 1969, U.S. Ct. Claims 1969, U.S. Ct. Appeals (9th cir.) 1969, U.S. Supreme Ct. 1969. Assoc. Graham & James, San Francisco, 1964-71, ptnr., 1971-94, Dezurick Edginton & Harrington LLP, Emeryville, Calif., 1994-98, Booth Banning LLP, San Francisco, 1999-2000; pvt. practice Point Richmond, Calif., 2000—. Author: Maritime Bankruptcy, 1989; editor-in-chief Maritime Practice and Procedure, vol. 29 Moore's Federal Practice, 1997, Maritime Desk Reference, 2001; contbr. numerous articles to profl. jours. With USN, 1957-60. Disting. U. Calif. alumni Order of Golden Bear. Mem. Maritime Law Assn. (chmn. practice and procedure com. 1991-95, bd. dirs. 1993-96), Swedish-Am. C. of C. (pres. Western Nat. 1988-90, 98-2000, nat. vice chmn. 1988-90, CFO, 1999—, bd. dirs. 1971—), Sierra Club (nat. outing com. 1964—, chmn. ins. com. 1991—, internat. trips 1992-95). Democrat. Methodist. Avocations: mountaineering, hiking, photography, model railroads. Office: Law Office of John A Edginton 124 Washington Ave Ste A-1 Point Richmond CA 94801-3979 Fax: (510) 235-4427. E-mail: jedginton@edg-law.com

EDIGER, ROBERT IKE, botanist, educator; b. Hutchinson, Kans., Apr. 2, 1937; s. Peter F. and Martha (Friesen) E.; m. Patricia L. Dickerson, Feb. 7, 1981; children: Madeline, Maureen, Alan, Shelly. B.A., Bethel Coll., 1959; M.S., Emporia State U., 1964; Ph.D., Kans. State U., 1967. Tchr. public schs., Ford, Kans., 1959-62, Hays, 1962-63; teaching and research asst. Kans. State U., 1964-67; asst. prof. dept. biol. scis. Calif. State U., Chico, 1967-71, asso. prof., 1971-74, prof., 1975-99, chmn. dept. biol. scis., 1974-77, dir.Eagle Lake field sta., 1967-73; ret., 1999. Mem. Am. Soc. Plant Taxonomists, Orgn. Biol. Field Stas. (pres. 1975), Calif. Bot. Soc., Calif. Native Plant Soc. Methodist. Home: 5359 Royal Oaks Dr Oroville CA 95966-3837 Office: Calif State U Dept Biol Scis Chico CA 95929-0001 E-mail: bpediger@aol.com

EDMONDS, CHARLES HENRY, publisher; b. Lakewood, Ohio, Sept. 4, 1919; s. Howard H. and Mary Frances (Galena) E.; student Woodbury Bus. Coll., 1939-40; m. Ruth Audrey Windfelder, Nov. 4, 1938; children: Joan Dickey, Charles Henry, Carolyn Anne, Dianne Marie. Owner, Shoreline Transp. Co., L.A., 1946-58; mgr. transp. Purity Food Stores, Burlingame, Calif., 1958-61; supr. Calif. Motor Express, San Jose, 1961-64; account exec. Don Wright Assos., Oakland, Calif., 1964-65; sales mgr. Western U.S., Shippers Guide Co., Chgo., 1965-70; pub. No. Calif. Retailer, San Jose, 1970-83; v.p. Kasmar Publs., 1983-88; pub. Retail Observer, 1990—. Recipient journalism awards various orgns. Republican. Roman Catholic. Contbr. articles to profl. jours. E-mail: retailobs@aol.com Home: 1442 Sierra Creek Way San Jose CA 95132-3618

EDMONDS, IVY GORDON, writer; b. Frost, Tex., Feb. 15, 1917; s. Ivy Gordon and Delia Louella (Shumate) E.; m. Reiko Mimura, July 12, 1956; 1 dau., Annette. Student pub. schs. Pub. rels. mgr. Northrop Corp., Anaheim, Calif., 1968-79, indsl. editor, Hawthorne, Calif., 1979-86. Freelance writer; author books including: Solomon In Kimono, 1957, Ooka the Wise, 1961, The Bounty's Boy, 1963, Hollywood RIP, 1963, Joel of the Hanging Gardens, 1966, Trickster Tales, 1966, Taiwan-the Other China, 1971, The Possible Impossibles of Ikkyo The Wise, 1971, The Magic Man, 1972, Mao's Long March, 1973, Motorcycling for Beginners, 1973, China's Red Rebel: Mao Tse-Tung, 1973, Micronesia, 1974, Pakistan, Land of Myster, Tragedy and Courage, 1974, Automotive Tuneups for Beginners, 1974, Ethiopia, 1975, The Magic Makers, 1976, The Shah of Iran, 1976, Allah's Oil: Mid-East Petroleum, 1976, Second Sight, 1977, Motorcycle Racing for Beginners, 1977, Islam, 1977, The Mysteries of Troy, 1977, Big U Universal in the Silent Days, Buddhism, 1978, D.D. Home, 1978, Bicycle Motocross, 1979, Hinduism, 1979, Girls Who Talked to Ghosts, 1979, The Magic Brothers, 1979, (with William H. Gebhardt) Broadcasting for Beginners, 1980, (with Reiko Mimura) The Oscar Directors, 1980, The Mysteries of Homer's Greeks, 1981, The Kings of Black Magic, 1981, Funny Car Racing for Beginners, 1982, The Magic Dog, 1982; author textbooks: (with Ronald Gonzales) Understanding Your Car, 1975, Introduction to Welding, 1975; also author pulp and soft cover fiction and nonfiction under names of Gene Cross and Gary Gordon and publishers house names. With USAAF, 1940-45, USAF, 1946-63. Decorated D.F.C., Air medals, Bronze Star. Home: 5801 Shirl St Cypress CA 90630-3326

EDMUNSON, JAMES L. political organization administrator; Chmn. Oreg. Dem. Party, Portland. Office: Oreg Dem Party 4545 SW Barbur Blvd Ste 105 Portland OR 97201-4005 Fax: 503-224-5335

EDSELL, PATRICK L. computer company executive; Pres. Spectra-Physics, Mountain View, Calif. Office: Spectra-Physics PO Box 7013 1335 Terra Bella Ave Mountain View CA 94039-7013

EDSON, WILLIAM ALDEN, electrical engineer, researcher; b. Burchard, Nebr., Oct. 30, 1912; s. William Henry and Pearl (Montgomery) E.; m. Saralou Peterson, Aug. 23, 1942; children: Judith Lynne, Margaret Jane, Carolyn Louise. B.S. (Summerfield scholar), U. Kans., 1934, M.S., 1935; D.Sc. (Gordon McKay scholar), Harvard U., 1937. Mem. tech. staff Bell Telephone Labs., Inc., N.Y.C., 1937-41, supr., 1943-45; asst. prof. elec. engring. Ill. Inst. Tech., Chgo., 1941-43; prof. physics Ga. Inst. Tech., Atlanta, 1945-46, prof. elec. engring., 1946-51, dir. sch. elec. engring., 1951-52; vis. prof., research asso. Stanford U., 1952-56, cons. prof., 1956; mgr. Klystron sub-sect. Gen. Electric Microwave Lab., Palo Alto, Calif., 1955-61; v.p., dir. research Electromagnetic Tech. Corp., Palo Alto, 1961-62, pres., 1962-70; sr. scientist Vidar Corp., Mountain View, Calif., 1970— 71; asst. dir. Radio Physics Lab., SRI Internat., Menlo Park, 1971-77; sr. prin. engr. Geosci. and Engring. Ctr., SRI Internat., 1977-2001; ret., 2001. Cons. high frequency sect. Nat. Bur. Standards, 1951-64; dir. Western Electronic Show and Conv., 1975-79 Author: (with Robert I. Sarbacher) Hyper and Ultra-High Frequency Engineering, 1943, Vacuum-Tube Oscillators, 1953. Life fellow IEEE (chmn. San Francisco sect. 1963-64, com. standards piezoelectricity 1950-67); mem. Am. Phys. Soc., Sigma Xi, Tau Beta Pi, Sigma Tau, Phi Kappa Phi, Eta Kappa Nu, Pi Mu Epsilon. Home: 23350 Sereno Ct Unit 29 Cupertino CA 95014-6543

EDSTROM, PAM, public relations executive; b. 1954; Pvt. practice, 1968-74; with Fred Meyer Savings and Loan, Portland, Oreg., 1974-77, Tektronix, Inc., Beaverton, 1977-81, Micro Soft, Redmond, Wash., 1981-83; sr. v.p. Waggener Edstrom, Inc., Portland, 1983-2000, exec. v.p., 2000—. Office: Waggener Edstrom Inc 3 Center Pointe Dr Ste 300 Lake Oswego OR 97035

EDWARDS, BRUCE GEORGE, retired ophthalmologist, naval officer; b. Idaho Springs, Colo., Apr. 6, 1942; s. Bruce Norwood and Evelyn Alice (Kohut) Edwards. BA, U. Colo., 1964; MD, U. Colo., Denver, 1968. Diplomate Am. Acad. Ophthalmology. Commd. ensign USN, 1964; advanced through grades to capt. U.S. Naval Hosp., 1980, intern, 1968-69; USN med. officer USS Long Beach (CGN-9), 1969-70; gen. med. officer U.S. Naval Hosp., Taipei, Taiwan, 1970-72, U.S. Naval Dispensary Treasure Island, San Francisco, 1972-73; resident in ophthalmology U.S. Naval Hosp., Oakland, Calif., 1973-76, U. Calif., San Francisco, 1973-76; mem. ophthalmology staff Naval Hosp., Camp Pendleton, Calif., 1976-83, ophthalmologist, chief of med. staff Naples, Italy, 1983-85; ophthalmology head Camp Pendleton Naval Hosp., 1985-97, dir. surg. svcs., 1990-92, dir. physician advisor quality assurance, 1985-86, ret., 1997. Vol. Internat. Eye Found., Harar, Ethiopia, 1975. Fellow Am. Acad. Ophthalmology (diplomate); mem. AMA, Calif. Med. Assn., Calif. Assn. Ophthalmologists, Am. Soc. Contemporary Ophthalmologists, Assn. U.S. Mil. Surgeons, Pan Am. Assn. Ophthalmology, Order of DeMolay (Colo. DeMolay of Yr. 1961, Idaho Springs Chevalier, Colo. State sec. 1961-62). Republican. Methodist. Avocations: piano, camping, hiking, biking, travel.

EDWARDS, CHARLES CORNELL, surgeon, research administrator; b. Overton, Nebr., Sept. 16, 1923; s. Charles Busby and Lillian Margaret (Arendt) E.; m. Sue Cowles Kruidenier, June 24, 1945; children: Timothy, Charles Cornell, Nancy, David. Student, Princeton U., 1941-43; B.A., U. Colo., 1945, M.D., 1948; M.S., U. Minn., 1956; L.L.D. (hon.), Phila. Coll. Pharmacy and Sci.; L.H.D. (hon.), Pa. Coll. Podiatry, U. Colo., LHD (hon.), 1993. Diplomate: Am. Bd. Surgery. Intern St. Mary's Hosp., Mpls., 1948-49; resident surgery Mayo Found., 1950-56; pvt. practice medicine specializing in surgery Des Moines, 1956-61; mem. surg. staff Georgetown U., Washington, 1961-62; also cons. USPHS; dir. div. socio-econ. activities A.M.A., Chgo., 1963-67; v.p., mng. officer health and sci. affairs Booz, Allen & Hamilton, 1967-69; commr. FDA, Washington, 1969-73; asst. sec. for health HEW, Washington, 1973-75; sr. v.p., dir. Becton, Dickinson & Co., 1975-77; pres. Scripps Clinic and Research Found., La Jolla, Calif., 1977-91; pres., CEO Scripps Insts. Medicine and Sci., La Jolla, 1991-93. Bd. dirs. Bergen Brunswig Corp., Molecular Biosys., Inc., No. Trust Bank, IDEC Pharms., Materia, Inc., Scripps Health Systems; bd. trustees Scripps Insts. Medicine & Sci.; trustee Scripps Rsch. Inst.; bd. regents Nat. Libr. Medicine, 1981-85; mem. Nat. Leadership Commn. on Health Care, 1986—; bd. govs. Hosp. Corp. Am., 1986-89; chmn. bd. dirs. San Diego Hospice. Trustee San Diego Hospice, San Diego YMCA. Lt. M.C. USNR, 1942-46. Recipient Disting. Svc. award U.S. Dept. Health, Edn., Welfare, Disting. Alumnus award Mayo Found., 1986, Humanity award Nat. Conf., 1994. Mem. Inst. Medicine, Am. Hosp. Assn. (hon.), Nat. Acad. Scis., Princeton Club, La Jolla Country Club, La Jolla Beach and Tennis Club. Office: Scripps Rsch Inst 10666 N Torrey Pines Rd La Jolla CA 92037-1027

EDWARDS, GEORGE KENT, lawyer; b. Ogden, Utah, Oct. 3, 1939; s. George and S. Ruth Edwards; m. Linda E. Brown; children: Scott M., Stacey R., Mark D. B.A., Occidental Coll., 1961; J.D., U. Calif.-Berkeley, 1964. Bar: Calif. 1965, Alaska 1966. Legislative counsel Alaska Legislature, 1964-66; ptnr. law firm Stevens, Savage, Holland, Erwin & Edwards, Anchorage, 1966-67; dep. atty. gen. Alaska, 1967-68; atty. gen., 1968-70; U.S. atty. Dist. Alaska, 1971-77; pvt. practice, 1977-81; shareholder Hartig Rhodes Norman Mahoney & Edwards, Anchorage, 1981—. Mem. Nat. Conf. Commrs. Uniform State Laws, 1968-70; chmn. Gov. Alaska Planning Coun. Adminstrn. Criminal Justice, 1968-70; guest lectr. bus. law U. Alaska, 1981-82; guest editorial columnist Anchorage Times, 1982-88. Co-author: Considerations in Buying or Selling a Business in Alaska, 1992. Pres. Greater Anchorage Area Young Reps., 1967; chmn. Carrs Great Alaska Shootout, 1995; pres. bd. dirs. Miss Alask Scholarship Pageant, 1980-84; bd. dirs. Anchorage Crime Stoppers, 1981-85; pres. Common Sense Alaska, 1982-85, 91—; bd. dirs., 1986—. Mem. ABA, Calif. Bar Assn., Alaska Bar Assn., Nat. Assn. Attys. Gen., Nat. Assn. Former U.S. Attys. (bd. dirs., pres.), Anchorage C. of C. (bd. dirs. 1989-96), Rotary (scholarship chair 1993, 95-98), Phi Delta Phi, Sigma Alpha Epsilon (Outstanding Sr. award Calif. Epsilon chpt. 1961). Home: 2113 Duke Dr Anchorage AK 99508-4553 Office: 717 K St Anchorage AK 99501-3330

EDWARDS, GLEN R. metallurgist; b. Monte Vista, Colo., July 21, 1939; married, 1959; 2 children. BS, Colo. Sch. Mines, 1961; MS, U. N.Mex., 1967; PhD in Math. Sci., Stanford U., 1971. Staff plutonium metall. Los Alamos (N.Mex.) Sci. Lab., 1963-67; asst. instr. math./sci. Stanford (Calif.) U., 1967-71; from asst. to assoc. prof. Naval Postgrad. Sch., 1971-76; assoc. prof. metall. engring. Colo. Sch. Mines, Golden, 1976-79, prof. metall. engring., 1979—, dir. ctr. welding and joining rsch., 1987—. Fellow Am. Soc. Metals Internat.; mem. Am. Inst. Mining & Metall. Engrs., Am. Welding Soc., Internat. Inst. Welding, Sigma Xi. Office: Colo Sch Mines Ctr Welding Joining Rs Golden CO 80401

EDWARDS, GLENN THOMAS, history educator; b. Portland, Oreg., June 14, 1931; s. Glenn Thomas E. and Marie Ann (Cheska) McMullen; m. Nannette Wilhelmina McAndie, June 15, 1957; children: Randall Thomas, Stephanie Lynn. B.A., Willamette U., 1953; M.A., U. Oreg., 1960, Ph.D., 1963. Asst. prof. San Jose State U., 1962-64, Whitman Coll., Walla Walla, Wash., 1964-68, assoc. prof., 1968-75, prof., 1976-98, ret., 1998. Cons. TV documentary Yakima Valley Mus. on William O. Douglas, Yakima, Wash., 1981-82; trustee Wash. Commn. of Humanities, Olympia, 1980-86. Author: Sowing Good Seeds: The Northwest Suffrage Campaigns of Susan B. Anthony, 1990, The Triumph of Tradition: The Emergence of Whitman College, 1859-1924, 1992; co-editor: Experiences in a Promised Land: Essays on Pacific Northwest History, 1986; contbr. articles to profl. jours. Mem. pub. edn. adv. com. State Supt. of Pub. Instrn., Olympia, 1975-78; mem. bd. trustees Wash. State Hist. Soc., 1983-92, Wash. Commn. for Humanities. Served with U.S. Army, 1954-56. Grantee Am Philos. Soc., 1971 Mem. Orgn. Am. Historians, Western History Assn., Oreg. Hist. Soc., Washington Hist. Soc. (photography cons. 1980). Congregationalist. Office: Whitman Coll Dept History Walla Walla WA 99362 E-mail: tomed@spiretech.edu

EDWARDS, KENNETH NEIL, chemical engineering executive; b. Hollywood, Calif., June 8, 1932; s. Arthur Carl and Ann Vera (Gomez) E.; children: Neil James, Peter Graham, John Evan. BA in Chemistry, Occidental Coll., 1954; MS in Chem. and Metall. Engring., U. Mich., 1955. Prin. chemist Battelle Meml. Inst., Columbus, Ohio, 1955-58; dir. new products rsch. and devel. Dunn-Edwards Corp., L.A., 1958-72; sr. lectr. organic coatings and pigments dept. chem. engring. U. So. Calif., L.A., 1976-80; CEO Dunn-Edwards Corp. Bd. dirs. Dunn-Edwards Corp., L.A.; cons. Coatings & Plastics Tech., L.A., 1972—. Contbr. articles to sci. jours. Recipient Judo Masters belt (6th dan), Korean Judo Assn., 2000. Mem. Am. Chem. Soc. (chmn. divisional activities 1988-89, exec. com. divsn. polymeric materials sci. and engring. 1963—, chair divsn. 1970, mem. devel. adv. com. 1996-99, Disting. Svc. award 1996, chair Disting. Svc. award selection 1997—, chair So. Calif. local sect. 1999), Alpha Chi Sigma (chmn. L.A. profl. chpt. 1962, counselor Pacific dist. 1967-70, grand profl. alchemist nat. v.p. 1970-76, grand master alchemist nat. pres. 1976-78, nat. adv. com. 1978—). Achievements include patents for air-dried polyester coatings and application, for process and apparatus for dispensing liquid colorants into a paint can, fluidic fillers, and for mechanical mixers. Home: Bottle Bay Rd Sagle ID 83860 also: 2926 Graceland Way Glendale CA 91206-1331 Office: Dunn Edwards Corp 136 W Walnut Ave Monrovia CA 91016-3444 E-mail: KNEatDE@aol.com

EDWARDS, KIRK LEWIS, medical services company executive; b. Berkeley, Calif., July 30, 1950; s. Austin Lewis and Betty (Drury) E.; m. Randi Edwards, Feb. 14, 1998; children: Elliott Tyler, Jonathan Bentley. BA in Rhetoric and Pub. Address, U. Wash., Seattle, 1972; postgrad., Shoreline Coll., 1976. Cert. bus. broker. From salesperson to mgr. Rede Realty, Lynnwood, Wash., 1973-77; br. mgr. Century 21/North Homes Realty, Lynnwood, 1977-79, Snohomish, 1979-81; pres., owner Century 21/Champion Realty, Everett, 1981-82, Champion Computers, Walker/Edwards Investments, Everett, 1981-82; br. mgr. Advance Properties, Everett, 1982-87; exec. v.p. Bruch & Vedrich Better Homes & Garden, Everett, 1987-88, dir. career devel., 1988-90; pres., CEO Century 21/Champion Realty, Everett, 1991-95, KR Bus. Brokers, Kirkland, Wash., 1995-2001; pres. Exec. Med. Svcs., Bellevue, 2001—. Named Top Business Broker In Washington Investment Brokers Assn., 1994-96. Mem. Snohomish County Camano Bd. Realtors (chmn. 1987-88), Snohomish County C. of C., Hidden Harbor Yacht Club, Mill Creek Country Club. Republican. Avocations: travel, water skiing, scuba diving. Office: KR Business Brokers 2285 116th Ave NE # 100 Bellevue WA 98004 E-mail: mrbzns@hotmail.com

EDWARDS, LINDA L. former elementary education educator; Tchr. Highland Park Elem. Sch., Lewistown, Mont.; ret., 1999. Named Mont. State Elem. Tchr. of Yr., 1993. Office: Highland Park Elem Sch 1312 7th Ave N Lewistown MT 59457-2112

EDWARDS, LYDIA JUSTICE, state official; b. Carter County, Ky., July 9, 1937; d. Chead and Velva (Kinney) Justice; m. Frank B. Edwards, 1968; children: Mark, Alexandra, Margot. Student, San Francisco State U. Began career as acct.; then Idaho state rep., 1982-86; treas. State of Idaho, 1987-99. Legis. asst. to Gov. Hickel, Alaska, 1967; conf. planner Rep. Gov.'s Assn., 1970-73; mem. Rep. Nat. Commn., 1972, del. to nat. conv., 1980, 96. Mem. Rep. Womens Fedn. Congregationalist.

EDWARDS, N. MURRAY, professional sports team owner; B Commerce, U. Saskatchewan; LLB, U. Toronto. bd. dirs. Can. Natural Resources, Ltd., Foremost Industries, Inc., Rio Alto Exploration, Ltd., Penn West Petroleum Ltd, Ensign Resource Svc. Group, Inc., Magellan Aerospace Corp., Imperial Metals Corp. Pres., CEO Edco Fin. Holdings, Ltd.; co-owner, chmn. Calgary Flames. Office: Calgary Flames PO Box 1540 Station M Calgary AB Canada T2P 3B9

EDWARDS, PATRICIA BURR, small business owner, counselor, consultant; b. Oakland, Calif., Feb. 19, 1918; d. Myron Carlos and Claire Idelle (Laingor) Burr; m. Jackson Edwards, Nov. 14, 1942; children: Jill Forman-Young, Jan Kurzweil. AB, U. So. Calif., 1939, MSEd, 1981. Prin. Constructive Leisure, L.A., 1968—. Spkr. in field; writer, prodr. counseling materials for career, leisure, life planning including computer software, audio cassettes and assessment surveys. Author: You've Got to Find Happiness: It Won't Find You, 1971, Leisure Counseling Techniques: Individual and Group Counseling Step-by-Step, 1975, 3d edit., 1980; (software) Leisure PREF, 1986, Over 50: Needs, Values, Attitudes, 1988, Adapting to Change: The NVAB Program, 1997; contbr. articles to profl. jours., mags. and books. Chmn. L.A. County Foster Families 50th Anniversary, 1962-64, L.A. Jr. League Sustainers, 1964-65, Hollywood Bowl Vols., L.A., 1960-61, Hollywood Bowl Patroness com., 1961—.

Mem. Am. Counseling Assn., Calif. Assn. for Counseling and Devel., Nat. Recreation and Park Assn., Assn. for Adult Devel. and Aging, Trojan League, Travellers Aid Soc. L.A., Jr. League L.A., First Century Families of L.A., Delta Gamma. Republican. Episcopalian. Avocations: family activities, singing, dancing, pets, learning.

EDWARDS, RALPH M. librarian; b. Shelley, Idaho, Apr. 17, 1933; s. Edward William and Maude Estella (Munsee) E.; m. Winifred Wylie, Dec. 25, 1969; children: Dylan, Nathan, Stephen. B.A., U. Wash., 1957, M.Library, 1960; D.L.S., U. Calif.-Berkeley, 1971. Libr. N.Y. Pub. Libr., N.Y.C., 1960-61; catalog libr. U. Ill. Libr., Urbana, 1961-62; br. libr. Multnomah County Libr., Portland, Oreg., 1964-67; asst. prof. Western Mich. U., Kalamazoo, 1970-74; chief of the Central Libr. Dallas Pub. Libr., 1975-81; city librarian Phoenix Pub. Libr., 1981-95, ret., 1996—. Author: Role of the Beginning Librarian in University Libraries, 1975. U. Calif. doctoral fellow, 1967-70; library mgmt. internship Council on Library Resources, 1974-75 Mem. ALA, Pub. Library Assn. Democrat. Home: 2884 Spring Blvd Eugene OR 97403-1662 E-mail: wedwards@efn.org

EDWARDS, RICHARD ALAN, retired lawyer; b. Portland, Oreg., June 28, 1938; s. Howard A. and Kay E. (Sheldon) E.; m. Renee Rosier, June 18, 1960; children: Teri Edwards Obye, Lisa Edwards Smith, Steve. BS, Oreg. State U., 1960; JD summa cum laude, Willamette U., 1968. Bar: Oreg. 1968, U.S. Dist. Ct. Oreg. 1968, U.S. Ct. Appeals (9th cir.) 1969. Various positions 1st Interstate Bank of Oreg., Portland, 1960-65; assoc. Miller, Nash, Wiener, Hager & Carlsen, Portland, 1968-74, ptnr., 1974—, mng. ptnr., 1991-96. Editor Willamette Law Jour., 1967-68. Mem. ABA (litigation sect. 1972), Oreg. State Bar (chairperson debtor-creditor sect. 1981-82, mem. various coms.). Republican. Presbyterian. Avocation: breeding and racing thoroughbred race horses.

EDWARDS, ROBIN MORSE, lawyer; b. Glens Falls, N.Y., Dec. 9, 1947; d. Daniel and Harriet Morse; m. Richard Charles Edwards, Aug. 30, 1970; children: Michael Alan, Jonathan Philip. BA, Mt. Holyoke Coll., 1969; JD, U. Calif., Berkeley, 1972. Bar: Calif. 1972. Assoc. Donahue, Gallagher, Thomas & Woods, Oakland, Calif., 1972-77, ptnr., 1977-89, Sonnenschein, Nath & Rosenthal, San Francisco, 1989—. Bd. dirs. Temple Sinai, 1997—. Mem. ABA, Calif. Bar Assn., Alameda County Bar Assn. (bd. dirs. 1978-84, v.p. 1982, pres. 1983), Alameda County Bar Found. (bd. dirs. 1998-2000). Jewish. Avocations: skiing, cooking. Office: Sonnenschein Nath Rosenthal 685 Market St 6th Flr San Francisco CA 94105-4202 E-mail: rme@sonnenschein.com

EDWARDS, SAMUEL ROGER, internist; b. Santa Barbara, Calif., Aug. 11, 1937; s. Harold S. and Margaret (Spaulding) E.; m. Marcia Elizabeth Dutton, June 17, 1961; children: Harold S. II, Charles Dutton. BA, Harvard U., 1960; MD, U. So. Calif., 1964. Intern Presbyn. Hosp., Phila., 1964-65; resident in internal medicine U Calif., San Francisco, 1968-70; fellow in cardiology Pacific Presbyn. Med. Ctr., San Francisco, 1970; pvt. practice specializing in internal medicine Santa Paula, Calif., 1971-94; med. dir. Santa Paula Convalescent, Twin Pines Convalescent Hosps., 1974-95; pres. med. staff Ventura (Calif.) County Med. Ctr., 1979-80, med. dir., 1983-95, hosp. adminstr., 1995—. Mem. clin. faculty UCLA Sch. Medicine, 1980-95; bd. dirs. Citizens State Bank of Santa Paula, 1975-97, chmn., 1994-97; bd. dirs. Limoneira Co., 1985—, Santa Barbara Bank and Trust, 1999—; chief dept. medicine Ventura County Gen. Hosp., 1975; chief med. staff Santa Paula Meml. Hosp., 1977. Lt. Comdr. USNR, 1966-68. Recipient Disting. Svc. award Ventura County Heart Assn., 1974. Fellow ACP; mem. AMA, Am. Coll. Hosp. Execs. Episcopalian. Home: 19789 E Telegraph Rd Santa Paula CA 93060-9693 Office: 243 March St Santa Paula CA 93060-2511

EDWARDS, SUSAN M. hotel executive; b. Bristol, Eng., Jan. 2, 1953; Student in English lit., 1970. Office mgr. Godfrey Davis Internat., San Francisco, 1970's; dir. sales Karageorgis Cruises, San Francisco, 1980's; regional sales dir., then nat. sales dir. Aston Hotels and Resorts, Hawaii, 1981-91, assoc. v.p., 1981-91; pres. Delfin Hotels & Resorts, Santa Cruz, Calif., 1991—. Avocation: dogs. Office: 2840 College Ave Ste A Berkeley CA 94705-2148

EFRON, BRADLEY, mathematics educator; b. St. Paul, May 24, 1938; s. Miles Jack and Esther (Kaufman) E.; m. Gael Guerin, July 1969 (div.); 1 child, Miles James; m. Nancy Troup, June 1986 (div.). BS in Math., Calif. Inst. Tech., 1960; PhD, Stanford U., 1964; DSc (hon.), U. Chgo., 1995; D (hon.), U. Carlos III de Madrid, 1998. Asst. and assoc. prof. stats. Stanford (Calif.) U., 1965-72, chmn. dept. stats., 1976-79, 1991-1994, chmn. math. scis., 1981—, prof. stats., 1974—, assoc. dean humanities and scis., 1987-90, endowed chair Max H. Stein prof. humanities and scis., 1991-94. Statis. cons. Alza Corp., 1971—, Rand Corp., 1962—. Author: Bootstrap Methods, 1979, Biostatistics Casebook, 1980. MacArthur Found. fellow, 1983; named Outstanding Statistician of Yr. Chgo. Statis. Assn., 1981; Wald and Rietz Lectr. Inst. Math. Stats., 1977, 81; recipient Fisher award, Chgo., 1996; recipient Parzen prize for statis. innovation, 1998. Fellow Inst. Math. Stats. (pres. 1987), Am. Statis. Assn. (Wilks medal 1990); mem. NAS, Am. Acad. Arts and Scis., Internat. Statis. Assn. Office: Stanford U Dept Stats Sequoia Hall Stanford CA 94305

EFRON, ROBERT, retired neurology educator, research institute administrator; b. N.Y.C., Dec. 22, 1927; s. Alexander and Rose (Kunitz) E.; m. Mary Louise Snyder, June 6, 1948 (div. 1966), children: Carol, Paul, Sonni; m. Barbara Klein, Dec. 30, 1967. BA, Columbia U., 1948; MD cum laude, Harvard U., 1952. Med. house officer Peter Bent Brigham Hosp., Boston, 1952-53; Moseley traveling fellow Harvard U., Boston, 1953-54; rsch. assoc. Nat. Hosp. Queen Sq., London, 1956-60; asst. prof. Boston U. Sch. Medicine, 1960-70; assoc. chief staff R & D VA Med. Ctr., Martinez, Calif., 1970—; prof. neurology U. Calif. Sch. Medicine, Davis, 1974—; pres. East Bay Inst. for Rsch. and Edn., Martinez, 1989—. MacEachran lectr. U. Alta., Can., 1989. Author: Decline and Fall of Hemisphere Assymmetry, 1990; contbr. articles to profl. jours. Lt. USNR, 1954-56. Fellow Acoustical Soc. Am.; mem. Phi Beta Kappa, Alpha Omega Alpha. Office: 2644 Carisbrook Dr Oakland CA 94611-1610

EGBERT, PETER ROY, ophthalmologist, educator; b. Indpls., Dec. 6, 1941; BA magna cum laude, DePauw U., Greencastle, Ind., 1963; MD, Yale U., 1967. Diplomate Nat. Bd. Med. Examiners, Am. Bd. Ophthalmology. Intern Cleve. Met. Gen. Hosp., 1967-68; resident in ophthalmology Yale U., New Haven, 1968-69, 71-73; acting asst. prof. surgery (ophthalmology Stanford (Calif.) U., 1973-74, dir. Ophthalmic Pathology Lab., 1973—, asst. prof. surgery, 1974-81; acting head divsn. ophthalmology Stanford U. Med. Ctr., 1980-82, assoc. prof. surgery, 1981-88, prof. ophthalmology, 1988—, chmn. dept. ophthalmology, 1992-97. Vis. prof. ophthalmology Govt. Hosp., San Pedro Sula, Honduras, 1974, Noor Eye Hosp., Kabul, Afghanistan, 1975, U. West Indies Med. Sch., Kingston, Jamaica, 1976, Princess Marina Hosp. - The Ctrl. Govt. Hosp., Gadorone, Botswana, 1978, Grenfell Regional Health Svcs., St. Anthony, Nfld., 1981, Govt. Hosp., Western Samoa, 1982, Project Orbis, Ismir, Turkey, 1985, Bamako, Mali, 1983, San Jose, Costa Rica, 1986, Port-au-Prince, Haiti, 1987, King Khaled Eye Hosp., Rihayd, Saudi Arabia, 1985, Korle-bu Teaching Hosp., U. Ghana, Accra, 1987, Leicester Royal Infirmary, Eng., 1987, Esperanca Hosp., Santarem, Brazil, 1987, Chinese Med. Sch., Hong Kong, Inst. Ophthalmology, Canton, Peking Med. Coll., Beijing, 1988, Nepal-Trilovan Teaching Hosp., 1990. Recipient Bordon prize DePauw U., 1960. Mem. Am. Acad. Ophthalmology, Am. Assn. Ophthalmic Pathologists, Am. Intra-Ocular Implant Soc., Assn. for Rsch. in Vision and Ophthalmology, Michael Hogan Eye Pathology Soc., No. Calif. Soc. to Prevent Blindness, Peninsula Eye Soc., Verhoeff Ophthalmic Pathology Soc., Alpha Omega Alpha, Phi Beta Kappa. Office: Stanford U Sch Medicine 300 Pasteur Dr Stanford CA 94305-5308

EGER, DENISE LEESE, rabbi; b. New Kensington, Pa., Mar. 14, 1960; d. Bernard D. and Estelle (Leese) E. BA in Religion, U. So. Calif., 1982; MA in Hebrew Letters, Hebrew Union Coll., L.A., 1985; Rabbi, Hebrew Union Coll., N.Y.C., 1988. Ordained rabbi, 1988. Chaplain Rabbi Beth Chayim Chadashim, L.A., 1988-92; founding rabbi Congregation Kol Ami, West Hollywood, Calif., 1992—. Columnist Edge mag., Lesbian News; contbr. articles to religious publs., chpts. to anthologies. Mem. cmty. adv. bd. Shanti Found.; treas. So. Calif. Bd. Rabbis; chair Task Force on Gays and Lesbians in the Rabbinate. Recipient Rainbow Key award City West Hollywood, L.A.C.E. Spirituality award L.A. Gay and Lesbian Ctr., Angel Amidst award City of West Hollywood. Mem. Cen. Conf. Am. Rabbis, Interfaith Clergy Assn. (past chair gays and lesbians bd.). Avocation: guitar. Office: Congregation Kol Ami 9056 Santa Monica Blvd Ste 100 West Hollywood CA 90069-7002

EGGERT, ROBERT JOHN, SR. economist; b. Little Rock, Dec. 11, 1913; s. John and Eleanora (Fritz) Lapp; m. Elizabeth Bauer, Nov. 28, 1935 (dec. Dec. 1991); children: Robert John, Richard F., James E.; m. Annamarie Hayes, Mar. 19, 1994. BS, U. Ill., 1935, MS, 1936; candidate in philosophy, U. Minn., 1938; LHD (hon.), Ariz. State U., 1988. Research analyst Bur. Agrl. Econs., U.S. Dept. Agr., Urbana, Ill., 1935; sec. War Meat Bd., Chgo., 1942-45, prin. marketing specialist, 1943; rsch. analyst U. Ill., 1935-36, U. Minn., 1936-38; asst. prof. econs. Kans. State Coll., 1938-41; asst. dir. mktg. Am. Meat Inst., Chgo., 1941-43, economist, assoc. dir., 1943-50; mgr. dept. mktg. rsch. Ford divsn. Ford Motor Co., Dearborn, Mich., 1951-53, mgr. program planning, 1953-54, mgr. bus. rsch., 1954-57, mgr. mktg. rsch. mktg. staff, 1957-61, mgr. mktg. rsch., mem. div. op. com., 1961-64, mgr. internat. mktg. rsch. mktg. staff, 1964-65, mgr. overseas mktg. rsch. planning, 1965-66, mgr. mktg. rsch. Lincoln-Mercury div., 1966-67; dir. agribus. programs Mich. State U., 1967-68; staff v.p. econ. and mktg. rsch. RCA Corp., N.Y.C., 1968-76; pres., chief economist Eggert Econ. Enterprises, Inc., Sedona, Ariz., 1976—. Pres., chief economist Sedona Sales Tax Collections, West Sedona, Ariz.; lectr. mktg. U. Chgo., 1947-49; chmn. Fed. Statistics Users Conf., 1960-61; adj. prof. bus. forecasting No. Ariz., 1976-79; mem. econ. adv. bd. U.S. Dept. Commerce, 1969-71, mem. census adv. com., 1975-78; mem. panel econ. advisers Congl. Budget Office, 1975-76; interim dir. Econ. Outlook Ctr. Coll. Bus. Adminstrn. Ariz. State U., Tempe, 1985-86, cons., 1985—; mem. Econ. Estimates Commn. Ariz., 1979—; apptd. Ariz. Gov.'s Commn. Econ. Devel., 1991—, vice chmn. investment adv. coun. Ariz. State Retirement System, 1993-98; trustee Marcus J. Lawrence Med. Ctr. Found., 1992-96, Flagstaff Inst.; chmn. market rsch. com. Gov.'s Strategic Partnership for Econ. Devel.; co-chmn. Ariz. Sr. Industries Cluster, 1995-97. Contbr. articles to profl. lit.; founder, editor emeritus: monthly Blue Chip Econ. Indicators, 1976—; exec. editor Ariz. Blue Chip, 1984—, Western Blue Chip Econ. Forecast, 1986—, Blue Chip Job Growth Update, 1990—, Mexico Consensus Econ. Forecast, 1993—, Sedona Sales Tax Collections, 1998—, National Consensus Forecast of Labor Employment, Compensation and Productivity, 2000-01. Mem. long range planning com. Ch. of Red Rocks, 1998-2001. Recipient Econ. Forecast award Chgo. chpt. Am. Statis. Assn., 1950, 60, 68; Seer of Yr. award Harvard Bus. Sch. Indsl. Econs., 1973, Golden Gloves Boxing award, U. Ill., 1935. Fellow Am. Statis. Assn. (chmn. bus. and econ. stats sect. 1957—, pres. Chgo. chpt. 1948-49), Nat. Assn. Bus. Economists (coun. 1969-72); mem. Coun. Internat. Mktg. Rsch. and Planning Dirs. (chmn. 1965-66), Am. Mktg. Assn. (dir., v.p. mktg. mgmt. divsn. 1972-73, nat. pres. 1974-75), Fed. Stats. Users Conf. (chmn. trustees 1960-61), Conf. Bus. Economists (chmn. 1972-74), Am. Quarter Horse Assn. (dir. 1966-73), Ariz. Econ. Roundtable, Am. Econs. Assn., Phoenix Econ. Club (hon.), Ariz. C. of C. (bd. dirs. 1991-95), Alpha Zeta. Republican. Office: Eggert Econ Enterprises Inc PO Box 4313 West Sedona AZ 86340-4313 Fax: (928) 282-2128. E-mail: eee@sedona.net

EGLEE, CHARLES HAMILTON, television and movie writer, producer; b. Boston, Nov. 27, 1951; s. Donald Read and Nancy (Hamilton) E.; m. Madeline Dalton, Feb. 29, 1984; children: Blythe Dalton, Eli Hamilton. BA in English, Yale U., 1974. Teaching asst. Yale U., New Haven, 1976; producer, writer for film Deadly Eyes Warner Bros., L.A., 1982; story editor for TV series St. Elsewhere MTM Prodns., Studio City, Calif., 1984-86; exec. story cons. for TV series Moonlighting ABC Circle Films, L.A., 1986-87, producer for TV series Moonlighting, 1987-89; exec. producer 20th Century Fox TV, 1989-91; writer, co-exec. producer "Civil Wars" Steven Bochco Prodns., 1991-93; writer L.A. Law, 1992; co-creator, exec. producer The Byrds of Paradise (Steven Bochco Prodns.), 1993-94; co-exec. producer N.Y.P.D. Blue (Steven Bochco Prodns.), 1994-95; co-creator, exec. prodr. Murder One (Steven Bochco Prodns.), 1995-97, Total Security (Steven Bochco Prodns.), 1997-98; co-creator, exec. prodr. TV series Dark Angel Cameron-Eglee Prodns., 1999—. Story editor (St. Elsewhere episode) Bye George, 1985 (Humanitas prize); co-writer (St. Elsewhere episode) Haunted, 1986 (Emmy nomination, Salute to Excellence Award nominee NAACP 1986), (Moonlighting episode) I Am Curious, Maddie, 1987 (Emmy nomination), N.Y.P.D. Blue, 1994 (Emmy award for best drama), Murder One, 1996 (People's Choice award for best new drama, Emmy nomination, best writing in one hour drama, pilot episode 1996, Golden Globe nomination 1996, best fgn. drama Brit. Acad. Film and TV, 1996), Dark Angel, 2001 (People's Choice award for best new drama 2001). Nominee Best Drama award Writers Guild Am., 1996. Mem. Acad. TV Arts and Scis., Writers Guild Am., Yale U. Alumni Fund, Mory's Assn. (New Haven). Democrat. Avocations: sailing, skiing, Am. art pottery, gardening.

EGUCHI, YASU, artist; b. Japan, Nov. 30, 1938; came to U.S., 1967; s. Chihaku and Kiku (Koga) E.; m. Anita Phillips, Feb. 24, 1968. Student, Horie Art Acad., Japan, 1958-65. Exhibited exhbns., Tokyo Mus. Art, 1963, 66, Santa Barbara Mus. Art, Calif., 1972-74, 85, Everson Mus. Art, Syracuse, N.Y., 1980, Nat. Acad. Art, N.Y.C., 1980—; one-man shows include Austin Gallery, Scottsdale, Ariz., 1968-87, Joy Tash Gallery, Scottsdale, 1989-99, Greystone Galleries, Cambria, Calif., 1969, 70, 72, Copenhagen Galleries, Calif., 1970-78, Charles and Emma Frye Art Mus., Seattle, 1974, 84, 98, Hammer Galleries, N.Y.C., 1977, 79, 81, 93, 2001, City of Heidenheim, Germany, 1980, Artique Ltd., Anchorage, 1981—, Heidenheim Mus. Art, 2000; pub. and pvt. collections, Voith Gmbh, Germany, City of Giengen and City of Heidenheim, Germany, represented, Deer Valley, Utah, Hunter Resources, Santa Barbara, Am. Embassy, Paris, Charles and Emma Frye Art Mus., Seattle, Nat. Acad. Art; author: Der Brenz Entlang, 1980; author: Tasu Eguchi, 2000; contbr. to jours in field. Active Guide Dogs for the Blind, San Raphael, Calif., 1976; active City of Santa Barbara Arts Council, 1979, The Eye Bank for Sight Restoration, N.Y., 1981, Anchorage Arts Council, 1981, Santa Barbara Mus. Natural History, 1989. Recipient Selective Artist award Yokohama Citizen Gallery, 1965; recipient Artist of Yr. award Santa Barbara Arts Council, 1979, Hon. Citizen award City of Heidenheim, 1980, The Adolph and Clara Obrig prize NAD, 1983, Cert. of Merit NAD, 1985, 87. Home: PO Box 30206 Santa Barbara CA 93130-0206

EHRHORN, RICHARD WILLIAM, electronics company executive; b. Marshalltown, Iowa, Jan. 21, 1934; s. Theodore Raymond and Zelda Elizabeth (Axtell) E.; m. Marilyn Patrick, Aug. 1, 1959; children: Scott Patrick, Kimberlee Dawn. BSEE, U. Minn., 1955; MSEE, Calif. Inst. Tech., 1958. Sr. engr. Gen. Dynamics Corp., Pomona, Calif., 1956-60; sr. rsch. engr. Calif. Inst. Tech. Jet Propulsion Lab., Pasedena, 1960-63; mgr. advanced devel. lab. Electronic Communications Inc., St. Petersburg, Fla., 1963-68; gen. mgr. Signal/One div., 1968-70; chmn., CEO Ehrhorn Tech. Ops., Inc., Colorado Springs, Colo., 1970-95; vice chmn. ASTeX/ETO, Inc., Colorado Springs, 1996-99; regent Liberty U., 1995—; chmn., CEO Alpha/Power, Inc., Longmont, Colo., 1996-2000. Chmn. bd. dirs. Ehrhorn Tech. Ops., Inc., Colorado Springs, 1970-95. Author: (with others) Principles of Electronic Warfare, 1959; patentee in field. Mem. IEEE (sr. life), Am. Radio Relay League, Radio Club Am., Quar. Century Wireless Assn. Home and Office: PO Box 6249 Breckenridge CO 80424-6249 E-mail: w4eto@earthlink.net

EHRLICH, ANNE HOWLAND, research biologist; b. Des Moines, Nov. 17, 1933; d. Winston Densmore and Virginia Lippincott (Fitzhugh) Howland; m. Paul Ralph Ehrlich, Dec. 18, 1954; 1 child: Lisa Marie Daniel. Student, U. Kans., 1952-55; LLD (hon.), Bethany Coll., 1990; doctorate (hon.), Oreg. State U., 1999. Technician Dept. Entomology U. Kans., Lawrence, 1955; rsch. asst. Dept. Biol. Scis. Stanford (Calif.) U., 1959-72, rsch. assoc., 1972-75, sr. rsch. assoc., 1975—; assoc. dir. Ctr. for Conservation Biology Stanford U., 1987—. Bd. dirs. Pacific Inst., Rocky Mountain Biol. Lab., Sierra Club, Ploughshares Fund. Author: (with others) Ecoscience: Population, Resources, Environment, 1977, The Golden Door, 1979, Extinction, 1981, Earth, 1987, The Population Explosion, 1990, Healing the Planet, 1991, The Stork and the Plow, 1995, Betrayal of Science and Reason, 1996; editl. bd. Pacific Discovery; contbr. articles to profl. jours. Named to Global 500 Roll of Honour for Environ. Achievement, UN, 1989, UNFP-Sasekawa prize, 1994, Heinz award, 1995, Tyler prize, 1998. Fellow Am. Acad. Arts & Scis., Calif. Acad. Scis. (hon.); mem. Am. Humanists Assn. (hon. life, Disting. Svc. 1985, Raymond B. Bragg award 1985). Avocations: flyfishing, hiking, reading. Home: Pine Hill Stanford CA 94305 Office: Stanford U Dept Biol Scis Stanford CA 94305

EHRLICH, PAUL RALPH, biology educator; b. Phila., May 29, 1932; s. William and Ruth (Rosenberg) E.; m. Anne Fitzhugh Howland, Dec. 18, 1954; 1 dau., Lisa Marie. AB, U. Pa., 1953; AM, U. Kans., 1955, PhD, 1957. Research assoc. U. Kans., Lawrence, 1958-59; asst. prof. biol. scis. Stanford U., 1959-62, assoc. prof., 1962-66, prof., 1966—, Bing prof. population studies, 1976—, dir. grad. study dept. biol. scis., 1966-69, 1974-76, pres. Ctr. for Conservation Biology, 1988—. Cons. Behavioral Rsch. Labs., 1963-67; corr. NBC News, 1989-92. Author: How to Know the Butterflies, 1961, Process of Evolution, 1963, Principles of Modern Biology, 1968, Population Bomb, 1968, 2d edit., 1971, Population, Resources, Environment: Issues in Human Ecology, 1970, 2d edit., 1972, How to Be a Survivor, 1971, Global Ecology: Readings Toward a Rational Strategy for Man, 1971, Man and the Ecosphere, 1971, Introductory Biology, 1973, Human Ecology: Problems and Solutions, 1973, Ark II: Social Response to Environmental Imperatives, 1974, The End of Affluence: A Blueprint for the Future, 1974, Biology and Society, 1976, Race Bomb, 1977, Ecoscience: Population, Resources, Environment, 1977, Insect Biology, 1978, The Golden Door: International Migration, Mexico, and the U.S., 1979, Extinction: The Causes and Consequences of the Disappearance of Species, 1981, The Machinery of Nature, 1986, Earth, 1987, The Science of Ecology, 1987, The Birder's Handbook, 1988, New World/New Mind, 1989, The Population Explosion, 1990, Healing the Planet, 1991, Birds in Jeopardy, 1992, The Birdwatchers Handbook, 1994, The Stork & the Plow, 1995, Betrayal of Science and Reason, 1996, World of Wounds, 1997, Human Natures, 2000, Wild Solutions, 2001; contbr. articles to profl. jours. Recipient World Wildlife Fedn. medal, 1987; co-recipient Crafoord prize in population biology and conservation biol. diversity, 1990, Volvo Environ. prize, 1993, World Ecology medal Internat. Ctr. Tropical Ecology, 1993, UN Sasakawa Environ. prize, 1994, Heinz prize for the environ., 1995, Tyler Environ. prize, 1998, Heineken prize for environ. sci., 1998, Blue Plant prize, 1999; MacArthur Prize fellow, 1990-95. Fellow Calif. Acad. Scis., Am. Acad. Arts and Scis., AAAS, Am. Philos. Soc., Entomology Soc. Am.; mem. Nat. Acad. Scis., Entomological Soc. Am., Soc. for Study Evolution, Soc. Systematic Zoology, Am. Soc. Naturalists, Lepidopterists Soc., Am. Mus. Natural History (hon. life mem.). Office: Stanford U Dept Biol Scis Stanford CA 94305

EHRLICH, THOMAS, law educator, educator; b. Cambridge, Mass., Mar. 4, 1934; s. William and Evelyn (Seltzer) E.; m. Ellen Rome, June 18, 1957; children— David, Elizabeth, Paul. AB, Harvard U., 1956, LLB, 1959; LLD (hon.), Villanova U., 1979, Notre Dame U., 1980, U. Pa., 1987. Bar: Wis. bar 1959. Law clk. Judge Learned Hand U.S. Ct. Appeals 2d Circuit, 1959-60; spl. asst. to legal adviser Dept. State, 1962-64; spl. asst. to under-sec. U.S. Dept. State, 1964-65; assoc. prof. law Stanford (Calif.) U., 1965-68, prof., 1968-75, also dean, 1971-75, Richard E. Lang dean and prof., 1973-75; pres. Legal Services Corp., Washington, 1976-79; dir. Internat. Devel. Coop. Agy., Washington, 1979-81; provost, prof. law U. Pa., Phila., 1981-87; pres., prof. law Ind. U., Bloomington and Indpls., 1987-94; vis. prof. Duke U., Durham, 1994; Disting. Univ. scholar Calif. State U., San Francisco, 1995-2000. Vis. prof. Stanford Law Sch., 1994-99; sr. scholar Carnegie Found. for Advancement of Tchg., 1997—. Author: (with Abram Chayes and Andreas F. Lowenfeld) The International Legal Process, 3 vols., 1968, (with Herbert L. Packer) New Directions in Legal Education, 1972, International Crises and the Role of Law, Cyprus, 1958-67, 1974; editor: (with Geoffrey C. Hazard Jr.) Going to Law School?, 1975, (with Mary Ellen O'Connell) International Law and the Use of Force, 1993, The Courage to Inquire, 1995, Philanthropy and the Nonprofit Sector in a Changing America, 1998, Civic Responsibility and Higher Education, 2000. Office: Carnegie Found Advancement of Tchg 555 Middlefield Rd Menlo Park CA 94025-3443

EIBERGER, CARL FREDERICK, lawyer; b. Denver, Jan. 17, 1931; s. Carl Frederick and Madeleine Anastasia (Ries) E.; children: Eileen, Carl III, Mary, James. BS in Chemistry magna cum laude, U. Notre Dame, 1952, JD magna cum laude, 1954; MBA, Denver U., 1959. Sole practice, 1954-55; ptnr. Rovira, DeMuth & Eiberger, Denver, 1957-69, Eiberger, Stacy, Smith & Martin, Denver, 1979-96; prin. Carl F. Eiberger & Assocs., Denver, 1996—. Chmn. CBA/DBA/Econs. of Law Practice Coms.; co-founder CBA/Steering Com. Labor Law Com., Denver; arbitrator Am. Arbitration Assn.; asst. bar examiner, 1963-68; lectr. on continuing legal edn. Contbr. articles to legal jours. Bd. dirs. Colo. Assn. Commerce and Industry; pres. Prospect Recreation and Park Dist.; founder Applewood Athletic Club, Jefferson County; gen. counsel Denver Symphony Orch. Recipient merit award Jefferson County Commrs., merit cert. Jefferson County Homeowners; named Man of the Yr. Notre Dame Club of Denver, Vol. of Yr. Channel 9TV, Denver., Citizen of Yr., Lions Club Internat. Mem. ABA, Colo. Bar Assn. (bd. govs.), Denver Bar Assn. (nominated pres.), Notre Dame Law Assn. (bd. dirs. 1965—, exec. com. 1998—), Gov. Adv. Coun. to Colo dept. of labor, Notre Dame Club (pres., bd. dirs.), Athletic Club (Denver), Rolling Hills Country Club. Roman Catholic. Home: 14330 Fairview Ln Golden CO 80401-2050 Office: 14330 Fairview Ln Golden CO 80401-2050

EICHELBERGER, JOHN CHARLES, volcanologist, educator; b. Syracuse, N.Y., Oct. 3, 1948; s. William Custer and Esther (Dorr) E.; m. Alice Palen, Dec. 27, 1969 (div. 1993); children: Laura Palen, Nathan William; m. Gail Davidson, Sept. 3, 1994; stepchildren: Jennifer Ruth March, Jody Elizabeth March. BS, MS in Geology, MIT, 1971; PhD in Geology, Stanford U., 1974. Staff mem. Los Alamos (N.Mex.) Nat. Lab., 1974-79; mem. tech. staff Sandia Nat. Labs., Albuquerque, 1979-89, disting. mem. tech. staff, 1989-90, supr. geochem. divsn., 1990-91; prof. volcanology U. Alaska, Fairbanks, 1991—. Group leader volcanology Geophys. Inst., 1991—; coord. scientist Alaska Volcano Obs., 1991—; chief scientist Katmai (Alaska) Sci. Drilling Project, 1988-94, Inyo Sci. Drilling Project,

Mammoth Lake, Calif., 1983-88; adj. prof. geochemistry N.Mex. Inst. Mines and Tech., Socorro, 1989-91. Editor Volcanology of Eos, Transactions of the Am. Geophys. Union, 1985-88; assoc. editor Jour. Geophys. Rsch., 1998—; contbr. more than 60 articles to profl. jours. Fellow Geol. Soc. Am.; mem. Am. Geophys. Union (life). Office: U Alaska Alaska Volcano Observatory Geophysical Inst Fairbanks AK 99775 E-mail: eich@gi.alaska.edu

EICHINGER, MARILYNNE HILDEGARDE, museum administrator; children: Ryan, Kara, Julia, Jessica, Talik. BA in Anthropology and Sociology magna cum laude, Boston U., 1965; MA, Mich. State U., 1971. With emergency and outpatient staff Ingham County Mental Health Ctr., 1972; founder, pres., exec. dir. Impression 5 Sci. and Art Mus., Lansing, Mich., 1973-85; pres. Oreg. Mus. Sci. and Industry, Portland, 1985-95; bd. dirs. Portland Visitors Assn., 1985-95; pres. Informal Edn. Products Ltd., 1995—, Portland, 1995—. Bd. dirs. N.W. Regional Edn. Labs., 1991-97; instr. Lansing (Mich.) C.C., 1978; ptnr. Eyrie Studio, 1982-85; condr. numerous workshops in interactive exhibit design, adminstrn. and fund devel. for schs., orgns., profl. socs. Author: (with Jane Mack) Lexington Montessori School Survey, 1969, Manual on the Five Senses, 1974; pub. Mich. edit. Boing mag. Founder Cambridge Montessori Sch., 1964; bd. dirs. Lexington Montessori Sch., 1969, Mid-Mich. South Health Sys. Agy., 1978-81, Cmty. Referral Ctr., 1981-85, Sta. WKAR, 1981-85; active Lansing "Riverfest" Lighted Boat Parade, 1980; mem. state Health Coordinating Coun., 1980-82; mem. pres.'s adv. coun. Portland State U., 1986—, mem. pres.' adv. bd., 1987-91; bd. dirs. Portland Visitors Assn., 1994-97. Recipient Diana Cert. Leadership, YWCA, 1976-77, Woman of Achievement award, 1991, Community Svc. award Portland State U., 1992. Mem. Am. Assn. Mus., Oreg. Mus. Assn., Assn. Sci. and Tech. Ctrs. (bd. dirs. 1980-84, 88-93), Mus. Store Assn., Direct Mktg. Assn., Zonta Lodge (founder, bd. dirs. East Lansing club 1978), Internat. Women's Forum, Portland C. of C. Office: Informal Edn Products Ltd 2525 SE Stubb St Milwaukie OR 97222

EICKHOFF, THEODORE CARL, epidemiologist; b. Cleve., Sept. 13, 1931; s. Theodore Henry and Clara (Strassen) E.; m. Margaret Heinecke, Aug. 24, 1952; children: Stephen, Mark, Philip. BA, Valparaiso U., 1953; MD, Case Western Res. U., 1957. Diplomate: Am. Bd. Internal Medicine. Intern, then resident Harvard Med. Services, Boston City Hosp., 1957-59; fellow in medicine Harvard Med. Sch.-Boston City Hosp., 1961-64; epidemiologist Center for Disease Control, 1964-67; prof. medicine U. Colo. Med. Ctr., 1975—, head div. infectious disease, 1967-80; vice chmn. dept. medicine U. Colo. Med. Center, 1976-81; dir. internal medicine Presbyn./St. Luke's Med. Ctr., 1981-92; dir. medicine Denver Gen. Hosp., 1978-81. Cons. FDA, Ctrs. for Disease Control, Am. Hosp. Assn.; mem. nat. commn. orphan diseases HHS, 1986-90, mem. vaccines adv. com., 1995-99. Contbr. articles to med. jours. Served with USPHS, 1959-67. Recipient Commr.'s Spl. Citation, FDA, 1990, Trustee's award Am. Hosp. Assn., 1993. Mem. ACP (Disting. Internist award Colo. chpt. 1995), Am. Fedn. Clin. Rsch., Am. Soc. Clin. Investigation, Assn. Am. Physicians, Infectious Diseases Soc. Am. (sec. 1978-82, pres. 1983-84, Finland Lectureship award 1995), Am. Epidemiol. Soc. (pres. 1985-86). Home: 15 S Franklin Cir Greenwood Village CO 80121-1245 Office: Univ Colo Health Sci Ctr Div Infectious Disease B 168 Denver CO 80262-0001 E-mail: theodore.eickhoff@uchsc.edu

EIDE, JOEL S. art consultant, appraiser; Dir. No. Ariz. U. Art Mus. and Galleries, 1975-98; prof. fine art No. Ariz. U., Flagstaff, 1998-99; fine art cons. Clarkdale, Ariz., 1999—. E-mial. Home: 1926 N Crescent Dr Flagstaff AZ 86001-1114 Office: PO Box 82 Sycamore Canyon Rd Clarkdale AZ 86324 E-mail: eideart@bmol.com

EIDE, TRACEY J. state legislator; m. Mark Eide; children: Joanna, Matthew. Mem. Wash. Ho. of Reps., Olympia, 1993-98, asst. majority whip, 1993-94, chair Federal Way Human Svcs. Commn., 1997-98; vice chair edn. com.; vice chair environ. quality and water resources com.; mem. Puget Sound Coun.; mem. transp. com.; majority asst. whip; mem. joint com. on children's oversight; co-chair commute trip reduction task force; mem. Wash. Senate, Dist. 30, Olympia, 1998—. Mem. Puget Sound. Coun.; alt. mem. Coun. State Govt., Western Water Policy Com.; mem. Wash. State Recycling Task Force. Recipient Disting. Leadership in Edn. award Fed. Way Sch. Dist., Emerging Leader award Nat. Conf. State Legislatures. Democrat. Office: 410 Legis Bldg Olympia WA 98504-0430

EIGLER, DONALD MARK, physicist; b. L.A., Mar. 23, 1953; s. Irving Baer and Evelin Muriel (Baker) E.; m. Roslyn Winifred Rubesin, Nov. 2, 1986. BA, U. Calif., San Diego, 1975, PhD in Physics, 1984. Rsch. assoc. U. Köln (Fed. Republic Germany), 1975-76, U. Calif., San Diego, 1977-84, postdoctoral rsch. assoc., 1984, assoc. rsch. physicist dept. physics, 1986; postdoctoral mem. tech. staff AT&T Bell Labs., Murray Hill, N.J., 1984-86; rsch. staff mem. IBM, San Jose, Calif., 1986-93, IBM fellow, 1993—. Alexander M. Cruickshank lectr. in phys. sci. (Gordon Rsch. Confs.), 1994. Co-winner 1993-94 Newcomb Cleveland prize AAAS; recipient Dannie Heineman prize Göttingen Acad. Scis., 1995, Outstanding Alumnus award U. Calif. San Diego alumni Assn., 1998, Nanoscience prize Conf. on Atomically Controlled Interfaces and Surfaces, 1999. Fellow AAAS, Am. Phys. Soc. (Davisson-Germer prize 2001). Office: IBM Almaden Rsch Ctr 650 Harry Rd San Jose CA 95120-6099

EIGSTI, ROGER HARRY, retired insurance company executive; b. Vancouver, Wash., Apr. 17, 1942; s. Harry A. and Alice E. (Huber) E.; m. Mary Lou Nelson, June 8, 1963; children: Gregory, Ann. BS, Linfield Coll., 1964. CPA, Oreg., Wash. Staff CPA Touche Ross and Co., Portland, Oreg., 1964-72; asst. to controller Safeco Corp., Seattle, 1972-78, controller, 1980, Safeco Life Ins. Co., Seattle, 1978-80; pres. Safeco Credit Co., Seattle, 1980-81, Safeco Life Ins. Co., Seattle, 1981-85; exec. v.p., CFO Safeco Corp., Seattle, 1985, CEO, chmn., 1985-2001. Bd. dirs. Ind. Colls. of Wash., Seattle, 1981-87, bus. dir. Seattle Repertory Theatre, 1981—, bd. dirs. 1981—. Mem. Am. Inst. CPA's, Life Office Mgmt. Assn. (bd. dirs. 1983—), Seattle C. of C. (chmn. metro budget rev. com. 1984—). Republican. Clubs: Mercer Island (Wash.) Country (treas., bd. dirs. 1981-84); Central Park Tennis. Home: 1503 Parkside Dr E Seattle WA 98112-3719

EILENBERG, LAWRENCE IRA, theater educator, artistic director; b. Bklyn., May 26, 1947; s. Jerome and Dorothy Vera (Natleson) E.; m. Diane Marie Eliasof, Nov. 25, 1973 (dec. Dec. 1984); children: David Joseph, Benjamin Alan; m. Judith Heiner, Nov. 10, 1990 (dec. Nov. 1994). BA, Cornell U., 1968; MPhil, Yale U., 1971, PhD, 1975. Jr. fellow Davenport Coll., Yale U., New Haven, 1971-72; asst. prof. theatre dept. Cornell U., Ithaca, N.Y., 1972-75; vis. asst. prof. in theatre U. Mich., Ann Arbor, 1975-77; asst. prof., then assoc. prof. U. Denver, 1977-82, 83; prof. San Francisco State U., 1983—, chmn. theatre arts dept., 1984-92; artistic dir. Magic Theatre, San Francisco, 1992-93, dramaturg, 1997—. Theatre corr. Sta. KCFR (NPR), Denver, 1979-82; literary mgr. Denver Ctr. Theatre Co., 1981-83; artistic dir. San Francisco New Vaudeville Festival, 1985-89; dramaturg One Act Theatre Co., San Francisco, 1986-88; bd. dirs. Theatre Bay Area, San Francisco, 1985-90, pres., 1987-89; co-dir. Congress of Clowns, 1994; speaker, lectr. in field. Editor Stage/Space mag., 1981-83; contbr. articles, book and theater revs. to profl. publs. U.S. del. Podium Festival of USSR, Moscow, 1989, Grantee Lilly Found., 1981, Idaho Humanities Assn., 1983, 84, 85, NEA, 1986, 92, Calif. Arts Coun., 1987, 88, 92; recipient Best Broadcast award Colo. Broadcasters Assn., 1982. Mem. Literary Mgrs. and Dramaturgs Am. (v.p. 1989-90), Nat. Assn. Schs. of Theatre (bd. accreditation, 1990-91, evaluator 1986—). Home: 2200 Leavenworth St Apt 606 San Francisco CA 94133-2293 Office: San Francisco State U Theatre Arts Dept 1600 Holloway Ave San Francisco CA 94132-1722

EINSTEIN, CLIFFORD JAY, advertising executive; b. L.A., May 4, 1939; s. Harry and Thelma (Bernstein) E.; m. Madeline Mandel, Jan. 28, 1962; children: Harold Jay, Karen Holly. BA in English, UCLA, 1961. Writer Norman, Craig and Kummel, N.Y.C., 1961-62, Foote, Cone and Belding, L.A., 1962-64; ptnr. Silverman and Einstein, L.A., 1965-67; pres., creative dir. Dailey and Assos., L.A., 1968-93, chmn., CEO, 1994—, also bd dirs. Dir. Campaign '80, advt. agy. Reagan for Pres., 1980; lectr. various colls.; founder, bd. dirs. First Coastal Bank; bd. dirs. The Jewish Cmty. Found. Contbr. articles to Advertising Age; prodr.: (play) Whatever Happened to Georgie Tapps, L.A. and San Francisco, 1980; film appearances include Real Life, Modern Romance, Defending Your Life, Face/Off, 1997; T.V. appearance in Bizarre, Super Dave Show. Bd. dirs. Rape Treatment Ctr., Santa Monica Med. Ctr., Discovery Fund for Eye Rsch.; vice-chmn. bd. Mus. Contemporary Art, L.A., 1994—. With U.S. Army, 1957. Recipient Am. Advt. award, 1968, 73, 79, Clio award, 1973, Internat. Broadcast Pub. Svc. award, 1970, 85, Nat. Addy award, 1979, Gov.'s award, 1987; named Creative Dir. of the West, Adweek Poll, 1982, Exec. of West, 1986, Western States Assn. Advt. Agys. Leader of Yr., 1992. Mem. AFTRA, ASCAP, SAG, Dirs. Guild Am., Am. Assn. Advt. Agys. (chmn. western region), Hillcrest Country Club, Calif. Club. Office: Dailey & Assocs 8687 Melrose Ave West Hollywood CA 90069-5701

EISCHEID, THEODORE J. toy company executive, lawyer; b. Des Moines, May 25, 1950; s. George Joseph and Juanita Margaret (Gambrall) E.; m. Jean Purcell, June 22, 1974; children: Nancy, Jennifer. BS, Iowa State U., 1972; M.Mgmt., Northwestern U., 1981; JD cum laude, Loyola U., Chgo., 1990. Bar: Ill. 1990; CPA, Ill. Audit asst. Arthur Andersen & Co., Chgo., 1972-74, audit sr., 1974-77, audit mgr., 1977-78; exec. v.p., CFO Glass Gorham Co., Skokie, Ill., 1978-80; controller Arvey Corp., Chgo., 1980-86, CFO, 1986-88; sr. v.p., CFO Revell-Monogram, Inc., Morton Grove, Ill., 1988-91, pres., 1991—. Dir. Revell-Monogram, Inc. Treas., bd. dirs. Ponds Homeowners Assn., Lake Forest, Ill., 1990—. Chief Justice Edward D. White scholar, Loyola U., Chgo., 1990. Mem. ABA, Ill. Bar Assn., Ill. Soc. CPAs, Fin. Execs. Inst., Toy Mfrs. of Am. (bd. dirs. 1991—). Roman Catholic. Office: EDUCATIONAL INSIGHTS,INC 16941 KEEGAN AVE Carson CA 90746

EISEN, HILDA, food products executive; b. Poland; came to U.S. in 1948. Owner Norco Ranch, Norco, Calif. Office: Norco Ranch Inc PO Box 910 Norco CA 92860-0910

EISENBERG, DAVID SAMUEL, molecular biologist, educator; b. Chgo., Mar. 15, 1939; s. George and Ruth E.; m. Lucy Tuchman, Aug. 25, 1963; children: Jenny, Nell. A.B., Harvard U., 1961; Phil.D., Oxford U., Eng., 1964. NSF postdoctoral fellow Princeton U., 1964-66; research fellow chemistry Calif. Inst. Tech., Pasadena, 1966-69; asst. prof. UCLA, 1968-71, assoc. prof., 1971-76, prof. chemistry, biochemistry, 1976—, assoc. dir. Molecular Biology Inst., 1981-85; dir. UCLA-DOE Lab. of Structural Biology and Molecular Medicine, 1993—. Author: (with W. Kauzmann) Structure and Properties of Water, 1969, (with D.M. Crothers) Physical Chemistry with Applications in the Life Sciences, 1979. Chmn. Citizens for West Los Angeles Veloway, 1977—; bd. dirs. Westlake Sch., 1983-89, Harvard-Westlake Sch., 1990-91. Recipient USPHS Career Devel. awardee, 1972-77; Rhodes scholar, 1961-64; Guggenheim fellow, 1985, Stein & Moore award, 1996, Repligen award, 1998. Fellow Biophys. Soc.; mem. NAS, Am. Acad. Arts and Scis., Am. Soc. Biol. Chemists, Am. Crystallographic Assn., Biophys. Soc. (councillor 1977-80), The Protein Soc. (pres. 1987-89, councillor 1989-94). Office: UCLA-DOE Lab Structural Biologyand Molecular Medicine PO Box 951570 Los Angeles CA 90095-1570

EISENBERG, MELVIN A. law educator; b. New York, Dec. 3, 1934; s. Max and Laura (Wallance) E.; m. Helen Garlitz, Feb. 5, 1956; children: Bronwyn, David Abram (dec. 1997). AB, SCL, Columbia U., 1956; LLB, SCL, Faye Diploma in Law, Harvard U., 1959; LLD (hon.), U. Milan, 1998. Bar: N.Y. 1960. Assoc. Kaye Scholer Fierman Hays & Handler, 1959-63, 64-66; corp. counsel City of N.Y., 1966; acting prof. U. Calif.-Berkeley, 1966-69, prof. law, 1969-83, Koret prof. law, 1983—. Vis. prof. Harvard U., 1969-70, U. Tokyo, 1992, Justin d'Atri vis. prof. law, bus. and society, Columbia U., 1998—; asst. counsel Pres. Commn. on Assassination Pres. Kennedy, Warren Commn., 1964; counsel mayor's task force on reorgn N.Y.C. govt., 1966; mem. mayor's task force on N.Y.C. transp. reorgn., 1966; mem. mayors' task force on mcpl. collective bargaining, 1966; reporter Am. Law Inst., principles of corporate governance: analysis and recommendations, 1980-84, chief reporter, 1984-94, Ammi Cutter chair, 1991-93; adviser, restatement 3d of agy. 1996—; adviser, restatement 2d of restitution, 1998—; prof.-in-residence, Cologne U., 1984, U. Milan, 1992; mem. ABA com. on corp. laws, 1992—; U. Iowa Inaugural lectr., 1987, Roy R. Ray lectr. So. Meth. U., 1993, Robert L. Levine Distg. Lectures, Fordham U., 1993; chmn. AALS contracts sect., 1989, AALS contracts workshop, 1986; chmn. AALS bus. assns. sect., 1998; visitor-in-residence U. Murdoch, U. Western Australia, 1992, McGill U., 1981; Sobeloff lectr. U. Md., 1994; Freehill, Hollingsdale and Page vis. fellow U. New South Wales, Australia, 1994. Author: The Structure of the Corporation, 1977 (Coif Triennial Book award honorable mention 1980), The Nature of the Common Law, 1988, (with L. Fuller) Basic Contract Law, 1996, Cases and Materials on Corporations and Other Business Organization, 2000; also numerous articles. Pres. Queen's Child Guidance Ctr., 1963-66. Recipient Disting. Teaching award U. Calif., Berkeley, 1990; Guggenheim fellow, 1971-72, Canterbury vis. fellow U. Canterbury, New Zealand, 1988, Kimber fellow York U., Toronto, Ont., Can., 1989; Fulbright Sr. scholar, Australia, 1987, Mellon scholar U. Pitts., 1989; named Cooley lectr. U. Mich., 1985; Manuel F. Cohen vis. scholar George Washington U. Sch. Law; Baron de Hirsch Meyer lectr. U. Miami Sch. Law; Wythe lectr. William and Mary Law Sch.; TePoel lectr. Creighton U. Sch. Law; Rabin fellow Yale Sch. Law.; recipient Faye Diploma Harvard U. Law Sch. Fellow AAAS; mem. ABA (com. on corp. law, 1992-99), Am. Law Inst., Am. Assn. Law Schs. (chair bus. assns. sect. 1999), Phi Beta Kappa. Home: 1197 Keeler Ave Berkeley CA 94708-1753 Office: U Calif Sch Law 331 Boalt Hl Berkeley CA 94720-0001 also: 201 E 79th St New York NY 10021-0830 also: Columbia U Law Sch 435 W 116th St New York NY 10027-7201 E-mail: eisenberg@law.berkeley.edu

EISENSHTAT, SIDNEY HERBERT, architect; b. New Haven, June 6, 1914; s. Morris and Ella (Sobole) E.; m. Alice D. Brenner, Dec. 19, 1937 (dec. Feb. 2001); children: Carole Oken, Abby Robyn. BArch, U. So. Calif., 1935. Registered architect, Calif. Prin. Sidney Eisenshtat & Assocs. FAIA, Beverly Hills, Calif., 1941—. Mem. architects panel Union Am. Hebrew Congregations; bd. dirs. Internat. Tech. Coop. Ctr., Tel Aviv; pres., chmn. bd. dirs. Beth Jacob Congregation; v.p. L.A. Assn. Jewish Edn.; chmn. bd., pres. West Coast Talmudical Sem.; co-chmn. Nat. Conf. Religious Architecture; cons. Great Synagogue, Jerusalem, Israel; chmn. bd. Torah U. (now Yeshiva of L.A.). Prin. works include House of the Book, Brandeis, Calif., 1970 (Landmark award 1979), Sinai Temple, Los Angeles, 1959 (25 yr. Landmark award 1984), Knox Presbyn. Ch., 1965 (Los Angeles Beauty award 1975), Wells Fargo Bldg., 1975 (Beverly Hills award 1978), Union Bank Bldg., 1960, Beverly Hills, Exec. Life Bldg., 1966, Beverly Hills, Hughes Aircraft Co. Hdqs. Bldg. and Computer Ctr., El Segundo, Calif., Friars Club, Los Angeles, 1961, Marlton Sch. for Deaf, Los Angeles, 1968, Sven Lokrantz School for Handicapped, Univ. Judaism Master Plan & Bldgs., Los Angeles, 1977, B'nai Zion Temple, El Paso, Tex., 1983, Temple Mt. Sinai, El Paso, 1962, Ctrl. Jewish Community Ctr., L.A., Bnai David Synagogue, Southfield, Mich., Hillel House, U. So. Calif.; whole body of archtl. work in permanent collection at U. So. Calif., Arts and Architecture Libr. as core collection of Jewish Architecture in America. Chmn., charter agy. pres. Bur. Jewish Edn. Greater L.A.; v.p., lifetime bd. mem. Jewish Fedn. Coun.; bd. dirs. Hebrew Immigration Soc.; v.p. Coun. Pres. Affiliated Orgns.; vice chmn. R-1 Commn., City of Beverly Hills. Recipient Nat. Sch. Adminstrs. award, 1966, Pub. Svc. award City of Beverly Hills, Nat. Disting. Svc. award Union Orthodox Jewish Congregations; honoree Bur. Jewish Edn. 60th Anniversary Celebration, Beth Jacob Congregation Banquet, 2001. Fellow AIA (honor award 1960, 66). Home and Office: 2736 Motor Ave Los Angeles CA 90064-3413

EISENSTADT, PAULINE DOREEN BAUMAN, investment company executive, state legislator; b. N.Y.C., Dec. 31, 1938; d. Morris and Anne (Lautenberg) Bauman; BA, U. Fla., 1960; MS (NSF grantee), U. Ariz., 1965; postgrad. U. N.Mex.; m. Melvin M. Eisenstadt, Nov. 20, 1960; children: Todd Alan, Keith Mark. Tchr., Ariz., 1961-65, P.R., 1972-73; adminstrv. asst. Inst. Social Research U. N.Mex., 1973-74; founder, 1st exec. dir. Energy Consumers N.Mex., 1977-81; dir., host TV program Consumer Viewpoint, 1980-82; host TV program N.Mex. Today and Tomorrow, 1992—; chmn. consumer affairs adv. com. Dept. Energy, 1979-80; v.p. tech. bd. Nat. Center Appropiate Tech., 1980—; pres. Eisenstadt Enterprises, investments, 1983—; mem. N.Mex. Ho. of Reps., 1985-92, chairwoman majority caucus, chair rules com. N.Mex. House of Reps., 1987—, chair sub. com. on children and youth, 1987; mem. exec. com., vice chair pvt. coun. Nat. Conf. State Legislators, 1987; mem. N.Mex. State Senate, 1996—, mem. senate fin. com., com. higher edn., com. econ. devel., sci. & tech., water & natural resources, electric deregulation com., chair conservation com.; vice chmn. Sandoval County (N.Mex.) Democratic Party, 1981—; mem. N.Mex. Dem. State Central Com., 1981—; N.Mex. del. Dem. Nat. Platform Com., 1984, Dem. Nat. Conv., 1984; pres. Sandoval County Dem. Women's Assn., 1979-81; vice chmn. N. Mex. Dem. Platform Com., 1984—; mem. Sandoval County Redistricting Task Force, 1983-84; mem. Rio Rancho Ednl. Study Com., 1984—; pres. Anti Defamation League, N. Mex., 1994-95; mem. N.Mex. First. Recipient Gov.'s award Outstanding N. Mex. Women, Commn. on the Status of Women and Gov. Bruce King, 1992. Author: Corrales, Portrait of a Changing Village, 1980. Mem. Kiwanis (1st woman mem. local club), Rio Rancho Rotary Club (pres. 1995—, Rotarian of the Year, 1995). Home: PO Box 658 Corrales NM 87048-0658

EISNER, MICHAEL DAMMANN, entertainment company executive; b. Mt. Kisco, N.Y., Mar. 7, 1942; s. Lester and Margaret (Dammann) E.; m. Jane Breckenridge; children: Breck, Eric, Anders. BA, Denison U., 1964. Began career in programming dept. CBS; asst. to nat. programming dir. ABC, 1966-68, mgr. spls. and talent, dir. program devel.-East Coast, 1968-71, dir. program devel. East Coast, 1968-71, dir. feature films and program devel. $D, 1969, v.p. daytime programming, 1971-75, v.p. program planning and devel., 1975-76, sr. v.p. prime time prodn. and devel., 1976; pres., chief operating officer Paramount Pictures, 1976-84; chmn., CEO Walt Disney Co., Burbank, Calif., 1984—. Governor Mighty Ducks of Anaheim, 1993. Trustee Denison U., Calif. Inst. Arts; bd. dirs. Am. Hosp. of Paris Found., UCLA Exec. Bd. for Med. Sci. Office: Walt Disney Co 500 S Buena Vista St Burbank CA 91521-0006

EITNER, LORENZ EDWIN ALFRED, art historian, educator; b. Brunn, Czechoslovakia, Aug. 27, 1919; came to U.S., 1935, naturalized, 1943; s. Wilhelm and Katherina (Thonet) E.; m. Trudi von Kathrein, Oct. 26, 1946; children: Christy, Kathy, Claudia. AB, Duke U., 1940; MFA, Princeton U., 1948, PhD, 1952. Research unit head Nuremberg War Crimes Trial, 1946-47; from instr. to prof. art U. Minn., Mpls., 1949-63; chmn. dept. art, dir. mus. Stanford U., Calif., 1963-89. Organizer exhbn. works of Gericault for museums of Los Angeles, Detroit and Phila., 1971-72 Author: The Flabellum of Tournus, 1944, Gericault Sketchbooks in the Chicago Art Institute, 1960, Introduction to Art, 1951, Neo-Classicism and Romanticism, 1969, Gericault's Raft of the Medusa, 1972, Gericault, His Life and Work, 1983 (Mitchell prize 1984, C.R. Morey award 1985), An Outline of 19th Century European Painting from David through Cezanne, 1987, French Nineteenth Century Paintings, 2000; (with others) The Arts in Higher Education, 1963, Stanford Mus. Art, The Drawing Collection, 1993; contbr. articles to profl. jours. Mem. Regional Area Arts Coun. San Francisco Bay Area. Officer OSS, AUS, 1943-46; sect. head ministries divsn. Nuremberg War Crimes Trial, 1946-47. Fulbright grantee, Belgium, 1952-53; Guggenheim fellow, Munich, Federal Republic Germany, 1956-57; recipient Gold Medal for Meritorious Service to Austrian Republic, 1990. Mem. AAAS, Am. Acad. Arts and Scis., Coll. Art Assn. Am. (bd. dirs., past v.p.), Phi Beta Kappa Home: 684 Mirada Ave Stanford CA 94305-8475 Office: Stanford U Art Dept Palo Alto CA 94305

EITZEN, DAVID STANLEY, sociologist, educator; b. Glendale, Calif., Aug. 4, 1934; s. David Donald and Amanda Emma (Heidebrecht) E.; m. Florine Kay Voran, May 29, 1956; children: Keith, Michael, Kelly. A.B. in History, Bethel Coll., 1956; M.S., Emporia State U., 1962; M.A. in Sociology, U. Kans., 1966, Ph.D. in Sociology, 1968. Recreational therapist Menninger Found., Topeka, 1956-58; tchr. Galva (Kans.) High Sch., 1958-60, Turner (Kans.) High Sch., 1960-65; asst. prof. sociology U. Kans., 1968-72, asso. prof., 1972-74; prof. sociology Colo. State U., Ft. Collins, 1974-95, prof. emeritus, 1995—. Author: Social Structure and Social Problems, 1974, Sociology of American Sport, 1978, In Conflict and Order: Understanding Society, 1978, Sport in Contemporary Society, 1979, Social Problems, 1980, Elite Deviance, 1981; Criminology: Crime and Criminal Justice, 1985, Diversity in American Families, 1987, Society's Problems: Sources and Consequences, 1989, Crime in the Streets and Crime in the Suites: Perspectives on Crime and Criminal Justice, 1989, The Reshaping of America: Social Consequences of the Changing Economy, 1989, Paths to Homelessness, 1994, Solutions to Social Problems: Lessons from Other Societies, 1997, Fair and Foul: Beyond the Myths and Paradoxes of Sport, 1999; editor Social Sci. Jour., 1978-84. Contbr. articles to profl. jours. NDEA fellow, 1965-67 Mem. Internat. Sociol. Assn., Am. Sociol. Assn., Midwest Sociol. Soc., Soc. Study Social Problems, Western Social Sci. Assn., Southwestern Social Sci. Assn., Internat. Com. for Sociology Sport., N.Am. Soc. for Sociology of Sport (pres. 1986-87). Democrat. Mennonite. Home: 924 Breakwater Dr Fort Collins CO 80525-3345 Office: Colo State U Dept Sociology Fort Collins CO 80523-0001

EIZENBERG, JULIE, architect; BArch, U. Melbourne, Australia, 1978; MArch II, UCLA, 1981. Lic. architect, Calif., reg. architect, Australia. Principal, architect Koning Eizenberg Architecture, Santa Monica, Calif., 1981—. Instr. various courses UCLA, MIT, Harvard U.; lectr. in field; jury member P/A awards. Exhbns. incl. Koning Eizenberg Architecture 3A Garage, San Francisco, 1996, "House Rules" Wexner Ctr., 1994, "The Architect's Dream: Houses for the Next Millenium" The Contemporary Arts Ctr., 1993, "Angels & Franciscans" Gagosian Gallery, 1992, Santa Monica Mus. Art, 1993, "Broadening the Discourse" Calif. Women in Environmental Design, 1990, "Conceptional Drawings by Architects" Bannatyne Gallery, 1991, Exhbn. Koning Eizenberg Projects Grad. Sch. Architecture & Urban Planning UCLA, 1990; prin. works include Digital Domain Renovation and Screening Room, Santa Monica, Lightstorm Entertainment Office Renovation and Screening Room, Santa Monica, Gilmore Bank Addition and Remodel, L.A., 1548-1550 Studios, Santa Monica, (with RTA) Materials Rsch. Lab. at U. Calif., Santa Barbara, Ken Edwards Ctr. for Cmty. Svcs., Santa Monica, Peck Park Cmty. Ctr. Gymnasium, San Pedro, Calif., Sepulveda Recreation Ctr., L.A. (Design award

AIA San Fernando Valley 1995, Nat. Concrete and Masonry award 1996, AIA Calif. Coun. Honor award 1996, L.A. Bus. Coun. Beautification award 1996, AIA Los Angeles Chpt. Merit Award, 1997), PS # 1 Elem. Sch., Santa Monica, Farmers Market, L.A. Additions and Master Plan (Westside Urban Forum prize 1991), Stage Deli, L.A., Simone Hotel, L.A. (Nat. Honor award AIA 1994), Boyd Hotel, L.A., Cmty. Corp. Santa Monica Housing Projects, 5th St. Family Housing, Santa Monica, St. John's Hosp. Replacement Housing Program, Santa Monica, Liffman Ho., Santa Monica, (with Glenn Erikson) Electric Artblock, Venice (Beautification award L.A. Bus. Coun. 1993), 6th St. Condominiums, Santa Monica, Hollywood Duplex, Hollywood Hills (Record Houses Archtl. Record 1988), California Ave. Duplex, Santa Monica, Tarzana Ho. (Award of Merit L.A. chpt. AIA 1992, AIA Calif. Coun. Merit Award, 1998, Sunset Western home Awards citation 1993-94), 909 Ho., Santa Monica (Award of Merit L.A. chpt. AIA 1991), 31st St. Ho., Santa Monica (Honor award AIACC 1994, Nat. AIA Honor award 1996), others. Recipient 1st award Progressive Architecture, 1987; named one of Domino's Top 30 Architects, 1989. Mem. L.A. County Mus. Art, Westside Urban Forum, Urban Land Inst., Architects and Designers for Social Responsibility, Mus. Contemporary Art, The Nature Conservancy, Sierra Club. Office: Koning Eizenberg Architecture 1454 25th St Santa Monica CA 90404-3008

EJABAT, MORY, communications executive; BS in Indsl. Engring., MS in Sys. Engring., Calif. State U.; MBA, Pepperdine U. V.p. Micom Sys. Inc., Ascend Comm., Alameda, Calif., 1990-92, exec. v.p., chief operating officer, 1992-95, pres., chief exec. officer, 1995-99; chmn., CEO Zhone Technologies, 1999—. Office: Zhone Technologies 7677 Oakport St Ste 1145 Oakland CA 94621-1932

EKANGER, LAURIE, retired state official; b. Salt Lake City, Mar. 4, 1949; d. Bernard and Mary (Dearth) E.; m. William J. Shupe, Nov. 6, 1973; children: Ben, Robert. BA in English, U. Oreg., 1973. Various pos. Mont. State Employment & Tng. Divsn., Helena, 1975-80, dep. adminstr., 1980-82; adminstr. Mont. State Purchasing Divsn., Helena, 1982-85, Mont. State Personnel Divsn., Helena, 1985-93; labor commr. Mont. Dept. Labor & Ind., Helena, 1993-97; dir. Mont. Dept. Pub. Health and Human Svcs., 1997-2000. Council chair State Employee Group Benefits Coun., 1985-93; bd. dirs. Pub. Employee Retirement Bd., 1988; mem. various state adv. couns. for health and human svcs. Home: 80 Pinecrest Rd Clancy MT 59634-9505

EKEGREN, E. PETER (PETE EKEGREN), state legislator; Farm implement dealer; mem. Mont. Senate, Dist. 44, Helena, 1998—; mem. bills and jour. com., taxation com., fish and game com. Mont. State Senate, mem. agr., livestock and irrigation com. Republican. Office: PO Box 862 Choteau MT 59422-0862

EKLUND, CARL ANDREW, lawyer; b. Aug. 12, 1943; s. John M. and Zara (Zerbst) E.; m. Nancy Jane Griggs, Sept. 7, 1968; children: Kristin, Jessica, Peter. BA, U. Colo., 1967, JD, 1971. Bar: Colo. 1971, U.S. Dist. Ct. Colo. 1971, U.S. Ct. Appeals (9th cir.) 1975, U.S. Ct. Appeals (10th cir.) 1978, U.S. Supreme Ct. 1978. Dep. dist. atty. Denver Dist. Attys. Office, 1971-73; ptnr. DiManna, Eklund, Ciancio & Jackson, Denver, 1975-81, Smart, DeFurio, Brooks & Eklund, Denver, 1982-84, Roath & Brega, P.C., Denver, 1984-88, Faegre & Benson, Denver, 1988-94, LeBoeuf, Lamb, Greene & MacRae LLP, Denver, 1994—. Mem. local rules com. Bankruptcy Ct. D.C., 1979-80; reporter Nat. Bankruptcy Conf., 1981-82; lectr. ann. spring meeting Am. Bankruptcy Inst., Rocky Mountain Bankruptcy Conf., Continuing Legal Edn. Colo., Inc., Colo. Practice Inst., Colo. Bar Assn., Nat. Ctr. Continuing Legal Edn., Inc., Profl. Edn. Sys., Inc., Comml. Law Inst. Am., Law Edn. Inst., Inc., Bur. Nat. Affairs, Inc., Practising Law Inst., So. Meth. U. Sch. Law, Continuing Edn. Svcs., Lorman Bus. Ctr., Inc. Author: The Problem with Creditors' Committees in Chapter 11: How to Manage the Inherent Conflicts without Loss of Function; contbg. author: Collier's Bankruptcy Practice Guide, Representing Debtors in Bankruptcy, Letters Formbook and Legal Opinion, Advanced Chapter 11 Bankruptcy Practice, mem. adv. bd. ABI Law Rev., 1993-2000; contbr. to law jours. Fellow Am. Coll. Bankruptcy; mem. ABA (bus. law and corp. banking sect. 1977—, bus. bankruptcy com. 1982—, subcom. on rules 1981—), Colo. Bar Assn. (bd. govs. 1980-82, corp. banking and bus. law sect. 1977—, ethics com. 1981-82, subcom. bankruptcy cts.), Am. Bankruptcy Inst. (dir. Rocky Mountain Bankruptcy Conf.), Denver Bar Assn. (trustee 1983-86). Office: LeBoeuf Lamb Greene & MacRae LLP 633 17th St Ste 2000 Denver CO 80202-3620

EKMAN, DONALD J. rental company executive; b. 1952; BA, U. Wash.; JD, Willamette U. Bar: Oreg. 1979. Ptnr. Ekman & Bowersox, 1992-93, v.p., gen. counsel Hollywood Entertainment Corp., Wilsonville, Oreg., 1993—, sr. v.p., gen. counsel, sec. Office: Hollywood Entertainment Corp Hollywood Video 9275 SW Peyton Ln Wilsonville OR 97070 Office Fax: 503-570-1680

ELAM, JASON, professional football player; b. Ft. Walton Beach, Fla., Mar. 8, 1970; m. Tamy; 1 child, Jason Jr. Student, U. Hawaii. Kicker Denver Broncos; player Pro Bowl, 1995, NCF Championship game, 1997, Super Bowl Championship Team, 1997. Avocation: Lic. pilot. Office: Denver Broncos 13655 Broncos Pkwy Englewood CO 80112-4150

ELDER, REX ALFRED, civil engineer; b. Pa., Oct. 4, 1917; s. George Alfred and Harriet Jane (White) E.; m. Janet Stevens Alger, Aug. 10, 1940; children: John A., Carol S., Susan A., William P. BSCE, Carnegie Inst. Tech., 1940; MS, Oreg. State Coll., 1942. Hydraulic engr. TVA, Norris, Tenn., 1942-48, dir. hydraulic lab., 1948-61, dir. engring. lab., 1961-73; engring. mgr. Bechtel Civil & Minerals Inc., San Francisco, 1973-85; cons. hydraulic engr., 1986—. Contbr. numerous articles on hydraulic structures, hydraulic model studies, reservoir stratification and water quality, hydraulic research and hydraulic machinery to profl. jours. Served with USN, 1945-46. Fellow ASCE (hon. 1993, James Laurie prize 1949, Hunter Rouse lectr. 1984, Hydraulic Structures medal 1991), NAE, Internat. Assn. Hydraulic Rsch. (hon.). Home and Office: 501 Via Casitas Apt 424 Greenbrae CA 94904-1947

ELDER, ROBERT LAURIE, newspaper editor; b. Nashville, June 23, 1938; s. Charles Jerome and Dorothea Eloise (Calhoun) E.; m. Betty Ann Doak, Sept. 1, 1958 (div. May 1969); children— Mark Christopher, Jeffrey Cathcart. B.A., Washington and Lee U., 1960; M.A., Vanderbilt U., 1966; postgrad., Stanford U., 1976-77. Reporter Nashville Tennessean, 1964-68; asst. dir. So. Newspaper Pubs. Assn. Found., Atlanta, 1969; reporter The Miami Herald, Fla., 1970-76; editor San Jose (Calif.) Mercury News, 1978—, v.p. editor, 1987—. Bd. dirs. RLM Ptnrs. Author: Crash, 1977. Bd. dirs. Santa Clara U. Ctr. for Applied Ethics, 1987—, Alliance for Cmty. Care, 1997, Nonprofit Devel. Ctr., 1997—. 1st lt. U.S. Army, 1960-62. Recipient Disting. Achievement award Fla. Soc. Newspaper Editors, 1973, White House Conf. on Librs. Pub. award, 1994, Pres. award Calif. Libr. Assn., 1995. Episcopalian Office: San Jose Mercury News 750 Ridder Park Dr San Jose CA 95190-0001

ELDREDGE, BRUCE BEARD, museum director; b. Van Wert, Ohio, July 1, 1952; s. Thomas Harte and Barbara Louise (Beard) E.; m. Janet Duncan Roth, May 17, 1975; children: Lindsay Katherine, Barbara Roth. BA, Ohio Wesleyan U., 1974; MA, Tex. Tech U., 1976; postgrad., SUNY, 1980-81. Dir. Geneva (N.Y.) Hist. Soc. and Mus., 1976-78, Schenectady (N.Y.) Mus., 1978-80; coord. art and humanities Capital Dist. Humanities Program, SUNY, Albany, 1980-81; dir. Frederic Remington Art Mus., Ogdensburg, N.Y., 1981-84, Muskegon (Mich.) Mus. Art, 1984-87, Tucson Mus. Art, 1987-89, Portsmouth (Va.) Mus's., 1991-93, Stark Mus. Art, Orange, Tex., 1993-96, Hubbard Mus. Am. West (formerly Mus. of the Horse), Ruidoso Downs, N.Mex., 1996—. Presenter Gov.'s Conf. on Tourism, Phoenix, 1989; mem. coun. Midwest Mus. Assn., 1986-87, chmn. program ann. meeting, Grand Rapids, Mich., 1987; chmn. Ruidoso Arts Commn., 1996—, Village Visioning Process, 1997—. Vice pres. Schenectady County coun. Boy Scouts Am., 1979-81, Seaway Valley coun., Canton, N.Y., 1982-84, West Mich. Shores coun., Grand Rapids, 1985-87, dist. com. Three Rivers coun., 1992-96, v.p. Three Rivers coun., 1995-96; bd. dirs. Orange Cmty. Concert Assn., 1995-96. Mem. Am. Assn. Mus., Tex. Assn. Mus. (sourcebook editor 1993-96), N.Mex. Mus. Assn. (membership chair), Kokopelli Club, Cree Meadows C.C., Rotary. Republican. Presbyterian. Home: 126 N Eagle Dr Ruidoso NM 88345-6831 Office: The Hubbard Mus PO Box 40 Ruidoso Downs NM 88346-0040 E-mail: bruce@ruidoso.k12.nm.us, eldredge@zianet.com

ELFVING, DON C. horticulturist; b. Albany, Calif., June 20, 1941; BS in Botany, U. Calif., Davis, 1964, MS in Horticulture, 1966; PhD in Plant Physiology, U. Calif., Riverside, 1971. From asst. prof. to assoc. prof. pomology Cornell U., Ithaca, N.Y., 1972-79; rsch. scientist Hort. Rsch. Inst. Ontario, Simcoe, Can., 1979-91, mgr. rsch. programs Vineland, Can., 1991-93; supt. tree fruit rsch. and extension ctr. Wash. State U., Wenatchee, 1993-97, horticulturist, 1997—. Cons. U.S. AID, 1977; cons. Internat. Agrl. Devel. Svc., Ark., 1981-82. Author: Training and Pruning of Apple and Pear Trees, 1992. Recipient U.P. Hedrick 1st Pl. award Am. Pomological Soc., 1992. Mem. Am. Soc. for Hort. Sci. (bd. dirs. 1993-95, chair publs. com. 1993-95), Internat. Dwarf Fruit Tree Assn. (R.F. Carlson Disting. lectr. 1993). Office: Tree Fruit Rsch & Ext Ctr 1100 N Western Ave Wenatchee WA 98801-1230

ELGIN, RON ALAN, advertising executive; b. Milw., Sept. 15, 1941; s. Carl John and Vivian Elaine (Phillips) E.; m. Bonnie Kay Visintainer, Dec. 3, 1968; 1 child, Alison. BA in Advt., U. Wash., 1965. With Cole & Weber, Seattle, 1965-81; pres. Elgin Syferd, Seattle, 1981-89; chmn. Elgin Syferd/Drake, Boise, Idaho, 1987—; pres., CEO Elgin DDB, 1989-99; pres. DDB Needham Retail, Seattle, 2000—. Chmn. Hornall Anderson Design Works, Seattle, 1982-91; ptnr. Christiansen & Fritsch Direct, Seattle, 1988-96; bd. dirs. Hart Crowser; bd. dirs. Ctrl. Media, Inc. Bd. dirs. Ronald McDonald House, Seattle, 1984—, Big Bros., Seattle, 1986—, Spl. Olympics, Seattle, 1987-90, Pacific N.W. Ballet, Seattle, 1988-98, Poncho, Seattle, 1991—, Odyssey, 1993-99, Swedish Hosp., 1995—; mem. adv. bd. U. Wash., Wash. State U. Lt. U.S. Army, 1965-69. Mem. Am. Assn. Advt. Agencies, Am. Mktg. Assn., Mktg. Comm. Execs. Internat. Office: Elgin DDB 1008 Western Ave Seattle WA 98104-1090

ELIAS, ROSALIND, mezzo-soprano; b. Lowell, Mass., Mar. 13, 1931; d. Salem and Shelahuy Rose (Namy) E.; m. Zuhayr Moghrabi. Student, New Eng. Conservatory Music, Accademia di Santa Cecilia, Rome; studies with, Daniel Ferro, N.Y.C. Singer New Eng. Opera, 1948-52, Met. Opera, 1954—; artistic dir. Am. Lyric Theatre. Debut with Boris Goldowsky, Boston, 1948; appeared in numerous roles including Cherubino, Dorabella, Rosina, Hansel, Cenerentola, Carmen, Amneris and Azucena (Verdi), Charlotte and Giulietta (Massenet), Herodias, 1987; originated role of Erika in Vanessa (Samuel Barber) and Cleopatra in Antony and Cleopatra (Barber); also appeared with Scottish Opera, Vienna Staatsoper, Glynbourne Festival, many others; prodr. Carmen, Cin., 1988, Il Barbiere di Siviglia, Opera Pacific, Costa Mesa, Calif., 1989; recs. for RCA and Columbia records include La Gioconda, La Forza del Destno, Il Trovatore, Falstaff, Madama Butterfly, Rigoletto, Der fliegende Holländer. Mem. Sigma Alpha Iota.

ELIASSEN, JON ERIC, utility company executive; b. Omak, Wash., Mar. 10, 1947; s. Marvin George and Helen Grace (Meyer) E.; m. Valerie A. Foyle, Aug. 14, 1971; 1 child, Michael T. BA in Bus., Wash. State U., 1970. Staff acct. Wash. Water Power Co., Spokane, 1970-73, tax acct., 1973-76, fin. analyst, 1976-80, treas., 1980-86, v.p. fin., CFO, 1986-96; sr. v.p., CFO Avista Corp., Spokane, 1996—. Bd. dirs. Itron Corp. Trustee Wash. State U. Found., Pullman, 1987, NW Mus. Art & Culture, 1998—; treas. Wash. State U. Found., 1995-97; trustee Spokane Symphony, 1989-95, treas., 1990-95, mem. endowment bd.; pres. Spokane Intercollegiate Rsch. & Tech. Inst. Found., 1996-2000; mem. Western Energy Inst. (bd. dirs., chair-elect); bd. dirs. Sirti. Mem. Fin. Exec. Inst. (bd. dirs., sec., past pres. Inland N.W. chpt. 1983—). Episcopalian. Avocations: skiing, traveling, bicycling, photography. Office: Avista Corp PO Box 3727 Spokane WA 99220-3727

ELIKANN, LAWRENCE S. (LARRY ELIKANN), television and film director; b. N.Y.C., July 4, 1923; s. Harry and Sadye (Trause) E.; m. Corinne Schuman; Dec. 6, 1947; children— JoAnne Jarrin, Jill Barad. B.A., Bklyn. Coll., 1943; E.E., Walter Harvey Coll., 1948. Tech. dir. NBC-TV, N.Y.C., 1948-64; comml. dir. VPI-TV, N.Y.C., 1964-66, Filmex-TV, N.Y.C., 1966-68, Plus two TV, N.Y.C., 1968-70. Dir. mini-series Last Flight Out, The Great L.A. Earthquake, The Big One, The Inconvenient Woman, Fever, Story Lady, One Against the Wind, Bonds of Love, I Know My First Name is Steven, Hands of a Stranger, Kiss of a Killer, God Bless the Child, Out of Darkness, Menendez—A Killing in Beverly Hills, Tecumseh—The Last Warrior, A Mother's Prayer, Blue River, "Unexpected Family", Lies He Told. Mem. Mus. Contemporary Art of L.A., L.A. County Mus.; mem. rsch. coun. Scripps Clinic and Rsch. Found. With Signal Corps, U.S. Army, 1943-46. Recipient Emmy award, 1978-79, 89, Golden Globe award, 1989, 91, 94, Christopher award 1973-76, 77, 78-79, 91, Chgo. Internat. Film Festival award 1977, Internat. Film and TV Festival of N.Y. award, 1977, Dir. of Yr. award Am. Ctrs. for Children, 1978; Humanitas prize, 1988, 94, 96. Mem. NATAS (gov. 1961-63), Dirs. Guild Am., Am. film Inst., Nat. Hist. Preservation Soc., Smithsonian Inst., Scripps Inst. (bd. dirs.), Acad. TV Arts and Scis.

ELINSON, HENRY DAVID, artist, language educator; b. Leningrad, USSR, Dec. 14, 1935; came to U.S., 1973; s. David Moses and Fraida Zelma (Ufa) E.; m. Ludmila Nicholas Tepina, Oct. 7, 1955; 1 child, Maria Henry. Student, Herzen State Pedagogical U., Leningrad, 1954-57; BA, Pedagogical Inst., Novgorod, USSR, 1958; MA, Pedagogical Inst., Moscow, 1963. Cert. educator. Spl. edn. tchr. Leningrad Sch. Spl. Edn., 1961-64; supr. dept. speech therapy Psychoneurological Dispensary, Leningrad, 1964-73; instr. Russian lang. Yale U., New Haven, 1975-76, Def. Lang. Inst., Presidio of Monterey, Calif., 1976-94. One-man shows include The Light and Motion Transmutation Galleries, N.Y.C., 1974, Thor Gallery, Louisville, 1974, Monterey (Calif.) Peninsula Art Mus., 1977, U. Calif. Nelson Gallery, Davis, 1978, Nahamkin Gallery, N.Y.C., 1978, Nahamkin Fine Arts, N.Y.C., 1980, Gallery Paule Anglim, 1981, 85, 87, Gallery Paule Anglim, San Francisco, 1991, 93, 96, 99, 2000, Dostoevsky's Mus., St. Petersburg, Russia, 1992, Mus. Art Santa Cruz, Calif., 1994, Duke U. Mus. Art, 1996, Mead Art Mus, 1998, Mus. of Non Conformist Art, St. Petersburg, Russia, 2000; exhibited in group shows at Bklyn. Coll. Art Ctr., 1974, CUNY, 1974, Galleria Il Punto, Genoa, Italy, 1975, New Art From the Soviet Union, Washington, 1977, Gallery Hardy, Paris, 1978, Mus. of Fine Art, San Francisco, 1979, Santa Cruz Mus. Fine Arts, 1994, V. Morlan Gallery Transylvania U., Lexington, Ky., 1995, numerous others; represented in permanent collections Mus. Fine Arts, San Francisco, Yale U. Art Gallery, Monterey Mus. Art, U. Calif. Art Mus., Berkeley, Bochum Mus., Germany, Check Point Charlie Mus., Berlin, State Russian Mus., Leningrad, Zimmerly Art Mus., Rutgers U., N.J., Duke U Mus. Art, 1996, Mead Art Mus., 1998, Mus. of St. Petersburg History, Mus. Non Conformist Art, State Hermitage, St. Petersburg, others. Mem. Underground Anti-Soviet Govt. Students' Orgn., 1957. Recipient Gold medal Art Achievement City of Milan, 1975. Avocations: travel, writing essays and short stories. Home: 997 Benito Ct Pacific Grove CA 93950-5333

ELIOT, THEODORE LYMAN, JR. international consultant; b. N.Y.C., Apr. 14, 1951; m. Patricia F. Peters. B.A., Harvard U., 1948, M.P.A., 1956; LL.D., U. Nebr., Omaha, 1975. With U.S. Fgn. Svc., 1949-78; spl. asst. to under sec. of state; to sec. treasury; country dir. for Iran Dept. State; exec. sec. State Dept.; also spl. asst. to sec. of state Dept. State; ambassador to Afghanistan; insp. gen. Dept. State., Washington; dean Fletcher Sch. Law and Diplomacy, Tufts U., 1979-85; exec. dir. Ctr. for Asian Pacific Affairs Asia Found., San Francisco, 1985-87. Bd. dirs. Neurobiol. Tech., Fiberstars, Cornell Lab. of Ornithology. Trustee Asia Found. Mem. Am. Acad. Diplomacy, Univ. Club (San Francisco).

ELKINS, CARL, food products executive; b. 1932; Attended, Taft Coll., 1955-57. Potato broker Higby & Sons, Bakersfield, Calif., 1957-60; office mgr. Sycamore Farms, Arvin, 1960-63; salesman, office and packing house mgr. Miller & Lux Corp., Bakersfield, 1963-72; pvt. practice, 1972-74; salesman Demont Packing Co., Victor, Calif., 1974-76; various positions Delta Packing Co., Lodi, 1976-99, pres.; now pres. Leeman Mettlar. With USAF, 1951-55. Office: Delta Packing Co 6021 E Kettleman Ln Lodi CA 95240-6400

ELKINS, DAVID J. political science educator; b. Ft. Madison, Iowa, July 29, 1941; BA, Yale U., 1963; MA, U. Calif., Berkeley, 1964, PhD, 1971. Asst. prof. polit. sci. U. B.C., Vancouver, Can., 1969-75, assoc. prof. Can., 1975-80, prof. Can., 1980—, head dept. polit. sci. Can., 1985-89, acting dean of arts, 1989-90. Vis. prof. Queen's U., Kingston, Ont., Can., 1984-85, U. Toronto, 1991. Author: Electoral Participation in a South Indian Context, 1975, Manipulation and Consent, 1993, Beyond Sovereignty, 1995; co-author: Survey Research, 1976, Small Worlds, 1980, Two Political Worlds, 1985; contbr. articles to profl. jours. Mem. Assn. Can. Studies Austrialia and New Zealand, Am. Polit. Sci. Assn., Am. Assn. Pub. Opinion Research, Can. Polit. Sci. Assn. (pres. 1988-89), Australasian Polit. Sci. Assn., Can. Civil Liberties Union, Can. Wildlife Fedn. Avocations: skiing, hiking. Home: 1355 Saturna Dr Parksville BC Canada V9P 2T5 Office: Univ BC Dept Polit Sci Vancouver BC Canada V6T 1Z1

ELKINS, GLEN RAY, retired service company executive; b. Winnsboro, La., May 23, 1933; s. Ceicel Herbert and Edna Mae (Lewallen) E.; m. Irene Kay Hildebrand, Aug. 25, 1951; children: Steven Breen, Douglas Charles, Karen Anne, Michael Glen; m. Diane Hodgson, Mar. 2, 1992. AA in Indsl. Mgmt, Coll. San Mateo, 1958. Successively mgr. production control, mgr. logistics, plant mgr., asst. v.p. ops. Aircraft Engring. and Maintenance Co., 1957-64; from mgr. field ops. to pres. Internat. Atlas Svcs. Co., Princeton, N.J., 1964-85; sr. v.p. Atlas Corp., Princeton; chmn., CEO, dir. Global Assocs., 1973-85; pres. Global Assocs. Internat. Ltd., 1975-84; pres., CEO Triad Am. Svcs. Corp., 1985-2000; pres. Pacific Mgmt. Svcs. Corp., TASC Enterprises Inc., dba Gottschall Engraving Co., 1993-2000; ret., 2000. Area chmn. Easter Seals drive, 1974; bd. dirs. Utah Children's Mus. With USN, 1950-54. Mem. Nat. Mgmt. Assn., Electronic Industries Assn., Lakeview Club, Willow Creek Country Club (past pres.). Home: 1445 Harvard Ave Salt Lake City UT 84105-1917 E-mail: greikinsut@aol.com

ELLEGOOD, DONALD RUSSELL, publishing executive; b. Lawton, Okla., June 21, 1924; s. Claude Jennings and Iva Claire (Richards) E.; m. Bettie Jane Dixon, Dec. 11, 1947; children— Elizabeth Nemi, Francis Hunter, Kyle Richards, Sarah Helen. B.A., U. Okla., 1948, M.A., 1950. Asst. editor U. Okla. Press, 1950-51; editor Johns Hopkins Press, 1951-54; dir. La. State U. Press, 1954-63, U. Wash. Press, Seattle, 1963—. Contbr. articles to profl. jours. Served to 1st lt. USAAF, 1943-46. Decorated Air medal, D.F.C. Mem. Am. Univ. Pubs. Group London (dir.), Am. Assn. Univ. Presses (pres.), Phi Beta Kappa. E-mail. Home: 17852 49th Pl NE Seattle WA 98155-4312 Office: U Wash Press PO Box 50096 Seattle WA 98145-5096 E-mail: DREedit@aol.com

ELLICKSON, BRYAN CARL, economics educator; b. Bklyn., Feb. 12, 1941; s. Raymond Thorwald and Loene (Gibson) E.; m. Phyllis Lynn Rutter, June 19, 1965; 1 child, Paul Bryan. BA, U. Oreg., 1963; PhD, MIT, 1970. From asst. prof. to assoc. prof. UCLA, 1968-83, prof., 1983—, chair econs. dept., 1996-99. Cons. Rand, Santa Monica, Calif., 1970—. Author: Competitive Equilibrium, 1993; contbr. articles to profl. jours. Rsch. grantee HUD, 1979-81, NSF, 1982-87. Mem. Am. Econ. Assn., Econometric Soc. Avocation: scuba diving. Home: 18409 Wakecrest Dr Malibu CA 90265-5620 Office: UCLA Dept Econs 405 Hilgard Ave Los Angeles CA 90095-1477 E-mail: ellickson@econ.ucla.edu

ELLINGSON, JON ERIC, state legislator; b. Rochester, N.Y., Aug. 21, 1948; m. Kathy Ellingson; 3 children. BA, Harvard U., 1970; MA, U. Mont., 1972; JD, U. Calif., 1974. Vol. Vista, 1970; atty., pvt. practice of law, 1975—; mem. Mont. Ho. of Reps., 1995-98, Mont. Senate, Dist. 33, Helena, 1998—; mem. taxation com., mem. edn. and cultural resources com. Mont. State Sanate, mem. fish and game com. Formerly bd. dirs. Missioula Specialized Transp. Sys., Regional Chem. Dependency Program; formerly bd. dirs. Missoula Mus. Arts; mem. adv. coun. Mont. Dept. Family Svcs. Democrat. Home: 430 Ryman St Missoula MT 59802-4249 E-mail: jee@mssl.uswest.net

ELLINGTON, JAMES WILLARD, retired mechanical design engineer; b. Richmond, Ind., May 26, 1927; s. Oscar Willard and Leola Lenora (Sanderson) E.; m. Sondra Elaine Darnell, Dec. 6, 1952 (dec. Jan. 1997); children: Ronald, Roxanna; m. Vada M. Jellsey, Oct. 10, 1998. BSME summa cum laude, West Coast U., L.A., 1978. Designer NATCO, Richmond, Ind., 1954-67; design engr. Burgmaster, Gardena, Calif., 1967-69; sr. mfg. engr. Xerox Co., El Segundo, 1969-84, cons. mem. engring. staff Monrovia, 1984-87; staff engr. Photonic Automation, Santa Ana, Calif., 1987-88; sr. mech. engr. Optical Radiation Co., Azusa, 1988; sr. staff engr. Omnichrome, Chino, 1988-96, ret., 1996. With USN, 1945-52. Mem. Soc. Mfg. Engrs. (sec. 1984). Republican. Baptist. Avocation: gardening.

ELLIOT, DAVID CLEPHAN, historian, educator; b. Larkhall, Scotland, Sept. 17, 1917; came to U.S., 1947, naturalized, 1954; s. John James and Edith Emily (Bell) E.; m. Nancy Franelle Haskins, Dec. 3, 1945 (dec.); children: Enid Frances, John Clephan, Nancy Elizabeth. M.A., St. Andrews U., 1939; A.M., Harvard U., 1948, Ph.D., 1951; M.A., Oxford U., 1956, postgrad. (Ford fellow), 1956-57. With Indian Civil Service, 1941-47; teaching fellow Harvard U., 1948-50; asst. prof. history Calif. Inst. Tech., Pasadena, 1950-53, asso. prof., 1953-60, prof., 1960-86, prof. emeritus, 1986—; chmn. Calif. Inst. Tech. (75th Anniversary), 1965-67, exec. officer for humanities and social scis., 1967-71. Trustee Westridge Sch., 1970-90, trustee emeritus, 1992—, pres., 1976-78. With Royal Arty., 1940. NATO fellow, 1980 Mem. Inst. Current World Affairs (gov. 1964-70, chmn. 1969-70, trustee 1979-82, hon. trustee 1992—). Home: 1251 Inverness Dr Pasadena CA 91103-1115 Office: Calif Inst Tech Div Humanities & Social Scis 1200 E California Blvd Pasadena CA 91125-0001 E-mail: DCE@HSS.Caltech.edu

ELLIOTT, CHARLES HAROLD, clinical psychologist; b. Kansas City, Mo., Dec. 30, 1948; s. Joseph Bond and Suzanne (Wider) E.; 1 child, Brian Douglas. BA, U. Kans., 1971, MA, 1974, PhD, 1976. Cert. clin. psychologist, N. Mex. Asst. prof. East Ctrl. U., Ada, Okla., 1976-79, U. Okla. Health Scis., 1979-85; assoc. prof. dept. psychiatry U. Okla., 1983-85, U. N. Mex.

Sch. Medicine, Albuquerque, 1985-87; adj. assoc. prof. dept. psychology U. N.Mex., Albuquerque, 1986—; faculty full appointment Fielding Inst., Santa Barbara, Calif., 1987—. Consulting editor Jour. Clin. Child Psychology, 1987-89; ad hoc reviewer to profl. jours., 1983—; cognitive therapist NIMH Collaborative Study of Depression, Okla. City, 1980-85. Co-author: (with Maureen K. Lassen) Why Can't I Get What I Want, 1998, (with Laura L. Smith) Why Can't I Be the Parent I Want to Be?, 1999, (with Laura L. Smith) Hollow Kids: Recapturing the Soul of a Generation Lost to the Self-Esteem Movement, 2001; guest editor Psychiatric Annals, 1992; contbr. numerous articles to profl. jours. Fellow Acad. Cognitive Therapy (founding); mem. APA, Biofeedback and Behavioral Medicine Soc. N.Mex. (pres. 1988), Assn. for Advancement of Behavior Therapy, Assn. for Advancement Psychology, Soc. Behavioral Medicine, Soc. Pediat. Psychology, N.Mex. Psychol. Assn. (bd. dirs. 1992-96). Home: 4200 Killington Rd NW Albuquerque NM 87114-5563 Office: 212 Gold Ave SW # 202 Albuquerque NM 87102-3320

ELLIOTT, DAVID DUNCAN, III, science research company executive; b. L.A., Aug. 4, 1930; s. David Duncan Elliott II and Mildred B. (Young) Mack; m. Arline L. Leckrone, Aug. 18, 1962; children: Lauren, Elliott Croft. BS, Stanford U., 1951; MS, Calif. Inst. Tech., 1953, PhD, 1959. Mem. tech. staff Lockheed Rsch. Lab., Palo Alto, Calif., 1959-61; postdoctoral fellow U. Paris., 1962; dept. head Aerospace Corp., El Segundo, Calif., 1961-70; sci. advisor Nat. Aeronautics and Space Coun., Washington, 1970-72; sr. staff mem. exec. office of pres. NSC, Washington, 1972-77; v.p. SRI Internat., Menlo Park, Calif., 1977-86; sr. v.p. Sci. Applications Internat. Corp., San Diego, 1986-91, Syst Control Tech., Palo Alto, Calif., 1991-94; corp. v.p. Sci. Applications Internat. Corp., Palo Alto, 1994-95; cons., 1995-99; cons. prof. Ctr. Internat. Security & Coop., Stanford (Calif.) U., 1999—. Mem. Army Sci. Bd., The Pentagon, Washington, 1982-89; cons. NRC, NAS, 1988—; mem. bd. visitors U. Calif., Davis, 1997—. Mem. editorial bd. Jour. Def. Rsch., 1988—. Recipient Outstanding Civilian Svc. award U.S. Army, 1989. Mem. AIAA, AAAS, Am. Phys. Soc., Am. Geophys. Union. Home: 2434 Sharon Oaks Dr Menlo Park CA 94025-6829 Office: CISAC Encina Hall Stanford CA 94305-6165

ELLIOTT, EMORY BERNARD, English language educator, educational administrator; b. Balt., Oct. 30, 1942; s. Emory Bernard and Virginia L. (Ulbrick) E.; m. Georgia Ann Carroll, May 14, 1966; children: Scott, Mark, Matthew, Laura, Constance. A.B., Loyola Coll., Balt., 1964; M.A., Bowling Green State U., 1966; Ph.D., U. Ill., 1972. Instr. Cameron Coll., Lawton, Okla., 1966-67, U.S. Mil Acad., West Point, N.Y., 1967-69; from asst. prof. to prof. English, Princeton U., N.J., 1972-89, chmn. Am. studies program, 1976-82, master Lee D. Butler Coll., 1982-86, chmn. English dept., 1987-89; Pres.'s chair English U. Calif., Riverside, 1989-91, disting. prof., 1992—, univ. prof., 2001—; dir. Ctr. for Ideas and Soc., 1996—. Writing cons. Bell Labs., Holmdel, N.J., 1975-79, RCA, Princeton, 1980-81; edn. cons. Western Electric Corp. Edn. Ctr., Hopewell, N.J., 1974-79 Author: Power and the Pulpit in Puritan New England, 1975, Puritan Influences in American Literature, 1979, Revolutionary Writers: Literature and Authority in the New Republic, 1982, The Literature of Puritan New England in The Cambridge History of American Literature, Vol. 1, 1994; editor: Dictionary of Literary Biography, 3 Vols., 1606-1810, 1983-84; editor: Columbia Literary History of the United States, 1988 (Am. Book award 1988), American Literature: A Prentice Hall Anthology 3 Vols., 1990, Columbia History of The American Novel, 1991, The Jungle, 1991, Wieland, 1994, Huckleberry Finn, 1998, Aesthetics and Difference: Cultural Diversity, Literature and the Arts, 2001; series editor Am. Novel Series, 1985—, Critical Studies in Contemporary Am. Fiction, 1987—; mem. editorial bd. Am. Quar., 1976-80, PMLA, 1990-92, Am. Lit., 1995—, Modern Fiction Studies, 1993—, Ill. Studies Lang. Lit., 1993—, Studies in Am. Puritan Spirituality, 1991—; mem. adv. com. Gale Bibliography of Am. Lit., 1981—; editor-at-large Am. Studies Internat., 1993—. Served to capt. U.S. Army, 1966-69. Fellow Woodrow Wilson Found., 1971-72, Am. Coun. Learned Socs., 1973, Guggenheim Found., 1976, Nat. Humanities Ctr. 1979-80, NEH, 1986-87, Inst. for Rsch. in the Humanities, 1991-92, Ford found., 1998-2000—, Rockefeller Found., 2000—; Richard Stockton preceptor Princeton U., 1975-78. Mem. MLA (chmn. Early Am. lit. div., Am. lit. div. 1991). Office: U Calif Dept English Riverside CA 92521-0001 E-mail: Emory.Elliott@ucr.edu

ELLIOTT, GORDON JEFFERSON, retired English language educator; b. Aberdeen, Wash., Nov. 13, 1928; s. Harry Cecil and Helga May (Kennedy) E.; m. Suzanne Tsugiko Urakawa, Apr. 2, 1957; children: Meiko Ann, Kenneth Gordon, Nancy Lee, Matthew Kennedy. AA, Grays Harbor Coll., 1948; BA, U. Wash., 1950; Cert. Russian, Army Lang. Sch., Monterey, Calif., 1952; MA, U. Hawaii, 1968. Lifetime credential, Calif. Community Coll. System. English prof. Buddhist U., Ministry of Cults, The Asia Found., Phnom Penh, Cambodia, 1956-62; English instr. U. Hawaii, Honolulu, 1962-68; dir., orientation English Coll. Petroleum and Minerals, Dhahran, Saudi Arabia, 1968-70; asst. prof., English/linguistics U. Guam, Mangilao, 1970-76; tchr., French/English Medford (Oreg.) Mid High Sch., 1976-77; instr., English Merced (Calif.) Coll., 1977-98, ret., 1998. Cons. on Buddhist Edn., The Asia Found., San Francisco, Phnom Penh, Cambodia, 1956-62; cons. on English Edn., Hawaii State Adult Edn. Dept., Honolulu, 1966-68; conf. on English Edn. in Middle East, Am. U., Cairo, Egypt, 1969; vis. prof. of English, Shandong Tchrs. U., Jinan, China, 1984-85. Co-author: (textbooks, bilingual Cambodian-English) English Composition, 1962, Writing English, 1966, (test) Standard English Recognition Test, 1976; contbr. articles to profl. jours. Mem. Statue of Liberty Centennial Commn., Washington, 1980-86, Heritage Found., Washington, Rep. Presdl. Task Force Founders' Wall, 2001, Lincoln Inst., Am. Near East Refugee Aid, Washington, Rep. Presdl. Task Force, 2001. Sgt. U.S. Army Security Agy., Kyoto, Japan, 1951-55. Tchr. Fellowship, U. Mich., Ann Arbor, 1956; recipient summer seminar stipend, Nat. Endowment For Humanities, U. Wash., Seattle, 1976, travel grants, People's Rep. of China, Beijing, 1984-85. Mem. NRA, Collegiate Press (editorial adv. bd.), Merced Coll. Found., Am. Assn. Woodturners, Elks. Republican. Avocations: swimming, woodturning, classical guitar, stamp/coin collecting, travel. Home: 680 Dennis Ct Merced CA 95340-2410 Office: Merced Coll 3600 M St Merced CA 95348-2806 E-mail: gjelliott@aol.com

ELLIOTT, JAMES HEYER, retired art museum curator, fine arts consultant; b. Medford, Oreg., Feb. 19, 1924; s. Bert R. and Marguerite E. (Heyer) E.; m. Judith Ann Algar, Apr. 23, 1966 (div.); children: Arabel Joan, Jakob Maxwell. BA, Willamette U., Salem, Oreg., 1947, DFA (hon.), 1978; AM, Harvard U., 1949; DFA (hon.), San Francisco Art Inst., 1991. James Rogers Rich fellow Harvard U., 1949-50; Fulbright grantee Paris, 1951-52; art critic European edit. N.Y. Herald-Tribune, 1952-53; curator, acting dir. Walker Art Center, Mpls., 1953-56; asst. chief curator, curator modern art Los Angeles County Mus. Art, 1956-63, chief curator, 1964-66; dir. Wadsworth Atheneum, Hartford, Conn., 1966-76, Univ. Art Mus., Berkeley, Calif., 1976-88, chancellor's curator, 1989-90, dir. emeritus, 1990—. Adj. prof. Hunter Coll., N.Y.C., 1968, U. Calif., Berkeley, 1976-90; commr. Conn. Commn. Arts, 1970-76; fellow Trumbull Coll., Yale U., 1971-75; mem. mus. arts panel Nat. Endowment Arts, 1974-77; bd. dirs. San Francisco Art Inst., 1980-90; art adv. com. Exploratorium, 1982-91; adv. com. Artists TV Access, 1987-90. Author: Bonnard and His Environment, 1964, James Lee Byars: Notes Towards a Biography, 1990. Trustee Marcia Simon Weisman Found., 1991—, 23 FIVE Found., San Francisco, 1993—, di Rosa Preserve, Napa, Calif., 1996—; mem. adv. bd. Artspace San Francisco, 1989—. With USNR, 1943-46. Mem. Am. Assn. Mus., Artists Space N.Y. (bd. dirs. 1980-84), Arts Club (Berkeley). Home: 13 Yellow Ferry Hbr Sausalito CA 94965-1327

ELLIOTT, JIM, state senator; b. Pottstown, Pa., Dec. 26, 1942; m. Tootie; 1 child, Elizabeth. BA, San Francisco State U., 1969; postgrad., U. Pa. Rancher; Dem. rep. Mont. Ho. of Reps., 1989-97; Dem. senator dist. 36 Mont. State Senate, 2000—. Mem. adminstrn., local govt. and edn. and cultural resources com. Mont. State Senate. Dist. supr. Green Mountain Conservation. Office: 100 Trout Creek Rd Trout Creek MT 59874 Fax: 406 827-3220. E-mail: jim@jimelliot.org

ELLIOTT, JOHN GREGORY, aerospace design engineer; b. Soerabaya, Dutch East Indies, Nov. 9, 1948; came to U.S., 1956; s. Frans Jan and Charlotte Clara (Rosel) E.; m. Jennifer Lee Austin, May 7, 1988. AA, Cerritos Coll., 1974; BS, Calif. State U., Long Beach, 1978. Design engr. Boeing Airplane Co., Long Beach, 1978-82, lead engr., 1983-89, sect. mgr. elect. installations group, 1989—. With USN, 1969-73. Mem. So. Calif. Profl. Engring. Assn., The Boeing Co. Tennis Club, The Boeing Co. Surf Club, The Boeing Co. Mgmt. Club. Republican. Presbyterian. Avocations: sailing, guitar, reading, remote-control gliders, painting. Office: Boeing Aircraft Co Long Beach Divsn Internal Mail Code 82-83 Long Beach CA 90846-0001 E-mail: john.g.elliott@boeing.com

ELLIOTT, LEE ANN, company executive, former government official; b. June 26, 1927; BA, U. Ill. V.p. Bishop, Bryant amd Assocs., Inc., 1979-81; mem. Fed. Election Commn., Washington, 1981-2000, chmn., 1884, 90, 96; pres. Form Meets Function Enterprises, Inc., Chandler, Ariz., 2000—. Lectr., author and inventor in field. Bd. dirs., pres. Chgo. Area Pub. Affairs Group; bd. dirs. Kids Voting, USA. Mem. Am. Med. Polit. Action Com. (asst. dir. 1961-70, assoc. exec. dir. 1970-79), Am. Assn. Polit. Cons. (bd. dirs.), Nat. Assn. Mfrs. (award of excellence), U.S. C. of C. (pub. affairs com.). Office: Form Meets Function Enterprises Inc 820 W Warner Rd Ste 123 Chandler AZ 85225-2940

ELLIOTT, STEVE, newspaper editor; Bur. chief AP, Phoenix, 1998—. Address: 500 N 3d St Ste 120 Phoenix AZ 85004

ELLIS, ALVIN, state legislator, farmer, rancher; b. Red Lodge, Mont., July 11, 1936; m. Maureen Ellis. BS in Animal Scis. Farmer, rancher; mem. Mont. State Ho. of Reps., 1991-98, Mont. Senate, Dist. 12, Helena, 1998—; mem. labor and employment rels. com., mem. taxation com. Mont. Senate; mem. edn. and cultural resources com. Mont. State Senate. Served to 2d lt. U.S. Army, also Res. Trustee Sch. Bd. Republican. Home: HC 50 Box 4840 Red Lodge MT 59068-9724

ELLIS, CARLENE, computer company executive; children: Stephanie, Jason. BS in Maths., U. Ga., 1969. Electrical engr. Western Electric; computer programmer U. Ga.; info. sys. officer City of Jacksonville; with Fairchild Camera & Instrument; mgr. planning and control corp. info. sys. Intel Corp., 1980-83, dir. sales and mktg. adminstrn., 1983-85, dir. corp. info. svcs., 1985-87, v.p. corp. info. sys., 1987-89, corp. officer, 1989, v.p. fin. and adminstrn., 1988-90, v.p. human resources, 1990-93; v.p. info. tech., 1993-98; v.p., dir. edn., 1999—. Dir. Merix Corp., fellow Am. Leadership Forum. Recipient Bus. Month's Corp. Women on the Move award, 1989, CIO 100 award, 1994, 96, 97, Bay Area's Most Powerful Corp. Women award San Francisco Chronicle, 1995. Mem. Delta Gamma. Office: Intel Corp PO Box 58119 2200 Mission College Blvd Santa Clara CA 95052-8119 E-mail: carlene.ellis@intel.com

ELLIS, ELDON EUGENE, surgeon; b. Washington, July 2, 1922; s. Osman Polson and Ina Lucretia (Cochran) E.; m. Irene Clay, June 26, 1948 (dec. 1968); m. Priscilla Dean Strong, Sept. 20, 1969 (dec. Feb. 1990); children: Paul Addison, Kathe Lynn, Jonathan Clay, Sharon Anne, Eldon Eugene, Rebecca Deborah; m. Virginia Michael Ellis, Aug. 22, 1992. BA, U. Rochester, 1946, MD, 1949. Intern in surgery Stanford U. Hosp., San Francisco, 1949-50, resident and fellow in surgery, 1950-52, 55; Schilling fellow in pathology San Francisco Gen. Hosp., 1955; ptnr. Redwood Med. Clinic, Redwood City, Calif., 1955-87, med. dir., 1984-87; semi-ret. physician, 1987—; med. dir. Peninsula Occupl. Health Assocs., San Carlos, Calif., 1991-94, physician, 1995-99, Sequoia Med. Clinic, Redwood City, Calif., 1999—. Asst. clin. prof. surgery Stanford U., 1970-80; dir. Sequoia Hosp., Redwood City, 1974-82. Pres. Sequoia Hosp. Found., 1983-92, bd. dirs.; pres., chmn. bd. dirs. Bay Chamber Symphony Orch., San Mateo, Calif., 1988-91; mem. Nat. Bd. Benevolence Evang. Covenant Ch., Chgo., 1988-93; mem. mgmt. com. The Samarkand Retirement Cmty., Santa Barbara, Calif., 1991-2000; past pres. Project Hope Nat. Alumni Assn., 1992-94, bd. dirs., 1994—; med. advisor Project Hope, Russia Commonwealth Ind. States, 1992. With USNR, 1942-46, 50-52. Named Outstanding Citizen of Yr., Redwood City, 1987. Mem. AMA, Calif. Med. Assn., Am. Coll. Chest Physicians, Am. Heart Assn. (v.p. 1974-75), Calif. Heart Assn. (pres. 1965-66), San Mateo County Heart Assn. (pres. 1961-63), San Mateo Med. Soc. (pres. 1969-70), San Mateo County Comprehensive Health Planning Coun. (v.p. 1969-70), San Mateo Surg. Soc., Stanford Surg. Soc., San Mateo Individual Practice Assn. (treas. 1984-97), Cardiovasc. Coun., Calif. Thoracic Soc., Commonwealth Club. Republican. Mem. Peninsula Convenant Ch. Home: 2305 Wooster Ave Belmont CA 94002-1549 Office: Sequoia Med Clinic 633 Veterans Blvd Redwood City CA 94063-1408 E-mail: eldonellis@hotmail.com

ELLIS, EMORY LEON, former biochemist; b. Grayville, Ill., Oct. 29, 1906; s. Walter Leon and Bertha May (Forman) W.; m. Marion Louise Faulkner, Sept. 17, 1930 (dec. Aug. 1994). BS, Calif. Inst. Tech., 1930, MS in Chemistry, 1932, PhD in Biochemistry, 1934. Registered profl. engr., Calif. Chemist U.S. FDA, L.A., 1934-35; rsch. assoc. CalTech, Pasadena, 1935-43; dept. head U.S. Navy Ordnance Test Sta., China Lake, Calif., 1943-54; dir. ordnance plan Rheem Ordnance Lab, Downey, 1954-57; project leader Inst. for Def. Analysis, Washington, 1957-63; cons. U.S. Navy Weapons Ctr., China Lake, 1966-68. Ptnr. Devcom, La Habra, Calif., 1965-68. Contbr. chpt. in books and articles to profl. jours. Recipient Naval Ordnance Devel. award USN, 1945, Alumni Disting. Svc. award Calif. Inst. Tech., 1970; Paul Harris fellow Rotary Internat., 1993. Mem. AAAS, Am. Chem. Soc., Tau Beta Pi, Sigma Xi. Avocations: writing essays, travel. Home: 506 Pioneer Ct Santa Maria CA 93454-3442

ELLIS, GEORGE EDWIN, JR. chemical engineer; b. Beaumont, Tex., Apr. 14, 1921; s. George Edwin and Julia (Ryan) E. BSChemE, U. Tex., 1948; MS, U. So. Calif., 1958, MBA, 1965, MS in Mech. Engring., 1968, MS in Mgmt. Sci., 1971, Engr. in Indsl. and Systems Engring., 1979. Rsch. chem. engr. Tex. Co., Port Arthur, 1948-51, Houston and Long Beach, Calif., 1952-53, Space and Info. Divsn., N.Am. Aviation Co., Downey, 1959-61, Magna Corp., Anaheim, 1961-62; chem. process engr. AiResearch Mfg. Co., L.A., 1953-57, 57-59; chem. engr. Petroleum Combustion & Engring. Co., Santa Monica, Calif., 1957, Jacobs Engring. Co., Pasadena, 1957, Sesler & Assocs., L.A., 1959; rsch. specialist Marquardt Corp., Van Nuys, Calif., 1962-67; sr. project engr. Conductron Corp., Northridge, 1967-68; info. systems asst. L.A. Dept. Water and Power, 1969-92. Instr. thermodynamics U. So. Calif., L.A., 1957. With USAAF, 1943-45. Mem. ASTM, ASME, AIChE, Nat. Assn. Purchasing Mgmt., Nat. Contract Mgmt. Assn., Am. Inst. Profl. Bookkeepers, Am. Soc. Safety Engrs., Am. Chem. Soc., Am. Soc. Materials, Am. Electroplaters and Surface Finishers Soc., Nat. Assn. Corrosion Engrs., Inst. Indsl. Engrs., Am. Prodn. and Inventory Control Soc., Am. Soc. Quality, Am. Indsl. Hygenists Assn., Steel Structure Painting Coun., Soc. Plastics Engrs., Inst. Mgmt. Accts., Soc. Mfg. Engrs., L.A. Soc. Coating Tech., Assn. Finishing Processes, Chem. Coatings Assn. Internat., Pi Tau Sigma, Phi Lambda Upsilon, Alpha Pi Mu. Home: 1344 W 20th St San Pedro CA 90732-4408

ELLIS, GEORGE RICHARD, museum administrator; b. Birmingham, Ala., Dec. 9, 1937; s. Richard Paul and Dorsie (Gibbs) E.; m. Sherroll Edwards, June 20, 1961 (dec. 1973); m. Nancy Enderson, Aug. 27, 1975; 1 son, Joshua. BA, U. Chgo., 1959, MFA, 1961; postgrad., UCLA, 1971. Art supr. Jefferson County Schs., Birmingham, 1962-64; asst. dir. Birmingham Mus. Art, 1964-66, UCLA Mus. Cultural History, 1971-81, assoc. dir., 1981-82; dir. Honolulu Acad. Arts, 1981—. Author various works on non-western art, 1971— . Bd. dirs. Children's Lit. Hawaii, Japan Am. Soc.; humanities adv. com. mem. Hawaii Pacific U., 1995—; cmty. adv. bd. Japanese Cultural Ctr., 1997—; sec.-treas. Social Sci. Club, 1985—. Recipient Ralph Altman award UCLA, 1968; recipient Outstanding Achievement award UCLA, 1980; fellow Kress Found., 1971 Mem. Pacific Arts Assn. (v.p. 1985-89, exec. bd. 1989—), Hawaii Mus. Assn. (v.p. 1986-87, pres. 1987-88, pres. 1996-97, 97-98), Assn. Art Mus. Dirs., Am. Assn. Mus., L.A. Ethnic Arts Coun. (hon.), Friends of Iolani Palace (bd. dirs.), Pacific Club. Office: Honolulu Academy Arts 900 S Beretania St Honolulu HI 96814-1495

ELLIS, JAMES REED, lawyer; b. Oakland, Calif., Aug. 5, 1921; s. Floyd E. and Hazel (Reed) E.; m. Mary Lou Earling, Nov. 18, 1944 (dec.); children: Robert Lee, Judith Ann (dec.), Lynn Earling, Steven Reed. B.S., Yale, 1942; J.D., U. Wash., 1948; LL.D., Lewis and Clark U., 1968, Seattle U., 1981, Whitman Coll., 1992. Bar: Wash. 1949, D.C. 1971. Ptnr. Preston, Thorgrimson, Horowitz, Starin & Ellis, Seattle, 1952-69, Preston, Thorgrimson, Starin, Ellis & Holman, Seattle, 1969-72, Preston, Thorgrimson, Ellis, Holman & Fletcher, Seattle, 1972-79; sr. ptnr. Preston, Thorgrimson, Ellis & Holman, Seattle, 1979-90, Preston, Thorgrimson, Shidler, Gates & Ellis, Seattle, 1990-92; ret., of counsel Preston, Gates & Ellis, Seattle, 1992—; chmn., CEO Wash. State Convention and Trade Ctr., Seattle, 1986—. Dep. pros. atty. King County, 1952; gen. counsel Municipality of Met. Seattle, 1958-79; dir., mem. exec. com. Key Bank of Wash., 1969-94, KIRO, Inc., 1965-95; dir. Blue Cross of Wash. and Alaska, 1989-98. Mem. Nat. Water Commn., 1970-73; mem. urban transp. adv. council U.S. Dept. Transp., 1970-71; mem. Wash. Planning Adv. Council, 1965-72; mem. Washington State Growth Strategies Commn., 1989-90; pres. Forward Thrust Inc., 1966-73; chmn. Mayors Com. on Rapid Transit, 1964-65; trustee Ford Found., 1970-82, mem. exec. com., 1978-82; bd. regents U. Wash., 1965-77, pres., 1972-73; trustee Resources for the Future, 1983-92; mem. council Nat. Mcpl. League, 1968-76, v.p., 1972-76; chmn. Save our Local Farmlands Com., 1978-79, King County Farmlands Adv. Commn., 1980-82; pres. Friends of Freeway Park, 1976-99; bd. dirs. Nat. Park and Recreation Assn., 1979-82; trustee Lewis and Clark U., 1988-94; pres. Mountains to Sound Greenway Trust, Inc., 1991—; trustee Henry M. Jackson Found., 1992—. 1st lt. USAAF, 1943-46. Recipient Bellevue First Citizen award, 1968, Seattle First Citizen award, 1968, Nat. Conservation award Am. Motors, 1968, Distinguished Service award Wash. State Dept. Parks and Recreation, 1968, Distinguished Citizen award Nat. Municipal League, 1969, King County Distinguished Citizen award, 1970, La Guardia award Center N.Y.C. Affairs, 1975, Environ. Quality award EPA, 1977, Am. Inst. for Public Service Nat. Jefferson award, 1974, State Merit medal State of Wash., 1990, Nat. Founders award Local Initiatives Support Corp., 1992, Henry M. Jackson Disting. Pub. Svc. medal, 1998, U. Wash. Alumnus Summa Laude Dignatus award, 1999. Fellow Am. Bar Found.; mem. ABA (ho. dels. 1978-82, past chmn. urban, state and local govt. law sect.), Nat. Assn. Bond Lawyers (com. standards of practice), Wash. Bar Assn., Seattle Bar Assn. (Pres.'s award 1993), D.C. Bar Assn., Am. Judicature Soc., Acad. Pub. Adminstrn., Coun. on Fgn. Rels., Mcpl. League Seattle and King County (past pres.), Order of Hosp. of St. John of Jerusalem, AIA (hon.), Order of Coif (hon.), Phi Delta Phi, Phi Gamma Delta, Rainier Club (Seattle). Home: 903 Shoreland Dr SE Bellevue WA 98004-6738 Office: 5000 Bank of America Tower 701 5th Ave Seattle WA 98104-7097 Fax: (206) 623-7022. E-mail: jamese@prestongates.com

ELLIS, JANICE RIDER, nursing educator, consultant; b. Sioux City, Iowa, Mar. 13, 1939; d. Evert Alvin and Lillian June (Hanson) Rider; m. Ivan R. Ellis, Aug. 3, 1959; children: Mark Allen, Anne Grace Ellis Wiley. BSN, U. Iowa, 1960; MN, U. Wash., 1971; Phd, U. Tex., 1990. RN, Wash. Staff nurse various hosps., Wash., Oreg., Iowa; prof., dir. nursing edn. Shoreline C.C., Seattle. Rschr. in field. Author textbooks; contbr. to profl. jours.; cons. in field. Mem. ANA, Nat. League Nursing, Wash. State Nurses Assn., Sigma Theta Tau, Phi Kappa Delta. Office: Shoreline C C 16101 Greenwood Ave N Seattle WA 98133-5667

ELLIS, JOHN MARTIN, German literature educator; b. London, May 31, 1936; came to U.S., 1966, naturalized, 1972; s. John Albert and Emily (Silvey) E.; m. Barbara Stephanie Rhoades, June 28, 1978; children: J. Richard, Andrew W., Katherine M., Jill E. B.A. with 1st class honours, U. London, 1959, Ph.D., 1965. Tutorial asst. German Univ. Coll., Wales, Aberystwyth, 1959-60; asst. lectr. U. Leicester, Eng., 1960-63; asst. prof. U. Alta., Edmonton, Can., 1963-66; mem. faculty U. Calif., Santa Cruz, 1966—, prof. German, 1970-94, prof. emeritus, 1994, dean grad. div., 1977-86. Vis. prof. U. Kent, Canterbury, Eng., 1970-71 Author: Schiller's Kalliasbriefe and the Study of His Aesthetic Theory, 1969, Kleist's Prinz Friedrich von Homburg: A Critical Study, 1970, Narration in the German Novelle, 1974, The Theory of Literary Criticism: A Logical Analysis, 1974, Heinrich von Kleist: Studies in the Character and Meaning of His Writings, 1979, One Fairy Story Too Many: The Brothers Grimm and Their Tales, 1983, Against Deconstruction, 1989, Language, Thought and Logic, 1993, Literature Lost: Social Agendas and the Corruption of the Humanities, 1997 (Peter Shaw Meml. award). Served with Brit. Army, 1954-56. Fellow Guggenheim Found., 1970-71; Fellow NEH, 1975-76, 92. Mem. NAS, ACLA, Am. Assn. Tchrs. German, Internat. Assn. Germanic Studies, Assn. Lit. Scholars and Critics (sec.-treas. 1994—). E-mail: gallusjme@aol.com

ELLIS, JOHN W. professional baseball team executive, utility company executive; b. Seattle, Sept. 14, 1928; s. Floyd E. and Hazel (Reed) R.; m. Doris Stearns, Sept. 1, 1953; children: Thomas R., John, Barbara, Jim. B.S., U. Wash., 1952, J.D., 1953. Bar: Wash. State bar 1953. Ptnr. Perkins, Coie, Stone, Olsen & Williams, Seattle, 1953-70; with Puget Sound Power & Light Co., Bellevue, Wash., 1970—, exec. v.p., 1973-76, pres., CEO, 1976-87, also dir., chmn., CEO, 1987-92, chmn. bd., 1992—, bd. dirs., 1993—; dir., chmn. Seattle br. Fed. Res. Bank of San Francisco, 1982-88; CEO, Seattle Mariners, 1992-99, chmn. emeritus, 1999—. Mem. Wash. Gov.'s Spl. Com. Energy Curtailment, 1973-74; mem. Wash. Gov.'s Coun. on Edn., 1991—; chmn. Pacific N.W. Utilities Coordinating Com., 1976-82; bd. dirs. Wash. Mut. Savs. Bank, Seattle, SAFECO Corp., Nat. Energy Found., 1985-87, FlowMole Corp., Assoc. Electric & Gas Ins. Svcs. Ltd.; chmn. Electric Power Rsch. Inst., 1984—; chmn., CEO, The Baseball Club of Seattle, L.P.; regent Wash. State U., 1992—. Pres. Bellevue Boys and Girls Club, 1969-71, Seattle/King County Econ. Devel. Council, 1984—; mem. exec. dirs. Seattle/King County Boys and Girls Club, 1972-75; bd. dirs. Overlake Hosp., Bellevue, 1974— , United Way King County, 1977— , Seattle Sci. Found., 1977— , Seattle Sailing Found., Evergreen Safety Council, 1981, Assn. Wash. Bus., 1980-81, Govs. Adv. Council on Econ. Devel., 1991—; chmn. bd. Wash. State Bus. Round Table, 1983, pres. United for Washington; adv. bd. Grad. Sch. Bus. Adminstrn. U. Wash., 1982—, Wash. State Econ. Ptnrship., 1984—; chmn. Seattle Regional Panel White Ho. Fellows, 1985—; trustee Seattle U., 1986—. Mem. ABA, Wash. Bar Assn., King County Bar Assn., Nat. Assn. Elec. Cos. (dir. 1977-79), Edison Electric Inst. (dir. 1978-80, exec. com. 1982, 2d vice chmn. 1987, 1st vice chmn. 1988, now chmn.), Assn. Edison Illuminating Cos. (exec. com. 1979-81), Seattle C. of C. (dir. 1980—, 1st vice chmn. 1987-88, chmn. 1988—), Phi Gamma Delta, Phi Delta Phi. Clubs: Rainier

(Seattle) (sec. 1972, v.p. 1984, pres. 1985), Seattle Yacht (Seattle), Corinthian Yacht (Seattle); Meydenbauer Bay Yacht (Bellevue), Bellevue Athletic. Lodge: Rotary (Seattle). Home: 901 Shoreland Dr SE Bellevue WA 98004-6738 Office: Seattle Mariners PO Box 4100 83 King St Seattle WA 98104-2860 also: Puget Sound Power & Light Co PO Box 97034 Bldg Bellevue WA 98009-9734

ELLIS, JOHNNY, state legislator; b. Springfield, Mo., Mar. 13, 1960; Student, U. Alaska, 1978-79; BA with honors, Claremont McKenna Coll., 1982. Owner Alaska Natural; co-owner Macuir Co.; mem. Alaska Ho. of Reps., 1986-92, Alaska Senate, Dist. H, Juneau, 1992—. Co-chair tourism working group, health task froce, adolescent pregnancy and parenting task force; commr. Western Interstate Commn. for Higher Edn. Active Fairview Cmty. Coun., Anchorage Econ. Devel. Corp., Mt. View Cmty. Ctr. Fundraising Dr., Mental Health Parity Task Force, 1998. Recipient Mayor's award for hist. preservation, Golden Key award A.R.C.A., Primary Health Care award, Adv. for Alaska's Children award, 1998; named Outstanding Rep., S.T.A.R. Mem. Am. Mktg. Assn. (Alaska chpt.). Democrat. Office: State Capitol 120 rth St Rm 9 Juneau AK 99801-1182 also: 716 W 4th Ave Ste 440 Anchorage AK 99501-2107 Fax: 907-465-2529/907-269-0172

ELLIS, ROBERT HARRY, retired television executive, university administrator; b. Cleve., Mar. 2, 1928; s. John George Ellis and Grace Bernice (Lewis) Ellis Kline; m. Frankie Jo Lanter, Aug. 7, 1954; children: Robert Harry Jr., Kimberley Kay Ellis Murphy, Shana Lee. BA, Ariz. State U., 1953; MA, Case Western Res. U., 1962. Newswriter, announcer Sta. KOY, Phoenix, 1953-55, continuity dir., 1955-61; dir., radio ops. Ariz. State U., Tempe, 1959-61; gen. mgr. Sta. KAET-TV, Tempe, 1961-87; assoc. v.p. Ariz. State U., Tempe, 1986-90. Exec. com. bd. dirs. Pub. Broadcasting Svc., Washington, 1972-77, 80-86; founder Pacific Mountain Network, Denver, 1972, pres., 1973-75; mem. ednl. telecomm. com. Nat. Assn. Ednl. Broadcasters, Washington, 1973-77, 80-86. Mem. Sister City, Tempe, Tempe Ctr. For the Handicapped, East Valley Mental Health Alliance, Mesa, Ariz., Ariz. Acad., State Ariz. Behavior Health Bd. of Examiners, 1991-92. Recipient Bd. Govs. award Pacific Mountain Network, 1987, achievement award Ariz. State U., 1997; named to Ariz. Broadcasters Hall of Fame, 1999. Mem. Nat. Assn. TV Arts and Scis. (life, v.p., bd. trustees 1969-70, bd. dirs. Phoenix chpt. 1986, silver circle award 1992), Nat. Assn. Pub. TV Stas. (bd. dirs. 1988-94), Tempe C. of C. (diplomate, bd. dirs. 1987-90), Sundome Performing Arts Assn. (bd. dirs. 1986-90), Ariz. Zool. Soc. (bd. dirs., sec. 1984-90), Ariz. State U. Alumni Assn. (life), Ariz. State U. Retirees Assn. (founder, pres. 1991-92), Tempe Conv. and Visitors Bur. (founder, sec./treas. 1988-93), Tempe Sports Authority (founder 1989-95), ASU Faculty Emeritus Orgn. (pres. 1992-93). Methodist. Avocations: tennis, racquetball, bridge.

ELLISON, CYRIL LEE, literary agent, retired publisher; b. N.Y.C., Dec. 11, 1916; m. Anne N. Nottonson, June 4, 1942. Assoc. pub., v.p. Watson-Guptill Publs., 1939-69, v.p., advt. dir., 1939-69, assoc. pub. Am. Artist mag.; exec. v.p. Communication Channels, Inc., N.Y.C., 1969-88; pub. emeritus Fence Industry, Access Control, Pension World, Trusts & Estates, Nat. Real Estate Investor, Shopping Center World; pres. Lee Comms., 1980—; assoc. Kids Countrywide, Inc., 1987-94; literary agent, 1994—. Pub. cons., book rep., advt. and mktg. cons., 1987-94; assoc. Mark Clements Rsch. N.Y., Inc., 1994—; pub. cons. Mag. Rsch. Mktg. Co., 1994—. Served with USAAF, 1942-46, PTO. Named Gray-Russo Advt. Man of Year Ad Men's Post Am. Legion, 1954; recipient Hall of Fame award Internat. Fence Industry Assn., 1985. Mem. Am. Legion (life, comdr. advt. men's post 1954, 64). Home: 6839 N 29th Ave Phoenix AZ 85017-1213 Office: Lee Communications 5060 N 19th Ave Phoenix AZ 85015-3210

ELLISON, DAVID R. career officer; BS, U.S. Naval Acad., 1970; MS, George Washington U., 1975; PhD in Bus. Adminstrn., Pa. State U., 1984; postgrad., Harvard U., 1989. asst. prof. U.S. Naval Acad., 1973-76. Ensign USN, 1970, advanced through ranks to rear adm.; various assignments to superintendent Naval Postgrad. Sch., 2000—. Decorated Def. Superior Svc. medal, Legion of Merit (3 awards), Bronze Star (with Combat V), Meritorious Svc. medal (3 awards), Navy Commendation medal, Navy Achievement medal, Coast Guard Achievement medal, others; fellow CNO Strategic Studies Group, Naval War Coll. Office: 1 University Cir Rm M11 Monterey CA 93943-5019

ELLISON, HERBERT JAY, history educator; b. Portland, Oreg., Oct. 3, 1929; s. Benjamin F. and Esther (Anderson) E.; m. Alberta M. Moore, June 13, 1952; children: Valery, Pamela. BA, U. Wash., 1951, MA, 1952; PhD (Fulbright fellow), U. London, 1955. Instr. history U. Wash., 1955-56; asst. prof. history U. Okla., 1956-62; asso. prof. history, chmn. Slavic studies program U. Kans., 1962-67, dir. NDEA Lang. and Area Center Slavic Studies, 1965-67, prof., 1965-68, asso. dean faculties internat. programs, 1967-68; prof. history, Russian and Eastern European studies U. Wash., 1968—, dir. div. internat. programs, 1968-72, vice provost for ednl. devel., 1969-72, dir. Inst. Comparative and Fgn. Area Studies, 1973-78, chmn. Russian and East European studies, 1979-83; sec. Kennan Inst. Advanced Russian Studies, Washington, 1983-85. Trustee Nat. Coun. for Russian and East European Rsch., 1983-87; dir. Russian rsch. Nat. Bur. Asian Rsch., 1990—, bd. dirs., 1993—; chmn. bd. dirs. Internat. Rsch. and Exchs. Bd., 1992-98; dir. The New Russia in Asia rsch. and conf. project, 1993-96; chmn. acad. coun. Kennan Inst. for Advanced Russian Studies, 1997-2001; bd. govs. Blakemore Found., 1998—. Author: History of Russia, 1964, Sino-Soviet Conflict, 1982, Soviet Policy Toward Western Europe, 1983, Japan and the Pacific Quadrille, 1987; co-author: Twentieth Century Russia, 1999; chief cons., exec. dir. (PBS/BBC TV series) Messengers from Moscow, 1995, (PBS TV spl.) Yeltsin, 2000 ; contbr. articles to profl. jours. Mem. AAUP, Am. Hist. Assn., Am. Assn. Advancement of Slavic Studies, Univ. Club. Home: 12127 SE 15th St Bellevue WA 98005-3821 Office: Univ Wash Jackson Sch Internat Study PO Box 353650 Seattle WA 98195-3650 E-mail: chellison@u.washington.edu

ELLISON, LAWRENCE J. computer software company executive; b. 1944; BS. With Amdahl, Inc., Santa Clara, Calif., 1967-71, systems architect; pres. systems div. Omex Corp., 1972-77; with Oracle Corp., Redwood, Calif., 1977—, chmn., CEO, 1978—, also bd. dirs. Recipient Disting. Info. Scis. award Assn. Info. Tech. Profls., 1996. Office: Oracle Corp 500 Oracle Pkwy MSC 5OPCEO Redwood Shores CA 94065-1675

ELLMAN, JONATHON ANTHONY, chemist; BS in Chemistry, MIT, 1984; PhD in Organic Chemistry, Harvard U., 1989. NSF postdoctoral fellow U. Calif., Berkeley, 1989-92, asst. prof., 1992-97, assoc. prof., 1997-98, prof., 1999—. Co-organizer NAS Symposium on Combinatorial Chemistry, 1997; sci. co-founder Sunesis Pharms., 1998; bd. dirs. Lake Tahoe Symposia. Assoc. editor Jour. Combinatorial Chemistry, 1998; guest editor spl. issue Combinatorial Chemistry, Accounts Chem. Rsch., 1996, Current Opinion in Chem. Biology, 1998; mem. editl. bd. Molecular Diversity, 1996-98. Recipient Burroughs Wellcome 1993 Hitchings award for drug design and discovery, 1993-97, Young Investigator award Arnold and Mabel Beckman Found., 1993-95, Young Investigator award NSF, 1993-98, Young Investigator award Office Naval Rsch., 1994-97, Cyanamid Faculty award, 1994, Burroughs Wellcome Fund New Initiatives in Malaria Rsch. award, 1997; named Procter and Gamble Young Investigator, 1994-96; grantee Eli Lilly, 1994-96; Predoctoral fellow NSF, 1984-87, postdoctoral fellow NSF, 1989-91, Alfred P. Sloan fellow, 1994-96; James Bryant Conant scholar, 1984, Texaco Philanthropist scholar, 1984. Mem. Am. Chem. Soc. (mem. long range planning com. medicinal chemistry divsn. 1996-98, Arthur C. Cope Scholar award 2000). Office: Dept Chemistry Univ Calif Berkeley CA

ELLMAN, MARK, chef, restaurant owner; b. L.A., Aug. 26, 1955; married; three children. Cook Texas Tommy's Hamburger Stand, San Fernando Valley, 1969; owner Can't Rock and Roll But Sure Can Cook, L.A., 1975, Avalon Restaurant, Maui, 1989, Maui Tacos, 1995—. Avocations: sailing, movies. Office: Avalon Restaurant 844 Front St Lahaina HI 96761-1626

ELLNER, CAROLYN LIPTON, university dean, consultant; b. Jan. 17, 1932; d. Robert Mitchell and Rose (Pearlman) Lipton; m. Richard Ellner, June 21, 1953; children: D. Lipton, Alison Lipton. AB cum laude, Mt. Holyoke Coll., 1953; AM, Columbia Tchrs. Coll., 1957; PhD with distinction, UCLA, 1968. Tchr., prof., administr. N.Y. and Md., 1957-62; prof. dir. tchr. edn., assoc. dean Claremont Grad. Sch., Calif., 1967-82; prof., dean sch. edn. Calif. State U., Northridge, 1982-98, dean emerita, 1998—. Pres., CEO On-the-Job Parenting. Co-author: Schoolmaking, 1977, Studies of College Teaching, 1983 (Orange County Authors award 1984). Trustee Ctr. for Early Edn., L.A., 1968-71, Oakwood Sch., L.A., 1972-78, Mt. Holyoke Coll., South Hadley, Mass., 1979-84; commr. Economy and Efficiency com., L.A., 1974-82, Calif. Commn. Tchr. Credentialing, 1987-90, 93—, vice chair, 1995-96, chair, 1996-98; bd. dirs. Found. for Effective Govt., L.A., 1982, Calif. Coalition for Pub. Edn., 1985-88, Valley Hosp. Found., 1992-94, Mt. Holyoke Alumnae Assn. Bd., 1993-96; founding dir. Decade of Edn., 1990; assoc. dir. New Devel. in Sci. Project NSF, 1985-94; bd. dirs., chair edn. com. Valley Industry and Commerce Assn., 1990-93, v.p. 1993-94; co-prin. dir. Mid South Calif. Arts Project, 1991-98; mem. coun., trustees L.A. Alliance for Restructing Now (LEARN), 1992-2000; bd. dirs. Inner City Arts Found., 1993-96; involved with L.A. Annenberg Met. Project (LAAMP); exec. bd. DELTA, 1995—, Calif. Subject Matter Projects, 1998—. Ford Found. fellow 1964-67, fellow Ednl. Policy Fellowship Program, 1989-90; recipient Office of Edn. award U.S. Office of Edn., 1969-72, Alumnae medal of honor Mt. Holyoke Coll., 1998; W.M. Keck Found. grantee, 1983, 94. Mem. ASCD, Am. Edn. Rsch. Assn., Am. Assn. Colls. for Tchr. Edn., Nat. Soc. for Study of Edn. E-mail: carolyn.ellner@csun.edu

ELLS, STEVE, food company executive; b. Indpls., Sept. 12, 1965; BA in Art History, U. Colo.-Boulder, 1988; grad., Culinary Inst. Am., 1990. Cook Stars Restaurant, San Francisco; founder, CEO Chiptole Mexican Grill, 1993—. Office: Chipotile Mexican Grill Corp Office 2401 E 1st Ave Denver CO 80206-5616

ELLSWORTH, FRANK L. non-profit executive; b. Wooster, Ohio, May 20, 1943; s. Clayton Sumner and Frances (Fuller) E.; 1 child, Kirstin Lynne. BA, Western Res. Coll., 1965; MEd, Pa. State U., 1967; MA, Columbia U., 1969; PhD, U. Chgo., 1976; LLD, Pepperdine U., 1997. Asst. dir. devel. Columbia Law Sch., 1968-70; dir. spl. projects, prof. lit. Sarah Lawrence Coll., N.Y., 1971; asst. dean Law Sch., U. Chgo., 1971-79, instr. social sci. collegiate div., 1975-79; pres., prof. polit. sci. Pitzer Coll., Claremont, Calif., 1979-91; pres. Ind. Colls. So. Calif., L.A., 1991-97; v.p. Capital Rsch. & Mgmt. Co., 1997—. Pres. Endowments, Inc. Author: The Foundation of the 21st Century, Law on the Midway, 1977, Student Activism in American Higher Education; contbr. articles to profl. jours. Trustee, chmn., exec. com. Japanese Am. Nat. Mus., Pitzer Coll., Ind. Colls. So. Calif., Southwestern U.; chmn. Am. Sch. Internat. Studies, Seattle, Global Ptnrs. Inst., Can. Global Ptnrs., Ctr. for the Preservation of Democracy. Recipient Disting. Young Alumnus award Case Western Res. U., 1981, True of Life award United Jewish Fund, 1991. Mem. History of Edn. Soc., Coun. for Advancement of Secondary Edn., Young Pres.'s Orgn., Ukiyo-e Soc., Asia Soc. Home: 254 La Mirada Rd Pasadena CA 91105-1019 Office: The Capital Group 333 S Hope St 33d Fl Los Angeles CA 90071-1406

ELLWOOD, PAUL MURDOCK, JR. health policy analyst, consultant; b. San Francisco, July 16, 1926; s. Paul Ellwood and Rebecca May (Logan) E.; divorced; children: David, Cynthia, Deborah. B.A., Stanford U., 1949, M.D., 1953. Dir. Kenny Rehab. Inst., Mpls., 1962-63; exec. dir. Am. Rehab. Found., Mpls., 1963-73; dir. Inst. Interdisciplinary Studies, Mpls., 1970-73; pres. InterStudy, health policy analysis Excelsior, Minn., 1973-85; pres. Paul Ellwood & Assocs., Excelsior, 1985-87; chmn. bd., pres. InterStudy, 1987-92; pres. Jackson Hole Group, Tenton Village, Wy., 1992—; founding dir. Found. for Accountability/Quality Measure for Healthcare, Portland, Oreg., 1997—. Dir., mem. exec. com. Jackson Hole Ski Corp., Wyo., 1972-87; clin. prof. phys. medicine and rehab., neurology and pediatrics U. Minn. Med. Sch.; cons. in health and delivery systems. Co-author: Assuring The Quality of Health Care, 1973; Co-editor: Handbook of Physical Medicine and Rehabilitation, 2d edit, 1971. Served with USNR, 1944-46. Recipient award Ministry Pub. Health, Republic Argentina, 1957; 1st award sci. exhibit Am. Acad. Neurology, 1958; citation President's Com. Employment Handicapped, 1962; Gold Key award Am. Congress Rehab., 1971; named Distinguished fellow Am. Rehab. Found., 1973 Mem. Inst. Medicine, Group Health Assn. Am. (dir. 1975-76), Nat. Health Council (dir. 1971-76), Assn. Rehab. Centers (pres. 1960-61, U.S. Healthcare Quality award 1991) Home: PO Box 165 Bondurant WY 82922-0165 Office: Jackson Hole Group PO Box 270 Bondurant WY 82922-0270

EL-MOSLIMANY, ANN PAXTON, paleoecologist, educator, writer; b. Fullerton, Calif., Aug. 2, 1937; d. Donald Dorn and Sarah Frances (Turman) Paxton; m. Mohammed Ahmad El-Moslimany, May 31, 1962; children: Samia, Ramsey, Rasheed. BS, N.Mex. State U., 1959; MS, Am. U., Beirut, 1961; PhD, U. Wash., 1983. Tchr. various schs., 1959-83, Kuwait U., 1984-86, Seattle Ctrl. C.C., 1986-90; prin., tchr. Islamic Sch. Seattle, 1989-99, curriculum coord., 1999—. Paleoecological rschr. Palynological Consultants, 1987—. Author: Zaki's Ramadan Fast, 1994; contbr. articles to sci. jours.; mem. adv. bd. Muslim Kaleidescope mag., Sisters mag. Mem. Amnesty Internat., Am. Quaternary Assn., Nat. Coun. Tchrs. Math., Geog. Alliance of Wash., Seattle Islamic Sisterhood. Home: PO Box 367 Seahurst WA 98062-0367 Office: Islamic Sch Seattle 720 25th Ave Seattle WA 98122-4902 E-mail: annelmoslimany@yahoo.com

ELROD, LU, music educator, actress, author; b. Chattanooga, Apr. 23, 1935; d. John C. Elrod and Helen Pauline (Kohn). MusB, Ga. State U., 1960; M in Music Edn., U. Ga., 1970, EdD, 1971; PhD, U. London, 1975. Prof. music, music coach U. Md., Balt., 1972-78, Calif. State U., L.A., 1978—. Singer with Dallas (Tex.) Opera, 1957. Appeared in movies Brewster's Millions, 1986, Major Pettigrew and Me, 1976, Seduction of Joe Tynan, 1977, Atlanta Child Murders, 1985, Children Don't Tell, 1986, For Love or Money, 1986, High School High, 1996, Wag the Dog, 1997, The Big Lebowski, 1998, Primary Colors, 1998, Lloyd the Ugly Kid, 1999, Beautiful, 1999, Glory Days, 2001; appeared on TV in Lazarus Syndrome, 1980, Hill Street Blues (Emmy award), 1988, Superior Court, 1988, TV Bloopers, 1989, Beakman's World (Emmy award), Dream On, 1993, Misery Loves Company, 1995, Caroline in the City, 1995, Louie, 1996, George and Alana, 1996, Maggie, 1998, Two Guys and a Girl, 2000, Glory Days, 2001; appeared in TV comms. Recipient Leadership Devel. award Ford Found., 1967, Leadership Fellows award Ford Found., 1968; Tift Coll. voice scholar, 1953, Baylor U. voice scholar, 1956; Lu Elrod scholarship named at Calif. State U., L.A., 1989. Mem. AAUP, AFTRA, SAG, Am. Guild Variety Artists, Calif. Faculty Assn., Coll. Music Soc. Avocations: philanthropy, fundraising. Office: Calif State Univ 5151 State University Dr Los Angeles CA 90032-4226 E-mail: lelrod@calstatela.edu

ELSBREE, LANGDON, English language educator; b. Trenton, N.J., June 23, 1929; s. Wayland Hoyt and Miriam (Jenkins) E.; m. Aimee Desiree Wildman, June 9, 1952; 1 child, Anita. BA, Earlham Coll., 1952; MA, Cornell U., 1954; PhD, Claremont Grad. Sch., 1963. Instr. in English Miami U., Oxford, Ohio, 1954-57, Harvey Mudd Coll., Claremont, Calif., 1958-59; instr. humanities Scripps Coll., Claremont, 1959-60; instr., prof. Claremont McKenna Coll., 1960-94, prof. emeritus, 1994; mem. grad. faculty Claremont Grad. Sch., 1965—. Part-time lectr. Calif. State U., L.A., 1968-70; vis. prof. Carleton Coll., 1987. Author: The Rituals of Life, 1982, Ritual Passages and Narrative Structures, 1991; co-author: Heath College Handbook, 6th-12th edits., 1967-90; guest editor D.H. Lawrence Rev., 1975, 87. Bd. dirs. Claremont Civic Assn., 1964-66; mem. founding com. Quaker Studies in Human Betterment, Greensboro, N.C., 1987. Fulbright Commn. lectr., 1966-67; grantee NEH, 1975, Claremont McKenna Coll., 1980, 82, 87. Mem. AAUP, MLA, Friends Assn. Higher Edn., D.H. Lawrence Soc. (exec. bd. 1990), Virginia Woolf Soc., Coll. English Assn., Sci. Fiction Rsch. Assn., Phi Beta Kappa. Democrat. Mem. Soc. of Friends. Avocations: traveling, reading, swimming, films, photography. Office: Claremont McKenna Coll Bauer Ctr 890 Columbia Ave Claremont CA 91711-3901 E-mail: lelsbree@earthlink.net

ELTON, KIM STEVEN, state legislator, pollster; b. Havre, Mont., Apr. 9, 1948; s. Claude Reginald and Shirley May (Hammer) E.; m. Mary Lou Cooper, Nov. 9, 1989. Reporter, editor Fairbanks (Alaska) Daily News-Miner, 1973-76; editor Juneau (Alaska) Empire, 1976-78; comml. fisherman Alaska, 1978-79; policy dir. Lt. Gov. Terry Miller, Juneau, 1979-82, contract writer, mem. legis. staff, 1983-89; from mem. staff to exec. dir. Alaska Seafood Mktg. Inst., Juneau, 1989-94; mem. Alaska Ho. of Reps., Juneau, 1994-98, Alaska Senate, Dist. B, Juneau, 1998—. Ptnr. Infomatrix, Juneau, 1994—. With U.S. Army, 1969-71, Vietnam. Democrat. Avocations: black and white photography, golf, hiking. Office: State Senate Rm 504 State Capitol Juneau AK 99801-1182

ELTRINGHAM, THOMAS JAMES GYGER, telecommunications professional; b. Riverside, Calif., Nov. 4, 1943; s. Thomas Lamar and May Katharyn (Gyger) E.; m. Hana Libuse Strachen, Jan. 21, 1966 (Feb. 1978); m. Lydia Rose Boss, Oct. 4, 1980; children: Glenn Alexander, Eric Douglas. HSST, Hubbard Coll., Copenhagen, 1969. Ordained to ministry. Minister Ch. of Scientology, L.A. and Clearwater, Fla., 1961-83; installations mgrs. Am. Sun, Inc., Commerce, Calif., 1984-86; v.p. ops. Power Ins. Inc., Santa Fe Springs, 1986-90; dir. L.D. Svcs., Inc., Santa Fe Springs, 1990-98; CEO GCC Telecomm. Inc., 1991-98; ret., 1998. Contbr. articles to profl. jours.; developer drug rehab. program, L.A., 1966. Chmn. bd. trustees Eltringham Family Found. Mem. Internat. Assn. Scientologists. Republican. Avocations: tennis, skiing, reading, computers, golf.

ELWAY, JOHN ALBERT, retired professional football player; b. Port Angeles, Wash., June 28, 1960; s. Jack Elway; m. Janet Elway; 2 daughters: Jessica Gwen, Jordan Marie. BA in Econs., Stanford U., 1983. Quarterback Denver Broncos, 1983-98; ret., 1998. Mem. Mayor's Council on Phys. Fitness, City of Denver; chmn. Rocky Mountain region Nat. Kidney Found. Played Super Bowl XXI, 1986, XXII, 1987, XXIV, 1989; named to Sporting News Coll. All-Am. team, 1980, 82, Sporting News NFL All-Pro team, 1987, Pro Bowl team, 1986, 87, 89, 91, 93, 94.

ELY, GARY G. utilities company executive; Grad., Brigham Young U.; postgrad., U. Idaho, Stanford U., Edison Elec. Inst. Leadership. With Avista Corp., Spokane, 1967—, v.p. mktg., 1986-91, v.p. natural gas, 1991-95, sr. v.p., 1996-97, pres., CEO, 1997—. Mem. State Bldg. Code Coun. Mem. Pacific Coast Gas Assn. (chmn. gas mgmt. exec. com., chmn. mktg. exec. com., bd. dirs.), N.W. Electric Light and Power Assn. (bd. dirs.), Spokane Valley C. of C. (exec. bd.), N.W. Gas Assn. (bd. dirs.). Office: Avista Corp 1411 E Mission Ave Spokane WA 99202-2600

ELY, PARRY HAINES, dermatologist, educator; b. Washington, Sept. 19, 1945; s. Northcutt and Marica (McCann) E.; m. Elizabeth Magee, June 24, 1969 (div. June 1998); children: Sims, Rebecca, Meredith, Tess. AB, Stanford U., 1967; MD, U. So. Calif., 1971. Diplomate Am. Bd. Dermatology, Am. Bd. Pathology; lic. dermatologist, Calif. Intern in medicine U. So. Calif.-L.A. County Med. Ctr., 1971-72, resident in dermatology, 1972-75; clin. prof. dermatology U. Calif., Davis, 1975—. Bd. dirs. Nevada City Wineries Mem. editl. bd. Calif. Physician, 1994—; manuscript reviewer Archives of Internal Medicine, 1988—, Annals of Internal Medicine, 1980—, Archives of Dermatology, 1977—; contbr. articles to med. jours. Fellow Am. Acad. Dermatology (asst. editor jour. 1988-94, manuscript reviewer 1994—), Am. Soc. Dermatopathology; mem. AMA, Internat. Soc. for Tropical Dermatology, Am. Fedn. for Clin. Rsch., Am. Soc. for Dermatologic Surgery, N.Am. Clin.. Dermatologic Soc., Calif. Med. Assn. (alt. del. 1995—, rep. to Calif. Telehealth/Telemedicine coord. project planning com. 1996—), Pacific Dermatologic Soc. (Nelson Paul Anderson Meml. Essay 1st pl. award 1979, Mini Presentation of Yr. award 1984), Noah Worcester Dermatol. Soc., Cutaneous Therapy Soc., Soc. Investigative Dermatology, Sacramento Valley Dermatol. Soc. (pres. 1990-91), Placer Nev. Med. Soc. (bd. dirs. 1978-79, 91-93, v.p. 1994, pres. 1995), Skin Cancer Found. (med. coun. 1987—), Tri-County Am. Cancer Soc. (bd. dirs. 1978-79, 91-92), Royal Soc. Medicine (London), Dermatology Found., Space Dermatology Found. (founding mem.), Shivas Irons Soc. (founding mem.) Office: Brunswick E # 7 10565 Brunswick Rd Grass Valley CA 95945-9053

EMANUEL, WILLIAM JOSEPH, lawyer; b. Hawthorne, Calif., Oct. 31, 1938; s. Lawrence John and Henrietta (Moser) E.; m. Elizabeth Wolfe, Mar. 14, 1964; children— Christina, Michael, Steven. A.B., Marquette U., 1960; J.D., Georgetown U., 1963. Bar: Nebr. 1963, Calif. 1965, U.S. Supreme Ct. 1976. Assoc. Musick, Peeler & Garrett, L.A., 1963-70, ptnr., 1970-76; ptnr. Morgan, Lewis & Bockius, L.A., 1976-97; ptnr. Jones, Day, Reavis & Pogue, L.A., 1998—; mem. labor rels.. com. Am. Hosp. Assn., also mem. spl. subcom. to analyze report of Nat. Commn. on Nursing, Comparable Worth Task Force; mem. adv. com. NLRB, 1994—. Author: (with Michael L. Wolfram) California Employment Law, A Guide to California Laws Regulating Employment in the Private Sector, 1989. Mem. ABA (mem. com. on devel. of law under Nat. Labor Relations Act sect. on labor and employment law), State Bar Calif. (labor and employment law sect.), Los Angeles County Bar Assn. (chmn. labor law sect. 1983-84, mem. exec. com. 1974-86), So. Calif. Labor Law Symposium (founding chmn. 1980, 81), Am. Soc. Hosp. Attys., State Bar Nebr. Contbr. articles to profl. jours. Office: Jones Day Reavis & Pogue 555 W 5th St Ste 4600 Los Angeles CA 90013-1025

EMENHISER, JEDON ALLEN, political science educator, academic administrator; b. Clovis, N.Mex., May 19, 1933; s. Glen Allen and Mary Opal (Sasser) E.; m. Patricia Ellen Burke, Jan. 27, 1954; 1 child, Melissa Mary Emenhiser Westerfield. Student, Am. U., 1954; BA, U. Redlands, 1955; PhD, U. Minn., 1962. Cert. community coll. adminstr., Calif. Instr. to prof. polit. sci. Utah State U., Logan, 1960-77, acting dean, 1973-74; prof. Humboldt State U., Arcata, Calif., 1977—, dean, 1977-86, acting v.p., 1984; chair Social Sci. Rsch. and Instrnl. Coun. Calif. State U., 1994-95; prof. Jr. Statesmen Summer Sch., Stanford U., 1989—. Vis. instr. U. Redlands, Calif., 1959-60; vis. prof. U. Saigon, Vietnam, 1964-65; asst. dean Colgate U., Hamilton, N.Y., 1972-73; staff dir. Utah Legislature, Salt Lake City, 1967, cons., 1968-77; dir. Bur. Govt. and Opinion Rsch., Logan, 1965-70; cons. USCG, McKinleyville, Calif., 1982; v.p. Exch. Bank, New Franklin, Mo., 1970-76; reader advanced placement exam. U.S. Govt. Coll. Bd., 1990-98; vis. fellow govt. divsn. Congl. Rsch. Svc. Libr. of Congress, 1996. Author: Utah's Governments, 1964, Freedom and Power in California, 1987; editor, contbr. Dragon on the Hill, 1970, Rocky Mountain Urban Politics, 1971; producer, dir. TV broadcasts The Hawks and the Doves, 1965-66; contbr. articles to profl. jours. Sec. Cache County Dem. Party, Logan, 1962-63; chmn. Mayor's Commn. on Govt. Orgn., Logan, 1973-74; campaign mgr. various candidates and issues, Logan, 1965-75; bd. dirs.

Humboldt Connections, Eureka, Calif., 1986-96, pres., 1989-92; elder Presbyn. ch. Sr. Fulbright-Hays lectr. Com. Internat. Exch. of Persons, Vietnam, 1964-65; Adminstrv. fellow Am. Coun. Edn., Colgate U., 1972-73; Paul Harris fellow Rotary Internat. Mem. Am. Polit. Sci. Assn., Western Polit. Sci. Assn., Am. Studies Assn., Phi Beta Kappa, Omicron Delta Kappa. Presbyterian. Avocations: gardening, photography, travel. Home: PO Box 250 Bayside CA 95524-0250 Office: Humboldt State U Dept Polit Sci Arcata CA 95521 E-mail: jae1@humboldt.edu

EMERSON, ALTON CALVIN, retired physical therapist; b. Webster, N.Y., Sept. 29, 1934; s. Homer Douglas and Pluma (Babcock) E.; m. Nancy Ann Poarch, Dec. 20, 1955 (div. 1972); children: Marcia Ann, Mark Alton; m. Barbara Irene Stewart, Oct. 6, 1972. BS in Vertibrate Zoology, U. Utah, 1957; cert. phys. therapy, U. So. Calif., 1959. Staff phys. therapist Los Angeles County Crippled Children's Services, 1958-65; pvt. practice phys. therapy Los Angeles, 1966-98; ret., 1998. Cons. City of Hope, Duarte, Calif., 1962-72; trustee Wolcott Found. Inc., St. Louis, 1972-86, chmn. bd. trustees, 1980-85. Recipient Cert. of Achievement, George Washington U., Washington, 1986. Mem. Masons (pres. Temple City High Twelve Club 1971, master Camellia 1973 (Hiram award Conejo Valley Lodge, 2001), pres. Calif. Assn. High Twelve Clubs 1986, internat. pres. High Twelve 1990-91, mem. High Twelve Internat., Pasadena Scottish Rite Bodies, Venerable Master, Lodge of Perfection 1998, KCCH, Legion Merit, coroneted 33, 2001), Royal Order Scotland, Al Malaikah Tmeple, Ancient Arabic order Nobles Mystic Shrine, DeMolay Legion of Honor, Order of DeMolay (hon. internat. supreme coun.), Conejo-Westlake Shrine Club (pres. 1996), Conejo Valley High Twelve Club 2000 (pres.), Divan 2000, Sigma Phi Epsilon. Home and Office: 287 W Avenida De Las Flores Thousand Oaks CA 91360-1808

EMERSON, BARRY D. computer company executive; b. 1958; BS in Acctg. (hons.), Calif. State U. Long Beach; MBA, UCLA Sch. Mgmt. CPA Arthur Anderson & Co.; mgr. corp. acctg. Wyle, 1984-86, corp. dir. fin. reporting, 1986-90, asst. corp. controller, 1990-92, controller, 1992-95, v.p., 1995—. Office: Elite Information Group Inc 5100 W Goldleaf Cir Ste 50 Los Angeles CA 90056

EMERSON, MARK, lumber company executive; CFO Sierra Pacific Industries, Redding, Calif. Office: Sierra Pacific Industries PO Box 496028 Redding CA 96049-6028

EMERSON, R. CLARK, priest, business administrator; b. L.A., Mar. 9, 1945; s. George Heins and Irma Furney (Sorter) E.; m. Katharine Ann Lawrence, June 27, 1980; children: Cynthia, Holly, Angela, William, Richard. BA, San Jose State U., 1966; MDiv, Ch. Div. Sch. of Pacific, 1972. Ordained deacon Episcopal Ch., 1972, ordained priest, 1973; cert. secondary tchr., Calif. Comml. tchr. Middletown (Calif.) High Sch., 1967-69; asst. to rector St. Francis Ch., Palos Verdes, Calif., 1972-76; adminstr. Power Transistor Co., Torrance, 1977-85; priest assoc. St. John's Ch., L.A., 1976-85; adminstr. Richard B. Belli Accountancy, San Jose, Calif., 1988-96; priest assoc. St. Luke's Ch., Los Gatos, 1985—. Contr. St. John's Well Child Ctr., L.A., 1985. Republican. Episcopalian. Avocations: steam railroading, antique automobiles, hot air ballooning.

EMERSON, RED, lumber company executive; CEO Sierra Pacific Industries, Redding, Calif. Office: Sierra Pacific Industries PO Box 496028 Redding CA 96049-6028

EMERSON, SHARON B. biology researcher and educator; b. Santa Monica, Calif., July 14, 1945; BA, U. Calif., Berkeley, 1966; MS, U. So. Calif., 1968, PhD, 1971. Rsch. assoc. Field Mus. Natural History, Chgo.; rsch. prof. Dept. Biology U. Utah. Rsch. assoc. Field Mus. Nat. History, Chgo. Recipient John D. and Katherine T. MacArthur fellowship, 1995, award for excellence in environ. health rsch. Lovelance Inst., Albuquerque, 1995. Mem. Am. Soc. Zoology (elected chair divsn. vertebrate morphology). Office: U Utah Dept Biology 257 S 1400 E Salt Lake City UT 84112-0840*

EMERT, GEORGE HENRY, academic administrator, biochemist; b. Tenn., Dec. 15, 1938; s. Victor K. Emert and Hazel G. (Shultz) Ridley; m. Billie M. Bush, June 10, 1967; children: Debra Lea Lipp, Ann Lanie Taylor, Laurie Elizabeth, Jamie Marie. BA, U. Colo., 1962; MA, Colo. State U., 1970; PhD, Va. Tech. U., 1973. Registered profl. chem. engr. Microbiologist Colo. Dept. Pub. Health, Denver, 1967-70; post doctoral fellow U. Colo., Boulder, 1973-74; dir. biochem. tech. Gulf Oil Corp., Merriam, Kans., 1974-79; prof. biochemistry, dir. biomass rsch. ctr. U. Ark., Fayetteville, 1979-84; exec. v.p. Auburn (Ala.) U., 1984-92; pres. Utah State U., Logan, 1992—, pres. emeritus, porf. biochemistry, 2001—. Adj. prof. microbiology U. Kans., Lawrence, 1975-79. Editor, author: Fuels from Biomass and Wastes, 1981; author book chpt.; contbr. articles to profl. jours.; poet. Mem. So. Tech. Coun., Raleigh, N.C., 1985-92; dir. Ala. Supercomputer Authority, Montgomery, 1987-92, Blue Cross Blue Shield Utah, 1996—, Utah Partnership Econ. Devel.; trustee, adv. bd. First Security Bank. Capt. U.S. Army, 1963-66, Vietnam. Named to Educators Hall of Fame, Lincoln Meml. U., 1988. Fellow Am. Inst. Chemists; mem. Rotary (Paul Harris fellow, pres., v.p. 1989-90), Phi Kappa Phi, Sigma Xi. Republican. Achievements include patent for method for enzyme reutilization. Office: Utah State U 1400 Old Main Hl Logan UT 84322-1400

EMIGH, MIKE, agricultural products company executive; b. 1948; BA in Acctg., U. Las Vegas, 1973. Plant contr. Johns Manville, Fresno, Calif., 1973-79; asst. contr. Sun Maid Growers of Calif., Inc., Kingsburg, 1979-84; sec., v.p., treas. Valley Fig Growers, Inc., Fresno, 1984-97, pres., 1997—. Office: Valley Fig Growers Inc 2028 S 3rd St Fresno CA 93702-4156

EMMANOUILIDES, GEORGE CHRISTOS, physician, educator; b. Drama, Greece, Dec. 17, 1926; came to U.S., 1955; s. Christos Nicholas and Vassiliki (Jordanopoulos) E.; married; children: Nicholas, Elizabeth, Christopher, Martha, Sophia. MD, Aristotelion U., 1951; MS in Physiology, UCLA, 1963. Diplomate Am. Bd. Pediatrics (pediatric cardiology and neonatal-perinatal medicine). Asst. prof. UCLA, 1963-69, assoc. prof., 1969-73, prof., 1973-95, prof. emeritus, 1995—. Chief divsn. pediatric cardiology Harbor UCLA Med. Ctr., Torrance, Calif., 1963-95. Co-author: Practical Pediatric Electrocardiography, 1973; co-editor: Heart Disease in Infants, Children and Adolescents, 2d edit., 1977, Moss' Heart Disease in Infants, Children and Adolescents, 3d edit., 1983, 4th edit., 1989, 5th edit., 1995, Neonatal Cardiopulmonary Distress, 1988; contbr. more than 70 articles in field to profl. jours. Served as 2d lt. M.C., Greek Army, 1953-55. Recipient Sherman Mellincoff award UCLA Sch. Medicine, 1982, several rsch. awards Am. Heart Assn., 1965-83. Fellow Am. Acad. Pediatrics (cardiology sect., chmn. 1978-80, Founders award 1996), Am. Coll. Cardiology; mem. Am. Pediatric Soc., Soc. for Pediatric Rsch., Hellenic-Am. Med. Soc. (pres.), Acad. of Athens (corr. mem.). Democrat. Greek Orthodox. Clubs: Hellenic Univ. (Los Angeles) (bd. dirs.). Avocation: gardening. Home: 4619 Browndeer Ln Rllng Hls Est CA 90275-3911 Office: Harbor-UCLA Med Ctr 1000 W Carson St Torrance CA 90502-2004 E-mail: [illegible]@ucla.edu

EMMANUEL, JORGE AGUSTIN, chemical engineer, environmental consultant; b. Manila, Aug. 28, 1954; came to U.S., 1970; s. Benjamin Elmido and Lourdes (Orozco) E.; 1 child, Andres Layanglawin. BS in Chemistry, N.C. State U., 1976, MSChemE, 1978; PhD in Chem. Engring., U. Mich., 1988. Registered profl. engr., Calif., environ. profl.; cert. hazardous materials mgr. Process engr. Perry Electronics, Raleigh, N.C., 1973-74; rsch. asst. N.C. State U., Raleigh, 1977-78; rsch. chem. engr. GE Corp. R & D Ctr., Schenectady, N.Y., 1978-81; Amoco rsch. fellow U. Mich., Ann Arbor, 1981-84; sr. environ. analyst TEM Assocs., Inc., Emeryville, Calif., 1988-91; pres. Environ. & Engring. Rsch. Group, Hercules, 1991—. Environ. cons. to the Philippines, UN Devel. Program, 1992, 94; rsch. assoc. U. Calif., Berkeley, 1988-90. Contbr. articles to profl. jours. Mem. Assn. for Asian Studies, Ann Arbor, 1982-88; sec. Alliance for Philippine Concerns, L.A., 1983-91; assoc. Philippine Resource Ctr., Berkeley, 1988-92; bd. dirs. ARC-Ecology, San Francisco, 1990—, Asia Pacific Ctr., Washington, 1995-2000; bd. advisors Urban Habitat, 1995—; chmn. bd. Filipino-Am. Coalition for Environ. Solutions, 2001—. N.C. State U. grantee, 1976, Phoenix grantee U. Mich., 1982. Mem. NSPE, AAAS, Air and Waste Mgmt. Assn., Calif. Acad. Scis., N.Y. Acad. Sci., Filipino-Am. Soc. Architects and Engrs. (exec. sec. 1989-90, Svc. award 1990). Avocations: classical guitar, ethnomusicology, Asian studies. Office: The Environ & Engring Rsch Group 628 2nd St Rodeo CA 94572-1111

EMMERICH, ROLAND, director, producer, writer; b. Stuttgart, Germany, Nov. 10, 1955; Prodr. The Thirteenth Floor, 1999, The High Crusade, 1994; dir. Raumpatrouille (TV series), 1998, Universal Soldier, 1992; dir., exec. prodr., writer Godzilla, 1998 (Best Dir. Audience award European Film Awards); exec. prodr. Godzilla The Series (TV series), 1998, Independence Day, 1996, Eye of the Storm, 1991; prodr., Moon 44, 1990; dir., writer Stargate, 1994 (Sci-Fi Universe Mag. Reader's Choice award), Hollywood-Monster, 1987, Joey, 1985, Das Arche Noah Prinzip, 1984; creator, exec. prodr. (TV series) The Visitor; editor, writer, dir. Franzmann, 1979; actor Die 120 Tage von Bottrop, 1997; exec. prodr., dir. The Patriot, 2000. Office: Creative Artists Agy 9830 Wilshire Blvd Beverly Hills CA 90212-1825

EMMERSON, MARK, paper/lumber company executive; CFO Sierra Pacific Ind., Redding, Calif. Office: Sierra Pacific Industries PO Box 496028 Redding CA 96049-6028 Office Fax: (530) 378-8109

EMMERSON, RED, sawmill owner; CEO Sierra Pacific Industries, Redding, Calif., 1949—. Office: Sierra Pacific Industries 19794 Riverside Ave Redding CA 96049-6028

EMMONS, ROBERT JOHN, corporate executive; b. Trenton, N.J., Sept. 18, 1934; s. Charles Glunk and Ruth Marie (Heilhecker) E.; m. Christine Young Bebb, July 13, 1980; children: Bradley Thomas, Cathy Lynne, Christopher Robert, Ryan Hunter. A.B. in Econs, U. Mich., 1956, M.B.A., 1960, J.D., 1964. V.p. Baskin-Robbins Co., Burbank, Calif., 1964-68; pres. United Rent-All, Los Angeles, 1968-69, Master Host Internat., Los Angeles, 1969-71; prof. Grad. Sch. Bus., U. So. Calif., 1971-82; pres. LTI Corp., Monterey, Calif., 1982-84; chmn., CEO, dir. Casino USA/SFI Corp., Santa Barbara, 1984-98; CEO Emmons Capital Investments, Santa Barbara, 1999—. Author: The American Franchise Revolution, 1970, The American Marketing Revolution, 1980; poetry Other Places, Other Times, 1974, Love and Other Minor Tragedies, 1980. Mem. AAUP, Am. Mktg. Assn., European Mktg. Assn., Am. Econ. Assn., Calif. Yacht Club (L.A.), Hawaii Yacht Club (Honolulu), The Valley Club of Montecito (Calif.), Useppa Island Club (Fla.), St. Petersburg Yacht Club (Fla.), The Calif. Club, Beta Gamma Sigma, Pi Kappa Alpha. Office: Emmons Capital Investments PO Box 50243 Santa Barbara CA 93150-0243

ENDERS, ALLEN COFFIN, anatomy educator; b. Wooster, Ohio, Aug. 5, 1928; s. Robert Kendal and Abbie Gertrude (Crandell) E.; m. Alice Hay, June 15, 1950 (div. Dec. 1975); children: Robert H., George C., Richard S., Gregory H.; m. Sandra Jean Schlafke, Aug. 5, 1976. AB, Swarthmore Coll., 1950; AM, Harvard U., 1952, PhD, 1955. From asst. prof. to assoc. prof Rice Inst., Houston, 1954-63; from assoc. prof. to prof. Washington U., St. Louis, 1963-75; prof., chmn. dept. human anatomy U. Calif., Davis, 1976-86, prof. cell biology and human anatomy, 1986—. Cons. NIH, Bethesda, Md., 1964-68, 70-73, 76-80, 83-93. Author: (with others) Bailey's Microscopic Anatomy, 1984; editor: Delayed Implantation, 1964; contbr. numerous articles on anatomy and reproduction to profl. jours. Nat. pres. Perinatal Research Soc., 1981. Grantee NIH, 1959-99. Fellow AAAS; mem. Am. Assn. Anatomists (v.p. 1980-82, pres. 1983-84), Soc. Study Reprodn., Am. Soc. Cell Biology. Home: 39707 Barry Rd Davis CA 95616-9415 Office: U Calif Sch Medicine Cell Biology & Anatomy Davis CA 95616

ENDICOTT, WILLIAM F. journalist; b. Harrodsburg, Ky., Aug. 26, 1935; s. William O. and Evelyn E.; m. Mary Frances Thomas, Dec. 27, 1956; children: Gene, Fran, Greg. Student, Am. U., 1955; BA in Polit. Sci., Transylvania U., 1957. With Lexington (Ky.) Leader, 1957; sports writer Louisville Courier-Jour., 1958-62; reporter Tulare (Calif.) Advance-Register, 1963; reporter, city editor Modesto (Calif.) Bee, 1963-66; city editor Sacramento Union, 1966-67; with Los Angeles Times, 1968-85; Capitol bur. chief Sacramento Bee, 1985-95, asst. mng. editor, 1995-98, dep. mng. editor, 1998-2000. Hearst vis. prof. U. Tex., 1993. Served with USMCR, 1957-58. Recipient various journalism awards Disting. Alumnus award Transylvania U., 1980 Episcopalian. Office: 21st and Q Sts Sacramento CA 95852

ENDRIZ, JOHN GUIRY, electronics executive, consultant; b. Oak Park, Ill., Jan. 10, 1942; s. John Daniel and Florence (Guiry) E.; m. Sally Jean Doubleday, July 19, 1975. BSEE, MSEE, MIT, 1965; PhD in EE, Stanford U., 1970. Guest rschr. Linkoping (Sweden) U., 1970-72; project mgr. R.C.A. Rsch. Lab., Princeton, N.J., 1972-77; engring. mgr. Varian Assocs., Palo Alto, Calif., 1977-88; v.p. engring. S.D.L., Inc., San Jose, 1988-97, v.p. power delivery bus. unit, 1997-99. Contbr. over 53 articles to profl. jours.; patentee more than 30 inventions. Mem. IEEE, S.P.I.E., Soc. Information Display. Home: 5 Heritage Ct Belmont CA 94002-2944

ENELOW, ALLEN JAY, psychiatrist, educator; b. Pitts., Jan. 15, 1922; s. Isadore M. and Rose (Kasdan) E.; m. Mary Cleveland, July 21, 1946 (div. Sept. 1965); children: David, James, Susan, Margaret, Patience, Abigail; m. Sheila Kearns, Oct. 1, 1966; stepchildren: Lauren, Lisa. A.B., W.Va. U., 1942; M.D., U. Louisville, 1944. Intern Michael Reese Hosp., Chgo., 1944-45; resident psychiatry Winter VA Hosp., Topeka, 1947-49; mem. staff Menninger Found. and Asso. Hosps., 1947-52; practice medicine specializing in psychiatry Beverly Hills, Calif., 1952-58, Pacific Palisades, 1956-64; faculty U. So. Calif., Los Angeles, 1960-67; prof., chmn. dept. psychiatry Mich. State U., East Lansing, 1967-72; prof. psychiatry U. of Pacific, 1972-78; chmn. dept. psychiatry Pacific Med. Center, San Francisco, 1972-82; clin. prof. psychiatry U. Calif., 1977-82, U. So. Calif., 1982-89, clin. prof. emeritus, 1989—. Cons. NIMH, VA, others; pres. VISTAS Lifelong Learning, Inc., Santa Barbara, Calif., 1999-2001. Author: Psychiatry in the Practice of Medicine, 1966, Interviewing and Patient Care, 1972, 3d edit., 1985, 4th edit., 1996, Elements of Psychotherapy, 1977; contbr. numerous articles to profl. jours. Served with M.C. AUS, 1945-47. Fellow Am. Psychiat. Assn. (life), ACP. Office: 1532 Anacapa St Santa Barbara CA 93101-1929

ENG, CATHERINE, health care facility administrator, physician, [illegible] educator; b. Hong Kong, May 20, 1950; came to U.S., 1953; d. Doi Kwong and Alice (Yee) E.; m. Daniel Charles Chan; 1 child, Michael B. BA, Wellesley Coll., 1972; MD, Columbia U., 1976. Diplomate Am. Bd. Internal Medicine, Am. Bd. Gastroenterology; cert. added qualifications geriatrics. Intern in internal medicine Presbyterian Hosp./Columbia, Presbyterian Med. Ctr., 1976-77, resident in internal medicine, 1977-79; fellow in gastroenterology/hepatology N.Y. Hosp./Cornell U. Med. Coll., 1979-81; instr. medicine Cornell U. Coll. Medicine, N.Y.C., 1980-81; staff physician On Lok Sr. Health Svcs., San Francisco, 1981-86, supervising physician, 1986-91, med. dir., 1992—. Asst. clin. prof. dept. family and cmty. medicine U. Calif., San Francisco, 1986-95, asst. clin. prof. dept. medicine, 1992-95; assoc. clinical prof. dept. medicine, Univ. Calif., San Francisco, 1995—; primary care specialist Program of All-inclusive Care for the Elderly, San Francisco, 1987-94; asst. chief dept. medicine Chinese Hosp., San Francisco, 1993-98, chmn. com. credentials, 1994—. Instr. BLS Am. Heart Assn., San Francisco, 1988-92; mem. nominating com. YWCA of Marin, San Francisco, San Mateo, 1991-95; mem. mgmt. com. YWCA-Chinatown/North Beach, San Francisco, 1989-95; bd. dirs. Chinatown Cmty. Children's Ctr., San Francisco, 1987-90. Durant scholar Wellesley Coll., 1972. Fellow ACP; mem. Am. Geriatrics Soc., Am. Soc. Aging, Am. Gastroent. Assn., Calif. Med. Assn. (assoc.), San Francisco Med. Soc. (assoc.), Sigma Xi, Alpha Omega Alpha. Avocations: reading, hiking. Home: 130 Dorchester Way San Francisco CA 94127-1110 Office: On Lok Sr Health Svcs 1333 Bush St San Francisco CA 94109-5691 E-mail: cathy@onlok.org

ENG, LAWRENCE FOOK, biochemistry educator, neurochemist; b. Spokane, Wash., Feb. 19, 1931; s. On Kee and Shee (Hue) E.; m. Jeanne Leong, Aug. 30, 1957; children: Douglas, Alice, Steven, Shirley. BS in Chemistry, Wash. State U., 1952; MS in Chemistry, Stanford U., 1954, PhD in Chemistry, 1962. Chief chemistry sect. path. and lab. med. svc. PAVA Health Care Sys., Palo Alto, Calif., 1961—; rsch. assoc. dept. pathology Sch. Medicine Stanford (Calif.) U., 1966-70, sr. scientist dept. pathology Sch. of Medicine, 1970-75, adj. prof., 1975-82, prof. dept. pathology Sch. of Medicine, 1982—. Mem. ad hoc neurol. sci. study sect. and neurology B study sect. NIH, 1976-79, mem. neurol. sci. study sect., 1978-83; mem. adv. bd. VA Office of Regeneration Rsch. Program, 1985-89; mem. VA Merit Rev. Bd. for Neurobiology, 1987-90; mem. Nat. Adv. Neurol. Disorders and Stroke Coun., 1991-94. Mem. editorial bd. Neurobiology, 1970-75, Jour. of Neurochemistry, 1978-85, Jour. of Neuroimmunology, 1980-83, Molecular and Chem. Neuropathology, 1982—, Glia, 1987—, Jour. for Neurosci. Rsch., 1991-2000, Neurochemical Rsch., 1993—. Capt. USAF, 1952-57. Mem. Am. Soc. for Neurochemistry (coun. 1979-83, 85-87, 93—, sec. 1987-93), Am. Soc. Biochemistry and Molecular Biology, Internat. Soc. for Neurochemistry, Soc. for Neurosci. Office: VAPA Health Care System Path & Lab Med Svc 3801 Miranda Ave Palo Alto CA 94304-1207

ENGDAHL, TODD PHILIP, newspaper editor; b. Jamestown, N.Y., Feb. 8, 1950; s. George Philip and Janice Marie (Wallin) E.; m. Caroline C.N. Schomp, Dec. 29 , 1973; children: Anders Justus Schomp, Mats Philip Schomp. BA, Pomona Coll., 1971; MS, Northwestern U., 1972. Reporter Oregonian, Portland, 1972-75; reporter Denver Post, 1975-80, asst. city editor, 1980-83, night city editor, 1983-85, Sunday editor, 1985-86, city editor, 1986-90, exec. city editor, 1990-95, new media editor, 1995—. Lectr. journalism Portland State U., 1974. Democrat. Lutheran. Avocations: reading, gardening, woodworking. Office: Denver Post PO Box 1709 Denver CO 80201-1709 E-mail: tengdahl@denverpost.com

ENGEL, THOMAS, chemistry educator; b. Yokohama, Japan, Apr. 2, 1942; came to U.S., 1947; s. George Walter and Juliane (Urban) E.; m. Esther Neeser, Aug. 23, 1979; 1 child, Alex. BS, Johns Hopkins U., 1963, MS, 1964; PhD, U. Chgo., 1969; Dr. rer. nat. habil., U. Munich, Fed. Republic Germany, 1979. Instr. Tech. U. Clausthal, Clausthal-Zellerfeld, Fed. Republic Germany, 1969-75, U. Munich, 1975-78; staff mem. IBM Rsch. Lab., Zurich, Switzerland, 1978-80; assoc. prof. chemistry U. Wash., Seattle, 1979-84, prof., 1984—, chmn. dept. chemistry, 1987-90. Contbr. papers and book chpts. to profl. publs. Recipient numerous grants NSF, Air Force Office Sci. Rsch., Office Naval Rsch, Am. Chem Soc. award in Colloid or Surface Chemistry, 1995. Mem. Am. Chem. Soc. (Surface Chemistry award 1995), Am. Vacuum Soc. Office: U Wash Dept Chemistry Bldg 10 Seattle WA 98195-0001 E-mail: engel@chem.washington.edu

ENGELBART, DOUG, engineering executive; b. Portland, Oreg., Jan. 30, 1925; BSEE, Oreg. State U., 1948, D (hon.), 1994; degree in engring., U. Calif., Berkeley, 1952; PhD in Elec. Engring., U. Calif., 1955. Electronic/radar tech. USN, 1944-46; elec. engr. NACA Ames Lab., Mountain View, Calif., 1948-51; asst. prof. elec. engring. U. Calif., Berkeley, 1955-56; rschr. Stanford (Calif.) Rsch. Inst. (now SRI Internat.), 1957-59, dir. augmentation rsch. ctr., 1959-77; sr. scientist Tymshare, Inc., Cupertino, Calif., 1977-84, McDonnell Douglas ISC, San Jose, 1984-89; dir. Bootstrap Project Stanford U., 1989-90; dir. Bootstrap Project, Palo Alto, Calif., 1990-91, Bootstrap Inst., Fremont, 1991—. Contbr. numerous articles to profl. jours. Recipient Lifetime Achievement award for Tech. Excellence, PC Mag., 1987, Disting. Alumni of Yr. award Oreg. STate U., 1987, Disting. Svc. and Outstanding Contbns. in Field citation Sigma Phi Epsilon, St. Louis, 1989, Lifetime Achievement award for Vision, Inspiration and Contbn., Electronic Networking Assn., San Francisco, 1990, Software Sys. award Assn. Computing Machinery, 1990, Am. Ingenuity award Nat. Assn. Mfrs.' Congress of Am. Industry, Washington, 1991, Disting. Alumnus award U. Calif., Berkeley, 1991, Lifetime Achievement award Dominican Coll. of San Rafael, Calif., 1991, Lifetime Achievement award Price Waterhouse, Washington, 1994, cert. of appreciation Smart Valley, Inc., 1994, Editors' Choice award MacUser Awards Ceremony, 1995, SoftQuad Web award World Wide Web Conf., Boston, 1995, cert. of merit The Franklin Inst. Com. on Sci. and the Arts, 1996, Spl. award Am. Soc. for Info. Sci., 1996, Jerome H. Lemelson-MIT prize for excellence in invention and innovation, 1997; named Pioneer of the Electronic Frontier, Electronic Frontier Found., Washington, 1992; Engelbart award established in his honor Internat. Conf. on Hypertext and Hypermedia, 1994. Fellow Nat. Acad. Arts and Scis.; mem. IEEE (treas., vice chmn., chmn. San Francisco chpt. profl. group on electronic computers 1957-59, Computer Pioneer award 1993), NAS (com. on augmentation of human intellect 1989, panel on future role of computers in rsch. librs. 1968-70), Nat. Acad. Engring., Computer Profls. for Social Responsibility (adv. bd.), The Tech. Ctr. of Silicon Valley (adv. coun.), Phi Kappa Phi, Tau Beta Pi, Sigma Tau, Eta Kappa Nu, Blue Key, Sigma Xi. Achievements include visionary and pioneering work in organizational augmentation, including strategies for continuous improvement, human-tool co-evolution and interactive collaborative hypermedia computing to support the knowledge-intensive work of groups and individuals; 7 patents relating to bi-stable gaseous plasma digital devices, 12 patents relating to all-magnetic digital devices, 1 patent for invention of the Mouse. Home: 89 Catalpa Dr Atherton CA 94027-2167 Office: Bootstrap Inst 6505 Kaiser Dr Fremont CA 94555-3614

ENGELBRECHT, RUDOLF, electrical engineering educator; b. Atlanta, Apr. 18, 1928; s. Walter and Dorothea (Succo) E.; m. Christel M. Kluth, Sept. 10, 1950; children— Richard, Rolf, Erika. B.S., Ga. Inst. Tech., 1951, M.S. in Elec. Engring., 1953; Ph.D. in Elec. Engring., Oreg. State U., 1979. Mem. tech. staff Bell Labs., Whippany, N.J., 1953-60, supr., Murray Hill, N.J., 1961-63, dept. head, 1964-69; dir. RCA Tech. Ctr., Somerville, N.J., 1970-72; group leader RCA Labs., Zurich, Switzerland, 1972-77; assoc. prof. Oreg. State U., Corvallis, 1977-93. Co-author: Microwave Devices, 1969; contbr. articles to profl. jours.; patentee in field. Named to Oreg. State U. Engring. Hall of Fame, 1998. Fellow IEEE (life, Centennial award 1984, Third Millennium medal 2000); [illegible] 1020 NW Douglas Pl Corvallis OR 97330-1005 Office: Oreg State U Dept Elec Computer Eng Corvallis OR 97331

ENGELHARDT, ALBERT GEORGE, physicist; b. Toronto, Ont., Can., Mar. 17, 1935; came to U.S., 1957, naturalized, 1965; s. Samuel and Rose (Menkes) E.; m. Elzbieta Szajkowska, June 14, 1960; children— Frederick, Leonard, Michael. B.A.Sc., U. Toronto, 1958; M.S., U. Ill., 1959, Ph.D. (grad. fellow), 1961. Research asst. elec. engring. U. Ill., Urbana, 1958-61;

staff research and devel. center engr. Westinghouse Electric Co., Pitts., 1961-70, mgr., 1966-69, fellow scientist, 1969-70; sr. research scientist, group leader Hydro-Que. Research Inst., Varennes, Can., 1970-74; mem. staff Los Alamos Sci. Lab., 1974-86; adj. prof. elec. engring. Tex. Tech. U., Lubbock, 1976—; pres., chief exec. officer, founder Enfitek, Inc., Los Alamos, N.Mex., 1982—. Vis. prof. U. Que., 1970-77 Contbr. articles to profl. jours. Group leader Boy Scouts Can., 1972-74. Mem. IEEE Nuclear and Plasma Scis. Soc., Am. Phys. Soc. Home and Office: 549 Bryce Ave Los Alamos NM 87544-3607 E-mail: agengelhardt@mailaps.org

ENGFER, SUSAN MARVEL, zoological park executive; b. Mpls., Dec. 6, 1943; d. Frederick Paul and Dorothy M. Engfer. BS, Albion Coll., 1965; MS, U. Wyo., 1968; postgrad., U. Calif., Santa Barbara, 1975-76; dipl., Sch. Profl. Mgmt. Devel. for Zoo and Aquarium Pers., 1981. Ranger, naturalist Grand Teton Nat. Park, Moose, Wyo., 1967; cancer rsch. technician U. Calif., Santa Barbara, 1967-68; zoo keeper Santa Barbara Zool. Gardens, 1968-70, edn. curator, 1970-72, asst. dir., 1972-88; pres., CEO Cheyenne Mountain Zool. Park, Colorado Springs, Colo., 1988—. Cons. oiled bird rehab. Union Oil and Standard Oil Co., 1968-70; master plan cons. Moorpark (Calif.) Coll., 1986-88; instr., bd. regents Sch. Profl. Mgmt. Devel. Zoo and Aquarium Pers., Wheeling, W.V., 1984-87. Author: North American Regional Studbook, Asian Small-Clawed Otter (Aonyx cinerea), 1987—. Fellow Am. Assn. Zool. Pks. and Aquariums (profl., bd. dirs. 1987-90, mem. accreditation commn. 1990—, chmn. accreditation commn. 1994-95); mem. Internat. Union Dirs. Zool. Gardens, Internat. Union Conservation of Nature and Natural Resources (mem. otter specialist group), Soc. Conservation Biology, Colo. Women's Forum, Rotary. Office: Cheyenne Mountain Zool Pk 4250 Cheyenne Mountain Zoo Rd Colorado Springs CO 80906-5755

ENGLEMAN, EPHRAIM PHILIP, rheumatologist; b. San Jose, Calif., Mar. 24, 1911; s. Maurice and Tillie (Rosenberg) E.; m. Jean Sinton, Mar. 2, 1941; children— Ephraim Philip, Edgar George, Jill. B.A., Stanford U., 1933; M.D., Columbia U., 1937. Intern Mt. Zion Hosp., San Francisco; resident U. Calif., San Francisco, Jos. Pratt Diagnostic Hosp., Boston; research fellow Mass. Gen. Hosp., Boston, 1937-42; practice medicine specializing in rheumatology San Francisco, 1948—; mem. faculty U. Calif. Med. Center, San Francisco, 1949—, clin. prof. medicine, 1965—; dir. Rosalind Russell Arthritis Center, 1979—. Mem. staff U. Calif., Mills Meml., Peninsula hosps.; Chmn. Nat. Commn. Arthritis and Related Diseases, 1975-76 Author: The Book on Arthritis: A Guide for Patients and Their Families, 1979; also articles, chpts. in books. Served to maj. M.C. USMCR, 1942-47. Nat. Inst. Arthritis grantee; recipient citation Arthritis Found., 1973; Ephraim P. Engleman Disting. Professorship in Rheumatology established in his honor U. Calif., San Francisco, 1991. Fellow ACP; Mem. Internat. League Against Rheumatism (pres. 1981-85), Am. Coll. Rheumatology (founding fellow, master, pres. 1962-63), Nat. Soc. Clin. Rheumatologists, AMA, Am. Fedn. Clin. Research; hon. mem. Japanese Rheumatism Soc., Spanish Rheumatism Soc., Uruguay Rheumatism Soc., Australian Rheumatism Assn., Chinese Med. Assn., French Soc. Rheumatology, Internat. League against Rheumatism, Gold-Headed Cane Soc. (U. Calif., San Francisco). Republican. Jewish. Club: Family (San Francisco). Office: U Calif Rosalind Russell Med Rsch Ctr Arthritis 350 Parnassus Ave Ste 600 San Francisco CA 94117-3608

ENGLISH, J. KALANI, state senator; Cert., Nat. Chengchi U., Taiwan, 1988; BA in Pacific Islands Studies, Hawai'i Loa Coll., 1989; Cert., East-West Ctr., 1991; MA in Pacific Islands Studies, U. Hawaii, 1995; Cert. Paralegal, Maui C.C., 1996; grad. Leadership Acad., Asian Pacific Am. Inst. Congl. Studies, 2000. Adminstrv. aide Office Hawaiian Affairs/State of Hawaii, 1991-92; case mgr. Hui No Ke Ola Pono, 1992-94; lectr. Maui C.C., 1991-94, Visitor Industry Tng. and Edn. Ctr., 1993-94; UN corr. Samoa News, 1994; assoc. editor Na Po'e Hawai'i Mag., 1994-95; advisor Permanent Mission of Federated States Micronesia to UN, 1993-96; chief of staff Hawaii State Senator Avery B. Chumbley, 1995-96; advisor polit. and devel. affairs Nat. Tropical Bot. Gardens, 1995-97; councilmem. Maui County Coun., County of Maui, 1997-2000; Dem. senator dist. 5 Hawaii State Senate, 2000—. Advisor U.S. Permanent Mission to UN, 1999; mem. Internat. Pushkin Bicentennial Com., 1999; head del. to Rapa Nui, 1999; mem. local govt. adv. com. U.S. EPA, 2000—; mem. ways and means, commerce, consumer protection, housing, health and human services, edn., water, land, energy and environ. coms. Hawaii State Senate, vice chair tourism, intergovtl. affairs. Contbr. articles to mags. and profl. jours. Mem. bd. dirs. Maui Arts and Culture Ctr., 1993—, Maui Econ. Devel. Bd., 1997-99, Hawaii Cultural Found., N.Y.C., 1996—, Honolulu Media Coun.; mem. Maui County Cable TV Pub. Access Consortium, 1997; mem. Coun. on Aging-County of Maui, 1998-2000; mem. exec. com., bd. dirs. Maui Visitor's Bur., 1999-2000. Mem. Maui C. of C. (bd. dirs.). Office: Hawaii State Senate State Capitol Rm 205 415 S Beretania St Honolulu HI 96813 Fax: 808 587 7230. E-mail: senenglish@Capitol.hawaii.gov

ENGLISH, STEPHEN FRANCIS, lawyer; b. Portland, Oreg., Jan. 17, 1948; BA with honors, U. Oreg., 1970; JD, U. Calif., San Francisco, 1973. Bar: Oreg. 1973; U.S. Dist. Ct. Oreg. 1973; U.S. Ct. Appeals (9th cir.) Oreg. 1980; U.S. Supreme Ct. 1982. Ptnr. Bullivant Houser Bailey, Portland, Oreg., 1983—. Mem. faculty Hastings Coll. Trial Advocacy, 1998—. Mem. ABA (vice-chair products liability com., 1996—, chair self insurers and risk mgrs. com. 1994-95, editor Self Insurers Newsletter 1987-89, chair non-profit, charitable and religious orgns. com. 1990-92), Multnomah County Bar Assn., Oreg. State Bar Assn. (chair litigation sect. 1990-91, exec. com. 1987-91), Am. Bd. of Trial Adv. (treas. Oreg. chpt. 1996-98, sec. Oreg. chpt. 1998—), Oreg. Assn. of Def. Counsel (chair products liability practice group 1997-98), Def. Rsch. Inst. Office: Bullivant Houser Bailey 300 Pioneer Tower 888 SW 5th Ave Portland OR 97204-2089

ENGLISH, STEPHEN RAYMOND, lawyer; b. Key West, Nov. 25, 1946; s. Jack Raymond and Jean Clyde (Peightal) E.; m. Molly Munger, Oct. 7, 1978; children: Nicholas, Alfred. BA, UCLA, 1975; JD, Harvard U., 1975. Bar: Calif. 1975, U.S. Dist. Ct. (cen. dist.) Calif. 1976, U.S. Dist. Ct. (so. dist.) Calif. 1978, U.S. Dist. Ct. (ea. dist.) Calif. 1988, U.S. Ct. Appeals (9th cir.) 1992. Assoc. Agnew, Miller & Carlson, L.A., 1975-78, Morgan, Lewis & Bockius, L.A., 1978-85, ptnr., 1985-98, English, Munger & Rice, L.A., 1998—. Lawyer rep. Ninth Cir. Jud. Conf., 1996-97. Pres. bd. dirs. Pub. Counsel, L.A., 1988-89, Inner City Law Ctr., L.A., 1992-93; bd. dirs. L.A. Legal Aid Found., 1999—. Mem. L.A. County Bar Assn. (mem. barristers exec. com. 1980-82, trustee 1990-92, chair pro bono coun. 1990-92, chair legal svcs. for poor 1993-95, mem. exec. com. litigation sect. 1994—, treas. litigation sect. 2001—), L.A. County Bar Found. (pres. 1998-99). Office: English Munger & Rice 801 S Grand Ave Ste 1900 Los Angeles CA 90017-4694

ENGLUND, ROBERT, actor, director, producer; b. Glendale, Calif., June 6, 1949; s. C. Kent and Janice (McDonald) E.; m. Nancy Ellen Booth, Oct. 1, 1988. Student, Oakland U., U. Calif., Northridge, UCLA, Royal Acad. Dramatic Arts, Rochester, Mich. Actor, dir., producer; resident artist Meadow Brook Theatre, Rochester, 1969-72, guest artist, 1973; resident actor Gt. Lakes Shakespeare Feestival, Cleve., 1970-71, Godspell, Cleve., 1971. Appeared as Freddy Krueger in A Nightmare on Elm Street, 1984, A Nightmare on Elm Street, Part 2: Freddy's Revenge, 1985, A Nightmare on Elm Street 3: Dream Warriors, 1987, A Nightmare on Elm Street 4: The Dream Master 1988, A Nightmare on Elm Street 5: The Dream Child, 1989, Freddy's Dead: The Final Nightmare, 1991, Wes Craven's New Nightmare, 1993; also appeared in films Buster and Billie, 1974, Hustle, 1975, Last of the Cowboys, 1976, Stay Hungry, 1976, A Star Is Born, 1976, Bloodbrothers, 1977, Big Wednesday, 1978, Dead and Buried, 1981, Don't Cry, It's Only Thunder, 1982, Never Too Young to Die, 1986, Phantom of the Opera, 1989, Dance Macabre, 1992, The Mangler, 1995, Tobe Hoopers Night Dreams, 1992, Ford Fairlane, 1990, Killer Tongue, 1996, Wishmaster, 1997, Disney's Meet the Deedles, 1997, Dee Snyder's Strangeland, 1997, Urban Legend, 1998, Nobody Knows Anything, 1999, The Prince and the Surfer, 1999, Wish You Were Dead, 2000, The Return of Caligostro, 2000, Python, 2000, Cold Sweat, 2000, Windfall, 2001, others; dir. 976-EVIL, 1988; appeared on TV in series Downtown, 1986-87, Freddy's Nighymares, 1987-89, Nightmare Cafe, 1992-93, Young Joe, the Forgotten Kennedy. 1977, The Ordeal of Patty Hearst, 1979, V, 1983, Hobson's Choice, 1983, I Want to Live, 1983, Hunter, 1985, Knight Rider, 1986, MacGyver, 1986, also on Police Woman, Soap, Charlie's Angels, Police Story, Married With Children, also others; TV films Mortal Fear, 1995, Unspoken Truth, 1996; also stage actor and producer. Mem. SAG, AFTRA, Actors Equity Assn., Dirs. Guild Am. Office: c/o Joe Rice Abrams Artists & Assocs 9200 W Sunset Blvd Ste 625 Los Angeles CA 90069-3508

ENGVALL, EVA, biochemist; b. Stockholm, Mar. 11, 1940; BSc, U. Stockholm, 1964, PhD in Immunology, 1975. Rsch. assoc. biochemistry Rsch. Lab. LKB, Stockholm, 1965-66, KABI AB, Stockholm, 1966-69; jr. rsch. sci. immunology U. Stockholm, 1969-75; fellow immunology U. Helsinki, 1975-76; fellow City Hope Med. Ctr., 1976-77, asst. rsch. sci. immunology, 1977-79; fellow European Molecular Biol. Orgn., 1975-77; scientist La Jolla (Calif.) Cancer Rsch. Found., 1979-96, Burnham Inst., La Jolla, 1996—. Recipient Biochemical Analysis award Ger. Soc. Clin. Chemistry 1976, Scientific Achievement award Edmund & Mary Shea Family Found., 1994. Mem. Am. Assn. Cancer Rsch., Am. Assn. Immunologists. Achievements include research in molecular interactions of extracellular matrix components. Office: Burnham Inst 10901 N Torrey Pines Rd La Jolla CA 92037-1062

ENNIS, THOMAS MICHAEL, management consultant; b. Morgantown, W.Va., Mar. 7, 1931; s. Thomas Edson and Violet Ruth (Nugent) E.; m. Julia Marie Dorety, June 30, 1956; children: Thomas John, Robert Griswold (dec.). Student, W.Va. U., 1949-52; AB, George Washington U., 1954; JD, Georgetown U., 1960. With Gov. Employees Ins. Co., Washington, 1956, 59, Air Transport Assn. Am., Washington, 1959-60; dir. ann. support program George Washington U., 1960-63; nat. dir. devel. Project HOPE, People to People Health Found., Inc., Washington, 1963-66; nat. exec. dir. Epilepsy Found. Am., Washington, 1966-74; exec. dir. Clinton, Eaton, Ingham Community Mental Health Bd., Lansing, Mich., 1974-83; nat. exec. dir. Alzheimer's Disease and Related Disorders Assn., Inc., Chgo., 1983-86; exec. dir., pres. The John Douglas French Alzheimers Found., L.A., 1986-96, pres. emeritus, 1996—. Clin. instr. dept. cmty. medicine and internat. health Georgetown U., 1967-74; adj. assoc. prof. dept. psychiatry Mich. State U., 1975-84; lectr. Univ. Ctr. for Internat. Rehab., 1977; cons. health and med. founds., related orgns.; cons. Am. Health Found., 1967-69, Reston, Va.-Georgetown U. Health Planning Project, 1967-70. Editl. bd. Am. Jour. Alzheimer's Disease, 1997—. Mem. adv. bd. Nat. Center for the Law and the Handicapped, 1971-74; advisor Nat. Reye's Syndrome Found.; mem. Nat. Com. for Research in Neurol. Disorders, 1967-72; mem. nat. adv. bd. Developmental Disabilities/Tech. Assistance System, U. N.C., 1971-78; nat. trustee Nat. Kidney Found., 1970-74, mem. exec. com. and bd. Nat. Capitol Area chpt., pres., 1972-74; bd. dirs. Nat. Assn. Pvt. Residential Facilities for Mentally Retarded, 1970-74; bd. dirs., mem. exec. com. Epilepsy Found. Am., 1977-84, Epilepsy Center Mich., 1974-83; nat. bd. dirs. Western Inst. on Epilepsy, 1969-72; bd. dirs., pres. Mich. Mid-South Health Systems Agy., 1975-78; sec. gen. Internat. Fedn. Alzheimer's Disease and Related Disorders, 1984-86; mem. panel Alzheimer's Disease Edn. and Referral Ctr., 1990-93; mem. Calif. State Coun. on Developmental Disabilities, 1997—; med. adv. bd. EdenCare Sr. Living Svcs., advisor Ctr. Aging, Washington, 1998—. World Rehab. Fund fellow Norway, 1980. Mem. Nat. Epilepsy League (bd. dirs. 1977-78), Mich. Assn. Cmty. Mental Health (pres. 1977-79), Nat. Coalition Rsch. Neurol. Disorders (dir. at-large 1991—), Scan Health Plan (bd. govs.), Phi Alpha Theta, Phi Kappa Psi. Home and Office: 23740 Killion St Woodland Hills CA 91367-5822

ENNIS, WILLIAM LEE, physics educator; b. Houston, Aug. 10, 1949; s. Arthur Lee and Helen Ennis; m. Constance Elizabeth Livsey, July 20, 1991. BS, Auburn (Ala.) U., 1974, BA, 1978. Rsch. tech. Nat. Tillage Lab., Auburn, Ala., 1974-76; tchr. Stanford Jr. H.S., Hillsborough, N.C., 1979-81; physics tchr., chmn. sci. dept. East H.S., Anchorage, 1981—. Chmn. Anchorage Sch. Dist. Physics Tchrs.; curriculum devel. sci. cons. Copper River Schs., Anchorage, 1991. Recipient Nat. Tchr. award Milken Family Found., 1999; named Tandy Tech. Outstanding Tchr., 1989-90, Tchr. of Excellence Brit. Petroleum, 1996, Brit. Petroleum Tchr. of Yr., 1996, Disting. Tchr., White House Commn. on Presdl. Scholars; Fermi Lab. scholar U.S. Dept. Energy, 1991. Mem. AAAS, Am. Assn. Physics Tchrs., Am. Phys. Soc., Nat. Sci. Tchrs. Assn., Alaska Sci. Tchrs. (life), Am. Mountain Guides Assn., Am. Alpine Club. Avocations: mountaineering, outdoor activities, sailing, computers. Office: East HS 4025 E Northern Lights Blvd Anchorage AK 99508-3588

ENOCH, JAY MARTIN, optometrist, educator; b. N.Y.C., Apr. 20, 1929; s. Jerome Dee and Stella Sarah (Nathan) E.; m. Rebekah Ann Feiss, June 24, 1951; children: Harold Owen, Barbara Diane, Ann Allison. BS in Optics and Optometry, Columbia U., 1950; postgrad., Inst. Optics U. Rochester, 1953; Ph.D. in Physiol. Optics, Ohio State U., 1956; DSc honoris causa, SUNY, 1993. Asst. prof. physiol. optics Ohio State U., Columbus, 1956-58; assoc. supr. Ohio State U. (Mapping and Charting Rsch. Lab.), 1957-58; fellow Nat. Phys. Lab., Teddington, Eng., 1959-60; rsch. instr. dept. ophthalmology Washington U. Sch. Medicine, St. Louis, 1958-59, rsch. asst. prof., 1959-64, rsch. assoc. prof., 1965-70, rsch. prof., 1970-74; fellow Barnes Hosp., St. Louis, 1960-64, cons. ophthalmology, 1964-74; rsch. prof. dept. psychology Washington U., St. Louis, 1970-74; grad. rsch. prof. ophthalmology and psychology Coll. Medicine U. Fla., Gainesville, 1974-80, grad. rsch. prof. physics, 1979-80; dir. Ctr. for Sensory Studies, 1976-80; dean Sch. Optometry, chmn. Grad. Group in Vision Sci. U. Calif., Berkeley, 1980-92, prof. optometry and vision sci., 1980-94, prof. of Grad. Sch., 1994—, prof. physiol. optics in ophthalmology San Francisco, 1980—. Exec. sec. subcom. on vision and its disorders of nat. adv.Nat. Inst. Neurol. Diseases and Blindness Coun., NIH, 1963-66; chmn. subcom. contact lens stds. Am. Nat. Stds. Inst., 1970-77; mem. nat. adv. eye coun. Nat. Eye Inst., NIH, 1975-77, 80-84; exec. com., com. on vision NAS-NRC, 1973-76; mem. U.S. Nat. Com. Internat. Commn. Optics, 1976-79; health scis. com. systemwide adminstrn. U. Calif., 1989-93, co-chmn. subcom. on immigrant health in Calif., 1993-94; mem. sci. adv. bd. Fight-for-Sight, 1988-92, Allergan Corp., 1991-93; mem. Lighthouse for Blind, N.Y., 1989-96, chair, 1995, Pisart award com. Contbr. chpts. and articles on visual sci., photoreceptor optics, perimetry, contact lenses, infant and aged vision, history of earliest lenses to profl. jours.; mem. editl. bd. Investigative Ophthamology, 1965-75, 83-88, Sight-Saving Rev., 1974-84, Sensory Processes, 1974-80, Vision Rsch., 1974-80, Internat. Ophthamology, 1977-93, Binocular Vision, 1984—, Clin. Vision Sci., 1986-93, Biomed. Optics, 1988-90; mem. editl. bd. optical scis. Springer-Verlag, Heidelberg, 1978-87, biomed. scis., 1988-95, Annals of Ophthalmology, 1997—; assoc. editor for vision Handbook of Optics, Optical Soc. Am., 1997-2001. Nat. sci. adv. bd. Retinitis Pigmentosa Found., 1977-95; U.S. rep. Internat. Perimetric Soc., 1974-90, also exec. com., chmn. Rsch. Group Standards; bd. dirs. Friends of Eye Rsch., 1977-88; trustee Illuminating Engring. Rsch. Inst., 1977-81; bd. dirs. Lighting Rsch. Bd., 1988-95; mem. bd. counselors U.C. San Francisco Sch. Dentistry, 1995—. 2d lt. U.S. Army, 1951-52. Recipient Career Devel. award NIH, 1963-73, Everett Kinsey award Contact Lens Assn. Ophthalmologists, 1991, Berkeley citation, Festschrift U. Calif. Berkeley, 1996. Fellow AAAS, Am. Acad. Optometry (Glenn A. Fry award 1972, Charles F. Prentice medal award 1974), Optical Soc. Am. (chmn. vision tech. sect. 1974-76, mem. book pub. com. 1996-2000), Am. Acad. Ophthalmology (honor award 1985); mem. Assn. for Rsch. in Vision and Ophthalmology (trustee 1967-73, pres. 1972-73, Francis I. Proctor medal 1977), Concilium Ophthalmologicum Universale (chmn. visual functions com. 1982-86), Am. Optometric Assn. (low vision sect., Vision Care award 1987), Internat. Perimetric Soc. (hon. mem.), Ocular Heritage Soc. (medal 1997), Cogan Ophthalmic History Soc., Cosmos Club (Washington), Sigma Xi. Home: 54 Shuey Dr Moraga CA 94556-2621 Office: U Calif Sch Optometry Berkeley CA 94720-2020 E-mail: jmenoch@socrates.berkeley.edu

ENOMOTO, JERRY JIRO, protective services official; b. San Francisco, Jan. 24, 1926; BA, U. Calif., Berkeley, 1949, MA, 1951. Counselor San Quentin Prison Calif. Dept. Corrections, 1952-54, parole officer, 1955-56, supr. San Quentin Prison, 1956-58, supr. Deuel Vocat. Inst., 1958-59, supr. counselor San Quinten Prison, 1959-60, assoc. warden Deuel Vocat Inst., 1960-65, chief classification svcs., 1965-70, deputy supt. Soledad Prison, 1970-71, warden Calif. Correctional Inst., 1971-74, acting supt. Calif. Inst. Women, 1974-75, dir., 1975-80; ind. cons., 1980-94; fed. ct. monitor, 1994; U.S. marshal Ea. Dist. Calif., 1994—. Pres., chmn. Japanese Am. Citizens League, 1987—. Mem. Am. Correctional Assn. Office: US Marshalls Office US Courthouse 501 I St Ste 5600 Sacramento CA 95814-7304

ENOS, KELLY D. telecommunications company financial executive; V.p. Sutro & Co., 1991-94, Oppenheimer & Co., Inc., 1994-95, Fortune Fin., 1995-96; ind. cons. mcht. banking field, 1996; CFO, Telecom., Inc., Santa Barbara, Calif., 1996—, treas., 1997—. Office: STAR Telecom Inc 223 E De La Guerra St Santa Barbara CA 93101-2206 Fax: 805-899-2972

ENRIGHT, CYNTHIA LEE, illustrator; b. Denver, July 6, 1950; d. Darrel Lee and Iris Arlene (Flodquist) E. BA in Elem. Edn., U. No. Colo., 1972; student, Minn. Sch. Art and Design, Mpls., 1975-76. Tchr. 3d grade Littleton (Colo.) Sch. Dist., 1972-75; graphics artist Sta. KCNC TV, Denver, 1978-79; illustrator No Coast Graphics, Denver, 1979-87; editorial artist The Denver Post, 1987—. Illustrator (mag.) Sesame St., 1984, 85; illustrator, editor "Tiny Tales" The Denver Post, 1991-94. Recipient Print mag. Regional Design Ann. awards, 1984, 85, 87, Phoenix Art Mus. Biannual award, 1979. Mem. Mensa. Democrat. Home: 1210 Ivanhoe St Denver CO 80220-2640 Office: The Denver Post 1560 Broadway Denver CO 80202-5177 E-mail: leeenright@aol.com

ENRIGHT, WILLIAM BENNER, judge; b. N.Y.C., July 12, 1925; s. Arthur Joseph and Anna Beatrice (Plante) E.; m. Bette Lou Card, Apr. 13, 1951; children— Kevin A., Kimberly A., Kerry K. BA, Dartmouth, 1947; LLB, Loyola U. at L.A., 1950. Bar: Calif. 1951; diplomate: Am. Bd. Trial Advs. Dep. dist. atty., San Diego County, 1951-54; ptnr. Enright, Levitt, Knutson & Tobin, San Diego, 1954-72; judge U.S. Dist. Ct. (so. dist.) Calif., San Diego, 1972-90, sr. judge, 1990—. Mem. adv. bd. Joint Legis. Com. for Revision Penal Code, 1970-72, Calif. Bd. Legal Specialization, 1970-72; mem. Jud. Council, 1972; Bd. dirs. Defenders, 1965-72, pres., 1972 Served as ensign USNR, 1943-46. Recipient Honor award San Diego County Bar, 1970; Extraordinary Service to Legal Professions award Mcpl. Ct. San Diego Jud. Dist., 1971 Fellow Am. Coll. Trial Lawyers, Am. Bar Found.; mem. ABA, San Diego County Bar Assn. (dir. 1963-65, pres. 1965), State Bar Calif. (gov. 1967-70, v.p. 1970, exec. com. law in a free soc. 1970—), Dartmouth Club San Diego, Am. Judicature Soc., Alpha Sigma Nu, Phi Delta Phi. Club: Rotarian. Office: US Dist Ct 4145 US Courthouse 940 Front St San Diego CA 92101-8994

ENRIQUEZ, CAROLA RUPERT, museum director; b. Washington, Jan. 2, 1954; d. Jack Burns and Shirley Ann (Orcutt) Rupert; m. John Enriquez, Jr., Dec. 30, 1989. BA in History cum laude, Bryn Mawr Coll., 1976; MA, cert. in mus. studies, U. Del., 1978. Pers. mgmt. trainee Naval Material Command, Arlington, Va., 1972-76; tchg. asst. dept. history U. Del., Newark, 1976-77; asst. curator/exhibit specialist Hist. Soc. Del., Wilmington, 1977-78; dir. Macon County Mus. Complex, Decatur, Ill., 1978-81, Kern County Mus., Bakersfield, Calif., 1981—. Pres. Kern County Mus Found., 1991—; advisor Kern County Heritage Commn., 1981-88; chmn. Hist. Records Commn., 1981-88; sec.-treas. Arts Coun. of Kern, 1984-86, pres., 1986-88; county co-chmn. United Way, 1981, 82; chmn. steering com. Calif. State Bakersfield Co-op Program, 1982-83; mem. cmty. adv. bd. Calif. State U.-Bakersfield Anthrop. Soc., 1986-88; bd. dirs. Mgmt. Coun., 1983-86, v.p., 1987, pres., 1988; bd. dirs. Calif. Coun. for Promotion of History, 1984-86, v.p., 1987-88, pres., 1988-90; mem. cmty. adv. bd. Calif. State U.-Bakersfiled Sociology Dept., 1986-88; mem. women's adv. com. Girls Scouts U.S., 1989-91; bd. dirs. Greater Bakersfield Conv. and Visitors Bur., 1993-95; co-chair 34th St. Neighborhood Partnership, 1994—. Hagley fellow Eleutherian Mills-Hagley found., 1977-78; Bryn Mawr alumnae reg. scholar, 1972-76. Mem. Calif. Assn. Mus. (reg. rep. 1991—, v.p. legis. affairs 1992—), Am. Assn. State and Local History (chair awards com. Calif. chpt. 1990, reg. vchair 1999—). Presbyterian. Office: Kern County Museum 3801 Chester Ave Bakersfield CA 93301-1345

ENSIGN, DONALD H. landscape architect; b. Salt Lake City, Sept. 5, 1936; s. C. Wesley and Mildred (Harker) E.; m. Kay Bateman, Sept. 9, 1959 (div. 1970); m. Nancy Ensign; children: Philip Wesley, Craig Allen, Michael Donald. B in Landscape Architecture, Utah State U., 1963; M in Landscape Architecture, U. Mich., 1968. Registered landscape architect, Mich., N.C. Landscape architect Frehner and Assocs., Salt Lake City, 1961-62; planner Roswell/Ensign and Assocs., Salt Lake City, 1962-66; instr. dept. landscape architecture and environ. planning Utah State U., Logan, 1963-66; planner Richard B. Wilkinson and Assocs., Ann Arbor, Mich., 1966-68; prin. Design Workshop, Inc., Aspen, Colo., 1970—; assoc. prof. sch. design N.C. State U., 1968-74, dir. basic design program, 1971-73. Prin. works include Aspen Inst., Grand Valley High Sch., Marolt Ranch, U. Mich., Utah State U., Estrella Lake Parks, Goodyear, Ariz., Fox River, Geneva, Ill., Lauder Residence, Aspen, Resort at Squaw Creek, Squaw Valley, Calif., 700 East Main, Aspen, Snowmass (Colo.) Club, Blackcomb Resort, Whistler, British Columbia, Early Winters Resort, Mazama, Wash., Grand Champions Resort, Aspen, many others. Avocations: fox hunting, cross country skiing, painting, golf, hiking. Office: Design Workshop 120 E Main St Aspen CO 81611-1714

ENSIGN, JOHN E. senator, former congressman; b. Roseville, Calif., Mar. 25, 1958; s. Mike and Sharon E.; m. Darlene Sciarretta Ensign; 1 child, Trevor. Student, UNLV; B in Gen. Sci., Oreg. State U., 1981; D of Veterinary Medicine, Colo. State U., 1985. Owner animal hosp., Las Vegas; gen. mgr. Gold Strike Hotel & Casino, 1991, Nev. Landing Hotel & Casino, 1992; mem. U.S. Congress from 1st Nev. dist., Washington, 1994-98; mem. ways and means com., subcom. health, subcom. human resources; mem. com. on resources, 1995-98. Candidate for U.S. Sen., 1998-99. Office: 9808 Moon Valley Pl Las Vegas NV 89134-6738*

ENSIGN, MICHAEL S. resort company executive; Gen. mgr. Circus Circus-Las Vegas; COO, exec. v.p. Circus-Circus Enterprises; also bd. dirs.; rejoined as COO, vice-chmn., 1995-98; CEO, chmn., 1998; CEO, COO, chmn. Mandalay Resort Group, Las Vegas, 1998—. Office: Mandalay Resort Group 3950 Las Vegas Blvd S Las Vegas NV 89119

ENSTROM, JAMES EUGENE, epidemiologist; b. Alhambra, Calif., June 20, 1943; s. Elmer Melvin, Jr. and Klea Elizabeth (Bissell) E.; m. Marta Eugenia Villanea, Sept. 3, 1978. B.S., Harvey Mudd Coll., Claremont, Calif., 1965; M.S., Stanford U., 1967; Ph.D. in Physics, 1970; M.P.H., UCLA, 1976. Research assoc. Stanford Linear Accelerator Center, 1970-71; research physicist, cons. Lawrence Berkeley Lab. U. Calif., 1971-75; Celeste Durand Rogers cancer research fellow Sch. Pub. Health, UCLA, 1973-75; Nat. Cancer Inst. postdoctoral trainee, 1975-76; cancer epidemiology researcher, 1976-81; assoc. research prof., 1981—. Program dir. for cancer control epidemiology Jonsson Comprehensive Cancer Center, 1978-88, research epidemiologist, 1988—, sci. dir. tumor registry, 1984-87, mem. dean's council, 1976—; cons. epidemiologist Linus Pauling Inst. Sci. and Medicine, 1976-94; cons. physicist Rand Corp., 1969-73, R&D Assos., 1971-75; mem. sci. bd. Am. Council on Sci. and Health, 1984—. Author papers in field. NSF predoctoral trainee, 1965-66; grantee Am. Cancer Soc., 1973—, Nat. Cancer Inst., 1979—; Preventive Oncology Acad. award, 1981-87. Fellow Am. Coll. Epidemiology; mem. Soc. Epidemiologic Research, Am. Heart Assn., Am. Pub. Health Assn., Am. Phys. Soc., AAAS, N.Y. Acad. Scis., Galileo Soc. Office: U Calif Sch Pub Health Los Angeles CA 90024

ENTHOVEN, ALAIN CHARLES, economist, educator; b. Seattle, Sept. 10, 1930; s. Richard Frederick and Jacqueline (Camerlynck) E.; m. Rosemary Fenech, July 28, 1956; children: Eleanor, Richard, Andrew, Martha, Nicholas, Daniel. B.A. in Econs, Stanford U., 1952; M.Phil. (Rhodes scholar), Oxford (Eng.) U., 1954; Ph.D. in Econs, MIT, 1956. Instr. econs. MIT, Cambridge, 1955-56; economist The RAND Corp., Santa Monica, Calif., 1956-60; ops. research analyst Office of Dir. Def. Research and Engring., Dept. Def., Washington, 1960; dep. comptroller, dep. asst. sec. U.S. Dept. Def., Washington, 1961-65, asst. sec. for systems analysis, 1965-69; v.p. for econ. planning Litton Industries, Beverly Hills, Calif., 1969-71; pres. Litton Med. Products, Beverly Hills, 1971-73; Marriner S. Eccles prof. pub. and pvt. mgmt. Grad. Sch. Bus. Stanford (Calif.) U., 1973-2000, prof. health care econs. Sch. Medicine, 1973-2000; sr. fellow Ctr. for Health Policy, Stanford U., 2000—. Cons. The Brookings Instn., 1956-60; vis. assoc. prof. econs. U. Wash., 1958; mem. Stanford Computer Sci. Adv. Com., 1968-73; cons. The RAND Corp., 1969— ; mem. vis. com. in econs. MIT, 1971-78; mem. vis. com. on environ. quality lab. Calif. Inst. Tech., 1972-77; mem. Inst. Medicine, Nat. Acad. Scis., 1972— ; mem. vis. com. Harvard U. Sch. Pub. Health, 1974-80; cons. Kaiser Found. Health Plan, Inc., 1973— ; vis. prof. U. Paris, 1985, London Sch. Hygiene and Tropical Medicine, 1998-99; vis. fellow St. Catherine's Coll., Oxford U., Eng., 1985, New Coll., 1998-99; dir. Hotel Investors Trust, 1986-87, PCS Inc., 1987-90, Caresoft, 1996—, Rx Intelligence, 2000—, eBeuX Inc, 2001—. Contbr. numerous articles on def. spending and on econs. and pub. policy in health care to profl. jours.; author: (with K. Wayne Smith) How Much is Enough? Shaping the Defense Program 1961-69, 1971, Health Plan: The Only Practical Solution to the Soaring Cost of Medical Care, 1980; editor: (with A. Myrick Freeman III) Pollution, Resources and the Environment, 1973, Theory and Practice of Managed Competition in Health Care Finance, 1988, In Pursuit of an Improving National Health Service, 1999. Bd. dirs. Georgetown U., Washington, 1968-73, Jackson Hole Group, 1993-96; bd. regents St. John's Hosp., Santa Monica, 1971-73; vis. com. Harvard U. Kennedy Sch. Govt. Rock Carling fellow Nuffield Trust, 1999; recipient President's award for disting. fed. civilian svc., 1963, Disting. Pub. Svc. medal Dept. Def., 1968, Baxter prize for health svcs. rsch., 1994, Bd. Dirs.' award Healthcare Fin. Mgmt. Assn., 1995, Ellwood award Found. for Accountability, 1998; chmn. Gov.'s Taskforce Managed Health Care Improvement, 1997-98. Mem. Am. Assn. Rhodes Scholars, Am. Acad. Arts and Scis., Integrated Healthcare Assn. (bd. dirs. 1999—), Phi Beta Kappa. Home: 1 McCormick Ln Atherton CA 94027-3033 Office: Stanford Univ Grad Sch Business Stanford CA 94305 E-mail: enthoven@stanford.edu

ENYEART, JAMES L. museum director; b. Auburn, Wash., Jan. 13, 1943; s. Lyle F. and Emma A. (Ham) E.; m. Roxanne Enyeart Malone, Sept. 7, 1964; children: Mara, Sascha, Megan. BFA, Kansas City Art Inst., 1965; MFA, U. Kans., 1972. Dir. Albrecht Gallery Art, St. Joseph, Mo., 1967-68; curator photography, assoc. prof. Spencer Mus. Art, U. Kans., 1968-76; exec. dir. Friends of Photography, Carmel, Calif., 1976-77; dir., adj. prof. art Ctr. for Creative Photography, U. Ariz., 1977-89; dir. Internat. Mus. Photography at George Eastman House, Rochester, N.Y., 1989-95; Anne and John Marion prof., dir. Marion Ctr. Photo. Art Coll. Santa Fe, 1995—. Prof. Photographic Arts, dir. Ann and John Marion Ctr., Coll. Santa Fe, 1995—; mem. numerous panels, adv. bds. and commns. in field, including peer panel, Nat. Endowment for Arts, Mus. Challenge Grants, 1993, adv. bd. Am. Photography Inst., NYU, 1991—, others; cons. in field. Author: Creative Camera, 1976, Francis Bruguiere, 1977, Jerry Uelsmann: Twenty-Five Years, A Retrospective, 1982, Edward Weston's California Landscapes, 1984 (Am. Inst. Graphic Arts award), Land, Sky, and All That Is Within: Visionary Photographers of the Southwest, 1998, The Nature of Photographs, 1998, others; (with R.D. Monroe, Philip Stokes) Three Classic American Photographs: Texts and Contexts, 1982; contbr. Edward Weston Omnibus, 1984, Contemporary Photographers, 1983, 2d rev. edit., 1986-87; editor: Decade by Decade: A Survey of Twentieth Century American Photography, 1989; co-editor: Henry Holmes Smith: Collected Writings 1935-1985, 1986; contbr. introductions to Andreas Feininger: A Retrospective, 1986, Aaron Siskind: Terrors and Pleasures, 1931-1980, 1982, W. Eugene Smith: Master of the Photographic Essay, 1981, Landscapes 1975-1979, 1981, Photography of the Fifties: An American Perspective, 1980, George Fiske, Yosemite Photographer, 1980, Peekamoose, 1973; editor Kans. Album, 1977, Heinecken, 1980, The Archive, 1988, Image, 1989—; designer print study rm. Spencer Mus. Art, U. Kans., 1976, Ctr. Creative Photography, U. Ariz., 1989; author, curator exhbn. Judy Dater: Twenty Years; represented in collections Albrecht Gallery, St. Joseph, Mo., Mus. Art, U. Kans., Bibliotheque Nationale, Paris, Internat. Mus. Photography at George Eastman House, Rochester, Sheldon Meml. Gallery, Lincoln, Nebr., Nat. Mus. Am. Art; numerous other publs. Commr. Kans. Arts Commn., 1973-74; selection com. Ariz. Gov's. Arts Awards, 1984; creative arts award com. Brandeis U., Waltham, Mass., 1990—; adv. bd. Aaron Siskind Found., 1981—, W. Eugene Smith Meml. Fund, Inc., 1983—; nom. com. MacArthur Found., 1982; rev. panel Bush Found. Fellowships, St. Paul, 1980. Recipient Josef Sudek medal Ministry Culture, Union Visual Arts, Czechoslovakia, 1989, Photokina Obelisk award, Fed. Republic Germany, 1982, Internat. Achievement award Photographic Soc. Japan, 1994, others; grantee NEA, 1973, 74, 75; Hon. Rsch. fellow U. Exeter, 1974, OAS fellow, 1966-67, John Simon Guggenheim Meml. fellow, 1987; fellow John S. and James L. Knight Found. Nat. Millennium Survey, 1998; named 100 Most Important People in Photography Am. Photo, 1998; grantee Nat. Endowment for the Arts, 1973—; other awards in field. Mem. Am. Assn. Art Mus. Dirs., Am. Assn. Art Mus., Am. Photography Inst. (adv. bd. 1991—), Am. Photog. Hist. Soc. (hon. life), Oracle (co-founder), Deutschen Gesellschaft fur Photographie (hon. mem.), others. Office: Coll Santa Fe Marion Ctr Photographic Art 1600 Saint Michaels Dr Santa Fe NM 87505-7615

ENZI, MICHAEL BRADLEY, senator, accountant; b. Bremerton, Wash., Feb. 1, 1944; s. Elmer Jacob and Dorothy (Bradley) E.; m. Diana Buckley, June 7, 1969; children: Amy, Bradley, Emily. BBA, George Wash. U., 1966; MBA, Denver U., 1968. Cert. profl. human resources, 1994. Pres. NZ Shoes, Inc., Gillette, Wyo., 1969-95, NZ Shoes of Sheridan, Inc., 1983-96; acctg. mgr. Dunbar Well Svc., Inc., Gillette, 1985-97; mem. Wyo. Ho. of Reps., Cheyne, 1987-91, Wyo. State Senate, Cheyne, 1991-96; senator from Wyo. U.S. Senate, 1997—. Chmn. bd. dirs. 1st Wyo. Bank, Gillette, 1978-88; chmn. Senate Revenue Com., 1992-96. Mayor City of Gillette, 1975-82; pres. Wyo. Assn. Mcpls., Cheyenne, 1980-82. Sgt. Wyo. Air NG, 1967-73. Mem. Wyo. Order of DeMolay (state master councilor 1963-64), Wyo. Jaycees (state pres. 1973-74), Masons (Sheridan and Gillette lodges), Scottish Rite, Shriners, Lions, Sigma Chi. Republican. Presbyterian. Avocations: fishing, bicycling, soccer. Home: 431 Circle Dr Gillette WY 82716-4903 Office: US Senate 201 Senate Russell Bldg Washington DC 20510-0001 E-mail: senator@enzi.senate.gov

EPEL, DAVID, biologist, educator; b. Detroit, Mar. 26, 1937; s. Jacob A. and Anna K. E.; m. Lois S. Ambush, Dec. 18, 1960; children: Andrea, Sharon, Elissa. A.B., Wayne State U., 1958; Ph.D., U. Calif.-Berkeley, 1963. Postdoctoral fellow Johnson Research Found., U. Pa., 1963-65; asst. prof. Hopkins Marine Sta., 1965-70; assoc. prof., then prof. Scripps Instn. Oceanography, 1970-77; Jane and Marshall Steel Jr. prof. marine scis. Hopkins Maine Sta., Stanford U., Pacific Grove, Calif., 1977—; acting dir. Hopkins Marine Sta., Pacific Grove, 1984-88. Co-dir. embryology course Marine Biol. Lab., Woods Hole, 1974-77. Mem. editl. bd. Acta Histochemica, Biol. Bull, Zygote. Bd. dirs. Rsch. Inst., Monterey Bay Aquarium, 1987-89, trustee, 1985-88. Guggenheim fellow, 1976-77, Overseas fellow Churchill Coll., Cambridge, Eng., 1976-77; recipient Allen Cox medal for fostering excellence in undergrad. rsch. Stanford U., 1995. Fellow AAAS (mem.-at-large, sect. G 1979-84, chmn. sect. on biol. scis. 1998—), Calif. Acad. Scis.; mem. Am. Soc. Cell Biology (mem. council 1978-80), Soc. Devel. Biology, Internat. Soc. Devel. Biology, Soc. Integrative and Comparative Biology (chairperson devel. and cell biology sect. 1990-92). Home: 25847 Carmel Knolls Dr Carmel CA 93923-8845 Office: Hopkins Marine Sta Pacific Grove CA 93950 E-mail: depel@stanford.edu

EPP, MENNO HENRY, clergyman; b. Lena, Man., Can., Apr. 11, 1932; s. Henry Martin and Anna (Enns) E.; m. Irma Mary Wiens, July 26, 1957 (dec. Sep. 1990); children: Charlene and Beverly (twins), Darrell; m. Elsie Neufeld, Apr. 10, 1993. BTh, Can. Mennonite Bible Coll., 1957; BA, Bethel Coll., 1964; MDiv, Assoc. Mennonite Bible Sem., 1971; D of Ministry, St. Stephens Coll., 1983. Tchr., prin. Bethel Bible Inst., Abbotsford, B.C., 1957-69; dir. Camp Squeah, Yale, 1963-69; youth pastor Bethel United Meth., Elkhart, Ind., 1969-71; pastor Foothills Mennonite Ch., Calgary, Alta., 1971-84, Leamington (Ont.) United Mennonite Ch., 1984-98; retired, 1998. Bd. dirs., chmn. Assoc. Mennonite Biblical Sem., Elkhart, 1977-89; moderator Conf. of Mennonites in Can., Winnipeg, 1990-96. Office: 242 Haight Pl Saskatoon SK Canada S7H 4W2

EPPERSON, STELLA MARIE, artist; b. Oakland, Calif., Nov. 6, 1920; d. Walter Peter and Martha Josephine (Schmitt) Ross; m. John Cray Epperson, May 10, 1941; children: Therese, John, Peter. Student, Calif. Coll. Arts & Crafts, 1939, 40-41, 56; postgrad., Art Inst., San Miguel d'Allende, Mex., 1972. Portrait artist Oakland Art Assn., 1956—, San Francisco Women Artists, 1962—, Marin Soc. Artists, Ross, Calif., 1971—. Art docent Oakland Mus., 1969-71, mem. women's bd., 1971—, art chmn. fund raiser, 1971-89, art guild chmn., 1965-69, chmn. exhbt. Japanese artists in Brazil, Kaiser Ctr., Oakland, for honoring artist Xavier Martinez, event honoring Neil Armstrong, Calif. Coll. Arts and Crafts. One-woman shows include Oakland Mus. Auction, 1993, Univ. Club, San Francisco, 1994; exhbns. include Women's Art Gallery, San Francisco, Kaiser Ctr., St. Mary's Coll. Hearst Gallery, numerous others; commd. portrait Mrs. Evangelina Macapagal, Malacalang Palace. Recipient San Francisco Women Artists, 1989, Oakland Art Assn., 1991, , 1997, , 2000, Marin Soc. Artists, 1992, Figurative Subject First award, Oakland Art Assn. Mem. Oakland Art Assn. (1st award in small format show 1998, 1999 Artistic award in Kaiser Ctr. Gallery Exhibit, Merit award 2000, Artistic award 2001), San Francisco Women Artists, Marin Art Assn., U. Calif. Berkeley Faculty Club, Orinda Country Club. Republican. Roman Catholic. Avocations: dress design, gourmet cooking, tennis. Home: 31 Valley View Rd Orinda CA 94563-1432

EPPLER, JEROME CANNON, private financial advisor; b. Englewood, N.J., Mar. 16, 1924; s. William E. and Aileen (Vaughan) E.; m. Debora Nye Eppler; children: Stephen Vaughan, William Durand, Margaret Nye, Elizabeth Scott, Edward Curtis. BSME, Tex. A&M U., 1946; MBA, U. Pa., 1949. With Gen. Electric Supply Corp., Newark, 1949-50; investment banker Equitable Securities Corp., Nashville, mgr. Houston, 1950-53; gen. ptnr. Cyrus J. Lawrence & Sons, N.Y.C., 1953-61; mem. N.Y. Stock Exch.; owner Eppler & Co., Denver, 1961; ltd. ptnr. Alex Brown & Sons, Balt., 1982-84; bd. dirs. Chgo. Milw. St. Paul & Pacific Ry., 1958-63, Chemex Pharms., 1984-88; prin. Olympic Capital Ptnrs., Seattle, 1995-2000. Dir. Advanced Rsch. Sys., Inc., Seattle, 1997-99, Pvt. Asset Mgmt., Inc., Bellevue, Wash.; chmn. bd. United Screen Arts, Inc., L.A., 1966-73; bd. dirs. VisionTek, Inc., Boulder, Colo., 1998-2001; chmn., bd. dirs. Life Ins. Co. Calif., 1967-77, I.S.I. Corp., 1967-77, Tessco Techs. Inc., Hunt Valley, Md., World Wide Life Assurance Co., London, 1972-77, Windsor Life Ins. Co., London, 1972-77; mem. indsl. adv. com. U. Calif., San Diego, 1978-93; dir. Telecredit, Inc., L.A., 1976-90, Brooktree Corp., San Diego, 1983-86, QTron, Inc., San Diego, 1995-97. Trustee emeritus Scripps Clinic and Research Found., La Jolla; former trustee Drew U. (N.J.), 1966-67, Morris Mus. Arts & Scis. (N.J.), 1954-76, Met. Opera Assn., 1980-82, Wharton Grad. Sch. Bus. N.Y., 1972-86. Lt. (j.g.) USNR, 1942-46. Mem. Wharton Grad. Bus. Sch. Club, Castle Pines Golf Club, River Bend Country Club (Tequesta, Fla.). Presbyterian. Office: Eppler & Co Castle Pines 1004 Hummingbird Dr Ste A Castle Rock CO 80104-9003

EPPS, MARY ELLEN, state legislator; b. Copperhill, Tenn., Dec. 25, 1934; Student, Regis Coll.; BS, Colo. Christian U. Former bus. owner; nurse/physician asst.; owner, founder Future Visions Video Prodn. Co.; mem. Colo. Ho. of Reps., Dist. 19, 1986-98, Colo. Senate, Dist. 11, Denver, 1998—; chair health, environment, welfare and instns. com.; mem. judiciary com., mem. transp. com. Edn. com. chair Am. Legis. Exch. Coun., Criminal Justice Task Force; leader Girl Scouts; active El Paso County Planning Commn.; vice-chair Social Svcs. Consumer Rev. Bd. Mem. AARP, VFW, Nat. Conf. State Legislatures (arts and tourism com.), Security Lioness Club, Optimists Club, Fountain Valley Lions Club, Am. Legion Aux., ENT Aero Club, Fountain Valley Teen Club. Republican. Home: 825 S Union Blvd Colorado Springs CO 80910-3466 Office: State Capitol 200 E Colfax Ave Ste 346 Denver CO 80203-1716

EPSTEIN, CHARLES JOSEPH, physician, medical geneticist, pediatrics and biochemistry educator; b. Phila., Sept. 3, 1933; s. Jacob C. and Frieda (Savransky) E.; m. Lois Barth, June 10, 1956; children: David Alexander, Jonathan Akiba, Paul Michael, Joanna Marguerite. A.B., Harvard U., 1955, M.D., 1959; DS, Northeastern Ohio U., 1997. Diplomate: Am. Bd. Medical Genetics. Intern in medicine Peter Bent Brigham Hosp., Boston, 1959-60, asst. resident in medicine, 1960-61; research assoc., med. officer and sect. chief Nat. Heart Inst. and Nat. Inst. Arthritis and Metabolic Diseases, NIH, Bethesda, Md., 1961-67; research fellow in med. genetics U. Wash., 1963-64; assoc. prof. pediatrics and biochemistry U. Calif., San Francisco, 1967-72, prof., 1972—, chief divsn. med. genetics. dept. pediatrics, 1967—, co-dir. program in human genetics, 1997—. Investigator Howard Hughes Med. Inst., 1976-81; mem. human embryology and devel. study sect. NIH, 1971-75; mem. mental retardation research com. Nat. Inst. Child Health and Devel., 1979-83, chmn., 1981-83; mem. com. for study inborn errors of metabolism NRC, 1972-75; mem. sci. adv. bd. Nat. Down Syndrome Soc., 1981-99, chmn., 1984-99, mem. nat. adv. bd., 1999—, also bd. dirs.; mem. recombinant DNA adv. com. NIH, 1985-90, mem. human gene therapy subcom., 1987-91, chmn. residency review com. med. genetics, 1993-99; Stanley Wright Meml. lectr. Western Soc. Pediatric Research, 1986; William Potter lectr. Thomas Jefferson U., 1987; George H. Fetterman lectr. U Pitts., 1989; faculty rsch. lectr. U. Calif., San Francisco, 1994; Mary Hulings Edens lectr., U. Tex. Med. Br., Galveston, 1996; Ida Cordelia Beam lectr., U. Iowa, 1998; Donald L. Thurston meml. lectr. Washington U., St. Louis, 1999. Author: The Consequences of Chromosome Imbalance: Principles, Mechanisms and Models, 1986; editor: Human Genetics, 1984-95, The Neurobiology of Down Syndrome, 1986, Oncology and Immunology of Down Syndrome, 1987, Am. Jour. Human Genetics, 1987-93, Molecular and Cytogenetic Studies of Non-disjunction, 1989, Molecular Genetics of Chromosome 21 and Down Syndrome, 1990, Morphogenesis of Down Syndrome, 1991, Down Syndrome and Alzheimer Disease, 1992, Phenotypic Mapping of Down Syndrome and other Aneuploid Conditions, 1993, Etiology and Pathogenesis of Down Syndrome, 1995; assoc. editor Rudolph's Textbook of Pediatrics, 18th edit., 1986, 20th edit., 1996; mem. editl. bd. Biology Reprodn., 1974-78, Cytogenetics and Cell Genetics, 1975-80; mem. editl. bd. Am. Jour. Med. Genetics, 1977—, sr. editor, 1995-99, adv. editor, 2000—; mem. editl. bd. Devel. Genetics, 1983-85, Jour. Embryology and Exptl. Morphology, 1983-85, Human Gene Therapy, 1990-98, Human Mutation, 1992-99, Human Genetics, 1995-99, Down Syndrome Quar., 1996—, Trends in Genetics, 1997—, Cmty. Genetics, 1998—, Annual Review of Human Genetics and Genomics, 1999—, Mechanisms of Aging and Development, 2000—. Served with USPHS, 1961-63. Recipient Henry A. Christian award Harvard Med. Sch., 1959, Rsch. Career Devel. award NIH, 1967-72, Nancy and Daniel Weisman Charitable Found. award, 1990, Lifetime Achievement award in genetic scis., March of Dimes Birth Defects Found, Col. Harland Sanders, 1995, 6th World Congress on Down Syndrome award, 1997, Disting. Rsch. award The Arc of the U.S., 1998, Premio Internat. Phoenix-Anni Verdi Perle Rsch. Genetiche, Italian Soc. Human Genetics, 1999. Fellow AAAS; mem. AMA, Am. Bd. Med. Genetics (bd. dirs. 1988-93, v.p. 1989, pres. 1990-91), Genetics Soc. Am., Am. Fedn. Clin. Rsch., Am. Soc. Human Genetics (bd. dirs. 1972-75, 87-93, 97-98, pres.-elect 1995, pres. 1996), Am. Soc. Biochemistry and Molecular Biology, Soc. Pediatric Rsch. (coun. 1972-75), Am. Coll. Med. Genetics (pres. elect 2001—), Western Soc. Clin. Investigation, Western Soc. Pediatric Rsch., Am. Soc. Clin. Investigation, Am. Soc. Cell Biology, Soc. Devel. Biology, Am. Pediatric Soc., Western Assn. Physicians (coun. 1993-95), Assn. Am. Physicians, Soc. Inherited Metabolic Disorders, Inst. Medicine (Nat. Acad. Scis.), Calif. Acad. Medicine, Phi Beta Kappa, Alpha Omega Alpha. Jewish. Achievements include research numerous publs. on human and med. genetics, devel. genetics and biochemistry. Office: U Calif Dept Pediatrics U585L San Francisco CA 94143-0001

EPSTEIN, DANIEL J. management consultant; Chmn., CEO Con Am Mgmt. Corp., San Diego, 1995—. Office: Con Am Mgmt Corp 1764 San Diego Ave San Diego CA 92110-1906

EPSTEIN, EDWARD LOUIS, lawyer; b. Walla Walla, Wash., Jan. 10, 1936; s. Louis and Marie (Barger) E.; m. Marilyn K. Young, Dec. 29, 1962; children: Lisa Marie, Rachel Ann. BA with great distinction, Stanford U., 1958; LLB magna cum laude, Harvard U., 1961. Bar: Oreg. 1962, U.S. Dist. Ct. Oreg. 1962, U.S. Ct. Appeals (9th cir.) 1963. Assoc. Stoel Rives LLP, Portland, Oreg., 1962-67, ptnr., 1967—. Past sec., bd. dirs. Portland Hosp. Facilities Authority; trustee Good Samaritan Hosp. and Med. Ctr., Portland, 1972-78, pres., 1978; past trustee Morrison Ctr. for Youth and Family Svcs., Oreg. Assn. Hosps. Found. Mem. ABA, Am. Bar Found., Am. Health Lawyers Assn., Oreg. Bar Assn., Multnomah County Bar Assn., Multnomah Athletic Club, Univ. Club, Harvard Law Rev., Phi Beta Kappa. Democrat. Office: Stoel Rives LLP 900 SW 5th Ave Ste 2600 Portland OR 97204-1268 E-mail: elepstein@stoel.com

EPSTEIN, EMANUEL, plant physiologist; b. Duisburg, Germany, Nov. 5, 1916; came to U.S., 1938, naturalized, 1946; s. Harry and Bertha (Lowe) E.; m. Hazel L. Leask, Nov. 26, 1943; children: Jared H. (dec.), Jonathan H. BS, U. Calif., Davis, 1940, MS, 1941; PhD, U. Calif., Berkeley, 1950. Plant physiologist Dept. Agr., Beltsville, Md., 1950-58; lectr., assoc. plant physiologist U. Calif.-Davis, 1958-65, prof. plant nutrition, plant physiologist, 1965-87, faculty rsch. lectr., 1980, prof. botany, 1974-87, prof. and plant physiologist emeritus (active), 1987—. Cons. to govt. and pvt. agys. Author: Mineral Nutrition of Plants: Principles and Perspectives, 1972; mem. editl. bd. Plant Physiology, 1962-71, 76-92, CRC Handbook Series in Nutrition and Food, 1975-84, The Biosaline Concept: An Approach to the Utilization of Underexploited Resources, 1978, Saline Agriculture: Salt-Tolerant Plants for Developing Countries, 1990, Plant Sci., 1981-89, Advances in Plant Nutrition, 1981-94, Soil Science and Plant Nutrition, 1998—; contbr. articles to profl. jours. With U.S. Army, 1943-46. Recipient Gold medal Pisa (Italy) U., 1962; Guggenheim fellow, 1958; Fulbright sr. research scholar, 1965-66, 74-75 Fellow AAAS (pres. Pacific divsn. 1990, Fifty-Yr. Life mem. award 1999); mem. Nat. Acad. Scis., Am. Soc. Plant Biologists (Charles Reid Barnes Hon. Life Membership award 1986), Japanese Soc. Plant Physiologists, Scandinavian Soc. Plant Physiology, Am. Inst. Biol. Scis., Common Cause, Save-the-Redwoods League, U. Calif. Davis Club, Nature Conservancy, Nat. Parks and Conservation Assn., Sigma Xi. Achievements include rsch., publs. on ion transport in plants, mineral nutrition and salt rels. of plants, salt tolerant crops, and silicon in plant biology. Office: UC Soils & Biogeochemistry Land Air & Water Resources 1 Shields Ave Davis CA 95616-8627 E-mail: eqepstein@ucdavis.edu

EPSTEIN, JOHN HOWARD, dermatologist; b. San Francisco, Dec. 29, 1926; s. Norman Neman and Gertrude (Hirsch) E.; m. Alice Thompson, Nov. 1953; children: Norman H., Janice A., Beverly A. BA, U. Calif., Berkeley, 1949, MD, 1952; MS, U. Minn., 1956. Diplomate Am. Bd. Dermatology (dir. 1974-84, pres. 1981-82). Intern Stanford U. Med. Ctr., 1952-53; resident in dermatology Mayo Clinic, Rochester, Minn., 1953-56; practice medicine specializing in dermatology San Francisco, 1956—; chief dermatology Mt. Zion Hosp., 1970-80. Clin. prof. U. Calif. Med. Sch., San Francisco, 1972— ; cons. Letterman Army Med. Center, U.S. Naval Hosp., San Diego. Chief editor Archives of Dermatology, 1973-78; asst. editor Jour. Am. Acad. Dermatology, 1978-88; contbr. over 260 articles to profl. jours. With USNR, 1944-46. Fellow ACP; mem. Am. Acad. Dermatology (pres. 1981-82, Silver award for exhibit 1962, Gold award 1969), Soc. Investigative Dermatology (v.p. 1979-80), Am. Dermatol. Assn. (bd. dirs. 1983-88, pres. 1990-91), N.Am. Dermatology Soc., Pacific Dermatol. Assn. (pres. 1985-86), Brit. Dermatol. Soc., Danish Dermatol. Soc., Polish Dermatol. Soc., San Francisco Dermatol. Soc. (pres. 1963-64), Am. Soc. Photobiology (councilor 1983-86), Academia Mexicana and Dermatologia (hon.), European Acad. Dermatology and Venerology (hon.), La Societe Francaise de Dermatologie & de Syphiligraphie, Spanish Dermatol. Soc. Office: 450 Sutter St Rm 1306 San Francisco CA 94108-4002

EPSTEIN, MARSHA ANN, public health administrator, physician; b. Chgo., Feb. 4, 1945; 1 child, Lee Rashad Mahmood. BA, Reed Coll., 1965; MD, U. Calif., San Francisco, 1969; MPH, U. Calif., Berkeley, 1971. Diplomate Am. Bd. Preventive Medicine. Intern French Hosp., San Francisco, 1969-70; resident in preventive medicine Sch. Pub. Health, U. Calif., Berkeley, 1971-73; fellow in family planning dept. ob-gyn. UCLA, 1973-74; med. dir. Herself Health Clinic, L.A., 1974-79; pvt. adult gen. practitioner L.A., 1978-82; dist. health officer L.A. County Pub. Health, L.A., 1982—. Part-time physician U. Calif. Student Health, Berkeley, 1970-73; co-med. dir. Monsenior Oscar Romero Free Clinic, L.A., 1992-93. Mem. APHA, Am. Coll. Physician Execs., Am. Med. Women's Assn., So. Calif. Pub. Health Assn., Calif. Acad. Preventive Medicine, L.A. County Med. Women's Assn. Democrat. Jewish. Avocations: dancing, native plants, meditating. Office: Burke Health Ctr 2509 Pico Blvd # 324 Santa Monica CA 90405-1828 E-mail: mepstein@dh.co.la.ca.us

EPSTEIN, SAMUEL, geologist, educator; b. Poland, Dec. 9, 1919; BSc, U. Man., Can., 1941, MSc, 1942; PhD in Phys. Chemistry, McGill U., Can., 1944; LLD (hon.), U. Man., 1980. Rsch. chemist Natural Rsch. Coun. Can., 1944-47; rsch. assoc. Inst. Nuclear Studies, U. Chgo., 1948-52, rsch. fellow, 1952-53, sr. rsch. fellow, 1953-54, assoc. prof., 1954-59; prof. geochemistry Calif. Inst. Tech., Pasadena, 1959-84, William E. Leonhard prof. geology, 1984—. Recipient Wollaston medal Geol. Soc., London, 1993. Fellow Am. Acad. Arts Scis., Am. Geophys. Union, European Union Geoscis. (hon. gdn., Urey medal 1995), Royal Soc. of Can. (fgn. fellow); mem. NAS, Geol. Soc. Am. (Arthur L. Day medal 1978), Geochem. Soc. (Goldschmidt medal 1977). Office: Calif Inst Tech Divsn Geol & Planetary Scis Pasadena CA 91125-0001 E-mail: epstein@gps.caltech.edu

EPTON, GREGG, performing company executive; b. Alberta, Can. Prodn. and tour. mgr. Alberta Ballet, Calgary, Can., 1987, gen. mgr. Can., 1989, exec. dir. Can., 1991—. Co-founder Alberta Ballet Sch., 1991. Mem. Can. Assn. Profl. Dance Orgns. (corp. sec. 1992-94).

ERASMUS, CHARLES JOHN, anthropologist, educator; b. Pitts., Sept. 23, 1921; s. Percy Thomas and Alice E.; m. Helen Marjorie O'Brien, Feb. 18, 1943; children: Thomas Glen, Gwendolyn. B.A., UCLA, 1942; M.A., U. Calif., Berkeley, 1950, Ph.D., 1955. Field ethnologist Smithsonian Instn., Colombia, 1950-52; applied anthropologist AID, Western S.Am., 1952-54; research assoc. culture exchange project U. Ill., Champaign-Urbana, 1955-59; vis. prof. anthropology Yale U., New Haven, 1959-60; assoc. prof. U. N.C., Chapel Hill, 1960-62, U. Calif., Santa Barbara, 1962-64, prof., 1964-87, prof. emeritus, 1987—, chmn. dept. anthropology, 1964-68. Author: Man Takes Control: Cultural Development and American Aid, 1961, In Search of the Common Good: Utopian Experiments Past and Future, 1977, Contemporary Change in Traditional Communities of Mexico and Peru, 1978. Served with USN, 1942-45. Home: 6190 Barrington Dr Santa Barbara CA 93117-1758 Office: U Calif Dept Anthropology Santa Barbara CA 93106

ERB, RICHARD A. state legislator, real estate executive; b. Chariton, Iowa, Dec. 26, 1928; married. BA in Bus. Mgmt., Eckerd Coll. Mem. Wyo. Ho. Reps., Cheyenne, 1992-96, Wyo. Senate, Dist. 24, Cheyenne, 1996—; mem. minerals, bus. and econ. devel. com. Wyo. Senate, Cheyenne, mem. corps., elections and polit. subdivisions com. Mem. Campbell County Airport Bd. Mem. Am. Legion, Rotary. Republican. Home: 1100 Warren Ave Gillette WY 82716-4804 Office: Wyo Senate State Capitol Cheyenne WY 82002-0001

ERB, RICHARD LOUIS LUNDIN, resort and hotel executive; b. Chgo., Dec. 23, 1929; s. Louis Henry and Miriam (Lundin) E.; m. Jean Elizabeth Easton, Mar. 14, 1959; children: John Richard, Elizabeth Anne, James Easton, Richard Louis II. BA, U. Calif., Berkeley, 1951, postgrad., 1952; student, San Francisco Art Inst., 1956. Cert. hotel adminstr. Asst. gen. mgr. Grand Teton Lodge Co., Jackson Hole, Wyo., 1954-62; mgr. Mauna Kea Beach Hotel, Hawaii, 1964-66; v.p., gen. mgr. Caneel Bay Plantation, Inc., St. John, V.I., 1966-75; gen. mgr. Williamsburg (Va.) Inn, 1975-78; exec. v.p., gen. mgr. Seabrook Island Co., Johns Island, S.C., 1978-80; v.p., dir. hotels Sands Hotel and Casino, Inc., Atlantic City, 1980-81; v.p., gen. mgr. Disneyland Hotel, Anaheim, Calif., 1981-82; COO Grand Traverse Resort, Grand Traverse Village, Mich., 1982-93; gen. mgr. Stein Eriksen Lodge, Deer Valley, Utah, 1993-96; pres. The Erb Group, 1996—. Pres. Spruce-Park Mgmt. Co., 1989; mem. adv. bd. travel and tourism Mich. State U., 1992-96; vice-chmn. Charleston (S.C.) Tourism Coun., 1979-81; bd. dirs. Anaheim Visitors and Conv. Bur., 1981-82, Grand Traverse Conv. and Visitors Bur., 1985-90, U.S. 131 Area Devel. Assn., 1983-93; sr. cons. Cayuga Hosp. Advisors, 1996—. Contbr. articles to trade jours. Vice-pres. V.I. Montessori Sch., 1969-71, bd. dirs., 1968-76; bd. dirs. Coll. of V.I., 1976-79; adv. bd. U. S.C., 1978-82, Calif. State Poly. Inst., 1981-82, Orange Coast C.C., 1981-82, Northwestern Mich. Coll., 1983-93; adv. bd. hospitality mgmt. program Ea. Mich. U., 1989-93; trustee Munson Med. Ctr., Traverse City, 1985-93; bd. dirs. Traverse Symphony Orch., 1984-88, N.A. Vasa, 1987-89; adv. panel Mich. Communities of Econ. Excellence Program, 1984-88; mem. hospitality adv. bd. Utah Valley State Coll., 1994-98. Lt. arty. U.S. Army, 1952-54. Named hon. prof. Mich. State U. Hotel Sch., 1992—. Fellow Edn. Inst.; mem. Am. Hotel and Motel Assn. (dir. 1975-77, , 90-94, exec. bd. 1991-94, Service Merit award 1976, Lawson Odde award 1993, Gold Medalist Membership award 1993, trustee Ednl. Inst. 1977-83, mktg. com., exec. com. 1978-83, chmn. projects and programs com. 1982-83, AH&MA resort com. 1986-96, AH&MA condominium com. 1985-96, chmn. ratings com. 1988-96, Ambassador award 1986, Blue Ribbon task force 1988-89, Resort Exec. of Yr. 1988), Caribbean Hotel Assn. (1st v.p. 1972-74, dir. 1970-76, hon. life mem., Extraordinary Service Merit award 1974), V.I. Hotel Assn. (pres. chmn. bd. 1971-76, Merit award 1973), Calif. Hotel Assn. (dir. 1981-82), Caribbean Travel Assn. (dir. 1972-74), Internat. Hotel Assn. (dir. 1971-73), S.C. Hotel Assn. (dir. 1978-82), Am. Hotel Assn. Edn. Inst., (Lamp of Knowledge award 1988), Va. Hotel Assn., Williamsburg Hotel Assn. (bd. dirs. 1975-78), Atlantic City Hotel Assn. (v.p. 1981-82), Atlantic City Casino Assn. (dir. 1981-82), Cornell Soc. Hotelmen, Mich. Travel and Tourist Assn. (bd. dirs. 1983-94, treas. 1986, sec. 1987, v.p. 1988, mktg. com. 1986-93, govtl. affairs com. 1986-93, chmn. edn. com. 1983-84, chmn. bd. 1989-90, Mich. Hotelier of Yr. 1991), Mich. Restaurant Assn. (bd. dirs. 1989-91, chmn. adminstrv. com. 1989-90), Mich. Gov.'s Task Force on Tourism, 1986-87, Grand Island Adv. Commn., Grand Traverse C. of C. (bd. dirs. 1984-89), Nat. Restaurant Assn., Utah Hotel and Motel Assn. (bd. dirs. 1994-96, treas. 1996), Leadership Grand Traverse (exec. com. 1984-92, fellow 1992), Park City Lodging Assn. (bd. dirs. 1993-96), Park City C. of C. (bd. dirs. 1994-97), Tavern Club, Rotary (Paul Harris fellow 1990), Beta Theta Pi. Congregationalist. E-mail: RichardErb@aol.com

ERGEN, CHARLIE, communications professional; BS in Bus. and Acctg., U. Tenn.; MBA, Wake Forest U. Founder, chmn., CEO Echostar Comms., Littleton, Colo., 1980—. Office: Echostar Comms 5701 S Santa Fe Littleton CO 80120

ERIBES, RICHARD, dean; Dean architecture and planning U. N.Mex., Albuquerque, 1996; dean Coll. Architecture U. Ariz., Tucson, 1997—. Office: U Ariz Sch Architecture PO Box 210075 Tucson AZ 85721-0075

ERICH, LOUIS RICHARD, physician; b. Shanghai, China, Nov. 7, 1928; (parents Am. citizens); s. Otis G. and Julia A. (Cunningham) E.; m. Lillian Annie McFeters, June 7, 1951; children: Jonathan, Kevin, Timothy, Janine. BA, Pacific Union Coll., 1950; MD, Loma Linda U., 1955. Diplomate Am. Bd. Ob-Gyn. Intern Spartanburg (S.C.) Gen. Hosp., 1955-56; resident in internal medicine Loma Linda Clin. Med. Ctr., 1965-66, resident in ob-gyn., 1970-73; physician Sonora (Calif.) Med. Group, Inc., 1977—. Capt. U.S. Army, 1956-58. Fellow Am. Coll. Ob-Gyn.

ERICKSEN, JERALD LAVERNE, retired engineering scientist, educator; b. Portland, Oreg., Dec. 20, 1924; s. Adolph and Ethel Rebecca (Correy) E.; m. Marion Ella Pook, Feb. 24, 1946; children: Lynn Christine, Randolph Peder. BS, U. Wash., 1947; MA, Oreg. State Coll., 1949; PhD, Ind. U., 1951; DSc (hon.), Nat. U. Ireland, 1984, Heriot-Watt U., 1988. Mathematician, solid state physicist U.S. Naval Research Lab., 1951-57; faculty Johns Hopkins U., 1957-83, prof. theoretical mechanics, 1960-83; prof. mechanics and math. U. Minn., Mpls., 1983-90; cons. Florence, Oreg., 1990—. Served with USNR, 1943-46. Recipient Bingham medal, 1968, Timoshenko medal, 1979, Engring. Sci. medal, 1987. Mem. Internat. Liquid Crystal Soc. (hon.), Nat. Acad. Engring., Soc. Rheology, Soc. Natural Philosophy, Soc. Interaction Mechanics and Math., Soc. Engring. Sci., Royal Irish Acad. (hon.). Home and Office: 5378 Buckskin Bob Dr Florence OR 97439-8320

ERICKSON, ARTHUR CHARLES, architect; b. Vancouver, B.C., Can., June 14, 1924; s. Oscar and Myrtle (Chatterson) E. Student, U. B.C., Vancouver, 1942-44; BArch., McGill U., Montreal, Que., Can., 1950; LLD (hon.), Simon Fraser U., Vancouver, 1973, U. Man., Winnipeg, Can., 1978, Lethbridge U., , 1981; D.Eng. (hon.), Novia Scotia Tech. Coll., McGill U., 1971; LittD (hon.), U. B.C., 1985, Frank Lloyd Wright Sch. Arch., 2001, MArch. Asst. prof. U. Oreg., Eugene, 1955-56; assoc. prof. U. B.C., 1956-63; ptnr. Erickson-Massey Architects, Vancouver, 1963-72; prin. Arthur Erickson Architects, Vancouver, 1972-91, Toronto, Ont., Can., 1981-91, Los Angeles, 1981-91, Arthur Erickson Archtl. Corp., Vancouver, 1991—. Prin. works include Can. Pavilion at Expo '70, Osaka (recipient first prize in nat. competition, Archtl. Inst. of Japan award for best pavilion), Robson Square/The Law Courts (honor award), Mus. of Anthropology (honor award), Eppich Residence (honor award), Habitat Pavilion (honor award), Sikh Temple (award of merit), Champlain Heights Cmty. Sch. (award of merit), San Diego Conv. Ctr., Calif. Plz., L.A., Fresno City Hall, Can. Embassy, Washington, MacMillan Bloedel Bldg., Roy Thompson Hall, Bank of Can., Koerner Libr., U.B.C. Liu Internat. Conf. Ctr., U. B.C. Scotibank Dance Ctr., Vancouver Internat. Glass Mus., Tacoma, Wash. Mem. com. on urban devel. Coun. of Can., 1971; bd. dirs. Can. Conf. of Arts, 1972; mem. design adv. coun. Portland Devel. Commn., Can. Coun. Urban Rsch.; trustee Inst. Rsch. on Pub. Policy. Capt. Can. Intelligence Corps., 1945-46. Recipient Molson prize Can. Coun. Arts, 1967, Triangle award Nat. Soc. Interior Design, Royal Bank Can. award, 1971, Gold medal Tau Sigma Delta, 1973, residential design award Can. Housing Coun., 1975, August Perret award Internat. Union Archiects Congress, 1975, Chgo. Architecture award, 1984, Gold medals Royal Archtl. Inst. Can., 1984, French Acad. Architecture, 1984, Pres. award excellence Am. Soc. Landscape Architects, 1979; named Officer, Order of Can., 1973, Companion Order of Can., 1981. Fellow AIA (hon., Pan Pacific citation Hawaiian chpt. 1963, Gold medal 1986), Royal Archtl. Inst. Can. (award 1980), Royal Inst. Brit. Archs. (hon.); mem. Archtl. Inst. B.C., Royal Inst. Scottish Archs. (hon.), Coll. d'arquitectos de España (hon.), Coll. d'architectos de Mex. (hon.), Royal Can. Acad. Arts (academician), Heritage Can., S.F.U. Faculty Club. Office: Arthur Erickson Archtl Corp 1672 W 1st Ave Vancouver BC Canada V6J 1G1

ERICKSON, LEIF B. federal judge; b. 1942; Law clk. Mont. Supreme Ct., 1967-68, pub. defender, 1969-70, dep. county atty., 1970-75, deputy city atty., 1979-85, judge 11th jud. dist., 1985-91; apptd. magistrate judge U.S. Dist. Ct. Mont., 1992. Office: Russell Smith Federal Bldg 201 E Broadway St Missoula MT 59802-4506 Fax: 406-542-7292. E-mail: leiferickson@9dc.mt.missoula

ERICKSON, ROBERT STANLEY, lawyer; b. Kemmerer, Wyo., Apr. 17, 1944; s. Stanley W. and Dorothy Marie (Johnson) E.; m. Alice Norman, Dec. 27, 1972; children: Robert Badger, Erin Elizabeth, Andrew Carl, Scott Stanley, Courtney Ellen, Brennan Marie. BS in Bus., U. Idaho, 1966; JD, U. Utah, 1969; LLM in Taxation, George Washington U., 1973. Bar: U.S. Supreme Ct. 1973, U.S. Ct. Appeals (9th cir.) 1980, U.S. Dist. Ct. Idaho 1973, U.S. Tax Ct. 1969, Idaho 1973, Utah 1969. Assoc. atty. Office of Chief Counsel, Dept. Treasury, Washington, 1969-73; assoc. Elam, Burke, Jeppesen, Evans & Boyd, Boise, Idaho, 1973-77; ptnr. Elam, Burke, Evans, Boyd & Koontz, Boise, 1977-81; spl. counsel Holme Roberts & Owen, Salt Lake City, 1981-83; ptnr. Hansen & Erickson, Boise, 1983-85, Hawley Troxell Ennis & Hawley, Boise, 1985—. Contbr. articles to profl. jours. Named Citizen of Yr., Boise Exch. Club, 1980. Fellow Am. Coll. of Trust and Estate Counsel (past Idaho chmn. 1993—); mem. ABA (sect. on taxation, com. state and local taxes), IRS/Western Region Bar Assn. (mem., past chmn. liaison com. Idaho co-chair local task force IRS non-filer program 1993), Idaho State Bar (founding chmn. taxation, probate and trust law sect.), Utah State Bar (tax and estate planning sect.), Boise Estate Planning Council, Idaho State Tax Inst. (exec. com., numerous other local and nat. coms.). Mem. LDS Ch. Office: Hawley Troxell Ennis & Hawley First Interstate Ctr 877 Main St Ste 1000 Boise ID 83702-5884

ERICKSON, WILLIAM HURT, retired state supreme court justice; b. Denver, May 11, 1924; s. Arthur Xavier and Virginia (Hurt) E.; m. Doris Rogers, Dec. 24, 1953; children: Barbara Ann, Virginia Lee, Stephen Arthur, William Taylor. Degree in petroleum engring., Colo. Sch. Mines, 1947; student, U. Mich., 1949; LLB, U. Va., 1950. Bar: Colo. 1951. Pvt. practice, Denver; state supreme ct. justice Colo. Supreme Ct., 1971-96, state supreme ct. chief justice, 1983-86; faculty NYU Appellate Judges Sch., 1972-85. Mem. exec. Commn. on Accreditation of Law Enforcement Agys., 1980-83; chmn. Pres.'s Nat. Commn. for Rev. of Fed. and State Laws Relating to Wiretapping and Electronic Surveillance, 1976. Chmn. Erickson Commn., 1997, Owens Columbine Rev. Commn., 2000-01; chmn. gov.'s Columbine Rev. Commn., 1999-2001. With USAAF, 1943. Recipient Disting. Achievement medal Colo. Sch. Mines, 1990. Fellow Internat. Acad. Trial Lawyers (former sec.), Am. Coll. Trial Lawyers, Am. Bar Found. (chmn. 1985), Internat. Soc. Barristers (pres. 1971); mem. ABA, (bd. govs. 1975-79, former chmn. com. on standards criminal justice, former chmn. coun. criminal law sect., former chmn. com. to implement standards criminal justice, mem. long-range planning com., action com. to reduce ct. cost and delay), Colo. Bar Assn. (award of merit 1989), Denver Bar Assn. (past pres., trustee), Am. Law Inst. (coun. 1973—), Practising Law Inst. (nat. adv. coun., bd. govs. Colo.), Freedoms Found. at Valley Forge (nat. coun. trustees, 1986—), Order of Coif, Scribes (pres. 1978). Home: 10 Martin Ln Englewood CO 80110-4821

ERICSON, BRUCE ALAN, lawyer; b. Buffalo, Feb. 28, 1952; s. Carl H. and Jean (Herman) E.; m. Elizabeth Whitney Burton, Feb. 6, 1988; children: John Cotton, Whitney Burton. AB, U. Pa., 1974; JD, Harvard U., 1977. Bar: Calif. 1977, U.S. Dist. Ct. (no. dist.) Calif, 1977, U.S. Dist. Ct. (ea. dist. and so. dist.) Calif. 1988, U.S. Dist. Ct. Ariz. 1992, U.S. Ct. Appeals (9th cir.) 1981, U.S. Ct. Appeals (11th cir.), 1991, U.S. Ct. Appeals (D.C. cir.) 1994, U.S. Supreme Ct. 1982. Assoc. Pillsbury, Madison & Sutro, San Francisco, 1977-84, ptnr., 1985—. Judge pro tem. San Francisco Mcpl. Ct., 1984—. Mem. ABA, San Francisco Bar Assn., Phi Beta Kappa. Republican. Club: Olympic (San Francisco). Avocations: skiing, squash. Office: Pillsbury Madison & Sutro LLP 235 Montgomery St Fl 16 San Francisco CA 94104-3104

ERICSON, RICHARD VICTOR, social science-law educator, university official; b. Montreal, Que., Sept. 20, 1948; s. John William and Elizabeth Mary (Hinkley) E.; m. Diana Lea McMillan, May 31, 1969; 1 child, Matthew Simon. BA, U. Guelph, Ont., 1969; MA, U. Toronto, 1971; PhD, Cambridge U., Eng., 1974, LittD, 1991. Asst. prof. U. Toronto, 1974-79, assoc. prof., 1979-82, prof. sociology, prof. criminology, 1982-93, dir. Ctr. of Criminology, 1992-93; prof. sociology, prof. law U. B.C., Vancouver, 1993—, prin. Green Coll., 1993—. Vis. rsch. prof. Coll. Pub. Programs Ariz. State U., Tempe, 1991; vis. fellow Inst. Criminology Cambridge U., 1979, 84-85, Churchill Coll. Cambridge U., 1979, 84-85, All Souls Coll., Oxford, 1998-99; vis. prof. U. Paris X-Nanterre, 1999; assoc. mem. Ctr. for Urban and Cmty. Rsch., Goldsmiths Coll., U. London, 2000—. Author: Making Crime (2d edit.), 1993; co-author: Negotiating Control, 1989, Representing Order, 1991, Policing the Risk Society, 1997. Hon. vis. fellow Green Coll., Oxford, 1993—, assoc. sr. fellow Massey Coll., Toronto, Ont., Can. Fellow Royal Soc. Can. Home: Principals Residence Green College at U BC Vancouver BC Canada V6T 1Z1 Office: Green College at U BC 6201 Cecil Green Park Rd Vancouver BC Canada V6T 1Z1

ERIKSEN, OTTO LOUIS, retired manufacturing company executive; b. Pitts., Jan. 28, 1930; s. Gabriel Soma and Catherine Lilian (Veatch) E.; m. Carmen Licano, July 4, 1981; children by previous marriage: Victor Soma, Catherine Ethel, Gregory Louis. Cert. in indsl. engring., Internat. Corr. Schs., 1965; student law, LaSalle U., 1966-68. Product line mgr. ITT Marlow Co., Midland Park, N.J., 1964-69; gen. mgr. ITT Jabsco, Costa Mesa, Calif., 1969-71; pres. ITT Marine & Recreation Components, Costa Mesa, 1971-83, ITT Jabsco Worldwide, 1983-90. Mem. Granite Falles and Desert Springs Golf Clubs (Surprise, Ariz.). Republican. Episcopalian.

ERISMAN, FRANK, lawyer; b. Lackawanna, N.Y., Mar. 6, 1943; s. Henry S. and Mary Lorraine (Conlin) E.; m. Judith A. Milano, Feb. 18, 1984; children: Porter, Melanie, Lindsay, Jacob. Degree in metall. engring., Colo. Sch. Mines, 1965; JD, U. Denver, 1968. Bar: Colo., 1968. Law clk. U.S. Ct. Appeals (5th cir.), Jacksonville, Fla., 1968-69; ptnr. Holme Roberts & Owen, L.L.P., Denver, 1969—. Mem. editorial bd. American Law of Mining, 2d edit., 1984; chmn. editorial bd. (periodical) The Public Land Resources Law Digest, 1985-88. Pres. bd. trustees Colo. Sch. Mines, Golden, 1996—; chmn. Colo. Sch. Mines Ann. Fund, 1990-91, Colo. Sch. Mines Pres.'s Coun., 1991-93; trustee Western Mus. of Mining & Industry, Colorado Springs, 1991-93. Recipient Disting. Achievement medal Colo. Sch. Mines, 1993. Mem. ABA (chmn. sect. of natural resources, energy and environ. law 1993-94), Colo. Bar Assn. (chmn. mineral law sect. 1991-92), Colo. Mining Assn. (bd. dirs. 1990-92), Rocky Mountain Mineral Law Found. (trustee, exec. bd. dirs. 1986-93, pres. 1997-98), Mining and Metallurgical Soc. Am. Avocations: gardening, hiking, fishing. Office: Holme Roberts & Owen LLP 1700 Lincoln St Ste 4100 Denver CO 80203-4541

ERNST, DONALD WILLIAM, producer; b. L.A., Jan. 25, 1934; s. William McKinley and Dorothy Elizabeth (Hast) E.; m. Janice Elaine Barber, Apr. 16, 1966; children: Stacey Dawn, Darci Lynn. BS in Civil Engring., UCLA, 1956. Apprentice editor Telemat, L.A., 1956-61; asst. editor Columbia Pictures, L.A., 1961-62, Metro-Goldwyn-Mayer, Culver City, Calif., 1962-64; film editor CBS, Studio City, 1964-72, Bakshi Prodns., L.A., 1972-79; sound editor Echo Films, L.A., 1979-82, Horta Editorial, Burbank, Calif., 1982-88; film editor Walt Disney Pictures, Glendale, 1988-89, prodn. exec., 1989—. Prodr.: (animated film) Roller Coaster Rabbit, 1990; co-prodr.: (animated film) Aladdin, 1992; exec. prodr.: (live action film) Homeward Bound: The Incredible Journey, 1993; producer Fantasia, 2000. Recipient Emmy awards TV Acad. Arts and Scis., 1977, 82. Mem. Am. Cinema Editors, Acad. Motion Picture Arts and Scis. Home: 25686 Moore Ln Stevenson Rnh CA 91381-1404 Office: Walt Disney Feature Animation 500 S Buena Vista St Burbank CA 91521-0006

ERNST, WALLACE GARY, geology educator; b. St. Louis, Dec. 14, 1931; s. Fredrick A. and Helen Grace (Mahaffey) E.; m. Charlotte Elsa Pfau, Sept. 7, 1956; children: Susan, Warren, Alan, Kevin. B.A., Carleton Coll., 1953; M.S., U. Minn., 1955; Ph.D., Johns Hopkins U., 1959. Geologist U.S. Geol. Survey, Washington, 1955-56; fellow (Geophys. Lab.), Washington, 1956-59; mem. faculty UCLA, 1960-89, prof. geology and geophysics, 1968-89, chmn. geology dept. (now earth and space scis. dept.), 1970-74, 78-82, dir. Inst. Geophysics and Planetary Physics, 1987-89; dean Stanford Sch. of Earth Scis., 1989-94; prof. geol. and environ. scis. Stanford (Calif.) U., 1989—, Benjamin M. Page prof., 1999—, dean Sch. of Earth Scis., 1989-94. Author: Amphiboles, 1968, Earth Materials, 1969, Metamorphism and Plate Tectonic Regimes, 1975, Subduction Zone Metamorphism, 1975, Petrologic Phase Equilibria, 1976, The Geotectonic Development of California, 1981, The Environment of the Deep Sea, 1982, Energy for Ourselves and Our Posterity, 1985, Cenozoic Basin Development of Coastal California, 1987, Metamorphic and Crustal Evolution of the Western Cordillera, 1988, The Dynamic Planet, 1990, Integrated Earth and Environmental Evolution of the Southwestern United States, 1998, Planetary Petrology and Geochemistry, 1999; editor: Earth Systems: Processes and Issues, 2000, (with R.G. Coleman) Tectonic Studies of Asia and the Pacific Rim--A Tribute to Benjamin M. Page, 2000, (with J.G. Liou) Ultrahigh-Pressure Metamorphism and Geodynamics in Collision-Type Orogenic Belts, 2000. Trustee Carnegie Instn. of Washington, 1990—. Recipient Miyashiro medal Geol. Soc. Japan, 1998. Mem. NAS (chmn. geology sect. 1979-82, sec. class I 1997—), AAAS (chair-elect), Am. Philos. Soc., Am. Geophys. Union, Am. Geol. Inst., Geol. Soc. Am. (pres. 1985-86), Am. Acad. Arts and Sci., Geochem. Soc., Mineral Soc. Am. (recipient award 1969, pres. 1979-80). Office: Stanford U Dept Earth & Environ Scis Green Earth Sci #209 Palo Alto CA 94303-1823

ERSKINE, JOHN MORSE, surgeon; b. San Francisco, Sept. 10, 1920; s. Morse and Dorothy (Ward) E. BS, Harvard U., 1942, MD, 1945. Diplomate Am. Bd. Surgery. Surg. intern U. Calif. Hosp., San Francisco, 1945-46; surg. researcher Mass. Gen. Hosp., Boston, 1948; resident in surgery Peter Bent Brigham Hosp., Boston, 1948-53; George Gorham Peters fellow St. Mary's Hosp., London, 1952; pvt. practice in medicine specializing in surgery San Francisco, 1954-98; asst. clin. prof. Stanford Med. Sch., San Francisco, 1956-59; asst., assoc. clin. prof. U. Calif. Med. Sch., San Francisco, 1959—. Surg. cons. San Francisco Vets. Hosp., 1959-73. Contbr. articles to profl. jours., chpts. to books. Founder No. Calif. Artery Bank, 1954-58, Irwin Meml. Blood Bank, San Francisco, commr., pres., 1969-74; bd. dirs. People for Open Space-Greenbelt Alliance, 1984-98, adv. coun., 1998—; chmn. adv. coun. Dorothy Enskine Open Space Fund. Capt. with U.S. Army, 1946-48. Fellow ACS; mem. San Francisco Med. Soc. (bd. dirs. 1968-72), San Francisco Surg. Soc. (v.p. 1984), Pacific Coast Surg. Assn., Am. Cancer Soc. (bd. dirs. San Francisco br. 1965-75), Calif. Med. Assn., Olympic Club, Sierra Club. Democrat. Unitarian. Avocations: mountaineering, tree farming, garden work, walking, reading. Home and Office: 233 Chestnut St San Francisco CA 94133-2452 E-mail: johnmerskine@aol.com

ERWIN, DONALD CARROLL, plant pathology educator; b. Concord, Nebr., Nov. 24, 1920; s. Robert James and Carol (Sexson) E.; m. Veora Marie Endres, Aug. 15, 1948; children: Daniel Erwin, Myriam Erwin Casey. Student, Wayne State (Nebr.) Tchrs.Coll, 1938-39; BSc, U. Nebr., 1949, MA, 1950; PhD, U. Calif.-Davis, 1953. Jr. plant pathologist U. Calif., Riverside, 1953-54, asst. plant pathologist, 1954-60, assoc. plant pathologist, 1960-66, prof. plant pathology, 1966—, emeritus prof., 1991. Sr. author: Phytophthora Diseases Worldwide, 1996; editor: Phytophthora: Its Biology, Taxonomy, Ecology and Pathology, 1983; contbr. articles to profl. jours. With U.S. Army, 1942-46; ETO. Nathan Gold fellow, 1949, Guggenheim fellow, 1959. Fellow Am. Phytopathol. Soc., Sigma Xi. Democrat. Roman Catholic. Office: U Calif Dept Plant Pathology Riverside CA 92521-0001

ERWIN, JOAN LENORE, artist, educator; b. Berkeley, Calif., Feb. 12, 1932; d. Ralph Albert and Dorothy Christine (Wuhrman) Potter; m. Byron W. Crider, Jan. 28, 1956 (div. May 1975); children: Susan Lynne Crider Adams, Gayle Leann Crider; m. Joseph G. Erwin Jr., May 28, 1976; children: Terry, Ray, Steve, Tim. BS, U. So. Calif., 1954; MS in Sch. Adminstrn., Pepperdine U., 1975. Cert. tchr., Calif.; registered occupational therapist. Calif. Occupational therapist Calif. State Hosp., Camarillo, 1955-56, Harlan Shoemaker Sch., San Pedro, Calif., 1956-57; tchr. Norwalk (Calif.) Sch. Dist., 1957-59, Tustin (Calif.) Sch. Dist., 1966-68,

Garden Grove (Calif.) Sch. Dist., 1968-92; freelance artist Phelan, Calif., 1976—; comml. artist Morningstar Creations, Fullerton, 1982-92; substitute tchr. Snowline Sch. Dist., Phelan, 1994—; owner, artist Plumfrog Creations, Phelan, 2000—. Artist Y.U.G.O., Los Alamitos, 1977-87; organizer 34th Annual Open Internat. Exbhn. Art, San Bernardino County Mus., 1999. Pet portrait artist, U.S. and Eng., 1978-85; author, artist Biblical coloring books, 1985-90; exhibited in group shows San Bernardino County Mus., Redlands, Calif., Riverside Art Mus. Bd. dirs. San Bernardino County Mus., Fine Arts Inst. Calif. Elks scholar, 1952-53; grantee Ford Found., 1957-58, Mentor Tchr. Program, 1986. Republican. Baptist. Avocations: gardening, travel. Home: 10080 Monte Vista Rd Phelan CA 92371-8371 E-mail: j.erwin3@verizon.net

ERWIN, STEVEN P. insurance company executive; BSc in Acctg. and Fin., Calif. State U.; MBA, U. Washington; student, Stanford U., Babson Coll. CPA. Treas. BayBanks, Inc., Boston, 1987-94; sr. v.p., CFO, treas. Old Nat. Bancorporation, 1994-97; CFO, exec. v.p. U.S. Bancorp, Portland, Oreg., 1994-97, 98. Auditor and other fin. positions Coopers & Lybrand, Lockhead Calif. Co., Gen. Electric Credit. Mem. Audit Com. Summit Design Inc. (bd. dirs., chmn.). Office: Health Net Inc 21650 Oxnard St Woodland Hills CA 91367

ERZBERGER, HEINZ, aeronautical engineer; Chief designer of Ctr.-Tracone Automation System Ames Rsch. Ctr., Moffet Field, Calif., sr. scientist for air traffic mgmt., 1996—. Recipient Hugh L. Dryden Lectureship in Rsch. award Am. Inst. of Aeronautics and Astronautics, 1997. Office: NASA Ames Rsch Ctr M/S 210-9 Moffett Field CA 94035

ESBER, EDWARD MICHAEL, JR. software company executive; b. Cleve., June 22, 1952; s. Edward Michael and Joanne Helen (Saah) E.; m. Margaret Renfrow, July 19, 1980; children: Dianne Michelle, Paul Andrew, Alexander Joseph. BS in Computer Engring., Case Western Res. U., Cleve., 1974; MSEE, Syracuse U., N.Y., 1976; MBA, Harvard U., Cambridge, 1978. Assoc. engr. IBM, Poughkeepsie, N.Y., 1974-76; mktg. mgr. Tex. Instruments, Lubbock, Tex., 1978-79; v.p. mktg. Visi Corp., San Jose, Calif., 1979-83; ptnr. Esber-Folk Assocs., Dallas, 1983-84; exec. v.p. mktg. and sales Ashton-Tate, Torrance, Calif., 1984, pres., COO, 1984—, pres., chief exec. officer, 1984—, chmn., chief exec. officer, 1986-90; pres., COO Creative Labs, Milpitas, 1993-94; chmn., CEO Creative Insights, Sunnyvale, 1994-95; CEO, pres. Solo Point, Los Gatos, 1995—, chmn. 1995-98. Bd. dirs. Quantum Inc., Portivity, Integrated Circuit Sys., Inc., Socket Comm. Trustee Case Western Res. U. Mem. Am. Electronic Assn. Republican. Office: The Esber Group 13430 Country Way Los Altos CA 94022-2434

ESCHBACH, JOSEPH WETHERILL, nephrology educator; b. Detroit, Jan. 21, 1933; s. Joseph William and Marguerite (Wetherill) E.; m. Mary Ann Charles, June 16, 1956; children: Cheryl Louise, Ann Elizabeth, Joseph Charles. BA, BS, Otterbein Coll., 1955; MD, Jefferson Med. Coll., 1959. Practitioner nephrology and internal medicine Minor and James Med., Seattle, 1965—; dir. home dialysis U. Wash., Seattle, 1965-72, clin. asst. prof. div. nephrology, 1967-70, clin. assoc. prof. div. nephrology, 1970-75, clin. prof. div. nephrology, 1975-85, clin. prof. divs. nephrology and hematology, 1985—. Cons. Ortho Pharm., Raritan, N.J., 1987-88, Amgen, Thousasnd Oaks, Calif., 1985-91. Co-editor: Erythropoietin: Molecular, Cellular and Clinical Biology, 1991; contbr. articles to jours. in field, chpts. to textbooks. Trustee First Ave. Svc. Ctr., 1976-86; pres. bd. trustees Northwest Kidney Ctr., Seattle, 1985-87 (Haviland award 1991). Recipient Disting. Svc. award Seattle Jaycees, 1979, Alumni Achievement award Otterbein Coll., 1991. Fellow ACP; mem. Inst. Medicine of NAS, AMA, Am. Soc. Nephrology, Internat. Soc. Nephrology, King County Med. Soc. (pres. 1987). Presbyterian. Avocations: squash, woodworking, singing. Home: 770 96th Ave SE Bellevue WA 98004-6502 Office: Minor & James Medical 515 Minor Ave Ste 300 Seattle WA 98104-2187

ESCUTIA, MARTHA, state senator; b. East Los Angeles, Calif. m. Leo Briones; 2 children. BA in Pub. Adminstrn. with honors, U. So. Calif; JD, GEorgetown U.; postgrad., Nat. Autonomous U., Mexico City. Sr. rsch. atty. Los Angeles County Superior Ct.; pvt. practice with law firm specializing in civil litigation, L.A.; mem. Calif. State Assembly, 1992-98, Calif. State Senate, 1998—, chmn. health and human svcs. com. V.p. govt. affairs and pub. policy United Way of L.A. Recipient numerous awards for pub. svc. Democrat. Office: Calif State Senate State Capitol Rm 5080 Sacramento CA 95814 also: Ste 125 12440 E Imperial Hwy Norwalk CA 90650

ESHELMAN, WILLIAM ROBERT, librarian, editor; b. Oklahoma City, Aug. 23, 1921; s. Cyrus Lenhert and Fern (Reed) E.; m. Mimi Blau, July 3, 1952 (div. Aug. 1956); m. Eve Kendall, June 21, 1957 (div. Apr. 1975); children: Ann, Benjamin, Zachary; m. Pat Rom, Dec. 29, 1977. BA, Chapman Coll., L.A., 1943; MA, UCLA, 1950; BLS, U. Calif. at Berkeley, 1951. Conscripted in civilian pub. service, Waldport, Oreg., 1943-46; ptnr. Untide Press, Pasadena, Calif., 1946-65; teaching asst. UCLA, 1949-50, library asst., 1950; faculty Los Angeles State Coll., 1951-65, asst. librarian, 1954-59, coll. librarian, 1959-65; librarian, prof. bibliography Bucknell U., 1965-68; editor Wilson Library Bull., 1968-78; pres. Scarecrow Press, Metuchen, N.J., 1979-86; proprietor The Press at the Camperdown Elm, Wooster, Ohio, 1987-93. Editor: Take Hold Upon the Future: Letters on Writers and Writing by William Everson and Lawrence Clark Powell, 1938-1946, 1994; author: No Silence! A Library Life, 1997; contbg. author: Perspectives on William Everson, 1992; mem. editl. bd. Choice, 1966-71. Bd. dirs. Grolier Edn. Corp., 1979-86; mem. adv. council edn. for librarianship U. Calif., 1961-64; mem. acad. senate Calif. State Colls., 1964-65. Mem. AAUP (v.p. L.A. State Coll. 1958-59, pres. 1964-65), ALA (winner Libr. Periodicals award 1960, editorial com. 1964-66, mem. coun. 1972-76, com. accreditation 1977-79), Calif. Libr. Assn. (chmn. intellectual freedom com., pres. so. dist. 1965, editor Calif. Libr. jour. 1960-63), Assn. Coll. and Rsch. Librs. (publs. com.), Assn. Calif. State Coll. Profs., ACLU, Friends Com. Legis., N.J. Libr. Assn. (hon.), Rounce and Coffin Club (L.A.; sec.-treas. 1953-56), Typophiles CLub (N.Y.C.). Home and Office: 3645 SW 52nd Pl Portland OR 97221-2113 E-mail: eshrom@aol.com

ESHLEMAN, VON RUSSEL, electrical engineering educator; b. Darke County, Ohio, Sept. 17, 1924; married; 4 children. BEE, George Washington U., 1949; MS, Stanford U., 1950, PhD in Elec. Engring., 1952. Rsch. assoc. Radio Propagation Lab. Stanford (Calif.) U., 1952-56, from instr. to prof. elec. engring., 1956-61, prof. elec. engring., co-dir. Ctr. Radar Astronomy, 1961-82, dir. Radioscience Lab., 1974-83. Cons. NAS, Nat. Bur. Stds., SRI Internat., Jet Propulsion Lab.; mem. Internat. Astronaut Congress, Internat. Astron. Union, Internat. Sci. Radion Union; dir. emeritus Watkins-Johnson Co.; mem. radio sci. team Galileo Mission to Jupiter, 1979—. Fellow AAAS, IEEE, Am. Geophys. Union, Royal Astronomy Soc.; mem. NAE. Achievements include rsch. in radar astronomy, planetary exploration, ionospheric and plasma physics, radio wave propagation, astronautics. Office: Stanford U Radar Astronomy Ctr Packard EE Bldg 309 Stanford CA 94305-9515 E-mail: eshleman@nova.stanford.edu

ESHOO, ANNA GEORGES, congresswoman; b. New Britain, Conn., Dec. 13, 1942; d. Fred and Alice Alexandre Georges; children: Karen Elizabeth, Paul Frederick. AA with honors, Canada Coll., 1975. Chmn. San Mateo County Dem. Ctrl. Com., Calif., 1978-82; chair Human Rels. Com., 1979-82; mem. U.S. Congress from 14th Calif. dist., 1993—; at-large minority whip; mem. energy and commerce com. Chief of staff Calif. Assembly Spkr. Leo McCarthy, 1981; regional majority whip No. Calif., 1993-94. Co-founder Women's Hall of Fame; chair San Mateo County (Calif.) Dem. Party, 1980; active San Mateo County Bd. Suprs., 1982-92, pres., 1986; pres. Bay Area Air Quality Mgmt. Dist., 1982-92; mem. San Francisco Bay Conservation Devel. Commn., 1982-92; chair San Mateo County Gen. Hosp. Bd. Dirs. Roman Catholic. Office: US Ho Reps 205 Cannon Ho Office Bldg Washington DC 20515-0001*

ESLER, JOHN KENNETH, artist; b. Pilot Mound, Man., Can., Jan. 11, 1933; s. William John and Jennie Mae (Thompson) E.; m. Annemarie Schmid, June 26, 1964; children— William Sean, John Derek. B.F.A., U. Man., B.Ed., 1962. Mem. faculty dept. art Alta. Coll. Art, 1964-68; mem. faculty U. Calgary, Alta., Can., 1968-80. Chmn. Print and Drawing Council Can., 1976-78 One-man exhbn., Gallery Moos, Toronto, Ont., 1978, Past and Present: One-Man Exhbn. Painting, Triangle Gallery, Calgary, Alberta, 1994, Retrospective/35 Years Printmaking, U. of C. Nickle Arts Mus., Calgary, Travelling exhbn., Sept. 1994; represented in permanent collections, Victoria and Albert Mus., London, Eng., Albright Knox Gallery, Buffalo, N.Y., Mus. Modern Art, N.Y.C., Nat. Gallery Can., Ottawa, Ont.; Author: Printing in Alberta. Life mem. Print and Drawing Coun. Can. Address: 5020 Viceroy Dr NW Calgary AB Canada T3A 0V5

ESPARZA, RICHARD R. museum director; b. Washington; m. Lauraine Brekke, Oct. 24, 1992; 4 children. BA in Philosophy, Calif. State U., Hayward, 1969; student, Met. State Coll., 1972-73. Asst. curator Colo. State Mus. Colo. State Hist. Soc., Denver, 1972-73; exec. dir. South Park City Mus., Fairplay, Colo., 1973-74, Ventura (Calif.) County Mus. History and Art, 1974-80, San Diego Hist. Soc., 1980-87, Santa Barbara (Calif.) Hist. Museums, 1987-89, Nev. Mus. Art, Reno, 1991-95; dir. Riverside (Calif.) Mcpl. Mus., 1995—. Faculty U. Calif. Santa Barbara Inst. Local History, 1981, Small Mus. Adminstrn. UCLA ext., 1981, Williamsburg Seminar for Historic Adminstrn., 1984. Mem. Riverside Downtown Assn. (bd. dirs.), Mission Inn Found. (bd. dirs.), Calif. Assn. Museums (bd. dirs.). Office: Riverside Mcpl Mus 3580 Mission Inn Ave Riverside CA 92501-3307

ESPLIN, KIMO, chemical company executive; CFO Huntsman Corp., Salt Lake City. Office: Huntsman Corp 500 Huntsman Way Salt Lake City UT 84108

ESPOSITO, JOSEPH JOHN, publishing company executive; b. Englewood, N.J., June 19, 1951; s. Ross and Ann (Tamborinno) E.; m. Kim Ann Loretucci. AB, Rutgers U., 1973, MA, 1977, M in Philosophy, 1978. Editor Rutgers U. Press, New Brunswick, N.J., 1978-81, Dover Publs., N.Y.C., 1981-82; v.p. spl. projects New Am. Libr., N.Y.C., 1982-85; pres. reference div. Simon & Schuster, N.Y.C., 1985-88; v.p. reference, pres. Fodor's Travel Publs. Random House Pub. Co., N.Y.C., 1988-90; with Ency. Britannica, 1990-96; pres. Merriam-Webster sub., 1990; CEO Ency. Britannica, 1995-96; pres., CEO Tribal Voice, Scotts Valley, Calif., 1997—. Mem. mgmt. bd. MIT Press. Mem. ACLU, Dictionary Soc. N.Am. Office: Tribal Voice 600 17th St # 700so Denver CO 80202-5402

ESQUIVEL, JOE G. food products executive; b. 1938; With Hanson Farms, Salinas, Calif., 1967-83; pres. Adobe Packing Co., Salinas, 1983—. Office: Adobe Packing Co PO Box 4940 Salinas CA 93912-4940

ESQUIVEL, MARY, agricultural products company executive; b. 1945; Homemaker, 1976; ct. interpreter State of Calif., Salinas, 1976-83; sec., treas. Adobe Packing Co., Salinas, 1983—. Office: Adobe Packing Co PO Box 4940 Salinas CA 93912-4940

ESSEX, LAUREN S. women's health care company executive; BA in Psychology and Bus., U. Rochester; MS in Mgmt., Northwestern U. Various brand mgmt. positions Helene Curtis, 1984-94, br. mgr., 1991-94; v.p. personal care products, sales and customer svc. La Costa Products Internat., 1994-96; v.p. mktg. Cosmederm Tech.s, Inc., 1996-98; v.p. mktg. self-care products Women First HealthCare, Inc., San Diego, 1998—. Office: Women First HealthCare Inc 12220 El Camino Real Ste 400 San Diego CA 92130-2091 Fax: 619-509-1353

ESTABROOK, REED, artist, educator; b. Boston, May 31, 1944; s. F. Reed and Nancy (Vogel) E.; 1 son, August. B.F.A., R.I. Sch. Design, Providence, 1969; M.F.A., Art Inst. Chgo., 1971. Instr. U. Ill., 1971-74; asst. prof. U. No. Iowa, Cedar Falls, 1974-78, assoc. prof., 1978-83, head dept. photog. program, 1974-83; advisor visual arts Iowa Arts Council, Des Moines, 1977-78, mem. art purchase com., 1977-78; chmn. photog. dept. Kansas City Art Inst., Mo., 1983-84; prof., coordinator Photo Dept. San Jose State U., 1984-89, 92-95. Bd. dirs. San Francisco Camera Work, 1987-90; Fulbright exch. tchr. Sheffield Poly., Eng., 1990-91. Exhibited one-man shows, Sioux City Art Ctr., Iowa, 1981, Klein Gallery, Chgo., 1982, James Madison U., Harrisonburg, Va., 1983, Orange Coast Coll., Costa Mesa, Calif., 1983, Portland State U., Oreg., 1983, others, group shows, Isetan Mus. of Art, Tokyo, 1993, U. Colo., Boulder, 1977, 82, Mus. Modern Art, N.Y.C., 1978, 82, 84, Santa Barbara Mus. Art, Calif., 1979, San Francisco Mus. Modern Art, 1982, 90, Hokkaido Obihito Mus. of Art, Tokyo, 1993, Royal Coll. Art, London, 1994, Mus. Fine Art, Santa Fe, N.Mex., 1994, 96, San Jose Inst. Contemporary Art, 1996, San Francisco Mus. Modern Art, 1996, Sheppard Gallery U. Nev., Reno, others; represented permanent collections, Mus. Modern Art, N.Y.C., Mpls. Inst. Arts, Hallmark Collection, Kansas City, Mo., Boise Gallery Art, Idaho, Walker Art Ctr., Mpls., R.I. Sch. Design, U. Colo., Fogg Mus. Art, Harvard U., Spencer Mus. Art, U. Kans., Lawrence, Internat. Mus. Photography, Rochester, N.Y., Art Inst. Chgo., Humbolt State U., Arcata, Calif., Smithsonian Instn., Washington, San Francisco Mus. Modern Art, J. Paul Getty Mus., Santa Monica, Calif., 2000. W.R. French fellow Art Inst. Chgo., 1971; Nat. Endowment for Arts fellow, 1976 Fellow Soc. Contemporary Photo; mem. Soc. for Photog. Edn. Home: 482 Chetwood St Oakland CA 94610-2649 Office: San Jose State U Sch Art & Design San Jose CA 95192-0001 E-mail: reede@pacbell.net

ESTEBAN, MANUEL ANTONIO, university administrator, educator; b. Barcelona, Spain, June 20, 1940; came to U.S., 1970; s. Manuel and Julia Esteban; m. Gloria Ribas, July 7, 1962; 1 child, Jacqueline. BA with 1st class honors in French, U. Calgary, Can., 1969, MA in Romance Studies, 1970; PhD in French, U. Calif., Santa Barbara, 1976. From asst. prof. to prof. French and Spanish langs. and lit. U. Mich., Dearborn, 1973-87, assoc. dean, 1984-86, acting dean coll. arts, scis., and letters, 1986-87; dean arts and scis. Calif. State U., Bakersfield, 1987-90; provost, v.p. acad. affairs Humboldt State U., Arcata, Calif., 1990-93; pres., prof. French and Spanish Calif. State U., Chico, 1993—. Bd. dirs. Calif. Joint Policy Coun. on Agr. and Edn., 1995—. Author: Georges Feydeau, 1983; contbr. books revs. and articles to profl. publs. Trustee Enloe Hosp. Woodrow Wilson fellow, 1969, doctoral fellow U. Calif., Santa Barbara, 1970-73, Can. Coun doctoral fellow, Govt. Can., 1970-73; Rackham grantee U. Mich., 1979, fellow, 1982-83. Mem. Am. Coun. Edn., Am. Assn. State Colls. and Univs., Greater Chico C. of C., Sierra Health Found. (bd. dirs. 1998—). Avocations: golf, woodworking, glassblowing. Office: Calif State Univ Pres Office Chico CA 95929-0001

ESTEP, JOHN HAYES, religious organization administrator, clergyman; b. Bellwood, Pa., June 30, 1930; s. Kenneth and Anna Emily Estep; m. Dorothy L. Nash, Aug. 21, 1951; children: Heidi Ann, John H. Jr. BA, Wheaton (Ill.) Coll., 1953; MDiv, Denver Sem., 1956, DD (hon.), 1980. Ordained to ministry Bapt. Ch., 1956. Asst. pastor Forest City Bapt. Ch., Rockford, Ill., 1956-62; pastor, sr. min. Calvary Bapt. Ch., Longmont, Colo., 1962-69; dir. ch. rels. Mission to the Americas, Wheaton, 1969-80, CEO, 1980-95. Bd. dirs. Colo. Christian U., Denver, 1964-71, Denver Sem., 1968-70. Mem. Nat. Assn. Evangelicals (officer 1988-96), Nat. Black Evang. Assn. (bd. dirs. 1992—). Avocations: golf, travel, reading, music. Office: CB Ministries 1501 W Mineral Ave Littleton CO 80120-5612 E-mail: jackecba@aol.com

ESTES, CARROLL LYNN, sociologist, educator; b. Fort Worth, May 30, 1938; d. Joe Ewing and Carroll (Cox) E.; 1 child, Duskie Lynn Gelfand Estes. AB, STanford U., 1959; MA, So. Meth. U., 1961; PhD, U. Calif., San Diego, 1972; DHL (hon.), Russell Sage Coll., 1986. Rsch. asst., asst. study dir. Brandeis U. Social Welfare Rsch. Ctr., 1962-63, rsch. assoc., 1964-65, project dir., 1965-67; vis. lectr. Florence Heller Grad. Sch., 1964-65; rsch. dir. Simmons Coll., 1963-64; asst. prof. social work San Diego State Coll., 1967-72; asst. prof. in residence dept. psychiatry U. Calif., San Francisco, 1972-75, assoc. prof. dept. social and behavioral scis., 1975-79, prof., 1979-92, chair dept. social and behavioral scis., 1981-93, coord. human devel. tng. program, 1974-75; dir. Aging Health Policy Rsch. Ctr., 1979-85, Inst. for Health and Aging, 1985-99. Faculty rsch. lectr. U. Calif., 1993. Author: The Decision-Makers: The Power Structure of Dallas, 1963; co-author: Protective Services for Older People, 1972, U.S. Senate Special Committee on Aging Report, Paperwork and the Older Americans Act, 1978, The Aging Enterprise, 1979 Fiscal Austerity and Aging, 1983, Long Term Care of the Elderly, 1985, Political Economy, Health and Aging, 1984, The Long Term Care Crisis, 1993, The Nation's Health, 1993, 6th edit., 2001, Critical Gerontology, 1999, Health Policy, 2001, Social Policy and Aging, 2001; contbr. articles to profl. jours. Mem. Calif. Commn. on Aging, 1974-77; cons. U.S. Senate Spl. Com. on Aging from 1976, Notch Commn. U.S. Commn. Social Security, 1993-94. Recipient Matrix award Theta Sigma Phi, 1964, award for contbns. to lives of older Californians, Calif. Commn. on Aging, 1977, Helen Nahm Rsch. award U. Calif., San Francisco, 1986, Woman Who Would Be Pres. League of Women Voters, 1998. Mem. Inst. Medicine of NAS, ACLU, Am. Sociol. Assn. (Disting. Scholar award Aging and Life Course 2000), Assn. Gerontology in Higher Edn. (pres. 1980-81, recipient Beverly award 1993, Tibbitts award 2000), Am. Soc. on Aging (pres. 1982-84, Leadership award 1986), Geronotol. Soc. Am. (Kent award 1992, pres. 1995-96), Older Women's League (v.p. 1994-97), Soc. Study Social Problems, Alpha Kappa Delta, Pi Beta Phi. Democrat. Office: U Calif San Francisco Inst Health & Aging 3333 California St Ste 340 San Francisco CA 94118-1944

ESTES, SHAWN, professional baseball player; b. San Bernardino, Calif., Feb. 18, 1973; Pitcher San Francisco Giants. Named All-Star. Office: San Francisco Giants Pac Bell Pk 24 Willie Mays Plz San Francisco CA 94107-2199

ESTRIN, GERALD, computer scientist, engineering educator, academic administrator; b. N.Y.C., Sept. 9, 1921; married; 3 children B.S., U. Wis., 1948, M.S., 1949, Ph.D. in Elec. Engring., 1951. Rsch. engr. Inst. Advanced Study, Princeton, N.J., 1950-53, 55-56; dir. electronic computing project Weizmann Inst. Sci., Israel, 1953-55; assoc. prof. engring. UCLA, 1956-58, prof., 1958-91, prof. emeritus, 1991—, chmn. dept. computer sci., 1979-82, 85-88. Mem. adv. bd. applied math. div. Argonne Nat. Lab., 1966-68, mem. assoc. univs. rev. com. for chmn., 1976-77, mem. adv. bd. applied math. div., 1974-80, adv. com. NASA Space Applications, 1983-86; dir. Computer Communications, Inc., 1966-67, Systems Engring. Labs., 1977-80; mem. internat. program com. Internat. Fedn. Info. Processing Congress, 1968; internat. program chmn. Jerusalem Conf. Info. Tech., 1971; mem. math. and computer sci. research adv. com. AEC; mem. sci. com., operating bd. Gould, Inc., Rolling Meadows, Ill., 1981-86; bd. govs. Weizmann Inst. Sci., 1971-96, gov. emeritus, 1996—. Lipsky fellow, 1954, Guggenheim fellow, 1963, 67; recipient Disting. Svc. award U. Wis., 1975, Jerusalem Conf. on Info. Tech. Spl. Recognition award, 1978, NASA Commendation, 1986, Computer Pioneer award IEEE Computer Soc., 1995. Fellow AAAS, IEEE (disting. spkr. 1980), Assn. Computing Machinery (nat. lectr. 1966-67). Office: UCLA BH4731 Dept Computer Sci Los Angeles CA 90095-0001 E-mail: gestrin@cs.ucla.edu

ESTRIN, JUDITH, computer company executive; BS in Maths. and Computer Sci., UCLA; MSEE, Stanford U. Co-founder Bridge Comms.; pres., CEO Network Computing Devices; chief tech. officer, sr. v.p. Cisco Sys., Inc., San Jose. Bd. dirs. Fed. Express, Sun Microsystems, Walt Disney Co. Office: Cisco Sys Inc 170 W Tasman Dr San Jose CA 95134-1706 Fax: 408-526-4100

ETCHART, MIKE, agricultural products company executive; b. 1961; V.p. Everkrisp Vegetables, Inc., Tolleson, Ariz. Office: Everkrisp Vegetables Inc PO Box 25 Tolleson AZ 85353-0025

ETCHESON, WARREN WADE, business administration educator; b. Bainbridge, Ind., May 15, 1920; s. Raymond W. and Rosetta (Evans) E.; m. Marianne Newgent, May 30, 1947; children: Denise Elene, Crayton Wade. BS, Ind. U., 1943; MA, U. Iowa, 1951, PhD, 1956. Adminstrv. sec., exec. sec., nat. sec. Delta Chi Nat. Fraternity, 1946-56; lectr. Santo Tomas U., Manila, 1946, U. Iowa, 1951-54; asst. prof. U. Wash., 1954-56, assoc. prof., 1956-60, prof. Sch. Bus. Adminstrn., 1960-90; assoc. dean Bus. Adminstrn., 1974-87. Fulbright prof. Istanbul, Turkey, 1963-64. Author: Pazarlama, 1964, Consumerism, 1972. Served to lt. U.S. Army, 1942-46. Mem. Alpha Kappa Psi, Phi Eta Sigma, Beta Gamma Sigma, Delta Chi. Home: 6625 NE 132nd St Kirkland WA 98034-1614 Office: Univ Wash Seattle WA 98195-0001

ETRA, DONALD, lawyer; b. N.Y.C., July 23, 1947; s. Harry and Blanche (Goldman) E.; m. Paula Renee Wiener, Dec. 28, 1985; children: Harry, Dorothy, Anna, Jonathan. BA, Yale U., 1968; MBA, JD, Columbia U., 1971. Atty. to Ralph Nader, Washington, 1971-73; trial atty. U.S. Dept. Justice, Washington, 1973-77, asst. U.S. atty. L.A., 1978-81; ptnr. Sidley & Austin, L.A., 1983-95, Law Offices of Donald Etra, L.A., 1995—. Co-author: Citibank, 1973. Office: Law Offices of Donald Etra 2029 Century Park East Ste 1020 Los Angeles CA 90067 E-mail: etralaw@aol.com

ETTENGER, ROBERT BRUCE, physician, nephrologist; b. Phila., Sept. 17, 1942; s.Ervin Earl and Sylvia (Goodstein) W.; m. Angela Joan Castellano Ettenger; children: Allison, Jessica. BA, U. Pa., 1964; MD, 1968. Maj. U.S. Army, El Paso, 1971-73; asst. prof. pediat. Children's Hosp. of L.A., 1976-80, Sch. Medicine UCLA, 1980-84, asst. prof., 1984-89, prof., 1989—, head divsn. pediat. nephrology dept. pediat., 1990—, vice chmn. clin. affairs, 1990—; dir. historcompatibility lab. UCLA Med. Ctr., 1987—. Mem., chairperson sub bd. nephrology Am. Bd. Pediat., Chapel Hill, N.C., 1986-91; cons. Immunosuppressive Adv. Com. Food and Drug Adminstrn., Bethesda, Md., 1994—, Biologics and Immune Response Modifiers, Food and Drug Adminstrn., Bethesda, 1994—; mem. biol. sci. adv. com. U.S. Renal Data Sys., Ann Arbor, Mich., 1993-2000. Mem. editl. bd. Transplantation, Pediat. Nephrology, Pediat. Transplantation; contbr. articles to profl. jours. Coach, mem. exec. bd. AYSO Soccer, Santa Monica, Calif., 1994—, Bobby Sox Softball, 1995-97, YWCA Basketball, 1995-2000; mem. adv. bd. Nat. Kidney Found., L.A., 1993—; mem. sports and phys. edn. adv. com. Santa Monica Sch. Dist. Recipient Ortho Biotech Lectureship Urologic Soc. for Transplantation, 1990, Continuing Svc. award Nat. Kidney Found., L.A., 1991, 92, 94. Fellow Internat. Soc. of Nephrology, Internat. Pediat. Nephrology Assn., Am. Acad. Pediat., Am. Soc. Transplant Physicians (pres. 1984-85), Am. Pediat.

Soc., Am. Soc. of Nephrology, Am. Soc. of Pediat. Nephrology, Soc. for Pediat. Rsch., Transplantation Soc (Best Drs. in Am. 1992, 96), United Network For Organ Sharing (regional councillor at region 5, bd. dirs. 2000—). Jewish. Avocations: distance running, youth sports. Office: UCLA Med Ctr A2-383 Dept Pediatrics 10833 Le Conte Ave Los Angeles CA 90095-3075

ETTINGER, HARRY JOSEPH, industrial hygiene engineer, project manager; b. N.Y.C., July 20, 1934; s. Morris and Pauline (Waxman) E.; m. June Kopf, June 14, 1958; children: Linda E., Steven E., Robert A. BCE, CCNY, 1956; MCE, NYU, 1958. Registered profl. engr., N.Mex.; cert. indsl. hygienist. Sanitary engr. USPHS, Bethesda, Md., 1958-61; staff mem. Los Alamos (N.Mex.) Nat. Lab., 1961-71, alt. group leader, 1971-74, group leader, 1974-80, program mgr., 1981-87; project dir. Occupational Safety and Health Adminstrn., Washington, 1987-89; tech. rsch. coord. Los Alamos (N.Mex.) Nat. Lab., 1989-91, program mgr., 1991-93, chief scientist environ., safety and health divsn., 1993-97, acting dep. divsn. dir., 1995-96, lab. assoc., 1997-99, cons., 1999—. Cons. divsn. reactor licensing USAEC, 1970-71, cons. EPA, 1972-74, various industries, 1970—; cons. to adv. com. on nuclear facility safety DOE, 1990-91; mem. adj. faculty U. Ark., Little Rock, 1969-90, San Diego State U., 1981-86; vis. faculty Tex. A&M U., College Station, 1981-99; faculty affiliate Colo. State U., Ft. Collins, 1983—; mem. exec. com. toxic substances rsch. and tchg. program U. Calif., 1984-90; mem. stds. steering group DOE Lab. Dirs. Environ. and Occupational Health, 1990-96. Contbr. jour. articles and tech. reports on indsl. hygiene, aerosol physics, respiratory protection. Active Los Alamos County Utility Bd., 1968-70, 78-82, chmn., 1970; vice chmn. Los Alamos County Planning and Zoning Commn., 1974-76, mem., 1972-76, 97-01. Fellow Am. Indsl. Hygiene Assn. (editl. rev. bd. 1979-87, 90-91, 95—, bd. dirs. 1987-90, v.p. 1991-92, pres.-elect 1992-93, pres. 1993-94, aerosol tech. com. 1968-78, 80-84, chmn. 1968-70, respirator com. 1995-98, Edward Baier award 1990); mem. Am. Acad. Indsl. Hygiene (editor newsletter 1997-01), Am. Assn. Aerosol Rsch., Am. Bd. Indsl. Hygiene (bd. dirs. 1979-85, chmn. 1983-85), Am. Conf. Govtl. Indsl. Hygiene (Meritorious Achievement award 1985), Internat. Soc. Respiratory Protection (bd. dirs. 1985-88, 95-97), Internat. Occupational Hygiene Assn. (bd. dirs. 1994-97). Democrat. Jewish. E-mail: Junee@rt66.com

EU, MARCH FONG, ambassador, former state official; b. Oakdale, Calif., Mar. 29, 1929; d. Yuen and Shiu (Shee) Kong; children by previous marriage: Matthew Kipling Fong, Marchesa Suyin Fong; m. Henry Eu, Aug. 31, 1973; stepchildren: Henry, Adeline, Yvonne, Conroy, Alaric. Student, Salinas Jr. Coll.; BS, U. Calif.-Berkeley, 1943; MEd, Mills Coll., 1947; EdD, Stanford U., 1956; postgrad., Columbia U., Calif. State Coll.-Hayward; LLD, Lincoln U., 1984; LLB (hon.), Western U., 1985; DHL (hon.), Northrup Coll., 1991; LLB (hon.), Pepperdine U., 1993. Chmn. divsn. dental hygiene U. Calif. Med. Center, San Francisco, 1948-56; dental hygienist Oakland (Calif.) Pub. Schs., 1948-56; supr. dental health edn. Alameda County (Calif.) Schs.; lectr. health edn. Mills Coll., Oakland; mem. Calif. Legislature, 1966-74, chmn. select com. on agr., foods and nutrition, 1973-74; mem. com. natural resources and conservation, com. commerce and pub. utilities, select com. med. malpractice; chief of protocol State of Calif., 1975-83, sec. of state, 1975-94; amb. to Federated States of Micronesia, Am. Embassy, Pohnpei, 1994—. Chmn. Calif. State World Trade Commn., 1983-87; ex-officio mem. Calif. State World Trade Commn., 1987—; spl. cons. Bur. Intergroup Relations, Calif. Dept. Edn.; ednl., legis. cons. Sausalito (Calif.) Pub. Schs., Santa Clara County Office Edn., Jefferson Elementary Union Sch. Dist., Santa Clara High Sch. Dist., Santa Clara Elementary Sch. Dist., Live Oak Union High Sch. Dist.; mem. Alameda County Bd. Edn., 1956-66, pres., 1961-62, legis. adv., 1963, Assembly Retirment Com., Assembly Com. on Govtl. Quality Com., Assembly Com. on Pub. Health; pres. Alameda County Sch. Bds. Assn., others; U.S. advisor Shenzhen Internat. Ent. Co., Ltd., Shenzhen, Guangzhou, China, 1997; internat. hon. advisor 4th World Chinese Entrepreneurs Conv., Vancouver, B.C., 1997; hon. chmn. Sino-Am. Inst. Human Resources, L.A., 1997; U.S. advisor Internat. Hort Exposition for 1999, Kunming, Yunnan, 1997; mem. exec. adv. bd. Asian Am. Policy Rev. Bd., Washington, 1998, others; adj. prof. continuing edn. Calif. State U., Sacramento, 2000; S.E. Asia advisor Startec Global Telecomm., Inc. Mem. adv. bd. for canonization of Father Junipero Sierra, Franciscan Fathers, Santa Barbara, Calif. Recipient Citizen of Yr. award Chinese-Am. United for Self Employment, 1996, Govt. Svc. award friends of Mus. of Chinese Am. History, L.A., 1997, Cmty. Svc. award Coll. of San Mateo, Ann. Humanitarian award Women's Ctr., Coll. of Law, San Diego, Asian Am. on the Move award for politics L.A. City Employees Asian Am. Assn., Outstanding Svc. to Cmty. award Irish-Israeli Italian Soc.. San Francisco, Disting. C.C. Alumni award Calif. C.C. and Jr. Coll. Assn., Outstanding Woman award Nat. Women's Polit. Caucus, Daisy award Calif. Landscape Contrs. Assn., 1980, Milton Shoong Hall of Fame Humanitarian award, 1981, Citizen of the Yr. award Coun. for Civic Unity of San Francisco Bay Area, 1982, Woman of the Yr., Dems. United, San Bernardino, 1986, Woman of Achievement Award of Distinction, San Gabriel Valley YWCA, 1987, Disting. svc. award Rep. of Honduras, 1987, Woman of the Yr. award Santa Barbara County Girls Club Coalition, 1987, Polit. Achievement award Calif. Dem. Party, Black Caucus, 1988, 1989 JFK Am. Leadership award Santa Ana Dem. Club, 1989, Cmty. Leadership award Torat-Haijun Hebrew Acad., 1990, Mother of the Yr. award No. Am. TV Corp., 1999, numerous others; March Fong Eu ann. achievement award named in her honor Nat. Notary Pub. Assn., 1998-99. Fellow Internat. Coll. Dentists; mem. Navy League (life), Am. Dental Hygienists Assn. (pres. 1956-57), No. Calif. Dental Hygienists Assn., Oakland LWV, AAUW (area rep. in edn. Oakland br.), Calif. Tchrs. Assn., Calif. Agrl. Aircraft Assn. (hon.), Calif. Sch. Bd. Assn., Alameda County Sch. Bd. Assn. (pres. 1965), Alameda County Mental Health Assn., Calif. Pub. Health Assn. Northern Divsn. (hon.), So. Calif. Dental Assn. (hon.), Bus. and Profl. Women's Club, Soroptimist (hon.), Hadassah (life), Ebell Club (L.A.), Chinese Retail Food Markets Assn. (hon.), Chinese Women's Assn. Singapore, Am. Assn. Singapore, Pilot Club Internat., Clara Barton Soc. Am. Red Cross (L.A. chpt.), Delta Kappa Gamma, Phi Alpha Delta (hon.), Phi Delta Gamma (hon.), others. Avocation: painting.

EUSTIS, ROBERT HENRY, mechanical engineer; b. Mpls., Apr. 18, 1920; s. Ralph Warren and Florence Louise E.; m. Katherine Vik Johnson, Mar. 20, 1943; children— Jeffrey Nelson, Karen V. B.M.E., U. Minn., 1942, M.S., 1944; Sc.D., M.I.T., 1953. Instr. U. Minn., 1942-44; research scientist NASA, 1944-47; asst. prof. M.I.T., 1947-51; chief engr. Thermal Research and Engring. Corp., 1951-53; mgr. heat and mech. sect. S.R.I. Internat., 1953-55; mem. faculty dept. mech. engring. Stanford U., 1955-90, prof., 1962, dir. high temperature gasdynamics lab, 1961-80, assoc. dean engring., 1984-88. Chmn. tech. adv. coun. Emerson Electric Corp.; prin Eustis Designs, 1990—. Contbr. articles to profl. jours. Recipient medal Soviet Sci. Acad., 1973 Fellow AIAA, ASME, AAAS; mem. Am. Soc. Engring. Edn. Home: 862 Lathrop Dr Palo Alto CA 94305-1053 Office: Stanford Univ Dept Mech Engring Stanford CA 94305 E-mail: rheustis@stanford.edu

EVANS, ANTHONY HOWARD, university president; b. Clay County, Ark., Sept. 24, 1936; s. William Raymond and Thelma Fay (Crews) E.; m. Lois Fay Kirkham, Aug. 29, 1959. BA, East Tex. Bapt. Coll., Marshall, 1959; MA, U. Hawaii, 1961; PhD, U. Calif.-Berkeley, 1966. Program officer Peace Corps, Seoul, Korea, 1970-72, chief program planning Washington, 1972-73, dir. planning office, 1973-75; asst. to pres. Eastern Mich. U., Ypsilanti, 1975-76, exec. v.p., 1976-79, acting pres., 1978-79, provost, v.p. acad. affairs, 1979-82; pres. Calif. State U., San Bernardino, 1982-97, trustee prof. San Marcos, 1997—. Mem. Orgn. Am. Historians, Phi Kappa Phi Home: 707 S Live Oak Park Rd Fallbrook CA 92028-3683

EVANS, BARTON, JR. analytical instrument company executive; b. Washington, Dec. 11, 1947; s. Barton and Viola (Gompf) E.; m. Harriet Andrea Neves, Nov. 20, 1983. BA in Econs., Claremont McKenna Coll., 1970; BS in Engring., MS in Engring., Stanford U., 1972. Sr. engr. Lockheed Missiles and Space Co., Sunnyvale, Calif., 1976-77, Dionex Corp., Sunnyvale, 1977-79, engring. mgr., 1979-81, dir. engring., 1981-83, v.p. engring., 1983-84, v.p. ops., 1984-93, sr. v.p., 1993-2001, exec. v.p., COO, 2001—. 1st lt. U.S. Army, 1972-75; col. USAR, 1976—. Mem. ASME, Civil Affairs Assn. (dir.), Psychol. Ops. Assn., Assn. U.S. Army, Res. Officers Assn. Achievements include co-inventor conductivity detector. Office: Dionex Corp 541 Lakeside Dr Sunnyvale CA 94085-4003

EVANS, BERNARD WILLIAM, geologist, educator; b. London, July 16, 1934; came to U.S., 1961, naturalized, 1977; s. Albert Edward and Marjorie (Jordan) E.; m. Sheila Campbell Nolan, Nov. 19, 1962. BSc, U. London, 1955; PhD, Oxford U., Eng., 1959. Asst. U. Glasgow, Scotland, 1958-59; departmental demonstrator U. Oxford, 1959-61; asst. research prof. U. Calif., Berkeley, 1961-65, asst. prof., 1965-66, assoc. prof., 1966-69; prof. geology U. Wash., Seattle, 1969—, chmn. dept. geol. scis., 1974-79. Contbr. articles to profl. jours. Recipient U.S. Sr. Scientist award Humboldt Found., Fed. Republic Germany, 1988-89; Fulbright travel award, France, 1995-96. Fellow Geol. Soc. Am., Mineral Soc. Am. (pres. 1993-94, award 1970), Geochem. Soc., Geol. Soc. London, Mineral. Soc. Gt. Britain, Swiss Mineral. Soc. E-mila. Home: 8001 Sand Point Way NE Apt 55C Seattle WA 98115-6399 Office: U Wash Dept Earth and Space PO Box 351310 Seattle WA 98195-1310 E-mail: evans@geology.washington.edu

EVANS, BEVERLY ANN, state legislator, school system administrator; b. Tod Park, Utah, Jan. 26, 1944; d. Elias Wilbur and Geraldine Vilate (Rigby) Cook; m. Stephen R. Evans, July 31, 1965; children: Lorie Ann, James. BS, Utah State U., 1965, MS, 1974. Tchr. Duchesne (Utah) Sch. Dist., 1965-70; instr. Utah Basin Applied Tech. Ctr., Roosevelt, Utah, 1970-73, adminstr., 1973—; instr. Utah State U., Logan, 1968—; mem. Utah Ho. of Reps., Salt Lake City, 1986-98, Nat. Nuclear Waste Task Force, 1987-88, Utah Senate, Dist. 26, Salt Lake City, 1998—. Cons. Utah State U., 1980—. Recipient Award of Merit, Nat. Safety Coun., Chgo., 1985-87, Alumni award Nat. 4-H, 1989, Bus. Woman of Yr award Utah BPW, 1990, Pub. Servant award Duchesne County C. of C., 1993. Mem., Amer. Vocational Assoc., Uintah Basin Education Ctr., Chamber of Commerce,Wasatch & Duchesne Counties. Republican. Mem. LDS Ch. Avocations: computers, outdoor activities, writing. Home: HC 65 Box 36 Altamont UT 84001-9704 Office: State Capitol Salt Lake City UT 84111

EVANS, BILL (JAMES WILLIAM EVANS), dancer, choreographer, educator, arts administrator; b. Lehi, Utah, Apr. 11, 1940; s. William Ferdinand and Lila (Snape) E.; married, Aug. 27, 1962 (div. 1965); 1 child, Thaïs. BA in English, U. Utah, 1963, MFA in Modern Dance, 1970; dance student various pvt. dance schs. and studios; cert. in laban and bartenieff, U. Utah, 1997. Apprentice Harkness Ballet Co., N.Y.C., 1966; mem. Chgo. Ballet and Lyric Opera Ballet, 1966-67; teaching asst. dept. ballet and modern dance U. Utah, 1967-68, faculty Virginia Tanner Creative Dance Program, 1968-73, asst. prof. modern dance, 1974-76, dancer, tchr., choreographer, artistic coordinator, mem. Repertory Dance Theatre, 1967-74; artistic dir. Dance Theatre Seattle, 1976-83; artistic dir., resident tchr., choreographer Winnipeg's Contemporary Dancers, Man., Can., 1983-84; assoc. prof., coord. dance program dept. kinesiology Ind. U., Bloomington, 1986-87, 87-88, artistic dir. Ind. Dance Theatre, 1986 88; head dance program dept. theatre and dance U. N.Mex., Albuquerque, 1988-93; prof. dance, 1993—; artistic dir. univ. Contemporary Dance Ensemble U. N.Mex., Albuquerque, 1989-93, dir., founder Univ. Youth Dance Camp, 1990, dir., founder Magnificio Youth Dance Groups, 1991-96. Artistic dir. Bill Evans Dance Co., toured U.S., Europe, Mex. 1975-99; Bill Evans Summer Insts. of Dance and Summer Festivals of Dance, Bill Evans Solo Dance Repertory, 1976—, Bill Evans Dance Co. Sch., Seattle; vis. prof. dance div. U. Wash., 1976-81; artistic advisor Fairmount Dance Theatre, Cleve., 1974-75; guest artist in residence Dance Dept., U. Utah; artist in resident Ill. U., Harvard U. Summer Sch., choreographer in residence Repertory Dance Theater; dir., choreographer N.Mex. Repertory Theatre, Santa Fe and Albuquerque; mem. Artists in Edn. Bank, Utah arts council; dance/movement specialist Artist-in-Schs. program Nat. Endowment for Arts; founder, dir. Celebrate Youth Summer Dance Inst., 1993-98; artistic coord. SW Am. Coll. Dance Festival, 1994; guest artist Kala Chhaya Cultural Ctr., India, 1993—; toured Karnataka, Maharastra, India. Freelance dancer, 1969—, including Berlin Ballet, 1969, Jacob's Pillow Dance Festival, Lee, Mass., 1973, Harvard U., 1973, 74, 90; choreographer over 170 works for various ballet and modern dance cos., 1967—; mem. editl. bd. Dance Connections, 1997. Am. Arts Alliance rep. before House and Senate appropriations coms., 1979. Served as officer U.S. Army, 1963-65. Recipient various choreographic awards, grants and fellowships from Nat. Endowment for Arts, 1972-75, 77-83, Utah Bicentennial Com., 1976, Art Found., Western States Arts Fedn., Wash. Arts Commn., King County Arts Commn., Seattle Arts Commn., Man. Arts Council, Ind. Arts Commn., N.Mex. Arts Div., U. N.Mex. Found., U. N.Mex. Coll. Fine Arts, Ind. U., Multidisciplinary Ventures Fund, U. N.Mex. Rsch. Allocations Com., City of Albuquerque, BRAVO award Albuquerque Arts Alliance, 1997, N.Mex. Gov.'s award for excellence and achievement in the arts, 2001; Guggenheim fellow, 1976-77, Am. Coll. Dance Fest., regional awards, 1986,87, 89-90, nat., 1986, 90; recipient Teaching Plaudit award nat. Dance Assn., 1981, scholar artist, 1997; named adjudicator and guest artist 1st Nat. Ballet Festival Regional Dance Am., 1997-99. Mem. Dancers, Inc. (adv. bd.), Nat. Dance Assn. (chair performance divsn. 1993—), Am. Coll. Dance Festival Assn. (bd. dirs. 1992—, U.S. rep. 1st internat. coll. dance festival Japan 1993). Office: U NM Dance Program Ctr for the Arts Dance Program Fine Art Ctr Albuquerque NM 87131-0001 E-mail: beran@unm.edu

EVANS, BOB OVERTON, electronics executive, director; b. Grand Island, Nebr., Aug. 19, 1927; s. Walter Bernard and Lillian (Overton) E.; m. Maria Bowman, Nov. 19, 1949; children: Cathleen L., Robert W., David D., Douglas B. B.E.E., Iowa State U., 1949. Electric operating engr. No. Ind. Pub. Service Co., Hammond, 1949-51; with IBM, 1951-84, v.p. devel. Data Systems div., 1962-64, pres. Fed. Systems div., 1965-69, pres. Systems Devel. div., 1970-74, pres. Systems Communication div., 1975-77; v.p. IBM engring., programming and tech., 1977-84; ptnr. Hambrecht and Quist, 1984-88; pres. Vanguard Internat. Semi-conductor Corp., 1995-96; mng. ptnr. Tech. Strategies and Alliances, Menlo Park, Calif., 1989—; chmn. Foothill Research, Inc., 1984-85; pres., CEO Interactive Voice Systems, Monrovia, Calif., 1997-99; chmn. Cambridge Tech. Group, McLean, Va., 1999—. Chmn. VCommand.com; pres., CEO Ridge Computers Inc., 1986-88; mem. Stark Draper Labs., Inc., Def. Sci. Bd.; mem. area bd. dirs. Md. Nat. Bank; cons. govt. agys.; bd. dirs. Santa Barbara Labs., Integrated CMOS Sys., Inc., V Mark Software, Cullinet Software, Micrognosis, Inc., Athena Sys., Planning Rsch. Corp., Cambridge Rsch. Assocs. Excellence in Comms. Corp.; mem. bd. overseers Superconductivity Super Collider, 1991-93. Mem. exec. bd. Nat. Capital Area coun. Boy Scouts Am., 1967-69; trustee Rensselaer Poly. Inst., 1972-84, N.Y. Pub. Libr., 1980-84; mem. elec. engring. vis. com. MIT, Cambridge, 1971-85. Lt. (j.g.) USNR, 1945-46. Recipient Disting. Pub. Svc. award NASA; Disting. Alumni citation Iowa State U., Disting. Achievement citation, 1991; Nat. medal of Tech., 1985; Republic of China VLSI Outstanding Contbn. award, 2001; named to Datamation Hall of Fame, 1987. Fellow IEEE (chmn. computer group conf. 1970, Armstrong award 1984), Assn. Computing Machines; mem. Nat. Acad. Engring., Profl. Group Electronic Computers, Nat. Security Indsl. Assn. (trustee), Armed Forces Communications and Electronics Assn. (trustee), Aerospace Industries Assn. (exec. bd.). Presbyterian. (elder). Achievements include designing and developing large digital electric computers. Home: 170 Robin Rd Hillsborough CA 94010-6632 Office: Tech Strategies & Alliances 3000 Sand Hill Rd # B-1S170 Menlo Park CA 94025-7113 E-mail: bevans@attglobal.net

EVANS, CASWELL ALVES, JR. dentist; BA, Franklin & Marshall Coll., 1965; DDS, Columbia U., 1970; MPH, U. Mich., 1972. Asst. prof. dentistry dept. dental ecology Sch. Dentistry, U. N.C., 1973-74; chief dental svc. and dir. rsch. and evaluation Healthco, Inc., 1973-74; clin. asst. prof. epidemiology and internat. health Sch. Pub. Health and Cmty. Med., Sch. Dentistry, U. Wash., 1974-85; asst. dir. health svc., dir. pub. health svc. L.A. County Dept. Health Svc., 1985-96, asst. dir., 1996—; assoc. prof. cmty. medicine Charles R. Drew U. Med. and Sci., 1986—. Chief dental svc. Seattle-King County Dept. Pub. Health, 1974-85, dir. ops., 1979; dir. King County Health Svc. Divsn., 1980-85; prin. investigator grant Nat. Cancer Inst.-NIH, 1986-91; co-prin. investigator, 1989-94; adj. prof. Sch. Dentistry, U. Calif., L.A., 1987—, Sch. Pub. Health, 1988—. Mem. APHA (pres. 1995), Inst. Medicine-NAS, Am. Assn. Pub. Health Dentistry. Office: LA County Dept Health Svcs 5555 Ferguson Dr Ste 100-26 Los Angeles CA 90022-5152

EVANS, CHARLES ALBERT, microbiology educator; b. Mpls., Feb. 18, 1912; s. Albert Grant and Susan Briery (Thompson) E.; m. Allie Ann Christman, Dec. 22, 1939; children: Nicholas J. (dec.), Susan Ethel, Thomas Charles, Carol Ann. BS, U. Minn., 1935, MD, 1937, PhD, 1943. Diplomate Am. B. Med. Microbiology. NRC fellow U. Rochester, 1941-42; rsch. supr. Minn. State Dept. Conservation, Mpls., 1942-43; asst. prof. dept. bacteriology U. Minn., Mpls., 1942-44, assoc. prof. dept. bacteriology, 1944-46; assoc. dir. Fred Hutchinson Cancer Rsch. Ctr., Seattle, 1971-75; prof. dept. microbiology U. Wash., Seattle, 1946-82, chmn., 1946-70, prof. emeritus, 1982—. Mem. nat. cancer coun. USPHS, Bethesda, Md., 1958-59,64-67; chmn. rsch. adv. coun. Am. Cancer Soc., 1967-70. Contbr. over 100 articles to profl. jours. Recipient numerous rsch. grants from NIH and Am. Cancer Soc. Mem. Am. Soc. for Microbiology (hon., pres. 1959-60), Soc. for Infectious Diseases (emeritus), Am. Assn. for Cancer Rsch. (emeritus), Am. Acad. Microbiology (mem. bd. govs. 1959-65, chmn. 1960-61). Avocations: birding, photography. Home: 7739 29th Ave NE Seattle WA 98115-4616 Office: U Wash Sch Medicine Dept Microbiology Seattle WA 98195-0001 E-mail: evansmic@u.washington.edu

EVANS, DON A. healthcare company executive; b. Jerome, Ariz., June 22, 1948; s. Rulon Cooper and Berniece (Ensign) E.; m. Susan Dahl, June 3, 1972; children: Emily, Austin, Adrienne, Alan. BS, Ariz. State U., Tempe, 1972; MS, U. Colo., 1974. Asst. adminstr. Nat. Jewish Hosp., Denver, 1974-80, LDS Hosp., Salt Lake City, 1980-84, COO, 1984-88; CEO Luth. Healthcare Network, Mesa, Ariz., 1988—; sr. group v.p. Banner Health Ariz., Mesa, 1999-2000, COO Phoenix, 2000—. Adj. prof. U. Minn., 1985-86. Fellow Am. Coll. Healthcare Execs. (regent for Ariz.); mem. Ariz. Hosp. Assn. (bd. dirs., chmn. bd. 1998-99). Republican. Office: 1441 N 12th St Phoenix AZ 85006-2837

EVANS, ERSEL ARTHUR, consulting engineer executive; b. Trenton, Nebr., July 17, 1922; s. Arthur E. and Mattie Agnes (Perkins) E.; m. Patricia A. Powers, Oct. 11, 1945 (div.); children: Debra Lynn (dec.), Paul Arthur. B.A., Reed Coll., Portland, Oreg., 1947; Ph.D., Oreg. State U., 1950. Registered profl. engr., Calif. With Gen. Electric Co., 1951-67, supr. ceramics research and devel. Wash., 1961-64; mgr. plutonium devel. Vallecitos Lab., Pleasanton, Calif., 1964-67; mgr. fuels and materials dept. Battelle Meml. Inst., Richland, Wash., 1967-70; with Westinghouse Electric Corp., 1970-87; v.p. Westinghouse Hanford Co., Richland, 1972-87, v.p., lab. tech. dir., 1985-87, ret., 1987, cons., 1987—. Mem. Tech. Assistance Adv. Group for Three Mile Island Recovery, 1981-86, mem. rev. Com. EBR-II, U. Chgo., 1989-91, 94—; mem. Japan Tech. Panel for Nuclear Power, NSF, 1989-90; mem. alt. applications of laser isotope separations tech. com. NRC, 1991-92, separations and tech. study, 1991-95, 96; del. Atlantic Coun. U.S.-Japan Conf. on Global Energy Issues, Maui, 1994, 96. Mem. vis. com. U. Wash. Served with USNR, 1943-45. Recipient Westinghouse Order of Merit; DuPont fellow, 1950-51; recipient Mishima award Am. Nuclear Soc., 1995. Fellow Am. Nuclear Soc. (Spl. Merit award 1964, Spl. Performance award 1980 Fed. Design Achievement award 1991, Walker Eisler medal 2001), Am. Inst. Chemists, Am. Soc. Metals, Am. Ceramic Soc.; mem. NAE, Phi Kappa Phi. Achievements include patents in field. Home and Office: Park Row # 45 701 Kettner Blvd San Diego CA 92101-5908 E-mail: ersel3@home.com

EVANS, GERALDINE ANN, academic administrator; b. Zumbrota, Minn., Feb. 24, 1939; d. Wallace William and Elda Ida (Tiedemann) Whipple; m. John Lyle Evans, June 21, 1963; children: John David, Paul William. AA, Rochester Community Coll., 1958; BS, U. Minn., 1960, MA, 1963, PhD, 1968. Cert. tchr., counselor, prin. and supt., Minn. Tchr. Hopkins (Minn.) Pub. Schs., 1960-63; counselor Anoka (Minn.) Pub. Schs., 1963-66; cons. in edn. Mpls., 1966-78; policy analyst Minn. Dept. Edn., St. Paul, 1978-79; dir. personnel Minn. Community Coll. System, St. Paul, 1979-82; pres. Rochester (Minn.) Community Coll., 1982-92; chancellor Minn. C.C. System, St. Paul, 1992-94; exec. dir. Ill. C.C. Bd., Springfield, 1994-96; chancellor San Jose (Calif.) Evergreen C.C. Dist., 1996—. Mem. San Jose Workforce Investment Bd., 2000—; mem. legis. and adv. com. Calif. C.C. League, 1998—. Vice chair, bd. dirs. Wayzata (Minn.) Sch. Bd., 1980-83; bd. dirs. Minn. Tech. Ctr., Rochester, 1991-92; sec.-treas. Coun. North Ctrl. Cmty. and Jr. Colls., 1990-92; moderator Mizpah United Ch. Christ, Hopkins, 1982; mem. Gov.'s Job Tng. Coun., St. Paul, 1983-94, chair, 1992-94; mem. ACE Commn. on Edn. Credit and Credentials, 1992-96; mem. Silicon Valley Pvt. Industry Coun., 1997-2000; mem. Workforce Silicon Valley, 1998—, chair youth com. 2000—; mem. Complete Count Com., U.S. Census, 2000. Winner Rochester C. of C. Athena award, 1990, San Jose YWCA Exec. award, 1998; Inst. Ednl. Leadership fellow, Washington, 1978-79. Mem. Nat. League Nursing (bd. assoc. degree accreditation rev. 1990-93, exec. com. 1993-96), Am. Assn. Cmty. Jr. Colls. (bd. dirs. 1984-87), North Ctrl. Assn. Cmty. and Jr. Colls. (evaluator 1985-96), Golden Gate Univ. (bd. trustees 1997—),Commonwealth Club Calif., Rotary. Congregationalist. Avocations: travel, gardening. E-mail: geraldine.evans@sjeccd.cc.ca.us

EVANS, HAROLD J. plant physiologist, biochemist, educator; b. Franklin, Ky., Feb. 19, 1921; s. James H. and Allie (Uhls) E.; m. Elizabeth Dunn, Dec. 14, 1946; children: Heather Mary, Pamela. B.S., U. Ky., 1946, M.S., 1948; Ph.D. (Cook-Vorhees fellow), Rutgers U., 1950. Asst. prof. botany N.C. State U., 1952-54, assoc. prof., 1954-57, prof., 1957-61; postdoctoral fellow Johns Hopkins U., Balt., 1952; prof. plant physiology Oreg. State U., Corvallis, 1961-88, Disting. prof. plant physiology, 1988-90, Disting. prof. plant physiology emeritus, 1990—. Dir. Lab. for Nitrogen Fixation, 1978-90; vis. prof. U. Sessex, Eng., 1967; George A. Miller vis. prof. U. Ill., Urbana, 1973; mem. panel for metabolic biology NSF, 1964-68; mem. U.S.-Japan Coop. Sci. Program, 1976. Editl. bd. Biofactors, 1989—; contbr. over 200 articles to profl. jours. Recipient Hoblitzelle Nat. award Tex. Research Found., 1964, Basic Research award Oreg. State U., 1965, NW Sci. award Gov. Oreg., 1967, von Humbolt Found. Sr. Rsch. award, 1991; named Disting. Alumnus U. Ky., 1975; recipient George G. Ferguson Disting. Prof. award and Milton Harris research award Oreg. State U., 1983 Fellow Am. Acad. Microbiology; mem. NAS, Am. Soc. Plant Physiologists (pres. 1971, trustee 1977—, Charles Reid Barnes award 1985), Sigma Xi (award 1968), Phi Kappa Phi. Democrat. Home: Apt C105 17320 Holy Name Dr Apt C105 Lake Oswego OR 97034 Office: Oreg State U Nitrogen Fixation Rsch Lab Corvallis OR 97331 E-mail: hjevans21@aol.com

EVANS, JAMES HANDEL, university administrator, architect, educator; b. Bolton, Eng., June 14, 1938; came to U.S., 1965. s. Arthur Handel and Ellen Bowen (Ramsden) E.; m. Carol L. Mulligan, Sept. 10, 1966; children: Jonathan, Sarah. Diploma of Architecture, U. Manchester, Eng., 1965; MArch., U. Oreg., 1967; postgrad., Cambridge (Eng.) U., 1969-70. Registered architect, Calif., U.K.; cert. NCARB. Assoc. dean. prof. architecture Calif. Poly. State U., San Luis Obispo, 1967-78; prof. art and design San Jose (Calif.) State U., 1979—, assoc. exec. v.p., 1978-81, interim exec. v.p., 1981-82, exec. v.p., 1982-91, interim pres., 1991-92, pres., 1992-95; vice chancellor Calif. State U System, Long Beach, CA, 1995-96; planning pres. Calif. State U. Channel Islands, Ventura, 1996-2001; pres. HE Cons. Inc., 2001—. Cons. Ibiza Nueva, Ibiza, Spain, 1977-80; vis. prof. Ciudad Universitaria, Madrid, 1977; vis. lectr. Herriott Watt U., Edinburgh, 1970; mem. adv. com. Army Command Staff Coll., Ft. Leavenworth, Kans., 1988. Trustee Good Samaritan Hosp., San Jose, 1987-90; bd. dirs. San Jose Shelter, 1988-90; dir. San Jose C. of C., 1991-94. Sci. Rsch. Coun. fellow Cambridge U., 1969-70. Fellow AIA; mem. Royal Inst. Brit. Architects, Assn. Univ. Architects. Avocation: golf. E-mail: jhevans@gte.net

EVANS, JANET, former Olympic swimmer; b. Placentia, Calif., Aug. 28, 1971; Degree in comms., U. So. Calif., 1994. 4 time Gold medalist, 400m Freestyle, 800m Individual Medley Seoul Olympic Games, 1988; Gold medalist, 800m Freestyle Barcelona Olympic Games, 1992, Silver medalist, 400m Freestyle, 1992; wubber 40th nat. title-400m Freestyle Phillips 66 Nat. Swimming Championships, Indpls., 1994; competed Atlanta Olympic Games, 1996; swimming coach U. So. Calif., host Janet Evans Invitational. Named U.S. Swimmer of Yr., 1987. Office: US Swimming Inc One Olympic Plaza Colorado Springs CO 80909-5724

EVANS, JOHN, state legislator, lawyer, educator; m. Mary Ann; 1 child, Evan. BA, U. Denver; MEd, PhD, Ga. State U.; JD, Valparaiso U. Bar: Colo., Ill, Ind., U.S. Supreme Ct. Mem. Colo. Senate, Dist. 30, Denver, 1998—; vice-chair health, environ., welfare and instns. com.; mem. judiciary com., mem. transp. com. Active Colo. State Bd. Edn.; chair, pres. Western Inst. for Agrl. Land Use; adv. bd. Gov.'s Manpower Devel. Commn.; organizer Rep. Leaders Initiative Forum; founder First Friday Breakfast Club, Rep. Forum Douglas County. Recipient Commendation medal Mil. Police Corps. Army, Cmty. Svc. award Optimist. Fellow Nat. Endowment for the Humanities; mem. Colo. Bar Assn. (bd. govs.), Nat. Orgn. on Legal Problems in Edn., Rotary Club. Republican. Avocations: skiing, fly fishing, hiking, carpentry. Home: 19130 E Molly Ave Parker CO 80134-7455 Office: State Capitol 200 E Colfax Ave Ste 346 Denver CO 80203-1716 E-mail: evansjo@sni.net

EVANS, KEITH EDWARD, government official, researcher; b. Pueblo, Colo., Apr. 26, 1940; s. C. Leslie and Clarabelle (Hammond) E.; m. Betty J. Watson, Aug. 21, 1960; children: Susan E., Steven C. BS in Wildlife Sci., Colo. State U., 1962, MS in Wildlife Sci., 1964; PhD in Wildlife Sci., Cornell U., 1971; postgrad., Fed. Exec. Inst., Charlottesville, Va., 1991. Range conservationist USDA Forest Svc., Rapid City, S.D., 1964-65, wildlife rsch. biologist, 1965-72, wildlife rsch. biologist, project leader Columbia, Mo., 1972-81, Am. Polit. Sci. Congl. fellow Washington, 1985-86, legis. asst., 1986-87, nat. range, wildlife and fish leader, 1987-89, asst. dir. Ogden, Utah, 1991-85, 89—. Contbr. over 50 articles to sci. jours. Recipient pub. svc. award North Utah Pub. Svc. Orgns., 1994. Mem. Nat. Audubon Soc. (past chpt. pres. and bd. dirs.). Avocations: bird watching, photography. Office: US Forest Svc Intermountain Rsch Sta 324 25th St Ste 4013 Ogden UT 84401-2394

EVANS, LOUISE, investor, retired psychologist, philanthropist; b. San Antonio; d. Henry Daniel and Adela (Pariser) E.; m. thomas Ross Gambrell, Feb. 23, 1960. BS, Northwestern U., 1949; MS in Clin. Psychology, Purdue U., 1952, PhD in Clin. Psychology, 1955. Lic. Marriage, Family and Child Counselor Calif.; Nat. Register of Health Svc. Providers in Psychology; lic. psychologist, Calif., N.Y. (inactive); diplomate Clin. Psychology, Am. Bd. Profl. Psychology. Intern clin. psychology Menninger Found. Topeka (Kans.) State Hosp., 1952-53; postdoctoral fellow clin. child psychology Menninger Clinic, Topeka, 1955-56; staff psychologist Kankakee (Ill.) State Hosp., 1954-55; head staff psychologist child guidance clinic Kings County Hosp., Bklyn., 1957-58; dir. psychology clinic Barnes-Renard Hosp.; instr. med. psychology Sch. Medicine Washington U., 1959-60; clin. rsch. cons. Episc. City Diocese, St. Louis, 1959-60; pvt. practice clin. and cons. psychology Fullerton, Calif., 1960-92; fellow Internat. Coun. Sex Edn. and Parenthood, 1984, Am. U., Washington. Psychol. cons. Fullerton Cmty. Hosp., 1961-81; staff cons. clin. psychology Martin Luther Hosp., Anaheim, Calif., 1963-70; nat. and internat. lectr clin. psychology schs. and profl. groups, 1950—; charperson, participant psychol. symposiums, 1956—; keynote spkr. clin. psychology civic and cmty. orgns., 1950—. Contbr. articles on clin. psychology to profl. pubs. Elected to Hall of Fame Ctrl. H.S., Evansville, Ind., 1966; recipient Svc. award Yuma County (Ariz.) Head Start Program, 1972, Statue of Victory Personality of Yr. award Centro Studi E. Ricerche Delle Nazioni, Italy, 1985, Alumni Merit award Northwestern U. Coll. Arts and Scis., 1997; named Miss Heritage, Heritage Publs., 1965. Fellow AAAS (emeritus), APA (clin. divsn. psychology of women divsn., divsn. psychotherapy, cons. divsn., dir. exec. bd. 1976-79), Acad. Clin. Psychology, Am. Assn. Applied and Preventative Psychology (charter), Royal Soc. Health England (emeritus), Internat. Coun. Psychologists (dir. 1977-79, sec. 1962-64, 73-76), Am. Orthopsychiat. Assn. (life), World Wide Acad. Scholars of N.Z. (life), Am. Psychol. Soc. (charter), L.A. Soc. Clin. Psychologists (exec. bd. 1966-67); mem. AAUP (emeritus), Calif. State Assn. (life, ins. com, 1961-65), L.A. County Psychol. Assn. (emeritus), Orange County Psychol. Assn. (charter founder, exec. bd. 1961-62), Orange County Soc. Clin. Psychologists (founder, exec. bd. 1963-65, pres. 1964-65), Am. Pub. Health Assn. (emeritus), Internat. Platform Assn., N.Y. Acad. Scis. (emeritus), Purdue U. Alumni Assn. (life mem., pres. coun., dean's club pacesetters, Citizenship award for Contbns. to Mental Health Fields 1975, Disting. Alumni award, 1993, Old Master, 1993), Northwestern U. 1851 Soc. (Coll. Arts and Scis. Merit award 1997), Ctr. Study Presidency, Soc. Jewelry Historians USA (charter), Alumni Assn. Menninger Sch. Psychiatry, Sigma Xi (emeritus), Pi Sigma Pi (pres. 1947-48, sec. 1946-47). Achievements include development of innovative theories and techniques of clinical practice; acknowledged pioneer in development of psychology as science and profession both nationally and internationally, and in marital and family therapy, and in consulting to hospitals and clinics. Office: PO Box 6067 Beverly Hills CA 90212-1067 Fax: 310-474-1361

EVANS, MAX JAY, historical society administrator; b. Lehi, Utah, May 11, 1943; s. Karl Robinson and Lucile (Johnson) E.; m. Mary Wheatley, June 16, 1967; children: David Max, Joseph Michael, Katherine Anne, Laura, Emily. BS, U. Utah, 1968; MS, Utah State U., 1971. Archivist LDS Ch. Hist. Dept., Salt Lake City, 1971-75; asst. ch. librarian, archivist Mormon Ch. Hist. Dept., Salt Lake City, 1975-77; dep. state archivist State Hist. Soc. Wis., Madison, 1977-86, library dir., 1986; dir. Utah State Hist. Soc., Salt Lake City, 1986—; acting dir. Utah State Archives, Salt Lake City, 1986-88. Archival cons. N.Y. State Archives, Albany, 1981, Wyo Dept. Archives and Hist., Cheyenne, 1982. Co-author: MARC for Archives and Manuscripts: A Compendium of Practice, 1985 (SAA Coker award 1986); articles in field. Trustee Middleton (Wis.) Pub. Libr., 1974-86, Am. West Heritage Found., 1995—; exec. sec. Utah Statehood Centennial Commn., 1988-93, Utah Pioneer Sesquicentennial Celebration Coord. Coun., 1994-98; chair Utah State Rcds. com., 1992—; bd. dirs. Rsch. Librs. Group, 1991-92; coun. mem. Am. Assn. for State and Local History, 1997—. Fellow Soc. Am. Archivists; mem. Utah State Hist. Soc. Mem. LDS Ch. Avocations: cross country and downhill skiing, bicycling, hiking, reading, movies. Office: Utah State Hist Soc 300 Rio Grande St Salt Lake City UT 84101-1106

EVANS, R. MONT, state legislator; b. Montpelier, Idaho, Jan. 9, 1947; m. Cheryl Evans; 4 children. BA in Polit. Sci. and History, Brigham Young U.; MSW, U. Utah. Social worker, adminstr. Utah Dept. Corrections; mem. Utah Ho. of Reps., 1986-96, Utah State Senate, 1996—, mem. transp. and pub. safety com., mem. transp. and environ. quality appropriations com., chair state and local affairs com. Mem. Riverton (Utah) City Coun., 1983-86; trustee, chmn. Riverton Arts Coun., 1983-87; trustee Riverton Hist. Soc.; mem., chmn. Riverton City Planing and Zoning Commn., 1982-84. Recipient Total Citizen award Utah C. of C., 1992. Republican. Mormon. Home: 1599 Big Var Way Riverton UT 84065-4003

EVANS, ROBERT VINCENT, sales and marketing executive; b. Mobile, Ala., Sept. 21, 1958; s. William Alexander Evans and Katherine Barbara (Doerr) Davidson; children: James Vernon, Chelsea Marie. BS in Computer Info. Systems, BS in Tech. Mgmt., Regis U., 1987; postgrad. in Mgmt., U. Wash., 1995. Electrician Climax (Colo.) Molybdenum Co., 1978-82; applications engr. Honeywell, Inc., Englewood, Colo., 1982-83, sales engr., 1983-87; systems engr. Apple Computer, Inc., Seattle, 1987-88, regional systems engring. mgr. Portland, Oreg., 1988-96, dist. sales mgr. Seattle, 1997—. Author: Anthology of American Poets, 1981. Dir. Operation Lookout, Seattle, 1989; mem. Rep. Nat. Com.; commr. dist. chmn. Boy Scouts Am. Recipient USMC Blues award, Marine Corps Assn. Leatherneck award, 1977, Denver Post Outstanding Svc. award, 1983, N.Y. Zool. Soc. Hon. medal, James West fellowship award, Paul Harris fellowship award, Silver Beaver award Boy Scouts Am., 1998. Mem. Am. Mgmt. Assn., Am. Platform Assn., Mensa, Rotary, Kiwanis. Republican. Mem. Northwest Cmty. Ch. Avocations: reading, church ministry, family activities. Office: Apple Computer Inc PO Box 40355 Bellevue WA 98015-4355

EVANS, RONALD ALLEN, lodging chain executive; b. Louisville, Apr. 5, 1940; s. William Francis and Helen Maxine (Hart) E.; m. Lynne Anne Ingraham, Aug. 25, 1979; children: Nicole Louise, Michele Lynne, Christopher Hart B.S. in Mgmt., Ariz. State U., 1963. Vice pres. Electronic Data Systems, Dallas, 1969-73; vice pres. First Fed. Savs., Phoenix, 1973-77, Community Fin. Corp., Scottsdale, Ariz., 1977-78; pres. Evans Mgmt. Services, Inc., Phoenix, 1978-84; pres., CEO Best Western Internat., Inc., Phoenix, 1979-98; dean Sch. Hotel and Restaurant Mgmt. No. Ariz. U., Flagstaff, 1998—. Served to lt. USNR, 1963-66 Decorated Bronze Star Republican. Episcopalian. Lodges: Masons (32 deg.), KT, Shriner Office: No Ariz U Sch Hotel & Restaurant Mgmt PO Box 5638 Flagstaff AZ 86011-0001

EVANS, THOMAS EDGAR, JR. title insurance agency executive; b. Toronto, Ohio, Apr. 17, 1940; s. Thomas Edgar and Sarah Ellen (Bauer) E.; m. Cynthia Lee Johnson, Feb. 23; children: Thomas Edgar, Douglas, Melinda, Jennifer. BA, Mt. Union Coll., 1963. Tchr., Lodi, Ohio, 1963-64; salesman Simpson-Evans Realty, Steubenville, 1964-65, Shadron Realty, Tucson, 1965-67; real estate broker, co-owner Double E Realty, Tucson, 1967-69; escrow officer, br. mgr., asst. county mgr., v.p. Ariz. Title Ins., Tucson, 1969-80; pres. Commonwealth Land Title Agy., Tucson, 1980-82, also dir.; pres. Fidelity Nat. Title Agy., 1982-90; bd. govs. Calif. Land Title Assn., 1990—; exec. v.p. Fidelity Nat. Title Ins. Co., 1990-92; v.p. Inland Empire Divsn. Fidelity Nat. Title, 1991-93, pres. Orange County divsn., 1993-2000, exec. v.p., regional mgr., 2000—. Bd. dirs. Western Fin. Trust Co., Fidelity Nat. Fin. Inc., Fidelity Nat. Title Ins. Co., Fidelity Nat. Title Agy. Pinal, The Griffin Co., Computer Market Place, Inc., e Market Place; bd. dirs., chmn. bd. Cochise Title Agy., TIPCO; v.p., dir. A.P.C. Corp. Named Boss of Yr., El Chaparral chpt. Am. Bus. Women's Assn., 1977. Mem. Calif. Land Title Assn. (pres. 1995-96), So. Ariz. Escrow Assn., So. Ariz. Mortgage Bankers Assn. (bd. dirs. 1982-85), Ariz. Mktg. Bankers Assn., Old Pueblo Businessmen's Assn. Tucson, Tucson Bd. Realtors, Ariz. Assn. Real Estate Exchangors (bd. dirs. 1968-69), Land Title Assn. Ariz. (pres. 1984), So. Ariz. Homebuilders Assn., Tucson Real Estate Exchangors (pres. 1968), Pacific Club, Ctr. Club, Old Pueblo Courthouse Club, La Paloma Club, Ventana Country Club, Centre Ct. Club, Coto de Casa Country Club, Elks Club, Pima Jaycees (dir. 1966), Sertoma (charter pres., chmn. bd. Midtown sect. 1968-70), Sunrise Rotary, Old Pueblo Club, South Coast Repertory (trustee 1996-2000), Blue Key, Sigma Nu. Home: 28861 Glen Rdg Mission Viejo CA 92692-4301 Office: 4050 Calle Real Ste 210 Santa Barbara CA 93110-3413

EVANS, TOMMY NICHOLAS, obstetrician/gynecologist, educator; b. Batesville, Ark., Apr. 12, 1922; s. James Rufus and Carrye Mae (Goatcher) E.; m. Jessica Ray Osment, June 12, 1945; 1 child, Laura Kathreen A.A., Mars Hill Jr. Coll., 1940; student, Duke U., 1940-41; A.B., Baylor U., 1942; M.D., Vanderbilt U., 1945. Intern U. Mich. Hosp., Ann Arbor, 1945-46, asst. resident ob-gyn, 1948, resident, 1948-49, jr. clin. instr., 1949-50, sr. clin. instr., 1950-51, instr., 1951-54, asst. prof., 1954-56, assoc. prof., 1956-60, prof., 1960-65; prof. ob-gyn Wayne State U., Detroit, 1965-83, dean Sch. Medicine, 1970-72, dir. C.S. Mott Ctr. Human Growth and Devel., 1973-83; sr. attending physician Hutzel Hosp., 1966-83, chief ob-gyn, 1966-82, vice chief of staff, 1967-70, chief of staff, 1970-74, trustee, 1975-78; mem. teaching, surgeon Harper-Grace Hosps., 1965-83, chief gynecology Harper div., 1970-83, chief ob-gyn, 1975-83; chief gynecology, sr. attending physician Detroit Receiving Hosp., 1965-83; chief gynecology U. Colo., Denver, 1983-89, vice chmn. ob-gyn., 1983-89, prof. emeritus ob-gyn., 1989—. Cons. pediatric surgery Children's Hosp.; cons. Sinai Hosp. William Beaumont Hosp., Wayne County Gen. Hosp.; past mem. med. adv. com. Detroit Med. Ctr. Corp. Bd. dirs. Alan Guttmacher Inst. Fellow Am. Assn. Ob-Gyn.; mem. Am. Coll. Obstetricians and Gynecologists (past exec. bd., past pres.), ACS (adv. council ob-gyn credentials com. 1983-85, bd. govs. 1982-86), Am. Fedn. Clin. Research, Am. Fertility Soc., Am. Gynecol. Club (past pres.), Am. Gynecol. Soc. (past pres.), Am. Gynecol. and Obstetrical Soc. (council), AMA, Am. Med. Soc. Vienna, Am. Pub. Health Assn., Am. Soc. Andrology (exec. council), Am. Soc. Study Sterility, Anthony Wayne Soc., Assn. Profs. Ob-Gyn (past chmn. nominating com.), Central Assn. Ob-Gyn (past pres.), Charlie Flowers Ob-Gyn Soc., Chgo. Gynecol. Soc., Continental Gynecol. Soc., Detroit Acad. Medicine, Detroit Cancer Club (past mem. program com.), Engring. Soc. Detroit, Greater Detroit Area Hosp. Council Inc., Internat. Fedn. Ob-Gyn (exec. bd.), Internat. Soc. Advancement Humanistic Studies in Gynecology, Miami Obstet. and Gynecol. Soc., Mich. Assn. Retarded Children, Mich. Cancer Found. (trustee), Mich. Council Study of Abortion, Mich. Soc. Ob-Gyn (past pres.), Mich. State Med. Soc. (past exec. council), Mich. United Cerebral Palsy Assn., Norman Miller Gynecol. Soc. (past pres.), Ob-Gyn Soc. N.Y., Planned Parenthood League, Pan Am. Med. Assn., Royal Soc. Medicine, Soc. Study of Reprodn., Soc. Ob-Gyn of Can., S. Atlantic Assn. Ob-Gyn, numerous others. Republican. Presbyterian. Office: 8146 E Whispering Wind Dr Scottsdale AZ 85255-2840

EVEN, RANDOLPH M. lawyer; b. 1943; BS, U. Calif.; JD, Calif. Western Sch. Law. Bar: Calif. 1969. Atty. Even, Crandall, Wade, Lowe & Gates and predecessor firm Genson, Even, Crandall & Wade, P.C., Woodland Hills, Calif. Mem. Am. Bd. Trial Advocates, Assn. So. Calif. Def. Counsel (bd. dirs. 1978-80, 93-98). Office: Even Crandall Wade Lowe & Gates 21031 Ventura Blvd Ste 801 Woodland Hills CA 91364-2240

EVENHUIS, HENK J. research company exxecutive; b. Ontario, Calif., Apr. 10, 1943; s. Kornelus and Harmina (Vermeer) E.; m. Cynthia Wheelus, Jan. 31, 1964; children: John, Karen. BS in Acctg., Calif. State Poly. U., Pomona, 1967; MBA in Fin., U. Santa Clara, 1976. V.p., CFO, Ferix Corp., Fremont, Calif., 1983-85, Trimedia Corp., Fremont, 1985-86, Corvus Systems Corp., San Jose, Calif., 1986-87; sr. v.p., CFO, Lam Rsch. Corp., Fremont, 1987—. Bd. dirs. Credence Corp., Fremont. Mem. Fin. Execs. Inst. (bd. dirs. Santa Clara, Calif. 1988-90). Avocations: skiing, golf. Office: FAIR, ISAAC & COMPANY, INC. 120 N REDWOOD DR. San Rafael CA 94903

EVERETT, PAMELA IRENE, legal management company executive, educator; b. L.A., Dec. 31, 1947; d. Richard Weldon and Alta Irene (Tuttle) Bunnell; m. James E. Everett, Sept. 2, 1967 (div. 1973); 1 child, Richard Earl. Cert. Paralegal, Rancho Santago Coll., Santa Ana, Calif., 1977; BA, Calif. State U.-Long Beach, 1985; MA, U. Redlands, 1988. Owner, mgr. Orange County Paralegal Svc., Santa Ana, 1979—; pres. Gem Legal Mgmt. Inc., Fullerton, Calif., 1986—; co-owner Bunnell Publs., Fullerton, 1992-96. Instr. Rancho Santiago Coll., 1979-96, chmn. adv. bd., 1980-85; instr. Fullerton Coll., 1989—, Rio Hondo Coll., Whittier, Calif., 1992-94; advisor Saddleback Coll., 1985—, North Orange County Regional Occupational Program, Fullerton, 1986—, Fullerton Coll. So. Calif. Coll. Bus. and Law; bd. dirs. Nat. Profl. Legal Assts. Inc., editor PLA News. Author: Legal Secretary Federal Litigation, 1986, Bankruptcy Courts and Procedure, 1987, Going Independent--Business Planning Guide, Fundamentals of Law Office Management, 1994. Republican. Avocation: reading. Office: 940 Manor Way Corona CA 92882 E-mail: Peverett@home.com

EVERETT-THORP, KATE, digital marketing executive; Grad. in Journalism, San Diego State U., 1991. TV reporter; media planner J. Walter Thompson U.S.A., San Francisco; v.p.-crusader advt. programs CNET, 1993; chmn. media measurement task force Internet Advt. Bur.; pres., CEO Lot21, San Francisco, 1998. Office: 548 4th St San Francisco CA 94107-1621

EVERHART, THOMAS EUGENE, retired university president, engineering educator; b. Kansas City, Mo., Feb. 15, 1932; s. William Elliott and Elizabeth Ann (West) E.; m. Doris Arleen Wentz, June 21, 1953; children: Janet Sue, Nancy Jean, David William, John Thomas. AB in Physics magna cum laude, Harvard, 1953; MSc, UCLA, 1955; PhD in Engring., Cambridge U., Eng., 1958. Mem. tech. staff Hughes Research Labs., Culver City, Calif., 1953-55; mem. faculty U. Calif., Berkeley, 1958-78, prof. elec. engring. and computer scis., 1967-78, Miller research prof., 1969-70, chmn. dept., 1972-77; prof. elec. engring., Joseph Silbert dean engring. Cornell U., Ithaca, N.Y., 1979-84; prof. elec. and computer engring., chancellor U. Ill., Urbana-Champaign, 1984-87; prof. elec. engring. and applied physics, pres. Calif. Inst. Tech., Pasadena, 1987-97, pres. emeritus Pasadena, 1997—. Fellow scientist Westinghouse Rsch. Labs., Pitts., 1962-63; guest prof. Inst. Applied Physics, U. Tuebingen, Germany, 1966-67, Waseda U., Tokyo, Osaka U., 1974; vis. fellow Clare Hall, Cambridge, U., 1975; chmn. Electron, Ion and Photon Beam Symposium, 1977; cons. in field; mem. sci. and ednl. adv. com. Lawrence Berkeley Lab., 1978-85, chmn., 1980-85; mem. sci. adv. com. GM, 1980-89, chmn., 1984-89, bd. dirs., 1989—; bd. dirs. Agilent Technologies Inc., Saint-Gobain Corp., Reveo, Inc., Raytheon Co., Hughes Electronics Co.; tech. adv. com. R.R. Donnelly & Sons, 1981-89; sr. sci. advisor W.M. Keck Found., 1997—; pro-vice chancellor Cambridge U., 1998. Chmn. Sec. of Energy Adv. Bd., 1990-93; bd. dirs. KCET, 1989-97, Corp. for Nat. Rsch. Initiatives, 1990—, Electric Power Rsch. Inst., 1998—; trustee Calif. Inst. Tech., 1998—; mem. bd. overseers Harvard U., 1999—. Marshall scholar Cambridge U., 1955-58, NSF sr. fellow, 1966-67, Guggenheim fellow, 1974-75. Fellow IEEE, AAAS, ASEE, Royal Acad. Engring.; mem. NAE (ednl. adv. bd. 1984-88, mem. com. 1984-89, chmn. 1988, coun. 1988-94, 96—), Microbeam Analysis Soc. Am., Electron Microscopy Soc. Am. (coun. 1970-72, pres. 1977), Coun. on Competitiveness (vice-chmn. 1990-96), Assn. Marshall Scholars and Alumni (pres. 1965-68), Athenaeum Club, California Club, Sigma Xi, Eta Kappa Nu. Home: PO Box 1639 Santa Barbara CA 93116-1639 Office: Calif Inst Tech Office Pres Emeritus/202-31 1200 E California Blvd Pasadena CA 91125-0001

EVERINGHAM, HARRY TOWNER, editor, publisher; b. Memphis, Aug. 14, 1908; s. William Kirby and Ida Pauline (Towner) E.; m. Margaret Sophia Johnson; children: Martha, Barbara, Richard Kirby. Student, Northwestern U., Evanston, Ill., 1936-39, U. Chgo., , 1940. Writer, dir. weekly radio drama WREC, Memphis, 1930-33; radio writer, producer Miles Lab., Chgo., Wade Advt. Agy., Chgo., 1934-35; v.p. Sehl Advt. Agy., Chgo., 1936-41; broadcasting Henry C. Lytton & Co., Chgo.; film producer, lectr. Employers Assn., Chgo., 1942; editor, pub. The Fact Finder, 1942—; pub. rels. dir. Ingalls-Shepard Div. Wyman Gordon Co., Harvey, Ill.; editor Forging Ahead Mag., 1942-45. Editor, pub. U.S.A.-Beyond the Crossroads, Chgo., The Am. Patriot, 1959-94; syndicated newspaper columnist, 1960-63. V.p. Greater Chgo. Churchmen, 1946-47; founder Pub. Club Chgo., 1942. Mem. Ariz. Breakfast Club (founder, pres.). Republican. Avocations: teaching, speaking, broadcasting. Office: We the People UNITED Box A Scottsdale AZ 85252

EVERROAD, JOHN DAVID, lawyer; b. Columbus, Ind., Jan. 6, 1940; s. Henry and Margaret L. (Eckleman) E.; m. Patricia Diane Hayworth, June 10, 1967; children: Andrew Quinn, Matthew Oldham. BA, Vanderbilt U., 1962, JD, 1969. Bar: Ariz. 1970, Calif. 1997. Atty. Fennemore Craig PC, Phoenix, 1969—. Mem. panels Nat. Inst. Trial Advocacy programs; lawyer Com. Uniform Jury Standards State of Ariz.; mem. faculty Continuing Edn. Legal Programs. Pres. Parochial Sch. Bd., Phoenix, 1972-78; mem. Christ Luth. Ch., Phoenix, 1969—, sec., 1986, 88-89, pres., 1979-80; bd. dirs. Combined Metro. Phoenix Arts and Scis., 1996-98. With USMC, 1962-66. Fellow ABA, Ariz. Bar Found. (founder), Maricopa County Bar Found. (founder); mem. Am. Bd. Trial Advocates, Maricopa County Bar Assn. (pres. 1992-93), Pima County Bar Assn., Ariz. State Bar Assn. (chmn. edit. bd. Jour., com. revisions uniform jury instructions 1984-89, Disciplinary com. 1984-90), Phi Delta Phi. Republican. Lutheran. Avocations: scuba, skiing, sport fishing, bow hunting. Home: 6625 N 3rd Dr Phoenix AZ 85013-1103 Office: Fennemore Craig PC 3003 N Central Ste 2600 Phoenix AZ 85012-2913

EVERS-WILLIAMS, MYRLIE, cultural organization administrator; b. Vicksburg, Miss., Mar. 17, 1933; m. Medgar Evers (dec. June 1963); 3 children; m. Walter Edward Williams (dec. 1995). Student, Alcorn State U.; BA in Sociology, Pomona Coll., 1968, honorary degree; cert., Simmons Coll.; honorary degree, Medgar Evers Coll., Spelman Coll., Columbia Coll., Chgo., Bennett Coll., Tougaloo Coll., Pomona Coll. Mem. staff, sec. NAACP; dir. planning Clarmont (Calif.) Colls., 1968-70; v.p. advt. & publicity Seligman & Latz, N.Y.C., 1973-75; dir. consumer affairs Atlantic Richfield Co.; commr. Pub. Works Bd., L.A., 1987-95; chmn. NAACP, 1995-98. Civil rights leader, lectr. Author: For Us the Living, 1967, Watch Me Fly, 1999; contbg. editor Ladies Home Jour. Candidate for Congress in Calif., 1970; candidate for L.A. City Coun., 1987; head So. Calif. Dem. Women's Divsn.; convener Nat. Women's Polit. Caucus; founder, chmn. Medgar Evers Inst. Named Woman of Yr., Glamour Mag., 1995, Ms. Mag., 1995, one of Women of Yr., Ladies Home Jour., 1996; recipient Mary Church Terrell award Delta Sigma Theta, 1996, Althea T.L. Simmons Social Action award, 1998; recipient Spingarn award, NAACP, Atlanta, 1998; recipient Trumpeter's award, Nat. Consumers League, New Orleans, 1998; named one of 200 most influential women, Vanity Fair mag., Jan. 1999. Office: MEW Assocs Inc 15 SW Colorado Ave Bend OR 97702-1150

EWELL, CHARLES MUSE, health care industry executive, consultant, publisher, educator; b. Richmond, Va., Jan. 12, 1937; s. Charles Muse Sr. and Virginia (Causey) E.; m. Loretta Ann Morris, Feb. 1960 (div. 1967); children— Charles Daniel, Elizabeth Morris; m. Valerie Ann White, Aug. 29, 1984 BS, MHA, Va. Commonwealth U.; PhD, U. Wis. Adminstr. for various hosps. in Midwest and East Coast, 1964-74; ptnr. Arthur Young & Co., Los Angeles, 1974-84; pres., chief exec. officer Am. Health Care Systems, San Diego, 1984-86; chmn. The Governance Inst., 1986—. Contbr. articles to profl. jours.; mem. editorial bd. various profl. jours. Chmn. men's bd. L.A. Philharm., 1982-83; bd. dirs. San Diego Symphony, 1986-90, Sharp Meml. Hosp., 1988-99. Mem. Valley Club (Sun Valley, Idaho), La Jolla Beach Club, La Jolla Country Club. Republican.

EWELL, MIRANDA JUAN, journalist; b. Beijing, Apr. 25, 1948; d. Vei-Chow and Hsien-fang Yolanda (Sun) J.; m. John Woodruff Ewell Jr., Feb. 20, 1971; children: Emily, David, Jonah. BA summa cum laude, Smith Coll., 1969; postgrad., Princeton U., 1971, U. Calif., Berkeley, 1981-82. Staff writer The Montclarion, Oakland, Calif., 1982-83; with San Jose (Calif.) Mercury News, 1984-99, staff writer; now correspondent San Jose (Calif.) Mercury News, San Francisco Bureau, 1990-95; correspondent in bus. San Jose Mercury News, 1997-99. Recipient Elsa Knight Thompson award Media Alliance, San Francisco, 1984, George Polk award L.I. U., N.Y., 1989, Heywood Brown award Newspaper Guild, Washington, 1989; Knight fellow Stanford U., 1995. Mem. Asian-Am. Journalists Assn.

EWERS, ANNE, opera company director; Gen. dir. Boston Lyric Opera, 1984-89, Utah Opera, Salt Lake City, 1990—. Panelist Nat. Endowment for Arts; freelance stage dir. San Francisco Opera, N.Y.C. Opera, Can. Opera Co., Minn. Opera, Vancouver Opera, numerous others. Dir. nearly fifty opera prodns. including La Giaconda, Un Ballo in Maschera, La Rondine, The Merry Widow, Ring Cycle, Salome, Dialogues des Carmelites, Eugene Onegin; dir. Dame Joan Sutherland's North American Farewell, Dallas Opera. Bd. dirs. Opera Am., 1993—. Office: Utah Opera 50 W 2nd S Ste 200 Salt Lake City UT 84101-1661

EWING, EDGAR LOUIS, artist, educator; b. Hartington, Nebr., Jan. 17, 1913; s. David E. and Laura (Buckendorf) E.; m. Suzanna Peter Giovan, Feb. 12, 1941. Grad., Art Inst. Chgo., 1935; studied, in France, Eng., Italy, 1935-37. Mem. faculty Art Inst. Chgo., 1937-43, U. Mich., Ann Arbor, 1946; asst. prof. fine arts U. So. Calif., 1946-54, assoc. prof., 1954-59, prof., 1959-78, Disting. prof. emeritus, 1978—; Mellon prof. Carnegie-Mellon U., Pitts., 1968-69. One-man shows M.H. DeYoung Meml. Mus. Art, San Francisco, 1948, Santa Barbara Mus. of Art, 1952, Long Beach Mus. Art, 1955, Dalzell Hatfield Galleries, Los Angeles, 1954, 56, 58, 61, 63, 65, Hewlett Gallery-Carnegie Mellon U., Pitts., 1969, Nat. Gallery, Athens, Greece, 1973, Los Angeles Mcpl. Art Gallery, 1974, Palm Springs (Calif.) Desert Mus., 1976-77, Fisher Gallery U. So. Calif., 1978, Fisher Gallery, U. So. Calif., 1993-94; group exhbns. Cin Art Mus., Corcoran Gallery Art, Washington, Denver Art Mus., Dallas Mus. Fine Arts, Fort Worth Art Ctr., Met. Mus., N.Y.C.; represented: San Francisco Mus. Art, Dallas Mus. Fine Arts, Ft. Worth Art Ctr., Met. Mus., N.Y.C., Sao Paulo (Brazil) Mus. Art, Wichita Art Mus., Fisher Gallery, U. So. Calif., 1994. Served with C.E., U.S. Army, 1943-46, PTO. Recipient Aberle Florscheim Meml. prize for Oil Painting, Art Inst. Chgo., 1943, Purchase award for oil painting Los Angeles County Mus. Art, 1952, Samuel Goldwyn award, 1957, Ahmanson Purchase award City of Los Angeles Exhbn., 1962, Disting. Prof. Emeritus award U. So. Calif., 1987; Edward L. Ryerson fellow, 1935; Louis Comfort Tiffany grantee, 1948-49, Jose Drudis Fund grantee, Greece, 1967; named one of 100 Artists-100 Yrs., Art Inst. Chgo., 1980. Mem. AAUP, Nat. Watercolor Soc. (v.p. 1952, pres. 1953) Democrat.

EWY, GORDON ALLEN, cardiologist, clinician, researcher, educator; b. Brenham, Kans., Aug. 5, 1933; s. Marvin John and Hazel Miller (Allen) E.; m. Priscilla Ruth Weldon; children: Kim Elizabeth, Gordon Stuart, Mark Allen. BA, U. Kans., 1955, MD, 1961. Resident, house officer Georgetown U. Hosp., Washington, 1961-64, cardiology fellow, 1964-65; instr. medicine Georgetown U., Washington, 1965-68, asst. prof., 1968-69, U. Ariz., Tucson, 1969-70, assoc. prof., 1970-75, prof. medicine, 1975—, chief cardiology, dir. cardiology fellowship program, 1982—, assoc. head dept. medicine, 1986-94, dir. Sarver Heart Ctr., 1991—. Editor: Cardiovascular Drugs and Management of Heart Disease, 1982, 93, Current Cardiovascular Drug Therapy, 1984; author numerous sci. publs.; contbr. numerous revs. to profl. jours., chpts. to books. Lt. (j.g.) USNR, 1955-57. Fellow ACP, Am. Heart Assn. (mem. clin. coun., nat. faculty advanced cardiac life support 1982-84, chmn. nat. programs subcom. 1982, bd. dirs. Ariz. chpt. 1975-82, 84-89, tchg. fellow 1970-75), Am. Coll. Cardiology (chmn. learning ctr. com. 1988-91, trustee 1992-97), Alpha Omega Alpha. Republican. Avocation: travel. Office: Ariz Health Scis Ctr 1501 N Campbell Ave Tucson AZ 85724-0001

EXNER, ADAM, archbishop; b. Killaly, Sask., Can., Dec. 24, 1928; Ordained priest Roman Catholic Ch., 1957, consecrated bishop, 1974. Bishop of Kamloops, B.C., Can., 1974-82; archbishop of Winnipeg Man., Can., 1982-91; archbishop of Vancouver B.C., Can., 1991—. Office: Vancouver Archdiocese 150 Robson St Vancouver BC Canada V6B 2A7

EYMANN, RICHARD CHARLES, lawyer; b. Hanover, N.H., June 6, 1945; BS, U. Oreg., 1968; JD, Gonzaga U., 1976. Bar: Wash. 1976, U.S. Dist. Ct. (ea. dist.) Wash. 1978, U.S. Ct. Appeals (9th cir.) 1987, U.S. Dist. Ct. (we. dist.) Wash. 1989, U.S. Supreme Ct. 1995. Ptnr. Feltman, Gebhardt, Eymann & Jones, Spokane, Wash., Eymann, Allison, Fennessy, Hunter & Jones, P.S., Spokane. Mem. ABA (founder, chmn. nat. appellate advocacy competition 1975-84, bd. advs. 1985-93), ATLA, Wash. State Bar Assn. (bd. govs. 1997-98, pres. elect 1998-99, pres. 1999-2000), Wash. State Trial Lawyers Assn. (bd. govs. 1984-86, 88-95, legis. steering com. 1990-96, membership chair 1984-85, v.p. East 1991-92, fin. com. 1994-95, Trial Lawyer of Yr. 1995, pres. 1996-97), Wash. Trial Lawyers for Pub. Justice (bd. dirs. 1994-98), Spokane County Bar Assn., Am. Inns of Ct. (barrister 1986, master of the bench 1990, Charles L. Powell & Inn pres. 1991-93). Office: Eymann Allison Fennessy Hunter & Jones PS 601 W Main Ave Ste 801 Spokane WA 99201 E-mail: eymann@eahjlaw.com

EYRE, DAVID R. orthopedics educator; BS in Biochemistry, U. Leeds, Eng., 1966; PhD, U. Leeds, 1969. Prof., dir. rsch. U. Wash. Med. Ctr., Seattle. Mem. AAAS, Internat. Soc. Matrix Biology (founder), Am. Acad. Orthopaedic Surgeons (assoc.), Orthopaedic Rsch. Soc., Biochem. Soc., Conn. Tissue Soc., Protein Soc., East Coast Connective Tissue Club. Achievements include research on connective tissue biochemistry, collagen chemistry, inborn skeletal diseaease, cartilage pathology, biochemistry of intervertebral disc, bone resorption and osteoporosis. Office: U Wash Med Ctr Dept Orthopaedics Box 356500 1959 NE Pacific St Seattle WA 98195-0001

EZRA, DAVID ALAN, federal judge; b. 1947; BBA magna cum laude, St. Mary's U., 1969, JD, 1972. Law clk. Office of Corp. Counsel City and County Honolulu, 1972; mem. firm Greenstein, Cowen & Frey, 1972-73, Anthony, Hoddick, Reinwald & O'Connor, 1973-80, Ezra, O'Connor, Moon & Tam, 1980-88; dist. judge U.S. Dist. Ct., Hawaii, 1988-98, chief judge, 1998—. Adj. prof. law Wm. S. Richardson Sch. Law, 1978—; exec. com. 9th cir. Jud. Conf. Co-editor, author: Hwaii Construction Law - What to Do and When, 1987; editor: Hawaii Collection Practices Manual. 1st lt. USAR 1971-77. Daugherty Fund scholar, 1971, San Antonio Bar Assn. Aux. scholar, 1972. Mem. ABA, U.S. Fed. Judges Assn. (bd. dirs., exec. com.), Dist. Judges Assn. (v.p. 9th cir.), Hawaii State Bar, Am. Arbitration Assn., Delta Epsilon Sigma, Phi Delta Phi. Office: US Dist Ct 300 Alamoana Blvd C-400 Honolulu HI 96850

FAAL, EDI M. O. lawyer; b. Gambia, Africa, 1954; came to U.S., 1974; BS, Fla. Internat. U.; Barrister at Law, Mid. Temple Inns Ct., London; JD, Western State U., Fullerton, Calif., 1982. Bar: U.K., Wales, Calif., Ind., U.S. Supreme Ct. Adj. prof. U. So. Calif. Law Ctr., L.A. Named Lawyer of Yr., Langston Bar Assn. L.A., 1994; recipient Pres.'s award L.A. Criminal Cts. Bar Assn., Legal Champion award Ohio Criminal Def. Bar Assn. Office: 221 N Figueroa St Ste 1200 Los Angeles CA 90012-2646

FAATZ, JEANNE RYAN, grant administrator; b. Cumberland, Md., July 30, 1941; d. Charles Keith and Myrtle Elizabeth (McIntyre) Ryan; children: Kristin, Susan. BS, U. Ill., 1962; postgrad. (Gates fellow), Harvard U., 1984; MA, U. Colo., Denver, 1985. Instr. Speech Dept. Met. State Coll., Denver, 1985-98; sec. to majority leader Colo. Senate, 1976-78; mem. Colo. Ho. Reps. from Dist. 1, 1979-98; dir. Colo. Sch.-to-Career, 1999—. Former House asst. majority leader. Past pres. Harvey Pk. (Colo.) Homeowners Assn., S.W. Denver YWCA Adult Edn. Club; S.W. met. coord. UN Children's Fund, 1969-74; mem. bd. mgrs. S.W. Denver YMCA. Home: 2903 S Quitman St Denver CO 80236-2208 Office: Governors Office State Capitol Denver CO 80203

FABE, DANA ANDERSON, state supreme court chief justice; b. Cin., Mar. 29, 1951; d. George and Mary Lawrence (Van Antwerp) F.; m. Randall Gene Simpson, Jan. 1, 1983; 1 child, Amelia Fabe Simpson. BA, Cornell U., 1973; JD, Northeastern U., 1976. Bar: Alaska 1977, U.S. Supreme Ct. 1981. Law clk. to justice Alaska Supreme Ct., 1976-77; staff atty. pub. defenders State Alaska, 1977-81; dir. Alaska Pub. Defender Agy., Anchorage, 1981—. Judge Superior Ct., Anchorage; justice Alaska Supreme Ct., Anchorage, 1996—, chief justice, 2000—. Named alumna of yr. Northeastern Sch. Law, 1983, alumni pub. svc. award, 1991. Office: Alaska Supreme Ct 303 K St Fl 5 Anchorage AK 99501-2013

FABER, MICHAEL WARREN, lawyer; b. N.Y.C., June 7, 1943; s. Carl Faber and Harriet Ruth Cohen; m. Adele Zolot, Apr. 16, 1975; children: Evan, Jenna. AB, Hunter Coll., 1964; JD, Fordham U., 1967. Bar: N.Y. 1967, D.C. 1972, U.S. Ct. Claims, 1972, U.S. Supreme Ct. 1972, Colo. 1993. Gen. atty. FCC, Washington, 1967-69, trial atty., 1969-71, atty. advisor to Commr. T.J. Houser, 1971; assoc. Peabody, Rivlin, Lambert & Meyers, Washington, 1971-73; ptnr. Peabody, Lambert & Meyers, Washington, 1973-84, Reid and Priest, Washington, 1984-93, mem. exec. com., 1986-92; prin. The Faber Group, Cascade, Colo., 1993-94; pres. USA Volleyball Ctrs. LLC, Colorado Springs, 1995-96; owner The Pantry Restaurant, Green Mountain Falls, 1996-2001. Cons. White House Office Telecomm. Policy, 1976; chmn. organizing com. Nat. Volleyball League. Bd. dirs. Washington Very Spl. Arts, 1986-93. Mem. N.Y. Bar Assn., D.C. Bar Assn., Fed. Bar Assn., Fed. Communications Bar Assn., Colo. Bar Assn.

FABER, SANDRA MOORE, astronomer, educator; b. Boston, Dec. 28, 1944; d. Donald Edwin and Elizabeth Mackenzie (Borwick) Moore; m. Andrew L. Faber, June 9, 1967; children: Robin, Holly. BA, Swarthmore Coll., 1966, DSc (hon.), 1986; PhD, Harvard U., 1972; DSc (hon.), Williams Coll., 1996. Asst. prof., astronomer Lick Obs., U. Calif., Santa Cruz, 1972-77, assoc. prof., astronomer, 1977-79, prof., astronomer, 1979—; univ. prof. U. Calif., Santa Cruz, 1996—. Mem. astronomy adv. panel NSF, 1975-77; vis. prof. Princeton U., 1978, U. Hawaii, 1983, Ariz. State U., 1985; Phillips visitor Haverford Coll., 1982; Feshbach lectr. MIT, Cambridge, Mass., 1990; Darwin lectr. Royal Astron. Soc., 1991; Marker lectr. Pa. State U., 1992; Bunyan lectr. Stanford U., 1992; Tomkins lectr. U. Calif., San Francisco, 1992; Mohler lectr. U. Mich., 1994; mem. Nat. Acad. Astronomy Survey Panel, 1979-81; chmn. vis. com. Space Telescope Sci. Inst., 1983-84; co-chmn. sci. steering com. Keck Obs., 1987-92, leader DEIMOS spectrograph team, 1993—; mem. Wide Field Camera team Hubble Space Telescope, 1985-97, user's com., 1990-92, mem. advanced radial camera selection team, 1995; mem. Calif. Coun. on Sci. and Tech., 1989-94, Nat. Acad. Com. on Astronomy and Astrophysics, 1993-95, Com. on Future Smithsonian Instn., 1994-95; mem. White House Space Sci. Workshop, 1996, Waterman Awards Com., NSF, 1997-99, Nat. Medal of Sci. selection com., 1999-2001; mem. Plumian Prof. selection com. Cambridge U., 1998—. Assoc. editor: Astrophys. Jour. Letters, 1982-87; editorial bd.: Ann. Revs. Astronomy and Astrophysics, 1982-87; contbr. articles to profl. jours. Trustee Carnegie Instn., Washington, 1985—; bd. dirs. Ann. Revs., 1989—, SETI Inst., 1997—; exec. com. Ann. Revs., 1998—. Recipient Bart J. Bok prize Harvard U., 1978, Director's Distinguished Lectr. award Livermore Nat. Lab., 1986; NASA Group Achievement award, 1993, DeVaucouleurs medal U. Tex., 1997; Carnegie Lectr. Carnegie Inst. Washington, 1988, 99; NSF fellow, 1966-71; Woodrow Wilson fellow, 1966-71; Alfred P. Sloan fellow, 1977-81; listed among 100 best Am. scientists under 40, Sci. Digest, 1984; Tetelman fellow, Yale U., 1987. Fellow Calif. Coun. on Sci. and Tech.; mem. NAS (vice chair adv. panel on cosmotology 1993), Am. Acad. Arts and Scis., Calif. Acad. Scis., 1998—, Am. Astron. Soc. (councilor 1982-84, Dannie Heineman prize 1986), Internat. Astron. Union, Phi Beta Kappa, Sigma Xi. Office: U Calif Lick Obs Santa Cruz CA 95064 E-mail: faber@ucolick.org

FABREGAS, J. ROBERT, retail appearel executive; M Bus. Adminstrn., Rutgers U. Exec. v.p. Credit Suisse, Los Angeles; exec. v.p., head corp. fin. Am. Savings Bank; pres., founder Stonepine Holdings, Ltd.; CFO, exec. v.p. Easyriders, Inc., 1999—. Office: Easyriders Inc. 28210 Dorothy Dr Agoura Hills CA 91301

FADELEY, EDWARD NORMAN, retired state supreme court justice; b. Williamsville, Mo., Dec. 13, 1929; m. Nancie Peacocke, June 11, 1953; children: Charles, Shira; m. Darian Cyr, Sept. 12, 1992. A.B., U. Mo., 1951; J.D. cum laude, U. Oreg., 1957. Bar: Oreg. 1957, U.S. Supreme Ct. 1968. Practice law, Eugene, Oreg., 1957-88; mem. Oreg. Ho. of Reps., 1961-63, Oreg. Senate, 1963-87, pres., 1983-85; justice Oregon Supreme Ct., 1989-98; ret., 1998. Mem. jud. working group Internat. Water Tribunal, Amsterdam, The Netherlands 1991-95; invitee Rio Environ. Conf., 1992, Indigenous Peoples of World Conf., New Zealand, 1993; adj. prof. law U. Oreg.; formerly gen. couns., bd. officer for rsch. corp., fin. instn.; founder, dir. N. Am. Hollis Internat. Law Ctr., 2001—. Advisor to past Pres.; chmn. Oreg. Dem. party, 1966-68; chmn. law and justice com. Nat. Conf. Legislators, 1977-78; adv. com. to State and Local Law Ctr., Washington; participants com. Washington Pub. Power Supply System, 1982-88; candidate for nomination for gov., 1986; bd. dirs. Wayne Morse Hist. Park; mgr. Stille Nacht Found., 1990—. Lt. USNR, 1951-54. Recipient First Pioneer award U. Oreg., 1980, Assn. Oreg. Counties award for leadership in the reform of state ct. system, 1982. Mem. ABA (internat. law, pub. utility law), Oreg. State Bar Assn. (chmn. uniform laws com. 1962-64), Order of Coif, Alpha Pi Zeta, Phi Alpha Delta. Democrat. Methodist. Avocations: canoeing, backpacking, hunting, riding, poetry.

FAERBER, CHARLES N. editor; b. Wakefield, R.I., July 11, 1944; BA, Dartmouth Coll., 1966; MS, San Diego State U., 1977. Newspaper reporter/editor, 1972-78; v.p. legis. affairs Nat. Notary Assn. Editor Nat. Notary mag., Notary Bull. Served with USN, 1967-72. Office: Nat Notary Assn Box 2402 9350 DeSoto Ave Chatsworth CA 91313-2402

FAGG, RUSSELL, judge, lawyer; b. Billings, Mont., June 26, 1960; s. Harrison Grover and Darlene (Bohling) F.; m. Karen Barclay, Feb. 15, 1992. BA, Whitman Coll., 1983; JD, U. Mont., 1986; MJS, U. Nev., 1999. Law clerk Mont. Supreme Ct., Helena, Mont., 1986-87; atty. Sandall Law Firm, Billings, 1987-89; city prosecutor City of Billings, 1989-91; dep. atty. Yellowstone County, Billings, 1991-94; mem. Montana State Legislator, Helena, 1991-94; judge State Dist. Ct. (13th dist.) Mont., Billings, 1995—. Dir. Midland Empire Pachyderm Club, 1988-94, pres. 1990-91; chmn. judiciary com. House of Reps., 1993-94. Named Outstanding Young Montanan, Mont. Jaycees, 1994. Avocations: hiking, fishing, skiing, reading. Home: 3031 Rimview Dr Billings MT 59102-0955 Office: PO Box 35027 Billings MT 59107-5027

FAGGIN, FEDERICO, electronics executive; b. Vicenza, Italy, Dec. 1, 1941; came to U.S., 1968, naturalized, 1978; s. Giuseppe and Emma (Munari) F.; m. Elvia Sardei, Sept. 2, 1967; children: Marzia, Marc, Eric. Grad., Perito Industriale Instituto A. Rossi, Vicenza, 1960; D.Physics, U. Padua, Italy, 1965. Sect. head Fairchild Camera & Instrument Co., Palo Alto, Calif., 1968-70; dept. mgr. Intel Corp., Santa Clara, 1970-74; founder, pres. Zilog Inc., Cupertino, 1974-80; v.p. computer systems group Exxon Enterprises, N.Y.C., 1981; co-founder, pres. Cygnet Technologies, Inc., Sunnyvale, Calif., 1982-86; co-founder, CEO Synaptics, Inc., San Jose, Calif., 1986-99, chmn., 1999—. Recipient Marconi Fellowship award, 1988, W. Wallace McDowell award IEEE Computer Soc., 1994, Kyoto prize, 1997; inducted Nat. Inventor's Hall of Fame, 1996. Achievements include developing silicon gate tech. for MOS fabrication, first microprocessor. Office: Synaptics Inc 2381 Bering Dr San Jose CA 95131-1125

FAGIN, DAVID KYLE, natural resources executive; b. Dallas, Apr. 9, 1938; s. Kyle Marshall and Frances Margaret (Gaston) F.; m. Margaret Anne Hazlett, Jan. 24, 1959 (dec. July 1999); children: David Kyle, Scott Edward. BS in Petroleum Engring., U. Okla., 1960; postgrad., Am. Inst. Banking, So. Meth. U. Grad. Sch. Bus. Adminstrn. Registered profl. engr., La., Okla., Tex. Trainee Exxon-Mobil (formerly Magnolia Petroleum Co.), 1955-56; jr. engr., engr., then ptnr. W.C. Bednar Petroleum Cons., Dallas, 1958-65; petroleum engr. Bank of Am. N.A. (formerly First Nat. Bank Dallas), Dallas, 1965-68; v.p. Rosario Resources Corp. (merged with AMAX Inc.), N.Y.C., 1968-75; pres. Alamo Petroleum Corp., 1968-82; exec. v.p. Rosario Resources Corp., N.Y.C., 1975-77, dir., 1975-80, pres., COO, 1977-82; chmn., dir., pres., CEO Fagin Exploration Co., Denver, 1982-86; pres., COO, bd. dirs. Homestake Mining Co., San Francisco, 1986-91; CEO & chmn. Golden Star Resources Ltd., Denver, 1992-96, dir., 1992—; chmn., CEO Western Exploration and Devel. Ltd., Denver, 1997-2000, dir., 1997-2001. Bd. dirs. several T. Rowe Price Mut. Funds, Balt., 1987—, Dayton Mining Co., Vancouver, B.C., 1988—, Mineral Info. Inst., 1989—, Canyon Resources Corp., 2000—. Bd. dirs. Denver Area coun. Boy Scouts Am., 1993—; bd. visitors U. Okla. Sch. Engring., 1995-98, 99—; Nat. Mining Hall of Fame and Mus., 1997—. Mem. AIME (chmn. Dallas sect. of Soc. Petroleum Engrs. 1975, chmn. investment fund 1979-82), Soc. Mining, Metallurgy and Exploration (dir. 1996-97), Soc. Petroleum Engrs., Mining and Metall. Soc. Am., Internat. Mining Profls. Soc. (dir., exec. com., v.p. 1999, pres. 2001—).

FAGUNDO, ANA MARIA, creative writing and Spanish literature educator; b. Santa Cruz de Tenerife, Spain, Mar. 13, 1938; came to U.S., 1958; d. Ramón Fagundo and Candelaria Guerra de Fagundo. BA in English and Spanish, U. Redlands, 1962; MA in Spanish, U. Wash., 1964, PhD in Comparative Lit., 1967. Prof. contemporary lit. of Spain and creative writing U. Calif., Riverside, 1967—. Vis. lectr. Occidental Coll., Calif., 1967; vis. prof. Stanford U., 1984. Author 10 books of poetry including Invention de la Luz, 1977 (Carbala de Oro Poetry prize Barcelona 1977), Obra Poetica: 1965-90, 1990, Isla En Si., 1992, Antologia, 1994, El Sol, La Sombra En El Instante, 1994, La Mirada de Los Sonambulos, 1994, Trasterrado Marzo, 1999; founder, editor Alaluz, 1969—. Grantee Creative Arts Inst., 1970-71, Humanities Inst., 1973-74; Summer faculty fellow U. Calif., 1968, 77; Humanities fellow, 1969. Mem. Am. Assn. Tchrs. Spanish and Portuguese, Sociedad Gen. de Autores de Espana. Roman Catholic. Avocations: tennis, jogging, walking. Home: 5110 Caldera Ct Riverside CA 92507-6002 Office: U Calif Spanish Dept Riverside CA 92521-0001

FAHEY, JOHN LESLIE, immunologist; b. Cleve., Sept. 8, 1924; MS, Wayne State U., 1949; MD, Harvard U., 1951. Intern medicine Columbia-Presbyn. Hosp., N.Y., 1951-52, asst. resident, 1952-53; clin. assoc. Nat. Cancer Inst., NIH, 1953-54, sr. investigator metabolism, 1954-63, chief immunology br., 1964-71; prof. medicine, microbiology and immunology, chmn. dept. Sch. Medicine UCLA, 1971-81; dir. Ctr. Interdisciplinary Rsch. Immunological Diseases UCLA, 1978—. Recipient Abbott Laboratories award Am. Society for Microbiology, 1995 Mem. Assn. Immunologists, Assn. Am. Physicians, Am. Soc. Microbiology, Clin. Immunology Soc. (founding pres.), Clin. Immunology Com. (pres.), Internat. Union Immunological Socs., Am. Assn. Cancer Rsch. Achievements include rsch. in immunology, AIDS, oncology. Office: UCLA Sch Medicine Dept Microbiology & Immunology Factor Bldg 12-262 Los Angeles CA 90095-0001

FAIR, JAMES STANLEY, hospital administrator; b. Delisle, Sask., Can., May 21, 1933; Bachelors degree, U. Sask., 1955; masters degree, U. Toronto, Ont., Can., 1968. Adminstrv. rschr. Toronto Gen. Hosp., 1967-68; asst. adminstr. Mckellar Gen. Hosp., Ft. William, Ont., 1968-72; dir. diagnostic svcs. Vancouver Gen. Hosp., B.C., Can., 1972-73; acting exec. dir. Gorge Road Hosp., Victoria, 1984, pub. adminstr., 1984-85; exec. dir. Victoria Gen. Hosp., 1973-84, Guelph (Ont.) Gen. Hosp., 1985-88; pres., CEO Fraser-Burrard Hosp., New Westminster, B.C., 1989-96, Simon Fraser Health Region, New Westminster, 1995—. Regent Am. Coll. Healthcare Execs. Western Can., 1998-99. Contbr. articles to profl. jours. Office: Simon Fraser Health Region 260 Sherbrooke St New Westminster BC Canada V3L 3M2

FAIRBANK, ROBERT HAROLD, lawyer; b. Northampton, Mass., Mar. 4, 1948; s. William Martin and Jane (Davenport) F.; m. Gail Lees, Feb. 16, 1992; children: Sarah Julia, David Kivy; stepchildren: Kristin Burdge, Lindsay Burdge. AB in Polit. Sci., Stanford U., 1972; MLS, U. Calif.-Berkeley, 1973; JD, NYU, 1977. Bar: Calif. 1977, U.S. Dist. Ct. (cen. and no. dists.) Calif. 1978, U.S. Dist. Ct. (so. dist.) Calif. 1993. Assoc. Gibson, Dunn & Crutcher, L.A., 1977-84, ptnr., 1985-96; co-founding ptnr. Fairbank & Vincent, 1996—. Lawyer rep., co-chair elect 9th circuit Jud. Conf. Ctrl. Dist., 2000—. Author: Effective Pretrial and Trial Motions, 1983, California Practice Guide: Civil Trials and Evidence (The Rutter Group 1993, with yearly updates); mem. editl. bd. NYU Law Rev., 1975-76. Named One of Top 100 Bus. Lawyers in L.A., L.A. Bus. Jour., 1995. Mem. Assn. Bus. Trial Lawyers (co-founder San Francisco and Orange County chpts., bd. govs. 1984-85, treas. 1986-87, sec. 1987-88, v.p. 1988-89, pres. 1989-90), L.A. County Bar Assn. (fed. cts. com. 1983-85), Jud. Coun. Calif. Adv. Com. on Local Rules (subcom. chair on civil trial rules). Office: Fairbank & Vincent 11755 Wilshire Blvd Ste 2320 Los Angeles CA 90025-1501 E-mail: rhf@fvlaw.com

FAIRBANKS, MARY KATHLEEN, data analyst, researcher; b. Manhattan, Kans., June 4, 1948; d. Everitt Edsel and Mary Catherine (Moran) F. BS, St. Norbert Coll., 1970; postgrad., Calif. Family Study Ctr., 1981-82. Neuropsychology researcher U.S. VA Hosp., Sepulveda, Calif., 1970-76; mgr. print shop Charisma In Missions, City of Industry, 1976-77; neuropsychology researcher L.A. County Women's Hosp., 1977-79; mem. tech. staff Computer Scis. Corp., Ridgecrest, Calif., 1979-81; systems programmer Calif. State U., Northridge, 1982-84; bus. systems analyst World

Vision, Monrovia, Calif., 1984-86; configuration analyst Teledyne System Co., Northridge, 1986-87; applications system analyst Internat. Telephone and Telegraph/Fed. Electric Corp., Altadena, Calif., 1987-88; supr. data analysts OAO Corp., Altadena, 1988—. Co-author, contbr.: Serotonin and Behavior, 1973, Advances in Sleep Research, vol. 1, 1974. Mem. St. Mary's Cath. Cmty. Theatre. Mem. OAO Mgmt. Assn., So. Calif. Application System Users Group, Digital Equipment Computer Users Soc. Roman Catholic. Avocations: photography, reading, music, hiking, camping. Home: 37607 Lasker Ave Palmdale CA 93550-7721 Office: OAO Corp 787 W Woodbury Rd Ste 2 Altadena CA 91001-5388 E-mail: fairbanks376@earthlink.net, mary.k.fairbanks@jpl.nasa.gov

FAIRFULL, THOMAS MCDONALD, museum director; b. Greensburg, Pa., Nov. 28, 1942; s. Tom and Margaret Jane (Heasley) F. BA, U. Pitts., 1964; MA, Duke U., 1972. Dir. 82d Airborne Divsn. Mus., Fort Bragg, N.C., 1975-78; instr. Campbell U., Buies Creek, 1976-78; dir. U.S. Army Mus. Hawaii, Honolulu, 1978—. Co-author: (with William R. Porter) History of the 3d Brigade 82d Airborne Divsn. 1969. Served to capt. U.S. Army, 1965-74, Vietnam. Recipient Bronze Star with oak leaf cluster, USA. Mem. Am. Mil. Inst., Hawaii Mus. Assn., Coun. Am.'s Mil. Past. Home: 1950 A 9th Ave Honolulu HI 96816-2906 Office: US Army Museum of Hawaii Stop 319 APVG-GAR-LM CRD DCA USAG Fort Shafter HI 96858

FAIRLEY, DARLENE, state legislator; m. Michael Fairley; 1 child, Andrew. BA in Polit. Sci., U. Wash. Owner Fairlook Antiques; mem. Wash. Senate, Dist. 32, Olympia, 1995—; chair labor and workforce devel. com.; mem. energy, tech. and telecom. com.; mem. ways and means com.; mem. adv. com. on minority and women's bus. enterprises; mem. water supply adv. com.; mem. joint com. on abstinence edn.; mem. organized crime adv. com. Mem. Lake Forest City Coun., 1992-95; vol. Cath. Relief Svcs.; mem. adv. bd. Lake Forest Park Stewardship Found.; vol. victim advocate Seattle Police Dept.; spl. advocate for abused children Snohomish County Juvenile Ct.; co-chair legis. com. Human Svcs. Roundtable of King County; founder Cuc Family Med. Clin., Vietnam; co-chair Lake Forest Park Telecom. and Electronic Access Com. Democrat. Office: 425 John Cherberg Bldg Olympia WA 98504-0001

FAISS, ROBERT DEAN, lawyer; b. Centralia, Ill., Sept. 19, 1934; s. Wilbur and Theresa Ella (Watts) F.; m. Linda Louise Chambers, Mar. 30, 1991; children: Michael Dean Faiss, Marcy Faiss Ayres, Robert Mitchell Faiss, Philip Grant Faiss, Justin Cooper. BA in Journalism, Am. U., 1969, JD, 1972. Bar: Nev. 1972, D.C. 1972, U.S. Dist. Ct. Nev. 1973, U.S. Supreme Ct. 1977, U.S. Ct. Appeals (9th cir.) 1978. City editor Las Vegas (Nev.) Sun, 1957-59; pub. info. officer Nev. Dept. Employment Security, 1959-61; asst. exec. sec. Nev. Gaming Commn., Carson City, 1961-63; exec. asst. to gov. State of Nev., Carson City, 1963-67; staff asst. U.S. Pres. Lyndon B. Johnson, White House, Washington, 1968-69; asst. to exec. dir. U.S. Travel Adminstrn., Washington, 1969-72; ptnr., chmn. adminstrv. law dept. Lionel, Sawyer & Collins, Las Vegas, 1973—. Mem. bank secrecy Act Adv. Group U.S. Treasury. Co-author: Legalized Gaming in Nevada, 1961, Nevada Gaming License Guide, 1988, Nevada Gaming Law, 1991, 95, 98. Recipient Bronze medal Dept. Commerce, 1972, Chris Schaller award We Can, Las Vegas, 1995, Lifetime Achievement award Nev. Gaming Attys. Assn., 1997; named One of 100 Most Influential Lawyers in Am. and premier U.S. gaming atty., Nat. Law Jour., 1997. Mem. ABA (chmn. gaming law com. 1985-86), Internat. Assn. Gaming Attys. (founding, pres. 1980), Nev. Gaming Attys. Office: Lionel Sawyer & Collins 300 S 4th St Ste 1700 Las Vegas NV 89101-6053

FAITHFULL, TIMOTHY WILLIAM, petroleum industry executive; b. Winchester, Hampshire, Eng., June 10, 1944; arrived in Can., 1999; s. Horace William and Mary Elizabeth Faithfull; m. Prudence Eyre String, July 7, 1973; children: Kaisi, William, Joseph. BA, Keble Coll., Oxford, Eng., 1967; MA, U. Oxford, 1972. Gen. mgr. Kenya Shell, Nairobi, 1989; area coord. Shell Internat., 1989-93; v.p. crude oil trading SITCO, Eng., 1993-96; chmn., CEO, Shell Ea. Petroleum Ltd., Singapore, 1996-99; pres., CEO, Shell Can. Ltd., Calgary, Alta., Can., 1999—, also bd. dirs. Can. Bd. trustees Starehe Boys Ctr., Kenya, 1995—. Mem. Calgary Petroleum Club, Calgary Golf and Country Club, United Oxford and Cambridge Univs. Club. Anglican. Avocations: sailing, golf. Office: Shell Can Ltd PO Box 100 400 4th Ave SW Calgary AB Canada T2P 2H5

FALBERG, KATHRYN E. pharmaceutical executive; B in Econs., UCLA, 1981, MBA in Fin. and Acctg., 1984. CPA. Various positions Applied Magnetics, 1984-93, v.p., CFO, treas., 1993-94; treas. Amgen, Inc., Thousand Oaks, Calif., 1995-96, asst. contr. sales and mktg., 1996, v.p. investor rels. dept. and corp. tax dept., 1996-98, sr. v.p. fin., CFO, 1998—. Edward Carter scholar UCLA, 1984. Office: Amgen Inc 1 Amgen Center Dr Thousand Oaks CA 91320-1799

FALEOMAVAEGA, ENI FA'AUAA HUNKIN, congressman; b. Vailoatai Village, Am. Samoa, Aug. 15, 1943; m. Hinanui Bambridge Cave; children: Temanuata Tuilua'ai, Taualai, Nifae, Vaimoana, Leonne. BA in Polit. Sci. and History, Brigham Young U., 1966; JD, U. Houston, 1972; LLM, U. Calif., Berkeley, 1973. Bar: Am. Samoa, U.S. Supreme Ct. Adminstrv. asst. Am. Samoa del. to Washington, 1973-75; staff counsel to house com. on interior and insular affairs U.S. House of Reps., Washington, 1975-81; dep. atty. gen. Am. Samoa, 1981-84, lt. gov., 1984-89; territorial del. from Am. Samoa U.S. Ho. Reps., 1988; rep. U.S. Congress from Samoa, 1989—; mem. internat. rels. com., resources com. Chmn. Gov.'s Task Force for Reorgn. of the Adminstrn., Am. Samoa Adv. Fisheries Council, 1985—, Gov.'s Adv. Com. on Grants Programs, 1985—; mem. nat. lt. gov.'s mission to Egypt, Jordan and Saudi Arabia, South Pacific Leaders Orientation Mission to Paris, 1987; leader Am. Samoa's del. to South Pacific Conf., Noumea New Caledonia, 1987; keynote speaker and leader Am. Samoa's del. to Pacific Trade/Investment Conf., 1986. With U.S. Army, 1966-69, including Vietnam, USAR, 1985—. Recipient Alumni Svc. award Brigham Young U., 1979; named Chieftain Faleomavaega, leone Village. Mem. Nat. Conf. of Lt. Govs., Nat. Assn. Secs. of State, Navy League of U.S., VFW, Nat. Am. Indian Prayer Breakfast Group, Lions (charter mem. Pago Pago chpt.), Go for Broke Assn. (life; pres. Samoa chpt.). Democrat, Office: US Ho Reps 2422 Rayburn HOB Washington DC 20515*

FALK, STEVEN B. newspaper publishing executive; Pres., CEO San Francisco Newspaper Agy. Office: San Francisco Newspaper Agy 925 Mission St San Francisco CA 94103-2905

FALKNER, FRANK TARDREW, physician, educator; b. Hale, Eng., Oct. 27, 1918; came to U.S., 1956, naturalized, 1963; s. Ernest and Ethel (Letten) F.; m. June Dixon, Jan. 1948; 2 children. M.D., Cambridge U., 1945. Diplomate: Am. Bd. Clin. Nutrition. Intern London Hosp., 1945; resident Guys Hosp., London, 1947-48, Children's Hosp., Cin., 1948-50; practice medicine specializing in pediatrics U.K. and Paris, 1948-56, Louisville, 1956-70, Yellow Springs, Ohio, 1971-79; chmn. dept. pediatrics U. Louisville, 1963-70; dir. Fels Research Inst., Yellow Springs, 1971-79; Fels prof. pediatrics, prof. obstetrics and gynecology U. Cin. Coll. Medicine, 1971-79; prof. child and family health U. Mich., 1979-81; prof. and chmn. maternal and child health U. Calif., Berkeley, 1981-89, prof. pediatrics San Francisco, 1981-89, prof. emeritus Berkeley, 1989—; San Francisco, 1989—. Editor-in-chief: International Child Health; syndicated columnist on children's and young people's health; contbr. articles to profl. jours. Fellowship to Am. Meml. Hosp. created in his name, 2000. Fellow Am. Acad. Pediatrics, Royal Coll. Physicians, Royal Coll. Pediat. and Child Health; mem. NAS (sr. mem. Inst. Medicine), Am. Pediatric Soc., Société Francaise de Pédiatrie. Home: 145 Forest Ln Berkeley CA 94708-1519 Office: U Calif Sch Pub Health Maternal And Child Health Berkeley CA 94720-0001 E-mail: ffalknermd@aol.com

FALKNER, JAMES GEORGE, SR. foundation executive; b. Spokane, Wash., Dec. 24, 1952; s. Albert Andrew and Amanda Rosalia (Reisinger) F.; m. Joleen Rae Ann Brown, June 22, 1974; children: James Jr., Jayson, Jerin, Jarret. BS in Acctg., U. Wash., 1975. CPA, Wash. CPA LeMaster & Daniels, Spokane, 1975-80; treas. Dominican Sisters Spokane, 1980-95; pres. Dominican Outreach Found., Spokane, 1995—. Bd. dirs. Dominican Network, Spokane, 1989-98, Dominican Health Svcs., 1989-98, Providence Svcs., Spokane, 1993-2000, Providence Svcs. Ea. Wash., 1998—, chmn. fin. com.; mem. bishop's fin. coun. Diocese of Spokane, 1990-96; mem. investment adv. com. Gonzaga Prep. H.S., 1995-99, Spokane Cath. Investment Trust, 1997—, chmn. investment com.; mem. investment adv. com. Sinsinawa Dominican Sisters, 1995—. Bd. dirs. sch. bd. St. Mary's Ch., Veradale, Wash., 1986-89, 90, sch. found., 1987-2000; mem. acctg. dept. adv. com. Spokane Falls C.C., 1989—. Mem.: Healthcare Fin. Mgmt. Assn. (bd. dirs. 1982—85), AICPA, Wash. State Soc. CPAs (Spokane Wash. bd. dirs., pres. 2000—01), Nat. Notary Assn. Avocations: coaching baseball, golf, soccer, carpentry. Office: Dominican Outreach Found 3102 W Fort George Wright Dr Spokane WA 99224-5203

FALKOW, STANLEY, microbiologist, educator; b. Albany, N.Y., Jan. 24, 1934; s. Jacob and Mollie (Gingold) F.; children from previous marriage: Lynn Beth, Jill Stuart; m. Lucy Stuart Tompkins, Dec. 3, 1983. BS in Bacteriology cum laude, U. Maine, 1955, DSc (hon), 1979; MS in Biology, Brown U., 1960, PhD, 1961; MD (hon.), U. Umea, Sweden, 1989. Asst. chief dept. bacterial immunity Walter Reed Army Inst. Rsch., Washington, 1963-66; prof. microbiology Med. Sch. Georgetown U., 1966-72; prof. microbiology and medicine U. Wash., Seattle, 1972-81; prof., chmn. dept. med. microbiology Stanford (Calif.) U., 1981-85, prof. microbiology, immunology & medicine, 1981—. Karl H. Beyer vis. prof. U. Wis., 1978-79; Sommer lectr. U. Oreg. Sch. Medicine, 1979, Kinyoun lectr. NIH, 1980; Rubbro orator Australian Soc. Microbiology, 1981; Stanhope Bayne-Jones lectr. Johns Hopkins U., 1982; mem. Recombinant DNA Molecule Com, task force on antibiotics in animal feeds FDA, microbiology test com. Nat. Bd. Med. Examiners. Author: Infectious Multiple Drug Resistance, 1975; editor: Jour. Infection and Immunity, Jour. Infectious Agents and Diseases. Recipient Ehrlich prize, 1981, Becton-Dickinson award in Clin. Microbiology, ASM, 1986, Altemeier medal Surg. Infectious Diseases Soc., 1990, Disting. Achievement in Infectious Disease Rsch. award Bristol-Myers Squibb, 1997; Bristol-Myers Squibb unrestricted infectious disease grantee. Fellow Am. Acad. Microbiology; mem. Inst. of Medicine, AAAS, Infectious Disease Soc. Am. (Squibb award 1979), Am. Soc. Microbiology, Genetics Soc. Am., Nat. Acad. Sci., Sigma Xi. Office: Stanford U Dept Microbiology and Immunology Fairchild D309A Stanford CA 94305-5402 E-mail: falkow@stanford.edu

FALLER, JAMES ELLIOT, physicist, educator; b. Mishawaka, Ind., Jan. 17, 1934; s. Elmer Edward and Leona Maxine (Forstbauer) F.; m. Jocelyne T. Bellenger, March 7, 1996; children: William Edward, Peter James. A.B. summa cum laude, Ind. U., 1955; M.A., Princeton U., 1957, Ph.D., 1963; M.A. (hon.), Wesleyan U., Middletown, Conn., 1972. Instr. Princeton U., 1959-62; mem. Joint Inst. Lab. Astrophysics, Boulder, Colo., 1963-66, fellow, 1972—; asst. prof. physics Wesleyan U., 1966-68, assoc. prof. physics, 1968-71, prof., 1971-72. Nat. Acad. Sci./NRC postdoctoral fellow, 1963-64; Sloan fellow, 1972-73; recipient Precision Measurement award Nat. Bur. Standards, 1970, Arnold O. Beckman award Instrument Soc. Am., 1970, Exceptional Sci. Achievement medal NASA, 1973, Gold medal Dept. Commerce, 1990, Fed. Lab. Consortium Tech. Transfer award, 1992. Mem. Am. Phys. Soc., AAAS, Am. Geophysical Union, Phi Beta Kappa, Sigma Xi. Home: 303 Hollyberry Ln Boulder CO 80305-5230 Office: JILA Univ Colorado Boulder CO 80309-0001

FALSTRUP, ASGER, electronics company executive; V.p. No. European region Ingram Micro, 1996-2000; sr. v.p. Ingram Micro, Inc., 2000—; pres. Ingram Micro Can., 2000—. Office: Ingram Micro Inc 1600 E St Andrew Pl Santa Ana CA 92705

FALUDI, SUSAN C. journalist, scholarly writer; Formerly with West Mag., San Jose, Calif., Mercury News; with San Francisco Bur., Wall St. Jour. Spkr. in field. Author: Backlash: The Undeclared War Against American Women, 1991 (National Book Critics Circle award for general non-fiction 1992); contbr. articles to mags. Recipient Pulitzer Prize for explanatory journalism, 1991. Office: care Sandra Dijkstra Literary Agy 1155 Camino Del Mar PMB 515 Del Mar CA 92014-2605

FAN, HUNG Y. virology educator, consultant; b. Beijing, Oct. 30, 1947; s. Hsu Yun and Li Nien (Bien) F. BS, Purdue U., 1967; PhD, MIT, 1971. Asst. research prof. Salk Inst., San Diego, 1973-81; asst. prof. U. Calif., Irvine, 1981-83, assoc. prof., 1984-88, prof., 1988—, dir. Cancer Rsch. Inst., 1985—, acting dean Sch. Biol. Scis., 1990-91. Editor Jour. of Virology, 1998—; contbr. more than 130 articles to profl. jours. NIH grantee, 1973—, grant review coms., 1973—; Woodrow Wilson Found. grad. fellow, 1967, Helen Hay Whitney Found. postdoctorate fellow, 1971. Fellow AAAS, Am. Acad. Microbiology; mem. Am. Soc. Microbiology, Am. Soc. Virology, Am. Assn. Cancer Rsch. Avocation: chamber music. Office: U Calif Cancer Rsch Inst Sch Biol Sci Irvine CA 92697-0001 E-mail: hyfan@uci.edu

FANCHER, MICHAEL REILLY, newspaper editor, newspaper publishing executive; b. Long Beach, Calif., July 13, 1946; s. Eugene Arthur and Ruth Leone (Dickson) F.; m. Nancy Helen Edens, Nov. 3, 1967 (div. 1982); children: Jason Michael, Patrick Reilly; m. 2d Carolyn Elaine Bowers, Mar. 25, 1983; Katherine Claire, Elizabeth Lynn. BA, U. Oreg., 1968; MS, Kans. State U., 1971; MBA, U. Wash., 1986. Reporter, asst. city editor Kansas City Star, Mo., 1970-76, city editor, 1976-78; reporter Seattle Times, 1978-79, night city editor, 1979-80, asst. mng. editor, 1980-81, mng. editor, 1981-86, exec. editor, 1986—, v.p., exec. editor, 1989-95; sr. v.p., 1995—. Bd. dirs. Blethen Maine Newspapers, Walla Walla Union-Bulletin, Yakima Herald Rep. Ruhl fellow U. Oreg., 1983 Mem. Am. Soc. Newspaper Editors, Soc. Profl. Journalists, Nat. Press Photographers Assn. (Editor of Yr. 1986). Office: Seattle Times PO Box 70 1120 John St Seattle WA 98111-0070 E-mail: mfancher@seattletimes.com

FANG, LI-ZHI, physicist, educator; b. Beijing, Feb. 12, 1936; came to U.S., 1991; s. Cheng-Pu and Peiji (Shi) F.; m. Shuxian Li, Oct. 6, 1961; children: Ke, Zhe. PhD in Physics, Peking U., 1956; PhD (hon.), Univ. Libre de Bruxelles, 1989, Univ. di Roma, La Sapienza, 1990, Coll. William and Mary, , 1991; DSc (hon.), U. Toronto, 1991, York U., Can., 1993; LHD (hon.), U. Wis., River Falls, 1992. Jr. rsch. fellow Inst. Modern Physics, Chinese Acad. Scis., Beijing, 1956-58; asst. prof. U. Sci. and Tech. of China, Beijing, 1958-63, lectr., 1963-77, prof. physics, 1978-87, dir. ctr. for astrophysics, 1980-87, v.p., 1984-87; prof., head of theoretical astrophysics group Beijing Astron. Obs., Chinese Acad. Scis., 1987-89; prof. physics and astronomy U. Ariz., Tucson, 1991—. Vis. fellow Academia dei Lincei, Rome, 1979; sr. vis. fellow Inst. Astronomy, Cambridge (Eng.) U., 1979-80, 90; vis. prof. Rsch. Inst. Fundamental Physics, Kyoto U., Japan, 1981-82; vis. fellow physics dept. U. Rome, 1983; assoc. mem. Internat. Ctr. for Theoretical Physics, Trieste, Italy, 1984-89; active Inst. for Advanced Study, Princeton, 1986, 91; vis. prof. dept. physics and astronomy Princeton (N.J.) U., 1991. Author or co-author of 20 books, including Creation of the Universe (with S.X. Li), 1989, Quantum Cosmology (with R. Ruffini), 1987, Bringing Down the Great Wall, 1991; editorial bd. 15 profl. jours., including Internat. Jour. Modern Physics, Modern Physics Letters A, Scienza, Nouvo Comento B.; contbr. more than 200 articles to profl. jours. Decorated officier l'Ordre des Arts et des Lettres (France); recipient numerous scientific awards in China including Nat. award for Sci. and Tech., 1978, Anhui Province award for sci. and tech., 1978, Yunnan Province award for sci. and tech., 1979, Innermongolia Autonomous Region award for sci. and tech., 1980, Chinese Acad. Scis. award, 1982; recipient other awards including First award Internat. Gravity Rsch. Found., 1985, Chinese Dem. Edn. Found. award, 1987, Peace Price of Politiken and Dagens Nyheter, 1989, Robert F. Kennedy Human Rights award, 1989, George Meany Human Rights award, 1990, Evelyn and Louis P. Smith First Amendment award, 1990, Freedom award Internat. Rescue Com., 1991, Human Rights award Internat. League Human Rights, 1991, Sidney Hook Meml. award Nat. Assn. Scholars, 1991, Human Courage award World Pub. Forum, 1993, Andrew Allen Liberty award Fgn. Policy Rsch. Inst., 1993, and numerous others. Mem. Am. Phys. Soc. (vice chair com. Internat. Freedom of Scis. 1993, chair 1994), Am. Astronomical Soc., Internat. Ctr. for Relativistic Astrophysics (mem. coun.), N.Y. Acad. Sci. (award 1988), Internat. Union for Pure and Applied Physics (commn. C19 on Astrophysics, commn. A.2). Achievements include development of theories that the distribution of galaxies might be described by a self-affinity geometry, that the clustering of large redshift quasars is less than that of small redshift quasars, that the topology of the cosmic spacetime is an important remains of the Planck era and the infrared cutoff in the primordial spectrum of density perturbations is probably an evidence of multiply connected topology of the universe, that the phase transitions of vacuum states play an important role in the generation of entropy in the early universe and in the formation of objects with abnormal matter states. Office: U Ariz Dept Physics Tucson AZ 85721-0001

FANGMEIER, DELMAR DEAN, retired agriculture and biosystems engineering educator, researcher; b. Hebron, Nebr., Oct. 27, 1932; s. August Henry and Louise Marie F.; m. Margaret-Ann Wagner, June 21, 1969; children: Kurt Joseph, Kristin Louise. BSA, U. Nebr., 1954, BS in Agrl. Engring., 1960, MS in Agrl. Engring., 1961; PhD in Engring., U. Calif., Davis, 1967. Registered profl. engr., Ariz., Calif. Agrl. engr. Agrl. Rsch. Svc., USDA, Lincoln, Nebr., 1960-61; asst. prof. U. Wyo., Laramie, 1966-68; assoc. prof. U. Ariz., Tucson, 1968-72, prof., 1972—. Cons. Colombian Cotton Growers, Bogota, 1987, SunCor Devel. Corp., Phoenix, 1990. Co-author: (textbooks) Soil and Water Conservation Engineering, Soil and Water Management Systems; contbg. author World Book Encyclopedia (Irrigation); also articles. Mem. coms. Sch. Dist., Tucson, 1980-87; pres. Homeowners' Assn., Tucson, 1987-88. Lt. U.S. Army, 1954-56. Rsch. grantee NSF, 1979, USDA, 1980, 87, U.S. Water Cons. Lab. Fellow ASCE; mem. Am. Soc. Agrl. Engrs. (paper award 1980), Am. Soc. for Engring. Edn., Guayule Rubber Soc. (pres. 1987). Avocations: reading, travel. Home and Office: 848 W Safari Dr Tucson AZ 85704-2848

FANSELOW, MICHAEL SCOTT, psychology educator; b. Bklyn, May 2, 1954; BS magna cum laude with honors, CUNY, Bklyn., 1976; PhD in Behavioral Psychology, U. Wash., 1980. Asst. prof. Rensselaer Poly. Inst., Troy, N.Y., 1980-81, Dartmouth Coll., Hanover, N.H., 1981-86, assoc. prof., 1986-88, UCLA, 1988-89, prof., 1989—. Recipient Troland Rsch. award NAS, 1995. Fellow AAAS, APA (Edwin B. Newman award 1979, D.O. Heb Young Scientist award 1983, Disting. Sci. award 1985). Office: UCLA Dept Psychology PO Box 951563 Los Angeles CA 90095-1563

FARBANISH, THOMAS, sculptor; b. Endicott, N.Y., Mar. 21, 1963; BFA, Rochester Inst. Tech., 1986. Asst. Artpark, Lewiston, N.Y., 1986, Wheaton Village, Millville, N.J., 1989; instr. Golden Glass Sch., Cin., 1990, Corning Bus. Devel. Ctr., 1991; faculty Tyler Sch. Art, Pa., 1991, Urban Glass, N.Y., 1992, Pilchuck Glass Sch., Stanwood, Wash., 1993-94, 97, gaffer, 1996-97; faculty Haystack Sch. Crafts, Maine, 1993, Penland Sch., N.C., 1993, Rochester (N.Y.) Inst. Tech., 1994, 97. Tchg. asst. Pilchuck Glass Sch., Stanwood, 1986, 87, 90, Saxe emerging artist in residence, 1988; lectr. in field. One-man and two-man shows include Snyderman Gallery, Phila., 1987, Sarah Squeri Gallery, Cin., 1990, AVA Gallery, Lebanon, N.H., 1992, Artspace, Kohler Art Ctr., Sheboygan, Wis., 1993, Robert L. Kidd Gallery, Birmingham, Mich., 1994, William Traver Gallery, Seattle, 1991, 94, 95, Heller Gallery, N.Y.C., 1995; group shows include Glass Gallery, Bethesda, Md., 1984, 85, Germanow Gallery, Rochester, 1984, Morris Mus., Morristown, N.J., 1985, Upton Hall Galleries, Buffalo, 1985, Courtyard Galleries, Balt., 1986, Huntington (W.Va.) Mus. Art, 1986, Heller Gallery, N.Y.C., 1986, 87, 91, 92, 94, 95, 97, Ward Gallery, 1987, Somerstown Gallery, Somers, N.Y., 1987, Snyderman Gallery, Pa., 1987, Am. Craft Mus., N.Y.C., 1988, So. Alleghenies Mus. Art, Loretto, Pa., 1988, Grohe Gallery, Boston, 1989, Robert L. Kidd Gallery, Birmingham, 1989, 96, William Traver Gallery, Seattle, 1990, 92, 93, Sotheby's, N.Y.C., 1990, Gallery Nakama, Tokyo, 1991, Lehman Gallery, N.Y.C., 1993, Christies, N.Y.C., 1993, Bellevue (Wash.) Art Mus., 1994, Habitat Galleries, Birmingham, 1994, Leedy Voulkos Gallery, Kansas City, Mo., 1995, Philabaum Gallery, Tucson, 1995, Huntsville (Ala.) Mus. Art, 1996; represented in permanent collections Huntsville Mus. Art, Am. Craft Mus., Prescott Collection, Wash., Huntington Mus. Art, Davis Wright and Jones, Wash., Wheaton (N.J.) Mus. Am. Glass, Pilchuck Glass Sch., Wash., Rochester Inst. Tech. Creative Glass Ctr. Am. fellow Wheaton Village, 1985, 90, Visual Artist fellow Nat. Endowment Arts, 1988, 94; Pilchuck Galss Sch. scholar, 1987; Mid Atlantic Arts Found. grantee, 1990. Office: c/o William Traver Gallery 110 Union St Ste 200 Seattle WA 98101-2028

FARBER, EUGENE MARK, research institute administrator; b. Buffalo, July 24, 1917; s. Simon and Mathilda Farber; m. Ruth Seiffert, Mar. 4, 1944; children: Nancy, Charlotte, Donald. BA, Oberlin (Ohio) Coll., 1939; MD, U. Buffalo, 1943; MS, U. Minn., 1946; DSc, Calif. Coll. Podiatric Medicine, 1973. Clin. asst., prof. dermatology Stanford (Calif.) U., 1949-50, asst. prof. pathology, 1949-50, clin. prof., dir. div. dermatology, 1950-598, prof., chmn. emeritus, 1959-86; pres. Psoriasis Rsch. Inst., Palo Alto, Calif., 1973—. Cons. Pacific Med. Ctr., San Francisco, 1982-84; nat. cons. to surgeon gen. USAF, Washington, 1957-64; cons. in dermatology Calif. State Dept. of Pub. Health, Sacramento, 1963-66; hon. prof. Dalian Med. U., People's Republic of China, 1999. Contbr. chpts. to book and articles to profl. jours. Recipient Physician's Recognition award AMA, 1982-85, 83-85, 91-94, Jose Marie Vargas award Cen. U. of Caracas, 1972, Mr. and Mrs. J.B. Taub Internat. Meml. award for Psoriasis Rsch., 1974, Disting. Svc. meda. Bd. Regents Uniformed Svcs. U., 1984, Order of Andres Bello, Banda de Honor, 1984, City of Paris medal, 1991, Most Disting. Alumni award U. Buffalo, 1998, Psoriasis Rsch. award Am. Skin Assn., 1999. Master Am. Acad. Dermatology (bd. dirs. 1957-60, others); mem. Am. Dermatol. Assn. (bd. dirs. 1974, hon. membership com. 1983-87), Assn. of Profs. of Dermatology (exec. bd., sec. 1977-80, pres. 1977-80, chairperson fin. com. 1980), Pacific Dermatology Assn. (bd. dirs. 1965-68, pres.-elect 1979-80, pres. 1980-81), Soc. for Investigative Dermatology (bd. dirs. 1957-62, pres. 1966-67, com. on hon. membership 1979—), Nat. Program for Dermatology, Space Dermatology Found. (v.p. 1986, pres. 1989-90), Chinese Assn. of the Integration of Traditional and Western Medicine (hon. advisor 1997), others. Home: 167 Ramoso Rd Portola Valley CA 94028-7327 Office: Psoriasis Rsch Inst 600 Town And Country Vlg Palo Alto CA 94301-2343

FARKAS, DANIEL FREDERICK, food science and technology educator; b. Boston, June 20, 1933; m. Alice Bridgetta Brady, Jan. 25, 1959; children: Brian Emerson, Douglas Frederick. BS, MIT, 1954, MS, 1955, PhD, 1960. Lic. chem. engr., Calif. Commd. U.S. Army, 1954, advanced through grades to major, 1968, ret., 1974; staff scientist Arthur D. Little, Cambridge, Mass., 1960-62; asst. prof. Cornell U. Agrl Expt. Sta., Geneva, 1962-66; rsch. leader We. regional rsch. ctr. USDA, Albany, Calif., 1967-80; prin. Daniel F. Farkas Assocs., Corvallis, Oreg., 1976—; prof., chair dept. food sci. U. Del., Newark, 1980-87; v.p. process R & D Campbell Soup Co., Camden, N.J., 1987-90; Jacobs-Root prof., head dept. food sci. and tech. Oreg. State U., Corvalis, 1990-2000, prof. emeritus, 2000—. Contbr. more than 50 articles to peer-reviewed sci. and tech. jours. Fellow Inst. Food Technologists; mem. AICE, Am. Chem. Soc. (profl.), Sigma Xi. Achievements include 5 U.S. patents for centrifugal fluidized bed food drying system, application of ultra-high hydrostatic pressure to food preservation. E-mail: dan.farkas.@orst.edu

FARLEY, JAMES NEWTON, manufacturing executive, engineer; b. Hutchinson, Kans., Nov. 8, 1928; s. James N. Farley and Elizabeth (Martin) Sanders; m. Nancy J. Hollabaugh, Apr. 30, 1956; children: Sarah Huskey, Timothy, Barbara Carré, James, Stuart. BSEE, Northwestern U., 1950. Registered profl. engr., Ill. Test engr. GE, Schenectady, N.Y., 1950-51; sales engr. Allen Bradley Co., Milw., 1953-54, Chgo., 1954-60; sales mgr. SpeedFam Corp., Skokie, Ill., 1960-64, pres. Des Plaines, 1964-87, chmn. bd. dirs., 1987-97; pres., CEO Speedfam-IPEC, Inc., Chandler, Ariz., 1987-92, CEO, chmn. bd. dirs., 1992-97, chmn. bd. dirs., 1997-2001. Bd. dirs. Lovejoy, Inc., Downers Grove, Ill., Extrude Hone Corp., Irwin, Pa., Berkley Process Control, Richmond, Calif., imortgage.com, Scottsdale, Ariz. With U.S. Army, 1951-53. Recipient Alumni Merit award Northwestern U., 1996. Mem. Assn. for Mfg. Tech., Econ. Club Chgo., Oriental Order of Groundhogs. Democrat. Episcopalian. Office: Speedfam-IPEC Inc 305 N 54th St Chandler AZ 85226-2405

FARLEY, KENNETH A. geochemist, educator; BS, Yale U.; PhD, U. Calif., San Diego, 1991. Prof. geochemistry Calif. Inst. Tech. Divsn. Geol. and Planetary Scis., Pasadena. Recipient James B. Macelwane medal, 1999, award for initiatives in sci. NAS, 2000. Office: Calif Inst Tech Divsn Geol & Planetary Scis MS 170-25 Pasadena CA 91125

FARLEY, THOMAS T. lawyer; b. Pueblo, Colo., Nov. 10, 1934; s. John Baron and Mary (Tancred) F.; m. Kathleen Maybelle Murphy, May 14, 1960; children: John, Michael, Kelly, Anne. BS, U. Santa Clara, 1956; LLB, U. Colo., 1959. Bar: Colo. 1959, U.S. Dist. Ct. Colo. 1959, U.S. Ct. Appeals (10th cir.) 1988. Dep. dist. atty. County of Pueblo, 1960-62; pvt. practice Pueblo, 1963-69; ptnr. Phelps, Fonda & Hays, Pueblo, 1970-75, Petersen & Fonda, P.C., Pueblo, 1975—. Bd. dirs. Pub. Svc. Co. Colo., Denver, Wells Fargo Pueblo, Wells Fargo Sunset, Health Net, Inc., Colo. Pub. Radio. Minority leader Colo. Ho. of Reps., 1967-75; chmn. Colo. Wildlife Commn., 1975-79, Colo. Bd. Agr., 1979-87; bd. regents Santa Clara U., 1987—; commr. Colo. State Fair; trustee Cath. Found. Diocese of Pueblo, Great Outdoors Colo. Trust Fund. Recipient Disting. Svc. award U. So. Colo., 1987, 93, Bd. of Regents, U. Colo., 1993. Mem. ABA, Colo. Bar Assn., Pueblo C. of C. (bd. dirs. 1991-93), Rotary. Democrat. Roman Catholic. Office: Petersen & Fonda PC 215 W 2d St Pueblo CO 81003-3251

FARMAN, RICHARD DONALD, energy company executive; b. San Francisco, Aug. 20, 1935; s. Carl Edward Jr. and Doris May (Muntz) F.; m. Suzanne Hotchkiss, Sept. 12, 1956; children: Michael H., Charles S. BA in Econs. cum laude, Stanford U., 1957, LLB, 1963. Bar: Calif. 1964. Pvt. practice law, Palo Alto, Calif., 1963-69; with Unionamerica, Inc., 1969-78, exec. v.p., sec., gen. counsel, 1969-75, exec. v.p. Unionamerica Ins. Group, 1976-78; v.p. Pacific Enterprises, 1978-82, pres. Pacific Lighting Energy Systems and Cen. Plants, Inc., 1982-86, vice chmn. So. Calif. Gas Co., L.A., 1987-88, chmn. bd., CEO, 1989-93, pres., COO, 1993-98, CEO, 1998; chmn., CEO Sempra Energy, San Diego, 1998—. Bd. dirs. Union Bank, Sentinel Group Funds, Inc., Nat. Bus.-Higher Edn. Forum. Lt. USN, 1957-60. Mem. Am. Gas Assn. (past chmn., bd. dirs., exec. com. 1988—), Pacific Coast Gas Assn., Interstate Nat. Gas Assn. Am., Nat. Petroleum Coun., L.A. Area C. of C. (bd. dirs., exec. com.), Calif. Club, L.A. Country Club, City Club on Bunker Hill. Republican. Avocations: golf, fishing, racquetball, music. Office: Sempra Energy 101 Ash St San Diego CA 92101-3017

FARMER, ROBERT LINDSAY, lawyer; b. Portland, Oreg., Sept. 29, 1922; s. Paul C. and Irma (Lindsay) F.; m. Carmen E. Engebretson, Sept. 8, 1943; children: Cort W., Scott L., Eric C. BS, UCLA, 1946; LLB, U. So. Calif., 1949. Bar: Calif. 1949. Since practiced in, L.A.; mem. Farmer & Ridley, L.A., 1949—. Trustee Edward James Found., West Dean Estate, Chichester, Eng. Served with AUS, 1943-46. Mem. ABA, Los Angeles County Bar Assn., Order of Coif, Beta Gamma Sigma, Kappa Sigma, Phi Delta Phi, Annandale Golf Club (Pasadena, Calif.). Home: 251 S Orange Grove Blvd Apt 1 Pasadena CA 91105-1766 Office: 444 S Flower St Los Angeles CA 90071-2901

FARMER, TERRY D(WAYNE), lawyer; b. Oklahoma City, May 1, 1949; s. Gayle V. and Allene (Edsall) F.; children: Grant L., Tyler M. BA, U. Okla., 1971, JD, 1974. Bar: Okla. 1974, N.Mex. 1975, U.S. Dist. Ct. N.Mex. 1976, U.S. Ct. Claims 1975, U.S. Ct. Appeals (10th cir.) 1977, U.S. Supreme Ct. 1980. Asst. trust officer First Nat. Bank of Albuquerque, 1974-75; assoc. Nordhaus, Moses & Dunn, Albuquerque, 1975-78, ptnr., 1978-80; dir. Moses, Dunn, Farmer & Tuthill, P.C., Albuquerque, 1980—. Pres. Albuquerque Lawyers Club, N. Mex., 1982-83. Fellow N.Mex. Bar Found.; mem. N.Mex. Bar Assn. (pres. Young Lawyers div., 1978-79), Okla. Bar Assn., N.Mex. Trial Lawyers. Office: Moses Dunn Farmer & Tuthill PC PO Box 27047 Albuquerque NM 87125-7047

FARNSWORTH, ELIZABETH, broadcast journalist; b. Mpls., Dec. 23, 1943; d. H. Bernerd and Jane (Mills) Fink; m. Charles E. Farnsworth, June 20, 1966; children: Jennifer Farnsworth Fellows, Samuel Thills. BA, Middlebury Coll., 1965; MA in History, Stanford U., 1966. Reporter, panelist PBS World Press, KQED, San Francisco, 1975-77; reporter InterNews, Berkeley, Calif., 1977-80; freelance TV and print reporter, San Francisco, 1980-91; fgn. corr. MacNeil/Lehrer News Hour, San Francisco, 1991-95; chief corr., prin. substitute anchor News Hour with Jim Lehrer, Arlington, Va., 1995-97, San Francisco, 1997-99, sr. corr., 1999—. Co-author: El Bloqueo Invisible, 1974; prodr., dir. documentary Thanh's War, 1991 (Cine Golden Eagle award); contbr. articles to various publs. Mem. adv. bd. Berkeley Edn. Found., 1990-95, U. Calif. Sch. Journalism, Berkeley; mem. nat. adv. bd. Ctr. Investigative Reporting, 2001-; bd. dirs. Media Alliance, San Francisco, 1985-87, Data Ctr., Oakland, Calif., 1993-95. Recipient Golden Gate award San Francisco Film Festival, 1984, Best Investigative Reporting award No. Calif. Radio, TV News Dirs.' Assn., 1986, Blue Ribbon, Am. Film and Video Festival, 1991. Mem. AFTRA, NATAS, World Affairs Coun. No. Calif. (bd. dirs. 1998—), Nat. Adv. Writers Corps, Phi Beta Kappa. Presbyterian. Avocations: gardening, hiking, writing poetry.

FARON, FAY CHERYL, private investigator, writer; b. Kansas City, Mo. d. Albert David and Geraldine Fay (Morgan) F. Student, Glendale (Ariz.) C.C., 1967-68, Ariz. State U., 1968-71, U. Ariz., 1971-72. Lic. pvt. investigator, Calif. Owner Monogramation, San Francisco, 1976-80; assoc. prodr. Sta. KGO-TV, San Francisco, 1980-81, Power/Rector, San Francisco, 1982-83; owner Office in the City, San Francisco, 1982-83, The Rat Dog Dick Detective Agy., San Francisco, 1983—. Lectr., guest spkr. San Francisco U., 1984—, San Francisco Assn. Legal Assts., 1984—, Commonwealth Club San Francisco, 1987, Calif. Collectors Coun., San Francisco, 1992—, Book Passage Mystery Writers Conf., 1997-99. Author: A Private Eye's Guide to Collecting a Bad Debt, 1991, Missing Persons, 1997; author/editor: The Instant National Locator Guide, 1991, 2nd edit., 1993, 3rd edit, 1996, Rip-Off, 1998; columnist Ask Rat Dog, 1993—; host, writer: (Court TV Crime Story Spl.) Rip-Offs and Scams, 2000. Co-founder, pres. bd. ElderAngels, San Francisco. Subject of Jack Olsen's book, Hastened to the Grave, 1998. Mem. Nat. Assn. Investigative Specialists, Nat. Assn. Bunco Investigators (asst.), Profls. Against Confidence Crimes (asst.), Sisters in Crime. Avocations: biking, camping, horseback riding, river rafting, travel.

FARQUHAR, JOHN WILLIAM, physician, educator; b. Winnipeg, Man., Can., June 13, 1927; came to U.S., 1934; s. John Giles and Marjorie Victoria (Roberts) F.; m. Christine Louise Johnson, July 14, 1968; children: Margaret F., John C.M.; children by previous marriage: Bruce E., Douglas G. A.B., U. Calif., Berkeley, 1949; M.D., U. Calif., San Francisco, 1952. Intern U. Calif. Hosp., San Francisco, 1952-53; resident, 1953-54, 57-58; postdoctoral fellow, 1955-57; resident U. Minn., Mpls., 1954-55; research asso. Rockefeller U., N.Y.C., 1958-62; asst. prof. medicine Stanford (Calif.) U., 1962-66, asso. prof., 1966-73, prof., 1978—; dir. Stanford Wellness Ctr., 1998—; C.F. Rehnborg prof. in disease prevention Stanford (Calif.) U., 1989-2000; dir. Stanford Ctr. Research in Disease Prevention, 1973-98; dir. collaborating ctr. for chronic disease prevention WHO, 1985-99; prof. health rsch. and policy, 1988—. Mem. staff Stanford U. Hosp.; chair Victoria Declaration Implementation com. Author: The American Way of Life Need Not Be Hazardous to Your Health, 1978, 2d edit., 1987, (with Gene Spiller) The Last Puff, 1990, The Victoria Declaration for Heart Health, 1992, How To Reduce Your Risk of Heart Disease, 1994, The Catalonia Declaration: Investing in Heart Health, 1996, Worldwide Efforts to Improve Heart Disease, 1997, (with Spiller) Diagnosis Heart Disease: Answers to Your Questions about Recovery and Lasting Helth, 2001; contbr. arti cles to profl. jours. Served with U.S. Army, 1945-46. Recipient James D. Bruce award ACP, 1983, Myrdal prize, 1986, Dana award for Pioneering Achievement in Health, Dana Found., 1990, Nat. Cholesterol award for Pub. Edn., Nat. Cholesterol Edn. Program of NIH, 1991, Rsch. Achievement award Am. Heart Assn., 1992, Order of St. George for Svc. to Autonomous Govt. of Catalonia, 1996, Joseph Stokes Preventive Cardiology award Am. Soc. Preventive Cardiology, 1999, Ancel Keys Meml. Lectr., Am. Heart Assn., 2000. Mem. NAS (Inst. Medicine), Am. Soc. Clin. Investigation, Am. Heart Assn. (coun. epidemiology and prevention), Soc. Behavioral Medicine (pres. 1991-92), Gold Headed Cane Soc., Sigma Xi, Alpha Omega Alpha. Episcopalian. Office: Stanford U Sch of Medicine Ctr Rsch in Disease Prevention 730 Welch Rd Palo Alto CA 94304-1506 Fax: 650-723-7018. E-mail: JFarquhar@SCRDP.stanford.edu

FARQUHAR, MARILYN GIST, cell biology and pathology educator; b. Tulare, Calif., July 11, 1928; d. Brooks DeWitt and Alta (Green) Gist; m. John W. Farquhar, June 4, 1952; children: Bruce, Douglas (div. 1968); m. George Palade, June 7, 1970. AB, U. Calif., Berkeley, 1949, MA, 1952, PhD, 1955. Asst. rsch. pathologist Sch. Medicine U. Calif., San Francisco, 1956-58, assoc. rsch. pathologist, 1962-64, assoc. prof., 1964-68, prof. pathology, 1968-70; rsch. assoc. Rockefeller U., N.Y.C., 1958-62, prof. cell biology, 1970-73, Sch. Medicine Yale U., New Haven, 1973-87, Sterling prof. cell biology and pathology, 1987-90; prof. pathology cell molecular medicine U. Calif., San Diego, 1990—, chair divsn. cellular and molecular medicine, 1991-99, prof. cellular & molecular medicine, chair dept. cellular & molecular medicine, 1999—. Mem. editorial bd. numerous sci. jours.; contbr. articles to profl. jours. Recipient Career Devel. award NIH, 1968-73, Disting. Sci. medal Electron Microscope Soc., 1987, Gomori medal Histochem. Soc., 1999. Mem. NAS, Am. Acad. Arts and Scis., Am. Soc. Cell Biology (pres. 1981-82, E.B. Wilson medal 1987), Am. Assn. Investigative Pathology (Rous Whipple award 2001), Am. Soc. Nephrology (Homer Smith award 1988). Home and Office: U Calif Sch Med 12894 Via Latina Del Mar CA 92014-3730

FARQUHARSON, WALTER HENRY, retired minister, religious organization administrator; b. Zealandia, Sask., Can., May 30, 1936; s. James and Jessie Ann (Muirhead) F.; m. Patricia Joan Caswell, Sept. 16, 1958; children: Scott, Michael, Catherine, Stephen. BA, U. Sask., Saskatoon, 1957, Diploma in Edn., 1969; BD, St. Andrew's Coll., Saskatoon, 1961, DD (hon.), 1975. Ordained to ministry United Ch. of Can., 1961. Min. Saltcoats-Bredenbury-Churchbridge Pastoral Charge, Sask., 1961-97. Moderator United Ch. of Can., 1990-92; exec. gen. coun., pres. Sask. Conf.; head Blue Heron House Bed and Breakfast Retreat, Counseling. Lyricist: (with composer Ron Klusmeier) For Nineveh's Sake, God's Gentle Gift, HHold the Child Gently, Stay with Us, (with composer Lori Erhardt) Little Red Wagon, Miracle Renewed; contbr. numerous hymns and religious songs. Recipient Commemorative medal 125th anniversary Confedn. Can. E-mial. Home: PO Box 126 Saltcoats SK Canada S0A 3R0 E-mail: farq.blueheron@sk.sympatico.ca

FARR, DONALD EUGENE, engineering scientist; b. Clinton, Iowa, July 1, 1933; s. Kenneth Elroy and Nellie Irene (Bailey) F.; m. Sally Joyce Brauer, Mar. 8, 1954; children: Erika Lyn Farr Leventis, Jolene Karyn Farr Walters. BA in Engring. Psychology, San Diego State U., 1961; MT with honors, Nat. U., 1974; postgrad., Calif. Pacific U., 1976-80. Human factors specialist Bunker Ramo Corp., Canoga Park, Calif., Germany, 1964-69; sr. design specialist Gen. Dynamics, San Diego, 1955-63, 69-76; tech. staff Sandia Nat. Labs., Albuquerque, 1977-80; group supr., sr. tech. advisor The Babcock and Wilcox Co., Lynchburg, Va., 1980-82; dir. human factors sys. Sci. Applications, Inc., Lynchburg, 1982-83; human engring. scientist Lockheed Calif. Co., Burbank, 1983-91; MANPRINT mgr. Teledyne Electronic Sys., Northridge, Calif., 1991-94; human engring. scientist, program mgr. Symvionics, Inc., Pasadena, 1994—. Ergonomics safety cons. govt., industry and academia, 1977—; instr. human factors/design psychology Art Ctr. Coll. of Design, Pasadena, Calif., 2000—. Contbr. articles to profl. jours. Precinct capt., voter registration vol. Rep. Party, 1963—; lectr., support group Am. Diabetes Assn., L.A., 1993—. With USN, 1952-53. Scholarship USN, 1953; recipient Admiral's award NSIA, 1963. Mem. Human Factors and Ergonomics Soc. (pres. San Diego, L.A. chpt.), Internat. Numismatic Soc. (pres. 1973-75), Am. Nuclear Soc. (human factors chair 1980-82), Am. Legion, NRA Golden Eagles (honor role). Lutheran. Avocations: bridge, numismatics, genealogy, computer graphics, travel. Home: 20054 Avenue Of The Oaks Newhall CA 91321-1361 Office: Symvionics Inc 3280 E Foothill Blvd Ste 200 Pasadena CA 91107-3187 E-mail: dfarr@earthlink.net

FARR, KEVIN M. consumer products executive; BS in Acctg., Mich. State U.; MBA in Fin. and Mktg., Northwestern U. CPA. With PricewaterhouseCoopers; sr. v.p., corp. contr. Mattell, Inc., El Segundo, Calif., 1991-2000, CFO, 2000—. Bd. dirs., treas. Children Affected by AIDS Found. Mem. AICPA, Calif. Soc. of CPAs. Office: Mattel Inc 333 Continental Blvd El Segundo CA 90245-5012

FARR, SAM, congressman; b. Calif., July 4, 1941; m. Shary Baldwin; 1 child, Jessica. BSc Biology, Willamette U., 1963; student, Monterey Inst. Internat. Studies, U. Santa Clara. Vol. Peace Corps, 1963-65; budget analyst, cons. Assembly com. Constl. Amendments; bd. suprs. Monterey (Calif.) County; rep. Calif. State Assembly, 1980-93; mem. U.S. Congress from 17th Calif. dist., 1993—; mem. appropriations com., agr. and military constrn. subcoms. Named Legislator of Yr. Calif. 9 times. Democrat. Avocations: photography, skiing, fly fishing, Spanish. Office: Ho of Reps 1221 Longworth Bldg Washington DC 20515-0517*

FARRAR, JOHN EDSON, II, business executive, consultant, investment adviser; b. Williamsport, Pa., Oct. 9, 1938; s. John Edson and Ruth (Price) F.; 1 child, John Edson III. BA in Psychology, Pasadena Coll., 1963; postgrad., U. Calgary (Alta.), 1967, pub. relations cert.; postgrad., Claremont Grad. Sch., 1963-64, U. Calif. at Riverside, 1968-71. Evaluating social services dir. Head Start dental rsch. project Loma Linda (Calif.) Sch. Dentistry, 1966-67; coordinator Head Start Riverside County Econ. Opportunity Bd., Riverside, Calif., 1967; dir. community relations San Bernardino County Welfare and Probation Depts., San Bernardino, 1968-73; publicity and promotions coordinator in charge tourism and indsl. devel. Econ. Devel. Dept. San Bernardino County, 1973; dir. pub. relations Middle East Boeing Comml. Airplane Co., Seattle, 1973-76, Northwest Hosp., Seattle, 1976-77; owner Craig & Farrar Pub. Relations and Advt., 1977-80; exec. v.p. Environ. Research and Devel. Corp., Seattle, 1980-82; owner Aamco Transmissions Ctr. of Bremerton, Wash., 1982-86; stockbroker Prudential-Bache Securities, Seattle, 1984-86; note broker Afamya, Ltd., London, 1986-87; ind. fin. and bus. cons. and broker Kent, Wash., 1987-93; pres. Professionally Managed Portfolios, Acton, Calif., 1993—. Lectr. mktg. pub. relations, investment techniques and options strategies Antelope Valley College and College of the Danyons, Valencia, Calif.; former chmn. dept. pub. relations and advt. City Coll., Seattle; instr. pub. relations U. Wash.; pub. relations cons. to pvt. bus., govt. Pres. bd. dirs. Frazee Community Center, 1970-71; bd. dirs., pub. relations chmn. Chief Seattle council Boy Scouts Am., promotions chmn. for camping in Southwestern U.S.; exec. bd. Seattle-King County Visitors and Conv. Bur.; mem. Republican Presdl. Task Force, 1982-84. Mem. Pub. Relations Soc. Am. (chpt. pres. 1971, 72, dist. chmn. govt. sect.), Calif. Social Workers Orgn. (v.p. 1970-71), Soc. for Internat. Devel., Nat. Pub. Relations Council Health and Welfare Services, Internat. Pub. Relations Assn., U.s.-Arab C. of C. Lodge: Rotary. E-mail: john@pmpmanagement.com

FARRAR, STANLEY F. lawyer; b. Santa Ana, Calif., 1943; BS, U. Calif., Berkeley, 1964, JD, 1967. Bar: Calif. 1968, N.Y. 1969. Mem. Sullivan & Cromwell, L.A. Mem. ABA (chmn. subcom. on bank holding cos. and nonbank activities banking law com. 1980-85, chmn. letters credit subcom. uniform comml. code com. 1982-88, sect. bus. law), State Bar Calif. (chmn. fin. instns. com. 1981-82). E-mila. Office: Sullivan & Cromwell 1888 Century Park E Los Angeles CA 90067-1710 E-mail: farrars@sullcrom.com

FARRELL, DENNIS, sports association executive; b. Orange, Calif., Feb. 23, 1951; s. Fred Bernard and Janet Louise (Crawford) F.; m. Charlene Louise Cassingham, Jan. 11, 1975; Timothy William, Michael Ted. AA in Liberal Arts, Santa Ana Coll., 1971; BA in Journalism, San Diego State U., 1973. Sports editor Saddleback Valley News, Mission Viejo, Calif., 1974-77; sports info. dir. Saddleback Coll., Mission Viejo, 1977-80; asst. commr. Pacific Coast Athletic Assn., Santa Ana, 1980-88; assoc. commr. Big West Conf., Santa Ana, 1988-92, commr. Irvine, 1992—. Mem. Collegiate Commrs. Assn. Avocations: golf, music. Office: Big West Conf 2 Corporate Park Ste 206 Irvine CA 92606-5115

FARRELL, JOSEPH, movie market analyst, producer, entertainment research company executive, writer, sculptor, designer; b. N.Y.C., Sept. 11, 1935; s. John Joseph and Mildred Veronica (Dwyer) F. A.B. summa cum laude, St. John's Coll., 1958; A.M., U. Notre Dame, 1959; J.D., Harvard U., 1965. Bar: N.Y. 1965. With firm Milbank, Tweed, Hadley & McCloy, N.Y.C., 1964-65; exec. assoc. Carnegie Corp. N.Y., 1965-66; exec. v.p., chief oper. officer Am. Council of Arts, 1966-71; cons. Rockefeller Bros. Fund, Spl. Projects, 1966-74, exec. v.p., 1974-77; vice chmn. Louis Harris & Assocs. (Harris Poll), N.Y.C., 1978; chmn., CEO, Nat. Rsch. Group, Inc., subs. VNU, L.A., London and Tokyo, 1978—. Movie market analyst and cons., 1978—; movie exec. producer, 1986—; sculptor, 1958—; designer Farbino Furniture, 1982—. Author, editor: Americans and the Arts, 1973, 75, Museums: USA, 1973, The Cultural Consumer, 1973, The U.S. Arts and Cultural Trend Data System, 1977; author: (novel) Birds of Prey, 1998; screenwriter The Foundation, Second Son, 1990—. Mem. Gov. N.Y. Task Force on Arts, 1975; founder, bd. dirs. Vol. Lawyers for Arts, 1968-76; bd. dirs. Arts and Bus. Coun. N.Y., 1973-76; bd. advisors Actors Studio, 1983-90. Woodrow Wilson fellow, 1958; named among Top 100 Influential People in Hollywood, Premiere mag., 1998, 99. Office: NRG 5900 Wilshire Blvd 29th Fl Los Angeles CA 90036-5013

FARRELL, KENNETH ROYDEN, economist; b. Ont., Can., Jan. 17, 1927; naturalized, 1958; s. William R. and Velma V. (Wood) F.; m. Mary Souter, Sept. 7, 1951; children: Janet, Betty, Deborah, Robert, Patricia, Lisa. BS, U. Toronto, Ont., 1950; MS, Iowa State U., 1955, PhD, 1958. Economist U. Calif., Berkeley, 1957-71; dep. adminstr. USDA, Washington, 1971-77, adminstr., 1977-81; dir. Nat. Ctr., Resources for the Future, Washington, 1981-87; v.p. U. Calif., Oakland, 1987-95, v.p. emeritus, 1995—. Economist Nat. Food Commn., Washington, 1965-66, Nat. Productivity Commn., Washington, 1972-73; mem. Presdl. Task Force, Washington, 1982; cons. Robert Nathan Assocs., 1983-84. Contbr. articles to profl. jours.; author (with others) books. Lt. Royal Can. Navy Reserve, 1946-48. Fulbright scholar U. Naples (Italy), 1963-64. Fellow AAAS, Am. Agrl. Econs. Assn. (bd. dirs. 1973-76, pres. 1976-77, named for Disting. Pub. Policy Contbn. 1980, 92); mem. Internat. Assn. Agrl. Econs., Commonwealth Club Calif., Phi Kappa Phi, Gamma Sigma Delta. Avocations: golf, gardening, literature. Office: Univ Calif 300 Lakeside Dr Ste 604 Oakland CA 94612-3534 E-mail: kenmar2001@aol.com, Kenneth.farrell@ucop.edu

FARRELL, THOMAS JOSEPH, insurance company executive, consultant; b. Butte, Mont., June 10, 1926; s. Bartholomew J. and Lavina H. (Collins) F.; m. Evelyn Irene Southam, July 29, 1951; children: Brien J., Susan M., Leslie A., Jerome T. Student, U. San Francisco, 1949. CLU. Ptnr. Affiliated-Gen. Ins. Adjusters, Santa Rosa, Calif., 1949-54; agt. Lincoln Nat. Life Ins. Co., Santa Rosa, 1954-57, supr., 1957-59, gen. agt., 1959-74; pres. Thomas J. Farrell & Assocs., 1974-76, 7 Flags Ins. Mktg. Corp., 1976-81, Farrell-Dranginis & Assocs., 1981-88, 88-90, cons., 1990. Specialist Dept. of Devel. Svcs., Calif.; pres., bd. dirs. Lincoln Nat. Bank, Santa Rosa, San Rafael. Pres. Redwood Empire Estate Planning Coun., 1981-82, Sonoma County Coun. for Retarded Children, 1956-59, Sonoma County Assn. for Retarded Citizens, City Santa Rosa Traffic and Parking Commn., 1963; specialist State of Calif. Dept. Devel. Svcs., 1990—; del. Calif. State Conf. Sml. Bus., 1980; mem. Santa Rosa City Schs. Compensatory Edn. Adv. Bd.; bd. dirs. Santa Rosa City Schs. Consumer Edn. Adv. Bd.; pres., nat. dir. United Cerebral Palsy Assn., 1954-55; nat. coord. C. of C. - Rotary Symposia on Employment of People with Disabilities, 1985-87; v.p. Vigil Light, Inc; chmn. bd. dirs. Nat. Barrier Awareness for People with Disabilities Found., Inc.; pres. Commn. on Employment of People with Disabilities, 1986-92; mem. Pres.'s Com. on Mental Retardation, 1982-86; chmn. Santa Rosa Cmty. Rels. Com., 1973-76; pres. Sonoma County Young Reps., 1953; past bd. dirs. Sonoma County Fair and Expn., Inc.; bd. dirs. Sonoma County Family Svc. Agy., Eldridge Found., North Bay Regional Ctr. for Developmentally Disabled; trustee Sonoma State Hosp. for Mentally Retarded. Recipient cert. Nat. Assn. Retarded Children, 1962, Region 9 U.S. HHS Cmty. Svc. award, 1985, Sonoma County Vendor's Human Svc. award 1986, Individual Achievement award Cmty. Affirmative Action Forum of Sonoma County, 1986. Mem. Nat. Assn. Life Underwriters, Redwood Empire Assn. CLU's (pres. 1974-75), Japanese-Am. Citizens League, Jaycees (Outstanding Young Man of Yr. 1961, v.p. 1955), Santa Rosa C. of C. (bd. dirs. 1974-75), Calif. PTA (hon. life), Rotary (Svc. Above Self award 1996). Home: 963 Wyoming Dr Santa Rosa CA 95405-7342

FARRELLY, BOBBY, writer, producer, director; b. Cumberland, R.I., 1958; Writer, prodr. Outside Providence, 1999; writer, co-prodr. Dumb and Dumber, 1994; exec. prodr., writer, dir. There's Something About Mary, 1998; writer, prodr. dir. Me, Myself and Irene, 1999; writer, dir. Stuck on You, 1999; writer Bushwacked, 1995; dir. Kingpin, 1996. Recipient Screenwriter of Yr. ShoWest Conv., 1999. Office: Creative Artists Agy c/o Adam Kantor 9830 Wilshire Blvd Beverly Hills CA 90212-1825

FARRELLY, PETER JOHN, screenwriter; b. Phoenixville, Pa., Dec. 17, 1956; s. Robert Leo and Mariann (Neary) F. BA, Providence Coll., 1979; MFA, Columbia U., 1987. Salesman U.S. Lines, Inc., Boston, 1979-81; bartender various libationary locales, Boston, 1981-85; screenwriter Paramount Columbia and Disney Studios, Los Angeles, 1985—. Author Outside Providence, 1988; co-writer (TV spls.) Our Planet Tonight, 1987, Paul Reiser: Out on a Whim, 1987; writer (film) Dumb & Dumber, 1994, Bushwhacked, 1995, There's Something About Mary, 1998; dir. (film) Dumb & Dumber, 1994, Kingpin, 1996, There's Something About Mary, 1998; prodr. There's Something About Mary, 1998, Outside Providence, 1999; writer, co-dir.: Me, Myself & Irene, 2000. Mem. Writers Guild Am. West. Roman Catholic.

FARRER, CLAIRE ANNE RAFFERTY, anthropologist, folklorist, educator; b. N.Y.C., Dec. 26, 1936; d. Francis Michael and Clara Anna (Guerra) Rafferty; 1 child, Suzanne Claire. BA in Anthropology, U. Calif., Berkeley, 1970; MA in Anthropology and Folklore, U. Tex., 1974, PhD in Anthropology and Folklore, 1977. Various positions, 1953-73; fellow Whitney M. Young Jr. Meml. Found., N.Y.C., 1974-75; arts specialist, grant adminstr. Nat. Endowment for Arts, Washington, 1976-77; Weatherhead resident fellow Sch. Am. Research, Santa Fe, 1977-78; asst. prof. anthropology U. Ill., Urbana, 1978-85; assoc. prof., coord. applied anthropology Calif. State U., Chico, 1985-89, prof., 1989—, master tchr., 1999-2000, dir. Multicultural and Gender Studies, 1994, Master tchr., 1999—2001. Cons. in field, 1974—; mem. film and video adv. panel Ill. Arts Coun., 1980-82; mem. Ill. Humanities Coun., 1980-82; vis. prof. U. Ghent, Belgium, 1990; named Hulbert Prof. S.W. Studies, Colo. Coll., Colorado Springs, 1997; bus. mgr. Calif. Folklore Soc., 1994-99. Author: Play and Inter-Ethnic Communication, 1990, Living Life's Circle: Mescalero Apache Cosmovision, 1991, Thunder Rides a Black Horse: Mescalero Apaches and the Mythic Present, 1994, 96; co-founder, co-editor Folklore Women's Commn., 1972; editor spl. issue Jour. Am. Folklore, 1975, 1st rev. edit., 1986; co-editor: Forms of Play of Native North Americans, 1979, Earth and Sky: Visions of the Cosmos in Native North American Folklore, 1992; contbr. numerous articles to profl. jours., mags. and newspapers, chpts. to books. Recipient numerous awards, fellowships and grants. Fellow Am. Anthrop. Assn., Am. Astronomy Assn. (history divsn.); mem. Authors Guild, Am. Ethnol. Soc., Am. Folklore Soc., Am. Soc. Ethnohistory. Mem. Soc. of Friends. Office: Calif State U Dept Anthropology Butte 311 Chico CA 95929-0001 E-mail: cfarrer@csuchico.edu

FARRIS, JEROME, federal judge; b. Birmingham, Ala., Mar. 4, 1930; s. William J. and Elizabeth (White) F.; widower; 2 children. BS, Morehouse Coll., 1951, LLD, 1978; MSW, Atlanta U., 1955; JD, U. Wash., 1958. Bar: Wash. 1958. Mem. Weyer, Roderick, Schroeter and Sterne, Seattle, 1958-59; ptnr. Weyer, Schroeter, Sterne & Farris and successor firms, Seattle, 1959-61, Schroeter & Farris, Seattle, 1961-63, Schroeter, Farris, Bangs & Horowitz, Seattle, 1963-65, Farris, Bangs & Horowitz, Seattle, 1965-69; judge Wash. State Ct. of Appeals, Seattle, 1969-79, U.S. Ct. of Appeals (9th cir.), Seattle, 1979-95, sr. judge, 1995—. Lectr. U. Wash. Law Sch. and Sch. of Social Work, 1976— ; mem. faculty Nat. Coll. State Judiciary, U. Nev., 1973; adv. bd. Nat. Ctr. for State Cts. Appellate Justice Project, 1978-81; founder First Union Nat. Bank, Seattle, 1965, dir., 1965-69; mem. U.S. Supreme Ct. Jud. Fellows Commn., 1997—; mem. Jud. Conf. Com. on Internat. Jud. Rels., 1997-2000. Del. The White House Conf. on Children and Youth, 1970; mem. King County (Wash.) Youth Commn., 1969-70; vis. com. U. Wash. Sch. Social Work, 1977-90; mem. King County Mental Health-Mental Retardation Bd., 1967-69; past bd. dirs. Seattle United Way; mem. Tyee Bd. Advisers, U. Wash., 1984-88, bd. regents, 1985-97, pres., 1990-91; trustee U. Law Sch. Found., 1978-84, Morehouse Coll., 1999—; mem. vis. com. Harvard Law Sch., 1996—. With Signal Corps, U.S. Army, 1952-53. Recipient Disting. Service award Seattle Jaycees, 1965, Clayton Frost award, 1966 Fellow Am. Bar Found. (chair of fellows 2000); mem. ABA (exec. com. appellate judges conf. 1978-84, 87-88, chmn. conf. 1982-83, del. jud. adminstrn. coun. 1987-88, sr. lawyers divsn. coun. 1998—), Wash. Council on Crime and Delinquency (chmn. 1970-72), Am. Bar Found. (bd. dirs. 1987, exec. com. 1989-97), State-Fed. Jud. Council of State of Wash. (vice-chmn. 1977-78, chmn. 1983-87), Order of Coif (mem. law rev.), U. Wash. Law Sch. Office: US Ct Appeals 9th Cir 1030 US Courthouse 1010 5th Ave Seattle WA 98104-1181

FARSON, RICHARD EVANS, psychologist; b. Chgo., Nov. 16, 1926; s. Duke Mendenhall and Mary Gladys (Clark) F.; m. Elizabeth Lee Grimes, May 21, 1954 (div. 1962); children: Lisa Page, Clark Douglas; m. 2d Dawn Jackson Cooper, Jan. 4, 1964 (div. 1990); children: Joel Andrew, Ashley Dawn, Jeremy Richard. BA, Occidental Coll., 1947, MA, 1951; postgrad., UCLA, 1948-50; PhD, U. Chgo., 1955. Dean Sch. Design Calif. Inst. Arts, Valencia, 1969-73; pres. Esalen Inst., Big Sur and San Francisco, 1973-75; faculty Saybrook Inst., San Francisco, 1975-79; pres. Western Behavioral Scis. Inst., La Jolla, Calif., 1958-68; chmn. bd. Western Behavior Scis. Inst., La Jolla, 1968-79, pres., 1979—. Dir. Internat. Design Conf., Aspen, Colo., 1971-2001, pres. 1976-80, 94-97. Editor: Science and Human Affairs, 1967; author: Birthrights, 1974, Management of the Absurd: Paradoxes in Leadership, 1996, (with others) The Future of the Family, 1969. Served to lt. j.g. USNR, 1955-57. Ford Found. fellow, Harvard U. Bus. Sch., 1953-54. Mem. Am. Psychol. Assn., Sigma Xi, Psi Chi Home: 252 Prospect St La Jolla CA 92037-4225 Office: Western Behavioral Science Inst PO Box 1049 La Jolla CA 92038 E-mail: rfarson@wbsi.org

FARWELL, HERMON WALDO, JR. parliamentarian, educator, former speech communication educator; b. Englewood, N.J., Oct. 24, 1918; s. Hermon Waldo and Elizabeth (Whitcomb) F.; A.B., Columbia, 1940; M.A., Pa. State U., 1964; m. Martha Carey Matthews, Jan. 3, 1942; children—Gardner Whitcomb, Linda Margaret (Mrs. Richard Hammer). Commd. USAF, 1940, advanced through grades to maj., various positions, 1940-66, ret., 1966; instr. aerial photography Escola Tecnica de Aviação, Brazil, 1946-48; faculty U. So. Colo., Pueblo, 1966-84, prof. emeritus speech communication, 1984—; cons., tchr. parliamentary procedure. Author: The Majority Rules-A Manual of Procedure for Most Groups: Parliamentary Motions: Majority Motions; editor The Parliamentary Jour., 1981-87, 91-93; contbr. articles to profl. jours. Mem. Am. Inst. Parliamentarians (nat. dir. 1977-87), Commn. on Am. Parliamentary Practice (chmn. 1976), Ret. Officers Assn., Nat. Assn. Parliamentarians, Am. Legion, VFW, Air Force Assn. Home and Office: 65 Macalester Rd Pueblo CO 81001-2052

FASI, FRANK FRANCIS, state legislator; b. East Hartford, Conn., Aug. 27, 1920; B.S., Trinity Coll., Hartford, 1942. Mem. Hawaii Senate, 1959—, Dem. mayor City and County of Honolulu, 1969-81, Rep. mayor, 1985-94; resigned, 1994; owner Property & Bus., Honolulu, 1995. Mem. Dem. Nat. Com. for Hawaii, 1952-56; del. 2d Constl. Conv., 1968; mem.-at-large Honolulu City Coun., 1965-69; non-partisan candidate for Mayor of Honolulu, 2000. Served to capt. USMCR. Mem. Pacific-Asian Congress Municipalities (founder, past pres., exec. dir.), VFW (former comdr. Hawaii dept.), AFTRA (past v.p.). Office: 401 Waiakamilo Rd Ste 201 Honolulu HI 96817-4955

FATHAUER, THEODORE FREDERICK, meteorologist; b. Oak Park, Ill., June 5, 1946; s. Arthur Theodore and Helen Ann (Mashek) F.; m. Mary Ann Neesan, Aug. 8, 1981. BA, U. Chgo., 1968. Cert. cons. meteorologist. Rsch. aide USDA No. Dev. Labs., Peoria, Ill., 1966, Cloud Physics Lab., Chgo., 1967; meteorologist Sta. WLW Radio/TV, Cin., 1967-68, Nat. Meteorol. Ctr., Washington, 1968-70, Nat. Weather Svc., Anchorage, 1970-80, meteorologist-in-charge Fairbanks, Alaska, 1980-98, lead forecaster, 1998—. Instr. U. Alaska, Fairbanks, 1975-76, USCG Aux., Fairbanks and Anchorage, 1974—; specialist in Alaska meteorology. Contbr. chpt to book Denali's West Buttress, 1997, Living With the Coast of Alaska, 1997; contbr. articles to weather mags. and jours. Bd. dirs. Fairbanks Concert Assn., 1988—; bd. dirs. No. Alaska Combined Fed. Campaign, 1996—, campaign chmn., 1996-97; bd. dirs. Friends U. Alaska Mus., 1993—, pres., 1993-95, sec. 1997-98; bd. visitors U. Alaska Fairbanks, 1995—; bd. dirs., sec. Fairbanks Symphony Assn., 1994—; bd. trustees U. Alaska Found., 1997—, mem. coll. fellows, 1993—, exec. com., 1997—, vice chair, 1998-99, chair, 2000—; mem. adv. bd. Salvation Army Fairbanks Corps, 1997—. Recipient Outstanding Performance award Nat. Weather Service, 1972, 76, 83, 85, 86, 89, Fed. Employee of Yr. award, Fed. Exec. Assn., Anchorage, 1978. Fellow Am. Meteorol. Soc. (TV and radio seals of approval), Royal Meteorol. Soc.; mem. AAAS, Am. Geophys. Union, Western Snow Conf., Arctic Inst. N.Am. (exec. sec. U.S. Corp. 1998—), Oceanography Soc., Can. Meteorol. and Oceanographic Soc., Greater Fairbanks C. of C., Am. Sailing Assn. Republican. Lutheran. Avocations: reading, music, skiing, canoeing. Home: PO Box 80210 Fairbanks AK 99708-0210 Office: Nat Weather Svc Forecast Office Internat Arctic Rsch Ctr U Alaska PO Box 757345 Fairbanks AK 99775-7345 E-mail: theodore.fathauer@noaa.gov

FAUCHER, DAVID F. federal judge; b. 1944; Apptd. part-time magistrate judge U.S. Dist. Ct. Hawaii, 1994. Address: Johnston Island PO Box 832 APO AP 96558 Fax: 808-622-3707

FAULSTICH, JAMES R. retired bank executive; b. St. Louis, Dec. 19, 1933; s. Robert C. and Eva D. (Mueller) F.; m. Gretchen Felthouse, July 28, 1956; children: Robert, Julie, Clairann. BS, Ind. U., 1958; JD, U. Chgo., 1961. Dep. legis. counsel State Oreg., Salem, 1961-67, ins. commr., 1967-69, asst. to gov., 1969-71; v.p. industry rels. Nat. Assn. Ind. Insurers, Des Plaines, Ill., 1971-77, dir. rsch., sr. v.p. industry rels., 1977-79; pres., CEO Fed. Home Loan Bank Seattle, 1979-99. Bd. dirs. Pentegra. Treas. Bd. of Social Compact, Washington; bd. dirs. Housing Partnership, Seattle, Seattle Ctr. Found.; mem. Higher Edn. Coordinating Bd.; trustee Seattle Opera. Mem. ABA, Am. Judicature Soc., Oreg. Bar Assn., Wash. Athletic Club, Rainier Club, Downtown Seattle Assn., Columbia Tower Club, Rotary. Home: 8101 SE 48th St Mercer Island WA 98040-4301 Office: Fed Home Loan Bank 1501 4th Ave Ste 1900 Seattle WA 98101-1693

FAULWELL, GERALD EDWARD, insurance company executive; b. San Francisco, May 13, 1942; s. Albert Jr. and Helen Marie (Thiel) F.; m. Constance Lee Danaher, Aug. 22, 1964 (div. Jan. 1982); children: Jeffrey, Jennifer, Heather, Cullen; m. Marita Girardo Tschirhart, Jan. 30, 1982. Student, Valley Coll., 1960-63; BA, UCLA, 1965. CPA, Tex. Acct. Farmers Group, Inc., L.A., 1966-67, sr. acct., 1967-69, acctg. specialist, 1969-72, acctg. mgr., 1972-78, mgmt. trainee, 1978-79, dir. corp. acctg., 1979-82, v.p. acctg., 1982-87, v.p., treas., 1988-92, v.p. strategic planning and budgets, 1993-95, sr. v.p. strategic planning and budgeting, 1996-97, sr. v.p., cfo, 1998—. Petty officer USN, 1960-64. Mem. AICPA, Tex. State Bd. Pub. Accountancy. Democrat. Roman Catholic. Avocations: golf, bowling. Home: 733 Oldstone Pl Simi Valley CA 93065-5336 Office: Farmers Group Inc 4680 Wilshire Blvd Los Angeles CA 90010-3807

FAUST, JAMES E. religious organization administrator. Mem. First Presidency, Ch. of Jesus Christ of Latter-day Saints. Office: LDS Church 47 E South Temple Salt Lake City UT 84150-9701

FAW, DUANE LESLIE, lay worker, law educator, retired career officer, writer; b. Loraine, Tex., July 7, 1920; s. Alfred Leslie and Noma Leigh (Elliott) F.; m. Lucile Elizabeth Craps, Feb. 20, 1943; children: Cheryl Leigh, Bruce Duane, Debra Leoma, Melanie Loraine. Student, N. Tex. State Coll., 1937-41; J.D., Columbia U., 1947. Bar: Tex. 1948, D.C. 1969, U.S. Supreme Ct. 1969. Commd. 2d lt. USMC, 1942, advanced through grades to brig. gen., 1969, bn. comdr., 1959-61, staff judge adv., 1961-64, policy analyst Marine Hdqrs., 1964-67, dep. chief of staff III Marine Amphibious Force, 1967-68, judge Navy Ct. Mil. Rev., 1968-69, dir. Judge Ad. Div. Marine Hdqrs., 1969-71, ret., 1971; prof. law Pepperdine U. Sch. Law, Malibu, Calif., 1971-85. Bible tchr. So. Presbyn. Ch., Denton, Tex., 1948-50, Camp Pendleton, N.C., 1959-61, Quantico, Va., 1962-63, United Meth. Ch., Arlington, Va., 1963-71; Bible tchr., elder Presbyn. Ch., Van Horn, Tex., 1950-52; lay spkr., Bible tchr. United Meth. Ch., Tustin, Malibu and Laguna Hills, Calif., 1972—, lay mem. ann. conf., 1974-81, 91, 95, 98. Author: The Paramony, 1986, The Joy of Spiritual Discovery, 1995; co-author: The Military in American Society, 1978. Gen. councilor URANTIA Brotherhood, 1979-88, gen. councilor of FELLOWSHIP, 1991-94; bd. dirs. Jesusonian Found., Boulder, 1988—, Touch for Health Found., Pasadena, Calif., 1988-94. Decorated Air medal with gold star, Navy Commendation medal with gold star, Legion of Merit with combat V with gold star; UN Cross of Gallantry with gold star; VN Honor medal 1st class. Mem. ABA (adv. com. mil. justice 1969-71, adv. com. lawyers in Armed Forces 1969-71), Fed. Bar Assn. (council), Judge Advs. Assn., Am. Acad. Religion, Soc. Bibl. Lit. Club: Masons. One of original 12 judges Navy Ct. Mil. Rev.; 1st gen. officer head Marine Corps Judge Advs. Home: Apt 3A 2399 Via Mariposa W Unit 3A Laguna Woods CA 92653-2052

FAY, ABBOTT EASTMAN, history educator; b. Scottsbluff, Nebr., July 19, 1926; s. Abbott Eastman and Ethel (Lambert) F.; m. Joan D. Richardson, Nov. 26, 1953; children: Rand, Diana, Collin. Grad., Scottsbluff (Nebr.) Jr. Coll.; BA, Colo. State Coll., 1949, MA, 1953; postgrad., U. Denver, 1961-63; cert. advanced study, Western State U., 1963. Tchr. Leadville (Colo.) Pub. Schs., 1950-52, elem. prin., 1952-54; prin. Leadville Jr. H.S., 1954-55; pub. info. dir., instr. history Mesa Coll., Grand Junction, Colo., 1955-64; asst. prof. history Western State Coll., Gunnison, 1964-76, assoc. prof. history, 1976-82, assoc. prof. emeritus, 1982—. Adj. faculty Adams State Coll., Alamosa, Colo., Mesa State Coll., Grand Junction, Colo., 1989—; propr. Mountaintop Books, Paonia, Colo.; bd. dirs. Colo. Assoc. Univ. Press; dir. hist. tours; columnist Valley Chronicle, Paonia, Best Years Beacon, Grand Junction, Guide Lines, Denver, The Historian, Fruita, Colo., Grand Mesa Byway News, Delta, Colo., Agewave: Get Up & Go!, Mpls.; profl. speaker in field; cons. Colo. Welcome Ctr., 1997—. Author: Mountain Academia, 1968, Writing Good History Research Papers, 1980, Ski Tracks in the Rockies, 1984, Famous Coloradans, 1990, I Never Knew That About Colorado, 1993, Beyond The Great Divide, 1999, To Think That This Happened in Grand County!, 1999, A History of Skiing in Colorado, 2000, More That I Never Knew About Colorado, 2000; playwright: Thunder Mountain Lives Tonight!; contbr. articles to profl. jours., freelance writer popular mags. Founder, coord. Nat. Energy Conservation Challenge; travel cons. Colo. State Welcome Ctr., 1997-99; project reviewer NEH, Colo. Hist. Soc.; steering com. West Elk Scenic & Historic Byway, Colo., 1994—; founder Leadville (Colo.) Assembly, pres., 1953-54; mem. Advs. of Lifelong Learning, 1994—. Named Top Prof. Western State Coll., 1969, 70, 71; fellow Hamline U. Inst. Asian Studies, 1975, 79; recipient Colo. Ind. Pubs. award, 1998. Mem. Western Writers Am., Rocky Mountain Social Sci. Assn. (sec. 1961-63), Am. Hist. Assn., Assn. Asian Studies, Western History Assn., Western State Coll. Alumni Assn. (pres. 1971-73), Internat. Platform Assn. Profl. Guides Assn. Am. (cert.), Rocky Mountain Guides Assn., Colo. Antiquarian Booksellers Assn., Am. Legion (Outstanding Historian award 1981), Phi Alpha Theta, Phi Kappa Delta, Delta Kappa Pi. Home: 1156 Bookcliff Ave Apt 4 Grand Junction CO 81501-8198

FAY-SCHMIDT, PATRICIA ANN, paralegal; b. Waukegan, Ill., Dec. 25, 1941; d. John William and Agnes Alice (Semerad) Fay; m. Dennis A. Schmidt, Nov. 3, 1962 (div. Dec. 1987); children: Kristin Fay Schmidt, John Andrew Schmidt. Student, L.A. Pierce Coll., 1959-60, U. San Jose, 1960-62, Western State U. of Law, Fullerton, Calif., 1991-92. Cert. legal asst., Calif. Paralegal Rasner & Rasner, Costa Mesa, Calif., 1979-82; paralegal, adminstr. Law Offices of Manuel Ortega, Santa Ana, 1982-92; sabbatical, 1992-94. Mem. editorial adv. bd. James Pub. Co., Costa Mesa, 1984-88. Contbg. author: Journal of the Citizen Ambassador Paralegal Delegation to the Soviet Union, 1990. Treas., Republican Women, Tustin, Calif., 1990-91; past regent, 1st vice regent, 2d vice regent NSDAR, Tustin, 1967—; docent Richard M. Nixon Libr. and Birthplace, 1993—, bd. dirs. Docent Guild, 1994-99; docent Orange County Courthouse Mus., 1992-94; chmn. Am. History Essay, 1999—. Mem. Orange County Paralegal Assn. (hospitality chair 1985-87). Roman Catholic. Avocations: theater, dance. Home: 13571 Hewes Ave Santa Ana CA 92705-2215 E-mail: gabriellex@pacbel.net

FEATHERSTONE, BRUCE ALAN, lawyer; b. Detroit, Mar. 2, 1953; s. Ronald A. and Lois R. (Bosshart) F.; children: Leigh Allison, Edward Alan. BA cum laude with distinction in Econs., Yale U., 1974; JD magna cum laude, U. Mich., 1977. Bar: Ill. 1977, Colo. 1983, U.S. Dist. Ct. (no. dist.) Ill. 1978, U.S. Dist. Ct. Colo. 1983, U.S. Ct. Appeals (5th cir.) 1980, U.S. Ct. Appeals (7th cir.) 1981, U.S. Ct. Appeals (10th cir.) 1983, U.S. Ct. Appeals (9th cir.) 1991, U.S. Ct. Appeals (fed. cir.), U.S. Supreme Ct. 1984. Assoc. Kirkland & Ellis, Denver, 1977-83, ptnr., 1983-96, Featherstone & Shea, LLP, Denver, 1996-99, Featherstone DeSisto LLP, Denver, 1999—. Articles editor U. Mich. Law Rev., 1976-77. Mem. ABA (litigation sect.), Assn. Trial Lawyers Am., Colo. Bar Assn., Colo. Trial Lawyers Assn., Colo. Def. Lawyers Assn., Denver Bar Assn., Order of Coif. Avocations: swimming, biking, running. Home: 725 Saint Paul St Denver CO 80206-3912 also: PO Box 1467 Denver CO 80201-1467 Office: Featherstone DeSisto LLP 600-17th St Ste 2400 Denver CO 80202-5402 E-mail: bfeatherstone@featherstonelaw.com

FEAVER, DOUGLAS DAVID, retired university dean, classics educator; b. Toronto, Ont., Can., May 14, 1921; came to U.S., 1948; s. Charles John and Margaret Adeline (Brett) F.; m. Margaret Ruth Seaman, June 10, 1950; children: David, John, Paul, Ruth, Peter. BA, U. Toronto, 1948; MA, Johns Hopkins U., 1949, PhD, 1951; postgrad., Am. Sch. Classical Studies, 1951-52. Instr. Yale U., New Haven, 1952-56; mem. faculty Lehigh U., Bethlehem, Pa., 1956—, prof. classics, 1966-84; internat. dean emeritus Coll. Humanities and Internat. Studies, Univ. of the Nations, Kailua, Kona, Hawaii, 1985-94, dean Kailua, Kona, Hawaii, 1994-98, dean emeritus Hawaii, 1998—. Jr. fellow Ctr. Hellenic Studies, 1967-68; ann. research prof. Am. Sch. Classical Studies, 1976-77; dir. Humanities Perspectives on Tech., 1972-75; cons. in field Author: El mundo en que vivio Jesus, 1972; contbr. articles to profl. jours. Served with RCAF, 1940-45. NEH scholar, 1971-84; cons. NEH, 1975— Presbyterian. Office: Univ of the Nations 75-5851 Kuakini Hwy Kailua Kona HI 96740-2199

FEAVER, GEORGE ARTHUR, political science educator; b. Hamilton, Ont., Canada, May 12, 1937; came to U.S., July 4, 1967; s. Harold Lorne and Doris Davies (Senior) F.; m. Nancy Alice Poynter, June 12, 1963 (div. 1978); m. Ruth Helene Tubbesing, Mar. 8, 1986 (div. 1991); children: Catherine Fergusson, Noah George, Anthea Jane, Elyria Beatta. B.A. with Honors, U. B.C., 1959; Ph.D., London Sch. of Econs., 1962. Asst. prof. Mt. Holyoke Coll., South Hadley, Mass., 1962-65; lectr., research assoc. London Sch. Econs. and Univ. Coll., London, 1965-67; assoc. prof. Georgetown U., Washington, 1967-68, Emory U., Atlanta, 1968-71, U.B.C., Vancouver, B.C., Canada, 1971-74, prof. Canada, 1974—. Vis. fellow Australian Nat. U., Canberra, 1987, London Sch. of Econ., 1991-92. Author: From Status to Contract, 1969; editor: Beatrice Webb's Our Partnership, 1975; editor: The Webbs in Asia: The 1911-12 Travel Diary, 1992; co-editor: Lives, Liberties and the Public Good, 1987; contbr. articles to profl. jours., books. Fellow Canada Council, 1970-71, 74-75, Am. Council Learned Socs., 1974-75, Social Scis. and Humanities Research Council of Canada, 1981-82, 86-91. Mem. Can. Polit. Sci. Assn., Am. Polit. Sci. Assn., Am. Soc. for Polit. and Legal Philosophy, Conf. for Study of Polit. Thought, Inst. Internat. de philosophie politique Club: Travellers' (London) Avocations: rambling, wine appreciation. Home: 4776 W 7th Ave Vancouver BC Canada V6T 1C6 Office: Univ British Columbia Dept Polit Sci Vancouver BC Canada V6T 1Z1 E-mail: feaver@unxg.ubc.ca

FEE, WILLARD EDWARD, JR. otolaryngologist; b. Portchester, N.Y., June 10, 1943; s. Willard E. and Jane Frances (Cromwell) F.; m. Caroline Fee, June 13, 1965; children: Heather, Adam. BS cum laude, U. San Francisco, 1965; MD magna cum laude, U. Colo., 1969. Intern Harbor Gen. Hosp., Torrance, Calif., 1969-70; resident in gen. surgery Wadsworth VA Hosp., L.A., 1970-71; resident in head and neck surgery UCLA Sch. Medicine, 1971-74; asst. prof. Stanford (Calif.) U. Med. Ctr., 1974-80, assoc. prof. otolaryngology, 1980-86, prof., 1986-2000, Edward C. & Amy H. Sewall prof., 1996—, chmn. dept., 1980-00. Dir. Am. Bd. of Otolaryngology, Houston, 1985—; chmn. med. sch. faculty senate Stanford U., 1992-94. Editl. bd. Archives in Otolaryngology, Chgo., 1984-95; contbr. numerous articles to profl. jours. Mem. Collegium ORLAS-US (chmn. 1995-2001), Paul H. Ward Soc., Inc. (pres. 1988-89), Am. Soc. Head and Neck Surgery (pres. 1989-90), Am. Acad. Otolaryngology and Head and Neck Surgery, Calif. Soc. Otolaryngology (pres. 1995-99), Alpha Omega Alpha. Home: 27299 Ursula Ln Los Altos CA 94022-3222 Office: Stanford U Med Ctr Divsn Otolaryngology Edwards R135 300 Pasteur Stanford CA 94305-5328

FEELEY, MALCOLM M. law educator, political scientist; b. North Conway, N.H., Nov. 28, 1942; s. John Aloysious and Mildred (McCollum) F.; divorced; children: Jacob, Miriam, Amin. B.A., Austin Coll., 1964; M.A., U. Minn., 1966, Ph.D., 1969. Asst. prof. NYU, N.Y.C., 1968-72; fellow, lectr. Yale U., New Haven, 1972-77; prof. U. Wis.-Madison, 1977-84; prof. law U. Calif.-Berkeley, 1984—. V.p. Silbert-Feeley Assn., New Haven, 1975-83; editorial advisor Longman Inc., N.Y.C., 1979—Author: The Process is the Punishment, 1979, The Policy Dilemma, 1981, Court Reform on Trial, 1983, Judicial Policy-Making, 1998; Editor: American Constitutional Law, 1985. Recipient Silver Gavel award ABA, 1980, cert. merit ABA, 1984; Hubert Humphrey fellow U. Minn., 1968 Mem. Law and Soc. Assn. (trustee 1975-80), Am. Polit. Sci. Assn. Democrat. Jewish Avocations: canoeing, hiking, reading. Office: U Calif Sch Law Boalt Hall Ctr Study Law Society Hl Berkeley CA 94720-0001

FEELEY, MICHAEL F. state legislator; b. Hackensack, N.J., 1933; m. Lesley A. Dahlkemper. B in Econs. magna cum laude, U. Colo., 1977; JD, U. Denver, 1982. Ptnr. Overton & Feeley; mem. Colo. State Senate, 1992, minority leader, mem. svcs. com., mem. legis. coun. Mem. gender and justice com. Colo. Supreme Ct. Active Gov.'s Colo. Edn. Goals Panel; ad hoc mem. Children's Campaign Legis. Com.; bd. mem. Colo. Guaranteed Student Loan Program, West Metro Fire Protection Dist. Sgt. USMC, 1971-74. Named Outstanding Legislator, Colo. Bankers Assn., Domestic

Violence Coun., Bldg. and Constrn. Trades Coun. Roman Catholic. Avocations: tennis, reading, CU football. Address: 13486 W Center Dr Lakewood CO 80228-2452 Office: State Capitol 200 E Colfax Ave Ste 274 Denver CO 80203-1716 also: 1120 Lincoln St Denver CO 80203-2139 Fax: 303-866-4543. E-mail: mike.freeley@state.co.us

FEENEY, ROBERT EARL, research biochemist; b. Oak Park, Ill., Aug. 30, 1913; s. Bernard Cyril and Loreda (McKee) F.; m. Mary Alice Waller, Dec. 3, 1954; children: Jane, Elizabeth. Student, Rochester (Minn.) Jr. Coll., 1932-33; BS in Chemistry, Northwestern U., 1938; MS in Biochemistry, U. Wis., 1939, PhD in Biochemistry, 1942. Diplomate Am. Bd. Nutrition. Rsch. assoc. Harvard U. Med. Sch., Boston, 1942-43; rsch. biochemist USDA Lab., Albany, Calif., 1946-53; prof. chemistry U. Nebr., Lincoln, 1953-60; prof. dept. food sci. and tech. U. Calif., Davis, 1960-84, prof. emeritus, rsch. biochemist, 1984—, interim dir. protein structure lab., 1990-91. Bd. dirs. Creative Chemistry Cons., Davis. Author: (with Richard Allison) Evolutionary Biochemistry of Proteins, 1969, (with Gary Means) Chemical Modification of Proteins, 1971, Professor On the Ice, 1974, Polar Journeys, 1998, The Role of Food and Nutrition in Early Exploration, 1998; editor: (with John Whitaker) Protein Tailoring for Food and Medical Uses, 1986. Capt. wound rsch. team M.C., U.S. Army, 1943-46. Recipient Superior Svc. award USDA, 1953, ; Feeney Peak, Antarctica named in his honor U.S. Bd. on Geog. Names, 1968. Mem. Am. Chem. Soc. (chmn. div. agrl. and food chemistry, 1978-79, award for disting. svc. in agrl. and food chemistry, 1978), Am. Soc. for Biochemistry and Molecular Biology, Inst. of Food Technologists, Explorers Club. Democrat. Avocations: polar sci., polar exploration author. Home: 780 Elmwood Dr Davis CA 95616-3517 Office: U Calif Dept Food Sci and Tech Cruess Hall Davis CA 95616

FEHER, GEORGE, physics and biophysics scientist, educator; b. Czechoslovakia, May 29, 1924; s. Ferdinand and Sylvia (Schwartz) F.; m. Elsa Rosenvasser, June 18, 1961; children— Laurie, Shoshanah, Paoli B.S. in Engring. Physics, U. Calif.-Berkeley, 1950, M.S. in Elec. Engring., 1951, Ph.D. in Physics, 1954; PhD (hon.), Hebrew U. Jerusalem, 1994. Research physicist Bell Telephone Labs., Murray Hill, N.J., 1954-60; vis. assoc. prof. Columbia U., N.Y.C., 1959-60; prof. physics U. Calif.-San Diego, 1960—. Vis. prof. biology MIT, Cambridge, 1967-68; William Draper Hawkins lectr. U Chgo., May 1986; Raymond and Beverly Sackler disting. lectr. U. Tel-Aviv, June 1986; vis. prof. Hebrew U. of Jerusalem, Israel, spring 1989, 93; bd. govs. Weizmann Inst. Sci., Rehovot, Israel, 1988. Author: Electron Paramagnetic Resonance with Applications to Selected Problems in Biology, 1970; contbr. numerous articles to profl. jous., chpts. to books Bd. govs. Technion-Israel Inst. Tech., 1968 Recipient Oliver E. Buckley Solid State Physics prize, 1976, Inaugural Annual award Internat. Electron Spin Resonance Soc., 1991; NSF fellow, 1967-68. Fellow AAAS, Internat. EPR/ESR Soc. (Zavoisky award 1996); mem. Am. Phys. Soc. (prize 1960, biophysics prize, 1982), Biophys. Soc. (nat. lectr. 1983), Nat. Acad. Scis., Am. Acad. Arts and Scis. (Rumford medal 1992), Sigma Xi Office: U Calif Dept Physics 9500 Gilman Dr Dept 319 La Jolla CA 92093-0319

FEHIR, KIM MICHELE, oncologist, hematologist; b. Chgo., Aug. 31, 1947; d. William Frank and Beatric Mae (Mc Glaughlin) Debelak; m. John Stephen Fehir, Dec. 24, 1974. BS, Mich. State U., 1969; MS, U. Ill., Chgo., 1973, PhD, 1975; MD, Rush Med. Sch., Chgo., 1978. Diplomate Am. Bd. Internal Medicine. Intern, resident John Hopkins Hosp., Balt., 1978-81; fellow in oncology Meml. Sloan Kettering Cancer Ctr., N.Y.C., 1981-83; dir. med. oncology Stehlin Oncology Clin., Houston, 1983—. Asst. prof. medicine Bayler Coll., Houston, 1983-98. Contbr. to profl. jours. Mem. AMA, Am. Med. Soc. Hematologist, Am. Med. Soc. Clin. Oncology. Republican. Avocations: running, climbing, skiing. Office: Med Assocs of Johnson County 497 W Lott St Buffalo WY 82834-1609 E-mail: kfehir@wyoming.com

FEHR, J. WILL, newspaper editor; b. Long Beach, Calif., Mar. 8, 1926; s. John and Evelyn (James) F.; m. Cynthia Moore, Sept. 4, 1951; children— Michael John, Martha Ann B.A. in English, U. Utah, 1951. City editor Salt Lake City Tribune, 1964-80, mng. editor, 1980-81, editor, 1981-91. Served to 1st lt. USAF, 1951-53 Mem. Am. Soc. Newspaper Editors, Sigma Chi Home: 468 13th Ave Salt Lake City UT 84103-3229 Office: Salt Lake City Tribune 143 S Main St Salt Lake City UT 84111-1924

FEHR, LOLA MAE, health facility administrator; b. Hastings, Nebr., Sept. 29, 1936; d. Leland R. and Edith (Wunderlich) Gaymon; m. Harry E. Fehr, Aug. 15, 1972; children: Dawn, Cheryl, Michael. RN, St. Luke's Hosp., Denver, 1958; BSN magna cum laude, U. Denver, 1959; MS, U. Colo., Boulder, 1975. Dir. staff devel. Weld County Gen. Hosp., Greeley, Colo., 1972-76, dir. nursing, 1976-80; exec. dir. Colo. Nurses Assn., Denver, 1980-89; dir. membership Assn. Oper. Rm. Nurses, Inc., Denver, 1989-90, exec. dir., 1990-99; pres. Fehr Cons. Resources, Frisco, Colo., 1999—; exec. dir. Am. Soc. Bariatric Physicians, 2000—. Editor Colo. Nurse, 1980-89. Recipient U. Colo. Alumni award, Colo. Nurses Assn. Profl. Nurse of the Yr. award. Mem. Am. Acad. Nursing, Nat. Assn. Parliamentarians, Am. Soc. Assn. Execs., Colo. Nurses Assn., Sigma Theta Tau.

FEIBELMAN, PETER JULIAN, physicist; b. N.Y.C., Nov. 12, 1942; s. Walter Leonard and Ilse Ruth Feibelman; m. Lorlys Rogers, Dec. 30, 1971; children: Camilla, Adam. BA, Columbia Coll., 1963; PhD, U. Calif., 1967. Fellow Centre d'Etudes Nucleaires Saclay, Gif-sur-Yvette, France, 1968, attaché de recherche du Ctr. Nat. Rsch. Sci. France, 1969; rshc. asst. prof. U. Ill., Urbana, 1969-71; asst. prof. SUNY, Stony Brook, 1971-74; disting. mem. tech. staff Sandia Nat. Labs., Albuquerque, 1974—. Author: (rev. vol.) Surface Electromagnetic Fields, 1982, A PhD Is Not Enough, 1993; mem. adv. editorial bd. Surface Sci., 1980—; divsn. assoc. editor Physical Rev. Letters. Precinct capt. Dem. Party, St. James, N.Y., 1973-74, Albuquerque, 1984-88. Recipient A. von Humboldt award A. von Humboldt Soc., 1980. Fellow Am. Physical Soc. (Davisson-Germer prize 1989), Am. Vacuum Soc. (Medard W. Welch award 1996). Democrat. Avocations: cycling, tennis. Office: Sandia Nat Labs Mail Stop 1413 Albuquerque NM 87185-1413

FEICHTINGER, MARK R. career officer; b. Eugene, Oreg., May 31, 1948; m. Nancy G. Feichtinger. Grad. with distinction, Northwestern U., Evanston, Ill., 1970; JD, U. Mich., 1978. Commd. ensign USN, 1970; advanced through ranks to rear adm. USNR; various assignments to sr. inspector, asst./mission effect.; dep. comdr. submarine force U.S. Pacific Fleet; ptnr. Stoel Rives LLP. Chair Clark County United Way Campaign, 1991-92; active 4-county United Way Bd.; chmn. bd. Clark County's Econ. Devel. Coun.; pres. Cmty. Found. for Southwest Washington. Decorated Navy Meritorious Svc. medal (4 times), Navy Commendation medal (2 times), Navy Achievement medal. Mem. Phi Beta Kappa. Avocations: cycling, reading, railroading, attending auto races. Office: 8060 SW Cedar St Portland OR 97225-2336

FEIDELSON, MARC, advertising executive; b. N.Y.C., Aug. 20, 1939; s. Robert and Ceil (Robbins) F.; m. Linda Sarnoff, June 11, 1964; children— Lee, Pamela. B.S. in Bus. Adminstrn., Boston U., 1961; M.A. in Psychology, CUNY, 1966. Media research analyst CBS-TV, N.Y.C., 1964-65; sr. media research analyst Ted Bates Advt., N.Y.C., 1966-67; media research dir. Benton & Bowles Advt., N.Y.C., 1967-70; media mgr. RCA Corp., N.Y.C., 1970-72; dir. advt. services Hunt-Wesson Foods, Fullerton, Calif., 1973-79; sr. v.p., media dir. Dailey & Assocs. Advt., Los Angeles, 1979— ; guest lectr. UCLA. Mem. Hollywood Radio and TV Soc., Los Angeles Media Dirs. Council (pres. 1981-82). Jewish. Guest editor Media Decisions mag., Apr. 1983. Office: Dailey & Assocs 8687 Melrose Ave West Hollywood CA 90069-5701

FEIG, STEPHEN ARTHUR, pediatrics educator, hematologist, oncologist; b. N.Y.C., Dec. 24, 1937; s. Irving L. and Janet (Oppenheimer) F.; m. Judith Bergman, Aug. 28, 1960; children: Laura, Daniel, Andrew. AB in Biology, Princeton U., 1959; MD, Columbia U., 1963. Diplomate Am. Bd. Pediatrics, Am. Bd. Hematology-Oncology. Intern Mt. Sinai Hosp., N.Y.C., 1963-64, resident in pediatrics, 1964-66; hematology fellow Children's Hosp. Med. Ctr., Boston, 1968-71, assoc. in medicine, 1971-72; asst. prof. pediatrics UCLA, 1972-77, chief div. hematology and oncology, sch. medicine, 1977—, assoc. prof., 1977-82, prof., 1982—, exec. vice chmn. dept. pediatrics sch. mediicne, 1994—. Cons. Olive View Med. Ctr., Van Nuys, Calif., 1973—, Valley Med. Ctr., Fresno, Calif., 1973—, Sunrise Hosp. dept. pediatrics, Las Vegas, Nev., 1980—; med. advisory com. Los Angeles chpt. Leukemia Soc. Am., 1978—; bd. trustees, 1984—; bd. dirs. Camp Ronald McDonald for Good Times; active numerous other pediatric hosp. and med. sch. coms. Reviewer Am. Jour. Pediatric Hematology/Oncology, Blood, Jour. Clin. Investigation, Pediatrics, Pediatric Rsch., Am. Jour. Diseases of Children, Jour. Pediatrics; contbr. articles to profl. jours.; editl. bd. Jour. Pediat. Hematology & Oncology, Stem Cells. Served with USNR, 1966-68. Mem. Am. Soc. Hematology, Soc. Pediatric Research, Am. Pediatric Soc., Internat. Soc. Exptl. Hematology, Am. Assn. Cancer Research. Jewish. Avocation: native arts. Office: UCLA Sch Medicine Dept Pediatrics 10833 Le Conte Ave Los Angeles CA 90095-3075

FEIGENBAUM, EDWARD ALBERT, computer science educator; b. Weehawken, N.J., Jan. 20, 1936; s. Fred J. and Sara Rachman; m. H. Penny Nii, 1975; children: Janet Denise, Carol Leonora, Sheri Bryant, Karin Bryant. BEE, Carnegie Inst. Tech., 1956, Ph.D. in Indsl. Adminstrn., 1960. From asst. prof. to assoc. prof. bus. adminstrn. U. Calif., Berkeley, 1960-64; from assoc. prof. computer sci. to prof. Stanford U., 1965-2000, prin. investigator heuristic programming project and knowledge sys. lab., 1965-2000, dir. Computation Ctr., 1965-68, chmn. dept. computer sci., 1976-81, Kumagai prof. computer sci., 1991-2000, emeritus, 2001—; pres. Intelli Genetics Inc., 1980-81; chmn., dir. Teknowledge, Inc., 1981-82; mem. tech. adv. bd. Intelli Genetics Inc., 1983-86; dir. IntelliCorp, 1984-90; chief scientist USAF, 1994-97; Kumagai prof. computer sci. Stanford (Calif.) U., 1997-2000. Cons. to industry, 1957—; mem. computer and biomath. scis. study sect. NIH, 1968-72, mem. adv. com. on artificial intelligence in medicine, 1974-92; mem. Math. Social Sci. Bd., 1975-78; computer sci. adv. com. NSF, 1977-80; mem. Internat. Joint Coun. on Artificial Intelligence, 1973-83; bd. dirs. Design Power Ind.; scientific adv. bd. USAF, 1997-2000; sci. advisor Air Force Office Sci. Rsch. Author: (with others) Information Processing Language V Manual, 1961, (with P. McCorduck) The Fifth Generation; author: (with R. Lindsay, B. Buchanan, J. Lederberg) Applications of Artificial Intelligence to Organic Chemistry: the Dendral Program; Editor: (with J. Feldman) Computers and Thought, 1963, (with A. Barr and P. Cohen) Handbook of Artificial Intelligence, 1981, 82, 89, (with Pamela McCorduck and H. Penny Nii) The Rise of the Expert Company: How Visionary Companies are using Artificial Intelligence to Achieve Higher Productivity and Profits; mem. editorial bd.: Jour. Artificial Intelligence, 1970-88. Trustee Charles Babbage Found. for the History of Info. Processing, U. Minn., 2000—; pres. Feigenbaum-Nii Found., 2000—. Recipient Exceptional Civilian Svc. award USAF, 1997, Meritorious Civilian Sci. award USAF, 2000; Fulbright scholar, 1959-60; Feigenbaum medal established in his honor World Congress on Expert Systems, 1991. Fellow AAAI, AAAS, Am. Coll. Med. Informatics, Am. Inst. Med. and Biol. Engring.; mem. Nat. Acad. Engring., Assn. Computing Machinery (nat. coun. 1966-68, chmn. spl. interest group on biol. applications 1973-76, A.M. Turing award 1994), Am. Assn. Artificial Intelligence (pres. 1980-81), Am. Acad. Arts and Scis., Cognitive Sci. Soc. (coun. 1979-82), Sigma Xi, Tau Beta Pi, Eta Kappa Nu, Pi Delta Epsilon. Home: 1017 Cathcart Way Palo Alto CA 94305-1048 Office: Stanford U Knowledge Systems Lab Gates Computer Sci Rm 220 Stanford CA 94305-9020

FEIMAN, THOMAS E. investment manager; b. Canton, Ohio, Dec. 21, 1940; s. Daniel Thaviu and Adrienne (Silver) F.; m. Marilyn Judith Miller, June 26, 1966; children: Sheri, Michael. BS in Econs., U. Pa., 1962; MBA, Northwestern U., 1963. CPA, Calif. Staff acct. Arthur Young & Co., L.A., 1963-66; field auditor IRS, L.A., 1966-68; pvt. practice acctg. Thomas Feiman, C.P.A., L.A., 1968-69; ptnr. Wideman & Feiman, C.P.A.s, L.A., 1969-74; pres. Wideman, Feiman, Levy, Sapin & Ko, L.A., 1974-93; investment mgr., v.p. Schroder Wertheim & Co., Inc., 1993-96; CFO Spinal Home Health Systems, Inc., L.A., 1983-85; fin. cons., v.p. Merrill Lynch, 1996—; pres., dir. Urol. Scis. Rsch. Found., 1993—. Sr. instr. UCLA Extension, 1967-84. Trustee Temple Israel of Hollywood, Calif., 1981-83, treas., 1983-84. Recipient cert. of award IRS, 1967. Mem. AICPA, Calif. Soc. CPAs, Northwestern Bus. So. Calif. Club (pres. 1977-80), Northwestern Alumni of So. Calif. Club (trustee 1977-92, treas. 1977-90 L.A.). Republican. Jewish. Office: Merrill Lynch 2029 Century Park E Ste 2800 Century City CA 90067-3014

FEINBERG, LAWRENCE BERNARD, university dean, psychologist; b. Bklyn., June 2, 1940; s. Robert Erwin and Geraldine F.; m. Lynn J. Feinberg; children: Ronald, Nancy, Jillian. B.A., U. Buffalo, 1961; M.S., SUNY, Buffalo, 1963, Ph.D., 1966. Lic. psychologist, Calif. cert. rehab. counselor. Lectr. dept. counselor edn. SUNY, Buffalo, 1965-66; prof. spl. edn. and rehab. Syracuse U., 1966-77, dir. rehab. edn., 1967-77; prof. counselor edn. San Diego State U., 1977—, adj. prof. public health, 1981-96, assoc. dean grad. div. and research, 1977-98, acting dean Coll. Edn., 1984-85, acting dean grad. div. and research, 1986-87, exec. dir internat. programs, 1988-98, assoc. v.p. for rsch. and tech., 1998—. Cons. psychologist VA Hosp., Syracuse, 1970-77; cons. Rehab. Services Adminstrn., HEW, Washington, 1976-77, Nat. Inst. Handicapped Research, U.S. Dept. Edn., 1982; chmn. Nat. Commn. Accreditation of Rehab. Edn., 1974-76; bd. dirs. Nat. Commn. Rehab. Counselor Cert., 1973-77 Author: (with others) Rehabilitation and Poverty: Bridging the Gap, 1969, Rehabilitation in the Inner City, 1970, Education for the Rehabilitation Services, 1974; cons. editor 6 profl. jours.; contbr. articles to profl. jours. Recipient 20 fed. grants, 4 nat. profl. service awards Fellow Am. Psychol. Assn. (treas. div. rehab. psychology 1980-83, pres. div. rehab. psychology 1984-85), Am. Psychol. Soc.; mem. Am. Rehab. Counseling Assn. (pres. 1973, dir. 1980-83), Am. Personnel and Guidance Assn. (dir. 1974), N.Y. State Rehab. Counseling Assn. (pres. 1970), Council Rehab. Counselor Educators (regional dir. 1969-71), Phi Beta Delta (pres. Delta chpt. 1987-89). Home: 5021 Bluff Pl El Cajon CA 92020-8212 Office: San Diego State U Grad Div And Rsch San Diego CA 92182

FEINGOLD, BENJAMIN S. broadcast executive; BA, Brandeis U.; MA, London Sch. Econs.; JD, U. Calif., San Francisco. With Kaye, Scholer, Fierman, Hays & Handler, N.Y.C.; corp. counsel, securities lawyer Sony Pictures Entertainment, 1988, v.p. entertainment transactions, 1989, sr. v.p. corp. devel.; pres. Sony Pictures Entertainment Columbia TriStar Home Video, Culver City, Calif., 1994—. Office: Sony Pictures Entertainment Columbia Tristar Home Video 10202 Washington Blvd Culver City CA 90232-3119

FEINSTEIN, DIANNE, senator; b. San Francisco, June 22, 1933; d. Leon and Betty (Rosenburg) Goldman; m. Bertram Feinstein, Nov. 11, 1962 (dec.); 1 child, Katherine Anne; m. Richard C. Blum, Jan. 20, 1980. BA History, Stanford U., 1955; LLB (hon.), Golden Gate U., 1977; D Pub. Adminstrn. (hon.), U. Manila, 1981; D Pub. Service (hon.), U. Santa Clara, 1981; JD (hon.), Antioch U., 1983, Mills Coll., 1985; LHD (hon.), U. San Francisco, 1988. Fellow Coro Found., San Francisco, 1955-56; with Calif. Women's Bd. Terms and Parole, 1960-66; mem. Mayor's com. on crime, chmn. adv. com. Adult Detention, 1967-69; mem. Bd. Suprs., San Francisco, 1970-78, pres., 1970-71, 74-75, 78; mayor City of San Francisco, 1978-88; senator from Calif. U.S. Senate, Washington, 1992—. Mem. exec. com. U.S. Conf. of Mayors, 1983-88; Dem. nominee for Gov. of Calif., 1990; mem. Nat. Com. on U.S.-China Rels., mem. judiciary com., rules and adminstrn Senate Dem. Policy Com., fgn. rels. com., now on appropriations com. Mem. Bay Area Conservation and Devel. Commn., 1973-78; mem. Senate Fgn. Rels. Com. Recipient Woman of Achievement award Bus. and Profl. Women's Clubs San Francisco, 1970, Disting. Woman award San Francisco Examiner, 1970, Coro Found. award, 1979, Coro Leadership award, 1988, Pres. medal U. Calif., San Francisco, 1988, Scopus award Am. Friends Hebrew U., 1981, Brotherhood/Sisterhood award NCCJ, 1986, Comdr.'s award U.S. Army, 1986, French Legion of Honor, 1984, Disting. Civilian award USN, 1987; named Number One Mayor All-Pro City Mgmt. Team City and State Mag., 1987. Mem. Trilateral Commn., Japan Soc. of No. Calif. (pres. 1988-89), Inter-Am. Dialogue, Nat. Com. on U.S.-China Rels. Office: US Senate 331 Hart Senate Office Bldg Washington DC 20510-0001*

FEINSTEIN, MICHAEL JAY, singer, pianist, musicologist, actor; b. Columbus, Ohio, Sept. 7, 1956; s. Edward and Florence Mazie (Cohen) F. Grad. high sch., Columbus, 1974. Personal archivist Ira Gershwin, L.A., 1977-83; asst. Harry Warren, L.A., 1979-81; recorded with Elektra, Angel. Accompanist Liza Minnelli, Rosemary Clooney, John Bubbles, Rose Marie, Jessie Matthews, Estelle Reiner, Leona Mitchell, 1980-84; singer, pianist Le Mondrian Hotel, West Hollywood, 1984-85, 87, York Hotel, San Francisco, 1985-87, Algonquin Hotel, N.Y.C., 1986, 87, The White House, Washington, 1986, 88, 89, Ritz Hotel, 1986, Mondavi Festival, 1986, Singers Salute to the Songwriter, L.A., 1986, 87, 88, 50th Anniversary George Gershwin Celebration, Hollywood Bowl, L.A., 1987, 100th Birthday Celebration for Irving Berlin, Hollywood Bowl, L.A., 1988 and Carnegie Hall, N.Y., 1988, Royal Command Performance, Palace Theatre, London, 1988, Dominion Theatre, London, 1989; Libr. of Congress Gerswhin Concert, 1989; performed with Houston Pops Orch., 1987, San Francisco Symphony & Pops Orch., 1987, 88, Liza Minnelli in European tour, 1987, Atlanta Symphony, 1988, Aspen Music Festival, Colo., 1988; appeared on Broadway and across country in show Michael Feinstein in Concert: Isn't it Romantic, 1988-89, Piano and Voice, 1990, Cole Porter 100th Birthday Concert Carnegie Hall, 1991; toured with Rosemary Clooney, 1991—; TV appearances include A Musical Toast: The Stars Shine for Pub. TV, 1986, Broadway Sings: The Music of Jule Styne, 1987, George Gershwin Remembered, 1987, Celebrating Gershwin: 'SWonderful, 1987, thirtysomething, 1987, The Two Mrs. Grenvilles, 1987, Nightline, 1988, A Grand Night: The Performing Arts Salute Pub. TV, 1988, Omnibus, 1989, An All-Star Salute to the Pres., 1989, Pat Sajak Show, 1989, Nightwatch, 1989, Royal Command Performance, BBS-TV, 1988, London TV Michael Feinstein in Concert BBC-TV, 1989, PBS-TV, Michael Feinstein in Concert, 1991, Wolf Trap 20th Anniversary Concert, 1991, PBS, Am. Masters-Cole Porter, 1990, others; film, Scenes from the Class Struggle in Beverly Hills; albums include Pure Gershwin, 1985, Live at the Algonquin, 1986, Remember: Michael Feinstein Sings Irving Berlin, 1987, Isn't it Romantic, 1987, Over There: Songs of War and Peace c. 1900-1920, 1989, The M-G-M Album, 1989, Michael Feinstein Sings the Burton Lane Songbook Vol. One, 1990, Michael Feinstein Sings the Jule Styne Songbook, 1991, Pure Imagination, 1991, Michael & George, 1998, Big City Rhythms, 1999; editor: Ira Gershwin Songbook; contbr. articles to Washington Post, N.Y. Times. Recipient Golden Laurel award San Francisco Coun. on Entertainment, 1985, 87, 88, N.Y.C. Seal of Recognition, 1987, Drama Desk award, 1988, Outer Critics Circle award, 1988; scholarships in his honor were established at Calif. State, Los Angeles and Queens Coll., N.Y.C. Mem. ASCAP, AFTRA, SAG, Am. Fedn. Musicians, Actor's Equity, Players Club. Office: care Buddy Morra Morra Brezner & Steinberg Los Angeles CA 90028

FEISS, GEORGE JAMES, III, financial services company executive; b. Cleve., June 24, 1950; s. George James Jr. and Bettie (Kalish) F.; m. Susan Margaret Cassel, May 30, 1981; children: Kalish Ilana Cassel-Feiss, Nika Catherine Cassel-Feiss. BA in Social Studies, Antioch Coll., 1973; MBA in Internat. Fin., Am. Grad. Sch. Internat. Mgmt., Phoenix, 1975. Registered investment advisor, Wash.; CFP Coll. Fin. Planning, Denver. Ptnr. Healthcare Cons., Seattle, 1976-80; pres. M2 Inc., Seattle, 1980—. Pres., CEO, Vivid Image Co., San Diego, 1994—; cons. Sta. KRAB, Seattle, 1988-89, Zion Christian Acad., Seattle, 1990—. Author: Mind Therapies/Body Therapies, 1979, Hope & Death in Exile - The Economics and Politics of Cancer in the United States, 1981. Bd. dirs. B'nai Brith, Seattle, 1988-91; mem. fin. com. Univ. Child Devel. Sch., Seattle, 1989—; mem. social action com. Am. Jewish Com., Seattle, 1992. Mem. Eastside Estate Planning Coun., Inst. for CFPs, Social Investment Forum, Social Venture Network. Avocations: sailing, skiing, travel, writing, sculpture. Office: M2 Inc 1122 E Pike St Seattle WA 98122-3916

FEJER, MARTIN M. physics educator; BA in Physics, Cornell U., 1977; PhD in Applied Physics, Stanford U., 1986. Acting asst. prof. applied physics Stanford (Calif.) U., 1986-89, asst. prof. applied physics, 1989-93, rsch. assoc. phys. sci., 1993-94, assoc. prof., 1994-2000, prof., 2000—, assoc. dir. Ctr. for Nonlinear Optical Materials. Fellow Optical Soc. Am. (W.R. Wood prize 1998); mem. IEEE, Am. Phys. Soc. Achievements include research on nonlinear optical materials and devices, guided waveoptics, microstructured ferroelectrics and semiconductors, photorefractive phenomena, optical characterization of materials and material synthesis processes. Office: Stanford U DL Ginzton Lab 316 Via Pueblo Mall Stanford CA 94305-4085 E-mail: fejer@stanford.edu

FELD, DONALD H. network consultant; b. Marshalltown, Iowa, Mar. 12, 1945; s. Donald C. and Wanda L. (Morgan) F.; m. Ruth L. Hensley, Aug. 29, 1965; children: Donald O., Derrick H. BSEE, Iowa State U., 1968; ME in Indsl. Engring./Ops. Rsch., U. Fla., 1975. Commd. 2d lt. USAF, 1968-94, advanced through grades to col., 1989, comdr. 95th Reconnaissance Squadron U.K., 1985-87; chief tactical sys. divsn. USAF Ctr. for Studies and Analysis, Pentagon, Washington, 1987-90, dir. resources directorate, 1990-91; chief flying tng. divsn. Air Edn. and Tng. Command, Randolph AFB, Tex., 1991-94; ret., 1994; v.p. Commonwealth Cons. Corp., Arlington, Va., 1994-96; network cons. Make Systems, Inc., Mountain View, Calif., 1996-99; dir. Nat. Lab., Enterprise Networking Sys., Inc., Redwood City, 1999—. Decorated DFC with 1 oak leaf cluster, Air Medal with 10 oak leaf clusters, Legion of Merit. Mem. IEEE, Air Force Assn. Avocations: water and snow skiing, computers, camping, golf, antique restoration. Office: Enterprise Networking Sys Inc 370 Convention Way Redwood City CA 94063 also: Make Systems Inc 1 Waters Park Dr Ste 250 San Mateo CA 94403-1163

FELDMAN, DEDE, state legislator; b. West Chester, Pa., Mar. 10, 1947; m. Mark M. Feldman. BA, U. Pa., 1968, MA, 1969. Tchr. pub. h.s., 1970-75; journalist, 1975-82; owner Dede Feldman & Co., Pub. Rels., 1985—; adj. coll. prof., 1980-92; comm. cons.; mem. N.Mex. Senate, Dist. 13, 1996—; mem. conservation com., mem. pub. affairs com. N.Mex. State Senate. Past chair Albuquerque Cmty. Adv. Group; mem. Shared Vision

Land Use and Transp. Caucus; mem. N.Mex. for Open Govt.; mem. North Valley Neighborhood Coalition; former precinct chair, ward chair Dem. Party, also former mem. state ctrl. com. Mem. N.Mex. Press Women (past pres. Albuquerque chpt.), N.Mex. Pub. Rels. Soc. Democrat. Office: 1821 Meadowview Dr NW Albuquerque NM 87104-2511 E-mail: dfeldman@state.nm.us

FELDMAN, JOEL SHALOM, mathematician; b. Ottawa, Ont., Can., June 14, 1949; s. Keiva and Anna (Ain) F. BS, U. Toronto, Ont., 1970; AM, Harvard U., 1971, PhD, 1974. Rsch. fellow Harvard U., Cambridge, Mass., 1974-75; Moore instr. MIT, Cambridge, 1975-77; prof. U. B.C., Vancouver, Can., 1977—; Aisenstadt chair lectr., Ctr. Rsch. Math. U. Montréal, 1999-2000. Assoc. editor Revs. Math. Physics, 1988—, Can. Jour. Math., 1994-98, Can. Math. Bull., 1994-98, Math Phys. EJ, 1995—, Ann. Henri Poincaré, 2000—; contbr. articles to profl. jours. Recipient Killam Rsch. prize U. B.C., 1988; Woodrow Wilson fellow, 1970. Fellow Royal Soc. Can. (John L. Synge award). Office: U BC Dept Math Vancouver BC Canada V6T 1Z2

FELDMAN, ROGER LAWRENCE, artist, educator; b. Spokane, Wash., Nov. 19, 1949; s. Marvin Lawrence and Mary Elizabeth (Shafer) F.; m. Astrid Lunde, Dec. 16, 1972; children: Kirsten B., Kyle Lawrence. BA in Art Edn., U. Wash., 1972; postgrad., Fuller Theol. Sem., Pasadena, Calif., 1972-73, Regent Coll., Vancouver, B.C., 1974; MFA in Sculpture, Claremont Grad. U., 1977. Teaching asst. Claremont (Calif.) Grad. U.; prof. art Biola U., La Mirada, Calif., 1989-2000, Seattle Pacific U., 2000—. Adj. instr. Seattle Pacific U., 1979, 80, 82, 83, Linfield Coll., 1978, Edmonds C.C., 1978-80, Shoreline C.C., 1978; guest artist and lectr. One-man shows include Art Ctr. Gallery, Seattle Pacific U., 1977, 83, 84, Linfield Coll., McMinnville, Oreg., 1979, Blackfish Gallery, Portland, 1982, Lynn McAllister Gallery, Seattle, 1986, Biola U., 1989, 93, Coll. Gallery, La. Coll., Pineville, 1990, Gallery W, Sacramento, 1991, 96, Aughinbaugh Gallery, Grantham, Pa., 1992, Riverside Art Mus., 1994, Azusa Pacific U., 1995, Cornerstone '96, Bushnell, Ill., 1996, Davison Gallery, Roberts Wesleyan Coll., Rochester, N.Y., 1997, Concordia U., Irvine, Calif., 1999, Northwestern Coll., St. Paul, 2000, Union U., Jackson, Tenn., 2001, F. Schaeffer Inst., St. Louis, 2001; group shows include Pasadena Artists Concern Gallery, 1976, Libra Gallery, Claremont, 1977, Renshaw Gallery, McMinnville, 1978, Cheney Cowles Mus., Spokane, 1979, 80, 83, Lynn McAllister Gallery, Seattle, 1985, Bumbershoot, Seattle, 1985, 86, 87, Pacific Arts Ctr., Seattle, 1987, Grand Canyon U., Phoenix, 1990, Connemara, Dallas, 1991, West Bend (Wis.) Gallery, 1992, L.A. Mcpl. Satellite Gallery, 1990, 93, Greenbelt 93, Northamptonshire, Eng., 1993, Claremont Sch. Theology, 1994, Queens Coll. Cambridge U., Eng., 1994, Jr. Arts Ctr. Gallery, Barnsdall Park, L.A., 1994, Bade Mus. Pacific Sch. of Religion, Berkeley, Calif., 1995, Ctrl. Arts Collective, Tucson, 1995, L.A. Mcpl. Gallery Barnsdall Art Park, 1996, Reconstructive Gallery Santa Ana, Ct., 1997, Guggenheim Gallery, Chapman U., Orange, Calif., 1997, Weaver Art Gallery, Bethel Coll., Mishawaka, Ind., 1998-, Concordia U. Art Gallery, Mequon, Wis., 1999, Palos Verdes Art Ctr., Calif., 1999, Grand Canyon U.,Phoenix, 2000, Tryon Ctr. Visual Arts, Charlotte, N.C., 2001, U. Dallas, Tex., 2001; comms. Wheaton, Pasadena, Calif., 1999, Renton Vocat. Tech Inst., 1987-89. Recipient King County Arts Commn. Individual Artist Project award, Seattle, 1988, Natl. Endowment for the Arts Individual Artist fellowship in Sculpture, 1986, David Gaiser award for sculpture Cheney Cowles Mus., 1980, Disting. Award for Harborview Med. Ctr. "Viewpoint", Soc. for Tech. Comm., 1987, Design award for "Seafirst News", Internat. Assn. Bus. Comm., 1987, Pace Setter award, 1987, others; Connemara Sculpture grant, 1990, Biola U., 1991. Office: Seattle Pacific U 3307 Third Ave West Seattle WA 98119 E-mail: rfeldman@spu.edu

FELDMAN, STANLEY GEORGE, state supreme court justice; b. N.Y.C., N.Y., Mar. 9, 1933; s. Meyer and Esther Betty (Golden) F.; m. Norma Arambula; 1 dau., Elizabeth L. Student, U. Calif., Los Angeles, 1950-51; LL.B., U. Ariz., 1956. Bar: Ariz. 1956. Practiced in, Tucson, 1956-81; ptnr. Miller, Pitt & Feldman, 1968-81; justice Ariz. Supreme Ct., Phoenix, 1982—, chief justice, 1992-97. Lectr. Coll. Law, U. Ariz., 1965-76, adj. prof., 1976-81. Bd. dirs. Tucson Jewish Community Council, U. Ariz. Found., 1999—. Mem. ABA, Am. Bd. Trial Advocates (past pres. So. Ariz. chpt.), Ariz. Bar Assn. (pres. 1974-75, bd. govs. 1967-76), Pima County Bar Assn. (past pres.), Am. Trial Lawyers Assn. (dir. chpt. 1967-76). Democrat. Jewish. Office: Ariz Supreme Ct 1501 W Washington St Phoenix AZ 85007-3222

FELDSTEIN, PAUL JOSEPH, management educator; b. N.Y.C., Oct. 4, 1933; s. Nathan and Sarah Feldstein; m. Anna Martha Lee, Dec. 24, 1968; children: Julie, Jennifer. BA in Econs., CCNY, 1955; MBA in Fin., U. Chgo., 1957, PhD in Econs., 1961. Dir. divsn. rsch. Am. Hosp. Assn., Chgo., 1961-64; prof. Sch. Pub. Health U. Mich., Ann Arbor, 1964-87; prof. Grad. Sch. Mgmt. U. Calif., Irvine, 1987—. Author: Health Care Economics, 5th rev. 1998, Health Policy Issues: An Economic Perspective on Health Reform, 2nd edit., 1999, The Politics of Health Legislation, 2nd edit., 1996; contbr. articles to profl. jours. 1st lt. inf. U.S. Army, 1955-57. Mem. Am. Econs. Assn. Avocations: jogging, biking. Office: U Calif Grad Sch Mgmt Irvine CA 92697-0001 E-mail: pfeldste@uci.edu

FELES, ARISTEDES, automotive parts manfacturing executive; Sr. acct. BDO Seidman, LLP, 1989-92; controller Edelbrock Corp., Torrance, Calif., 1992-97, dir., v.p. fin., 1997—. Office: Edelbrock Corp 2700 California St Torrance CA 90503

FELIX, RICHARD E. academic administrator; Pres. Azusa (Calif.) Pacific U., 1985—. Office: Azusa Pacific U Office of President 901 E Alosta Ave Azusa CA 91702-2769

FELL, JAMES FREDERICK, lawyer; b. Toledo, Nov. 18, 1944; s. George H. Fell and Bibianne C. (Hebert) Franklin; children from a previous marriage: Jennifer A., Brian F.; m. Betty L. Wenzel, May 23, 1981. BA, U. Notre Dame, 1966; JD, Ohio State U., 1969. Bar: N.Y. 1970, Calif. 1972, Idaho 1978, Wash. 1981, Oreg. 1984, U.S. Ct. Appeals (9th cir.) 1983, U.S. Dist. Ct. Idaho 1978. Assoc. Breed, Abbott & Morgan, N.Y.C., 1969-72; ptnr. McKenna & Fitting, L.A., 1972-78; atty. Office Atty. Gen., State of Idaho, Boise, 1978-79; dir. policy and administrn. Idaho Pub. Utilities Commn., Boise, 1979-81; gen. counsel, dep. dir. Northwest Power Planning Coun., Portland, Oreg., 1981-84; ptnr. Stoel Rives LLP, Portland, 1984—. Mem. ABA (pub. utility law sect.), Oreg. State Bar (pub. utility law sect.). Office: Stoel Rives LLP 900 SW 5th Ave Ste 2600 Portland OR 97204-1268

FELLER, DAVID E. law educator, arbitrator; b. 1916. AB, Harvard U., 1938, LLB, 1941. Bar: Mass. 1941, D.C. 1942. Lectr. law and econs. U. Chgo., 1941-42; atty. U.S. Dept. Justice, Washington, 1946-48; law clk. U.S. Supreme Ct., 1948-49; assoc. gen. counsel CIO, Washington, 1949-53, United Steelworkers, Washington, 1949-60; gen. counsel ind. union dept. AFL-CIO, Washington, 1961-66, United Steelworkers, 1961-65; ptnr. Goldberg Feller & Bredhoff, Washington, 1955-60, Feller, Bredhoff & Anker, 1961-65, Feller & Anker, 1965-67, John H. Boalt prof. emeritus U. Calif.-Berkeley Sch. Law. Editor Harvard Law Rev. Bd. dirs. NAACP Legal Def. and Edn. Fund, 1960-97; pres. Council Univ. Calif. Faculty Assns., 1973-89. Mem. Nat. Acad. Arbitrators (v.p. 1985-87, pres. 1992-93), Fed. Mediation and Conciliation Service Roster of Arbitrators, ABA (sec. labor law sect. 1972-73), Phi Beta Kappa. Home: 728 Santa Barbara Rd Berkeley CA 94707-2005 Office: U Calif Sch of Law Boalt Hall Berkeley CA 94720-7200

FELLER, RALPH PAUL, dentist, educator; b. Quincy, Mass., Aug. 31, 1934; s. Paul Frederich and Frances Elizabeth (Hubert) F.; children: Lynne Anne Feller Grenier, Paul Herbert, Wendy Elizabeth. BS, Tufts U., 1956, DMD, 1964; MS, U. Tex., Houston, 1975; MPH, Loma Linda U., 1981. Asst. prof. Harvard U., Boston, 1965-71; assoc. prof. U. Tex. Med. Br., Houston, 1971-75; clin. investigator VA Med. Ctr., Houston, 1971-75, chief dental svc. Lyons, N.J., 1975-77, Loma Linda, Calif., 1977-95; assoc. prof. Fairleigh Dickinson U., Hackensack, N.J., 1975-77; prof., dir. clin. rsch. ctr. Loma Linda U. Sch. Dentistry, 1995—. Cons. Johnson & Johnson, East Windsor, N.J., 1980-85, Oral-B Labs., Inc., Redwood City, Calif., 1986-92, Richardson-Vicks, Shelton, Conn., 1988-92, Colgate-Polmolive Co., Piscataway, N.J., 1988—. Contbr. articles to profl. jours. Col. USAR, 1960-95, ret. Mem. ADA (Achievement award 1995), Internat. Assn. Dental Rsch. (numerous offices 1964—), am. Coll. Prosthodontists, Am. Assn. Dental Schs., Calif. Dental Assn., Assn. Mil. Surgeons U.S., Rotary. Avocations: boating, golf. Home: 30832 Alta Mira Dr Redlands CA 92373-7402 Office: Loma Linda U Sch Dentistry Loma Linda CA 92350-0001 Fax: (909) 558-0328. E-mail: rpfeller@aol.com

FELSINGER, DONALD E. utilities corporation executive; BSME, U. Ariz. Exec. v.p. SDG&E (subs. Enova Corp.), 1993-96, pres., CEO, 1996-98, Enova Corp., 1998; group pres., unregulated affils. Sempra Energy (merger of Pacific Enterprises/Enova Corp.), San Diego, 1998—. Bd. dirs. Edison Electric Inst. Bd. dirs. U.S.-Mexico C. of C., Greater San Diego C. of C., Inst. of the Americas, San Diego Holiday Bowl. Office: Sempra Energy 101 Ash St San Diego CA 92112

FELTON, JEAN SPENCER, physician; b. Oakland, Calif., Apr. 27, 1911; s. Herman and Tess (Davidson) F.; m. Janet E. Birnbaum, June 27, 1937 (dec.); children: Gary, Keith, Robin; m. Suzanne E. Colvin, Sept. 2, 1990. AB, Stanford U., 1931, MD, 1935. Diplomate: Am. Bd. Preventive Medicine, Am. Bd. Indsl. Hygiene. Intern Mt. Zion Hosp., San Francisco, 1934-35, resident in surgery, 1935-36, Dante Hosp., San Francisco, 1936-38; practice medicine San Francisco, 1938-40; guest lectr. indsl. sociology U. Tenn. at Knoxville, 1946-53; med. dir. Oak Ridge Nat. Lab., 1946-53; cons. dept. medicine, prof. dept. preventive medicine, pub. health U. Okla. Med. Sch., 1953-58; cons. indsl. hygiene Okla. State Dept. Health, 1953-58; past cons. VA, St. Louis area; prof. occupational health U. Calif. Schs. Medicine and Pub. Health, Los Angeles, 1958-68; dir. occupational health service Dept. Personnel, County Los Angeles, 1968-74; med. dir. occupational health Naval Regional Med. Center, Long Beach, Calif., 1974-78; clin. prof. community medicine U. So. Calif., 1968-82, clin. prof. emeritus, 1982—; clin. prof. medicine U. Calif., Irvine, 1975—. Cons. occupational health NASA, USN, VA, AEC, USPHS, Social Security Adminstrn., 1955-62; Fellow through Distinction faculty occupational medicine Royal Coll. Physicians, London, 1997—. Author: (with A. H. Katz) Health and Community, 1965, Man, Medicine, and Work, 1965, Occupational Medical Management, 1990; bd. dirs. Excerpta Medica, Sect. XXXV, The Netherlands; mem. editl. panel Occupational Medicine, London, 1994—; contbr. articles to med. jours. Past mem. youth svc. com. Oak Ridge Welfare Coun., 1946-53; past mem. Tenn. Commn. on Childen, Welfare Svcs. Dept.; chmn., mem. adv. bd. Oak Ridge; past mem. Gov.'s Com. on Utilization Physically Handicapped Pres.'s Com. on Employment People with Disabilities, 1947-94. Lt. col. M.C., 1940-46. Decorated Army Commendation Ribbon, 1946; recipient Citation for Excellence in Med. Authorship by Am. Assn. Indsl. Physicians and Surgeons, 1948; Knudsen award Indsl. Med. Assn., 1968; Physician of Yr. award Calif. Gov.'s Com. on Employment of Handicapped, 1979; Physician of Yr. award Pres.'s Com. on Employment of Handicapped, 1979 Fellow Am. Coll. Preventive Medicine (pres. 1966-67), Am. Acad. Occupational Medicine, Am. Occupational Med. Assn. (Meritorious Svc. award 1965, Health Achievement in Industry award 1983), Am. Pub. Health Assn., Collegium Ramazzini (coun. of fellows 1994—); mem. AMA (sec., vice chmn. sect. preventive and indsl. medicine and pub. health 1949-53, chmn. sect. 1953), Am. Indsl. Hygiene Assn., Nat. Rehab. Assn. So. Calif. (dir.), So. Calif. Ind. Hygiene Assn. (past pres.), Am. Coll. Occupational Medicine (Robert A. Kehoe award 1989), New Eng. Occupational Med. Assn. (Harriet F. Hardy award 1989), Soc. Occupational Medicine (hon.). Unitarian. Achievements include preparing standard operating procedure of U.S. Army indsl. med. program at San Francisco Port of Embarkation (adopted by the U.S. Army Chief of Transp. for use by all Ports of Embarkation). Home: PO Box 246 45150 Cypress Dr Mendocino CA 95460-9796 Office: U Calif Dept Medicine Nelson Rsch Ctr Bldg Med Sci Complex Irvine CA 92717 E-mail: jfelton@mcn.org

FENIMORE, GEORGE WILEY, management consultant; b. Bertrand, Mo., 1921; BBA in Fin., Northwestern U., 1941; LLB, Harvard U., 1947; postgrad., UCLA, 1955; LLD (hon.), Southwestern U., 1992. Bar: Mich. 1948. Asst. to dir. planning Ford Motor Co., Dearborn, Mich., 1947-48; exec. to v.p. and gen. mgr. Hughes Aircraft Co., Culver City, Calif., 1948-53; adminstrv. mgr. tech. products Packard Bell Electronics Co., 1954-55; with TRW, Inc., Los Angeles, 1955-64; v.p., gen. mgr. TRW Internat., Los Angeles, 1959-64; v.p. internat. ops. Bunker Ramo Corp., Los Angeles, 1964-65; dir. public relations, then corp. sec. Litton Industries, Inc., Beverly Hills, Calif., 1965-73, v.p., corp. sec., 1973-81, sr. v.p., corp. sec., 1981-86, mgmt. cons., 1986—; sr. v.p. Peck Jones Constrn., Beverly Hills. Past chmn. bd. Southwestern U. Sch. Law; mem. Calif. Tchrs. Retirement Bd. Bd. dirs. Children's Bur. L.A., Child Shelter Homes a Rescue Effort; sec. French Found. for Alzheimer's Rsch.; mem. Calif. Fair Polit. Practices Commn., 1986-91; mem. United Way Emergency Food Sys. Study Task Force; elder, chmn. fin. com. Westwood Presbyn. Ch.; past trustee Sheldon Jackson Coll., Sitka, Alaska; mem. Beverly Hills Mayor's Econ. Adv. Com. and MOVE com. Maj. USAAF, WW II. Recipient Citizen of Yr. award Beverly Hills Lions Club, 1976, Spirit Honoree Beverly Hills Edn. Found., 1986, Beverly Hills YMCA, 1988, Brentwood/San Vicente C. of C., 1987, Hon. Citizen award Beverly Hills City Coun., 1986, Guardian Angel award Child S.H.A.R.E., 1989, Highest award for Lifetime Svc. to Cmty., Key to City of Beverly Hills, 1990, State Gold award Calif. Tchrs. Assn., 1993. Mem. Am. Soc. Corp. Secs. (dir., past nat. dir., past pres. Los Angeles Group), Beverly Hills C. of C. (past pres., Citizen of Yr. award 1979, chmn. edn. com., bd. dirs., David Orgell Meml. award 1990), Mandeville Canyon Assn. (past pres.), Bar Assn. Mich., L.A. Country Club, Rotary (past pres. Beverly Hills, Paul Harris fellow, William C. Ackerman trophy 1986), Shriners. Presbyterian. Office: 10866 Wilshire Blvd Los Angeles CA 90049

FENNELL, DIANE MARIE, marketing executive, process engineer; b. Panama, Iowa, Dec. 11, 1944; d. Urban William and Marcella Mae (Leytham) Schechinger; m. Leonard E. Fennell, Aug. 19, 1967; children: David, Denise, Mark. BS, Creighton U., Omaha, 1966. Process engr. Tex. Instruments, Richardson, 1974-79; sr. process engr. Signetics Corp., Santa Clara, Calif., 1979-82; demo lab. mgr. Airco Temescal, Berkeley, 1982-84; field process engr. Applied Materials, Santa Clara, 1984-87; mgr. product mktg. Lam Rsch., Fremont, Calif., 1987-90; dir. sales and mktg. Ion & Plasma Equipment, Fremont, 1990-91; pres. FAI, Half Moon Bay, 1990-96; v.p. mktg. Tegal Corp., Petaluma, 1997-99; v.p. mktg./sales Semicaps, Inc., Santa Clara, 1999—. Founder, coord. chmn. Plasma Etch User's Group, Santa Clara, 1984-87, tchr. computer course Hatch Sch., Half Moon Bay, Calif., 1982-83. Founder, bd. dirs. Birth to Three program Mental Retardation Ctr., Denison, Tex., 1974-75; fund raiser local sch. band, Half Moon Bay, 1981-89; community rep. local sch. bd., Half Moon Bay, 1982-83. Mem. Am. Vacuum Soc., Soc. Photo Instrumnentation Engrs., Soc. Women Engrs., Material Rsch. Soc., Commonwealth Club. Avocations: hiking, reading, gardening. Home: 441 Alameda Ave Half Moon Bay CA 94019-3337

FENNELLY, JANE COREY, lawyer; b. N.Y.C., Dec. 12, 1942; d. Joseph and Josephine (Corey) F. BA, Cornell U., 1964; MLS, UCLA, 1968; JD, Loyola U., L.A., 1974. Bar: Calif. 1974, U.S. Dist. Ct. (ctrl. and so. dists.) Calif. 1974, U.S. Dist. Ct. (ea. dist.) Calif. 1977, U.S. Dist. Ct. (no. dist.) Calif. 1980, N.Y. 1982, Colo. 1993, Ariz. 1995. Ptnr. Graham & James, 1976-83; with legal dept. Bank of Am., L.A., 1973-76, Wyman, Bautzer, Kuchel & Silbert, L.A., 1983-87, Dennis, Shafer, Fennelly & Creim (merged with Bronson & McKinnon), L.A., 1987-96; with Squire, Sanders & Dempsey, Phoenix, 1996-98, Fennelly & Assocs., Phoenix, 1998—. Mem. ABA, N.Y. State Bar Assn., Am. Bankruptcy Inst., Calif. Bankruptcy Forum, L.A. County Bar Assn. (bd. dirs., mem. exec. com. comml. law and bankruptcy sect. 1989-92), Maricopa County Bar Assn., Scottsdale Bar Assn., Fin. Lawyers Conf. (pres. bd. dirs. 1983-84, mem. bd. govs. 1984—). Home: 15356 W Pasadena Dr Surprise AZ 85374 Office: 2916 N 7th Ave Ste 208 Phoenix AZ 85013 E-mail: jane.fennelly@azbar.org

FENNER, PETER DAVID, communications executive; b. Newark, Apr. 18, 1936; s. John David and Janice (Gleason) F.; m. Nancy Carrell Royce, Aug. 1958; children: Guy David, Karl Gleason, James Andrew. BS in Indsl. Engring., Lehigh U., 1958; MSBA, MIT, 1975. Field engr. Factory Mut.Engring., Montclair, N.J., 1958-61; assignments in engring., d.p., and software devel. Western Electric Co., Inc., N.J., N.Y., Mo., Colo., Calif., Mass., 1961-82; regional v.p. AT&T Network Systems (now Lucent Techs.), Balt. and Bethesda, Md., 1982-85; v.p. product planning, Morristown AT&T Network Systems, Balt. and Bethesda, 1986-88, pres. Transmission Systems, 1989-92; mgmt. cons., 1993-95; CEO, COM 21, Milpitas, Calif., 1996-2001. Bd. dirs. SBS Techs., Albuquerque, BitMicro, Fremont, Calif., Active Strategies, Pa. Sloan fellow MIT, Cambridge, 1974-75. Mem. Westhampton Yacht Squadron, Westhampton Country Club. Avocations: sailing, tennis. Home and Office: 215 Hanna Way Menlo Park CA 94025-3583

FENNESSEY, PAUL VINCENT, pediatrics and pharmacology educator, research administrator; b. Oct. 3, 1942; m. Susan Blackwell; children: Shirley, Karl, Shaun. BS in Chemistry, U. Okla., 1964; PhD of Organic Analytical Chemistry, MIT, 1968. Rsch. asst. U. Okla., Norman, 1963-64; predoctoral fellow MIT, Cambridge, 1964-69; asst. prof. pediat. and pharmacology U. Colo. Health Sci. Ctr., Denver, 1975-81, co-dir. mass spectral ctr., 1980, assoc. prof. pediat. and pharmacology, 1981-90, prof. pediat. and pharmacology, 1990—, vice chair pediat., 1991—. Contbr. articles to profl. jours. Asst. program scientist Viking Project, Martin Marietta Corp., Denver, 1969-72, program scientist, 1972-74. Recipient NSF Undergrad. Rsch. award, 1963-64, Merck award in Organic Chemistry, 1963; fellow Woodrow Wilson, 1964-65, NIH, 1964-68. Mem. Am. Chem. Soc., Am. Soc. Mass Spectrometry, Nat. Acad. Clin. Biochemists, Soc. Inherited Metabolic Diseases, Am. Soc. Pharmacology and Exptl. Therapeutics, Internat. Soc. Study Xenobiotics, Sigma Xi. Home: 13009 S Parker Ave Pine CO 80470-9617 Office: U Colo Health Sci Ctr 4200 E 9th Ave # C232 Denver CO 80220-3706 Fax: (303) 315-0080. E-mail: paul.fennessey@echsc.edu

FENNING, LISA HILL, lawyer, mediator, former federal judge; b. Chgo., Feb. 22, 1952; d. Ivan Byron and Joan (Hennigar) Hill; m. Alan Mark Fenning, Apr. 3, 1977; 4 children. BA with honors, Wellesley Coll., 1971; JD, Yale U., 1974. Bar: Ill. 1975, Calif. 1979, U.S. Dist. Ct. (no. dist.) Ill., U.S. Dist. Ct. (no., ea., so. & cen. dists.) Calif., U.S. Ct. Appeals (6th, 7th & 9th cirs.), U.S. Supreme Ct. 1989. Law clk. U.S. Ct. Appeals 7th cir., Chgo., 1974-75; assoc. Jenner and Block, Chgo., 1975-77, O'Melveny and Myers, L.A., 1977-85; judge U.S. Bankruptcy Ct. Cen. Dist. Calif., L.A., 1985-2000; mediator JAMS, Orange, Calif., 2000-01; ptnr. Dewey Ballantine LLP, L.A., 2001—. Bd. govs. Nat. Conf. Bankruptcy Judges, 1989-92; pres. Nat. Conf. of Women's Bar Assns., N.C., 1987-88, pres.-elect, 1986-87, v.p., 1985-86, bd. dirs.; lectr., program coord. in field; bd. govs. Nat. Conf. Bankruptcy Judges Endowment for Edn., 1992-97, Am. Bankruptcy Inst., 1994-2000; mem., bd. advisors Nat. Jud. Edn. Program to Promote Equality for Women and Men in the Cts., 1994—. Mem., bd. advisors: Lawyer Hiring & Training Report, 1985-87; contbr. articles to profl. jours. Durant scholar Wellesley Coll., 1971; named one of Am's. 100 Most Important Women Ladies Home Jour., 1988, one of L.A.'s 50 Most Powerful Women Lawyers, L.A. Bus. Jour., 1998. Fellow Am. Bar Found., Am. Coll. Bankruptcy (bd. regents 1995-98); mem. ABA (standing com. on fed. jud. improvements 1995-98, mem. commn. on women in the profession 1987-91, Women's Caucus 1987—, Individual Rights and Responsibilities sect. 1984—, bus. law sect. 1986—, bus. bankruptcy com.), Nat. Assn. Women Judges (nat. task force gender bias in the cts. 1986-87, 93-94), Nat. Conf. Bankruptcy Judges (chair endowment edn. bd. 1994-95), Am. Bankruptcy Inst. (nominating com. 1994-95, bd. steering com. stats. project 1994-96), Calif. State Bar Assn. (chair com. on women in law 1986-87), Women Lawyers' Assn. L.A. (ex officio mem., bd. dirs., chmn., founder com. on status of women lawyers 1984-85, officer nominating com. 1986, founder, mem. Do-It-Yourself Mentor Network 1986-96), Phi Beta Kappa. Democrat. Office: Dwery Ballantine LLP 333 S Grand Ave 26th Fl Los Angeles CA 90071 E-mail: Lfenning@deweyballantine.com

FENTON, DONALD MASON, retired oil company executive; b. L.A., May 23, 1929; s. Charles Youdan and Dorothy (Mason) F.; m. Margaret M. Keehler, Apr. 24, 1953; children: James Michael, Douglas Charles. BS, U. Calif., L.A., 1952, PhD, 1958. Chemist Rohm and Haas Co., Phila., 1958-61; sr. rsch. chemist Union Oil Co., Brea, Calif., 1962-67, rsch. assoc., 1967-72, sr. rsch. assoc., 1972-82, mgr. planning and devel., 1982-85; mgr. new tech. devel. Unocal, Brea, 1985-92. Cons. AMSCO, 1967-73; co-founder, 1st chmn. Petroleum Environ. Rsch. Forum; chmn. bd. dirs. Calif. Engring. Found., 1991-92. With U.S. Army, 1953-55. Inventor in field. Fellow Am. Inst. Chemists, Alpha Chi Sigma; mem. Am. Chem. Soc. Achievements include more than 100 patents in field; co-invention of unisulf process. Home: 2861 E Alden Pl Anaheim CA 92806-4401

FENTON, LEWIS LOWRY, lawyer; b. Palo Alto, Calif., Aug. 20, 1925; s. Norman and Jessie (Chase) F.; m. Gloria J. Palmieri, Aug. 21, 1978; children: Lewis Lowry, Juanita F. Donnelly, Daniel Norman, Pamela Chase. B.A., Stanford U., 1948, LL.B., 1950. Bar: Calif. 1950, U.S. Dist. Ct. (no. dist.) Calif. Atty. Calif. Dept. Pub. Works, 1950-52; chmn., bd. dirs. Hoge, Fenton, Jones & Appel, Inc., Monterey, San Luis Obispo and San Jose, 1952-93; counsel Fenton & Keller, P.C., Monterey, 1993—, Hoge, Fenton, Jones & Appel, Inc., San Jose, 1993—. Bd. dirs. 1st Nat. Bank Monterey County, 1984— (chmn. 1987-90). Mem. bldg. com. Community Hosp. Monterey Peninsula, Carmel, 1961-62; found. dir. Monterey Jazz Festival, 1958; past bd. dirs. Monterey Peninsula Coll., pres. 1971-72, Monterey Inst. Fgn. Studies; past pres. and bd. dirs. York Sch., Monterey, Calif., 1960-74, chmn. bd., 1992—; bd. dirs. Monterey Bay Aquarium, Community Found. Monterey County, chmn., 1998—; bd. visitors Stanford Law Sch. Served to 2d lt. USAAF, 1942-46. Fellow Am. Coll. Trial Lawyers, Internat. Acad. Trial Lawyers; mem. ABA, Calif. Bar Assn., Santa Clara Bar Assn., Monterey County Bar Assn. (pres. 1963, 1st Chief Justice Gibson award), [illegible] Advocacy, Nat. Assn. R.R. Counsel, Internat. Assn. Def. Counsel, Def. Research Inst., Am. Judicature Soc., Am. Acad. Hosp. Attys., Am. Bd. Trial Advs. (adv.), Stanford U. Alumni Assn. (pres. 1966-67), Calif. Med. Legal Nat. Health Lawyers Assn. Episcopalian (vestryman, sr. warden 1956-58). Clubs: Cypress Point, Old Capital, Pacheco, Pacific Union. Home and Office: PO Box 791 Monterey CA 93942-0791 E-mail: LFenton@fentonkeller.com, [illegible]

FENTON, NOEL JOHN, venture capitalist; b. New Haven, May 24, 1938; s. Arnold Alexander and Carla (Mathiasen) F.; m. Sarah Jane Hamilton, Aug. 14, 1965; children: Wendy, Devon, Peter, Lance. B.S., Cornell U., 1959; M.B.A., Stanford U., 1963. Research asst. Stanford (Calif.) U., 1963-64; v.p. Mail Systems Corp., Redwood City, Calif., 1964-66; v.p., gen. mgr. products div. Acurex Corp., Mountain View, 1966-72, pres., chief exec. officer, dir., 1972-83, Covalent Systems Corp., Sunnyvale, 1983-86; mng. gen. ptnr. Trinity Ventures Ltd., 1986—. Bd. dirs. Requisite Tech., Inc., Netigy, Inc., LoopNet, Inc., SciQuest, Inc., Medchannel, Inc., ChipData, Inc. Chmn. adv. coun. resource Ctr. for Women, chmn. bd. dirs. 1987-88; mem. San Jose Econ. Devel. Task Force, 1983, Young Pres.'s Orgn., 1976-88, Pres. Reagan's Bus. Adv. Panel; mem. World Pres.'s Orgn., 1988—, dir., 1994-2000. Lt. (j.g.) USN, 1959-61. Mem. Am. Electronics Assn. (chmn. 1978-79, dir. 1976-80), Santa Clara County Mfrs. Group (dir. 1980-83), Chief Execs. Orgn., Stanford Bus. Sch. Alumni Assn. (pres. 1976-77, dir. 1971-76), Stanford Alumni Assn. (exec. bd. 1985-89). Republican. Epsicopalian. Home: 247 Mapache Dr Portola Vally CA 94028-7354 Office: Trinity Ventures Bldg 4 3000 Sand Hill Rd Ste 160 Menlo Park CA 94025-7113

FENVES, GREGORY L. engineering educator; Prof. civil engring. U. Calif., Berkeley. Recipient Walter L. Huber Civil Engring. Rsch. prize ASCE, 1995. Office: U Calif Dept Civil Engring 760 Davis Hall Berkeley CA 94720-1710

FENWICK, JAMES HENRY, editor; b. South Shields, Eng., Mar. 17, 1937; came to U.S., 1965; s. James Henry and Ellen (Tinmouth) F.; m. Suzanne Helene Hatch, Jan. 27, 1968. BA, Oxford U., Eng., 1960. Freelance lectr., writer, 1960-65; assoc. editor Playboy mag., Chgo., 1965-71; planning and features editor Radio Times, BBC, London, 1971-77, U.S. rep. N.Y.C., 1978-87; sr. editor Modern Maturity mag., Lakewood, Calif., 1987-90, exec. editor, 1990-91, editor, 1991-98; contbg. editor Get Up and Go!, Age Wave Comm., Lakewood, 1998-99; editor Next Mag., Palm Springs, 2000—.

FENZL, TERRY EARLE, lawyer; b. Milw., Mar. 19, 1945; s. Earle A. and Elaine A. (Chandler) F.; m. Barbara Louise Pool, June 24, 1967; children: Allison, Andrew, Ashley. BBA, U. Wis., 1966; JD, U. Mich., 1969. Bar: Ariz. 1970, U.S. Dist. Ct. Ariz. 1970, U.S. Ct. Claims 1970, U.S. Ct. Appeals (9th cir.) 1973, U.S. Supreme Ct. 1973, U.S. Dist. Ct. (no. dist.) Calif. 1983. Assoc. Brown & Bain, P.A. and predecessor firms, Phoenix, 1969-74, ptnr., 1975—. Mem. ABA, Ariz. State Bar Assn., Maricopa County Bar Assn., Ariz. Town Hall. Democrat. Mem. United Ch. of Christ. Home: 6610 N Central Ave Phoenix AZ 85012-1014 Office: Brown & Bain PA PO Box 400 Phoenix AZ 85001-0400 E-mail: fenzl@brownbain.com

FEOLA, LOUIS, broadcast executive; Pres. MCA/Universal Home Video, Inc., North Hollywood, Calif., 1983-98, Universal Family & Home Entertainment Prodn., North Hollywood, 1998—. Office: Universal Family & Home Entertainment Prodn Bldg 13200 100 Universal City Plz Universal Cty CA 91608-1002

FERBER, NORMAN ALAN, retail executive; b. N.Y.C., Aug. 25, 1948; m. Rosine Abergel; children: Robert, Lauren, Richard. Student, Bklyn. Coll., 1965-68, L.I.U., 1968-70. Buyer, mdse. mgr. Atherton Industries, N.Y.C., 1976-79; v.p., mdse. mgr. Raxton Corp., N.Y.C., 1979-82; v.p. Fashion World, N.Y.C., 1982; v.p merchandising, mktg. and distbn. Ross Stores Inc., Newark, 1984-87, exec. v.p., COO, 1987-88, pres., CEO, 1988-93, chmn., CEO, 1993-96, chmn., 1996—. Office: Ross Stores Inc PO Box 728 8333 Central Ave Newark CA 94560-3440

FERBER, ROBERT RUDOLF, physics researcher, educator, science administrator; b. June 11, 1935; s. Rudolf F. and Elizabeth J. (Robertson) F.; m. Eileen Merhaut, July 25, 1964; children: Robert Rudolf, Lynne C. BSEE, U. Pitts., 1958; MSEE, Carnegie-Mellon U., 1966, PhD in Semiconductor Physics, 1967. Registered profl. engr., Pa. Mgr. engring. dept. WRS Motion Picture Labs., Pitts., 1954-58, sec., 1959-76, v.p., 1976-79; sr. engr. Westinghouse Rsch. Labs., Pitts., 1956-67; mgr. nuclear effects group Westinghouse Elec. Corp., Pitts., 1967-71, mgr. adv. engr. energy projects East Pittsburgh, 1971-77; photovoltaic materials and collector rsch. mgr. Jet Propulsion Lab., Pasadena, Calif., 1977-85, SP100 Project contract tech. mgr., 1985-90, asst. project mgr. Spaceborne Imaging Radar, 1990-96, Earth Observing Sys. microwave limb sounder radiometer mgr., 1995-99, mgr. Herschel HIFI project amplifier devel. task mgr., 2000—. V.p. Executaire Inc., Pitts., 1960-64; pres. Tele-Cam Inc., Pitts., 1960-78. Editor: Transactions of the 9th World Energy Conf. 1974, Digest of the 9th World Energy Conf., 1974. Contbr. articles to profl. jours.; patentee in field. Mem. Franklin Regional Sch. Dist. Bd., Murrysville, Pa., 1975-77. Fellow Buhl Found., 1965-66, NDEA, 1976-77. Mem. IEEE (sr.), ASME (chmn. 1986 Solar Energy divsn. conf.). Republican. Lutheran. Home: 5314 Alta Canyada Rd La Canada Flintridge CA 91011-1606 Office: NASA Jet Propulsion Lab 4800 Oak Grove Dr Pasadena CA 91109-8001 E-mail: robert.r.ferber@jpl.nasa.gov

FERGUS, GARY SCOTT, lawyer; b. Racine, Wis., Apr. 20, 1954; s. Russell Malcolm and Phyl Rose (Muratore) F.; m. Isabelle Sabina Beekman, Sept. 28, 1985; children: Mary Marckwald Beekman Fergus, Kirkpatrick Russell Beekman Fergus. SB, Stanford U., 1976; JD, U. Wis., 1979; LLM, NYU, 1981. Bar: Wis. 1979, Calif. 1980. Assoc. Brobeck, Phleger & Harrison, San Francisco, 1980-86, ptnr., 1986-2000, mng. ptnr. products liability, ins. coverage, environ. and antitrust/appellate practices, 1996-2000, ptnr. internet and E-commerce team, 2000—, sr. ptnr. e-commerce anti-trust group, 2000—. Energy Arch. computerized case mgmt. sys. Vol. San Francisco Leadership. Mem. ABA. Home: 3024 Washington St San Francisco CA 94115-1618 Office: Brobeck Phleger & Harrison 1 Market Plz Ste 341 San Francisco CA 94105-1420

FERGUSON, ELDON EARL, retired physicist; b. Rawlins, Wyo., Apr. 23, 1926; s. George Earl and Bess (Pierce) F. B.S., Okla. U., 1949, M.S., 1950, Ph.D., 1953. Physicist U.S. Naval Research Lab., Washington, 1954-57; prof. physics U. Tex., Austin, 1957-62; dir. aeronomy lab. NOAA, Dept. Commerce, Boulder, Colo., 1962-95, ret., 1995. Served with U.S. Army, 1944-45. Guggenheim Found. fellow, 1960; Humboldt fellow, 1979-80; recipient Will Allis prize Am. Physical Society, 1994 Mem. Am. Phys. Soc., Am. Geophys. Union. Office: 325 Broadway St Boulder CO 80305-3337

FERGUSON, LLOYD ELBERT, retired manufacturing engineer; b. Denver, Mar. 5, 1942; s. Lloyd Elbert Ferguson and Ellen Jane (Schneider) Romero; m. Patricia Valine Hughes, May 25, 1963; children: Theresa Renee, Edwin Bateman. BS in Engring., Nova Internat. Coll., 1983. Cert. hypnotherapist, geometric tolerance instr. Crew leader FTS Corp., Denver, 1968-72; program engr. Sundstrand Corp., Denver, 1972-87, sr. assoc. project engr., 1987-90, sr. liaison engr., 1990-93; sr. planning engr. Hamilton Sundstrand Corp., Denver, 1990-2000; ret., 2000. V.p. Valine Corp. Lic. practitioner of religious sci. United Ch. of Religious Sci., L.A.; team capt. March of Dimes Team Walk, Danver, 1987; mem. AT&T Telephone Pioneer Clowns for Charity. Recipient recognition award AT&T Telephone Pioneers, 1990 Mem. Soc. Mfg. Engrs. (chmn. local chpt. 1988, zone chmn. 1989, achievement award 1984, 86, recognition award 1986, 90, appreciation award 1988), Nat. Mgmt. Assn. (cert., program instr. 1982—, honor award 1987, 90), Am. Indian Sci. and Engring. Soc., Colo. Clowns. Mem. United Ch. of Religious Sci. Home: 10983 W 76th Dr Arvada CO 80005-3481

FERGUSON, MARGARET ANN, tax consultant; b. Steuben County, Ind., Mar. 24, 1933; d. Leo C. and Ruth Virginia (Engle) Wolf; m. Billy Hugh Ferguson, Feb. 15, 1955 (dec. Oct. 1971); children: Theresa Ruth, Scott Earl, Wade Leo, Luke, Angela, Cynthia, Brenda. AA in Psychology/Social Svs., Palomar Coll., San Marcos, Calif., 1977; BA in Behavioral Sci., Nat. U., Vista, Calif., 1980. Enrolled agt. Office mgr., adminstr. asst. Better Bus. Bur., San Diego, 1979-82; tax technician IRS, Oceanside, Calif., 1982-84, problem resolution tax specialist, 1985-87, revenue agt., 1987-90; pvt. cons. Vista, 1991—. Instr. adult edn. Vista Unified Sch. Dist., 1990-99; mem. adv. com. of nat. cemetery sys. Dept. Vet. Affairs, 1991-98, adv. coun. IRS, 1999—. Mem. AAUW (treas.), Calif. Assn. Ind. Accts., Calif. Soc. Enrolled Agts. (dir. Palomar chpt. 1993-95, 2000-01, 1st v.p. 1998-2000), Inland Soc. Tax Cons., Assn. Homebased Bus., Gold Star Wives Am., Inc. (regional pres. 1989-90, chpt. pres. 1992-93, 96-97, nat. pres. 1993-95). Avocations: lace making, needle work, gardening, writing. Home and Office: 1161 Tower Dr Vista CA 92083-7144 E-mail: gswtax@aol.com

FERGUSON, WARREN JOHN, federal judge; b. Eureka, Nev., Oct. 31, 1920; s. Ralph and Marian (Damele) F.; m. E. Laura Keyes, June 5, 1948; children: Faye F., Warren John, Teresa M., Peter J. B.A., U. Nev., 1942; LL.B., U. So. Calif., 1949; LL.D. (hon.), Western State U., San Fernando Valley Coll. Law. Bar: Calif. 1950. Mem. firm Ferguson & Judge, Fullerton, Calif., 1950-59; city atty. for cities of Buena Park, Placentia, La Puente, Baldwin Park, Santa Fe Springs, Walnut and Rosemead, 1953-59; mcpl. ct. judge Anaheim, 1959-60; judge Superior Ct., Santa Ana, 1961-66, Juvenile Ct., 1963-64, Appellate Dept., 1965-66; U.S. dist. judge Los Angeles, 1966-79; judge U.S. Circuit Ct. (9th cir.), Los Angeles, 1979-86; sr. judge U.S. Ct. Appeals (9th cir.), Santa Ana, 1986—; faculty Fed. Jud. Ctr., Practising Law Inst., U. Iowa Coll. Law, N.Y. Law Jour. Assoc. prof. psychiatry (law) Sch. Medicine, U. So. Calif.; assoc. prof. Loyola Law Sch. Served with AUS, 1942-46. Decorated Bronze Star. Mem. Phi Kappa Phi, Theta Chi. Democrat. Roman Catholic. Office: US Courthouse 411 W 4th St Ste 10-80 Santa Ana CA 92701-4500 E-mail: judge_ferguson@ca9.uscourts.gov

FERINI, ROBERT PAT, agricultural products company executive; b. 1963; With Betteravia Farms, Santa Maria, Calif.; now ptnr. Office: Betteravia Farms PO Box 5845 Santa Maria CA 93456-5845

FERNANDEZ, FERDINAND FRANCIS, federal judge; b. 1937; BS, U. So. Calif., 1958, JD, 1963; LLM, Harvard U., 1963. Bar: Calif. 1963, U.S. Dist. Ct. (cen. dist.) Calif. 1963, U.S. Ct. Appeals (9th cir.) 1963, U.S. Supreme Ct. 1967. Elec. engr. Hughes Aircraft Co., Culver City, Calif., 1958-62; law clk. to dist. judge U.S. Dist. Ct. (cen. dist.) Calif., 1963-64; pvt. practice law Allard, Shelton & O'Connor, Pomona, Calif., 1964-80; judge Calif. Superior Ct. San Bernardino County, 1980-85, U.S. Dist. Ct. (cen. dist.) Calif., L.A., 1985-89, U.S. Ct. Appeals (9th cir.), L.A., 1989—. Lester Roth lectr. U. So. Calif. Law Sch., 1992. Contbr. articles to profl. jours. Vice chmn. City of La Verne Commn. on Environ. Quality, 1971-73; chmn. City of Claremont Environ. Quality Bd., 1972-73; bd. trustees Pomona Coll., 1990—. Fellow Am. Coll. Trust and Estate Counsel; mem. ABA, State Bar of Calif. (fed. cts. com. 1966-69, ad hoc com. on attachments 1971-85, chmn. com. on adminstrn. of justice 1976-77, exec. com. taxation sect. 1977-80, spl. com. on mandatory fee arbitration 1978-79), Calif. Judges Assn. (chmn. juvenile cts. com. 1983-84, faculty mem. Calif. Jud. Coll. 1982-83, faculty mem. jurisprudence and humanities course 1983-85), Hispanic Nat. Bar Assn., L.A. County Bar Assn. (bull. com. 1974-75), San Bernardino County Bar Assn., Pomona Valley Bar Assn. (co-editor Newsletter 1970-72, trustee 1971-78, sec.-treas. 1973-74, 2d v.p. 1974-75, 1st v.p. 1975-76, pres. 1976-77), Estate Planning Coun. Pomona Valley (sec. 1966-76), Order of Coif, Phi Kappa Phi, Tau Beta Pi. Office: US Ct Appeals 9th Cir 125 S Grand Ave Ste 602 Pasadena CA 91105-1621

FERRARIO, JOSEPH A. retired bishop; Educator St. Charles Coll., Catonsville, Md., St. Mary's Sem., Baltimore, Catholic U., Washington, D.C., U. of Scranton, Pa. Ordained Roman Catholic priest, 1951; ord. aux. bishop of Honolulu, titular bishop of Cuse, 1978, bishop of Honolulu, 1982-94. Office: Diocese of Honolulu 1184 Bishop St Honolulu HI 96813-2838

FERRARO, JOHN, city official; b. Los Angeles County, May 14, 1924; s. Dominico and Lucia Ferraro; m. Margaret Ferraro, 1982; 1 child, Luckey. BS, U. So. Calif., 1948; LLD, Southwestern U., 1981. Mem. L.A. Police Commn., 1953-66, pres., three terms; city councilman 4th dist. L.A. City Coun., 1966—, pres. Pro-Tempore, 1975-77, pres., 1977-81, 87—, chmn. rules and election com., mem. energy and natural resources com., vice-chmn. intergovtl. rels. com.; past pres. Meml. Coliseum Commn.; mem. sanitation dist. Los Angeles County; mem. interagy. AWMD implementation & so. Calif. water coms. Past pres., bd. dirs. League of Calif. Cities; bd. dirs. L.A. Museum Contemporary Art, Wilshire YMCA, Gene Autry Western Heritage Museum. With USN. Named All-Am Football Player, U. So. Calif., 1944, Citizen of Yr. L.A. Marathon, 1996; named to Nat. Football Found. Hall of Fame, 1974, U. So. Calif. Hall of Fame, 1995; recipient Heritage award L.A. City Assn., 1992. Ind. Cities Assn. (alt., past pres.), So. Calif. Assn. Govts., Rotary. Roman Catholic. E-mail: jferraro@council.lacity.org

FERRARO, ROBERT, customer service executive; BS, U. Nev., Reno, 1957, MS, 1959. Asst. county agt. U. Nev., Fallon, 1959-63, Lovelock, 1963-70; mgr. electrocytic sys. Pacific Engring. and Prodn. of Nev., Henderson, 1970-85; mgr. Pepcon sys. Pepcon Sys. Inc., Las Vegas, Nev., 1985-96; mgr. customer rels. Ampac, Las Vegas, 1996—. Pres. boulder City (Nev.) Mus. and Hist. Assn., 1980—; city councilman Boulder City, mayor. Address: Boulder City/Hoover Dam Mus PO Box 60516 Boulder City NV 89006-0516

FERREIRA, ARMANDO THOMAS, sculptor, educator; b. Charleston, W.Va., Jan. 8, 1932; s. Maximiliano and Placeres (Sanchez) F.; children: Lisa, Teresa. Student, Chouinard Art Inst., 1949-50, Long Beach City Coll., 1950-53; B.A., UCLA, 1954, M.A., 1956. Asst. prof. art Mt. St. Mary's Coll., 1956-57; mem. faculty dept. art Calif. State U., Long Beach, 1957—, prof., 1967—, chmn. dept. art, 1971-77, assoc. dean Sch. Fine Arts, acting dean Coll. Arts. Lectr., cons. on art adminstrn. to art schs. and universities, Brazilian Ministry Edn. One-man shows include, Pasadena Mus., 1959, Long Beach Mus., 1959, 69, Eccles Mus., 1967, Clay and Fiber Gallery, Taos, 1972; exhibited in group shows at L.A. County Art Mus., 1958, 66, Wichita Art Mus., 1959, Everson Mus., 1960, 66, San Diego Mus. Fine Arts, 1969, 73, Fairtree Gallery, N.Y.C., 1971, 74, L.A. Inst. Contemporary Art, 1977, Utah Art Mus., 1978, Bowers Mus., Santa Ana, Calif., 1980, No. Ill. U., 1986, Beckstrand Gallery, Palos Verdes (Calif.) Art Ctr., 1987, U. Madrid, 1993; permanent collections include Utah Mus. Art, Wichita Art Mus., Long Beach (Calif.) Mus. Art, State of Calif. Collection; vis. artist, U. N.D., 1974. Fulbright lectr. Brazil, 1981 Fellow Nat. Assn. Schs. Art and Design (dir.); mem. Internat. Video Network (dir.), Assn. Calif. State Univ. Profs.

FERRELL, STEPHEN J. career officer; BS, Baker U. Commd. 2d lt. U.S. Army, advanced through grades to brig. gen., early assignments include platoon leader Colo., flight platoon leader 48th aviation co. Nelligen, Germany, comdr. assault helicopter co. Ft. Lewis, Wash., ops. rsch. staff officer Alexandria, Va., brigade S-3, aviation brigad 3d armored divsn. Hanau, Germany; exec. officer 3d bn. 227th aviation regiment Hanau; bn. comdr. Desert Shield/Desert Storm Hunter Army Airfield, Ga.; dir. ops. testing and experimentation command Ft. Hood, Tex.; comdr. 4th brigade 4th infantry divsn. Ft. Hood, 1996; dir. plans U.S. Space Command, U.S. Army, Peterson AFB, Colo., also comdr. U.S. Army Element. Decorated Bronze Star, Legion of Merit, meritorious svc. medal withoak leaf cluster, air medal, others. Master aviator.

FERRIOLI, TED, state legislator; b. Spokane, Wash., Feb. 15, 1951; m. Mary Ferrioli. BA, Oreg. U. Exec. dir. Malheur Timber Operators, Inc.; mem. Oreg. Legislature, Salem, 1996—, mem. agr. and natural resources com., mem. joint com. on ways and means, mem. stream restoration and species recovery com., chair transp. com. Pres. Creswell City Coun.; bd. dirs. Cmty. Substance Abuse Consortium. Republican. Office: 750 W Main St John Day OR 97845-1037 E-mail: ferrioli.sen@state.or.us

FERRIS, RUSSELL JAMES, II, freelance writer; b. Rochester, N.Y., June 11, 1938; s. Russell James and Phyllis Helen (Breheny) F.; m. Ilma Maria dos Santos, June 29, 1968. Student, St. Bonaventure U., 1956-59; BS, U. Rochester, 1967; MS, Emerson Coll., 1989; PhD, Universal Life Ch., 1983. Cert. social worker. Film inspector City of Rochester, 1962-67; social worker Tulare County, Visalia, Calif., 1967-69, Alameda County, Oakland, 1969-71; ghostwriter self-employed, San Francisco, 1971—. Author: Crescendo, 1972 and 14 other novels. With USAR, 1956-68. Recipient Botany fellowship Emerson Coll., 1989. Mem. Assn. U.S. Army, Air Force Assn., Ret. Officers Assn. (life), Res. Officers Assn. (life), Am. Mensa Inc. Libertarian. Roman Catholic. Avocation: aviculture. Home and Office: 202 Font Blvd San Francisco CA 94132-2404

FERRY, DAVID KEANE, electrical engineering educator; b. San Antonio, Oct. 25, 1940; s. Joseph Jules and Elizabeth (Keane) F. m. Darleen Heitkamp; Aug. 25, 1962; children: Lara Annette, Linda Renee. BSEE, Tex. Tech U., 1962, MSEE, 1963; PhD, U. Tex., 1966. Lectr. U. Tex., Austin, 1966; postdoctoral fellow U. Vienna, Austria, 1966-67; asst. prof., then assoc. prof. Tex. Tech U., Lubbock, 1967-73; sci. officer Office Naval Rsch., Arlington, Va., 1973-77; prof., head elec. engring. Colo. State U., Ft. Collins, 1977-83; Regent's prof., dir. Ctr. for Solid State Electronics Rsch. Ariz. State U., Tempe, 1983-89, Regent's prof., chair elec. computing engring., 1989-92, Regent's prof., 1992—. Mem. microelectronics panel NRC, Washington, 1977-79; mem. materials rsch. coun. Def. Advanced Rsch. Projects Agy., Arlington, 1982-98; mem. supercomputer adv. group NSF, Washington, 1984-87. Author: (with D. R. Fannin) Physical Electronics, 1971; (with L. A. Akers and E. W. Greeneich) Ultra Large Scale Integrated Microelectronics, 1988, Semiconductors, 1991, (with R.O. Grondin) Physics of Submicron Devices, 1991, Quantum Mechanics, 1995, 2d edit., 2000, (with S.M. Goodnick) Transport in Nanostructures, 1997, Semiconductor Transport, 2000; numerous pub. sci. articles; editor: GaAs Technology, 1985, GaAs Technology II, 1989; (with J. R. Barker and C. Jacoboni) Physics of Nonlinear Transport in Semiconductors, 1979, (with J.R. Barker and C. Jacoboni) Granular Nonelectronics, 1991, (with C. Jacoboni) Quantum Transport in Semiconductors, 1992, (with C. Jacoboni, A.P. Jauho, H.L. Grubin) Quantum Transport in Ultrasmall Devices, 1995, (with J.P. Bird) Electronic Materials and Devices, 2001, Semiconductor Transport, 2001; patentee in field. Fellow IEEE (Cledo Brunetti prize for advancements in nanoelectronics 1999), Am. Phys. Soc.; mem. Sigma Xi. Avocations: photography, skiing. Office: Ariz State U Elec Dept Tempe AZ 85287

FERRY, MILES YEOMAN, state legislator; b. Brigham City, Utah, Sept. 22, 1932; s. John Yeoman and Alta (Cheney) F.; m. Suzanne Call, May 19, 1952; children: John, Jane Ferry Stewart, Ben, Helen, Sue Ferry Thorpe. BS, Utah State U., 1954. Rancher, Corinne, Utah, 1952; pres. J.Y. Ferry & Son, Inc.; mem. Utah Ho. of Reps., 1965-66, Utah Senate, 1967-84, minority whip, 1975-76, minority leader, 1977-78, pres. senate, 1979-84; mem. presdl. advisor commn. on intergovtl. affairs, 1984; mem. governing bd. Council State Govts., 1983-84. V.p. Legis./Exec. Consulting Firm, 1994—; chmn. Corinne Cemetery Dist., 1989—. Pres. Brigham Jr. C. of C., 1956-61, Nat. Conf. of State Legislators, 1984, v.p., 1982, pres.-elect, 1983, pres., 1984; v.p. Utah Jr. C. of C., 1960-61; nat. dir. Utah Jaycees, 1961-62; pres. Farm Bur. Box Elder County, 1958-59; food and agr. commr. USDA, commr. agr. State of Utah, 1985-93. Recipient award of merit Boy Scouts Am., 1976, Alumnusi of Yr. award Utah State U., 1981, award of merit Utah Vocat. Assn., 1981, Friend of Agr. award Utah Farm Bur., 1988, Cert. Appreciation USDA, 1988, Contbn. to Agr. award Utah-Idaho Farmers Union, 1989, Disting. Svc. award Utah State U., 1993, 94; named Outstanding Young Man of Yr., Brigham City Jr. C. of C., 1957, Outstanding Nat. Dir. U.S. Jaycees, 1963, Outstanding Young Man in Utah, Utah Jr. C. of C., 1961, Outstanding Young Farmer, 1958, One of 3 Outstanding Young Men of Utah, 1962, Rep. Legislator of Yr., 1984, One of 10 Outstanding Legislators of Yr., 1984. Mem. SAR, Sons Utah Pioneers, Gov.'s Cabinet, Utah Commn. Agr., Fed. Rsch. Com., Nat. Assn. State Depts. Agr. (bd. dirs. 1989), Western Assn. of State Depts. of Agr. (v.p. 1990-91, pres. 1991-92), Western U.S. Agr. Trade Assn. (sec. treas-elect 1987-88, pres. 1989-90), Utah Cattlemen's Assn., Nat. Golden Spike Assn. (dir. 1958—), Phi Kappa Phi, Pi Kappa Alpha. Republican. Address: 815 N 6800 W Corinne UT 84307-9737 E-mail: leg.ex.con@worldnet.att.net

FERRY, RICHARD MICHAEL, executive search firm executive; b. Ravenna, Ohio, Sept. 26, 1937; s. John D. and Margaret M. (Jeney) F.; m. Maude M. Hillman, Apr. 14, 1956; children: Richard A., Margaret L., Charles Michael, David W., Dianne E., Ann Marie. BS, Kent State U., 1959. CPA. Cons. staff Peat, Marwick, Mitchell, Los Angeles, 1965-69, ptnr., 1969; founder, chmn. Korn/Ferry Internat., Los Angeles, 1969—. Bd. dirs. Mellon/1st Bus. Bank, L.A., Avery Dennison, Pasadena, Calif., Dole Food Co., Calif., Pacific Life Ins. Co., Newport Beach, Calif. Trustee St. John's Health Ctr., Santa Monica, Calif.; bd. dirs. Cath. Charities, L.A., Calif. Cmty. Found., Hugh O'Brien Youth Leadership; pres. Catholic Edn. Found., L.A. Republican. Roman Catholic. Office: Korn/Ferry Internat 1800 Century Park E Ste 900 Los Angeles CA 90067-1512

FERY, JOHN BRUCE, former real estate property manager; b. Bellingham, Wash., Feb. 16, 1930; s. Carl Salvatore and Margaret Emily (Hauck) F.; m. Delores Lorraine Carlo, Aug. 22, 1953; children: John Brent, Bruce Todd, Michael Nicholas. BA, U. Wash., 1953; MBA, Stanford U., 1955; D of Law (hon.), Gonzaga U., 1982; D of Nat. Resources (hon.), U. Idaho, 1983. Asst. to pres. Western Kraft Corp., 1955-56; prodn. mgr., 1956-57; with Boise Cascade Corp., Idaho, 1957-94, pres., CEO, 1972-78, chmn. bd., CEO, 1978-94, chmn., 1994-95; with F&C Corp., Boise, 1996—. Bd. dirs. Albertsons, Inc., The Boeing Co.; active mem. Bus. Coun. Dir. Idaho Community Found. With USN, 1950-51. Named Most Outstanding Chief Exec. Officer Fin. World, 1977, 78, 79, 80. Mem. Am. Forest and Paper Assn. (exec. com., bd. dirs.), Arid Club, Hillcrest Country Club. Office: F&C Corp Rocky Mountain Mgmt PO Box 15407 Boise ID 83715-5407 also: 2700 Airport Way Boise ID 83705-5068

FESTINGER, RICHARD, music educator, composer; b. Newton, Mass., Mar. 1, 1948; s. Leon and Mary (Ballou) F.; m. Karen Cummings Rosenak; stepchildren: Jacob Rosenak, Max Rosenak. Student, Stanford U., 1965-68; student jazz arrangement and composition, Berklee Coll. Music, 1970-72; BM magna cum laude, San Francisco State U., 1976; MA in Music, U. Calif., Berkeley, 1978, PhD in Music, 1983; postgrad., Calif. State U., Hayward, 1984-85; postgrad. studies in Computer Engring., Calif. State U., San Jose, 1985; postgrad. studies in Computer Sci., Stanford U., 1985-86, 91. Lectr. music theory U. Calif., Berkeley, 1982-83, Davis, 1989-90; assoc. prof. music San Francisco State U., 1990—, dir. theory and composition, dir. Electronic Music Studio, 1992—. Asst. conductor U.

Calif. Symphony Orch., 1980-82; vis. asst. prof. music Dartmouth Coll., 1984; rsch. affiliate Ctr. for Computer Rsch. Music and Acoustics, Stanford U., vis. scholar, 1996, 97; pres. bd. dirs., artistic dir. music ensemble EARPLAY, San Francisco, 1987-91, 94; resident Edward Macdowell Colony, 1983, 85; music panelist New England Found. for Arts, 1983, dir., Composition program, Summer Arts Festival, Calif. State U., 1996, 97. Published music includes Triptych for solo flute, 1979, Impromptu for clarinet and piano, 1985, Septet for flute, clarinet, violin, viola, violoncello, percussion and piano, 1987, Variations for Piano, 1988, Two Little Piano Pieces, 1992, A Serenade for Six for flute, clarinet/bass, clarinet, violin, violoncello, percussion and piano, 1993, Twinning for violin and piano, 1994, String Quartet for two violins, viola and violoncello, 1994, Violuminescence for violin solo and chamber orchestra, 1995, Windsongs for flute, oboe, clarinet, horn and bassoon, 1996, Trionometry for flute, clarinet/bass clarinet and piano, 1996, Tapestries for violin, violoncello and piano, 1997, After Blue for flute/piccolo, clarinet/bass clarinet, violin, violoncello, percussion and piano, 1998; recordings and include Triptych for unaccompanied flute, Live at Pangaea Improvisations, vols. I and II, 1986, Richard Festinger Chamber Music, Septet, 1996, A Serenade for Six, 1998; commissions include Alter Ego Ensemble, Rome, Italy, 1999-2000, San Francisco Contemporary Music Players, Barlow Found., 2000-01, N.Y. New Music Ensemble, 1999-2000, Cygnus Ensemble, 2000-01, others. Recipient George Ladd Grand Prix de Paris, 1978, Nicolo di Lorenzo prize in music composition, 1981, Roslyn Schneider Eisner award, 1982, Prometheus Orch. Composition Competition award for piano concerto, 1982, Walter Hinrichsen award Am. Acad. Arts and Letters, 1993; Composition Assistance grantee Am. Music Ctr., 1982, Regents fellow U. Calif., 1976; Meet the Composer grantee, 1984, 91, Rsch. and Profl. Devel. grantee San Francisco State U., 1991, 93-94, Alfred Hertz Meml. fellow, 1977, Edward MacDowell Colony Norlin/MacDowell fellow, 1982, Wellesley Composers Conf. fellow, 1993, June in Buffalo Conf. fellow, 1994; Jerome Found. commn., 1990, San Francisco Contemporary Music Players commn., 1992, N.Y. New Music Ensemble commn., 1993, Alexander String Quartet commn., 1994, Fromm Found. commn., 1995, City Winds commn., 1996, Laurel Trio commn., 1997, Koussevitzky Music Found. commn., 1997, Left Coast Ensemble commn., 1998, Calif. Assn. Profl. Music Tchrs. commn., U. Calif. Davis commn. Office: San Francisco State U 1600 Holloway Ave San Francisco CA 94132-1722 Fax: 415-338-3294. E-mail: raf@sfsu.edu

FETTER, ALEXANDER LEES, theoretical physicist, educator; b. Phila., May 16, 1937; s. Ferdinand and Elizabeth Lean Fields (Head) F.; m. Jean Holmes, Aug. 4, 1962 (div. Dec. 1994); children: Anne Lindsay, Andrew James. AB, Williams Coll., 1958; BA, Balliol Coll., Oxford U., 1960; PhD, Harvard U., 1963. Miller rsch. fellow U. Calif., Berkeley, 1963-65; mem. faculty dept. physics Stanford U., 1965—, prof., 1974—, chmn. dept. physics, 1985-90, assoc. chmn. dept. physics, 1998-99, assoc. dean undergrad. studies, 1976-79, assoc. dean humanities and sci., 1990-93, dir. Hansen Exptl. Physics Lab., 1996-97, dir. lab. for adv. materials, 1999—; vis. prof. Cambridge U., 1970-71; Nordita vis. prof. Tech. U., Helsinki, Finland, 1976. Author: (with J.D. Walecka) Quantum Theory of Many Particle Systems, 1971, Theoretical Mechanics of Particles and Continua, 1980. Alumni trustee Williams Coll., 1974-79. Rhodes scholar, 1958-60; NSF fellow, 1960-63; Sloan Found. fellow, 1968-72; Recipient W.J. Gores award for excellence in teaching Stanford U., 1974 Fellow Am. Physics Soc. (chmn. div. condensed matter physics 1991), AAAS; mem. Sigma Xi. Home: 904 Mears Ct Palo Alto CA 94305-1029 Office: Stanford U Physics Dept Stanford CA 94305-4060

FETTER, TREVOR, healthcare industry executive; married; 2 children. BS in Econs., Stanford U.; MBA, Harvard U. With investment banking divsn. Merrill Lynch Capital Mkts.; sr. v.p. MGM/UA Comm. Co., 1988; exec. v.p., CFO Metro-Goldwyn-Mayer, Inc., Tenet Healthcare Corp., Santa Barbara, Calif., 1995-2000; chmn., CEO Broad Ln., Inc., San Francisco, 2000—. Chmn. bd. Santa Catalina Island Conservancy; trustee Santa Barbara Zool. Garden; bd. dirs. iVillage Corp. Office: Broad Ln Inc 40 Gold St San Francisco CA 94133

FETTERLY, LYNN LAWRENCE, real estate broker, developer; b. Ogdensburg, N.Y., Oct. 21, 1947; s. Keith C. and Florence E. Fetterly; m. Melody Bulriss, July 23, 1971; children: Kim Marie, Adam Lynn. AAS, Canton (N.Y.) Coll., 1967; BS, SUNY, Albany, 1969; MA, U. Detroit, 1972; cert. in mgmt., U. So. Calif., L.A., 1984. Auditor Arthur Andersen & Co., Rochester, N.Y., 1969-70; asst. v.p. Security Pacific Nat. Bank, L.A., 1972-75, Security Pacific Corp., L.A., 1976-77, Citibank, N.A., Rochester, 1977-81; v.p. regional mgr. Security Pacific Nat. Bank, N.Y.C., 1981-84; pres., CEO Security Pacific EuroFinance, Inc., London, 1984-88; vice chmn. Security Pacific Fin. Svcs. Sys., Inc., San Diego, 1988-90; pres., COO Security Pacific Fin. Svcs. System, Inc., San Diego, 1991-92; ind. real estate broker/developer, 1993—. With USAR, 1969-75. Mem. Dayton Valley Country Club. Republican. Presbyterian. Avocations: golf, tennis.

FETTERS, DORIS ANN, retired secondary education educator; b. Bklyn. d. John Joseph and Loreta Gertrude (Stratford) F. BA, Calif. State Coll., L.A., 1952. Cert. gen. secondary tchr. Tchr. Temple City (Calif.) H.S., 1954-55, L.A. City Schs., 1955-56; vice consul 3d sec. of embassy Dept. of State, Washington, 1957-60; tchr. U. Rafael Landivar, Guatemala, 1960-63, L.A. Unified Schs., 1964-90. Mem. Am. Fedn. Tchrs., United Tchrs. L.A. Democrat. Roman Catholic. Avocations: gardening, arts and crafts, reading.

FETTERS, NORMAN CRAIG , II, banker; b. Pitts., Aug. 27, 1942; s. Karl Leroy and Hazel (Lower) F.; m. Linda Wood, Aug. 14, 1965; children— Eric Craig, Kevin Edward, Brian Allan AB, Westminster Coll., 1964; MBA, U. Pitts., 1965. Various positions to v.p. Security Pacific Nat. Bank, Los Angeles, 1965-66, 69-74, v.p., 1974-82; sr. v.p. Security Pacific Bank Washington, Seattle, 1982-92, SeaFirst Bank, Seattle, 1992-93; sr. v.p., dir. Security Pacific Savs. Bank, Seattle, 1993-94; v.p. Key Bank of Wash., Seattle, 1994-96, sr. v.p., 1996-99; v.p., credit officer Fed. Home Loan Bank of Seattle, 1999—. Served to lt. U.S. Army, 1966-69 Mem. Robert Morris Assocs., Lions Club (pres. 1988-89). Presbyterian (elder). Avocations: cross-country skiing, travel, hiking, photography. Office: Fed Home Loan Bank of Seattle 1501 4th Ave Ste 1900 Seattle WA 98101-1693 E-mail: cfetters@fhlbsea.com

FEUERSTEIN, HOWARD M. lawyer; b. Memphis, Sept. 16, 1939; s. Leon and Lillian (Kapell) F.; m. Tamra Lynn Saperstein, May 19, 1968; children: Laurie, Leon. BA, Vanderbilt U., 1961, JD, 1963. Bar: Tenn. 1963, Oreg. 1965. Law clk. to justice U.S. Ct. Appeals (5th cir.), Montgomery, Ala., 1963-64; teaching fellow Stanford U., 1964-65; assoc. Davies, Biggs et al (now Stoel Rives LLP), Portland, Oreg., 1965-71; ptnr. Stoel Rives LLP, Portland, 1971—. Mem. Oreg. Gov.'s Task Force on Land Devel. Law, 1974; bd. realtors Condominium Study Com., Oreg., 1975-76. Editor-in-chief Vanderbilt Law Rev., 1962-63. Trustee Congregation Beth Israel, Portland, 1977-83; bd. dirs. Jewish Family & Child Service, Portland, 1975-81, Young Musicians and Artists Inc., 1991-96. Recipient Founder's medal Vanderbilt Law Sch., 1963. Mem. ABA, Oreg. State Bar, Community Assn. Inst. (bd. dirs. Oreg. chpt. 1980-86), Am. Coll. Real Estate Lawyers. Office: Stoel Rives LLP 900 SW 5th Ave Ste 2600 Portland OR 97204-1268 E-mail: hmfeuerstein@stoel.com

FIBIGER, JOHN ANDREW, life insurance company executive; b. Copenhagen, Apr. 27, 1932; came to U.S., 1934, naturalized, 1953; s. Borge Rottboll and Ruth Elizabeth (Wadmond) F.; m. Barbara Mae Stuart, [illegible] Minn., 1953, M.A., 1954; postgrad., U. Wis. With Lincoln Nat. Life Ins. Co., Ft. Wayne, Ind., 1956-57; with Bankers Life Ins. Co. Nebr., Lincoln, 1959-73, sr. v.p. group, 1972-73; with New Eng. Mut. Life Ins. Co., Boston, 1973-89, vice chmn., pres., chief operating officer, 1981-89; with Transam Life Cos., 1991-94; exec. v.p., CFO, then pres. Transamerica Occidental Life Ins. Co., L.A., 1994-95, chmn., 1995-97. Past vice chmn. Actuarial Bd. for Counseling and Discipline; bd. dirs. Transamerica Life Can. Life trustee, past chmn. Mus. Sci., Boston, 1989-91; past overseer New Eng. Med. Ctr., Boston Symphony Orch.; bd. dirs. Menninger Found., v.p., bd. dirs. L.A. Chamber Orch.; past chmn. Menninger Fund; bd. dirs. U. So. Calif. Sch. Gerontology; past trustee Calif. Mus. Sci. and Industry. Fellow Soc. Actuaries (past bd. dirs.); mem. Nat. Acad. Social Ins. (founding mem.), Am. Acad. Actuaries (past pres.), Assn. Calif. Life Cos. (past bd. chmn.). E-mail: fibij@aol.com

FICKINGER, WAYNE JOSEPH, communications executive; b. Belleville, Ill., June 23, 1926; s. Joseph and Grace (Belton) F.; m. Joan Mary Foley, June 16, 1951; children: Michael, Joan, Jan, Ellen, Steven. BA, U. Ill., 1949; MS, Northwestern U., 1950. Overnight editor United Press, Chgo., 1950-51; spl. project writer Sears-Roebuck & Co., Chgo., 1951-53; account exec. Calkins & Holden Advt. Agy., Chgo., 1953-56; account supr. Foote, Cone & Belding Advt. Agy., Chgo., N.Y.C., 1956-63; sr. v.p. J. Walter Thompson Co., Chgo., 1963-72, exec. v.p., dir. U.S. Western div., 1972-75, pres. N.Am. divsn., 1975-78; pres., chief operating officer J. Walter Thompson Co. Worldwide, 1978-79; pres. JWT Group, Inc., 1979-82, trustee retirement fund, dir., mem. exec. com., 1980-82; mng. dir. Spencer Stuart & Assocs., 1982-83; vice chmn., dir. Bozell, Jacobs, Kenyon & Eckhardt Inc., Chgo., 1984-89; pres. Mid-Am. Com., Chgo., 1989-93; exec. v.p., dir. Monroe Comm. Corp., 1992—; v.p., dir. Adams Comm., 1994—. Mem. adv. bd. Phase One Inc.; bd. dirs. Alford Group, Inc. Fundraising cons. Nat. Mental Health Assn., 1970; comm. counselor Cook County (Ill.) Rep. Orgn., 1970; bd. dirs. Off-the-Street Club, Chgo., 1974-77, Mundelein Coll., 1985-91, United Cerebral Palsy, 1986, Chgo. Conv. and Tourists Bur., 1986-90, Columbia Coll., Chgo., 1990-95, Fermi Inst. Hadron Therapy, 2000—; chmn. Chgo. Funding Statue of Liberty, 1986, March of Dimes, 1987, Mayor's Chgo. Tourism Com., 1990-92; mem. steering com. El Valor, 1997-98. With USNR, 1943-46. Recipient Five-Year Meritorious Service award A.R.C., 1963, Service award Mental Health Assn., 1970 Mem. Am. Assn. Advt. Agys., Council on Fgn. Relations (Chgo. com.), Sigma Delta Chi, Alpha Delta Sigma. Clubs: Exmoor Country (Highland Park, Ill.); N.Y. Athletic; Mid-Am. (Chgo.), Internat. (Chgo.). Office: 350 S Beverly Dr Ste 300 Beverly Hills CA 90212-4817 E-mail: wfick@webtv.net

FIDEL, JOSEPH A. state legislator; b. Bibo, N.Mex., Oct. 14, 1923; married. Grad., St. Michael's H.S. Real estate broker; bank dir., ins. agt.; mem. N.Mex. Senate, Dist. 30, Sante Fe, 1973—; vice chair fin. com.; mem. corps. and transp. com. N.Mex. Senate. County assessor, 1950-54, 62-66; mem. City Coun., 1953-60; mem. Sch. Bd., 1959-71. Mem. Elks (life), K.C. (charter mem.). Democrat. Office: PO Box 968 Grants NM 87020-0968

FIDEL, RAYA, library science educator; b. Tel Aviv, Jan. 18, 1945; came to U.S., 1977; BSc, Tel Aviv U., 1970; MLS, Hebrew U., Jerusalem, 1976; PhD, U. Md., 1982. Tchr. Adult Edn. Ctr., Jerusalem, 1971-72; br. libr. Hebrew U., Jerusalem, 1972-77; asst. prof. libr. sci. U. Wash., Seattle, 1982-87, assoc. prof. libr. sci., 1987-2000, prof. Info. Sch., 2000—. Vis. libr. Duke U. Libr., Durham, N.C., 1992-93. Author: Database Design, 1987; editor Advances in Classification, 1991-94 (award 1992-94); contbr. articles to profl. publs. Recipient Research award Am. Society for Information Science, 1994 Mem. AAUP (chair U. Wash. chpt. 1990-92, pres. state conf. 1992-97), IEEE Computer Soc., Assn. Computing Machinery, Am. Soc. Info. Sci. (dir.-at-large 2000—). Home: 5801 Phinney Ave N Seattle WA 98103-5862

FIELD, HAROLD, state finance administrator; Sec. N.Mex. Fin. & Adminstrn. Dept., Sante Fe. Office: NMex Fin & Adminstrn Dept 180 Bataan Meml Bldg Sante Fe NM 87503

FIELD, JOHN LOUIS, architect; b. Mpls., Jan. 18, 1930; s. Harold David and Gladys Ruth (Jacobs) F.; m. Carol Helen Hart, July 23, 1961; children: Matthew Hart, Alison Ellen. BA, Yale U., 1952, MArch, 1955. Individual practice architecture, San Francisco, 1959-68; v.p. firm Bull, Field, Volkmann, Stockwell, Architects, San Francisco, 1968-83; ptnr. Field/Gruzen, Architects, San Francisco, 1983-86, Field Paoli Architects, San Francisco, 1986—. Guest lectr. Stanford, 1970; chmn. archtl. council San Francisco Mus. Art, 1969-71; mem. San Francisco Bay Conservation and Devel. Commn., Design Rev. Bd., 1980-84; founding chmn. San Francisco Bay Architects Review, 1977-80 Co-author, producer, dir.: film Cities for People (Broadcast Media award 1975, Golden Gate award San Francisco Internat. Film Festival 1975, Ohio State award 1976); film The Urban Preserve (Calif. Council AIA Commendation of excellence 1982); co-design architect: design for New Alaska Capital City (winner design competition). Recipient Archtl. Record award, 1961, 1972; AIA, Sunset mag. awards, 1962, 64, 69; No. Calif. AIA awards, 1967, 82; Calif. Council AIA award, 1982; certificate excellence Calif. Gov.'s Design awards, 1966; Homes for Better Living awards, 1962, 66, 69, 71, 77; Albert J. Evers award, 1974, Best Bldg. award Napa (Calif.) C. of C., 1987, Design award Internat. Council Shopping Ctrs., 1988, Stores of Excellence award Nat. Mall Monitor, 1989, 92, 93, Pacific Coast Builders Gold Nugget award, 1989, 91, Urban Design award Calif. Coun. AIA, 1991, 93. Fellow AIA (com. on design); mem. Nat. Coun. Archtl. Registration Bds., Urban Land Inst. (Design award 1995), Yale Club, Lambda Alpha. Office: Field Paoli Architects 1045 Sansome St Ste 206 San Francisco CA 94111-1315 E-mail: jlf@fieldpaoli.com

FIELD, RICHARD CLARK, lawyer; b. Stanford, Calif., July 13, 1940; s. John and Sally Field; m. Barbara Faith Butler, May 22, 1967 (dec. Apr. 1984); 1 child, Amanda Katherine; m. Eva Sara Halbreich, Dec. 1, 1985. BA, U. Calif., Riverside, 1962, JD, Harvard U., 1965. Bar: Calif. 1966, U.S. Supreme Ct., 1971, U.S. Ct. Appeals (9th cir.) 1979. Assoc. Thompson & Colegate, Riverside, 1965-69; ptnr. Adams, Duque & Hazeltine, Los Angeles, 1970-89, mem. mgmt. com., 1981-84, chmn. litigation dept., 1985-89; ptnr. Cadwalader, Wickersham & Taft, Los Angeles, 1989-97, McCutchen, Doyle, Brown & Enersen, LLP, Los Angeles, 1997—. Bd. dirs. ARC, L.A., 1984-93, 97—. Mem. ABA (litigation, torts and ins. practice sects., bus. torts com., products, gen. liability and consumer law com.), Los Angeles County Bar Assn. (trial lawyers sect.), Assn. Bus. Trial Lawyers (bd. govs. 1978-82), Am. Arbitration Assn. (comml. arbitration panel). Episcopalian. Office: McCutchen Doyle Brown & Enersen LLP 355 S Grand Ave Ste 4400 Los Angeles CA 90071-3106

FIELD, TED (FREDERICK FIELD), film and record industry executive; b. Chgo. s. Marshall Field IV and Katherine W. Fanning; 6 children. Student, U. Chgo., Pomona Coll. Former race car driver; founder, chmn. [illegible] scope, Geffen, A&M Records; former co-owner Field Enterprises, Chgo.; owner Panavision, 1985-87. Co-producer (films) Critical Condition, 1987, Outrageous Fortune, 1987, Three Men and a Baby, 1987, Revenge of the Nerds II, 1987, Cocktail, 1988, The Seventh Sign, 1988, An Innocent Man, 1989; co-exec. producer (films) Bill and Ted's Excellent Adventure, 1989, Renegades, 1989; producer Revenge of the Nerds, 1984, Turk 182, 1985, [illegible] Opus, 1996, Runaway Bride, 1999; exec. producer The First Power, 1990, Bird on a Wire, 1990, What Dreams May Come, 1998, Very Bad Things, 1998; exec. producer Hand That Rocks The Cradle, 1992; co-exec. producer (TV films) The Father Clements Story, Everybody's Baby: The Rescue of Jessica McClure, A Mother's Courage. Avocations: chess, martial arts. Office: Interscope Communications 10900 Wilshire Blvd Ste 1400 Los Angeles CA 90024-6532

FIELDER, DAVID R. medical research administrator; V.p. rsch. Calif. Pacific Med. Ctr. Research Inst., San Francisco. Office: Calif Pacific Med Ctr Rsch Inst 2340 Clay St San Francisco CA 94115-1932

FIELDING, ELIZABETH BROWN, education educator; b. Ligonier, Ind., Feb. 17, 1918; d. Herbert Benjamin and Roberta (Franklin) B.; m. Frederick Allan Fielding, May 23, 1942 (wid. July 1962); children: Elizabeth Enndriss Fielding, Frederick Allan Fielding, Jr. BA, Smith Coll., 1939; MA, U. San Francisco, 1975. Cert. tchr. com. colls., Calif. Field staff mem. San Francisco Bay Girl Scout Assn., 1963-69; exec. dir. Tri-City Project on Aging, Rodeo, Calif., 1970-73; tchr., cons. various univs., 1974—. Mem. curriculum com. U. Calif., Berkeley, 1979-80; chair edn. programs Diablo Valley Found. on Aging, Walnut Creek, Calif., 1980s. Author: The Memory Manual: 10 Simple Things You Can Do to Improve Your Memory After 50, 1999, Teacher's Guide to The Memory Manual, 2000; contbr. articles to profl. jours. Chair Mental Health Task Force, County Coun. for Aging, Contra Costa County, 1974-76; mem. Sr. Svcs. Commn., City of Lafayette, Calif., 1981—; pres. bd. dirs. Calif. Specialists on Aging, Calif., 1976-79. Mem. Western Gerontol. Assn. (now Am. Soc. on Aging), Nat. Transactional Analysis Assn., Internat. Coun. on the Aging, Authors Guild, Calif. Writers Club. Avocations: writing fiction, genealogy, art appreciation, bird watching. Home: 3170 Plymouth Rd Lafayette CA 94549-3236

FIELDING, JONATHAN E. pediatrician; b. Oct. 4, 1942; BA, Williams Coll., 1964; MA, MD, Harvard Coll., 1969, MPH, 1971; MBA, U. Pa., 1977. Diplomate Am. Bd. Pediats., Am. Bd. Preventive Medicine. Josiah Macy fellow Harvard U., Cambridge, Mass., 1969; intern, resident Boston Children's Hosp., 1969-71; fellow Harvard U., Boston, 1971; resident in pediats. Georgetown U. Med. Ctr., Washington, 1971-72, prin. med. svcs. nat. officer Job Corps, 1971-73; commr. pub. health Commonwealth of Mass., 1975-79; prof. health svcs. & pediats. UCLA, 1979—; dir. pub. health L.A. County, 1997—. Spl. asst. to dir. Bur. Cmty. Health Svcs. Health Svcs. & Mental Health Adminstrn. HEW, 1971-73; co-dir. Ctr. Health Enhancement Edn. & Rsch., 1979-84; co-dir. Ctr. for Healthier Children, Families & Cmtys., 1985—; lectr. Harvard U., Boston, 1973-75, Boston U., 1975-79, Brandeis U., 1975-79, Northwestern U., 1975-79; vis. lectr. UCLA, 1977; rsch. assoc. Urban Rsch. Ctr. Hunter Coll. CUNY, 1978; vis. prof. Nordic Sch. Pub. Health, Sweden, 1980, 83, 93. Editor: Ann. Revs. Pub. Health, 1995—; asst. editor Mercy-Rosenau Pub. Health and Preventive Medicine 1992-98, 14th edit. Fellow Assn. Health Svcs.; mem. NAS Inst. Medicine, Am. Acad. Pediats., Am. Assn. Pub. Health Physicians, Am. Med. Peer Rev. Assn., Am. Pub. Health Assn., Assn. Health Svcs. Medicine, Am. Heart Assn., Am. Coll. Preventive Medicine (pres. 1997—). Office: UCLA Sch Pub Health Ctr Health Sci 61 253A Los Angeles CA 90095-0001

FIELDS, ANTHONY LINDSAY AUSTIN, health facility administrator, oncologist, educator; b. St. Michael, Barbados, Oct. 21, 1943; arrived in Can., 1968; s. Vernon Bruce and Marjorie (Pilgrim) F.; m. Patricia Jane Stewart, Aug. 5, 1967. MA, U. Cambridge, 1969; MD, U. Alta., 1974. Diplomate Am. Bd. Internal Medicine. Sr. specialist Cross Cancer Inst., Edmonton, Alta., Can., 1980-85, dir. dept. medicine Can., 1985-88, dir. Can., 1988-2000; v.p. med. affairs and cmty. oncology Alta. Cancer Bd., 2000—. Asst. prof. medicine U. Alta., Edmonton, 1980-84, assoc. prof., 1984-98, prof., 1998—, dir. divsn. med. oncology, 1985-89, dir. divsn. oncology, 1988-93; v.p. Nat. Cancer Inst. Can., 2000—. Fellow ACP (gov. Alta. chpt.), Royal Coll. Physicians and Surgeons Can. (specialist cert. med. oncology, internal medicine); mem. Can. Assn. Med. Oncologists (pres. 1994-96), Am. Soc. Clin. Oncology, Am. Fedn. Clin. Rsch., Can. Soc. for Clin. Investigation, Can. Med. Assn. Avocation: photography. Office: # 1220 10405 Jasper Ave Edmonton AB Canada T5J 3N4

FIELDS, BERTRAM HARRIS, lawyer; b. Los Angeles, Mar. 31, 1929; s. H. Maxwell and Mildred Arlyn (Ruben) F.; m. Lydia Ellen Minevitch, Oct. 22, 1960 (dec. Sept. 1986); 1 child, James Eldar, m. Barbara Guggenheim, Feb. 21, 1991. B.A., UCLA, 1949; J.D. magna cum laude, Harvard U., 1952. Bar: Calif. 1953. Practiced in, Los Angeles, 1955—; assoc. firm Shearer, Fields, Rohner & Shearer, and predecessor firms, 1955-57, mem. firm, 1957-82; ptnr. Greenberg, Glusker, Fields, Claman & Machtinger, 1982—. Author: (as D. Kincaid) The Sunset Bomber, 1986, The Lawyer's Tale, 1992, (as B. Fields) Royal Blood Richard III and the Mystery of the Princes, 1998; mem. bd. editors: Harvard Law Rev., 1953-55. Bd. dirs. U. So. Calif. Annenberg Sch. Comm. 1st. lt. USAF, 1953-55, Korea. Mem. ABA, L.A. County Bar Assn., Coun. Fgn. Rels. Achievements include being the subject of profiles Calif. Mag., Nov. 1987, Avenue Mag., Mar. 1989, Am. Film Mag., Dec. 1989, Vanity Fair Mag., Dec. 1993, Harvard Law Sch. Bull., spring 1998, London Sunday Telegraph, June 1999, Sunday New York Post, July 1999. Office: Greenberg Glusker Fields Claman & Machtinger Ste 2000 1900 Avenue Of The Stars Los Angeles CA 90067-4590

FIELDS, DEBBI, cookie franchise executive; m. Randy Fields (div.); 5 children; m. Michael Rose. Founder, Mrs. Fields Original Cookies, Salt Lake City. Office: Mrs Fields Original Cookies 2855 Cottonwood Pkwy Ste 400 Salt Lake City UT 84121-7050

FIELDS, HOWARD LINCOLN, neurology and physiology educator; b. Chgo., Dec. 12, 1939; s. Charles and Mae (Pinkert) F.; m. Carol Margaret Felts, Dec. 31, 1966; children: Rima Tamar, Gabriel Charles. Research neurologist Walter Reed Research Inst., Washington, 1967-70; clin. fellow Harvard Med. Sch., Boston, 1970-72; asst. prof. U. Calif., San Francisco, 1973-78, assoc. prof., 1978-82, prof., 1982—; vice chmn. neurology, 1993—; dir. Wheeler Ctr. for Neurobiology of Addiction. Cons. NIH, Bethesda, Md., 1979-84; vis. fellow Clare Hall Coll., Cambridge (Eng.) U., 1979; vis. prof. Royal Soc. Medicine, 1988. Editor: (book) Recent Advances in Pain Research and Therapy, 1985, Core Curriculum for Professional Education in Pain, 1991, 2d edit., 1995; author: Pain, 1987, Pain Syndromes in Neurology, 1990, Pharmacotherapy of Pain, 1994; contbr. 200 articles to profl. jours. Recipient rsch. career devel. award NIH, merit award Nat. Inst. Drug Abuse, Kerr award Am. Pain Soc., 1997. Mem. Internat. Assn. Study of Pain (program chmn. 1981-84, sec. 1990-93, editor-in-chief IASP Press 1993—), Am. Soc. Clin. Investigation, Am. Acad. Neurology (Cotzias lecture award 2000), Am. Neurol. Assn. (councillor 1991, program com. 1991), Soc. for Neurosci., Inst. Medicine of NAS. Office: U Calif Dept Neurology PO Box 453 San Francisco CA 94143-0001

FIFE, DENNIS JENSEN, chemistry educator, career officer; b. Brigham [illegible] Marie Gunther, June 22, 1972; children: Kimball, Kellie, Keith, Kurt, Katie, Kenton. BS in Chemistry, Weber State U., Ogden, Utah, 1969; MBA, Inter-Am. U., San German, P.R., 1973; MS in Chemistry, Utah State U., 1978, PhD in Phsy. Chemistry, 1983. Assoc. chemist Thiokol Chem. Corp., Brigham City, 1969; commd. 2d lt. USAF, 1969, advanced through grades to lt. col.; pilot, instr., flight examiner Hurricane Hunters, Ramey [illegible] Squadron, Ogden, Utah, 1979-81; instr. chemistry USAF Acad., Colorado

Springs, Colo., 1977-79, asst. prof., 1983-85, assoc. prof., 1985-90, prof., 1990; pres. Select Pubs., Inc., Colorado Springs, 1985-90, also chmn. bd. dirs., 1990; mgr. analytical labs. dept. Thiokol Corp., Brigham City, Utah, 1990—. Author: How to Form a Colorado Corporation, 1986; contbr. articles to profl. jours. Active Boy Scouts Am., 1981—, sustaining mem. Rep. Nat. Com., Washington, 1983— Decorated Air medal with oak leaf cluster: NSF research grantee, 1967-68. Mem. Internat. Union Pure and Applied Chemistry (affiliate), Am. Chem. Soc., Phi Kappa Phi. Republican. Mormon. Avocations: racketball, fly fishing, hunting. Office: Thiokol Propulsion PO Box 707 Brigham City UT 84302-0707

FIFIELD, MARVIN G. psychologist, educator; BA in Music, Idaho State U., 1956, MEd in Ednl. Adminstrn., 1958; EdD in Counseling, Wash. State U., 1963. Lic. psychologist, Idaho; cert. sch. psychologist, Utah, Idaho; cert. sch. counselor, Utah, Idaho. Dir. rsch. and spl. svcs. Pocatello (Idaho) Sch. Dist., 1964-66; dir. Ctr. for MR Study Idaho State U., Pocatello, 1967-69; postdoctoral fellow Columbia Tchr. Coll., N.Y.C., summer 1970; chmn. dept. spl. edn. Utah State U., Logan, 1969-72, dir. Affiliated Devel. Ctr. for Handicapped Persons, 1972-86, dir. Affiliated Ctr. for Persons with Disabilities, 1987—, dir. Utah Assistive Tech. Program, 1989—, prof. dept. spl. edn. and psychology, 1989—; profl. staff mem. Com. on Labor and Human Resources U.S. Senate, Washington, 1986-87. Vocat. expert HEW/Social Security Adminstrn., Washington, 1968—; UAF liaison cons. HEW/OHDS Divsn. Devel. Disabilities, Washington, 1975-78; expert cons., tchr. trainer WHO Pan Am. Sanitary Bur., Santiago, Chile, 1979; cons. in evaluation tng. and psychol. svcs. Diné Ctr. for Human Devel., Navajo C.C., Ariz., 1980-86; curriculum and psychol. cons. Assn. Venezolena de Padres y Amigos de Ninos Excepcionales, Caracas, 1981-86. Contbr. articles to profl. jours.; author 18 books, chpts. in books, monographs. Vice chmn. Idaho Mental Retardation and Mental Health Planning Coun., 1963-65; adv. bd. Intermountain Regional Med. Program, 1972-76; mem. Utah Gov.'s Coun. for Persons with Disabilities, 1978—; chmn. Senator Hatch's Adv. Com. on Disability Issues, 1981—; chmn. bd. dirs. OPTIONS for Independence, No. Utah, 1987-91; exec. com. Utah Legis. Task Force on Svcs. for Persons with Handicaps, 1990-91; bd. dirs. Utah Legal Ctr. for Persons with Disabilities, 1991—; active ARC. Mem. APA (mem. divsn. counseling psychology, ednl. psychology and sch. psychology), Am. Assn. Univ. Affiliated Proglrams (pres. 1984-85, bd. dirs. 1995—), Rehab. Engring. Soc. N.Am. (co-chair ann. conv. 1996), Am. Assn. on Mental Retardation, Nat. Assn. Retarded Citizens, Utah Cerebral Palsy Assn., Phi Delta Kappa. Office: Utah State U Ctr Persons with Disabilities UMC 680C Logan UT 84322-0001 E-mail: marv@cpo2.usu.edu

FIFLIS, TED JAMES, lawyer, educator; b. Chgo., Feb. 20, 1933; s. James P. and Christine (Karakitsos) F.; m. Vasilike Pantelakos, July 3, 1955; children: Christina Eason, Antonia Fowler, Andreanna Lawson. BS, Northwestern U., 1954; LLB, Harvard U., 1957. Bar: Ill. 1957, Colo. 1975, U.S. Supreme Ct. 1984. Pvt. practice law, Chgo., 1957-65, mem. faculty U. Colo. Law Sch., Boulder, 1965—, prof., 1968—. Vis. prof. NYU, 1968, U. Calif., Davis, 1973, U. Chgo., 1976, U. Va., 1979, Duke U., 1980, Georgetown U., 1982, U. Pa., 1983, Am. U., 1983, Harvard U., 1988; Lehmann disting. vis. prof. Washington U., St. Louis, 1991; cons. Rice U.; arbitrator AT&T divesture disputes, 1984-87. Author: (with Homer Kripke, Paul Foster) Accounting for Business Lawyers, 1970, 3rd edit., 1984, Accounting Issues for Lawyers, 1991; editor-in-chief Corp. Law Rev., 1977-88; contbr. articles to profl. jours. Mem. ABA, Am. Assn. Law Schs. (past chmn. bus. law sect.), Colo. Bar Assn. (mem. coun. sect. of corp., banking and bus. law 1974-75), Am. Law Inst. (chmn. com. on rsch. proposed fed. securities code), Colo. Assn. Corp. Counsel (pres. 1998-99). Greek Orthodox. Home: 1340 Bluebell Ave Boulder CO 80302-7832 Office: Univ Of Colo Law Sch Boulder CO 80309-0001

FIGLEY, MELVIN MORGAN, radiologist, physician, educator; b. Toledo, Dec. 5, 1920; s. Karl Dean and Margaret (Morgan) F.; m. Margaret Jane Harris, Mar. 16, 1946; children: Karl Porter, Joseph Dean, Mark Thompson. Student, Dartmouth, 1938-41; MD magna cum laude (John Harvard fellow), Harvard, 1944. Diplomate: Am. Bd. Radiology (trustee 1967-72). Intern, then resident internal medicine Western Res. U., 1944-46; resident radiology U. Mich., 1948-51, instr., asst. prof., asso. prof. radiology, 1950-58; practice specializing in radiology Seattle, 1958-86; prof. radiology, chmn. dept. U. Wash., 1958-78, prof. radiology and medicine, 1979-85, emeritus prof. radiology and medicine, 1986—. Mem. radiation study sect. NIH, 1963-67; mem. com. on radiology Nat. Acad. Scis.-NRC, 1964-69, chmn., 1968-69 Editor: Am. Jour. Roentgenology, 1976-85; contbr. articles profl. jours. Bd. dirs. James Picker Found., 1970-80. Served to capt. M.C. AUS, 1946-48. John and Mary R. Markle scholar, 1952-57 Fellow Am. Coll. Radiology (Gold medal 1987), Royal Coll. Radiologists (hon., London), Royal Australian Coll. Radiologists (hon.); mem. Royal Soc. Medicine (hon.), Assn. Univ. Radiologists (pres. 1966, Gold medal 1983), Am. Roentgen Ray Soc. (exec. council 1970-88, pres. 1983-84, Gold medal 1986), N. Am. Soc. Cardiac Radiology (pres. 1974), Fleischer Soc. (pres. 1986-87), Radiol. Soc. N.Am. (Gold Medal 1986), AMA, Boylston Med. Soc., Wash. Heart Assn. (past trustee), Soc. Chmn. Acad. Radiology Depts. (exec. council 1969-71), Phi Beta Kappa, Sigma Xi, Alpha Omega Alpha, Sigma Alpha Epsilon. Episcopalian. Home: PO Box 859 Grantham NH 03753-0859

FIGUEROA, LIZ, state senator; b. San Francisco; children: AnaLisa, Aaron. Ed., Coll. San Mateo. Owner, oeprator Figueroa Employment Cons., 1981-98; mem. Union Sanitary Dist., pres., 1985; mem. Calif. State Senate, 1998—, mem. bus. and professions com. Mem. Hispanic Cmty. Affairs Coun.; mem. Fermont Adult Sch. Adv. Bd.; bd. dirs. Legal Assistance for Srs.; local bd. dirs. Selective Svc. Sys.; mem. adv. bd. Peninsula Coll. Law. Named Outstanding Legislator by several orgns. Mem. Calif. Elected Women's Assn. for Edn. and Rsch. (bd. dirs.). Democrat. Office: Calif State Senate State Capitol Rm 2057 Sacramento CA 95814 also: 43271 Mission Blvd Fremont CA 94539-5826

FILIPPOU, FILIP C. engineering educator; b. Thessaloniki, Greece, July 14, 1955; m. Lucia L. Longhi, 1984; children: Pauline, Romina. Diploma, Tech. U., Munich, Germany, 1978; PhD in Civil Engring., U. Calif., Berkeley, 1983. Asst. prof. U. Calif., Berkeley, 1983-89, assoc. prof. structural engring., 1989-98, now prof. structural engring., 1998—. Engr. Tylin Int, 1983-84; NSF presdl. young investigator, 1987; vis. prof. U. Rome, Italy, 1988, Ecole Normale Superieure, Cachan, France, 1999, 2000. Fellow Am. Concrete Inst.; mem. ASCE (Alfred Noble prize 1988, Walter L. Huber Civil Engring. rsch. prize 1994), Prestressed Concrete Inst., Earthquake Engring. Rsch. Inst. Achievements include research in analysis and behavior of reinforced and prestressed concrete structures under normal and extreme loadings; development of models and effective simulation strategies; design guidelines for structures, particularly, under earthquake loads. Office: U Calif Dept Civil Engring 731 Davis Hall Berkeley CA 94720-1711 E-mail: filippou@ce.berkeley.edu

FILLIUS, MILTON FRANKLIN, JR. food products company executive; b. N.Y., Nov. 17, 1922; s. Milton Franklin and Georgiana (Bergh) F.; m. Nelma Chauncey, May 11, 1996; children by previous marriage: Julie, Karen, Anthony, Donald. BA, Hamilton Coll., 1946; JD, U. Mich., 1949; LHD (hon.), Hamilton Coll., 1996. Bar: Calif. 1950, U.S. Supreme Ct. 1950. Adminstrv. asst. to banker in, San Diego, 1949-51; treas., gen. mgr. Nat. Steel and Shipbldg. Co., San Diego, 1951-56, exec. v.p., gen. mgr., 1956-62; exec. v.p. Westgate-Calif. Corp., 1962-65; chmn. Vita-Pakt Citrus Products Co., 1966-90. Mem. State Bar of Calif., San Diego C. of C. (pres. 1962-64), Theta Delta Chi, Phi Alpha Delta. Home: 18163 Viceroy Dr San Diego CA 92128-1302 Office: Vita-Pakt Citrus Products Co PO Box 309 Covina CA 91723-0309

FILNER, BOB, congressman; b. Pitts., Sept. 4, 1942; m. Jane Merrill; children: Erin, Adam. BA in Chemistry, Cornell U., 1963; MA in History, U. Del., 1969; PhD in History, Cornell U., 1973. Prof. history San Diego State U., 1970-92; legis. asst. Senator Hubert Humphrey, 1974, Congressman Don Fraser, 1975; spl. asst. Congressman Jim Bates, 1984; city councilman 8th dist. City of San Diego, 1987-92, dep. mayor, 1992; mem. U.S. Congress from 50th Calif. dist., 1993—; mem. transp. and infrastructure com., vets. affairs com. Pres. San Diego Bd. Edn., 1982, mem.-elect 1979-83; chmn. San Diego Schs. of the Future Commn., 1986-87. Democrat. Office: US Ho of Reps 2463 Rayburn Hob Washington DC 20515-0001*

FILO, DAVID, computer communications executive; b. Moss Bluff, La. Co-founder, chief yahoo Yahoo!, Santa Clara, Calif., 1994—. Office: Yahoo Inc 3420 Central Expy Ste 201 Santa Clara CA 95051-0703

FILOSA, GARY FAIRMONT RANDOLPH V., II, multimedia executive, financier; b. Wilder, Vt., Feb. 22, 1931; s. Gary F.R. de Marco de Varra and Rosaline M. (Falzarano) Filosa; m. Catherine Moray Stewart (dec.); children: Marc Christian Bazire de Villadon III, Gary Fairmont Randolph de Varra III. Grad., Mt. Hermon Sch., 1950; PhB, U. Chgo., 1954; BA, U. Americas, Mex., 1967; MA, Calif. Western U., 1968; PhD, U.S. Internat. U., 1970. Sports reporter Claremont Daily Eagle, Rutland Herald, Vt. Informer, 1947-52; pub. The Chicagoan, 1952-54; account exec., editor house publs. Robertson, Buckley & Gotsch, Inc., Chgo., 1953-54; account exec. Fuller, Smith & Ross, Inc., N.Y.C., 1955; prodr./host Weekend KCET Channel 13, N.Y.C., 1955-67; editor Apparel Arts mag. (now Gentlemen's Quar.), Esquire, Inc., N.Y.C., 1955-56; chmn. bd., CEO, pres. Filosa Publs. Internat., N.Y.C., 1956-63; pub. Teenage, Rustic Rhythm, Teen Life, Mystery Digest, Top Talent, Rock & Roll Roundup, Celebrities, Stardust, Personalities, Campus monthly mags.; pres., chmn. bd. Teenarama Records, Inc., N.Y.C., 1956-62; chmn. bd., pres. Produciones Mexicanes Internationales (S.A.), Mexico City, 1957-68; assoc. pub. Laundromatic Age, N.Y.C., 1958-59; ptnr. with Warner LeRoy purchase of Broadway plays for Hollywood films, N.Y.C., 1958-61; pres. Montclair Sch., 1958-60, Pacific Registry, Inc., L.A., 1959-61; exec. prodr. Desilu Studios, Inc., Hollywood, Calif., 1959-61; exec. asst. to Benjamin A. Javits, 1961-62; propr. Gino's of Hollywood, 1961-70; dean adminstrn. Postgrad. Ctr. for Mental Health, N.Y.C., 1962-64; chmn. bd., CEO Filosa Films Internat., Beverly Hills, Calif., 1962—; pres. Amateur Athletes Internat., Iowa City, 1996-2000; chmn. bd., pres. Cinematografica Americana Internationale (S.A.), Mexico City, 1964-84; pres. Casa Filosa Corp., Palm Beach, Fla., 1982-87; dir. Cmty. Savs., North Palm Beach, 1982-87. V.p. acad. affairs World Acad., San Francisco, 1967-68; asst. to provost Calif. Western U., San Diego, 1968-69; assoc. prof. philosophy Art Coll., San Francisco, 1969-70; v.p. acad. affairs, dean of faculty Internat. Inst., Phoenix, 1968-73; chmn. bd. dirs., pres. Universite Universelle, 1970-73, 2000—; bd. dirs., v.p. acad. affairs, dean Summer Sch., Internat. C.C., L.A., 1970-72; chmn. bd., pres. Social Directory Calif., 1967-75, Am. Assn. Social Registries, L.A., 1970-76; pres. Social Directory U.S., N.Y.C., 1974-76; pres. Herbert Hoover Forum, Iowa City, 1996-2000; chmn. bd. dirs. Internat. Soc. Social Registers, Paris, 1974—; surfing coach U. Calif. at Irvine, 1975-77; v.p. Xerox-Systemic, 1979-80; CEO Internat. Surfing League, Palm Beach, 1987-95, Santa Barbara, Calif., 1996—; chmn., CEO Filosa Harrop Internat., Phoenix, 1987-89; pres. Amateur Athletes Internat., Iowa City, 1996-2000; nationally syndicated columnist Conservations with Am., 1997 2000. Editor: Sci. Digest, 1961-62; composer: (lyrics) The Night Discovers Love, 1952, That Certain Something, 1953, Bolero of Love, 1956; author: (stage play) Let Me Call Ethel, 1955, The Bisexual, 1961, Technology Enters 21st Century, 1966, (mus.) Feather Light, 1966, No Public Funds for Nonpublic Schools, 1968, Creative Function of the College President, 1969, The Surfers Almanac, 1977, The Filosa Newsletter, 1986-92, The Sexual Continuum, 1990, Traveltalk, 1991, God's Own Prince, 1995, Holy Hawai'i, 1996, (biography) A Plague on Paradise, 1994, (TV series) Danny Thomas Show, 1963, Surfing USA, 1977, Payne of Florida, 1985, Honolulu, 1991, The Gym, 1992, Sales Pitch, 1992, 810 Ocean Avenue, 1992, One Feather, 1992, Conversations with America, 1989, All American Beach Party, 1989, Riding High, 2000, Dreamsport, 2000, Icons, 2000; contbr. numerous articles, editorials, to profl. jours., newspapers, and encys., including Life, Look, Sci. Digest, Ency. of Sports, World Book Ency., New York Times, Cedar Rapids Gazete, L.A. Times, others. Trustee Univ. of the Ams., Pueblo, Mex., 1986-2000; candidate for L.A. City Coun., 1 959; chmn. Educators for Re-election of Ivy Baker Priest, 1970; mem. So. Calif. Com. for Olympic Games, 1977-84. With AUS, 1954-55. Recipient DAR Citizenship awrd, 1959, Silver Conquistador award Am. Assn. Social Registers, 1970, Ambassador's Cup U. Ams., 1967, resolution Calif. State Legis., 1977, Duke Kahanamoku Classic surfing trophy, 1977, gold pendant Japan Surfing Assn., 1978, Father of Olympic Surfing award Internat. Athletic Union, 1995, Father of Surfing trophy Amateur Athletes Internat., 1997, Father of Surfing trophy Internat. Surfing Fedn., 2000; inducted into Rock & Roll Mus. & Hall of Fame, Cleve., 1995. Mem. NAACP, NCAA (bd. dels. 1977-82), AAU (gov. 1978-82), Am. Acad. Motion Picture Arts and Scis., Internat. Surfing Com., U.S. Surfing Com. (founder 1960—), Internat. Surfing League (founder, chmn., CEO 1988—), Internat. Surfing Fedn. (pres. 1960—), Am. Assn. UN, Authors League, Authors Guild, Alumni Assn. U. Ams. (pres. 1967-70), Surf Club of the Palm Beaches (pres. 1983-94), Sierra Club, Surfing Hui of Hawaii, Internat. Soc. Bibliotherapists (Paris, pres. 1997—), Lords Corybantes (Berlin) (life pres. 1966—), Commonwealth Club (San Francisco), Town Hall (L.A.), Calif. Club (L.A.), Sigma Omicron Lambda (founder, pres. 1965-92). Episcopalian. Home: PO Box 2893 Palm Beach FL 33480-2883 Office: PO Box 299 Beverly Hills CA 90213-0299

FILS, ELLIOTT, advertising executive; CFO Rodgers & Assocs., L.A. Office: Rodgers & Assocs 1875 Century Park E Ste 300 Los Angeles CA 90067-2504

FILSHIE, MICHELE ANN, editor; b. Hartford, Conn., Mar. 5, 1964; d. Joseph James Fitzgibbons and Judith Ann (Bennett) Small; m. Glenn Filshie, May 24, 1986 (div. 1997). BA in English, U. Western Ont., London, 1986. Asst. to the pub. Black Sparrow Press, Santa Rosa, Calif., 1991—. Pres., bd. dirs. Sonoma County People for Econ. Opportunity, Santa Rosa, Calif., 1999-2001; candidate West Sonoma County Union H.S. Dist. Sch. Bd., 1998, elected trustee, 2000. Recipient Write Women Back into History award Nat. Women's History Project, Windsor, Calif., 1995. Mem. NOW (pres. Sonoma County chpt. 1994-96), Nat. Women's Polit. Caucus, Sebastopol C. of C., Rotary Club of Sebastopol Sunrise (past dir.). Democrat. Avocation: dance. Office: Black Sparrow Press 24 10th St Santa Rosa CA 95401-4714 E-mail: books@blacksparrowpress.com

FINCH, CALEB ELLICOTT, neurobiologist, educator; b. London, July 4, 1939; came to U.S., 1939; s. Benjamin F. and Faith (Stratton) Campbell; m. Doris Nossamen, Oct. 11, 1975; stepsons: Michael, Alec Tsongas. BS, Yale U., 1961; PhD, Rockefeller U., 1969. Guest investigator Rockefeller U., N.Y.C., 1969-70; asst. prof. Cornell U. Med. Coll., N.Y.C., 1970-72; asst. prof. biology, gerontology U. So. Calif., L.A., 1972-75, assoc. prof., 1975-78, prof., 1978—, ARCO and William Kieschnick prof. neurobiology of aging, 1985—, Univ. prof., 1989—. Mem. editl. bd. Jour. Gerontology, 1979-86, Neurobiology of Aging, 1982—, Synapse, 1992—, Exp. Gerontol., 1997—; contbr. more than 350 articles to profl. jours.; author: Longevity, Senescence and the Genome, 1990, (with R. Ricklefs) Aging: A Natural History, 1995, (with T. Kirkwood) Chance, Development and Aging, 2000. Recipient Allied Signal Inc. award Achievement in Biomed. Aging, 1988, Rsch. award Alzheimer's Assn. L.A., 1989, Am. Aging Assn., 1994, Cherkin award UCLA, 1991, Sandoz Premier prize IAG, 1996, prize for longevity rsch. IPSEN Found., 1996, award for leadership in comms. IASIA, 1996, Irving Wright award AFAR, 1999; NIH rsch. grantee, 1972—. Fellow AAAS, Gerontol. Soc. Am. (chmn. biology sect. 1992-93, Robert W. Kleemeier award 1984); mem. Neurosci. Soc., Endocrine Soc., Neuroendocrine Soc., Psychoneuroendocrine Soc., Iron Mountain String Band (fiddler 1963—). Home: 2144 Crescent Dr Altadena CA 91001-2112 Office: U So Calif Gerontology Ctr University Park Los Angeles CA 90007

FINDLEY, JOHN A., JR. publisher; b. Fulton, Mo., Feb. 25, 1951; s. John Allen and Naomi Joan (Reker) F.; m. Oneida Lynn Blackwell, Dec. 4, 1993; children: John III, Hugh. Student, U. Mo., 1973; AB, Westminster Coll., 1973. Sales rep. Kingdom Daily News, Fulton, 1973-74; adv. rep. Colo Daily Press-Telegram, Boulder, 1974-76; advt. sales rep. Dallas Times Herald, 1976-77, advt. sales mgr., 1977-80, dir. consumer mktg., 1981-83, dir. circulation, 1983, dir. retail advt., 1983-84; regional sales mgr. Times Mirror Nat. Mktg., 1984-86; v.p. mktg. So. Conn. Newspapers, Stamford, 1986-88, sr. v.p. mktg. and prodn., 1989-93; pres. Charleston (W.Va.) Newspapers, 1993-97; pub., CEO Long Beach (Calif.) Press-Telegram, 1998—. Bd. govs. Calif. State U., Long Beach; bd. dirs. Long Beach coun. Boy Scouts Am., Long Beach Found., Long Beach Venture Forum. Mem. Newspaper Assn. Am., Sigma Chi. Office: 604 Pine Ave Long Beach CA 90844-0003 E-mail: jack.findley@press-telegram.com

FINE, CHARLES LEON, lawyer; b. Waukegan, Ill., Jan. 30, 1932; s. David M. and Henrietta (Goodman) F.; m. Penny J. Haines, Aug. 30, 1958; children: Karen L., Andrew H. BS, U. Wis., 1955; LLB, JD, Am. U., 1961. Bar: Mich. 1962, Ariz. 1981, U.S. Supreme Ct. 1971. Newscaster, news editor WKOW Radio and TV, Madison, Wis., 1953-58; editor, writer U.S. Bur. Pub. Roads, Washington, 1958-61; trial, staff atty. U.S. NLRB, Washington, Detroit, 1961-63; atty, assoc. Griffith & Griffith law firm, Detroit, 1963-69; atty., ptnr. Clark, Hardy, Lewis & Fine, Detroit, Birmingham, 1969-81; assoc. prof. law U. Detroit Sch. Law, 1976-80; ptnr. O'Connor, Cavanagh, et al, Phoenix, 1981-96, Streich Lang, 1996-2000, Littler Mendelson, 2000—. Cons. Met. Detoit Bur. Sch. Studies, 1970-80, Employer's Assn. Detroit, 1970-80. Assoc. editor Washington Coll. Law Rev., 1960; co-editor, author: Ariz. Employment Law Handbook, 1994; contbr. articles to legal jours. and chpts. to books. Mem. Ariz. Supreme Ct. Commn. on Minorities, 1996-2000; pres. Meadowlake Homeowners Assn., Birmingham, Mich., 1972-73; bd. dirs. Sch. Law Inst., Detroit, 1976-77; atty., advisor Gov.'s Office, Mich., 1979-80; cons. Cmty. Legal Svcs., Phoenix, 1986—. 1st lt. U.S. Army, 1955-57. Recipient Best Advocate award Nat. Moot Ct. Competition, Washington, 1960, Order of Barristers award Nat. Honor Soc., 1978; scholarship fund in his name U. Detroit Sch. of Law, 1979. Fellow Coll. Labor and Employment Lawyers; mem. Am. Employment Law Coun., Ariz. Bar Assn., Mich. Bar Assn., Am. Arbitration Assn. (arbitrator, employment arbitration panelist 1995—), Ariz. Insl. Rels. Assn. Avocations: badminton, hiking, swimming, reading. Home: 9041 N 33rd Way Phoenix AZ 85028-4968 Office: Littler Mendelson 2425 E Camelback Rd Ste 900 Phoenix AZ 85016 Fax: 602-241-3221. E-mail: CFINE@Littler.com

FINE, JAMES STEPHEN, physician; b. St. Paul, June 14, 1946; s. Ralph Irving and Beverlee Lois (Rockler) F.; m. Meredith Ann Blehert, June 20, 1970; children: Zachary, Esther, Gabriel. BA in Math., U. Minn., 1968, MD, 1972, MS in Biometry, Health Info. Systems, 1977. Intern in medicine St. Paul-Ramsey Hosp., 1972-73; residency U. Minn., Mpls., 1973-77; assoc. prof., dir. info. and specimen processing div. U. Wash. Hosp., Seattle, 1977-94, chmn. lab. medicine, 1994— Mem. Am. Assn. Clin. Chemistry, Acad. Clin. Lab. Physicians and Scientists (Gerald T. Evans award 2001), Computer Soc. of IEEE, Am. Med. Informatics Assn., Wash. State Med. Assn., King County Med. Soc. Office: U Wash Hosp Box 357110 1959 NE Pacific Ave NW 120 Seattle WA 98195

FINE, MARJORIE LYNN, lawyer; b. Bklyn., Aug. 14, 1950; d. Percy and Sylvia (Bernstein) F.; m. John Kent Markley, May 6, 1979; children: Jessica Paige Markley, Laura Anne Markley. BA, Smith Coll., 1972; JD, U. Calif., 1977. Bar: Calif. 1977. Assoc. to ptnr. Donahue Gallagher Woods & Wood, Oakland, Calif., 1977-87; sr. counsel Bank of Am., San Francisco, 1987-89; assoc., gen. counsel Shaklee Corp., San Francisco, 1989-90; gen. counsel, v.p. Shaklee U.S., Inc., San Francisco, 1990-94, Shaklee U.S., Shaklee Technica, 1995-99, 1999—, Yamanouchi Pharma Techs., Inc., 1999-2001; gen. counsel, sr. v.p. Shaklee Corp., 2001 . Judge pro tem Oakland Piedmont Emeryville Mcpl. Ct., 1982-89; fee arbitrator Alameda Co. Bar Assn., 1980-87. Mem. ABA, Calif. Bar Assn., Calif. Employment Law Coun. (bd. dirs. 1993—). Jewish. Office: Shaklee Corp 4747 Willow Rd Pleasanton CA 94588-2740

FINEGOLD, SYDNEY MARTIN, microbiology educator; b. N.Y.C., Aug. 12, 1921; s. Samuel Joseph and Jennie (Stein) F.; m. Mary Louise Saunders, Feb. 8, 1947 (dec. June 1994); children: Joseph, Patricia, Michael; m. Gloria Weiss, Feb. 18, 1996. A.B., UCLA, 1943; M.D., U. Tex., 1949. Diplomate: Am. Bd. Med. Microbiology (mem. bd. 1979-85), Am. Bd. Internal Medicine. Intern USPHS, Galveston, Tex., 1949-50; fellow in medicine U. Minn. Med. Sch., 1950-52, research fellow, 1951-52; resident medicine Wadsworth Hosp., VA Ctr., Los Angeles, 1953-54; instr. medicine U. Calif. Med. Ctr., Los Angeles, 1955-57, asst. clin. prof., 1957-59, asst. prof., 1959-62, assoc. prof., 1962-68, prof., 1968—, prof. microbiology and immunology, 1983—; chief chest and infectious disease sect. Wadsworth Hosp., 1957-61, chief infectious disease sect., 1961-86, assoc. chief staff for research and devel., 1986-92; staff physician infectious disease sect. VA Med. Ctr., L.A., 1992—. Mem. pulmonary disease research program com. VA, 1961-62, infectious disease research program com., 1961-65, merit rev. bd. (infectious diseases), 1972-74, med. research program specialist, 1974-76, adv. com. on infectious disease, 1974-87; mem. NRC-Nat. Acad. Sci. Drug Efficacy Study Group, 1966-69; mem. subcom. on gram-negative anaerobic bacilli Internat. Com. on Nomenclature Bacteria, 1966—, chmn., 1972-78; mem. adv. panel U.S. Pharmacopoeia, 1970-75; chmn. working group on anaerobic susceptibility test methods Nat. Com. Clin. Lab. Standards, 1987-97, advisor, 1998—. Mem. editl. bd. Calif. Medicine, 1966-73, Applied Microbiology, 1973-74, Western Jour. Medicine, 1974-77, Am. Rev. Respiratory Disease, 1974-76, Jour. Clin. Microbiology, 1975-85, Infection, 1976—, Jour. Infectious Disease, 1979-82, 84-85, Antimicrobial Agts. Chemotherapy, 1980-89, Diagnostic Microbiology and Infectious Diseases, 1982-90; editor Revs. of Infectious Diseases, 1990-91, Clin. Infectious Diseases, 1992-2000; sect. editor: infectious diseases vols. Clin. Medicine, 1978-82, Microbiol. Ecology in Health and Disease, 1987-90; assoc. editor, consulting editor Anaerobe, 1994—. editor-in-chief, 1998—. Vice chmn. UCLA Acad. Senate, 1986-87, chair, 1987-88. Served with USMCR; Served with USNR, 1943-46; to 1st. lt. AUS, 1952-53. Co-recipient V.A. Williams S. Middleton award for biomed. rsch., 1984; recipient Profl. Achievement award UCLA, 1987, Mayo Soley award Western Soc. Clin. Investigation, 1988, Disting. Alumnus award U. Tex. Med. Br., 1988, UCLA Med. Alumni Assn. Med. Scis. award, 1990, Hoechst Roussel award Am. Soc. Microbiology, 1992, medal Helsinki U., Finland, 1996, Lifetime Achievement award Infectious Disease Assn. Calif., 1995, Wm. H. Oldendorf Lifetime Achievement awrd VA Med. Ctr., 1996, Lifetime Achievement award Internat. Soc. Anaerobic Bacteriology, 1998, Becton Dickinson award in Clin. Microbiology, 1999; organism named Finegoldia magna, 1999. Master ACP; fellow APHA, AAAS, Am. Acad. Microbiology,

Infectious Diseases Soc. Am. (councilor 1976-79, pres.-elect 1980-81, pres. 1981-82, exec. com. 1980-83, Bristol award 1987, Soc. citation 1999); mem. Assn. Am. Physicians, Am. Soc. Microbiology (chmn. subcom. on taxonomy of Bacteroidaceae 1971-74, 1st annual Alex Sonnen Wirth award 1986), Am. Thoracic Soc., Western Soc. Clin. Rsch., Western Assn. Physicians, Wadsworth Med. Alumni Assn. (past pres.), Anaerobe Soc. of the Ams. (interim pres. 1992-94, pres. 1994-96), Soc. Intestinal Microbiology Ecology and Disease (interim pres. 1982-83, pres. 1983-87), Va. Soc. Physician in Infectious Diseases (pres. 1986-88), Am. Fedn. Clin. Rsch., Sigma Xi, Alpha Omega Alpha. Democrat. Jewish. Home: 11715 Folkstone Ln Los Angeles CA 90077-1311 Office: Infectious Disease Sect VA Med Ctr Wilshire & Sawtelle Blvds Los Angeles CA 90073 E-mail: sidfinegol@aol.com

FINGARETTE, HERBERT, philosopher, educator; b. Bklyn., Jan. 20, 1921; m. Leslie J. Swabacker, Jan. 23, 1945; 1 dau., Ann Hasse. B.A., UCLA, 1947, Ph.D., 1949; LHD, St. Bonaventure U., 1993. Mem. faculty U. Calif.-Santa Barbara, 1948—, Phi Beta Kappa Romanell prof. philosophy, 1983—; William James lectr. religion Harvard U., 1971; W.T. Jones lectr. philosophy Pomona Coll., 1974; Evans-Wentz lectr. Oriental religions Stanford U., 1977; Gramlich lectr. human nature Dartmouth Coll., 1978; cons. NEH; Raphael Demos lectr. Vanderbilt U., 1985. Disting. tchr. U. Calif.-Santa Barbara, 1985, faculty research lectr., 1977. Author: The Self in Transformation, 1963, On Responsibility, 1967, Self Deception, 1969, Confucius: The Secular as Sacred, 1972, The Meaning of Criminal Insanity, 1972, Mental Disabilities and Criminals Responsibility, 1979, Heavy Drinking: The Myth of Alcoholism as a Disease, 1988, Rules, Rituals, and Responsibility: Essays Dedicated to Herbert Fingarette, 1991, Death: Philosophical Soundings, 1996. Washington and Lee U. Lewis law scholar, 1980; fellow NEH, NIMH, Walter Meyer Law Research Inst., Battelle Research Ctr., Addiction Research Ctr., Inst. Psychiatry, London; fellow Ctr. for Advanced Studies in Behavioral Sci., Stanford, 1985-86. Mem. Am. Philos. Assn. (pres. Pacific divsn. 1977-78). Home: 1507 APS Santa Barbara CA 93103 Office: U Calif Dept Philosophy Santa Barbara CA 93106

FINK, JOSEPH RICHARD, academic administrator; b. Newark, Mar. 20, 1940; s. Joseph Richard and Jean (Chorazy) F.; m. Donna Gibson, 1965 (div. 1986); children: Michael, Taryn; m. Christine Gaudenzi, oct. 4, 1992; children: Madison, Joseph. AB, Rider U., 1961; PhD in Am. History, Rutgers U., 1971; DLitt (hon.), Rider U., 1982, Coll. of Misericordia, 1992, Golden Gate U., 1994. Asst. then assoc. prof history Immaculata (Pa.) Coll., 1964-72, adminstrv. asst. to pres., 1969-72; dean of Arts & Scis. City Colls. Chgo., 1972-74; pres. Raritan Valley Coll., Somerville, N.J., 1974-79, Coll. Misericordia, Dallas, 1979-88, Dominican U of Calif, San Rafael, 1988—. Pres. Regional Planning Coun. Higher Edn., Region 3/Northeastern Pa., 1986-88. Mem. exec. com. Philharm. Soc. Northeastern Pa., 1986-89; bd. dirs. Marin Symphony, 1989-99, San Francisco Ballet, 1994-97, Ind. Coll. No. Calif., 1992—, Marin Forum, 1991—, Guide Dogs for the Blind, 1994-97; bd. dirs. Am. Land Conservancy, 1995—, exec. com.; mem. campaign cabinet United Way San Francisco, 1990; bd. dirs. North Bay Coun., 1993—, chmn., 1996, exec. com. Mem. Nat. Assn. Ind. Colls. and Univs. (secretariat 1986), Nat. Assn. Intercollegiate Athletics (pres.'s adv. coun. 1986), Am. Coun. on Higher Edn. (commn. leadership devel. higher edn. 1978-82, commn. on internat. edn. 1993-96, acad. adminstrn. fellow 1974-75), Assn. Mercy Colls. (pres. 1985-87, exec. com. 1981-87), Coun. for Ind. Colls. (bd. dirs. 1989-92), Am. Hist. Assn., World Affairs Coun. No. Calif. (bd. dirs. 1990-96), Commonwealth Club Calif. (quar. chmn. 1989, chmn. Marin County chpt. 1989—, bd. dirs. 1992—, exec. com. 1997—). Home: 900 Green St San Francisco CA 94133-3600 Office: Dominican Coll of San Rafael 50 Acacia Ave San Rafael CA 94901-2230

FINK, RICHARD A. lawyer; b. 1940; BA, MBA, Stanford U. Sr. exec. v.p., dir. corp. devel. Glendale (Calif.) Fed. Bank; dir. corp. devel. Glendale Fed. Bank, Glendale. Office: Glendale Fed Bank 414 N Central Ave Glendale CA 91203-2002

FINK, ROBERT RUSSELL, music theorist, former university dean; b. Belding, Mich., Jan. 31, 1933; s. Russell Foster and Frances (Thornton) F.; m. Ruth Joan Bauerle, June 19, 1955; children: Denise Lyn, Daniel Robert. B.Mus., Mich. State U., 1955, M.Mus., 1956, Ph.D., 1965. Instr. music SUNY, Fredonia, 1956-57; instr. Western Mich. U., Kalamazoo, 1957-62, asst. prof., 1962-66, assoc. prof., 1966-71, prof., 1971-78, chmn. dept. music, 1972-78; dean Coll. Music U. Colo., Boulder, 1978-93; retired, 1994. Prin. horn Kalamazoo Symphony Orch., 1957-67; accreditation examiner Nat. Assn. Schs. Music, Reston, Va., 1973-92, grad. commr., 1981-89, chmn. grad. commn., 1987-89, assoc. chmn. accreditation commn., 1990-91, chmn., 1992. Author: Directory of Michigan Composers, 1972, The Language of 20th Century Music, 1975; composer: Modal Suite, 1959, Four Modes for Winds, 1967, Songs for High School Chorus, 1967; contbr. articles to profl. jours. Bd. dirs. Kalamazoo Symphony Orch., 1974-78, Boulder Bach Festival, 1983-90. Mem. Coll. Music Soc., Soc. Music Theory, Mich. Orch. Assn. (pres.), Phi Mu Alpha Sinfonia (province gov.), Pi Kappa Lambda. Home: 643 Furman Way Boulder CO 80305-5614 E-mail: Robert.Fink@colorado.edu

FINKBEINER, WILLIAM, state legislator; m. Kristin Finkbeiner; children: Connor, Anna. BA in Anthropology, Whitman Coll. Mem. Wash. Senate, Dist. 45, Olympia, 1998—; mem. edn. com. Wash. Legislature, Olympia, mem. higher edn. com., mem. transp. com., mem. info. svcs. bd., mem. gov.'s task force on telecom., mem. Pacific N.W. Econ. Region Networking subgroup, mem. Pacific N.W. Econ. Region exec. com. Bd. dirs. Eastside Multi-Svc. Ctr. Mem. Kirkland C. of C. Republican. Office: 201 Irving Newhouse Ofc Olympia WA 98504-0001

FINLAY, JAMES CAMPBELL, retired museum director; b. Russell, Man., Can., June 12, 1931; s. William Hugh and Grace Muriel F.; m. Audrey Joy Barton, June 18, 1955; children: Barton Brett, Warren Hugh, Rhonda Marie. BSc, Brandon U., 1952; MSc in Zoology, U. Alta., 1968. Geophysicist Frontier Geophys. Ltd., Alta., 1952-53; geologist, then dist. geologist Shell Can., Ltd., 1954-64; chief park naturalist and biologist Elk Island (Can.) Nat. Park, 1965-67; dir. hist. devel. and archives, dir. hist. and sci. service, dir. Nature Center, dir. interpretation and recreation City of Edmonton, Alta., 1967-92; founder Fedn. Alta. Naturalists, 1969. Author: A Nature Guide to Alberta, Bird Finding Guide to Canada; (with Joy Finlay) Ocean to Alpine-A British Columbia Nature Guide, A Guide to Alberta Parks. Recipient Order of the Bighorn, Govt. of Atla., 1987, Heritage award Environment Can., 1990, Loran Goulden award Fedn. Alta Naturalists, 1991, Can. 125th Anniversary award, 1993; named to Edmonton Hist. Hall of Fame, 1976. Mem. Can. Mus. Assn. (pres. 1976-78), Alta. Mus. Assn. (founding mem., past pres.), Am. Mus. Assn. (past council), Am. Ornithol. Union. Home: 270 Trevlac Pl RR 3 Victoria BC Canada V9E 2C4

FINLAYSON, BRUCE ALAN, chemical engineering educator; b. Waterloo, Iowa, July 18, 1939; s. Rodney Alan and Donna Elizabeth (Gilbert) F.; m. Patricia Lynn Hills, June 9, 1961; children: Mark, Catherine, Christine. BA, Rice U., 1961, MS, 1963; PhD, U. Minn., 1965. Asst. prof. to assoc. prof. U. Wash., Seattle, 1967-77, prof. dept. chem. engring. and applied math., 1977-82, Rehnberg prof. dept. chem. engring., 1983—, chmn. dept. chem. engring., 1989-98. Vis. prof. Univ. Coll., Swansea, Wales, U.K., 1975-76, Denmark Tekniske Hojskole, Lyngby, 1976, Universidad Nacional del Sur, Bahia Blanca, Argentina, 1980; Gulf vis. prof. Carnegie Mellon U., 1986; trustee Computer Aids to Chem. Engring. Edn., Austin, Tex., 1980-92; mem. bd. on chem. sci. and tech. NRC, 1990-92. Mem. editorial bd. Internat. Jour. Numerical Methods in Fluids, Swansea, 1980—, Numerical Heat Transfer, 1981—, Numerical Methods for Partial Differential Equations, 1984—, Chem. Engring. Edn., 1991—; author: The Method of Weighted Residuals and Variational Principles, 1972, Nonlinear Analysis in Chemical Engineering, 1980, Numerical Methods for Problems with Moving Prints, 1992. Lt. USNR, 1965-67. Mem. AIChE (CAST divsn. programming 1981-85, William H. Walker award 1983, bd. dirs. CAST divsn. 1984-86, vice chmn. 1987-88, chmn. 1989, bd. dirs. 1992-94, editorial bd. 1985-91, v.p. 1999, pres. 2000, past pres. 2001), Am. Chem. Soc., Am. Soc. Engring. Edn. (dir. Summer Sch. for Chem. Engring. Faculty 1997), Soc. Indsl. and Applied Math., Soc. Rheology, Nat. Acad. Engring. Home: 6315 22nd Ave NE Seattle WA 98115-6919 Office: U Wash Dept Chem Engring PO Box 351750 Seattle WA 98195-1750 E-mail: ravenna@mindspring.com, finlayson@cheme.washington.edu

FINLEY, DOROTHY HUNT, beverage distribution company executive; b. Douglas, Ariz. d. John P. and Salley E. (Stewart) Hunt; m. Harold Walter Finley, June 29, 1946 (dec. 1983); 1 child, John H. BA, MEd, U. Ariz. Cert. tchr., sch. adminstr., Ariz. Tchr. Tucson Unified Sch. Dist., 1943-46, 55-58, supervising tchr., 1958-60, sch. prin., 1960-80; pres., dir. Finley Distbg. Co., Inc., Tucson, 1983—. Bd. dirs. Tucson YWCA, 1984, Tucson area Girl Souts U.S., 1985, Tucson chpt. Planned Parenthood, 1987; founder, pres. Women's Studies Orgn. U. Ariz., Tucson, 1986; chair Met. Tucson Conv. and Visitors Bur. Mem. Ariz. Whgolesale Beer and Liquor Assn., Pima County Wholesale Beer and Liquor Assn., Tucson Key Club, U. Ariz. Alumni Club, Pi Lambda Theta, Delta Kappa Gamma. Republican. Episcopalian. Avocations: golf, cards, needlepoint, travel. Office: Finley Distbg Co Inc 2104 S Euclid Ave Tucson AZ 85713-3653

FINNBERG, ELAINE AGNES, psychologist, editor; b. Bklyn., Mar. 2, 1948; d. Benjamin and Agnes Montgomery (Evans) F.; m. Rodney Lee Herndon, Mar. 1, 1981; 1 child, Andrew Marshal. BA in Psychology, L.I. U., 1969; MA in Psychology, New Sch. for Social Rsch., 1973; PhD in Psychology, Calif. Sch. Profl. Psychology, 1981. Diplomate Am. Bd. Forensic Examiners, Am. Bd. Forensic Medicine, Am. Bd. Med. Psychotherapists and Psychodiagnosticians, Am. Bd. Disability Analysts, Am. Bd. Psychol. Specialties, Prescribing Psychologists Register; lic. psychologist, Calif. Rsch. asst. in med. sociology Cornell U. Med. Coll., N.Y.C., 1969-70; med. abstractor USV Pharm. Corp., Tuckahoe, N.Y., 1970-71, Coun. for Tobacco Rsch., N.Y.C., 1971-77; editor, writer Found. of Thanatology Columbia U., N.Y.C., 1971-76, cons. family studies program cancer ctr. Coll. Physicians & Surgeons, 1973-74; dir. grief psychology and bereavement counseling San Francisco Coll. Mortuary Scis., 1977-81; rsch. assoc. dept. epidemiology and internat. health U. Calif., San Francisco, 1979-81, asst. clin. prof. dept. family and cmty. medicine, 1985-93, assoc. clin. prof., dept. family and cmty. medicine, 1993—; active med. staff Natividad Med. Ctr., Salinas, Calif., 1984—, chief psychologist, 1984-96. Profl. adv. coun. Am. Bd. Disability Analysts; asst. chief psychiatry svc. Natividad Med. Ctr., 1985-96, acting chief psychiatry, 1988-89, vice-chair medicine dept., 1991-93, sec.-treas. med. staff, 1992-94; cons. med. staff Salinas Valley Meml. Hosp., 1991—, Mee Meml. Hosp., 1996-97; dir. tng. Monterey Psychiat. Health Facility, 1996-97, chief clin. staff, 1996-97; expert cons. Calif. Bd. Psychology. Editor: The California Psychologist, 1988-95; editor Jour. of Thanatology, 1972-76, Cathexis, 1976-81. Govs. adv. bd. Agnews Devel. Ctr., San Jose, Calif., 1988-96, chair, 1989-91, 94-95. Fellow Prescribing Psychologists Register (diplomate); mem. APA, Nat. Register Health Svc. Providers in Psychology, Calif. Psychol. Assn. (Disting. Svc. award 1989), Soc. Behavioral Medicine, Mid-Coast Psychol. Assn. (sec. 1985, treas. 1986, pres. 1987, Disting. Svc. to Psychology award 1993), Forensic Mental Health Assn. Calif., Western Psychol. Assn., Assn. Advancement Behavior Therapy, Am. Med. Writers Assn., Assn. Treatment Sexual Abuses, Soc. for Personality Assessment, Internat. Rorschach. Soc., Internat. Soc. Police Surgeons.

FINNEGAN, CYRIL VINCENT, retired university dean, zoology educator; b. Dover, N.H., July 17, 1922; emigrated to Can., 1958; s. Cyril Vincent and Hilda A. (McClintock) F.; children: Maureen A., Patrick S., Cathaleen C., Kevin S., Eileen D., Gormlaith R., Michaeleen S., Mairead B., Conal E. B.S., Bates Coll., Lewiston, Maine, 1946; M.S., U. Notre Dame, 1948, Ph.D., 1951. From instr. to asst. prof. St. Louis U., 1952-56; asst. prof. U. Notre Dame, South Bend, Ind., 1956-58; from asst. prof. to prof. zoology U. B.C., Vancouver, 1958-88, emeritus, 1988—, assoc. dean sci., 1972-79, dean sci., 1979-85, dean emeritus, 1988—, assoc. acad. v.p., 1986-88. Contbr. articles to sci. jours. Served to sgt F.A. and C.E. AUS, 1942-45, NATOUSA, CBI. Postdoctoral research fellow NIH, 1952-53; Killum sr. fellow, 1968-69 Mem. Soc. Devel. Biology, Can. Soc. Cell Biology, Tissue Culture Assn., Internat. Soc. Develop. Biology, Sigma Xi Roman Catholic. Office: U BC Dept Zoology Faculty of Science Vancouver BC Canada V6T 1Z4

FINNELL, MICHAEL HARTMAN, corporate executive; b. L.A., Jan. 27, 1927; s. Jules Bertram and Maribel Hartman (Schumacher) F.; m. Grace Vogel, Sept. 11, 1954 (div. June 1964); children: Lesley Finnell Blanchard, Carter Hartman, Hunter Vogel. Student, Asheville (N.C.) Sch., 1939-44; BA, U. Toronto, 1950; MBA, Harvard U., 1952; HHD (hon.), Capital U., Columbus, Ohio, 1980. Sec.-treas. Triad Oil Co. Ltd., 1952-62, v.p., dir., 1962-65; pres. Devon-Palmer Oils Ltd., 1963-65; v.p., dir. Can. Hydrocarbons, Ltd., 1967-71, pres., 1971-72. Trustee Capital U., Columbus, 1982-94; life trustee Columbus Mus. of Art; pres. Tamarack Corp., 1978—, Montreal River Internat. Silver Mines, 1972—. Mem. Calif. Club (L.A.), Annandale Golf Club (Pasadena, Calif.), Ranchmen's Club, Calgary Petroleum Club, Calgary Golf and Country Club, La Grulla Gun Club (Baja, Calif.), Nantucket (Mass.) Yacht Club. Home: 724 Holladay Rd Pasadena CA 91106-4115 Office: Tamarack Corp 625 Fair Oaks Ave Ste 288 South Pasadena CA 91030-2668

FINNIE, IAIN, mechanical engineer, educator; b. Hong Kong, July 18, 1928; s. John and Jessie Ferguson (Mackenzie) F.; m. Joan Elizabeth Roth, July 28, 1969; 1 dau., Shauna. B.S. with honors, U. Glasgow, 1949; M.S., MIT, 1951, M.E., 1952, Sc.D., 1954; D.Sc. (hon.), U. Glasgow, 1974. With Shell Devel. Co., 1954-61, engr., to 1961; mem. faculty dept. mech. engring. U. Calif., Berkeley, 1961—, prof., 1963—. Vis. prof. Cath. U. Chile, 1965, Ecole Polytechnique, Lausanne, Switzerland, 1976, 87. Author: Creep of Engineering Materials, 1959; contbr. articles to profl. jours. Guggenheim Found. fellow, 1967-68 Mem. Nat. Acad. Engring., ASME (hon., Nadai award 1982). Home: 2901 Avalon Ave Berkeley CA 94705-1401 Office: U Calif 6179 Etcheverry Berkeley CA 94720-0001 E-mail: finnie@me.berkeley.edu

FINNIGAN, ROBERT EMMET, business owner; b. Buffalo, May 27, 1927; s. Charles M. and Marie F. (Jacobs) F.; m. Bette E. van Horn, Apr. 1, 1950; children: Michael, Patrick, Robert E. Jr., Joan, Shawn, Thomas, Matthew. BS, U.S. Naval Acad., 1949; MS, U. Ill., 1954, PhD, 1957. Commd. lt. USAF, 1949, advanced through grades to capt., 1954; sr. scientist Livermore Lab., U. Calif., 1959, U. Calif. Lawrence Livermore Lab., 1957-62; sr. rsch. scientist Stanford Rsch. Inst., Menlo Park, Calif., 1962-63; dir. Electronic Assocs. Inc., Palo Alto, 1963-67; founder, vice chmn., sr. v.p. Finnigan Corp., San Jose, 1967-92, vice chmn. emeritus cons., 1992—. Mem. panel NAS, Washington, 1986-89; bd. dirs. Strategic Diagnostics, Inc., Newark, Del., Informed Diagnostics, Sunnyvale, Calif.; advisor to Environ. Tech. Fund, Chase H&Q, San Francisco. Author: Identification and Analysis of Organic Pollutants in Water, 1976, Advances in Identification and Analysis of Organic Pollutants in Water, 1981. Chmn., co-founder U.S. Nat. Working Group on Pollution, Internat. Orgn. for Legal Metrology, Washington, 1990-97. [illegible] Coll. of Engring., U. Ill., 1980, Winston Churchill medal of wisdom, 1999; named Pioneer in Analytical Instrumentation-Mass Spectrometry, Soc. for Analytical Chemists of Pitts. and Pitts. Conf. on Analytical Chemistry, 1994, Instrumentation Hall of Fame, Pitts., Conf. on Analytical Chemistry and Analytical Chem. Soc., 1999; named to Wisdom Hall of Fame, 1999. Mem. IEEE (sr.), Am. Soc. for Mass Spectrometry (bd. dirs.), Am. Electronic Assn. (bd. dirs. 1982-84, 87, chmn., co-founder environ. and occupational health com.). Avocations: wine, hiking, snowshoeing. Office: Finnigan Corp 355 River Oaks Pkwy San Jose CA 95134-1991 Home Fax: 650-941-2086

FIORINA, CARLETON S. (CARLY . FIORINA), computer company executive; b. Austin, Tex., Sept. 6, 1954; married. BA in Medieval History and Philosophy, Stanford U., 1976; MBA, U. Md., 1980; MSc, MIT, 1989; postgrad., UCLA. Account exec. Long Lines AT&T, 1980, sr. v.p. Global Mktg., pres. Atlantic and Canadian Region; v.p. Corp. Ops. Lucent Technologies, group pres. Global Svc. Provider; pres., CEO Hewlett-Packard, Palo Alto, 1999—, chmn. bd. dirs., 2000—. Bd. dirs. Kellogg Co., Merck & Co., Inc., Power Up; elected U.S. China Bd. Trade. Named one of Fortune Mag. Most Powerful Women in Am. Bus. Office: Hewlett-Packard 3000 Hanover St Palo Alto CA 94304-1181

FIORINO, JOHN WAYNE, podiatrist; b. Charleroi, Pa., Sept. 30, 1946; s. Anthony Raymond and Mary Louise (Caramela) F.; m. Susan K. Bonnett, May 2, 1984; children: Jennifer, Jessica, Lauren, Michael. Student, Nassau Coll., 1969-70; BA in Biology, U. Buffalo, 1972; Dr. Podiatric Medicine, Ohio Coll. Podiatric Medicine, 1978. Cert. primary podiatric medicine Am. Podiatric Med. Specialties Bd.; diplomate Am. Bd. Medical Spltys. in Podiatry. Salesman E. J. Korvettes, Carle Place, N.Y., 1962-65; orderly Nassau Hosp., Mineola, 1965-66; operating room technician-trainee heart-lung machine L.I. Jewish-Hillside Med. Center, New Hyde Park, 1967-69; pharmacy technician Feinmel's Pharmacy, Roslyn Heights, 1969-70; mgr., asst. buyer Fortunoffs, Westbury, 1972-73; bd. certified perfusionist L.I. Jewish-Hillside Med. Center, New Hyde Park, 1973-74; clin. instr. cardiopulmonary tech. Stony Brook (N.Y.) Univ., 1973-74; operating room technician Cleve. Met. Hosp., 1975; lab. technician Univ. Hosp., Cleve., 1976-78; surg. resident Mesa Gen. Hosp., 1978-79, staff podiatrist, 1979—; pvt. practice podiatry Mesa, 1979—. Staff podiatrist Sacaton (Ariz.) Hosp., 1979—, Mesa Gen. Hosp., 1979, Valley Luth. Hosp., Mesa, 1985, Chandler Community Hosp., 1985, Desert Samaritan Hosp., Mesa, 1986; podiatrist U.S. Govt. Nat. Inst., Sacaton, 1980-87, Indian Health Services, Sacaton, 1980-87; cons. staff Phoenix Indian Med. Ctr., 1985. Served with USN, 1966-67. Mem. Am. Podiatry Assn., Ariz. Podiatry Assn. (treas. 1984-86), Acad. Ambulatory Foot Surgery, Am. Coll. Foot Surgeons (assoc.), Mut. Assn. Profls., Am. Acad. Pain Mgmt. (cert.), Phi Delta, Alpha Gamma Kappa. Home: 2624 W Upland Dr Chandler AZ 85224-7870 Office: 5520 E Main St Mesa AZ 85205-8793

FIRESTONE, MORTON H. business management executive; b. Chgo., Feb. 4, 1935; s. William and Lillian (Kliot) F.; m. Roberta (Bobbie) Schwartz, Feb. 3, 1957; children: Jeffrey, Scott, Dan. BS, U. Calif., Davis, 1957; MBA, U. So. Calif., 1971. V.p. Security Pacific Nat. Bank, Los Angeles, 1957-77; chmn. bd., chief fin. officer, corp. sec. Elixir Industries, 1977-87, also dir.; pres. Garden Ins., 1978-87, Club Wholesale Concepts, Inc., 1986-87; chmn. bd., chief exec. officer Rondure Industries, 1987-90; pres. Lin Mor Corp., Woodland Hills, Calif., 1990—. Bd. dirs. Robert Burns & Sons, Inc. Past chmn. Los Angeles-Eilat Sister City Com. Mem. Fin. Execs. Inst., Beta Gamma Sigma. Lodges: Optimist (past pres. Hollywood), Kiwanis (past pres. West Hollywood). Office: Lin Mor Corp PO Box 571025 Tarzana CA 91357-1025 E-mail: mort@linmorecorp.com

FIRESTONE, ROY, sportscaster; b. Miami Beach, Fla., Dec. 8, 1953; s. Bernard and Regina Firestone; m. Midori Firestone, 1987; 2 children. Diploma in Mass Communications, U. Miami, 1974. Sports reporter Sta. WTVJ-TV, Miami, Fla., 1973-75, Sta. WPLG-TV, Miami, 1975-77; sports reporter, anchor Sta. KCBS-TV, Los Angeles, 1977-85, color analyst, football telecasts, 1978-79; host Mazda SportsLook ESPN, 1980-97, play-by-play football announcer, 1987—. Host (syndicated TV show) Sports Comedy Around the World, Up Close Prime Time, Up Close, 1991-95, SportsLook, 1980-90, Into the Night, 1992; halftime commentator ESPN, 1988; play-by-play commentator NFL, 1987; appeared in movies Jerry Maguire, The Scout; comedy appearances include Late Night with David Letterman, The Tonight Show, Nightline, others. Recipient 4 L.A. Emmy awards Acad. TV Arts and Scis., Excellence in Sports Broadcast Journalism award Northeastern U., 1990, 2 Golden Mike awards, Best Sportscast award L.A. Press Club, 1981; named Best Program Interviewer, CableACE awards, 1996, Best Sports Host, 1986, 88, 91. Office: ESPN 6251 Afton Pl Los Angeles CA 90028-8204

FIRSTENBERG, JEAN PICKER, film institute executive; b. N.Y.C., Mar. 13, 1936; d. Eugene and Sylvia (Moses) Picker; m. Paul Firstenberg, Aug. 9, 1956 (div. July 1980); children: Debra, Douglas BS summa cum laude, Boston U., 1958. Asst. producer Altman Prodns., Washington, 1965-66; media advisor J. Walter Thompson, N.Y.C., 1969-72; asst. for spl. projects Princeton (N.J.) U., 1972-74, dir. publs., 1974-76; program officer Markle Found., N.Y.C., 1976-80; dir., CEO Am. Film Inst., L.A., Washington, 1980—. Bd. dirs. Trans-Lux Corp.; former chmn. nat. adv. bd. Peabody Broadcasting Awards; bd. dirs. Trans-Lux Corp. Former trustee Boston U.; mem. adv. bd. Will Rogers Inst., N.Y.C.; chmn., bd. advisors Film Dept. N.C. Sch. of Arts. Recipient Alumni award for disting. service to profession Boston U., 1982; seminar and prodn. chairs at directing workshop for women named in her honor Am. Film Inst., 1986 Mem. Women in Film (Crystal award 1990), Trusteeship for Betterment of Women, Acad. Motion Picture Arts and Scis. Office: Am Film Inst 2021 N Western Ave PO Box 27999 Los Angeles CA 90027-0999

FISCH, MICHAEL J. publisher; b. Fairmont, Minn., 1952; Pres., CEO THe Bakersfield Californian, 1992; pres., publisher Honolulu Advt. Inc., 1998—. Office: PO Box 3110 Honolulu HI 96802-3110

FISCHER, ALFRED GEORGE, geology educator; b. Rothenburg, Germany, Dec. 10, 1920; came to U.S., 1935; s. George Erwin and Thea (Freise) F.; m. Winnifred Varney, Aug. 26, 1939; children: Joseph Fred, George William, Lenore Ruth Fischer Walsh. Student, Northwestern Coll., Watertown, Wis., 1935-37; BA, U. Wis., 1939, MA, 1941; PhD, Columbia U., 1950. Instr. Va. Poly. Inst. and State U., Blacksburg, 1941-43; geologist Stanolind Oil & Gas Co., Kans. and Fla., 1943-46; instr. U. Rochester, N.Y., 1947-48; from instr. to asst. prof. U. Kans., Lawrence, 1948-51; sr. geologist Internat. Petroleum, Peru, 1951-56; prof. geology Princeton (N.J.) U., 1956-84, U. So. Calif., Los Angeles, 1984—. Co-Author: Invertebrate Fossils, 1952, The Permian Reef Complex, 1953, Electron Micrographs of Limestone, 1967; editor: Petroleum and Global Tectonics, 1975. Recipient Verrill medal Yale U. Fellow Geol. Soc. Am. (Penrose medal 1993), Geol. Soc. London (hon., Lyell medal 1992), Soc. Econ. Paleontologists (hon., Twenhofel medal); mem. AAAS, NAS, U.S. Nat. Acad. Sci., Am. Assn. Petroleum Geologists, Paleontol. Soc. (medal 1995), German Geol. Soc. (Leopold van Buch medal), Geol. Union (Gustav Steinmann medal 1992), Mainz Acad. Sci. Lit. (corr.), Lincei Acad. Rome [illegible] Office: U So Calif Dept Earth Scis Univ Park Los Angeles CA 90089-0001

FISCHER, EDMOND HENRI, biochemistry educator; b. Shanghai, Republic of China, Apr. 6, 1920; came to U.S., 1953; s. Oscar and Renée (Tapernoux) F.; m. Beverley B. Bullock. Lic. es Sciences Chimiques et Biologiques, U. Geneva, 1943, Diplome d'Ingenieur Chimiste, 1944, PhD, 1947; D (hon.), U. Montpellier, France, 1985, U. Basel, Switzerland, 1988, Med. Coll. of Ohio, , 1993, Ind. U., 1993, U. Bochum, Germany, 1994. Pvt. docent biochemistry U. Geneva, 1950-53; research assoc. biology Calif. Inst. Tech., Pasadena, 1953; asst. prof. biochemistry U. Wash., Seattle, 1953-56, assoc. prof., 1956-61, prof., 1961-90, prof. emeritus, 1990—. Mem. exec. com. Pacific Slope Biochem. Conf., 1958—59, pres., 1975; mem. biochemistry study sect. NIH, 1959—64; symposium co-chmn. Battelle Seattle Rsch. Ctr., 1970, 73, 78; mem. sci. adv. bd. Biozentrum, U. Basel, , Switzerland, 1982—86, Weizmann Inst. Sci., Rehovot, Israel, 1998—, bd. govs. , 1997—; mem. sci. adv. bd. Principe Felipe Sci. Mus., Valencia, Spain, 1998—, Friedrich Miescher Inst., Ciba-Geigy, Basel, 1976—84, chmn., 1981—84; mem. bd. sci. govs. Scripps Rsch. Inst., La Jolla, Calif., 1987—, Basel Inst. for Immunology, 1996—. Contbr. numerous articles to sci. jours. Mem. sci. council on basic sci. Am. Heart Assn., 1977-80, sci. adv. com. Muscular Dystrophy Assn., 1980-88. Recipient Lederle Med. Faculty award, 1956-59, Guggenheim Found. award, 1963-64, Disting. Lectr. award U. Wash., 1983, Laureate Passano Found. award, 1988, Steven C. Beering award, 1991, Nobel prize in Physiology or Medicine, 1992. Fellow Am. Acad. Arts and Scis.; mem. NAS, AAAS, AAUP, Am. Soc. Biol. Chemists (coun. 1989-93), Am. Chem. Soc. (adv. bd. biochemistry divsn. 1962, exec. com. divsn. biology 1969-72, monograph adv. bd. 1971-73, editl. adv. bd. Biochemistry, 1961-66, assoc. editor 1966-91), Swiss Chem. Soc. (Werner medal), Spanish Royal Acad. Scis. (fgn. assoc.), Venice Inst. Sci., Arts and Letters (fgn. assoc.), Japanese Biochem. Soc. (hon.), Royal Acad. Medicine and Surgery (hon., Cadiz, Spain), Korean Acad. Sci. and Tech. (hon.). Achievements include cellular regulation by phosphorylation/dephosphorylation cycle. Office: U Washington Med Sch PO Box 357350 Seattle WA 98195-7350 E-mail: efischer@u.washington.edu

FISCHER, JOEL, social work educator; b. Chgo., Apr. 22, 1939; s. Sam and Ruth (Feiges) F.; m. Renee H. Furuyama; children: Lisa, Nicole BS, U. Ill., 1961, MSW, 1964; D in Social Welfare, U. Calif., Berkeley, 1970. Prof. sch. social work U. Hawaii, Honolulu, 1970—. Vis. prof. George Warren Brown Sch. Social Work, Washington U., St. Louis, 1977, U. Wis. Sch. Social Welfare, Milw., 1978-79, U. Natal, South Africa, 1982, U. Hong Kong, 1986; cons. various orgns. and univs. Author: (with Harvey L. Gochros) Planned Behavior Change: Behavior Modification in Social Work, 1973, Handbook of Behavior Therapy with Sexual Problems, vol. I, 1977, vol. II, 1977, Analyzing Research, 1975, Interpersonal Helping: Emerging Approaches for Social Work Practice, 1973, The Effectiveness of Social Casework, 1976, (with D. Sanders and O. Kurrem) Fundamentals of Social Work Practice, 1982, Effective Casework Practice: An Eclectic Approach, 1978, (with H. Gochros) Treat Yourself to a Better Sex Life, 1980, (with H. Gochros and J. Gochros) Helping the Sexually Oppressed, 1985, (with Martin Bloom) Evaluating Practice: Guidlines for the Helping Professional, 1982, (with Kevin Corcoran) Measures for Clinical Practice, 1987, (with Daniel Sanders) Visions for the Future: Social Work and Pacific-Asian Perspectives, 1988, (with Martin Bloom and John Orme) Evaluating Practice, 2nd edit., 1995, (with Kevin Corcoran) Measures for Clinical Practice, 2nd edit., vol. 1, 1994, Couples, Children, Families, vol. 2, 1994, Adults, 1994, East-West Connections: Social Work Practice Traditions and Change, 1992, (with Martin Bloom and John Orme) Evaluating Practice, 3d edit., 1999, (with Martin Bloom and John Orme) Teacher's Manual for Evaluating Practice, 1999; (with Kevin Corcoran) Measures for Clinical practice, 3d edit, vol. 1, 2000, Couples, Children and Families, Adults, vol. 2, 2000, (with Martin Bloom and John Brine) Evaluating Practice, 4th edit., 2001, Teacher's Manual for Evaluations Practice, 2nd edit., 2001; mem. editl. bd. 12 profl. jours.; contbr. over 150 articles, revs., chpts. and papers to profl. jours. Bd. dirs. U. Hawaii Profl. Assembly. With U.S. Army, 1958. Mem. Hawaii Com. for Africa, Nat. Assn. Social Workers, Coun. Social Work Edn., Acad. Cert. Social Workers, Nat. Conf. Social Welfare, AAUP, Unity Organizing Com., Hawaii People's Legis. Coalition, Bertha Reynold Soc. Democrat. Home: 1371-4 Hunakai St Honolulu HI 96816-5501 Office: U Hawaii Sch Social Worl Menken Hall Honolulu HI 96822-2217 E-mail: jfischer@hawaii.edu

FISCHER, MICHAEL LUDWIG, environmental executive; b. Dubuque, Iowa, May 29, 1940; s. Carl Michael and Therese Marie (Stadler) F.; m. Jane Pughe Rogers; children: Christina Marie, Steven Michael. BA in Polit. Sci., Santa Clara U., 1964; M in City and Regional Planning, U. Calif., Berkeley, 1967; grad. exec. program in environ. mgmt., Harvard U., 1980. Planner City of Mountain View, Calif., 1960-65; assoc. Bay Area Govts., 1966-67; planner County of San Mateo, Calif., 1967-69; assoc. dir. San Francisco Planning and Urban Rsch. Assn., nonprofit civic orgn., 1969-73, exec. dir. North Cen. region Calif. Coastal Zone Conservation Commn., San Rafael, 1973-76; chief dep. dir. Gov.'s Office Planning and Rsch., Sacramento, 1976-78; exec. dir. Calif. Coastal Commn., San Francisco, 1978-85; sr. assoc. Sedway Cooke Assocs., environ. cons., San Francisco, 1985-87; exec. dir. Sierra Club, San Francisco, 1987-93; resident fellow John F. Kennedy Sch. Govt., Inst. Politics, Harvard U., Cambridge, Mass., 1993; sr. cons. Natural Resources Def. Coun., San Francisco, 1993-95; exec. officer Calif. Coastal Conservancy, Oakland, 1994-97; program officer environ. William & Flora Hewlett Found., Menlo Park, Calif., 1997—. Lectr. dept. city and regional planning U. Calif., Berkeley, 1984; mem. and former chair environ. com. adv. coun. Calvert Social Investment Fund, 1989-99; mem. Harvard Commn. Global Change Info. Policy, 1993—; mem. com. on impact of maritime facility devel. NAS/NRC, 1975-78; mem. nat. sea grant review panel Nat. Oceanic and Atmospheric Adminstrn., 1998—, bd. mem. High Country News Found., 2000—. Co-author Calif. state plan, An Urban Strategy for Calif., 1978, Building a New Municipal Railway, 1973, Oral History, Coastal Commn. Yrs., 1973-85, Oral History, Sierra Club Yrs., 1987-93; author intro. Ansel Adams: Yosemite, 1995; contbr. papers to profl. publs. Recipient Life Achievement award Assn. Environ. Profls., 1986, Disting. Leadership award. Am. Soc. Pub. Adminstrn., 1987, Outstanding Nat. Leadership award Coastal States Orgn., 1990, Exemplary Pub. Svc. award San Francisco Bay Conservation and Devel. Commn., 1997, Spl. Recognition award Calif. State Legis., 1998. Mem. Nat. Resources Def. Coun., Calif. Planning and Conservation League (bd. dirs. 1970-76), Alliance Ethnic and Environ. Orgn. (founding bd. dirs. 1991-93), The Oceanic Soc. (bd. dirs. 1983-88), Am. Inst. Cert. Planners, Sierra Club, Friends of the Earth (bd. dirs. 1988-94), League for Coastal Protection, Save San Francisco Bay Assn., Am. Youth Hostels, Inc. (bd. dirs. 1985-87), Yosemite Restoration Trust (bd. dirs. 1990-97, pres. 1995-97), Lambda Alpha. Office: William & Flora Hewlett Found 525 Middlefield Rd Menlo Park CA 94025-3460 E-mail: fischer@igc.org, mfischer@hewlett.org

FISCHER, ROBERT EDWARD, meteorologist; b. Bethlehem, Pa., Aug. 4, 1943; s. Frederic Philip and Muriel Winifred (Johnson) F. BS cum laude, U. Utah, 1966; MS, Colo. State U., 1969. Meteorologist Nat. Weather Svc., Fairbanks, Alaska, 1973—. Contbr. articles to profl. jours. Vol. classical music program prodr. Sta. KUAC-FM, Fairbanks. Recipient Nat. Oceanic and Atmospheric Adminstrn. Unit citation, 1989. Fellow Royal Meteorol. Soc.; mem. Am. Meteorol. Soc. (Charles L. Mitchell award 1985), Nat. Weather Assn. (Outstanding Operational Performance award 1987), Assn. Lunar and Planetary Observers, Am. Assn. Variable Star Observers, Royal Astron. Soc. Can., Sigma Xi, Phi Kappa Phi. Avocations: running, photography, astronomy, bird watching. Home: PO Box 82210 Fairbanks AK 99708-2210 Office: Nat Weather Svc Forecast IARC Bldg 930 Kuyukuk Dr U Alaska Fairbanks AK 99775-3745

FISET, STEPHANE, professional hockey player; b. Montreal, Que., Can., June 17, 1970; m. Isabelle; 1 child, Karolane. Goaltender Que., 1988-96, L.A. Kings, 1996—. Recipient Can. Hockey Goaltender of Yr. award. Avocations: movies, cards. Office: LA Kings Staples Ctr 1111 S Figueroa St Los Angeles CA 90015-1300

FISETTE, SCOTT MICHAEL, landscape and golf course architect; b. Orange, Tex., May 17, 1963; s. Roderick John and Addie Faye (Byrnes) F.; m. Keali'i Kane; children: Shane Roderick, Hayley Kaimalie. BS in Landscape Architecture, Tex. A&M U., 1985. Registered landscape architect, Tex., Hawaii, Commonwealth of No. Mariana Islands. Project architect Dick Nugent Assocs., Long Grove, Ill., 1985-90; prin., pres. Fisette Golf Designs, Kaneohe, Hawaii, 1991—. Mem. Golf Course Supts. Assn. Am., Am. Soc. Landscape Architects, Nat. Golf Found., Hawaii Turf Grass Assn. (bd. dirs. 1991-96), Donald Ross Soc. Avocations: golf, fishing, water skiing, softball. Office: Fisette Golf Designs PO Box 1433 Kaneohe HI 96744-1433

FISH, BARBARA, psychiatrist, educator; b. N.Y.C., July 31, 1920; d. Edward R. and Ida (Citrin) F.; m. Max Saltzman, Dec. 12, 1953; children: Mark, Ruth Saltzman Deutsch. B.A. summa cum laude, Barnard Coll., Columbia U., 1942; M.D., NYU, 1945. Diplomate Am. Bd. Psychiatry and Neurology, Am. Bd. child psychiatry. Intern Bellevue Hosp., N.Y.C., 1945-47, resident in pediatrics, 1948-49, resident in psychiatry, 1949-52; resident in pediatrics N.Y. Hosp., N.Y.C., 1947-48; practice medicine specializing in child psychiatry N.Y.C., 1952-65; instr. psychiatry Med. Coll Cornell U., N.Y.C., 1955-60, instr. pediatrics, 1955-56, asst. prof. clin. pediatrics, 1956-60; child psychiatrist dept. pediatrics N.Y. Hosp.-Cornell Med. Center, 1955-60; mem. faculty William A. White Inst. Psychoanalysis, N.Y.C., 1957-66; assoc. prof. psychiatry sch. medicine NYU, N.Y.C., 1960-70, prof., 1970-72; adj. prof. N.Y. U., 1972—, dir. child psychiatry med. ctr., 1960-72; prof. psychiatry and behavioral sci. UCLA, 1972-89, Della Martin prof. psychiatry and behavioral sci., 1989-91, Della Martin prof. psychiatry and behavioral sci. emeritus, 1991—. Mem. advisory com. mental health services for children N.Y.C. Community Mental Health Bd., 1963-72; mem. profl. advisory com. on children N.Y. State Dept. Mental Hygiene, 1966-72; mem. com. cert. child psychiatry Am. Bd. Psychiatry and Neurology, 1969-77; mem. clin. program projects research rev. com. NIMH, 1976-78. Contbr. articles on the antecedents of schizophrenia and other severe mental disorders, and on the psychiat. diagnosis and treatment of children; mem. editorial bd.: Jour. Am. Acad. Child Psychiatry, 1966-71, Jour. Autism and Childhood Schizophrenia, 1971-74, Child Devel. Abstracts and Bibliography, 1974-82, Archives Gen. Psychiatry, 1975-84. Recipient Woman of Sci. award UCLA, 1978; NIMH grantee, 1961-72, 78-88, Harriett A. Ames Charitable Trust grantee, 1961-66, William T. Grant Found. grantee, 1977-83, Scottish Rite schizophrenia rsch. grantee, 1979-87. Fellow Am. Psychiat. Assn. (Agnes McGavin award 1987), Am. Acad. Child Psychiatry, Am. Coll. Neuropsychopharmacology (charter); mem. Am. Psychopath. Assn. (v.p. 1967-68), Assn. for Research in Nervous and Mental Diseases, Soc. Research in Child Devel., Psychiat. Research Soc. Home: 16428 Sloan Dr Los Angeles CA 90049-1157 Office: UCLA Neuropsychiat Inst 760 Westwood Plz Los Angeles CA 90095-8353 E-mail: bfish@ucla.edu

FISHBURNE, JOHN INGRAM, JR. obstetrician/gynecologist, educator; b. Charleston, S.C., Aug. 18, 1937; m. Jean Crawford, June 10, 1971; children: John Ingram III, Barron Crawford, Virginia Heyward. AB, Princeton U., 1959; MD, Med. Coll. S.C., 1963. Diplomate Am. Bd. Ob Gyn. (sub. specialty maternal-fetal medicine). Surg. intern Duke U. Hosp., Durham, N.C., 1963-64; resident in ob-gyn. U. N.C., Chapel Hill, 1966-70, resident in anesthesiology, 1970-72, instr. dept. ob-gyn., 1970-71, asst. prof., 1971-74, assoc. prof., 1974-75, asst. prof. dept. anesthesiology, 1972-75; assoc. prof. dept. ob-gyn. Bowman Gray Sch. Medicine, Wake Forest U., Winston-Salem, N.C., 1975-78, prof., 1978-83, assoc. prof. anesthesiology, dept. anesthesiology, 1975-83; prof., chmn. dept. ob-gyn. U. Okla. Health Scis. Ctr., Oklahoma City, 1983-97, adj. prof. dept. anesthesiology, 1983-97, chmn. search com. for chair pathology dept., 1987-88, chmn. search com. for chair family medicine dept., 1993-94; residency program dir. dept ob-gyn. Maricopa Med. Ctr., Phoenix, 1997—. Dir. maternal-fetal medicine dept. ob-gyn. Forsyth Meml. Hosp., Winston-Salem, 1977-83; vis. prof. U. W.I., Kingston, Jamaica, 1973-74, African-Health Tng. Instns. Project Nairobi, Kenya, 1975; cons. devel. mission U.S. AID, Dacca, Bangladesh, 1980, Assn. Vol. Surg. Contraception World Fedn. Health Agys., Manila, 1984, Singapore, 1986, Zhordania Inst., Tbilisi, Republic of Georgia, 1992, 93, 97, Ivanovo, Russia, 1994, Almaty, Kazakhstan, 1994, St. Petersburg, Russia, 1995, Khojand, Tahjikistan, 1995, Odessa, Ukraine, 1995, Chechenov, Moldova, 1996, L'viv Ukraine; oral examiner Am. Bd. Ob-Gyn, 1980—; chmn. Gov.'s Task Force on Perinatal Care, 1984-86; mem. steering com. Robert Wood Johnson Healthy Futures of Okla., 1988-92; trustee Am. Assn. for Gynecologic Laparascopists, 1980-81; presenter numerous sci. papers and lectures local, nat. and internat. profl. meetings. Author: (with others) The Prostaglandins, 1972, Endocrine-Metabolic Drugs, 1974, Gynecologic Laparoscopy: Principles and Techniques, 1974, Laparoscopy, 1977, Endoscopy in Gynecology, 1978, Clinics in Perinatology, 1982, Obstetric Anesthesia, 1982, Clinical and Diagnostic Procedures Obstetrics and Gyncecology, Part B, 1984, Advances in Clinical Obstetrics and Gynecology, Medical Economics Books, 1985, Clinical Obstetrics, 1987, Danforth's Obstetrics and Gynecology, 1994, 98, Bonica's Obstetric Analgesia and Anesthesia, 1995; contbr. update series Am. Coll. Obstetricians and Gynecologists; editorial bd. Obstetrics and Gynceology, 1985-89; author self instructional programs in field; contbr. numerous articles to profl. jours. Capt. USAFR, 1964-66. Clin. fellow Am. Cancer Soc. U. N.C., 1968-69, clin. fellow obstet. anesthesia Pub. Health Svc. U. Hosps. Case Western Res. U., 1969; tng. rsch. grantee NIH Med. U. S.C., 1961-62. Fellow ACOG (spl. interest rep. for obstet. anesthesia 1974-78, learning resources commn. 1981-82, mem. personal rev. of learning in ob-gyn. task force for obstetrics 1981-82, chair obs. IV, 1996-98, chair edn. commn. 1996-98, chair residency rev. com. ob/gyn. Accreditation Coun. for Grad. Med. Edn. 1994-97, dir., mem. exec. com. Accreditation Coun. for Grad. Med. Edn. 2000-2004, vice chair coun. of residency rev. com. chairs 1996, chair accreditation coun. for grad. med. edn. coun. res. rev. com. chairs, 1997-98), Am. Coll. Anesthesiologists (assoc. examiner 1974); mem. Am. Soc. Anesthesiologists, Maternal & Fetal Medicine Soc. (rep. liaison com. ob.-gyn. 1983-89, bd. dirs. 1981-84), S. Atlantic Assn. Obstetricians and Gynecologists (assoc.), Perinatal Rsch. Soc., Oklahoma City Ob-Gyn. Soc., Okla. County Med. Soc., Okla. Anesthesia Soc., Internat. Soc. Advancement Humanistic Studies in Medicine, Cen. Assn. Obstetricians and Gynecologists, Continental Gynecol. Soc., So. Med. Assn., Am. Gynecol. and Obstet. Soc., Med. Alumni Assn., Med. U. S.C. (Disting. Alumnus award 1989), Alpha Omega Alpha. Episcopalian. Home: 7060 N Hillside Dr Paradise Valley AZ 85253-2813 Office: Maricopa Med Ctr Dept Ob-Gyn 2601 E Roosevelt St Dept Ob Phoenix AZ 85008-4973 E-mail: jfishburne@home.com, john.fishburne@hcs.maricopa.gov

FISHER, DELBERT ARTHUR, physician, educator; b. Placerville, Calif., Aug. 12, 1928; s. Arthur Lloyd and Thelma (Johnson) F.; m. Beverly Carne Fisher, Jan. 28, 1951; children: David Arthur (dec.), Thomas Martin, Mary Kathryn. BA, U. Calif., Berkeley, 1950; MD, U. Calif., San Francisco, 1953. Diplomate Am. Bd. Pediat. (examiner 1971-80, mem. subcom. on pediat. endocrinology 1976-79). Intern, resident in pediat. U. Calif. Med. Ctr., San Francisco, 1953-55; resident in pediat. U. Oreg. Hosp., Portland, 1957-58; from asst. prof. to assoc. prof. pediat. Med. Sch. U. Ark., Little Rock, 1960-67, prof. pediat., 1967-68, UCLA, 1968-73, prof. pediat. and medicine Med. Sch., 1973-91, prof. emeritus, 1991—; chief, pediat. endocrinology Harbor-UCLA Med. Ctr., 1968-75, rsch. prof. devel. and perinatal biology, 1975-85, chmn. pediat., 1985-89, sr. scientist Rsch. and Edn. Inst., 1991—; dir. Walter Martin Rsch. Ctr., 1986-91; pres. Nichols Inst. Reference Labs, San Juan Capistrano, Calif., 1991-93; pres. acad. assocs., chief sci. officer Nichols Inst., San Juan Capistrano, 1993-94, Quest Diagnostics-Nichols Inst., San Juan Capistrano, 1994-97, sr. sci. officer, 1997-98, chief sci. officer, 1998-99; v.p. sci. and innovation Quest Diagnostics Inc., 1999—. Cons. genetic disease sect. Calif. Dept. Health Svcs., 1978-98; mem. organizing com. Internat. Conf. Newborn Thyroid Screening, 1977-88. Co-editor: Pediatric Thyroidology, 1985, 8 other books; editor-in-chief Jour. Clin. Endocrinology and Metabolism, 1978-83, Pediat. Rsch., 1984-89; contbr. over 550 articles to profl. jours., chpts. to numerous books. Capt. M.C., USAF, 1955-57. Recipient Career Devel. award NIH, 1964-68, Disting. Scientist award Clin. Ligand Assay Soc., 2001. Mem. Inst. Medicine NAS, Nat. Acad. Clin. Biochemistry, Am. Acad. Pediat. (Borden award 1981), Soc. Pediat. Rsch. (v.p. 1973-74), Am. Pediat. Soc. (pres. 1992-93, John Howland medal 2001), Endocrine Soc. (pres. 1983-84, Williams Leadership award 1998)), Am. Thyroid Assn. (pres. 1988-89), Am. Soc. Clin. Investigation, Assn. Am. Physicians, Lawson Wilkins Pediatric Endocrine Soc. (pres. 1982-83), Western Soc. Pediat. Rsch. (pres. 1983-84), Clin. Ligand Assay Soc. (Disting. Scientist award 2001), Phi Beta Kappa, Alpha Omega Alpha. Home: 24582 Santa Clara Ave Dana Point CA 92629-3031 Office: Quest Diagnostics-Nichols Inst 33608 Ortega Hwy San Juan Capistrano CA 92675-2042

FISHER, DONALD G. casual apparel chain stores executive; b. 1928; married. B.S., U. Calif., 1950. With M. Fisher & Son, 1950-57; former ptnr. Fisher Property Investment Co.; co-founder, pres. The Gap Stores Inc., San Bruno, Calif., dir., now chmn., founder, 1996—. Office: The Gap Stores 1 Harrison St San Francisco CA 94105-1602

FISHER, FREDERICK HENDRICK, oceanographer emeritus; b. Aberdeen, Wash., Dec. 30, 1926; s. Sam (Sverre) and Astrid K. Fisher; m. Julie Gay Saund, June 17, 1955 (dec. 1993); children: Bruce Allen, Mark Edward, Keith Russell, Glen Michael; m. Shirley Mercedes Lippert, Oct. 10, 1994. BS, U. Wash., 1949, PhD, 1957. Tchg. asst. U. Wash., 1949-53; rsch. asst. UCLA, 1954-55; grad. rsch. physicist Marine Phys. Lab., Scripps Inst. Oceanography, 1955-57, rsch. physicist, rsch. oceanographer, 1958-91, assoc. dir., 1975-87, dep. dir., 1987-93, acting assoc. dir., 1993-94, rsch. oceanographer emeritus, 1997—; rsch. fellow acoustics Harvard U., 1957-58. Dir. rsch. in reverse osmosis and desalination Havens Industries, San Diego, 1963-64; prof., chmn. dept. physics U. R.I., Kingston, 1970-71; mem. governing bd. Am. Inst. Physics, 1984-90. Assoc. editor: Jour. Oceanic Engring., 2001—. Mem. San Diego County Dem. Ctrl. Com., 1956-57, 60-62. Midshipman U.S. Naval Acad., 1945-47, with USNR, 1945. NCAA nat. tennis doubles champion, 1949; named to U. Wash. Athletic Hall of Fame, 1989; recipient Disting. Svc. award IEEE Oceanic Engring. Soc., 1991, Disting. Tech. Achievement award IEEE/OES, 1996, 3d Millenium Medal IEEE, 2000. Fellow (emeritus) Acoustical Soc. Am. (assoc. editor jour. 1969-76, v.p. 1980-81, pres. 1983-84, Am.'s Finest Acousticians award San Diego chpt. 1997); mem. IEEE (life sr., editor Jour. Oceanic Engring. 1988-91, assoc. editor 2001—), Marine Tech. Soc., The Oceanographic Soc., Seattle Tennis Club. Achievements include co-designer and project scientist ocean research platform FLIP, 355' long manned spar buoy with 300' draft in vertical position, 1960-62; co-discoverer of boric acid as cause of low frequency sound absorption in the ocean; measured effect of pressure on sound absorption and electrical conductivity of magnesium and calcium sulfate and other salts related to high frequency sound absorption in the ocean; conducted sound propagation measurements at long range 30-800 miles in the ocean. Home: 5034 Park West Ave San Diego CA 92117-1046 Office: Scripps Instn Oceanography Marine Phys Lab La Jolla CA 92093-0701 E-mail: fhf@mpl.ucsd.edu

FISHER, JOEL MARSHALL, political scientist, legal consultant, educator; b. Chgo., June 24, 1935; s. Dan and Nell (Kolvin) F.; children: Sara Melinda, Matthew Nicholas. AB, U. So. Calif., 1955; LLB, MA, U. Calif.-Berkeley; PhD in Govt., Claremont Grad. U., 1968. Orgn. dir. Republican Citizens Com. of U.S., Washington, 1964-65; dir. arts and scis. state legis. divs. Rep. Nat. Com., Washington, 1968-69; asst. dep. counsel to pres. U.S. White House, 1969-70; dep. asst. sec. econ. and social affairs U.S. Dept. State, Washington, 1969-71; vis. prof. comparative and internat. law Loyola U. Sch. Law, L.A., 1972-73; dir. World Bus. Inst., L.A., 1974-75; prof. constl. law Southwestern U. Sch. Law, L.A., 1974-76; dir. World Trade Inst. So. Calif., 1976-84; prof. internat. law, asst. dean Whitter Coll. Sch. Law, L.A., 1977-80; prin. Ziskind, Greene and Assocs., 1980-83; v.p. Wells Internat., 1983-84; pres. LawSearch Inc., 1984-91; v.p. Clarke Cos., 1991-93; pres. Fisher Group, 1993—; adj. prof. Calif. Internat. U., L.A., 1993-99. Spl. projects Hollywood Palace, 1998—, ofcl. visitor The European Communities, 1974, 76, wine instr., AILA/culinary arts, 1999—; mem. U.S. dels. UN confs., 1969-71; chmn. Strategy for Peace Conf. Panel on U.S. and UN, 1972—; coord. Series on the Contemporary Am. Presidency, 1972-73; cons. Robert Taft Inst., 1977-82, World Trade Inst. N.Y., 1977-80; chair Bid Renewal Steering Com., Hollywood Entertainment Dist.; bd. dirs. Vine St. Assn., Hollywood Neighborhood Coun. Co-author two books; contbr. articles to profl. jours. Mem. steering com. Calif. Com. for Reelection of Pres., 1972; nat chmn. Community Leaders for Ford, 1976; trustee Rep. Assocs., 1978—, exec. com., 1986—; mem. vestry, sr. warden St. Michael and All Angeles Ch., Studio City, Calif., 1983-86, 89-93, mem. diocesan coun. L.A., 1986-88, chmn. budget com. 1987; bd. dirs. Corp. of the Cathedral, 1988-91; mem. com. on constitution and canons, 1993—. Fellow Nobel Found., 1958; Falk fellow, 1961-62 Mem. Am. Polit. Sci. Assn. (state legis. fellow 1970-73). Home: 4358 Mammoth Ave Apt 26 Sherman Oaks CA 91423-3692 Office: 1735 Vine St Hollywood CA 90028-5248

FISHER, JOHN RICHARD, engineering consultant, former naval officer; b. Columbus, Ohio, Dec. 28, 1924; s. Don Alfred and Katherine Buchanan (Galigher) F.; m. Kitson Overmyer, Oct. 2, 1946; children: Scott Owen, Lani Kitson. BS, U.S. Naval Acad., 1946; BCE, MCE, Rensselaer Poly. Inst., 1950; grad. Advanced Mgmt. Program, Harvard, 1971. Registered profl. engr., S.C. Commd. ensign U.S. Navy, 1946, advanced through grades to rear adm., 1972; service in North Africa, Cuba, The Philippines, Antarctica, Vietnam, Australia; comdr. 30th Seabee Rgt., Vietnam, 1968-69; dep. comdr. Naval Facilities Engring. Command; also comdr. Chesapeake divsn. constrn. facilities U.S. Naval Acad. and Omega Nav. System, 1969-73; comdr. Pacific divsn. Naval Facilities Engring. Command, Constrn. Facilities Diego Garcia, 1973-77; ret., 1977; v.p. Raymond Internat., Inc., 1977-81, sr. group v.p., 1981-83, exec. v.p., 1983-86. Pres. Cmty. Hosp. Assn. Mid-Am., Scottdale, Ariz., 1985-96; past sr. warden St. Anthony Episcopal Ch. Decorated DSM, Legion of Merit with combat V (2). Fellow Am. Soc. Mil. Engrs.; mem. ASCE, Navy League U.S. (nat. pres. 1999-2001), The Moles, Outrigger Canoe Club (Honolulu), Army-Navy Country Club (Arlington, Va.), Tau Kappa Epsilon (nat. pres. 1993-95), Tau Beta Pi. Home: 10615 E Arabian Park Dr Scottsdale AZ 85258-6021 Office: PO Box 5585 Scottsdale AZ 85261-5585 E-mail: jFisher@navyleague.org

FISHER, JOSEPH STEWART, management consultant, consultant; b. Athens, Pa., Mar. 3, 1933; s. Samuel Royer and Agnes Corinne (Smith) F.; m. Anita Ann Coyle, May 15, 1954; 1 child, Samuel Royer. BS in Tech. Mgmt., Regis U., 1981; postgrad., U. Colo., 1986-87, Iliff Sch. Theology, 1988-89. With IBM Corp., Kingston, Syracuse & Endicott, N.Y., 1956-60, Boulder, 1960-87; cons., sole propr. Fisher Enterprises, Boulder, 1975—. Bd. dirs. Vervcraft Inc., Loveland, Colo. Leadership devel. Boy Scouts Am., 1975—, chmn. long range planning, 1982-86, chaplain, 1991—; bd. dirs. Longs Peak Coun., 1983-87, Colo. Crime Stoppers, 1983-88; exec.

dir. Caring About People, Inc., Colo., 1990—; v.p. Helplink, Inc., Boulder, 1991—. With USN, 1952-56, Korea. Recipient Silver Beaver award Boy Scouts Am., Boulder, 1978, God and Svc. award Boy Scouts Am. and United Meth. Ch., 1991, OES Rose award 1994; James E. West fellow Boy Scouts Am., 1997. Mem. Am. Soc. Indsl. Security (cert. CPP, treas. 1985), Colo. Crime Prevention Assn. (cert. CPS), Mason (treas. Columbia lodge #14 1969-85, 90—), Royal Arch. Masons, Commandery Knights Templar of York Rite, Scottish Rite (32nd degree), Shriners. Republican. Methodist. Avocations: scouting, church and masonic. Home and Office: 4645 Bedford Ct Boulder CO 80301-4017

FISHER, LAWRENCE N. lawyer; BA, U. So. Calif., 1965, JD, 1968. Bar: Calif. 1969. Assoc. ptnr. Hahn & Han, 1969-74; tax counsel Fluor Corp., Irvine, Calif., 1974-76; sr. tax counsel Flour Corp., Irvine, 1976-78; v.p. adminstrn. Fluor Arabia Ltd., 1978-79; v.p., corp. law and asst. sec. Fluor Corp., Irvine, 1984—. Office: Fluor Corp 1 Enterprise Aliso Viejo CA 92656-2606

FISHER, LOUIS MCLANE, JR. management consultant; b. Balt., July 25, 1938; s. Louis McLane and Betty Taylor (Griswold) F.; m. Sue Jane Roderick, Jan. 2, 1977; children: Kathy, Mark, Matthew, Andy; stepchildren: Rolf (dec.), Sonja, Kirsten. B.A. magna cum laude, Hampden-Sydney Coll., 1961; postgrad., U. Va., 1961-62; M.B.A., U. Oreg., 1963. Exec. trainee First Nat. Bank Oreg., Portland, 1963, investment analyst, 1964; owner. Bus. Consulting Svcs., Corvallis, Oreg., 1964-65; administrv. mgr. CH2M HILL, Denver, 1965-70, treas., 1970-75, exec. v.p., 1975-94; pres. Quaere, Littleton, Colo., 1995—. Guest lectr. Oreg. State U.; bd. dirs. Open Door Inc., Iotech Inc., OMI Inc., Indsl. Design Corp., Power Interests Holding Corp., Coleman Sperryn-Jones, Mariott Resort, Bahamas, GCSI Tissuscan Tech., Grand Masters of Lacrosse, PSMA, Merrick Engring. Contbr. articles to profl. jours. Bd. dirs. Corvallis Arts Ctr. Fellow Profl. Svcs. Mgmt. Assn. (cert. profl. svcs. mgr.; bd. dirs. 1975-78, pres. 1976-77, chmn. coll. fellows 1980—); mem. Am. Mgmt. Assn., Am. Cons. Engrs. Coun., Nat. Assn. Corp. Dirs., Fin. Execs. Inst., Western Regional Coun. (treas. 1987-88), Denver C. of C., Corvallis Area C. of C. (bd. dirs., v.p. 1971), Met. Club, Châine de Rôtisseurs. Republican. Episcopalian. Clubs: Metropolitan. Home: 6093 S Bellaire Way Littleton CO 80121-3171 Office: Quaere 5250 E Arapahoe Rd Ste F7 Littleton CO 80122-2361

FISHER, LUCY J. motion picture company executive; b. N.Y.C., Oct. 2, 1949; d. Arthur Bertram and Naomi (Kislak) F.; m. Douglas Z. Wick, Feb. 16, 1986; children: Sarah, Julia, Tessa. BA, Harvard U., 1971. V.p. prodn. 20th Century Fox, L.A., 1979-80; v.p. worldwide prodns. Zoetrope Studios, Burbank, Calif., 1980-81; v.p., sr. prodn. exec. Warner Bros. Pictures, Burbank, 1981-87, sr. v.p., 1987-89, exec. v.p. prodn., 1989-96; vice chmn. Columbia Tristar Motion Picture Co., Culver City, Calif., 1996-2000; producer Red Wagon Productions, Culver City, 2000[]. Office: Sony Pictures Entertainment Astaire Bldg Rm 1312 10202 Washington Blvd Culver City CA 90232-3119

FISHER, MATTHEW P. A. physicist; Rsch. physicist Inst. Theoretical Physics, Santa Barbar, Calif. Recipient Initiatives in Rsch. award NAS, 1997. Office: U California Inst Theoretical Physics 522 University Rd Santa Barbara CA 93106-0002

FISHER, NANCY LOUISE, pediatrician, medical geneticist, former nurse; b. Cleve., July 4, 1944; d. Nelson Leopold and Catherine (Harris) F.; m. Larry William Larson, May 30, 1976 (div. Oct. 2000); 1 child, Jonathan Raymond. Student, Notre Dame Coll., Cleve., 1962-64; BSN, Wayne State U., 1967; postgrad., Calif. State U., Hayward, 1971-72; MD, Baylor Coll. of Medicine, 1976; M in Pub. Health, U. Wash., 1982, certificate in ethics, 1993. Diplomate Am. Bd. Pediatrics, Am. Bd. Med. Genetics. RN coronary care unit and med. intensive care unit Highland Gen. Hosp., Oakland, Calif., 1970-72; RN coronary care unit Alameda (Calif.) Hosp., 1972-73; intern in pediatrics Baylor Coll. of Medicine, Houston, 1976-77, resident in pediatrics, 1977-78; attending physician, pediatric clinic Harborview Med. Ctr., Seattle, 1980-81; staff physician children and adolescent health care clinic Columbia Health Ctr., Seattle, 1981-87, founder, dir. of med. genetics clinic, 1984-89; maternal child health policy cons. King County div. Seattle King County Dept Pub. Health, 1983-85; dir. genetic svcs. Va. Mason Clinic, 1986-89; dir. med. genetic svcs. Swedish Hosp., 1989-94; pvt. practice Seattle, 1994-97; med. cons. supr. office of managed care Wash. State Dept. Social and Health Svcs., Olympia, 1996-97; med. dir. Medicaid Dept. of Social and Health Svcs., Wash., 1997-99; assoc. med. dir. Govt. Programs Regence Blue Shield, 1999; med. dir. Regence Blue Shield, 2000—. Nurses aide psychiatry Sinai Hosp., Detroit, 1966-67; charge nurse Women's Hosp., Cleve., 1967; research asst. to Dr. Shelly Liss, 1976; with Baylor Housestaff Assn., Baylor Coll. Medicine, 1980-81; clin. asst. prof. grad. sch. nursing, U. Wash., Seattle, 1981-85, clin. asst. prof. dept. pediatrics, 1982-92, clin. assoc. prof. dept. pediatrics, 1992—; com. appointments include Seattle CCS Cleft Palate Panel, 1984-97; bd. dirs., first v.p. King County Assn. Sickle Cell Disease 1985-86, acting pres. 1986, pres. 1986-87; hosp. affiliation include Childrens Orthopedic Hosp. and Med. Ctr., Seattle, 1981—, Virginia Mason Hosp., Seattle, 1985-89, Harborview Hosp., Seattle, 1986—. Contbr. articles to profl. jours. Active Seattle Urban League, 1982-96, 101 Black Women, 1986-94; bd. dirs. Seattle Sickle Cell Affected Family Assn., 1984-85, Am. Heart Assn., 2001—; mem. People to People Citizen Ambassador Group; sec. Shala Com. on Infant Mortality, 1993—, Twins Com. Inst. of Medicine, 1995-2000; Evaluation, Rsch. and Planning Group Ethical Legal & Social Implications Nat. Human Gerome Rsch. Inst., 1997-2000. Served to lt. USN Nurse Corps, 1966-70. Fellow Am. Coll. Medicine Genetics (founder); mem. Am. Acad. Physician Execs., Student Governing Body and Graduating Policy Com. Baylor Coll. Medicine (founding mem. 1973-76), Loans and Scholarship Com. Baylor Coll. Medicine (voting mem. 1973-76), Am. Med. Student Assn., Student Nat. Med. Assn., Admission Com. Baylor Coll. Medicine (voting mem. 1974-76), AMA, Am. Med. Women's Assn., Am. Acad. Pediatrics, Am. Pub. Health Assn., Am. Soc. Human Genetics, Nat. Speakers Assn., Wash. State Assn. Black Providers of Health Care, Soc. Health and Human Values, Wash. State Soc. Pediatrics, Seattle C. of C. (mem. Leadership Tomorrow 1988—), Wash. State Med. Assn. (women in medicine com., interspecialty coun., telemedicine com.), Sigma Gamma Rho, Phi Delta Epsilon. E-mial. Office: PO Box 21267 MS-S515 Seattle WA 98111-3267 E-mail: nfisher@regence.com

FISHER, RAYMOND CORLEY, judge, lawyer; b. Oakland, Calif., July 12, 1939; s. Raymond Henry and Mary Elizabeth (Corley) F.; m. Nancy Leigh Fairchilds, Jan. 22, 1961; children: Jeffrey Scott, Amy Fisher Ahlers. BA, U. Calif., Santa Barbara, 1961; LLB, Stanford U., 1966. Bar: Calif. 1967, U.S. Ct. Appeals (9th cir.) 1967, U.S. Dist. Ct. (no. and cen. dists.) Calif. 1967, U.S. Ct. Claims 1967, U.S. Supreme Ct. 1967. Law clk. to Hon. J. Skelly Wright U.S. Ct. Appeals (D.C. cir.), Washington, 1966-67; law clk. to Hon. William J. Brennan U.S. Supreme Ct., Washington, 1967-68; ptnr. Tuttle & Taylor, L.A., L.A., 1968-88; sr. litigation ptnr. Heller, Ehrman, White & McAuliffe, L.A., 1988-97; assoc. atty. gen. U.S. Dept. of Justice, Washington, 1997-99; judge U.S. Ct. Appeals (9th cir.), 1999—. Exec. com. 9th Cir. Jud. Conf., 1989-91; mem. Am. Law Inst., So. Calif. ADR Panel, CPR Inst. for Dispute Resolution. Pres. Stanford Law Rev., 1965-66. Spl. asst. to Gov. of Calif., Sacramento and L.A., 1978—; dir. Constl. Rights Found., L.A., 1978-97, pres., 1983-87; pres. L.A. City Bd. Civil Svc. Commn., 1987-88; dep. gen. counsel Christopher Commn., L.A., 1991-92; pres. L.A. City Bd. Police Commrs., 1996-97. With USAR, 1957. Fellow Am. Coll. Trial Lawyers, Am. Bar Found.; mem. ABA, Fed. Bar Assn. (exec. com. 1990-96), Calif. State Bar, L.A. County Bar Assn., Chancery Club, Order of Coif. Office: US Ct Appeals 125 S grand Ave Rm 402 Pasadena CA 91105

FISHER, ROBERT, retail executive; MBA, Stanford U. Store mgr. The Gap, Inc., 1980-85, exec. v.p., mdse., Banana Republic, 1985-89, pres., Banana Republic, 1989-90, bd. dirs., 1990—, exec. v.p., 1992—, COO, 1992-93, 95-97, CFO, 1993-95. Office: The Gap Inc 1 Harrison St San Francisco CA 94105-1602

FISHER, ROBERT ALAN, laser physicist; b. Berkeley, Calif., Apr. 19, 1943; s. Leon Harold and Phyllis (Kahn) F.; children: Andrew Leon, Derek Martin. AB, U. Calif., Berkeley, 1965, MA, 1967, PhD, 1971. Programmer Stanford (Calif.) linear accelerator Stanford U., Stanford University, 1965; staff mem. Granger Assocs., Palo Alto, Calif., 1966; lectr. U. Calif., Davis, 1972-74; physicist Lawrence Livermore Lab., Calif., 1971-74; laser physicist Los Alamos (N.Mex.) Nat. Lab., 1974-86. Cons. to R.A. Fisher Assocs., Santa Fe, N.Mex., 1986—; instr. Engring. Tech., Inc., 1982—; mem. Air Force ABCD Panel, 1982; program com. mem. Internat. Quantum Electronics Conf., 1982, 1986; vice chmn. Gordon Conf. on Lasers and Non-linear Optics, 1981; chmn. Soc. Photo-Optical Instrumentation Engrs. conf. on Optical Phase Conjugation/Beam Combining/Diagnostics, 1987—; mem. Air Force Red Team for Space-Based Laser, 1983-86, HEDS II SDI Red Team, 1986; U.S. Ballistic Missile Office Options Team, 1986; mem. secretariat SDI Red/Blue Sensor Teams, 1986, SDI GBL Red/Blue Team Interaction, 1987-88; mem. architecture panel SDI SDS Phase 1, 1990, Air Force Laser 21 Working Group, 1990. Assoc. editor Optics Letters, 1984-86, Applied Optics, 1984-91; editor: Optical Phase Conjugation, 1973; contbr. articles to profl. jours. Vol. coach elem. sch. chess team Pojoaque Elem. Sch. (winner nat. elem. championship 1984), Santa Fe, 1984. Fellow Optical Soc. Am. (guest editor jour. spl. issue on optical phase conjugation), SPIE (bd. dirs. 2002—); mem. IEEE (sr.). Avocations: restoring old houses, skiing, music. Home and Office: PO Box 9279 Santa Fe NM 87504-9279

FISHER, ROBERT MORTON, foundation administrator, university administrator; b. St. Paul, Oct. 15, 1938; s. S.S. and Jean Fisher; m. Elinor C. Schectman, June 19, 1960; children: Laurie, Jonathan. AB magna cum laude, Harvard Coll., 1960; JD, Harvard U., 1963; PhD, London Sch. Econs, Polit. Sci., 1967; LLD, West Coast U., L.A., 1981; DHL, Profl. Sch. Psychology, San Francisco, 1986; DPS, John F. Kennedy U., Orinda, Calif., 1988. Rsch. assoc. Mass. Mental Health Ctr., Cambridge, 1957-62; rsch. asst. Ctr. Study Juvenile Delinquency, Cambridge, 1961-63; spl. asst. to chief psychologist British Prison Dept. Home Office, London, 1963-67; prof. Sch. Criminology U. Calif., Berkeley, 1965-71; profl. race car driver, 1972-77; pres. John F. Kennedy U., Orinda, Calif., 1974-85; exec. dir. 92d St. YMHA, N.Y.C., 1984-85; dir., CEO The San Francisco Found., 1987-97. Mayor, councilman Lafayette, Calif., 1968-76; mem. Minn. and Calif. Bar Specialty: charitable gift planning; CEO Fisher Cos., 1997—. Scholar-in-residence Rockefeller Found., Bellagio, 1994; Polit. Sci. vis. fellow London Sch. Econs. and Polit. Sci., 1994; named Outstanding Fundraising Exec. Nat. Soc. Fund Raising Execs. Home and Office: 85 Southwood Dr Orinda CA 94563-3026

FISHER, STEVEN KAY, neurobiology educator; b. Rochester, Ind., July 18, 1942; s. Stewart King and Hazel Madeline (Howell) F.; m. Dinah Dawn Marschall, May 2, 1971; children: Jenni Dawn, Brian Andrew, Steven William. BS, Purdue U., 1964, MS, 1966; postgrad., Johns Hopkins U., 1967-69; PhD, Purdue U., 1969. Postdoctoral fellow Johns Hopkins U., Balt., 1969-71; prof. U. Calif., Santa Barbara, 1971—, dir. Inst. Environ. Stress, 1985-88, dir. Neurosci. Rsch. Inst., 1989-2001. Cons. Ultrastructure Tech., Goleta, Calif., 1984—, Regeneron Pharms., Inc., 1993, 94, Amgen, Inc., 1994, 95; mem. NIH Visual Scis. A2 Study Sect. Contbr. numerous articles to profl. jours. Recipient Devel. award NIH, 1980-84, M.E.R.I.T. award NIH, 1989-99; NIH grantee, 1971—. Mem. AAAS, Assn. Rsch. in Vision and Ophthalmology (mem. program com. 1979-80, K-12 edn. com. 1997-2001), Soc. Neurosci., Am. Soc. Cell Biology, Electron Microscopy Soc. Am. Avocations: music, gardening, literature, swing dancing, weight lifting. Home: 6890 Sabado Tarde Rd Goleta CA 93117-4305 Office: U Calif Neuroscience Research Institute Santa Barbara CA 93106-5060 E-mail: fisher@lifesci.uscb.edu

FISHER, THOMAS E. energy company executive; BSME, Tex. A&M U., 1966. Various engring. and mgmt. positions Unocal Corp., El Segundo, Calif., 1966-87, divsn. v.p., 1987-94, sr. v.p. corp. new ventures, comml. affairs, 1994—. Office: Unocal Corp 2141 Rosecrans Ave Ste 4000 El Segundo CA 90245

FISHER, WESTON JOSEPH, economist; b. Glendale, Calif., 29 Aug. s. Edward Weston and Rosalie Eloise (Bailey) F. BS, U. So. Calif., l962, MA, l965, MS, l97l, PhD, 1989. Sr. mgr. Naval Undersea Ctr., Pasadena, Calif., l964-69; chief exec. officer, prin. Ventura County, Ventura, 1969-73; So. Calif. dir. County Suprs. Assn., L.A., l974-75; coord. govtl. rels. So. Calif. Assn. Govts., L.A., 1975-78; devel. dir. Walter H. Leimert Co., L.A., l979-90. Bd. dirs. Gray Energy Corp., L.A., Mission Inn Group, Riverside, Calif., Coun. of Leaders and Specialists - UN, Peterson Oil and Gas. Mem. Gov.'s Adv. Coun. for Econ. growth, Channel Islands Conservancy. Mem. Medieval Acad. Am., El Dorado Country Club, Univ. Club, South Coast Yacht Club, Cave Creek Club, Lambda Alpha. Republican. Avocation: medieval and U.S. history. Home: 14373 Tawya Rd Apple Valley CA 92307-5545

FISHER, WILLIAM G.E. state legislator, rental investor, assisted living facility owner; b. Artesia, Calif., Mar. 24, 1936; m. Darlene F. Fisher; children: William G.E., Darryl E., Rhonda M. BA in Bibl. Langs., Walla Walla Coll., 1965; postgrad., Andrews U., Berrien Springs, Mich., 1966-67, Eastern Wash. State Coll., Cheney, 1968. Mem. Oreg. Ho. of Reps., 1992-96, Oreg. Senate, 1996—. Chmn. Health and Human Svcs. Com., Oreg. Senate, 1997—, vice chmn. Agr. and Natural Resources Com., 1997, mem. Trade and Econ. Devel. Com., 1997-99, mem. Agr. and Natural Resources Com., 1997-99, mem. Ways and Means (Human Resources sub-com.), 1999, mem. Edn. Com., 2001. Bd. dirs. Riverside Ctr., 1996—, Douglas County Coun. on Alcoholism, 1971-76; mem. Douglas County Pers. Rev. Bd., 1973; bd. dirs. Roseburg Jr. Acad., 1986-89, chmn. bd., 1987-88; mem. Western States Legis. Forestry Task Force, 1993-95; mem. Gov.'s Commn. on Sr. Svcs., 1995-97, reappointed, 1998, 2001; Douglas County Precinct Committeeman, 1990, 92, 94, 96, 98, 2000; sec. Douglas County Rep. Exec. com., 1990-93. Served with U.S. Army, 1958-60, also Res. Fellow Am. Coll. Health Care Adminstrs.; mem. Am. Health Care Assn., Oreg. Health Care Assn. (bd. dirs. 1971-73, v.p. 1974-89), Am. Legion, Douglas Timber Operators, Oreg. Farm Bur., Kiwanis Club Roseburg (bd. dirs. 1981), NRA (life), Oreg. State Shooting Assn. (life), Oreg. Hunters Assn., Roseburg Rod and Gun Club (life), Am. Assn. Ret. Persons, Sr. Citizens Inc., Aircraft Owners and Pilots Assn., Oreg. Pilots Assn., Exptl. Aircraft Assn., Antique Aircraft Assn., Stearman Restorers Assn., Harley Owners Group, Am. Motorcycle Assn., others. Seventh-day Adventist. Office: Oreg State Capitol 900 Court St NE # S-209 Salem OR 97310-0001 also: 3329 NE Stephens St Roseburg OR 97470-1259 Fax: (541) 672-0862. E-mail: billfisher@mcsi.net, pisher.sen@state.or.us

FISHMAN, ARNIE, marketing executive, consultant, film producer; b. Bklyn., 1965; married; 3 children. BS, CUNY, 1965, postgrad. in Pscholog, 1966. Rsch. asst. Liberman Rsch, N.Y.C., 1966, v.p., 1971; founder Lieberman Rsch. Worldwide, L.A., 1973—, also chmn. bd. dirs. Founder, chmn. bd. dirs. Interviewing Svc. Am., 1982—; expert witness Fed. Trade Commn.; spkr. in field; cons. in field. Office: Lieberman Rsch Worldwide 1900 Ave Of Stars Ste 1550 Los Angeles CA 90067-4483

FISHMAN, JOSHUA AARON, sociolinguist, educator; b. Phila., July 18, 1926; s. Aaron S. and Sonia (Horwitz) F.; m. Gella Jeanne Schweid, Dec. 23, 1951; children: M. Manuel, David Elliot, Avrom Avi. B.S., M.S. (Mayor Phila. competitive scholar 1944-48), U. Pa., 1948; Ph.D., Columbia U., 1953; Ped.D. (hon.), Yeshiva U., 1968; LittD (hon.), Free U. Brussels, 1986. Tchr. elem. and secondary Yiddish secular schs., 1945-50; ednl. psychologist, sr. research asso. dept. research and experimentation Jewish Edn. Com. N.Y., 1951-54; from lectr. to vis. prof. psychology CCNY, 1955-58; research assoc. to dir. research Coll. Entrance Exam. Bd., 1955-58; assoc. prof. human relations and psychology U. Pa., 1958-60; prof. psychology and sociology, dean Grad. Sch. Edn. Yeshiva U., 1960-66, disting. univ. research prof. social scis. Ferkauf Grad. Sch. Psychology, 1966-88, emeritus, 1988—, univ. v.p. acad. affairs, 1973-76; vis. rschr., vis. prof. Stanford (Calif.) U., 1990—. Cummings lectr. McGill U., 1979; Linguistics Soc. Am. prof. Linguistics Inst., 1980; disting. vis. prof. Monash U., Melbourne, Australia, summers 1985, 2000; mem. com. on sociolinguistics Social Sci. Rsch. Coun.; adviser, cons. Am. Jewish Congress, Nat. Scholarship Svc. and Fund for Negro Students, Coll. Entrance Exam. Bd., Am. Assn. Jewish Edn., Ministry of Fin., Republic of Ireland; cons. Ctr. for Applied Linguistics, Internat. Rsch. Ctr. on Bilingualism, Secretariat Linguistic Policy Basque Govt., 1986—, Maori Lang. Commn., 1995—; vis. prof. linguistics L.I. U., 2000, NYU, 1998—, Grad. Ctr. CUNY, 1999—; bd. dirs. Consortium for Study of Lang. Problems, 2001—. Author: Studies on Polish Jewry, 1974, Sociology of Bilingual Education, 1976, The Spread of English, 1977, Advances in the Study of Societal Multilingualism, 1978, Never Say Die: A Thousand Years of Yiddish in Jewish Life and Letters, 1981, Bilingual Education for Hispanic Students in the U.S., 1982, The Rise and Fall of the Ethnic Revival, 1985, Readings in the Sociology of Jewish Languages, 1985, Ethnicity in Action, 1985, The Fergusonian Impact (2 vols.), 1986, Ideology, Society and Language, 1987, Language and Ethnicity in Minority Sociolinguistic Perspective, 1988, Yiddish: Turning to Life, 1991, Reversing Language Shift, 1991, The Earliest Stage of Language Planning, 1993, Post-Imperial English, 1996, In Praise of the Beloved Language, 1997, The Multilinges Apple: Languages in New York City, 1997, Handbook of Language and Ethnic Identity, 1999, Can Threatened Languages Be Saved?, 2000, also numerous profl. publs. including Afn shvel, 1980—, Forverts, 1996—; assoc. editor: Jour. Ednl. Sociology, 1963-65, Yivo Ann., 1970-77, Yidishe Sprakh, 1970—; editor: Yivo Bleter, 1974-77; editor Jour. Social Issues, 1964-69; editor: (series) Contribution to the Sociology of Lang., 1971—, Internat. Jour. Sociology of Lang., 1973—, (series) Contribution to the Sociology of Jewish Languages, 1985-88. Pres.'s scholar E.C. Morris fellow Columbia Tchrs. Coll., 1952-53, postdoctoral rsch. tng. fellow Social Sci. Rsch. Coun., 1954-55, fellow Ctr. Advanced Study Behavioral Scis., 1963-64, Princeton Inst. Advanced Study fellow, 1975-76, fellow Netherlands Inst. Advanced Study, 1982-83, Israel Inst. Advanced Studies, 1983, Nat. Fgn. Lang. Ctr., 1995-96; NSF European Conf. grantee, 1960, Office of Edn. grantee, 1960-63, 66-68, 72-74, 79-80, Social Sci. Rsch. Coun. European Conf. grantee, 1961, NIMH grantee, Latin Am., 1963, 66, NSF grantee, Europe, 1966, 79-83, Ford Found. grantee, 1969-72, 75-76, Meml. Found. Jewish Culture grantee, 1970-71, 78-79, 82-83, Nat. Inst. Edn. grantee, 1978-79, 79-81; sr. specialist Inst. Advanced Projects, East-West Ctr., 1968-69; sr. assoc. Multicultural-Bilingual divsn. Nat. Inst. Edn., 1976-77. Fellow APA, Am. Sociol. Assn., Am. Anthrop. Assn.; mem. AAAS, Am. Ednl. Rsch. Assn., Linguistic Soc. Am., Yivo Inst. Jewish Rsch., Nat. Assn. Bilingual Edn. (Man of Yr. 1992), TESOL, AAUP, Terralingua. Office: Stanford U Ctr Ednl Rsch at Stanford Stanford CA 94305

FISHMAN, ROBERT ALLEN, neurologist, educator; b. N.Y.C., May 30, 1924; s. Samuel Benjamin and Miriam (Brinkin) F.; m. Margery Ann Satz, Jan. 29, 1956 (dec. May 29, 1980); children: Mary Beth, Alice Ellen, Elizabeth Ann.; m. Mary Craig Wilson, Jan. 7, 1983. A.B., Columbia U., 1944; M.D., U. Pa., 1947. Mem. faculty Columbia Coll. Physicians and Surgeons, 1954-66, asso. prof. neurology, 1962-66; asst. attending neurologist N.Y. State Psychiat. Inst., 1955-66, Neurol. Inst. Presbyn. Hosp., N.Y.C., 1955-61, asso., 1961-66; co-dir. Neurol. Clin. Research Center, Neurol. Inst., Columbia-Presbyn. Med. Ctr., 1961-66; prof. neurology U. Calif. Med. Ctr., San Francisco, 1966-94, chmn. dept. neurology, 1966-92, prof. emeritus, 1994—. Cons. neurologist San Francisco Gen. Hosp., San Francisco VA Hosp., Letterman Gen. Hosp.; dir. Am. Bd. Psychiatry and Neurology, 1981-88, v.p., 1986, pres., 1987 Author: Cerebrospinal Fluid in Diseases of the Nervous System, 1992; chief editor Annals of Neurology, 1993-97; contbr. articles to profl. jours. Nat. Multiple Sclerosis Soc. fellow, 1956-57; John and Mary R. Markle scholar in med. sci., 1960-65; recipient Disting. Alumnus award U. Pa. 1996. Mem. Am. Neurol. Assn. (pres. 1983-84), Am. Fedn. for Clin. Research, Assn. for Research in Nervous and Mental Diseases, Am. Acad. Neurology (v.p. 1971-73, pres. 1975-77), Am. Assn. Physicians, Am. Soc. for Neurochemistry, Soc. for Neurosci., N.Y. Neurol. Soc., Am. Assn. Univ. Profs. Neurology (pres. 1972-73), AAAS, Am. Epilepsy Soc., N.Y. Acad. Scis., AMA (sec. sect. on nervous and mental diseases 1964-67, v.p. 1967-68, pres. 1968-69), Alpha Omega Alpha (hon. faculty mem.) Home: 205 Paradise Dr Tiburon CA 94920-2534 Office: U Calif Med Ctr 794 Herbert C Moffitt Hosp San Francisco CA 94143-0001 E-mail: raf530@aol.com, aon@itsa.ucsf.edu

FISK, HAYWARD D. lawyer; BS, U. Kans., 1965, JD, 1968; LLM, U. Mo., 1971. Bar: Kans. 1968, Pa. 1972, D.C. 1986. V.p., gen. counsel, sec. Sprint Corp., 1971-82, v.p., Wash. counsel, 1982-88, v.p., assoc. gen. counsel, 1988-89; v.p., gen. counsel, sec. Computer Scis. Corp., El Segundo, Calif., 1989—. Legal advisor Nat. Legal Ctr. for Pub. Interest, 1991—; chmn. bd. dirs. Atlantic Legal Found. Bd. editors The Computer Lawyer, 1989—. Office: Computer Scis Corp 2100 E Grand Ave El Segundo CA 90245-5024

FITCH, ROBERT MCLELLAN, business and technology consultant; b. Shanghai, China, Apr. 30, 1928; came to U.S., 1937; s. George A. and Geraldine (Townsend) F.; m. Reta Peck, Aug. 21, 1955; children: David H.A., Douglas G., Christopher M. AB, Dartmouth Coll., 1949; PhD, U. Mich., 1954. Prof. U. Conn., Storrs, 1962-83; v.p. corp. rsch. SC Johnson Wax, Racine, Wis., 1983-85, sr. v.p. R & D, 1985-89; pvt. practice cons., 1990—. Author: Polymer Colloids, A Comprehensive Introduction, 1997; editor: Polymer Colloids, 1971, Polymer Colloids II, 1980; contbr. over 100 articles to profl. jours.; patentee in field. Mem. adv. team Nat. Inst. for Sci. Edn., 1995-2000; chmn. Taos Talking Pictures, 1998-2000. Recipient Disting. Svc. award Am. Chem. Soc., 1987; named to S.E. Wis. Educator's Hall of Fame, 1992. Fellow AAAS. Avocations: bonsai culture, skiing, scuba diving.

FITCH, WALTER M(ONROE), molecular biologist, educator, evolutionist; b. San Diego, May 21, 1929; s. Chloral Harrison Monroe and Evelyn Charlotte (Halliday) F.; m. Eleanor E. McLean, Sept. 1, 1952 (div. Mar. 28, 1988); children: Karen Allyn, Kathleen Leslie, Kenton Monroe; m. Chung-Cha Ziesel, Sept. 9, 1989. AB, U. Calif., Berkeley, 1953, PhD, 1958. USPHS postdoctoral fellow U. Calif. Berkeley, 1958-59, Stanford U., Palo Alto, Calif, 1959-61; lectr. Univ. Coll., London, 1961-62; asst. prof. U. Wis.-Madison, 1962-67, assoc. prof., 1967-72, prof., 1972-86, U. So. Calif., L.A., 1986-89, U. Calif.-Irvine, 1989—, prof., chmn. dept. ecology and evolutionary biology, 1990-95; prof., 1995—. Vis. Fulbright lectr. London, 1961-62; NIH vis. prof. Hawaii, 1973-74; Macy Found. vis. prof. U. Calif., L.A., 1981-82; vis. prof. U. So. Calif., L.A., 1985, U. Cambridge, England., 1998-99, Isaac Newton Inst. Math., England, 1998-99. Editor-in-chief Molecular Biology and Evolution, 1983-93; editor Classification Literature, 1975-80; assoc. editor Jour. Molecular Evolution, 1976-80; contbr. articles to profl. jours. Mem. Cupertino Planning Commn. Calif. 1960-61, Madison Planning Commn., 1965-68; mem

Dane County Regional Planning Commn., 1968-73; chmn. Madison Reapportionment, 1979-81. Grantee NIH and NSF, 1962—. Fellow AAAS; mem. NAS, Am. Philos. Soc., Am. Acad. Arts and Scis., Am. Soc. for Biochemistry and Molecular Biology, Am. Chem. Soc., Am. Soc. Naturalists, Biochem. Soc. (Eng.), Genetics Soc. Am., Soc. Study Evolution, Soc. Systematic Biology, Soc. for Molecular Biology and Evolution (pres. 1992-93), Linnean Soc. (London). Office: U Calif Dept Ecol & Evol Biology Irvine CA 92697-0001 E-mail: wfitch@uci.edu

FITZGERALD, JAMES MICHAEL, federal judge; b. Portland, Oreg., Oct. 7, 1920; s. Thomas and Florence (Linderman) F.; m. Karin Rose Benton, Jan. 19, 1950; children: Dennis James, Denise Lyn, Debra Jo, Kevin Thomas. BA, Willamette U., 1950, LLB, 1951; postgrad., U. Wash., 1952. Bar: Alaska 1953. Asst. U.S. atty., Ketchikan and Anchorage, Alaska, 1952-56; city atty. City of Anchorage, 1956-59; legal counsel to Gov. Alaska, Anchorage, 1959; commr. pub. safety State of Alaska, 1959; judge Alaska Superior Ct., 3d Jud. Dist., 1959-69, presiding judge, 1969-72; assoc. justice Alaska Supreme Ct., Anchorage, 1972-75; judge U.S. Dist. Ct. for Alaska, Anchorage, from 1975, formerly chief judge, now sr. judge. Mem. advisory bd. Salvation Army, Anchorage, 1962— , chmn., 1965-66; mem. Anchorage Parks and Recreation Bd., 1965-77, chmn., 1966. Served with AUS, 1940-41; Served with USMCR, 1942-46. Office: US Dist Ct 222 W 7th Ave Box 50 Anchorage AK 99513-7564

FITZGERALD, JOAN, principal; Prin. Xavier Coll. Prep. Sch., 1975—. Recipient Blue Ribbon Sch. award 1990-91. Office: Xavier Coll Prep Sch 4710 N 5th St Phoenix AZ 85012-1738

FITZ-GERALD, JOAN, state senator; Dem. senator dist. 13 Colo. State Senate, 2000—. Mem. edn. com. Colo. State Senate, chair bus., labor and fin. com. Office: Colo State Senate 200 E Colfax Rm 330 Denver CO 80203 Fax: 303 526-2052

FITZGERALD, JOHN CHARLES, JR. investment banker; b. Sacramento, May 23, 1941; s. John Charles and Geraldine Edith (McNabb) F.; m. Mildred Ann Kilpatrick, June 26, 1965; children: Geraldine Kathrine, Erec John. BS, Calif. State U., Sacramento, 1964; MBA, Cornell U., 1965. Dir. corp. planning Bekins Co., L.A., 1966-73; mgr. corp. planning Ridder Publs., Inc., L.A., 1973-75; CFO City of Inglewood, Calif., 1975-77; treas./contr. Inglewood Redevel. Agy., 1975-77; v.p. mcpl. fin. White, Weld & Co., Inc., L.A., 1977-78; v.p. pub. fin. paine Webber Jackson & Curtis, L.A., 1978-79; v.p. and mgr. for Western region, mcpl. fin. dept. Merrill Lynch Capital Markets, L.A., 1979-82, mng. dir. Western region, mcpl. fin. dept., 1982-86; mng. dir. Seidler-Fitzgerald Pub. Fin., L.A., 1986—; sr. v.p. The Seidler Cos., Inc., L.A., 1986—, also bd. dirs., mem. exec. com. Instr. fin./adminstrn. El Camino Coll., Torrance, Calif., 1977-80. Chmn. bd. dirs., exec. com., treas., chmn. fundraising com. L.a. chpt. Am. Heart Assn., 1977—; bd. dirs. Daniel Freeman Hosps. Inc., Corondelet Health Care corp.; trustee Mt. St. Mary's Coll., L.A., 1992—; bd. dirs. Tau Kappa Epsilon Ednl. Found., Indpls., 1995—; bd. dirs. Calif. Soc. for Biomed. Rsch., 1998; alumni coun. mem. Johnson Grad. Sch. Mgmt. Cornell U., real estate coun. Mem. Fin. Execs. Inst., Mcpl. fin. Officers, League Calif. Cities, So. Calif. Corp. Planners Assn. (past pres.), L.A. Bond, Lido Isle Yacht Club, Jonathan Club, The Calif. Club, Lake Arrowhead Country Club, Rotary, Beta Gamma Sigma. Address: PO Box 765 27447 Bayshore Dr Lake Arrowhead CA 92352

FITZGERALD, TIKHON (LEE R. H. FITZGERALD), bishop; b. Detroit, Nov. 14, 1932; s. LeRoy and Dorothy Kaeding (Higgins) F. AB, Wayne State U., 1958. Ordained deacon, 1971, priest, 1978, bishop Eastern Orthodox, 1987. Enlisted U.S. Army, 1954-57; commd. 2 lt. USAF, 1960, advanced through grades to capt., 1971; air staff, 1966-71; released, 1971; protodeacon Holy Virgin Mary Russian Orthodox Cathedral, L.A., 1972-78, rector, archpriest, 1979-87; bishop of San Francisco and the West Orthodox Ch. in Am., L.A., 1987—. Recipient Order of St. Vladimir II Class, Patriarch Aleksy of Moscow, 1993. Democrat. Home: 649 Robinson St Los Angeles CA 90026-3612 Office: Orthodox Ch Am Diocese of the West 650 Micheltorena St Los Angeles CA 90026-3623

FITZPATRICK, LOIS ANN, library administrator; b. Yonkers, N.Y., Mar. 27, 1952; d. Thomas Joseph and Dorothy Ann (Nealy) Sullivan; m. William George Fitzpatrick, Jr., Dec. 1, 1973; children: Jennifer Ann, Amy Ann. BS in Sociology, Mercy Coll., 1974; ML, Pratt Inst., 1975. Clk. Yonkers Pub. Libr., 1970-73, libr. trainee, 1973-75, libr. I, 1975-76; reference libr. Carroll Coll. Libr., Helena, Mnt., 1976-79, acting dir., 1979, dir., 1980—; asst. prof. Carroll Coll., Helena, 1979-89, assoc. prof., 1989-99, prof., 2000—. Bd. dirs. Mont. Shares; chmn. arrangements Mont. Gov.'s Pre White House Conf. on Libraries, Helena, 1977-78; mem. steering com. Reference Point coop. program for librs., 1991; mem. adv. com. Helena Coll. of Tech. Libr., 1994—; adv. coun. Mont. Libr. Svcs., 1996—; mem. Networking Task Force, Laws Revision Task Force; pres. elect Helena Area Health Sci. Libraries Cons., 1979-84, pres., 1984-88; bd. dirs. Mont. FAXNET. Co-chmn. interst group OCLC; chmn. local arrangements Mont. Gov.'s Pre White House Conf.; mem. adv. bd. Helena Coll. Tech.; bd. dirs. Mont. Race for the Cure, ACLU-MT, 1999—. Mem. Mont. Libr. Assn. (task force for White House conf. 1991, chair govt. affairs com. 2000—, EdLINK-MT 1997-99, 2000—), Soroptimist Internat. of Helena (2d v.p. 1984-85, pres. 1986-87). Home: 1308 Shirley Rd Helena MT 59602-6635 Office: Carroll Coll Jack & Sallie Corette Libr 1601 N Benton Ave Helena MT 59625-0001 E-mail: lfitzpat@carroll.edu

FITZPATRICK, THOMAS MARK, lawyer; b. Anaconda, Mont., June 12, 1951; s. Marcus Leo and Natalie Stephanie (Trbovich) F. BA, U. Mont., 1973; JD, U. Chgo., 1976. Bar: Ill. 1976, Wash. 1978. Asst. to pres.-elect ABA, Chgo., 1976-77, asst. to pres., 1977-78; assoc. Karr, Tuttle, Campbell, Seattle, 1978-85, ptnr., 1985-89, Stafford, Frey, Cooper, Seattle, 1989-99; asst. chief civil divsn. Snohomish County Prosecuting Atty.'s Office, Everett, Wash., 1999—. Editor: ABA: A Century of Service, 1979. Fellow Am. Bar Found.; mem. ABA (chmn. lawyer and media conf. 1985-88, profl. discipline com. 1988-94, LRIS com. 1994-97, chmn. nat. conf. groups 1982-85, ho. of dels. 1990—, state del. 1993-98, bd. govs. 1998—), Wash. Bar Assn. (pres. young lawyer divsn. 1986-87), Snohomish County Bar Assn., Seattle-King County Bar, U. Chgo. Law Sch. Alumni Assn. (bd. dirs., Seattle regional pres. 1980-86). Roman Catholic Home: 7345 13th Ave NW Seattle WA 98117-5306 Office: Snohomish County Civil Divsn Prosecuting Attys Office 2918 Colby Ave Ste 203 Everett WA 98201-4011

FITZSIMMONS, COTTON (LOWELL COTTON FITZSIMMONS), professional basketball executive, broadcaster, former coach; b. Hannibal, Mo., Oct. 7, 1931; s. Clancy and Zelda Curry (Gibbs) F.; m. JoAnn D'Andrea, Sept. 2, 1978 (div.); 1 child, Gary. B.S., Midwestern Univ., Wichita Falls, Tex., 1956, M.A., 1957. Head coach, athletic dir. Moberly Jr. Coll, Moberly, Mo., 1958-67; head coach Kans. State U., Manhattan, 1967-70, NBA Phoenix Suns, 1970-72, 1988-94, 96-97, dir. player personnel, 1987-88; head coach NBA Atlanta Hawks, 1972-76; dir. player personnel NBA Golden State Warriors, Oakland, Calif., 1976-77; head coach NBA Buffalo Braves, 1977-78, NBA Kansas City Kings, Mo., 1978-84, NBA San Antonio Spurs, 1984-87; sr. exec. v.p. Phoenix Suns, 1992—, head coach. Coach Schick Rookies, 45th ann. All Star Game, America West Arena. Recipient Coach of the Yr. award Nat. Jr. Coll. Athletic Assn., 1966, 67, Coach of the Yr. award Big 8 Conf., 1970, Coach of the Yr. award NBA, 1979, 89, Coach of the Yr. award Sporting News, St. Louis, 1979, 89; inducted into Mo. Sports Hall of Fame, Springfield, Mo., 1981, Nat. Jr. Coll. Basketball Hall of Fame, Hutchinson, 1985 Fellow Nat. Assn. Basketball Coaches Avocations: golf, fishing. Office: Phoenix Suns 201 E Jefferson St Phoenix AZ 85004-2412

FIX, WILBUR JAMES, department store executive; b. Velva, N.D., Aug. 14, 1927; s. Jack J. and Beatrice D. (Wasson) F.; m. Beverly A. Corcoran, Sept. 20, 1953; children: Kathleen M., Michael B., Jenifer L. BA, U. Wash., 1950. Credit mgr. Bon Marche, Yakima, Wash., 1951-54, controller, ops. mgr. Boise, Idaho, 1954-58, sr. v.p. Seattle, 1970-76, exec. v.p., 1976-77, pres., chief exec. officer, 1978-87; chmn., chief exec. officer, sr. v.p. Allied Stores Corp., 1987-93; chmn. Fix Mgmt. Group, 1993—. Chmn. Wash. Retail Coun., 1983-84; bd. dirs. Bldg. Materials Holding Corp., Vans, Inc., Nsite Software Inc.; mem. adv. coun. Inst. for Retail Studies, Col. of the Desert, Palm Desert, Calif., Corp. Coun. of the Arts, Seattle. Mem. pres.'s adv. com. Allied Stores Corp., N.Y., 1968-72; mem. citizens adv. com. Seattle Pub. Schs., 1970-71; v.p. Citizens Council Against Crime; chmn. Seattle King County Conv. & Visitors Bur., 1990. With AUS, 1946-47. Mem. Nat. Retail Mchts. Assn., Controllers Congress, Seattle Retail Controllers Group (past pres.), Fin. Execs. Inst., Western States Regional Controllers Congress (past pres.), Seattle C. of C. (exec. com., bd. dirs.), Assn. Wash. Bus. (fin. adv.), Downtown Seattle Devel. Assn. (exec. com., trustee), Wash. Round Table, Wash. Athletic Club, Mission Hills Country Club (Rancho Mirage, Calif.), Elks, Pi Kappa Alpha, Alpha Kappa Psi, Phi Theta Kappa. Episcopalian. Address: 149 Racquet Club Dr Rancho Mirage CA 92270-1461 Office: The Bon Marché 3rd And Pine St Seattle WA 98181-0001 also: 5403 W Mercer Way Mercer Island WA 98040-4635 E-mail: b2fix@aol.com

FIXMAN, MARSHALL, chemist, educator; b. St. Louis, Sept. 21, 1930; s. Benjamin and Dorothy (Finkel) F.; m. Marian Ruth Beatman, July 5, 1959 (dec. Sept. 1969); children: Laura Beth, Susan Ilene, Andrew Richard; m. Branka Ladanyi, Dec. 7, 1974. A.B., Washington U., St. Louis, 1950; Ph.D., MIT, 1954. Jewett postdoctoral fellow chemistry Yale U., 1953-54; instr. chemistry Harvard U., 1956-59; sr. fellow Mellon Inst., Pitts., 1959-61; prof. chemistry, dir. Inst. Theoretical Sci., U. Oreg., 1961-64, prof. chemistry, research asso. inst., 1964-65; prof. chemistry Yale U., New Haven, 1965-79; prof. chemistry and physics Colo. State U., Ft. Collins, 1979-2000, prof. emeritus, 2000—. Mem. editorial bd. Jour. Chem. Physics, 1962-64, Jour. Phys. Chemistry, 1970-74, Macromolecules, 1970-74, Accounts Chem. Rsch. 1982-85, Jour. Polymer Sci. B, 1991-93; assoc. editor Jour. Chem. Physics, 1994—. Wwith U.S. Army, 1954-56. Fellow Alfred P. Sloan Found., 1961-63; recipient Governor's award Oreg. Mus. Sci. and Industry, 1964 Mem. NAS, Am. Acad. Arts and Scis., Am. Chem. Soc. (award pure chemistry 1964, award polymer chemistry 1991), Am. Phys. Soc. (high polymer physics award 1980), Fedn. Am. Scientists. Office: Colo State U Dept Chemistry Fort Collins CO 80523-0001 E-mail: mf@fibm.mfbl.colostate.edu

FLAGG, NORMAN LEE, retired advertising executive; b. Detroit, Jan. 21, 1932; s. Frank and Harriet (Brown) F.; m. Carolanne Flagg; children: James, Suzanne. BFA, U. Miami, Miami, Fla., 1958. Advt. supr. Smithkline Beckman, Phila., 1970-75, creative dir., 1975-80; owner Illusions Restaurants, Bryn Maur, Pa., 1979-87, Illusions Restaurant, Tucson, 1984-88. Author: Shooting Blanks, 1994. With USMC, 1954-56. Recipient Diana awards Whlse Druggest Assn. 1977, Aesculapius award Modern Medicine 1978. Mem. Acad. Magical Arts.

FLAHERTY, LOIS TALBOT, editor, psychiatrist, educator; b. Nashville, Apr. 28, 1942; BA, Wellesley Coll., 1963; MD, Duke U., 1968. Diplomate Nat. Bd. Med. Examiners. Intern D.C. Gen. Hosp., 1968-69; resident in psychiatry Georgetown U. Hosp., 1969-71; resident in child psychiatry Johns Hopkins Hosp., 1971-73; pvt. practice Cross Keys, Md., 1973-81; dir. tng. divsn. child and adolescent psychiatry U. Md., 1981-89, assoc. prof. med. sch. divsn. child and adolescent psychiatry, 1982-93, dir. divsn. child and adolescent psychiatry, 1984-92, adj. assoc. prof., 1994—; clin. assoc. prof. psychiatry U. Pa., 1997-2000; pvt. practice Blue Bell, Pa., 1994-99; editor Adolescent Psychiatry, 2000—. Instr. depts. psychiatry and pediatrics Johns Hopkins U. Sch. Medicine, 1973-92; attending staff psychiatrist family, child and adolescent divsn. Sinai Hosp. Balt., 1974-77; staff child psychiatrist Walter P. Carter Ctr., 1977-78, dir. child and adolescent svcs., 1978-92, acting dir. impatient adolescent unit, 1979-80; clin. asst. prof. U. Md., 1977-81; cons. Northwest Drug Alert Sinai Hosp. Balt., 1971-72, St. Vincent's Child Care Ctr., 1973-78, Children's Guild, Inc., 1975-82, SSA, Balt., 1985, many others. Contbr. chpts. to books and articles and book revs. to profl. jours. NIMH grantee, 1983-86. Fellow Am. Psychiat. Assn., Am. Soc. for Adolescent Psychiatry; mem. Am. Acad. Child Psychiatry, Am. Coll. Psychiatrists, Group for Advancement of Psychiatry, Pa. Psychiatr. Soc., Pa. Soc. for Adolescent Psychiatry, Pa. Regional Coun. for Child and Adolescent Psychiatry. Office: Lois T Flaherty 18765 Kenlake Pl NE Kenmore WA 98028-3236

FLAKE, JEFF, congressman; b. Snowflake, Ariz. m. Cheryl, 15 yrs.; 5 children. BA in Internat. Rels., MA in Polit. Sci., Brigham Young U. Worked in pub. rels., Wash., DC, 1987; exec. dir. Found. Democracy, Nambia, Goldwater Instit., Ariz., 1992; mem. 107th Congress, 1st Ariz. dist., 2001—. Mem. House Judiciary com.; serving on House Internat. Rels. com. Office: 512 Cannon House Office Bldg Washington DC 20515-0301*

FLANAGAN, JOHN MICHAEL, editor, publisher; b. Bangor, Maine, Mar. 8, 1946; s. Joseph F. and Dorothy Elizabeth (Albert) F.; m. Mary Katherine Fastenau, June 22, 1990. Student, U. Notre Dame, 1963-65; BJ, U. Mo., 1971. With The News-Jour. papers, Wilmington, Del., 1971-84, mng. editor, 1982-84; editor Marin Ind. Jour., San Rafael, Calif., 1984-87; exec. editor Honolulu Star-Bulletin, 1987-93; editor, pub. Honolulu Star-Bull., 1993—. With U.S. Army, 1965-68. Office: Honolulu Star Bull PO Box 3080 Honolulu HI 96802-3080

FLANAGAN, ROBERT JOSEPH, economics educator; b. New Haven, Dec. 16, 1941; s. Russell Joseph and Anne (Macauley) F.; m. Susan Rae Mendelsohn, Aug. 23, 1986. BA, Yale U., 1963; MA, U. Calif., 1966, PhD, 1970. Economist U.S. Dept. Labor, Washington, 1963-64; asst. prof. labor econs. Grad. Sch. Bus. U. Chgo., 1969-75; assoc. prof. labor econs. Grad. Sch. Bus. Stanford (Calif.) U., 1975-86; sr. staff economist Coun. of Econ. Advisors, Washington, 1978-79; sr. fellow The Brookings Instn., Washington, 1983-84; prof. labor econs. Grad. Sch. Bus., Stanford (Calif.) U., 1987-92, Matsushita prof. internat. labor econs. and econ. policy, 1993—, assoc. dean, 1996-99. Cons. OECD, Paris, 1988, U.S. Civil Rights Commn., Washington, 1982-83, NOAA, Washington, 1981; vis. scholar IMF, 1994, Australian Nat. U., 1990, 2000. Author: Labor Relations and Litigation Explosion, 1987; (with others) Unionism, Economic Stabilization and Income Policy, 1982, Economics of the Employment Relationship, 1989, numerous others; contbr. articles to profl. jours. Mem. Am. Econs. Assn., Indls. Rels. Rsch. Assn. Office: Stanford U Grad Sch Bus Palo Alto CA 94305

FLANIGAN, JAMES J(OSEPH), journalist; b. N.Y.C., June 6, 1936; s. James and Jane (Whyte) F.; m. Patricia Quatrine, Nov. 28, 1997; children: Michael, Siobhan Jane. BA, Manhattan Coll., 1961. Fin. writer N.Y. Herald Tribune, 1957-66; bur. chief, asst. mng. editor Forbes Mag., 1966-86; bus. columnist, sr. econs. editor L.A. Times, 1986—. Office: LA Times 202 W 1st St Los Angeles CA 90012 E-mail: jim.flanigan@latimes.com

FLATTERY, THOMAS LONG, lawyer, legal administrator; b. Detroit, Nov. 14, 1922; s. Thomas J. and Rosemary (Long) F.; m. Gloria M. Hughes, June 10, 1947 (dec.); children: Constance Marie, Carol Dianne Lee, Michael Patrick, Thomas Hughes, Dennis Jerome, Betsy Ann Sprecher; m. Barbara J. Balfour, Oct. 4, 1986. BS, U.S. Mil. Acad., 1947; JD, UCLA, 1955; LLM, U. So. Calif., 1965. Bar: Calif. 1955, U.S. Patent and Trademark Office 1957, U.S. Customs Ct. 1968, U.S. Supreme Ct. 1974, Conn. 1983, N.Y. 1984. With Motor Products Corp., Detroit, 1950, Equitable Life Assurance Soc., Detroit, 1951, Bohn Aluminum & Brass Co., Hamtramck, Mich., 1952; mem. legal staff, asst. contract adminstr. Radioplane Co. (divsn. Northrop Corp.), Van Nuys, Calif., 1955-57; successively corp. counsel, gen. counsel, asst. sec. McCulloch Corp., L.A., 1957-64; sec., corp. counsel Technicolor, Inc., Hollywood, Calif., 1964-70; successively corp. counsel, asst. sec., v.p., sec. and gen. counsel Amcord, Inc., Newport Beach, 1970-72; v.p., sec., gen. counsel Schick Inc., L.A., 1972-75; counsel, asst. sec. C.F. Braun & Co., Alhambra, Calif., 1975-76; sr. v.p., sec., gen. counsel Automation Industries, Inc. (now PCC Tech. Industries Inc. a unit of Penn Cen. Corp.), Greenwich, Conn., 1976-86; v.p., gen. counsel G&H Tech., Inc. (a unit of Penn Cen. Corp.), Santa Monica, Calif., 1986-93; temp. judge Mcpl. Ct. Calif. L.A. Jud. Dist. and Santa Monica Unified Cts., 1987—; settlement officer L.A. Superior and Mcpl. Cts., 1991—; pvt. practice, 1993—. Panelist Am. Arbitration Assn., 1991—; jud. arbitrator and mediator Alternative Dispute Resolution Programs L.A. Superior and Mcpl. Cts, 1993—, Calif. Ct. Appeals 2d Appellate Dist., 1999—; mem. L.A. Supr. Ct. Alternative Dispute Resolution com., 2001—. Contbr. articles to various legal jours. Served to 1st lt. AUS, 1942-50. Mem. ABA, Nat. Assn. Secs. Dealers, Inc (bd. arbitrators 1996, mediators 1997), State Bar Calif. (co-chmn. corp. law dept. com. 1978-79, lectr. continuing legal edn. program), L.A. County Bar Assn. (chmn. corp. law dept. com. 1966-67), Century City Bar Assn. (chmn. corp. law dept. com. 1979-80), Conn. Bar Assn., Santa Monica Bar Assn. (trustee 1999—, chmn. alt. dispute resolution sect. 2000—), N.Y. State Bar Assn., Am. Soc. Corp. Secs. (L.A. regional group pres. 1973-74), L.A. Intellectual Property Law Assn., Am. Ednl. League (trustee 1988—, sec. 1998—), West Point Alumni Assn., Army Athletic Assn., Friendly Sons St. Patrick, Jonathan Club (dir. 1996-99), Braemar Country Club, Phi Alpha Delta. Roman Catholic. Home and Office: 439 Via De La Paz Pacific Palisades CA 90272-4633 E-mail: flatteryl@earthlink.net

FLEISCHAKER, GORDON HENRY, JR. pediatrician; b. Louisville, July 1, 1928; s. Gordon H. and Agnes Rose (Shatzen) F.; m. Barbara Lorraine Draeger, Aug. 15, 1954; children: Rachel, Judith, James. BA in Zoology, U. Louisville, 1949, MD, 1953. Intern Univ. Hosp., Madison, Wis., 1953-54; resident in pediatrics The Childrens Hosps., Denver, 1956-58; fellow in pediatric rheumatology State U. Iowa, Iowa City, 1958-60; practice medicine specializing in pediatrics Denver, 1960—. Assoc. clin. prof. pediatrics U. Colo. Sch. of Med., Denver, 1960—; mem. active med. staff The Children's Hosp., Denver. Served to capt. MC, USAF, 1953-56. Fellow Am. Acad. Pediats.; mem. AMA, AAAS, Colo. Med. Soc., Clear Creek Valley Med. Soc. Office: G H Fleischaker MD 4485 Wadsworth Blvd Wheat Ridge CO 80033-3318 E-mail: PeeDaTrx@aol.com

FLEISCHER, EVERLY BORAH, academic administrator; b. Salt Lake City, June 5, 1936; s. Arthur and Clare (Katzenstein) F.; m. Harriet Eve Perlysky, June 14, 1959; children: Deborah, Adam Joseph. BS, Yale U., 1958, MS, 1959, PhD, 1961. Asst. prof., then assoc. prof. chemistry U. Chgo., 1961-69; prof. U. Calif., Irvine, 1970-80, dean phys. sci., 1975-80; prof. chemistry, dean Coll. Arts and Scis. U. Colo., Boulder, 1980-88; exec. vice chancellor, prof. chemistry U. Calif., Riverside, 1988-94; program exec. Am. Acad. Arts and Scis., Western Ctr., 1996. Author articles on metalloporphyrins, bioinorganic chemistry. NSF fellow, 1959-61; Alfred P. Sloan fellow, 1962-66; recipient Univ. Svc. award U. Calif., Irvine, 1980. Fellow AAAS; mem. Am. Chem. Soc., Sigma Xi, Alpha Chi Sigma. Home: 8 Tivoli Ct Newport Beach CA 92657-1533 Office: Univ California Dept Chemistry Irvine CA 92697-0001 E-mail: ebfleisc@chem.ps.uci.edu

FLEISCHER, GERALD ALBERT, industrial engineer, educator; b. St. Louis, Jan. 7, 1933; s. Louis Saul and Rita Bashkow F.; m. Ann Ivancic, Dec. 17, 1960 (div. 1992); children: Laural Andrea, Adam Steven; m. Carolyn M. Boyum, Apr. 13, 1993. BS, St. Louis U., 1954; MS, U. Calif., Berkeley, 1959; PhD, Stanford U., Calif., 1962. Ops. analyst Consolidated Freightways, Menlo Park, Calif., 1959-60; instr. Stanford U., 1961-63; asst. prof. U. Mich., Ann Arbor, 1963-64; assoc. prof. engring. U. So. Calif., Los Angeles, 1964-71, prof. engring., 1971-97, univ. marshal, 1981-87, pres. faculty senate, 1986-87, prof. emeritus, 1998—. Author: Capital Allocation Theory, 1969, Risk and Uncertainty, 1975, Contingency Table Analysis, 1981, Engineering Economy, 1984, Introduction to Engineering Economy, 1994; contbr. to Handbook of Industrial Engineering, 1992, Industrial Engineering Handbook, 1992. Served to lt. (J.G.) USN, 1954-57 Ford Found. fellow, 1960-62, Fulbright sr. lectr. Edcuador, 1974; fellow Inst. Advancement of Engring., 1976 Fellow Inst. Indsl. Engrs. (region v.p. 1984-86); mem. Am. Soc. Engring. Edn., Inst. Mgmt. Scis.

FLEISCHMANN, ERNEST MARTIN, music administrator; b. Frankfurt, Germany, Dec. 7, 1924; came to U.S., 1969; s. Gustav and Antonia (Koch) F.; children: Stephanie, Martin, Jessica. B of Commerce, U. Cape Town, South Africa, 1950, MusB, 1954; postgrad., South African Coll. Music, 1954-56; MusD (hon.), Cleve. Inst. Music, 1987. Gen mgr. London Symphony Orch., 1959-67; dir. Europe CBS Masterworks, 1967-69; exec. v.p., mng. dir. L.A. Philharm. Assn. and Hollywood Bowl, 1969-98; artistic cons. L.A. Philharm. Assn., 1998—; pres. Fleischmann Arts, Intl. Arts Mgmt. Cons. Svc., 1998—; artistic dir. Ojai Festival, 1998—. Mem. French Govt. Commn. Reform of Paris Opera, 1967-68; steering com. U.S. nat. commn. UNESCO Conf. Future of Arts, 1975. Debut as condr. Johannesburg (Republic of South Africa) Symphony Orch., 1942; asst. condr. South African Nat. Opera, 1948-51, Cape Town U. Opera, 1950-54; condr. South African Coll. Music Choir, 1950-52, Labia Grand Opera Co., Cape Town, 1953-55; music organizer Van Riebeeck Festival Cape Town, 1952; dir. music and drama Johannesburg Festival, 1956; contbr. to music publs. Recipient award of Merit, L.A. Jr. C. of C., John Steinway award, Friends of Music award, Disting. Arts Leadership award U. So. Calif., 1989, L.A. Honors award, L.A. Arts Coun., 1989, Live Music award Am. Fedn. Musicians Local 47, 1991, Disting. Authors/Artists award U. Judaism, 1994, Treasures of L.A. award, Ctrl. City Assn. L.A., 1996, Los Amigos de Los Angeles award, L.A. Conv. and Vis. Bur., 1996, Comdrs. Cross of Order of Merit, Germany, 1997, Officer, Ordre des Arts et Lettres Legion of Honor, France, 1998, Knight, First Class, of the Order of the White Rose of Finland, Jan., 1999; Honored by Mayor and City Coun. as First living Cultural Treasure of Los Angeles, 1998, Gold Baton award Am. Symphony Orch. League, 1999. Mem. Assn. Calif. Symphony Orchs., L.A. Philharm. Assn. (bd. dirs. 1984—). Office: Fleischmann Arts 707 Wilshire Blvd Ste 1850 Los Angeles CA 90017-3507 E-mail: artsernest@aol.com

FLEISCHMANN, PAUL, religious organization administrator, minister; b. June 20, 1946; s. Leonard and Viola (Tyler) F.; m. Anntoinette Jordan, June 14, 1973; children: Todd Paul, Tyler Jonathan. BA, Seattle Pacific Coll., 1968; MDiv, Western Bapt. Sem., Portland, Oreg., 1975; postgrad., Internat. Christian Grad. U., San Bernardino, Calif. Ordained to ministry, Conservative Bapt. Assn., 1981. Youth pastor Ballard Bapt. Ch., Seattle, 1965-67; campus staff Seattle Youth for Christ, 1967-68; high sch. ministry staff Campus Crusade for Christ, various locations, 1968-88; exec. dir. Nat. Network of Youth Ministries, San Diego, 1982—. Home missionary, 1968—; youth ministry cons., 1974—; officer Bd. Deacons, 1980-82, 88-93, mem. Bd. Christian Edn., 1980-82, ch. planter, 1988-93; adj. prof. Christian edn. Western Bapt. Sem., Portland, Oreg., 1981-83; chmn. Youth Ministry Exec. Coun., 1992—, Atlanta 96 Youth Leaders Conf., 1993-96;

chmn. Challenge 2000 Alliance. Author: Where to Turn for Help in Youth Ministry, 1996; exec. editor: Insight for Student Discipleship, 1979-83; contbg. author: Working with Youth, 1982; editor: Discipling the Young Person, 1985; exec. editor Network News, 1983—; contbr. articles to profl. jours.; contbg. author: Magnet Effect, 1995, Reaching a Generation for Christ, 1997. Dir. Continental Singers Choir and Orch., 1977, Nat. Conv. on High Sch. Discipleship, 1979-83; asst. dir. Youth Congress '85, Washington. Recipient Gold Medallion, Evang. Christian Pubrs. Assn., 1986. Office: Nat Network of Youth Min 12335 World Trade Dr Ste 16 San Diego CA 92128-3791

FLEISHER, MARK, political organization administrator; Student, U. N.Mex. Chair. Arizona Democratic Party, Phoenix. Chmn. Dem. Party Ariz. State, 1997—. Mem. Assn. State Dem. Chairs (chmn.). Address: Ariz Democratic Party 13610 N Black Canyon Hwy Phoenix AZ 85029-1373

FLEMING, ARTHUR WALLACE, physician, surgeon; b. Johnson City, Tenn., Oct. 1, 1935; s. Smith Goerge and Vivian (Richardson) F.; m. Dolores E. Caffey, Apr. 8, 1978; children: Arthur Jr., Robyn, Jon, Mark, Bernadette, Robert, Erik. Student, Ill. State U., 1953-54; BA, Wayne State U., 1958-61; MD cum laude, U. Mich., 1961-65. Diplomate Am. Bd. Surgery, Am. Bd. Thoracic Surgery. Intern Walter Reed Gen. Hosp., Washington, 1965-66, resident in gen. surgery, 1966-70, resident in thoracic and cardiovascular surgery, 1970-72; research tng. fellowship Walter Reed Army Inst. of Research, Walter Reed Army Med. Ctr., Washington, 1973-74, mem. staff dept. surgery, 1974-76, chief div. exptl. surgery, 1976-77, dir. dept. surgery, 1977-83; assoc. prof. surgery Uniformed Service U. of Health Scis., Bethesda, Md., 1978-83, clin. assoc. prof. surgery, 1983—; program dir. gen. surgery residency tng. program Martin L. King, Jr./Drew Med. Ctr., Los Angeles, 1983—, dir. trauma ctr., 1983-99, chief surgery, 1983—; clin. prof. surgery UCLA, 1983—; chmn. dept. surgery, prof. surgery Charles R. Drew U. Medicine & Sci., Los Angeles, 1983—. Contbr. numerous articles to profl. jours. Served with USN, 1954-62. Recipient Hoff Medal, 1974, Gold Medal for paper Southeastern Surg. Congress, 1977, Letter of Commendation Commanding Gen. U.S. Army Med. Research and Devel. Command, 1981, Surgeon Gen's. "A" prefix, 1981, Commendation Compton City Council, 1985, Recognition award King-Drew Hosp. Social Service, 1985. Mem. ACS., Nat. Assn. Minority Med. Educators (western region), Golden State Med. Soc., Nat. Med. Assn., Charles R. Drew Med. Soc., Am. Heart Assn., Soc. Surg. Chmn., Assn. Program Dirs. in Surgery, Soc. Thoracic Surgeons, Assn. Acad. Surgery, Am. Assn. Blood Banks, Southeastern Surg. Congress, Am. Fedn. Clin. Research, Assn. Mil. Surgeons. Democrat. Roman Catholic. Avocations: golf, classical music, carpentry crafts. Office: Charles R Drew U Medicine & Sci 12021 Wilmington Ave Los Angeles CA 90059-3019

FLEMING, BRICE NOEL, retired philosophy educator; b. Hutchinson, Kans., July 29, 1928; s. Augustus Brice and Anna (Noel) F.; m. Barbara Warr, Dec. 20, 1965. B.A., Harvard U., 1950; D.Phil., Oxford (Eng.) U., 1961. Asst. lectr. Manchester (Eng.) U., 1956-57; instr. Yale U., 1957-59, 1960-62; asst. prof. U. Calif. at Santa Barbara, 1962-65, assoc. prof., 1965-69, prof., 1969-91, prof. emeritus, 1991—. Served with AUS, 1951-53. Office: U Calif Dept Philosophy Santa Barbara CA 93106

FLEMING, CAROLYN ELIZABETH, religious organization administrator, interior designer; b. Sept. 24, 1946; d. Jerry J. and Mary Josephine (Korten) Maly; m. Roger Earl Fleming, May 26, 1974; children: Karl Joseph, Briana Danika. Student, Texarkana Jr. Coll., 1963-65, Okla. State U., 1965-66; BS in Interior Design, U. Tex., 1970. Asst. to designer Planning/Design Cons., Inc., Tulsa, 1970-72; pvt. cons. Texarkana, Tex., 1972-73; with Anchorage Neuro-Spinal Clinic, 1987-90, 91-96; sec. Nat. Tchg. Com. Bahais of Alaska, Anchorage, 1976-89, mem., 1989-92, Baha'i materials promotion com., Anchorage, 1987-89, Nat. Spirituality Assembly, Bahais of Alaska, 1992-97, sec. gen., CEO, 1994-96; chmn. Anchorage Bahais Local Spiritual Assembly, 1990-92; mem. Texarkana Bahai Local Spirituality Assembly, 1985, Oceanview (Alaska) Bahai Local Spiritual Assembly, 1986-87; rec. sec. Chena Valley (Alaska) Local Spiritual Assembly Bahais, 1997; mem. internat. goals com. Nat. Spiritual Assembly Bahais of Alaska, Inc., 1997-2000; adminstrv. asst. to treas. in corp. offices Alaska Comm. Sys. Group, Inc., 2000—, adminstrv. asst. to treas. and v.p., 2000, adminstrv. asst. to v.p. investor rels., 2000-2001, adminstrv. asst. to CFO and treas., 2001—, v.p. investor rels., 2001—, v.p. sales and mktg.-Corp. office, 2001—. Coord. Interdenominational Cultural Unity Conf. for Anchorage Area, 1986. Vol. Rural Comty. Action Program, 1986-87, Alaska Coun. on Prevention Alcohol and Drug Abuse, 1987, Spirit Days, 1987-88; trainee Parent and Youth Mediation Program, 1990; mem. Anchorage Local Spiritual Assembly, 1998; asst. aux. bd. for Bahai Oceanview Comty., 1989-92; mem. Arts Coun., Valdez, Alaska, 1974-76, Beyond Beijing Coalition, Anchorage, 1995-96. Mem. ACS (contbns. and donations com. 2000-2001), Assn. Interior Designers, Alaska Women's Coalition (v.p. 2000—), Bus. and Profl. Women's Orgn., Beta Sigma Phi. Mem. Baha'i Faith. Office: PO Box 101997 Anchorage AK 99510-1997

FLEMING, GRAHAM RICHARD, chemistry educator; b. Barrow-in-Furness, Lancashire, Eng., Dec. 3, 1949; came to U.S., 1979; s. Maurice Norman and Ena (Winter) F.; m. Jean McKenzie, Sept. 16, 1977; 1 child, Matthew. BS with honors, U. Bristol, Eng., 1971; PhD in Phys. Chemistry, U. London, 1974. Rsch. fellow Calif. Inst. Tech., Pasadena, 1974-75; univ. rsch. fellow U. Melbourne, Australia, 1975, Australian Rsch. Grants Commn. rsch. asst. Australia, 1976; Leverhulme fellow Royal Instn., London, 1977-79; asst. prof. U. Chgo., 1979-83, assoc. prof., 1983-85, prof., 1985-87, A.H. Compton Disting. Svc. prof., 1987-97, chmn. dept. chemistry, 1988-90; prof. U. Calif., Berkeley, 1997—; dir. phys. bioscis. divsn. Lawrence Berkeley Nat. Lab., 1997—. Co-chmn. Ultrafast Phenomena V Meeting, Snowmass, Colo., 1986; co-dir. Inst. Bioengring., Biotech., Quantitative Biomedicine, U. Calif., Berkeley, San Francisco, Santa Cruz. Author: Chemical Applications of Ultrafast Spectroscopy, 1986; mem. editl. bd. Chem. Physics Letters, Jour. of Phys. Chemistry, Chem. Physics; contbr. 235 rsch. articles to profl. publs. Recipient Coblentz award Coblentz Soc., 1985; Alfred P. Sloan Found. fellow, 1981, J.S. Guggenheim fellow, 1987; Dreyfus tchr.-scholar, 1982. Fellow Am. Acad. Arts and Scis., Royal Soc. London; mem. Optical Soc. Am., Inter-Am. Photochem. Soc. (award 1996), Royal Soc. Chemistry (Marlow medal 1981, Tilden medal 1991, Centenary medal 1996), Am. Chem. Soc. (Nobel Laureate Signature award for grad. edn. in chemistry 1995, Peter Debye award in phys. chemistry 1998, Harrison Howe award 1999). Avocation: mountaineering. Office: Univ of Calif-Berkeley Dept Chemistry B84 Hildebrand # 1460 Berkeley CA 94720-0001

FLEMING, JOSEPH CLIFTON, JR. dean, law educator; b. Atlanta, July 24, 1942; s. Joseph Clifton Sr. and Claudia Leola (Duncan) F.; m. Linda Wightman, May 27, 1964; children: Allison, Erin, Anne, Matthew Clifton, Stephen Joseph, Michael Grant. BS, Brigham Young U., 1964; JD, George Washington U., 1967. Bar: Wash. 1967, U.S. Dist. Ct. (we. dist.) Wash. 1967, U.S. Tax Ct. 1969, U.S. Ct. Appeals (9th cir.) 1970, Utah 1979. Assoc. Bogle & Gates, Seattle, 1967-73; assoc. prof. Law Sch. U. of Puget Sound, Tacoma, 1973-74, Brigham Young U., Provo, Utah, 1974-76, prof. Law Sch., 1976-98, assoc. dean Law Sch., 1986—, Ernest L. Wilkinson prof. Law Sch., 1998—; Fulbright prof. faculty law U. Nairobi, Kenya, 1977-78; prof. in residence Office of Chief Counsel IRS, Washington, 1985-86. Vis. prof. U. Queensland, Brisbane, Australia, 1997, 99. Author: Estate and Gift Tax, 1975, Tax Aspects of Buying and Selling Corporate Businesses, 1984, Tax Aspects of Forming and Operating Closely Held Corporations, 1992, Federal Income Tax: Doctrine, Structure and Policy, 1995, 2nd edit., 1999; notes editor George Washington U. Law Rev., 1966-67; contbr. numerous articles to profl. jours. Bishop Ch. of Jesus Christ of LDS, Orem, Utah, 1981-85. Mem. ABA (subcom. chair tax sect. corp. tax com. 1979-83, chair tax sect. com. on teaching taxation 1992-94), Am. Law Inst. (tax adv. group 1988-94, 98-2001). Office: Brigham Young U J Reuben Clark Law Sch PO Box 28000 Provo UT 84602-8000

FLEMING, REX JAMES, meteorologist; b. Omaha, Apr. 25, 1940; s. Robert Leonard and Doris Mae (Burrows) F.; m. Kathleen Joyce Ferry, Sept. 3, 1969; children: Thane, Manon, Mark, Noel. B.S., Creighton U., 1963; M.S., U. Mich., 1968, Ph.D., 1970. Commd. lt. U.S. Air Force, 1963, advanced through grades to capt., 1972; research scientist Offutt AFB, Nebr., 1963-67; sci. liaison to Nat. Weather Service for Air Weather Service, Suitland, Md., 1970-72; resigned, 1972; mgr. applications mktg. advanced sci. computer Tex. Instruments, Inc., Austin, 1972-75; dir. U.S. Project Office for Global Weather Expt., NOAA, Rockville, Md., 1975-80, Spl. Research Projects Office, 1980-82, Office of Climate and Atmospheric Research, 1983-84, Internat. Tropical Ocean and Global Atmosphere Project Office and Nat. Storm Program Office, 1984-86; pres. Tycho Tech. Inc., Boulder, Colo., 1986-87, Creative Concepts, Boulder, 1987-91; sr. mgr., coord. FAA rsch. Nat. Ctr. for Atmospheric Rsch., 1991-92, vis. scientist, 1987-88; NOAA, Boulder, 1993-2001; program mgr. U. Corp. for Atmospheric Rsch., 2001—. Contbr. articles to profl. jours. Recipient Gold Medal award Dept. Commerce, 1980 Fellow AAAS; mem. Am. Meteorol. Soc. (chmn. probability and statistics com. 1976-77), The Planetary Soc., Am. Geophys. Union (sec. atmospheric scis. sect. 1984-86). Republican. Home: 7225 Spring Dr Boulder CO 80303-5115 Office: NCAR PO Box 3000 Boulder CO 80307-3000

FLEMING, TERRI, newspaper editor; b. 1955; BS in Comm. Journalism, So. Ill. U., 1979. Copy editor, features writer Colorado Springs (Colo.) Sun, 1979-81; news editor, copy editor, designer The Gazette Telegraph, Colorado Springs, 1982-87, design dir., 1987-91, dep. mng. editor, 1991-96; mng. editor The Gazette, Colorado Springs, 1996-2000, acting editor, 2000—. Various editor positions Auckland (New Zealand) Herald, Christchurch (New Zealand) Press, Fiji times, 1980-81; copy editor Thousand Oaks (Calif.) News chronicle, 1981-82. Mem. Am. Soc. Newspaper Editors, Soc. Newspaper Design, Soc. Profl. Journalists, Associated Press Mng. Editors. Avocations: mountain biking, gardening, dance, travel, voluntarism. Office: The Gazette 30 S Prospect St Colorado Springs CO 80903-3671

FLEMMING, STANLEY LALIT KUMAR, family practice physician, mayor, state legislator; b. Rosebud, S.D., Mar. 30, 1953; s. Homer W. and Evelyn C. (Misra) F.; m. Martha Susan Light, July 2, 1977; children: Emily Drisana, Drew Anil, Claire Elizabeth Misra. AAS, Pierce Coll., 1973; BS in Zoology, U. Wash., 1976; MA in Social Psychology, Pacific Luth. U., 1979; DO, Western U., 1985. Diplomate Am. Coll. Family Practice; cert. ATLS. Intern Pacific Hosp. Long Beach (Calif.), 1985-86; resident in family practice Pacific Hosp. Long Beach, 1986-88; fellow in adolescent medicine Children's Hosp. L.A., 1988-90; clin. preceptor Family Practice Residency Program Calif. Med. Ctr., U. So. Calif., L.A., 1989—; clin. instr. Sch. Medicine U. So. Calif., L.A., 1989-90; clin. instr. Western U. Health Sci., Pomona, Calif., 1989-90, clin. asst. prof. Family Medicine, 1987—; exam. commr., expert examiner Calif. Osteo. Med. Bd., 1987-89; med. dir. Cmty. Health Care Delivery System Pierce County, Tacoma, 1990—; mayor City of University Place. Clin. instr. U. Wash. Sch. Medicine, 1990—; bd. dirs. Calif. State Bd. Osteo. Physicians Examiners, 1989—, cons., 1989. Mayor, City of University Place, Wash. Col. M.C., U.S. Army, 1976—, Named one of Outstanding Young Men of Am., U.S. Jaycees, 1983, 85, Intern of Yr. Western U. Health Sci. Coll., 1986, Resident of Yr., Greater Long Beach Assn., 1988, Alumnus of Yr., Pierce Coll., 1993, 97; recipient Pumerantz-Weiss award, 1985. Mem. Fedn. State Bds. Licensing, Am. Osteopathic Assn., Am. Acad. Family Practice, Soc. Adolescent Medicine, Assn. Military Surgeons U.S., Assn. U.S. Army (chpt. pres.), Soc. Am. Military Engrs. (chpt. v.p.), Calif. Med. Assn., Wash. Osteopathic Med. Assn. (Physician of Yr. 1993), Calif. Family Practice Soc., Long Beach Med. Assn. (com. mem.), N.Y. Acad. Sci., Calif. Med. Review Inc., Sigma Sigma Phi, Am. Legion. Episcopalian. Home: 7619 Chambers Creek Rd W University Place WA 98467-2015 Office: Family Health Ctr University Place WA 98466

FLETCHER, BETTY BINNS, federal judge; b. Tacoma, Mar. 29, 1923; B.A., Stanford U., 1943; LL.B., U. Wash., 1956. Bar: Wash. 1956. Mem. firm Preston, Thorgrimson, Ellis, Holman & Fletcher, Seattle, 1956-1979; judge U.S. Ct. Appeals (9th cir.), Seattle, 1979—, sr. judge, 1998-. Mem. ABA (Margaret Brent award 1992), Wash. State Bar Assn., Am. Law Inst., Fed. Judges Assn. (past pres.), Order of Coif, Phi Beta Kappa. Office: US Ct Appeals 9th Cir 1010 5th Ave Ste 1000 Seattle WA 98104-1196*

FLETCHER, HOMER LEE, librarian; b. Salem, Ind., May 11, 1928; s. Floyd M. and Hazel (Barnett) F.; m. Jacquelyn Ann Blanton, Feb. 7, 1950; children— Deborah Lynn, Randall Brian, David Lee. B.A., Ind. U., 1953; M.S. in L.S, U. Ill., 1954. Librarian Milw. Pub. Library, 1954-56; head librarian Ashland (Ohio) Pub. Library, 1956-59; city librarian Arcadia (Cal.) Pub. Library, 1959-65, Vallejo (Calif.) Pub. Library, 1965-70, San Jose, Calif., 1970-90; ret. San Jose, 1990. Contbr. articles to profl. jours. Pres. S. Solano chpt. Calif. Assn. Neurol. Handicapped Children, 1968-69; mem. Presbyn. Ch. Sunnyvale, 1997. Served with USAF, 1946-49. Mem. ALA (intellectual freedom com. 1967-72), Calif. Library Assn. (pres. pub. libraries sect. 1967), Phi Beta Kappa. Democrat. Presbyterian. Home: 7921 Belknap Dr Cupertino CA 95014-4973 E-mail: sigdigdat@aol.com

FLETCHER, JAMES ALLEN, video company executive; b. Toledo, Sept. 18, 1947; s. Allen Rae and Ruth Helen (Scharf) F.; m. Kathy Jane Barrett, Jan. 25, 1975. AS, West Coast U., 1977, BSEE, 1979. Cert. Microsoft Systems Engr., 2000. Electronic technician Hughes Aircraft Co., El Segundo, Calif., 1970-72; engring. technician Altec Corp., Anaheim, 1972-75, Magna Corp., Santa Fe Springs, 1975-76, Odetics Inc., Anaheim, 1976-79, electronic engr., 1979-86; pres., founder F & B Technologies, Orange, Calif., 1986—. Cert. systems engr. Microsoft, 2000. Sgt. U.S. Army, 1967-69. Mem. Soc. Motion Picture and TV Engrs., Mensa. Libertarian. Avocations: record collecting, automobile restoration and customization. Office: F & B Technologies 630 N Tustin St Ste 1516 Orange CA 92867-7127

FLETCHER, WILLIAM A. federal judge, law educator; b. 1945; BA, Harvard U., 1968, Oxford U., 1970; JD, Yale U., 1975. Law clk. to presiding justice U.S. Dist. Ct. Calif., San Francisco, 1975-76; law clk. to Justice J. Brennan U.S. Supreme Ct., D.C., 1976-77; acting prof. law U. Calif., Berkeley, 1977-84, prof. law, 1984—; judge U.S. Ct. Appeals (9th cir.), San Francisco, 1998—. Office: 95 7th St San Francisco CA 94103*

FLETTNER, MARIANNE, opera administrator; b. Frankfurt, Germany, Aug. 9, 1933; d. Bernhard J. and Kaethe E. (Halbritter) F. Bus. diploma, Hessel Bus. Coll., 1953. Sec. various cos., 1953-61, Pontiac Motor Div., Burlingame, Calif., 1961-63, Met. Opera, N.Y., 1963-74, asst. co. mgr., 1974-79; artistic adminstr. San Diego Opera, 1979—. Avocations: travel, hiking, swimming, cooking. Home: 4015 Crown Point Dr San Diego CA 92109-6270 Office: San Diego Opera 1200 Third Ave 18th Fl San Diego CA 92101-4112 E-mail: marianne.flettner@sdopera.com

FLICK, WILLIAM FREDRICK, surgeon; b. Lancaster, Pa., Aug. 18, 1940; s. William Joseph and Anna (Volkl) F.; m. Jacqueline Denise Phaneuf, May 21, 1966; children: William J., Karen E., Christopher R., Derrick W., Brian A. BS, Georgetown U., 1962, MD, 1966; MBA, U. Colo., 1990. Cert. Am. Bd. Surgeons, 1976. Self employed surgeon, Cheyenne, Wyo., 1973-84; pres., surgeon Cheyenne Surgical Assocs., 1984-94; med. dir. Blue Cross Blue Shield of Wyo., Cheyenne, 1994—. Trustee Laramie County Sch. Dist. #1, Cheyenne, 1988-92. Maj., chief of surgery USAF, 1971-73. Fellow ACS; mem. Am. Coll. Physician Execs., Nat. Assn. Managed Care. Republican. Roman Catholic. Office: Blue Cross Blue Shield Wyo 400 House Ave Cheyenne WY 82007-1468

FLINN, PAUL ANTHONY, materials scientist; b. N.Y.C., Mar. 25, 1926; s. Richard A. and Anna M. (Weber) F.; m. Mary Ellen Hoffman, Aug. 20, 1949; children: Juliana, Margaret, Donald, Anthony, Patrick. AB, Columbia Coll., 1948, MA, 1949; ScD, MIT, 1952. Asst. prof. Wayne U., Detroit, 1953-54; research staff Westinghouse Research Lab., Pitts., 1954-63; prof. Carnegie-Mellon U., Pitts., 1964-78; sr. staff scientist Intel Corp., Santa Clara, Calif., 1978-95; cons. prof. dept. material sci. and engring. Stanford (Calif.) U., 1985—. Vis. prof. U. Nancy, France, 1967-68, U. Fed. do Rio Grand du Sol, Porto Allegro, Brazil, 1975, Argonne (Ill.) Nat. Lab., 1977-78, Stanford (Calif.) U., 1984-85. Contbr. sci. articles to profl. jours. Served with USN, 1944-46, PTO. Fellow Am. Phys. Soc.; mem. Metall. Soc., Materials Rsch. Soc., Phi Beta Kappa, Tau Beta Pi. Office: Stanford U Dept Material Sci & Engring Stanford CA 94305-2205

FLORY, CURT ALAN, research physicist; BS in Physics with distinction, Stanford U., 1975; MS in Physics, U. Wash., 1977; PhD in Physics, U. Calif., Berkeley, 1981. Prin. lab. scientist, rsch. physicist Agilent Technologies, Palo Alto, Calif., 1984—; postdoct. SLAC, 1981-84. Recipient Indsl. Physics prize Am. Inst. Physics, 1993-94. Fellow Am. Phys. Soc. Office: Agilent Technolgies 3500 Deer Creek Rd # 26M Palo Alto CA 94304-1317 E-mail: curt_flory@agilent.com

FLOSS, HEINZ G. chemistry educator, scientist; b. Berlin, Aug. 28, 1934; s. Friedrich and Annemarie F.; m. Inge Sauberlich, July 17, 1956; children: Christine, Peter, Helmut, Hanna. BS in Chemistry, Technische Universitat, Berlin, 1956, MS in Organic Chemistry, 1959; PhD in Organic Chemistry, Technische Universitat, Munich, W. Ger., 1961, Habilitation in Biochemistry, 1966; DSc (hon.), Purdue U., 1986; Dr. (h.c.), U. Bonn, 2001. Hilfsassistent Technische Universitat, Berlin, 1958-59; hilfsassistent Technische Hochschule, Munich, 1959-61, wissenschaftlicher asst. and dozent, 1961-66; on leave of absence at dept. biochemistry and biophysics U. Calif.-Davis, 1964-65; assoc. prof. Purdue U., 1966-69, prof., 1969-77, Lilly Disting. prof., 1977-82, head dept. medicinal chemistry, 1968-69, 74-79; prof. chemistry Ohio State U., Columbus, 1982-87, chmn. dept. chemistry, 1982-86; prof. chemistry U. Wash., Seattle, 1987—, adj. prof. medicinal chemistry and microbiology, 1988—, adj. prof. biochemistry, 1988-99, prof. emeritus, 2001—. Vis. scientist ETH Zurich, 1970; vis. prof. Tech. U. Munich, 1980, 86, 95; mem. bio-organic and natural products study sect. NIH, 1989-93; mem. internat. adv. Natural Product Reports, 1997—. Mem. editorial bd. Lloydia-Jour. Natural Products, 1971—, BBP-Biochemie und Physiologie der Pflanzen, 1971-84, Applied and Environ. Microbiology, 1974-84, Planta Medica, 1978-83, Jour. Medicinal Chemistry, 1979-83, Applied Microbiology and Biotech., 1984-88, Jour. Basic Microbiology, 1989—. Recipient Lederle faculty award, 1967, Mead Johnson Undergrad. Rsch. award, 1968, rsch. career and devel. award USPHS, 1969-74, Volwiler award, 1979, Humboldt sr. scientist, 1980, Newby-McCoy award 1981, award in microbial chemistry Kitasato Inst. and Kitasato U., 1988, White Magnolia Commemoration award and medal, Shanghai, 1995. Fellow Acad. Pharm. Scis. (Research Achievement award in natural products 1976), AAAS; mem. Am. Chem. Soc., Am. Soc. Biol. Chemistry and Molecular Biology, Am. Soc. Microbiology, Am. Soc. Pharmacognosy (Rsch. award 1988), Phytochem. Soc. N.Am., Sigma Xi (Faculty Research award 1976) Office: Univ Wash Box 351700 Seattle WA 98195-1700

FLOURNOY, JOHN CHARLES, SR. training specialist, retired career officer; b. Florala, Ala., Nov. 30, 1936; s. Q. P. and Alice Ruby (Cope) F.; m. Charlene Reneé Lett, June 7, 1957; children: Jamie Lynn, John Charles Jr., Jeffrey Allan. BS, Auburn (Ala.) U., 1959. Commd. 2d lt. USAF, 1959, advanced through grades to col.; dep. chief of staff for ops. 23rd Air Force; USAF, Scott AFB, 1983-86, dir. ops. Scott AFB; dep. chief of staff for ops. 23d Air Force, Hurlburt Field, Fla., 1986-88; site mgr., tng. mgr. Raytheon Sys., Kirkland AFB, N.Mex., 1988-98, tng. analyst, Air Force Rsch. Lab., 1998-99; cons. Air Force Rsch Lab, Albuquerque, 1999—. Recipient German Gratitude medal Fed. Republic of Germany, 1962; decorated Leigon of Merit, 1988. Mem. Jolly Green Assn. (1st v.p. 1983-84, pres. 1985-86), Order of Daedalians (former flight capt.), Tanker/Airlift Assn., USAF Helicopter Pilot Assn., Air Commando Assn., Air Rescue Assn. (dir. pub. rels.). Republican. Avocations: fishing, walking, coin collecting, camping. Home: 6817 Medinah Ln NE Albuquerque NM 87111-6419 E-mail: flournoy@swcp.com

FLOWERREE, ROBERT EDMUND, retired forest products company executive; b. New Orleans, Jan. 4, 1921; s. Robert E. and Amy (Hewes) F.; m. Elaine Dicks, Sept. 22, 1943; children: Ann D., John H., David R. B.A., Tulane U., 1942. Vice pres. Georgia-Pacific Corp., 1956-63, exec. v.p. pulp, paper and chem. ops., 1963-75, pres., 1974-76, chmn., chief exec. officer, 1976-83, chmn., 1983-84, ret., 1984, Kilgore Corp. Past bd. dirs. Ga. Gulf Corp. Emeritus adminstr. Tulane U., New Orleans; life trustee Lewis and Clark Coll., Portland, Oreg. Served to lt. USNR, 1942-46. Recipient Disting. Alumnus award Tulane U., 1978 Clubs: Knights of Malta; Arlington (Portland), Waverley Country (Portland); Boston (New Orleans); Links (N.Y.C.). Office: 805 Broadway Ste 2290 Portland OR 97205

FLOWERS, WILLIAM HAROLD, JR. lawyer; b. Chgo., Mar. 22, 1946; s. William Harold and Ruth Lolita (Cave) F.; m. Pamela Mays, Sept. 13, 1980. BA, U. Colo., 1967, JD, 1971. Bar: Colo. 1973, U.S. Dist. Ct. Colo. 1973, U.S. Ct. Appeals (10th cir.) 1978, U.S. Supreme Ct. 1985, U.S. Ct. Appeals (4th cir.) 1994. Atty. Pikes Peak Legal Svcs., Colorado Springs, Colo., 1973; ptnr. Tate, Tate & Flowers, Denver, 1973-76; dep. dist. atty. Office Adams County Dist. Atty., Brighton, Colo., 1977-78; ptnr. Taussig & Flowers, Boulder, 1978-81; pvt. practice Boulder, 1981-89; ptnr. Holland & Hart, LLP, Denver, 1989-97, Hurth Yeager & Sisk, LLP, 1997—. Mem. Boulder County Cmty. Corrections Bd., 1985-90. Mem. Boulder Bd. Zoning Adjustment, 1973-78, chmn., 1977-78; mem. Boulder Growth Task Force, 1980-82; mem. exec. bd. Longs Peak coun. Boy Scouts Am., 1983-98; bd. dirs. Sta. KGNU, Boulder County Broadcasting, 1981-84. Mem.: ATLA (creative com. 2001—, chair-elect state dels. 2001—, pres. Coun. of Presidents 2001—), Nat. Bar Assn. (regional dir. 1983—86, bd. govs. 1983—96, v.p. 1990—91), Colo. Criminal Def. Bar (bd. dirs. 1982—83), Colo. Trial Lawyers Assn. (past pres. 1999—2000, exec. com. 2001—, bd. dirs. 1989—), Boulder County Bar Assn. (civil litigation com. 1978—, criminal law com. 1979—), Sam Cary Bar Assn. (pres. 1987), U. Colo. Boulder Alumni Assn. (bd. dirs. 1987—96, pres. 1994—95), U. Colo. Found. (bd. dirs. 1995—). Democrat. Methodist. Office: Hurth Yeager & Sisk LLP PO Box 17850 4860 Riverbend Rd Boulder CO 80308

FLOYD, SHELLY L. computer company executive; b. Oklahoma City, 1950; Grad., Grinnell Coll., 1972, U. London, 1974; MBA, Stanford U., 1977. Contbg. editor Technologic Ptnrs.; v.p. Salomon Bros.; spl. limited ptnr. L.F. Rothschild, Unterberg, Towbin; with Intel Corp., Santa Clara, Calif., 1997—, v.p. fin. Office: Intel Corp PO Box 58119 2200 Mission College Blvd Santa Clara CA 95052-8119 E-mail: shelly.floyd@intel.com

FLYNN, JOAN MAYHEW, librarian; b. Mpls., Sept. 13, 1927; d. Oscar Koehler and Mabel Victoria (Stein) Mayhew; m. Elliot Colter Dick, Jr., Aug. 19, 1950 (div. May 1966); children: Emily Diane Dick Tuttle, Elliot Mayhew Dick; m. Paul James Flynn, Nov. 4, 1967. BMus, U. Minn., 1950; MLS, U. Hawaii, 1972, cert. in advanced libr. and info. studies, 1986. Circulation clk., 1972-75; reference libr., 1975-85; dir. acad. support svcs., head Sullivan Libr. Chaminade U. of Honolulu, 1986—. Mem. Interlibr. Cooperation Coun., 1990, 91; supr. vocal music Forest Lake (Minn.) Pub. Schs. Asst. dir. races Norman Tamanaha Meml., 1982, dir. 1983; bd. dirs. Hawaii Kai Fun Runners. Mem. ALA, Hawaii Libr. Assn., MidPac Road Runners Assn. (bd. dirs.), Hawaii Masters Track Club, Beta Phi Mu, Pi Lambda Theta, Sigma Alpha Iota. Avocations: running, biking, swimming, weight lifting, reading. Home: 130 Opihikao Way Honolulu HI 96825-1125 Office: Chaminade U 3140 Waialae Ave Honolulu HI 96816-1578

FLYNT, LARRY CLAXTON, publisher; b. Magoffin County, Ky., Nov. 1, 1942; s. Larry Claxton and Edith (Arnett) F.; m. Althea Leasure, Aug. 21, 1976; children: Tonya, Lisa, Teresa, Larry Claxton, III. Student public schs., Saylersville, Ky. Factory worker Gen. Motors, Dayton, Ohio, 1958, 64-65; owner, operator Hustler Club, Dayton, Columbus, Toledo, Akron and Cleve., 1970-74; owner, pub. Hustler and Chic mags., Los Angeles, 1974—; owner, operator Flynt Distbg. Co., Los Angeles, 1976—. Served with U.S. Army, 1958; Served with USN, 1959-64.

FOCHT, MICHAEL HARRISON, health care industry executive; b. Reading, Pa., Sept. 16, 1942; s. Benjamin Harrison and Mary (Hannahoe) F.; m. Sandra Lee Scholwin, May 14, 1964; 1 child, Michael Harrison Archtl. estimator Caloric Corp., Topton, Pa., 1964-65, cost acct., 1965-66, indsl. engr., 1966-68, mgr. wage rates and standards, 1968-70; indsl. engr. Am. Medicorp. Inc., Fort Lauderdale, Fla., 1970-71, exec. dir. midwest region Chgo., 1977-78; asst. adminstr. Cypress Community Hosp., Pompano Beach, Fla., 1971-73, adminstr., 1975-77, Doctor's Hosp. Hollywood, 1973-75; v.p. Medfield Corp., St. Petersburg, 1978-79; v.p. ops. hosp. group Nat. Med. Enterprises, Inc., Los Angeles, 1979-81, regional sr. v.p. hosp. group Tampa, Fla., 1981-83, pres., chief exec. officer internat. group Los Angeles, 1983-86, pres. chief exec. officer hosp. group, 1986-91, sr. exec. v.p., dir. ops., 1991-93, pres., 1993-95; pres., COO Tenet Healthcare Corp., Santa Barbara, 1995—. Mem. Fedn. Am. Hosps. (bd. govs. 1983—), Fla. League Hosps. (bd. dirs. 1982-83) Republican. Roman Catholic Home: PO Box 703 Santa Ynez CA 93460-0703 Office: Tenet Healthcare Corp 3820 State St Santa Barbara CA 93105-3112

FODOR, STEPHEN P. A. chemical company executive; BS in Biology, Wash. State U., 1978, MS in Biochemistry, 1981; MA in Chemistry, Princeton U., 1983, PhD in Chemistry, 1985. NIH postdoctoral fellow dept. chemistry U. Calif., Berkeley, 1986-89; sr. scientist optical techs. Affymax Rsch. Inst., Palo Alto, Calif., 1989-92, dir. phys. scis., 1992-93; chmn., CEO Affymetrix, Inc., Santa Clara, 1993—. Contbr. over 40 articles to profl. jours. Recipient Chemistry Tchg. award Princeton U., 1982, Assn. Princeton Grad. Alumni Tchg. honor, 1983, Postdoctoral fellow NIH, 1986-89, Alumni Achievement award Wash. State U., 1992, Intellectual Property Owner's Disting. Inventor of Yr. award, 1993, Chiron Corp. Biotechnology Rsch. award Am. Acad. Microbiology, 1997, Gabbay award in Biotech. in Medicine, 1998, Achievement award Assn. for Lab. Automation, 1998. Mem. AAAS (Newcomb-Cleveland award 1992), Am. Chem. Soc., Biophysical Soc. Office: Affymetrix Inc 3380 Central Expy Santa Clara CA 95051-0704

FOGEL, JEREMY DON, judge; b. San Francisco, Sept. 17, 1949; s. Daniel and Gladys (Caplan) F.; m. Kathleen Ann Wilcox, Aug. 20, 1977; children: Megan, Nathaniel. AB, Stanford U., Palo Alto, Calif., 1971; JD, Harvard U., 1974. Bar: Calif. 1974, U.S. Dist. Ct. (no. dist.) Calif. 1974. Atty. Smith, Johnson, Fogel and Ramo, San Jose, 1974-78; dir. atty. Mental Health Advocacy Project, San Jose, 1978-81; exec. dir. Santa Clara County Bar Assn. Law Found., San Jose, 1980-81; judge Santa Clara County Mcpl. Ct., San Jose, 1981-86, Santa Clara County Superior Ct., San Jose, 1986-98, U.S. Dist. Ct. (no. dist.) Calif., 1998—. Faculty Calif. Continuing Jud. Studies Prog., Berkeley, 1987—; trainer of judges and lawyers in case mgmt. and mediation, Jordan, Bangladesh, Hong Kong, Israel, 1989-2001. Contbr. articles to profl. jours. Recipient Service award, Mental Health Assn., Santa Clara County, 1980, Honors award Legal Advocates Children and Youth, 1997; named Judge of Yr., Consumer Attys. Calif., 1997. Mem. Calif. Judges Assn. (v.p. 1990-91, exec. bd. 1988-91, chair jud. ethics com. 1987-88, discipline and disability com. 1991-93, jud. discipline adv. panel 1992-98, Pres.'s award 1997). Office: US Dist Ct 280 S 1st St Rm 4050 San Jose CA 95113-3095 E-mail: jeremy_fogel@cand.uscourts.gov

FOGEL, PAUL DAVID, lawyer; b. Santa Monica, Calif., Sept. 19, 1949; s. Phillip and Betty (Distler) F.; m. Yvette Chalom, Feb. 11, 1981; 1 child, Daniele. AB, U. Calif.-Berkeley, 1971; postgrad., U. Paris II, 1972-73; JD, UCLA, 1976. Bar: Calif. 1976, U.S. Dist. Ct. (ctrl. dist.) Calif. 1977, U.S. Dist. Ct. (no. dist.) Calif. 1987, U.S. Supreme Ct. 1990, U.S. Ct. Appeals (9th cir.) 1981. Grad. fellow Ctr. for Law in Pub. Interest, L.A., 1976-77; dep. state pub. def. State Pub. Defender, L.A., 1977-79; Fulbright fellow U. Paris II Law Sch., 1979-80; dep. state pub. def. State Pub. Def., San Francisco, 1980-82; sr. supervising atty. Calif. Supreme Ct., San Francisco, 1982-87; assoc. Hinton & Alfert, Walnut Creek, Calif., 1987-88, Crosby, Heafey, Roach & May, San Francisco, 1988-89, ptnr., 1990—. Lectr. Am. law USIA, Washington, 1980, 87, 99; lectr. U. Calif. Berkeley Boalt Hall Sch. Law, 1995, practitioner-advisor, 1991-94, 96—. Mem. Am. Acad. Appellate Lawyers, Calif. Acad. Appellate Lawyers, Calif. State Bar Assn. (chmn. appellate cts. com. 1990-91), Bar Assn. San Francisco (chair appellate practice sect. 1999-2000), Amnesty Internat. Office: Crosby Heafey Roach & May 2 Embarcadero Ctr Ste 2000 San Francisco CA 94111-4191 E-mail: pfogel@chrm.com

FOGELBERG, DANIEL GRAYLING, songwriter, singer; b. Peoria, Ill., Aug. 13, 1951; s. Lawrence Peter and Margaret Young (Irvine) F. Student, U. Ill., 1969-71. Founder Hickory Grove Music, Full Moon Prodns., 1971; v.p. Full Moon Prodns. Co.; freelance record producer, studio musician. Recordings: Homefree, 1972, Souvenirs, 1974, Captured Angel, 1975, Netherlands, 1977, (with Tim Weisberg) Twin Sons of Different Mothers, 1979, Phoenix, 1980, The Innocent Age, 1981, Greatest Hits, 1982, Windows & Walls, 1983, High Country Snows, 1985, Exiles, 1987, Dan Fogelberg Live-Greetings From the West, 1991, River of Souls, 1993, No Resemblance Whatsoever, 1995. Mem. ASCAP, AFTRA, Telstar.

FOGELMAN, ALAN MARCUS, internist; b. Bklyn., 1940; BA in Zoology, UCLA, 1962, MD, 1966. Diplomate Am. Bd. Internal Medicine. Intern UCLA Hosp., 1966-67, resident, 1967-68, 70-71, fellow cardiology, 1971-73, prof. medicine, exec. chair dept. medicine. With USN, 1968-70. Mem. ACP, Am. Coll. Cardiology. Office: UCLA Sch Medicine 10833 Le Conte Ave Los Angeles CA 90095-3075

FOGERTY, JOHN CAMERON, musician, composer; b. Berkeley, Calif., May 28, 1945; Singer, guitarist Creedence Clearwater Revival, 1968-72; solo performer, 1973—; albums include (with Creedence Clearwater Revival) Creedence Clearwater Revival, 1968, Bayou Country, 1969, Willy & the Poor Boys, 1969, Green River, 1969, Cosmo's Factory, 1970, Pendulum, 1970, Creedence Gold, 1972, Mardi Gras, 1972, More Creedence Gold, 1973, Live in Europe, 1973, Chronicle, Vol. 1, 1976, Vol. 2, 1986, Down on the Corner, 1976, Hot Stuff, 1977, Greatest Hits, 1979, Concert, 1980, Creedence Country, 1981, Rollin' on the River, 1988, Travelin' Band, 1990; (solo) Blue Ridge Rangers, 1973, John Fogerty, 1975, Hoodoo, 1976, Centerfield, 1985, Knockin' on Your Door, 1986, Eye of the Zombie, 1986, Blue Moon Swamp, 1997. Inducted to Rock and Roll Hall of Fame, 1993. Office: Warner Bros 3300 Warner Blvd Burbank CA 91505-4694

FOGG, RICHARD LLOYD, food products company executive; b. Boston, Jan. 22, 1937; s. Lloyd Clark and Mildred Ann (Cass) F.; m. Carolyn Ann Kane, Feb. 12, 1966; children— Amanda C., Jennifer S., Timothy L. AB, Bowdoin Coll., Brunswick, Maine, 1959; MBA, Cornell U., 1961. With brand mgmt. dept. Procter & Gamble Co., Cin., 1961-66; dir. mktg. mgmt. Hunt-Wesson Foods, Fullerton, Calif., 1967-76; sr. v.p. Amfac Food Group, Portland, Oreg., 1977; pres. subs. Fisher Cheese Co., Wapakoneta, Ohio, 1978-83; group v.p., COO Land O'Lakes Dairy Foods, Mpls., 1983-93; pres., CEO Orval Kent Food Co., Wheeling, Ill., 1994-96; pvt. investor, 1997—. Mem. Am. Mktg. Assn. Fax: (707) 939-7859. E-mail: sonomafogg@aol.com

FOHRER, ALAN J. utilities company executive; CFO Edison Internat., Rosemead, Calif.; chmn., pres., CEO Edison Mission Energy, Irvine. Office: Edison Mission Energy 18101 Van Karman Ave Irvine CA 92612

FOHRMAN, BURTON H. lawyer; b. Chgo., July 9, 1939; s. Max and Helen (Naparty) F.; m. Raleigh S. Newman, Dec. 12, 1975. AB cum laude, U. So. Calif., Los Angeles, 1960; JD, UCLA, 1963. Bar: Calif. 1964. Pvt. practice, Riverside, Calif., 1964-66; mng. ptnr. Redwine and Sherrill, Riverside, 1966-83; ptnr. Jones, Day, Reavis and Pogue, L.A., 1983-92, former chmn. gen. real estate sect.; ptnr. White & Case, 1992—. Editor Calif. Real Property Jour., 1978-83. Mem. State Bar Calif. (chmn. real property sect. 1983), Los Angeles County Bar Assn. (chmn. real property fin. com. 1979-80, exec. com. real property sect. 1980-83), Daini Bar Assn. Office: 1-19-1 Kanda-Nishikicho Chiyoda-ku Tokyo 101-0054 Japan E-mail: bfohrman@whitecase.com

FOK, AGNES KWAN, cell biologist, educator; b. Hong Kong, Dec. 11, 1940; came to U.S., 1962; d. Sun and Yau (Ng) Kwan; m. Fok, June 8, 1965; children: Licie Chiu-Jane, Edna Chiu-Joan. BA in Chemistry, U. Great Falls, 1965; MS in Plant Nutrition and Biochemistry, Utah State U., 1966; PhD in Biochemistry, U. Tex., Austin, 1971. Asst. rsch. prof. pathology U. Hawaii, Honolulu, 1973-74, Ford Found. postdoctoral fellow, anatomy dept., 1975, asst. rsch. prof., 1975-82, assoc. rsch. prof., 1982-88, rsch. prof. Pacific Biomed. Rsch. Ctr., 1988-96, grad. faculty, dept. microbiology, 1977—, dir., 1994-96, dir., prof. biology program, 1996—. Contbr. articles to profl. jours. Mem. Am. Soc. for Cell Biology, Soc. for Protozoologists, Sigma Xi (treas. Hawaii chpt. 1979—). Avocations: reading, gardening, hiking, sewing. Office: U Hawaii Biology Program Honolulu HI 96822

FOLBERG, HAROLD JAY, lawyer, mediator, educator, university dean; b. East St. Louis, Ill., July 7, 1941; s. Louis and Matilda (Ross) F.; m. Diana L. Taylor, May 1, 1983; children: Lisa, Rachel, Ross. BA, San Francisco State U., 1963; JD, U. Calif., Berkeley, 1968. Bar: Oreg. 1968. Assoc. Rives & Schwab, Portland, Oreg., 1968-69; dir. Legal Aid Service, Portland, 1970-72; exec. dir. Assn. Family and Conciliation Cts., Portland, 1974-80; prof. law Lewis and Clark Law Sch., Portland, 1972-89; clin. asst. prof. child psychiatry U. Oreg. Med. Sch., 1976 89; judge pro-tem Oreg. Trial Cts., 1974-89; dean, prof. U. San Francisco Sch. Law, 1989-99, prof. law, 1999—. Chair jud. coun. Calif. Task Force on Alternative Dispute Resolution and the Jud. Sys., 1998-99; Rockefeller Found. scholar in residence Bellagio, Italy, 1996; vis. prof. U. Wash. Sch. Law, 1985-86; mem. vis. faculty Nat. Jud. Coll., 1975-88; mem. Nat. Commn. on Accreditation for Marriage and Family Therapists, 1984-90; cons. Calif. Jud. Coun., U.S. Dist. Ct. (no. dist.) Calif. Author: Joint Custody and Shared Parenting, 1984, 2d edit., 1991; (with Taylor) Mediation-A Comprehensive Guide to Resolving Conflicts without Litigation, 1984; (with Milne) Divorce Mediation-Theory and Practice, 1988; mem. editorial bd.Family Counts Rev., Jour. of Divorce, Conflict Resolution Quar.; contbr. articles to profl. jours. Bd. dirs. Internat. Bioethics Inst., 1989-95, Oreg. Dispute Resolution Adv. Coun., 1988-89. Mem. ABA (chmn. mediation and arbitration com. family law sect. 1980-82), Oreg. State Bar Assn. (chmn. family and juvenile law sect. 1979-80), Am. Bd. Trial Advs., Multnomah Bar Assn. (chmn. bd. dirs. legal aid svc. 1973-76), Am. Arbitration Assn. (mem. panel of arbitrators), Internat. Soc. Family Law, Assn. Family and Conciliation Cts. (pres. 1983-84), Assn. Marriage and Family Therapists (disting. mem.), Am. Assn. Law Schs. (chmn. alternative dispute resolution sect. 1988), Acad. Family Mediators (bd. dirs., pres. 1988), Assn. Conflict Resolution, World Assn. Law Profs. (sec.-gen. 1995-2000). Office: U San Francisco Sch Law 2130 Fulton St San Francisco CA 94117-1080 E-mail: folbergj@usfca.edu

FOLDEN, NORMAN C. (SKIP FOLDEN), information systems executive, consultant; b. San Francisco, July 28, 1933; BS in Math./English/Engring., U.S. Mil. Acad., 1956. With IBM, various locations, 1966-83, U.S. program mgr. I/S tech. Sommers, N.Y., 1983-86; owner Folden Mgmt. (Palladin Advocacy), Westchester, 1986-91, Folden Mgmt., Las Vegas, 1991—. Author: Drug Criminalization: Organized Crime Cash Cow, Prime Cause of U.S. Victim Crime and Threat to National Sovereignty, 1996, Delegation of Legislative Authority, 1997, Payback to Lippo Group or Grand Coincidence at Grand Staircase, 1997, Kosovo Negotiations Provisions-Five by Five Plan, 1999, ICTY Charges and Submission, 1999. Mem. Internat. Platform Assn., Assn. Grads. U.S. Mil. Acad., Little Big Horn Assocs., Calif. Scholarship Fedn., Team Marcus. Avocations: ancient history/teachings/exploration, organized crime and drug policy, antiquities, constitutional law. Home and Office: 4329 Silvercrest Ct North Las Vegas NV 89032-0116 E-mail: sfolden@ix.netcom.com

FOLEY, JACK (JOHN WAYNE HAROLD FOLEY), poet, writer, editor; b. Neptune, N.J., Aug. 9, 1940; s. John Harold and Juana (Terio) F.; m. Adelle Joan Abramowitz, Dec. 21, 1961; 1 child, Sean Ezra. BA, Cornell U., 1963; MA, U. Calif., Berkeley, 1965. Exec. prodr.-in-charge poetry program Sta. KPFA-FM, Berkeley, 1988—; editor-in-chief Poetry USA, Oakland, Calif., 1990-95. Resident artist The Djerassi Program, 1994. Author: (poetry and prose) Letters/Lights-Words for Adelle, 1987; (poetry) Gershwin, 1991, Adrift, 1993; (prose) O Her Blackness Sparkles! The Life and Times of the Batman Art Gallery, San Francisco, 1960-65, 1995, Exiles, 1996, O Powerful Western Star, 2000, Foley's Books: California Rebels, Beats, and Radicals, 2000; (with Ivan Arquelles) New Poetry From California: Dead, Requiem, 1998, Advice to the Lovelorn, 1998; contbr. (film jour.) Bright Lights; contbg. editor: Poetry Flash, 1992—; performances of poetry with wife Adelle, 1985—; columnist Foley's Books, The Alsop Rev., 1998—. Woodrow Wilson fellow U. Calif., 1963-65; Poetry grant Oakland Arts Coun., 1992-95. Mem. MLA, Poets and Writers, Nat. Poetry Assn. (sec. San Francisco 1989-95), PEN Oakland (program dir. 1990-97). Avocations: playing guitar, tap dancing, writing songs. Home and Office: 2569 Maxwell Ave Oakland CA 94601-5521 E-mail: JASFOLEY@aol.com

FOLEY, JOHN V. water company executive; Chmn. Met. Water Dist. of So. Calif., L.A., bd. dirs. Office: Office of the Bd of Dirs PO 54153 Los Angeles CA 90054-0153

FOLEY, L(EWIS) MICHAEL, real estate executive; b. Detroit, Nov. 30, 1938; s. Raymond B. and Mabel (White) F.; m. Pamela Wagner, June 16, 1962; children: Michael D., Kimberly B., Robin E. BS in Sci. Engring., U. Mich., 1960; MBA in Fin. and Mktg., Harvard U., 1964. Lic. real estate broker. Pres. Econ. Devel. Corp., Detroit, 1969-71; v.p. Chrysler Realty Corp., Troy, Mich., 1972-77; exec. v.p. Bell and Howell Video Group, Chgo., 1977-79; v.p. fin., chief fin. officer Bell and Howell Corp., Chgo., 1979-80; sr. v.p. Homart Devel. Co., Chgo., 1981-84, exec. v.p., 1984-93; sr. exec. v.p. Coldwell Banker Real Estate Group Inc., Chgo., 1986-93; chmn., CEO Sears Savs. Bank, Chgo., 1989-93; sr. v.p., CFO Coldwell Banker Corp., 1995-96. Chmn. Borrowers Choice Corp., 1992-93; bd. dirs. BRE Properties, Inc. Author: Management of Racial Integration in Business, 1965. Vestry, jr. warden St. James by the Sea Episcopal Ch. Mem. Internat. Council Shopping Ctrs. (v.p., trustee), Sigma Alpha Epsilon. Episcopalian. Office: 5824 Camino de la Costa La Jolla CA 92037-6551 E-mail: lfoley1@san.rr.com

FOLEY, PATRICK, air courier company executive; Chmn., CEO DHL Airways, Redwood City, Calif., 1988-1999. Office: DHL Corp 333 Twin Dolphin Dr Redwood City CA 94065-1496

FOLEY, RIDGWAY KNIGHT, JR. lawyer, writer; b. Portland, Oreg., Oct. 7, 1937; s. Ridgway Knight and Eunice Alberta (Ammer) F. BS magna cum laude, Lewis & Clark Coll., 1959; JD, U. Oreg., 1963. Bar: Oreg. Assoc. Mautz, Souther, Spaulding, Kinsey & Williamson, Portland, 1964-71; gen. ptnr. Schwabe, Williamson & Wyatt (and predecessor firms), Portland, 1972-84, sr. ptnr., 1985-92; ptnr., shareholder Foley & Duncan, P.C., Portland, 1993-96; of counsel Greene & Markley PC, Portland, 1997—, med. office mgr., 1999—. Com. mem. Multnomah Lawyer Com., 1964-68, 90-93, chair, 1992-93. Contbr. more than 100 articles, essays to profl. jours., 1962—; lectr. profl. orgns., 1970—; Trustee Found. Econ. Edn., Inc., Irvington-on-Hudson, N.Y., 1974-91, 93-96; founding dir. Paulist Fathers Cath. Ctr., Portland, 1978-85. Mem. ABA, Oreg. State Bar, Multnomah County Bar (dir. 1993-97), University Club (Portland), Mt. Hood Philos. Soc. (founding trustee, officer 1972-85), Lang Syne Soc., Geneal. Forum of Oreg., Order of Coif. Episcopalian. Avocations: writing, lecturing, genealogy, publishing, history. Office: Greene & Markley PC 1515 SW 5th Ave Ste 600 Portland OR 97201-5449

FOLEY, WILLIAM PATRICK, II, title insurance company executive; b. Austin, Tex., Dec. 29, 1944; s. Robert P. Foley; m. Carol J. Johnson, Nov. 15 1969; children: Lindsay, Robert P. II, Countney Diane, William P. III. BS, U.S. Mil. Acad., 1967; MBA, Seattle U., 1970; JD, U. Wash., 1974. Assoc. Streich, Lang, Weeks, Cardon & French P.A., Phoenix, 1974-76; ptnr., pres., dir. Foley, Clark & Nye P.A., Phoenix, 1976-84; pres. chief exec. officer Land Resources Corp., Scottsdale, Ariz., 1983-84; chmn. bd., pres., CEO Fidelity Nat. Title Ins. Co., Irvine, Calif., 1981—; also bd. dirs. Fidelity Nat. Title Ins., Irvine; chmn. Checkers Drive-In Restaurants, Inc., Clearwater, Fl. Chmn. bd., dir., pres., chief exec. officer Fidelity Nat. Fin., Inc., Fidelity Nat. Title Ins. Co. of Calif., Fidelity Nat. Title Ins. Co. of Tenn., Fidelity Nat. Title Ins. Co. of Tex., So. Title Holding Co., Pacific Western Aviation, Inc., Western Am. Exch. Corp., Western Pacific Property & Casualty Agy., Inc., Fidelity Appraisal Group, Inc., Folco Devel. Corp., Western Pacific Acquisitions, Inc., Bristol Investment Corp.; chmn. bd., dir. Western Fin. Trust Co., Rocky Mountain Aviation, Inc.; chmn. bd. dir., chief exec. officer Fidelity Nat. Title Agy., Inc. Fidelity Nat. Title Agy. of Maricopa County, Inc., Fidelity Nat. Title Agy. of Pinal County, Inc., Fidelity Nat. Title Co. of El Paso, Fidelity Nat. Title Co. of Oreg., Ramada Inn Old Town Mgmt., Inc.; numerous other chairmanships and directorships in fin. industry. Address: Checkers Drive-In Restaurants PO Box 18800St Clearwater FL 33762 Office: Fidelity Nat Title Ins 2390 E Camelback Rd Phoenix AZ 85016-3448

FOLICK, JEFFREY M. healthcare systems company executive; married; three children. BS in Bus., Calif. State U., L.A. Chief fin. officer Vly. Presbyn. Hosp.; pres. Peak Health Plan, Calif.; v.p. Secure Horizons PacifiCare Health Sys., 1989-94, exec. v.p., chief fin. officer, 1994-98, pres., COO Calif., 1998—. Chmn. allocation com., bd. dirs. PacifiCare Found.; bd. dirs. Long Term Health Group. Office: PacifiCare Health Sys 3120 W Lake Center Dr Santa Ana CA 92704-6917

FOLKMAN, DAVID H. retail, wholesale and consumer products consultant; b. Jackson, Mich., Nov. 6, 1934; s. Jerome D. and Bessie (Schomer) F.; m. Susan Kleppner, June 22, 1958, children: Louis, Sarah, Karen, Jeffrey. A.B., Harvard U., 1957, M.B.A., 1960. Mdse. mgr. Foley's, Houston, 1957-69; v.p. dir. stores Famous-Barr, St. Louis, 1969-74; sr. v.p., gen. mdse. mgr. Macy's Calif., San Francisco, 1974-82; pres., chief exec. officer Emporium Capwell, San Francisco, 1982-87; gen. ptnr. U.S. Venture Ptnrs., Menlo Park, Calif., 1987-90; venture ptnr., 1991-93; pres., chief exec. officer Laurel Burch, Inc., San Francisco, 1990-91; retail investor, cons., 1991-93; CEO Esprit de Corp, San Francisco, 1993-95; prin., Regent Pacific Mgmt. Corp., Cupertino, Calif., 1995—. Instr. U. Houston, 1968-69, Wash. U., St. Louis, 1970-73; bd. dirs. Regent Pacific Mgmt. Corp., Accrue Software, Inc., Shoe Pavilion, Inc.; pres., CEO ON-SITE Dental Care, Inc., 1999—. Mem. Harvard Club (N.Y.C.). E-mail: dfolkman@pacbell.net

FOLLETT, ROBERT JOHN RICHARD, publisher; b. Oak Park, Ill., July 4, 1928; s. Dwight W. and Mildred (Johnson) F.; m. Nancy L. Crouthamel, Dec. 30, 1950; children: Brian L., Kathryn R., Jean A., Lisa W. AB, Brown U., 1950; postgrad., Columbia U., 1950-51. Editor Follett Pub. Co., Chgo., 1951-55, sales mgr., 1955-58, gen. mgr. ednl. div., developer first multi-racial textbook program, first textbooks for disadvantaged, first beginning-to-read books, 1958-68, pres., 1968-78; chmn., dir. Follett Corp., 1979-94. Pres. Alpine Guild, Inc., 1977—; dir. Assn. Am. Pubs., 1972-79; chmn. Rocky Mountain Resource Ctr., Inc., 1997—, Sch. Pubs., 1971-73; dir. Ednl. Systems Corp.; mem. Ill. Gov.'s Commn. on Schs., 1972; pres. Alpine Rsch. Inst., Adv. Coun. on Edn. Stats., 1975-77; chmn. Book Distbn. Task Force of Book Industry, 1978-81; adv. coun. Krannert Sch. of Mgmt., 1988-93; pres. Soda Creek Open Space Assn. Inc., 1994—; dir. Continental Divide Land Trust, 1996—; mem. adv. bd. Ctr. for Living Democracy, 1997-2000; mem. Consortium on Renewing Edn., 1997-2000; lectr. Denver U. Pub. Inst., 1997—; chmn. Open Space for Summit, 1999. Author: Your Wonderful Body, 1961, What to Take Backpacking and Why, 1977, How to Keep Score in Business, 1978, The Financial Side of Book Publishing, 1982, rev. edit., 1988, Financial Feasibility in Book Publishing, 1988, rev. edit., 1996. Bd. dirs. Village Mgr. Assn., 1964-84, Cmty. Found. Oak Park and River Forest, 1959-86, Fund for Justice, 1974-77, For Character, 1983-93, Ctr. Book Rsch., 1985-88; trustee Inst. Ednl. Data Systems, 1965—, Snake River Found., 2001—; elected mem. Rep. State Com. from 7th dist. Ill., 1982-90, vice chmn., 1986-90; chmn. Ill. Reps. Strategic Planning Com., 1986-87; Presdl. Elector, 1988; pres. Keystone Citizens League, 1997—; mem. Keystone Mountain Responsibility Team, 1998-2000; hon. co-chair Colo. Mountain Coll. Campaign, 1998-99; mem. Wildlife/Wetlands Citizens Adv. Group, 2001—. Served in AUS, 1951-53. Mem. Chgo. Pubs. Assn. (pres. 1976-94), Mid.-Am. Pubs. Assn. (mng. dir., 1987-88, dir. 1988-93), Rocky Mountain Book Pubs. Assn., Am. Book Coun. (v.p. 1987-88), Ill. C. of C. (chmn. edn. com. 1977-79), Soc. Midland Authors, Sierra Club, River Forest Tennis Club, Rotary Club Summit County. Office: Alpine Guild Inc PO Box 4848 Dillon CO 80435-4848 E-mail: bob@alpineguild.com

FOLLETT, RONALD FRANCIS, soil scientist; b. Laramie, Wyo., June 26, 1939; s. Roy Lawrence and Frances (Hunter) F.; m. Dorothy Mae Spangle, Jan. 1, 1967; children: William, Jennifer, Michael. BS, Colo. State U., 1961, MS, 1963; PhD, Purdue U., 1966. Rsch. soil scientist Agrl. Rsch.

Svc., USDA, Mandan, N.D., 1968-75, nat. rsch. program leader Beltsville (Md.) and Ft. Collins (Colo.), 1976-86, rsch. leader soil-plant-nutrient rsch. unit Ft. Collins, 1986—; postdoctoral rsch. U.S. Plant-Soil-Nutrition Lab., Ithaca, N.Y., 1975-76. Co-author: The Potential of U.S. Cropland to Sequester Carbon and Mitigate the Greenhouse Effect, 1998; editor: Soil Fertility and Organic Matter as Critical Components of Production Systems, 1987, Nitrogen Management and Ground Water Protection, 1989, Managing Nitrogen for Ground Water Quality and Farm Profitablity, 1991, The Potential of U.S. Grazing Lands to Sequester Carbon and Mitigate the Greenhouse Effect, 2000; guest editor spl. issue Jour. Containmant Hydrol.; contbr. over 150 articles to profl. jours. Officer 1st Presbyn. Ch., Mandan, then Ft. Collins, 1972—; adult leader local Boy Scouts Am., Beltsville, then Ft. Collins, 1975—. Capt. arty., U.S. Army, 1966-68; maj. Res. Recipient Disting. Svc. award USDA, 1984, 92, 2000,Superior Svc. award, 2000; cert. of merit, 1990, 99, cert. of appreciation, 1992. Fellow Soil Sci. Soc. Am. (divsn. chmn. bd. dirs. 1985-88), Am. Soc. Agronomy, Soil and Water Conservation Soc. Am. Avocations: working with youth, skiing, fishing, gardening. Office: USDA Agrl Rsch Svc Soil-Plant-Nutrient Rsch Unit PO Box E Fort Collins CO 80522-0470 E-mail: rfollett@lamar.colostate.edu

FOLLETTE, WILLIAM ALBERT, electronics company executive; b. Tampa, Fla., Dec. 29, 1946; s. Harold Albert and Louise Olga (Mehm) F.; m. Barbara Ann Cunneen, June 8, 1968; children: Kelly, James, William T. BBA, U. Notre Dame, 1968; MBA, Ariz. State U., 1978. Prodn. control analyst Motorola, Mesa, Ariz., 1974-77; successively bus. planner, bus. planning mgr., dir. strategic planning Sperry Corp., Phoenix, 1977-87; dir. bus. and strategic planning, group dir. quality Honeywell Inc., Phoenix, 1987—. Pres. Phoenix chpt. Planning Forum. Maj. USAFR, 1968-90. Republican. Roman Catholic. Avocations: skiing, golf, flying. Home: 5041 E Cortez Dr Scottsdale AZ 85254-4634 Office: Honeywell Inc Comml Flight Sys Group 21111 N 19th Ave Phoenix AZ 85027-2700

FOLLICK, EDWIN DUANE, law educator, chiropractic physician; b. Glendale, Calif., Feb. 4, 1935; s. Edwin Fulfford and Esther Agnes (Catherwood) F.; m. Marilyn K. Sherk, Mar. 24, 1986 BA, Calif. State U., L.A., 1956, MA, 1961, Pepperdine U., , 1957, MPA, 1977; PhD, DTh, St. Andrews Theol. Coll., Sem. of Free Prot. Episc. Ch., London, 1958; MS in Libr. Sci., U. So. Calif., 1963, MEd in Instructional Materials, 1964, AdvMEd in Edn. Adminstrn., 1969; postgrad., Calif. Coll. Law, 1965; LLB, Blackstone Law Sch., 1966, JD, 1967; DC, Cleve. Chiropractic Coll., L.A., 1972; PhD, Academia Theatina, Pescara, 1978; MA in Organizational Mgmt., Antioch U., L.A., 1990. Tchr., libr. adminstr. L.A. City Schs., 1957-68; law librarian Glendale U. Coll. Law, 1968-69; coll. librarian Cleve. Chiropractic Coll., L.A., 1969-74, dir. edn. and admissions, 1974-84, prof. jurisprudence, 1975—, dean student affairs, 1976-92, chaplain, 1985—, dean of edn., 1989—; assoc. prof. Newport U., 1982; extern prof. St. Andrews Theol. Coll., London, 1961; dir. West Valley Chiropractic Health Ctr., 1972-2000, West Valley Chiropractic Consulting, 2001—. Contbr. articles to profl. jours. Chaplain's asst. U.S. Army, 1958-60. Decorated cavaliere Internat. Order Legion of Honor of Immaculata (Italy); Knight of Malta, Sovereign Order of St. John of Jerusalem; Knight Grand Prelate, comdr. with star, Order of Signum Fidei; comdr. chevalier Byzantine Imperial Order of Constantine the Gt.; comdr. ritter Order St. Gereon; chevalier Mil. and Hospitaller Order of St. Lazarus of Jerusalem (Malta); numerous others. Mem. ALA, NEA, Am. Assn. Sch. Librarians, L.A. Sch. Libr. Assn., Calif. Sch. Libr. Assn., Assn. Coll. and Rsch. Librarians, Am. Assn. Law Librarians, Am. Chiropractic Assn., Internat. Chiropractors Assn., Nat. Geog. Soc., Internat. Platform Assn., Phi Delta Kappa, Sigma Chi Psi, Delta Tau Alpha. Democrat. Episcopalian. Home: 6435 Jumilla Ave Woodland Hills CA 91367-2833 Office: 590 N Vermont Ave Los Angeles CA 90004-2115 also: 7022 Owensmouth Ave Canoga Park CA 91303-2005 E-mail: follicke@cleveland.edu

FOLTZ, CRAIG B. astronomer, educator; b. Shamokin, Pa., June 28, 1952; m. Sharon Burrier, Aug. 30, 1980; children: Rachel Elizabeth, Robin Amelia. BA in Physics summa cum laude, Dartmouth Coll., 1974; PhD in Astronomy, Ohio State U., 1979. Postdoctoral fellow dept. astronomy Ohio State U., 1979-80, instr. dept. physics, 1980, instr. dept. astronomy, 1980, rsch. assoc. dept. astronomy, 1981; rsch. assoc. Steward Obs., U. Ariz., 1983, astronomer, 1990—; asst. prof. dept. astronomy U. Ill., 1983-84; staff astronomer Multiple Mirror Telescope Obs., U. Ariz., Tucson, 1984-90, acting dir., 1990-91, 96-97, dep. dir., 1990-96, dir., 1997—. Project scientist 6.5m Telescope Project, 1989-94, dir., 1996—; vis. scholar Inst. Astronomy, Cambridge U., 1995; astroner Smithsonian Astrophys. Obs., 1990—; lectr. in field. Contbr. articles to profl. jours. Grantee NSF, 1987-90, 90-94, 92-95, 94-98, 94-98, 1998-2001, NASA, 1991-92, STScI, 1993-96, 94-96, 94-96, 96-97, 1999-2000, Smithsonian, 1994-99; Alfred P. Sloan scholar Dartmouth Coll., 1970-74; univ. fellow Ohio State U., 1974-78. Mem. Internat. Astron. Union, Am. Astron. Soc., Astron. Soc. of the Pacific, Phi Beta Kappa, Phi Kappa Phi. Achievements include research of QSO absorption lines and the intergalactic medium, distribution of Quasi-Stellar objects, gravitational lenses, emission lines in QSOs and active galactic nuclei, astronomical instrumentation. E-mai. Office: Multiple Mirror Telescope Obs Rm 460a Steward Obs Bldg Univ Ariz Tucson AZ 85721-0465 Fax: 520-670-5740. E-mail: cfoltz@as.arizona.edu, cfoltz@cfa.harvard.edu

FONDAHL, JOHN WALKER, civil engineering educator; b. Washington, Nov. 4, 1924; s. John Edmund and Mary (DeCourcy) F.; m. Doris Jane Plishker, Mar. 2, 1946; children: Lauren Valerie, Gail Andrea, Meredith Victoria, Dorian Beth. BS, Thayer Sch. Engring., Dartmouth, 1947, MSCE, 1948. Instr., then asst. prof. U. Hawaii, 1948-51; constrn. engr. Winston Bros. Co., Mpls., 1951-52; project engr. Nimbus Dam and Powerplant project, Sacramento, 1952-55; mem. faculty Stanford U., 1955—, prof. civil engring., 1966-90, Charles H. Leavell prof. civil engring., 1977-90, prof. emeritus, 1990—. Author reports in field. Served with USMCR, 1943-46. Recipient Golden Beaver award Heavy Constrn. Industry, 1976 Fellow ASCE (Constrn. Mgmt. award 1977, Peurifoy Constrn. Rsch. award 1990), Project Mgmt. Inst. (hon. life, Fellow award 1981); mem. Nat. Acad. Engring., Nat. Acad. Constrn., Phi Beta Kappa. Achievements include patent in field. Home and Office: 12810 Viscaino Rd Los Altos Hills CA 94022-2520 E-mail: fondahlj@aol.com

FONG, HIRAM LEONG, former senator; b. Honolulu, Oct. 15, 1906; s. Lum Fong and Chai Ha Lum; m. Ellyn Lo; children, Hiram, Rodney, Merie-Ellen Fong Gushi, Marvin-Allan (twins). AB with honors, U. Hawaii, 1930, LLD, 1953; JD, Harvard U., 1935; LLD, Tufts U., 1960, Lafayette Coll., 1960, Lynchburg Coll., 1970, Lincoln U., 1971, U. Guam, 1974, St. John's U., 1975, Calif. Western Sch. Law, 1976, Tung Wu (Soochow) U., Taiwan, 1978, China Acad., 1978; LHD, L.I. U., 1968. With supply dept. Pearl Harbor Navy Yard, 1924-27; chief clk. Suburban Water System, 1930-32; dep. atty. City and County of Honolulu, 1935-38; founder, ptnr. law firm Fong, Miho, Choy & Robinson, until 1959; founder, chmn. bd. emeritus Finance Factors, Grand Pacific Life Ins. Co.; founder, chmn bd. Finance Investment Co., Market City, Ltd., Fin. Enterprises Ltd.; pres. Ocean View Cemetery, Ltd.; owner, operator Sen. Fong's Plantation and Gardens, Honolulu. Dir. numerous firms Honolulu [illegible] China Airlines. Mem. Hawaii Legislature, 1938-54, speaker, 1948-54; mem. U.S. Senate, 1959-77, Post Office and Civil Service Com., Judiciary Com., Appropriations Com., Spl. Com. on Aging; U.S. del. 150th Anniversary Argentine Independence, Buenos Aires, 1960, 55th Interparliamentary Union (World) Conf., 1966, Ditchley Found. Conf., 1967, U.S.-Can. Inter-Parliamentary Union Conf., 1961, 65, 67, 68, Mex.-U.S. Interparliamentary Conf., 1969, [illegible] 1971; mem. Commn. on Revision Fed. Ct. Appellate System, 1975—; Active in civic and service orgns.; v.p. Territorial Constl. Conv., 1950; del. Rep. Nat. Conv., 1952, 56, 60, 64, 68, 72; founder, chmn. bd. Fin. Factors Found.; founder, pres. Hiram & Ellyn Fong Found.; founder, pres., chmn. bd. Market City Found.; hon. co-chmn. McKinley High Sch. Found., 1989; bd. visitors U.S. Mil. Acad., 1971—, U.S. Naval Acad., 1974—. Served from 1st lt. to maj. USAAF, 1942-44; ret. col. USAF Res. Recipient award NCCJ, 1960, Meritorious Svc. citation Nat. Assn. Ret. Civil Employees, 1963, Horatio Alger award, 1970, citation for outstanding svc. Japanese Am. Citizens League, 1970, award Am. Acad. Achievement, 1971, Outstanding Svc. award Orgn. Chinese Ams., 1973, award Nat. Soc. Daus. Founders and Patriots Am., 1974, cert. Pacific Asian World, 1974, Citizen Among Citizens award Boys & Girls Clubs of Hawaii, 1991, Disting. Alumnus award U. Hawaii Alumni Assn., 1991, Kulia I Ka Nu'u award Pub. Schs. Hawaii Found., 1992, Dedication and Support Svc. award McKinley Found., 1995, ABOTA-Hawai'i Ha'aheo award, 1997; named to Jr. Achievement Hawaii Bus. Hall of Fame, 1995; decorated Order of Brilliant Star with Grand Cordon Republic of China, 1976, Order of Diplomatic Svc. Merit, Gwanghwan Medal Republic of Korea, 1977; Univ. of Hawaii Colls. of Arts and Scis. Hiram L. Fong Endowment in Arts and Scis., 1995; recipient nat. Outstanding Citizen Achievement award Orgn. Chinese Ams., Inc., 1996; named Model Chinese Father of Yr., United Chinese Soc., 1996. Mem. Am. Legion, VFW, Lambda Alpha Internat. (Aloha chpt.), Phi Beta Kappa. Congregationalist. Home: 1102 Alewa Dr Honolulu HI 96817-1507 Office: Fax: (808) 522-2027

FONG, MATTHEW KIPLING, state official; b. Oakland, Calif., Nov. 20, 1953; s. Chester and March Fong; m. Paula Fong, May 28, 1978; children: Matthew II, Jade. Grad., U.S. Air Force Acad., 1975; MBA, Pepperdine U., 1982; JD, Southwestern Law. Sch., 1985. Former vice chmn. State Bd. Equalization; treas. State Calif., L.A., -1999; atty. L.A., 1999—. Regent Pepperdine U., Children's Hosp. L.A.; Rep. nominee State Controller, 1990. Lt. col. Air Force Res. Office: Sheppard Mullin Richter & Hampton 333 S Hope St Fl 48 Los Angeles CA 90071-1406

FONTENOTE-JAMERSON, BELINDA, museum director; Pres. Mus. African Am. Art, L.A. Office: Mus African Am Art 4005 S Crenshaw Blvd Fl 3 Los Angeles CA 90008-2534

FOOTE, CHRISTOPHER SPENCER, chemist, educator; b. Hartford, Conn., June 5, 1935; s. William J. and Dorothy (Bennett) F.; m. Judith L. Smith; children: Jonathan, Thomas. BS magna cum laude, Yale U., 1957; Fulbright scholar, U. Goettingen, 1957-58; AM, Harvard U., 1959, PhD, 1961. NSF predoctoral fellow Harvard U., 1958-61; instr. chemistry UCLA, 1961-62, asst. prof., 1962-66, assoc. prof., 1966-69, prof., 1969—, chmn. dept., 1978-81. Cons. Chevron, Procter and Gamble; acad. adv. bd. Indsl. Rsch. Inst., 1997—. Sr. editor Accounts of Chem. Rsch., 1995—. Recipient Humboldt sr. scientist award, 1986-87; Sloane fellow, 1965-67; Guggenheim fellow, 1967-68. Fellow AAAS; mem. Am. Chem. Soc. (Baeklund medal, Tolman award 1996, Arthur C. Cope scholar 1994), Chem. Soc. London, Am. Soc. Photobiology (coun. 1978-81, pres. 1988-89, Rsch. award 2000), German Chem. Soc., Phi Beta Kappa, Sigma Xi, Phi Lambda Upsilon. Home: 930 Berkeley St Santa Monica CA 90403-2308 Office: U Calif Dept Chemistry & Biochemistr Los Angeles CA 90095-1569

FORBES, DAVID CRAIG, musician; b. Seattle, Feb. 12, 1938; s. Douglas James and Ruby A. (Niles) F.; m. Sylvia Sterling, Aug. 29, 1965 (div. Apr. 1973); 1 child, Angela Rose. Grad., USN Sch. Music, 1957; student, Western Wash. U., 1960-64. Prin. horn La Jolla (Calif.) Civic Orch., 1958-60, Seattle Worlds Fair Band, 1962, Seattle Opera Co., 1964—, Pacific Northwest Ballet, Seattle, 1964—; asst. prin. horn Seattle Symphony Orch., 1964—; prin. horn Pacific Northwest Wagner Fest., Seattle, 1975—. Instr. horn Western Wash. State U., 1969-81, Cornish Inst., Seattle, 1964-78. Served with USN, 1956-60. Mem. NARAS, Internat. Horn Soc. Avocations: piano, golf, fishing. Home: 9050 15th Ave NW # 2 Seattle WA 98117-3429

FORCE, RONALD WAYNE, librarian; b. Sioux City, Iowa, Sept. 7, 1941; s. Robert N. and Madeline (Heine) F.; m. Jo Ellen Hitch, May 31, 1964; children: Emily, Alicia. BS, Iowa State U., 1963; MA, U. Minn., 1968; MS, Ohio State U., 1975. Asst. to head dept. libs. Ohio State U., Columbus, 1968-70, head engring. librs., 1970-72, head edn./psychology libr., 1972-79; asst. dir. pub. svcs. Wash. State U. Librs., Pullman, 1979-82; asst. sci. libr. U. Idaho Libr., Moscow, 1982-84, pub. svcs. libr., 1984-85, humanities libr., 1985-88, assoc. dean libr. svcs., 1988-91, dean libr. svcs., 1991—. Mem. adv. coun. Libr. Svcs. and Constrn. Act. Author: Guide to Literature on Biomedical Engineering, 1972; contbr. articles to profl. jours. Mem. Sacajawea Coun. Campfire Bd., 1980-85, mem. Pullman Dist. Campfire Com., fin. com., 1980-82, chair, 1983-84, treas., 1985, Sacajawea County Self-Study Com., 1986; mem. adv. bd. N.W. Net Info. Resources, 1994-95, 2000—; mem. Idaho Network Adv. Com., 1993-95; mem. LSCA Adv. Coun., 1989-95. Mem. ALA, Idaho Libr. Assn. (2d v.p. 1997-98, 1st v.p. 1998-99, pres. 1999-2000). Home: 545 N Blaine St Moscow ID 83843-3626 Office: U Idaho Libr Moscow ID 83844-2371

FORD, ANABEL, research anthropologist, archaeologist; b. L.A., Dec. 22, 1951; d. Joseph B. Ford and Marjorie Henshaw; m. Michael A. Glassow, May 4, 1974. BA in Anthropology, U. Calif., Santa Barbara, 1974, MA in Anthropology, 1976, PhD in Anthropology, 1981. Teaching asst. dept. anthropology & environ. studies U. Calif., Santa Barbara, 1975-80, rsch. asst. archaeologist office of pub. archaeology, 1980-81, lectr. dept. archaeology, 1982—, asst. rsch. archaeologist Social Process Rsch. Inst., 1982-87, founding dir. MesoAmerican Rsch. Ctr., 1987, asst. rsch. archaeologist Community Orgn. Rsch. Inst., 1987-91, assoc. rsch. archaeologist, 1991-98, dir. MesoAm. Rsch. Ctr., 1991-98, rsch. archeologist Inst. Social, Behavioral and Econ. Rsch., 1998—; assoc. rsch. archaeologist Inst. Social, Behavioral and Econ. Rsch., 1991-98, rsch. archaeologist, 1998—. Vis. asst. prof. dept. anthropology UCLA, 1987-89; guest lectr. various univs. including Ariz. State U., U. Ariz., Boston U., Columbia U., Harvard U., La. State U., Trent U., UCLA, York U., Univ. Nacional Autonoma de México; co-participant USIA, 1995-96; active commn. Centroamericana de Ambiente Y Desarrollo, 1996; active Mac Arthur World Environment and Resources Program, 1997; active Inst. for Internat. Edn., 1998; program initiator Ford Found., 1998;co-dir. Rsch. Across Disciplines, 1999. Contbr. over 50 articles to profl. jours.; presenter over 40 papers at profl. meetings & symposia; author various manuscripts. Pub. lectr. various schs. and orgns.; supr. Vol. Lab. and Field Program, 1978—. Humanities fellow U. Calif.-Santa Barbara (UCSB), 1989-90, 90-91; Fulbright rsch. scholar, 1986, 90; grantee UCSB, L.S.B. Leakey Found., NSF, NEH, Heinz Found., Wenner-Gren, CIRMA, CIES/USIS, Univ. Rsch. Expeditions Program, Ford Found., Fulbright-Hays Found; recipient Rolex award for Enterprise, 2000; named Educator of Yr. Goleta Chamber, 2000, Calif. State Assembly, 2000, Calif. State Senate, 2000; recipient Outstanding Cmty. Svc. award U.S. Senate, 2000, certificate of recognition Amigos de El Pilar Belize/Guatemala, 2000. Mem. AAAS, Am. Anthropol. Assn., Soc. for Am. Archaeology, Assn. for Field Archaeology, Sociedad Mexicana de Antropologia, So. Calif. Mesoamerican Network, UCSB Affiliated Faculty Women, [illegible] Studies, Sigma Xi. Office: U Calif Inst Soc Behav & Econ Rsch MesoAmerican Rsch Ctr Santa Barbara CA 93106 E-mail: ford@sscf.uscb.edu, elpilar@btl.net

FORD, BETTY BLOOMER (ELIZABETH FORD), former First Lady of United States, health facility executive; b. Chgo., Apr. 8, 1918; d. William Stephenson and Hortense (Neahr) Bloomer; m. Gerald R. Ford (38th Pres. U.S.), Oct. 15, 1948; children: Michael Gerald, John Gardner, Steven Meigs, Susan Elizabeth. Student, Sch. Dance Bennington Coll., 1936, 37; LL.D. (hon.), U. Mich., 1976. Dancer Martha Graham Concert Group, N.Y.C., 1939-41; fashion dir. Herpolsheimer's Dept. Store, Grand Rapids, Mich., 1943-48; dance instr. Grand Rapids, 1932-48. Chmn. bd. dirs. The Betty Ford Ctr., Rancho Mirage, Calif. Author: autobiography The Times of My Life, 1979, Betty: A Glad Awakening, 1987. Bd. dirs. Nat. Arthritis Found. (hon.); trustee Martha Graham Dance Ctr., Eisenhower Med. Ctr., Rancho Mirage; hon. chmn. Palm Springs Desert Mus.; nat. trustee Nat. Symphony Orch.; bd. dirs. The Lambs, Libertyville, Ill. Episcopalian. Home: PO Box 927 Rancho Mirage CA 92270-0927

FORD, CHRIS, professional basketball coach; b. Atlantic City, Jan. 11, 1949; m. Kathy Ford; children: Chris, Katie, Anthony, Michael. Ed., Villanova Univ. Player Detroit Pistons, NBA, 1973-78, Boston Celtics, NBA, 1978-82, broadcaster, 1982-83, asst. coach, 1983-90, head coach, 1990-95, Milw. Bucks, NBA, 1996-98, L.A. Clippers, NBA, 99-2000. Mem. NBA Championship teams, as player, 1981, as coach, 1984, 86. Office: Los Angeles Clippers 3939 S Figueroa St Los Angeles CA 90037-1200

FORD, DONALD HAINLINE, lawyer; b. Chgo., Dec. 5, 1906; . Matthew Henry and Ethel (Griffith) F.; m. Siri Ann Enegren (dec.), Aug. 22, 1934; children— Carol Ann (Mrs. Raymond D. McMullin), Barbara Jean (Mrs. Robert A. Harrington), Richard Donald; m. Norma R. Ford, Dec. 28, 1998. B.S., Oreg. State U., 1929; J.D., U. Mich., 1932. Bar: Calif. bar 1933. Park ranger Lassen Volcanic Nat. Park, 1931-32; assoc. firm Overton, Lyman & Prince, Los Angeles, 1933-41, partner, 1941—. Dir. W.W. Henry Co., Macpherson Oil Co. Served with USAAF, 1941-46; col. USAF; Ret. Decorated Bronze Star; Cloud and Banner spl. class (China). Mem. ABA, Calif. Bar, Los Angeles County Bar Assn. Presbyterian. Lodge: Rotary Office: 520 S Grand Ave Fl 7 Los Angeles CA 90071-2600

FORD, GERALD J. bank executive; B in Econs., So. Meth. U., 1966, JD, 1969. Bar: Tex. Chmn., CEO First Gibralter Bank, Tex., 1988-93; chmn. bd. dirs. First Madison Bank; pres., owner Madison Fin., Inc.; founder First United Bank Group, Inc.; chmn., CEO First Nationwide Bank, 1994, Calif. Fed. Bank, 1997, Golden State Bancorp, 1998—. Named Among 40 Most Generous, Fortune Mag., 1998. Office: Golden State Bancorp Inc 135 Main St San Francisco CA 94105-1812

FORD, GERALD RUDOLPH, JR. thirty eighth President of the United States; b. Omaha, July 14, 1913; s. Gerald R. and Dorothy (Gardner) F.; m. Elizabeth Bloomer, Oct. 15, 1948; children: Michael, John, Steven, Susan. A.B., U. Mich., 1935; LL.B., Yale U., 1941; LL.D., Mich. State U., Albion Coll., Aquinas Coll., Spring Arbor Coll. Bar: Mich. 1941. Practiced law at, Grand Rapids, 1941-49; mem. law firm Buchen and Ford; mem. 81st-93d Congresses from 5th Mich. Dist., 1949-74, elected minority leader, 1965; v.p. served under Pres. Richard Nixon U.S., U.S., 1973-74; pres. U.S., 1974-77. Del. Interparliamentary Union, Warsaw, Poland, 1959, Belgium, 1961, Bilderberg Group Conf., 1962; dir. The Travelers, Inc.; adv. dir. Tex. Commerce Bancshares, Inc., Am. Express Co.; mem. internat. adv. coun. Inst. Internat. Studies. Served as lt. comdr. USNR, 1942-46. Recipient Grand Rapids Jr. C. of C. Distinguished Service award, 1948; Distinguished Service Award as one of ten outstanding young men in U.S. by U.S. Jr. C. of C., 1950; Silver Anniversary All-Am. Sports Illustrated, 1959; Distinguished Congressional Service award Am. Polit. Sci. Assn., 1961, Medal of Freedom, 1999, Congressional Gold Medal, 1999, Profile in Courage award, 2001. Mem. Am., Mich. State, Grand Rapids bar assns., Delta Kappa Epsilon, Phi Delta Phi. Republican. Episcopalian. Clubs: University (Kent County), Peninsular (Kent County). Lodge: Masons. Office: PO Box 927 Rancho Mirage CA 92270-0927

FORD, JAMES CARLTON, human resources executive; b. Portland, Mar. 10, 1937; s. John Bernard and Margaret (Reynolds) F.; m. Carolyn Tadina, Aug. 22, 1959; children: Scott, Michele, Mark, Brigitte, Deidre, John. BA in History, U. Portland, 1960; MS in Edn., Troy State U., 1969; MPA, U. Puget Sound, 1976. Cert. sen. profl. in human resources. Commd. 2d lt. USAF, 1960, advanced through grades to lt. col., 1976, adminstr., tng. officer, 1960-70, personnel mgmt. officer, 1971-76; dep. inspector gen. U.S. Air Force Acad., Colorado Springs, Colo., 1977-80, ret., 1980; employment mgr. Western Fed. Savs. (name changed to Bank Western), Denver, 1980-82, v.p. human resources, 1982-88, sr. v.p. mgmt. svcs., 1988-92; dir. career mgmt. AIM Exec., Inc., Cons. Svcs., 1992-95; owner Orgn. Strategies, Inc., Cons., 1995—. Bd. dirs. Rocky Mountain chpt. Am. Inst. Banking, Denver, 1988-92; adj. prof. U. Colo., Colorado Springs, 1978-79, USAF Acad., Colorado Springs, 1978-80; adv. bd. U. Colo. Contemporary Mgmt. Program, Regis Coll. Career Svcs.; mem. faculty U. Phoenix, Colo., 1995—; mediator Pikes Peak Better Bus. Bur., 1995—. Mediator Neighborhood Justice Ctr., Colorado Springs, 1980; vol. allocations com. Pikes Peak United Way, Colorado Springs, 1978-79; vol. campaign exec. Mile Hi United Way, Denver, 1986-89; vol. mgmt. cons. Tech. Assistance Svc., Denver, 1991. Mem. Assn. for Mgmt. of Orgn. Design, Soc. for Human Resource Mgmt. (state dir. certification 1996-97). Republican. Roman Catholic. Office: Orgn Strategies Inc 975 Tari Dr Colorado Springs CO 80921-2256

FORD, PETER C. chemistry educator; b. Salinas, Calif., July 10, 1941; s. Clifford and Thelma (Martin) F.; children: Vincent, Jonathan; m. Mary E. Howe-Grant. BS with honors, Calif. Inst. Tech., 1962; MS, Yale U., 1963, PhD, 1966. Postdoctoral fellow Stanford U., 1966-67; asst. prof. chemistry U. Calif., Santa Barbara, 1967-72, assoc. prof. chemistry, 1972-77, prof. chemistry, 1977—. Grad. advisor dept. chemistry U. Calif., 1980-81, co-grad. advisor, 1985-92, 99—, chmn., 1994-96; vis. fellow Australian Nat. U., 1974; guest prof. H.C. Oersted Inst., Denmark, 1981; lectr. U. Berne, Switzerland, 1989, MITI-ASTI, Japan, 1990; guest investigator radiation biology br. Nat. Cancer Inst., 1994. Contbr. to profl. jours. Fellow NIH, 1963-66, NSF, 1966-67, Sterling fellow Yale U., 1963, sr. fellow Fulbright Found., 1974; Dreyfus Found. Tchr. scholar, 1971-76; recipient Alexander von Humboldt-Stiftung U.S. Sr. Scientist Rsch. award, 1992, Richard C. Tolman medal Am. Chem. Soc., 1993. Fellow AAAS. Achievements include research in the photochemical, photocatalytic and photophysical mechanisms of transition metal complexes and with homogeneous catalysis mechanisms as probed by modern kinetics techniques; the bioinorganic chemistry of metal nitrosyl complexes. Office: Univ of California Dept of Chemistry 552 University Rd Santa Barbara CA 93106-0001

FOREMAN, DALE MELVIN, lawyer, state official; b. Los Angeles, May 1, 1948; s. C. Melvin and Sylvia (Ahnlund) F.; m. Gail Burgener, June 24, 1972; children: Mari Elizabeth, Ann Marie, James Sterling. AB cum laude, Harvard U., 1970, JD, 1975. Bar: Wash. 1976, U.S. Dist. Ct. (we. dist.) Wash. 1977, U.S. Ct. Claims 1977, U.S. Dist. Ct. (ea. dist.) Wash. 1981, U.S. Ct. Appeals (9th cir.) 1981, Calif. 1986, U.S. Ct. Appeals (3rd cir.) [illegible] & Foreman, Wenatchee, Wash., 1975-81, Jardine, Foreman & Arch, Wenatchee, 1981-88; sr. ptnr. Foreman, Arch, Dodge, Volyn & Zimmerman, Wenatchee, 1988—; mem. 12th legis. dist. Wash. Ho. of Reps., 1993-96, majority leader, 1995-97. Mem. Spl. Adv. Commn. on Pub. Opinion, U.S. Dept. of State, 1970-72. Author: Washington Trial Handbook, 1988, Dental Law, 1989, How to Become an Expert Witness, 1989, Crucify Him! A Lawyer Looks at the Trial of Jesus, 1989. Chmn. Chelan County Rep. Cen. Com., Wenatchee, 1977-79, 82-84; bd. dirs. Am. and Fgn. Christian Union, N.Y.C., 1985—, Greater

Wenatchee Community Found., 1987—. Mem. ABA, Assn. Trial Lawyers Am., Wash. State Bar Assn., State Bar Calif., Wash. State Trial Lawyers Assn. (bd. govs. 1990—), Harvard Club, Rotary. Presbyterian. Avocation: horticulture. Home: 323 Chatham Hill Rd Wenatchee WA 98801-5931 Office: Foreman Arch Dodge & Volyn 124 N Wenatchee Ave # A Wenatchee WA 98801-2239

FORESTER, BERNARD I. recreational equipment company executive; b. 1928; B.S. in Bus. Adminstrn., U. Ariz., 1950. Audit mgr. Price Waterhouse & Co., 1950-64; chief fin. officer, dir. Republic Corp., 1964-66; exec. v.p., gen. mgr. K2 Inc. (formerly Anthony Industries Inc.), City of Commerce, Calif., 1966-67; pres. K2 Industries (formerly Anthony Industries Inc.), City of Commerce, 1967-90, chief exec. officer, 1973-95, chmn. bd., 1975—, also bd. dirs. With AUS, 1946-48. Office: K2 Inc 4900 S Eastern Ave Ste 200 Los Angeles CA 90040-2959

FORGAN, DAVID WALLER, retired career officer; b. Chgo., Sept. 28, 1933; s. Harold Nye and Ruth Ada (Waller) F.; m. Shirley Dobbins, Oct. 18, 1958; children— Bruce Dobbins, Todd Macmillan B.S. in Mktg., U. Colo., 1955; M.S. in Mgmt., George Washington U., 1966. Commd. 2d lt. U.S. Air Force, 1956, advanced through grades to maj. gen., 1985, various positions worldwide, 1956-77, dir. programs hdgrs. tactical air command Va., 1977-79, dir. force devel. Washington, 1979-80, dep. comdr. spl. ops. command Fort Bragg, N.C., 1980-82; asst. chief staff ops. Allied Forces Central Europe, Brunssum, The Netherlands, 1982-85; dep. chief staff ops. U.S. Air Force Europe, Ramstein Air Base, Fed. Republic Germany, 1985-87; comdr. Sheppard Tech. Tng. Ctr. Sheppard AFB, Tex., 1987-89; ret., 1989. Decorated Silver Star, D.F.C. (3), Legion of Merit, Air medal, Def. Disting. Svc. medal, Def. Superior Svc. medal; Aero Cross of Merit (Spain). Mem. Delta Tau Delta Republican Avocations: military history, skiing, golf. Home: 4935 Newstead Pl Colorado Springs CO 80906-5978

FORGANG, DAVID M. curator; b. N.Y.C., Mar. 26, 1947; s. Joseph Hyman and Clarice (Ishbia) F.; m. Joyce Enid Blumenthal, June 15, 1968 (div. May 1979); children: Adam, Bradley. B in Anthropology, U. Ariz., 1968, M in Anthropology, 1971. Mus. curator So. Ariz. Group Nat. Pk. Svc., Phoenix, 1971-77, regional curator we. region San Francisco, 1977-82, curator Yosemite (Calif.) Mus., 1982—. Pres. Yosemite Renaissance Art Competition, 1983-94; dir. Yosemite Artist in Residence Program, 1985—. Mariposa County advisor El Portal (Calif.) Town Planning Adv. Bd., 1984-94. Recipient Unit Award citation US Dept. Interior, 1974. Democrat. Jewish. Avocations: fishing, canoeing, hunting, gardening. Office: Nat Pk Svc PO Box 577 Yosemite National Park CA 95389-0577

FORMBY, BENT CLARK, immunologist; b. Copenhagen, Apr. 3, 1940; naturalized, 1991; s. John K. and Gudrun A. (Dinesen) F.; m. Irene Menck-Thygesen, June 28, 1963 (div. May 1980); children: Rasmus, Mikkel; m. Florence G. Schmid, June 28, 1980. BA in Philosophy summa cum laude, U. Copenhagen, 1959, PhD in Biochemistry, 1968, DSc, 1976. Asst. prof. U. Copenhagen, 1969-73, assoc. prof., 1973-79, prof., 1979-83; vis. prof. U. Calif., San Francisco, 1979-84; sr. scientist, dir. lab. of immunology Sansum Med. Rsch. Found., Santa Barbara, Calif., 1984-99; dir. rsch. The Rasmus Inst. Med. Rsch., Santa Barbara, 2000—. Cons. Cell Tech., Inc., Boulder, Colo., 1989—, Immunex Corp., Seattle, 1989—; med. adv. bd. Biocellular Rsch. Orgn., Ltd., London, Childrens Hosp. of Orange County, Lautenburg Ctr. for Gen. and Tumor Immunology, Hebrew U., Hadassah Med. Sch., Jerusalem, 1993—. Co-author: Lightsout, 2000; editor: Fetal Islet Transplantation, 1988, 2d edit. 1995; contbr. articles to profl. jours.; patentee on non-invasive glucose measurement, BH55 Hyaluronidase. Grantee Juvenile Diabetes Found., 1987, 88, E.L. Wiegand Found., 1993, Santa Barbara Cottage Hosp. Rsch., 1993-94, Breast Cancer Rsch. U. Calif., 1995-96, 96-97, 97-98. Mem. N.Y. Acad. Scis., Am. Diabetes Assn. (grantee 1985, 86, 89, pres. Santa Barbara chpt. 1995), Am. Fedn. Clin. Rsch., European Assn. for the Study of Diabetes. Avocations: painting, swimming. Office: The Rasmus Inst Med Rsch 1620 Eucalyptus Hill Rd Santa Barbara CA 93103-2812 E-mail: FRMBY43012@aol.com

FORNESS, STEVEN ROBERT, educational psychologist; b. Denver, May 13, 1939; s. Robert E. and Rejeana C. (Houck) F. BA in English, U. No. Colo., 1963, MA in Ednl. Psychology, 1964; EdD in Spl. Edn., UCLA, 1968. Tchr. Santa Maria High Sch., Calif., 1964-66; counselor Sch. Edn. UCLA, 1966-68; spl. educator Neuropsychiat. Inst., 1968—, chief ednl. psychology child outpatient dept., 1970—, mem. mental retardation research ctr., 1970—, prof. dept. psychiatry, 1972—, prin. inpatient sch., 1976—, dir. mental retardation and developmental disabilities tng. program, 1985-92. Grant rev. panelist U.S. Dept. Edn., 1974-2000; cons. Nat. Assn. Exceptional Children, Venezuela, 1974-2000; commn. ednl. psychology Calif. State Bd. Behavioral Scis. Examiners, 1977-99. Specialist in classroom observation tech. early identification of children with learning and behavior disorders; author publs. including (with Frank Hewett) Education of Exceptional Learners, 3d edit., 1984, (with K. Kavale) Science of Learning Disabilities, 1985, (with Kavale and Bender) Handbook of Learning Disabilities, vols. I, II and III, 1987, 88; (with K. Kavale) Nature of Learning Disabilities, 1995, Efficacy of Special Education, 1999; cons. editor various jours. Sr. scholar Shaklee Inst. on Spl. Edn., 1996-2001. Fulbright scholar Ministry of Edn., Portugal, 1976 Fellow Internat. Acad. Rsch. in Learning Disabilties, Am. Assn. Mental Retardation; mem. Tchr. Educators of Children with Behavior Disorders (pres. 1985-86), Coun. Children with Behavior Disorders (pres. 1987-88, Leadership award 1995), Am. Assn. Univ. Affiliated Programs in Developmental Disabilities (interdisciplinary coun. 1972-89), Internat. Coun. for Exceptional Children (del. Assembly 1988-91, Wallin award 1992, Excellence in Tchr. Edn. award 1995, honors com. 1999-2002), Acad. on Mental Retardation (exec. com. 1989-91), Nat. Mental Health and Spl. Edn. Coalition (co-chair of Definition Task Force 1987-2000), Am. Psychiat. Assn. (DSM IV subcom. on learning disorders 1988-94), Profl. Group for Attention and Related Disorders (com. profl. advisors 1990-91), Midwest Symposium on Behavioral Disorders (Leadership award 1993), Am. Acad. Child and Adolescent Psychiatry (co-chmn. practice parameters on learning disabilities 1996-98, Sidney Berman award on learning disorders 2000), Knights of Malta (Order of St. John 1994). Home: 11901 W Sunset Blvd Los Angeles CA 90049-4240 Office: UCLA Dept Psychiatry 760 Westwood Plz Los Angeles CA 90095-8353

FORRESTER, BRAD, management consultant; Pres. Con Am Mgmt. Corp., San Diego, 1997—. Office: Con Am Mgmt Corp 1764 San Diego Ave San Diego CA 92110-1906

FORSBERG, PETER, professional hockey player; b. Ornskoldsvik, Sweden, July 20, 1973; Profl. hockey player MODO Hockey Swedish League, 1990-94, Swedish Olympic Team, 1994, Quebec Nordiques, Colo. Avalanche, 1994—. Named to Swedish League All-Star team, 1991-92; named Swedish League Player of Yr., 1993-94, NHL Rookie of Yr., Sporting News, 1994-95; recipient Calder Meml. award 1994-95; mem. Gold Medal winning Swedish Olympic Team, 1994. Office: c/o Colorado Avalanche 1635 Clay St Denver CO 80204-1743

FORSTER, JULIAN, physicist, consultant; b. N.Y.C., Aug. 31, 1918; s. Meyer Kivetz and Rose (Sommer) F.; m. Frieda Bain, July 2, 1941; children: Jeffrey M., Laura Gherman. BS in Physics, CCNY, 1940. Registered nuclear engr., Calif. Sr. physicist US Naval 4th Dist., Phila., 1941-56; sr. nuclear engr. GE, San Jose, Calif., 1956-70, sr. project mgr. nuclear energy dept., 1970-80; sr. mgmt. tech. Quadrex Corp., Campbell, 1980-85, cons., 1985-96, GE-NE, 1996—. Contbr. articles to profl. jours. Commr. Fine Arts, San Jose, 1987-95. Fellow IEEE (life, emeritus; standards bd. 1970—, computer soc. 1985—, nuclear scis. soc. 1963—, power engrng. soc. 1975—, coord. pace divsn. IV 1993-2000, chmn. awards and recognition com. 1986-95, Divsnl. Profl. Achievment award 1994, Standards Bd. Spl. Achievement award 1995, Stds. Dist. Svc. award 2000, 3d Millennium medal of Honor 2000); mem. Internat. Electro Tech. Com. (nuclear power com. SC45A 1969—, R.F. Shea Svc. award 1992). Democrat. Jewish. Avocations: music, wine, fine arts, golf. Home: 6962 Castlerock Dr San Jose CA 95120-4704 Office: GE NE MC/334 175 Curtner Ave San Jose CA 95125-1014 Fax: 408-925-2923. E-mail: jay.forster@gene.ge.com

FORSTER, MERLIN HENRY, foreign languages educator, writer, researcher; b. Delta, Utah, Feb. 24, 1928; s. Henry and Ila Almeda (Rawlinson) F.; m. Vilda Mae Naegle, Apr. 25, 1952; children: Celia Marlene, David Merlin, Angela, Daniel Conrad, Elena Marie. BA, Brigham Young U., 1956; MA, U. Ill., 1957, PhD, 1960. Instr. in Spanish U. Tex., Austin, 1960-61, asst. prof., 1961-62; asst. prof. Spanish and Portuguese U. Ill., Urbana, 1962-65, assoc. prof., 1965-69, prof., 1969-78, dir. Latin Am. studies, 1972-78; prof., chmn. dept. Spanish and Portuguese, U. Tex., Austin, 1978-87; disting. prof. Latin Am. lit. Brigham Young U., Provo, Utah, 1987-98, chmn. dept. Spanish and Portuguese, 1989-93, prof. emeritus, 1998—. Dir. summer seminars NEH, 1978, 89, 90, 93, 96, 98. Author: Los Contemporáneos, 1964, Fire and Ice, 1976, Historia de la Poesia Hispanoamericana, 1981; editor: Index to Mexican Journals, 1966, Tradition and Renewal, 1975, De la Crónica a la Nueva Narrativa, 1986, Vanguardism in Latin American Literature: An Annotated Bibliographical Guide, 1990, La vanguardia literaria en Mexico y la América Central, 2000 Rsch. grantee Social Sci. Rsch. Coun., Mexico City, 1965, Fulbright-Hays, Buenos Aires, 1971, NEH, Austin, 1986-87, Am. Coun. Learned Socs. and German Acad. Exch. Svc., 1993-94; fellow Ctr. for Advanced Study, Urbana, 1976-77. Mem. MLA, Latin Am. Studies Assn., Am. Assn. Tchrs. Spanish and Portuguese, Internat. Inst. Iberoam. Lit. (pres. 1981-83, 94-96). Mem. LDS Ch. Avocations: classical music, quartet singing, gardening, woodworking. Office: Brigham Young Univ Dept Spanish and Portuguese Provo UT 84602

FORSYTH, BEN RALPH, academic administrator, medical educator; b. N.Y.C., Mar. 8, 1934; s. Martin and Eva Forsyth; m. Elizabeth Held, Aug. 19, 1962; children: Jennifer, Beverly, Jonathan. Attended, Cornell U., 1950-53; MD, NYU, 1957. Diplomate Am. Bd. Internal Medicine. Intern, then resident Yale Hosp., New Haven, 1957-60; postdoctoral fellow Harvard U. Med. Shc., Boston, 1960-61; rsch. assoc. NIH, Bethesda, Md., 1963-66; assoc. prof. med. microbiology, prof. med. coll. U. Vt., Burlington, 1966-90, assoc. dean div. health scis., 1971-85, assoc. v.p. acad. affairs, 1977-78, v.p. adminstrn., 1978-85, sr. v.p., 1985-90; sr. exec. asst. to pres. Ariz. State U., Tempe, 1990—, prof. health adminstrn. and policy, 1991—, interim v.p. adminstrv. svcs., 1991-93; interim provost Ariz. State U. West, Phoenix, 1992-93, Ariz. State U. East, Mesa, 1994-96; provost, v.p. Ariz. State U. West, Phoenix, 1993-96. Sr. cons. Univ. Health Ctr., Burlington, 1986-90. Contbr. articles to profl. jours. V.p., chmn. United Way Planning Com., Burlington, 1974-75, Ops. Com., 1975-76, bd. dirs., officer, 1977-89; bd. trustees U. Vt., Burlington, 1996—; mem. New England Bd. Higher Edn. Com., Burlington, 1985-89; chmn. U. Vt. China Project Adv. Bd., Burlington, 1989-90. Lt. comdr. USN, 1962-63. Sinsheimer Found. faculty fellow, 1966-71. Fellow ACP, Infectious Diseases Soc. Am.; mem. Phi Beta Kappa, Alpha Omega Alpha. Avocations: hiking, gardening, travel. Office: Arizona State Univ PO Box 872203 Tempe AZ 85287-2203 E-mail: forsyth@asu.edu

FORSYTH, G. FRED, electronics company executive; BS magna cum laude, U. N.H.; MBA, Babson Coll. Former corp. sr. v.p., pres. Profl. Products Divsn. Iomega Corp.; former sr. exec. Apple Computers, Digital Equipment Corp., GE; corp. v.p., pres. Solectron Ams. Solectron Corp., Milpitas, Calif., 1999—. Office: Solectron Corp 847 Gibraltar Dr Milpitas CA 95035

FORSYTH, RAYMOND ARTHUR, civil engineer, consultant; b. Reno, Mar. 13, 1928; s. Harold Raymond and Fay Exona (Highfill) F.; m. Mary Ellen Wagner, July 9, 1950; children: Lynne, Gail, Alison, Ellen. BS, Calif. State U., San Jose, 1952; MCE, Auburn U., 1958. Jr. engr., asst. engr. Calif. Divsn. Hwys., San Francisco, 1952-54; assoc. engr., sr. supervising, prin. engr. Calif. Dept. Transp., Sacramento, 1961-83, chief geotech. br., 1972-79, chief soil mechanics and pavement br., 1979-83; chief Transp. Lab., Sacramento, 1983-89. Cons., lectr. in field; geotech. engr. cons., 1989—. Contbr. articles to profl. jours. Served with USAF, 1954-56. Fellow ASCE (pres. Sacramento sect., chmn. Calif. coun. 1980-81); mem. Transp. Rsch. Bd. (chmn. embankments and earth slopes com. 1976-82, chmn. soil mechanics sect. 1982-88, chmn. group 2 coun. 1988-91), ASTM. Home: 5017 Pasadena Ave Sacramento CA 95841-4149 E-mail: slvrfox800@aol.com

FORTH, KEVIN BERNARD, beverage distributing industry consultant; b. Adams, Mass., Dec. 4, 1949; s. Michael Charles and Catherine Cecilia (McAndrews) F.; m. Deborah Newport; children: Melissa, Brian. AB, Holy Cross Coll., 1971; MBA with distinction, NYU, 1973. Divsn. rep. Anheuser-Busch, Inc., Boston, 1973-74, dist. sales mgr. L.A., 1974-76, asst. to v.p. mktg. staff St. Louis, 1976-77; v.p. Straub Distbg. Co., Ltd., Orange, Calif., 1977-81, pres., 1981-93, chmn., CEO, 1986-93, also bd. dirs. Beverage industry cons., 1994—. Commr. Orange County Sheriff's Adv. Coun., 1988—; mem. adv. bd. Rancho Santiago C.C. Coll. Dist., 1978-80; bd. dirs. Children's Hosp. of Orange County Padrinos Found., 1983-85, St. Joseph's Hosp. Found., Orange County Sports Hall of Fame, 1980-89; exec. com., bd. dirs. Nat. Coun. on Alcoholism, 1980-83; mem. pres. coun. Holy Cross Coll., 1987-91; bd. dirs., pres. Calif. State Fullerton Titan Athletic Found., 1983-85, 89-90; mem. Calif. Beer Wholesalers Assn., dir., 1978-89, v.p., 1984, chmn., 1985; bd. dirs. Freedom Bowl, 1984-93, v.p., 1984-85, pres., 1986, chmn., 1986-87, Anaheim Vis. and Conv. Bur., 1989-93; bd. dirs. Orangewood Children's Found., 1988-93; mem. Calif. Rep. State Ctrl. Com., 1988-93, Orange County Probation Dept. Cmty. Involvement Bd., 1992-93. Recipient Founders award Freedom Bowl, 1993; Benjamin Levy fellow NYU, 1971-73. Mem. Nat. Beer Wholesalers Assn. (bd. dirs. 1986-93, asst. sec. 1989-90, sec. 1989-91, vice-chmn. 1992, chmn. 1993; Lifetime Achievement Service award, 2001), Industry Environ. Coun., Holy Cross Alumni Assn., NYU Alumni Assn., Sports Car Club Am. (Ariz. state champion 1982), Holy Cross Club (So. Calif.), Beta Gamma Sigma. Roman Catholic. Home and Office: 27750 Tamara Dr Yorba Linda CA 92887-5840

FORTMANN, STEPHEN PAUL, medical educator, researcher, epidemiologist; b. Burbank, Calif., Oct. 13, 1948; s. Daniel John and Mary (Van Halteren) F.; married; children: Nicolas, Michele. AB, Stanford U., 1970; MD, U. Calif., San Francisco, 1974. Diplomate Am. Bd. Internal Medicine, Am. Coll. Epidemiology. Clin. instr. Stanford (Calif.) U. Sch. Medicine, 1979-83, asst. prof., 1983-90, assoc. prof., 1990-99, prof., 1999—. Advisor World Health Orgn., Geneva, 1980-86. Contbr. articles to profl. jours. Fellow ACP, Am. Heart Assn. (coun. on epidemiology and prevention), Am. Coll.Epidemiology, Soc. Behavioral Medicine. Avocations: photography, running. Office: Stanford U Sch Medicine 1000 Welch Rd Palo Alto CA 94304-1811 E-mail: fortmann@stanford.edu

FORTSON, EDWARD NORVAL, physics educator; b. Atlanta, June 16, 1936; s. Charles Wellborn and Virginia (Norval) F.; m. Alix Madge Hawkins, Apr. 3, 1960; children— Edward Norval, Lucy Frear, Amy Lewis B.S., Duke U., 1957; Ph.D., Harvard U., 1963. Research fellow U. Bonn., Federal Rep. Germany, 1965-66; research asst. prof. physics U. Wash., Seattle, 1963-65, asst. prof., 1966-69, assoc. prof., 1969-74, prof., 1974—. Fulbright travel grantee, 1965-66; Nat. Research Council fellow Oxford, Eng., 1977; Guggenheim fellow, 1980-81 Fellow AAAS, Am. Phys. Soc.; mem. NAS. Office: U Wash Dept Physics PO Box 351560 Seattle WA 98195-1560

FORWARD, ROBERT L(ULL), physicist, businessman, consultant, writer; b. Geneva, Aug. 15, 1932; s. Robert Torrey and Mildred (Lull) F.; m. Martha Neil Dodson, Aug. 29, 1954; children— Robert Dodson, Mary Lois, Julie Elizabeth, Eve Laurel BS in Physics, U. Md., 1954, PhD, 1965; MS in Applied Physics, UCLA, 1958. With Hughes Aircraft Co., 1956-87, assoc. mgr. theoretical studies dept., 1966-67, mgr. exploratory studies dept., 1967-74; sr. scientist Hughes Research Labs., Malibu, Calif., 1974-87; owner, chief scientist Forward Unltd., Clinton, Wash., 1987—; ptnr., chief scientist Tethers Unlimited, 1994-97; v.p., chmn. bd. dirs., sec., treas., chief scientist Tethers Unltd., Inc., 1997—. Popular sci. writer and lectr. Author: (sci. fiction) Dragon's Egg, 1981, The Flight of the Dragonfly, 1983, Starquake, 1985, Rocheworld, 1986, Martian Rainbow, 1991, Timemaster, 1992, Camelot 30K, 1993, (with Julie Forward Fuller) Return to Rocheworld, 1993, Rescued from Paradise, 1995, (with Martha Dodson Forward) Marooned on Eden, 1993, Ocean under the Ice, 1994, Saturn Rukh, 1997, (nonfiction) (with Joel Davis) Mirror Matter: Pioneering Antimatter Physics, 1988, Future Magic, 1988, Indistinguishable from Magic, 1995; contbr. numerous articles to sci. jours. Capt. USAF, 1954-56. Hughes fellow, 1956-62. Fellow AIAA (assoc.), Brit. Interplanetary Soc.; mem. Am. Phys. Soc., Author's Guild, Sci.-Fiction and Fantasy Writers' Am., Sigma Xi, Sigma Pi Sigma. Home and Office: 8114 S Pebble Ct Clinton WA 98236-9240 E-mail: Bob@ForwardUnlimited.com

FORYST, CAROLE, computer electronics executive; b. Chgo., 08 Apr. d. James M. and Marie V. Foryst; m. Anthony H. Cordesman, Feb. 14, 1976; children: Justin G., Alexander Scott. Student, Rosary Coll., 1958-61, Cite Universite de Grenoble, France, 1961, Hunter Coll., , 1964-67, Roosevelt U., 1970-71. Fin. reporter Chgo. Sun-Times, 1969-72, L.A. Times, 1972; staff asst. to sec. U.S. Dept. Treasury, Washington, 1973-76; dep. dir. pub. affairs U.S. Dept. Interior, Washington, 1976; asst. v.p. Assn. Am. R.R.'s, Washington, 1977-78; v.p. AMTRAK, Washington, 1979-81; assoc. adminstr. budget and policy Urban Mass Transp. Adminstrn., Washington, 1981-84; comml. real estate broker Barnes, Morris & Pardoe, Washington, 1984-88, Larry Hogan & Assocs., Inc., Landover, Md., 1988-93; mortgage broker Mortgage Investment Corp., Vienna, 1993-94, Windsor Mortgage Co, McLean, 1994-95; v.p. ops. Floating Images Inc., Westbury, N.Y., 1997-98, DynaFirm, Inc., Los Alamos, N.Mex., 1998-99, CEO, 1999-2000. Mem. fin. svc. com. Treas. Dept., Fed. Credit Union, 1991-93, Pub. Internat. Bus. Insights, 1991-93, Hotels and Comm. Real Estate Co., 1993-. Republican Home: PO Box 1114 Corrales NM 87048-1114 Office: PO Box 1114 Corrales NM 87048-1114

FOSSLAND, JOEANN JONES, professional speaker, personal coach; b. Balt., Mar. 21, 1948; d. Milton Francis and Clementine (Bowen) Jones; m. Richard E. Yellott III, 1966 (div. 1970); children: Richard E. IV, Dawn Joeann; m. Robert Gerard Fossland Jr., Nov. 25, 1982. Student, Johns Hopkins U., 1966-67; cert., Hogan's Sch. Real Estate, 1982. Cert. values coach, behaviors coach, 1998, GRI; master cert. coach. Owner Kobble Shop, Indiatlantic, Fla., 1968-70, Downstairs, Atlanta, 1971; seamstress Aspen (Colo.) Leather, 1972-75; owner Backporch Feather & Leather, Aspen and Tucson, 1975-81; area mgr. Welcome Wagon, Tucson, 1982; realtor assoc. Tucson Realty & Trust, 1983-85; mgr. Home Illustrated mag., Tucson, 1985-87; asst. pub., gen. mgr. Phoenix, Scottsdale, Albuquerque, Tricities Tucson Homes Illustrated, 1990-93; pres. Advantage Solutions Group, Cortaro, Ariz., 1993—. Power leader Darryl Davis Seminars Power Program, 1995—; personal and profl. coach.; instr. Women's Coun Realtors, 1999—. Designer leather goods (Tucson Mus. Art award 1978, Crested Butte Art Fair Best of Show award 1980); author: Personal and Professional Coaching: Coach University, Certified Training Program, 1996. Voter registrar Recorder's Office City of Tucson, 1985-91; bd. dirs. Hearth Found., Tucson, 1987-96, pres., 1994; bd. dirs. Ariz. Integrated Residential & Ednl. Svcs., Inc., 1989-95, pres. 1994-95). Mem. NAFE, Internat. Fedn. Coaches (master cert. coach), Women's Coun. Realtors (leadership tng. grad. designation, pres. Tucson chpt. 1995, Ariz. state gov. 1997-98, v.p. Region IV, 2000, Tucson Affiliate of Yr. award 1991, Ariz. State Mem. of Yr. 1999), Tucson Assn. Realtors (Affiliate of Yr. award 1988). Democrat. Presbyterian. Avocations: tennis, gardening, reading, travel, public speaking. Office: Advantage Solutions Group PO Box 133 Cortaro AZ 85652-0133 E-mail: joeann@joeann.com

FOSTER, COLLEEN, library director; BA in English Lit., Coll. Notre Dame, Belmont, Calif., 1967; MLS, U. Denver, 1968. Br. reference libr. San Francisco Pub. Libr., 1968-69; reference libr. Stockton-San Joaquin County Pub. Libr., Calif., 1969-77, audiovisual libr., 1977-78, br. supr., 1978-81, libr. divsn. mgr. for adult svcs., 1990-92, dep. dir. libr. svcs., 1992-94, dir. libr. svcs., 1994—. Five gallon blood donor, Delta Blood Bank; mem. League of Women Voters of San Joaquin County, 1981—, sec., 1983-84, mem. speakers bureau, pros and cons presenter, 1985—, voter editor (newsletter), 1984-88, voter distbn. coord., 1991-97, participant candidates' forum, 1984-92, bd. dirs., 1983-84, 88-90, mem. League Study Com.; mem. Leadership Stockton, Class of 1995; reading tutor vol. Marshall Middle Sch. HOSTS (Help One Student to Suceed), 1996—. Mem. ALA, ACLU, NOW, MADD, Calif. Libr. Assn. (coun. mem. 1984-91, chair Coun. Rules Com. 1986, 88-89, bd. dirs. Calif. Soc. Librs. 1987-89, chair Bylaws Reorganization Com. 1990, mem. future of the profession task force, 1995, sec., treas. Calif. County Librs. Assn. 1995, mem. assembly 1995-98, mem. Conf. Planning Com. 1996, Fin. Com. 1996-98, Exec. Com. 1997-98, Mgmt. Svcs. Divsn. Excellence in Libr. Mgmt. award 1997), Habitat for Humanity, So. Poverty Law Ctr., Amnesty Internat., Greenpeace, Nature Conservancy, World Wildlife Found., Sierra Club, Rotary (Stockton chpt., vol. Asparagus Festival 1994—, Rotary Read-in 1994—, Su Salud Health Fair 1995). Office: Stockton-San Joaquin County Pub Libr 605 N El Dorado St Stockton CA 95202-1907 Fax: 209-937-8683

FOSTER, DAVID RAMSEY, soap company executive; b. London, May 24, 1920; (parents Am. citizens); s. Robert Bagley and Josephine (Ramsey) F.; m. Anne Firth, Aug. 2, 1957 (dec. June 1994); children: Sarah, Victoria; m. Alexandra Chang, May 24, 1996. Student in econs., Gonville and Caius Coll., Cambridge (Eng.) U., 1938. With Colgate-Palmolive Co. and affiliates, 1946-79; v.p., gen. mgr. Europe Colgate-Palmolive Internat., 1961-65, v.p., gen. mgr. household products divsn. parent co., 1965-68, exec. v.p., 1968-70, pres., 1970-75, CEO, 1971-79, chmn., 1975-79. Author: Wings Over the Sea, 1990. Trustee Woman's Sport Found. Served to lt. comdr. Royal Naval Vol. Res., 1940-46. Decorated Disting. Svc. Order, D.S.C. with bar, Mentioned in Despatches (2); recipient Victor award City of Hope, 1974, Herbert Hoover Meml. award, 1976, Adam award, 1977, Harriman award Boys Club N.Y., 1977, Charter award St. Francis Coll., 1978, Walter Hagen award, 1978, Patty Berg award, 1986, Commr.'s award LPGA, 1995. Mem. Soc. Mayflower Descs., Hawks Club (Cambridge U.), Royal Ancient Golf Club (St. Andrews, Scotland), Royal Cinque Ports Golf Club (life), Sunningdale Golf Club, Sankaty Head Golf Club, Racquet and Tennis Club (N.Y.C.), Mission Hills Country Club, Bally Bunion Golf Club (life). Home: 540 Desert West Dr Rancho Mirage CA 92270-1310

FOSTER, DAVID SCOTT, lawyer; b. White Plains, N.Y., July 13, 1938; s. William James and Ruth Elizabeth (Seltzer) F.; m. Eleanore Stalker, Dec. 21, 1959; children: David Scott, Robert McEachron. BA, Amherst Coll., 1960; LLB, Harvard U., 1963. Bar: N.Y. 1963, D.C. 1977, Calif. 1978. Jud. law clk. U.S. Dist. Ct. (so. dist.) N.Y., 1963-64; assoc. Debevoise & Plimpton, N.Y.C., 1964-72; internat. tax counsel U.S. Treasury Dept., Washington, 1972-77; ptnr. Brobeck, Phleger & Harrison, San Francisco, 1978-90, Coudert Bros., San Francisco, 1990-91, Thelen, Reid & Priest LLP, San Francisco, 1991—. Mem. ABA, San Francisco Bar Assn., Internat. Fiscal Assn., Western Pension and Benefits Confs., St. Francis Yacht Club (San Francisco). Presbyterian. Office: Thelen Reid & Priest LLP 101 2nd St Ste 1800 San Francisco CA 94105-3659

FOSTER, JAMES HENRY, advertising and public relations executive; b. Kansas City, Mo., May 14, 1933; s. Wendell F. and Lillian M. (East) F. BA, Drake U., 1955, postgrad., 1957. Reporter, editor Des Moines (Iowa) Register, 1951-61; pub. rels. and advt. exec. J. Walter Thompson Co., N.Y.C., 1961-73, 79-99, v.p., 1970-73; sr. v.p., gen. mgr. Brouillard Comm. divsn., N.Y.C., 1979-81, exec. v.p., gen. mgr., 1981-84, pres., CEO, 1984-94; chmn., CEO Brouillard Comm., 1994-97, chmn., 1997-99, chmn. emeritus, 1999—; v.p. pub. affairs Western Union Corp., Uppper Saddle River, 1973-79; pres. Reputation Mgmt. Strategies, Durango, Colo., 1999—, Music in the Mountains, Inc., Durango, 2000—, also bd. dirs. Bd. dirs. Fort Lewis Coll. Found., 1999—. Mem. Union League Club (N.Y.C.), Petroleum Club (Durango). Presbyterian. Office: Reputation Mgmt Strategies 1472 E Third Ave Durango CO 81301-5244

FOSTER, JOHN STUART, JR. physicist, former defense industry executive; b. New Haven, Sept. 18, 1922; s. John Stuart and Flora (Curtis) F.; m. Frances Schnell, Dec. 28, 1978; children: Susan, Cathy, Bruce, Scott, John. BS, McGill U., 1948; PhD in Physics, U. Calif., Berkeley, 1952; DSc (hon.), U. Mon., 1979. Dir. Lawrence Livermore (Calif.) Lab., 1952-65; dir. def. rsch. and engring. Dept. Def., Washington, 1965-73; v.p. TRW Energy Systems Group, Redondo Beach, Calif., 1973-79; v.p. sci. and tech. TRW Inc., Cleve., 1979-88, also bd. dirs. Chmn. Def. Sci. Bd., 1989-93; chmn. Pilkington Aerospace; chmn. Tech. Strategies & Alliances. Decorated knight Comdr.'s Cross, Badge and Star of Order of Merit (Federal Republic of Germany); comdr. Legion of Honor (France); recipient Ernst Orlando Lawrence Meml. award AEC, 1960, Disting. Pub. Svc. medal Dept. Def., 1969, 73, 93, Cromwell medal, 1972, Enrico Fermi Award, U.S. Dept. of Energy, 1992, Eugene Fubini award, U.S. Dept. Def., 1998. Mem. NAE (Founders award 1989), AIAA, Am. Def. Preparedness Assn., Nat. Security Indsl. Assn. Office: TRW Inc 1 Space Park Blvd Bldg E1-5010 Redondo Beach CA 90278-1071

FOSTER, KENNITH EARL, life sciences educator; b. Lamesa, Tex., Jan. 20, 1945; s. John Hugh and Mamie (Hyatt) F.; children: Sherry, Kristi. BS, Tex. Tech. U., 1967; MS, U. Ariz., 1969, PhD, 1972. Prof. and dir. Office of Arid Lands Studies, U. Ariz., Tucson, 1983—. Contbr. articles to profl. jours. Grantee NASA, NSF, USDA, U.S. AID, industry, 1983—. Home: 651 S Avenida Princesa Tucson AZ 85748-6858 Office: Univ of Ariz Office of Arid Lands Studies 1955 E 6th St Tucson AZ 85719-5224

FOSTER, KENT B. telephone company executive. Pres., Gen. Telephone Co. Northwest Inc., Everett, Wash.; pres. GTE Telephone Ops., Irving, Tex., CEO, Ingram Micro Inc., Santa Ana, CA, 2000—. Office: Ingram Micro Inc 1600 E Saint Andrew Pl Santa Ana CA 92799-5125

FOSTER, LAWRENCE, concert and opera conductor; b. Los Angeles, 1941; Student, Bayreuth Festival Masterclasses; studied with, Fritz Zweig. Debut as condr., Young Musicians' Found., Debut Orch., 1960; condr., mus. dir., 1960-64, condr., San Francisco Ballet, 1961-65, asst. condr., Los Angeles Philharmonic Orch., 1965-68, chief guest condr., Royal Philharmonic Orch., Eng., 1969-75, guest condr., Houston Symphony, 1970-71, condr. in chief, 1971-72, music dir., 1972-78, Orch. Philharmonique of Monte Carlo, 1979, gen. music dir., Duisburg & Dusseldorf Opera (Ger.), 1982-86, former music dir. Lausanne Chamber Orch., 1991-96, music dir. Aspen (Colo.) Music Festival and Sch.; currently music dir. Orquestra Ciutat de Barcelona; artistic dir. Bucharest Festival and Competition; guest condr. orchs. in, U.S., Europe, Australia and Japan; recorded, condr. world premiere Paul McCartney's Standing Stone, 1997; (Recipient Koussevitsky Meml. Conducting prize 1966, Eleanor R. Crane Meml. prize Berkshire Festival, Tanglewood, Mass. 1966); condr. Jerusalem Symphony Orch., 1990; regular guest condr. Dutsche Opera, Berlin, L.A. Opera. Address: ICM Artists Ltd c/o Jenny Vogel 8942 Wilshire Blvd Beverly Hills CA 90211-1934

FOSTER, MARY CHRISTINE, motion picture and television executive; b. L.A., Mar. 19, 1943; d. Ernest Albert and Mary Ada (Quilici) F.; m. Paul Hunter, July 24, 1982. BA, Immaculate Heart Coll., Los Angeles, 1967; M of Journalism in TV News Documentary, UCLA, 1968. Dir. research and devel. Metromedia Producers Corp., Los Angeles, 1968-71; dir. devel. and prodn. services Wolper Prodns., Los Angeles, 1971-76; mgr. film programs NBC-TV, Burbank, Calif., 1976-77; v.p. movies and mini series Columbia Pictures TV, Burbank, 1977-81, v.p. series programs, 1981; v.p. program devel. Group W. Prodns., L.A., 1981-87; agt. The Agency, Los Angeles, 1988-90, Shapiro-Lichtman Agy., Los Angeles, 1990-99; ret., ind. prodr., 1999—. Lectr. in field, 1970—. Creator: (TV series) Sullivan, 1985, Auntie Mom, 1986. Trustee Immaculate Heart H.S., L.A., 1980—; mem. comty. devel. com. Immaculare Heart Cmty., 2001—; mem. exec. com. Humanitas Awards, Human Family Inst., 1985—, L.A. Roman Cath. Archdiocesan Comms. Commn., L.A., 1986-90, Catholics in Media, 1992—. Mem. Women in Film (bd. dirs. 1974-78), Nat. Acad. TV Arts and Scis. Democrat.

FOSTER, NORMAN HOLLAND, geologist; b. Iowa City, Oct. 2, 1934; s. Holland and Dora Lucinda (Ransom) F.; m. Janet Lee Grecian, Mar. 25, 1956; children: Kimberly Ann, Stephen Norman. BA, U. Iowa, 1957, MS, 1960; PhD, U. Kans., 1963. Instr. geology U. Iowa, 1958-60; sr. geologist, geol. specialist, exploration team supr. Sinclair Oil Corp. and Atlantic Richfield Co., Casper, Wyo., also Denver, 1962-69; dist. geologist Trend Exploration Ltd., 1969-72, v.p., 1972-79; ind. geologist Denver, 1979—; instr. geology U. Kans., 1960-62. Chmn., pres., CEO Voyager Exploration, Inc., Denver, 1995—; guest lectr. geology Colo. Sch. Mines, 1972—, U. Colo., 1972—, U. Iowa, 1975—, U. Kans., 1975—; adv. bd. U. Kans., 1982—, U. Iowa, 1988—, U. Colo., 1990—; chmn. fin. com. 28th Internat. Geol. Congress, 1987-89, ofcl. U.S. rep., Washington, 1989; dir. MarkWest Hydrocarbon, Inc., Denver, 1996—. Assoc. editor Guidebook to Geology and Energy Resources of Piceance Basin, Colorado, 1974, Mountain Geologist, 1967-68, 71-85, editor, 1968-70; co-editor, compiler Treatise of Petroleum Geology, 1984—; contbr. papers on geology to profl. publs. Served to capt. inf. AUS, 1957. Recipient Haworth Disting. Alumni award dept. geology U. Kans., 1977, Disting. Alumni award dept. geology U. Iowa, 1992. Fellow Geol. Soc. Am.; mem. Am. Assn. Petroleum Geologists (del. 1972-75, 79-82, disting. lectr. 1976-77, pres. Rocky Mountain sect. 1979-80, treas. 1982-84, adv. coun. 1985-88, chmn. astrogeology com. 1984-88, nat. pres. 1988-89, found. trustee 1979—, hon. mem. 1993—, Levorsen award 1980, Disting. Svc. award 1985, founder astrogeology com. 1984, mem. 1984—, mem. resource evaluation com. 1992—), Rocky Mountain Assn. Geologists (sec. 1970, 1st v.p. 1974, pres. 1977, best paper award 1975, Explorer of Yr. award 1980, Disting. Svc. award 1981, hon. mem. 1983—), Soc. Econ. Paleontologists and Mineralogists, Am. Inst. Profl. Geologists, Soc. Ind. Profl. Earth Scientists, Soc. Exploration Geophysicists, Soc. Petroleum Engrs., Nat. Acad. Scis. (bd. earth scis. and resources, U.S. nat. com. geology, com. earth resources, com. adv. to U.S. Geol. Survey 1989-92), Colo. Sci. Soc., Sigma Xi, Sigma Gamma Epsilon. Republican. Mem. Christian Ch. Office: 1625 Broadway Ste 370 Denver CO 80202-4746

FOTSCH, DAN ROBERT, elementary education educator; b. St. Louis, May 17, 1947; s. Robert Jarrel and Margaret Louise (Zimmermann) F.; m. Jacquelyn Sue Rotter, June 12, 1971; children: Kyla Michelle, Jeffrey Scott, Michael David. BS in Edn. cum laude, U. Mo., 1970; MS in Edn., Colo. State U., 1973. Cert. K-12 phys. edn. and health tchr. Mo., Colo. Tchr. phys. edn., coach North Callaway Schs., Auxvasse, Mo., 1970-71; grad. teaching asst., asst. track coach Colo. State U., Ft. Collins, 1971-73; tchr. elem. phys. edn., coach Poudre R-1 Sch. Dist., Ft. Collins, 1973—; tchr. on spl. assignment Elem. Phys. Edn. Resource, 1990; adminstrv. asst. Moore Sch., Ft. Collins, 1990—, acting prin., 1997, tchr. on spl. assignment dist. phys. edn. coord., 1998, k-12 coord. dist. phys. edn., 1998—. Co-dir. Colo. State U. Handicapped Clinic, Ft. Collins, 1973-93; dir. Moore Elem. Lab. Sch., Ft. Collins, 1979—; dir. Colo. State U. Super Day Camp, 1979—; presenter for conf. in field. Contbr. articles to profl. jours. State dir. Jump Rope for Heart Project, Denver, 1981. Recipient Scott Key Acad. award, Sigma Phi Epsilon, 1969, Honor Alumni award, Coll. of Profl. Studies of Colo. State U., 1983; grantee Colo. Heart Assn., 1985; recipient Coaching Excellence award Ft. Collins Soccer Club, 1991-92. Mem. NEA, AAHPERD (exec. bd. mem. coun. on phys. edn. for children 1983-86, reviewer Jour. Phys. Edn., Recreation and Dance 1984—, fitness chairperson, conv. planner 1986), ASCD, Poudre Edn. Assn., Colo. Edn. Assn., Colo. Assn. Health, Phys. Edn., Recreation and Dance (pres. 1979-82, Tchr. award 1977, Honor award 1985), Internat. Platform Assn., Ctrl. Dist. Alliance for Health, Phys. Edn., Recreation and Dance (elem. divsn. chairperson for phys. edn. 1989—), Phi Delta Kappa (found. rep. 1985), Phi Epsilon Kappa (v.p. 1969, pres. 1970). Republican. Avocations: marathons, triathlons, racketball, volleyball, swimming (Colo. State Swimming Championship Village Green Team, 1987, 89). Home: 2807 Blackstone Dr Fort Collins CO 80525-6190 Office: Moore Elem Sch 1905 Orchard Pl Fort Collins CO 80521-3210

FOUSTE, DONNA H. association executive; b. N.Y.C., Feb. 26, 1944; d. Donald Lynn and Edna (Parker) Ham; m. James Edward Fouste, Nov. 2, 1980. AA in Mgmt. and Supervision, Coastline Community Coll., Fountain Valley, Calif., 1980; BS in Organizational Behavior, U. San Francisco, 1985, MS in Orgnl. Devel., 1988. Officer mgr., bus. mgr. Fulwider, Patton, Rieber, Lee & Utecht, L.A., 1971-79, 89-91; patent adminstrn. specialist Discovision Assocs., Costa Mesa, Calif., 1979-82; law office mgr. City of Anaheim, 1982-89; exec. dir. Orange County Bar Assn., Santa Ana, 1992—. Instr. Rancho Santiago Coll., Santa Ana, with legal asst. program, 1987—; instr. U. Calif., Irvine, 1997; mem. adv. bd. Pub. Svc. Inst., Santa Ana, 1986-88. Patron Friends of South Coase Repertory, Costa Mesa, Calif., 1985; mem. applause chpt. Performing Arts Ctr., Costa Mesa, 1986-87. Recipient Silver medal in Chess Corp. Challenge, 1988, Tribute to Women award YWCA, 1997, Spirit of Volunteerism award Vol. Ctr. of Greater Orange County, 1996. Mem. Assn. Legal Adminstrs., Nat. Assn. Bar Execs. (membership chair 1999), State Bar Calif. (minimum continuing legal edn. com.), Am. Soc. Assn. Execs., So. Calif. Soc. Assn. Execs., Execs. of Calif. Law Assns. Avocations: gourmet cooking, skiing, gardening. Office: Orange County Bar Assn PO Box 17777 Irvine CA 92623-7777

FOUTZ, CLAUDIA, state agency administrator; BS in Econs., U. Calif., Davis. Audit divsn. chief Calif. State Employment Devel. Dept.; chief dep. dir. Calif. Dept. Consumer Affairs; exec. officer Calif. State Bd. Pharmacy; exec. dir. Calif. Optometric Assn., Ariz. Bd. Med. Examiners, Phoenix. Pres.-elect Nat. Coun. Licensure, Enforcement and Regulation. Mem. Calif. Soc. Assn. Execs. (mem. strategic planning com.). Office: Ariz Bd Med Examiners 1651 E Morten Ave Ste 210 Phoenix AZ 85020-4613

FOWLER, REGGIE, retail executive; CEO, pres. Spiral Inc., Chandler, Ariz. Office: Spiral Inc 7100 W Erie St Chandler AZ 85226-2424

FOWLER, THOMAS KENNETH, physicist; b. Thomaston, Ga., Mar. 27, 1931; s. Albert Grady and Susie (Glynn) F.; m. Carol Ellen Winter, Aug. 18, 1956; children: Kenneth, John, Ellen. B.S. in Engring, Vanderbilt U., 1953, M.S. in Physics, 1955; Ph.D. in Physics, U. Wis., 1957. Staff physicist Oak Ridge Nat. Lab., 1957-65, group leader plasma theory, 1961-65; staff physicist Gen. Atomic Co., San Diego, 1965-67, head plasma physics divsn., 1967; group leader plasma theory Lawrence Livermore Lab., Livermore, Calif., 1967-69, div. leader, 1969-70, assoc. dir. magnetic fusion, 1970-87; prof., chmn. dept. nuclear engring. U. Calif., Berkeley, 1988-94, prof. emeritus, 1995—. Calif. Coun. Sci. Tech. fellow, 1997—. Fellow Am. Phys. Soc. (chmn. plasma physics div. 1970); mem. Nat. Acad. Scis., Sigma Xi, Sigma Nu. Home: 221 Grover Ln Walnut Creek CA 94596-6310 Office: U Calif 4167 Etcheverry Hall Berkeley CA 94720-1731

FOWLER, VINCENT R. dermatologist; b. South Bend, Ind., Dec. 15, 1944; s. Vincent R. and Miriam Frances (Alward) F.; m. Madeline M. Morales, Apr. 26, 1975; children: Debra, Michael, Peter. BA in Pscyhology, Calif. State U., L.A., 1969; MD, U. Autonoma Guadalajara, Mex., 1973. Diplomate Am. Bd. Dermatology; lic. Calif. Intern Long Beach (Calif.) Med. Ctr., 1974-75; resident in internal medicine SUNY Med. Ctr., Stonybrook, N.Y., 1975-78; resident in dermatology Letterman Army Med. Ctr., Presido San Francisco, Calif., 1978-80; chief medicine/dermatology Reynolds Army Hosp., Fort Sill, Okla., 1980-82; chief dermatology W. L.A. Kaiser Med. Ctr., 1982—. Asst. clin. prof. UCLA Sch. Medicine, 1984—. Major Army Med. Corps., 1978-82. Fellow Am. Acad. Dermatology; mem. L.A. Met. Dermatol. Soc. Avocations: surfing, skiing, tennis. Office: Kaiser W LA Med Ctr 5971 Venice Blvd Los Angeles CA 90034-1713

FOWLER, WILLIAM MAYO, JR. rehabilitation medicine physician; b. Bklyn., June 16, 1926; BS, Springfield Coll., 1948, MEd, 1949; MD, U. So. Calif., L.A., 1957. Diplomate Am. Bd. Phys. Medicine and Rehab. Intern UCLA, 1958, resident in pediatrics, 1959, resident in phys. medicine, rehab., 1963; chmn. dept. phys. medicine, rehab. U. Calif., Davis, 1968-82, mem. faculty dept. phys. medicine, rehab., 1972-91, prof. emeritus, 1991—. Fellow Am. Acad. Phys. Medicine and Rehab. (pres. 1981, Krusen award 1994), Am. Coll. Sports Medicine; mem. Assn. Acad. Physiatrists. Office: U Calif Davis Dept Phys Med Rehab One Shields Ave Davis CA 95616

FOX, KENNETH L. retired newspaper editor, writer; b. Kansas City, Mo., Mar. 18, 1917; s. Henry Hudson and Margaret Patience (Kiely) F.; m. Mary Harbord Manville, June 20, 1975. A.B., Washington U., St. Louis, 1938; student, U. Kansas City, 1939-40. With Kansas City Star, 1938-78, asso. editor, 1966-78. News analyst Sta. WDAF, Kansas City, 1948-53; war corr., Vietnam and Laos, 1964, corr., No. Ireland, 1973 Served to col. AUS, 1940-46, vet. Normandy Invasion, Battle of the Bulge, Liberation of Paris, 1944. Decorated Bronze Star, Commendation medals with Oak Leaf Cluster; recipient 1st place editl. div. nat. aviation writing contest, 1957, 58, 59, 60, 67, Disting. Alumnus award Washington U. (St. Louis), 1998; named Aviation Man of Yr. for Kansas City, 1959; Kenneth L. Fox Day proclaimed by Gov. of Ariz., 1998. Mem. Am. Legion, 40 and 8, Res. Officers Assn., Ret. Officers Assn., Mil. Order World Wars, Phi Beta Kappa, Beta Theta Pi, Pi Sigma Alpha, Sigma Delta Chi. Clubs: Kansas City Press; Ariz. Home: 9796 E Ironwood Dr Scottsdale AZ 85258-4728

FOX, MICHAEL J. museum director; Pres., CEO Mus. of No. Ariz., Flagstaff. Office: Mus of No Ariz 3101 N Fort Valley Rd Flagstaff AZ 86001-8348

FOX, NED, professional sports team owner; BS in Accounting, U. So. Calif., 1969, MBA, 1971. With real estate Arthur Andersen & Co., 1971-78; sr. ptnr. Maguire Thomas Ptnrs., 1978-93. Founder, co-mng. dir. CommonWealth Ptnrs., L.A., 1993—; adv. com. U. So. Calif. Grad. Sch. Bus.; adv. coun. U. So. Calif. Sch. Arts & Architecture. Exec. com., bd. dirs. L.A. Convention & Vis. Bur., 1993—; chmn. real estate/constrn. com. L.A. County Music Ctr Unified Fund Campaign, 1992-93; urban devel./mixed-use coun. Urban Land Inst.; vol. Boy Scouts Am. Mem. Am. Inst. Cert. CPAs. Office: Sacramento Kings One Sports Pkwy Sacramento CA 95834 also: Commonwealth Ptnrs 633 W 5th St Ste 5610 Los Angeles CA 90071-3502

FOX, ROBERT AUGUST, food company executive; b. Norristown, Pa., Apr. 24, 1937; s. August Emil and Elizabeth Martha (Deimling) F.; m. Linda Lee Carnesale, Sept. 19, 1964; children: Lee Elizabeth, Christina Carolyn. B.A. with high honors, Colgate U., 1959; M.B.A. cum laude, Harvard U., 1964. Unit sales mgr. Procter & Gamble Co., 1959-62; gen. sales mgr. T.J. Lipton Co., 1964-69; v.p. mktg. Can. Dry Corp., 1969-72; pres., chief exec. officer, dir. Can. Dry Internat., 1972-75; exec. v.p., dir. Hunt-Wesson Foods, Inc., 1975-78; pres., chief exec. officer, dir. R.J. Reynolds Tobacco Internat. S.A., 1978-80; chmn., chief exec. officer, dir. Del Monte Corp., San Francisco, 1980-85; vice chmn. Nabisco Brands, Inc., East Hanover, N.J., 1986-87; pres., chief oper. officer Continental Can Co., Norwalk, Conn., 1988-90; chmn., chief exec. officer Clarke Hooper Am., Irvine, Calif., 1990-92, also bd. dirs.; pres. Revlon Internat., N.Y.C., 1992; pres., CEO Foster Farms, Livingston, Calif., 1993—. Bd. dirs. New Perspective Fund, Growth Fund Am., Income Fund Am., Am. Balanced Fund, New World Fund, Crompton Corp., Fundamental Investors; trustee Euro-Pacific Growth Fund. Trustee Colgate U. Mem. San Francisco C. of C. (bd. dir., pres. 1984), Pacific Union Club, The Olympic Club. Office: Foster Farms PO Box 457 PO Box 457 Livingston CA 95334-0457

FOX, STUART IRA, physiologist; b. Bklyn., June 21, 1945; s. Sam and Bess F.; m. Ellen Diane Berley; 1 child, Laura Elizabeth. BA, UCLA, 1967; MA, Calif. State U., L.A., 1967; postgrad., U. Calif., Santa Barbara, 1969; PhD, U. So. Calif., 1978. Rsch. assoc. Children's Hosp., L.A., 1972; prof. physiology L.A. City Coll., 1972-85, Calif. State U., Northridge, 1979-84, Pierce Coll., 1986—. Cons. McGraw-Hill, 1976—. Author: Computer-Assisted Instruction in Human Physiology, 1979, Laboratory Guide to Human Physiology, 2d edit., 1980, 9th edit., 2002, Textbook of Human Physiology, 1986, 7th edit., 2002, Human Anatomy and Physiology, 1986, 5th edit., 1999, Perspectives on Human Biology, 1991, Laboratory Manual for Anatomy and Physiology, 1986, 5th edit., 1999; contbg. author: Biology, 5th edit., 1999, Synopsis of Anatomy and Physiology, 1997. Mem. AAAS, Am. Physiol. Soc., Am. Anatomy & Physiology Soc., Sigma Xi. Home: 5556 Forest Cove Ln Agoura Hills CA 91301-4047 Office: Pierce Coll 6201 Winnetka Ave Woodland Hills CA 91371-0001

FOXLEY, CECELIA HARRISON, commissioner; BA in English, Utah State U., 1964; MA in English, U. Utah, 1965, PhD in Ednl. Psychology, 1968. English tchr. Olympus H.S., Salt Lake City, 1965-66; asst. prof. edn., assoc. dir. student activities U. Minn., Mpls., 1968-71; from asst. prof. to assoc. prof., asst. dean Coll. Edn. U. Iowa, Iowa City, 1971-81; prof. psychology Utah State U., Logan, 1981-85, from asst. v.p. student svcs. to assoc. v.p. for student svcs. and acad. affairs, 1981-85; assoc. commr. for acad. affairs Utah State Bd. Regents, Salt Lake City, 1985-93, commr., 1993—. Utah rep. Am. Coun. on Edn. Office Women in Higher Edn., 1982-92; mem. nat. adv. coun. on nurse tng. U.S. Dept. Health and Human Svcs., 1987-91; mem. nat. adv. bd. S.W. Regional Ctr. for Drug Free Schs., 1988-93; mem. edn. bd. Utah Alliance for Edn. and Humanities, 1989-93; mem. prevention subcom. Utah Substance Abuse Coordinating Coun., 1991-93; mem. exec. bd. U.S. West Comm., 1995—; mem. adv. bd. Salt Lake Buzz, 1995—; active Consortium for Women in Higher Edn. Bd., 1981-85, Utah State Libr. Bd., 1990-93, Compact for Faculty Diversity, 1994—; presenter in field; cons. in field. Author: Recruiting Women and Minority Faculty, 1972, Locating, Recruiting, and Employing Women, 1976, Non-Sexist Counseling: Helping Women and Men Redefine Their Roles, 1979; co-author: The Human Relations Experience, 1982; editor: Applying Management Techniques, 1980; co-editor: Multicultural Nonsexist Education, 1979; author chpts. to books; contbr. articles to profl. jours. Grantee Utah State Dept. Social Svcs., 1984-85, 85-86; recipient Pres. Leadership award Assn. Utah Women Edn. Adminstrs., 1990, Disting. Alumni award Utah State U., 1991. Mem. APA, Am. Assn. Counseling and Devel., Am. Coll. Pers. Assn., Nat. Forum Sys. Chief Acad. Officers, State Higher Edn. Exec. Officers (mem. exec. com. 1994—), Western Interstate Cooperative Higher Edn. (mem. exec. com. 1994—). Office: Utah State Bd Regents 355 W North Temple Salt Lake City UT 84180-1114

FOXLEY, WILLIAM COLEMAN, cattleman; b. St. Paul, Jan. 7, 1935; s. William Joseph and Eileen (Conroy) F. BA, U. Notre Dame, 1957. Pres., chmn. bd. Foxley Cattle Co., Omaha, 1960—. Chmn. bd. Mus. Western Art, Denver. Served with USMCR, 1957-60. Republican. Roman Catholic. Office: Foxley Cattle Co 10795 Tiarra Santa Blvd San Diego CA 92124

FOY, ROBERT W(ILLARD), water service company executive; b. San Francisco, Sept. 18, 1936; m. Barbara B. Barron, Oct. 21, 1967; children: Matthew S., Peter A. BS with honors in Bus. and Indsl. Mgmt., San Jose State U., 1959. Mgmt. trainee, purchasing agt. Continental Group Inc. (formerly Continental Can Co.), Stockton, Calif., 1962-64; with Pacific Storage Co., Stockton, 1964-96, pres., CEO, 1977-96; chmn. bd. dirs. Calif. Water Svc. Co., San Jose, 1996—. Reid Travel Assocs.; mem. bd. agts. com. Bekins Van Line Co. Mem. selection com. Military Acad. 14th Congl. Dist.; vol. adv. com. State Calif. Atty. Gen. Office, San Joaquin County Grand Jury; chmn. presdl. task force U. Pacific; bd. dirs. Boy's Club, San Joaquin County (Calif.) Better Bus. Bur., San Joaquin County Mental Health Assn.; chmn. Stockton parole adv. com. State Calif.; pres. United Way, St. John's Episcopal Ch., Stockton, San Joaquin Employer's Coun.; chmn. bd. commrs. Stockton Port Dist.; chmn. bd. trustees St. Joseph's Med. Ctr.; co-chmn. Make Brighter Tomorrows campaign A Safe Place for Battered Women; chmn. Congressman Norman D. Shumway Campaign, 1978-90; hon. chmn. San Joaquin/Calaveras unit Am. Cancer Soc.; active San Jose State U. Spartan Found. Capt. (infantry) USAR. Recipient Conservative of Yr. award Norman D. Shumway-Lincoln Club Cen. Calif., 1987, Disting. Alumnus award Sch. Bus. San Jose State U., 1981. Mem. Cen. Valley Purchasing Agts. Assn. (chmn.), Nat. Def. Transp. Assn., Am. Soc. Pub. Adminstrn. (mem. com. on rels. bus., industry), Calif. Moving and Storage Assn. (pres., sec.-treas., v.p.), Nat. Moving and Storage Assn. (chmn. bd. dirs.), Greater Stockton C. of C. (bd. dirs., pres.), West Lane Tennis Club, Yosemite Club (pres.), Pioneer Mus. and Haggin Gallery Mus. Club (pres.), San Jose State U. Alumni Assn., San Jose State U. Quarterback Club. Republican. Avocations: backpacking, reading, wine collecting, San Jose State intercollegiate athletics. Address: 933 W Monterey Ave Stockton CA 95204-3028 Office: Calif Water Svc Co 1720 N 1st St San Jose CA 95112-4598

FOY, THOMAS PAUL, lawyer, retired state legislator, retired banker; b. Silver City, N.Mex., Oct. 19, 1914; s. Thomas J. and Mary V. Foy; m. Joan Carney, Nov. 17, 1948 (dec. June 1994); children: Celia, Thomas Paul Jr. (dec.), Muffet (Mary Ann), J. Carney, James B. BS in Commerce, Notre Dame U., 1938, JD, 1939. Bar: N.Mex. 1946. Dist. atty. N.Mex. 6th Jud. Dist., Silver City, 1949-57; atty. Village of Bayard, N.Mex., 1954-68, Village of Ctrl., 1960-70; v.p., counsel, bd. dirs. Sunwest Bank, Silver City,

1946-84, chmn. bd. dirs., 1969-84, chmn. emeritus, 1984-97; state rep. Dist. 39 State of N.Mex., Grant-Hidalgo, 1971-98; chmn. jud. com. N.Mex. State Legis., Santa Fe, 1984-98; pres. Foy & Vesely and Foy, Foy & Castillo, Silver City, 1946-99, Foy Law Firm PC, 1999—. 1st lt. U.S. Army, 1941-46; prisoner of war, PTO, 1942-45. Decorated Bronze Star, Purple Heart, Asiatic-Pacific Ribbon with 3 oak leaf clusters; recipient Citizen of Yr. award Silver City-Grant County C. of C., 1965, Dedication to Advancement award Trial Lawyers Assn., 1993, N.Mex. Disting. Svc. medal, 1994. Mem. ABA, N.Mex. Bar Assn. (bar commr. 1967-85, v.p. N.Mex. bar commn. 1978-79, Disting. Svc. of Laws award 1987), Am. Judicature Soc., Bataan Vets. Orgn. (state comdr. 1965-66, 98-99), KC (Grand Knight 1936-37), VFW (state comdr. 1959-60), Lions (dist. gov. 1956-57), Elks. Democrat. Roman Catholic. Avocations: football, baseball, travel, conventions. Office: The Foy Law Firm PC 210 W Broadway St Silver City NM 88061-5353

FRACKMAN, RUSSELL JAY, lawyer; b. N.Y.C., July 3, 1946; s. Sam and Doris (Wasserberg) F.; m. Myrna D. Morganstern, Aug. 3, 1980; children: Steven Howard, Abigail Zoe. BA in History, Northwestern U., 1967; JD cum laude, Columbia U., 1970. Bar: Calif. 1971, U.S. Dist. Ct. (ctrl., ea. and no. dists.) Calif., U.S. Ct. Appeals (2d and 9th cirs.), U.S. Supreme Ct. Assoc. Mitchell, Silberberg & Knupp, L.A., 1970-76, ptnr., 1976—, chmn. litigation dept., 1994-96. Lectr. on intellectual property and entertainment law various instns. including Practising Law Inst., L.A. Copyright Soc., Beverly Hills Bar Assn., U. So. Calif. Sch. Law, Am. Film Mktg. Assn., Calif. Copyright Conf. Bd. editors Columbia Law Rev., 1969-70; contbr. articles and revs. to legal jours. Co-chmn. internat. leadership devel. forum CARE, 1990; bd. trustees CARE Found., 1991—, Twitty, Milsap, Sterban Found., 1988-92. Mem. ABA (chmn. copyright subcom. litigation sect. 1990-93, lectr. various confs.), Am. Film Mktg. Assn. (mem. arbitration tribunal). Democrat. Jewish. Office: Mitchell Silberberg & Knupp 11377 W Olympic Blvd Los Angeles CA 90064-1625

FRAGNER, MATTHEW CHARLES, lawyer; b. N.Y.C., Jan. 12, 1954; s. Berwyn N. and Marcia R. (Salkind) F.; m. Mariann Donahue, June 19, 1983; children: Rachel Jade, Jaron Roark, Bailyn Natalie, Talia Colby. BA, Yale U., 1975; JD, U. Calif., Berkeley, 1978. Bar: Calif. 1978, U.S. Tax Ct. 1979, U.S. Ct. Appeals (9th crct.) 1979. Atty. Thomas Shafran & Wasser, L.A., 1978-83; ptnr. Shafran & Fragner, L.A., 1984-87, Lane & Edson, L.A., 1987-88, Mayer Brown & Platt, L.A., 1989-92, Sonnenschein Nath & Rosenthal, L.A., 1992-2000; pres. Somnolence, Inc., L.A., 1989—; gen. cousel, dir. investments Citadel Capital Mgmt. Corp., 2000—; founder, chmn. Tools to Talent Non Profit Corp., 2001—. Lectr. U. So. Calif., 1994-99; founder, chmn. Tools to Talent Nonprofit Corp. Active Berkeley (Calif.) Law Found., 1978-83. Mem. Los Angeles County Bar Assn. (chair comml. devel. and leasing subsect.). Office: Citadel Capital Mgmt Corp 333 S Grand Ave Ste 3030 Los Angeles CA 90071 E-mail: mfragner@pacbell.net

FRAKES, RODNEY VANCE, plant geneticist, educator; b. Ontario, Oreg., July 20, 1930; s. Wylic and Pearl (Richardson) F.; m. Ruby L. Morey, Nov. 27, 1952; children: Laura Ann, Cody Joe. BS, Oreg. State U., 1956, MS, 1957; PhD, Purdue U., 1960. Instr. dept. agronomy Purdue U., West Lafayette, Ind., 1959-60; asst. prof. dept. crop sci. Oreg. State U., Corvallis, 1960-64, assoc. prof., 1964-69, prof., 1969—, assoc. dean research, 1981-88, emeritus dean of rsch., prof. emeritus crop sci., 1989—. Author numerous papers and abstracts; contbr. to books in field Served with USCG, 1950-53 Named Man of Yr., Pacific Seedsmen's Assn., 1972; recipient Elizabeth P. Ritchie Disting. Prof. award Oreg. State U., 1980. Fellow Am. Soc. Agronomy, Crop Sci. Soc. Am.; mem. AAAS, Soc. Research Adminstrs., Nat. Council Univ. Research Adminstrs., Western Soc. Crop Sci. (pres. 1978), Model A Ford Club of Am., Model T Ford Club of Am., Rotary. Avocations: antique autos, Am. history, amateur radio. Home: 2625 NW Linnan Cir Corvallis OR 97330 1221 Office: Oreg State U Rsch Office Corvallis OR 97331

FRAKNOI, ANDREW, astronomy educator, astronomical society executive; b. Budapest, Hungary, Aug. 24, 1948; came to U.S., 1959; naturalized; s. Emery I. and Katherine H. (Schmidt) F.; m. Lola Goldstein, Aug. 16, 1992; 1 child, Alexander. B.A. in Astronomy, Harvard U., 1970; M.A. in Astrophysics, U. Calif.-Berkeley, 1972. Instr. astronomy and physics Cañada Coll., Redwood City, Calif., 1972-78; exec. dir. Astron. Soc. of Pacific, San Francisco, 1978-92; chmn. dept. astronomy Foothill Coll., Los Altos, Calif., 1992—. Part-time prof. San Francisco State U., 1980-92; fellow Com. for Sci. Investigation of Claims of Paranormal, 1984—; bd. dirs. Search for Extra Terrestrial Intelligence Inst., Mountain View, Calif., 1984—; host radio program Exploring the Universe Sta. KGO-FM, San Francisco, 1983-84. Author: Resource Book for the Teaching of Astronomy, 1978, (with others) Effective Astronomy Teaching and Student Reasoning Ability, 1978, Universe in the Classroom, 1985, (with T. Robertson) Instructor's Guide to the Universe, 1991, (with others) Exploration of the Universe, 1995, (with others) Voyages Through the Universe, 1997, (with others) Voyages to the Planets, 2000; editor: The Planets, 1985, Interdisciplinary Approaches to Astronomy, 1985, The Universe, 1987, The Universe at Your Fingertips Resource Notebook, 1995, Cosmos in the Classroom, 2000 ; editor Mercury Mag., 1978-92, The Universe in the Classroom Newsletter, 1985-92; assoc. editor: The Planetarian, 1986-88; columnist monthly column on astronomy San Francisco Examiner, 1986-87 and others. Bd. dirs. Bay Area Skeptics, San Francisco, 1982-91. Recipient award of merit Astron. Assn. No. Calif., 1980, award Astron. League, 1993, Klumpke-Roberts award, 1994, Annenberg Found. prize in astronomy edn., 1994; Asteroid 4859 named Asteroid Fraknoi, 1992. Mem. AAAS (astronomy sect. com. 1988-92), Am. Astron. Soc. (astronomy edn. adv. bd. 1988—), Astron. Soc. Pacific, Am. Assn. Physics Tchrs., Nat. Assn. Sci. Writers, No. Calif. Sci. Writers Assn. (program chmn. 1983-85). Avocations: music, astronomy, science, literature. Office: Foothill Coll Dept Astronomy 12345 El Monte Rd Los Altos CA 94022-4504 E-mail: fraknoi@fhda.edu

FRAME, LARRY A. electronics executive; BSEE, U. Wyo.; MBA, Santa Clara U. Mgr. test equipment design Lockheed Missiles and Space Co.; with Litton Industries, Inc., Woodland Hills, Calif., 1964-67, v.p. Salt Lake City, 1967-87, v.p. program mgmt. Woodland Hills, Calif., 1987-90, corp. v.p., 1990-94, sr. v.p., group exec. navigation, guidance & control sys., 1994—. Office: Litton Industries Inc 21240 Burbank Blvd Woodland Hills CA 91367-6675

FRAME, TED RONALD, lawyer; b. Milw., June 27, 1929; s. Morris and Jean (Lee) F.; m. Lois Elaine Pilgaim, Aug. 15, 1954; children: Kent, Lori, Nancy, Owen. Student, UCLA, 1946-49; AB, Stanford U., 1950; LLB, 1952. Bar: Calif. 1953. Gen. agri-bus. practice, Coalinga, Calif., 1953—; sr. pntr. Frame & Matsumoto and predecessor , Coalinga, 1965—. Trustee Baker Mus.; dir. West Hills Coll. Found. Mem. ABA, Calif. Bar Assn., Fresno County Bar Assn., Kings Co. Bar Assn., Am. Agrl. Law Assn., Coalinga C. of C. (past pres.), Masons, Shriners, Elks. Avocations: bicycling, hiking. Home: 1222 Nevada St Coalinga CA 93210-1239 Office: 201 Washington St Coalinga CA 93210-0895 E-mail: lawriam@lightspeed.net

FRANCHINI, GENE EDWARD, state supreme court justice; b. Albuquerque, May 19, 1935; s. Mario and Lena (Vaio) F.; m. Glynn Hatchell, Mar. 22, 1969; children: Pamela, Lori (dec.), Gina, Joseph James, Nancy. BBA, Loyola U., 1955; degree in adminstrn., U. N.Mex., 1957; JD, Georgetown U., 1960; LLM, U. Va., 1995. Bar: N.Mex. 1960, U.S. Dist. Ct. N.Mex. 1961, U.S. Ct. Appeals (10th cir.) 1970, U.S. Supreme Ct. 1973. Ptnr. Matteucci, Gutierrez & Franchini, Albuquerque, 1960-70, Matteucci, Franchini & Calkins, Albuquerque, 1970-75; judge State of N.Mex. 2d Jud. Dist., Albuquerque, 1975-81; atty.-at-large Franchini, Wagner, Oliver, Franchini & Curtis, Albuquerque, 1982-90; chief justice N.Mex. Supreme Ct., Santa Fe, 1990-99, justice, 1999—. V.p. bd. dirs. Conf. Chief Justices, 1997-98. Chmn. Albuquerque Pers. Bd., 1972, Albuquerque Labor Rels. Bd., 1972, Albuquerque Interim Bd. Ethics, 1972. Capt. USAF, 1960-66. Recipient Highest award Albuquerque Human Rights Bd., 1999. Mem. Am. Bd. Trial Advocates, N.Mex. Trial Lawyers (pres. 1967-68), N.Mex. Bar Assn. (bd. dirs. 1976-78), Albuquerque Bar Assn. (bd. dirs. 1976-78, Outstanding Judge award 1997). Democrat. Roman Catholic. Avocations: fishing, hunting, golf, mushroom hunting. Home: 4901 Laurene Ct NW Albuquerque NM 87120-1026 Office: NMex Supreme Ct PO Box 848 Santa Fe NM 87504-0848

FRANCIS, CHARLES K. medical educator; b. Newark, May 24, 1939; BA, Dartmouth Coll., 1961; MD, Jefferson Med. Coll., 1965. Med. intern Phila. Gen. Hosp., 1965-66; med. resident Boston City Hosp., Tufts U., 1969-70; clin. fellow cardiology Tufts Circulation Lab., 1970-71; clin. and rsch. fellow cardiology Mass. Gen. Hosp., 1971-72, sr. med. resident, 1972-73; chief cardiac catheterization lab. divsn. cardiology Martin Luther King Jr. Gen. Hosp., L.A., 1973-74, chief cardiology divsn., 1974-77; dir. cardiology divsn. Mt. Sinai Hosp., Hartford, Conn., 1977-80; assoc. dir. hypertension svc., assoc. prof. medicine, dir. cardiac catheterization lab. Yale Med. Sch., Hartford, 1980-87; dir. dept. medicine Harlem Hosp. Ctr., N.Y.C., 1987-98; prof. clin. medicine Columbia U. Coll. Physicians and Surgeons, 1987-98; pres. Charles R. Drew U. Med. and Sci., 1998—. Clin. instr. medicine Sch. Medicine, Tufts U., 1970-71; tchg. fellow Harvard Med. Sch., 1971-72, clin. fellow, 1972-73; asst. prof. medicine Charles R. Drew Postgrad. Med. Sch. & Sch. Medicine, U. So. Calif., 1973-77; asst. prof. medicine, dir. Burgdorf Hypertension Clin., Med. Sch., U. Conn., 1977-80; mem. cardiac adv. comty. Nat. Heart, Lung & Blood Inst., NIH, 1977-79; asst. prof. medicine Sch. Medicine, Yale U., 1980-81, assoc. prof., 1981-87. Fellow ACP, Am. Coll. Cardiology; mem. Inst. Medicine-NAS, Am. Fedn. Clin. Rsch., Am. Heart Assn., Assn. Black Cardiologists (chmn. bd. 1994—). Address: Charles Drew U of Med & Sci 1621 E 120th St Los Angeles CA 90059-3025

FRANCIS, CURT, computer company executive; B in Engring. and Applied Sci., Yale U.; MSEE, MIT; MBA, Harvard U. Cons. Boston Consulting Group, 1976-80; with Advanced Micro Devices, 1980-93, v.p. corp. planning and devel., 1995-98, v.p. corp. operational planning; v.p. corp. devel. Sun Microsys., 1993-95, Quantum Corp., Milpitas, Calif. Office: Quantum Corp 500 Mccarthy Blvd Milpitas CA 95035-7909

FRANCIS, MERRILL RICHARD, lawyer; b. Iowa City; children: Kerry L., David M., Robin A. B.A. magna cum laude, Pomona Coll., 1954; J.D., Stanford U., 1959. Bar: Calif. 1960, Supreme Ct. 1970. Ptnr. Sheppard, Mullin, Richter & Hampton, L.A., 1959-00, of counsel, 2001—. Mem. Fellows of Contemporary Art, 1980—. Served to lt. (j.g.) U.S. Navy, 1954-56. Fellow Am. Bar Found., Am. Coll. Bankruptcy (chmn. 9th cir. admissions coun. 1992-95, 2001—, bd. dirs. 1995—, chair bd. regents 1995-01); mem. ABA (bus. law sect., chmn. secured creditors com. 1981-85, chmn. bus. bankruptcy com. 1986-89, chmn. Task Force on Fed. Ct. Structure 1990-93, mem. Coun. Bus. Law sect. 1991-95, chmn. ad hoc com. on brown bag programs 1994-97, sr. lawyers divsn., chmn. sr. housing and real estate practice com. 2001—, chmn. ad hoc com. bankruptcy ct. structure and insolvency process com. 2001—), State Bar of Calif. (mem. debtor/creditor and bankruptcy com. of bus. law sect. 1978-79), L.A. County Bar Assn. (mem. real property sect., exec. com. 1970-80, mem. comml. law and bankruptcy sect., sect. chmn. 1976-77), Fin. Lawyers Conf. (bd. govs. 1970—, pres. 1972-73), La Canada-Flintridge C. of C. and Cmty. Assn. (pres. 1971-72), Order of the Coif, Jonathan Club, Phi Beta Kappa. Office: Sheppard Mullin Richter & Hampton 333 S Hope St Fl 48 Los Angeles CA 90071-1406 E-mail: mfrancis@smrh.com

FRANCIS, NORM, computer software executive, accountant; BSc in computer science, U. B.C. CPA. Co-owner Basic Software Group (acquired by Computer Assocs. Internat., 1979; pres, CEO Pivotal Software Inc., North Vancouver, B.C., Can. Lectr. in field. Office: Pivotal Software Inc 300-224 W Esplanade North Vancouver BC Canada V7M3MG

FRANCIS, PHILIP L. retail executive; Grad., U. Ill., Ind. U. Corp. v.p. wholesale Roundy's, Pewaukee, Wis.; sr. leadership positions Cardinal Health, Jewel Cos.; pres., COO Shaw's Supermkts., E. Bridgewater, Mass., 1991-98; pres., CEO PETsMART, Inc., Phoenix, 1998—; chmn. Mem. Greater Phoenix Leadership. Office: PetsMart 19601 N 27th Ave Phoenix AZ 85027

FRANCIS, ROBERT, professional hockey coach; m. Deborah Francis; children: Kelley, Kristine, Ryan. Student, U. N.H. Hockey player Detroit Red Wings, 1980-86; player/asst. coach Salt Lake Golden Eagles, 1986-87, asst. coach, 1987-88, head coach, 1989-93, Calgary Flames, 1993-94, Bruins AHL affiliate in Providence; asst. coach Boston Bruins, 1997-99; head coach Phoenix Coyotes, 1999-. Office: Phoenix Coyotes Cellular One Ice Den 9375 E Bell Rd Scottsdale AZ 85260-1500

FRANCIS, TIMOTHY DUANE, chiropractor; b. Chgo., Mar. 1, 1956; s. Joseph Duane and Barbara Jane (Sigwalt) F. Student, U. Nev., 1974-80, We. Nev. C.C., 1978; BS, L.A. Coll. Chiropractic, 1982, Dr. of Chiropractic magna cum laude, 1984; postgrad., Clark County C.C., 1986—; MS in Bio/Nutrition, U. Bridgeport, 1990. Diplomate Internat. Coll. Applied Kinesiology, Am. Acad. Pain Mgmt., Am. Naturopathic Med. Bd.; cert. kinesiologist, applied kinesiology tchr.; lic. chiropractor, Calif., Nev. Instr. dept. recreation and phys. edn. U. Nev., Reno, 1976-80; from tchng. asst. to lead instr. dept. principles & practice L.A. Coll. Chiropractic, 1983-85; pvt. practice Las Vegas, 1985—. Asst. instr. Internat. Coll. Applied Kinesiology, 1990, chmn. exam review com., 1993, chmn. syllabus review com., 1994; adj. faculty The Union Inst. Coll. of Undergrad. Studies, 1993; joint study participant Nat. Olympic Tng. Ctr., Beijing, China, 1990. Mem. editl. rev. bd. Alternative Medicine Rev., 1996; contbr. articles to profl. jours. including Internat. Coll. Applied Kinesiology. Charles F. Cutts scholar, 1980. Fellow Internat. Acad. Clin. Acupuncture, British Inst. Homeopathy (homeopathy diploma 1993); mem. Am. Chiropractic Assn. (couns. on sports injuries, mutrition, roentgenology, technic, and mental health), Nev. State Chiropractic Assn., Nat. Strength and Conditioning Assn., Gonsted Clin. Studies Soc., Found. for Chiropractic Edn. and Rsch., Internat. Chiropractors Assn., Internat. Coll. Applied Kinesiology, Internat. Fedn. Practitioners Natural Therapeutics, Nat. Inst. Chiropractic Rsch., Nat. Strength and Conditioning Assn., Am. Naturopathic Med. Assn., Nat. Acad. Rsch. Biochemists, Phi Beta Kappa, Phi Kappa Phi (v.p. 1979-80, Scholar of the Yr. award, 1980), Delta Signa. Republican. Roman Catholic. Avocations: karate, weightlifting. Home: 3750 S Jones Blvd Las Vegas NV 89103-2259

FRANCISCO, IRVING, national monument administrator; b. Ft. Defiance, Ariz., July 6, 1952; Student, Yavapai Coll., Coconino Coll., No. Ariz. U. Pk. ranger U.S. Pks. Svc., 1972-93; chief ranger Navajo Nat. Monument, Tonalea, Ariz., 1993—. Office: Navajo National Monument HC 71 Box 3 Tonalea AZ 86044-9708

FRANCKE, UTA, medical geneticist, genetics researcher, educator; b. Wiesbaden, Germany, Sept. 9, 1942; came to U.S., 1969; d. Kurt and Gertrud Müller; m. Bertold Richard Francke, May 27, 1967 (div. 1982); m. Heinz Furthmayr, July 27, 1986. MD, U. Munich, Fed. Republic Germany, 1967; MS, Yale U., 1985. Diplomate Am. Bd. Pediatrics, Am. Bd. Med. Genetics (bd. dirs. 1981-84). Asst. prof. U. Calif., San Diego, 1973-78; assoc. prof. Yale U., New Haven, 1978-85, prof., 1985-88; prof. genetics Stanford (Calif.) U., 1989-00. Investigator Howard Hughes Med. Inst., Stanford, 1989—, mem. sci. rev. bd., Bethesda, Md., 1986-88; mem. mammalian genetics study sect. NIH, Bethesda, 1990-94; bd. dirs. Am. Soc. Human Genetics, Rockville, Md., 1981-84. Profl. advisor March of Dimes Birth Defects Found., White Plains, N.Y., 1990, Marfan Assn., Port Washington, N.Y., 1991. Mem. Inst. Medicine of NAS (fgn. assoc.), Human Genome Orgn., Soc. for Pediatric Rsch., Soc. for Inherited Metabolic Disorders, Am. Soc. Human Genetics (pres. 1999). Avocation: piloting. Office: Stanford U Med Sch Howard Hughes Med Inst Beckman Ctr Stanford CA 94305-5323 E-mail: francke@cmpgm.stanford.edu

FRANICH, STEVEN, automotive company executive; CEO, owner Marty Franich Auto Ctr., Watsonville, Calif. Office: Marty Franich Auto Ctr 550 Auto Center Dr Watsonville CA 95076

FRANK, ANTHONY MELCHIOR, federal official, former financial executive; b. Berlin, Germany, May 21, 1931; came to U.S., 1937, naturalized, 1943; s. Lothar and Elisabeth (Roth) F.; m. Gay Palmer, Oct. 16, 1954; children: Tracy, Randall BA, Dartmouth Coll., 1953, MBA, 1954; postgrad. in fin., U. Vienna, 1956. Asst. to pres., bond portfolio mgr. Glendale (Calif.) Fed. Savs. Assn., 1958-61; v.p., treas. Far West Fin. Corp., Los Angeles, 1962; adminstrv. v.p., v.p. savs. First Charter Fin. Corp., Beverly Hills, Calif., 1962-66; pres. State Mut. Savs. and Loan Assn., Los Angeles, 1966-68, Titan Group, Inc., N.Y.C. and Los Angeles, 1968-70, INA Properties, Inc., 1970-71, Citizens Savs. & Loan, San Francisco, 1971-73, vice chmn., chief exec. officer, 1973-74; chmn. bd., pres., chief exec. officer FN Fin. Corp., 1974-88; postmaster gen. U.S. Postal Svc., 1988-92; founding chmn. Belvedere Capital Ptnrs., San Francisco. Also pres., vice chmn., industry dir. Fed. Home Loan Bank San Francisco, 1972-77; trustee, treas. Blue Shield of Calif., from 1976-88; bd. dirs. Temple Inland, Schwab, Bedford Property Investors Inc., Crescent Real Estate Equities. Chmn., bd. dirs. Calif. Housing Fin. Agy., Sacramento, 1978-86; trustee Am. Conservatory Theater; chmn. bd. visitors Sch. Architecture and Planning UCLA, 1971-86; bd. overseers Tuck Sch.; del. Calif. Dem. Conv., 1968. Served with AUS, 1954-56 Mem. SAG, Chief Execs. Orgn., World Bus. Forum, Dartmouth Club No. Calif., Bohemian Club. Office: Belvedere Capital Ptnrs One Maritime Plz Ste 825 San Francisco CA 94111-6114

FRANK, JOHN PAUL, lawyer, writer; b. Appleton, Wis., Nov. 10, 1917; s. Julius Paul and Beatrice (Ullman) F.; m. Lorraine Weiss, May 11, 1944; children: John Peter, Gretchen, Karen, Andrew, Nancy. B.A., U. Wis., 1938, M.A., LL.B., 1940; J.S.D., Yale U., 1946; LL.D., Lawrence U., 1981; HHD, Ariz. State U., 1997. Bar: Wis. 1940, D.C. 1966, Ariz. 1954, U.S. Supreme Ct. 1954. Law clk. U.S. Supreme Ct. Justice Hugo L. Black, 1942; asst. to sec. interior, 1943; to atty. gen., 1944-45; asst. prof. law Ind. U., 1946-49; asso. prof. law Yale, 1949-54; vis. lectr. law U. Wash., 1966, U. Ariz., 1967, Ariz. State U., 1969, 72; with firm Covington & Burling, Washington, 1947, Arnold & Porter, Washington, 1948, 53; mem. firm Lewis & Roca, Phoenix, 1954—. Mem. adv. com. civil procedure Jud. Conf. U.S., 1960-70; chmn. U.S. Circuit Judge Nominating Commn.-9th Circuit Panel, South, 1977; mem. exec. com. Adv. Com. on Appellate Justice; mem. Ariz. Commn. Appellate Ct. Appointments, 1974-85; chmn. sr. adv. bd. 9th Cir. Ct. Appeals. Author: Mr. Justice Black, 1949, Cases on Constitutional Law, 1950, Cases on the Constitution, 1951, My Son's Story, 1952, Marble Palace, 1958, Lincoln as a Lawyer, 1961, Justice Daniel Dissenting, 1964, The Warren Court, 1964, American Law: The Case for Radical Reform, 1969, Clement Haynsworth, The Senate and the Supreme Court, 1991; also articles. Dem. precinct committeeman, 1956-86; counsel Ariz. Dem. Com., 1962-67, 79-99. Recipient Lewis F. Powell, Jr. award, Am. Inns of Ct. Found., 1997. Fellow Am. Bar Found.; mem. ABA, Maricopa County Bar Assn., Am. Law Inst. (coun.), Ariz. Club. Office: Lewis and Roca 40 N Central Ave Ste 1900 Phoenix AZ 85004-4429 E-mail: jfrank@lrlaw.com

FRANKE, WILLIAM AUGUSTUS, corporate executive; b. Bryan, Tex., Apr. 15, 1937; s. Louis John and Frances (Hanna) F.; m. Carolyn Diane Franke; children: Catherine Anne, Paige Estelle, Brian Hanna, David Parker, Rebecca. BA, Stanford U., 1959, LLB, 1961. Bar: Wash. 1961. With MacGillivray, Jones, Clark & Schiffner, Spokane, 1962-69; ptnr. S.W. Forest Industries, Phoenix, 1970-86; CEO, S.W. Forest Industries (merged with Stone Container Corp.), Phoenix, 1978, chmn. bd. dirs., 1986—; pres., owner Franke & Co., Inc., Phoenix, 1987—; chmn., CEO Am. West Airlines, Inc., Phoenix, 1994—, Am. West Holdings, Corp., Phoenix, 1995—. Chmn. bd., CEO America West Airlines Inc, Phoenix, 1994—. Served to capt. U.S. Army, 1961-62. Mem. ABA, Wash. Bar Assn., Chief Execs. Orgn. Episcopalian. Clubs: Paradise Valley Country, Desert Mountain Country. Home: 7701 N Saguaro Dr Paradise Valley AZ 85253-3043 Office: America West Holdings Corp 2525 E Camelback Rd Ste 800 Phoenix AZ 85016-4230

FRANKISH, BRIAN EDWARD, film producer, director; b. Columbus, Ohio, July 28, 1943; s. John (Jack) Fletcher Frankish and Barbara Aileen (Tondro) Gray; m. Tannis Rae Benedict, Oct. 13, 1985; children: Merlin L. Reed III, Michelle Lynn Reed. AA, Chaffey Coll., 1964; BA, San Francisco State U., 1967. Freelance producer, L.A.; prin. Frankish-Benedict Entertainment, L.A. Prodr. (film) Vice Squad, 1981, (TV series) Max Headroom, 1987; assoc. prodr.: (films) Elephant Parts, 1981, Strange Brew, 1982, The Boy Who Could Fly, 1985, In the Mood, 1986, Stuart Little, 1999; exec. prodr., unit prodn. mgr. (film) Field of Dreams, 1989, Flight of the Intruder, 1990, American Me, 1991, Life As A House, 2001; prodr. visual effects for film Turbulence, 1996; prodr., dir. (theatrical play) Timing is Everything, 1991; 1st asst. dir.: (TV shows) Big Shamus, 1979, Skag, 1979, Why Me?, 1983, Making Out, 1984, Berrengers, 1984, (films) Strange Brew, 1982, Uncle Joe Shannon, 1978, Savage Harvest, 1980, Dead and Buried, 1980, Spring Break, 1982, Brainstorm, 1982-83, The Last Starfighter, 1983, The New Kids, 1983, Aloha Summer, 1984, The Best of Times, 1985, Odd Jobs, 1985, The Fugitive, 1993, Demolition Man, 1993, Roswell, 1994; unit prodn. mgr. Second Serve, 1986, The Net, 1995, Stuart Little, 1999; distbr.'s rep. and completion bond rep. Made in Heaven, 1986; prodn. mgr.: The Net, 1995; other prodn. credits include: Play it Again, Sam, 1971, Everything You Always Wanted to Know About Sex..., 1972, Time to Run, 1972, Haunts, 1975, Mahogany (Montage), 1975, King Kong, 1976, The Betsy, 1977. Mem. Dirs. Guild Am., Calif. Yacht Club.

FRANKLIN, EVE, state legislator; b. N.Y., Aug. 14, 1954; m. Les Nilson. BSN, Earlham Coll.; MSN, Herbert H. Lehman Coll. Formerly nurse-educator; mem. Mont. Senate, Dist. 21, Helena, 1991—; minority whip Mont. Senate, 1997-98, mem. joint appropriation subcom. on gen. govt. and transp., mem. fish and game com., mem. fin. and claims com., mem. pub. health, welfare and safety com. Democrat. Home: 2707 Dawn Dr Great Falls MT 59404-3633

FRANKLIN, GENE FARTHING, engineering educator, consultant; b. Banner Elk, N.C., July 25, 1927; s. Burnie D. and Delia (Farthing) F.; m. Gertrude Stritch, Jan. 1952; children: David M., Carole Lea. BSEE, Ga. Inst. Tech., 1950; MSEE, MIT, 1952; DEngSc, Columbia U., 1955. Asst. prof. Columbia U., N.Y.C., 1955-57; prof. elec. engring. Stanford (Calif.) U., 1957-95, prof. emeritus, 1995—. Cons. IBM, Rochester, Minn., 1982-94. Author: Sampled-Data Control, 1958, Digital Control, 1980, 3d edit., 1997, Feedback Control, 1986, 4th edit., 2001. With USN, 1945-47. Recipient Edn. award Am. Automatic Control Coun., 1985. Fellow IEEE (life), Control Soc. of IEEE (Bode lectr. 1994). Democrat. Office: Stanford U Dept Elec Engring Stanford CA 94305

FRANKLIN, JOEL NICHOLAS, mathematician, educator; b. Chgo., Apr. 4, 1930; m. Patricia Anne; 1 dau., Sarah Jane. B.S., Stanford, 1950, Ph.D., 1953. Research asso. N.Y. U., 1953-55; asst. prof. math. U. Wash, 1955; mem. faculty Calif. Inst. Tech., 1957—, prof. applied sci., 1966-69, prof. applied math., 1969—. Author: Matrix Theory, 1968, Methods of Mathematical Economics, 1980, also articles. Mem. Am. Math. Soc., Soc. Indsl. and Applied Math., Phi Beta Kappa. Home: 1763 Alta Crest Dr Altadena CA 91001-2130 Office: Calif Inst Tech 217 50 Pasadena CA 91125-0001

FRANKLIN, JON DANIEL, writer, journalist, educator; b. Enid, Okla., Jan. 12, 1942; s. Benjamin Max and Wilma Irene (Winburn) F.; m. Nancy Sue Creevan, Dec. 12, 1959 (div. 1976, dec. 1987); children: Teresa June, Catherine Cay; m. Lynn Irene Scheidhauer, May 20, 1988. B.S. with high honors, U. Md., 1970; LHD (hon.), U. Md., Balt. County, 1981, Coll. Notre Dame, Balt., 1982. With USN, 1959-67; reporter/editor Prince Georges (Md.) Post, 1967-70; sci. and feature writer Balt. Evening Sun, 1970-85; assoc. prof. U. Md. Coll. Journalism, 1985-88, prof., 1988-89; prof., chmn. dept. journalism Oreg. State U., Corvallis, 1989-91; prof. creative writing, dir. U. Oreg., Eugene, 1991-98; sci. writer, spl. assignments editor Raleigh News and Observer, Raleigh, N.C., 1998-2001; Philip Merrill prof. journalism U. Md., College Park, 2001—. Author: Shocktrauma, 1980, Not Quite a Miracle, 1983, Guinea Pig Doctors, 1984, Writing for Story, 1986, The Molecules of the Mind, 1987. pub.: *Bylines*, WriterL. Recipient James T. Grady medal Am. Chem. Soc., 1975, Pulitzer prize for feature writing, 1979, Pulitzer prize for explanatory journalism, 1985, Carringer award Nat. Mental Health Assn., 1984, Penney-Mo. Spl. award for health reporting, 1985; named to Newspaper Hall of Fame, Md.-Del.-D.C. Press Assn. Mem. Nat. Assn. Sci. Writers (bd. dirs.), Soc Profl. Journalists, The Writers Guild.

FRANKLIN, MARC ADAM, law educator; b. Bklyn., Mar. 9, 1932; s. Louis A. and Rose (Rosenthal) F.; m. Ruth E. Korzenik, June 29, 1958 (dec. Dec. 2000); children: Jonathan, Alison. AB, Cornell U., 1953, LLB, 1956. Bar: N.Y. 1956. Assoc. Proskauer Rose Goetz & Mendelsohn, N.Y.C., 1956-57; law clk to Hon. Carroll C. Hincks, New Haven, 1957-58, to Earl Warren, U.S. Supreme Ct., Washington, 1958-59; prof. law Columbia U., 1959-62, Stanford U., Calif., 1962-76, Frederick I. Richman prof. law, 1976—. Author: Biography of a Legal Dispute, 1968, Dynamics of American Law, 1968, Cases and Materials on Tort Law and Alternatives, 1971, (with R.L. Rabin) 7th edit., 2001, Mass Media Law, 1977, (with D.A. Anderson and F.H. Cate) 6th edit., 2000, The First Amendment and the Fourth Estate, 1977, (with T.B. Carter and J.B. Wright) 8th edit., 2001, The First Amendment and the Fifth Estate, 1986, (with T.B. Carter and J.B. Wright) 5th edit., 1999. Fellow Ctr. for Advanced Study in Behavioral Scis., 1968-69; Fulbright rsch. scholar Victoria U., Wellington, N.Z., 1973 Home: 1000 Green St #704 San Francisco CA 94133 Office: Stanford U Law Sch Nathan Abbott Way Stanford CA 94305

FRANKLIN, MICHAEL HAROLD, arbitrator, lawyer, consultant; b. Los Angeles, Dec. 25, 1923; m. Betty Chernow, 1989; children from previous marriage: Barbara, John, James, Robert. A.B., UCLA, 1948; LL.B., U. So. Calif., 1951. Bar: Calif. 1951. Practiced in, Los Angeles, 1951-52; pvt. practice, 1951-52; atty. CBS, 1952-54, Paramount Pictures Corp., 1954-58; exec. dir. Writers Guild Am. West, Inc., 1958-78; nat. exec. dir. Dirs. Guild Am., Inc., 1978-88. Mem. Fed. Cable Adv. Commn. Served with C.E. AUS, 1942-46. Mem. Order of Coif.

FRANKLIN, ROSA G. state legislator, retired nurse; m. James Franklin; 3 children. RN, Good Samaritan Waverly Hosp., Columbia, S.C., 1948; BA in Biology and English, U. Puget Sound, 1968; MA in Social Scis. and Human Rels., Pacific Luth. U., 1974; postgrad., U. Wash., 1974. Ret. nurse; mem. Wash. Senate, Dist. 29, Olympia, 1993—; mem. labor and workforce devel.; vice-chair health and long-term care com.; mem. human svcs. and corrections com.; vice-chair rules com., mem. coun. on aging com.; Dem. whip Wash. Senate, Olympia, 1997, majority whip, 1999-01, pres. pro tem, 2001. Mem. Tacoma Urban League, Safe Streets, South End Neighborhood for Family Safety, Hunger Walk '93; mem. adv. com. Cancer Screening Program for Targeted Populations; bd. dirs. Cascade Blood Bank; bd. advisors Health Edn. Coun. Named Outstanding Vol. Stafford Study Club, Hon. Citizen award Citizen of Tacoma, Dem. Woman of Yr. Wash. State Fedn. Dem. Women, Thurgood Marshall award African Am. Port of Tacoma, Lifetime Achievement award Wash. Dem. Party, 2000. Mem. LWV, NAACP, Wash. Assn. C.C. Women's Programs, Pierce County Nurses Assn, Alpha Kappa Alpha. Democrat. Office: 309410 Legislative Bldg Olympia WA 98500 E-mail: franklin_no@leg.wa.gov

FRANKLIN, WILLIAM EMERY, international business educator; b. Sedalia, Mo., Apr. 6, 1933; s. Russell George and Edith Mae (Van Dyke) Franklin; m. Beverly Jean Feig, Mar. 25, 1933 (div. 1963); children: Stephen, Julia, Angela. BS in Bus., U. Mo., 1954; postgrad., Harvard U., 1982. With forestry ops. Weyerhaeuser Co., Longview, Wash., 1954; pres. Weyerhaeuser Far East Ltd., Hong Kong, 1980-96, Franklin Internat., Ltd., Seattle, 1996—. Chmn. Weyerhaeuser China Ltd.; pres. Weyerhaeuser Korea; mem. U.S.-Japan Bus. Coun., Pacific Basin Econ. Coun.; bd. dirs. NCR Japan Ltd.; mem. Eisenhower Fellowship Com., adv. com. on investment and devel. U.S. Dept. State; past chmn. forestry working group industry coop. program of UN-FAO, com. on internat. trade U.S. Dept. Commerce; adj. prof. U. Puget Sound, Am. Grad. Sch. Internat. Mgmt.; guest lectr. U. Internat. Bus. Econs., Beijing, Columbia U., Internat. U. of Japan, Seattle U. Trustee Pacific N.W. Ballet; chmn. Far East Coun. Friends of Scouting. Mem. Am. C. of C. in Japan (pres.), Yomiuri Internat. Econ. Soc. (bd. dirs.), Coun. Fgn. Rels., World Affairs Coun., U.S.-Asian Bus. Coun., Fgn. Corrs. Club, Tokyo Lawn Tennis Club, Tokyo Club. Avocations: tennis, music, sailing.

FRANZKE, RICHARD ALBERT, lawyer; b. Lewistown, Mont., Mar. 7, 1935; s. Arthur A. and Senta (Clark) F.; divorced; children: Mark, Jean, Robert. BA in Polit. Sci., Willamette U., 1958, JD with honors, 1960. Bar: Oreg. 1960, U.S. Dist. Ct. Oreg., 1960, U.S. Supreme Ct., 1961. Ptnr. Stoel, Rives, Portland, 1960—. Bd. dirs., chmn. various coms. Assn. Gen. Contractors Am., Portland, 1972-79; mem. com. on legis. affairs Assn. Builders & Contractors, Portland, 1983—. Author: A Study of the Construct by Contract Issue, 1979. Mem. Gov.'s Task Force on Reform of Worker's Compensation, Salem, Oreg., 1980-81; atty. gen.'s com. on Pub. Contracting. Recipient SIR award Assn. Gen. Contractors, 1979, Nat. Winner Outstanding Oral Argument award U.S. Moot Ct., 1959. Mem. ABA (sect. pub. contract law), Oreg. Bar (law sch. liaison, com. on practice and procedure specialization), Multnomah County Bar Assn. Republican. Avocations: antique autos, antique furniture, boating. Home: 14980 SW 133rd Ave Tigard OR 97224-1646 Office: Stoel Rives 900 SW 5th Ave Ste 2300 Portland OR 97204-1229 E-mail: rafranzke@stoel.com

FRANZMANN, ALBERT WILHELM, wildlife veterinarian, consultant; b. Hamilton, Ohio, July 19, 1930; s. Wilhelm Heinreich and Louise Marie (Schlichter) F.; m. Donna Marie Grueser, Dec. 13, 1953; children: Karl Wilhelm, Louise Ann. DVM, Ohio State U., 1954; PhD, U. Idaho, 1971. Diplomate Am. Coll. Zool. Medicine (hon.). Veterinarian Tiffin (Ohio) Animal Hosp., 1956-59; gen. practice vet. medicine Hamilton, 1959-68; NDEA rsch. fellow U. Idaho, Moscow, 1968-71; wildlife cons. F-2 Wildlife Cons., Moscow, 1971-72; dir. Kenai Moose Rsch. Ctr. Alaska Dept. Fish and Game, Soldotna, 1972-87; cons. AWF Profl. Svcs. Affil. assoc. prof., U. Alaska, Fairbanks, 1972-87; bd. dirs. Internat. Wildlife Vet. Svc. Inc., Laramie, Wyo., Hamilton Tool co., Bd. of Game State of Alaska, Alaska [illegible] to profl. jours., 15 chpts. to books. Bd. dirs. N.Am. Moose Found. Capt. USAF, 1954-56. Named Disting. Moose Biologist, N.Am. Moose Conf., Prince George, B.C., Can.,1983; recipient Disting. Alumnus award Ohio State U. Coll. Vet. Medicine, Lifetime Conservation award Kenai Penisula chpt. Safari Club Internat., 2001. Mem. AVMA, Am. Assn. Wildlife Veterinarians (pres. 1979-81), Wildlife Disease Assn. (council 1980-81, Emeritus award 1996), Am. Assn. Zoo Veterinarians, Am. Coll. Zool. Medicine (hon. diplomate), The Wildlife Soc. (cert. wildlife biologist, Einarsen award N.W. sect.), Phi Zeta, Xi Sigma Pi. Republican. Lodge: Elks. Avocations: photography, hunting, fishing, travel, exploration. Home and Office: PO Box 666 Soldotna AK 99669-0666

FRASCA, ROBERT JOHN, architect; b. Niagara Falls, N.Y., May 10, 1933; s. John and Jean Marie (Delgross) F.; m. Marilyn Margaret Buys, Sept. 23, 1937; children: Jason Robert, Andrea Melina. BArch, U. Mich., 1957; M in City Planning, MIT, 1959. Registered architect, Oreg., Wash., Calif., N.Y., Ariz., Utah. Ptnr. in charge of design Zimmer Gunsul Frasca Partnership, Portland, Oreg., 1966—, chief exec. officer, 1979—. Design commn. U. Wash.; vis. prof. architecture U. Mich., U. Calif., Berkeley; design juror numerous nat., state and chpt. AIA awards programs. Prin. works include Justice Ctr., 1983, KOIN Ctr., 1985, Vollum Inst. for Advanced Biomed. Rsch., 1986, Oreg. Conv. Ctr., 1990, Oreg. Mus. of Sci. and Industry, 1992, Fred Hutchinson Cancer Rsch. Ctr., 1993; contbr. articles to profl. jours. and mags. Charter adv. bd. mem. Portland State U., 1987—; trustee Nat. Bldg. Mus., Washington; bd. dirs. Assn. for Portland Progress. Fellow AIA; mem. Arlington Club (Portland), Multnomah Athletic Club, Century Club (N.Y.). Clubs: Arlington (Portland), Multnomah Athletic. Office: Zimmer Gunsul Frasca 320 SW Oak St Ste 500 Portland OR 97204-2737

FRASER, BRAD, playwright, theatrical director, screenwriter; b. Edmonton, Alta., Can., June 28, 1959; Works include: (plays) Two Pariahs At A Bus Stop In A Large City Late At Night, Mutants, Wolfboy, 1981, Rude Noises (For A Blank Generation), 1982, Chainsaw Love, 1985, Return Of The Bride, 1985, Unidentified Human Remains and the True Nature of Love, 1989 (Floyd S. Chalmers award for best new Can. play), Blood Buddies, Prom Night of the Living Dead, The Ugly Man, 1992, Poor Super Man, 1994 (Floyd S. Chalmers award for best new Can. play); (screenplay) Love and Human Remains, 1993. Office: Int'l Arts Entertainment 8899 Beverly Blvd Ste 800 Los Angeles CA 90048-2428

FRASER, BRUCE DOUGLAS, JR. architect, artist; b. Corvallis, Oreg., Dec. 1, 1948; s. Bruce Douglas and Betty Adele (Lively) F.; m. Laura Jane Wells, June 18, 1972. BArch, Calif. Poly. State U., 1972. Registered architect, Calif. Artist, illustrator Hopkins Assocs., San Luis Obispo, Calif., 1972-73; planner U.S. Peace Corps, Mashhad, Iran, 1973-75; mem. archtl. staff Meyer-Merriam Assocs., San Luis Obispo, 1975-77; prin. MDW Assocs., San Luis Obispo, 1977-85, Merriam-Fraser Architecture and Planning, San Luis Obispo, 1985-87, Archtl. Office Bruce Fraser, San Luis Obispo, 1987—. Chair Bldg. Appeals Bd., Pismo Beach, Calif., 1990, Planning Commn., Pismo Beach, 1991-92, vice chair, 1990. Recipient various design awards Obispo Beautiful Assn., 1977—, Downtown Assn., 1990—. Mem. AIA (v.p. Calif. Ctrl. Coast chpt. 1985, pres. 1986). Office: Archtl Office of Bruce Fraser AIA 971 Osos St San Luis Obispo CA 93401-3212

FRASER, CATHERINE ANNE, Canadian chief justice; b. Campbellton, N.B., Can., Aug. 4, 1947; d. Antoine Albert and Anne (Slevinski) Elias; m. Richard C. Fraser, Aug. 17, 1968; children: Andrea Claire, Jonathan James. BA, U. Alta., Can., 1969, LLB, 1970; ML, U. London, 1972. Assoc., ptnr. Lucas, Bishop & Fraser, Edmonton, Alta., 1972-89; justice Ct. Queen's Bench Alta., Edmonton, 1989-91, Ct. Appeal Alta., Edmonton, 1991-92, chief justice Alta. and NW Ter., 1992—. Dir. Can. Inst. Adminstrn. Justice, 1991-95. Recipient Tribute to Women award YWCA, 1987. Mem. Can. Bar Assn., Edmonton Bar Assn., Law Soc. Alta. Office: Ct Appeal Alta Law Courts Bldg Edmonton AB Canada T5J OR2

FRASER, KAREN, state legislator; m. Tim Malone; 1 child, Hiromi. BA in Sociology, U. Wash., 1966, MPA, 1969. Thurston County commr., 1981-88; mayor City of Lacey, 1976-80, mem. coun., 1973-80; mem. Wash. Senate, Dist. 22, Olympia, 1988—; chair environ. quality and water resources com.; mem. energy, tech., and telecoms. com.; mem. ways and means com.; mem. joint com. on pension policy Wash. Senate, Olympia, 1995—, exec. com. Asia and Pacific parliamentarians conf., 1994-97, co-chair legis. internat. caucus, 1994—, mem. capitol campus design adv. com., 1995—, senate ecology and parks com. chair, 1993-96; chair com. on natural resources, environ. and water. Bd. dirs. Wash. Wildlife and Recreation Coalition; mem. com. Olympic Trials Legacy, 1998—; chair Nisqually River Coun.; founding bd. dirs. Nisqually River Basic Land Trust; trustee State Capital Hist. Assn.; host com. Women's Olympic Marathon Trials Assn., chair chair, 1984; past v.p., treas. Tumwater area coun. Boy Scouts Am. Recipient Legislator of Yr. award Wash. Fedn. State Employees, 1993, Silver Beaver award Boys Scouts Am., Toll Fellow Coun. State Govts., 1993, Legislator of Yr. Wash. Health Care Assn., 1996, Puget Sound Hero, People for Puget Sound., 1995, Woman of Distinction award Pacific Peaks Girl Scouts USA Coun., 1995, Cert. Appreciation Jud. Staff Bd. Indsl. Ins. Appeals, Wash. Fedn. State Employees, 1998, Disting. Leadership Recognition award Assn. Wash. Housing Authorities, 1998, Program Leadership award Nisqually River Mgmt. Program, 1998, Legis. Citation of Merit award Wash. Recreation and Parks Assn., 1998. Mem. Wash. State Assn. Counties (pres. 1987-98). Democrat. Avocations: outdoor recreation, sailing, hiking, marathon running. Office: 417 John Cherberg Bldg Olympia WA 98504-0001

FRASER, KATHLEEN JOY, poet, creative writing educator; b. Tulsa, Mar. 22, 1935; d. James Ian and Marjorie Joy (Axtell) F.; m. Jack Marshall, July 10, 1960 (div. 1970); 1 child, David Ian; m. Arthur Kalmer Bierman, June 30, 1984 BA in English Lit., Occidental Coll., 1958; doctoral equivalency, San Francisco State U., 1976. Vis. prof. writing, lectr. in poetry The Writer's Workshop, U. Iowa, Iowa City, 1969-71; writer in residence Reed Coll., Portland, Oreg., 1971-72; dir. Poetry Center San Francisco State U., 1972-75, prof. creative writing, 1972-92. Founder-dir. Am. Poetry Archives, San Francisco, 1973-75; founder-editor How(ever), Jour. for poets/scholars interested in modernism and women's innovative writing, 1983-91. Author: (children's book) Stilts, Somersaults and Headstands, 1967; (poetry) What I Want (New and Selected Poems), 1974, New Shoes, 1978, Something (even human voices in the foreground) A Lake, 1984, Notes Preceding Trust, 1988, When New Time Folds Up, 1993, Il Cuore: The Heart, Selected Poems 1970-95, 1997. Recipient Frank O'Hara Poetry prize, 1964; Nat. Endowment for Arts fellow, 1978, Guggenheim fellow, 1981.

FRASER, MARGOT, consumer products company executive; b. Bremen, Germany; Pres., founder Birkenstock Footprint Sandals, Inc., 1972—. Inductee Footwear News Hall of Fame. Office: Birkenstock Footprint Sandals 8171 Redwood Blvd Novato CA 94945-1403

FRASER, MARTIN, automobile parts executive; Exec. v.p. merchandising, distbn. and comml. CSK Auto Corp., Phoenix, pres., COO, 2000—. Office: CSK Auto Corp. 645 E Missouri Ave Ste 400 Phoenix AZ 85012

FRASIER, S. DOUGLAS, medical educator; b. L.A., Nov. 29, 1932; m. Robin D'Arvin; children: Karen Lynn, Eric Marc, Sara Leslie. BA, U. Calif., L.A., 1953; MD with highest honors, U. Calif., 1958. Diplomate [illegible] pediat. Strong Meml. Rochester (N.Y.) Mcpl. Hosps., 1958-59; asst. resident pediat. U. Calif. Hosps., L.A., 1959-61; postdoc. trainee U. Calif., L.A., 1963-65; from asst. prof. to prof. pediat. U. So. Calif. Sch. Medicine, L.A., 1965-86; prof. pediat. UCLA Sch. Medicine, L.A., 1986—. Attending physician Children's Mercy Hosp., Kansas City, Mo., 1962-63, L.A. county-Harbor Gen. Hosp., Torrance, Calif., 1965-67; endocrine cons. Pacific State Hosp., Pomona, Calif., 1965-69, tng. cons., 1965-70; med. adv. Human Growth Found. L.A. Chpt., 1967-74, chmn. adv. com., 1967-72, co-chmn. rsch. com., 1972-75; med. adv. bd. Nat. Pituitary Agy., 1971-74; chief divsn. pediat. endocrinology, L.A. County-U. So. Calif. Med. Ctr., 1967-86, physician, 1967-86, dir. pediat. endocrine and diabetic clinics., 1967-72; exec. asst. Calif. Student Health Project, L.A., 1967-68, faculty dir., 1968-69; coord. curriculum U. So. Calif. Sch. Medicine, L.A., 1969-76, assoc. dean student affairs, 1970-76, vice-chair dept. pediat., 1986—; assoc. attending physician divsn. endocrinology/metabolism children's Hosp. L.A., 1976-79, cons., 1979-82; cons. Calbiochem Corp., 1969-78, Hoechst-Roussel Pharmaceutical Corp., 1978-79, maternal and child health br. genetics disease sect. Calif. Dept. Health Scis., 1978—, Soreno Labs., Inc., 1979-94, growth hormone program Can. Med. Rsch. Coun., 1981, program on drugs AMA, 1985; endocrine cons. Lanterman State Hosp., Pomona, 1980-82; chief pediat. Olive View-UCLA Med. Ctr., Sylmar, Calif., 1986—; mem. med. staff UCLA Med. Ctr., L.A., 1986—; vis. lectr. Milwaukee Children's Hosp., 1977; vis. prof. U. Ariz. Sch. Medicine, 1978, Kapiolani/Children's Med. Ctr., Honolulu, 1983, U. Montreal/Hosp. Sainte-Justine, 1988, Australasian Pediat. Endocrine Group, 1990, Tripler Army Hosp., Honolulu, 1993; mem., chmn. various other hosp. coms. Mem. editl. bd. Jour. Pediat. Endocrinology; rev. Pediats., Jour. Pediats., Jour. Clin. Endocrinology and Metabolism, Am. Jour. Diseases Children, Pediat. Rsch., Med. Letter, Metabolism, Endocrine Revs. Capt. U.S. Army Med. Corps, 1961-63. Fellow U. Calif. Sch. Medicine, L.A., 1955-56, Cecil E. Vesy scholar, 1956-58; recipient Sheard-Sanford prize Am. Soc. Clin. Pathologists, 1958. Mem. L.A. Pediat. Soc., Am. Acad. Pediat., Western Soc. Pediat. Rsch. (chmn. nominating com. 1975-76), Endocrine Soc., Lawson Wilkins Pediat. Endocrine Soc. (membership com. 1971-74, chmn. membership com. 1973-74, dir. 1978-82, ad hoc com. uses human growth hormone 1981-87, 88-90, pres.-elect 1988-89, chmn. awards com. 1988—, pres. 1989-90, past pres. 1990-91, chmn. drug and therapeutic com., 1990-94), Soc. Pediat. Rsch., Am. Pediat. Soc. Home: 10428 Lorenzo Pl Los Angeles CA 90064-4449 Office: UCLA-Ssch of Med Dept Pediatrics/Endocrin 10833 Le Conte Ave Los Angeles CA 90095-3075

FRASURE, EVAN S. state legislator; b. Pocatello, Idaho, Mar. 20, 1951; m. Analyn Frasure; children: Kent, Evan, Lena, Jessica. BA in Edn., Idaho State U. Grocery store owner, 1981-83; real estate broker, mgr. Coldwell Banker, 1983-87; exec. dir. Melaleuca, Inc., 1987—; elected rep. Idaho Ho. of Reps., Boise, 1990-92; mem. Idaho Senate, Dist. 34, Boise, 1992—. Chair transp. com., mem. local govt. and tax., fin., and resources and environment coms.; vice chair, energy and transp. com., Nat. Conf. State Legislators. Mem. Am. Legis. Exch. Coun. Republican. Mormon. Office: State Capitol PO Box 83720 Boise ID 83720-3720

FRAUENFELDER, HANS, physicist, educator; b. Neuhausen, Switzerland, July 28, 1922; came to U.S., 1952, naturalized, 1958. s. Otto and Emma (Ziegler) F.; m. Verena Anna Hassler, May 16, 1950; children: Ulrich Hans, Kätterli Anne, Anne Verena. Diploma, Swiss Fed. Inst. Tech., 1947, Ph.D. in Physics, 1950. Asst. Swiss Fed. Inst. Tech., 1946-52; asst. prof. physics U. Ill. at Urbana, 1952-56, assoc. prof., 1956-58, prof., 1958-92, prof. emeritus, 1992—; mem. staff Los Alamos (N.Mex.) Nat. Labs., 1992—. Guggenheim fellow, 1958-59, 73; vis. scientist CERN, Geneva, Switzerland, 1958-59, 63, 73. Author: The Mossbauer Effect, 1962, (with E.M. Henley) Subatomic Physics, 1974, 2d edit., 1991, Nuclear and Particle Physics, 1975; contbr. articles to profl. jours. Recipient Humboldt award, 1987-88. Fellow AAAS, Am. Phys. Soc. (Biol. Physics prize 1992), N.Y. Acad. Sci.; mem. Royal Swedish Acad. Scis., NAS, Am. Inst. Physics (chmn. governing bd. 1986-93), Am. Acad. Arts and Sci., Am. Philos. Soc., Acad. Leopoldina. E-mail: frauenfelder@lanl.gov

FRAUNFELDER, FREDERICK THEODORE, ophthalmologist, educator; b. Pasadena, Calif., Aug. 16, 1934; s. Reinhart and Freida Fraunfelder; m. Yvonne Marie Halliday, June 21, 1959; children— Yvette Marie, Helene, Nina, Frederick, Nicholas. BS, U. Oreg., 1956, MD, 1960, postgrad. (NIH postdoctoral fellow), 1962. Diplomate Am. Bd. Ophthalmology (bd. dirs. 1982-90). Intern U. Chgo., 1961; resident U. Oreg. Med. Sch., 1964-66; NIH postdoctoral fellow Wilmer Eye Inst., Johns Hopkins U., 1967; chmn. dept. ophthalmology U. Ark. Health Scis. Ctr., 78-98, prof., 1978—; prof., chmn. dept. ophthalmology Oreg. Health Scis. U. Dir. Casey Eye Inst., 1992-98, Nat. Registry Drug-Induced Ocular Side Effects, 1976—; vis. prof. ophthalmology Moorfields Eye Hosp., London, 1974. Author: Drug-Induced Ocular Side Effects and Drug Interactions, 1976, 5th edit., 2001, Current Ocular Therapy, 1985, 5th edit., 2001, Recent Advances in Ophthalmology, 8th edit., 1985; assoc. editor: Jour. Toxicology: Cutaneous and Ocular, 1984—; mem. editl. bd. Am. Jour. Ophthalmology, 1982-92, Ophthalmic Forum, 1983-90, Ophthalmology, 1984-89; contbr. over 200 articles on lens and eye toxicity rsch. to med. jours. Served with U.S. Army, 1962-64. FDA grantee, 1976-86; Nat. Eye Inst. grantee, 1970-87. Mem. AMA, ACS, Am. Acad. Ophthaolmology, Assn. Univ. Profs. in Ophthalmology (pres. 1976), Am. Ophthalmol. Soc., Am. Coll. Cryosurgery (pres. 1977), Assn. Research in Ophthalmology. Lutheran. Clubs: Lions, Elks. Home: 13 Cellini Ct Lake Oswego OR 97035-1307 Office: Casey Eye Inst 3375 SW Terwilliger Blvd Portland OR 97201-4197

FRAUTSCHI, STEVEN CLARK, physicist, educator; b. Madison, Wis., Dec. 6, 1933; s. Lowell Emil and Grace (Clark) F.; m. Mie Okamura, Feb. 16, 1967; children: Laura, Jennifer. B.A., Harvard U., 1954; Ph.D., Stanford U., 1958. Research fellow Kyoto U., Japan, 1958-59, U. Calif.-Berkeley, 1959-61; mem. faculty Cornell U., 1961-62, Calif. Inst. Tech., Pasadena, 1962—, prof. theoretical physics, 1966—, exec. officer physics, 1988-97, master student houses, 1997—. Vis. prof. U. Paris, Orsay, 1977-78 Author: Regge Poles and S-Matrix Theory, 1963, The Mechanical Universe, 1986. Guggenheim fellow, 1971-72 Mem. Am. Phys. Soc. Achievements include research and publications on Regge poles, bootstrap theory, cosmology. Home: 1561 Crest Dr Altadena CA 91001-1838 Office: 1201 E California Blvd Pasadena CA 91125-0001

FRAZIER, G. REX, real estate executive; Grad., U. Utah. CPA, Utah. Audit supr. Touche Ross & Co.; dir. fin. Fairfax, v.p. fin., exec. v.p., pres., COO, 1986—; pres., COO, JP Realty Inc., Salt Lake City, 1993—, also bd. dirs. Office: JP Realty Inc 35 Century Park Way Salt Lake City UT 84115-3507

FRÉCHET, JEAN MARIE JOSEPH, chemistry educator; b. Chalon, France, Aug. 18, 1944; came to U.S., 1967; s. Victor H. and Renée F.; m. Janet R. Manning, Nov. 25, 1967; children: Jacques Christopher, Marc Alexander. MSc, SUNY, Syracuse, 1969, PhD, 1971, Syracuse U., , 1971. Asst. prof. chemistry U. of Ottawa, Can., 1973-78, assoc. prof. chemistry Can., 1978-82, prof. chemistry Can., 1982-87; IBM prof. chemistry Cornell U., Ithaca, N.Y., 1987-95, P.J. Debye chair chemistry, 1996 [illegible] prof. chemistry U. Calif., Berkeley, 1996—. Vis. scientist IBM Rsch. Lab., San Jose, Calif., 1979, 83; vice dean grad. studies and rsch. U. Ottawa, 1983-87; cons. Xerox Corp., 1979-88, Allied Signal Corp., Morristown, 1986-93, Exxon Corp., Linden, N.J., 1988—, E.I. duPont de Nemours, Wilmington, 1990-93, Loctite, 1993—, Pharmacia, 1993-95, Miles, 1994, Bayer, 1996—, Symyx, 1996—, Rhone Poulenc, 1994-99, Pharmacopeia, [illegible] Ont. Ctr. for Materials Rsch., Toronto. Contbr. numerous articles to profl.

jours.; patentee in field. Recipient Award Internat. Union Pure and Applied Chemistry, 1983, Polymer Soc. of Japan, 1986, A.K. Doolittle award, 1986, Coop. Rsch. award Am. Chem. Soc., 1994, Applied Polymer Chem. award Am. Chem. Soc., 1996, 2000, Kosar Meml. award Soc. Imaging Sci. Tech., 1999, Polymer Chem. award Am. Chem. Soc., 2000; A.C. Cope scholar Am. Chem. Soc., 2001; numerous grants for rsch. Fellow AAAS; mem. Nat. Acad. Scis., Nat. Acad. of Engring., Am. Acad. of Arts and Scis. Avocation: oenophile. Office: U Calif 718 Latimer Hl Berkeley CA 94720-0001

FREDERICK, DOLLIVER H. merchant banker; b. Edmonton, Alta, Can., Apr. 2, 1944; s. Henry and Gladys (Ganske) F.; m. Joan B. Dickau, Aug. Student, Alta Coll., U. Alta; No. Alta Inst. Tech.., 1965. With Imperial Oil Ltd., Edmonton, 1965-72; sr. analyst mktg. Toronto, Ont., Can., 1972-73; corp. devel. mgr. Hees Internat. (formerly Bovis Corp. Ltd.), 1973-75, copr. v.p., 1975-79; pres., chief operating officer Gen. Supply Co. Can. (1973) Ltd., 1975-79, Equipment Fed. Que. Ltd., 1975-79; pres. CEO, dir. CanWest Investment Corp., Toronto, Ont., 1979-81; chmn. exec. com., dir. Na-Churs Plant Food Co., Marion, Ohio, 1979-81, Macleod-sTedman, Inc., Winnipeg and Toronto, 1980-81; chmn., pres. CEO, dir. Cochran-Dunlop Lt., 1982-87, Frederick Capital Corp. (Can.) Inc., 1981—; pres., CED, dir. Comterm Inc., 1989-90; pres., CEO, dir. Electrohome Ltd., 1985-87. Mem. Can. Coun. of Christians and Jews (dir., the Nat. Conf., 1997—), Southern Counties Oil Co, 1997—, Cardlock Fuels System, 1997—, PNEC Corp., 1997—, Flint Fuels, 1997. Mem. Engineers Club of Toronto;, adv. bd. mem. Noram Capital Mgmt.; mem. Assn. Corp. Growth, World Pres.'s Orgn., CChief Executive Org., Nat., Can. Club N.Y., Pacific Club. Republican. Office: Frederick Capital Corp 5000 Birch St Ste 3000 Newport Beach CA 92660-2140 E-mail: dhfrederich@frederichcapital.com

FREDERICK, SHERMAN, publishing executive; Pub. Las Vegas (Nev.) Rev.-Jour.; pres. Donrey Media Group. Office: Las Vegas Rev-Journal 1111 W Bonanza Rd Las Vegas NV 89106-3545

FREDERICKS, DALE EDWARD, communications company executive; b. Springfield, Ill., Mar. 12, 1943; m. Jean Schmidt, June 8, 1968; children: Michael J., Amy C. BS with honors, Bradley U., 1965; JD, U. Ill., 1968. Bar: D.C. 1969, Calif. 1971, U.S. Supreme Ct. 1978. Gen. counsel Summit Fidelity and Surety Co., Minneapolis, 1988-93, Hampton Ct. Holdings, Inc., San Francisco, 1989-93; ptnr. Sheppard, Mullin, Richter & Hampton, 1991-96, mng. ptnr. San Francisco office, 1993-95; CEO C5 Comm. LLC, Incline Village, Nev., 1999—. Pres. Sangamon Properties Co., Incline Village, Nev., Sangamon Devel. Co., Sangamon Energy Co., Lafayette, Calif. Capt. USMCR, 1968-72. Mem. ABA (antitrust law and litigation sects.), Calif. Bar Assn., San Francisco Bar Assn., Internat. Bar Assn., World Trace Club. Republican. Avocation: golf, real estate development. Office: C5 Comm LLC 937 Tahoe Blvd Incline Village NV 89451

FREDERICKS, PATRICIA ANN, real estate executive; b. Durand, Mich., June 5, 1941; d. Willis Edward and Dorothy (Plowman) Sexton; m. Ward Arthur Fredericks, June 12, 1960; children: Corrine Ellen, Lorraine Lee, Ward Arthur II. BA, Mich. State U., 1962; cert. mediator, U. Calif., 1999. Cert. Grad. Real Estate Inst., residential broker, residential salesperson; cert. real estate broker. Assoc. Stand Brough, Des Moines, 1976-80; broker Denton, Tucson, 1980-83; broker-trainer Coldwell Banker, Westlake Village, Calif., 1984-90; broker, br. mgr. Brown, Newbury Park, 1990-94; dir. tng. Brown Real Estate, Westlake Village, 1994-95; gen. mgr., dir. mktg. Coldwell Banker Town & Country Real Estate, Newbury Park, 1994—; dir. mktg. Coldwell Banker Town and Country, 1995—. Bd. sec. Mixtec Corp., Thousand Oaks, 1984—. Contbr. articles to profl. jours. Pres. Inner Wheel, Thousand Oaks, 1991, 96-97; bd. dirs. Community Leaders Club, Thousand Oaks, 1991, Conejo Future Found., Thousand Oaks, 1989-92, Wellness Community Ventura Valley, 1994—. Mem. ABA, Calif. Assn. Realtors (dir. 1988-95 regional chairperson 1995, vice chairperson expn. 1997, chair Calif. Expo 1998), Conejo Valley Assn. Realtors (sec., v.p., pres.-elect 1989-92, pres. 1993, Realtor of Yr. 1991), Pres.'s Club Mich. State U., Com. 100, Cmty. Concerts Assn., Alliance for the Arts, Conejo Valley Symphony Guild, Wellness Cmty., Indian Wells Country Club, North Ranch Country Club, Sherwood Country Club, Aviation Country Club Calif. E-mail: classybker@aol.com

FREDMANN, MARTIN, ballet artistic director, educator, choreographer; b. Balt., Feb. 3, 1943; s. Martin Joseph and Hilda Adele (Miller) F.; m. Kaleriya Fedicheva, Jan. 2, 1973 (div.); m. Patricia Renzetti, June 12, 1980. Student, Nat. Ballet Sch., Washington, 1962-64, Vaganova Sch., Leningrad, 1972. Prin. dancer The Md. Ballet, Balt., 1961-64; dancer The Pa. Ballet, Phila., 1964-65, Ballet of the Met. Opera Co., N.Y.C., 1965-66; prin. dancer Dortmund (Fed. Republic Germany) Ballet, 1973-75, Scapino Ballet, Amsterdam, Holland, 1975-76; tchr. German Opera Ballet, West Berlin, Fed. Republic Germany, 1979, Netherlands Dance Theater, 1979, Royal Swedish Ballet, 1980, San Francisco Ballet, 1981; tchr., coach Australian Ballet, 1982; tchr. Tokyo City Ballet, Hong Kong Ballet, 1985, 86, 87, London Festival Ballet, 1981-83; dir. ballet Teatro Comunale, Florence, Italy, 1984-85; artistic dir. Tampa (Fla.) Ballet, 1984-90; artistic dir. in alliance with The Tampa Ballet Colo. Ballet, Denver, 1987-90, artistic dir., 1987—. Tchr. German Opera Ballet, 1982, Ballet Rambert, London, Bat Dor summer course, Israel, 1983, Cullberg Ballet, Sweden, 1983, Hong Kong Acad. For Performing Arts, 1985, 86, 87, 89, 91, Tokyo City Ballet, 1985, 86, 87, 89, 90, Ballet West, 1990, Nat. Ballet Korea, 1991, Dance Divsn. Tsoying High Sch., Kaohsiung, Taiwan, R.O.C., 1992; guest lectr., tchr. Cen. Ballet China, Beijing Dancing Acad., P.L.A. Arts Coll., Beijing, 1990; tchr. Legat Sch., 1978, examiner, 1980; tchr. Eglevsky Sch., N.Y.C., 1980; asst. dir., ballet master Niavaron Cultural ctr., Tehran, Iran, 1978; tchr. Ballet Arts Sch. Carnegie Hall, N.Y.C., 1979-81, choreographer Estonia Nat. Theatre, USSR, 1991; dir. Marin Ballet, Calif., 1981. Choreographer Romeo and Juliet, 1983, Sachertorte, 1984, A Little Love, 1984, Ricordanza, 1986, Cinderella, 1986, Coppelia, 1987, The Nutcracker, 1987, Beauty and the Beast, 1988, Masquerade Suite, 1989, Silent Woods, 1989, The Last Songs, 1991, Centenial Suite, 1994. Recipient Mayor's award Denver, 1996, Dance Mag. award, 1999, Boufils-Stanton Found. award, 2000. Mem. Am. Guild Mus. Artists, Fla. State Dance Assn., Nat. Assn. Regional Ballet. Avocations: cooking, cook book collecting, travel, opera. Home: 836 E 17th Ave Apt 3A Denver CO 80218-1449 Office: Colo Ballet 1278 Lincoln St Denver CO 80203-2114

FREDRICKSON, GEORGE MARSH, history educator; b. Bristol, Conn., July 16, 1934; s. George Fredrickson and Gertrude (Marsh) F.; m. Helene Osouf, Oct. 16, 1956; children: Anne, Laurel, Thomas, Caroline. A.B., Harvard U., 1956, Ph.D., 1964. Instr. history Harvard U., Cambridge, Mass., 1963-66; assoc. prof. history Northwestern U., Evanston, Ill., 1966-71, prof., 1971-84, William Smith Mason prof. Am. history, 1979-84; Edgar E. Robinson prof. U.S. history Stanford U., Calif., 1984—. Fulbright prof. Moscow U., 1983, Harmsworth prof. Am. history Oxford U., 1988-89. Author: The Inner Civil War, 1965, 2d edit., 1993, The Black Image in the White Mind, 1971, 2d edit., 1987 (Anisfield-Wolf award 1972), White Supremacy, 1981 (Ralph Waldo Emerson award 1981, Merle Curti award, 1982, Pulitzer prize finalist 1982), The Arrogance of Race, 1988, Black Liberation, 1995, The Comparative Imagination, 1997; co-author: America: Past and Present, 5th edit., 1998; editor: A Nation Divided, 1975. Served to lt. USN, 1957-60. Guggenheim fellow, 1967-68; NEH fellow, 1973-74; Ctr. for Advanced Studies in Behavioral Scis. fellow, 1977-78; NEH fellow, 1985-86; Ford sr. fellow DuBois Inst., Harvard U., 1993. Fellow Soc. Am. Historians, Am. Antiquarian Soc., Am. Acad. Arts and Scis.; mem. Am. Hist. Assn., Orgn. Am. Historians (pres. 1997-98), So. Hist. Assn. Home: 741 Esplanada Way Palo Alto CA 94305-1013 Office: Stanford Univ Dept History Stanford CA 94305 E-mail: fredrick@stanford.edu

FREDRICKSON, GLENN HAROLD, chemical engineering and materials educator; b. Washington, May 8, 1959; BS in Chem. Engring. with honors, U. Fla., 1980; MS in Chem. Engring., Stanford U., 1981, PhD in Chem. Engring., 1984. Mem. tech. staff AT&T Bell Labs., Murray Hill, N.J., 1984-89, disting. mem. tech. staff, 1989-90; assoc. prof. dept. chem. engring. and engring. materials dept. U. Calif., Santa Barbara, 1990-91, dir. Macromolecular Sci. and Engring. Ctr., prof. dept. chem. engring. and engring. materials dept., 1991—, vice-chair chem. engring., 1996-98, chair chem. engring., 1998—. Allan P. Colburn lectr. U. Del., 1991; George T. Piercy disting prof. chem. engring. and materials sci. U. Minn., Mpls., 1992; vis. rsch. prof. Miller Inst. U. Calif., Berkeley, 1993; lectr. in field. Mem. editorial bd. Jour. Polymer Sci. physics edit., 1992—, Macromolecules, 1994-96; mem. internat. editorial adv. bd. Acta Polymerica, 1992—. Exxon Teaching fellow Stanford U., 1982-84, Alfred P. Sloan Rsch. fellow, 1992; recipient Presdl. Young Investigator award NSF, 1990, Camille and Henry Dreyfus Tchr.-Scholar award, 1991. Fellow Am. Phys. Soc. (publs. com. 1992-94, John H. Dillon medal Divsn. High Polymer Physics 1992), Am. Inst. Chem. Engrs., 1999 (Alpha Chi Sigma award); mem. Phi Kappa Phi. Office: U Calif Chem Engring Eng II Rm 3329 Santa Barbara CA 93106-5080

FREED, PETER QUENTIN, amusement park executive; b. Salt Lake City, Jan. 8, 1921; s. Lester David and Jasmine (Young) F.; children: David Wicker, Michael Stahle, Howard Eldred, Anne, Kristen, Jennifer. BA with hons., U. Utah, 1947. Pres. Freed Co., 1952-74; exec. v.p. Amusement Svc., Salt Lake City, 1947—. V.p. Terrace Co., Salt Lake City, from 1952; exec. v.p. Patio Gardens, Farmington, Utah, from 1956; v.p. Westworld Corp., Salt Lake City, from 1974, Pioneer Village Campground, Farmington, from 1975; dir. Pioneer Village, Farmington; pres. Lagoon Corp., Salt Lake City, 1974— . Mem. Union Sta. Theatre Bd. With USNR, 1942-45. Mem. Nat. Assn. Amusement Parks, Utah Mus. Assn., Salt Lake Tennis Club, New Yorker Club. Republican. Christian Scientist. Home: 642 Aloha Rd Salt Lake City UT 84103-3329 Office: Lagoon Theme Park 375 N Lagoon Dr Farmington UT 84025-2554

FREEDLAND, RICHARD ALLAN, retired biologist, educator; b. Pitts., May 9, 1931; s. Milton and Gertrude (Davis) F.; m. Beverly Jane Pachefsky, June 22, 1958; children: Howard M., Judith L., Stephen J. BS, U. Pitts., 1953; MS, U. Ill., 1955; PhD, U. Wis., 1958. Research assoc. U. Wis., Madison, 1958-60; lectr. U. Calif., Davis, 1960-61, asst. prof., 1961-65, assoc. prof., 1965-69, prof. physiol. chemistry, 1969-74, prof., chmn. physiol. scis., 1974-93. Wellcome vis. prof. U. Ga., Athens, 1990-91. Author: A Biochemical Approach to Nutrition, 1977, Biochemistry: A Short Course, 1997; mem. editorial bd. Archives Biochemistry and Biophysics, 1978—, Jour. Biol. Chemistry, 1985-91, Fedn. Am. Socs. for Exptl. Biology Jour., 1991-94; assoc. editor Jour. of Nutrition, 1984-88, editor, 1988-89. Fulbright scholar, Australia, 1987-88. Fellow AAAS, Am. Soc. Nutrition Sci.; mem. Am. Soc. Biol. Chemists. Office: U Calif Dept Molecular BioSci Davis CA 95616 E-mail: rafreedland@ucdavis.edu

FREEDMAN, BART JOSEPH, lawyer; b. New Haven, Sept. 27, 1955; s. Lawrence Zelic and Dorothy (Robinson) F.; m. Esme Detweiler, Sept. 28, 1985; children: Luke Edward, Samuel Meade, Benjamin Zelic. BA, Carleton Coll., 1977; JD, U. Pa., 1982. Bar: Wash. 1984, U.S. Dist. Ct. (we. dist.) Wash. 1984, U.S. Ct. Appeals (9th cir.) 1985, U.S. Dist. Ct. (ea. dist.) Wash. 1988. Law clk. to chief justice Samuel Roberts Supreme Ct. Pa., Erie, 1982-83; asst. city solicitor City of Phila., 1984, assoc. Perkins Coie, Seattle, 1984-90; ptnr. Preston Gates & Ellis, Seattle, 1990—. Editor: Natural Resource Damages, 1993. Bd. dirs. Seattle Metrocenter YMCA, 1988-97, chmn. 1993-97; bd. dirs. Leadership Tomorrow, 1996-97; chair Sierra Club Inner City Outings Program, Seattle, 1986-90; chmn. bd. advisors Earth Svc. Corps/YMCA, Seattle, 1990-97. Mem. ABA (com. on corp. counsel 1985-95), Wash. State Bar Assn., Seattle-King County Bar Assn. (participant neighborhood legal clinics 1985-94). Office: Preston Gates & Ellis 701 5th Ave Ste 5000 Seattle WA 98104-7078 E-mail: bartf@prestongates.com

FREEDMAN, DAVID AMIEL, statistics educator, consultant; b. Montreal, Que., Can., Mar. 5, 1938; came to U.S., 1958; s. Abraham and Goldie (Yelin) F.; children: Deborah, Joshua. B.Sc., McGill U., Montreal, 1958; M.A., Princeton U., 1959, Ph.D., 1960. Prof. stats. U. Calif.-Berkeley, 1961—, Miller prof., 1991, chmn. dept. stats., 1981-86. Cons. Bank of Can., Ottawa, 1971-72, WHO, 1973, Carnegie Commn., 1976, Dept. Energy, 1978-87, Bur. Census, 1983, 98, Dept. Justice, 1984, 89-92, 96, Brobeck, Phleger & Harrison, 1985-89, Skadden Arps, 1986, County of Los Angeles, 1989, Fed. Jud. Ctr., 1993—. Author: Markov Chains, 1971, Brownian Motion and Diffusion, 1971, Approximating Countable Markov Chains, 1972, Mathematical Methods in Statistics, 1977, Statistics, 1978, 3d edit., 1997; contbr. numerous articles to profl. pubis. Fellow Can. Council, 1960, Sloan Found., 1964 Mem. Am. Acad Scis. Home: 901 Alvarado Rd Berkeley CA 94705-1551 Office: U Calif-Berkeley Dept Stats Berkeley CA 94720-0001

FREEDMAN, DAVID NOEL, religious studies educator; b. N.Y.C., May 12, 1922; s. David and Beatrice (Goodman) F.; m. Cornelia Anne Pryor, May 16, 1944; children: Meredith Anne, Nadezhda, David Micaiah, Jonathan Pryor. Student, CCNY, 1935-38; AB, UCLA, 1939; BTh, Princeton Theol. Sem., 1944; PhD, Johns Hopkins U., 1948; LittD, U. Pacific, 1973; ScD, Davis and Elkins Coll., 1974. Ordained to ministry Presbyn. Ch., 1944; supply pastor in Acme and Deming, Wash., 1944-45; tchg. fellow, then asst. instr. Johns Hopkins U., 1946-48; asst. prof., then prof. Hebrew and Old Testament lit. Western Theol. Sem., Pitts., 1948-60; prof. Pitts. Theol. Sem., 1960-61, James A. Kelso prof., 1961-64; prof. Old Testament San Francisco Theol. Sem., 1964-70, Gray prof. Hebrew exegesis, 1970-71, dean of faculty, 1966-70, acting dean of sem., 1970-71; prof. Old Testament Grad. Theol. Union, Berkeley, Calif., 1964-71; prof. dept. Nr. Ea. studies U. Mich., Ann Arbor, 1971-92, Thurnau prof. Bibl. studies, 1984-92, dir. program on studies in religion, 1971-91; prof., endowed chair in Hebrew Bibl. studies U. Calif., San Diego, 1987—, dir. religious studies program, 1989-97. Danforth vis. prof. Internat. Christian U., Tokyo, 1967; vis. prof. Hebrew U., Jerusalem, 1977, Macquarie U., N.S.W., Australia, 1980, U. Queensland (Australia), 1982, 84, U. Calif., San Diego, 1985-87; Green vis. prof. Tex. Christian U., Ft. Worth, 1981; dir. Albright Inst. Archeol. Rsch., 1969-70, dir., 1976-77; centennial lectr. Johns Hopkins U., 1976; Dahood lectr. Loyola U., 1983; Soc. Bibl. Lit. meml. lectr., 1983, Smithsonian lectr., 1984; prin. bibl. cons. Reader's Digest, 1984, 88, 89, 90, 94; disting. faculty lectr. Univ. Mich., 1988; Stone lectr. Princeton Theol. Sem., 1989; Mowinckel lectr., Oslo U., 1991; lectr. Uppsala U., Sweden, 1991; vis. lectr. Brigham Young Ctr. Near Eastern Studies, Jerusalem, 1993. Author: Pottery, Poetry and Prphecy, 1980, The Unity of the Hebrew Bible, 1991 (paperback edit., 1993), Divine Commitment and Human Obligation, 1997, Psalm 119, 1999, The Nine Commandments, 2000; co-author: (with J.D. Smart) God Has Spoken, 1949, (with F.M. Cross, Jr.) Early Hebrew Orthography, 1952, (with John M. Allegro) The People of the Dead Sea Scrolls, 1958, (with R.M. Grant) The Secret Sayings of Jesus, 1960, (with F.M. Cross, Jr.) Ancient Yahwistic Poetry, 1964, rev. edit., 1975, 97, (with M. Dothan) Ashdod I, 1967, The Published Works of W.F. Albright, 1975, (with L.G. Running) William F. Albright: Twentieth Century Genius, 1975, 2d edit., 1991, (with B. Mazar, G. Cornfeld) The Mountain of the Lord, 1975, (with W. Phillips) An Explorer's Life of Jesus, 1975, (with G. Cornfeld) Archaeology of the Bible: Book by Book, 1976, Pottery, Poetry and Prophecy, 1980, (with K.A. Mathews) The Paleo-Hebrew Leviticus Scroll, 1985, The Unity of the Hebrew Bible, 1991, (with D. Forbes and F. Andersen) Studies in Hebrew and Aramaic Orthography, 1992, (with Sara Mandell) The Relationship between Herodotus' History and Primary History, 1993, (with J. Geoghegan and M. Homar) The Nine Commandments, 2000; co-author, editor: (with F. Andersen) Anchor Bible Series Hosea, 1980, Anchor Bible Series Amos, 1989, Micah, 2000; editor: (with G.E. Wright) The Biblical Archaeologist, Reader I, 1961, (with E.F. Campbell, Jr.) The Biblical Archaeologist, Reader 2, 1964, Reader 3, 1970, Reader 4, 1983, (with W.F. Albright) The Anchor Bible, 1964—, including, Genesis, 1964, James, Peter and Jude, 1964, Jeremiah, 1965, Job, 1965, 2d edit., 1973, Proverbs and Ecclesiastes, 1965, I Chronicles, II Chronicles, Ezra-Nehemiah, 1965, Psalms I, 1966, John I, 1966, Acts of the Apostles, 1967, II Isaiah, 1968, Psalms II, 1968, John II, 1970, Psalms III, 1970, Esther, 1971, Matthew, 1971, Lamentations, 1972, 2d edit., 1992, To the Hebrews, 1972, Ephesians 1-3, 4-6, 1974, I and II Esdras, 1974, Judges, 1975, Revelation, 1975, Ruth, 1975, I Maccabees, 1976, I Corinthians, 1976, Additions, 1977, Song of Songs, 1977, Daniel, 1978, Wisdom of Solomon, 1979, I Samuel, 1980, Hosea, 1980, Luke I, 1981, Joshua, 1982, Epistles of John, 1983, II Maccabees, 1983, II Samuel, 1984, II Corinthians, 1984, Luke II, 1985, Judith, 1985, Mark, 1986, Haggai-Zechariah 1-8, 1987, Ecclesiasticus, 1987, 2 Kings, 1988, Amos, 1989, Titus, 1990, Jonah, 1990, Leviticus I, 1991, Deuteronomy I, 1991, Numbers 1-20, 1993, Romans, 1993, Jude and 2 Peter, 1993, Zechariah 9-14, 1993, Zephaniah, 1994, Colossians, 1995, Joel, 1995, James, 1995, Obadiah, 1996, Tobit, 1996, Ecclesiastes, 1997, Ezekiel 21-37, 1997, Galatians, 1997, Malachi, 1998, Acts of the Apostles, 1998, Exodus 1-18, 1999, Jeremiah 1-20, 1999, Mark 1-8, 2000, Numbers 21-36, 2000, 1 Peter, 2001, Isaiah 1-39, 2000, Thessalonians 1&2, 2000, Leviticus 17-22, 2000, Proverbs 1-9, 2000, Micah, 2000, Philemon, 2000, Timothy 1&2, 2001, Hebrews, 2001, Leviticus 23-27, 2001; editor Anchor Bible Ref. Libr., Jesus Within Judaism, 1988, Archaeology of the Land of the Bible, 1990, The Tree of Life, 1990, A Marginal Jew Vol. 1, 1991, The Pentateuch, 1991, The Rise of Jewish Nationalism, 1992, History and Prophecy, 1993, Jesus and the Dead Sea Scrolls, 1993, The Birth of the Messiah, 1993, The Death of the Messiah, 2 vols., 1994, Introduction to Rabbinical Literature, 1994, A Marginal Jew, vol. 2, 1994, The Scepter and the Star, 1995, An Introduction to the New Testament, 1997, Education in Ancient Israel, 1998, Warrior, Dancer, Seductress, Queen, 1998, A History of the Synoptic Problem, 1999, Archaeology of the Land of the Bible, vol. 2, 2001, editor: Eerdmans Critical Commentary, 1 and 2 Timothy, 1999, Philemon, 2000, Biblical Resource Series, The Parables of Jesus, 2000, The Rivers of Paradise, 2000, Eerdmans Dictionary of the Bible, 2000, Bible in its World Series: David's Secret Demons, 2001, (with J. Greenfield) New Directions in Biblical Archaeology, 1969, (with J.A. Baird) The Computer Bible, 1971, A Critical Concordance to the Synoptic Gospels, 1971, An Analytic Linguistic Concordance to the Book of Isaiah, 1971, I, II, III John: Forward and Reverse Concordance and Index, 1971, A Critical Concordance to Hosea, Amos, Micah, 1972, A Critical Concordance of Haggai, Zechariah, Malachi, 1973, A Critical Concordance to the Gospel of John, 1974, A Synoptic Concordance of Aramaic Inscriptions, 1975, A Linguistic Concordance of Ruth and Jonah, 1976, A Linguistic Concordance of Jeremiah, 1978, Syntactical and Critical Concordance of Jeremiah, 1978, Synoptic Abstract, 1978, I and II Corinthians, 1979, Zechariah, 1979, Galatians, 1980, Ephesians, 1981, Philippians, 1982, Colossians, 1983, Pastoral Epistles, 1984, 1 & 2 Thessalaians, 1985, Density Plots in Ezekiel, 1986, Exodus, 1987, Hebrews, 1988, Ruth, 1989, James, 1991, 1 & 2 Peter, 1991, 1, 2 & 3 John and Jude, 1991, Psalms, Job and Proverbs, 1992, Apocalypse, 1993, The Pentateuch, 1995, Aramaic Inscriptions, 1975, (with T. Kachel) Religion and the Academic Scene, 1975, Am. Schs. Oriental Research publs; co-editor: Scrolls from Qumran Cave I, 1972, Jesus: The Four Gospels, 1973, Pomegranates and Golden Bells, 1995; Reader's Digest editor: Atlas of the Bible, 1981, Family Guide to the Bible, 1984, Mysteries of the Bible, 1988, Who's Who in the Bible, 1994, The Bible Through the Ages, 1996, Complete Guide to the Bible, 1998; gen. editor: (facsimile edit.) Complete Guide to the Bible, 1998; The Leningrad Codex, 1998; assoc. editor Jour. Bible Lit., 1952-54, editor, 1955-59; cons. editor Interpreter's Dictionary of the Bible, 1957-60, Theologisches Wörterbuch des Alten Testaments, 1970-92, English Translation Theological Word-Book of the Old Testament, 1975—; editor in chief The Anchor Bible Dictionary, 6 vols., 1992; co-editor (with W.H. Propp and Baruch Halpern) The Hebrew Bible and Its Interpreters, 1990; contbr. numerous articles to profl. jours. Recipient prize in New Testament exegesis Princeton Theol. Sem., 1943, Carey-Thomas award for Anchor Bible, 1965, Layman's Nat. Bible Com. award, 1978, 3 awards for Anchor Bible Bibl. Archaeol. Soc., 1993; William H. Green fellow in Old Testament, 1944, William S. Rayner fellow Johns Hopkins U., 1946, 47, Guggenheim fellow, 1959, Am. Assn. Theol. Schs. fellow, 1963; Am. Coun. Learned Socs. grantee-in-aid, 1967, 76. Fellow U. Mich. Soc. Fellows (sr., chmn. 1980-82); mem. Soc. Bibl. Lit. (pres. 1975-76), Am. Oriental Soc., Am. Schs. Oriental Rsch. (v.p. 1970-82, editor bull. 1974-78, editor Bibl. Archeologist 1976-82, dir. publs. 1974-82), Archaeol. Inst. Am., Am. Acad. Religion, Bibl. Colloquium (sec.-treas. 1960-90). Office: U Calif San Diego Dept History 0104 9500 Gilman Dr Dept 0104 La Jolla CA 92093-5004 E-mail: dnfreedman@ucsd.edu

FREEDMAN, JONATHAN BORWICK, journalist, writer, lecturer, educator; b. Rochester, N.Y., Apr. 11, 1950; s. Marshall Arthur and Betty (Borwick) F.; children: Madigan, Nicholas; m. Isabelle Rooney, 1999; 1 child, Genevieve. AB in Lit. cum laude, Columbia Coll., N.Y.C., 1972. Reporter AP of Brazil, Sao Paulo and Rio de Janeiro, 1974-75; editorial writer The Tribune, San Diego, 1981-90; syndicated columnist Copley News Service, San Diego, 1987-89; free-lance opinion writer L.A. Times, 1990—; free-lance editorial writer N.Y. Times, 1990-91; dir. Hope Lit. Project, 1998—. Dist. vis. lectr. and adj. faculty San Diego State U., 1990—; mem. U.S.-Japan Journalists Exch. Program, Internat. Press Inst., 1985. Author, illustrator: The Man Who'd Bounce the World, 1979; author: The Editorials and Essays of Jonathan Freedman, 1988, Wall of Fame, 2000; contbg. author: Best Newspaper Writing, From Contemporary Culture, 1991, (nonfiction) From Cradle to Grave: The Human Face of Poverty in America, 1993; freelance columnist, 1979-81; dir. (TV documentary) Pedaling Hope, 1998; contbr. articles to N.Y. Times, Chgo. Tribune, San Francisco Examiner, Oakland Tribune, others. Moderator PBS, San Diego, 1988; bd. dirs. Schs. of the Future Commn., San Diego, 1987. Recipient Copley Ring of Truth award, 1983, Sigma Delta Chi award, 1983, San Diego Press Club award, 1984, Spl. citation Columbia Grad. Sch. Journalism, 1985, Disting. Writing award Am. Soc. Newspaper Editors, 1986, Pulitzer prize in Disting. Editorial Writing, 1987; Cornell Woolrich Writing fellow Columbia U., 1972, Eugene C. Pullian Editorial Writing fellow Sigma Delta Chi Found., 1986, Media fellow Hoover Instn., Stanford, Calif., 1991, Kaiser Media fellow, 1995, Peacemaker award San Diego Mediation Ctr., 1999, one of 45 Am. Heroes, Esquire mag., 1998. Mem. Soc. Profl. Journalists (Disting. Svc. award 1985, Casey medal for meritorious journalism 1994), Nat. Conf. Editl. Writers, Authors Guild, Phi Beta Kappa. Jewish. Avocations: skiing, tai chi. Office: 755 Genter St La Jolla CA 92037-5459

FREEDMAN, LOUIS, vintager executive; CFO E&J Gallo Winery, Modesto, Calif. Office: E&J Gallo Winery 600 Yosemite Blvd Modesto CA 95354

FREEDMAN, MICHAEL HARTLEY, mathematician, educator; b. Los Angeles, Apr. 21, 1951; s. Benedict and Nancy (Mars) F.; 1 child by previous marriage, Benedict C.; m. Leslie Blair Howland, Sept. 18, 1983; children: Hartley, Whitney, Jake. Ph.D., Princeton U., 1973. Lectr. U. Calif., 1973-75; mem. Inst. Advanced Study, Princeton, N.J., 1975-76; prof. U. Calif., San Diego, 1976-97, Charles Lee Powell chair math., 1985—; sr. rsch. scientist Microsoft Corp., 1997—. Author: Classification of Four Dimensional Spaces, 1982; assoc. editor Jour. Differential Geometry, Math. Rsch. Letters and Topology, 1982—, Annals of Math., 1984-91, Jour. Am. Math. Soc., 1987—. MacArthur Found. fellow, 1984-89; named Calif. Scientist of Yr., Calif. Mus. Assn., 1984; recipient Veblen prize Am. Math. Soc., 1986, Fields medal Internat. Congress of Mathematicians, 1986, Nat. Medal of Sci., 1987, Humboldt award, 1988; Guggenheim fellow, 1989, 94. Mem. Nat. Acad. Scis., Am. Assn. Arts and Scis., N.Y. Acad. Sics., Guggenheim Fellowship award, 1994. Avocation: technical rock climber (soloed Northeast ridge Mt. Williamson winter 1970, Great Western boulder climbing champion 1979). Office: Microsoft Rsch One Microsoft Way Redmond WA 98052

FREEDMAN, SARAH WARSHAUER, education educator; b. Wilmington, N.C., Feb. 23, 1946; d. Samuel Edward and Miriam (Miller) Warshauer; m. S. Robert Freedman, Aug. 20, 1967; 1 child, Rachel Karen. BA in English, U. Pa., 1967; MA in English, U. Chgo., 1970; MA in Linguistics, Stanford U., 1976, PhD in Edn., 1977. Tchr. English Phila. Sch. Dist., 1967-68, Lower Merion H.S., 1968-69; instr. English U. N.C., Wilmington, 1970-71; instr. English and linguistics Stanford U., 1972-76; asst. and assoc. prof. English San Francisco State U., 1977-81; asst. prof. edn. U. Calif., Berkeley, 1981-83, assoc. prof. edn., 1983-89; dir. Nat. Ctr. for the Study of Writing and Literacy, 1985-96; prof. edn. U. Calif., 1989—. Resident Bellagio Conf. and Study Ctr., Rockefeller Found., 1997; mem. nat. task force Nat. Writing Project, 1998—. Author: Response to Student Writing, 1987, Exchanging Writing, Exchanging Cultures, Lessons in School Reform from the United States and Great Britain, 1994, (with E.R. Simons, J.S. Kalnin, A Casareno and M-Class teams) Inside City Schools, Investigating Literacy in Multi-cultural Classrooms, 1999; editor: The Acquisition of Written Language: Response and Revision, 1985; contbr. chpts. to books and articles to profl. jours. Recipient Richard Meade award for Pub. Rsch. in Tchr. Edn. Nat. Coun. Tchrs. English, 1989, 94, Ed Fry book award, 1996, 2000, Multicultural Book award, Nat. Assn. Multicultural Edn., 2000; fellow Nat. Conf. on Rsch. in English, 1986, Ctr. Advanced Study Behavioral Scis., 1999-00; Spencer Found. grantee, 1996-99, Rockefeller Found. grantee Bryn Mawr Coll., 1992, Nat. Ctr. for Study of Writing and Literacy grantee Office Ednl. Rsch. and Improvement, 1985-95, Minority Undergrad. Rsch. Program grantee U. Calif., 1988, 89, 92, 93, numerous other grants. Mem. Nat. Coun. Tchrs. English (mem. standing com. on rsch. 1981-87, ex-officio 1987—, chair bd. trustees rsch. found. 1990-93, co-chair rsch. assembly 1999—), Am. Ednl. Rsch. Assn. (chair spl. interest group on rsch. in writing 1983-85, numerous other coms.), Linguistic Soc. Am., Am. Assn. Applied Linguistics, Internat. Reading Assn. Office: U Calif Dept Edn Berkeley CA 94720-0001

FREEDMAN, STANLEY MARVIN, manufacturing company executive; b. Frederick, Md., Aug. 26, 1923; s. Jacob Menaham and Ethel (Freiman) F.; m. Lynn Maureen Katchen, Apr. 24, 1957 (dec.); children: Rita, Lynn, Michael, Richard, Jon, Jack; m. Lottie Carnell, Dec. 31, 1994 (div.). Student, Georgetown U., 1944; AB in English, High Point Coll., 1946. Owner, operator retail bus., Bound Brook, N.J., 1949-63; dir. mktg. Franklin State Bank, Somerset, 1963-65; program dir. mktg. div. Am. Mgmt. Assn. N.Y.C., 1965-67; exec. dir. Internat. Bus. Forms Industries, Washington, 1967-69; dir. communications, dir. office machines group Bus. Equipment Mfrs. Assn., Washington, 1969-72; div. pres. Litton Industries, Hampton, Va., 1972-74, group v.p., paper, printing and forms group Virginia Beach, 1974-86. Cons. bus. planning and devel; univ. lectr., 1986-91; dir. Somerset County Savs. & Loan; exec. in residence U. Wis. Grad. Sch. Bus., 1973; entrepreneur in residence U. of the Pacific, Stockton, Calif., 1996. Mem. Bound Brook Bd. Edn., 1955-63; trustee Raritan Valley Hosp., Somerset, N.J., 1960-62; chmn. Urban Devel., Bound Brook, N.J., 1963; mem. def. conversion team AID, Warsaw, Poland, 1995-96. Served with U.S. Army, 1943-46, PTO. Mem. Am. Transfer Print Assn. (conf. bd.), Am. Mgmt. Assn. Home and Office: 7046 E Soaring Eagle Way Scottsdale AZ 85262-7108 E-mail: stanrlmrjj@earthlink.net

FREELAND, ROBERT FREDERICK, retired librarian; b. Flint, Mich., Dec. 20, 1919; s. Ralph V. and Susan Barbara (Goetz) F.; m. June Voshel, June 18, 1948; children: Susan Beth Visser, Kent Richard. BS, Eastern Mich. U., 1942; postgrad., Washington & Lee U., 1945; MS, U. So. Calif., 1948, postgrad., 1949, U. Mich., 1950-52, Calif. State U., 1956-58, UCLA, 1960; LittD (hon.), Linda Vista Bible Coll., 1973. Music supr. Consol. Schs. Warren, Mich., 1946-47; music dir. Carson City (Mich.) Pub. Schs., 1948-49; librarian, audio-visual coord. Ford Found., Edison Inst., Greenfield Village, Dearborn, Mich., 1950-52, Helix High Sch. Library, 1952-77; librarian, prof. library sci. Linda Vista Bible Coll., 1976—; reference libr. San Diego Pub. Libr. System, 1967-97. Cons. edn., libr. and multimedia. Editor book and audio-visual aids review, Sch. Musician, Dir. and Teacher, 1950-75. Former deacon and elder Christian Reform Ch., libr., 1969-72, Classis archivist, 1991—; pub. affairs officer, sr. program officer, moral leadership officer Sq. 57 GP III, Calif. wing CAP. With USAAF, 1942-46. Named Scholar Freedoms Found., Valley Forge, Pa., 1976-80. Mem. NEA (life), ALA, Nat. Music Camp, Calif. Tchrs. Assn., Music Libr. Assn. So. Calif. (adviser exec. bd.), Calif. Libr. Assn. (pres. Palomar chpt. 1972-73), Sch. Libr. Assn. Calif. (treas. 1956-73), Calif. Media and Libr. Educators (charter mem.), Am. Legion (Americanism chmn. 22d dist. San Diego County, chmn. oratorical contest com. La Mesa post), Ret. Officers Assn., San Diego Aero Space Mus., San Diego Mus. Art, Alumnia Assn. Ea. Mich. U. Home: 4800 Williamsburg Ln Apt 223 La Mesa CA 91941-4651 E-mail: 112527.676@compuserve.com

FREEMAN, GORDON RUSSEL, chemistry educator; b. Hoffer, Sask., Can., Aug. 27, 1930; s. Winston Spencer Churchill and Aquila Maud (Chapman) F.; m. Phyllis Joan Elson, Sept. 8, 1951; children: Mark Russel, Michèle Leslie. B.A., U. Sask., 1952, M.A., 1953; Ph.D., McGill U., 1955; D.Phil., Oxford (Eng.) U., 1957. Postdoctoral fellow Centre D'Etudes Nucléaires, Saclay, France, 1957-58; asst. prof., then assoc. prof. chemistry U. Alta. (Can.), Edmonton, 1958-65, prof., 1965 95, chmn. div. phys. and theoretical chemistry, 1965-75, dir. radiation rsch. ctr., 1968-95, prof. emeritus, 1995—; exec. Chem. Inst. Can., 1974-80, chmn. phys. chemistry div., 1976-78, councillor, 1978-80. Contbr. over 440 articles to jours., chpts. to books on radiation chemisty and chemical physics. Research grantee Nat. Research Council Can., 1959-78; research grantee Natural Scis. and Engring. Research Council Can., 1978-98, Def. Research Bd. Can., 1965-72 Mem. Chem. Inst. Can., Am. Phys. Soc., Can. Soc. History & Philosophy Sci., Can. Assn. Archaeologists. Achievements include current research in archaeoastronomy and sociology. Office: U Alta U Alta Chemistry Dept Edmonton AB Canada T6G 2G2 E-mail: k.np@ualberta.ca

FREEMAN, LINTON CLARKE, sociology educator; b. Chgo., July 4, 1927; s. Willis and Kathryn Clarke (Kieffer) F.; m. Sue Carole Feinberg, Aug. 2, 1958; children: Stacey Elizabeth Vanhanswyk, Michael Andrew. B.A., Roosevelt U., Chgo., 1952; M.A., U. Hawaii, 1953; Ph.D., Northwestern U., 1956. Asst. prof., then assoc. prof. sociology Syracuse (N.Y.) U., 1956-67; prof. sociology and computer sci. U. Pitts., 1967-69; prof. sociology and info. sci. U. Hawaii, 1969-72; Lucy G. Moses distinguished prof. sociology Lehigh U., Bethlehem, Pa., 1973-79; prof. Sch. Social Scis., U. Calif., Irvine, 1979—, dean, 1979-82; Killam sr. lectr. sociology and anthropology Dalhousie U., Halifax, N.S., Can., 1972; directeur d'Etudes Associé Maison des Sciences de l'Homme, Paris, 1991. Ward supr. Onondaga County (N.Y.) Bd. Suprs., 1966-68 Author: Elementary Applied Statistics, 1965, Patterns of Local Community Leadership, 1968; co-author: Residential Segregation Patterns, 1970; editor: Social Networks; contbr. to profl. jours. Served with USNR, 1944-46. Home: 2705 Temple Hills Dr Laguna Beach CA 92651-2037 Office: U Calif Sch Social Scis Irvine CA 92697-1500 E-mail: lin@aris.ss.uci.edu

FREEMAN, MARSHALL, publishing executive; BA in Econs., Stanford U., 1955. Advt. sales McGraw-Hill, N.Y.C., Boston, L.A., 1957-63; from salesman to chmn., CEO Miller Freeman Publs., San Francisco, 1963-98, chmn., 1998—. Office: Miller Freeman Inc 600 Harrison St Ste 400 San Francisco CA 94107-1391

FREEMAN, MILTON MALCOLM ROLAND, anthropology educator; b. London, Apr. 23, 1934; came to Can., 1958; s. Louis and Fay (Bomberg) F.; m. Mini Christina Aodla; children: Graham, Elaine, Malcolm. BS, Reading U., Eng., 1958; postgrad., U. Coll., London, 1962-64; PhD, McGill U., 1965. Research scientist No. Affairs Dept., Ottawa, Ont., Can., 1965-67; asst. prof. Meml. U., St. John's, Nfld., Can., 1967-71, assoc. prof. Can., 1971-72; dir. Inuit Land Use Study, Hamilton, Ont., 1973-75; prof. anthropology McMaster U., Hamilton, 1976-81; Henry Marshall Tory prof. U. Alta., Edmonton, Can., 1982-99, prof. emeritus, 1999—, adj. prof. East Asian studies Can., 1993—. Adj. prof. environ. studies U. Waterloo, Ont., 1977-81; sr. sci. advisor Indian and No. Affairs, Ottawa, 1979-81; chmn. No. Sci. Network, UNESCO-MAB, 1983-87; sr. rsch. scholar Can. Circumpolar Inst., U. Alta., 1990—; McLean prof. Trent U., Peterborough, Can., 1995; chmn. UNESCO-MAB No. Sci. Network, 1983-88. Author: People Pollution, 1974, Cultural Anthropology of Whaling, 1989, Recovering Rights, 1992, Inuit, Whaling, and Sustainability, 1998; editor: Inuit Land Use and Occupancy Report, 1976, Procs. Internat. Symposium on Renewable Resources and the Economy of the North, 1981, Japanese Small-type Coastal Whaling, 1988, Endangered Peoples of the Arctic, 2000; co-editor: Adaptive Management of Marine Resources in the Pacific, 1991, Elephants and Whales: Resources for Whom?, 1994. Bd. dirs. Sci. Inst. N.W.T., 1985-87; chmn. adv. bd. Circumpolar Inst., 1990—; chmn. Man-Environ. Commn., Internat. Union Anthrop. and Ethnol. Scis., 1977-82. Fellow Am. Anthropol. Assn., Arctic Inst. Soc. Applied Anthropology; mem. Soc. Applied Anthropology Can. (pres. 1984-85). Home: 305 10710 80th Ave Edmonton AB Canada T6E 1V8 Office: U Alta Can Circumpolar Inst Edmonton AB Canada T6G 0H1 E-mail: milton.freeman@ualberta.ca

FREEMAN, PATRICIA ELIZABETH, library and education specialist; b. El Dorado, Ark., Nov. 30, 1924; d. Herbert A. and M. Elizabeth (Pryor) Harper; m. Jack Freeman, June 15, 1949; 3 children. BA, Centenary Coll., 1943; postgrad., Fine Arts Ctr., 1942-46, Art Students League, 1944-45; BSLS, La. State U., 1946; postgrad., Calif. State U., 1959-61, U. N.Mex., 1964-74; EdS, Peabody Coll., Vanderbilt U., 1975. Libr. U. Calif., Berkeley, 1946-47; libr. Albuquerque Pub. Schs., 1964-67, ind. sch. libr. media ctr. cons., 1967—. Painter lithographer; one-person show La. State Exhibit Bldg., 1948; author: Pathfinder: An Operational Guide for the School Librarian, 1975, Southeast Heights Neighborhoods of Albuquerque, 1993; compiler, editor: Elizabeth Pryor Harper's Twenty-One Southern Families, 1985; editor: SEHNA Gazette, 1988-93, N.Mex. AAUW, 1999—. Mem. task force Goals for Dallas-Environ., 1977-82; pres. Friends of Sch. Librs., Dallas, 1979-83; v.p., editor Southeast Heights Neighborhood Assn., 1988-93. With USAF, 1948-49. Honoree AAUW Ednl. Found., 1979, 96; vol. award for outstanding service Dallas Ind. Sch. Dist., 1978; AAUW Pub. Service grantee 1980. Mem. ALA, AAUW (dir. Dallas 1976-82, Albuquerque 1983-85, N.Mex. 1999—), LWV (sec. Dallas 1982-83, editor Albuquerque 1984-88), Nat. Trust Historic Preservation, Friends for the Pub. Libr., Colorado Springs Fine Arts Ctr., N.Mex. Symphony Guild, Alpha Xi Delta. Home: 612 Ridgecrest Dr SE Albuquerque NM 87108-3365

FREEMAN, RALPH CARTER, investment banker, management consultant; b. La Grange, Ga. s. Ralph Carter and Alice (Cordell) F.; m. Carole Stephens, July 31, 1957 (div. 1977); children: Carter III, Allyson, Stephens, LeAnna; m. Nancy Lynn Brown, Apr. 8, 1977. BBA, Emory U., 1959. CPA, Mont.; cert. mgmt. cons.; real estate broker, Calif. From mem. staff to ptnr. Pannell Kerr Forster, Atlanta, Honolulu, 1959-72; mgmt. cons. Touche Ross & Co., Honolulu, Am. Samoa, Asia, South Pacific, 1972-75; pres. FP Industries, Inc., Hawaii, Mont., Ga., 1975-85, Janas Consulting, Huntsville, Ala., 1986-90; prin. Janas Assocs. Investment Bankers, Orange County, San Diego, Houston, 1999—, Orange County, Houston, 1999—. Founder Peoples Bank LaGrange, Ga., 1966; founding investor Bank of Newnan, Ga., 1988. Contbr. articles to profl. jours. and nat. trade mags. Mem. Inst. Mgmt. Cons. (cert., bd. dirs., treas. 1999-2000), All Cities Resource Group, Turnaround Mgmt. Assn., L.A. Venture Assn., Sigma Alpha Epsilon. Avocations: fishing, tennis, camping.

FREEMAN, RUSSELL ADAMS, lawyer; b. Albany, N.Y., July 22, 1932; s. Russell Marvin and Edith (Adams) F.; m. Elizabeth Frances McHale, June 30, 1956; children: Lynn, James. BA, Amherst Coll., 1954; JD, Albany (N.Y.) Law Sch., 1957; LLM, U. So. Calif., 1966. Bar: N.Y. 1957, Calif. 1960. Practiced in, Albany, 1957-59; with Security Pacific Nat. Bank, L.A., 1959-92, v.p., 1968-72, counsel, 1968-74, head legal dept., 1968-74; sr. v.p. Security Pacific Corp., L.A., 1972-81, exec. v.p., 1981-92, gen. counsel, 1972-92; sr. counsel O'Melveny & Myers, L.A., 1992-94. Bd. govs. Fin. Lawyers Conf., 1972-74; faculty Pacific Coast Banking Sch., 1980-81; lectr. in field, 1965-94. Contbr. articles to profl. publns. Trustee Flintridge Prep. Sch., La Canada, Calif., 1978-80. Mem. ABA (mem. banking com.), Am. Bankers Assn. (mem. govt. rels. com. 1981-84, del. to Leadership Conf. 1984-86, 90-92), Assn. Banking Holding Cos., Calif. Bankers Assn. (dir., chmn. govt. rels. group 1979-81, 86-88, dir. and chmn. fed. govt. rels. 1985-86, Almon B. McCallum award for disting. and meritorious legal svc. 1986), Calif. Bankers Clearing House Assn. (chmn. pub. policy adv. com. 1980-81, 88-89), Calif. State Bar, L.A. County Bar Assn. past chmn. comml. law and bankruptcy sect., Outstanding Corp. Counsel award 1989, corp. law dept. sect., Constl. Rights Found. (bd. dirs. 1986-94).

FREEMAN, TOM M. lawyer; b. Wauwatosa, Wis., Oct. 5, 1952; s. Max and Betty J. (Zimmerman) F.; m. Judith Casper, June 23, 1974; children: Sarah Carolyn, Benjamin Robert. BA with honors, U. Wis., 1974; JD cum laude, Harvard U., 1977. Bar: Wis. 1977, Ill. 1978, Calif. 1980, U.S. Dist. Ct. (we. dist.) Wis. 1977, U.S. Ct. Appeals (7th cir.) 1978, U.S. Dist. Ct. (no. dist.) Calif. 1980, U.S. Ct. Appeals (9th cir.) 1982. Law clk. Wis. Supreme Ct., Madison, 1977-78; staff atty. U.S. Ct. Appeals (7th cir.), Chgo., 1978-80; assoc. Brobeck, Phleger, Harrison, LLP, San Francisco, 1980-85. Democrat. Jewish. Office: Brobeck Phleger & Harrison LLP Spear St Tower 1 Market San Francisco CA 94105 E-mail: tfreeman@brobeck.com

FREESTONE, THOMAS LAWRENCE, state legislator; b. Mesa, Ariz., July 15, 1938; s. Herbert L. and Margaret (Heywood) F.; m. Phyllis Rogers, Jan. 14, 1961; children: Jeanne Freestone Palmer, Crystal Freestone Davis, Michael Phillip. Student Brigham Young U., 1956-57, Ariz. State U., 1957-58, Mesa C.C., 1964. Constable East Mesa Justice precinct Maricopa County, 1968-72, chief dep. recorder, 1972-74; mgr. Maricopa County Auto Lic. Bur., Mesa, 1972-74; recorder Maricopa County, 1974-78, mem. bd. suprs., 1978—; pres. Freestone Travels, Inc., Mesa, 1979-83. Mem. Ariz. Jail Assn., Ariz. Jail Standards Adv. Com., various Ariz. Joint Legis. Coms.; past chmn. Rep. State Election Bd.; past precinct committeeman Dist. 29, 21.; del. Conf. on Security and Cooperation in Europe. Mem. Ariz. State Legis. Jt. Study Com. on County Issues, Corp. Commn. Citizens Com.; active Mesa United Way; bd. dirs. Mesa Hist. and Archaeol. Soc., Morrison Found., Mesa, PreHab Found., Mesa, Luth. Healthcare Network, Mesa, Mesa Community Coll. Ho-Chief Found., Cystic Fibrosis Found., March of Dimes, Mesa YMCA; scoutmaster, explorer post advisor Boy Scouts Am. Recipient Outstanding Citizen award Valley Radio, United Way award, 1981, MARC Ctr. award for Outstanding Svc., 1981, Key to City of Mesa, 1992; named Outstanding Citizen of Yr., 1990. Mem. Nat. Assn. Counties (criminal justice and pub. safety steering com. 1884—), Ariz. Assn. Counties, Maricopa Assn. Govts., Nat. Recorders and Clerks Assn., Ariz. Assn. County Recorders (legis. steering com.), Nat. Assn. Election County Officials, Trunk 'N Tusk Club, Mesa C. of C., Chandler C. of C. Republican. Mem. Ch. of Jesus Christ of Latter-Day Saints. Avocations: raquetball, football, bodybuilding. Office: Ariz Senate 1700 W Washington St Phoenix AZ 85007-2812

FREI, BRENT R. computer software executive; BS in Engrg., Dartmouth Coll., Hanover, N.H., 1989; MS, Dartmouth Coll. Mech. engr. Motorola Corp., 1989-90; progammer analyst Microsoft Info. Tech. Group, 1991-94; dir. ONYX, 1994—, pres., sec., treas., 1995-98, pres., CEO, Chmn., 1998—. Office: ONYX Software Corp 3180 139th Ave SE Ste 500 Bellevue WA 98005-4091

FREIHEIT, CLAYTON FREDRIC, zoo director; b. Buffalo, Jan. 29, 1938; s. Clayton John and Ruth (Miller) F. Student, U. Buffalo, 1960; DHL (hon.), U. Denver, 1996. Caretaker Living Mus., Buffalo Mus. Sci., 1955-60; curator Buffalo Zool. Gardens, 1960-70; dir. Denver Zool. Gardens, 1970—. Contbr. articles to profl. jours. Named Outstanding Citizen, Buffalo Evening News, 1967 Mem. Internat. Union Dirs. Zool. Gardens, Am. Assn. Zool. Pks. and Aquariums (pres. 1967-68 Outstanding Svc. award). Home: 3855 S Monaco Pky Denver CO 80237-1271 Office: Denver Zool Gardens City Park Denver CO 80205

FREIMAN, PAUL E. pharmaceutical company executive; b. 1932; BS, Fordham U., 1955. Formely exec. v.p. pharm. and agribusiness Syntex USA Inc., pres., co-chief exec. officer, now pres., chief exec. officer, bd. dirs.; also pres. Syntex Corp., Palo Alto, Calif.; pres. and CEO Neurobiological Technologies Inc., Richmond, CA, 1997—. Office: Neurobiological Technologies Inc 1387 Marina Way S Richmond CA 94804-3746

FREIMARK, ROBERT (BOB FREIMARK), artist; b. Doster, Mich., Jan. 27, 1922; s. Alvin O. and Nora (Shinaver) F.; m. Mary Carvin (dec.); 1 son, Matisse Jon; m. Lillian Tihlarik; 1 child, Christine Gay. B.E., U. Toledo, 1950; M.F.A., Cranbrook Acad. Art, 1951. Prof. art emeritus San Jose State U., 1964-86; W.I.C.H.E. prof. Soledad State Prison, 1967. Established artist in residence program Yosemite Nat. Park,1984-85, Fire Clay and Tile, Aromas, Calif., 1998; artist in residence Museo Regla, Cuba, 2000. Guest artist Harvard U., 1972-73; first Am. to make tapestries in Art Protis technique at Atelier Vlnena, Brno, Czechoslovakia.; contbr. to profl. publs.; Numerous solo shows including, Minn. Inst. Arts, Toledo Mus. Art, Salpeter Gallery, Morris Gallery, N.Y.C., Des Moines Art Center, Santa Barbara Mus., Moravska Mus., Czechoslovakia, Brunel U., London, Amerika Haus, Munich, Stuttgart, Regensburg, Joslyn Ctr. for Arts, Torrance, Calif, Stanford U., San Jose (Calif.) Mus. Art, Triton Mus., Santa Clara, Calif., Guatemalteco, Guatemala City, Dum Umeni Brno, CSFR, Strahov Closter, Prague, 1990, Walter Bischoff Gallery, Stuttgart, 1990, Kunstler aus den USA, Kunsthaus Ostbayern and Amerika Haus, Stuttgart, 1991, Max Planck Inst., Munich, The Gag Theatre, Prague, 1992, Haus Wiegand, Munich, 1993, San Jose State U., 1994, Viva!, Tokyo, 1994, Gallery Q, Sacramento, 1997, Parish Gallery, Wash. D.C., 1997, Barton Gallery, Sacramento, Calif., 1997; Galeria Galiano Havana, 1998, Galerie Weber, Viechtach, Germany, 1998, Point Gall., Brno, Czech Rep., 1998, Galerie Divadlo, Uherske Hradiste, C.R., 1998, Marco Polo Galleries, Carmel, Calif., 2001, exhibited in group shows, Art Inst. Chgo., 1952, Pa. Acad. Fine Arts, 1953 (Lambert Fund prize), Detroit Inst. Arts, 1956, Mich. State U., 1956, N.A.D., 1956, Boston Print Symposium, 1997, Internat. Print Exhibition Portland (Oreg.) Art Mus., 1997, Honolulu Acad. Art, 1998, Internat. Graphic Triennial, Krakow, Poland, 1998, Internat. Small Engraving Salon, Florean Mus., Romania, Art Expo, N.Y.C., 2000, Internat. Woodprint Assn., Kyoto, Japan, 1999, Bklyn. Mus., Mus. Modern Art, Michael Stone Collection, D.C., Contempo Collection, Tokyo, Havana Bienale, 2000, others, L.A., Boston, San Francisco, Omaha, Oklahoma City, Des Moines, Dallas, Phoenix, San Jose, Havana, Tokyo, Manila, Rio de Janeiro, Mexico City, Sao Paulo, Brasilia, Buenos Aires, Prague, exhbn. 50 States toured, European Mus., 1970-71, represented in collections, Pa. Acad. Fine Art, Boston Mus. Fine Arts, Fogg Mus., Butler Inst. Am. Art, Ford Motor Co., South Bend Art Assn., Joslyn Art Mus., Seattle Art Mus., Ga. Mus., Huntington Gallery, Des Moines Art Center, Smithsonian Instn., Libr. Congress, L.A. County Art Inst., Brit. Mus., Nat. Gallery, Prague, Birmingham (Eng.) Mus., Moravske Mus., Brno, Czechoslovakia, Bibliotheque Nationale, Paris, Harn Mus., Gainsville, Fla., Portland Mus. Art (complete prints), Nat. Mus., Washington, Natl. Mus. of Cuba, La Habana, Nat. Mus. Costa Rica, San Jose, Nat. Mus. Egypt, Cairo, others; numerous tapestries in pub. and pvt. collections, created tapestry representing U.S. for Olympic Games, Moscow, 1980; produced film El Día Tarasco, 1982; prodr. video documentary: Arte Cubano (Contemporary Art and Culture in Cuba, 1999, 2000; guest artist, Joslyn Meml. Mus., 1961, instr. painting and drawing, Ohio U., 1955-59, artist in residence, Des Moines Art Center, 1959-63, dir., Crystal Lake Art Center, Frankfort, Mich., (1955-57), guest lectr., one man show, Columbia U., 1963, solo exhibit, Northamerican Cultural Inst., Mexico City, 1963; guest artist, Riverside Art Center, 1964, Agora Vienna, Austria, 1994; curated exhibit Stuttgart, 1993; founder Bob & Lil Freimark Collection Portland Art Mus.; contbr. to craft and fibre publs. Served with USNR, 1939-46. Recipient 2d award for oil Northwest Territorial exhibit, 1954, Roulet medal Toledo Mus. Art, 1957, 1st award Print Exhbn., 1958, purchase award Midwest Biennial and Northwest Printmakers, Jurors award Berkeley Art Ctr, 1996; Calif. State Coll. Sys. spl. creative leave edit. serigraphs; elected to New Talent in U.S.A., 1957; Ohio U. rsch. grantee, 1958-59, Ford Found. grantee, 1965; Western Interstate Commn. for Higher Edn. grantee, 1967, San Jose State Coll. Found. grantee, 1966, 67, 68, 69, 70, 71, 85; designated ofcl. U.S. Bicentennial Exhbn. Amerika Hausen, Fed. Republic Germany, 1976; donated Bob & Lil Freimark Collection, Mexican Arts & Crafts, Gavilan Coll., Gilroy, Calif., 1996; represented by Parish Gallery, Washington, Triad Gallery, Seal Rock, Oreg., Haus Wiegand, Munich, Art Foundry Gallery, Sacramento, Greg Barlon Gallery, Sacramento. Achievements include being subject of TV interview, 1993. Home: 539A Dougherty Ave Morgan Hill CA 95037-9241 Office: Grass Valley Studios Morgan Hill CA 95037 E-mail: bfreimar@pacbell.net

FREITAG, PETER ROY, transportation specialist; b. L.A., Dec. 19, 1943; s. Victor Hugo and Helen Veronica (Burnes) F. Student, U. Fla., 1961-63, George Washington U., 1964-65. Chief supr. Eastern Airlines, L.A., 1965-77; tariff analyst, instr. United Airlines, San Francisco, 1977-84; mng. ptnr. Bentdahl, Freitag & Assoc., San Francisco, 1984-86; v.p. ops. PAD Travel, Inc., Mountain View, Calif., 1985-86; travel mgr. Loral Aerospace Corp, San Jose, 1986-95; pres. Capital Fin. Ptnrs. Corp., San Francisco, 1995—. Co-editor: (textbook) International Air Tariff and Ticketing, 1983. Vol. San Francisco Bay chpt. Oceanic Soc., 1984-95. Mem. Silicon Valley Bus. Travel Assn., Bay Area Bus. Travel Assn. Episcopalian. Avocations: travel, cooking, oenology, hiking. Office: Capital Fin Ptnrs Corp 3145 Geary Blvd Ste 708 San Francisco CA 94118-3316

FRENCH, KIRBY ALLAN, transportation engineer, computer programmer; b. San Angelo, Tex., Oct. 12, 1948; s. Leland Wayne French and Helen Lois (Stennett) French-Vance; m. Verda Jane Amyl Schaffer, Oct. 11, 1970; children: Tammy Lyrae, Adrian Allyn. Diploma in Computer Programming, Mkt. Tng. Inst., 1968. Transp. engr. Calif. Dept. Transp., San Bernardino, 1969-98; ret., 1998. Author: Speed Math, 1991, Trigonometric Formulas, 1991, Speed Reading, 1994, Microsoft Word 6 Macros for Spec Writers, 1996, Power Macintosh Apple Script Programs, 1996. Avocations: computer programming, writing, painting, Star Trek conventions. Home: 1257 Poplar St San Bernardino CA 92410-2522

FRENCH, LAURENCE ARMAND, social science educator, psychology educator; b. Manchester, N.H., Mar. 24, 1941; s. Gerald Everett and Juliette Teresa (Boucher) F.; m. Nancy Picthall, Feb. 13, 1971. BA cum laude, U. N.H., 1968, MA, 1970, PhD, 1975; postdoctorate, SUNY, Albany, 1978; PhD, U. Nebr., 1981; MA, Western N.M. U., 1994. Diplomate Am. Bd. Forensic Medicine, Am. Bd. Forensic Examiners, Am. Bd. Psychol. Specialties in Forensic Psychology & Neuropsychology, Am. Coll. Advanced Practice Psychologists; lic. psychologist, Ariz. Instr. U. So. Maine, Portland and Gorham, 1971-72; asst. prof. Western Carolina U., Cullowhee, N.C., 1972-77, U. Nebr., Lincoln, 1977-80; psychologist I N.H. Hosp., Concord, 1980-81; psychologist II Laconia (N.H.) State Sch., 1981-88; sr. psychologist N.H. Divsn. for Children & Youth Svcs., Concord, 1988-89; prof., chair dept. social scis. Western N.Mex. U., Silver City, 1989—. Psi Chi Nat. Honor Soc. in psychology Western N.Mex. faculty adviser; adj. assoc. prof. U. So. Maine, 1980-84; cons. N.C. Dept. Mental Health, 1977-77, Nebr. Indian Commn., Lincoln, 1977-80, Cherokee (N.C.) Indian Mental Health Program, 1974-77; cons. alcohol program Lincoln Indian Ctr., 1977-80; prof. adv. bd. Internat. Coll. Prescribing Psychologists. Author: The Selective Process of Criminal Justice, 1976, (with Richard Crowe) Wee Wish Tree: Special Qualla Cherokee Issue, 1976, (with Hornbuckle) Cherokee Perspective, 1981, (with Letman et al) Contemporary Issues in Corrections, 1981, Indians and Criminal Justice, 1982, Psychocultural Change and the American Indian, 1987, The Winds of Injustice, 1994, Counseling American Indians, 1997, The Qualla Cherokee Surviving in Two Worlds, 1998, Addictions and Native Americans, 2000; spl. issue editor Quar. Jour. Ideology, Vol. II, 1987; editl. bd. Jour. Police and Criminal Psychology; contbr. articles to profl. jours. Commr. Pilsbury Lake Village Dist., Webster, N.H., 1985-90. With USMC, 1959-63, Badge of Honor, Republic of China, 1998. Recipient Hon. medal Rep. China, 1998, Nat. Int. Drug Abuse 1st Leadership in Rsch. award, 1999; Dissertation Yr. fellow U. N.H. 1971-72, Nebr. U. System grad. faculty fellow, 1978. Fellow APA, Prescribing Psychologists Register (diplomate), Soc. Psychol. Study Social Issues, Am. Coll. Forensic Examiners (diplomate); mem. Nat. Assn. Sch. Psychologists, Veterans Foreign Wars (life), Am. Soc. Criminology (life), Internat. Coll. Prescribing Psychologists Inc. (profl. adv. bd.), Nat. Assn. Alcohol and Drug Abuse Counselors (nat. chmn., clin. issue com. 1996-98), N.Mex. Alcohol and Drug Abuse Counselors Assn. (educator of the yr. award 1997), Phi Delta Kappa (treas. 1990-91, pres. 1991-92). Office: Western NMex U Dept Social Scis Silver City NM 88062 E-mail: frenchl@silver.wnmu.edu

FREUD, NICHOLAS S. lawyer; b. N.Y.C., Feb. 6, 1942; s. Frederick and Fredericka (von Rothenburg) F.; m. Elsa Doskow, July 23, 1966; 1 child, Christopher. AB, Yale U., 1963, JD, 1966. Bar: N.Y. 1968, Calif. 1970, U.S. Tax Ct. 1973. Ptnr. Chickering & Gregory, San Francisco, 1978-85, Russin & Vecchi, San Francisco, 1986-93, Jeffer, Mangels, Butler & Marmaro, LLP, San Francisco, 1993—. Mem. joint adv. bd. Calif. Continuing Edn. of Bar, chair taxation subcom. 1987-87; mem. fgn. income adv. bd. Tax Management Internat. Jour., mem. bd. advs. The Jour. of Internat. Taxation; mem. adv. bd. NYU Inst. on Fed. Taxation; academician Internat. Acad. Estate and Tax Law. Author: (with Charles G. Stephenson and K. Bruce Friedman) International Estate Planning, rev. edit., 1997; contbr. articles to profl. jours. Fellow Am. Coll. of Tax Counsel (cert. specialist in taxation law) mem. ABA (tax sect. vice chair adminstrn. 2000—, vice-chair coun. dir. 1995-97, chair com. on U.S. activities of foreigners and tax treaties 1989-91, vice chair 1987-89, chair subcom. on tax treaties 1981-87), Calif. State Bar Assn. (taxation sect. exec. com. 1981-85, vice chair 1982-83, chair 1983-84, vice chair income tax com. 1981-82, chair 1982-83, vice chair personal income tax subcom. 1979-80, chair 1980-81, co-chair fgn. tax subcom. 1978-79), N.Y. State Bar Assn. (taxation sect., mem. com. on U.S. activities of fgn. taxpayers and fgn. activities of U.S. taxpayers), Bar Assn. of San Francisco, Bar Assn. of City of N.Y., San Francisco Tax Club (pres. 1988), San Francisco Internat. Tax Group. Office: Jeffer Mangels Butler & Marmaro LLP 1 Sansome St Fl 12 San Francisco CA 94104-4430 E-mail: nsf@jmbm.com

FREUDENBERGER, KENT W. freight company executive; Exec. v.p. mktg. Airborne Freight Corp., Seattle, 1989—. Office: Airborne Freight Corp PO Box 662 3101 Western Ave Seattle WA 98111-0662

FREUDENTHAL, DAVID D. prosecutor; U.S. atty. for Wyo. U.S. Dept. Justice, Cheyenne, 1994—. Office: US Atty Dist Wyo 2120 Capitol Ave Rm 4002 Cheyenne WY 82001-3633

FREUDENTHAL, STEVEN FRANKLIN, lawyer, political organization chairman; b. Thermopolis, Wyo., June 8, 1949; s. Lewis Franklin and Lucille Iola (Love) F.; m. Janet Mae Mansfield, Aug. 30, 1969 (div. Sept. 1996); children: Lynn Marie, Kristen Lee; m. Barbara A. Crofts, Jan. 1, 1998; stepchildren: Shane C., Jeanne N. B.A., Trinity Coll., Hartford, Conn., 1971; J.D., Vanderbilt U., 1975. Bar: Wyo. 1975, U.S. Supreme Ct. 1981. Tax acct. Conn. Gen. Life Ins. Co., Hartford, Conn., 1971-72; asst. atty. gen. Wyo. Cheyenne, 1975-77; atty. gen. Wyo. Cheyenne, 1981-82; state planning coordinator Office Gov. Wyo., Cheyenne, 1977-78; dep. under sec. Dept. Interior, Washington, 1978-79, exec. asst. to sec., 1979-80; ptnr Sherman & Howard, Cheyenne, Wyo., 1980-81; ptnr. Herschler, Freudenthal, Salzburg & Bonds, Cheyenne, 1983—; mem. Wyo. Ho. Reps., 1987-91. Trustee United Med. Ctr., 1990-97, pres., 1993-96; bd. dirs. Cheyenne LEADS, 1990-93; chmn. Wyo. Dem. Party, 1999-2001. Office: 314 E 21st St PO Box 387 Cheyenne WY 82003-0387 E-mail: steve@wyolaw.com

FREUND, FREDRIC S. real estate broker, property manager; b. Denver, Sept. 23, 1930; AB, Brown U., 1952. Sr. v.p. Hanford, Freund & Co., San Francisco, 1956—. Past adv. dir. Western Investment Real Estate Trust; bd. dirs. Berkeley Antibody Co.; instr. real estate mgmt. U. Calif. Ext.; guest lectr. Stanford U. Sch. Bus. Adminstrn. Commr. Calif. Senate Adv. Commn. on Cost Control in State Govt.; mem. citizens adv. com. Bldg. Inspection Dept., San Francisco. Mem. Am. Soc. Real Estate Counselors (CRE, pres. no. Calif. 1987-88), San Francisco Assn. Realtors (pres. 1974-75, Realtor of Yr. 1975), Bldg. Owners & Mgrs. Assn. San Francisco, Realtors Nat. Mktg. Inst. (CCIM), Inst. Real Estate Mgmt. (CPM). Office: Hanford Freund & Co 47 Kearny St Ste 300 San Francisco CA 94108-5582 Fax: 415-296-0725. E-mail: ffreund@hanfordfreund.com

FREY, CHARLES FREDERICK, surgeon, educator; b. N.Y.C., Nov. 15, 1929; s. Charles N. and Julia (Leary) F.; m. Jane Louise Tower, July 20, 1957; children: Jane Elizabeth, Susan Ann, Charles Frederick, Robert Tower, Nancy Louise. BA, Amherst Coll., 1951; MD, Cornell U., 1955. Diplomate Am. Bd. Surgery. Intern Cornell Med. Ctr., N.Y.C., 1955-56, asst. resident, 1956-57, 59-61, 1st asst. resident, 1962, chief resident, 1963; instr. surgery U. Mich., Ann Arbor, 1964-65, asst. prof. surgery, 1965-68, assoc. prof., 1968-72, prof., 1972-76, U. Calif., Davis, 1976—, vice. chmn. dept. surgery, 1976-81, exec. vice-chmn. dept., 1981-95, emeritus prof. surgery, vice chmn. dept. surgery, 1998—; mem. staff VA Hosp., Martinez, Calif., chief surg. service, 1976-80; attending surgeon Sutter Hosps., Sacramento. Surg. cons. U. Mich., 1966-76, VA, 1971—, Highway Safety Research Inst., 1973-76. Assoc. editor, mem. editorial bd. The Pancreas, Internat. Jour. of Pancreatology; mem. editorial bd. Western Jour. Medicine, Jour. Gastrointestinal Surgery; contbr. numerous articles to profl. jours. Served to capt. USAF, 1957-59. Fellow ACS (chief regional com. on trauma 1976-89, disaster preparedness com. 1978—, med. motion picutres com. 1981-91, allied health com. 1981-82, program com. No. Calif. chpt., 1981—, credentials com. No. Calif. chpt. 1982—, mem. bd. govs. 1989-94, gov. 1988-94, adv. com. on ambulatory surgery, chmn. ambulatory surg. care com. 1990-94, pres. No. Calif. chpt. 1995-96), Am. Assn. Surgery Trauma; mem. AMA, Calif. Med. Assn., El Dorado-Scarmento Med. Soc., Am. Fedn. Clin. Rsch., Am. Assn. Automotive Medicine (bd. dirs. 1970-74), Internat. Assn. Accident and Traffic Medicine, Am. Trauma Soc. (founding, standards devel. com. 1978—, v.p. Calif. divsn. 1979—, bd. dirs. 1980—), Calif. Trauma Soc. (trustee 1977—), Nat. Trauma Com. of ACS (chmn. membership com. 1980-84, exec. com. 1981-85), Assn. Acad. Surgery, Am. Surg. Assn., Brazilian Surg. Soc., Western Surg. Assn., Ctrl. Surg. Assn. (membership com. 1971-73), Pacific Coast Surg. Assn., Sacramento Surg. Soc. (pres. 1994), Assn. VA Surgeons (publs., program coms. 1981—), Soc. Univ. Surgeons, Soc. Surgery Alimentary Tract (constn. and by-laws com. 1969—, chmn. 1972-76, v.p. 1995-96), Internat. Assn. Pancreatology (mem. editl. bd. 1986, steering com.), Internat. Biliary Assn., Am. Gastroenterology Assn., Pancreas Club (chmn. 1975-96). Home and Office: Green Springs Ct Rescue CA 95672 E-mail: cffreymd@pacbell.net

FREY, JULIA BLOCH, French language educator, art historian educator; b. Louisville, July 25, 1943; d. Oscar Edgeworth and Jean Goldthwaite (Russell) Bloch; m. Roger G. Frey, Dec. 27, 1968 (div. Mar. 1976); m. Ronald Sukenick, Mar. 9, 1992. BA, Antioch Coll., 1966; MA, U. Tex., 1968; MPhil, Yale U., 1970, PhD, 1977. Instr. Brown U., Providence, 1972-73; chargé de cours U. Paris, 1974-75; lectr. Yale U., New Haven, 1975-76; prof. U. Colo., Boulder, 1999—; prof. Inst. Internat. Comparative Law, U. San Diego, Paris, 1979-89, adminstrv. dir., 1989; prof. French, art history U. Colo., Boulder, 1976-98, dir. undergrad. studies, 1985-95, assoc. chmn. for grad. studies, 1996-97, 98-99, chmn., 1999—. Guest prof. Sarah Lawrence Coll., Bronxville, N.Y., 1983; curator Toulouse-Lautrec Met. Mus. Art Denver Art Mus., 1999. Author: Toulouse-Lautrec, a life, 1994, Toulouse-Lautrec l'homme qui aimait les femmes, 1996; editor: Gustave Flaubert's La Lutte du Sacerdoce et de L'Empire (1837), 1981; contbr. articles and monographs to profl. publs., chpts. to books; translator: René. Recipient Conn. Grad. Study award, 1970-73; grantee NDEA, 1967, Brown U. Research and Travel, 1973, Boulder Arts Com., 1979, 80, Ctr. for Applied Humanities, 1985, S.W. Inst. for Research on Women, 1985-86, NEH, 1986; fellow NDEA, 1966-68, Yale U., 1968-72, Gilbert Chinard, Inst. Français de Washington, 1977, Big 12 2000, Humanities Rsch. Ctr., Australian Nat. U., 2000; Pen Ctr. USA West Lit. award for non-fiction, 1995; Finalist Nat. Book Critics Cir. award for Biography, 1994. Mem. MLA, PEN U.S.A., Coll. Art Assn., Yale Club. Unitarian. Home: 200 Rector Place Apt 26B New York NY 10280 Office: U Colo Dept French and Italian PO Box 238 Boulder CO 80309-0238 E-mail: freyj@spot.colorado.edu

FREY, VIOLA, sculptor, educator; b. Lodi, Calif., Aug. 15, 1933; AA, Delta Coll.; BFA, Calif. Coll. Arts and Crafts; MFA, Tulane U. Prof. ceramics Calif. Coll. Arts and Crafts, 1965—; chmn. dept. ceramics Noni Eccles Treadwell Ceramic Arts Ctr. One woman shows at Whitney Mus. Am. Art, 1984, Moore Coll. Art, Phila., 1984; exhibited sculpture in numerous shows including Calif. State U., Fullerton, 1977, San Francisco Mus. Modern Art, 1978, A Century of Ceramics in the U.S. Everson Mus. Art, Syracuse, N.Y., 1979, Renwick Mus., Washington, 1979, Cooper-Hewitt Mus., N.Y., 1979, Crocker Art Mus., Sacramento, Oakland (Calif.) Mus., St. Louis Mus. Art, Huntsville (Ala.) Mus. Art, Seattle Art Mus. Grantee Nat. Endowment Arts, 1978, 86. Office: c/o Rena Bransten Gallery 77 Geary St San Francisco CA 94108-5723

FREY, WILLIAM RAYBURN, healthcare educator, consultant; b. Springfield, Tenn., July 20, 1948; s. Rayburn and Elma Faye (Nunley) F.; m. Carol Jackson, Jan. 2, 1971. BS in Occupational Therapy, U. Ill., Chgo., 1971; MEd, Ga. State U., 1973; MHA, Washington U., St. Louis, 1976; PhD, Ohio State U., 1987. Registered occupational therapist. Asst. prof. U. Ill., Chgo., 1974; hosp. adminstr. The Toledo Hosp., 1975-81; instr. Ohio State U., Columbus, 1981-85; hosp. adminstr. Nat. Med. Enterprises, York, Pa., 1985-87; assoc. prof. Slippery Rock (Pa.) U., 1987-88; prof. Coll. St. Francis, Joliet, Ill., 1988-92, St. Mary's Coll., Moraga, Calif., 1992—. Cons. Commn. on Accreditation of Rehab. Facilities, Samuel Merritt Coll., Nat. Med. Enterprises. Author: Cross National Perspective on Health Care Reform, 1995, A Binational Study of the Role of Information-Technology in National Healthcare Systems, 2001; (jours.) Health Care Mgmt. Rev., Archives of Phys. Medicine and Rehab., Jour. of Head Trauma Rehab., Jour. of Allied Health. Juror Acad. Med. Films; bd. dirs. Easter Seals Rehab., Quincy Found. for Med. Rsch., 1997—; pres. Child Abuse Prevention, hon. adv. bd., 1982. Capt. U.S. Army, 1971-73. Fellow Am. Coll. Healthcare Execs.; mem. Am. Hosp. Assn., Am. Occupational Therapy Assn., Assn. Univ. Programs Health Adminstrn. Avocations: acting, musical comedy. Office: St Marys College PO Box 4700 Moraga CA 94575-4700

FREYD, JENNIFER JOY, psychology educator; b. Providence, Oct. 16, 1957; d. Peter John and Pamela (Parker) F.; m. John Q. Johnson, June 9, 1984; children: Theodore, Philip, Alexandra. BA in Anthropology magna cum laude, U. Pa., 1979; PhD in Psychology, Stanford U., 1983. Asst. prof. psychology Cornell U., 1983-87, mem. faculty coun. of reps., 1986-87; assoc. prof. psychology U. Oreg., Eugene, 1987-92, prof., 1992—, mem. dean's adv. com., 1990-91, 92-93, mem. exec. com. Ctr. for the Study of Women in Soc., 1991-93, mem. child care com., 1987-89, 90-91; fellow Ctr. for Advanced Study in the Behavioral Scis., 1989-90. Elected mem. faculty coun. of reps. Cornell U., 1986-87; mem. dean's adv. com. U. Oreg., 1990—, exec. com. Ctr. for Rsch. Study of Women in Soc., 1991-92, Inst. of Cognitive and Decision Scis., 1991-94. Author: Betrayal Trauma: The Logic of Forgetting Childhood Abuse, 1996 (Disting. Publ. award Assn. of Women in Psychology 1997, Pierre Janet award Internat. Soc. for Study Dissociation 1997); co-editor: (with A.P. De Prince) Trauma and Cognitive Science: A Meeting of Minds, Science, and Human Experience, 2001; mem. editl. bd. Jour. Exptl. Psychology: Learning, Memory, and Cognition, 1989-91, Gestalt Theory, 1985—, Jour. of Aggression, Maltreatment, and Trauma, 1997—; guest reviewer Am. Jour. Psychology, Am. Psychologist, others; contbr. articles to profl. jours. Recipient Graduate fellowship NSF, 1979-82, Univ. fellowship Stanford U., 1982-83, Presdl. Young Investigator award NSF, 1985-90, IBM Faculty Devel. award, 1985-87, fellowship Ctr. for Advanced Study in the Behavioral Scis., 1989-90, John Simon Meml. fellowship Guggenheim Found., 1989-90, Rsch. Scientist Devel. award NIMH, 1989-94, Pierre Janet award Internat. Soc. for the Study of Dissociation, 1997; other rsch. funding. Fellow AAAS, APA (liaison divsn. 35 to sci. directorate 1996—), Am. Psychol. Soc.; mem. Psychonomic Soc., Assn. for Women in Psychology, Sigma Xi. Office: U Oreg 1227 Dept Psychology Eugene OR 97403-1227

FREYD, WILLIAM PATTINSON, fund raising executive, consultant; b. Chgo., Apr. 1, 1933; s. Paul Robert Freyd and Pauline Margaret (Pattinson) Gardiner; m. Diane Marie Carlson, May 19, 1984. BS in Fgn. Svc., Georgetown U., 1960. Field rep. Georgetown U., Washington, 1965-67; campaign dir. Tamblyn and Brown, N.Y.C., 1967-70; dir. devel. St. George's Ch., N.Y.C., 1971; assoc. Browning Assocs., Newark, 1972-73; regional v.p. C.W. Shaver Co., N.Y.C., 1973-74; founder IDC, Henderson, Nev., 1974—. Inventor PHONE/MAIL program. Bd. dirs. Nev. Symphony Orch., 1994-99, N.J. Symphony Orch., 1991-94; apptd. Nev. Charitable Solicitation Task Force, 1994, pres.'s circle adv. coun. U.S. Naval Acad., 2000. Mem. Assn. Fundraising Profls. (nat. treas. 1980-81, pres. N.Y. chpt. 1974-76, cert. 1982), Am. Assn. Fund Raising Counsel (sec. 1984-86), World Fund Raising Coun. (bd. dirs. 1995-99, treas. 1998-99), Georgetown U. (regional club coun.), N.Y. Yacht Club, Union League Club N.Y., Masons, Nassau Club, Circumnavigators Club. Achievements include the invention of the Phone Mail Program. Office: IDC 5-521 IDC Ctr 2920 N Green Valley Pkwy Henderson NV 89014-0406 E-mail: wfreyd@aol.com, wfreyd@goidc.com

FREYERMUTH, CLIFFORD L. structural engineering consultant; BS in Civil Engring., State U. Iowa, 1956, MS in Structural Engring., 1958. Registered structural engr., Ariz. Consulting engr. structural design Ned L. Ashton, 1955-57; grad. teaching asst. structural mechanics State U. Iowa, 1957-58; with bridge divsn. Ariz. State Hwy. Dept., 1958-64; with Portland Cement Assn., Chgo., Skokie, Ill., 1964-71; dir. post-tensioning divsn. Prestessed Concrete Inst., 1971-76; mgr. Post-Tensioning Inst., 1976-88; pres. Clifford L. Freyermuth, Inc., 1988—. Mem. cable-stayed bridges com. Post-Tensioning Inst, editor various publs.; prin. investigator Nat. Coop. Hwy Rsch. Project, Washington, 1988. Contbr. articles to profl. jours. Recipient Martin P. Korn award Prestressed Concrete Inst., 1969, George C. Zollman award Precast/Prestressed Concrete Inst., 1999. Fellow Am. Concrete Inst. (prestressed concrete com., standard bldg. code com., bd. dirs. 1991—, Henry C. Turner medal 1992); mem. ASCE (prestressed concrete com.), Internat. Assn. Bridge and Structural Engrs., Structural Engrs. Assn. Ariz., Chi Epsilon. Office: Clifford L Freyermuth Inc 9201 N 25th Ave Ste 150B Phoenix AZ 85021-2721 E-mail: asbi@earthlink.net

FRIBERG, GEORGE JOSEPH, electronics company executive; m. Mary Seymour; children: Fane George, Felicia Lynn Friberg Clark. BSME, U. N.Mex., 1962, MBA, 1982, postgrad. Sales engr. Honeywell, L.A., 1962-64; liaison engr. ACF Industries, Albuquerque, 1964-66; quality assurance mgr. data sys. divsn. Gulton Industries Inc., Albuquerque, 1966-72, mgr. mfg. Femco divsn. Irwin (Pa.), High Point (N.C.), 1972-77, v.p. mfg. data sys. divsn. Albuquerque, 1977-86; pres., CEO Tetra Corp., Albuquerque, 1986-92, also bd. dirs.; pres., CEO Laguna Industries Inc., Albuquerque, 1992-96; dir. programs Tech. Ventures Corp., Albuquerque, 1996—. Adj. prof. U. N.Mex. Mgmt. Tech., 1998—; bd. dirs. Noonday, Inc. Mem. editl. bd. N.Mex. Bus. Jour., 1995-97. Mem. N.Mex. R & D Gross Receipts Task Force, 1988-89; mem. Econ. Forum of Albuquerque; bd. dirs. Technet, 1983-97, pres., 1983-84, 88-89; bd. dirs. Lovelace Insts., 1988—, U. N.Mex. R.O. Anderson Bus. Sch. Found., 1988-92, N.Mex. Bus. Innovation Ctr., 1986-92, U. N.Mex. Found., 1999—, Golden Apple Found., 1998—, N.Mex. Natural History Mus. Found., 1999—, N.Mex. First, 2001—; grad. Leadership N.Mex., 1998; mem. mech. engring. adv. coun. U. N.Mex., 1999—. Inducted Anderson Sch. of Bus. Hall of Fame, 1996; recipient Zia award U. N.Mex., 1998, Regents medal U. N.Mex., 1998, Lockheed Martin Nova award, 1998, Albuquerque High Harrington award, 2000. Mem. Albuquerque C. of C. (bd. dirs. 1985—, polit. action com. 1983-84, chair Buy N.Mex. chpt. 1986-87, vice chmn. econ. affairs planning coun. 1987—, chmn. bd. 1990-91), N.Mex. Alumni Lettermen's Club, U. N.Mex. Alumni Assn. (bd. dirs. 1995-2001, pres.-elect 1997, pres. 1997-98). Home: 13234 Sunset Canyon Dr NE Albuquerque NM 87111-4220

FRICK, OSCAR LIONEL, physician, educator; b. N.Y.C., Mar. 12, 1923; s. Oscar and Elizabeth (Ringger) F.; m. Mary Hubbard, Sept. 2, 1954. A.B., Cornell U., 1944, M.D., 1946; M.Med. Sci., U. Pa., 1960; Ph.D., Stanford U., 1964. Diplomate. Am. Bd. Allergy and Immunology (chmn. 1967-72). Intern Babies Hosp., Columbia Coll. Physicians and Surgeons, N.Y.C., 1946-47; resident Children's Hosp., Buffalo, 1950-51; pvt. practice medicine specializing in pediatrics Huntington, N.Y., 1951-58; fellow in allergy and immunology Royal Victoria Hosp., Montreal, Que., Can., 1958-59; fellow in allergy U. Calif.-San Francisco, 1959-60, asst. prof. pediatrics, 1964-67, assoc. prof., 1967-72, prof., 1972—, dir. allergy tng. program, 1964—; fellow immunology Inst. d'Immunobiologie, Hosp. Broussais, Paris, France, 1960-62. Contbr. articles papers to profl. publs. Served with M.C., USNR, 1947-49. Mem. Am. Assn. Immunologists, Am. Acad. Pediatrics (chmn. allergy sect. 1971-72, Bret Ratner award 1982), Am. Acad. Allergy (exec. com. 1972— , pres. 1977-78), Internat. Assn. Allergology and Clin. Immunology (exec. com. 1970-73, sec. gen. 1985—), Am. Pediatric Soc. Club: Masons. Home: 370 Parnassus Ave San Francisco CA 94117-3609

FRICK, Mr. See GROEBLI, WERNER FRITZ

FRIDLEY, ROBERT BRUCE, agricultural engineering educator; b. Burns, Oreg., June 6, 1934; s. Gerald Wayne and Gladys Winona (Smith) F.; m. Jean Marie Griggs, June 12, 1955; children: James Lee, Michael Wayne, Kenneth Jon BSME, U. Calif., Berkeley, 1956; MS in Agrl. Engring., U. Calif., Davis, 1960; PhD in Agrl. Engring., Mich. State U., East Lansing, 1973; D (hon.), U. Poly., Madrid, 1988. Asst. specialist U. Calif., Davis, 1956-60, prof. agrl. engring., 1961-78, acting assoc. dean engring., 1972, chmn. dept. agrl. engring., 1974-76, dir. aquaculture and fisheries program, 1985-89, exec. assoc. dean agrl. and environ. scis., 1989-94, prof. emeritus, 1994—; dept. mgr. R & D Weyerhaeuser Co., Tacoma, 1977-85. Vis. prof. Mich. State U., East Lansing, 1970-71; NATO vis. prof. U. Bologna, Italy, 1975; bd. agrl. and natural resources NRC, 2000—. Co-author: Principles and Practices for Harvesting and Handling Fruits and Nuts, 1973; contbr. articles to profl. jours.; patentee in field. Recipient Charles G. Woodbury award Am. Soc. Hort. Sci., 1966, Alumni citation Calif. Aggie Alumni Assn., 1990. Fellow Am. Soc. Agrl. Engrs. (Young Rschrs. award 1971, Concept of Yr. award 1976, Outstanding Paper award 1966, 68, 69, 76, 86, Disting. Svc. award 1988, 97, 99, pres. 1997-98, v.p. Found. 1989-93, pres. Found. 1993-96); mem. NAE. Office: U Calif 150 Mrak Hall Davis CA 95616

FRIED, BURTON DAVID, physicist, educator; b. Chgo., Dec. 14, 1925; s. Albert O. and Bertha (Rosenthal) F.; m. Sally Rachel Goldstein, Aug. 17, 1947; children— Joel Ethan, Jeremy Steven. BS, Ill. Inst. Tech., 1947; MS, U. Chgo., 1950, PhD, 1952. Instr. physics Ill. Inst. Tech., 1947-52; research physicist Lawrence Berkeley Lab. of U. Calif., 1952-54; sr. staff physicist TRW Systems, Los Angeles, 1954-86; dir. research lab. (Ramo-Wooldridge Computer Div.), Los Angeles, 1961-63; prof. physics UCLA, 1963—. Served with USNR, 1944-46. Fellow Am. Phys. Soc. (chmn. plasma physics div. 1978-79); mem. Sigma Xi. Achievements include research and publs. on theoretical elementary particle and plasma physics. Home: 223 Desert Holly Dr Palm Desert CA 92211-7410 Office: UCLA Dept Physics 405 Hilgard Ave Los Angeles CA 90095-9000 E-mail: fried@physics.ucla.edu

FRIED, ELAINE JUNE, insurance company executive; b. L.A., Oct. 19, 1943; m. Howard I. Fried, Aug. 7, 1966; children: Donnoven Michael, Randall Jay. Grad., Pasadena (Calif.) H.S.; various coll. courses. Agt., office mgr. Howard I. Fried Agy., Alhambra, Calif., 1975—. V.p. Sea Hill, Inc., Pasadena, 1973-95; spkr. on psycho-social aspects of diabetes, insurance, diabetes, ins. medicine. Contbr. articles to profl. jours. Publicity chmn., unit telephone chmn. San Gabriel Valley unit Am. Diabetes Assn., past chmn., vol. lobbyist, mem. patient edn. com. region II Calif. chpt., 1998; past publicity chmn. San Gabriel Valley region Women's Am. Orgn. for Rehab. Tng. (ORT); chmn. spl. events publicity, Temple Beth Torah Sisterhood, Alhambra, membership chmn., 1991-92, v.p. membership, 1991-93; former mem. bd. dirs., pub. rels. com., pers. com. Vis. Nurses Assn., Pasadena and San Gabriel Valley; chmn. outside Sisterhood publicity Congregation Shaarei Torah, 1993—, pub. rels. chmn., 1993—, membership v.p., 1999—, mem. mktg. com. 2001—. Recipient Vol. award So. Calif. affiliate Am. Diabetes Assn., 1974-77, 25 Yr. Vol. Svc. award, 1996, cert. of appreciation, 1987; co-recipient Ner Tamid Temple Beth Torah. Mem. ORT, Hadassah, Greater Pasadena Assn. Ins. and Fin. Advisors (co-v.p. cmty. affairs 1998-2000). Home: 404 N Hidalgo Ave Alhambra CA 91801-2640 E-mail: howie1818@aol.com

FRIED, JOHN H. chemist; b. Leipzig, Germany, Oct. 7, 1929; s. Abraham and Frieda F.; m. Heléne Gellen, June 26, 1955; children: David, Linda, Deborah. AB, Cornell U., 1951, PhD, 1955. Steroid chemist, research assoc. Merck and Co., Rahway, N.J., 1956-64; with Syntex Research, Palo Alto, Calif., 1964-92, dir. inst. organic chemistry, 1967-74, exec. v.p., 1974-76, pres., 1976-92; sr. v.p. Syntex Corp., 1981-86, vice chmn., 1986-92; dir. Corvas Internat., Inc., 1992-99, chmn., 1997-99. Chmn. Alexion Pharms., Inc., 1992—; pres. Fried & Co., Inc., 1992—. Mem. Am. Chem. Soc. Office: 20 Faxon Forest Atherton CA 94027-4067

FRIEDEN, CLIFFORD E. lawyer; b. L.A., Mar. 8, 1949; s. Sidney S. and Norma (Stern) F.; m. Dinah S. Baumring, June 20, 1971; children: Jamie, Kari, Curtis. BA, UCLA, 1971; JD, U. Calif., Berkeley, 1974. Bar: Calif. 1974, U.S. Dist. Ct. (so. dist.) Calif. 1974, U.S. Dist. Ct. (cen. dist.) Calif. 1977. Ptnr. Rutan & Tucker, Costa Mesa, Calif., 1974—. Active Orange County chpt. ARC, 1995-2001. Mem. Orange County Bar Assn. (del. state conv. 1983-95, chair judiciary com. 1987-88, bd. dirs. 1989-91), Phi Beta Kappa. Avocations: basketball, jogging. Office: Rutan & Tucker PO Box 1950 611 Anton Blvd Ste 1400 Costa Mesa CA 92626-1931

FRIEDENBERG, RICHARD MYRON, radiology educator, physician; b. N.Y.C., May 6, 1926; s. Charles and Dorothy (Steg) F.; m. Gloria Geshwind, Jan. 22, 1950; children: Lisa, Peter, Amy. A.B., Columbia, 1946; M.D., L.I. Coll. Medicine, 1949. Diplomate: Am. Bd. Radiology. Intern in medicine Maimonides Hosp., Bklyn., 1949-50; resident in radiology Bellevue Hosp., N.Y.C., 1950-51, Nat. Cancer fellow, 1951-52; fellow radiology Columbia-Presbyn. Hosp., 1952-53; cons. radiologist 3d Air Force, London, Eng., 1953-55; asst. prof. radiology Albert Einstein Coll. Medicine, 1955-66, assoc. clin. prof. radiology, 1966-68; dir., chmn. dept. radiology Bronx Lebanon Hosp. Center, 1957-68; prof., chmn. dept. radiology N.Y. Med. Coll., 1968-80; emeritus prof. U. Calif., Irvine, 1992—. Dir. radiology Flower Fifth Ave Hosp., Met. Hosp. Ctr., Bird S. Coler Hosp., N.Y.C., Westchester County Med. Ctr., all 1968-80; prof., chmn. dept. radiol. scis. U. Calif., Irvine, 1980-92. Author: (with Charles Ney) Radiographic Atlas of the Genitourinary System, 1966, 2d edit., 1981; Contbr. (with Charles Ney) articles to profl. jours. Fellow Am. Coll. Radiology, N.Y. Acad. Medicine; mem. Assn. Univ. Radiologists, Radiol. Soc. N.Am., Am. Roentgen Ray Soc., N.Y. Acad. Scis., Assn. Am. Med. Colls., AMA, Soc. Chairmen Acad. Radiology Depts. (past pres.), N.Y. Roentgen Soc. (past pres.), Orange CTY Radiology Soc. (past pres.). Home: 18961 Castlegate Ln Santa Ana CA 92705-2801 Office: U Calif Dept Radiology Irvine CA 92697-0001 E-mail: rmfriede@uci.edu

FRIEDLANDER, CHARLES DOUGLAS, space consultant; b. N.Y.C., Oct. 5, 1928; s. Murray L. and Jeane (Sottosanti) F.; m. Diane Mary Hutchins, May 12, 1951; children: Karen Diane, Lauren Patrice, Joan Elyse. BS, U.S. Mil. Acad., 1950; exec. mgmt. program, NASA, 1965; grad., Command and Staff Coll. USAF, 1965, Air War Coll. USAF, 1966. Commd. 2d lt. U.S. Army, 1950, advanced through grades to 1st lt., officer inf. Korea, 1950-51, resigned, 1954; mem. staff UN Forces, Trieste, Italy, 1953-54; chief astronaut support office NASA, Cape Canaveral, Fla., 1963-67; space cons. CBS News, Cape Canaveral, 1967-69; exec. asst. The White House, Washington, 1969-71. V.p. bd. dirs. Internat. Aerospace Hall of Fame, San Diego; space program cons., various cos., Boca Raton, Fla., 1967-69; mem. staff First Postwar Fgn. Ministers Conf., Berlin, 1954; radio/TV cons. space program. Author: Buying & Selling Land for Profit, 1961, Last Man at Hungnam Beach, 1952. V.p. West Point Soc., Cape Canaveral, Fla., 1964. Served to lt. col. USAFR, maj. USAR. Decorated Bronze Star V, Combat Inf. badge; co-recipient Emmy award CBS TV Apollo Moon Landing, 1960; recipient medal of honor N.Y.C., 1951. Mem. Explorer's Club, West Point Soc., Chosin Few Survivors Korea, NASA Alumni League, Nat. Space Soc. Avocations: fishing, travel.

FRIEDLANDER, SHELDON KAY, chemical engineering educator; b. N.Y.C., Nov. 17, 1927; s. Irving and Rose (Katzewitz) F.; m. Marjorie Ellen Robbins, Apr. 16, 1934; children: Eva Kay, Amelie Elise, Antonia Zoe, Josiah. BS, Columbia U., 1949; SM, MIT, 1951; PhD, U. Ill., 1954. Asst. prof. chem. engring. Columbia U., N.Y.C., 1954-57, Johns Hopkins, Balt., 1957-59, assoc. prof. chem. engring., 1959-62, prof. chem. engring., 1962-64; prof. chem. engring., environ. health engring. Calif. Inst. Tech., Pasadena, 1964-78; prof. chem. engring. UCLA, 1978—, Parsons prof., 1982—, chmn. dept. chem. engring., 1984-88, chmn. steering com. Ctr. for Clean Tech., 1989-92. Chmn. EPA Clean Air Sci. Adv. Com., 1978-82. Author: Smoke, Dust, and Haze: Fundamentals of Aerosol Dynamics, 2nd edit., 2000. Served with U.S. Army, 1946-47. Recipient Sr. Humboldt prize Fed. Republic of Germany, 1985, Internat. prize Am. Assn. for Aerosol Rsch./Gesellschaft für Aerosolforschung/Japan Assn. for Aerosol Sci. and Tech., Fuchs Meml. award, 1990, Christian Junge award European Aerosol Assn., 2000; Fulbright scholar, 1960-61; Guggenheim fellow, 1969-70. Mem. NAE, Am. Inst. Chem. Engrs. (Colburn award 1959, Alpha Chi Sigma award 1974, Walker award 1979, Lawrence K. Cecil award in environ. chem. engring. 1995), Am. Assn. for Aerosol Research (pres. 1984-86). Office: UCLA Dept Chem Engring 5531 Boelter Hl Los Angeles CA 90095-0001

FRIEDMAN, ALAN E. lawyer; b. N.Y.C., May 5, 1946; BA, Amherst Coll., 1967; JD, Stanford U., 1970. Bar: Calif. 1971. Ptnr. Tuttle & Taylor, L.A., 1970—. Note editor: Stanford Law Rev., 1969-70 Office: Tuttle & Taylor 355 S Grand Ave Fl 40 Los Angeles CA 90071-1560

FRIEDMAN, GARY DAVID, epidemiologist; b. Cleve., Mar. 8, 1934; s. Howard N. and Cema C. F.; m. Ruth Helen Schleien, June 22, 1958; children: Emily, Justin, Richard. Student, Antioch Coll., 1951-53; BS in Biol. Sci., U. Chgo., 1956, MD with honors, 1959; MS in Biostats., Harvard Sch. Pub. Health, 1965. Diplomate Am. Bd. Internal Medicine. Intern, resident Harvard Med. Svcs., Boston City Hosp., 1959-61; 2d yr. resident Univ. Hosps. Cleve., 1961-62; med. officer heart disease epidemiology study Nat. Heart Inst., Framingham, Mass., 1962-66; chief epidemiology unit, field and tng. sta., heart disease ctrl. program USPHS, San Francisco, 1966-68; sr. epidemiologist divsn. rsch. Kaiser Permanente Med. Care Program, Oakland, Calif., 1968-76, asst. dir. epidemiology and biostats., 1976-91, dir., 1991-98, sr. investigator, 1998-99, adj. investigator, 1999—; cons. prof. Dept. Health Rsch. and Policy Stanford U. Sch. Medicine, 1998—. Rsch. fellow, then rsch. assoc. preventive medicine Harvard Med. Sch., 1962-66; lectr. dept. biomedical and environ. health scis., sch. pub. health U. Calif. Berkeley, 1968—; lectr. epidemiology and biostatics U. Calif. Sch. Medicine, San Francisco, 1980—, asst. clin. prof. 1967-75, assoc. clin. prof., 1975-92 depts. medicine and family and community medicine; mem. U.S.-USSR working group sudden cardiac death Nat. Heart, Lung and Blood Inst., 1975-82, com. on epidemiology and veterans follow-up studies Nat. Rsch. Coun., 1980-85, subcommittee on twins, 1980—, epidemiology and disease ctrl. study sect. NIH, 1982-86, U.S. Preventive Svcs. Task Force, 1984-88, scientific rev. panel on toxic air contaminants State of Calif., 1988—, adv. com. Merck Found./Soc. Epidemiol. Rsch., Clin. Epidemiology Fellowships, 1990-94; sr. advisor expert panel on preventive svcs. USPHS, 1991-96. Author: Primer of Epidemiology, 1974, 2d edit., 1980, 3d edit., 1987, 4th edit., 1994; assoc. editor, then mem. editl. bd. Am. Jour. Epidemiology, 1988-96, 99—; mem. editl. bd. HMO Practice, 1991-98, Jour. Med. Screening, 1997—; contbr. over 270 articles to profl. jours., chpts. to books; composer: Autumn for oboe and piano (First prize Composers Today Competition Music Tchrs. Assn. Calif. 1999), Fugue for Four Winds (Second prize Music Tchrs. Assn. Calif. 2000). Oboist San Francisco Civic Symphony, 1990—, Symphony Parnassus, 1994—, Bohemian Club Band, 1994—; bd. dirs. Chamber Musicians No. Calif., Oakland, 1991-98. Sr. surgeon USPHS, 1962-68. Recipient Roche award for Outstanding Performance as Med. Student; Merit grantee Nat. Cancer Inst., 1987, Outstanding Investigator grantee, 1989, 94; named to Disting. Alumni Hall of Fame Cleve. Heights High Sch., 1991. Fellow Am. Heart Assn. (chmn. com. on criteria and methods 1969-71, chmn. program com. 1973-76, coun. epidemiol.), Am. Coll. Physicians; mem. APHA, Am. Epidemiol. Soc. (mem. com. 1982-86, pres.-elect 1998, pres. 1999), Am. Soc. Preventive Oncology, Internat. Epidemiol. Assn., Internat. Soc. Twin Studies, Soc. Epidemiologic Rsch.(exec. Com., 1998—), Med. Biological Alumni Assn. U. Chgo. (Disting. Svc. award 2000), Phi Beta Kappa, Alpha Omega Alpha, Delta Omega. Achievements include research on cancer, cardiovascular disease, gallbladder disease, effects of smoking, alcohol and medicinal drugs, evaluation of health screening tests. Office: Stanford U Sch Medicine Dept Health Rsch and Policy Redwood Bldg Rm T210 Stanford CA 94305-5405 E-mail: gdf@leland.stanford.edu

FRIEDMAN, GEORGE JERRY, aerospace engineer, executive; b. N.Y.C., Mar. 22, 1928; s. Sander and Ruth (Oberlander) F.; m. Ruthanne Goldstein, Sept. 7, 1953; children— Sanford, Gary, David BS, U. Calif.-Berkeley, 1949; MS, UCLA, 1956, PhD, 1967. Registered profl. mech. engr., controls engr., Calif. Mech. engring. assoc. Dept. Water and Power, Los Angeles, 1949-56; devel. engr. Servo Mechanisms, Hawthorne, Calif., 1956-60; v.p. Northrop Corp., Los Angeles, 1960-94; exec. v.p., rsch. dir. Space Studies Inst., Princeton, N.J., 1994—. Mem. indsl. adv. group NATO, Brussels, 1977-78; guest lectr. UCLA, 1983—, Calif. State U., Northridge, 1983—, dir. trust fund, 1984-89; cons. to sci. adv. bd. USAF, Washington, 1985—, bd. govs. Aerospace and Elec. Sys. Soc., L.A., 1985—, v.p. publs., 1999; adj. prof. U. So. Calif., L.A., 1994—; pres. Internat. Coun. on Sys. Engring., 1994, fellow 1998. Contbr. articles to profl. jours. Served as pfc. U.S. Army, 1950-52 Recipient Engring. Excellence award San Fernando Valley Engring. Council, 1983 Fellow IEEE (Baker award 1970), AIAA (assoc.; chmn. planetary def. subcom. 1995-97); mem. Am. Def. Preparedness Assn. (exec. com., preparedness award 1985). Democrat. Jewish Home and Office: 5084 Gloria Ave Encino CA 91436-1529 E-mail: gfriedma@usc.edu

FRIEDMAN, K. BRUCE, lawyer; b. Buffalo, Jan. 1, 1929; s. Bennett and Florence Ruth (Israel) F.; m. Lois G. Rosoff, June 15, 1986. A.B., Harvard U., 1950; LL.B., Yale U., 1953. Bar: N.Y. 1955, D.C. 1956, Calif. 1958. Atty. CAB, Washington, 1955-57; practiced in San Francisco, 1958—; mem. firm Zang, Friedman & Damir, 1969-78, Cotton, Seligman & Ray, 1978-79, Friedman, McCubbin, Spalding, Bilter, Roosevelt & Montgomery, San Francisco, 1980—. Lectr. law U. Calif. Law Sch., Berkeley, 1966-76; Pres. Econ. Roundtable San Francisco, 1964. Bd. dirs. San Francisco chpt. Am. Jewish Com., 1960-76; trustee World Affairs Council No. Calif., San Francisco, 1970-76; pres. San Francisco Estate Planning Council, 1973-74; regional dir. for No. Calif. Asso. Harvard Alumni, 1981-84; bd. dirs. Am. Coll. Trust and Estate Counsel Found., 2000—. Served with U.S. Army, 1953-55. Fellow Am. Coll. Trust and Estate Counsel, Am. Bar Found.; mem. ABA, State Bar Calif., San Francisco Bar Assn., Internat. Acad. Estate and Trust Law (treas. 1996—), Am. Law Inst., San Francisco Com. on Fgn. Rels., U. Calif. San Francisco Found., Univ. Club, Calif. Tennis Club, Commonwealth Club Calif., Harvard Club of San Francisco (pres. 1976-78), Rotary. Jewish. Office: Friedman McCubbin Spalding Bilter Roosevelt & Montgomery 425 California St Ste 2200 San Francisco CA 94104-2207 E-mail: kbrucefriedman@fomlaw.com

FRIEDMAN, KENNI, healthcare company official, councilwoman; BA, UCLA, 1963, MBA, 1964. Councilwoman City of Modesto, Calif., 1991-99, vice mayor, 2000—; mem. bd. Sutter-affiliated Meml. Hosps. Assn., Sacramento, chmn. bd., 1993-95; bd. dirs. Sutter Health Inc., Sacramento. Bd. dirs. Sutter Gould Med. Found., Modesto; active League Calif. Cities, United Way Sanislaus County, Modesto Symphony Assn.; former mem. state bd. dirs. and nat. bd. dirs. LWV; mem. policy bd. San Juaquin Valley Unified Air Pollution Control Dist. Mem. Modesto C. of C. (bd. dirs.). Office: Sutter Health Inc One Capitol Mall Sacramento CA 95814

FRIEDMAN, LAWRENCE M. law educator; b. Chgo., Apr. 2, 1930; s. I. M. and Ethel (Shapiro) F.; m. Leah Feigenbaum, Mar. 27, 1955; children: Jane, Amy. AB, U. Chgo., 1948, JD, 1951, LLM, 1953; LLD (hon.), U. Puget Sound, 1977, CUNY, 1989, U. Lund, Sweden, 1993, John Marshall Law Sch., , 1995, U. Macerata, Italy, 1998. Mem. faculty St. Louis U., 1957-61, U. Wis., 1961-68; prof. law Stanford U., 1968—, Marion Rice Kirkwood prof., 1976—; David Stouffer Meml. lectr. Rutgers U. Law Sch., 1969; Sibley lectr. U. Ga. Law Sch., 1976; Wayne Morse lectr. U. Oreg., 1985; Childress meml. lectr. St. Louis U., 1987. Jefferson Meml. lectr. U. Calif., 1994; Higgins vis. prof. Lewis and Clark U., 1998; Tucker lectr. Washington & Lee Univ., 2000. Author: Contract Law in America, 1965, Government and Slum Housing, 1968, A History of American Law, 1973, 2d edit., 1985, The Legal System: A Social Science Perspective, 1975, Law and Society: An Introduction, 1977, (with Robert V. Percival) The Roots of Justice, 1981, American Law, 1984, Total Justice, 1985, Your Time Will Come, 1985, The Republic of Choice, 1990, Crime and Punishment in American History, 1993; co-editor: (with Stewart Macaulay) Law and the Behavioral Sciences, 1969, 2d edit., 1977, (with Harry N. Scheiber) American Law and the Constitutional Order, 1978, Legal Culture and the Legal Profession, 1996, (with Stewart Macaulay and John Stookey) Law and Society: Readings on the Social Study of Law, 1995, (with George Fisher) The Crime Conundrum, 1997, The Horizontal Society, 1999; contbr. articles to profl. jours. Served with U.S. Army, 1953-54. Recipient Triennial award Order of Coif, 1976, Willard Hurst prize, 1982, Harry Kalven prize, 1992, Silver Gavel award ABA, 1994, Rsch. award, Am. Bar. Found., 2000, Am. Bar Found. rsch. award, 2001; Ctr. for Advanced Study in Behavioral Sci. fellow, 1974-75, fellow Inst. Advanced Study, Berlin, 1985. Mem. Law and Soc. Assn. (pres. 1979-81), Am. Acad. Arts and Scis., Am. Soc. for Legal History (v.p. 1987-89, pres. 1990-91), Soc. Am. Historians (hon. life mem. rsch. com. sociology of law). Home: 724 Frenchmans Rd Palo Alto CA 94305-1005 Office: Stanford U Law Sch Nathan Abbott Way Stanford CA 94305-9991 E-mail: lmf@leland.stanford.edu

FRIEDMAN, MILTON, economist, educator, writer; b. Brooklyn, N.Y., July 31, 1912; s. Jeno Saul and Sarah Ethel (Landau) F.; m. Rose Director, June 25, 1938; children: Janet, David. AB, Rutgers U., 1932, LLD (hon.), 1968; AM, U. Chgo., 1933; PhD, Columbia U., 1946; LLD (hon.), St. Paul's (Rikkyo) U., 1963, Loyola U., 1971, U. N.H., 1975, Harvard U., 1979, Brigham Young U., 1980, Dartmouth Coll., 1980, Gonzaga U., 1981; DSc (hon.), Rochester U., 1971; LHD (hon.), Rockford Coll., 1969, Roosevelt U., 1975, Hebrew Union Coll., L.A., 1981, Jacksonville U., , 1993; LittD (hon.), Bethany Coll., 1971; PhD (hon.), Hebrew U., Jerusalem, 1977; DCS (hon.), Francisco Marroquín U., Guatemala, 1978; D honoris causa, Econ. U. Prague, 1997. Assoc. economist Nat. Resources Com., Washington, 1935-37; mem. research staff Nat. Bur. Econ. Research, N.Y.C., 1937-45, 1948-81; vis. prof. econs. U. Wis., Madison, 1940-41; prin. economist, tax research div. U.S. Treasury Dept., Washington, 1941-43; assoc. dir. research, statis. research group, War Research div. Columbia U., N.Y.C., 1943-45; assoc. prof. econs. and statistics U. Minn., Mpls., 1945-46; assoc. prof. econs. U. Chgo., 1946-48, prof. econs., 1948-62, Paul Snowden Russell disting. service prof. econs., 1962-82, prof. emeritus, 1983—; Fulbright lectr. Cambridge U., 1953-54; vis. Wesley Clair Mitchell research prof. econs. Columbia U., N.Y.C., 1964-65; fellow Ctr. for Advanced Study in Behavioral Sci., 1957-58; sr. research fellow Hoover Inst., Stanford U., 1977—. Mem. Pres.'s Commn. All-Vol. Army, 1969-70, Pres.'s Commn. on White House Fellows, 1971-74, Pres.'s Econ. Policy Adv. Bd., 1981-88; vis. scholar Fed. Res. Bank, San Francisco, 1977. Author: (with Carl Shoup and Ruth P. Mack) Taxing to Prevent Inflation, 1943, (with Simon S. Kuznets) Income from Independent Professional Practice, 1946, (with Harold A. Freeman, Frederic Mosteller, W. Allen Wallis) Sampling Inspection, 1948, Essays in Positive Economics, 1953, A Theory of the Consumption Function, 1957, A Program for Monetary Stability, 1960, Price Theory: A Provisional Text, 1962, (with Rose D. Friedman) Capitalism and Freedom, 1962, (with R.D. Friedman) Free to Choose, 1980, Tyranny of the Status Quo, 1984, Two Lucky People: Memoirs, 1998, (with Anna J. Schwartz) A Monetary History of the United States, 1867-1960, 1963, (with Schwartz) Monetary Statistics of the United States, 1970, Monetary Trends in the U.S. and the United Kingdom, 1982, Inflation: Causes and Consequences, 1963, (with Robert Roosa) The Balance of Payments: Free vs. Fixed Exchange Rates, 1967, Dollars and Deficits, 1968, the Optimum Quantity of Money and Other Essays, 1969, (with Walter W. Heller) Monetary vs. Fiscal Policy, 1969, A Theoretical Framework for Monetary Analysis, 1972, (with Wilbur J. Cohen) Social Security, 1972, An Economist's Protest, 1972, There's No Such Thing as a Free Lunch, 1975, Price Theory, 1976, (with Robert J. Gordon et al) Milton Friedman's Monetary Framework, 1974, Tax Limitation, Inflation and the Role of Government, 1978, Bright Promises, Dismal Performance, 1983, Monetarist Economics, 1991, Money Mischief, 1992, (with Thomas S. Szasz) Friedman & Szasz on Drugs: Essays on the Free Market and Prohibition, 1992; editor: Studies in the Quantity Theory of Money, 1956; bd. editors Am. Econ. Rev., 1951-53, Econometrica, 1957-69; adv. bd. Jour. Money, Credit and Banking, 1968-94; columnist Newsweek Mag., 1966-84, contbg. editor, 1971-84; contbr. articles to profl. jours. Chmn. bd. dirs. Milton and Rose D. Friedman Found.; mem. adv. bd. Calif. Parents for Ednl. Choice, 1999—. Decorated Grand Cordon of the 1st Class Order of the Sacred Treasure (Japan); recipient Nobel prize in econs., 1976, Pvt. Enterprise Exemplar medal Freedoms Found., 1978, Presdl. medal of Freedom, 1988, Nat. Medal of Sci., 1988, Prize in Moral-Cultural Affairs, Instn. World Capitalism, 1993; named Chicagoan of Yr., Chgo. Press Club, 1972, Educator of Yr., Chgo. Jewish United Fund, 1973, Source award for lifetime achievement The Primary Source, Tufts U., 1997, Robert Maynard Hutchins History Maker award for distinction in edn. Chgo. Hist. Soc., 1997, Templeton Honor Rolls Lifetime Achievement award, 1997, Goldwater award, 1997. Fellow Inst. Math. Stats., Am. Statis. Assn., Econometric Soc.; mem. NAS, Am. Econ. Assn. (exec. com. 1955-57, pres. 1967; John Bates Clark medal 1951), Am. Enterprise Inst. (adv. bd. 1956-79), Western Econ. Assn. (pres. 1984-85), Royal Economic Soc., Am. Philos. Soc., Mont Pelerin Soc. (bd. dirs. 1958-61, pres. 1970-72), Quadrangle Club. Office: Stanford U Hoover Instn Stanford CA 94305-6010

FRIEDMAN, MORTON LEE, lawyer; b. Aberdeen, S.D., Aug. 4, 1932; s. Philip and Rebecca (Feinstein) F.; m. Marcine Lichter, Dec. 20, 1955; children— Mark, Philip, Jeffrey. Student, U. Mich., 1950-53; A.B., Stanford U., 1954, LL.B., 1956. Bar: Calif. bar 1956. Mem. firm Kimble, Thomas, Snell, Jamison & Russell, Fresno, 1957, Busick & Busick, Sacramento, 1957-59; sr. partner firm Friedman, Collard & Poswall (name now Friedman & Collard), Sacramento, 1959—. Lectr. various law schs. and seminars; mem. Calif. Bd. Continuing Edn. Pres. Mosaic Law Congregation, 1977-80, 97-99; v.p. Sacramento Jewish Fedn., 1980-82; chmn. Sacramento campaign United Jewish Appeal, 1981; dir., former nat. v.p. Am. Israel Pub. Affairs Com.; mem. bd. Calif. State U. Inst., 1995-99; bd. dirs. Nat. Bd. AntiDefamation League. 1st lt. USAF, 1956. Recipient Sacramento Businessman of Yr. award Sacramento Met. C. of C., 1991, Best Lawyers in Am. award, Outstanding Philanthropists award Nat. Soc. Fund Raising Execs., 1999; Fulbright candidate Stanford Law Sch., 1956. Fellow Am. Coll. Trial Lawyers; mem. ABA, ATLA, Calif. Bar Assn., Sacramento County Bar Assn. (pres. 1976, Lawyer of Yr. 1999), Calif. Trial Lawyers Assn. (v.p. 1973-75), Capitol City Lawyers Club (past pres.), Am. Bd. Trial Advocates (adv., pres. 1977, Calif. Trial Lawyer of Yr. 1988), West Sacramento C. of C. (dir.), Order of Coif. Democrat. Home: 1620 McClaren Dr Carmichael CA 95608-5936 Office: Friedman & Collard 7750 College Town Dr Ste 300 Sacramento CA 95826-2386

FRIEDMAN, NATHAN BARUCH, medical educator; b. N.Y.C., Jan. 30, 1911; s. Emanuel David and Rose (Borgenicht) F.; widower; children: MaryLou, Emily. BS, Harvard U., 1930; MD, Cornell U., 1934. Intern, resident Harlem and Bellevue Hosps., 1935; intern Montefiore Hosp., 1936-37; resident U. Chgo., 1938-39; fellow Harvard U., 1940; instr. Stanford (Calif.) U., 1941; dir. labs. Cedars Hosp., L.A., 1948-69, sr. cons., 1969—; clin. prof. U. So. Calif., L.A., 1950-90, emeritus prof., 1990. Maj. AUS, 1942-46. Home: 15150 Mulholland Dr Los Angeles CA 90077-1619 Office: Cedars Sinai Med Ctr 8700 Beverly Blvd Los Angeles CA 90048-1865

FRIEDMAN, PAUL JAY, radiologist, educator; b. N.Y.C., Jan. 20, 1937; s. Louis Alexander and Rose (Solomon) F.; m. Elisabeth Clare Richardson, June 18, 1960; children: Elizabeth Ruth Coley, Deborah Anne Yeager, Matthew Alexander Xu-Friedman, Rachel Clare Lentz. BS, U. Wis., 1955; postgrad., Oxford (Eng.) U., 1957-58; MD, Yale U., 1960. Intern Einstein Med. Sch., N.Y.C., 1960-61; resident in radiology Columbia-Presbyn. Hosp., N.Y.C., 1961-64; asst. prof., assoc. prof. U. Calif. San Diego Med. Sch., 1968-75, prof. radiology, 1975-2001, from assoc. dean to dean acad. affairs, 1982-95, prof. emeritus, 2001—. Cons. VA Hosp.; vis. scholar Inst. Med./NAS, AAMC, 1988-89; adv. com. on rsch. integrity Dept. Health & Human Svcs., 1991-93; cons. 26th, 27th and 28th edit. Stedman's Med. Dictionary; specialist in chest radiology and rsch. ethics, tenure and retirement issues; bd. dirs. Am. Coun. Edn., 1996-97. Mem. editl. bd. Investigative Radiology, 1976-87, Am. Jour. Roentgenology, 1986-88; contbr. articles to profl. jours. Bd. dirs. La Jolla Symphony Assn., 1987-92. Lt. comdr. M.C., USNR, 1964-66. Markle scholar acad. medicine, 1969-74; Picker Found. advanced acad. fellow and scholar, 1966-69 Fellow Am. Coll. Chest Physicians, Am. Coll. Radiology; mem. AAUP, Assn. of Am. Med. Colls. (disting. svc. mem.), Internat. Soc. for Magnetic Resonance in Medicine, Assn. Univ. Radiologists (rep. to coun. acad. socs. Assn. Am. Med. Colls. 1985-97), Soc. for Computer Applications in Radiology, Fleischner Soc. (pres. 1994-95), Radiol. Soc. N.Am., Roentgen Ray Soc., Nat. Conf. Lawyers and Scientists, Phi Beta Kappa, Alpha Omega Alpha. Avocations: choral singing, computers, gardening. Home: 5644 Soledad Rd La Jolla CA 92037-7048 Office: U Calif Sch Medicine Dept Radiology 200 W Arbor Dr San Diego CA 92103-9000

FRIEDMAN, ROBERT LEE, film company executive; b. N.Y.C., Mar. 1, 1930; s. Edward A. and Claire (Seidenberg) F.; m. Marlene Saltz; children: Marc, Lisa. Sales Universal Pictures, N.Y.C., 1948-52, 54-59; exec. v.p., distbn. & mktg. United Artists Corp., N.Y.C., 1959-79; pres., distbn. Columbia Pictures, Burbank, Calif., 1979-82; pres. AMC Entertainment Internat., L.A., 1984-92, pres. motion picture group, 1992-99; pres. RLF Entertainment, Beverly Hills, Calif., 1999—; CEO, pres. Stereo Vision Entertainment, Beverly Hills, 2000—. Radio announcer The Bob Friedman Hour, 1952-54; cons. RLF Prodns., Beverly Hills, Calif., 1982-84; entertainment advisor, cons. Chanin Capital Ptnrs. Exec. prodr., appeared in (motion picture) 9 Deaths of the Ninja, 1984; appeared in (motion picture) Stardust Memories, 1980. Bd. dirs., chmn. Entertainment Industry com. Century City C. of C., L.A., 1988—; chmn. Will Rogers Hosp., 1980-81, also bd. dirs.; bd. dirs. Dare Am.; mem. vision fund The Lighthouse for the Blind. With U.S. Army, 1952-54. Named Man of Yr. N.Y. State Nat. Assn. Theatre Owners, 1981, Va., Md., Washington D.C. Assn. Theatre Owners,

1980. Mem. Acad. Motion Picture Arts & Scis. (bd. dirs. endowment fund, 1979—), Variety Club Am. (L.A.), Motion Picture Pioneers Am., Motion Picture Assocs. Found. (pres. 1970-73), L.A.-Century City C. of C. (Citizen of Yr., 1994) Avocations: going to movies, playing tennis, exercising, photography, spending time with my wife and grandchildren. Office: RLF Entertainment 2216 Summitridge Dr Beverly Hills CA 90210-1526

FRIEDMAN, SHELLY ARNOLD, cosmetic surgeon; b. Providence, Jan. 1, 1949; s. Saul and Estelle (Moverman) F.; m. Andrea Leslie Falchook, Aug. 30, 1975; children: Bethany Erin, Kimberly Rebecca, Brent David, Jennifer Ashley. BA, Providence Coll., 1971; DO, Mich. State U., 1982. Diplomate Nat. Bd. Med. Examiners, Am. Bd. Dermatology. Intern Pontiac (Mich.) Hosp., 1982-83, resident in dermatology, 1983-86. Assoc. clin. prof. dept. internal med. Mich. State U., 1984-89, adj. clin. prof., 1989—; med. dir. Inst. Cosmetic Dermatology, Scottsdale, Ariz., 1986—; pres. Am. Bd. Hair Restoration Surgery. Contbr. aritcles to profl. jours. Mem. B'nai B'rith Men's Council, 1973, Jewish Welfare Fund, 1973. Am. Physicians fellow for medicine, 1982. Mem. AMA, Am. Osteopathic Assn., Am. Assn. Cosmetic Surgeons, Am. Acad. Cosmetic Surgery, Internat. Soc. Dermatologic Surgery, Internat. Acad. Cosmetic Surgery, Am. Acad. Dermatology, Am. Soc. Dermatol. Surgery, Frat. Order Police, Sigma Sigma Phi. Jewish. Avocations: karate, horseback riding. Office: Scottsdale Inst Cosmetic Dermatology 5206 N Scottsdale Rd Scottsdale AZ 85253-7006

FRIEDMAN, SYDNEY M. anatomy educator, medical researcher; b. Montreal, Que., Can., Feb. 17, 1916; s. Jacob and Minnie (Signer) F.; m. Constance Livingstone, Sept. 23, 1940. B.Sc., McGill U., Montreal, Can., 1938, M.D., C.M., 1940, M.Sc., 1941, Ph.D., 1946. Med. licentiate, Que. Teaching fellow anatomy McGill U., Montreal, Que., Can., 1940-42, asst. prof. anatomy Can., 1944-48, assoc. prof. anatomy Can., 1948-50; prof., head dept. anatomy U. B.C., Vancouver, Can., 1950-81, prof. anatomy Can., 1981-85, prof. emeritus Can., 1985—. Mem. panel on shock Def. Research Bd., Ottawa, Can., 1955-57; sci. subcom. Can. Heart Found., 1962-66, Am. Heart Assn., 1966-68, B.C. Heart Found., Vancouver, founding mem. Author: Visual Anatomy. Served as flight lt. RCAF, 1943-44. Recipient Premier award for rsch. in aging CIBA Found., 1955, Outstanding Svc. award Heart Found. Can., 1981, Disting. Achievement award Can. Hypertension Soc., 1987; Commemorative medal 125th Anniversary Can. Confedn.; Pfizer travel fellow Clin. Rsch. Inst., Montreal, 1971. Fellow Royal Soc. Can., Coun. High Blood Pressure Rsch.; mem. Am. Anatomical Assn. (exec. com. 1970-74), Can. Assn. Anatomists (pres. 1965-66, J.C.B. Grant award 1982), Internat. Soc. Hypertension, Am. Physiol. Soc., Royal Vancouver Yacht Club, Vancouver Club. Avocation: painting. Home: 4916 Chancellor Blvd Vancouver BC Canada V6T 1E1 Office: U BC Dept Anatomy 2177 Wesbrook Mall Vancouver BC Canada V6T 1Z3

FRIEDMANN, THEODORE, physician; b. Vienna, June 16, 1935; s. Eric and Rochelle (Bewar) F.; m. Ingrid Anna Stromberg, Jan. 3, 1965; children: Eric, Carl. BA, U. Pa., 1956, MD, 1960, MA, 1994. Diplomate Nat. Bd. Med. Examiners. Staff scientist NIH, Bethesda, Md., 1965-68; from asst. to full prof. pediatrics U. Calif. San Diego, La Jolla, 1970—, prof. pediatrics, dir. gene therapy, bd. dirs. Vis. scientist Salk Inst., La Jolla, 1968-70; Newton Abraham vis. prof., fellow Lincoln Coll., U. Oxford, Eng., 1994; mem. Congrl. Biomed. Ethics Adv. Com., U.S. Congress, Washington, 1989-92; mem. Exptl. Vriology Study Sect./NIH, Washington, 1986-90. Author: (monograph) Gene Therapy: Fact and Fiction, 1993; editor: (book series) Molecular Genetic Medicine, 1989—; patentee in gene therapy. Avocation: music. Office: Univ Calif San Diego CMG Gilman Dr 9500 Gilman Dr La Jolla CA 92093-5004 E-mail: tfriedmann@ucsd.edu

FRIEDRICHS, EDWARD CHARLES, architect; BA, Stanford U., 1965; MArch, U. Pa., 1968. Lic. architect Calif., Nev., Utah, Hawaii, N.Y., N.J., Ind. Architect M. Arthur Gensler Jr. & Assocs., San Francisco, 1969—, dir. projects, 1973-76, mng. prin. L.A., 1976-95; pres. Gensler, San Francisco, 1995—, CEO, 2000—, also bd. dirs., mem. mgmt. com. Pres., bd. govs. West L.A. County coun. Boy Scouts Am.; mem. exec. bd. San Francisco Bay Area Coun., Boy Scouts Am. Fellow AIA, Internat. Interior Design Assn.; mem. Internat. Facility Mgmt. Assn., Nat. Coun. Archtl. Registration Bds., Urban Land Inst. Office: Gensler 600 California St San Francisco CA 94108-2704

FRIEMAN, EDWARD ALLAN, academic administrator, educator; b. N.Y.C., Jan. 19, 1926; s. Joseph and Belle (Davidson) F.; m. Ruth Paula Rodman, June 19, 1949 (dec. May 1966); children: Jonathan, Michael, Joshua; m. Joy Fields, Sept. 17, 1967, children: Linda Gatchell, Wendy. BS, Columbia U., 1946, MS in Physics, 1948; PhD in Physics, Poly. Inst. Bklyn., 1952. Prof. astrophys. scis., dep. dir. Plasma Physics Lab. Princeton U., N.J., 1953-79; dir. energy rsch. Dept. Energy, Washington, 1979-81; exec. v.p. Sci. Applications Internat. Corp., La Jolla, Calif., 1981—; dir. Scripps Instn. Oceanography, La Jolla, 1986-96; vice-chancellor marine scis. U. Calif., San Diego, 1986-96, rsch. prof., dir. emeritus, 1996—. Vice-chmn. White House Sci. Coun., 1981-89, Def. Sci. Bd., Washington, 1984-90; mem. Joint Oceanog. Insts., Inc., 1986—, chmn., 1991—; chmn. supercollider site evaluation com. NRC, 1987-89; sci. adv. com. GM, 1987-93, corp. Charles Stark Draper Lab., Inc., 1989—, Sec. Energy Adv. Bd., 1990—, v.p. Space Policy adv. bd., 1992—; bd. dirs. Sci. Applications Internat. Corp.; chmn. NASA Earth Observing Sys. Engring. Rev., 1991-92, v.p.'s space policy adv. bd., 1992—; chmn. Pres.'s Com. on Nat. Medal Sci., 1992-93; chmn. bd. global change NAS/NRC, 1993-94, chmn. bd. on sustainable devel., 1995—; active Joint Oceanog. Insts., Inc., 1986—, chmn., 1991-94; spl. study group NRAC, 1995—; mem. law and policy adv. bd. Ctr. for Oceans, 1994—; mem. Def. Sci. Bd. Task Force on Future Submarines, 1997—. Contbr. articles to profl. jours. With USN, 1943-46, PTO. Recipient Disting. Service medal Dept. Energy, Compass Disting. Achievement Award, Marine Technology Soc., 1995; Disting. Alumni award Poly. Inst. Bklyn.; NSF sr. postdoctoral fellow; Guggenheim fellow Fellow Am. Phys. Soc. (Richtmyer award); mem. AAAS, NAS, Am. Philos. Soc., Cosmos Club (Washington). Avocations: piano, tennis, literature. Home: 1001 Genter St Ph 6 La Jolla CA 92037-5539 Office: Univ Calif San Diego Inst Geophys & Plan Physics 1241 Cave St La Jolla CA 92037-3602

FRIERY, THOMAS P. city treasurer; m. Linda Friery; three children. BS in Acctg., Dyke Coll., 1965; Corp. Cash Mgmt. Cert., Wharton Sch.'s Entrepreneurial, Ctr. Cert. Calif. Mcpl. Treas. Fin. and investment specialist State Auditor Gen., Calif., 1974-76; treasury divsn. mgr. Washington Pub. Power Supply System, Richland, 1976-78; city treas. City of Sacramento, 1978—. Mem. Calif. Mcpl. Treas. Assn. (past prest., chair legis. com.). Avocations: golf, fishing. Office: Office City Treas 926 J St Ste 300 Sacramento CA 95814-2706

FRIES, JAMES FRANKLIN, internal medicine educator; b. Normal, Ill., Aug. 25, 1938; s. Albert Charles and Orpha (Loreen) F.; m. Sarah Elizabeth Tilton, Aug. 27, 1960; children: Elizabeth Ann, Gregory James. AB, Stanford U., 1960; MD, Johns Hopkins U., 1964. Diplmate Am. Bd. Internal Medicine. Intern Johns Hopkins Hosp., Balt., 1964-65, resident in medicine, 1965-66, fellow connective tissue disease divsn., 1966-68; resident in medicine Stanford (Calif.) U. Sch. Medicine, 1968-69, instr. in medicine, 1969-71, asst. prof. medicine, 1971-77, assoc. prof. medicine, 1978-93, prof. medicine, 1993—. Dir. Arthritis, Rheumatism, Aging Med. Info. Sys., Stanford, 1975—; bd. dirs. Healthtrac Found., Menlo Park, Calif.; chmn. Healthtrac, Inc., 1984—; exec. com. The Health Project, 1992—. Author: Take Care of Yourself, 1975, 7th edit., 2000, Prognosis, 1981, Living Well, 1997, 4th edit., 1999, Taking Care of Your Child, 1999, The Arthritis Helpbook, 5th edit., 1999, Arthritis, 5th edit., 1999; mem. editl. bd. Jour. Rheumatology, Jour. Clin. Rheumatology, Computers Biomed. Rsch. Named Best Med. Specialist in U.S. Town and Country mag., 1984, Best Dr. in U.S. Good Housekeeping mag., 1991, one of Best Drs. in Am. Woodward-White, 1995; recipient C. Everett Koop Nat. Health award, 1994. Fellow ACP, Am. Coll. Rheumatology, Am. Coll. Med. Info. Avocations: running, expedition mountain climbing. Home: 135 Farm Rd Woodside CA 94062-1210 Office: Stanford U Sch Medicine 1000 Welch Rd Ste 203 Palo Alto CA 94304-1808 E-mail: jff@stanford.edu

FRIESE, ROBERT CHARLES, lawyer; b. Chgo., Apr. 29, 1943; s. Earl Matthew and Laura Barbara (Mayer) F.; m. Chandra Ullom; children: Matthew Robert, Mark Earl, Laura Moore. AB in Internat. Rels., Stanford U., 1964; JD, Northwestern U., 1970. Bar: Calif. 1972. Dir. Tutor Applied Linguistics Ctr., Geneva, 1964-66; atty. Bronson, Bronson & McKinnon, San Francisco, 1970-71, SEC, San Francisco, 1971-75; ptnr. Shartsis, Friese & Ginsburg, San Francisco, 1975—. Pres., bd. dirs. Custom Diversification Fund Mgmt., Inc., 1993—; dir.-co-founder Internat. Plant Rsch. Inst., Inc., San Carlos, Calif., 1978-86. Chmn. bd. suprs. Task Force on Noise Control, 1972-78; chmn. San Franciscans for Cleaner City, 1977; exec. dir. Nob Hill Neighbors, 1972-81; bd. dirs. Nob Hill Assn., 1976-78, Palace Fine Arts, 1992-94, San Francisco Beautiful, 1986—, pres., 1988-2000; chmn. Citizens Adv. Com. for Embarcadero Project, 1991—; mem. major gifts com. Stanford U.; bd. dirs. Presidio Heights Neighborhood Assn., 1993—, pres., 1996-98; bd. dirs. Inst. of Range and the American Mustang, 1990—. Mem. ABA, Assn. Bus. Trial Lawyers (bd. dirs.), Calif. Bar Assn., Bar Assn. San Francisco (bd. dirs. 1982-85, chmn. bus. litigation com. 1978-79, chmn. state ct. civil litigation com. 1983-90, new courthouse com. 1993—), Lawyers Club of San Francisco, Mensa, Calif. Hist. Soc., Commonwealth Club, Swiss-Am. Friendship League (chmn. 1971-79). Office: Shartsis Friese & Ginsburg 1 Maritime Plz Fl 18 San Francisco CA 94111-3404 E-mail: rcf@sfglaw.com

FRIESECKE, RAYMOND FRANCIS, health company executive; b. Mar. 12, 1937; s. Bernhard P. K. and Josephine (De Tomi) F. BS in Chemistry, Boston Coll., 1959; MSCE, MIT, 1961. Product specialist Dewey & Almy Chem. divsn. W. R. Grace & Co., Inc., Cambridge, Mass., 1963-66; market planning specialist USM Corp., Boston, 1966-71; mgmt. cons. Boston, 1971-74; dir. planning and devel. Schweitzer divsn. Kimberly-Clark Corp., Lee, Mass., 1974-78; v.p. corp. planning Butler Automatic, Inc., Canton, 1978-80; pres. Butler-Europe Inc., Greenwich and Munich, Conn., Germany, 1980; v.p. mktg. and planning Butler Greenwich Inc., 1980-81; pres. Strategic Mgmt. Assocs., San Rafael, Calif., 1981-96; chmn. Beyond Health Corp., 1994—, Health-E-America Found., 2000—. Bd. dirs. Better Physiology, Ltd.; corp. clk., v.p. Bldg. R&D, Inc., Cambridge, 1966-68. Host, prodr.: The Ounce of Prevention Show, Sta. KEST, San Francisco, 1994-98, Stas. KBZS and WNN, 1998—, Stas. WRPT and WSRO, 1999—, KYCY, 2001—; author: Management by Relative Product Quality, The New Way to Manage; pub.: Beyond Health News, 1995—; contbr. articles to profl. jours. State chmn. Citizens for Fair Taxation, 1972-73; state co-chmn. Mass. Young Reps., 1967-69; chmn. Ward 7 Rep. Com., Cambridge, 1968-70; vice-chmn. Cambridge Rep. City Com., 1966-68; bd. dirs. Kentfield Rehab. Hosp. Found., 1986-88, chmn., 1988-91; Rep. candidate Mass. Ho. of Reps., 1964, 66; pres. Marin Rep. Coun., 1986-91; chmn. Calif. Acad., 1986-88; sec. Navy League Marin Coun., 1984-91, v.p., 1994-2000; bd. dirs. The Marin Ballet, 1996-98; bd. dirs. Insts. for Behavioral Physiology, Seattle, 1999-2000. 1st lt. U.S. Army, 1961-63. Mem. NRA, Nat. Health Fedn., Am. Chem. Soc., Physicians Com. for Responsible Medicine, Marin Philos. Soc. (v.p. 1991-92), Ctr. for Sci. in Pub. Interest, Health Medicine Forum, Assn. of Am. Physicians and Surgeons, Orthomolecular Health Medicine Soc., The World Affairs Coun. Home: 141 Convent Ct San Rafael CA 94901-1335 Office: 777 Grand Ave Ste 205 San Rafael CA 94901-3509

FRIMMER, PAUL NORMAN, lawyer; b. N.Y.C., June 8, 1945; s. William and Irene (Alper) F.; m. Carol S. Zucker, June 9, 1968; children: Tracey, Scott. BS, Queens Coll., N.Y.C., 1966; JD cum laude, Fordham U., 1969. Bar: N.Y. 1969, Calif. 1971. Assoc. Stroock and Stroock, and Lavan, N.Y.C., 1969-71; ptnr. Irell and Manella, L.A., 1971—. Panelist Calif. Continuing Edn. of Bar, 1972, co-chmn. various sects. 73, 75, 76, 80, 86; instr. advanced profl. program U. So. Calif., 1977-80; lectr. 6th and 14th Insts. Estate Planning U. Miami Law Ctr., 1972, 80, Practicing Law Inst.-ABA programs, 1973-91, 31st Inst. Fed. Taxation U. So. Calif., 1979, other bar assn. groups on estate planning, probate, taxation, charitable giving and community property. Contbr. numerous articles to profl. jours. Nat. trustee, asst. sec. Leukemia Soc. Am., Inc., 1976-86, 91—, trustee, chmn. planned giving com. L.A. chpt., chpt. pres., 1973-86; trustee L.A. Children's Mus., 1982-86. Fellow Am. Coll. Trust and Estate Counsel, Internat. Acad. Probate and Trust Law; mem. ABA (real property, probate and trust law sect. com. charitable giving, trusts and founds., chmn. disclaimer task force), Calif. Bar Assn. Avocations: tennis, skiing. Office: Irell & Manella 1800 Avenue Of The Stars Los Angeles CA 90067-4276

FRISBEE, DON CALVIN, retired utilities executive; b. San Francisco, Dec. 13, 1923; s. Ira Nobles and Helen (Sheets) F.; m. Emilie Ford, Feb. 5, 1947; children: Ann, Robert, Peter, Dean. BA, Pomona Coll., 1947; MBA, Harvard U., 1949. Sr. investment analyst, asst. cashier investment analysis dept. 1st Interstate Bank Oreg., N.A., Portland, 1949-52; treas. PacifiCorp, Portland, 1958-60, then v.p., exec. v.p., pres., 1966-73, chief exec. officer, 1973-89, chmn., 1973-94; chmn. emeritus PacifiCorp., Portland, 1994-97. Bd. dirs. Wells Fargo Bank. Chmn. bd. trustees Reed Coll.; trustee Safari Game Search Found., High Desert Mus.; mem. cabinet Columbia Pacific coun. Boy Scouts Am.; founder Oreg. chpt. Am. Leadership Forum; mem. exec. com. Oreg. Partnership for Internat. Edn. 1st lt. AUS, 1943-46. Mem. Arlington Club, Univ. Club Multnomah Athletic Club, City Club. Office: 310 SW 4th Ave Ste 510 Portland OR 97204

FRISCH, JOSEPH, mechanical engineer, educator, consultant; b. Vienna, Austria, Apr. 21, 1921; came to U.S., 1940, naturalized, 1946; s. Abraham and Rachel (Lieberman) F.; m. Joan S. Frisch, May 26, 1962; children—Nora Theresa, Erich Martin, Jonathan David BSME, Duke U., 1946; MS, U. Calif., 1950. Registered profl. engr., Calif. Mem. faculty U. Calif.-Berkeley, 1947—, asst. prof. mech. engring., 1951-57, assoc. prof. mech. engring., 1957—, prof. mech. engring., 1963—, asst. dir. Inst. Engring. Rsch., 1961-63, chmn. div. mech. design, 1966-70, assoc. dean, 1972-75. Cons. to indsl. and govtl. labs. Contbr. articles to profl. jours. Fellow ASME (life); mem. Phi Beta Kappa, Sigma Xi, Tau Beta Pi, Pi Tau Sigma Club: U. Calif.-Berkeley Faculty. Office: U Calif Dept Mech Engring Berkeley CA 94720-1740

FRISCHKNECHT, LEE CONRAD, retired broadcasting executive; b. Brigham City, Utah, Jan. 4, 1928; s. Carl Oliver and Geniel (Lund) F.; m. Sara Jean McCulloch, Sept. 3, 1948; children: Diane Frischknecht Etherington, Jill Frischknecht Taylor, Ellen Frischknecht DePola, Amy Frischknecht Blodgett. BS in Speech, Utah State U., 1951; MA in Radio-TV, Mich. State U., 1957. Announcer sta. KID Radio, Idaho Falls, Idaho, 1951-52; producer-director sta. WKAR-TV, East Lansing, Mich., 1953-57, prodn. mgr., 1958-59, program mgr., 1960-61, gen. mgr., 1962-63; dir. sta. rels. Nat. Ednl. TV, N.Y.C., 1964-67; dir. univ. rels. Utah State U., 1969-70; dir. network affairs Nat. Pub. Radio, Washington, 1971, v.p., 1972, pres., 1973-77; communications cons., 1978—; mgr. ed. telecommunications sta. KAET-TV, Phoenix, 1980-86, asst. gen. mgr., 1987-93. Assoc. prof. radio-TV, Mich. State U., 1962-63; assoc. prof. speech Utah State U., 1968-69; lectr. Ariz. State U., 1981-82. Bd. dirs. Nat. Pub. Radio, 1973-78, Ariz. Sch. Svcs. Through Ednl. Tech., 1984-93, PSSC Legacy Fund, 1993—; bd. dirs. Pub. Svc. Satellite Consortium, 1982-90, chmn., 1987-90. Recipient Outstanding Alumnus in Communications award Mich. State U., 1973, Meritorious Svc. award in Communications, Brigham Young U., 1974, Disting. Svc. award Pacific Mountain Network, 1987. Mem. LDS Ch. Home: 8100 E Camelback Rd # 180 Scottsdale AZ 85251-2729

FRISON, GEORGE CARR, education educator; BA, U. Wyo., 1963; MA, U. Mich., 1965, PhD, 1967. Prof. of anthropology U. Wyo., 1967-95, prof. emeritus, 1995—; dir. archeol. excavations State of Wyo. Mem. NAS, Soc. for Am. Archaeology (pres. 1983-85).

FRITZ, LYNN C. transportation executive; With Fritz Cos., Inc., 1965—, various sr. exec. positions, 1970—, CEO, chmn. of bd. Bd. regents Pepperdine U.; trustee Monterey Inst. Internat. Studies; dir. Exploratorium, San Francisco. Office: Fritz Cos Inc 706 Mission St Fl 9 San Francisco CA 94103

FRITZ, RENE EUGENE, JR. manufacturing executive; b. Prineville, Oreg., Feb. 24, 1943; s. Rene and Ruth Pauline (Munson) F.; m. Sharyn Ann Fife, June 27, 1964; children: Rene Scott, Lanz Eugene, Shay Steven, Case McGarrett. BS in Bus. Adminstrn., Oreg. State U., 1965. Sales mgr. Renal Corp., Albany, Oreg., 1965-66, Albany Machine and Supply, 1965-66; pres. Albany Internat. Industries Inc., 1966-85, Wood Yield Tech. Corp., 1972-85, Albany Internat. DISC, 1972-85, Automation Controls Internat. Inc., 1975-85; co-founder, chmn. Albany Titanium Inc., 1981-89; prin. Torwest Capital, 1989; founder, pres. WY Tech. Corp., 1984-89, R. Fritz & Assocs., 1987-89. Pres. Chief Execs. Forum, 1989—, Fritz Grup Inc., 1989—; fin. planner, investment banker M&A, Vancouver, Wash., 1991—; chmn. Stormwater Treatment LLC, CSF Treatment Sys.; chmn. NTP, Wilsonville, Oreg., 1999—, Dentamax, Inc., Vancouver, 1999—, Human Capital Oreg./Wash., Vancouver, 1999—, MindNautilus, Inc., Portland, 2000—. Patentee computer controlled machinery. Pres. Oreg. World Trade Coun., 1982—; trustee U.S. Naval Acad. Found., Annapolis, Md., 1988—. Mem. Oreg. State Alumni, Forest Products Rsch. Soc., Young Pres. Orgn., Rotary, Elks. Presbyterian. E-mail: rfritz@ceforum.com

FROEBE, GERALD ALLEN, lawyer; b. The Dalles, Oreg., Feb. 16, 1935; s. Earl Wayne and Ethelene Alvina (Ogle) F.; m. Olivia Ann Tharaldson, Aug. 31, 1958; children: Dana Lynn, Heidi Ann. BBA, U. Oreg., 1956, LLB, 1961; LLM, NYU, 1962. Bar: N.Y. 1962, Oreg. 1962, U.S. Dist. Ct. Oreg. 1962. Auditor Arthur Andersen & Co., Seattle, 1956-58; lawyer, ptnr. Miller, Nash, Wiener, Hager & Carlsen, Portland, Oreg., 1962—. Editor-in-chief Oreg. Law Rev., Eugene, 1960-61. Republican. Christian. Avocations: hiking, travel. Home: 1109 SW Ardmore Ave Portland OR 97205-1004 Office: 1109 SW Ardriove Ave Portland OR 97205

FROHNMAYER, DAVID BRADEN, academic administrator; b. Medford, Oreg., July 9, 1940; s. Otto J. and MarAbel (Fisher) B. F.; m. Lynn Diane Johnson, Dec. 30, 1970; children: Kirsten (dec.), Mark, Kathryn (dec.), Jonathan, Amy. AB magna cum laude, Harvard U., 1962; BA, Oxford (Eng.) U., 1964, MA (Rhodes scholar), 1971; JD, U. Calif., Berkeley, 1967; LLD (hon.), Willamette U., 1988; D Pub. Svc. (hon.), U. Portland, 1989. Bar: Calif. 1967, U.S. Dist. Ct. (no. dist.) Calif. 1967, Oreg. 1971, U.S. Dist. Ct. Oreg. 1971, U.S. Supreme Ct. 1981. Assoc. Pillsbury, Madison & Sutro, San Francisco, 1967-69; asst. to sec. Dept. HEW, 1969-70; prof. law U. Oreg., 1971-81, spl. asst. to univ. pres., 1971-79; atty. gen. State of Oreg., 1981-91; dean Sch. Law U. Oreg., 1992-94, pres., 1994—. Chmn. Conf. Western Attys. Gen., 1985-86; chmn. Am. Coun. Edn. Govtl. Rels. commn, 1996-98; bd. dirs. Umpqua Holding Co. Mem. Oreg. Ho. of Reps, 1975-81; mem. coun. pub. reps. NIH, 1999-2000; bd. dirs. Fred Hutchinson Cancer Rsch. Ctr., 1994-2000, Nat. Marrow Donor Program, 1987-99, Fanconi Anemia Rsch. Fund, Inc., Tax Free Trust of Oreg. Fund; active Oreg. Progress Bd. Recipient awards Weaver Constl. Law Essay competition Am. Bar Found., 1972, 74, Advocacy award Research!Am., 1999, Albert B. Sabin Heroes of Sci. award Ams. for Med. Progress Ednl. Found., 2000; Rhodes scholar, 1962. Mem. ABA (Ross essay winner 1980), Oreg. Bar Assn., Calif. Bar Assn., Nat. Assn. Attys. Gen. (pres. 1987, Wyman award 1987), Round Table Eugene, Order of Coif, Phi Beta Kappa, Rotary. Republican. Presbyterian. Home: 2315 McMorran St Eugene OR 97403-1750 Office: U Oreg Johnson Hall Office Pres Eugene OR 97403 E-mail: pres@oregon.uoregon.edu

FROHNMAYER, JOHN EDWARD, lawyer, legal scholar, ethicist, writer; b. Medford, Oreg., June 1, 1942; s. Otto J. and Marabel (Braden) F.; m. Leah Thorpe, June 10, 1967; children: Jason Otto, Jonathan Aaron. BA in Am. History, Stanford U., 1964; MA in Christian Ethics, U. Chgo., 1969; JD, U. Oreg., 1972. Bar: Oreg. 1972, Mont. 1995. Assoc. Johnson, Harrang & Mercer, Eugene, Oreg., 1972-75; ptnr. Tonkon, Torp, Galen, Marmaduke & Booth, Portland, 1975-89; 5th chmn. Nat. Endowment for the Arts, Washington, 1989-92; writer, lectr. on art, ethics and politics, 1992—; pvt. practice Oreg., 1972-89, Bozeman, Mont., 1995—. Mem. Oreg. Arts Commn., 1978-85, chmn., 1980-84; bd. dirs. Internat. Sculpture Symposium, eugene, 1974; chmn. screening com. Oreg. State Capitol Bldg., 1977. Author: Leaving Town Alive, 1993, Out of Tune: Listening to The First Amendment, 1994; editor-in-chief Oreg. Law Rev., 1971-72; singer; appeared in recital, oratorio, mus. comedy and various other mus. prodns. Trustee Holladay Park Pla.; founding mem. chamber choir Novum Cantorum; bd. dirs. Chamber Music Northwest, Western States Arts Found.; mem. Nat. Endowment for the Arts Opera-Mus. Theater, 1982, 83. With USN, 1966-69. Sr. fellow Freedom Forum, 1993; recipient People for the Am. Way Ann. 1st Amendment award, 1992, Oreg. Gov. Arts award, 1993, Intellectual Freedom award Mont. Libr. Assn., 1997, Citation of Merit, Mu Phi Epsilon, 1998. Fellow Am. Leadership Forum; mem. ABA (com. comml. transactions litigation), Oreg. State Bar Assn. (chmn. bar com. domestic law 1975-76, procedure and practice com. 1984-85), Multnomah County Bar Assn., City Club Portland (bd. dirs.), Sta. L. Rowing Club (sec.), Order of the Coif (legal hon. 1972). Home and Office: 14080 Lone Bear Rd Bozeman MT 59715-6620 E-mail: frohn@wtp.net

FROMAN, SANDRA SUE, lawyer; b. San Francisco, June 15, 1949; d. Jay and Beatrice Froman. AB with honors, Stanford U., 1971; JD, Harvard U., 1974. Bar: Calif. 1974, U.S. Dist. Ct. (cen. dist.) Calif. 1974, U.S. Dist. Ct. (so. dist.) Calif. 1976, U.S. Dist. Ct. (no. dist.) Calif., U.S. Ct. Claims 1979, U.S. Tax Ct. 1984, Ariz. 1985, U.S. Dist. Ct. Ariz. 1985, U.S. Ct. Appeals (9th cir.) 1986, U.S. Supreme Ct. 1986. Assoc. Loeb & Loeb, L.A., 1974-80, ptnr., 1981-84; assoc. Bilby & Schoenhair, P.C., Tucson, 1985, shareholder, 1986-89; ptnr. Snell & Wilmer, Tucson, 1989-99. Vis. asst. prof. law U. Santa Clara, Calif., 1983-85; mem. Pima County Commn. on Trial Ct. Appointments, 1996-98. Trustee Firearms Civil Rights Legal Def. Fund, 1992-98, NRA Found., pres. 1997-2000; bd. dirs., 2d v.p. NRA, 1992—. Mem. Ariz. Bar Found. (pres. 1996—), Wildlife for Tomorrow Found. (pres. 1999—). Office: Ste 140 200 W Magee Rd Tucson AZ 85704-6492

FRONTERA, MICHAEL P. municipal official; b. Newburgh, N.Y., May 22, 1969; BA, SUNY, Binghamton, 1991; JD, U. Ariz., 1994. Election specialist City Clk.'s Office City of Tucson (Ariz.), 1993-95; info. dir. Denver Election Commn. City of Denver, 1996-97, exec. dir. Denver Election Commn., 1997-99; client support mgr. Sequoia Pacific, Denver,

1999—, installation mgr. Mem. Election Ctr. 96. Recipient Am. Jurisprudence award in Constl. Law Lawyers Coop. Publishing, 1991. Mem. ABA, Colo. Bar Assn., Denver Bar Assn., Internat. Assn. Clks., Recorders, Election Officials & Treasurers, Colo. State Assn. County Clks. & Recorders. Office: Sequoia Pacific 410 17th St Ste 1950 Denver CO 80202-4432

FROST, EVERETT LLOYD, anthropologist, academic administrator; b. Salt Lake City, Oct. 17, 1942; s. Henry Hoag Jr. and Ruth Salome (Smith) F.; m. Janet Owens, Mar. 26, 1967; children: Noreen Karyn, Joyce Lida. BA in Anthropology, U. Oreg., 1965; PhD in Anthropology, U. Utah, 1970. Field researcher in cultural anthropology, Taveuni, Fiji, 1968-69; asst. prof. in anthropology Ea. N.Mex. U., Portales, 1970-74, assoc. prof., 1974-76, asst. dean Coll. Liberal Arts and Scis., 1976-78, dean acad. affairs and grad. studies, 1978-80, v.p. for planning and analysis, dean rsch., 1980-91, dean grad. studies, 1983-88, pres., 1991-2001, pres. emeritus, prof. anthropology emeritus, 2001—. Cons., evaluator N. Ctrl. Assn. Accreditation Agy. for Higher Edn., 1989-93—, mem. rev. bd., 1993-95—; bd. dirs. Quality N.Mex., 1st Savs. Bank of Clovis and Portles, N.Mex., Plains Regional Med. Ctrs., Clovis and Portales; bd. mem. emeritus N.Mex. First; commr., pres. Western Interstate Commn. for Higher Edn., 1993-2002; pres. Lone Star Athletic Conf. Pres.'s Commn., 1992-93; chmn. rsch. com. N.Mex. First, 1989-91. Chmn. N.Mex. Humanities Coun., 1980-88; mem. N.Mex. Gov.'s Commn. on Higher Edn., 1983-86; mem. exec. bd. N.Mex. First, 1987-92; bd. dirs. Roosevelt Gen. Hosp., Portales, 1989-92; pres. bd. dirs. San Juan County Mus. Assn., Farmington, 1979-82; vice chair Portales Pub. Schs. Facilities Com., 1990-91. NDEA fellow, 1969-70; grantee NEW, 1979-80, NSF, 1968-69, Fiji Forbes, Ltd., 1975-76, others. Fellow Am. Anthropol. Assn., Am. Assn. Higher Edn., Soc. Coll. and Univ. Planning, Assn. Social Anthropologists Oceania, Anthropol. Soc. Washington, Sch. Am. Rsch., Western Assn. Grad. Deans, Current Anthropology (assoc.) Polynesian Soc., Phi Kappa Phi.

FROST, STERLING NEWELL, arbitrator, mediator, management consultant; b. Oklahoma City, Dec. 21, 1935; s. Sterling Johnson and Eula Dove (Whitford) F.; m. Patricia Joyce Rose, Aug. 18, 1957; children: Patricia Diane Wiscarson, Richard Sterling, Lindy Layne Harrington. BS Indsl. Engring., U. Okla., Norman, 1957; MS Indsl. Engring., Okla. State U., 1966. Registered profl. engr., Okla., Calif. Asst. mgr. acctg. Western Electric, Balt., 1972-73; mgr. indsl. engring. Chgo., 1973-75; mgr. devel. engring., 1975-76; mgr. acct. mgmt. San Francisco, 1976-78; dir. staff Morristown, N.J., 1978-79; gen. mgr. distbn. & repair AT&T Techs., Sunnyvale, Calif., 1979-85; area v.p. material mgmt. svcs. AT&T Info. Systems, Oakland, 1985-87; ops. v.p. material mgmt. svcs. San Francisco, 1988-89; dir. configuration ops. Businessland, Inc., San Jose, Calif., 1989-90; dir. svcs. support, 1990-91; exec. v.p. Isotek, Tiburon, Calif., 1991; v.p., gen. mgr. Tree Fresh, San Francisco, 1991-92; CFO Prima Pacific, Iinc., Tiburon, 1992-93; mgmt. cons., arbitrator/mediator Sterling Solutions, Santa Cruz, 1993—. Bd. dirs. Contract Office Group, San Jose, 1983—, chmn., 1984—. Bd. dirs. Santa Clara County YMCA, San Jose, Calif., 1981-84, bd. dirs., Northern Calif. Medication Assn., 1995-99. Recipient Man of Day citation Sta. WAIT Radio, Chgo. Mem. Nat. Soc. Prof. Engrs. (chmn. edn. com. 1969-70), Am. Inst. Idsl. Engrs. (pres. bd. dirs. 1966-68), Okla. Soc. Profl. Engrs. (v.p. 1968-69), No. Calif. Mediation Assn. (bd. dirs. 1996-98), Am. Arbitration Assn., Soc. Profls. in Dispute Resolution. Republican.

FRUCHTER, JONATHAN SEWELL, research scientist, geochemist; b. San Antonio, June 5, 1945; s. Benjamin and Dorothy Ann (Sewell) F.; m. Cecelia Ann Smith, Mar. 31, 1973; children: Diane, Daniel. BS in Chemistry, U. Tex., 1966; PhD in Geochemistry, U. Calif., San Diego, 1971. Research assoc. U. Oreg., Eugene, 1971-74; research scientist Battelle Northwest, Richland, Wash., 1974-79, mgr. research and devel., 1979-87, staff scientist, 1987-91, 94—, tech. group leader, 1991-94. Contbr. numerous articles to profl. jours. Recipient R&D 100 Awd., 1998. Mem. AAAS, Am. Chem. Soc., Phi Beta Kappa, Phi Kappa Phi. Avocations: fishing, skiing, boating. Office: Battelle NW PO Box 999 Richland WA 99352-0999

FRUMKIN, SIMON, political activist and columnist; b. Kaunas, Lithuania, Nov. 5, 1930; came to U.S., 1949; s. Nicholas and Zila (Oster) F.; m. Rhoda Hirsch, June 1953 (div. 1978); children: Michael Alan, Larry Martin; m. Kathy Elizabeth Hoopes, June 22, 1981 (dec. 1994); m. Ella Zousman, Dec. 11, 1995. BA, NYU, 1953; MA in History, Calif. State U., Northridge, 1964. Pres., chief exec. officer Universal Drapery Fabrics, Inc., Los Angeles, 1953-87; chmn. Southern Calif. Council for Soviet Jews, Studio City, 1969—. Lectr. Simon Wiesenthal Ctr. for Holocaust Studies, Los Angeles, 1980—; chmn. Union of Councils for Soviet Jews, 1972-73. Columnist Heritage, numerous other So. Calif. newspapers, 1980—; corr. to columnist Panorama, U.S.A. Russian Lang., 1985—; contbr. articles to newspapers. Pres. Media Analysis Found., Los Angeles, 1988; chmn. Ams. for Peace and Justice, 1972-74; mem. Pres.' Senatorial Inner Circle, U.S. Senatorial Club. Honored by Calif. Govt., Los Angeles City Council, Los Angeles Office of City Atty., numerous Jewish orgns. Mem. Assn. Soviet Jewish Emigre's (pres. 1987—), Zionist Orgn. Am., Am. Israel Polit. Action Com., Russian Republican Club, Mensa. Avocations: writing, photography, skiing, fitness. Home and Office: 3755 Goodland Ave Studio City CA 91604-2313

FRY, DAVID, electronics executive; CII, CFO Fry's Electronics, Inc., San Jose, Calif. Mng. gen. ptnr. San Jose SaberCats. Office: Fry's Electronics Inc 600 E Brokaw Rd San Jose CA 95112

FRY, EARL HOWARD, political scientist, educator; b. Oakland, Calif., May 19, 1947; s. Harvey Wallace and Alice (Horlacher) F.; m. Elaine Fisher, May 29, 1971; children: Christopher, Lisa, Leanna, Kimberly, Steven, Kristen. BA, BA, Brigham Young U., 1971, MA, 1972; PhD, UCLA, 1976. Fulbright prof. U. Sorbonne, Paris, 1974-75; asst. prof. Boise State U., Idaho, 1976-79; assoc. prof. SUNY, Plattsburgh, 1979-80, Brigham Young U., Provo, Utah, 1980-83, prof. dept. Polit. Sci., Endowed prof. Canadian studies, 1989—, dir. the Washington Seminar, 1999-2000; spl. asst. Office U.S. Trade Rep., Washington, 1983-84. Asst. dir. Brigham Young U.-U Grenoble Semester Abroad Program, 1972; vis. rschr. UN, Geneva, 1974; asst. prof. Boise State U., 1976-79; chmn. BSU Faculty Rsch. com., 1977-78; vis. prof. U. B.C., 1977; prin. investigator Idaho Internat. Trade directory Pacific northwest Regional Commn., 1979; assoc. prof. SUNY Plattsburgh, 1979-80, dir. Internat. Edn., Canadian Studies, 1979-80; vis. prof. U. Montreal, 1989, Ecole des Hautes Etudes en Scis. Sociales, Paris, 1990; review com. Internat. Proposals U.S. Dept. Edn., 1985-88; Utah State Tax Commn. Task Force on Unitary Taxation, 1985; chmn. Canadian Studies, Brigham Young U., 1980—; Univ. rep. Atlantic Coun. U.S., 1987—; fellowship com. Coun. Fgn. Rels., 1989-93, fellow 1983-84; dir. Grad. Studies, Rsch., Publs., David M. Kennedy Ctr. Internat. Studies, 1987-90; Fulbright Commn. review com., 1991; vis. fellow Ams. Soc., N.Y.C., 1991-93; acad. assoc. Atlantic Coun., Washington, 1987—; dir. The Washington Seminar, 1999-2000; lectr., cons. and spkr. in field. Author: Financial Invasion of the U.S.A., 1980, Canadian Government and Politics in Comparative Perspective, 1983, The Canadian Political System, 1991, Canada's Unity Crisis: Implications for U.S.-Canadian Economic Relations, 1992; co-author Idaho's Foreign Relations: The Transgovernmental Linkages of an American State, 1978, The Other Western Europe: A Comparative Analysis of the Smaller Democracies, 1980, The Other Western Europe, 1983, America the Vincible: U.S. Foreign Policy for the Twenty-First Century, 1994, The Expanding Role of State and Local Governments in U.S. Foreign Affairs, 1998; co-editor The Canada/U.S. Free Trade Agreement: The Impact on Service Industries, 1988, Investment in the North American Free Trade Area: Opportunities and Challenges, 1992; gen. editor Canadian Studies Curriculum Guide, 1980; contbr. numerous articles to profl. jours. Bd. dirs. Fulbright Assn., 1995-98. Recipient Can. Studies Sr. Fellowship award, 1983, Karl G. Maeser Rsch. and Creative Arts award, 1989; rsch. grantee Coll. Family, Home and Social Scis., 1986, 88, 89, 92; rsch. and conf. grantee Can. govt., 1985-92; Fulbright lectr. U. Paris (La Sorbonne), 1974-75; Bissell-Hyde-Fulbright chair U. Toronto, 1995-96; Elliot/Winant Lecture fellow UK, 1993, Coun. Fgn. Rels. Internat. Affairs fellow, 1983, David M. Kennedy Rsch. fellow Brigham Young U., 1985-86, Rsch. grantee, 1987-89; Atlantic Coun. Travel grantee, 1988; Presdl. fellow Am. Grad. Sch. Internat. Mgmt., 1993. Mem. Internat. Polit. Sci. Assn., Assn. Can. Studies in U.S. (Washington v.p. 1989-91, pres. 1991-93, exec. coun. 1985—, Bissell-Hyde Fulbright chair U. Toronto 1995-96), Fulbright Assn. (bd. dirs. 1995-97), Coun. Fgn. Rels. Mem. LDS Ch. Office: Brigham Young U Dept Pol Scis Provo UT 84602 E-mail: earl_fry@byu.edu

FRY, JOHN, electronics executive; CEO Fry's Electronics Inc., San Jose, Calif., 1985—. Office: Frys Electronics Inc 600 E Brokaw Rd San Jose CA 95112-1006

FRY, MICHAEL GRAHAM, historian, educator; b. Brierley, Eng., Nov. 5, 1934; s. Cyril Victor and Margaret Mary (Copley) F.; m. Anna Maria Fulgoni; children: Michael Gareth, Gabrielle, Margaret Louise. B.Sc. in Econs. with honors, U. London, 1956, Ph.D., 1963. Dir. Norman Paterson Sch. Internat. Affairs, Carleton U., Ottawa, Ont., 1973-77; dean, prof. internat. relations Grad. Sch. Internat. Studies, U. Denver, 1978-81; dir., prof. Sch. Internat. Relations, U. So. Calif., Los Angeles, 1981—. Vis. prof. Middle East Center, U. Utah, 1979, U. Leningrad, 1976 Author: Illusions of Security: North Atlantic Diplomacy, 1918-1922, 1972, Freedom and Change, 1975, Lloyd George and Foreign Policy, Vol. I, The Education of a Statesman, 1890-1916, 1977, Despatches from Damascus, 1933-39, 1986, History and International Studies, 1987, History, The White House and the Kremlin: Statesmen as Historians, 1991, Power, Personalities and Policies, 1992, The North Pacific Triangle: Canada Japan and the U.S. at Century's End, 1998. NATO rsch. fellow, 1970-71, rsch. fellow Annenberg Program, Washington, 1986-87; grantee Can. Coun. Fellow Royal Hist. Soc.; mem. Soc. Historians Am. Fgn. Rels. Roman Catholic. Home: 1358 Cassins St Carlsbad CA 92009-4856 Office: U So Calif Sch Internat Rels Los Angeles CA 90089-0001

FRYE, HELEN JACKSON, federal judge; b. Klamath Falls, Oreg., Dec. 10, 1930; d. Earl and Elizabeth (Kirkpatrick) Jackson; m. William Frye, Sept. 7, 1952; children: Eric, Karen, Heidi; 1 adopted child, Hedy; m. Perry Holloman, July 10, 1980 (dec. Sept. 1991). BA in English with honors, U. Oreg., 1953, MA, 1960, JD, 1966. Bar: Oreg. 1966. Public sch. tchr., Oreg., 1956-63; with Riddlesberger, Pederson, Brownhill & Young, 1966-67, Husband & Johnson, Eugene, 1968-71; trial judge State of Oreg., 1971-80; U.S. dist judge Dist. Oreg. Portland, 1980-95; sr. judge U.S. Dist. Ct., Portland, 1995—. Mem. Phi Beta Kappa. Office: 1107 US Courthouse 1000 SW 3rd Ave Portland OR 97204-2930

FU, KAREN KING-WAH, radiation oncologist; b. Shanghai, China, Oct. 15, 1940; came to U.S., 1959, naturalized, 1975; d. Ping Sen and Lein Sun (Ho) F. Student, Ind. U., 1959-61; A.B., Barnard Coll., Columbia U., 1963, M.D., 1967. Cert. radiation oncologist. Intern Montreal Gen. Hosp., Que., Can., 1967-68; resident Princess Margaret Hosp., Toronto, Ont., Can., 1968-69, Stanford U. Hosp., Calif., 1969-71; instr. U. Utah, 1971-72; clin. instr. U. Calif., San Francisco, 1972-73, asst. prof., 1973-76, assoc. prof., 1976-82, prof., 1982—, vice chmn., 1994-95, rsch. assoc. Cancer Research Inst., 1973-96. Contbr. articles to profl. jours. Mem. San Francisco Opera Guild, San Francisco Symphony Assn., San Francisco Ballet, Calif. Acad. Sci., De Young Mus. Grantee Am. Cancer Soc., 1982, 86, NIH, 1982, 87. Fellow Am. Coll. Radiology; mem. Am. Soc. Therapeutic Radiologists, Am. Med. Women's Assn., Calif. Radiation Therapy Assn., Calif. Radiol. Soc., No. Calif. Acad. Clin. Oncology, Radiation Research Soc., Am. Soc. Clin. Oncologists, Assn. Women in Sci. Office: U Calif San Francisco Dept Radiation Oncology PO Box 226 San Francisco CA 94143-0001

FU, LEE-LUENG, oceanographer; b. Taipei, Republic of China, Oct. 10, 1950; s. Yi-Chin and Er-Lan (Chen) F.; m. Cecilia C. Liu, Mar. 26, 1977; 1 child, Christine. BS, Nat. Taiwan U., Taipei, 1972; PhD, MIT, 1980. Postdoctoral assoc. MIT, Cambridge, Mass., 1980; mem. tech. staff Jet Propulsion Lab., Pasadena, Calif., 1981-85, tech. group supr., 1986-93, project scientist, 1988—, lead scientist/ocean scis., 1994, sr. rsch. scientist, 1994. Chmn. TOPEX/POSEIDON sci. working team NASA, Washington, 1988—, mem. NSCAT sci. working team, 1986—; mem. sci. steering com. U.S. World Ocean Experiment Circulation, 1998—, U.S. Global Ocean Observing System, 1998—. Contbr. articles to profl. publs. Recipient Laurels award Aviation Week and Space Tech., 1993, CNES medal French Space Agy., 1994, Exceptional Scientific Achievement medal NASA, 1996. Mem. AAAS, Am. Geophys. Union, Am. Meteorol. Soc., Oceanography Soc. Office: Jet Propulsion Lab MS 300-323 4800 Oak Grove Dr Pasadena CA 91109-8001

FUCALORO, ANTHONY FRANK, dean; b. Bklyn., Apr. 17, 1943; s. Gaetano Atillio and Josepina (Noto) F.; m. Liliane Marie-Louise Rigas, June 25, 1967; children: Nicole Antionette, Cristina Veronique. BS, Poly. Inst., Bklyn., 1964; PhD, U. Ariz., 1969. Assoc. N.Mex. State U., Las Cruces, 1969-71; vis. asst. prof. U. New Orleans, 1971-74; prof. chemistry Claremont (Calif.) McKenna Coll., 1974-93, v.p., pres., dean faculty, 1991—. Cons. Occidental Petroleum, Irvine, Calif., Ill. Tool Works, Chgo., Jet Propulsion Lab., Pasadena, Calif. Contbr. articles to profl. jours. Mem. Am. Chem. Soc. (soc. advisor to Congressman David Dreier). Office: Claremont McKenna Coll Bauer Ctr 500 E 9th St Claremont CA 91711-5903

FUCHS, RENATO, bioengineer; BChemE, U. de Valle, Columbia, 1967; MS in Biochem. Engring., MIT, 1969, PhD in Biochem. Engring., 1974. Various mgmt. positions Schering-Plough; sr. v.p. pharm. devel. Centocor, St. Louis, 1988-93, Leiden, Holland, 1988-93; sr. v.p. mfg. and devel. ops. Chiron Corp., Emeryville, Calif., 1993—. Mem. NAE. Office: Chiron Corp 4560 Horton St Emeryville CA 94608-2916

FUCHS, VICTOR ROBERT, economics educator; b. N.Y.C., Jan. 31, 1924; s. Alfred and Frances Sarah (Scheiber) F.; m. Beverly Beck, Aug. 29, 1948; children: Nancy, Fredric, Paula, Kenneth. BS, NYU, 1947; MA, Columbia U., 1951, PhD, 1955. Internat. fur broker, 1946-50; lectr. Columbia U., N.Y.C., 1953-54, instr., 1954-55, asst. prof. econs., 1955-59; assoc. prof. econs. NYU, 1959-60; program assoc. Ford Found. Program in Econ. Devel. and Adminstrn., 1960-62; prof. econs. Grad. Ctr., CUNY, 1968-74; prof. community medicine Mt. Sinai Sch. Medicine, 1968-74; prof. econs. Stanford U. and Stanford Med. Sch., 1974-95, Henry J. Kaiser Jr. prof., 1988-95, prof. emeritus, 1995—; v.p. research Nat. Bur. Econ. Research, 1968-78, mem. sr. research staff, 1962—. Author: The Economics of the Fur Industry, 1957; (with Aaron Warner) Concepts and Cases in Economic Analysis, 1958, Changes in the Location of Manufacturing in the United States Since 1929, 1962, The Service Economy, 1968, Production and Productivity in the Service Industries, 1969, Policy Issues and Research Opportunities in Industrial Organization, 1972, Essays in the Economics of Health and Medical Care, 1972, Who Shall Live? Health, Economics and Social Choice, 1975, expanded edit., 1998, (with Joseph Newhouse) The Economics of Physician and Patient Behavior, 1978, Economic Aspects of Health, 1982, How We Live, 1983, The Health Economy, 1986, Women's Quest for Economic Equality, 1988, The Future of Health Policy, 1993, Individual and Social Responsibility: Child Care Education, Medical Care, and Long-term Care in America, 1996.; contbr. articles to profl. jours. Served with USAAF, 1943-46. Fellow Am. Acad. Arts and Scis., Am. Econ. Assn. (disting.; pres. 1995); mem. Inst. Medicine of NAS, Am. Philos. Soc., Sigma Xi, Beta Gamma Sigma. Home: 796 Cedro Way Stanford CA 94305-1032 Office: NBER 204 Alta Rd Stanford CA 94305-8006

FUERSTENAU, DOUGLAS WINSTON, mineral engineering educator; b. Hazel, S.D., Dec. 6, 1928; s. Erwin Arnold and Hazel Pauline (Karterud) F.; m. Margaret Ann Pellett, Aug. 29, 1953; children: Linda (dec.), Lucy, Sarah, Stephen. BS, S.D. Sch. Mines and Tech., 1949; MS, Mont. Sch. Mines, 1950; ScD, MIT, 1953; Mineral Engr., Mont. Coll. Mineral Sci. and Tech., 1968; hon. doctorate degree, U. Liege, Belgium, 1989; D of Technology (hon.), Lulea U. Tech., Sweden, 2001. Asst. prof. mineral engring. MIT, 1953-56; sect. leader, metals research lab. Union Carbide Metals Co., Niagara Falls, N.Y., 1956-58; mgr. mineral engring. lab Kaiser Aluminum & Chem. Corp., Permanente, Calif., 1958-59; assoc. prof. metallurgy U. Calif., Berkeley, 1959-62, prof. metallurgy, 1962-86, P. Malozemoff prof. of mineral engring., 1987-93, prof. grad. sch., 1994—, Miller rsch. prof., 1969-70, chmn. dept. materials sci. and mineral engring., 1970-78; hon. prof. Huainan Inst. Tech., 2000—. Mem. Nat. Mineral Bd., 1975-78; Am. rep. Internat. Mineral Processing Congress Com., 1978-97. Editor: Froth Flotation-50th Anniversary Vol., 1962; co-editor-in-chief: Internat. Jour. of Mineral Processing, 1974-98, hon. editor-in-chief, 1998—; contbr. articles to profl. jours. Recipient Alexander von Humboldt Sr. Am. Scientist award, Germany, 1984, Frank F. Aplan award The Engring. Found., 1990, Internat. Mineral Processing Congress Lifetime Achievement award, 1995; Rsch. fellow Japan Soc. Promotion Sci., 1993; Douglas W. Fuerstenau professorship established at S.D. Sch. of Mines and Tech., 1998. Mem. NAE, AIChE, Am. Inst. Mining and Metall. Engrs. (chmn. mineral processing divsn. 1967, Robert Lansing Hardy gold medal 1957, Rossiter W. Raymond award 1961, Robert H. Richards award 1975, Antoine M. Gaudin award 1978, Mineral Industry Edn. award 1983, Henry Krumb disting. lectr. 1989, hon. 1989), Soc. Mining Engrs. (bd. dirs. 1968-71, Disting. mem.), Am. Chem. Soc., Russian Fedn. Acad. Natural Scis. (fgn. mem.), Sigma Xi, Theta Tau. Congregationalist. Home: 1440 Le Roy Ave Berkeley CA 94708-1912 E-mail: dwfuerst@socrates.berkeley.edu, fuerstenau@home.com

FUGATE, IVAN DEE, banker, lawyer; b. Blackwell, Okla., Dec. 9, 1928; s. Hugh D. and Iva (Holmes) F.; m. Lois Unita Rossow, June 3, 1966; children: Vickie Michelle, Roberta Jeanne, Douglas B., Thomas P. AB, Pittsburg (Kans.) State U., 1949; LLB, U. Denver, 1952, JD, 1970. Bar: Colo. 1952. Exec. sec., mgr. Jr. C. of C. of Denver, 1950-52; also sec. Colo. Jr. C. of C.; individual practice law Denver, 1954—; chmn. bd., pres. Green Mountain Bank, Lakewood, Colo., 1975-82; chmn., pres. Western Nat. Bank Denver (now Vectra Bank of Colorado); chmn. exec. com. North Valley Bank, Thornton, Colo., 1962—, chmn., pres., 1981-2000, chmn., 2000—; founder, chmn. emeritus Ind. State Bank of Colo. (now Bankers Bank of West), 1978—, Ind. Bankers of Colo., 1973—. Former bd. dirs. Kit Carson State Bank, Colo.; sec. First Nat. Bank, Burlington, Colo.; owner, farms, ranches, Kans., Colo.; instr. U. Denver Coll. Law, 1955-60; mem. Colo. Treas's. Com. Investment State Funds, 1975—. Treas. to Rep. Assos., Colo., 1959-61, trustee, 1959-64. Maj. USAR, 1952-54. Mem. ABA, Colo. Bar Assn., Denver Bar Assn. (trustee 1962-65), Colo. Bankers Assn. (bd. dirs.), Colo. Cattlemen's Assn., Ind. Bankers Assn. Am. (pres. 1978, adminstrv. com., exec. coun. 1976—, bd. dirs. fed. legis. com., chmn. spl. tax com., instr. One Bank Holding Co. seminars 1976—), Denver Law Club, Petroleum Club, Denver Athletic Club, Lakewood Country Club, Phi Alpha Delta. Methodist. Home: 12015 W 26th Ave Lakewood CO 80215-1110 Office: North Valley Bank Bldg PO Box 29429 9001 Washington St Denver CO 80229-4363

FUHLRODT, NORMAN THEODORE, retired insurance executive; b. Wisner, Nebr., Apr. 24, 1910; s. Albert F. and Lena (Schafersman) F.; student Midland Coll., 1926-28; A.B., U. Nebr., 1930; M.A., U. Mich., 1936; m. Clarice W. Livermore, Aug. 23, 1933; 1 son, Douglas B. Tchr., athletic coach high schs., Sargent, Nebr., 1930-32, West Point, Nebr., 1932-35; with Central Life Assurance Co., Des Moines, 1936-74, pres., chief exec. officer, 1964-72, chmn. bd., chief exec. officer, 1972-74, also dir. Named Monroe St. Jour. Alumnus of Month, U. Mich. Grad Sch. Bus. Adminstrn. Gen. chmn. Greater Des Moines United campaign United Community Service, 1969-70. Former bd. dirs. Des Moines Center Sci. and Industry. Fellow Soc. Actuaries. Home: 760 E Bobier Dr # 116B Vista CA 92084-3806

FUJII, SHARON M. federal agency administrator; BA, U. Washington, 1966, M in Social Work, 1969; PhD, Brandeis U., 1975. Sr. v.p. Gerontological Planning Assn., 1975-77; prin. investigator Pacific-Asian Elderly Rsch. Project, 1977-79; program analyst Office of Refugee Resettlement, 1978-79, regional dir., 1979-80; regional dir., adminstrn. for children and families Dept. Health and Human Svcs., 1980-86; regional adminstr., adminstrn. for children and families, 1986—. Mem. Pres. Fed. Coun. on Aging, 1975-78. Health, Edn. and Welfare fellow, 1978-79. Office: Dept Health & Human Svcs 50 United Nations Plz Rm 450 San Francisco CA 94102-4912

FUJINAMI, ROBERT SHIN, neurology educator; b. Salt Lake City, Dec. 8, 1949; BA, U. Utah, 1972; PhD, Northwestern U., Chgo., 1977. Instr. microbiology and immunology Northwestern U., Chgo., 1973-76; rsch. fellow immunopathology Scripps Clinic and Rsch. Found., La Jolla, Calif., 1977-80, rsch. assoc. immunopathology, 1980-81, asst. mem., asst. prof. dept. immunology, 1981-85, vis. investigator dept. immunology, 1985-89; vis. investigator dept. neuropharmacology divsn. virology Scripps Rsch. Inst. (formerly Scripps Clinic and Rsch. Found.), La Jolla, 1989-90; rsch. immunopathologist dept. pathology U. Calif., San Diego, 1980-82, assoc. prof. pathology, 1985-90; prof. neurology U. Utah, Salt Lake City, 1990—, adj. prof. dept. pathology divsn. cell biology and immunology, 1991—. Mem. Weber immunology adv. com., dept. pathology U. Utah, Salt Lake City, 1991—, mem. neurosci. steering com., 1992-96, mem. biosafety com., 1992-96, chmn., 1994-96, chmn. safety com., dept. neurology, 1993—, chmn. promotion, retention and tenure com., 1993-96, mem. univ. promotions and tenure adv. com., 1995-98, chair oversight com. Fluorescence Activated Cell Sorter (FACS) Sch. Medicine, 1996-99, mem. univ. rsch. com., 1999—, disting. rsch. award subcom., 1999—, senate task force on RPT procedures, 1999—, adv. com. core facilities Huntsman Cancer Inst., 1999—, dir. grad. studies pathology PhD program, 1999—, chmn. tenured faculty rev. com., dept. neurology, 1999—. Contbr. chpts. to books, 110 articles to profl. jours. Recipient New Investigator award NIH, 1981-83; NIH scholar, 1989-96. Fellow AAAS; mem. Nat. Multiple Sclerosis Soc. (bd. dirs. Utah chpt. 1992-99—, Hary M. Weaver Neurosci. award 1982-86). Office: U Utah Dept Neurology 30 N 1900 E Salt Lake City UT 84132-0001

FUJIOKA, ROGER SADAO, microbiologist, researcher; b. Pearl City, Hawaii, May 11, 1938; s. Nobuichi and Hisayo (Ihoshi) F.; m. Ruby Nanaye Yamashita, July 2, 1966; 1 child, Ryan Makoto. BS in Med. Tech., U. Hawaii, 1960, MS in Microbiology, 1966; PhD in Virology, U. Mich., 1970. Assoc. research U. Hawaii, Honolulu, 1963-66, rsch. microbiologist, 1972—; predoctoral fellow U. Mich., Ann Arbor, 1966-70; postdoctoral fellow Baylor Coll. Medicine, Houston, 1970-71. Sec.-treas. Hawaii Water Pollution Control, Honolulu, 1986—; mem. com. Standard Methods, Washington, 1986—. Contbr. articles to profl. jours. Served to capt. USAR, 1960-66. Grantee Sea Grant Coll. Program, 1976-84, Office Water United

States Geol. Survey, 1978—, Office Naval Research, 1985—, Dept. Health, 1986—, all in Honolulu. Mem. AAAS, Am. Soc. Microbiology, Water Environment Fedn., Am. Water Works Assn., Soc. for Applied Bacteriology, Internat. Assn. on Water Quality. Avocation: tennis. Office: U Hawaii Water Resources Research Ctr Holmes Hall 283 2540 Dole St Honolulu HI 96822-2303

FUKAI, ROBERT D. energy executive; m. Vicky Fukai; children: Chris, Kelly, Collin, Kathryn. BA in Acctg., BBA, Wash. State U., 1972. Various Avista Corp., Spokane, Wash., 1972-83, exec. asst., mgr. purchasing and materials svcs., 1983-85, asst. v.p. ops., 1985, v.p. ops., 1985-92, v.p. corp. svcs. and human resources, 1992-96, v.p. external rels., 1996—. Bd. dirs. Spokane Sch. Dist. # 81; commr. State Wash. Commn. Nat. and Cmty. Svc.; bd. regents Wash. State U.; chmn. Spokane Physicians & Hosp. Cmty. Orgn., Spokane County Health Improvement Partnership. Office: Avista Corp 1411 E Mission Ave Spokane WA 99202-2600

FUKUNAGA, CAROL A. state legislator, lawyer; b. Dec. 12, 1947; BA, JD, U. Hawaii. Pvt. practice, Honolulu; mem. Hawaii Ho. of Reps., Honolulu, 1978-82, 86-92, Hawaii Senate, Dist. 12, Honolulu, 1992—; co-chair ways and means com., mem. health and human svcs. Hawaii Senate, Honolulu, mem. labor and environment com. Exec. officer Office of the Lt. Gov., Honolulu, 1982-86; hearings officer Hawaii Pub. Employees Rels. Bd.; mem. coord. com. Hawaii Dem. Action, 1985; platform co-chair State Dem. Conv., 1984; bd. dirs. Hawaiian Air; mem. Japanese Am. Citizens League, Sex Abuse Treatment Ctr. Mem. Hawaii Women Lawyers. Democrat. Office: State Capitol 415 S Beretania St Rm 210 Honolulu HI 96813-2407

FULGINITI, VINCENT, university dean; b. Phila., 1931; AB in Psychology, Temple U., 1953, MD, 1957, MS in pediatrics, 1961. Intern Phila. Gen. Hosp., 1957-58; resident in pediatrics Christophers Hosp. for Children, 1958-61, chief resident, 1960-61; NIH fellow pediatric infectious diseases U. Colo. Sch. Medicine, Denver, 1961-62, from asst. prof. to assoc. prof. pediatrics, 1962-69; prof., chmn. dept. pediatrics U. Ariz. Coll. Med., Tucson, 1969-85, vice dean for acad. affairs, 1985-89, acting dean, 1988-89; dean Tulane U. Sch. Medicine, New Orleans, 1989-93; chancellor U. Colo. Health Sci. Ctr., Denver, 1993-98, prof. pediats., 1998—. Editor Am. Jour. Diseases of Children, 1983-93. Chmn. Nat. Vaccine Adv. Com., 1990-94. Mem. AAAS, AMA, Am. Pediatric Soc. (pres. 1990), Am . Assn. Physician., Am. Pub. Health Assn., Soc. Pediatric Rsch. Office: U Colo Health Scis Ctr Childrens Hosp 1056 E 19th Ave Denver CO 80218-1007

FULKERSON, RICHARD, state agency administrator; BA in Bus. Adminstrn., Chadron State Coll., 1974; postgrad., U. Nebr., Omaha, 1981-83, cert. bus. computing, 1986. Nat. accreditation fed. thrift regulator. Mgr. Chicago Lumber Co., Omaha, 1977-82; v.p., contr. Midwest Fed. Savs. and Loan Assn., Nebraska City, Nebr., 1983-86; asst. dir. Fed. Home Loan Bank Topeka, 1986-89, Office Thrift Supervision, Overland Park, Kans., 1989-95; dir. examinations Colo. Divsn. Banking, Denver, 1995-96; Colo. State Bank commr. Dept. Regulatory Agys., Denver, 1996—. Office: Regulatory Agys Dept 1560 Broadway Ste 1175 Denver CO 80202-5152

FULKERSON, WILLIAM MEASEY, JR. college president; b. Moberly, Mo., Oct. 18, 1940; s. William Measey and Edna Frances (Pendleton) F.; m. Grace Carolyn Wisdom, May 26, 1962; children: Carl Franklin, Carolyn Sue. BA, William Jewell Coll., 1962; MA, Temple U., 1964; PhD, Mich. State U., 1969. Asst. to assoc. prof. Calif. State U., Fresno, 1981—; asst. to pres. Calif. State U.-Fresno, 1971-73; assoc. exec. dir. Am. Assn. State Colls., Washington, 1973-77; acad. v.p. Phillips U., Enid, Okla., 1977-81; pres. Adams State Coll., Alamosa, Colo., 1981-94, State Colls. in Colo., 1994—. Interim pres. Met. State Coll., Denver, 1987-88, Western State Coll., 1996. Author: Planning for Financial Exigency, 1973; contbr. articles to profl. jours. Commr. North Ctrl. Assn., Chgo., 1980—; bd. dirs. Acad. Collective Bargaining Info. Svc., Washington, 1976, Office for Advancement Pub. Negro Colls., Atlanta, 1973-77, Colo. Endowment for Humanities, 1988-2000, pres., 1998-99. Named Disting. Alumni William Jewell Coll., 1982, Outstanding Alumnus Mich. State U. Coll. Comm., Arts & Scis., 1987. Mem. Am. Assn. State Colls. and Univs. (parliamentarian, bd. dirs. 1992-94), Am. Coun. on Edn. (bd. dirs.), Assn. Pub. Coll.s and Univs. Pres.s (pres. 1994-95), Nat. Assn. Sys. Heads, Alamosa C. of C. (dir., pres. 1984 Citizen Yr. award), Rotary. Office: State Colls Colo 1580 Lincoln St Ste 750 Denver CO 80203-1505

FULLENWIDER, NANCY VRANA, music composer, dance educator, pianist; b. Sheridan, Wyo., May 9, 1940; d. Jacob Allen and Edith Martha (Tripp) Fullenwider; m. Linsfred Leroy Vrana, Apr. 26, 1980. BA summa cum laude, U. Denver, 1962, MA, 1971, postgrad., 1974. Prin. dancer, instr. Colo. Ballet and Colo. Ballet Ctr., Denver, 1958-80; owner, instr. Idaho Springs (Colo.) Sch. Ballet, 1962-67, Sch. Ballet, Parker, Colo., 1974-79. Curriculum developer Career Edn. Ctr., Denver Pub. Schs., 1973; grad. asst. U. Denver, 1974; guest artist, choreographer, composer Young Audiences, Denver, 1975-80; instr. ballet Ballet Arts Ctr., Denver, 1992-98, Colo. Dance Ctr., Littleton, 1992—; music dir., accompanist for Western Chamber Ballet, Denver, 1994-98, Colo. Ballet, 1999, Arvada Ctr., 1998, Ballet Arts, 1998, Internat. Sch. Ballet, 2000. Composer (CD's) To the Pointe, 1997, Brava!, 1999, Curtain Call, 2000; commissioned ballet works performed at Auditorium Theatre, Denver, 2000, Arvada Ctr. for Performing Arts, Colo., 1991, Aurora (Colo.) Fox Arts Ctr., 1989-92, Buell Theatre, Colo., 1993, Cleo Parker Robinson Dance Theatre, Colo., 1992, Colo. Springs Fine Arts Ctr., 1991, Houston Fine Arts Ctr., Colo., 1971, San Luis Arts Festival, Colo., 1990, Bonfils Theatre, Colo., 1971, Denver Civic Theatre, 2000, Auditorium Theatre, Denver, 2000, (TV series) Providence, 2000. Grantee Douglas County Schs., Colo., 1998. Mem. Phi Beta Kappa, Alpha Lambda Delta. Avocations: hiking, fly fishing, theatre, concerts.

FULLER, ROBERT KENNETH, architect, urban designer; b. Denver, Oct. 6, 1942; s. Kenneth Roller and Gertrude Ailene (Heid) F.; m. Virginia Louise Elkin, Aug. 23, 1969; children: Kimberly Kirsten, Kelsey Christa. BArch, U. Colo., 1967; MArch and Urban Design, Washington U., St. Louis, 1974. Registered profl. architect, Colo. Archtl. designer Fuller & Fuller, Denver, Marvin Hatami Assocs., 1968-69; architect, planner Urban Research and Design Ctr., St. Louis, 1970-72; urban designer Victor Gruen & Assocs., 1973-75; prin. Fuller & Fuller Assocs., Denver, 1975—. Past pres. Denver East Ctrl. Civic Assn., Country Club Hist. Dist.; bd. dirs. Cherry Creek Steering Com., Cherry Creek Found.; pres. Horizon Adventures, Inc.; permanent sec.-treas. Ednl. Fund, Colo. Soc. Archs. Sgt. USMCR, 1964-70. Mem. AIA (past pres. Denver chpt.), Colo. Arlberg Club (past pres.), Rocky Mountain Vintage Racing Assn., Phi Gamma Delta, Delta Phi Delta. Home: 2244 E 4th Ave Denver CO 80206-4107 Office: 3320 E 2nd Ave Denver CO 80206-5302

FULLER, WILLIAM P. foundation administrator; b. Calif. BA, Stanford U., 1960, MA in Polit. Sci., 1964, PhD in Devel. Econs. and Edn., 1970; MBA, Harvard U., 1962. Program officer UNICEF, Cairo, Egypt, 1962-64, planning officer and asst. to dep. dir. N.Y.C., 1964-66, regional planning officer Beirut, Lebanon, 1966-67; cons. economist for Nigeria, Ghana, Morocco World Bank/UNESCO Program, Paris, 1970-71; planning and rsch. advisor funded by Ford Found. Nat. Edn. Commn., Bangkok, Thailand, 1971-76; vis. lectr. U. Chgo., 1976; rep. Ford Found., Dhaka, Bangladesh, 1977-81; mission dir. Sr. Fgn. Svc. USAID, Indonesia, 1981-87, dep. asst. adminstr. bur. for Asia and Near East, 1987-89; pres. The Asia Found., San Francisco, 1989—. Bd. dirs. Overseas Devel. Coun., Washington, Inst. for the Future, Stanford, Calif.; vice chmn. World Affairs Coun. No. Calif., San Francisco. Recipient Pres.'s Meritorious Svc. award, 1985, '87. Fellow Asia Pacific Ctr., Stanford U.; mem. Nat. Com. U.S.-China Rels. Office: The Asia Found 465 California St Fl 14 San Francisco CA 94104-1804

FULLMER, DANIEL WARREN, former psychologist, educator; b. Spoon River, Ill., Dec. 12, 1922; s. Daniel Floyd and Sarah Louisa (Essex) F.; m. Janet Satomi Saito, June 1980; children: Daniel William, Mark Warren. B.S., Western Ill. U., 1947, M.S., 1952; Ph.D., U. Denver, 1955. Post-doctoral intern psychiat. div. U. Oreg. Med. Sch., 1958-61; mem. faculty U. Oreg., 1955-66; prof. psychology Oreg. System of Higher Edn., 1958-66; faculty Coll. Edn. U. Hawaii, Honolulu, 1966-95, retired, 1995, prof. emeritus, 1974—; pvt. practice psychol. counseling. Cons. psychologist Grambling State U., 1960-81; founder Free-Family Counseling Ctrs., Portland, Oreg., 1959-66, Honolulu, 1966-74; co-founder Child and Family Counseling Ctr., Waianae, Oahu, Hawaii, Kilohana United Meth. Ch., Oahu, 1992, v.p., sec., 1992; pres. Human Resources Devel. Ctr., Inc., 1974—; chmn. Hawaii State Bd. to License Psychologists, 1973-78. Author: Counseling: Group Theory & System, 2d. edit., 1978, The Family Therapy Dictionary Text, 1991, MANABU, Diagnosis and Treatment of a Japanese Boy with a Visual Anomaly, 1991; co-author: Principles of Guidance, 2d. edit., 1977; author (counselor/cons. training manuals) Counseling: Content and Process, 1964, Family Consultation Therapy, 1968, The School Counselor-Consultant, 1972, Family Therapy as the Rites of Passage, 1998; editor: Bulletin, Oreg. Coop Testing Service, 1955-57, Hawaii P&G Jour., 1970-76; assoc. editor: Educational Perspectives, U. Hawaii Coll. Edn. Served with USNR, 1944-46. Recipient Francis E. Clark award Hawaii Pers. Guidance Assn., 1972, Thomas Jefferson award for Outstanding Pub. Svc., 1993; named Hall of Fame Grambling State U., 1987. Mem. Am. Psychol. Assn., Am. Counseling Assn. (Nancy C. Wimmer award 1963), Masons. Methodist. Office: 1750 Kalakaua Ave Apt 809 Honolulu HI 96826-3725

FULLMER, STEVEN MARK, systems engineer; b. San Francisco, Mar. 15, 1956; s. Thomas Patrick and Patricia Ann (Carroll-Boyd) F.; m. Rhonda Lynnette Bush, Nov. 8, 1992; children: Wesley Stevenson, Sierra Marin. BA in Chemistry, BA in Biology, Willamette U., 1978; MBA, Ariz. State U., 1993. Sr. engr., project leader Honeywell Large Computer Products, Phoenix, 1981-86; bank officer, cons., infosecurity cons. First Interstate Bank/Wells Fargo Bank, Phoenix, 1987-96; project mgr. Wells Fargo Bank, 1996; systems engr. AG Comm. Systems, 1996—. Cons. J.A. Boyd & Assoc., San Francisco, 1985-96, ImaginInc. Consulting, Phoenix, 1985—. Contbr. articles to profl. jours. Mem. exec. bd. Grand Canyon coun. Boy Scouts Am., scoutmaster, 1983-88, commr., 1988-92, dist. chmn., 1995-96; founder, lt. comdr. Maricopa County Sheriff's Adj. Posse, 1982-93; pres. Heard Mus. Coun., 1995-96; dept. head, lead Liberty Wildlife. Recipient Order of Merit Boy Scouts Am., 1988, Nat. Disting. Commr. award Boy Scouts Am., 1990, Nat. Founder's award Boy Scouts Am., 1991, Silver Beaver award Boy Scouts Am., 1994. Mem. Am. Inst. for Cert. Computer Profls. (cert. data processor 1985), Mensa, KC (membership dir. 1988), SAR, Knights Cross (Sovereign Order of St. Stanislas), Phi Lambda Upsilon, Phi Eta Sigma, Kappa Sigma, Alpha Chi Sigma, Sigma Iota Epsilon, Beta Gamma Sigma. Republican. Roman Catholic. Avocations: Am. Indian history, science fiction, scuba diving, hiking, camping. Office: AG Comm Systems 2500 W Utopia Rd Phoenix AZ 85027-4129 E-mail: fullmers@agcs.com

FUNG, YUAN-CHENG BERTRAM, bioengineering educator, writer; b. Yuhong, Changchow, Kiangsu, China, Sept. 15, 1919; came to U.S., 1945, naturalized, 1957; s. Chung Kwang and Lien (Hu) F.; m. Luna Hsien-Shih Yu, Dec. 22, 1949; children: Conrad Antung, Brenda Pingsi. BS, Nat. Central U., Chungking, China, 1941, MS, 1943; PhD, Calif. Inst. Tech., 1948. Research fellow Bur. Aero. Research China, 1943-45; research asst., then research fellow Calif. Inst. Tech., 1946-51, mem. faculty, 1951-66, prof. aeros., 1959-66; prof. bioengrng. and applied mechanics U. Calif., San Diego, 1966—. Cons. aerospace indsl. firms, 1949—; prof. (hon.) 15 univs. China. Author: The Theory of Aeroelasticity, 1955, 69, 93, Foundations of Solid Mechanics, 1965, A First Course in Continuum Mechanics, 1969, 77, 93, Biomechanics, 1972, Biomechanics: Mechanical Properties of Living Tissues, 1980, 1993, Biodynamics: Circulation, 1984, Biomechanics: Circulation, 1996, Biomechanics: Motion, Flow, Stress and Growth, 1990, Selected Works on Biomechanics and Aeroelasticity by Y.C. Fung, 1997, Classical and Computational Solid Mechanics, 2001, Introduction to Bioengineering, 2001; also papers; editor Jour. Biorheology, Jour. Biomech. Engrng. Bd. trustees (hon.) Chongqing U.; chair (hon.), bd. trustees Nanjing U., China. Recipient Achievement award Chinese Inst. Engrs., 1965, 68, 93, Landis award Microcirculatory Soc., 1975, Poiseuille medal Internat. Soc. Biorheology, 1986, Engr. of Yr. award San Diego Engrng. Soc., 1986, von Karman medal ASCE, 1976, ALZA award Biomed. Engrng. Soc., 1989, Borelli award Am. Soc. Biomechanics; Guggenheim fellow, 1958-59, Melville medal Am. Soc. of Mechanical Engineers, 1994. Fellow AIAA, ASME (hon., Lissner award 1978, Centennial medal 1978, Worcester Reed Warner medal 1984, Timoshenko medal 1991, Melville medal 1994); mem. NAS, NAE, Inst. Medicine, Soc. Engrng. Sci., Microcirculatory Soc., Am. Physiol. Soc., Nat. Heart Assn., Acad. Sinica, Chinese Acad. Scis. (fgn. mem.), Basic Sci. Coun., Sigma Xi. Home: 2660 Greentree Ln La Jolla CA 92037-1148 Office: U Calif Dept Bioengrng 9500 Gilman Dr La Jolla CA 92093-0412

FUNK, WILLIAM HENRY, retired environmental engineering educator; b. Ephraim, Utah, June 10, 1933; s. William George and Henrietta (Hackwell) F.; m. Ruth Sherry Mellor, Sept. 19, 1964 (dec.); 1 dau., Cynthia Lynn; m. Lynn Bridget Robson, Mar. 30, 1996. B.S. in Biol. Sci, U. Utah, 1955, M.S. in Zoology, 1963, Ph.D. in Limnology, 1966. Tchr. sci., math. Salt Lake City Schs., 1957-60; research asst. U. Utah, Salt Lake City, 1961-63; head sci. dept. N.W. Jr. High Sch., Salt Lake City, 1961-63; mem. faculty Wash. State U., Pullman, 1966-99, assoc. prof. environ. engrng., 1971-75, prof., 1975-99, chmn. environ. sci./regional planning program, 1979-81; dir. Environ. Research Center, 1980-83, State of Wash. Water Research Ctr., 1981-99; ret., 1999. Cons. U.S. Army C.E., Walla Walla, Wash., 1970-74, Harstad Engrs., Seattle, 1971-72, Boise Cascde Corp., Seattle, 1971-72, Wash. Dept. Ecology, Olympia, 1971-72, ORB Corp., Renton, Wash., 1972-73, U.S. Civil Svc., Seattle, Chgo., 1972-74; mem. High Level Nuclear Waste Bd., Wash., 1986-89; mem. Wash. 2010 Com., 1989; mem. Pure Water 2000 Steering Com., 1990, Inst. Resource Mgmt.; co-founder Terrene Inst., Washington, 1991, pres., 1993—. Author publs. on water pollution control and lake restoration. Served to capt. USNR, 1955-88. Grantee NSF Summer Inst., 1961, U.S. Army C.E., 1970-74, 94-96, 97-98, Office Water Resources Rsch., 1971-72, 73-76, EPA, 1980-83, 93-94, 95-96, U.S. Geol. Survey, 1983-94, 95-96, 97-98, 99-00, Nat. Parks Svc., 1985-87, Colville Confederated Tribes, 1990-92, Nez Pierce Tribe, 1992-95, Wash. Conservation Commn., 1992-95, Clearwater Co., 1992-93, Idaho Dept. Environ. Quality, 1995-96, U.S. Bur. Reclamation, 1995-98; USPHS fellow, 1963; recipient Pres.'s Disting. Faculty award Wash. State U., 1984. Mem. Naval Res. Officers Assn. (chpt. pres. 1969), Res Officers Assn. (U.S. Naval Acad. info. officer 1973-76), N.Am. Lake Mgmt. Soc. (pres. 1984-85, Secchi Disk award 1988), Pacific N.W. Pollution Control Assn. (editor 1969-77, pres.-elect 1982-83, pres. 1983-84), Water Pollution Control Fedn. (Arthur S. Bedell award Pacific N.W. assn. 1976, nat. bd. dirs. 1978-81, bd. dirs. Rsch. Found. 1990-92), Nat. Assn. Water Inst. Dirs. (chair 1985-87, bd. dirs. univ. council on water resources 1986-89), Wash. Lakes Protection Assn. (co-founder 1986, Friend of Lakes award 1999), Am. Water Resources Assn. (v.p. Wash. sect. 1988), Am. Soc. Limnology and Oceanography, Am. Micros. Soc., N.W. Sci. Assn., North Am. Lake Mgmt. Soc. (co-founder 1972), Sigma Xi, Phi Sigma. Home: 330 SW Kimball Ct Pullman WA 99163-2176

FUNKHOUSER, LAWRENCE WILLIAM, retired geologist; b. Napoleon, Ohio, June 9, 1921; s. Edward A. and Margaret M. (Reinking) F.; m. Jean Garnet Cooper, June 1, 1946; children: Donald W., Thomas E., David P., Karen J. AB in Geology, Oberlin Coll, 1943; MS in Geology, Stanford U., 1948; DSc (hon.), Oberlin Coll., 1990. Geologist, dist. geologist The Calif. Co., New Orleans, 1948-58, div. exploration supt., 1958-61; div. exploration supt., v.p. exploration Standard Oil Co. Tex., Midland and Houston, 1961-66; v.p. exploration Standard Oil Co. Calif., San Francisco, 1968-73, dir., v.p. exploration, 1973-77; dir., v.p. exploration and prodn. Chevron Corp., San Francisco, 1978-86, ret., 1986; v.p., dir. Energy Exploration Mgmt. Co., Houston, 1989-92. Mem. Nat. Research Council Commn. on Physical Sci., Math. and Resources, 1987-90. Mem. Am. Assn. Petroleum Geologists (hon., pres.-elect 1986-87, pres. 1987-88), Am. Assn. Petroleum Geologists Found. (chmn. 1991-2001), Geol. Soc. Am., Phi Beta Kappa, Sigma Xi. Presbyterian Home: 283 Park Ln Atherton CA 94027-5448 Office: PO Box 1088 Menlo Park CA 94026-1088 E-mail: lwfsexpl@aol.com

FURBUSH, DAVID MALCOLM, lawyer; b. Palo Alto, Calif., Mar. 25, 1954; s. Malcolm Harvey and Margaret (McKittrick) F. BA, Harvard U., 1975, JD, 1978. Bar: Calif. 1978, U.S. Dist. Ct. (no. dist.) Calif. 1978, U.S. Ct. Appeals (9th cir.) 1987, U.S. Supreme Ct. 1990. Assoc. Chickering & Gregory, San Francisco, 1978-81, Brobeck, Phleger & Harrison, San Francisco, 1981-85, ptnr. Palo Alto, Calif., 1985—. Office: Brobeck Phleger & Harrison Two Embarcadero Pl 2200 Geng Rd Palo Alto CA 94303-3322

FURIMSKY, STEPHEN, JR. freelance writer; b. Coalton, Ill., Aug. 4, 1924; s. Stephen Sr. and Anna (Petricko) F.; m. Dorothy Conrad, June 8, 1946 (dec. Nov. 1989); children: Stephen III, Karen Ann Segal, Daniel Michael, Melany; m. Janet Fay Green, Dec. 16, 1991; step-children: Bruce Emerson, Peni Emerson, Kara Welliver, Beth Emerson Levine. AB, U. Chgo., 1951; MS in Internat. Affairs, George Washington U., 1967; grad., Air War Coll., 1967. Instr. in polit. sci. Craven C.C., New Bern, N.C., 1975-80; owner San Diego Sod, San Marcos, Calif., 1981-84; spl. advocate juvenile ct. Voices for Children, San Diego, 1985-91; sports editor, health and fitness editor Enterprise Newspaper, Fallbrook, Calif., 1989-91. Candidate state senate, N.C., 1978. Col. USMC, 1942-73. Decorated Legion of Merit, D.F.C., Bronze Star, Air medal, Cross of Gallantry (Vietman). Mem. VFW (life), Am. Legion, The Order of Daedalians, Mil. Order of World Wars. Republican. Eastern Orthodox. Avocation: shark tooth fossil collecting. Home: 58 Desert Rain Ln Henderson NV 89074-2915

FURLOW, MARY BEVERLEY, English language educator; b. Shreveport, La., Oct. 14, 1933; d. Prentiss Edward and Mary Thelma (Hasty) F.; divorced, 1973; children: Mary Findley, William Prentiss, Samuel Christopher; m. William Peter Cleary, Aug. 1, 1989. BA, U. Tenn., 1955, MEd, 1972; MA, Governors State U., 1975; cert. advanced study, U. Chgo., 1987. Mem. faculty Chattanooga State C.C., 1969-73, Moraine Valley C.C., Palos Hills, Ill., 1974-78; mem. English faculty Pima C.C., Tucson, 1978—. Cons. in field. Contbr. author: Thinking on the Edge, 1993. Named one of Outstanding Educators of Am., 1973. Fellow Internat. Soc. Philos. Enquiry; mem. DAR, Internat. Soc. Appraisers, Internat. Soc. Philos. Enquiry, Ariz. Antiquarian Guild, Cincinatus Soc., Jr. League, Mensa, Holmes Socs., Clan Chattan Soc., Daus. of Confederacy, Alpha Phi Omega (Tchr. of Yr. 1973), Pi Beta Phi. Democrat. Episcopalian. Home: 1555 N Arcadia Ave Tucson AZ 85712-4010 Office: Pima CC 8202 E Poinciana Dr Tucson AZ 85730-4645 E-mail: beverleyF@aol.com

FURR, RANDY W. electronics manufacturing executive; CPA. With Gen. Signal Corp.; v.p., gen. mgr. Gen. Signal Thinfilm Co.; v.p., CFO Aquarius Systems Inc. N.Am., 1992, Sanmina, San Jose, Calif., 1992-96, pres., COO, 1996—. Office: Sanmina Corp 2700 North 1st St San Jose CA 95134

FURST, ARTHUR, toxicologist, educator; b. Mpls., Dec. 25, 1914; s. Samuel and Doris (Kolochinsky) F.; m. Florence Wolovitch, May 24, 1940; children: Carolyn, Adrianne, David Michael, Timothy Daniel. AA, L.A. City Coll., 1935; AB, UCLA, 1937, AM, 1940; PhD, Stanford U., 1948; ScD, U. San Francisco, 1983. Mem. faculty, dept. chemistry San Francisco City Coll., 1940-47; asst. prof. chemistry U. San Francisco, 1947-49, assoc. prof. chemistry, 1949-52; assoc. prof. medicinal chemistry Stanford Sch. Medicine, 1952-57, prof., 1957-61; with U. Calif. War Tng., 1943-45, San Francisco State Coll., 1945; rsch. assoc. Mt. Zion Hosp., 1952 82; clin. prof. pathology Columbia Coll. Physicians and Surgeons, 1969-70; dir. Inst. Chem. Biology; prof. chemistry U. San Francisco, 1961-80, prof. emeritus, 1980—, dean grad. div., 1976-79. Vis. fellow Battelle Seattle Research Center, 1974; Michael vis. prof. Weizmann Inst. Sci., Israel, 1982; cons. toxicology, 1980—; cons. on cancer WHO; mem. com., bd. mineral resources NRC; emeritus mem. scientific advisory bd. Golden Neo Life Diamite Internat., Fremont, Calif. Author: Toxicologist as Expert Witness, 1997; contbr. over 300 articles to profl. and ednl. jours. Recipient Klaus Schwartz Commemorative medal Internat. Toxicological Congress, Tokyo, 1986, Profl. Achievement award UCLA Alumni Assn., 1992, Henry Hall Clay award U. San Francisco, 1977; ann. lectureship named in his honor Stanford U. Health Libr. Fellow Acad. Toxicological Scis. (diplomate), AAAS, Am. Coll. Nutrition, Am. Coll. Toxicology (nat. sec., pres. 1985), N.Y. Acad. Scis., Am. Inst. Chemists; mem. Am. Soc. Pharmacology and Exptl. Therapeutics, Am. Chem. Soc., Am. Assn. Cancer Research, Soc. Toxicology, Sigma Xi, Phi Lambda Upsilon. Achievements include research activities on organic synthesis, chemotherapy cancer, carcinogenesis of metals and hydrocarbons. Home: 23500 Cristo Rey Dr Unit 211D Cupertino CA 95014-6524 Office: U San Francisco Inst Chem Biology San Francisco CA 94117-1080 Fax: 650-967-4488. E-mail: artfurst@aol.com

FURTAN, WILLIAM HARTLEY, director scientific organization; b. Peebles Saskatchewan, Canada; BSA in Agrl. Econs. with honors, U. Saskatchewan, Canada, 1971; MSc in Agrl. Econs., U. Saskatchewan, 1973; PhD in Agrl. Econs., Purdue U., 1975. From asst. to prof. in Dept. Agrl. Econs. U. Saskatchewan, Saskatoon, Canada, 1976—, dept. head Dept. Agrl. Econs., 1981-89. Dir., pres. Canadian Agrl. Econs. Soc.; dir. Saskatchewan Water Corp., Prairie Malt Corp., Saskatchewan Natural Product Mktg. Coun.; Dep. Minister Agrl. and Food, Saskatchewan province, 1993-95; dir. Ctr. for Studies in Agrl., Law and the Environ.; visiting scholar U. Chgo., 1983. Author (with K.K. Klein): The Economics of Agricultural Research in Canada, 1986; contbr. chpts. to books, articles to profl. jours.; presenter in field. Office: U Saskatchewan Coll Agrl Agrl Bldg Rm 3E70 Coll Dr Saskatoon SK Canada

FURTH, FREDERICK PAUL, lawyer; b. West Harvey, Ill., Apr. 12, 1934; s. Fred P. and Mamie (Stelmach) F.; children: Darby, Ben Anthony, Megan Louise; m. Peggy Wollerman, July 19, 1986. Student, Drake U., 1952-53; BA, U. Mich., 1956, JD, 1959; postgrad., U. Berlin, 1959, U. Munich, Fed. Republic Germany, 1960. Bar: Mich. 1959, N.Y. 1961, D.C. 1965, U.S. Supreme Ct. 1965, Calif. 1966. Assoc. Cahill, Gordon, Reindel & Ohl, N.Y.C., 1960-64; with Kellogg Co., Battle Creek, Mich., 1964-65; assoc. Joseph L. Alioto, San Francisco, 1965-66; sr. ptnr. The Furth Firm, San Francisco, 1966—. Bd. dirs. Robert Half Internat.; chmn., propr. Chalk Hill Winery. Trustee, chmn. bd. Furth Family Found., San Francisco; bd.

dirs. Franklin and Eleanor Roosevelt Inst., 1996—, The Ctr. for Democracy, Washington; chmn. Internat. Jud. Conf., Strasbourg, France. Mem. ABA, Internat. Bar Assn., N.Y. Bar Assn., San Francisco Bar Assn., State Bar Calif., Assn. of Bar of City of N.Y., St. Francis Yacht Club, Olympic Club. Office: The Furth Firm 201 Sansome St San Francisco CA 94104-2303 E-mail: fpfurth@aol.com

GABBE, STEVEN GLENN, obstetrician/gynecologist, educator; b. Newark, Dec. 1, 1944; s. Charles Paul and Marcia May Gabbe; m. Jessica Gabbe, June 26, 1966 (div. 1980); children: Amanda, Daniel; m. Patricia Temple, July 26, 1981. BA, Princeton U., 1965; MD, Cornell U., 1969; MA (hon.), U. Pa., 1983. Diplomate Am. Bd. Ob-Gyn (examiner 1980—), Am. Bd. Maternal-Fetal Medicine (examiner 1979-89). Intern in medicine N.Y. Hosp., N.Y.C., 1969-70; rsch. fellow reproductive medicine Boston Hosp. for Women, 1970-71, resident in ob-gyn, 1972-74; rsch. fellow in biol. chemistry Harvard Med. Sch., Boston, 1970-71, clin. fellow ob-gyn., 1972-74; asst. prof. ob-gyn U. So. Calif., L.A., 1975-77; assoc. prof. U. Colo. Sch. Medicine, Denver, 1977-78; assoc. prof. ob-gyn. and pediatrics U. Pa. Sch. Medicine, Phila., 1978-87, prof. radiology, 1987; mem. staff Hosp. of U. Pa., Phila., 1978-87, dir. Jerrold R. Golding divsn. fetal medicine, 1978-87, mem. med. bd. and numerous coms., 1984-87; prof. U. Pa. Sch. Nursing, Phila., 1982-87; prof., chmn. dept. ob-gyn Ohio State U. Coll. Medicine, Columbus, 1987-96; prof., chmn. dept. ob/gyn. U. Wash. Sch. Medicine, Seattle, 1996—; dir. Jerrold R. Golding divsn. fetal medicine Hosp. of U. Pa., Phila., 1978-87, mem. med. bd. and numerous coms., 1984-87. Vis. prof. ob-gyn King's Coll. Hosp., London, 1985-86; dir. maternal and infant care program Phila. Dept. Health, Disease Prevention and Health Promotion, 1982-87; mem. maternal and infant care adv. coun. Dept. Pub. Health, Phila., 1983-87; mem. subcom. on pregnancy and weight gain NRC, NAS, 1981; mem. internat. sci. bd. Reproductive Toxicology Ctr., 1984—; bd. dirs., med. adv. bd. Diabetes Treatment Ctrs. Am., 1984, others; mem. Coun. Univ Chairs of Ob-Gyn., 1996—. Author: Clinical Obstetrics and Gynecology: Diabetes and Pregnancy, 1985, Clinical Obstetrics and Gynecology: Obstetric Ultrasound Update, 1988; (with J.R. Niebyl and J.L. Simpson) Obstetrics: Normal and Problem Pregnancies, 1986, 2d edit., 1991; contbr. numerous articles to profl. jours. and chpts. to books; editor i chief Am. Jour. Perinatology, 1983—; mem. numerous editorial bds. Mem. Pa. Diabetes Task Force, 1981-87, Ohio Diabetes Task Force, 1987—; bd. dirs. UNITE, Jeanes Hosp., 1980-87. Recipient Sr. Resident's award for Excellence in Tng., L.A. County Women's Hosp., 1976, Disting. Tchr. award from Graduating Class, U. Wash., 1999; grantee Juvenile Diabetes Found., 1981, HHS, 1984, 1985, Diabetes Treatment Ctrs. Am., 1986. Fellow Am. Coll. Obstetricians and Gynecologists (mem. PROLOG self assessment program task force 1981-82, chmn. 1986, mem. PROLOG subcom. 1986—); mem. Am. Gynecol. and Obstet. Soc., Am. Inst. Ultrasound in Medicine, Perinatal Rsch. Soc., Soc. Gynecologic Investigation, Soc. Perinatal Obstetricians (v.p. 1986, pres. 1987-88, bd. dirs. 1983-88, chmn. credentials, constn. and by-laws com. 1983-87), Am. Diabetes Assn. (mem. nat. rsch. bd. 1981-83, chmn. coun. on diabetes in pregnancy 1985, com. on food and nutrition 1976-80), Juvenile Diabetes Found. (mem. med. sci. rev. com., med. sci. adv. bd. 1981-83), Phila. Neonatal Soc., Obstet. Soc. Phila. (program chmn. 1986-87), Phila. Perinatal Soc. (pres. 1982-84), Columbus Ob-Gyn Soc., Pa. Diabetes Acad. (acad. steering com. 1986—, editorial rev. com. 1986—), Union League (Phila.), Phi Beta Kappa, Alpha Omega Alpha. Avocations: sports, running. Office: U Wash Dept Ob-Gyn Box 356460 Seattle WA 98195-6460

GABEL, KATHERINE, academic administrator; b. Rochester, N.Y., Apr. 9, 1938; d. M. Wren and Esther (Conger) G.; m. Seth Devore Strickland, June 24, 1961 (div. 1965). AB, Smith Coll., Northampton, Mass., 1959; MSW, Simmons Coll., 1961; PhD, Syracuse U., 1967; JD, Union U., 1970; bus. program, Stanford U., 1984. Psychol. social worker Cen. Island Mental Health Ctr., Uniondale, N.Y., 1961-62; psychol. social worker, supt. Ga. State Tng. Sch. for Girls, Atlanta, 1962-64; cons. N.Y. State Crime Control Coun., Albany, 1968-70; faculty Ariz. State U., Tempe, 1972-76; supt. Ariz. Dept. of Corrections, Phoenix, 1970-76; dean, prof. Smith Coll., 1976-85; pres. Pacific Oaks Coll. and Children's Sch., Pasadena, Calif., 1985-98; we. regional leader Casey Family Program, Pasadena, 1998—. Advisor, del. UN, Geneva, 1977; mem. So. Calif. Youth Authority, 1986-91. Editor: Master Teacher and Supervisor in Clinical Social Work, 1982; author report Legal Issues of Female Inmates, 1981, model for rsch. Diversion program Female Inmates, 1984, Children of Incarcerated Parents, 1995. Vice chair United Way, Northampton, 1982-83; chair Mayor's Task Force, Northampton, 1981. Mem. Nat. Assn. Social Work, Acad. Cert. Social Workers, Nat. Assn. Edn. Young Children, Western Assn. Schs. and Colls., Pasadena C. of C., Athenaeum, Pasadena Rotary Club. Democrat. Presbyterian. Avocations: collecting, S.W. Indian art, aviary. E-mail: kgabel@casuj.org

GABLER, LEE, talent agency executive; Co-chmn. Creative Artists Agy. Office: Creative Artists Agy 9830 Wilshire Blvd Beverly Hills CA 90212-1825

GABOW, PATRICIA ANNE, internist; b. Starke, Fla., Jan. 8, 1944; m. Harold N. Gabow, June 21, 1971; children: Tenaya Louise, Aaron Patrick. BA in Biology, Seton Hill Coll., 1965; MD, U. Pa. Sch. Medicine, 1969. Diplomate Am. Bd. Internal Medicine, Am. Bd. Nephrology, Nat. Bd. Med. Examiners; lic. Colo. Internship in medicine Hosp. of U. of Pa., 1969-70; residency in internal medicine Harbor Gen. Hosp., 1970-71; renal fellowship San Francisco Gen. Hosp. and Hosp. of U. Pa., 1971-72, 72-73; instr. medicine divsn. renal diseases, asst. prof. U. Colo. Health Scis. Ctr., 1973-74, 74-79, assoc. prof. medicine divsn. renal diseases, prof., 1979-87; chief renal disease, clin. dir. dept. medicine Denver Gen. Hosp., 1973-81, 76-81, dir. med. svcs., 1981-91; CEO, med. dir. Denver Health and Hosps., 1992—. Intensive care com. Denver Gen. Hosp., 1976-81, med. records com., 1979-80, ind. rev. com., 1978-81, continuing med. edn. com., 1981-83, animal care com., 1979-83; student adv. com. U. Colo. Health Scis. Ctr., 1982-87, faculty senate, 1985, 86, internship adv. com., 1977-92; exec. com. Denver Gen. Hosp., 1981—, chmn. health resources com., 1988-90, chmn. pathology search com., 1989, chmn. faculty practice plan steering com., 1990-92. Mem. editorial bd. EMERGINDEX, 1983-93, Am. Jour. of Kidney Disease, 1984-96, Western Jour. of Medicine, 1987-98, Annals of Internal Medicine, 1988-91, Jour. of the Am. Soc. of Nephrology, 1990-97; contbr. numerous articles, revs. and editorials to profl. publs., chpts. to books. Mem. Mayor's Safe City Task Force, 1993; mem. sci. adv. bd. Polycystic Kidney Rsch. Found., 1984-96, chmn., 1991; mem. sci. adv. bd. Nat. Kidney Found., 1991-94; mem. Nat. Pub. Health and Hosps. Inst. Bd., 1993-2001. Recipient Sullivan award for Highest Acad. Average in Graduating Class, Seton Hill Coll., 1965, Pa. State Senatorial scholarship, 1961-65, Kaiser Permanente award for Excellence in Teaching, 1976, Ann. award to Outstanding Woman Physician, 1982, Kaiser Permanente Nominee for Excellence in Teaching award, 1983, Seton Hill Coll. Disting. Alumna Leadership award, 1990, Florence Rena Sabin award U. Colo., 2000, Nathan Davis award AMA, 2000, named one of The Best Doctors in Am., 1994-95; grantee Bonfils Found., 1985-86, NIH, 1985-90, 91-96, 96-2000. Mem. Denver Med. Soc., Colo. Med. Soc., Am. Soc. Nephrology, Internat. Soc. Nephrology, Am. Coll. Physicians, Am. Fedn. Clin. Rsch., Am. Physiol. Soc., Polycystic Kidney Disease Rsch. Found. (sci. advisor 1984-96), Western Assn. Physicians, Nat. Kidney Found. (sci. adv. bd. 1987-91), Women's Forum of Colo. Inc., Assn. Am. Physicians. Roman Catholic. Office: Denver Health 660 Bannock St Denver CO 80204-4506

GABRIEL, DONALD EUGENE, science educator; b. Brush, Colo., May 24, 1944; s. Max and Vera Ellen (Coleman) G.; m. Evonne Kay Asheim, Sept. 27, 1964; children: Shawn Lee, Dawn Kay. AA, Northeastern Jr. Coll., Sterling, Colo., 1964; BA, Colo. State Coll., 1967; MA, U. No. Colo., 1972. Cert. secondary chemistry tchr. Tchr. sci. and math. Brush (Colo.) H.S., 1967—. Adv. bd. mem. Colo. Sci. and Engring. Fair, Fort Collins, 1980—; ea. zone chairperson Colo.-Wyo. Jr. Acad. Sci., Fort Morgan, Colo., 1980—; co-dir. Morgan-Washington BiCounty Sci. Fair, Fort Morgan, 1975—. Contbr. articles to profl. jours. Pres. South Platte Valley BOCES, Fort Morgan, 1993-99, v.p., 1991-93; Eagle Scout reviewer Boy Scouts Am., Fort Morgan, 1990—; sec., treas. Brush Pub. Schs., 1995-99. Grantee Tandy Corp., 1989, Joslin Needhams Found., 1990; recipient Presdl. award NSF, 1994; named Milken Nat. Educator, Milken Found., 1991, Tandy Tech. Scholars Outstanding Tchr., 1994-95, Pub. Svc. Co. of Colo. Classroom Connection awards, 1993-99, S. Platte Valley Bd. of Coop. Ednl. Svcs. grants, 1995-98. Mem. Nat. Sci. Tchrs. Assn. (Presdl. award 1994), Colo. Assn. Sci. Tchrs. (regional dir. 1993-96, Outstanding Tchr. 1990). Republican. Lutheran. Avocations: arrowhead hunting, rock hounding. Home: 26137 MCR S 2 Brush CO 80723 Office: Brush HS PO Box 585 Brush CO 80723-0585

GADDES, RICHARD, performing arts administrator; b. Wallsend, Northumberland, Eng., May 23, 1942; s. Thomas and Emilie Jane (Rickard) G. L.T.C.L. in piano, L.T.C.L. for sch. music; G.T.C.L., Trinity Coll. Music, London, 1964; D. Mus. Arts (hon.), St. Louis Conservatory, 1983; D.F.A. (hon.), U. Mo.-St. Louis, 1984; D.Arts (hon.), Webster U., 1986. Founder, mgr. Wigmore Hall Lunchtime Concerts, 1965; dir. Christopher Hunt and Richard Gaddes Artists Mgmt., London, 1965-66; bookings mgr. Artists Internat. Mgmt., London, 1967-69; artistic adminstr. Santa Fe Opera, 1969-78, assoc. gen. dir., 1995—; gen. dir. Opera Theatre of St. Louis, 1975-85, bd. dirs., 1985—. Bd. dirs. Grand Ctr., Inc., 1988—, pres., 1988-95; bd. dirs. William Matheus Sullivan Found. Mem. bd. advisors Royal Oak Found. Recipient Lamplighter award, 1982, Mo. Arts award, 1983, St. Louis award, 1983, Human Relations award Jewish-Am. Com., St. Louis, 1985, Nat. Inst. for Music Theatre award, 1986, Cultural Achievement award Young Audiences, 1987. Office: Santa Fe Opera PO Box 2408 Santa Fe NM 87504-2408

GAETANO, JOY M. human resources executive; V.p. human resources U.S. Filter Corp., Palm Desert, Calif., 1996—. Office: US Filter Corp 40-004 Cook St Palm Desert CA 92211

GAFFNEY, DONALD LEE, lawyer; b. Phoenix, July 7, 1952; s. Leroy H. and Myriam (Brazeal) G.; m. Debby Dunn, May 31, 1974; children: Brian, Colin, Caitlin. BA, Austin Coll., 1974; JD, U. Tex., 1977. Bar: Ariz. 1979, U.S. Ct. Appeals (9th cir.) 1979, U.S. Ct. Appeals (10th cir.) 1984, U.S. Supreme Ct. 1984. Ptnr. Streich & Lang, Phoenix, 1977-89, Snell & Wilmer, Phoenix, 1988—. Adj. prof. Ariz. State U. Law Sch., Tempe, 1983-84. Co-author: Bankruptcy, 1987; note comment and book review editor: Tex. Law Review 1976-77; contbr. to profl. jours. Mem. Gov.'s Task Force Ctrl. Ariz. Project, 1993. Austin scholar. Mem. ABA, Am. Arbitration Assn. (com. panel), Comml. Law League of Am. (bankruptcy com. 1980-84), State Bar Ariz. (chmn. bankruptcy sect., 1982-84, com. on bankruptcy rules 1979-81, uniform comml. code com. 1980—) , Phi Delta Phi. Democrat. Roman Catholic. Office: Snell & Wilmer 1 Arizona Ctr Phoenix AZ 85004-0001

GAGE, B. TIMOTHY, state finance department administrator; Dir. Calif. Fin. Dept., Sacramento. Office: Calif Fin Dept State Capitol Rm 1145 Sacramento CA 95814

GAILLARD, MARY KATHARINE, physics educator; b. New Brunswick, N.J., Apr. 1, 1939; d. Philip Lee and Marion Catharine (Wiedemayer) Ralph; children: Alain, Dominique, Bruno. BA, Hollins (Va.) Coll., 1960; MA, Columbia U., 1961; Dr du Troiseme Cycle, U. Paris, Orsay, France, 1964, Dr-es-Sciences d'Etat, 1968. With Ctr. Nat. Rsch. Sci., Orsay and Annecy-le-Vieux, France, 1964-84, head rsch. Orsay, 1973-80, Annecy-le-Vieux, 1979-80, dir. rsch., 1980-84; prof. physics, sr. faculty staff Lawrence Berkeley lab. U. Calif., Berkeley, 1981—. Morris Loeb lectr. Harvard U., Cambridge, Mass., 1980; Chancellor's Disting. lectr., U. Calif., Berkeley, 1981; Warner-Lambert lectr. U. Mich., Ann Arbor, 1984; vis. scientist Fermi Nat. Accelerator Lab., Batavia, Ill., 1973-74, Inst. for Advanced Studies, Santa Barbara, Calif., 1984, U. Calif., Santa Barbara, 1985; group leader L.A.P.P., Theory Group, France, 1979-81, Theory Physics div. LBL, Berkeley, 1985-87; sci. dir. Les Houches (France) Summer Sch., 1981; cons., mem. adv. panels U.S. Dept. Energy, Washington; cons. Nat. Sci. Bd., 1996-97, bd. dirs., 1997—. Co-editor: Weak Interactions, 1977, Gauge Theories in High Energy Physics, 1983; contr. articles to profl. jours. Recipient Thibaux prize U. Lyons (France) Acad. Art & Sci., 1977, E.O. Lawrence award, 1988, J.J. Sakurai prize for theoretical particle physics, APS, 1993; Guggenheim fellow, 1989-90. Fellow Am. Acad. Arts and Scis., Am. Philos. Soc. (mem. various coms., chairperson com. on women, J.J. Saburai prize 1993); mem. AAAS, NAS, Nat. Sci. Bd. Office: U Calif Dept Physics Berkeley CA 94720-0001

GAINES, FRANCIS PENDLETON, III, judge; b. Lexington, Va., Sept. 24, 1944; s. Francis Pendleton Jr. and Dorothy Ruth (Bloomhardt) G.; m. Mary Chilton, Dec. 19, 1967 (div. Aug. 1992); children: Elizabeth Chilton, Edmund Pendleton, Andrew Cavett. Grad., Woodberry Forest Sch., Va., 1962; BA in Hist., U. Ariz., 1967; LLB, U. Va., 1969. Bar: U.S. Dist. Ct. (Ariz.) 1969, Ariz. 1969, U.S. Ct. Appeals (9th cir.) 1972, U.S. Supreme Ct. 1975. Assoc. Evans, Kitchel & Jenckes, Phoenix, 1969-75, ptnr., 1975-89, Fennemore Craig, Phoenix, 1989-99; judge Superior Ct. of Ariz., Phoenix, 1999—. Panel arbitrators N.Y. Stock Exch., 1984-99, NASD, 1984-99; judge pro tem Ariz. Ct. Appeals, 1994-95, Maricopa County (Ariz.) Superior Ct., 1994-99; mem. State Bar Disciplinary Hearing Com., 1991-94, chair, 1995-97; mem. nat. litig. panel U. Va. Sch. Law; mem. Ariz. Commn. on Judicial Performance Review, 2001—; lectr. and panelist CLE programs. Author: Punitive Damages-A Railroad Trial Lawyers Guide, 1985. Sr. warden All Saints' Episcopal Ch., 1994-97, parish chancellor, 1997-99, diversity preceptor, 1999—; standing com. Episcopal Diocese of Ariz., 1997—; chmn. bd. govs. All Saints' Day Sch., Phoenix, 1990-91. Fellow Am. Bar Found., Ariz. Bar Found.; mem. ABA, State Bar Ariz. (civil practice and procedure com. 2000—), Maricopa County Bar Assn., Nat. Assn. Railroad Trial Coun. (exec. com. Pacific region, v.p. 1997-98), Securities Industry Assn., Univ. Club, U. Ariz. Pres.'s Club. Republican. Episcopalian. Office: Superior Ct Ariz 201 W Jefferson St Phoenix AZ 85003-2205

GAITHER, JAMES C. lawyer; b. Oakland, Calif., Sept. 3, 1937; s. Horace Rowan Jr. and Charlotte Cameron (Castle) G.; m. Susan Good, Apr. 30, 1960; children: James Jr., Whitaker, Reed, Kendra. BA in Econs., Princeton U., 1959; JD, Stanford U., 1964. Bar: Calif. 1964, U.S. Dist. Ct. D.C. 1965, U.S. Dist. Ct. (no. dist.) Calif. 1965, U.S. Ct. Appeals (D.C. cir., 7th cir., 9th cir.), 1965, U.S. Supreme Ct. Law clk. to chief justice Earl Warren, Washington, 1964-65; spl. asst. to asst. atty. gen. John W. Douglas, Washington, 1965-66; staff asst. Pres. Lyndon B. Johnson, Washington, 1966-69; atty. Cooley Godward LLP, San Francisco, 1969-71, ptnr., 1971—, mng. ptnr., 1984-90, sr. counsel, 2001—; mng. dir. Sutter Hill Ventures, 2001—. Cons. to sec. HEW, 1977, chmn. ethics adv. bd., 1977-80; bd. dirs. Basic Am. Inc., San Francisco, Blue Martini Software, Inc., San Mateo, Levi Strauss & Co., San Francisco, Siebel Sys., San Mateo; nVidia Corp., Santa Clara; chmn. James Irvine Found.; former vice chair Carnegie Endowment for Internat. Peace; dir. Hewlett Found.; former trustee The RAND Corp. Note editor Stanford Law Rev., 1963-64. Former pres. bd. trustees, Stanford (Calif.) U.; mem. exec. com. bd. vis. Sch. Law Stanford U.; former chmn. bd. trustees Branson Sch., Ross, Calif., Ctr. for Biotech. Rsch. San Francisco; past trustee Family Svc. Agy. San Francisco, St. Stephens Parish Day Sch., Belvedere, Calif., The Scripps Rsch. Inst.; past trustee, chmn. protem Marin Cmty. Found, Marin County, Calif.; past pres. bd. trustees Marin County Day Sch., Corte Madera; past pres. bd. trustees Marin Ednl. Found., San Rafael; past treas., trustee Rosenberg Found.; past v.p., trustee, vice chmn. San Francisco Devel. Fund; past chmn. Dean's Adv. Coun. Stanford Law Sch., chmn. capital campaign; Inst. Capt. USMC, 1959-61. Recipient Disting. Pub. Svc. award HEW, 1977, Stanford Assocs. award Stanford U., 1989, 97; named Entrepreneur of Yr. Harvard Bus. Sch., 1979. Fellow Am. Acad. Arts and Scis.; mem. ABA, Calif. Bar Assn., San Francisco Bar Assn., Order of Coif, Phi Delta Phi (province 12). Democrat. Presbyterian. Avocations: tennis, hiking, camping, fishing, photography. Office: Cooley Godward LLP 1 Maritime Plz Fl 20 San Francisco CA 94111-3510

GALANOS, JAMES, retired fashion designer; b. Phila., Sept. 20, 1924; s. Gregory D. and Helen (Gorgoliatos) G. With Hattie Carnegie, 1944; asst. to designer Columbia Pictures Corp., Hollywood, Calif., 1946-47; trainee Robert Piguet, Paris, France, 1947-48; founder, designer Galanos Originals, L.A., 1951-99. Exhbns. include restrospectives Costume Council of Los Angeles County Mus. Art, 1974, Fashion Inst. Tech., 1976, Costume Inst. Mus. Fine Arts, Houston, 1987, Galanos Retrospective, 1951-92, 1997, Cleve. Hist. Soc., 1996, 45 yr. career retrospective Los Angeles County Mus. Art, 1997. Recipient award for distinguished service in field of fashion Neiman-Marcus, 1954; Am. Fashion Critics award Met. Mus. Art, Costume Inst., 1954; Return award, 1956; Hall of Fame, 1959; Creativity award Internat. Achievements Fair, 1956; Filene's Young Talent design award Boston, 1958; Cotton Fashion award, 1958; Lifetime Achievement award Council Fashion Designers Am., 1985; Stanley award Fashion Collectors of Dallas Hist. Soc., 1986; Otis-Parsons Design Achievement award, 1987, first Annual award for Design Excellence Costume Com. Chgo. Hist. Soc., 1992; Recognition award outstanding contbn. to the World of Fashion. Office: 2254 S Sepulveda Blvd Los Angeles CA 90064-1812

GALANTER, RUTH, city official; Grad., U. Mich.; MA, Yale U. Chair South Coast Regional Coastal Commn.; city coun. 6th dist. L.A., 1987—. Mem. Am. Pub. Health Assn. Office: City Hall 200 N Main St Rm 515 Los Angeles CA 90012-4103

GALANTI, RICHARD A. wholesale business executive; CFO Costco Wholesale, Issaqyah, Wash. Office: Costco Wholesale 999 Lake Dr Ste 200 Issaquah WA 98027-5367

GALBRAITH, JAMES MARSHALL, lawyer, business executive; b. Iowa City, Oct. 4, 1942; s. John Semple and Laura (Huddleston) G.; m. Margaret Rodi, Aug. 19, 1966; children: Margaret Laura, Katherine Lou, Robert James. BA, Pomona Coll., 1964; JD, Stanford U., 1967. Bar: Calif. 1968. Assoc. Gibson, Dunn & Crutcher, Los Angeles, 1967-68; ptnr. Rodi, Pollock, Pettker, Galbraith & Cahill, Los Angeles, 1968-84, of counsel, 1984—; pres. Bell Helmets Internat., Inc., San Marino, Calif., 1980-84; ptnr. Palm Properties Co., San Marino, 1979—. Pres., dir. Van de Kamp's Bakers, Inc., San Marino, 1985-87; ptnr. Huntington Hotel Assocs., San Marino, 1986-95; pres. Crestmont Fin. Svcs., Inc., 1991—, Crestmont Industries, LLC, 1996—. Author: In the Name of the People, 1977, The Money Tree, 1982, Fear of Failure, 1993, Patient Power, 1995; mem. bd. editors Stanford Law Rev., 1965-67. Trustee Pomona Coll., 1987-89, hon. trustee, 1989—; trustee, mem. exec. com. Children's Hosp. L.A., 1986-91, hon. trustee, 1991—; mem. Soc. of Fellows, Huntington Libr. Art Gallery and Bot. Gardens, 1982—; mem. Young Pres. Orgn., 1979-93. Mem. State Bar Calif., Phi Beta Kappa. Episcopalian. Clubs: California (L.A.), Valley Hunt (Pasadena). Home: 1640 Oak Grove Ave San Marino CA 91108-1109 Office: 2600 Mission St San Marino CA 91108-1676

GALBRAITH, JOHN ROBERT, insurance company executive; b. Portland, Oreg., Oct. 18, 1938; s. Maurice Kerr and Margaret Ione (Veach) G.; m. Maureen McKovich, Oct. 2, 1971 (div. Mar. 1978); children: Margaret Maureen, Marc Ryan; m. Betty Jean Irelan, Dec. 11, 1987. BA, Willamette U., 1960; MBA, U. Washington, 1962. CPA, Oreg. Staff acct. Ernst & Young, Portland, 1962-65; treas. First Pacific Corp., Portland, 1965-71; v.p., treas. Geo McKovich Cos., Palm Beach, Fla. and L.A., 1971-80; v.p., chief fin. officer SAIF Corp., Salem, Oreg., 1980-82; exec. v.p., CFO Liberty N.W. Ins. Corp., Portland, 1983—, bd. dir. Bd. dir. Helmsman Mgmt. Svcs. N.W., Inc., Portland, 1987—. Bd. dirs. Liberty Health Plan, Inc., Portland, 1992—. With Army N.G., 1957-66. Mem. AICPAs, Fin. Exec. Inst., Fla. Ins. CPAs, Calif. Soc. CPAs, Oreg. Soc. CPAs, Multnomah Athletic Club. Republican. Home: 3324 Sandhurst Rd Birmingham AL 35223-2806 Office: Liberty NW Ins Corp One Liberty Ctr Portland OR 97232-2038

GALE, ARNOLD DAVID, pediatric neurologist, consultant; b. Chgo., Nov. 2, 1949; s. Benjamin and Revelle Frances (Steinman) G.; m. Sharon Ann Stone, 1997. AB summa cum laude, Stanford U., 1971; MD, Johns Hopkins U., 1976. Diplomate Am. Bd. Pediatrics, Nat. Bd. Med. Examiners; med. lic., Calif. Resident in pediatrics Mass. Gen. Hosp., Boston, 1976-78; postdoctoral fellow Johns Hopkins Hosp., Balt., 1978-79, resident in neurology, 1979-82; asst. prof. pediatrics and neurology George Washington U. Sch. Medicine, Washington, 1982-89; dir. neurology tng. program Children's Hosp. Nat. Med. Ctr., Washington, 1982-89; clin. assoc. prof. neurology, neurological scis. and pediatrics Sch. of Med. Stanford U., Stanford, Calif., 1989—; med. info. officer Muscular Dystrophy Assn., Tucson, 1992—. Cons. neurologist Vaccine Injury Program U.S. Dept. HHS, Rockville, Md., 1989—, Inst. Vaccine Safety Sch. Hygiene and Pub. Health Johns Hopkins U., Balt., 1998—, Anthrax Vaccine Expert Com., 1999—; adv. panel FDA, Rockville, 1983-89; vis. lectr. U. Pitts. Sch. Medicine, 1981—. Author: Pediatric Emergency Medicine, 1989; contbr. articles to profl. jours. Support group coord. Muscular Dystrophy Assn., San Jose, Calif., 1989—; mem. Pres.'s Com. Employment of People Disabilities, Washington, 1992—; med. adv. bd. Multiple Sclerosis Soc., Santa Clara, Calif., 1990—; v.p. Muscular Dystrophy Assn., Tucson, 1992-94, bd. dirs., 1993-96. Recipient Nat. Rehab. award Allied Svcs., Scranton, Pa., 1994. Fellow Am. Acad. Pediatrics; mem. Am. Acad. Neurology, Am. Soc. Neurol. Investigation (founding mem.), Am. Acad. Immunotherapy, Child Neurology Soc., Calif. Children's Lobby, Nat. Alumni Coun. (Johns Hopkins U.), Phi Beta Kappa, Alpha Omega Alpha. Jewish. Avocations: writing, travel. Office: 335 Elan Village Ln Unit 107 San Jose CA 95134-2540 E-mail: adgale@jhu.edu

GALE, ROBERT PETER, physician, scientist, researcher; b. N.Y.C., Oct. 11, 1945; s. Harvey Thomas and Evelyn (Klein) G.; m. Tamar Tishler, June 2, 1976; children: Tal, Shir, Elan. BA, Hobart Coll., 1966; MD, SUNY, Buffalo, 1970; PhD, UCLA, 1976; DSc (hon.), Albany Med. Coll., 1987; LHD (hon.), Hobart Coll., 1987; D of Pub. Svc. (hon.), MacMurray Coll., 1988. Diplomate Am. Bd. Internal Medicine, Am. Bd. Med. Oncology, Am. Bd. Hematology. Resident in hematology and oncology UCLA, 1972-74, prof. medicine, 1974—; dir. bone marrow and stem cell transplantation Salick Health Care, Inc., 1993—. Chmn. Internat. Bone Marrow Transplant Registry, Milw., 1982—; pres. Armand Hammer Ctr. for Advanced Studies in Nuc. Energy and Health; sci. dir. Ctr. for Advanced Studies in Leukemia, L.A.; mem. Am. Com. on U.S.-Soviet Rels. Author 20 books, 700 articles on hematology, oncology, immunology and transplantation. Recipient Presdl. award N.Y. Acad. Scis., 1986, Olender Peace prize, 1986, Emmy award NATAS, Scientist of Distinction award Weizmann Inst. Sci., 1988; Bogart fellow and scholar Leukemia Soc. Am., 1976-81. Fellow ACP; mem. Transplantation Soc., Am. Soc. Hematology,

Am. Assn. Immunology, Internat. Soc. Hematology, Soc. Exptl. Hematology, Am. Soc. Clin. Oncology, Am. Assn. Cancer Rsch., Russian Acad. Med. Sci. (hon.). Home: 2316 Donella Circle Los Angeles CA 90077-1801 Office: 11693 San Vicente Blvd # 335 Los Angeles CA 90049-5105

GALL, DONALD ALAN, data processing executive; b. Reddick, Ill., Sept. 13, 1934; s. Clarence Oliver and Evelyn Louise (McCumber) G.; m. Elizabeth Olmstead, June 25, 1960 (div. 1972); children: Christopher, Keith, Elizabeth; m. Kathleen Marie Insogna, Oct. 13, 1973; 1 child, Kelly Marie. BSME, U. Ill., 1956; SM, MIT, 1958, ME, 1960, ScD, 1964. Rsch. engr. GM, Detroit, 1956-57; staff engr. Dynatech Corp., Cambridge, Mass., 1959-60, mgr. ctr. systems, 1962-63; asst., assoc. prof. Carnegie-Mellon U., Pitts., 1964-69; rsch. assoc. prof. surgery and anesthesiology U. Pitts. Sch. Medicine, 1969-73; vis. fellow IBM Research Lab., Rueschlikon, Switzerland, 1970-71; pres. Omega Computer Systems, Inc., Phoenix, 1973—; CEO Omega Legal Systems, Inc., Phoenix, 1995—; bd. dirs. TTI Technologies, Inc., Omaha, 1996—. Chmn. bd. dirs. M Tech. Assn. Contbr. articles to profl. jours.; inventor fuel injection system. Bd. dirs. Scottsdale Boys and Girls Club, 1982-93; mem. Scottsdale Head Honchos, 1978-87; mem. Verde Vaqueros, 1987—. Recipient Taylor medal Internat. Conf. on Prodn. Rsch., Disting. Alumnus award dept. mech. and indsl. engring. U. Ill., 1997. Mem. AAAS, ASME, M Tech Assn. (exec. dir., bd. dirs. 1996-98, chmn. bd. dirs. 1998—), Sigma Xi, Pi Tau Sigma, Tau Beta Pi, Phi Kappa Phi. Avocations: horseback riding, skiing, golf. Home: 9833 E Cortez St Scottsdale AZ 85260-6012 Office: Omega Computer Sys Inc 3875 N 44th St Ste 200 Phoenix AZ 85018-5486 E-mail: dgall@omegalegal.com

GALL, MEREDITH DAMIEN (MEREDITH MARK DAMIEN GALL), education educator, writer; b. New Britain, Conn., Feb. 18, 1942; s. Theodore A. and Ray (Ehrlich) G.; m. Joyce Pershing, June 12, 1968; 1 child, Jonathan. AB, EdM, Harvard U., 1963; PhD, U. Calif., Berkeley, 1968. Sr. research assoc. Far West Lab. for Ednl. Research and Devel., San Francisco, 1968-75; assoc. prof. edn. U. Oreg., Eugene, 1975-79, prof., 1980—, co-dir. mid./secondary edn., 1999—. Author: Handbook for Evaluating and Selecting Curriculum Materials, 1981, (with K.A. Acheson) Techniques in the Clinical Supervision of Teachers, 4th edit., 1997, (with J.P. Gall) Making the Grade, rev. 2d edit., 1993, (with W.R. Borg and J.P. Gall) Educational Research: An Introduction, 6th edit., 1996, (with J.P. Gall, D.R. Jacobsen, and T.L. Bullock) Tools for Learning: A Guide to Teaching Study Skills, 1990, (with W.R. Borg and J.P. Gall) Applying Educational Research, 4th edit., 1999; editor: (with B.A. Ward) Critical Issues in Educational Psychology, 1974; cons. editor Jour. Ednl. Rsch., Jour. Rsch. in Rural Edn., Forum for Reading, Jour. Exptl. Edn. USPH fellow, 1963-64. Fellow Am. Psychol. Assn.; mem. ASCD, Am. Ednl. Research Assn., Oreg. Ednl. Research Assn. (pres. 1985-86), Phi Delta Kappa (Dist. I Meritorious award 1978). Home: 4810 Mahalo Dr Eugene OR 97405-4609 Office: U Oreg Coll Edn Eugene OR 97403

GALLAGHER, DENNIS JOSEPH, municipal official, state senator, educator; b. July 1, 1939; s. William Joseph and Ellen Philomena (Flaherty) G.; children: Meaghan Kathleen, Daniel Patrick. BA, Regis Coll., 1961; MA, Cath. U. Am., 1968; postgrad. (Eagleton fellow), Rutgers U., 1972, 86. With locals of Internat. Assn. Theatrical and Stage Employees, Denver and Washington, 1956-63; tchr. St. John's Coll. H.S., Washington, 1964-66, Heights Study Ctr., Washington, 1965-67, Regis U., Washington, 1967; mem. Colo. Ho. of Reps. from 4th Dist., 1970-74, Colo. Senate, 1974-95; councilman dist. 1, Denver, 1995—. Chmn. Dem. Caucus, 1982-84, Dem. Whip, 1985-87. Mem. Platte Area Reclamation Com., 1973-75; mem. Denver Anti-Crime Coun., 1976-77; trustee Denver Art Mus.; bd. dirs. Cath. Cmty. Svcs.; past mem. Colo. Commn. on Aging; past mem. Colo. State Adv. Coun. on Career Edn.; mem. Victim Assistance Law Enforcement Bd., Denver, 1984-88; bd. dirs. Denver Am. Ireland Fund. Named Gates Found. fellow Harvard U.; recipient Jacques Ellul award Media Ecology Assn., 2001. Mem. Colo. Fedn. Tchrs. (pres. local 1333, 1972-74), Colo. Calligrapher's Guild, Colo. History Group, James Joyce Reading Soc., Speech Comm. Assn. Colo., Western States Comm. Assn. Democrat. Roman Catholic. Home: 5097 Meade St Denver CO 80221-1033 Office: Regis U Dept Comm 3333 Regis Blvd Dept Comm Denver CO 80221-1099 also: 458 City and County Bldg Denver CO 80202 also: 4404 Lowell Blvd Denver CO 80211-1367 Fax: 720-865-9540. E-mail: dgallagh@regis.edu

GALLAGHER, JOSEPH FRANCIS, marketing executive; b. N.Y.C., May 15, 1926; s. Joseph O'Neil and Nora (Shea) G.; m. Anne Decker, June 17, 1950; children: June, Virginia, Aline. Student, U. Va., 1947-50. Advanced to pres., dir. Erwin Wasey, Inc., Los Angeles, 1968-80; pres. JFG, Inc., Oildale, Calif., 1981—. Served with USNR, 1944-46. Mem. Phi Gamma Delta, Delta Sigma Rho. Home: 5088 Ovalo Laguna Hills CA 92653-1801 Office: JFG Inc Oildale CA 93388

GALLAGHER, MICHAEL L. lawyer; b. LeMars, Iowa, Apr. 14, 1944; BA, Ariz. State U., 1966, JD, 1970. Bar: Ariz. 1970. Judge pro tem Maricopa County Superior Ct., 1979, Ariz. Ct. Appeals, 1985; mem. adv. bd. AMEC, Inc. Chmn. gov.'s adv. com. profl. football, 1981-87, mayor's adv. com. profl. sports, 1984-91; bd. dirs. Maricopa County Sports Authority, 1989; bd. visitors law sch. Ariz. State U., 1979; dir. Valley of the Sun YMCA, chmn., 1995, Phoenix Suns Charities; trustee Peter Kiewit Found.; dir. Ariz. Pub. Svc. Co., Omaha World Herald Co., Pinnacle West Capital Corp., Vincor. Fellow Internat. Acad. Trial Lawyers; mem. Am. Bd. Trial Advocates (pres. Phoenix chpt. 1988). Office: Gallagher & Kennedy PC 2575 E Camelback Rd Phoenix AZ 85016-4240 E-mail: mlg@gknet.com

GALLAGHER, THOMAS EDMUND, hotel executive, lawyer; AB magna cum laude, Holy Cross Coll., 1966; JD cum laude, Harvard Univ., 1969. Bar: Calif. 1970. Assoc. Gibson, Dunn and Crutcher, 1969—70, 1973—77, ptnr., 1977—92, with, 1977—79, 1979—83, 1983—87, N.Y.C., 1988—92; legis. asst. US Senate , 1970—72; pres., CEO The Griffin Group, Inc., 1992—97; pres., CEO Resorts Internat./Griffin Gaming and Entertainment, Atlantic City, 1995—96; exec. v.p., chief adminstrv. officer, gen. counsel Hilton Hotels Corp., Beverly Hills, Calif., 1997-2000; pres. & CEO Park Place Entertainment Corp. (NYSE-PPE), Las Vegas, 2000—. Office: Park Place Entertainment Corp 3930 Howard Hughes Pky Las Vegas NV 89109

GALLAGHER, TIM, parks and recreation director; b. Burbank, Calif., Jan. 30, 1953; BS, UCLA, 1974; MS, Calif. State U., 1977. Dir. parks and recreation City of Yreka (Calif.), 1979-85; mgr. parks and open spaces County of San Luis Obispo (Calif.), 1985-97; dir. parks and recreation City of Stockton (Calif.), 1997—. Office: City Stockton 6 E Lindsay St Stockton CA 95202-1912

GALLAGHER, TIM, newspaper editor; Editor Ventura (Calif.) County Star, 1995—, pres., editor. Office: Ventura County Star 5250 Ralston St Ventura CA 93003-7392

GALLEGLY, ELTON WILLIAM, congressman; b. Huntington Park, Calif., Mar. 7, 1944; married; four children. Student, Calif. State U., L.A. Businessman, real estate broker, Simi Valley, Calif., from 1968; mem. Simi Valley City Coun., 1979; mayor City of Simi Valley, 1980-86; mem. 100th-106th Congresses from the 21st (now 23d) Calif. dist., 1986—; chmn. internat. rels. subcom. on Europe; judiciary com.; resources com. Mem. Congl. Human Rights Caucus, Congl. Fire Svcs. Caucus, Congl. Task Force on Tobacco and Health, Congl. Task Force on Alzheimers Disease, other congl. caucuses include Automotive, Fight and Control Methamphetamine, Friends of Animals, Wine caucus, Diabetes caucus, Fairness caucus, House Renewable Energy and Energy Efficiency caucus, Older Ams. caucus; chmn. Task Force on Urban Search and Rescue; past vice-chmn., chmn. Ventura County Assn. govts., Calif. Bd. dirs. Moorpark Coll. Found. Office: US Ho Reps 2427 Rayburn Hob Washington DC 20515-0001

GALLI, DARRELL JOSEPH, management consultant; b. Ft. Bragg, Calif., Nov. 10, 1948; s. Joseph Germain and Esther Edith (Happajoki) G.; B.A. in Transp./Internat. Bus., San Francisco State U., 1975; BS in Computer Info. Systems, 1985; MBA Golden Gate U., 1980; m. Rondus Miller, Apr. 23, 1977 (div. 1981); 1 dau., Troyan Hulda. With Pacific Gas & Electric Co., Santa Cruz, Calif., 1972-73; with Calif. Western R.R., Ft. Bragg, 1975-77, Sheldon Oil Co., Suisun, Calif, 1978-80; mgr. House of Rondus, Suisun, 1974-79; mgmt. cons., Suisun City, 1979—; instr. Solano Coll., 1979-81, Golden Gate U., 1981; mem. faculty U. Md. European div., Heidelberg, W.Ger., 1982-88; owner, mgr. Old Stewart House Bed and Breakfast, Fort Bragg, Calif., 1990—; lectr. Coll. Redwoods, Ft. Bragg, 1989—; coord. Small Bus. Mgmt. Seminar, 1980. Asst. coordinator Sr. Citizens Survey for Solano Coll. and Sr. Citizens Center, 1980; mem. Ft. Bragg City Coun., 1994—. Served with U.S. Army, 1969-71. Lic. Calif. real estate agt. Mem. Am. Assn. M.B.A. Execs., World Trade Assn., Bay Area Elec. R.R. Assn. Democrat. Episcopalian. Club: Odd Fellows. Home and Office: 511 Stewart St Fort Bragg CA 95437-3226

GALLINGER, LORRAINE D. prosecutor; b. Sept. 2, 1948; BS, U. Wyo., 1970; JD, Cath. U. Am., 1975. Bar: D.C., Mont. 1st asst. U.S. atty. Dept. Justice, Billings, Mont., 1976-85, 91, sr. litigation counsel, chief civil divsn., 1985-91, acting U.S. atty., 1991-93; first asst. U.S. Attys. Office, Billings, 1993—. Instr. Atty. Gen. Advocacy Inst. Recipient Dir.'s Superior Performance award AUSA, 1988. Office: US Attys Office PO Box 1478 Billings MT 59103-1478

GALLIVAN, JOHN WILLIAM, publisher; b. Salt Lake City, June 28, 1915; s. Daniel and Frances (Wilson) G.; m. Grace Mary Ivers, June 30, 1938 (dec.); children: Gay, John W. Jr., Michael D., Timothy. B.A., U. Notre Dame, 1937. With Salt Lake Tribune, 1937—, promotion mgr., 1942-48, asst. pub., 1948-60, pub., 1960-84; pres. Kearns-Tribune Corp., 1960-86, chmn. bd., 1984-99; dir., exec. com. Tele-Communications, Inc., 1989-2000. Pres. Silver King Mining Co., 1960-97. Pres. Utah Symphony, 1964-65. Mem. Sigma Delta Chi, Bohemian Club (San Francisco). Clubs: Nat. Press (Washington); Alta (Salt Lake City), Salt Lake Country (Salt Lake City), Rotary (Salt Lake City). Home: 1664 White Pine Canyon Rd Park City UT 84060 Office: Kearns Tribune Corp 143 S Main St Salt Lake City UT 84111-1924

GALLO, ERNEST, vintner; b. 1909; widowed. Co-owner, chmn. bd. dirs. E & J Gallo Winery, Modesto, Calif., 1933—. Office: E & J Gallo Winery 600 Yosemite Blvd Modesto CA 95354

GALLO, JOAN ROSENBERG, lawyer; b. Newark, Apr. 28, 1940; BA in Psychology, Boston U.; postgrad. studies in Counseling, We. Md. Coll.; postgrad studies in Clin. Pyschology, We. Grad. Sch. Psychology; JD magna cum laude, U. Santa Clara, 1975. Bar: Calif. 1975. Assoc. with Cynthia Mertens U, Santa Clara, Calif., 1975-76; sr. law clk. U.S. Dist. Ct., 1976-78; assoc. Decker and Collins, San Jose, 1978-79; from dep. city atty. to city atty. City of San Jose, 1979-2000; ptnr. Terra Law LLP, San Jose, 2000—. Mem. Psi Chi. Office: Terra Law LLP 60 S Market St Ste 200 San Jose CA 95113-2333 E-mail: jgallo@terra-law.com

GALLO, JON JOSEPH, lawyer; b. Santa Monica, Calif., Apr. 19, 1942; s. Philip S. and Josephine (Sarazan) G.; m. Jo Ann Broome, June 13, 1964 (div. 1984); children: Valerie Ann, Donald Philip; m. Eileen Florence, July 4, 1985; 1 child, Kevin Jon. BA, Occidental Coll., 1964; JD, UCLA, 1967. Bar: Calif. 1968, U.S. Ct. Appeals (9th cir.) 1968, U.S. Tax Ct. 1969. Assoc. Greenberg, Glusker, Fields, Claman & Machtinger, L.A., 1967-75, ptnr., 1975—. Bd. dirs. USC Probate and Trust Conf., L.A., 1980—, UCLA Estate Planning Inst., chmn. 1992—. Contbr. articles to profl. jours. Fellow Am. Coll. Trust and Estate Counsel; mem. ABA (chair Generation Skipping Taxation com. 1992-95, co-chair life ins. com. 1995—), Internat. Acad. Estate and Trust Law, Assn. for Advanced Life Underwriting (assoc. mem.). Avocation: photography. Office: Greenberg Glusker Fields Claman & Machtinger LLP Ste 2100 1900 Avenue Of The Stars Los Angeles CA 90067-4502

GALLO, JOSEPH E. vintner; b. 1941; Various positions Gallo Sales Co., South San Francisco, 1962—, now pres. Office: Gallo Sales Co Inc 30825 Wiegman Rd Hayward CA 94544-7893

GALSTER, RICHARD W. engineering geologist; b. Seattle, May 13, 1930; BS in Geology, U. Wash., 1951, MS, 1956. Geologist Grant County (Wash.) Pub. Utilities Dist., 1954-55; geologist Seattle dist. U.S. Army Corps. Engrs., 1955-85; dist. geologist, 1973-85; cons. engring. geologist, 1985—. Recipient Dept. of Army Decoration for Meritorious Civilian Svc., 1985. Fellow Geol. Soc. Am. (chmn. engring. geology divsn. 1978-79, E.B. Burwell award 1993, Disting. Practice award 1995), Assn. Engring. Geologists (hon., pres. 1982-83, Claire P. Holdredge award 1991). Home and Office: PO Box 908 Edmonds WA 98020-0908 E-mail: georichgal@connectexpress.com

GALVAN, ELIAS GABRIEL, bishop; b. San Juan Acozac, Puebla, Mexico, Apr. 9, 1938; came to U.S., 1956; s. Elias and Olga (Peralta) G.; m. Zoraida Freytes, July 12, 1986, 1 child, Elias Gabriel. BA, Calif. State U., Long Beach; D in Religion, Sch. Theology Claremont. Ordained deacon United Meth. Ch., 1964, ordained elder, 1970. Asst. pastor Asbury United Meth. Ch., L.A., 1964-66; pastor City Ter. United Meth. Ch., L.A., 1966-69, All Nations United Meth. Ch., L.A., 1969-71; exec. dir. ethnic planning dept. United Meth. Ch., L.A., 1971-74, dist. supt. Santa Barbara Dist., 1974-80, coun. dir. Pacific and Southwest Conf., 1980-84, bishop United Meth. Ch., Phoenix area, 1984-96, now bishop, Seattle. 1st Hispanic bishop elected by United Meth. Ch. Avocation: tennis. Office: 2112 3d Ave Ste 301 Seattle WA 98121-2391

GALVAN, JOE H. federal judge; Bar: N.Mex. Magistrate judge for N.Mex., U.S. Magistrate Ct., Las Cruces, 1991—. Office: US Magistrate Ct B-201C US Courthouse 200 E Griggs Ave Las Cruces NM 88001-3523

GAMBLE, PATRICK K. career officer; BA in Math., Tex. A&M U., 1967; MBA, Auburn U., 1978; Grad., Air Command and Staff Coll., Maxwell AFB, 1978; Disting. Grad., Air War Coll., Maxwell AFB, 1984. Commd. 2d lt. USAF, 1967, advanced through ranks to gen., 1998; various assignments to dep. chief of staff air/space opers. Hdqtrs. USAF/The Pentagon, Washington, 1997-98; comdr. Pacific Air Forces, Hickam AFB, 1998—. Contbr. articles to profl. jours. Decorated Def. Disting. Svc. medal with one oak leaf cluster, Disting. Svc. medal, Legion of Merit, Disting. Flying Cross, Meritorious Svc. medal with two oak leaf clusters, Air medal with 13 oak leaf clusters, Air Force Commendation medal, Presdl. Unit citation with oak leaf cluster, Vietnam Svc. medal with three svc. stars, Republic of Vietnam Gallantry Cross with svc. star, Republic of Vietnam Gallantry Cross with Palm, NATO medal, others. Office: PACAF/CC 25 E St Ste G214 Hickam AFB HI 96853-5400

GAMBOA, GEORGE CHARLES, oral surgeon, educator; b. King City, Calif., Dec. 17, 1923; s. George Angel and Martha Ann (Baker) G.; m. Winona Mae Collins, July 16, 1946; children: Cheryl Jan Gamboa Granger, Jon Charles, Judith Merlene Gamboa Hiscox. Pre-dental cert., Pacific Union Coll., 1943; DDS, U. Pacific, 1946; MS, U. Minn., 1953; AB, U. So. Calif., 1958, EdD, 1976. Diplomate Am. Bd. Oral and Maxillofacial Surgery. Fellow oral surgery Mayo Found., 1950-53; clin. prof. grad. program oral and maxillofacial surgery U. So. Calif., L.A., 1954-99; assoc. prof. Loma Linda (Calif) U., 1958-99, chmn. dept. oral surgery, 1960-63; pvt. practice oral and maxillofacial surgery San Gabriel, Calif., 1955-93. Dir. So. Calif. Acad. Oral Pathology, 1995—. Mem., past chmn. first aid com. West San Gabriel chpt. ARC. Fellow Am. Coll. Dentists, Am. Coll. Oral and Maxillofacial Surgeons (founding fellow), Pierre Fauchard Acad., Am. Inst. Oral Biology, Internat. Coll. Dentists, So. Calif. Acad. Oral Pathology (pres. 2001); mem. Am. Assn. Oral and Maxillofacial Surgeons, Internat. Assn. Oral Surgeons, So. Calif. Soc. Oral and Maxillofacial Surgeons, Western Soc. Oral and Maxillofacial Surgeons, Am. Acad. Oral and Maxillofacial Radiology, Marsh Robinson Acad. Oral Surgeons, Profl. Staff Assn. L.A. County-U. So. Calif. Med. Ctr. (exec. com. 1976-99), Am. Cancer Soc. (Calif. div., profl. edn. subcom. 1977-90, pres. San Gabriel-Pomona Valley unit 1989-90), Am. Dental Assn. (sci. session chmn. sect. on anesthesiology, 1970), Calif. Dental Soc. Anesthesiology (pres. 1989-94), Calif. Dental Found. (pres. 1991-93), Calif. Dental Assn. (jud. coun. 1990-96), So. Calif. Acad. Oral Pathology (dir. 1995—, pres. 2000-01), San Gabriel Valley Dental Soc. (past pres.), Xi Psi Phi, Omicron Kappa Upsilon, Delta Epsilon. Seventh-Day Adventist. Home: 1102 Loganrita Ave Arcadia CA 91006-4535

GAMBRELL, THOMAS ROSS, investor, retired physician, surgeon; b. Lockhart, Tex., Mar. 17, 1934; s. Sidney Spivey and Nora Katherine (Rheinlander) G.; m. Louise Evans, Feb. 23, 1960. Student summa cum laude, U. Tex., 1953, MD, 1957. Intern Kings County Hosp., Bklyn., 1957-58; company physician Hughes Aircraft, Fullerton, Calif., 1958-65, Chrysler Corp., Anaheim, 1962-65, L.A. Angels Baseball Team, Fullerton, 1962-64; pvt. practice medicine Fullerton, 1958-91. With St. Jude Hosp., Anaheim Meml. Hosp., Fullerton Cmty. Hosp., Martin Luther Hosp.; mem. utilization rev. com. St. Mary's Convalescent Hosp., Fullerton Convalescent Hosp., Sunhaven and Fairway Convalescent Hosp.; owner Ranching (Citrus) & Comml. Devel., Ariz., Tex., N.Y., 1962-94. Contbr. articles to profl. jours. Organizer of care for needy elderly, North Orange County, 1962-65; sponsor numerous charity events. Fellow Am. Acad. Family Physicians; mem. AMA, Am. Geriats. Soc., Calif. Med. Assn., Tex. Med. Assn., Tex. Alumni Assn., Orange County Med. Assn., Mayflower Soc., Plantagenet Soc., Sons of Confederacy, SAR, Order Royal Descendants Living in Am. (col., listed in Living Descendants of Blood Royal), Order Crown (col.), Baronial Order Magna Carta, Order of Aesculaepius, Phi Eta Sigma, Delta Kappa Epsilon, Phi Chi. Avocations: collecting, travel, history. Office: PO Box 6067 Beverly Hills CA 90212-1067

GANAS, PERRY SPIROS, physicist; b. Brisbane, Australia, June 20, 1937; came to U.S., 1968, naturalized, 1975; s. Arthur and Lula (Grivas) G. B.S., U. Queensland, Australia, 1961; Ph.D., U. Sydney, 1968. Postdoctoral research asso., instr. U. Fla., 1968-70, vis. asst. research prof., 1972, vis. assoc. prof. physics, 1978, vis. assoc. research prof., 1979-80; prof. physics Calif. State U., Los Angeles, 1970—. Lectr. U. So. Calif., 1985-86, East L.A. Coll., 1988—; vis. prof. physics UCLA, summer 1987, 91, 92; referee Astrophys. Jour., Astron. and Astrophysics. Contbr. articles to profl. jours. Mem. AAUP, Congress of Faculty Assns., Am. Phys. Soc., Sigma Xi. Home: 11790 Radio Dr Los Angeles CA 90064-3615 Office: Calif State U Physics Dept Los Angeles CA 90032 E-mail: pganas@calstatela.edu

GANDARA, DANIEL, lawyer; b. L.A., July 7, 1948, s. Henry and Cecilia (Contreras) G.; m. Juleann Cottini, Aug. 26, 1972; children: Mario, Enrico. BA, UCLA, 1970; JD, Harvard U., 1974. Bar: Calif. 1974, Wash. 1978. Asst. city atty. City of L.A., 1974-77; staff atty. FTC, Seattle, 1977-79; ptnr. Lane, Powell, Moss & Miller, Seattle, 1979-87, Graham & Dunn, Seattle, 1987-93, Vandeberg, Johnson & Gandara, Seattle, 1993—. Mem. ABA, Wash. State Bar Assn., King County Bar Assn., Hispanic Nat. Bar Assn., Wash. State Hispanic C. of C., Seattle Athletic Club. Democrat. Roman Catholic. Home: 2010 E Lynn St Seattle WA 98112-2620

GANN, PAMELA BROOKS, academic administrator; b. 1948; BA, U. N.C., 1970; JD, Duke U., 1973. Bar: Ga. 1973, N.C. 1974. Assoc. King & Spalding, Atlanta, 1973, Robinson, Bradshaw & Hinson, P.A., Charlotte, N.C., 1974-75; asst. prof. Duke U. Sch. Law, Durham, 1975-78, assoc. prof., 1978-80, prof., 1980-99, dean, 1988-99; pres. Claremont McKenna Coll., Claremont, Calif., 1999—. Vis. asst. prof. U. Mich. Law Sch., 1977; vis. assoc. prof. U. Va., 1980 Author: (with D. Kahn) Corporate Taxation and Taxation of Partnerships and Partners, 1979, 83, 89; article editor Duke Law Jour. Mem. Am. Law Inst., Coun. Fgn. Rels., Order of Coif, Phi Beta Kappa Office: Claremont McKenna Coll Office Pres 500 E 9th St Claremont CA 91711-5903

GANNON, JOHN, computer company executive; BS, USAF Acad.; MBA, So. Ill. U.; grad. Internat. Sr. Mgrs. program, Harvard Bus. Sch. With Measurement Sys. Internat., Inc., 1976-81, Hewlett-Packard Co., mktg. mgr. mass storage group, 1991, gen. mgr. worldwide digital audio tape bus. Eng., gen. mgr. worldwide comml. desktop personal computer bus. Grenoble, France; exec. v.p. worldwide sales and corp. mktg. Quantum Corp., Milpitas, Calif., 1998, pres. hard disk dr. group. With USAF; USAFR, 1976-92. Office: Quantum Corp 500 Mccarthy Blvd Milpitas CA 95035-7909

GANONG, WILLIAM F(RANCIS), physiologist, physician; b. Northampton, Mass., July 6, 1924; s. William Francis and Anna (Hobbet) G.; m. Ruth Jackson, Feb. 22, 1948; children: William Francis III, Susan B., Anna H., James E. AB cum laude, Harvard U., 1945, MD magna cum laude, 1949; DSc (hon.), Med. Coll. Ohio, 1995. Intern, jr. asst. resident in medicine Peter Bent Brigham Hosp., Boston, 1949-51, asst. in medicine and surgery, 1952-55; research fellow medicine and surgery Harvard U., 1952-55; asst. prof. physiology U. Calif., San Francisco, 1955-60, assoc. prof., 1960-64, prof., 1964-82, Jack D. and Deloris Lange prof., 1982-91, Lange prof. emeritus, 1991—, faculty research lectr., 1968, vice chmn. dept., 1963-68, chmn., 1970-87. Cons. Calif. Dept. Mental Hygiene. Author: Review of Medical Physiology, 20th edit., 2001, Physiology: A Study Guide, 3d edit., 1989; editor: (with L. Martini) Neuroendocrinology, vol. I, 1966, vol. II, 1967, Frontiers in Neuroendocrinology, 1969, 71, 73, 76, 78, 80, 82, 84, 86, 88, (with S. McPhee, V. Lingappa and J. Lange) Pathophysiology of Disease, 1995, 3d edit., 2000; editor-in-chief Neuroendocrinology, 1979-84; co-editor Frontiers in Neuroendocrinology, 1990-2002. Served with U.S. Army, 1943-46; served to capt. M.C. 1951-52. Recipient Boylston Med. Soc. prize Harvard U., 1949, A.A. Berthold medal, 1985, Lifetime Achievement award High Blood Pressure Rsch. Coun., Am. Heart Assn., 1995; named Disting. Svc. mem. Am. Assn. Med. Colls., 1988. Fellow AAAS; mem. Am. Physiol. Soc. (pres. 1977-78), Assn. Chairmen Depts. Physiology (pres. 1976-77), Am. Soc. for Gravitational and Space Biology (bd. dirs. 1984-87), Soc. Exptl. Biology and Medicine (councillor 1989-93), Endocrine Soc., Chilean Endocrine Soc. (corr.), Internat. Brain Rsch. Orgn., Soc. for Neurosci., Internat. Soc. Neuroendocrinology (hon., v.p. 1976-80). Home: 710 Hillside Ave Albany CA 94706-1022 Office: U Calif Dept Physiology San Francisco CA 94143-0444

GANTZ, DAVID ALFRED, lawyer, university official; b. Columbus, Ohio, July 30, 1942; s. Harry Samuel and Edwina (Bookwalter) G.; m. Susan Beare, Aug. 26, 1967 (div. Feb. 1989); children: Stephen David, Julie Lorraine; m. Catherine Fagan, Mar. 28, 1992. AB, Harvard U., 1964; JD, Stanford U., 1967, M in Jud. Sci., 1970. Bar: Ohio 1967, D.C. 1971, Ariz. 1995, U.S. Ct. Internat. Trade 1983, U.S. Ct. Appeals (9th cir.), U.S. Supreme Ct. 1972. Asst. prof. law U. Costa Rica, San Jose, 1967-69; law clk. U.S. Ct. Appeals, San Francisco, 1969-70; asst. legal advisor U.S. Dept. State, Washington, 1970-77; ptnr. Cole & Corrette, Washington, 1977-83, Oppenheimer Wolff & Donnelly, Washington, 1983-90, Reid & Priest, Washington, 1990-93, of counsel, 1993-97, Dorsey & Whitney, 1997-99; prof. law, dir. grad. studies U. Ariz. Coll. Law, Tucson, 1993—; assoc. dir. Nat. Law Ctr. for Inter-Am. Free Trade, 1993—. Panelist U.S.-Can. Free Trade Agreement, 1989-92, Am. Arbitration Assn., 1996—, NAFTA, 1994—; judge OAS Adminstrv. Tribunal, 1987-95; adj. prof. Georgetown U. Law Ctr., 1982-93. Contbr. numerous articles on internat. law to profl. jours. Pres. Potomac River Sports Found., 1992-94. Mem. ABA, Am. Soc. Internat. Law, Potomac Boat Club (Washington, bd. dirs. 1986-93). Home: 7112 N Corte Del Anuncio Tucson AZ 85718-7333 Office: Ariz James E Rogers Coll Law 1201 E Speedway Blvd Tucson AZ 85719 E-mail: gantz@nt.law.arizona.edu

GANULIN, JUDY, public relations professional; b. Chgo., May 2, 1937; d. Alvin and Sadie (Reingold) Landis; m. James Ganulin, June 23, 1957; children: Stacy Ganulin Clark, Amy Ganulin Lowenstein. BA in Journalism, U. Calif., Berkeley, 1958. Copywriter-sec. Joe Connor Advt., Berkeley, 1958; exec. sec. Prescolite Mfg. Co., Berkeley, 1958-59; info. officer Office of Consumer Counsel, Sacramento, 1959-61; pub. rels. positions various polit. campaigns, Fresno, Calif., 1966; adminstrv. asst., editor, mktg. Valley Pubs., Fresno, 1971-80; staff asst. to county supr. Bd. Suprs., Fresno, 1980-82; field rep. Assemblyman Bruce Bronzan, Fresno, 1982-84; prin. Judy Ganulin Pub. Rels., Fresno, 1984—. Speaker new bus. workshop SBA/Svc. Corps Ret. Execs., Fresno, 1990—. Active Hadassah, Fresno, 1975—; pres. Temple Beth Israel Sisterhood, Fresno, 1976; panelist campaign workshop Nat. Women's Polit. Caucus, Fresno, 1994, publicity chmn. Ctrl. Calif. chpt. 1999-2000; bd. dirs. Temple Beth Israel, Fresno, 1972-75, Planned Parenthood Ctrl. Calif., Fresno, 1986-91, Empty Bowls, Sr. Companion Program; mem. Art and Wine Festival Com., 1999-2000, Valley Women's Polit. Fund. Mem. Pub. Rels. Soc. Am. (accredited pub. rels. practitioner, pres. Fresno/Ctrl. Valley chpt. 1994), Am. Mktg. Assn. (pres. ctrl. Calif. chpt.-ctrl. 1987-88), Calif. Press Women, Fresno Advt. Fedn., Pub. Rels. Roundtable (v.p., pres. 1991-93), Fresno C. of C. (mem. mktg. com. 1988—). Democrat. Avocations: traveling, reading, cooking. Office: Judy Ganulin Pub Rels 1117 W San Jose Ave Fresno CA 93711-3112

GARABEDIAN, CHARLES, artist; b. Detroit, 1923; MFA, UCLA, 1961. Solo shows include LaJolla (Calif.) Mus. Art, 1966, CeJee Gallery, N.Y., 1966, 67, Eugenia Butler Gallery, L.A., 1970, Newspace Gallery, L.A., 1974, Whitney Mus. Am. Art, N.Y.C., 1976, Broxton Gallery, L.A., 1976, L.A. Louver Gallery, Venice, Calif., 1979, 83, 86, 89, 90, 92, 94, 96, LaJolla Mus. Contemporary Art, 1981, Ruth S. Schaffner Gallery, Santa Barbara, Calif., 1982, Rose Art Mus., Waltham, Mass., 1983, Hirschl & Adler Modern Mus., N.Y.C., 1984, Gallery Paule Anglim, San Francisco, 1985, 93, 98, numerous others; exhibited in group shows at numerous mus. including Rose Art Mus., The High Mus., Atlanta, 1980, Emanuel Walter Gallery, San Francisco, 1981, LaJolla Mus. Contemporary Art, 1981, Mizumo Gallery, L.A., 1981, Mandeville Art Gallery, San Diego, Oakland Mus. Art, 1981, Brooke Alexander Gallery, N.Y., 1982, Kunst Mus., Luzern, 1983, Fresno Art Ctr., 1983, Tibor de Nagy Gallery, N.Y.C., 1983, Hirshhorn Mus. and Sculpture Garden, Smithsonian Instn., Washington, 1984, Newport Harbor Art Mus., Calif., 1984, El Museo Rufino Tamayo, Mexico City, 1984, L.A. Mcpl. Art Gallery, 1984, L.A. Louver, Venice, 1985, Whitney Mus. Art, 1986, DiLaurenti Gallery, N.Y., 1986, R.C. Erpf Gallery, N.Y., 1987, N.Y. State Mus., Albany, 1987, Richard Green Gallery, 1988, Bklyn. Mus. Art, 1989, James Corcoran Gallery, 1991, Riva Yares Gallery, Scottsdale, Ariz., 1994, Hirschl & Adler Mus., 1996, Mcpl. Art Gallery L.A., 1997; pub. collections include Met. Mus. Art, N.Y.C., Whitney Mus. Am. Art, Mus. Contemporary Art, L.A., Rose Art Mus., San Diego Mus. Contemporary Art, L.A. County Mus. Art Staff sgt. USAF, 1942-45. John Simon Guggenheim Meml. Found. fellow, 1979, Nat. Endowment for the Arts fellow, 1977. Dealer: L A Louver 45 Venice Blvd Venice CA 90291

GARAGIOLA, JOE, JR. baseball team executive; m. Noel Garagiola; children: Meredith, Valerie, Natalie, Christopher. BA cum laude, U. Notre Dame, 1972; JD, Georgetown U., 1975. Bar: Ariz., Calif., N.Y. Gen. counsel, asst. to pres. N.Y. Yankees, N.Y.C.; ptnr. Gallagher and Kennedy, Phoenix, 1982—; chmn. bd. dirs. Phoenix Met. Sports Found., 1985-87; v.p., gen. mgr. Ariz. Diamondbacks (profl. baseball expansion team), 1995—. Vice chmn. Gov.'s Cactus League Task Force, Phoenix, mem. Mayor's profl. baseball com.; chmn. Maricopa County (Ariz.) Sports Authority, Ariz. Baseball Commn. Bd. dirs. Am. West Airlines Ednl. Found., Phoenix Meml. Hosp. Recipient Inst. Human Rels. award, Am. Jewish Com., 1998. Office: c/o Ariz Diamondbacks 401 E Jefferson St Phoenix AZ 85004-2438

GARBARINO, JOSEPH WILLIAM, labor arbitrator, economics and business educator; b. Medina, N.Y., Dec. 7, 1919; s. Joseph Francis and Savina M. (Volpone) G.; m. Mary Jane Godward, Sept. 18, 1948; children: Ann, Joan, Susan, Ellen. B.A., Duquesne U., 1942; M.A., Harvard U., 1947, Ph.D., 1949. Faculty U. Calif., Berkeley, 1949—, prof., 1960-88, dir. Inst. Bus. and Econ. Research, 1962-88, prof. emeritus, 1988—. Vis. lectr. Cornell U., 1959-60, UCLA, 1949, SUNY, Buffalo, 1972; Fulbright lectr. U. Glasgow, Scotland, 1969; vis. scholar U. Warwick; mem. staff Brookings Instn., 1959-60; vis. lectr. U. Minn., 1978; labor arbitrator. Author: Health Plans and Collective Bargaining, 1960, Wage Policy and Long Term Contracts, 1962, Faculty Bargaining: Change and Conflict, 1975, Faculty Bargaining in Unions in Transition. Served with U.S. Army, 1942-45, 51-53. Decorated Bronze Star. Democrat. Roman Catholic. Home: 7708 Ricardo Ct El Cerrito CA 94530-3344

GARBER, ALAN MICHAEL, physician, educator, economist; b. Ill., 1955; s. Harry Garber; m. Anne Yahanda, Oct. 9, 1988. AB in Econs. summa cum laude, Harvard Coll., 1976, AM in Econs., 1977, PhD, 1982; MD, Stanford U., 1983. Diplomate Am. Bd. Internal Medicine. Cons. Inst. Medicine, Washington, 1979-80; clin. fellow Med. Sch. Harvard U., Boston, 1983-86, rsch. fellow John F. Kennedy Sch. Govt. Cambridge, Mass., 1986; staff physician VA Palo Alto (Calif.) Health Care System, 1986—; rsch. assoc. Nat. Bur. Econ. Rsch., Palo Alto, Calif., 1986—, dir. health care program Cambridge, 1990—; asst. prof. Stanford (Calif.) U., 1986-93, assoc. prof., 1993-98, dir. Ctr. Health Policy/Ctr. Primary Care and Outcomes Rsch., 1997—, prof., 1998—; contractor Office Tech. Assessment, Washington, 1987-88, 89-92. Fellow NSF, 1976, Henry J. Kaiser faculty fellow Kaiser Found., 1989-92. Fellow ACP, Assn. Health Svcs. Rsch.; mem. Inst. Medicine of NAS, Soc. Med. Decision Making (trustee 1989-91), Am. Econ. Assn., Assn. Health Svcs. Rsch., Am. Fedn. Clin. Rsch. (nat. councillor 1991-96), Soc. Gen. Internal Medicine. Office: Primary Care Outcomes Rsch Ctr Health Policy 179 Encina Commons Stanford CA 94305-6019

GARCETTI, GILBERT I. prosecutor; BS, U. So. Calif., L.A.; JD, UCLA, 1968. Dist. atty. County of Los Angeles, 1983—. Office: County Los Angeles Dist Attys Office 210 W Temple St Rm 18-709 Los Angeles CA 90012-3210

GARCHIK, LEAH LIEBERMAN, journalist; b. Bklyn., May 2, 1945; d. Arthur Louis and Mildred (Steinberg) Lieberman; m. Jerome Marcus Garchik, Aug. 11, 1968; children— Samuel, Jacob B.A., Bklyn. Coll., 1966. Editorial asst. San Francisco Chronicle, 1972-79, writer, editor, 1979-83, editor This World, 1983-84, columnist, 1984—; also author numerous book and movie reviews, features and profiles. Author: San Francisco; the City's Sights and Secrets, 1995; panelist (radio quiz show) Mind Over Matter; gossip reporter Bay TV; contbr. articles to mags. Vice pres. Golden Gate Kindergarten Assn., San Francisco, 1978; pres. Performing Arts Workshop, San Francisco, 1977-79; bd. dirs. Home Away From Homelessness, 1994-99. Recipient 1st prize Nat. Soc. Newspaper Columnists, 1992. Mem. Deutsche Music Verein, Newspaper Guild. Democrat. Jewish Home: 156 Baker St San Francisco CA 94117-2111 Office: San Francisco Chronicle 901 Mission St San Francisco CA 94103-2905 E-mail: lgarchik@sfchronicle.com

GARCIA, CARLOS M. financial services company executive; V.p. fin., chief acctg. officer Countrywide Credit Ind., Inc., Calabasas, Calif., 1984-86, sr. v.p., 1986-90, mng. dir., chief acctg. officer, 1990-95, mng. dir. fin., CFO, CAO, 1995-99, COO, mng. dir. fin., 1999-00, dir. CHL, 2000—. Office: Countrywide Credit Ind Inc 4500 Park Granada Calabasas CA 91302

GARCIA, DANIEL PETER, real estate manager; BBA, Loyola U., L.A., 1970; MBA, U. So. Calif., 1971; JD, UCLA, 1974. Ptnr. Munger, Tolles & Olson, L.A.; sr. v.p., worldwide corp. real estate Warner Bros., 1991—; sr. v.p., corp. real estate Warner Music Group, 1996—. Contbr. articles on urban policy issues including land use, housing, development and urban planning to profl. jours. Hearing examiner L.A. City Police Commn., 1975-76; pres. L.A. Planning Commn., 1978-88; mem. L.A. Bd. Police Commrs.; apptd. 1993 by Mayor Riordan to Airport Commn.; transferred 1994 to Bd. Commns. L.A. Cmty. Redevel. Agy. (chmn.); transferred back to Airport Commn., 1995 (pres.); trustee Rockefeller Found.; mem. nat bd. dirs. Kaiser Found. Hosps. and Health Plans. Platoon sgt. combat infantry U.S. Army, 1967-69, Vietnam. Decorated Purple Heart with 2 oak leaf clusters, Silver Star, Bronze Star with oak leaf cluster, Air medal. Planning Assn. regional, state, nat. awards for excecellence in pub. planning. Office: Warner Bros 4000 Warner Blvd Bldg 137 Burbank CA 91522-0002

GARCIA, DAVID, agricultural products executive; b. 1953; Graduate, U. Wyo., 1975. With We. Nuclear Mining, Lander, Wyo., 1976-78, Diamond Fruit Growers, Inc., Hood River, Oreg., 1978—; now contr. Office: Diamond Fruit Growers Inc PO Box 180 Hood River OR 97031-0060

GARCIA, EDWARD J. federal judge; b. 1928; AA, Sacramento City Coll., 1951; LLB, U. Pacific, 1958. Dep. dist. atty. Sacramento County, 1959-64, supervising dep. dist. atty., 1964-69, chief dep. dist. atty., 1969-72; judge Sacramento Mcpl. Ct., 1972-84, U.S. Dist. Ct. (ea. dist.) Calif., Sacramento, 1984-96, sr. judge, 1996—. Served with U.S. Army Air Corps, 1946-49. Office: US Dist Ct US Courthouse Clk Office 501 I St Rm 4-200 Sacramento CA 95814-7300

GARCIA, F. CHRIS, academic administrator, political science educator, public opinion researcher; b. Albuquerque, Apr. 15, 1940; s. Flaviano P. and Crucita A. Garcia; m. Sandra D. Garcia; children: Elaine L., Tanya C. BA, U. N.Mex., 1961, MA in Govt., 1964; PhD in Polit. Sci., U. Calif., Davis, 1972. Asst. prof. polit. sci. U. N.Mex., Albuquerque, 1970-74, assoc. prof., 1974-78, prof., 1978—, asst. dir. divsn. govt. rsch., 1970-72, assoc. dean Coll. Arts and Scis., 1975-80, dean Coll. Arts and Scis., 1980-86, v.p. acad. affairs, 1987-90, provost, 1993, 98-2000; founder Zia Rsch. Assocs., Inc., Albuquerque, 1973-94, also chmn. bd. dirs. Cons.-evaluator North Ctrl. Assn., 1994—. Author: Political Socialization of Chicano Children, 1973, La Causa Politica, 1974, The Chicano Political Experience, 1977, State and Local Government in New Mexico, 1979, New Mexico Government, 1976, 81, 94, Latinos and the Political System, 1988, Latino Voices, 1992, Pursuing Power, 1997. Mem. edn. com. Good Govt. Group; mem. charter rev. com. City of Albuquerque, 1999. Mem. Western Polit. Sci. Assn. (pres. 1977-78), Am. Polit. Sci. Assn. (v.p. 1994-95, mem. exec. coun. 1984-86, sec. 1992-93, disting. svc. award 2001), Am. Assn. Pub. Opinion Rsch., Coun. Colls. of Arts and Sci. (bd. dirs. 1982-85), Nat. Assn. State Univs. and Land Grant Colls. (mem. coun. acad. affairs 1987-90, mem. exec. com. 1989), Western Social Sci. Assn. (mem. exec. coun. 1973-76), Phi Beta Kappa, Phi Kappa Phi, Gold Key. Home: 1409 Snowdrop Pl NE Albuquerque NM 87112-6331 Office: U N Mex Polt Sci Dept Social Scis Bldg 2053 Albuquerque NM 87131-0001 E-mail: cgarcia@unm.edu

GARCIA, JUNE MARIE, librarian; b. Bryn Mawr, Pa., Sept. 12, 1947; d. Roland Ernest and Marion Brill (Hummel) Traynor; m. Teodosio Garcia, July 17, 1928; children: Gretchen, Adrian. BA, Douglass Coll., 1969; MLS, Rutgers U., 1970. Reference libr. New Brunswick (N.J.) Pub. Libr., 1970-72, Plainfield (N.J.) Pub. Libr., 1972-75; br. mgr. Phoenix Pub. Libr., 1975-80, extension svcs. adminstr., 1980-93; dir. San Antonio Pub. Libr., 1993-99; CEO, CARL Corp., Denver, 1999-2001; v.p., chief amb. TLC/CARL, Denver, 2001—. Recipient Productivity Innovator award City of Phoenix, 1981. Mem. ALA (life, coun. 1986-90, 93-2001, pres. Pub. Libr. Assn. 1991-92, new stds. task force 1983-87, goals, guidelines and stds. com. 1986-90, chairperson 1987-90, resource allocation com. 1998-99), Freedom to Read Found. (bd. dirs.), Ariz. State Libr. Assn. (pres. 1984-85, Libr. of Yr. award 1986, Pres.'s award 1990), Beta Phi Mu. Office: TLC/CARL 3801 E Florida Ave Ste 300 Denver CO 80210-2542

GARCIA, LORENZO F. federal judge; b. 1947; BA with honors, Coll. of Santa Fe, 1969; JD, U. N.Mex., 1973. Bar: N.Mex. Judge N.Mex. Dist. Ct., Santa Fe, N.Mex. Ct. Appeals, Santa Fe; designated justice N.Mex. Supreme Ct.; magistrate judge for N.Mex., U.S. Dist. Ct., Albuquerque, 1992—. Mem. editl. bd. N.Mex. Law Rev. With U.S. Army. Office: US Dist Ct US Courthouse 333 Lomas Blvd NW Albuquerque NM 87102-2272

GARCIA, MARY JANE MADRID, state legislator; b. Dona Ana, N. Mex., Dec. 24, 1936; d. Isaac C. and Victoria M. Garcia. AA, San Francisco City Coll., 1956; BS, N.Mex. State U., 1982, BA in Anthropology, 1983, MA in Anthropology, 1985. Interpretor, translator to USAF Capt., Hotel Balboa, Madrid, Spain, 1962-63; exec. sec. to city mgr. City of Las Cruces, N.Mex., 1964-65; adminstrv. asst. RMK-BRJ, Saigon, Socialist Rep. Vietnam, 1966-72; owner Billy the Kid Gift Shop, Mesilla, N.Mex., 1972-81; pres., owner Victoria's Night Club, Las Cruces, 1981—; state senator Dist. 38 N.Mex. With archaeol. excavations N.Mex. State U. Anthropology Dept., summer 1982, spring 1983; bd. dirs., sec-treas. Dona Anna Mutual Domestic Water Assn.; mem. Subarea Council Health Systems Agy., 1979; bd. dirs. Sun Country Savings Bank, Las Cruses, 1985; treas. Toney Anaya for U.S. Senate, 1978; active Toney Anaya for N.Mex. Gov., 1979-82. Mem. N.Mex. Retail Liquor Assn. Democrat. Roman Catholic. Address: Majority Whip 226 Issac Garcia Rd PO Box 22 Dona Ana NM 88032-0022

GARCIA, MONICAE, communications equipment company executive; Pres., CEO Complas Inc., Corona, Calif., 1989—. Mentor U. Calif., Irvine; co-founder Corona (Calif.) Mfrs. Coun. Recipient Women of Achievement award YWCA, 1998. Office: Complas Inc 255 Airport Cir Corona CA 92880-2527

GARCIA, RICHARD J. bishop; b. Jan. 24, 1947; Aux. bishop Sacramento Roman Cath. Ch., 1997—. Office: Diocese Sacramento 2110 Broadway Sacramento CA 95818

GARDINER, JOHN JACOB, leadership educator, writer, philosopher, speaker; b. Tel Aviv, Feb. 6, 1946; came to U.S., 1952; s. Leon and Zipora (Shalev) Zucker; m. Joanna Meredith Winslow, 1967 (div. 1998); children: James, Katharine. BA, U. Fla., 1967, PhD, 1973; postgrad., U. Oreg., 1978, Stanford U., 1983. Tchr., dept. chair Keystone Heights (Fla.) Sch., 1968-72; instr., asst. to v.p. acad. affairs U. Fla., Gainesville, 1973-75; asst. prof. edn. The Citadel, Charleston, S.C., 1975-77; prof., dept. chair Okla. State U., Stillwater, 1979-91, Seattle U., 1991—. Assoc. in edn. Harvard U., 1985; vis. asst. prof. Fla. State U., Tallahassee, 1977-78, U. Oreg., Eugene, 1978-79; chair bd. Pacific N.W. Postdoctoral Inst., Seattle, 1995—; bd. dirs. Conflict Resolution Inst., Human Connection Inst., Ctr. for Advanced Study of Leadership, U. Md., College Park; co-founder All Russia Leadership Devel. Ctr., Novosibirsk, 1999-2000. Co-author: UNESCO Guide, 1991, Insights on Leadership, 1998. Permanent fund chair dist. 5030 Rotary, Seattle, 1996-2001. Recipient Svc. to State award Gov. and Ho. of Reps., 1991; fellow W. K. Kellogg Found., 1972-73; grantee James McGregor Burns Leadership Acad. Ctr. for Advanced Study of Leadership, 1998. Mem. Am. Coun. Edn. (bd. dirs. Nat. Leadership Group 1985-96), Assn. Study of Higher Edn. (bd. dirs. 1983-85), Am. Ednl. Rsch. Assn. (bd. dirs. divsn. J 1983-85), Vashon Island Rotary Club (pres. 2000-01, Rotary dist. 5030 asst. gov. 2001—). Episcopalian. Avocations: walking, reading, gardening, public speaking. Office: Seattle U 510 Loyola Hall Broadway and Madison Seattle WA 98122

GARDINER, T(HOMAS) MICHAEL, artist; b. Seattle, Feb. 5, 1946; s. Thomas Scott Gardiner and Carolyn Virginia (Harmer) Bolin; m. Kelly Michelle Floyd, Mar. 7, 1981 (div. Dec. 1983); m. Diana Phyllis Shurtlieff Rainwater, Sept. 26, 1986; children: Rita Em, Nigel Gus. BA in Philosophy, Sulpician Sem. N.W., Kenmore, Wash., 1969; student, Cornish Inst. Arts, 1971-73. Seaman Tidewater Barge, Camas, Wash., 1969; pari-mutuel clk. Longacres Racetrack, Renton, 1969-92; dock worker Sealand, Inc., Seattle, 1970. Tchr. Coyote Jr. H.S., Seattle, 1989-95, Sch. Visual Concepts, Seattle, 1990-95; tchr., vis. artist Ctrl. Wash. U., Ellensburg, 1991. Represented in permanent collections Microsoft Corp., Steel Rives LLP, Stokes Lawrence PS, Seattle Water Dept., Nordstrom, Seattle City Light, Sultan (Wash.) Sch. Dist., King County Portable Works Collection, SAFECO Ins. Co., Seattle, City of Portland Collection, 1988, Highline Sch. Dist., Seattle; commns. include ARTp Metro Art Project, Seattle, interior painting Villa del Lupo restaurant, Vancouver, B.C., Can.; illustrations included in The New Yorker Mag., Am. Illustration 13, The Seattle Times. Recipient Best Design award Print Mag., 1985; Nat. Endowment for Arts Fellowship grantee, 1989. Democrat. Roman Catholic. Home and Office: 3023 NW 63rd St Seattle WA 98107-2566 E-mail: gardiner@speakeasy.org

GARDNER, FREDERICK BOYCE, library director; b. Hopkinsville, Ky., Mar. 12, 1942; s. Boyce and Alleen Louise (Brown) G. BA, U. Ky., 1964; MA, Ind. U., Bloomington, 1966. Head librarian U. Ky. Hopkinsville Community Coll., Hopkinsville, 1966-69; head, readers service CUNY, Manhattan Community Coll., N.Y.C., 1969-71; reference librarian Calif. Inst. of the Arts, Valencia, Calif., 1971-84, head, pub. svcs., 1974-87, dir. computer svcs., 1984-87, acting dir., 1987-88, dean of the library, 1988—. Del. Calif. Conf. on Networking, Pomona, 1985; mem. Calif. Networking Task Force, 1990-95; mem. governing bd. Statewide Calif. Electronic Llbr. Consortium, 2000-01. Sec. Sequoia String Quartet Found., L.A., 1977-87. Capt. USAF, 1968-69. Mem. ALA, Assn. Coll. and Rsch. Librs., Santa Clarita Interlibr. Network (pres. 1989-91), Calif. Pvt. Acad. Librs. (exec. bd. 1988-91, 96—, chmn. 1990), Total Interlibr. Exch. (v.p. 1980-81, pres. 1981-82, chmn. 1983-86, cons. 1983-85), Calif. Libr. Assn., Performing Arts Librs. Network (chmn. 1991), West Hollywood Chorale (exec. com. 1997-98). Avocations: music, computers, hiking. Office: Calif Inst Arts 24700 McBean Pky Santa Clarita CA 91355-2397

GARDNER, GEORGIA ANNE, state legislator; 2 children. Mem. Wash. Senate, Dist. 42, Olympia, 1998—; vice chair transp. com. Wash. Legislature, Olympia, mem. agr. and rural econ. devel. com., mem. commerce, trade, housing and fin. instns. com., vice chair state and local govt. com., mem. legis. transp. com., mem. joint legis. audit and rev. com., mem. joint adminstrv. rules rev. com., mem. Nat. Conf. State Legis. Fed. Budget and Tax. com. Bd. dirs. Bellingham/Whatcom County Conv. and Vis. Bur.; mem. Blaine County Planning Commn.; founding bd. dirs., treas. Computers for Kids; mem. United Meth. Ch.; mem. Blaine City Coun., 1990-97, Whatcom County Charter Rev. Commn., 1995. Recipient Thomas L. George award Blaine Woman of Yr., Westside Record Jour., 1999. Mem. Assn. Wash. Cities, Kiwanis. Democrat. Avocations: water color painting, traveling. Office: 424 John Cherberg Bldg Olympia WA 98504-0001

GARDNER, JAMES HARKINS, venture capitalist; b. Evanston, Ill., July 15, 1943; s. James Floyd and Charlotte (Hoban) G.; m. Shirley Jane Bisset, June 22, 1968 (div. 1980); 1 child, Warren Lee; m. Shannon Lee Greer, Nov. 19, 1982; 1 child, Charlotte Greer. BS, Purdue U., 1965; MBA, Harvard U., 1968. V.p. Geomet, Inc., Rockville, Md., 1970-78; pres. Risk Mgmt. Resources, Inc., San Francisco, 1979-91; COO KinderCare Learning Ctrs., Inc., Montgomery, Ala., 1991-93; pres., COO, dir., Discovery Zone, Inc, 1994-95; mng. gen. ptnr., Media Venture Ptnrs., 1995—; CEO HBS Funding, Inc. dba Great City Traders, 1998—; del. White House Conf. on Small Bus., 1986; treas. No. Calif. With USPHS, 1968-70. Mem. Nat. Fedn. Ind. Bus. (Calif. guardian coun., dir. Calif. polit. action com., fed. liaison 1988-91), Ind. Adminstrs. Assn. (bd. dirs. 1989-91, v.p. 1991), Commonwealth Club Calif. (San Francisco), Masons, Sigma Nu. Office: Great City Traders PO Box 885166 San Francisco CA 94188-5166

GARDNER, JOHN WILLIAM, writer, educator; b. Los Angeles, Oct. 8, 1912; s. William and Marie (Flora) G.; m. Aida Marroquin, Aug. 18, 1934; children: Stephanie Gardner Trimble, Francesca Gardner. A.B., Stanford U., 1935; Ph.D., U. Calif., 1938, LL.D. (hon.), 1959; hon. degrees from various colls., univs.; hon. fellow, Stanford U., 1959. Teaching asst. in psychology U. Calif., 1936-38; instr. psychology Conn. Coll., 1938-40; asst. prof. psychology Mt. Holyoke Coll., 1940-42; head Latin-Am. sect. FCC, 1942-43; mem. staff Carnegie Corp. of N.Y., 1946-47, exec. assoc., 1947-49, v.p., 1949-55, pres., 1955-65, cons., 1968-77; pres. Carnegie Found. Advancement of Teaching, 1955-65; sec. U.S. Dept. HEW, 1965-68; chmn. Urban Coalition, 1968-70; founder and chmn. Common Cause, 1970-77; chmn. Pres.'s Commn. on White House Fellowships, 1977-80; co-founder, chmn. Independent Sector, 1980-83, dir. leadership studies program, 1984-89; Miriam and Peter Haas prof. pub. svc. Stanford (Calif.) U., 1989-96. Cons. prof. Stanford Sch. Edn., 1996—; mem. Pres. Kennedy's Task Force on Edn., 1960; chmn. U.S. Adv. Commn. Internat. Ednl. and Cultural Affairs, 1962-64, Pres. Johnson's Task Force on Edn., 1964, White House Conf. Edn., 1965; dir. N.Y. Telephone Co., 1961-65, Shell Oil Co., 1962-65, Am. Airlines, 1968-71, Time, Inc., 1968-72 Author: Excellence, 1961, rev. edit., 1984, Self-Renewal, 1964, rev. edit, 1981, No Easy Victories, 1968, The Recovery of Confidence, 1970, In Common Cause, 1972, Morale, 1978, On Leadership, 1990; editor: To Turn the Tide (John F. Kennedy); co-editor: Know or Listen to Those Who Know, 1975, reissued as Quotations of Wit and Wisdom, 1980. Chmn. Nat. Civic League, 1994-96; trustee N.Y. Sch. Social Work, 1949-55, Met. Mus. Art, 1957-65, Stanford U., 1968-82, Rockefeller Bros. Fund, 1968-77, Jet Propulsion Lab., 1978-82, Enterprise Found., 1982-91. Served to capt. USMC, 1943-46. Recipient USAF Exceptional Svcs. award, 1956; Presdl. Medal of Freedom, 1964; Nat. Acad. Scis. Pub. Welfare medal, 1966; U.A.W. Social Justice award, 1968; Eem. Legacy award Anti-Defamation League, 1968; AFL-CIO Murray Green medal, 1970. Office: Stanford Sch Edn Stanford CA 94305-3084

GARDNER, MURRAY BRIGGS, pathologist, educator; b. Lafayette, Ind., Oct. 5, 1929; s. Max William and Margaret (Briggs) G.; m. Alice E. Danielson, June 20, 1961; children: Suzanna, Martin, Danielson, Andrew. B.A., U. Calif., Berkeley, 1951; M.D., U. Calif., San Francisco, 1954. Intern Moffitt Hosp., San Francisco, 1954-55; resident in gen. practice Sonoma County Hosp., Santa Rosa, Calif., 1957-59; resident in pathology U. Calif. hosps., San Francisco, 1959-63; faculty U. So. Calif. Sch. Medicine, Los Angeles, 1963-81, prof. pathology, 1973-81, U. Calif., Davis Sch. Medicine, 1981—, chmn. dept. pathology, 1982-90. Contbr. chpts. to books, numerous articles in field to profl. jours. Served to lt. M.C. USNR, 1957-59. NIH grantee, 1968— Fellow AAAS; mem. Coll. Am. Pathologists, Internat. Acad. Pathology. Home: 8313 Maxwell Ln Dixon CA 95620-9662 Office: Ctr of Comparative Medicine U Calif Davis Davis CA 95616 E-mail: mbgardner@ucdavis.edu

GARDNER, SHERYL PAIGE, gynecologist; b. Bremerton, Wash., Jan. 24, 1945; d. Edwin Gerald and Dorothy Elizabeth (Herman) G.; m. James Alva Beat, June 20, 1986. BA in Biology, U. Oreg., 1967, MD cum laude, 1971. Diplomate Am. Bd. Ob-Gyn. Intern L.A. County Harbor Gen. Hosp., Torrance, Calif., 1971-72, resident in ob-gyn., 1972-75; physician Group Health Assn., Washington, 1975-87; pvt. practice Mililani, Hawaii, 1987—. Med. staff sec. Wahiawa (Hawaii) Gen. Hosp., 1994-95. Mem. Am. Coll. Ob-Gyn., Am. Soc. Colposcopy and Cervical Pathology, Hawaii Med. Assn., N.Am. Menopause Soc., Sigma Kappa, Alpha Omega Alpha. Democrat. Avocation: supporter numerous environ., peace and social concern groups. Office: 95-1249 Meheula Pkwy Ste B10A Mililani HI 96789-1763

GARDNER, WILFORD ROBERT, physicist, educator; b. Logan, Utah, Oct. 19, 1925; s. Robert and Nellie (Barker) G.; m. Marjorie Louise Cole, June 9, 1949; children: Patricia, Robert, Caroline. BS, Utah State U., 1949; MS, Iowa State U., 1951, PhD, 1953. Physicist U.S. Salinity Lab., Riverside, Calif., 1953-66; prof. U. Wis., Madison, 1966-80; physicist, prof., head dept. soil and water sci. U. Ariz., Tucson, 1980-87; dean coll. natural resources U. Calif., Berkeley, 1987-94; dean emeritus, 1994—; adj. prof. Utah State U., 1995—. Author: Soil Physics, 1972. Served with U.S. Army, 1943-46. NSF sr. fellow, 1959; Fulbright fellow, 1971-72. Fellow AAAS, Am. Soc. Agronomy; mem. Internat. Soil Sci. Soc. (pres. physics commn. 1968-74), Soil Sci. Soc. Am. (pres. 1990, Rsch. award 1962), Nat. Acad. Scis.

GARDOM, GARDE BASIL, lieutenant governor of British Columbia; b. Banff, Alta., Can., July 17, 1924; s. Basil and Gabrielle Gwladys (Bell) G.; m. Theresa Helen Eileen Mackenzie, Feb. 11, 1956; children: Kim Gardom Allen, Karen Gardom MacDonald, Edward, Brione Gardom MacDonald, Brita Gardom McLaughlin. BA, LLB, U. B.C., Vancouver, 1949. Bar: called to bar 1949. With Campbell, Brazier & Co., 1949; sr. partner Gardom & Co., Vancouver, 1960-75; apptd. Queen's Counsel, 1975; mem. B.C. Legis. Assembly for Vancouver-Point Grey, B.C., 1966-87; atty. gen. B.C., 1975-79; min. intergovtl. rels., 1979-86; policy cons. Office of Premier, 1986-87; agt. gen. for B.C. London, 1987-92; mem. Premier's Econ. Adv. Coun., 1988-91; apptd. lt.-gov. B.C., 1995—. Dir. Crown Life Ins. Co., 1993-95. Named to B.C. Sports Hall of Fame, 1995; named Freeman of City of London, 1992; hon. col. British Columbia Regiment. Mem. Can. Bar Assn., B.C. Law Soc., Vancouver Lawn Tennis and Badminton Club, Union Club of B.C., Royal Overseas Club, Phi Delta Theta. Anglican. Office: Govt House 1401 Rockland Ave Victoria BC Canada V8S 1V9

GAREY, DONALD LEE, pipeline and oil company executive; b. Ft. Worth, Sept. 9, 1931; s. Leo James and Jessie (McNatt) G.; m. Elizabeth Patricia Martin, Aug. 1, 1953; children: Deborah Anne, Elizabeth Laird. BS in Geol. Engring., Tex. A&M U., 1953. Registered profl. engr., Tex. Reservoir geologist Gulf Oil Corp., 1953-54, sr. geologist, 1956-65; v.p., mng. dir. Indsl. Devel. Corp. Lea County, Hobbs, N.Mex., 1965-72, dir., 1972-86, pres., 1978-86; v.p., dir. Minerals, Inc., Hobbs, 1966-72, pres., dir., 1972-86, CEO, 1978-82; mng. dir. Hobbs Indsl. Found. Corp., 1965-72, dir., 1965-76; v.p. Llano, Inc., 1972-74, exec. v.p., COO, 1974-75, pres., 1975-86, CEO, also dir., 1978-82; pres., CEO Pollution Control, Inc., 1969-81. Pres. NMESCO Fuels, Inc., 1982-86; chmn., pres., CEO Estacado, Inc., 1986—, Natgas Inc., 1987—; pres. Llano Co2, Inc., 1984-86; cons. geologist, geol. engr., Hobbs, 1965-72. Chmn. Hobbs Manpower Devel. Tng. Adv. Com., 1965-72; mem. Hobbs Adv. Com. for Mental Health, 1965-67; chmn. N.Mex. Mapping Adv. Com., 1968-69; mem. Hobbs adv. bd. Salvation Army, 1967-78, chmn., 1970-72; mem. exec. bd. Conquistador coun. Boy Scouts Am., Hobbs, 1965-75; vice chmn. N.Mex. Gov's Com. for Econ. Devel., 1968-70; bd. regents Coll. Southwest, 1982-85. Capt. USAF, 1954-56. Mem. AIPG, AAPG, SPE of AIME. Home: 315 E Alto Dr Hobbs NM 88240-3905 Office: Broadmoor Tower PO Box 5587 Hobbs NM 88241-5587

GARFIELD, ERNEST, bank consultant; b. Colorado River, Ariz., July 14, 1932; s. Emil and Carmen (Ybarra) G.; m. Betty Ann Redden, Apr. 18, 1953; children: Laural, Jeffery Alan. BS, U. Ariz., 1975; B of Internat. Mgmt., Am. Grad. Sch., Phoenix, 1975, M of Internat. Mgmt., 1976. Owner Garfield Ins. Agy., Tucson, 1962-70; senator State of Ariz., Phoenix, 1967-68, dep. treas., 1970-71, treas., 1971-74; commr. Ariz. Corp. Commn., Phoenix, 1974-79; chmn. United Bancorp Systems, Inc., Phoenix, 1979—, Interstate Bank Developers, Inc., Scottsdale, 1994—. Chmn. The White House Conf. on Energy, Com. on Energy Policy of Nat. Assn. Regulatory Utility Commn.; pres. Western Conf. Pub. Svc. Commns.; mem. Ad Hoc Com. on Regulatory Reform, Electric and Nuclear Energy Com. Mem. Ariz. Kidney Found., Multiple Sclerosis Soc., Rep. Senatorial Inner Circle, 1989; mem. Pres. Bush Task Force, 1989; mem. adv. bd. St. Joseph's Hosp., Phoenix; mem. establishment com. Pima County Jr. Coll., Tucson; mem. orgn. com. Pima County Halfway House, Tucson; chmn. Ariz. Gov. Commn. on Rape Prevention, 1988, Nat. Commn. on Rape Prevention, 1990—; commr. Ariz. Gov. Commn. on Violence Against Women, 1993—; active Ariz. Gov.'s Sexual Assault Task Force; dir. Ariz. Sexual Assault Network; bd. dirs. Ariz. Cactus-Pine coun. Girl Scouts U.S.; mem. Men Against Violence Network. With U.S. Army, 1952-55. Recipient Outstanding Young Men Ariz. award, Press Club award; named to U.S. Arty. Hall of Fame, 1999. Mem. Ariz.-Mexican C. of C., Thunderbird Internat. Banking Inst. (mem. adv. coun. 1990—). Republican. Roman Catholic. Avocation: graphology. Home and Office: 8442 N 72nd Pl Scottsdale AZ 85258-2762

GARFIELD, LEONARD, museum director; Archtl. hist. State of Wash., preservation programs coord.; with King County Office Cultural Resources; exec. dir. Mus. History and Industry, Seattle, 1998—. Office: MOHAI 2700 24th Ave E Seattle WA 98112-2031

GARLAND, CEDRIC FRANK, epidemiologist, educator; b. La Jolla, Calif., Nov. 10, 1946; s. Cedric and Eva (Caldwell) Garagliano. BA, U. So. Calif., 1967; MPH, UCLA, 1970, DPH, 1974. Asst. prof. Johns Hopkins U., Balt., 1974-81; prof. Sch. Medicine U. Calif., La Jolla, 1981—. Contbr. chpts. to books, articles to profl. jours. Recipient Aristotle award for acad. excellence UCLA, 1974, Golden Apple award for Tchg. Excellence Johns Hopkins U., 1980, Environ. Health Coalition Disting. Svc. award, 1984, NIH Rsch. Career award, 1982. Fellow Am. Coll. Epidemiology; mem. Physicians for Social Responsibility (chmn. info. resources 1982—), Soc. Epidemiol. Rsch., Sierra Club (chmn. Save Our Shore 1982—, Disting. Achievement award 1984). Roman Catholic. Achievements include work with Dr. Frank Garland and Dr. Edward Gorham who together played a role in establishing the association between deficiency of vitamin D and calcium, and risk of intestinal, breast, and ovarian cancer; this group also played a role in establishing that ultraviolet A is a cause of human melanoma. Office: U Calif Dept 0631C Dept Family & Preventive Medicine 9500 Gilman Dr La Jolla CA 92093-5003

GARLICK, LARRY, executive; BSEE, MSEE, Stanford U. V.p. distributed systems Xerox Corp.; vaious positions including v.p. Sun Microsystems; chmn., pres., CEO Pemedy Corp., Mountain View, Calif., 1990—. Office: 1505 Salado Dr Mountain View CA 94043-1110

GARMANY, CATHARINE DOREMUS, astronomer; b. N.Y.C., Mar. 6, 1946; d. Edwin and Janet (MacMaster) Doremus; children: Richard, Jeffrey. BS, Ind. U., 1966; MS, U. Va., 1968, PhD, 1971. Rsch. assoc. U. Va., Charlottesville, 1971-73; rsch. assoc. Joint Inst. for Lab Astrophys. U. Colo., Boulder, 1977-84, sr. rsch. assoc. Joint Inst. for Lab Astrophys., 1984-2000; dir. Fiske Planetarium, 1991-2000; dir. astronomy Astronomy, Oracle, Ariz., 2000—. Contbr. articles to profl. jours. Recipient Annie J. Cannon award AAUW, AAS, 1976; grantee NASA, NSF. Office: Biosphere 2 Atronomy Bldg 32540 S Biosphere Rd Oracle AZ 85623 E-mail: katy@astro.bio2.edu

GARN, EDWIN JACOB (JAKE GARN), former senator; b. Richfield, Utah, Oct. 12, 1932; s. Jacob Edwin and Fern (Christensen) G.; m. Hazel Rhae Thompson, Feb. 2, 1957 (dec. 1976); children: Jacob Wayne, Susan Rhae, Ellen Marie, Jeffrey Paul; m. Kathleen Brewerton, Apr. 8, 1977; children: Matthew Spencer, Christopher Brook, Jennifer Kathleen. B.S., U. Utah, 1955. City commr., Salt Lake City, 1968-72; mayor Salt Lake City, 1972-74; U.S. Senator from Utah, 1974-93; vice chmn. Huntsman Corp., Salt Lake City, 1993-99; mng. dir. Summit Ventures LLC, Salt Lake City, 1999—. Bd. dirs. Dean Witter InterCapital, N.Y.C., Franklin Covey, Salt Lake City. Served to lt. USNR, 1956-60; brig. gen. Utah Air N.G., 1963-79; payload specialist, space shuttle mission 51D, 1985. Recipient Tom McCoy award Utah League Cities and Towns, 1972, Wright Bros. Meml. trophy, 1992. Mem. Utah League Cities and Towns (pres. 1971-72, dir. 1968—), Nat. League Cities (1st v.p. 1973-74, hon. pres. 1975), Sigma Chi. Mem. LDS Ch. Office: Summit Ventures LLC 1 Utah Ctr #600 201 S Main St Salt Lake City UT 84111-2215

GARNER, CARLENE ANN, fundraising consultant; b. Dec. 17, 1945; d. Carl A. and Ruth E. (Mathison) Timblin; m. Adelbert L. Garner, Feb. 17, 1964; children: Bruce A., Brent A. BA, U. Puget Sound, 1983. Adminstrv. dir. Balletacoma, 1984-87; exec. dir. Tacoma Symphony, 1987-95; prin. New Horizon Cons., Tacoma, 1995-98; co-owner Stewardship Devel., 1998—. Cons. Wash. PAVE, Tacoma, 1983-84. Treas. Coalition for the Devel. of the Arts, 1992-94; pres. Wilson High Sch. PTA, Tacoma, 1983-85; chmn. Tacoma Sch. Vol. Adv. Bd., 1985-87; pres. Emmanuel Luth. Ch., Tacoma, 1984-86, chmn. future steering com., 1987-93; sec.-treas. Tacoma-Narrows Conf., 1987-98; vice chmn. Tacoma Luth. Home, 1996-98; pub. mem. Wash. State Bd. Pharmacy, 1993-98. Mem. N.W. Devel. Officers Assn. (chair Tacoma/Pierce County com. 1994-96), Jr. Women's Club Tacoma (pres. 1975-76, pres. Peninsula dist. 1984-86), Gen. Fedn. Women's Club-Wash. State (treas. 1988-90, 3d v.p. 1990-92, 2d v.p. 1992-94, 1st v.p. 1994-96, pres. 1996-98, Clubwoman of Yr. 1977, Outstanding FREE chmn. Gen. Fedn. 1982), Commencement Bay Woman's Club (pres. 1990-92), Gen. Fedn. of Women's Club (bd. dirs., chair nat. conv. 1995, state pres. 1996-98, chair cmty. improvement program 1998-2000, treas. 2000—). Lutheran. Office: Stewardship Devel 1115 N Cheyenne St Tacoma WA 98406-3624 E-mail: cagarner@mindspring.com

GARNER, DONALD K. lawyer; b. 1944; BS, MBA, U. So. Calif. Bar: Calif. 1971. Ptnr. Bryan Cave LLP, Santa Monica, Calif. Office: Bryan Cave LLP 120 Broadway Ste 500 Santa Monica CA 90401-2386

GARNETT, KATRINA A. information technology executive; b. Brisbane, Australia, Oct. 17, 1961; BS, SUNY; MBA, Webster U., Geneva, Switzerland. CEO, pres. Cross Worlds Software, Burlingame, Calif., 1996—. Office: Cross Worlds Software 577 Airport Blvd Ste 800 Burlingame CA 94010-2024

GAROFALO, DAVID, mayor; Mayor City of Hunting Beach, Calif. Office: City Hall 2000 Main St Huntington Beach CA 92648-2702

GAROFALO, JANEANE, actress, comedienne; b. Newton, N.J., Sept. 28, 1964; BA in History and Am. Studies, Providence Coll. TV appearances include The Ben Stiller Show, 1992-93, The Larry Sanders Show, 1992-97, Saturday Night Live, 1994-95, Comedy Product, 1995, emcee, prodr., (movies) Late for Dinner, 1991, Armistead Maupin's Tales of the City, 1993, Reality Bites, 1994, Bye Bye Love, 1995, Cold Blooded, 1995, The Truth about Cats and Dogs, 1996, HBO 1 Hour Special, 1997; appearances include (films) The Cable Guy, 1996, Larger Than Life, 1996, Sweethearts, 1997, Touch, 1997, Romy and Michele's High School Reunion, 1997, Cop Land, 1997, Clay Pigeons, 1997, The Matchmaker, 1997, Permanent Midnight, 1998, Dog Park, 1998, Half Baked, 1998, Thick as Thieves, 1999, Steal This Movie, 1999, The Minus Man, 1999, Dogma, 1999, Can't Stop Dancing, 1999, 200 Cigarettes, 1999, Mystery Men, 1999. Office: c/o Messina Baker Entertainment 955 Carrillo Dr Ste 100 Los Angeles CA 90048-5400 also: UTA Inc 9560 Wilshire Blvd Fl 5 Beverly Hills CA 90212-2401

GARON, CLAUDE FRANCIS, laboratory administrator, researcher; b. Baton Rouge, Nov. 5, 1942; s. Ivy Joseph and Janith (Latil) G.; m. Sally Sheffield; children: Michele, Anne, Julie. BS, La. State U., 1964, MS, 1966; PhD, Georgetown U., 1970. Predoctoral fellowship La. State U., Baton Rouge, 1964-66; predoctoral traineeship Georgetown U., Washington, 1966-69; postdoctoral fellowship Nat. Inst. Allergy and Inf. Diseases, Bethesda, Md., 1971-73, staff fellowship, 1971-73, sr. staff fellowship, 1973-74, rsch. microbiologist, 1974-81; head electron microscopy Rocky Mountain Labs., Hamilton, Mont., 1981-85, chief pathobiology, 1985-89, chief lab. vectors and pathogens, 1989-94, chief microscopy br., 1994—. Bd. govs. Ctr. Excellence in Biotech., Missoula, Mont., 1988—; faculty affiliate U. Mont., 1989—. Mem. editorial bd. Jour. Clin. Microbiology, 1993; assoc. editor Jour. Spirochetal and Tick-borne Diseases, 1993. Bd. dirs. Internat. Heart Inst. of Mont. Found., 1995. Recipient award of merit NIH, 1979, Dirs. award, 1988, Lyme Disease Found prize, 1996. Mem. Am. Soc. for Microbiology, Am. Soc. Biochemistry and Molecular Biology, Microscopy Soc. Am., Am. Soc. Rickettsiology, Pacific N.W. Electron Microscopy Soc., Lions (pres. Hamilton 1989-90). Office: Rocky Mountain Labs Microscopy Br 903 S 4th St Hamilton MT 59840-2999 E-mail: claude_garon@nih.gov

GARRETT, JAMES JOSEPH, lawyer; b. L.A., Dec. 17, 1939; s. Joseph Robert and Catherine Agnes (Cavanaugh) G.; m. Mary Isabel McNeil, June 22, 1963 (div.); children: Sean, Drew, Craig; m. Maria Pamela Rivera, July 26, 1980; children: Joshua, Matthew. AB, Stanford U., 1961; JD, Harvard U., 1964. Bar: Calif. 1965. Ptnr. Morrison & Foerster, San Francisco, 1966—. Author: Antitrust Compliance, 1978; gen. editor and contbg. author: World Antitrust Law and Practice, 1995; author chpt.: A Guide to Foreign Investment in the United States, 1992. Capt. U.S. Army, 1964-66. Mem. ABA, Calif. Bar Assn. Roman Catholic. Avocations: collecting historical newspapers, running, fly fishing, backpacking. Office: Morrison & Foerster Ste 450 101 Ygnacio Valley Rd Walnut Creek CA 94596-4094

GARRISON, P. GREGORY, diversified financial services company executive; Chmn. entertainment, media and comm., also mng. ptnr. Price Waterhouse L.L.P.-U.S., L.A. Office: Price Waterhouse Cooper 350 S Grand Ave Los Angeles CA 90071-3406

GARRISON, WILLIAM LOUIS, civil engineering educator; b. Nashville, Apr. 20, 1924; s. Sidney Clarence and Sara (Elisabeth) McMurry; s. Marcia Fordyce Stanley, Aug. 31, 1938; children: Sara, Ann, Helen, Deborah, James, Jane, John. BS, Peabody Coll., 1946, MS, 1947; PhD, Northwestern U., 1950. From asst. prof. to prof. dept. geography U. Wash., Seattle, 1950-60; prof. dept. geography, civil engring. Northwestern U., Evanston, Ill., 1960-67, dir. transp. ctr., 1965-67; dir. ctr. for urban studies U. Ill., Chgo., 1967-69; Weidlein Prof. Environ. Engring. U. Pitts., 1969-73; dir. Inst. for Transp. Studies U. Calif., Berkeley, 1973-81, prof. civil engring., 1981—. Cons. U.S. Bur. Pub. Rds., Washington, 1960-68; bd. govs. Regional Sci. Research Inst., Phila., 1964—; adv. com. on econs. NSF, Washington, 1958-63; panel on values of social sci. research Nat. Sci. Bd., Washington, 1963-64. Author: Geographical Impact of Highway Improvements, 1960, Tomorrow's Transportation, 2000; author, editor Jour. Transp. Tech., 1985; editor: Quantitative Geography, 1969; articles in field. Served to capt. USAF, 1943-46. Recipient Disting. award U. Coun. of Transp. Rsch. Ctrs., 1999. Mem. Transp. Research Bd. (chmn. 1972-73, Roy C. Crum award 1973), Regional Sci. Assn. (pres. 1960), ASCE, Assn. Am. Geographers (Outstanding research award 1958), AAAS. E-mial. Home: 10 Rancho Diablo Dr Lafayette CA 94549-2722 Office: U Calif Dept Civil Engring Berkeley CA 94720-0001 E-mail: garrison@newton.berkeley.edu

GARRITY, RODMAN FOX, psychologist, educator; b. Los Angeles, June 10, 1922; s. Lawrence Hitchcock and Margery Fox (Pugh) G.; m. Juanita Daphne Mullan, Mar. 5, 1948; children: Diana Daphne, Ronald Fox. Student, Los Angeles City Coll., 1946-47; B.A., Calif. State U., Los Angeles, 1950; M.A., So. Meth. U., Dallas, 1955; Ed.D., U. So. Calif., 1963. Tchr. elem. sch. Palmdale (Calif.) Sch. Dist., 1952-54; psychologist, prin. Redondo Beach (Calif.) City Schs., 1954-60; asst. dir. ednl. placement lectr., ednl. adviser U. So. Calif., 1960-62; asso. prof., coordinator credentials programs Calif. State Poly. U., Pomona, 1962-66, chmn. social sci. dept., 1966-68, dir. tchr. preparation center, 1968-71, coordinator grad. program, 1971-73, prof. tchr. preparation center, 1968—, coordinator spl. edn. programs, 1979—. Cons. psychologist, lectr. in field. Pres. Redondo Beach Coordinating Council, 1958-60; mem. univ. rep. Calif. Faculty Assns., 1974-76. Served with Engr. Combat Bn. AUS, 1942-45. Mem. Prins. Assn. Redondo Beach (chmn. 1958-60), Nat. Congress Parents and Tchrs. (hon. life), Am. Psychol. Assn., Calif. Tchrs. Assn. Democrat. Office: Calif State U Dept Special Edn Pomona CA 91768

GARRUTO, JOHN ANTHONY, cosmetics executive; b. Johnson City, N.Y., June 18, 1952; children: James, Christopher, Catherine, Gabrielle. BS in Chemistry, SUNY, Binghamton, 1974; AAS in Bus. Adminstrn., Broome Coll., 1976. Rsch. chemist Lander Co. Inc., Binghamton, 1974-77, rsch. dir. St. Louis, 1977-79, Olde Worlde Products, High Point, N.C., 1979-81; v.p. rsch. and devel. LaCosta Products Internat., Carlsbad, Calif., 1981-89; chief ops. officer Randall Products Internat., Carlsbad, 1989-91; pres. Dermasearch Internat., 1991-92; chief tech. officer Innovative Bioscis. Corp., Oceanside, Calif., 1992-95; v.p. rsch. Garden Botanika, Oceanside, 1995-99; pres., founder Free Radical Tech., 1999—. Cons. Trans-Atlantic Mktg., Binghamton, 1975-78; instr. cosmetic sci UCLA, 1991—, UCLA Ext.; lectr. to cosmetic industry. Patentee in field. Mem. AAS, Soc. Cosmetic Chemists (newsletter editor 1980-81, publicity chmn. 1984—, edn. chmn. 1987, employment chmn. 1994—, chmn. elect 1999-00, chmn. 2000, nat. elections com. 2001), Inst. for Food Technologists (sec. beauty industry west), Pacific Tech. Exch., Fedn. Am. Scientists, N.Y. Acad. Scis.

GARRY, JAMES B. historian, naturalist, storyteller, writer; b. Taylor, Tex., Apr. 28, 1947; s. Mahon Barker and Grace (Dellinger) G. BS, U. Mich., 1970, MS, 1975. Part-time wilderness guide, naturalist Triangle X Ranch, Moose, Wyo., 1969-75; community organizer, media cons., tchr. Hobart St. Project, Detroit, 1974-75; media specialist, lobbyist Powder River Basin Resource Coun., Sheridan, Wyo., 1975-76; pvt. practice media and polit. cons. Big Horn, 1976-78; video and film artist-in-residence Wyo. Coun. on the Arts/Sheridan Coll., Sheridan, 1978-80; mem. staff Great Plains Lore and Natural History, Big Horn, 1980—. Storyteller Buffalo Bill Hist. Ctr., Cody, Wyo., 1980—; tchr. Yellowstone (Wyo.) Inst., summers 1986—; tour study leader, rsch. collaborator Smithsonian Instn., Washington, 1984—. Co-author: Writing About Wildlife, 1974; author, editor. Buck: Stories by Lloyd Buck Bender, 1984, This Ol' Drought Ain't Broke Us Yet But We're All Bent Pretty Bad, 1992, The First Liar Never Has a Chance: Curly, Jack and Bill (and Other Characters of the Hills, Brush and Plains), 1994; storyteller in field. 2d lt. U.S. Army, 1970. Recipient Spl. Heritage award Old West Trail Found., 1983; named one of Individual Humanist of Yr., Wyo. Coun. for Humanities, 1986. Democrat. Roman Catholic. Avocation: nature. Home: PO Box 2165 Cody WY 82414-2165 Office: Great Plains Lore & Natural History PO Box 2165 Cody WY 82414-2165

GARSH, THOMAS BURTON, publisher; b. New Rochelle, N.Y., Dec. 12, 1931; s. Harry and Matilda (Smith) G.; m. Beatrice J. Schmidt; children: Carol Jean, Thomas Burton, Janice Lynn. B.S., U. Md., 1955. Edn. rep. McGraw Hill Book Co., N.Y.C., 1959-68; mktg. mgr. D.C. Heath & Co., Boston, 1969-71; dir. mktg. Economy Co., Oklahoma City, 1971-72; sr. v.p. Macmillan Pub. Co., N.Y.C., 1972-78; pres. Am. Book Co., N.Y.C., 1978-81; founder, pres., dir. Am. Ednl. Computer, Inc., Palo Alto, Calif., 1981-86. Founder, chmn., chief exec. officer OmnyEd Corp., Palo Alto, 1987-91; pres. Silver Burdett & Ginn divsn. of Simon and Schuster, 1991-92; dir. Fifty Plus Fitness Assn., Palo Alto, Calif. Publ. Homes and Land of Santa Clara, 1998—. Mem. county council Boy Scouts Am., 1963-65; mem. ch. council on Interracial Affairs, 1966-68, pres., 1967; vice-chmn. Madison County Democratic Party, 1967. Mem. Assn. Am. Pubs., Profl. Bookman's Assn., Omicron Delta Kappa, Sigma Alpha Epsilon. Club: Cazenovia Country (founder). Home: 401 Old Spanish Trl Portola Valley CA 94028

GARSTANG, ROY HENRY, astrophysicist, educator; b. Southport, Eng., Sept. 18, 1925; came to U.S., 1964; s. Percy Brocklehurst and Eunice (Gledhill) G.; m. Ann Clemence Hawk, Aug. 11, 1959; children: Jennifer Katherine, Susan Veronica. B.A., U. Cambridge, 1946, M.A., 1950, Ph.D., 1954, Sc.D., 1983. Research assoc. U. Chgo., 1951-52; lectr. astronomy U. Coll., London, 1952-60; reader astronomy U. London, 1960-64, asst. dir. Obs., 1959-64; prof. astrophysics U. Colo., Boulder, 1964-94, chair faculty assembly, 1988-89, prof. emeritus, 1994—; chmn. Joint Inst. for Lab. Astrophysics, 1966-67. Cons. Nat. Bur. Standards, 1964-73; v.p. commn. 14 Internat. Astron. Union, 1970-73, pres., 1973-76; Erskine vis. fellow U. Canterbury, N.Z., 1971; vis. prof. U. Calif., Santa Cruz, 1971. Editor: Observatory, 1953-60; Contbr. numerous articles to tech. jours. Recipient Excellence in Svc. award U. Colo., 1990 Fellow Am. Phys. Soc., AAAS, Optical Soc. Am., Brit. Inst. Physics, Royal Astron. Soc.; mem. Am. Astron. Soc., Royal Soc. Scis. Liege (Belgium). Achievements include rsch. on atomic physics and astrophys. applications; calculation of atomic transition probabilities, atomic spectra in very high magnetic fields and magnetic white dwarf stars; modelling of light pollution. Home: 830 8th St Boulder CO 80302-7409 Office: U Colo Boulder CO 80309-0440 E-mail: garstang@earthlink.net

GARTNER, HAROLD HENRY, III, lawyer; b. L.A., June 23, 1948; s. Harold Henry Jr. and Frances Mildred (Evans) G.; m. Denise Helene Young, June 7, 1975; children: Patrick Christopher, Matthew Alexander. Student, Pasadena City Coll., 1966-67, George Williams Coll., 1967-68, Calif. State U., Los Angeles, 1969; JD cum laude, Loyola U., Los Angeles, 1972. Bar: Calif. 1972, U.S. Dist. Ct. (cen. dist.) Calif. 1973, U.S. Ct. Appeals (9th cir.) 1973. Assoc. Hitt, Murray & Caffray, Long Beach, Calif., 1972; dep. city atty. City of L.A., 1972-73; assoc. Patterson, Ritner & Lockwood, L.A., 1973-79; mng. ptnr. all offices Patterson, Ritner, Lockwood, Gartner & Jurich, L.A., Ventura, Bakersfield, and San Bernardino, Calif., 1991—. Instr. law Ventura Coll., 1981. Recipient Am. Jurisprudence award Trusts and Equity, 1971. Mem. ABA, Am. Bd. Trial Advocates, Calif. Bar Assn., Ventura County Bar Assn., Nat. Assn. Def. Counsel, Assn. Am. Bd. Trial Advocates, So. Calif. Def. Counsel, Ventura County Trial Lawyers Assn. Republican. Club: Pacific Corinthian Yacht. Avocations: sailing, scuba diving, flying. Home: 6900 Via Alba Camarillo CA 93012-8279 Office: Patterson Ritner Lockwood Gartner & Jurich 260 Maple Ct Ste 231 Ventura CA 93003-3570 E-mail: hgartner@dock.net

GARVENS, ELLEN JO, art educator, artist; b. Omro, Wis., Aug. 15, 1955; d. Leonard Kenneth and Eugenia Mary (Wetter) G.; m. James Patrick Phalen, Oct. 18, 1988; children: Cole Garvens Phalen, Mason Garvens Phalen. BS in Art, U. Wis., 1979; MA, U. N. Mex., 1982, MFA, 1987. Asst. prof. of art Oberlin (Ohio) Coll., 1990-94; assoc. prof. art U. Wash., Seattle, 1994—. Artist: one person shows include: Humboldt State, 2000, Jayne H. Baum Gallery, N.Y.C., 1986, 89, 93, Wooster (Ohio) Mus. of Art, U. R.I., Kingston. Recipient Wis. Women in Arts award Madison, 1978, Fullbright Hays scholarship Internat. Comm. Agy., Washington, 1979-80; grantee, NEA, Washington, 1986, HC Powers grant, Oberlin Coll., 1991, Royalty Rsch. Fund grant, U. Wash., 1996, Artist Trust Washington State fellowship, 2000—. Home: 19518 67th Ave NE Kenmore WA 98028-3447 Office: U Wash Sch of Art PO Box 353440 Seattle WA 98195-3440 E-mail: elgarv@u.washington.edu

GARVEY, DANIEL CYRIL, mechanical engineer; b. Chgo., Nov. 25, 1940; s. Cyril and Genei Marie (McCarthy) G; children: Michael Daniel, Erin T. BSME, Marquette U., Milw., 1963; MSME, IIT, Chgo., 1965. With Kearney & Trecker Corp., Milw., 1960-63, A C Electronics div. Gen. Mtrs. Corp., Milw., 1965-68; vibration and control sys. engr. Woodward Governor Co., Ft. Collins, Colo., 1970-99; cons. engr. DCG Power Systems, 1999—. Reviewer tech. papers IEEE, 1980—; contbr. articles to profl. jours.; patentee in field. Recipient Arch T. Colwell Merit award, SAE, 1984, Internal Combustion Engine award ASME, 1990. Mem. IEEE (sr.), Soc. Automotive Engrs., Instrument Soc. Am. Home: 5205 Mail Creek Ln Fort Collins CO 80525-3812

GARVEY, JOANNE MARIE, lawyer; b. Oakland, Calif., Apr. 23, 1935; d. James M. and Marian A. (Dean) G. AB with honors, U. Calif., Berkeley, 1956, MA, 1957, JD, 1961. Bar: Calif. bar 1962. Assoc. firm Cavaletto, Webster, Mullen & McCaughey, Santa Barbara, Calif., 1961-63, Jordan, Keeler & Seligman, San Francisco, 1963-67, ptnr., 1968-88, Heller, Ehrman, White & McAuliffe, 1988—. Bd. dirs. Mexican-Am. Legal Def. and Ednl. Fund; chmn. Law in a Free Soc., Continuing Edn. of Bar; mem. bd. councillors U. So. Calif. Law Center. Recipient Paul Veazy award YMCA, 1973, Internat. Women's Yr. award Queen's Bench, 1975, honors Advs. for Women, 1978, CRLA award, Boalt Hall Citation award, 1998, Judge Lowell Jensen Cmty. Svc. award, 2001. Fellow Am. Bar Found.; mem. ABA (gov., state del., chmn. SCLAID, chmn. delivery of legal svcs.), Calif. State Bar (v.p., gov., tax sect., del., Jud Klein award, Joanne Garvey award), San Francisco Bar Assn. (pres., pres. Barristers), Am. Law Inst., Calif. Women Lawyers (founder), Order of Coif, Phi Beta Kappa. Democrat. Roman Catholic. Home: 16 Kensington Ct Kensington CA 94707-1010 Office: 333 Bush St San Francisco CA 94104-2806 E-mail: jgarvey@hewm.com

GARY, JAMES FREDERICK, business and energy advising company executive; b. Chgo., Dec. 28, 1920; s. Rex Inglis and Mary Naomi (Roller) G.; m. Helen Elizabeth Gellert, Sept. 3, 1947; children: David Frederick, John William, James Scott, Mary Anne. BS, Haverford (Pa.) Coll., 1942. With Wash. Energy Co. and predecessors, Seattle, 1947-67; v.p. Wash. Energy Co., 1956-67; pres., CEO Pacific Resources Inc., Honolulu, 1967-79, chmn., CEO, 1979-84, chmn., 1985, chmn. emeritus, 1986—, internat. bus. and energy advisor, 1987-2001. Chmn. bd. dirs. Inter Island Petroleum, Inc.; bd. dirs. The Salk Inst. Coun., La Jolla, Dole Food Co., Inc. Mem. Pacific Coast Gas Assn., 1965-75, pres., 1974-75; pres. Chief Seattle coun. Boy Scouts Am., 1966-67, Aloha coun., 1973-74, mem. nat. coun., 1964—, v.p. Western region, 1978-85, pres., 1985-91, also bd. dirs.; chmn. Aloha United Way, 1978, pres., 1979-80, chmn., 1980; mem. bd. regents U. Hawaii, 1981-89; trustee Hawaii Loa Coll., 1968-85, Linfield Coll., McMinnville, Oreg., 1983-89; mem. bd. mgrs. Haverford Coll., 1983-92; bd. dirs. Rsch. Corp. of U. Hawaii, 1971-77, chmn., 1974-77, Hawaii Ednl. Coun.; bd. dirs., officer, trustee Oahu Devel. Conf., Hawaii Employers Coun., Friends of East-West Ctr., Honolulu Symphony Soc., East-West Ctr. Internat. Found.; chmn. Hawaii Comty. Found., 1987-92, mem. bd. govs., 1987-94; mem. bd. regents Chaminade U., 1991-93. Capt. AUS, 1942-46. Recipient Pres.' trophy Pacific Gas Assn., 1960, Disting. Eagle award Boy Scouts Am., 1972, Silver Beaver award, 1966, Silver Antelope award, 1976, Silver Buffalo award, 1988. Mem. Am. Gas Assn. (bd. dirs. 1970-74), Nat. LP-Gas Assn. (bd. dirs. 1967-70), Am. Petroleum Inst., Inst. Gas Tech. (trustee 1975-86), Hawaii Econ. Coun., Nat. Petroleum Coun., Hawaii Dist. Export Coun., Japan-Hawaii Econ. Coun., U.S Nat. Com. for Pacific Econ. Cooperation, Pacific Basin Econ. Coun. (chmn. U.S. com. 1985-86), Japan-Am. Soc. Honolulu, Ctr. for Strategic and Internat. Studies-Pacific Forum, Honolulu Commn. on Fgn. Rels., Hawaii C. of C. (chmn. 1979). Episcopalian. Clubs: Pacific Union (San Francisco); Oahu Country, Waialae Country, Outrigger Canoe, Pacific, Plaza (Honolulu); Seattle Tennis, Wash. Athletic Rainier (Seattle)

GARZA, ELIZEO, director solid waste management, Tucson; b. Chgo., July 21, 1951; BA, U. Tex., 1972; MEd, Antioch U., 1976. Asst. dir. neighborhood ctr. City of Tucson, 1974-79, planner, dep. asst. dir., 1979-93, dir. solid waste mgmt., 1993—. Mem. Solid Waste Assn. N. Am.. Office: City Tucson Office Solid Waste Mgmt PO Box 27210 Tucson AZ 85726-7210

GARZA, OSCAR, newspaper editor; Daily calendar editor-arts L.A. Times, Calif. Office: Los Angeles Times Times Mirror Sq Los Angeles CA 90053

GASICH, WELKO ELTON, retired aerospace executive, management consultant; b. Cupertino, Calif., Mar. 28, 1922; s. Elija J. and Catherine (Paviso) G.; m. Patricia Ann Gudgel, Dec. 28, 1973; 1 child, Mark David A.B. cum laude in Mech. Engring. (Bacon scholar), Stanford U., 1943, M.S. in Mech. Engring., 1947, cert. in fin. and econs. (Sloan exec. fellow), 1967; Aero. Engr., Calif. Inst. Tech., 1948. Aerodynamicist Douglas Aircraft Co., 1943-44, supr. aeroelastics, 1947-51; chief aero design Rand Corp., 1951-53; chief preliminary design aircraft divsn. Northrop Corp., Los Angeles, 1953-56, dir. advanced systems, 1956-61, v.p., asst. gen. mgr. tech., 1961-66, corp. v.p., gen. mgr. Northrop Ventura divsn., 1967-71, corp. v.p., gen. mgr. aircraft divsn., 1971-76, corp. v.p., group exec. aircraft group, 1976-79, sr. v.p. advanced projects, 1979-85, exec. v.p. programs, 1985-88, ret., 1988; aerospace cons. Encino, Calif., 1988—. Author: 40 Years of Ferrari V-12 Engines, 1990; patentee in field. Chmn. adv. council Stanford Sch. Engring., 1981-83; past mem. adv. council Stanford Grad. [illegible] United Way, 1964; chmn. Scout O Rama Los Angeles council Boy Scouts Am., 1964; chmn. explorer scout exec. com., 1963-64. Served to lt. USN, 1944-46 Fellow AIAA, Soc. Automotive Engrs.; mem. NAE, Navy League, Stanford Grad. Sch. Bus. Alumni Assn. (pres. 1971), Conquistadores del Cielo Club, Bel Air Country Club. Republican. Office: 3517 Caribeth Dr Encino CA 91436-4103

GASKILL, HERBERT LEO, accountant, engineer; b. Seattle, July 1, 1923; s. Leo Dell and Vesta Rathbone (Dahlen) G.; m. Margaret Helen Jenkins, Mar. 1, 1944 (div.); children: Margaret V., Herbert Leo; m. Opal Jordan, June 13, 1992; 1 child, Ann. BS, MSChE, U. Wash., 1949, MBA, 1976. CPA, Wash. Asst. prof. and exec. officer dental materials Sch. Dentistry, U. Wash., 1950-56; ops. analyst The Boeing Co., Seattle, 1958-71, mktg. cons. govt. programs, 1972-74; pvt. practice acctg. Seattle, 1976-80; hazardous waste mgr. Boeing Co., Seattle, 1980-86; project mgr. Western Processing Remediation, 1986-95; ret., 1995. Contbr. articles to profl. jours. Active Seattle Art Mus., Pacific N.W. Aviation Hist. Found. Lt. (j.g.) USNR, 1941-46. TAPPI fellow, 1956, U. Wash. Engring. Exptl. Sta. fellow, 1957. Mem. Wash. Soc. CPAs. Home: 1236 NE 92nd St Seattle WA 98115-3135

GAST, NANCY LOU, retired chemical company executive; b. Appleton, Wis., Aug. 13, 1941; d. Harvey William Gast and June Louella (Mohr) Webster. Med. technologist Palo Alto/Stanford (Calif.) Hosp., 1963-65, St. Vincent Hosp., Portland, Oreg., 1965-70, chemistry supr., 1970-81; tech. rep. DuPont-Diagnostic Systems, Claremont, Calif., 1981-83, sales rep. Wilmington, Del., 1983-85, account rep. Claremont, Calif., 1985-87, acct. mgr., 1987-96, exec. coun. med. products sales, 1995-96, territory mgr., 1996; account rep. Dade Internat., Inc., Deerfield, Ill., 1996-98. Bd. dirs. Housecall Providers, Inc. Vol. med. technologist Health Help Ctr., Portland, 1984-88; bd. dirs. Assocs. ofSisters of Holy Names of Jesus and Mary, 1984-93, co-dir, 1994—; bd. dirs. Housecall Providers, Inc., 2000—. Mem. Am. Soc. Med. Technologists, Assn. Oreg. Med. Technologists (treas. 1976-78, chmn. sci. assembly for industry 1992-95), Am. Soc. Clin. Pathologists (cert. med. technologist assoc.). Republican. Roman Catholic. Office: 5727 SW Corbett Ave Portland OR 97201-3705

GASTIL, RUSSELL GORDON, geologist, educator; b. San Diego, June 25, 1928; s. Russell Chester and Frances (Duncan) G.; m. Emily Janet Manly, Sept. 13, 1958; children— Garth Manly, Mary Margaret, George Christopher, John Webster. A.B, U. Calif. at Berkeley, 1950, Ph.D., 1954. With Shell Oil Co., 1954, Canadian Javelin Co., 1956-58; lectr. U. Calif. at Los Angeles, 1958-59; faculty San Diego State U., 1959—, prof. geology, 1965—, chmn. dept., 1969-72. Publisher: We Can Save San Diego, 1975; Contbr. papers to profl. lit. Democratic candidate U.S. Ho. of Reps., 1976; mem. Calif. Dem. Central Com., 1977-78; coordinator 41st Congl. dist. Common Cause, 1977; pres. Grossmont-Mt. Helix Improvement Assn., 1978-80; mem. San Diego County Air Pollution Hearing Bd., 1977-80. Fellow Geol. Soc. Am. (vice chmn. Cordilleran sect. 1967, gen. chmn. ann. meeting San Diego 1991); mem. AAAS, Soc. Econ. Mineralogists and Paleontologists, Am. Geophys. Union. Home: 9435 Alto Dr La Mesa CA 91941-4226 Office: San Diego State U Dept Geol Scis San Diego CA 92182

GATES, BILL (III WILLIAM HENRY GATES), software company executive; b. Seattle, Oct. 28, 1955; s. William H. and Mary M. (Maxwell) G.; m. Melinda French, January 1, 1994. Grad. high sch., Seattle, 1973; student, Harvard U., 1973-75. With MITS, from 1975; founder, chmn. bd. Microsoft Corp., Redmond, Wash., 1976-99, former chief exec. officer, 1999—, chief software architect, 1999—. Author: The Future, 1994, The Road Ahead, 1995, Business at the Speed of Thought, 1999. Recipient Howard Vollum award, Reed Coll., Portland, Oreg., 1984, Nat. medal Tech. U.S. Dept. Commerce Tech. Adminstrn., 1992; named CEO of Yr., Chief Executive mag., 1994. Office: Microsoft Corp 1 Microsoft Way Redmond WA 98052-8300

GATES, BRUCE CLARK, chemical engineer, educator; b. Richmond, Calif., July 5, 1940; s. George Laurence and Frances Genevieve (Wilson) G.; m. Jutta M. Reichert, July 17, 1967; children: Robert Clark, Andrea Margarete. BS, U. Calif., Berkeley, 1961; PhD in Chem. Engring., U. Wash., 1966. Rsch. engr. Chevron Rsch. Co., Richmond, Calif., 1967-69; from asst. prof. to assoc. prof. U. Del., Newark, 1969-77, prof. chem. engring., 1977-85, H. Rodney Sharp prof., 1985-92, assoc. dir. Ctr. Catalytic Sci. & Tech., 1977-81, dir. Catalytic Ctr. Sci. & Tech., 1981-88; prof. chem. engring. U. Calif., Davis, 1992—. Author: Catalytic Chemistry, 1992; co-author: Chemistry of Catalytic Processes, 1979; co-editor: Metal Clusters in Catalysis, 1986, Surface Organometallic Chemistry, 1988, Advances in Catalysis, 1996—. Fulbright Rsch. grantee Inst. Phys. Chemistry U. Munich, 1966-67, 75-76, 83-84, 90-91; recipient Sr. Rsch. award Humboldt Found., U. Munich, 1998, Sr. Humboldt Found. fellow Inst. Phys. Chemistry, U. Munich, 1998-99. Mem. AIChE (Alpha Chi Sigma award 1989, William H. Walker award 1995), Am. Chem. Soc. (Del. sect. award 1985, Petroleum Chemistry award 1993), Catalysis Soc. N.Am. (bd. dirs. 1997—). Achievements include research in catalysis, surface chemistry and reaction kinetics, chemical reaction engineering, petroleum and petrochemical proccesses, catalysis by solid acids, zeolites, soluble and supported transition-metal complexes and clusters, catalytic hydroprocessing. Office: U Calif Dept Chem Engring & Materials Sci Davis CA 95616 E-mail: bcgates@ucdavis.edu

GATES, CHARLES CASSIUS, rubber company executive; b. Morrison, Colo., May 27, 1921; s. Charles Cassius and Hazel LaDora (Rhoads) G.; m. June Scowcroft Swaner, Nov. 26, 1943; children: Diane, John Swaner. Student, MIT, 1939-41; BS, Stanford U., 1943; DEng (hon.), Mich. Tech. U., 1975, Colo. Sch. of Mines, 1985. With Copolymer Corp., Baton Rouge, 1943-46; with Gates Rubber Co., Denver, 1946-96, v.p., 1951-58, exec. v.p., 1958-61, chmn. bd., 1961-96, CEO; chmn. bd. The Gates Corp., Denver, 1982-96, CEO, 1982-96, also bd. dirs., pres., 1994-96; chmn. Cody Co., Denver, 1996—, Gates Capital Mgmt., LLC, Denver, 1996—. Bd. trustees Gates Found. Trustee Denver Mus. Natural History, Calif. Inst. Tech., Pasadena, Denver Art Mus. Found., Graland Country Day Sch. Found. Recipient Cmty. Leadership and Svc. award Nat. Jewish Hosp., 1974; Mgmt. Man of Year award Nat. Mgmt. Assn., 1965; named March of Dimes Citizen of the West, 1987; inductee Colo. Bus. Hall of Fame, 1998. Mem. Conf. Bd. (dir.), Conquistadores del Cielo, Denver Country Club, Outrigger Canoe Club, Waialae Country Club, Boone and Crockett Club, Club Ltd., Old Baldy Club, Country Club of Colo., Roundup Riders of Rockies, Shikar-Safari Internat., Augusta Nat. Golf Club, Castle Pines Golf Club, The Wigwam Club. Office: Cody Co Ste 680 3773 Cherry Creek North Dr Denver CO 80209-3816

GATES, MILO SEDGWICK, retired construction company executive; b. Omaha, Apr. 25, 1923; s. Milo Talmage and Virginia (Offutt) G.; m. Anne Phleger, Oct. 14, 1950 (dec. Apr. 1987); children: Elena Motlow, Susan Gates Suman, Virginia Lewis, Anne Symington, Milo T.; m. Robin Templeton Quist, June 18, 1988; stepchildren: Robert L. Quist, Catherine Brisbin, Sarah Mazzocco. Student, Calif. Inst. Tech., 1943-44; B.S., Stanford U., 1944, MBA, 1948. With Swinerton & Walberg Co., San Francisco, 1955—, pres., 1976—, chmn., 1988-96, ret. Bd. dirs., trustee Children's Hosp. San Francisco; trustee Grace Cathedral, San Francisco; bd. dirs. Calif. Acad. Scis. Lt. (j.g.), USNR, 1944-46. Mem. Pacific-Union Club, Bohemian Club. Republican. Home: 7 Vineyard Hill Rd Woodside CA 94062-2531

GATES, MIMI GARDNER, museum administrator; Dir. Seattle Art Mus. Wash. Office: Seattle Art Mus PO Box 22000 Seattle WA 98122-9700

GATES, SUSAN INEZ, magazine publisher; b. San Francisco, Jan. 14, 1956; d. Milo Sedgwick and Anne (Phelger) G. BA in English/French magna cum laude, U. Colo., 1978; MS in Journalism, Columbia U., 1983. With GEO Mag., N.Y.C., 1978-79, New York Mag., N.Y.C., 1981-82; dir. Ladd Assocs., N.Y.C., 1983-85, McNamee Cons., N.Y.C., 1986-88; founding pub. BUZZ mag., L.A., 1989-97; co-chmn. Mind Over Media, Sherman Oaks, Calif., 1997—. Contbg. writer San Francisco Chronicle and Examiner Book Rev., 1983-86. So. Calif. adv. bd. Natural Resources Def. Coun., L.A., 1989-96. Mem. Advt. Club of L.A. (bd. dirs. 1995-98), Phi Beta Kappa. E-mail: sgates@cncdsl.com

GATTI, JIM, editor; b. Detroit, July 4, 1943; m. Carol A. Gatti; children: Theresa, Julie, Thomas, John. BA in English, Wayne State U., 1966. News editor Detroit News, city editor, asst. mng. editor, dep. mng. editor; editor Honolulu Advertiser, 1995—. With U.S. Army, 1966-68. Recipient Silver Gavel, ABA, Robert F. Kennedy Pub. Svc. award. Office: Honolulu Advertiser 605 Kapiolani Blvd Honolulu HI 96813-5129

GAUFF, LISA, broadcast journalist; b. Seattle; d. Joseph F. and Patricia A. (Lee) G. BA in Comm., U. Wash., 1987; MA in Journalism & Pub. Affairs, Am. U., 1988. Pub. info. asst. King County Coun., Seattle, 1985-86; reporter Sta. KUOW-FM, Seattle, 1985-86; news anchor Sta. KCMU-FM, Seattle, 1986-87; TV field prodr. Group W/Newsfeed Network, Washington, 1988-89; anchor, reporter Capitol TV, Washington, 1989-90, Newschannel 8, Washington, 1991-93; prodr., writer Sta. WJLA-TV, Washington, 1990-91; weekend anchor Sta. WHTM-TV, Harrisburg, Pa., 1993-94; morning anchor Sta. WJW-TV, Cleve., 1994-97; traffic anchor Sta. KNX-AM, L.A., 1998—. Freelance reporter KCBS-TV, KABC-TV, UPN-TV, Fox TV, Sunworld, Satellite News, Media Gen., NPR Radio, Shadow Broadcasting, 1988-89; ind. video prodr., 1989-91. Host, editor TV documentary Coming to Terms, 1993. Bd. dirs. NE Ohio AAU Baseball Com., 1995-96; moderator Ohio Acad. Decathalon, Cleve., 1995, 96; vol. United Way, Cleve., 1995, 96; honorary chair Women's Ctr. Greater Cleve., 1995; celebrity spokesperson Cleve. Christian Home for Children, 1995. Recipient John Merriman award Writer's Guild Am., 1988, Appreciation cert. United Negro Coll. Fund, 1995, 96; named One of 20 Top Women in Media, Washington D.C. Tchrs. Assn., 1993. Mem. NATAS, AFTRA. Avocations: art history, skiing, quiz shows. Office: Sta KNX-AM 6121 W Sunset Blvd Los Angeles CA 90028-6423

GAULKE, MARY FLORENCE, library administrator; b. Johnson City, Tenn., Sept. 24, 1923; d. Gustus Thomas and Mary Belle (Bennett) Erickson; m. James Wymond Crowley, Dec. 1, 1939; 1 son, Grady Gaulke (name legally changed); m. 22nd, Bud Gaulke, sept. 1, 1945 (dec. Jan. 1978); m. 3rd, Richard Lewis McNaughton, Mar. 21, 1983 (div. 1995). BS in Home Econs., Oreg. State U., 1963; MS in L.S., U. Oreg., 1968; Phd in Spl. Edn., 1970. Cert. std. pers. supr., std. handicapped learner, Oreg. Head dep. home econs. Riddle Sch. Dist. (Oreg.), 1963-66; libr., cons. Douglas County Intermediate Edn. Dist., Roseburg, Oreg., 1966-67; head resident, head counselor Prometheus Project So. Oreg. coll.ect, Ashland, summers 1966-68; supr. librs. Medford Sch. Dist. (Oreg.), 1970-73; instr. psychology So.Oreg. Coll., Ashland, 1970-73; libr. supr. Roseburg Sch. Dist., 1974-91; resident psychologist Black Oaks Boys Sch., Medford, 1970-75. Mem. Oreg. Gov.'s Coun. Librs., 1979. Author: Vo-Ed Course for Junior High, 1965; Library Handbook, 9167, Instructions for Preparation of Cards for All materials Cataloged for Libraries, 1971, Handbook for Training Library aides, 1972. Coord. Laubach Lit. Workshops for High Sch. Tutors, Medford, 1972. Fellow Internat. Biog. Assn. (life); mem. ALA, So Oreg. Libr. Fedn. (sec. 1971-73), Oreg. Libr. Assn., Pacific N.W. Libr. Assn., Am. Biog. Inst. (lifetime dep. gov. 1987—), Internat. Biog. Ctr. (hon., adv. coun. 1990), Delta Kappa Gamma (pres. 1980-82), Delta Kappa Gamma (pres. 1980-82), Phi Delta Kappa (historian, rsch. rep.). Democrat. Methodist. Home: 976 29th St Vero Beach FL 32960-6905 Office: 119 Orchard Ln Ashland OR 97520-9627 also: 15200 Birch St Long Beach WA 98631 Fax: (360) 642-5712; (561) 770-1112. E-mail: mumgg@earthlink.net

GAUS, CLIFTON R. healthcare executive; MHA, U. Mich.; ScD, Johns Hopkins U. Mem. faculty Johns Hopkins U. Sch. Pub. Health, Balt., Georgetown U. Med. Sch., Washington; assoc. adminstr. policy, planning and rsch. Health Care Financing Adminstrn.; former adminstr. Agy Health Care Policy amd Rsch. HHS; sr. v.p. for R & D, Kaiser Permanente, Oakland, Calif.; exec. vice pres., chief admin. ofcr. Well Point Health Networks, Inc., Thousand Oaks. Co-founder, past. pres., bd. dirs. Assn. Health Svcs. Rsch. Office: Well Point Health Networks Inc One Well Point Way Thousand Oaks CA 91362

GAUSS, JOHN A. career officer; b. Salem, Mass. BS in Engring. and Physics, Cornell U., 1969; M of Philosophy, Naval Postgrad. Sch., 1976, PhD in Electronics Engring. Commd. ensign USN, 1969, advanced through ranks to rear adm.; various assignments to comdr. Def. Info. Systems Agy., Arlington, Va., 1994-97; dir. Allied & Fleet Requirements Divsn. Space, Info. Warfare Command & Control Directorate, Washington, 1997—. Decorated Def. Disting. Svc. medal, Legion of Merit (3 times), Meritorious Svc. medal, Navy Achievement medal. Office: 4301 Pacific Hwy San Diego CA 92110-3127

GAVALAS, GEORGE R. chemical engineering educator; b. Athens, Greece, Oct. 7, 1936; s. Lazaros R. and Belouso A. (Matha) G. BS, Nat. Tech. U., 1958; MS, U. Minn., 1962, PhD, 1964. Asst. prof. chem. engring. Calif. Inst. Tech., 1964-67, asso. prof., 1967-75, prof., 1975—. Cons. in field. Author: Nonlinear Differential Equations of Chemically Reacting Systems, 1968, Coal Pyrolysis, 1983; contbr. articles to profl. jours. Mem. AIChE (Tech. award 1968, Wilhelm award 1983), Am. Chem. Soc., N.Am. Membrane Soc. Home: 707 S Orange Blvd # F Pasadena CA 91105-1779 Office: Caltech 210-41 Pasadena CA 91125-0001 E-mail: garalas@cheme.caltech.edu

GAY, E(MIL) LAURENCE, lawyer; b. Bridgeport, Conn., Aug. 10, 1923; s. Emil D. and Helen L. (Mihalich) G.; m. Harriet A. Ripley, Aug. 2, 1952; children: Noel L., Peter C., Marguerite S., Georgette A. BS, Yale U., 1947; JD magna cum laude, Harvard U., 1949. Bar: N.Y. 1950, Conn. 1960, Calif. 1981, Hawaii 1988. Assoc. Root, Ballantine, Harlan, Bushby & Palmer, N.Y.C., 1949-51; mem. legal staff U.S. High Commr. for Germany, Bad Godesberg, 1951-52; law sec., presiding justice appellate div. 1st dept. N.Y. Supreme Ct., N.Y.C., 1953-54; assoc. Debevoise, Plimpton & McLean, N.Y.C., 1954-58; v.p., sec.-treas., gen. counsel Hewitt-Robins, Inc., Stamford, Conn., 1958-65; pres. Litton Gt. Lakes Corp., N.Y.C., 1965-67; sr. v.p. finance AMFAC, Inc., Honolulu, 1967-73, vice chmn., 1974-78; fin. cons. Burlingame, Calif., 1979-82; of counsel Pettit & Martin, San Francisco, 1982-88, Goodsill, Anderson, Quinn & Stifel, Honolulu, 1988—. Editor Harvard Law Rev., 1948-49. Pres. Honolulu Symphony Soc., 1974-78; trustee Loyola Marymount U., 1977-80, San Francisco Chamber Soloists, 1981-86, Honolulu Chamber Music Series, 1988—; officer, dir. numerous arts and ednl. orgns. 2d lt. AUS, 1943-46. Mem. ABA, State Bar of Hawaii, Pacific Club (Honolulu), Nat. Assn. of Securities Dealers, Am. Arbitration Assn. (mem. arbitration panels), Phi Beta Kappa. Republican. Roman Catholic. Avocations: music, arts. Home: 1159 Maunawili Rd Kailua HI 96734-4641 Office: Goodsill Anderson Quinn & Stifel PO Box 3196 Honolulu HI 96801-3196

GAYNOR, C.W. paper company executive; BS, Iowa State U.; MBA, Ariz. State U., 1974. Fin. mgr. Weyerhaeuser Co., Tacoma, 1974, v.p. gen. mgr. Saskatchewan disvn., sr. v.p. Canada, 1998—. Dir. exec. com. Coun. Forest Industries. Served in U.S. Navy. Mem. Can. Pulp & Paper Assn. (bd. dirs.). Office: Weyerhaeuser Co PO Box [illegible] Tacoma [illegible]

GAYNOR, JOSEPH, chemical engineer, technical-management consultant; b. N.Y.C., Nov. 15, 1925; s. Morris and Rebecca (Schnapper) G.; m. Elaine Bauer, Aug. 19, 1951; children: Barbara Lynne, Martin Scott, Paul David, Andrew Douglas. B in Chem. Engring., Poly. Inst., 1950; MS, Case Western Res. U., 1952, PhD, 1955. Rsch. asst. Case Inst., Cleve., 1952-55; with Gen. Engring. Labs. GE, Schenectady, N.Y., 1955-66, mgr. R & D sect., 1962-66; group v.p. rsch. Bell & Howell Co., 1966-72; mgr. comml. devel. group, mem. pres.' office Horizons Rsch., Inc., Cleve., 1972-73; pres. Innovative Tech. Assocs., Ventura, Calif., 1973—; mem. nat. materials adv. bd. com. NAS; chmn. conf. com. 2d internat. conf. on bus. graphics, 1979; program chmn. 1st internat. congress on advances in non-impact printing techs., 1981; mem. adv. com. 2d internat. congress on advances in non-impact printing techs., 1984; chmn. publs. com. 3rd internat. congress on advances in non-impact printing techs., 1986; chmn. internat. conf. on hard copy media, materials and processes, 1990. Editor: Electronic Imaging, 1991, Procs. Advances in Non-Impact Printing Technologies, Vol. I, 1983, Vol. II, 1988, 3 spl. issues Jour. Imaging Tech., Proc. Hard Copy Materials Media and Processes Internat. Conf., 1990; patentee in field. Served with U.S. Army, 1944-46. Fellow AAAS, AIChE, Imaging Sci. and Tech. Soc. (sr., gen. chmn. 2nd internat. conf. on electrophotography 1973, chmn. bus. graphics tech. sect. 1976—, chmn. edn. com. L.A. chpt. 1978—), Am. Soc. Photobiology, Sigma Xi, Tau Beta Pi, Phi Lambda Upsilon, Alpha Chi Sigma. Home: 108 La Brea St Oxnard CA 93035-3928 Office: Innovative Tech Assocs 3639 Harbor Blvd Ste 203E Ventura CA 93001-4255

GAZELL, JAMES ALBERT, public administration educator; b. Chgo., Mar. 17, 1942; s. Albert James and Ann Marion (Bloch) G. BA in Polit. Sci. with honors, Roosevelt U., 1963, MA in Polit. Sci., 1966; PhD in Govt., So. Ill. U., 1968. Instr. Roosevelt U., Chgo., 1965, 67, So. Ill. U., Carbondale, 1966-68; asst. prof. San Diego State U., 1968-72, assoc. prof., 1972-75, prof., 1975—. Cons. County San Diego, 1973, Ernst and Ernst, Detroit, 1973, Wadsworth Pub. Co., 1995, McGraw-Hill Pub. Co., 1997. Author books; contbr. articles to profl. jours.; assoc. editor Encyclopedia of Public Administration and Public Policy, 1999; mem. editl. bd. Internat. Jour. Pub. Adminstrn., Internat. Jour. Orgnl. Theory and Behavior. Mem. ACLU, Am. Soc. Pub. Adminstrn., Nat. Ctr. for State Cts., Nat. Assn. Ct. Mgmt., Nat. Assn. for Ct. Mgmt. Home: 4319 Hilldale Rd San Diego CA 92116-2135 Office: San Diego State U 5500 Campanile Dr San Diego CA 92182-0002

GEBB, SHELDON ALEXANDER, lawyer; b. Long Beach, Calif., Jan. 12, 1935; AB, U. Calif., Berkeley, 1957; LLB, U. Calif., 1963. Bar: Calif. 1964. Mng. ptnr. Baker & Hostetler, L.A., Long Beach and Beverly Hills, Silicon Valley, Calif. Chmn. bd. trustees Southwestern U. Sch. Law, 1985-91 Mem. ABA, State Bar Calif., Maritime Law Assn. U.S. Office: Baker & Hostetler 600 Wilshire Blvd Los Angeles CA 90017-3212

GEBHARD, BOB, professional baseball team executive; Gen. mgr. Colorado Rockies, 1991-99. Office: Colo Rockies 2001 Blake St Denver CO 80205-2008

GEBHART, CARL GRANT, security broker; b. Santa Monica, Calif., Jan. 24, 1926; s. Carl V. and Hazel (Grant) G.; m. Margaret Mary del Bondio, Nov. 29, 1952 (dec. Feb. 1989); children: Elizabeth G. Gebhart-Hardin, Peggy G. McFarland, Julia Ann Seamon. B.A. in Journalism, U. So. Calif., 1947; M.B.A. in Fin, Harvard U., 1949. Registered rep. Mitchum, Jones & Templeton, Inc., Los Angeles, 1949-56, gen. partner, 1956-62, sr. v.p., sec., dir., 1962-73; v.p. investments Paine Webber, Los Angeles, 1973—; financial reporter radio sta. KABC, Los Angeles, 1968-73. Mem. L.A. Soc. Fin. Analysts (v.p. 1959), Spring St. Forum (pres. 1962), Petroleum Club (L.A.), Univ. Club L.A., Univ. Assocs. U. So. Calif. (life), Tennis Patrons Santa Monica (life), Beach Club (Santa Monica), Phi Beta Kappa, Phi Kappa Phi, Phi Eta Sigma, Chi Phi, Sigma Delta Chi. Republican. Presbyterian. Home: 749 Amalfi Dr Pacific Palisades CA 90272-4509 Office: 777 S Figueroa St Los Angeles CA 90017-5800

GEBLER, DAVID B. finance company executive; b. Binghamton, N.Y., Oct. 6, 1949; s. Norman Frederick and Dorothy (Dedrick) G.; m. Catherine Hopkins, Oct. 7, 1978; children: Anna, Kathleen. BS, Clarkson U., 1971; postgrad., U. N.C., 1971-72; Dde, U. Mich., 1977, MS, 1979. Various positions Ford Motor Co./Ford Motor Credit Co., Dearborn, Mich., 1972-81; mgr. Ford Motor Credit Co., Dearborn, 1981-89; pres. U.S. Airlease Inc./U.S. Leasing Internat., San Francisco, 1989-90; exec. v.p. Transp. Financing/U.S. Leasing Internat., San Francisco, 1990—; pres. Airlease Ltd., San Francisco, 1989—. Capt. U.S. Army, 1971-81. Mem. Nat. Assn. Security Dealers (registered rep.). Office: Airlease Ltd 555 California St San Francisco CA 94104

GECHT, GUY, publishing company executive; b. 1965; BS in Computer Sci. and Math., Ben Gurion U., Israel. Various to v.p. and gen. mgrs. server products Electronics for Imaging, Inc, Foster City, Calif., 1995-2000, CEO, 2000—. Office: Electronics for Imaging Inc 303 Velocity Way Foster City CA 94404

GEDDES, GARY LEE, wildlife park director; b. Peoria, Ill., Aug. 23, 1950; s. Robert and Mary O. (McCartney) G.; m. Debbie L. Lush, Sept. 7, 1974; children: Jake Austin, Cody Robert, Katelyn Jane. AS, Ill. Cen. Jr. Coll., 1970; BA in Zoology, So. Ill. U., 1972. Dir. Wildlife Prairie Park, Hanna City, Ill., 1973-81, N.W. Trek Wildlife Park, Eatonville, Wash., 1981—, Point Defiance Zoo & Aquarium, Tacoma. Co-chmn. bd. dirs. Region 6 Tourism Coun., Olympia, Wash., 1984-86; vice chmn. Bates Vocat. Sch. Tourism Adv. Bd.; exec. bd. mem. Regional Tourism Coun., Olympia, Wash., 1983-88. Leader Boy Scouts Am.; bd. dirs. Ctr. for Wildlife Conservation. Fellow Am. Assn. Zool. Parks and Aquariums, Audobon Soc. (bd. dirs. Tahoma chpt.). Avocations: mountain climbing, camping, cross-country skiing, gardening. Office: Northwest Trek Wildlife Pk 11610 Trek Dr E Eatonville WA 98328-9502 Address: Point Defiance Zoo & Aquarium 5400 N Pearl St Tacoma WA 98407

GEDDES, ROBERT L. state legislator; b. Preston, Idaho, Nov. 14, 1955; m. Tammy Geddes; children: Megan, Emily, Lizabeth, Robert W., Jess. Student, Ricks Coll.; BS in Geology, Utah State U. Geologist; environ. specialist; mem. Idaho Senate, Dist. 32, Boise, 1994—. Vice chair local govt. and tax. com., mem. agrl. affairs, resources and environment, and state affairs coms.; assoc. bd. mem. Caribou County Soil Conservation Dist. Past chair Caribou County Rep. com. Mem. Am. Inst. Mining (past chair Snake River sect.). Republican. Office: State Capitol PO Box 83720 Boise ID 83720-3720

GEE, CHUCK YIM, dean; b. San Francisco, Aug. 28, 1933; s. Don Yow Elsie (Lee) G. AA, City Coll. of San Francisco, 1953; BSBA, U. Denver, 1957; MA, Mich. State U., 1958; PhD (hon.), China Acad. Chin. Cultural U., 1972; D of Pub. Svc. (hon.), U. Denver, 1991. Assoc. dir. Sch. of Hotel and Restaurant Adminstn. U. Denver, 1958-68; cons. East West Ctr., Honolulu, 1968-74; assoc. dean and prof. Sch. of Travel Industry Mgmt. U. Hawaii, 1968-75, dean and prof. Sch. Travel Industry Mgmt., 1976-99, interim dean Coll. Bus. Adminstrn., 1998-99, dean emeritus, 2000—. Vis. prof. Sch Bus. and Commerce, Oreg. State U., 1975; hon. prof. Nankai U., Tianjin, China, 1987—, Shanghai Inst. Tourism, 1994—, Dept. Tourism Huaqiao U., Xiamen, China, 1995—; cons. Internat. Sci. and Tech. Inst., Washington, 1986-90; trustee Pacific Asia Travel Assn. Found., San Francisco; chmn. Govs. Tourism Tng. Coun., Honolulu, 1989-92, chmn., 1992-96, chmn. industry coun. PATA, 1994-96, PATA Human Resource Devel. Coun., 1996-99, chmn. PATA Coun. on Ednl. Devel. and Certification, 2000—; mem. State Workforce Devel. Coun., 1997-98, Pacific Asia Travel Assn. Human Resource Devel. Coun, 1996-98; acad. Inst. Cert. Travel Agts., Wellesley, Mass., 1989—; mem. Coun. on Hotel, Restaurant and Edn., Honolulu Commn. on Fgn. Rels., Pacific Asian Affairs Coun.; sr. acad. adv. China Tourism Assn. Cons., Inc., 1993—; adv. World Tourism Orgn. Internat. Tourism Edn. and Tng. Ctr., 1991-2000; external examiner sch. accountancy and bus. Nanyang Tech. U., Singapore, 1996-98; bd. dirs. ProjectonNet.com. Author: Resort Development and Management, 1988, 2d edit., The Story of PATA, 2d edit., co-editor, 2001; co-author: The Travel Industry, 1988, 3d edit., 1997, Professional Travel Agency Management, 1990, International Hotels: Development and Management, 1994; editor: International Tourism: A Global Perspective, 1997; mem. adv. bd. Asian Hotelier mag., 1997-99, Get2Hawaii.com, 2001—. Bd. dirs. Hawaii Visitors Bur., 1993-95, Kaukini Med. Ctr., Honolulu, 1986-95, KMC, 1996—, Travel and Tourism Adv. Bd., U.S. Dept. Commerce, Washington, 1982-90, Pacific Rim Found., Honolulu, 1987-93; vice-chmn. Tourism Policy Adv. Coun., Dept. Bus. and Econ. Devel., Honolulu, 1978-92; chmn. Kaukini Geriatric Care, Inc., bd. dirs., 1992-95; trustee Pata Found., 1984-95, Kuakini Health System, 1988—; consulting com. Beijing Inst. Tourism, 1992—; v.p. Hawaii Vision 2020, 1992-93; mem. Mayor's Task Force on Waikiki Master Plan, 1992-93; mem. workforce devel. coun. Hawaii Dept. of Labor and Indsl. Rels., 1996-98; bd. dirs. Cyberspace Enterprises, Hawaii Dept. Edn., 1997—. With U.S. Army, 1953-55. Recipient NOAH award Acad. Tourism Orgns., 1987, Gov.'s Proclamation honors State of Hawaii, 1998; named State Mgr. of Yr., State of Hawaii, 1995; named to list of 100 Who Made a Difference in Hawaii during 20th Century, Star Bull., 1999. Mem. Acad. for Study of Tourism, Pacific Asia Travel Assn. (bd. dirs. 1993-96, 99—, chmn. industry coun. 1994-96, 50th Anniversary Hall of Honors, Grand award for individual edn. 1991, Life award 1990, Presdl. award 1986), Travel Industry Am. (Travel Industry Hall of Leaders award 1988), China Tourism Assn. (award of excellence in tourism edn. 1992), C. of C. of Hawaii, Soc. for Advancement of Food Svc. Rsch., Chaine des Rotisseurs, Golden Key. Office: U Hawaii Sch Travel Industry Mgmt 2560 Campus Rd Honolulu HI 96822-2217 E-mail: cgee@hawaii.edu

GEE, GAVIN M. state government official; Dir. dept. finance State of Idaho, Boise. Office: 700 W State St Fl 2 Boise ID 83702-5822

GEFFEN, DAVID, recording company executive, producer; b. Bklyn., Feb. 21, 1943; s. Abraham and Batya (Volovskaya) Geffen , U of Texas, Austin, Brooklyn Coll. of CUNY. Agt. with William Morris, N.Y.C., 1964-68; agt. with Ashley Famous, 1968; exec. V.P. and agent Creative Management Associates, 1969; founder (with Laura Nyro) and pres. Tuna Fish publishing co.; pres. Asylum Records, 1970-73, Geffen-Roberts, Inc., 1970-71, Elektra-Asylum Records, 1973-76; founder and pres. Geffen Records, L.A., 1980-89; v.p. Warner Bros. Pictures, 1975; chmn. Geffen Records, L.A.; head Geffen Film Co.; vice-chmn. Warner Brothers Pictures, 1974; exec. asst. to chmn. Warner Communications, 1977; co-founder Dreamworks SKG, Universal City, 1995—. Mem. music faculty Yale U., 1978; apptd. Regent U. Calif., Gov. Calif., 1980-87. Producer films including After Hours, Lost in America, Personal Best, 1982, Risky Business, 1983, Little Shop of Horrors, 1986, Social Security, 1986, Beetlejuice, 1988, Men Don't Leave, 1990, Interview with the Vampire, 1994; co-producer Master Harold...and the Boys, 1982, Cats, 1982, Good, 1982, Dreamgirls, 1983, Madam Butterfly, 1988 (9 Tony award, Best Play); musical Miss Saigon. Bd. dirs. Los Angeles County Art Mus. Avocations: collector modern art. Office: Dreamworks SKG 100 Universal City Plz Bldg 477 Universal City CA 91608

GEHRES, JAMES, lawyer; b. Akron, Ohio, July 19, 1932; s. Edwin Jacob and Cleora Mary (Yoakam) G.; m. Eleanor Agnew Mount, July 23, 1960. BS in Acctg., U. Utah, 1954; MBA, U. Calif.-Berkeley, 1959; JD, U. Denver, 1970, LLM in Taxation, 1977. Bar: Colo. 1970, U.S. Dist. Ct. Colo. 1970, U.S. Tax Ct. 1970, U.S. Supreme Ct. 1973, U.S. Ct. Appeals (10th cir.) 1978, U.S. Ct. Claims 1992. Atty. IRS, Denver, 1965-80, atty. chief counsel;s office, 1980—. Contbr. articles to profl. jours. Treas., dir. Colo. Fourteeners Initiative. With USAF, 1955-58, capt. Res. ret. Mem. ABA, Colo. Bar Assn., AICPA, Colo. Soc. CPAs, Am. Assn. Atty.-CPAs, Am. Judicature Soc., Order of St. Ives, The Explorers Club, Am. Alpine Club, Colo. Mountain Club (bd. dirs.), Colo. Mountain Club Found. (bd. dirs., pres.), Beta Gamma Sigma, Beta Alpha Psi. Democrat. Office: 935 Pennsylvania St Denver CO 80203-3145

GEHRING, GEORGE JOSEPH, JR. dentist; b. Kenosha, Wis., May 24, 1931; s. George J. and Lucille (Martin) G.; m. Ann D. Carrigan, Aug. 2, 1982; children: Michael, Scott. DDS, Marquette U., 1955. Pvt. practice dentistry, Long Beach, Calif., 1958—. Author: The Happy Flosser. Chmn. bd. Long Beach affiliate Calif. Heart Assn.; mem. Long Beach Grand Prix com. of 300; ind. candidate for pres. of the U.S., 1988, 92, 2000. Served with USNR, 1955-58. Fellow Internat. Coll. of Dentists, Am. Coll. Dentists; mem. Harbor Dental Soc. (dir.), Pierre Fauchard Acad., Delta Sigma Delta, Rotary. Home: 1230 E Ocean Blvd Unit 603 Long Beach CA 90802-6908

GEHRY, FRANK OWEN, architect; b. Toronto, Ont., Can., Feb. 28, 1929; came to U.S., 1947; s. Irving and Thelma (Caplan) G.; children: Leslie, Brina; m. Berta Aguilera, Sept. 11, 1975; children: Alejandro, Samuel B. in Architecture, U. So. Calif., 1954; postgrad., Harvard U., 1956-57. Registered profl. architect, Calif. Designer Victor Gruen Assocs., L.A., 1953-54, planning, design and project dir., 1958-61; project designer, planner Pereira & Luckman, L.A., 1957-58; prin. Frank O. Gehry & Assocs., Santa Monica, Calif., 1962—. Architect Loyola Law Sch., L.A., 1978-92, Temporary Contemporary Mus., L.A., 1983, Calif. Aerospace Mus., L.A., 1984, Frances Goldwyn Regional Br. Libr., Hollywood, Calif., 1986, U.C.I. Info. and Computer Sci./Engring. Rsch. Lab. and Engring. Ctr., Irvine, Calif., 1986-88, Vitra Internat. Mfg. Facility and Design Mus., Weil am Rhein, Germany, 1989, Chiat/Day Hdqs., Venice, Calif., 1991, Am. Ctr., Paris, 1994, Advanced Tech. Labs. Bldg., Iowa City, 1992, U. Toledo Ctr. for Visual Arts, 1992, Walt Disney Concert Hall, L.A., Frederick R. Weisman Art Mus., Mpls., 1993, Vitra Internat. Hdqs., Basel, Switzerland, 1994, Disney Ice, Anaheim, Calif., 1995, EMR Communication and Tech. Ctr., Bad Oeynhausen, Germany, 1995, Team Disneyland Adminstrn. Bldg., Anaheim, 1996, Nationale-Nederlanden Bldg., Prague, Czech Republic, 1996, Guggenheim Mus., Bilbao, Spain, 1997, Experience Music Project, Seattle, 2000, Weatherfield Sch. Mgmt., Cleve., 2000. Trustee Hereditary Disease Found., Santa Monica, Calif., 1970— Recipient Arnold W. Brunner Meml. prize in architecture, 1983, Eliot Noyes Design chair Harvard U., 1983, Charlotte Davenport Professorship in architecture Yale U., 1982, 85, 87-89, Pritzker Architecture prize, 1989, Wolf prize in art, 1992, Praemium Imperiale, 1992, Dorothy and Lilian Gish award, 1994, Nat. Medal of Arts, 1998. Office: Frank O Gehry & Assocs 1520B Cloverfield Blvd Santa Monica CA 90404-3502*

GEIDUSCHEK, E(RNEST) PETER, biophysics and molecular biology educator; b. Vienna, Austria, Apr. 11, 1928; came to U.S., 1945, naturalized, 1946; s. Sigmund and Frieda (Tauber) G.; m. Joyce Barbara Brous; 2 children B.A., Columbia U., 1948; A.M., Harvard U., 1950, Ph.D., 1952. Instr. chemistry Yale U., New Haven, 1952-53, 55-57; asst. prof. chemistry U. Mich., Ann Arbor, 1957-59; asst. prof. biophysics U. Chgo., 1959-62, assoc. prof., 1962-64, prof., 1964-70; prof. biology U. Calif., San Diego, 1970-94, rsch. prof., 1994—, chmn. dept., 1981-83, 94. Cons. USPHS, 1963-69, NIH, 1991-94, 98—. Editl. bd. Biophys. Jour., 1967-69, Ann. Revs. Biophysics and Bioengring., 1971-74, Virology, 1972—, Sci., 1977-84, Seminars in Virology, 1990-98, Ency. Virology, 1990—. Served with U.S. Army, 1953-55 Recipient rsch. award Am. Postgrad. Med. Assn., 1962, USPHS, 1962, Order of Merit of Italian Republic; Guggenheim fellow, 1964-65. Fellow AAAS, Am. Acad. Microbiology; mem. NAS, Am. Acad. Arts and Scis., Am. Soc. Biochemistry and Molecular Biology (pub. affairs com. 1988-90), Am. Soc. Microbiology, Am. Soc. Virology (coun. 1985-87). Office: U Calif Dept Biology Ctr Molecular Genetics La Jolla CA 92093

GEIER, PHILIP OTTO, III, college president; b. Cin., 1948; s. Philip O. Jr. and Susanne (Ernst) G.; m. Amy Yeager, Dec. 27, 1975; children: Katherine, Elizabeth, Christopher. BA in Am. Civilization with honors, Williams Coll., 1970; attended, U. Paris, 1973; MA in History, Syracuse U., 1975, PhD in Am. Studies and History, 1980. Instr. history and Am. studies Dickinson Coll., Carlisle, Pa., 1976-77; Fulbright lectr. U. Paris-Sorbonne, 1977-78; interim exec. dir. French-Am. Found., N.Y.C., 1978-79; assoc. dir. Am. Farm Sch., Thessaloniki, Greece, 1979-82; v.p. external affairs World Learning, Brattleboro, Vt., 1982-93; pres., dir. Armand Hammer United World Coll., Montezuma, N.Mex., 1993—. Bd. dirs. Fulbright Prize Com., Washington, Pine Manor Coll., Thornburg Found. Realty, Info. Markets Corp.; chair social Svcs. and Internat. Exch. Commn. 2d U.S.-USSR Emerging Leaders Summit, Moscow and Sochi, 1990, del. to 1st Commn., Phila., 1988; mem. Coun. Fgn. Rels., Pacific Coun. on Internat. Policy, L.A. 2d lt. Supply Corps, USN, 1970-72, Vietnam. Fulbright award Fed. Republic of Germany, 1988. Avocations: international relations, outdoor recreation. Office: United World Coll PO Box 248 Montezuma NM 87731-0248

GEIS, GERALD E. state legislator, trucking company executive; b. Ten Sleep, Wyo., Aug. 31, 1933; s. Nicholas Eugene and Hazel Irene (Harvard) G.; m. Irma Lungrun, 1993; children: Elizabeth Pike, Cheryl. Student, pub. schs., Worland, Wyo. Pres. Geis Trucking, Worland, Wyo., 1951—. Mem. Worland City Coun., Wyo. Senate. Mem.: Nat. Conf. State Legislators. Republican. Roman Catholic. Home: 600 Holly Ave Worland WY 82401-3925

GEISER, THOMAS CHRISTOPHER, lawyer; b. Bern, Switzerland, Aug. 13, 1950; came to U.S., 1952; s. Henry Abraham and Pia Margaret (Tschudin) G.; m. Catherine Barlow Yeakle, Oct. 20, 1973 (div. Mar. 1983); m. Donna Lea Schweers, Jan. 3, 1987; 1 child, Kelsey Schweers. BA, U. Redlands, Calif., 1972; JD, U. Calif., San Francisco, 1977. Bar: Calif. 1978. Atty. Internat. Bur. Fiscal Documentation, Amsterdam, The Netherlands, 1977-78; assoc., ptnr. Hanson, Bridgett, Marcus, Vlahos & Stromberg, San Francisco, 1979-85; ptnr. Epstein, Becker, Stromberg & Green, San Francisco, 1985-90, Brobeck, Phleger & Harrison, San Francisco, 1990-93; sr. v.p., gen. counsel, sec. WellPoint Health Networks Inc., Woodland Hills, Calif., 1993-96, exec. v.p., gen. counsel, sec., 1996—. Mem. Am. Health Lawyers Assn., Calif. Soc. Health Care Attys., Order of Coif. Office: WellPoint Health Networks Inc 1 Wellpoint Way Thousand Oaks CA 91362-3893

GEISTFELD, RONALD ELWOOD, retired dental educator; b. St. James, Minn., Nov. 9, 1933; s. Victor E. and Viola (Becker) G.; m. Lois N. Tolzman Wilkens, June 15, 1955 (div. June 1974); m. Annette L. Swenson, Jan. 14, 1977; children: Shari, Mark, Steven, Ann, Leah, Erik. AA, Bethany Jr. Coll., 1952; BS, U. Minn., 1954, DDS, 1957. Pvt. practice dentistry, Northfield, Minn., 1959-72; clin. asst. prof. dentistry U. Minn. Sch. Dentistry, Mpls., 1969-72, assoc. prof., 1972-82, chmn. dept. operative dentistry, 1978-87, prof., 1982-97, prof. emeritus, 1997; dir. quality programs Pentegra Dental Group, Inc., 1998-2000. Dental cons. Hennepin County Med. Ctr., Mpls., 1975-96, VA Hosp., Mpls., 1977-96, VA Hosp., St. Cloud, Minn., 1978-96, Human Performance and Informatics Inst., Atama, Japan, 1990-95, K-9 Dental Sys. Quidnunc Australia Pty. Ltd., 1994-95, Metro Dental Group, Mpls., 1995-2000, The Dentists Ins. Co., 1995-99, VGM Expert Systems, 1996-98, Met. Life Ins. Co., 1996—, Pentegra Ltd., 1997-2000; mem. resource faculty for Bush faculty devel. program on excellence and diversity in teaching U. Minn., 1993-94. Pres. PTA, Northfield, 1965, Arts Guild, Northfield, 1968; bd. dirs., chairperson Rice County Health and Sanitation Bd., Faribault, Minn., 1966-74; bd. dirs. Northfield Bd. Edn., 1969-74; pres. Roseville Luth. Ch., 1987-88. Capt. U.S. Army, 1957-59. Am. Coll. Dentists fellow, 1972; recipient Prof. of Yr. award Century Club, 1996-97. Mem. Am. Dental Assn. (chairperson operative dentistry sect. 1979-80, curriculum cons. 1981-88, grants and spl. projects request evaluator 1988-92, Am. fund for Dental Health, edit. review bd. JADA 1992-96), Minn. Dental Assn. (ethics com. 1969-76, chairperson sci. and ann. sessions com. 1984-86, spkr. house del. 1992-96, del. to ADA 1992-96, bd. dirs. 1992-96), Mpls. Dist. Dental Soc. (program chairperson 1978-79, peer rev. com. 1988-92, bd. dirs. 1979-80, 87-89, MDA del. 1989-92), Minn. Acad. Restorative Dentistry (pres. 1979-80), Minn. Acad. Gnathological Rsch. (pres. 1986-87), Am. Assn. Dental Schs. (chairperson operative dentistry sect. 1984-85, edit. rev. bd. 1984-88), Acad. Operative Dentistry (exec. council 1978-81, rsch. com. 1987-89), Am. Acad. Gold Foil Operators, Northfield C. of C. (treas. and chairperson 1968-70), Delta Sigma Delta, Omicron Kappa Upsilon (Theta chpt.). Lodge: Rotary (pres. Northfield 1972-73).

GELBER, DON JEFFREY, lawyer; b. L.A., Mar. 10, 1940; s. Oscar and Betty Sheila (Chernitsky) G.; m. Jessica Jeasun Song, May 15, 1967; children: Victoria, Jonathan, Rebecca, Robert. Student UCLA, 1957-58, Reed Coll., 1958-59; AB, Stanford U., 1961, JD, 1963. Bar: Calif. 1964, Hawaii 1964, U.S. Dist. Ct. (cen. and no. dists. Calif.) 1964, U.S. Dist. Ct. Hawaii 1964, U.S. Ct. Appeals (9th cir.) 1964, U.S. Supreme Ct. 1991. Assoc. Greenstein, Yamane & Cowan, Honolulu, 1964-67; reporter Penal Law Revision Project, Hawaii Jud. Council, Honolulu, 1967-69; assoc. H. William Burgess, Honolulu, 1969-72; ptnr. Burgess & Gelber, Honolulu, 1972-73; prin. Law Offices of Don Jeffrey Gelber, Honolulu, 1974-77; pres. Gelber & Wagner, Honolulu, 1978-83, Gelber & Gelber, Honolulu, 1984-89, Gelber, Gelber, Ingersoll, Klevansky & Faris, Honolulu, 1990—; legal counsel Hawaii State Senate Judiciary Com., 1965; adminstrv. asst. to majority floor leader Hawaii State Senate, 1966, legal counsel Edn. Com., 1967, 68; majority counsel Hawaii Ho. of Reps., 1974; spl. counsel Hawaii State Senate, 1983. Contbr. articles to legal publs. Mem. State Bar Calif., ABA (sect. bus. law), Am. Bankruptcy Inst., Hawaii State Bar Assn. (sect. bankruptcy law, bd. dirs. 1991-93, pres. 1993). Clubs: Pacific, Plaza (Honolulu). Office: Gelber Gelber Ingersoll Klevansky & Faris 745 Fort Street Mall Ste 1400 Honolulu HI 96813-3877

GELLER, STEPHEN ARTHUR, pathologist, educator; b. Bklyn., Apr. 26, 1939; s. Sam John and Alice (Podber) G.; m. Kate Eleanor DeJong, June 24, 1962; children: David Phillip, Jennifer Lee. BA, Bklyn. Coll., 1959; MD, Howard U., 1964. Diplomate Am. Bd. Pathology, Nat. Bd. Med. Examiners. Intern Lenox Hill Hosp., N.Y.C., 1964-65; resident in pathology Mt. Sinai Hosp., N.Y.C., 1965-69; chief lab. Naval Hosp., Beaufort, S.C., 1969-71; asst. prof. pathology Mt. Sinai Med. Ctr., N.Y.C., 1971-75, assoc. prof., 1975-78, prof., 1978-84; chmn. dept. pathology Cedars-Sinai Med. Ctr., L.A., 1984—; prof. pathology UCLA, 1984—. Co-author: Histopathology, 1989; contbr. articles to profl. jours. Recipient Excellence in Teaching award CUNY, 1974. Fellow Coll. Am. Pathologists, Am. Soc. Clin. Pathologists; mem. Am. Assn. Study of Liver Diseases, Hans Popper Hepatopathology Soc., Calif. Soc. Pathologists (sec. 1989-91, v.p. 1991-93, pres. 1994-96), L.A. Soc. Pathologists (v.p. 1989-91, pres. 1992), N.Y. Pathol. Soc., Alpha Omega Alpha. Democrat. Jewish. Avocations: music, writing fiction. Office: Cedars Sinai Med Ctr 8700 Beverly Blvd Los Angeles CA 90048-1865 E-mail: geller@cshs.org

GELLERT, JAY M. health/medical products executive; BA, Stanford U. Sr. v.p., COO Calif. Healthcare System, 1985-88; pres., CEO Bay Pacific Health Corp., 1988-91; dir. Shattuck Hammond Ptnrs. Inc.; pres., COO Health Systems Internat. Inc., Health Net, Inc. (formerly Found. Health Systems Inc.), 1998, pres., CEO, 1999—. Office: Health Net Inc 21650 Oxnard St Woodland Hills CA 91367-4901

GELLIN, GERALD ALAN, dermatologist; b. Bklyn., May 24, 1934; m. Lucille E. Gellin. AB, U. Pa., 1954; MD, NYU, 1958. Diplomate Am. Bd. Dermatology. Chief sect. dermatology VA Hosp., Bklyn., 1964-67; clin. prof. U. Calif. Med. Ctr., San Francisco, 1969—. Chief dermatology divsn. VA Hosp., Bklyn., 1963-67, San Francisco Gen. Hosp., 1969-73, Calif. Pacific Med. Ctr., 1986—. Contbr. articles to profl. jours. With USPHS, 1967-69. Fellow ACP. Office: 3838 California St San Francisco CA 94118-1522

GELLMAN, GLORIA GAE SEEBURGER SCHICK, marketing professional; b. La Grange, Ill., Oct. 5, 1947; d. Robert Fred and Gloria Virginia (McQuiston) Seeburger; m. Peter Slate Schick, Sept. 25, 1978 (dec. 1980); 2 children; m. Irwin Frederick, Gellman, Sept. 9, 1989; 3 children. BA magna cum laude, Purdue U., 1969; student, Lee Strasberg Actors Studio; postgrad., UCLA, U. Calif.-Irvine. Mem. mktg. staff Seemac, Inc. (formerly R.F. Seeburger Co.); v.p. V.I.P. Properties, Inc., Newport Beach, Calif.; pres. Glamglo Prodns. Host radio show Orange County Art Bytes, Sneak Previews from the Orange County Performing Arts Ctr. Profl. actress, singer, artist, writer; TV and radio talk show hostess, Indpls.; performer radio and TV commls.; feature writer arts and entertainment column H mag. Mem. Orange County Philharm. Soc., bd. dirs. women's com.; mem. Orange County Master Chorale, Orange County Performing Arts Ctr., v.p., treas. Crescendo chpt. OCPAC Ctr. Stars, 1st v.p. membership; bd. dirs. Newport Harbor (Calif.) Art Mus., v.p. membership, mem. acquisition coun.; bd. dirs., mem. founders soc. Opera Pacific, mem. exec. com. bd. dirs.; patron Big Bros./Big Sisters Starlight Found.; mem. Visionaries Newport Harbor Mus., Designing Women of Art Inst. Soc. Calif.; past pres. Opera Pacific Guild Alliance; past pres. Spyglass Hill Philharm. Com.; v.p. Pacific Symphony Orch. League, chair endowment sect., spl. events chair; bd. dirs. Pacific Symphony Orch., v.p. cmty. affairs; mem. Calif. State Libr. Found. Bd., U. Calif. Irvine Found. Bd., mem. devel. com., honors com., pub. affairs and advocacy com.; mem. social scis. dean's adv. coun. U. Calif., Irvine; chmn. adv. coun. Cold War Studies Ctr., Chapman U.; chmn. numerous small and large fundraisers; mem. com. Red Cross; mem. Fashionables of Chapman U.; bd. dirs. Sta. KOCE PBS TV. Recipient Lauds and Laurels award U. Calif., Irvine, 1994, Gellman Courtyard Sculpture honoring contbn. to Sch. of Humanities, U. Calif., Irvine. Mem. AAUW, AFTRA, SAG, Internat. Platform Assn., Actors Equity, U. Calif.-Irvine Chancellor's Club, U. Calif.-Irvine Humanities Assocs. (founder, pres., bd. dirs.), Mensa, Orange County Mental Health Assn., Seneca Network, Balboa Bay Club, U. Club, Club 39, Islanders, Covergirls, Pacific Symphony Supper Club (founder), Alpha Lambda Delta, Delta Rho Kappa. Republican. Home: PO Box 1993 Newport Beach CA 92659-0993 E-mail: glamglo@aol.com

GELL-MANN, MURRAY, theoretical physicist, educator; b. N.Y.C., Sept. 15, 1929; s. Arthur and Pauline (Reichstein) Gell-M.; m. J. Margaret Dow, Apr. 19, 1955 (dec. 1981); children: Elizabeth, Nicholas; m. Marcia Southwick, June 20, 1992; 1 stepson, Nicholas Levis. BS, Yale U., 1948; PhD, Mass. Inst. Tech., 1951; ScD (hon.), Yale U., 1959, U. Chgo., 1967, U. Ill., 1968, Wesleyan U., 1968, U. Turin, Italy, 1969, U. Utah, , 1970, Columbia U., 1977, Cambridge U., 1980; D (hon.), Oxford (Eng.) U., 1992, So. Ill. U., 1993, U. Fla., 1994, So. Meth. U., 1999. Mem. Inst. for Advanced Study, 1951, 55, 67-68; instr. U. Chgo., 1952-53, asst. prof., 1953-54, assoc. prof., 1954, Calif. Inst. Tech., Pasadena, 1955-56, prof., 1956-67, R.A. Millikan prof. physics, 1967-93, R.A. Millikan prof. emeritus, 1993—; disting. fellow Santa Fe Inst., 1993—, co-chmn. sci. bd. 1985-2000. Vis. prof. MIT, spring 1963, CERN, Geneva, 1971-72, 79-80, U. N.Mex., 1995—; vis. assoc. prof. Columbia U., 1954; overseas fellow Churchill Coll., 1966; mem. Pres.'s Sci. Adv. Com., 1969-72, Pres.'s Com. of Advisors on Sci. and Tech., 1994-2001; mem. sci. and grants com., Leakey Found., 1977-80; chmn. bd. trustees Aspen Ctr. for Physics, 1973-79; founding trustee Santa Fe Inst., 1982, chmn. bd. trustees, 1982-85, co-chmn. sci. bd. 1993-2000, prof., disting. fellow, 1993—; cons. Inst. Def. Analysis, Arlington, Va., 1961-70, Rand Corp., Santa Monica, Calif., 1956; mem. physics panel NASA, 1964, Coun. Fgn. Rels., 1975—, Los Alamos (N.Mex.) Sci. Lab., 1956—, Lab. fellow, 1982—; mem. adv. bd. Network Physics, 1999—. Author: (with Y. Ne'eman) Eightfold Way, 1964, The Quark and the Jaguar, 1994. Citizen regent Smithsonian Instn., 1974-88; trustee Wildlife Conservation Soc., 1994—; bd. dirs. J.D. and C.T. MacArthur Found., 1979—, Calif. Nature Conservancy, 1984-93; bd. dirs. AeroVironment, Inc., 1971—; chmn. Lovelace Insts., 1993-95. NSF post doctoral fellow, vis. prof. Coll. de France and U. Paris, 1959-60; recipient Dannie Heineman prize Am. Phys. Soc., 1959; E.O. Lawrence Meml. award AEC, 1966; Franklin medal, 1967; Carty medal Nat. Acad. Scis., 1968; Rsch. Corp. award, 1969; named to UN Environ. Program Roll of Honor for Environ. Achievement, 1988; Nobel prize in physics, 1969, Erice prize, 1990. Fellow Am. Phys. Soc.; mem. NAS, AAAS, Am. Acad. Arts and Scis. (v.p., chmn. Western ctr. 1970-76), Council on Fgn. Relations, French Phys. Soc. (hon.), Am. Philos. Soc., Conservation Internat. (sci. adv. com. 1993), Royal Soc. London (fgn.), Pakistan Acad. Scis. (fgn.), Indian Acad. Scis. (fgn.), Russian Acad. Scis. (fgn.). Clubs: Cosmos (Washington); Century Assn., Explorers (N.Y.C.); Athenaeum (Pasadena) Address: Santa Fe Institute 1399 Hyde Park Rd Santa Fe NM 87501-8943

GELPI, ALBERT JOSEPH, English educator, literary critic; b. New Orleans, July 19, 1931; s. Albert Joseph and Alice Marie (Delaup) G.; m. Barbara Charlesworth, June 14, 1965; children: Christopher Francis Cecil, Adrienne Catherine Ardelle. A.B., Loyola U., New Orleans, 1951; M.A., Tulane U., 1956; Ph.D., Harvard U., 1962. Asst. prof. Harvard U., 1962-68; assoc. prof. Stanford U., 1968-74, prof. Am. lit., 1974-99, Wm. Robertson Coe prof. Am. lit., 1978-99, Coe prof. emeritus, 1999—, chmn. Am. studies program, 1980-83, 94-97, asso. dean grad. study and research, 1980-85, chmn. English dept., 1985-88. Author: Emily Dickinson: The Mind of the Poet, 1965, The Tenth Muse: The Psyche of the American Poet, 1975, A Coherent Splendor: The American Poetic Renaissance 1910-1950, 1987; editor: The Poet in America: 1650 to the Present, 1974, (with Barbara Charlesworth Gelpi) Adrienne Rich's Poetry, 1975, Wallace Stevens: The Poetics of Modernism, 1985, (with Barbara Charlesworth Gelpi) Adrienne Rich's Poetry and Prose, 1993, Denise Levertov: Selected Criticism, 1993, The Blood of the Poet: Selected Poems of William Everson, 1994; editor Cambridge Studies in American Literature and Culture, 1981-91, Living in Time: The Poetry of C. Day Lewis, 1998. Served with U.S. Army, 1951-53. Guggenheim fellow, 1977-78 Mem. MLA, Am. Lit. Assn. Democrat. Roman Catholic. Home: 870 Tolman Dr Palo Alto CA 94305-1026 Office: Stanford U Dept English Stanford CA 94305

GELWIX, MAX D. chemical company executive; BS, Colo. State U. Exec. v.p. Arthur J. Gallagher & Co., 1979-96; pres. Maxell Enterprises, 1996-97; v.p. Eco Soil Sys., Inc., San Diego, 1998-00, pres., COO, 2000—. Office: Eco Soil Sys Inc 10740 Thornmint Rd San Diego CA 92127

GENGLER, SUE WONG, health educator, evaluation consultant, speaker, trainer; b. Hong Kong, Apr. 6, 1959; came to U.S., 1966; d. Tin Ho and Yuet Kum (Chan) Wong; m. Clayton J. Gengler, 1995. BS, UCLA, 1981; MPH, Loma Linda (Calif.) U., 1990; DrPH, Loma Linda U., 1995. Cert. health edn. specialist. Asst. to the dir. Project Asia Campus Crusade for Christ, San Bernardino, Calif., 1982-83, Campus Crusade for Christ-Internat. Pers., San Bernardino, 1983-90; health educator San Bernardino County Pub. Health, 1990-92; community lab. instr., rsch. asst. dept. health promotion and edn. Loma Linda (Calif.) U. Sch. Pub. Health, 1992-95; behaviorist/educator Anaheim Hills Med. Group/St. Jude Heritage Med. Group, Anaheim, Calif., 1995-96; direct svcs. dir. Alternatives to Domestic Violence, Riverside, 1997—2001; evaluation cons., domestic violence sect. Maternal and Child Health br. Calif. Dept. Health Svcs., 1999—; health edn. mgr., 2001—. Mem. Minority Health Coalition, San Bernardino, 1990-92, Com. for the Culturally Diverse, San Bernardino, 1990-92; vol. Am. Cancer Soc.; chair Gt. Am. Smokeout, Inland Empire, 1991; bd. dirs. Family Svcs. Agy., San Bernardino, 1994-96. Selma Andrews scholar Loma Linda U., 1994; named Outstanding Young Woman of Yr., 1983, Hulda Crooke Scholar, Loma Linda U., 1989; recipient Am. Cancer Soc. Rose award, 1991 (Calif.), Gaspar award, 1991 (nat.), Chief's award of Excellence Corona Police Dept. Mem. APHA, Nat. Coun. for Internat. Health, Soc. Pub. Health Edn. Avocations: travel, reading, volleyball, calligraphy, music. E-mail: advsgengler@yahoo.com

GENGOR, VIRGINIA ANDERSON, financial planning executive, educator; b. Lyons, N.Y., May 2, 1927; d. Axel Jennings and Marie Margaret (Mack) Anderson; m. Peter Gengor, Mar. 2, 1952 (dec.); children: Peter Randall, Daniel Neal, Susan Leigh. AB, Wheaton Coll., 1949; MA, U. No. Colo., 1977. Chief hosp. intake svc. County of San Diego, 1966-77; cheif Kearny Mesa Dist. Office, 1977-79; chief Dept. Children of Ct., 1979-81, chief child protection svcs., 1981-82; regisrtered rep. Am. Pacific Securities, San Diego, 1982-85; registered tax preparer State of Calif., 1982—; registered rep. (prin.) Sentra Securities, 1985—; assoc. Pollock & Assocs., San Diego, 1986-86; pres. Gengor Fin. Advisors, 1986—. Cons. instr. Nat. Ctr. for Fin. Edn., San Diego, 1986-88; instr. San Diego Community Coll., 1985-88. Mem. allocations panel United Way, San Diego, 1976-79; children's cir. Child Abuse Prevention Found., 1989—; chmn. com. Child Abuse Coord. Coun., San Diego, 1979-83; pres. Friends of Casa de la Esperanza, San Diego, 1980-85, bd. dirs., 1980—; 1st v.p. The Big Sis. League, San Diego, 1985-86, pres., 1987-89. Mem. NAFE, AAUW (bd. dirs.), Inst. Cert. Fin. Planners, Internat. Assn. Fin. Planning, Inland Soc. Tax Cons., Nat. Assn. Securities Dealers (registered prin.), Nat. Ctr. Fin. Edn., Am. Bus. Women's Assn., Navy League, Freedoms Found., Valley Forge, Intenrat. Platform Assn. Presbyterian. Avocations: community service, travel, reading. Home: 6462 Spear St San Diego CA 92120-2929 Office: Gengor Fin Advisors 4950 Waring Rd Ste 7 San Diego CA 92120-2700 E-mail: vgengor@home.com

GENINI, RONALD WALTER, history educator, historian; b. Oakland, Calif., Dec. 5, 1946; s. William Angelo and Irma Lea (Gays) G.; m. Roberta Mae Tucker, Dec. 20, 1969; children: Thomas, Justin, Nicholas. BA, U. San Francisco, 1968, MA, 1969. Cert. secondary edn. tchr., Calif.; adminstrv. svcs. credential. Tchr. Ctrl. Unified Sch. Dist., Fresno, Calif., 1970—. Judge State History Day, Sacramento, 1986-94; mem. U.S. history exam. devel. team Golden State, San Diego, 1989-93; securer placement of state-registered landmarks. Author: Romualdo Pacheco, 1985, Darn Right It's Butch, 1994, Theda Bara, 1996; contbr. articles to profl. jours.; cited as authority on Theda Bara by Ency. Brit. Online Am. Women in History, 1999, also on Romualdo Pacheco by Biog. Directory of Am. Congress. Bd. dirs. Fresno Area 6 Neighborhood Coun., 1973-74, Fresno City and County Hist. Soc., 1975-78, St. Anthony's sch. bd., Fresno, 1980-84; mem. Good Company Players, Fresno, 2000—. Named one of Outstanding Young Educators Am., Fresno Jaycees, 1978; recipient recognition for Tchr. Cares award Calif. State Assembly and Fresno City Coun., 1996. Mem. Calif. Hist. Soc. Democrat. Avocations: writing history 19th century Calif. and early Hollywood, motion picture scriptwriter, commercial acting. Home: 1486 W Menlo Ave Fresno CA 93711-1305 Office: Ctrl HS 2045 N Dickenson Ave Fresno CA 93722-9643 E-mail: rgenini@hotmail.com

GENN, NANCY, artist; b. San Francisco; d. Morley P. and Ruth W. Thompson; m. Vernon Chathburton Genn; children: Cynthia, Sarah, Peter. Student, San Francisco Art Inst., U. Calif., Berkeley. Lectr. on art and papermaking Am. Ctrs. in Osaka, Japan, Nagoya, Japan, Kyoto, Japan, 1979-80; guest lectr. various univs. and art mus. in U.S., 1975—; vis. artist Am. Acad. in Rome, 1989, 94. One woman shows of sculpture, paintings include, De Young Mus., San Francisco, 1955, 63, Gumps Gallery, San Francisco, 1955, 57, 59, San Francisco Mus. Art, 1961, U. Calif., Santa Cruz, 1966-68, Richmond (Calif.) Art Center, 1970, Oakland (Calif.) Mus., 1971, Linda/Farris Gallery, Seattle, 1974, 76, 78, 81, Los Angeles Inst. Contemporary Art, 1976, Susan Caldwell Gallery, N.Y.C., 1976, 77, 79, 81, Nina Freudenheim Gallery, Buffalo, 1977, 81, Annely Juda Fine Art, London, 1978, Inoue Gallery, Tokyo, 1980, Toni Birckhead Gallery, Cin., 1982, Kala Inst. Gallery, Berkeley, Calif., 1983, Ivory/Kimpton Gallery, San Francisco, 1984, 86, Eve Mannes Gallery, Atlanta, 1985, Richard Iri Gallery, L.A., 1990, Harcourts Modern and Contemporary Art, San Francisco, 1991, 93, 96, Am. Assn. Advancement of Sci., Washington, 1994, Anne Reed Gallery, Ketchum, Id., 1995, Michael PeTronko Gallery, N.Y., 1997, Mills Coll. Art Mus., Oakland, Calif., 1999, Takada Gallery, San Francisco, 1999, 2000; group exhbns. include San Francisco Mus. Art, 1971, Aldrich Mus., Ridgefield, Conn., 1972-73, Santa Barbara (Calif.) Mus., 1974, 75, Oakland (Calif.) Mus. Art, 1975, Susan Caldwell, Inc., N.Y.C., 1974, 75, Mus. Modern Art, N.Y.C., 1976, traveling exhbn. Arts Coun. Gt. Britain, 1983-84, Inst. Contemporary Arts, Boston, 1977, J.J.Brookings Gallery, San Francisco, 1997, Portland (Oreg.) Art Mus., 1997—, Takada Gallery, San Francisco, 1999, 2000; represented in permanent collections Mus. Modern Art, N.Y.C., Albright-Knox Art Gallery, Buffalo, Libr. of Congress, Washington, Nat. Mus. for Am. Art, Washington, L.A. County Mus. Art, Art Mus. U. Calif., Berkeley, McCrory Corp., N.Y.C., Mus. Art, Auckland, N.Z., Aldrich Mus., Ridgefield, Conn., (collection) Bklyn. Mus., (collection) U. Tex., El Paso, Internat. Ctr. Aesthetic Rsch., Torino, Italy, Cin. Art Mus., San Francisco Mus. Modern Art, Oakland Art Mus., L.A. County Mus., City of San Francisco Hall of Justice, Harris Bank, Chgo., Chase Manhattan Bank, N.Y.C., Modern Art Gallery of Ascoli Piceno, Italy, Mills Coll. Art Mus., Oakland, Calif., Mills Coll. of Art, Oakland, Calif., Leighton Gallery, Blue Hill, Maine, various mfg. cos., also numerous pvt. collections; commd. works include, Bronze lectern and 5 bronze sculptures for chancel table, 1st Unitarian Ch., Berkeley, Calif., 1961, 64, bronze fountain, Cowell Coll., U. Calif., Santa Cruz, bronze menorah, Temple Beth Am, Los Altos Hills, Calif., 1981, 17, murals and 2 bronze fountain sculptures, Sterling Vineyards, Calistoga, Calif., 1972, 73, fountain sculpture, Expo 1974, Spokane, Wash; vis. artist Am. Acad., Rome, 1989. U.S./Japan Creative Arts fellow, 1978-79; recipient Ellen Branston award, 1952; Phelan award De Young Mus., 1963; honor award HUD, 1968 Home: 1515 La Loma Ave Berkeley CA 94708-2033

GENNARO, ANTONIO L. biology educator; b. Raton, N.Mex., Mar. 18, 1934; s. Paul and Mary Lou (Gasperetti) G.; m. Virginia Marie Sullivan, May 15, 1955 (div. 1979); children: Theresa Ann, Carrie Marie, Janelle Elizabeth; m. Marjorie Lou Cox, Sept. 27, 1980. BS, N.Mex. State U., 1957, MS, 1961, PhD, 1965. Tchr. biology Las Cruces (N.Mex.) H.S., 1957-58; asst. prof. biology St. John's U., Collegeville, Minn., 1964-65; prof. biology Eastern N.Mex. U., Portales, 1965—. Bd. trustees N.Mex. Mus. Natural History, 1996—. Served to capt. U.S. Army, 1958-59; USAR, 1959-66. Recipient presdl. faculty award Eastern N.Mex. U., 1970, pres.'s faculty award for excellence in rsch., 1988, spirit of east award, 1995, outstanding sci. award N.Mex. Acad. Sci., 1975, disting. faculty emeritus, 1998. Mem. Southwestern Naturalists (treas. 1974-78), Am. Soc. Mammalogists, Herpetologists League, Sigma Xi, Phi Kappa Phi (pres. 1970-74).

GENRICH, MARK L. public relations executive; b. Buffalo, Aug. 28, 1943; m. Allison Forbes, 1967; children: Audrey, Liza, Colby. BA, Bucknell U., 1966. Editl. writer Palladium-Item, Richmond, Ind., 1970; writing exec. Bruce Eberle & Assocs., Inc., Vienna, 1975-77; dep. editor editl. pgs. Phoenix Gazette, 1977-96; editl. writer, columnist The Ariz. Republic, Phoenix, 1996-98; dir. Warne Ctr. Goldwater Inst., Phoenix, 1998-2000; pub. rels. dir. Quest Comm. Internat., Inc., 2000—. Participant U.S. Army War Coll., Carlisle, Pa., U.S. Naval War Coll., Newport, R.I.; participant arms control, disarmament programs including Space & Arms talks, Geneva; chmn. New Tech. Com., Journalism in Edn. Com.; mem. various coms. Creator, host cable TV program focus on polit. figures; regional editor The Masthead. Grantee European Cmty. Visitor Programme, 1993; recipient highest honors editl. writing, newspaper design Ariz., Western Region; highest honor Maricopa County Bar Assn.; Hoover Inst. media fellow, 1985. Mem. Nat. Conf. Editl. Writers (bd. dirs., included vol. Editl. Excellence), First Amendment Cong. (bd. dirs.), Soc. Profl. Journalists/Sigma Delta Chi, ABA (com. prisons, sentencing). Avocations: coaching competitive soccer, tennis, photography, riding. Home: 130 W Pine Valley Dr Phoenix AZ 85023-5283 Office: Quest Comm Internat Inc 3033 N Third St Phoenix AZ 85012

GENTILE, JOSEPH F. lawyer, educator; b. San Pedro, Calif., Jan. 15, 1934; s. Ernest B. and Icy Otie (Martin) G.; m. Kathleen McMahon, Aug. 11, 1976; children— Kim Yvonne, Kevin James, Kelly Michele, Kristien Elyse, Kerri Nicole. B.A. cum laude, San Jose State U., 1955; J.D., U. La Verne, 1966; cert. in indsl. rels., UCLA, 1959; teaching credential, Calif. C.C., 1972; M.Pub. Adminstrn., U. So. Calif., 1976. Bar: Calif. 1967, U.S. Supreme Ct. 1972. Mem. indsl. relations staff Kaiser Steel Corp., Fontana Works, 1957-62; labor relations counsel Calif. Trucking Assn., Burlingame, Calif., 1964-68; acting dir. indsl. relations, labor relations counsel McDonnell Douglas Corp., Santa Monica, 1968-70; sr. partner Nelson, Kirshman, Goldstein, Gentile & Rexon, Los Angeles, 1970-76; individual practice, 1976—; Evening instr. bus. econs., indsl. relations U. Calif., 1969-94; evening instr. personnel and indsl. relations San Bernardino Valley Coll., 1969-72; evening instr. transp. Mt. San Antonio Coll., 1972-74; lectr. labor law Loyola U., 1973-74; lectr. Grad. Sch. Pub. Adminstrn., U. So. Calif., 1976-80; adj. prof. law Pepperdine U., 1981—; chmn. Employee Relations Commn., Los Angeles County, 1979—. Mem. arbitration panel Fed. Mediation and Conciliation Service, Calif. Conciliation Service; mem. employee rels. bd. L.A. City, 2000—. Contbr. articles to profl. jours. Served with AUS, 1955-57. Mem. ABA, Calif. Bar Assn., Los Angeles County Bar Assn. (past chmn. exec. com. labor law sect.), Am. Arbitration Assn. (chmn. regional adv. coun., arbitration panel, nat. bd. dirs. 1985-91), Phi Sigma Alpha, Phi Alpha Delta. Office: PO Box 491117 Los Angeles CA 90049-9117

GENTRY, DONALD WILLIAM, mine engineering executive; b. St. Louis, Jan. 18, 1943; s. William Henry and Roberta Elizabeth (Bardelmeier) G.; m. Sheila Carol Schuepbach, Aug. 21, 1965; children: Tara Cassandre, Chad Ryan. B.S.E., U. Ill., 1965; M.S., U. Nev., 1967; Ph.D., U. Ariz., 1972. Asst. prof. mining engring. Colo. Sch. Mines, Golden, 1972-74, assoc. prof., 1974-77, asst. to dean faculty, assoc. prof., 1977-78, asst. to dean faculty, 1978-79, prof. mining engring., 1978-83, dean undergrad. studies, 1983-84, dean engring. and undergrad. studies, 1990-95, head dept. mining engring., 1995-98, prof. mining-engring., 1998—; pres., CEO PolyMet Mining Corp., Golden, 1998—, also bd. dirs. Contbr. articles to profl. jours. Mem. Nat. Acad. Engring., Soc. Mining Engrs. of AIME (pres. 1993), AIME (dir. Colo. sect. 1982-83, Krumb lectr. 1987, pres. 1996, Krumb lectr. 1987, Mineral Industry Edn. award 1991, Daniel C. Jackling award 1998), Nat. Acad. Engring. (elected 1996), Sigma Tau, Sigma Gamma Epsilon Republican. Lutheran. Home: 6590 Ridgeview Dr Morrison CO 80465-2700 Office: PolyMet Mining Corp 13949 W Colfax Ave Ste 205 Golden CO 80401-3209

GEORGE, ALEXANDER LAWRENCE, political scientist, educator; b. Chgo., May 31, 1920; s. John and Mary (Sargis) G.; m. Juliette Lombard, Apr. 20, 1948; children: Lee Lawrence, Mary Lombard. AM, U. Chgo., 1941, PhD, 1958; DHL (hon.), U. San Diego, 1987; PhD (hon.), U. Lund, Sweden, 1994. Rsch. analyst OSS, 1944-45; dep. chief rsch. br. Info. Control divsn. Office Mil. Govt. for Germany, 1945-48; specialist study of decision-making and internat. rels. RAND Corp., Santa Monica, Calif., 1948-68, head dept. social sci., 1961-63; prof. polit. sci. and internat. rels. Stanford (Calif.) U., 1968—. Lectr. U. Chgo., 1950, Am. U., 1952-56; chmn. com. on Conflict Resolution NRC/NAS, 1995—. Author: (with Juliette L. George) Woodrow Wilson and Colonel House: A Personality Study, 1956, Propaganda Analysis, 1959, The Chinese Communist Army in Action, 1967; (with others) The Limits of Coercive Diplomacy, 1971; (with Richard Smoke) Deterrence in American Foreign Policy: Theory and Practice, 1974 (Bancroft prize for Deterrence in Am. Fgn. Policy 1975), Towards A More Soundly Based Foreign Policy: Making Better Use of Information, 1976, Presidential Decisionmaking in Foreign Policy, 1980, Managing U.S.-Soviet Rivalry, 1983; (with Gordon Craig) Force and Statecraft, 1983, 3rd edit., 1995; editor: (with others) U.S.-Soviet Security Cooperation: Achievements, Failures, Lessons, 1988, Avoiding War: Problems of Crisis Management, 1991, Forceful Persuasion, 1992, Bridging the Gap: Theory and Practice of Foreign Policy, 1993; (with William E. Simons) The Limits of Coercive Diplomacy, 2d. edit., 1994; (with Juliette L. George) Presidential Personality and Performance, 1998. Mem. Carnegie Commn. on Preventing Deadly Conflict, 1993-97. Fellow Ctr. Advanced Study Behavioral Scis., 1956-57, 76-77, NIMH, 1972-73, MacArthur Prize, 1983-88, Disting. fellow U. S. Inst. Peace, 1990-91, 91-92; Founds. Fund for Rsch. in Psychiatry grantee, 1960, NSF rsch. grantee, 1971-73, 75-77; recipient award for behavioral rsch. relevant to prevention of nuclear war NAS, 1997, Johan Skytte prize in polit. sci., Uppsala U., Swden, 1998; Carnegie Corp. grantee, 1999. Mem. Am. Acad. Arts and Scis., Coun. on Fgn. Rels., Am. Polit. Sci. Assn., Internat. Studies Assn. (pres. 1973-74), Am. Philos. Soc., Phi Beta Kappa. Home: 944 Lathrop Pl Stanford CA 94305-1060 E-mail: algeorge@stanford.edu

GEORGE, AUBREY WESTMORELAND, library director; b. Marshall, Tex., May 20, 1950; BA, Stephen F. Austin U., 1972, MA in Polit. Sci., 1974; MLS, N. Tex. State U., 1975. Asst. dir. Corpus Christi (Tex.) Pub. Libr., 1975-91; mgr. pub. svc. Spokane (Wash.) Pub. Libr., 1991-96, dep. dir., 1996, dir., 1996—. Mem. Am. Libr. Assn., Wash. Libr. Assn. Office: Spokane Pub Libr 906 W Main Ave Spokane WA 99201-0976

GEORGE, DONALD WARNER, online columnist and editor, freelance writer; b. Middlebury, Conn., June 24, 1953; s. Lloyd Foster and Vivian (Minor) G.; m. Kuniko Ninomiya, Apr. 24, 1982; children: Jennifer Ayako, Jeremy Naoki. BA, Princeton U., 1975; MA, Hollins (Va.) Coll., 1977. Tchg. fellow Athens (Greece) Coll., 1975-76, Internat. Christian U., Tokyo, 1977-79; TV talk show host Japan Broadcasting Corp., Tokyo, 1977-79; freelance writer, 1980-81; travel writer San Francisco Examiner, 1981-82, sr. editor Calif. Living mag., 1982-85, sr. editor Image mag., 1985-87, travel editor, 1987-95; cyber columnist, Global Network Navigator American Online, Berkeley, Calif., 1995-96; editor Salon Wanderlust Online Travel Mag., 1997-2000; travel editor Lonely Planet Publs., 2001—. Recipient gold award Pacific Asia Travel Assn., 1987-94). Mem. Soc. Am. Travel Writers (Lowell Thomas award 1987-94). Office: Lonely Planet 150 Linden St Oakland CA 94607 E-mail: dgeorge@salm.com

GEORGE, GARY, state legislator, farmer; b. Dos Palos, Calif., Nov. 17, 1946; m. Kathy George. Student, Fresno State U. Mem. Oreg. Legislature, Salem, 1996—, chair agr. and natural resources com., mem. edn. com., mem. transp. com., mem. water and land use com., mem. subcom. on natural resources. Mem. Yamhill Budget Com. Republican. Office: 15195 NE Ribbon Ridge Rd Newberg OR 97132-6715 E-mail: george.sen@state.or.us

GEORGE, KATTUNILATHU OOMMEN, physician, educator; Diploma in Medicine and Surgery, C.H. Med. Coll. and Hosp., 1965; Bachelor of Medicine and Surgery, Coun. Homoeopathic Medicine West Bengal, India, 1975; MSW, Am. Christian Theol. Sem., 1980; M in Marriage, Family and Child Counseling, Calif. Christian Inst., 1982; grad., Acupuncture Acad. Oriental Medicine, Fla., 1983; Diploma in Acupuncture, Acupuncture Rsch. Inst., L.A., 1986. Resident Hahnemann Mission Hosp., Quilon, Kerala, India, 1965-67, med. officer India, 1965-67; chief med. examiner pharmacology, clin. medicine and pharmacy Travancore-Cochin Med. Coun. Homoeopathic Medicine, 1967-76; chief med. officer Fellowship Hosp., India; chief med. officer, dir. Fellowship Clinic and Pharm., India; resident Pub. Health Ctr., L.A., 1978-80, Family Svcs. Am., Tustin, Calif., 1979-80; practicing homoeopathic physician; founding pres., dean, dir., prof. homoeopathic medicine with health scis. Samuel Hahnemann Sch. Homoeopathic Medicine, L.A. Internat. U., 1983—; pres. Hahnemannian Rsch. Ctr., Inc., Irvine, Calif., 1985—. Nutrition cons. Biochemical Analysis Clinic, 1978-80, Shaw Health Ctr., 1982—; instr. homoeopathic medicine Calif. Acupuncture Coll., Westwood, 1979-80; counselor, cons. New Hope Counseling Ctr., Garden Grove, Calif., 1980-81; mem. faculty coll. acupuncture L.A. U., 1980-81, Western U., Phoenix, 1982, grad. sch. Calif. Christian Inst., 1982-87; cons. Indsl. Med. Clinic and Potner's Med. Group, L.A., 1981-88; instr., bd. dirs. Acupuncture Rsch. Inst., 1982—; conductor seminars, trainer in field. Author: Twelve Energy Supplements for Health and Nutrition, 1979, A Comprehensive Therapeutics in Homoeopathy for Physicians, 1984, Twelve Energy Medicine, 1980, How to Balance your Body Dynamically, Ways to Change the Health Care Crisis in America, 1985; contbr. articles to profl. jours. Mem. Homoeopathic Med. Assn. Am. (founding pres., bd. dirs. 1988—), Nat. Ctr. Homoeopathy (bd. dirs. 1988), Homoeopathic Med. Assn. India, All-India Homoeopathic Med. Assn., All-India Homoeopathic Pharm. Assn. (exec. adv. mem.), Hahnemann Med. Soc. Am., Fla. State Soc. Homoeopathic Physicians, Internat. Homoeopathic Med. Orgn., Med. Acupuncture Rsch. Inst. (bd. dirs. 1977—), Internat. Homoeopathic Med. League, Soc. Ultramolecular Medicine. Office: Hahnemann Research Ctr Inc 18818 Teller Ave Ste 230 Irvine CA 92612-1680

GEORGE, LLOYD D. federal judge; b. Montpelier, Idaho, Feb. 22, 1930; s. William Ross and Myrtle (Nield) G.; m. LaPrele Badouin, Aug. 6, 1956; children: Douglas Ralph, Michele, Cherie Suzanne, Stephen Lloyd. BS, Brigham Young U., 1955; JD, U. Calif., Berkeley, 1961. Ptnr. Albright, George, Johnson & Steffen, 1969-71, George, Steffen & Simmons, 1971-74; judge U.S. Bankruptcy Ct. (Nev. dist.), 1974-84, U.S. Dist. Ct. Nev., 1984—, chief judge, sr. judge, 1997—. Justice of Peace Clark County, Nev., 1962-69. With USAF, 1955-58. Office: US Dist Ct Foley Fed Bldg Rm 316 300 Las Vegas Blvd S Fl 3 Las Vegas NV 89101-5833

GEORGE, RICHARD LEE, oil company executive; b. Colo., May 16, 1950; s. Albert H. and Betty Lou (McDill) G.; m. Julie G. White, June 4, 1972; children: Zachary Ryan, Matthew Shane, Emily Christine. BS in Engring., Colo. State U., 1973; JD, U. Houston, 1977; grad. program for mgmt. devel., Harvard Bus. Sch., 1984. Bar: Tex. 1978; registered profl. engr., Tex. Dep. mng. dir. Sun Oil Britain, London, 1982-86, dist. mgr. Aberdeen, Scotland, 1986-87; v.p. internat. E. and P. Sun Exploration & Prodn., Dallas, 1987-88; mng. dir. Sun Internat. Exploration & Prodn., London, 1988-91; pres., COO Suncor, Inc., North York, Ont., Can., 1991, pres., CEO Can., 1991-93, chmn., pres., CEO Can., 1993-94; pres., CEO. Bd. dirs. Dofasco Inc., Enbridge Inc., Santa Fe Internat., Inc.; mem. Bus. Coun. Nat. Issues. Active Can. Inst. for Advanced Rsch. Office: Suncor Enerty Inc 112-4th Ave SW Box 38 Calgary AB Canada T2P 2V5

GEORGE, ROBERT D. technology corporation executive; b. 1956; BA in Econs., Drew U.; MBA, Duke U. Various fin. and opers. positions Zurn Industries, Elgin Electronics, and Xerox Corp.; treas., controller Esterline Technologies Corp., Bellevue, Wash., 1997-99, chief fin. officer, v.p., 1999—. E-mail: www.esterline.com. Office: Esterline Technologies Corp 10800 NE 8th St Ste 600 Bellevue WA 98004-4471

GEORGE, RONALD M. state supreme court chief justice; b. L.A., Mar. 11, 1940; AB, Princeton U., 1961; JD, Stanford U., 1964. Bar: Calif. 1965. Dep. atty. gen. Calif. Dept. Justice, 1965-72; judge L.A. Mcpl. Ct., L.A. County, 1972-77, Superior Ct. Calif., L.A. County, 1977-87, supervising judge criminal divsn., 1983-84; assoc. justice 2d dist., divsn. 4 Calif. Ct. Appeal, L.A., 1987-91; assoc. justice Calif. Supreme Ct., San Francisco, 1991-96, chief justice, 1996—. Mem. Calif. Judges Assn. (pres. 1982-83). Avocations: hiking, skiing, running. Office: Calif Supreme Court 350 Mcallister St Fl 5 San Francisco CA 94102-4713

GEORGE, RUSSELL LLOYD, lawyer, legislator; b. Rifle, Colo., May 28, 1946; s. Walter Mallory and Eleanora (Michel) G.; m. Neal Ellen Moore, Nov. 24, 1972; children: Russell, Charles, Thomas, Andrew. BS in Econs., Colo. State U., 1968; JD, Harvard Law Sch., 1971. Bar: Colo. Shareholder Stuver & George, P.C., Rifle, 1976—. State rep. dist. 57 Colo. Gen. Assembly, 1993—, speaker of the House, Colo Gen.Assembly. Fellow Colo. Bar Found.; mem. Colo. Bar Assn., Rotary Internat., Masonic Lodge. Republican. Methodist. Home: 1300 E 7th St Rifle CO 81650-2123 Office: Stuver & George PC PO Box 907 120 W 3rd St Rifle CO 81650-2297

GEORGE, SARAH B. museum director; Dir. Utah Mus. of Natural History and Hansen Planetarium, Salt Lake City. Office: Utah Mus Natural History U Utah 1390 E Pres Cir Salt Lake City UT 84112

GEORGE, THOM RITTER, conductor, composer; b. Detroit, June 23, 1942; s. Robert Murray and Virginia Flowers (Ritter) G.; m. Patricia Imogene Dengler , Aug. 14, 1965; children: Samantha, Clara, Alexander. MusB, Eastman Sch. Music, 1964, MusM, 1968; D in Mus. Arts, The Cath. U. Am., 1970. Lectr. music The Cath. U. Am., Washington, 1966-70; music dir., condr. Quincy (Ill.) Symphony Orch., 1970-83; lectr. music John Wood Community Coll., Quincy, 1980-83; music dir., condr. Idaho State Civic Symphony, Pocatello, 1983—; assoc. prof. Idaho State U., Pocatello, 1983-88, prof., 1988—. Composer: Concerto for Bass Trombone, 1964, Proclamations, 1965, Sextet, 1980, numerous others. Bd. dirs. Civic Music Assn., Quincy, 1970-74; bd. sec. Vol. Action Ctr., Quincy, 1976-78. Served with USN, 1966-70. Recipient citation Quincy Coll., 1973, Sigvald Thompson award Fargo (N.D.) Madison Symphony, 1975, Composer-in-Residence Elkhorn Music Festival, Sun Valley, Idaho, 1986. Mem. ASCAP, Am. String Tchrs. Assn., Nat. Band Assn. Lodges: Rotary (Quincy membership chmn. 1975-83, mem. Pocatello fine arts com. 1985—). Avocations: reading, traveling, photography. Office: Idaho State U Dept Music PO Box 8099 Pocatello ID 83209-0001

GEORGE, TIMOTHY G. metallurgist; BS in Metallurgy, U. Pitts., 1980; postgrad., U. N.Mex.; M in Mgmt./Human Rels./Orgnl. Behavior, U. Phoenix, 1990. With Kennametal Inc. Latrobe Rsch. Lab.; joined Dept. Energy Los Alamos (N.Mex.) Nat. Lab., 1983, head Actinide Ceramics Group, 1993, head Radioisotope Heat Source Program, 1993, head Cassini Heat Source Prodn. Project, 1993, project leader Nuc. Fuels Demonstration, 1997, acting dep. dir. Nuc. Materials Tech. Divsn., dir. Nuc. Materials Tech. Divsn., 1999—. Contbr. articles to profl. jours. Recipient James F. Lincoln Arc Welding Found. award, 1995; co-recipient Schreiber-Spence Space Achievement award Inst. for Space and Nuc. Power Studies, 1998. Office: Los Alamos Nat Lab Nuc Materials Divsn PO Box 1663 MSE500 NMT-DO Los Alamos NM 87545 E-mail: tgeorge@lanl.gov

GEORGE, VANCE, conductor; b. Bremen, Ind., Sept. 30, 1933; BA in Music Edn., Goshen Coll., Ind., 1955; Grad., Bhatkande Sch. Music and Dance, India, 1959; student, Goethe Inst., Germany, 1961; MusM in Conducting, Ind. Univ., 1963, Mus D in Conducting, 1965; Mus D (hon.), Kent State U., 1998. Chorus master Opera Theater, Ind. Univ., Bloomington, Ind., 1963-65; dir. Women's Chorus, Ind. Univ., Bloomington, 1963-65; dir. choral activities Univ. Wis., Madison, 1965-71; instr. Choral Inst., Am. Choral Found., Madison, 1967, 69; dir. choral activities Kent State Univ., Ohio, 1971-82; assoc. chorus conductor Cleveland Orch. Chorus, Cleveland Orch. Chamber Chorus, 1977-83; prof. conducting Festival of the Rockies, Whitefish, Mont., 1987; conductor Phoenix Bach Soc., Ariz., 1988-90; dir. San Francisco Symphony Chorus, Calif., 1983—. Bd. dirs. Choris Am.; former chmn. Cleve. Orch. Chorus, Sch. of the Cleve. Orch.; guest chorus dir. Kent State Univ. Chorus, Canton Symphony Orch., 1976-77, 80-81; vis. assoc. prof. Univ. Calif., Berkeley, 1983, 85, 87, 88. Condr. San Francisco Symphony, San Francisco Symphony Chorus, oratorio, seasonal concerts, pops, Asian Youth Orch., Asian Youth Chorus, Ein Deutsches Requiem (Grammy award Best Choral Performance 1995); studies in U.S., Europe, Canada, India. Recipient Grammy award for Best Choral Performance, 1992, 95; nominee Grammy award Mahler Symphony #2, 1994. Mem. IFCM, ACDA, Pi Kappa Lambda. Office: San Francisco Symphony Chorus 201 Van Ness Ave Ste 107 San Francisco CA 94102-4595 E-mail: vygeorg@aol.com

GEORGES, MAURICE OSTROW, retired lawyer; b. Portland, Oreg., Nov. 6, 1921; s. Thomas T. and Daisy P. (Ostrow) G.; m. Evelyn Stella Scher, Nov. 25, 1948; children: Andra R., Emily A. Georges Gottfried, Daniel O. AB, Reed Coll., 1947; LLB, Columbia U., 1950. Bar: Calif. 1951, Oreg. 1951. Assoc. in law U. Calif., Berkeley, 1950-51; assoc. King, Miller, Anderson, Nash & Yerke, Portland, 1951-56; ptnr. Miller Nash, Portland, 1956-92; of counsel Miller, Nash, Wiener, Hager & Carlsen (and predecessors), Portland, 1992-97. Contbr. articles to legal jours. Trustee Reed Coll., Portland, 1966-82; dir. Portland Opera Assn., 1983-89; v.p., dir. Contemporary Crafts Assn., 1969-72, Cmty. Music Ctr., Portland, 1974-76, Oreg. Humanities Coun., 1994-97. Staff sgt. AUS, 1942-46, ETO. Mem. ABA, Oreg. Bar Assn. (chmn. tax sect. 1960-61), Tualatin Country Club (pres. 1964-66), Astoria Golf and Country. Office: Miller Nash Wiener Hager 111 SW 5th Ave Ste 3500 Portland OR 97204-3699

GEORGES, ROBERT AUGUSTUS, emeritus educator, researcher, writer; b. Sewickley, Pa., May 1, 1933; s. John Thomas and Pauline Pantzis G.; m. Mary Virginia Ruth, Aug. 11, 1956; 1 child, Jonathan Gregory. BS, Ind. U. of Pa., 1954; MA, U. Pa., 1961; PhD, Indiana U., 1964. Tchr. Bound Brook (N.J.) High Sch., 1954-56, Southern Regional High Sch., Manahawkin, N.J., 1958-60; asst. prof. U. Kans., Lawrence, 1963-66, UCLA, 1966-70, assoc. prof., 1970-76, prof., 1976-94; prof. emeritus, 1994—. Vice chmn. Folklore and Mythology Program UCLA, 1966-82, chmn. 1983-86. Author: Greek-American Folk Beliefs and Narratives, 1980; co-author: People Studying People: The Human Element in Fieldwork, 1980, American and Canadian Immigrant and Ethnic Folkore: An Annotated Bibliography; co-author: Folkloristics: An Introduction, 1996; editor: Studies on Mythology, 1968; translator: Two Studies on Modern Greek, Folklore by Stilpon P. Kyriakides, 1968; contbr. numerous articles to folklore periodicals. With U.S. Army, 1956-58. NDEA fellow, 1962-63, Guggenheim fellow, 1969-70. Fellow Am. Folklore Soc.; mem. Calif. Folklore Soc. Home: 906 Fiske St Pacific Palisades CA 90272-3841 E-mail: rgeorges@ucla.edu

GERAGHTY, JOHN VINCENT, public relations consultant; b. Seattle, Feb. 23, 1934; s. John V. and Gladys I (Johnson) G.; children: Marcella Maile, Sheila Leek, Brigid Krause, Nora Lipton. BA in Comm., U. Wash., 1956; MPA (hon.), Ea. Washington U., 1994. Reporter Spokane (Wash.) Daily Chronicle, 1959-62; sec. to mayor/coun. City of Spokane, 1962-64; county commr. Spokane (Wash.) County, 1964-71; vp. guest rels. EXPO '74 Corp., Spokane, 1971-74; publisher, owner The Falls Newspaper, Spokane, 1974-76; v.p. Haworth & Anderson, Inc., Spokane, 1976-83; owner, pres. Jack Geraghty & Assocs., Spokane, 1983—; prin. Alliance Pacific, Inc., Spokane, 1985—; mayor City of Spokane, 1994-98. Bd. dirs., past pres. Future Spokane, 1983-89; cons. Citizens League of Greater Spokane. Bd. dirs. and past pres., Spokane Cmty. Mental Health Ctr., 1980-95; mem. and past chmn. bd. trustees Ea. Wash. U., Cheney, Wash., 1985-97; mem. and vice chair Spokane Centennial Projects Com., 1988. Mem. Pub. Rels Soc. Am. (pres. Spokane chpt. 1983), Spokane Pub. Rels. Coun. (past pres.), Spokane Club, Beta Theta Pi. Democrat. Roman Catholic. Avocations: golf, sailing, cooking. Home: PO Box 251 Spokane WA 99210-0251 Office: Jack Geraghty Assoc 621 W Mallon Ave Spokane WA 99201-2163

GERARD, SUSAN, state senator; Bachelors degree, Drake U.; MBA, Ariz. State U. Rep. rep. dist. 18 Ariz. Ho. of Reps.; Rep. senator dist. 18 Ariz. State Senate, 2000—. Mem. banking and ins. and govt. coms. Ariz. State Senate, chmn. health com.; mem. Fleming Fellows Bd., Nat. Conf. State Legislators Nat. Forum for State Health Policy Leadership, Ariz. Acad. Town Hall; mem. pub. health adv. bd. CDC. Mem. AIDS Task Force, Phoenix, Marcus House Bd.; bd. dirs. Mingus Mountain Estate Residential Ctr. Recipient Outstanding Leadership award Ariz. Assn. Managed Care Plans, Freedom of Info. award Ariz. Newspaper Assn. Office: Ariz State Senate State Capitol Rm 303 1700 W Washington Phoenix AZ 85007-2890 E-mail: sgerard@azleg.state.az.us

GERATY, LAWRENCE THOMAS, academic administrator, archaeologist; b. St. Helena, Calif., Apr. 21, 1940; s. Thomas Sinclair and Hazel Mae (McVicker) G.; m. Gillian Anne Keough, Aug. 5, 1962; children: Brent, Julie. BA, Pacific Union Coll., 1962; MA, Andrews U., 1963, BD, 1965; PhD, Harvard U., 1972. Pastor 7th Day Adventist Ch., Calif., 1962-66; instr. old testament Andrews U., Berrien Springs, Mich., 1966-72, asst. prof. archaeology and history, 1972-76, assoc. prof. archaeology and history, 1976-80, prof., 1980-85; curator S.H. Horn Archaeol. Mus., Berrien Springs, 1976-85; dir. Inst. Archaeology Andrews U., Berrien Springs, 1981-85; pres. Atlantic Union Coll., Lancaster, Mass., 1985-93, La Sierra U., Riverside, Calif., 1993—. Project dir. Excavation of Tell Hesban, Jordan, 1973-76, Madaba Plains Project, Jordan, 1984—; v.p. Am. Ctr. of Oriental Rsch., Amman, 1985—. Editor, contbr. articles to profl. jours. Bd. dirs. Thayer Symphony Orch., Lancaster, Mass., 1985-93; mem. Edn. Forum of Clinton, Mass., 1990-93. Fulbright fellow, 1970-71, Robert H. Pfeiffer fellow, 1970-71; grantee Ford Found., 1969-70, Ctr. Field Rsch., 1976, NEH, 1979. Mem. Soc. Bibl. Literature (pres. 1988-90), Archeol. Inst. Am., Clinton C. of C. (bd. dirs. 1985-92), Riverside C. of C. (bd. dirs. 1996—), Raincross Club, Employers Group (bd. dirs. 1996—). Seventh-Day Adventist. Office: La Sierra U Office Pres 4700 Pierce St Riverside CA 92505-3332

GERBA, CHARLES PETER, microbiologist, educator; b. Blue Island, Ill., Sept. 10, 1945; s. Peter and Virginia (Roulo) G.; m. Peggy Louise Scheitlin, June 6, 1970; children: Peter, Phillip. BS in Microbiology, Ariz. State U., 1969; PhD in Microbiology, U. Miami, 1973. Postdoctoral fellow Baylor Coll. Medicine, Houston, 1973-74, asst. prof. microbiology, 1974-81; assoc. prof. U. Ariz., Tucson, 1981-85, prof., 1985—. Cons. EPA, Tucson, 1980—, World Health Orgn., Pan Am. Health Orgn., 1989—; advisor CRC Press, Boca Raton, Fla., 1981—. Editor: Methods in Environmental Virology, 1982, Groundwater Pollution Microbiology, 1984, Phage Ecology, 1987, Pollution Sci., 1996; contbr. numerous articles to profl. and sci. jours. Mem. Pima County Bd. Health, 1986-92; mem. sci. adv. bd. EPA, 1987—. Recipient McKee medal Water Environ. Fedn., 1996; named Outstanding Research Scientist U. Ariz., 1984, 92, Outstanding Rsch. Team, 1994. Fellow AAAS (environ. sci. and engring.), Am. Acad. Microbiology, Am. Soc. Microbiology (divsn. chmn. 1982-83, 87-88, pres. Ariz. chpt. 1984-85, councilor 1985-88); mem. Internat. Assn. Water Pollution Rsch. (sr. del. 1985-91), Am. Water Works Assn. (A.P. Black award 1997), Water Quality Assn. (Hom. Mem. award 1998). Achievements include research in environmental microbiology, colloid transport in ground water, wastewater reuse and risk assessment. Home: 1980 W Paseo Monserrat Tucson AZ 85704-1329 Office: U Ariz Dept Microbiol & Immunol Wat Tucson AZ 85721-0001 E-mail: gerba@ag.arizona.edu

GERBER, WILLIAM NORMAN, motion picture executive; b. Las Vegas, Nev., Apr. 30, 1957; s. Roy Herbert and Constance Doris Gerber. West coast dir. Nemporer Records, Los Angeles, 1978-79; exec. v.p. Lookout Mgmt., Los Angeles, 1979-84; prin. owner Gerber/Rodkin Co., Los Angeles, 1985-86; v.p. theatrical prodn. divsn. Warner Bros., Inc., Burbank, 1986-98, co-pres. worldwide theatrical prodn. Calif., 1998; prodr. Gerber Pictures, 1998. Office: Gerber Pictures 9465 Wilshire Blvd Beverly Hills CA 90212-2612 Fax: 310 385-5881

GERBERDING, WILLIAM PASSAVANT, retired university president; b. Fargo, N.D., Sept. 9, 1929; s. William Passavant and Esther Elizabeth Ann (Habighorst) G.; m. Ruth Alice Albrecht, Mar. 25, 1952; children: David Michael, Steven Henry, Elizabeth Ann, John Martin. B.A., Macalester Coll., 1951; M.A., U. Chgo., 1956, Ph.D., 1959. Congl. fellow Am. Polit. Sci. Assn., Washington, 1958-59; instr. Colgate U., Hamilton, N.Y., 1959-60; research asst. Senator E.J. McCarthy, Washington, 1960-61; staff Rep. Frank Thompson, Jr., Washington, 1961; faculty UCLA, 1961-72, prof., chmn. dept. polit. sci., 1970-72; dean faculty, v.p. for acad. affairs Occidental Coll., Los Angeles, 1972-75; exec. vice chancellor UCLA, 1975-77; chancellor U. Ill., Urbana-Champaign, 1978-79; pres. U. Wash., Seattle, 1979-95. Bd. dirs. Wash. Mut. Bank, Safeco Corp., Seattle; cons. Dept. Def., 1962, Calif. Assembly, 1965; chair Inst. Medicine, Clin. Rsch. Roundtable, 2000—. Author: United States Foreign Policy: Perspectives and Analysis, 1966; co-editor, contbg. author: The Radical Left: The Abuse of Discontent, 1970. Trustee Macalester Coll., 1980—83, 1996—2001, Gates Cambridge Trust, U. Cambridge, England, 2000—. With USN, 1951—55. Recipient Distinguished Teaching award U. Calif., Los Angeles, 1966; Ford Found. grantee, 1967-68 Office: Univ Wash PO Box 352800 Seattle WA 98195-2800

GERBRACHT, ROBERT THOMAS (BOB GERBRACHT), painter, educator; b. Erie, Pa., June 23, 1924; s. Earl John and Lula Mary (Chapman) G.; m. Delia Marie Paz, Nov. 27, 1952; children: Mark, Elizabeth, Catherine. BFA, Yale U., 1951; MFA, U. So. Calif., 1952. Cert. tchr., Calif. Art tchr. William S. Hart Jr. and Sr. High Sch., Newhall, Calif., 1954-56; stained glass artist Cummings Studios, San Francisco, 1956-58; art tchr. McKinley Jr. High Sch., Redwood City, Calif., 1958-60, Castro Jr. High Sch., San Jose, 1960-79; portrait artist, tchr. San Jose, San Francisco, 1979—; represented by John Pence Gallery, San Francisco. Instr. art Coll. of Notre Dame, Belmont, Calif., 1955-60, San Jose City Coll., 1967-71, Notre Dame Novitiate, Saratoga, 1976-79, U. Calif., Santa Cruz, 1980-81; art cons. Moreland Sch. Dist., Campbell, Calif., 1979-80; instr. nationwide workshops, Calif., Colo., Fla., Kans., Mass., Nebr., Nev., N.Mex., N.Y., Oreg., S.C., Vt., Wash., Wis., Mex., 1980—; presenter guest portrait demonstrations to numerous art assns. and clubs, San Francisco area including The Commonwealth Club of Calif., 1992 and The Acad. of Art Coll., 1998. Exhibited in Charles and Emma Frye Mus. Fine Art, Seattle, Rosicrucian Mus., San Jose, Calif., San Jose Mus. of Art, Denver Art Mus., Erie Mus. Art, Triton Mus. of Art, Santa Clara, Calif., Commonwealth Club Calif., 1992, San Francisco Acad. of Art Coll., 1998, 2000, Israel, Austria, China; represented in permanent collection Triton Mus. Art, Santa Clara, Calif.; portraits include Marie Gallo, Mrs. Bruce Jenner, Austin Warburton, Rev. Jack La Rocca, Rev. Cecil Williams; subject of articles in Today's Art and Graphics, Art and Antique Collector, Am. Artist, U.S. ART, Pastel Jour., Internat. Artist, Pastel Artist Internat.; work reproduced and included in Best of Pastel, Best of Oil Painting, 1996, Pastel Highlights, 1996, Portrait Inspirations, The Best of Portrait Painting, 1997, Best of Pastel 2, 1998. Cpl. U.S. Army, 1943-46. Recipient Am. Artist Achievement award Tchr. of Pastels, 1993, Gold medal Amsterdam Art Competition, 1998. Mem. Pastel Soc. Am. (master pastellist), Pastel Soc. West Coast (advisor, Best of Show 1988), Soc. Western Artists (trustee 1989-97, Best of Show 1982, 85, 90, Best Portrait award 1984, Best of Show Nat. Open Exhbn. 1999), Oil Painters Am. Home and Office: 1301 Blue Oak Ct Pinole CA 94564-2145

GERGIANNAKIS, ANTHONY EMMANUEL **See ANTHONY, METROPOLITAN OF THE DARDANELLES**

GERHARDT, HEINZ ADOLF AUGUST, retired aircraft design engineer; b. Biedenkopf, Hessen, Germany, Jan. 31, 1934; came to U.S., 1962; s. Heinrich Ludwig and Emilie Henriette (Schuechler) G.; m. Heide Hanne Waltraud von Ryschkowsky, Sept. 3, 1962; children: Heinrich, Friederike, Helmar. MS in Mech. Engring., Tech. U. Darmstadt, Germany, 1961. Engr. Heinkel AG, Munich, 1962; from engr. to mgr. advanced aerodesign Northrop Corp., Hawthorne, Calif., 1962-91, prin. engr., 1991-99; ret., 1999. Patentee in field. Recipient Otto Lilienthal prize Wissenschaftliche Gesellschaft fuer Luftfahrt, 1954, Aerodynamic award Am. Inst. of Aeronautics and Astronautics, 1994 Mem. AIAA (assoc. fellow, Aerodynamics award 1994), Soc. Automotive Engrs., Deutsche Gesellschaft fuer Luft und Raumfahrt. Avocations: flying, sailplanes, swimming, hiking.

GERINGER, JAMES E. governor; b. Wheatland, Wyo., Apr. 24, 1944; m. Sherri Geringer; children: Jen, Val, Rob, Meri, Beckie. BS in Mechanical Engring., Kans. State U., 1967. Commd. officer USAF; with contract administration Mo. Basin Power Project's Laramie River Sta., 1977-79; elected mem. Wyo. Legislature, 1982; farm owner, 1987—; Governor State of Wyoming, 1994—. Participant in various space devel. programs, Calif., devel. variety Air Force and NASA space boosters including launches of reconnaissance satellites, the NASA Viking Mars lander, an upper stage booster for the space shuttle and the Global Positioning Satellite System; chief of computer programming at a ground receiving station for early warning satellites. Mem. Nat. Fedn. Ind. Bus., Am. Legion, Farm Bur., Farmer's Union, Rotary, Lions, Ducks Unlimited, Pheasants Forever, C. of C. Lutheran. Office: Office Gov 200 W 24th St Rm 124 Cheyenne WY 82002-0001*

GERKEN, WALTER BLAND, insurance company executive; b. N.Y.C., Aug. 14, 1922; s. Walter Adam and Virginia (Bland) G.; m. Darlene Stolt, Sept. 6, 1952; children: Walter C., Ellen M., Beth L., Daniel J., Andrew P., David A. BA, Wesleyan U., 1948; MPA, Maxwell Sch. Citizenship and Pub. Affairs, Syracuse, 1958. Supr. budget and adminstrv. analysis, Wis., Madison, 1950-54; mgr. investments Northwestern Mut. Life Ins. Co., Milw., 1954-67; v.p. finance Pacific Mut. Life Ins. Co., L.A., 1967-69, exec. v.p., 1969-72, pres., 1972-75, chmn. bd., 1975-87, chmn. exec. com. Los Angeles, 1987-95, also dir.; sr. advisor Boston Consulting Group. Bd. dirs. Mullin Cons., Inc.; vice-chmn. Global Fin. Group, 2000—. Bd. dirs. Keck Found.; trustee emeritus Occidental Coll. L.A., Wesleyan U., Middletown, Conn.; bd. dirs. Nature Conservancy Calif.; mem. Calif. Citizens Budget Com., Calif. Commn. Campaign Fin. Reform, Calif.

Commn. on Higher Edn.; bd. dirs., former chair Exec. Svc. Corps. So. Calif.; v.p. Orange County Cmty. Found.; mem. adv. bd. The Maxwell Sch. Citizenship and Pub. Affairs, Syracuse U. Decorated D.F.C., Air medal. Mem. Calif. Club, Dairymen's Country Club (Boulder Junction, Wis.), Automobile Club So. Calif. (bd. dirs.), Pauma Valley Country Club, Edison Internat., Times Mirror Co. Office: Pimco Advisors LP 800 Newport Center Dr Newport Beach CA 92660-6309 E-mail: wgerken@pimcoadvisors.com

GERMAN, DONALD FREDERICK, physician; b. San Francisco, Oct. 2, 1935; m. Marilyn Sue King; children: Susan, Charles, Donald. BS, U. San Francisco, 1956; MD, U. Calif., San Francisco, 1960. Diplomate Am. Bd. Pediats., Am. Bd. Allergy and Immunology. Intern Kaiser Found. Hosp., San Francisco, 1960-61, resident in pediats., 1963-65, resident, fellow in allergy, 1966-68; staff pediatrician Kaiser Med. Ctr., Santa Clara, Calif., 1965-66, staff allergist, 1968-69; chief dept. allergy Kaiser Permanente Med. Ctr., San Francisco, 1969-99, allergy staff physician, 1999—. Clin. prof. pediatrics U. Calif. Med. Sch., San Francisco, 1991—. Capt. USAF, 1961-63. Fellow Am. Acad. Pediats., Am. Coll. Allergy and Immunology, Am. Acad. Allergy and Immunology; mem. Calif. Soc. Allergy and Immunology (pres.). Avocations: running, hiking, fly fishing, travel. Office: Kaiser Permanente Med Ctr Allergy Dept 1635 Divisadero St Ste 101 San Francisco CA 94115-3000 also: Asthma and Allergy Clinic of Maria # 110 1030 Sir Francis Drake Blvd Northfield CA 94904 E-mail: Dfgerman@aol.com

GERMAN, WILLIAM, newspaper editor; b. N.Y.C., Jan. 4, 1919; s. Sam and Celia (Norack) G.; m. Gertrude Pasenkoff, Oct. 12, 1940 (dec. 1998); children: David, Ellen, Stephen. B.A., Bklyn. Coll., 1939; M.S., Columbia U., 1940; Nieman fellow, Harvard U., 1950. Mng. editor KQED, Newspaper of the Air, 1968; editor Chronicle Fgn. Service, 1960-77; reporter, asst. fgn., news, mng., exec. editor, editor San Francisco Chronicle, 1940-2000, editor emeritus, 2000—. Lectr. U. Calif., Berkeley, 1946-47, 68-70 Editor: San Francisco Chronicle Reader, 1962. Bd. trustees World Affairs Coun. Served with AUS, 1943-45. Mem. AP Mng. Editors Assn., Am. Soc. Newspaper Editors, Commonwealth Club of Calif. (pres. 1995). Home: 150 Lovell Ave Mill Valley CA 94941-1883 Office: San Francisco Chronicle 901 Mission St San Francisco CA 94103-2905 E-mail: wgerman@sfchronicle.com

GEROU, PHILLIP HOWARD, architect; b. Natick, Mass., July 20, 1951; s. James Francis and Enid (Meymaris) G.; m. Cheri Rodgers, Nov. 24, 1979; children: Gregory Bedford, Sara Christine. BArch, U. Nebr., 1974, MArch, 1975. Designer, owner Gerou & Assocs. Ltd., Evergreen, Colo., 1986—. Design cons. Kilimanjaro Children's Hosp., Tanzania, 1988-91, World Alpine Ski Championships, Vail, Colo., 1988. Pres. Colo. Soc. of Architects Ednl. Fund., Denver, 1986; del. State Rep. Assembly, Denver, 1986; trustee Rockland Community Ch., Denver, 1986-89. Recipient Citation award Nat. Assn. of Remodeling Industry, 1991, 96, Design Excellence Wood, Inc., 1990, Citation award, 1990. Fellow AIA (pres. Colo. chpt. 1986, bd. dirs. 1981-87, nat. dir. 1991-94, nat. v.p. 1995, dir. Nat. Ethics Coun. 1997—, chmn., 2001—, conf. chair Western Mtn. region design conf. 1990, Spl. Recognition award 1990), Nat. Coun. Archtl. Adminstrn. Bds. (examiner 1985). Republican. Mem. United Ch. of Christ. Avocations: skiing, travel, architectural design.

GERRITSEN, MARY ELLEN, vascular and cell biologist; b. Calgary, Alta., Can., Sept. 20, 1953; came to U.S., 1978; d. Thomas Clayton and Alice Irene (Minton) Cooper; m. Paul William Gerritsen, May 24, 1975 (div. 1977); m. Thomas Patrick Parks, Oct. 11, 1980; children: Kristen, Madelene. BSc summa cum laude, U. Calgary, 1975, PhD, 1978. Postdoctoral fellow U. Calif., San Diego, 1978-80; asst. prof. N.Y. Med. Coll., Valhalla, 1981-86, assoc. prof., 1986-90; sr. staff scientist Pharm. divsn. Bayer Corp., West Haven, Conn., 1990-93, head inflammation exploratory rsch., 1990-96, prin. staff scientist, 1993-97; vis. scientist Harvard U., 1996, assoc. dir. Cardiovascular Rsch., 2000—. Cons. Insite Vision, Alameda, Calif., 1987-89, Boehringer Ingelheim Pharms., Ridgefield, Conn., 1985-88; adj. assoc. prof. N.Y. Med. Coll., 1990-99. Mem. editorial bd. Microvascular Rsch., 1988-96, Am. Jour. Physiology, 1993—, Am. Jour. Cardiovascular Pathology, 1996—, Circulation Rsch., 1997-99, Endothelium, 1999—; editor-in-chief Microcirculation, 1993-98; cons. editor, 1998—; editor N.Am. Vascular Biology Orgn. Newsletter; contbr. articles to profl. jours. I. W. Killam Found. fellow, 1976, Med. Rsch. Coun. Can. fellow, 1978. Mem. Am. Soc. for Pharmacology and Exptl. Therapeutics, Am. Physiol. Soc., Assn. Rsch. on Vision and Ophthalmology, Am. Soc. Investigational Pathology, Soc. Leukocyte Biology, Am. Soc. Cell Biology, Microcirculatory Soc. (mem. coun. 1989-92, chairperson publs. com. 1991-93, Mary Weideman award 1985, Young Investigator award 1984), N.Am. Vascular Biology Orgn. (mem. steering com. 1993, mem. coun. 1994-97, editor-in-chief newsletter 1994-97, sec.-treas. 1997-99, pres.-elect 1999). Avocations: running, step aerobics, horticulture. Office: Genentech Inc MS 42 1 Dna Way South San Francisco CA 94080-4990

GERSTELL, A. FREDERICK, aggregates, asphalt and concrete manufacturing executive; b. 1938; AB, Princeton U., 1960. Vice pres. mktg., dir. Alpha Portland Cement Co., 1960-75; v.p. Calif. Portland Cement Co., L.A., 1975-81, pres., chief operating officer, 1981-84, CalMat Co., L.A., 1984-88, pres., chief exec. officer, chief operating officer, 1988-90, chmn.bd., pres., chief exec. officer/chief operating officer, 1990-96, chmn. bd., CEO, 1996-98, vice chmn., dir., 1998—. Trustee emeritus The Lawrenceville (N.J.) Sch. With USAR 1960-66. Mem. Merchants and Mfrs. Assn. (dir.), Nat. Stone Assn. (bd. dirs., vice chmn., exec. com.), Calif. C. of C. (bd. dirs.), Ameron, Inc. (dir.). Office: CalMat Co 3200 N San Fernando Rd Los Angeles CA 90065-1415

GERSTENBERGER, DONNA LORINE, humanities educator; b. Wichita Falls, Tex., Dec. 26, 1929; d. Donald Fayette and Mabel G. AB, Whitman Coll., 1951; MA, U. Okla., 1952, PhD, 1958. Asst. prof. English U. Colo., Boulder, 1958-60; prof. U. Wash., 1960-96, prof. emeritus, 1996—, chmn. undergrad. studies, 1971-74, assoc. dean Coll. Arts and Scis., dir. Coll. Honors and Office Undergrad. Studies, 1974-76, chmn. dept. English, 1976-83, vice chmn. faculty senate, 1984-85, chmn. faculty senate, 1985-86. Cons. in field; bd. dirs. Am. Lit. Classics; mem. grants-in-aid com. Am. Coun. Learned Socs.; chmn. region VII, Mellon Fellowships in Humanities, 1982-92; mem. adv. com. Grad. Record Exams, 1990-93, Coun. Internat. Exch. of Scholars, 1992-95. Author: J.M. Synge, 1964, 2d edition, 1988, The American Novel: A Checklist of Twentieth Century Criticism, vols. I and II, 1970, Directory of Periodicals, 1974, The Complex Configuration: Modern Verse Drama, 1973, Iris Murdoch, 1974, Richard Hugo, 1983; editor: Microcosm, 1969, Swallow Series in Bibliography, 1974—; assoc. editor: Abstracts of English Studies, 1958-68; founder, editor jour. Seattle Rev., 1983-96. Bd. dirs. N.W. Chamber Orch., Seattle, 1975-78, Wash. Friends Humanities, 1991—; trustee Wash. Commn. Humanities, 1985-91, pres., 1988-90; mem. vis. com. Lehigh U., 1987-92; pres. Am. Commn. for Irish Studies/West, 1989-91. Grantee Am. Council Learned Socs., 1962, 88, Am. Philos. Soc., 1963 Mem. MLA, Am. Com. Irish Studies. Office: U Wash Box 354330 Dept English Seattle WA 98195-4330

GERSTING, JUDITH LEE, computer science educator, researcher; b. Springfield, Vt., Aug. 20, 1940; d. Harold H. and Dorothy V. (Kinney) MacKenzie; m. John M. Gersting, Jr., Aug. 17, 1962; children: Adam, Jason. BS, Stetson U., 1962; MA, Ariz. State U., 1964, PhD, 1969. Assoc. prof. computer sci. U. Ctrl. Fla., Orlando, 1980-81; asst. prof. computer sci. Ind. U.-Purdue U., Indpls., 1970-73, assoc. prof., 1974-79, prof., 1981-93; prof. computer sci. U. Hawaii, Hilo, 1994—. Staff scientist Indpls. Ctr. for Advanced Rsch., 1982-84. Author: Mathematical Structures for Computer Science, 1999, Visual Basic Programming, 1996; contbr. articles to computer sci. jours. Mem. Assn. for Computing Machinery, IEEE Computer Soc. Avocations: youth soccer, reading. Office: U Hawaii 200 W Kawili St Hilo HI 96720-4075 E-mail: gersting@hawaii.edu

GERTH, DONALD ROGERS, university president; b. Chgo., Dec. 4, 1928; s. George C. and Madeleine (Canavan) G.; m. Beverly J. Hollman, Oct. 15, 1955; children: Annette, Deborah. BA, U. Chgo., 1947, AM, 1951, PhD, 1963. Field rep. S.E. Asia World Univ. Svc., 1950; asst. to pres. Shimer Coll., 1951; Admissions counselor U. Chgo., 1956-58; assoc. dean students, admissions and records, mem. dept. polit. sci. San Francisco St. U., San Francisco, 1958-63; assoc. dean instnl. relations and student affairs Calif. State Univ., 1963-64; chmn. commn. on extended edn. Calif. State Univs. and Colls., 1977-82; dean of students Calif. State U., Chico, 1964-68, prof. polit. sci., 1964-76, assoc. v.p. for acad. affairs, dir. internat. programs, 1969-70, v.p. acad. affairs, 1970-76; co-dir. Danforth Found. Research Project, 1968-69; coordinator Inst. Local Govt. and Public Service, 1968-70; pres., prof. polit. sci. and public adminstrn. Calif. State U., Dominguez Hills, 1976-84, pres., prof. govt. and adminstrn. Sacramento, 1984—. Past chair Accrediting Commn. for Sr. Colls. and Univs. of Western Coll. Assn.; chmn. admissions coun. Calif. State U.; bd. dirs. Ombudsman Found., L.A., 1968-71; com. continuing edn. Calif. Coordinating Coun. for Higher Edn., 1963-64; lectr. U. Philippines, 1953-54, Claremont Grad. Sch. and Univ. Ctr., 1965-69; chair Sacramento World Trade Ctr.; chmn. Calif. State U. Inst. Co-author: The Learning Society, 1969; author, editor: An Invisible Giant, 1971; contbg. editor Education for the Public Service, 1970, Papers on the Ombudsman in Higher Education, 1979. Mem. pers. commn. Chico Unified Sch. Dist., 1969-76, chmn., 1971-74; adv. com. on justice pgorams Butte Coll., 1970-76; mem. Varsity Scouting Coun., 1980-84; chmn. United Way campaign Calif. State Univs., L.A. County, 1981-82; bd. dirs. Sacramento Area United Way, campaign chmn., 1991-92, exec. com., 1991-96, vice chmn., 1992-94, chmn.-elect, 1994-95, chmn., 1995-96; mem. bd. dirs. South Bay Hosp. Found., 1979-82; mem. The Cultural Commn., L.A., 1981-84; mem. com. govtl. rels. Am. Coun. Edn. Capt. USAF, 1952-56. Mem. Internat. Assn. Univ. Pres. (pres. 1996-99), Am. Polit. Sci. Assn., Am. Soc. Pub. Adminstrn., Soc. Coll. and Univ. Planning, Western Govtl. Rsch. Assn., World Affairs Coun. No. Calif., Assn. Pub. Adminstrn. Edn. (chmn. 1973-74), Western Polit. Sci. Assn., Am. Assn. State Colls. and Univs. (bd. dirs.), Calif. State C. of C. (edn. com.), Assn. Governing Bds. of Univs. and Colls., Calif. State U. Inst. (chmn. bd. dirs.), UN Ednl., Sci. and Cultural Orgn. (mem. adv. com.), UN Univ. Coun., World Trade Ctr. Sacramento, (chmn.), Sacramento Club (bd. dirs.), Comstock Club. Democrat. Episcopalian. Avocations: tennis, skiing, reading. Home: 417 Websters Ct Roseville CA 95747-8339 Office: Calif State U 6000 J St # 206 Sacramento CA 95819-2605

GERWICK, BEN CLIFFORD, JR. construction engineer, educator; b. Berkeley, Calif., Feb. 22, 1919; s. Ben Clifford and Bernice (Coultrap) G.; m. Martelle Louise Beverly, July 28, 1941 (dec. Jan. 1995); children: Beverly (Mrs. Robert A. Brian), Virginia (Mrs. Roy Wallace), Ben Clifford III, William; m. Ellen Chaney Lynch, May 18, 1996. B.S., U. Calif., 1940. With Ben C. Gerwick, Inc., San Francisco, 1946—, pres., 1952-88, chmn., 1988-2000, sr. tech. cons., 2000—; exec. v.p. Santa Fe-Pomeroy, Inc., 1968-71; prof. civil engring. U. Calif., Berkeley, 1971-89, prof. emeritus, 1989—. Sponsoring mgr. Richmond-San Rafael bridge substructure, 1953-56, San Mateo-Hayward bridge, 1964-66; lectr. constrn. engring. Stanford U., 1962-68; cons. major bridge and marine constrn. projects; cons. engr. for ocean structures and overwater bridges, also offshore structures in U.S., North Sea, Arctic Ocean, Japan, Australia, Indonesia, Arabian Gulf, Hong Kong, Europe, Can., S.E. Asia, S.Am.; mem. U.S. Arctic Rsch. Commn., 1990-95. Author: Russian-English Dictionary of Prestressed Concrete and Concrete Construction, 1966, Construction of Prestressed Concrete Structures, 1971, 2d edit., 1996, Construction and Engineering Marketing for Major Project Services, 1981, Construction of Marine and Offshore Structures, 1986, 2nd edit., 2000; contbr. articles to profl. jours. Chmn. Marine Bd., Nat. Rsch. Coun., 1978-80. Served with USN, 1940-46; comdr. Res. ret. Recipient Golden Beaver award Beavers Constrn. Soc., 1974, Mörsch medal Deutsche Beton Verein, Weisbaden, Germany, 1978, Blakely Smith ocean engring. medal Soc. Naval Architects and Marine Engrs., 1981, Lockheed Ocean Engring. award Marine Tech. Soc., 1982, U. Calif. Berkeley Citation, 1989; named One of Top Engrs. in Past 125 Yrs., Engring. News Record, 2000, Internat. award Japan Soc. Civil Engring., 2001. Fellow ASCE (hon. mem., Karp award 1976, G. Brooks Earnest award 1980, Peurifoy award 1989, Pres.'s award 1989, Disting. Constructor award 2000, Ralph B. Peck Lectr. award 2001, Outstanding Lifetime Achievement award 2001), Am. Concrete Inst. (hon. mem., dir. 1960, Turner award 1974, Corbetta award 1981, Franklin Inst. Brown award 1984, Offshore Tech. Rsch. Ctr. Honors award 1992), Deep Founds. Inst. (Disting. Svc. award 1996), Internat. Assn. Bridge and Structural Engrs.; mem. NAE, Fédn. Internat. de la Precontrainte (pres. 1974-78, now hon. pres., Freyssinet medal 1982), Prestressed Concrete Inst. (pres. 1957-58, hon.), Japan Soc. Civil Engrs. (Internat. award 2001). Congregationalist. Clubs: Bohemian (San Francisco); Claremont Country (Oakland), World Trade Club (San Francisco). Home: 5727 Country Club Dr Oakland CA 94618-1717 Office: Ben C Gerwick Inc 20 California St Fl 4 San Francisco CA 94111-2607 E-mail: bcg@gerwick.com

GESCHKE, CHARLES M. computer scientist, computer company executive; b. Cleve., Sept. 11, 1939; married, 1964; 3 children. AB, Xavier U., 1962, MS, 1963; PhD in Computer Sci., Carnegie-Mellon U., 1972. Instr. math. John Carroll U., 1963-68; rsch. scientist computer sci. Palo Alto Rsch. Ctr., Xerox Corp., 1972-80, mgr. Imaging Sci. Lab., 1980-87; co-founder Adobe Sys. Inc., Mountain View, Calif., 1982, pres., chmn. bd., 1987-2000. Mem. NAE, Assn. Computer Math., Math. Assn. Am. Achievements include research in programming languages; machine design for efficient emulation of higher level languages; computer imaging and graphics.

GESHELL, RICHARD STEVEN, lawyer; b. Colorado Springs, Colo., Aug. 6, 1943; s. Peter Steven and Ann Elizabeth (Irwin) G.; m. Carol Ann Reed, Sept. 6, 1965; 1 child, Carmen Marie. BA in Chemistry, Ariz. State U., 1965; JD, U. Nebr., 1968. Bar: Nebr. 1968, U.S. Dist. Ct. Nebr. 1968, Hawaii 1983, U.S. Dist. Ct. Hawaii 1983, U.S. Ct. Appeals (9th cir.) 1984, U.S. Supreme Ct. 1986. With Robak and Geshell, Columbus, Nebr., 1968-83; ptnr. R. Steven Geshell, Honolulu, 1983—. Lawyer; b. Colorado Springs, Colo., Aug. 6, 1943; s. Peter Steven and Ann Elizabeth (Irwin) G.; m. Carol Ann Reed, Sept. 6, 1965; 1 child, Carmen Marie. BA in Chemistry, Ariz. State U., 1965; JD, U. Nebr., 1968. Bar: Nebr. 1968, U.S. Dist. Ct. Nebr. 1968, Hawaii 1983, U.S. Dist. Ct. Hawaii 1983, U.S. Ct. Appeals (9th cir.) 1984, U.S. Supreme Ct. 1986. Mem. Robak and Geshell, Columbus, Nebr., 1968-83; ptnr. R. Steven Geshell, Honolulu, 1983—. Served to capt. USAR, 1974-83. Mem. Hawaii Bar Assn., Blue Key (pres. 1964-65), Elks (chief forum 1984, trustee), Phi Sigma Kappa. Republican. Capt. USAR, 1974-83. Mem. Hawaii Bar Assn., Blue Key (pres. 1964-65), Elks (chief forum 1984, trustee), Phi Sigma Kappa. Republican. Home: 1155 Kaluanui Rd Honolulu HI 96825-1357 Office: Ste #116 6600 Kalanianaole Hwy Honolulu HI 96825 E-mail: geshell@lava.net

GEST, HOWARD DAVID, lawyer; b. Bergenfield, N.J., Jan. 24, 1952; m. Lucy Acevedo; 1 child, Aaron. AB in Econs., U. Calif., Berkeley, 1974; JD, Hastings Coll., 1977. Bar: Calif. 1977. Staff atty. U.S. Ct. Appeals (9th cir.), San Francisco, 1977-78; asst. U.S. atty. Cen. Dist. Calif., L.A., 1978-83; ptnr. Sidley & Austin, L.A., 1983-99, Burhenn & Gest, L.A., 2000—. Office: Burhenn & Gest LLP Ste 2200 624 S Grand Ave Los Angeles CA 90017 E-mail: hgest@burhenngest.com

GESTON, MARK SYMINGTON, lawyer; b. Atlantic City, June 20, 1946; s. John Charles and Mary Tobiatha (Simmington) G.; m. Gayle Francis Howard, June 12, 1971 (div. Aug. 1972); m. Marijke Havinga, Aug. 14, 1976; children: Camille LaCroix, Robert L. LaCroix, Emily S. Geston. AB in History, Kenyon Coll., 1968; JD, NYU, 1971. Bar: Idaho, U.S. Ct. Appeals (9th cir.). AB in History with high honors Eberle & Berlin, Boise, Idaho, 1971—. Author: Lords of the Starship, 1967, Out of the Mouth of the Dragon, 1969, The Day Star, 1972, The Seige of Wonder, 1975, Mirror to the Sky, 1992, The Stronghold If, 1973; contbr. stories to Amazing Stories, Fantasy and Sci. Fiction. Recipient prize for achievement in lit., Kenyon Coll., 1968; named Root-Tilden fellow NYU, 1968-71. Mem. Idaho State Bar Assn., Phi Beta Kappa. Avocation: writing. Office: Eberle & Berlin PO Box 1368 Boise ID 83701-1368

GETIS, ARTHUR, geography educator; b. Phila., July 6, 1934; s. Samuel J. and Sophie Getis; m. Judith M. Marckwardt, July 23, 1961; children: Hilary Hope Tarazi, Victoria Lynn, Anne Patterson Tibbetts. BS, Pa. State U., 1956, MS, 1958; PhD, U. Wash., 1961. Asst. instr. geography U. Wash., 1960-61; asst. prof. Mich. State U., 1961-63; faculty Rutgers U., New Brunswick, N.J., 1963-77, prof. geography, 1969-77, dir. grad. programs in geography, 1970-73, chmn. New Brunswick geography dept., 1971-73; prof. geography U. Ill., Urbana-Champaign, 1977-90, San Diego State U., 1990—, doctoral program coord., 1990-92, Stephen/Mary Birch Found. Endowed Chair of Geog. Studies, 1992—, Albert W. Johnson Univ. Rsch. Lectureship, 1995; head dept. U. Ill., 1977-83, dir. Sch. Social Scis., 1983-84; centennial fellow Pa. State U., 1996; A. Robinson lectr. Ohio State U., 1999. Vis. lectr. Bristol U., Eng., 1966-67, UCLA, summers 1968, 74, U. B.C., 1969; vis. prof. Princeton U., 1971-74; vis. disting. prof. San Diego State U., 1989; mem. Regional Sci. Research Group, Harvard U., 1970; panelist NSF, 1981-83 Author: (with B. Boots) Models of Spatial Processes, 1978, Point Pattern Analysis, 1988, (with J. Getis and J.D. Fellmann) Geography, 1981, Human Geography, 7th edit., 2001, Introduction to Geography, 7th edit., 2000, (edited with J. Getis) The United States and Canada, 1995, 2d edit., 2001, The Tyranny of Data, 1996, (edited with M.M. Fischer) Recent Developments in Spatial Analysis, 1997; co-editor Jour. Geographical Systems, 1992—; contbg. editor, assoc. editor: Jour. Geography, 1972-74; mem. editl. bd. Nat. Geog. Rsch., 1984-90, Rsch. and Exploration, 1991-95, Geog. Analysis, 1991—, Papers in Regional Sci., 1999—, Annals of Regional Sci., 1999—; contbr. articles to profl. jours. Mem. Urbana Zoning Bd. Appeals, 1980-84; co-pres. Univ. High Sch. Parent-Faculty Orgn., 1982-83; bd. dirs. Univ. Consortium for Geog. Info. Scis., 1997—, pres.-elect, 2001—. Rutgers U. faculty fellow, 1970; East-West Center sr. fellow, 1974; NSF grantee, 1983-85, 1992-94; recipient Walter Isard award N.Am. Regional Sci. Coun., 1997. Mem. Assn. Am. Geographers (grantee 1964-65, vis. scientist 1970-72, chair math. models and quantitative methods splty. group 1991-92), Western Regional Sci. Assn. (bd. dirs. 1992-97, pres. 1998—), Regional Sci. Assn. (pres. N.E. sect. 1973-74, bd. dirs. 1998—), Internat. Inst. Brit. Geographers, Internat. Geog. Union (sec. commn. math. models 1988-96), Sigma Xi. Home: 5135 Jumilla St San Diego CA 92124-1503 Office: San Diego State U Dept Geography San Diego CA 92182 E-mail: arthur.getis@sdsu.edu

GETREU, SANFORD, city planner; b. Mar. 9, 1930; s. Isadore and Tillie (Kuchinsky) G.; m. Gara Eileen Smith, Dec. 8, 1952 (div. Feb. 1983); children: David Bruce, Gary Benjamin, Allen Dana; m. Kelly Heim, Aug. 8, 1988. BA in Arch., Ohio State U., 1953; MA in Regional Planning, Cornell U., 1955. Resident planner Mackesey & Reps., consultants, Rome, 1955-56; planning dir. Rome, 1956-57; dir. gen. planning Syracuse, N.Y., 1957-59; dep. commr. planning, 1959-62; commr. planning, 1962-65; planning dir. San Jose, Calif., 1965-74; urban planning cons., 1974—. Pres. Sanford Getreu, AICP, Inc., vis. lectr., critic Cornell U., 1960-65, Syracuse U., 1962-65, Stanford, 1965, San Jose State Coll., 1965, Santa Clara U., Calif. State Poly. Coll., DeAnza Coll., San Jose City Coll., U. Calif. at Berkeley; pres. planning dept. League of Calif. Cities, 1973-74; advisor State of Calif. Office of Planning and Research. Past bd. dirs. Theater Guild, San Jose, Triton Mus., San Jose. Mem. Am. Soc. Cons. Planners, Am. Planning Assn., Am. Inst. Cert. Planners, Bay Area Planning Dirs. Assn. (v.p. 1965-74, mem. exec. com. 1973-74), Assn. Bay Area Govts. (regional planning com. 1967-74), Rotary. Home and Office: 105 Coronado Ave Los Altos CA 94022-2222

GETTING, IVAN ALEXANDER, physicist, former aerospace company executive; b. N.Y.C., Jan. 18, 1912; s. Milan and Harriet (Almasy) G.; m. Dorothea Louise Gracy, Oct. 2, 1937 (dec. Sept. 1976); children: Nancy Louise Secker, Ivan Craig, Peter Alexander; m. Helen Avery, Jan. 9, 1977. SB, MIT, 1933; DPhil, Oxford U., 1935; DSc (hon.), Northeastern U., 1954, U. So. Calif., 1986. Jr. fellow Harvard U., Cambridge, Mass., 1935-40; mem. staff, head divsn. 8 radiation lab. MIT, Cambridge, 1940-45, assoc. prof. elec. engring., 1945-46, prof., 1946-50; asst. for devel. planning, dep. chief of staff USAF, Washington, 1950-51; v.p. engring and research Raytheon Corp., Waltham, Mass., 1951-60; pres., chief exec. officer The Aerospace Corp., El Segundo, Calif., 1960-77. Cons. USAF, USN, U.S. Army, NRC, Dept. Def., others, 1945—. Contbr. articles to profl. jours.; patentee in field. Dir. Los Angeles World Affairs Council, 1961—. Fellow AIAA (hon.), IEEE (pres. 1978), Am. Inst. Physics, Am. Acad. Arts and Scis.; mem. Nat. Acad. Engring., L.A. Yacht Club, Cosmos Club.

GETTY, GORDON PETER, composer, philanthropist; b. Los Angeles, Dec. 20, 1933; s. J. Paul and Ann Rork (Light) G.; m. Ann Getty; 4 children. Studied, voice with Easton Kent, piano with Robert Vetlesen, theory with Sol Joseph, 1961-62; BS, San Francisco Conservatory Music, hon. music degree, 1981, Pepperdine U., 1985; hon. doctorate, Mannes Coll. Music, N.Y.C., 1986. Former cons. Getty Oil Co., dir.; former chmn. LSB Leakey Found., Pasadena, Calif., now trustee. Works include opera in two acts Plump Jack, commnd. by Globe Shakespeare Ctr., London, performed by San Francisco Symphony, 1985, also Scene One broadcast live from Davies Symphony Hall, San Francisco, Mar. 1985; Emily Dickinson Song Cycle The White Election, 30 performances U.S. and abroad, 1981-85, also broadcast live from Nat. Gallery Art, Washington, 1985; Victorian Scenes, performed San Francisco Girls Chorus U. Calif., Berkeley, WInifred Baker Choral, 1985; Nine Piano Pieces performed by Stewart Gordon, 1985; A Cappella Choruses and Piano Works broadcast live Georgetown U., Washington, Apr., 1985; author monograph on White Election, poems My Uncle's House, 1984, other poetry. Adv. dir. Met. Opera, 1977—; trustee Mannes Coll. Music, 1982—; dir. San Francisco Symphony, 1979—. Recipient Golden Plate award Am. Acad. Achievement, 1985, Achievement Arts award Northwood Inst., 1985. Office: Rork Music Publ 1 Embarcadero Ctr Ste 1050 San Francisco CA 94111-3698

GETZ, WAYNE MARCUS, biomathematician, researcher, educator; b. Johannesburg, Republic of South Africa, Apr. 26, 1950; came to U.S., 1979; m. Jennifer Bryna Gonski, Feb. 15, 1972; children: Stacey Lynn, Trevor Russell. BSc with honors, U. Witwatersrand, South Africa, 1972, PhD, 1976; DSc, U. Cape Town, South Africa, 1995. Rsch. scientist Coun. for Sci. and Indsl. Rsch., Pretoria, South Africa, 1974-79; biomathematician U. Calif., Berkeley, 1979—, prof. entomology, 1987-93, prof. environ. sci., 1993—; [illegible] 1997—; [illegible] prof., 1998—. Cons. Nat. Marine Fisheries Svc., 1980-89. Author: (with R. Haight) Population Harvesting: Demographic Models of Fish, Forest, and Animal Resources, 1989; editor Oxford U. Press book series Biol. Resource Mgmt., 1983-97; mem. editl. bd. Ecol. Applications, 1994-96, Annales Zoologica Fennici; contbr. articles to profl. jours. Rsch. grantee NSF, NIH, Whitehall Found., Alfred P. Sloan Found., Def. Advanced Rsch. Programs Adminstrn.; Alexander von Humboldt U.S. Sr. Scientist awardee,

1993. Fellow AAAS, Calif. Acad. Scis.; mem. Internat. Soc. for Neuroethology, Soc. Am. Naturalist, Internat. Soc. for Ecol. Modelling, Internat. Neurol. Network Soc., Ecology Soc. Am., Resource Modelling Assn. (pres. 1995-96, bd. dirs. 1992-98), Soc. for Math. Biology. Office: Univ Calif Dep Env Sci Policy Mgmt Berkeley CA 94720-0001

GEYMAN, JOHN PAYNE, physician, educator; b. Santa Barbara, Calif., Feb. 9, 1931; s. Milton John and Betsy (Payne) G.; m. Eugenia Clark Deichler, June 9, 1956; children: John Matthew, James Caleb, William Sabin. A.B. in Geology, Princeton U., 1952; M.D., U. Calif., San Francisco, 1960. Diplomate: Am. Bd. Family Practice. Intern L.A. County Gen. Hosp., 1960-61; resident in gen. practice Sonoma County Hosp., Santa Rosa, Calif., 1961-63; pvt. practice specializing in family practice Mt. Shasta, 1963-69; dir. family practice residency program Community Hosp. Sonoma County, Santa Rosa, 1969-71; assoc. prof. family practice, chmn. divsn. family practice U. Utah, 1971-72; prof., vice chmn. dept. family practice U. Calif., Davis, 1972-77; prof., chmn. dept. family medicine U. Wash., 1977-90, prof. family medicine, 1990-93; prof. family medicine emeritus, 1993—. Author: The Modern Family Doctor and Changing Medical Practice, 1971, Family Practice: Foundation of Changing Health Care, 1980, 2d edit., 1985, Flight as a Lifetime Passion: Adventures, Misadventures and Lessons, 2000; editor: Content of Family Practice, 1976, Family Practice in the Medical School, 1977, Research in Family Practice, 1978, Preventive Medicine in Family Practice, 1979, Profile of the Residency Trained Family Physician in the U.S, 1970-79, Funding of Patient Care, Education and Research in Family Practice, 1981, The Content of Family Practice: Current Status and Future Trends, 1982, Archives of Family Practice, 1980, 81, 82; founding editor Jour. Family Practice, 1973-90; editor Jour. Am. Bd. Family Practice, 1990—; co-editor: Behavioral Science in Family Practice, 1980, Evidence-Based Clinical Practice: Concepts and Approaches, 2000, Textbook of Rural Medicine, 2000, Health Care in America: Can Our Ailing System Be Healed? 2002; editor: Family Practice: An International Perspective in Developed Countries, 1983. Served to lt. (j.g.) USN, 1952-55, PTO. Recipient Gold-headed Cane award U. Calif. Sch. Medicine, 1960, Alumnus of Yr., 1998. Mem. Am. Acad. Family Physicians, Soc. Tchrs. Family Medicine, Inst. Medicine of Nat. Acad. Scis. Unitarian. Home: 53 Avian Ridge Ln Friday Harbor WA 98250-8895 Office: Univ Wash Sch Medicine Dept Family Medicine PO Box 354696 Seattle WA 98195-4696

GHAUSI, MOHAMMED SHUAIB, electrical engineering educator, university dean; b. Kabul, Afghanistan, Feb. 16, 1930; came to U.S., 1951, naturalized, 1963; s. Mohammed Omar and Homaira G.; m. Marilyn Buchwold, June 12, 1961; children: Nadjya, Simine. B.S. summa cum laude, U. Calif., Berkeley, 1956, M.S., 1957, Ph.D., 1960. Prof. elec. engring. NYU, 1960-72; head elec. scis. sect. NSF, Washington, 1972-74; prof., chmn. elec. engring. dept. Wayne State U., Detroit, 1974-77; John F. Dodge prof. Oakland U., Rochester, Mich., 1978-83, dean Sch. Engring. and Computer Sci., 1978-83; dean Coll. Engring., U. Calif., Davis, 1983-96, interim vice chancellor rsch., vice provost, dean grad., 1996-97. Mem. adv. panel NSF, 1989. Author: Principles and Design of Linear Active Circuits, 1965, Introduction to Distributed-Parameter Networks, 1968, Electronic Circuits, 1971, Modern Filter Design: Active RC and Switched Capacitor, 1981, Electronic Devices and Circuits: Discrete and Integrated, 1985, Design of Analog Filters, 1990, also numerous articles.; cons. editor Van Nostrand Rinehold Pub. Co., 1968-71. Mem. disting. alumni rev. panel Elec. Engring. and Computer Sci. programs U. Calif., Berkeley, 1973; mem. external bd. visitors U. Pa., 1974. Recipient Outstanding Alumnus award in Elec. Engring. and Computer Sci., U. Calif., 1998. Fellow IEEE (chmn. edn. medal com. 1990-92, Centennial medal, Alexander von Humboldt prize, circuits and systems soc. edn. award); mem. Circuits and System Soc. (v.p. 1970-72, pres. 1976), N.Y. Acad. Scis., Engring. Soc. Detroit, Sigma Xi, Phi Beta Kappa, Tau Beta Pi, Eta Kappa Nu. Office: U Calif Office of Dean Coll Engring Davis CA 95616 E-mail: msghausi@uc.davis.edu

GHEZ, ANDREA MIA, astronomy and physics educator; b. N.Y.C., June 16, 1965; d. Gilbert and Susanne (Gayton) G.; m. Tom La Tourette, May 1, 1993. BS, MIT, 1987; MS, Calif. Inst. Tech., 1989, PhD, 1993. Hubble postdoctoral fellow U. Ariz., Tucson, 1992-93; vis. rsch. scholar Inst. Astronomy, Cambridge, England, 1994; asst. prof. physics and astronomy UCLA, 1994-97, assoc. prof. physics and astronomy, 1997—. Recipient Young Investigator award NSF, 1994, Fullam Dudley award, 1995; fellow Pacific Telesis, 1991, Sloan fellow, 1996, Packard fellow, 1996, Pierce prize, 1998, Maria Goeppert-Meyer award, Am. Phys. Soc., 1999. Mem. Am. Astron. Soc., AAUW (Anne Jump Cannon award 1994), Phi Beta Kappa. Achievements include discovery of formation of young low mass stars in multiple star systems, production of the first diffraction limited image with the keck 10-m telescope (the largest telescope in the world), and measurement of stellar motions which indicate the presence of a supermassive black hole at the center of our own galaxy. Home: 224 Barlock Ave Los Angeles CA 90049 Office: UCLA Dept Astronomy 405 Hilgard Ave Los Angeles CA 90095-1562

GHIL, MICHAEL, atmospheric scientist, geophysicist; b. Budapest, Hungary, June 10, 1944; s. Louis and Ilona V. (Dobo) Cernat; m. Michèle J. Denizot, July 8, 1982; children: Emmanuel A., Mirella J. BSc cum laude, Technion-Israel Inst. Tech., Haifa, Israel, 1966, MSc in Mech. Engring., 1971; MS, NYU, 1973, PhD in Math., 1975. Rsch. asst. to instr. Technion-Israel Inst. Tech., Haifa, 1966-71; rsch. assoc. NASA Goddard Inst. Space Studies, N.Y.C., 1975-76; rsch. asst. prof. math. Courant Inst. Math. Scis., N.Y.C., 1976-79, rsch. assoc. prof. atmos. sci., 1979-82, rsch. prof., 1982-86; prof. atmos. sci. and geophysics UCLA, 1985—. Chmn. dept. atmospheric scis., UCLA, 1988-92; dir. Climate Dynamics Ctr., UCLA, 1986-92, Inst. Geophys. Planet Phys. UCLA, 1992—; disting. vis. scientist Jet Propulsion Lab, Calif. Inst. Tech./NASA, Pasadena, Calif., 1988—; Condorcet chair Ecole Normale Supérieure, Paris, 1995; Elf-Aquitaine/CNRS chair Acad. Scis., Paris, 1996, Collège de France, Paris, 1997. Author: Topics in GFD: Atmospheric Dynamics, Dynamo Theory and Climate Dynamics, 1987; editor: Turbulence and Predictability in Geophysical Fluid Dynamics and Climate Dynamics, 1985, Dynamic Meteorology: Data Assimilation Methods, 1981, Natural Climate Variability on Decade-to-Century Time Scales, 1995, Data Assimilation in Meteorology and Oceanography: Theory and Practice, 1997. Mem. adv. bd. Calif. Space Inst., San Diego, 1986-90; chmn. sci. adv. coun. Climate Sys. Modeling Program, Boulder, Colo., 1988—; bd. dirs. New Sun Found. Geneva, 1994-99, bd. govs. Weizmann Inst. Sci. Rehovot, Israel, 1995-2000. Fellow Am. Meteorol. Soc. (profl. com. 1989-92), Am. Geophys. Union, mem. Nat. Rsch. Coun. (climate rsch. com. 1989-98), Soc. for Indsl. and Applied Math., Acad. Europaea (fgn.), Sigma Xi. Democrat. Jewish. Avocations: hiking, climbing, squash, skiing, swimming, arts, literature, music, languages. Office: UCLA Inst Geophys Planet Phys 405 Hilgard Ave Los Angeles CA 90095-9000

GHISELIN, BREWSTER, author, English language educator emeritus; b. Webster Groves, Mo., June 13, 1903; s. Horace and Eleanor (Weeks) G.; m. Olive F. Franks, June 7, 1929; children: Jon Brewster, Michael Tenant. A.B., UCLA, 1927; M.A., U. Calif.-Berkeley, 1928, student, 1931-33, Oxford U., Eng., 1928-29; LHD, U. Utah, 1994. Asst. in English U. Calif., Berkeley, 1931-33; instr. English U. Utah, 1929-31, 34-38, lectr., 1938-39, asst. prof., 1939-46, assoc. prof., 1946-50, prof., 1950-71, prof. emeritus, 1971, Disting. Rsch. prof., 1967-68. Dir. Writers' Conf., 1947-66; poetry editor Rocky Mt. Rev., 1937-46; assoc. editor Western Rev., 1946-49; lectr. creativity, cons. Inst. Personality Assessment and Research, U. Calif., Berkeley, 1957-58; editorial adv. bd. Concerning Poetry, 1968— Author: Against the Circle, 1946, The Creative Process, 1952, new paperback edit., 1985, 95, The Nets, 1955, Writing, 1959, Country of the Minotaur, 1970, (with others) The Form Discovered: Essays on the Achievement of Andrew Lytle, 1973, Light, 1978, Windrose: Poems, 1929-1979, 1980, (with others) Contemporary Authors, 1989; (poems) Flame, 1991. Bd. advisors Silver Mountain Found. Ford Found. fellow, 1952-53; recipient award Nat. Inst. Arts and Letters, 1970; Blumenthal-Leviton-Blonder prize Poetry mag., 1973; Levinson prize, 1978; William Carlos Williams award Poetry Soc. Am., 1981; Gov.'s award for arts Utah Arts Council, 1982; LHD hc, U of Utah, 1994. Mem. MLA, Utah Acad. Scis., Arts and Letters (Charles Redd award), Phi Beta Kappa, Phi Kappa Phi. Home: 1115 Jefferson Way Laguna Beach CA 92651-3022

GHOSH, SAMBHUNATH (SAM GHOSH), civil engineering educator; BS, U. Calcutta; MS, U. Ill.; PhD, Ga. Inst. Tech. Engr. Wiedeman & Singleton, Atlanta, 1971-85; with Gas Technology, Chgo.; prof. civil engring. U. Utah, Salt Lake City; prof. civil, agrl. and geol. engring. N.Mex State U., Las Cruces. Recipient Ill. Energy award, 1985, Utah Gov.'s award for energy innovation, 2986, John Ericsson award in Renewable Energy U.S. Dept. Energy, 1994, George Bradley Gascoigne medal Water Environment Found., 1996. Home: 1281 Federal Heights Dr Salt Lake City UT 84103-4325 E-mail: saghosh@nmsu.edu, ghoshsanbhunath@hotmail.com

GHYMN, ESTHER MIKYUNG, English educator, writer; b. Seoul; d. Yong Shik and Kyung hee (Park) Kim; m. Kyung-Il Ed Ghymn; children: Jennifer, Eugene. MA, U. Hawaii; MAT, U. Pitts.; PhD, U. Nev., Reno, 1990. Lectr. English, U. Nev., Reno, 1993—, ESL coord., 1996—, mem. ethnic studies bd., 1998—. Author: The Shapes and Styles of Asian American Prose Fiction, 1990, Images of Asian American Women Writers, 1995; editor APANN News, Asian Am. Studies, Identity, Images, Issues Past and Present, 2000. Bd. dirs. Asian Americans N. Nev., 1992-95, Multicultural Office, Truckee Meadows C.C., Reno, 1994-96, mem. steering com. Access to Success, 1996; mem. affirmative action adv. bd. U. Nev., Reno, 1998, ethnic studies bd., 1997—, women's studies bd., 1998—, chair liaison com., 1998—, chair lang. com., 1999—; series editor Peter Lang Pub. Mem. Phi Beta Delta (sec.). Avocations: teaching, writing, reading, travel. E-mail: emg@admin.unr.edu

GIAMBI, JASON GILBERT, professional baseball player; b. West Covina, Calif., Jan. 8, 1971; m. Dana, Nov. 9, 1996. Grad., Long Beach State U. 1st baseman Milw. Brewers, 1989-92, U.S. Olympic Team, 1992, Oakland (Calif.) A's, 1992—. Recipient Bronze medal Pan Am. Games, Havana, Cuba, 1991. Avocations: off-roading, WWF. Office: c/o Oakland A's 7677 Oakport St Ste 200 Oakland CA 94621-1933

GIANNINI, VALERIO LOUIS, investment banker; b. N.Y.C., Feb. 7, 1938; s. Gabriel M. and Luisa M. (Casazza) G.; m. Linda Martin, Oct. 6, 1979; children: Martin Louis, Alexander Elliot, Charles Gabriel. BSE, Princeton U., 1959. With Kidder Peabody & Co., N.Y.C., 1961-64; sr. cons. IIT Research Inst., Chgo., 1964-66; sec. Giannini-Voltex, L.A., 1966-68; pres. V.L. Giannini & Co., L.A., 1968-76; chmn. Namco Chems., Inc., 1975; dir. White House ops., Washington, 1977-78; dep. spl. asst. to Pres. for adminstrn. White House, 1979-80; dep. asst. sec. Dept. Commerce, Washington, 1980-81; prin. Cumberland Investment Group, N.Y.C., 1981-87; pres. Numex Corp., 1986-87; CEO, Geneva Bus. Network, Inc., Irvine, Calif., 1987-90. Founder Eurosearch Ptnrs., Newport Beach, Calif., 1990; prin. Newcap Ptnrs., 1995; bd. dirs. Meridian Health, Inc., Dudek & Assocs., iMet Technologies, Inc.; adj. prof. Argyros Sch. Bus., Chapman U., 2001. Pres. Lido Jr. Sailing Found., 2000—. Lt. USNR, 1959-61. Mem. N.Y. Yacht Club, Newport Harbor Yacht Club.

GIANNOTTA, STEVEN LOUIS, neurosurgery educator; b. Detroit, Apr. 4, 1947; s. Louis D. and Betty Jane (Root) G.; m. Sharon Danielak, June 13, 1970; children: Brent, Nicole, Robyn. Student, U. Detroit, 1965-68; MD, U. Mich., 1972. Diplomate Am. Bd. Neurol. Surgeons. Surg. intern U. Mich., Ann Arbor, 1972-73, neurosurg. resident, 1973-78; asst. prof. neurosurgery UCLA, 1978-80, U. So. Calif., Sch. Medicine, L.A., 1980-83, assoc. prof. neurosurgery, 1983-89, prof. neurosurgery, 1989—. Bd. dirs. Am. Bd. Neurol. Surgery, 1995-2001, sec., 1999-2000. Fellow ACS, Am. Heart Assn. (stroke coun., rsch. grantee 1980, 84), So. Calif. Neurol. Soc. (pres. 1993-94), Congress Neurol. Surgeons (sec. 1986-89, v.p. 1993_, Soc. Clin. Neuroscis. (L.A. pres. 1992-93). Democrat. Roman Catholic. Avocations: golf, skiing, sports cars. Office: Dept Neurosurgery Box 239 1200 N State St Los Angeles CA 90033-1029

GIANNULLI, MOSSIMO, designer, apparel business executive; Owner, chmn. bd. Mossimo Inc., Irvine, Calif. Office: Mossimo Inc 2450 White Rd Fl 2 Irvine CA 92614-6250

GIBALDI, MILO, dean; b. N.Y.C., Dec. 17, 1938; s. Ignatius and Angela G.; m. Florence D'Amato, Dec. 26, 1960; 1 child, Ann Elizabeth. BS, Coll. Pharmacy, Columbia U., 1960, PhD, 1963. Asst. prof. pharmacy Columbia U., N.Y.C., 1963-66; asst. prof. pharmaceutics SUNY, Buffalo, 1966-67, assoc. prof., 1967-70, prof., 1970-78, chmn. dept., 1970-78; prof. pharmaceutics U. Wash., Seattle, 1978—; dean U. Wash. Sch. Pharmacy, Seattle, 1978-95, dean emeritus, 1995—. Cons. Bur. Drugs, FDA, 1970-72, VA, Washington, 1971-72; vis. prof. U. Rochester, 1972-74; program dir. clin. pharmacokinetics and biopharmaceutics NIH, 1973-78, pharmacology study sect., 1976-80; sci. adv. bd. G.D. Searle & Co., 1978—. Author: (with Donald Perrier) Pharmacokinetics, 1976; contbr. articles to profl. jours. Fellow Acad. Pharm. Scis., AAAS; mem. Am. Chem. Soc., Am. Pharm. Assn., Acad. Soc. Clin. Pharmacology, Am. Soc. Pharmacology and Exptl. Therapeutics, N.Y. Acad. Scis., Am. Assn. Colls. Pharmacy, Nat. Acad. Scis. (mem. Inst. Medicine 1986), Health Scis. U. Wash. (assoc. v.p. 1983), Sigma Xi, Rho Chi. Office: U Wash Sch Pharmacy Dept Pharmaceutics Box 357610 Seattle WA 98195-7610

GIBBON, TIM, communications executive; Chmn., pres., CEO JWT Specialized Comm., Inc., L.A. Office: JWT Specialized Comm Inc 6500 Wilshire Blvd Fl 21 Los Angeles CA 90048-4920

GIBBONS, JAMES ARTHUR, congressman; b. Reno, Dec. 16, 1944; s. Leonard A. and Matilda (Hancock) G.; m. T. Dawn Sanders-Snelling, June 21, 1986; children: Christopher, Jennifer, James A. Jr. BS in Geology, U. Nev., Reno, 1967, MS in Mining Geology, 1973; JD, Southwestern U., 1979. Bar: Nev. 1982, U.S. Dist. Ct. Nev. 1982. Hydrologist U.S. Fed. Water Master, Reno, 1963-67; geologist Union Carbide Co., Reno, 1972-75; comml. pilot Western Airlines, Inc., L.A., 1979-88; pilot Delta Airlines, Salt Lake City, 1988-96; sr. land mgr., atty. Homestake Mining Co., Reno, 1980-82; pvt. practice Reno, 1982—; mem. U.S. Congress from Nev. 2d dist., 1997—; mem. house resource com., armed svcs. com. Environ. atty. Alaskan Wilderness Soc., Anchorage, 1982-83; mem. Congressional Com. on Nat. Security, 1997—, Resources, 1997—, Intelligence, 1997—, Vets. Affair, 1999—. Contbr. articles to profl. pubs. Mem. Nev. Coun. on Econ. Edn., 1986; mem. Nev. State Assembly, 1988-94. Lt. col. Nev. Air Nat. Guard, Persian Gulf, 1990-91; with USAF, 1967-72. Decorated DFC. Mem. Assn. Trial Lawyers of Am., Nev. Trial Lawyers Assn., Rocky Mt. Mineral Law Found., Comml Law League Am., Am. Inst. Mining Engrs., Nev. Landman's Assn. (chmn. 1981-82, cons. atty. 1982-83). Republican. Avocation: flying. Office: US Ho Reps 100 Cannon Ho Office Bldg Washington DC 20515-0001 E-mail: mail.gibbons@mail.house.gov

GIBBONS, JAMES FRANKLIN, electrical engineering educator; b. Leavenworth, Kans., Sept. 19, 1931; s. Clifford Hugh and Mary Jewel (Petty) G.; m. Mary Lynn Krywick; children: Robert, Sally, Laura B.S., Northwestern U., 1953; Ph.D., Stanford U., 1956. Prof. elec. engring. Stanford U., Calif., 1956-84, 96—, Reid Weaver Dennis prof. elec. engring., 1983-84, 96—, dean Sch. Engring., 1984-96, Frederick Emmons Terman prof. engring., 1984-96. Bd. dirs. Centigram, Cisco Systems, Raychem Corp., Menlo Park, Calif., Lockheed Martin, Bethesda, Md., El Paso (Tex.) Energy; founder, chmn. Sera Learning Techs.; cons. Shockley Transistor Corp., 1957-63, Fairchild Semiconductor, 1964-71, Avantek, Inc., 1964-91; chmn. grad. fellowship panel NSF, 1967-70; mem. Newman com. HEW Task Force on Higher Edn., 1969-74; mem. ednl. tech. panel Pres. Sci. Adv. Com., 1971-73; Fulbright guest lectr. European univs.; vis. prof. nuclear physics dept. Oxford U., 1970-71; vis. prof. U. Tokyo, 1971; cons. electronics br. Atomic Energy Research Establishment, 1971; mem. sci. team for exchanges on ion implanation and beam processing U.S. Nat. Acad. Scis., 1971, 76, 77, 79, 81. Author: (with J. G. Linvill) Transistors and Active Circuits, 1961, (with P. E. Gray, D. DeWitt and A. R. Boothroyd) SEEC Vol. 2: Physical Electronics and Models of Transistors, 1964, Semiconductor Electronics, 1966; editor: Fundamentals of Electronic Science, 1970-78; contbr. articles to profl. jours.; inventor tutored video instruction technique Recipient Western Electric Fund award Am. Soc. Engring. Edn., 1971, award for Outstanding Achievement, No. Calif. Solar Energy Assn., 1975, Founder's prize Tex. Instruments, 1983, Outstanding Alumni award Northwestern U., 1985, Rappaport award IEEE Electron Devices Soc., 1990, Univ. Rsch. award Semicondr. Industry Assn., 1996, Medal of Achievement award Am. Electronics Assn., 1966; NSF and NAS fellow, 1953-56; Fulbright fellow Cambridge (Eng.) U., 1956-57; NSF postdoctoral fellow, 1963-64; inducted Santa Clara County Bus. Hall of Fame, 1997, Silicon Valley Engring. Hall of Fame, 1997. Fellow IEEE (Jack A. Morton award 1980, Edn. medal 1985, Solid State Sci. and Tech. award Electrochem. Soc. 1989); mem. Nat. Acad. Engring., Nat. Acad. Sci., Swedish Acad. Engring. Scis., Norwegian Acad. Tech. Scis., Am. Acad. Arts and Scis., Sigma Xi, Tau Beta Pi (award for outstanding undergrad. engring. teaching 1976), Eta Kappa Nu. Home: 320 Tennyson Ave Palo Alto CA 94301-3835 Office: Elec Engring Dept CISX-201X Paul G Allen Bldg Stanford CA 94305-4075

GIBBONS, LEEZA, television talk show host, entertainment reporter; m. Stephen Meadows; children: Lexi, Troy. Student, U. S.C. CEO Leeza Gibbons Enterprises; co-host Entertainment Tonight, Hollywood, Calif., 1984—, John and Leeza, Hollywood, 1993; host, exec. prodr. Leeza, 1993—; host/exec. prodr. syndicated radio programs Entertainment Tonight on Radio with Leeza Gibbons, The Entertainment Report, The Top 25 Countdown with Leeza Gibbons, The Leeza Gibbons' Superstar Music Spl. Host Miss Universe Pageant, The Hollywood Christmas Parade; host, co-prodr. (series) Growing Up Together; film appearances include Robocop, 1987, Robocop 2, 1990, Soapdish, 1991, The Player, 1992, Last Action Hero, 1993. Office: Paramount TV 5555 Melrose Ave Los Angeles CA 90038-3112

GIBBS, ANTONY (TONY), film editor; Editor: (films) The Loneliness of the Long Distance Runner, 1962, A Taste of Honey, 1962, Tom Jones, 1963, The Luck of Ginger Coffey, 1964, The Knack...And How to Get It, 1965, The Loved One, 1965, Petulia, 1968, Performance, 1970, Walkabout, 1971, (with Robert Lawrence) Fiddler on the Roof, 1971, Jesus Christ Superstar, 1973, Rollerball, 1975, The Sailor Who Fell from Grace with the Sea, 1976, A Bridge Too Far, 1977, (with Graeme Clifford) F.I.S.T., 1978, Yesterday's Hero, 1979, (with George Trirogoff) Butch and Sundance: The Early Days, 1979, (with Anne V. Coates and Stanley Warnow) Ragtime, 1981, The Dogs of War, 1981, Bad Boys, 1983, Dune, 1984, Agnes of God, 1985, Tai-Pan, 1986, Russkies, 1987, Stealing Home, 1988, (with Lou Lombardo) In Country, 1989, The Runner, 1990, The Taking of Beverly Hills, 1992, The Man Without a Face, 1993, Don Juan DeMarco, 1995, Ronin, 1998, Reindeer Games, 2000, (TV movies) Devlin, 1992, A Case for Life, 1996, Crime of the Century, 1996, George Wallace, 1997, James Dean, 2001. Office: 15691 Royal Ridge Rd Sherman Oaks CA 91403-4208 E-mail: SeymourPrd@aol.com

GIBBS, RONALD STEVEN, obstetrician/gynecologist; b. Phila., Mar. 31, 1943; MD, U. Pa., 1969. Intern Hartford (Conn.) Hosp., 1969-70; resident ob.-gyn. U. Pa. Hosp., Phila., 1970-74; fellow maternal-fetal medicine U. Tex. Health Ctr., San Antonio, 1976-78; obstetrician-gynecologist Univ. Hosp. U. Colo., Denver, 1989—; prof., chmn. dept. ob.-gyn. U. Colo., Denver, 1989—. Dir., treas, Am. Bd. of Obstetric and Gyn, Residency Review Com. Mem. ACOG, AMA, Am. Gynecologic and Obstetric Soc. (sec.), Infectious Disease Soc. Am., Infectious Disease Soc. Ob/Gyn, Soc. Gynecologic Investigation, Soc. Perinatal Obstetric (bd. dirs.). Office: U Colo Health Sci Ctr 4200 E 9th Ave # Denver CO 80220-3706

GIBBS, WILLIAM HAROLD, finance company executive; b. Evanston, Ill., Apr. 10, 1950; s. Harold William and Margaret Rose (Heidbreder) G. BS, Ariz. State U., 1973; MBA, U. Ill., 1975. CPA. Mgr. Price Waterhouse, Phoenix, 1975-82; chief fin. officer Apollo Group Inc., Phoenix, 1983-87; pres. U. Phoenix, 1987-98; sr. v.p. Apollo Group, Inc., Phoenix, 1998—. Office: Apollo Group Inc 4615 E Elwood St Phoenix AZ 85040-1958

GIBLETT, ELOISE ROSALIE, hematology educator; b. Tacoma, Jan. 17, 1921; d. William Richard and Rose (Godfrey) G. B.S., U. Wash., 1942, M.S., 1947, M.D. with honors, 1951. Mem. faculty U. Wash. Sch. Medicine, 1957—, research prof., 1967-87, emeritus research prof., 1987—. Asso. dir., head immunogenetics Puget Sound Blood Center, 1955-79, exec. dir., 1979-87, emeritus exec. dir., 1987—; former mem. several research coms. NIH. Author: Genetic Markers in Human Blood, 1969; editorial bd. numerous jours. including Blood, Am. Jour. Human Genetics, Transfusion, Vox Sanguinis; Contbr. over 200 articles to profl. jours. Recipient fellowships, grants, Emily Cooley, Karl Landsteiner, Philip Levine and Alexander Wiener immunohematology awards, distinguished alumna award U. Wash. Sch. Med., 1987. Fellow AAAS; Mem. Nat. Acad. Scis., Am. Soc. Human Genetics (pres. 1973), Am. Soc. Hematology, Am. Assn. Immunologists, Brit. Soc. Immunology, Internat. Soc. Hematologists, Am. Fedn. Clin. Research, Western Assn. Physicians, Assn. Am. Physicians, Sigma Xi, Alpha Omega Alpha. Home: 6533 53rd Ave NE Seattle WA 98115-7748 Office: Puget Sound Blood Ctr 921 Terry Ave Seattle WA 98104-1256

GIBNEY, FRANK BRAY, publisher, editor, writer, foundation executive; b. Scranton, Pa., Sept. 21, 1924; s. Joseph James and Edna May (Wetter) G.; m. Harriet Harvey, Dec. 10, 1948 (div. 1957); children: Alex, Margot; m. Harriet C. Suydam, Dec. 14, 1957 (div. 1971); children: Frank, James, Thomas; m. Hiroko Doi, Oct. 5, 1972; children: Elise, Josephine. BA, Yale U., 1945; DLitt (hon.), Kyung Hee U., Seoul, Korea, 1974. Corr., assoc. editor Time mag., N.Y.C., Tokyo and London, 1947-54; sr. editor Newsweek, N.Y.C., 1954-57; staff writer, editorial writer Life mag., N.Y.C., 1957-61; pub., pres. SHOW mag., N.Y.C., 1961-64; pres. Ency. Brit. (Japan), Tokyo, 1965-69, TBS-Brit., Tokyo, 1969-75, vice chmn., 1976-99; v.p. Ency. Brit., Inc., Chgo., 1975-79; vice chmn., bd. editors Ency. Brit., Chgo., 1978—; pres. Pacific Basin Inst., Pomona Coll., Claremont, Calif., 1979—. Prof. Pomona Coll., 1997—; bd. dirs. U.S. Com. for Pacific Econ. Cooperation, 1988—, v.p., 1993-95; cons. com. on space and aeros. U.S. Ho. of Reps., Washington, 1957-59; vice chmn. Japan-U.S. Friendship Commn., 1984-90, U.S.-Japan Com. Edn. and Cultural Interchange, 1984-90. Author: Five Gentlemen of Japan, 1953, The Frozen Revolution, 1959, (with Peter Deriabin) The Secret World, 1960, The Operators, 1961, The Khrushchev Pattern, 1961, The Reluctant Space Farers, 1965, Japan:

The Fragile Super-Power, 1975, 3rd edit., 1996, Miracle by Design, 1983, The Pacific Century, 1992, Korea's Quiet Revolution, 1993; co-author: The Battle for Okinawa, 1995; editor: The Penkovskiy Papers, 1965, Senso, 1995, Unlocking The Bureaucrats' Kingdom, 1998, The Nanjing Massacre, 1999. Served to lt. USNR, 1942-46. Decorated Order of the Rising Sun 3d Class Japan, Order of Sacred Treasure 2d Class Japan. Mem. Council on Fgn. Relations, Tokyo Fgn. Corr. Club, Am. C.of C. (Tokyo), Japan-Am. Soc., Japan Soc. Roman Catholic. Clubs: Century Assn., Yale (N.Y.C.); Tokyo; Tavern, The Arts (Chgo.). Home: 1901 E Las Tunas Rd Santa Barbara CA 93103-1745 E-mail: tgibney@silcom.com

GIBSON, BENJAMIN FRANKLIN, physicist; b. Madisonville, Tex., Sept. 3, 1938; s. Mitchell Osler and Christine (Bennett) G.; m. Margaret Alice Ferguson, July 20, 1968; children: James M., Michael W., Stuart W. BA, Rice U., 1961; PhD, Stanford U., 1966. Postdoctoral fellow Lawrence Livermore (Calif.) Nat. Lab., 1966-68; rsch. assoc. NAS, Nat. Bur. Stds., Gaithersburg, Md., 1968-70, CUNY, Bklyn., 1970-72; group leader, T-5 Los Alamos (N.Mex.) Nat. Lab., 1982-86, staff mem., 1972—; detailee Dept. of Energy Divsn. Nuclear Physics, 1980-81. Program adv. com. MIT Bates Electron Accelerator, Boston, 1985-89, 98—; mem. subatomic physics grant selection com. Can. Natural Scis. and Engring. Rsch. Coun., 1994-96, theory rev. panel NSF, 1997, 98. Co-editor: Three-body Force in the Three-Nucleon System, 1986, Procs. of LAMPF Workshop on pi K Physics, 1991, New Vistas in Physics with High-Energy Pion Beams, 1993, Properties and Interactions of Hyperons, 1994, Baryons '95, 1996, 20 Years of Meson Factory Physics: Accomplishments and Prospects, 1997; assoc. editor Phys. Review C, 1988—, mem. editl. bd., 1978-79, 87-88; mem. editl. bd. FEW Body Sys., 1986—; contbr. articles to profl. jours. Recipient Sr. Scientist Rsch. award Alexander von Humboldt Found., 1992; Japan Soc. Promotion of Sci. rsch. fellow Tohoku U., 1984; vis. fellow U. Melbourne, Australia, 1986, Flinders U., Adelaide, Australia, 1987, Murdoch fellow Inst. for Nuclear Theory, U. Wash., Seattle, 1992. Fellow Am. Phys. Soc., Few-Body Sys. Topical Group (vice chmn. 1990-92, chmn. 1992-93, divsn. nuclear physics sec.-treas. 1995—). Achievements include patents in field of epithermal-neutron well logging. Office: T-16 MSB283 Los Alamos NM 87545-0001 E-mail: bfgibson@lanl.gov

GIBSON, ELISABETH JANE, principal; b. Salina, Kans., Apr. 28, 1937; d. Cloyce Wesley and Margaret Mae (Yost) Kasson; m. William Douglas Miles, Jr., Aug. 20, 1959 (div.); m. Harry Benton Gibson Jr., July 1, 1970. AB, Colo. State Coll., 1954-57; MA, San Francisco State Coll., 1967-68; EdD, U. No. Colo., 1978; postgrad., U. Denver, 1982. Cert. tchr., prin., Colo. Tchr. elem. schs., Santa Paula, Calif., 1957-58, Salina, Kans., 1958-63, Goose Bay, Labrador, 1963-64, Jefferson County, Colo., 1965-66, Topeka, 1966-67; diagnostic tchr. Ctrl. Kans. Diagnostic Remedial Edn. Ctr., Salina, 1968-70; instr. Loretta Heights Coll., Denver, 1970-72; co-owner Ednl. Cons. Enterprises, Inc., Greeley, Colo., 1974-77; resource coord. region VIII Resource Access Project Head Star Mile High Consortium, Denver, 1976-77; exec. dir. Colo. Fedn. Coun. Exceptional Children, Denver, 1976-77; asst. prof. Met. State Coll., Denver, 1979; dir. spl. edn. N.E. Colo. Bd. Coop. Edn. Svcs., Haxtun, Colo., 1979-82; prin. elem. jr. h.s. Elizabeth, 1982-84; prin., spl. projects coord. Summit County Schs., Frisco, 1985-92; prin. Frisco Elem. Sch., 1985-91. Cons. Mont. Dept. Edn., 1978-79, Love Pub. Co., 1976-78, Colo. Dept. Inst., 1974-75, Colo. Dept. Edn., 1984-85, mem. proposal reading com., 1987—; pres. Found. Exceptional Children, 1980-81; pres. bd. dirs. N.E. Colo. Svcs. Handicapped, 1981-82; bd. dirs. Dept. Ednl. Specialists, Colo. Assn. Sch. Execs., 1982-84; mem. Colo. Title IV Adv. Coun., 1980-82; mem. Mellon Found. grant steering com. Dolo. Dept. Edn., 1984-85; mem. Colo. Dept. Edn. Data Acquisition Reporting and Utilization Com., 1983, Denver City County Commn. for Disabled, 1978-81; chmn. regional edn. com. 1970 White House Conf. Children and Youth; bd. dirs. Advs. for Victims of Assault, 1986-91; mem. adv. bd. Alpine Counseling Ctr., 1986-92; mem. placement alternatives commn. Dept. Social Svcs., 1986—; mem. adv. com. Colo. North Ctrl. Assn., 1988-91; sec. Child Care Resource and Referral Agy., 1992—; mem. Child Care Task Force Summit County, 1989-92; mem. tchr. cert. task force Colo. State Bd. Edn., 1990-91; chmn. Summit County Interagy. Coord. Coun., 1989-93. Co-author: (with H. Padzensky) Goal Guide: A minicourse in writing goals and behavioral objectives for special education, 1975, Assaying Student Behavior: A minicourse in student assessment techniques, 1974; contbr. articles to profl. jours. Recipient Vol. award Colo. Child Care Assn., 1992, Ann. Svc. award Colo. Fedn. Coun. Exceptional Children, 1981; San Francisco State Coll. fellow, 1967-68. Mem. ASCD, Nat. Assn. Elem. Sch. Prins., Colo. Assn. Retarded Citizens, North Ctrl. Assn. (state adv. com. 1988-91), Order Ea. Star, Kappa Delta Pi, Pi Lambda Theta, Phi Delta Kappa. Republican. Methodist. Home: 4505 S Yosemite St Unit 114 Denver CO 80237-2520 Office: Orchard Valley Learning Ctr 15100 E Orchard Rd Aurora CO 80016-3001

GIBSON, JAMES B. mayor; BA, Brigham Young U., 1972; JD, Calif. Western, 1975. Gen. counsel Am. Pacific Corp.; ptnr. Rooker and Gibson Law Firm; now mayor City of Henderson, Nev., 1997—. Office: City Hall 240 S Water St Rm 203 Henderson NV 89015-7296 E-mail: jbg@gty.ci.henderson.nv.us

GIBSON, VIRGINIA LEE, lawyer; b. Independence, Mo., Mar. 5, 1946; BA, U. Calif., Berkeley, 1972; JD, U. Calif., San Francisco, 1977. Bar: Calif. 1981. Assoc. Pillsbury, Madison & Sutro, San Francisco, 1980-83; ptnr. Chickering & Gregory, San Francisco, 1983-85, Baker & McKenzie, San Francisco, 1985—. Mem. ABA (tax sect.), Nat. Assn. Stock Plan Profls., Nat. Ctr. for Employee Ownership, Calif. Bar Assn. (exec. com. tax sect. 1985-88), San Francisco Bar Assn. (internat. taxation sect.), Western Pension and Benefits Conf. (pres. San Francisco chpt. 1989-91, program com. 1984-88). Office: Baker & McKenzie 2 Embarcadero Ctr Ste 2400 San Francisco CA 94111-3909

GIDEON, FRANCIS C., JR. career officer; BS in Engring. Scis., USAF Acad., 1966; grad., Squadron Officer Sch., 1970, Indsl. Coll. Armed Forces, 1971; MS in Sys. Mgmt., Air Force Inst. Tech., 1974; grad., Air Command and Staff Coll., 1979, Air War Coll., 1981; exec. devel. program, U. Pitts., 1988; grad., Def. Sys. Mgmt. Coll., 1990. Cert. program mgmt. level II, test and evaluation level III. Commd. 2d lt. USAF, 1966, advanced through grades to maj. gen., 1994; pilot tng., 1966-67; pilot F-100 Phan Rang, Vietnam, 1968-69; pilot F-100, F-4 RAF Lakerhealth, England, 1969-73; pilot Air Force Inst. Tech., 1973-74; F-4 test pilot 6512th Test Squadron, Edwards AFB, Calif., 1975-76; test pilot, ops. officer A-10 Joint Test Force, Edwards AFB, 1976-80; chief devel. plans aircraft divsn. Air Force Sys. Command, Andrews AFB, Md., 1981; dep. dir. Devel. Plans Tactical Sys. Directorate, Andrews AFB, 1982-84; chief F-15 projects and test divsn. F-15 Sys. Program Office, Wright-Patterson AFB, Ohio, 1984-85; dir. Fighter Attack Sys. Program Office, Wright-Patterson AFB, 1985-86, Strike Sys. Program Office, Wright-Patterson AFB, 1986-87; comdr. 4950th Test Wing, Wright-Patterson AFB, 1987-88, Fgn. Aerospace Sci. and Tech. Ctr., Wright-Patterson AFB, 1988-92; vice comdr. Sacramento Air Logistics Ctr., McClellan AFB, Calif., 1992-93; dir. of ops. Hdqs. Air Force Materiel Command, Wright-Patterson AFB, 1993-97; chief of safety USAF, comdr. Hdqs. Air Force Safety Ctr., Kirtland AFB, N.Mex., 1997—. Decorated Disting. Svc. medal, Legion of Merit with oak leaf cluster, D.F.C. Office: HQ USAF/SE 9700 G Ave SE Ste 240 Kirtland AFB NM 87117-5670

GIEDT, BRUCE ALAN, paper company executive; b. Fargo, N.D., May 7, 1937; s. Alexander and Alice Mildred (Rognaldson) G.; m. Suzanna Tae Abbott, Apr. 30, 1963; children: Alex, Jeffrey, Marybeth; m. 2d, Gail Ann Platt. BA, U. Wash., 1959; MBA, Harvard U., 1965. From regional sales mgr. to v.p. service products bus. units Crown Zellerbach Corp., San Francisco, 1965—; pres. Champion Paper Distbrs., Inc., Riverside, Calif., 1981-87, Pioneer Packaging, Phoenix, 1987—, Woodale, Ill., 1997—. Author: The Future of Commercial Arbitration, 1965. V.p. exec. com. Keep Riverside AHead, econ. devel. com., bd. dirs.; exec. com. mem. Riverside C. of C., devel. com. Served to Capt. USAF, 1959-63. Evans scholar Western Golf Assn., 1967. Mem. Am. Paper Inst. (past com. chmn.). Republican. Lutheran. Lodge: Elks. Home: 704 Foothills East cir Payson AZ 85541 Office: 730 E University Dr Phoenix AZ 85034-6509

GIEM, ROSS NYE, JR. surgeon; b. Corvallis, Oreg., May 23, 1923; s. Ross Nye and Goldie Marie (Falk) G.; children: John, David, Paul, James, Ross N. III, Matthew John, Julie. Student, U. Redlands, Walla Walla Coll.; BA, MD, Loma Linda U. Diplomate Am. Bd. Surgery. Intern Sacramento Gen. Hosp., 1952-53; resident in ob-gyn Kern County Gen. Hosp., Bakersfield, Calif., 1956-57, resident in gen. surgery, 1957-61; practice medicne specializing in gen. surgery Sullivan, Mo., 1961-70; staff emergency dept. Hollywood Presbyn. Med. Ctr., 1971-73, Meml. Hosp., Belleville, Ill., 1973-87, St. Elizabeth Hosp., Belleville, 1973-90, St. Luke Hosp., Pasadena, 1973-89, Doctors Hosp., Montclair, Calif., 1990-93, Harriman Jones Med. Group, Long Beach, 1993—. Instr. nurses, physicians, paramedics, emergency med. technicians, 1973-91. Served with AUS, 1943-46. Fellow ACS, Am. Coll. Emergency Physicians; mem. AMA, Ill. Med. Assn., Pan Am. Med. Assn., Pan Pacific Surg. Assn., Royal Coll. Physicians (Eng.).

GIESEN, JOHN WILLIAM, advertising executive; b. St. Paul, Apr. 5, 1928; s. William J. and Salome Anna (Shopnitz) G.; m. Mary Lou Gilbertson, May 20, 1950; children: Cynthia, John, Lee Ann, Gregory, David, Laurie. Student, St. Thomas Coll., 1948-50, U. Minn., 1950-52, St. Paul Sch. Assoc. Arts, 1951-53. Advt. rep. St. Paul Dispatch-Pioneer Press, 1950-54; advt. mgr. Bruce Pub. Co., St. Paul, 1954-56; nat. advt. mgr. Duluth Herald News Tribune, 1956-60; account exec. N.W. Ayer & Son, Inc., Chgo., 1960-64, acct. supr., 1964-66; account exec. Leo Burnett, Inc., Chgo., 1966-68, v.p. account supr., 1968-74; exec. v.p. Barickman Advt., Denver, 1974-77, chmn. exec. com., 1977-82; pres. Doyle Dane Bernbach Advt., Denver, 1982-86, DDB Needham Worldwide, Denver, 1986-88, chmn., 1988-89; pres., chief exec. officer The Advt. Consortium, Inc., Denver, 1989-94; pres., CEO The Giesen Group, Inc., Denver, 1994—. Chmn. Sts. Faith-Hope Charity Elem. Sch. Bd., Winnetka, Ill., 1972-74, Rocky Mountain Council 4 A's, 1985; hon. bd. Colorado Spl. Olympics, 1988. With U.S. Army, 1946-48, res. 1949-60. Mem. Denver Advt. Fedn. (dir. 1980-82, pres.-elect 1987). Republican. Roman Catholic. Home and Office: 6186 E Princeton Ave Englewood CO 80111-1035 E-mail: jwgiesen@concentric.net

GIFFARD, ROBIN P. computer engineer, industrial physicist; With Hewlett-Packard Co., Palo Alto, Calif. Recipient Indsl. Applications prize Am. Inst. Physics, 1993-94. Office: Hewlett-Packard Co 3000 Hanover St Palo Alto CA 94304-1181

GIFFIN, GLENN ORLANDO, II, music critic, writer, newspaper editor; b. Denver, Feb. 27, 1943; s. Glenn Orlando and E. Louise (Mosler) G. B.Mus., U. Colo., 1965; M.A. in Librarianship, U. Denver, 1967. Scriptwriter, broadcaster radio Sta. KRNW-FM, Boulder, 1965-67; asst. music critic San Francisco Chronicle, 1968; asst. music librarian Norlin libraries U. Colo., 1968-70; music critic, staff writer Denver Post, 1970-73, music editor, 1973-88, book page editor, music critic, 1988-98, editor Colo. Living, Writing/Entertainment, 1998—, entertainment columnist. Host Soundings, Sta. KOA Radio 1985-86; curator Carson-Brierly Dance Library U. Denver, 1986—. Rockefeller Found. fellow, 1966-68; Corbett Found. fellow, 1969; Nat. Endowment for Arts grantee Dance Criticism Inst., Conn. Coll., summer 1971; named Outstanding Alumnus U. Colo., 1985. Mem. Music Library Assn., Am. Musicol. Soc., Dance Critics Assn., Music Critics Assn., Sigma Delta Chi. Office: Denver Post PO Box 1709 1560 Broadway Denver CO 80201-1709

GIFFIN, SANDRA LEE, nursing administrator; b. Tacoma, July 16, 1957; d. Clayton Eugene and Carol Lee (Fisher) Peterson; m. Herbert Kent Giffin, May 6, 1989. Diploma, Tacoma Gen. Hosp. Sch. Nursing, 1978; BSN magna cum laude, Pacific Luth. U., 1980; MS, Oreg. Health Scis. U., 1994. Cert. in nursing adminstrn. Staff nurse Mary Bridge Children's Hosp., 1978-81, evening nurse supr., infection control nurse, 1981-83, asst. med./surg. nurse mgr., 1983-84, med./surg. nurse mgr., 1984-89; dept. dir. Oreg. Poison Ctr. Oreg. Health Scis. U., Portland, 1989—, instr., Sch. Nursing, 1994—, dept. dir. nurse cons. program, 1995-2000, interim dir. physician cons. program, 2000. Presenter in field. Author/presenter abstracts in field. Sec. Rocky Butte Neighborhood Assn., 1996; sec. bd. dirs. Make A Wish Found. Oreg., 1989-96; mem. adv. bd. Oreg. Safe Kids Coalition; active Oreg. Interagy. Hazardous Comm. Coun., Oreg. Sch. Health Edn. Coalition. Grantee Agy. for Toxic Substances and Disease Registry/Am. Assn. Poison Control Ctrs., 1992, Oreg. State Health Divsn., 1993-94. Mem. Am. Acad. Ambulatory Care Nursing, Am. Assn. Poison Control Ctrs., N.W. Orgn. Nursing Execs. (apptd. mem. commn. on health care policy 2000). Avocations: skiing, reading, bicycling, travel, cooking. Office: Oreg Poison Ctr 3181 SW Sam Jackson Park Rd Portland OR 97201-3011

GIFFORD, ERNEST MILTON, biologist, educator; b. Riverside, Calif., Jan. 17, 1920; s. Ernest Milton and Mildred Wade (Campbell) G.; m. Jean Duncan, July 15, 1942; 1 child, Jeanette A.B., U. Calif., Berkeley, 1942, Ph.D., 1950; grad., U.S. Army Command and Gen. Staff Sch., 1965. Asst. prof. botany, asst. botanist expt. sta. U. Calif.-Davis, 1950-56, assoc. prof. botany, assoc. botanist, 1957-61, prof. botany, botanist, 1962-87, prof. emeritus, 1988—, chmn. dept. botany and agrl. botany, 1963-67, 74-78. Author: (with A. S. Foster) Morphology and Evolution of Vascular Plants, 3d edit., 1989, (with T. L. Rost) Mechanisms and control of Cell Division, 1977; editor in chief Am. Jour. Botany, 1975-79; advisor to editor Ency. Brit.; contbr. articles on anatomy, ultrastructure and morphogenesis of higher plants to profl. jours. Served to maj. U.S. Army, 1942-46; ETO; to col. USAR, 1946-73. Decorated Bronze Star medal; named disting. contbr. Ency. Brit., 1964; NRC fellow Harvard U., 1956; Fulbright research scholar, France, 1966; John Simon Guggenheim Found. fellow, France, 1966; NATO sr. postdoctoral fellow, France, 1974; recipient Acad. Senate Disting. Teaching award U. Calif.-Davis, 1986. Mem. Bot. Soc. Am. (v.p. 1981, pres. 1982, merit award 1981), Internat. Soc. Plant Morphologists (v.p. 1980-84), Am. Inst. Biol. Scis., Sigma Xi. Office: U Calif Divsn Biol Scis Sect Plant Biology Davis CA 95616-8536

GIFFORD, GERALD FREDERIC, retired science educator; b. Chanute, Kans., Oct. 24, 1939; s. Gerald Leo and Marion Lou (Browne) G.; m. Cinda Jean Lowman, June 26, 1982. Student, Kans. U., 1957-60; BS in Range Mgmt., Utah State U., 1962, MS in Watershed Mgmt., 1964, PhD in Watershed Sci., 1968. Asst. prof. watershed sci. Utah State U., Logan, 1967-72, assoc. prof., 1972-80, prof., 1980-84, chmn. watershed sci. unit, 1967-84, dir. Inst. Land Reclamation, 1982-84; head range, wildlife and forestry U. Nev., Reno, 1984-92, chmn. environ. and resource sci. dept., 1992-94. Exchange scientist NSF, Canberra, Australia, 1974; cons. Smithsonian Inst., Nat. Park Service, Office of Tech. Assessment, Tex. Tech U., U. Minn., Bur. Land Mgmt. AMAX Coal Co., Nat. Commn. Water Quality, 1967—. Author: Rangeland Hydrology, 1981; assoc. editor Arid Soil Rsch and Rehab., 1985-90, Jour. of Range Mgmt., 1982-87, 91-95; contbr. papers to profl. pubs. Named Tchr. of Yr., U. Nev. Coll. Agr., 1996. Mem. Am. Water Resources Assn., Soil and Water Conservation Soc. Avocations: racquetball, antiques, garage sales. Home: 3880 Squaw Valley Cir Reno NV 89509-5663 Office: U Nev Environ and Resource Scis 1000 Valley Rd Reno NV 89512-2815 E-mail: fredandcinda@aol.com

GIFFORD, JOHN F. consumer products company executive; Founded AMD, Sunnyvale, Calif., 1969, Maxim Integrated Products, Sunnyvale, 1983, chmn., pres., CEO Calif., 1992—. Office: Maxim Integrated Products 120 San Gabriel Dr Sunnyvale CA 94086-5150

GILB, CORINNE LATHROP, history educator; b. Lethbridge, Alta., Can., Feb. 19, 1925; d. Glen Hutchison and Vera (Passey) Lathrop; m. Tyrell Thompson Gilb, Aug. 19, 1945 (dec. 2001); children: Lesley Gilb Taplin, Tyra. BA, U. Wash., 1946; MA, U. Calif., Berkeley, 1951, law student, 1950-53; PhD, Harvard U., 1957. History lectr. Mills Coll., Oakland, 1957-61; prof. humanities San Francisco State U., 1964-68; rsch. assoc. U. Calif., Berkeley, 1953-68; prof. history Wayne State U., Detroit, 1968-94, co-dir. Liberal Arts Urban Studies program, 1976-86; dir. planning City of Detroit, 1979-85; pres. Atherton Press, Calif., 1997—. Spl. cons. Calif. Legislature, 1963, 64; vis. scholar Hoover Instn., Stanford U., fall 1993; UN Nongovtl. Orgn. rep. Internat. Orgn. for Unification of Terminological Neologisms, 1995—. Author: Conformity of State to Federal Income Tax, 1964, Hidden Hierarchies, 1966, Toward Holistic History, 2000, The World's Earliest Cities, 2001. Guggenheim fellow, 1957; grantee Social Sci. Rsch. Coun. Mem. Internat. Soc. Comparative Study of Civilizations (five terms exec. coun., 1st v.p. 1995-98), No. Calif. World Affairs Coun., various acad. assns. Presbyterian. E-mail: cgilb@msn.com

GILBERT, DONALD ROY, lawyer; b. Phila., June 6, 1946; BA, Stanford U., 1968; JD, U. Calif., 1971. Bar: Calif. 1972, Ariz. 1972. Ptnr., dir. Fennemore Craig, Phoenix, 1972—. Mem. ABA, State Bar Ariz., State Bar Calif., Maricopa County Bar Assn. Office: Fennemore Craig 3003 N Central Ste 2600 Phoenix AZ 85012-2913

GILBERT, JAMES FREEMAN, geophysics educator; b. Vincennes, Ind., Aug. 9, 1931; s. James Freeman and Gladys (Paugh) G.; m. Sally Bonney, June 19, 1959; children: Cynthia, Sarah, James. BS, MIT, 1953, PhD, 1956; D honoris causa, Utrecht U., 1994. Research assoc. MIT, Cambridge, 1956-57; asst. research geophysicist Inst. Geophysics and Planetary Physics at UCLA, 1957, asst. prof. geophysics, 1958-59; sr. research geophysicist Tex. Instruments, Dallas, 1960-61; prof. Inst. Geophysics and Planetary Physics at U. Calif. San Diego, La Jolla, 1961—, assoc. dir., 1976-88; chmn. grad. dept. Scripps Inst. Oceanography, La Jolla, 1988-91. Chmn. steering com. San Diego Supercomputer, 1984-86. Contbr. numerous articles to profl. jours. Recipient Arthur L. Day medal Geol. Soc. Am., 1985, Internat. Balzan prize , 1990; Fairchild scholar Calif. Inst. Tech., Pasadena, 1987; fellow NSF, 1956, Guggenheim, 1964-65, 72-73, Overseas fellow Churchill Coll. U. Cambridge, Eng., 1972-73. Fellow AAAS, Am. Geophys. Union (William Bowie med. 1999); Nat. Acad. Scis., European Union Geoscis. (hon.); mem. Seismology Soc. Am., Am. Math. Soc., Royal Astron. Soc. (recipient Gold medal 1981), Acad. Nat. dei Lincei (fgn.), Sigma Xi. Home: 780 Kalamath Dr Del Mar CA 92014-2630 Office: U Calif Inst Geophysics Planetary Physics 0225 La Jolla CA 92093 E-mail: fgilbert@ucsd.edu

GILBERT, JEROME B. consulting environmental engineer; Consulting engr. pvt. practice, Orinda, Calif., 1991—. Gordon Fair award Am. Acad. Environ. Engring., 1993. Mem. Nat. Acad. Engring. Office: 324 Tappan Ter Orinda CA 94563-1343

GILBERT, JOHN HUMPHREY VICTOR, speech scientist, educator; b. Bath, Somerset, Eng., Mar. 19, 1941; s. Daniel and Nancy (Johns) G.; m. Carolyn; children: Eliot Daniel, Oliver Gaius, Kristen. Grad., U. London; PhD, Purdue U., 1966. Asst. prof. U. B.C., 1966-69, assoc. prof., 1969-74, prof., 1974—, Med. Research Council postdoctoral scholar, 1969-74, head div. audiology and speech sci., dir. Sch. Audiol. Speech Sci., 1980-88, acting dir. Sch. Rehab. Medicine, 1985-88; coord. health scis. Univ. B.C., Vancouver, Can., 1995—. Mem. study sect. NIH, 1983; mem. senate U. B.C., 1984-87, 96—, chair senate libr. com. 93-99, vice-chair senate, 2000-2001; chmn. adv. com. B.C. Med. Svcs. Found., 1981-2000, chmn., pres. com. lectures, 1986-90; mem. health and welfare com. Vancouver Found.; bd. dirs. B.C. Rsch. Found., deputy chair, 1998—; mem. adv. com. Cmty. Care Found., 1994-2000. Mem. editl. bd. Cambridge U. Press, J. Child Lang. Fulbright scholar Purdue U., 1963-66; David Ross Rsch. fellow, 1965-66, sr. fellow Green Coll., U. B.C., 1996—; recipient Killam Tchg. prize U. B.C., 1995; named Outstanding Alumnus, Purdue U., 1993. Mem. Can. Assn. Audiologists and Speech Lang. Pathologists (pres. 1984-85, chmn. com. on examinations 1986-88, medal for outstanding profl. achievement 1988), Internat. Assn. Child Lang. (exec. coun. 1983-89), Vancouver Club. Home: 3350 W 37th Ave Vancouver BC Canada V6N 2V6 Office: Univ BC Health Sci Office Rm 400 IRC 2194 Health Mall Vancouver BC Canada V6T 1Z3 E-mail: john.gilbert@ubc.ca

GILBERT, NEIL ROBIN, social work educator, writer, consultant; b. N.Y.C., Sept. 18, 1940; s. Alan and Ida (Bedzin) G.; m. Barbara Diane Feinstein, June 2, 1963; children: Evan Mallory, Jesse Arthur, George Nathaniel, Nicole. BA, Bklyn. Coll., 1963; MSW, U. Pitts., 1965, PhD, 1968. Caseworker Interdepartmental Service Ctr., N.Y.C., 1963; dir. research Mayor's Com. on Human Resources, Pitts., 1967-69; prof. sch. social welfare U. Calif., Berkeley, 1969—, chmn. doctoral program, 1983—, acting dean sch. social welfare, 1986, 95-97, Milton and Gertrude Chernin prof. social welfare and social svcs., 1989—. Advisor Jour. Social Policy, 1982—. Author: Clients or Constituents, 1970, Capitalism and the Welfare State, 1983, (with others) Dimensions of Social Welfare Policy, 1974, 2d rev. edit., 1986, Dynamics of Community Planning, 1978, (with Barbara Gilbert) The Enabling State, 1989, Protecting Young Children from Sexual Abuse, 1989, Practical Program Evaluation, 1990, (with Jill Berrick) With the Best of Intentions, 1992, Welfare Justice, 1995; editor Social Welfare Series, 1977-83, Social Worker and Social Welfare Series, 1977—. Trustee Head Royce Sch., 1990-96; chair bd. dirs. Seneca Ctr. Fellow NIMH, 1966, U.N. Research Inst. for Social Devel., 1975; Fulbright scholar, U.S. Info. Agy, 1981; Fulbright Research fellow, London, 1981, Fulbright Western European scholar, 1987; recipient Medallion of Distinction U. Pitts., 1987. Mem. Nat. Assn. Social Workers, Assn. Pub. Policy Analysis and Mgmt. Avocations: skiing, moutaineering. Office: U Calif Sch Social Welfare Haviland Hl Berkeley CA 94720-0001

GILBERT, PAUL H. engineering executive, consultant; b. Healdsburg, Calif., Apr. 23, 1936; s. Lindley D. and Beatrice G.; m. Elizabeth A. Gilbert, July 13, 1963; children: Christopher, Gregory, Kevin. BSCE, U. Calif., Berkeley, 1959, MSCE, 1960. Registered profl. engr. in 17 states. Project mgr. Calif. State Water Project, Sacramento, 1959-68; officer U.S. Army Corp Engrs., Heidleberg, Germany, 1960-61, capt. Germany, 1961-68; project mgr. Parsons Brinckerhoff, N.Y.C., 1969-73, regional mgr./ptnr. San Francisco, 1973-85, dir. N.Y.C., 1973-98, chmn. bd., 1990-98, sr. v.p., 1973—, project dir. supercollider design and constrn., 1990-95; vice chmn. Parsons Brinckerhoff Internat. Inc., 1993—. Laser Interferometer Gravitational-Wave Observatory reviewer NSF, Washington, 1992-99; program mgmt. advisor Railtrack West Coast Modernization Project, London, U. Calif. new campus devel., Merced, GM Warren (Mich.) Design Ctr. modernization; NRC spl. com. on rev. and oversight com. U.S. Dept. Energy Project Mgmt. Program, 1999—; mem. U. Calif. Pres. Coun. Project Mgmt. Panel for the UC Managed Three Nat. Labs., 2000—;

prin.-in-charge of award winning projects Glenwood Canyon I-70 tunnels, San Francisco Ocean Outfall, Seattle Bus. Tunnel, Hood Canal Floating Bridge and West Seattle High Level and Low Level Swing Bridges, others. Contbr. articles to profl. jours. Trustee Assoc. Univs. Inc.; mem. pres.'s coun. project mgmt. panel U. Calif., 2000—. Named disting. engring. alumnus U. Calif., Berkeley, 1998. Fellow ASCE (Rickey medal 1969, Constrn. Mgmt. award 1994, Lincoln Art Welding award 1966); mem. NAE, Project Mgmt. Inst., Soc. Am. Mil. Engrs., Moles, Nat. Acad. of Engring. Republican. Roman Catholic. Office: Parsons Brinkerhoff 999 3rd Ave Ste 2200 Seattle WA 98104-4020 E-mail: gilbert@pbworld.com

GILBERT, RICHARD JOSEPH, economics educator; b. N.Y.C., Jan. 14, 1945; s. Michael N. and Esther (Dillon) G.; m. Sandra S. Waknitz, Sept. 7, 1974; children: Alison, David. BEE with honors, Cornell U., 1966, MEE, 1967; MA in Econs., PhD, Stanford U., 1976. Rsch. assoc. Stanford U., Calif., 1975-76; from assist. prof. to assoc. prof. econs. U. Calif., Berkeley, 1976-83; assoc. prof engring-econ. systems Stanford U., 1982-83; prof. econs. U. Calif., Berkeley, 1983—, dir. energy rsch. inst., 1983-93, prof. bus. adminstrn., 1990—; dep. asst. atty. gen. antitrust divsn. U.S. Dept. Justice, 1993-95. Prin. Law & Econ. Cons. Group, Berkeley, 1989—. Contbr. numerous articles to profl. jours.; editor scholarly jours. Adv. U.S. Dept. Energy, Washington, 1983—, World Bank, Washington, 1980—, NSF, Washington, 1985—, Calif. Inst. Energy Efficiency, Berkeley, 1990—. Fulbright scholar Washington, 1989; vis. scholar Cambridge U., 1979, Oxford U., 1979. Mem. Tau Beta Pi, Eta Kappa Nu, Sigma Xi. Office: U Calif Dept Economics Berkeley CA 94720-0001

GILBERT, SCOTT, advertising executive; Co-chmn. bd., CEO Team One Advertising, El Segundo, Calif.; pres., CEO Sachi & Sachi, L.A. Office: Sachi & Sachi 3501 Sepulveda Blvd Torrance CA 90505-2538

GILBERTSON, OSWALD IRVING, marketing executive; b. Bklyn., Mar. 23, 1927; s. Olaf and Ingeborg (Aase) Gabrielsen; m. Magnhild Hompland, Sept. 11, 1954; 1 child, Jan Ivar. Cert. electrotechnician, Sorlandets Teknise Skole, Norway, 1947; BSEE, Stockholms Teknisa Inst., Stockholm, Sweden, 1956. Registered profl. engr., Vt. Planning engr. test equipment design and devel. Western Electric Co., Inc., Kearny, N.J., 1957-61, planning engr. new prodn., 1963-67, engring. supr. test equipment, 63-67, engring. supr. submarine repeaters and equalizers, 1967-69; engring. mgr. comm. cables ITT Corp., Oslo, Norway, 1969-71; mktg. mgr. for ITT's Norwegian co. Std. Telefon og Kabelfabrik A/S (STK), 1971-87, STK factory rep., 1987-89, Alcatel Kabel Norge AS Factory rep., 1989-92, Alcatel Can. Wire Inc. Factory rep., 1992-95; divsn. mgr. Eswa Heating Sys., Inc., 1980-87, pres., 1987-89. Author: Electrical Cables for Power and Signal Transmission, 2000; patentee in field. With AUS, 1948-52. Named Hon. Norwegian Consul, 1981—; apptd. Knight 1st Class Norwegian Order Merit, 1989. Mem. IEEE, Norwegian Soc. Profl. Engrs., Soc. Norwegian Am. Engrs., Sons of Norway. Home and Office: 6240 Brynwood Ct San Diego CA 92120-3805

GILBERTSON, ROBERT G. computer company executive; b. Madison, Wis., May 18, 1941; s. Palmer B. and Agnes E. (Ericson) G.; m. Ellen L. Podell; children: David Scott, Jeffrey Allan. Student, MIT, 1959-62; MBA, U. Chgo., 1970; PhD, Stanford U., 1973. Arch. designer various firms, 1963-66; mktg. exec. IBM, Chgo., White Plains, N.Y., 1966-71; asst. prof. Harvard Grad. Sch. Bus., Cambridge, Mass., 1973-78; sr. v.p. Data Archs. Inc., Waltham, 1978-83; pres., CEO, Channel Net Corp., Southport, Conn., 1983-85, Data Switch Corp., Shelton, 1985-92, CMX Sys. Inc., Wallingford, 1993-96, also bd. dirs.; pres., CEO Network Computing Devices, Inc., Mountain View, Calif., 1996—. Bd. dirs. Network Computing Devices, DSL.Net; adj. prof. Brandeis U., Walthama, 1976-80. Contbr. articles to profl. jours. Bd. dirs. Griffin Hosp., Seymour, Conn., 1987-92, Conn. Bus. Industry Assn., 1995-96; bd. dirs., vice chmn. Mfr. Assn. Conn., 1992-96. Named Turnaround Mgr. of Yr., 1988. Mem. IEEE, Am. Electronics Assn. (treas., sec., chmn. 1991-92), Assn. for Computing Machinery, Soc. Info. Mgmt., Inst. Mgmt. Scis., Conn. Com. Bus. Opportunity, Def. Diversified and Indsl. Policy, S.W. Area Commerce and Industry Assn. (bd. dirs. 1988-93 (chmn. regional transp. coun. 1990-93). Lutheran. Avocations: tennis, racquetball, skiing, golf, bridge.

GILBERTSON, ROBERT LEONARD, plant pathology educator; BS, U. Mass., 1978, MS, 1981; PhD, Colo. State U., 1985. Contbr. numerous articles to profl. jours. Recipient Novartis award Am. Phytopathol. Soc., 1998. Achievements include research in the molecular characterization, detection, and genetics of plant viruses, particularly geminiviruses. Office: U Calif 4208 Storer Hall 1 Shields Ave Davis CA 95616-5200 E-mail: rlgilbertson@ucdavis.edu

GILBERTZ, LARRY E. state legislator, entrepreneur; b. Gillette, Wyo., Feb. 3, 1929; s. Jacob A. and Lena E. (Schlautmann) G.; m. Verna Ann Howell, June 18, 1955; children: Katerine, L.D., Susan, Jay. Mgr. Gilbertz Ranch, Gillette, 1953-62, owner, 1963—; sr. ptnr. Gilbertz Co., Gillette, 1971—; pres. Gilbertz Enterprises, Gillette, 1988—; mem. Wyo. Senate, Cheyenne, 1993—. Chmn. U. Wyo. Exptl. Farm, Campbell County, 1970-74. Treas. Sch. Bd. Dist. # 9, Campbell County, 1969-71; active Sch. Dist. Reorgn., Campbell County, 1970, Wyo. Ct. Reform, 1971. With U.S. Army, 1951-53, PTO. Recipient Performance Testing award U. Wyo., 1969-74, Chem. Weed Control award, 1969-74. Mem. Am. Farm Bur., Am. Legis. Exch. Coun., Am. Legion. Republican. Roman Catholic. Avocation: world travel. Home: 3934 Highway 50 Gillette WY 82718-9201

GILCHRIST, JAMES BEARDSLEE, banker; b. Cleve., Apr. 1, 1939; s. Hart D. and Alice (Beardslee) G.; m. Lewayne Dorman, Sept. 14, 1963; children: Hart D., Matthew J. AB, Dartmouth Coll., 1961; LLB, Stanford U., 1964; grad. with honors, Pacific Coast Banking Sch., U. Wash., 1970. Bar: Wash. 1964, Colo. 1964. Dep. pros. atty., King County, Wash., 1964-65; with Seattle First Nat. Bank, 1965-93, v.p., 1973-93, trust officer, 1970-77, corp. sec., 1977-82; sec. Seafirst Corp., 1977-82, mgr. instl. trust dept., 1982-85, mgr. personal trust dept., 1985-93; ptnr. Trust Concepts, 1993—. Instr. Am. Inst. Banking, Seattle Community Coll., 1976-78 Mem. candidate evaluation team Seattle Mcpl. League, 1976-79, chmn., 1979; mem. adv. com. Mercer Island Sch. Bd., 1979-81; bd. dirs. Mercer Island Schs. Found., 1981-85; mem. Dartmouth Coll. Alumni Coun., 1987-90. Mem. Wash. Bar Assn., Am. Soc. Corp. Secs. (chpt. pres. 1980-81, corp. practices com. 1981-83, dir. 1982-84), Corp. Trustees Assn. of Wash. (chmn. 1988-91), Seattle Estate Planning Coun. (mem. exec. com. 1987-89, chmn. seminar 1975).

GILDRED, THEODORE E. former diplomat, real estate developer; b. Mexico City, 1935; m. Heidi Coppin. Grad., Stanford U., 1959; postgrad., Sorbonne, U. Heidelberg; grad. Sch. Internat. Rels. and Pacific Area Studies, U. Calif. Pres. Gildred Found., 1967; founder Torrey Pines Bank (now Wells Fargo Bank), San Diego, 1979; U.S. amb. to Argentina, 1986-89; founder, chmn. bd. The Lomas Santa Fe Group, San Diego, 1989—. Bd. dirs. N.Am. Airlines, Grad. Sch. Internat. Rels. and Pacific Area Studies, U. Calif., San Diego, Security Pacific Nat. Bank; spkr. in field. Recipient hon. command pilot wings Ecuadorian Air Force, Orden de Mayo al Mèrito, en Grado de Gran Cruz, Pres. Carlos Menem, Argentina, 1992. Office: The Lomas Santa Fe Group Ste 200 265 Santa Helena Solana Beach CA 92076-1508 Fax: 858-755-6821. E-mail: Tgildred@lsfg.com

GILES, GERALD LYNN, psychology, learning enhancement, computer educator; b. Manti, Utah, Jan. 2, 1943; s. Bert Thorne and Sarah Jenett (Carlen) G.; m. Sharon Ruth Bleak, June 12, 1967; children: Kim, David, Kristie, Becky, Michael, Andrew, Brent, Amber. BA, U. Utah, 1968, MA, 1971. Tchr. Granite Sch. Dist., Salt Lake City, 1968-72; prof. Salt Lake C.C., Salt Lake City, 1972—. Cons. QUE Enterprises, Salt Lake City, 1976—; faculty U. Phoenix, Salt Lake City, 1986—; presenter in field. Author: The Vicious Circle of Life, 1988. Chmn. Rep. voting dist., Salt Lake City, 1984-86; bishop LDS Ch., 1986-91; adviser Explorer Scouts. Named Outstanding Tchr. of Yr., 1986; recipient Teaching Excellence award, 1986, Excellence award Nisod, 1994, Local Svc. aard UAACCE, 1998, SLCC Outstanding Contbn. award, 2000. Mem. ASCD, Nat. Assn. Devel. Edn., Coll. Reading and Learning Assn., Southwestern Assn. Devel. Edn. (pres.), Utah Assn. Adult Cmty. and Continuing Edn. (Local Svc. award 1998). Avocations: videotaping, computers, writing, public speaking and presentation. Home: 4342 Beechwood Rd Taylorsville UT 84123-2206 Office: Salt Lake C C PO Box 30808 Salt Lake City UT 84130-0808 E-mail: gilesge@home.com

GILES, ROBERT EDWARD, JR. lawyer; b. Bremerton, Wash., Dec. 17, 1949; s. Robert Edward Sr. and Alice Louise (Morton) G.; m. Barbara Susan Miller, Aug. 21, 1971; children: Steven, William, Thomas, James. BA in Fin., U. Washington, 1971, JD, 1974. Bar: Wash. 1974, U.S. Tax Ct. 1974. From assoc. to fin. ptnr. Perkins Coie, Seattle, 1974-86, mng. ptnr., 1986—. Bd. dirs. Jr. Achievement, Seattle, 1984—; bd. dirs., sec. Wash. Coun. for Econ. Edn., 1981-91; v.p., chief Seattle coun. Boy Scouts Am., 1996—. Capt. U.S. Army, 1974. Mem. ABA, Wash. State Bar Assn., Greater Seattle C. of C. (trustee 1994-97). Avocations: hiking, climbing. Home: 22018 NE 137th St Woodinville WA 98072-5802 Office: Perkins Coie 1201 3rd Ave Fl 40 Seattle WA 98101-3029

GILGER, PAUL DOUGLASS, architect; b. Mansfield, Ohio, Oct. 13, 1954; s. Richard Douglass and Marilyn Joan (Hawkins) G. BArch, U. Cin., 1978. Registered architect, Ohio. Architect Soulen & Assocs., Mansfield, Ohio, 1976-81, PGS Architecture/Planning, Los Gatos, Calif., 1981-82, Bottomline Systems, Inc., San Francisco, 1983-85; pvt. practice San Francisco Bay Area, 1985-90; set designer Nomad Prodns. Scenic Studios, San Francisco, 1985-87; architect James Gillam, Architect, San Francisco, 1987-90, Hedgpeth Architects, Santa Rosa, Calif., 1990—, Home Planners, Inc., Tucson, 1994—. Booking mgr. 1177 Club, San Francisco, 1985-86, City Cabaret, San Francisco, 1986-87; bd. dirs San Francisco Coun. Entertainment, 1987-90; project architect Lucasfilm Movie Studio Indsl. Light and Magic, San Rafael, Calif., 1991. Author: "The Best of Times", the Jerry Herman Musical Revue. Recipient Ohio Cmty. Theatre Assn. award, 1980, Theatrewest Acting award, 1983, 3 Bay Area Critics Cir. award, 1984, 85, 4 Cabaret Gold awards San Francisco Coun. Entertainment, 1985, 86, 3 Hollywood Dramalogue awards, 1985, 5 awards. 1996; San Francisco Focus award, 1985. Avocations: travel, piano, automobiles. paul.hedgpetharchitects.com. Home: 530 Juilliard Park Dr Santa Rosa CA 95401-6312 Office: Hedgpeth Architects 2321 Bethards Dr Santa Rosa CA 95405-8536 E-mail: gilger@sonic.net

GILHOOLY, DAVID JAMES, III, artist; b. Auburn, Calif., Apr. 15, 1943; s. David James and Gladys Catherine (Schulte) G.; m. Camille Margot Chang, Aug. 23, 1983; children: David James, Andrea Elizabeth, Abigail Margaret, Peter Rodney, Hakan Yuatutsu, Kiril Shintora, Sorqan Subetei. BA, U. Calif., Davis, 1965, MA, 1967. Tchr. San Jose (Calif.) State Coll., 1967-69, U. Sask. (Can.), Regina, 1969-71, York U., Toronto, Ont., Can., 1971-75, 76-77, U. Calif.-Davis, summer 1971, 75-76, Calif. State U.-Sacramento, summers 1978-79; lectr. in field. One-man shows include San Francisco Museum Art, 1967, M. H. deYoung Meml. Mus., San Francisco, 1968, Matrix Gallery, Wadsworth Athenuem, Hartford, Conn., 1976, Mus. Contemporary Art, Chgo., 1976, Vancouver (B.C., Can.), Art Gallery, 1976, ARCO Co. for Visual Arts, Los Angeles, 1977, Mus. Contemporary Craft, N.Y.C., 1977, E.B. Crocker Art Mus., Sacramento, 1980, St. Louis Mus. Art, 1981, Smith-Anderson Gallery, Palo Alto, 1985, San Jose Mus. Art, 1992, De Saisset Mus., Santa Clara U., 1999, Hallie Ford Mus. Art, Salem, Oreg., 2000; group shows include U. Calif.-Berkeley Art Mus., 1967, Inst. Contemporary Art, Boston, 1967, Whitney Mus. Am. Art, N.Y.C., 1970, 74, 81, Musee d'art de la Ville Paris, 1973, Chgo. Art Inst., 1975, San Francisco Mus. Art and Nat. Collection Fine Art, Washington, 1976-77, Stedelijk Mus., Amsterdam, The Netherlands, 1979, Everson Mus. Art, Syracuse, N.Y., 1979, Whitney Mus. Am. Art, N.Y.C., 1981, Palm Springs Desert Art Mus., 1984, Oakland Mus., 1985, Stanford Mus. Art, 1987, Inst. Contemporary Art, Boston, 1994, DeSaisset Mus., Santa Clara, Calif., 1999, Hallie Ford Mus., Salem, Oreg., 2000; represented in permanent collections S. Bronfman Collection Can. Art, Montreal, Que., San Francisco Mus. Art, Phila. Mus. Art, Vancouver Art Gallery, Art Gallery Greater Victoria (B.C.), Albright-Knox Art Gallery, Buffalo, San Antonio Mus. Art, Oakland (Calif.) Mus. Art, Stedelijk Mus., Stanford U., Palo Alto, Calif., Australian Nat. Gallery, Canberra, Govt. Can., Calgary, Alta., Whitney Mus. Am. Art, Eugene (Oreg.) Ctr. Performing Arts. Can. Council grantee, 1975, 78. Mem. Royal Can. Acad. Republican. Mem. Ch. of Scientology. Office: 4385 Yaquina Bay Rd Newport OR 97365-9618 E-mail: dgilhooly@earthlink.net

GILL, DAVID, food products executive; b. 1949; Student, Cal Poly San Luis Obispo, 1970-75. With Almaden Vineyards, Napa Valley, Calif., 1975-78; ptnr. Rio Farms, Oxnard, 1978—. Office: Rio Farms 1051 Pacific Ave Oxnard CA 93030

GILL, GEORGE WILHELM, anthropologist; b. Sterling, Kans., June 28, 1941; s. George Laurance and Florence Louise (Jones) G.; m. Pamela Jo Mills, July 26, 1975 (div. 1988); children: George Scott, John Ashton, Jennifer Florence, Bryce Thomas. BA in Zoology with honors (NSF grantee), U. Kans., 1963, MPhil Anthropology (NDEA Fellow, NSF, 1970, PhD in Anthropology, 1971. Diplomate Am. Bd. Forensic Antropology. Mem. faculty U. Wyo., Laramie, 1971—, prof. anthropology, 1985—. Chair dept. anthropology, 1993-96; forensic anthropologist law enforcement agys., 1972—; sci. leader Easter Island Anthrop. Expdn., 1981; chmn. Rapa Nui Rendezvous: Internat. Conf. Easter Island Rsch., U. Wyo., 1993. Author: articles, monographs; edotor: (with S. Rhine) Skeletal Attribution of Race, 1990. Served to capt. U.S. Army, 1963-67. Recipient J.P. Ellbogen meritorious classroom teaching award, 1983; rsch. grantee U. Wyo., 1972, 78, 82, Nat. Geog. Soc., 1980, Center for Field Rsch. 1980, Kon-Tiki Mus., Oslo, 1987, 89, 94, 96, World Monuments Fund, 1989. Diplomate Am. Bd. Forensic Anthropology (bd. dirs. 1985-90). Fellow Am. Acad. Forensic Scis. (sec. phys. anthropology sect. 1985-87, chmn. 1987-88); mem. Am. Assn. Phys. Anthropologists, Plains Antrop. Soc., Wyo. Archael. Soc. Republican. Presbyterian. Home: 649 Howe Rd Laramie WY 82070-6885 Office: U Wyo Dept Anthropology Laramie WY 82071 E-mail: ggill@uwyo.edu

GILL, GORDON N. medical educator; b. Dec. 19, 1937; BA in Chemistry/Lit., Vanderbilt U., 1960, MD, 1963. Diplomate Am. Bd. Internal Medicine with subspecialty in endocrinology and metabolism. Intern in internal medicine Vanderbilt U. Hosp., Nashville, 1963-64; resident Yale-New Haven Hosp., 1964-66; fellow postdoctoral fellow metabolism/endocrinology NIH/Yale U., 1966-68; spl. postdoctoral rsch. fellow NIH/U. Calif., San Diego, 1968-69; asst. prof. medicine U. Calif., San Diego, 1969-73, assoc. prof., 1973-78, prof. medicine, 1978—, chief divsn. endocrinology dept. medicine, 1971-83, chief divsn. endocrinology/metabolism, 1983-95, assoc. chair sci. affairs, 1992-95, chmn. faculty basic biomed. scis., 1995—, dean sci. affairs, 2001—. Chmn. endocrinology study sect. NIH, 1979-80, chmn. task force on endocrinology, 1978, dir. tng. grant on exptl. endocrinology and metabolism, 1978—; prin. investigator interdisciplinary program to study macromolecules regulating growth and oncogenesis U. Calif., San Diego, 1988-95; chmn. Gordon Conf. on Hormone Action, 1979, Gordon Conf. on Peptide Growth Factors, 1990; mem. sci. adv. bd. BioCryst, 1990—; sci. and med. adv. bd. chair Whittier Inst., 1991-95; sci. adv. bd. Liver Ctr., U. Calif., San Francisco, 1991-95, Charles E. Culpepper Found., 1992—, Coun. for Tobacco Rsch. USA, 1991-97, ICN Pharms., 1992—; internat. adv. bd. dept. molecular and structural biology U. Grenoble, France, 1993—; S. Richardson Hill vis. prof. U. Ala., Birmingham, 1991; Berlin lectr. Northwestern U. Sch. Medicine, 1994. Editl. bd. Jour. Cyclic Nucleotide and Protein Phosphorylation Rsch., 1974-84, Endocrinology, 1978-82, Am. Jour. Physiology, Cell Physiology, 1981-87, Jour. Biol. Chemistry, 1983-88, Jour. Cellular Biochemistry, 1984-89, Ann. Rev. Medicine, 1986-91, Analytical Biochemistry, 1980-92; editor Molecular and Cellular Endocrinology, 1974-92; cons. editor Jour. Clin. Investigation, 1992-97; sect. editor: Endocrinology, Best and Taylor Physiological Basis of Medical Practice, 11th and 12th edits., Endocrinology and Metabolism, Cecil's Textbook of Medicine, 20th edit. Bd. dirs. Med. Rsch. and Edn. Found., The Agouron Inst., 1985—; mem. biochemistry and endocrinology sci. adv. com. Am. Cancer Soc., 1989-91; adv. com. Markey Charitable Trust, 1990-97; peer rev. com. Am. Heart Assn., 1991-96. Helen Hay Whitney Found. fellow, 1969-73; NIH Rsch. Career Devel. awardee, 1969-73, Merit award. Fellow ACP, Am. Acad. Arts and Scis.; mem. AAAS, Assn. Am. Physicians, Am. Fedn. Clin. Rsch., Am. Soc. Clin. Investigation, Am. Soc. Biol. Chemistry and Molecular Biology, Endocrine Soc., Western Assn. Physicians, Western Soc. for Clin. Investigation, Am. Soc. for Cell Biology, Phi Beta Kappa, Alpha Omega Alpha. Office: Univ Calif 9500 Gilman Dr La Jolla CA 92093-5003

GILL, MARGARET GASKINS, lawyer; b. St. Louis, Mar. 2, 1940; d. Richard Williams and Margaret (Cambage) Gaskins; m. Stephen Paschall Gill, Dec. 21, 1961; children: Elizabeth, Richard. BA, Wellesley Coll., 1962; JD, U. Calif., Berkeley, 1965. Bar: Calif. 1966. Assoc. Pillsbury, Madison & Sutro, San Francisco, 1966-72, ptnr., 1973-94, mem. mgmt. com., 1973-94, head corp. securities group, mem. assoc., rev. com., 1981-91, chair asoc., rev. com., 1988-91; sr. v.p. legal, external affairs & sec. AirTouch Communications, San Francisco, 1994—. Referee Calif. State Bar Ct., 1979-82; bd. dirs. Consolidated Freightways. Mem. steering com. Trinity Episcopal Ch., Menlo Park, Calif., 1980-82, com. to revise constitution, Diocese Calif., 1981-82; trustee St. Luke's Hosp. Found., San Francisco, 1983-93; mem. adv. coun. Ch. div. Sch. of the Pacific, 1986; bd. dirs. Episcopal Diocese Calif., 1989—; trustee San Francisco Ballet, 1991—; bd. dirs., gen. counsel United Way Bay Area, San Francisco, 1993-94. Fellow Am. Bar Found.; mem. ABA (spl. com. on internat. practice 1979-82, spl. com. negotiated acquisition 1988-90), Calif. Bar Assn. (corp. com. 1982-85, chairperson 1985, exec. com. 1985-88, vice chairperson 1987-88, chair nominating com. bus. law sect. 1988), San Francisco Bar Assn. Republican. Episcopalian. Office: AirTouch Communications One Calif St San Francisco CA 94111

GILL, STEPHEN PASCHALL, retired physicist, mathematician; b. Balt., Nov. 13, 1938; s. Robert Lee and Charlotte (Olmsted) G.; m. Margaret Ann Gaskins, Dec. 21, 1961; children: Elizabeth Olmsted, Richard Paschall. B.S., MIT, 1960; M.A., Harvard U., 1961, Ph.D., 1964. Cons. hypersonic aerodynamics Raytheon Corp., Bedford, Mass., 1963-64; research physicist Stanford Research Inst., Menlo Park, Calif., 1964-65, head high energy gasdynamics, 1965-68, Physics Internat. Co., San Leandro, 1968-70, mgr. shock dynamics dept., 1970-72; founder, pres. Artec Assocs., Inc., Hayward, 1972-77, chief scientist, 1977-91; founder, pres. Votan Corp., Hayward, 1979-91, chief scientist, chmn. bd., 1981-85; ret., 1999. Founder, chief scientist Magnetic Pulse Inc., 1985-99. Mem. San Francisco Symphony Assn.; mem. San Francisco Mus. Art. Mem. IEEE, Am. Phys. Soc., Am. Math. Soc., MIT Alumni Assn., Sigma Xi, Delta Kappa Epsilon. Republican. Episcopalian. Clubs: MIT. Home: 32 Flood Cir Atherton CA 94027-2151 E-mail: stephen_p_gill@hotmail.com

GILLAN, KAYLA J. lawyer; JD, U. Calif., Davis, 1984. Gen. counsel Calif. Pub. Employees Ret. Sys., Sacramento, 1996—. Named one of Top 50 Women Lawyers Nat. Law Jour., 1998. Office: Calif Pub Employees Ret Sys Lincoln Plz 400 P St Sacramento CA 95814-5345

GILLESPIE, GERALD ERNEST PAUL, comparative literature educator, writer; b. Cleve., July 12, 1933; s. Francis and Nora Veronica (Quinn) G.; m. Adrienne Amalia Galante, Sept. 5, 1959. AB, Harvard U., 1956; postgrad., U. Tübingen, Germany, 1956-57; MA, Ohio State U., 1958, PhD, 1961; postgrad., U. Munich, 1960-61. Asst. prof. U. So. Calif., L.A., 1961-65; assoc. prof., then prof. SUNY, Binghamton, 1965-74; vis. prof. U. Pa., Phila., 1969, NYU, 1970; prof. Stanford (Calif.) U., 1974—. Vis. prof. U. Minn., Mpls., 1978, Peking U., Beijing, 1985, U. East Anglia, Norwich, Eng., 1988, U. Munich, 1993. Author: German Baroque Poetry, 1971, Evolution of the European Novel, 1987, Garden and Labyrinth of Time, 1988; author, editor: Herkommen und Erneuerung, 1976, Studien zum Werk D.C. von Lohenstein, 1983, German Theater Before 1750, 1992, Romantic Drama, 1994, Narrative Ironies, 1997, Mallarmé in the Twentieth Century, 1998; translator, editor: Night Watches, 1972, Puss-in-Boots, 1974, Bohemian Lights, 1976; editor: Littérature Comparée, Littérature Mondiale, 1991, Visions in History, 1995, Powers of Narration, 1995; mem. editl. bd. Comparative Lit., 1977—, Internationales Archiv, 1975—, Utrecht Studies in Comparative Lit., 1987—, Recherche Littéraire, 1991—, Literary Imagination, 1998—; co-editor German Life and Letters, 1987—. Andrew Mellon Found. fellow, 1966-67; John S. Guggenheim Found. fellow, 1967-68; NEH sr. fellow, 1973-74; vis. fellow Clare Hall, Cambridge U., Eng., 1979 Mem. MLA (mem. exec. com. comparative studies in romanticism and the 19th century 1982-87, mem. nat. program com. 1985-88, mem. exec. com. classical studies and modern lit. 1986-91), Internat. Comparative Lit. Assn. (sec. 1979-85, mem. editl. bd. bull. 1979-85, v.p. 1985-88, pres. 1994-97), Berliner Wissenschaftliche Gesellschaft (corr.), Am. Comparative Lit. Assn., Brit. Comparative Lit. Assn., Renaissance Soc. Am., Assn. of Literary Scholars and Critics (coun. 1998—), Calif. Assn. Scholars.

GILLESPIE, MARILYN, museum administrator; Dir. Las Vegas Natural History Mus., 1991—. Pres. Bd. Mus. and Attractions, Nev., sec. 1997—. Vol. promoting environ. concerns, homelessness issues, spl. edn. Mem. Am. Assn. Mus., Nev. Mus. Assn., Allied Arts Coun., S.W. Marine Educators Assn., Kiwanis Club (bd. dirs. Las Vegas Territory, program dir. Uptown). Office: Las Vegas Natural History Mus 900 Las Vegas Blvd N Las Vegas NV 89101-1112

GILLETTE, EDWARD LEROY, radiation oncology educator; b. Coffeyville, Kans., May 21, 1932; s. Harold R. and Laura Belle (McLaughlin) G.; m. Carol J. Peterson, June 2, 1956 (div. Oct. 1981); children: William R., Jeffrey S., Timothy E., Jennifer L.; m. Sharon L. McChesney, Nov. 26, 1988. BS, DVM, Kans. State U., 1956; MS, Colo. State U., 1961, PhD, 1965. From instr. to prof. radiology and radiation biology Colo. State U., Ft. Collins, 1959-72, prof., 1972-2000, prof., chmn. emeritus, 2000—, dir. comparative oncology, 1974-98, chmn. dept. radiol. health scis., 1989-98, assoc. dean rsch. Coll. Vet. Medicine and Biomed. Sci., 1997-98; adj. clin. prof. dept. radiation oncology UCLA Med. Sch., 1998—. Adj. prof. dept. radiation oncology Duke U. Med. Coll., Durham, N.C.; bd. dirs. The Children's Hosp. Kempe Rsch. Ctr., Denver, 1984-90; vis. scientist M.D. Anderson Cancer Ctr. U. Tex., 1988. Assoc. editor Radiation Rsch., 1979-82, 86-90; assoc. editor, Internat. Jour. of Radiation Oncology Biology and Physics, 1990-95, mem. editl. bd., 1995—; contbr. articles to profl. jours. Bd. dirs. Colo. State Sci. Fair, 1984-90. 1st lt. U.S. Army, 1956-58. Recipient Outstanding Svc. to the Vet. Profession award Am.

Animal Hosp. Assn., 1984, Ralston-Purina rsch. award, 1988, Kans. State U. Alumni Assn. Medallion award, 1999; U. Tex. fellow, 1968-69. Mem. AVMA, Am. Coll. Vet. Radiology (cert., pres. 1973-74), Am. Coll. Vet. Internal Medicine, Oncology (cert.), Am. Cancer Soc. (mem. exec. com. Colo. divsn. 1978-82, bd. dirs. Colo. divsn. 1984-90, pres. Larimer County chpt. 1977-81), Vet. Cancer Soc. (pres. 1982-84), Radiation Rsch. Soc. (councilor 1988-91), Am. Soc. Therapeutic Radiology and Oncology, Am. Assn. Cancer Rsch., Colo. State U. Alumni Assn. (Honor Alumnus award 1985). Republican. Avocation: reading. Office: Colo State U Dept Radiol Health Sci Fort Collins CO 80523-0001

GILLETTE, FRANKIE JACOBS, retired savings and loan executive, social worker, government administrator; b. Norfolk, Va., Apr. 1, 1925; d. Frank Walter and Natalie (Taylor) Jacobs; m. Maxwell Claude Gillette, June 19, 1976. BS, Hampton U., 1946; MSW, Howard U., 1948. Lic. clin. social worker; cert. jr. coll. tchr., life. Youth dir. YWCA, Passaic, N.J., 1948-50; dir. program Ada S. McKinley Community Ctr., Chgo., 1950-53; program dir. Sophie Wright Settlement, Detroit, 1953-64; dir. Concerted Services Project, Pittsburg, Calif., 1964-66, Job Corps Staff Devel., U. Calif., Berkeley, 1966-69; spl. program coordinator U.S. Community Services Adminstrn., San Francisco, 1969-83; pres. G & G Enterprises, San Francisco, 1985—. Chmn. bd. dirs. Time Savs. and Loan Assn., San Francisco, 1986-87. Commr. San Francisco Human Rights Commn., 1988-93; bd. dirs. Urban Econ. Devel. Corp., 1980-93, San Francisco Conv. and Visitors Bur.; trustee Fine Arts Mus. of San Francisco, 1993—; chmn. San Francisco-Abidjan Sister City Com., 1990—. Mem. Nat. Assn. Negro Bus. and Profl. Women's Clubs (pres. 1983-87), The Links, Inc., Delta Sigma Theta, Inc. Office: G & G Enterprises 85 Cleary Ct Apt 4 San Francisco CA 94109-6518

GILLETTE, RICHARD GARETH, neurophysiology educator, researcher; b. Seattle, Feb. 17, 1945; s. Elton George and Hazel I. (Hand) G.; m. Sally A. Reams, Feb. 17, 1978 (div. Nov. 1988); 1 child, Jesse Robert. BS, U. Oreg., 1968; MS, Oreg. Health Sci. U., 1976, PhD, 1993. Rsch. asst. dept. otolaryngology Oreg. Health Sci. U., Portland, 1969-72, grad. rsch. asst., 1973-80; instr. neurosci. Western State Chiropractic Coll., Portland, 1981-85, asst. prof. neurosci., 1985-93, assoc. prof. neurosci., 1993-99, prof. neurosci., 1999—. Lectr. neurosci. sch. optometry Pacific U., Forest Grove, Oreg., 1985-86; grad. rsch. asst. Neurol. Sci. Inst. OHSU, Portland, 1988-93, vis. scientist, 1993—. Contbr. articles to profl. jours. NIH Predoctoral Tng. fellow Oreg. Health Sci. U., 1973-76, Tarter fellow Med. Rsch. Found. Oreg., 1989; NIH grantee, 1990-99. Mem. AAAS, Soc. for Neurosci., Am. Pain Soc., Internat. Assn. for Study of Pain. Avocations: history studies, vocal music performance. Office: WSCC 2900 NE 132nd Ave Portland OR 97230-3014 E-mail: rgillette@wschiro.edu

GILLETTE, W. MICHAEL, state supreme court justice; b. Seattle, Dec. 29, 1941; s. Elton George and Hazel Irene (Hand) G.; m. Susan Dandy Marmaduke, 1989; children: Kevin, Saima, Ali, Quinton. AB cum laude in German, Polit. Sci., Whitman Coll., 1963; LLB, Harvard U., 1966. Bar: Oreg. 1966, U.S. Dist. Ct. Oreg. 1966, U.S. Ct. Appeals (9th cir.) 1966, Samoa 1969, U.S. Supreme Ct. 1970, U.S. Dist. Ct. Vt. 1973. Assoc. Rives & Rogers, Portland, Oreg., 1966-67; dep. dist. atty. Multnomah County, Portland, 1967-69; asst. atty. gen. Govt. of Am. Samoa, 1969-71, State of Oreg., Salem, 1971-77; judge Oreg. Ct. Appeals, Salem, 1977-86; assoc. justice Oreg. Supreme Ct., Salem, 1986—. Avocation: officiating basketball.

GILLIAM, EARL B. federal judge; b. Clovis, N.Mex., Aug. 17, 1931; s. James Earl and Lula Mae G.; m. Rebecca L. Prater; children: Earl Kenneth, Derrick James. B.A., Calif. State U., San Diego, 1953; J.D., Hastings Coll. Law, 1957. Bar: Calif. 1957. Dep. dist. atty. San Diego, 1957-62; judge San Diego Mcpl. Ct., 1963-74, Superior Ct. Calif., San Diego County, 1975-80, U.S. Dist. Ct. (so. dist.) Calif., San Diego, 1980-93, sr. judge, 1993-2001. Head Trial Practice Dept. Western State U. Law Sch., San Diego, 1969—. Recipient Trial Judge of Yr. award San Diego County Trial Lawyers Assn., 1981. Office: US Dist Ct Ste 5195 US Ct House 940 Front St San Diego CA 92101-8994

GILLIS, JOHN SIMON, psychologist, educator; b. Washington, Mar. 21, 1937; s. Simon John and Rita Veronica (Moran) G.; m. Mary Ann Wesolowski, Aug. 29, 1959; children: Holly Ann, Mark, Scott. B.A., Stanford U., 1959; M.S. (fellow), Cornell U., 1961; Ph.D. (NIMH fellow), U. Colo., 1965. Lectr. dept. psychology Australian Nat. U., Canberra, 1968-70; sr. psychologist Mendocino (Calif.) State Hosp., 1971-72; asso. prof. dept. psychology Tex. Tech U., Lubbock, 1972-76; prof. psychology Oreg. State U., Corvallis, 1976—, chmn. dept. psychology, 1976-84, 97—. Cons. VA, Ciba-Geigy Pharms., USIA, UN High Commn. for Refugees; commentator Oreg. Ednl. and Pub. Broadcasting System, 1978-79; Fulbright lectr., India, 1982-83, Greece, 1992, Kyrgyzstan, 2001; vis. prof. U. Karachi, 1984, 86, U. Punjab, Pakistan, 1985, Am. U., Cairo, 1984-86. Contbr. articles to profl. jours. Served with USAF, 1968-72. Ciba-Geigy Pharms. grantee, 1971-82 Mem. Am. Psychol. Assn., Western Psychol. Assn., Oreg. Psychol. Assn. Roman Catholic. Home: 7520 NW Mountain View Dr Corvallis OR 97330-9106 Office: Oreg State U Dept Psychology Corvallis OR 97331 E-mail: jgillis@orst.edu

GILLIS, STEVEN, biotechnology company executive; b. Phila., Apr. 25, 1953; s. Herbert and Rosalie Henrietta (Segal) G.; m. Anne Cynthia Edgar, June 26, 1976; children: Sarah Milne, Bradley Stirling. BA cum laude, Williams Coll., 1975; PhD, Dartmouth Coll., 1978. Lectr. in biology Dartmouth Coll., Hanover, N.H., 1977-78; research assoc. Dartmouth Med. Sch., Hanover, 1978-79; assoc. researcher Meml. Sloan-Kettering, N.Y.C., 1979-80; asst. prof. U. Wash., Seattle, 1980-83; exec. v.p., dir. R & D Immunex Corp., Seattle, 1982—, pres., chief oper. officer, 1988—, chief exec. officer, 1990-94, also bd. dirs.; adj. prof. U. WA, Seattle, 1990-97; pres and CEO Corixa Corp., Seattle, 19946, Seattle, 1994—. Adj. assoc. prof. U. Wsah., 1982-90, adj. prof., 1990—. Editor: Lymphokines, 1985, Recombinant Lymphokines and Their Receptors, 1987; contbr. articles to profl. jours. Asst. mem. Fred Hutchinson Cancer Ctr., Seattle, 1980-82, affiliate investigator, 1982—. Recipient Internat. Immunopharmacology award, 1983. Mem. Am. Assn. Immunologists, N.Y. Acad. Scis., Am. Assn. Arts and Scis., Columbia Tower Club (Seattle). Avocations: golf, swimming. Office: Corixa Corp 1124 Columbia St Ste 200 Seattle WA 98104-2040

GILLMOR, HELEN, federal judge; b. 1942; BA, Queen's Coll. of CUNY, 1965; LLB magna cum laude, Boston U., 1968. With Ropes & Gray, Boston, 1968-69, Law Offices of Alexander R. Gillmor, Camden, Maine, 1970, Torkildson, Katz, Jossem, Fonseca, Jaffe, Moore & Hetherington, Honolulu, 1971-72; law clk. to Chief Justice William S. Richardson Hawaii State Supreme Ct., 1972; dep. pub. defender Office of Pub. Defender, Honolulu, 1972-74; dist. ct. judge per diem Family Ct. (1st cir.) Hawaii, 1977-83; per diem judge Dist. Ct., 1st circuit, 1983-85; pvt. practice Honolulu, 1985-94; district judge U.S. Dist. Ct. Hawaii, 9th circuit, 1994—. Counsel El Paso Real Estate Investment Trust, 1969; lectr. U.S. Agy. Internat. Devel., Seoul, South Korea, 1969-70, Univ. Hawaii, [illegible] Honolulu HI 96850-0001

GILLOM, JENNIFER, professional basketball player; b. June 13, 1964; Basketball player Italian League, Milan, 1987-91, Ancona, 1991-94, Messina, 1995-96, Athens, Greece, 1996-97, Phoenix Mercury, WNBA, 1997—. Recipient Gold medal Pan Am. Games, 1987, Olympic Games, 1988; named to All WNBA 1st Team, 1988. Office: Phoenix Mercury 201 E Jefferson St Phoenix AZ 85004-2412

GILMAN, JOHN JOSEPH, research scientist; b. St. Paul, Dec. 22, 1925; s. Alexander Falk and Florence Grace (Colby) G.; m. Pauline Marie Harms, June 17, 1950 (div. Dec. 1968); children: Pamela Ann, Gregory George, Cheryl Elizabeth; m. Gretchen Marie Sutter, June 12, 1976; 1 son, Brian Alexander. BS, Ill. Inst. Tech., 1946, MS, 1948; PhD, Columbia, 1952. Research metallurgist Gen. Electric Co., Schenectady, 1952-60; prof. engrng. Brown U., Providence, 1960-63; prof. physics and metallurgy U. Ill., Urbana, 1963-68; dir. Materials Research Center Allied Chem. Corp., Morristown, N.J., 1968-78; dir. Corp. Devel. Center, 1978-80; mgr. corp. research Amoco Co. (Ind.), Naperville, Ill., 1980-85; assoc. dir. Lawrence Berkeley Lab./U. Calif., Calif., 1985-87; sr. scientist Lawrence Berkeley Lab., 1987-93; adj. prof. UCLA, 1993—. Author: Micromechanics of Flow in Solids, 1969, Inventivity-The Art and Science of Research Management, 1992; editor: The Art and Science of Growing Crystals, 1963, Fracture of Solids (with D.C. Drucker), 1963, Atomic and Electronic Structures of Metals, 1967, Metallic Glasses, 1973, Energetic Materials, 1993; editl. bd. Jour. Applied Physics, 1969-72; contbg. editor Materials Tech., 1994-99; contbr. over 300 papers, articles to tech. jours. Served as ensign USNR, 1943-46. Recipient Mathewson gold medal Am. Inst. Metal Engrs., 1959, Disting. Service award Alumni Assn. Ill. Inst. Tech., 1962, Application to Practice award, 1985. Fellow Am. Phys. Soc., The Materials Soc., Am. Soc. for Metals (Campbell lectr. 1966); mem. Nat. Acad. Engring., Phi Kappa Phi, Tau Beta Pi. Home: 2852 Forrester Dr Los Angeles CA 90064-4662 Office: UCLA 6532 Boelter Hl Los Angeles CA 90095-0001 E-mail: gilman@seas.wda.edu

GILMAN, NELSON JAY, library director; b. Los Angeles, Mar. 30, 1938; s. Louis L. and Alice (Cohen) G.; children: Justine C., Seth F.; m. Lixia Zhao. BS, U. So. Calif., 1959, MS, 1960; MLS, U. Calif., Berkeley, 1964. Tchr. math. dept. Pasadena (Calif.) H.S., 1960-61, Tamalpais H.S., Mill Valley, Calif., 1962-63; intern library adminstrn. UCLA, 1964-65, asst. to librarian, 1965-66, asst. to biomedical librarian, 1966-67, asst. biomedical librarian, 1967-69; assoc. dir. Pacific Southwest Regional Med. Library Svc., UCLA, 1969-71; dir. L.A. County/U. So. Calif. Med. Ctr. Libraries, 1974-79; asst. prof. dept. med. edn. U. So. Calif. Sch. Medicine, L.A., 1971—, dir. Norris Med. Library, 1971—, dir. Health Scis. Librs., 1984—, assoc. dir. devel. and demonstration ctr., 1981—; assoc. dean librs., dir. planning for teaching libr. U. So. Calif., 1989-90; interim dir. Ctrl. Libr. System, 1990-91. Cons. HEW, San Francisco, 1973-76, NIH, Washington, 1970-71. Assoc. editor U. So. Calif. Sch. Medicine Info. Systems Research Program, 1984-87; contbr. articles to profl. jours. With USAR, 1961-67. Mem. Am. Library Assn., Am. Soc. Info. Sci., Assn. Acad. Health Scis. Library Dirs. (bd. dirs. 1980-83), Med. Library Assn. (bd. dirs. 1977-79). Democrat. Jewish. Avocation: gardening. Home: 615 22nd St Santa Monica CA 90402-3121 Office: U So Calif Norris Med Library 2003 Zonal Ave Los Angeles CA 90089-0001

GILMORE, TIMOTHY JONATHAN, paralegal; b. Orange, Calif., June 24, 1949; s. James and Margaret (Swanson) G.; m. Blanche Jean Panter, Sept. 3, 1984; children: Erin, Sean and Brian (twins). BA, St. Mary's Coll., Moraga, Calif., 1971; grad., Denver Paralegal Inst., 1996. Adminstrv. asst. Gov. Ronald Reagan, Sacramento, 1971-73; salesman Penn Mutual, Anaheim, 1973-76; asst. devel. dir. St. Mary's Coll., Moraga, 1976-81; devel. dir. St. Alphonsus Hosp., Boise, Idaho, 1981-83; adminstr. Blaine County Hosp., Hailey, 1983-86; exec. dir. Poudre Hosp. Found., Ft. Collins, Colo., 1986-87; nat. recruiting dir. Power Securities Corp., Denver, 1987-89; cons. Horn, Fagan & Lund Exec. Search Cons., Ft. Collins, 1989; v.p. Jackson & Coker Locum Tenens, Inc., Denver, 1990-93; pres. Gilmore and Assocs., Ft. Collins, Colo., 1993-98; paralegal Brownstein, Hyatt & Farber PC, Denver, 1998—. Republican. Mem. LDS Ch. Avocation: fishing. Home and Office: 1527 River Oak Dr Fort Collins CO 80525-5537 E-mail: TG1527FC@aol.com

GILTNER, PHIL, food distributing executive; CFO Shamrock Foods, Phoenix. Mem. Ariz. Bus. Leadership Assn. (founding pres., spkr.). Office: Shamrock Foods 2228 N Black Canyon Hwy Phoenix AZ 85009

GIMPLE, W. THOMAS, sales executive; BSBA, U. So. Calif. Pres. Iwerks Touring Techs., Inc. (subs. Iwerks Entertainment), 1991-95; exec. v.p. Iwerks Entertainment, Inc., 1995-96; pres., CEO, dir. Tickets.com, CEO, co-chmn., dir., 1999—. Office: Tickets.com Inc 555 Anton Blvd Fl 12 Costa Mesa CA 92626-7811

GINN, SAM L. telephone company executive; b. Saint Clair, Ala., Apr. 3, 1937; s. James Harold and Myra Ruby (Smith) G.; m. Meriann Lanford Vance, Feb. 2, 1963; children: Matthew, Michael, Samantha. B.S., Auburn U., 1959; postgrad., Stanford U. Grad. Sch. Bus., 1968. Various positions AT&T, 1960-78; with Pacific Tel. & Tel. Co., 1978—, exec. v.p. network, 1979-81, exec. v.p. services, 1981-82, exec. v.p. network services, 1982, exec. v.p., strategic planning and adminstrn., 1983, vice chmn. bd., strategic planning and adminstrn., 1983-84; vice chmn. bd., group v.p. PacTel Cos. Pacific Telesis Group, San Francisco, 1984-86; pres. Air Touch Commn., San Francisco, 1984-87; vice chmn. bd., pres., chief exec. officer PacTel Corp. Pacific Telesis Group, San Francisco, 1986; pres., chief operating officer Pacific Telesis Group, San Francisco, 1987-88, former chmn., pres., chief exec. officer; chmn. Air Touch Commn., San Francisco, 1993—, now chmn. bd., CEO. Mem. adv. bd. Sloan program Stanford U. Grad. Sch. Bus., 1978-85, mem. internat. adv. council Inst. Internat. Studies; bd. dir. 1st Interstate Bank, Chevron Corp., Safeway, Inc. Trustee Mills Coll., 1982— . Served to capt. U.S. Army, 1959-60. Sloan fellow, 1968 Republican. Clubs: Blackhawk Country (Danville, Calif.); World Trade, Pacific-Union; Rams Hill Country (Borrego Springs, Calif.), Bankers. Office: Air Touch Commn 1 California St San Francisco CA 94111-5401

GINSBURG, GERALD J. lawyer, business executive; b. Poughkeepsie, N.Y., Aug. 29, 1930; s. Abraham and Anna (Murkoff) G.; children: Jason Andrew, Stephanie Carla. B.S., Syracuse U., 1952; J.D., Bklyn. Law Sch., 1958. Bar: N.Y. 1959. Pub. acct., 1954-59; v.p. fin. and ops., dir. Sheffield Watch Corp., N.Y.C., 1959-70, dir., 1967-70; exec. v.p., dir. Kurt Orban Co., Wayne, N.J., 1971-83; pres., dir. Pacific Marine Holdings Corp., 1983-87; pres. J&S Cons., Walnut Creek, CAlif. Dir. Ramapo Fin. Corp., Pilgrim State Bank Served with USNR, 1952-53. Mem. ABA, N.Y. Bar Assn. Office: PO Box 5314 Walnut Creek CA 94596-1314

GIOTTONINI, JAMES B. city official; b. Stockton, Calif., 1945; BS, Calif. State U., San Jose, 1968; MBA, Calif. State U., Sacramento, 1977. Dir. pub. works Town of Morgan Hill, Calif., 1978-82; city engr. City of Stockton, 1982-89, acting dir. pub. works, 1989, dir. pub. works, 1989—. Mem. ASCE. Office: City Stockton Dept Pub Works Rm 317 425 N El Dorado St Stockton CA 95202-1997

GIOVANIELLI, DAMON VINCENT, physicist, consulting company executive; b. Teaneck, N.J., May 8, 1943; s. Dominick John and Marie Concetta (Conti) G.; m. Eleanor Ruth Rand, Aug. 18, 1968; children: Kira, Tina. AB, Princeton U., 1965; PhD in Physics, Dartmouth Coll., 1970. [illegible] Los Alamos (N.Mex.) Nat. Lab., 1972-93, dep. assoc. dir. fusion rsch. and applications, 1984-85, tech. asst. to assoc. dir. for def. rsch. and applications, 1985-87, leader physics div., 1987-93, program dir. for strategic def. policy, liaison-new programs, 1992-93; ret., 1993; pres. Sumner Assocs., Sante Fe, 1993—; chmn. bd. dirs. La Mancha Co., 1997—. With J. Robert Oppenheimer Meml. Com. Contbr. articles to sci. jours. Mem. alumni schs. com. Princeton U. Fellow AAAS, mem. AIAA, Am. Phys. Soc. (program com. div. plasma physics 1978-79, chmn. nominating com. 1980, mem. exec. com. 1982-83), Am. Def. Preparedness Assn., Fusion Power Assocs., U.S. Space Found., Sigma Xi. Episcopalian. Home: 12 Loma Del Escolar Los Alamos NM 87544-2524 Office: Sumner Assocs 100 Cienega St Ste D Santa Fe NM 87501-2003

GIOVINCO, JOSEPH, nonprofit administrator, writer; b. San Francisco, Oct. 12, 1942; s. Joseph Bivona Giovinco and Jean Andrews; m. Sally Garey, Aug. 31, 1970 (div. Mar. 1982); 1 child, Gina Lorraine. BA, U. Oreg., 1964; MA in History, San Francisco State U., 1968; PhD in History, U. Calif., Berkeley, 1973. Asst. prof. history SUNY, Albany, 1974-76; instr. multicultural studies Sonoma State U., Cotati, Calif., 1976-79; exec. dir. Hist. Mus. Found., Sonoma County, Santa Rosa, 1977-80; exec. dir. no. Calif. affiliate Am. Diabetes Assn., San Francisco, 1980-81; exec. dir. San Francisco Sch. Vols., 1981-85, Calif. Hist. Soc., San Francisco, 1985-87; dir. Ctr. Advancement & Renewal of Educators, San Francisco, 1988—. Contbr. articles to profl. publs. Fellow, NEH and Harvard U., 1973; recipient scholarship U. Minn. Ctr. for Immigration History, Mpls., 1975; Rockefeller Found. grantee, 1977; recipient Covello prize Italian Am. Hist. Assn., 1976; named Alumnus of Yr., San Francisco State U., 1987. Roman Catholic. Avocations: rose gardening, classical music. Office: Ctr Advancement & Renewal Educators 25550 25th Ave San Francisco CA 94116

GIRARD, NETTABELL, lawyer; b. Pocatello, Idaho, Feb. 24, 1938; d. George and Arranetta (Bell) Girard Student, Idaho State U., 1957-58; BS, U. Wyo., 1959, JD, 1961. Bar: Wyo. 1961, D.C. 1969, U.S. Supreme Ct. 1969. Practiced in, Riverton, 1963-69; atty.-adviser on gen. counsel's staff HUD; assigned Office Interstate Land Sales Registration, Washington, 1969-70; sect. chief interstate land sales Office Gen. Counsel, 1970-73; ptnr. Larson & Larson, Riverton, 1973-85; pvt. practice Riverton, 1985—. Guest lectr. at high schs.; condr. seminar on law for layman Riverton br. A.A.U.W., 1965; condr. course on women and law; lectr. equal rights, job discrimination, land use planning. Editor Wyoming Clubwoman, 1966-68; bd. editors Wyo. Law Jour., 1959-61; writer Obiter Dictum column Women Lawyers Jour., Dear Legal Advisor column Solutions for Seniors, 1988-94; featured in Riverton Ranger, 1994; also articles in legal jours. Chmn. fund dr. Wind River chpt. ARC, 1965; chmn. Citizens Com. for Better Hosp. Improvement, 1965; chmn. subcom. on polit. legal rights and responsibilities Gov.'s Commn. on Status Women, 1965-69, mem. adv. com., 1973-93; rep. Nat. Conf. G ovs. Commn., Washington, 1966; local chmn. Law Day, 1966, 67, county chmn. Law Day, 1994, 95, 96, 97; mem. state bd. Wyo. Girl Scouts USA, sec. 1974-89, mem. nat. bd., 1978-81; state vol. adv. Nat. Found., March of Dimes, 1967-69; legal counsel Wyo. Women's Conf., 1977; gov. apptd. State Wyo. Indsl. Siting Coun., 1995—. Recipient Spl. Achievement award HUD, 1972, Disting. Leadership award Girl Scouts U.S.A., 1973, Franklin D. Roosevelt award Wyo. chpt. March of Dimes, 1985, Thanks Badge award Girl Scout Coun., 1987, Women Helping Women award in recognition of effective advancement status of women Riverton Club of Soroptimist Internat., 1990, Spl. award plaque in appreciation and recognition of 27 yrs. of svc. to State of Wyo., Wyo. Commn. for Women, 1964-92, Appreciation award Wyo. Sr. Citizens and Solutions for Srs., 1994, Arts in Action Pierrot award for outstanding musician, 1998. Mem. AAUW (br. pres.), Wyo. Bar Assn., Fremont County Bar Assn. (Spl. Recognition cert. 1997), D.C. Bar Assn., Women's Bar Assn. D.C., Internat. Fedn. Women Lawyers, Am. Judicature Soc., Assn. Trial Lawyers Am., Wyo. Trial Lawyers Assn., Nat. Assn. Women Lawyers (del. Wyo., nat. sec. 1969-70, v.p. 1970-71, pres. 1972-73), Wyo. Fedn. Women's Clubs (state editor, pres.-elect 1968-69, treas. 1974-76), Prog. Women's Club (pres.-elect. 1994-95), Riverton Chautaqua Club (pres. 1965-67), Riverton Civic League (pres. 1987-89), Kappa Delta, Delta Kappa Gamma (state chpt. hon.). Home: PO Box 687 Riverton WY 82501-0687 Office: 513 E Main St Riverton WY 82501-4440

GIRARD, ROBERT DAVID, lawyer; b. Pitts., Aug. 2, 1946; s. Oscar L. and Ruth (Alpern) G. AB, UCLA, 1967; LLB, Yale U., 1970. Bar: Calif. 1971, U.S. Dist. Ct. (cen. dist.) Calif. 1971. Ptnr. Musick, Peeler & Garrett, L.A., 1970-85, Girard, Ellingsen, Christensen & West, L.A., 1985-88, Jones, Day, Reavis & Pogue, L.A., 1988-92, Musick Peeler & Garrett, L.A., 1992-98; with Sonnenschein Nath & Rosenthal, L.A., 1998—. Bd. dirs. Calif. Pediatric Ctr., L.A., 1980—, chmn., 1998—. Mem. ABA, L.A. County Bar Assn., Am. Acad. Hosp. Attys., Nat. Health Lawyers Assn., Calif. Health Care Lawyers Assn. (bd. dirs. 1982-85), Jonathan, Phi Beta Kappa. Office: Sonnenschein Nath & Rosenthal 601 S Figueroa St Ste 1500 Los Angeles CA 90017-5720

GIRARDEAU, MARVIN DENHAM, physics educator; b. Lakewood, Ohio, Oct. 3, 1930; s. Marvin Denham and Maude Irene (Miller) G.; m. Susan Jessica Brown, June 30, 1956; children— Ellen, Catherine, Laura. B.S., Case Inst. Tech., 1952; M.S., U. Ill., 1954; Ph.D., Syracuse U., 1958. NSF postdoctoral fellow Inst. Advanced Study, Princeton, 1958-59; research assoc. Brandeis U., 1959-60; staff mem. Boeing Sci. Research Labs., 1960-61; research assoc. Enrico Fermi Inst. Nuclear Studies, U. Chgo., 1961-63; assoc. prof. physics, research asso. Inst. Theoretical Sci., U. Oreg., Eugene, 1963-67, prof. physics, research assoc., 1967—, dir., 1967-69, chmn. dept. physics, 1974-76, prof. emeritus, 1995—; rsch. prof. optical scis. U. Ariz., 2000—. Contbr. articles to profl. jours. Recipient Humboldt Sr. U.S. Scientist award, 1984-85. NSF research grantee, 1965-79; ONR research grantee, 1981-87, 99—. Fellow Am. Phys. Soc.; mem. AAUP. Achievements include research on quantum-mech. many-body problems, statis. mechanics, atomic, molecular and chem. physics; Bose-Einstein condensation of atomic vapors, coherent control of quantum systems. Home: 288 N Bent Ridge Dr Green Valley AZ 85614-5949 Office: Optical Scis Ctr Univ Arizona Tucson AZ 85721-0001 E-mail: girardeau@optics.arizona.edu

GIRARDELLI, RONALD K. food products executive; b. 1949; BA, Oreg. State U., 1971. With Blue Cross, Portland, Oreg., 1971-73; pres. Diamond Fruit Growers, Inc., 1973—. Office: Diamond Fruit Growers Inc PO Box 180 Hood River OR 97031-0060

GIRAUD, RAYMOND DORNER, retired language professional; b. N.Y.C., Aug. 26, 1920; s. Gabriel and Mabel (Dorner) G.; m. Lise Kurzmann, Feb. 1, 1948. B.A., Coll. City N.Y., 1941; M.A., U. Chgo., 1949; Ph.D., Yale, 1954. Instr. English and French Ill. Inst. Tech., 1946-49; instr., then asst. prof. French Yale, 1952-58; mem. faculty Stanford, 1958—, prof. French, 1962—, chmn. dept. French and Italian, 1968-72; prof. emeritus, 1986. Author: The Unheroic Hero, 1957, Flaubert, A Collection of Critical Essays, 1964. Served with AUS, 1942-45. Decorated Chevalier, Ordre des Palmes Académique, 1967; Guggenheim fellow, 1961-62. Home: 2200 Byron St Palo Alto CA 94301-4007 Office: Stanford U Dept French Italian Stanford CA 94305 E-mail: giraud2200@webtv.net

GIRVIGIAN, RAYMOND, architect; b. Detroit, Nov. 27, 1926; s. Manoug and Margaret G.; m. Beverly Rae Bennett, Sept. 23, 1967; 1 son, Michael Raymond. AA, UCLA, 1947; BA with honors, U. Calif., Berkeley, 1950; M.A. in Architecture, U. Calif.-Berkeley, 1951. With Hutchason Architects, L.A., 1952-57; owner, prin. Raymond Girvigian, L.A., 1957-68, South Pasadena, Calif., 1968—. Co-founder, advisor L.A. Cultural [illegible] Washington, 1966-70; co-founder, mem. Calif. Hist. Resources Commn.,

1970-78; co-founder, chmn. governing bd. Calif. Hist. Bldgs. Code, 1976-91, chmn. adminstrv. law, 1992—, chmn. emeritus, 1993—; chmn. Calif. State Capitol Commn., 1985-98, chmn. emeritus, 1998—. Co-editor, producer: film Architecture of Southern California for Los Angeles City Schs, 1965; historical monographs of HABS Landmarks, Los Angeles, 1958-80; historical monographs of Califs. State Capitol, 1974, Pan Pacific Auditorium, 1980, L.A. Meml. Coliseum, 1984, Powell Meml. Libr., UCLA, 1989; designed: city halls for Pico Rivera, 1963, LaPuente, 1966, Rosemead, 1968, Lawndale, 1970 (all Calif.); hist. architect for restoration of Calif. State Capitol, 1975-82, Workman/Temple Hist. Complex, City of Industry, Calif., 1974-81, Robinson Gardens Landmarks, Beverly Hills, Calif., 1983-92, Pasadena (Calif.) Ctrl. Libr., 1982-92, 95—, Mt. Pleasant House Mus., Heritage Sq., L.A., 1972-95. With U.S. Army, 1944-46. Recipient Outstanding Achievement in Architecture award City of Pico Rivera, Calif., 1968, Neasham award Calif. Hist. Soc., 1982, Preservationist of Yr. award Calif. Preservation Found., 1987, L.A. Mayor's award for archtl. preservation, 1987, Gold Crown award for advancement of arts Pasadena Arts Coun., 1990, Golden Palm award Hollywood Heritage, 1990; named Hist. Architect Emeritus, Calif. Legislature, 1998, commendation for state and national career achievemtns hist. preservation, Calif. Legislature, 1998; co-recipient honor award for rehab. Los Altos Apts., Calif. Preservation Found., 1999. Fellow AIA, 1972 (Calif. state preservation chmn. 1970-75, state preservation coord. 1970-89, co-recipient nat. honor award for restoration Calif. State Capitol 1983, co-recipient honor award for restoration Pasadena Cen. Libr., Pasadena chpt. 1988); mem. Soc. Archtl. Historians, Nat. Trust for Historic Preservation, Calif. Preservation Found., Calif. Hist. Soc., Xi Alpha Kappa. Democrat. Episcopalian. Office: PO Box 220 South Pasadena CA 91031-0220

GISH, NORMAN RICHARD, energy industry executive; b. Eckville, Alta., Can., Oct. 13, 1935; s. Robert Bruce and Lillian (Foster) G.; m. Joan Ann Thompson, Sept. 5, 1959; children— David Cole, Carolyn Nancy, Graeme Christopher. B.A., U. Alta., 1957; LL.B., U. B.C., 1960. Asst. trade commr. Fgn. Trade Service of Canadian Govt., Ottawa, 1961-62, Hong Kong, 1962-65; exec. B.C. Forest Products, Ltd., Vancouver, 1965-77; chmn. B.C. Energy Commn., 1977-80; v.p. Turbo Resources Ltd., 1980-83, chmn., pres., CEO, 1983-85; pres., CEO North Can. Oils Ltd., 1986-93; mng. dir. Emergo China Ltd & Fracmaster China Ltd, Beijing, China, 1994-96; chmn., dir. Alliance Pipeline, Ltd., Calgary, Alta., Can., 1997-99, dir., chmn. pres., CEO Can., 1999—. Chmn., dir. ICG Propane Inc., Calgary. Home: 8405-400 Eau Claire Ave SW Calgary AB Canada T2P 4X2 Office: Alliance Pipeline Ltd 1200 605-5 Ave SW Calgary AB Canada T2P 3H5

GIST, RICHARD D. federal judge; b. 1940; BS, U. Wyo., 1963, JD, 1965. Pvt. practice, Casper, Wyo., Lander, 1970; U.S. magistrate judge Lander, 1971—; alt. judge Lander Mcpl. Ct., 1974-79; commr. Wyo. Dist. Ct. 9th Jud. Dist., Fremont County, 1982-92. With U.S. Army, 1966-70. Office: 150 N 3rd St Ste A Lander WY 82520-2809 Fax: 307-332-2759

GITT, CYNTHIA E. lawyer; b. York, Pa., Nov. 14, 1946; BA, Wheaton Coll., 1968; JD with high honors, George Washington U., 1971. Bar: D.C. 1971, Calif. 1974, Mich. 1976, U.S. Supreme Ct. 1976, Ariz. 1978. Legis. asst. to Hon. Bella Abzug, 1971; trial atty. Equal Employment Opportunity Commn., Washington, San Francisco, 1971-75; asst. prof. Wayne State Law Sch., Detroit, 1975-77; atty. Morgan, Lewis & Bockus, L.A., 1977-84; mem. Ford & Harrison, L.A., 1984-91, Epstein, Becker & Green, L.A., 1991—. Mem. ABA (labor and employment sect.), Assn. Trial Lawyers Am., State Bar Calif., D.C. Bar, Los Angeles County Bar Assn. (sect. labor law, sect. litigation), Order Coif. Office: Epstein Becker & Green 1875 Century Park E Ste 500 Los Angeles CA 90067-2506

GITTES, RUBEN FOSTER, urological surgeon; b. Mallorca, Spain, Aug. 4, 1934; s. Archie and Cicely Mary (Foster) G.; m. K.S. Zipf, June 10, 1955 (div.); m. Rita R. Drum, Feb. 21, 1976 (div.); m. Vera Gomes, Feb. 9, 1996; children: Julia S., Frederick T., George K., Robert F. Grad., Phillips Acad., Andover, Mass., 1952; AB, Harvard U., 1956, MD, 1960. Intern, then resident in surgery and urology Mass. Gen. Hosp., Boston, 1960-67; asst. prof. UCLA Med. Sch., 1968-69; assoc. prof., then prof., chief urology U. Calif. at San Diego Med. Sch., 1969-75; prof. urol. surgery Harvard U. Med. Sch., chmn. Harvard program urology Longwood area, 1975-87; chmn. dept. surgery Scripps Clinic and Rsch. Found., La Jolla, Calif., 1987-98. Mem. study sects., task forces NIH, 1973— Author, editor publs. in field. Served with USPHS, 1963-65. NIH grantee, 1969— Mem. AAAS, Endocrine Soc., Soc. Univ. Surgeons, Soc. Univ. Urologists, Am. Assn. Genito-Urinary Surgeons, Clin. Soc. Genito-Urinary Surgeons, A.C.S., Am. Surg. Assn., Am. Urol. Assn., Am. Soc. Transplant Surgeons, Soc. Ancient Numismatics, Phi Beta Kappa, Alpha Omega Alpha. Office: Scripps Clinic & Rsch Found 10666 N Torrey Pines Rd La Jolla CA 92037-1092

GITTINGER, D. WAYNE, lawyer; b. Kellogg, Idaho, Jan. 22, 1933; s. Daniel Reese and Evelyn Caroline (Knudson) G.; 1 child, Marni; m. Anne Elizabeth Nordstrom, Dec. 17, 1984; stepchildren: John Hopen, Susan Dunn. BA, U. Wash., 1955, JD, 1957. Bar: Wash. 1957, U.S. Ct. Appeals (9th cir.) 1957, Tax Ct. of U.S., U.S. Supreme Ct. Teaching assoc. Northwestern U. Law Sch., Chgo., 1957-58; ptnr. Lane Powell Spears Lubersky, Seattle, 1959—. Bd. dirs. Nordstrom, Inc. Active U. Wash. Alumni Assn., 1965—. Lt. USCGR, 1958-67. Mem. Vintage Club, Seattle Golf Club, Seattle Yacht Club, 101 Club, Overlake Golf and Country Club (past pres. 1978-79). Republican. Avocations: golf, yachting. Office: Lane Powell Spears Lubersky 1420 5th Ave Ste 4100 Seattle WA 98101-2338 E-mail: gittingerw@lanepowell.com

GIULIANI, DAVID, personal care products company executive; CEO Optiva Corp., Bellevue, Wash. Office: Optiva Corp PO Box 5000 Snoqualmie WA 98065-5000

GIULIANO, NEIL GERARD, mayor, former academic administrator; b. Bloomfield, N.J., Oct. 26, 1956; s. Jacqueline Ann (Enright) G. BA, Ariz. State U., 1979, MEd, 1983. Pres. Circle K. Internat., Chgo., 1977-78, conv. cons., 1983-91; counselor disabled students Ariz. State U., Tempe, 1980-81, pres. associated students, 1982-83, coord. leadership devel., 1983-87, constituent dir., 1988-91, dir. fed. and community rels., 1991—; pres. Valley Achievement, Tempe, 1987—. Speaker, trainer in field. Mem. Tempe City Coun., 1990—; bd. dirs. Tempe Community Coun., 1990—, Valley Big Bros.-Big Sisters, Tempe, 1987—; pres. Tempe Leadership, Inc., 1990-91; mem. gov.'s task force on drug abuse, 1990—. Recipient Selected Participant award Ctr. for the Study of the Presidency Symposium, Washington, 1983. Mem. Tempe C. of C., Kiwanis (pres. 1986-87), Sigma Nu (conv. cons. 1988), Key Club Internat. (conv. cons. 1983-87). Republican. Roman Catholic. Avocations: reading, rock climbing, tennis. Home: 2074 E Balboa Dr Tempe AZ 85282-4005

GIVAN, BOYD EUGENE, aircraft company executive; With Boeing Co, Seattle, 1986-98, sr. v.p., CFO, 1991-98. Office: Boeing Co PO Box 3707 Seattle WA 98124-2207

GLACKIN, WILLIAM CHARLES, arts critic, editor; b. Sacramento, July 10, 1917; s. William Martin and Anita Ivy (Derr) G.; m. Helen Bateman, 1941 (div. 1960); children: Christine, Nancy; m. Sandra May Littlewood, Jan. 27, 1962; 1 child, Brendan. BS, St. Mary's Coll., Calif., 1939; postgrad., U. Calif., Berkeley, 1939-41. Tchr. Sacramento City Schs., 1941-43; reporter UPI, Sacramento, 1946-48; critic Sacramento Bee, 1948—, arts editor, 1948-76. Dir. criticism workshops Nat. Coll. Theater Festival, Sacramento, 1980's, various theater groups, Sacramento, 1948-62. Author: (musical) Anita, 1955. Sgt. U.S. Army, 1943-46. Nominated Pulitzer prize in criticism, 1980; named Conservator of Am. Arts Am. Conservatory Theater Found., 1984. Mem. Am. Newspaper Guild, Am. Theater Critics Assn., Music Critics Assn. Avocations: golf, tennis. Office: Sacramento Bee 2100 Q St PO Box 95852 Sacramento CA 95852

GLAD, DAIN STURGIS, aerospace engineer, consultant; b. Santa Monica, Calif., Sept. 17, 1932; s. Alma Emanuel and Maude LaVerne (Morby) G.; m. Betty Alexandra Shainoff, Sept. 12, 1954 (dec. 1974); 1 child, Dana Elizabeth; m. Carolyn Elizabeth Giffen, June 8, 1979. BS in Engrng., UCLA, 1954; MSEE, U. So. Calif., 1963. Registered profl. engr., Calif. Elec. engr. Clary Corp., San Gabriel, Calif., 1957-58; with Aerojet Electro Systems Co., Azusa, 1958-72, 75-84; with missile systems divsn. Rockwell Internat., Anaheim, 1973-75; with support systems divsn. Hughes Aircraft Co., 1984-90; with Electro-Optical Ctr. Rockwell Internat. Corp., 1990-94; cons., 1994—. Operating mgr., V.C.D. Techs. LLC, 1997—. Contbr. articles to profl. jours. With USN, 1954-56; lt. j.g. Res., 1956-57. Mem. IEEE. Home: 1701 Marengo Ave South Pasadena CA 91030-4818 E-mail: dglad@socal.rr.com, vcdtech@earthlink.net

GLAD, SUZANNE LOCKLEY, retired museum director; b. Rochester, N.Y., Oct. 2, 1929; d. Alfred Allen and Lucille A. (Watson) Lockley; m. Edward Newman Glad, Nov. 7, 1953; children: Amy, Lisanne Glad Lantz, William E. BA, Sweet Briar Coll., 1951; MA, Columbia U., 1952. Exec. dir. New York State Young Reps., N.Y.C., 1951-57; mem. pub. rels. staff Dolphin Group, L.A., 1974-83; scheduling sec. Gov.'s Office, Sacramento, 1983-87; dep. dir. Calif. Mus. Sci. and Industry, L.A., 1987-94; ret. Mem. Calif. Rep. League, Pasadena, 1969—; mem. Assistance League of Flintridge, 1970—, Flintridge Guild Children's Hosp., 1969-89. Mem. Sweet Briar Alumnae of So. Calif. (pres. 1972), Phi Beta Kappa, Tau Phi. Episcopalian. Avocations: reading, gardening.

GLADWELL, DAVID L. state legislator; b. Ogden, Utah, Apr. 19, 1947; m. Ruth Ann. BA in English, U. Utah, 1971, JD, 1974. Atty., 1974—; mem. Utah State Senate, Sale Lake City, 2001—. Mem. Utah State Bar Assn. Office: PO Box 12069 Ogden UT 84412 Fax: 801-626-2423. E-mail: dgladwel@le.sate.ut.us*

GLANCY, DOROTHY JEAN, lawyer, educator; b. Glendale, Calif., Sept. 24, 1944; d. Walter Perry and Elva T. (Douglass) G.; m. Jon Tobias Anderson, June 8, 1979. BA, Wellesley Coll., 1967; JD, Harvard Law Sch., 1970. Bar: D.C. 1971, Calif. 1976, U.S. Dist. Ct. D.C. 1971, U.S. Ct. Appeals (D.C. cir.) 1972. Assoc. Hogan & Hartson, Wash., 1971-73; counsel U.S. Senate Judiciary Subcomm. on Constitutional Rights, Wash., 1973-74; fellow in Law & Humanities Harvard U., Cambridge, Mass., 1974-75; asst. to assoc. prof. law Santa Clara U., Calif., 1975-82, prof. law, 1984—; vis. prof. law U. Arizona, Tucson, 1979; asst. gen. counsel U.S. Dept. of Agr., 1982-83. Cons. Commn. Fed. Paperwork, Wash., 1976; dir. summer Law Study Program in Hong Kong, 1985-90; advisor Restatement, Third Property: Servitudes, 1986-97. Dir. legal rsch. project regarding privacy and intelligent trnsp. systems Fed. Hwy. Adminstrn., 1993-95; bd. dirs. Presidio Hts. Assn. Neighbors, 1990—. Fellow Wellesley Coll., Harvard U. Mem. ABA (chair ethics com. of sect. on natural resources, energy and environ. law, 1993-95, coun. mem. 1995-98), State Bar Calif. (mem. environ. law sect., adv. exec. com. 1993-96, advisor 1996—), Am. Assn. Law Schs. (chair environ. law sect. 1992-93, chair property sect. 1996-97), Am. Law Inst., Calif. Women Lawers, Soc. Am. Law Tchrs., Phi Beta Kappa. Democrat. Avocations: gardening, travel. Office: Santa Clara U Sch Law Santa Clara CA 95053-0001

GLASER, DONALD ARTHUR, physicist; b. Cleveland, Ohio, Sept. 21, 1926; s. William Joseph Glaser. BS, Case Inst. Tech., 1946, ScD, 1959; PhD, Calif. Inst. Tech., 1949. Prof. physics U. Mich., 1949-59; prof. physics U. Calif., Berkeley, 1959—, prof. physics, molecular and cell biology, divsn. neurobiology, 1964—. Recipient Henry Russel award U. Mich., 1955, Charles V. Boys prize Phys. Soc., London, 1958, Nobel prize in physics, 1960, Gold Medal award Case Inst. Tech., 1967, Golden Plate award Am. Acad. of Achievement, 1989; NSF fellow, 1961, Guggenheim fellow, 1961-62, fellow Smith-Kettlewell Inst. for Vision Rsch, 1983-84. Fellow AAAS, Fedn. Am. Scientists, The Exploratorium (bd. dirs.), Royal Soc. Sci., Royal Swedish Acad. Sci., Assn. Rsch. Vision and Ophthalmology, Neurosci. Inst., Am. Physics Soc. (prize 1959); mem. Nat. Acad. Scis., Am. Assn. Artificial Intelligence, N.Y. Acad. Sci., Internat. Acad. Sci., Am. Philos. Soc., Sigma Xi, Tau Kappa Alpha, Theta Tau. Home: 41 Hill Rd Berkeley CA 94708-2131 Office: U Calif Dept Molecular & Cell Biology 337 Stanley Hl Berkeley CA 94720-0001

GLASER, EDWIN VICTOR, rare book dealer; b. N.Y.C., June 7, 1929; s. Simon and Dorothy (Goldwater) G.; m. Janice Briggs, May 1, 1959 (div. 1975); children: Peter, Daniel. BA, U. N.Mex., 1950; MS, Columbia U., 1951. Reporter Providence Jour.-Bulletin, 1951-55; sales mgr. R.E.C. Corp., New Rochelle, N.Y., 1955-69; owner Edwin V. Glaser Rare Books, Sausalito, Calif., 1969—. Faculty mem., antiquarian book seminar, U. Denver, 1979—. Contbr. numerous articles to profl. jours. Mem. Antiquarian Booksellers Assn. Am. (pres. 1986-87, gov.). Office: Glaser Rare Books PO Box 155 Napa CA 94559

GLASER, ROB, communications company executive; CEO and chmn. Progressive Networks, Seattle; CEO Real Networks, Seattle, 1997—. Office: Real Networks 2601 Elliott Ave Ste 1000 Seattle WA 98121-3307

GLASER, ROBERT JOY, retired physician, foundation executive; b. St. Louis, Sept. 11, 1918; s. Joseph and Regina G.; m. Helen Louise Hofsommer, Apr. 1, 1949 (dec. Oct. 1999); children: Sally Louise, Joseph II, Robert Joy. SB, Harvard U., 1940, MD magna cum laude, 1943; DS (hon.), U. Health Scis.-Chgo. Med. Sch., 1972, Temple U., 1973, U. N.H., 1979, U. Colo., 1979; LHD, Rush Med. Coll., 1973; DS, Mt. Sinai Med. Sch., 1984; DS (hon.), Washington U., 1988, Thomas Jefferson U., 1991; DHL, Johns Hopkins U., 2000. Med. intern Barnes Hosp., St. Louis, 1944, asst. resident physician, 1945-46, resident physician, 1946-47, asst. physician, 1949-57; asst. resident physician Peter Bent Brigham Hosp., Boston, 1944-45; NRC fellow med. scis. Wash. U. Med. Sch., 1947-49, instr. medicine, 1949-50, asst. prof., 1950-56, asst. dean., 1947, 53-55, assoc. prof., 1956-57, assoc. dean, 1955-57; dean, prof. medicine Med. Sch. U. Colo., 1957-63, v.p. for med. affairs, 1959-63; vis. physician Washington U. Med. Service, St. Louis City Hosp., 1950, chief service, 1950-53, cons., 1953-57; attending physician Colo. Gen. Hosp., Denver, 1957-63; prof. social medicine Harvard U., Boston, 1963-65; pres. Affiliated Hosps. Ctr., Inc., 1963-65; v.p. med. affairs, dean Sch. Medicine, prof. medicine Stanford U., 1965-70, acting pres., 1968, cons. prof., 1972-97, prof. emeritus, 1997—; bd. dirs. Henry J. Kaiser Family Found., 1970-83, pres., chief exec. officer, 1972-83; attending physician Columbia-Presbyn. Med. Ctr., N.Y.C., 1971-72, clin. prof. medicine, 1971-72; dir. for med. sci. Lucille P. Markey Charitable Trust, 1984-97, trustee, 1989-97. Bd. dirs. Maxygen, Hanger Orthopedic Group; cons. medicine VA Hosp., Denver, 1957-63, Fitzsimons Army Hosp., Aurora, Colo., 1957-63, Lowry AFB, Denver, 1957-63; mem. nat. adv. council NIMH, 1970-72, Harvard Fund Council, 1953-56, Harvard Med. Alumni Council, 1956-59; assoc. mem. streptococcal commn. Armed Forces Epidemiologic Bd., 1958-61; chmn. com. study nat. needs biomed. and behavioral research personnel Nat. Acad. Scis.-NRC, 1974-77; mem. vis. com. Med. Sch. Harvard U., 1968-74, Sch. Pub. Health, 1971-77; bd. visitors Charles Drew Postgrad. Med. Sch., 1972-79; mem. com. on med. affairs Yale U., 1969-82, adv. bd. Sch. Orgn. and Mgmt., 1976-84; vis. com. Tufts Med. Sch., 1974-84. Editor: Pharos, 1962-97, editor emeritus, 1997—; contbr. articles to sci. jours. and chpts. to books. Bd. regents Georgetown U., 1976-78; bd. dirs. Kaiser Found. Hosps., Kaiser Found. Health Plan, 1967-79, Council on Founds., 1974-79, Packard Humanities Inst., 1987—; trustee Commonwealth Fund, 1969-88, v.p., 1970-72; trustee David and Lucille Packard Found., 1984-96, Pacific Sch. Religion, 1972-77, Washington U., St. Louis, 1979-87, 88—, Albert and Mary Lasker Found., 1998—; trustee Palo Alto Med. Found., 1974—, vice chmn., 1991-2000, trustee emeritus, 2000—; mem. Sloan Commn. on Govt. in Higher Edn., 1977-79. Master ACP; fellow AAAS, Am. Acad. Arts and Scis. (exec. bd., v.p. 1972-76), Am. Philos. Soc., Royal Coll. Physicians of London; mem. Am. Clin. and Climatological Assn. (pres. 1982-83), Am. Fedn. Clin. Research (chmn. midwestern sect. 1954-55), Central Soc. Clin. Rsch. (councillor 1955-58), Am. Soc. Clin. Investigation, Assn. Am. Med. Colls. (asst. sec. 1956-60, chmn. com. edn. and research 1958-63, mem. exec. council 1959-63, 76-79, v.p. 1963-64, chmn. exec. council and assembly 1968-69, Abraham Flexner award Disting. Svc. award), Assn. Am. Physicians, Western Assn. Physicians (councillor 1960-63), Am. Soc. Exptl. Pathology, Nat. Inst. Allergy and Infectious Disease (tng. grant com. 1957-60), Inst. Medicine, Nat. Acad. Sci. (mem. exec. com. 1971-73, chmn. membership com. 1970-72, acting pres. 1970-71), N.Y. Acad. Medicine (John Stearns award for lifetime achievement in medicine 2000), Harvard Med. Sch. Alumni (pres. 1993-1994), Harvard Club (N.Y.C.), Century Club, Sigma Xi, Alpha Omega Alpha (bd. dirs. 1963-77).

GLASER, WILLIAM E. state legislator; b. Long Beach, Calif., Jan. 4, 1940; m. Patsy Glaser. Student, Calif. schs. In constrn. bus.; mem. Mont. State Ho. of Reps., 1985-90, Mont. Senate, Dist. 8, Helena, 1997—; vice chair edn. and cultural resources com. Mont. State Senate, mem. local govt. com., mem. taxation com. Republican. Home: 1402 Indian Creek Rd Huntley MT 59037-9348

GLASGOW, WILLIAM JACOB, lawyer, venture capitalist, business executive; b. Portland, Oreg., Sept. 29, 1946; s. Joseph Glasgow and Lena (Friedman) Schiff; m. Renée Vonfeld, Aug. 30, 1969; children: Joshua, Andrew. BS magna cum laude, U. Pa., 1968; JD magna cum laude, Harvard U., 1972. Bar: Oreg. 1972, U.S. Dist. Ct. Oreg. 1972, U.S. Ct. Appeals (9th cir.) 1978. Assoc. Rives, Bonyhadi & Drummond, Portland, 1972-76, ptnr., 1976-79; mng. ptnr. Perkins Coie, Portland, 1983-88; sr. v.p., gen. counsel PacifiCorp Fin. Svcs. Inc., Portland, 1988-89, chmn., CEO, 1989-95; sr. v.p. PacifiCorp, Portland, 1992-93, sr. v.p., CFO, 1993-95; pres. PacifiCorp Holdings Inc., Portland, 1992-95; pres., dir. NERCO, Inc., Portland, 1992-93; dir. Pacific-Telecom, Inc., 1992-93; co-chmn. Shaw, Glasgow & Co. LLC, 1995-96; pres., CEO BCN Data Sys. (a Bechtel/CellNet Data Sys. joint venture), Portland, 1996-2000, Madrona Venture Group LLP, Portland, 2000—; ret. PacifiCorp, Portland, 1996. Pres. bd. trustees Oreg. Mus. Sci. and Industry, Portland, 1981; pres. N.W. Fin. Symposium, Portland, 1985; trustee Oreg. Art Inst., 1990-92, 94—, Oreg. Grad. Inst. Sci. and Tech., 1991—, Discovery Inst., 1992—; pres. Portland Met. Sports Authority, 1992—; v.p. NIKE World Masters Games, 1994—; bd. dirs. Internat. World Masters Games, 1994—. Mem. Oreg. Bar Assn., Portland C. of C. (bd. dirs. 1983), Harvard Law Sch. Alumni Assn. (pres. Oreg. chpt. 1981). Democrat. Home: 3088 SW Fairmount Blvd Portland OR 97201-1439

GLASS, CHRISTOPHER KEVIN, physician; b. Oakland, Calif., Aug. 13, 1955; s. William Charles and Arden Barbara (Raysor) G.; m. Renee Fitzmorris; children: Erin Rose, Bryan James, Megan Christine, Sean William. BA Biophysics, U. Calif., Berkeley, 1977; MD, PhD Biology, U. Calif. San Diego, 1984. Intern dept. medicine Brigham & Women's Hosp., Boston, 1984-85, resident dept. medicine, 1985-86; fellow div. endocrinology U. Calif. San Diego, La Jolla, 1986-89, asst. prof. medicine, 1989-95, assoc. prof. medicine and cellular and molecular medicine, 1995-99, prof. medicine and cellular and molecular medicine, 1999—. Cons. Parke-Davis, Ann Arbor, Mich., 1994-95, Ligand Pharms., San Diego, 1994-95. Contbr. articles to profl. jours. Recipient Wilson S. Stone award M.D. Anderson, Houston, 1989, Lucille P. Markey scholarship, Lucille P. Markey Trust, Miami, 1987. Fellow Am. Heart Assn. (Established Investigator award 1995); mem. Endocrine Soc. (Ernst Oppenheimer award 2000), Am. Soc. for Clin. Investigation, Fedn. Am. Soc. of Exptl. Biologists. Achievements include the discovery that retinoic acid receptors bind to DNA as hetrodimers; discovery of allosteric interactions betwen retinoic acid and retinoid x receptors, nuclear receptor co-activators and corepressors; discovery of antiinflammatory and antiatherogenic properties of the peroxisome proliferator-activated receptor gamma. Office: U Calif San Diego 9500 Gilman Dr 0651 La Jolla CA 92093-5003 E-mail: cglass@ecsd.edu

GLASS, JEAN ANN, special education services professional; b. Phoenix, Mar. 15, 1934; d. James Leslie Giffin and Helen Lucille Griffith; m. Dwaine Charles Glass, Nov. 26, 1952; children: Michael James, Stephen Charles, Daphne Ann, Diona Lynn, Helen Louise, Geoffrey Giffin. Student, U. Nev., 1950-52; AA in Psychology, Mt. San Antonio Coll., 1973, AS in Mental Health, 1974; BA in Behavioral Sci., Calif. Poly. U., 1975; MA in Spl. Edn., Calif. State U., L.A., 1979, MA in Psychology, 1983; MS in Devel. Disabilities Programming, U. La Verne, 1981, postgrad., 1981-99, Azusa Pacific U., 1989. Instr. devel. disabled Chaffey C.C., Alta Loma, Calif., 1975-79; program dir. sch.- age parenting and infant devel. El Monte (Calif.) Union High Sch. Dist., 1981-95, tchr., 1981—. Family life educator Nat. Coun. Family Rels., Mpls., 1988—; therapeutic recreation specialist Nat. Coun. Therapeutic Recreation, Thiells, N.Y., 1975—; rschr., psychiat. technician Frank D. Lanterman State Hosp. and Devel. Ctr., Pomona, Calif., 1981-94. Sec.-gen. World Cultural Conv., 2001—. Recipient cert. of commendation State of Calif., 1985, City of El Monte, 1993, 2000, cert. internat. fellowship 27th Internat. Millennium Congress on Arts and Comm., 2000. Mem. DAR, AAUW, Nat. Geneal. Soc., Coun. Exceptional Children, Archaeol. Survey Assn. So. Calif., Inc., Bibl. Archaeology Soc., The Planetary Soc., Natural Resources Def. Coun., L.A. World Affairs Coun., El Monte Cmty. Cultural Commn.'s Sister City Assn., Pomona Valley Personal Ancestral File Users Group, Covina Valley Hist. Soc., San Gabriel/Pomona Valley Alumnae Panhellenic Assn., Conna Valley Hist. Soc. (sec. gen.), Calif. Fedn. Chaparral Poets, Gamma Phi Beta. Republican. Mem. LDS Ch. Avocations: genealogy, archaeology, history, the arts. Office: El Monte Union H S Dist 3537 Johnson Ave El Monte CA 91731-3290 E-mail: Jeanann7@earthlink.net

GLASSER, CHARLES EDWARD, university president; b. Chgo., Apr. 3, 1940; s. Julius J. and Hilda (Goldman) G.; m. Hannah Alex, Mar. 8, 1987; children: Gemma Maria, Julian David. BA in History, Denison U., 1961; MA in Polit. Sci., U. Ill., 1967; JD, John F. Kennedy U., 1970. Bar: Calif. 1970, U.S. Ct. Appeals (9th cir.) 1970. Pvt. practice Hineser, Spellberg & Glasser, Pleasant Hill, Calif., 1971-77; dean Sch. Law John F. Kennedy U., Orinda, 1977-83, pres., 1990—; v.p., gen. counsel Western Hosp. Corp., Emeryville, 1983-90. Author: The Quest for Peace, 1986. Mem. Calif. Bar Assn. Office: John F Kennedy U 12 Altarinda Rd Orinda CA 94563-2603

GLASSEY, KATHERINE, software company executive; BS in Ops. Rsch., Cornell U. Sr. cons. mgmt. cons. divsn. Arthur Young & Co. (now Ernst & Young, LLP), co-founder decision support sys. gorup; mgr. application devel. and cons. orgns. Metaphor Computer Sys., Inc., hardware and software co.; chief tech. officer Brio Tech., Palo Alto, Calif. Office: Brio Tech 3460 W Bayshore Rd Palo Alto CA 94303-4227 Fax: 650-856-8020

GLASSHEIM, JEFFREY WAYNE, allergist, immunologist, pediatrician; b. Far Rockaway, N.Y., Sept. 16, 1958; s. Ronald Alan and Glenda (Deitch) G.; m. Paulette Renèe, Apr. 16, 1989; children: Elyssa Gwen, Brenna Chase. BA, Temple U., 1980; DO, U. New. Eng., 1984. Diplomate Am. Bd. Allergy and Clin. Immunology, Am. Bd. Pediatrics. Commd. 2d lt. U.S. Army, 1980, advanced through grades to maj., 1989, resigned, 1992; intern Winthrop-Univ. Hosp., Mineola, N.Y., 1984-85; resident Madigan Army Med. Ctr., Tacoma, 1985-87; fellow Fitzsimons Army Med. Ctr. and Nat. Jewish Ctr. Immunology, Aurora, Colo., 1990-91, chief fellow allergy-clin. immunology, 1990-91; chief allergy-clin. immunology and immunizations svcs. Silas B. Hays Army Community Hosp., Fort Ord, Calif., 1991-93; resigned USAR, 1993; pvt practice Fresno, 1993—; dir. allergy-immunology dept. Pediatric Med. Group of Fresno, Calif., 1994-95; dir. allergy-immunology Northwest Med. Group, Fresno, 1995-97; pvt. practice allergy and immunology, 1997—. Contbr. articles to profl. jours. Fellow Am. Acad. Pediatrics (allergy and immunoogy sect.), Am. Acad. Allergy Asthma and Immunology, Am. Coll. Allergy, Asthma and Immunology; mem. AMA, Am. Osteo. Assn., Am. Physicians Fellowship for Medicine in Israel, Calif. Soc. Allergy, Asthma and Clin. Immunology, Ctrl. Calif. Allergy Soc., Fresno-Madera Med. Soc., Calif. Med. Assn., Osteo. Physicians and Surgeons of Calif. Republican. Jewish. Avocations: meteorology, sports, reading/current events, gardening, walking. Office: Valley Med Plz Herndon 1646 E Herndon Ave Ste 106 Fresno CA 93720-3305 Fax: 559-490-0237. E-mail: glasjw@aol.com

GLATZER, ROBERT ANTHONY, marketing and sales executive; b. N.Y.C., May 19, 1932; s. Harold and Glenna (Beaber) G.; m. Paula Rosenfeld, Dec. 20, 1964; m. Mary Ann Murphy, Dec. 31, 1977; children: Gabriela, Jessica, Nicholas. BA, Haverford Coll., 1954. Br. store dept. mgr. Bloomingdale's, N.Y.C., 1954-56; media buyer Ben Sackheim Advt., N.Y.C., 1956-59; producer TV commls. Ogilvy, Benson & Mather Advt., N.Y.C., 1959-62; dir. broadcast prodn. Carl Ally Advt., N.Y.C., 1962-63; owner Chronicle Prodns., N.Y.C., 1963-73; dir. Folklife Festival, Smithsonian Inst., Washington, 1973, Expo 74 Corp., Spokane, Wash., 1973-74; pres. Robert Glatzer Assocs., Spokane, 1974— ; ptnr. Delany/Glatzer Advt., Spokane, 1979-84; dir. sales/mktg. Pinnacle Prodns., Spokane; adj. faculty Ea. Wash. U., 1987—. Bd. dirs. Riverfront Arts Festival, 1977-78; bd. dirs. Comprehensive Health Planning Council, 1975-78, Spokane Quality of Life Council, 1976-82, Allied Arts of Spokane, 1976-80, Art Alliance Wash. State, 1977-81, Spokane chpt. ACLU, 1979-83, Wash. State Folklife Council, 1983—, chair 1998—; commr. Spokane Arts, 1987—; mem. Spokane Community Devel. Bd., 1988—; mem. Shorelines Update Commn., 1988—; mem. Wash. State Small Bus. Improvement Coun., 1994—, chair 1998—. Recipient CINE Golden Eagle award (2). Mem. Dirs. Guild Am. Democrat. Jewish. Author: The New Advertising, 1970; co-scenarist Scorpio and other TV prodns.

GLAUTHIER, T. J. non-profit CEO; b. Durham, N.C., Jan. 3, 1944; s. Theodore and Martha May (Myers) G.; m. Carrie L. Bostrom, June 11, 1966 (div. 1973); children: Jeff, Paul, Tad; m. M. Brigid O'Farrell, July 9, 1977; 1 child, Patrick O. AB, Claremont (Calif.) Men's Coll., 1965; MBA, Harvard Bus. Sch., 1967. Cons. Peat, Marwick, Livingston, L.A., 1967-68; with Applied Computer Tech., L.A., 1968-70; cons. Applied Decision Systems, Cambridge, Mass., 1970-74; v.p. Temple, Barker & Sloane, Inc., Lexington, 1974-90; head Pub. Policy Practice, 1980-90; head Washington office, 1986-90; dir. energy and climate change World Wildlife Fund, Washington, 1990-93; assoc. dir. nat. resources, energy and sci. U.S. Office Mgmt. and Budget, Washington, 1993-98; dep. sec. & COO U.S. Dept. Energy, 1999-2001; pres. & CEO Electricity Innovation Inst., Palo Alto, CA, 2001—. Mng. public and private partnerships for electricity tech. R&D. Pres. Lake Barcroft Assn., 1989-94; assoc. Lake Barcroft Watershied Improvement Dist., 1989—; del. Va. State Dem. Conv., 1993, 97. Democrat. Unitarian. Home: 6304 Crosswoods Cir Falls Church VA 22044-1302 Office: Electricity Innovation Inst 3412 Hillview Ave Palo Alto CA 94304 E-mail: tjj@e2ionline.org, tjglauthier@aol.com

GLAZER, GARY MARK, radiology educator; b. Feb. 13, 1950; m. Diane Glazer; children: Daniel I., David A. AB, U. Mich., 1972; MD, Case Western Res. U., 1976. Intern in internal medicine U. Calif., San Francisco, 1976-77, resident in diagnostic radiology, 1977-80, clin. instr., fellow in diagnostic radiology, 1980-81; asst. prof. radiology, dir. div. body computed tomography U. Mich., Ann Arbor, 1981-84, assoc. prof. radiology, 1984-87, dir. divs. magnet resonance imaging and body computed tomography, 1984-89, assoc. prof. cancer ctr., 1986-87, prof. radiology, prof. cancer ctr., 1987-89; prof., chmn. dept. radiology Stanford (Calif.) Sch. Medicine, 1989—. Cons., assoc. editor, reviewer Radiology; cons., reviewer Jour. Computer Assisted Tomogrphy; cons., chmn., reviewer, mem. editorial bd. Radiographics; contbr. articles to profl. publs. Fellow Am. Cancer Soc., 1980-82, Clarence Heller Found., 1980-81. Mem. Am. Roentgen Ray Soc., Radiology Soc. N.Am., Soc. Magnetic Resonance in Medicine, Fred Jenner Hodges Soc., Soc. Magnetic Resonance Imaging, Alpha Omega Alpha. Office: Stanford Sch Med Dept Radiology Stanford CA 94305

GLAZER, MICHAEL, lawyer; b. L.A., Oct. 10, 1940; BS, Stanford U., 1962; MBA, Harvard U., 1964; JD, U. Calif., L.A., 1967. Bar: Calif. 1967, D.C. 1980. Law clk. to Hon. Roger J. Traynor Calif. Supreme Ct., 1967-68; commr. L.A. Dept. of Water & Power, 1973-76; chmn. Calif. Water Commn., 1976-78; asst. adminstr. nat. oceanic and atmospheric adminstrn. U.S. Dept. of Commerce, 1978-80; dir. Met. Water Dist. of So. Calif., 1984-91; ptnr. Paul, Hastings, Janofsky & Walker LLP, L.A. Articles editor U. Calif. at L.A. Law Rev., 1966-67. Mem. State Bar Calif. (com. on corps. 1986-87), L.A. County Bar Assn. (chair fed. securities regulation com. 1988-90, chair exec. com. bus. and corp. law sect. 1995-96), Order of the Coif, Phi Beta Kappa. Office: Paul Hastings Janofsky & Walker LLP 555 S Flower St Los Angeles CA 90071-2300

GLAZIER, RON, zoological park administrator; Dir. Santa Ana Zoo, Santa Ana, Calif. Office: Santa Ana Zoo 1801 E Chestnut Ave Santa Ana CA 92701-5001

GLEASON, JOHN H. real estate development company executive; BS in Mktg., U. So. Calif. Gen. contractor, Ariz., Calif., Nev., Tex., Southeast states, 29 years; pres. The Foothills Del Webb Corp., Phoenix, 1988-90, sr. v.p. project planning & devel. Office: Del Webb Corp 6001 N 24th St Phoenix AZ 85016-2018

GLENN, CONSTANCE WHITE, art museum director, educator, consultant; b. Topeka, Oct. 4, 1933; d. Henry A. and Madeline (Stewart) White; m. Jack W. Glenn, June 19, 1955; children: Laurie Glenn Buckle, Caroline Glenn Galey, John Christopher. BFA, U. Kans., 1955; grad., U. Mo., 1969; MA, Calif. State U., 1974. Dir. Univ. Art Mus. & Mus. Studies program, from lectr. to prof. Calif. State U., Long Beach, 1973—. Art cons. Archtl. Digest, L.A., 1980-89. Author: Jim Dine Drawings, 1984, Roy Lichtenstein: Landscape Sketches, 1986, Wayne Thiebaud: Private Drawings, 1988, Robert Motherwell: The Dedalus Sketches, 1988, James Rosenquist: Time Dust: The Complete Graphics 1962-92, 1993, The Great American Pop Art Store: Multiples of the Sixties, 1997; contbg. author: Encyclopedia Americana, 1995—, The Grove Dictionary of Art, 1989—, Double Vision: Photographs from the Strauss Collection, 2001, Carrie Mae Weems: The Hampton Project, 2000. Vice-chair Adv. Com. for Pub. Art, Long Beach, 1990-95; chair So. Calif. adv. bd. Archives Am. Art, L.A., 1980-90; mem. adv. bd. ART/L.A., [illegible] Profession award Calif. Mus. Photography, 1986, Disting. Scholarly and Creative Achievement award, Calif. State U. Long Beach, Women of Distinction award Soroptimist Internat., 1999. Mem. Am. Assn. Mus., Assn. Art Mus. Dirs. (trustee), Coll. Art Assn., Art Table, Long Beach Pub. Corp. for the Arts (arts adminstr. of yr. 1989), Kappa Alpha Theta. Office: Univ Art Mus 1250 N Bellflower Blvd Long Beach CA 90840-0006

GLENN, GUY CHARLES, pathologist; b. Parma, Ohio, May 13, 1930; s. Joseph Frank and Helen (Rupple) G.; m. Lucia Ann Howarth, June 13, 1953; children: Kathryn Holly, Carolyn Helen, Cynthia Marie. BS, Denison U., 1953; MD, U. Cin., 1957. Diplomate Am. Bd. Pathology, Am. Bd. Radioisotopic Pathology. Intern Walter Reed Army Med. Ctr., Washington, 1957-58; resident in pathology Fitzsimmons Army Med. Ctr., Denver, 1959-63; commd. 2d lt. U.S. Army, 1956; advanced through grades to col., 1977; demonstrator pathology Royal Army Med. Coll., London, 1970-72; chief dept. pathology Fitzsimmons Army Med. Ctr., Denver, 1972-77. Past pres. med. staff St. Vincent Hosp., Billings, Mont.; past mem. governing bd. Mont. Health Systems Agy. Contbr. articles to profl. jours. Fellow Coll. Am. Pathologists (chmn. chemistry resources com., chmn. commn. sci. resources, mem. budget com., coun. on quality assurance, chmn. practice guidelines com., outcomes com., bd. govs., chmn. nominating com.), Am. Soc. Clin. Pathology, Am. Registry Pathology (bd. dirs.), Soc. Med. Cons. to Armed Forces, Midland Empire Health Assn. (past pres.), Rotary (bd. dirs. local chpt.). Home: 3225 Jack Burke Ln Billings MT 59106-1113 E-mail: gundlglenn@myavista.com

GLENN, JEROME T. secondary school principal; Prin. San Lorenzo (Calif.) High Sch., to 1999; dir. secondary edn. San Lorenzo (Calif.) Sch. Dist., 1999—. Recipient Blue Ribbon Sch. award U.S. Dept. Edn., 1990-91. Office: San Lorenzo Dist Ednl Svcs 15510 Usher St San Lorenzo CA 94580-1641

GLENNY, LYMAN ALBERT, retired education educator; b. Trent, S.D., Jan. 26, 1918; s. Walter and Ann (Henning) G.; m. Carolyn Joy Ballou, Dec. 19, 1942 (div. Mar. 1977); children— Terence Alan, Celia Joy, Colleen Marie; m. Helen S. Thompson, June 24, 1978 (dec. Aug. 1986). B.S., U. Minn., 1947; M.A., U. Colo., 1948; Ph.D., State U. Iowa, 1950. Instr. U. Iowa, 1948-50; from asst. prof. to prof. Sacramento State Coll., 1950-62; assoc. dir. Ill. Bd. Higher Edn., 1962-65, exec. dir., 1965-69; prof. higher edn. U. Calif., Berkeley, 1969-83, dir. Ctr. for Research and Devel. in Higher Edn., 1969-76. Dir. Nebr. Study Adminstrn. Higher Edn., 1960 Author: Autonomy of Public Colleges, 1959, Coordinating Higher Education for the 70's, 1971, State Budgeting for Higher Education: Interagency Conflict and Consensus, 1976, Issues in Higher Education: A Six Nation Analysis, 1980, State Coordination of Higher Education: The Modern Concept, 1985, (with J. R. Kidder) State Tax Support of Higher Education: Revenue Appropriation Trends and Patterns, 1963-73, 1973, (with T. K. Dalglish) Public Universities, State Agencies, and the Law: Constitutional Autonomy in Decline, 1973, (with others) Presidents confront reality: From edifice complex to university without walls, 1975, (with Janet Ruyle) Trends in State Revenue Appropriations for Higher Education, 1968-78, (with F.M. Bowen) Uncertainty in Public Higher Education, 1980, Signals for Change: Stress Indicators, 1980, Quality and Accountability, 1981, also other publs. on state budgeting for higher edn.; editor: Statewide Planning for Post-Secondary Education, 1971; contbr. articles, chpts. to profl. publs.; bd. editors: Western Polit. Quar, 1959-62. Served to capt. U.S. Army, 1941-46, 51-52. Mem. AAUP, Am. Assn. Higher Edn., Am. Soc. Public Adminstrn., Assoc. Inst. Research, State Higher Edn. Exec. Officers Assn. (Oho) (hon.), Western Polit. Sci. Assn. Home: 3123 Lippizaner Ln Walnut Creek CA 94598-4606 Office: U Calif Tolman Hall Berkeley CA 94720

GLICK, EARL A. retired lawyer; b. Chgo., Feb. 20, 1930; s. Simon and Eva (Cohen) G.; m. Janet Esther Klein, Aug. 22, 1953; children: Michael J., Daniel H., Linda J. Richardson, Steven B. BS, U. Ill., 1951; JD, Northwestern U., 1953. Bar: Ill. 1953, Calif. 1962. Asst. atty. gen. State of Ill., Chgo., 1953-57; ptnr. Gerwin & Glick, Chgo., 1957-61, Gendel, Raskoff, Shapiro & Quittner, L.A., 1962-90, Orrick, Herrington & Sutcliffe, L.A., 1990-2000; gen. counsel S & S Corp., Beverly Hills, Calif., 1961-62; ret., 2000; of counsel Murphy Noell Capital, LLC, Westlake Village, Calif., 2000—. Bd. govs. Fin. Lawyers Conf., L.A., 1965-2000. Fellow Am. Coll. Comml. Fin. Lawyers; mem. ABA (chair program com. fin. svcs. subcom., 1993-96). Republican. Jewish. Avocations: travel, walking, reading. Home: 5560 Ostin Ave Woodland Hills CA 91367-3976 E-mail: eglick@socal.rr.com

GLICK, MILTON DON, chemist, university administrator; b. Memphis, July 30, 1937; s. Lewis S. and Sylvia (Kleinman) G.; m. Peggy M., June 22, 1965; children: David, Sander. AB cum laude, Augustana Coll., 1959; PhD, U. Wis., 1965. Asst. prof. chemistry Wayne State U., Detroit, 1966-70, assoc. prof., 1970-74, prof., 1974-83, chmn. dept., 1978-83; dean arts & scis. U. Mo., Columbia, 1983-88; provost Iowa State U., Ames, 1988-91, interim pres., 1990-91; sr. v.p., provost Ariz. State U., Tempe, 1991—. Contbr. articles to profl. jours. Fellow dept. chemistry Cornell U., Ithaca, N.Y., 1964-66. Office: Ariz State U Office Provost 2803 Adm A210 PO Box 872803 Tempe AZ 85287 E-mail: glick@asu.edu

GLICKENHAUS, MIKE, radio station executive; BA in Mktg./Comm., SUNY, Albany, 1975. Sales rep. Fidelity Union Life Ins. Co., San Diego, 1976-78; account mgr. S.C. Enterprises, Long Beach/San Diego, 1978-80; account exec. Sta. XTRA-FM, XTRA-AM Noble Broadcast Group, San Diego, 1980-83, local sales mgr., 1983-85, gen. sales mgr. Sta. XTRA-FM, 1985-88, v.p./gen. mgr., 1988-91, exec. v.p./gen. mgr. Sta. XTRA-FM, XTRA-AM, KWNK-AM (L.A.), 1991-96; market gen. mgr. Jacor Comm., San Diego, 1996-97, co-market mgr. FM stas., v.p./gen. mgr. FM stas., 1997—; gen. mgr. VETRA-FM, San Diego. Office: VETRA-FM/Jacor Comm Clear Channel Comm 4891 Pacific Hwy San Diego CA 92110-4003

GLICKMAN, DAVID, telecommunications industry executive; BA, U. Pa.; MA in Psychology, U. Calif., L.A. Prin., owner Oliver D. World; founder, chmn. Justice Telecom, Culver City, Calif., 1993—, TelePacific, 1998—. Founder Calif. Assn. Entrepreneurs; bd. dirs. L.A. Philharmonic; vice chmn. Hollywood Bowl. Mem. L.A. Philharmonic, Hollywood Bowl. Office: TelePacific Comms 515 S Flower St 49th Fl Los Angeles CA 90071 Fax: 310-526-2077

GLICKMAN, HARRY, professional basketball team executive; b. Portland, Oreg., May 13, 1924; s. Sam and Bessie (Karp) G.; m. Joanne Carol Matin, Sept. 28, 1958; children: Lynn Carol, Marshall Jordan, Jennifer Ann. B.A., U. Oreg., 1948. Press agt., 1948-52; pres. Oreg. Sports Attractions, 1952—; mgr. Multnomah (Oreg.) Civic Stadium, 1958-59; pres. Portland Hockey Club, 1960-73; former exec. v.p. basketball team Portland Trail Blazers, now pres. emeritus. Trustee B'nai B'rith Jr. Camp, 1965; bd. dirs. U. Oreg. Devel. Fund. Served with AUS, 1943-46. Named to Oreg. Sports Hall of Fame, 1986. Mem. Portland C. of C. (bd. dirs. 1968-72), Sigma Delta Chi, Sigma Alpha Mu. Jewish. Office: Portland Trail Blazers 1 Center Ct Ste 200 Portland OR 97227-2103

GLOCK, CHARLES YOUNG, sociologist, writer; b. N.Y.C., Oct. 17, 1919; s. Charles and Philippine (Young) G.; m. Margaret Schleef, Sept. 12, 1950; children: Susan Young, James William. B.S., N.Y. U., 1940; M.B.A., Boston U., 1941; Ph.D., Columbia U., 1952. Research asst. Bur. Applied Social Research, Columbia U., 1946-51, dir., 1951-58, lectr., then prof. sociology, 1956-58; prof. sociology U. Calif. at Berkeley, 1958-79, prof. emeritus, 1979—, chmn., 1967-68, 69-71; dir. Survey Research Center, [illegible] Yale U., 1968. Co-author: Wayward Shepherds, The Anatomy of Racial Attitudes, Anti-Semitism in America, American Piety; sr. author: Adolescent Prejudice, To Comfort and To Challenge, Religion and Society in Tension, Christian Beliefs and Anti-Semitism, The Apathetic Majority; contbg. editor Rev. Religious Rsch. Sociological Analysis; editor: The New Religious Consciousness, Survey Research in the Social Sciences, Beyond the Classics, Religion in Sociological Perspective, Prejudice U.S.A., Unison-Newsletter of One Voice, 1990-96; contbr. numerous articles on social scis. Active parish edn. Luth. Ch. Am., 1970-72; mem. mgmt. com. Office Rsch. and Planning, 1973-80; bd. dirs. Pacific Luth. Theol. Sem., 1962-74, 80-86, Inst. Rsch. in Social Behavior, 1962-90, Interplayers, 1990-92, Sandpoint Christian Connection, 1995-97; pres. Cornerhouse Fund, 1982-92, One Voice, 1994-95, bd. dirs., 1995-97; mem. adv. com. Office Rsch. and Evaluation Evang. Luth. Ch. Am., 1988—; mem. history com. Soc. Study of Religion, 1993-94. Capt. USAAF, 1942-46. Decorated Bronze Star, Legion of Merit; recipient Roots of Freedom award Pacific bd. Anti-Defamation League, 1977, Garman-Hidy award for Disting. Contbn. to Life of Luth. Ch. in the West, 1999; Berkeley citation U. Calif., Berkeley, 1979; Rockefeller fellow, 1941-42; fellow Center Advanced Study Behavioral Scis., 1957-58; fellow Soc. for Religion in Higher Edn., 1968-69 Fellow Soc. Sci. Study Religion (Western rep., pres. 1968-69); mem. Am. Assn. Pub. Opinion Research (v.p., pres. 1962-64, pres. Pacific chpt. 1959-60), Am. Sociol. Assn. (v.p. 1978-79), Religious Research Assn., Sociol. Research Assn. Home: 319 S 4th Ave Sandpoint ID 83864-1219

GLOVER, FRED WILLIAM, artificial intelligence and optimization research director, educator; b. Kansas City, Mo., Mar. 8, 1937; s. William Cain and Mary Ruth (Baxter) G.; m. Diane Tatham, June 4, 1988; 1 child, Lauren Glover; children from previous marriage: Dana Reynolds, Paul Glover. BBA, U. Mo., 1960; PhD, Carnegie-Mellon U., 1965. Asst. prof. U. Calif., Berkeley, 1965-66; assoc. prof. U. Tex., Austin, 1966-69; prof. U. Minn., Mpls., 1969-70; John King prof. U. Colo., Boulder, 1970-87, US West chair in sys. sci., 1987-98, Media One chair in sys. sci., 1998—; rsch. dir. Artificial Intelligence Ctr., Boulder, 1984-90, Hearin Ctr. for Enterprise Sci., U. Miss., 2000—. Invited disting. lectr. Swiss Fed. Inst. Tech., Lausaunne, 1990—, IMAG Labs., U. Grenoble, France, 1991, U. Canterbury, New Zealand, 1997, U. Paris, 1998; vis. Regents Chair in Engring., U. Tex., Austin, 1989; cons. U.S. Congress, 1984, Nat. Bur. Stds., 1986, also over 70 U.S. corps. and govt. agys., 1965—; lectr. NATO, France, Italy, Germany, Denmark, 1970, 78, 80, 82, 89, Inst. Decision Scis., 1984; bd. dirs. Heuristec, Boulder, OptTek, Boulder, Decision Analysis, Rsch. & Computation, Austin, 1971-83; head, rsch. assoc. Global Optimization Space Contrn. Ctr., Boulder, 1988—; rsch. prin. U. Colo.-U.S. West Joint Rsch. Initiative, 1990—; prin. investigator Air Force Office Sci. Rsch., Office Naval Rsch., 1990—; invited rsch. scholar U. B.C., 1994. Author: Netform Decision Models, 1983 (DIS award 1984), Tabu Search I, 1989, Tabu Search II, 1990, Tabu Search (book and special vols.) 1993, 97, 98, Ghost Image Processes for Neural Networks, 1993, Linkages with Artificial Intelligence, 1990, Network Models in Optimization and Their Application in Practice, 1992, also others; contbr. over 300 articles on math. optimization and artificial intelligence to profl. jours. Participant Host Vis. Exchange, Nat. Acad. Scis., 1981; mem. grants com. Queen Elizabeth II fellowships, Australia and U.S., 1984; mem. U.S. nat. adv. bd. Univ. Rsch. Initiative on Combinatorial Optimization. Recipient Internat. Achievement award Inst. Mgmt. Scis., 1982, Energy Rsch. award Energy Rsch. Inst., 1983, Univ. Disting. Rsch. Lectr. award U. Colo., 1988, Rsch. Excellence prize Ops. Rsch. Soc., 1989, Nat. Best Theoretical/Empirical Rsch. Paper award Decision Scis. Inst., 1993, Computer Sci. Rsch. Excellence award Ops. Rsch. Soc. Am., 1994, Nat. Rsch. Excellence award Comp. Sci. Ops. Rsch. Soc., 1994, John Von Neumann Theory award INFORMS, 1998; named first U.S. West Disting. fellow, 1987. Fellow AAAS, Am. Inst. Decision Scis (lectr. 1984, Outstanding Achievement award 1984), Am. Assn. Collegiate Schs. Bus., ICC Inst.; mem. Alpha Iota Delta. Achievements include design of software systems used throughout the U.S. and abroad. Office: U Colo Coll Bus Box 419 Boulder CO 80309-0419

GLOVER, KAREN E. lawyer; b. Nampa, Idaho, Apr. 14, 1950; d. Gordon Ellsworth and Cora (Frazier) G.; m. Thaddas L. Alston, Aug. 17, 1979; children: Samantha Glover Alston, Evan Glover Alston. AB magna cum laude, Whitman Coll., 1972; JD cum laude, Harvard U., 1975. Bar: Wash. 1975, U.S. Dist. Ct. (we. dist.) Wash. 1975. Assoc. Preston, Thorgrimson Ellis & Holman, Seattle, 1975-80; ptnr. Preston Gates & Ellis, Seattle, 1981—. Chmn. bd. dirs. Cmty. Health Info. Sys., 2001—. Chmn. bd. dirs. United Way King County, Seattle, 1993-94; trustee Whitman Coll., Walla Walla, Wash., 1998—, King County Libr. Sys., Seattle, 1992—. Mem. Wash. State Bar Assn. (corp. and tax sects.), Seattle Pension Roundtable, Columbia Tower Club, Sand Point Country Club, Rainier Club. Episcopalian. Office: Preston Gates & Ellis 701 5th Ave Fl 50 Seattle WA 98104-7097

GLOVER, THOMAS T. federal judge; Apptd. chief bankruptcy judge we. dist. U.S. Dist. Ct. Wash., 1985. Office: 315 Park Place Bldg 1200 6th Ave Seattle WA 98101-3123 Fax: 206-553-0187

GLOVSKY, MYRON MICHAEL, medical educator; b. Boston, Aug. 15, 1936; m. Carole Irene Parks; five children. BS magna cum laude, Tufts U., 1957, MD, 1962. Bd. cert. Nat. Bd. Med. Examiners, Am. Bd. Allergy & Immunology, Am. Bd. Diagnostic Lab. Immunology. Intern Balt. (Md.) City Hosp., 1962-63; resident New Eng. Med. Ctr., Boston, 1965-66; spl. NIH fellow allergy and immunology Walter Reed Army Inst. Rsch., Washington, 1966-68; fellow hematology and immunology U. Calif., San Francisco, 1968-69; staff physician dept. internal medicine So. Calif. Permanente Med. Group, L.A., 1969-72, dir. allergy & immunology lab., 1970-84, chief dept. allergy and clin. immunology, co-dir. residency program in allergy & clin. immunology, 1974-84, dir. pheresis unit, 1978-80; dir. L.A. County Gen. Hosp./U. So. Calif. Asthma Clinic; prof. medicine, head allergy and immunology labs. pulmonary divsn., head allergy and clin. immunology divsn. pulmonary medicine. U. So. Calif., Sch. Medicine, 1984-89, prof. pathology, 1986-89; clin. prof. medicine, clin. prof. pathology U. So. Calif., 1989—; dir. asthma and allergy referral ctr. Huntington Meml. Hosp., Pasadena, 1989—. Head fellowship and career devel. program Nat. Heart Inst., NIH, Bethesda, Md., 1963-65, fellowship bd. mem., 1964-65; vis. assoc. in chemistry Calif. Inst. Tech., Pasadena, 1977—; acad. assoc. complement and allergy Nichols Inst., San Juan Capistrano, Calif., 1980—, med. dir. immunology, 1980-89; clin. prof. medicine U. Calif., L.A., 1983-84; vis. prof. clin. scholars program Eli Lilly & Co., Indpls., 1988; mem. steering com. Aspen Allergy Conf., 1988—. With USPHS, 1963-65. Fellow Am. Acad. Allergy; mem. AAAS, Am. Assn. Immunologists, Am. Thoracic Soc., Am. Fedn. for Clin. Rsch., Am. Coll. Allergy, Reticuloendothelial Soc., L.A. Soc. Allergy and Clin. Immunology (pres. 1979-80), Collegium Internat. Allergolicum. Home: 1961 Oak St South Pasadena CA 91030-4957 Office: Huntington Meml Hosp Asthma & Allergy Ctr 39 Congress St Ste 302 Pasadena CA 91105-3022 E-mail: yksvolg@aol.com

GLUECK, MARY AUDREY, retired psychiatric and mental health nurse; b. Bridgetown, Barbados; came to U.S., 1952; d. Hubert and Christina Cumming; m. Stephen G. Glueck (dec.). Grad. sch. nursing, St. Joseph's Mercy Hosp., Georgetown, Guyana; paralegal diploma, 2000. RN, Calif. Asst. nursing educator in new employee orientation San Mateo County Gen. Hosp., San Mateo, Calif., also facilitator video insvcs. for nursing staff, tchr. safety and emergency response procedures to staff, ret., 1998. [illegible] Ct Union City CA 94587-4853 E-mail: maryg57@juno.com

GLYNN, ROBERT D., JR. electric power and gas industry executive; b. Orange, N.J., 1942; BSME, Manhattan Coll.; MS in Nuclear Engring., L.I. U.; postgrad., U. Mich., Harvard U. With L.I. Lighting Co., 1964-72; exec. v.p., prin., dir. Woodward Clyde Cons., 1972-84; with PG&E Corp., San Francisco, 1984—, CEO, pres., 1997—, chmn. bd., 1998—. Chmn. bd. dirs. Pacific Gas and Electric Co. subs. PG&E Corp. Bd. govs. San Francisco Symphony. Office: PG&E Corp One Market St Spear Tower Ste 2400 San Francisco CA 94105

GNANT, RANDALL, state legislator; b. Milw., Oct. 15, 1945; m. Leslie Gnant. Mem. Ariz. Senate, Dist. 28, Phoenix, 1994—; chmn. appropriations com.; mem. commerce, agr. and natural resources com.; mem. fin. instns. and retirement com. Active Ariz. Visitors and Conv. Bur., Valley of the Sun Visitor and Conv. Bur.; precinct committeeperson and exec. bd. mem. Mem. Scottsdale C. of C., Lions, Phi Sigma Kappa. Republican. Office: State Capitol Bldg #110 1700 W Washington St # 110 Phoenix AZ 85007-2812 also: 7527 N Del Norte Dr Scottsdale AZ 85258-3564 E-mail: rgnant@azleg.state.az.us

GOBAR, ALFRED JULIAN, economic consultant, educator; b. Lucerne Valley, Calif., July 12, 1932; s. Julian Smith and Hilda (Millbank) G.; m. Sally Ann Randall, June 17, 1957; children: Wendy Lee, Curtis Julian, Joseph Julian. BA in Econs., Whittier Coll., 1953, MA in History, 1955; postgrad., Claremont Grad. Sch., 1953-54; PhD in Econs., U. So. Calif., 1963. Asst. pres. Microdot Inc., Pasadena, Calif., 1953-57; regional sales mgr. Sutorbilt Corp., L.A., 1957-59; mkt. rsch. assoc. Beckman Instrument Inc., Fullerton, Calif., 1959-64; sr. marketing cons. Western Mgmt. Consultants Inc., San Diego, 1964-66; ptnr., prin., chmn. bd. Darley/Gobar Assocs., Inc., San Diego, 1966-73; pres., chmn. bd. Alfred Gobar Assocs., Inc., Placentia, Calif., 1973—. Asst. prof. finance U. So. Calif., L.A., 1963-64; assoc. prof. bus. Calif. State U., L.A., 1963-68, 70-79, assoc. prof. Calif. State U.-Fullerton, 1968-69; mktg., fin. adviser 1957—; bd. dirs. Quaker City Bancorp, Inc.; pub. spkr. seminars and convs. Contbr. articles to profl. publs. Trustee Whittier Coll., 1992—. Home: 1100 W Valencia Mesa Dr Fullerton CA 92833-2219 Office: 721 W Kimberly Ave Placentia CA 92870-6343 E-mail: agobar@gobar.com

GODAGER, JANE ANN, social worker; b. Blue River, Wis., Nov. 29, 1943; d. Roy and Elmyra Marie (Hood) G. BA, U. Wis., 1965; MSW, Fla. State U., 1969. Lic. clin. social worker. Social worker III State of Wis. Dept Corrections, Wales, 1965-71; supervising psychiat. social worker I State of Calif., San Bernardino, 1972-75, La Mesa, 1975-77, psychiat. social worker San Bernardino, 1978-85; supr. mental health services Riverside (Calif.) County Dept. Mental Health, 1985-86; mental health counselor Superior Ct. San Bernardino County, 1986—. Former mem. adv. bd. Grad. Sch. Social Work Calif. State U., San Bernardino, Mental Health Assn.; mem. County Hosp. Re-Use Com. Mem. Nat. Assn. Social Workers, Acad. Cert. Social Workers (diplomate), Kappa Kappa Gamma Alumnae Assn. Avocations: travel, reading, music. Office: Office Mental Health Counselor Superior Ct-HCMC 400 N Pepper Ave Colton CA 92324-1801

GODDARD, JAMES RUSSELL, producer, writer, actor; b. Anaheim, Calif., May 8, 1955; s. Russell Nathaniel and Marilyn (Carson) G.; m. Laurie Lynn Ragsdale, June 5, 1982; children: Aaron Russell, Joshua James, Nathaniel Carson. AA, Cypress Coll., 1976; student, Calif. State U., Fullerton, 1976-77. Prodr., writer Creation Artists, Anaheim, 1976—, R & R Prodns., Chatsworth, Calif., 1990—, Love Letters Live Prodns., 1998—. Founder, prodr. Creation Theatrical Co., Anaheim & Riverside, 1976—, Actors Promotional Svcs., Hollywood, Calif., 1989—; stage mgr. Super Bowl Half-Time Show, Encore! Three Tenors, 1993. Author: (screenplays) Son of the Morning, 1988, Wait In Silence, 1990, Final Fade Out, 1993; producer/writer Jack and Charmian London, 2000; (indsl. film) Recycling Kids, 1990; appeared in 98 TV and film prodns., 1977—, teleplays include The Yellow Kite (co-writer), 1999, Flawed from Inception, 1999; various positions in over 500 profl. entertainment prodns., 1976—; prodr., writer: Jack & Charmian, 2000. Leader Boy Scouts Am., Anaheim, 1970-74, asst. scoutmaster, Corona, Calif., 1997—; crisis counselor Melodyland Hotline Ctr., Anaheim, 1976-80; mem. Jack London Found., Glen Ellen, Calif.; mgr. Little League Baseball, various locations. Co-recipient Disneyland Cmty. Svc. award Disneyland, 1976-78; recipient Walter Knott Americanism award Walter Knott Assn. Mem. SAG (mem. ethics com. 1992), Nat. Forensics League, Nat. Thespians Soc. Republican. Avocations: backpacking, archery, trains, writing. E-mail: windmill. E-mail: filmworks@hotmail.com

GODDARD, JOHN WESLEY, cable television company executive; b. Aberdeen, Wash., May 4, 1941; s. Fred G. and Winifred (Vaughan) G.; m. Susan Ehrhart, Dec. 29, 1962 (div. Oct. 1978); 1 child, John Wesley Jr.; m. Joan Marie McGiff, Sept. 13, 1980. Grad., Stanford U.; MBA in Fin., U. Calif., Berkeley. Asst. mgr. Tele-Vue Systems Inc., Dublin, 1966, mgr., 1967-69, contr., 1969-74, pres., 1974-78; exec. v.p. Viacom Cable, Pleasanton, Calif., 1978-80, pres., 1980—. Dir. Viacom Internat. Inc., N.Y.C., 1983-87; treas. Nat. Cable TV Assn., Washington, 1984, sec., 1985-86, vice chmn., 1987, chmn., 1988, bd. dirs., 1981—. Republican. Episcopalian. Office: Viacom Cable 2166 Rheem Dr Pleasanton CA 94588-2613

GODDEN, JEAN W. columnist; b. Stamford, Conn., Oct. 1, 1933; d. Maurice Albert and Bernice Elizabeth (Warvel) Hecht; m. Robert W. Godden, Nov. 7, 1952 (dec. Dec. 1985); children: Glenn Scott, Jeffrey Wayne. BA, U. Wash., 1974. News editor Univ. Dist. Herald, Seattle, 1951-53; bookkeeper Omniarts Inc., Seattle, 1963-71; writer editorial page Seattle Post-Intelligencer, Seattle, 1974-80, editorial page editor, 1980-81, bus. editor, 1981-83, city columnist, 1983-91, Seattle Times, 1991—. Author: The Will to Win, 1980, Hasty Put Ins, 1981. Communicator of the Yr. U. Wash. Sch. of Comm., 1995. Mem. LWV (dir. 1969-71), Wash. Press Assn. (Superior Performance award 1979), Soc. Profl. Journalists, Mortarboard, City Club, Phi Beta Kappa. Office: The Seattle Times PO Box 70 Seattle WA 98111-0070

GOEDDE, JOHN W. state senator; b. Chelan, Wash., May 20, 1949; m. Sandy Goedde; children: Brian, Melissa. BA, Wash. State U., 1972. Mgr. Country Club, 1973-79; salesman Panhandle Ins. Agy., 1979-83, pres., 1983—; Rep. senator dist. 3 Idaho State Senate, 2000—. Precinct committeeman Kootenai County Rep. Ctrl. Com., 1986—, state committeeman, 1995-96; co-founder Kootenai Charities, 1994—; committeeman adv. com. State Ins. Fund Agts., 1994—; pres. Idaho Jaycee Internat. Senate, 1994-95; co-chair resolutions com. Rep. State Conv., 1996; trustee Coeur d'Alene Sch. Dist. # 271, 1997— Mem. Ind. Ins. Agts. Idaho (exec. committeeman 1999), Coeur d'Alene Ind. Ins. Agts. Assn. (pres. 1985), Coeur d'Alene Area C. of C. (chair 1992), Coeur d'Alene Sunrise Rotary (charter). Office: 3959 Jonquil Ct Coeur d'Alene ID 83815 also: Idaho State Senate 700 W Jefferson Boise ID 83720-0081 Fax: 664-9336. E-mail: goedde@icehouse.net

GOEHRING, KENNETH, artist; b. Evansville, Wis., Jan. 8, 1919; s. Walter A. and Ruth I. (Rossman) G.; m. Margretta M. MacNicol, Dec. 1, 1945. Student, Cass Tech. Inst., 1933-35, Meinzinger Sch. Applied Art, 1945-46, Colorado Springs Fine Arts Ctr., 1947-50. Works have appeared in over 100 exhibitions in 17 states and 20 museums; 17 one-man shows; exhibitor, Terry Inst., Miami, Symphony Hall, Boston, de Cordova Mus., Fitchburg Mus., Mass., Farnsworth Mus., Maine, Corcoran, Washington, Joslyn Meml. Mus., Nebr., Detroit Inst. Arts, Nebr. Galleries, Stanford U. Galleries, Calif, De Young Mus., San Francisco, Denver Art Mus., Okla. Art Ctr., La Jolla Art Ctr., Calif., Colorado Springs Fine Arts Ctr., 1998, 99, Boulder Mus. Avant Garde Art, 1999, others; represented in permanent collections, Sheldon Art Ctr., Lincoln, Nebr., Colorado Springs Fine Arts Ctr., Foothills Gallery, Golden Colo., Canon City Fine Arts Ctr., Colo., Washburn U. Gallery, Wichita, Kans., Swedish Consulate, Washington, El Pomar Found., Colo. Springs, in many pvt. collections throughout U.S. Purchase awards include Colorado Springs Fine Arts Ctr., 1958; Washburn U., 1957; Am. Acad. Design, 1977 Address: 2017 W Platte Ave Colorado Springs CO 80904-3429

GOEI, BERNARD THWAN-POO (BERT GOEI), architectural and engineering firm executive; b. Semarang, Indonesia, Jan. 27, 1938; came to U.S., 1969; naturalized, 1976; s. Ignatius Ing-Khien Goei and Nicolette Giok-Nio Tjioe; m. Sioe-Tien Liem, May 26, 1966; children: Kimberley Hendrika, Gregory Fitzgerald. BA in Fine Arts, Bandung Inst. Tech. State U. Indonesia, 1961, MA in Archtl. Space Planning, 1964; postgrad., U. Heidelberg, Germany, 1967-68. Co-owner, chief designer Pondok Mungil Interiors Inc., Bandung, 1962-64; dept. mgr., fin. advisor Gumarna Architects, Engrs. and Planners, Inc., Bandung, Jakarta, Indonesia, 1964-67; shop supr., model maker Davan Scale Models, Toronto, Ont., Can., 1968-69; chief archtl. designer George T. Nowak Architects and Assocs., Westchester, Calif., 1969-72; sr. archtl. designer Krisel & Shapiro Architects and Assocs., L.A., 1972-74; sr. supervising archtl. designer The Ralph M. Parsons A/E Co. (now Parsons Infrastructure and Tech. Group Inc.), Pasadena, Calif., 1974—. V.p. United Gruno U.S.A. Corp. Import/Export, Monterey Park, Calif., 1980-89. Mem. Rep. Presdl. Task Force, Washington, 1982—, Nat. Rep. Senatorial Com., Washington, 1983—, Nat. Rep. Congrl. Com., Washington, 1981—, Rep. Nat. Com., Washington, 1982—; active Am. Indonesian Cath. Soc. Recipient Excellent Design Achievement commendation Magneto-Hydro-Dynamics Program, 1976, Strategic Def. Initiative "Star Wars" Program, 1988, USAF Space Shuttle Program, West Coast Space-Port, 1984; scholar U. Heidelberg, 1967-68. Mem. NRA, Am. Air Gunner Assn., Tech. Comm. Soc., Indonesian Am. Soc., Dutch Am. Soc., Second Amendment Found., The Right to Keep and Bear Arms Com. Republican. Roman Catholic. Avocations: fire arms and daggers, photography, hi-tech electronics, stamps and coins, world travel. Home: 154 Ladera St Monterey Park CA 91754-2125 Office: Parsons Infrastructure & Tech Group Inc 100 W Walnut St Pasadena CA 91124-0001

GOELTZ, THOMAS A. lawyer; BA in Econs. summa cum laude, DePauw U., 1969; JD magna cum laude, Mich. U., 1973. Assoc. Riddell, Williams, Ivie, Bullitt & Walkinshaw, Seattle, 1973-75; dep. prosecuting atty. civil divsn. King County Prosecuting Atty.'s Office, Seattle, 1976-79; prin. Cohen, Keegan & Goeltz, Seattle, 1979-86; ptnr. Davis Wright Tremaine, Seattle, 1986—. Cons. state and local govt. agencies on environ. land use issues; adv. shoreline mgmt. City of Seattle; part-time lectr. Law Sch. U. Wash., Seattle, 1976-79. Editor Mich. Law Rev. Active Gov. Task Force on Regulatory Reform, 1993-95. Mem. ABA (urban, state & local govt. law sect.), Wash. State Bar Assn. (real property sect., past chair land use and environ. law sect.), Seattle-King County Bar Assn., Am. Coll. Real Estate Lawyers, Nat. Assn. Indsl. and Office Park, ICSC, Order of Coif. Office: Davis Wright Tremaine 2600 Century Sq 1501 4th Ave Seattle WA 98101-1688

GOEN, BOB, television show host; b. Dec. 1, 1954; Grad., San Diego State U. DJ Stint Sta. KPRO-FM, Riverside, Calif., 1977-81; achor, reporter, prodr., writer, editor Sta. KESQ-TV, Palm Springs, 1981-86; game show host Perfect Match, 1986, The Home Shopping Game, Blackout; daytime host Wheel of Fortune, 1989-92; game show host The Hollywood Game, 1992; co-host Entertainment Tonight, 1996—. Host Miss Universe, Miss USA, Miss Teen USA, 1993—.

GOETSCHEL, ROY HARTZELL, JR. mathematician, researcher; b. Oak Park, Ill., Apr. 19, 1930; s. Roy Hartzell and Elizabeth Wilhelmina Johanna (Gaude) G.; m. Jane Peterson, June 6, 1971. BS, Northwestern U., 1954; MS, DePaul U., 1958; PhD, U. Wis., 1966. Asst. prof. math. Sonoma State U. of Calif., Rohnert Park, Calif., 1966-69; prof. math. U. Idaho, Moscow, 1969-97, prof. emeritus math., 1997—. Author: Advanced Calculus, 1981; contbr. articles to Fuzzy Sets and Systems. Mem. N.Y. Acad. Scis. Achievements include introduction and development of concept of fuzzy darts and fuzzy dart representations of fuzzy numbers; introduction of the topic of fuzzy hypergraphs including methodology and applications (especially Hebbian structures) to the literature through papers published in Fuzzy Sets and Systems; conceptualization and development of the basis of a fuzzy matroid theory. Avocation: music (vocal and instrumental). Home: 1721 Atsirk St Moscow ID 83843-9302

GOETZEL, CLAUS GUENTER, metallurgical engineer; b. Berlin, July 14, 1913; came to U.S., 1936; s. Walter and Else (Baum) G.; m. Lilo Kallmann, Nov. 19, 1938; children: Rodney G., Vivian L. Holley. Dipl.-Ing., Technische Hochschule, Berlin, 1935; PhD, Columbia U., 1939. Registered profl. engr., Calif. Research chemist, lab. head Hardy Metall. Co., 1936-39; tech. dir., works mgr. Am. Electro Metal Corp., 1939-47; v.p., dir. research Sintercast Corp. Am., 1947-57; adj. prof. NYU, N.Y.C., 1945-57, sr. research scientist, 1957-60; cons. scientist Lockheed Missiles & Space Co., Sunnyvale, Calif., 1960-78; cons. metall. engring. Portola Valley, 1978—; lectr., vis. scholar Stanford (Calif.) U., 1961-88. Vis. prof. Tech. Univ. Karlsruhe, Germany, 1978-80. Author: Treatise on Powder Metallurgy, 5 vols., 1949-63; co-author: (with Lilo Goetzel) Dictionary of Materials and Process Engineering, vol. 1 English-German, 1995, vol. 2, German-English, 1997; inventor or co-inventor of over 40 U.S. patents; contbr. over 50 articles to profl. jours. and handbooks. Recipient Alexander von Humboldt Sr. U.S. Scientist award, Fed. Republic Germany, 1978. Fellow AIAA (assoc.), Am. Soc. Materials Internat.; mem. AIME (life), Am. Powder Metallurgy Inst. (sr.), Materials Sci. Club N.Y. (life, past pres.), Inst. Materials (life, London).

GOFORTH, NATHAN DAN, protective services official; b. Phoenix, Sept. 12, 1951; s. Nathan and Mabel Lettie (Deal) G.; m. Lori Ann Petersen (div. 1984). AA in Bus. Adminstrn., Glendale Community Coll., Ariz., 1974, AA in Adminstrn. Justice, 1976; BS in Pub. Programs, Ariz. State U., 1985. Second asst. mgr. Smittys Big Town, Phoenix, 1967-73, sales rep., 1975-76; sr. inventory auditor Motorola Semiconductor, Phoenix, 1973-74; police officer City Glendale, Ariz., 1976—. Interpreter for deaf Glendale Police Dept., 1976—, peer counselor, 1989—, field tng. officer, 1980—; vol. tchr. Glendale Community Coll. Police Res. Acad., 1989-94. Res. hwy. patrolman Ariz. Dept. Pub. Safety, Phoenix, 1975-76; advisor Glendale Explorer Post 469, 1978—, instl. head, 1992; bd. dirs. Theater Works, 1994-97, v.p., 1995-97. Recipient Dedication to DAV award, 1990-91, Cert. of Appreciation award Independence High Sch., 1990, Outstanding Vol. Svc. award MADD, 1991. Mem. NRA, Ariz. State U. Alumni Assn., Internat. Police Assn., Frat. order of Police (treas. 1990-94, v.p. 1994-95, 96-00, trustee 1995—), Ariz. Cts. Assn., Critical Incident Stress Debriefing (S.W. region), Sons of Am. Legion. Avocations: volleyball, racquetball, camping, traveling Europe. Office: Glendale Police Dept 6835 N 57th Dr Glendale AZ 85301-3218

GOGUEN, JOSEPH AMADEE, computer science educator; b. Pittsfield, Mass., June 28, 1941; s. Joseph Amadee and Helen Almira (Stratton) G.; m. Nancy Hammer (div. 1974); children: Healfdene, Heather; m. Kathleen Morrow (div. 1994); 1 child, Alice. BA, Harvard U., 1963; MA, U. Calif., Berkeley, 1967, PhD, 1968. Tutor Bur. of Study Coun. Harvard U., 1961-62; instr. dept. math. U. Calif., Berkeley, 1963-65; asst. prof. com. on info. sci. U. Chgo., 1968-73; rsch. fellow math. scis. dept. IBM T.J. Watson Rsch. Ctr., Yorktown Heights, N.Y., 1971-72; mng. dir., gen. ptnr. Structural Semantics, Palo Alto, Calif., 1978—; asst. prof. computer sci. dept. UCLA, 1973-74, assoc. prof. computer sci. dept., 1974-79, prof. computer sci. dept., 1979-81; sr. staff scientist computer sci. lab. SRI Internat., 1981-88; prof. computing sci., fellow St. Anne's Coll. Oxford (Eng.) U., 1988-96; prof. computer sci. and engring. U. Calif., San Diego, 1996—, dir. program in advanced mfg., 1996-98, dir. Lab. for Meaning and Computation, 1996—. Programming and digital design technician GE Def. Electronics Div., Pittsfield, 1959, 60; scientist applied rsch. lab. Sylvania Electronic Systems, Waltham, Mass., 1962, 63; cons. Krohn-Rhodes Rsch. Inst., 1966, 67, IBM, NCR, Hughes Aircraft, Westinghouse Electric, several other corps.; acad. staff Naropa Inst., Boulder, Colo., 1974, 75, 77, 78; vis. assoc. prof. U. Colo., Boulder, 1974, 75, 77, 78; sr. vis. fellow dept. artificial intelligence U. Edinburgh, Scotland, 1976, 77. Mem. editl. bd. Math. Structures in Computer Sci., 1990—, Internat. Foundations of Computer Sci., 1988—, Cambridge Tracts in Theoretical Computer Sci., 1987—, Future Computer Sys., 1985, Jour. Computer and Sys. Scis., 1981—, Internat. Jour. Fuzzy Sets and Sys., 1977-97; editor in chief Jour. Consciousness Studies, 1993—; referee for profl. jours.; author (with others) Requirements Engineering: Social and Technical Issues, 1994, Algebraic Semantics of Imperative Problems, 1995; contbr. over 200 articles to profl. jours. Recipient NASA Cert. of Recognition, 1990. Fellow Japan Soc. for Promotion Sci.; mem. Assn. for Computing Machinery (software engring., artificial intelligence, programming langs., automata and computability theory), IEEE (tech. coms. on computer architecture, data engring., founds. of computing, com. on pub. policy), European Assn. for Theoretical Computer Sci., Math. Assn. Am., Computer Profls. for Social Responsibility, Am. Math. Soc. Buddhist. Avocations: poetry, meditation, philosophy. Office: U Calif San Diego 9500 Gilman Dr La Jolla CA 92093-5004

GOIN, PETER JACKSON, art educator; b. Madison, Wis., Nov. 26, 1951; children: Kari, Dana. BA, Hamline U., 1973; MA, U. Iowa, 1975, MFA, 1976. Prof. art U. Nev., Reno, 1984—. Author: Tracing the Line: A Photographic Survey of the Mexican-American Border, 1987, Nuclear Landscapes, 1991, Arid Waters: Photographs from the Water in the West Project, 1992, Stopping Time: A Rephotographic Survey of Lake Tahoe, 1992, Humanature, 1996, Atlas of the West, 1997, A Doubtful River, 2000; one-man shows include Duke U. Mus. Art, Durham, N.C., 1992, Phoenix Mus. Art, 1992, Indpls. Mus. Art, 1992, Savannah (Ga.) Coll. Art and Design, 1992, Nev. Humanities Com. Traveling Exhibit, 1992, NICA, Las Vegas, Nev., 1997, Mus. for Photographie, Braunschweig, Germany, 1997, U. Oreg. Mus. of Art, Eugene, 1997, Nev. Mus. Art, Reno, 1996, 99, Princeton (N.J.) U. Art Mus., 1996, Whitney Mus. Am. Art, N.Y.C., 1996, Museet for Fotografie, Denmark, 1999, Recipient Millennium award for Excellence in Arts, Nev., 1999; grantee NEA, 1981, 90. Office: Univ Nev Dept Art Reno NV 89557-0001 E-mail: pgoin@unr.edu

GOIN, SUZANNE, food company executive, chef; b. L.A., Sept. 25, 1966; BA in History, Brown U.; apprenticeship, Ma Maison, L.A. Line cook Chez Panisse, Berkeley, Calif., 1990-92, Arpege Brigade, Paris, 1993; sous chef Olives, Boston, 1993; exec. chef Alloro, Boston, 1994-96, Campanile, L.A., 1997-98. Named Best New Chef Boston mag., 1994. Office: Lucques 8474 Melrose Ave West Hollywood CA 90069-5313

GOINGS, CALVIN, state legislator; b. Pullyap, Wash. m. Amy Morrison, 1999. AAS, Pierce Coll.; BAS in Polit. Sci., Pacific Luth. U. Mem. Wash. Legislature, Olympia, 1995—, majority asst. floor leader, 1999, vice chair energy, tech., and telecoms. com., vice chair transp. com., mem. edn. com., mem. jud. com., mem. rules com. Dir. Wash. Credit Union Found. Commr. Pierce County Fire Dist. No. 6, Ctrl. Pierce Fire and Rescue, 1991-97; mem. Ezra Meeker Hist. Soc.; trustee Pierce Coll. Found.; mem. Friends of the South Hill Libr. Assn., South Hill Cmty. Coun.; former chair Summit/Frederickson Bus. Coun., Am. Heart Assn., Puyallup Jaycees; mem. adv. bd. Pierce County Sheriff's Dept.; summer games tournament organizer, dir., Pierce County Spl. Olympics; mem. task force Pierce County Emergency Med. Svcs., Canyon Rd. Corridor Transp.; chair Crown Valley Estates Neighborhood Assn.; v.p. Pierce County Fire Commrs. Assn.; mem. long-range strategic planning com. Pierce Coll. Democrat. Office: 410 John Cherberg Bldg Olympia WA 98504-0001

GOLAY, FRANK H., JR. lawyer; b. Chgo., 1948; BA, Cornell U., 1970, MAT, 1972, JD, 1977. Bar: N.Y. 1978. Ptnr. Sullivan & Cromwell, L.A. Office: Sullivan & Cromwell 1888 Century Park E Los Angeles CA 90067-1702

GOLD, ANNE MARIE, library director; b. N.Y.C., Feb. 24, 1949; d. James Raymond and Marion Rita (Magner) Scully; m. Steven Louis Gold, Aug. 9, 1974; 1 child, Lauren Z. BA in English, St. Lawrence U., 1971; MS in Libr. Svc., Columbia U., 1972. Libr. N.Y. Pub. Libr., N.Y.C., 1972-74, Oakland (Calif.) Pub. Libr., 1975-80, Solano County Libr., Fairfield, Calif., 1980-90, dir. libr. svcs., 1986-90; county libr. Contra Costa County Libr., Pleasant Hill, 1990-98; exec. dir. Stanford (Calif.) State Libr., 1998—. Mem. Lafayette Sch. Dist. Sch. Bd., 1993-97. Mem. ALA, Pub. Libr. Assn. (bd. dirs. 1992-93, met. librs. sect., pres. 1992-93), Libr. Adminstrn. and Mgmt. Assn. (various coms.), Calif. Libr. Assn. (coun. mem. 1985-87, 90-92, exec. bd. 1991-92, co-chair legis. com. 1992-94, pres. 1998, Mem. of Year award, 1994), Calif. Inst. Librs. (v.p. 1990-91), Restructuring Calif. Pub. Librs. Task Force (1994-95). Office: Cecil H Green Libr Stanford U Stanford CA 94305-6004 E-mail: amgold@sulmail.stanford.edu

GOLD, ARNOLD HENRY, judge; b. Santa Monica, Calif., Apr. 12, 1932; s. Louis and Rose (Shalat) G.; m. Gloria Victor; children: Jeffrey Alan, Kenneth Clarke, Susan Elizabeth. AB with distinction, Stanford U., 1953, JD, 1955. Bar: Calif. 1955, U.S. Dist. Ct. (so., ctrl. and no. dists.) Calif. 1955, U.S. Ct. Appeals (9th cir.) 1955, U.S. Supreme Ct. 1955. Law clk. to Hon. John W. Shenk Supreme Ct. of Calif., San Francisco, 1955-56; assoc. atty. Loeb & Loeb, L.A., 1956-61; pvt. practice Beverly Hills, Calif., 1961-70; ptnr. Pachter, Gold & Schaffer, and predecessors, L.A., 1970-88; judge Calif. Superior Ct. for County of L.A., 1988-2001, supervising judge probate dept., 1993-94. Chmn. probate and mental health com. Calif. Judges Assn., 1995-96; lectr. Calif. Jud. Edn. and Rsch. Probate and Mental Health Insts., 1994-2001, Civil Practice Inst., 1993, Family Law Inst., 1992; lectr. Calif. Continuing Edn. of Bar, 1969, 76-77, 79-82, 84-88, 92; mem. Calif. Atty. Gen's Com. on Charitable Reporting Standards, 1970-71, Calif. Atty. Gen.'s Task Force on Charitable Solicitation Legis., 1975-78, Calif. Jud. Coun. Probate and Mental Health Adv. Com., 1997—; mem. exec. com. Stanford Law Soc. So. Calif., 1973-77 Co-author: Probate Module, California Civil Practice, 1993; contbg. author: California Family Law Handbook, California Nonprofit Corporations Handbooks; mng. editor, bd. editors Stanford Law Rev., 1954-55. Mem. ABA, State Bar Calif. (vice chmn. conf. dels. 1986-87), L.A. County Bar Assn. (trustee 1981-83), Los Angeles County Bar Found. (bd. dirs. 1985-91), Mulholland Tennis Club, Phi Beta Kappa, Alpha Epsilon Pi, Phi Alpha Delta, Delta Sigma Rho. E-mail: judgeagold@aol.com

GOLD, BETTY VIRGINIA, artist; b. Austin, Tex., Feb. 15, 1935; d. Julius Ulisses and Jeffie Mae (Meek) Lee; 1 child, Laura Lee Gold Bousquet. Student, U. Tex. Lectr. Gazi U., Ankara, Turkey, 1988, NAshida Gallery, Nara, Japan, 1989, Met. State Coll. Denver, 1992, Downey Mus., Calif., 1993, Foothills Art Ctr., Golden, Colo., 1994, Triskel Art Ctr., Cork, Ireland, 1994, ARmand Hammer Mus., L.A., 1994, Austin Art Mus., 1996. One-woman shows include Sol Del Rio Gallery, San Antonio, 1971, Parkcrest Gallery, Austin, 1972, Rubicon Gallery, L.A., 1973, Downtown Gallery, Honolulu, 1974, Esther Robles Gallery, L.A., 1975, Laguna Gloria Art Mus., Austin, 1976, Charles W. Bowers Meml. Mus., Santa Ana, Calif., 1977, Phoenix Art Mus., 1979, Baum-Silverman Gallery, L.A., 1988, Del. Art Mus., Wilmington, 1981, Univ. Art Mus., Austin, 1981, Decias Art, LaJolla, Calif., 1982, Patrick Gallery, Austin, 1983, Jan Baum Gallery, L.A., 1984, Boise State U., 1985, Purdue U., West Lafayette, Ind., 1986,

Walker Hill Art Ctr., Seoul, Korea, 1987, Nishida Gallery, Nara, Japan, 1989, Armeson Fine Arts, Ltd., Vail, Colo., 1991, Downey Mus., Calif., 1993, ARt Mus. South Tex., Corpus Christi, 1995, Austin Art Mus., Austin, 1996, The Czech Mus. Fine Arts, Prague, 1998, Elite Gallery, Venice, 1998, others; group shows include Enhol Gallery, Dallas, 1971, Bestart Fallery, Houston, 1972, Gargoyle, Inc., Aspen, Colo., 1975, Aronson Gallery, Atlanta, 1976, Shidoni Gallery, Sante Fe, N.Mex., 1977, Elaine Horwich Gallery, Scottsdale, Ariz., 1981, Fordham U., Bronx, 1983, Nat. Mus. Contemporary Art, Seoul, 1987, John Thomas Gallery, Santa Monica, Calif., 1989, La Quinta Sculpture Park, Calif., 1994, Bova Gallery, L.A., 1995, Museo Nacional Centro de Arte Reina Sofia, Madrid, Spain, 1997, Threshold Gallery, Santa Monica, 1998, others; represented in permanent installations at RCA Bldg., Chgo., Cedars Sinai Hosp., L.A., Sinai Temple, L.A., Hawaii State Fond. Arts, Apollo Plastic Corp., Chgo., Houston First Savs., Pepperdine U., Malibu, Calif., No. Ill. U., Dekalb, Mus. Nacional-Centro de Arte Reina Sofia, Madrid, Texas U., Austin, City of Palma de Mallorca (1999), Spain, Duke U. Med. Ctr. (1999), others. Fax: 310-399-3745. E-mail: bgold1324@earthlink.net

GOLD, CAROL SAPIN, international management consultant, speaker; b. N.Y.C. d. Cerf Saul and Muriel Louise (Fudin) Rosenberg; children: Kevin Bart Sapin, Craig Paul Sapin, Courtney Byrens Sapin. BA, U. Calif., Berkeley, 1955. Asst. credit mgr. Union Oil Co., 1956; with U.S. Dept. State, 1964-66; mem. dept. pub. rels. Braun & Co., L.A., 1964-66; corp. dir. pers. tng. Gt. Western Fin. Corp., L.A., 1967-71; pres. Carol Sapin Gold & Assocs., L.A., 1971—. Bd. dirs. Marathon Nat. Bank, L.A.; cons., profl. spkr., Bath, Eng., 1987-90; cons., Can., Mex., India, Australia, New Zealand; host radio program The Competitive Edge; mem. expdn. to Syria and Jordan, 1994, to Morocco, 1995; mem. WORID Bus. Acad.; instr. Learning Annex; presenter Expertise Forum Presentations, Malaysia, Bangkok, 1997; instr. Asian program U. So. Calif., 1998. Author: Solid Gold Customer Relations, Travel for Scholars, Paris, 1999; featured in tng. films Power of Words; Author: Cassette Libraries, Sound Selling. Bd. dirs. Ctr. Theatre Group, Town Hall, Music Ctr., Odyssey Theater; asst. dir. Burnhill Prodns., 1992—, Cabaret, Palisades Theatre; dir. Improv Corp.; vol. Exec. Svc. Corp., 1996—. Mem. ASTD, Am. Film Inst. Assn., Sales and Mktg. Execs., Nat. Spkrs. Assn., Nat. Platform Assn., Women in Bus., KCET Women's Coun., Exec. Svc. Corps, World Affairs Coun., Blue Ribbon, Women in Arts, Women in Film, Manuscript Soc. Forum Scotland, Plato Soc., Brandeis Univ. Women, Sierra Club (Toure de Mt. Blanc), Supreme Ct. Hist. Soc. Avocation: collecting famous manuscripts. Office: PO Box 11447 Marina Del Rey CA 90295 E-mail: cconsult@aol.com

GOLD, RICK L. federal agency administrator; b. Rexburg, Idaho, June 25, 1946; s. Raymond Russell and Thelma (Lee) G.; m. Anamarie Sanone, May 14, 1988; children: Nanette Phillips, Russell. BSCE, Utah State U., 1968, MSCE, 1970. Registered profl. engr., Colo., Mont., Utah. Hydraulic engr. U.S. Bur. Reclamation, Provo, Utah, 1969-73, project hydrologist Durango, Colo., 1973-75, regional hydrologist Billings, Mont., 1975-81, spl. asst. to regional dir. Washington, 1981-82, asst. planning officer Billings, 1982-83, projects mgr. Durango, Colo., 1983-88, regional planning officer Salt Lake City, 1988-90, asst. regional dir., 1990-94, deputy regional dir., 1994—. Mem. water quality com. Internat. Joint Commn. Study on Garrison Divsn. Unit, Billings, 1975-77; fed. negotiator Cost Sharing and Indian Water Rights Settlement, Durango, 1986-88; chmn. Cooperating Agy. on Glen Canyon Dam EIS, Salt Lake City, 1990-94. Contbr. articles to profl. jours.; author papers. Mem. Rotary Internat., Durango, 1985-87; bd. dirs. United Way of La Plata County, Durango, 1983-88; chmn. Combined Fed. Campaign, La Plata County, 1985; bd. dirs. U.S. Com. on Irrigation and Drainage, 1994-2000. Mem. ASCE. Office: US Bur Reclamation 125 S State St Salt Lake City UT 84138-1102

GOLD, STANLEY PHILLIP, diversified investments executive; b. 1942; AB, U. Calif., 1964; JD, U. So. Calif., 1967. Ptnr. Gang Tyre and Brown, 1967-85, Shamrock Holdings Inc., Burbank, Calif., 1985—; pres., CEO, Shamrock Holdings, Burbank. Office: Shamrock Holdings Inc 4444 W Lakeside Dr Burbank CA 91505-4054 E-mail: sgold@shamrock.com

GOLDBERG, AUBREY, lawyer; b. Suffolk, Va., Dec. 2, 1940; s. Meyer R. and Miriam (Pear) G.; m. Joanne Holland, Aug. 25, 1963; children: Devon Jon, Jennifer Jonine. BA, Coll. William & Mary, 1963, JD, 1966. Bar: Va. 1966, Nev. 1968, U.S. Dist. Ct. Nev. 1968, U.S. Ct. Appeals (9th cir.) 1985. Ptnr. Greenman, Goldberg, Raby & Martinez, Las Vegas, 1970—; settlement judge Nev. Supreme Ct., 1997—. Served to capt. USAF, 1966-70 Vietnam; lt. col. USAFR. Mem. ABA, Nev. Bar Assn. (bd. govs. 1986-93, pres. 1992-93), Clark County Bar Assn. (pres. 1978, 1st annual pres. award 1985), Las Vegas C. of C., Assn. Trial Lawyers Am., Nev. Trial Lawyers Assn. Democrat. Jewish. Avocations: tennis, weight lifting, jogging. Office: Greenman Goldberg Raby & Martinez 601 S 9th St Las Vegas NV 89101-7012

GOLDBERG, DAVID THEO, law educator, writer; b. Pretoria, South Africa, Jan. 8, 1952; came to U.S., 1978; s. Isidore and Florence (Lief) G.; m. Alena Luter, June 25, 1984; 1 child, Gabriel Dylan. BA in Econs. and Philosophy, U. Cape Town, South Africa, 1973, BA in Philosophy with honors, 1975, MA in Philosophy, 1978; PhD in Philosophy, CUNY, 1985. Adj. asst. prof. NYU, N.Y.C., 1984-87, Hunter Coll., CUNY, 1984-87; co-pres. Metafilms, N.Y.C., 1982-88; asst. prof. Drexel U., Phila., 1987-90; asst. prof. justice studies Ariz. State U., Tempe, 1990-92, assoc. prof., 1992-94, prof., dir., chair Sch. Justice Studies, 1995-2000; dir. Humanities Rsch. Inst. U. Calif., 2000—, prof. African Am. studies and criminology, law and soc., 2000—. Author: Ethical Theory and Social Issues, 1989, Racist Culture: Philosophy and the Politics of Meaning, 1993, Racial Subjects: Writing on Race in America, 1997, The Racial State, 2001; editor: Anatomy of Racism, 1990, Multiculturalism: A Critical Reader, 1994; co-editor: Social Identities: A Journal of Race, Nation and Culture, Jewish Identity, 1993, Race Critical Themes, 2001, Blackwell Companion to Racial and Ethnic Studies, 2001, Between Law and Culture, 2001; co-dir. film The Island, 1982. Grantee N.Y. State Coun. on Arts, 1981, NSF, 1991, ACLS, 1988. Mem. Am. Philos. Assn. (mem. com. on Blacks 1992—), Law and Soc. Assn., Greater Phila. Philosophy Consortium (colloquia com. 1989-90), Soc. for Philosophy and Pub. Affairs (exec. com. 1987-88). Avocations: reading, swimming, surfing. Office: Ariz State U Sch Justice Studies Tempe AZ 85287

GOLDBERG, FRED SELLMANN, advertising executive; b. Chgo., Jan. 22, 1941; s. Sydney Norman and Birdie (Cohen) G.; m. Jerrilyn Toby Tager, Apr. 12, 1964; children— Robin Lynn, Susanne Joy B.S., U. Vt., 1962; M.B.A., NYU, 1964. Mktg. research mgr. P. Ballantine & Sons, Newark, 1964-67; sr. v.p., mgmt. supr. Young & Rubicam, N.Y.C., 1967-78, sr. v.p., gen. mgr. Los Angeles, 1978-82; exec. v.p., gen. mgr. Chiat-Day, Inc., San Francisco, 1982-85; exec. v.p., chief operation officer Chiat-Day, Advt., L.A., 1985-87; pres., chief exec. officer San Francisco office Chiat-Day, Inc., San Francisco; vice chmn. Chiat/Day Advt., Inc., L.A., 1987-90; founder, chmn., CEO Goldberg Moser O'Neill Advt., San Francisco, 1990—. Republican. Jewish. Avocations: tennis, music, running. Office: Goldberg Moser O'Neill 600 Battery St San Francisco CA 94111-1802

GOLDBERG, JACKIE, councilwoman; b. L.A. 1 child, Brian. Tchr. Compton and L.A. Unified Sch. Dists.; instr. Calif. State U.; city councilwoman City of L.A., 1993—. Chairwoman Personnel Com.; vice chairwoman Intergovt. Rels. Office: LA City Coun 200 N Main St Ste 408 Los Angeles CA 90012-4117

GOLDBERG, LEE WINICKI, furniture company executive; b. Laredo, Tex., Nov. 20, 1932; d. Frank and Goldie (Ostrowiak) Winicki; m. Frank M. Goldberg, Aug. 17, 1952; children: Susan, Arlene, Edward Lewis, Anne Carri. Student, San Diego State U., 1951-52. With United Furniture Co., Inc., San Diego, 1953-83, corp. sec., dir., 1963-83, dir. environ. interiors, 1970-83; founder Drexel-Heritage store Edwards Interiors subs. United Furniture, 1975; founding ptnr., v.p. FLJB Corp., 1976-86; founding ptnr., sec., treas. Sea Fin., Inc., 1980; founding ptnr. First Nat. Bank San Diego, 1982. Den mother Boy Scouts Am., San Diego, 1965; vol. Am. Cancer Soc., San Diego, 1964-69; chmn. jr. matrons United Jewish Fedn., San Diego, 1958; del. So. Pacific Coast region Hadassah Conv., 1960, pres. Galilee group San Diego chpt., 1960-61; supporter Marc Chagall Nat. Mus., Nice France, U. Calif. at San Diego Cancer Ctr. Foun., Smithsonian Instn., Los Angeles County Mus., San Diego Mus. Contemporary Art, San Diego Mus. Art; pres. San Diego Opera, 1992-94. Recipient Hadassah Service award San Diego chpt., 1958-59; named Woman of Dedication by Salvation Army Women's Aux., 1992, Patron of Arts by Rancho Santa Fe Country Friends, 1993. Democrat. Jewish.

GOLDBERG, MARK ARTHUR, neurologist; b. N.Y.C., Sept. 4, 1934; s. Jacob and Bertha (Grushlawska) G.; 1 child, Jonathan. BS, Columbia U., 1955; PhD, U. Chgo., 1959, MD, 1962. Resident neurology N.Y. Neurol. Inst., N.Y.C., 1963-66; asst. prof. neurology Columbia U. Coll. Phys. and Surgs., N.Y.C., 1968-71; assoc. prof. neurology and pharmacology UCLA, 1971-77, prof. neurology and pharmacology, 1977—; chair dept. neurology Harbor UCLA Med. Ctr., Torrance, 1977—. Contbr. articles to profl. jours., chpts. to books. Capt. U.S. Army, 1966-68. Fellow Am. Neurol. Assn., Am. Acad. Neurology; Am. Soc. Neurochemistry, Assn. Univ. Profs. Neurology. Avocation: oriental cusine.

GOLDBERG, MICHAEL ARTHUR, land policy and planning educator; b. Bklyn., Aug. 30, 1941; s. Harold and Ruth (Abelson) G.; m. Rhoda Lynne Zacker, Dec. 22, 1963 (div. 1987); children: Betsy Anne, Jennifer Heli; m. Deborah Nelson, Sept. 7, 1991. B.A. cum laude, Bklyn. Coll., 1962; M.A., U. Calif., Berkeley, 1965, Ph.D., 1968. Acting instr. Sch. Bus. Adminstrn., U. Calif., Berkeley, 1967-68; asst. prof. Faculty of Commerce and Bus. Adminstrn., U. B.C., Vancouver, 1968-71, assoc. prof., 1971-76, prof., 1976—, assoc. dean, 1980-84, dean, 1991-97, Herbert R. Fullerton prof. urban land policy, 1981—. Mem. Vancouver Econ. Adv. Commn., 1980-82, Can. dept. Fin. Deposit Ins. adv. group, 1992-94, Can. dept. Internat. Trade, Strategic Adv. Group on Internat. Trade in Fin. Svcs., 1991-96; vice chmn. B.C. Real Estate Found., 1985-87, chmn. 1987-91; mem. IFC Vancouver, 1985—, vice chmn., 1985-88, chmn., 1988-89, exec. dir., 1989-91; bd. dirs. Imperial Parking Ltd., 1991-94, VLC Properties Ltd., 1991-93, Redekop Properties, 1993-2000, Catamaran Ferries, Inc., 1996-97, Sinorank Petroleum, 1996-98; vice chmn. Can. Fedn. Deans of Mgmt. and Adminstrv. Scis., 1991-92, chair, 1992-94, Securities Industry Policy Adv. Con., 1995—; pub.-pvt. partnership task force, 1995-96; mem. investment com. B.C. Workers' Compensation Bd., 1997—. Author: (with G. Gau) Zoning: Its Costs and Relevance for 1980's, 1980, The Housing Problem: A Real Crisis?, 1983, (with P. Chinloy) Urban Land Economics, 1984, The Chinese Connection, 1985, (with J. Mercer) The Myth of the North American City, 1985, On Balance, 1989; editor: Recent Perspectives in Urban Land Economics, 1976, (with P. Horwood) North American Housing Markets into the Twenty-first century, 1983, (with E. Feldman) The Rites and Wrongs of Land Use Policy, 1988. Trustee Temple Sholom, 1980-84. Can. Coun. fellow, 1974-75, Social Scis. and Humanities Rsch. Coun. fellow, 1979-80, 84-85, Lincoln Inst. Land Policy fellow, 1979-80, Urban Land Inst. fellow, 1984—, Homer Hoyt Inst. fellow, 1988—; recipient Can. 125th anniversary medal for service to Can., 1993; named hon. life mem. Real Estate Inst. B.C., 1999. Mem. Canadian Regional Sci. Assn., Am. Real Estate and Urban Econs. Assn. (dir. 1978—, pres. 1984), B.C. Automobile Dealers Assn. (dir. 2000—), Vancouver Bd. Trade, Real Estate Inst. British Columbia (hon.), Lambda Alpha. Home: 1986 W 15th Ave Vancouver BC Canada V6J 2L3 Office: U BC Faculty Commerce & Bus Vancouver BC Canada V6T 1Z2

GOLDBERG, MITCHEL R. federal judge; b. 1943; BA, U. Colo., 1965, JD, 1968. With Rosen & Goldberg, Santa Ana, Calif., 1971-80; pvt. practice, 1981-88; apptd. bankruptcy judge cen. dist. U.S. Dist. Ct. Calif., 1988. With U.S. Army, 1969-70. Office: 3420 12th St Riverside CA 92501-3801

GOLDBERG, MORRIS, internist; b. Jan. 23, 1928; s. Saul and Lena (Schanberg) G.; m. Elaine Shaw, June 24, 1956; children: Alan Neil, Seth David, Nancy Beth. BS in Chemistry cum laude, Poly. Inst. Bklyn., 1951; MD, SUNY, Bklyn., 1956. Diplomate Am. Bd. Internal Medicine. Intern Jewish Hosp., Bklyn., 1956-57, resident, 1957-58, 61-62, renal fellow, 1958-59; practice medicine specializing in internal medicine N.Y.C., 1962-71, Phoenix, 1971—. Instr. to asst. clin. prof. internal medicine State U. N.Y. Coll. Medicine, Bklyn., 1962-71; clin. investigator, metabolic research unit Jewish Hosp. Bklyn., 1962-71; cons. in field; mem. staff Phoenix Bapt., Good Samaritan, St. Joseph's Hosp., Vets. Affairs Med. Ctr., Phoenix. Contbr. articles to med. jours. Capt. M.C., U.S. Army, 1959-61. Fellow ACP; mem. AMA, Am. Soc. Internal Medicine, Am. Coll. Nuclear Physicians (charter mem.), Am. Soc. Nephrology, Am. Soc. Hypertension (charter mem.), Ariz. Med. Assn., 38th Parallel Med. Soc., S. Korea, Ariz., Maricopa County Med. Assn., Sigma Xi, Phi Lambda Upsilon, Alpha Omega Alpha. Office: Vets Affairs Med Ctr 650 E Indian School Rd Phoenix AZ 85012-1839

GOLDBERG, ROBERT LEWIS, preventive and occupational medicine physician, internet executive; b. Phila., Aug. 13, 1953; MD, Jefferson Med. Coll., 1976. Diplomate Am. Bd. Preventive Medicine (trustee 1995—, vice-chair occupational medicine 1997—). Resident in family medicine Scenic Gen. Hosp., Modesto, Calif., 1976-77; intensive resident occupl. medicine U. Calif., San Francisco, 1987-88; pres., med. dir. Valley Occupl. Med. Group, Modesto, 1978-98; med. dir. De la Cruz Occupl. Healthcare, Santa Clara, Calif., 1995-98; chief med. officer U.S. Healthworks of Calif., 1998-99; asst. prof. family medicine Sch. Medicine U. Calif., Davis, 1997—, asst. clin. prof. medicine Sch. Medicine San Francisco, 1998—; gen. mgr. Healthcare Learning Solutions DigitalThink, Inc., San Francisco, 1999—. Mem. Inds. Med. Coun. State of Calif., 1993-2000. Fellow Am. Coll. Occupl. Medicine; mem. Am. Coll. Occupl. and Environ. Medicine (bd. dirs., 2d v.p., 1997, 1st v.p. 1998, pres. 2000). Office: DigitalThink Inc 1098 Harrison St San Francisco CA 94103-4521

GOLDBERGER, MARVIN LEONARD, physicist, educator; b. Chgo., Oct. 22, 1922; s. Joseph and Mildred (Sedwitz) G.; m. Mildred Ginsburg, Nov. 25, 1945; children: Samuel M., Joel S. B.S., Carnegie Inst. Tech., 1943; Ph.D., U. Chgo., 1948. Research assoc. Radiation Lab., U. Calif., 1948-49; research assoc. Mass. Inst. Tech., 1949-50; asst.-assoc. prof. U. Chgo., 1950-55, prof., 1955-57; Higgins prof. physics Princeton U., 1957-77, chmn. dept., 1970-76, Joseph Henry prof. physics, 1977-78; pres. Calif. Inst. Tech., Pasadena, 1978-87; dir. Inst. Advanced Study, Princeton, N.J., 1987-91; prof. physics UCLA, 1991-93, U. Calif., San Diego, 1993-2000, dean divsn. natural scis., 1994-99, prof. emeritus, 2000—. Mem. President's Sci. Adv. Com., 1965-69; chmn. Fedn. Am. Scientists, 1971-73. Fellow Am. Phys. Soc., Am. Acad. Arts and Scis.; mem. Nat. Acad. Scis., Am. Philos. Soc., Council on Fgn. Relations. E-mail: mgoldberger@ucsd.edu

GOLDBLATT, HAL MICHAEL, photographer, accountant; b. Long Beach, Calif., Feb. 6, 1952; s. Arnold Phillip and Molly (Stearns) G.; m. Shawn Naomi Doherty, Aug. 27, 1974; children: Eliyahu Yonah, Tova Devorah, Raizel, Shoshana, Reuven Lev, Eliezer Noach, Esther Bayla, Rochel Leah, Zalman Ber, Perle Sara. BA in Math., Calif. State U., Long Beach, 1975. Owner Star Publs., Las Vegas, 1975—; treas. Goldblatt, Inc., Las Vegas, 1980—; pres. SDG Computer Svc., Las Vegas, 1985—; chief fin. officer Martin & Mills Ltd., Las Vegas, 1992-93; controller Amland Devel., Las Vegas, 1993-95; CFO Stewart Constrn., Las Vegas, 1995-96; CEO Goldblatt, Inc., Las Vegas, 1996-97; cost acct. Ameristar Casinos, Inc., Las Vegas, 1997-99; dir. spl. projects Chabad So. Nev., Las Vegas, 1999-2000; dir. photography Lightons Creations, Las Vegas, 2000—; contr. Nev. Hand, Las Vegas, 2001—. Photographer: (photo essays) Mikveh Yisroel, 1978, Chassidic Fabrengen, 1979, A Day at Disneyland, 1985, Shavous Trek, 1997, Garth Brooks World Tour, 1998, Care for Kids Telethon, 1998, 99, Chanukah - Festival of Lights, 1998-00; prodr., engr.: (audio cassettes) From the Heart of My Dreams, 1980, Middle Class Dreams, 1981, Uforatzta Trio, 1982. Founder, pres. Jews for Judaism, Long Beach, 1975-82, v.p., 1983—; fundraising chmn. Friends of Lubavitch, Long Beach, 1977; bd. dirs. Congregation Lubavitch, Long Beach, 1987, 91-92; treas. Actor's Repertory Theatre, 1995-98, mem. adv. bd., 1998—. Recipient Gold Press Card award Forty Niner Newspaper, 1973, 74, Floyd Durham Meml. award for Outstanding Community Svc., 1973, Georgie award Actor's Repertory Theatre, 1995, ART Disting. Svc. award, 1996. Office: Nev Hand Ste 18 2450 E Chandler Ave Las Vegas NV 89120-4059 Fax: 702-739-3305. E-mail: hgoldblatt@nevadahand.org

GOLDEN, T. MICHAEL, state supreme court justice; b. 1942; BA in History, U. Wyo., 1964, JD, 1967; LLM, U. Va., 1992. Bar: Wyo. 1967, U.S. Dist. Ct. 1967, U.S. Ct. Appeals (10th cir.) 1967, U.S. Supreme Ct. 1970. Mem. firm Brimmer, MacPherson & Golden, Rawlins, Wyo., 1971-83, Williams, Porter, Day & Neville, Casper, 1983-88; justice Wyo. Supreme Ct., Cheyenne, 1988—, chief justice, 1994—, assoc. justice. Mem. Wyo. State Bd. Law Examiners, 1977-82, 86-88. Capt. U.S. Army 1967-71. Office: Wyo Supreme Ct Bldg PO Box 1737 2301 Capitol Ave Cheyenne WY 82002

GOLDFARB, TIMOTHY MOORE, hospital administrator; b. Jerome, Ariz., Dec. 15, 1949; married. B, Ariz. State U., 1975, MHA, 1978. Adminstrv. resident Univ. Med. Ctr., Tucson, 1977-78, mgr. patient accts., 1978-79; asst. adminstr. Tucson Gen. Hosp., 1979, Univ. Med. Ctr., Tucson, 1979-83, assoc. adminstr., 1983-84; assoc. hosp. dir. Oreg. Health Scis. Univ. Hosp., Portland, 1984-89, health care sys. dir., 1989—. Office: Oreg Health Scis Univ Hosp 3181 SW Sam Jackson Park Rd Portland OR 97201-3011

GOLDHABER, GERSON, physicist, educator; b. Chemnitz, Germany, Feb. 20, 1924; came to U.S., 1948, naturalized, 1953; s. Charles and Ethel (Frisch) G.; m. Judith Margoshes, May 30, 1969; children: Amos Nathaniel, Michaela Shally, Shaya Alexandra M.Sc., Hebrew U., Jerusalem, 1947; Ph.D., U. Wis., 1950; PhD honoris causus, U. Stockholm, 1986. Instr. Columbia U., N.Y.C., 1950-53; acting asst. prof. physics U. Calif., Berkeley, 1953-54, asst. prof., 1954-58, assoc. prof., 1958-63, prof. physics, 1963-92, prof. physics emeritus, 1992—; Miller research prof. Miller Inst. Basic Sci. U. Calif.-Berkeley, 1958-59, 75-76, 84-85, prof. Grad. Sch., 1994—; Morris Loeb lectr. in physics Harvard U., 1976-77. Named Calif. Scientist of Yr., 1977, Sci. Assoc., CERN, 1986; Ford Found. fellow CERN, 1960-61; Guggenheim fellow CERN, 1972-73 Fellow AAAS, Am. Phys. Soc. (Panofsky prize 1991), Sigma Xi; mem. Royal Swedish Acad. Sci. (fgn.), Nat. Acad. Sci. Office: Lawrence Berkeley Nat Lab Physics Ms 50 208 Berkeley CA 94720-0001 Fax: 510 486-6738. E-mail: gerson@lbl.gov

GOLDIE, RAY ROBERT, lawyer; b. Dayton, Ohio, Apr. 1, 1920; s. Albert S. and Lillian (Hayman) G.; m. Dorothy Roberta Zafman, Dec. 2, 1941; children: Marilyn, Deanne, Dayle, Ron R. Student, U. So. Calif., 1943-44, JD magna cum laude, 1957; student, San Bernardino Valley Coll., 1950-51. Bar: Calif. 1957; cert. specialist estate planning, trusts and probate law, Calif. Bd. Legal Specialization. Elec. appliance dealer, various locations, 1944-54; dep. atty. gen. State Bar of Calif., L.A., 1957-58, 1957-58; pvt. practice San Bernardino, Calif., 1958-87, Rancho Mirage, 1987—. Pres. Trinity Acceptance Corp., 1948-53. Mem. World Peace Through Law Ctr., 1962—; regional dir. Legion Lex U. So. Calif. Sch. Law 1959-75; chmn. San Bernardino United Jewish Appeal, 1963; v.p. United Jewish Welfare Fund, San Bernardino, 1964-66; Santa Anita Hosp., Lake Arrowhead, 1966-69; bd. dirs. San Bernardino Med. Arts Corp.; trustee McCallum Theater, Bob Hope Cultural Ctr., 1996-99, Friends of Cultural Ctr. Found.; bd. dirs. Palm Canyon Theater, 1998—; legal counsel Lake Arrowhead Skating Found., 1998. Fellow Internat. Acad. Law and Sci.; mem. ABA, Assn. Naval Aviation Desert Storm Sqdn. (adminstrv. officer, sec.), San Bernardino County Bar Assn., Riverside County Bar Assn., State Bar Calif. (cert. specialist estate planning, probate and trust law), Am. Judicature Soc., Am. Soc. Hosp. Attys., Calif. Trial Lawyers Assn. (v.p. chpt. 1965-67, pres. 1967-68), Am. Arbitration Assn. (nat. panel arbitrators), Coachella Valley Desert Bar Assn. (chmn. taxation and estate planning, trusts, wills and probate com. 1992-94), Order of the Coif, Lake Arrowhead Country Club (pres. 1972-73, 80-81), Lake Arrowhead Yacht Club, Club at Morningside (CFO 1992-93, sec. 1993-94), Nu Beta Epsilon (pres. 1956-57). E-mail: ray r. Home and Office: 1 Hampton Ct Rancho Mirage CA 92270-2585 E-mail: goldie@earthlink.net

GOLDING, SUSAN, mayor; b. Muskogee, Okla., Aug. 18, 1945; d. Brage and Hinda Fay (Wolf) G.; children: Samuel, Vanessa. Cert. Pratique de Langue Francaise, U. Paris, 1965; BA in Govt. and Internat. Rels., Carleton Coll., 1966; MA in Romance Philology, Columbia U., 1974. Asssoc. editor Columbia U. Jour. of Internat. Affairs, N.Y.C., 1968-69; teaching fellow Emory U., Atlanta, 1973-74; instr. San Diego Community Coll. Dist., 1978; assoc. pub., gen. mgr. The News Press Group, San Diego, 1978-80; city council mem. City of San Diego, 1981-83; dep. sec. bus., transp., housing State of Calif., Sacramento, 1983-84; county supr. dist. 3 County of San Diego, 1984-92; mayor City of San Diego, 1992—. Chmn. San Diego Drug Strike Force, 1987-88, Calif. Housing Fin. Agy., Calif. Coastal Commn.; bd. dirs. San Diego County Water Authority; trustee So. Calif. Water Com., Inc.; founder Mid City Comml. Revitalization Task Force, Strategic Trade Alliance, 1993, Calif. Big 10 City Mayors, 1993; mem. Gov. Calif. Mil. Base Reuse Task Force, 1994; established San Diego World Trade Ctr., 1993, San Diego City/State/County Regional Permit Assistance Ctr., 1994; mem. adv. bd. U.S. Conf. of Mayors, 1994; chair Gov. Wilson's Commn. on Local Governance for 21st Century. Bd. dirs. Child Abuse Prevention Found., San Diego Conv. and Vis. Bur., Crime Victims Fund, United Cerebral Palsy, San Diego Air Quality Bd., San Diego March of Dimes, Rep. Assocs.; adv. bd. Girl Scouts U.S.; trustee So. Calif. Water Comm.; mem. Rep. State Cen. Com.; co-chair com. Presidency George Bush Media Fund, Calif.; chair San Diego County Regional Criminal Justice Coun., race rels. com. Citizens Adv. Com. on Racial Intergration, San Diego Unified Sch. Dist.; hon. chair Am. Cancer Soc's. Residential Crusade, 1988. Recipient Alice Paul award Nat. Women's Polit. Caucus, 1987, Calif. Women in Govt. Achievement award, 1988, Willie Velasquez Polit. award Mex. Am. Bus. and Profl. Assn., 1988, Catalyst of Chance award Greater San Diego C. of C., 1991, Woman Who Means Bus. award San Diego Bus. Jour., 1994, Internat. Citizen award World Affairs Coun., 1994; named One of San Diego's Ten Outstanding Young Citizens, 1981, One of Ten Outstanding Rep. County Ofcls. in U.S.A., Rep. Nat. Com., 1987, San Diego Woman of Achievement Soroptimists Internat., 1988. Mem. Nat. Assn. of Counties (chair Op. Fair Share, mem. taxation and fin. com.), Nat. Women's Forum. Jewish. Office: Office of Mayor PMB #285 7770 Regents Rd #113 San Diego CA 92122-1967 E-mail: COMMERCE@GOLDING.ORG

GOLDMAN, ALLAN BAILEY, lawyer; b. Auburn, N.Y., Jan. 1, 1937; s. Charles and Rose Hortense (Abrahams) G.; m. Eleanor Ruth Levy, May 26, 1963; children: Jennifer Brooke Horwitz, Andrea Allison Gellert. AB magna cum laude, Harvard U., 1958, JD, 1963; LHD (hon.), Hebrew Union Coll.-Jewish Inst. Religion, 1992. Bar: Calif. 1964, D.C. 1977, U.S. Supreme Ct. 1977. Assoc. Wyman, Bautzer, Kuchel & Silbert, Beverly Hills, Calif., 1963-67, ptnr. L.A., 1967-91, Katten Muchin & Zavis, L.A., 1991—. Judge pro-tem Calif. Mcpl. and Small Claims Cts.; arbitrator Calif. Superior Ct. Contbr. articles to profl. jours. Chmn. Attys. for Brown for Gov., officer Brown for Pres., 1976; founder L.A. Com. for Civil Rights Under Law, Mus. Contemporary Art., L.A., Fraternity of Friends of L.A. Music Ctr.; trustee Calif. Mus. Sci. and Industry, 1981-89, St. John's Hosp. and Health Ctr. Found., 1978—, exec. com., 1979-89, bd. dirs., 1989-95, treas., 1990-94, chmn., 1994-95; chmn. nat. bd. trustees Union of Am. Hebrew Congregations, 1987-91; bd. govs. Hebrew Union Coll.-Jewish Inst. Religion, 1988—, bd. overseers L.A. campus, 1981-85, 88—; trustee SKirball Cultural Ctr., 1997—; pres. Leo Baeck Temple, L.A., 1975-77, Coun. of Synagogue Assn. of Greater L.A., 1983—; mem. Conf. Pres.'s Major Jewish Orgns., 1987-91; mem. synagogue funding com. Jewish Fedn. Coun. of Greater L.A., 1979, chmn., 1985-88; Calif. Commn. Jud. Nominees Evaluation, 1999—. Lt. USNR, 1958-60. Mem. Calif. Bar Assn., D.C. Bar Assn., Regency Club. Democrat. Jewish. Avocations: trekking, running, tennis. Home: 347 Conway Ave Los Angeles CA 90024-2603 Office: Katten Muchin Zavis Ste 1400 1999 Avenue Of The Stars Los Angeles CA 90067-6115 E-mail: allan.goldman@kmz.com

GOLDMAN, BENJAMIN EDWARD, lawyer; b. N.Y.C., Feb. 25, 1940; s. William Wolfe and Blanche (Kallenburg) G.; m. Lynda Ann Schwartz, July 27, 1950; children: Brian Edward, Victoria Beth, Adam Edward BS, NYU, 1965; JD, Fordham U., 1968; LLM, Georgetown U., 1970. Bar: N.Y. 1968, D.C. 1972, U.S. Dist. D.C., U.S. Ct. Appeals (D.C., 4th, 5th and 9th cirs.), Calif. 1986, U.S. Dist. Ct. (cen. dist.) Calif. 1986. Atty., advisor to chmn. NLRB, Washington, 1968-72; assoc. Arent, Fox, Kitner, Plotkin, Kahn, Washington, 1972-75; ptnr. Feldman, Krieger, Goldman, Tisch, Washington, 1976-83, Memel, Jacobs, Pierno, Gersh & Ellsworth, L.A., 1984-87, Graham and James, L.A., 1987-2001, Squire, Sanders & Dempsey LLP, L.A., 2001—. Mem. com. on devel. law under NLRB Act, 1968—; speaker Healthcare Fin. Mgmt. Assn., Calif., 1987, Nat. Health Edn. Conf. on AIDS, 1987, Inst. Corp. Counsel, 1986, Hosp. Coun. N. Calif., 1985, others. Contbr. articles to profl. jours. Mem. ABA (forum com. on health law 1983, mem. labor and employment law sect. 1968—), Nat. Health Lawyers Assn. (speaker ann. healthlaw update 1985), Calif. Bar Assn., N.Y. Bar Assn., D.C. Bar Assn., Am. Acad. Hosp. Attys. Office: Squire Sanders & Dempsey LLP 801 S Figueroa St Fl 14 Los Angeles CA 90017-2573 E-mail: bgoldman@ssd.com

GOLDMAN, GERALD HILLIS, beverage distribution company executive; b. Omaha, July 26, 1947; s. Lester Jack and Lilyan Haykin (Weiskopf) G.; m. Cathy Evelyn Brightman, Dec. 15, 1973; children: Lori, Jeffrey. BSBA, U. Nebr., 1969; MBA, U. So. Calif., 1975. C.P.A., Calif., Nebr. Sr. acct. Arthur Andersen & Co., Los Angeles, 1969-72, exec. v.p., CFO CORE-MARK Internat., Inc., Richmond, B.C., Can., 1972-86, exec. v.p. Can., 1986-87; pres. Gen. Acceptance Corp., Los Angeles, 1986-87; CFO, sr. v.p. fin. and ops. Alaska Distbrs., Inc., Seattle, 1987—. Mem. AICPA, Calif. Soc. CPAs, Fin. Execs. Inst.

GOLDMAN, WILLIAM, writer; b. Chgo., Aug. 12, 1931; s. M. Clarence and Marion (Weil) G.; m. Ilene Jones, Apr. 15, 1961; children: Jenny, Susanna. BA, Oberlin Coll., 1952; MA, Columbia U., 1956. Author: The Temple of Gold, 1957, Your Turn to Curtsy, My Turn to Bow, 1958, Soldier in the Rain, 1960, Boys and Girls Together, 1964, No Way to Treat a Lady, 1964, The Thing of It Is, 1967, Father's Day, 1971, The Princess Bride, 1973, Marathon Man, 1974, Wigger, 1974, Magic, 1976, Tinsel, 1979, Control, 1982, The Silent Gondoliers, 1983, The Color of Light, 1984, Heat, 1985, Brothers, 1987; (non-fiction) The Season: A Candid Look At Broadway, 1969, Adventures in the Screen Trade, 1983; (with Mike Lupica) Wait Until Next Year, 1988, Hype and Glory, 1990, Four Screenplays, 1995, Five Screenplays, 1997, Which Lie Did I Tell, 2000; (essays) The Big Picture, 1999; (play, with James Goldman) Blood Sweat and Stanley Poole, 1961; (musical comedy, with James Goldman and John Kander) A Family Affair, 1962; (screenplay) Masquerade, 1965, Harper, 1966, Butch Cassidy and The Sundance Kid, 1969 (Acad. award best original screenplay 1970), The Hot Rock, 1972, The Stepford Wives, 1974, The Great Waldo Pepper, 1975, Marathon Man, 1976, All the President's Men, 1976 (Acad. award best screenplay adaptation 1977), A Bridge Too Far, 1977, Magic, 1978, The Princess Bride, 1987, Heat, 1987, Misery, 1990, The Year of the Comet, 1992, Memoirs of an Invisible Man, 1992, Chaplin, 1992, Maverick, 1994, Ghost and the Darkness, 1996, Absolute Power, 1997, Hearts in Atlantis, 2001. Recipient Laurel Award for lifetime achievement in screenwriting, 1983. Office: c/o William Morris 151 El Courino Dr Beverly Hills CA 90212-1804

GOLDREICH, PETER MARTIN, astrophysics and planetary physics educator; b. N.Y.C., July 14, 1939; s. Paul and Edith (Rosenfield) G.; m. Susan Kroll, June 14, 1960; children: Eric, Daniel. BS in Physics, Cornell U., 1960, PhD in Physics, 1963. Instr. Cornell U., summers 1961-63; post-doctoral fellow Cambridge U., 1963-64; asst. prof. astronomy and geophysics UCLA, 1964-66, assoc. prof., 1966; assoc. prof. planetary sci. and astronomy Calif. Inst. Tech., 1966-69, prof. planetary sci. and astronomy, 1969—, Lee DuBridge prof. astrophysics and planetary physics, 1981—. Recipient Chapman medal Royal Astron. Soc., 1985, Gold medal, 199; named Calif. Scientist of Yr. 1981, Nat. Medal of Science, 1995; Woodrow Wilson hon. fellow, 1960-61, fellow NSF, 1961-63, Sloan Found., 1968-70 National Medal of Science, 1995. Mem. NAS (fellow 1972), Am. Acad. Arts and Scis. (fellow 1973), Am. Astron. Soc. (Henry Norris Russell lectr., Dick Brouwer award 1986, George P. Kuiper prize divsn. planetary sci. 1992). Office: Calif Inst Tech Msc 150-21 1200 E California Blvd Pasadena CA 91125-0001

GOLDSMITH, BRAM, banker; b. Chgo., Feb. 22, 1923; s. Max L. and Bertha (Gittelsohn) G.; m. Elaine Maltz; children: Bruce, Russell. Student, Herzl Jr. Coll., 1940, U. Ill., 1941-42. Asst. v.p. Pioneer-Atlas Liquor Co., Chgo., 1945-47; pres. Winston Lumber and Supply Co., East Chicago, Ind., 1947-50; v.p. Medal Distilled Products, Inc., Beverly Hills, Calif., 1950-75; pres. Buckeye Realty and Mgmt. Corp., Beverly Hills, 1952-75; exec. v.p. Buckeye Constrn. Co., Inc., Beverly Hills, 1952-75; chmn. bd., CEO City Nat. Corp., Beverly Hills, 1975-95; CEO City Nat. Bank, 1975-96, chmn., 1975-95, CNC, 1995—. Mem., bd. dirs. L.A. Philharm. Assn.; bd. dirs. Cedars/Sinai Med. Ctr.; pres. Jewish Fedn. Coun. Greater L.A., 1969-70; nat. chmn. United Jewish Appeal, 1970-74; regional chmn. United Crusade, 1976; co-chmn. bd. dirs. NCCJ; chmn. Am. com. Weizman Inst. Sci. With signal corps U.S. Army, 1942-45. Mem. Masons, Hillcrest Country Club, Balboa Bay Club. Office: City Nat Corp 400 N Roxbury Dr Beverly Hills CA 90210

GOLDSMITH, DONALD WILLIAM, lawyer, astronomer, writer; b. Washington, Feb. 24, 1943; s. Raymond William and Selma Evelyn (Fine) G.; m. Rose Marien, Apr. 10, 1975 (div. 1978); 1 child, Rachel Evelyn. BA, Harvard U., 1963; PhD, U. Calif., Berkeley, 1969, JD, 1983. Asst. prof. earth and space sci. SUNY, Stony Brook, 1972-74; vis. prof. Niels Bohr Inst., Copenhagen, 1977; vis. instr. physics Stanford (Calif.) U., 1983; vis. lectr. astronomy U. Calif., Berkeley, 1980-88, vis. assoc. prof., 1990-93; assoc. Pillsbury, Madison and Sutro, San Francisco, 1985-87. Cons. Cosmos TV program, Los Angeles, 1978-80; pres. Interstellar Media Publs., Berkeley, 1978—. Author: Nemesis, 1985, The Evolving Universe, 1985, Supernoval, 1989, Space Telescope, 1989, The Astronomers, 1991, The Hunt for Life on Mars, 1997, Worlds Unnumbered, 1997, The Ultimate Einstein, 1997, The Ultimate Planets, 1998, Voyage to the Milky Way, 1999, The Runaway Universe, 2000; (with others) The Search for Life in the Universe, 1980, 2d edit. 1992, Cosmic Horizons, 1982, Mysteries of the Milky Way, 1991; co-writer (TV programs) Is Anybody Out there, 1986, The Astronomers, 1991. Recipient 1st prize popular essays in astronomy Griffith Obs./Hughes Aircraft Corp., L.A., 1983, Best Popular Writing by a Scientist award Am. Inst. Physics, 1986, Klumpke-Roberts award for lifetime achievement Astronomy Soc. Pacific, 1990, Annenberg Found. award for edn. Am. Astron. Soc., 1995. Home: 2153 Russell St Berkeley CA 94705-1006

GOLDSMITH, JERRY, composer; b. L.A., Feb. 10, 1929; m. Carol Sheinkopf. Student, Los Angeles City Coll.; studies with, Jakob Gimpel, Mario Castelnuovo-Tedesco; MusD, Berklee Coll. Music, 1990. Composer: (radio scores) Romance, Suspense, CBS Radio, (TV scores) Twilight Zone, Gen. Elec. Theatre, Doctor Kildare, Gunsmoke, Climax, Playhouse 90, Studio One, Star Trek: Voyager (Emmy award, 1995), (film scores, partial list) (debut) Black Patch, 1956, Lonely Are The Brave, 1961, Freud (Acad. award nomination), 1962, The Stripper, 1962, Lilies of the Field, 1963, The Prize, 1963, Seven Days in May, 1963, In Harm's Way, 1964, The Man From UNCLE, 1965, Von Ryan's Express, 1965, A Patch of Blue (Acad. award nomination), 1965, The Blue Max, 1965, Our Man Flint, 1965, Seconds, 1965, Stagecoach, 1965, The Sand Pebbles (Acad. award nomination), 1966, In Like Flint, 1967, Planet of the Apes (Acad. award nomination), 1968, The Ballad of Cable Hogue, 1969, Tora! Tora! Tora!, 1970, Patton (Acad. award nomination), 1970, Wild Rovers, 1971, The Other, 1972, The Red Pony (Emmy award), 1972, Papillon (Acad. award nomination), 1973, QB VII (Emmy award), 1974, Chinatown (Acad. award nomination), 1974, The Reincarnation of Peter Proud, 1974, Logan's Run, 1975, The Wind and the Lion (Acad. award nomination), 1976, The Omen (Acad. award winner, Grammy award nomination, two N.B. nominations), 1976, Islands in the Stream, 1976, Mac Arthur, 1977, Coma, 1977, The Boys from Brazil (Acad. award nomination), 1978, Damien-Omen II, 1978, Alien, 1979, Babe (Emmy award), Masada (Emmy award), 1981, Star Trek: The Motion Picture (Acad. award nomination), 1979, The Final Conflict, 1981, Outland, 1981, Raggedy Man, 1981, Mrs. Brisby: The Secret of NIMH, 1982, Poltergeist (Acad. award nomination, Edgar Allan Poe award), 1982, First Blood, 1982, Twilight Zone-The Movie, 1983, Psycho II, 1983, Under Fire (Acad. award nomination), 1983, Gremlins (Saturn award), 1984, Legend (European version), 1985, Explorers, 1985, Rambo: First Blood II, 1985, Poltergeist II: The Other Side, 1986, Hoosiers (Acad. award nomination), 1986, Innerspace, 1987, Extreme Prejudice, 1987, Rambo III, 1988, Criminal Law, 1989, The 'Burbs, 1989, Leviathan, 1989, Star Trek V: The Final Frontier, 1989, Total Recall, 1990, Gremlins 2: The New Batch, 1990, The Russia House, 1990, Not Without My Daughter, 1991, Sleeping With the Enemy, 1991, Medicine Man, 1991, Love Field, 1992, Mom and Dad Save the World, 1992, Basic Instinct, 1992 (Acad. award nomination, Golden Globe nomination), Mr. Baseball, 1992, Forever Young, 1992, Matinee, 1992, The Vanishing, 1993, Dennis the Menace, 1993, Malice, 1993, Rudy, 1993, Six Degrees of Separation, 1993, Angie, 1994, Bad Girls, 1994, The Shadow, 1994, I.Q., 1994, The River Wild, 1994, First Knight, 1995, Congo, 1995, Powder, 1995, City Hall, 1995, Executive Decision, 1996, Chain Reaction, 1996, The Ghost and the Darkness, 1996, Star Trek: First Contact, 1996, Fierce Creatures, 1996, L.A. Confidential, 1997 (Acad. award nomination, Golden Globe nomination), Air Force One, 1997, The Edge, 1997, Deep Rising, 1997, U.S. Marshals, 1998, Mulan, 1998 (Acad. award nomination, Golden Globe nomination), Small Soldiers, 1998, Star Trek: Insurrection, 1998, The Mummy, 1999, The 13th Warrior, 1999, The Haunting, 1999, Hollow Man, 2000, Along Came a Spider, 2000; debuted as concert condr. with Christus Apollo, So. Calif. Chamber Symphony, 1969; guest condr. Royal Philharm. Orch., London, 1975, 87, Glendale Symphony, 1975, USAF Band, 1976, 83, Okla. Symphony Orch., 1983, San Diego Pops Orch., 1985, London Philharmonia, 1987, Pitts. Symphony, 1988, Ala. Symphony, 1988, Nat. Symphony, Washington, 1988, Indpls. Symphony, 1989, Ft. Worth Symphony, 1989, London Symphony, 1989, 99, 2000, Utah Symphony, 1990, 91, El Paso (Tex.) Symphony, 1990, Syracuse Symphony, 1990, Toronto (Ont., Can.) Symphony, 1990, Balt. Symphony, 1990, New World Symphony, Miami, Fla., 1991, 2000, Cin. Symphony, 1991, Memphis Symphony, 1992, Milw. Symphony, 1993, Detroit Symphony, 1993, 2000, Oulu (Finland) City Orchestra, 1993, Colo. Symphony, 1993, Madrid (Spain) Symphony, 1993, BBC Concert Orchestra, Eng., 1994, San Diego Symphony Orchestra, 1994, Toledo Symphony, 1995, San Jose Symphony, 1997, Pasadena POPS Orch., 1997, New York FILMharmonic Orchestra., 1998, Seville (Spain) Symphony, 1998, Kanagawa (Japan) Philharmonic Orchestra., 1998, 2000, Royal Scottish National Orchestra, 1999, Budapest Festival Orch., 1999, L.A. Philharmonic, 1999, Barcelona (Spain) Symphony, 1999; ballet scores include Othello, 1971, A Patch of Blue, 1970, Capricorn One, 1989; premier Music For Orchestra with St. Louis Symphony, 1971-72. Recipient Max Steiner award Nat. Film Soc., 1982, 1st ann. Richard Kirk award BMI, 1987, Golden Score award Am. Soc. Music Arrangers, 1990, Career Achievement award Soc. for Preservation of Film Music, 1993, 1st Am. Music Legend award from Variety, 1995, 18 Acad. award nominations, 7 Emmy award nominations, 7 Grammy award nominations, 9 Golden Globe nominations. Office: c/o Savitsky & Co 1901 Ave Of Stars Ste 1450 Los Angeles CA 90067-6087

GOLDSMITH, WERNER, mechanical engineering educator; b. Düsseldorf, Rhineland, Germany, May 23, 1924; came to U.S., 1938; s. Siegfried and Margarethe (Grunewald) G.; m. Adrienne Kessler (div.); children: Stephen M., Andrea Jo; m. Penelope I. Alexander, Oct. 5, 1973; 1 child, Remy M. BSME, U. Tex., 1944, MSME, 1945; PhDME, U. Calif., Berkeley, 1949. Registered mech. and safety engr., Calif. Engr. Westinghouse Electric Co., Pitts. and Phila., 1945-47; instr. div. engring. design U. Calif., Berkeley, 1947-49, asst. prof., 1949-55, assoc. prof. dept. mech. engring., 1955-60, prof., 1960-87, prof. emeritus in active svc., 1988-97, prof. Grad. Sch., 1997—; mech. engr. U.S. Naval Weapons Ctr., China Lake, Calif., 1951—. Instr. math. U. Pitts., 1945-46; lectr. in engring. U. Pa., Phila., 1946-47; engring. cons. govt., industry, legal profession, Berkeley, 1953—; chmn. head injury com. NIH, Bethesda, Md., 1966-70; cons. Fuze div. U.S. Army, Picatinny Arsenal, N.J., 1970-76; panel mem. Nat. Rsch. Coun. Rev. Armanent and Materials Disectorate of Army Rsch. Labs.; vis. prof. Technion, Haifa, Israel, Nat. Poly. U., Athens, Greece, Tokyo Inst. Tech., East China Inst. Tech., Nanjing, 1968—, T.H., Eindhoven, Holland, Inst. Su. Matériaux et Construction Mécanique, St. Ouen, France; cons. mech. engring. dept. U. Calif., San Diego, 1997—. Author: A History of the Department of Mechanical Engineering, University of California, Berkeley, 1997; (monograph) Impact, 1960, reprint, 1999; co-author, co-editor: Introduction to Bioengineering, 1996; contbr. over 225 articles on impact, wave propagation, rock mechanics, biomechanics, head and neck injuries, protective devices, exptl. mechs. to profl. jours.; also numerous tech. reports. Guggenheim fellow, 1953-54, Fulbright rsch. fellow U.S. Dept. State, 1974-75, 81-82, Lady Davies fellow Lady Davies Trust Fund, 1986; named Outstanding Engring. Grad. by U. Calif. Berkeley Engring. Alumni Assn., 2001. Fellow Am. Acad. Mechanics (spl. issue internat. jour. Impact honoring 70th birthday 1994); mem. ASME (hon., chair West Coast applied mechanics divsn. 1960, hon. mem. 1997, honoree 3-day symposium Applied Mechanics/Materials divsns. 1995), NAE, Faculty Club (Berkeley). Avocations: tournament bridge, collecting old maps, stamp collecting, classical music. Home and Office: 450 Gravatt Dr Berkeley CA 94705-1506 Office: U Calif Dept Mech Engring Berkeley CA 94720-0001 Fax: (510) 486-8050. E-mail: goldsmth@me.berkeley.edu

GOLDSTEIN, AVRAM, pharmacology educator; b. N.Y.C., July 3, 1919; s. Israel and Bertha (Markowitz) G.; m. Dora Benedict, Aug. 29, 1947; children— Margaret, Daniel, Joshua, Michael. A.B., Harvard, 1940, M.D., 1943. Intern Mt. Sinai Hosp., N.Y.C., 1944; successively instr., assoc., asst. prof. pharmacology Harvard U., 1947-55; prof. dept. pharmacology Stanford U., Palo Alto, Calif., 1955-89, exec. head dept., 1955-70, prof. emeritus, 1989—. Dir. Addiction Research Found., Palo Alto, Calif., 1973-87. Author: Biostatistics, Principles of Drug Action, 1965, ADDICTION: From Biology to Drug Policy, 2001. Served from 1st lt. to capt., M.C. AUS, 1944-46. Mem. AAAS, NAS and Inst. Medicine, Am. Acad. Arts and Scis., Am. Soc. Pharmacology and Exptl. Therapeutics, Am. Soc. Biol. Chemists. Office: Stanford U Sch Medicine Edwards Bldg Rm 354 300 Pasteur Dr Stanford CA 94305

GOLDSTEIN, BARRY BRUCE, biologist, food company executive, lawyer; b. N.Y.C., Aug. 2, 1947; s. George and Pauline (Kolodner) G.; m. Jacqueline Barbara Aboulafia, Dec. 21, 1968; children: Joshua, Jessica. BA, Queens Coll., 1968; MA, CCNY, N.Y.C., 1974; PhD, CUNY, N.Y.C., 1980; JD, U. N.Mex., 1994. Microbiologist CPC Internat., Yonkers, N.Y., 1968-71; rsch. scientist U. Tex., Austin, 1977-80; v.p. SystemCulture Inc., Honolulu, 1980-83; bioenergy/aquaculture program mgr. N.Mex. Solar Energy Inst., Las Cruces, 1983-89; pres. Ancient Seas Aquaculture Inc., Roswell, N.Mex., 1989-92, Desert Seas Aquaculture Inc., Roswell, 1990-92, Hawaii Shellfish Co., Las Cruces, 1991—; prin. mem. tech. staff Sandia Nat. Labs., Albuquerque, 1994—. Editl. bd. Natural Resources Jour.; contbr. articles to profl. jours. Recipient Nat. Energy Innovation award Dept. Energy, Washington, 1985; Grad. fellow CUNY, 1971, Jesse Smith Noyes fellow, 1975, Regents scholar SUNY, 1964. Mem. World Aquaculture Soc., Am. Bar Assn., N.Mex. State Bar Assn. Avocations: aquaculture, reading. Office: 5117 Roanoke Ave NW Albuquerque NM 87120-4542 E-mail: bgoldst@sandia.gov

GOLDSTEIN, DAVID BAIRD, energy program director, physicist; b. Cleve., June 29, 1951; s. Laurence and Gloria Reta (Baumgarten) G.; m. Julia Beth Vetromile, May 17, 1980; children: Elianna Louise, Abraham Micah. AB in Physics, U. Calif., Berkeley, 1973; PhD in Physics, U. Calif., 1978. Rsch. asst. Lawrence Berkeley (Calif.) Lab., 1975-78, staff scientist, 1978-80; sr. scientist, dir. energy program Natural Resources Def. Coun., San Francisco, 1980—. Sub-com. chair standing standards project com. 90.1 ASHRAE, Atlanta, 1983-96; vice-chmn. bd. Consortium for Energy Efficiency, Inc., Sacramento, 1991-93, 99—, advisor, 1993-96; initiator and advisor Super Efficient Refrigerator Program, Inc., 1991-96. Contbr. articles to profl. jours. Recipient Champion of Energy Efficiency award Am. Coun. for an Energy Efficient Economy, 1988, 94. Fellow Am. Phys. Soc. (Leo Szilard award 1998); mem. Inst. for Market Transformation (initiator, bd. dirs., chmn. 1995—), New Bldgs. Inst. (treas. 1998-99, v.p. 1999-2000, pres. 2000—), Phi Beta Kappa, Sigma Xi. Jewish. Avocations: travel, hiking, music, photography. Home: 1240 Washington St San Francisco CA 94108-1041 Office: Natural Resources Def Coun 71 Stevenson St Ste 1825 San Francisco CA 94105-2964 E-mail: dgoldstein@nrdc.org

GOLDSTEIN, EDWARD DAVID, lawyer, former glass company executive; b. N.Y.C., July 12, 1927; s. Michael and Leah (Kirsh) G.; m. Rhoda Gordon, Apr. 18, 1950; children: Linda, Ellen, Ruth, Michael. BA, U. Mich., 1950, JD with distinction, 1952. Bar: Calif. 1952. Assoc. Orrick, Dahlquist, Herrington & Sutcliffe, San Francisco, 1952-54, Johnston & Johnston, San Francisco, 1954-56; with legal dept. Ohio Match Co., Hunt Foods & Industries, 1956-58; asst. gen. mgr., sales mgr. Glass Containers Corp., Fullerton, Calif., 1958-62, v.p., gen. mgr., 1962-68, pres., CEO, 1968-83. Chmn. bd. Knox Glass Co., Fairmount Glass Cos., 1967-68; gen. counsel FHP, Internat., FHP, Inc., 1985-87. Chmn. bd. trustees St. Jude Hosp., Fullerton, 1984-88. Served with USNR, 1945-46. Mem. ABA, State Bar Calif., Orange County Bar Assn., Nat. Health Lawyers Assn., Am. Arbitration Assn., Am. Coll. Legal Medicine (assoc.-in-law), Calif. Soc. Healthcare Attys. Home: 2230 Yucca Ave Fullerton CA 92835-3320 Office: 110 E Wilshire Ave Fullerton CA 92832-1900 E-mail: edgatty@aol.com

GOLDSTEIN, JACK, health science executive, microbiologist; b. N.Y.C., June 7, 1947; s. Arnold L. and Rachel (Vogel) G.; m. Laurie Ann Sacks, Aug. 28, 1969; 1 child, Justin T. BA, Rider Coll., Trenton, N.J., 1969; MS, St. John's U., Jamaica, N.Y., 1974, PhD, 1976. Diplomate Am. Bd. Med. Microbiology. Asst. dir. microbiology Queens Hosp. Ctr., Jamaica, 1976-81; dir. diagnostic labs. API div. Sherwood Med. Co., Plainview, N.Y., 1981-83; v.p. research and devel. MicroScan div. Baxter Travenol, Sacramento, 1983-86; group v.p. Ortho Diagnostic Systems Inc. div. Johnson & Johnson Co., Raritan, N.J., 1986-88; group v.p., gen. mgr. infectious disease bus. Ortho Diagnostic Systems, Inc. div. Johnson & Johnson Co., Raritan, 1988-92; exec. v.p. worldwide Ortho Diagnostic Sys. Inc. divsn. Johnson & Johnson Co., Raritan, 1992-93, pres. Ortho Diagnostic Sys. Inc. divsn., 1993-97; pres., CEO Applied Imaging Corp., Santa Clara, Calif., 1997-2001, chmn. bd., 2001—; gen. ptnr. Windamere Venture Ptnrs., San Diego, 2001—. Mem. exam. com. Am. Bd. Med. Microbiology, Washington, 1984-91. Mem. editl. bd. Jour. Clin. Microbiology, Wasington, 1983-91; contbr. articles to profl. jours. Mem. Am. Soc. Microbiology, Am. Soc. Clin. Chemistry, Beta Beta Beta. Avocations: reading, skiing. Office: Applied Imaging Corp 2380 Walsh Ave Santa Clara CA 95051-1301

GOLDSTEIN, KENNETH F. entertainment executive, software executive; b. Detroit, Mar. 10, 1962; s. Earl Goldstein and Sarita (Bow) Snow. BA in Philosophy and Theater, Yale U., 1984. Freelance writer, TV and film producer, L.A., 1984-89; writer, producer Cinemaware Corp., Westlake Village, Calif., 1989-91; designer, producer Philips Interactive Media, L.A., 1991-92; exec. publisher Carmen Sandiego series Broderbund Software, Inc., Novato, Calif., 1992-96, v.p. entertainment, gen. mgr. divsn. Red Orb Entertainment Myst, Riven Series, 1996-98, Journeyman Project series, Warlords series, 1996-98; sr. v.p., gen. mgr. Disney Online, 1998-2000; exec. v.p., mng. dir. Walt Disney Internet Group, 2000—. Author: (screenplays) 8, 1992-95; designer (software programs) Carmen Sandiego: Jr. Detective Edition, 1994 (Software Publs. Assn. award 1995), Reading Galaxy, 1994 (Family PC, Mac World awards 1996), In the 1st Degree, 1995 (Software Publs. Assn. award 1996). Vol. Olive Crest Treatment Ctr., 1986, Free Arts for Abused Children, 1988; sec. bd. trustees Full Circle Programs, Marin County, Calif., 1992-98. Recipient Pub. Svc. awards, Olive Crest Treatment Ctrs., 1986, Free Arts for Abused Children, 1988; named one of Top 100 Multimedia Producers, Multimedia Producer Mag., 1995, Best of What's New in Computers, Electronics, Popular Sci. Mag., 1995, Upside Mag. Elite 100, Honorable Mention Digital Entertainment, 1998, Best of Festival award Interant. Web Awards, 2000, Modalis Rsch. Excellence award, 2001. Mem. Writers Guild of Am. West, Acad. Interactive Arts and Scis (founding mem., bd. govs. L.A.), Yale Univ. Alumni (schs. com. 1988—), Computer Game Developers Assn. Avocations: skiing, health and fitness, reading lit. and non-fiction. Office: Disney Online 500 S Buena Vista St Burbank CA 91521-0001

GOLDSTEIN, MARY KANE, physician; b. N.Y.C., Oct. 24, 1950; d. Edwin Patrick and Mary Kane; m. Yonkel Noah Goldstein, June 24, 1979; children: Keira, Gavi. Philosophy degree, Columbia U., 1973, MD, 1977; MS in Health Svcs. Rsch., Stanford U., 1994. Resident Duke U. Med. Ctr., Durham, N.C., 1977-80; asst. prof. medicine U. Calif., San Francisco, 1980-84, staff physician Cowell Student Health Ctr. Santa Cruz, 1984-85; clin. instr. dept. family and cmty. preventive medicine Stanford U., Santa Cruz, 1984-85; staff physician Mid-Peninsula Health Svc., Palo Alto, Calif., 1986-88; dir. grad. med. edn. divsn. gerontol. Stanford (Calif.) U., 1986-93, Agy. for Health Care Policy Rsch. fellow Sch. Medicine, 1991-94, asst. prof. medicine, 1996-99, assoc. prof. medicine, 1999—, program dir. Ctr. for Primary Care and Outcomes Rsch., 1998—, Faculty fellow Inst. for Rsch. on Women and Gender, 2000; sect. chief for gen. internal medicine Palo Alto (Calif.) VA Med. Ctr., 1994-96, rsch. assoc. health svcs. R&D, 1996—; assoc. dir. clin. svcs. The VA Geriatric Rsch. Edn. and Clinical Ctr., Palo Alto, 1999—; asoc. prof. Stanford (Calif.) U. Editor Computer Ctr. Pubs., N.Y.C., 1971-72; computer programmer Columbia U., N.Y.C., 1972-73; governing coun. evidence-based practice ctr. U. Calif., Stanford, 1998—. Author chpt. to book; contbr. articles to profl. jours. Recipient Clin. Practice Guildelines for Hypertension award, VA Hlth. Svc. Rsch. & Devel., 1997, Practice Guidelines Multisite Study award, 2000, Intelligent Critiquing of Med. Records award, NIH/NLM, 2001. Fellow Am. Geriat. Soc. (bd. dirs. 1996—); mem. Am. Bd. Family Practice (bd. dirs. 1993-98), Am. B. Internal Medicine, Geriatric Test Com., Am. Bd. Family Practice. Office: VA Palo Alto Health Care Sys GRECC 182B 3801 Miranda Ave Palo Alto CA 94304-1207 E-mail: goldstein@stanford.edu

GOLDSTEIN, MICHAEL GERALD, lawyer, director; b. St. Louis, Sept. 21, 1946; s. Joseph and Sara G. (Finkelstein) G.; m. Ilene Marcia Ballin, July 19, 1970; children: Stephen Eric, Rebecca Leigh. BA, Tulane U., 1968; JD, U. Mo., 1971; LLM in Taxation, Washington U., 1972. Bar: Mo. 1971, U.S. Dist. Ct. (ea. dist.) Mo. 1972, U.S. Tax Ct. 1972, U.S. Ct. Appeals (8th cir.) 1974, U.S. Supreme Ct. 1976. Atty. Morris A. Shenker, St. Louis, 1972-78; ptnr. Lashly, Caruthers, Baer & Hamel and predecessor, St. Louis, 1979-84, Suelthaus & Kaplan, P.C. and predecessors, St. Louis, 1974-91; ptnr., chmn. dept. tax & estate planning Husch & Eppenberger, 1991-99; pres., CEO 1st Fin. Resources, 1999—; sr. v.p. EPS Fin. Solutions Corp., 1999-2000. Adj. prof. tax law Washington U. Sch. Law, 1986-97; planning com. Mid-Am. Tax Confs., chmn. ALI/ABA Tax Seminar; lectr., author taxation field. Author: BNA Tax Mgmt. Portfolios, ABA The Insurance Counselor Books; contbr. articles to profl. jours. Bd. dirs. Jewish Family and Children's Svc. St. Louis, 1980—, pres., 1986-88; bd. dirs. Jewish Fedn. of St. Louis; trustee United Hebrew Temple, 1986-88; grad. Jwish Fedn. St. Louis Leadership Devel. Coun.; co-chmn. lawyers divsn. Jewish Fedn. St. Louis Campaign, 1981-82, Leadership St. Louis, 1988-89. Capt. USAR, 1970-78. Fellow Am. Coll. Tax Counsel, Am. Coll. Trust and Estate Counsel; mem. ABA (chmn. tax seminar, group editor newsletter for taxation sect.), Am. Law Inst., Mo. Bar Assn., Bar Assn. Met. St. Louis, St. Louis County Bar Assn. Home: 2011 Yacht Mischief Newport Beach CA 92660-6713 Office: 18101 Von Karman Ste 540 Irvine CA 92612

GOLDSTEIN, MICHAEL L. neurologist; b. Chgo., June 14, 1945; s. Charles and Dorothy (Mack) G.; m. Barbara Joan Kaplan, June 18, 1967; children: Rachel, Elizabeth, Adam. AB, Princeton, 1966; MD, U. of Chgo., 1970. Intern Stanford U., 1970-71; resident in neurology Beth Israel Hosp., Boston, 1971-74; fellow in neurology Harvard U. Med. Sch., 1971-74; chief resident in neurology Children's Hosp., Boston, 1973-74; with Western Neurol. Assoc., Salt Lake City. Cons. Soc. Sec., Balt., 1990-91; bd. dirs., edn. comm. chmn. Rowland Hall, St. Marks Sch., Salt Lake City, 1986-92; examiner Am. Bd. Psychiatry and Neurology, 1987—; clin. assoc. prof. U. Utah Med. Sch., Salt Lake City, 1977—. Co-author: Managing Attention Disorders, 1990, Parent's Guide to ADD, 1993; co-producer: Educating Inattentive Children, 1992, It's Just Attention Disorder, 1993. Pres. synagogue, Salt Lake City, 1985-86. Fellow Am. Acad. Pediat., Am. Acad. Neurology (chair practice com, 1995-2000, treas. 2001—). Office: Western Neurol Assn 1151 E 3900 S Salt Lake City UT 84124-1216

GOLDSTEIN, MICHAEL SAUL, sociologist; b. N.Y.C., Aug. 1, 1944; s. Abraham J. and Rose G.; m. Laura Geller, Dec. 23, 1979 (div. May 1992); children: Joshua, Adam, Elana. BA, Queens Coll., Flushing, N.Y., 1965; MA, Brown U., Providence, 1967, PhD, 1971. Lectr. Brown U., Providence, 1970-71; asst. prof. Sch. Pub. Health, UCLA, 1971-78, assoc. prof., 1978-88, prof., 1988—, chair dept. community health, 1988-91. Author: The Health Movement, 1992; author, editor: 50 Simple Things You Can Do to Save Your Life, 1992. Mem. APHA, Am. Sociol. Assn. Soc. for Study Social Problems, Hastings Inst. Soc. Ethics and the Life Scis. Office: UCLA Sch Pub Health po bOX 95177 Los Angeles CA 90024

GOLDSTEIN, MORRIS, retired entertainment company executive; b. Pitts., Feb. 2, 1945; s. Irving and Clara (Caplan) G.; m. Diane Donna Davis, Aug. 21, 1966 (div. Nov. 1985); children: Jonathan, Julie; m. Kathy Evelyn Niemeier, July 7, 1990. BS, Carnegie Inst. Tech., 1967; MBA, U. Pa., 1979. Sales rep. computer divsn. RCA, Cherry Hill, N.J., 1968-70; sales mgr. Sedgwick Printout Sys., Princeton, 1970-76, pres., 1976-80; v.p. Courier-Jour. Louisville Times, 1980-81; mgr. bus. devel. Ziff-Davis Pub., N.Y.C., 1982-2000; pres. Information Access Corp. divsn., Foster City, Calif., 1982-2000; pres., COO Imagination Network Inc., Oakhurst, 1994; sr. v.p. Ziff-Davis Pub., Foster City, 1994; CEO Info. Access Co., A Thomson Corp. Co., Foster City, 1995-96, Thomson Tech. Ventures, San Mateo, 1997; pres., CEO Alliance Gaming Inc, Las Vegas, Nev., 1997-99; pres. entertainment bus. divsn. InnoVentry LLC, Las Vegas, 1999-2000; ret., 2000. Dep mayor Mt. Laurel Twp., N.J., 1974-78. Home: 3581 E Maule Ave Las Vegas NV 89120-2918

GOLDSTEIN, SIR NORMAN, dermatologist; b. Bklyn. July 14, 1934; s. Joseph H. and Bertha (Docteroff) G.; B.A., Columbia Coll., 1955; M.D., SUNY, 1959; m. Ramsay, Feb. 14, 1980; children: Richard, Heidi. Intern, Maimonides Hosp., N.Y.C., 1959-60; resident Skin and Cancer Hosp., 1960-61, Bellevue Hosp., 1961-62, NYU. Postgrad. Center, 1962-63 (all N.Y.C.); ptnr. Honolulu Med. Group, 1967-72; practice medicine specializing in dermatology, Honolulu, 1972—; clin. prof. dermatology U. Hawaii Sch. Medicine, 1973—; bd. dirs. Pacific Laser. Bd. dirs. Skin Cancer Found., 1979—; trustee Dermatol. Found., 1979-82, Hist. Hawaii Found., 1981-87; pres. Hawaii Theater Ctr., 1985-89, Hawaii Med. Libr., 1987; mem. Oahu Heritage Council, 1986-94. Served with U.S. Army, 1960-67. Recipient Henry Silver award Dermatol. Soc. Greater N.Y., 1963; Husik award NYU, 1963; Spl. award Acad. Dermatologia Hawaiiana, 1971, Outstanding Scientific Exhibit award Calif. Med. Assn., 1979, Special award for Exhibit Am. Urologic Assn., 1980, Svc. to Hawaii's Youth award Adult Friends for Youth, 1991, Nat. Cosmetic Tattoo Assn. award, 1993, Cmty. Svc. award Am. Acad. Dermatology, 1993; named Physician of Yr., Hawaii Med. Assn., 1993. Fellow ACP, Am. Acad. Dermatology (Silver award 1972), Am. Soc. Lasers Medicine & Surgery, Royal Soc. Medicine; mem. Internat. Soc. Tropical Dermatologists (Hist. and Culture award), Soc. Investigative Dermatologists, AAAS, Am. Soc. Photobiology, Internat. Soc. Cryosurgery, Am. Soc. Micropigmentation Surgery, Pacific and Asian Affairs Council, Navy League, Assn. Hawaii Artists, Biol. Photog. Assn., Health Sci. Communication Assn., Internat. Pigment Cell Soc., Am. Med. Writers Assn., Physicians Exchange of Hawaii (bd. dirs.), Am. Coll. Cryosurgery, Internat. Soc. Dermatol. Surgery, Am. Soc. Preventive Oncology, Soc. for Computer Medicine, Am. Assn. for Med. Systems and Info., Japan Am. Soc. Hawaii (bd. dirs.), Pacific Telecom Council, Hawaii State Med. Assn. (mem. public affairs com.), Hawaii Dermatol. Soc. (sec.-pres.), Hawaii Public Health Assn., Pacific Dermatol. Assn., Pacific Health Research Inst., Honolulu County Med. Soc. (gov.), Nat. Wildlife Fedn., C. of C., Preservation Action, Am. Coll. Sports Medicine, Rotary, Hemlock Soc. USA (med. bd.), Hawaii Govs. Blue Ribbon Panel on Living and Dying with Dignity, Ancient Gaelic Nobilitary Soc. (named Knight of the Niadh Nask, 1995), Outrigger Canoe Club, Plaza Club (pres. bd. dirs. 1990-92), Chancellor's Club, Oahu Country Club. Editor: Hawaii Med. Jour.; contbr. articles to profl. jours. Office: Tan Sing Bldg 1128 Smith St Honolulu HI 96817-5197

GOLDSTEIN, PAUL, lawyer, educator; b. Mount Vernon, N.Y., Jan. 14, 1943; s. Martin and Hannah (Shimberg) G.; m. Jan Thompson, Aug. 28, 1977 B.A., Brandeis U., 1964; LL.B. Columbia U., 1967. Bar: N.Y. 1968, Calif. 1978. Asst. prof. law SUNY-Buffalo, 1967-69, assoc. prof., 1969-71, prof., 1972-75; vis. assoc. prof. Stanford U., Calif., 1972-73, prof. law, 1975—, Stella W. and Ira S. Lillick prof. law, 1985—; of counsel Morrison and Foerster, San Francisco, 1988—. Author: Changing the American Schoolbook--Law, Politics and Technology, 1978, Real Estate Transactions--Cases and Materials on Land Transfer, Development and Finance, 1980, 3d edit. (with G. Korngold), 1993, Real Property, 1984, Copyright, 4 vols., 2d edit., 1996, Copyright, Patent, Trademark and Related State Doctrines--Cases and Materials on the Law of Intellectual Property, Rev. 4th edit., 1999, Copyright's Highway: From Gutenberg to the Celestial Jukebox, 1995, International Copyright Law, 2001, International Intellectual Property Law, 2001. Mem. Assn. Litteraire et Artistique Internationale, Copyright Soc. U.S.A. Office: Stanford U Law Sch Nathan Abbott Way Stanford CA 94305 E-mail: paulgold@stanford.edu

GOLDSTEIN, WALTER ELLIOTT, biotechnology executive; b. Chgo., Nov. 28, 1940; s. Henry Harold and Dorothy (Davidson) G.; m. Paula G. Copen, Feb. 18, 1962; children: Susan, Marc. BS in Chem. Engring., Ill. Inst. Tech., 1961; MBA, Mich. State U., 1968; MSChemE, U. Notre Dame, 1971, PhDChemE, 1973. Registered profl. engr., Ind. Process devel. engr. Linde div. Union Carbide, Tonawanda, N.Y., 1961-64; assoc. project engr. Miles Labs., Elkhart, Ind., 1964-67, assoc. rsch. scientist, 1967-72, rsch. scientist, 1972-73, rsch. supr., 1973-76; mgr. chem. engring. rsch. & pilot svcs. Chem. Engring. Rsch. & Pilot Svcs., Elkhart, 1976-78, dir., 1978-82; chem. engring. rsch. v.p. Biotech. Group, Elkhart, 1982-87; v.p. R&D ESCAgenetics Corp., San Carlos, Calif., 1987-94; pres. Goldstein Cons. Co., Foster City, 1994—; co-founder Transcyte Corp., Inc., 1996—, Phytonic Corp., 2001—. Adj. prof. chem. engring. U. Notre Dame, 1974-75, San Jose State U., 1995—; cons. Bernard Wolnak, Chgo., 1987 Contbr. chpts. to books; inventions and publs. in chem. engring., pharm., food, diagnostics and biotech. field. Vice-pres. B'nai B'rith, South Bend., Ind., 1978-89. Mem. AAAS, Am. Chem. Soc., Am. Soc. Pharmocognosy, Soc. for Competitive Intelligence Profls., Am. Inst. Chem. Engrs., N.Y. Acad. Scis., Inst. Food Technologists, Sigma Xi. Jewish. Avocations: reading, computers, outdoor sports, social/charitable causes. E-mail: goldconsul@aol.com

GOLDSTINE, STEPHEN JOSEPH, college administrator; b. San Francisco, Nov. 16, 1937; s. Edgar Nathan and Regina Thelma (Benno) G.; m. Emily Raechel Miller Keeler, Apr. 12, 1981; children: Rachel, Bettina, Simone Massimiliana Student, Calif. Sch. Fine Arts, 1951, 58; B.A., U. Calif., Berkeley, 1961, postgrad. in philosophy, 1962-67. Teaching asst. rhetoric dept. U. Calif., Berkeley, 1963-66; asst. prof. St. Mary's Coll., Moraga, Calif., 1964-70, chmn. art dept., 1969-70; cons. Freeman & Gossage, San Francisco, 1967-69; dir. neighborhood arts program Art Commn. City and County San Francisco, 1970-77; exec. sec. Mayor's Interagency Com. for Arts, San Francisco, 1971-75; founding dir. Performing Arts for the Third Age, San Francisco, 1973; co-dir. Rockefeller Tng. Fellowships in Mus. Edn., San Francisco, 1975; pres. San Francisco Art Inst., 1977-86; dir. grad. programs Calif. Coll. Arts and Crafts, 1986—; visiting faculty San Francisco State U. Sr. cons. Daniel Solomon Architects and Planners, 1988; mem. chancellor's adv. bd. Univ. Art Mus., U. Calif., Berkeley, 1979—, exec. com., trustee San Francisco Arts Edn. Found., 1985—; mem. prominent orgns. panel Calif. Arts Coun., 1981, vice chmn., 1983, chmn., 1985-87; chmn. invited session Am. Philos. Assn. (pacific div.), 1986, lectr. UCLA, 1976, Stanford U., 1966, Harvard U., 1976, 71; docent Lycee Internat. Franco-Americain, 1993—. Editor: Western Round Table on Modern Art, 1993; co-prodr., co-dir. (film) Walz um die Wände hoch zu gehen, 1999. Conductor The Art Orch., Calif. Palace of the Legion of Honor, 1997. Democrat. Jewish. Home: 1331 Green St San Francisco CA 94109-1926 Office: Calif Coll Arts Crafts 1111 Eighth St San Francisco CA 94107-2206 E-mail: mrgoldstine@earthlink.net

GOLDWATER, BERT M. federal judge; Apptd. bankruptcy judge U.S. Dist. Ct. Nev., 1995. Office: Fed Bldg US Courthouse 300 Booth St Rm 1109 Reno NV 85909

GOLITZ, LOREN EUGENE, dermatologist, pathologist, clinical administrator, educator; b. Apr. 7, 1941; s. Ross Winston and Helen Francis (Schupp) G.; m. Deborah Burd Frazier, June 18, 1966; children: Carrie Campbell, Matthew Ross. MD, U. Mo., Columbia, 1966. Diplomate Am. Bd. Dermatology, Nat. Bd. Med. Examiners. Intern USPHS Hosp., San Francisco, 1966-67, med. resident, 1967-69, resident in dermatology S.I., N.Y., 1969-71, dep. chief dermatology, 1972-73; vis. fellow dermatology Columbia-Presbyn. Med. Ctr., N.Y.C., 1971-72; asst. in dermatology Coll. Physicians Surgeons, Columbia, N.Y.C., 1972-73; vice-chmn. Residency Rev. Com. for Dermatology, 1983-85; assoc. prof. dermatology, pathology Med. Sch. U. Colo., Denver, 1974-88, prof., 1988-97, clin. prof. pathology, dermatology, 1997—. Chief dermatology Denver Gen. Hosp., 1974-97; med. dir. Ambulatory Care Ctr., Denver Gen. Hosp., 1991-97. Mem. editl. bd. Jour. Cutaneous Pathology, Jour. Am. Acad. Dermatology, Advances in Dermatology (editl. bd. Current Opinion in Dermatology); contbr. articles to med. jours. Fellow Royal Soc. Medicine; mem. AMA (residency rev. com. for dermatology 1982-89, dermatopathology test com. 1979-85), AAAS, Am. Soc. Dermatopathology (sec., treas. 1985-89, pres.-elect 1989, pres. 1990), Am. Acad. Dermatology (chmn. coun. on clin. and lab. svcs., coun. sci. assembly 1987-91, bd. dirs. 1987-91, chmn. joint dermatopathology com.), Soc. Pediat. Dermatology (pres. 1981), Soc. Investigative Dermatology, Pacific Dermatol. Assn. (exec. com. 1979-89, sec.-treas. 1984-87, pres. 1988), Noah Worcester Dermatol. Soc. (publs. com. 1980, membership com. 1989-90), Colo. Dermatol. Soc. (pres. 1978), Am. Bd. Dermatology Inc. (chmn. part II test com. 1989—, exec. com. 1993—, v.p. 1994, pres.-elect 1995, pres. 1996, dir. Emeritus, cons. to bd. 1997—), Colo. Med. Soc., Denver Med. Soc., Denver Soc. Dermatopathology, Am. Dermatol. Assn., Women's Dermatologic Soc., So. Med. Assn., Internat. Soc. Pediat. Dermatology, Am. Contact Dermatitis Soc., Am. Soc. Dermatologic Surgery, Physicians Who Care, Am. Bd. Med. Specialties (del.), N.Y. Acad. Scis., Brit. Assn. Dermatologists (hon.), Brazilian Soc. Dermatology (hon.), U. Mo. Med. Alumni Orgn. (bd. govs. 1993—). Home: 130 S Elm St Denver CO 80246-1131 Office: Dermatopathology Svc PO Box 6218 Denver CO 80206-0218

GOLLEHER, GEORGE, food company executive; b. Bethesda, Md., Mar. 16, 1948; s. George M. and Ruby Louise (Beecher) G.; div.; 1 child, Carly Lynn. BA, Calif. State U., Fullerton, 1970. Supr. acctg. J.C. Penney, Buena Park, Calif., 1970-72; systems auditor Mayfair Markets, Los Angeles, 1973, v.p., CFO, 1982-83; controller Fazio's, Los Angeles, 1974-78; group controller Fisher Foods, Ohio, 1978-79; v.p. fin. Stater Bros. Markets, Colton, Calif., 1979-82; sr. v.p., CFO Boys Markets Inc., Los Angeles, 1983-95; CEO Ralph Grocery Co., Compton, Calif., 1995-99; pres., COO Fred Meyer Inc., Portland, Oreg., 1997-99; chmn. Farrs Supermarkets, Albuquerque, 2001—. Office: Farrs Supermarkets 4411 The 25 Way NE Albuquerque NM 87109

GOLOMB, SOLOMON WOLF, mathematician, electrical engineer, educator, university official; b. Balt., May 31, 1932; s. Elhanan Hirsh and Minna (Nadel) G. A.B., Johns Hopkins U., 1951; M.A., Harvard U., 1953, Ph.D., 1957; postgrad., U. Oslo, 1955-56; DSc (hon.), Dubna Internat. U., Russia, 1995; DHL (hon.), Hebrew Union Coll., L.A., 1996. Mem. faculty Boston U., 1954-55, Harvard U., 1954-55, UCLA, 1957-61, Calif. Inst. Tech., 1960-62; sr. research engr. Jet Propulsion Lab., Pasadena, Calif., 1956-58, research group supr., 1958-60, asst. chief telecommunications research sect., 1960-63; assoc. prof. U. So. Calif., L.A., 1963-64, prof. elec. engring. and math., 1964—, vice provost for research, 1986-89, univ. prof., 1993—, dir. tech. Annenberg Ctr. for Comms., 1995-98, Viterbi prof. comms., 1997—. Cons. to govt. and industry Author: Digital Communications with Space Applications, 1964, 81, Polyominoes, 1965, rev. edit., 1994, Shift Register Sequences, 1967, 82, Basic Concepts in Information Theory and Coding, 1994; contbr. articles to profl. jours. Recipient Presdl. medal U. So. Calif., 1985, Lomonosov medal Russian Acad. Sci., 1994, Kapistsa medal Russian Acad. Natural Scis., 1995. Fellow IEEE (Shannon award Info. Theory Soc. 1995), AAAS; mem. NAE, AAUP, Internat. Sci. Radio Union, Russian Acad. Natural Scis. (fgn.), Am. Math. Soc., Math. Assn. Am., Soc. Indsl. and Applied Math., Golden Key, Phi Beta Kappa, Sigma Xi, Pi Delta Epsilon, Eta Kappa Nu, Phi Kappa Phi. Office: U So Calif Univ Park Dept Elec Engring Eeb 504A Los Angeles CA 90089-0001

GOLTZ, ROBERT WILLIAM, physician, educator; b. St. Paul, Sept. 21, 1923; s. Edward Victor and Clare (O'Neill) G.; m. Patricia Ann Sweeney, Sept. 27, 1945; children: Leni, Paul Robert. B.S., U. Minn., 1943, M.D., 1945. Diplomate: Am. Bd. Dermatology (pres. 1975-76). Intern Ancker Hosp., St. Paul, 1944-45; resident in dermatology Mpls. Gen. Hosp., 1945-46, 48-49, U. Minn. Hosp., 1949-50; practice medicine specializing in dermatology Mpls., 1950-65; clin. instr. U. Minn. Grad. Sch., 1950-58, clin. asst. prof., 1958-60, clin. assoc. prof., 1960-65, prof., head dept. dermatology, 1971-85; prof. medicine and dermatology U. Calif., San Diego, 1985—, acting chair divsn. dermatology, 1995-97; prof. dermatology, head div. dermatology U. Colo. Med. Sch., Denver, 1965-71. Former editorial bd.: Archives of Dermatology; editor: Dermatology Digest. Served from 1st lt. to capt., M.C. U.S. Army, 1946-48. Mem. Assn. Am. Physicians, Am. Dermatol. Assn. (dir. 1976-79, pres. 1985-86), Am. Soc. Dermatopathology (pres. 1981), Am. Dermatologic Soc. Allergy and Immunology (pres. 1981), AMA (chmn. sect. on dermatology 1973-75), Dermatology Found. (past dir.), Minn. Dermatol. Soc., Soc. Investigative Dermatology (pres. 1972-73, hon. 1988), Histochem. Soc., Am. Acad. Dermatology (pres. 1978-79, past dir.) (hon.), Brit. Assn. Dermatology (hon.), Chilean Dermatology Soc. (hon.), Colombian Dermatol. Soc. (corr. mem.), Can. Dermatol. Soc. (hon. mem.), Pacific Dermatol. Soc. (hon.-mem.), S. African Dermatol. Soc. (hon. mem.), N.Am. Clin. Dermatol. Soc., Assn. Profs. Dermatology (sec.-treas. 1970-72, pres. 1973-74), West Assn. Physicians. Home: 6097 Avenida Chamnez La Jolla CA 92037-7404 Office: U Calif San Diego Med Ctr Divsn Dermatology H-8420 200 W Arbor Dr San Diego CA 92103-1911

GOMES, WAYNE REGINALD, academic administrator; b. Modesto, Calif., Nov. 15, 1938; s. Frank C. and Mary (Rogers) G.; m. Carol L. Gerlach, Sept. 2, 1964 (deceased); children: John Charles, Regina Carol. BS, Calif. Poly. State U., 1960; MS, Wash. State U., 1962; PhD, Purdue U., 1965. Asst. prof. dairy sci. Ohio State U., Columbus, 1965-69, assoc. prof. dairy sci., 1969-72, prof. dairy sci., 1972-81; prof., head dept. dairy sci. U. Ill., Urbana, 1981-85, prof., head dept. animal scis., 1985-89, acting dean Coll. Agr., 1988-89, dean, 1989-95; v.p. agr. and natural resources U. Calif. System, Oakland, 1995—. Fulbright prof. Zagreb U., Yugoslavia, 1974; vis. scholar Kyoto U., Japan, 1980; mem. bd. on agr. and natural resources NRC. Editor: The Testis, Vols. 1-4, 1970-77; contbr. over 100 articles to jours. and chpts. to books. Mem. Coun. for Agrl. Sci. and Tech., Am. Soc. of Animal Sci., Am. Dairy Sci. Assn., Soc. for Study of Reprodn., Endocrine Soc., others. Lodge: Rotary. Office: U Calif 1111 Franklin St Oakland CA 94607-5201

GOMO, STEVEN J. technical communications product company executive; BSBA, Oreg. State U.; MBA, Santa Clara U. Numerous positions to gen. mgr. inkjet mfg. ops. Hewlett-Packard Co., 1974-98; sr. v.p., CFO Silicon Graphics Inc., Mountain View, Calif., 1998—. Bd. dirs. Hello Direct Inc. Office: Silicon Graphics Inc 1600 Amphitheatre Pkwy Mountain View CA 94043-1351

GONG, HENRY, JR. physician, researcher; b. Tulare, Calif., May 23, 1947; s. Henry and Choy (Low) G.; m. Janice Wong; children: Gregory, Jaimee. BA, U. of the Pacific, 1969; MD, U. Calif., Davis, 1973. Diplomate Am. Bd. Internal Medicine, 1977, Pulmonary Disease subspecialty bd., 1980. Resident in medicine Boston U., 1973-75; fellow in pulmonary medicine UCLA Med. Ctr., 1975-77; asst. prof., then assoc. prof. Sch. Medicine UCLA, 1977-89, prof. medicine, 1989-93; assoc. chief pulmonary div. UCLA Med. Ctr., 1985-92; chief Environ. Health Svc. Rancho Los Amigos Med. Ctr., 1993—; prof. medicine U. So. Calif., 1993—, prof. preventive medicine, 1997—. Dir. Environ. Exposure Lab., UCLA, 1988-93; chmn. dept. medicine Rancho Los Amigos Med. Ctr., 1996—; mem. pub. health and socio-econs. task force South Coast Air Quality Mgmt. Dist., El Monte, Calif., 1989-90. Contbr. over 300 articles to rsch. publs., chpts. to books; editorial bd. Jour. Clin. Pharmacology, 1983—, Am. Jour. Critical Care, 1992—, Arch Environ. Health, 2000—. Elder on session Pacific Palisades Presbyn. Ch., 1984-86, 89-91. Fellow Am. Coll. Chest Physicians (pres. Calif. chpt. 1991-92), Am. Coll. Clin. Pharmacology; mem. Am. Thoracic Soc., Am. Fedn. Clin. Rsch., Western Soc. Clin. Investigation, Phi Eta Sigma. Avocation: travel. Office: Environ Health Svc Rancho Los Amigos Med Ctr 7601 Imperial Hwy Downey CA 90242-3456

GONG, MAMIE POGGIO, elementary education educator; b. San Francisco, June 26, 1951; d. Louis and Mary Lee (Lum) G.; m. Andy Anthony Poggio. BA, U. Calif., Berkeley, 1973, postgrad., 1981-83, MEd, 1982. Tchr. Oakland (Calif.) Unified Sch. Dist., 1974-84, Palo Alto (Calif.) Unified Sch. Dist., 1984-91. Cons., writer Nat. Clearinghouse for Bilingual Edn., Washington, 1984; cons. ARC Assocs., Oakland, 1983; rsch. asst. dept. edn. Stanford U., 1987-89. Co-author: Promising Practices: A Teacher Resource, 1984. Recipient Kearney Found. award, 1969, others. Mem. Tchrs. English to Speakers Other Langs. (presenter 1990 conf.), Calif. Assn. Tchrs. English to Speakers Other Langs. Democrat. Office: Palo Alto Unified Sch Dist 25 Churchill Ave Palo Alto CA 94306-1099

GONICK, HARVEY CRAIG, nephrologist, educator; b. Winnipeg, Man., Can., Apr. 10, 1930; s. Joseph Wolfe and Rose (Chernick) G.; m. Gloria Granz, Dec. 16, 1967; children: Stefan, Teri, Julie, Suzanne. BS in Chemistry, UCLA, 1951; MD, U. Calif., San Francisco, 1955. Diplomate Am. Bd. Internal Medicine, Am. Bd. Nephrology. Intern Peter Bent Brigham Hosp., 1955-56; fellow in nephrology Mass. Meml. Hosp., 1956-57; fellow in nephrology, resident in internal medicine Wadsworth VA Hosp., Los Angeles, 1959-61, clin. investigator, 1961-64, chief metabolic balance unit, 1964-67; instr. medicine Sch. Medicine, UCLA, 1961-64, asst. prof., 1964-69, assoc. prof., 1969-72, adj. assoc. prof., 1972-76, adj. prof., 1976—, assoc. chief div. nephrology, 1965-72, co-dir. Bone and Stone Clinic, 1972-76, coordinator postgrad. nephrology edn., 1975-78; mem. staff St. John's Hosp., Santa Monica, Calif., Century City Hosp., L.A., med. dir. dialysis unit, 1972-79, chief medicine, 1978-79; mem. staff Cedars-Sinai Med. Ctr., L.A., dir. trace element lab., 1979-96, clin. chief nephrology, 1983-85, coord. renal tng., dir. hypertension rsch., 1996—; practice medicine specializing in nephrology Los Angeles, 1972-94. Co-founder, med. dir. Berkeley East Dialysis Unit, Santa Monica, 1971-75; co-founder, cons. Kidney Dialysis Care Units Inc., Lynwood, Calif., 1971-78; co-dir. Osteoporosis Prevention and Treatment Ctr., Santa Monica, 1987-93; mem. numerous adv. coms. to state and fed. agys., 1969-83. Contbr. articles to profl. jours.; editor: Current Nephrology, 1977-96. Served to capt. M.C., USAF, 1957-59. Fellow Charles Nelson Fund, Kaiser Found., NIH; recipient Oliver P. Douglas Meml. award Los Angeles County Heart Assn., 1959, Vis. Scientist award Deutscher Academischer Austauschendienst, 1978. Fellow ACP; mem. AMA, AAAS, Internat. Soc. Nephrology (organizing com. internat. cong. 1984), Am. Soc. Nephrology, European Dialysis and Transplant Assn., Soc. Exptl. Biology and Medicine, Calif. Med. Assn., Los Angeles County Med. Assn., Nat.

Kidney Found. (active ann. conf. 1963-65, sec. nat. med. adv. coun. 1969-70, regional rep. and legis. com. nat. med. adv. coun. 1970-73, grantee 1963), So. Calif. Kidney Found. (chmn. sci. adv. coun. 1968-70, co-chmn. legis. com. 1970-73, bd. dirs. 1974-83, honoree 1979), Am. Soc. Bone and Mineral Rsch., Am. Coll. Toxicology, Soc. Toxicology, Am. Heart Assn. (renal sect. of coun. on circulation), Am. Fedn. Clin. Rsch., Western Soc. Clin. Rsch., Western Assn. Physicians, Phi Beta Kappa, Sigma Xi, Alpha Omega Alpha, Phi Eta Sigma, Alpha Mu Gamma, Phi Lambda Upsilon. Avocation: tennis. Office: Cedars Sinai Med Ctr Ste 995 W Tower 8700 Beverly Blvd Los Angeles CA 90048-1865

GONSER, THOMAS HOWARD, lawyer, former bar association executive; b. Berkeley, Calif., May 8, 1938; s. William Adam and Alice Gertrude (Lease) G.; m. Stephanie Jane Griffiths, Nov. 27, 1960; children: Thomas Howard, Catherine Ruth. AA, U. Calif., Berkeley, 1958, BA in Polit. Sci., 1960, JD, 1965. Bar: Calif. 1965, Idaho 1970. Atty. S.P. Co., San Francisco, 1965-68; asst. gen. counsel Boise Cascade Corp., Idaho, 1969-72, assoc. gen. counsel, 1972-81, asst. sec., 1972-81; exec. dir. ABA, Chgo., 1981-87, exec. v.p., COO, 1987, also bd. dirs. Author: The Bar Foundation, 1979. Served with U.S. Army, 1960-62. Fellow Am. Bar Found.; mem. Internat. Bar Assn. (dep. sec. gen. 1982-86), Am. Law Inst., Nat. Conf. Bar Founds. (pres. 1980-81), Nat. Ctr. Preventive Law (trustee 1988—), ABA (chmn. task force on preventive law 1996—), Econ. Club Chgo. Methodist. Office: T H Gonser & Associates 4841 E Harbor Dr Friday Harbor WA 98250-9322

GONZALES, RICHARD L. protective services official; AA in Fire Sci. Tech., Red Rocks C.C., 1988; BS summa cum laude in Bus. Adminstrn., Regis U., 1991; MA, Harvard U., 1991; student, U. Colo. Firefighter Denver Fire Dept., 1972-75, mem. fire prevention bureau, dist. 5 roving officer, 1976-79, mem. training divsn., 1980-81, dist. roving officer firefighter, 1981-82, capt. firefighter pumper 2 and 27, 1982-85, asst. chief, 1985-87, chief fire dept., 1987—. Mem. Nat. Fire Protective Assn. Urban Fire Forum, Internat. Assn. Fire Chiefs, Metro Fire Chiefs Assn., Denver Metro Fire Chiefs Assn., Colo. State Fire Chiefs Assn., Urban Fire Forum, IAFF Local 858 Negotiating Team; bd. trustees Nat. Fire Protection Assn., 1992-95. Mem. adv. bd. U. Colo. Denver Sch. of Pub. Affairs, Red Rocks C.C., Denver Ptnrs., KAZY Denver Marathon; bd. trustees Nat. Multiple Sclerosis Soc.; bd. dirs. Rocky Mountain Poison Drug Found., Chic Chicana, Golden Gloves Charity. Recipient Outstanding Achievement award Hispanics of Colo., 1987; named Young Firefighter of the Yr., 1981. Office: Denver Fire Dept 745 W Colfax Ave Denver CO 80204-2612

GONZALES, RICHARD STEVEN, broadcast executive; b. San Diego, Apr. 25, 1954; s. Lawrence Avila and Catalina Victoria (Salvaterra) G.; m. Tara Norcross Siler, Oct. 12, 1991; 1 child, Diego Siler. BA in Psychology and Social Relations, Harvard U., 1977. Pub. affairs dir. KPFA-FM, Berkeley, Calif., 1979-85; frelance prod. KQED-TV, San Francisco, 1986; fgn. affairs corr., State Dept. Nat. Pub. Radio, Washington, 1986-90, White House corr., 1990-93, congl. corr., 1993-94, reporter, nat. affairs corr., for All Things Considered, Morning Edition and Weekend Edition San Francisco, 1995—. Documentary: Street Children in Maputo, 1988. Co-founder Familias Unidas, Richmond, Calif., 1980. Recipient Media award World Hunger Inc., N.Y.C., 1988, Thomas Starke award World Affairs Coun. No. Calif., San Francisco, 1984; John S. Knight fellow Stanford U., 1994-95. Office: Nat Pub Radio 2601 Mariposa St San Francisco CA 94110-1426

GONZALES, RON, mayor, former county supervisor; b. San Francisco; m. Alvina Gonzales; 3 children: Miranda, Rachel, Alejandra. BA in Community Studies, U. Calif., Santa Cruz. Formerly with Sunnyvale (Calif.) Sch. Dist., City of Santa Clara, Calif.; then human resource mgr. Hewlett Packard Co.; market program mgmt. cons. state and local govts.; mem. city coun. City of Sunnyvale, 1979-87, mayor, 1982, 87; mem. bd. suprs. Santa Clara County, 1989-96; edn. program mgr. Hewlett Packard Co., 1996-98; mayor San Jose, Calif., 1999—. Bd. chair, 1993; bd. transit suprs. Santa Clara County, 1989—; bd. dirs. Joint Venture: Silicon Valley, The Role Model Program, Bay Area Biosci. Ctr., Am. Leadership Forum, Santa Clara County. Office: City Hall Office Mayor 801 N 1st St Rm 600 San Jose CA 95110-1704

GONZALES, STEPHANIE, state official; b. Santa Fe, Aug. 12, 1950; 1 child, Adan Gonzales. Degree, Loretto Acad. for Girls. Office mgr. Jerry Wood & Assocs., 1973-86; dep. sec. of state Santa Fe, 1987-90; sec. of state Santa Fe, 1991-99; state dir. rural devel. U.S. Dept. of Agriculture, Albuquerque, 1999—. Bd. dirs. N.Mex. Pub. Employees Retirement, N.Mex. State Convassing Bd., N.Mex. Commn. Pub. Records. Mem. exec. bd. N.Mex. AIDS Svc.; mem. Commn. White House Fellowships. Mem. Nat. Assn. Secs. State, United League United Latin Am. Citizens (women's coun.), Nat. Assn. Latin Elected and Appointed Ofcls. Office: Rural Devel State Office 6200 Jefferson St NE Rm 255 Albuquerque NM 87109-3434

GONZALEZ, ARTHUR PADILLA, artist, educator; b. Sacramento, July 22, 1954; s. John and Rita (Padilla) G.; m. Christine Carol Ciavarella, Feb. 11, 1988; stepchild, Nick Port. BA, Calif. State U., Sacramento, 1977, MA, 1979; MFA, U. Calif., Davis, 1981. Vis. artist La. State U., Baton Rouge, 1982-83, U. Ga., Athens, summer 1984, R.I. Sch. Design, Providence, 1985; asst. prof. U. Calif., Davis, 1985-86, Berkeley, 1987-88; vis. artist, instr. San Francisco Art Inst., 1990-91; assoc. prof. art Calif. Coll. Arts & Crafts, Oakland, 1991—. Mem. adv. bd. Calif. Craft Mus., San Francisco, 1994-95; juror Sacramento Met. Arts Commn., 1994-95. One-person shows include Sharpe Gallery, N.Y.C., 1984, 85, 86, 88, Phyllis Kind Gallery, N.Y.C., 1995, Susan Cummins Gallery, Mill Valley, Calif., 1997. Recipient awards Nat. Endowment for Arts, 1982, 84, 86, 90, Virginia Groot award, 1997. Democrat. Avocation: Polynesian dance. Home: 1713 Versailles Ave Alameda CA 94501-1650 Office: Calif Coll Arts & Crafts 5212 Broadway Oakland CA 94618-1426

GONZALEZ, IRMA ELSA, federal judge; b. 1948; BA, Stanford U., 1970; JD, U. Ariz., 1973. Law clk. to Hon. William C. Frey U.S. Dist. Ct. (Ariz. dist.), 1973-75; asst. U.S. atty. U.S. Attys. Office Ariz., 1975-79, U.S. Attys. Office (ctrl. dist.) Calif., 1979-81; trial atty. antitrust divsn. U.S. Dept. Justice, 1979; assoc. Seltzer Caplan Wilkins & McMahon, San Diego, 1981-84; judge U.S. Magistrate Ct. (so. dist.) Calif., 1984-91; ct. judge San Diego County Superior Ct., 1991-92; dist. judge U.S. Dist. Ct. (so. dist.) Calif., San Diego, 1992—. Adj. prof. U. San Diego, 1992; trustee Calif. Western Sch. Law; bd. visitors Sch. Law U. Ariz. Mem. Girl Scout Women's Adv. Cabinet. Mem. Lawyers' Club San Diego, Thomas More Soc., Inns of Ct. Office: Edward J Schwartz US Courthouse 940 Front St Ste 5135 San Diego CA 92101-8911

GONZÁLEZ-TRUJILLO, CÉSAR AUGUSTO, Chicano studies educator, writer; b. L.A., Jan. 17, 1931; s. José Andalón and Camerina (Trujillo) González; m. Bette L. Beattie, Aug. 30, 1969. BA, Gonzaga U., 1953, MA, Licentiate in Philosophy, 1954; MST, Licentiate in Sacred Theology, U. Santa Clara, 1961; postgrad., UCLA, 1962-65. Tchr. Instituto Regional Mex., Chihuahua, Mex., 1954-57; community devel. specialist Centro Laboral Méx., México D.F., Mex., 1965-68; supr. ABC Headstart East L.A., L.A., 1968-69; employment counselor Op. SER, San Diego, 1969-70; prof., founding chair dept. Chicano studies San Diego Mesa Coll., 1970-99, prof. emeritus, 1999—. Founding chairperson Raza Consortium, San Diego, 1971-72; cons. Chicano Fedn. San Diego, Inc., 1987-89. Author poetry, short fiction and criticism, 1976—. Mem. Ednl. Issues Coordinating Com., L.A., 1968-69; founding bd. dirs. Mex.-Am. Adv. Com. to Bd. of Edn., L.A., 1969. Fulbright-Hays fellow, Peru, 1982, NEH fellow, 1984; recipient Cmty. Svc. award Chicano Fedn. San Diego Inc., 1982, Teaching Excellence award Nat. Inst. Staff and Orgnl. Devel., 1993, Outstanding Tchr. San Diego Mesa Coll., 1985, 95, Editor's Choice award Poet Mag., 1993, Cesar Chavez Social Justice award, 1994, Latina Latino Indigenous People Coalition award, 1995; named Outstanding Tchr. and Scholar, Concilio of Chicano Studies for San Diego, Imperial Valley and Baja, Calif., 1990; Spl. Congl. recognition Congressman Bob Filner, 1995; AVID Writer of the Yr. award San Diego Imperial Counties, 1997, Premio Aztla'n, 2000. Mem. Am. Fedn. Tchrs., Centro Cultural De La Raza (past bd. dirs.), Poets and Writers, Asociación Internacional de Hispanistas. Democrat. Roman Catholic. Avocations: reading, travel. Office: San Diego Mesa Coll 7250 Mesa College Dr San Diego CA 92111-4902

GOODALL, JACKSON WALLACE, JR. restaurant company executive; b. San Diego, Oct. 29, 1938; s. Jackson Wallace and Evelyn Violet (Koski) G.; m. Mary Esther Buckley, June 22, 1958; children: Kathleen, Jeffery, Suzanne, Minette. BS, San Diego State U., 1960. With Foodmaker, Inc., San Diego, 1963—, pres., 1970—, CEO, 1979—, also chmn. bd. dirs. Founder, bd. dir. Grossmont Bank, La Mesa, Calif.; bd. dirs. Thrifty Drug Stores Inc., Van Camp Seafood Inc., Ralcorp.; owner, dir., bd. dirs. San Diego Padres Baseball Club. Bd. dirs. Greater San Diego Sports Assn.; mem. Pres.'s Coun. San Diego State U.; chmn. Child Abuse Prevention Found.; dir. San Diego Hall Champions. Recipient Golden Chain award, 1982, Silver Plate award Internat. Foodsvc. Mfg. Assn., 1985; named Disting. Alumni of Yr. San Diego State U., 1974, 89, Golden Chain Operator of Yr. Multi Unit Food Svc. Operators, 1988, State of Israel Man of Yr., 1987, Citizen of Yr. City Club of San Diego, 1992, Marketer of Yr. Acad. Mktg. Sci., 1992, Manchester Cmty. Svc. award, 1997; inducted into San Diego Bus. Hall of Fame, 1992. Mem. Am. Restaurant Assn., Fairbanks Ranch Country Club (founder), Univ. Club of San Diego, San Diego Intercollegiate Athletic Coun., Kadoo Club of N. Am., La Jolla Country Club. Republican. Office: Foodmaker Inc 9330 Balboa Ave San Diego CA 92123-1516

GOODALL, LEONARD EDWIN, public administration educator; b. Warrensburg, Mo., Mar. 16, 1937; s. Leonard Burton and Eula (Johnson) G.; m. Lois Marie Stubblefield, Aug. 16, 1959; children: Karla, Karen, Greg. BA, Central Mo. State U., 1958; MA, U. Mo., 1960; PhD (Kendrick C. Babcock fellow), U. Ill., 1962; AA (hon.), Schoolcraft Coll., 1977. Asst. prof. polit. sci., asst. dir. Bur. Govt. Research, Ariz. State U., Tempe, 1962-65, bur. dir., 1965-67; assoc. prof. polit. sci., assoc. dean faculties U. Ill. at Chgo. Circle, 1968-69, vice chancellor, 1969-71; chancellor U. Mich., Dearborn, 1971-79; pres. U. Nev., Las Vegas, 1979-85, prof. mgmt. and pub. adminstrn., 1985—. Cons. Ariz. Acad., Phoenix, 1964-67; dir. Peace Corps tng. program for Chile, 1965; vice chmn. bd. Comml. Bank of Nev., 1993-98; chmn. bd. Colonial Bank Nev., 1998—. Contributing editor, Canadian Moneysaver, 1997—; Author: The American Metropolis: Its Governments and Politics, 1968, rev. edit., 1975, Gearing Arizona's Communities to Orderly Growth, 1965, State Politics and Higher Education, 1976, When Colleges Lobby States, 1987, Managing Your TIAA-CREF Retirement Accounts, 1990, The World Wide Investor, 1991, Nevada Government and Politics, 1996; editor: Urban Politics in the Southwest, 1967. Mem. univ. exec. com. United Fund, 1966-67; v.p. Met. Fund, Inc.; mem. Mich. Gov.'s Commn. Long Range Planning, 1973-75, Tempe Planning and Zoning Commn., 1965-67, New Detroit Com., 1972-79; mem. Wayne County (Mich.) Planning Commn., 1973-79, vice chmn., 1976-79; mem. exec. bd. Clark County chpt. NCCJ, 1979-86; bd. dirs. Nev. Devel. Authority, 1980-86, Boulder Dam coun. Boy Scouts Am., 1980-89; bd. dirs. Nev. Power Co. Consumer Adv. Coun., 1984-90, chmn., 1986-89. Served with AUS, 1959. Mem. Am. Polit. Sci. Assn., Am. Soc. Pub. Adminstrn. (chpt. pres. 1989-90), Western Govtl. Rsch. Assn. (exec. coun. 1966-68), Dearborn C. of C. (dir. 1974-79), Phi Sigma Epsilon, Phi Kappa Phi Found. (bd. dirs. 1994-96). Lodge: Rotary. Home: 6530 Darby Ave Las Vegas NV 89146-6518 Office: U Nev Dept Pub Adminstrn Las Vegas NV 89154 E-mail: patgoodall@aol.com

GOODALL, STEPHEN C. marketing professional; Grad. in psychology, grad. in bus. adminstrn.; MBA, U. So. Calif. With J.D. Power and Assocs., 1979—, founder Detroit br. Calif., pres, COO, 1996—. Office: JD Power & Assocs 30401 Agoura Rd Agoura Hills CA 91301-2084

GOODBY, JEFFREY, advertising agency executive; Grad., Harvard Univ., 1973. Political reporter, Boston; began advt. career with J. Walter Thompson; with Hal Riney & Ptnrs. San Francisco; co-chmn., creative dir. Goodby, Silverstein & Ptnrs., San Francisco, 1983—. Office: Goodby Silverstein & Ptnrs 720 California St San Francisco CA 94108-2404

GOODCHILD, MICHAEL, geographer, educator; Prof. geography U. Calif., Santa Barbara. Recipient Scholarly Distinction in Geography award Can. Assn. Geographers, 1990. Office: U Calif Nat Ctr Geog Info & Analysis Santa Barbara CA 93106-4060

GOODE, BARRY PAUL, lawyer; b. N.Y.C., Apr. 11, 1948; s. Hy and Charlotte (Langer) G.; m. Erica Tucker, Sept. 1, 1974; children: Adam, Aaron. AB magna cum laude, Kenyon Coll., 1969; JD cum laude, Harvard U., 1972. Bar: Mass. 1972, Calif. 1975, Hawaii 1995, U.S. Dist. Ct. Mass. 1972, U.S. Dist. Ct. (no. dist.) Calif. 1975, U.S. Dist. Ct. (ctrl. dist.) Calif. 1983, U.S. Dist. Ct. Hawaii 1995, U.S. Ct. Appeals (9th cir.) 1976, U.S. Ct. Appeals (6th cir.) 1999, U.S. Supreme Ct. 1986. Spl. asst. Sen Adlai E. Stevenson III, Washington, 1972-74; assoc. McCutchen, Doyle, Brown & Enersen, San Francisco, 1974-80, ptnr., 1980-2001; legal affairs sec. Gov. Gray Davis, 2001—. Co-author: Federal Litigation Guide, 1985. Advisor Gov.'s Com. to Review Water Law, San Francisco, 1979; bd. dirs. Stanford Pub. Interest Law Found., 1979-82; bd. dirs. Coro No. Calif., 1997—. Mem. San Francisco Bar Assn. (exec. com. environ. law sect. 1989-91), Am. Law Inst. Office: Gov Gray Davis State Capitol Sacramento CA 95814

GOODE, ERICA TUCKER, internist; b. Berkeley, Calif., Mar. 25, 1940; d. Howard Edwin and Mary Louise (Tucker) Sweeting; m. Bruce Tucker (div. 1971); m. Barry Paul Goode, Sept. 1, 1974; children: Adam Nathaniel, Aaron Benjamin. BS summa cum laude, U. Calif., Berkeley, 1962, MPH, 1967; MD, U. Calif., San Francisco, 1977. Diplomate Am. Bd. Internal Medicine. Chief dietitian Washington Hosp. Ctr., Washington, 1968; pub. health nutritionist Dept. Human Resources, Washington, 1969-73; intern Children's Hosp. (now Calif. Pacific Med. Ctr.), San Francisco, 1977-78, resident, 1978-80, chief med. resident internal medicine, 1979-80; pvt. practice internal medicine San Francisco, 1980—. Expert witness med.-legal issues, Calif., 1990—; lectr., tchr. med. house staff Calif. Pacific Med. Ctr. Hosp., 1982—; assoc. prof. medicine U. Calif., San Francisco, 1984—. Contbr. articles to profl. publs. Co-chair Physicians for Clinton, No. Calif., 1992, 96. Mem. ACP, Calif. Med. Assn., Calif. Soc. Internal Medicine, San Francisco Med. Soc., U. Calif. Alumni Assn. (del.), Alpha Omega Alpha (named Best Doctor's list 1998-2001). Office: Health & Healing Clinic 2300 California St Ste 200 San Francisco CA 94115-2754 E-mail: goodeE.@sutterhealth.org

GOODENOUGH, KEITH, state legislator; b. Winstead, Conn., July 22, 1956; BS in Forestry, U. Mont. Vol. Peace Corps, Guatemala, 1980-82; mem. Wyo. Ho. Reps., Cheyenne, Wyo. Senate, Dist. 28, Cheyenne, 1996—; mem. jud. com. Wyo. Senate, Cheyenne, mem. agr., pub. lands, and water com., mem. resources com., mem. labor, health, and social svcs. com. Mem. Powder River Basin Resource Coun.; mem. Domestic Violence Polit. Action project. Mem. NRA, Wyo. Soc. for Social Change. Democrat. Office: PO Box 1852 Casper WY 82602-1852

GOODING, CHARLES ARTHUR, radiologist, physician, educator; b. Cleve., Feb. 28, 1936; s. Joseph J. and Florence G. (Pitt) G.; m. Gretchen Wagner, June 19, 1961; children: Gunnar, Justin, Britta. BA, Western Res. U., 1957; MD, Ohio State U., 1961. Intern Ohio State U. Hosp., 1961-62; resident in radiology Peter Bent Brigham Hosp., Children's Hosp. Med. Center, both Boston, 1963-65; rsch. fellow radiology Harvard Med. Sch., Boston, 1962, tchg. fellow, 1965-66; Harvard Med. Sch. fellow Hosp. for Sick Children, London, Karolinska Hosp., Stockholm, 1966; faculty U. Calif. Med. Center, San Francisco, 1967—, prof. radiology and pediatrics, 1976—, exec. vice-chmn. dept. radiology, 1974—. Pres. Radiology Rsch. and Edn. Found., 1973—, Radiology Outreach Found., 1988—; hon. mem. faculty Francesco Maroquin U. Sch. Medicine, Guatemala City. Contbr. chpts. to books.; Editor: Pediatric Radiology, 1973— ; editor: Diagnostic Radiology, 1972—; contbr. articles to profl. jours. Capt. M.C. USAR, 1967-68. Recipient Outstanding Alumni award Brigham Women's Hosp. Harvard Med. Sch., Disting. Alumnus award Ohio State U., 1986, Case Western Res. U., 1999, Beclere medal Internat. Soc. Radiology; named to Disting. Alumni Hall of Fame Cleve. Heights H.S., 1999, Top Pediat. Radiologist San Francisco mag. Fellow Am. Coll. Radiology, Coll. Radiologists (hon.), Royal Coll. Radiologists London (hon.), Armenian Radiol. Soc. (hon.); mem. Am. Roentgen Ray Soc., Assn. Univ. Radiologists, European Soc. Pediat. Radiologists (hon.), Pacific Coast Pediat. Radiologists Assn., Radiol. Soc. N.Am., Polish Radiology Soc. (hon.), Hungarian Radiology Soc. (hon.), San Francisco Med. Soc., Soc. Pediat. Radiology (v.p. 1994, pres. 1997 pres. SPR rsch. and edn. found. 1993-96, chmn., bd. dirs. 1998), Rocky Mountain Mountain Radiol. Soc. (hon.), Australian Soc. for Pediatric Imaging (hon.), Chinese Radiol. Soc. (hon.), Swiss Radiol. Soc. (hon.), Malaysian Radiol. Soc. (hon.), Vietnamese Radiol. Soc. (hon.), (French Soc. of Radiology (hon.), Indian Radiol. and Imaging Soc. (hon.), Radiol. Soc. of Pakistan (hon.), Indonesian Radiol. Soc. (hon.), Mongolian Nat. Radiol. Assn. (hon.), Nepal Radiol. Soc. (hon.), Armenian Med. Diagnostic Assn. (hon.), Brazilian Coll. Radiology (hon.), Cuban Radiol. Soc. (hon.). Office: U Calif Med Ctr Dept Radiology San Francisco CA 94143-0628

GOODING, GRETCHEN ANN WAGNER, physician, educator; b. Columbus, Ohio, July 2, 1935; d. Edward Frederick and Margaret (List) Wagner; m. Charles A. Gooding, June 19, 1961; children: Gunnar Blaise, Justin Mathias, Britta Meghan. BA magna cum laude, St. Mary of the Springs Coll., Columbus, 1957; MD cum laude, Ohio State U., 1961. Diplomate Am. Bd. Diagnostic Radiology. Intern Univ. Hosps., Columbus, 1961-62; rsch. fellow Boston City Hosp., 1962-63, Boston U., 1963-65; with dept. radiology U. Calif., San Francisco, 1975—, assoc. prof. in radiology, 1981-85, prof., vice chmn., 1986—; asst. chief radiology VA Med. Ctr., San Francisco, 1978-87, chief radiology, 1987—, chief ultrasonography, 1975—. Chair com. acad. pers. U. Calif., San Francisco, 1993-94, bd. dirs. commn. accreditation vascular labs., 1993-96. Co-editor Radiologic Clinics of N.Am., 1993—; mem. editl. bd. San Francisco Medicine, 1986—, Applied Radiology, 1987-89, Current Opinion in Radiology, 1992-93, The Radiologist, 1993—, Emergency Radiology, 1993—, Jour. Clin. Ultrasound, 1997—; guest editor Emergency Radiology, 1999; contbr. articles to profl. jours. Recipient Recognition award Inter Societal Commn. for Accreditation of Vascular Labs., 1997. Fellow Am. Coll. Radiology (mem. commn. on ultrasound 1984-00), Am. Inst. Ultrasound in Medicine (bd. govs. 1981-84, chair conv. program 1986-88, Presdl. Recognition award 1984), Am. Soc. Emergency Radiology, Soc. Radiologists U.S.; mem. AMA, San Francisco Med. Soc. (chmn. membership com. 1992-94, bd. dirs. 1996—), RSNA (course com. 1984-88, tech. exhibit com. 1992-96), Bay Area Ultrasound Soc. (pres. 1979-80), Soc. Radiologists Ultrasound (chair membership com. 1991-93, chair corp. com. 1996-97), ARRS, AUR, CRS, Calif. Med. Assn., Am. Assn. Women Radiologists (pres. 1984-85, trustee 1991-94), VA Chiefs of Radiology Assn. (pres.-elect, pres. 1994-95), San Francisco Radiol. Soc. (pres. 1990-91), Hungarian Radiol. Soc. (hon.), Pakistan Radiol. Soc. (hon.), Cuba Radiol. Soc. (hon.). Office: VA Med Ctr Radiology Svc 4150 Clement St San Francisco CA 94121-1545

GOODLAD, JOHN INKSTER, education educator, writer; b. North Vancouver, B.C., Can., Aug. 19, 1920; s. William James and Mary (Inkster) G.; m. Evalene M. Pearson, Aug. 23, 1945; children: Stephen John, Mary Paula. Teaching certificate, Vancouver Normal Sch., 1939; BA, U. B.C., 1945, MA, 1946; PhD, U. Chgo., 1949; DPS (hon.), Brigham Young U., 1995; LHD (hon.), Nat. Coll. Edn., 1967, U. Louisville, 1968, So. Ill. U., 1982, Bank Street Coll. Edn., 1984, Niagara U., 1989, SUNY Coll. Brockport, 1991, Miami U., 1991, Linfield Coll., 1993, W.Va. U., 1998; LLD (hon.), Kent State U., 1974, Pepperdine U., 1976, Simon Fraser U., 1983, U. Man., 1992; DEd (hon.), Eastern Mich. U., 1982, U. Victoria, 1998; LittD (hon.), Montclair State U., 1992; PedD (hon.), Doane Coll., 1995; LHD (hon.), U. Nebr., Lincoln, 1999, U. So. Maine, 2001. Tchr. Surrey Schs., B.C., 1939-41, prin., 1941-42; dir. edn. Provincial Sch. For Boys, B.C., 1942-46; cons. curriculum Atlanta Area Tchr. Edn. Service, 1947-49; assoc. prof. Emory U., 1949-50; prof., dir. div. tchr. edn. Agnes Scott Coll. and Emory U., 1950-56; prof., dir. U. Chgo. Center Tchr. Edn., 1956-60; prof., dir. Univ. Elem. Sch. UCLA, 1960-85, dean Grad. Sch. Edn., 1967-83; prof. U. Wash., Seattle, 1985-91; prof. emeritus, 1991—; dir. Ctr. for Ednl. Renewal U. Wash., Seattle, 1986-2000; pres. Inst. for Ednl. Inquiry, Seattle, 1992—. Chmn. Coun. on Coop. Tchr. Edn., Am. Coun. Edn., 1959-62; dir. rsch. Inst. for Devel. of Ednl. Activities, 1966-82; mem. governing bd. UNESCO Inst. for Edn., 1971-79. Author: (with others) The Elementary School, 1956, Educational Leadership and the Elementary School Principal, 1956, (with Robert H. Anderson) The Nongraded Elementary School, 1959, rev. edit., 1963, reprinted, 1987, (with others) Computers and Information Systems in Education, 1966, Looking Behind the Classroom Door, 1970, rev. edit., 1974, Toward a Mankind School, 1974, The Conventional and the Alternative in Education, 1975, Curriculum Inquiry: The Study of Curriculum Practice, 1979, Planning and Organizing for Teaching, 1963, School Curriculum Reform, 1964, The Changing School Curriculum, 1966, School, Curriculum and the Individual, 1966, The Dynamics of Educational Change, 1975, Facing the Future, 1976, What Schools Are For, 1979, A Place Called School, 1983, Teachers for Our Nation's Schools, 1990, Educational Renewal: Better Teachers, Better Schools, 1994, In Praise of Education, 1997; author, editor: The Changing American School, 1966, (with Harold S. Shane) The Elementary School in the United States, 1973, (with M. Frances Klein and Jerrold M. Novotney) Early Schooling in the United States, 1973, (with Norma Feshback and Alvima Lombard) Early Schooling in England and Israel, 1973, (with Gary Fenstermacher) Individual Differences and the Common Curriculum, 1983, The Ecology of School Renewal, 1987, (with Kenneth A. Sirotnik) School-University Partnerships in Action, 1988, (with Pamela Keating) Access to Knowledge, 1990, (with others) The Moral Dimensions of Teaching, 1990, Places Where Teachers Are Taught, 1990, (with Thomas C. Lovitt) Integrating General and Special Education, 1992, (with Timothy J. McMannon) The Public Purpose of Education and Schooling, 1997, (with Roger Soder and Timothy J. McMannon) Developing Democratic Character in the Young, 2001; mem. bd. editors Sch. Rev, 1956-58, Jour. Tchr. Edn, 1958-60; contbg. editor: Progressive Edn, 1955-58; mem. editorial adv. bd. Child's World, 1952-80; chmn. editorial adv. bd. New Standard Ency, 1953— ; chmn. ednl. adv. bd. Ency. Brit. Ednl. Corp, 1966-69; contbr. chpts. to books, articles to profl. jours. Recipient Disting. Svc. Medal Tchrs. Coll., Columbia U., 1983, Outstanding Book award Am. Ednl. Rsch. Assn., 1985, Disting. Contbns. to Ednl. Rsch. award 1993; named Faculty Rsch. Lectr. U. Wash., 1987-88, faculty of High Distinction, UCLA, 1987; Edward C. Pomeroy award, Amer. Assn. of Coll. for Teacher Edn., 1995, Disting. Svc. award Coun. Chief State Sch. Officials, 1997, Harold W. McGraw, Jr. Prize in Edn., 1999, Edn. Commn.

State James Bryant Conant award, 2000. Fellow Internat. Inst. Arts and Letters; mem. Nat. Acad. Edn. (charter; sec.-treas.), Am. Ednl. Rsch. Assn. (past pres., award for Disting. Contbns. to Ednl. Rsch. 1993), Nat. Soc. Coll. Tchrs. Edn. (past pres.), Nat. Soc. for Study of Edn. (dir.), Am. Assn. Colls. for Tchr. Edn. (pres. 1989-90). Office: U Wash Coll Edn PO Box 353600 Seattle WA 98195-3600

GOODMAN, COREY SCOTT, neurobiology educator, researcher; b. Chgo., June 29, 1951; s. Arnold Harold and Florence (Friedman) G.; m. Marcia M. Barinaga, Dec. 8, 1984. BS, Stanford U., 1972; PhD, U. Calif., Berkeley, 1977. Postdoctoral fellow U. Calif., San Diego, 1979; asst. prof. dept. biol. scis. Stanford (Calif.) U., 1979-82, assoc. prof., 1982-87; prof. neurobiology and genetics U. Calif., Berkeley, 1987—, Evan Rauch prof. neurosci., 1999—. Investigator Howard Hughes Med. Inst., 1988—, dir. Helen Wills Neurosci. Inst., 1999—. Mem. editl. bd. Cell, Neuron; assoc. editor Devel.; contbr. more than 200 articles to profl. jours. Recipient Charles Judson Herrick award, 1982, Alan T. Waterman award Nat. Sci. Bd., 1983, Javits Neurosci. Investigator award NIH, 1985, 92, NIH Merit award, 1985, Found. IPSEN Neuronal Plasticity prize, 1996, J. Allyn Taylor Internat. prize in medicine, 1996, Gairdner Found. Internat. award for achievment in med. sci., 1997, Ameritec Found. Basic Rsch. Toward Cure Paralysis prize, 1997, Wakeman award for rsch. in neurosci., 1998, March-Of-Dimes Prize in Devel. Biology, 2001. Fellow Am. Acad. Arts and Scis.; mem. NAS, Am. Philos. Soc. Office: U Calif Howard Hughes Med Inst Dept Molecular & Cell Biology Life Sci Addition Rm 519 Berkeley CA 94720-0001 E-mail: goodman@uclink4berkeley.edu

GOODMAN, JOHN M. construction executive; b. Omaha, Apr. 5, 1947; BS in Acctg., Calif. State U., Long Beach, 1970; JD, Pepperdine U., 1974. CPA, Calif.; cert. real estate broker, Calif.; cert. ins. agt., Calif.; lic. contractor, Calif. Sr. v.p., CEO, dir. Lewis Homes Mgmt. Corp., Upland, Calif. Office: Lewis Operating Corp PO Box 670 Upland CA 91785-0670

GOODMAN, JOSEPH WILFRED, electrical engineering educator; b. Boston, Feb. 8, 1936; s. Joseph and Doris (Ryan) G.; m. Hon Mai Lam, Dec. 5, 1962; 1 dau., Michele Ann. B.A., Harvard U., 1958; M.S. in E.E., Stanford U., 1960, Ph.D., 1963; DSc (hon.), U. Ala., 1996. Postdoctoral fellow Norwegian Def. Rsch. Establishment, Oslo, 1962-63; rsch. assoc. Stanford U., 1963-67, asst. prof., 1967-69, assoc. prof., 1969-72, prof. elec. engring., 1972-99; vis. prof. Univ. Paris XI, Orsay, France, 1973-74; dir. Info. Sys. Lab. Elec. Engring. Stanford U., 1981-83, chmn. dept. of elec. engring., 1988-96, William E. Ayer prof. elec. engring., 1988-99, sr. assoc. dean engring., 1996-98, acting dean engring., 1999, prof. emeritus, 2000—. Cons. to govt. and industry, 1965—; v.p. Internat. Comm. for Optics, 1985-87, pres., 1988-90, past pres., 1991-93. Author: Introduction to Fourier Optics, 1968, 2nd edit. 1996, Statistical Optics, 1985, (with R. Gray) Fourier Transforms: An Introduction for Engineers; editor: International Trends in Optics, 1991; contbr. articles to profl. jours. Recipient F.E. Terman award Am. Soc. Engring. Edn., 1971, Frederic Ives Medal, 1990, Optical Soc. Am., Ester Hoffman Beller award Optical Soc. of Am., 1995. Fellow AAAS, Optical Soc. Am. (dir. 1977-83, editor jour. 1978-83, Max Born award 1983, Frederick Ives award 1990, Esther Hoffman Beller medal 1995, v.p. 1990, pres.-elect 1991, pres. 1992, past pres. 1993), IEEE (edn. medal 1987), Soc. Photo-optical Instrumentation Engrs. (bd. govs. 1979-82, 88-90, Dennis Gabor award 1987), Am. Acad. Arts & Scis.; mem. NAE, Electromagnetics Acad. Home: 570 University Ter Los Altos CA 94022-3523 Office: Stanford U Dept Elec Engring Stanford CA 94305 E-mail: goodman@ee.stanford.edu

GOODMAN, MAX A. lawyer, educator; b. Chgo., May 24, 1924; s. Sam and Nettie (Abramowitz) G.; m. Marlyene Monkarsh, June 2, 1946; children: Jan M., Lauren A. Packard, Melanie Murez. AA, Herzl Jr. Coll., 1943; student, Northwestern U., 1946-47; JD, Loyola U., 1948; LLD (hon.), Southwestern U. Sch. Law, 2000. Bar: Calif. 1948; cert. family law specialist, 1980, 85, 90. Pvt. practice, L.A., 1948-53; ptnr. Goodman, Hirschberg & King, L.A., 1953-81; prof. Southwestern U. Sch. Law, L.A., 1966—. Lectr. Calif. Continuing Edn. of the Bar, 1971—; editorial cons. Bancroft Whitney, San Francisco, 1986—. Contbr. articles to profl. jours. Served to cpl. U.S. Army, 1943-45. Mem. ABA (chmn. law sch. curriculum com. family law sect. 1987-88, family law sect. 1987-88, 97-98), State Bar Calif. (del. conf. dels. 1972, 80-87, 91, exec. com. family law sect. 1981-85), Los Angeles County Bar Assn. (chmn. family law sect. 1971-72, editor family law handbook 1974-89). Avocation: contract bridge. Office: Southwestern U Sch Law 675 S Westmoreland Ave Los Angeles CA 90005-3905

GOODMAN, MURRAY, chemistry educator; b. N.Y.C., July 6, 1928; m. Zelda Silverman; Aug. 26, 1951; children: Andrew, Joshua, David. BS magna cum laude with honors in Chemistry, Bklyn. Coll., 1949; PhD, U. Calif., Berkeley, 1953; DSc honoris causa, CUNY, Staten Island, 1995; DSc (hon.), U. Ioannina, Greece, 1995. Asst. prof. Polytechnic Inst., Bklyn., 1956-60, assoc. prof., 1960-64, prof. chemistry, 1964-71, dir. polymer rsch. inst., 1967-71; prof. chemistry U. Calif.-San Diego, La Jolla, 1971—, chmn. dept. Chemistry, 1976-81. Vis. prof. U. Alta., Can., 1981, Lady Davis Vis. Prof., Hebrew U., Jerusalem, 1982; William H. Rauscher lectr. Rensselaer Poly. Inst., 1982; BioMega lectr. McGill U., 1998. Editor-in-chief Biopolymers Jour., 1963—; contbr. numerous articles to profl. jours. Recipient Alumnus medal Bklyn. Coll., 1964, Scoffone medal U. Padova, 1980, Humboldt award 1986-87, Max-Bergmann medal 1991, Givaudan-Roure award Assn. Chemo-reception Scis., 1992, Ralph Hirschmann award for peptide chemistry Am. Chem. Soc., 1997, Chem. Pioneer award Am. Inst. Chemists, 1997; NRC fellow Cambridge (Eng.) U., 1955-56. Fellow AAAS; mem. Internat. Union Pure Applied Chemistry, Am. Chem. Soc. (Herman F. Mark Polymer Chemistry award 2000, Arthur C. Cope Scholar award 2001), Am. Peptide Soc. (pres.; Pierce award 1989), Am. Soc. Biol. Chemists, Chem. Soc., Biophys. Soc., Protein Soc., Russian Acad. Scis. (fgn.), Phi Beta Kappa, Sigma Xi. Office: U Calif San Diego Dept Chem Biochem 6223 A Pacific Hall La Jolla CA 92093-0343

GOODMAN, OSCAR BAYLIN, mayor, lawyer; b. Phila., July 26, 1939; s. A. Allan and Laura (Baylin) G.; m. Carolyn Goldmark, June 6, 1962; children: Oscar B. Jr., Ross C., Eric A., Cara Lee. BA, Haverford Coll., 1961; JD, U. Pa., 1964. Bar: Nev., U.S. Ct. Appeals. Ptnr. Goodman, Chesnoff and Keach, Las Vegas, 1965—; mayor City of Las Vegas, 1998—. Mem. Nat. Assn. Criminal Def. Lawyers (pres. 1983). Jewish. Office: Off of the Mayor 400 Stewart Ave Las Vegas NV 89101-2927 also: Goodman Chesnoff & Keach 520 S 4th St Las Vegas NV 89101-6524

GOODMAN, PHYLLIS L. public relations executive; b. N.Y.C., Sept. 7, 1946; d. Bernard Jacob and Claire (Rosenberg) Goodman. BS, Cornell U., 1967. Ext. home economist Nassau County Ext. Svc., Mineola, N.Y., 1967-68; editl. asst. Funk & Wagnalls, N.Y.C., 1968-69; sr. v.p. Glick & Lorwin, Inc., N.Y.C., 1969-80, Sci. and Medicine, N.Y.C., 1980-82; v.p. Hill and Knowlton, Inc., N.Y.C., 1982-85; assoc. v.p. comm. and pub. affairs St. Luke's-Roosevelt Hosp. Ctr., N.Y.C., 1985-92; owner Goodman Pub. Rels., Albuquerque, 1993-95; v.p. corp. comm. Sun Healthcare Group, Inc., Albuquerque, 1995-2000; v.p. mktg. and comm. St. Vincent Hosp., Santa Fe, 2000-01. Mem. com. pub. affairs Greater N.Y. Hosp. Assn., 1988-92. Bd. dirs. Chamber Music Albuquerque, 1998—. Mem. Am. Coll. Healthcare Execs., Am. Soc. Health Care Mktg. and Pub. Rels. (treas. N.Mex. chpt. 1993-94), Pub. Rels. Soc. Am. (accredited, pres. N.Mex. chpt. 1996), Healthcare Pub. Rels. and Mktg. Soc. Greater N.Y. (pres. 1990-91), Westside C. of C. N.Y.C. (bd. dirs. 1986-92), Pi Lambda Theta. Office: [illegible] NM 87109-4373

GOODMAN, SAM RICHARD, electronics company executive; b. N.Y.C., May 23, 1930; s. Morris and Virginia (Gross) G.; m. Beatrice Bettencourt, Sept. 15, 1957; children: Mark Stuart, Stephen Manuel, Christopher Bettencourt. BBA, CCNY, 1951; MBA, NYU, 1957, PhD, 1968. Chief acct. John C. Valentine Co., N.Y.C., 1957-60; mgr. budgets and analysis Gen. Foods. Corp., White Plains, N.Y., 1960-63; budget dir. Crowell Collier Pub. Co., N.Y.C., 1963-64; v.p., chief fin. officer Nestle Co., Inc., White Plains, 1964; chief fin. officer Aileen, Inc., N.Y.C., 1973-74, Ampex Corp., 1974-76; exec. v.p. fin. and adminstrn. Baker & Taylor Co. div. W.R. Grace Co., N.Y.C., 1976-79, Magnuson Computer Systems, Inc., San Jose, Calif., 1979-81; v.p., chief fin. officer Datamac Computer Systems, Sunnyvale, 1981; pres. Nutritional Foods Inc., San Francisco, 1983-84; chmn., chief exec. officer CMX Corp., Santa Clara, Calif., 1984-88; dir., sr. v.p. Masstor Systems Corp., Santa Clara, 1988—; pvt. cons. Atherton, Calif., 1990—; sr. mgmt. cons. Durkee/Sharlit, 1991—; pres. Mayfair Packing Co., 1991—; mng. dir. Quincy Pacific Ptnrs., L.P., 1992—; pres., CEO Mayfair Packing Co., San Jose, Calif., 1991-94; pvt. cons. BMG Assocs., 1994—. Lectr. NYU Inst. Mgmt., 1965-67; asst. prof. mktg. Iona Coll. Grad. Sch. Adminstrn., 1967-69; prof. Golden Gate U., 1974—; prof. fin. and mktg. Pace U. Grad. Sch. Bus. Adminstrn., 1969-79. Author 7 books, including Controller's Handbook; contbr. articles to jours. Lt. (j.g.) USNR, 1951-55. Mem. Fin. Execs. Inst., Nat. Assn. Accts., Am. Statis. Assn., Am. Econs. Assn., Planning Execs. Inst., Am. Arbitration Assn., Turnaround Mgmt. Assn. Home and Office: 60 Shearer Dr Atherton CA 94027-3957 E-mail: bgoodman@cbnorcal.com

GOODMAN, STUART B. medical educator; b. Toronto, May 15, 1951; married. BS, U. Toronto, 1973, MD, 1978; MS, Inst. Med. Sci./U. Toronto, 1982; PhD in Med. Sci., U. Lund, 1994. Diplomate Am. Bd. Orthopaedic Surgery. Intern Toronto Gen. Hosp., 1978-79; resident orthopaedic surgery U. Toronto, 1979-84; rsch. fellow Hosp. for Sick Children, Toronto, 1979-80; orthopaedic arthritis and trauma fellow Wellesley Hosp./Sunnybrook Med. Ctr., Toronto, 1984-85; acting asst. prof., attending orthopaedic surgeon Stanford U. and Med. Ctr., 1985, asst. prof., attending orthopaedic surgeon, 1985-92; chief of orthopaedic trauma, asst. dir. surg. arthritis Stanford U. Med. Ctr., 1986-90, assoc. faculty - biomechan. engring. program, 1990—, assoc. prof. with tenure, dept. function restoration, 1992-98; head Divns. of Orthopedic Surgery Stanford U. Sch. Medicine, 1994—, assoc. chmn. functional restoration, 1997—, prof. functional restoration, 1998—. Vis. prof., lectr. numerous regional, nat. and internat. orgns. Editl. bd. Orthopaedic Capsule and Comment, 1990-92, Jour. of Arthroplasty, The Joint Letter, Jour. Biomed. Material Rsch., Jour. Applied Biomaterials; reviewer for 20 jours. in field; contbr. articles to profl. jours. and publs. Fellow ACS, Am. Acad. Orthopaedic Surgeons; mem. Royal Coll. Physicians and Surgeons of Can., Acad. Orthopaedic Soc., Assn. Bone and Joint Surgery, Orthopaedic Trauma Assn., Knee Soc., Soc. for Biomaterials, Can. Orthopaedic Assn., Calif. Orthopaedic Assn., Calif. Med. Assn., Santa Clara Orthopaedic Assn., Santa Clara Med. Assn. Office: Stanford Med Ctr Divsn Ortho Surg Sch of Medicine R-144 Stanford CA 94305-5341

GOODSTEIN, DAVID LOUIS, physics educator; b. Bklyn., Apr. 5, 1939; s. Sam and Claire (Axel) G.; m. Judith R. Koral, June 30, 1960; children: Marcia, Mark. BS, Bklyn. Coll., 1960; PhD, U. Wash., 1965. Research instr. U. Wash., Seattle, 1965-66; research fellow Calif. Inst. Tech., Pasadena, 1966-67, asst. prof., 1968-71, asso. prof., 1971-76, prof., 1976—, vice-provost, 1987—, Frank J. Gilloon disting. teaching and svc. prof., 1995—. Vis. scientist Frascati Nat. Lab., Italy, 1971— . Author: States of Matter, 1975, (with J. Goodstein) Feynman's Lost Lecture, 1996; mem. editl. bd. Il Nuovo Cimento, 1987—; contbr. articles to profl. jours.; project dir., host physics TV course The Mechanical Universe. Bd. dirs. Calif. Coun. Sci. and Tech., 1989—, Sierra Monolithics; sci. adv. com. David and Lucille Packard Found., 1988—. NSF postdoctoral fellow, 1967-68; Sloan Found. fellow, 1969-71; recipient Oersted medal, 1999, John P. McGovern Sci. and Soc. award, 2000. Fellow AAAS; mem. Am. Phys. Soc., Am. Inst. Physics. Office: Calif Inst Tech Dept Physics Pasadena CA 91125-0001 E-mail: dg@caltech.edu

GOODWIN, ALFRED THEODORE, federal judge; b. Bellingham, Wash., June 29, 1923; s. Alonzo Theodore and Miriam Hazel (Williams) G.; m. Marjorie Elizabeth Major, Dec. 23, 1943 (div. 1948); 1 son, Michael Theodore; m. Mary Ellin Handelin, Dec. 23, 1949; children: Karl Alfred, Margaret Ellen, Sara Jane, James Paul. B.A., U. Oreg., 1947; J.D., 1951. Bar: Oreg. 1951. Newspaper reporter Eugene (Oreg.) Register-Guard, 1947-50; practiced in Eugene until, 1955; circuit judge Oreg. 2d. Jud. Dist., 1955-60; assoc. justice Oreg. Supreme Ct., 1960-69; judge U.S. Dist. Ct. Oreg., 1969-71, U.S. Ct. Appeals for (9th cir.), Pasadena, Calif., 1971-88, chief judge, 1988-91, sr. judge, 1991—. Editor Oreg. Law Rev., 1950-51. Bd. dirs. Central Lane YMCA, Eugene, 1956-60, Salem (Oreg.) Art Assn., 1960-69; adv. bd. Eugene Salvation Army, 1956-60, chmn., 1959. Served to capt., inf. AUS, 1942-46, ETO. Mem. Am. Judicature Soc., Am. Law Inst., ABA (ho. of dels. 1986-87), Order of Coif, Phi Delta Phi, Sigma Delta Chi, Alpha Tau Omega. Republican. E-mila. Office: US Ct Appeals 9th Cir PO Box 91510 125 S Grand Ave Pasadena CA 91105-1621 E-mail: alfred_goodwin@ca9.uscourts.gov

GOODWIN, DORIS HELEN KEARNS, history educator, writer; b. Rockville Centre, N.Y., Jan. 4, 1943; d. Michael Alouisius and Helen Witt (Miller) Kearns; m. Richard Goodwin, 1975; three sons. BA magna cum laude, Colby Coll., 1964; PhD, Harvard U., 1968. Intern Dept. State, D.C., 1963, Ho. of Reps., 1965; rsch. assoc. U.S. Dept. Health, Edn., and Welfare, 1966; spl. asst. to Willard Wirtz U.S. Dept. Labor, 1967; spl. asst. to President Lyndon B. Johnson, 1968; asst. prof. Harvard U., Cambridge, 1969-71, assoc. prof. govt., 1972, historian. Spl. cons. to President Johnson, 1969-73; asst. dir. Inst. Politics, 1971—; hostess "What's the Big Idea", WGBH-TV, Boston, 1972; polit. analyst news desk, WBZ-TV, Boston, 1972; mem. Women's Polit. Caucus, Mass., 1972, Faculty Coun. Harvard U., 1971, Dem. Party Platform Com., 1972; trustee Wesleyan U., Colby Coll., Robert F. Kennedy Found. Author: Lyndon Johnson and the American Dream, 1976, The Fitzgeralds and the Kennedys: An American Saga, 1987, No Ordinary Time: Franklin and Eleanor Roosevelt-The Homefront in World War II, 1994 (Pulitzer Prize for history 1995); contbr.: Telling Lives: The Biographer's Art, 1979; forward: Mortal Friends: A Novel, 1992. Named Fulbright fellow, 1966, White House fellow, 1967. Mem. Am. Polit. Sci. Assn., Coun. Fgn. Relations, Women Involved, Group for Applied Psychoanalysis, Signet Soc., Phi Beta Kappa (outstanding young women of yr. award 1966), Phi Sigma Iota. Roman Catholic. Office: c/o Dori Lawson Soldier Creek Assoc 642 Gladstone St Sheridan WY 82801-5109

GOODWIN, MARTIN BRUNE, radiologist; b. Vancouver, B.C., Can., Aug. 8, 1921; came to U.S., 1948; m. Cathy Dennison, Mar. 7, 1980; 1 child, Suzanne; stepchildren: Chuck Glikas, Dianna; 1 child from previous marriage, Nancijane Goodwin Hilling. BSA in Agriculture, U. B.C., 1943, postgrad., 1943-44; MD, CM, McGill U. Med. Sch., Montreal, Can., 1948. Diplomate Am. Bd. Med. Examiners, lic. Med. Coun. Can.; cert. diagnostic and therapeutic radiology Am. Bd. Radiology; cert. Am. Bd. Nuclear Medicine. Intern Scott & White Hosp., Temple, Tex., 1948-49; fellow radiology Scott & White Clinic, 1949-52, mem. staff, 1952-53; instr. U. Tex., Galveston, 1952-53; radiologist Plains Regional Med. Ctr., Clovis, N.Mex., Portales, pres. med. staff; chief radiology De Baca Gen. Hosp., Ft. Sumner; cons. Cannon AFB Hosp., Clovis; pvt. practice radiology Clovis, Portales, Ft. Sumner and Tucumcari, 1955—. Adj. prof. health scis. Ea. N.Mex. U., 1976-77; adj. clin. prof. health scis. We. Mich. U., 1976-78 [illegible] former chmn. N.Mex. Health and Social Svcs. Bd.; mem. Regional Health Planning Coun.; treas. Roosevelt County Rep. Ctrl. Com. Capt. U.S. Army M.C., 1953-55; Col. USAF M.C., 1975-79. Fellow AAAS, Am. Coll. Radiology, Am. Coll. Radiology (past councillor); mem. Am. Soc. Thoracic Radiologists (founder), Radiol. Soc. of N.Am. (past councillor), N.Mex. Med. Soc. (various coms., chmn. joint practice com., councillor bd. dirs.), N.Mex. Radiol. Soc. (past pres.), N.Mex. Thoracic Soc. (past pres.), N.Mex. Med. Review Assn. (bd. dirs. 1970-93), N.Mex. Med. Soc. Found. for Med. Care (bd. dirs. 1975—, former v.p., former treas.), County Med. Soc. (past pres., past v.p., past sec.), Clovis C. of C. (chmn. civic affairs com., bd. dirs.), Clovis Elks Lodge (past exalted ruler), Clovis Noonday Lions Club (past sec.). Republican. Presbyterian. Home: 505 E 18th St Portales NM 88130-9201

GOODWIN, NANCY LEE, corporate executive; b. Peoria, Ill., Aug. 11, 1940; d. Raymond Darrell and Mildred Louise (Brown) G. B.A. (Nat. Meth. scholar, Nat. Merit scholar), MacMurray Coll., 1961; M.A., U. Colo., 1963; Ph.D., U. Ill., 1971. Tchr. Roosevelt Jr. High Sch., Peoria, 1961-62; counselor U. Ill., Urbana, 1963-66, staff assoc., asst. prof. edn. measurement Chgo., 1967-71; asst. v.p., assoc. prof. stats. Fla. Internat. U., Miami, 1971-78; pres. Greenfield (Mass.) Community Coll., 1978-82, Arapahoe Community Coll., Colo., from 1982; corp. owner MTF Enterprises; prof. Nat. U.; owner C.A.T.S. Inc., 1987—; corp. mgr. DRM Enterprises. Dir. Cons. Mid-Am. Computer Corp., First Chance Network U.S. Office Edn., 1972-78 Mem. Com. on Ill. Govt., Higher Edn. Task Force; mem. Vol. Action Center, Miami, 1972-78; active Girl Scouts U.S.A.; mem. Franklin/Hampshire Area Service Planning Team, 1978; incorporator Franklin County (Mass.) United Way, Farren Meml. Hosp.; adv. Franklin County Public Hosp.; bd. dirs. Women's Inst. Fla., Franklin County Arts Council, Franklin County Devel. Corp., Western Welcome Week, Inc.; bd. dirs., mem. fin. monitoring com. New Eng. Soy Dairy, 1980. Recipient Merit award Chgo. Tchrs. Assn., 1969; citation Girl Scouts U.S.A., 1973 Mem. NEA, Am. Assn. Higher Edn., Am. Edni. Research Assn., Assn. Instl. Research, Centennial C. of C. (dir. 1983) Home: 5228 Del Rey Ave Las Vegas NV 89146-1414

GORDLEY, JAMES RUSSELL, law educator; b. 1946; BA, U. Chgo., 1967, MBA, 1968; JD, Harvard U., 1970. Fellow U. Florence Inst. Law, Italy, 1970-71; assoc. Foley, Hoag & Eliot, Boston, 1971-72; fellow comparative law Harvard U., Cambridge, Mass., 1973-78; acting prof. U. Calif., Berkeley, 1978-81, prof., 1981—, Shannon Cecil Turner prof. jurisprudence, 1995—. Fellow Deutsche Forschungsgemeinschaft, 1983, sr. NATO fellow, 1991, Guggenheim fellow, 1995-96, Fulbright fellow, 1996. Fellow Am. Acad. Arts and Scis. Office: U Calif Sch Law Boalt Hall Berkeley CA 94720

GORDLY, AVEL LOUISE, state legislator, community activist; b. Portland, Oreg., Feb. 13, 1947; d. Fay Lee and Beatrice Bernice (Coleman) G.; 1 child, Tyrone Wayne Waters. BS in Adminstrn. of Justice, Portland State U., 1974; Grad. John F. Kennedy Sch. Govt., Harvard U., 1995; grad., U. Oreg. Pacific Program, 1998. Phone co. clk. Pacific West Bell, Portland, 1966-70, mgmt. trainee, 1969-70; work release counselor Oreg. Corrections Divsn., Portland, 1974-78, parole and probation officer, 1974-78; dir. youth svcs. Urban League of Portland, 1979-83; dir. So. Africa program Am. Friends Svc. Com., Portland, 1983-89, assoc. exec. sec., dir. Pacific N.W. region, 1987-90; freelance writer Portland Observer, Portland, 1988-90; program dir. Portland House of Umoja, 1991; mem. Oreg. Ho. of Reps., Portland, 1991-96, mem. joint ways and means com., adv. mem. appropriations com., rules and reorgn. com., low income housing com., energy policy rev. com., others; mem. Oreg. Senate from 10th dist., Salem, 1997—; mem. crime and corrections com., trades econ. devel. com. Oreg. Senate, 1997, mem. joint ways and means com. on pub. safety, 1997, mem. joint ways and means com. on edn., 1999. Mem. joint ways and means com. on edn., mem. gov. drug and violent crime policy bd., mem. Oreg. liquor control commn. task force, mem. sexual harrassement task force, mem. Hanford waste bd., mem. Gov.'s Commn. for Women, Gov.'s Drug and Violent Crime Policy Bd.; originator, producer, host Black Women's Forum, 1983-88; co-producer, rotating host N.E. Spectrum, 1983-88. Mem. corrections adv. com. Multnomah Cmty.; mem. adv. com. Oregonians Against Gun Violence; mem. Black Leadership Conf.; treas., bd. dirs. Black United Fund; co-founder, facilitator Unity Breakfast Com.; co-founder Sisterhood Luncheon; past project adv. bd. dirs. Nat. Orgn. Victims Assistance; past citizen chmn. Portland Police Bur.; past mem. coordinating com. Portland Future Focus Policy Com.; past coord. Cmty. Rescue Plan; past vice chmn. internat. affairs Black United Front; past sec. Urban League Portland, past vice chmn. and exec. com.; past adv. com. Black Ednl. Ctr.; past vice chmn. Desegregation Monitoring; also past adv. com., past chmn. curriculum com., founder African Am. Leg. Issues Roundtable; founder Black Women Gathering; other past orgn. coms.; elected state senate First African Am. Woman, 1996. Recipient Outstanding Cmty. Svc. award NAACP, 1986, Outstanding Women in Govt. award YWCA, 1991, Girl Scout-Cmty. Svc. award, 1991, N.W. Conf. of Black Studies-Outstanding Progressive Leadership in the African-Am. Cmty. award, 1986, Cmty. Svc. award Delta Sigma Theta, 1981, Joint Action in Cmty. Svc.-Vol. and Cmty. Svc. award, 1981, Quality of Life Photography award Pacific Power & Light Co., 1986, Am. Leadership Forum Sr. fellow, 1988, Equal Opportunity award, Urban League, 1996, Outstanding Alumni, 1996, PSU, Causa '98 En Defensa de la Comunidad award, 1997, Matrix award Assn. for Women in Comm., 1999, Pres.'s award Portland Oreg. Visitors Assn., 1999, Legacy award, Black United Fund, 2000. Mem. NAACP. Avocations: reading group, mentoring, photography, walking.

GORDON, BASIL, mathematics educator; b. Balt., Dec. 23, 1932; s. Basil and Helen (Williams) G. MA, Johns Hopkins, 1953; PhD, Calif. Inst. Tech., 1956. Instr. Calif. Inst. Tech., 1956-57; asst. prof. math. U. Calif. at Los Angeles, 1959-63, assoc. prof., 1963-67, prof., 1967-93; prof. emeritus, 1993—. Editor: Pacific Jour. Mathematics, 1969-70, 72-73, Jour. Combinatorial Theory, 1970—, Ramanujan Jour., 1997—; contbr. articles to profl. jours. Served with AUS, 1957-59. Alfred P. Sloan fellow, 1962-64 Mem. Math. Assn. Am., Pi Mu Epsilon. Achievements include rsch. on number theory, combinatorics, group theory, and function theory. Home: 526 Palisades Ave Santa Monica CA 90402-2722 Office: 405 Hilgard Ave Los Angeles CA 90095-9000 E-mail: bg@math.ucla.edu

GORDON, DARRIEN X. JAMAL, professional football player; b. Shawnee, Okla., Nov. 14, 1970; Student, Stanford U. Cornerback, punt returner San Diego Chargers, 1993-97; with Denver Broncos, 1997-98, Oakland Raiders, 1998—. Mem. AFC Championship Tesm, 1994; leader in punt return average AFC, 1994. Office: c/o Oakland Raiders 1220 Harbor Bay Pkwy Alameda CA 94502-6570

GORDON, DAVID ELIOT, lawyer; b. Santa Monica, Calif., Mar. 8, 1949; s. Sam and Dee G.; m. Mary Debora Lane, Mar. 5, 1978. BA, Harvard U., 1969, JD, 1972. Bar: Calif. 1972. Ptnr. O'Melveny & Myers, L.A., 1980—. Adj. prof. Loyola Law Sch., 2000—. Founder, editor ERISA Litigation Reporter; contbr. articles on tax and employee benefits to profl. jours. Trustee Ctr. for Early Edn., 1997—. Fellow Los Angeles County Bar Found. (life, pres. 1984-85, bd. dirs. 1980-86); mem. ABA (employee benefits com. 1986—), Am. Coll. Tax Counsel, Los Angeles County Bar Assn. (tax sect., pres. 1990-91). Republican. Avocations: tennis, squash, racquetball. Office: O'Melveny & Myers 400 S Hope St Los Angeles CA 90071-2899

GORDON, JOSEPH HAROLD, lawyer; b. Tacoma, Mar. 31, 1909; s. Joseph H. and Mary (Obermiller) G.; m. Jane Wilson, Sept. 12, 1936 (dec.); [illegible] Jan. 7, 1967. BA, Stanford, 1931; LLB, JD, U. Wash., 1935. Bar: Wash. 1935.

Since practiced in, Tacoma; ptnr. Gordon & Gordon, Tacoma, 1935-50, Henderson, Carnahan, Thompson & Gordon, Tacoma, 1950-57, Carnahan, Gordon & Goodwin, Tacoma, 1957-70, Gordon, Thomas, Honeywell, Malanca, Peterson & Daheim, Tacoma, 1970—. Mem. ABA (ho. dels. 1951-2000, bd. govs. 1962-72, treas. 1965-72), Wash. State Bar Assn., Tacoma Bar Assn. (past pres.) Presbyn. (elder). Clubs: Rotary, Tacoma, Tacoma Golf and Country. Home: 2819 N Junett St Tacoma WA 98407-6345 Office: Gordon Thomas Honeywell Malanca Peterson & Daheim PO Box 1157 2200 Wells Fargo Plz Tacoma WA 98401-1157 E-mail: gordsr@gth-law.com

GORDON, JUDITH, communications consultant, writer; b. Long Beach, Calif. d. Irwin Ernest and Susan (Pearlman) G.; m. Lawrence Banka, May 1, 1977. BA, Oakland U., 1966; MS in Libr. Sci., Wayne State U., 1973. Researcher Detroit Inst. of Arts, 1968-69; libr. Detroit Pub. Libr., 1971-74; caseworker Wayne County Dept. Social Svcs., Detroit, 1974-77; advt. copywriter Hudson's Dept. Store, Detroit, 1979; mgr. The Poster Gallery, Detroit, 1980-81; mktg., corp. communications specialist Bank of Am., San Francisco, 1983-84, mgr., consumer pubs., 1984-86; prin. ACTIVE VOICE, San Francisco, 1986—. Contbr. edit. The Artist's Mag., 1988-93; contbr. to book Flowers: Gary Bukovnik, Watercolors and Monotypes, Abrams, 1990. Vol. From the Heart, San Francisco, 1992, Bay Area Book Festival, San Francisco, 1990, 91, Aid & Comfort, San Francisco, 1987, Save Orch. Hall, Detroit, 1977-81, NOW sponsored abortion clinic project. Recipient Nat. award Merit. Soc. Consumer Affairs Profls. in Bus., 1986, Bay Area Best award Internat. Assn. Bus. Communicators, 1986, Internat. Galaxy awards, 1992, 95, 97, Internat. Mercury awards, 1995, Charles Schwab Excellence in Svc. award, 2000. Mem. AAUW, Internat. Assn. Bus. Communicators, Nat. Writers Union, Freelance Editl. Assn., Clarity, Achenbach Graphics Arts Coun., Women's Nat. Book Assn., Assn. for Women in Comms., FIMA West (bd. dirs.), ZYZZYVA (bd. dirs.). Office: 899 Green St San Francisco CA 94133-3756 E-mail: activvduo@msn.com

GORDON, KEN, state senator; b. Detroit, Feb. 6, 1950; div.; children: Ben, Windy. BA, U. Mich., 1971; JD, Boston U., 1975. Pub. defender State of Colo., 1976-80; atty., 1981-93; adj. prof. polit. sci., 1983—; Dem. rep. dist. 9 Colo. Ho. of Reps., 1992-2000; Dem. senator dist.35 Colo. State Senate, 2000—. Mem. appropriations, agr., livestock and natural resources and state affairs coms. Colo. State Senate, exec. com. legis. coun. Exec. dir. Rocky Mountain Forum, 1983-85; committeeman Dem. Party, 1982-84, dist. capt., 1986-87; bd. dirs. Colo. Environ. Coalition, 1998-2000. Mem. Colo. Bar Assn., Colo. Trial Lawyers Assn. Jewish. Office: 3141 S Jasmine Way Denver CO 80222 also: Colo State Senate 200 E Colfax Rm 222 Denver CO 80203 Fax: 303 756-2134; 303 866-2291. E-mail: kgordon@sni.net, Kgordon@netone.com

GORDON, LARRY JEAN, political science educator, public health administrator; b. Tipton, Okla., Oct. 16, 1926; s. Andrew J. and Deweylee (Stewart) G.; m. Nedra Callender, Aug. 26. 1950; children: Debra Gordon Dunlap, Kent, Gary. Student, U. Okla., 1943-44; BS, U. N.Mex., 1949, MS, 1951; MPH, U. Mich., 1954. High sch. sci. tchr., N.Mex., 1949-50; various positions N.Mex. Dept. Health, 1950-55; commd. officer USPHS, 1957—, advanced through grades to Dir. Grade (Navy capt.), dir. Albuquerque Environ. Health Dept., 1955-68, 82-86; dir. Environ. Improvement Agy., Santa Fe, 1968-73; adminstr. for health and environ. programs N.Mex. HHS Dept., Santa Fe, 1976-78; dir. N.Mex. Sci. Lab. System, Albuquerque, 1973-76; dep. sec. N.Mex. Health and Environ. Dept., Santa Fe, 1978-82, sec., 1987-88; vis. prof. pub. adminstrn. U. N.Mex., Albuquerque, 1988—, adj. prof. polit. sci., 1997—, sr. fellow Inst. for Pub. Policy, 1997—. Chmn. N.Mex. Water Quality Commn., 1971-73. Asst. editor Jour. Environ. Health, 1975-78; cons. editor Environ. News Digest, 1970-82; editl. cons. Jour. Pub. Health Policy, 1980-96, Underwriters Labs., 1996; contbr. over 220 articles to profl. jours. Recipient Samuel J. Crumbine award for Outstanding Devel. of Comprehensive Program for Environ. Sanitation, 1959 and 65, Sanitarians Disting. Service award Internat. Assn. Milk, Food, and Environ. Sanitarians, 1962, Outstanding Contrbn. award N.Mex. Assn. Pub. Health Sanitarians, 1967, Boss of Yr. award Santa Fe chpt. Nat. Secs. Assn., 1970, Walter F. Snyder award For Achievement in Environ. Quality, 1978, Commendation for Leadership in Health Care N.Mex. Hosp. Assn., 1981, N.Mex. Outstanding Pub. Svc. award, 1988, Zimmerman award U. N.Mex. Alumni, 1993, L.A. County Breslow award L.A. County Dept. Health Svcs., 1994, Outstanding Leadership in Environ. Adminstrn. award Am. Soc. for Pub. Adminstrn., 1994. Mem. APHA (exec. bd. 1975-82, pres. 1980-81, John J. Sippy Meml. award 1962, other coms., Sedgwick award 1987), Am. Acad. Sanitarians (founder, David Calvin Wagner Excellence award 1984), N.Mex. Pub. Health Assn. (past pres., Disting. Svc. award 1970, Spl. award, 1978, D.A. Larrazola award 1989), N.Mex. Environ. Health Assn., (past pres.), Am. Lung Assn. N.Mex. (bd. dirs. 1982-94, Clinton P. Anderson award for Oustanding Contbn. to Lung Health 1987), Nat. Accreditation Coun. Environ. Health Curricula, Nat. Audubon Soc. (pres. coun. 1982-86), U. Mich. Sch. Pub. Health Alumni Assn. (bd. govs. 1985-88, Outstanding Alumnus award 1995), Royal Soc. Promotion of Health, London (hon.), N.Mex. Soc. Pub. Adminstrn. (Disting. Pub. Adminstr. award 1996), Delta Omega, Phi Kappa Phi, Phi Sigma. Republican. Avocations: fishing, boating, golf. Home: 1674 Tierra Del Rio NW Albuquerque NM 87107-3259 Office: Univ NMex Polit Sci Dept Albuquerque NM 87131-0001 E-mail: lgordon@flash.net

GORDON, LEONARD, sociology educator; b. Detroit, Dec. 6, 1935; s. Abraham and Sarah (Rosen) G.; m. Rena Joyce Feigelman, Dec. 25, 1955; children: Susan Melinda, Matthew Seth, Melissa Gail. B.A., Wayne State U., 1957; M.A., U. Mich., 1958; Ph.D., Wayne State U., 1966. Instr. Wayne State U., Detroit, 1960-62; research dir. Jewish Community Council, Detroit, 1962-64; dir. Mich. area Am. Jewish Com., N.Y.C., 1964-67; asst. prof. Ariz. State U., Tempe, 1967-70, assoc. prof., 1970-77, prof., 1977—, chmn. dept. sociology, 1981-90, assoc. dean for acad. programs Coll. Liberal Arts and Scis., 1990-2001, rsch. prof., 2001—. Cons. OEO, Maricopa County, Ariz., 1968 Author: A City in Racial Crisis, 1971, Sociology and American Social Issues, 1978, (with A. Mayer) Urban Life and the Struggle To Be Human, 1979, (with R. Hardert, M. Laner and M. Reader) Confronting Social Problems, 1984, (with J. Hall and R. Melnick) Harmonizing Arizona's Ethnic and Cultural Diversity, 1992. Sec. Conf. on Religion and Race, Detroit, 1962-67; mem. exec. bd. dirs. Am. Jewish Com., Phoenix chpt., 1969-70. Grantee NSF, 1962, Rockefeller found., 1970, 84. Fellow Am. Sociol. Assn. (chair task force on current knowledge on hate/bias acts on coll. and univ. campuses 2000—); mem. AAUP, Pacific Sociol. Assn. (v.p. 1978-79, pres. 1980-81), Soc. Study Social Problems (chair C. Wright Mills award com. 1988, treas. 1989-96), Ariz. State U. Alumni Assn. (faculty dir. 1981-82). Democrat. Jewish. Home: 13660 E Columbine Dr Scottsdale AZ 85259-3753 Office: Ariz State U Coll Liberal Arts & Scis Acad Programs Office Tempe AZ 85287

GORDON, MALCOLM STEPHEN, biology educator; b. Bklyn., Nov. 13, 1933; s. Abraham and Rose (Walters) G.; m. Diane M. Kestin, Apr. 16, 1959 (div. Sept. 1973); 1 child, Dana Malcolm; m. Marjorie J. Weinzweig, Jan. 28, 1976 (dec. Mar. 1990); m. Carol A. Cowen, July 19, 1992. BA with high honors, Cornell U., 1954; PhD, Yale U., 1958. Instr. UCLA, 1958-60, asst. prof., 1960-65, assoc. prof., 1965-68, prof. biology, 1968—, dir. Inst. Evolutionary and Environ. Biology, 1971-76, chmn. interdept. com. Environ. Sci. Engring. Program, 1984-88; asst. dir. rsch. Nat. Fisheries Ctr. and Aquarium, U.S. Dept. of Interior, Washington, 1968-69. Vis. prof. zoology Chinese U. Hong Kong, 1971-72; mem. panel on marine biology, panel on oceanography Pres.'s Sci. Adv. Com., 1965-66; mem. nat. adv com. R/V Alpha Helix, Scripps Inst. Oceanography, 1969-73; mem. com. on Latimeria, NAS, 1969-72; mem. tech. adv. com. Santa Monica Bay Restoration Project, EPA, 1988—; mem. tech. adv. group on milkfish reprodn. AID, 1984-92; chmn. Commn. on Comparative Physiology, Internat. Union Physiol. Sci., 1993—; co-founder Inst. of Environment, UCLA, 1997. Author coll. textbooks, technical books; mem. editorial bd. Fish Physiol. Biochem. Jour., 1986—, Jour. Exptl. Zool., 1990-93; contbr. articles to sci. jours. Active community orgns. on environ., civil liberties. NSF fellow Yale U., 1958; Fulbright fellow U.K., 1957-58; Guggenheim fellow Italy and Denmark, 1961-62; Sr. Queen's fellow in marine sci. Australia, 1976; Irving-Scholander Meml. lectr., U. Alaska-Fairbanks, 2000. Fellow AAAS; mem. Am. Physiol. Soc. (mem. exec. com. pub. affairs 1989-92), Am. Soc. Ichthyologists and Herpetologists, Soc. Integrative Comparative Biology (chmn. divsn. ecology 1979-80, chmn. divsn. comparative biochem. physiology 1988-89), Soc. for Exptl. Biology. Home: 2801 Glendower Ave Los Angeles CA 90027-1118 Office: UCLA Dept Organismic Biology PO Box 951606 Los Angeles CA 90095-1606 E-mail: msgordon@ucla.edu

GORDON, MILTON ANDREW, academic administrator; b. Chgo., May 25, 1935; s. Herrmann Andrew Gordon and Ossie Bell; m. Margaret Faulwell, July 18, 1987; children: Patrick Francis, Vincent Michael; 1 stepchild, Michael Faulwell. BS, Xavier U. La., New Orleans, 1957; MA, U. Detroit, 1960; PhD, Ill. Inst. Tech., 1968; postgrad., Harvard U., 1984. Teaching asst. U. Detroit, 1958-59; mathematician Lab. Applied Scis. U. Chgo., 1959-62; part-time tchr. Chgo. Pub. Sch. System, 1962-66; assoc. prof. math. Loyola U., Chgo., 1966-67; dir. Afro-Am. Studies Program Loyla U., Chgo., 1971-77; dean Coll. Arts and Scis., prof. math. Chgo. State U., 1978-86; v.p. acad. affairs, prof. math. Sonoma State U., Rohnert Park, Calif., 1986-90; pres., former prof. math. Calif. State U., Fullerton, 1990—. Bd. dirs. Associated We. Univs., Inc.; hon. admissions counselor United States Naval Acad., 1979; mem. exec. coun. Calif. State U., 1990; rep. for Calif. univs.Am. Assn. State Colls. and Univs., 1992; commn. on leadership devel. Am. Coun. on Edn., 1992; nat. task force on gender equality Nat. Collegiate Athletic Assn., 1992-94, pres.'s commn., 1994—; commr. joint commn. on accoutability reporting project Am. Assn. of State Colls. and Univs./Nat. Assn. of State Univs. and Land Grant Colls., 1994—, Am. Assn. Applied Ethics. Contbr. articles to profl. jours. Chmn. Archdiocese of Chgo. Sch. Bd., 1978-79; bd. govs. Orange County Community Found., Costa Mesa, Calif., 1990—, NCCJ, 1991—; bd. dirs. United Way of Orange County, Irvine, Calif., 1991, Pacific Symphony Orch., Santa Ana, 1993—; bd. adv. St. Jude Med. Ctr., Fullerton, Calif., 1992, Partnership 2010, Orange County, 1994, Black Leadership in Orange County, 1995—; bd. dirs. Orange County Bus. Coun., 1996—. Recipient cert. of appreciation Community Ch. Santa Rosa, Calif., 1988, Tree of Life award Jewish Nat. Fund, 1994, Humanitarian of Yr. award North Orange County YMCA, 1995; named Adminstr. of Yr., Chgo. State U., 1979. Mem. Am.conf. Acad. Deans (chmn. bd. dirs. 1983-85), Am. Assn. Univ. Adminstrs. (bd. dirs. 1983-86), Calif. Coalition of Math., Sigma Xi, Phi Beta Delta. Roman Catholic. Avocations: photography, sports, walking, movies. Office: Calif State Univ 800 N State College Blvd PO Box 6810 Fullerton CA 92834-6810

GORDON, ROBERT EUGENE, lawyer; b. L.A., Sept. 20, 1932; s. Harry Maurice and Minnie (Shaffer); 1 child, Victor Marten. BA, UCLA, 1954; LLB, U. Calif., Berkeley, 1959, JD, 1960; cert., U. Hamburg, Fed. Republic Germany, 1960. Bar: Calif. 1960. Assoc. Lillick, Geary, McHose, Roethke & Myers, Los Angeles, 1960-64, Schoichet & Rifkind, Beverly Hills, Calif., 1964-67; ptnr. Baerwitz & Gordon, Beverly Hills, 1967-69, Ball, Hunt, Hart, Brown & Baerwitz, Beverly Hills, 1970-71; of counsel Jacobs, Sills & Coblentz, San Francisco, 1972-78; ptnr. Gordon & Hodge, San Francisco, 1978-81; sole practice San Francisco, 1981-84, Sausalito, Calif., 1985-89; pvt. practice Corte Madera, 1989—. Adj. prof. entertainment law Hastings Coll. of Law, San Francisco, 1990-91, U. Calif., Berkeley, 1992. Served to 1st lt. U.S. Army, 1954-56. Mem. ABA (forum com. on entertainment and sports law), Los Angeles Copyright Soc. (bd. trustees 1970-71), Copyright Soc. of the USA. Avocations: cycling, skiing. Home: 35 Elaine Ave Mill Valley CA 94941-1014 Office: 5725 Paradise Dr Ste 250 Corte Madera CA 94925-1212

GORDON, STEPHEN MAURICE, manufacturing company executive, rancher; b. Chgo., Aug. 20, 1942; s. Milton A. and Elinor (Loeff) G.; m. Helene Lindow, Feb. 11, 1978 (div. Mar. 1998); 2 children: Hallie Lindow, Lacey Edison; m. Marilee Ann Enright, Mar. 21, 1998. Student, Middlebury Coll., 1960-61; B.A., U. Chgo., 1964; J.D., N.Y. U., 1967; D.I.L., Cambridge (Eng.) U., 1968. Bar: N.Y. State 1968. Aide to Vice Pres. Hubert Humphrey, Democratic Nat. Com., Washington, 1968; assoc. firm Marshall, Bratter, Greene, Allison & Tucker, N.Y.C., 1968-70; sr. rsch. assoc. Halle & Stieglitz, Inc., N.Y.C., 1970-72, v.p., 1972-75, pres., 1975-79; pres., chief exec. officer Irvin Industries Inc., N.Y.C., 1979-89, pres. Diamond G Ranch Inc., Dubois, Wyo. Chmn. bd. dirs. Vincennes Steel Corp. Mem. Nat. Wildlife Art Mus. (dir., treas.), MacLean-Fogg (dir.), Am. Red Angus Assn., Young Pres.' Orgn., Beta Gamma Sigma, Psi Upsilon. Home: Diamond G Ranch Dunoir Rd Dubois WY 82513 Office: PO Box 25009 Jackson WY 83001-7000

GORDON, WILLIAM CHARLES, college administrator; m. Kathryn Gordon; children: Jason, Scott, Kate, Jonathan. Bachelor's degree, Master's degree, Wake Forest U.; PhD in Exptl. Psychology, Rutgers U. Asst. prof. psychology SUNY, Binghamton, 1973-78; tchr. psychology dept. U. N.Mex., Albuquerque, 1978, chair psychology dept., 1990, interim dean Coll. Arts and Scis., 1992, dean, 1993, provost, v.p. for acad. affairs, 1996, interim pres., 1998—; pres., 1999. Office: U N Mex Albuquerque NM 87131-0001

GORDY, BERRY, entrepreneur, record company executive, motion picture executive; b. Detroit, Nov. 28, 1929; children from a previous marriage: Berry IV, Hazel Joy, Terry James, Kerry A., Sherry R., Kennedy W., Stefan K., Rhonda Ross-Kendrick. Founder, C.O.B. Motown Record Corp., from 1961; chmn. bd. dirs. The Gordy Co.; exec. producer motion pictures; chmn. bd. dirs. West Grand Media, 1998—; founder, COB Jobete Music Co., Inc., 1997—. Dir. motion picture Mahogany, 1975; exec. producer films Lady Sings the Blues, 1972, Bingo Long Traveling All-Stars and Motor Kings, 1975, The Last Dragon, 1984; author: To Be Loved: The Music, the Magic, the Memories of Motown, 1994. Recipient Bus. Achievement award Interracial Coun. for Bus. Opportunity, 1967, 2d Ann. Am. Music award for outstanding contbn. to mus. industry, 1975, Whitney M. Young Jr. award L.A. Urban League, 1980, NARAS Trustees award, 1991, Am. Legend award ASCAP Pop Music Awards, 1998, star on Hollywood Walk of Fame, 1996, Rainbow/Push Wall St. Project Millennium award, 2000; inducted into Leading Entrepreneurs of Nation Babson Coll., 1978, Rock and Roll Hall of Fame, 1988, Jr. Achievement Nat. Bus. Hall of Fame, 1998; Gordon Grand fellow Yale U., 1985. Mem. Guild Am. (bd. dirs.). Office: West Grand Media Inc Ste 1110 6255 W Sunset Blvd Los Angeles CA 90028-7412

GORE, ANDREW, editor-in-chief periodical; Contbg. editor early Mac pubs.; products editor Macintosh News; with Compyuter Reseller News; exec. editor, sr. new editos, exec. editor/news MacWeek; mgr. editl. dept. MacUser, 1996-97; editor-in-chief Mac World, San Francisco, 1997—. Co-author: Power Book, The digital Nomad's Guide, AT&T EO Personal Communicator, Newton's Law. Office: Mac World 301 Howard St San Francisco CA 94105-2252

GOREN, HOWARD JOSEPH, biochemistry educator; b. Bialocerkwe, Ukraine, Apr. 9, 1941; came to Can., 1940's; s. Morris Mordechai and Bracha (Nissenbaum) G.; m. Frances Claire, Sept. 18, 1965; children: Robyn Pearl, Jeffrey Michael. B.Sc., U. Toronto, Ont., Can.; Ph.D., SUNY, Buffalo. Postdoctoral fellow Weizman Inst, Rehovot, Israel, 1968-70; asst. prof. U. Calgary, Alta., Can., 1970-75, assoc. prof. Can., 1975-82, prof. Can., 1982—, chmn. univ. biochemistry group Can., 1987-91. Vis. scientist NIH, Bethesda, Md., 1977-78; vis. prof. Harvard Med. Sch., Boston, 1984-85, 1999-2000, U. Calif. San Francisco, 1992-93. Asst. editor Molecular Pharmacology, 1974-77; contbr. articles to profl. jours. Mem. AAAS, Am. Soc. Biochemistry and Molecular Biology, Am. Soc. Pharmacology and Exptl. Therapeutics, Can. Soc. Biochem., Cellular and Molecular Biology, Am. Diabetes Assn. Avocations: running, curling. Office: U Calgary 3330 Hospital Dr Calgary AB Canada T2N 4N1 E-mail: goren@ucalgary.ca

GORENBERG, ALAN EUGENE, physician; b. Japan, Apr. 30, 1959; s. Daniel and Louise Gorenberg; m. Ladan Hariri. BS in Biology, U. Calif., Irvine, 1981; MD, Loma Linda U., 1986. Diplomate Am. Bd. Internal Medicine, Am. Bd. Allergy and Immunology. Pvt. practice, San Bernardino, Calif., 1991—, Victorville, 1991—; asst. clin. prof. medicine Loma Linda (Calif.) U. Sch. Medicine, 1996—, Western U. Sch. Medicine, 1997—. Office: 2130 N Arrowhead Ave Ste 101 San Bernardino CA 92405-4023 also: 12408 Hesperia Rd Ste 7 Victorville CA 92392-5839

GORES, THOMAS C. lawyer; b. Milw., Sept. 24, 1948; s. Kenneth W. and Carolyn (Camblin) G.; m. Ann P. Pacelli, June 13, 1970; children: Lauren, Jake, Kathryn. BA, U. Notre Dame, 1970, JD, 1973; LLM, U. Miami, 1977. Bar: Wash. 1973, U.S. Tax Ct. 1973. Assoc., then ptnr. Bogle & Gates, Seattle, 1973-78, ptnr., 1978-93, Gores & Blais, Seattle, 1993-2001, Perkins Coie LLP, 2001—. Fellow Am. Coll. Trust and Estate Counsel; mem. Wash. State Bar Assn., Seattle Estate Planning Coun. (pres.). Office: Gores & Blais 1420 5th Ave Ste 2600 Seattle WA 98101-1357 E-mail: tgores@goresblais.com

GORHAM, FRANK DEVORE, JR. petroleum company executive; b. St. Louis, June 4, 1921; s. Frank DeVore and Lillian (Hawley) G.; m. Marie Ellis Kelly, Sept. 1, 1947; children— Frank DeVore III, Daniel Kelly, Timothy Walker, Robert Hawley II, Mark Linton. AB, U. Mo., 1943. Petroleum geologist Creole Petroleum Co., Venezuela, 1946-49; dist. geologist Pure Oil Co., Denver, 1949-50; chief geologist Pubco Petroleum Corp., Albuquerque, 1950-60, exec. v.p., 1960-65, pres., 1965-73, Questa Petroleum Inc., 1973—; owner Cuesta Prodn. Co., 1973—, Riva Ridge Ranch, 1979—; mng. ptnr. Sindbad Partnership, 1990—. Served to capt. AUS, 1943-46, MTO. Decorated Silver Star. Fellow Geol. Soc. Am., Explorers Club, Am. Assn. Petroleum Geologists (pres. Rocky Mountain sect. 1959) Home: 218 16th St SW Albuquerque NM 87104-1154 Office: Ste 1300 Sandia Savs Bldg Albuquerque NM 87102

GORHAM, RAMSAY L. state legislator; b. Rocky Mount, N.C., July 11, 1951; BA, Converse Coll., S.C. Artist; mem. N. Mex. Senate, Dist. 10., Sante Fe, 1996—; mem. edn. com., mem. rules com. Republican. Office: 805 Salamanca St NW Albuquerque NM 87107-5619

GORMAN, JOSEPH GREGORY, JR. lawyer; b. Chgo., Sept. 27, 1939; s. Joseph Gregory Sr. and Genevieve C. (Smith) G.; m. Mary (Molly) O'Donovan, Mar. 23, 1968; children: Jennifer Ann Gorman Patton, Joseph Gregory III. BA, U. Calif., Berkeley, 1961; MBA, UCLA, 1963, JD, 1966. Bar: U.S. Dist. Ct. (cen. dist.) Calif. 1967, U.S. Ct. Appeals (9th cir.) 1967, U.S. Tax Ct. Assoc., ptnr. Sheppard, Mullin, Richter & Hampton LLP, L.A., 1966—. Chair death and gift tax com. Los Angeles County Bar Assn., 1974-76, probate & trust law sect., 1980-81; chair death and gift tax com. Calif. State Bar, 1976-77; co-founder U. So. Calif. Probate & Trust Conf., 1974—; mem. adv. bd. Miami Inst. Estate Planning, 1978—. Contbr. articles to profl. jours. Served with USAR, Calif. NG, 1962-68. Fellow Am. Coll. Trust and Estate Counsel, Academician, The Internat. Acad. of Estate and Trust Law. Republican. Roman Catholic. Clubs: Annandale Golf (Pasadena); Jonathan (Los Angeles). Office: Sheppard Mullin Richter & Hampton LLP 333 S Hope St Fl 48 Los Angeles CA 90071-1448 E-mail: jgorman@smrh.com

GORMAN, MICHAEL JOSEPH, library director, educator; b. Witney, Oxfordshire, Eng., Mar. 6, 1941; came to U.S. 1977; s. Philip Denis and Alicia F. (Barrett) G.; m. Anne Gillett, Mar. 6, 1962 (div. 1992); children— Emma, Alice Student, Ealing Sch. Librarianship, 1964-66. Dir. gen. services dept. Univ. Library U. Ill., Urbana, 1977-88, acting univ. librarian, 1986-87; prof. library adminstrn. U. Ill., Urbana, 1977-88; vis. prof. U. Chgo. Library Sch., 1984, 86-88, U. Calif., Berkeley, 1989-91; dean libr. svcs. Calif. State U., Fresno, 1988—. Vis. lectr. U. Ill. Grad. Sch. Library Sci., Urbana, 1974-75; bibliog. cons. Brit. Library Planning Secretariat, 1972-74; head cataloguing Brit. Nat. Bibliography 1969-72. Author: A Study of the Rules for Entry and Headings in the Anglo-American Cataloguing Rules, 1967, 68, Format for Machine Readable Cataloguing of Motion Pictures, 1973, Concise AACR2, 1980, 3d edit., 1999, Technical Services Today and Tomorrow,1990, 2nd edit., 1998, Future Libraries (with Walt Crawford) 1995, Our Singular Strengths: Meditations for Librarians, 1998, Our Enduring Values, 2000; others; editor: Anglo-American Cataloguing Rules, 2d edit., 1978, rev., 1988, Catalogue and Index, 1973, Non Solus, 1981, Crossroads, 1986, Convergence, 1990; contbr. articles to profl. jours., chpts. to books Recipient Blackwell scholarship award, 1997. Fellow Brit. Libr. Assn.; mem. ALA (Margaret Mann citation 1979, mem. coun. 1991-95, Melvil Dewey medal 1992, Highsmith award 2001), Libr. Info. and Tech. Assn. (mem.-at-large exec. bd. 1982-85, pres. 1999-2000). Office: Calif State U Henry Madden Libr 5200 N Barton Ave Fresno CA 93740-8014

GORMAN, MICHAEL STEPHEN, construction executive; b. Tulsa, Aug. 3, 1951; s. Lawrence Matthew and Mary Alice (Veith) G.; m. Sheryl Lane McGee, Feb. 19, 1972; children: Kelley Lane, Michael Ryan. Student, Colo. State U., 1970, 71. With McGee Constrn. Co., Denver, 1972-74, with sales and estimating dept., 1974-78, gen. mgr., 1978-80, pres., owner, 1980-91; pres. Wisor Group, Boulder, 1990—; prin. TechKnowledge. Cons., author, columnist in remodeling and custom home building; mortgage banker, ins. cons., 1995—; presenter seminars in field. Mem. Nat. Assn. Remodeling Industry (chmn. membership svcs. com. 1987-91, bd. dirs. 1982-91, regional v.p. 1987-89, nat. sec. 1990-91, Man of Yr. 1982, Regional Contractor of Yr. 1988). Avocations: running, sailing, skiing, pilot.

GORNEY, RODERIC, psychiatry educator; b. Grand Rapids, Mich., Aug. 13, 1924; s. Abraham Jacob Gorney and Edelaine (Roden) Harburg; m. Carol Ann Sobel, Apr. 13, 1986. BS, Stanford U., 1948, MD, 1949; PhD in Psychoanalysis, So. Calif. Psychoanalytic Inst., 1977. Diplomate Am. Bd. Psychiatry and Neurology. Pvt. practice psychiatry, San Francisco, 1952-62; asst. prof. UCLA, 1962-71, assoc. prof., 1971-73, prof. psychiatry, 1980—, dir. psychosocial adaptation and the future program, 1971—. Faculty So. Calif. Psychoanalytic Inst. Author: The Human Agenda, 1972. Served with USAF, 1943-46. Fellow AAAS, Acad. Psychoanalysis, Am. Psychoanalytic Assn., Am. Psychiatric Assn. (essay prize 1971), Group for Advancement of Psychiatry. Avocation: music. Office: UCLA Neuropsychiatric Inst 760 Westwood Plz Los Angeles CA 90095-8353 E-mail: preadapt@ucla.edu

GORONKIN, HERBERT, physicist; b. Pitts., Jan. 9, 1936; s. Sander (Tammie) and Mae (Shulman) G.; children: David, Jeffrey, Michael; m. Pamela Louise Cooper, Oct. 4, 1980; children: Rebecca Louise, Theresa Louise, James David. BA, Temple U., 1961, MA, 1962, PhD, 1973. Physicist Internat. Resistance Co., Phila., 1963-65; sr. research physicist Honeywell Inc., Ft. Washington, Pa., 1965-66; sect. head Am. Electronic

Labs., Colmar, 1966-69; project engr. Gen. Electric Co., Syracuse, N.Y., 1969-75; mgr. semiconductor ops. Varian Assocs., Beverly, Mass., 1975-77; from mgr. high speed devices to chief scientist Phoenix copr. rsch. labs. Motorola Inc., Phoenix, 1977-88, mgr. to dir. phys. rsch. lab., 1988-99; v.p. phys. rsch. labs. Phys. Scis. Rsch. Labs., Phoenix, 1999—. Chmn. Workshop on Compound Semicondr. Microwave Materials and Devices, 1984-86, Quantum Electronics, Quantum Functional Devices and Compound Semicondr. Devices, 1986, Advanced Hetrostructure Workshop, 1994; program chair Internat. Symposium on Compound Semicondrs., 1994, gen. chair, 1997. Contbr. articles to profl. jours., chpts. to books; patentee in field. Served with USAF, 1954-57. Recipient Motorola Disting. Innovator award, 1993, Motorola Master Innovator award, 1995, Motorola Dan Noble fellow, 1996; named IEEE Phoenix Sect. Sr. Engr. of Yr., 1993. Fellow IEEE (IEDM compound semiconductor tech. program com. 1983-86); mem. Am. Phys. Soc., Sigma Xi. Avocations: hiking, Japanese, cooking. Home: 8641 S Willow Dr Tempe AZ 85284-2473 Office: Motorola Inc 7700 S River Pkwy Tempe AZ 85284-1806 E-mail: herb.goronkin@motorola.com

GORSUCH, EDWARD LEE, chancellor; Degree in Econ. and Cmty. Devel., U. Mo. Dir. Inst. Social and Econ. Rsch., 1976-94; dean Sch. Pub. Affairs U. Alaska, Anchorage, 1988-94, chancellor, 1994—. Bd. dirs. Commonwealth North; mem. adv. bd. Alaska Airlines Anchorage Cmty.; mem. civilian adv. bd. ALCOM; mem. Fiscal Policy Coun. Alaska. Office: U Alaska Anchorage Chancellor's Office 3211 Providence Dr Anchorage AK 99508-8060 E-mail: aychanc@uaa.alaska.edu

GORTNER, SUSAN REICHERT, nursing educator; b. San Francisco, Dec. 23, 1932; d. Frederick Leet and Erida Louise (Leuschner) R.; m. Willis Alway Gortner, Aug. 25, 1960 (dec. Sept. 1993); children: Catherine Willis, Frederick Aiken. AB, Stanford U., 1953; M Nursing, Western Res. U., 1957; PhD, U. Calif., Berkeley, 1964; postgrad., Stanford U., 1983. Staff nurse, instr., supr. Johns Hopkins Hosp. Sch. Nursing, Balt., 1957-58; instr. to asst. prof. Sch. Nursing U. Hawaii, Honolulu, 1958-64; staff scientist, rsch. adminstr. div. nursing USPHS, Bethesda, Md., 1966-78; assoc. dean rsch. Sch. Nursing U. Calif., San Francisco, 1978-86, acting chmn. dept. family health, 1982, prof. dept. family health care nursing, 1978-94; prof. emerita, 1994—; fellow, assoc. mem. faculty Inst. Health Policy U. Calif., San Francisco, 1979-94, mem. affiliated faculty Inst. for Aging and Health, 1981-94, adj. prof. internal medicine dept. gen. medicine, 1989-94, dir. cardiac recovery lab. Sch. Nursing, 1987-95, spl. asst. to dean, 1993-94. Fulbright lectr., rsch. scholar Norwegian Fulbright Commn., Oslo, 1988; invited prof. U. Montreal, 1991; vis. prof. U. Alta., Edmonton, Can., 1995. Contbr. articles, papers to profl. publs., chpts. to books. Health advisor N. Fork Assn., Soda Springs, Calif., 1981—. Disting. scholar Nat. Ctr. Nursing Rsch., 1990; named Disting. Alumna Frances Payne Bolton Sch. Nursing, 1983. Fellow Am. Acad. Nursing (Living Legend award 2001); mem. ANA (chair exec. com., coun. nurse rsch. com. 1976-80, cabinet on nursing rsch. 1984-86), Am. Heart Assn. (coun. cardiovasc. nursing exec. com. 1987-91, coun. epidemiology 1989—, Katharine Lembright award 1991, fellow cardiovasc. nursing coun. 1992), Sigma Theta Tau (Alpha Eta chpt., Margretta M. Styles award 1994). Office: U Calif 4th And Parnassus N411Y San Francisco CA 94143-0001 E-mail: sgortner@pacbell.net

GORTON, SLADE, attorney, former senator; b. Chicago, Ill., Jan. 8, 1928; s. Thomas Slade and Ruth (Israel) G.; m. Sally Jean Clark, June 28, 1958; children: Tod, Sarah Jane, Rebecca Lynn. AB, Dartmouth Coll., 1950; LLB with honors, Columbia U., 1953. Bar: Wash. 1953. Assoc. law firm, Seattle, 1953-65; ptnr. law firm, 1965-69; atty. gen. State of Wash., Olympia, 1969-81; ptnr. Davis, Wright & Jones, Seattle, 1987-89; senator from Wash. U.S. Senate, 1981-87, 1989-2001; of counsel Preston, Gates & Ellis, Seattle and Washington, 2001—. Mem. Wash. Ho. of Reps., 1959-69, majority leader, 1967-69, nat. Rep. senatorial com., Indian affairs, budget com., appropriations com., commerce/sci. and transp. com., energy and natural resources com.; chmn. commerce, sci. and transp. subcom. on aviation, chmn. com. on appropriations subcom. on interior. Trustee Pacific Sci. Center, Seattle, found. mem., 1977-78; mem. Pres.'s Consumer Adv. Council, 1975-77; mem. Wash. State Law and Justice Commn., 1969-80, chmn., 1969-76; mem. State Criminal Justice Tng. Commn., 1969-80, chmn., 1969-76. Served with AUS, 1946-47; to 1st lt. USAF, 1953-56; col. USAFR (ret.). Mem. ABA, Wash. Bar Assn., Nat. Assn. Attys. Gen. (pres. 1976-77, Wyman award 1980), Phi Delta Phi, Phi Beta Kappa. Clubs: Seattle Tennis, Wash. Athletic (Seattle). Office: Preston Gates & Ellis LLP 701 5th Ave Ste 5000 Seattle WA 98104-7011*

GOSSARD, ARTHUR CHARLES, physicist, researcher; b. Ottawa, Ill., June 18, 1935; s. Arthur Paul and Mary Catherine (Lineberger) G.; m. Marsha Jean Palmer, Jan. 8, 1965; children: Girard Christopher, Elinore Suzanne. B.A., Harvard U., 1956; Ph.D., U. Calif., Berkeley, 1960. Solid state physicist, disting. mem. tech. staff AT&T Bell Labs., Murray Hill, N.J., 1960-87; prof. materials and electrical and computer engring. U. Calif., Santa Barbara, 1987—. Author tech. papers magnetic resonance, magnetism, transition metals, molecular beam epitaxy, quantum structures, semiconductors. Sr. fellow Humboldt Found. Fellow IEEE, Am. Phys. Soc. (Oliver Buckley condensed matter physics prize 1984, James McGroddy prize for New Materials 2001); mem. NAS, Nat. Acad. of Engring. Office: U Calif Materials Dept Santa Barbara CA 93106 E-mail: gossard@engineering.ucsb.edu

GOTH, HARVEY L. construction company executive; Former v.p. Blackfield Hawaii Corp. (subs. Pacific Enterprises); former pres. Malama Pacific Corp. (subs. Hawaiian Electric Industries); sr. v.p. acquisition and development Schuler Homes, Inc., Honolulu. Office: Schuler Homes Inc 828 4th St Mall Fl 4 Honolulu HI 96813-4321

GOTHOLD, STUART EUGENE, school system administrator, educator; b. L.A., Sept. 20, 1935; s. Hubert Eugene and Adelaide Louise (Erickson) G.; m. Jane Ruth Soderberg, July 15, 1955; children: Jon Ernest, Susan Louise, Eric Arthur, Ruth Ann. BA, Whittier Coll., 1956, MA in Edn., 1961, LLD (hon.), 1988; EdD, U. So. Calif., 1974. Tchr. grades 1-9 El Rancho Sch. Dist., Pico Rivera, Calif., 1956-61, prin. jr. h.s., 1961-66; curriculum cons. L.A. County Office Edn., 1966-70; asst. supt. South Whittier (Calif.) Sch. Dist., 1970-72, supt., 1972-77; asst. supt. L.A. County Office Edn., Downey, 1977-78, chief dep. supt., 1978-79, supt., 1979-94; clin. prof. U. So. Calif., L.A., 1994—. Mem. adv. bd. Nat. Ctr. Fgn. Lang., 1984—; charter mem. Edn. Insights, Detroit, 1990—; bd. dirs. Fedco, KCET. Author: (book) Inquiry, 1970, Decisions-A Health Edn. Curriculum, 1971. Recipient Alumni Merit award USC, 1993, Alumni Achievement award Whittier Coll., 1986; named Dist. Educator Calif. State U., 1993. Republican. Roman Catholic. Avocations: tennis, choral singing, photography, hiking. Home: 10121 Pounds Ave Whittier CA 90603-1649 Office: U So Calif Wph 902 C Los Angeles CA 90089-0031 E-mail: gothold@usc.edu

GOTO SABAS, JENNIFER, state official; BA, U. Hawaii, 1983; JD, Georgetown U., 1986. Bar: Va. 1986. Legal rsch. and writing instr. Cath. U. Law Sch., 1986-87; legis. asst. Joint Chief of Staff-Office US Senator Daniel K. Inouye, Washington, 1987-90, dep. chief of staff, 1990-91, chief of staff Honolulu, 1993—. Adj. instr. legal rsch. and writing Am. U. Sch. of Law, 1988. Office: Office Sen Daniel K Inouye Prince Kuhin Bldg Fed Bldg Rm 7-212 Honolulu HI 96850

GOTTFRIED, IRA SIDNEY, management consulting executive; b. Bronx, N.Y., Jan. 4, 1932; s. Louis and Augusta (Champagne) G.; m. Judith Claire Rosenberg, Sept. 19, 1954; children: Richard Alan, Glenn Steven, David Aaron. BBA, CCNY, 1953; MBA, U. So. Calif., 1959. Lic. airline transport pilot. Sales mgr. Kleerpak Plastics, North Hollywood, Calif., 1956-57; head sys. and procedures Hughes Aircraft Co., Culver City, 1957-60; mgr. corp. bus. sys. The Aerospace Corp., El Segundo, 1960-61; dir. adminstrn. Eldon Industries, Inc., Hawthorne, 1962; mgr. info. sys. Litton Industries, Inc., Woodland Hills, 1963-64; exec. v.p. Norris & Gottfried, Inc., L.A., 1964-69; pres. Gottfried Cons., Inc., L.A., 1970-85; exec. ptnr. PriceWaterhouseCoopers, LLP, L.A., 1985-88, ret., 1988. V.p. Cresap/Towers Perrin, 1988-90; pres., dir. Gottfried Cons. Internat. 1990—; vice chmn. ACME Inc., 1984-85; dir., mem. exec. com. Blue Cross of Calif., 1968-77. Contbr. articles to profl. jours. Bd. dirs. ARC, Westside Amateur Radio Club, Univ. Synagogue, 1986-92. With USNR, 1953-56. Recipient Pres.'s award United Hosp. Assn. Mem. Inst. Mgmt. Cons. (life), Am. Arbitration Assn., Assn. Info. Tech. Profls. (life), Alpha Phi Omega (life), Brentwood Country Club, Palm Valley Country Club. Jewish. Avocations: amateur radio operator (K6IRA), pilot, railroading. Home: 12118 La Casa Ln Los Angeles CA 90049-1530

GOTTHOLD, WILLIAM EUGENE, emergency physician; b. Long Beach, Calif., Sept. 20, 1942; BA, Trinity U., 1964; MD, Tulane U., 1969. Cert. emergency medicine. Intern Letterman Army Med. Ctr., San Francisco, 1969-70, resident in gen. surgery, 1970-72; mem. staff Ctrl. Wash. Hosp., Wenatchee, 1978—; physician dir. clin. mgmt. Wenatchee (Wash.) Valley Clinic. Mem. AMA, Am. Coll. Emergency Physicians, Wash. State Med. Assn., Am. Bd. Emergency Medicine (cert., dir.). Office: Wenatchee Valley Clinic 820 N Chelan Ave Wenatchee WA 98801-2028 E-mail: wgotthold@wvclinic.com

GOTTLIEB, JOSEPH ABRAHAM See BISHOP, JOEY

GOTTLIEB, LESLIE, geneticist, educator; BA in English Lit., Cornell U., 1957; PhD in Botany, U. Mich., 1969. Prof. genetics dept. evolution and ecology U. Calif., Davis. Contbr. articles to profl. jours. Recipient Merit award Bot. Soc. Am., 2000. Achievements include research on molecular genetics and evolution of phosphoglucose isomerase in plants, particularly in the wildflower Clarkia; research on genetic basis for large morphological differences between closely related plant species and subspecies. Office: U Calif Davis 5310 Storer Hall One Sheilds Ave Davis CA 95616 E-mail: ldgottlieb@ucdavis.edu

GOTTLIEB, SHERRY GERSHON, author, editor; b. L.A., Apr. 6, 1948; d. Harry L. and Evelyn Jellen) Gershon; m. David Neil Gottlieb, Aug. 12, 1971 (div. 1973). BA in Dramatic Arts, U. Calif., Berkeley, 1969. Exec. sec. Budget Films, L.A., 1970-72; script reader United Artists, L.A., 1971-74; owner A Change of Hobbit bookstore, L.A. and Santa Monica, Calif., 1972-91, Career Boost Résumés, Ventura, 1999—. Class coord. UCLA Extension, 1982. Author: Hell No, We Won't Go! Resisting the Draft During the Vietnam War, 1991, Love Bite, 1994, Worse Than Death, 2000. Named Spl. Guest of Honor, Westercon, 1979. Mem. PEN USA. Democrat. Avocations: reading, cooking, Scrabble, Trivial Pursuit, travel. E-mail: writer@wordservices.com

GOTTSCHLING, DANIEL E. molecular research biologist; Rsch. biologist U. Chgo.; now prin. investigator Fred Hutchinson Cancer Rsch. Ctr., Seattle. Recipient Molecular Biology award NAS, 1995. Office: Fred Hutchinson Cancer Rsch Ctr 1100 Fairview Ave N Seattle WA 98109-4417

GOUGH, DENIS IAN, geophysics educator; b. Port Elizabeth, Cape, South Africa, June 20, 1922; came to Can., 1966; s. Frederick William and Ivy Catherine (Hingle) G.; m. Winifred Irving Nelson, June 2, 1945; children— Catherine Veronica, Stephen William Cyprian B.Sc., Rhodes U., Grahamstown, Republic of South Africa, 1943, M.Sc., 1947, D.Sc. (hon.), 1990; Ph.D., U. Witwatersrand, Johannesburg, Republic of South Africa, 1953. Research officer Nat. Phys. Lab., Johannesburg, S. Africa, 1947, sr. research officer S. Africa; lectr. Univ. Coll. Rhodesia, Salisbury, 1958, sr. lectr.; assoc. prof. geophysics Southwest Ctr. for Advanced Studies, Dallas, 1964-66; prof. geophysics U. Alta., Edmonton, Can., 1966-87, prof. emeritus Can., 1987—, dir. Inst. Earth and Planetary Physics Can., 1975-80. Contbr. numerous articles to profl. jours. Royal Soc. Can. fellow, 1972 Fellow Royal Astron. Soc. (Chapman medal 1988), Am. Geophys. Union; Geol. Assn. Can.; mem. Can. Geophys. Union (past pres., J. Tuzo Wilson medal 1983), Internat. Assn. Geomagnetism and Aeronomy (pres. 1983-87), S. African Geophys. Assn. (Rudolf Krahmann medal 1989). Avocations: reading, music, poetry. Office: Univ Alta Dept Physics Edmonton AB Canada T6G 2J1 E-mail: iangough@incentre.net

GOULD, DAVID, lawyer; b. L.A., Feb. 19, 1940; s. Erwin and Beatrice (Altman) G.; m. Bonnie Becker, Feb. 12, 1967; children: Julie M., Michael. AB, U. Calif., L.A., 1962; LLB, U. Calif., Berkeley, 1965. Bar: Calif. 1965, U.S. Dist. Ct. (cen., so., ea. and no. dists.) Calif. 1966, U.S. Ct. Appeals (9th cir.) 1967, U.S. Supreme Ct. 1995. Dep. atty. gen. Calif. Dept. of Justice, L.A., 1965-68; assoc. Loeb & Loeb, L.A., 1968-73, Danning, Gill, Gould, Diamond & Spector, L.A., 1974-76, ptnr., 1976-92, McDermott, Will & Emery, L.A., 1992—. Adj. assoc. prof. Southwestern U. Sch. of Law, L.A., 1978-80; adj. prof. Pepperdine U. Sch. of Law, Malibu, Calif., 1982. Co-author: Local Bankruptcy Practice Manual for the Central District of California, 2d edit., 1990—. Fellow Am. Coll. Bankruptcy; mem. ABA (bus. bankruptcy com. sect. on bus. law 1982—, vice chair rules subcom. 1986-92, chair 1992—), Calif. Bar Assn. (debtor/creditor rels. and bankruptcy com. 1984-87, chair 1987-88, advisor 1988-89, uniform comml. code com. 1988-92, bankruptcy cons. group bd. legal specialization 1989-93), L.A. County Bar Assn. (fed. cts. com. 1987—, chair bankruptcy 1989-90), Calif. Bankruptcy Forum (bd. dirs. 1995—, treas. 1998-99, sec. 1999—), L.A. Bankruptcy Forum (bd. trustees 1989, sec. 1990—, pres. 1993-94, lawyer rep. cen. dist. Calif. to 9th cir. jud. conf.). Avocations: trap and skeet shooting. Office: McDermott Will & Emery 2049 Century Park E Ste 3400 Los Angeles CA 90067-3208

GOULD, MARTHA BERNICE, retired librarian; b. Claremont, N.H., Oct. 8, 1931; d. Sigmund and Gertrude Heller; m. Arthur Gould, July 29, 1960; children: Leslie, Stephen. BA in Edn., U. Mich., 1953; MS in Library Sci., Simmons Coll., 1956; cert., U. Denver Library Sch. Community Analysis Research Inst., 1978. Childrens librarian N.Y. Pub. Libr., 1956-58; adminstr. library services act demonstration regional library project Pawhuska, Okla., 1958-59; cons. N.Mex. State Libr., 1959-60; childrens librarian then sr. childrens librarian Los Angeles Pub. Libr., 1960-72; acctg. dir. pub. srvices, reference librarian Nev. State Libr., 1972-74; pub. services librarian Washoe County (Nev.) Libr., 1974-79, asst. county librarian, 1979-84, county librarian, 1984-94; ret., 1994. Cons. Nev. State Libr. and Archives, 1996—; part-time lectr. in libr. adminstrn. U. Nev.; cons. Nev. State Libr. and Archives; acting dir. Nev. Ctr. for the Book; chair Nat. Commn. in Librs. & Info. Sci., 2000—. Co-editor: Nevada Women's History Project Annotated Bibliography, 1999; contbr. articles to jours. Exec. dir. Kids Voting USA, Nev., 1996; treas. United Jewish Appeals, 1981; bd. dirs. Temple Sinai, Planned Parenthood, 1996-97, Truckee Meadows Habitat for Humanity, 1995-98; trustee RSVP, North Nevadans for ERA; No. Nev. chmn. Gov.'s Conf. on Libr., 1990; mem. bd. Campaign for Choice, No. Nev. Food Bank, Nev. Women's Fund (Hall of Fame award 1989); mem. No. Nev. NCCJ, Washoe County Quality Life Task Force, 1992—, Washoe County Elections Taskforce, 1999—; bd. dirs. KUNR Pub. Radio, 1999—, chair bd. dirs., 2000—; chair Nat. Commn. Librs. & Info. Sci., 2000—; chair Sierra (Nev.) Comty. Access TV; presdl. appointee vice-chair Nat. Comn. on Librs. and Info. Sci., 1993—; mem. adv. bd. Partnership Librs. Washoe County; co-chair social studies curriculum adv. task force Washoe County Sch. Dist.; mem. Nev. Women's History Project Bd.; chair Downtown River Corridor Com., 1995-97; vice chair Dem. Party Washoe County; v.p. Nev. Diabetes Assn. for Children and Adults, 1998—; adv. bd. Fleischmann Planetarium, 1999—. Recipient Nev. State Libr. Letter of Commendation, 1973, Washoe County Bd. Commrs. Resolution of Appreciation, 1978, ACLU of Nev. Civil Libertarian of Yr. 1988, Freedom's Sake award AAUW, 1989, Leadership in Literacy award Sierra chpt. Internat. Reading Assn., 1992, Woman of Distinction award 1992, Nev. Libr. Assn. Libr. of Yr., 1993. Mem. ALA (bd. dirs., intellectual freedom roundtable 1977-79, intellectual freedom com. 1979-83, coun. 1983-86), ACLU (bd. dirs. Civil Libertarian of Yr. Nev. chpt. 1988, chair gov.'s conf. for women 1989), Nev. Libr. Assn. (chmn. pub. info. com. 1972-73, intellectual freedom com. 1975-78, govt. rels. com. 1978-79, v.p., pres.-elect 1980, pres. 1981, Spl. Citation 1978, 87, LIbr. of Yr. 1993). E-mail: mgould@powernet.net

GOULD, RONALD MURRAY, judge; b. St. Louis, Oct. 17, 1946; s. Harry H. and Sylvia C. (Sadofsky) G.; m. Suzanne H. Goldblatt, Dec. 1, 1968; children: Daniel, Rebecca. BS in Econs., U. Pa., 1968; JD, U. Mich., 1973. Bar: Wash. 1975, U.S. Dist. Ct. (we. dist.) Wash. 1976, U.S. Ct. Appeals (9th cir.) 1980, U.S. Supreme Ct. 1981, U.S. Dist. Ct. (ea. dist.) Wash. 1982, U.S. Ct. Appeals (fed. cir.) 1986. Law clk. to hon. Wade H. McCree Jr. U.S. Ct. Appeals (6th cir.), Detroit, 1973-74; law clk. to hon. justice Potter Stewart U.S. Supreme Ct., Washington, 1974-75; assoc. Perkins Coie, Seattle, 1975-80, ptnr., 1981-99; judge U.S. Ct. Appeals (9th cir.), Seattle, 2000—. Editor-in-chief Mich. Law Rev., 1972-73; editor: Washington Civil Procedure Deskbook, 1981, author with others, 1986, 92. Exec. bd. chief Seattle coun. Boy Scouts Am., Seattle, 1984—; mem. cmty. rels. coun. Jewish Fedn. of Greater Seattle, 1985-88; bd. dirs. econ. devel. coun. Seattle and King County, 1991-94; citizens cabinet mem. Gov. Mike Lowry, Seattle, 1993-96; bd. trustees Bellevue Cmty. Coll., 1993-99, chair bd. 1995-96. Fellow ABA (antitrust sect., litigation sect.); mem. Wash. State Bar Assn. (bd. govs. 1988-91, pres. 1994-95), King County Bar Assn. (Award for Disting. Svc. 1987), Supreme Ct. Hist. Soc., 9th Jud. Cir. Hist. Soc. (bd. dirs. 1994—). Jewish. Avocations: reading, chess. Office: US Courthouse 1200 6th Ave Fl 21 Seattle WA 98101-3123

GOULD, ROY WALTER, engineering educator; b. Los Angeles, Apr. 25, 1927; s. Roy Walter Gould and Rosamonde Belle (Stokes) Termain; m. Ethel Stratton, Aug. 23, 1952; children: Diana Stratton, Robert Clarke. BS, Calif. Inst. Tech., 1949, PhD, 1956; MS, Stanford U., 1950. With Calif. Inst. Tech., Pasadena, 1955—, exec. officer for applied physics, 1972-79, chmn. div. engring. and applied sci., 1979-84, Simon Ramo prof. engring., 1979-96, prof. emeritus, 1996—. Dir. div. controlled thermonuclear research U.S. Energy Research Devel. Agy., Washington, 1970-72. Contbr. 85 research papers to profl. pubs. Served with USN, 1945-46. Fellow IEEE, Am. Phys. Soc. (James Clerk Maxwell prize in plasma physics 1994); mem. NAS, Am. Acad. Arts and Scis., Nat. Acad. Engring. Office: Calif Inst Tech Dept Engring Applied Sci Ms 128 95 Pasadena CA 91125-0001 E-mail: rwgould@caltech.edu

GOULDTHORPE, KENNETH ALFRED PERCIVAL, publisher, state official; b. Jan. 7, 1928; came to U.S., 1951, naturalized, 1956; s. Alfred Edward and Frances Elizabeth Finch (Callow) G.; m. Judith Marion Cutts, Aug. 9, 1975; children: Amanda Frances, Timothy Graham Cutts. Student, U. Westminster, 1948-49; diploma, City and Guilds of London, 1949; student, Washington, 1951-52. Staff photographer Kentish Mercury, London, 1949-50, St. Louis Post-Dispatch, 1951-55, picture editor, 1955-57; nat. and fgn. corr. Life mag., Time, Inc., N.Y.C., 1957-61, Paris Bur., 1961-65, regional editor Australia-New Zealand, 1966-68, editl. dir. Latin Am., 1969-70; editor Signature mag., N.Y.C., 1970-73; mng. editor Penthouse mag., N.Y.C., 1973-76, pub. cons., 1976-79; editor, exec. pub. Adventure Travel mag., Seattle, 1979-80; sr. ptnr. Pacific Pub. Assocs., Seattle, 1979-80; editor, pub. Washington mag., 1984-89; vice-chmn. Evergreen Pub Co., 1984-89; dir. tourism State of Wash., 1989-91. Pub., cons., writer, 1991—; dir. Grand Fir Pub. Corp., 1994—; tchr. design, editl. techniques Parsons Sch. Design, N.Y.C.; lectr., contbr. elementary schs. lit. progs. Author: Design for Music, 1998; contbr. articles, photographs to nat. mags., books by Life mag. With Royal Navy, 1946-48. Decorated Naval Medal and bar; recipient awards of excellence Nat. Press Photographers Assn., AP and UP, 1951-57, Pres.'s medal Ea. Wash. U., 1986; certs. excellence Am. Inst. Graphic Arts, 1971, 72, 73, Comm. Arts, 1980, 81, 84; Spl. award N.Y. Soc. Publs. Designers, 1980; nominated for Pulitzer Prize for coverage of Andrea Doria disaster, 1956. Mem. Regional Pubs. Assn. (v.p., pres., Best Typography award 1985, Best Spl. Issue 1989), Western Publs. Assn. (Best Consumer Mag. award, Best Travel Mag. awards 1980, Best Regional and State Mag. award 1985, 86, 88, Best New Publ. award 1985, Best Column award 1985, Best Signed Essay 1986, 87, Best Four-Color Layout 1985, Best Four Color Feature Design), City and Regional Mag. Assn. (William Allen White Bronze awards), Time/Life Alumni Soc., Assn. Washington Gens. (gen. of state 1995, bd. dirs.), Sigma Delta Chi. Episcopalian. Home: 3049 NW Esplanade Seattle WA 98117-2624 E-mail: kgouldthorpe@earthlink.net

GOULET, ROBERT GERARD, singer, actor; b. Lawrence, Mass., Nov. 26, 1933; s. Joseph and Jeannette (Gauthier) G.; m. Louise Longmore, 1956 (div.); 1 child, Nicolette; m. Carol Lawrence, 1963 (div.); children: Christopher, Michael; m. Vera Chochrovska Novak, 1982. Student, Royal Conservatory Music, Toronto, Ont. Made Broadway debut in Camelot, 1960; numerous stage appearances including: Carousel, 1955, Finian's Rainbow, 1956, Gentlemen Prefer Blondes, 1956, The Pajama Game, 1957, The Beggar's Opera, 1958, Bell's Are Ringing, 1959, Meet Me in St. Louis, 1960, The Happy Time, 1968 (Tony award); (Broadway plays) I Do I Do, 1970, Carousel, 1979, On a Clear Day, 1980, Kiss Me Kate, 1981, South Pacific, 1986-88, Fantasticks, 1990, Camelot as King Arthur, 1990, 92-94; (nat. tour and Broadway) South Pacific, 1995, Moon Over Buffalo, 1996, Man of La Mancha, 1996-97; star in ABC-TV series Blue Light, 1966; numerous TV spls. and guest TV appearances including The Big Valley, 1967, Police Story, 1970, Mission Impossible, 1972, Police Woman, 1975, Cannon, 1976, The Dream Merchants, 1980, Matt Houston, 1983, Glitter, 1984, Murder, She Wrote, 1985, Finder of Lost Love, 1985, Mr. Belvedere, 1986, 88, 89, 90, (CBS pilot) Make My Day, 1991, In the Heat of the Night, 1992, Based on a Untrue Story, 1992, Burke's Law, 1994, Get Smart, 1994, ESPN Coll. Basketball Commls., 1995-97; star films Honeymoon Hotel, 1964, I'd Rather Be Rich, 1964, I Deal in Danger, 1966, Underground, 1970, Atlantic City, 1981, Beetlejuice, 1988, Scrooged, 1989, Naked Gun II 1/2, 1991, Mr. Wrong, 1996, (voice) Toy Story 2, 1999, The Last Producer, 2000, G-Men From Hell, 2000; has recorded over 60 albums. Recipient numerous awards including World Theatre award, Tony award, Grammy award Best New Artist, 1962, Grammy award Gold Album for My Love Forgive Me, 1964. Fellow (hon.) Toronto Royal Conservatory Music. Fellow Royal Conservatory Music (hon.). Office: Rogo & Rove Inc 3110 Monte Rosa Ave Las Vegas NV 89120-3040

GOURLEY, RONALD ROBERT, architect, educator; b. St. Paul, Oct. 5, 1919; s. Robert Thomas and Eva Jeane (Caudle) G.; m. Phyllis Mary McDonald, Apr. 10, 1950; children: Robert McDonald, Karen Ellen, Geoffrey James. BArch, U. Minn., 1943; MArch, Harvard U., 1948. Instr. architecture MIT, Cambridge, 1948-53; vis. prof. Royal Acad., Copenhagen, Denmark, 1952; prof. architecture Harvard U., 1953-70; ptnr., co-founder Sert, Jackson & Gourley, Cambridge, 1958-64, Integrated Design Svcs. Group, Cambridge, 1966-72; ptnr. Gourley/Richmond, 1972-76, Gourley, Richmond & Mitchell, 1976-82; tech. coord. Boston Archtl. Ctr., 1976-77; prof. architecture U. Ariz., Tucson, 1977-90, dean Coll.

Architecture, 1977-87, pres. Architecture Lab., 1986-89, dean, prof. emeritus, 1990—, disting. vis. prof. architecture, 1990—; pvt. practice Cambridge, 1954-58, 64-66, Tucson and Chilmark, 1990—. Prin. works include U. N.H. Meml. Union Bldg., Harvard U. Married Student Housing (Nat. Honor award AIA 1965), Cunningham Found. Bldg., Radcliffe Coll. Faculty Housing (Nat. Honor award AIA 1973), Brookline (Mass.) Pub. Libr., Kingston Housing for Elderly, Wheaton Coll. Libr., Mass. Hosp Sch. Recreation Bldg. With AUS, 1944-46. Inducted to Hall of Fame, The Humboldt Complex, St. Paul, 1995. Fellow AIA; mem. Boston Archtl. Ctr. (hon.). Home: 2522 E 3rd St Tucson AZ 85716-4115 also: Box 177 Middle Road Martha's Vineyard Chilmark MA 02535 Office: U Ariz Coll Architecture Tucson AZ 85721-0001

GOUTERMAN, MARTIN PAUL, chemistry educator; b. Phila., Dec. 26, 1931; s. Bernard and Melba (Buxbaum) G.; 1 child, Mikaelin BlueSpruce. B.A., U. Chgo., 1951, MS, 1955, Ph.D. in Physics (NSF Predoctoral fellow), 1958. Faculty Harvard U., Cambridge, Mass., 1958-66, postdoctoral fellow to asst. prof. chemistry dept.; mem. faculty U. Wash., Seattle, 1966—, prof. chemistry, 1968-99, prof. emeritus, 2000—. Fellow Am. Inst. Physics; mem. Am. Chem. Soc., Sigma Xi. Achievements include research and publications in spectroscopy and quantum chemistry of porphyrins and their use as luminescence sensors for biomedical and aeronautical application, in particular pressure sensitive paint; developed BS degree program in biochemistry and a chemistry minors program. Office: U Wash Chemistry Box 351700 Seattle WA 98195-1700

GOVEDARE, PHILIP BAINBRIDGE, artist, educator; b. Yuba City, Calif., Oct. 5, 1954; s. Philip Wright and Virginia (Pease) G.; m. Christine Lambert; 1 child, Eloise. BFA, San Francisco Art Inst., 1980; MFA, Tyler Sch. of Art, Phila., 1984. Instr. Tyler Sch. of Art, Phila., 1985-88, asst. prof., 1988-91, Univ. of Wash., Seattle, 1991-96, assoc. prof., 1996—. Mem. program com. Sch. of Art Wash. U., 1993—; chmn. painting U. Wash.,1993-95. Represented by Francine Seders Gallery, Seattle. Recipient fellowship NEA, Washington, 1993; grantee Pa. Coun. on the Arts, Harrisburg, 1988, Pollock Krasner Found., N.Y.C., 1991. Home: 4702 35th Ave NE Seattle WA 98105-3004 Office: Univ Wash Sch Art M-10 Seattle WA 98103

GOWDY, FRANKLIN BROCKWAY, lawyer; b. Burlington, Iowa, Dec. 27, 1945; s. Franklin Kamm and Dorothy Faye (Brockway) G.; m. Jennifer June McKenrick, Nov. 27, 1982; stepchildren: Jeffrey F. Hammond, Tracy Lawrence, Jonathan R. Hammond, Julie E. Rawls. BA in Polit. Sci., Stanford U., 1967; JD, U. Calif., Berkeley, 1970. Bar: U.S. Dist. Ct. (no. dist.) Calif. 1971, U.S. Ct. Appeals (9th cir.) 1971, U.S. Supreme Ct. 1979, U.S. Dist. Ct. (cen. dist.) Calif. 1984. Assoc. Brobeck, Phleger & Harrison, San Francisco, 1971-78, ptnr., 1978—. Fellow Am. Coll. Trial Lawyers; mem. ABA, Calif. Bar Assn., San Francisco Bar Assn., Assn. Bus. Trial Lawyers (bd. govs.). Home: 3428 Shangrila Rd Lafayette CA 94549-2423 Office: Brobeck Phleger Harrison LLP Spear St Tower 1 Market Plz San Francisco CA 94105-1420 E-mail: fgowdy@brobeck.com

GOYAN, MICHAEL DONOVAN, stockbroker, investment executive; b. Eureka, Calif., Sept. 18, 1938; s. Gerald Hazen and Lucille (Johnson) G.; children: Michael Donovan, Kevin Lee. A.B., Occidental Coll., 1960. Stockbroker, allied mem. William R. Staats, Los Angeles, 1961-74; ptnr., stockbroker Crowell, Weedon & Co., L.A., 1974-89; sr. v.p. investments PaineWebber Inc., L.A., 1989—. Mem. hearing bd. N.Y. Stock Exchange, 1970— Bd. dirs. Inst. Internat. Edn., Los Angeles and N.Y.C., 1972-78, West Coast nat. trustee. Mem. Newcomen Soc., Long Beach Yacht Club, L.A. Bond Club (bd. dirs. 1970—, pres. 1983-84), Calif. Club, Ingomar Club (Eureka), Kappa Beta Phi (bd. dirs. 1985—).

GOZON, RICHARD C. paper distribution executive; b. Pitts., Oct. 9, 1938; s. Frank J. and Helen (Franklin) G.; m. Fran A. Burmeister, June 21, 1940; children: Cheryl, Michael, Diana. BS in Bus., Valparaiso U., 1960; advanced mgmt. program, Harvard U., 1978. With sales dept. Champion Internat., Hamilton, Ohio, 1959-61; dir. sales Nationwide Papers, Chgo., 1961-72; pres. Rourke Eno Paper Co., Hartford, Conn., 1972-78; exec. v.p. Unisource Corp., Phila., 1978-79, pres., 1979-85; v.p. Alco Standard Corp., Phila., 1982, dir., 1983, exec. v.p., chief oper. officer, 1987, pres., chief oper. officer, 1988—; pres. Alco Paper & Office Products, Phila., 1983, Paper Corp. of Am., Phila., 1985-87; exec. v.p., chief exec. officer Alco Standard Corp., Valley Forge, Pa., 1988—. Bd. dirs. Alco Standard Corp., Phila.; trustee Richard Roberts Real estate Growth Trus I, Avon, Conn.; dir. U.G.I. Corp. Dir., World Affaris Coun. of Phila. Mem. Sales & Mktg. Execs. Club. Republican. Lutheran. Clubs: Merion Golf (Ardmore, Pa.); Pine Valley golf (Clementon, N.J.); Harvard Bus. Sch. Avocations: golf, tennis, skiing. Home: 4922 Canterwood Dr NW Gig Harbor WA 98332-8856 Office: Weyerhaeuser Co PO Box 2999 33663 Weyerhaeuser Way S Tacoma WA 98477

GRABER, SUSAN P. federal judge; b. Oklahoma City, July 5, 1949; d. Julius A. and Bertha (Fenyves) G.; m. William June, May 3, 1981; 1 child, Rachel June-Graber. BA, Wellesley Coll., 1969; JD, Yale U., 1972. Bar: N.Mex. 1972, Ohio 1977, Oreg. 1978. Asst. atty. gen. Bur. of Revenue, Santa Fe, 1972-74; assoc. Jones Gallegos Snead & Wertheim, Santa Fe, 1974-75, Taft Stettinius & Hollister, Cin., 1975-78; assoc., then ptnr. Stoel Rives Boley Jones & Grey, Portland, Oreg., 1978-88; judge, then presiding judge Oreg. Ct. Appeals, Salem, 1988-90; assoc. justice Oreg. Supreme Ct., Salem, 1990-98; judge U.S. Ct. Appeals (9th cir.), Portland, 1998—. Mem. Gov.'s Adv. Coun. on Legal Svcs., 1979-88; bd. dirs. U.S. Dist. Ct. of Oreg. Hist. Soc., 1985—, Oreg. Law Found., 1990-91; mem. bd. visitors Sch. Law, U. Oreg., 1986-93. Mem. Oreg. State Bar (jud. adminstrn. com. 1985-87, pro bono com. 1988-90), Ninth Cir. Jud. Conf. (chair exec. com. 1987-88), Oreg. Jud. Conf. (edn. com. 1988-91, program chair 1990), Oreg. Appellate Judges Assn. (sec.-treas. 1990-91, vice chair 1991-92, chair 1992-93), Am. Inns of Ct. (master), Phi Beta Kappa. Office: US Ct Appeals 9th Cir Pioneer Courthouse 555 SW Yamhill St Portland OR 97204-1336*

GRABER, WILLIAM RAYMOND, pharmaceutical executive; b. Vancouver, Wash., Apr. 10, 1943; s. R. Archie and Josephine N. (Martin) G.; m. Mary Lynn McArthur, June 19, 1965; children: Kristine, Kathleen, Timothy. BA in Math., Wash. State U., 1965. Fin. mgr. GE, 1965-91; contr. The Mead Corp., Dayton, Ohio, 1991—; CFO, sr. v.p. McKesson HBOC, San Francisco, 2000—. Avocations: golf, jogging. Home: 145 Las Vegas Rd Orinda CA 94563-1954

GRACE, JOHN ROSS, chemical engineering educator; b. London, Can., June 8, 1943; s. Archibald John and Mary Kathleen (Disney) G.; m. Sherrill Elizabeth Perley, Dec. 20, 1964; children— Elizabeth, Malcolm. B.E.Sc., U. Western Ont., 1965; Ph.D., Cambridge (Eng.) U., 1968. From asst. prof. to prof. chem. engring. McGill U., Montreal, Que., 1968-79; sr. research engr. Surveyor Nenniger & Chenevert Inc., 1974-75; prof. chem. engring. U. B.C., Vancouver, 1979—, head dept. chem. engrin., 1979-87, dean faculty grad. studies, 1990-96, prof. chem. and biol. engring., 2000—, Can. rsch. chair, 2001—. Cons. in field Co-author: Bubbles, Drops and Particles, 1978; co-editor: Fluidization, 1980, Fluidization VI, 1989, Circulating Fluidized Beds, 1997; editor Chem. Engring. Sci., 1984-90; contbr. articles to profl. jours. NRC sr. indsl. fellow; Athlone fellow; Can. Coun. Killam Res. fellow, 1999. Fellow Royal Soc. Can., Can. Acad. Engring., Chem. Inst. Can. (v.p. 1994-95, pres. 1995-96); mem. Can. Soc. Chem. Engring. (pres., Erco award, R.S. Jane award), Assn. Profl. Engrs. B.C., Instn. Chem. Engrs. Office: 2216 Main Mall Vancouver BC Canada V6T 1Z4 E-mail: jgrace@chml.ubc.ca

GRACE, SUE, state legislator; b. Milw., Jan. 31, 1958; m. Vincent Grace. BA, Marquette U. Mem. Ariz. Ho. of Reps., 1991-96; mktg. specialist; mem. Ariz. Senate, Phoenix, 1996-. Named Legis. of Yr., Mental Health Assn., 1991. Mem., Paradise Valley Chamber of Commerce, United Fund Council, Phoenix Mountaineers. Republican. Office: Ariz State Senate Rm 303 1700 W Washington St Phoenix AZ 85007-2812 Address: 2102 E Redfield Rd Phoenix AZ 85022-4659

GRADINGER, GILBERT PAUL, plastic surgeon; b. Waterloo, Iowa, 1930; MD, Wash. U., 1956. Diplomate Am. Bd. Plastic Surgery (sec.-treas. 1993, chmn. 1994). Intern U. Calif. Hosp., San Francisco, 1956-57, resident in surgery, 1957-59, chief resident in plastic surgery, 1960-61; resident in plastic surgery Franklin Hosp., San Francisco, 1959-60; plastic surgeon Peninsula Hosp. Med. Ctr., Burlingame, Calif.; clin. prof. plastic surgery U. Calif., San Francisco, prof. plastic surgery. Fellow ACS; mem. Am. Assn. Plastic Surgeons, Am. Soc. Plastic Surgery, Calif. Soc. Plastic Surgeons. Office: Ste 420 2330 Post St San Francisco CA 94115-3000 E-mail: gilg800@cs.com

GRAF, ERVIN DONALD, municipal official; b. Crow Rock, Mont., Mar. 9, 1930; s. Emanuel and Lydia (Bitz) G.; m. Carolyn Sue Robinson, Mar. 15, 1956 (div. 1958); m. Eleanor Mahlein, Apr. 13, 1959 (dec. Oct. 1990); children: Debra, Belinda, Corrina, Melanie (dec.), Ervin Jr. (dec.). Enlisted U.S. Army, 1948; served two tours of duty in Vietnam; ret. U.S. Army, 1972; with office and maintenance staff Greenfields Irrigation Dist., Fairfield, Mont., 1972-77, sec. to Bd. Commrs., 1977-95; ret., 1995. Decorated Bronze star with oak leaf cluster. Mem. Am. Legion (all offices Post #80 and Dist. 8 incl. dist. comdr.). Democrat. Lutheran. Avocations: bowling, coin collecting, fishing, camping. Home: 211 6th St N Box 565 Fairfield MT 59436-0565

GRAF, HANS, conductor; b. Austria, Feb. 15, 1949; Studied with Franco Ferrera and Arvid Jansons. Music dir. Mozarteum Orch., Salzburg, Austria, 1984-94, Calgary Philharm. Orch., 1995—; apptd. music dir. Orch. Nat. de Bordeaux-Aquitaine and Opera de Bordeaux, 1998—. Guest condr. Vienna Symphony, Vienna Philharm., Orchestre Nat. de France, Leningrad Philharm., Pitts. Symphony, Boston Symphony. Office: Calgary Philharmonic Orchestra 205 8th Ave SE Calgary AB Canada T2G 0K9

GRAF, RUDY J. communications company executive; Mgmt. AT&T; reg. v.p. Metromedia Telecomms.; pres., COO Centennial Cellular Corp., 1991-99; CEO, pres. and COO Citizens Comms., 1999—. Office: Electric Lightwave Inc 4400 NE 77th Ave Vancouver WA 98662

GRAFE, WARREN BLAIR, cable television executive; b. N.Y.C., June 22, 1954; s. Warren Edward and Maree Lee (Ahn) G.; m. Pamela Arden Rearick, Mar. 8, 1980 (div. Nov. 1982). Student, Kendall Coll., 1974-75, U. Wis., Platteville, 1975-76; BA, Ind. U., 1979. Sales rep. Sta. WGTC-FM, Bloomington, Ind., 1979-84, account exec., coop. cord., 1980-84; nat. sales rep. Stas. WTTS-WGTC, Bloomington, 1984; sales rep. Sta. KLFF-KMZK, Phoenix, 1985; account exec. Rita Sanders Advt. and Pub. Rels. Agy., Tempe, Ariz., 1985, Am. Cable TV, Phoenix, 1985-86, Dimension Media Svcs., Phoenix, 1986-89, Greater Phoenix Interconnect, 1989-95, CableRep/Phoenix, 1995-99, CableRep/Ariz., Phoenix, 1999—. Recipient Nat. Sales awards, Cable TV Advt. Bur., 1986, 87, 91, 94, 96, 98, finalist, 1995, 99, 2000; named one of Cable's Best Top Ten Cable Advt. Sales Reps. in Country, Cable Avails, 1995. Mem. Tempe C. of C. (ambassador 1986), Chandler (Ariz.) C. of C., Mesa (Ariz.) C. of C. Home: 9616 N 26th Pl Phoenix AZ 85028-4708 Office: CableRep Ariz 2020 N Central Ave Ste 400 Phoenix AZ 85004-4510

GRAFF, CYNTHIA STAMPER, health care executive; b. Fairbanks, Alaska, May 22, 1953; d. Marshall Bernard and Nell (Buntyn) Stamper; m. Grant H. Van de Walker, July 13, 1974 (div. 1980); m. Dennis Alan Graff, July 10, 1990. BS in Fin., Calif. State U., Long Beach, 1975; LLB, York U., Toronto, 1985. Pres. MC Fin., Inc., Salt Lake City, 1976-82; founder, pres. The Road Butler, Toronto, 1985-86; house counsel Polyvoltec Inc., Toronto, 1986-87; v.p. Lindora Med. Clinics, Costa Mesa, Calif., 1988-91; pres. Lindora, Inc., Costa Mesa, 1992—. Mem. Am. Soc. Bariatric Physicians, Young Pres.'s Orgn. Republican. Avocations: golf, skiing, reading. Office: Lindora Med Clinics 3505 Cadillac Ave Ste N-2 Costa Mesa CA 92626-1466

GRAFF, PAT STUEVER, secondary education educator; b. Tulsa, Mar. 24, 1955; d. Joseph H., Sr. and Joanne (Schneider) Stuever; m. Mark A. Rumsey; children: Earl, Jr., Jeremy. BS in Secondary Edn., Okla. State U., 1976; postgrad., U. N.M., 1976-87. Cert. tchr. lang. arts, social studies, journalism, French, N.Mex. Substitute tchr. Albuquerque Pub. Schs., 1976-78; tchr. Cleveland Mid. Sch., Albuquerque, 1978-86, La Cueva H.S., Albuquerque, 1986—, co-chair English dept., 1996—, chair sch. restructuring coun., 1999-2001. Adviser award winning lit. mag. El Tesoro, sch. newspapers The Edition, Huellas del Oso; instr. journalism workshops, N.Mex. Press Assn., Ind. U., Bloomington, Nat. Scholastic Press, Mpls., Kans. State U., Manhattan, Interscholastic Press League, Austin, Tex., St. Mary's U., San Antonio, Ala. Scholastic Press Assn.; keynote spkr. at numerous confs. in Ohio, Ind., Kans., S.C., Okla., Ala., N.Mex., Tex., and N.Y.; reviewer of lang. and textbooks for several cos.; instr. Homework Hotline, Dial-A-Tchr., N.Mex., 1991—; textook evaluator Holt Pub., Inc., 1991. Author: Journalism Text, 1983; contbg. author: Communication Skills Resource Text, 1987, Classroom Publishing/Literacy, 1992; contbr. articles to profl. jours. Troop leader Girl Scouts U.S., 1979-90, coord. various programs, asst. program com. chmn. Chaparral Coun., 1988-89, chmn. adult recognition task force, 1991-96, bd. dirs., 1991-98; active PTA Gov. Bent Elem. Sch., 1983-86, v.p., 1985-86, Osuna Elem. Sch., 1986-92, N.Mex. PTA, 1994—; pub. various children's lit. mags., 1987—, pub. parent's newsletter, 1986—; newsletter layout editor Albuquerque Youth Soccer Orgn., 1985-88; active YMCA youth and govt. model legis., faculty advisor La Cueva del., 1986—, press corps advisor, 1987—; asst. den. leader Boy Scouts Am., 1987-88, den leader, 1988-91. Recipient Innovative Teaching award Bus. Week mag., 1990, Svc. commendatin Coll. Edn. Alumni Assn., Okla. State U., 1990, Alumni Recognition award, 1993, Mem. Yr. Svc. award Bernalillo County Coun. Internat. REading Assn., Thanks to Tchrs. award Apple Computers, 1990, Spl. Recognition Albuquerque C. of C., 1992; named Spotlighted Mem. Phi Delta Kappa, 1990, Spl. Recognition Advisor Dow Jones Newspaper Fund, 1990, Nat. H.S. Journalism Tchr. of Yr., 1995, Disting. Advisor, 1991, U.S. West Tchr. Yr. finalist, 1991, N.Mex. Pubs. Adviser of Yr., 1991, N.Mex. State Tchr. of Yr., 1993, finalist Nat. Tchr. Yr., 1993, finalist Am. Tchr. Awards, Disney, 1998; named USA Today All-Am. Tchr., 1999; grantee Phi Delta Kappa 1989, 91, Geraldine R. Dodge Found., 1990, 92, 95-97, Learn and Serve Am., 1999. Mem. ASCD (Focus on Excellence award 1990, editor newsletter 1991-92, focus on excellence awards com. 1992-94), Nat. Assn. Secondary Sch. Prins. (breaking ranks tchr. rep.), Nat. Alliance High Schs. (tchr. rep. 1997-2000), Nat. Coun. Tchrs. English (nat. chair com. English Tchrs. and Pubs. 1988-91, nat. chair assembly for advisors of student pubs., regional rep. Tex., La., N.Mex., standing com. affiliates 1991-94, nat. chair, 1995-98), Secondary Sect. Com. 1999—, Nat. Sch. Pub. Rels. Assn. (Zia chpt., contest winner 1991-94, Pres.'s award 1993), Nat. Fedn. Press Women, Journalism Edn. Assn. (judge nat. contests 1988—, mem. nat. cert. bd. 1989-99, presenter nat. convs. 1989—, cert. journalism educator 1990, master journalism educator 1991, issues seminar planning com. 1990, chair 1991, nat. conf. chmn. 1997-99), Journalism Edn. Assn. (nat. bd. 1991—), N.Mex. Coun. Tchrs. English (regional coord. Albuquerque 1983-86, chair state confs. 1985-87, editl. bd. N.Mex. English Jour. 1986-88 (editor, 1999—), adv. mgr. 1989-90, state pres. 1987-88, chair English Humanities expo com. 1988-99, chair facilities for Fall conf. 1988-93, Svc. award 1989, Outstanding H.S. English Tchr. N.Mex. 1991), N.Mex. Scholastic Press Assn. (state v.p. 1985-89, coord. workshop 1986, editor newsletter 1986-89, asst. chair state conf. 1988, 89, state bd. dirs. 1991—, state v.p. 1992-95, state pres. 1995-97), N.Mex. Press Women (state scholarship chair 1994, publicity chair 1995-96, state treas. 1996-1998, state v.p., 1998-99), Albuquerque Press Women (Communicator of Achievement award 1993, v.p. 1994, pres. 1995), Quill & Scroll (adv. La Cueva chpt. 1986—, judge nat. newspaper rating contest 1988-97), AAUW (chpt. newsletter editor 1995-2001, local v.p. 1997-99, state program v.p. 1997-99, state media chair, 2000—), Pi Lambda Theta (Ethel Mary Moore award Outstanding Educator 1993), N.M. Goals 2000 (panel mem. 1994-97), Delta Kappa Gamma . Roman Catholic. Avocations: soccer, running, hiking, travel, skiing. Home: 8101 Krim Dr NE Albuquerque NM 87109-5223 Office: La Cueva H S 7801 Wilshire Ave NE Albuquerque NM 87122-2807 Fax: 505-797-2250. E-mail: pgraff@aol.com

GRAHAM, BEARDSLEY, management consultant; b. Berkeley, Calif., Apr. 24, 1914; s. Reuben Jacob and Kate Ellen (Beardsley) G.; m. Frances Rose McSherry, June 17, 1951 (div. Mar. 1967); children: McSherry, Heather; m. Lorraine Juliana Shaw, Oct. 22, 1973. BS in Chemistry, Physics and Math., U. Calif., Berkeley, 1935; postgrad. in Electronics, U. Calif., 1938-40, Columbia U., 1941-42; postgrad. in Chemistry, Tufts U., 1942-43. Registered profl. engr., Ariz., Calif., Ky.; lic. real estate broker, Calif. Instr. Edison Elec. Sch., Berkeley; frameman Pacific Tel. & Tel. co., San Francisco, 1937-39; chief engr. Golden Gate Internat. Expn. RCA Mfg. Co., 1939-40; devel. engr. NBC, Hollywood, Calif., N.Y.C., 1940-42; staff mem. radiation lab MIT, Cambridge, 1942-44; chief engr., head dept. spl. products devel. labs. Eclipse-Pioneer div. Bendix Aviation Corp., Teterboro, N.J., and Pacific div., Detroit, 1946-51, chief engr. rsch. labs., tech. cons. to v.p. rsch.; asst. chmn. engring. dept. Stanford Rsch. Inst., Menlo Park, Calif., 1951-56; pres. Spindletop Rsch., 1961-67; exec. v.p. Sequoia Process Corp., Redwood City, Calif., 1956-57; spl. asst. comml. satellites Lockheed Aircraft Corp., Palo Alto and Sunnyvale, Calif., 1957-61, mgr. satellite systems planning Air Force Satellite Systems Program, mgr. specialty sales dept.; pres. Spindletop Rsch. Inc., Lexington, Ky., 1961-67; cons. Lockheed Aircraft Corp., Palo Alto and Sunnyvale, Calif., 1967—; pvt. practice mgmt. cons. Bend, Oreg., 1967—. Pioneer in fields of new techs. and svcs. including econ. devel., air pollution and environ. qualities, nuclear weapons and power, satellite systems; bd. dirs., incorporator (selected by Pres. Kennedy) Communication Satellite Corp., 1962-64; founding chmn. bd. Videorecord Corp. Am.; mem. adv. com. on isotope and radiation devel. AEC, Ky., Atomic Energy and Space Authority, Ky. adv. com. on nuclear energy; rsch. prof. elec. engring. U. Ky., 1965; active in Microwave Communications Inc. (now MCI), Aetna Life Inc., numerous other. Papers on file at Bancroft Libr., U. Calif. at Berkeley. V.p. Bend Urban Area Planning Commn., 1983-87; vice chmn. engring. tech. adv. com. Cen. Oreg. Community Colls., 1983—, Citizens Com. for Cityhood, Yucca Valley, Calif., 1977; mem. energy adv. com. League Oreg. Cities, 1983-87; active various other civic orgns.; treas., bd. govs. ocm. for art Stanford U., 1956; mem. Bend Traffic-Saftey Com., 1987, Cent. Oreg. Coun. on Higher Edn., 1983—. Named to Hon. Order Ky. Cols. Fellow IEEE (life), AIAA (assoc.); mem. Internat. Solar Energy Soc. (founding sec., bd. dirs. 1953-66), Solar Energy Assn. Oreg. (parliamentarian 1986, exec. bd.), International Club (Washington), Arizona Club, University Club (L.A.). Democrat. Home and Office: 214 Hillcrest Pl Baker City OR 97814-4132

GRAHAM, BILL, opera company director; Artistic dir. Spokane (Wash.) Opera, Spokane, Wash. Vet. dir. over 50 shows ranging from grand opera to musical theatre; active vocal coach. Office: Spokane Opera 643 S Ivory St Ste 2 Spokane WA 99202-2362

GRAHAM, DENIS DAVID, marriage and family therapist, educational consultant; b. Santa Rosa, Calif., Oct. 21, 1941; s. Elbert Eldon and Mildred Bethana (Dyson) G.; m. Margaret Katherine Coughlan, Aug. 31, 1968; children: Kathleen Ann, Todd Cameron (dec.). BS in Tel. Edn., U. Nev., 1964, MEd, 1973, MA, 1982. Cert. for ednl. pers.; lic. marriage and family therapist, Nev. Tchr. vocat. bus. edn. Earl Wooster H.S., Reno, 1964-66, chmn. dept. bus. edn., 1966-67; stare supr. bus. and office edn. Nev. Dept. Edn., Carson City, 1967-70, adminstr. vocat. edn. field svcs., 1970-74, asst. dir., 1974-78, vocat. edn. cons., 1978-85; edn. curriculum specialist Washoe County Sch. Dist., Reno, 1985-89, curriculum coord., 1989-94, ret., 1994; pres. Midpoint Inc., 1995—. Marriage and family counselor Severance & Assocs., Carson City, 1983-85, Mountain Psychiat. Assocs., 1985-87; mem. tng. and youth employment coun. S.W. Regional Lab. for Ednl. R&D, Los Alamitos, Calif., 1982, mem. career edn. coun., 1980-81. Editor Coun. of Chief State Sch. Officers' Report: Staffing the Nation's Schools: A National Emergency, 1984; contbr. articles to profl. jours. Bd. dirs. U. Nev.-Reno Campus Christian Assn., 1988-90, 97-99; mem. adv. com. Truckee Meadows C.C., Reno, 1988-94; mem. Gov.'s Crime Prevention Com., Carson City, 1979-83, Atty. Gen.'s Anti-Shoplifting Com., Carson City, 1974-78, Gov.'s Devel. Disabilities Planning Coun., Carson City, 1977-79; bd. dirs. Jr. Achievement No. Nev., 1989-92, sec., mem. exec. com., 1990-91; bd. dirs. Friends of the Coll. of Edn., U. Nev., Reno, 1995-99. Recipient award for svc. Bus. Edn. Assn. No. Nev., 1973, Svc. award YMCA, 1962, 63, Helping Hand award Procter R. Hug H.S., 1993-94. Mem. ACA, Am. Vocat. Assn., Nat. Assn. Vocat. Edn. Spl. Needs Pers. (Outstanding Svc. award Region V 1982), Am. Assn. Marriage and Family Therapy, Nev. Vocat. Assn. (Outstanding Svc. award 1991, Bill Trabert Meml. award Excellence in Occup. Edn. 1994), Internat. Assn. Marriage and Family Counselors, U. Nev. Reno Alumni Assn. (exec. com. 1971-75), Phi Delta Kappa, Phi Kappa Phi. Democrat. Methodist. Home: 3056 Bramble Dr Reno NV 89509-6901 Office: PO Box 33034 Reno NV 89533-3034 E-mail: denisg2348@aol.com

GRAHAM, HOWARD HOLMES, financial executive; b. Greensburg, Pa., Apr. 24, 1947; s. Howard B. and Dorothy (Holmes) G.; m. Roberta A. Grant, June 8, 1968 (div. Feb. 1984); m. Linda A. Cossarek, Mar. 14, 1987; children: Christina Ross, John Howard. BS, Carnegie Mellon U., 1968; MBA, U. Chgo., 1973. CPA, Ill. Various positions Zenith Electronics Corp., Glenview, Ill., 1973-81, dir. acctg., 1981-82, v.p. fin. svcs., 1982-87, v.p. fin., 1987-88; sr. v.p. fin. Wyse Tech. Inc., San Jose, Calif., 1988-90, Informix Corp., Menlo Park, 1990-96; sr. v.p. fin. and adminstrn., CFO, Siebel Sys., San Mateo, 1997—. Capt. U.S. Army, 1968-71, Vietnam. Decorated Bronze Star; recipient Elijah Watt Sells award Am. Inst. CPA's, 1982. Mem. La Rinconada Country Club, Beta Gamma Sigma. Office: Siebel Systems 1855 S Grant St San Mateo CA 94402-7016

GRAHAM, JAN, state attorney general; b. Salt Lake City; BS in Psychology, Clark U., Worcester, Mass., 1973; MS in Psychology, U. Utah, 1977, JD, 1980. Bar: Utah. Ptnr. Jones, Waldo, Holbrook & McDonough, Salt Lake City, 1979-89; soliciter gen. Utah Atty. Gen.'s Office, Salt Lake City, 1989-93; atty. gen. State of Utah, 1993—. Adj. prof. law U. Utah Law Sch.; bar commr. Utah State Bar, 1991; master of bench Utah Inns Ct. VII; mem. Utah Commn. on Justice in 21st Century; bd. dirs. Jones, Waldo, Holbrook & McDonough; bd. trustees Coll. Law U. Utah (pres.). Fin. devel. chair YWCA; chair Ctrl. Bus. Improvement Dist.; mem. Salt Lake City Olympic Bid Com. 1988 Games. Named Woman Lawyer Yr. Utah, 1987. Mem. Am. Arbitration Assn. (nat. panel arbitrators), Women Lawyers Utah (co-founder, mem. exec. com.). Office: Attorney Generals Office 236 State Capitol Building Salt Lake City UT 84114-1202

GRAHAM, PATRICK J. state agency administrator; BS, Mont. State; MS, Univ. Idaho. With State Mont. Fish, Wildlife and Parks Dept., 1977-93, dir., 1993-2000.

GRAHAM, RONALD LEWIS, mathematician; b. Taft, Calif., Oct. 31, 1935; s. Leo Lewis and Margaret Jane (Anderson) G.; children: Cheryl, Marc. Student, U. Chgo., 1951-54; BS, U. Alaska, 1958; MA, U. Calif., Berkeley, 1961, PhD, 1962; LLD (hon.), Western Mich. U., 1984; DSc, St. Olaf Coll., 1985, U. Alaska, 1988. Mem. tech. staff Bell Labs., Murray Hill, N.J., 1962—, head dept. discrete math., 1968—, dir. Math. Scis. Rsch. Ctr., 1983—, adj. dir. rsch., info. scis. divsn., 1987-95; prof. Rutgers U., 1987—; chief scientist AT&T Labs. Rsch., Florham Park, N.J., 1996-98; Jacobs Endowed chair computer and info. sci. U. Calif., San Diego, 1999—. Regents' prof. UCLA, 1975; vis. prof. computer sci. Stanford U., 1979, 81, Princeton (N.J.) U., 1987, 89; Irwin and Joan Jacobs prof. computer sci. U. Calif. San Diego, La Jolla, 1998—. Author: Ramsey Theory, 1980, Concrete Mathematics, 1989, Erdös on Graphs, 1998. Served with USAF, 1955-59. Recipient Polya prize, 1975; Euler prize, 1993; named Scientist of Yr. World Book Encyclopedia, 1981; scholar Ford Found., 1958, Fairchild Found. Disting. scholar Calif. Inst. Tech., 1983; fellow NSF, 1961, Woodrow Wilson Found., 1962. Fellow AAAS, N.Y. Acad. Scis., Assn. Computing Machinery; mem. NAS (treas. 1996—), Am. Math. Soc. (pres. 1993-94), Math. Assn. Am., Soc. Indsl. and Applied Math., Am. Acad. Arts and Scis., Internat. Jugglers Assn. (past pres.). Office: U Calif San Diego CSE La Jolla CA 92093-0114

GRAHAM, STEPHEN MICHAEL, lawyer; b. Houston, May 1, 1951; s. Frederick Mitchell and Lillian Louise (Miller) G.; m. Joanne Marie Sealock, Aug. 24, 1974; children: Aimee Elizabeth, Joseph Sealock, Jessica Anne. BS, Iowa State U., 1973; JD, Yale U., 1976. Bar: Wash. 1977. Assoc. Perkins Coie, Seattle, 1976-83, ptnr., 1983-2000, Orrick, Herrington & Sutcliffe LLP, Seattle, 2000—. Bd. dirs. Wash. Spl. Olympics, Seattle, 1979-83, pres., 1983; mem. Seattle Bd. Ethics, 1982-88, chmn., 1983-88; mem. Seattle Fair Campaign Practices Commn., 1982-88; trustee Cornish Coll. Arts, 1986-91, mem. exec. com., 1989-91; trustee Arboretum Found., 1994-96; mem. exec. com. Sch. Law, Yale U., 1988-92, 93-97; bd. dirs. Perkins Coie Cmty. Svc. Found., 1988-91; trustee Seattle Repertory Theatre, 1993-95; trustee Seattle Children's Theatre, 1996-98, mem. exec. com., 1997-98; bd. dirs. Wash. Biotech. and Biomed. Assn., 1996—, mem. exec. com., 1997—; trustee Fred Hutchinson Cancer Rsch. Ctr., 1999-2001, Sr. Citizens Ctr. Mem. ABA, Wash. State Bar ASsn., Seattle-King County Bar Assn., Wash. Athletic Club, Rainier Club. Episcopalian. Office: Orrick Herrington & Sutcliffe Ste 900 719 Second Ave Seattle WA 98104-7063

GRAINGER, JOHN R. medical association administrator; COO Laidlaw, 1997-99; pres., CEO Am. Med. Response, Aurora, Colo., 1999—. Office: Am Med Response 2821 S Parker Rd Aurora CO 80014-2735

GRAINGER, MICHAEL J. data processing executive; BS in Acctg., U. Montevallo, Ala. CPA, Calif. CFO Coble Systems, Inc., Nashville, 1980-86, Book Group, Sullivan Graphics, Inc., 1986-90; v.p., contr. Ingram Industries, Inc., Nashville, 1990-96, CFO, 1996; exec. v.p., worldwide CFO Ingram Micro Inc., Santa Ana, Calif., 1996—. Office: Ingram Micro Inc PO Box 25125 1600 E St Andrew Pl Santa Ana CA 92799-5125

GRALAPP, MARCELEE GAYL, librarian; b. Winfield, Kans., Nov. 2, 1931; d. Benjamin Harry and Lelia Iris (Compton) G. BA, Kans. State Tchrs. Coll., 1952; MA, U. Denver, 1963. Children's libr. Hutchinson (Kans.) Pub. Libr., 1952-57, Lawrence (Kans.) Pub. Libr., 1957-59; assoc. libr. Boulder (Colo.) Pub. Libr., 1959-66, libr. dir., 1966—. Vis. faculty U. Denver, 1965-66, 67, Kans. State Tchrs. Coll., Emporia, 1965. Chmn. state plan for libr. devel. Librs.-Colo., 1974; city staff liaison Boulder Arts Commn., 1979—; bd. dirs. Boulder Ctr. for Visual Arts, 1975-79. Recipient Gov.'s award Colo. Coun. on Arts and Humanities, 1981; named Woman of Yr., Bus. and Profl. Women, 1997. Mem. ALA, Colo. Libr. Assn. (Lifetime Achievement award 1992), Delta Kappa Gamma. Democrat. Home: 3080 15th St Boulder CO 80304-2614 Office: Boulder Pub Libr PO Drawer H 1000 Canyon Blvd Boulder CO 80302-5120

GRAN, ROBERT, engineering company executive; b. 1941; PhD, Calif. Inst. Tech., 1970. Sec. head TRW Sys., Redondo Beach, Calif., 1970-73; sr. rsch. engr., divsn. mgr. Flow Rsch. Inc., L.A., 1973-76; chief sci. Dynamics Tech., Inc., Torrance, Calif., 1976—. Office: Dynamics Tech Inc 21311 Hawthorne Blvd Ste 300 Torrance CA 90503-5691

GRANATO, CATHERINE (CAMMI GRANATO), professional hockey player; b. Downers Grove, Ill., Mar. 25, 1971; Student, Providence Coll., R.I., 1989-93, Concordia U., , 1994-97. Hockey player U.S. Nat. Team, 1992—. Recipient ice hockey Gold medal Olympic Games, Nagano, Japan, 1998. Office: USA Hockey Inc 1775 Bob Johnson Dr Colorado Springs CO 80906-4090

GRANCHELLI, RALPH S. company executive; b. Framingham, Mass., Jan. 2, 1955; s. Ralph S. and Avon L. (Chadwick) G. ASEE, Wentworth Inst. Tech., Boston, 1975; postgrad., U. Mass., 1975-78. Nat. sales mgr. Teledyne Semiconductor Co., Mountain View, Calif., 1981-85; v.p. Elantec, Inc., Milpitas, 1985—. Office: Elantec Inc 675 Trade Zone Blvd Milpitas CA 95035-6803

GRAND, TAMARA C. zoology researcher; b. Port Moody, B.C., Can., June 7, 1967; BS in Zoology with honors, U. Western Ont., Can., 1989; MS in Biology, Concordia U., Montreal, Quebec, 1992; PhD in Behavioral Scis., Simon Fraser U., Burnaby, B.C., Can., 1997. Rsch. asst. zoology dept. U. Western Ont., 1989; rsch. asst. biology dept. Concordia U., Montreal, 1990; researcher U. B.C., Vancouver, Can. Instr. Simon Fraser U., 1993, coop. edn. tchg. asst., 1994-96; coord. Pacific Ecology Conf., Bamfield Marine Sta., Vancouver Is., B.C., 1994; presenter, lectr. in field. Contbr. numerous articles to profl. jours. Ont. scholar, 1985, postgrad. scholar N.S.E.R.C., 1990-92, 93-95; ; Simon Fraser Spl. grad. rsch. fellow, 1993, grad. fellow, 1997, postdoct. fellow N.S.E.R.C., 1998—; recipient Alice Wilson award Royal Soc. Can., 1998 Mem. Soc. Canadian Women in Sci. and Tech., Animal Behavior Soc., Soc. Am. Naturlists, Internat. Soc. Behavioral Ecology. Achievements include researchin examining the effects of individual differences in vulnerability to predators on habitat choice in three-spine stickebacks, incorporating population dynamics and morphological evolution into a game theroetic model of habitat choice, experimentally measuring selection by predators on stickleback morphology, using comparative analyses to investigate the relationship between territory size and body size in fishes. Office: U BC Dept Zoology 6270 University Blvd Vancouver BC Canada V6T 1Z4 E-mail: grand@zoology.ubc.ca

GRANDIN, TEMPLE, industrial designer, science educator; b. Boston, Aug. 29, 1947; d. Richard McCurdy and Eustacia (Cutler) G. BA in Psychology, Franklin Pierce Coll., 1970; MS in Animal Sci., Arizona State U., 1975; PhD in Animal Sci., U. Ill., Urbana, 1989; D (hon.), McGill U., 1999. Livestock editor Ariz. Farmer Ranchman, Phoenix, 1973-78; equipment designer Corral Industries, Phoenix, 1974-75; ind. cons. Grandin Livestock Systems, Urbana, 1975-90, Fort Collins, Colo., 1990—; lectr., asst. prof. animal sci. dept. Colo. State U., Fort Collins, 1990—. Chmn. handing com. Livestock Conservation Inst., Madison, Wis., 1976—; surveyor USDA. Author: Emergence Labelled Autistic, 1986, Recommended Animal Handling Guidelines for Meat Packers, 1991, Livestock Handling and Transport, 1993, 2nd edit., 2000, Thinking in Pictures, 1995, Genetics and the Behavior of Domestic Animals, 1998, Beef Cattle Behavior Handling and Facilities Design, 2000; contbg. editor Meat and Poultry mag., 1987-98; contbr. articles to profl. jours.; patentee in field. Named One of Processing Stars of 1990 Nat. Provisioner, 1990, Woman of Yr. in Svc. to Agr. Progressive Farmer, 1999; recipient Meritorious Svcs. award Livestock Conservation, Madison, Wis., 1986, Disting. Alumni award Franklin Pierce Coll., 1989, Industry Innovators award Meat Mktg. and Tech. Mag., 1994, Brownlee award for internat. leadership in sci. publ. promoting respect for animals Animal Welfare Found. of Canada, 1995, Harry Roswell award Scientists Ctr. for Animal Welfare, 1995, Humane Ethics in Action award Geraldine R. Dodge Found., 1998, Forbes award Nat. Meat Assn., 1998, Founders award Am. Soc. Prevention Cruelty Animals, 1999, Humane award Am. Vet. Med. Assn., 1999, , 1999, Joseph Wood Krutch award, Humane Soc. of U.S., 2001. Mem. Autism Soc. Am. (bd. dirs. 1988—, Trammel Crow award 1989), Am. Soc. Animal Sci. (Animal Mgmt. award 1995), Am. Soc. Agrl. Cons. (bd. dirs. 1981-83), Am. Soc. Agrl. Engrs., Am. Meat Inst. (supplier mem., Industry Advancement award 1995), Am. Registry of Profl. Animal Scis. Republican. Episcopalian. Achievements include design of stockyards and humane restraint equipment for major meat packing companies in the U.S., Canada and Australia. Home: Grandin Livestock Systems 2918 Silverplume Dr Apt C3 Fort Collins CO 80526-2402 Office: Colo State U Animal Sci Dept Fort Collins CO 80523-0001

GRANIRER, EDMOND ERNEST, mathematician, educator; b. Constanza, Romania, Feb. 19, 1935; s. Jacob G. M.Sc., Hebrew U., Jerusalem, 1959, Ph.D., 1962. Mem. faculty dept. math. U. Ill., 1962-64, Cornell U., 1964-65, U. B.C., Vancouver, 1965-66, 67—, prof. math., 1970-97, prof. emeritus, 1997—; faculty U. Montreal, 1966-67. Contbr. articles to profl. jours. Grantee NSERC, 1996. Fellow Royal Soc. Can.; mem. Can. Math. Soc., Am. Math. Soc. Office: U BC Dept Math Vancouver BC Canada V6T 1Z2

GRANNEMAN, VERNON HENRY, lawyer; b. Chico, Calif., Aug. 2, 1953; s. Vern Henry and Mary Elizabeth (Riley) G.; m. Stephanie Sampson, Aug. 19, 1978; children: Kelly, Michael. BA, Santa Clara U., 1975, JD, 1978. Bar: Calif. 1978, U.S. Dist. Ct. (no. dist.) Calif. 1978, U.S. Dist. Ct. (cen. dist.) Calif. 1984, U.S. Dist. Ct. (so. and ea. dists.) Calif. 1985. Assoc. atty. Ruffo Ferrari & McNeil, San Jose, Calif., 1978-81, Pillsbury, Madison & Sutro (merger with Ruffo Ferrari & McNeil), San Jose, 1981-85, ptnr., 1986-96, O'Donnell, Rice, Davis, Alexander & Granneman, San Jose, 1996-97, Genesis Law Group, LLP, San Jose, 1997-99, Skjerven, Morrill, MacPherson LLP, San Jose, 1999—. Mem. ABA, Internat. Found. Employee Benefit Plans (arbitration com. 1991-94), Santa Clara County Bar, Santa Clara Univ. Law Alumni (bd. dirs. 1986-92). Democrat. Roman Catholic. Office: Skjerven Morrill MacPherson LLP 25 Metro Dr Ste 700 San Jose CA 95110-1349

GRANNUCI, LEO, retired marketing professional; Sr. v.p. mktg. and sales Core-Mark Internat., South San Francisco, Calif.; retired. Office: Core Mark Internat 395 Oyster Point Blvd Ste 415 South San Francisco CA 94080-1932

GRANT, ALAN J. business executive, educator; b. Chgo., Dec. 18, 1925; s. Hugo Bernard and May (Gardner) G.; m. Margaret Stewart, Dec. 21, 1946; children: Pamela Rose, Deborah May, Bruce David. BSEE, Ill. Inst. Tech., 1946, MSEE, 1948; EdD, U. San Diego, 1992. Instr. elec. engring. Ill. Inst. Tech., Chgo., 1946-49; with N.Am. Aviation, Inc. (Autonetics), Anaheim, Calif., 1949-64, v.p., gen. mgr. computer and data systems div., 1962-64; pres. Lockheed Electronics Co. div. Lockheed Aircraft Corp., Plainfield, N.J., 1965-69; also v.p. parent co.; exec. v.p. Aerojet-Gen. Corp., El Monte, Calif., 1970-74; chmn., pres. Wavecom Industries, Sunnyvale, 1974-78, Primark Corp., San Mateo, 1975-80; chmn., chief exec. officer Internat. Rotex, Inc., Reno, 1980-86; dir. UNC Resources Inc, Falls Church, Va., 1974-81; chmn. Atasi Corp., San Jose, Calif., 1982-85; gen. ptnr. EMC Venture Ptnrs., San Diego, 1984-86; pres. Grant Venture Mgmt. Co., Coronado, Calif., 1986-96; chmn. Am. Innovision, San Diego, 1986-92, SalePoint Systems Corp., San Diego, 1987-92. Adj. prof. managerial scis. U. Nev., Reno, 1976-87, mgmt. San Diego State U., 1986-90; pres. Corp. Mgmt. Assocs., 1996—; adj. prof., dir. Ctr. for Entrepreneurship, Calif. State U., Long Beach, 1999—; adj. prof. entrepreneurship Calif. State U., Hayward, 2001—. Paul T. Babson prof. entrepreneurship Babson Coll., Babson Park, Mass., 1992-94. Mem. Am. Electronics Assn. (chmn. 1973, dir. 1970-74). Office: Corp Mgmt Assocs 778 Wimbledon Ln Livermore CA 94550-1750 E-mail: agrant105@home.com

GRANT, LEWIS O. agricultural products executive, meteorology educator; b. Washington, Mar. 29, 1923; s. Lewis F. and Rita J. (Jacqmain) G.; m. Patricia Jean Lovelock, July 23, 1949; children: Ann, Nancy, Brenda, Andrew, Laura. BS, U. Tulsa, Okla., 1947; MS, Calif. Inst. Tech., Pasadena, 1948. Meteorological cons. Water Resources Devel. Corp., Pasadena, Calif., 1948-54, Denver, 1948-54; rschr. and rsch. dir. Am. Inst. Aerological Rsch., Denver, 1954-59; asst. prof., assoc. prof., prof. atmospheric sci. dept. Colo. State U., Ft. Collins, 1959-93, emeritus prof., 1993—; pres. Piedmont Farms, Inc., Wellington, Colo., 1975-98, Grant Family Farms, Wellington, 1998—. Cons. Colo. Legis., Denver, 1971-73; bd. dirs. adv. com. Integrated Pest Mgmt. Contb. to profl. jours. Scout master, com. chmn. Boy Scouts of Am.; pres. Partner Communities, Ft. Collins, Colo., 1988; elder Presbyn. Ch., 1980—; 1st lt. U.S. Field Artillery and USAF, 1943-46. Recipient Vincent J. Schaefer award Weather Modification Assn., 1991, Soil and Water Conservation award Ft. Collins Soil Conservation Dist., 1994. Fellow Am. Meterological Assn.; mem. Nat. Acad. Sci. (sect. chmn. 1975-76, mem. climate com.), Organic Farming Rsch. Found. (bd. mem. 1995—). Republican. Presbyterian. Avocation: organic farm-scale gardening. Office: Grant Family Farms 1020 W County Road 72 Wellington CO 80549-1912 also: Colo State U Dept Atmospheric Sci Fort Collins CO 80523-0001

GRANT, RAYMOND THOMAS, arts administrator; b. Yonkers, N.Y., Nov. 1, 1957; s. Kieran J. and Rita B. (Benedek) G.; m. Susan Mary McLoughlin, Nov. 6, 1993; children: 1 child, Kieran John. B of Music Edn., U. Kans., 1980; MA in Arts Adminstrn., NYU, 1984. Cert. music edn. tchr. Intern John F. Kennedy Ctr. for the Performing Arts, Washington, 1980; band dir. Lawrence (Kans.) Pub. Schs., 1980-81; dir. spl. projects 92nd St. YM-YWHA, N.Y.C., 1983-85; gen. mgr. Am. Symphony Orch., N.Y.C., 1985-91; pres. Raymond T. Grant, Ltd., 1989-93; dir. Tisch Ctr. for the Arts of the 92d St. Y, N.Y.C., 1991-92; mgr. program devel. performing arts and film The Disney Inst., Celebration, Fla., 1993-96; programming cons. Walt Disney Attractions, Inc., 1996-98; dir. arts and culture Salt Lake Organizing Com. for Olympic Winter Games of 2002, 1998—; artistic dir. 2002 Cultural Olympiad. Guest lectr., spkr. King's Coll., NYU, N.Y.C., 1990, The Hartt Sch., U. Hartford, U. No. Iowa, Ind. U., 1997, The Sch. of the Art Inst. of Chgo., 1998, Va. Tech., 1998, U. Utah, 2000; mem. adv. com. Carnegie Hall Profl. Tng. Workshops, 1990-91; programming cons. Imperial Tombs of China Exhbn., Orlando (Fla.) Mus. Art, 1997—. Bd. dirs. Kans. Alliance for Arts Edn., Lawrence, 1981, Concerts for Young People, Lawrence, 1981, Negro Spiritual Scholarship Found., Orlando, Fla., 1997—; mem. adv. bd. N.Y. Youth Symphony, 1986; panel mem. presenting and commissioning program, challenge grant program NEA, 1993, site visitor presenting and commissioning program, 1994: mem. [illegible] cultural affairs Fla. Dept. State, 1994-95, 96; facilitator, mem. panel Martin Luther King, Jr. Forum, Diocese of Orlando, Orlando Mus. Art, 1997, 98. Power Found. scholar U. Kans., 1979; Stella Wolcott Aten grantee U. Kans., 1978, Scholarship Found. grantee, N.Y.C., 1980. Mem. Rocky Mountain Elk Found., Blue Mountain Sportsman Ctr., Ducks Unltd. Roman Catholic. Avocation: handgun shooting. Office: Salt Lake Organizing Com Olympic Winter Games 2002 299 S Main St Ste 1200 Salt Lake City UT 84111-2081 Home: 2188 Wilson Ave Salt Lake City UT 84108-3022 E-mail: raymond.grant@saltlake2002.com

GRANT, RICHARD EARL, medical and legal consultant; b. Spokane, Wash., Aug. 27, 1935; s. Conrad Morrison and Sylva Celeste (Sims) G.; m. Susan Kimberly Hawkins, Mar. 17, 1979; children: Paaqua A., Camber Do'otsie O. BSc cum laude, U. Wash., 1961; MEd, Whitworth Coll., 1974; PhD, Wash. State U., 1980. Cert. ins. rehab. specialist; cert. case mgr. Supr. nursing Providence Hosp., Seattle, 1970-72; asst. prof. nursing Wash. State U., Spokane, 1972-78; dir. nursing Winslow (Ariz.) Meml. Hosp., 1978-79; adminstr. psychiat. nursing Ariz. State Hosp., Phoenix, 1979-80; asst. prof. Ariz. State U., Tempe, 1980-83; assoc. prof. Linfield Coll., Portland, Oreg., 1983-86, Intercollegiate Ctr. for Nursing Edn., Spokane, 1986-88; sr. med. care coord. Fortis Corp., Spokane, 1988-92; med. svcs. cons. CorVel Corp., Spokane, 1992-94; owner Richard Grant & Assoc., Spokane, 1995-99; med./voc. case mgr. Genex Svcs., Seattle, 1999—. Cons. Ariz. State Hosp., 1980-82, Pres.'s Commn., Washington, 1981-83, U. No. Colo., Greely, 1985-86; area med. svcs. cons., 1992—. Author: The God-Man-God Book, 1976, Publications of the Membership (Conaa), 1983, 3d rev. edit., 1985, 4th rev. edit., 1988, Predetermined Careplan Handbook-Nursing, 1988, Duhikya: The Hopi Healer, 1996; contbr. articles to profl. jours. Judge Student Space Shuttle Project, Portland, 1983, N.W. Sci. Expo, Portland, 1983. With U.S. Army, 1953-56. Grantee NIMH, U. Wash., 1961; named one of top Hopi Scholars, Hopi Tribe, Second Mesa, Ariz., 1981. Mem. AAAS, Nat. League for Nursing, Wash. League for Nursing (v.p. 1988-90), Coun. on Nursing and Anthropology (editor 1982-90), N.Y. Acad. Scis., Case Mgmt. Soc. Am., Sigma Theta Tau. Avocations: painting, scuba diving. E-mail: dr.regrant@home.com

GRANT, WILLIAM WEST, III, banker; b. N.Y.C., May 9, 1932; s. William West and Katherine O'Connor (Neelands) G.; m. Rhondda Lowery, Dec. 3, 1955. BA, Yale U., 1954; postgrad., NYU Grad. Sch. Bus., 1958, Columbia U. Grad. Sch. Bus., 1968, Harvard U. Grad. Sch. Bus., 1971. With Bankers Trust Co., N.Y.C., 1954-58, br. credit adminstr., 1957-58; with Colo. Nat. Bank, Denver, 1958-93, pres., 1975-86, chmn. bd., 1986-93. Chmn. bd. Colo. Capital Advisors, 1989-94; bd. dirs. Barrett Resources Corp. Trustee Gates Found. Denver, Midwest Rsch. Inst., Kansas City, Episc. Ch. Found., Nat. Trust for Hist. Preservation; bd. dirs. Mountain State Employers Coun. Mem. Met. Denver C. of C. Episcopalian. Clubs: Denver Country, Denver. Home: 545 Race St Denver CO 80206-4122 Office: KRMA-TV 1089 Bannock St Denver CO 80204-4067

GRASSHOFF, ALEX, writer, producer, director; b. Boston; Student, Tufts Coll., U. So. Calif. Writer, producer, dir.: TV series Rockford Files, CHiPs, Nightstalker. Recipient Acad. award nomination for Really Big Family, 1966; recipient Acad. award nomination for Journey to the Outer Limits, 1974, Acad. award for documentary Young Americans, 1968, Emmy award for Journey to the Outer Limits, 1974, Emmy award for The Wave, 1982 Office: 7845 Torreyson Dr West Hollywood CA 90046-1228

GRASSO, MARY ANN, theater association executive; b. Rome, Nov. 3, 1952; d. Vincent and Rose Mary (Pupa) Grasso. BA in Art History, U. Calif., Riverside, 1973; MLS, U. Oreg., 1974. Dir. Warner Rsch. Collection, Burbank, Calif., 1975-84; mgr. CBS TV/Docudrama, Hollywood, 1984-88; v.p., exec. dir. Nat. Assn. Theatre Owners, North Hollywood, 1988—. Instr. theatre arts UCLA, 1980-85, Am. Film Inst., L.A., 1985-88. Screen credits: The Scarlet O'Hara Wars, This Year's Blonde, The Silent Lovers, A Bunnies Tale, Embassy. Apptd. commr. Burbank Heritage Commn. Mem. Bus. and Profl. Women's Assn. (Woman of Achievement award 1983), Retinitis Pigmentosa Internat. (The Vision award 1996), Friends of Tripod, Acad. Motion Picture Arts and Scis., Found. of the Motion Picture Pioneers, Phi Beta Kappa. Democrat. Avocations: traditional music and dance, environ. activities, tennis, yoga. Office: Nat Assn Theatre Owners 4605 Lankershim Blvd Ste 340 North Hollywood CA 91602-1875

GRAUBART, JEFFREY LOWELL, lawyer; b. Chgo., Aug. 18, 1940; s. John H. and Florence R. G.; m. Mary Linda Carey, June 24, 1973; children: Joshua Gordon, Noah Carey. BS in Fin., U. Ill., 1962; JD, Northwestern U., Chgo., 1965. Bar: Ill. 1965, Calif. 1968, N.Y. 1980. Assoc. Curtis Friedman & Marks, Chgo., 1965-67, Capitol Records, Inc., Los Angeles, 1968-70; prin. Hadfield, Jorgensen, Graubart & Becker, San Francisco, 1970-81; counsel Frankfurt, Garbus, Klein & Selz, P.C., N.Y., 1981-85; prin. Strote, Graubart & Ashley, P.C., Beverly Hills, Calif. and N.Y., 1986-87; counsel Cohen & Luckenbacher, L.A., 1988-90, Engel & Engel, L.A., 1991-92; pvt. practice L.A., 1992—. Sec. Paramount Growers, Inc., Delano, Calif., 1968-70; v.p., dir. London Internat. Artists, Ltd., Los Angeles, 1969-70, Jazz Images, Inc., N.Y.C., 1983-86; adj. prof. NYU, 1982-85; lectr. Columbia U. Sch. Law, N.Y.C., 1982-85, UCLA, 1988—, U. So. Calif., 1988—. Contbr. articles to profl. jours. and mags. Counsel San Francisco Jazz Found., 1980-81. Recipient Deems Taylor award ASCAP, 1981. Mem. NARAS (San Francisco chtp. legal counsel 1973-93, gov. 1973-85, gov. and legal counsel N.Y. chpt. 1982-85, gov. L.A. chpt. 1988-92), Calif. Copyright Conf. (dir. 1995—), Internat. Fedn. Festival Orgns. (dir. 1994—), Inter-Pacific Bar Assn., Beverly Hills Bar Assn. (chair internat. law sect. 1995—), Internat. Radio and TV Soc., Country Music Assn., Assn. of the Bar of the City of N.Y., Soc. Preservation of Film Music (trustee 1989—), v.p. 1991-94). Lodges: B'nai Brith (N.Y. and Los Angeles); Golden Gate (San Francisco) (v.p. 1974-75), Entertainment Industry Unit L.A. (founder, trustee 1988—). Office: Ste 1425 1900 Avenue of the Stars Los Angeles CA 90067-3013

GRAUSAM, JEFFREY LEONARD, lawyer; b. Newark, Sept. 21, 1943; s. John G. and Angela (D'Addario) G.; m. Anne Jenks Boynton, Dec. 20, 1969; children: Daniel Carpenter, Elizabeth Wiley. BA, Wesleyan U., 1965; JD, U. Chgo., 1968; LLM in Taxation, NYU, 1975. Bar: Calif. 1969, N.Y. 1970, U.S. Supreme Ct. 1981. Law clk. to chief justice Roger J. Traynor Supreme Ct., State of Calif., San Francisco, 1968-69; assoc. Debevoise, Plimpton, Lyons & Gates, N.Y.C., 1969-75; officer, mem. firm Tuttle & Taylor, Inc., L.A., 1975-89; ptnr. Morgan, Lewis & Bockius, LLP, L.A., 1989—. Editor-in-chief law rev. U. Chgo., 1967-68. Dir. Libr. Found. L.A., 1993-98, 99—. Mem. L.A. County Bar Assn. (exec. com. taxation sect. 1994-95), Order of Coif. Avocation: cycling. Office: Morgan Lewis & Bockius LLP 300 S Grand Ave Fl 22 Los Angeles CA 90071-3109

GRAVES, EARL WILLIAM, JR. journalist; b. Kodiak, Alaska, June 30, 1950; s. Earl William Graves, Sr. and Lola (Olson) Raab; m. Karin Ann Steichen, July 30, 1972; children: Emma, Mark, Max. BA in English with honors, U. Puget Sound, 1972; MA in English, Western Wash. State U., 1976. Tchr. English Naselle (Wash.) High Sch., 1972-74, Clatskanie (Oreg.) High Sch., 1975-77; police reporter Coeur d'Alene (Idaho) Press, 1978-79, city editor, 1980-82, mng. editor, 1983-84; sr. reporter Bulletin, Bend, Oreg., 1984-86; edn. reporter News and Observer, Raleigh, N.C., 1986-87; state edn. reporter News and Observer/Raleigh Times, 1987-89; edn. reporter The Oregonian, Portland, 1990—. Author: Poisoned Apple, 1995. Recipient Outstanding Svc. award N.C. chpt. Phi Delta Kappa, 1988, Third Prize Sr. Journalism Feature Reporting award Inst. for So. Studies, 1989, N.C. Sch. Bell award N.C. Assn. Educators, 1989, Benjamin Fine award Nat. Assn. Secondary Sch. Prins., 1989, First Pl. Gen. News Reporting award N.C. Press Assn., 1990, First Pl. Edn. Reporting award Pacific Northwest Excellence in Journalism, Soc. Profl. Journalists, 1991, 92, 2001, Media award Assn. Retarded Children Oreg., 1992, Seconad Pl. Spot News Reporting award Best of West, 1992, Second Pl. Best Writing award Oreg. Newspaper Pubs. Assn., 1993, Excellence in Edn. award Oreg. Assn. Supervision and Cirriculum Devel., 1993; Nieman fellow Harvard

U., 1998-99. Mem. Edn. Writers Assn. (pres., sec., bd. dirs. 1990—, Spl. Citation Nat. Awards for Edn. Reporting 1987, 91, Second Pl. Newspaper Series award 1989, Second Pl. Nat. Awards Edn. Reporting 1989). Democrat. Avocations: gardening, photography, outdoors, running, travel. Office: Oregonian 1320 SW Broadway Portland OR 97201-3499

GRAVES, KAREN LEE, high school counselor; b. Twin Falls, Idaho, Dec. 9, 1948; d. Isaac Mason and Agnes Popplewell; m. Frederick Ray Graves, Apr. 2, 1987. BA, Idaho State U., 1971; MEd, Coll. of Idaho, 1978. Cert. tchr. secondary edn., english 7-12, vocat. home econs. 7-12, pupil pers. svcs. K-12, Idaho. Tchr. Filer (Idaho) Sch. Dist., 1971-74, 76-80, Twin Falls (Idaho) Sch. Dist., 1974-76; counselor Mountain Home (Idaho) Sch. Dist., 1980—, dept. chairperson, dir. Bldg. coord. student assistance program, parent vols., mem. multi-disciplinary team. Sponsor mem. Rocky Mountain Elk Found. Mem. NEA, ACA, ASCD, Am. Sch. Counseling Assn., Idaho Counseling Assn., Idaho Sch. Counseling Assn., Idaho Edn. Assn., Idaho Affiliation Supervision and Curriculum Devel., Mountain Home Edn. Assn. Avocations: painting ceramics, crafting, stamping, reading, crossword puzzles. Home: 1105 Maple Dr Mountain Home ID 83647-2027 Office: Mountain Home H S 300 S 11th E Mountain Home ID 83647-3235 E-mail: graves_kp@sd193.k12.id.us

GRAVES, RAY, lawyer; b. Seattle, Feb. 23, 1924; s. Ralph Raymond and Naomi (Capron) G.; m. Joan Catherine Kikkert, May 19, 1946; children: Valerie Ann, Jon Carlton. BA, Wash. State Coll., 1950; JD, Duke U., 1952. Bar: Wash. 1952. Pvt. practice, Tacoma, 1952-60; of counsel McGavick, Graves, P.S. (and predecessor), 1960—. Mem. Wash. Bd. Bar Examiners, 1968-76. Contbr. articles to profl. jours. Served with USMCR, 1943-46. Mem. Wash. Bar Assn., Order of Coif, Tacoma Club. Republican. Presbyterian. Club: Tacoma Country and Golf. Home: 11005 80th Avenue Ct SW Lakewood WA 98498-5600 Office: 1102 Broadway Tacoma WA 98402-3525

GRAY, ALFRED ORREN, retired journalism educator; b. Sun Prairie, Wis., Sept. 8, 1914; s. Charles Orren and Amelia Katherine (Schadel) G.; m. Nicolin Jane Plank, Sept. 5, 1947; children— Robin, Richard B.A., U. Wis.-Madison, 1939, M.A., 1941. Reporter-correspondent-intern U. Wis.-Madison and Medford newspapers, 1937-39; free-lance writer, 1938-41, 51-57; intelligence investigator U.S. Ordnance Dept., Ravenna, Ohio, 1941-42; hist. editor, chief writer U.S. Ordnance Service, ETO, Paris and Frankfurt, Germany, 1944-46; asst. prof. journalism Whitworth Coll., Spokane, Wash., 1946-48, assoc. prof., 1948-56, head dept. journalism, adviser student publs., 1946-80, prof., 1956-80, prof. emeritus, 1980—, chmn. div. bus. and communications arts, 1958-66, chmn. div. applied arts, 1978-79; rschr. writer Spokane, 1980—; dir. Whitworth News Bur., 1952-58. Prin. researcher, writer 12 hist. and ednl. projects. Author: The History of U.S. Ordnance Service in the European Theater of Operations, 1942-46, Not by Might, 1965, Eight Generations From Gondelsheim: A Genealogical Study, 1980; co-author: Many Lamps, One Light: A Centennial History, 1984; editor: The Synod Story, 1953-55; mem. editl. adv. bd. Whitworth Today mag., 1989-90; contbr. articles to newspapers, mags., jours.; reader Am. Presbyns.: The Jour. of Presbyn. History, 1992-94. Scoutmaster Troop 9, Four Lakes Coun., Boy Scouts Am., Madison, Wis., 1937-41; chmn. Pinewood Addition Archtl. Com., Spokane, 1956— ; dir. Inland Empire Publs. Clinic, Spokane, 1959-74; mem. ho. of dels. Greater Spokane Council of Chs., 1968-71; judge Goodwill Worker of Yr. awards Goodwill Industries Spokane County, 1972; vice-moderator Synod Wash.-Alaska, Presbyn. Ch. (U.S.A.), 1966-67; bd. dirs. Presbyn. Hist. Soc., 1984-90, 91-94, exec. com., 1986-90, chmn. hist. sites com., 1986-90; mem. Am. Bd. Mission Heritage Commn. for Sesquicentennial of Whitman Mission, 1986; elder Spokane 1st Presbyn. Ch., 1962—, clk. of session, 1984-86, mem. Inland Empire Presbytery Com. for Bicentennial of Gen. Assembly, 1988-89; mem. com. justice and peacemaking Presbytery of the Inland Northwest, 1988-95; mem. Care and Equipping of Congregations Com., 1995—; Dem. precinct official, Spokane, 1988-92. Served with AUS, 1942-46. Decorated Bronze Star and Army Commendation medals; recipient citation Nat. Coun. Coll. Publ. Advisers, 1967, Outstanding Teaching of Journalism award Whitworth Coll. Alumni Assn., 1972; named Disting. Newspaper Adviser in U.S. among colleges and univs., Nat. Coun. Coll. Publ. Advisers, 1979. Mem. Assn. for Edn. in Journalism and Mass Comms., Ea. Wash. Hist. Soc., Coll. Media Advisors (hon.), N.Am. Mycol. Assn., U. Wis. Alumni Assn. Half Century Club, Phi Beta Kappa (pres. profl. chpt. 1949-50, 67-68, 70-71), Sigma Delta Chi, Phi Eta Sigma. Democrat. Avocations: genealogy, travel. Home: 304 W Hoerner Ave Spokane WA 99218-2124 E-mail: aograyjour@aol.com

GRAY, BRUCE, computer and electronics company executive; Pres. Xicor, Milpitas, Calif. Office: Xicor 1511 Buckeye Dr Milpitas CA 95035-7431

GRAY, HARRY BARKUS, chemistry educator; b. Woodburn, Ky., Nov. 14, 1935; s. Barkus and Ruby (Hopper) G.; m. Shirley Barnes, June 2, 1957; children: Victoria Lynn, Andrew Thomas, Noah Harry Barkus. BS, Western Ky. U., 1957; PhD, Northwestern U., 1960, DSc (hon.), 1984, U. Chgo., 1987, U. Rochester, 1987, U. Paul Sabatier, 1991, U. Göteborg, 1991, U. Firenze, 1993, Columbia U., 1994, Bowling Green State U., 1994, Ill. Wesleyan, 1995, Oberlin Coll., 1996, U. Ariz., 1997. Postdoctoral fellow U. Copenhagen, 1960-61; faculty Columbia U., 1961-66, prof., 1965-66; prof. chemistry Calif. Inst. Tech., Pasadena, 1966—, now Arnold O. Beckman prof. chemistry and dir. Beckman Inst. Vis. prof. Rockefeller U., Harvard U., U. Iowa, Pa. State U., Yeshiva U., U. Copenhagen, U. Witwatersrand, Johannesburg, South Africa, U. Canterbury, Christchurch, New Zealand, U. Hong Kong ;George Eastman prof. Oxford U., U.K., 1997-98; cons. govt., industry; Kistiakowsky lectr. Harvard U., 1999. Author: Electrons and Chemical Bonding, 1965, Molecular Orbital Theory, 1965, Ligand Substitution Processes, 1966, Basic Principles of Chemistry, 1967, Chemical Dynamics, 1968, Chemical Principles, 1970, Models in Chemical Science, 1971, Chemical Bonds, 1973, Chemical Structure and Bonding, 1980, Molecular Electronic Structures, 1980, Braving the Elements, 1995. Recipient Franklin Meml. award Stanford U., 1967, Fresenius award Phi Lambda Upsilon, 1970, Shoemaker award U. Louisville, 1970, award for excellence in teaching Mfg. Chemists Assn., 1972, Centenary medal of Royal Soc. Chemistry, 1985, Nat. Medal of Sci., 1986, Alfred Bader Bioinorganic Chemistry award, 1990, Gold medal Am. Inst. Chemists, 1990, Linderstrom-Lang Prize, 1992, Priestley award Dickinson Coll., 1991, Chandler medal Columbia U., 1999, Harvey prize Technion Israel Inst. Tech., 2000; named Calif. Scientist of Yr., 1988, Achievement Rewards for Coll. Scis. Man of Sci., 1990; Guggenheim fellow, 1972-73; Phi Beta Kappa scholar, 1973-74. Fellow AAAS; mem. NAS, Am. Chem. Soc. (award pure chemistry 1970, award inorganic chemistry 1978, award for disting. service in advancement of inorganic chemistry 1984, Harrison Howe award 1972, Remsen Meml. award 1979, Tolman medal 1979, Pauling medal 1986, Priestley medal 1991, Willard Gibbs medal 1992), Royal Swedish Acad., Royal Soc. (London), Am. Philos. Soc., Royal Danish Acad. Scis. and Letters, Alpha Chi Sigma, Phi Lambda Upsilon. Home: 1415 E California Blvd Pasadena CA 91106-4101 Office: Calif Inst Tech 139-74 1200 E California Blvd Pasadena CA 91125-0001

GRAY, JAMES N. computer scientist; BS, PhD, U. Calif. Sys. rschr. Bell Labs, Murray Hill, N.J.; ops. sys. rschr. T.J. Watson Rsch. Lab IBM, database rschr. Calif.; rschr. Tandem Computers, Cupertino, Digital Equipment Corp.; sys. rschr. Microsoft Corp.; sr. rschr., disting. engr. Scaleable Servers Rsch. Group Microsoft Bay Area Rsch. Ctr., San Francisco, 1995—. Vis. scholar U. Calif., Berkeley; pres. Adv. Com. on Info. Tech.; mem. adv. bd. Sch. Engring., Stanford U. Editor: Morgan Kaufmann Data Management Series, Data Mining and Knowledge Discovery; moderator database sect. Computer Sci. Online Rsch. Repository; past editor in chief and endowment bd. VLDB Jour. Recipient Turing award Assn. Computer Machinery. Fellow Assn. Computing Machinery; mem. NAE, NRC (mem. computer sci. and telecomm. bd.). Office: Microsoft Rsch 301 Howard St Fl 8 San Francisco CA 94105 E-mail: gray@microsoft.com

GRAY, KARLA MARIE, state supreme court chief justice; BA, MA in African History, Western Mich. U.; JD, Hastings Coll. of Law, San Francisco, 1976. Bar: Mont. 1976, Calif. 1977. Law clk. to Hon. W. D. Murray U.S. Dist. Ct., 1976-77; staff atty. Atlantic Richfield Co., 1977-81; pvt. practice law Butte, Mont., 1981-84; staff atty., legis. lobbyist Mont. Power Co., Butte, 1984-91; justice Supreme Ct. Mont., Helena, 1991-2000, chief justice, 2000—. Mem. Mont. Supreme Ct. Gender Fairness Task Force. Fellow Am. Bar Found., Am. Judicature Soc., Internat. Women's Forum; mem. State Bar Mont., Silver Bow County Bar Assn. (past pres.), Nat. Assn. Women Judges. Avocations: travel, reading, piano, family genealogy, cross-country sking. Office: Supreme Ct Mont PO Box 203001 Helena MT 59620-3001

GRAY, MARVIN LEE, JR. lawyer; b. Pitts., May 9, 1945; s. Marvin L. and Frances (Stringfellow) G.; m. Jill Miller, Aug. 14, 1971; children: Elizabeth Ann, Carolyn Jill. AB, Princeton U., 1966; JD magna cum laude, Harvard U., 1969. Bar: Wash. 1973, U.S. Supreme Ct. 1977, Alaska 1984. Law clk. to judge U.S. Ct. Appeals, N.Y.C., 1969-70; law clk. to justice U.S. Supreme Ct., Washington, 1970-71; asst. U.S. atty. U.S. Dept. Justice, Seattle, 1973-76; ptnr. Davis Wright Tremaine, Seattle, 1976—, mng. ptnr., 1985-88. Staff counsel Rockefeller Commn. on CIA Activities in U.S., Washington, 1974; lectr. trial practice U. Wash. Law Sch., Seattle, 1979-80. Lay reader Episcopal Ch. of Ascension, Seattle, 1982-94. Capt. USAF, 1971-73. Fellow Am. Coll. Trial Lawyers; mem. ABA, Am. Law Inst. Office: Davis Wright Tremaine 1501 4th Ave Ste 2600 Seattle WA 98101-1688

GRAY, PATRICIA JOYCE, legal administration; b. Carlsbad, N.Mex., Feb. 5, 1951; d. Owen Corbett and Bobby Jo (Jones) G.; m. Patrick A. Edwards, Oct. 29, 1981 (div. June 1990). Student, U. Nev., Las Vegas, 1974-77. Receptionist, clk. Nationwide Fin., Las Vegas, 1969-70; dep. clk. U.S. Bankruptcy Ct. for Dist. Nev., Las Vegas, 1970-74, chief dep. clk., 1974-75, chief clk., 1975-79, clk. of ct., 1979—. Mem. bankruptcy work measurement subcom. of com. on adminstrn. bankruptcy system Jud. Conf. U.S., 1989-91; mem. tng. and edn. com. U.S. Bankruptcy Cts. Adminstrv. Office U.S. Cts., 1990-91; mem. Bankruptcy Work Measurement subcom. of Clerk's adv. com. Adminstrv. Office U.S. Cts., 1992-93, local rules subcom. Dist. Nev., 1991—. Mem. Space and Facilities Ad Hoc Task Force on Personnel of Adminstrv. Office of U.S. Cts., 1994-95, 9th Cir. Task Force on Race, Religious, and Ethnic Fairness, 1994-97; mem. bd. dirs. of Clark County, Nev. chpt. ARC, 1994-98. Mem. Nat. Conf. Bankruptcy Clks., Fed. Ct. Clks. Assn. Rebublican. Avocations: reading, pottery, gardening. Office: US Bankruptcy Ct Foley Fed Bldg 300 Las Vegas Blvd S Las Vegas NV 89101-5833

GRAY, PAUL RUSSELL, electrical engineering educator; b. Jonesboro, Ark., Dec. 8, 1942; BS, U. Ariz., 1963, MS, 1965, PhD, 1969. Prof. dept. elec. engring. and computer sci. U. Calif., Berkeley, dean Coll. Engring., 1996-2000, exec. vice chancellor, provost, 2000—. Recipient Solid-State Circuits award IEEE, 1994. Fellow IEEE (Baker prize 1980, Morris N. Liebmann Meml. award 1983); mem. NAE. Office: U Calif Office Chancellor 200 California Hall Berkeley CA 94720-1502

GRAY, PHILIP HOWARD, former psychologist, writer; b. Cape Rosier, Maine, July 4, 1926; s. Asa and Bernice (Lawrence) G.; m. Iris McKinney, Dec. 31, 1954; children: Cindelyn Gray Eberts, Howard. M.A., U. Chgo., 1958; Ph.D., U. Wash., 1960. Asst. prof. dept. psychology Mont. State U., Bozeman, 1960-65, assoc. prof., 1965-75, prof., 1975-92; ret., 1992. Vis. prof. U. Man., Winnipeg, Can., 1968-70, U. N.H., 1965, U. Mont., 1967, 74, Tufts U., 1968, U. Conn., 1971; pres. Mont. Psychol. Assn., 1968-70 (helped write Mont. licensing law for psychologists); chmn. Mont. Bd. Psychologist Examiners, 1972-74; spkr. sci. and geneal. meetings on ancestry of U.S. presidents; presenter, instr. grad. course on serial killers and the psychopathology of murder; founder Badger Press of Mont., 1998. Organizer folk art exhbns. Mont. and Maine, 1972-79; author: The Comparative Analysis of Behavior, 1966, (with F.L. Ruch and N. Warren) Working with Psychology, 1963, A Directory of Eskimo Artists in Sculpture and Prints, 1974, The Science That Lost Its Mind, 1985, Penobscot Pioneers vol. 1, 1992, vol. 2, 1992, vol. 3, 1993, vol. 4, 1994, vol. 5, 1995, vol. 6, 1996, Mean Streets and Dark Deeds: The He-Man's Guide to Mysteries, 1998, Ghoulies and Ghosties and Long-leggety Beastics: Imprinting Theory Linking Serial Killers, Child Assassins, Molesters, Homosexuality, Feminism and Day Care, 1998, Egoteria of a Psychologist: Poetry, Letters, Memos from Nether Montana, 2001; contbr. numerous articles on behavior to psychol. jours.; contbr. poetry to lit. jours. With U.S. Army, 1944-46. Decorated EAME medal Ctrl. Europe and Rhineland Campaigns, Victory medal WWII; recipient Am. and Can. research grants. Fellow AAAS, APA, Am. Psychol. Soc., Internat. Soc. Rsch. on Aggression; mem. NRA (life), SAR (v.p. Sourdough chpt. 1990, pres. 1991-2001, trustee 1989, 2001, v.p.-gen. intermountain dist. 1997-98, pres. state soc. 1998-99), Nat. Geneal. Soc., New Eng. Hist. Geneal. Soc., Gallatin County Geneal. Soc. (charter, pres. 1991-93), Deer Isle-Stonington Hist. Soc., Internat. Soc. Human Ethology, Descs. Illegitimate Sons and Daus. of Kings of Britain, Piscataque Pioneers, Order Desc. Colonial Physicians and Chirugiens, Flagon and Trencher, Order of the Crown of Charlemagne, Bozeman Rifle and Pistol Club. Republican. Avocations: collecting folk art, first and signed editions of novels, pistol shooting. Home: 1207 S Black Ave Bozeman MT 59715-5633 E-mail: phgray@mcn.net

GRAY, RICHARD MOSS, retired college president; b. Washington, Jan. 25, 1924; s. Wilbur Leslie and Betty Marie (Grey) G.; m. Catherine Claire Hammond, Oct. 17, 1943; children: Janice Lynn Gray Armstrong, Nancy Hammond Gray Schultz. BA, Bucknell U., 1942; MDiv summa cum laude, San Francisco Theol. Sem., 1961; PhD, U. Calif., Berkeley, 1972; doctorate degree (hon.), World Coll. West, 1988. Writer, creative dir. N.W. Ayer & Son, Phila., 1942-58; univ. pastor Portland State U., Oreg., 1961-68; founder, pres. World Coll. West, Petaluma, Calif., 1973-88, pres. emeritus, 1988—. Bd. dirs. World Centre, San Francisco, Life Plan Ctr.; founder Presidio World Coll., 1992—. Author poetry Advent, 1989. Bd. dirs. Citizens Found. Marin, San Rafael, Calif., 1988—, Marin Ednl. Found.; ruling elder Presbyn. Ch. U.S.A. Named Disting. Alumnus of Yr. San Francisco Theol. Sem., 1988, Marin Citizen of Yr. Citizens Found., 1988; recipient Svc. to Humanity award Bucknell U., 1992. Mem. Phi Beta Kappa. Avocations: song-writing, poetry.

GRAY, ROBERT M(OLTEN), electrical engineering educator; b. San Diego, Nov. 1, 1943; s. Augustine Heard and Elizabeth DuBois (Jordan) G.; m. Arlene Frances Ericson; children: Timothy M., Lori A. BS, MS, MIT, 1966; PhD, U. So. Calif., 1969. Elec. engr. U.S. Naval Ordinance Lab., White Oak, Md., 1963-65, Jet Propulsion Lab., Pasadena, Calif., summers 1966, 67; asst. prof. elec. engring. Stanford (Calif.) U., 1969-75, assoc. prof., 1975-80, prof., 1980—, dir. Info. Systems Lab., 1984-87, vice chair dept. elec. engring., 1993—. Author: Probability, Random Processes and Ergodic Properties, 1988, Source Coding Theory, 1990, Entropy and Information Theory, 1990; co-author: Random Processes, 1986, Vector Quantization and Signal Compression, 1992, Fourier Transforms, 1995; assoc. editor Math. of Control and System Sci. jour., 1987—; contbr. articles to profl. jours. Fireman La Honda (Calif.) Vol. Fire Brigade, 1970-80, pres., 1971-72; coach Am. Youth Soccer Orgn., La Honda, 1971-78, commr., 1976-78. Japan Soc. for Promotion Sci. fellow, 1981, Guggenheim fellow, 1982, NATO/CNR fellow, 1990. Fellow IEEE (Centennial medal 1984, 3d Millennium medal 2000), Inst. Math. Stats.; mem. Info. Theory Soc. IEEE (assoc. editor Trans. 1977-80, editor in chief 1980-83, paper prize 1976, Golden Jubilee award for technol. achievement 1998), Signal Processing Soc. IEEE (sr. award 1983, soc. award 1993, program co-chmn. 1997 Internat. Conf. on Image Processing, Tech. Achievement award 1998), Soc. Ingenieurs et Scientifiques de France. Avocations: maritime and Gilded Age history, hiking, computers. Home: PO Box 160 La Honda CA 94020-0160 Office: Stanford U Dept Elec Engring Stanford CA 94305 E-mail: rmgray@stanford.edu

GRAY, THOMAS STEPHEN, journalist, writer; b. Burbank, Calif., Aug. 22, 1950; s. Thomas Edgar and Lily Irene (Ax) G.; m. Barbara Ellen Bronson, Aug. 27, 1977; children: Jonathan Thomas, Katherine Marie. BA, Stanford U., 1972; MA in English, UCLA, 1976. Tchg. assoc. UCLA, 1976-77; reporter L.A. Daily News, 1977-79, editl. writer, 1979-84, editl. page editor, 1984-95; sr. editor Investor's Bus. Daily, L.A., 1995-98. Author: Teach Yourself Investing Online, 1999, Investing Online for Dummies—Quick Reference, 2000, Online Investing Bible, 2001. Recipient 1st Place award Editl. Writing Greater L.A. Press Club, 1988, Inland Daily Press Assn., 1993. E-mail: tsgray@qwestisp.net

GRAY, WALTER P., III, archivist, consultant; b. San Francisco, Aug. 8, 1952; s. Walter Patton II and Elsie Josephine (Stroop) G.; m. Mary Amanda Helmich, May 23, 1980. BA in History, Calif. State U., Sacramento, 1976. Rschr. Calif. State R.R. Mus., Sacramento, 1977-80, curator, 1980-81, 85-90, archivist, 1981-85, mus. dir., 1990-98; Calif. state archivist, 1998—. Cons. in field, 1976—. Contbr. articles to profl. jours. Democrat. Buddhist. Avocations: woodworking, antique automobiles, photography. Office: California State Archives 1020 O St Sacramento CA 95814-5704

GRAY, WILLIAM MASON, meteorologist, atmospheric science educator; b. Detroit, Oct. 9, 1929; BA, George Washington U., 1952; MS, U. Chgo., 1959, PhD, 1964. Rsch. asst. meteorologist U. Chgo., 1957-61; asst. meteorologist Colo. State U., Ft. Collins, 1961-64, from asst. to assoc. prof., 1964-74, prof. atmospheric scis., 1974—, sci. team prin. investigator. NSF Rsch. grantee, 1965-66, 70-71; Jule G. Charney award Am. Meteorol. Assn., 1994, Banner I. Miller award, 1994, Jack E. Cermak award, 1992, Neil Frank award Nat. Hurricane Conf., 1995, Man of Sci. award Colo. chpt. Achievement Reward Coll., 1995; named Person of Week ABC TV, 1995. Mem. Am. Meteorol. Assn. (Jule G. Charney Award, 1994). Office: Colo State U Dept Atmospheric Scis Fort Collins CO 80523-0001

GRAYBILL, DAVID WESLEY, chamber of commerce executive; b. Council Bluffs, Iowa, Apr. 8, 1949; s. John Donald and Dorothy Lorraine (King) G.; m. Kortney Loraine Steinbeck, Aug. 17, 1974; 1 child, Darcy Lorraine. BA in Journalism, U. Iowa, 1971; MA in Mgmt. and Leadership Studies, City U., 1999. Cert. econ. developer, Chamber exec. Adminstrv. asst. Iowa City C. of C., 1972-74; exec. v.p. Brighton (Colo.) C. of C., 1974-77; pres. Fremont (Nebr.) C. of C., 1977-83; pres., chief exec. officer Tacoma-Pierce County C. of C., 1983—. Pres. Nebr. C. of C. Execs., 1981-82; treas. NE Nebr. Econ. Devel. Dist., 1980-83. Charter mem. Gov.'s Small Bus. Improvement Com., Wash., 1984-86; presiding elder Tacoma (Wash.) Reorganized LDS Ch. Mem. Am. Econ. Devel. Coun. (bd. dirs. 1985-87), Am. C. of C. (bd. dirs. 1990-94), Wash. C. of C. Execs. (pres. 1988-89, bd. dirs. 1988-90, 98—), Rotary (bd. dirs. Tacoma 1985-87). Office: Tacoma Pierce County C of C PO Box 1933 Tacoma WA 98401-1933

GRAYSMITH, ROBERT, political cartoonist, author; b. Pensacola, Fla., Sept. 17, 1942; s. Robert Gray and Frances Jane (Scott) Smith; m. Melanie Krakower, Oct. 15, 1975 (div. Sept. 1980); children— David Martin, Aaron Vincent, Margot Alexandra. B.A., Calif. Coll. Arts and Crafts, 1965. Polit. cartoonist: Oakland (Calif.) Tribune, 1964-65, Stockton (Calif.) Record, 1965-68, San Francisco Chronicle, 1968-83 ; author: (non-fiction) Zodiac, 1986,Trailside, 1986, The Sleeping Lady, 1990, The Murder of Bob Crane, 1993, Unabomber: A Desire to Kill, 1997, The Bell-Tower, A True Detective Story of Gas-lit SanFrancisco, 1998, Ghost Fleet, 1999; illustrator (children's book by Penny Wallace) I Didn't Know What to Get You, 1993. Recipient 2d place Fgn. Press Awards 1973, World Population Contest 1976. Democrat. Presbyterian. Office: San Francisco Chronicle 901 Mission St San Francisco CA 94103-2905

GRAYSTON, J. THOMAS, medical and public health educator; b. Wichita, Kans., Sept. 6, 1924; s. Jesse T. and Luzia B. (Thomas) G.; children: Susan, Jesse, David; m. M. Nan Bryant, June 7, 1980. Student, Carleton Coll., 1942-43; B.S., U. Chgo., 1947, M.D., 1948, M.S., 1952. Diplomate: Am. Bd. Internal Medicine, Am. Bd. Preventive Medicine. Intern Albany (N.Y.) Med. Sch., 1948-49; Seymour Coman fellow preventive medicine U. Chgo., 1949-50, asst. resident medicine, 1950-51; epidemiologist epidemic intelligence service USPHS, U. Kans. Med. Center, 1951-53; chief resident medicine U. Chgo., 1953-54, instr. medicine, 1953-55; fellow Nat. Found. Infantile Paralysis, 1954-56; asst. prof. medicine U. Chgo., 1955-60, asso. prof., 1960; chief div. microbiology and epidemiology U.S. Naval Med. Research Unit 2, Taipei, Taiwan, 1957-60, cons., 1960-79; prof. preventive medicine, chmn. dept. Sch. Medicine, U. Wash., 1960-70, founding dean Sch. Pub. Health and Community Medicine, 1970-71, v.p. for health scis., 1971-83, prof. dept. epidemiology, 1970—, adj. prof. pathobiology, 1982—; mem. exec. com. Regional Primate Research Center, 1964-70, research affiliate, 1967-70; attending physician medicine Univ. Hosp., Seattle, 1960-70. Asso. mem. commn. acute respiratory diseases Armed Forces Epidemiol. Bd., 1962-65, mem., 1965-73; mem. research and engring. adv. panel biology and medicine Dept. Def., 1963-67; sci. group trachoma research WHO, 1963; virology and rickettsiology study sect. NIH, 1963-67; mem. internat. centers com. Nat. Inst. Allergy and Infectious Diseases, 1967-71; mem. expert adv. panel on Trachoma, WHO, 1970-88; chmn. exec. com., mem. nat. adv. council on health professions edn. NIH, 1972-75 Contbr. numerous articles to profl. jours. Fellow Am. Coll. Preventive Medicine (v.p. gen. preventive medicine 1970-71, regent 1971-74), Am. Pub. Health Assn. (governing bd. 1978-80); mem. Am. Assn. Immunologists, Am. Assn. Physicians, Am. Epidemiol. Soc. (pres. 1982-83), Am. Fedn. Clin. Research, Am. soc. Microbiology, Am. Soc. Clin. Investigation, Am. Soc. Tropical Medicine and Hygiene, Assn. Acad. Health Centers (dir. 1975-80, pres. 1978-79), Assn. Tchrs. Preventive Medicine, Infectious Diseases Soc., Internat. Epidemiol. Assn., Soc. Exptl. Biology and Medicine, Inst. Medicine of Nat. Acad. Scis., Western Assn. Physicians, Western Soc. Clin. Rsch. Office: U Washington Dept Epidemiology Ms 357236 Seattle WA 98195-0001

GRAZER, BRIAN, film company executive; Co-chair Imagine Films Entertainment. Prodr. films including: Night Shift, 1982, Splash, 1984, Real Genius, 1985, Spies Like Us (with George Folsey Jr.), 1985, Armed & Dangerous (with James Keach), 1986, Like Father, Like Son (with David Valdes, 1987, Parenthood, 1989, Cry Baby (with Jim Abrahams, 1990, Kindergarten Cop (with Ivan Reitman), 1990, Closet Land (with Ron Howard), 1991, The Doors (with Nicholas Clainos & Mario Kassar), 1991, Backdraft (with Raffaella DeLaurentiis), 1991, My Girl, 1991, Far and Away (with Ron Howard), 1992, Boomerang (with Warrington Hudlin), 1992, Housesitter, 1992, CB4 (with Sean Daniel), 1993, For Love or Money, 1993, The Paper (with Frederick Zollo), 1994, My Girl 2, 1994, Greedy, 1994, The Cowboy Way, 1994, Apollo 13 (with Ron Howard),

1995 (Acad. Award Nom. Best Picture, 1996), Sgt. Bilko, 1996, Ransom, 1996, Bowfinger, 1999, Beyond the Mat, 1999, Curious George, 2000, Nutty Professor II: The Klumps, 2000, How the Grinch Stole Christmas, 2000, Wonderland (TV series), 2000. Office: Imagine Films Entertainment 9465 Wilshire Blvd Fl 7 Beverly Hills CA 90212-2606

GREAT, DON CHARLES, composer, music company executive; b. Medford, Oreg., Mar. 11, 1951; s. Donald Charles Sr. and Anna Marie (Huff) G.; m. Andrea Louise Gerber, Oct. 31, 1970. Student, UCLA, 1975-76, 83-86, Dick Grove Sch. Music, 1983-87. Freelance songwriter Metro-Goldwyn-Mayer Records, 20th Century Records, Bell Records, L.A., 1968—; pres. Don Great Music, Inc., L.A., 1972—. Composer music for TV shows and feature films including Who's the Boss? (ABC), 227 (NBC), The Jeffersons (CBS), Gimme a Break (NBC), A Different World (NBC), Facts of Life (NBC), Unsolved Mysteries (NBC), Amen (NBC), Freddie's Nightmares (Lorimar-Warner Bros. TV), Saved By the Bell (NBC Disney), One Day at a Time (CBS), Married With Children (Fox/Columbia Pictures), Small Wonder (Fox TV), 1978—, Different Strokes (NBC), BJ and the Bear (NBC), Silverspoons (NBC), Sheriff Lobo (NBC), Incredible Hulk (CBS), Sanford (NBC), Real People (NBC), Crimetime After Primetime (CBS), The Promised Land (CBS), Candid Camera, Tales From the Crypt, In Living Color (Fox-TV), Laugh-In, Baby Races, Walker: Texas Ranger (CBS), Sex And The City (HBO), Girl Interrupted (Columbia Pictures), The Visitor (Fox), Thelma and Louise; composer music score Pres. Reagen Libr. Video, Pres. Carter Presdl. Libr. CD-ROM, 1994. Mem. Broadcast Music, Inc. (Best Music Score of Yr. award 1986, named TV Composer of Yr. 1986). Avocations: playing piano, going for Sunday drives. E-mail: dgreatmxx@aol.com

GREAVER, HARRY, artist; b. L.A., Oct. 30, 1929; s. Harry Jones and Lucy Catherine (Coons) G.; m. Hanne Synnestvedt Nielsen, Nov. 30, 1955; children— Peter, Paul, Lotte. BFA, U. Kans., 1951, MFA, 1952. Assoc. prof. art U. Maine, Orono, 1955-66; exec. dir. Kalamazoo Inst. Arts, 1966-78; dir. Greaver Gallery, Cannon Beach, Oreg., 1978—. Mem. visual com. Mich. Coun. Arts, 1976-78. One-man exhbns. include Baker U., Baldwin, Kans., 1955, U. Maine, Orono, 1958, 59, Pacific U., 1985; group exhbns. include U. Utah Mus. Fine Arts, 1972-73, Purdue U., 1977, Drawings/U.S.A, St. Paul, 1963, San Diego Mus., 1971, Rathbun Gallery, Portland, Oreg., 1988; 10-yr. print retrospective Cannon Beach Arts Assn., 1989, 20-yr. retrospective, 1998. Mem. adv. bd. Haystack Ctr. for the Arts, Cannon Beach, 1988-91. Recipient Purchase award Nat. Endowment Arts, 1971; grantee U. Maine, 1962-64 Mem. Cannon Beach Arts Assn., 1986-88. Address: PO Box 120 Cannon Beach OR 97110-0120

GREAVES, JAMES LOUIS, art conservator; b. Middletown, Conn., Jan. 25, 1943; s. Wellington North and Mabel (Frazer) G.; divorced; 1 child, Stephen Frazer. BS in Biology, Coll. William and Mary, 1965; MA in Art History, NYU; Diploma in Art Conservation, Inst. Fine Arts, 1970. Conservation intern Los Angeles County Mus., 1968-70, conservator, 1970, asst. head conservator, 1977-79, acting head conservator, 1979-81, sr. paintings conservator, 1981-85; owner, cons. Conservation Svcs., Santa Monica, Calif., 1985—. Chief conservator Detroit Inst. Arts, 1970-77; cons. conservator Art Gallery of Huntington Library, San Marino, Calif., 1979-91; part-time instr. art conservation for sr. and grad. level art historians, UCLA and Calif. State U., Fullerton, 1979-83. Fellow Internat. Inst. Conservation, Am. Inst. Conservation; mem. Western Assn. Art Conservators (past pres.).

GREBER, ROBERT MARTIN, retired financial investments executive; b. Phila., Mar. 15, 1938; s. Joseph and Golda (Rubin) G.; m. Judith Ann Pearlstein, Dec. 23, 1962; children: Matthew, Jonathan. B.S. in Fin., Temple U., 1962; grad., Sch. Mgmt. and Strategic Studies, 1982-84. Account exec. Merrill Lynch, Phila., 1962-68; portfolio mgr. v.p. Afuture Funds Inc., Lima, Pa., 1968-70; instl. account exec. Merrill Lynch, Phila., 1970-75, officer, mgr.-v.p. Los Angeles, 1975-79; chief fin. officer Lucasfilm Ltd., Los Angeles, 1979-80, pres., CEO San Rafael, Calif., 1980-84, Diagnostic Networks, Inc., San Francisco, 1984-87; ptnr. Leon A. Farley Assocs., San Francisco, 1988-90; pres., COO, Pacific Stock Exch., San Francisco, 1990-95, chmn., CEO, 1996-99; ret., 1999. Bd. dirs. Bay View Capital Group. Bd. dirs. KQED Pub. Broadcasting Sys., San Francisco, 1983, chmn. bd., 1988; bd. dirs. Film Inst. No. Calif., Marin Symphony Orch., 1981-83, Sonic Solutions, 1993—; trustee Western Behavior Scis. Inst., La JOlla, 1982-89; vice chmn. Assn. Am. Pub. TV, 1992-94; trustee Beryl Buck Inst. for Edn., 1990-93. With Army NG, 1959-60.

GREEN, BARTLEY CROCKER, advertising executive; m. Nancy Green; 4 children. Grad., U. Utah, 1981. Various positions, including maj. accounts mgr. San Mateo Times Newspaper Group; retail sales rep. San Francisco Newspaper Agy., 1986, advt. dir., then retail advt. mgr., v.p. for advt., 1996—. Featured as one of 20 Under 40 salute to newspaper profls. Presstime Mag. Mem. Newspaper Assn. Am. (com. mem.), Calif. Newspaper Advt. Execs. Assn. (past pres.), San Francisco Rotary Club. Office: San Francisco Examiner 110 5th St San Francisco CA 94103-2918

GREEN, CAROL H. lawyer, educator, journalist; b. Seattle, Feb. 18, 1944; BA in History/Journalism summa cum laude, La. Tech. U., 1965; MSL, Yale U., 1977; JD, U. Denver, 1979. Reporter Shreveport (La.) Times, 1965-66, Guam Daily News, 1966-67; city editor Pacific Jour., Agana, Guam, 1967-68, reporter, editl. writer Guam, 1968-76, legal affairs reporter Guam, 1977-79; asst. editor editl. page Denver Post, 1979-81, house counsel, 1980-83, labor rels. mgr., 1981-83; assoc. Holme Roberts & Owen, 1983-85; v.p. human resources and legal affairs Denver Post, 1985-87, mgr. circulation, 1988-90; gen. mgr. Distbn. Systems Am., Inc., 1990-92; dir. labor rels. Newsday, 1992-95, dir. comm. & labor rels., 1996-97; v.p. Weber Mgmt. Cons., 1997-98; v.p. human resources Denver Post, 1998-2000, Denver Newspaper Agy., 2000—. 1985 speaker for USIA, India, Egypt; mem. Mailers Tech. Adv. Com. to Postmaster Gen., 1991-92. Recipient McWilliams award for juvenile justice, Denver, 1971, award for interpretive reporting Denver Newspaper Guild, 1979. Mem. ABA (forum on comm. law), Colo. Bar Assn. (bd. govs. 1985-87, chair BAR-press com. 1980), Newspaper Assn. Am. (mem. human resources and labor rels. com.), Denver Bar Assn. (co-chiar jud. sel. and benefits com. 1982-85, 2st v.p. 1986), Colo. and Internat. Women's Dorum, Leadership Denver, Human Resources Planning Soc., Soc. Human Resources Mgmt., Indsl. Rels. Rsch. Assn., Colo. Assn. Human Resources Assn., Huntington Camera Club. Epsicopalian.

GREEN, CORDELL, computer scientist, educator; b. Ft. Worth, Dec. 26, 1941; s. William and Rebecca (Glickman) G.; m. Christine Louise Ochs, June 21, 1979; children— Jeffrey Adam, Laura Leah. B.A., B.S., Rice U., 1964, M.S., 1965; Ph.D., Stanford U., 1969. Research mathematician Artificial Intelligence Group, Stanford Research Inst., 1966-69; research and devel. program mgr. Info. Processing Techniques Office, ARPA, 1970-71; asst. prof. computer sci. Stanford U., 1971-78, cons. prof. computer sci., 1979— ; chief scientist computer sci. dept. Systems Control Inc., Palo Alto, Calif., 1979-81; dir., chief scientist Kestrel Inst., Palo Alto, 1981— ; cons. in field. Served to capt. U.S. Army, 1969-71. Air Force Office Sci. Research grantee, 1978-83; NSF grantee, 1980-83; Rome Air Devel. Ctr. grantee, 1982-83. Mem. Assn. for Computing Machinery (artificial intelligence area editor jour. 1972-79), Advanced Research Projects Agy. (grantee 1973-83). Contbr. articles to profl. jours.; mem. editorial bd. Jour. Cognitive Sci., 1977-80; researcher in field of computer sci. Office: 1801 Page Mill Rd Palo Alto CA 94304-1216

GREEN, CUMER L. lawyer; b. Moscow, Oct. 6, 1941; s. Leon Grant and Gwen Pratt G.; m. JoAnne Ames; children: Scott, Cliff, Holly, Stephen, Chris. BS in Bus., U. Idaho, 1963, MA in Acctg., JD, U. Idaho, 1969. Bar: Idaho 1969; U.S. Dist. Ct. Idaho, 1969, U.S. Ct. Appeals (9th cir.) 1971, U.S. Tax Ct. 1971, U.S. Dist. Ct. (cen. dist.) Calif. 1987; CPA, Idaho. Assoc. Eberle & Berlin, Boise, 1969-71; pvt. practice Boise, 1971-72; ptnr. Green & Bithell, Boise, 1972-75, Green & Frost, Boise, 1973-75, Green & Cantrill, Boise, 1975-80, Green & Sullivan, Boise, 1980-81; owner Green Law Offices, Boise, 1981-88, 91-01; ptnr. Green & Nyman, Boise, 1988-90. Treas. Ford for Pres., Boise; chmn. Gov's Task Force on Local Govt. Revenue Problems, 1970; prin. sponser Law Inst., Boise, 1992—. With USMC, 1959-60. Mem. ABA, Nat. Bd. Sch. Attys., Idaho State Bar Assn. (commr. 1995-98, pres. 1998), Idaho State Code Commn. (commr. 1998—), Phi Alpha Delta. Republican. Avocation: jogging, skiing. Office: PO Box 2597 Boise ID 83701-2597 E-mail: clgreen@micron.com

GREEN, HARRY WESTERN, II, geology-geophysics educator; b. Orange, N.J., Mar. 13, 1940; s. Harry Buetel and Mabel (Hendrickson) G.; children from previous marriage: Mark, Stephen, Carolyn, Jennifer; m. Maria Manuela Marques Martins, May 15, 1975; children: Alice, Miguel, Maria. AB in Geology with honors, UCLA, 1963, MS in Geology and Geophysics, 1967, PhD in Geology and Geophysics with distinction, 1968. Postdoctoral research assoc. materials sci. Case Western Res. U., Cleve., 1968-70; asst. prof. geology U. Calif., Davis, 1970-74, assoc. prof., 1974-80, prof., 1980-92, chmn. dept., 1984-88, prof. geology and geophysics Riverside, 1993-99, disting. prof. geology and geophysics, 1999—, dir. Inst. Geophysics and Planetary Physics, 1993-95, 2001, dir. analytical electron microscopy facility, 1994—, vice chancellor for rsch., 1995-2000. Exch. scientist U. Nantes, France, 1973, vis. prof., 1978-79; vis. prof. Monash U., Melbourne, Australia, 1984; specialist advisor World Bank Program, China U. of Geoscis., Wuhan, 1988; adj. sr. rsch. scientist Lamont-Doherty Earth Obs., Columbia U., 1989-95, Vetlesen vis. prof., 1991-92; expert advisor geophysics rev. panel NSF, 1991-94; co-founder Gordon Conf. on Rock Deformation, 1995, chmn. 2d conf., 1997; hon. faculty China U. Geoscis., Wuhan, 1998; vis. scientist Carnegie Inst. Washington, 2000. Contbr. articles to books and profl. jours. Grantee NSF, 1969—, Dept. Energy, 1988-94. Fellow AAAS, Mineral Soc. Am., Am. Geophys. Union (N.L. Bowen award 1994, Francis Birch lectr. 1995); mem. Materials Rsch. Soc., Sigma Xi. Achievements include discovery of a new mechanism of deep earthquakes and exhumation of rocks from great depth in subduction zones. Avocations: travel, hiking. Office: U Calif Inst Geophysics & Planetar Physics Riverside CA 92521-0001 E-mail: harry.green@ucr.edu

GREEN, JONATHAN WILLIAM, museum administrator and educator, artist, writer; b. Troy, N.Y., Sept. 26, 1939; s. Alan Singer and Frances (Katz) G.; m. Louise Lockshin, Sept. 16, 1962 (div. 1985); children: Raphael, Benjamin; m. Wendy Hughes Brown, Aug. 12, 1988. Student, MIT, 1958-60, Hebrew U., 1960-61; BA, Brandeis U., 1963, postgrad., 1964-67; MA, Harvard U., 1967. Photographer Jonathan Green, Photography, Boston, 1966-76, Ezra Stoller Assocs., Mamaroneck, N.Y., 1967-68; prof. MIT, Cambridge, Mass., 1968-76, dir. Creative Photography Lab, 1974-76; editor Aperture Books and Periodical, N.Y.C., 1972-76; prof. Ohio State U., Columbus, 1976-90; dir. Univ. Gallery Fine Arts, Columbus, 1981-90; founding dir. Wexner Ctr. for the Arts, Columbus, 1981-90; dir. Calif. Mus. Photography, U. Calif., Riverside, 1990—, prof., 1990—. Cons. Nat. Endowment for Arts, Washington, 1975-76, 85, 88, 94, Harry N. Abrams, Pubs., N.Y.C., 1982-84, Oxford U. Press, N.Y.C., 1977-82, Polaroid Corp., Cambridge, 1976; co-founder Visible Lang. Workshop, MIT Media Lab., 1973. Author: American Photography, 1984 (Nikon Book of Yr. award 1984, Benjamin Citation 1986), The Snapshot, 1974 (N.Y. Type Dirs. Club award 1974), Camera Work: A Critical Anthology, 1973 (Best Art Book award 1973), Continuous Replay: The Photographs of Arnie Zane, 1999 (Am. Assn.'s Mus.'s Publ. award 1999); editor, essayist Re-framing History in Jean Ruiter Photo Works, 1985-1995, 1996, The Garden of Earthly Delights: Photographs by Edward Weston and Robert Mapplethorpe, 1995, New Photographs by Pedro Meyer: Truths & Fictions, An Interactive CD-ROM, 1993, 5 Celebrations of Leslie J. Payne in Leslie Payne: Visions of Flight, 1991, Algorithms for Discovery, 1989, Pink Noise: Three Conversations concerning a Collaborative acoustic Installation with Philip Glass, Richard Serra, Kurt Munacsi, 1987, Rudolf Baranik Elegies: Sleep Napalm Night Sky, 1987, Straight Shooting in America, 1985, James Friedman: Rephotographing the History of the World in James Friedman, Color Photographs 1979-1982, 1982, Aperture in the 50's: The Word and the Way, in Afterimage, 1979, others; represented in permanent collections Mus. Fine Arts, Boston, Mus. Fine Art, Houston, Cleve. Mus. Art, Va. Mus. Fine Art, Richmond, Princeton U. Art Mus., Bell System Collection, Moderna Museet, Stockholm, Ctr. for Creative Photography, Tucson, De Saisset Art Gallery and Mus., Internat. Ctr. Photography, N.Y.C., MIT, Mpls. Inst. Arts; photographs pub.: American Images: New Work by Twenty Contemporary Photographers, 1979, Aperture, 1972, 73, 74, 25 Years of Record Houses, 1981, Architectural Record, Architecture and Urbanism, Progressive Architecture, A Field Guide to Modern American Architecture. Danforth fellow, 1963-67, NEA Photographer fellow, 1978, AT & T fellow, 1979. Office: UCR Calif Mus Photography Downtown Hist Pedestrian Mall 3824 Main St Riverside CA 92501-3624

GREEN, JOSHUA, III, retired banker; b. Seattle, June 30, 1936; s. Joshua, Jr. and Elaine (Brygger) G.; m. Pamela K. Pemberton, Nov. 1, 1974; children: Joshua IV, Jennifer Elaine, Paige Courtney. B.A. in English, Harvard U., 1958. With Peoples Nat. Bank Wash., Seattle, 1960-88, exec. v.p., 1972-75, pres., 1975—, chief exec. officer, 1977-78, chmn. bd., 1979-88, U.S. Bank Washington (merger PeoplesBank and Old Nat. Bank), 1988-96; chmn., CEO Joshua Green Corp., Seattle, 1996—. Bd. dirs., chmn., CEO, Joshua Green Corp., U.S. Bancorp, Safeco, Port Blakely Tree Farms, Virginia Mason Hosp. Found., Virginia Mason Hosp. Rsch. Pres. Joshua Green Found.; trustee Downtown Seattle Assn., Corp.Coun. for the Arts. Mem. Seattle C. of C., U. Club, Rainier Club, Seattle Tennis Club, Wash. Athletic Club. Home: 1932 Blenheim Dr E Seattle WA 98112-2308 Office: Joshua Green Corp 1425 4th Ave Ste 420 Seattle WA 98101-2218

GREEN, LARRY ALTON, physician, educator; b. Ardmore, Okla., Mar. 27, 1948; s. Thomas Alton and Mary Lou (Gauntt) G.; m. Margaret Joyce Ball, Mar. 27, 1971; children: Nathaniel, Katherine. BA, U. Okla., 1969; MD, Baylor Coll. Medicine, Houston, 1973. Diplomate Am. Bd. Family Practice. Intern then resident U. Rochester, Highland Hosp., N.Y., 1973-76; asst. prof. U. Colo., Denver, 1977-82, assoc. prof., 1982-85, prof., 1985—, chmn. dept., 1985-99, Woodward-Chisholm chair, 1989-99, dir. AAFP Ctr. for Policy Studies in Family Practice and Primary Care, 1998—. Vis. prof. various univs., U.S., New Zealand, U.K., Republic of South Africa, 1982—; dir. residency Mercy Med. Ctr., Denver, 1980-85; found. pres. Ambulatory Sentinel Practice Network, Denver. Contbr. articles to profl. jours. Elder Presbyn. Ch., Denver, With USPHS, 1976-77. Grantee USPHS, 1978—, Kellogg Found., 1982-87. Mem. Assn. Depts. Family Medicine (pres. 1987-89), N.Am. Primary Care Rsch. Group (bd. dirs. 1989-93, pres. 1997—), Am. Acad. Family Physicians, Soc. Tchrs. Family Medicine, Inst. Medicine. Avocation: fly fishing. Office: U Colo Health Scis Ctr Dept of Family Medicine 1180 Clermont St Denver CO 80220-6716 also: Ctr Policy Studies Family Practice & Primary Care 2023 Massachusetts Ave NW Washington DC 20036-1011

GREEN, LYDA N. state legislator; b. Livingston, Tex., Oct. 16, 1938; m. Curtis Green; children: Shelton, Kristie, Brad. BBA, Sam Houston State U., 1959; Slingerland lang. cert., U. Alaska, 1988. Tchr. West H.S., 1962-63; adminstrv. asst. Pan Am. Petroleum, AMOCO, 1963-65; co-owner Anchorage Racquet Club, 1978-88; instrs. asst. U. Alaska, Anchorage, 1991; adj. instr. Mat-Su C.C., 1991-93; mem. Alaska Senate, Dist. N, Juneau, 1994—. Former mem. Gov.'s Coun. on Disabilities and Spl. Edn., 1991-94; mem. spl. edn. regulations task force Dept. Edn., 1993-94; active First Bapt. Ch. Recipient Defender of Freedom award NRA, Legislator Appreciation award 4-H; named Legislator of Yr., Alaska Farm Bur., 1996. Mem. Soroptimists, Palmer Pioneer Lions, C. of C. Republican. Avocations: reading, piano, tennis, sewing, dyslexia. Office: State Capitol 120 4th St Rm 125 Juneau AK 99801-1142 also: 600 E Railroad Ave Ste 1 Wasilla AK 99654-8135 Fax: 907-465-3805/907-376-3157. E-mail: green@legis.state.ak.us

GREEN, PETER, former mayor, biological sciences educator; BSc in Biology, St. Benedict's Coll., 1952; BS in Theology, St. Gregory's Sem., 1956; BS in Zoology, U. Okla., 1959; MS in Zoology, Okla. State U., 1961, PhD in Ecology, 1964. Acad. dean St. Gregory's Coll., Shawnee, Okla., 1964-69, founding pres., 1968, pres., 1969-70; prof. biol. scis. Golden West Coll., Huntington Beach, Calif., 1970—; mayor City of Huntington Beach, 1998-99; mem. Huntington Beach City Council, 1999—. Post-doctoral fellow higher edn. U. Okla., Norman, 1970; cons. Environ. Planners, Linesch and Assocs., Long Beach, Calif., Wintersburg High Sch. Sci. Program, 1982-83; coun. mem. City of Huntington Beach, 1984—, mayor pro tempore, 1989-90. Contbr. articles to profl. jours. Chmn. curriculum com. for regional accreditation Golden West Coll., 1975-76, resdl. search com., 1977, parliamentarian, senator at large Acad. Senate of Golden West Coll., 1976-78, pres., 1978-79; liaison allied arts bd., libr. bd., environ. rev. bd., A & R design com., pub. facilities corp., toxic waste com. Huntington Beach City Coun., 1989—; rep. state-wide environ. issues com. Orange County div. Calif. League of Cities, 1988—; founding chmn. bd. Bolsa Chica Found., 1983—. NSF grantee, 1965, 68-69, 70-71, Kellogg grantee, 1966, 67; fellow Golden West Coll., 1973-77; named one of Outstanding Educators of Am., 1969-70, 74-75. Mem. Bosa Chica Conservancy (founding bd. mem. 1990), Amigos De Bolsa Chica (governing bd. mem., past pres. 1975-84). Office: City Hall Mayor & City Coun Office 2000 Main St Huntington Beach CA 92648-2702

GREEN, RICHARD E. real estate company executive; married; two children. BS in Acctg. and Fin., San Jose State U. With Price Waterhouse & Co., May Ctrs., Inc., 1968-80, exec. v.p.; co-pres. Westfield Group, L.A., 1980—. Bd. dirs. UCLA Armand Hammer Mus. of Art and Cultural Ctr. Office: 11601 Wilshire Blvd Fl 12 Los Angeles CA 90025-1770

GREEN, RICHARD FREDERICK, astronomer; b. Omaha, Feb. 13, 1949; m. Joan Auerbach; children: Alexander Simon, Nathaniel Martin. AB in Astronomy magna cum laude, Harvard U., 1971; PhD in Astronomy, Calif. Inst. Tech., 1977. Physics lab instr. Harvard U., Cambridge, 1970-71; NSF trainee Calif. Inst. Tech., Pasadena, 1971-72, grad. teaching asst. in astronomy, 1972-74, grad. rsch. asst. in astronomy, 1974-77, rsch. fellow in astronomy, 1977-79; asst. astronomer Steward Observatory, U. Ariz., Tucson, 1979-83, Kitt Peak Nat. Observatory, Tucson, 1983-85, assoc. astronomer, 1986-90, astronomer, 1990—, dir., 1997—; acting dir. Nat. Optical Astronomy Observatories, Tucson, 1992-93, acting dep. dir., 1993-94, dep. dir., 1994-99. Rsch. asst. Smithsonian Astrophys. Observatory, 1970-71; adj. asst. prof. Steward Observatory, U. Ariz., 1983-85, adj. assoc. astronomer and prof., 1986-90, adj. astronomer, 1990—; mem. users' com. Internat. Ultraviolet Explorer Satellite, NASA, 1979-81, chair proposal rev. panel, 1986-88, 93, final sci. program com., 1993, mem. sci. team Far Ultraviolet Spectroscopic Explorer Satellite, 1981—, Space Telescope Imaging Spectrograph, 1982—, guest observer working group Extreme Ultraviolet Explorer Satellite, 1988-92, chair proposal rev. panel ROSAT Guest Observer Program, 1989, 92, ROSAT Users' Coms., 1990-93, chair HST Cycle 2 Porposal Rev. Panel, mem. time allocation com., 1991, STSDAS users' com., 1991-92, Hubble Space Telescope Program Rev., 1997; mem. panel ultraviolet and optical astronomy from space, astronomy survey com. Nat. Acad. Scis., 1989-90; mem. panel HST and Beyond AURA, 1994-95; mem. proposal rev. panels NSF, 1996-97; instrument scientist Gemini 8-m Telescopes Project, 1991-92; mem. U.S. Gemini sci. adv. com., Gemini (Internat.) sci. com. U.S. Gemini Project Office, 1991-93, acting U.S. Gemini Project scientist, 1992-93, mem. instrument forum, optical instrumentation sci. working group, chair multi-object spectrograph critical design rev., 1997. Nat. Merit scholar; Hon. scholar Harvard U. Mem. AAAS (astronomy divsn. nominating com. 1992, coun. astronomy rep. com. coun. affairs 1995-97), Am. Astronomical Soc., Internat. Astronomical Union, Astronomical Soc. of the Pacific, Phi Beta Kappa. Office: Kitt Peak Nat Observatory 950 N Cherry Ave PO Box 26732 Tucson AZ 85726-6732

GREEN, ROBERT LEONARD, hospital management company executive; b. Los Angeles, Mar. 20, 1931; s. Leonard H. and Helene (Rains) G.; m. Susan Wolf, June 9, 1957; children— Wendy, Julie B.A., Stanford U., 1952, LL.B., 1956. C.P.A., Calif. Acct. John F. Grieder, San Francisco, 1957-59; assoc. Heller, Ehrman, White & McAuliffe, San Francisco, 1959-61; pres. Sutter Capital Co., San Francisco, 1961-69; chmn. bd. Community Psychiat. Ctrs., San Francisco, 1969-89, VIVRA, 1989-94, pres., 1989-92; chmn. Edn. Ptnrs., San Francisco, 1994-2000. Trustee Sta. KQED-Pub. TV, San Francisco, 1981-91, Mus. Modern Art, 1984-89, Mt. Zion Hosp., 1985-86. 1st lt. U.S. Army, 1954-56 Avocations: bicycling, golf. Office: 2601 Mariposa St San Francisco CA 94110-1426

GREEN, TRAVIS, professional hockey player; b. Castlegar, B.C., Can., Dec. 20, 1970; m. Sherry Ragan, July 18. Center New York Islanders, 1989-98, Mighty Ducks of Anaheim, 1998-99, Phoenix Coyotes, 1999—. Mem. Team Canada at World Championships, Vienna, 1995-96/ Office: Phoenix Coyotes 2 North Central Ste 1930 Phoenix AZ 85004

GREEN, WILLIAM PORTER, lawyer; b. Jacksonville, Ill., Mar. 19, 1920; s. Hugh Parker and Clara Belle (Hopper) G.; m. Rose Marie Hall, Oct. 1, 1944; children: Hugh Michael, Robert Alan, Richard William. BA, Ill. Coll., 1941; JD, Northwestern U., Evanston, Ill., 1947. Bar: Ill. 1947, Calif. 1948, U.S. Dist. Ct. (so. dist.) Tex. 1986, U.S. Ct. Customs and Patent Appeals, U.S. Patent and Trademark Office 1948, U.S. Ct. Appeals (fed. cir.) 1982, U.S. Ct. Appeals (5th and 9th cir.), U.S. Supreme Ct. 1948, U.S. Dist. Ct. (cen. dist.) Calif. 1949, (so. dist.) Tex.1986. Pvt. practice, L.A., 1947—; mem. Wills, Green & Mueth, L.A., 1974-83; of counsel Nilsson, Robbins, Dalgarn, Berliner, Carson & Wurst, L.A., 1984-91; of counsel Nilsson, Wurst & Green L.A., 1992—. Del. Calif. State Bar Conv., 1982—, chmn., 1986. Bd. editors Ill. Law Rev., 1946; patentee in field. Mem. L.A. world Affairs Coun., 1975—; deacon local Presbyn. Ch., 1961-63. Mem. ABA, Calif. State Bar, Am. Intellectual Property Law Assn., L.A. Patent Law Assn. (past. sec.-treas., mem. bd. govs.), Lawyers Club L.A. (past treas., past sec., mem. bd. govs., pres. 1985-86), Los Angeles County Bar Assn. (trustee 1986-87), Am. Legion (past post comdr.), Northwestern U. Alumni Club So. Calif., Big Ten Club So. Calif., Town Hall Calif. Club, PGA West Golf Club (La Quinta, Calif.), Phi Beta Kappa, Phi Delta Phi, Phi Alpha. Republican. Home: 3570 Lombardy Rd Pasadena CA 91107-5627 Office: 707 Wilshire Blvd Ste 3200 Los Angeles CA 90017-3514 E-mail: wpgreen@aol.com

GREENAN, THOMAS J. lawyer; b. Great Falls, Mont., July 13, 1933; s. Phil G. and Ada E. (Collins) G.; m. Helen Louise Shepard, June 1, 1957; children: Gregory, Kathleen, Timothy, Maureen, Daniel. Grad. Gonzaga U., 1955, JD, 1957. Bar: Wash. 1957, U.S. Dist. Ct. (we. dist.) Wash. 1959,

U.S. Ct. Appeals (9th cir.) 1961, U.S. Supreme Ct. 1970. Asst. atty. gen. State of Washington, 1957-60, 62-63; assoc. Ferguson & Burdell (subsequently Schwabe, Williamson, Ferguson & Burdell), Seattle, 1963-68; ptnr. Ferguson & Burdell, Seattle, 1968-95, Gordon, Thomas, Honeywell, Malanca, Peterson & Daheim, Seattle, 1995—. Lectr. on antitrust and civil practice and procedure. Trustee Gonzaga U., Spokane, Wash., 1984—, chmn., 1991-92. Fellow Am. Coll. Trial Lawyers (regent 1990-93, sec. 1993-95); mem. ABA, Wash. State Bar Assn. (chmn. antitrust sect. 1980-81, chmn. disciplinary bd. 1983-84, chmn. character and fitness com. 1991-92), Seattle-King County Bar Assn., Fed. Bar Assn. (pres. we. dist. Wash. 1982-83), Am. Judicature Soc., Wash. Athletic Club, Broadmoor Golf Club (Seattle; pres. 1988-89), KC. Democrat. Roman Catholic. Office: Gordon Thomas Honeywell Malanca Peterson & Daheim 600 University St Ste 21OO Seattle WA 98101-1176

GREENBAUM, JAMES RICHARD, liquor distributing company executive, real estate developer; b. Cleve., July 3, 1933; s. Harold and Miriam (Lion) G.; m. Peggy Strauss, Jan. 29, 1955; children: Robert Strauss, James R., Clifford Harold. B.A., Tulane U., 1955. V.p. Strauss Distbrs., Ark., 1961—. Bd. dirs. S&D Realty, Little Rock. Bd. dirs. Palm Springs Desert Mus., Jewish Fedn. Palm Springs, Betty Ford Ctr., Rancho Mirage, Calif. Lt. U.S. Army, 1955-57. Mem. Beaver Creek Club (Colo.), Tamarisk Club (Rancho Mirage, Calif.), Country Club of Rockies (Vail, Colo.), Club at Morningside (Rancho Mirage), Tamarisk Country Club, Zeta Beta Tau. Jewish (past pres., bd. dirs. temple). Office: 1 Hawkeye Pk 69844 US Highway 111 Ste H Rancho Mirage CA 92270-2849

GREENBERG, ALLAN, advertising and marketing research consultant; b. N.Y.C., Dec. 8, 1917; s. Solomon and Rose (Honik) G.; m. Rosalie Katz, Nov. 7, 1943; children— Barbara L. Gutman, Roy J. B.S., CCNY, 1942; postgrad., U. Wis., 1944, New Sch. for Social Research, 1946-54. Assoc. Psychol. Corp., N.Y.C., 1937-38; research analyst Serutan, Inc., Jersey City, 1939-41; research mgr./asst. dir. research Grey Advt., Inc., N.Y.C., 1948-55; sr. v.p., dir. research and planning Doyle Dane Bernbach, Inc., N.Y.C., 1955-74; research cons. to advt. agys. and mfrs., 1974—. Former chmn. tech. rsch. com. Advt. Rsch. Found.; former pres. joint coun. Empire Blue Cross/Blue Shield-HMO. Author: (with Mary Joan Glynn) A Study of Young People; booklet, 1966; contbr. articles to profl. jours. Former pres. mems. coun. Cmty. Health Program Queens-Nassau; mem. Profls. and Execs. in Retirement Group at Hofstra U. With AUS, 1942-45. Lodge: B'nai Zion (past mem. nat. exec. bd.; past pres. L.I. region) Home and Office: 5333 Zelzah Ave Apt 140 Encino CA 91316-2207 E-mail: agreen3102@aol.com

GREENBERG, BYRON STANLEY, newspaper and business executive, consultant; b. Bklyn., June 17, 1919; s. Albert and Bertha (Getleson) G.; m. Helena Marks, Feb. 10, 1946; children: David, Eric, Randy. Student, Bklyn. Coll., 1936-41. Circulation mgr. N.Y. Post, 1956-62, circulation dir., 1962-63, bus. mgr., 1963-72, gen. mgr., COO, 1973-79; sec., dir. N.Y.. Post Corp., 1966-75, treas., dir., 1975-76, v.p., 1976-81. V.p., dir. Leisure Systems, Inc., 1978-80; pres., chief exec. officer, dir. Games Mgmt. Services, Inc., 1979-80 Bd. dirs. 92d St YMHA, 1970-71, Friars Nat. Found., 1981-82. Served with AUS, 1942-45. Mem. Friars Club. Home and Office: 2560 S Grade Rd Alpine CA 91901-3612

GREENBERG, DANIEL, electronics rental company executive; b. Mpls., May 14, 1941; s. Mayer and Ruth (Cooperman) G.; m. Susan L. Steinhauser, Oct. 19, 1985. BA, Reed Coll., 1962; JD, U. Chgo., 1965. Staff atty. State of Calif. Dept. Water Resources, 1965-67; various positions, then pres., ceo Telecor, Inc., 1967-79; with Electro Rent Corp., Van Nuys, Calif., 1973—, chmn., chief exec. officer, 1979—. Bd. dirs. House of Fabrics, N.Y.C. Trustee Reed Coll., Craft and Folk Art Mus.; former mem. visiting com. U. Chgo. Law Sch.; former mem. adv. com. Dept. Commerce, Fgn. Comml. Svc. Mem. Am. Bus. Conf. (charter, past bd. dirs.), Sierra Club Legal Def. Fund, Inc.(chmn. 1991-94). Office: Electro Rent Corp 6060 Sepulveda Blvd Van Nuys CA 91411-2512

GREENBERG, DAVID ETHAN, communications consultant; b. N.Y.C., Oct. 8, 1949; s. Abraham M. and Norma B. (Jacovitz) G.; m. Kerri Shwayder, Apr. 24, 1983; children: Alison Leigh, Zachary Scott. BA cum laude, Columbia U., 1971; JD, Harvard U., 1975. Bar: Colo. 1975. Speechwriter Gov. Richard D. Lamm, Denver, 1977-78, legal counsel, 1978-79; dir. mktg. Colo. Ski Country U.S.A., Denver, 1979-82; sr. ptnr. GBSM, Denver, 1982—. Adj. assoc. prof. U. of Colo., Denver, 1984-89. Columnist, The Denver Post, 1985-88. Spl. asst. to adminstr. for communications EPA, Washington, 1989; pres. Children's Mus. Denver, 1988; vice chair Colo. Ocean Journey Aquarium, 1994—; mem. Colo. Commn. Higher Edn., 1993—; trustee Clayton Coll. Found. Nat. Merit Scholar, N.Y.C., 1967; White House fellow, 1988-89. Office: GBSM Inc 535 16th St Denver CO 80202-4235

GREENBERG, EDWARD SEYMOUR, political science educator, writer; b. Phila., July 1, 1942; s. Samuel and Yetta (Kaplan) G.; m. Martha Ann Baker, Dec. 24, 1964; children: Joshua, Nathaniel. BA, Miami (Ohio) U., 1964, MA, 1965; PhD, U. Wis., 1969. Asst. prof. polit. sci. Stanford (Calif.) U., 1968-72; assoc. prof. Ind. U., Bloomington, 1972-73; prof. U. Colo., Boulder, 1973—, dir. research program polit. and econ. change Inst. Behavioral Sci., 1980—, chair dept. polit. sci., 1985-88. Author: Serving the Few, 1974, Understanding Modern Government, 1979, Capitalism and the American Political Ideal, 1985, The American Political System, 1989, Workplace Democracy, 1986 (Dean's Writing award Social Scis. 1987), The Struggle for Democracy, 1993, 95, 97, 99, brief edit., 1996, 99, 2001; contbr. articles to profl. jours. Recipient fellowship In Recognition of Disting. Tchg., 1968, Jeffrey Pressman award Policy Studies Assn.; grantee Russell Sage Found., 1968, U. Wis., 1968, NSF, 1976, 82, 85, NIH, 1991-94, 96-2001. Mem. Internat. Polit. Sci. Assn., Am. Polit. Sci. Assn., Western Polit. Sci. Assn. (mem. exec. bd. 1986-89). Avocations: skiing, reading, bicycling, travel. Home: 755 11th St Boulder CO 80302-7512 Office: U Colo Inst Behavioral Sci PO Box 487 Boulder CO 80309-0487 E-mail: edward.greenberg@colorado.edu

GREENBERG, KATE, telecommunications industry executive; CFO Justice Tech. Corp., Culver City, Calif., Fastpoint Canon, L.A., 1999—. Office: Fastpoint Canon 5777 Century Blvd Ste 60 Los Angeles CA 90045 Fax: (310) 526-2100

GREENBERG, LENORE, public relations professional; b. Flushing, N.Y. d. Jack and Frances Orenstein. BA, Hofstra U.; MS, SUNY. Dir .pub. rels. Bloomingdale's, Short Hills, N.J., 1977-78; dir. comms. N.J. Sch. Bds. Assn., Trenton, 1978-82; dir pub. info. N.J. State Dept. Edn., Trenton, 1982-90; assoc. exec. dir. Nat. Sch. Pub. Rels. Assn., Arlington, Va., 1990-91; pres. Lenore Greenberg & Assocs., Inc., 1991—. Adj. prof. pub. rels. Rutgers U. Freelance feature writer N.Y. Times. Mem. bd. assocs. McCarter Theatre, Princeton, N.J.; mem. Franklin Twp. Zoning Bd. Adjustment; mem. Franklin Twp. Human Rels. Commn.; chair Somerset County LWV; instr. Bus. Vols. for the Arts. Recipient award Am. Soc. Assn. Execs., award Women in Comms., award Internat. Assn. Bus. Communicators; Gold Medallion awrd Nat. Sch. Pub. Rels. Assn. Mem. Pub. Rels. Soc. Am. (accredited; pres. N.J. State chpt., nat. nominating and accreditation coms., Silver Anvil award), Nat. Health/Edn. Consortium. Home and Office: 30971 Carrara Rd Laguna Niguel CA 92677-2757

GREENBERG, MYRON SILVER, lawyer; b. L.A., Oct. 17, 1945; s. Earl W. and Geri (Silver) G.; m. Shlomit Gross; children: David, Amy, Sophie, Benjamin. BSBA, UCLA, 1967; JD, 1970. Bar: Calif., 1971, U.S. Dist. Ct. (middle dist.) Calif. 1971, U.S. Tax Ct. 1977; cert. splst. in taxation law bd. legal specialization State Bar Calif.; CPA, Calif. Staff acct. Touche Ross & Co., L.A., 1970-71; assoc. Kaplan, Livingston, Goodwin, Berkowitz, & Selvin, Beverly Hills, Calif., 1971-74; ptnr. Myron S. Greenberg, a Profl. Corp., Larkspur, 1982—. Professorial lectr. tax. Golden Gate U.; instr. U. Calif., Berkeley, 1989—; mem. taxation law adv. commn. Calif. Bd. Legal Specialization, 1998—, chair, 2001. Author: California Attorney's Guide to Professional Corporations, 1977, 79; bd. editors UCLA Law Rev., 1969-70. Mem. San Anselmo Planning Commn., 1976-77; mem. adv. bd. cert. program personal fin. planning U. Calif., Berkeley, 1991—. Mem. AHA (bd. dirs. Marin county chpt. 1984-90, pres. 1988-89), ABA, AICPAs, L.A. County Bar Assn., Marin County (Calif.) Bar Assn. (bd. dirs. 1994-2001, pres. 1999), Real Estate Tax Inst. Calif. Cont. Edn. Bar (planning com.), Larkspur C. of C. (bd. dirs. 1985-87), Calif. Bd. Legal Specialization, 2001. Democrat. Jewish. Office: # 205 700 Larkspur Landing Cir Larkspur CA 94939-1711 E-mail: msg@eplaw.com

GREENBERGER, ELLEN, psychologist, educator; b. N.Y.C., Nov. 19, 1935; d. Edward Michael and Vera (Brisk) Silver; m. Michael Burton, Aug. 26, 1979; children by previous marriage— Kari Edwards, David Silver. BA, Vassar Coll., 1956; MA, Harvard U., 1959, PhD, 1961. Instr. Wellesley (Mass.) Coll., 1961-63, asst. prof., 1963-67; sr. research scientist Johns Hopkins U., Balt., 1967-76; prof. psychology and social behavior U. Calif., Irvine, 1976—. Author: (with others) When Teenagers Work, 1986; contbr. articles to profl. jours. USPHS fellow, 1956-59; Margaret Floy Washburn fellow, 1956-58; Ford Found. grantee, 1979-81; Spencer Found. grantee, 1979-81, 87, 88-91. Fellow APA, Am. Psychol. Soc.; mem. Soc. Rsch. in Child Devel., Soc. Rsch. on Adolescent Devel. Office: U Calif 3340 Social Ecology II Irvine CA 92697-7085 E-mail: egreenbe@uci.edu

GREENBERGER, MARTIN, technologist, information scientist, educator; b. Elizabeth, N.J., Nov. 30, 1931; s. David and Sidelle (Jonas) G.; m. Ellen Danica Silver, Feb. 2, 1959 (div. June 1974); children: Kari Edwards, David Silver; m. Liz Attardo, Dec. 11, 1982; children: Beth Jonit, Jonah Ben, Jilly Sal. AB, Harvard U., 1955, AM, 1956, PhD, 1958. Teaching fellow, resident adviser, staff mem. Computation Lab., Harvard U., Cambridge, 1954-58; mgr. applied sci. Cambridge IBM, 1956-58; asst. prof. mgmt. Mass. Inst. Tech., Cambridge, 1958-61, assoc. prof., 1961-67; prof., chmn. computer sci., dir. info. processing Johns Hopkins U., Balt., 1967-72; prof. math. scis., sr. research assoc. Center for Met. Planning and Research, 1972-75, prof. math. scis., 1978-82; IBM chair in tech. and info. systems UCLA Anderson Grad. Sch. Mgmt., 1982—; dir. UCLA Ctr. Digital Media, 1995-2000; pres. Council for Tech. and the Individual, 1985—; sr. fellow Milken Inst., 1999—. Mgr. systems program Electric Power Research Inst., Palo Alto, Calif., 1976-77; Isaac Taylor vis. prof. Technion-Israel Inst. Tech., Haifa, 1978-79; vis. prof. Internat. Energy Program, Grad. Sch. Bus., Stanford U., 1980; vis. prof. MIT Media Lab., 1988-89, Harvard u., 2001; mem. computer sci. and engring. bd. NAS, 1970-72; chmn. COSATI rev. group NSF, 1971-72; mem. evaluation com. Internat. Inst. for Applied Systems Analysis, Laxenburg, Austria, 1980; mem. adv. panels, Office Tech. Assessment, GAO, U.S. Congress; mem. adv. com. Getty Info. Inst.; mem. adv. bd. Safeguard Scientifics, Kinecta Corp.; cons. IBM, AT&T, CBS, Rand Corp., Morgan Guaranty, Arthur D. Little, TRW, Munger TollesBolt, Beranek & Newman, Brookings Inst., Resources for Future, Electric Power Rsch. Inst., Atlantic Richfield, Rockwell Internat., Security Pacific Corp., John F. Kennedy Sch. of Govt. Harvard U., Bell Atlantic Corp., Sony Corp., Applied Minds, Mitchell Silberberg and Knupp, Am. Online, Kirkland and Ellis, Vertex Pharmaceuticals. Author: (with Orcutt, Korbel and Rivlin) Microanalysis of Socioeconomic Systems: A Simulation Study, 1961; (with Jones, Morris and Ness) On-Line Computation and Simulation: The OPS-3 System, 1965; (with Crenson and Crissey) Models in the Policy Process: Public Decision Making in the Computer Era, 1976; (with Brewer, Hogan and Russell) Caught Unawares: The Energy Decade in Retrospect, 1983; editor: Management and The Computer of the Future, 1962, republished as Computers and the World of the Future, 1964; Computers, Communications, and the Public Interest, 1971; (with Aronofsky, McKenney and Massy) Networks for Research and Education, 1973; Electronic Publishing Plus: Media for a Technological Future, 1985, Technologies for the 21st Century, Vol. 1, On Multimedia, 1990, Vol. 3, Multimedia in Review, 1992, Vol. 5, Content and Communication, 1994, Vol. 7, Scaling Up, 1996. Mem. overseers' vis. com. Harvard U., 1975-81; founder and mem. working groups Energy Modeling Forum, Stanford U., 1978-81; mem. adv. com. Nat. Center Analysis of Energy Systems Brookhaven Nat. Lab., 1976-80, chmn., 1977; mem. rev. com. Energy and Environment div. Lawrence Berkeley Lab., 1983, applied sci. div., 1986-88; chmn. forum on electronic pub. Washington program Annenberg, 1983-84; co-founder ICC Forum, 1985; chmn. CTI Roundtable, 1990-99; trustee Educom, Princeton, N.J., 1969-73, chmn. council, 1969-70. With USAF, 1952-54, USAFR, 1954-60. NSF fellow, 1955-56; Guggenheim fellow U. Calif., Berkeley, 1965-66. Fellow AAAS (v.p., chmn. sect. T 1973-75); mem. Phi Beta Kappa, Sigma Xi. Office: UCLA Anderson Grad Sch Mgmt Los Angeles CA 90095-1481 E-mail: mg@ucla.edu

GREENE, ALBERT LAWRENCE, healthcare executive; b. N.Y.C., Dec. 10, 1949; s. Leonard and Anne (Birnbaum) G.; m. Jo Linda Anderson, Sept. 3, 1972; children: Stacy, Jeremy. BA, Ithaca Coll., 1971; MHA, U. Mich., 1973. Adminstrv. asst. Harper Hosp., Detroit, 1973-74, asst. adminstr., 1974-77, assoc. adminstr., 1977-80; adminstr. Grace Hosp., Detroit, 1980-84, Harper Hosp., Detroit, 1984-87; pres., CEO Sinai Samaritan Med. Ctr., Milw., 1988-90, Alta Bates Med. Ctr., Berkeley, Calif., 1990-98; CEO Sutter Health East Bay Svc. Area, Berkeley, 1998-99, HealthCtrl., Emeryville, 1999—. Bd. dirs. Sierra Health Svcs., Lumisys Corp., QuadraMed Corp.; chmn. Calif. Assn. Hosps. and Health Sys., 1998. Trustee Huron Valley Hosp., Milford, Mich., 1984-87. Mem. Am. Coll. Healthcare Execs., Young Pres. Orgn., Blackhawk Country Club, Lakeview Club. Avocations: tennis, golf. Home: 3819 Cottonwood Dr Danville CA 94506-6007 Office: HealthCtrl 6001 Shellmound St Ste 800 Emeryville CA 94608-1924

GREENE, ALVIN, service company executive, management consultant; b. Pitts., Aug. 26, 1932; s. Samuel David and Yetta (Kroff) G.; BA, Stanford U., 1954, MBA, 1959; m. M. Louise Sokol, Nov. 11, 1977; children: Sharon, Ami, Ann, Daniel. Asst. to pres. Narmco Industries, Inc., San Diego, 1959-62; adminstrv. mgr., mgr. mktg. Whittaker Corp., L.A., 1962-67; sr. v.p. Cordura Corp., L.A., 1967-75; chmn. bd. Sharon-Sage, Inc., L.A., 1975-79; exec. v.p., chief operating officer Republic Distbrs., Inc., Carson, Calif., 1979-81, also dir.; chief operating officer Memel, Jacobs & Ellsworth, 1981-87, 87—; pres. SCI Cons., Inc.; dir. Sharon-Sage, Inc., True Data Corp.; vis. prof. Am. Grad. Sch. Bus., Phoenix, 1977-81. Chmn. bd. commrs. Housing Authority City of L.A., 1983-88 . Served to 1st lt., U.S. Army, 1955-57. Mem. Direct Mail Assn., Safety Helmet Mfrs. Assn., Bradley Group. Office: 11990 San Vicente Blvd Ste 300 Los Angeles CA 90049-6608

GREENE, C. MICHAEL, art association administrator; Pres., CEO NARAS, Santa Monica, Calif. Office: NARAS 3402 Pico Blvd Santa Monica CA 90405-2118

GREENE, DAVID LEE, physical anthropologist, educator; b. Denver, Aug. 23, 1938; s. Ralph Francis and Dorothy Elizabeth (Allen) G.; m. Kathleen Ann Kerger, Sept. 4, 1962; 1 son, Andrew David. BA, U. Colo., 1960, MA, 1962, PhD in Anthropology (NSF fellow). Asst. prof. anthropology and orthodontics SUNY, Buffalo, 1964-65; asst. prof., head dept. anthropology U. Wyo., 1965-67; asst. prof. U. Colo., Boulder, 1967-69, asso. prof., 1969-71, prof., 1971—, chmn. dept. anthropology, 1974-77, 81-83, 1990-91. Dir. NSF Summer Inst. in Anthropology, 1970-71; outside grad. examiner U. Toronto, 1974, field rsch. in Sudan, 1963-64, Micronesia, 1969, Brazil, 1986, 88. Author: Genetics, Dentition and Taxonomy, 1967, (with G.J. Armelagos) The Wadi Halfa Mesolithic Population, 1972; contbr. articles to profl. jours. NSF grantee, 1978-80 Fellow Am. Anthrop. Assn.; mem. Am. Assn. Phys. Anthropologists, AAAS, Sigma Xi. Office: U Colo Dept Anthropology Boulder CO 80309-0001

GREENE, ENID, former congresswoman; b. San Rafael, Calif., Oct. 5, 1958; BS in Pol. Sci., U. Utah, 1980; JD, Brigham Young U., 1983. Caseworker, rsch. asst. U.S. Rep. Dan Marriott, R., 1980; atty. Ray, Quinney & Nebeker, 1983-90; dep. chief of staff Gov. Norman H. Bangerter, 1990-92; corp. counsel Novell, Inc., 1993-94; mem. 104th Congress from 2nd Utah dist., Washington, 1995-97; atty. Smith & Glauser, Salt Lake City, 1998—. Office: Smith & Glauser 2180 S 1300 E Salt Lake City UT 84106-2813

GREENE, FRANK SULLIVAN, JR. investment management executive; b. Washington, Oct. 19, 1938; s. Frank S. Sr. and Irma O. Greene; m. Phyllis Davison, Jan. 1958 (dec. 1984); children: Angela, Frank, Ronald; m. Carolyn W. Greene, Sept. 1990. BS, Washington U., St. Louis, 1961; MS, Purdue U., 1962; PhD, U. Santa Clara, Calif., 1970. Part-time lectr. Washington U., Howard U., Am. U., 1959-65; pres., dir. Tech. Devel. Corp., Arlington, Tex., 1985-92; pres. Zero One Systems Inc. (formerly Tech. Devel. of Calif.), Santa Clara, Calif., 1971-87, Zero One Systems Group subs. Sterling Software Inc., 1987-89. Asst. chmn., lectr. Stanford U., 1972—74; bd. dirs. ZNYX Corp., Epicentric, Inc., Quippe Tech., Broadware; mng. mem. New Vista Capital, LLC, Palo Alto, Calif., 1993—; pres. Networked Picture Sys. Inc., 1989—91, chmn., 1991—94. Author two indsl. textbooks; also articles; patentee in field. Bd. dirs. NCCJ, Santa Clara, 1980—, NAACP, San Jose chpt., 1986-89, Am. Musical Theatre of San Jose, 1995—; bd. regents Santa Clara U., 1983-90, trustee, 1990-2000; mem. adv. bd. Urban League, Santa Clara County, 1986-89, East Side Union High Sch., 1985-88. Capt. USAF, 1961-65. Mem IEEE, IEEE Computer Soc. (governing bd. 1973-75), Assn. Black Mfrs. (bd. dirs. 1974-80), Am. Electric Assn. (indsl. adv. bd. 1975-76), Fairchild Rsch. and Devel. (tech. staff 1965-71), Bay Area Purchasing Coun. (bd. dirs. 1978-84), Security Affairs Support Assn. (bd. dirs. 1980-83), Sigma Xi, Eta Kappa Nu, Sigma Pi Phi.

GREENE, HERBERT BRUCE, lawyer, investor; b. N.Y.C., Apr. 13, 1934; s. Joseph Lester and Shirley (Kasen) G.; m. Judith Jean Metricks, Dec. 31, 1958; children: Pamela S., Scott L. AB, Harvard U., 1955; JD, Columbia U., 1958. Bar: N.Y. 1959, Conn. 1975. Asst. U.S. atty So. Dist. N.Y., Dept. Justice, N.Y.C., 1958-61; assoc. Kaye, Scholer, Fierman, Hays & Handler, N.Y.C., 1961-66; asst. to gen. counsel CIT Fin. Corp., N.Y.C., 1966-67; group gen. counsel Xerox Corp., Rochester, N.Y., 1967-68, v.p. adminstrn., 1968-71; sr. v.p. Xerox Edn. Group, Stamford, Conn., 1971-75; v.p., gen. counsel, sec. Lone Star Industries, Inc., Greenwich, 1976-79, sr. v.p., asst. to chmn., 1979-82; chmn., CEO Earle and Greene & Co., Westport, 1982-96, Portland, Oreg., 1997—. Mem. Phi Delta Phi. Republican. Home: 4233 SW Redondo Ave Portland OR 97201-1380 Office: Herbert B Greene & Co 4233 W Redondo Ave Portland OR 97201-1380

GREENE, JOHN M. physicist; b. Pitts., Sept. 22, 1928; s. John W. and Frances M. Greene; m. Alice Andrews; 1 child, Emily. BS, Calif. Inst. Tech., 1950; PhD, U. Rochester, 1956. Physicist Princeton (N.J.) Plasma Physics Lab., 1956-82, Gen. Atomics Co., San Diego, 1982—. Recipient James Clerk Maxwell prize Am. Phys. Soc., 1992, Plasma Physics Rsch. Excellence award Am. Phys. Soc., 1992. Office: General Atomics Co PO Box 85608 San Diego CA 92186-5608

GREENE, JOHN THOMAS, judge; b. Salt Lake City, Nov. 28, 1929; s. John Thomas and Mary Agnes (Hindley) G.; m. Dorothy Kay Buchanan, Mar. 31, 1955; children: Thomas Buchanan Greene, John Buchanan Greene, Mary Kay Greene Platt. BA in Polit. Sci., U. Utah, 1952, JD, 1955. Bar: Utah 1955, U.S. Dist. Ct. (10th cir.) 1955, U.S. Supreme Ct. 1966. Pvt. practice, Salt Lake City, 1955-57; asst. U.S. atty. Salt Lake City, 1957-59; ptnr. Marr, Wilkins & Cannon (and successor firms), Salt Lake City, 1959-75; ptnr., pres., chmn. bd. dirs. Greene, Callister & Nebeker, Salt Lake City, 1975-85; judge U.S. Dist. Ct., Salt Lake City, 1985—. Author: (manual) American Mining Law, 1960; contbr. articles to profl. jours. Chmn. Salt Lake City Cmty. Coun., 1970-75, Utah State Bldg. Authority, Salt Lake City, 1980-85; Regent Utah State Bd. Higher Edn., Salt Lake City, 1982-86. Recipient Order of Coif U. Utah, 1955, Merit of Honor award, 1994, Utah Fed. Bar Disting. Svc. award, 1997. Fellow ABA Found. (life); ABA ho. of dels. 1972-92, bd. govs. 1987-91; mem. Dist. Judges Assn. (pres. 10th cir. 1998-2000), Utah Bar Assn. (pres. 1971-72, Judge of Yr. award 1995), Am. Law Inst. (life, panelist and lectr. 1980-85, advisor 1986-98); Phi Beta Kappa. Mormon. Avocations: travel, reading, tennis. Office: US Dist Ct 350 S Main St Ste 447 Salt Lake City UT 84101-2180 E-mail: JTGJR@hotmail.com

GREENE, SHECKY, entertainer; b. Chgo., Apr. 8, 1926; s. Carl and Bessie (Harris) Greenfield; m. Nalani Kele, Dec. 6, 1972. Student public schs., Chgo. Entertainer in night clubs, 1947— , on TV, 1953— , also in movies, night club appearances at all major clubs throughout, U.S., 1947— , night club appearances, Las Vegas, 1953— ; films include The Love Machine, 1970, Tony Rome, 1967; co-star: TV series Combat, 1956; host: TV series Johnny Carson and Merv Griffin TV shows; co-host: numerous TV guest appearances on talk, variety and game shows Mike Douglas TV show; author all materials and songs for appearances. Recipient Las Vegas Best Lounge Entertainer award, 1972, 1st Jimmy Durante award as best comedian Miami, Fla., 1975; named Comedy Performer of Yr. South Fla. Entertainment Writers Assn., 1978, Male Comedy Star of Yr. Las Vegas Acad. Variety and Cabaret Artists, 1977 Jewish. Club: Las Vegas Country. Office: Marlin Management 743 Uclan Dr Burbank CA 91504-3938

GREENLAW, ROGER LEE, interior designer; b. New London, Conn., Oct. 12, 1936; s. Kenneth Nelson and Lyndell Lee (Stinson) G; children: Carol Jennifer, Roger Lee. BFA, Syracuse U., 1958. Interior designer Cannell & Chaffin, 1958-59, William C. Wagner, Arch., L.A., 1959-60, Gen. Fireproofing Co., L.A., 1960-62, K-S Wilshire, Inc., L.A., 1963-64; dir. interior design Calif. Desk Co., L.A., 1967-67; sr. interior designer Bechtel Corp., L.A., 1967-70; sr. interior designer, project mgr. Daniel, Mann, Johnson & Mendehall, L.A., 1970-72, Morganelli-Heumann & Assocs., L.A., 1972-73; owner, prin. Greenlaw Design Assocs., Glendale, Calif., 1973-76, Greenlaw Interiro Planning & Design, 1996—. Lectr. UCLA; mem. adv. curriculum com. Mt. San Antonio Coll., Walnut, Calif., Fashion Inst. Design, L.A.; bd. dirs. Calif. Legis. Conf. Interior Design, treas., 1992-94, v.p., 1990-92, pres., 1994-98. Past scoutmaster Verdugo coun. Boy Scouts Am.; pres. bd. dirs. Unity Ch., La Crescenta, Calif., 1989-91. Mem. ASID (treas. Pasadena chpt. 1983-84, 1st v.p. 1985, pres. 1986-87, chmn. So. Calif. regional conf. 1985, nat. dir. 1987-89, nat. com. legis., nat com. jury for catalog award, spkr. ho. dels., nat. bd. dirs., medallist award, regional v.p., nat. chair ethics com., nat. exec. com., v.p., treas. 1992 Calif. legis. conf. interior design, chmn. stds. task force, pres. 1994-98), Glendale C. of C. (bd. dirs. 1998), Adm. Farragut Acad. Alumni Assn., Kiwanis (bd. dirs.), Delta Upsilon. Republican. Home: 2100 Valderas Dr Apt F Glendale CA 91208-1340 Office: 2155 Verdugo Blvd Montrose CA 91020-1628 E-mail: greenlawdesign@juno.com

GREENLEAF, JOHN EDWARD, research physiologist; b. Joliet, Ill., Sept. 18, 1932; s. John Simon and Julia Clara (Flint) G.; m. Carol Lou Johnson, Aug. 28, 1960. MA, N.Mex. Highlands U., 1956; BA in Phys. Edn., U. Ill., 1955, MS, 1962, PhD in Physiol., 1963. Tchg. asst. N.Mex. Highlands U., Las Vegas, Nev., 1955-56; engring. draftsman Allis-Chalmers Mfg. Co., Springfield, Ill., 1956-57; tchg. asst. in phys. edn. U. Ill., Urbana, 1957-58, rsch. asst. in phys. edn., 1958-59, tchg. asst. in human anatomy and physiology, 1959-62; summer fellow NSF, 1962; pre-doctoral fellow NIH, 1962-63; rsch. physiologist Space Scis. Directorate, NASA, Ames Rsch. Ctr., Moffett Field, Calif., 1963-66, 67—; postdoctoral fellowship Karolinska Inst., Stockholm, 1966-67. Adj. prof. biology dept. San Francisco State U., 1988—; adj. prof. dept. exercise sci. U. Calif., Davis, 1996—; Japan Soc. for Promotion of Sci. vis. prof. Kyoto Prefectural U. Medicine, 1997; mem. internat. adv. bd. Medicina Sportiva. Mem. editorial bd. Jour. Applied Physiology, 1989-99, Med. Sci. Sports Exercise, 2000—; contbr. articles to profl. jours. Pub. dir. N.Mex. Highlands U. Found., 1999—. Served with U.S. Army, 1952-53. Recipient Disting. Alumni award N.Mex. Highlands U., 1990, Disting. Alumni award dept. molecular and integrative physiology U. Ill., 1998, Am. Coll. Sports Medicine Citation award, 1999; exch. fellow NAS, 1973-74, 77, 89, NIH, 1980. Fellow Am. Coll. Sports Medicine (trustee 1984-87), Aerospace Med. Assn. (Harold Ellingson award 1981-82, Eric Liljencrantz award 1990), NASA Ames Assn.; mem. AIAA, Am. Physiol. Soc. (mem. com. on coms. 1984-87, long range planning com. 1987-90, internat. physiol. com. 1997-00), Polish Soc. Sports Medicine (hon.), Shooting Sports Rsch. Coun. (internat. shooters devel. fund 1984), Sigma Xi. Achievements include patents in field. Home: 12391 Farr Ranch Ct Saratoga CA 95070-6527 Office: NASA Ames Rsch Ctr Life Sci Div MS 221A-2 Moffett Field CA 94035-1000 E-mail: jgreenleaf@mail.arc.nasa.gov

GREENLICK, MERWYN RONALD, health services researcher; b. Detroit, Mar. 12, 1935; s. Emanuel and Fay G.; m. Harriet, Aug. 19, 1956; children— Phyllis, Michael, Vicki. B.S., Wayne State U., 1957; M.S., U. Mich., 1961, Ph.D., 1967. Pharmacist, Detroit, 1957-60; spl. instr., instr. pharmacy adminstrn. Coll. Pharmacy Wayne State U., 1958-62; dir. of research n.w. region Kaiser-Permanente, Portland, 1964-95; v.p. (research) Kaiser Found. Hosps., 1981-95; sr. fellow Ctr. for Advanced Study in the Behavioral Scis., Stanford, Calif., 1995-96; adj. prof. sociology and social work Portland State U., 1965—; clin. prof. preventive medicine and pub. health Oreg. Health Scis. U., 1971-89, prof., acting chair preventive medicine and pub. health, 1990-93, prof., chair preventive medicine and pub. health, 1993-2000, emeritus prof., 2000—. Mem. Gov.'s Commn. on Health Care, 1988; cons. Gov.'s Health Manpower Coun. Bd. dirs. Washington County Community Action Orgn., 1966-70; pres. Jewish Edn. Assn., Portland, 1976-78; bd. dirs. Jewish Fedn., 1975-79. USPHS trainee, 1962-63, 63-64 Fellow APHA, NAS, Inst. Medicine; mem. AAAS, Assn. Health Svcs. Rsch. (Disting. Fellow, Pres.'s award 1995), N.W. Health Found. (bd. dirs. 1997—). Jewish. Home: 712 NW Spring Ave Portland OR 97229-6913 Office: Oreg Health Svcs U CB 669 3181 SW Sam Jackson Park Rd Portland OR 97201-3011

GREENSPAN, DEBORAH, dental educator; 2nd BDS, U. London, 1960, BDS, 1964, DSc, 1991; fellow in Dental Surgery (hon.), Royal Coll. Surgeons, Edinburgh, 1994; LDS, Royal Coll. Surgeons, Eng., 1964; ScD (hon.), Georgetown U., 1990. Registered dental practioner, U.K.; diplomate Am. Bd. Oral Medicine. Vis. lectr. oral medicine U. Calif., San Francisco, 1976-83, asst. clin. prof., 1983-85, assoc. clin. prof., 1985-89, clin. prof., 1989-96, prof. clin. oral medicine, 1996—. Lectr. in oral biology, U. Calif., San Francisco, 1972, clin. dir. Oral AIDS Ctr., 1987—, active Sch. Dentistry coms. including admissions com., 1985—, chair task force on infection control, 1987—; cons. Joint FDI/WHO Working Group on AIDS, 1989—, EEC, 1990, WHO, 1990, 91, Dept. Health State Calif., 1991, others; ad hoc reviews Epidemiology and Disease Control Sect. Div. Rsch. Grants NIH, 1987—; mem. programs adv. com. Nat. Inst. Dental Rsch., 1989—, mem. spl. ad hoc tech. rev. panel, 1991, mem. panel Fed. Drug Adminstrn., 1991-94; other svc. to govtl. agys.; participant numerous sci. and profl. workshops, meetings, and continuing edn. courses, numerous radio, TV, and press interviews concerning AIDS and infection control in dentistry. Author: (with J.S. Greenspan, Pindborg, and Schiødt), AIDS and the Dental Team, 1986 (transl. German, French, Italian, Spanish, Japanese), AIDS and the Mouth, 1990, (with others) San Francisco General Hospital AIDS Knowledge Base, 1986, Dermatologic Clinics, 5th edit., 1987, Infectious Disease Clinics of North America, 2nd. edit., 1988, Oral Manifestations of AIDS, 1988, Contemporary Periodontics, 1989, Opportunistic Infections in AIDS Patients, 1990, AIDS Clinical Review, 1990, Oral Manifestations of Systemic Disease, 1990, others; mem. editl. bd. rev. Jour. Am. Coll. Dentists, 1991; mem. editl. bd. Oral Diseases, 1999; ad hoc referee Jour. Oral Pathology, 1983—, Cancer, 1985—, Jour. Acad. Gen. Dentistry, 1986—, European Jour. Cancer & Clin. Oncology, 1986, Archives of Dermatology, 1988—, Jour. AMA, 1988—, AIDS, 1991; contbr. numerous articles to profl. jours. Mem. dental subcom. of profl. edn. com. Calif. div. Am. Cancer Soc., 1982-90, profl. health care providers task force, 1991. Nat. Cancer Inst. fellow, 1978-79, Am. Coll. Dentists fellow, 1988; recipient Woman of Distinction award, London, 1986, Commendation cert. Asst. Sec. for Health, 1989; named Seymour J. Kreshover lectr. Nat. Inst. Dental Rsch., 1989, Hon. Lectr. United Med. and Dental Schs. of Guys and St. Thomas Hosps., U. London, 1991. Fellow AAAS, Royal Soc. Medicine, Royal Coll. Surgeons; mem. ADA (vis. lectr. speaker's bur. 1988—, cons. coun. on dental therapeutics 1988—, mem. coun. sci. affairs 1999—), Am. Assn. Dental Rsch. (session chair 1986-87, constitution com. 1988-91, chair 1990-91, pres. San Francisco sect. 1990—, treas. 1992—), Am. Acad. Oral Pathology, Am. Soc. Microbiology, Am. Assn. Women Dentists, Am. Acad. Oral Medicine, Am. Assn. Dental Schs., Internat. Assn. Dental Rsch. (pres. exptl. pathology group 1989-90, other coms. and offices), Internat. Assn. Oral Pathologists, Calif. Dental Assn., San Francisco Dental Soc., Internat. AIDS Soc., Inst. of Medicine. Achievements include rsch. on oral candidiasis in HIV infection, on HIV-associated salivary gland disease, on oral hairy leukoplakia, and on the prevalence of HIV-associated gingivitis and periodontitis in HIV-infected patients. Office: U Calif Sch Dentistry Dept Stomatology S 612 PO Box 422 San Francisco CA 94143-0001

GREENSPAN, FRANCIS S. physician; b. Perth Amboy, N.J., Mar. 16, 1920; s. Philip and Francis (Davidson) G.; m. Bonnie Jean Fisher, Oct. 25, 1945; children: Richard L., Robert H., Susan L. B.A., Cornell U., 1940, M.D., 1943. Diplomate: Am. Bd. Internal Medicine. Mem. endocrinology staff U. Calif.-San Francisco; chief endocrinology Stanford (Calif.) Hosp., 1949-59; chief thyroid clinic U. Calif. Med. Ctr., San Francisco, 1959—; practice medicine specializing in endocrinology San Francisco; now clin. prof. medicine and radiology U. Calif. Med. Ctr.; chief staff U. Calif. Hosps. and Clinics, San Francisco, 1976-78. Editor: Textbook of Endocrinology; contbr. articles to med. jours. Served with USNR, 1944-45. Mem. San Francisco Med. Soc., Calif. Med. Assn., AMA, Endocrine Soc., Am. Thyroid Assn., Western Soc. Clin. Research, Western Assn. Physicians, Calif. Acad. Medicine. Office: U Calif Med Ctr 350 Parnassus Ave Ste 609 San Francisco CA 94117-3608

GREENSPAN, JOHN S. dental and medical educator, scientist, administrator; b. London, Jan. 7, 1938; came to U.S., 1976; s. Nathan and Jessie (Dion) G.; m. Deborah, Dec. 1962; children: Nicholas J., Louise C. BSC in Anatomy with 1st class honors, U. London, 1959, B in Dental Surgery, 1962, PhD in Exptl. Pathology, 1967; ScD (hon.), Georgetown U., 1990. Licentiate in dental surgery Royal Coll. of Surgeons of Eng. Asst. house surgeon in conservation and periodontology Royal Dental Hosp. London, 1962; asst. lectr. oral pathology Sch. of Dental Surgery Royal Dental Hosp. of London, U. London, 1963-65, lectr. oral pathology Sch. of Dental Surgery, 1965-68, sr. lectr. oral pathology Sch. of Dental Surgery, 1968-75; prof. oral biology and oral pathology Sch. of Dentisty, U. Calif., San Francisco, 1976—, vice chmn. dept. oral medicine and hosp. dentistry, 1977-82, chmn. div. oral biology, 1981-89, coord. basic scis. Sch. of Dentistry, 1982-96; chmn. dept. stomatology U. Calif., San Francisco, 1989—. Cons. oral pathology St. John's Hosp. and Inst. of Dermatology, London, 1973-76; cons. dental surgeon St. George's Hosp., 1972-76; prof. dept. pathology Sch. Medicine U. Calif., San Francisco, 1976—; dir. U. Calif. AIDS Specimen Bank, San Francisco, 1982—, U. Calif. Oral AIDS Ctr., San Francisco, 1987—; assoc. dir. dental clin. epidemiology program U. Calif., San Francisco, 1987—; dir. U. Calif. AIDS Clin. Rsch. Ctr., San Francisco, 1992—; Burroughs Wellcome vis. prof. Royal Soc. Medicine, U.K., 1996-97; presenter, lectr. Author: (with others) Opportunistic Infections in Patients with the Acquired Immunodeficiency Syndrome, 1989, Contemporary Periodontics, 1989, Gastroenterology Clinics of North America, 1988, Perspectives on Oral Manifestations of AIDS, 1988, AIDS: Pathogenesis and Treatment, 1988, others; contbr. articles to profl. jours.; editorial cons. Achives of Oral Biology, 1968—, Jour. of Calif. Dental Assn., 1980—; editoral adv. bd. Jour. of Dental Rsch., 1977—; editorial bd. AIDS Alert, 1987-89, Brit. Dental Jour., 1998—; sr. editor Oral Diseases, 1994-98. Rsch. grantee NIH-Nat. Inst. Dental Rsch., 1978-82, 86—, U. Calif. Task Force on AIDS, 1983—, rsch. com. Royal Dental Hosp., London, 1964-76, Med. Rsch. Coun. of U.K., 1974-77, chmn. U. Calif. San Francisco Acad. Senate, 1983-85; Nuffield dental scholar, 1958-59; fellow Am. Coll. Dentists, 1982—, AAAS, 1985—; recipient Seymour J. Kreshover Lecture award Nat. Inst. Dental Rsch., NIH, 1989, Rsch. in Oral Biology award Internat. Assn. Dental Rsch., 1992. Fellow Royal Coll. Pathologists, Royal Coll. Surgeons Faculty of Dental Surgery, Inst. Medicine of Nat. Acad. Scis.; mem. ADA, AAAS, Am. Assn. Dental Rsch. (pres. 1988-89), Internat. Assn. Dental Rsch. (pres. 1996-97), Royal Soc. Medicine (U.K.), Pathological Soc. (U.K.), Oral Pathology Soc. (U.K.), Am. Acad. Oral Pathology, Bay Area Tchrs. Oral Pathology, Internat . Assn. Oral Pathologists, San Francisco Dental Soc., Calif. Dental Assn., Calif. Soc. Oral Pathologists Histochem. Soc., Am. Assn. Pathologists. Avocations: skiing, gardening, travel, wine. Office: U Calif Dept Stomatology PO Box 422 San Francisco CA 94143-0001

GREENSTEIN, MARLA NAN, lawyer; b. Chgo., Jan. 20, 1957; d. Charles Allen and Lenore (Gould) G. Cert., Oxford U., Eng., 1978; AB, Georgetown U., 1979; JD, Loyola U., 1982. Bar: Ill. 1982, Alaska 1997, U.S. Dist. Ct. (no. dist.) Ill. 1982, U.S. Ct. Appeals (7th cir.) 1983. Sr. staff atty. Am. Judicature Soc., Chgo., 1982-85, Alaska Jud. Council, Anchorage, 1985-89; exec. dir. Ala. Commn. Jud. Conduct, Anchorage, 1989—. Cons. Com. on Cts. and Justice, Chgo., 1985. Author: Handbook for Judicial Nominating Commissioners, 1984. Mem. ABA (chair lawyers conf. jud. divsn. 1996-97), Assn. Jud. Disciplinary Counsel (bd. dirs. 1992—), Am. Judicature Soc. (bd. dirs. 1992-97, exec. com. 1997—), Pi Sigma Alpha. Avocations: photography, drawing. Office: Commn Jud Conduct 310 K St Ste 301 Anchorage AK 99501-2064

GREENSTEIN, MARTIN RICHARD, lawyer; b. Boston, Dec. 29, 1944; s. Paul and Sarah Greenstein; m. Judith Stevens; children: Stacey, Marc, Seth, Andrew. BSEE magna cum laude, Tufts U., 1965; MSEE, Princeton U., 1966; JD with highest honors, John Marshall Law Sch., 1971. Bar: Ill. 1971, N.Y. 1982, Calif. 1982, U.S. Patent Office 1971, U.S. Supreme Ct. 1981. Mem. tech. staff Bell Telephone Labs., Naperville, Ill., 1965-70, mem. patent staff, 1970-71; assoc. firm Baker & McKenzie, Chgo., 1971-78, ptnr., 1978-89, Palo Alto, Calif., 1989-93, TechMark, Trademark and Intellectual Property Law, San Jose, 1993—. Instr. John Marshall Law Sch., Chgo., 1972-76 Editorial bd. The Trademark Reporter, 1976-92. Trustee Village of Lisle, 1980-83; bd. dirs. Ill. Software Assn. and Ctr., 1984-87 Mem. ABA, State Bar Calif., Internat. Trademark Assn., Am. Intellectual Property Law Assn., Tau Beta Pi, Eta Kappa Nu. Home: 1709 Whitham Ave Los Altos CA 94024 Office: TechMark 16th Fl 55 S Market St San Jose CA 95113-2327

GREENSTEIN, MERLE EDWARD, import and export company executive; b. Portland, Oreg., June 22, 1937; s. Sol and Tillie Germaine (Schnitzer) G.; m. Nasi Jenab; children: Todd Aaron, Boback Emad, Lela Emad. BA, Reed Coll., 1959. Pres. Acme Trading and Supply Co., Portland, 1963-82; chmn. MMI Group, Portland, 1982-91, Internat. Devel. Assocs., Portland, 1991—. Com. mem. ISRI, Washington, 1987-89; mem. dist. export coun. U.S. Dept. Commerce, 1980—, mem. first USA trade Missions to Vietnam, 1996. Chmn. fin. Portland Opera, 1966; bd. dirs. Met. YMCA, 1964-67; del. to China, State of Oreg. Ofcl. Trade Mission, 1979; chmn. Western Internat. Trade Group, 1981-82; mem. State of Oreg. Korea Commn., 1985-90; fin. chmn. Anne Frank exhibit, Portland; joint chmn. bldg. campaign Oreg. Mus. Sci. and Industry; bd. dirs. Waverly Children's Home; bd. cons. Unilearn Corp., Oreg. Youth Leadership Sem.; chmn. fin. Oreg. Holocaust Mem.; mem. Food Bank Relocation Com.; mem. property task force com. Oreg. Food Bank, also mem. capital campaign cabinet; bd. dirs. Metro. Family Svc.; treas. AJC; fin. chmn. Anne Frank Exhibit Return, 2001; mem. Oreg. Mentoring Group. Recipient President's E for Export, U.S. Dept. Commerce, 1969; named Citizen of the Week, City of Portland, 1953. Mem. Rolls Royce Owners Club (London), City Club, Tualatin Country Club, Masons, Shriners. Avocations: antique autos, Arabian horses, cross country skiing. Office: Internat Devel Assocs 6731 NE 47th Ave Portland OR 97218-1205 E-mail: merlenasi@yahoo.com

GREENSTEIN, MICHAEL STEVEN, editor, writer; b. N.Y.C., Feb. 17, 1949; s. Stanley Theodore and Rosalie (Levy) G. BA, Syracuse U., 1970, MS, 1974. Writer N.Y. State Assembly, Albany, 1970-71; editor in chief Syracuse New Times, 1971-75, 85-98, editl. dir., 1998—; freelance writer Syracuse, 1975-85, Seattle, 1999—. Editor Wash. State Visitors' Guide, 2000—; adj. prof. Syracuse U., 1976-97. Author: Music Industry and the Media, 1976, Syracuse University Basketball Trivia, 1988. Recipient Best Sports Story award Syracuse Press Club, 1980, Best Criticism award, 1981, Syracuse Press Club Lifetime Achievement award, 1997, Best Scenic Photo award, 1998. Mem. Psi Upsilon (trustee Pi chpt. 1975-87). Avocations: hiking, rock music, canoeing, sports. Home: 3635 43rd Ave W Seattle WA 98199-1805 E-mail: mikegreenstein@aol.com

GREENWALD, ARTHUR M. federal judge; b. 1936; BBA, UCLA; JD, Southwestern Sch. Law. Asst. U.S. atty. L.A., 1964-87; apptd. bankruptcy judge cen. dist. U.S. Dist. Ct. Calif., 1987. Mem. FBA, Am. Judicature Soc., Calif. Soc. CPAs, L.A. County Mus., KCET Pub. Broadcasting Sys. Office: 21041 Burbank Blvd Ste 324 Woodland Hills CA 91367-6606 Fax: 818-587-2949

GREENWOOD, COLLETTE P. municipal official, finance officer; b. Summit, Ill. BA, Ea. Wash. U., 1980. With acctg. dept. Montgomerty Ward, Spokane, Wash., 1976-90; acctg. clk. water, hydro City of Spokane, 1979-93, budget acctg., 1993-96, dir. of office of mgmt. & bufget, 1996—. Recipient Class of 1998 award Leadership Spokane Spokane C. of C. Mem. Nat. Mgmt. Assn. (elected dir. 1999), Govt. Fin. Officers Assn., Wash. Fin. Officers Assn. Office: City Spokane 808 W Spokane Falls Blvd Spokane WA 99201-3333

GREENWOOD, M. R. C. college dean, biologist, nutrition educator; b. Gainesville, Fla., Apr. 11, 1943; d. Stanley James and Mary Rita (Schmeltz) Cooke; m. (div. 1968); 1 child, James Robert. AB summa cum laude, Vassar Coll., 1968; PhD, Rockefeller U., 1973; LHD (hon.), Mt. St. Mary Coll., 1989. Rsch. assoc. Inst. of Human Nutrition, Columbia U., N.Y.C., 1974-75, adj. asst. prof., 1975-76, asst. prof., 1976-78; assoc. prof. dept. biology Vassar Coll., Poughkeepsie, N.Y., 1978-81, prof. biology, 1981-86, dir. animal model, CORE Lab. of Obesity Rsch. Ctr., 1985-89, dir. undergrad. rsch. summer inst., 1986-88, dir. Howard Hughes biol. scis. network program, 1988, chmn. of biology dept., John Guy Vassar prof. natural scis., 1986-89; prof. nutrition and internal medicine, dean grad. studies U. Calif., Davis, 1989-96, chancellor Santa Cruz, 1996—. Mem. nutrition study sect. NIH, 1983-87; mem. NRC; assoc. dir. for sci. White House Office Sci. and Tech., 1993-95. Editor: Obesity, Vol. 4, 1983; contbr. over 250 articles and abstracts to profl. jours., 1974-89. Recipient Rsch. Career Devel. award NIH, 1978-83; Mellon scholar-in-residence St. Olaf Coll., Northfield, Minn., 1978; N.Y. State Regents fellow, 1968. Mem. Inst. Medicine of Nat. Acad. Scis. (chair food and nutrition bd., diet and health subcom. 1986—), N.Am. Soc. for Study of Obesity (pres. 1987-88), Am. Inst. Nutrition (BioServ 1982), Am. Physiol. Soc., The Harvey Soc., Am. Diabetes Assn., Internat. Assn. for Study of Obesity (treas. 1991—). Home: University House Santa Cruz CA 95064 Office: U Calif Chancellor Office 296 McHenry Libr Santa Cruz CA 95064-1077

GREENWOOD, RICHARD A. protective services official; m. Dessa Rae Greenwood; 4 children. BS in Criminal Justice, Weber State U.; grad., FBI Nat. Acad., 1992. Trooper Metro-Dade Police Dept., Miami, 1972-76; with Utah Hwy. Patrol, 1976—, trooper, 1976-86, sgt., accident reconstrn. specialist, adminstrv. asst. to supt., 1990-91, lt., comdr. protective svcs. at the state capitol, comdr. exec. protection, 1992, supt., 1993—. Office: Utah Hwy Patrol Box 141100 4501 S 2700 W Salt Lake City UT 84114

GREER, HOWARD EARL, retired career officer; b. Tyler, Tex., May 1, 1921; s. Earl Abner and Ollie (Lightfoot) G.; m. Dale Price, Nov. 1, 1986; children— Margaret, Darby, David, Briand, Holly, Howard. Student, Tyler Jr. Coll., 1939-40; B.S., U.S. Naval Acad., 1943; M.B.A., George Washington U., 1965. Commd. ensign U.S. Navy, 1943, advanced through grades to vice adm., 1975; comdr. Aircraft Carrier Hancock, 1967-69, Carrier Force, Vietnam, (4 tours), Naval Air Forces, U.S. Atlantic Fleet, Norfolk, Va., 1975-78. Mem. CEDAM Internat. Decorated D.S.M. (2), Legion of Merit (4), Knights of Malta Order St. John of Jerusalem. Mem. Assn. Naval Aviation, Golden Eagles (early pioneer naval aviators), Tailhook Assn., Naval Res. Assn., Lomas Santa Fe Country Club. Republican. Methodist. Home: 8539 Prestwick Dr La Jolla CA 92037-2025

GREER, MONTE ARNOLD, endocrinologist, educator; b. Portland, Oreg., Oct. 26, 1922; s. William Wallace and Rose (Rasmussen) G.; m. Peggy Johnson, Dec. 31, 1943; children: Susan Elizabeth, Richard Arnold. Student, Oreg. State U., 1940-43; AB, Stanford U., 1944, MD, 1947. Intern San Francisco Gen. Hosp., 1946-47; rsch. fellow endocrinology New England Med. Ctr., Boston, 1947-49; resident internal medicine Mass. Meml. Hosp., Boston, 1949-50; rsch. assoc. in endocrinology New England Med. Ctr. Hosp., 1950-51; sr. investigator, sr. asst. surgeon USPHS, Nat. Cancer Inst., NIH, Bethesda, Md., 1951-55; chief radioisotope unit D.C. Gen. Hosp., Washington, 1951-55; clin. asst. prof. medicine UCLA, 1955-56; chief radioisotope svc. VA Hosp., Long Beach, Calif., 1955-56; head div. endocrinology Oreg. Health Scis. U. (formerly U. Oreg. Med. Sch.), Portland, 1956-80, assoc. prof., 1956-62, prof. medicine, 1962—, prof. physiology, 1992—, head divsn. endocrinology, metabolism and clin. nutrition, 1980-84, head sect. endocrinology, 1984-90. Author: (with H. Studer) The Regulation of Thyroid Function in Iodine Deficiency, 1968, (with P. Langer) Antithyroid Drugs and Naturally Occurring Goitrogens, 1977; editor: The Thyroid Gland, 1990, (with D.H. Solomon) The Thyroid, 1974; mem. editorial bd. Endocrinology, 1960-72, Neuroendocrinology, 1965-76, Endocrine Regulations, 1971—; contbr. articles to profl. jours. Mem. Thyroid Task Force NIH Com. for Evaluation of Endocrinology and Metabolic Diseases, 1977-80, Endocrinology Study Sect., NIH, 1977-80. Pharmacol. and Endocrinology fellowship study sect. NIH, 1968-72; recipient Oppenheimer award Endocrine Soc., 1958, Rsch. Career award NIH, 1962-81, Discovery award Med. Rsch. Found. Oreg., 1985, DeMolay Legion of Honor award, 1988. Mem. AAAS, Am. Fedn. for Clin. Rsch. (chmn. Western sect. 1958-59), Western Soc. for Clin. Rsch. (v.p. 1963-64, pres. 1967-68), Endocrine Soc. (mem. council 1965-68, v.p. 1976-77), Am. Thyroid Assn. (v.p., dir. 1974-77, pres. 1980, Disting. Service award 1985), Am. Soc. Clin. Investigation, Soc. Exptl. Biology and Medicine, Western Assn. Physicians (sec.-treas. 1974-77), Assn. Am. Physicians, Internat. Brain Rsch. Orgn., Internat. Soc. Neuroendocrinology, European Thyroid Assn., Japan Endocrine Soc. (hon.), Czechoslovak Endocrine Soc. (hon.), Rotary, Sigma Chi. Office: Oreg Health Scis U Portland OR 97201

GREEVER, MARGARET QUARLES, retired mathematics educator; b. Wilkensburg, Pa., Feb. 7, 1931; d. Lawrence Reginald and Ella Mae (LeSueur) Quarles; m. John Greever, Aug. 29, 1953; children: Catherine Patricia, Richard George, Cynthia Diane. Cert. costume design, Richmond Profl. Inst., 1952; student, U. Va., 1953-56; BA in Math., Calif. State U., L.A., 1963; MA in Math., Claremont Grad. Sch., 1968. Cert. tchr. specializing in Jr. Coll. math., Calif. Tchr. math. Chaffey Unified H.S. Dist., Alta Loma, Calif., 1963-64, L.A. Unified Sch. Dist., 1964-65, Chino (Calif.) Unified Sch. Dist., 1965-81; from asst. prof. to prof. Chaffey Coll., Rancho Cucamonga, 1981-96, phys. sci. divsn. chmn. Alta Loma, 1985-92, dean, phys., life, health sci., 1992-96. Mem. AAUW (pres. local chpt. 1998-2000), Orcas Island Garden Club (treas. 1997-2000, pres.-elect 2000, pres. 2001), Orcas Island Yacht Club, Pi Lambda Theta. Avocations: quilting, cooking, sewing, gardening.

GREGG, CHARLES THORNTON, research company executive; b. Billings, Mont., July 27, 1927; s. Charles Thornton and Gertrude (Hurst) G.; m. Elizabeth Whitaker, Dec. 20, 1947; children: Paul, Diane, Brian, Elaine. BS in Physics, Oreg. State U., 1952, MS in Organic Chemistry, 1955, PhD in Biochemistry, 1959. Postdoctoral fellow Nat. Cancer Inst., Johns Hopkins Sch. Med., Balt., 1959-63; mem. staff Los Alamos (N.Mex.) Nat. Lab., 1963-85; sr. scientist Mesa Diagnostics, Los Alamos, 1985-86; v.p. rsch. Los Alamos Diagnostics, 1986-90; pres. Innovative Surg. Tech. Inc., 1991—. Pres. Bethco, Inc., 1972—; vis. prof. The Free U., Berlin, 1973-74; cons. internat. tech. div. Los Alamos Nat. Lab., 1985-90. Author: Plague, 1978, The Virus of Love, 1983, Tarawa, 1985; patentee bacterial identification apparatus, safe surg. knife. Bd. dirs. Friends of Mesa Pub. Libr., Los Alamos, 1981-83, County Libr. Los Alamos, 1983-85, Los Alamos Arts Coun., 1985-87, bd. dir., Lukens Med. Corp., 1996-97. Served in U.S. Navy, 1944-46. Fellow AAAS; mem. Am. Soc. Biochemistry and Molecular Biology, Am. Soc. Microbiology, Sigma Xi, Sigma Pi Sigma, Phi Lambda Upsilon. Democrat. Unitarian. Avocation: hiking. Office: 190 Central Park Sq Los Alamos NM 87544-4001 E-mail: cgregg1@yahoo.com

GREGOIRE, CHRISTINE O. state attorney general; b. Auburn, Wash. m. Michael Gregoire; 2 children. BA, U. Wash.; JD cum laude, Gonzaga U., 1977. Clerk, typist Wash. State Adult Probation/ Parole Office, Seattle, 1969; caseworker Wash. Dept. Social and Health Scis., Everett, 1974; asst. atty. gen. State of Wash., Spokane, 1977-81, sr. asst. atty. gen., 1981-82, dep. atty. gen. Olympia, 1982-88; dir. Wash. State Dept. Ecology, 1988-92; atty. gen. State of Wash., 1992—. Dir. Wash. State Dept. Ecology, 1988-92. Chair Puget Sound Water Quality Authority, 1990-92, Nat. Com. State Environ. Dirs., 1991-92, States/B.C. Oil Spill Task Force, 1989-92. Recipient Conservationist of Yr. award Trout Unlimited/N.w. Steelhead & Salmon Coun., 1994, Gov.'s Child Abuse Prevention award, 1996, 5th Annual Myra Bradwell award, 1997, Wyman award, 1997-98, Bd. of Gov.'s award for professionalism WSBA, 1997, Kick Butt award The Tobacco Free Coalition of Pierce County, 1997, award Wash. State Hosp. Assn., 1997, Citizen Activist award Gleitsman Found., 1998, Woman of Achievement award Assn. for Women in Comm. Matrix Table, 1999, WSTLA Pub. Justice award, 1999, Excellence in Pub. Health award Wash. State Assn. Local Pub. Health Ofcls., 1999, Women in Govt. award Good

Housekeeping, 1999, Woman of Yr. award Am. Legion Aux., 1999, Spl. Recognition award Wash. State Nurses Assn., 2000; named one of 25 Most Influential Working Mothers, Working Mother mag., 2000. Mem. Nat. Assn. Attys. Gen. (consumer protection and environment com., energy com., children and the law subcom.). Office: Attorney Generals Office PO Box 40100 Olympia WA 98504

GREGOR, DOROTHY DEBORAH, librarian; b. Dobbs Ferry, N.Y., Aug. 15, 1939; d. Richard Garrett Heckman and Marion Allen (Richmond) Stewart; m. A. James Gregor, June 22, 1963 (div. 1974). BA, Occidental Coll., 1961; MA, U. Hawaii, 1963; MLS, U. Tex., 1968; cert. in Library Mgmt., U. Calif., Berkeley, 1976. Reference libr. U. Calif., San Francisco, 1968-69; dept. libr. Pub. Health Libr. U. Calif., Berkeley, 1969-71, tech. services libr., 1973-76; reference libr. Hamilton Libr., Honolulu, 1971-72; head serials dept. U. Calif., Berkeley, 1976-80, assoc. univ. libr. tech. svcs. dept., 1980-84, univ. libr., 1992-94; chief Shared Cataloging div. Libr. of Congress, Washington, 1984-85; univ. libr. U. Calif.-San Diego, La Jolla, 1985-92, OCLC asst. to pres. for acad. and rsch. libr. rels., 1995-98. Instr. sch. libr. and info. studies U. Calif., Berkeley, 1975, 76, 83; cons. Nat. Libr. of Medicine, Bethesda, Md., 1985, Ohio Bd. Regents, Columbus, 1987; trustee Online Computer Libr. Ctr., 1988-96; dir. Nat. Coordinating Com. on Japanese Libr. Resources, 1995-98. Mem. ALA, Libr. Info. Tech. Assn., Program Com. Ctr. for Rsch. Librs. (bd. chair 1992-93, Hugh Atkinson award 1994). E-mail: dgregor@mcn.org

GREGORY, CALVIN, insurance service executive; b. Bronx, N.Y., Jan. 11, 1942; s. Jacob and Ruth (Cherchian) G.; m. Rachel Anna Carver, Feb. 14, 1970 (div. Apr. 1977); children— Debby Lynn, Trixy Sue; m. 2d, Carla Deane Deaver, June 30, 1979. AA, L.A. City Coll., 1962; BA, Calif. State U.-L.A., 1964; MDiv, Fuller Theol. Sem., 1968; MRS, Southwestern Sem., Ft. Worth, 1969; PhD in Religion, Universal Life Ch., Modesto, Calif., 1982; DDiv (hon.), Otay Mesa Coll., 1982. Notary pub., real estate lic., casualty lic., Calif.; ordained to ministry Am. Baptist Conv., 1970. Youth minister First Bapt. Ch., Delano, Calif., 1964-65, 69-70; youth dir. St. Luke's United Meth. Ch., Highland Park, Calif., 1969-70; tchr. polit. sci. Maranatha High Sch., Rosemead, Calif., 1969-70; aux. chaplain U.S. Air Force 750th Radar Squadron, Edwards AFB, Calif., 1970-72; pastor First Bapt. Ch., Boron, Calif., 1971-72; ins. agt. Prudential Ins. Co., Ventura, Calif., 1972-73, sales mgr., 1973-74; casualty ins. agt. Allstate Ins. Co., Thousand Oaks, Calif., 1974-75; pres. Ins. Agy. Placement Svs., Thousand Oaks, 1975— ; head youth minister Emanuel Presbyn. Ch., L.A., 1973-74; owner, investor real estate, U.S., Wales, Eng., Can., Australia. Counselor YMCA, Hollywood, Calif., 1964, Soul Clinic-Universal Life Ch., Inc., Modesto, Calif., 1982. Mem. Apt. Assn. L.A., Life Underwriter Tng. Coun., Forensic Club (L.A.), X32 Club (Ventura, Calif.), Kiwanis (club spkr. 1971). Republican. Office: Ins Agy Placement Svc PO Box 4407 Thousand Oaks CA 91359-1407

GREGORY, HEROLD LA MAR, chemical company administrator; b. Farmington, Utah, Nov. 9, 1923; s. Elijah B. and Julia Ellen (Tree) G.; m. Mary Ethel Eccles, Aug. 15, 1951; children— Vicki McGregor, Walter E., Suellen Winegar. B.A., U. Utah, 1949. Exec. dir. Utah Symphony, Salt Lake City, 1957-86; asst. to chmn. Huntsman Corp., 1986—. Pres. East German mission Ch. of Jesus Christ of Latter-day Saints, Berlin, 1953-57, mission sec., 1949-51; assoc. prof. arts adminstrn. U. Utah, 1976-85 Mem. Mormon Tabernacle Choir, 1978-85, adminstrv. asst. 1987—; mem. Utah Symohony Chorus, 1985—; sec. Utah Symphony Bd., 1957—, Tanner Gift of Music Trust, 1983—. With AUS, 1943-45. Home: 3215 Skycrest Cir Salt Lake City UT 84108-1611 Office: 500 Huntsman Way Salt Lake City UT 84108-1235

GREGORY, JAMES, retired actor; b. N.Y.C., Dec. 23, 1911; s. James Gillen and Axemia Theresa (Ekdahl) G.; m. Ann Catherine Miltner, May 25, 1944. Grad. high sch. Actor, 1936—. Actor: (summer stock prodns.) Deer Lake, Pa., 1936-37, 39, Millbrook, N.Y., 1938, Braddock Heights, Md., 1940, Buck's County Playhouse, New Hope, Pa., 1941, Ivy Tower Playhouse, Spring Lake, N.J., 1951, (Broadway shows) Key Largo, 1939, Journey to Jerusalem, 1940, In Time to Come, 1941, Dream Girl, 1945, All My Sons, 1947, Death of a Salesman, 1948-49 (played Biff on Broadway with 5 Willy Lomans), Dead Pigeon, 1954, Fragile Fox, 1955, Desperate Hours, 1956-57, (films) The Young Strangers, 1955, Al Capone Story, 1955, Gun Glory, 1956, Nightfall, 1956, The Big Caper, 1956, A Distant Trumpet, 1961, Underwater Warrior, 1962, PT-109, 1965, The Sons of Katie Elder, 1967, The Manchurian Candidate, 1967, Captain Newman, M.D, 1967, Million Dollar Duck, 1968, Clam Bake, 1967, Secret War of Harry Frigg, 1968, Beneath the Planet of the Apes, 1970, The Hawaiians, 1970, Shoot Out, 1971, The Late Liz, 1971, $1,000,000. Duck, 1971, The Strongest Man in the World, 1974, The Main Event, 1979, Wait Til Your Mother Gets Home, 1982, X-15, Death of a Salesman, also 5 Matt Helm pictures, (TV shows) Big Valley, Bonanza, Gunsmoke, Rawhide, Playhouse 90, Climax, Alfred Hitchcock Presents, Twilight Zone, Quincy, as Inspector Luger in Barney Miller, Mr. Belvedere, 1986. Served with USNR, USMCR, 1942-45, PTO. Mem. Soc. Preservation and Encouragement Barber Shop Quartet Singing Am. Club: Hollywood Hackers, Golf. Home: 55 Cathedral Rock Dr Unit 33 Sedona AZ 86351-8624

GREGORY, LEONARD, publishing executive; Mng. editor Pueble (Colo.) Chieftan, exec. editor. Office: Pueblo Chieftan 825 W 6th St Pueblo CO 81003-2390

GREGORY, NORMAN WAYNE, chemistry educator, researcher; b. Albany, Oreg., June 23, 1920; s. Arthur Donald and Edith Florence (Self) G.; m. Lillian Virginia Larson, May 21, 1943; children: Norman Wayne Jr., Martha Jean, Brian Neil. Student, Lower Columbia Jr. Coll., 1936-38; B.S., U. Wash., Seattle, 1940, M.S., 1941; Ph.D., Ohio State U., 1943. Research chemist Radiation Lab., U. Calif., Berkeley, 1944-46; instr. U. Wash., Seattle, 1946-47, asst. prof., 1947-53, assoc. prof., 1953-57, prof. chemistry, 1957-89, prof. emeritus, 1989—, chmn. dept., 1970-75. Author: Physical Chemistry, 1964; contbr. articles to profl. jours. Mem. Am. Chem. Soc. (chmn. Puget Sound sect. 1964, treas. 1962), Sigma Xi Office: U Wash PO Box 351700 Seattle WA 98195-1700

GREIF, AVNER, economics educator; b. 1955; m. Estee; 3 children. BA, Tel Aviv U., 1981, MA, 1985, Northwestern U., 1988, PhD, 1989. Assoc. prof. econs. Stanford U., Calif. Author: Genoa and the Mghribi Traders; Historical and Comparative Institutional Analysis, 1998; contbr. articles to profl. jours. MacArthur fellow John D. and Catherine T. MacArthur Found., 1998 Mem. Am. Econs. Assn., ASSHA, EHA, Cliometrics Soc. Achievements include research in economic history; use of game theory and other modelling techniques to demonstrate the connection of random beliefs, institutions and social ties to cultural norms of trust and reciprocity in order to understand the conditions leading to social conflict and cooperation. Office: Stanford U Econs Dept Ralph Candan Econs Bldg Stanford CA 94305-6072 E-mail: avner@leland.stanford.edu

GREIG, WILLIAM TABER, JR. publishing company executive; b. Mpls., Apr. 16, 1924; s. William Taber and Margaret Naomi (Buckbee) G.; m. Doris Jane Walters, June 23, 1951; children: Kathryn Ann Greig Rowland, William Taber, III, Gary Stanley, Doris Jane. B.Arch., U. Minn., 1945. Jr. exec. Bur. Engraving, Mpls., 1946-48; partner, mgr. Praise Book Publns., Mound, Minn., 1948-50; v.p., exec. v.p., gen. mgr. Gospel Light Publs., 1950-76, pres., owner Calif., 1976—, chmn., 1983—. Bd. dirs. Lighthouse Ptnrs. Bookstores, Gospel Lit. Internat.; founder, chmn. bd. St. Petersburg (Russia) Pub. Ruling elder Presbyn. Ch. (U.S.A.); bd. dirs., chmn. Joy of Living Bible Studies, 1978—; trustee Concerts of Prayer Internat., 1988—; chmn. John Perkins Found., 1990—; founding trustee Internat. Bd. Reconciliation. Served to lt. (j.g.) USNR, 1943-46. Mem. Evang. Christian Pubs. Assn. (co-founder 1974, bd. dirs., pres. 1981-83) Republican. Clubs: Tower. Home: 347 Lupine Way Ventura CA 93001-2201 Office: Gospel Light Publs 2300 Knoll Dr Ventura CA 93003-7383

GRESHAM, ZANE OLIVER, lawyer; b. Mobile, Ala., Dec. 16, 1948; S. Charles Brandon and Lillian Ann (Oliver) G.; m. Marian Gan, Mar. 3, 1988. BA cum laude, Johns Hopkins U., 1970; JD magna cum laude, Northwestern U., 1973. Bar: Calif. 1973. Assoc. Morrison & Foerster, San Francisco, 1973-79, ptnr., 1980—, co-chair land use and environ. law group, 1987-97, co-chair airports and aviation law group, 1996—; chair Latin Am. Group, 1998—. Dir., v.p. (Latin Am.) Internat. Private Water Assn., 1999—; dir. Fromm Inst., 2000—. Cons. editor: Environ. Compliance and Litigation Strategy. Pres. San Francisco Forward, 1980-85; bd. dirs. Regional Inst. Bay Area, Richmond, Calif., 1989-95, Regional Parks Found., Oakland, Calif., 1992—, pres., 1995; spl. counsel Grace Cathedral, San Francisco, 1991—; dir., exec. v.p. Pan Am. Soc. Calif., 1995-97, pres. 1998—; vice chmn. Nat. Youth Sci. Found., 1997—. Mem. State Bar Calif., Urban Land Inst., Lambda Alpha. Avocations: opera, sketching. Office: Morrison & Foerster 425 Market St Ste 3100 San Francisco CA 94105-2482 E-mail: zgresham@mofo.com

GRESSAK, ANTHONY RAYMOND, JR. sales executive; b. Honolulu, Jan. 22, 1947; s. Anthony Raymond and Anne Tavares (Ferreira) G.; m. Catherine Streb, Apr. 11, 1981; children: Danielle Kirsten, Anthony Raymond III, Christina Michelle. AA, Utah State U., 1967; postgrad., U.S. Army Inf. Officers Candidate Sch., 1968. Restaurant mgr. Ala Moana Hotel, Honolulu, 1970-72; gen. mgr. Fred Harvey, Inc., Ontario, Calif., 1972-73; regional mgr. So. Calif., 1972-73, regional mgr. tollway ops., 1973; divisional mgr. Normandy Lane, 1973; resident mgr. Royal Inns of Am., San Diego, 1974; food and beverage dir. Asso. Inns & Restaurant Co. of Am. (Aircoa), Big Sky, Mont., 1974-75; condominium mgr. Big Sky, 1975; asst. gen. mgr. Naples (Fla.) Bath and Tennis Club, 1975-76; food and beverage dir. Nat. Parks, Grand Canyon, Ariz., 1976-77; gen. mgr. Grand Canyon Nat. Park Lodges, 1977-79; divisional v.p. food services The Broadway, Carter Hawley Hale, Inc., Los Angeles, 1979-82; exec. v.p. Silco Corp., Los Angeles, 1982-84; mktg. mgr. Interstate Restaurant Supply, 1984-85; dir. mktg. and merchandising S.E. Rykoff & Co., Los Angeles, 1986-91; nat. accounts sales mgr. healthcare and hospitality Rykoff-Sexton, Inc., L.A., 1991-93; v.p. distbr. sales The Cheesecake Factory Bakery Inc., Calabasas, Calif., 1993—. Maitre de table Chaine des Rotisseurs-Los Angeles; mem. edn. culinary steering com. Los Angeles Trade Tech. Coll. With U.S. Army, 1967-70. Decorated Silver Star, Bronze Star, Purple Heart; South Vietnamese Cross of Gallantry. Mem. Nat. Restaurant Assn. (assoc.), Internat. Order DeMolay (life, chevalier), Smithsonian Assocs., Am. Culinary Fedn. (assoc., Presdl. Medallion award 1991), Calif. Restaurant Assn. (assoc.), Les Toques Blanches Internat. Roman Catholic. Home: 20301 Minnehaha St Chatsworth CA 91311-2540 Office: The Cheesecake Factory 26950 Agoura Rd Agoura Hills CA 91301-5335 E-mail: tgressak@thecheesecakefactory.com

GRETZKY, WAYNE DOUGLAS, retired hockey player, businessman; b. Brantford, Ont., Can., Jan. 26, 1961; s. Walter and Phyllis G.; m. Janet Jones, July 16, 1988; 3 children: Paulina, Ty Robert, Trevor Douglas. Center Peterborough Petes, Jr. Ont. Hockey Assn., 1977-78, Sault Ste. Marie Greyhounds, 1977-78, Indpls. Racers, World Hockey Assn., 1978, Edmonton Oilers (Alta., Can.), NHL, 1988, Los Angeles Kings, NHL, 1988-96, Saint Louis Blues, NHL, 1996, N.Y. Rangers, NHL, 1996-99, ret., 1999; investor Los Arcos Sports LLC/Phoenix Coyotes, 1999—. Player NHL All-Star game, 1980-86, 1988-94; mem. Stanley Cup championship teams, 1984, 85, 87, 88. Player NHL All-Star first team, 1980-92, 1990-91; named Rookie of Yr. World Hockey Assn., 1978-79, Sportsman of Yr. Sports Illus., 1982, Sporting News NHL Player of the Year, 1980-81, 86-87, Sporting News All-Star team, 1980-81, 86-87, 90-91, Sporting News Man of the Year, 1981, All-Star game MVP, 1983, 89, Canadian Athlete of the Year, 1985, Dodge Performer of the Year, 1984-85, 1986-87; recipient Art Ross Meml. trophy NHL, 1981-87, 89-90, 90-91, 93-94, Conn Smythe trophy, 1985, 88, William Hanley trophy, 1977-78, Lemms Family award, 1977-78, Hart Meml. trophy, 1974-80, Lady Byng Meml. tropy, 1979-80, 90-91, 91-92, 93-94, Lester B. Pearson award, 1982-82, 84-85, 86-87, Emery Edge award, 1983-84, 84-85, 86-87, Lester Patrick trophy, 1993-94; holder NHL career scoring record. Achievements include being the record holder for points, goals, assists, overtime assists and others. Office: c/o Phoenix Coyotes Cellular One Ice Den 9375 E Bell Rd Scottsdale AZ 85260-0101

GREY, BRAD, producer, agent; Mgr., prodr. Brillstein-Grey Entertainment, Beverly Hills, Calif., now chmn., CEO. Prodr. (films) The Burning, 1981; del. prodr. Opportunity Knocks, 1990; exec. prodr. (films) The Celluloid Closet, 1995, Cat and Mouse, 1995, Happy Gilmore, 1996, The Cable Guy, 1996, Bulletproof, 1996, The Replacement Killers, 1998, Dirty Work, 1998, (TV movie) Don't Try This at Home!, 1990, (TV series) The Larry Sanders Show, 1992, Mr. Show, 1995, The Naked Truth, 1995, The Steve Harvey Show, 1996, Just Shoot Me!, 1997, Alright Already, 1997, C-16: FBI, 1997. Office: Brillstein Grey Entertainment 9150 Wilshire Blvd Ste 350 Beverly Hills CA 90212-3453

GREY, ROBERT DEAN, academic administrator, biology educator; b. Liberal, Kans., Sept. 5, 1939; s. McHenry Wesley and Kathryn (Brown) G.; m. Alice Kathleen Archer, June 11, 1961; children: Erin Kathleen, Joel Michael. BA, Phillips U., 1961; PhD, Washington U., 1966. Asst. prof. Washington U., St. Louis, 1966-67; from asst. prof. to full prof. zoology U. Calif., Davis, 1967—, chmn. dept., 1979-83, dean biol. scis., 1985—, interim exec. vice chancellor, 1993-95, provost, exec. vice chancellor, 1995—. Author: (with others) A Laboratory Text for Developmental Biology, 1980; contbr. articles to profl. jours. Recipient Disting. Tchg. awrd Acad. Senate U. Calif., Davis, 1977, Magnar Ronning award for tchg. Associated Students U. Calif., Davis, 1978, Disting. Alumnus award Phillips U., 1991. Mem. Am. Soc. Cell Biology, Soc. Developmental Biology, Phi Sigma. Avocations: music, hiking, gardening. Office: U Calif 573 Mrak Hall 1 Shields Ave Davis CA 95616-5200

GREYSON, CLIFFORD RUSSELL, internist; b. N.Y.C., 1958; AB, Harvard Coll., 1980; MSEE, Stanford U., 1985, MD, 1987. Cert. internal medicine and cardiovascular diseases, critical care medicine. Resident in internal medicine Stanford U. Hosp., 1987-90, fellow in critical care, 1990-91; fellow in cardiovasc. disease U. Calif., San Francisco, 1991-95, faculty cardiology divsn., 1995-99, U. Colo. Health Scis. Ctr., Denver, 1999—. Co-dir. med. intensive care unit San Francisco VA Med. Ctr., 1998-99. Elected to city coun. Town of Woodside, Calif., 1995. Recipient Clinician Scientist award Am. Heart Assn., 1995-96, Clin. Investigator Devel. award NIH, 1996—. Fellow Am. Coll. Cardiology; mem. ACP. Office: Denver VA Med Ctr Cardiology 111B 1055 Clermont St Denver CO 80220-3808

GRIECO, PAUL ANTHONY, chemistry educator; b. Framingham, Mass., Oct. 27, 1944; married; 4 children. BA, Boston U., 1966; MA, Columbia U., 1967, PhD in Organic Chemistry, 1970. NSF fellow Harvard U., 1970-71; from asst. prof. to prof. chemistry U. Pitts., 1971-80; prof. chemistry Ind. U., Bloomington, 1980-85, Earl Blough prof. chemistry, 1985—, chmn. dept., 1988-97; head of chemistry and biochemistry dept. Mont. State U., 1999—. William P. Timmie lectr. Emory U., 1977; Abbott lectr. Yale U., 1984; H.C. Brown lectr. Purdue U., 1984; Disting. lectr. U. Wyo., 1986; Conv. Intercantonale Romande pour L'Enseignement du Troisième Cycle en Chimie, Switzerland, 1987; Centennial lectr. Abbott Labs., Chgo., 1988; H. Martin Friedman lectr. Rutgers U., 1988; Centennial Anniversary lectr. 1st Internat. Conf. on Organic Chem. Nomenclature, Geneva, 1992. Fellow Alfred P. Sloan Found., 1974-76, Japan Soc. Promising Scientists, 1978-79; recipient Ernest Guenther award, 1982, NIH-Nat. Cancer Inst. Merit award, 1988. Mem. Am. Chem. Soc. (Akron sect. award 1982, Arthur C. Cope Scholar award 1990, award for creative work in synthetic organic chemistry 1991, lectr. French.-Am. socs. meeting in France 1992), Royal Soc. Chemistry, Chem. Soc. Japan, Swiss Chem. Soc. Achievements include rsch. in the devel. of new synthetic methods for constrn. of complex natural products. Office: Mont State U Dept Biochem & Chem 108 Gains Hl Bozeman MT 59717-0001

GRIEGO, PHIL A. state legislator; b. Santa Fe, Aug. 5, 1948; JD, Coll. Santa Fe. CEO Am. Surety Title; rancher; mem. N.Mex. Senate, Dist. 39, Sante Fe, 1996—; mem. conservation com., mem. fin. com. N.Mex. Senate. Democrat. Office: PO Box 10 San Jose NM 87565-0010

GRIEP, DAVID MICHAEL, astronomical scientist, researcher; b. Mpls., Oct. 13, 1957; s. Richard Arthur Sr. and Carole Elaine (Bengal) G.; m. Carolina May Von Gnechten, Nov. 19, 1994. BS in Astrophysics, U. Minn. Inst. Tech., 1979; MS in Astronomy, U. Minn., 1981. Rsch. assoc. Inst. Astronomy U. Hawaii, Hilo, 1982—. Office: Univ Hawaii Inst Astronomy PO Box 4729 Hilo HI 96720-0729

GRIER, JAMES EDWARD, hotel company executive, lawyer; b. Ottumwa, Iowa, Sept. 7, 1935; s. Edward J. and Corinne (Bailey) G.; m. Virginia Clinker, July 4, 1959; children: Michael, Susan, James, John, Thomas. BSc, U. Iowa, 1956, JD, 1959. Bar: Iowa 1959, Mo. 1959. Mng. ptnr. Hillix, Brewer, Hoffhaus & Grier, Kansas City, Mo., 1964-77, Grier & Swartzman, Kansas City, 1977-89; pres. Doubletree Hotels Corp., Phoenix, 1989-94; chmn. Sonoran Hotel Capital, Inc., Phoenix, 1994-96; mng. ptnr. Copa Investments, 1996—, Gainey Hotel Co., 1996—. Bd. dirs. Iowa Law Sch. Found., Iowa City, St. Joseph Healthcare Ariz., Phoenix, Homeward Bound, Phoenix. Home: 3500 E Lincoln Dr Phoenix AZ 85018-1010 Office: Copa Investments 7300 E Gainey Suites Dr Ste 169 Scottsdale AZ 85258-2061 E-mail: jegrier@mindspring.com

GRIESEMER, ALLAN DAVID, retired museum director; b. Mayville, Wis., Aug. 13, 1935; s. Raymond John and Leone Emma (Fisher) G.; m. Nancy Jean Sternberg, June 6, 1959; children: David, Paul, Steven. AB, Augustana Coll., 1959; MS, U. Wis., 1963; PhD, U. Nebr., 1970. Curator; coordinator ednl. services U. Nebr., Lincoln State Museum, 1965-77, assoc. prof., assoc. dir., 1977-79, acting dir., 1980-81, assoc. dir. and coordinator, 1981-82, interim dir., 1982-84; dir. San Bernardino County Mus., Calif., 1984-97, dir. emeritus, 1997—; mem. faculty dept. geology U. Nebr., Lincoln, 1968-80; lectr. geology U. Nebr., Lincoln State Mus., 1968-80; CEO, dir., curator Mousley Mus. Natural History, San Bernardino County Mus., Yucaipa, Calif., 1984-97; ret., 1997. Adj. prof. Calif. State U., San Bernardino, 1986. Contbr. articles to sci. jours., mus. publs., 1965— . Bd. dirs. Redland Music Assn., Prospect Pk., Fortnightly Club, Inland Harvest, Calif. Desert Studies Consortium, Redlands Cmty. Hosp. Found.; mem. adv. bd. Redlands Cmty. Hosp., brd. mem., Habitat Humanity San Bernardino, adv. mem., Montessori in Red Lands. Recipient Hon. award Sigma Gamma Epsilon, 1958 Mem. Paleontol. Soc., Nebr. Mus. Conf. (pres. 1976-79), Nebr. Geol. Soc., Nebr. Acad. Scis., Mountain Plains Conf., Mountain Plains Mus. Assn. (pres. 1979), Am. Assn. Museums (v.p. 1983), Rotary (bd. dirs.). Lutheran. Home: 306 La Colina Dr Redlands CA 92374-8247

GRIEVE, ROBERT BURTON, parasitologist, educator; b. Torrington, Wyo., Oct. 27, 1951; s. Burton William and Eulah Ann (Scott) Grieve; m. Marcia Ann Mika, Jan. 16, 1982; children: Jonathon Robert, Megan Mika, Madeline Reno. BS in Microbiology, U. Wyo., 1973, MS in Microbiology, 1975; PhD in Parasitology, U. Fla., 1978. Postdoctoral assoc., then rsch. assoc. Cornell U., Ithaca, N.Y., 1978-81; asst. prof. U. Pa., Phila., 1981-84; assoc. prof. U. Wis., Madison, 1984-87, Colo. State U., Ft. Collins, 1987-90, prof. parasitology, 1990—; v.p. R & D, chief sci. officer, CEO Heska Corp., Ft. Collins, 1991—. Assoc. investigator USAF, Keesler AFB, Miss., 1979-84; adviser WHO, Geneva, 1984; cons. NIH, 1985, 88. Patentee heartworm diagnosis procedure; contbr. articles to profl. jours. Recipient Ralston Purina Small Animal Rsch. award, 1991. Mem. AAAS, Am. Soc. Parasitologists (editorial bd., Henry Baldwin Ward medal 1990, pres. 1996-97), Am. Soc. Tropical Medicine and Hygiene, Am. Assn. Immunologists (assoc. editor 1991-95), Am. Assn. Veterinary Parasitologists (chair nominating com. 1987-88), Sigma Xi, Alpha Zeta. Home: 38501 WCR21 Fort Collins CO 80524 Office: Heska Corp 1613 Prospect Pkwy Fort Collins CO 80525-9769

GRIFFEN, AGNES MARTHE, library administrator; b. Ft. Dauphin, Madagascar, Aug. 25, 1935; d. Frederick Stang and Alvilde Margrethe (Torvik) Hallanger; m. Thomas Michael Griffen (div. Nov. 1969); children: Shaun Helen Griffen D'Antoni, Christopher Patrick, Adam Andrew; m. John H.P. Hall, Aug. 26, 1980. BA cum laude in English, Pacific Luth. U., 1957; MLS, U. Wash., 1965; Urban Exec. cert., MIT, 1976; postgrad., Harvard U., 1993. Cert. librarian, Wash., Md., Ariz. Area children's libr. King County Libr. Sys., Seattle, 1965-68, coord. instl. librs., 1968-71, dep. libr. for staff and program devel., 1971-74; dep. libr. dir. Tucson Pub. Libr., 1974-80; dir. Montgomery County Dept. Pub. Librs., Rockville, Md., 1980-96; libr. dir. Tucson-Pima Pub. Libr., 1997—. Lectr. Grad. Libr. Sch., U. Ariz., Tucson, 1976-77, 79; vis. lectr. Sch. Librarianship, U. Wash., Seattle, 1983. Contbr. articles to library periodicals and profl. jours. Active Md. Humanities Coun., Balt., 1986-92, Ariz. Humanities Coun., Phoenix, 1977-80; charter mem. Exec. Women's Coun. of So. Ariz., Tucson, 1979-80; mem. coun. Nat. Capital Area Pub. Access Network, 1992-94, pres. bd., 1993-94. Recipient Helping Hand award Md. Assn. of the Deaf, 1985, Cert. Recognition Montgomery County Hispanic Employees Assn., 1985; Henry scholar U. Washington Sch. Librarianship, 1965. Mem. ALA (exec. bd. 1989-93, divsn. pres. pub. libr. assn. bd. 1981-82, councilor-at-large 1972-76, 86-93, chmn. com. on program evaluation and support 1987-88, legis. com. 1998—), Md. Libr. Assn., Ariz. Libr. Assn. Democrat. Home: 1951 N El Moraga Dr Tucson AZ 85745-9070 Office: Tucson-Pima Public Library PO Box 27470 Tucson AZ 85726-7470 E-mail: agriffe1@ci.tucson.az.us

GRIFFEY, LINDA BOYD, lawyer; b. Keokuk, Iowa, Aug. 6, 1949; d. Marshall Coulter and Geraldine Vivian (White) Boyd; m. John Jay Griffey, June 24, 1972. BS in Pharmacy, U. Iowa, 1972; JD, Duke U., 1980. Bar: Calif. 1980; lic. pharmacist, Iowa, N.C. Pharmacist Davenport (Iowa) Osteo. Hosp., 1972-75, Wagner Pharmacy, Clinton, Iowa, 1975-77, Durham (N.C.) County Gen. Hosp., 1977-80; assoc. O'Melveny & Myers, L.A., 1980-88, ptnr., 1988—. Spkr., writer in field of employee benefits and exec. compensation; former pres. L.A. chpt. Western Pension and Benefits Conf., 1998-99. Active L.A. Philharm. Bus. & Profl. Assn.; bd. dirs. Hillsides Home for Children, Pasadena Playhouse. Mem. ABA (employee benefits com. tax sect.), Am. Law Inst., L.A. County Bar Assn. (former chair employee benefits com. 1994-95), L.A. Duke Bar Assn. (pres. 1987-90, 91-92), Rotary (L.A. chpt. bd. dirs. 1995-97). Avocations: golf, reading, swimming. Office: O'Melveny & Myers 400 S Hope St Los Angeles CA 90071-2899 E-mail: lgriffey@omm.com

GRIFFIN, GLORIA JEAN, elementary school educator; b. Emmett, Idaho, Sept. 10, 1946; d. Archie and Marguerite (Johnson) G. AA, Boise (Idaho) Jr. Coll., 1966; BA, Boise Coll., 1968; MA in Elem. Curriculum, Boise State U., 1975. Cert. advanced elem. tchr., Idaho. Tchr. music, tutor, Boise; sec. Edward A. Johnson, atty., Boise; tchr. Head Start, Boise; elem.

tchr. Meridian (Idaho) Sch. Dist., 1968—. Developer multi-modality individualized spelling program; co-developer program for adapting curriculum to student's individual differences. Author: The Culture and Customs of the Argentine People As Applied to a Sixth Grade Social Studies Unit. Sec. PTA. Named Tchr. of Yr., Meridian Sch. Dist., 1981. Mem. NEA, Idaho Edn. Assn., Meridian Edn. Assn. (bldg. rep.), Idaho Reading Coun., Horizons Reading Coun., Alpha Delta Kappa (rec. sec.). Office: Silver Sage Elem Sch 7700 Snohomish St Boise ID 83709-5975

GRIFFIN, JEAN (ALVA JEAN GRIFFIN), entertainer; b. Detroit, June 1, 1931; d. Henry Bethel White and Ruth Madelyn (Gowen) Durham; m. Francis Jay Griffin, July 8, 1958 (dec.); stepchildren: Patra, Rodney; 1 adopted child, Donald; children: Rhonda Jean, Sherree Lee. Student, Anderson Coll., 1952-53; DD (hon.), Ministry of Salvation, Chula Vista, Calif., 1990, Ministry of Salvation, , 1990. Ordained minister, 1990. Supr. Woolworth's, Detroit, 1945-46; operator, supr. Atlantic Bell Tel. Co., Detroit, 1947-51, Anderson, Ind., 1952-56; sec. to div. mgr. Food Basket-Lucky Stores, San Diego, 1957-58; owner, mgr. Jay's Country Boy Markets, Riverside, Calif., 1962-87; entertainer, prodr., dir., singer Mae West & Co., 1980—. Past owner The Final Touch, Colorado Springs; owner Omega Communique Co., 1997—; tchr. art Grant Sch., Riverside, 1964-65; tchr., adviser Mental Retarded Sch., Riverside, 1976-77; instr. Touch for Health Found., Pasadena, Calif., 1975-79; cons., hypnotist, nutritionist, Riverside, 1976-79; mem., tchr. Psi field parapsychology. Writer children's stories and short stories. Mem. Rep. Presdl. Task Force, 1983. Recipient svc. award Rep. Presdl. Task Force, 1986. Mem. Parapsychology Assn. Riverside (pres. 1981-82). Mem. Ch. of Religious Science New Thought. Avocations: arts and crafts, photography, hiking, horseback riding, travel. Home: 201 W Chapel Rd Sedona AZ 86336-7031

GRIFFIN, JEFF, mayor; Mayor City of Reno, Nev. Office: City Reno 490 S Center St Reno NV 89501-2105

GRIFFIN, KEITH BROADWELL, economics educator; b. Colon, Republic of Panama, Nov. 6, 1938; came to U.S., 1988; s. Marcus Samuel Griffin and Elaine Ann (Broadwell) Fabick; m. Dixie Beth, Apr. 2, 1956; children: Janice, Kimberley. BA, Williams Coll., 1960, DLitt (hon.), 1980; PhB, Oxford U., Eng., 1962, PhD, 1965. Fellow and tutor in econs. Magdalen Coll. Oxford (Eng.) U., 1965-76, fellow Magdalen Coll., 1977-79, pres., 1979-88, hon. fellow, 1988; acting warden, dir. Queen Elizabeth House, Inst. Commonwealth Studies, 1973, 77-78, warden, dir., 1978-79; prof. U. Calif., Riverside, 1988—, chmn. dept. econs., 1988-93, Presdl. prof., 1988-90, Disting. prof., 1997—. Vis. prof. Inst. Econs. and Planning U. Chile, 1962-63, 64-65; chmn. bd. UN Rsch. Inst. for Social Devel., 1988-95, sr. cons., 1971-72; mem. UN com. for devel. planning, 1987-94; mem. coun. UN Univ., 1986-92, chmn. fin. and budget com., 1988-90; mem. Marshall Aid Commemoration Commn., 1984-88; mem. World Commn. on culture and Devel., 1994-95; chief ILO Employment Adv. Mission to Ethiopia, 1982; econ. advisor Govt. of Bolivia, 1989-91; pres. Devel. Studies Assn., U.K., 1978-80; chief rural and urban employment policies br. ILO, 1975-76; cons. ILO on rurual devel. in Ecuador, 1974; sr. adviser OECD Devel. Centre, Paris, 1986-91; adviser to Inter-Am. Com. for Alliance for Progress on copper expansion programme in Chile, 1968, to FAO/ICO, IBRD World Coffee Study in Guatemala, El Salvador and Colombia, 1967; rsch. advisor Pakistan Inst. Devel. Econs., Karachi, 1965, 70; expert on agrl. planning to Govt. of Algeria, acting chief FAO Mission, Algiers, 1963-64; cons. IBRD on land reform on Morocco, 1973; head UN Devel. Program Poverty Alleviation Mission to Mongolia, 1994; head ILO Social Policy Review Mission to Uzbekis, 1995; cons. on econ. reform in Vietnam, UNDP, 1997; head ILO Employment and Social Protection Mission to Kazakstan, 1997; head UNDP mission to Mongolia, 2001. Author: Underdevelopment in Spanish America, 1969, 2d edit., 1971, Spanish edit., 1972, The Green Revolution: An Economic Analysis, 1972, The Political Economy of Agrarian Change, 1974, 2d edit., 1979, Spanish edit., 1982, Hindi edit., 1983, Land Concentration and Rural Poverty, 1976, 2d edit., 1981, Spanish edit., 1983, International Inequality and National Poverty, 1978, Spanish edit., 1984, World Hunger and the World Economy, 1987, Alternative Strategies for Economic Development, 1989, 2d edit., 1999, Chinese edit., 1992, Studies in Globalization and Economic Transitions, 1996, Studies in Development Strategy and Systemic Transformation, 2000; co-author: Comercio Internacional y Politicas de Desarrollo Economico, 1967, Planning Development, 1970, Spanish edit., 1975, The Transition to Egalitarian Development, 1981, Globalization and the Developing World, 1992, Implementing a Human Development Strategy, 1994; editor: Financing Development in Latin America, 1971, Institutional Reform and Economic Development in the Chinese Countryside, 1984, The Economy of Ethiopia, 1992, Poverty and the Transition to a Market Economy in Mongolia, 1995, Social Policy and Economic Transformation in Uzbakistan, 1996, Economic Reform in Vietnam, 1998; co-editor: Ensayos Sobre Planificacion, 1967, Growth and Inequality in Pakistan, 1972, The Economic Development of Bangladesh, 1974, Human Development and the International Development Strategy for the 1990s, 1990, The Distribution of Income in China, 1993, also numerous articles. Vis. fellow Oxford Ctr. Islamic Studies, 1998. Fellow AAAS; mem. Am. Econ. Assn. Avocation: travel. Office: Univ Calif Dept Econs Riverside CA 92521-0001

GRIFFIN, MERV EDWARD, former entertainer, television producer, entrepreneur; b. San Mateo, Calif., July 6, 1925; s. Mervyn Edward and Rita (Robinson) G.; m. Julann Elizabeth Wright, May 18, 1958 (div. June 1976); 1 son, Anthony Patrick. Student, San Mateo Coll., 1942-44; L.H.D., Emerson Coll., 1981. Owner Teleview Racing Patrol Inc., Miami, Fla., Video Racing Patrol Inc., Seattle, Beverly Hilton Hotel, Beverly Hills, Calif., The Scottsdale (Ariz.) Hilton, Wickenburg (Ariz.) Inn; chmn. bd. Griffin Group, Inc., Beverly Hills, Givenchy Hotel and Spa, Palm Springs, Calif., Blue Moon Hotel, So. Beach, Miami Beach, Fla.; owner Merv Griffin Entertainment, Beverly Hills, 1996—, Cleran's Manor Ho., Galway, Ireland. Performer Merv Griffin Show radio sta. KFRC, San Francisco, 1945-48, vocalist Freddy Martin's Orch., 1948-52; contract player, star So This is Love, Warner Bros., 1953-55; TV master ceremonies, 1958—, Merv Griffin Show, NBC-TV, 1962-63, Westinghouse Broadcasting Co., 1965-69, CBS-TV, 1969-72, syndication, 1972-86; currently exec. producing: Wheel of Fortune, Jeopardy. Club: Bohemian (San Francisco). Office: The Griffin Group 9860 Wilshire Blvd Beverly Hills CA 90210-3115 also: 780 3rd Ave Rm 1801 New York NY 10017-2024

GRIFFIN, WILLIAM RAY, consulting and publishing company executive; b. S.D., June 11, 1949; Cert. sr. carpet insp., hard & resilient wood floor care specialist, bldg. cleaning and small bus. mgmt. specialist. Pres. Cleaning Cons. Svcs. Inc., Seattle, 1975—. Author 10 books; contbr. more than 200 articles to profl. jours. Mem. Internat. Sanitary Supply Assn., Assn. Specialists in Cleaning and Restoration, Bldg. Svc. Contractors Assn., Bldg. Owners and Mgrs. Assn. Office: Cleaning Cons Svcs Inc PO Box 1273 Seattle WA 98111-1273 Fax: 206-622-6876. E-mail: wgriffin@cleaningconsultants.com

GRIFFITH, OSBIE HAYES, chemistry educator; b. Torrance, Calif., Sept. 14, 1938; s. Osbie and Mary Belle (Neathery) G.; m. Karen Hedberg; 2 sons B.A., U. Calif.-Riverside, Riverside, 1960; Ph.D., Calif. Inst. Tech., 1964; postgrad., Stanford U., 1965. NAS-NRC postdoctoral Stanford U., Eugene, 1965; asst. prof. chemistry U. Oreg., Eugene, 1966-69, assoc. prof., 1969-72; prof. chem. Inst. Molecular Biology, 1972—. Co-editor: Lipid-Protein Interactions, 1982; mem. edtl. bd. Biophysical Jour., 1974-78, Chemistry & Physics of Lipids, 1974-95, Microscopy and Microanalysis, 1995—; contbr. articles to profl. jours. Scholar Camille and Henry Dreyfus Found., 1970; Career Devel. award Nat. Cancer Inst., 1972-76; fellow Sloan Found., 1967-69, Guggenheim Found., 1972-76; Faculty Achievement award for Teaching Excellence, Burlington No. Found., 1987, Dean's Devel. award, 1991, Creativity Extension NSF, 1992. Mem. Am. Chem. Soc., Biophys. Soc., Microscopy Soc. Am. Home: 2550 Charnelton St Eugene OR 97405-3216 Office: U Oreg Inst Molecular Biology Eugene OR 97403 E-mail: hayes@molbio.uoregon.edu

GRIGG, NEIL S. civil engineering educator; Grad., U.S. Mil. Acad., 1961; MS in Civil Engring., Auburn U., 1965; PhD in Civil Engring., Colo. State U., 1969. Dir. Colo. Water Resources Rsch. Inst., Internat. Sch. Water Resources, Colo. State U., 1988-91; asst. sec. natural resources State of N.C., 1979-81, dir. environ. mgmt., 1980-81; dir. U. N.C. Water Resources Rsch. Inst., 1979-82; co-founder Sellards & Grigg, Inc., Denver; prof., head dept. civil engring. Colo. State U., Fort Collins, 1991—. Organizer confs.; advocate pub. works edn. and rsch.;mem. working groups Nat. Coun. on Pub. Works Improvement; mem. Edn. Found. Com. on Govt. Affairs, 1992 U.S.-Japan Infrastructure Delegation, Top Ten Selection Panel, Coun. on Internat. Collaboration; pres. Ft. Collins Water Bd., 1991—. Contbr. articles to profl. jours. Fellow ASCE (chair exec. com., water resources planning and mgmt. divsn. 1995, chmn. water pricing task com. 1990-92, founding chair WP&M Divsn. Urban Water Com. 1986-88, chair tech. coun. on rsch. 1983-85, chmn. urban water resources rsch. coun. 1978-79, nat. water policy com. 1981, chmn. nat. environ. systems policy com. 1983), Am. Pub. Works Assn. (bd. dirs., chair mgmt. practices evaluation com.), Am. Water Works Assn., Ft. Collins C. of C. (chmn. water com. 1989—). Office: Colo State U Dept Civil Engring Fort Collins CO 80523-0001

GRIGGS, GAIL, former marketing executive; b. 1937; Grad., U. Oreg., U. Chgo. Instr. Chgo. Art Inst., Roosevelt U., Chgo., Evergreen State U., Olympia, Wash.; with Griggs-Anderson, Inc., 1979-99; now pres. Griggs-Anderson, Inc./Gartner Group. Office: Griggs Anderson Inc Gartner Group 308 SW 1st Ave Fl 4 Portland OR 97204-3400

GRIGGS, GARY BRUCE, science administrator, oceanographer, geologist, educator; b. Pasadena, Calif., Sept. 25, 1943; s. Dean Brayton and Barbara Jayne (Farmer) G.; m. Venetia Gina Bradfield, Jan. 11, 1980; children: Joel, Amy, Shannon, Callie, Cody. BA in Geology, U. Calif., Santa Barbara, 1965; PhD in Oceanography, Oreg. State U., 1968. Registered geologist, Calif.; cert. engr. geologist, Calif. Rsch. asst., NSF grad. fellow in oceanography Oreg. State U., 1965-68; from asst. prof. to prof. earth scis. U. Calif., Santa Cruz, 1969—; Fulbright fellow Inst. for Ocean & Fishing Rsch., Athens, Greece, 1974-75; oceanographer Joint U.S.A.-N.Z. Rsch. Program, 1980-81; chair earth scis. U. Calif., Santa Cruz, 1981-84, assoc. dean natural scis., 1992-95; dir. Inst. of Marine Scis., 1991-2000. Vis. prof. Semester at Sea program U. Pitts., 1984-96; guest lectr. World Explorer Cruises, 1987; chair marine coun. U. Calif., 1999—; bd. govs. Consortium for Oceanographic Rsch. and Edn., 1995—. Author: (with others) Geologic Hazards, Resources and Environmental Planning, 1983, Living with the California Coast, 1985, Coastal Protection Structures, 1986, California's Coastal Hazards, 1992; mem. editl. bd. Jour. of Coastal Rsch., Geology; contbr. numerous articles to profl. jours. Mem. Am. Geophys. Union, Am. Geol. Inst., Coastal Found. Achievements include research in coastal processes; coastal erosion and protection; coastal engineering and hazards; sediment yield, transport and dispersal; geologic hazards and land use. Office: U Calif Inst Marine Scis Santa Cruz CA 95064 E-mail: griggs@emerald.ucsc.edu

GRIGSBY, FREDERICK J., JR. human resources executive; BBA, Ctrl. State U.; grad. exec. program, U. Va. Various positions in human resources Westinghouse; v.p. human resources Thermo King Corp., 1995-98; v.p. human resources and adminstrn. Fluor Corp., Aliso Viejo, Calif., 1998—. Diversity bd. dirs. Westinghouse Savannah River Co. Bd. dirs. Exec. Leadership Found. Mem. Nat. Black MBA Assn., Ctrl. State Alumni Assn., Human Resources Mgmt. Soc. (human resources exec. coun.), Kappa Alpha Psi. Office: Fluor Corp One Enterprise Dr Aliso Viejo CA 92656-2606

GRILL, LAWRENCE J. lawyer, accountant, corporate/banking executive; b. Chgo., Nov. 5, 1936; s. Samuel S. and Evelyn (Wollack) G.; m. Joan V. Krimston, Dec. 16, 1961; children: Steven Eric, Elizabeth Anne. B.S. with honors, U. Ill., 1958; postgrad., U. Chgo., 1959-60; LL.B., Northwestern U., 1963. Bar: Ill. 1963, Calif. 1965; C.P.A., Ill. Audit and tax mgr. Arthur Anderson & Co., Chgo., 1958-60; with firm Aaron, Aaron, Schimberg & Hess, Chgo., 1963-64, Gendel, Raskoff, Shapiro & Quittner, Los Angeles, 1964-66; sec., gen. counsel Traid Corp., Los Angeles, 1966-69; v.p., sec., gen. counsel Kaufman & Broad, Inc., Los Angeles, 1969-78; pres. Kaufman & Broad Asset Mgmt., dir. subs.; v.p., sec., gen. counsel AM Internat., Inc., Century City, 1979-82, dir. subs.; sr. v.p., group ops. officer, dir. subs. Wickes Cos., Inc., Santa Monica, 1982-85; acting chief exec. officer, chief operating officer, mem. exec. com. Barco of Calif., Gardena, 1985-86; pres. Lawrence J. Grill & Assocs., L.A., Calif., 1985-94; pres., CEO Pan Am. Bank and United Pan Am. Fin. Corp., San Mateo, 1994-2000, also bd. dirs. Chmn., pres., CEO Universal Savs. Bank, Orange, Calif., 1988-90; cons. bd. dirs. World Trade Bank, N.A., 1992, Marathon Nat. Bank, 1992-93; spl. advisor to Fed. Home Loan Bank Bd. San Francisco, Fed. Deposit Ins. Co. for Distressed Savs. Instns., 1986-88; arbitrator Am. Arbitration Assn. Served with AUS, 1958-59. Home: 48437 Vista Palomino La Quinta CA 92253 Office: 1300 S El Camino Real San Mateo CA 94402-2963 E-mail: Larg36@yahoo.com

GRILLER, GORDON MOORE, legal administrator; b. Sioux City, Iowa, Feb. 3, 1944; s.Joseph Edwards and Arlene (Searles) G. m. Helen Mary Friederichs, aug. 20, 1966; children: Heather, Chad. BA in Political Sci., U. Minn., 1966, MA in Pub. Affairs, 1969. Mgmt. analyst Hennepin County Adminstr., Mpls., 1968-72; asst. court adminstr. Hennepin County Municipal Ct., Mpls., 1972-77, ct. adminstr., 1977-78; judicial dist. adminstr. 2nd Dist. Ct. Minn., St. Paul, 1978-87; ct. adminstr. Superior Ct. Ariz., Phoenix, 1987—. Bd. dirs. Nat. Ctr. State Cts., 1997—, Nat. Conf. Metro Cts., 1999—. Vice-chmn. Bloomington Sch. Bd., Minn., 1981-87. Sgt. USAAF, 1968-74 Res. Recipient Warren E. Burger award Inst. Ct. Mgnt.,1988, Leadership Fellows award Bush Leadership Program, 1974. Mem. Nat. Assn. Trial Ct. Adminstrs.(pres. 1983-84), Ariz. Ct. Assn., Nat. Assn Ct. Mgmt., Am. Judicature Soc., (bd. dirs. 1997—). Lutheran. Avocations: running, kyaking, racquetball, scuba diving. Home: 8507 E San Jacinto Dr Scottsdale AZ 85258-2576 Office: Superior Ct Ariz 201 W Jefferson St Fl 4 Phoenix AZ 85003-2243

GRILLO, LEO, actor, photographer, animal rescuer; b. Lawrence, Mass., Feb. 6, 1949; s. Leo F. Sr. and Carmela M. (DeLucia) G.; m. Stacy Grillo; children: Erica, Meguire. BS in speech, Emerson Coll., Boston, 1970. Actor, Glendale, Calif., 1965—; pres., founder Dedication and Everlasting Love to Animals Inc., Glendale, 1979—, Living Earth Prodns., 1990—, Horse Rescue Am., 1991—; founder, pres. DELTA Rescue India; pres. Leo Grillo Prodns. Inc., 1995. Author: (with others) Landscam, 1988, Is This the Place?; producer, host Safe House, (TV show) Delta Rescue Story; actor (feature film) The Crap Game, The Rescuer. Mem. Screen Actors' Guild, AFTRA, Actors Equity Assn. Office: DELTA Rescue PO Box 9 Glendale CA 91209-0009

GRILLY, EDWARD ROGERS, physicist; b. Cleve., Dec. 30, 1917; s. Charles B. and Julia (Varady) G.; m. Mary Witholter, Dec. 14, 1942 (dec. 1971); children: David, Janice; m. Juliamarie Andersen Langham, Feb. 1, 1973. BA, Ohio State U., 1940, PhD, 1944. Rsch. scientist Carbide & Carbon Chemicals Corp., Oak Ridge, Tenn., 1944-45; asst. prof. Chemistry U. N.H., Durham, 1946-47; mem. staff U. Calif. Nat. Lab., Los Alamos, N.Mex., 1947-80, cons., 1980—. Contbr. articles to books and profl. jours. Mem. N.Mex. House of Reps., Santa Fe, 1967-70, Los Alamos County Coun., Los Alamos, 1976-78. Mem. Am. Physical Soc., Kiwanis Club, Los Alamos Golf Club (pres. 1974-75). Republican. Avocation: golf. Home: 705 43rd St Los Alamos NM 87544-1807

GRILLY, GERALD E. publisher; Publ. Anchorage Daily News, 1978-93; CEO Denver Post, 1993-98, publ., 1998—. Office: 1560 Broadway Denver CO 80202-6000

GRIMES, DUANE D. state legislator; b. Spokane, Wash., Sept. 17, 1957; m. Connie Grimes; 3 children. Student, Colo. Aero. Tech.; BA, Bob Jones U., 1983, postgrad. Pilot, aircraft insp.; pers. officer Mont. Dept. Revenue; mem. Mont. Senate, Dist. 20, Helena, 1998—; mem. legis. adminstrn. com., mem. local govt. com. Mont. Senate, mem. pub. health, welfare/safety com., mem. judiciary com. Republican. Home: 4 Hole In The Wall Clancy MT 59634-9516

GRIMLEY, JANET ELIZABETH, newspaper editor; b. Oelwein, Iowa, Dec. 3, 1946; d. Harold E. and Ida Mae (Anderson) Teague; m. Terry L. Grimley, June 15, 1968; 1 child, Brynn Sara Mae Grimley. BA, U. Iowa, Iowa City, 1969; attended, U. Wash., Seattle, 1979-82. Asst. mng. editor Seattle Post-Intelligencer; publs. dir. Marycrest Coll., Davenport, Iowa, 1969-70; reporter Quad-Cities Times, Davenport, 1970-74, Seattle Post-Intelligence, Seattle, 1974-76, feature editor, 1976-95, asst. mng. editor, 1995—. Past pres. Am. Assn. Sunday and Feature Editors; mem. Newspaper Features Coun. Mem. Shoreline Strategic Planning Com., Seattle, 1993, Shorewood Site Coun., 1997-99, Shorewood Boosters; co-chair Shoreline Capitol/Bond Com., Seattle, 1994, Einstein Site Coun., Seattle, 1994-96; bd. dirs. Ctr. for Human Svcs. Mem. Junior League of Seattle (bd. dirs. 1989-90, exec. bd. 1991-92), City Club Seattle. Avocations: sailing, skiing, gardening. Office: Seattle Post Intelligencer 101 Elliott Ave W Ste 200 Seattle WA 98119-4295

GRIMM, BOB, food products executive; b. 1954; With Grimmway Enterprises, Inc., Bakersfield, Calif., 1975—, v.p., 1975-98, pres., 1998—. Office: Grimmway Enterprises Inc PO Box 81498 Bakersfield CA 93380-1498

GRIN, LEONID, conductor; b. Dniepropetrovsk, Ukraine, June 19, 1947; came to U.S., 1981; s. Gavriil and Ita (Sklar) Grinshpun; m. Marina Gusak, Apr. 25, 1970; children: Radmila, Daniel. BMus, Dniepropetrovsk Music Coll., 1966; MusM, Onesin's Music Inst., 1971; MusM in Conducting, Moscow State Conservatory, 1975, DMus, 1977. Assoc. condr. Moscow Philharm. Symphony Orch., 1977-79; prof. conducting U. Houston, 1983-86; prin. guest condr. Tampere (Finland) Philharm Orch., 1988-90, music dir., condr., 1990-94, San Jose (Calif.) Symphony Orch., 1992—. Guest condr. various orchs. in Denmark, Sweden, Norway, Finland, Eng., Scotland, Israel, Germany, The Netherlands, Italy, Belgium, Spain, Portugal, New Zealand, USA, Can., many others. Recs. include music by Tchaikovsky, Procofrev, Shostakovitch, all 6 symphonies by Erkki Mellartin. Office: San Jose Symphony Orchestra 495 Almaden Blvd San Jose CA 95110

GRINDAL, MARY ANN, former sales professional; b. Michigan City, Ind., Sept. 9, 1942; d. James Paxton and Helen Evelyn (Koivisto) Gleason; m. Bruce Theodore Grindal, June 12, 1965 (div. Sept. 1974); 1 child, Matthew Bruce. BSBA, Ind. U., 1965. Sec. African studies program Ind. U., Bloomington, 1965-66; rsch. aide Ghana, West Africa, 1966-68; exec. sec. divsn. biol. scis. Ind. U., Bloomington, 1968-69; office asst. Dean of Students office Middlebury (Vt.) Coll., 1969-70; exec. sec. Remo, Inc., North Hollywood, Calif., 1974-76; sec., asst. to product mgrs. in cosmetic and skin care Redken Labs., Canoga Park, 1976-79; various sec. and exec. sec. positions L.A., 1979-81, 85-89; exec. sec. Sargent Industries, Burbank, Calif., 1981-85; sales asst. Chyron Graphics, Burbank, 1989-97; adminstrv. sec. divsn. instructional svcs. Burbank Unified Sch. Dist., 1998—. Author of poems and essays. Mem. U.S. Navy Meml. Found. Mem. DAR (chpt. registrar 1988-91, chpt. regent 1991-94, chpt. chmn. pub. rels. and pub. 1994-2001, chpt. chaplain 1994-2001, mem. spkrs. staff 1995—, state chmn. Am. Heritage 1994-96, state chmn. Calif. DAR scholarship com. 1996-98), Daus. of Union Vets. of Civil War, 1861-65, Inc., Nat. Soc. Dames of the Ct. of Honor (state chaplain 1997-2001). Lutheran. Avocations: travel, writing, genealogy.

GRINELL, SHEILA, science center administrator; b. N.Y.C., July 15, 1945; d. Richard N. and Martha (Mimiless) G.; m. Thomas E. Johnson, July 15, 1980; 1 child, Michael; stepchildren: Kathleen, Thomas. BA, Radcliffe Coll., 1966; MA, U. Calif., Berkeley, 1968. Co-dir. exhibits and programs The Exploratorium, San Francisco, 1969-74; promotion dir. Kodansha Internat., Tokyo, 1974-77; traveling exhbn. coord. Assn. Sci. Tech. Ctrs., Washington, 1978-80, exec. dir., 1980-82, project dir. traveling exhbn. Chips and Changes, 1982-84; assoc. dir. N.Y. Hall of Sci., 1984-87; pres., CEO Ariz. Sci. Ctr., Phoenix, 1993—. Cons. Optical Soc. Am., 1987, Nat. Sci. Ctr. Found., 1988, Interactive Video Sci. Consortium, 1988, Assn. Sci. Tech. Ctrs., 1988-89, Found. for Creative Am., 1989-90, Am. Assn. for World Health, 1990, Children's TV Workshop, 1991, Sciencenter, 1991, SciencePort, 1991, The Invention Factory, 1992, N.Y. Bot. Garden, 1992-93. Author: Light, Sight, Sound, Hearing: Exploratorium '74, 1974; editor A Stage for Science, 1979, A New Place for Learning Science: Starting and Running A Science Center, 1992, (with Mark St. John) Vision to Reality: Critical Dimensions in Science Center Development, Vol. I, 1993, II, 1994. Fulbright teaching asst., 1966; hon. Woodrow Wilson fellow, 1967 Fellow AAAS; mem. Am. Assn. Mus., Phi Beta Kappa. Office: Ariz Sci Ctr 600 E Washington St Phoenix AZ 85004-2303 E-mail: grinells@azscience.org

GRINNELL, ALAN DALE, neurobiologist, educator, researcher; b. Mpls., Nov. 11, 1936; s. John Erle and Swanhild Constance (Friswold) G.; m. Verity Rich, Sept. 30, 1962 (div. 1975); m. Feelie Lee, Dec. 23, 1996. BA, Harvard U., 1958, PhD, 1962. Jr. fellow Harvard U., 1959-62; research assoc. biophysics dept. Univ. Coll. London, 1962-64; asst. research zoologist UCLA, 1964-65, from asst. prof. to prof. dept. biology, 1965-78, prof. physiology, 1972—; dir. Jerry Lewis Neuromuscular Research Ctr. UCLA Sch. Medicine, 1978—; head Ahmanson Lab. Cellular Neurobiology UCLA Brain Research Inst, 1977—; dir. tng. grant in cellular neurobiology UCLA, 1968—, rsch. assoc. Fowler Mus. Cultural History, 1990—, chmn. dept. physiol. sci., 1997—. Author: Calcium and Ion Channel Modulation, 1988, Physiology of Excitable Cells, 1983, Regulation of Muscle Contraction, 1981, Introduction to Nervous Systems, 1977, others; contbr. editorial revs. to profl. jours., pub. houses, fed. granting agys. Guggenheim fellow, 1986; recipient Sr. Scientist award Alexander von Humboldt Stiftung, 1975, 79, Jacob Javits award NIH, 1986. Mem. AAAS (mem.-at-large neurosci. steering group 1998—), Muscular Dystrophy Assn. (mem. med. adv. com. L.A. chpt. 1980-92), Soc. for Neurosci. (councilor 1982-86), Am. Physiol. Soc. (mem. neurophysiol. steering com. 1981-84), Soc. Fellow, Phi Beta Kappa, Sigma Xi, others. Avocations: music, anthropology, archaeology, travel. Home: 510 E Rustic Rd Santa Monica CA 90402-1116 Office: UCLA Sch Medicine Jerry Lewis Neuromuscular Los Angeles CA 90095-0001 E-mail: adg@ucla.edu

GRINSTEIN, GERALD, transportation executive; b. 1932; married B.A., Yale U., 1954; LL.B., Harvard U., 1957. Bar: D.C., Wash. Counsel to merchant marine and transp. subcoms., chief counsel U.S. Senate Commerce Com., Washington, 1958-67; adminstrv. asst. U.S. Senator Warren G. Magnuson, Washington, 1967-69; ptnr. Preston Thorgrimson Ellis & Holman, 1969-83; chmn. bd. Western Air Lines Inc., Los Angeles, 1983-84, pres., COO, 1984-85, CEO, 1985-86, chmn., CEO, 1986-87; vice chmn. Burlington Northern Inc., Ft. Worth, 1987-88; pres., CEO Burlington Northern, Inc., Ft. Worth, 1989-90, chmn., CEO, 1990-95; pres., CEO, Burlington No. R.R. Co., 1989-90; chmn., CEO Burlington Northern R.R. Co., 1990-95; chmn. Delta Air Lines, Inc., 1997-99, also bd. dirs.; chmn. Agilent Techs., 1999—. Bd. dirs. Imperial Sugar Corp., Paccar, Inc., Vans Inc., Expedia.com, The Pittston Co. Office: 1000 2nd Ave Ste 3700 Seattle WA 98104-1053

GRISEZ, JAMES LOUIS, physician, plastic surgeon; b. Modesto, Calif., Feb. 25, 1935; s. John Francis and Josephine Marie (Tournahu) G.; m. Diane Madeline Skidmore, Mar. 7, 1989; children: James, Stephen, Suzanne, Kathleen. MD, St. Louis Sch. Medicine, 1960. Diplomate Am. Bd. Plastic and Reconstructive Surgery. Intern D.C. Gen. Hosp., Washington, 1960-61; resident med. ctr. Georgetown U., Washington, 1961-64; resident plastic and reconstructive surgery ctr. St. Francis Meml. Hosp., San Francisco, 1964-66; military surgeon Brook Army Med Ctr., San Antonio, 1966, Second Gen. Hosp., Landstuhl, Germany, 1966-69; pvt. practice Napa, Calif., 1969-82, Salinas, 1982-90, Kailua-Kona, Hawaii, 1990-93, South Valley Plastic Surgery, Gilroy, Calif., 1993—. Active staff mem. St. Louise Regional Hosp.; chief of staff South Valley Hosp., Hazel Hawkins; chief staff St. Helena Hosp., 1977-78, exec. com. 1973-80; radio talk show host All About Plastic Surgery, sta. KRNY, 1986-88. Contbr. articles to med. jours. Mem. Am. Cancer Soc. (pres. 1988-90), Am. Soc. Plastic Surgeons, Calif. Soc. Plastic and Reconstructive Surgeons, Hawaii Plastic Surgery Soc. Home: 8675 Muir Dr Gilroy CA 95020-3725 Office: 8375 Church St Gilroy CA 95020-4406

GRISSOM, GARTH CLYDE, lawyer, director; b. Syracuse, Kans., Jan. 24, 1930; s. Clyde and Bernice Minnie (Eddy) G.; m. Elena Joyce Kerst, Aug. 17, 1958; children: Colin, Grady, Cole, Kent. B.S., Kans. State U., 1951; LL.B., Harvard U., 1957. Bar: Colo. 1957, U.S. Dist. Ct. (fed. dist.) Colo., 1957, U.S. Ct. Appeals (10th crct.) 1957, U.S. Supreme Ct. 1989. Ptnr., mem., counsel Sherman & Howard, L.L.C., Denver, 1963—. Sec., counsel, trustee Mile High United Way, Denver, 1985-88; trustee Kans. State U. Found., Manhattan, 1962-89; mem. Colo. Gov.'s Commn. on Life and the Law, 1990-99, chmn., 1996-99. Mem. ABA, Colo. Bar Assn., Denver Bar Assn. (pres. 1985-86, award of merit 1994), Rotary (sec. Denver 1983-84, bd. dirs. 1983-86, pres. 1989-90), Pi Kappa Alpha (pres. 1968-70). Home: 1777 Larimer St Apt 1610 Denver CO 80202-1548 Office: Sherman & Howard LLC 633 17th St Ste 3000 Denver CO 80202-3665

GRITTON, EUGENE CHARLES, nuclear engineer, department chairman; b. Santa Monica, Calif., Jan. 13, 1941; s. Everett Mason and Matilda (Benne) G.; children from previous marriage: Dennis Mason, Kathleen Wanda; m. Gwendolyn O. Gritton. BS, UCLA, 1963, MS, 1965, PhD, 1966. Research engr., def. systems analyst RAND, Santa Monica, Calif., 1966-73, project leader advanced undersea tech. program, 1973-76, program dir. marine tech., 1974-76, program dir. applied sci. and tech., 1976-94, head dept. phys. scis., 1975-77, head engrng. and applied scis. dept., 1977-86, RAND resident scholar for tech., 1990-93, dep. v.p. Nat. Security Rsch. Divsn., 1986-93, dep. v.p. Rsch. Ops. Group, 1986-90, dir. Acquisition and Tech. Policy Ctr., 1994—; acting dir. Nat. Security Rsch. Divsn., 1997-98. Vis. lectr. dept. mech. engrng. U. So. Calif., L.A., 1967-72; vis. lectr. dept. energy and kinetics UCLA, 1971, 73; mem. Def. Sci. Bd. Study, 1996, 98. Recipient Engrng. Alumnus of Yr. award UCLA Sch. Engrng. and Applied Sci., 1985-86; AEC fellow, 1963, NSF Coop. Grad. fellow, 1964-66. Mem. Am. Nuclear Soc. (mem. exec. com. aerospace and hydrospace div. 1974-75), AIAA Home: 3616 The Strand # C Manhattan Beach CA 90266-3276 Office: RAND PO Box 2138 1700 Main St Santa Monica CA 90407-2138 E-mail: gene_gritton@rand.org

GROBE, CHARLES STEPHEN, lawyer, accountant; b. Columbus, Ohio, May 5, 1935; s. Harry A. and Bertha S. (Swartz) G.; m. Ila Silverman, Aug. 30, 1964; children— Eileen, Kenneth. B.S., U. Calif. at Los Angeles, 1957; J.D., Stanford, 1961. Bar: Calif. 1962; CPA, Calif. Tax accountant, Beverly Hills, Calif., 1961-63; tax atty. Los Angeles, 1963—. Author: Guide to Investing Pension and Profit-Sharing Trust Funds, 1973, Guardianship, Conservatorship and Trusts on Behalf of Persons Who Are Mentally Retarded— An Assessment of Current Applicable Laws in the State of California, 1974, Using an Individual Retirement Savings Plan and the Related Rollover Provisions of the Pension Reform Act of 1974, 1975, Guide to Setting Up a Group Term Life Insurance Program Under IRC Section 79, 1976, Practical Estate Planning, 1988, Planning for Incapacity, 1989, Planning to Reduce the Generation Skipping Tax, 1989, Estate Planning Considerations for Community Property Interests, 1990, Legal and Tax Problems of Joint Tenancy as a Form of Ownership, 1990, The Tax Economics of Using the Generating Skipping Tax Exemptions, 1992, The Tax Economics of Gifting Property, 1992, Saving Estate Taxes with Life Insurance and a Life Insurance Trust, 1992, Family Wealth Transfer Planning, The Tax Economics of a Qualified Personal Residence Trust, also articles. Capt. AUS, 1957-64. Mem. ABA, State Bar Calif., L.A. County Bar Assn., Beverly Hills Bar Assn., Calif. Soc. CPAs. Home: 501 N Cliffwood Ave Los Angeles CA 90049-2621 Office: 12110 Wilshire Blvd Los Angeles CA 90025-1104

GROBSTEIN, RUTH H. health facility administrator; 3 children. BA, NYU, 1945; PhD in Biology, Yale U., 1957; MD, UCLA, 1976. Postdoctoral fellow Yale Med. Sch., Calif., mem. staff microbiology; prin. investigator U. Calif., San Diego, resident in radiation oncology San Francisco; divsn. head radiation oncology Scripps Clin., La Jolla. Dir. The Ida M. and Cecil H. Green Cancer Ctr. Grantee Atomic Energy Commn., 1966, Nadonal Inst. Health, 1966. Office: Scripps Clinic Torrey Pines 10666 N Torrey Pines Rd La Jolla CA 92037-1092

GROCE, AUGUSTUS BEN, paper company executive; BS in Pulp and Paper Tech., N.C. State U., 1963. Various mgmt. positions Boise Cascade Corp., Boise, Idaho, 1979-91, v.p. Maine opers., 1991-93, v.p. paper mfg., engrng., transp. and procurement, 1993-94, sr. v.p. mfg. paper divsn., 1994-2000, sr. v.p., gen. mgr. paper divsn., 2000—. Office: Boise Cascade Corp 1111 W Jefferson St Boise ID 83728-0071

GRODSKY, GEROLD MORTON, biochemistry educator; b. St. Louis, Jan. 18, 1927; s. Louis and Goldie B.; m. Kayla Deane Wolfe, Dec. 6, 1952; children: Andrea, Jamie. BS, U. Ill., 1946, MS, 1947; PhD, U. Calif., Berkeley, 1954; postgrad., Cambridge (Eng.) U., 1954-55. Prof. biochemistry U. Calif. Med. Sch., 1961-92, prof. emeritus (active status), 1992—. Vis. prof. U. Geneva, 1968-69, U. paris VII, 1989; Somogyi Meml. lectr., 1972, Helen Martin lectr., 1976, Herman Rosenthal lectr., 1986; cons. various pharm. houses; cons. UCSF Diabetes Program Project, 1993—. Mem. editl. bd. Diabetes, 1965-73, 86-90, Am. Jour. Physiology, 1977-94, Diabetologia, 1990-92, Endocrinology, 1992-96; founding adv. editor: Diabetes Tech. and Therapy, 1998—, Diabetes New World (China); contbr. chpts. to books; contbr. over 200 articles on diabetes and storage, secretion of insulin to profl. jours. Mem. med. adv. bd. Juvenile Diabetes Found., 1974-77, 80-85; program dir. NIH Diabetic Animal Program, 1978-82, chmn. diabetes rsch. adv. bd. to Sec. Health, 1982-87. Lt. (s.g.) USNR, 1944-54. Recipient David Rumbough Internat. award Juvenile Diabetes Found., 1984, Williams-Levine award, 1990, NIH Merit award, 1987, Juvenile Diabetes Found. endowed Grodsky award for basic rsch. in diabetes, 1994—; named as one of 1000 most cited world scientists. Mem. Internat. Diabetes Found., Am. Soc. Biol. Chemists, Soc. Exptl. Biology, Am. Fedn. Clin. Rsch., European Diabetes Assn., Endocrine Soc., Am. Diabetes Assn. (rsch. bd. 1974-77, chmn. rsch. policy com. 1977, bd. dirs. Calif. chpt. 1989-91, nat. grant rev. com. 1992-96), Calif. Tennis Club, Harborpoint Club Home: 3969 Washington St San Francisco CA 94118-1613 Office: U Calif Sch Medicine Metabolic Unit PO Box 0540 San Francisco CA 94143-0001

GRODY, MARK STEPHEN, public relations executive; b. Milw., Jan. 1, 1938; s. Ray and Betty (Rothstein) G.; m. Karen Goldstein, Mar. 6, 1965 (div. 1972); 1 child, Laura; m. Susan Tellem, Mar. 25, 1979 (div. 1989); 1 child, Daniel. BS, U. Wis., 1960. Pub. rels. exec. GM, Detroit, 1961-74; v.p. pub. affairs Nat. Alliance of Businessmen, Washington, 1973-74; v.p. Carl Terzian & Assocs., L.A., 1974-75; chmn. Mark Grody Assocs. and Grody Tellem Comm., Inc. (now The Rowland Co.), L.A., 1975-90; pres. Mark Grody Assocs., L.A., 1990-93; exec. v.p., gen. mgr. Ogilvy Pub. Rels., L.A., 1993-96; pres. Mark Grody Assocs., L.A., 1996—. Ptnr. Mktg. Golf Resources, L.A., 1996-99, thegolfspot.com, 1998; founder corporate-egolf.com, L.A., 1999—. Co-author: Corporate Golf: How to Play the Game for Business Success, 1996. Capt. U.S. Army, 1960. Mem. Internat. Network Golf (bd. dirs.), Pub. Rels. Soc. Am., The Lakes Country Club. Avocations: golf, bridge. E-mail: mgrody@aol.com

GRODY, WAYNE WILLIAM, physician; b. Syracuse, N.Y., Feb. 25, 1952; s. Robert Jerome and Florence Beatrice (Kashdan) G.; m. Gaylen Ducker, July 8, 1990. BA, Johns Hopkins U., 1974; MD, Baylor Coll. Medicine, 1977, PhD, 1981. Diplomate Am. Bd. Pathology, Am. Bd. Med. Genetics; lic. physician, Calif. Intern/resident UCLA Sch. Medicine, 1982-85, postdoctoral fellow, 1985-86, asst. prof., 1987-93, assoc. prof., 1993-97; prof., 1997—. Panelist Calif. Children's Svcs., 1987—, U.S. FDA, Washington, 1989—; mem. DNA tech. com. Pacific Southwest Regional Genetics Network, Berkeley, Calif., Coll. Am. Pathologists, Am. Coll. Med. Genetics, NIH Task Force on Genetic Testing, others, 1987—; med., tech. cons. and writer Warner Bros., NBC, Tri-Star, CBS, Twentieth Century Fox, Universal, others, 1987—; mem. molecular genetics com. Coll. Am. Pathology, Am. Coll. Med. Genetics, Assn. Molecular Pathology, others; also TV/movie consulting and writing. Contbg. editor: MD Mag., 1981-91; assoc. editor Diagnostic Molecular Pathology, 1993—; contbr. articles to profl. jours., books, websites. Recipient best paper award L.A. Soc. Pathology, 1984, Joseph Kleiner Meml. award Am. Soc. Med. Technologists, 1990; Basil O'Connor scholar March of Dimes Birth Defects Found., 1989, Nakamura Lecturship Scripps Clinic, 1996, Moss Lectureship LSU, 1998, Stop Cancer Fdn. Rsch. Award, 1998, Am.'s top Doctors, 2001. Mem. AAAS, AMA, Am. Soc. Clin. Pathology (DNA workshop dir. 1988—), Am. Soc. Human Genetics, Coll. Am. Pathologists (scholar award 1987), Soc. Inherited Metabolic Disorders, Soc. Pediat. Rsch., Am. Coll. Med. Genetics (mem. DNA com.). Democrat. Jewish. Achievements include application of molecular biology to clinical diagnosis, molecular genetics research and AIDS research. Avocation: classical music. Office: UCLA Sch Medicine Divsn Med Genetics and Molecular Pathology Los Angeles CA 90095-1732 E-mail: wgrody@mednet.ucla.edu

GROEBLI, WERNER FRITZ (MR. FRICK), professional ice skater, realtor; b. Basel, Switzerland, Apr. 21, 1915; s. Fritz and Gertrud (Landerer) G.; m. Yvonne Baumgartner, Dec. 30, 1954. Student architecture, Swiss Fed. Inst. Tech., 1934 35. Lic. realtor, Calif. Chmn. pub. relations com. Profl. Skaters Guild Am., 1972— Performed in ice shows, Patria, Brighton, Eng., 1937; command performance in, Marina, London, 1937, Symphony on Ice, Royal Opera House, 1937; mem. Ice Follies, 1939-81, partner (with Hans Mauch) in comedy team Frick & Frack, 1939-53; solo act as Mr. Frick (assisted by comedy team), 1955-81; numerous TV appearances including Snoopy on Ice, 1973, Snoopy's Musical on Ice, 1978, Sportsworld, NBC-TV, 1978, Donnie and Marie Osmond Show, 1978, Mike Douglas Show, 1978, Dinah Shore Show, 1978; films include Silver Skates, 1942, Lady Let's Dance, 1943, Jinxed, 1981; interviewed by Barbara Walters NBC Today, 1974; appeared in Christmas Classics on Ice at Blue Jay Ice Castle, 1991. Served with Swiss Army, 1934-37. Named Swiss jr. skating champion, 1934; named to Madison Sq. Garden Hall of Fame for 10,000 performances in Ice Follies, 1967, U.S. Figure Skating Assn. World Hall of Fame, 1984; recipient Hall of Fame Ann. award Ice Skating Inst. Am. Mem. Profl. Skaters Guild Am. Lasted 15,000 performances in Ice Follies; originator of "Frick" cantilever spread-eagle skating movement; comedic choreography consultant. Address: PO Box 7886 Incline Village NV 89452-7886

GROENING, MATTHEW, writer, cartoonist; b. Portland, Oreg., Feb. 15, 1954; s. Homer Philip and Margaret Ruth (Wiggum) G.; m. Deborah Lee Caplan; 2 children. BA, Evergreen State Coll., 1977. Cartoonist Life in Hell weekly comic strip (syndicated by Acme Features Syndicate), Sheridan, Oreg., 1980—; pres. Matt Groening Prodns., Inc., L.A., 1988—, Bongo Entertainment, Inc., L.A., 1993—. Cartoonist for tv cartoon Futurama, 1999. Named New Pub. of Yr. Diamond Distbn. Gem awards, 1993.

GROFF, JOANN, organization administrator; b. Ft. Leonardwood, Mo., Oct. 10, 1956; d. Barry T. Groff and Ann (Ferry) Ragsdale. Student, Georgetown U., 1974-76; BS in Bus. Adminstrn., Babson Coll., Wellesley, Mass., 1978. Office mgr. Morgan Smith for Congress, Northglenn, Colo., 1978; fair and rodeo asst. Adams County Commrs., Brighton, 1979; mktg. devel. officer Columbine Title Co., Lakewood, 1979-80; exec agt., loan officer Wells Fargo Credit Corp., Englewood, 1981-84; pub. banking rep. Cen. Bank of Denver, 1985-89; mem. Colo. Ho. of Reps., Denver, 1983-89, chmn. audit com., 1989; fin. com.; dir. Leadership Giving Mile High United Way, 1991-92; pres. Colo. Retail Coun., 1992—. Past pres. Westminster Cmty. Artist Series; mem. bd. Pub. Svc. Credit Union, Colo. State Dem. Com., 1980-93, Colo. State Exec. Com., 1988-93, del. Nat. Conv., 1980, 84, alt. del., 1976; bd. dirs. Westminster (Colo.) Cmty. Artist Series, Marycrest H.S.; apptd. mem. Colo. State Bd. Equalization, 1994—. Colo. Transp. Com., 1999—. Roman Catholic. Office: Colo Retail Coun 451 E 58th Ave Denver CO 80216-1404 E-mail: jag@coloradoretail.org

GROGAN, JAMES J. real estate company executive; Grad. cum laude, Coll. of the Holy Cross, 1976; grad., U. Cin., 1979. Mng. atty. Gallagher and Kennedy, Phoenix; sr. exec. v.p. UDC Homes; pres., CEO Samoth Capital Corp. and Samoth USA Inc., Scottsdale, Ariz., 1998—, Sterling Financial Corp., Scottsdale. Bd. dirs. AMERCO. Bd. trustees Coll. of the Holy Cross. Office: Sterling Financial Group 6900 E 2d St Scottsdale AZ 85251

GROSCOST, JEFF, state legislator, small business owner; b. Tooele, Utah, Apr. 29, 1961; m. Dana Groscost; 4 children. Student, Ariz. State U., Mesa C.C., Brigham Young U. Mem. Ariz. Ho. of Reps., 1993—, past chmn. ways and means com., past mem. appropriations com., past mem. block grants com., past mem. joint legis. budget com., past mem. joint legis. tax com., past majority whip, past chmn. apropriations sub-com. gen. gov., past com. states rights and mandates, house spkr. Gem broker; mem. adv. bd. Gov.'s Motion Picture and TV. Bd. dirs. S.W. Shakespeare Fest.; vol. youth coach Mesa Family YMCA, East Valley; chmn. Cub pack com. Boy Scouts Am. Mem. State Bd. Chartered Schs., Constl. Def. Coun. LDS. Office: State Capitol 1700 W Washington St Phoenix AZ 85007-2812 also: 2425 E Florian Ave Mesa AZ 85204-5401 Fax: 602-542-0102. E-mail: igroscos@azleg.state.az.us

GROSE, ANDREW PETER, foundation executive; b. Washington, July 16, 1940; s. Peter Andrew and Mildred (Holston) G.; m. Jacqueline Stamm, Aug. 17, 1963; children: Peter Andrew II, Tracey Christine. BS with high honors, U. Md., 1962, MA, 1964. Mem. legis. staff Fla. Ho. of Reps., Tallahassee, 1972-74; rsch. dir. Nev. Legislature, Carson City, 1974-83; chief of staff Office of Gov. Nev., Carson City, 1983-84, dir. econ. devel., 1984-90; dir. Western region Coun. of State Govt., San Francisco, 1990-95; pres. Westrends, 1990-95; CFO Pub. Policy Inst. Calif., 1995—. Mem. exec. com. Nat. Conf. State Legislatures, Denver, 1982-83. Author: Florida Model City Charter, 1974; mem. editl. bd. Nev. Rev. of Bus. and Econs., Reno, 1976-90. Chair trustees Temple United Meth. Ch., San Francisco, 1998—. Capt. USAF, 1964-70, to brig. gen., Res. Recipient Spl. citation Nev. Libr. Assn., Carson City, 1981. Mem. Air Force Assn., Res. Officers Assn., Nat. Assn. State Devel. Agys. (1st v.p.), Western Govt. Rsch. Assn. (pres. 1993-95), Kiwanis (pres. 1981-82, bd. dirs. 1994-97, treas. 1997-2000, pres. 2001-2002). Democrat. Home: 405 Hazelwood Ave San Francisco CA 94127-2129 Office: Public Policy Inst Calif 500 Washington St Ste 800 San Francisco CA 94111-2934 E-mail: grose@ppic.org

GROSECLOSE, WANDA WESTMAN, retired elementary school educator; b. Clarks, Nebr., Oct. 5, 1933; m. B. Clark Groseclose; children: D. Kim, Byron C. Jr., Eric P., A. Glenn. B degree, Brigham Young U., 1976; M in Tchg., St. Mary's Coll., Moraga, Calif., 1981. Cert. tchr., Calif., life credential. 5th grade tchr. Brentwood (Calif.) Union Sch. Dist., 1977-97; ret. Art tchr., mentor tchr. Contra Costa County Program of Excellence. Author: American Music in Time, In the Shadow of Our Ancestors. Mem. human rels. bd. dirs. City of Livermore, Calif., 1968-70. Republican. Mem. LDS Ch. Avocations: oil painting, sewing, gardening, genealogy. Home: 83 Payne Ave Brentwood CA 94513-4701 E-mail: grosclose@ecis.com

GROSFIELD, LORENTS, state legislator; b. Billings, Mont., Aug. 27, 1944; m. Sydney Grosfield. Student, St. Olaf Coll., Minn.; BA in Bus. Adminstrn., Colo. State U. Farmer, cattle rancher; supr. Conservation Dist.; mem. Mont. Senate, Dist. 13, Helena, 1990—; chair judiciary com., vice chair com. on coms. Mont. Senate; mem. natural resources com. Mont. State Senate. Mem. Mont. Bd. Natural Resources, 1989-90. Served with U.S. Army, Vietnam. Republican. Home: HC 87 Box 2145 Big Timber MT 59011-9703

GROSS, ALLEN JEFFREY, lawyer; b. Wheeling, W.Va., May 2, 1948; s. Arthur and Bertyl (Kahn) G.; m. Carolyn McGuire, May 2, 1982; children: Alexander, Lindsay. BS, Ohio State U., 1970; JD, Georgetown U., 1974. Bar: Pa. 1974, U.S. Dist. Ct. (ctrl. and we. dists.) Pa., Calif. 1989, U.S. Dist. Ct. (no., so. and ctrl. dists.) Calif. 1989, U.S. Ct. Appeals (3d and 6th cirs.). Ptnr. Morgan, Lewis & Bockius, Phila., 1974-89, Orrick, Harrington & Sutcliffe, L.A., 1989-93; now with Mitchell, Silberberg & Knupp, L.A. Mem. Corp. Counsel Inst. adv. bd. Georgetown U. Law Ctr. Author: Survey of Wrongful Discharge Cases in the United States, 1979, Employee Dismissal Laws, Forms, Procedures, 1986, 2d edit. 1992. Fellow Coll. Labor and Employment Lawyers Inc.; mem. ABA (chair trial advocacy supcom. 1989-93, employee rights and responsibilities com. 1991—, co-chair Nat. Advocacy Inst. 1992), Calif. Bar Assn., Pa. Bar Assn. (mgmt. chair Employee Rights Responsibilities com., Sect. Insts. Spl. Programs sub-com.), L.A. County Bar Assn. Office: Mitchell Silberberg & Knupp 11377 W Olympic Blvd Los Angeles CA 90064-1625

GROSS, CAROL A. biochemist, educator; Prof. U. Calif., San Francisco. Office: UC San Francisco PO Box 512 San Francisco CA 94143-0001

GROSS, EDWARD, retired sociologist, educator, lawyer; b. Nagy Genez, Romania; s. Samuel and Dora (Levi) G.; m. Florence Rebecca Goldman, Feb. 18, 1943; children: David P., Deborah L., Allison. BA, U. B.C., Can., 1942; MA, U. Toronto, Ont., Can., 1945; PhD, U. Chgo., 1949; JD, U. Wash., 1991. Prof. Wash. State U., Pullman, 1947-51, 53-60; prof. U. Wash., Seattle, 1951-53, 65-89, prof. emeritus, 1990—; prof. sociology U. Minn., Mpls., 1960-65. Vis. prof. Australian Nat. U., Canberra, 1971, U. Queensland, U. New South Wales, Griffith U., Australia, 1977; invited lectr. Cen. China Poly. Inst., 1987; lectr. arts and scis. honor program U. Wash., 1998—. Author: Work and Society, 1958, University Goals and Academic Power, 1968, Changes in University Organization, 1964-71, The End of a Golden Age: Higher Education in a Steady State, 1981, Organizations in Society, 1985, Embarrassment in Everyday Life, 1994; contbg. author: Handbook of Sociology and Encyclopedia of Sociology, 2d edit.; former assoc. editor Social Problems, Symbolic Interaction, Can. Jour. Sociology; contbr. numerous articles to profl. jours. Trustee Temple Beth Am, Seattle, 1993-97. Fulbright scholar Australia, 1977, 87. Mem. Pacific Sociol. Assn. (pres. 1971, coun. 1983-85). Office: U Wash Dept Sociology Seattle WA 98195-0001 E-mail: egross@uwahington.edu

GROSS, KEN, transportation executive; Co-owner The Gilbert Cos., Commerce, Calif., 1987—. Office: The Gilbert Cos 4940 Triggs St Los Angeles CA 90022-4832 Fax: 323-526-9856

GROSS, RICHARD EDMUND, education educator; b. Chgo., May 25, 1920; s. Edmund Nicholas and Florence (Gallistel) G.; m. Jane Clare Hartl, May 25, 1943; children: Kathryn Ann, Elaine Clare, Edmund Ralph, John Richard. BS, U. Wis., 1942, MS, 1946; EdD, Stanford U., 1951. Jr. personnel officer FSA, Milw., 1942-43; tchr. Central High Sch., Madison, Wis., 1943-48; instr. Menlo Sch. and Coll., Menlo Park, Calif., 1948-51; asso. prof. Fla. State U., 1951-55; mem. faculty Sch. Edn., Stanford U., 1955—, prof., 1965—, chmn. curriculum and tchr. edn., 1977-90. Chief cons. central com. social studies Calif. Dept. Edn., 1958-60; Fulbright lectr. tchr. edn. U. Wales, Swansea, 1961-62; guest prof. Am. Inst., U. Frankfurt, Germany, 1968-69; ednl. adviser World Bank Pilot Center project U. Santiago, Spain, 1973; vis. prof. Monash U., Melbourne, Australia, 1976; curriculum cons. to schs., 1952— ; guest lectr. Taiwan Tchrs. Inst., Taipei, 1990, Seoul Nat. U., Republic of Korea, 1995; Bicentennial lectr. U. Alaska, Anchorage, 1987; adv. bd. Edn. Policy Com., 1958-68; chmn. nat. advisory bd. E.R.I.C. Social Sci. Center, U. Colo., 1969-71; dir. social studies, adviser Addison-Wesley Publs., 1970-83; bd. dirs. Calif. Inst. Internat. Studies, Inst. Devel. Human Resources; co-dir. nat. citizenship edn. study, 1985-93. Author: How to Handle Controversial Issues, 1952, The Problems Approach and the Social Studies, 1955, The Sociology of the School, 1957, The United States Congress, 1957, Educating Citizens for Democracy, 1958, The Heritage of American Education, 1962, British Secondary Education, 1965, Civics in Action, 1966, Man's World: A Physical Geography, 1966, The History of Education: A Timeline, 1967, Teaching the Social Studies, 1969, Profile of America, 1971, Quest for Liberty, 1971, Teaching Social Studies Skills, 1973, The Human Experience, 1974, Social Studies for Our Times, 1978, American Citizenship: How We Govern, 1979, Learning to Live in Society, 1980, What Should We Be Teaching in the Social Studies, 1983, Ciencias Sociales, 1983, What Chinese Children Have Learned about the United States, 1990, Social Science Perspectives on Citizenship, 1990, Designing Effective Instruction for Secondary Social Studies, 1998; editor: Phi Delta Kappa Bi-centennial Fast-Backs, 1976, Calif. Social Sci. Rev, 1962-68; contbr. articles to encys., profl. jours.; creator Scholastic World-Affairs Multitext Publs, 1963; K. and E. overhead viewer transparencies for U.S. History, 1964. Mem. ASCD, AAUP, NEA, Nat. Coun. Social Studies (pres. 1967, Career Rsch. award 1990), Nat. Soc. Study Edn., Am. Acad. Polit. and Social Sci., History of Edn. Soc., World Assn. Civic Edn. (exec. com.), Phi Alpha Theta, Kappa Delta Tau, Phi Delta Kappa (Hilda Taba hon. award, 1988). Home: 26304 Esperanza Dr Los Altos CA 94022-2653 Office: Stanford Univ Cubberley Hall Stanford CA 94305

GROSS, RUTH TAUBENHAUS, physician; b. Bryan, Tex., June 24, 1920; d. Jacob and Esther (Hirshenson) Taubenhaus; m. Reuben H. Gross, Jr., Aug. 22, 1942; (div. June 1952); 1 son, Gary E. BA, Barnard Coll., 1941; MD, Columbi U., 1944. Intern, Charity Hosp., New Orleans, 1944; resident in pediatrics Tulane U., New Orleans, 1945, Columbia U., N.Y.C., 1946, 47; instr. Radcliffe Infirmary, Oxford, Eng., 1949-50; instr. pediatrics Stanford (Calif.) U., 1950-53, asst. prof., 1953-56, assoc. prof., 1956-60, prof., 1973-92, prof. emerita, 1992; acting exec. pediatrics, 1957-59, assoc. dean student affairs, 1973-75, dir. div. gen. and ambulatory pediatrics, 1975-85, dir. Stanford-Children's Ambulatory Care Ctr., 1980-85, nat. study dir. Infant Health and Devel. Program, 1983-92; assoc. prof. pediatrics, co-dir. div. human genetics Albert Einstein Coll. Medicine, Yeshiva U., N.Y.C., 1960-64, prof. pediatrics, 1964-66; clin. prof. pediatrics U. Calif. Med. Ctr., San Francisco, 1966-73; dir. dept. pediatrics Mt. Zion Hosp. and Med. Ctr., San Francisco, 1966-73. Commonwealth fellow human genetics Instituto de Genetica, Pavia, Italy, 1959-60. Mem. Inst. Medicine, NAS, Am. Fedn. Clin. Rsch., Am. Pediatric Soc., Soc. Pediatric Rsch., Am. Acad. Pediatrics, Ambulatory Pediatric Assn., Soc. Rsch. in Child Devel., Phi Beta Kappa, Alpha Omega Alpha, Sigma Xi. Contbr. articles to profl. jours.

GROSSER, BERNARD IRVING, psychiatry educator; b. Boston, Apr. 19, 1929; s. John and Katherine (Russman) G.; children: Steven, Mark, Minda; m. Karen Grosser. BA, U. Mass., 1950; MS, U. Mich., 1953; MD, Case-Western Res. U., 1959. Diplomate Am. Bd. Psychiatry and Neurology. Intern U. Utah, 1959-60, resident in psychiatry, 1960-65; asst. prof. psychiatry U. Utah Sch. Medicine, Salt Lake City, 1967-71, assoc. prof., 1971-75, prof., 1975—, chmn. dept., 1978—. Mem. pre-clin. and clin. psychopharm. rev. com. NIMH, Washington, 1974-79, 80-84, mem. sci. adv. bd., 1984-88; mem. merit rev. bd. VA, Washington, 1988-91; sr. sci. advisor Alcohol, Drug Abuse and Mental Health Adminstrn., Washington, 1987-88; ad hoc mem. Mental Health Clin. Rsch. Ctr. rev. com. NIMH, 1997, ad hoc mem. mental health clin. contracts rev. com., 1998, ad hoc mem. spl. emphasis panel, 2000. Contbr. chpts. to books, articles to profl. jours. Capt. USAF, 1965-67. Grantee NIMH, 1959-84, FDA, 1985-88; recipient Exemplary psychiatrist award Nat. Alliance for Mentally Ill, 1997. Fellow Am. Psychiat. Assn. (life); mem. Internat. Soc. Psychoneuroendocrinology (treas. 1974-88), Utah Psychiat. Assn. (pres. 1995-96), Psychiat. Rsch. Soc. (pres. 1986-87), Am. Coll. Neuropsychopharmacology, Soc. Neurosci., N.Y. Acad. Scis., Collegium Internat. Neuropsychopharmacologicum, Am. Assn. Psychiatry Dept. Chairmen (coun. 1997-2000). Republican. Jewish. Home: 511 Perrys Hollow Rd Salt Lake City UT 84103-4245 Office: U Utah Sch Medicine Dept Psychiatry 50 N Medical Dr Salt Lake City UT 84132-0001

GROSSER, T.J. administrator, developer, fundraiser; b. Milw., Oct. 17, 1938; s. Owen Henry and Ethel Clare (Hathazy) G.; m. Mary Janet McClanahan, Apr. 3, 1976; children: Paul Howard, Julie Anne, Philip Owen, Peter John, Elizabeth Michelle. BA, U. Wis., 1958, MA, 1962, EdD, 1971; DD (hon.), Union Theol. Sem., Richmond,Va., 1972. Min. edn. Cross Luth. Ch., Milw., 1957-62; assoc. Christ Luth. Ch., Oshkosh, Wis., 1962-65; preacher/tchr. Trinity Luth. Ch., Santa Barbara, Calif., 1966-71; pres. Amigos de las Ams., Houston, 1972-79, Vols. in Internat. Svc. & Awareness, L.A., 1980-84; v.p. Pacific Clinics, Pasadena, Calif., 1985-87; pres., chief exec. officer Children's Aid Internat., San Diego, 1987-97; pres., CEO Angelcare, 1998—. Bd. dirs. Am. Devel. Found., Washington, 1981-95; bd. dirs., pres. End Hunger Network, L.A., 1983-87; bd. dirs., v.p. Ind. Charities of Am., San Francisco, pres., 1988—; bd. dirs. Children's Charities Am.; advisor numerous internat. and religious agys. Contbr. 200 articles to profl. jours. Advisor African Refugee Ctr., L.A., 1989—; worker priest Hope Luth. Ch., Hollywood, Calif., 1983—. Named Educator of Yr. Am. Luth. Ch., Mpls., 1966, exec. of Yr. Coun. Internat. Vol. Orgn., Geneva, 1975, 76; recipient Papal medal Pope John Paul II, Rome, 1979. Mem. Fund Raising Execs., Rotary (Paul Harris fellow) 1987). Democrat. Avocations: reading, speaking, travel, promoting internat. adoptions. Home: 6457 Elmhurst Dr San Diego CA 92120-3959 Office: Anglecare PO Box 600370 San Diego CA 92160-0370 E-mail: tjgrosser@angelcare.org

GROSSINGER, RICHARD SELIG, publisher, writer, editor; b. N.Y.C., Nov. 3, 1944; s. Paul Leonard and Martha Washington (Rothkrug) G.; m. Lindy Downer Hough, June 21, 1966; children: Robin, Miranda. BA, Amherst Coll., 1966; MA, U. Mich., 1968, PhD in Anthropology, 1975. Lectr. in anthropology-geography U. Maine, Portland, 1970-72; mem. faculty dept. cultural history Goddard Coll., Plainfield, Vt., 1972-77; founder, editor, pub. Io mag., 1965—, North Atlantic Books, Berkeley, Calif. Mem. adv. bd. animal rights group Between the Species, 1985—, Mars Project, 1987; speaker Angels, Aliens and Archetypes Conf., San Francisco, 1987. Author: Solar Journal: Oecological Sections, 1970, Spaces Wild and Tame, 1971, Book of the Earth and Sky, 1971, Mars: A Science Fiction Vision, 1971, The Continents, 1973, Early Field Notes From the All-American Revival Church, 1973, The Windy Passage from Nostalgia, 1974, The Book of Being Born Again into the World, 1974, Martian Homecoming at the All-American Revival Church, 1974, The Long Body of the Dream, 1974, Book of the Cranberry Islands, 1974, The Provinces, 1975, The Unfinished Business of Doctor Hermes, 1976, Planet Medicine from Stone Age Shamanism to Post-Industrial Healing, 1980, The Night Sky, 1981, Embryogenesis, 1986, Waiting for the Martian Express, 1989, New Moon, 1996, Out of Babylon, 1997, Homopaint: The Great Riddle, 1998, Embryogenesis: Species, Gender, and Identity, 2000; author major essay The Dream Work in Dreams are Wiser Than Men, 1987; editor: (with Kevin Kerrane) Baseball I Gave You All The Best Years of My Life, 1977, Ecology and Consciousness, 1978, Alchemy: pre-Egyptian Legacy, Millennial Promise, 1979, The Alchemical Tradition in the Late Twentieth Century, 1983, The Temple of Baseball, 1985, Planetary Mysteries: Megaliths, Glaciers, The Face on Mars and Aboriginal Dreamtime, 1986, The Dreamlife of Johnny Baseball, 1987. NIH fieldwork fellow, 1969; Nat. Endowment for Arts writer's fellow, 1976 Mem. Soc. for Study Native Arts and Scis. (dir. 1980—) E-mail: char2@lmi.net

GROSSMAN, ELMER ROY, pediatrician; b. L.A., Jan. 30, 1929; s. Harry and Reta (Frankel) G.; m. Rosalind Nagin, June 24, 1951 (div. 1976); children— Deena, Marianna; m. Pamela Canfield Antoncich, July 29, 1976; stepchildren: Camilla Sutter, Michael A. Antoncich. A.B., U. Calif.-Berkeley, 1949; M.D., U. Calif. Sch. Medicine, San Francisco, 1953. Intern Orange County Gen. Hosp., Orange, Calif., 1953-54; resident U. Calif. Hosps., San Francisco, 1957-59; practice medicine specializing in pediatrics Berkeley Pediatric Med. Group, Calif, 1959-92. Assoc. clin. prof. health and med. scis. U. Calif.-Berkeley, 1978-80; clin. prof. pediatrics emeritus U. Calif. Sch. Medicine, San Francisco; chmn. dept. pediatrics Alta Bates Hosp., Berkeley, 1972-74, chmn. infant care ethics com., 1984-90. Author: Everyday Pediatrics, 1993, Everyday Pediatrics for Parents, 1996; columnist The Everyday Pediatrician; contbr. articles to profl. jours. Mem. Berkeley Schs. Master Plan Com., 1966-68, Berkeley Schs. Child Care Com., 1968-70; pres. Temple Beth El, Berkeley, 1970-72. Served to capt. USAF, 1954-56 Fellow Am. Acad. Pediatrics; mem. Alameda-Contra Costa Med. Assn., Physicians for Social Responsibility, Physicians for a Nat. Health Program. Democrat. Jewish Avocations: wine making; gardening. Home and Office: 899 Euclid Ave Berkeley CA 94708-1305 E-mail: elmergrossman@home.com

GROSSMAN, GEORGE STEFAN, library director, law eductor; b. Poltar, Czechoslovakia, May 31, 1938; m. Suzi Herczeg, 1960; 1 child, Zoltan B.A., U. Chgo., 1960; LL.B., Stanford U., 1966; M.A. in Library Sci., Brigham Young U., 1971. Bar: Calif. 1966, Minn. 1974. Tech. processes law librarian U. Pa., 1966-68; assoc. prdf. law, law librarian U. Utah, 1968-70, prof., law librarian, 1970-73; prof., dir. law library U. Minn., 1973-79, Northwestern U., Chgo., 1979-93; prof., dir. law libr. U. Calif., Davis, 1993—. Cons. to univs. Author: Legal Research: Historical Foundations of the Electronic Age, 1994, The Spirit of American Law, 1999; contbr. articles to legal jours. Mem. Indian rights com. ACLU, 1973-92, pres. Utah affiliate, 1972-73, bd. dirs. Ill. affiliate, 1982-87. Mem. Am. Assn. Law Libraries, Internat. Assn. Law Libraries. Office: U Calif Sch Law Libr King Hall 400 Mrak Dr Davis CA 95616 Fax: 530-752-8959

GROSSMAN, LAWRENCE MORTON, nuclear engineering educator; b. N.Y.C., Aug. 2, 1922; married; 1 child. B.Chem. Engring., City Coll. N.Y., 1942, M.Sc. (Standard Oil Co. Calif. fellow), 1944; Ph.D. in Engring. Sci., U. Calif. at Berkeley, 1948. Chem. engr. E.I. du Pont de Nemours & Co., Niagara Falls, N.Y., 1942-43; instr. mech. engring. U. Calif., Berkeley, 1944-46, lectr., 1946-48, asst. prof., 1948-54, assoc. prof. mech. engring., 1954-59, prof., 1959—, chmn. dept. nuclear engring., 1969-74. Fulbright lectr. U. Delft, 1952-53; NSF Sr. research fellow Saclay Nuclear Research Center, France, 1961-62; NATO sr. fellow, 1974 Recipient Berkeley Citation, 1991. Mem. A.A.A.S., Am. Nuclear Soc. Office: U Calif Etcheverry Hl Berkeley CA 94720-0001 E-mail: grossman@nuc.berkeley.edu

GROSSMAN, WILLIAM, medical researcher, educator; b. N.Y.C., 1940; MD, Yale U., 1965. Intern Peter Bent Brigham Hosp., Boston, 1965-66, resident in medicine, 1968-69, rsch. fellow in cardiology, 1969-71; dir. cardiac catheterization labs. N.C. Meml. Hosp., Chapel Hill, 1971-75, Peter Bent Brigham Hosp., Boston, 1975-81; chief cardiovasc. divsn. Beth Israel Hosp., Boston, 1981-94; tchg. fellow in medicine Harvard U., Boston, 1968-71, assoc. prof., 1975-81, prof., 1981-84, Herman Dana prof. medicine, 1984-94; exec. dir. cardiovasc. rsch. Merck & Co., West Point, Pa., 1994-95, v.p., 1996-97; prof. medicine U. Calif., San Francisco, 1997—, chief cardiology, 1997—. Adj. prof. U. Pa., 1995-97. Served as sr. asst. surgeon USPHS, 1966-68. Fellow Am. Coll. Cardiology, Am. Heart Assn., Assn. Am. Physicians, Am. Physiol. Soc., Am. Soc. Clin. Investigation. Office: UCSF Med Ctr Dept Cardiology Box 0124 San Francisco CA 94143-0124

GROSSMANN, RONALD STANYER, lawyer; b. Chgo., Nov. 9, 1944; s. Andrew Eugene and Gladys M. Grossmann; m. Jo Ellen Hanson, May 11, 1968; children: Kenneth Frederick, Emilie Beth. BA, Northwestern U., 1966; JD, U. Mich., 1969. Bar: Oreg., 1969. Law clk. Oreg. Supreme Ct., Salem, 1969-70; assoc. Stoel Rives LLP, Portland, Oreg., 1970-76; ptnr. Stoel Rives Boley Jones & Grey, Portland, 1976—. Mem.: ABA, Oreg. Bar Assn., Am. Coll. Employee Benefits Coun. Office: Stoel Rives LLP 900 SW 5th Ave Ste 2600 Portland OR 97204-1268 E-mail: rsgrossmann@stoel.com

GROSZ, PHILIP J. lawyer; b. Oshkosh, Wis., Feb. 1, 1952; s. Joseph Otto and Marjorie (Berkhoel) G.; m. Linda Marie Ondrejka, Dec. 29, 1973. BA with honors, U. Wis., 1973; JD, Yale Law Sch., 1977. Bar: Calif. Ptnr. Loeb & Loeb, L.A., 1983-92, mng. ptnr., 1992-96. Founder, bd. dirs. Love is Feeding Everyone, L.A., 1983-94. Mem. Calif. Bar Assn. Democrat. Office: Loeb & Loeb 10100 Santa Monica Blvd Los Angeles CA 90067-4164

GROTEN, BARNET, energy company executive; b. Bklyn., Oct. 25, 1933; s. Irving and Pearl G.; m. Iris Diane Brand, Aug. 1955; children: Eric Allen, Kurt David, Jessica Amy. BS, Bklyn. Coll., 1954; PhD, Purdue U., 1961. Joined Exxon Co., various locations, 1961; dir. rsch. and bus. devel. Tex. Eastern Corp., Houston, 1977-87; exec. v.p. Tex. Eastern Devel., Inc., 1980-87; sec. Gulf Univs. Research Consortium, 1980-81; chmn. bd. Gulf Univs. Rsch. Consortium, 1982-83; exec. dir. Energy Ctr. U. Okla., Norman, 1987-91; v.p. Energy Internat., Inc., Bellevue, Wash., 1991-99; pres. Grait Techs., LLC, Bellevue, 1999—, Power Genix Systems, Inc., Bellevue, 2001—. Contbr. articles to profl. jours. Mem. Gov.'s Energy Adv. Coun.; chmn. Natural Gas Vehicle Task Force. Office: Grait Techs LLC 13706 NE 36th Pl Bellevue WA 98005-1413 E-mail: barnet@wolfenet.com

GROTH, ALEXANDER JACOB, political science educator; b. Warsaw, Poland, Mar. 7, 1932; came to U.S., 1947; s. Jacob and Maria (Hazenfuss) Goldwasser; m. Marilyn Ann Wineburg, Dec. 15, 1961; children: Stevin James, Warren Adrian. BA magna cum laude, CCNY, 1954; MA, Columbia U., 1955, PhD, 1960. Instr. polit. sci. Trinity Coll., Hartford, Conn., 1957-58, CUNY, 1960-61; asst. prof. Harpur Coll., Binghamton, N.Y., 1961-62, U. Calif., Davis, 1962-71, prof., 1971—. Cons. Ency. Am., Danbury, Conn., 1965—. Author: Comparative Politics, 1971, Major Ideologies, 1971, 2d rev. edit., 1983, People's Poland, 1972, Progress and Chaos, 1984, Lincoln: Authoritarian Savior, 1995, Democracies Against Hitler, 1999; co-author: Contemporary Politics: Europe, 1976, Comparative Resource allocation, 1984, Public Policy Across Nations, 1985; editor: Revolution and Political Change, 1996; contbr. numerous articles to encys., scholarly jours. Recipient Ward medal dept. govt. CCNY, 1954, T. R. Dye award, 2000; grantee Am. Co. Learned Socs. and Social Sci. Research Council, 1965-66. Mem. Western Polit. Sci. Assn., Policy Studies Assn., Far West Slavic Assn., Phi Beta Kappa. Republican. Avocations: baseball, baseball history, research and writing. Business e-mail: ajgroth@ucdavis.edu. Personal e-mail: marilynag@aol.com. Home: 1848 Rushmore Ln Davis CA 95616-6654 Office: U Calif Dept Polit Sci Davis CA 95616

GROUNDS, VERNON CARL, seminary administrator; b. Jersey City, July 19, 1914; s. John and Bertha Barbara (Heimburg) G.; m. Ann Barton, June 17, 1939; 1 child, Barbara Ann Grounds Owen. BA, Rutgers U., 1937; BD, Faith Theol. Sem., 1940; PhD, Drew U., 1960; DD (hon.), Wheaton Coll., 1954; LHD (hon.), Gordon Coll., 1977. Pastor Paterson (N.J.) Gospel Tabernacle, 1935-45; dean, prof. theology Bapt. Bible Sem., Johnson City, N.Y., 1945-51; dean Denver Conservative Bapt. Sem., 1951-55, pres., 1955-79, chancellor, 1979—. Author: Yes, But How?, Emotional Problems and the Gospel, Evangelicalism and Social Responsibility, The Reason for Our Hope, Revolution and the Christian Faith; contbg. editor Christianity Today, 1980—. Sec. Evangelical Theol. Soc., Lynchburg, Va., 1963-76; bd. dirs. Radio Bible Class Ministries. Home: 3455 S Corona St Apt 513 Englewood CO 80110-2878 Office: Denver Sem PO Box 10,000 Denver CO 80250

GROVE, ANDREW S. electronics company executive; b. Budapest, Hungary, 1936; married; 2 children B.S., CCNY, 1960, DSc (hon.), 1985; Ph.D., U. Calif.-Berkeley, 1963; DEng (hon.), Worcester Poly. Inst., 1989. With Fairchild Camera and Instrument Co., 1963-67; pres., COO, Intel Corp., Santa Clara, Calif., 1967-87, pres., CEO, 1987-98, also bd. dirs., chmn. bd., 1998—. Recipient medal Am. Inst. Chemists, 1960, Merit cert. Franklin Inst., 1975, Townsend Harris medal CCNY, 1980, Enterprise award Profl. Advt. Assn., 1987, George Washington award Am. Hungarian Found., 1990, Citizen of Yr. award World Forum Silicon Valley, 1993, Exec. of Yr. award U. Ariz., 1993, Achievement medal Am. Electronics Assn., 1993, Heinz Family Found. award for tech. and economy, 1995, John von Neumann medal Am. Hungarian Assn., 1995, Steinman medal City Coll. N.Y., 1995, Statesman of the Yr. award Harvard Bus. Sch., 1996, Internat. Achievement award World Trade Club, 1997, Cinema Digital Technols. award Internat. Film Festival, 1997, Cinema Digital Tech. award Cannes Film Festival, 1997, Tech. Leader of Yr. award Industry Week, 1997, Man of Yr. award Time mag., 1997; named CEO of Yr. CEO mag., 1997. Fellow IEEE (Achievement award 1969, J.J. Ebers award 1974, Engring. Leadership Recognition award 1987, Computer Entrepreneur award 1997), Acad. Arts and Scis.; mem. Nat. Acad. Engring. (award 1979). Office: Intel Corp PO Box 58119 2200 Mission College Blvd Santa Clara CA 95054-1549

GROVES, MARTHA, newspaper writer; Computer writer L.A. Times, 1992-93, staff writer, 1985—. Office: LA Times Times Mirror Sq Los Angeles CA 90053

GRUB, PHILLIP DONALD, business educator; b. Medical Lake, Wash., Aug. 8, 1931; s. Carl Dryer and Barbara Rosalie (Johnson) G. BA in Econs. and Bus. Edn. with honors, Eastern Wash. State U., 1953; MBA (Scottish Rite Found. fellow), George Washington U., 1960, DBA (Am. Security and Trust scholar), 1964; DBus (hon.), U. Internat. Bus. and Econs., Beijing, 1986. Pres. Phillip D. Grub, Inc., Spokane, Wash., 1953-54; pvt. practice, 1956-62; co-owner, co-mgr. 7G Ranch, Medical Lake, 1962-70; assoc. prof., dir. programs in internat. bus. George Washington U., Washington, 1964-70, chmn. dept. bus. adminstrn., 1968-70, prof. bus. adminstrn., 1971-73, Aryamehr prof. multinat. mgmt., 1974-94, Aryamehr prof. emeritus, 1994—, spl. asst. to pres., 1974-80; chmn. Phillip Grub and Assocs., 1994—; disting. internat. exec. in residence Ea. Washington U., Cheney, 1997—. Cons. Summa Group, Jakarta, Indonesia, 1991-92; mgmt. cons. to industry and govts.; sr. ptnr. C & P Properties, Medical Lake, Wash., 1988—; mem. Md.-D.C. Export Expansion Coun., 1968-89; vis. prof. internat. bus. adminstrn., acting dir. Ohio World Trade Edn. Ctr., Cleve. State U., 1972-73; dir., chmn. exec. com. Diplomat Nat. Bank, 1978-80; mem. bd. adv. Donaldson, Luftkin & Jenrette, 1980-83; bd. dirs. U.S.-Japan Culture Ctr.; dir. Washington World Trade Inst., 1983-91, pres., 1983-86; dir. U.S. Vietnam Ednl. Found., 1990—; sr. advisor Shanghi Ctr. Internat. Studies, 1987—. Author: A Guide to Personnel Development, 1966, A Handbook for Term Papers, Theses and Dissertations, 1967, American-East European Trade: Controversy, Progress, Prospects, 1968; (with Norma M. Loeser) Executive Leadership: The Art of Successfully Managing Resources, 1969, Management U.S.A., 1968; (with Mika S. Kaskimies) International Marketing in Perspective, 1971; (with Ashok Kapoor) The Multinational Enterprise in Transition, 1972, 3d edit., 1986; (with Ghadar and Khambata) Asia Dimensions of International Business, 1982, Foreign Investment Analysis: Cases and Country Studies, 1986, Global Business Management in the 1990's, 1990, Foreign Direct Investment in China, 1991, The Re-Emerging Securities Market in China, 1992, Vietnam, The New Investment Frontier in Southeast Asia, 1992, (with Dara Khambata) The Multinational Enterprise: Strategies for Global Competitiveness, 1993, Global Business Strategies for the Year 2000, 1995; contbr. articles to profl. jours. Bd. dirs. U.S. Forestry, 1987-90; sr. advisor Shanghai Ctr. Internat. Studies, 1987—. With U.S. Army, 1954-56. Named a Univ. Prof. in Peoples Republic of China, 1986. Mem. Acad. Internat. Bus. (pres. 1975-77), Acad. Mgmt., Am. Mgmt. Assn., U.S.-Japan Culture Soc. (bd. dirs., exec. sec.), Fellows Acad. Internat. Bus., Masons, Alpha Kappa Psi, Beta Gamma Sigma. Home: 4810 S Saint Andrews Ln Spokane WA 99223-4304 Office: C & P Properties PO Box 220 Medical Lake WA 99022-0220 E-mail: drpdgrub@gateway.net

GRUBB, DAVID H. construction company executive; b. Jan. 22, 1936; married BSCE, Princeton U.; MSCE, Stanford U. With Swinerton and Walberg Co., San Francisco, 1964—, then exec. v.p. Structural divsn., exec. v.p. ops., pres., also bd. dirs.; pres. Swinerton Incorp., 1993-96, CEO and chmn. bd. Chmn. bd. Swinerton Builders, SW Indsl., Inc., Westwood Swinerton Constrn., Swinerton Property Svcs., Inc.; vice chmn. William P. Young Construction, Inc., Bud Bailey Constrn., Inc.; chmn. Harbison-Mahony-Higgins Builders, Inc. Office: Swinerton Incorp 580 California St Ste 1200 San Francisco CA 94104-1045

GRUBB, EDGAR HAROLD, financial services industrial executive; b. Harrisburg, Pa., May 8, 1939; s. Harold E. and Ruth (Longenecker) G.; m. Patricia A. Kerwin, Dec. 14, 1963; children: Dennis, Lisa, Mary, Jennifer. BS, Pa. State U., 1961; MBA, Calif. State U., Fullerton, 1967. CPA, Calif. Cons. mgr., auditor Coopers & Lybrand, San Francisco and L.A., 19678-72; group contr. Crown Zellerbach Corp., San Francisco, 1972-75, gen. mgr. packaging papers, 1976-77, dir. planning, 1978-80, v.p. consumer, 1981-82, v.p., contr., 1983-84, sr. v.p., chief fin. officer, 1984-86, Lucky Stores, Inc., Dublin, 1986-89; sr. v.p. Transam. Corp., 1989-93, CFO, 1993-99. Bd. dirs. Goodwill Industries of Alameda/Contra Costa/Solano Counties. Trustee Mills Coll., Oakland, Calif. Capt. USMC, 1961-65. Mem. AICPA, Calif. Soc. CPA's, Fin. Execs. Inst. Roman Catholic. Home: 41 Comistas Ct Walnut Creek CA 94598-4523 Office: Transamerica Corp 600 Montgomery St Ste 2300 San Francisco CA 94111-2770

GRUBBS, ROBERT HOWARD, chemistry educator; b. Calvert City, Ky., Feb. 27, 1942; s. Henry Howard and Faye (Atwood) G.; m. Helen Matilda O'Kane; children— Robert B., Brendan H., Kathleen M. B.S., U. Fla., 1963, M.S., 1965; Ph.D., Columbia U., 1968. NIH postdoctoral fellow Stanford U., Calif., 1968-69; asst. prof. Mich. State U., East Lansing, 1969-73, assoc. prof., 1973-78; prof. chemistry Calif. Inst. Tech., Pasadena, 1978—, Victor and Elizabeth Atkins prof., 1989. Contbr. articles to profl. publs.; patentee in field. Fellow Sloan Found., 1974-76, Alexander von Humboldt Found., 1975; Dreyfus Found. scholar, 1975-78; recipient award in Polymer Chem. Am. Chem. Soc., 1995. Mem. AAAS, NAS, Am. Chem. Soc. (Organic Chemistry award 1989, Polymer Chemistry award 1995, Benjamin Franklin medal in chemistry 2000, Herman F. Mark polymer chemistry award 2000, Herbert C. Brown award for creative rsch. in synthetic methods 2001). Democrat. Home: 1700 Spruce St South Pasadena CA 91030-4721 Office: Calif Inst Tech Dept Chemistry 164 30 Pasadena CA 91125-0001

GRUBE, JAMES R. federal judge; b. 1942; BA, U. Santa Clara, 1964; JD, U. Calif., 1967. Asst. dist. atty. City and County of San Francisco, 1970-75; with Murray & Grube, Palo Alto, Calif., 1975-79, Campeau & Grube, San Jose, 1980-88; apptd. bankruptcy judge no. dist. U.S. Dist. Ct. Calif., 1988. With U.S. Army, 1968-69. Mem. ABA, Am. Bankruptcy Inst., Nat. Conf. Bankruptcy Judges, U.S. Dist. Ct. for State Bar of Calif., No. Dist. of Calif. Histo. Soc., Santa Clara County Bar Assn., Bay Area Bankruptcy Forum, Bench and Bar Hist. Soc. of Santa Clara County. Office: US Bankruptcy Ct Rm 3035 280 S 1st St San Jose CA 95113-3002

GRUBER, JOHN BALSBAUGH, physics educator, university administrator; b. Hershey, Pa., Feb. 10, 1935; s. Irvin John and Erla R. (Balsbaugh) G.; m. Judith Anne Higer, June 20, 1961; children: David Powell, Karen Leigh, Mark Balsbaugh. B.S., Haverford (Pa.) Coll., 1957; Ph.D., U. Calif. at Berkeley, 1961. NATO postdoctoral fellow Inst. Tech. Physics, Tech. U. Darmstadt, Germany, 1961-62, gastdozent, 1961-62; asst. prof. physics U. Calif. at Los Angeles, 1962-66; asso. prof. physics Wash. State U., Pullman, 1966-71, prof. chem. physics, 1971-75; asst. dean Wash. State U. (Grad. Sch.), 1968-70, assoc. dean, 1970-72; prof. physics, dean Coll. Sci. and Math., N.D. State U., Fargo, 1975-80; prof. physics and chemistry, v.p. for acad. affairs Portland (Oreg.) State U., 1980-84; prof. physics San Jose State U., 1984—, acad. v.p., 1984-86, v.p. devel., 1986, dir. Inst. for Modern Optics, 1992—, chmn. dept. physics, 2001—. Vis. prof. Joint Ctr. Grad. Study, Richland, Wash., 1964, 65, 66, Ames Lab., Dept. of Energy, Iowa State U., 1976-80; Disting. vis. prof. U.S. Navy Naval Weapons Ctr., China Lake, Calif., 1984-93, Stanford U., 1993—; invited lectr., U.S., Can., Europe, 1966—; cons. in laser physics and spectroscopy Aerospace Corp., El Segundo, Calif., 1962-65, Douglas Aircraft and McDonnell Douglas Astronautics Co., Santa Monica, Calif., 1963-69, N.Am. Aviation, Space and Info. Systems, Downey, Calif., 1964-66, Battelle Northwest, Richland, Wash., 1964-69, Los Alamos (N.Mex.) Sci. Lab., 1969-71, 73-74; mem. task force lunar exploration sci. Apollo, NASA, 1964-69, 71-73; cons. Harry Diamond Labs. U.S. Army, 1981—, U.S. Army Rsch. Lab., IBM, 1985-90, GTE, 1986-89, Lasergenics, 1986—, Night Vision Lab. U.S. Army, Ft. Belvoir, 1988—, Deltron, 1990-91, Rey Tech Corp., 1998—, Laser Sci. and Tech., 1999—, Bicron Corp., 2000—, Spectragen Corp., 2000; mem. Rare Earth Rsch. Conf. Com., 1976-83, exec. com., 1977-83, sec. bd. dirs., 1979-84; gen. conf. chmn. XIV Internat. Rare Earth Rsch. Conf., 1979, Novel Laser Sources and Materials, 1982; exec. sec. Internat. Frank H. Spedding Award, 1979, 83, Willig award, 1986, Internat. Spencer prize for outstanding contbrn. to sci., 1987, Pres.'s Scholar, 1994-95, Outstanding Achievement awards U.S. Dept. Def., 1995, 96, 98, Nom. U.S. Asst. Sec. Def. (Spl. Ops.), 1986-87; chmn. U.S. Navy/ASEE Postdoctoral Selection Bd., 1988—, U.S. Nat. Inst. Sci. and Tech. Postdoctoral Selection Bd., 1989-91; mem. rev. panel U.S. Navy/ASEE Grad. Fellowship Program, 1990—; chmn., mem. NASA/ASEE program rev. bd., 1994-98; chmn. Internat. Conf. on Novel Laser Sources and Applications, San Jose, Calif., 1993, chmn. Battelle U.S. Dept. Def. Scholarship Prgram, 1994—; mem. Battelle Sci. Bd. for selection of grad. scholarship fellows, 1998-99; vis. scholar Stanford U., 1993—. Contbr. articles to profl. jours., chpts. to books; holder numerous patents in laser sci. and tech. Trustee Symphony Bd. Fargo-Moorhead Symphony Orch., 1978-80; pres. Franklin Elementary Sch. PTA, Pullman, 1973-74; pres. elect PTA coordinating council, City of Pullman, 1974-75; v.p. Horace Mann Elementary Sch. PTA, Fargo, 1975-76, pres., 1976-77; mem. PTA coordinating council, City of Fargo, 1976-77, N.D. State Bd. PTA; chmn. Univ., Coll. and Pub. Sch. Relations Bd., 1979-80; active Boy Scouts Am.; trustee Pullman Pub. Library, 1973-75, N.D. Symphony Orchestras Assn., 1978-80; mem. planning commn. City of Pullman, 1972-75; bd. dirs. Westminster Found., 1982-84. Recipient Outstanding Merit and Performance award San Jose State U., 1990, San Jose State Pres.'s Scholar award, 1994-95, Dist. Tchr./scholar award, 1996, 97, 99, Disting. Performance award in the field of lasers and electro-optics U. Chgo., 1995, Citation for Svc. and Achievement Dept. of Def., 1996, Award for Rsch. into night vision devices U.S. Army, 1997, Outstanding World Leadership in Sci. award Acad. Scis., Poland, 1998; grantee AEC-ERDA, 1963-75, NSF, 1966-72, 76-78, 92—, U.S. Army Rsch. Office, Durham, 1979-80, Am. Chem. Soc. Petroleum Rsch. Funds, 1979-80, Dept. Energy, 1979-84, Dept. Def., 1984—, Office Naval Rsch., 1987—, Office Naval Tech., 1988-93, Dept. Def., DARPA, 1998—; fellow NASA Ames Lab., 1993-95; vis. scholar Stanford U., 1993—. Fellow Am. Soc. Engring. Edn. (disting.), Am. Phys. Soc. (chmn. nat. mtg. sessions), Am. Acad. Spectral Scis.; mem. AAAS, IEEE (sec. lasers and electro-optics 1995-96), NSF (reviewer and panel mem. divsn. material sci. 1994—), N.Y. Acad. Scis., N.D. Acad. Sci., Oreg. Acad. Sci., Acad. Scis. of Ukraine, Nat. Acad. Scis. (com. on lasers and electro-optics), Coun. Colls. Arts and Scis., Optical Soc. No. Calif. (v.p. 1992, pres. 1993), Lasers and Electro-optics Soc. (mem. program com. nat. meeting 1995), Internat. Soc. Optical Engring. (bd. dirs. 1993), Phi Beta Kappa, Sigma Xi, Phi Kappa Phi, Sigma Pi Sigma, Phi Sigma Iota. Presbyterian (ruling elder). Clubs: Mason (Shriner), Kiwanian. Home: 5870 Meander Dr San Jose CA 95120-3839 E-mail: jbgruber@email.sjsu.edu

GRUDEN, JON, professional football coach; b. Sandusky, Ohio, Aug. 17, 1963; Student, U. Dayton. Asst. coach U. Tenn., 1986-87, U. Southeast Mo., 1988-89, San Francisco 49ers, 1990, U. Pitts., 1991, Green Bay Packers, 1992-94; offensive coord. Phila. Eagles, 1994-97; head coach Oakland Raiders, 1998—. Office: Oakland Raiders 1220 Harbor Bay Pkwy Alameda CA 94502-6570

GRUDZIELANEK, MARK JAMES, professional baseball player; b. Milw., June 30, 1970; Student, Trinidad (Colo.) Jr. Coll. Selected 11th round free-agt. draft Montreal Expos, 1994, shortstop, 3d baseman, 2d baseman, 1995-99; infielder L.A. Dodgers, 1999—. Selected Nat. League All-Star Team, 1996. Office: LA Dodgers Dodger Stadium 1000 Elysian Park Ave Los Angeles CA 90012-1112

GRUMBACH, MELVIN MALCOLM, physician, educator; b. N.Y.C., Dec. 21, 1925; s. Emanuel and Adele (Weil) G.; m. Madeleine F. Butt, Dec. 1, 1951; children: Ethan Malcolm, Kevin Lawrence, Anthony Havemeyer. Grad., Columbia U., 1945, MD, 1948; DM (honoris causa), U. Geneva, 1991; D honoris causa, U. René Descartes Paris V, 2000. Diplomate Am. Bd. Pediatrics, Am. Bd. Pediatric Endocrinology (com. mem. 1975-79). Resident in pediatrics Babies Hosp., Presbyn. Hosp., N.Y.C., 1949-51; vis. fellow Oak Ridge Inst. Nuclear Studies, 1952; postdoctoral fellow, asst. pediatrics Johns Hopkins Sch. Medicine, 1953-55; mem. faculty Columbia U. Coll. Physicians and Surgeons, N.Y.C., 1955-65, assoc. prof. pediatrics, 1961-65; asst. attending pediatrician to assoc. attending pediatrician, head pediatric endocrine div. and postdoctoral tng. program pediatric endocrinology Babies Hosp. and Vanderbilt Clin., Columbia-Presbyn. Med. Ctr., 1955-65; prof. pediatrics, chmn. dept. U. Calif. Sch. Medicine, San Francisco, 1966-86, first Edward B. Shaw prof. pediatrics, 1983-94, Edward B. Shaw prof. emeritus pediatrics (active), 1994—, acting dir. Lab. Molecular Endocrinology, 1987-89; dir. pediatric svc. U. Calif. Hosps., 1966-86. Vis. prof. Vanderbilt U., 1961, Emory U., 1962, U. Western Ont., 1962, U. N.C., 1963; Alpha Omega Alpha lectr. State U. N.Y. Downstate Med. Ctr., 1961, U. Calif. at San Francisco, 1966; univ. lectr. U. Zurich, 1971; Clausen vis. prof. U. Rochester, 1972; Richard E. Weitzman vis. prof. UCLA, 1981; Culpeper vis. prof. U. N.C., 1982; Frederick Moll lectr. U. Wash., 1979; Kenneth C. Haltalin vis. prof. U. Tex.-Dallas, 1983; Eley lectr. Harvard U. Med. Sch., Children's Med. Ctr., Boston, 1979; domestic lectr. Jour. Pediatrics Edn. Found., 1962, 79; Mali Dittman lectr. U. Chgo., 1980; Frederick M. Kenny lectr. Children's Hosp. Pitts., 1981; Winthrop award lectr. Am. Fertility Soc., 1981; Grover Powers lectr. Yale U., 1981; univ. lectr. Assembly of Profs., Coll. de France, Paris, 1979; Meredith Campbell lectr. Am. Urol. Assn., 1982; Prader lectr. Tel Aviv U. Med. Sch., 1982; Hopkins-Maryland lectr., 1983; Felton Bequests prof. Royal Childrens Hosp., Melbourne, 1983; Sandoz lectr. Can. Soc. Clin. Investigation, 1983; vis. prof. U. Minn., 1984, Royal Soc. Medicine, London, 1985, Joint Endocrine Societies of Great Britain, Oxford; John Lind lectr. Karolinska Inst., Stockholm, 1984; Bilderback lectr. Oreg. Health Scis. U., 1986; Mathew Steiner lectr. Northwestern U., Children's Meml. Hosp., 1989, Gurson lectr. U. Istanbul, 1991, Maranon Symposium lectr. Universidad Autonoma de Madrid, Spain, 1991, Judson Van Wyk lectr. U. N.C., 1993, James Etteldorf lectr. La Bonheur Children's Hosp. U. Tenn., 1994, lectr. Australasian Pediatric Endocrine Soc., 2000; U.S. Plenary lect. X Asia Oceania Congress Endocrinology, Beijing, 1994, VIII Asia Oceania Congress of Endocrinology, Bangkok, 1986; Robert N. Ganz lectr. Mass. Gen. Hosp., 1996, Brigham and Women's Hosp. and Children's Med. Ctr., Boston, 1999; cons. Letterman Gen. Hosp., 1966-94, Children's Hosp., San Francisco, U.S. Naval Hosp., Oakland, Calif., 1966-94, HEW, NIH, Nat. Bd. Med. Examiners, 1964-68; mem. human embryology and devel. study sect. NIH, 1962-66, endocrinology study sect., 1967-71; bd. sci. counselors Nat. Inst. Child Health and Human Devel., 1971-75; mem. gen. clin. rsch. ctrs. com., div. rsch. resources NIH, 1976-80; mem. com. for rev. NIH Clin. Ctr., 1984-85, nat. adv. coun. Nat. Inst. Child Health and Human Devel., NIH, 1991-96; mem. sci. adv. com., clin. rsch. adv. com. Nat. Found.-March of Dimes, 1969-94, chmn. clin. rsch. adv. com., 1974-82, Basil O'Connor starter scholar rsch. award comm., 1995-99; mem. awards com. Lita Annenberg Hazen Award for Excellence in Clin. Rsch., 1981-86; mem. sci. adv. bd. Scripps Clinic and Rsch. Found., 1977-78; mem. sci. adv. bd. Princesse Marie Christine Found., Brussels, 1981-91, U. Mich. Ctr. for Human Growth and Devel., 1982-89; mem. adv. bd. Nat. Pituitary Agy., 1965-69, NIH Evaluation of Endocrinology and Metabolic Diseases, 1977-79; mem. sci. adv. bd. U. Colo. Health Scis. Barbara Davis Ctr., 1986-93; Dean's Bd. of Vis., Mt. Sinai Sch. of Medicine, 1986-87; mem. sci. adv. bd. Hosp. for Sick Children, Toronto, 1984-88, Children's Hosp. of Los Angeles, 1987-92; sci. and med. adv. bd. Whittier Inst. Diabetes and Endocrinology, 1987-92; mem. sci. adv. coun. Cin. Children's Hosp. Rsch. Found., 1997-98; pres. bd. trustees Internat. Pediatric Rsch. Found., Inc., 1984-89; mem. sci. coun. Aid Pour la Recherche Medicale a l'enfance, Paris, 1981-89; del. to Chinese Acad. of Med. Scis., 1986; vis. prof. Peking Union Med. Coll. and Hosp., 1986; vis. prof. U. Hong Kong, 1986. Assoc. editor, mem. editorial bd. Jour. Clin. Endocrinology, 1957-70; adv. editor Jour. Pediatrics, 1966-73; editorial bd., 1973-79; assoc. editor Pediatric Rsch., 1970-84, Barnett Pediatrics, 14th-15th edits., Rudolph Pediatrics, 16th-21st edits., Current Topics in Experimental Endocrinology; mem. internat. editorial bd. pediatrics and pediatric surgery: Excerpta Medica, 1974—; editorial bd. Biology of Reproduction, 1968-70; editorial com. Endocrinologic Clinica Metabolismo, 1981—; editorial bd. Pediatrics in Rev., 1982-84, Jour. Endocrinol. Investigation, 1982-90, Endocrine Revs., 1984-88, Jour. Pediatric Endocrinology Metabolism, 1984—, Trends in Endocrinology, 1989—, Monographs on Endocrinology, Springer-Verlag, 1975-90, Clinical Pediatric Endocrinology (Jour. of the Japanese Soc. for Pediatric Endocrinology), 1992—, Jour. Endocrine Genetics, 1999—; contbr. articles to med. and sci. books and jours. Served to capt. M.C. USAF, 1951-53. Postdoctoral fellow Nat. Found. Infantile Paralysis, 1953-55; recipient Joseph M. Smith prize Columbia U., 1962; Career Scientist award Health Research Coun. City N.Y., 1961-66; Silver medal Bicentennial Columbia Coll. Physicians and Surgeons, 1967, Gold medal, 1988; Clin. Endocrinology Trust medal (U.K.), 1985, Centennial Medallist award Babies Hosp., Columbia-Presbyn. Med. Ctr., 1987, Borden award, Am. Acad. Pediatrics, 1971, Collège de France medal, 1979, Robert H. Williams Disting. Leadership award, Endocrine Soc., 1980, Winthrop award, Am. Fertility Soc., 1981, Fred Conrad Koch award Endocrine Soc., 1992, Lifetime Achievement award Am. Acad. Pediatrics, 1996, John Howland award Am. Pediatric Soc., 1997. Fellow Am. Acad. Arts and Scis., Am. Acad. Pediatrics, N.Y. Acad. Scis., AAAS; mem. NAS, Am. Pediatric Soc. (pres.-elect 1988-89, pres. 1989-90), Inst. Medicine of Nat. Acad. Scis. (com. on the Future of Pub. Health, 1985-87, com. to study AIDS rsch. program of NIH, 1989-91, com. on understanding biology of sex and gender differences 2000-2001), Assn. Med. Sch. Pediatric Dept. Chairmen (exec. coun. 1967-72, pres. 1973-75, task force on Pediatric Scientist Tng. Program, 1984-91, chmn. selection com. 1986-91), Am. Soc. Clin. Investigation, Assn. Am. Physicians, Am. Soc. Human Genetics, Harvey Soc., Lawson Wilkins Pediatric Endocrine Soc. (pres. 1975-76), Western Soc. Pediatric Rsch. (pres. 1978-79), Soc. Pediatric Rsch., Teratology Soc., Endocrine Soc. (coun. 1968-71, 80-83, pres. elect 1980-81, pres. 1981-82, Internat. Endocrine Soc. (del. to central com. 1976-92; exec. com. 1984-92, hon. pres. 2000—), Soc. Study Reprodn., European Soc. Pediatric Endocrinology (corr.), Société Française de Pediatrie (corr.), Internat. Neuroendocrinology Soc., Argentine Soc. Endocrinology and Metabolism (hon.), Can. Soc. Endocrinology and Metabolism (hon.), Japanese Soc. Pediatric Endocrinology (hon.), Western Assn. Physicians, Calif. Acad. Medicine, Western Soc. Clin. Rsch., Pacific Coast Fertility Soc. (hon.), Israel Endocrine Soc. (hon.), Sigma Xi, Alpha Omega Alpha. Club: University (N.Y.C.). Office: U Calif Sch Medicine Dept Pediatrics San Francisco CA 94143-0434 E-mail: grumbac@itsa.ucsf.edu

GRUSHOW, SANDY, broadcast executive; BA in Communication, UCLA, 1983. Former v.p. creative advtg. 20th Century Fox Film Corp.; sr. v.p. advtg. and promotion Fox Broadcasting Co., 1988-90, exec. v.p. programming and scheduling, 1990-91; exec. v.p. Fox Entertainment Group, 1991-92, pres., 1992-95, Tele-TV Media, 1995-97, Twentieth Century Fox TV, LA, 1997—; chmn. Fox Entertainment Group. Office: Fox Entertainment Group PO Box 900 Beverly Hills CA 90213-0900

GUADARRAMA, BELINDA, executive; B of Econs., Trinity U.; post-grad., U. Tex. Pres. CEO GC Micro Corp., 1986—. Chair NASA Minority Bus. Resource Adv. Com., 1997-99. Recipient Adminstrs. Excellence award U.S. Small Bus. Adminstrn., 1997; named 1 of 4 Women Who Could Be Pres., LLWV, San Francisco, 1998, U.S. Dept. Commerce NAt. Minority Female Entrepreneur of Yr., 1997. Mem. Hispanic Bus. CEO Roundtable, Calif. Hispanic C. of C. (Outstanding Bus. Mem. of Yr. award 1997). Office: GC Micro 25 Leveroni Ct Novato CA 94949-5726

GUALANDRIS, FABIO LUIGI, company executive; b. Bergamo, Lombardia, Italy, Mar. 9, 1959; s. Angelo and Lory (Bertozzi) G.; m. Lucia Riceputi, Sept. 23, 1986 (div. 1992); m. Paola Luisa Cagnoni, June 25, 1992. Dottore in Fiscia, U. Milan, Italy, 1983. Scientist Ctrl. R&D SGS-Thomson, Milan, 1984-87, engr. mgr., 1987-89, mfg. mgr., 1989-91, ops. mgr., 1991-96; automotive dir. STM, 1996-97; pres. and CEO Semitool, Inc., Kalispell, Mont., 1998—. Rschr. CNR, Milan, 1983. Patentee in field; contbr. articles to profl. jours. Mem. IEEE. Avocations: playing the flute, horseback riding, climbing, gardening, photography. Home: Residenza Delle Botteghe 20090 Milano Segrate Italy Office: Semitool Inc 655 W Reserve Dr Kalispell MT 59901-2127

GUAY, GORDON HAY, federal agency administrator, marketing educator, consultant; b. Hong Kong, Aug. 1, 1948; came to U.S., 1956; s. Daniel Bock and Ping Gin (Ong) G. AA, Sacramento City Coll., 1974; BS, Calif. State U., Sacramento, 1976, MBA, 1977; PhD, U. So. Calif., 1981. Mgmt. assoc. U.S. Postal Svc., Sacramento, 1980-82, br. mgr., 1982-83, fin. mgr., 1983-84, mgr. quality control, 1984-86, mgr. tech. sales and svcs. divsn., 1986-91, dir. mktg. and comm., 1991-95, postmaster, 1996—. Assoc. prof. bus. adminstrn., mktg. and mgmt. Calif. State U., Sacramento, 1981-85; prof. mktg. Nat. U., San Diego, 1984—; pres. Gordon Guay and Assocs., Sacramento, 1979—; cons. Mgmt. Cons. Assocs., Sacramento, 1977-79. Author: Marketing: Issues and Perspectives, 1983; also articles to profl. jours. With U.S. Army, 1968-70. Recipient Patriotic Svc. award U.S. Treasury Dept., San Francisco, 1985. Fellow Acad. Mktg. Sci.; mem. NEA, AAUP, Am. Mgmt. Assn., Am. Mktg. Assn. (Outstanding Mktg. Educator award 1989), Am. Soc. Pub. Adminstrn., Soc. Advancement Mgmt. (Outstanding Mem. 1976), Assn. MBA Execs. Democrat. Avocations: teaching, golf, tennis, fishing, camping. E-mail: erudite@juno.com

GUBLER, DUANE J. research scientist, administrator; b. Santa Clara, Utah, June 4, 1939; s. June and Thelma (Whipple) G.; m. Bobbie J. Carroll, Mar. 1, 1958; children: Justin Chase, Stuart Jefferson. BS, Utah State U., 1963; MS, U. Hawaii, 1965; ScD, Johns Hopkins U., 1969; AS, So. Utah State U., 1962, DSc (hon.), 1988. Asst. prof. pathobiology Sch. Hygiene Johns Hopkins U., Balt. and Calcutta, 1969-71; assoc. prof. tropical medicine Sch. Medicine U. Hawaii, Honolulu, 1971-75; head virology dept. Naval Med. Rsch. Unit Number 2, Jakarta, Indonesia, 1975-78; assoc. prof. entomology and microbiology U. Ill., Urbana, 1978-79; rsch. microbiologist divsn. vector-borne viral diseases Ctrs. for Disease Control and Prevention, Fort Collins, Colo., 1980-81, dir. San Juan (P.R.) Labs., 1981-89, dir. divsn. vector-borne infectious diseases Colo., 1989—. Cons. NRC, 1972, South Pacific Commn., 1972-76, WHO, Geneva, 1974—, AID, Washington, 1977—, Pan Am. Health Orgn., 1981—, Internat. Devel. Rsch. Ctr., Ottawa, Can., 1977—, Rockefeller Found., N.Y.C., 1987—, numerous nat. ministries of health, 1972—; Bailey K. Ashford meml. lectr. U. P.R. Sch. Medicine, 1999. Contbr. numerous articles to profl. jours. Lt. USN, 1975-77; capt. USPHS. Recipient Commendation medal, 1984, Outstanding Svc. medal, 1988, Meritorious Svc. medal, 1991, Outstanding Unit citation, 1995, 98, 2000, Outstanding Alumni award for sci. and rsch. Johns Hopkins U. Sch. Pub. Health, 1997, Chuck Alexander Operational award La. Mosquito Control Assn., 1998, Disting. Svc. award Dept. HHS, 2001, Charles Shepard award in Sci., Ctr. for Disease Control, 2001; selected as one of 90 Illustrious Alumni in celebration of U. Hawaii's 90th year, 1997, Woodward Lectr. award USN Preventive Medicine Unit, 2000. Mem. AAAS, Am. Soc. Tropical Medicine (Charles Franklin Craig lectr. 1988, pres.-elect 1998, pres. 2000), Am. Soc. Parasitologists, Am. Mosquito Control Assn., Entomol. Soc. Am. (highlights in med. entomology lecture 1979, 95), Soc. Vector Ecologists, Infectious Disease Soc. Am., Rotary (Rotarian of Yr. San Juan chpt. 1986, Meritorious Svc. award Rotary Found., Evanston, Ill. 1990, Svc. Above Self award Fort Collins Club 1999). Home: 717 Dartmouth Trl Fort Collins CO 80525-1522 Office: USPHS Ctrs Disease Control & Prevention PO Box 2087 Fort Collins CO 80522-2087 E-mail: dgubler@cdc.gov

GUBLER, WALTER DOUGLAS, plant pathology educator; BS, So. Utah State Coll.; MS, U. Ark.; PhD, U. Calif., Davis. Prof. plant pathology U. Calif., Davis. Contbr. more than 85 articles to profl. jours. Mem. Am. Phytopathological Soc., Am. Soc. Enol. Vitie. Office: U Calif Dept Plant Pathology Davis CA 95616 E-mail: wdgubler@ucdavis.edu

GUDEA, DARLENE, publishing company executive; Group pub. Call Ctr./CRM group Advanstar Tech. Comms., Santa Ana, Calif., 2000—. Office: Advanstar Comms 201 Sandpointe Ave Ste 600 Santa Ana CA 92707-8700 Fax: 714-513-8640. E-mail: dgudea@advanstar.com

GUENTHER, HERB, state legislator, executive assistant; b. Mineola, Apr. 9, 1941; m. Sharon Guenther; children: Brandon, Chris, Cathy, D.J. AA, Glendale C.C., 1969; BS, Ariz. State U., 1971. With photogrammetry and mapping divsn. Ariz. Hwy. Dept.; with rsch. divsn. Ariz. Game and Fish Dept.; with U.S. Bur. Reclamation; exec. asst. Wellton Mohawk Irrigation and Drainage Dist.; commr. Ariz. Game and Fish Commn., 1994-99; mem. Ariz. Senate, Dist. 5, Phoenix, 1999—; mem. appropriations com., mem. transp. com.; mem. joint legis. audit com.; mem. govt. and environ. stewardship com. Active Yuma Dist. Adv. Coun., Bur. Land Mgmt.; mem. Yuma Clapper Rail Endangered Species Recovery Team, U.S. Dept. Interior, mem. Devil's Hole Pupfish Endangered Species Recovery Team, alt. Colorado River Fishes Recovery Team; bd. mem. Mohawk Valley Sch. Dist.; trustee Yuma Regional Med. Ctr.; dir. EXCEL Group, Inc., 1992-99. With USAF, 1963-67. Named Paul Harris fellow Rotary Internat., Legislator of Yr., Nat. Coun. Stae Legislatures, 1988, Water Statesmen of Yr., Agri-Bus. Coun., 1992, Legislator of Yr. Mem. Nat. Water Resource Assn., Coun. State Govts. (Western Legis. Conf. water policy com. chair 1987-90, vice-chair, 1990-91, chmn. 1991-92), Colorado River Water Users Assn. (Ariz. dir. 1992—, v.p. 1996-97, pres. 1998, 99), Antelope-Welton Rotary Club (pres. 1986). Democrat. Office: State Capitol Bldg 1700 W Washington St Ofc 314 Phoenix AZ 85007-2812 E-mail: hguenthe@azleg.state.az.us

GUERIN, CHARLES ALLAN, museum director, artist; b. San Francisco, Feb. 27, 1949; s. John Warren and Charlene (Roovaart) G.; m. Katherine Riccio. BFA, No. Ill. U., 1971, MA, 1973, MFA, 1974. Co-dir. Guerin Design Group, Colorado Springs, Colo., 1972-77; dir. exhbns. Colorado Springs Fine Arts Ctr., 1977-80, curator fine arts, 1980-86; dir. U. Wyo. Art Mus., Laramie, 1986—. Author catalogues including various Colorado Springs Fine Arts Ctr. catalogues; contbg. author The Encyclopedia of Crafts, 1974; exhbns. include Purdue U. West Lafayette, Ind., 1974, 76, DePauw U., Greencastle, Ind., 1976, Colorado Springs Fine Arts Ctr., 1977, Mus. of Fine Arts, Santa Fe, N.Mex., 1978, Wis. State U., Platteville, 1972, Suburban Fine Arts Ctr., Highland Park, Ill., 1974, Colo. Woodworking Invitational, Silver Plume, 1977, Colo. Craft Invitational, Arvada, 1981, Leslie Levy Gallery, Scottsdale, Ariz., 1983, Robischon Gallery, Denver, 1983, Adams State Coll., Alamosa, Colo., 1984, U. Wyo. Art Mus., 1986—, Elaine Horwitch Gallery, Scottsdale, 1990; represented in permanent collections Lloyds of London, Dallas, Art Inst. Chgo., Marriott Hotel, Albany, N.Y., Ill. State Mus., Springfield, U.S. West Corp., Denver, Thresholds, Chgo., others. Grantee Nat. Endowment for the Arts, Ill. Arts Council, 1973. Mem. Coll. Art Assn. Am., Am. Assn. Mus., Western Mus. Conf. Office: U Wyo Art Mus PO Box 3807 U Laramie WY 82071-3807

GUEST, CHRISTOPHER, actor, director, screenwriter; b. New York City, Feb. 5, 1948; m. Jamie Lee Curtis; 1 child. Grad., High Sch. Music and Art, N.Y.C.; student, Bard Coll., NYU. Appeared in Broadway plays Room Service (debut) 1970, Moonchildren, 1972; Off-Broadway plays include National Lampoon's Lemmings (also writer), 1973, East Lynne, 1975; films (actor) The Hospital, 1971, The Hot Rock, 1972, Death Wish, 1974, The Fortune, 1975, La Honte de la Jungle, 1975, Girlfriends, 1978, The Last Word, 1979, The Long Riders, 1980, The Missing Link, 1980, Heartbeeps, 1981, This is Spinal Tap, (also writer), 1984, Little Shop of Horrors, 1986, Beyond Therapy, 1987, The Princess Bride, 1987, Sticky Fingers, 1988, A Few Good Men, 1992, Small Soldiers (voice), 1998; film dir.; The Big Picture, 1989, Edwards and Hunt, 1997, Almost Heroes, 1998; film actor/dir.: Dogumentary, 2000; dir. tv movie: D.O.A., 1999; TV series: Saturday Night Live with Howard Cosell, 1975, Saturday Night Live, 1984-85; TV movies: It Happened One Christmas, 1977, Haywire, 1980, Million Dollar Infield, 1982, A Piano for Mrs. Cimino, 1982; TV specials: The Lily Tomlin Special (also writer, Emmy award 1976), 1975, Billion Dollar Bubble, 1977, How to Survive the 70's and Maybe even Bump into Happiness, 1978, Close Ties, 1983, Martin Short Concert for the North Americas, 1985, Billy Crystal-Don't Get me Started, 1986; TV director of Johnny Appleseed segment Tall Tales and Legends, The Attack of the 50 Foot Woman, 1993; actor, dir., composer, writer (film) Waiting for Guffman, 1996; albums: Six albums with National Lampoon, This is Spinal Tap, 1984, Break like the Wind (with Spinal Tap), 1992. Office: CU 8383 Wilshire Blvd Ste 850 Beverly Hills CA 90211-2420

GUGGENHIME, RICHARD JOHNSON, lawyer; b. San Francisco, Mar. 6, 1940; s. Richard E. and Charlotte G.; m. Emlen Hall, June 5, 1965 (div.); children: Andrew, Lisa, Molly; m. Judith Perry Swift, Oct. 3, 1992. AB in Polit. Sci. with distinction, Stanford U., 1961; JD, Harvard U., 1964. Bar: Calif. 1965, U.S. Dist. Ct. (no. dist.) Calif. 1965, U.S. Ct. Appeals (9th cir.) 1965. Assoc. Heller, Ehrman, White & McAuliffe, 1965-71, ptnr., 1972—. Spl. asst. to U.S. Senator Hugh Scott, 1964; bd. dirs. Comml. Bank of San Francisco, 1980-81, Global Savs. Bank, San Francisco, 1984-86, North Am. Trust Co., 1996-99. Mem. San Francisco Bd. Permit Appeals, 1978-86; bd. dirs. Marine World Africa USA, 1980-86; mem. San Francisco Fire Commn., 1986-88, Recreation and Parks Commn., 1988-92; chmn. bd. trustees San Francisco Univ. H.S., 1987-90; trustee St. Ignatius Prep. Sch., San Francisco, 1987-96; dir. Olympic Club, 2000—. Mem. Am. Coll. Probate Counsel, San Francisco Opera Assn. (bd. dirs.), Bohemian Club, Wine and Food Soc. Club, Olympic Club (dir. 1999—), Chevaliers du Tastevin Club (San Francisco), Thunderbird Country Club (Rancho Mirage, Calif.). Home: 2621 Larkin St San Francisco CA 94109-1512 Office: Heller Ehrman White & McAuliffe 333 Bush St San Francisco CA 94104-2806

GUICE, JOHN THOMPSON, retired career officer; b. Kosciusko, Miss., Nov. 5, 1923; s. Gustave Nathaniel and Anne Mae (McCool) G.; m. Charlotte Webb, Mar. 8, 1949; children— John Thompson, James G., Steven L., Thomas A., Joseph D. B.S. in Engring, U.S. Mil. Acad., 1947; M.S. in Internat. Relations, George Washington U., 1966; disting. grad., Air Command and Staff Coll., 1962, Air War Coll., 1966. Commd. 2d lt. U.S. Army, 1947; advanced through grades to maj. gen. USAF, 1974; tactical and interceptor pilot, 1947-55; officer Air N.G. and N.G., 1956—; dep. dir. Air N.G., 1974-77, dir., 1977-81, ret., 1981. Decorated Legion of Merit, Air Force D.S.M. Mem. Air Force Assn., N.G. Assn., Sigma Chi. Home: 4901 N Calle Luisa Tucson AZ 85718-4925

GUILBEAU, ERIC J. biomedical engineer, electrical engineer, educator; b. Tullos, La., June 5, 1944; BS, La. Tech. U., 1967, MS, 1968, PhD in Chem. Engring., 1971. Rsch. assoc. chem. engring. La. Tech. U., 1971-72, rsch. assoc. biomed. engring., 1972-73, from asst. to assoc. prof., 1973-77; prof. chem. and biomed. engring. Ariz. State U., Tempe, 1973-77, assoc. prof., 1977-81, prof. chem. and biomed. engring., 1981—, dir. bioengring., 1990—. Affiliate med. staff St. Joseph's Hosp., Phoenix, 1977. M. AICE, Am. Chem. Soc., Internat. Soc. Study Oxygen Transport to Tissue,

Biomed. Engring. Soc., Soc. Biomat. Achievements include research in biomedical engineering, development of transducers for measurement of cellular biological parameters, research in transport phenomena in physiological systems, investigation of myocardial protection techniques, development of pericardial substitutes. Office: Ariz State U Coll Engring ECG 202 Tempe AZ 85287

GUILD, CLARK JOSEPH, JR. lawyer; b. Yerington, Nev., May 14, 1921; s. Clark Joseph and Virginia Ellen (Carroll) G.; m. Elizabeth Ann Ashley, July 20, 1945 (div. 1977); children: Clark J. III, Jeffrey S., Daniel E. (dec.), Jann Cademartori. BA, U. Nev., 1943; JD, Georgetown U., 1948. Bar: Nev. 1948, D.C. 1948, U.S. Dist. Ct. (no. dist.) Nev. 1948, U.S. Ct. Appeals (D.C. cir.) 1948, U.S. Supreme Ct. 1959, U.S. Ct. Appeals (9th cir.) 1984. Ptnr. Guild, Hagen & Clark, Ltd., Reno, Nev., 1953-88, Guild, Russell, Gallgher & Fuller Ltd., Reno (formerly Guild, Hagen & Clark Ltd.), 1988—. Pres. YMCA, Reno, 1954, 64; regent U. Nev. System, 1972. Capt. inf. U.S. Army, 1942-46. Recipient Disting. Nevadan award U. Nev., 1989. Fellow Am. Coll. Trial Lawyers; mem. ABA, State Bar Nev., Clark County Bar Assn., Washoe County Bar Assn. (pres. 1959-60), Masons, Elks. Democrat. Episcopalian. Office: Guild Russell Gallagher & Fuller Ltd 100 W Liberty St Reno NV 89501-1962

GUILES, EDWIN A. utilities company executive; With Sempra Energy, 1972—, various mgmt. positions, sr. v.p. energy supply, 1993-97; sr. v.p. Enova Corp.; pres. San Diego Gas and Electric, 1998-2000; group pres. Sempra Energy, 2000—. Chmn. San Diego Gas and Electric, So. Calif. Gas. Co., 2000—. Office: Sempra Energy 101 Ash St San Diego CA 92101-3017

GUILFORD, ANDREW JOHN, lawyer; b. Santa Monica, Calif., Nov. 28, 1950; s. Howard Owens and Elsie Jennette (Hargreaves) G.; m. Loreen Mary Gogain, Dec. 22, 1973; children: Colleen Catherine, Amanda Joy. AB summa cum laude, UCLA, 1972, JD, 1975. Bar: Calif. 1975, U.S. Dist. Ct. (cen. dist.) Calif. 1976, U.S. Ct. Appeals (9th cir.) 1976, U.S. Supreme Ct. 1979, U.S. Dist. Ct. (so. dist.) Calif. 1981, U.S. Dist. Ct. (no. and ea. dists.) Calif. 1990. Assoc. Sheppard, Mullin, Richter & Hampton, L.A. and Orange County, Calif., 1975-82, ptnr. Orange County, 1983—. Lectr. The Rutter Group, Encino, Calif., 1983—, Continuing Edn. of the Bar, Berkeley, 1978—, Hastings Ctr. for Advocacy, San Francisco, 1988; judge pro tem, arbitrator Calif. Superior Ct., 1983—; mem. commn. future legal profession and state bar. Author UCLA Law Review, 1975. Mem. Amicus Publico, Santa Ana, Calif., 1986; bd. dirs. Constl. Rights Found., 1990, Pub. Law Ctr. Orange County, 1990—, Baroque Music Festival, 1992-96, NCCJ, 1995-99, UCLA Law Alumni Assn., 1992-95; subdeacon, warden, del. Episcopal Ch. Recipient resolution of commendation Calif. Assembly, Outstanding Svc. award Poverty Law Ctr., 1991; co-recipient President's Pro Bono award State Bar; Regents scholar U. Calif., Berkeley, 1968-72. Fellow Am. Coll. Trial Lawyers; mem. ABA, FBA, Assn. Bus. Trial Lawyers (founding officer Orange County chpt.), Am. Arbitration Assn. (arbitrator large complex case program 1993—), Calif. Bar Assn. (pres. 1999-2000, lectr. continuing edn. of bar 1978—, bd. govs. 1996-2000), Orange County Bar Assn. (bd. dirs. 1985-87, officer 1988-90, pres. 1991, chmn. bus. litigation sect. 1983, state bar conv. 1986, 87, law-motion com. 1982, standing com. trial ct. delay reduction 1987-93), 9th Cir. Jud. Conf. (rep. 1990-93, 99—), Phi Beta Kappa (sec.-treas. 1978-80, v.p. 1980-84), Pi Gamma Mu, Sigma Pi. Republican. Avocations: theater, photography, sports, gardening, poetry. Home: 23 Via Terracaleta Coto De Caza CA 92679-4016 Office: Sheppard Mullin Richter & Hampton 650 Town Center Dr Fl 4 Costa Mesa CA 92626-1993

GUILLEMIN, ROGER C. L. physiologist; b. Dijon, France, Jan. 11, 1924; came to U.S., 1953, naturalized, 1963; s. Raymond and Blanche (Rigollot) G.; m. Lucienne Jeanne Billard, Mar. 22, 1951; children: Chantal, Francois, Claire, Helene, Elizabeth, Cecile. B.A., U. Dijon, 1941, B.Sc., 1942; M.D., Faculty of Medicine, Lyons, France, 1949; Ph.D., U. Montreal, 1953; Ph.D. (hon.), U. Rochester, 1976, U. Chgo., 1977, Baylor Coll. Medicine, 1978, U. Ulm, Germany, 1978, U. Dijon, France, 1978, Free U. Brussels, , 1979, U. Montreal, 1979, U. Man., Can, 1984, U. Turin, Italy, 1985, Kyung Hee U., Korea, 1986, U. Paris, Paris, 1986, U. Barcelona, Spain, 1988, U. Madrid, , 1988, McGill U., Montreal, Can., 1988, U. Claude Bernard, Lyon, France, 1989, Laval U., Quebec, Can., 1996, Sherbrooke U., Quebec, 1997, U. Franche-Comté, France, 1999. Intern, resident univs. hosps., Dijon, 1949-51; asso. dir., asst. prof. Inst. Exptl. Medicine and Surgery, U. Montreal, 1951-53; asso. dir. dept. exptl. endocrinology Coll. de France, Paris, 1960-63; asst. prof. physiology Baylor Coll. Medicine, 1953-57, assoc. prof., 1957-63, prof., dir. labs. neuroendocrinology, 1963-70, adj. prof., 1970—; resident fellow, chmn. labs. neuroendocrinology Salk Inst., La Jolla, Calif., 1970-89, adj. rsch. prof., 1989-94; Disting. Scientist Whittier Inst., 1989-97, med. and sci. dir., 1993-94; adj. prof. medicine U. Calif., San Diego, 1995-97; disting. prof. Salk Inst., La Jolla, Calif., 1997—. Bd. dirs. ICN Pharms. Decorated chevalier Legion d'Honneur (France), 1974, officer, 1984; recipient Gairdner Internat. award, 1974; U.S. Nat. Medal of Sci., 1977; co-recipient Nobel prize for medicine, 1977; recipient Lasker Found. award, 1975; Dickson prize in medicine, 1976; Passano award sci., 1976; Schmitt medal neurosci., 1977; Barren Gold medal, 1979; Dale medal Soc. for Endocrinology U.K., 1980, Ellen Browning Scripps Soc. medal Scripps Meml. Hosps. Found., 1988, Disting. Scientist award Nat. Diabetes Rsch. Coalition. Fellow AAAS; mem. NAS, Am. Physiol. Soc., Am. Peptide Soc. (hon.), Assn. Am.Physicians, Endocrine Soc. (pres. 1986), Soc. Exptl. Biology and Medicine, Internat. Brain Rsch. Orgn., Internat. Soc. Rsch. Biology Reprodn., Soc. Neuro-scis., Am. Acad. Arts and Scis., French Acad. Scis. (fgn. assoc.), Academie Internationale de Medecine (fgn. assoc.), Swedish Soc. Med. Scis. (hon.), Academie des Scis. (fgn. assoc.), Academie Royale de Medecine de Belgique (corr. fgn.), Internat. Soc. Neurosci. (charter), Western Soc. Clin. Rsch., Can. Soc. Endocrinal Metabolism, (hon.), Club of Rome. Office: The Salk Inst 10010 N Torrey Pines Rd La Jolla CA 92037-1099*

GUINASSO, VICTOR, delivery service executive; BS, U. of San Francisco, 1977. Exec. v.p., coo DHL Corp., 1982—; pres. & CEO DHL Airways, Redwood City, Calif., 1999-2001, chmn., 2000-2001; pres., CEO DHL Worldwide Express Inc., San Francisco, 2001—. Office: DHL Worldwide Express 50 California St San Francisco CA 94111*

GUINN, KENNY C. governor; b. Garland, Ark., Aug. 24, 1936; married BA, MA, Calif. State U.; EdD, Utah State U. Supt. Clark County Sch. Dist.; v.p. adminstrn. Nev. Savs. and Loan Assn. (PriMerit Bank), 1978-80, pres., chief operating officer, 1980-85, chief exec. officer, 1985-92, now chmn. bd.; pres. Southwest Gas Corp., 1987-88, chmn., chief exec. officer, 1988-93; chmn. bd. S.W. Gas Corp.; gov. State of Nev., Carson City, 1999—. Office: Governors Office 101 N Carson St Carson City NV 89701*

GUINN, STANLEY WILLIS, lawyer; b. Detroit, June 9, 1953; s. Willis Hampton and Virginia Mae (Pierson) G.; m. Patricia Shirley Newgord, June 13, 1981; children: Terri Lanae, Scott Stanley. BBA with high distinction, U. Mich., 1979, MBA with distinction, 1981; MS in Taxation with distinction, Walsh Coll., 1987; JD cum laude, U. Mich., 1992. CPA, Mich.; cert. mgmt. acct., Mich. Tax mgr. Coopers & Lybrand, Detroit, 1981-87; tax cons. Upjohn Co., Kalamazoo, 1987-89; litigation atty. Brobeck, Phleger & Harrison, 1992-94, Coughlan, Semmer & Lipman, San Diego, 1994-95; consumer fin. atty. Bank Am. NT & SA, San Francisco, 1995-98, GreenPoint Credit, LLC, San Diego, 1998—. Served with USN, 1974-77. Mem. AICPA, ABA, Calif. State Bar Assn., Inst. Cert. Mgmt. Acctg., Phi Kappa Phi, Beta Gamma Sigma, Beta Alpha Psi, Delta Mu Delta. Republican. Mem. Christian Ch. Avocations: tennis, racquetball, running. Home: 3125 Crystal Ct Escondido CA 92025-7763 Office: GreenPoint Credit 10089 Willow Creek Rd San Diego CA 92131-1603 E-mail: stan.guinn@greenpoint.com

GUINOUARD, DONALD EDGAR, psychologist; b. Bozeman, Mont., Mar. 31, 1929; s. Edgar Arthur and Venabell (Ford) G.; m. Irene M. Egeler, Mar. 30, 1951; children: Grant M., Philip A., Donna I. BS, Mont. State U., Bozeman, 1954; MS, Mont. State U., 1955; EdD, Wash. State U., Pullman, 1960; postdoctoral, Stanford U., 1965; grad., Indsl. Coll. of the Armed Forces, 1964, Air War Coll., 1976. Lic. psychologist, Ariz., counselor, Wash., Mont.; cert. secondary tchr. and sch. adminstr., Wash., Mont.; diplomate Am. Psychotherapy Assn., Am. Bd. Forensic Counselors, Am. Bd. Psychol. Specialities. Advanced through grades to col. USAFR, 1946-84, ret., 1984; dir. counseling Consol. Sch. Dist., Pullman, Wash., 1955-60; assoc. prof. Mont. State U., Bozeman, 1960-66; field selection officer Peace Corps, U.S., S.Am., 1962-68; prof. counseling, counseling psychologist Ariz. State U., Tempe, 1966-90; prof. emeritus, 1990; co-owner Forensic Cons. Assocs., Tempe, 1970—; pvt. practice, 1990—. Admissions liaison officer USAF Acad., Colo. Springs, 1967-84; assessment officer Fundamental Edn. Ctr. for the Devel. of the Latin American Community, Patzcuaro, Mex., 1963-64; expert witness on vocat. and psychol. disability for fed. and state cts. Contbr. articles to profl. jours. Mem. Ariz. Psychol. Assn., Am. Assn. Counseling & Devel., Reserve Officers Assn., Am. Psychotherapy Assn., Am. Coll. Forensic Examiners. Democrat. Methodist. Avocations: photography, woodworking, camping, fishing, silversmithing. Home and Office: 112 E Cairo Dr Tempe AZ 85282-3606 E-mail: donaldg516@aol.com

GUINOUARD, PHILIP ANDRE, restaurant executive; b. Pullman, Wash., Apr. 9, 1960; s. Donald Edgar and Irene (Egeler) G.; m. Miquela Teresa Padilla, Feb. 16, 1988; children: Mia, Angela, Alyssa. Student, Mesa (Ariz.) Community Coll. Dir. quality Garcia's, Phoenix, 1978-84; area spr. El Pollo Asado Inc., Phoenix, 1985-89; gen. mgr. Quinto Patio, Evergreen, Colo., 1989-90, Garcia's, Littleton, 1990—, Quila's Fresh Mexican Cantina, 1993-94; field tng. mgr. Internat. House of Pancakes, 1994-95; pres., CEO Sub & Munch, 1995-2000; pres. S.W. Automated Payment Svc. LLC, 1997—. Mem. Tempe (Ariz.) C. of C. Mem. Colo. Restaurant Assn., Income Builders Internat. (life), Tempe (Ariz.) C. of C., Better Bus. Bureau. Avocations: sports, photography. Home: 1714 W Manor St Chandler AZ 85224-5105 E-mail: pguinouard@uswest.net, phil@allpaymentsolutions.com

GUIRE, RONALD W. electronics company executive; Exec. v.p., CFO, bd. dirs. Exar Corp., Fremont, Calif. Chmn. bd. dirs. XeTel Corp., Austin, Tex. Office: Exar Corp 48720 Kato Rd Fremont CA 94538

GUITTAR, LEE JOHN, retired newspaper executive; b. St. Louis, May 4, 1931; s. LeRoy and Edna Mae (Johnston) G.; m. Elizabeth Madden Shedrick, Aug. 23, 1980; children: David Lee, Stephen Joseph, Mitchell John, Jeanne Marie Kessler, Richard Laughran; step-children: Elisabeth F. Shedrick, Kathryn S. Shedrick, Daniel C. Shedrick. AB, Columbia U., 1953; postgrad., U. Mass., 1962; MA, Columbia U., 1993. With Gen. Electric Co., 1955-65, mgr. community and govt. relations programs, 1963-65; mgr. employee and pub. relations Tidewater Oil Co., N.Y.C., 1965-66; from personnel dir. to circulation dir. Miami (Fla.) Herald, 1967-71; v.p., bus. mgr. Detroit Free Press, 1972-74, v.p., gen. mgr., 1974-75, pres., dir., 1975-77; pub. Dallas Times Herald, 1977-80; Publisher The Denver Post, 1980-83; chmn. Denver Post, 1983; pres. U.S.A. Today, 1984-86; v.p. group exec. newspapers The Hearst Corp., N.Y.C., 1986-98; editor, pub. San Francisco Examiner, 1995-98, ret., 1998. Lt. (j.g.) USNR, 1953-55, Korea. Mem. Farm Neck Golf Club (Martha's Vineyard, Mass.), Phi Beta Kappa. Republican. Roman Catholic.

GULCHER, ROBERT HARRY, aircraft company executive; b. Columbus, Ohio, Aug. 26, 1925; s. Alban H. and Beatrice (Plohr) G.; m. Barbara Witherspoon, June, 1949 (div.); 1 child, Robert; m. Anne Cummings, Dec. 14, 1959 (dec.); children: Jeffrey, Donald; m. Suzanne K. Kane, Apr. 12,1969; children: Andrew, Kristin. B.S., U.S. Marine Acad., 1945; B.E.E., Ohio State U., 1950. Third asst. engr. Am. Petroleum Transp. Co., N.Y.C., 1945-46; engr. Capital Elevator & Mfg. Co., Columbus, Ohio, 1949-51, Columbus div. N. Am. Aviation, 1951-53, various mgmt. engring. positions, 1953-66; chief engr. Columbus div. Rockwell Internat., 1966-79, v.p. rsch. and engring. N.Am. aircraft ops. Calif., 1979-85, v.p. advanced programs N.Am. aircraft ops., 1985-87, v.p., program mgr. nat. aerospace plane, 1987-90, v.p. hypersonic programs Calif., 1990-91; retired, 1991; aerospace cons., 1992—. Trustee Little Co. of Mary Hosp. Found., 1992—, chmn. bd. trustees, 1996-97; trustee coun. LCMH Hosp., 1997—. Fellow AIAA, IEEE (sr. mem.); mem. Rotary Internat. Republican. Lutheran. E-mail: rgulcher@aol.com

GUMP, BARRY HEMPHILL, chemistry and food science educator; b. Columbus, Ohio, Nov. 12, 1940; BS, Ohio State Univ., 1962; PhD, Univ. Calif., 1966. Rsch. assoc. Bureau Sci., Food & Drug Adminstrn., Washington, 1966-67; asst. prof. to assoc. prof. Calif. State Univ., 1967-74, prof. chemistry, 1974—, prof. enol., 1981—. Vis. scientist Bioorg. Standards Sec. Analysis Divsn., Nat. Inst. Sci. and Tech., 1974-76; Fulbright lectr. U. Repub. Montivideo, Uruguay, 1983; assoc. referee for sulfur dioxide in wine, AOAC, 1986. Mem. Am. Chem. Soc., Am. Soc. Enology and Viticulture. Achievements include research separation methods in chemistry, especially chromatographic methods; analytical methods development, trace components in foods and wine; characterization of grape juice concentrates. Office: Calif State U Fresno Dept Chemistry Fresno CA 93740-8034 E-mail: barryg@csufresno.edu

GUMPEL, GLENN J. association executive; Pres. internat. and global bus. affairs Universal Studios Recreation Group, Universal City, Calif.; pres. Internat. Global Affairs; exec. v.p., chief adminstrv. officer MCA Recreation divsn. Universal Studios Recreation Group. Mem. Dirs. Guild Am. Office: Universal Studios Recreation Group Universal City Plaza LRW 11 Universal City CA 91608

GUND, GEORGE, III, financier, professional sports team executive; b. Cleve., May 7, 1937; s. George and Jessica (Roesler) G.; m. Mary Theo Feld, Aug. 13, 1966; children: George, Gregory. Student, Western Res. U., Menlo (Calif.) Sch. Bus. Engaged in personal investments, San Francisco, 1967—; cattle ranching Lee, Nev., 1967—; partner Calif. Seals, San Francisco, 1976-77; pres. Ohio Barons, Inc., Richfield, 1977-78; chmn. bd. Northstar Fin. Corp., Bloomington, Minn., from 1978; formerly chmn. bd. Minn. North Stars, Bloomington; chmn., co-owner San Jose Sharks, NHL, San Jose, CA, 1991—; co-owner Cleve. Cavaliers; film prodr. Caipirinha Prodns., San Francisco. Dir. Ameritrust Cleve., vice chmn. Gund Investment Corp., Princeton, N.J.; chmn. North Stars Met Center Mgmt. Corp., Bloomington; v.p. hockey Sun Valley Ice Skating, Inc., Idaho Chmn. San Francisco Internat. Film Festival, 1973— ; mem. sponsors council Project for Population Action; adv. council Sierra Club Found.; mem. internat. council Mus. Modern Art, N.Y.C.; collectors com. Nat. Gallery Art; bd. dirs. Calif. Theatre Found., Bay Area Ednl. TV Assn., San Francisco Mus. Art, Cleve. Health Museum, George Gund Found., Cleve. Internat. Film Festival, Sun Valley Center Arts and Humanities, U. Nev. Reno Found., Sundance Inst. Served with USMCR, 1955-58. Clubs: Calif. Tennis (San Francisco), University (San Francisco), Olympic (San Francisco); Union (Cleve.), Cleve. Athletic (Cleve.), Kirkland Country (Cleve.), Rowfant (Cleve.); Ranier (Seattle). Office: 39 Mesa St Ste 300 San Francisco CA 94129-1019

GUNDERSEN, WAYNE CAMPBELL, management consultant, oil and gas consultant; b. Elgin, Ill., May 27, 1936; s. LeRoy Arthur and Jean Ellen (Campbell) G.; m. Gail Andrews, Mar. 21, 1959; children: Thomas Dexter, Lori Ann, Kathy Lee. BS, U. Nebr., 1959, MS, 1961. Advisor fgn. ops. Standard Oil of Calif., San Francisco, 1974-76; asst. to v.p. Chevron Overseas Petroleum, San Francisco, 1976-80; dir. oil and gas Kaiser Aluminum & Chem. Corp., Oakland, Calif., 1980-81; v.p., gen. mgr. Kaiser Energy, Inc., Oakland, 1983-85, pres., 1985-87; v.p. Kaiser Aluminum and Chem. Corp., Oakland, 1983-87; pres. Kaiser Aluminum Exploration Co., Oakland, Kaiser Exploration and Mining Co., Oakland, 1985-87; cons. in oil and gas., 1987—. Chmn. bd., chief exec. officer The Petroleum Synergy Group, Inc., 1988—; mem. geology adv. bd. U. Nebr., Lincoln, 1984-87. Co-authored articles in field. Pres. Parents Club Foothill Sch., Walnut Creek, Calif., 1978-79. Named Man-of-Yr., New Orleans Jaycees, 1973; Sinclair fellow, 1960-61. Mem. Am. Assn. Petroleum Geologists. Republican. Methodist. E-mail: renooilman@aol.com

GUNDERSON, CLEON HENRY, management consultant corporation executive; b. Great Falls, Mont., June 5, 1932; s. Leon H. and Mona (Emmett) G.; m. Virginia Ellen Hudson, Aug. 26, 1972; children: Craig H., Robert S., Laura E. BS, Inst. Tech., Dayton, Ohio, 1971, Mont. State U., , 1957; MAPA, U. Okla., 1975. Communications engr. Mountain States Tel & Tel, Helena, Mont., 1953-54; aerospace engr. Boeing Co., Seattle, 1957-58; commd. 2d lt. USAF, 1958, advanced to col., 1974, ret., 1976; pres. Precision Prodn. & Engring., Walla Walla, Wash., 1976-79, Western Skies Energy Systems, Spokane, 1979-88, Computer Central, Olympia, 1988-90, C.H. Gunderson & Assocs., Littlerock, 1990—. Mem. Am. Inst. Elec. Engrs., Seattle, 1957-60, Am. Inst. Indsl. Engrs., Spokane, 1982-85. Inventor heatexchange solar panels, comml. solar panels. Past pres. Tumwater Liions Club. Decorated Silver Stars, Disting. Flying Crosses, Purple Heart, Air medals. Mem. Soc. Mfg. Engrs. (sr. mem.), Soc. Mil. Engrs., Nat. Assn. Small Businesses, Toastmasters Internat., Walla Walla C. of C., Canto Blanco Gun Club (Madrid, v.p. 1973-75, Scott Air Force Base Gun Club (v.p. 1975-76), Spokane Gun Club, Evergreen Gun Club (Littlerock). Republican. Avocations: hunting, fishing, competitive shooting. Home: 7136 Holmes Island Rd SE Olympia WA 98503-3436 Office: C H Gunderson & Assocs PO Box 246 Littlerock WA 98556-0246 E-mail: lvgunder@juno.com

GUNDERSON, ELMER MILLARD, state supreme court justice, law educator; b. Mpls., Aug. 9, 1929; s. Elmer Peter and Carmaleta (Oliver) G.; m. Lupe Gomez, Dec. 29, 1967; 1 son, John Randolph. Student, U. Minn., U. Omaha, 1948-53; LL.B., Creighton U., 1956; LL.M., U. Va., 1982; LL.D., Calif. Western Sch. Law; student appellate judges seminar, N.Y. U., 1971; LL.D., U. Pacific. Bar: Nebr. 1956, Nev. 1958. Atty.-adviser FTC, 1956-57; pvt. practice Las Vegas, 1958-71; justice Nev. Supreme Ct., 1971-89, now sr. justice. Instr. bus. law So. regional div. U. Nev.; lectr., author bulls. felony crimes for Clark County Sheriff's Dept.; counsel Sheriff's Protective Assn.; mem. legal staff Clark Council Civil Def. Agy.; legal counsel Nev. Jaycees. Compiler, annotator: Omaha Home Rule Charter; project coordinator: Jud. Orientation Manual, 1974. Chmn. Clark County Child Welfare Bd., Nev. central chpt. Nat. Multiple Sclerosis Soc.; hon. dir. Spring Mountain Youth Camp. Served with U.S. Army. Recipient A.J.S. Herbert Harley award Mem. Am., Nebr., Nev. bar assns.; Mem. Inst. Jud. Adminstrn., Am. Law Inst., Am. Trial Lawyers Assn., Am. Judicature Soc., Phi Alpha Delta, Alpha Sigma Nu. Office: Nev Supreme Ct 100 N Carson St Carson City NV 89701-4717

GUNDY-BURLET, KAREN, research scientist; B of Engring., U. Calif., Berkeley; M of Aeronautical Engring., PhD, Stanford U. Rsch. scientist, computational fluid dynamics NASA Ames Rsch. Ctr., Moffett Field, Calif. Sponsor high sch. students Space Biology Program. Fellow Stanford U. Office: NASA Ames Rsch Ctr Moffett Field CA 94035

GUNN, GILES BUCKINGHAM, English educator, religion educator; b. Evanston, Ill., Jan. 9, 1938; s. Buckingham Willcox and Janet (Fargo) G.; m. Janet Mears Varner, Dec. 29, 1969 (div. July 1983); 1 child, Adam Buckingham; m. Deborah Rose Sills, July 9, 1983; 1 child, Abigail Rose. BA, Amherst Coll., 1959; student, Episc. Theol. Sch., Cambridge, Mass., 1959-60; MA, U. Chgo., 1963, PhD, 1967. Prof. religion and lit. U. Chgo., 1966-74; prof. religion and am. studies U. N.C., Chapel Hill, 1974-85; prof. English and Religion U. Fla., 1984-85; prof. English U. Calif., Santa Barbara, 1985—, chmn. English dept., 1993-97, chmn. global and internat. studies, 1998—. Vis. asst. prof. religion Stanford U., Palo Alto, Calif., 1973; Benedict Disting. vis. prof. religion Carleton Coll., Northfield, Minn., 1977; William R. Kenan Disting. vis. prof. humanities Coll. William and Mary, Williamsburg, Va., 1983-84; Humanities Disting. vis. prof. U. Colo., 1989; Eric Yoegelin Disting. prof. Am. Studies, U. Munich, 1994-95; dir. NEH summer sems. for coll. and univ. tchrs., 1979, 81, 85, 94, for sch. tchrs., 1987, 88, 89, 91; cons. Libr. of Am. Author: F.O. Matthiessen, The Critical Achievement, 1975, The Interpretation of Otherness: Literature, Religion and the American Imagination, 1979, The Culture of Criticism and The Criticism of Culture, 1987, Thinking Across the American Grain: Ideology, Intellect, and the New Pragmatism, 1992, Beyond Solidarity: Pragmatism and Difference in a Globalised World, 2001; editor: Literature and Religion, 1971, Henry James, Senior: A Selection of His Writings, 1974, New World Metaphysics: Readings on the Religious Meaning of the American Experience, 1981, The Bible and American Arts and Letters, 1983, Church, State, and American Culture, 1984, Early American Writing, 1994, William James, Pragmatism and Other Writings, 2000; co-editor: Redrawing the Boundaries: The Transformation of English and American Literary Studies, 1992; contbr. numerous articles to profl. jours. Bd. dirs. Fund for Santa Barbara. Edward John Noble Leadership grantee, 1959-63; Amherst-Doshisha fellow, Kyoto, Japan, 1960-61, Kent fellow, Danforth Found., 1963-65, Guggenheim fellow, 1978-79, Nat. Endowment for Humanities fellow, 1990, U. Calif. Pres.'s Rsch. fellow, 1990; Phi Beta Kappa vis. scholar, 2000-01. Mem. MLA, Am. Acad. Religion (dir. research and pubs. 1974-77), Am. Studies Assn., Soc. Religion, Arts and Contemporary Culture, Soc. Am. Phil., Nat. Critics Book Circle. Democrat. Avocations: walking, motorcycling, traveling. Home: 2744 Macadamia Ln Montecito CA 93108-1658 Office: U Calif Dept English Santa Barbara CA 93106

GUNSUL, BROOKS R. W. architect; b. Seattle, Aug. 7, 1928; s. Frank Justus and Phyllis (Webster) G.; m. Marilyn Thompson, Aug. 26, 1950; children: Robin, Karen, David, Jana. B.S. in Archtl. Engring., Wash. State U., 1952. Registered architect, Oreg., Wash., Ill., N.Y. Architect Stewart & Richardson architect, Portland, 1952-57, Scott & Payne, Portland, 1957-59, Wolff & Zimmer, 1959-65; ptnr. Wolff, Zimmer Gunsul. Frasca, Portland, 1966-77, Zimmer Gunsul Frasca, Portland, 1977—, Seattle, 1987—, L.A., 1988—. Mem. adv. com. Wash. State U. Dept. Architecture, Pullman, 1983-93, found. adv. bd., 1994-96; dir., founder Architecture Found., Portland, 1980-88; trustee Wash. State U. Found. Contbr. articles to profl. jours. Chmn. adv. com. Oreg. Maritime Ctr. and Mus.; trustee Wash. State U. Found. With U.S. Army, 1946-47. Recipient Wash. State U. Achievement award, 1991. Fellow AIA (Firm of Yr. award 1991), Portland Yacht Club, Multnomah Athletic Club. Office: Zimmer Gunsul Frasca Partnership 320 SW Oak St Ste 500 Portland OR 97204-2737

GUNTHER, GERALD, lawyer, educator; b. Usingen, Germany, May 26, 1927; came to U.S., 1938, naturalized, 1944; s. Otto and Minna (Floersheim) Gutenstein; m. Barbara Kelsky, June 22, 1949; children: Daniel Jay, Andrew James. BA, Bklyn. Coll., 1949; MA, Columbia, 1950; LLB, Harvard, 1953; LLD (hon.), Ill. Inst. Tech., 1987, Bklyn. Law Sch., 1990, Bklyn. Coll. of CUNY, 1990, Duquesne U., 1995, Valparaiso U., 1996. Bar: N.Y. 1955. Law clk. Judge Learned Hand, 1953-54, Chief Justice Earl Warren, 1954-55; assoc. Cleary, Gottlieb, Friendly & Hamilton, N.Y.C., 1955-56; assoc. prof. law Columbia U., N.Y.C., 1956-59, prof., 1959-62; prof. law Stanford U., 1962-72, Wm. Nelson Cromwell prof., 1972-95, prof. emeritus, 1995—; lectr. polit. sci. Bklyn. Coll., 1949-50. Author: John Marshall's Defense of McCulloch versus Maryland, 1969, (with K.M. Sullivan) Constitutional Law, 14th edit., 2001, Learned Hand: The Man and the Judge, 1994, 95, (with K.M. Sullivan) First Amendment Law, 1999; mem. editl. bd. Found. Press, 1972—, Stanford Univ. Press, 1983-86; mem., Overseers' Com. to visit The Harvard Law Sch., 1974-80, 1995-2001; mem. adv. bd. and editl. bd. Ency. of Am. Constn., 1983-86; contbr. articles to profl. jours. Recipient Disting. Alumnus award Bklyn. Coll., 1961, Learned Hand medal for excellence in fed. jurisprudence Fed. Bar Coun., 1988, Richard J. Maloney prize for disting. contbns. to legal edn. Bklyn. Law Sch., 1990, Erwin N. Griswold Triennial prize Supreme Ct. Hist. Soc., 1995, Bernard Witkin medal State Bar Calif., 1995, Triennial award (for Hand biography) Order of the Coif, 1999; Guggenheim fellow, 1962-63; Ctr. Advanced Study in Behavioral Scis. fellow, 1969-70; Fulbright-Hays lectr. Ghana, 1970; NEH fellow, 1980-81, 85-86. Fellow AAAS; mem. Am. Philos. Soc., Am. Law Inst., Am. Hist. Assn. (mem. com. Littleton-Griswold Fund, 1968-73), U.S. Assn. Constnl. Law (bd. dirs. 1997—). Office: Stanford U Law Sch Bldg Lawsh 559 Nathan Abbott Way Stanford CA 94305-8610 E-mail: ggunther@Stanford.edu

GUNTHEROTH, WARREN GADEN, pediatrician, educator; b. Hominy, Okla., July 27, 1927; s. Harry William and Callie (Cornett) G.; m. Ethel Haglund, July 3, 1954; children: Kurt, Karl, Sten. M.D., Harvard U., 1952. Diplomate: Am. Bd. Pediatrics, Am. Bd. Pediatric Cardiology, Nat. Bd. Med. Examiners. Intern Peter Bent Brigham Hosp., Boston, 1952-53; fellow in cardiology Children's Hosp., Boston, 1953-55, resident in pediatrics, 1955-56; rsch. fellow physiology and biophysics U. Wash. Med. Sch., Seattle, 1957-58, mem. faculty, 1958—, prof. pediatrics, 1969—, head divsn. pediatric cardiology, 1964-91. Author: Pediatric Electrocardiography, 1965, How to Read Pediatric ECGs, 1981, 3d edit., 1992, Crib Death (Sudden Infant Death Syndrome), 1982, 3d edit., 1995, Climbing With Sasha, a Washington Husky, 1995; also numerous articles; mem. editl. bd. Am. Heart Jour., 1977-80, Circulation, 1980-83, Am. Jour. Noninvasive Cardiology, 1985-94, Jour. Am. Coll. Cardiology, 1988-94, Am. Jour. Cardiology, Jour. Noninvasive Cardiology, 1996-00; sect. editor Practice of Pediatrics, 1979-87. Served with USPHS, 1950-51. Spl. research fellow NIH, 1967. Mem. Soc. Pediatric Rsch., Biomed. Enging. Soc. (charter), Am. Heart Assn. (chmn. N.W. regional med. rsch. adv. com. 1978-80), Cardiovascular System Dynamics Soc. (charter), Am. Coll. Cardiology. Democrat. Home: 13201 42nd Ave NE Seattle WA 98125-4626 Office: U Wash Med Sch Dept Pediatrics PO Box 356320 Seattle WA 98195-6320 E-mail: wgg@u.washington.edu

GUNTY, CHRISTOPHER JAMES, newspaper editor; b. Hometown, Ill., Oct. 13, 1959; s. Harold Paul and Therese Agnes (Kohs) G.; m. Nancy Louise Blanton, July 10, 1982; children: William, Amy, Timothy. BA, Loyola U., Chgo., 1981. Circulation mgr. The Chgo. Catholic, 1981-83, assoc. mnging. editor, 1983, mng. editor, 1983-85; editor, mng. editor The Catholic Sun, Phoenix, 1985-96; assoc. pub. The Cath. Sun, Phoenix, 1996—. Author: He Came to Touch Us, 1987; co-author videotape script The Pope in Arizona, 1987; contbg. author: (anthologies) Freedom of Journalist, 1990, Mission and Future of the Catholic Press, 1998; contbr. articles to spl. Catholic news svcs. as well as papers where employed. Mem. Fiesta Bowl Com., Phoenix, 1987-92; bd. dirs. Catholic Journalism Scholarship Fund, 1990—, pres., 1995-96, 99-2001. Named Honoree Summer U. Internat. Cath. Union of the Press, Switzerland, 1988. Mem. Cath. Press Assn. (bd. dirs. 1988-99, sec. 1990-92, v.p. 1994-96, pres. 1996-98, St. Francis de Sales award 2000), Assoc. Ch. Press, Ariz. Newspapers Assn., Soc. Profl. Journalists. Roman Catholic. Avocations: bicycling, sci. fiction. Office: The Catholic Sun 400 E Monroe St Phoenix AZ 85004-2336

GUPTA, KULDIP CHAND, electrical and computer engineering educator, researcher; b. Risalpur, India, Oct. 6, 1940; came to U.S., 1982; s. Chiranjiva Lal and Gauran (Agarwal) G.; m. Usha Agarwal, Apr. 4, 1971; children: Parul, Sandeep, Anjula. BSc, Punjab U., Chandigarh, India, 1958; BE, Indian Inst. Sci., Bangalore, India, 1961, ME, 1962; PhD, Birla Inst. Tech. Sci., Pilani, India, 1969. Asst. prof. Punjab Enging. Coll., Chandigarh, 1964-65, Birla Inst. Tech. and Sci., Pilani, 1968-69; asst. prof., then prof. Indian Inst. Tech., Kanpur, India, 1969-84; prof. U. Colo., Boulder, 1983—. Vis. assoc. prof. U. Waterloo, Ont., 1975-76, vis. prof. Swiss Fed. Tech. Inst., Lausanne, 1976, Zurich, 1979, Tech. I. Denmark, Lynby, 1976-77, U. Kans., Lawrence, 1982-83, Indian Inst. Sci., 1993-94; advisor, cons. UN Devel. Programme, People's Republic of China, 1987, India, 1990, 94-95; cons. UNIDO project, India, 1993, Indian Telephone Industries, 1993-94. Author: CAD of Microwave Circuits, 1981, Chinese transl., 1986, Russian transl., 1987, Microstrip Lines and Slotlines, 1979, 2d edit., 1996, Microwaves, 1979, Spanish transl., 1983; editor, author: Microwave Integrated Circuits, 1974, Microstrip Antenna Design, 1988, Analysis and Design of Planar Microwave Components, 1994; founding editor Internat. Jour. Microwave Millimeter-Wave Computer Aided Enging., 1991—; contbr. articles to profl. jours. and chpts. to books; patentee in field. Bd. dirs. Hindu U. of Am. Fellow IEEE (guest editor spl. issue IEEE Transactions on Microwave Theory and Tech. 1988), Instn. Electronics and Telecommunication Engrs. India (guest editor jour. July 1982) Hindu. Office: U Colo PO Box 425 Boulder CO 80309-0425

GUPTA, MADHU SUDAN, electrical engineering educator; b. Lucknow, India, June 13, 1945; came to U.S., 1966; s. Manohar Lal and Premvati Gupta; m. Vijaya Lakshmi Tayal, July 9, 1970; children: Jay Mohan, Vineet Mohan; m. Manorama Vyas, May 29, 1985. BS, Lucknow U., India, 1963; MS, Allahabad U., India, 1966, Fla. State U., , 1967; MA, U. Mich., 1968, PhD, 1972. Registered profl. engr., Ont. Asst. prof. elec. enging. Queen's U., Kingston, Ont., Can., 1972-73, MIT, Cambridge, 1973-78, assoc. prof. elec. enging., 1978-79, U. Ill., Chgo., 1979-84, prof. elec. enging., 1984-87, dir. grad. studies, 1980-83; vis. prof. elec. and computer enging. U. Calif., Santa Barbara, 1985-86; sr. staff engr. Hughes Aircraft Co., 1987-95; prof. elec. enging., chmn. dept. elec. enging. Fla. State U., Tallahassee, 1995-2000; prof. elec. enging., RF comm. sys. industry chair San Diego State U., 2000—; dir. Comm. Sys. and Signal Processing Inst., 2000—. Cons. Lincoln Lab. MIT, Lexington, 1976-79, Hughes Research Labs., Malibu, Calif., 1986-87. Editor: Electrical Noise, 1977, Teaching Engineering, 1987, Noise in Circuits and Systems, 1988; contbr. articles to profl. jours.; editor in chief IEEE Microwave & Guided Wave Letters, 1998-2000. Lilly fellow, 1974-75. Fellow IEEE; mem. IEEE Microwave Soc. (vice chmn. 1984-85, chmn. 1986-87). Achievements include patents in field. Office: San Diego State U Dept Elec Enging 5500 Campanile Dr San Diego CA 92182-1309 E-mail: m.gupta@ieee.org

GUPTA, SUDHIR, immunologist, educator; b. Bijnor, India, Apr. 14, 1944; came to U.S., 1971; s. Tej S. and Jagdishwari Gupta; m. Abha, Jan. 28, 1980; children: Ankmalika Abha, Saurabh Sudhir. MD, King George's Med. Coll., Lucknow, India, 1966, PhD, 1970. Diplomate Am. Bd. Allergy and Immunology, Am. Bd. Diagnostic Lab. Immunology, Clin. Immunology Bd., Royal Coll. Physicians and Surgeons Can. Intern King George's Med. Coll., Lucknow, 1966, resident in medicine, 1967-70; teaching faculty fellow dept. medicine Tufts U. Med. Sch., Boston, 1971-72; vis. fellow in medicine Columbia U., N.Y.C., 1972-74; rsch. fellow Sloan-Kettering Inst. Cancer Rsch., N.Y.C., 1974-76, asst. prof., 1976-78, assoc. prof., 1978-82; instr. Cornell U., N.Y.C., 1976-77, asst. prof., 1977-79, assoc. prof., 1979-82; prof. medicine U. Calif., Irvine, 1982—, prof. microbiology and molecular genetics, 1984—, prof. pathology, 1986—, prof. neurology, 1988—, vice chair Dept. Medicine, 1994—. Mem. adv. panel FDA, Washington, 1989—; sci. advisor Inst. Immunopathology, Kohn, Germany, 1990—; mem. allergy-immunology subcom. NIH, Bethesda, Md., 1985-89; vis. prof. Hematologic Rsch. Found., Roslyn, N.Y., 1992. Editor-in-chief Jour. Clin. Immunology, 1980—; editor: Immunology of Clinical and Experimental Diabetes, 1984, Mechanisms of Lymphocyte Activities and Immune Regulation I-VII, 1985-98, New Concepts in Immunbodeficiency Diseases, 1993, Multidrug Resistance in Cancer, 1996, Immunology of HIV Infections, 1996. Pres. Nargis Dutt Meml. Found., So. Calif., 1990; vice-chair AIDS Task Force, Orange County (Calif.) Med. Assn., 1987-95; mem. Indo-Am. Republican Club, Orange County, 1991—. Recipient Arthur Manzel Rsch. award R.A. Cooke Inst., N.Y.C., 1976, Outstanding Achievement award in med. scis. Nat. Fedn. Asian Indians in N.Am., 1986, Lifetime Achievement award Jeffrey Modell Found., N.Y.C., 1990, Disting. Scientists award Assn. Scientists Indian Origin in Am., 1994, Disting. Physician award Indian Med. Assn. Master ACP; fellow Royal Coll. Physicians and Surgeons Can., Am. Soc. Medicine (London); mem. Am. Assn. Immunologists. Achievements include description of the presence of K+ channels in human T cells, their role in T cell function and assn. with exptl. autoimmune diseases, reversal of multidrug resistance of cancer cells by cyclosporin A both in vitro and in vivo, described a new human intracisternal retrovirus associated with CD4+ cell deficiency without HIV infection; increased apoptosis in T cells in human aging. Office: U Calif Dept Medicine C240 Med Sci I Irvine CA 92697-0001 Fax: 949-824-4362. E-mail: sgupta@uci.edu

GUPTA, VINITA, communications executive; B Enging in electronics, U. Roorkee; MS in elec. enging., UCLA. Engr. GTE Lenkurt; enging. mgmt. Bell No. Rsch. Inc., 1978-85; chairperson Digital Link Corp., Sunnyvale, Calif., 1985—. Office: Quick Eagle Networks 217 Humboldt Ct Sunnyvale CA 94089-1300 Fax: 408-745-6250

GUPTA, YOGENDRA M. physicist, educator; b. New Delhi, July 24, 1949; came to U.S., 1968; s. Brij M. and Prabha (Garg) G.; m. Barbara MacKay, June 21, 1975; children: Anjuli Monica, Sonia Michelle. BS in Physics, Chemistry and Math., BITS, Pilani, India, 1966, MS in Physics, 1968; PhD in Physics, Wash. State U., 1972. Postdoctoral research assoc. Wash. State U. and Brown U., Providence, 1973-74; from physicist to sr. physicist SRI Internat., Menlo Park, Calif., 1975-81, cons., 1981—; from assoc. prof. to prof. Wash. State U., Pullman, 1981—; dir. Inst. for Shock Physics. Editor: Shock Waves in Condensed Matter, 1986; contbr. articles to profl. jours. Mem. AAAS, Am. Phys. Soc., Am. Acad. Mechanics, Phi Kappa Phi. Office: Wash State U Dept Physics Pullman WA 99164-0001 E-mail: ymgupta@wsu.edu

GURALNICK, MICHAEL J. medical research administrator; Dir. Child Development adn Mental Retardation Ctr., U Wash., Seattle, 1986—. Office: Ctr Human Devel & Disability Box 357920 Seattle WA 98195-7920

GURASH, JOHN THOMAS, insurance company executive; b. Oakland, Calif., Nov. 25, 1910; s. Nicholas and Katherine Restovic Gurash; 1 child John N. Student Loyola Univ. Sch. Law, 1934. With Pacific Employers Ins. Co., 1944—53; pres., organizer Meritplan Ins. Co., 1953—59; exec. vpres. Pacific Employers Ins. Co., 1959—60, pres., 1960—68, chmn. bd., 1968—76; vpres. Ins. Co. N. Am., 1966—70; exec. vpres. INA Corp., 1968 69, dir., 1968—69, chmn., 1969—74, pres., 1969—74, CEO, 1969—74, chmn., 1974—75, CEO, 1974—75, chmn. bd., 1975, chmn. exec. comt., 1975—79; chmn. bd. CertainTeed Corp. and Saint Gobain Corp. , 1978—92, chmn. emeritus, 1992—; chmn. Horace Mann Educators Corp., Springfield, Ill., 1989—96, chmn. emeritus, 1996—; dir. St. Gobain Corp., chmn. bd. dirs., 1991—92; trustee emeritus Occidental Col., Los Angeles; former trustee Orthopaedic Hosp., Los Angeles; dir. Weingart Found., bd. dirs. Insurance company executive; b. Oakland, Calif., Nov. 25, 1910; s. Nicholas and Katherine (Restovic) G.; student Loyola U. Sch. Law, Los Angeles, 1936, 38-39; m. Katherine Mills, Feb. 4, 1934; 1 child, John N. With Am. Surety Co. N.Y., 1930-44, with Pacific Employers Ins. Co., 1944-53; pres., organizer Meritplan Ins. Co., 1953-59; exec. v.p. Pacific Employers Ins. Co., 1959-60, pres., 1960-68, chmn., bd., 1968-76; v.p. Ins. Co. N. Am., 1966-70; exec. v.p., dir. INA Corp., 1968-69, chmn., pres., CEO, 1969-74, chmn., CEO, 1974-75, chmn. bd., 1975, chmn. exec. com., 1975-79; chmn. bd. CertainTeed Corp. and Saint Gobain Corp., 1978-92, chmn. emeritus, 1992—; chmn. Horace Mann Educators Corp., Springfield, Ill., 1989-96, chmn. emeritus, 1996—; dir. St. Gobain Corp., chmn. bd. dirs., 1991-92. Trustee emeritus Occidental Coll., L.A.; former trustee Orthopaedic Hosp., Los Angeles; dir. Weingart Found. Bd. dirs. Weingart Found. Office: 1000 Wilshire Blvd Ste 610 Los Angeles CA 90017-2463 E-mail: jtgurash@aol.com

GURFEIN, PETER J. lawyer; b. N.Y.C., Sept. 13, 1948; m. Pamela Hedin, June 23, 1976; children: Diana, William, Eva. BA, NYU, 1969; JD, George Washington U., 1973. Bar: N.Y. 1976, U.S. Supreme Ct. 1976, US. Dist. Ct. (so. and ea. dists.) N.Y. 1976, U.S. Ct. Appeals (2d cir.) 1979, Internat. Ct. Trade 1979, U.S. Ct. Appeals (9th cir.) 1986, Calif. 1986, U.S Dist. Ct. (no., ea., so. and cen. dists.) Calif. 1987, D.C. 1993. Project dir. Commn. on Correctional Facilities and Scs. ABA, Washington, 1973-76; asst. dist. atty., spl. narcotics prosecutor Dist. Atty.'s Office N.Y. County, N.Y.C., 1976-81; assoc. Zalkin, Rodin & Goodman, N.Y.C., 1981-83, Moses & Singer, N.Y.C., 1983-86; ptnr. Morrison & Foerster, San Francisco, 1986-92, Sonnenshein, Nath & Rosenthal, L.A. and San Francisco, 1993-2000; with Akin, Gump, Strauss, Hauer & Feld, LLP, L.A., 2001—. Editor-in-chief The Calif. Bankruptcy Jour., 1995-2000; contbr. articles to handbooks and profl. jours. Mem. Bar Assn. San Francisco (chmn. bankruptcy and comml. law sect. 1993), L.A. County Bar Assn.; dir. L.A. Bankruptcy Forum, 1995—. Office: Akin Gump Strauss Hauer & Feld LLP Ste 2400 2029 Century Park E Los Angeles CA 90067 E-mail: pgurfein@akingump.com

GURIAN, MAL, telecommunications executive; b. N.Y.C., Nov. 17, 1926; s. George Joseph and Rose (Graff) G.; m. Gloria Dickler; children: Randy Harlan, Nancy Ellen Newman. Ptnr. Mal Gurian Assocs., N.Y.C., 1946-77; v.p. Radio Telephone Corp., N.Y.C., 1960-83; sr. v.p. Aerotron, Inc., Raleigh, N.C., 1965-81; v.p. Oki Advanced Comm., Hackensack, N.J., 1981-84; pres. Oki Telecom, Fairlawn, 1984-88, Cartell, Inc., Romulus, Mich., 1988, Cellcom Cellular Corp., Fairfield, N.J., 1989-91; CEO Universal Cellular, Inc., Anaheim, Calif., 1992; chmn., CEO Global Link Comm., Inc., Irvine, 1993—; pres., CEO Authentix Network, Inc., Tucson, 1995-98, 99—, chmn., 1998-2001; pres., CEO SimplySay, LLC, Tucson, 2001—. Pres. Ea. Profl. Photographers Assn., N.Y.C., 1951-53; exec. advisor TRW Wireless Commn., Sunnyvale, Calif., 1994; advisor Sims Comms., Inc., Delray Beach, Fla., 1994-98; arbitrator Am. Arbitration Assn., 1994—; bd. dirs. Rangestar Internat., San Jose, Calif. Life mem. Old Tappan (N.J.) First Aid Corp., 1966—. Cpl. USMC, 1943-46. Decorated Air medal; recipient Alexander S. Popov Hon. Medal award St. Petersburg Electrotech. U., Russia, 1995. Fellow and life mem. Radio Club Am. (life mem., v.p. 1976-92, exec. v.p. 1993, pres. 1994, pres. emeritus 1995—, Spl. Svcs. award 1986, Sarnoff citation 1988, Fred Link award 1989); mem. Am. Assn. Pub. Safety Comm. Officers, Nat. Assn. Bus. and Ednl. Radio (bd. dirs. 1977-84, Chmn.'s award 1986).

GURNEY, DANIEL SEXTON, race car manufacturing company executive, racing team executive; b. L.I., Apr. 13, 1931; s. John R. and Roma (Sexton) G.; m. Evi B., July 7, 1969; children: Justin B., Alexander R.; children by previous marriage: John, Lyndee, Danny, Jimmy. Grad., Menlo Jr. Coll., 1951. Profl. race car driver, 1955-70; pres., owner Dan Gurney's All Am. Racers, Inc. (doing bus. as); Dan Gurney Eagle Racing Cars, U.S.A., Santa Ana, Calif., 1964-65; mgr. Eagle Racing Team (Indpls. 500 winners 1968, 73, 75, U.S. Auto Club Nat. Championship winners 1968, 74), Formula A Championship winners 1968, 69); TV sports commentator. Mem. Automobile Competition Com. for U.S.A.; car owner, builder Fed Ex Championship Series, Santa Ana, Calif. Served with U.S. Army, 1952-54, Korea. Recipient numerous racing awards including GTO driving championship Internat. Motor Sports Assn. (driver Chris Cord), 1987, GTO Mfrs.' championship Interrnat. Motor Sports Assn. (mfr. Toyota), 1987, Norelco Cup championship (driver Willy T. Ribbs), 1987, IMSA Camel GTP championship, 1992, 93, IMSA mfrs. championship for Toyota, 1992, 93. Mem. Screen Actors Guild, AFTRA, U.S. Auto Club, Sports Car Club Am., U.S. C. of C., Championship Auto Racing Teams, Inc., Soc. Automotive Engrs., Fedn. Internationale de L'Automobile, Internat. Motor Sports Assn. Clubs: Balboa Bay, Eagle.

GURNIS, MICHAEL CHRISTOPHER, geological sciences educator; b. Boston, Oct. 22, 1959; s. George Albert and Barbara (Dempsey) G. BS, U. Ariz., 1982; PhD, Australian Nat. U., Canberra, 1987. Rsch. fellow in geophysics Calif. Inst. Tech., Pasadena, 1986-88, assoc. prof. geophysics, 1994-96; asst. prof. geol. scis. U. Mich., Ann Arbor, 1988-93, assoc. prof., 1993—; asst. dir. Seismological Lab. Calif. Inst. Tech., Pasadena, 1995—, prof. geophysics, 1996—. Recipient Presdl. Young Investigator award NSF, 1989, fellowship David and Lucile Packard Found., 1991. Fellow Am. Geophys. Union (Macelwance medal 1993), Geol. Soc. Am. (sr., Donath medal 1993). Achievements include research in the linkage of sedimentary rocks deposited in the interiors of continents to geodynamic processes within the earth; global dynamics, mantle convection, plate tectonics, sea level changes, evolution of mantle and crust; computational and visual fluid mechanics. Office: Calif Inst Tech Seismol Lab-252-21 Pasadena CA 91125-0001

GUST, ANNE BALDWIN, lawyer; b. Grosse Pointe Farms, Mich., Mar. 15, 1958; d. Rockwell Thomas Jr. and Anne Elizabeth (Baldwin) G. BA, Stanford U., 1980; JD, U. Mich., 1983. Bar: Calif. 1983, U.S. Dist. Ct. (no. dist.) Calif. 1983, U.S. Ct. Appeals (9th cir.) 1983. Assoc. Orrick, Herrington & Sutcliffe, San Francisco, 1983-86, Brobeck, Phleger & Harrison, San Francisco & Palo Alto, Calif., 1986—. Contbr. articles to labor trade jours. Mem. ABA (labor subcom.), Calif. Bar Assn. Office: The Gap Inc 1 Harrison St San Francisco CA 94105

GUSTAFSON, ALICE FAIRLEIGH, lawyer; b. Houston, Dec. 1, 1946; d. William H. and Mary Davis (McCord) Bell; m. Charles R. Gustafson, May 30, 1971. BA in Econs., Wellesley (Mass.) Coll., 1968; JD, U. Puget Sound, 1976. Bar: Wash. 1976. Various positions U.S. Dept. HEW, various locations, 1968-75; assoc. Graham & Dunn, Seattle, 1977-83, ptnr., 1983—. Bd. dirs. King County Am. Cancer Soc., Seattle, 1983-85, Women & Bus., Inc., Seattle, 1984-87; mem. nominating com. YWCA Seattle-King County, 1985-88. Mem. ABA, Wash. State Bar Assn. (chair Bench-Bar-Press com. 1988-90), Seattle-King County Bar Assn. (trustee young lawyers divsn. 1980-83, treas. 1985-87), N.W. Comm. Lawyers, Met. Seattle Urban League (bd. dirs. 1991-93). Avocations: sailing, bicycling, skiing. Home: 13560 Riviera Pl NE Seattle WA 98125-3845 Office: Graham & Dunn 1420 5th Ave Fl 33 Seattle WA 98101-4087

GUSTAFSON, KIRK, performing company executive; Student, U. Colo.; D in Mus. Arts, U. Wash. Music dir. Grand Junction (Colo.) Symphony Orch., 1981—. Guest condr. Rogue Valley (S.D.) Symphony, Salt Lake Symphony, Boulder Philharmonic, Arapahoe Philharmonic, Arvada Chamber Orch., Colo. Festival Orch.; soloist various orchs.; lectr. Mesa State Coll. Boeing fellow U. Wash. Office: Grand Junction Symphony Orch PO Box 3039 Grand Junction CO 81502-3039

GUSTAFSON, RANDALL LEE, city manager; b. Sidney, Nebr., Nov. 11, 1947; s. Robert John and Hilda Lydia (Sims) G.; m. Cynthia Ann Taylor, Oct. 18, 1974. Student, U. Kans., 1965-68, Rockhurst Coll., 1968-70; BS in Pub. Adminstrn., Upper Iowa U., 1992; MS in Pub. Adminstrn., PhD in Pub. Adminstrn., Hamilton U., 1998. City mgr. City of Bonner Springs, Kans., 1970-77; bus. owner Lambquarters, Dix, Nebr., 1977-83; city mgr. City of Aurora, Mo., 1983-85, City of Sterling, Colo., 1985—. Bd. dirs. Logan Area Devel. Co., Sterling. Bd. dirs. Fire and Police Pension Assn. Colo., Denver, 1987-95, 13th Jud. Dist. Cmty. Corrections, Brush, Colo., 1988-90; mem. Colo. Mcpl. League Policy Com., Denver, 1987-89. Recipient Disting. Svc. award Jaycees, 1976. Mem. Internat. City Mgmt. Assn. (award for excellence in honor of Mark E. Keane 1999), Colo. Assn. City Mgmt., Am. Soc. for Pub. Adminstrn., Govs. Fin. Assn., Rotary, Elks, Mensa. Republican. Lutheran. Office: Centennial Sq Sterling CO 80751

GUSTAVSON, CARRIE, museum director; Dir. Bisbee (Ariz.) Mining and Hist. Mus., 1992—. Office: Bisbee Mining & Hist Mus PO Box 14 Bisbee AZ 85603-0014

GUTHRIE, MICHAEL B. health facility administrator; b. Aug. 10, 1946; BA, Amherst Coll., 1968; MD, U. Pa., 1972; MBA, U. Colo., 1985. Diplomate Nat. Bd. Med. Examiners. Coord. Emergency Attending Svc., Phila., 1975-76; dir. profl. edn. Colo. State Hosp., Pueblo, 1977-79; chief psychiatry Penrose Hosps., Pueblo, 1977-79, exec. com. med. staff, 1977-88, dir. med. affairs, 1979-83, v.p. med. affairs, med. dir., 1983-87; v.p. bus. devel. Penrose-St. Francis Healthcare, Pueblo, 1987-91; COO Interstate Health Svcs., 1990-92; pres. Health Care Providers, 1990-92; sr. v.p., COO Penrose-St. Francis Healthcare Sys., 1991-92; pres., CEO Good Samaritan Health Sys., San Jose, Calif., 1992—. Bd. dirs., trustee-at-large Healthcare Forum. Contbr. articles to profl. jours. Fellow APA, Am. Coll. Physician Execs.; mem. Am. Hosp. Assn. (Physician Marketer of Yr. 1990), VHA-Pacific (bd. dirs. 1993—, vice-chair 1994-95). Office: Premier Practice Mgmt 12225 El Camino Real San Diego CA 92130-2006

GUTJAHR, ALLAN LEO, mathematics educator, researcher; b. Hosmer, S.D., Mar. 20, 1938; s. Christian E. Gutjahr and Emma Preszler; m. Ellen Troxel, Nov. 21, 1959 (div. 1978); children: Kurt, Eric, Kristin; m. Margaret Rae Sjostedt, Aug. 15, 1981; children: Ted, Meghan. Student, Cen. Wash. Coll., 1958-59; BS in Math., U. Wash., 1962; MSE, Johns Hopkins U., 1963; PhD in Stats., Rutgers U., 1970. Tech. staff Bell Labs., Holmdel, N.J., 1962-71; prof. math. N.Mex. Tech. U., Socorro, 1971-99, prof. emeritus, 1999—, chmn. dept. math., 1985-88, assoc. v.p. acad. affairs, 1990-92, v.p. rsch. and econ. devel., 1992-97. Vis. rschr. Ecole Des Mines, Paris, 1978, U.S. Geol. Survey, Denver, 1978, Stanford U., fall 1989, U. Poly. Catalonia, Barcelona, fall 1997. Contbr. articles to profl. jours. Bd. dirs. V.I.A. With U.S. Army, 1956-58. Recipient Disting. Tchg. award N.Mex. Tech. U., 1987, Disting. Rsch. award Nimex Tech. U., 1999. Fellow Am. Geophys. Union; mem. Math. Assn. Am., Am. Statis. Assn., Internat. Assn. of Math. Geol., Sigma Xi. Avocations: reading, writing, jogging. Home: 445 Aquina Ct Belen NM 87002-6345

GUTSCHE, STEVEN LYLE, physicist; b. St. Paul, Nov. 10, 1946; s. Lyle David and Phyllis Jane (Stubstad) G.; divorced; children: Kristina, Angela; m. Marilyn D. Maloney, Oct. 4, 1980; children: Taylor Steven, Daniel Mark. BS, U. Colo., 1968; MS, U. Calif., Santa Barbara, 1970. Physicist USN Pacific Missile Range, Point Mugu, Calif., 1968-71; staff scientist

Mission Rsch. Corp., Santa Barbara, 1971-76, group leader, 1977-79, div. leader, 1979—, v.p., 1987-89; pres., 1989—; also bd. dirs. Mission Rsch. Corp., Santa Barbara. Contbr. articles to tech. publs. Presbyterian. Avocations: collecting oriental rugs, soccer, long distance running, reading. Office: Mission Rsch Corp 735 State St Santa Barbara CA 93101-3351

GUTTMAN, IRVING ALLEN, opera stage director; b. Chatham, Ont., Can., Oct. 27, 1928; s. Shea and Bernetta (Schaffer) G. Opera student, Royal Conservatory Music, Toronto, 1947-52; LittD (hon.), U. Winnipeg, 1996. Asst. to Herman Geiger Torel of Can. Opera Co., Toronto, 1948-52; dir., under Pauline Donalda Montreal (Que., Can.) Opera Guild, 1959-68; artistic dir. Edmonton Opera, Manitoba Opera. Mem. adv. com. Can. Coun. Founding artistic dir., Vancouver (B.C., Can.) Opera Assn., 1960-74, artistic dir., Edmonton (Alta., Can.) Opera Assn., from 1966, Man. (Can.) Opera Assn., Winnipeg, from 1972; dir. numerous TV productions of opera, including first full-length TV opera for, CBC French Network, 1953, operatic productions for numerous U.S. opera cos., also Can. and European cos.; founding artistic dir., Opera Group, Courtenay Youth Music Camp; author: The Unlikely Pioneer-David Watmough, 1987. Decorated Centennial medal, Queen Elizabeth Jubilee medal, Order of Can., Alberta Govt. award of Excellence, 1989, Gov. Gen.'s Can.'s 125th medal for contbn. to arts in Can., Opera Am. Achievement award for 25 yrs. of disting. svc., 1996; named to Edmonton Hall of Fame, 1989, Vancouver Hall of Fame, 1994, Montreal Hall of Fame, 1996. Mem. Canadian Equity, Am. Guild Musical Artists.

GUY, ANDREW A. lawyer; b. Kansas City, Mo., May 11, 1952; AB summa cum laude, Princeton U., 1974; JD, U. Va., 1979. Bar: Wash. 1979. With firm Bogle & Gates, P.L.L.C., Seattle, 1979—, ptnr., 1987—. Mem. ABA (litigation sect.), Wash. State Bar Assn. (litigation sect.), King County Bar Assn. (litigation sect., creditors' rights, real property, probate and trust sects.). Office: Bogle & Gates PLLC Two Union Sq 810 3rd Ave Ste 604 Seattle WA 98104-1645

GUY, ARTHUR WILLIAM, electrical engineering educator, researcher; b. Helena, Mont., Dec. 10, 1928; s. Arthur Jack and Evelyn (Hebb) G.; m. Vivian Ruth Walker, June 12, 1952; children: William, Sandra, Fred, Arla. BSEE, U. Wash., 1955, MSEE, 1957, PhDEE, 1966. Rsch. asst. elec. engring. dept. U. Wash., Seattle, 1956-57; rsch. engr. Boeing Airplane Co., Seattle, 1957-63; cons. engr. rehab. medicine U. Wash., Seattle, 1963-65, rsch. engr. elec. engring. dept., 1964-66, prof. elec. engring. dept., rehab. medicine, 1966-83, prof., dir. bioelectromagnetics rsch. lab. Ctr. for Bioengineering, 1983-91, prof. emeritus, 1991—. Cons. Bioelectromagnetics Cons., Seattle, 1991-2000; mem. telecomms. facilities adv. com. Seattle City Coun., 1991-92; mem. Sci. Adv. Group on Wireless Tech., 1993-95; active Wireless Tech. Rsch., L.L.C., 1993-97. Contbr. articles to profl. jours. Mem. Electromagnetic Field Task Force State Dept. Health, Olympia, Wash., 1991-92. Sgt. USAF, 1947-52. Recipient Achievement award Westinghouse Co., 1954, spl. award for the decade internat. Power Inst. for Med. and Biol. Rsch., 1980. Fellow AAAS, IEEE (life, vice chair SCC 28 stds. bd. 1989-94, mem. COMAR 1974-89, 92-98, chair COMAR 1987-89); mem. Nat. Coun. on Radiation Protection and Measurements (hon.), Bioelectromagnetic Soc. (charter mem., pres. 1984, d'Arsenval award 1987). Methodist. Home and Office: 18122 60th Pl NE Kenmore WA 98028-8901

GUY, RICHARD P. retired state supreme court justice; b. Coeur d'Alene, Idaho, Oct. 24, 1932; s. Richard H. and Charlotte M. Guy; m. Marilyn K. Guy, Nov. 16, 1963; children: Victoria, Heidi, Emily. JD, Gonzaga U., 1959. Bar: Wash. 1959, Hawaii 1988. Former judge Wash. Superior Ct., Spokane, from 1977; chief justice Wash. Supreme Ct., Olympia, 1998—. Capt. USAS. Mem. Wash. State Bar, Spokane County Bar Assn. Roman Catholic. Office: Wash Supreme Ct Temple Justice PO Box 40929 Olympia WA 98504-0929

GUYMON, GARY LEROY, civil engineering educator, consultant; b. Farmington, N.Mex., Nov. 5, 1935; s. Leland W. and Grace E. (Cumming) G.; m. Lucinda A. Kemmis, June 11, 1988; children by previous marriage: Gary Jr., Richard, Marisa, Michael. BS, U. Calif., Davis, 1966, MS, 1967, PhD, 1970. Asst. civil engr. Calif. Dept. Water Resources, L.A., 1955-66; asst. rsch. engr. U. Calif., Davis, 1969-71; assoc. prof. U. Alaska, Fairbanks, 1971-74; prof. U. Calif., Irvine, 1974-94, chmn. dept. civil engring., 1984-88, prof. emeritus, 1994—. Mem. coordinating bd. U. Calif. Water Resources Ctr., Berkeley, 1985-89; del. Univs. Coun. on Water Resources, Carbondale, Ill., 1980-94. Author: Unsaturate Zone Hydrology, 1994; contbr. numerous articles to profl. jours.; assoc. editor Advances in Water Resources, Southampton, U.K., 1981-89. Fellow ASCE; mem. Am. Geophys. Union, U.S. Com. on Large Dams, Phi Beta Kappa, Tau Beta Pi, Chi Epsilon. Republican. Avocations: woodworking, physical fitness. Office: U Calif Dept Civil & Environ Engring Irvine CA 92717

GUZE, PHYLLIS ARLENE, internist, educator, academic administrator; MD, U. So. Calif., 1971. Resident in internal medicine Harbor UCLA Med. Ctr., fellow; dean of edn. UCLA, 1991-95, prof. medicine, vice chair, 1985—; chief dept. medicine VA Greater LA Healthcare Systems, L.A., 1985—. Contbr. numerous articles to profl. jours. Recipient Disting. Tchr. award in clin. scis. Assn. Am. Med. Colls., 1995, Sherman M. Melinkoff Faculty award UCLA Sch. Medicine, 1995, Luckman Disting. Tchg. award, 1996, Disting. Tchr. award Alpha Omega Alpha, 1995. Mem. ACP, Am. Bd. of Internal Medicine (cert. com.), Assn. of Program Dirs. in Internal Medicine, Assn. of VA Chiefs of Medicine. Office: VA Greater LA Healthcare Sys West LA 11301 Wilshire Blvd # Mc111 Los Angeles CA 90073-1003

GUZY, MARGUERITA LINNES, middle school education educator; b. Santa Monica, Calif., Nov. 19, 1938; d. Paul William Robert and Margarete (Rodowski) Linnes; m. Stephen Paul Guzy, Aug. 25, 1962 (div. 1968); 1 child, David Paul. AA, Santa Monica Coll., 1959; student, U. Mex., 1959-60; BA, UCLA, 1966, MA, 1973; postgrad. in psychology, Pepperdine U., 1988-92; cert. bilingual competence, Calif., 1994. Cert. secondary tchr., quality review team ednl. programs, bilingual, Calif. Tchr. Inglewood (Calif.) Unified Sch. Dist., 1967—, chmn. dept., 1972-82, mentor, tchr., 1985-88; clin. instr. series Clin. Supervision Levels I, II, Ingelwood, 1986-87; clin. intern Chem. Dependency Ctr., St. John's Hosp., Santa Monica, 1988-92; lectr. chem. and codependency St. John's Hosp., Santa Monica, 1992—. Tchr. Santa Monica Coll., 1975-76; cons. bilingual edn. Inglewood Unified Sch. Dist., 1975—, lead tchr. new hope program at-risk students, 1992; cons. tchr. credentialing fgn. lang. State of Calif., 1994; sch. rep. restructuring edn. for state proposal, 1991-93; mem. Program Quality Rev. Team Pub. Edn., Calif., 1993; mem. Supt.'s Com. for Discrimination Resolution, 1994-95, tech. com. for integrating multimedia in the classroom, 1997—. Author: Elementary Education: "Pygmalian in the Classroom", 1975, English Mechanics Workbook, 1986. Recipient Teaching Excellence cert. State of Calif., 1986; named Tchr. of Yr., 1973, 88. Mem. NEA, Calif. Tchrs. Assn., Inglewood Tchrs. Assn. (local rep. 1971-72, tchr. edn. and profl. svcs. com. 1972-78), UCLA Alumnae Assn. (life), Prytanean Alumnae Assn. (bd. dirs. 1995-96, 1960's rep., 2d v.p. membership 1996-98). Republican. Avocations: reading, travel, swimming, dancing, cooking. Office: Monroe Magnet Mid Sch 10711 S 10th Ave Inglewood CA 90303-2015 E-mail: mlguzy@earthlink.net

GUZZO, GLENN, newspaper editor; V.p. news Knight Ridder Inc., 1989-93; editor The Philadelphia Inquirer, Ft. Worth Star-Telegram; mng. editor Akron Beacon Jour., 1993-99; editor Denver Post, 1999—. Office: Denver Post 1560 Broadway Denver CO 80202-5177

GWINN, CASEY, city attorney San Diego, California; m. Beth Gwinn; 3 children. BA in Polit. Sci. with honors, Stanford U., 1982; JD, UCLA, 1985. Bar: Calif. 1995. Dep. city atty. City of San Diego, 1985-88, head dep. city atty., 1988-95, prin. asst. to city atty., 1995-96, asst. atty., 1996, atty., 1996—. Faculty Nat. Coll. Dist. Attys., Nat Judges Conf. on Domestic Violence, Nat. Navy Family Advocacy Conf., Nat. U.S. Marine Corps Love and Violence Conf., Calif. Dist. Attys. Assn. Contbr. articles to profl. jours. Adv. bd. Home Start, San Diego Ctr. for Children, Children' Edn. with Care; founder San Diego Task Force on Domestic Violence. Recipient Gov.'s Recognition award, 1990, Diogenes award Pub. Rels. Soc. Am., 1990, Recognition award Nat. Coun. Juvenile and Family Ct. Judges, 1993, State Resolution, Calif. Assembly, 1994; named 1 of Top 45 Pub. Lawyers in Am., American Lawyer. Mem. ABA, Calif. Dist. Attys. Assn., San Diego County Bar Assn., League of Calif. Cities, City Atty. Dept. Office: City Atty Office 1200 3rd Ave Ste 1620 San Diego CA 92101-4178

GWINN, MARY ANN, newspaper reporter; b. Forrest City, Ark., Dec. 29, 1951; d. Lawrence Baird and Frances Evelyn (Jones) G.; m. Richard A. King, June 3, 1973 (div. 1981); m. Stephen E. Dunnington, June 10, 1990. BA in Psychology, Hendrix Coll., 1973; MEd in Spl. Edn., Ga. State U., 1975; MA in Journalism, U. Mo., 1979. Tchrs. aide DeKalb County Schs., Decatur, Ga., 1973-74, tchr., 1975-78; reporter Columbia (Mo.) Daily Tribune, 1979-83, Seattle Times, 1983—, internat. trade and workplace reporter, 1992-96, book editor, 1996-98, asst. city editor, 1996-98, book editor, 1998—. Instr. ext. divsn. U. Wash., Seattle, 1990; journalism instr., Seattle U., 1994. Recipient Charles Stewart Mott Found. award for edn. reporting, 1980, C.B. Blethen award for enterprise reporting Blethen Family, Seattle, 1989, Pulitzer Prize for nat. reporting, 1990. Mem. Newspaper Guild. Avocations: writing fiction, gardening, reading, wilderness camping. Office: Seattle Times PO Box 70 Seattle WA 98111-0070

GWINN, MARY DOLORES, business developer, philosopher, writer, speaker; b. Oakland, Calif., Sept. 16, 1946; d. Epifanio and Carolina (Lopez) Cruz; m. James Monroe Gwinn, Oct. 23, 1965; 1 child, Larry Allen. Student, Monterey Peninsula Jr. Coll., 1965. Retail store mgr. Consumer's Distbg. divsn. May Co., Hayward, Calif., 1973-78; mktg. rep. Dale Carnegie Courses, San Jose, 1978-79; founder, pres. Strategic Integrations, Ariz.'s Innovative Bus. Devel. Ctr., Scottsdale, 1985—, Gwinn Genius Inst., Scottsdale, 1998—. Speaker St. John's Coll. U. Cambridge, England, 1992, INC. Mag., U.S.A., 1996, Clemson Univ., 1996, Antelope Valley Coll., Lancaster, Calif., 1998; founder, pres. Internat. Inst. for Conceptual Edn., Scottsdale, 1993—; chairperson Keble Coll., Oxford (Eng.) U., 1997; spkr. Willard Internat. Hotel, Washington, 2000. Founder new fields of study Genestics and NeuroBus.; profiled the Thought Process of Genius; conceived Whole Brain Business Theory, 1985; author: Genius Leadership Secrets from the Past for the 21st Century, 1995; writer bus. column Gwinn on Bus., IMAGE Networker, Pa., 1996; contbr. articles to profl. jours. Chairperson Keble Coll., Oxford (Eng.) U. Republican. Avocations: reading, imagination games, playing with grandchildren. Home and Office: 5836 E Angela Dr Scottsdale AZ 85254-6410

GWYNN, ANTHONY KEITH (TONY GWYNN), professional baseball player; b. L.A., May 9, 1960; m. Alicia; children: Anthony, Anisha Nicole. Student, San Diego State U. Player minor league teams, Walla Walla and Amarillo, Hawaii, 1981-82; outfielder San Diego Padres, 1982—. Winner Nat. League batting title, 1984, 87, 88, 89, 95; recipient Gold Glove award, 1986-87, 89-91; mem. All-Star team, 1984-87, 89-96; named MVP N.W. League, 1981, Sporting News Nat. League Silver Slugger team, 1984, 86-87, 89, 94, Sporting News Nat. League All-Star Team, 1984, 86-87, 89, 94. Office: San Diego Padres Qualcomm Stadium PO Box 2000 San Diego CA 92112-2000

GYANI, MOHAN, communications company executive; b. Goa, India, June 15, 1951; MBA with distinction, San Francisco State U., 1978. V.p., contr. Pacific Bell; v.p., treas. Pacific Telesis; CFO for internat. subs. AirTouch Comm., San Francisco, v.p. fin., treas., 1994-95, exec. v.p., CFO, 1995-99; exec. v.p., CFO wireless svcs. unit AT&T, Redmond, Wash., 2000, pres., CEO wireless svcs. unit, 2000—. Former lectr. San Francisco State U.; participant Pvt. Sector Coun.; bd. dirs. PCS Prime Co. Inc., Mannesman Arcor. Mem. exec. bd. Boy Scouts Am. Office: AT&T Wireless Group 7277 164th Ave NE Bldg 1 Redmond WA 98052-7823

GYLSETH, DORIS (LILLIAN) HANSON, retired librarian; b. Helena, Mont., May 26, 1934; d. Richard E. and Lillie (Paula) Hanson; m. Arlie Albeck, Dec. 26, 1955 (div. Apr. 1964); m. Hermann M. Gylseth, Apr. 29, 1983 (dec. Aug. 1985). BS in Edn., Western Mont. Coll. Edn., 1958; MLS, U. Wash., 1961. Tchr. Helena Sch. Dist., 1955-56, Dillon (Mont.) Elem. Sch., 1957-59, Eltopia (Wash.) Unified Sch. Dist., 1959-60; sch. libr. Shoreline Sch. Dist., Seattle, 1960-64, Dept. of Def., Chateauroux, France, Hanau, Fed. Republic Germany, Tachikawa, Japan, 1964-68, Long Beach (Calif.) Unified Sch. Dist., 1968-70; br. libr. Long Beach Pub. Libr., 1970-74, coord. children's svcs., 1974-85; libr. Long Beach (Calif.) Unified Sch. Dist., 1986-94; realtor Century 21, All Pacific, 1994-96. Bd. dirs. Children's Svcs. divsn. Calif. Libr. Assn., 1985, Literary Guild of Orange County, 1993—; co-chmn. Long Beach Authors Festival, 1978-86; mem. planning coun. Third Pacific Rim Conf. on Children's Lit., UCLA, 1986. Mem. So. Calif. Coun. on Lit. for Children and Young Poeple (bd. dirs. 1974-88, pres. 1982-84), Helen Fuller Cultural Carrousel (bd. dirs. 1985—), Friends of Long Beach Pub. Libr. (bd. dirs. 1988—), Zonta (pres. 1978-80). Avocations: cats, traveling. Home: 5131 Kingscross Rd Westminster CA 92683-4832

HAAK, HAROLD HOWARD, university president; b. Madison, Wis., June 1, 1935; s. Harold J. and Laura (Kittleson) H.; m. Betty L. Steiner, June 25, 1955; children— Alison Marie, Janet Christine. B.A., U. Wis., 1957, M.A., 1958; Ph.D., Princeton U., 1963. From asst. prof. to assoc. prof. polit. sci., pub. adminstrn. and urban studies San Diego State Coll., 1962-69, dean coll. profl. studies, prof. pub. adminstrn. and urban studies, 1969-71; acad. v.p. Calif. State U., Fresno, 1971-73, pres., 1980-91, pres. emeritus, 1991—, trustee prof., 1991-2000, trustee, prof., vice chancellor acad. affairs, 1992-93; v.p. U. Colo., Denver, 1973, chancellor, 1974-80; pres. Fresno Pacific U., 2000—. Trustee William Saroyan Found., 1981-91; mem. NCAA Pres. Commn., 1987-91; bd. dirs. Fresno Econ. Devel. Corp., 1981-91, Cmty. Hosps. Ctrl. Calif., 1989-92; mem. bd. visitors Air Univ.; mem. Army adv. panel on ROTC affairs, 1988-92; vice chair Calif. Commn. on Agr. and Higher Edn., 1993-96; bd. dirs. Pacific Luth. Theol. Sem. Recipient U. Colo. medal, 1980. Mem. Phi Beta Kappa, Phi Kappa Phi. Office: Fresno Pacific U Pres Office 1717 S Chestnut Ave Fresno CA 93702

HAAN, STEVEN WILLIAM, physics researcher; b. Denver, Nov. 21, 1951; BS in Math. and Physics with honors, Calvin Coll., 1973; PhD in Physics, U. Md., 1977. Rsch. assoc. Nat. Bur. Stds., Gaithersburg, Md., 1977-79; lectr., rsch. assoc. dept. chem. U. Calif., Berkeley, 1979-81; staff physicist X-Divsn. Lawrence Livermore (Calif.) Nat. Lab., 1981-85, assoc. divsn. leader X-Divsn., 1985—. Recipient Alan Berman Rsch. Publ. award Naval Rsch. Lab., 1994. Fellow Am. Phys. Soc. (Excellence in Plasma Physics Rsch. award 1995, Edward Teller medal 1995). Home: 401 Fernando Ct San Ramon CA 94583-1721 Office: Lawrence Livermore Nat Lab PO Box 808 L-23 Livermore CA 94551-0808

HAAS, BRADLEY DEAN, pharmacy director, clinical pharmacist, consultant; b. Albion, Nebr., Nov. 24, 1957; s. Ernest Duane Jr. and Joy Lou (Fusselman) H. Student, Kearney State Coll., 1976-78; PharmD with distinction, U. Nebr. Coll. Pharmacy, Omaha, 1981. Registered pharmacist, Nebr., Colo.; cert. hosp. pharmacy residency, basic life support instr. and provider, advanced cardiac life support instr. and provider. Resident hosp. pharmacy U. Nebr. Med. Ctr., Omaha, 1981-82; intensive care clin. pharmacist Mercy Med. Ctr., Denver, 1982-85; home care pharmacist Am. Abbey Homecare, Englewood, Colo., 1985; pharmacy dir. Charter Hosp. of Aurora, 1989-90; clin pharmacy coord. Porter Meml. Hosp., Denver, 1987-92; asst. dir. clin. pharmacy svcs. Luth. Med. Ctr., Wheat Ridge, Colo., 1992-94; dir. pharmacy Integrated Pharmacy Solutions, Inc./Pru Care Pharmacies, Denver, 1994-96; sr. med. info. scientist AstraZeneca L.P. (formerly Astra Merck), 1996—. Cons. Porter Meml. Hosp. Chronic Pain Treatment Ctr., 1987-89, Charter Hosp., 1989-90; adj. asst. prof. pharmacy U. Colo., 1983-96; mem. leadership adv. coun. sch. pharmacy U. Colo., 1987-89; mem. State Colo./ Medicare D.U.R. Com., 1992-96. Author, co-author in field. Vol. Colo. Hosp. Pharmacists Week, Poison Prevention Week, KUSA-TV Health Fair; active Colo. Trust. Named Disting. Young Pharmacist of the Year Marion Labs., Colo., 1987, one of Outstanding Young Men of Am., 1987; recipient Acad. Scholarship U. Nebr. Med. Ctr, 1978-81, Excellence in Pharmacy Practice award U. Colo. Sch. Pharmacy, 1988; Marjorie Merwin Simmons Meml. scholar U. Nebr. Found. Fund., 1980; scholar VFW, 1978-81. Mem. Am. Soc. Health-Sys. Pharmacists (state chpt. grants program selection com. 1989, nominations com. 1990-91, ho. of dels. 1987, 90-92), Acad. Managed Care Pharmacy, Colo. Managed Care Pharmacy Dirs., Colo. Soc. Health-Sys. Pharmacists (presdl. officer 1987-89, chmn. numerous couns. and coms., Hosp. Pharmacy Practitioner Excellence award 1988, 89), LoDo Sertoma Club (charter mem., sec. 1999-2000, v.p. sponsoreship 2000-2001, v.p. programs 2001-2002). Avocations: snow/water skiing, bicycling, photography, golf, community service activities. Office: AstraZeneca LP 10115 Granite Hill Dr Parker CO 80134-9515 E-mail: bradley.haas@astrazeneca.com

HAAS, CHARLIE, screenwriter; b. Bklyn., Oct. 22, 1952; s. Philip and Eunice (Dillon) H.; m. Barbara K. Moran, Dec. 21, 1981. BA, U. Calif., Santa Cruz, 1984. Editorial dir. Warner Bros. Records, Burbank, Calif., 1974-76; contbg. editor New West Mag., Beverly Hills, 1976-80; freelance writer L.A., 1976-80, Oakland, Calif., 1980—. Co-author: (movies) Over the Edge, 1979, Tex, 1982, Gremlins 2, 1990, Matinee, 1993, Runaway Daughters, 1994; contbr. articles to mags. Mem. Friends of Oakland Parks & Recreation, Friends of Oakland Pub. Libr. Avocations: fountain pens, mountain bikes.

HAAS, PETER E., SR. apparel company executive; b. San Francisco, Dec. 20, 1918; s. Walter A. and Elise (Stern) H.; m. Josephine Baum, Feb. 1, 1945; m. Mimi Lurie, Aug., 1981; children: Peter E., Michael Stern, Margaret Elizabeth. Student, Deerfield Acad., 1935-36; A.B., U. Calif., 1940; MBA cum laude, Harvard, 1943. With Levi Strauss & Co., San Francisco, 1945—, exec. v.p., 1958-70, pres., 1970-81, CEO, 1976-81, chmn. bd., 1981-89, chmn. exec. com., 1989—, also bd. dirs.; chmn. exec. com., bd. dirs. Levi Strauss Assocs. Inc. Holding Corp. Dir. emeritus AT&T. Trustee San Francisco Found., 1984—; assoc. Smithsonian Nat. Bd., 1988—; bd. dirs. No. Calif. Grantmakers, 1989—; former mem. exec. com. Strive for Five; former mem. Golden Gate Nat. Recreation Area Adv. Com.; Former pres. Jewish Welfare Fedn.; former trustee Stanford U.; former dir., vice chmn. San Francisco Bay Area Council; former trustee United Way of San Francisco Bay Area; former pres. Aid to Retarded Children; former bd. govs. United Way of Am. Recipient Alexis De Tocqueville Soc. award, United Way Am., 1985; named CEO of Yr., Fin. World mag., 1981, Bus. Statesman of Yr., Harvard Bus. Sch., 1982; Baker scholar, 1940. Office: Levi Strauss & Co 1155 Battery St San Francisco CA 94111-1256

HAAS, RAYMOND P. lawyer; b. Corpus Christi, Tex., Dec. 9, 1942; BA cum laude, Yale U., 1964, LLB, 1967. Bar: Calif. 1967. Law clk. to Hon. Roger J. Traynor Supreme Ct. of Calif., 1967-68; atty. Howard, Rice, Nemerovski, Canady, Falk & Rabkin, San Francisco. Trustee San Francisco U. High Sch., 1973-78, 85-88, chmn., 1973-76, treas., 1986-88; trustee Pacific Presbyn. Med. Ctr., 1979-91, vice chmn. 1986-91. Mem. ABA (forum com. on franchising, antitrust law sect., bus. law sect., internat. law sect., patent, copyright and trademarks sect., sci. and tech. sect.), State Bar Calif., Bar Assn. San Francisco (computer law sect.), Licensing Execs. Soc., Computer Law Assn., Order of Coif. Office: Howard Rice Nemerovski Canady Falk & Rabkin 3 Embarcadero Ctr Ste 7 San Francisco CA 94111-4074

HAAS, ROBERT DOUGLAS, apparel manufacturing company executive; b. San Francisco, Apr. 3, 1942; s. Walter A. Jr. and Evelyn (Danzig) H.; m. Colleen Gershon, Jan. 27, 1974; 1 child, Elise Kimberly. BA, U. Calif., Berkeley, 1964; MBA, Harvard U., 1968. With Peace Corps, Ivory Coast, 1964-66; fellow White House, Washington, 1968-69; assoc. McKinsey & Co., 1969-72; with Levi Strauss & Co., San Francisco, 1973—, sr. v.p. corp. planning and policy, 1978-80, pres. new bus. group, 1980, pres. operating groups, 1980-81, exec. v.p., COO, 1981-84, pres., CEO, 1984-89, CEO, chmn. bd., 1989-99, chmn. bd. dirs., 2000. Pres. Levi Strauss Found., mem. global leadership team. Hon. dir. San Francisco AIDS Found.; trustee Ford Found.; bd. dirs. Bay Area Coun.; past bd. dirs. Am. Apparel Assn. White House fellow, 1968-69 Mem. Brookings Inst. (trustee), Bay Area Com., Conf. Bd., Coun. Fgn. Rels., Trilateral Commn., Calif. Bus. Roundtable, Meyer Friedman Inst. (bd. dirs.), Phi Beta Kappa. Office: Levi Strauss & Co 1155 Battery St San Francisco CA 94111-1256

HACH-DARROW, KATHRYN, water testing company executive; m. Clifford Hach. Chair, CEO Hach Co., Ames, Iowa, 1947-98, chair, 1999—. Office: Hach Company Loveland CO 80538

HACKER, THOMAS OWEN, architect; b. Dayton, Ohio, Nov. 4, 1941; s. Homer Owen and Lydia (McLean) H.; m. Margaret (Brooks) Stewart, Mar. 21, 1965; children: Jacob, Sarah, Alice. BA, U. Pa., 1964, MArch, 1967. Registered arch., Oreg.; registered Nat. Coun. Archtl. Registration Bds. Intern architect Office of Louis I. Kahn, Phila., 1964-70; mem. faculty architecture U. Pa., Phila., 1967-69, U. Oreg., Eugene, 1970-84; design prin. Thomas Hacker and Assocs. Architects P.C., Portland, Oreg., 1983—. Vis. profl. architecture, U. Oreg., 1985—. Prin. works include Biomed. Info. Comm. Ctr., Oreg. Health Scis. U., Sch. Nursing, Oreg. Health Scis. U., Portland Art Mus., High Desert Mus., Bend, Oreg.; designer crystal vase for Steuben Inc., Spokane Pub. Libr., Yellowstone Art Mus., Billings, Mont., Lewis & Clark Coll. Signature Project, Multnomah County Librs., Columbia Gorge Interpretive Ctr., Portland State U. Urban Ctr., Whitman Coll. Penrose Meml. Libr., Portland 1st Unitarian Ch., Bend Pub. Libr. Office: 34 NW 1st Ave Ste 406 Portland OR 97209-4017 Home: 2762 SW Montgomery Dr Portland OR 97201-1693

HACKETT, ROBERT JOHN, lawyer; b. N.Y.C., Feb. 6, 1943; s. John P. and Marie S. (Starace) H.; m. Anita Carlile, Apr. 19, 1969; children: Robert J. Jr., John Peter, Kathryn Marie. AB, Rutgers U., 1964; JD, Duke U., 1967. Bar: N.Y. 1967, Ariz. 1972. Assoc. Milbank, Tweed, Hadley, McCloy, N.Y.C., 1967-71; ptnr. Evans, Kitchel & Jenckes, Phoenix, 1971-89; dir. Fennemore Craig, Phoenix, 1989—, course dir. seminar on mergers and acquisitions, 1996, 99. Mem. editl. bd. Duke Law Jour. Bd. dirs. Xavier Coll. Prep. Mem. ABA (com. on fed. securities regulation), State Bar Ariz. (past chmn. securities regulation sect.), Maricopa County Bar Assn., Assn. Corp. Growth (past bd. dirs., past pres. Ariz. chpt.), Phoenix Duke U. Law Alumni Club (past pres.), Pi Sigma Alpha. Republican. Roman Catholic. E-mail: rhackett@fclaw.com

HACKWOOD, SUSAN, electrical and computer engineering educator; b. Liverpool, Eng., May 23, 1955; came to U.S., 1980; d. Alan and Margaret Hackwood. BS with honors, DeMontfort U., Eng., 1976; PhD in Solid State Ionics, DeMontfort U., Eng., 1979; PhD (hon.), Worcester Poly. Inst., 1993; DSc (hon.), DeMontfort U., 1993. Rsch. fellow DeMontfort U., Leicester, Eng., 1976-79; postdoctoral rsch. fellow AT&T Bell Labs., Homdel, N.J., 1980-81, mem. tech. staff, 1981-83, supr. robotics tech., 1983-84, dept. head robotics tech., 1984-85; prof. elec. and computer engrng. U. Calif., Santa Barbara, 1985-89, dir. Ctr. Robotic Systems in Microelectronics, 1985-89, dean Bourns Coll. Engrng. Riverside, 1990-95; exec. dir. Calif. Coun. on Scis. and Tech., Riverside, 1995—. Editor Jour. Robotic Systems, 1983, Recent Advances in Robotics, 1985; contbr. over 100 articles to tech. jours.; 7 patents in field. Fellow AAAS, IEEE (sr.). Office: 5262 King St Riverside CA 92506-1623

HACKWORTH, MICHAEL L. electronics company executive; m. Joan. B of Engrng., Santa Clara U. Various positions Fairchild Semiconductor, Motorola; various positions including sr. v.p. Signetics Corp. (now Philips Semiconductors); chmn., pres., CEO Cirrus Logic, Fremont, Calif., 1985—. Named Semiconductor Entrepreneur of Yr. Ernst & Young, 1990. Office: 3100 W Warren Ave Fremont CA 94538-6423

HACKWORTH, THEODORE JAMES, JR. city official; b. Denver, Nov. 7, 1926; s. Theodore James and Thelma B. (Hill) H.; m. Doris Evelyn Larson, Dec. 31, 1947; children: James Robert, Joan Evelyn Grady, Linda Jean Hoffman. BA, U. Denver, 1955. Sales mgr. Continental Baking Co., Denver, 1950-64; mktg. exec. Sigman Meat Co., Denver, 1964-76; v.p. sales Pierce Packing Co., Billings, Mont., 1976-79; city councilman City of Denver, 1979—, pres., 1983-84. Cons. EPA. Contbr. articles to EPA jours. Mem. Denver pub. schs. bd. edn., 1971-77; dir. Urban Drainage and Flood Control Dist., 1981-84; dir. Met. Wastewater Reclamation Dist., 1982—, sec., 1984-85, chmn. elect, 1988-89, chmn., 1989-91; mem. Denver Regional Council Govts., 1979-94, vice chmn., 1981-83, chmn., 1984-86; neighborhood commr. Boy Scouts Am., 1968-69, Western Dist. commr., 1970-71; pres. Harvey Park Improvement Assn., 1969; chmn. Denver Met. Library Task Force, 1982. Served with USAF, 1945-47. Recipient Individual Achievement award for pub. svc. Assn. Met. Sewerage Agys., 1996, Paul Swalm Lifetime Achievement award Denver County Reps., 1998. Mem. Nat. Assn. Regional Coun. (bd. dirs., chmn. surface trans. task force, pres. 1987-89, Tom Bradley Regional Leadership award 1993), Mt. Vernon Country Club. Republican. Home: 3955 W Linvale Pl Denver CO 80236-2212 Office: Ste 304 3110 S Wadsworth Blvd Denver CO 80227-4810 E-mail: 1invaleplace@MSN.com, Hackwot@CI.Denver.CO.us

HADAS, ELIZABETH CHAMBERLAYNE, editor; b. Washington, May 12, 1946; d. Moses and Elizabeth (Chamberlayne) H.; m. Jeremy W. Heist, Jan. 25, 1970 (div. 1976); m. Peter Eller, Mar. 21, 1984 (div. 1998). AB, Radcliffe Coll., 1967; postgrad., Rutgers U., 1967-68; MA, Washington U., St. Louis, 1971. Editor U. N.Mex. Press, Albuquerque, 1971-85, dir., 1985-2000, spl. acquisitions editor, 2000—. Mem. Assn. Am. Univ. Presses (pres. 1992-93). Democrat. Home: 2900 10th St NW Albuquerque NM 87107-1111 Office: U New Mexico Press 1720 Lomas Blvd NE Albuquerque NM 87106-3807 E-mail: ehadas@unm.edu

HADDA, JANET RUTH, Yiddish language educator, lay psychoanalyst; b. Bradford, Eng., Dec. 23, 1945; came to U.S., 1948; d. George Manfred and Annemarie (Kohn) H.; m. Allan Joshua Tobin, Mar. 22, 1981; stepchildren: David, Adam. BS in Edn., U. Vt., 1966; MA, Cornell U., 1969; PhD, Columbia U., 1975. Prof. Yiddish UCLA; rsch. psychoanalyst So. Calif. Psychoanalytic Inst., L.A., 1988—, tng. and supervising analyst, 1995—, Inst. Contemporary Psychoanalysis, 1993—. Author: Yankev Glatshteyn, 1980, Passionate Women, Passive Men: Suicide in Yissish Literature, 1988, Isaac Bashevis Singer: A Life, 1997; editl. bd. Prooftexts, Yivo Ann; contbr. articles to profl. jours. Mem. MLA, Assn. Jewish Studies, Am. Psychoanalytic Assn., Inst. Contemporary Psychoanalysis, So. Calif. Psychoanalytic Inst., Phi Beta Kappa. Office: UCLA Dept English 1335 Rolfe Hl Los Angeles CA 90095-0001

HADDAD, EDWARD RAOUF, civil engineer, consultant; b. Mosul, Iraq, July 1, 1926; came to U.S., 1990. s. Raouf Sulaiman Haddad and Fadhila (Sulaiman) Shaya; m. Balquis Yousef Rassam, July 19, 1961; children: Reem, Raid. BSc, U. Baghdad, Iraq, 1949; postgrad., Colo. State U., 1966-67; PhD (hon.), 1995. Project engr., cons. Min. Pub. Works, Baghdad, 1949-63; arbitrator Engring. Soc. & Ct., Kuwait City, Kuwait, 1963-90, tech. advisor Royal Family, Kuwait, 1987-90; cons. pvt. practice Haddad Engrng., Albuquerque, 1990-95; owner, pres. Overseas Contacts-Internat. Bus. and Consulting, Albuquerque, 1995—. Organizer reps abroad, Kuwait, 1990. Pres. Parents Assn., U. N.Mex., 1995. Recipient Hon. medal Pope Paul VI of Rome, 1973, Men of Achievement award Internat. Biog. Ctr., 1994. Mem. ASCE, NSPE, ABA (assoc.), Am. Arbitration Assn. (mem. adv. bd.), Sierra Cath. Internat. (trustee), Lions (bd. dirs. 1992), Inventors Club (bd. dirs. 1992), KC (chancellor 1992). Address: 1425 Monte Largo Dr NE Albuquerque NM 87112-6378 E-mail: edward.haddad@yahoo.com

HADDON, SAM ELLIS, lawyer; b. West Monroe, La., June 19, 1937; s. James Charlie and Letha (Daughtry) H.; m. Betty G. Loyd, Dec. 22, 1958; children: Elizabeth Anne Haddon Alexander, Steven Craig Haddon, Allison Lee Haddon Conover. BS, Rice U., 1959; student, Border Patrol Acad., El Paso, Tex., 1959-60, Treasury Law Enforcement Sch., Washington, 1961; JD with honors, U. Mont., 1965. Bar: Mont. 1965, U.S. Ct. Appeals (9th cir.) 1966, U.S. Dist. Ct. Mont. 1966, U.S. Supreme Ct. 1975. Immigration patrol insp. U.S. Border Patrol, 1959-61; agt. Fed. Bur. Narcotics, 1961-62; rsch. asst. in law U. Mont., 1964-65; law clk. to judge U.S. Dist. Ct., 1965-66; assoc. Anderson, Symmes, Forbes, Peete and Brown, Billings, Mont., 1966-69; ptnr. Boone, Karlberg, and Haddon, Missoula, 1969—. Instr. U. Mont. Sch. Law, 1971-99; chmn. Mont. Supreme Ct. Commn. on Rules of Evidence, 1975—; mem. Mont. Supreme Ct. Comm. on Practice, 1986—, chmn., 1996—; judge pro tem Mont. Dist. Ct. 4th Jud. Dist., 1975; spl. master Mont. Supreme Ct., 1978; del. Jud. Conf. 9th Cir., 1975, rep., 1977-80. Editor-in-chief Mont. Law Rev., 1964-65. Fellow Am. Coll. Trial Lawyers; mem. ABA, Am. Acad. Appellate Lawyers, Am. Judicature Soc. (bd. dirs. 1976-79), Am. Bd. Trial Advocates, Am. Law Inst., Mont. Bar Assn. (chmn. sect. young lawyers 1967-68, exec. com. 1968-69), State Bar Mont. (trustee 1976-78), Western Mont. Bar Assn. Office: Boone Karlberg & Haddon 300 Central Sq 201 W Main St Missoula MT 59802-4326

HADFIELD, TOMI SENGER, hospital administrator; b. Ft. Lee, Va., Dec. 8, 1954; d. Joseph Anthony and Vesta Ilene (Murray) Senger; m. Hal Burton Hadfield, June 6, 1975; children: Bradie Suzanne, Michael Burton, Evan Scott. Cert. in bus., U. N.D., 1975; BA in Bus., U. Calif., Riverside, 1979; M in Health Adminstrn., Chapman Coll., 1989. Project mgr. Control Data Corp., Mpls., 1980-84; asst. hosp. adminstr. Riverside Gen. Hosp., 1987—. Membership campaign cabinet Arthritis Found., Riverside, 1988, YWCA, Riverside, 1988, United Way, Riverside, 1988-89. Fellow Nat. Assn. Pub. Hosps.; mem. Calif. Assn. Pub. Hosps., So. Calif. Healthcare Mktg. Assn., Jr. League Riverside (v.p.), Medi-Trans (bd. dirs.), Riverside C. of C. (v.p. 1989—), Women in Healthcare. Avocations: travel, skiing, volunteer, family. Home: 1395 Rimroad Riverside CA 92506-5558 Office: Riverside Gen Hosp 26520 Cactus Ave Moreno Valley CA 92555-3911

HADLEY, MARLIN LEROY, direct sales financial consultant; b. Mankato, Kans., Jan. 5, 1931; s. Charles LeRoy and Lillian Fern (Dunn) H.; m. Clarissa Jane Payne, Sept. 17, 1949; children: Michael LeRoy, Steven Lee. B.S., U. Denver, 1953; postgrad., Harvard U., 1966. Pres. Jewel Home Shopping Service div. Jewel Cos., Inc., Barrington, Ill., 1953-72; pres., chief exec. officer, dir. Beeline Fashions, Inc., Bensenville, 1972-82; chmn. bd. HAS Originals, Blairstown, NJ, 1984—; fin., bus. cons. Pres., dir. Beeline Real Estate Corp., Act II Jewelry, Inc., Home Galleries, Inc.; dir. Goulder Co., Inc., Climax Spltys., Inc. Club: Economics (Chgo.). Home and Office: 4298 W Lake Cir Littleton CO 80123

HADLEY, PAUL BURREST, JR. (TABBIT HADLEY), domestic engineer; b. Louisville, Apr. 26, 1955; s. Paul Burrest and Rose Mary (Ruckert) H. Grad. in Computer Ops. and Programming, No. Ky. Vocat. Sch., 1975. Floor mgr. reconciling dept. Cen. Trust Co., Cin., 1974-76; freelance photographer Ky., Ohio, Colo., 1975—; chef mgr. The Floradora, Telluride, Colo., 1978-96; domestic engr. Telluride Resort Accomodations , 1996—, The River Club, 2001. Pres. Tabbit Enterprises; freelance recipe writer, Telluride, 1978—; Author poetry (Golden Poet award 1989, Silver Poet award 1990); actor: (plays) Of Mice and Men, The Exercise, Crawling Arnold, A Thousand Clowns, The Authentic Life of Billy The Kid, others. Actor The Plunge Players, Telluride; v.p. Telluride Coun. for Arts and Humanities, 1989. Mem. Plan Internat. USA, Christian Children's Fund. Avocations: mountain climbing, hiking, photography, travel. Home: PO Box 923 Telluride CO 81435-0923

HADLEY, WILLIAM MELVIN, college dean; b. San Antonio, June 4, 1942; s. Arthur Roosevelt and Audrey Merle (Barrett) H.; m. Dorothy J. Hadley, Jan. 21, 1967 (div. July 1989); children: Heather Marie, William Arthur; m. Jane F. Walsh, Oct. 13, 1990. BS in Pharmacy, Purdue U., West Lafayette, Ind., 1967, MS in Pharmacology, 1971, PhD in Toxicology, 1972. Teaching and grad. asst. Purdue U., West Lafayette, 1967-72; asst. prof. U. N.Mex., Albuquerque, 1972-76, assoc. prof., 1976-82, prof., 1982—, asst. dean Coll. Pharmacy, 1984-86, acting dean Coll. Pharmacy, 1985, dean Coll. Pharmacy, 1986—. Vis. scientist Lovelace Inhalation Toxicology Inst., Albuquerque, 1981, adj. scientist, 1991—; mem. adv. bd. Waste Edn. Rsch. Consortium, Las Cruces, N.Mex., 1989—; mem. NIH Proposal Rev. Panels, Bethesda, Md., 1983-84; mem. Gov.'s PCB Expert Adv. Panel, Santa Fe, 1985-86; toxicology cons. numerous law firms N.Mex.; mem. sci. adv. bd. Carlsbad Environ. Monitoring Ctr., 1992-97; mem. sci. adv. com. S.W. Regional Spaceport, Las Cruces, 1992-94. Mem. steering com. United Fund, U.N.Mex., 1987, key person, 1988-97. NIH grantee, 1974-80, 83-87. Mem. AAAS, Am. Pharm. Assn., Am. Assn. Colls. of Pharmacy, Soc. Toxicology (pres. Rocky Mt. chpt. 1990-91), Western Pharmacology Soc., Southwestern Assn. Toxicologists. Achievements include research in biotransformation of xenobiotics with special emphasis on nasal tissue; the effects of heavy metals on biotransformation with emphasis on cadmium; the toxic effects of xenobiotics on the immune system. Office: U NMex Coll Pharmacy Albuquerque NM 87131-5691 E-mail: wmhadley@unm.edu

HAERLE, PAUL RAYMOND, judge; b. Portland, Oreg., Jan. 10, 1932; s. George William and Grace (Soden) H.; m. Susan Ann Wagner, May 30, 1953 (div. Apr. 1973); children: Karen A. Haerle D'Or, David A.; m. Michele A. Monson, June 1, 1991. AB, Yale U., 1953; JD, U. Mich., 1956. Bar: Calif. 1956, U.S. Supreme Ct. 1962. Assoc. Thelen, Marrin, Johnson & Bridges, San Francisco, 1956-64, ptnr., 1965-67, 69-94, mng. ptnr., 1990-93; appointments sec. Office of Gov., State of Calif., Sacramento, 1967-69; assoc. justice Calif. Ct. Appeal (1st dist.), San Francisco, 1994—. Lawyer rep. 9th Cir. Jud. Conf., 1985-88. Editor-in-chief Mich. Law Rev., 1955-56 Presdl. elector, 1972; del. Rep. Nat. Conv., 1972; vice chmn. Calif. Rep. Com., 1973-75, chmn., 1975-77; mem. Rep. Nat. Com., 1975-77; trustee World Affairs Coun. No. Calif., 1997—. Fellow Am. Coll. Trial Lawyers; mem. Yale Club of San Francisco, Order of Coif. Avocations: tennis, travel, hiking. Office: Calif Ct Appeal 350 McAllister St San Francisco CA 94102-3600

HAFEY, JOSEPH MICHAEL, health association executive; b. Annapolis, Md., June 25, 1943; s. Edward Earl Joseph and Verna (Hedlund) H.; m. Mary Kay Miller, Dec. 30, 1978; children: Erin Catherine, Ryan Michael. BA, Whittier Coll., 1965; MPA, UCLA, 1967. Sr. asst. health officer HHS, Washington, 1967 69; dir. govt. relations Alliance for Regional Community Health, St. Louis, 1969-71; exec. dir. Contra Costa Comprehensive Health Assn., Richmond, Calif., 1971-74, Bay Area Comprehensive Health Planning Coun., San Francisco, 1974-76, Western Ctr. for Health Planning, San Francisco, 1976-86, Western Consortium for Pub. Health, Berkeley, 1980-95; pres., CEO Pub. Health Inst. (formerly Calif. Pub. Health Found.), 1985—. Chmn. Contra Costa Pub. Health Adv. Body, Martinez, Calif., 1987-93; founder Calif. Coalition for Future of Pub. Health, Sacramento, 1988—; co-founder Calif. Healthy Cities Program, Berkeley, 1987—. Chmn. United Way Com. for the Uninsured, San Francisco, 1985-93; bd. dirs. Eugene O'Neill Found., 1980-89. With USPHS, 1967-69. Recipient fellowship WHO, Geneva, 1987. Mem. Am. Pub. Health Assn. (governing coun. 1984-87), Am. Health Planning Assn. bd. dirs., chmn. annual meeting 1982). Avocations: jogging, tennis, skiing, collecting political campaign buttons. Home: 1749 Toyon Rd Lafayette CA 94549-2111 Office: Pub Health Inst 2001 Addison St Ste 200 Berkeley CA 94704-1103

HAFTER, ERVIN R. psychology educator; Prof. dept. psychology U. Calif., Berkeley. Office: U Calif Dept Psychology Berkeley CA 94720-0001

HAFTER, RUTH ANNE, library director, educator; b. N.Y.C., Apr. 18, 1935; BA in History and Econs. cum laude, Brandeis U., 1956; cert. Bus. Adminstrn., Harvard-Radcliffe U., 1957; MLS, Columbia U., 1963; PhD in Libr. and Info. Studies, U. Calif., Berkeley, 1984. Supr. sch. librs. Halifax County, N.S., Can., 1965-66; asst. edn. libr. Harvard U., Cambridge, Mass., 1967-68; univ. libr. St. Mary's U., Halifax, N.S., Can., 1969-75; libr. dir. Sonoma State U., Rohnert Park, Calif., 1978-86, San Jose (Calif.) State U., 1986-91, prof. div. libr. and info. sci., 1987-99, prof. emeritus, 1999—. Instr. St. Mary's U., 1972-75, Sonoma State U., 1982-85, U. Calif., Berkeley, 1975-78, 85-86; cons. Ministry of State Urban Affairs, Can., 1975, Sonoma County Hist. Records, 1979-80; coord. Geysers Info. Project., 1980-81; project humanist Calif. Coun. for Humanities, 1981-83; dir. Indochinese Cultures project Nat. Endowment for Humanities, 1983-84, Videodisc Work Shop Calif. State U., 1987—, Online Pub. Catalog Implementation, 1989; pres. Beethoven Ctr. San Jose State U., 1987-88. Author: Academic Librarians and Cataloging Networks: Visibility, Quality and Professional Status, 1986, (with George Rawlyk) Acadian Education in Nova Scotia, 1970; contbr. articles to profl. jours. Mem. Mayor Feinstein's com. on Teaching of Holocaust, San Francisco, 1986, adv. com. Foothill Coll. Libr. Tech. Asst. Program, 1987—, San Jose Pub. Libr. Found., 1987—, bd. govs. 1987-89, exec. bd. Friends of San Jose Pub. Libr., 1989—, Calif. State Libr. Networking Task Force, 1989—, adv. bd. dirs. Frances Gullard Child Devel. Ctr., 1990—; pres. alumni bd. Sch. Libr. and Info. Sci, U. Calif., Berkeley, 1993-94. Inst. Ethnography grantee Dept. Edn., 1994-95. Mem. ALA (com. on accreditation, field site vis. bd. 1982—, libr. career resource network 1987—, program com. reference and adult svcs. div. 1989—), Coop. Libr. Agy. Systems and Svcs. (bd. govs. 1988—, acad. librs. rep.), Calif. Acad. and Rsch. Librs. (pres. 1983-84), Calif. Libr. Assn. (legis. network 1988—, chair continuing edn. com. 1997), North Bay Coop. Assn. (exec. com. 1984-85), Phi Kappa Phi. Home: 177 19th St Apt 1E Oakland CA 94612-4653

HAGEDORN, BOB, state senator; b. Elizabeth City, N.C., Feb. 16, 1952; div.; 1 child, Robert. BS, U. Colo., 1974, BS, 1979. Pub. adminstr., 1980-83, 87-88; pub. rels. and mktg., 1983-87, 88-90; instr. Met. State Coll., 1990—; Dem. rep. dist. 42 Colo. Ho. of Reps., 1992-2000; Dem. senator dist. 29 Colo. State Senate, 2000—. Mem. health, environ, instns. and welfare, state vets. and mil. affairs coms. Colo. Ho. of Reps.; mem. agr. and natural resources com. Colo. State Senate, vice chmn. health, environ, children and families com. Mem. Dem. Bus. Coalition Colo., Dem. Leadership Coun., Downtown Aurora Bus. Assn. Mem. Soc. Profl. Journalists, Aurora C. of C. Presbyterian. Office: 1278 Sable Blvd Aurora CO 80011 also: Colo State Senate State Capitol 200 E Colfax Rm 271 Denver CO 80203 Fax: 303 866 2302. E-mail: bhagedor@sni.net

HAGEE, MICHAEL W. career officer; BS in Engrng. with distinction, U.S. Naval Acad., 1968; MSEE, U.S. Naval Postgrad. Sch., 1969; MA in Nat. Security/Strategic Studies, Naval War Coll., 1987; Grad., Command and Staff Coll., 1982, U.S. Naval War Coll., 1987. Commd. 2d lt. USMC, 1968, advanced through grades to brig. gen., 1996—; command positions include 1st Btn., 8th Marines, 1988-90; commanding officer 11th Marine Expeditionary Unit, 1992-93; various to exec. asst. to asst. commandant USMC, 1993-94; dir. Character Devel. Divsn. U.S. Naval Acad., 1994-95; sr. mil. asst. to dep. sec. of def. Office of Sec. of Def., Washington, 1995-96; exec. asst. to dir. CIA, Washington, 1995-96; dep. dir. opers. Hdqtrs., U.S. European Command, Stuttgart, Germany, 1996-98; dir. strategic planning and policy U.S. Pacific Command, 1998—. Decorated Def. Disting. Svc. medal, Legion of Merit with two gold stars, Bronze Star with Combat "V", Def. Meritorious Svc. medal, Meritorious Svc. medal with one gold star, Navy Achievement medal with one gold star, Combat Action Ribbon, Nat. Intelligence Disting. Svc. medal. Office: HQ USCINCPAC/JO1PA 1st Marine Div PO Box 64031 Camp H M Smith HI 96861-4031

HAGELSTEIN, WILLIAM C. advertising executive; With Kenyon & Eckhardt, Detroit, 1971-76, Parker Advs., Calif., 1976-78, Needham Harper Worldwide, 1978, v.p., 1979-83, sr. v.p., mgmt. dir., group acct. dir., 1983-88; exec. v.p., mng. dir. Foote Cone & Belding, Orange, Calif., 1988-95; exec. v.p. Rubin Postaer & Assocs., Santa Monica, 1996—. Vol. Nat. History Mus. L.A. County, Orange County chpt. ARC, bd. dirs., mem. exec. com. Mem. Am. Advt. Fedn. (bd. dirs.), Young Pres. Orgn. Office: Rubin Postaer & Assocs 1333 2d St Santa Monica CA 90401

HAGEN, DAVID WARNER, judge; b. 1931; BBA, U. Wis., 1956; LLB, U. San Francisco, 1959. Bar: Washoe County 1981, Nev. 1992. With Berkley, Randall & Harvey, Berkeley, Calif., 1960-62; pvt. practice Loyalton, 1962-63; with Guild, Busey & Guild (later Guild, Hagen and Clark Ltd. and Guild & Hagen Ltd.), Reno, 1963-93; judge U.S. Dist. Ct. Nev., Reno, 1993—, chmn. 9th Cir. Art. III, judge edn. com., 1998-2000. Lectr U. Nev., 1968-72; acting dean Nev. Sch. of Law, 1981-83, adj. prof., 1981-87; mem. Nev. Bd. Bar Examiners, 1972-91, chmn., 1989-91; chmn. Nev. Continuing Legal Edn. Com., 1967-75; mem. Nev. Uniform Comml. Code Com. S/sgt. USAF, 1949-52. Fellow Am. Coll. Trial Lawyers (state chmn. 1983-85); mem. VFW, Nev. Bar Assn., Calif. Bar Assn., Washoe County Bar Assn., Am. Bd. Trial Advocates (advocate), Nat. Maritime Hist. Soc., U.S. Sailing Assn. Office: US Dist Ct Fed Bldg & US Courthouse 400 S Virginia St Reno NV 89501-2193

HAGEN, NICHOLAS STEWART, medical educator, consultant; b. Plentywood, Mont., Aug. 6, 1942; s. William Joseph and June Janette (Reuter) H.; m. Mary Louise Edvalson, July 26, 1969; children: Brian Geoffrey, Lisa Louise, Eric Christopher, Aaron Daniel, David Michael. BS in Chemistry, Ariz. State U., 1964; MBA in Internat. Bus., George Washington U., 1969; MD, U. Ariz., 1974. Lic. physician Ariz., Utah, Idaho.; diplomate Nat. Bd. Med. Examiners. Intern., resident Good Samaritan Hosp., Phoenix, 1974-75; pvt. practice Roy, Utah, 1975-77; dir. clin. rsch. Abbott Labs., North Chicago, Ill., 1977-84; v.p. med. affairs Rorer Group, Inc., Ft. Washington, Pa., 1984-88; clin. prof. Ariz. State U., Tempe, 1988-90. Pres. Southwestern Clin. Rsch., Tempe, 1987—, Travel Profl. Internat., Tempe, 1989-98; mem. Ariz. Bd. Med. Student Loans, 1998—. Author: Valproic Acid: A Review of Pharmacologic Properties and Clinical Use in Pharmacologic and Biochemical Properties of Drug Substances, 1979; contbr. articles to med. jours.; patentee in field. Bishop Ch. Jesus Christ of Latter-day Saints, Gurnee, Ill., 1981-84; various positions with local couns. Boy Scouts Am., 1988—; active Rep. campaigns, Mesa, Ariz., 1988—; 2d vice chmn. Maricopa County Rep. Assembly, 1997-99; dist. republican chmn., 1996 98; mem. governing bd. East Valley Inst. Tech., 1998—. Lt. comdr. USCG, 1965-69. Joan Mueller-Etter scholar Ariz. State U., 1960, Phelps-Dodge scholar Ariz. State U., 1961; NASA fellow Brigham Young U., 1964. Mem. Am. Coll. Sports Medicine, Eagle Forum, Nat. Right-to-Life Assn., Utah Hist. Soc., Nat. Geneal. Soc., Bucks County Geneal. Soc., Sons of Norway, Soc. Descendants Emigrants from Numedal, Hallingdal and Hedmark, Norway, Blue Key, Archons, Kappa Sigma (treas. Greater Phoenix alumni chpt. 1999—), Beta Beta Beta, Alpha Epsilon Delta, Phi Eta Sigma, Sophos. Republican. Mormon. Avocations: genealogy, swimming, philately, medieval history, art collecting. Office: 2251 N 32d St Lot 20 Mesa AZ 85213-2445

HAGENSTEIN, WILLIAM DAVID, forester, consultant; b. Seattle, Mar. 8, 1915; s. Charles William and Janet (Finigan) H.; m. Ruth Helen Johnson, Sept. 2, 1940 (dec. 1979); m. Jean Kraemer Edson, June 16, 1980 (dec. 2000). BS in Forestry, U. Wash., 1938; MForestry, Duke, 1941. Registered profl. engr., Wash., Oreg. Field aid in entomology U.S. Dept. Agr., Hat Creek, Calif., 1938; logging supt. and engr. Eagle Logging Co., Sedro-Woolley, Wash., 1939; tech. foreman U.S. Forest Svc., North Bend, 1940; forester West Coast Lumbermen's Assn., Seattle and Portland, Oreg., 1941-43, 45-49; sr. forester FEA, South and Central Pacific Theaters of War and Costa Rica, 1943-45; mgr. Indsl. Forestry Assn., Portland, 1949-80, exec. v.p., 1956-80, hon. dir., 1980-87; pres. W.D. Hagenstein and Assocs., Inc., Portland, 1980—. H.R. MacMillan lectr. forestry U. B.C., 1952, 77; Benson Meml. lectr. U. Mo., 1966; S.J. Hall lectr. indsl. forestry U. Calif. at Berkeley, 1973; cons. forest engr. USN, Philippines, 1952, Coop. Housing Found., Belize, 1986; mem. U.S. Forest Products Trade Mission, Japan, 1968; del. VII World Forestry Congress, Argentina, 1972, VIII Congress, Indonesia, 1978; mem. U.S. Forestry Study Team, West Germany, 1974; mem. sec. Interior's Oreg. and Calif. Multiple Use Adv. Bd., 1975-76; trustee Wash. State Forestry Conf., 1948-92, Keep Oreg. Green Assn., 1957—, v.p., 1970-71, pres., 1972-73; adv. trustee Keep Wash. Green Assn., 1957-95; co-founder, dir. World Forestry Ctr., 1965-89, v.p., 1965-79; hon. Dir. for Life, 1990. Author: (with Wackerman and Michell) Harvesting Timber Crops, 1966; Assoc. editor: Jour. Forestry, 1946-53; columnist Wood Rev., 1978-82; contbr. numerous articles to profl. jours. Trustee Oreg. Mus. Sci. and Industry, 1968-73. Served with USNR, 1933-37. Recipient Hon. Alumnus award U. Wash. Foresters Alumni Assn., 1965, Forest Mgmt. award Nat. Forest Products Assn., 1968, Western Forestry award Western Forestry and Conservation Assn., 1972, 79, Gifford Pinchot medal for 50 yrs. Outstanding Svc., Soc. Am. Foresters, 1987, Charles W. Ralston award Duke Sch. Forestry, 1988, Lifetime Achievement award Oreg. Soc. Am. Foresters, 1995; Honored as only surviving co-founder World Forestry Ctr., 2000. Fellow Soc. Am. Foresters (mem. coun. 1958-63, pres. 1966-69, Golden Membership award 1989); mem. Am. Forestry Assn. (life, hon. v.p. 1966-69, 74-92, William B. Greeley Forestry award 1990), Commonwealth Forestry Assn. (life), Internat. Soc. Tropical Foresters, Portland C. of C. (forestry com. 1949-79, chmn. 1960-62), Nat. Forest Products Assn. (forestry adv. com. 1949-80, chmn. 1972-74, 78-80), West Coast Lumbermen's Assn. (v.p. 1969-79), David Douglas Soc. Western N. Am., Lang Syne Soc., Hoo Hoo Club, Xi Sigma Pi (outstanding alumnus Alpha chpt. 1973). Republican. Home: 3062 SW Fairmount Blvd Portland OR 97201-1439 Office: 921 SW Washington St Ste 803 Portland OR 97205-2826

HAGER, JOHN PATRICK, metallurgy engineering educator; b. Miles City, Mont., Oct. 2, 1936; s. John Herman and Agnes C. (Hart) H.; m. Mary Anna McCloskey, Aug. 26, 1961; children: Patrick, Michael, Charles, Justine, Brendan, Thomas, John Jr. BS, Mont. Sch. Mines, 1958; MS, Mo. Sch. Mines, 1960; ScD, MIT, 1969. Asst. scientist AVCO Corp., Wilmington, Mass., 1961; instr. MIT, Cambridge, 1961-64, research asst., 1964-66; asst. prof. Colo. Sch. Mines, Golden, 1966-69, assoc. prof., 1969-71, dept. head, prof., 1971-74, prof. metallurgy, 1971—, St. Joe Mineral's Corp. prof. extractive metallurgy, 1974-87, Hazen research prof. extractive metallurgy, 1988—. Mem. TMS-AIME. Republican. Roman Catholic. Home: 2054 Crestvue Cir Golden CO 80401-1763 Office: Colo Sch Mines Dept Metal & Materials Engring Golden CO 80401

HAGER, MICHAEL W. museum director; m. Denise Hager; children: Amy, Brian. BA in Biology, Grinnell Coll.; PhD in Geology, U. Wyo. Prof. geology Augustana Coll., 1973-78; dir. Mus. of the Rockies, 1978-89, Va. Mus. Natural History, 1989-91; exec. dir. San Diego Natural History Mus., 1991—. Mus. cons. Exec. prodr. (film) Baja California, 2000. Bd. dirs. Elem. Inst. Sci. and Harborside Sch.; head cultural com. Binational Com. Edn. and Culture, San Diego/Tijuana. Mem. Assn. Sci. Mus. Dirs. (pres.). Office: San Diego Natural History Mus PO Box 121390 San Diego CA 92112-1390 Fax: 619-232-0248. E-mail: mhager@sdnhm.org

HAGGEN, DONALD E. food products executive; CEO Haggen Foods, Bellingham, Wash., co-chmn., 1996—. Office: Haggen's Inc PO Box 9704 Bellingham WA 98227-9704

HAGGERTY, ANCER LEE, judge; b. 1944; BS, U. Oreg., 1967; JD, Hastings Coll. Law, 1973. Law clk. Metro. Pub. Defender, Portland, 1972, 73, staff atty., 1973-77; assoc. Souther, Spaulding, Kinzey, Williamson and Schwabe, 1977-82, Schwabe, Williamson & Wyatt, 1983-88; judge Multnomah County Dist. Ct., 1989-90, Multnomah County Cir. Ct., 1990-93; dist. judge U.S. Ct. Appeals (9th cir.), Portland, 1994—. Mem. Gov.'s task force evaln.Oreg. Liquor Control Commn., 1978, Jud. Conduct Com., 1989-92; coord. Multnomah County Bar Pro Bono program, 1983-88; mem. Oreg. State Bd. Bar Examiners, 1979-82. Coach, practice judge mock ct. team Jefferson H.S.; asst. coach Whitaker 7th and 8th grade Pop Warner football teams. 1st lt. USMC, 1967-70, Vietnam. Decorated Silver Star medal, Purple Heart; recipient award Alumni Assn. U. Oreg., Local Hero award Martin Luther King, Jr. Elem. Sch. Fifth Grade, 1993. Mem. ABA, Am. Bridge Assn., Oreg. State Bar Assn., Nat. Bar Assn., Lloyd Ctr. Racquet Club, Marine Corps League, Phoenix Bridge Club. Address: US District Ct 1000 SW 3rd Ave Portland OR 97204-2930

HAGGERTY, CHARLES A. former electronics executive; Student, U. St. Thomas. Pres., chief exec. officer, chmn. bd. dirs. IBM, 1964-92; pres., COO Western Digital Corp., Irvine, Calif., 1992-96. Office: Western Digital Corp 8105 Irvine Center Dr Irvine CA 92618-2937

HAHN, BETTY, artist, photographer, educator; b. Chgo., Oct. 11, 1940; d. Eugene Joseph and Esther Josephine (Krueger) H.; widowed. A.B., Ind. U., 1963, M.F.A., 1966. Asst. prof. photography Rochester (N.Y.) Inst. Tech., 1969-75; prof. art U. N.Mex., Albuquerque, 1976-97, prof. emeritus, 1997—. One-woman shows include Smithsonian Instn., Washington, 1969, Ctr. Photographic Studies, Louisville, 1971, Focus Gallery, San Francisco, 1974, Sandstone Gallery, Rochester, N.Y., 1978, Blue Sky Gallery, Portland, Oreg., 1978, Susan Spiritus Gallery, Newport Beach, Calif., 1977, 82, Witkin Gallery, N.Y.C., 1973, 79, Washington Project for the Arts, 1980, Ctr. Creative Photography, Tucson, 1981, Columbia Coll. Gallery, Chgo., 1982, Port Washington Pub. Library, N.Y., 1984, Mus. Fine Arts, Mus. N.Mex, Santa Fe, 1986, Lehigh U., 1988, U. Mass., Amherst, 1989, Andrew Smith Gallery, Santa Fe, 1991, U. N.Mex. Art Mus., Albuquerque, 1994. Named Honored Educator, Soc. for Photog. Edn., 1984; Nat. Endowment Arts grantee, 1977-78, 82-83; N.Y. State Council Arts grantee, 1976 Mem. Soc. Photog. Edn., Coll. Art Assn., Evidence Photographers Internat. Council Office: Univ N Mex Art Dept Albuquerque NM 87131-0001

HAHN, ELLIOTT JULIUS, lawyer; b. San Francisco, Dec. 9, 1949; s. Leo Wolf and Sherry Marion (Portnoy) H.; m. Toby Rose Mallen; children: Kara Rebecca, Brittany Atira Mallen, Michael Mallen, Adam Mallen. BA cum laude, U. Pa., 1971, JD, 1974; LLM, Columbia U., 1980. Bar: N.J. 1974, Calif. 1976, D.C. 1978, U.S. Dist. Ct. N.J. 1974, U.S. Dist. Ct. (cen. dist.) Calif. 1976, U.S. Supreme Ct. 1980. Assoc. von Malitz, Derenberg, Kunin & Janssen, N.Y.C., 1974-75; law clk. L.A. County Superior Ct., 1975-76; atty. Atlantic Richfield Co., L.A., 1976-79; prof. Summer in Tokyo program Santa Clara Law Sch., 1981-83; assoc. prof. law Calif. Western Coll. Law, San Diego, 1980-85; atty. Morgan, Lewis & Bockius, L.A., 1985-87; assoc. Whitman & Ransom, L.A., 1987-88, ptnr., 1989-93, Sonnenschein Nath & Rosenthal, L.A., 1993-97, Hahn & Bolson LLP, 1997—. Vis. scholar Nihon U., Tokyo, 1982; vis. lectr. Internat. Christian U., Tokyo, 1982; adj. prof. law Southwestern U. Sch. Law, 1986-93, Pepperdine U. law Sch., 1986-93, U. So. Calif. Law Sch., 1997-98; lectr. U. Calif., Davis, Law Sch. Orientation in U.S.A. Law Program, 1994-97. Author: Japanese Business Law and the Legal System, 1984; contbr. chpt. on Japan to The World Legal Ency.; internat. law editor Calif. Bus. Law Reporter. Vice-chmn. San Diego Internat. Affairs Bd., 1981-85; bd. dirs. San Diego-Yokohama Sister City Soc., 1983-85, L.A.-Nagoya Sister City Soc., 1986-1996; mem. master planning com. City of Rancho Palos Verdes, Calif., 1989-91; advisor, exec. com. Calif. Internat. Law Sect., 1990-91, 95, appointee exec. com., 1991-94, vice-chmn., 1992-93, chair, 1993-94; appointee, trustee Palos Verdes Libr. Dist., 1993-94; bd. dirs. Internat. Student Ctr. UCLA, 1996—, pres., 2000-01. Mem. ABA, State Bar Calif., L.A. County Bar Assn. (bd. dirs. internat. sect., exec. com. Internat. Legal Sec. 1987—, sec. 1995-96, 2d v.p. 1996-97, 1st v.p. 1997-98, chmn. 1998-99, appointee Pacific rim com. 1990-98, chmn. 1991-92, 95-98, trustee 1997-98), Assn. Asian Studies, U. Pa. Alumni Club (pres. San Diego chpt. 1982, pres. coun. Phila. 1983), Anti Defamation League, Japanese-Am. Soc. (book rev. editor Seattle 1983-85). Jewish. Office: Hahn & Bolson LLP 1000 Wilshire Blvd # 1600 Los Angeles CA 90017-2457 E-mail: ehahn@hahnbolsonllp.com

HAHN, ERWIN LOUIS, physicist, educator; b. Sharon, Pa., June 9, 1921; s. Israel and Mary Hahn; m. Marian Ethel Failing, Apr. 8, 1944 (dec. Sept. 1978); children: David L., Deborah A., Katherine L.; m. Natalie Woodford Hodgson, Apr. 12, 1980. B.S., Juniata Coll., 1943, D.Sc., 1966; M.S., U. Ill., 1947, Ph.D., 1949; D.Sc., Purdue U., 1975, U. Stuttgart, Germany, 2001; DrRerNat, U. Stuttgart, 2001. Asst. Purdue U., 1943-44; research assoc. U. Ill., 1950; NRC fellow Stanford, 1950-51, instr., 1951-52; research physicist Watson IBM Lab., N.Y.C., 1952-55; assoc. Columbia U., 1952-55; faculty U. Calif., Berkeley, 1955—, prof. physics, 1961—, assoc. prof., then prof. Miller Inst. for Basic Rsch., 1958-59, 66-67, 85-86. Eastman vis. prof. Balliol Coll., Oxford, Eng., 1988-89; cons. Office Naval Rsch., Stanford, 1950-52, AEC, 1955—; spl. cons. USN, 1959; adv. panel mem. Nat. Bur. Stds., Radio Stds. div., 1961-64; mem. NAS/NRC com. on basic rsch.; advisor to U.S. Army Rsch. Office, 1967-69; faculty rsch. lectr. U. Calif., Berkeley, 1979. Author: (with T.P. Das) Nuclear Quadrupole Resonance Spectroscopy, 1958. Served with USNR, 1944-46. Fellow Guggenheim Found., 1961-62, 69-70, NSF, 1961-62; recipient prize Internat. Soc. Magnetic Resonance, 1971, Humboldt Found. award, 1977, 94, Alumni Achievement award Juniata Coll., 1986, citation U. Calif., Berkeley, 1991; co-winner prize in physics Wolf Found., 1984; named to Calif. Inventor Hall of Fame, 1984; vis. fellow Brasenose Coll., Oxford U., 1969-70, life hon. fellow, 1984—. Fellow AAAS, Internat. Soc. Electron Paramagnetic Resonance, Am. Phys. Soc. (past mem. exec. com. div. solid state physics, Oliver E. Buckley prize 1971), Soc. Magnetic Resonance in Medicine (hon.), The Inst. of Physics Great Britain; mem. NAS (co-recipient Comstock prize in electricity, magnetism and radiation 1993), Slovenian Acad. Scis. and Arts (fgn.), French Acad. Scis. (fgn. assoc.), Berkeley Fellows, Royal Soc. U.K. (fgn. mem.). Home: 69 Stevenson Ave Berkeley CA 94708-1732 Office: U Calif Dept Physics 367 Birge Berkeley CA 94720-0001

HAHN, HAROLD THOMAS, physical chemist, chemical engineer; b. N.Y.C., May 31, 1924; s. Gustave Hahn and Lillie Martha (Thomas) H.; m. Bennie Joyce Turney, Sept. 5, 1948; children: Anita Karen, Beverly Sharon, Carol Linda, Harold Thomas Jr. Student, Hofstra U., 1941-43; BSChemE, Columbia U., 1943-44; PhD in Chemistry, U. Tex., 1950-53. Chem. engr. Manhattan Dist. U.S. Army, Los Alamos, N.Mex., 1945-47; chem. engr. U. Calif., Los Alamos, 1947-50; sr. scientist Gen. Electric Co., Hanford, Wash., 1953-58; sect. chief, chem. research dept. Phillips Petroleum Co., Idaho Falls, Idaho, 1958-64; sr. staff scientist Lockheed Missiles & Space Co., Palo Alto, Calif., 1964-92; private cons., 1992—. Contbr. articles to profl. jours.; patentee in field. Pres. Edgemont Gardens PTA, Idaho Falls, 1963-64; commr. cub scout div. Stanford area council Boy Scouts Am., Palo Alto, 1973-76, also cubmaster pack 36, 1973-80, chmn. troops 36 and 37, 1975-77; mem. adminstrv. bd. Los Altos Meth. Ch. Served to col. U.S. Army, 1944-46, with res., 1946-84, col. res. ret. Humble Oil Co. fellow, 1952, Naval Bur. Ordnance fellow, 1953. Fellow Am. Inst. Chemists; mem. AIAA, Magnetics Soc. IEEE (elected sr. mem.), Calif. Acad. Scis., Internat. Platform Assn., Am. Chem. Soc., Sigma Xi, Phi Lambda Upsilon, Kappa Rho. Home and Office: 661 Teresi Ln Los Altos CA 94024-4162

HAHN, HELENE B. motion picture company executive; b. N.Y.C. BA, Hofstra U.; JD, Loyola U., Calif., 1975. Bar: Calif. 1975. V.p. bus. affairs Paramount Pictures Corp., L.A., sr. v.p. bus. affairs, 1983-84; sr. v.p. bus. and legal Walt Disney Studios, Burbank, Calif., 1984-87, exec. v.p., 1987-94; with Dreamworks, 1994—. Recipient Frontrunner award in bus. Sara Lee Corp., 1991, Big Sisters Achievement award, 1992, Clairol Mentor award, 1993, Women in Bus. Magnificent Seven award, 1994.

HAHN, JAMES KENNETH, lawyer; b. L.A., July 3, 1950; s. Kenneth and Ramona Hahn; m. Monica Ann Teson, May 19, 1984; children: Karina Natalie, Jackson Kenneth. BA in English magna cum laude, Pepperdine U., 1972, JD, 1975. Bar: Calif. 1975. Law clk. L.A. County Dist. Atty.'s Office; city pros. L.A. City Atty.'s Office, 1975-79; pvt. practice Marina del Rey, 1979-81; city contr. City of L.A., 1981-85, city atty., 1985—. Office: City LA Atty Office 1800 City Hall E 200 N Main St Los Angeles CA 90012-4110

HAHN, WOODY, sports association executive; Grad., Wash. State U. Athletic dir. Ea. Mont. Coll., until 1987; commr. Great Northwest Conf., 1988—, Continental Divide Conf., 1989—, Pacific West Conf., Billings, Mont. Active NCAA West Region Men's Basketball Adv. Com. Mem. Nat. Assn. Collegiate Dirs. Athletics, Volleyball Coaches' Assn., Basketball Coaches' Assn., NCAA Divsn. II Commrs. Assn. Office: Pacific West Conf PO Box 2002 Billings MT 59103-2002

HAIGHT, DAVID B. religious organization administrator. s. Hector C. and Clara Tuttle Haight; m. Ruby Olson, three children. Attended Utah State U; Former Mayor, Palo Alto, Calif.; Asst. to the twelve 1970-76, Apostle, Quorum of the Twelve, 1976—, Mormon Ch., Salt Lake City; Comdr. Navy, WW2. Office: LDS Church 50 E North Temple Salt Lake City UT 84150-0002 also: Bonneville Internat Corp Broadcast House 55 E 3rd S Salt Lake City UT 84111-2201

HAIGHT, JAMES THERON, lawyer, corporate executive; b. Racine, Wis., Dec. 10, 1924; s. Walter Lyman and Geraldine (Foley) H.; m. Patricia Aloe, Apr. 26, 1952; children: Alberta, Barbara, Catherine, Dorothy, Elaine. Student, U. Nebr., 1943-44, U. Bordeaux, France, 1947; diplome d'Etudes, U. Paris, 1948; B.A., U. Wis., 1950, LL.B., 1951. Bar: D.C. 1952, U.S. Supreme Ct. 1955, Calif. 1968. Atty. Covington & Burling, Washington, 1951-56, Goodyear Tire & Rubber Co., Goodyear Internat. Corp., Akron, Ohio, 1956-61; gen. counsel, sec. George J. Meyer Mfg. Co., Milw., 1961-66; sr. v.p., sec., chief corp. counsel Thrifty Corp., L.A., 1966-92, spl. counsel, 1992-96. Adv. bd. Edward Roybal Inst. Applied Gerontology, Calif. State U., L. A. Fellow Am. Bar Found. (life); mem. ABA (vice chmn. internat. law sect. 1965-67, chmn. 1974-75), Calif. Bar Assn., Pasadena Bar Assn., Am. Soc. Corp. Secs., Order of Coif. Home and Office: 1390 Ridge Way Pasadena CA 91106-4514

HAIGHT, WARREN GAZZAM, investor; b. Seattle, Sept. 7, 1929; s. Gilbert Pierce and Ruth (Gazzam) H.; m. Suzanne H., Sept. 1, 1951; children— Paula Lea, Ian Pierce; m. Ottina Mehau, June 25, 1985 A.B. in Econs, Stanford U., 1951. Asst. Treas. Hawaiian Pineapple Co., Honolulu, 1955-64; v.p., treas. Oceanic Properties, Inc., Honolulu, 1964-67, pres., dir., 1967-85, chmn., 1983-85; pres. Hawaii, Castle & Cooke Inc., 1983-85, Warren G. Haight & Assocs., 1985—; chmn. Molokai Ranch, Ltd., 1996-2001, Pacific Island Resources, LLC, 2000—. Bd. dirs. Round Hill Enterprises, Inc., Las Positas Land Co., Inc., Baldwin Pacific Properties, Inc., Hawaii Project Mgmt., Inc., Transamerica Realty Advisors, Inc., Queen Emma Corp., Queens Devel. Corp., Dole Corp., Standard Fruit and Steamship Co., Inc., Bumble Bee Seafoods, Inc. Bd. dirs. Downtown Improvement Assn., Oahu Devel. Conf., Hawaii Island Econ. Devel. Bd., Econ. Devel. Corp. Honolulu, Intellect, Inc., Hawaii Resort Developers Conf., Homeless Solutions, Inc., Mutual Housing of Hawaii, Inc.; mem. Transit Coalition, Honolulu, Govs. Com. on Econ. Futures; pres., bd. dirs. Land Use Rsch. Found. of Hawaii, Pacific Found. for Cancer Rsch., Hawaii Nature Ctr.; mem. policy adv. bd. for elderly affairs State of Hawaii. Lt. USNR, 1951-55. Mem. Housing Coalition, Calif. Coastal Council. Clubs: Outrigger Canoe, Round Hill Country, Plaza, Pacific Home: 319 Lala Pl Kailua HI 96734-3224 Office: 220 S King St Ste 1465 Honolulu HI 96813-4542 E-mail: haighthawaii@aol.com

HAILE, ALLEN CLEVELAND, educator and administrator; b. Forbes Rd., Pa., Aug. 26, 1930; s. Wesley Matthew and Mary Olivia (Hall) H.; m. Barbara Honey, Dec. 30, 1975; children: Mark, Brice, Scott, Marybeth, Jonathan, Courtney. AB, U. Nebr., Omaha, 1959; MS, U. So. Calif., 1966, MPA, PhD, U. So. Calif., 1971. Commd. 2d lt. USAF, 1953, advanced through grades to lt. col., retired, 1973; v.p. urban affairs Pepperdine U., L.A., 1969-73; sr. rschr. Dept. Info. Scis. Rand Corp., Santa Monica, Calif., 1972-73; regional rep. Pacific Basin U.S. Sec. Commerce, L.A., 1977-81; dept. mgr. human resources devel. Bechtel Civil, Inc., Jubail City, 1981-85, mgr. bus. devel. for bldgs. and infrastructure ops., 1985-87, mgr. mktg., 1987-89, mgr. infrastructure devel. Pacific Rim countries, 1991—; dean Coll. of Bus. Calif. Poly State U., San Luis Obispo, 1993-94, dir. cmty. and govt. rels., 1994—. Adj. prof. Golden Gate Univ., 1992. V.p., bd. dirs. San Luis Obispo ARC, C. of C.; pres. Filipino Am C. of C., 1991; bd. dirs. United Way, San Luis Obispo, Econ. Forecast Project, San Luis Obispo, Larkin St. Youth Ctr., San Francisco Edn. Fund Ct. Appointed Spl. Advocates for Children, Western Govtl. Rsch. Assn., pres. 1989; pres. San Francisco Social Svcs. Commn. 1989, San Francisco Planning and Urban Rsch. Assn., 1992. Decorated DFC and seven air medals. Mem. Am. Soc. Pub. Adminstrn. (bd. trustees found., chmn. constitution revision com. 1988, 89). Home: 1022 Islay St San Luis Obispo CA 93401-4026 Office: Calif Poly State U Office Corp Govt Rels San Luis Obispo CA 93407

HAINES, RICHARD FOSTER, retired psychologist; b. Seattle, May 19, 1937; s. Donald Hutchinson and Claudia May (Bennett) H.; m. Carol Taylor, June 17, 1961; children: Cynthia Lynn, Laura Anne. Student, U. Wash., 1955-57; BA, Pacific Luth. Coll., Tacoma, 1960; MA, Mich. State U., 1962, PhD, 1964. Predoctoral rsch. fellow NIH, 1964; Nat. Acad. Sci. postdoctoral resident rsch. assoc. Ames Rsch. Ctr./NASA, Moffett Field, Calif., 1964-67, rsch. scientist, 1967-86, chief of space human factors office, 1987-88, rsch. scientist Rsch. Inst. Advanced Computer Sci., 1988-90; assoc. prof. dept. psychology San Jose State U., 1988-89; computer scientist RECOM Techs., Inc., Moffett Field, Calif., 1993-2000, Raytheon Corp., 2000—; ret., 2001. Rsch. cons. to NASA Foothill Coll.; cons. Stanford U. Sch. medicine, 1966-67, TRW-Systems Group, 1969-70; mem. adv. com. on vision NRC; founding mem. advanced tech. applications com. Calif. Coun. AIA and NASA, 1975-80; mem. adv. bd. Space Scis. Ctr.-Foothill Coll., 1976-78; bd. advisors Fund for UFO Rsch., Washington; chmn. bd. Novosibirsk Christian Pub.-Calif., 1993—; chief scientist Nat. Aviation Reporting Ctr. on Anomalous Phenomena, 2001—. Author: UFO Phenomena and the Behavioral Scientist, 1979, Observing UFOs, 1980, Melbourne Episode: Case Study of a Missing Pilot, 1987, Advanced Aerial Devices Reported During the Korean War, 1990, Night Flying, 1992, Project Delta, 1994, Close Encounters of the Fifth Kind, 1999; mem. editl. and sci. bd. Jour. UFO Studies, Internat. UFO Reporter, Cuadernos de Ufologica; contbr. articles to profl. jours. Mem. Palo Alto (Calif.) Mayor's Com. on Youth Activities, 1967; chmn. adv. coun. Christian Cmty. Progress Corp., Menlo Park (Calif.); v.p., dir. Ctr. Counseling for Drug Abuse, Menlo Park; bd. dirs., chmn. sci. adv. team Threshold Found.; founding co-dir. Joint Am.-Soviet Aerial Anomaly Fedn., 1991—. Named Alumnus of Yr., Pacific Luth. U., 1972 Fellow Aerospace Med. Assn. (assoc.); mem. Optical Soc. Am., Soc. for Sci. Exploration, Sigma Xi. Achievements include patents for device of advanced detection of glaucoma, optical projector of vision performance data for design engineers, visual simulator optical alignment device, grooming aid for use by astronauts in space. Home: 325 Langton Ave Los Altos CA 94022-1055

HAIR, KITTIE ELLEN, secondary educator; b. Denver, June 12, 1948; d. William Edward and Jacqueline Jean (Holt) H. BA, Brigham Young U., 1971; MA in Social History, U. Nev., Las Vegas, 1987, cert. paralegal, 1995. cert. tchr., Nev. Health educator Peace Corps, Totota, Liberia, 1971-72; tchr. Clark County Sch. Dist., Las Vegas, Nev., 1972-77, 1979—, chair dept. social studies, 1993-95; missionary Ch. Jesus Christ Latter-Day Saints, Alta., Can., 1977-79. Assessor Nat. Bd. Profl. Tchg. Standards. Recipient Outstanding Faculty award U. Nev./Southland Corp., Las Vegas, 1991; named Educator of Yr. Kiwanis Club, 1998-99. Mem. Phi Kappa Phi, Phi Alpha Theta, Delta Kappa Gamma (pres. Chi State, Iota chpt. 1996-98). Democrat. Avocations: collecting western and Native American art, gardening. Office: Advanced Technologies Acad 2501 Vegas Dr Las Vegas NV 89106-1643 E-mail: Khair@atech.org

HAISCH, BERNARD MICHAEL, astronomer, researcher; b. Stuttgart-Bad Canstatt, Federal Republic of Germany, Aug. 23, 1949; s. Friedrich Wilhelm and Gertrud Paula (Dammbacher) H.; m. Pamela S. Eakins, July 29, 1977 (div. 1986); children: Katherine Stuart, Christopher Taylor; m. Marsha A. Sims, Aug. 23, 1986. Student, St. Meinrad (Ind.) Coll., 1967-68; BS in Astrophysics, Ind. U., 1971; PhD in Astronomy, U. Wis., 1975. Rsch. assoc. Joint Inst. Lab. Astrophysics, U. Colo., 1975-77, 78-79; vis. scientist space rsch. lab. U. Utrecht, The Netherlands, 1977-78; rsch. scientist Lockheed Rsch. Lab., Palo Alto, Calif., 1979-83, staff scientist, 1983-99; dep. dir. Ctr. for EUV Astrophysics U. Calif., Berkeley, 1992-94; dir. Calif. Inst. Physics and Astrophysics, 1999—. Guest investigator Internat. Ultraviolet Explorer, Einstein Obs., Exosat, ROSAT Obs., EUVE Obs., Astro-D (ASCA), X-Ray Timing Explorer, 1980—; vis. fellow Max Planck Inst. Extraterr. Physik, Garching, Germany, 1991-94. Editor-in-chief Jour. Sci. Exploration, 1988—, Solar and Stellar Flares, 1989; sci. editor The Astrophys. Jour., 1993—; monograph The Many Faces of the Sun, 1999; mem. editl. bd. Solar Physics, 1992-95, Speculations in Sci. and Tech., 1995—; contbr. articles to profl. jours. Fellow Royal Astron. Soc., AIAA (assoc.); mem. AAAS (patron), Internat. Astron. Union, Am. Astron. Soc., European Astron. Soc., Am. Assn. Physics Tchrs., Sigma Xi, Phi Beta Kappa, Phi Kappa Phi. Avocations: Tae Kwon Do, international folk dance, downhill skiing, songwriting. Office: Calif Inst Physics and Astrophysics 366 Cambridge Ave Palo Alto CA 94306-1506 E-mail: haisch@calphysics.org

HAKE, RALPH F. construction company executive; b. Cin. BBA, U. Cin.; MBA, U. Chgo. V.p. adminstrn.l. Mead Corp., Escababa, Mich., 1980-84, dir. corp. devel. Dayton, Ohio, 1984-87; various fin. and ops. positions including corp. v.p., contr. Whirlpool Corp., Benton Harbor, Mich., from 1987, pres. Bauknecht appliance group, exec. v.p. N.Am. appliance group, sr. exec. v.p. ops., until 1997, sr. exec. v.p., CFO, 1997-1999; exec. v.p., CFO Fluor Corp., Aliso Viejo, Calif., 1999—. With U.S. Army, 1971-73. Mem. NAM (bd. dirs.). Office: Fluor Corp 1 Enterprise Dr Aliso Viejo CA 92650-2606

HAKIMI, S. LOUIS, electrical and computer engineering educator; b. Meshed, Iran, Dec. 16, 1932; came to U.S., 1952, naturalized, 1967; s. A. Moshe and Miriam (Nabavian) H.; m. Mary Yomtob, Aug. 22, 1965; children: Alan, Carol, Diane. B.S. in Elec. Engring., U. Ill., Urbana, 1955, M.S. in Elec. Engring., 1957, Ph.D. in Elec. Engring., 1959. Asst. prof. elec. engring. U. Ill., 1959-61; assoc. prof. Northwestern U., Evanston, Ill., 1961-66, prof., 1966-86, chmn. dept. elec. engring., 1972-77; prof. U. Calif., Davis, 1986—, chmn. elec. and computer engring., 1986-96. Assoc. editor Networks, 1975-90, adv. editor, 1990—; assoc. editor IEEE Transactions on Circuits and Systems, 1975-77; bd. adv. editors Transp. Sci., 1985—. Fellow IEEE (life); mem. Soc. Indsl. and Applied Math., Sigma Xi, Tau Beta Pi, Phi Kappa Phi. Home: 27017 E El Macero Dr El Macero CA 95618-1008 Office: U Calif Dept Elec & Computer Engring Davis CA 95616

HAKKILA, EERO ARNOLD, retired nuclear safeguards technology chemist; b. Canterbury, Conn., Aug. 4, 1931; s. Jack and Ida Maria (Lillquist) H.; m. Margaret W. Hakkila; children: Jon Eric, Mark Douglas, Gregg Arnold. BS in Chemistry, Cen. Conn. State U., 1953; PhD in Analytical Chemistry, Ohio State U., 1957. Staff mem. Los Alamos (N.Mex.) Nat. Lab., 1957-78, assoc. group leader safeguard systems, 1978-80, dep. group leader, 1980-82, group leader, 1982-83, project mgr. internat. safeguards, 1983-87, program coord., 1987-95; ret., 1995. Editor: Nuclear Safeguards Analysis, 1978; contbr. numerous articles to profl. jours. Fellow Am. Inst. Chemists; mem. N.Mex. Inst. Chemists (pres. 1971-73), Am. Chem. Soc., Am. Nuclear Soc. (exec. com. fuel cycle and waste mgmt. div. 1984-86), Inst. Nuclear Materials Mgmt. Avocations: skiing, fishing, rockhounding, golf. E-mail: a. Office: Los Alamos Nat Lab PO Box 1663 MS E541 Los Alamos NM 87544-0600 E-mail: hakkila@msn.com

HALAMANDARIS, HARRY, aerospace executive; b. Sunnyside, Utah, Sept. 26, 1938; s. Gust and Olga (Konakis) H.; m. Sandra Susan Hansen, Aug. 4, 1961; children: Chris Harry, Gina Lee. AS, Carbon Coll., 1958; BS in Math., Utah State U., 1960, BSEE, 1961, MSEE, 1962. Instr. West Coast U., L.A., 1964-68; mem. tech. staff Hughes Aircraft, Culver City, Calif.,

1962-65; sr. mem. tech. staff Litton Guidance & Controls, Woodland Hills, 1965-69; gen. mgr., exec. v.p. Satellite Positioning Corp., Encino, 1969-72; pres., asst. group exec. Teledyne Systems, Northridge, 1972-89; dir. corp. tech. Teledyne Industries, Inc., L.A., 1989-94; group exec. Kaiser Aerospace and Electronics, Van Nuys, Calif., 1994-95; exec. v.p., COO Litton Industries, Inc., 1995-2000, sr. v.p., group exec., 2000—. Mem. adv. coun. Coll. Ea. Utah; industry adv. bd. U. So. Calif., Calif. State U., L.A.; bd. dirs. Econ. Devel. Corp., 1992-94. Contbr. over 30 articles to profl. jours. Mem. bd. govs. Pacific Boys Lodge, Woodland Hills, Calif., 1986-88; aerospace chmn. United Way, L.A., 1988-89. NSF fellow, 1961-62. Mem. Am. Electronics Assn. (bd. dirs., exec. com. 1984-94, pres. Roundtable exec. com. 1989-92), Utah State Alumni, Masons, Sigma Xi (officer, v.p. 1960-61), Phi Kappa Phi, Tau Betta Pi. Democrat. Greek Orthodox. Avocations: racquetball, gardening, sports. Home: 21041 Nashville St Chatsworth CA 91311-1447 Office: Litton Industries Inc 21240 Burbank Blvd Woodland Hills CA 91367-6675

HALBACH, EDWARD CHRISTIAN, JR. law educator, educator; b. Clinton, Iowa, Nov. 8, 1931; s. Edward Christian and Lewella (Sullivan) H.; m. Janet Elizabeth Bridges, July 25, 1953; children: Kristin Lynn, Edward Christian III, Kathleen Ann, Thomas Elliot, Elaine Diane. BA, U. Iowa, 1953, JD, 1958; LLM, Harvard U., 1959; LLD, U. Redlands, 1973. Assoc. prof. Sch. Law, U. Calif. at Berkeley, 1959-62, prof., 1963—, dean, 1966-75. Co-author: Materials on Decedents' Estates and Trusts, 1965, 73, 81, 87, 93, 2000, Materials on Future Interests, 1977, Death, Taxes and Family Property, 1977, California Will Drafting, 1965, 77, 92; author: Use of Trusts in Estate Planning, 1975, 81, 84, 86, 91, Fundamentals of Estate Planning, 1983, 86, 87, 89, 91, 93, 95, Summary of the Law of Trusts, 1990, 1998, Principles and Techniques of Estate Planning, 1995; reporter Uniform Probate Code, 1969, Restatement 3d Trusts Prudent Investor Rule, 1991; also articles. 1st lt. USAF, 1954-56. Mem. ABA (chmn. various coms. sect. individual rights and responsibilities and sect. real property probate adn trust law, dir. probate and trust divsn., sect. chmn.), Iowa Bar Assn., Am. Law Inst. (reporter Restatement 3d Trusts, advisor Restatement 2d, 3d Property), Am. Acad. Polit. and Social Scis., Am. Bar Found., Am. coll. Trust and Estate Counsel, Am. Coll. Tax Counsel, Internat. Acad. Estate and Trust Law (v.p., exec. com., pres.). Home: 679 San Luis Rd Berkeley CA 94707-1725 Office: U Calif Sch Law Boalt Hall Berkeley CA 94720

HALBER, DIANE, professional figure skater; b. Torrance, Calif., May 13, 1977; Competitive history include placing 19th in the Nat. Sr., 1997, 3rd place Pacific Coast Sr., 1997, 4th place Southwest pacific Sr., 1997, 5th place, 1996, 1st place Nat. Collegiate, 1996, others. Office: 20 1st St Colorado Springs CO 80906-3624

HALE, BRUCE DONALD, retired marketing professional; b. Oak Park, Ill., Dec. 21, 1933; s. Edward Garden and Mildred Lillian (Pelc) H.; m. Nancy Ann Novotny, July 2, 1955 (div. 1976); children: Jeffrey Bruce, Karen Jill Hale; m. Connie Luella Green Gunderson, Apr. 21, 1979. BA in Econs., Wesleyan U., Middletown, Conn., 1955. Trainee Caterpillar Tractor Co., Peoria, Ill., 1955-56, dealer tng. rep., 1956-59, dist. rep. Albuquerque, 1959-62; asst. sales mgr. Rust Tractor Co., Albuquerque, 1962-65, gen. sales mgr. Albuqerque, 1965-71, v.p. sales, 1971-81, v.p. mktg., 1981-96; ret., 1996. Mem. Am. Mining Congress, Soc. Mining Engrs., Associated Contractors N.Mex., Associated Equipment Distbrs., Rocky Mountain Coal Mining Inst., N.Mex. Mining Assn., Albuquerque Country Club. Avocations: golf, fishing, music, classic cars. Home: 9508 Layton Pl NE Albuquerque NM 87111-1368

HALE, DAVID FREDRICK, health care company executive; b. Gadsden, Ala., Jan. 8, 1949; s. Millard and Mildred Earline (McElroy) H.; m. Linda Carol Sadorski, Mar. 14, 1975; children: Shane Michael, Tara Renee, Erin Nicole, David Garrett. BA, Jacksonville State U. Dir. mktg. Ortho Pharm. Corp. divsn. Johnson & Johnson, Raritan, N.J., 1978-80; v.p. mktg. BBL Microbiology Sys. divsn. Becton Dickinson & Co., Cockeysville, Md., 1980-81, v.p., gen. mgr., 1981-82; sr. v.p. mktg. and bus. devel. Hybritech, Inc., San Diego, 1982, pres., 1983-86, CEO, 1986-87; pres., CEO, bd. dirs. Gensia Sicor, Inc., San Diego, 1987-97, Women First HealthCare, Inc., 1998-2000, CancerVax Corp., Carlsbad, Calif., 2000—. Bd. dirs. LMA N.Am., Metabasis Therapeutics, Santarus, Inc., Children's Hosp., Francis Parker Sch., San Diego Econ. Devel. Corp., Biocom San Diego; founder CONNECT. Mem. World Pres.'s Orgn., Chief Exec.'s Orgn. Republican. Episcopalian. Home: PO Box 8925 17079 Circa del Sur Rancho Santa Fe CA 92067 Office: CancerVax Corp 5931 Darwin Ct Carlsbad CA 92008

HALE, KAREN, state legislator; b. June 24, 1958; m. Jon Martin Hale. BS in Mass. Comm., U. Utah. Formerly pub. and editor; formerly vol. in neighborhood schs.; mem. Utah Senate, Dist. 7, Salt Lake City, 1998—; mem. trans. and pub. safety com., edn. com.; mem. pub. edn. appropriations com. Utah State Senate. Chair pub. rels. Sugarhouse Sesquicentennial Celebration, 1997; statewide edn. chair Earth Day Utah, 1990. Democrat. Home: 2564 Maywood Dr Salt Lake City UT 84109-1614

HALE, KAYCEE, research marketing professional; b. Mount Hope, W.Va., July 18, 1947; d. Bernard McFadden and Virginia Lucille (Mosley) H. AA, Compton Coll., 1965; BS, Calif. State U., Dominguez Hills, 1981. Fashion model O'Bryant Talent Agy., L.A., 1967-77; faculty mem. L.A. Trade-Tech. Coll., 1969-71, Fashion Inst., L.A., 1969-77, L.A., 1975—; pres. The Fashion Co., L.A., 1970-75; co-host The Fashion Game TV Show, L.A., 1982-87; exec. dir. Fashion Inst. Design and Merchandising Resource & Rsch. Ctr., L.A., 1975—, Fashion Inst. Design and Merchandising Mus. and Libr., L.A., 1977-98. Lectr. in field, internat., 1969—. Author: (brochure) What's Your I.Q. (Image Quotient)?; (tape) Image Builders; contbg. editor Library Management in Review; columnist The Public Image, 1990; contbr. Bowker Annual 1990-91, (newsletter) Northeast Library System, 1991. Adv. bd. Calif. State U., Long Beach, 1988-91. Mem. ALA, Spl. Librs. Assn. (pres. elect 1986—, pres. 1987-88, bd. dirs. So. Calif. chpt. 1985—), Spl. Librs. Adv. Coun. (pub. rels. com. 1987-89), SLA Libr. Mgmt. Div. (chmn.-elect 1987-88, chmn. 1988-89, pres.'s task force on image of libr./info. profl.), Textile Assn. L.A. (bd. dirs. 1985-87), Calif. Media and Libr. Educators Assn., Am. Mktg. Assn., Western Mus. Conf., Am. Mus. Assn., Costume Soc. Am. Office: Fashion Inst Design & Merchandising 919 S Grand Ave Los Angeles CA 90015-1421

HALE, NATHAN ROBERT, architect; b. Battle Creek, Mich., July 20, 1944; s. Nathan Shirley and Gertrude Anges (Barnes) H.; m. CarolAnn Purrington, May 28, 1966; children: Marilyce, Maile, Martha. BA, Syracuse U., 1967, BArch, 1971. Dir. Archs. Hawaii, Honolulu, 1971—. Served with AUS, 1968-70, Vietnam. Mem. AIA (bd. dirs. 1984, pres. 1992), Hawii C. of C. (exec. com. 1994-99), Econ. Devel. Corp. Honolulu (chair 1993-96, bd. dirs. 1982—), Rotary Club (bd. dirs. 1986-88), Friends of Children's Advocacy Ctr. (pres. 1991, 93, bd. dirs., 1986—). Office: Architects Hawaii Ltd Pacific Tower 300 1001 Bishop St Honolulu HI 96813-3429

HALE, PATRICIA S. state legislator; m. Tom Hale; 5 children. Degree in mktg., U. N.C.; degree in econs., U. Richmond. Dir. strategic intiatives Fluor Daniel Hanford; mem. Wash. Senate, Dist. 8, Olympia, 1994—; majority whip Wash. Senate, Olympia, 1997, Rep. caucus chair, 1999. Bd. Tri-Cities Cancer Ctr. Found., United Way, Tri-Cities Vis. and Conv. Bur., Wash. State Hist. Soc.; co-chair Mission Impossible com. March of Dimes; fundraising co-chair Boys and Girls Club; co-chair Walk Am., 1996; campaign chair Benton/Franklin United Way, 1997. Recipient Top Notch award for Comms. Excellence Rockwell Internat., Total Quality Achievement award Westinghouse Hanford Co., 1989, Nat. Mgmt. award Westinghouse Electric Corp., 1990. Mem. Rotary, Kennewick C. of C. (former dir.), Pvt. Indsl. Coun. (past vice chair and econ. devel. com. chair 1997). Republican. Office: 303 Legislative Bldg Olympia WA 98504-0001

HALES, ALFRED WASHINGTON, mathematics educator, consultant; b. Pasadena, Calif., Nov. 30, 1938; s. Raleigh Stanton and Gwendolen (Washington) H.; m. Virginia Dart Greene, July 7, 1962; children—Andrew Stanton, Lisa Ruth, Katherine Washington B.S., Calif. Inst. Tech., 1960, Ph.D., 1962. NSF postdoctoral fellow Cambridge U., Eng., 1962-63; Benjamin Peirce instr. Harvard U., 1963-66; faculty mem. UCLA, 1966-92, prof. math., 1973-92, prof. emeritus, 1992—; dir. Inst. Def. Analyses, Ctr. Comms. Rsch., La Jolla, Calif., 1992—. Cons. Jet Propulsion Lab., La Canada, Calif., 1966-70, Inst. for Def. Analyses, Princeton, N.J. and LaJolla, Calif., 1964-65, 76, 79-92; vis. lectr. U. Wash., Seattle, 1970-71; vis. mem. U. Warwick Math. Inst., Coventry, Eng., 1977-78, Math. Sci. Rsch. Inst., Berkeley, 1986-87. Co-author: Shift Register Sequences, 1967, 82; contbr. articles to profl. jours. Bd. trustees Math. Sci. Rsch. Inst., Berkeley, 1995-99. Mem. Am. Math. Soc., Math. Assn. Am., Soc. Indsl. and Applied Math. (Polya prize in combinatorics 1972), Sigma Xi Clubs: Pasadena Badminton. Office: Ctr for Comm Rsch 4320 Westerra Ct San Diego CA 92121-1969 E-mail: hales@ccrwest.org

HALEY, GEORGE PATRICK, lawyer; b. Bad Axe, Mich., Sept. 23, 1948; s. Glen Kirk and Bernice (Cooper) H.; m. Theresa L. Thomas, Dec. 24, 1975. BS, U. Mich., 1970; MS, U. Calif., Berkeley, 1971; JD, Harvard U., 1974. Bar: Calif. 1974, U.S. Dist. Ct. (no. dist.) Calif. 1974, U.S. Dist. Ct. (ea. dist.) Calif. 1980. Assoc. Pillsbury Winthrop LLP, San Francisco, 1974-81, ptnr., 1982—. Prof. U. Shanghai, Shanghai-San Francisco Sister City Program, 1986—. Author numerous articles uniform commercial code, project fin. Dir. Calif. Shakespeare Festival, Berkeley, 1986-93; dir. Nat. Writing Project, 1996—. Mem. ABA (chmn. com. 1976-93), Am. Coll. Comml. Fin. Lawyers, State Bar Calif. (chmn. fin. instns. com. 1980, commercial code com. 1988). Republican. Methodist. Avocations: tai chi chuan, golf, cooking. Home: 1825 Marin Ave Berkeley CA 94707-2414 E-mail: ghaley@pillsburywinthrop.com

HALEY, JOHN DAVID, petroleum consulting company executive; b. Denver, Mar. 16, 1924; s. Peter Daniel and Margaret Dorothy (O'Haire) H.; m. Annie Loretta Breeden, June 20, 1951; children: Laura, Patricia, Brian, Sharon, Norine, Kathleen. Profl. engr., Colo. Sch. Mines, 1948. Registered profl. engr., Colo., Okla. Petroleum engr. Creole Petroleum, Venezuela, 1948-50; field engr. Texaco Inc., La., 1950-52; staff engr. Carter Oil (Exxon), Tulsa, 1954-56; petroleum cons. Earlougher Engring., Tulsa, 1956-61; v.p. prodn. Anschutz Corp., Denver, 1962-86; v.p. Circle A Drilling, Denver, 1967-78; dir. Circle A Mud, Denver, 1983-86; pres. Greylock Pipeline, Denver, 1983-86, Anschutz Pipeline, Denver, 1984-86, Haley Engring. Inc., 1987—. Mem. Pres.'s Coun., Colo. Sch. Mines, 1985—; bd. dirs. AlumniAssn., 1992-97, pres., 1995; bd. dirs. CSM Found., 1996-98; Rep. committeeman, Littleton, Colo. Lt. comdr. USNR, 1943-46, 52-54. Recipient Outstanding Alumnus award Alumni Assn., 1997. Mem. Soc. Petroleum Engrs. (bd. dirs. Denver chpt. 1965), Soc. Petroleum Evaluation Engrs. (bd. dirs. 1992-95), Ind. Petroleum Assn. Mountain States, Am. Petroleum Inst. (citation for svc.), Internat. Assn. Drilling Contractors, Rocky Mountain Oil and Gas Assn. (bd. dirs. 1988-2000), Soc. Profl. Well Log Analysts, Petroleum Club (Denver chpt.). Roman Catholic. Home: 561 E Caley Dr Littleton CO 80121-2212

HALFORD, RICK, state legislator; b. Boston, Sept. 17, 1944; m. Rona Halford; children: Stacy, Katy, Tina, Kellen, Alec. BA in History and Polit. Sci., Alaska Meth. U. Owner, operator Halford Guide Svc.; mem. Alaska Ho. of Reps., 1978-82, Alaska Senate, Dist. M, Juneau, 1982—; pres. Alaska Senate, 1993—; chair resources com., vice-chair judiciary com.; mem. com. on coms., transp. com., legis. budget & audit com. Dir. State Legis. Leaders Found. Staff sgt. Alaska Air Nat. Guard, 1968-75. Mem. NRA (life), Nat. Conf. State Legislatures, Alaska Outdoor Coun., Chugiak/Eagle River C. of C., Greater Wasilla C. of C. Republican. Avocations: flying, children, outdoor activities. Office: State Capitol 120 4th St Rm 121 Juneau AK 99801-1142 Fax: 907-465-4928

HALGREN, LEE A. academic administrator; Pres., v.p. acad. and student affairs State Coll. Colo., Denver, 1995—. Office: The State Coll Colo 1580 Lincoln St Ste 750 Denver CO 80203-1505 E-mail: halgrenl@mscd.edu

HALKETT, ALAN NEILSON, lawyer; b. Chungking, China, Oct. 5, 1931; came to U.S., 1940; s. James and Evelyn Alexandrina (Neilson) H.; m. Mary Lou Hickey, July 30, 1955; children— Kent, James, Kate B.S., UCLA, 1953, LL.B., 1961. Bar: Calif. 1962. Mem. firm Latham & Watkins, L.A., 1961-95, mem. exec. com., 1968-72, chmn. litigation dept., 1980-86, chmn. succession com., 1986-87. State chmn. Am. Coll., Calif., 1992-94; designee CPR panel Disting. Neutrals, 1994—. Served to lt. USN, 1954-58 Fellow Am. Coll. Trial Lawyers; mem. Calif. Bar Assn., Nat. Arbitration Forum, Def. Orientation Conf. Assn., Chancery Club, UCLA Law Alumni Assn. (pres. 1968), Order of Coif. Republican. Clubs: Jonathan (Los Angeles); Palos Verdes Country (Palos Verdes Estates, Calif.) Avocations: golf; old cars. Office: Latham & Watkins 633 W 5th St Ste 4000 Los Angeles CA 90071-2005 E-mail: mhalkett@gateway.net

HALKIN, HUBERT, mathematics educator, research mathematician; b. Liege, Belgium, June 5, 1936; came to U.S., 1960; s. Leon E. and Denise (Daude) H.; m. Carolyn Mulliken, June 22, 1964 (div. 1971); children: Christopher, Sherrill-Anne; m. Katherine Hodges, Dec. 24, 1988. Ingenieur, U. Liège, 1960; PhD, Stanford U., 1963. Tech. staff Bell Telephone Labs., Whippany, N.J., 1963-65; assoc. prof. math. dept. U. Calif., San Diego, 1965-69, prof., 1969—, dept. chmn., 1981-87. Editor Jour. Optimization Theory and Applications, 1968—, Revue Française d'Automatique de Recherche Operationnelle, 1973—. Guggenheim fellow, 1971-72. Mem. Sierra Club. Club: Sierra. Office: U Calif San Diego Dept Math La Jolla CA 92093 E-mail: hhalkin@ucsd.edu

HALL, ADRIENNE A. international marketing executive, venture capitalist consultant; b. L.A. d. Arthur E. and Adelina P. Kosches; m. Maurice Hall; children: Adam, Todd, Stefanie, Victoria; adopted and foster children: Joe Kwan, Carlos Moreno. B.A., UCLA. Founding ptnr. Hall & Levine Advt., L.A., 1970-80; vice chmn. bd. Eisaman, Johns & Laws Advt. Inc., L.A., Houston, Chgo., N.Y.C., 1980-94; pres., CEO The Hall Group, Beverly Hills, Calif., 1994—. Co-founder, chair, bd. dirs. Women, Inc.; chair, adv. bd., Women's Pres. Orgn., 1999—, co-chair, State Econ. Network, 2000—; chmn. Eric Bovy Inc., 1986-89, Hall Partnership, Venture Capital; bd. dirs. Calif. Mfrs. Assn., Calif. Life Corp., Inc.; mem. adv. bd. Global Asset Mgmt., The Edison Co. Trustee UCLA; bd. regents Loyola-Marymount U., 1990—, Natl. Bus. Counc., Wash. D.C.; mem. The Founders of Music Ctr.; mem. women's leadership bd. Kennedy Sch. Govt., Harvard U.; adv. bd., The Gas Co. (Sempra Energy), 1999—, Global Asset Mgmt.; commr. L.A. County Arts Commn.; commr. Calif. Gov.'s Commn. on Econ. Devel., task force Rebuild L.A.; chair, adv. bd. Leading Women Entrepreneurs of the World; bd. dirs. United Way, ARC, Exec. Svc. Corps, The Com. of 200, Shelter Partnership; trustee Nat. Health Found., Women's Enterprise Devel. Corp.; gov. Town Hall; mem. adv. coun. Girls' Clubs Am.; mem. adv. bd. Girl Scouts U.S., Asian Pacific Women's Adv. Bd., Coalition of 100 Black Women, Nat. Network of Hispanic Women, Women of Color, Women in Bus., Downtown Women's Ctr. and residence, Leadership Am., Washington, L.A., Food Bank; mem. exec. bd. Greater L.A. Partnership for Homeless. Recipient Nat. Headliner award Women in Comm., 1982, Profl. Achievement award UCLA Alumni, 1979, Award for Cmty. Svc., 1994, Asian Pacific Network Woman Warrior award, 1994, Woman of the Yr. award Am. Advt. Fedn., 1973, Ad Person of West award Mktg. and Media Decisions, 1982, Bus. Woman of Yr. award Boy Scouts Am., 1983, Women Helping Women award Soroptimists Internat., 1984, 1st ann. portfolio award for exec. women, 1985, Communicator of Yr. award Ad Women, 1986, Leader award YWCA, 1986, L.A. Women's Found. Mentor award, 1997; named Bus. Leader of Yr., L.A. Bus. Coun., 1999. Mem. Internat. Women's Forum (Woman Who Made a Difference award 1987), Am. Assn. Advt. Agys. (bd. dirs. 1980, chmn. bd. govs. western region), Western States Advt. Agys. Assn. (pres. 1975), Hollywood Radio and TV Soc. (dir.), Nat. Advt. Rev. Bd., Overseas Edn. Fund, Com. 200 (western chmn.), Women in Communications, Orgn. Women Execs., Calif. Women's Forum (founder, chmn. The Trusteeship), Rotary (L.A. 5 chpt.), Internat. Bus. Fellows (mem. adv. bd.), Women's Econ. Alliance, Nat. Assn. Women Bus. Owners (adv. bd.), L.A. Area C. of C. (alumni dir.). Clubs: Calif. Yacht; Stock Exchange, Los Angeles Advt. (pres.) (Los Angeles). Lodge: Rotary. E-mail: aahall@earthlink.net

HALL, ANTHONY ELMITT, crop ecologist; b. Tickhill, Yorkshire, Eng., May 6, 1940; came to U.S., 1964; s. Elmitt and Mary Lisca (Schofield) H.; m. Bretta Reed, June 20, 1965; children: Kerry, Gina. Student, Harper Adams Agrl. Coll., Eng., 1958-60; student in agrl. engring., Essex Inst. Agrl. Engring., Eng., 1960-61; BS in Irrigation Sci., U. Calif., Davis, 1966, PhD in Plant Physiology, 1970. Farmer Dyon House, Austerfield, Eng., 1955-58; extension officer Ministry of Agr., Tanzania, 1961-63; research asst. U. Calif., Davis, 1964-70, asst. research scientist, 1971; research fellow Carnegie Inst., Stanford, Calif., 1970; prof. U. Calif., Riverside, 1971—, cons. agrl. devel., 1974—, chmn. dept botany and plant scis., 1994-97. Author: Crop Responses to Environment, 2001; editor: Agriculture in Semi-Arid Environments, 1979, Stable Isotopes and Plant Carbon-Water Relations, 1993; mem. editl. adv. bd. (jour.) Field Crops Rsch., Vigna Crop Germplasm Com. USDA; contbr. articles to profl. jours. Recipient BIFAD chair's award for scientific excellence, 2000, USDA Sec.'s Honor award plant breeding rsch., 2001. Fellow Am. Soc. Agronomy, Crop Sci. Soc. Am.; mem. Am. Soc. Plant Physiologists, Scandinavian Soc. Plant Physiology, Alpha Zeta, Gamma Sigma Delta (Disting. Achievement in Agr. award of merit 1999), Phi Beta Kappa, Phi Kappa Phi. Achievements include design (with others) of a steady state porometer for measuring stomatal conductance; research on the physiology and breeding of heat and chilling tolerant, pest resistant and drought adapted cowpea cultivars including developing cowpea variety CB27. Office: U Calif Dept Botany & Plant Scis Riverside CA 92521-0001

HALL, BLAINE HILL, retired librarian; b. Wellsville, Utah, Dec. 12, 1932; s. James Owen and Agnes Effie (Hill) H.; m. Carol Stokes, 1959; children: Suzanne, Cheryl, Derek. BS, Brigham Young U., 1960, MA, 1965, MLS, 1971. Instr. English, Brigham Young U., Provo, Utah, 1963-72, humanities librarian, 1972-96. Book reviewer Am. Reference Book Ann., 1984-2000. Author: Collection Assessment Manual, 1985, Saul Bellow Bibliography, 1987, Jerzy Kosinski Bibliography, 1991, Jewish American Fiction Writers Bibliography, 1991, Conversations with Grace Paley, 1997; editor: Utah Libraries, 1972-77 (periodical award ALA 1977); contbr. articles to profl. jours. Bd. dirs. Orem (Utah) Pub. Libr., 1977-84; mem. Orem Media Rev. Commn., 1984-86; chmn. Utah Adv. Commn. on Librs. With U.S. Army, 1953-54, Korea. Mem. ALA (coun. 1988-92), Utah Libr. Assn. (pres. 1980-81, Disting. Svc. award 1989), Mountain Plains Libr. Assn. (bd. dirs. 1978-83, editor newsletter 1978-83, pres. 1994-96, grantee 1979, 80, Disting. Svc. award 1991), Phi Kappa Phi. Mormon. Avocations: writing, photography, carpentry, family history, reading. Home: 230 E 1910 S Orem UT 84058-8161 E-mail: bhall11@worldnet.att.net

HALL, BRENDA, human resources executive; CEO Hall, Kinion and Assocs., Cupertino, Calif. Office: Hall Kinion & Assocs 19925 Stevens Creek Blvd Cupertino CA 95014-2305

HALL, CLARENCE ALBERT, JR. geologist, educator; b. L.A., Jan. 5, 1930; s. Clarence Albert and Margaret Olive (Fabrick) H.; children: Eric Robert, Kris Delorah. BS, Stanford U., 1952, MS, 1953, PhD, 1956. Instr. U. Oreg., Eugene, 1954-55; mem. faculty UCLA, 1956—, prof. geology, chmn. dept. geology, 1974-76, chmn. dept. geophysics and space physics, 1976, chmn. dept. earth and space scis., 1976-78, dean of phys. scis., 1983-94; dir. White Mountain Rsch. Sta. U. Calif. Systemwide, 1979-95. Contbr. articles to profl.jours.; editor Jour. Paleontology, 1971-71. Fulbright rsch. fellow in Italy, 1963-64, 70-71; recipient Dibblee medal, 1998. Fellow Geol. Soc. Am., Paleontol. Soc. Office: UCLA Dept Earth & Scis Los Angeles CA 90095-1567 E-mail: hall@ess.ucla.edu

HALL, CYNTHIA HOLCOMB, federal judge; b. Los Angeles, Feb. 19, 1929; d. Harold Romeyn and Mildred Gould (Kuck) Holcomb; m. John Harris Hall, June 6, 1970 (dec. Oct. 1980) A.B., Stanford U., 1951, J.D., 1954; LL.M., NYU, 1960. Bar: Ariz. 1954, Calif. 1956. Law clk. to judge U.S. Ct. Appeals 9th Circuit, 1954-55; trial atty. tax div. Dept. Justice, 1960-64; atty.-adviser Office Tax Legis. Counsel, Treasury Dept., 1964-66; mem. firm Brawerman & Holcomb, Beverly Hills, Calif., 1966-72; judge U.S. Tax Ct., Washington, 1972-81, U.S. Dist. Ct. for central dist. Calif., Los Angeles, 1981-84; cir. judge U.S. Ct. Appeals (9th cir.), Pasadena, Calif., 1984—, sr. judge, 1997—. Served to lt. (j.g.) USNR, 1951-53. Office: US Ct Appeals 9th Cir 125 S Grand Ave Pasadena CA 91105-1621

HALL, DAVID RAMSAY, architect; b. Lansing, Mich., Oct. 24, 1945; s. Harold Wendell and Sarah Katherine (Schlademan) H.; m. Catherine Anne Weeks, Dec. 23, 1967; children: Sarah Catherine, Rebecca Jane. BArch, Wash. State U., 1968. Registered architect, Wash. Designer, draftsman Earl Flansburgh & Assocs., Cambridge, Mass., 1968-70, NBBJ, Seattle, 1970, Mel Streeter & Assoc., Seattle, 1971-72; designer, ptnr. Henry Klein Partnership, Architects, Mt. Vernon, Wash., 1972—. Author, designer, contbr. articles to profl. publs. Commr. Dike Dist. # 19, Skagit County, Wash., 1984-95; mem. adv. bd. Wash. State U., Pullman, 1990-96; bd. dirs. Self Help Housing, Mt. Vernon, 1980-84. Recipient Progressive Architecture Design award, 1972, Honor award Cedar Shake & Shingle, 1991, Am. Wood Coun., 1993, Sunset Mag. Western Home award. 1995. Mem. AIA (bd. dirs. N.W. chpt. 1985-88, Honor award Seattle chpt. 1991, N.W. chpt. 1991, 94, 96, 97, 98, Commendation award Seattle chpt. 1987). Avocations: watercolor painting, photography, hiking, gardening, fishing. Home: 5871 Farm To Market Rd Bow WA 98232-9254 Office: Henry Klein Partnership 314 Pine St Ste 205 Mount Vernon WA 98273-3852

HALL, DON ALAN, editor, writer; b. Indpls., Aug. 7, 1938; s. Oscar B. and Ruth Ann (Leak) H.; m. Roberta Louise Bash, Apr. 30, 1960; children: Alice Leigh, Nancy Elizabeth. B.A., Ind. U., 1960, M.A., 1968. News editor Rock Springs (Wyo.) Daily Rocket-Miner, 1960-63; mag. editor, picture editor Waukegan News-Sun, Ill., 1964-66; reporter, copy editor Salem Capital Jour., Oreg., 1966-70; free lance journalist Victoria, B.C., Can., 1970-74; copy editor, sci. writer, music reviewer Corvallis (Oreg.) Gazette-Times, 1974-78, copy desk chief, 1978-82, news editor, 1983-84, author weekly opinion column, 1985-87; author weekly nature column for Oreg. newspapers, 1976-85; instr. dept. journalism Oreg. State U., 1984-87. Author: On Top Of Oregon, 1975, Bird in the Bush, 1986; editor Mammoth Trumpet, Center for the Study of the First Americans, 1991-2001. Recipient Westinghouse-AAAS sci. writing award, 1977 Home and Office: 620 NW Witham Dr Corvallis OR 97330-6535

HALL, GORDON R. retired state supreme court chief justice; b. Vernal, Utah, Dec. 14, 1926; s. Roscoe Jefferson and Clara Maud (Freestone) H.; m. Doris Gillespie, Sept. 6, 1947; children: Rick Jefferson, Craig Edwin. B.S., U. Utah, 1949, LL.B., 1951. Bar: Utah 1952. Solo practice, Tooele, Utah, 1952-69; county atty. Tooele County, 1958-69; judge 3d Jud. Dist. Utah, 1969-77; assoc. justice Supreme Ct. Utah, 1977-81, chief justice, 1981-94; of counsel Snow, Christensen & Martineau, Salt Lake City, 1994-98. Chmn. Utah Jud. Coun., 1983-94; pres. Conf. Chief Justices, 1988-89; chmn. Nat. Ctr. State Cts., 1988-89; pres. Utah Assn. Counties, 1965; mem. Pres.'s Adv. Com. OEO, 1965-66. Served with U.S. Maritime Svc., 1944-46. Mem. ABA, Utah Bar Assn. Office: Snow Christensen & Martineau 250 N Sandrun Rd Salt Lake City UT 84103-2239

HALL, HENRY KINGSTON, JR. chemistry educator; b. N.Y.C., Dec. 7, 1924; s. Henry Kingston and Agnes (Furrer) H.; m. Alene Winifred Brown, Mar. 9, 1951; children: Joan, Douglas, Lillian. BS, Poly. Inst. Bklyn., 1944; MS, Pa. State U., 1946; PhD, U. Ill., 1949. Sr. research chemist textile fibers dept. E.I. DuPont de Nemours & Co., Inc., Wilmington, Del., 1952-65, group leader central research dept., 1965-69; prof. chemistry U. Ariz., Tucson, 1969-96, chmn. dept., 1970-73, emeritus prof., 1996—. Cons. Eastman Kodak Co., Rochester, Ticona Corp., Summit, N.J.; vis. prof. Imperial Coll., London, 1976, Max Planck Inst. for Polymer Rsch., Mainz, Federal Republic of Germany, Jan.-June, 1988; sr. vis. fellow Japan Soc. for Promotion Sci., summer 1981 Contbr. articles profl. jours. Recipient Japan Award for Disting. Svc. in Advancement of Polymer Sci., Soc. Polymer Sci., 1996. Mem. Am. Chem. Soc. (PMSE divsn. award for industry-univ. coop. 1997, Award for Polymer Chemistry 1996, H.F. Mark award 2000). Achievements include research in mechanisms of organic reactions and synthesis of new high polymers. Office: U Ariz Dept Chem PO Box 210041 Tucson AZ 85721-0041

HALL, HOWARD PICKERING, engineering and mathematics educator; b. Boston, July 8, 1915; s. George Henry and Elizabeth Isabel (McCallum) H.; m. Ellen Marguerite Ide, June 25, 1945 (dec. 1984); children: Charlotte McCallum, Stephanie Wilson, Lindsey Louise, Gretchen Elizabeth. AB, Harvard U., 1936, MS, 1937, DSc, 1951. Registered structural engr., Ill., 1953. Instr., civil engring. Brown U., Providence, 1937-38; structural analyst Mark Linenthal, Engr., Boston, 1938-39; instr., asst. prof., assoc. prof. civil engring. Northwestern U., Evanston, Ill., 1939-56; design engr, field engr. Porter, Urquart, Skidmore, Owings, Merrill, Casablanca, Fr. Morocco, 1951-53; dean, sch. engring., acad. v.p. Robert Coll., Istanbul, Turkey, 1956-68; dir. of studies, acting headmaster St. Stephen's Sch., Rome, 1968-72; prof. math. Iranzamin Internat., Tehran, Iran, 1973-80; math. tchr. Vienna Internat. Sch., 1980-83, Copenhagen Internat. Sch., 1983-86. Cons. S.J. Buchanan, Bryan, Tex., Eng., 1955. Contbr. articles to profl. jours. Served to Capt. U.S. Army, 1942-46, ETO. Recipient Clemens Herschel award Boston Soc. Civil Engrs., 1954. Mem. Sigma Xi. Home: 301 SW Lincoln St Apt 1401 Portland OR 97201-5033

HALL, HOWARD TRACY, chemist; b. Ogden, Utah, Oct. 20, 1919; s. Howard and Florence (Tracy) H.; m. Ida Rose Langford, Sept. 24, 1941; children— Sherlene, Howard Tracy Jr., David Richard, Elizabeth, Virginia, Charlotte, Nancy. A.S., Weber Coll., 1939; B.S., U. Utah, 1942, M.S., 1943, Ph.D., 1948; D.Sc. (hon.), Brigham Young U., 1971; HHD (hon.), Weber State U., 1987. Registered patent agt. Chemist U.S. Bur. Mines, Salt Lake City, 1942-44, 46; research asso. Gen. Electric Research Lab., Schenectady, 1948-55; dir. research, prof. chemistry Brigham Young U., 1955-67, disting. prof. chemistry, 1967-80, disting. prof. emeritus, 1980—. Chmn. Novatek Indsl. Diamond Mfg. Co., Provo. Contbr. articles to profl. jours.; patentee in field. Served as ensign USNR, 1944-46. Co-recipient Research medal Am. Soc. Tool Mfg. Engrs., 1962; Modern Pioneers Creative Industry award NAM, 1965; Engring. Materials Achievement award Am. Soc. Metals, 1973; Man of Yr. award Abrasive Engring. Soc., 1980; Alfred P. Sloan Found. research fellow, 1959-63 Fellow Am. Inst. Chemists (Chem. Pioneer award 1970), AAAS; mem. Am. Chem. Soc. (Creative Invention award 1972), Am. Phys. Soc. (co-winner Internat. Prize for New Materials 1977), Sigma Xi, Phi Kappa Phi. Achievements include pioneering in synthesizing of diamond. Home: 1711 Lambert Ln Provo UT 84604-1858 Office: Brigham Young Univ Dept Chemistry Provo UT 84602

HALL, JEROME WILLIAM, research engineering educator; b. Brunswick, Ga., Dec. 1, 1943; s. William L. and Frances K. H.; m. Loretta E. Hood, Aug. 28, 1965; children: Jennifer, Bridget, Bernadette. BS in Physics, Harvey Mudd Coll., 1965; MS in Engring., U. Wash., 1968, PhDCE, 1969. Registered profl. engr., D.C., N.Mex., Va. Asst. prof. civil engring. U. Md., College Park, 1970-73, assoc. prof., 1973-77, U. N.Mex., Albuquerque, 1977-80, prof., 1980—, dir. bur. engring. research, 1981-88, asst. dean engring., 1985-88, chmn. dept. of civil engring., 1990-97. Cons. in field. Contbr. articles to profl. jours. Recipient Teetor award Soc. Automotive Engrs., 1975; Pub. Partnership award Alliance For Transportation Rsch., 1997. Fellow Inst. Transp. Engrs. (pres. N.Mex. sect. 1984-86, sec.-treas. western dist. 1987-88, v.p. 1988-89, pres. 1989-90, internat. bd. dirs. 1993-95); mem. Transp. Rsch. Bd. (chmn. com. 1986-92, chmn. group coun. 1992-95, panel chmn. 1990—), Am. Soc. Engring. Edn., Am. Rd. and Transp. Builders Assn., Nat. Assn. County Engrs. Republican. Roman Catholic. Office: U NMex Civil Engring Dept Albuquerque NM 87131-1351 E-mail: jerome@unm.edu

HALL, JOHN LEWIS, physicist, researcher; b. Denver, Aug. 21, 1934; s. John Ernest and Elizabeth Rae (Long) H.; m. Marilyn Charlene Robinson, Mar. 1, 1958; children: Thomas Charles, Carolyn Gay, Jonathan Lawrence. BS in Physics, Carnegie Mellon U., 1956, MS in Physics, 1958, PhD in Physics, 1961; PhD (hon.), U. Paris XIII, 1989. Postdoctoral rsch. assoc. Nat. Bur. Standards, Washington, 1961-62, physicist Boulder, Colo., 1962-75, sr. scientist, 1975—. Cons. Los Alamos (N.Mex.) Sci. Labs., 1963-65; lectr. U. Colo., Boulder, 1977—; cons. numerous firms in laser industry, 1974—. Contbr. articles to profl. jours.; patentee in laser tech.; editor: Laser Spectroscopy 3, 1977. Recipient IR-100 award IR Mag., 1975, 77, Gold medal Nat. Bur. Stds., 1974, Stratton award, 1971, E.U. Condon award, 1979, Gold medal Dept. Commerce, 1969, Presdl. Meritorious Exec. award, 1980, Meritorious Alumnus award Carnegie Mellon U., 1985, Humbolt Sr. Scientist award Munich, 1989, A.V. Astin award NIST, 2000; Sherman Fairchild Disting. scholar Calif. Tech., 1992. Fellow Optical Soc. Am. (bd. dirs. 1980-82, Charles H. Townes award 1984, Frederic Ives medal 1991), Am. Phys. Soc. (Davisson-Germer award 1988, Arthur L. Schawlow prize 1993); mem. NAS, Comite Consultatif pour la Definition du Metre. Office: JILA Nat Bur Standards 325 Broadway St Boulder CO 80303-3337 E-mail: jhall@jila.colorado.edu

HALL, LARRY D. energy company executive, lawyer; b. Hastings, Nebr., Nov. 8, 1942; s. Willis E. and Stella W. (Eckoff) H.; m. Jeffe D. Bryant, July 5, 1985; children: Scott, Jeff, Mike, Bryan. BA in Bus., U. Nebr., Kearney; JD, U. Nebr. Bar: Nebr., Colo. Ptnr. Wright, Simmons, Hancock & Hall, Scottsbluff, Nebr., 1967-71; atty., asst. treas. KN Energy Inc., Hastings, 1971-73, dir. regulatory affairs, 1973-76, v.p. law divsn. Lakewood, Colo., 1976-82, sr. v.p., 1982-85, exec. v.p., 1985-88, pres., COO, 1988-94, pres., CEO, 1994—, also bd. dirs., 1988-94, chmn., CEO, pres., 1996-99; mng. dir. CPS Investments. Bd. dirs. Colo. Assn. Commerce and Industry, Gas Rsch. Inst., Colo. Alliance for Bus., MLA, Intrasar, Inc., Health Arising; chmn. Natural Gas Coun., 1998. Dir. Boy Scouts Am. Colo. Mem. ABA, Colo. Assn. Commerce and Industry (bd. dirs.), Interstate Natural Gas Assn. Am. (chmn. 1997), Midwest Gas Assn., CAB (bd. dirs.), Fed. Energy Bar Assn., Nebr. Bar Assn., Colo. Bar Assn., Pres. Assn., Midwest Gas Assn. (chmn.), Hiwan Country Club, Desert Mountain, Elks, Club 30. Presbyterian. Avocations: skiing, golf, photography. Home: 1892 Sugarbush Dr Evergreen CO 80439-9415 Office: KN Energy Inc PO Box 15265 Lakewood CO 80215

HALL, LEE BOAZ, publishing company consultant, author; b. Little Rock, Oct. 8, 1928; s. Graham Roots and Louise (Boaz) H.; m. Mary Louise Reed, Nov. 29, 1951 (div.); children: Gwendolyn, Ann Valerie, Graham; m. Sarah Moore, Dec. 15, 1978. B.A., Yale U., 1950. Reporter Ark. Gazette, Little Rock, 1950-51; officer Dept. Def., Washington, 1951-52, W.Ger., 1952-53; reporter Washington Post, 1953-55; with Life mag., 1955-70, bur. chief Latin Am., 1958-59, Paris, 1963-66; editor Life en Espanol, 1966-69; editor internat. edits. Life, N.Y.C., 1970; pres. Tomorrow Pub. Co., N.Y.C., 1970-72; sr. v.p. internat. pub. Playboy Enterprises, Inc., Chgo., 1972-86; pres. Int Pub., Inc., 1986—, Donlee, Inc., Little Rock, 1986—. Author: International Magazine and Book Licensing, 1983. Served with U.S. Army, 1950-51. Mem. Federation Internationale de la Presse Periodique (liaison), Coral Casino, Montecito Country Club. Home and Office: 3 Hunt Dr PO Box 763 Summerland CA 93067-0763 E-mail: LeeBHall@aol.com

HALL, PAUL J. lawyer; b. San Diego, Jan. 13, 1951; AB with highest honors, U. Calif., Santa Cruz, 1972; postgrad, Yale U.; JD, U. Calif., Berkeley, 1975. Bar: Calif. 1975. Mem. Manatt, Phelps & Phillips, L.A., 1975-94, Stein & Lubin LLP, San Francisco, 1995-98, Lillick & Charles LLP, San Francisco, 1998—. Bd. regents U. Calif., 1992-93, regent designate, 1991-92. Trustee U. Calif. Santa Cruz Found., 1986—. Mem. Calif. State Bar, Boalt Hall Alumni Assn. (bd. dirs. 1983-90, treas. 1985-86, sec. 1986-87, v.p. 1987-89, pres.-elect 1989-90, pres. 1990-91), U. Calif. Santa Cruz Alumni Assn. (bd. dirs. 1983-90, pres. 1986-90). Address: Lillick & Charles 2 Embarcadero Ctr Ste 2700 San Francisco CA 94111-3996

HALL, ROBERT EMMETT, JR. investment banker, realtor; b. Sioux City, Iowa, Apr. 28, 1936; s. Robert Emmett and Alvina (Faden) H.; m. De Phan. BA, U. S.D., 1958, MA, 1959; MBA, U. Santa Clara, 1976; grad., Am. Inst. Banking, Realtors Inst. Grad. asst. U. S.D., Vermillion, 1958-59; mgr. ins. dept., asst. mgr. installment loan dept. Northwestern Nat. Bank Sioux Falls, S.D., 1959-61, asst. cashier, 1961-65; asst. mgr. Crocker Nat. Bank, San Francisco, 1965-67, loan officer, 1967-69, asst. v.p., asst. mgr. San Mateo (Calif.) br., 1969-72; v.p., western regional mgr. Internat. Investments & Realty, Inc., Washington, 1972—; owner Hall Enterprises Co., San Jose, Calif., 1976—; pres. Alamaden Oaks Realtors, Inc., 1976—. Instr. West Valley Coll., Saratoga, Calif., 1972-82, Grad. Sch. Bus., U. Santa Clara (Calif.), 1981-82, Evergreen Valley Coll., San Jose, Calif. Treas. Minnehaha Leukemia Soc., 1963, Lake County Heart Fund Assn., 1962, Minnehaha Young Rep. Club, 1963. Mem. Am. Inst. Banking, Calif. Assn. Realtors (vice chmn.), Alamaden Country Club, Elks, Rotary (past pres.), KC, Beta Theta Pi. Home: 6951 Castlerock Dr San Jose CA 95120-4705 Office: Hall Enterprises 100A Crown Blvd San Jose CA 95120-2903

HALL, ROBERT ERNEST, economics educator; b. Palo Alto, Calif., Aug. 13, 1943; s. Victor Ernest and Frances Marie (Gould) H.; m. Susan E. Woodward; children: Christopher, Anne, Jonathan, Andrew. BA, U. Calif.-Berkeley, 1964; PhD, MIT, 1967. Asst. prof., acting assoc. prof. U. Calif., Berkeley, 1967-70; from assoc. prof. to prof. MIT, Cambridge, 1970-78; prof., sr. fellow Stanford U. (Calif.), 1978—, Robert and Carole McNeil joint prof. and sr. fellow, 1998. Dir. econ. fluctuation program Nat. Bur. Econ. Research, Cambridge, 1978— ; adv. com. Congl. Budget Office, Washington, 1993—. Author: Macroeconomics, 1985, 5th rev. edit., 1997, Booms and Recessions in a Noisy Economy, 1990, The Rational Consumer: Theory and Evidence, 1990, Flat Tax, 1995, Economics, 1997, 2d rev. edit., 2000, Digital Dealing, 2001; editor: Inflation, 1983. Woodrow Wilson fellow, 1964; Ford Found. faculty rsch. fellow, 1969 Fellow Econometric Soc., Am. Acad. Arts and Scis.; mem. Am. Econs. Assn., Am. Statis Assn. Democrat. Office: Stanford U Hoover Instn Stanford CA 94305 E-mail: hall@hoover.stanford.edu

HALL, TENNIEBEE M. editor; b. Bakersfield, Calif., May 21, 1940; d. William Elmer and Lillian May (Otis) Hall; m. Harold Robert Hall, Feb. 20, 1965. BA in Edn., Fresno State Coll., 1962; AA, Bakersfield Coll., 1960. Cert. tchr., Calif. Tchr. Edison (Calif.) Sch. Dist., 1962-65; substitute tchr. Marin and Oakland Counties (Calif.), Berkeley, 1965-66; engring. asst. Pacific Coil Co., Inc., Bakersfield, 1974-81; editor United Ostomy Assn., Inc., Irvine, Calif., 1986-91. Co-author: Treating IBD, 1989, Current Therapy in Gastroenterology, 1989; author, designer: Volunteer Leadership Training Manuals, 1982-84; editor: Calif. Parliamentarian, 1999—; contbr. articles to Ostomy Quar., 1973—. Mem. Pacific Beach Town Coun., San Diego, 1977—; campaign worker Maureen O'Connor (1st woman mayor of city), San Diego, 1986; mem. Nat. Digestive Diseases Adv. Bd., NIH, Washington, 1986-91; mem. planning and devel. bd. Scripps Clinic and Rsch. Found. Inflammatory Bowel Disease Ctr., San Diego, 1993—; various vol. activities, 1966-74, 81-86. Recipient Outstanding Svc. award VA Vol. Svc., Bur. of Vets. Affairs, Washington, 1990. Mem. Nat. Assn. Parliamentarians, United Ostomy Assn. Inc. (regional program dir. 1980-84, pres. 1984-86, Sam Dubin award 1983, Industry Adv. award 1987), Crohn's and Colitis Found. Am. (nat. trustee 1986-95, nat. v.p. 1987-92). Avocations: travel, volunteerism. Home and Office: 8585 Via Mallorca Unit 7 La Jolla CA 92037-2585

HALL, TERRY, air transportation executive; CFO U.S. Airways Group Inc., Arlington, Va.; sr. v.p., CFO Gen. Corp., Inc., Ranchero Cordova, Calif., 1999—. Office: Gen Corp Inc Hwy 50 & Aerojet Rd PO Box 537012 Ranchero Cordova CA 95853-7012

HALL, WILLIAM E. engineering and construction company executive; b. Washington, Sept. 5, 1942; s. George W. and Jane F. (Brogger) H.; m. Lavinia Swift, Sept. 21, 1974; children: Deborah A., Douglas E., L. Jane, Elizabeth D. BSChemE, Va. Poly. Inst. and State U., 1963, MSChemE, 1964; postgrad., Stanford U., 1991. Process engr. Stone & Webster Engring. Co., Boston, 1967-70, project mgr. London, 1970-76, N.Y.C., 1976-78, regional bus. devel. mgr. Houston, 1978-79; prin. project mgr. RM Parsons Co., Pasadena, Calif., 1979-81, sr. v.p., 1989-92; pres. Ralph M. Parsons Co., Pasadena, 1992—; prin. project mgr. Saudi Arabia Parsons Ltd., Yanbu, 1981-84, mng. dir., 1984-89. Bd. dirs. Proye Parsons, Caracas, Venezuela, Latisa; alt. dir. Constrn. Industry Inst., Austin, Tex., 1990-92, dir. 1992—. CHmn. Tournament of Life, Pasadena, 1990-92. Mem. Am. Inst. Chem. Engrs. Republican. Lutheran. Avocations: golf, bridge. Office: Ralph M Parsons Co 100 W Walnut St Pasadena CA 91124-0002 also: Parsons Energy & Chemicals Group Inc 5 E Greenway Plz Houston TX 77046-0500

HALL, ZACH WINTER, academic administrator; b. Atlanta, Sept. 15, 1937; s. Dixon Winter and Marjorie Elizabeth (Owens) H.; m. Anne Browning, June 1958 (div. Aug. 1960); m. Marion Nestle, Dec. 1973 (div. June 1985); m. Julie Ann Giacobassi, Nov. 9, 1987. BA, Yale U., 1958; PhD, Harvard U., 1966. Asst. prof., then assoc. prof. Harvard Med. Sch., Boston, 1968-76; prof. U. Calif., San Francisco, 1976-94; dir. Nat. Inst. Neurol. Disorders and Stroke, Bethesda, Md., 1994-97; assoc. dean for rsch. U. Calif. San Francisco, 1997-98, vice chancellor rsch., 1998-2000, exec. vice chancellor, 2000—. Mem. Med. Adv. Bd., Chevy Chase, Md., 1995-99, Howard Hughes Med. Inst.; Alexander Forbes lectr. Grass Found., 1994; David Nachmanson lectr. Weigmann Inst., Rehovath, Israel, 1996. Author, editor: Molecular Neurobiology, 1992; editor jour. Neuron, 1988-94. Fellow AAAS; mem. Am. Acad. Arts and Scis., Inst. Medicine. Office: U Calif San Francisco Sch Medicine Parnassus Ave San Francisco CA 94143-0001

HALLA, BRIAN L. electronics company executive; b. Springfield, Ill., 1946; BSEE, U. Nebr., 1969. Applications engr. Control Data Corp., 1969-74; dir. mktg. Intel Corp., 1974-78; exec. v.p. LSI Logic, 1988-96; chmn. bd., pres., CEO Nat. Semiconductor Corp., Santa Clara, Calif., 1996—. Mem. Semi-Conductor Indsl. Assn. (bd. dirs.). Office: National Semiconductor Corp 2900 Semiconductor Dr Santa Clara CA 95051-0695

HALLE, BRUCE T. automotive products company executive; b. Springfield, Mass., 1930; Student, Ea. Mich. U., 1948-50, BBA, 1956, Phd (hon.). Various entry level positions including landscaping, janitor; owner Discount Tire Co., Ann Arbor, 1960, now CEO largest ind. tire dealer in N.Am. Scottsdale. Discount Tire Co. has 290 stores in 12 states. Supporter March of Dimes, Am. Heart Assn., Am. Cancer Soc., Am. Liver Found., ARC, Muscular Dystrophy Assn., Ariz. Boys and Girls Clubs, Ariz. Opera League, Phoenix Symphony, Crisis Nursery, Scottsdale Symphony and Children's Urban Survival Program, Phoenix; contbr. funds for new bldgs., Eastern Mich. U. With USMC, 1950-53. Recipient Gold Plate award, Am. Acad. Achievement, 1994; hon. chmn. Muscular Dystrophy Assn. event, 1994; entrepreneurial fellow U. Ariz. Mem. Beta Gamma Sigma.

HALLECK, CHARLES WHITE, lawyer, photographer, former judge; b. Rensselaer, Ind., July 6, 1929; s. Charles Abraham and Blanche (White) H.; m. Carolyn L. Wood, Dec. 23, 1950 (div. Oct. 1969); children: Holly Louise, Charles White, Todd Alexander, Heather Leigh, Heidi Lynne, William Hemsley, Hope Leslie; m. Jeanne Wahl, May 16, 1970. A.B., Williams Coll., 1951; J.D., George Washington U., 1957; LL.D. (hon.), St. Joseph's Coll., 1971; AA in Photography, Foothill Coll., Los Altos Hills, Calif., 1996. Asst. U.S. atty. for D.C., 1957-59; assoc. Hogan and Hartson, Washington, 1959-65; judge Superior Ct. D.C., 1965-77; mem. firm Lamb, Halleck & Keats, Washington, 1977-80; sole practice, 1980-86; photojournalist, 1986-99; fine art photographer, 1999—. Served with USNR, 1951-55; to lt. Res. (ret.). Mem. Beta Theta Pi, Phi Delta Phi.

HALLENBECK, HARRY C. architect; Dir. State of Calif., Sacramento, 1997; dir. planning and design svc. Vanir Constrn. Mgmt., Inc., Sacramento, 1997—. Recipient Edward C. Kemper award Archtl. Inst. Am., 1994. Office: Vanir Constrn Mgmt Inc 980 9th St Ste 900 Sacramento CA 95814-2725 also: 7485 Rush River Dr # 333 Sacramento CA 95831-5259

HALLENBECK, KENNETH LUSTER, numismatist; b. Ann Arbor, Mich., Oct. 20, 1931; s. Kenneth Luster and Ethel (Apfel) H.; m. June Eugenia Miekka, July 2, 1955; children: Kevin L., Thomas G., Scott A., Sheryl A. AB in Geography, U. Mich., 1955. Planning analyst Lincoln Nat. Life Ins. Co., Ft. Wayne, Ind., 1957-70, sr. planning analyst, 1970-72, asst. mgr. policy issue, 1972-77; bd. govs. Am. Numismatic Assn., Colorado Springs, Colo., 1971-87, mus. curator, 1977-82, v.p., 1987-89, pres., 1989-91; pres., owner Ken Hallenbeck Coin Gallery, Inc., Colorado Springs, 1983—. Apptd. by Pres. Nixon to U.S. Assay Commn. 1974; testified before Congl. subcom. on coinage and consumer affairs for commemorative coinage, mem. design selection com. for Olympic coin designs, 1992. Contbr. numerous articles to mags. Mem. Rep. Cen. Com., Ft. Wayne, 1972-77, Better Bus. Bur., Colorado Springs; alternate del. to Rep. County and 5th Congl. Dist. Caucuses. With U.S. Army, 1955-57. Fellow Life Mgmt. Inst.; mem. Colorado Springs C. of C., Tokens and Medals Soc. (past pres.), Masons, also numerous local, regional and nat. coin clubs. Republican. Congregationalist. Avocations: numismatics, western history. Office: Ken Hallenbeck Coin Gallery Inc 711 N Nevada Ave Colorado Springs CO 80903-1007

HALLER, EUGENE ERNEST, materials scientist, educator; b. Basel, Switzerland, Jan. 5, 1943; s. Eugene and Maria Anne Haller; m. Marianne Elisabeth Schlittler, May 26, 1973; children: Nicole Marianne, Isabelle Cathrine. Diploma in Physics, U. Basel, 1967, PhD in Physics, 1970. Postdoctoral asst. Lawrence Berkeley (Calif.) Lab., 1971-73, staff scientist, then sr. staff scientist, 1973-80, faculty sr. scientist, 1980—; assoc. prof. U. Calif., Berkeley, 1980-82, prof. materials sci., 1982—. Co-chmn. Materials Rsch. Soc. Symposia, Boston, 1982, 89, Internat. Conf. on Shallow Levels in Semiconductors, Berkeley, 1984, 94; chair 20th Internat. Conf. on Defects in Semicondrs., 1999; mem. rev. com. instrument div. Brookhaven Nat. Lab., Upton, N.Y., 1987-93; mem. Japanese tech. panel on sensors NSF-Nat. Acad. Sci., Washington, 1988; vis. prof. Imperial Coll. Sci., Tech. and Medicine, London, 1991. Editorial adv. bd. Jour. Phys. and Chem. Solids, 1993—, Material Sci. Founds., 1998—; contbr. to numerous profl. publs. U.S. Sr. scientist award Alexander von Humboldt Soc., Germany, 1986, Max-Planck Rsch. award, 1994; rsch. fellow Miller Inst. Basic Rsch., Berkeley, 1990, 2001. Fellow Am. Phys. Soc. (James C. McGroddy prize in new materials 1999); mem. AAAS, Materials Rsch. Soc., Swiss Phys. Soc., Sigma Xi. Achievements include patents in surface passivation of semiconductors, synthesis of crystalline carbon nitride potentially a superhard material, and far infrared germanium laser. Office: U Calif Berkeley 553 Evans Hall Berkeley CA 94720-1775 Fax: 510-486-5530. E-mail: eehaller@lbl.gov

HALLIDAY, JOHN MEECH, investment company executive; b. St. Louis, Oct. 16, 1936; s. William Norman and Vivian Viola (Meech) H.; m. Martha Layne Griggs, June 30, 1962; children: Richard M., Elizabeth Halliday Traut. BS, U.S. Naval Acad., 1958; MBA, Harvard U., 1964. Dir. budgeting and planning Automatic Tape Control, Bloomington, Ill., 1964-66; dir. planning Ralston-Purina, St. Louis, 1966-67, v.p. subsidiary, 1967-68, dir. internat. banking, 1967-68; v.p. Servicetime Corp., St. Louis, 1968-70; assoc. R.W. Halliday Assocs., Boise, Idaho, 1970-87. V.p. Sawtooth Comm. Corp., Boise, 1970-73, Comdr. Corp., 1979-81; pres., CEO, bd. dirs. ML, Ltd., San Francisco, 1979—, H.W.L. Inc., San Francisco, 1985-93; pres. Halliday Labs., Inc., 1980-91; exec. v.p., bd. dirs. Franchise Fin. Corp. Am., Phoenix, 1980-85; bd. dirs., v.p. Harvard Bus. Sch. Assn. No. Calif., 1980-87; pres., CEO, bd. dirs. Cycletorl Diversified Industries, Inc., 1992—; guest lectr. U. Calif. Berkeley, 1991-2000, Calif. Bus.-Higher Edn. Forum, 1995-98; sponsor Halliday lectr. in astronomy, U. Calif. Santa Cruz, 2000—. Pres. Big Bros. San Francisco, 1978-81; trustee, pres. U. Calif.-Santa Cruz Found., 1988—; mem. ad hoc com. on corrections Calif. State Senate, 1995-96; fellow bd. visitors and fellows viticulture and enology U. Calif., Davis, 1999—. Mem. Restaurant Assn. (v.p. 1969-70), Olympic Club (San Francisco), Scott Valley Tennis Club (Mill Valley, Calif.). Republican. Episcopalian. Home: 351 Corte Madera Ave Mill Valley CA 94941-1013 Office: 55 New Montgomery St Ste 317 San Francisco CA 94105-3426 E-mail: jhalli8835@aol.com

HALLIGAN, MIKE, state legislator; b. July 9, 1949; m. Leslie Halligan. BS, MA, JD, U. Mont. Atty.; mem. Mont. Senate, Dist. 34, Helena, 1981—; minority leader Mont. Senate, 1995-98; chair select com. on impelemtnation of CI-75; mem. ethics com., mem. conf. com., mem. judiciary com.; mem. agr., livestock and irrigation com., mem. rules com. Served with U.S. Army. Democrat. Office: PO Box 9121 Missoula MT 59807-9121

HALLIN, DANIEL CLARK, communications educator; b. Palo Alto, Calif., June 11, 1953; BA in Polit. Sci. with honors, U. Calif., Berkeley, 1973, MA in Polit. Sci., 1974, PhD in Polit. Sci., 1980. Fellow Freedom Forum Media Studies Ctr., Columbia U., N.Y.C., 1991-92; prof. dept. comm., adj. prof. polit. sci. U. Calif., San Diego, 1980—, chairperson, 1994-97. Assoc. Ctr. for War, Peace and News Media; presenter, keynote spkr. various ednl. symposia and confs., most recently at Seoul Nat. U., 1997, Westminster U., London, 1998, Nat. U., Athens, Greece, 1998, Budapest, 2000, U. Leipzig, 2000, U. Munich, 2000, U. Calif. Berkeley, 2000, U. Perugia, 1999; Merkator prof. Inst. Medienwissenschaft U. Dusseldorf, 2000. Author: The "Uncensored War": The Media and Vietnam, 1989, The Presidency, The Press and the People, 1992, We Keep America on Top of the World: Television Journalism and the Public Sphere, 1994; contbr. chpt. to: Critical Theory and Public Life, 1985, Political Communication: Approaches, Studies, Assessments, 1987, Reading the News, 1986, Watching Television, 1986, Is the Cold War Over? Images of the USA and the USSR in Soviet and American Media, 1991, Comparatively Speaking, 1992, Viewing War: How the Media Handled the Persian Gulf, 1994; co-contbr. chpt. to: Taken by Storm: The Media, Public Opinion and U.S. Foreign Policy in the Gulf War, 1994, Mass Media and Society, 1996, Dewesternizing Media Studies, 2000, Tabloid Tales, 2000; mem. editl. bd. Polit. Comm.; contbr. articles and revs. to profl. publs. Pres. Binat. Assn. Schs. of Comm. of the Californias, 1997-99; bd. dirs. Internat. Comm. Assn. Recipient 1st prize media studies project essay contest Woodrow Wilson Internat. Ctr. for Scholars, 1990. Mem. Am. Polit. Sci. Assn., L.Am. Studies Assn., Internat. Comm. Assn., Union for Dem. Comm. Home: 3315 31st St San Diego CA 92104-4619 Office: Univ Calif San Diego Dept Comm 0503 La Jolla CA 92093 E-mail: dhallin@ucsd.edu

HALLOCK, C. WILES, JR. athletic official; b. Denver, Feb. 17, 1918; s. Claude Wiles and Mary (Bassler) H.; m. Marjorie Louise Eldred, Mar. 23, 1944; children: Lucinda Eldred Hallock Rinne, Michael Eldred. A.B., U. Denver, 1939. Sports info. dir. U. Wyo., 1949-60, track coach, 1952-56; sports info. dir. U. Calif., Berkeley, 1960-63; dir. pub. relations Nat. Collegiate Athletic Assn., 1963-68; dir. Nat. Collegiate Sports Services, 1967-68; commr. Western Athletic Conf., 1968-71; exec. dir. Pacific-8 Conf. (now Pacific-10 conf.), San Francisco and Walnut Creek, Calif., 1971-83; historian Pacific 10 Conf., 1983. Mem. Laramie (Wyo.) City Council, 1958-60. Served to lt. comdr. USNR, World War II. Decorated Air medal; mem. Nat. Football Found. and Hall of Fame Honors Ct. Mem. Nat. Collegiate Athletic Assn., Nat. Assn. Collegiate Dirs. Athletics (Corbett award 1983), Collegiate Commrs. Assn., Coll. Sports Info. Dirs. Am. (Arch Ward award 1963), Football Writers Assn. Am. (past dir.), U.S. Basketball Writers Assn., Lambda Chi Alpha. Presbyn. Home: 235 Western Hills Dr Pleasant Hill CA 94523-3167 Office: 800 S Broadway Walnut Creek CA 94596-5218 E-mail: i4claude@aol.com

HALLORAN, MICHAEL JAMES, lawyer; b. Berkeley, Calif., May 20, 1941; s. James Joseph and Fern (Ogden) H.; m. Virginia Smedberg, Sept. 6, 1964; children: Pamela, Peter, Shelley. BS, U. Calif., Berkeley, 1962, LLB, 1965. Bar: Calif. 1966, D.C. 1979, Wyo. 1996. Assoc. Keatinge & Sterling, L.A., 1965-67, Pillsbury, Madison & Sutro, San Francisco, 1967-72, ptnr., 1973-90, 97—, mng. ptnr. Washington, 1979-82; exec. v.p., gen. counsel BankAm. Corp. and Bank of Am., San Francisco, 1990-96. Mem. legal adv. com. N.Y. Stock Exch., 1993-96; bd. overseers Inst. Civil Justice, 1994-98; chair sect. corp. securities banking and emerging cos. Pillsbury Madison & Sutro, 1997-2000. Editor: Venture Capital and Public Offering Negotiation, 1982—. Mem. corp. governance, shareholder rights and securities transactions com. Calif. Senate Comm., 1986-98; bd. dirs. Am. Conservatory Theater, 1994-2000. Mem. ABA (chmn. state regulation of securities com. 1981-84, mem. coun. of sect. of bus. law 1986-90, chmn. banking law com. 1992-96, mem. corp. laws com. 1997—), Bar Assn. San Francisco (bd. dirs. 1993-96). Avocations: skiing, golf, fishing, hiking. E-mail: halloran. Office: Pillsbury Madison & Sutro LLP 50 Fremont St Fl 10 San Francisco CA 94105-2233 also: 2550 Hanover St Palo Alto CA 94304-1115 E-mail: mj@pillsgurylaw.com

HALLY, TERRY L. aerospace executive; BA, Bemidji State U.; JD, U. Minn. Asst. city atty., chief prosecutor City of Rochester, 1978; with LeFevre, Lefler, et. al.; sr. corp. counsel Republic Airlines; v.p., gen. mgr., COO Northwest Aircraft, Inc., 1990; v.p., treas. United Airlines, 1990 93; v.p., CFO Tyco Internat., 1993-95; v.p. fin., CFO Apogee Enterprises, Inc., 1995-97; sr. v.p. fin., CFO U.S. Airways, 1997-99; sr. v.p., CFO Aerojet, Sacramento, 1999—. Office: Aerojet PO Box 537012 Sacramento CA 95853-7012

HALMOS, PAUL RICHARD, mathematician, educator; b. Budapest, Hungary, Mar. 3, 1916; came to U.S., 1929; s. Alexander Charles and Paula (Rosenberg) H.; m. Dorothy Moyer, Jan. 1, 1934 (div. Mar. 1945); m. Virginia Templeton Pritchett, Apr. 7, 1945. BS, U. Ill., 1934, MS, 1935, PhD, 1938; DSc (hon.), U. St. Andrews, Scotland, 1984; D Math. (hon.), U. Waterloo, Can., 1990. Instr. U. Ill., Urbana, 1938-39, assoc., 1942-43; fellow, asst. Inst. for Advanced Study, Princeton, N.J., 1939-42; asst. prof. Syracuse (N.Y.) U., 1943-46; from asst. prof. to prof. U. Chgo., 1946-61; prof. U. Mich., Ann Arbor, 1961-68; prof., chmn. dept. U. Hawaii, Honolulu, 1968-69; prof., then Disting. prof. Ind. U., Bloomington, 1969-85; prof. Santa Clara (Calif.) U., 1985-96, prof. emeritus, 1996—. Author: Finite Dimensional Vector Spaces, 1942, Measure Theory, 1950, A Hilbert Space Problem Book, 1967, I Want to Be a Mathematician, 1985, others. Mem. Math. Assn. Am. (Haimo award for Dist. Coll. & Univ. Teaching of Mat., 1994), Am. Math. Soc., others. Avocations: photography, walking. Home: 110 Wood Rd Apt I-203 Los Gatos CA 95030-6720 Office: Santa Clara U Dept Math Santa Clara CA 95053-0001

HALPERIN, ROBERT MILTON, retired electrical machinery company executive; b. Chgo., June 1, 1928; s. Herman and Edna Pearl (Rosenberg) H.; m. Ruth Levison, June 19, 1955; children: Mark, Margaret, Philip. Ph.B., U. Chgo., 1949; B.Mech. Engring., Cornell U., 1949; M.B.A., Harvard U., 1952. Engr. Electro-Motive div. Gen. Motors Corp., La Grange, Ill., 1949-50; trust rep. Bank of Am., San Francisco, 1954-56; adminstr. Dumont Corp., San Rafael, Calif., 1956-57; vice chmn., bd. dirs. Raychem Corp., Menlo Park, 1957-94. Chmn. bd. dirs. Avid Tech. Inc.; bd. dirs. Vitria Tech. Inc. Bd. trustees U. Chgo.; bd. dirs. Harvard Bus. Sch. Pub. Co., Stanford U. Hosp. and Clinics. Lt. USAF, 1952-63. Mem. Harvard Club of N.Y.C. Office: 2929 Campus Dr Ste 400 San Mateo CA 94403

HALPERIN, STUART, entertainment company executive; b. Bklyn., June 20, 1963; Newswriter CNN; various mktg. positions New Line Cinema, 20th Century Fox Internat., Universal Pictures; co-founder, exec. v.p. Hollywood.com, Santa Monica, Calif; exec. v.p. mktg. MovieTickets.com, Hollywood, 2000—. Office: MovieTickets.com Freeman Bldg 202 5555 Melrose Ave Hollywood CA 90038

HALPERN, BARRY DAVID, lawyer; b. Champaign, Ill., Feb. 25, 1949; s. I.L. and Trula M. H.; m. Cynthia Ann Zedler, Aug. 4, 1972; children: Amanda M., Trevor H. BA, U. Kans., 1971, JD, 1973. Bar: Kans. 1973, Fla. 1975, Ariz. 1978, Colo. 1991, U.S. Dist. Ct. Kans. 1973, U.S. Dist. Ct. Ariz. 1978, U.S. Supreme Ct. 1976. Ptnr. Snell & Wilmer, Phoenix, 1978—. Bd. dirs. Crisis Nursery, Phoenix, 1987, Friends of Foster Children, Phoenix, 1987, Phoenix Symphony; pres. Combined Orgn. Met. Phoenix Arts and Scis., 1996-97, bd. dirs., 1997-2000, mem. exec. com., 1998-2001; mem. Gov.'s Task Force Edn. Reform, 1991. Mem. ABA, State Bar Ariz., State Bar, Fla., State Bar Kans., State Bar Colo., Maricopa County Bar Assn. (chmn. med.-legal com. 1995-96), Phoenix C. of C. (health care coun. 1993-96). Office: Snell & Wilmer 1 Arizona Ctr Phoenix AZ 85004-2202

HALPRIN, ANNA SCHUMAN (MRS. LAWRENCE HALPRIN), dancer; b. Wilmette, Ill., July 13, 1920; d. Isadore and Ida (Schiff) Schuman; m. Lawrence Halprin, Sept. 19, 1940; children: Daria, Rana. Student, Bennington Summer Sch. Dance, 1938-39; BS in Dance, U. Wis., 1943, PhD (hon.), 1994; PhD in Human Services (hon.), Sierra U., 1987. Presenter opening invocation STate of the World Forum by spl. invitation from Mikhail S. Gorbachev. Author: Moving Toward Life, Five Decades of Transformative Dance, Dance as a Healing Art, A Teachers' Guide and Support Manual for People with Cancer; performances at Kennedy Ctr., Washington, Yerba Buena Ctr. for Arts, San Francisco, Joyce Theatre, N.Y.C., 2001—; 80th yr. retrospective performance Cowell Theatre, San Francisco. Bd. dirs. East West Holistic Healing Inst.; mem. Gov.'s Coun. on Phys. Fitness and Wellness. Recipient award Am. Dance Guild, 1980, Guggenheim award, 1970-71, Woman of Wisdom award Bay Area Profl. Women's Network, Tchr. of Yr. award Calif. Tchrs. Assn., 1988, Lifetime Achievement award in visual and performing arts San Francisco Bay Guardian newspaper, 1990, Women of Achievement, Vision and Excellence award, 1992, Balasaraswati/Joy Ann Dewey Bieneke chair for disting. tchg. Am. Dance Festival, 1996, Lifetime Achievement in Modern Dance award Am. Dance Festival, 1997, Lifetime Achievement award Calif. Arts Coun., 2000, Breast Cancer Watch, 2001; Person of Yr. in field of Dance award Ballet-ranz, Berlin; named to Isadora Duncan Hall of Fame, Bay Area Dance Coalition, 1986; Nat. Endowment Arts Choreographers grantee, 1976, NEA choreography grantee, 1977, San Francisco Found. grantee, 1981, Calif. Arts. Coun. grantee, 1990—; inductee Marin Women's Hall of Fame, 1998. Fellow Am. Expressive Therapy Assn.; mem. Assn. Am. Dance, Conscientious Artists Am., San Francisco C. of C. Home and Office: 15 Ravine Way Kentfield CA 94904-2713

HALSTEAD, BRUCE WALTER, biotoxicologist; b. San Francisco, Mar. 28, 1920; s. Walter and Ethel Muriel (Shanks) H.; m. Joy Arloa Mallory, Aug. 3, 1941 (div.); m. Terri Lee Holcomb, June 25, 1988; children by previous marriage: Linda, Sandra, David, Larry, Claudia, Shari. A.A., San Francisco City Coll., 1941; B.A., U. Calif.-Berkeley, 1943; M.D., Loma Linda U., 1948. Research asst. in ichthyology Calif. Acad. Scis., 1935-43; instr. Pacific Union Coll., 1943-44; mem. faculty Loma Linda (Calif.) U., 1948- 58; research assoc. Lab. Neurol. Research, Sch. Medicine, 1964—; dir. World Life Research Inst., Colton, Calif., 1959—, Internat. Biotoxicol. Center; research assoc. in ichthyology Los Angeles County Mus., 1964-66; instr. Walla Walla Coll., summers 1964-65. Cons. to govt. agys., pvt. corps; mem. editorial staff Exerpta Medica, 1959-63, Toxicon, 1962-67; mem. joint group experts on sci. aspects marine pollution UN; Dir. Nat. Assn. Underwater Instrs., Internat. Underwater Enterprises, Internat. Bots., Inc. Author: Poisonous and Venomous Marine Animals of the World, 7 vols., 1966; others.; contbr. 300 articles to profl. jours. Fellow AAAS, Internat. Soc. Toxicology (a founder), N.Y. Acad. Scis., Royal Soc. Tropical Medicine and Hygiene; mem. Am. Inst. Biol. Scis., Am. Micros. Soc., Am. Soc. Ichthyologists and Herpetologists, Am. Soc. Limnology and Oceanography, Inst. Radiation Medicine (hon. cons.), Chinese Acad. Mil. Med. Sci., numerous others. Republican. Adventist. Office: World Life Rsch Inst 210 Sliger Rd Mentone CA 92359-9735

HALSTED, CHARLES HOPKINSON, internist; b. Cambridge, Mass., Oct. 2, 1936; s. James Addison and Isabella (Hopkinson) H.; m. June 7, 1959, (div. 1986); children: John, Michael, Ellen; m. Ann Wyant, Dec. 20, 1986. BA, Stanford U., 1958; MD, U. Rochester, 1962; post grad., Cleve. Metro Gen. Hosp., 1966, John Hopkins U., 1970. Diplomate Am. Bd. Internal Medicine. Asst. prof. John Hopkins U., Balt., 1971-74, U. Calif., Davis, 1974-76, assoc. prof., 1976-80, prof., 1980—, dir. div. clin. nutrition and metabolism, 1983-97. Dir. Clin. Nutrition Rsch. Unit, NIH, Davis, Calif., 1985—. Editor: Nutrition in Organ Failure, 1989; co-editor The Laboratory in Clinical Medicine, 1981; editor-in-chief Am. Jour. Clin. Nutrition, 1997—; contbr. articles to profl. jours. Surgeon USPHS, 1966-68. Fellow ACP; mem. Am. Soc. Clin. Nutrition (pres. 1988-89), Am. Soc. Clin. Investigation, Am. Gastroentrological Assn., Am. Soc. for Study Liver Diseases, Western Assn. Physicians, Am. Bd. Nutrition (pres. 1990—), Calif. Acad. Medicine. Office: U Calif Sch Medicine TB 156 Davis CA 95616

HALVER, JOHN EMIL, nutritional biochemist; b. Woodinville, Wash., Apr. 21, 1922; s. John Emil and Helen Henrietta (Hansen) H.; m. Jane Loren, July 21, 1944; children: John Emil, Nancylee Halver Hadley, Janet Ann Halver Fix, Peter Loren, Deborah Kay Halver Hanson. BS, Wash. State U., 1944, MS in Organic Chemistry, 1948; PhD in Med. Biochemistry, U. Wash., 1953. Plant chemist Assoc. Frozen Foods, Kent, Wash., 1946-47; asst. chemist Purdue U., 1948-49; instr. U. Wash., Seattle, 1949-50, affiliate prof., 1960-75; prof. U. Wash. Sch. Fisheries, 1978-92; prof. emeritus U. Wash., 1992—. Condr. research on vitamin and amino acid requirements for fish; identified aflatoxin B1 as specific carcinogen for rainbow trout hematoma, identified vitamin C2 for fish; dir. Western Fish Nutrition Lab., U.S. Fish and Wildlife Service, Dept. Interior, Cook, Wash., 1950-75, sr. scientist, nutrition, Seattle, 1975-78; cons. FAO, UNDP, Internat. Union Nutrition Scientists, Nat. Fish Research Inst., Hungary, World Bank, Euroconsult, UNDP, IDRC; affiliate prof. U. Oreg. Med. Sch., 1965-69; vis. prof. Marine Sci. Inst., U. Tex., Port Arkansas; pres. Fisheries Devel. Technology, Inc., 1980-90, Halver Corp., 1978—. Capt. U.S. Army, World War II; col. USAR. Decorated Purple Heart, Bronze Star with oak leaf cluster, Meritorious Service Conduct medal. Fellow Am. Inst. Fishery Research Biologists, Am. Inst. Nutrition; mem. Soc. Exptl. Biol. Medicine, Nat. Acad. Sci., Am. Sci. Affiliation, Am. Chem. Soc., Am. Fishery Soc., World Aquaculture Soc., Hungarian Acad. Sci., Phi Lambda Upsilon, Pi Mu Epsilon, Alpha Chi Sigma. Methodist (lay leader 1965-70). Club: Rotary. Home: 16502 41st Ave NE Seattle WA 98155-5610 Office: U Wash Box 355100 Sch Fisheries Seattle WA 98195-5100 E-mail: halver@u.washington.edu

HALVORSEN, CLAY A. construction executive; V.p., gen. counsel, sec. Standard Pacific Corp., Costa Mesa, Calif., 1997—. Office: Standard Pacific Corp 1565 W MacArthur Blvd Costa Mesa CA 92626

HALVORSON, ARDELL DAVID, soil scientist, researcher; b. Rugby, N.D., May 31, 1945; s. Albert F. and Karen Halvorson; m. Linda Halvorson; children: Renae, Rhonda. BS, N.D. State U., 1967; MS, Colo. State U., 1969, PhD, 1971. Soil scientist Agr. Rsch. Svc., USDA, Sidney, Mont., 1971-83, Akron, Colo., 1983-88, rsch. leader, 1988-94; lab. dir. USDA-Agr. Rsch. Svc., Mandan, N.D., 1994-97, soil scientist Ft. Collins, Colo., 1997—. Contbr. numerous articles to profl. publs. Fellow Am. Soc. Agronomy (assoc. editor 1983-87), Soil Sci. Soc. Am. (chmn. divsn. S-8 1989), Soil and Water Conservation Soc. (chpt. pres. 1991); mem. Crop Sci. Soc. Am. Office: USDA ARS PO Box E Fort Collins CO 80522-0470 E-mail: adhalvor@lamar.colostate.edu

HALVORSON, FRANK ELSWORTH, sales executive; b. Stockton, Calif., Feb. 5, 1956; s. William Elsworth and Lorraine (Rogers) H.; m. Lori Thom, Sept. 30, 1980; children: Amanda Rose, Lauren Elizabeth. Student, U. the Pacific, 1979. Dist. mgr. Oldsmobile div. Gen. Motors, St. Louis, Fresno, Calif. and San Francisco, 1979-83; gen. mgr., v.p. Prospect Motors Inc., Jackson, Calif., 1983—, pres. County chmn. membership drive Boy Scouts Am., 1987. Mem. Soc. Sales Execs. (Gen. Motors Div.). Republican. Roman Catholic. Lodges: Rotary, Moose. Avocations: golf, fishing, hunting. Office: Prospect Motors Inc 645 Hwy 49 & 88 PO Box 1360 Jackson CA 95642-1360

HALVORSON, MARJORY, opera director; Pvt. studies with, Sister Marietta Coyle, Jerry Daniels, Dolores Ravich. Dir. vocal studies Whitworth Coll., Spokane; artistic dir. Spokane Opera, Spokane. Dir. vocal master classes iwth Thomas Hampson, Richard Miller, Dale Moore, John Shirley-Quirk, James Maddalena, Armen Guzlimien; tchr. pvt. lesons in voice, vocal pedagogy, diction and lit.; director opera workshop. Named Woman of Achievement in Arts and Culture, City of Spokane, 1996; recipient outstanidng cmty. svc. award Westminster United Ch. of Christ. Office: Spokane Opera 643 S Ivory St Spokane WA 99202-2362

HALVORSON, WILLIAM, former automotive executive; b. 1932; Mgr. sales Chase Chevrolet, Stockton, Calif., 1953-75; sec.-treas. Prospect Motors, Inc., Jackson, 1975-82, pres., 1982-99. Office: Prospect Motors Inc PO Box 1360 Jackson CA 95642-1360

HAM, GARY MARTIN, psychologist; b. Lincoln, Nebr., Feb. 6, 1940; s. Wendell E. and Sally Bertha (Lind) H.; children: Jeffery M. BS in Psychology, Wash. State U., 1963, MS in Psychology, 1965; PsyD, Newport U., 1988. Diplomate Am. Psychotherapy Assn., Am. Bd. Psychol. Spltys. in Med. Psychology; lic. psychologist, Calif.; cert. tchr., Calif, counselor. Clin. psychologist Riverside (Calif.) County Dept. Mental Health, 1967—. Tchr., cons., pub. speaker, researcher Riverside County Dept. Mental Health, 1967—; instr. U. Calif. Riverside, Chapman U. Clin. psychologist Riverside County, Critical Incidents Disaster Response Team, 1985—, ARC Disaster Team. 1st lt. USAF, 1964-67. Mem. AAS, AAAS, APA, ASCD, Am. Mental Health Counselors Assn., Am. Critical Incident Stress Found., Calif. Psychol. Assn., Air Force Soc. Psychologists, Am. Coll. Forensic Examiners, Psi Chi, Sigma Phi Epsilon. Office: Riverside County Dept Mental Health PO Box 52567 Riverside CA 92517-3567

HAM, LEE EDWARD, civil engineer; b. San Francisco, Dec. 19, 1919; s. Lloyd Burley and Helen Mary (Atkinson) H.; 6, 1942; children by previous marriage; Elizabeth, Peter, Charles, Barbara; m. Elizabeth Chapman, Aug. 29, 1986. B.C.E., U. Calif., Berkeley, 1942. Civil engr. Wilsey & Broughton, S., San Francisco, 1946-52; v.p. Wilsey & Ham, Foster City, Calif., 1952-57, pres., 1957-84, chmn. bd. dirs., 1985-88, pres., chmn. bd., 1988—, founder, 1998. Past bd. dirs. Calif. Health Systems, Mills Peninsula Corp. Author: The Corporate New Town, 1971. Vice pres. Western region Boy Scouts Am. Served with U.S. Army, 1941-46. Decorated Bronze Star; recipient Eminent Engr. award Tau Beta Pi, 1988. Fellow ASCE, Am. Cons. Engrs. Council; mem. Lambda Alpha. Achievements include designing new town of Foster City, 1960. Home: 225 Roblar Ave Hillsborough CA 94010-6845 Office: 383A Vintage Park Dr Foster City CA 94404-1135

HAMADA, DUANE TAKUMI, architect; b. Honolulu, Aug. 12, 1954; s. Robert Kensaku and Jean Hakue (Masutani) H.; m. Martha S.P. Lee, Dec. 22, 1991; children; Erin, Robyn, David. BFA in Environ. Design, U. Hawaii, 1977, BArch, 1979. Registered architect, Hawaii, Guam, Florida, Puerto Rico, Saipan. Intern Edward Sullam, FAIA & Assocs., Honolulu, 1979-80; assoc. Design Ptnrs., Inc., Honolulu, 1980-86; prin. AM Ptnrs., Inc., Honolulu, 1986-98; dir. Design Ptnrs. Inc., Honolulu, 1998—. Chmn. 31st Ann. Cherry Blossom Festival Fashion Show, Honolulu, 1982, 32d Ann. Cherry Blossom Festival Cooking Show, 1983, mem. steering com., 1982, 83. Recipient Gold Key award for Excellence in Interior Design Am. Hotel and Motel Assn., 1990, Renaissance '90 Merit award Nat. Assn. Home Builder's Remodeler Coun., Merit award Honolulu mag., 1990, Cert. of Appreciation PACDIV USN, 1992, Gold Nugget award of Merit, 1997. Mem. AIA (jury student awards 1997, 98, jury profl. awards 1999), Constrn. Specifications Inst., Nat. Coun. Archtl. Registration Bds., Colegio de Arcquitectos de P.R., Japanese C. of C. Hawaii, Hawaiian Astron. Soc. Avocations: astronomy, music. Office: Design Ptnrs Inc 1580 Makaloa St Ste 1100 Honolulu HI 96814-3240 E-mail: dpinc@aloha.com

HAMAN, RAYMOND WILLIAM, lawyer; b. St. Maries, Idaho, Jan. 22, 1927; s. William and Eva Kate (Colliver) H.; m. Phyllis Maxine Garrett, June 24, 1948; children: Lorinda Ann, Bradley Lawrence (dec.). Student, Whitman Coll., 1947-49; JD, Washington and Lee U., 1952. Bar: Wash., 1952, U.S. Dist. Ct. (we. dist.) Wash. 1952, U.S. Ct. Appeals (9th cir.), U.S. Supreme Ct. Assoc. Evans, McLaren, Lane, Powell & Beeks, Seattle, 1952-59, ptnr., 1959-66, Lane Powell Moss & Miller, Seattle, 1966-89, Lane Powell Spears Lubersky, Seattle, 1989-91, of counsel, 1991-2001. Legal counsel Gov. Daniel J. Evans, Olympia, Wash., 1965, 67; mem. statute Law Com., 1966-95, chmn. 1988-95. Trustee, past pres. Lighthouse for the Blind, Inc., Seattle, 1964—; bd. dirs. Mercer Island (Wash.) Sch. Dist., 1967-72, Island County (Wash.) United Way, 1993—, pres., 1997-98; mem. Vestry St. Augustine's Episcopal Ch., 1999—. With USMC, 1945-46, PTO. Mem. Wash. Bar Assn., Order of the Coif. Republican. Episcopalian. Home: PO Box 926 Langley WA 98260-0926 Office: Lane Powell Spears Lubersky 1420 5th Ave Ste 4100 Seattle WA 98101-2338

HAMANN, DENNIS, food products executive; CFO Young's Mkt., Orange, Calif. Office: Youngs Market 2164 N Batavia St Orange CA 92865-3109

HAMBRECHT, WILLIAM R. retired venture capitalist; b. 1935; married; 5 children. Student, Princeton U. Broker Francis I. DuPont & Co., San Francisco; mng. ptnr. Hambrecht & Quist, San Francisco, 1968-97, past pres., CEO, chmn. bd. dirs., ret., 1997; founder, CEO W.R. Hambrecht & Co., San Francisco, 1997—. Bd. dirs. People Express, Inc., Internet Travel Network, Adobe Sys. Inc., Calyx and Corolla, LXR Biotech. Inc. Bd. dirs. pub. radio and TV sta. KQED Inc., San Francisco. Address: 539 Bryant St Ste 100 San Francisco CA 94107-1269

HAMBURGER, ROBERT N. pediatrics educator, consultant; b. N.Y.C., Jan. 26, 1923; s. Samuel B. and Harriet (Newfield) H.; m. Sonia Gross, Nov. 9, 1943; children: Hilary, Debre (dec.), Lisa. BA, U. N.C., 1947; MD, Yale U., 1951. Diplomate Am. Bd. Pediatrics, Am. Bd. Allergy and Immunology. Instr., asst. clin. prof. sch. medicine Yale U., New Haven, 1951-60; assoc. prof. biology U. Calif. San Diego, La Jolla, 1960-64, assoc. prof. pediatrics, 1964-67, prof., 1967-90, prof. emeritus, 1990—, asst. dean sch. medicine, 1964-70, lab. dir., 1970-98, head fellows tng. program allergy and immunology divsn., 1970-90; pres., CEO RNA and Co., Inc., 1997—. Cons. various cos., Calif., Sweden, Switzerland, 1986—. Author 1 book; contbr. articles to profl. jours.; patentee allergy peptides, allergen detector. Vol. physician, educator Children of the Californias, Calif. and Baja California, Mex., 1993—, Baker Sch. Free Clinic, 1999—. 1st lt. Air Corps, U.S. Army, 1943-45. Grantee NIH and USPHS, 1960-64, 64-84; Fulbright fellow, 1980, Disting. fellow Am. Coll. Allergy, Asthma, Immunology, 1986. Mem. U. Calif. San Diego Emeriti Assn. (pres. 1992-94). Avocations: flying, skiing, writing. Office: U Calif San Diego Revelle Coll Sch Medicine La Jolla CA 92093-0950 E-mail: rhamburger@ucsd.edu

HAMEL, MICHAEL A. career officer; BS in Aero. Engring., USAF Acad., 1972; MBA, Calif. State U., Dominguez Hills, 1974; grad., Squadron Officer Sch., 1975, Air Command and Staff Coll., 1980. Commd. 2d lt. USAF, 1972, advanced through grades to brigadier gen.; staff devel. planner Space and Missile Sys. Orgn., L.A. AFB, 1972-75; missile analyst fgn. tech. divsn. Lowry AFB, Colo., 1975-77; mission dir. Aerospace Data Facility, Buckley Air N.G. Base, 1977-79; air staff tng. officer R&D Hdqs. USAf, Washington, 1979-80; project mgr., manned spaceflight engr. Office of Sec. of Air Force for Spl. Projects, L.A. AFB, 1980-86; program element monitor, exec. officer Hdqs. USAF, Washington, 1986-90; chief plans divsn. Hdqs. Air Force Space Command, Peterson AFB, Colo., 1991-94; comdr. 750th Space Group, Onizuka Air Sta., Calif., 1994-95; vice comdr. 21st Space Wing, Peterson AFB, 1995-96; mil. adviser to v.p. The White House, Washington, 1996-98; vice comdr. Space and Missile Sys. Ctr., L.A. AFB, 1998-99; dir. requirements Air force Space Command HQ, Peterson AFB, Colo., 1999—. Decorated Def. Superior Svc. medal, Legion of Merit, Meritorious Svc. medal with 3 oak leaf clusters. Office: HAFSC 775 Loring Ave Colorado Springs CO 80914-1184

HAMILTON, BEVERLY LANNQUIST, investment management professional; b. Roxbury, Mass., Oct. 19, 1946; d. Arthur and Nancy Lannquist. BA cum laude, U. Mich., 1968; postgrad., NYU, 1969-70. Prin. Auerbach, Pollak & Richardson, N.Y.C., 1972-75; v.p. Morgan Stanley & Co., N.Y.C., 1975-80, United Techs., Hartford, Conn., 1980-87; dep. comptr. City of N.Y., 1987-91; pres., ret. ARCO Investment Mgmt Co, L.A., 1991-2000; also v.p. Atlantic Richfield Co., L.A. Bd. dirs. Mass. Mut. Investment Mgmt., Emerging Markets Growth Fund; trustee The Commonfund, Monterey Inst. Internat. Studies; investment writer Rockefeller Found., U. Mich., Unilever (The Netherlands) Pension Fund, CSFB Sport Venture Capital. Trustee Hartford Coll. for Women, 1981-87, Stanford Univ. Mgmt. Co., 1991-99; bd. dirs. Inst. for Living, 1983-87. Mem. NCCJ (bd. dirs. 1987-91). Address: 5485 Quail Meadows Dr Carmel CA 93923-7971

HAMILTON, CHARLES HOWARD, metallurgy educator; b. Pueblo, Colo., Mar. 17, 1935; s. George Edwin and Eva Eleanor (Watson) H.; m. Joy Edith Richmond, Sept. 7, 1968; children: Curtis Gene, Krista Kathleen, Brady Glenn. BS, Colo. Sch. Mines, 1959; MS, U. So. Calif., 1965; PhD, Case Western Res. U., 1968. Research engr. Space div. Rockwell Internat., Downey, Calif., 1959-65, mem. tech. staff Los Angeles div., 1968-75; tech. staff, phys. metallurgy Sci. Ctr., Thousand Oaks, Calif., 1975-77, group mgr. metals processing, 1977-79, prin. scientist, 1979-81, dir. materials synthesis and processing dept., 1982-84; assoc. prof. metallurgy Wash. State U., Pullman, 1984-87, prof., 1987-2000, prof. emeritus, 2000—. Chmn. Rockwell Corp. tech. panel, materials research and engring; co-organizer 1st Internat. Symposium Superplastic Forming, 1982, Internat. Conf. on Superplasticity and Superplastic Forming, 1988. Sr. editor Jour. Materials Shaping Tech.; dep. editor Scripta Metallurgica et Materialia, 1989-94; contbr. tech. articles to profl. publs.; patentee advanced metalworking and tech. Named Rockwell Engr. of Yr., 1979; recipient IR 100 award Indsl. Research mag., 1976, 80. Fellow Am. Soc. Metals; mem. AIME (shaping and forming com.), Sigma Xi. Home: PO Box 2064 McCall ID 83638

HAMILTON, DARDEN COLE, state legislator, flight test engineer; b. Pitts., Nov. 28, 1956; s. Isaac Herman Hamilton and Grace Osborne (Fish) Thorp; m. Linda Susanne Moser, Aug. 7, 1976; children: Christopher Moser Hamilton, Elijah Cole Hamilton. BS in Aeronautics, St. Louis U., Cahokia, Ill., 1977; postgrad., Ariz. State U. Lic. pilot, airframe and power mechanic. Engr. McDonnell Douglas Aircraft Co., St. Louis, 1977-80; group leader, engring. Cessna Aircraft Co., Wichita, Kans., 1980-83, sr. flight test engr., 1983-85, Allied-Signal Aerospace Co., Phoenix, 1986-92, flight test engr. specialist, 1992-98, prin. engr., 1998—; mem. Ariz. Senate, Dist. 16, Phoenix, 1998—; vice chair transp. com., mem. appropriations com. Ariz. Senate, Phoenix, 1999-2000, mem. fin. com., mem. health com., 1999-2000, chmn. rules com., appropriations sales com., 2000—, vice chmn. natural resources, agr. and environ. com., 2000—, mem. edn. com., 2000—. Editor Family Proponent Newsletter, 1994-98. Mem. Ariz. Gov.'s Constnl. Commemoration Com., 1997-99; bd. dirs. Ariz. House and Senate Chaplaincy, 1997-98, chmn. bd. advisors, 1998-2000; Desert Sky precinct committeeman Glendale Rep. Com.; vol. coord. legis. dist. 16 campaign John Shadegg for Congress, 1994-96; mem. adult edn. dept. Rivers Cmty. Ch.; del. Ariz. dist. 16 Ariz. Rep. Conv., 1995—; resolutions com. Ariz. Rep. Com., Ariz. govs. mil. base retention task force, 1999—; chmn. Ariz. Senate domestic violence task force, 1999—, Ariz. Space Commn., 2000—. Mem. NRA (life, cert. instr.), Soc. Flight Test Engrs., Am. Helicopter Soc., Am. Legis. Exch. Coun., Ariz. State Rifle and Pistol Assn. (life). Avocations: horses, target shooting, camping. Home: 5533 W Christy Dr Glendale AZ 85304-3889 Office: Allied-Signal Aerospace Co 111 S 34th St Phoenix AZ 85034-2802 Address: Ariz State Senate Rm 304 1700 W Washington St Phoenix AZ 85007

HAMILTON, DAVID MIKE, publishing company executive; b. Little Rock, 1951; s. Ralph Franklin and Mickey Garnette H.; m. Carol Nancy McKenna, Oct. 25, 1975; children: Elisabeth Michelle, Caroline Ellen. BA, Pitzer Coll., 1973; MLS, UCLA, 1976. Cert. tchr. library sci., Calif. Editor Sullivan Assocs., Palo Alto, Calif., 1973-75; curator Henry E. Huntington Library, San Marino, 1976-80; mgr. prodn., mktg. William Kaufmann Pubs., Los Altos, 1980-84; pres. The Live Oak Press, Palo Alto, 1984—. Cons. editor, gen. ptnr. Sensitive Expressions Pub. Co., Palo Alto, 1985-98; consulting dir. AAAI Press, 1994—; mng. editor and pub. AI Mag. Author: To the Yukon with Jack London, 1980, The Tools of My Trade, 1986, Making A Digital Book, 1994; contbg. editor and webmaster AAAI world-wide web site, 1995—; contbg. author Small Press jour., 1986, Making a Digital Book, 1995, (books) Book Club of California Quarterly, 1985, Research Guide to Biography and Criticism, 1986. Sec. vestry Trinity Parish, Menlo Park, 1986, bd. dirs., 1985-87; trustee Jack London Ednl. Found., San Francisco; bd. dirs. ISYS Forum, Palo Alto, 1987-96; pres. site coun., mem. supt.'s adv. com. Palo Alto Unified Sch. Dist.; mem. Wellesley Coll. Parent's Coun., 1997—. Mem. ALA, Coun. on Scholarly, Med. and Ednl. Publs., Am. Assn. Artificial Intelligence (bd. dirs., dir. publs.), Authors Guild, Bookbuilders West (book show com. 1983), Author's Guild, Soc. Tech. Comm. (judge 1984), Assn. Computing Machinery (chmn. pub. com. 1984), Soc. Scholarly Pubs. (program com. 1999), Sierra Club (life), Commonwealth Club, Book Club Calif. Democrat. Episcopalian. Avocations: backpacking, camping, hiking, book collecting. Office: The Live Oak Press PO Box 60036 Palo Alto CA 94306-0036 E-mail: mhamilton@aol.com, mhamilton@liveoakpress

HAMILTON, FREDERIC CRAWFORD, oil company executive; b. Columbus, Ohio, Sept. 25, 1927; s. Ferris F. and Jean (Crawford) H.; m. Jane C. Murchison, Feb. 14, 1953; children: Christy, Frederic C., Crawford M., Thomas M. Grad., Lawrenceville Sch., 1945, Babson Coll., 1947. Pres. Hamilton Bros. Oil Co., Denver, 1957—, Hamilton Bros. Can. Gas Co., Ltd., Calgary, Alta., 1968—; chmn. bd. Hamilton Bros. Oil and Gas (Gt. Brit.), Ltd., London, Eng., 1964—, Hamilton Bros. Petroleum Corp., Denver; chmn., chief exec. officer, pres. Hamilton Oil Corp.; chief exec. ofcr. Denver Art Mus., Denver. Bd. dirs. Gates Learjet Corp., IntraWest Fin. Corp., U.S. Trust Co., Skandinaviska, Enskilda Banken Internat. Corp.; adv. bd. Volvo Internat. Served with USAAF, 1944-46. Mem. Am. Petroleum Inst. (bd. dirs.). Office: Hamilton Oil Corp 1560 Broadway Denver CO [illegible] Denver Art Museum 100 W 14th Ave Denver CO 80204

HAMILTON, HARRY LEMUEL, JR. educator; b. Charleston, S.C., May 26, 1938; s. Harry Lemuel and Velma Fern (Bell) H.; m. LaVerne McDaniel, June 26, 1965 (div. 1978); children: David M., Lisa L; m. Mary MacIntyre, May 10, 1997. BA in Physics, Beloit Coll., 1960; MS in Meteorology, U. Wis., 1962, PhD in Meteorology, 1965. Asst. prof. atmospheric sci. SUNY, Albany, 1965-71, assoc. prof., 1971-90, dir. ednl. opportunity program, 1968-71, chairperson atmospheric sci., 1976-83, dean undergrad. studies, assoc. v.p. acad. affairs, 1983-88; rsch. scientist GE, Schenectady, N.Y., 1973-75; sr. v.p., provost Chapman U., Orange, Calif., 1990-2000, prof. atmospheric sci., 2000—. Trustee Beloit (Wis.) Coll., 1972—, Newport Beach Pub. Libr., 2001—; bd. dirs. Albany Med. Ctr., 1988-90, Mohawk Hudson Cmty. Found., 1988-90; pres. Empire State Inst. for Performing Arts, Albany, 1986-90; bd. dirs. world affairs coun. Orange County, 1995—; treas. Arts Orange County, 1995-2000; bd. dirs. Discovery Sci. Ctr., 1998-2000. Mem. Am. Meteorol. Soc., Am. Assn. for Higher Edn. Office: Chapman U 1 University Dr Orange CA 92866-1005 E-mail: hamilton@chapman.edu

HAMILTON, JAMES WILLIAM, lawyer; b. Omaha, Sept. 6, 1932; s. James William and Mary (Morgans) H.; m. Carol Lorraine Kircher, July 10, 1954; children: Theodore, Evelyn, Bonnie. BA, Stanford U., 1954, LLB, 1959. Bar: Calif. 1960, D.C. 1983. Assoc. Paul, Hastings, Janofsky & Walker, L.A., 1959-65, ptnr., 1965-93, sr. counsel, 1993—, ptnr. Costa Mesa, Calif., 1974-82, 85-93, Washington, 1982-85, of counsel, 1993—. Bd. dirs. Nat. Bank So. Calif., Newport Beach. Bd. dirs. Art Inst. So. Calif., Laguna Beach, Opportunity Internat., Chgo.; bd. visitors Stanford U. Law Sch., 1978-81, 96—. 1st lt. USAF, 1954-56. Mem. ABA, Los Angeles County Bar Assn. (chmn. corp. sect. 1973-74, editor bull. 1970-71), Orange County Bar Assn., Big Canyon Country Club (Newport Beach), Ironwood Country Club (Palm Desert, Calif.), Phi Gamma Delta. Republican. Presbyterian. Avocations: golf, skiing, swimming. Home: 895 Cliff Dr Laguna Beach CA 92651-1410 Office: Paul Hastings Janofsky & Walker 695 Town Center Dr Fl 17 Costa Mesa CA 92626-1924

HAMILTON, JOAN NICE, editor-in-chief periodical; b. Chgo., 1948; d. William and Dorothy Nice. Grad., Pomona Coll., 1970. Former editor High Country News; editor Climbing Mag.; editor-in-chief Sierra Mag., San Francisco. Contbr. articles to Audubon, Defenders, Nat. Wildlife Mags. Office: Sierra Mag 85 2nd St San Francisco CA 94105-3459

HAMILTON, JOE, communications company executive; BA in Math., Fordham U.; MBA in Fin., U. Calif., Berkeley. Numerous positions including sr. v.p. capital markets divsn. Crocker Nat. Bank; chief adminstrv. officer, CFO Grubb & Ellis Co.; exec. dir. Brobeck, Phleger & Harrison Law Firm; C.O.O. and pres. Cunningham Comm., Inc., Palo Alto, Calif. Bd. dirs. Cunningham Comm., Inc. Office: 1510 Page Mill Rd Palo Alto CA 94304-1125

HAMILTON, JUDITH HALL, computer company executive; b. Washington, June 15, 1944; d. George Woods and Jane Fromm (Brogger) Hall; m. Stephen T. McClellan, Oct. 29, 1988. BA, Ind. U., 1966; postgrad., Boston U., 1966-68; postgrad. Exec. Sch. Mgmt., UCLA, 1980-81. Programmer System Devel. Corp., Santa Monica, Calif., 1968-69, dir. programming, 1975-80; systems analyst Daylin, Inc., Beverly Hills, 1969-71; systems mgr. Audio Magnetics, Gardena, 1971-73; pres. Databasics, Inc., Santa Monica, 1973-75; v.p. Computer Scis. Corp., El Segundo, Calif., 1980-87; ptnr. Ernst & Young, L.A., 1987-89, N.Y.C., 1989-91; sr. v.p., gen. mgr. Locus Computing Corp., L.A., 1991-92; pres., CEO Dataquest, Inc., a Dun & Bradstreet Corp., San Jose, Calif., 1992-95, First Floor Software, Mountain View, 1996-98, Classrm. Connect, El Segundo, 1999—. Dir. Lante Corp. Classroom Connect; bd. dirs. R.R. Donnelley, Software.com, Lante, Inc., Evolve, Inc. Bd. dirs. Wildlife Conservation Soc. No. Calif., 1994—, Cmty. Breast Health Project 1994-99. Mem. Assn. Data Processing Svc. Orgns. (bd. dirs., chmn.), Info. Tech. Assn. Am., Commonwealth Club Silicon Valley (bd. dirs. 1997-99), Kappa Alpha Theta. Office: Classroom Connect Ste 400 8000 Marina Blvd Brisbane CA 94005

HAMILTON, MARK R. academic administrator; BS, U.S. Mil. Acad., 1967; Ma in English lit., Fla. State U., 1973; grad., Armed Forces Staff Coll., U.S. Army War Coll. Comdr. Division Artillery, Fort Richardson, 1988-90; chief staff Alaskan Command, Elmendorf AFB, 1992-93; dep. dir. force structure, resource and analysis Joint Staff, Washington, 1995-97; head recruiting U.S. Army, Fort Knox, Ky., 1997-98; pres. U. Alaska, Fairbanks, 1998—. Office: U Alaska PO Box 755000 Fairbanks AK 99775-5000

HAMILTON, PATRICIA ROSE, artist agent; b. Phila., Oct. 21, 1948; d. William Alexis and Lillian Marie (Sloan) Hamilton. BA, Temple U., 1970; MA, Rutgers U., 1971. Sec. to curator Whitney Mus., N.Y.C., 1971-73; sr. editor Art in Am., 1973; curator exhbns. Crispo Gallery, 1974-75; dir. Hamilton Gallery, 1976-84; artist's agt., 1984—. Democrat. Avocations: tennis, swimming, cooking. Home and Office: 6753 Milner Rd Los Angeles CA 90068-3214 E-mail: pathamilton@earthlink.net

HAMILTON, SCOTT SCOVELL, professional figure skater, former Olympic athlete; b. Toledo, Aug. 28, 1958; adopted s. Ernest Scovell and Dorothy (McIntosh) H. Grad. high sch., Bowling Green, Ohio, 1976; student, Metro State Coll., 1979. Nat. spokesman Discover Card youth programs, 1995—. Amateur competitive career includes Nat. Figure Skating Championships: jr. men's 1st pl., 1976, sr. men's 9th pl., 1977, 3d pl., 1978, 4th pl., 1979, 3d pl., 1980, 1st pl., 1981, 82, 83, 84, Mid-Western Figure Skating Championships: sr. men's 3d pl., 1977, 78, 79, Norton Skate Championships (now Skate Am.): men's divsn. 1st pl., 1979, 80, 81, 82, South Atlantic Figure Skating Championships: sr. men's divsn. 1st pl., 1980, Eastern Figure Skating Championships: sr. men's 1st pl., 1980, 81, 82, 83, 84, World Figure Skating Championships: men's divsn. 5th pl., 1980, 1st pl. 81, 82, 83, 84, Nat. Sports Festival Championships: 1st pl. men's divsn., 1981; Winter Olympics: men's divsn. 5th pl., Lake Placid, N.Y., 1980, 1st pl., Sarajevo, Yugoslavia, 1984, Nippon Hoso Kykai Figure Skating Championships, men's divsn. 1st pl., 1982, Golden Spin of Zagreb Championships, men's divsn. 1st pl., 1983; Profl. competitive career includes Nutrasweet/NBC-TV World Profl. Figure Skating Championships mens. divsn., 1st pl., 1984, 86, 2d pl., 85, 87, 88, 89, 91; World Challenge Champions/ABC-TV men's divsn., 2d pl., 1985, 1st pl., 1986; U.S. Open men's divsn. 1st pl., 1990, 2d pl., 1991, Diet Coke Profl. Skaters Championship men's divsn. 1st pl., 1992, Hershey's Kisses Pro-Am. Figure Skating Championships 2d Place Men's divsn. 1993, Sun Valley Men's Outdoor Championship 2d pl., 1994, The Gold Championship men's divsn. 1st pl., 1994, Can. Profl. Skating Championship men's divsn. 1st pl., 1994, Fox's Rock and Roll Skating Championship men's divsn. 1st pl., 1994; profl. performances include Nat. Arena Tour Ice Capades, 1984-85, 85-86, star Scott Hamilton's Am. Tour, 1986-87, 1990-91, co-star Concert On Ice, Harrah's Hotel, Lake Tahoe, Nev., 1987, spl. guest star Festival On Ice, Nat. Theatre Tour, 1987, star Discover Card Stars On Ice Nat. Arena Tour, 1987-88, 88-89, star Festival On Ice, Harrah's Hotel, 1988, guest star ABC-TV spl. Ice Capades With Kirk Cameron, 1988, A Very Special Christmas, ABC-TV, 1988, An Olympic Calgary Christmas, ABC-TV, 1988, star and mus. comedy and acting debut Broadway On Ice, Harrah's Hotel and Nat. Theatre Tour, 1989; CBS-TV Sports Figure Skating Commentator 1984-91 various skating competitions and CBS-TV coverage Winter Olympics, Albertville, France, 1992, Lillehammer, Norway, 1994; star, dir., producer Scott Hamilton's Celebration On Ice, Sea World of Calif., 1988, Scott Hamilton's Time Traveler: An Odyssey On Ice, Sea World of Calif., 1990, host, guest star TV spl. A Salute To Dorothy Hamill, 1988; star, co-producer Discover Card Stars On Ice, Nat. Arena Tour, 1989-91; guest star CBS-TV spl. Disney's Christmas on Ice, 1990; co-producer, star Discover Card Stars on Ice Nat. Arena Tour, 1991-92; co-host, star HBO TV spl. Vail Skating Festival, 1992; co-prodr., star Discover Card Stars on Ice Nat. Arena Tour, 1992-93, 93-94, 94-95, Canadian Nat. Tour, 1995; guest TV spl. A Disney Christmas on Ice, 1992, CBS-TV spl. Disney on Ice, 1992, HBO-TV spl. Vail Skating Festival, 1993, Skates of Gold I, Boston, 1993, Skates of Gold II, Cin., 1994, CBS-TV Disney Fantasy on Ice, 1993, CBS-TV spl. Nancy Kerrigan & Friends, 1994, CBS-TV spl. Disney's Greatest Hits, 1994, CBS-TV spl. Dreams on Ice, 1995; creator original concepts in arena figure skating. Cons. Friends of Scott Hamilton Found. named in his honor to fundraise and benefit youth oriented causes throughout U.S., 1988, Scott Hamilton's Friends and Legends 1st Annual Celebrity Charity Golf Tournament, Ford's Colony, Williamsburg, Va., 1991; participant fund-raising Athletes for Reagan, March of Dimes, Am. Cancer Soc., Spl. Olympics, Starlight Found., United Way Adoption Home Socs., Make A Wish Found, Big Bros., 1984—, Athletes For Bush, Adult and Ped. AIDS Rsch., Edn. and Funding, 1988—, Homeless, 1989—, Great Am. Workout for Pres.'s Coun. Phys. Fitness & Sports, 1990, 92; nat. spokesman Discover Card youth programs, 1995—. Winner Olympic Gold medal, Sarajevo, 1984; U.S. Olympic Com. awards and honors include carrier Am. Flag in opening ceremonies Lake Placid, 1980, Figure Skating Athlete of Yr., 1981, 82, 83, 84, Athlete of Yr., 1981, Olympic Spirit award, 1987; recipient Olympia award Southland Corp., 1984, Achievement award March of Dimes, 1984, Colo. Athlete of Yr. award Denver Athletic Club, 1984, Most Courageous Athlete award Phila. Sportswriters Assn., 1985, Profl. Skater of Yr. award Am. Skating World mag., 1986, Jacques Favart award Internat. Skating Union, 1988, The Crown Royal Achievement award from House of Seagrams and Jimmy Heuga Ctr., 1991, Clairol's Personal Best award, 1991, Spirit of Giving award U.S. Figure Skating Assn., 1993, 9th Ann. Great Sports Legends award Nick Buonoconti Fund The Miami Project, 1994, Ritter F. Shumway award U.S. Figure Skating Assn., 1994; inducted U.S. Olympic Hall of Fame, 1990, World Figure Skating Hall of Fame, 1990; honoree nat. com. for adoption, 1992. Hon. mem. Phila. Skating Club, Humane Soc. Republican. Avocation: golf. Office: 13041 Ventura Blvd Studio City CA 91604-2237 Address: CBS Sports CBS Inc 7800 Beverly Blvd Los Angeles CA 90036-2188

HAMILTON, STEVEN G. lawyer; b. 1939; BS, Mont. State U., 1962; JD, UCLA, 1966. Pvt. practice, 1966-68; asst. gen. counsel Garrett Corp., L.A., 1968-80, v.p., gen. counsel, 1980-88; v.p., legal and gen. counsel Alaska Airlines, Inc., Seattle, 1988—. Office: Alaska Airlines PO Box 68900 Seattle WA 98168-0900

HAMILTON, W. W. religious organization administrator; Gen. sec. The Church of God in Christ, Memphis. Office: Church God in Christ Office Gen Sec 1620 Broadway Ave Seaside CA 93955-5121

HAMLIN, DOUG, publishing executive; V.p. group pub. Motor Trend, subs. Petersen Pub. Co., L.A. Office: Petersen Pub Co LLC 6420 Wilshire Blvd Los Angeles CA 90048-5502

HAMMAR, LESTER EVERETT, health care manufacturing executive, retired; b. Tillamook, Oreg., Dec. 15, 1927; s. Leo E. and Harriet L. (Parsons) H.; m. Margrit Steigl, May 9, 1964; children: Lawrence, Thomas, Stephanie. B.S., Oreg. State U., 1950; M.B.A., Washington U., 1964. With Montsanto Co., 1952-69; controller Monsanto-Europe, 1966-69; v.p., controller Smith Kline & French Labs., Phila., 1969-72, Abbott Labs., North Chgo., Ill., 1972-88; ret. Bd. trustees Asia House Investments; project mgr. Exec. Svc. Corp. Chgo. Mem. audit com. City of Lake Forest; ruling elder, clk. of session 1st Presbyn. Ch. of Lake Forest; bd. dirs. Haven, Clara Abbott Fund; bd. dirs. Teton County Housing Authority. 1st lt. F.A., AUS, 1951-52. Mem. Fin. Execs. Inst., Am. Mgmt. Assn. (former chmn. fin. coun., bd. mem.), 100 Club of Lake Country Club. Home and Office: 634 Academy Woods Dr Lake Forest IL 60045

HAMMAR, SHERREL LEYTON, medical educator, dean; b. Caldwell, Idaho, May 21, 1931; m. Shirley; children: Kathryn M., David Jefferson. BA, Coll. Idaho, 1953; MD, U. Wash., 1957. Intern Mpls. Gen. Hosp., 1957-58; resident U. Wash., Seattle, 1958-60; instr. dept. pediatrics U. Wash. Sch. Medicine, Seattle, 1962-64, asst. prof. dept. pediatrics, 1964-69, assoc. prof. dept. pediatrics, 1969-71, U. Hawaii, Honolulu, 1971-73; prof. U. Hawaii Sch. Medicine, Honolulu, 1973—; interim dean John A. Burns Sch. Medicine U. Hawaii, Honolulu, 1996-99. Chief adolscent clinic U. Wash., 1964-65, acting dir. clin. tng. unit devel. & mental health ctr., 1964, asst., 1965-71, acting dir. clin. tng. unit child devel. and mental retardation ctr., 1970-71; dir. ambulatory pediatric svcs., chief adolscent medicine Kauikeolani Children's Hosp., Honolulu, 1971-72, dir. med. svcs. and tng., 1972-73, chief pediatrics, 1973—, dir. pediatric med. edn., 1979—; chmn. dept. pediatrics U. Hawaii, 1973-97, residency program dir., 1973-97; cons. in field. Contbr. articles to profl. jours. Fellow U. Wash., 1960-62. Fellow APHA, Am. Acad. Pediatrics (com. youth 1967-73, 75-81, sect. adolscent health, exec. coun. 1978-80, com. early childhood, adoption & dependent care 1990-92, task force on AIDS 1990-92); mem. AMA (med. sch. sect.), Western Soc. Pediatric Rsch., Hawaii Med. Assn., Ambulatory Pediatric Assn., Seattle Pediatric Soc., Honolulu County Med. Soc., Alpha Omega Alpha. Office: U Hawaii John A Burns Sch Med Kapiolani Med Ctr 1319 Punahou St Rm 740 Honolulu HI 96826-1001 E-mail: hammars@postoffice.att.net

HAMMARGREN, LONNIE, former lieutenant governor; b. Dec. 25, 1937; married. BA, U. Minn., 1958, MA in Psychol., 1960, BS, MD, U. Minn., 1964, MS in Neurosurgery, 1974. Diplomate Am. Bd. Neurological Surgery; med. license Nev., Minn. Flight surgeon for the astronauts NASA Manned Space Craft Ctr.; former lt. gov., pres. of the senate State of Nev., 1995-98; med. pvt. practice Las Vegas, 1998—. Assoc. clin. prof. neurosurgery U. Nev. Sch. Medicine, Reno; clin. assoc. prof. surgery U. Calif., San Diego, 1982; chair Commn. Econ. Devel., Commn. Tourism; bd. dirs. Nev. Dept. Transp. Bd. regents U. and C.C. Sys. Nev., 1988-94; adv. bd. mem. Gov.'s com. for Employment of Handicapped; mem. State Bd. Edn., 1984-88; bd. mem. March of Dimes, Aid to Adoption of Spl. Kids. Mem. Spinal Cord Injury Program of Nev. (pres.), Cancer Soc., Aerospace Med. Assn., U Med. Ctr. Rehabilitation Unit (dir.), U. Med. Ctr. (chmn. neurosurgery dept.), Help Them Walk Again Found. (Nat. Dir.), Spina Bifida and Hydrocephalus Soc. (med. dir.), Internat. Ctr. for Rehabilitation Engring. (med. dir.), Pacific World Med. Found. (treas.), Paramed. and Emergency Care Bd. (adv.). Office: 3196 S Maryland Pkwy Ste 106 Las Vegas NV 89109-2312

HAMMER, SUSAN W. educational foundation executive, former mayor; b. Altadena, Calif., Dec. 21, 1938; d. James Nathan and Katrine (Krutzsch) Walker; m. Philip Hammer, Sept. 4, 1960; children: Philip, Hali, Matthew. BA in History, U. Calif., Berkeley, 1960. Svc. rep. Pacific Telephone Co., Berkeley, 1960-61; staff asst. Peace Corps, Washington, 1962-63; councilwoman City of San Jose, Calif., 1980-81, 83-90, spl. asst. to mayor, 1981-82, vice mayor, 1985-87, mayor, 1991-99; CEO Synopsys Outreach Found. and Synopsys Silicon Valley Sci. and Tech. Championship, 1999—. Chair, pres. Adv. Com. on Trade Policy and Negotiations, 1994—. Bd. dirs. San Jose Mus. Art, 1971-90, pres., 1978-80; mem. governing bd. NCCJ, 1978—; mem. adv. bd. Cmty. Found. Santa Clara County, 1978—; mem. Santa Clara County Transp. Com., 1976-77, Santa Clara County Juvenile Justice Commn., 1980, Victim-Witness Adv. Bd., 1977-90, Children's Health Coun., San Jose, 1981-89, Santa Clara Valley Leadership Program, 1986-90, Childrens Shelter Project, 1991—, Am. Leadership Forum, [illegible] on Trade Policy and Negotiation; mem. San Jose Fine Arts Commn., 1980;

v.p. Calif. Bd. Edn., 1999— Recipient Rosalie M. Stern Community Svc. award U. Calif., 1975, Disting. Citizen of San Jose award Exch. Club, 1979, Investment in Leadership award Coro Found., 1985, Tzedek award for honor, compassion and community svc. Temple Emanu-El, 1987, Recognition award YWCA, Santa Clara County, 1989, resolution of commendation Assn. for Responsible Alcohol Control, 1990, Woman of Achievement award The Women's Fund, 1990, Dox Quixote award Nat. Hispanic U., 1991, Friends of Bay Area Mcpl. Elections Com. award, 1991. Democrat.

HAMMERGREN, JOHN H. pharmaceutical company executive; BSBA, U. Minn.; MBA, Xavier U. With Baxter Healthcare Corp./Am. Hosp. Corp. and Lyphomed Inc., 1981-91; pres. med./surgical divsn. Kendall Healthcare Products Co., Mansfield, Mass., 1991-96; corp. exec. v.p., pres., CEO supply mgmt. bus. McKesson HBOC, Inc., 1996-99, co-pres. & co-CEO, 1999—. Office: McKesson HBOC Inc One Post St San Francisco CA 94104

HAMMES, MICHAEL NOEL, automotive company executive; b. Evanston, Ill., Dec. 25, 1941; s. Ferdinand Edward and Winifred Hammes; m. Lenore Lynn Forbes, Jan. 3, 1964; children: Michael, Nicole, Karl, Erik, Heide. BS, Georgetown U., 1963; MS, NYU, 1965. Exec. dir. internat. bus. Ford Internat. Automotive Ops., Dearborn, Mich., 1975-78; pres. Ford Mex. SA, Mexico City, 1978-83; v.p. truck ops. Ford Europe, Warley, Essex, Eng., 1983-86; pres. internat. ops. Chrysler Corp., 1986-90; corp. vice chmn., pres. worldwide consumer product ops. Black & Decker Corp., 1990-93; chmn., CEO The Coleman Co., 1993-97; CEO Guide Corp., Anderson, Ind., 1998-2000; pres., CEO Sunrise Medical Inc., Carlsbad, Calif., 2000—. Bd. dirs., chmn. audit com. Sunrise Med. Inc., 1998—. Office: Sunrise Med Inc 2382 Faraday Ave Ste 200 Carlsbad CA 92008-7220

HAMMOND, CHARLES AINLEY, clergyman; b. Asheville, N.C., Aug. 7, 1933; s. George Bradley and Eleanor Maria (Gantz) H.; m. Barbro Stigsdotter Laurell, July 16, 1960; children: Stig Bradley, Inga Allison. B.A., Occidental Coll., Los Angeles, 1955; B.D., Princeton Theol. Sem., 1958; D.D., Missouri Valley Coll., 1981, Wabash Coll., 1982. Ordained to ministry United Presbyn. Ch., 1958; pastor chs. in Pa. and Calif., 1958-75; exec. presbyter Presbytery Wabash Valley, West Lafayette, Ind., 1975-87, Presbytery Phila., 1987-98; int. pastor Presbyn. Ch., New Providence, N.J., 1998-99, 1st Presbyn. Ch., Salt Lake City, 1999-2001. Moderator 192d gen. assembly United Presbyn. Ch., 1980-81; chmn. Gen. Assembly Mission Coun., 1982-83. Author: Newtonian Polity in an Age of Relativity, 1977, Seven Deadly Sins of Dissent, 1979. Sec. Hallam (Pa.) Borough Planning Commn., 1962-64, Westchester Cmty. Plans, L.A., 1966-68, Pasadena (Calif.) Planning Commn., 1971-75; chmn. pvt. land use com., 1972-73, chmn. pub. land use com., 1973-74; mem. gen. assembly coun. Presbyn. Ch. (U.S.A.), 1983-91; bd. dirs. Met. Coun. Chs. of Phila., 1990-95; trustee Beaver Coll., 1991-99; gen. assembly Permanent Jud. Com., 1995-2001; mem. bd. corporators Pres. Min. Found. Recipient Disting. Alumnus award Princeton Theol. Sem., 1981. Mem. Assn. Presbyn. Ch. Educators, Friends of Old Pine (trustee). Republican.

HAMMOND, JUDY MCLAIN, business services executive; b. Downey, Calif., June 24, 1956; d. Ernest Richard and Bernice Elaine (Thompson) McLain; m. Dennis Francis Hammond, Aug. 15, 1981. BS in Mgmt., Pepperdine U., 1982; MBA, U. So. Calif., 1986. Br. mgr. Kelly Svcs., Encino, Calif., 1978-81; mktg. mgr. Payco Am. Corp., Encino, 1981-83, GC Svcs. Corp., Santa Ana, Calif., 1983-86; pres. Resource Mgmt. Svcs. Inc., Norwalk, 1986—; founder, CEO The Debt Marketplace, Inc., Norwalk, 1994—; sr. v.p. DebtAuction.com, 2000—. Cons., expert in collection and recovery. Author: Collect More From Collection Agencies. Mem. Toastmasters, Merchants Rsch. Coun. (bd. dirs.). Avocations: scuba diving, underwater photography. Office: 10440 Pioneer Blvd Ste 2 Santa Fe Springs CA 90670-8235 E-mail: judy.hammond@debtmarketplace.com

HAMMOND, LARRY AUSTIN, lawyer; b. Wichita, Kans., Sept. 17, 1945; BA, U. Tex., 1967, JD, 1970. Bar: Calif. 1971, Ariz. 1975. Law clk. to Hon. Carl McGowan U.S. Ct. Appeals (D.C. cir.), 1970-71; law clk. to Hon. Hugo L. Black U.S. Supreme Ct., 1971, law clk. to Hon. Lewis F. Powell Jr., 1971-73; asst. spl. prosecutor Watergate spl. prosecution force U.S. Justice Dept., 1973-74, dep. asst. atty. gen. office legal counsel, 1977-80; mem. Osborn Maledon P.A., Phoenix, 1995—. Adj. prof. law Ariz. State U., 1977, 85—, U. Ariz., 1983, U. Mex., 1983; judge pro tempore Ariz. Ct. Appeals, 1992. Editor-in-chief Tex. Law Rev., 1969-70. Mem. ABA, Order of Coif. Office: Osborn Maledon PO Box 36379 Phoenix AZ 85067-6379

HAMMOND, R. PHILIP, chemical engineer; b. Creston, Iowa, May 28, 1916; s. Robert Hugh and Helen Hammond; m. Amy L. Farmer, Feb. 28, 1941 (div. 1969); children: Allen L., David M., Jean Phyllis, Stanley W.; m. Vivienne Fox, 1972. BSChemE, U. So. Calif., 1938; Ph.D. in Phys. and Inorganic Chemistry (Naval Research fellow), U. Chgo., 1947. Registered profl. engr., Ill., Calif. Chief chemist Lindsay Chem. Co., West Chicago, Ill., 1938-46; group leader Los Alamos Sci. Lab., 1947-62, assoc. div. leader reactor devel. div., 1960-62; dir. nuclear desalination program Oak Ridge Nat. Lab., 1962-73; adj. prof. U. Calif. at Los Angeles, 1972—; head energy group R & D Assos. Corp., Santa Monica, Calif., 1973-83; desalination cons., 1987—; leader advanced sea water evaporator design Met. Water Dist. of So. Calif., L.A., 1989-98. Author articles on nuclear power reactors, nuclear wastes, reactor safety econs., energy centers, metallurgy of plutonium and refractory metals, rare earths, radiation chemistry, remote control engring.; contbr. to fusion energy concept using underground containment, to Ency. Brit. Mem. U.S. delegation Conf. on Peaceful Uses Atomic Energy, Geneva, Switzerland, 1955, 65, 71, IAEA Panel on Desalination, Vienna, Austria, 1964, 65, 66, 71; mem. U.S. team to USSR on desalination, 1964. Mem. Am. Nuclear Soc. (charter), Am. Chem. Soc., Am. Inst. Chem. Engrs., Sigma Xi, Phi Kappa Phi, Phi Lambda Upsilon. Achievements include patents for improved safety for high speed rail transport, for devices for preventing collisions at sea and for storing nuclear waste; origination of advanced concepts in sea water evaporator construction, and efficient coupling to nuclear energy sources; design (with others) of advanced reactor containment system capable of withstanding melt-down accidents with zero leakage, and of automotive engine using liquid air and liquid natural gas as fuel. Home and Office: PO Box 3971 Laguna Hills CA 92654-3971

HAMREN, NANCY VAN BRASCH, bookkeeper; b. L.A., Feb. 2, 1947; d. Milton Carl and Winifred (Taylor) Van Brasch; m. Jerome Arthur Hamren, Feb. 14, 1981; children: Emily Allison, Meredith Ann. Student, Pasadena City Coll., 1964-65, San Francisco State Coll., 1966-67, U. Oreg., 1975-79. Bookkeeper/office mgr. Springfield Creamery, Eugene, Oreg., 1969—, also bd. dirs. Originator Nancy's Yogurt, Nancy's Cultured Dairy Products. Active mem. Oreg. Shakespearean Festival, Ashland, 1986, Planned Parenthood, Sta. KLCC-PBS Radio; bd. dirs. BRING Recycling, sec. bd. dirs. Mem. Oreg. Dairy Assn., Audubon Soc., N.Am. Truffling Soc., The Wilderness Soc., Oreg. Pub. Broadcasting, Buhl (Idaho) Arts Coun., Conservation Internat, Provender Alliance (pres. bd. dirs.). Democrat. Avocations: gourmet cooking, gardening, walking, wine tasting. Home: 1315 Ravenwood Dr Eugene OR 97401-1912 Office: Springfield Creamery 29440 Airport Rd Eugene OR 97402-9524 E-mail: nhamren@uswest.net

HAN, JIAHUAI, medical researcher; BS in Biochemistry, Beijing U., 1982, MS in Protein Biochemistry, 1988; PhD in Molecular Biology, U. Brussels, 1990. Rsch. fellow Dept. Internal Medicine and Howard Hughes Med. Inst., U. Tex. Southwestern Med. Ctr., Dallas, 1987-92; rsch. assoc. Dept. Immunology, The Scripps Rsch. Inst., La Jolla, Calif., 1992-93, sr. rsch. assoc., 1993-96, asst. mem., 1996—. Contbr. articles to profl. jours. Recipient Established Investigator award Am. Heart Assn., 1995. Office: Scripps Rsch Inst IMM-9 10550 N Torrey Pines Rd La Jolla CA 92037-1000

HANABUSA, COLLEEN, state legislator, lawyer; b. Honolulu, 1952; m. June and Isao Hanabusa. BA in Econs. and Sociology, U. Hawaii, 1973, MA in Sociology, 1975, JD, 1977. Labor atty., Honolulu; legal rschr. Madison, Wis., 1978; mem. Hawaii Senate, Dist. 21, Honolulu; chair water, land and Hawaiian affairs com. Hawaii Senate, Honolulu, mem. commerce and consumer protection com., mem. govt. ops. and housing com. Advisor Arnold Morgado for Mayor Canmpaign, 1994. Recipient 2d runner-up Hawaii Jr. Miss Pageant, 1969. Avocation: reading murder mysteries. Office: State Capitol 415 S Beretania St Honolulu HI 96813-2407 Fax: (808) 586-7797

HANAUER, JOE FRANKLIN, real estate executive; b. Stuttgart, Fed. Republic Germany, July 8, 1937; came to U.S., 1938; s. Otto and Betty (Zurndorfer) H.; m. Jane Boyle, Oct. 20, 1972; children: Jill, Wendy, Jason, Elizabeth. BS, Roosevelt U., 1963. Pres. Thorsen Realty, Oak Brook, Ill., 1974-80; sr. v.p. Coldwell Banker, Newport Beach, Calif., 1980-83, pres., 1984, chmn. bd., CEO, 1984-88; prin. Combined Investments LP, Laguna Beach, 1989—; chmn. bd. dirs. Grubb & Ellis Co., San Francisco, 1993-97. Bd. dirs. MAF Bancorp, Chgo., Grubb & Ellie Co., Chgo., Homestore-.com.; chmn. policy adv. bd. Joint Ctr. for Housing Studies Harvard U., 1995-96. Bd. dirs. Chgo. Chamber Orch., 1976—; trustee Roosevelt U. Mem. Nat. Assn. Realtors (exec. com.). Home: 105 S La Senda Dr Laguna Beach CA 92651-6731 Office: Combined Investments LP 361 Forest Ave Ste 200 Laguna Beach CA 92651-2146

HANAWALT, PHILIP COURTLAND, biology educator, researcher; b. Akron, Ohio, Aug. 25, 1931; s. Joseph Donald and Lenore (Smith) H.; m. Joanna Thomas, Nov. 2, 1957 (div. Oct. 1977); children: David, Steven; m. Graciela Spivak, Sept. 10, 1978; children: Alex, Lisa. Student, Deep Springs Coll., 1949-50; BA, Oberlin Coll., 1954; MS, Yale U., 1955, PhD, 1959; ScD (hon.), Oberlin Coll., 1997. Postdoctoral fellow U. Copenhagen, Denmark, 1958-60, Calif. Inst. Tech., Pasadena, 1960-61; rsch. biophysicist, lectr. Stanford U., Calif., 1961-65, assoc. prof., 1965-70, prof., 1970—, Howard H. and Jessie T. Watkins univ. prof., 1997—, chmn. dept. biol. scis. Calif., 1982-89; faculty dept. dermatology Stanford Med. Sch., 1979—. Mem. physiol. chemistry study sect. NIH, Bethesda, Md., 1966-70, mem. chem. pathology study sect., 1981-84; mem. sci. adv. com. Am. Cancer Soc., N.Y.C., 1972-76, Coun. for Extramural Grants, 1998-2001; chmn. 2d ad hoc senate com. on professoriate Stanford U., 1988-90; mem. NSF fellowship rev. panel, 1985; mem. carcinogen identification com. Calif. EPA, 1995-98; mem. toxicology adv. com. Burroughs-Welcome Fund, 1995-2000, chmn., 1997-2001; mem. sci. adv. bd. Fogarty Internat. Ctr., NIH, 1995-99; chmn. Gordon Conf. on Mutagenesis, 1996; chmn. Gordon Conf. on Mammalian DNA Repair, 1999; mem. bd. on radiation effects rschr. NAS Commn. on Life Scis., 1996-98; trustee Oberlin Coll., 1998—. Author: Molecular Photobiology, 1969; author, editor: DNA Repair: Techniques, 1981, 83, 88, Molecular Basis of Life, 1968, Molecules to Living Cells, 1980; mng. editor DNA Repair Jour., 1982-93; assoc. editor Jour. Cancer Rsch., Molecular Carcinogenesis, Environ. Health Perspectives, Biotechniques; bd. rev. editors Sci.; contbr. more than 400 articles to profl. jours. Recipient Outstanding Investigator award Nat. Cancer Inst., 1987-2001, Excellence in Tchg. award No. Calif. Phi Beta Kappa, 1991, Environ. Mutagen Soc. Ann. Rsch. award, 1992, Peter and Helen Bing award for Disting. Tchg., 1992, Am. Soc. for Photobiology Rsch. award, 1996, Internat. Mutation Rsch. award, 1997, Ellison Found. Sr. scholar award, 2001—; Hans Falk lectr. Nat. Inst. Environ. Health Scis., 1990, Severo Ochoa Meml. Hons. lectr. NYU, 1996, IBM-Princess Takamatsu lectr. Japan, 1999; Fogarty sr. rsch. fellow, 1993. Fellow AAAS, Am. Acad. Microbiology; mem. NAS, Am. Assn. Cancer Rsch. (bd. dirs. 1994-97), Am. Soc. for Photobiology, Genetics Soc., Biophys. Soc. (exec. bd. 1969-71), Am. Soc. Biochemistry and Molecular Biology, Environ. Mutagen Soc. (pres. 1993-94), Radiation Rsch. Soc., Sigma Xi. Achievements include co-discovery of DNA excision-repair and transcription-coupled DNA repair; research on role of DNA change in human genetic disease and aging. Home: 317 Shasta Dr Palo Alto CA 94306-4542 Office: Stanford U Dept Biol Scis Herrin Biology Labs 371 Serra Mall Stanford CA 94305-5020

HANCOCK, JOHN WALKER, III, banker; b. Long Beach, Calif., Mar. 8, 1937; s. John Walker and Bernice H.; m. Elizabeth Hoien, June 20, 1959; children: Suzanne, Donna, Randy, David. BA in Econs, Stanford U., 1958, MBA, 1960. With Security Pacific Nat. Bank, L.A., 1960-92, v.p., 1968-77, sr. v.p., 1977-84, exec. v.p., 1984-92; pres. Bancap Investment Group, Long Beach, Calif., 1992—. Bd. dirs. Harbor Bank; chmn. Meml. Med. Ctr.; commr. Port of Long Beach. Bd. dirs. Long Beach Symphony, Meml. Hosp., Long Beach City Coll. Found. Mem. Stanford U. Alumni Assn., Calif. Club (L.A.), Va. Country Club, Balboa Bay Club, Pacific Club, Bohemian Club. Republican. Home: 258 Roycroft Ave Long Beach CA 90803-1717 Office: Bancap Investment Group 6265 E 2d St Long Beach CA 90803-4613

HANCOCK, LONI, mayor; b. N.Y.C., 1940; children: Leita, Mara. BA, Ithaca Coll.; MA, Wright Inst. Mem. Berkeley City Council, 1971-79, Berkeley's Waterfront Adv. Commn., 1984-86; mayor City of Berkeley, 1986—; region IX rep. US Dept. of Edn., San Francisco. Mem. Bay Area Air Quality Mgmt. Dist., 1990—, Alameda County Congestion Mgmt. Agy., 1991—. Mem. Berkeley Parent Nursery Schs., 1964-68, Berkeley Citizens Action Com., 1975-93; mem., past pres. New Dem. Forum, 1982—; v.p. Berkeley Office of Econ. Opportunity, 1969-71, Local Gov. Commn., Literacy Vols. of Am., Youth Project; past regional dir. of ACTION, 1977-80; exec. dir. Shalan Found., San Francisco, 1981-86; mem., co-founder LeConte Neighborhood Assn,. 1969-71. Mem. Sierra Club, Nat. Women's Polit. Caucus. Office: Dept Edn 50 United Nations Plz Rm 205 San Francisco CA 94102-4912

HANCOCK, N(EWELL) LES(LIE), accountant; b. Pitts., Apr. 13, 1943; s. Newell Francis and Mildred Helen (Bouverot) H.; m. Margaret Ann Kendrick, Nov. 30, 1968; children: Michelle Lynn, Jennifer Ann, Marie Noelle. BSBA, U. Denver, 1966; postgrad., various schs., 1969—. CPA, Colo. Supr. Pannell, Kerr, Forster, Denver and Atlanta, 1969-78; mgr. Wolf & Co. of Colo., Inc., Denver, 1978-79, 83-84; supr. Kafoury, Armstrong & Co., Reno, 1979-82; pvt. practice acctg. Arvada, Colo. and Reno, 1982—; mgr. Ashby, Armstrong & Co., Denver, 1984-87; asst. contr. 1st Resorts Inc. and Great Am. Mgmt. Group Inc., Lakewood, Colo., 1987-89; team leader subcontract audit Nat. Renewable Energy Lab., Golden, 1989—. Served to 1st lt. U.S. Army, 1966-69. Mem. AICPA, Colo. Soc. CPAs (report rev. com. 1984-90, pvt. co. practice com. 1990-93, accountancy regulation com. 1993-94, mem. rels. com. 1994-96, mem. svcs. com. 1996-97), Nev. Soc. CPAs (bd. dirs. Reno chpt. 1982-83, auditing stds. com. 1981-82, vice chmn. acctg. principles com. 1981-83), Hospitality Accts. Assn. (sec. 1976-77). Republican. Baptist. Avocations: summer sports, collections. Office: PO Box 740535 Arvada CO 80006-0535

HAND, CADET HAMMOND, JR. marine biologist, educator; b. Patchogue, N.Y., Apr. 23, 1920; s. Cadet Hammond and Myra (Wells) H.; m. Winifred Werdelin, June 6, 1942; children: Cadet Hammond III, Gary Alan. B.S., U. Conn., 1946; M.A., U. Calif. at Berkeley, 1948, Ph.D., 1951. Instr. Mills Coll., 1948-50, asst. prof., 1950-51; research biologist Scripps Inst. Oceanography, 1951-53; mem. faculty U. Calif. at Berkeley, 1953—, prof. zoology, 1963-85, prof. emeritus, 1985—; dir. Bodega Marine Lab., 1961-85; Cons. NIH, 1964-66, NSF, 1964-69; mem. atomic safety and licensing bd. panel Nuclear Regulatory Commn., 1971-92, adminstrv. judge atomic safety and licensing bd. panel, 1980-92. NSF sr. postdoctoral fellow, 1959-60; Guggenheim fellow, 1967-68 Contbr. articles to profl. jours. Fellow Calif., Wash. acads. scis.; mem. No. Calif. Malacozool. Soc. (pres. 1963-87), Soc. Systematic Zoology, Ecol. Soc. Am., Ray Soc. (Gt. Britain), Am. Soc. Zoologists (chmn. div. invertebrate zoology 1977-78), Am. Soc. Limnology and Oceanography. Home: PO Box 1016 Bodega Bay CA 94923-9769 Office: Bodega Marine Lab Bodega Bay CA 94923

HAND, DALE L. pharmacist; b. Boise, Idaho, Oct. 21, 1947; s. Robert Ray and Evelyn Mabel (McKenzie) H.; m. Gloria J. Lassen, Dec. 19, 1970; children: Travis D., Jason D. Student, Walla Walla Coll., 1965-66; B Pharmacy, Idaho State U., 1970; MS in Health Svcs. Adminstrn., Coll. St. Francis, Joliet, Ill., 1985. Intern Clinic Pharmacy, Pocatello, Idaho, 1968-70; pharmacognosy lab. tchng. asst. Idaho State U., 1969-70; hosp. pharmacy internship St. Luke's Hosp., Boise, 1970-71, clin. staff pharmacist, 1971-77; various to dir. pharmacy svcs. Porter Meml. Hosp., Denver, 1981-92, adminstrv. dir. dept. pharm. care, 1992—; pharmacy extern preceptor U. Colo., 1981—. Cons. pharmacist McNamara Hosp. and Nursing Home, Fairplay, Colo., 1981-83; cons. Edn. Design, Inc., 1993—; lectr. in field.; chmn. various hosp. coms. Contbr. articles to profl. jours. Bd. dirs. Arapahoe Sertoma, 1991-98. Mem. Am. Soc. Health Sys. Pharmacists, Colo. Soc. Health Sys. Pharmacists. Avocations: golf, softball, snow-skiing, landscape design, music. Home: 7269 W Chestnut Dr Littleton CO 80128-5699 Office: Porter Adventist Hosp 2525 S Downing St Denver CO 80210-5817 E-mail: dalehand@centura.org

HANDLER, EVELYN, science administrator; b. Budapest, Hungary, May 5, 1933; U.S. citizen; m. 1965; two children. BA, Hunter Coll., 1954; MSc, NYU, 1962, PhD in Biology, 1963; LHD (hon.), Rivier Coll., 1982, U. Pitts., 1987, Hunter Coll., 1988. Rsch. assoc. Sloan-Kettering Inst., 1958-60, Merck Inst. Therapeutic Rsch., 1958-60; lectr. Hunter Coll., 1962-64, from asst. to prof. biol. sci., 1965-80, dean sci. and math., 1977-80; pres. U. N.H., 1980-83, Brandeis U., 1983-91; exec. dir. Calif. Acad. Scis., San Francisco, 1994-98; ret. Vis. scientist Karolinska Inst., 1971-72; evaluator Com. Higher Edn., Middle States Assn., 1972—; vice chmn. univ. faculty senate CUNY, 1974-76; generalist, mem. Am. Coun. Pharm. Edn., 1978-83; bd. dirs. New Eng. Life Ins. Co., Student Loan Corp. Trustee Bay Area Biosci. Ctr., 1995—, Mills Coll., 1995—. Sr. fellow Carnegie Found. Advanced Tchg., 1990-92; scholar in residence Harvard U., 1991-92, assoc. in edn. 1992-93; rsch. grantee NIH, 1964-69, 73-76, NSF, 1965-67, 70-72, CUNY, 1972-74. Fellow AAAS, N.Y. Acad. Sci.; mem. Internat. Soc. Hematology, Harvey Soc. Office: Calif Acad Scis Golden Gate Park San Francisco CA 94118

HANDY, ROBERT MAXWELL, lawyer; b. Buffalo, Apr. 1, 1931; s. John Abner and Yvonne Fernande (Blaise) H.; m. Berniece Emily Reist, July 2, 1955; children: Mary, Robert, David. B.S., Trinity Coll., 1953; M.S., Northwestern U., 1958, Ph.D., 1962; J.D., Ariz. State U., 1984. New product devel. research mgr. Westinghouse Electric Co., Pitts., 1961-69; product mgr. Semiconductor div. Motorola, Inc., Phoenix, 1969-72, corp. dir. research, 1972-75; exec. dir. Ariz. Solar Energy Research Commn., 1975-76; dir. bus. and tech. planning Integrated Circuits div. Motorola, Inc., Mesa, Ariz., 1976-80, sr. patent counsel Phoenix, 1980-88, group patent counsel, 1988-94; intellectual property counsel Ea. Europe, Mid. East, and Africa Motorola GmbH, Weisbaden, Germany, 1995-98; pvt. practice Gilbert, Ariz., 1999—. Instr. Carnegie Mellon U., 1967. Served to lt. (j.g.) USNR, 1954-57. Royall A. Cabell fellow, 1959-60 Mem. ABA, IEEE, Am. Phys. Soc., Phi Beta Kappa. Office: 1700 E Lakeside Dr #17 Gilbert AZ 85234-4978

HANES, JOHN GRIER, lawyer, state legislator; b. Cheyenne, Wyo., 1936; s. Harold H. and Mary Elizabeth H.; m. Liv Paul; children: Greg, Clint. BS in Bus. Adminstrn., U. Wyo., 1958, JD, 1960. Bar: Wyo. 1960, U.S. Ct. Appeals (10th cir.) 1960, U.S. Ct. Mil. Appeals, 1960, U.S. Supreme Ct. 1964. Dep. sec. of state State of Wyo., 1963-65; prin. Burke Woodard & Bishop, Cheyenne, 1965-90, of counsel, 1990—; atty. Wyo. Senate, 1967-71; mcpl. judge City of Cheyenne, 1970-73; mem. Burke, Woodard & O'Donnell, Cheyenne, Wyo., until 1990; of counsel Burke & Woodard, P.C. and predecessor firms, Cheyenne, 1990—; mem. Wyo. Ho. of Reps., 1993-99, Wyo. Senate, 1999—. Vol. Cheyenne Frontier Days; mem. Heels; Rep. precinct committeeman, 1976-94. With U.S. Army JAGC. Mem. C. of C., Rotary (pres. 1982-83, dist. gov. 1990-91), Sigma Nu. Avocations: outdoor sports, travelling. Home: 848 Creighton St Cheyenne WY 82009-3231 Office: 1720 Carey Ave 600 Boyd Bldg Cheyenne WY 82001-4429

HANF, JAMES ALPHONSO, poet, government official; b. Chehalis, Wash., Feb. 3, 1923; s. William G. and Willa DeForest (Davis) H.; m. Ruth G. Eyler, Aug. 16, 1947; 1 child, Maureen Ruth. Grad. Centralia Jr. Coll., 1943, DLitt (hon.) World U. Ariz., 1980 Naval architect technician P.F. Spaulding, naval architects, Seattle, 1955-56, Puget Sound Bridge & Dredge Co. (Wash.), 1953-55, Puget Sound Naval Shipyard, 1951-53, 56-93; cons. Anderson & Assocs., ship bldg.; cons. The Rsch. Bd. Advs., Am. Biographical Inst., Inc.; guest lectr. on poetry and geneal. rsch. methods to various lit. socs., 1969—; contbr. hundreds of poems to lit. jours., anthologies and popular mags.; poetry editor Coffee Break, 1977-82. Recipient Poet Laureate Recognition award Internat. Biog. Centre of Cambridge, Eng., grand prize World Poetry Soc. Conv., 1985, 86, , 90, Golden Poet award World of Poetry in Calif., 1985-90, Silver Poet award Calif. sponsored nat. contest, 1989, numerous other awards. Judge poetry contest, Australia and India, 1985; named Man of Yr. Abaas, 1989—; named Internat. Eminent Poet Internat. Poet Acad. of Madras, India, 1987. Mem Internat. Poetry Soc. (Poet Laureate Wash. State award 1981), World of Poetry Soc. (Golden Poet award 1985-88, Poet Laureate award 1979), Kitsap County Writers Club (pres. 1977-78), Internat. Fedn. Tech. Engrs., Nat. Hist. Locomotive Soc., Kitsap County Hist. Soc., Puget Sound Geneal. Soc., Western World Haiku Soc., Olympic Geneal. Soc. (pres. 1974-75), N.Y. Poetry Forum, World Poets Resource Ctr., Literarische Union, Académie Européenne des Scis., Des Arts Et Des Letters (corr.), Internat. Soc. Poets Md. (hon. charter), Internat. Platform Assn., Calif. Fedn. Chaparral Poets, World Sadhak Soc. (hon.), Nat. Libr. Poetry (hon. mem.). Baptist. Home: PO Box 374 Bremerton WA 98337-0075

HANF, MICHAEL W. construction executive; CFO DPR Construction, Redwood City, Calif. Office: DPR Construction 1450 Veterans Blvd Redwood City CA 94063 Office Fax: (650) 474-1451

HANIFEN, RICHARD CHARLES, bishop; b. Denver, June 15, 1931; s. Edward Anselm and Dorothy Elizabeth (Ranous) H. B.S., Regis Coll., 1953; S.T.B., Cath. U., 1959, M.A., 1966; J.C.L., Pontifical Lateran U., Italy, 1968. Ordained priest Roman Catholic Ch., 1959; asst. pastor Cathedral Parish, Denver, 1959-66; sec. to archbishop Archdiocese Denver, 1968-69, chancellor, 1969-76; aux. bishop of Denver, 1974-83; 1st bishop of Colorado Springs, Colo., 1984—. Office: Bishop Colo Springs 29 W Kiowa St Colorado Springs CO 80903-1403

HANLEY, FRANK L. surgeon, educator; MD, Tufts U. Diplomate Am. Bd. Surgery, Am. Bd. Thoracic Surgery. Resident U. Calif., San Francisco. Mem. Am. Assn. for Thoracic Surgery (adv. editl. bd.), Congenital Heart Surgeons' Soc. Data Ctr., Soc. of Thoracic Surgeons, Thoracic Surgery Dirs. Assn. Office: U Calif Dept Surgery Rm S-549 San Francisco CA 94143-0001 Fax: 415 476-9678. E-mail: marlene_charles@pedcardgateway.ucsf.edu

HANLEY, HOWARD JAMES MASON, research scientist; b. Hove, Sussex, Aug. 19, 1937; arrived in U.S., 1962; s. Charles Edward Mason and Evelyn Agnes (Palmer) H.; m. Janet Mary Kettlewell, July 29, 1964; 1 child, Elizabeth Mary. BSc, London U., 1959, PhD, 1963. Rsch. assoc. Dept. Chemistry, Pa. State U., State College, 1963-65; phys. chemist Nat. Bur. of Stds., Boulder, 1965-83; fellow Nat. Inst. of Stds. and Tech., Boulder, 1983—. Adj. prof. Dept. Chem. Engring., U. Colo., 1974—, vis. prof. 1969; vis. rsch. fellow Australian Nat. U., 1973-74, 78-79, 87, 88, 92; vis. scientist Inst. Laue-Langevin, Grenoble, France, 1984, 85; fellow Wissenschaftskolleg zu Berlin, Berlin Inst. Advanced Studies, 1989-90; rsch. adv. com. Nat. Bur. Stds., 1980-83; Australian Nuclear Sci. and Tech. Orgn. vis. prof. Rsch. Sch. Chemistry, Australian Nat. U., 1998—. Author: Transport Phenomena in Fluids, 1969, Turner in Dorset, 1992; cons. editor Marcel Dekker Inc., N.Y., 1968—; editor NIST Jour. of Rsch., 1975-88; adv. editor Internat. Jour. of Thermophysics, 1981—; contbr. articles to profl. jours. Recipient Silver medal U.S. Dept. of Commerce, 1982, Gold medal, 1985; recipient Humboldt Rsch. prize, 1992. Fellow Royal Chem. Soc.; mem. ASME (com. thermophys. properties 1980-94, chmn. 1980-85), Internat. Union Pure and Applied Chemistry (transport properties com. 1976-88, com. on quantum fluids), MaryLeBone Cricket Club. Avocations: landscape art, English literature, social history, music, cricket. Office: Nat Inst Stds Tech 325 Broadway Boulder CO 80303-3337 E-mail: howard.hanley@nist.gov

HANLON, EDWARD, JR. career officer; b. Watertown, Minn., Dec. 4, 1944; BSBA, Southea. Okla. U., 1966; MS, Pepperdine U., 1977, U. Minn., 1981. Commd. 2nd lt. USMC, 1967, advanced through grades to maj. gen., 1996, officer Republic of Vietnam, 1968-69; asst. legal officer, pub. affairs officer, co. exec. officer USMC Hdqrs., Washington, 1969-72; various adminstrv. and tchg. assignments USMC, 1972-85; dir. personal svcs. USMC Recruit Depot, San Diego, 1985-86; asst. chief of staff for plans and ops. USMC Hdqrs. FMF Europe, London, 1987-90; fleet marine officer U.S. Atlantic Fleet, 1990-92; commdg. officer 10th Marines, 2nd Marine Divsn., 1992-93; dep. comdr. Naval Striking and Support Forces So. Europe, Naples, Italy, 1993-96; dir. Expeditionary Warfare Divsn. Office of Chief of Naval Ops., The Pentagon, Washington, 1996-98; comdg. gen. USMC, Camp Pendleton, Calif., 1998—. Decorated Legion of Merit with Gold Star. Office: USMC PO Box 555010 Cmp Pendleton CA 92055-5010

HANNA, DEANNA, state senator; b. Flatonia, Tex. BS, Tex. Women's U.; MS, U. Colo. Clin. instr. Sch. Nursing, Tex. Woman's U., 1966-67; staff nurse Meth. Hosp., 1967-68; sch. nurse Denver Pub. Schs., 1968—; Dem. senator dist. 21 Colo. State Senate, 2000—. Appointed to Optometric State Regulatory Bd., 1983-88; mem. health, environ., children and families coms. Colo. State Senate, vice chair agr. and natural resources coms. Chair precinct Jefferson County, Colo., 1970—; bd. dirs. Kids in Need of Dentistry, 1980-86; trustee Denver Pub. Schs. Retirement Bd., 1990—; mem. cmty. budget steering com. Denver Pub. Schs., 1991-95. Mem. Colo. Assn. Sch. Nurses (chair/legis. chair 1986-92), Denver Classroom Tchrs. Assn. (polit. action chair 1997—). Office: 9536 W Ohio Pl Lakewood CO 80226 also: Colo State Senate 200 E Colfax Rm 332 Denver CO 80203 E-mail: deannahanna2000@yahoo.com

HANNA, NABIL, biomedical engineer; b. 1944; PhD in Immunology, Hebrew U., Israel. Lectr. Hebrew U., Israel, 1973-78; rsch. sci. NCI-Frederick Cancer Rsch. Ctr., 1978-81; dir. SmithKline Beecham, 1981-90; chief sci. officer IDEC Pharm. Corp., San Diego, 1991—. Office: IDEC Pharm Corp 3010 Science Park Rd PO Box 909080 San Diego CA 92191-9080

HANNA, WILLIAM JOHNSON, electrical engineering educator; b. Longmont, Colo., Feb. 7, 1922; s. William Grant and Anna Christina (Johnson) H.; m. Katherine Fagan, Apr. 25, 1944 (dec. 1993); children: Daniel August, Paul William; m. Helen Yeager McCarty, Sept. 19, 1996. BSEE, U. Colo., 1943, MS, 1948, D in Elec. Engring., 1951. Registered profl. engr., Colo., Kans. Mem. faculty U. Colo., 1946-91, prof. elec. engring., 1962-91, prof. emeritus, 1991—. Cons. in field; mem. Colo. Bd. Engring. Examiners, 1973-85; with Ponderosa Assocs., Lafayette, Colo. Author articles, reports. Served to 1st lt. AUS, 1943-46. Recipient Faculty Recognition award Students Assn. U. Colo., 1956, 61, Alfred J. Ryan award, 1978, Archimedes award Calif. Soc. Profl. Engrs., 1978, Outstanding Engring. Alumnus award U. Colo., 1983, Faculty Service award, 1983; named Colo. Engr. of Yr. Profl. Engrs. Colo., 1968; named to Hon. Order of Ky. Cols. Mem. IEEE, Am. Soc. Engring. Edn., Nat. Soc. Profl. Engrs. (pres. Colo. 1967-68), Nat. Coun. Engring. Examiners (pres. 1977-78, Disting. Svc. award with spl. commendation 1990), AIEE (chmn. Denver 1961-62) Republican. Presbyterian. Club: Masons. Home and Office: 27 Silver Spruce Nederland Star Rt Boulder CO 80302-9604

HANNAH, DAVID H. metal products executive; BSBA, U. So. Calif. CPA. Mgr. audit divsn. Ernst & Whinney, L.A., 1973-81; CFO Reliance Steel & Aluminum, L.A., 1981-87, v.p., 1987-92, dir., exec. v.p., CFO, 1992-95, pres., 1995—, CEO, 1998—. Office: Reliance Steel & Aluminum 2550 E 25th St Los Angeles CA 90058

HANNEMAN, LE ROY C., JR. real estate executive; With Del Webb Corp., Phoenix, 1976—, pres., COO, 1998—, CEO, 1999—. Office: Del Webb Corp 60001 N 24th Ar Phoenix AZ 85016

HANNON, LENN L. state legislator, insurance agent; b. Roseburg, Oreg., July 4, 1943; m. Dixie Hannon. Student, So. Oreg. State Coll. Mem. Oreg. Legislature, Salem, 1974—, mem. joint com. on ways and means, mem. subcom. on pub. safety/regulation, chair subcom. on transp. and econ. devel., mem. transp. com. Republican. Home: 240 Scenic Dr Ashland OR 97520-2622 E-mail: hannon.sen@state.or.us

HANRAHAN, PATRICK M. computer scientist; PhD, U. Wis., 1986. Canon USA prof. dept. computer scientist Stanford (Calif.) U. Mem. NAE. Office: Stanford U Rm 3B Gates Computer Sci Bldf 370 Stanford CA 94305-4070

HANSCHEN, PETER WALTER, lawyer; b. San Francisco, July 7, 1945; s. Walter A. and Dorothy E. (Watkins) H.; m. Brenda C. Hanschen, Feb. 7, 1987. BA, San Francisco State U., 1967; JD, U. Calif.-Berkeley, 1971. Bar: Calif. 1972, U.S. Supreme Ct. 1985, U.S. Ct. Appeals D.C. Cir. 1975. Assoc. Lawler, Felix & Hall, L.A., 1971-73; atty. Pacific Gas Transmission Co., San Francisco, 1973-76, Pacific Gas & Elec. Co., San Francisco, 1976-79; gen. counsel Pacific Gas Transmission, San Francisco, 1979-83; asst. gen. counsel Pacific Gas & Elec. Co., San Francisco, 1983-88; ptnr. Graham & James, San Francisco, 1988-99, Morrison & Foerster, San Francisco, 1999—. Mem. ABA, Internat. Bar Assn., Fed. Energy Bar Assn., Counsel of Calif. Pub. Utilities. Avocations: golf, gardening, sports. Office: Morrison & Foerster LLP 425 Market St Ste 3100 San Francisco CA 94105-2482 E-mail: phanschen@mogo.com

HANSELL, DEAN, lawyer; b. Bridgeport, Conn., Mar. 24, 1952; BA, Denison U., 1974; JD, Northwestern U., 1977. Bar: Ill. 1977, U.S. Dist. Ct. (no. dist.) Ill. 1977, U.S. Ct. Appeals (7th cir.) 1978, U.S. Ct. Appeals (D.C. cir.) 1978, U.S. Ct. Appeals (9th cir.) 1979, Calif. 1980, U.S. Dist. Ct. (cen. dist.) Calif. 1981, U.S. Dist. Ct. (so. dist.) Calif. 1989, U.S. Supreme Ct. 1998. Asst. atty. gen. for environ. control State of Ill., Chgo., 1977-80; atty. FTC, L.A., 1980-83; assoc. Lillick, McHose & Charles, L.A., 1983-84, Donovan Leisure Newton & Irvine, L.A., 1984-86; ptnr. LeBoeuf, Lamb, Greene & MacRae, L.A., 1986-01, mng. ptnr., 2001—. Adj. assoc. prof. Southwestern U. Sch. Law, L.A., 1982-86; mem. Ill. Solar Resources Adv. Panel, 1978-80; judge pro tem L.A. County Mcpl. Ct., 1987-97, L.A. County Superior Ct., 1989—; mem. adv. bd. Fayette Haywood Legal Svcs., Tenn., 1979-83, Nat. Inst. for Citizen Edn. in Law, 1989-94. Mem. editl. bd. L.A. Lawyer Mag., 1995—, Internat. Reins. Dispute Reporter, 1996—; contbr. articles to profl. jours. Bd. dirs. Jewish Fed. Coun. Met. L.A. Region, 1984-87, Project LEAP, Legal Elections in All Precincts, Chgo., 1976-80, Martin Luther King, Jr. Ctr. Nonviolence, L.A., 1991-95, L.A. Pub. Libr. Found., 1997—; commr. L.A. Bd. Police Commrs., 1997—. Mem. L.A. County Bar Assn. (mem. exec. com. antitrust sect. 1982-92, chair 1989-90), Calif. Bar Assn., Phi Beta Kappa, Omicron Delta Kappa. Office: LeBoeuf Lamb Greene & MacRae 725 S Figueroa St Ste 3600 Los Angeles CA 90017-5436 E-mail: dhansell@llgm.com

HANSEN, ALEXANDER E. advertising agency executive; Pres., CEO Bravant LLC, L.A.; ptnr. Tatum CFO Ptnrs., LLP, L.A. Office: Tatum CFO Ptnrs LLP 555 W 5th St Fl 31 Los Angeles CA 90013-1010 E-mail: alex.hansen@bravant.com

HANSEN, CURTIS LEROY, federal judge; b. 1933; BS, U. Iowa, 1956; JD, U. N.Mex., 1961. Bar: N.Mex. Law clk. to Hon. Irwin S. Moise N.Mex. Supreme Ct., 1961-62; ptnr. Snead & Hansen, Albuquerque, 1962-64, Richard C. Civerolo, Albuquerque, 1964-71, Civerolo, Hansen & Wolf, P.A., 1971-92; dist. judge U.S. Dist. Ct., N.Mex., 1992—. Mem. State Bar N.Mex., Albuquerque Bar Assn., Am. Coll. Trial Lawyers, Am. Bd. Trial Advocates, Albuquerque Country Club. Office: US Courthouse Chambers 660 333 Lomas Blvd NW Albuquerque NM 87102-2272

HANSEN, GLEN ARTHUR, scientist, researcher; b. Thermopolis, Wyo., June 28, 1961; s. Glen Arthur and Ilene Lois (Haynes) H.; m. Paula Dee Rathbun, May 23, 1998. AAS in Petroleum Engring. Tech., Casper Coll., 1982; BS in Petroleum Engring., U. Wyo., 1985; MS in Mech. Engring., U. Nebr., 1991; PhD in Computer Sci., U. Idaho, 1996. Rsch. asst. U. Nebr., Lincoln, 1989-90, tchg. asst., 1990-91; sr. engr. Idaho Nat. Engring. Lab., Idaho Falls, 1991-95, engring. specialist, 1995-96; tech. staff mem. Los Alamos Nat. Lab., 1996—, project leader, 1997—; prin. investigator Los Alamos (N. Mex.) Nat. Lab., 1998—. Mem. IEEE, ASME, Am. Nuclear Soc. (Idaho chpt.), Soc. Indsl. Applied Math., Assn. Computing Machinery. Home: 945 San Ildefonso Rd # 57 Los Alamos NM 87544-2849 Office: Los Alamos National Lab PO Box 1663 Los Alamos NM 87545-0001

HANSEN, H. REESE, dean, educator; b. Logan, Utah, Apr. 8, 1942; s. Howard F. and Loila Gayle (Reese) H.; m. Kathryn Traveller, June 8, 1962; children: Brian T., Mark T., Dale T., Curtis T. BS, Utah State U., 1964; JD, U. Utah, 1972. Bar: Utah, 1974. Atty. Strong, Poelman & Fox, Salt Lake City, 1972-74; from asst. prof. to assoc. prof. Brigham Young U., Provo, Utah, 1974-79, prof., 1979—. from asst. dean to assoc. dean, 1974-89, dean, 1989—. Commr. ex officio Utah State Bar, Salt Lake City, 1989—; commr. Nat. Conf. Commrs. on Uniform State Laws, 1988-95. Co-author: Idaho Probate System, 1977, Utah Probate System, 1977, Cases and Text on Laws of Trusts, 6th edit., 1991; editor: Manual for Justices of Peace--Utah, 1978; contbr. articles to profl. jours. Mem. LDS Ch. Office: Brigham Young U 348A Jrcb Provo UT 84602-1029

HANSEN, JAMES LEE, sculptor; b. Tacoma, June 13, 1925; s. Hildreth Justine and Mary Elizabeth Hansen; m. Annabelle Hair, Aug. 31, 1946 (dec. Sept. 1993); children: Valinda Jean, Yauna Marie; m. Jane Lucas, May 13, 1994. Grad., Portland Art Mus. Sch. Faculty Oreg. State U., Corvallis, 1957-58, U. Calif., Berkeley, 1958, Portland State U., 1964-90. One-man shows include Fountain Gallery, Portland, Oreg., 1966, 69, 77-81, U. Oreg. Art Mus., Eugene, 1970, Seligman (Seders Gallery), Seattle, 1970, Portland Art Mus., 1971, Cheney Cowles Meml. Mus., Spokane, Wash., 1972, Polly Freidlander Gallery, Seattle, 1973, 75-76, Smithsonian Instn., Washington, 1974, Hodges/Banks Gallery (now Linda Hodges Gallery), Seattle, 1983, Abanté Gallery, Portland, 1986, 88, 92, Maryhill Mus. of Art, Goldendale, Wash., 1997-98, Bryan Ohno Gallery, Seattle, 1997, 99, Mus. Northwest Art, La Conner, Wash., 1999; exhibited in group shows at N.W. Ann. Painters and Sculptors, Seattle, 1952-73, Oreg. Ann. Painters and Sculptors, Portland Art Mus., 1952-75, Whitney Mus. Am. Art, N.Y.C., 1953, Santa Barbara (Calif.) Mus. Art, 1959-60, Denver Art Mus., 1960, San Francisco Art Mus., 1960, Smithsonian Instn., Washington, 1974, Wash. State U., Pullman, 1975, Benton County Hist. Mus., 1998; represented in permanent collections Graphic Arts Center, State Capitol, Olympia, Wash., U. Oreg., Eugene, Salem (Oreg.) Civic Center, Clark Coll., Vancouver, Wash., Portland Art Mus., Transit Mall, Portland, Seattle Art Mus., Gresham Town Fair (Oreg.), Oreg. Health Scis. U., Portland, Vancouver Sculpture Park, others; represented by Abanté Gallery, Portland, Hansen Studio, Vancouver, Peter Bartlow Gallery, Chgo., Bryan Ohno Gallery, Seattle. Address: 28219 NE 63rd Ave Battle Ground WA 98604-7107

HANSEN, JAMES VEAR, congressman; b. Salt Lake City, Aug. 14, 1932; s. J. Vear and Sena H.; m. Ann Burgoyne, 1958; children: Susan, Joseph James, David Burgoyne, Paul William, Jennifer. BS, U. Utah, 1960. With Framington City Coun., 1960-72, Utah State Legis., 1972-80; mem. Utah Ho. of Reps., 1973-80; spkr. of the house U.S. Ho. of Reps., 1979-80; mem. U.S. Congress from 1st Utah dist., Washington, 1981—; mem. nat. security com., resource com. Pres. James V. Hansen Ins. Agy., Woodland Springs Devel. Co. Office: Ho of Reps 242 Cannon Ho Office Bldg Washington DC 20515-0001

HANSEN, MATILDA, former state legislator; b. Paullina, Iowa, Sept. 4, 1929; d. Arthur J. and Sada G. (Thompson) Henderson; m. Robert B. Michener, 1950 (div. 1963); children: Eric J., Douglas E.; m. Hugh G. Hansen (dec.). BA, U. Colo., 1963; MA, U. Wyo., 1970. Tchr. history Englewood (Colo.) Sr. High Sch., 1963-65; dir. Albany County Adult Learning Ctr., Laramie, Wyo., 1966-78, Laramie Plains Civic Ctr., 1979-83; treas. Wyo. Territorial Prison Corp., Laramie, 1988-93, also bd. dirs. Bd. dirs. Wyo. Territorial Park. Author: (textbooks) To Help Adults Learn, 1975, Let's Play Together, 1978. Legislator Wyo. Ho. of Reps., Cheyenne, 1975-95, minority whip, 1987-88, asst. minority leader, 1991-92, 93-94; mem. mgmt. coun. Wyo. State Legislature, Cheyenne, 1983-84; chair Com. for Dem. Legislature, Cheyenne, 1990-94, Wyo. State Dems., 1995-99. GE fellow in econs. for high sch. tchrs., 1963; named Pub. Citizen of Yr., Wyo. Assn. Social Workers, 1980-81. Mem. LWV Wyo. (v.p. 1966-68), LWV Laramie (bd. dirs. 1966-72, Nat. Conf. State Legislators (vice chair human resources 1983, nat. exec. com. 1990-94), Laramie Area C. of C., Laramie Women's Club, Faculty Women's Club. Mem. Soc. of Friends. Avocations: gardening, quilting, mountaineering. Home and Office: 1306 E Kearney St Laramie WY 82070-4142

HANSEN, ROBERT CLINTON, electrical engineering consultant; b. St. Louis, 1926; m. 1952; 2 children BS, U. Mo., 1949, D of Eng. (hon.), 1975; MS, U. Ill., 1950, PhD, 1955. Rsch. assoc. antenna lab. U. Ill., 1950-55; sr. staff engr. microwave lab. Hughes Aircraft Co., 1955-59; sr. staff engr. telecomm. lab. Space Technol. Labs., 1959-60; dir. test mission analysis office Aerospace Corp., Calif., 1960-67; head electronics divsn. KMS Technol. Ctr., 1967-71; pres., cons. R.C. Hansen, Inc., Tarzana, Calif., 1971—. Mem. commn. B, Internat. Sci. Radio Union Editor: Microwave Scanning Antennas, 1964-65, Significant Phased Array Papers, 1973, Geometric Theory of Diffraction, 1981, Moment Methods in Antennas and Scattering, 1990; author: Phased Array Antennas, 1998. Recipient Disting. Alumnus award U. Ill. Elect. Engring. Dept., 1981, Disting. Alumnus Svc. medal, 1986. Fellow IEEE (pres. antennas and propagation soc. 1964, 80), Aerospace & Electronic Sys. Soc. (Barry Carlton award 1991, AP Disting. Achievement award 1994), Inst. Elec. Engrs. (London); mem. NAE, Am. Phys. Soc. Office: RC Hansen Inc PO Box 570215 Tarzana CA 91357

HANSEN, THOMAS CARTER, college athletics conference commissioner; b. Seattle, Nov. 30, 1937; s. Herbert and Marjorie Jean (Jordan) H.; m. Melva Marie Fuhr, Oct. 11, 1962; children: Sarah Marie Hansen Reeves, Bryan Thomas. BA, U. Wash., 1959. Reporter The Columbian, Vancouver, Wash., 1959-60; dir. pub. rels. Pacific-10 Conf., San Francisco, 1960-67, NCAA, Kansas City, Mo., 1967-71, asst. exec. dir., 1971-83; commr. Pacific-10 Conf., Walnut Creek, Calif., 1983—. Author: (chpt.) Administration for Athletic Programs, 1987. Mem. Kiwanis Club, Vancouver, 1959-60, San Francisco, 1960-67, Kansas City, 1967-83. Mem. Nat. Assn. Collegiate Dirs. of Athletics (exec. com. 1988-92, Adminstrv. Excellence award 1994), Collegiate Commrs. Assn. (pres. 1992, 93), Football Found. Hall of Fame (honors ct. 1994-01, Contbns. to Football award 2001). Republican. Lutheran. Avocations: golfing, reading, music. Office: Pacific 10 Conf 800 S Broadway Ste 400 Walnut Creek CA 94596-5278

HANSEN, TOM, lawyer; Ptnr. Hansen Jacobson & Teller, Beverly Hills, Calif. Office: Hansen Jacobson Teller Hoberman 450 N Roxbury Dr Fl 8 Beverly Hills CA 90210-4222

HANSEN, WAYNE W. lawyer; b. Clintonville, Wis., June 7, 1942; s. William W. and Berniece M. (Kuehn) H.; m. Carolyn M. Lemke, Dec. 21, 1969; children: Drew D., Janna J. BBA, U. Wis., 1965, JD, 1967. Bar: Wis. 1967, U.S. Dist. Ct. (we. dist.) Wis. 1971, U.S. Ct. Appeals (7th cir.) 1972, U.S. Dist. Ct. (ea. dist.) Wis. 1975, Wash. 1979, U.S. Dist. Ct. (we. dist.) Wash. 1979, U.S. Ct. Appeals (9th cir.) 1982, U.S. Dist. Ct. (ea. dist.) Wash. 1986. Atty. NLRB, Mpls., 1967-70, Schmitt Nolan Hansen & Hartley, Merrill, Wis., 1970-79; ptnr. Lane Powell Spears Lubersky, Seattle, 1979-98; mng. ptnr. Jackson Lewis Schnitzler & Krupman, Seattle, 1998—. Contbg. author: Developing Labor Law, 1971, Doing Business in Washington State*Guide for Foreign Business, 1989. Office: Jackson Lewis Schnitzler & Krupman 1420 5th Ave Ste 2000 Seattle WA 98101-1348

HANSON, CURTIS, director, writer; b. Mar. 24, 1945; Dir., screenwriter (film) Sweet Kill, 1972, The Bedroom Window, 1988; dir., co-producer (film) The Little Dragons, 1977; dir. (film) The Arousers, 1970, Losin' It, 1983, Bad Influence, 1990, The Hand That Rocks the Cradle, 1992, The River Wild, 1994, L.A. Confidential, 1997, Wonder Boys, 1999; screenwriter: The Dunwich Horror, 1970, The Silent Partner, 1978, White Dog, 1982, Never Cry Wolf, 1983; actor (TV) Hitchcock: Shadow of a Genius, 1999. Office: United Talent Agy 9560 Wilshire Blvd Fl 5 Beverly Hills CA 90212-2400

HANSON, GEORGE, music director, conductor; m. Dawn Hanson. Degree, Ind. U. Resident conductor Atlanta Symphony; asst. to Leonard Bernstein Vienna Stae Opera; asst. Giuseppe Patane La Scala, Covent Garden, Munich Opera Houses; mus. dir. Anchorage Symphony; asst. conductor N.Y. Philharmonic; conductor Tucson Symphony Orchestra. Appeared with sixty orchestras and operas in sixteen countries. Named Winner of the Leopold Stokowski Competition at Carnegie Hall, N.Y.C., Hungarian Internat. Coducting Competition, Budapest, Young Musician of 1990 Musical Am. Address: Tucson Symphony Orchestra TSO 2175 N 6th Ave Tucson AZ 85705-5606

HANSON, GERALD WARNER, retired county official; b. Alexandria, Minn., Dec. 25, 1938; s. Lewis Lincoln and Dorothy Hazel (Warner) H.; m. Sandra June Wheeler, July 9, 1960; 1 child, Cynthia R. AA, San Bernardino Valley (Calif.) Coll., 1959; BA, U. Redlands (Calif.), 1979; MA, U. Redlands, 1981; EdD, Pepperdine U., 1995. Cert. advanced metrication specialist. Dep. sealer San Bernardino (Calif.) County, 1964-80, div. chief, 1980-85, dir. weights and measures, 1985-94; CATV cons. City of Redlands, 1996—, City of Yucaipa, 1998-99. Substitute tchr. Redlands Unified Sch. Dist., 1996—. Chmn. Redlands Rent Rev. Bd., 1985-99; bd. dirs. House Neighborly Svc., Redlands, 1972-73, Boys Club, Redlands, 1985-86; mem. Redlands Planning commn., 1990-98. With USN. Fellow U.S. Metric Assn. (treas. 1986-88, 92—); mem. NRA (life), Nat. Conf. on Weights and Measures (life, asst. treas. 1986-94), Western Weights and Measures Assn. (life, pres. 1987-88), Calif. Assn. Weights and Measures Ofcls. (life, 1st v.p. 1987), Calif. Rifle and Pistol Assn. (life), Masons, Shriners, Kiwanis (treas. Redlands club 1983-95), Over the Hill Gang (San Bernardino, newsletter editor 1998-2000). Avocations: golf, digital photography, mechanics, microcomputers. Home: 225 E Palm Ave Redlands CA 92373-6131 E-mail: doctorjer@hotmail.com

HANSON, JANICE CRAWFORD, artist, financial analyst; b. Norwalk, Conn., Oct. 8, 1952; d. Arthur James and Jean Alice (MacKinnon) Crawford; m. Jeffrey Becker Hanson, May 29, 1976; children: Forrest James, Shane Crawford. BA, Wellesley Coll., 1974; MBA, U. Denver, 1979. CFA. Sec. to assoc. dean Yale Sch. of Music, New Haven, 1975-76; adminstrv. asst. to dir. of internships Inst. Policy Scis. Duke U., Durham, N.C., 1976-78; fiscal analyst Denver Water Bd., 1979-84; fin. analyst Englewood, Colo., 1984; part-time fin. analyst Jeffrey B. Hanson M.D., P.C., Granger, Ind., 1989-92; part-time watercolorist Englewood, Colo., 1989—. Exhibitions include group shows Watercolor West Exhbn., Riverside, Calif., 1995, 1999, Western Colo. Watercolor Soc. Nat. Juried Exhbn., Grand Junction, Colo., 1994, 1995, 1996, 2000, Rocky Mountain Nat. Watermedia Exhbn., Golden, Colo., 1996, 1998, Pikes Peak Watercolor Soc. Internat. Exhbn., Colo. Springs, Colo., 1997, 1998, 2000, Am. Women Artists Nat. Juried Competition, Taos, N.Mex., 1999, Nat. Watercolor Soc. Annual Exhbn., Brea, Calif., 2001. Vol. Denver Dumb Friends League, 1986-88, Cherry Creek Schs., Englewood, Colo., 1992—. Recipient Best of Show award Nat. Greeley Art Mart, 1994, Platinum award, Nat. Greeley Art Mart, 1995, Dean Witter award for originality Colo. Watercolor Soc. State Juried Exhbn., 1996, WinsorNewton Merchandise award, 1999, Daler-Rowney award Pikes Peak Watercolor Soc. Internat. Exhbn., 2000; Am. Women Artists scholar, 1999. Mem.: Nat. Watercolor Soc. (signature), Assn. for Investment Mgmt. and Rsch., Watercolor West (assoc.), Colo. Watercolor Soc. (signature), Western Colo. Watercolor Soc. (signature), Denver Soc. Security Analysts. Avocations: running, fiber arts, needlework, photography.

HANSON, JOHN J. lawyer; b. Aurora, Nebr., Oct. 22, 1922; s. Peter E. and Hazel Marion (Lounsbury) H.; m. Elizabeth Anne Moss, July 1, 1973; children from their previous marriages— Mark, Eric, Gregory. A.B., U. Denver, 1948; LL.B. cum laude, Harvard U., 1951. Bar: N.Y. bar 1952, Calif. bar 1955. Asso. firm Dewey, Ballantine, Bushby, Palmer & Wood, N.Y.C., 1951-54; ptnr. firm Gibson, Dunn & Crutcher, L.A, 1954—, mem. exec. com., 1978-87, adv. ptnr., 1991—. Contbr. articles to profl. jours.

Trustee Palos Verdes (Calif.) Sch. Dist., 1969-73. Served with U.S. Navy, 1942-45. Fellow Am. Coll. Trial Lawyers; mem. Am. Bar Assn., Los Angeles County Bar Assn. (chmn. antitrust sect. 1979-80), Bel Air Country Club. Home: 953 Linda Flora Dr Los Angeles CA 90049-1630 Office: Gibson Dunn & Crutcher 333 S Grand Ave Ste 4400 Los Angeles CA 90071-3197

HANSON, LARRY KEITH, plastics company executive; b. Hawkins, Wis., Aug. 14, 1932; s. Harold and Clara Pauline (Lund) H.; m. Patricia Rosalie Sammarco, Aug. 6, 1955; children: Lawrence Keith, John Steven, James Paul. BS, U.S. Mcht. Marine Acad., 1955. Engr. Curtis-Wright Corp., Woodridge, N.J., 1955-58; sales engr. Gits Bros. Mfg. Co., Chgo., 1958-66, Aeroquip Corp., Burbank, Calif., 1966-70; exec. v.p. Furon Co., Laguna Niguel, 1970-97; mng. dir. Furon SA/NV subs. Furon Co., Kontich, Belgium, 1983-90; exec. v.p. Furon Co., Laguna Niguel, Calif., 1990-97; retired, 1997; cons. (part-time) Furon Co., Laguna Niguel, 1997—. Patentee in field. Mem. ASME, Soc. Automotive Engrs. Avocations: fly fishing, drawing, inventions.

HANSON, MARIAN W. state legislator; b. Santa Maria, Calif., Jan. 17, 1933; m. Darrel Hanson; 4 children. Rancher, Ashland, Mont.; mem. Mont. Ho. of Reps., Helena, 1983-2000, spkr. of ho. pro tem, 1993-97. County mem. Local Govt. Study Commn. Republican. Home: PO Box 237 Ashland MT 59003-0237 Office: Mont Ho of Reps State Capitol Helena MT 59620

HANSON, RICHARD E. paper company executive; BS in Indsl. Mgmt., U. Oreg., 1965. With Weyerhaeuser Co., Tacoma, 1970-98, sr. v.p. timberlands, 1998—. Bd. dirs. Oreg. Forest Industries Coun., also operating com.; adv. com. Oreg. State U. Forest Rsch. Lab. Trustee Oreg. Zoo; mem. founder's cir. Stop Oreg. Litter & Vandalism. Office: Weyerhaeuser Co PO Box 2999 Tacoma WA 98477-2999

HAPKA, CATHERINE M. Internet executive; BS, U. Minn.; MBA, U. Chgo. Gen. mgr. Gen. Electric, 1984-87; pres. Data Svcs., 1989-91; pres., COO Interprise, U.S. West Comms., 1991-94, exec. v.p., 1994-96; pres., CEO, chmn. and founder Rhythms NetConnections, Englewood, Colo., 1997—.

HARA, GEORGE, software company executive; b. Osaka, Japan, Oct. 10, 1952; s. Nobutaro and Mitsuko (Kuroda) H.; m. Junko Hara, Oct. 8, 1988. LLB, Keio U., Tokyo, 1975; MS in Engring., Stanford U., 1981, MABA in Bus. Fin. officer UN Capital Devel. Fund, N.Y.C., 1980-81; founder, pres. Gekee Fiberoptics Inc., Palo Alto, Calif., 1981-83; pres. Data Control Ltd., Osaka, 1984-85; v.p. Pacific Catalyst Group, L.A., 1984—; gen. ptnr. Japan Incubation Capital, Tokyo, 1985-88; pres., chief exec. officer Data Control Ltd., Osaka, Tokyo and Palo Alto, 1985—; founder, mng. ptnr. DEFTA, Palo Alto and San Francisco, 1986—. Founder, advisor Control Tech. Ltd., Osaka, 1986—; bd. dirs. Wollongong Group Inc., Palo Alto, IDA Bldg. (USA) Corp., San Francisco, Plantec Inc., Tokyo, Borland Internat.; chief exec. advisor Hankyo Corp., Osaka., 1989—. Advisor coll. bus. U. San Francisco, 1987—, advisor to pres., 1988—; advisor to gov. Prefecture of Osaka, 1986-88; active task force for econ. devel. Osaka Kansai Keizaid-oyukai, 1981; bd. dirs. Mctadigm Found., Calif. Mem. Archaeol. Inst. Am., Japan-Cen. Am. Soc. (pres. 1976-78), Shotosha Found. (chmn. 1977—), Japan Software Rsch. Found. (bd. dirs. 1988—), Networking Japan (pres. 1985), Alliance Japan (pres. 1986, chmn. 1989), Alliance 90 (chmn. 1990), Smithsonian Inst., Calif. Acad. Sci., Stanford Assn. Japan, U.S.-Japan High Tech. Trade and Strategic Alliance Com. (pres. 1989—) Ccn. Am. Mita Assn., Kansai Stanford Assn. (mus. soc. officer), Nat. Venture Capital Assn. Office: DEFTA Ptnrs 111 Pine St Ste 1410 San Francisco CA 94111-5616 also: One Embarcadero Ctr San Francisco CA 94111

HARAD, GEORGE JAY, manufacturing company executive; b. Newark, Apr. 24, 1944; m. Beverly Marcia Harad, June 12, 1966; children: Alyssa Dawn, Matthew Corde. BA, Franklin and Marshall Coll., 1965; MBA with high distinction, Harvard Bus. Sch., 1971. Staff cons. Boston Cons. Group, 1970-71; asst. to sr. v.p. housing Boise Cascade Corp., 1971, asst. to v.p. Calif., 1971; fin. mgr. Boise Cascade Realty Group, Palo Alto, 1972-76; mgr. corp. devel. Boise Cascade Corp., Boise, ID, 1976-80, dir. retirement funds, risk mgmt., 1980-82, v.p., contr., 1982-84, sr. v.p., chief fin. officer, 1984-89, exec. v.p., chief fin. officer, 1989-90, exec. v.p. paper, 1990-91, pres., COO ID, 1991-94, pres., CEO, 1994-95, chmn., bd. dirs., 1995; chmn., dir. Boise Cascade Office Products Corp.; CEO, chmn. Boise Cascade Corp., Boise, ID, 1995—. Bd. dirs. Allendale Ins. Co.; bd. govs. Nat. Coun. of Paper Industry for Air and Stream Improvement Inc. Founder, pres. Boise Coun. for Gifted and Talented Students, 1977-79; bd. dirs. Boise Philharm. Assn., 1983-84; dir. bd. trustees Coll. Idaho, 1986-91. Grad. Prize fellow Harvard Grad. Sch. Arts and Scis., 1965-69, Frederick Roe fellow Harvard U. Sch. Bus., 1971; George F. Baker scholar, 1970 71. Mem. NAM (bd. dirs.), Am. Forest and Paper Assn. (bd. dirs., mem. exec. com. 1984-94), Century Club (Boston), Arid Club, Crane Creek Country Club. Office: Boise Cascade Corp PO Box 50 Boise ID 83728-0050

HARALICK, ROBERT MARTIN, electrical engineering educator; b. N.Y.C., Sept. 30, 1943; s. David and Yetta (Stier) H.; m. Joy Gold, Aug. 20, 1967 (div. July 1977); 1 child, Tammy-Beth; m. Linda G. Shapiro, Feb. 12, 1978 (div. Aug. 1992); 1 child, Michael Aaron; m. Ihsin T. Phillips, Dec. 1993. BA, U. Kans., 1964, BS, 1966, MS, 1967, PhD, 1969. Asst. prof. elec. engring. U. Kans., Lawrence, 1969-71, assoc. prof., 1971-75, prof., 1975-78, Va. Poly. Inst. and State U., 1979-84; v.p. rsch. Machine Vision Internat., Ann Arbor, Mich., 1984-86; Boeing Clairmont Egtvedt prof. elec. engring., adj. prof. computer sci. U. Wash., Seattle, 1986-2000; pres. Mnemonics Inc., 1979—; disting. prof. computer sci. Grad. Ctr. CUNY, 2001—. Co-dir. NATO Advanced Study Inst. Image Processing, 1978; co-chmn. NATO Advanced Study Inst. on Image Processing, 1980, Robust Computer Vision Workshop, 1990, 92, 94; vice chmn. 5th Internat. Conf. on Pattern Recognition, Miami, 1980; dir. NATO Advanced Study Inst. on Pictorial Data Analysis, 1982; adj. prof. Ctr. Bioengring. U. Wash., Seattle, 1988—; program chmn. 10th annual ICPR Conf. on Pattern Recognition Systems and Applications, 1990; program co-chmn. Internat. Conf. on Document Analysis and Recognition, 1991, vice chmn., 1997; co-chmn. Evaluation and Validation of Computer Vision Algorithm, 1998. Author: (with T. Creese) Differential Equations for Engineers, 1977; Pictorial Data Analysis, 1983, (with L. Shapiro) Computer and Robost Vision, Vol I and II, 1992, The Inner Meaning of Hebrew Letters, 1995, (with M. Glazerson) The Torah Codes and Israel Today, 1996; editor: (with J. C. Simon) Issues in Digital Image Processing, 1980, Digital Image Processing, 1981; assoc. editor Computer Vision, Graphics and Image Processing, 1975-93, Pattern Recognition, 1977-93, Communication of the ACM, Image Processing, 1982-92, IEEE Transactions on Systems, Man and Cybernetics, 1979-88, IEEE Transactions on Image Processing, 1992-96, Jour. of Electronic Imaging, 1994—; mem. editl. bd. IEEE Transactions on Pattern Analysis and Machine Intelligence, 1981-84, IEEE Expert, 1986-90, Machine Vision and Applications, 1987—, Real Time Imaging, 1994—, mem. adv. bd.; mem. adv. program com. Structural & Syntactic Pattern Recognition, 1990; contbr. over 525 articles to profl. jours.; digital computer art exhbns. include William Rockhill Nelson Gallery, Kansas City, Mo., 1971, Nat. History Mus., U. Kans., 1971, Dulin Gallery Art, 1971 (2 purchase awards), Nat. Invitational Print Show, U. R.I., 1972, Fla. State U., 1972, San Diego State Coll., 1972. Recipient Dow Chem. Young Outstanding Faculty award Am. Soc. Engring. Educators, 1975, Outstanding Young Elec. Engrs. Honorable Mention award Eta Kappa Nu, 1975, Best Paper award 5th Ann. Symposium on Automatic Imagery Pattern Recognition, 1975, Best Paper award Pattern Recognition Soc., 1989; NSF faculty fellow, 1977-79. Fellow IEEE, IAPR; mem. IEEE Computer Soc. (chmn. pattern analysis and machine intelligence tech. com. 1975-82, acoustics, signal and speech processing, sys., man and cybernetics, pattern recognition tech. subcom. 1975-81, data structures and pattern recognition subcom. 1975-81, biomed. pattern recognition subcom. 1975-81, internat. assn. for pattern recognition gov. bd. 1986—, pres. 1996-98, program com. pattern and image processing conf. 1978, 4th internat. joint conf. on pattern recognition 1978, conf. B-pattern recognition methods and sys. program com. 11th internat. conf. on pattern recognition 1992, structural and syntactic pattern recognition 1992, 2d internat. conf. on document analysis and recognition 1993, chairperson various workshops and confs., Cert. Appreciation award 1978, 84), Pattern Recognition Soc., Internat. Assn. for Pattern Recognition (pres. 1996-98), Am. Assn. Artificial Intelligence, Assn. Computing Machinery. Avocation: hammered dulcimer. Home: 207 Woodside Dr Hewlett NY 11557 E-mail: haralick@mahigc.cuny.edu

HARARI, ELI, computer company executive; PhD in Solid State Scis., Princeton U. Co-founder, pres., CEO Wafer Scale integration; pres., CEO San Disk Corp., Sunnyvale, Calif. Patentee in field. Office: 140 Caspian Ct Sunnyvale CA 94089-1000

HARARY, FRANK, mathematician, computer scientist, educator; b. N.Y.C., Mar. 11, 1921; s. Joseph and Mary (Laby) H.; children: Miriam, Natalie, Judith, Thomas, Joel, Chaya (dec.). B.A., Bklyn. Coll., 1941, M.A., 1945; Ph.D., U. Calif., Berkeley, 1948; M.A. status, U. Oxford, Eng., 1973; D.Sc., M.Sc. in Math. (hon.), U. Aberdeen, Scotland, 1975; Fil.Dr. in Social Scis. (hon.), U. Lund, Sweden, 1978; M.A. status, U. Cambridge, Eng., 1981; D.Sc. (hon.) in Computer Sci., U. Exeter, Eng., 1992. Mem. faculty dept. math. U. Mich., Ann Arbor, 1948-86, prof., 1964-86, prof. emeritus, 1987—; faculty assoc. Research Center for Group Dynamics, Inst. Social Research, 1950-82; Disting. vis. prof. math. and computer sci. N. Mex. State U., Las Cruces, 1986, Disting. prof. computer sci., 1987—. Mem. Inst. Advanced Study, Princeton, N.J., 1957-59; vis. prof. math. Princeton U., 1958-59, Univ. Coll. London, 1962-63; sr. rsch. behavioural sci. Tavistock Inst. Human Rels., London, 1962-63; vis. prof. stats. London Sch. Econs., 1966-67; vis. prof. psychology U. Melbourne, 1969; vis. prof. combinatorics U. Waterloo, Ont., Can., fall 1970; vis. prof. psychology U. Ctrl., Caracas, Venezuela, 1979; vis. prof. elec. engring. U. Chile, Santiago, 1970; vis. prof. math. U. Copenhagen, 1970, Technion, Haifa, Israel, 1973, U. Niamey, Niger, 1975, U. Newcastle, Australia, 1976, U. Tartu, Estonia, 1989, U. Catania, Italy, 1988, Ain Shams U., Cairo, 1992, U. Rome, 1992, 93; vis. prof. compuer sci. U. Jyvaskyla, Finland, 1992, 96; fellow Wolfson Coll., U. Oxford, 1973-74, Churchill Coll., Cambridge U., 1980-81; vis. prof. civil engring. Columbia U.; vis. prof. chemistry U. Paris, 1971, U. Basel, Switzerland, 1974, Texas A&M U., Galveston, 1993; vis. prof. geography U. Lagos, Nigeria, 1975; vis. prof. Tallinn Bot. Gardens, Estonian Acad. Scis., 1989; vis. prof. computer sci. Alexander the Great U. of Macedonia, Thessaloniki, Greece, 1993, 96, U. Tampere, Finland, 1993, Tallinn Tech. U., Estonia, 1993; vis. prof. econs. Aristotle U. Thessaloniki, 1993; vis. prof. mech. engring. Nat. Cheng Kung U., Tainan, Taiwan, 1988, 96; colloquium lectr. Edinburgh Math. Soc., St. Andrews, 1972; inaugural lectr. S.E. Asian Math. Soc., Singapore, 1972; lectr. Malaysian Math. Soc., Penang, Malaysia, 1974; lectr. Inst. Mgmt. Scis. & Ops. Rsch. Soc. Am., Phila., 1958, OR Soc. Am., Inst. Radio Engrs., N.Y.C., 1958, AAAS, N.Y.C., 1960, Linguistic Soc. Am., N.Y.C., 1960, Am. Math. Soc., N.Y.C., 1960, 1st Caribbean Combinatorial Conf., Kingston, Jamaica, 1970, Bridgetown, Barbados, 1977, Soc. Indsl. and Applied Math., Santa Barbara, Calif., 1968, 3rd Conf. Info. Retrieval, Elsinore, Denmark, 5th Brit. Combinatorial Conf., Aberdeen, Scotland, 1975, 7th S.E., Conf. on Graph Theory and Computing, Baton Rouge, 1977, 88, 96Ont. Math. Meetings, St. Catherine, 1977, Bremer Konferenz zur Chemie, Bremen, Germany, 1978, European Assn. for Theoretical Computer Sci., Udine, Italy, 1978, Math. Assn. Am., Bradenton, Fla., 1974, Valparaiso, Ind., 1980, Holland, Mich., 1980, Brookings, S.D., 1983, Serbian Chem. Soc., Kragujevac, Yugoslavia, 1980, Greek Math. Soc., Athens, 1983, Assn. for Math. Applied to Econ. and Social Scis., Catania, Sicily, 1983, Conf. on Graph Theory, Steiner Systems and Their Applications, Santa Tecla, Sicily, 1986, 89, Calcutta Math Soc., 1986, Indian Math Soc., Allahabad, 1986, Hong Kong Math Soc., 1986, 1st Japan Conf. on Graph Theory, Hakone, 1986, 1st China-U.S. conf. on Graph Theory, Jinan, 1986, China, Chem. Soc. Japan, Shizuoka, 1987, 30th Anniversary Conf. of Thessaloniki Grad. Sch. Bus. Adminstrn., 1987, 1st Internat. Conf. on Artificial Intelligence, Hong Kong, 1988, 7th Sunbelt Conf. on Social Networks, Tampa, Fla., 1989, 4th Internat. Conf. On Mathematical Chemistry, Galveston, Tex., 1989, 9th Conf. on Discrete Math., Clemson U., 1989, 13th Conf.,London, 14th, Charleston, 1996, 16th, U. Miss., 1996, Internat. Confs. on Graph Theory, Western Mich. U., Kalamazoo, 1968-92, 2d Balkan Conf. OR, Thessaloniki, 1993, 1st Pan-Hellenic Conf. on computers and math., Ioannina, Greece, 1993; disting. vis. lectr. U. Cen. Fla., Orlando, 1984, 90; invited Reunion of Nobel Laureates, Lindau, Germany, 1989, disting. scientist in residence N.Y. Acad. Scis., 1977; Humboldt Found. fellow, Munich, Germany, summers 1978, 79; dir. summer schs. NATO, Frascati, Italy, 1962, Varenna, Italy, 1964; participant numerous internat. symposia in honor of 70th birthday including Estonian Math. Soc., Tartu and Kaariku, 1991, Graphs and Hypergraphs, Varenna, Italy, 1991, Graph Theory and Applications, Durban and Itala, South Africa, 1991, Graph Theory and Theoretical Chemistry, U. Sask., Saskatoon, Can., 1991, Graph Theory and Computer Sci., Monterrey, Guadalajara, Mex., 1991, Graph Theory and Mech. Engring. Taiwan, 1991. Editor, founder: Jour. Combinatorial Theory, 1966—; editor: Discrete Mathematics, 1970—, Jour. Math. Sociology, 1970-78, Bull. Calcutta Math. Soc, 1976—, Jour. Combinatorics, Info. and Systems Scis, 1976—; editor, founder: Jour. Graph Theory, 1977—, Social Networks, 1978-81, Networks, 1979—, Discrete Applied Mathematics, 1979—, Math. and Computer Modelling, 1980—, Caribbean Jour. Math. and Computing Scis., 1980—, Math. Social Scis., 1980-87, Jour. Information and Optimization Scis., 1987-89, Applied Math. Letters, 1988—, Computers and Math. with Application, 1988—, Jour. Mathematical Chemistry, 1991-93, Proyecciones, 1992—; author: (with R. Norman and D. Cartwright) Structural Models, 1965, Graph Theory, 1969, (with E. Palmer) Graphical Enumeration, 1973; (with Per Hage) Structural Models in Anthropology, 1983, (with F. Buckley) Distance in Graphs, 1990, (with P. Hage) Exchange in Oceania, 1991, Island Networks, 1996; editor: A Seminar on Graph Theory, 1967, Graph Theory and Theoretical Physics, 1967, Proof Techniques in Graph Theory, 1969, New Directions in the Theory of Graphs, 1973, (with R. Bari) Graphs and Combinatorics, 1974, Topics in Graph Theory, 1979, (with J. S. Maybee) Graphs and Applications, 1985. Mem. Am. Math. Soc., London Math Soc., Glasgow Math Soc., Edinburgh Math Soc., Can. Math Soc., S.E. Asian Math Soc., Malaysian Math Soc., Calcutta Math Soc. (v.p. 1978—), Math. Assn. Am., Soc. for Indsl. and Applied Math, Allahabad Math. Soc. Office: NMex State U Dept Computer Sci Las Cruces NM 88003-8001

HARBAUGH, JAMES JOSEPH, professional football player; b. Toledo, Dec. 23, 1963; Degree in comm., U. Mich., 1987. Quarterback Chgo. Bears, 1987-93, Indpls. Colts, 1994-98, Balt. Ravens, 1998-99, San Diego Chargers, 1999—. Selected to Pro Bowl, 1995. Office: San Diego Chargers PO Box 609609 San Diego CA 92160-9609

HARBAUGH, JOHN WARVELLE, geologist, educator; b. Madison, Wis., Aug. 6, 1926; s. Marion Dwight and Marjorie (Warvelle) H.; m. Josephine Taylor, Nov. 24, 1951 (dec. Dec. 25, 1985); children: Robert, Dwight, Richard; m. Audrey Wegst, Oct. 21, 2000. BS, U. Kans., 1948, MS, 1950; PhD, U. Wis., 1955. Prodn. geologist Carter Oil Co., Tulsa, 1951-53; prof. geol. sci. Stanford U., 1955-99, prof. emeritus, 1999—. Author: (with G. Bonham Carter) Computer Simulation in Geology, 1970, (with D.M. Tezlaff) Simulating Clastic Sedimentation, 1989, (with P. Martinez) Simulating Nearshore Environments, 1993, (with R. Slingerland and K. Furlong) Simulating Clastic Sedimentary Basins, 1994, (with J.C. Davis and J. Wendebourg) Computing Risk for Oil Prospects: Principles and Programs, 1995, (with J. Wendebourg) Simulating Oil Entrapment in Clastic Sequences, 1997. Recipient Haworth Disting. Alumni award U. Kans., 1968, Krumbein medal Internat. Assn. Math. Geologists, 1986. Fellow Geol. Soc. Am.; mem. Am. Assn. Petroleum Geologists (Levorsen award 1970, Disting. Svc. award 1987, Disting. Edn. award Pacific sect. 1999). Republican. Home: 683 Salvatierra St Stanford CA 94305-8539 Office: Stanford U Dept Geol Scis 229 Geology Bldg Stanford CA 94305-2115 E-mail: harbaugh@pangea.stanford.edu

HARCOURT, MICHAEL FRANKLIN, retired premier of Province of British Columbia, lawyer, educator; b. Edmonton, Alta., Can., Jan. 6, 1943; s. Frank Norman and Stella Louise (Good) H.; m. Mai-Gret Wibecke Salo, June 26, 1971; 1 son, Justen Michael. BA, U. B.C., 1965, LLB, 1968. Bar: B.C. 1969. Founder dir. Vancouver Cmty. Legal Assistance Soc., 1969-71; ptnr. firm Lew, Fraser & Harcourt, 1971-79; pres. Housing and Econ. Devel. Cons. Firm, Vancouver, from 1977; alderman City of Vancouver, 1972-80, mayor, 1980-86; mem. Legis. Assembly, 1986-96; leader New Dem. Party of B.C., 1987-96; premier Province of B.C., 1991-96, ret., 1996; former leader of opposition, leader of govt.; sr. assoc. Sustainable Devel. Inst., Vancouver, B.C., 1996—. Asst. dir. Justice Devel. Commn., Vancouver; dir. Housing Corp. B.C.; adj. prof. faculty grad. studies U. B.C., 1996—; bd. dirs. Vancouver Internat. Airport, Vancouver Port Authority. Bd. dirs. Asia-Pacific Found. Mem. Law Soc. B.C., Nat. Rountable Environ. and Economy (chmn. fgn. rels. com.), Jericho Tennis Club. New Democrat. Mem. United Ch. Can. Avocations: tennis, golf, skiing, jogging, basketball. Office: HU B5-2202 Main Mall Vancouver BC Canada V6T1Z4

HARDAWAY, PENNY (ANFERNEE DEON HARDAWAY), professional basketball player; b. Memphis, July 18, 1972; Grad., Memphis State U. Guard, forward Orlando Magic, 1993-99, Phoenix Suns, 1999—. Appeared in film Blue Chips, 1994. Named to Newcomer of Yr. in the BMC, 1992-93, NBA All-Rookie First Team, 1993, Eastern Conf. All-Star Team, 1994-95, 95-96, All NBA First Team, 1995, Dream Team III, 1996; Nat. H.S. Player of Yr. award Paracle Mag., 1990-91; 1st team All Am. Memphis State U., 1992-93; honored by retiring of Jersey at Memphis State U., 1994. Mem. Eastern Conf. Champions Orlando Magic, 1994-95. Office: Phoenix Suns 201 E Jefferson St Phoenix AZ 85004-2412

HARDEN, HARVEY, state agency administrator; b. Blackwell, Okla., July 6, 1940; BBA, Walla Walla Coll., 1963; MBA in Bus. Edn., Ea. Washington U., 1969. Bus. instr. Rainer (Wash.) Sch. Dist., 1966-67; mem. testing staff Spokane Civil Svc. Dept., 1968-70, mem. classification staff, 1970-77, director, 1977—. Mem. Internat. Pers. Mgmt. Assn. Office: City of Spokane Civil Svc Dept 808 W Spokane Falls Blvd Spokane WA 99201-3333

HARDER, VIRGIL EUGENE, business administration educator; b. Ness City, Kans., July 19, 1923; s. Walter J. and Fern B. (Pausch) H.; m. Dona Maurine Dobson, Feb. 4, 1951; children— Christine Elaine, Donald Walter. B.S., M.A., U. Iowa, 1950; Ph.D., U. Ill., 1958. Instr. bus. adminstrn. U. Ill., Urbana, 1950-55; asst. prof. U. Wash., Seattle, 1955-59, assoc. prof., 1959-67, prof., 1967-86, prof. emeritus, 1986—, asso. dean sch. bus. adminstrn., 1966-74; dir. Inst. Fin. Edn. Sch. for Exec. Devel., Seattle, 1974-83. Served with AUS, 1943-45. Fellow Am. Bus. Communications Assn. (pres. 1965) Club: Trail Blazers. Office: U Wash Sch Bus Adminstrn Seattle WA 98195-0001

HARDER, WENDY WETZEL, communications executive; b. Oceanside, Calif., Feb. 14, 1951; d. Burt Louis and Marjorie Jean (Evans) W.; m. Peter N. Harder, Dec. 1, 1984; 1 child, Jonathan Russell. AA, Palomar Coll., 1971; BA in Communications, U. So. Calif., 1973; MBA, Pepperdine U., 1988. Pub. rels. dir. Orange County Community Devel. Coun., Santa Ana, Calif., 1975-76; assoc. producer Sta. KOCE-TV, Huntington Beach, 1976-77, reporter, 1977-79, anchor, assoc. producer, 1979-82; sr. adminstr. communications Mission Viejo (Calif.) Co., 1983-84, mgr. corp. affairs, 1984-85, dir. corp. affairs, 1985-91, v.p. corp. affairs, 1991-93, v.p. mktg. and corp. comm., 1993-97; dir. cmty. rels. Soka Univ. Am., 1998—. 1st v.p. Aliso Viejo (Calif.) Cmty. Found., 1988-93, pres., 1993-97, Saddleback Coll. Found., Mission Viejo, 1989-94; co-chmn. The Ctr. on Tour-Schs. Com., Orange County, Calif., 1989-92; v.p. Found. for Vocat. Visions, 1996—, pres., 2000—; bd. dirs. Dunaj Internat. Dance Ensemble, Orange County, 1985—. Recipient Golden Mike award Radio & TV News Assn., 1981; co-recipient Best Spl. Event award, Pub. Rels. Soc. Am., 1986, Golden Mike award Radio & TV News Assn., 1979. Mem. Pub. Rels. Soc. Am., Orange County Press Club (Best Feature Release award 1983), Phi Beta Kappa. Republican. Lutheran. Avocations: folk dancing, reading. Office: Soka Univ Am 1 University Dr Aliso Viejo CA 92656 E-mail: wwharder@soka.edu

HARDESTY, ROBERT ALAN, plastic surgeon; b. St. Helena, Calif., Apr. 24, 1953; m. Marti F. Baum; children: Ashley, Bradford, Chelsea. BA, Loma Linda U., 1974, MD, 1978. Diplomate Am. Bd. Surgery, Am. Bd. Plastic Surgery. Resident in gen. surgery Loma Linda (Calif.) U. Med. Ctr., 1979-83; resident in plastic surgery U. Pitts. Med. Ctr., 1984-86; fellow in craniofacial surgery Children's Hosp., Washington U., St. Louis, 1986-87; instr. dept. surgery, dept. emergency medicine Loma Linda U. Sch. Medicine, 1983-84; instr. in surgery, divsn. plastic and reconstructive surgery Washington U., 1986-87; asst. prof. dept. surgery, divsn. plastic and reconstructive surgery Loma Linda U. Sch. of Medicine, 1987-90; assoc. prof. dept. pediatrics Loma Linda U. Sch. Medicine, 1995—; prof. surgery, chief divsn. plastic/reconstructive surgery Loma Linda U. Sch. of Medicine, 1990—; prof. oral maxillofacial surgery and pediats. Sch. Dentistry Loma Linda U., 1995—, mem. numerous coms., 1987—; divsn. chief plastic & reconstructive surgery Loma Linda Med. Ctr. Apptd. to various hosps. including Loma Linda Community Hosp., 1987—, Jerry L. Pettis VA Med. Ctr., Loma Linda, 1987—, Riverside (Calif.) Gen. Hosp., 1987—, San Bernardino (Calif.) County Med. Ctr., 1990—; chmn. various symposiums; lectr., rschr. in field. Guest editor: Clinics in Plastic Surgery, 1993; mem. internat. editorial adv. bd. Jour. Reconstructive Microsurgery, 1990-91, 91-92, 92-93; contbr. articles to profl. jours., chpts. to books. Recipient Clin. Resident Competition Second Prize award Robert H. Ivy Soc. Plastic and Reconstructive Surgeons, 1986, First prize Ohio Valley Soc. Plastic Surgery, 1986, Second prize Pitts. Acad. Medicine, 1986, Traveling Fellow award Royal Coll. Surgeons, 1991-92; Rsch. grantee Valley Lab, 1988, Plastic Surgery Ednl. Found., Am. Soc. Aesthetic Plastic Surgery, 1988, 93, Maxillofacial Surgeons Found., 1992; grantee Loma Linda U. Med. Ctr., 1989, NIH, 1989-92, Am. Cleft Palate-Craniofacial Assn., 1991, The Aesthetic Soc., 1992, Nat. Inst. Dental Rsch., 1992; Craniofacial Seed grantee Loma Linda U., 1992. Fellow ACS; mem. AMA, AAAS, Am. Acad. Pediatrics (plastic surgery sect.), Am. Assn. Clin. Anatomists, Am. Assn. Pediatric Plastic Surgeons, Am. Burn Assn., Am. Cleft Palate-Craniofacial Assn., Am. Soc. Maxillofacial Surgeons, Am. Soc. Plastic and Reconstructive Surgeons, Internat. Confedn. Plastic, Reconstructive and Aesthetic Surgery, Pan-Pacific Surg. Assn., Tri-County Surg. Soc., Calif. Med. Assn., Calif. Soc. Plastic Surgeons, San Bernardino County Med. Soc., Aesthetic Surgery Edn. and Rsch. Found., Adventist Internat. Med. Soc., Assn. Acad. Chairmen of Plastic Surgery, Lipoplasty Soc. N.Am., Loma Linda Med.- Dental Soc., Walter E. Macpherson Soc., Plastic Surgery Rsch. Coun., Wound Healing Soc., Alpha Omega Alpha. Home: 1515 W Cypress Ave Redlands CA 92373-5614 Office: Loma Linda U Health Care Divsn Plastic Surgery 11370 Anderson St Ste 2100 Loma Linda CA 92354-3450

HARDIN, WAYNE, automotive executive; CEO, chair Santa Monica (Calif.) Ford. Office: Santa Monica Ford 1230 Santa Monica Blvd Santa Monica CA 90404-1798 Fax: 310-394-8115

HARDING, KAREN ELAINE, chemistry educator; b. Atlanta, Sept. 5, 1949; d. Howard Everett and Ruth Evangeline (Lund) H.; m. Bruce Roy McDowell, Aug. 30, 1975. BS in Chemistry, U. Puget Sound, Tacoma, 1971; MS in Environ. Chemistry, U. Mich., 1972; postgrad., Evergreen State Coll., 1972, 84, Yale U., 1986, Columbia U., 1991. Chemist Environ. Health Lab., Inc., Farmington, Mich., 1972-73, U. Mich. Med. Sch., Ann Arbor, 1973-75; instr. chemistry Schoolcraft Coll., Livonia, Mich., 1975-77; chair chemistry dept. Pierce Coll., Tacoma, 1977—. Adj. prof. U. Mich., Dearborn, 1974-77; instr. S.H. Alternative Learning Ctr., Tacoma, 1980-83, Elderhostel, Tacoma, 1985-89; mem. exec. com. Chemlinks project NSF. Mem. County Solid Waste Adv. Com., Tacoma, 1989—, Superfund Adv. Com., Tacoma, 1985-89, Sierra Club, Wash., 1989—; mem., past pres. Adv. Com. Nature Ctr., Tacoma, 1981-87. Faculty Enhancement grantee Pierce Coll., 1990; recipient Nat. Teaching Excellence award, 1991. Mem. NW Assn. for Environ. Studies (treas. 1985—), Am. Chem. Soc., Ft. Steilacoom Running Club (race dir. 1986—). Avocations: running, skiing, backpacking, bicycling, reading. Office: Pierce Coll 9401 Farwest Dr SW Tacoma WA 98498-1919

HARDISON, DEE, mayor; Tchr. spl. edn. Torrance Unified Sch. Dist., 1980-89, program specialist, 1989-94; mem. Torrance City Coun., 1986-94; mayor City of Torrance, 1994—. Office: 3031 Torrance Blvd Torrance CA 90503-5015

HARDMON, LADY, professional athlete; b. Sept. 12, 1970; Guard Utah Starzz, 1997-99, Sacramento Monarchs, 1999—. Named to All-SEC team, 1990, 92, SEC All-Tournament team, 1990, 92, Hon. Mention Kodak All-Am.; winner bronze medal World Univ. Games in Buffalo, 1993, gold medal, 1992; played in 1989 Jr. World Championship. Avocations: working out, speaking to young people at church. Office: Sacramento Monarchs Utah Starzz One Sports Pky Sacramento CA 95834

HARDWICK, DAVID FRANCIS, pathologist, department chairman; b. Vancouver, B.C., Can., Jan. 24, 1934; s. Walter H. W. and Iris L. (Hyndman) H.; m. Margaret M. Lang, Aug. 22, 1956; children: Margaret F., Heather I., David J. MD, U. B.C., 1957, LLD, 2001. Intern Montreal (Que., Can.) Gen. Hosp., 1957-58; resident Vancouver Gen. Hosp., 1958-59, Children's Hosp., Los Angeles, 1959-62; research assoc. U. So. Calif., 1961-62; clin. instr. U. B.C., Vancouver, 1963-65, asst. prof. pathology, 1965-69, assoc. prof., 1969-74, prof., 1974—, head dept. pathology, 1976-90, assoc. dean rsch. and planning, 1990-96; dir. labs. Children's Hosp., Vancouver, 1969-92, Vancouver Gen. Hosp., 1976-90; chmn. M.A.C., Children's Hosp., 1970-87; interinstitutional planning U. B.C. Medicine, 1996-98, spl. advisor on planning, 1999—. Adj. prof. Chinese U. Hong Kong; mem. U. B.C. Senate, 1966-71. Author: Acid Base Balance and Blood Gas Studies, 1968, Intermediary Metabolism of Liver, 1971, Directing the Clinical Laboratory, 1990; contbr. numerous articles to profl. publs. Bd. dirs. Children's and Women's Hosp., B.C., 1998—, Women's Hosp. Found., 1997—, B.C. Transplant Found., 1993—. Recipient Queen's Centennial medal Govt. Can., 1978, U. B.C. Faculty Citation Teaching award, 1987, Wallace Wilson Leadership award, 1990, William Boyd Lectureship award Canadian Assn. Path, 1994, Sydney Israels Founders award B.C. Rsch. Inst. Children and Family, 1997, Univ. medal for Outstanding Svc., U. B.C., 1997; Sydney Farber lectr., Soc. Ped. Path., 1998. Fellow Royal Coll. Physicians (Can.), Coll. Am. Pathologists; mem. Internat. Acad. Pathology (pres. 1996, v.p. N.Am. 1998—), Can. Med. Assn., B.C. Assn. Lab. Medicine, B.C. Med. Assn., N.Y. Acad. Sci., Soc. Pediat. Pathology, Internat. Acad. Pathology (Disting. Svc. award 1994), U.S. Acad. Pathology, Can. Assn. Pathology, B.C. Transplant Soc. (chmn. bd. 2000—), Alpha Omega Alpha. Home: 727 W 23rd Ave Vancouver BC Canada V5Z 2A7 Office: U BC Dept Pathology 2211 Wesbrook Mall Vancouver BC Canada V6T 1W5 E-mail: david.f.hardwick@ubc.ca

HARDY, CHARLES LEACH, federal judge; b. L.A., Jan. 24, 1919; s. Charles Little and Dorothy (Leach) H.; m. Jean McRae, Jan. 26, 1947; children: Charles M., Caroline, Catherine, John L. Julianne, Eileen, Sterling A., Steven W., Janette. BS, U. Ariz., 1947, LLB, 1950. Bar: Ariz. 1949. Pvt. practice, Phoenix, 1949-66; dep. county atty. Maricopa County, Ariz., 1952-55; asst. atty. gen. State of Ariz., 1956-59; judge Ariz. Superior Ct., 1966-80; U.S. dist. judge Ariz. Dist., Phoenix, 1980—; now sr. judge. Pres. Young Democratic Clubs Ariz., 1956-57, nat. committeeman, 1957-58; chmn. Maricopa County Dem. Cen. Com., 1958-59; mem. Ariz. Bd. Crippled Children's Services, 1965. Served with F.A. AUS, 1941-45. Decorated Bronze Star. Mem. ABA, Am. Judicature Soc., State Bar Ariz., Maricopa County Bar Assn. Mem. LDS Ch. Office: US Dist Ct US Courthouse & Fed Bldg Rm 7025 3017 US Courthouse Phoenix AZ 85025-0005

HARDY, DEBORAH WELLES, history educator; b. Milw., Nov. 2, 1927; d. Frank M. and Doris (Berger) Hursley; widowed; children: Scott, Jonathan, Bridget. Student, Swarthmore Coll., 1945-47; BA, Stanford U., 1949; MA, U. Calif., 1950; PhD, U. Wash., 1968. TV writer, 1964-72; mem. faculty U. Wyo., Laramie, 1967-93, prof. history, 1978-93, head dept., 1980-85, prof. emeritus, 1993—. Free-lance TV writer, 1964-74; mem. Wyo. Council Humanities, 1972-76. Author: Petr. Tkachev: The Critic as Jacobin, 1977, Wyoming University: The First Hundred Years, 1986, Land and Freedom: The Origins of Russian Terrorism, 1987; also articles. Grantee Social Sci. Research Council, summer 1971, Am. Philos. Soc., 1976; Internat. Research and Exchanges Bd. scholar, 1987. Mem. Am. Hist. Assn., Am. Assn. Advancement of Slavic Studies, Western Social Sci. Assn., Western Slavic Assn., Phi Beta Kappa. Home: 2450 E Park Ave Laramie WY 82070-4858 Office: U Wyo Dept History Laramie WY 82071

HARDY, WALTER NEWBOLD, physics educator, researcher; b. Vancouver, B.C., Mar. 25, 1940; s. Walter Thomas and Julia Marguerite (Mulroy) H.; m. Sheila Lorraine Hughes, July 10, 1959; children: Kevin James, Steven Wayne. BSc in Math and Physics with honors, U. B.C., 1961; PhD in Physics, Univ. B.C., 1965. Postdoctral fellow Centre d'Etudes Nucleaires de Saclay, France, 1964-66; mem. tech. staff N.Am. Rockwell, Thousand Oaks, Calif., 1966-71; assoc. prof. physics U. B.C., 1971-76, prof., 1976—. Vis. scientist Ecole Normale Superieure, Paris, 1980-81, 85, 95. Contbr. articles to sci. jours.; patentee precision microwave instrumentation. Recipient Stacie prize NRC of Can., 1978, Gold medal B.C. Sci. Coun., 1989, Killam prize Can. Coun., 1999; Rutherford Meml. scholar, 1964; Alfred P. Sloan fellow, 1972-74; Can. Coun. Rsch. fellow, 1984-86. Mem. Can. Assn. Physicists (Herzberg medal 1978, gold medal for achievement in physics, 1993, Brockhouse medal 1999), Am. Phys. Soc. Office: U BC Dept Physics Astronomy Vancouver BC Canada V6T 1Z1

HARDY, WAYNE RUSSELL, insurance and investment broker; b. Denver, Sept. 5, 1931; s. Russell Hinton and Victoria Katherine (Anderson) [illegible] Russell Hardy, Jann Miller Hardy. BSCE, U. Colo., 1954; MS in Fin. Svcs., Am. Coll., 1989. CLU; chartered fin. cons. Western dist. mgr. Fenestra, Inc., San Francisco, 1956-63; ins. and investment broker John Hancock Fin. Svs., Denver, 1963—, Wayne R. Hardy Assocs., Denver, 1963—. Speaker convs. and sales seminars, 1977, 81, 84, 85, 89; v.p. CLU assn. John Hancock, 1979-80, chmn. agt.'s adv. com., 1983-84; active State of [illegible] 1964-89. Chmn. Colo. Coun. Camera Clubs, Denver, 1962; bd. dirs. Porter Charitable Found., Denver, 1983-85; deacon, class pres. South Broadway Christian Ch., 1961-65; mem. Denver Art Mus., Denver Botanic Gardens, Rocky Mountain Estate Planning Coun., Mensa, Alliance Francaise. Capt. U.S. Army, 1954-56, Korea, USAR, 1956-80. Mem. Am. Soc. CLU and ChFC (pres. Rocky Mountain chpt. 1990-91), Nat. Assn. Life Underwriters (pres. Denver chpt. 1983-84, Nat. Quality award 1968—, expert witness ins. litigation, Disting. Life Underwriters award 1970-83), Screen Actors Guild, Million Dollar Round Table (life), U. Colo. Alumni (bd. dirs. 1990-92), U. Colo. Alumni C Club (bd. dirs. 1972-74), Univ. Club, Greenwood Athletic Club, Village Tennis Club, Rocky Mountain Optimist Club (pres. 1984-85). Republican. Avocations: tennis, photography, foreign languages, art, travel. Home and Office: 6178 E Hinsdale Ct Englewood CO 80112-1534

HARGRAVE, SARAH QUESENBERRY, consulting company executive; b. Mt. Airy, N.C., Dec. 11, 1944; d. Teddie W. and Lois Knight (Slusher) Quesenberry. Student, Radford Coll., 1963-64, Va. Poly. Inst. and State U., 1964-67. Mgmt. trainee Thalhimer Bros. Dept. Store, Richmond, Va., 1967-68; Cen. Va. fashion and publicity dir. Sears Roebuck & Co., Richmond, 1968-73, nat. decorating sch. coord. Chgo., 1973-74, nat. dir. bus. and profl. women's programs, 1974-76; v.p., treas., program dir. Sears-Roebuck Found., Chgo., 1976-87, program mgr. corp. contbns. and memberships, 1981-84, dir. corp. mktg. and pub. affairs, 1984-87; v.p. personal fin. svcs. and mktg. Northern Trust Co., Chgo., 1987-89; pres. Hargrave Consulting, 1989—. Spkr., seminar leader in field. Bd. dirs. Am. Assembly Collegiate Schs. Bus., 1979-82, mem. vis. com., 1979-82, mem. fin. and audit com., 1980-82, mem. task force on doctoral supply and demand, 1980-82; mem. Com. for Equal Opportunity for Women, 1976-81; chmn., 1978-79, 80-81; mem. bus. adv. coun. Walter E. Heller Coll. Bus. Adminstrn., Roosevelt U., 1979-89; co-dir. Ill. Internat. Women's Yr. Ctr., 1975. Named Outstanding Young Women of Yr. Ill., 1976; named Women of Achievement State Street Bus. and Profl. Woman's Club, 1978 Mem. ASTD, Eddystone Condominium Assn. (v.p. 1978-86), Profl. Women's Network. Home and Office: 34 Fairlawn Ave Daly City CA 94015-3425

HARGREAVES, GEORGE HENRY, civil and agricultural engineer, researcher; b. Chico, Calif., Apr. 2, 1916; s. Carey and Luella May (Raymond) H.; m. Elizabeth Ann Gardner, Aug. 9, 1941 (dec. Dec. 1948); 1 child, Margaret Ann Hargreaves Stolpmann; m. Sara Etna Romero, Jan 6, 1951; children: Mark Romero, Sonia Maria Hargreaves Hart, George Leo. BS in Soils, U. Calif., Berkeley, 1939; BSCE, U. Wyo., 1943. Civil engr. U.S. Bur. Reclamation, Sacramento, 1946-48; reclamation engr. U.S. Army C.E., Greece, 1948-49; engr. AID, Greece, Peru, Haiti, Philippines, Brazil and Colombia, 1950-68; chief civil engr. engring. br. Natural Resources divsn. Inter-Am. Geudetic Survey, Ft. Clayton, C.Z., 1968-70; rsch. engr. in irrigation Utah State. U., Logan, 1970-86; rsch. Internat. Irrigation Ctr., 1980-86, rsch. prof. emeritus, 1986—. Author: World Water for Agriculture, 1977; co-author: Irrigation Fundamentals, 1998, Fundamentos Del Riego, 2000; contbr. numerous articles to profl. jours. Lt. (j.g.) USNR, 1943-46, PTO. Recipient Royce J. Tipton award 1987. Fellow ASCE (chmn. surface water com. 1974-75); mem. Am. Soc. Agrl. Engrs. (chmn. Rocky Mountain sect. 1974), Internat. Commn. Irrigation and Drainage (chmn. U.S. com. on crops and water use 1992-96, chmn. U.S. com. on history of irrigation, drainage and flood control 1999—). Achievements include development of methodology used by the International Water Management Institute in the IWMI World Water and Climate Atlas, providing worldwide climate data and an index of rainfall adequacy for agricultural production. Home: 1660 E 1220 N Logan UT 84341-3040 Office: Utah State U Internat Irrigation Ctr Dept Biol Irrigation Engring Logan UT 84322-4150

HARGROVE, DON, state legislator; b. Bozeman, Mont., Mar. 16, 1933; s. Ora Augustus and Helen Victoria (Dringle) H.; m. Eloise Marilyn Fellbaum, Aug. 20, 1955; children: Mark, Dan, David. BS, Mont. State U., 1956; MS, U. So. Calif., L.A., 1966. Commd. 2d lt. USAF, 1956, advanced through grades to col., 1976, comdr. 41st Mil. Airlift Squadron, comdr. 63d Mil. Airlift Group, def. attache to Bolivia; mem. Mont. Senate, Dist. 16, Helena, 1995—; maj. whip, 1999-2000. Aviation advisor Colombian Nat. Narcotics Police, 1986-91. Republican. Home: 37 Big Chief Trl Bozeman MT 59718-9419 Office: PO Box 1 Belgrade MT 59714-0001

HARGROVE, JAMES E. state legislator; b. Portland, Oreg., Oct. 5, 1953; m. Laurie Hargrove; children: Jimmy-Jack, Jewel, Daniel. BS in Forest Mgmt., Oreg. State U. Mem. Wash. Senate, Dist. 24, Olympia, 1993—; chair human svcs. and corrections com.; mem. jud. com.; mem. natural resources, parks and recreation com. Mem. Grays Harbor Econ. Devel. Coun., Hoquiam Little League. Mem. Grays Harbor C. of C. Democrat. Office: 412A Legislative Bldg Olympia WA 98504-0001

HARGROVE, JOHN JAMES, bankruptcy judge; b. Bay Shore, N.Y., May 4, 1942; s. John A. and Cecelia L. Hargrove; m. Jane A Nagle, Oct. 21, 1967; children: David, Kristin, Kelly, Kathryn. BAin Polit. Sci., U. Notre Dame, 1964, JD, 1967. Bar: N.Y. 1968, Calif. 1971. Atty. Gant & Asaro, San Diego, 1972-76; ptnr. Weeks, Willis, Hoffman & Hargrove, San Diego, 1976-79, Strauss, Kissane, Davis & Hargrove, San Diego, 1979-83, Britton & Hargrove, San Diego, 1983-84; prin. John J. Hargrove & Assocs., San Diego, 1984-85; judge U.S. Bankruptcy Ct., San Diego, 1985—, chief bankruptcy judge. Adj. prof. Calif. Western Sch. Law, 1986. Coach University City Bobby Sox Softball Team; lector Our Mother of Confidence Roman Cath. Ch.; trustee U. Notre Dame, 1987-89. Lt. col. USMCR, 1968-90. Mem. U. Notre Dame Alumni Assn. (bd. dirs. 1985-89, pres. 1988-89). Republican. Avocations: basketball, softball, running. Office: US Bankruptcy Ct So Dist Calif 325 W F St San Diego CA 92101-6989 Fax: 619-557-6925

HARGROVE, LINDA, professional basketball coach; m. Ed Hargrove; children: Brian, Tara. BS magna cum laude, Southwestern Coll., 1975; MEd, Wichita State U., 1985. Head coach Cowley County C.C. Tigers, 1972-89, Wichita State U. Shockers, 1989-98; head coach, dir. player pers. Colo. Xplosion, Am. Basketball League, Denver, 1998—; head coach Portland Fire, WNBA, 1999—. Asst. coach 1990 U.S. Sr. Nat. Women's Team, 1989, 1992 U.S. Olympic Team; cons. WNBA Orlando Miracle; mem. USA Basketball Sr. Nat. Team Com. Inductee Southwestern Coll. Athletic Hall of Fame, 1992. Mem. Women's Basketball Coaches Assn. (bd. dirs., Midwest divsn. I rep.). Office: Portland Fire One Center Ct Ste 150 Portland OR 97227

HARKEN, ALDEN HOOD, thoracic surgeon; b. Boston, 1941; MD, Case Western Reserve U., 1967. Diplomate Am. Bd. Surgeons, Am. Bd. Thoracic Surgeons. Intern Peter Bent Brigham Hosp., Boston, 1967-68, resident surgery, 1968-70, resident thoracic surgery, 1971-73; fellow cardio-vascular surgery Boston Children's Hosp., 1970-71; surgeon U. Colo. Hosp., Denver; prof., chmn. surgery dept. U. Colo. Sch. Medicine, Denver, 1983—; part time pvt. practice surgery Denver. Mem. Am. Assn. Thoracic Surgeons, Soc. Univ. Surgeons. Office: U Colo Med Sch Dept Surg 4200 E 9th Ave Denver CO 80220-3706

HARLAN, NANCY MARGARET, lawyer; b. Santa Monica, Calif., Sept. 10, 1946; d. William Galland and Betty M. (Miles) Plett; m. John Hammack, Dec. 01, 1979; children: Laryssa Maria Rebello, Leea Elyce. BS magna cum laude, Calif. State U., Hayward, 1972; JD, U. Calif., Berkeley, 1975. Bar: Calif. 1975, Fed. Bar, U.S. Dist. Ct. (ctrl. dist. 9th cir.) 1976. Assoc. Poindexter & Doutr+248, L.A., 1975—80; residential counsel [illegible] 1980—81; sr. counsel for real estate subs. law dept. Pacific Lighting Corp. [illegible] [illegible] [illegible] [illegible] [illegible] Santa Ana, 1981—87; sr. v.p., gen. counsel The Presley Cos., 1987—. Bd. dirs. La Casa; exec. v.p. student body U. Calif., Berkeley, 1974—75. Mem.: ABA, NAFE, State Bar Calif., L.A. County Bar Assn., Orange County Bar Assn. (dir. corp. counsel sect. 1982—), Bus. and Profl. Women, Calif. Women Lawyers Assn., Orange County Women Lawyers Assn., L.A. Women Lawyers Assn. Office: William Lyon Homes Inc 4490 Von Karman Ave Newport Beach CA 92660-2008

HARLAN, NEIL EUGENE, retired healthcare company executive; b. Cherry Valley, Ark., June 2, 1921; s. William and Mary Nina (Ellis) H.; m. Martha Almlov, Sept. 27, 1952; children: Lindsey Beth, Neil Eugene, Sarah Ellis. Student, U. Edinburgh, Scotland, 1946; BS, U. Ark., 1947, LLD, 1969; MBA, Harvard U., 1950, DBA, 1956. Mem. faculty Grad. Sch. Bus. Adminstrn. Harvard U., 1951-62, asst. prof., 1954-58, assoc. prof., 1958-61, prof., 1962; asst. sec. Air Force Washington, 1962-64; exec. v.p. Anderson, Clayton & Co., 1964-67; dir. McKinsey & Co., Inc., 1967-74, McKesson Corp., San Francisco, 1974-93, chmn., CEO, 1984-86, 89-90. Author: Management Control in Air Frame Subcontracting, 1956, (with R.H. Hassler) Cases in Controllership, 1958, Cases in Accounting Policy, 1961, Managerial Economics, 1962. Chmn. San Francisco Ballet, 1982-85; trustee exec. com. World Affairs Coun. No. Calif., 1983—; vice-chmn., dir. Nat. Park Found., 1986-92; bd. govs. San Francisco Symphony, 1985-88; mem. Calif. Com. on Campaign Fin., Calif. Bus. Roundtable, 1984-87; vis. com. Harvard Bus. Sch., 1984-87. Served with AUS, 1943-46. Mem. Webhannet Golf Club, Edgecomb Tennis Club (Kennebunk Beach, Maine), Bohemian Club, Pacific Union Club (San Francisco), Links Club (N.Y.C.). Home: 1170 Sacramento St Apt 13D San Francisco CA 94108-1953 Office: McKesson Corp 1 Post St Ste 3200 San Francisco CA 94104-5292

HARLAN, ROBERT DALE, information studies educator, academic administrator; b. Hastings, Nebr., Aug. 4, 1929; s. Hugh Allan and Madge Keister (Newmyer) H. BA, Hastings Coll., 1950; MA in Library Sci., U. Mich., 1956, MA, 1958, PhD, 1960. Head book order sect. Library U. Mich., Ann Arbor, 1956-58, lectr., 1960; asst. prof. Sch. Library Sci. U. So. Calif., Los Angeles, 1960-63; asst. prof. library and info. studies U. Calif., Berkeley, 1963-70, assoc. prof., 1970-76, prof., 1976-94, prof. emeritus, 1994—; assoc. dean Sch. Library and Info. Studies, 1971-74, 77-82; acting dean Sch. Library and Info. Studies U. Calif., Berkeley, 1985-86. Vis. assoc. prof. Sch. Libr. Sci. UCLA, summer 1973; cons. NEH, Washington; proprietor Park Hills Press. Author: John Henry Nash, 1970, Bibliography of the Grabhorn and Grabhorn-Hoyem Presses, 1977, George L. Harding, 1978, The Colonial Printer: Two Views, 1978, Chapter Nine, 1982, William Doxey's Publishing Venture: At the Sign of the Lark, 1983, The Two Hundredth Book, 1993; chmn. edit. bd. catalogues and bibliographies series U. Calif. Press, 1982-99; contbr. numerous articles and revs. to profl. jours. Rackham pre-doctoral fellow, U. Mich., 1958-60, summer faculty fellow U. Calif., Berkeley, 1964; grantee Assn. Coll. and Research Libraries, 1960, 63. Mem. Bibliog. Soc. Am., Bibliog. Soc. U. Va., Am. Soc. 18th Century Studies, Will Cather Pioneer Meml. Soc., Fine Press Book Assn., Book of Calif. Club (bd. dirs. 1982-88, sec. bd. 1987-88). Office: U Calif Sch Info Mgmt Berkeley CA 94720-0001

HARLEY, ROBISON DOOLING, JR. lawyer, educator; b. Ancon, Panama, July 6, 1946; s. Robison Dooling and Loyde Hazel (Goehenauer) H.; m. Suzanne Purviance Bendel, Aug. 9, 1975; children: Arianne Erin, Lauren Loyde. BA, Brown U., 1968; JD, Temple U., 1971; LLM, U. San Diego, 1985. Bar: Pa. 1971, U.S. Ct. Mil. Appeals 1972, Calif. 1976, U.S. Dist. Ct. (cen. and so. dists) Calif. 1976, N.J. 1977, U.S. Dist. Ct. N.J. 1977, U.S. Supreme Ct. 1980, D.C. 1981, U.S. Ct. Appeals (9th cir.) 1982, U.S. Dist. Ct. (ea. dist.) Pa. 1987, U.S. Ct. Appeals (3rd cir.) 1986. Cert. criminal law specialist Calif. Bd. Legal Specialization, 1981, recertified 1986, 91, 96; cert. criminal trial adv. Nat. Bd. Trial Advocacy, 1982, recertified, 1987, 92, 97. Asst. agy. dir. Safeco Title Ins. Co., L.A., 1975-77; ptnr. Cohen, Stokke & Davis, Santa Ana, Calif., 1977-85; prin. Harley Law Offices, Santa Ana, Calif., 1985—; adj. prof. Orange County Coll. Trial Advocacy, adj. prof., paralegal program U. Calif., trial adv. programs U.S. Army, USN, USAF, USMC; judge pro-tem Orange County Cts. Author: Orange County Trial Lawyers Drunk Driving Syllabus; contbr. articles to profl. jours. and reports. Bd. dirs. Orange County Legal Aid Soc. Served to lt. col. JAGC, USMCR, 1975-94; trial counsel, def. counsel, mil. judge, asst. staff judge adv. USMC, 1971-75, regional def. counsel Western Region, 1986-90, instr., program coord. Army, Navy, Air Force, Marines, Coast Guard Trial Adv. Programs worldwide. Recipient Commendation medal U.S. Navy, Nat. Defense Svc. medal, Reserve medal, 23 Certs. of Commendation and/or Congratulations. Mem. ABA, ATLA, Orange County Bar Assn. (judiciary com., criminal law sect., adminstrn. of justice com.), Orange County Trial Lawyers Assn., Calif. Trial Lawyers Assn., Calif. Attys. for Criminal Justice, Calif. Pub. Defenders Assn., Nat. Assn. for Criminal Def. Attys., Assn. Specialized Criminal Def. Advs., Orange County Criminal Lawyers Assn. (found. com.), Res. Officers Assn., Marine Corps Reserve Officers Assn., Marine Corps Assn. Republican. Avocations: sports, physical fitness, reading. Home: 31211 Paseo Miraloma San Juan Capistrano CA 92675-5505 Office: Harley Law Offices 825 N Ross St Santa Ana CA 92701-3419

HARMAN, JANE, congresswoman, lawyer; b. N.Y.C., June 28, 1945; d. A. N. and Lucille (Geier) Lakes; m. Sidney Harman, Aug. 30, 1980; children: Brian Lakes, Hilary Lakes, Daniel Geier, Justine Leigh. BA, Smith Coll., 1966; JD, Harvard U., 1969. Bar: D.C. 1969, U.S. Ct. Appeals (D.C. cir.) 1972, U.S. Supreme Ct. 1975. Spl. asst. Commn. of Chs. on Internat. Affairs, Geneva, Switzerland, 1969-70; assoc. Surrey & Morse, Washington, 1970-72; chief legis. asst. Senator John V. Tunney, Washington, 1972-73; chief counsel, staff dir. Subcom. on Rep. Citizen Interests, Com. on Judiciary, Washington, 1973-75; adj. prof. Georgetown Law Ctr., Washington, 1974-75; chief counsel, staff dir. Subcom. on Constl. Rights, Com. on Judiciary, Washington, 1975-77; dep. sec. to cabinet The White House, Washington, 1977-78; spl. counsel Dept. Def., Washington, 1979; ptnr. Manatt, Phelps, Rothenberg & Tunney, Washington, 1979-82, Surrey & Morse, Washington, 1982-86; of counsel Jones, Day, Reavis & Pogue, Washington, 1987-92; mem. 103rd-105th, 107th Congresses from 36th Calif. dist., 1992-98, 2001—; mem. nat. security com., intelligence com. 103rd-105th Congresses from 36th Calif. dist.; mem. U.S. Ho. of Reps., 2001—. Regents prof. UCLA, 1999-2000; mem. vis. coms. Harvard Law Sch., 1976-82, Kennedy Sch. Govt., 1990-96. Counsel Dem. Platform Com., Washington, 1984; vice-chmn. Ctr. for Nat. Policy, Washington, 1981-90; chmn. Dem. Nat. Com. Nat. Lawyers' Coun., Washington, 1986-90; bd. dirs. Planned Parenthood, 1998-2000—, Venice (Calif.) Family Clinic, 1998-2000. Mem. Phi Beta Kappa. Democrat. Office: 811 N Catalina Ave Ste 1302 Redondo Beach CA 90277 also: 229 Cannon HOB Washington DC 20515

HARMON, DANIEL PATRICK, classics educator; b. Chgo., May 3, 1938; s. Bernard Leonard and Dorothy Mildred (Lesser) H. AB, Loyola U., Chgo., 1962; MA, Northwestern U., 1965, PhD, 1968; postdoctoral, Am. Sch. Classical Studies in Athens, 1975. Acting asst. prof. U. Wash., Seattle, [illegible] classics and comparative lit., 1976-84, prof. classics, 1984—, chmn. classics, 1976-91; dir. U. Wash. Rome Ctr., 1992-2000. Contbr. articles and revs. to profl. jours. Mem. Am. Philol. Assn., Archaeol. Inst. Am., Société des Études Latines, County Louth (Ireland) Archaeol. and Hist. Soc., Classical Assn. Pacific Northwest (pres. 1974-75). Avocations: painting, photography, music. Home: 3149 NE 83rd St Seattle WA 98115-4751 [illegible] E-mail: dph@u.washington.edu

HARMON, DAVID, finance company executive; b. 1938; MBA, Mich. State U., 1965. With Electronic Memories and Magnetics, Hawthorne, Calif., 1965-78; CEO El Camino Resources Ltd., Woodland Hills, 1978—; with El Camino Resources Internat., Woodland Hills, 1986—. Office: 21051 Warner Center Ln Woodland Hills CA 91367-6509

HARNISH, JOHN J. manufacturing executive; Gen. mgr. Tractor & Equipment Co., Sidney, Mont., 1977-82, pres. Williston, N.D., 1982—, CEO, 1984—. Office: Tractor & Equipment Co 17025 W Valley Hwy Tukwila WA 98188-5519

HAROLD, ROBERT, apparel executive; With NIKE, Inc., Beaverton, Oreg., 1984—, interim CFO, acctg. officer, 1998-99. Office: NIKE Inc One Bowerman Dr Beaverton OR 97005-6453

HARP, JOHN G. state legislator; b. Vancouver, Wash., Sept. 26, 1952; m. Kathy Harp. Ed., Missoula Bus. Coll. Contractor, bus. exec.; mem. Mont. Ho. of Reps., 1981-88, Mont. State Senate, 1988—, chair rules com., minority whip, 1993-94, majority leader, 1995. Mem. Evergreen Sch. Bd. Mem. Evergreen Lions Club. Republican. Home: 633 Sylvan Ct Kalispell MT 59901-5077

HARPENDING, HENRY COSAD, anthropologist, educator; b. Penn Yan, N.Y., Jan. 13, 1944; married, 1966; 2 children; married 1995; 1 child. AB, Hamilton Coll., 1964; MA, Harvard U., 1965, PhD in Anthropology, 1972. Asst. prof. anthropology Yale U., 1971-72; from asst. prof. to prof. anthropology U. N.Mex., 1972-85; prof. anthropology Pa. State U., 1986-97, U. Utah, 1997—. Mem. Nat. Acad. Sci., Am. Assn. Anthrop. Genetics, Human Behaviour Evolution Soc. Office: U Utah Dept Anthropology Stuart Salt Lake City UT 84112

HARPER, ANTHONY, counselor, singer; b. Clarksville, Tenn., Jan. 6, 1952; s. Hal L. and Kathryn A. (Reding) H.; m. Mary K. McGrane, July 1972 (div. Nov. 1974); 1 child, Amy; m. Mary J. Breshears, Aug., 1980. BA, USNY, 1984; MEd, Coll. Idaho, 1986; postgrad., Liberty U., Calif. Coast U., 1989—; PhD, Calif. Coast U., 1996. Tv switcher engr. KISU TV, Pocatello, Idaho, 1977-78, KIFI TV, Idaho Falls, 1979; singer various locations, 1978—; co-founder, exec. dir., counselor Shiloh Counseling Ctr., Boise, Idaho, 1987—. Guest spkr. in field; co-founder, exec. dir. Children of Hope Family Hosp., 1997—. Author: (test and manual) Spiritual Relationship Scale, 1990. Republican. Avocations: playing trumpet, piano, hiking, ice skating. Office: PO Box 1829 Boise ID 83701-1829 E-mail: aharper1952@juno.com

HARPER, JUDSON MORSE, university administrator, consultant, educator; b. Lincoln, Nebr., Aug. 25, 1936; s. Floyd Sprague and Eda Elizabeth (Kelley) H.; m. Patricia Ann Kennedy, June 15, 1958; children: Jayson K., Stuart H., Neal K. B.S., Iowa State U., 1958, M.S., 1960, Ph.D., 1963. Registered profl. engr., Minn. Instr. Iowa State U., Ames, 1958-63; dept. head Gen. Mills, Inc., Mpls., 1964-69, venture mgr., 1969-70; prof., dept. head agrl. and chem. engring. Colo. State U., Ft. Collins, 1970-82, v.p. rsch. and info. tech., 1982-2000, interim pres., 1989-90, spl. asst. to the pres., 2000—. Cons. USAID, Washington, 1972-74, various comml. firms., 1975—; Lady Davis scholar Technion, Haifa, Israel, 1978-79. Author: Extrusion of Foods, 1982, Extrusion Cooking, 1989; editor newsletter Food, Pharm. & Bioengring. News, 1979-83, LEC Newsletter, 1976-89; contbr. articles to profl. publs.; patentee. Mem. sch. bd. St. Louis Park, Minn., 1968-70. Recipient Disting. Svc. award Colo. State U., 1977, Fulbright-Hayes scholar, 1978, Svc. award Centro de Investigaviones y Asistencia Technologica de Estado de Chihuahua, Chichuahua, Mex., 1980, Food Engring. award Dairy and Food Industry Supply Assn. and Am. Soc. Agrl. Engrs., 1983, Cert. of Merit, USDA Office Internat. Coop. and Devel., 1983, Cert. of Merit, Consejo Nacional de Ciencia y Technologie en Mexico, Mexico City, 1984, Profl. Achievement Citation Iowa State U., 1986, Cert. Appreciation Chinese Inst. of Food Tech., 1987, Charles Lory Pub. Svc. award, 1993, Hammer award The Nat. Performance Rev., 1994. Fellow Inst. Food Technologists (Internat. award 1990), AAAS; mem. Am. Inst. Chem. Engring. (dir. 1981-84), Am. Soc. Agrl. Engrs. (com. chmn. 1973-78, hon. engr. Rocky Mountain region), Am. Chem. Soc., Am. Soc. Engring. Edn. (com. chmn. 1976-77). Mem. Ind. United Methodist Ch. Home: 1818 Westview Rd Fort Collins CO 80524-1891 Office: Colo State U Spl Projects Office Fort Collins CO 80523-2046 E-mail: judson.harper@colostate.edu

HARPER, RICHARD HENRY, film producer, director; b. San Jose, Calif., Sept. 15, 1950; s. Walter Henry and Priscilla Alden H.; m. Ann Marie Morgan, June 19, 1976; children: Christine Ann, Paul Richard, James Richard. Show designer Walt Disney Imagineering, Glendale, Calif., 1971-76; motion picture producer, dir. Harper Films, Inc., La Canada, 1976—. Producer, dir. (films) Impressions de France, Disney World, Fla., 1982, Magic Carpet Round the World, Disneyland, Tokyo, 1983, American Journeys, Disneyland, Calif., 1985, Collecting America, Nat. Gallery Art, Washington, 1988, Hillwood Mus., Washington, 1989, Journey Into the 4th Dimension for Sanrio World, Journey Into Nature for Sanrio World, Japan, 1990, Masters of Illusion, Nat. Gallery of Art, Washington, 1992. Recipient more than 150 awards world-wide for outstanding motion picture prodn. including Silver trophy Cannes Internat. Film Festival, 2 Gold awards Internat. Festival of the Ams., 1981, 82, 14 Golden Eagle C.I.N.E. awards, 1977-92, Emmy award Nat. Acad. TV Arts and Scis., 1993-. Mem. Acad. of Motion Picture Arts and Scis.

HARPER, STEVEN V. state senator; b. Tampa, Fla., Oct. 19, 1943; m. Sharron Harper; 4 children. BGS, U. Nebr., 1976. Commd. 2d lt. USAF, 1963, advanced through grades, 1993; Rep. rep. dist. 53 Oreg. Ho. of Reps., 1996-2000; Rep. senator dist. 30 Oreg. State Senate, 2000—. Mem. gen. govt. com. Oreg. Ho. of Reps. Mem. Rotary, C. of C. Baptist. Office: Oreg State Senate H-295 State Capitol Salem OR 97310 E-mail: harper.rep@state.or.us

HARRIGAN, ROSANNE CAROL, dean, nursing educator; b. Miami, Feb. 24, 1945; d. John H. and Rose (Hnatow) Harrigan; children: Dennis, Michael, John. BS, St. Xavier Coll., 1965; MS in Nursing, Ind. U., 1974, EdD in Nursing and Edn., 1979. Staff nurse, recovery rm. Mercy Hosp., Chgo., 1965, evening charge nurse, 1965-66; head nurse Chgo. State Hosp., 1966-67; nurse practitioner Health and Hosp. Corp. Marion County, Indpls., 1975-80; assoc. prof. Ind. U. Sch. Nursing, Indpls., 1978-82; nurse practitioner devel. follow-up program Riley Hosp. for Children, Indpls., 1980-85; chief nursing sect. Riley Hosp. Child Devel. Ctr., Indpls., 1982-85; prof. Ind. U. Sch. Nursing, Indpls., 1982-85; chmn., prof. maternal child health Loyola U. Niehoff Sch. Nursing, Chgo., 1985-92; dean U. Hawaii, Honolulu, 1992—; nurse practitioner Waimanalo (Hawaii) Health Ctr., 1999—. Lecturer Ind. U. Sch. Nursing, 1974-75, chmn. dept. pediatrics, family and women's health, 1980-85; adj. prof. of pediatrics Ind. U. Sch. Med., 1982-85; editorial bd. Jour. Maternal Child Health Nursing, 1984-86, Jour. Perinatal Neonatal, 1985—, Jour. Perinatology, 1989—, Loyola U. Press, 1988—; adv. bd. Symposia Medicus, 1982-84, Proctor and Gamble Rsch. Adv. Com. Blue Ribbon Panel; scientific review panel NIH, 1985; mem. NIH nat. adv. coun. nursing rsch., 2000-, ; cons. in field. Contbr. articles to profl. jours. Bd. dirs. March of Dimes Cen. Ind. Chpt., 1974-76, med. adv., 1979-85; med. and rsch. adv. March of Dimes Nat. Found., 1985—, chmn. Task Force on Rsch. Named Nat. Nurse of Yr. March of Dimes, 1983; faculty research grantee Ind. U., 1978, Pediatric Pulmonary Nursing Tng. grant Am. Lung Assn., 1982-85, Attitudes, Interests and Competence of Ob-Gyn Nurses Rsch. grant Nurses Assn. Am. Coll. Ob-Gyn., 1986, Attitudes, Interests and Priorities of Neonatal Nurses Rsch. grant Nat. Assn. Neonatal Nurses, 1987, Biomedical Rsch. Support grant, 1988; Doctoral fellow Am. Lung Assn. Ind. Tng. Program, 1981-86. Mem. AAAS, ANA (Maternal Child Nurse of Yr. 1983), Assn. Women's Health, Obstetrical and Neonatal Nursing (chmn. com. on rsch. 1983-86), Am. Nurses Found., Nat. Assn. Neonatal Nurses, Nat. Perinatal Assn. (bd. dirs. 1978-85, rsch. com. 1986), Midwest Nursing Rsch. Soc. (theory devel. sect.), Ill. Nurses Assn. (commn. rsch. chmn. 1990-91), Ind. Nurses Assn., Hawaii Nurses Assn., Ind. Perinatal Assn. (pres. 1981-83), N.Y. Acad. Sci., Ind U. Alumni Assn. (Disting. Alumni 1985), Sigma Xi, Pi Lambda Theta, Sigma Theta Tau (chpt. pres. 1988-90).

HARRINGTON, CHARLENE ANN, sociology and health policy educator; b. Concordia, Kans., Sept. 28, 1941; d. Lyman K. and Maxine (Boucher) Harrington; m. Ben Yerger, Aug. 28, 1976. BSN, U. Kans., Kansas City, 1963; MA in Cmty. Health, U. Wash., 1968; PhD in Sociology and Higher Edn., U. Calif., Berkeley, 1975. Staff nurse Good Samaritan Hosp., Portland, Oreg., 1963-64; sch. nurse U.S. Army Dependent Schs., Heilbronn, Germany, 1964-65; pub. health nurse Seattle King County and Group Health, Seattle, 1966-68; asst. prof., nursing program U. Kans., Kansas City, 1968-70; dep. dir., spl. asst. Calif. State Dept. Health, Sacramento, 1975-78; dir. Golden Empire Health Planning Agy., Sacramento, 1978-80; sr. rschr. Inst. for Health and Aging, U. Calif., San Francisco, 1980-83, asst. prof. Sch. Nursing, 1983-85, assoc. prof. dept. social and behavioral scis. Sch. Nursing, 1985-89, prof., vice chair dept. social and behavioral scis., 1989-93; chair dept. social and behavioral scis. U. Calif., San Francisco, 1994-96, prof. social and behavioral scis., 1997—. Assoc. dir. Inst. for Health and Aging, U. Calif., San Francisco, 1981-94; cons. Nat. Coalition for Nursing Home Reform, Washington, 1987—; com. on regulation nursing homes Inst. Medicine, 1984-86, com. on nursing staff, 1994-96. Author: Long Term Care, 1985, Health Policy and Nursing, 2d edit., 1996; contbr. chpts. to books, articles to profl. jours. Fellow Am. Acad. Nursing (chair commn. on health policy 1991-93); mem. ANA, APHA, Nursing Econs. (bd. dirs. 1985-93), Inst. Medicine (com. nurse staffing 1995-96, roundtable of quality 1997-98, com. on quality in long-term care 1997—), Am. Sociol. Assn. (sect. coun. mem. 1992-94), Elected Inst. of Medicine (com. on longterm care quality 1998—, round table on quality 1997-98), Sigma Theta Tau. Democrat. Avocation: gardening. Office: U Calif Sch Nursing 3333 California St San Francisco CA 94143-0001

HARRINGTON, DAN W. state senator; b. Butte, Mont., Feb. 12, 1938; m. Pat Harrington; children: Kathleen, Dan, Kevin. BS, Western Mont. Coll., 1960. Cert. tchr., Mont. Tchr. Sch. Dist. No. 1, Butte, 1961-97; Dem. rep. dist. 38 Mont. Ho. of Reps., 1976-2000; Dem. senator dist. 38 Mont. State Senate, 2000—. Majority whip Mont. Ho. of Reps., 1983, minority whip, 1995-99. Pres. Silver Bow Young Dems., 1960-62; del. Mont. Constl. Conv., 1971-72; chair Silver Bow County Dem. Com., 1970-90; pres. Silver Bow Dem. Burrows Club, 1997—. Mem. Butte Tchrs. Union. Roman Catholic. Office: 1201 N Excelsior Ave Butte MT 59701-8505 also: Mont State Senate Capitol Station Helena MT 59620

HARRINGTON, MARY EVELINA PAULSON (POLLY HARRINGTON), religious journalist, writer, educator; b. Chgo. d. Henry Thomas and Evelina (Belden) Paulson; m. Gordon Keith Harrington, Sept. 7, 1957; children: Jonathan Henry, Charles Scranton. BA, Oberlin Coll., 1946; postgrad., Northwestern U., Evanston, Ill., Chgo., 1946-49, Weber State U., Ogden, Utah, 1970s, 80s; MA, U. Chgo.-Chgo. Theol. Sem., 1956. Publicist Nat. Coun. Chs., N.Y.C., 1950-51; mem. press staff 2d assembly World Coun. Chs., Evanston, Chgo., 1954; mgr. Midwest Office Communication, United Ch. of Christ, Chgo., 1955-59; staff writer United Ch. Herald, N.Y.C., St. Louis, 1959-61; affiliate missionary to Asia, United Ch. Bd. for World Ministries, N.Y.C., 1978-79; freelance writer and lectr., 1961—; corr. Religious News Svc., 1962—. Prin. lectr. Women & Family Life in Asia series to numerous librs., Utah, 1981, 81-82; pub. rels. coord. Utah Energy Conservation/Energy Mgmt. Program, 1984-85; tchr. writing Ogden Cmty. Schs., 1985-89; adj. instr. writing for publs. Weber State U., 1986—; instr. Acad. Lifelong Learning, Ogden, 1992—, Eccles Cmty. Art Ctr., Ogden, 1993-94; dir. comm. Shared Ministry, Salt Lake City, 1983-97; chmn. comm. Intermountain Conf., Rocky Mountain Conf., Utah Assn. United Ch. of Christ, 1970-78, 82—, Ind. Coun. Chs., 1960-63, United Ch. of Christ, Ogden, 1971—; dir. comm. United Chs., 1971-78, Christ Congl., Ogden, 1980—; chmn. comm. Ch. Women United Utah, 1974-78, Ogden rep., 1980—; hostess Northern Utah, 1998. Editor: Sunshine and Moonscapes: An Anthology of Essays, Poems, Short Stories, 1994, (booklet) Family Counseling Service: Thirty Years of Service to Northern Utah, 1996; contbr. numerous articles and essays to religious and other publs. Pres. T.O. Smith Sch. PTA, 1976-78, Ogden City Coun. PTA, 1983-85; assoc. dir. Region II, Utah PTA, Salt Lake City, 1981-83, mem. State Edn. Commn., 1982-87; chmn. state internat. hospitality and aid Utah Fedn. Women's Clubs, 1982-86; v.p. Ogden dist., 1990-92, pres. Ogden dist., 1992-96, state resolutions com., 1996—; trustee Family Counseling Svc. No. Utah, Ogden, 1983-95, emeritus trustee, 1995—; Utah rep. to nat. bd. Challenger Films, Inc., 1986—; state pres. Rocky Mountain Conf. Women in Mission, United Ch. of Christ, 1974-77, sec., 1981-84, vice moderator Utah Assn., 1992-94; chair pastor-parish rels. com. United Ch. of Christ Congl., Ogden, 1999—, chmn. search com., 1995-96. Recipient Ecumenical Svc. citation Ind. Coun. Chs., 1962, Outstanding Local Pres. award Utah PTA, 1978, Outstanding Latchkey Child Project award, 1985, Cmty. Svc. award City of Ogden, 1980, 81, 82, Celebration of Gifts of Lay Woman Nat. award United Ch. of Christ, 1987, Excellence in the Arts in Art Edn. award Ogden City Arts Commn., 1993, Spirit of Am. Woman in Arts and Humanities award Your Cmty. Connection, Ogden, 1994, Heart and Hand award United Ch. of Christ, Ogden, 2001; Utah Endowment for Humanities grantee, 1981, 81-82. Mem. Nat. League Am. Penwomen (chmn. Utah conv. 1973, 11 awards for articles and essays 1987-95, 1st pl. news award 1992, 1st pl. short stories 1997, 3d pl. articles 1997), AAUW (state edn. rep. 1982-86, parliamentarian Ogden br. 1997—), League of Utah Writers (Publ. Quill award 1998). Democrat. Avocation: building miniature world of peace each Christmas by family in the home. Home and Office: 722 Boughton St Ogden UT 84403-1152 E-mail: gkHarrington1@home.com

HARRINGTON, ROGER FULLER, electrical engineering educator, consultant; b. Buffalo, Dec. 24, 1925; s. Henry Bassett and Emilie (Fuller) H.; m. Juanita L. Crawford, Aug. 7, 1954; m. Sandra, Judith, Alan, Laura. BS, Syracuse U., 1948, MS, 1950; PhD, Ohio State U., 1952. Instr. Syracuse U., N.Y., 1948-50, asst. prof., 1952-56, assoc. prof., 1956-60, prof., 1960-94, dir. Electromagnetics Ctr., 1982-94. Vis. prof. U. Ill., Urbana, 1959-60, U. Calif., Berkeley, 1964, E. China Normal U., 1983, Ecole Poly. Fédéral de Lausanne, Switzerland, 1991; guest prof. Tech. U. Denmark, Lyngby, 1969; cons. in field. Author: Introduction to EM Engineering, 1956, Time-Harmonic EM Fields, 1961, Field Computation by Moment Methods, 1968. Served with USN, 1944-46. Rsch. fellow Ohio State U., Columbus, 1950-52; Fulbright lectr., Denmark, eng., 1969; named Disting. Alumni Ohio State U., 1970; recipient Chancellor's Citation Syracuse U., 1984, URSI van der Pol Gold medal, 1996, jubilee medal Nicola Tesla Found., 1998. Mem. IEEE (Centennial medal 1984, Disting. Achievement award 1989, Electromagnetics award 2000, Third Millennium medal 2000), AAUP, Sigma Xi, Sigma Nu. Home: 5424 N Strada De Rubino Tucson AZ 85750-6061 Office: U Ariz Dept Elec Computer Engring Tucson AZ 85721-0001

HARRIS, BARBARA S. editor-in-chief; Editor-in-chief Shape mag. Weider Publ., Woodlands Hills, Calif. Office: Weider Publ 21100 Erwin St Woodland Hills CA 91367-3712

HARRIS, BILL H. computer software company executive; BA in Am. Studies, Middlebury Coll.; MBA, Harvard U. With Time, Inc.; exec. v.p. U.S. News & World Report; pres., CEO Intuit, Inc. (formerly ChipSoft, Inc.), Mountain View, Calif., 1991-93, chmn., 2000—. Office: 2535 Garcia Ave Mountain View CA 94043-1111

HARRIS, DALE RAY, lawyer; b. Crab Orchard, Ill., May 11, 1937; s. Ray B. and Aurelia M. (Davis) H.; m. Toni K. Shapkoff, June 26, 1960; children: Kristen Dee, Julie Diane. BA in Math., U. Colo., 1959; LLB, Harvard U., 1962. Bar: Colo. 1962, U.S. Dist. Ct. Colo. 1962, U.S. Ct. Appeals (10th cir.) 1962, U.S. Supreme Ct. 1981. Assoc. Davis, Graham & Stubbs, Denver, 1962-67, ptnr., 1967—, chmn. mgmt. com., 1982-85. Spkr., instr. various antitrust and comml. litig. seminars; bd. dirs. Lend-A-Lawyer, Inc., 1989-94. Mem. campaign cabinet Mile High United Way, 1986—87, chmn., atty. adv. com., 1988, sec., legal counsel, trustee, 1989—94, 1996—2001, mem. exec. com., 1989—2001, chmn. bd. trustees, 1996, 1997; trustee The Spaceship Earth Fund, 1986—89, Legal Aid Found. Colo., 1989—95, 2000—01; mem. devel. coun. U. Colo. Arts and Scis. dept., 1985—93; area chmn. law sch. fund Harvard U., 1978—81; bd. dirs. Colo. Jud. Inst., 1994—, vice chari, 1998; bd. dir. Colo. Lawyers Trust Account Found., 1996—2001; steering com. Youth-At-Work, 1994, School-To-Work, 1995; mem. jud. adv. coun. Colo. Supreme Ct., 2001—. With reserves USAR, 1962—68. Recipient Williams award, Rocky Mountain Arthritis Found., 1999. Fellow: Am. Bar Found. (Colo. state chmn. 1998—); mem.: Denver Law Club (pres. 1976—77, Lifetime Achievement award 1997), The Two Percent Club (exec. com. 1994—), Univ. Club, Rotary (Denver), Colo. Forum, Citizens Against Amendment 12 Com. (exec. com. 1994), Phi Beta Kappa, ABA (antitrust and litigation sects.), Colo. Bar Found. (pres.-elect 1992—93), Colo. Bar Assn. (chmn. antitrust com. 1980—84, coun. corp. banking and bus. law sect. 1978—83, bd. govs. 1991—95, bd. govs. 1999—, chmn. family violence task force 1996—2000, pres.-elect 1999—2000, pres. 2000—01, co-chair multi-disciplinary practice task force 1999—2000, chmn. profl. reform initiative task force 2001—), Denver Bar Assn. (chmn. centennial com. 1990—91, pres. 1993—94, bd. trustees 1992—95, Merit award 1997), Colo. Assn. Corp. Counsel (pres. 1973—74). Home: 2032 Bellaire St Denver CO 80207-3722 Office: Davis Graham & Stubbs 1550 17th St Ste 500 Denver CO 80202-1202 E-mail: dale.harris@dgslaw.com

HARRIS, DARRYL WAYNE, publishing executive; b. Emmett, Idaho, July 29, 1941; s. Reed Ingval and Evelyn Faye (Wengreen) H.; m. Christine Sorenson, Sept. 10, 1965; children: Charles Reed, Michael Wayne, Jason Darryl, Stephanie, Ryan Joseph. B.A., Brigham Young U., 1966. Staff writer Deseret News, Salt Lake City, 1965, Post-Register, Idaho Falls, 1966-67; tech. editor Idaho Nuclear Corp., Idaho Falls, 1967-68; account exec. David W. Evans & Assos. Advt., Salt Lake City, 1968-71; pres. Harris Pub., Inc., Idaho Falls, 1971—; pub. Potato Grower of Idaho mag., 1972—, Snowmobile West mag., 1974—, Sugar Producer mag., 1974—, Blue Ribbon mag., 1987-90; Modstock mag., 1992—; pub. SnowAction mag., 1987—, Western Guide to Snowmobiling, 1988—, Houseboat Mag., 1990—, Pontoon and Deck Boat Mag., 1995—. Campaign mgr. George Hansen for Congress Com., 1974, 76; campaign chmn. Mel Richardson for Congress Com., 1986; 1st counselor to pres. Korean Mission, Ch. Jesus Christ of Latter-day Saints, Seoul, Korea, 1963, area public communications dir., Eastern Idaho, 1976-86; pres. Korea Seoul Mission, 1997-2000; High Priest, LDS Ch., 1987-91, high coun. Idaho Falls Ammon Stake, 1987-91, Ammon 8th Ward Bishopric, 1991-96; founder Blue Ribbon Coalition, 1987; v.p. Teton Peaks Council Boy Scouts Am., 1987-92; publicity chmn. Upper Snake River Scout Encampment, 1988; founder , pres. Our Land Soc., 1989-92. Mem. Agr. Editors Assn., Internat. Snowmobile Industry Assn. (Best Overall Reporting journalism award 1979, 80), Western Publs. Assn., World Champion Cutter and Chariot Racing Assn. (historian 1966-80), Nat. Snowmobile Found. (founder 1988), Kappa Tau Alpha. Lodge: Idaho Falls Kiwanis (pres. 1978, Disting. Club Pres. award 1978). Office: Harris Pub Inc 520 Park Ave Idaho Falls ID 83402-3516

HARRIS, DAVID THOMAS, immunology educator; b. Jonesboro, Ark., May 9, 1956; s. Marm Melton and Lucille Luretha (Buck) H.; m. Francoise Jacqueline Besencon, June 24, 1989; children: Alexandre M., Stefanie L., Leticia M. BS in Biology, Math. and Psychology, Wake Forest U., 1978, MS, 1980, PhD in Microbiology and Immunology, 1982. Fellow Ludwig Inst. Cancer Rsch., Lausanne, Switzerland, 1982-85; rsch. asst. prof. U. N.C., Chapel Hill, 1985-89; assoc. prof. U. Ariz., Tucson, 1989-96, prof., 1996—. Cons. Teltech, Inc. Mpls., 1990—, Advanced Biosci. Resources, 1994-95; bd. sci. advisors Cryo-Cell Internat., 1992-95; bd. dirs. Ageria, Inc., Tuscon; dir. Cord Blood Stem Cell Bank, 1992—; mem. Ariz. Cancer Ctr., Steele Meml. Children's Rsch. Ctr., Ariz. Arthritis Ctr. Program, sci. adv. bd. Cord Blood Registry, Inc., chief sci. div. Cord Blood Registry, Inc. Co-author chpts. to sci. books, articles to profls. jours.; reviewer sci. jours.; co-holder 7 scientific patents. Grantee local and fed. rsch. grants, 1988—. Mem. AAAS, Am. Assn. Immunologists, Reticuloendothelial Soc., Internat. Soc. Hematotherapy and Graft Engring., Internat. Soc. Devel. and Comparative Immunology, Scandanavian Soc. Immunology, Sigma Xi, Democrat. Mem. Ch. of Christ. Avocations: tennis, hiking, jogging, skiing, travel. Office: U Ariz Dept Microbiology Bldg 90 Tucson AZ 85721-0001 E-mail: davidh@U.Arizona.edu

HARRIS, DAVID W. state agency administrator; m. Linda Harris; two children. Grad., Ea. N.Mex. U., 1971. Trainee analyst Legis. Fin. Com., 1972; asst. fin. dir. State Hwy. Dept.; dir. property control divsn. Dept. Fin. and Adminstrn., sec. natural resources dept.; sec. fin. and adminstrn. N.Mex. Dept. Fin. and Adminstrn., until 2000. Exec. officer State Bd. Fin.; mem. State Investment Coun., Pub. Sch. Capital Outlay Coun., N.Mex. Fin. Authority, N.Mex. Cmty. Assistance Coun. With USAF, Korea. Recipient N.Mex. Disting. Pub. Svc. award, 1997. Office: Fin and Adminstrn 180 Bataan Memorial Bldg Santa Fe NM 87503-0001

HARRIS, DONALD J. economics educator; b. Jamaica; BA, London U., 1960; PhD, U. Calif., Berkeley, 1965. Asst. prof. econs. U. Ill., Urbana, 1965-67; assoc. prof. U. Wis., Madison, 1968-72; prof. Stanford (Calif.) U., 1972—. Econ. cons. UN, N.Y.C., 1966-67, Inter-Am. Devel. Bank, Washington, 1993-94; vis. fellow Cambridge (Eng.) U., 1966, 68, 77, 82, assoc. fellow Trinity Coll., 1982; disting. vis. prof. Yale U., New Haven, 1977-78; Fulbright scholar, Brazil, 1990-91, Mex., 1992. Author: Capital Accumulation and Income Distribution, 1978, Japanese ed., 1982, Spanish edit., 1984, Jamaica's Export Economy, 1997; mem. bd. editors Jour. Econ. Lit., 1979-84; contbr. articles to profl. jours. Ford Found. fellow, 1984-85. Mem. Am. Econ. Assn., Nat. Econ. Assn. Avocations: music, theater. Office: Stanford U Dept Econs Stanford CA 94305

HARRIS, EDWARD D., JR. physician; b. Phila., July 7, 1937; children: Ned, Tom, Chandler. A.B., Dartmouth Coll., 1958, grad. with honors, 1960; M.D. cum laude, Harvard U., 1962. Diplomate Am. Bd. Internal Medicine and Rheumatology (chmn. subsplty. bd. in rheumatology 1986-88). Intern Mass. Gen. Hosp., Boston, 1962-63, asst. resident, 1963-64, sr. resident, 1966-67, clin. research fellow arthritis unit, 1967-69; asst. prof. Harvard Med. Sch., Boston, 1970; from asst. prof. to prof. Dartmouth Med. Sch., Hanover, N.H., 1970-83, Eugene W. Leonard prof., 1979-83, chief connective tissue disease sect., 1970-83; mem. staff Mary Hitchcock Meml. Hosp., 1970-83; chief med. service Middlesex Gen. U. Hosp., New Brunswick, N.J., 1983—; asst. prof. Harvard U. Med. Sch., Boston, 1970; prof., chmn. medicine U. Medicine and Dentistry N.J.-Rutgers U. Med. Sch., New Brunswick, 1983-88; Arthur L. Bloomfield prof. medicine Stanford U. Sch. Medicine, 1988-95, chmn. dept. medicine, 1988-95, George DeForest Barnett prof. medicine, 1988—. Chief med. svc. Stanford U. Hosp., 1988-95; dir. Ctr. for Musculoskeletal Diseases, Stanford,

1996—; pres. med. staff, Stanford U. Hosp., 1997-99; med. dir. Internat. Med. Svc., 1997—. Editor The Pharos, 1997—. Fellow ACP (gov. No. Calif. chpt. ACP-Am. Soc. Internal Medicine 2000—); mem. Am. Rheumatism Assn. (numerous coms. 1967— , pres. 1985-86), Alpha Omega Alpha (exec. sec. 1997—, editor The Pharos 1997—). Office: Stanford U 1000 Welch Rd Ste 203 Palo Alto CA 94304-1808 E-mail: madera@stanford.edu

HARRIS, EVA, molecular biology educator; b. N.Y.C., Aug. 6, 1965; BA, Harvard U., 1987; PhD in Molecular and Cell Biology, U. Calif., Berkeley, 1993. Dir. applied molecular biology/appropriate technol. transfer program U. Calif., San Francisco, 1993—, asst. adj. prof., 1997-98, asst. prof. Sch. Pub. Health Berkeley, 1998—. John D. and Catherine T. MacArthur Found. fellow, 1997. Mem. AAAS, Am. Soc. Microbiology. Office: U Calif Sch Pub Health 239 Warren Hl Berkeley CA 94720-0001*

HARRIS, FRED R. political science educator, former senator; b. Walters, Okla., Nov. 13, 1930; s. Fred Byron and Alene (Person) H.; m. LaDonna Crawford, Apr. 8, 1949 (div. 1981); children: Kathryn, Byron, Laura.; m. Margaret S. Elliston, Sept. 5, 1982. B.A. in Polit. Sci, U. Okla., 1952, J.D. with distinction, 1954. Bar: Okla. bar 1954. Founder, sr. partner firm Harris, Newcombe, Redman & Doolin, Lawton, Okla., 1954-64; mem. Okla Senate, 1956-64, U.S. Senate from Okla., 1964-73; prof. polit. sci. U. N.Mex., Albuquerque, 1976—. Author: Alarms and Hopes, 1969, Now Is The Time, 1971, The State of the Cities: Report of the Commission on Cities in the 70's, 1972, Social Science and National Policy: The New Populism, 1973, Potomac Fever, 1977, America's Democracy, 1980, 3d edit., 1985, Readings on the Body Politic, 1987, Deadlock or Decision, 1993, In Defense of Congress, 1994; co-author: America's Legislative Processes, 1983, Understanding American Government, 1988, Quiet Riots, 1988, America's Government, 1990, Locked in the Poorhouse, 1998. Mem. Nat. Adv. Commn. Civil Disorders, 1967-68; Chmn. Democratic Nat. Com., 1969-70. Mem. Order of Coif, Phi Beta Kappa. Office: U New Mexico Dept Polit Sci Albuquerque NM 87131-0001 E-mail: fharris@unm.edu

HARRIS, HOWARD JEFFREY, marketing and printing company executive; b. Denver, June 9, 1949; s. Gerald Victor and Leona Lee (Tepper) H.; m. Michele Whealen, Feb. 6, 1975; children: Kimberly, Valerie. BFA with honors, Kansas City Art Inst., 1973; M of Indsl. Design with honors, Pratt Inst., 1975; postgrad. Graphic Arts Rsch. Ctr., Rochester Inst. Tech., 1977; Cert. Mktg. Exec., U. Utah, 1987. Indsl. designer Kivett & Myers, Architects, 1970-71, United Rsch. Corp., Denver, 1971-72; indsl. designer, asst. to v.p., pres. JFN Assocs., n.Y.C., 1972-73; dir. facility planning Abt & Assocs., Cambridge, Mass., 1973-74; pres., COO EagleDirect, Denver, 1974—; pres. Eagle Direct, Denver. Vol., chmn. bd. dirs. Stepping Stones. Recipient Small Bus. Person of Yr. award for State of Colo., SBA, 1997. Mem. Indsl. Designers Soc. Am., Graphic Arts Tech. Found., Direct Mktg. Assn., Cable TV Adminstrn. and Mktg. Assn., Mail Advt. Assn., Am. Avt. Fedn., Nat. Assn. Print Leadership (bd. dirs., chmn. mktg. com.). Democrat. Jewish. Office: 5105 E 41st Ave Denver CO 80216-4420

HARRIS, JAY TERRENCE, newspaper editor; b. Washington, Dec. 3, 1948; s. Richard James and Margaret Estelle (Burr) H.; m. Eliza Melinda Dowell, June 14, 1969 (div.); 1 child, Taifa Akida; m. Anna Christine Harris, Oct. 25, 1980; children: Jamarah Kai, Shala Marie. BA, Lincoln U., 1970, LHD (hon.), 1988. Reporter Wilmington (Del.) News-Jour., 1970-73, spl. project editor, 1974-75; instr. journalism and urban affairs Medill Sch. Journalism, Northwestern U., Evanston, Ill., 1973-75, asst. prof., 1975-82, asst. dean, 1977-82; nat. corr. Gannett News Service, Washington, 1982-84, columnist Gannet newspapers and USA Today, 1984-85; exec. editor Phila. Daily News, 1985—; v.p. Phila. Newspapers, Inc., 1987—; chmn., pub. San Jose Mercury News, 1995—. Asst. dir. Frank E. Gannett Urban Journalism Ctr., Northwestern U., 1977-82; founder, exec. dir. Consortium for Advancement of Minorities in Journalism Edn., Evanston, 1978-81; dir. Dow Jones Newspaper Fund, Princeton, N.J., 1980— ; bd. visitors John S. Knight Profl. Journalism Fellowships, Palo Alto, Calif., 1982— ; head Minorities and Communication Div. Assn. for Edn. in Journalism, 1982-83 Author: (annual census) Minority Employment in Daily Newspapers, 1978-82; co-author series articles on drug trafficking in Wilmington, 1972 (Pub. Service awards AP Mng. Editors Assn. 1972, Greater Phila. chpt. Sigma Delta Chi 1973) Past mem. bd. advisors Sch. Journalism U. Mo. Frank E. Gannett Urban Journalism fellow, 1973-74; recipient Pub. Service award Greater Phila. chpt. Sigma Delta Chi, 1973; Pub. Service award AP Mng. Editors Assn., 1972; Spl. Citation Nat. Urban Coalition, 1979; Par Excellence Disting. Service in Journalism award Operation PUSH, 1984; Drum Maj. for Justice award Southern Christian Leadership Conf., 1985 Mem. Am. Soc. Newspaper Editors (chmn. readership and rsch. com.), Women in Communication, Nat. Assn. Black Journalists, Omega Psi Phi Office: San Jose Mercury News 750 Ridder Park Dr San Jose CA 95190-0001

HARRIS, JEREMY, mayor; s. Ann Harris; m. Ramona Sachiko Akui Harris. BA, BS in Marine Biology, U. Hawaii, 1972; M in Population and Environmental Biology and Urban Ecosystems, U. Calif., Irvine. Lectr. oceanography, biology Kauai C.C.; instr. on reef walks on Kauai U. Hawaii Sea Grant Program; del. Hawaii Constl. Conv., 1978; chmn. Kauai County Council; exec. asst. to Mayor Frank F. Fasi City and County of Honolulu, 1985-86, mng. dir. of Honolulu, 1986-94, mayor, 1994—. Named Pub. Adminstr. of Yr. Am. Soc. Pub. Adminstrn., 1993, 94; recipient Merit award Internat. Downtown Assn., others. Office: Office Mayor Honolulu Hale 530 S King St Honolulu HI 96813

HARRIS, MARK O. state legislator; b. Omaha, Nov. 26, 1950; m. Michele Harris. BS, U. Albuquerque, 1975. Mem. Wyo. Ho. Reps., Cheyenne, 1989-92, Wyo. Senate, Dist. 14, Cheyenne, 1992—; mem. appropriations com. Wyo. Senate, Cheyenne, mem. travel, recreation, wildlife, and cultural com., minority caucus chair, 1995-96. With USNR, 1971-73. Mem. U.S. Steelworkers Am., Nat. Eagle Scout Assn., N.Am. Hunting Club. Democrat. Office: PO Box 345 Green River WY 82935-0345 also: Wyo Senate State Capitol Cheyenne WY 82002-0001 E-mail: mharris@senate.wyoming.com

HARRIS, PHILIP ROBERT, management and space psychologist; b. Bklyn., Jan. 22, 1926; s. Gordon Roger and Esther Elizabeth (Delahanty) H.; m. Dorothy Lipp, July 3, 1965 (dec. 1997). B.B.A., St. John's U., 1949; M.S. in Psychology, Fordham U., 1952, Ph.D., 1956; spl. student, NYU, 1948-49, Syracuse U., 1961. Lic. psychologist U. of State of N.Y., 1959, N.Y. Dir. guidance St. Francis Prep. Sch., N.Y.C., 1952-56; dir. student personnel, v.p. St. Francis Coll., N.Y.C., 1956-63; exec. dir. Assn. Human Emergency-Thomas Murray Tng. Program, 1964-66; vis. prof. Pa. State U., 1965-66; vis. prof., cons. Temple U.; sr. assoc. Leadership Resources Inc., 1966-69; v.p. Copley Internat. Corp., La Jolla, Calif., 1970-71; pres. Mgmt. and Orgn. Devel. Inc. (now Harris Internat. Ltd.), La Jolla, 1971—; edn. dir. Air/Space Am., 1988; sr. scientist Netrologic, Inc., La Jolla, Calif., 1990-93. Rsch. assoc. Calif. Space Inst., U. Calif., San Diego, 1984-90; adj. prof. Pepperdine U., U. No. Colo.; acad. adv. Command Coll., Commn. on Peace Officers Stds. and Tng. State of Calif., Dept. Justice, 1986-94; past cons. Westinghouse, N.V. Philips, I.B.M., Computer Sci. Corp. Control Data, govt. agys.; chmn. bd. dirs. United Socs. in Space, Inc., 1993-97. Author: Effective Management of Change, 1976, Improving Management Communicatio Skills, 1978, Managing Cultural Differences, 1979, 5th edit., 2000, New Worlds, New Ways, New Management, 1983, Managing Cultural Synergy, 1982, Management in Transition, 1985, Living and Working in Space, 1992, 2d edit., 1996, High Performance Leadership, 2d edit., 1994, New Work Culture, 1998; co-author: Transcultural Leadership, 1993, Developing Global Organizations, 1993, 2d edit., 2001, Multicultural Management 2000, 1998, Multicultural Law Enforcement, 1995, 2nd edit., 2001; editor: Innovations in Global Consultation, 1980, Global Strategies in Human Resource Development, 1983; author (series) New Work Culture, 3 vols., 1994-98; co-editor Manging Cultural Differences Series Butterworth-Heinemann, 1979—; mem. editl. bd. European Bus. Rev.; founding editor emeritus Space Governance Jour., 1993-98; contbr. 225 articles to profl. jours. V.p. Bklyn. Downtown Renewal Effort, 1957-59. Named to Gulf Pub. Author Hall of Fame, 1999; Fulbright prof. to India U.S. State Dept., 1962; NASA faculty fellow, 1984. Fellow AIAA (assoc.); mem. ASTD (Torch award 1975), Aviation Space Writers Assn. (journalism awards 1986, 88, 89, 93), World Bar Assn. (Space Humanitarian award1992), Nat. Space Soc., United Socs. in Space (dir. emeritus), Soc. for Human Performance in Extreme Environments, La Jolla Beach and Tennis Club. Independent. Home and Office: 2702 Costebelle Dr La Jolla CA 92037-3524 E-mail: philharris@aol.com

HARRIS, RICHARD A. film editor; Works include: (films) Downhill Racer, 1969, Dusty and Sweets McGee, 1971, The Christian Licorice Store, 1971, The Candidate, 1972, Chandler, 1972, Catch My Soul, 1974, Smile, 1975, The Bad News Bears, 1976, Semi-Tough, 1977, The Bad News Bears Go To Japan, 1978, An Almost Perfect Affair, 1979, The Island, 1980, The Toy, 1982, The Survivors, 1983, Fletch, 1985, Tiger Town, 1985, The Golden Child, 1986, Wildcats, 1986, The Couch Trip, 1988, Fletch Lives, 1989, L.A. Story, 1991, The Bodyguard, 1992, Terminator 2: Judgement Day, 1991 (Acad. award nomination, Emmy nomination), True Lies, 1994 (Emmy nomination); (TV films) A Mother's Courage: The Mary Thomas Story, 1990, My Boyfriend's Back, 1990, Indictment: The McMartin Trial (Emmy award, Outstanding Individual Achievement in Editing for a Mini Series of a Spl. 1995, ADB Cable ACF award 1995); editor (films) Last Action Hero, 1993, Titanic, 1997. Address: 3001 Old Calzada Rd Santa Ynez CA 93460-9527

HARRIS, RICHARD EUGENE VASSAU, lawyer; b. Detroit, Mar. 16, 1945; s. Joseph S. and Helen Harris; m. Milagros A. Brito; children: Catherine, Byron. AB, Albion Coll., 1967; JD, Harvard U., 1970; postdoctoral, Inst. Advanced Legal Studies, London, 1970-71. Bar: Calif. 1972. Assoc. Orrick, Herrington, Rowley & Sutcliffe, San Francisco, 1972-77; ptnr. Orrick, Herrington & Sutcliffe, San Francisco, 1978-98; pvt. practice Richard E. V. Harris Law Office, Oakland, Ca., 1998—. Faculty Calif. Tax Policy Conf., 1987, 95; spkr. univ., govtl. and profl. groups. Knox fellow Harvard U., 1970-71. Mem. ABA (urban state and local govt. sect. 1983-88, vice chmn. govt. liability com. 1982-84, antitrust law sect. state action com. 1981—, BOULDER task force 1983-84, internat. com. 1994—, litigation sect. corp. counsel com., subcom. chmn. 1980-82, 83—, vice chmn. 1982-83, tax litigation com. 1992—, co-chmn. Nat. Insts. Antitrust Liability 1983, 85, bus. law sect., SEC investigation atty.-client privilege waiver task force 1988, corp. counsel com., 1995—, conflicts of interest task force 1993-96, conflicts of interest com., 1996—, tax sect., state and local taxes com. 1989—, Ctr. for Profl. Responsibility, ABA Ethics 2000 adv. group 1999—), Am. Law Inst. (cons. restatements of law unfair competition 1991-94, governing lawyers 1991-99, torts 1993—, agy. 1996—, trusts 1996—), Bar Assn. San Francisco (ethics com., 1980—).

HARRIS, ROBERT ADRON, pharmacologist; b. El Paso, Tex., Nov. 23, 1945; s. James Buford and Maurine Harris; m. Diane Snell. BS in Chemistry, N.Mex. State U., 1967; MS in Chemistry, U. Ariz., 1970; PhD in Pharmacology, U. N.C., 1973. Postdoctoral fellow U. Calif., San Francisco, 1973-76; asst. prof. pharmacology Sch. Medicine U. Mo., Columbia, 1976-81, assoc. prof. pharmacology, 1981-83; rsch. pharmacologist Truman Meml. VA Hosp., Columbia, 1979-83; assoc. prof. pharmacology Sch. Medicine U. Colo., Denver, 1983-88, prof. pharmacology, 1988—, acting chmn. dept. pharmacology, 1989-90; assoc. rsch. career scientist VA Med. Ctr., Denver, 1983-88, rsch. career scientist, 1988—; faculty mem. Inst. Behavioral Genetics U. Colo., Boulder, 1992—. Sci. dir. VA Alcohol Rsch. Ctr., Denver, 1992—. Co-editor Internat. Rev. Neurobiology, 1992—; contbr. over 180 articles to sci. jours. Grantee VA Med. Ctr., 1979—, NIH, 1994—; recipient Merit award NIH, 1989—. Mem. AAAS, Am. Soc. Pharmacology and Exptl. Therapeutics, Soc. for Neurosci., Rsch. Soc. for Alcoholism (pres. 1993-95). Office: U Colo Health Scis Ctr 4200 E 9th Ave # 236 Denver CO 80220-3706

HARRIS, ROBERT DALTON, history educator, researcher, writer; b. Jamieson, Oreg., Dec. 24, 1921; s. Charles Sinclair and Dorothy (Cleveland) H.; m. Ethel Imus, June 26, 1971. BA, Whitman Coll., Walla Walla, Wash., 1951; MA, U. Calif., Berkeley, 1953, PhD, 1959. Tchg. asst. U. Calif., Berkeley, 1956-59; instr. history U. Idaho, Moscow, 1959-61, asst. prof., 1961-68, assoc. prof., 1968-74, prof. history, 1974-86, prof. emeritus, 1986—. Author: (Book) Necker, Reform Statesman of Ancient Regime, 1979, Necker & Revolution of 1789, 1986. 1st lt., U.S. Army, 1942-46; Ballet Folk of Moscow, Idaho, (bd. dirs., 1971-73), Historian, First United Methodist Church, Moscow, Idaho, 1989—. Mem. Am. Hist. Assn., Am. Assn. of U. Prof. Democrat. Methodist. Avocations: social dancing, violinist. Home: 928 E 8th St Moscow ID 83843-3851 E-mail: roberth@uidaho.edu

HARRIS, ROBERT M. college president; BA in Anthropology, U. Calif., Santa Barbara, 1970; MA with honors, U. Kans., 1973, PhD with honors, 1975. Life cert. cmty. coll. instr. spl. edn., counselor, supr., psychology instr., chief adminstr. Dir. Kansas state demographic studies U. Kans. Med. Ctr., United Way of Wyandotte County, 1973-75; sr. clin. rehab. psychologist Casa Colina Hosp. for Rehab. Medicine, Pomona, Calif., 1976, program mgr., 1976-77; dist. specialist programs for students devel. disabilities Chaffey C.C., Alta Loma, Calif., 1977-79, dist. dir. spl. edn., 1981, acting assoc. dean student svcs., 1981, acting supt., pres., 1985, v.p., bus. and student svcs., 1985-86, v.p. student svcs., 1981-87; pres. Sacramento City Coll., 1987—. Cons. and presenter in field. Contbr. articles to profl. publs. Bd. dirs. United Way, Sacramento, bd. chair 1998—. Named Affirmative Action Officer of Yr., 1980-81; doctoral fellow U. Kans., 1974-75; recipient various grants. Mem. Assn. of Calif. C.C. Adminstrs., Calif. C.C. Chief Student Svcs. Adminstrs. Assn. (v.p. southern sect.), Nat. Assn. of Student Pers. Adminstrs., Am. Psychol. Assn. (divsn. 22 rehab. psychology), Calif. Assn. of Post-Secondary Educators for the Disabled, Easter Seal Soc. of Superior Calif. (bd. dirs.). Office: Sacramento City Coll 3835 Freeport Blvd Sacramento CA 95822-1318

HARRIS, ROBERT NORMAN, advertising and communications educator; b. St. Paul, Feb. 11, 1920; s. Nathan and Esther (Roberts) H.; m. Paula Nidorf, May 2, 1992; children: Claudia, Robert Norman, Randolph B. B.A., U. Minn., 1940. A founder Toni Co., div. Gillette Co., 1940-55; exec. v.p. Lee King & Ptnrs., Chgo., 1955-60, Allen B. Wrisley Co., Chgo., 1960-62, North Advt., Chgo., 1962-72; pres. Robert Piguet, Ltd., Chgo., 1972-73, Westbrook/Harris, Inc., Chgo., 1973-77; exec. v.p., gen. mgr. Creamer Inc., Chgo., 1977-81; pres. The Harris Creative Group, Inc., 1981—; prof. advt. and mass communications San Jose State U. (Calif.), 1983-92. Bd. dirs. KTEH Pub. Broadcasting Sys. Found., San Jose, 1987-99, CHM Villages Golf and Country Club CATV Sys., 1995-99. Mem. NATAS, Am. Mktg. Assn., Am. Advt. Fedn., Am. Assn. Advt. Agys., Sons in Retirement (bd. dirs. 1986-90).

HARRIS, ROBERT W. lawyer; b. Hindsdale, Ill., Feb. 5, 1948; BA, U. Kans., 1970; JD, U. Denver, 1973. Bar: Colo. 1973. Formerly ptnr. Hall & Evans, Denver; pres., sr. ptnr. Harris, Karstaedt, Jamison & Powers, P.C., Englewood, Colo., 1995—. Mem. ABA. Office: Harris Karstaedt Jamison & Powers 383 Inverness Dr S Ste 400 Englewood CO 80112-5864

HARRIS, STEPHEN ERNEST, electrical engineering and applied physics educator; b. Bklyn., Nov. 29, 1936; s. Henry and Anne (Alpern) H.; m. Frances Joan Greene, June 7, 1959; children: Hilary Ayn, Craig Henry. B.S., Rensselaer Poly. Inst., 1959; M.S., Stanford U., 1961, Ph.D., 1963. Mem. tech. staff Bell Telephone Labs., Murray Hill, N.J., 1959-60; coop. student Sylvania Electric Systems, Mountain View, Calif., 1961-63; prof. elec. engring. Stanford U., 1963-79, prof. elec. engring. and applied physics, 1979—, dir. Edward L. Ginzton Lab., 1983-88, Kenneth and Barbara Oshman prof., 1988—. Chair Dept. Applied Physics, Stanford U., 1993-96. Recipient Alfred Noble prize ASCE, 1965, Curtis McGraw rsch. award Am. Soc. Engring. Edn., 1973, Davies medal for engring. achievement Rensselaer Poly. Inst., 1984, Einstein prize, 1991, Optical Soc. Am. Teaching award, 1992, Frederic Ives medal Optical Soc. Am., 1999, IEEE/LEOS Quantum Electronics award, 1994. Fellow Am. Assn. Advancement Sci., Am. Acad. Arts & Scis., IEEE (David Sarnoff award 1978), Optical Soc. Am. (Charles Hard Townes award 1985), Am. Phys. Soc.; mem. Nat. Acad. Engring., Nat. Acad. Scis. Office: Stanford Univ Edward L Ginzton Lab 450 Via Palou Mall Stanford CA 94305-4085

HARRIS, SUSAN LOUISE, financial services company executive; AB, UCLA, 1978; JD, U. So. Calif., 1981. Bar: Calif. 1981. Assoc. Lillick, McHose & Charles, 1981-85; sr. v.p., gen. counsel corp. affairs, sec. SunAmerica, Inc., L.A., 1985—. Office: SunAmerica Inc 1 Sun America Ctr Los Angeles CA 90067-6121

HARRIS, T. GEORGE, editor; b. Simpson County, Ky., Oct. 4, 1924; s. Garland and Luna (Byrum) H.; m. Sheila Hawkins, Oct. 31, 1953 (dec. Jan. 1977); children: Amos, Anne, Crane, Gardiner; m. Ann Rockefeller Roberts, Mar. 3, 1979 (div. Apr. 1993); children: Clare, Joseph, Mary Louise and Rachel Pierson; m. Jeannie Pinkerton, Sept. 12, 1998; 1 child, A.J. Clancy. Student, U. Ky., 1946; BA, Yale U., 1949. Reporter Clarksville (Tenn.) Leaf-Chronicle, 1942; corr. Time, 1949-55; Chgo. bur. chief Time-Life-Fortune, 1955-58, San Francisco bur. chief, 1960-62; sr. editor Look mag., 1962-68; editor in chief Psychology Today mag., 1969-76, 88-90, US, 1977; founding editor Am. Health mag., AH Fitness Bull., 1980-90; cons. editor U. Calif., San Diego, 1993—; editor Harvard Bus. Rev., Boston, 1992-93, Spirituality & Health - The Soul Connection, 1996-98, USCD-Connect Telecom Weekly Online, 2000—. Editor Bodywatch, PBS Network; bd. sci. advisors Inst. for the Advancement Health, ABC's 20-20 program.. Cons. editor Sci. & Spirit, Next, Runner, Somatics, Aware, Industry Week, Psychologia Contemporanea, Man the Mystery, Japan, Modern Maturity, Psychologie Heute mags., Addison-Wesley Pub. Co., Abby Press of Benedictine Order, Age Wave; editor-in-residence U. Calif., San Diego; columnist, cons. Beliefnet.com. Bd. dirs. Am. Health Found., Nat. Vol. Ctrs., Rockefeller Bros. Fund, Go Code Corp.; med. adv. com. Nat. YMCA; regent Cathedral of St. John the Devine. 2d lt. on Bastogne battlefield, F.A., AUS, WWII. Decorated Bronze Star, Air medal with 2 clusters; nominated Croix de Guerre; recipient Econ. Journalism prize U. Mo. Brotherhood award NCCJ, 1973, 85, Mag. of Yr. editing award Columbia U., Psychology Today, 1975, Am. Health, 1983, Am. Psychology Fedn. award for Lifetime Contbn., 1983, FMI-Esther Peterson award for nutrition edn., 1990, Centennial award APA, 1992, Disting. Svc. award Psychosomatic Soc., 1995, Nat. Fitness Leader award, '91 Dist. Svc. medal Inst. for Adv. Health, Pres. medal APA, 2001; named Outstanding Young Man of Chgo., 1955, Ky. Col., Am. Fitness Leader, 1987, Mag. Profl. of Yr. 2000, Educators in Journalism and Mass Media; named to Ky. Hall of Fame. Mem. Yale Club (N.Y.C.), Century Assn., La Jolla Beach and Tennis Club, Phi Beta Kappa. Episcopalian. Home and Office: 8115 Paseo Del Ocaso La Jolla CA 92037-3140 Fax: 858-459-0838

HARRIS, THEODORE EDWARD, mathematician, educator; b. Phila., Jan. 11, 1919; s. Julius and Hazel (Rosenfield) H.; m. Constance Ruth Feder, June 29, 1947; children: Stephen Joel, Marcia Faye. Student, So. Meth. U., 1935-37; BA, U. Tex., Austin, 1939; MA, Princeton U., 1946, PhD, 1947; D of Tech. (hon.), Chalmers Inst. of Tech., Gothenburg, Sweden, 1989. With Rand Corp., 1947-66, chmn. dept. math., 1959-66; prof. math. U. So. Calif., 1966-89, prof. emeritus, 1989—. Vis. asst. prof. UCLA, 1949-50; vis. assoc. prof. Columbia, 1953; vis. prof. Stanford U., 1963; lectr. U. So. Calif., 1989-97. Author: The Theory of Branching Processes, 1963; Editor: Annals of Math. Statistics, 1955-58. Served to maj. USAAF, 1942-45. Recipient Albert S. Raubenheimer disting. faculty award, 1985, disting. emeritus award U. So. Calif., 1990. Fellow AAAS, Inst. Math. Stats. (pres. 1966-67); mem. Am. Math. Soc., Nat. Acad. Scis., Phi Beta Kappa, Sigma Xi. Jewish. E-mail: THARRIS2MTHA.USC.EDU. Office: Univ So Calif Dept Math 1042 W 36th St # Pl155 Los Angeles CA 90089-0094 Fax: 213-740-2424

HARRIS, WALTER EDGAR, chemistry educator; b. Wetaskiwin, Alta., Can., June 9, 1915; s. William Ernest and Emma Louise (Humbke) H.; m. Phyllis Pangburn, June 14, 1942; children: Margaret Anne, William Edgar. BS, U. Alta., 1938, MS, 1939; PhD, U. Minn., 1944; DSc (hon.), U. Waterloo, 1987, U. Alta., 1991. Research fellow U. Minn., 1943-46; prof. analytical chemistry U. Alta., Edmonton, 1946-80, chmn. dept. chemistry, 1974-79, chmn. Pres.'s Adv. Com. on Campus Revs., 1980-90. Author: (with H.W. Habgood) Programmed Temperature Gas Chromatography, 1965, (with B. Kratchovil) Chemical Separations and Measurements, 1974, Teaching Introductory Analytical Chemistry, 1974, An Introduction to Chemical Analysis, 1981, Risk Assessment, 1997, (with H.A. Laitinen) Chemical Analysis, 1975; contbr. numerous articles to profl. jours. Decorated Order of Can., 1998; recipient Outstanding Achievement award U. Minn., 1973; Govt. Alta. Achievement award, 1974 Fellow AAAS, Royal Soc. Can.; mem. Chem. Inst. Can. (Fisher Sci. Lecture award 1969, Chem. Edn. award 1975), Am. Chem. Soc., Sigma Xi. Home: Ste 515 11148-84 Ave Edmonton AB Canada T6G 0V8 Office: U Alta Dept Chem Edmonton AB Canada T6G 2G2 E-mail: Walter.Harris@ualberta.ca

HARRIS, WARREN LYNN, development engineer; b. Albuquerque, May 8, 1966; s. Jerry Dale and Viola Guadalupe (Gutierrez) H., m. Clarissa Cosgrove, Apr. 1, 1998, 1 child: Tiffany Bellan. BS, Ariz. State U., 1988. Programming mgr. I.P.C. Computer Svcs., Inc., Tempe, Ariz., 1985-89; software sys. engr. Intel Corp., Chandler, 1990; dir. software R & D Pics, Inc., Tempe, 1990-91; dir. software R & D parics divsn. Ansoft Corp., Tempe, 1991-94, devel. engr. Phoenix, 1994—. Mem. IEEE, Assn. for Computing Machinery, Mortar Bd., Golden Key, Upsilon Pi Epsilon. Avocations: racquetball, model building, chess, pool, Star Trek collecting. Office: Ansoft Corp 4949 W Phelps Rd Glendale AZ 85306-1426

HARRISON, ETHEL MAE, financial executive; b. Ft. Dodge, Iowa, June 11, 1931; d. Arthur Melvin and Grace Gwendolyn (Hall) Cochran; m. Cleo Arden Goss, June 17, 1951 (div. 1962); m. Clarence Hobert Harrison, Dec. 23, 1965 (dec. Feb. 1993). Dipl., Internat. Corres. Schs., Riverside, Calif., 1986. Tax preparer Goss Tax Svc., Riverside, 1953-61, H & R Block, Inc., Riverside, 1972-84, supr./bookkeeper, 1974-79; owner, pres. Ethel Harrison's Tax Svc., Riverside, 1984—. Mem. NAFE, Riverside Tax Cons. Assn. (sec. 1988—), Am. Soc. Profl. and Exec. Women, Am. Inst. Profl. Bookkeepers, Soc. of Calif. Tax Profls., Nat. Assn. Tax Cons., Nat. Soc. Tax Profls., Nat. Assn. Tax Preparers, Inland Soc. Tax Cons., Nat. Taxpayers Union. Avocations: camping, fishing, photography, auto racing. Home and Office: 10460 Gramercy Pl Riverside CA 92505-1300

HARRISON, JOHN CONWAY, state supreme court justice; b. Grand Rapids, Minn., Apr. 28, 1913; s. Francis Randall and Ethlyn (Conway) H.; m. Ethel M. Strict; children: Nina Lyn, Robert Charles, Molly M., Frank R., Virginia Lee LLD, George Washington U., 1940. Bar: Mont. 1947, U.S. Dist. Ct. 1947. County atty. Lewis and Clark County, Helena, Mont., 1934-60; justice Mont. Supreme Ct., Helena, 1961-98, ret., 1998. Pres.

Mont. TB Assn., Helena, 1951-54, Am. Lung Assn., N.Y.C., 1972-73, Mont. coun. Boy Scouts Am., Great Falls, Mont., 1976-78. Col. U.S. Army Mem. ABA, Mont. Bar Assn., Kiwanis (pres. 1953), Sigma Chi. Home: 215 S Cooke St Helena MT 59601-5143

HARRISON, MARK ISAAC, lawyer; b. Pitts., Oct. 17, 1934; s. Coleman and Myrtle (Seidenman) H.; m. Ellen R. Gier, June 15, 1958; children: Lisa, Jill. AB, Antioch Coll., 1957; LLB, Harvard U., 1960. Bar: Ariz. 1961, Colo. 1991. Law clk. to justices Ariz. Supreme Ct., 1960-61; ptnr. Harrison, Harper, Christian & Dichter, Phoenix, 1966-93, Bryan Cave, LLP, Phoenix, 1993—. Adj. prof. U. Ariz. Coll. Law, 1995-97, Ariz. State Coll. Law, 2001—; nat. bd. visitors, 1996—. Co-author: Arizona Appellate Practice, 1966; editorial bd. ABA/BNA Lawyers Manual on Profl. Conduct, 1983-86; contbr. articles to profl. jours. Fellow Am. Bar Found., Am. Acad. Appellate Lawyers (pres. 1993-94); mem. ABA (chmn. commn. pub. understanding law 1984-87, standing com. profl. discipline 1976-84, chmn. 1982-84, chmn. coord. com. on professionalism 1987-89, com. on women in the profession, ethics com. 1999—, Michael Franck Profl. Responsibility award 1996), Assn. Profl. Responsibility Lawyers (pres. 1992-93), Maricopa County Bar Assn. (pres. 1970), Am. Bd. Trial Advocates, State Bar Ariz. (bd. govs. 1971-77, pres. 1975-76), Ariz. Bar Found. (pres. 1991), Am. Inns of Ct. (master, pres. Sandra Day O'Connor chpt. 1993-94), Nat. Conf. Bar Pres. (pres. 1977-78), Western States Bar Conf. (pres. 1978-79), Am. Judicature Soc. (exec. com. 1983-86, bd. dirs. 1983-87), Ariz. Civil Liberties Union, Ariz. Policy Forum (bd. dirs. 2000—), , Harvard Law Sch. Assn. (nat. exec. coun. 1980-84), Am. Law Inst. (nat. coun., lawyers com. for human rights), Law Coll. Assn. U. Ariz. (bd. dirs. 1999—). E-mila. Office: Bryan Cave 2 N Central Ave Ste 2200 Phoenix AZ 85004-4406 E-mail: ellenmark@aol.com, miharrison@bryancave.com

HARRISON, WALTER ASHLEY, physicist, educator; b. Flushing, N.Y., Apr. 26, 1930; s. Charles Allison and Gertrude (Ashley) H.; m. Lucille Prince Carley, July 17, 1954; children: Richard Knight, John Carley, William Ashley, Robert Walter. B. Engring. Physics, Cornell U., 1953; M.S., U. Ill., 1954, Ph.D., 1956. Physicist Gen. Elec. Research Labs., Schenectady, 1956-65; prof. applied physics Stanford (Calif.) U., 1965-2001, prof. emeritus, 2001—, chmn. applied physics dept., 1989-93, prof. emeritus, 2001—. Scientific adv. bd. Max Planck Inst., Stuttgart, Germany, 1989-92. Author: Pseudopotentials in the Theory of Metals, 1966, Solid State Theory, 1970, Electronic Structure and the Properties of Solids, 1980, Elementary Electronic Structure, 1999, Applied Quantum Mechanics, 2000; editor: the Fermi Surface, 1960, Proceedings of the International Conference on the Physics of Semiconductors, 1985, Proceedings of the International Conference on Materials and Mechanisms of High-Temperature Superconductivity, 1989. Guggenheim fellow, 1970-71; recipient von Humboldt sr. U.S. scientist award, 1981, 89, 94; vis. fellow Clare Hall, Cambridge U., 1970-71. Fellow Am. Phys. Soc. Home: 817 San Francisco Ct Stanford CA 94305-1021 Office: Stanford U Dept Applied Physics Stanford CA 94305-4045 E-mail: walt@stanford.edu

HARSHA, PHILIP THOMAS, aerospace engineer; b. N.Y.C., Feb. 22, 1942; s. Palmer and Catherine (Redinger) H.; m. Jean Ann Quinn, Oct. 23, 1965; children: Peter Charles, Evan Michael. BS in Engring. Sci., SUNY, Stony Brook, 1962, MS in Engring. Sci., 1964; PhD in Aerospace Engring., U. Tenn., 1970. Combustion rsch. engr. GE, Cin., 1964-67; lead rsch. engr. Aro, Inc., Arnold Engring. Devel. Ctr., Tenn., 1969-74; rsch. specialist R & D Assoc., Marina Del Rey, Calif., 1974-76; divsn. mgr. Sci. Applications Internat. Corp., Chatsworth, 1976-85; chief aero. scientist Lockheed Aero. Sys. Group, Burbank, 1985-88; chief project engr. Rocketdyne divsn. Rockwell Internat., Canoga Park, 1988-90; dep. program dir. Nat. Aero-Space Plane Program, 1990-95; program mgr. Boeing North Am., Inc., Seal Beach, Calif., 1994—. Contbr. articles to profl. jours. Recipient Disting. Alumnus award U. Tenn. Space Inst., 1984. Mem. AIAA, ASME, N.Y. Acad. Sci., Sigma Xi. Republican. Methodist. Home: 1607 Ocean Ave Seal Beach CA 90740-6548 Office: The Boeing Co 2401 E Wardlow Rd Long Beach CA 90807-5309

HART, EDWARD LEROY, poet, educator; b. Bloomington, Idaho, Dec. 28, 1916; s. Alfred Augustus and Sarah Cecilia (Patterson) H.; m. Eleanor May Coleman, Dec. 15, 1944 (dec. Dec. 1990); children: Edward Richard, Paul LeRoy, Barbara, Patricia; m. Leah Yates Bryson, Apr. 30, 1993. BS, U. Utah, 1939; MA, U. Mich., 1941; DPhil (Rhodes scholar), Oxford (Eng.) U., 1950. Instr. U. Utah, Salt Lake City, 1946; asst. prof. U. Wash., Seattle, 1949-52, Brigham Young U., Provo, Utah, 1952-55, assoc. prof., 1955-59, prof., 1959-82, prof. emeritus, 1982—. Vis. prof. U. Calif., Berkeley, 1959-60, Ariz. State U., summer 1968. Author: Minor Lives, 1971, Instruction and Delight, 1976, Mormom in Motion, 1978; (poems) To Utah, 1979, Poems of Praise, 1980; More Than Nature Needs, 1982, God's Spies, 1983; contbr. articles to profl. jours. Lt. USNR, 1942-46. Am. Philos. Soc. grantee, 1964; First prize in poetry and biography Utah State Arts Coun., 1973, 75; Fulbright-Hays sr. lectr. Pakistan, 1973-74; recipient Charles Redd award Utah Acad., 1976, Coll. Humanities Disting. Faculty award Brigham Young U., 1977, presdl. citation Brigham Young U. Commencement, 1998. Fellow Am. Coun. Learned Socs., Found. Econ. Edn.; mem. Phi Beta Kappa, Phi Kappa Phi. Democrat. Mormon. Home: 1401 Cherry Ln Provo UT 84604-2848 Office: Brigham Young U Dept English Provo UT 84602

HART, FREDERICK MICHAEL, law educator; b. Flushing, N.Y., Dec. 5, 1929; s. Frederick Joseph and Doris (Laurian) H.; m. Joan Marie Monaghan, Feb. 13, 1956; children: Joan Marie, Ellen, Christiane, F. Michael, Margaret, Andrew, Brigid, Patrick. B.S., Georgetown U., 1951, J.D., 1955; LL.M., N.Y. U., 1956; postgrad., U. Frankfurt, Germany, 1956-57. Lectr., dir. food law program N.Y. U., N.Y.C., 1957-58, asst. prof., 1958-59; prof. law Albany Law Sch., Union U., 1959-61, Boston Coll., 1961-66, Law Sch., U. N.Mex., Albuquerque, 1966—, dean, 1971-79, acting dean, 1985-86; dir. Law Sch., U. N.Mex. (Indian Law Center), 1967-69; vis. prof. U. Calif., Davis, spring 1981. Pres., chmn. bd. trustees Law Sch. Admission Test Council, 1974-76 Author: Forms and Procedures Under the Uniform Commercial Code, 1963, Uniform Commercial Code Reporter-Digest, 1965, Handbook on Truth in Lending, 1969, Commercial Paper Under the U.C.C, 1972, Student Guide to Secured Transactions, 1985, Student Guide to Sales, 1987; editor: Am. Indian Law Newsletter, 1968-70. Served to lt. USAF, 1951-53. Mem. ABA (law sch. accreditation com. 1986-93, skills tng. com. 1995-98, nominating com. 1987), Order of Coif, Phi Delta Phi. Roman Catholic. Home: 1505 Cornell Dr NE Albuquerque NM 87106-3703 Office: U NMex Sch Law 1117 Stanford Dr NE Albuquerque NM 87106-3700

HART, JOHN EDWARD, lawyer; b. Portland, Oreg., Nov. 21, 1946; s. Wilbur Elmore and Daisy Elizabeth (Bowen) H.; m. Bianca Mannheimer, Mar. 29, 1968 (div. 1985); children: Ashley Rebecca, Rachel Bianca, Eli Jacob; m. Serena Callahan, Nov. 9, 1991; 1 child, Katelyn Elizabeth. Student, Oreg. State U., 1965-66; BS, Portland State U., 1971; JD, Lewis and Clark Coll., 1974. Bar: Oreg. 1974, U.S. Dist. Ct. Oreg. 1974, U.S. Ct. Appeals (9th cir.) 1975. Ptnr. Schwabe, Williamson and Wyatt, Portland, 1973-92, Hoffman, Hart & Wagner, Portland, 1992—. Adj. faculty U. Oreg. Dental Sch., 1987—; legal cons. Oreg. Chpt. Obstetricians, Gynecologists, Portland, 1985—, Am. Cancer Soc. Mammography Project, 1987—. Contbr. articles to profl. jours. Co-chmn. Alameda Sch. Fair, Portland, 1983. With U.S. Army, 1967-68. Mem. ABA, Am. Coll. Trial Lawyers, Am. Bd. Trial Advocates (pres. 1995) Am., Inns of Ct., Oreg. State Bar Assn., Oreg. Assn. Def. Counsel (pres. 1989), Multnomah Athletic Club. Democrat. Presbyterian. Avocations: jogging, weight lifting, outdoor activities. Office: Hoffman Hart & Wagner 1000 SW Broadway Ste 2000 Portland OR 97205-3072

HART, JOHN H. communications professional; Former positions in network architecture/product devel. with Control Data Corp., South Cen. Bell, So. Bell.; former v.p. engring. and advanced devel. Vitalink Comms. Corp.; sr. v.p., chief tech. officer 3Com Corp. Mem. IEEE. Office: 3Com Corp 5400 Bayfront Plz Santa Clara CA 95054-3601

HART, JOHN LEWIS (JOHNNY HART), cartoonist; b. Endicott, N.Y., Feb. 18, 1931; s. Irwin James and Grace Ann (Brown) H.; m. Bobby Jane Hatcher, Apr. 26, 1952; children: Patti Sue, Perri Ann. Ed. pub. schs. Free-lance cartoonist, 1954-58; commerical artist GE, Johnson City, NY, 1957-58; syndicated cartoonist, 1958—. Comic strip, B.C., nationally syndicated, 1958—, (with Brant Parker) The Wizard of Id, 1964—; collections include: Hey B.C., 1958, Hurray for B.C., 1958, Back to B.C., 1959, B.C. Strikes Back, 1961, What's New B.C., 1962, B.C.- Big Wheel, 1963, B.C. is Alive and Well, 1964, The King is a Fink, 1964, Take a Bow, B.C., 1965, The Wonderous Wizard of Id, 1965, B.C. on the Rocks, 1966, The Peasants are Revolting, 1966, B.C. Right On, 1967, B.C. Cave In, 1967, Remember the Golden Rule, 1967, There's A Fly in My Swill, 1967, The Wizard's Back, 1968, B.C., 1972, B.C. Cartoon Book, 1973. Served with USAF, 1950-53, Korea. Recipient Best Humor Strip awards, Nat. Cartoonists Soc., 1967-71; Reuben Award, Nat. Cartoonist Soc., 1969, named Outstanding Cartoonist of Year, 1968; Yellow Kid award, 1970; Internat. Congress Comics for best cartoonist, Lucca, Italy; Best Humor Strip award, French Comics Council, 1971; Public Service Award, NASA, 1972. Mem. Nat. Comics Council, Nat. Cartoonists Soc. Achievements include premiering nationally pub. cartoon in Sat. Eve. Post, 1954. Office: care Creators Syndicate 5777 W Century Blvd Ste 700 Los Angeles CA 90045-5675

HART, JOSEPH H. bishop; b. Kansas City, Mo., Sept. 26, 1931; Ed., St. John Sem., Kansas City, St. Meinrad Sem., Indpls. Ordained priest Roman Catholic Ch., 1956; consecrated titular bishop of Thimida Regia and aux. bishop Cheyenne Wyo., 1976; apptd. bishop of Cheyenne, 1978. Office: Bishops Residence Chancery Office PO Box 1468 Cheyenne WY 82003-0426

HART, MARY, television talk show host; b. Sioux Falls, S.D., Nov. 8, 1951; m. Burt Sugarman, Apr. 8, 1989; 1 child. BA, Augustana College, 1972. Co-host, prodr. Danny's Day, Oklahoma City; co-host PM Mag., L.A., 1978, The Regis Philbin Show, N.Y.C., 1981-92, Entertainment Tonight, Hollywood, 1982—; co-owner Customer's Last Stand. Host: Tournament of Roses Parade, Macy's Thankgiving Day Parade; other TV appearences include (miniseries) Hollywood Wives, 1985, Circus of the Stars, Good Morning America, Blossom, Coach; exec. prodr., host Mary Hart Presents: Love in the Public Eye, 1990, Mary Hart Presents: Power in the Public Eye, 1990; musical debut Dolly, ABC-TV; headliner, dancer, singer, Las Vegas debut Golden Nugget, 1988, Resorts Internat., Atlantic City; videos include: Shape Up with Mary Hart, 1989, Mary Hart: Fit and Firm, 1990. Office: Paramount TV 5555 Melrose Ave Los Angeles CA 90038-3112

HARTENBACH, DAVID LAWRENCE, school system administrator; b. St. Louis, Dec. 6, 1934; s. Henry Charles and Loretta S. (Schwarz) H. BA, St. Louis U., 1958, MEd, 1960; EdD in Sacred Theology, U. No. Colo., 1981. Cert. adminstr., Colo. Adminstrv. intern St. Louis U. H.S., 1966-67, asst. prin., 1967-68; prin. Regis H.S. Archdiocese of Denver, 1968-70; prin. Benton Harbor (Mich.) H.S., 1970-72; prin. W.C. Hinkley H.S. Aurora (Colo.) Pub. Schs., 1972-77, exec. dir. H.S.'s, 1977-86, assoc. supt. instrn., 1986-89, assoc. supt. aux., 1989-93, supt. schs., 1993—. Mem. state com. Colo. North Ctrl. Assn., Greeley, 1976-83. Membership chmn. Centennial Dist. Unit PTA, Aurora, 1993—; mem. human rels. com. City of Aurora, 1978-84. Named Colo. Supt. of Yr., Nat. Sch. Bds. Assn., 1995; grantee Ford Found., 1965-66, Nat. Acad. Rsch. in Vocat. Edn., 1979. Mem. ASCD, Nat. Assn. Secondary Sch. Prins. (nat. com. large secondary schs. 1980-83, adminstrv. intern J. Lloyd Trump grantee 1966-67), Am. Assn. Sch. Adminstrs., Colo. Assn. Sch. Bds., Colo. Assn. Sch. Execs., Kiwanis (past pres. Centennial chpt.). Avocations: golfing, fishing, sports, music. Office: Aurora Pub Schs 1085 Peoria St Aurora CO 80011-6203

HARTER, CAROL CLANCEY, university president, English language educator; m. Michael T. Harter, June 24, 1961; children: Michael R., Sean P. BA, SUNY, Binghamton, 1964, MA, 1967, PhD, 1970; LHD, Ohio U., 1989. Instr. SUNY, Binghamton, 1969-70; asst. prof. Ohio U., Athens, 1970-74, ombudsman, 1974-76, v.p., dean students, 1976-82, v.p. for adminstrn., assoc. prof., 1982-89; pres., prof. English SUNY, Geneseo, 1989-95; pres. U. Nev., Las Vegas, 1995—. Co-author: (with James R. Thompson) John Irving, 1986, E.L. Doctorow, 1990; author dozens of presentations and news columns; contbr. articles to profl. jours. Bd. dirs., mem. exec. com. NCAA, 2000—. Mem. CIEE (bd. dirs. 1997—). Office: U Nev Office Pres 4505 S Maryland Pkwy # 1001 Las Vegas NV 89154-1001 E-mail: harter@ccmail.nevada.edu

HARTER, LAFAYETTE GEORGE, JR. economics educator emeritus; b. Des Moines, May 28, 1918; s. Lafayette George and Helen Elizabeth (Ives) H.; m. Charlotte Mary Toshach, Aug. 23, 1950; children— Lafayette George III, James Toshach, Charlotte Helen. B.A. in Bus. Adminstrn, Antioch Coll., 1941; M.A. in Econs, Stanford, 1948, Ph.D., 1960. Instr. Menlo Coll., Menlo Park, Calif., 1948-50; instr. Coll. of Marin, Kentfield, 1950-60; prof. econs. dept. Oreg. State U., 1960-85, prof. emeritus, 1985—, chmn. dept., 1967-71. Mem. panel arbitrators Fed. Mediation and Conciliation Svc., 1965-84, Oreg. Conciliation Svc., 1967-84; mem. Univ. Ctrs. for Rational Alternatives. Author: John R. Commons: His Assault on Laissez-faire, 1962, Labor in America, 1957, Economic Responses to a Changing World, 1972; editorial bd. Jour. Econ. Issues, 1981-84. Assoc. campaign chmn. Benton United Good Neighbor Fund, 1970-72, campaign chmn., v.p., 1972-73, pres., 1973-74, vice chmn.; pub. mem. Adv. Commn. on Unemployment Compensation, 1972, 73, chmn., 1974-78; Bd. dirs. Oreg. Coun. Econ. Edn., 1971-89; pub. mem. local profl. responsibilities Oreg. State Bar Assn., 1980-83; pub. mem. Oreg. Coun. on Ct. Procedures, 1985-93, bd. mem. Community Econs. of Corp., Community Econ. Stabilization Corp. Lt. comdr. USNR, 1941-46. Mem. AAUP, Am. Arbitration Assn. (pub. employment disputes panel 1970-92), Am. Western Econ. Assns., Indsl. Rels. Rsch. Assn., Am. Assn. for Evolutionary Econs., Oreg. State Employees Assn. (v.p. faculty chpt. 1972, pres. 1973), Am. Assn. Ret. Persons (pres. local chpt. 1992-93), Corvallis Retirement Village (fin. com., bd. dirs.). Democrat. Mem. United Ch. of Christ (moderator 1972, 73; mem. fin. com. Oreg. conf. 1974-82, dir. 1978-81, mem. personnel com. 1983-85). Home: 3755 NW Van Buren Ave Corvallis OR 97330-4952

HARTKE, STEPHEN PAUL, composer, educator; b. Orange, N.J., July 6, 1952; s. George William Hartke, Jr. and Priscilla Nancy (Redfearn) Elfrey; m. Lisa Louise Stidham, Sept. 12, 1981; 1 child, Alexander Stidham. BA magna cum laude, Yale U., 1973; MA, U. Pa., 1976; PhD, U. Calif., Santa Barbara, 1982. Advt. mgr. Theodore Presser Co., Bryn Mawr, Pa., 1977-78; advt. and art dir. European Am. Music Corp., Clifton, N.J., 1978-79; ednl. dir. Carl Fischer Inc., N.Y.C., 1980; Fulbright prof. composition U. São Paulo, Brazil, 1984-85; prof. composition Sch. Music U. So. Calif., L.A., 1987—. Vis. composer Coll. Creative Studies U. Calif., Santa Barbara, 1981-83, 85-87; composer-in-residence L.A. Chamber Orch., 1988-92. Composer: Caoine, 1980, Sonata-Variations for violin and piano, 1984 (Kennedy Friedheim award 1985), Oh Them Rats Is Mean In My Kitchen, 1985, Pacific Rim for orch., 1988, The King of the Sun, 1988, Symphony Number 2, 1990, Concerto for violin and orch., 1992, Wulfstan at the Millennium, 1995, The Ascent of the Equestrian in a Balloon, 1995, Sons of Noah, 1996, The Horse with the Lavender Eye, 1997, Piano Sonata, 1998, The Rose of the Winds, 1998; recordings on CRI, New World Records, ECM EMI record labels. Recipient Acad. award AAAL, 1993, Rome prize Am. Acad. in Rome, 1992, Stoeger award Lincoln Ctr. Chamber Music Soc., 1997; Composer-in-Residence grantee Nat. Endowment for Arts (1990, 91), Commn. grantee Koussevitzky Music Found., 1992, Fromm Found. Commn. grantee, 1994, Inst. for Am. Music Commn. grantee; Guggenheim fellow, 1997. Mem. Opera Am., Am. Mus. Ctr. Office: U So Calif Sch Music 308 University Park Los Angeles CA 90089-0001

HARTL, JOHN GEORGE, film critic; b. Wenatchee, Wash., June 28, 1945; s. David and Georgiann (MacLean) H. BA in Journalism, U. Wash., 1967. Film critic Seattle Times, 1966-2001; freelance writer Seattle, 2001—. Avocations: swimming, reading, camping. Office: Seattle Times PO Box 70 Fairview Ave N & John St Seattle WA 98111-0070 E-mail: johnhart.@yahoo.com

HARTLEY, BOB, hockey coach; b. Hawkesbury, Ont., Can., Sept. 7, 1960; m. Micheline; children: Kristine, Steve. Coach Hawkesbury Hawks, 1987-91; head coach Laval Titans, 1991-93, Cornwall Aces, 1993-94, 1994-95; coach Hershey Bears, 1996-98; head coach Colo. Avalanche, 1998—. Office: care Colo Avalanche Pepsi Ctr Arena 1000 Chopper Cir Denver CO 80204-5808

HARTLEY, JAMES EDWARD, lawyer; b. Orange, N.J., Nov. 4, 1949; s. George and Carolyn (Stewart) H.; m. Judy Franklin, Mar. 1, 1986; 1 child, Jonathan. BA, U. Calif., Berkeley, 1971, JD, 1974. Bar: Colo. 1974, U.S. Dist. Ct. Colo. 1974, U.S. Ct. Appeals (10th cir.) 1975, U.S. Supreme Ct. 1981, U.S. Ct. Appeals (Fed. cir.) 1993. Assoc. Holland & Hart, Denver, 1974-80, ptnr., 1980—. Adj. prof. Denver U. Law Sch., 1985-86. Co-author: Private Litigation Under Section 7 of the Clayton Act: Law and Policy, 1989, Antitrust Pitfalls in Outpatient Services, 1992, Rule of Reason Monograph, 1999, State Antitrust Practice and Procedure, 1999; asst. editor: ABA Antitrust Law Jour., 1994-98. Mem. ABA (chair ann. rev. antitrust law devels. 2000), Nat. Health Lawyers Assn., Colo. Bar Assn., Denver Bar Assn., Order of Coif, Phi Beta Kappa. Home: 2540 Briarwood Dr Boulder CO 80305-6804 Office: Holland & Hart LLP 555 17th St Ste 3200 Denver CO 80202-3950

HARTLEY, MARY, state legislator; b. Bronx, N.Y., Aug. 16, 1954; m. John Hartley; three children. Student, Air Force C.C. Mem. Ariz. Senate, Dist. 20, Phoenix, 1994—; mem. family svcs. com., mem. health com. Active Alhambra Elem. Sch. Dist. Governing Bd., DES Child Care Adv. Com., Ariz. State PTA, Kids Voting, Coalition for Tobacco Free Ariz. Recipient award of excellence All Ariz. Sch. Bd., 1995. Mem. MADD, Nat. Assn. for Partnership Edn. (award 1992), Sierra Club, Audubon Coun. Democrat. Office: State Capitol Bldg 1700 W Washington St Ofc 315 Phoenix AZ 85007-2812 also: 4118 W San Juan Ave Phoenix AZ 85019-2008 E-mail: mhartley@azleg.state.az.us

HARTMAN, HOWARD LEVI, mining engineering educator, consultant; b. Indpls., Aug. 7, 1924; s. Howard Levi and Catherine Gladys (Miller) H.; m. Bonnie Lee Sherrill, June 8, 1947; children: Sherilyn Hartman Knoll, Greg Alan. Student, Colo. Sch. Mines, 1942-44; BS, Pa. State U., 1946, MS, 1947; PhD, U. Minn., 1953. Registered profl. engr., Colo. Instr. Pa. State U., University Park, 1947-48, prof., dept. head and assoc. dean, 1957-67; mining engr. Phelps Dodge Corp., Bisbee, Ariz., 1948-49; state mine dust engr. Mine Inspector's Office, Phoenix, 1949-50; instr. U. Minn., Mpls., 1950-54; from asst. prof. to assoc. prof. Colo. Sch. Mines, Golden, 1954-57; prof., dean Calif. State U., Sacramento, 1967-71, Vanderbilt U., Nashville, 1971-80; Drummond endowed chair mining engring. U. Ala., Tuscaloosa, 1980-89, consulting mining engr., 1989—. Chmn. Fed. Metal and Nonmetallic Mine Safety Bd. Rev., Washington, 1971-75; Warren lectr. U. Minn., 1965; Disting. lectr. Can. Inst. Mining and Metallurgy, 1966; cons. engr. Standard Oil N.J., Tulsa, 1961-64, Ingersoll-Rand Co., Bedminster, N.J., 1964-66, Inst. for Technol. Research, São Paulo, Brazil, 1977, 85, Bechtel Corp., San Francisco, 1982-85. Author, editor various books including: Mine Ventilation and Air Conditioning, 1971, 82, 97, Introductory Mining Engineering, 1987; contbr. articles to profl. jours.; sr. editor SME Mining Engineering Handbook, 1992. Mem. Human Rights Commn., Nashville, 1975-79. Served to lt. (j.g.) USNR, 1942-44. Recipient Faculty Svc. award Nat. Univ. Continuing Edn. Assn., 1985, Howard N. Eavenson award Soc. Mining, Metallurgy and Exploration, 1992, Jackling award, 1990, Alumni Scholar medal Pa. State U., 1996. Mem. Soc. Mining, Metallurgy and Exploration (disting. mem., chmn. com., Mineral Industries Edn. award 1965, Book Pub. award 1982, Hartman Mine Ventilation award 1989), mem. Am. Soc. Engring. Edn., Met. Opera Guild, Nat. Acad. Engring., Sigma Xi, Kappa Sigma. Democrat. Presbyterian (elder). Club: Yosemite Assn. (El Portal, Calif.). Avocations: hiking, opera, color photography. Home: 4052 Alex Ln Carmichael CA 95608-6728

HARTMAN, ROBERT LEROY, artist, educator; b. Sharon, Pa., Dec. 17, 1926; s. George Otto and Grace Arvada (Radabaugh) H.; m. Charlotte Ann Johnson, Dec. 30, 1951; children: Mark Allen, James Robert. BFA, U. Ariz., 1951, MA, 1952; postgrad., Colo. Springs Fine Arts Center, 1947, 51, Bklyn. Mus. Art Sch., 1953-54. Instr. architecture, allied arts Tex. Tech. Coll., 1955-58; asst. prof. art U. Nev., Reno, 1958-61; mem. faculty dept. art U. Calif., Berkeley, 1961—, prof., 1972-91, prof. emeritus, 1991—, chmn. dept., 1974-76. Mem. Inst. for Creative Arts, U. Calif., 1967-68 One man exhbns. include, Bertha Schafer Gallery, N.Y.C., 1966, 69, 74, Santa Barbara Mus. Art, 1973, Cin. Art Acad., 1975, Hank Baum Gallery, San Francisco, 1973, 75, 78, San Jose Mus. Art, 1983, Bluxome Gallery, San Francisco, 1984, 86, U. Art Mus., Berkeley, 1986, Instituto D'Arte Dosso Dossi, Ferrara, Italy, 1989, Victor Fischer Galleries, San Francisco, 1991, Triangle Gallery, San Francisco, 1992, 93, 95, 97, 99, 2000, 01, Augusta State U., 1998, Mary Pauline Gallery, Augusta, Ga., 2001; group exhbns. include Richmond Mus., 1966, Whitney Mus. Biennial, 1973, Oakland Mus., 1976, San Francisco Arts Commn. Gallery, 1985 (award), Earthscape Expo '90 Photo Mus., Osaka, Japan, 1990, In Close Quarters, American Landscape Photography Since 1968, Princeton Art Mus., 1993, Facing Eden: 100 Years of Landscape Art in The Bay Area, San Francisco, 1995, Colorado Springs Fine Arts Ctr., 1998; represented in permanent collections, Nat. Collections Fine Arts, Colorado Springs Fine Arts Center, Corcoran Gallery, San Francisco Art Inst., Roswell Mus., Princeton Art Mus. U. Calif. humanities research fellow, 1980 Office: U Calif Dept Art Berkeley CA 94720-0001

HARTMAN, SUSAN P(ATRICE), adult education administrator; Dir. adult edn. Front Range C.C., Westminster, Colo., 1995—. Recipient Regional Person of Yr. award, 1992. Office: Cmty Learning Ctr Front Range Community Coll Westminster CO 80031

HARTMANN, WILLIAM KENNETH, astronomy scientist; b. June 6, 1939; m. Gayle Harrison, Mar. 22, 1970; 1 child, Amy. BS in Physics, Pa. State U., 1961; MS in Geology, U. Ariz., 1965, PhD in Astronomy, 1966. Asst. prof. Lunar and Planetary Lab., U. Ariz., 1967-70; assoc. and sr. scientist IIT Research Inst., 1970-72; sr. scientist Planetary Sci. Inst., Sci. Applications Internat. Corp., Tucson, 1972-95, Planetary Sci. Inst., San Juan Rsch. Inst., 1995—. Co-investigator 1971 Mariner 9 Mars Mission, 1971-72, Mars Observer Mission, 1991, Mars Global Surveyor Mission, 1996, Russian Mars 96 Mission; vis. assoc. prof. Inst. for Astronomy, U. Hawaii; affiliate faculty U. Hawaii at Hilo, 1990—, U. Ariz., 1993—; cons. Smithsonian Air and Space Mus., 1977; photog. cons. House Select Com. on Assassinations, 1978-79; mem. various coms. NASA, 1978—; co-organizer Kona Conf. on Origin of Moon, 1984; mem. com. on planetary exploration NRC, 1984-87. Author: Astronomy: The Cosmic Journey, 1978, last edit., 1993, Moons and Planets. 1972, 4th edit., 1999, Out of the Cradle, 1984, Cycles of Fire, 1987, The History of Earth, 1991, Mars Underground, 1997; co-author: The Grand Tour: A Traveller's Guide to the Solar System, 1981, last edit., 1993; co-editor: Origin of the Moon, 1986, Desert Heart, 1989; prin. editor: In the Stream of Stars: The Soviet-American Space Art Book, 1990; also numerous tech. articles to sci. publs. Co-winner 1965-66 Ninninger Meteorite award; Asteroid 3341 named Hartmann in honor of his rsch. on solar system evolution; 1st recipient Carl Segan medal Am. Astron. Soc., 1997. Office: Planetary Sci Inst 620 N 6th Ave Tucson AZ 85705-8331

HARTSBURG, CRAIG WILLIAM, professional hockey coach; b. Stratford, Ont., Can., June 29, 1959; Grad. H.S., Sault Ste. Marie, Ont., Can. Profl. hockey player Minn. North Stars, 1979-89, asst. coach, 1989-90, Phila. Flyers, 1990-94; head coach Chgo. Blackhawks, 1995-98, Mighty Ducks of Anaheim, 1998—. Recipient Max Kaminsky Meml. trophy, 1978-77; named OHA All-Star 2d team, 1978-77; played in NHL All-Star Game, 1980, 82, 83. Office: Mighty Ducks Anaheim 2695 E Katella Ave PO Box 61077 Anaheim CA 92803-6177

HARTSHORN, TERRY O. health facility administrator; b. 1944; Adminstrv. sec. Centinela Valley Hosp., Inglewood, Calif., 1965-68, adminstrv. asst., 1969; adminstr., cons. Community Health Svc., USPHS, L.A., 1969-71; adminstr. Luth. Hosp. Soc. So. Calif., L.A., 1971-73, Moore-White Med. Clinic, L.A., 1973-76; chmn. Pacificare Health Systems, Inc., Cypress, Calif., 1977—, chmn., pres., CEO Burbank, 1993—; chmn. bd., pres., CEO UniHealth Am., Inc., Burbank, 1993—. Office: Pacificare Health 3120 Lake Center Dr. Burbank CA 92704

HARTSOUGH, GAYLA ANNE KRAETSCH, management consultant; b. Lakewood, Ohio, Sept. 16, 1949; d. Vernon W. and Mildred E. (Austin) Kraetsch; m. James N. Heller, Aug. 20, 1972 (div. 1977); m. Jeffrey W. Hartsough, Mar. 12, 1983; 1 child, Jeffrey Hunter Kraetsch Hartsough. BS, Northwestern U., 1971; EdM, Tufts U., 1973; MEd, PhD, U. Va., 1978. Vol. VISTA, Tenn., 1970-71; asst. tchr. Perkins Sch. for the Blind, Watertown, Mass., 1971-72; resource tchr. Fairfax (Va.) County Pub. Schs., 1972-76; asst. dir. ctr. U. Va., Charlottesville, 1976-78; sr. program officer Acad. for Edn. Devel., Washington, 1978-80; mng. cons. Cresap/Towers Perrin, Washington and L.A., 1980-86; pres. KH Consulting Group, L.A., 1986—. Mem. nat. adv. coun. Northwestern U. Sch. Speech, Evanston, Ill., 1992—; cons. in field. Contbr. more than 20 articles to profl. jours. Co-founder L.A. Higher Edn. Roundtable, L.A., 1987-94; mem. nat. adv. coun., co-chair for Sch. of Speech Campaign $1 Billion, Northwestern U.; mem. Coun. 100 Northwestern U., 1999—. Recipient Outstanding Woman of Achievement award Century City C. of C., 1991. Mem. Orgn. Women Execs. (past pres., bd. dirs. L.A. 1986-95). Home: 15624 Royal Ridge Rd Sherman Oaks CA 91403-4207 Office: KH Consulting Group 1901 Ave Of Stars Ste 1900 Los Angeles CA 90067-6020 Fax: 310-203-5419. E-mail: khcggak@aol.com

HARTUNG, THOMAS F. state legislator; b. Eugene, Oreg., June 11, 1927; m. Beverly Hartung; 5 children. BS in Agr. Econs., Oreg. State U., 1950; postgrad., U. Oreg. Agrl. cons.; owner Hartung Meat Co.; mem. Oreg. Legislature, Salem, 1971—, chair edn. com., mem. rev. com., mem. subcom. on edn. Past chair Beaverton Sch. Bd.; co-founder Beaverton Edn. Found.; past chair Oreg. Ethics Commn. Republican. Protestant. Home: 13975 NW Burton Rd Portland OR 97229-4326 Office: S-212 State Capitol Salem OR 97310-0001

HARTWELL, LELAND HARRISON, geneticist, educator; b. Los Angeles, Oct. 30, 1939; s. Majorie (Taylor) H.; m. Theresa Naujack. BS, Calif. Inst. Tech., 1961; PhD, MIT, 1964. Postdoctoral fellow Salk Inst., 1964-65; asst. prof. U. Calif., Irvine, 1965-67, assoc. prof., 1967-68, U. Washington, Seattle, 1968-73, prof., 1973—; pres., dir. Fred Hutchison Cancer Rsch. Ctr., Seattle, 1997—. Rsch. prof. Am. Cancer Soc., 1990—. Recipient Eli Lilly award, 1973, NIH Merit award, 1990, GM Sloan award, 1991, Hoffman LaRoche Mattia award, 1991, Gairdner Found. Internat. award, 1992, Simon Shubitz award U. Chgo., 1992, Brandeis U. Rosenstiel award, 1993, Sloan Kettering Cancer Ctr. Katherine Berkan Judd award, 1994, Genetics Soc. of Am. medal, 1994, MGH Warren Triennial prize, 1995, Keith Porter award Am. Soc. Cell Biology, 1995, Carnegie Mellon Dickson award, 1996, Louisa Gross Horwitz prize Columbia U., 1995, Albert Lasker Basic Med. Rsch. award Albert and Mary Lasker Found., 1998, Brinker Internat. award for basic sci. Susan G. Komen Breast Cancer Found., 1998, Disting. Alumni award Calif. Inst. Tech., 1999, City of Medicine award, 1999, medal of honor Am. Cancer Soc., 1999, Léopold Giffuel prize Assn. pour la Recherche sur le Cancer, France, 2000, The Massry prize The Meira and Shaul G. Massry Found.; Guggenheim fellow, 1983-84; Am. Bus. Cancer Rsch. grantee, 1983—; Am. Cancer Soc. scholar; laureate Passano Found., 1996. Mem. NAS, AAAS, Am. Soc. Microbiology, Am. Soc. Cell Biology, Genetics Soc. Am. (pres. 1990). Office: Fred Hutchinson Cancer Rsch Ctr 1100 Fairview Ave N Seattle WA 98109-4417

HARUTUNIAN, ALBERT T(HEODORE), III, judge; b. San Diego, May 15, 1955; s. Albert Theodore Jr. and Elsie Ruth H.; m. Rebecca Blair, Oct. 16, 1999. BA, Claremont McKenna Coll., 1977; JD, U. Calif., Berkeley, 1980. Bar: Calif. 1980, U.S. Dist. Ct. (so. dist.) Calif. 1980, U.S. Ct. Apppeals (9th cir.) 1982, U.S. Supreme Ct. 1984. Law clk. to Hon. Howard B. Turrentine U.S. Dist. Ct., San Diego, 1980-81; assoc. Luce, Forward, Hamilton & Scripps, San Diego, 1982-87, ptnr., 1988-95; judge San Diego Mcpl. Ct., 1995-98, San Diego Superior Ct., 1998—. Spl. counsel standing com. on discipline U.S. Dist. Ct. Calif., San Diego, 1983-85; chmn. San Diego Bar Labor and Employment Sect., 1988-89; chmn. fed. cts. com. Calif. State Bar, 1989-90. Bd. dirs. ARC San Diego chpt., 1992—, Crime Victims Fund, 1995-97; bd. govs. Muscular Dystrophy Assn., San Diego, 1985; mem. LEAD Inc., San Diego, 1986—; planning com. San Diego United Way, 1986-92. Named one of Outstanding Young Men of Am., 1983; recipient Outstanding Service award 9th Cir. Jud. Conf., 1986. Mem. ABA, Calif. State Bar Ct. (referee 1985-88), Am. Arbitration Assn. (arbitrator 1986-95), Calif. Judges Assn. (mem. criminal law and procedure com. 1997-2000), Boalt Hall Alumni Assn. (bd. dirs. 1994-97), Claremont McKenna Coll. Alumni Assn. (founding dir. San Diego chpt. 1984-2000), Rotary (bd. dirs. San Diego club 1995—). Republican. Avocations: music, golf. Office: San Diego Superior Ct PO Box 122724 San Diego CA 92112-2724

HARVEY, BRYAN LAURENCE, crop science educator; b. Newport, Gwent, Wales, U.K., Nov. 1, 1937; came to Can., 1948; s. Laurence W.J. And Irene E.D. (Stoneman) H.; m. Eileen Bernice Pfeifer, Sept. 24, 1961; children: Donald, James. BSA, U. Sask., 1960, MSc, 1961; PhD, U. Calif., Davis, 1964. Asst. prof. crop sci. U. Guelph, Ont., Can., 1964-66; from asst. prof. to prof. crop sci. U. Sask., Saskatoon, 1966—, head dept. crop sci. and plant ecology, 1983-94, head dept. horticulture, 1994-97, univ. coord. agrl. rsch., 1997—. Dir. Crop Devel. Ctr., 1983-94, asst. dean Coll. Agr., 1980-83; vis. prof. U. Nairobi, Kenya, 1975; dir. accreditation Agr. Inst. Can., 1996—; chmn. Can. Expert Com. Grain Breeding, 1984-89 Exec. Can. Agrifood Rsch. Coun., 2000—, Bd. Genome Prairie, 2000—, Can. Expert Com. on Plant gene resources, 1986-93, Can. Adv. Co. on Variety Registration, 1987-95, Can. Prairie Registration Recommending Com. for Grain, 1989-95, Can. Adv. Com. on Plant Breeders Rights, 1986—, Barley Devel. Coun., 1994-96, Can. Com. on Crops, 1996—, Can. Agrifood Rsch. Coun., 1993—. Contbr. articles to sci. jours. on plant genetics. Recipient Outstanding Svc. award [illegible] of the Am. 1996, Significant Sci. Contbn. award Can. Seed Trade Assn., 1997. Fellow Agrl. Inst. Can. (pres. 1994-95, Fellowship award 1990), Am. Soc. Agronomy, Crop Sci. Soc. Am.; mem. Assn. Faculties of Agr. Can. (pres. 1982-83), Barley Genetics Congress (pres. 1986-91, 96-2000), Am. Barley Workers (pres. 1970-74), Can. Seed Growers Assn. (hon. life), Sask. Seed Growers Assn. (hon. life), Rotary (pres. 1987-89). Developed 42 varieties of barley. Office: U Sask 211 Kirk Hall 117 Sci Pl Saskatoon SK Canada S7N 5C8 E-mail: harvey@duke.usask.ca

HARVEY, DONALD, artist, educator; b. Walthamston, Eng., June 14, 1930; s. Henry and Annie Dorothy (Sawell) H.; m. Elizabeth Clark, Aug. 9, 1952; children— Shan Mary, David Jonathan. Art tchrs. diploma, Brighton Coll. Art, 1951. Art master Ardwyn Grammar Sch., Wales, 1952-56; mem. faculty dept. art U. Victoria, B.C., Can., 1961-95, now prof. emeritus painting. One man exhbns. include, Albert White Gallery, Toronto, 1968, retrospective, Art Gallery of Victoria, 1968; represented in permanent collections, Nat. Gallery Can., Montreal Mus., Albright-Knox Mus., Seattle Art Mus. Mem. accessions com. Art Gallery of Victoria, 1969-72. Can. Council fellow, 1966 Mem. Royal Can. Acad. of Arts (full academician), Can. Group Painters, Can. Painters and Etchers. Home: 1025 Joan Crescent Victoria BC Canada V8S 3L3

HARVEY, ELINOR B. child psychiatrist; b. Boston, Jan. 11, 1912; d. William and Florence (Maysles) H.; m. Donald K. Freedman, July 2, 1936; children: Peter, F. Kenneth. BS cum laude, Jackson Coll., 1933; MD, Tufts U., 1936. Diplomate Am. Bd. Psychiatry and Neurology, Nat. Bd. Med. Examiners. Intern New Eng. Hosp. Women and Children, Roxbury, Mass., 1936-37; resident Sea View Hosp., Staten Island, N.Y., 1937-39; adminstrv. and indsl. physician Assoc. Hosp. Svc. N.Y., 1939-41; house physician, resident Henry St. Settlement House, N.Y.C., 1939-41; pvt. practice Arlington, Va., 1941-43; pvt. practice as pediatrician Newport News, 1943-46; clinician Westchester County Health Dept., White Plains, N.Y., 1947; pediatrician Arrowhead Clinic, Duluth, Minn., 1947-48; resident in psychiatry VA Hosp., Palo Alto, Calif., 1949-52; resident in child psychiatry child guidance clinic Children's Hosp. San Francisco, 1952-53, fellow in child psychiatry, 1953-54; pvt. practice as child and family psychiatrist Berkeley, Calif., 1954-68, Juneau, Alaska, 1968-77. Instr. Am. Univ. Washington, 1941—43; clinician prenatal clinics Arlington County Health Dept. , Arlington, 1941—43; clinician Planned Parenthood , Wash., 1941—43; mem. adv. bd. emergency maternal and infant care program C's. Bur., Wash., 1942—48; instr. pediatrics schs. nursing Buxton and Riverside Hosps. , 1943—46; consult pediatrician Community Hosp. and Clin, Two Harbors, Minn., 1947—48; mem. courtesy staff Herrick Hosp. , Berkeley , Calif., 1955—68, Bartlett Mem. Hosp. , Juneau, 1968—77; consult. US Bur. Indian Affairs Dept. Educ., Alaska, 1968—76, Southeast Regional Mental Health Clin., Juneau, 1975—77, Mars & Kline Psychiat. Clin. and Hosp., Port-Au-Prince, Port-Au-Prince, Haiti, 1977—78, Navajo Area Indian Health Serv. , Gallup, N.Mex., 1980—, Brookside Hosp., San Pablo, Calif., 1980—84, San Pablo, 1984—; instr. mental health and mental illness Alaska Homemaker-Home Health Aide Servs., Juneau C.C., 1968—77, 1984—99; coord. State Alaska Program Continuing Educ. Mental Health , 1974—76; clin. assoc. prof. dept. psychiat. and behavioral scis. Univ. Washington, 1976—77; vol. child and family psychiatrist Baptist Mission, Fermathe, Haiti, 1977—79; instr. child develop. Mars and Kline Pscychiat. Clin and Hosp., 1977—78; mem. hosp. staff Gallup (NM) Indian Med. Cent., 1980—; consult. Brazelton neonatal behavioral assessment Navajo Area Indian Health Serv. , 1982—; consult. infant-parent program Brookside Hosp., 1984—; demonstrator Brazelton neonatal behavioral assessment scale Cent. Recursos Educatius Deficients Visuals Catalunya, Barcelona, 1992; active Child Protection Agency, Juneau; mem. planning bd. Coordinated Child Care Cent. , Juneau; presenter in field. Author: (with others) Annual Progress in Child Psychiatry and Child Development, 10th ann. edit., 1977, Expanding Mental Health Intervention in Schools, Vol. I, 1985, Psychiatric House Calls, 1988, The Indian Health Service Primary Care Provider, 1991; contbr. articles to profl. jours. Mem. comprehensive health planning coun. City and Borough of Juneau. Grantee NIMH, 1958-63. Fellow Am. Psychiat. Assn. (life), Am. Acad. Child and Adolescent Psychiatry (life, mem. task force Am. Indian children); mem. No. Calif. Psychiat. Assn. (Outstanding Achievement award 1996), Internat. Assn. Child Psychiatry, World Fedn. Mental Health, Internat. Assn. Circumpolar Health, Soc. Reproductive and Infant Psychology, Phi Beta Kappa. Home and Office: 1547 Buckeye Ct Pinole CA 94564-2124

HARVEY, JOSEPH PAUL, JR. orthopedist, educator; b. Youngstown, Ohio, Feb. 28, 1922; s. Joseph Paul and Mary Justinian (Collins) H.; m. Martha Elizabeth Toole, Apr. 12, 1958; children: Maryalice, Martha Jane, Frances Susan, Helen Lucy, Laura Andre. Student, Dartmouth Coll., 1939-42; MD, Harvard U., 1945. Diplomate: Nat. Bd. Med. Examiners. Intern Peter Bent Brigham Hosp., Boston, 1945-46; resident Univ. Hosp., Cleve., 1951-53, Hosp. Spl. Surgery, N.Y.C., 1953-54; instr. orthopedics Cornell Med. Coll., N.Y.C., 1954-62; mem. faculty Sch. Medicine, U. So. Calif., Los Angeles, 1962-92; prof. orthopedic surgery U. So. Calif., 1966-92, prof. emeritus, 1992—; chmn. sect. orthopedics Keck Sch. Medicine, U. So. Calif., 1964-78. Dir. dept. orthopedics U. So. Calif.-Los Angeles County Med. Center, 1964-79, mem. staff, 1979— Editor-in-chief: Contemporary Orthopedics, 1978-96. Served to capt. AUS, 1946-48. Exchange orthopedic fellow Royal Acad. Hosp., Upsala, Sweden, 1957 Fellow Western Orthop. Assn., Am. Acad. Orthop. Surgery, A.C.S., Am. Soc. Testing Materials; mem. AMA, Calif. Med. Assn., Los Angeles County Med. Assn., Am. Rheumatism Assn., Am. Orthop. Assn., Internat. Soc. Orthopedics and Traumatology. Club: Boston Harvard. Home: 432 Arlington Dr Pasadena CA 91105-2850

HARWOOD, BRIAN DENNIS, securities industry executive; b. London, Feb. 3, 1932; arrived Can., 1953; s. William Henry and Catherine Mary (O'Brien) H.; m. Diane Louise McLean, Sept. 1, 1988. Ed. pvt. schs., London. Fgn. exch. cashier Thos. Cook & Sons, London, 1949-50, 52-53; to br. mgmt. Bank of Montreal, Vancouver and Montreal, Can., 1953-62, 64-70; lending officer Security First Nat. Bank, L.A., 1963-64; with Canaccord Capital Corp (formerly L.O.M. Western Securities Ltd.), Vancouver, 1970—, exec. v.p., 1975-87, pres., chief oper. officer, 1987-94; vice chmn., 1994—, Can. Investor Protection Fund, also bd. dirs. Sgt. Brit. Army, 1950-52. Mem. Investment Dealers Assn. Can. (bd. dirs., nat. and exec. coms. 1989-94), Vancouver Stock Exch. (bd. govs. 1985-94, vice chmn. 1989, chmn. 1991-93), Royal Vancouver Yacht Club. Avocations: boating, reading, walking, cycling. Office: Canaccord Capital Corp 609 Granville St PO Box 10337 Vancouver BC Canada V7Y 1H2

HARWOOD, IVAN RICHMOND, retired pediatric pulmonologist; b. Huntington, W.Va., July 3, 1939; BA, Dartmouth Coll., 1961; MD, U. W.Va., 1965. Diplomate Nat. Bd. Med. Examiners; lic. physician, Calif., Can.; cert. Am. Bd. Pediatrics. Intern in pediatrics U. W.Va. Hosp., Morgantown, 1965-66; resident in pediatrics Yale-New Haven (Conn.) Hosp., 1966-68, sr. resident outpatient dept., 1968-69; chief pediatrics USAF Hosp. 3646, Del Rio, Tex., 1968-70; asst. prof. pediatrics U. Calif. Med. Ctr., San Diego, 1971-78, chief pediatric pulmonary div., 1972-93, dir. pediatric intensive care unit, 1972-78, assoc. adj. prof. pediatrics, 1978-86, prof., 1987—. Mem. patient care rev. and numerous other coms. U. Calif. Med. Ctr., 1976—; co-dir. Cystic Fibrosis Ctr., San Diego, 1972-73, dir., 1973; mem. Cystic Fibrosis Young Adult Com., Atlanta, 1974-80, chmn., 1976-80, Cystic Fibrosis Ctr. Com., 1986-89, vice-chmn., 1990-94; mem. San Diego County Tuburculosis Control Bd., 1974-78; dir. Cystic Fibrosis Ctr. Children' s Hosp. and Health Ctr., San Diego, 1995—; presenter, lectr. in field. Producer: (videos) Issues in Cystic Fibrosis Series; mem. rev. bd., CF Film, 1980; contbr. chpts. to books, and numerous articles to profl. jours. Mem. Air Quality Adv. Com., State of Calif., 1974-80; mem. Genetically Handicapped Persons Program Adv. Com., Calif., 1977-87; mem. adv. bd. Grossmont Coll. Inhalation Therapy Sch., San Diego, 1975-76; mem. inpatient adolscent adv. com., Mercy Hosp., 1982-85. U. Calif. fellow in pediatric cardiology, 1970-71; recipient 1st Prize Internat. Rehab. Film Library Competition, 1980. Mem. Calif. Med. Assn. (patient care audit com. 1975-78), Nat. Cystic Fibrosis Found. (mem. adv. com. 1976-80, planning ad hoc com. 1976-77, patient registry subcom. 1986-90), San Diego Found. for Med. Care (major med. rev. com. 1978-84), San Diego Lung Assn. (pediatric com. 1976-80, chmn. Project Breath-Easy 1976-78). Home: PO Box 431 Jamul CA 91935-0431

HASBROOK, A. HOWARD, safety engineer, consultant; b. Trenton, N.J., July 15, 1913; s. Albert Howard and Mabel (Naar) H.; m. Christel Anna Schneider, 1938 (div. 1955); children: Barbara Elaine, Howard Richard Jay; m. Virginia Randolph Whiting, 1955. Grad. H.S., DuBois, Pa. Safety engr., Calif. Flight instr., engring. test pilot USAAF, 1942-45; agrl., charter, airline & test pilot, comml. flight examiner, 1945-50; assoc. dir. Av-CIR Cornell U., 1950-55, dir. Av-CIR and aviation crash injury rschr., 1955-60; chief crash safety, sr. rsch. scientist FAA Civil Aeromed. Inst., 1960-67, chief flight performance, sr. rsch. scientist, 1968-75. Aviation safety cons., profl. engr., accident investigator, analyst & reconstructionist, rsch. pilot, engring. test pilot, flight instr., 1975—, also accident prevention counselor FAA, 1975—, assoc. prof. Embry-Riddle Aerospace U., 1982, expert witness in accident litigation. Presenter lectures/tech. papers before numerous orgns.; contbr. more than 200 tech. papers & reports to profl. jours. Served with U.S. Army, 1933-34. A. Howard Hasbrook sect. established in his honor by Wright State U. Med. Sch. Libr., 1990; recipient Flight Safety Found. award, 1958, Gen. Spruance award, 1970, Harry G. Mosely award, 1972; named to Ariz. Aviation Hall of Fame, 1992, OX5 Aviation Pioneers Hall of Fame, 1995; fellow in aerospace medicine, 1972. Fellow Aerospace Med. Assn. (Hasbrook award named in his honor); mem. Internat. Soc. Air Safety Investigators, Quiet Birdmen, OX-5 Aviation Pioneers, Nat. Forensic Ctr. Home and Office: Safety Engring & Rsch HC 30 Box 813 Prescott AZ 86305-7484

HASELTINE, JAMES LEWIS, artist, consultant; b. Portland, Oreg., Nov. 7, 1924; s. William Ambrose and Clara Thusnelda (Scharpf) H.; m. Jane Winsberg, Nov. 14, 1948 (div. 1953); m. Margaret Ann Wilson, Aug. 15, 1955; children: Thomas, Jean, Kay, Suzanne, Angela. Student, Ark. State Coll., 1943-44, Reed Coll., 1946-47, Mus. Art Sch., 1947, 49, Art Inst. Chgo., 1947-48, Bklyn. Mus. Sch., 1950-51. Dir. Salt Lake Art Ctr., Salt Lake City, 1961-67; exec. dir. Wash. State Arts Commn., Olympia, Wash., 1967-80; prof. artist, 1950—. Vis. lectr. art history U. Utah, Salt Lake City, 1964-65; panel mem. Nat. Endowment for the Arts, Washington, 1969-80; various art cons. positions, 1980—. Author: 100 Years of Utah Painting, 1965 (Mormon History Assn. award 1965); paintings and prints represented in permanent collectinos Portland ArtMus., Oakland Art Mus., Mus. Art U. Oreg., Mus. Fine Arts U. Utah, Tacoma Art Mus., Willamette U., Salem, Oreg. Mem. search com. for pres. Evergreen State Coll., Olympia, 1984; trustee Portland Art Mus., 1953-55. With U.S. Army, 1942-46, ETO. Mem. Western Assn. Art Mus. (pres. 1964-66), Artists Equity Assn. (nat. dir. 1955-58, chmn. Oreg. chpt. 1953-55), Western States Arts Found. (bd. dirs. 1975-77), Brit.-Am. Art Assn. (trustee 1980-84). Home and Office: 3820 Sunset Beach Dr NW Olympia WA 98502-3542

HASELTON, RICK THOMAS, lawyer; b. Albany, Oreg., Nov. 5, 1953; s. Shirley (Schantz) H. AB, Stanford U., 1976; JD, Yale U., 1979. Chair Oreg. State Bd. Bar Examiners, 1988-89, bd. dirs., 1986-88; mem. adv. com. on rules of practice 9th Cir. Ct., 1991-93. Law clk. U.S. Ct. Appeals (9th cir.) Oreg., Portland, 1979-80; from assoc. to ptnr. Lindsay, Hart, Neil & Weigler, Portland, 1979-93; sole practice Portland, 1993-94; assoc. judge Oreg. Ct. Appeals, Salem, 1994—. Chair Multnomah County Legal Aid, Portland, 1985-86, bd. dirs., 1982-87. Mem. ABA, Oreg. Bar Assn., ACLU (cooperating atty. 1982-94), Phi Beta Kappa. Jewish. Office: 300 Justice Blvd Salem OR 97310-0001

HASHE, JANIS HELENE, editor; d. James William and Arlene Florence (Houses) H. AA with honors, Cabrillo Coll., 1974; BA summa cum laude, San Francisco State, 1976; MA, San Jose State, 1982. Asst. editor Sunset Trade Publs., L.A., 1988-89, assoc. editor, 1989-90; editor Western Grocery News, L.A., 1990-95; sr. editor L.A. Parent Mag., Burbank, Calif., 1995—, nat. column editor. Author: (radio play) A Knot in the Heart, 1990; writer essays. Vol. Braille Inst., L.A., 1988—; block capt. Crime Watch Catalina, L.A., 1990-91. Scholar Am. Assn. U. Women, 1972. Mem. Nat. Writers Union, New One-Act Theatre Ensemble (artistic dir., 1985-88, pres., bd. dirs. 1995—). Democrat. Buddhist. Office: L A Parent Mag 443 Irving Dr Burbank CA 91504-2447

HASHIMOTO, CHRISTINE L. physician; b. Chgo., June 29, 1947; d. Shigeru and Kiyo (Sato) H. BA, Oberlin Coll., 1968; MD, Med. Coll. of Pa., 1973. Clin. instr. internal medicine, emergency medicine Med. Coll. and Hosp. of Pa., Phila., 1976-77; asst. prof. medicine Health Service Ctr. U. Colo., Denver, 1977-80, clin. asst. prof. medicine, 1980-87; staff physician emergency dept. St. Joseph Hosp., Denver, 1980-88, Rose Med. Ctr., Denver, 1988-91, Luth. Med. Ctr., Wheatridge, Colo., 1991—. Mem. Colo. Med. Soc., Denver Med. Soc., Am. Coll. Emergency Physicians. Office: Luth Med Ctr 8300 W 38th Ave Wheat Ridge CO 80033-6005

HASKAYNE, RICHARD FRANCIS, petroleum company executive; b. Calgary, Alta., Can., Dec. 18, 1934; s. Robert Stanley and Bertha (Hesketh) H.; m. Lee Mary Murray, 1958 (dec. 1993); m. Lois P. Heard, 1995. B.Comm., U. Alta., 1956; postgrad., U. Western Ont., 1968, LLD, U. Calgary, U. Alta. Chartered acct., Alta. With Riddell, Stead & Co., chartered accts., Calgary, 1956-60; corp. acctg. supr. to v.p. fin. Hudson's Bay Oil & Gas Co., Ltd., Calgary, 1960-73; compt. Canadian Arctic Gas Study Ltd., 1973-75; sr. v.p. to pres. Hudson's Bay Oil & Gas Co. Ltd., Calgary, 1975-81; pres., chief exec. officer Home Oil Co., Ltd., Calgary, 1981-91, also bd. dirs.; chmn. bd. NOVA Corp., Calgary, 1992-98. Pres., CEO Interprovencial Pipe Line Co., 1987—91, Interhome Energy, 1989—91; bd. dirs., chmn. bd. Fording Inc.; bd. dirs. Alta. Energy, Inc.; chmn. bd. dirs. Transcanada Pipelines; bd. dirs. Weyerhaeuser Co.; chmn. bd. TransAlta Corop., 1996—98, TransCan Pipeline Ltd., 1998—, MacMillan Biodel Ltd., 1996—99; dir. emeritus CIBC. Chmn. emeritus bd. govs. U. Calgary. Recipient award Officer of the Order of Can., 1997. Fellow Fin. Execs. Inst., Inst. Corp. Dirs.; mem. Calgary Petroleum Club (past pres.), Calgary Golf and Country Club, Earl Grey Golf Club, Ranchmen's Club, U. Calgary Chancellor's Club, The York Club, Libr. Club, Commerce Club, Alta Inst. Chartered Accts., Kappa Sigma Office: 2030 Bankers Hall 855 2d St SW Calgary AB Canada T2P 4J8

HASLAM, GERALD WILLIAM, writer, educator; b. Bakersfield, Calif., Mar. 18, 1937; s. Fredrick Martin and Lorraine Hope (Johnson) H.; m. Janice Eileen Pettichord, July 1, 1961; children: Frederick W., Alexandra R., Garth C., Simone B., Carlos V. BA, San Francisco State U., 1963, MA, 1965; PhD, Union Grad. Sch., 1980. Instr. English San Francisco State U., San Francisco, 1966-67; asst. prof. English Sonoma State U., Rohnert Park, Calif., 1967-70, assoc. prof. English, 1970-74, prof. English, 1971-97, emeritus prof. English, 1997—; prof. Fromm Inst./U. San Francisco, 2001—; adj. prof. Union Grad. Sch., Cin., 1984—. The Nat. Faculty, Atlanta, 1984—. Editor various anthologies; author various booklets, monographs, film scripts, (fiction) Okies: Selected Stories, 1973, Masks: A Novel, 1976, The Wages of Sin: Collected Stories, 1980, Hawk Flights: Visions of the West, 1983, Snapshots: Glimpses of the Other California, 1985, The Man Who Cultivated Fire and Other Stories, 1987, That Constant Coyote: California Stories, 1990, Condor Dreams and Other Fictions, 1994, The Great Tejon Club Jubilee, 1996, Manuel and the Madman, 2000, Straight White Male, 2000, (non-fiction) Voices of a Place,

1987, Coming of Age in California, 1990, The Other California, 1990, The Great Central Valley: California's Heartland, 1993, Workin' Man Blues: Country Music in California, 1999, Coming of Age in California, 2d enlarged edit., 2000. With U.S. Army, 1958-60. Creative Writing fellow Calif. Arts Coun., 1989; recipient Benjamin Franklin award, 1993, Bay Area Book Reviewers' Non-fiction award, 1994, Commonwealth Club medal for Calif., 1994, Merit award Assn. State & Local History, 1994, Commendation citation, 2001; Fulbright sr. lectr., 1986-87, Josephine Miles award, 1990, Ralph J. Gleason award, 2000, Carey McWilliams award, 2001, Western States Book Fiction award, 2001. Mem. NAACP, Great Valley Ctr. (adv. bd.), Western Lit. Assn. (bd. dirs., past pres., Disting. Achievment award 1999), Calif. Studies Assn. (steering com., founding mem.), Calif. Hist. Assn., Calif. Tchrs. Assn., San Francisco State U. Alumni Assn. (life), Union Inst. Alumni Assn., Multi-Ethnic Lit. of U.S. (founding mem.), Robinson Jeffers Assn. (founding mem.), Sierra Club, The Nature Conservancy, Calif. Trout (founding mem.), Tulare Basin Archeology Group, Defenders of Wildlife, Common Cause, Yosemite Assn. (bd. dirs.). Roman Catholic. Avocations: bicycling, hiking, fishing. Office: Sonoma State U 1801 E Cotati Ave Rohnert Park CA 94928-3609 E-mail: ghaslam@sonic.net

HASLAM, ROBERT THOMAS, III, lawyer; b. Taunton, Mass., May 4, 1946; s. Robert Thomas and Marcella Neale (Compton) H.; m. Mary Ashley Brayton, June 14, 1969; children: Laurel Ashley, Julia Compton. BS Aeronautics and Astronautics, MIT, 1968; JD, Hastings Coll., 1976. Bar: Calif., 1976. Atty., ptnr. Heller, Ehrman, Mnelo Park, Calif., 1976—. Capt. USAF 1969-73. Mem. ABA (co-chair litigation, intellectual property sect. 1993—). Avocations: tennis, soccer. Home: 838 University Ave Palo Alto CA 94301-2131 Office: Heller Ehrman 275 Middlefield Rd Menlo Park CA 94025-3506

HASS, ROBERT L. writer, educator; b. San Francisco, 1941; Prof. Dept. English U. Calif., Berkeley. Author: (books of poetry) Sun Under Wood: New Poems, 1996, Human Wishes, 1989, Praise, 1979, Field Guide, 1973; co-translator vols. of poetry with Czeslaw Milosz including: Facing the river, 1995; author/editor essays and translation including: The Essential Haiku: Versions of Basho, Buson, and Issa, 1994, Twenthieth Century Pleasures: Prose on Poetry, 1984 (Nat. Book Critics Circle award). Bd. dirs. Internat. Rivers Network. Apptd. Poet Laureate of U.S., 1995; MacArthur "Genius" fellow; named Educator of the Yr., N.Am. Assn. on Environ. Edn., 1997. Office: Steven Barclay Agy 321 Pleasant St Petaluma CA 94952-2648 E-mail: bobhass@uclink4.berkeley.edu

HASSLEIN, GEORGE JOHANN, architectural educator; b. Los Angeles, Aug. 31, 1917; s. August Theodore and Lena (Matranga) H.; m. Neva B. Henderson, Oct. 13, 1945 (dec. Dec. 1963); children: Vaughn, Tracey; m. Marilyn L. Collins, Sept. 10, 1966 (dec. Dec. 1967). BArch, U. So. Calif., 1946. Registered architect, Calif. With Army Engrs., Costa Rica, 1942-44; archtl. designer firm Welton Becket (architect), Los Angeles, 1948-50; mem. faculty Calif. State Poly. Coll., San Luis Obispo, 1949—, prof., head dept. archtl. engring., 1952-68, founding dean Sch. Architecture and Environ. Design, 1968-84, prof., 1984—. Archtl. adviser bd. trustees Calif. State Univs. and Colls., 1961-84; mem. AID mission to Argentina, 1963; regent Roofing Industry Ednl. Inst., 1979—; mem. del. Archtl. Educators to Republic of China, 1979; commr. Calif. State Bd. Archtl. Examiners, 1961—, Western Assn. Sch. and Colls., 1980—. Mem. acad. and planning coms. Channel Island U., 2000. Recipient Achievement award L.A. C. of C., 1981; health, edn. and welfare travel grantee to Israel, 1965. Fellow AIA (Distinguished service award edn. 1971, 99, Excellence in Edn. award 1977); mem. Am. Arbitration Assn., Scarab, Delta Phi Delta, Tau Sigma, Alpha Rho Chi also: 2333 Helena St San Luis Obispo CA 93401-4511 E-mail: ghasslei@calpoly.edu

HASTINGS, DOC, congressman; b. Spokane, Wash., Feb. 7, 1941; m. Claire Hastings; 3 children. Student, Columbia Basin Coll., Ctrl. Wash. U. Mem. Wash. State Ho. of Reps., 1979-87; pres. Columbia Basin Paper & Supply, 1983-94; mem. U.S. Congress from 4th Wash. dist., 1995—; mem. rules com., budget com., standards of official conduct com., asst. majority whip. Bd. dirs. Yakima Fed. Savings & Loan; chmn. Franklin County Republican Com., 1974-78 Office: US House Reps 1323 Longworth Ho Office Bldg Washington DC 20515-0001*

HASTINGS, EDWARD WALTON, theater director; b. New Haven, Apr. 14, 1931; s. Edward Walton and Madeline (Cassidy) H. B.A., Yale, 1952; postgrad., Royal Acad. Dramatic Art, London, 1953, Columbia U., , 1955-56. Bd. dirs. Asian/Am. Theater Co., 1986, Arts Internat., 1987, Eugene O'Neill Found., 1993; guest instr. Shanghai Drama Inst., 1984. Dir. Australian premiere Hot L Baltimore, 1975, Shakespeare's People nat. tour, 1983, Nothing Sacred, Hong Kong, 1992, Come Back Little Sheba, Gogol Theater, Moscow, 1995, Dial M for Murder nat. tour, 1995, Beggars Opera, Santa Fe Opera, 2000, others; exec. dir. Am. Conservatory Theatre, San Francisco, 1965-80, artistic dir., 1986-92; freelance dir., 1980-86. Served with U.S. Army, 1953-55. Mem. Coll. of Fellows of the Am. Theatre. Club: Elizabethan (New Haven). Office: Am Conservatory Theatre 30 Grant Ave San Francisco CA 94108-5800

HASTINGS, L(OIS) JANE, architect, educator; b. Seattle, Mar. 3, 1928; d. Harry and Camille (Pugh) H.; m. Norman John Johnston, Nov. 22, 1969. B.Arch., U. Wash., Seattle, 1952, postgrad. in Urban Planning, 1958. Architect Boeing Airplane Co., Seattle, 1951-54; recreational dir. Germany, 1954-56; architect (various firms), Seattle, 1956-59, pvt. practice architecture, 1959-74; instr. archtl. drafting Seattle Community Coll., part-time 1969-80; owner/founder The Hastings Group Architects, Seattle, 1974—; lectr. design Coll. Architecture, U. Wash., 1975; incorporating mem. Architecta (P.S.), Seattle, 1980, pres., from 1980. Mem. adv. bd. U. Wash. YWCA, 1967-69; mem. Mayor's Com. on Archtl. Barriers for Handicapped, 1974-75; chmn. regional public adv. panel on archtl. and engring. services GSA, 1976; mem. citizens adv. com. Seattle Land Use Adminstrn. Task Force, from 1979; AWIU guest of Soviet Women's Con., 1983; speaker Pacific Rim Forum, Hong Kong, 1987; guest China Internat. Conf. Ctr. for Sci. and Tech. of the China Assn. for Sci. and Tech., 1989; mem. adv. com. Coll. architecture and urban planning U. Wash., 1993; mem. accreditation team U. Oreg. Coll. Architecture, 1991, N.J. Inst. Tech. Sch. Architecture, 1992; jurur Home of the Yr. ann. award AIA/Seattle Times, 1996. Design juror for nat. and local competitions, including Red Cedar Shingle/AIA awards, 1977, Current Use Honor awards, AIA, 1980, Exhibit of Sch. Architecture award, 1981; Contbr. to: also spl. features newspapers, articles in profl. jours. Sunset mag. Mem. bd. Am. Women for Internat. Understanding, del. to, Egypt, Israel, USSR, 1971, Japan and Korea, 1979, USSR, 1983; mem. Landmarks Preservation Bd. City of Seattle, 1981-83; mem. Design Constrn. Rev. Bd. Seattle Sch. Dist., 1985-87; mem. mus. con. Mus. History and Industry, 1987—; leader People to People del. women architects to China, 1990. Recipient AIA/The Seattle Times Home of Month Ann. award, 1968; Exhbn. award Seattle chpt. AIA, 1970; Environ. award Seattle-King County Bd. Realtors, 1970, 77,; AIA/House and Home/The American Home Merit award, 1971, Sp. Honor award Wash. Aggregates and Concrete Assn., 1993, Prize bridge Am. Inst. Steel Contrn., 1993; Honor award Seattle chpt. AIA, 1977, 83; Women Achievement award Past Pres. Assembly, 1983, Washington Women and Trading Cards, 1983; Nat. Endowment for Arts grantee, 1977; others; named to West Seattle High Sch. Hall of Fame, 1989, Woman of Achievement Matrix Table, 1994; named Woman of Distinction, Columbia River Girl Scout Coun., 1994. Fellow AIA (pres. Seattle chpt. 1975, pres. sr. coun. 1980, state exec. bd. 1975, N.W. regional dir. 1982-87, Seattle chpt. found. bd. 1985-87, Bursar Coll. Fellows 1989-90, Coll. of Fellows historian 1994—, internat. rels. com. 1988-92, vice chancellor 1991, chancellor 1992, Seattle chpt. medal 1995), Internat. Union Women Architects (v.p. 1969-79, sec. gen. 1985-89, del. UIA Congress, Montreal 1990), Am. Arbitration Assn. (arbitrator 1981—), Coun. of Design Professions, Assn. Women Contrs., Suppliers and Design Cons., Allied Arts Seattle, Fashion Group, Tau Sigma Delta, Alpha Rho Chi (medal). Office: The Hastings Group Architects 603 Stewart St Ste 915 Seattle WA 98101-1264

HATCH, CHARLES R. university dean; BS in Forest Mgmt., U. Mont., 1964; M in Forestry, Forest Mensuration, Oreg. State U., 1966; PhD in forest Mensuration/Stats., U. Minn., 1971. Grad. asst. Oreg. State U. Sch. Forstry, Corvallis, 1965-66; instr. U. Minn. Sch. Forestry, St. Paul, 1967-71; asst. prof. dept. forestry So. Ill. U., Carbondale, 1971-73; assoc. prof. Coll. Forestry, Wildlife and Range Scis., U. Idaho, Moscow, 1973-77, prof., 1977—, program dir. continuing edn. in forest ecology/silviculture, 1977-82, assoc. dean rsch., assoc. dir. forestry, wildlife, 1979-83, head dept. forest resources, 1987-89, assoc. dean rsch., internat. programs, dir. experiment sta., 1994-95; dean now U. Idaho, Coll. Natural Resources, Moscow, 1995—. Forestry advisor U.S. AID, New Delhi, India, 1983-87; chief of party forestry planning and devel. project Winrock Internat., Islamabad, Pakistan, 1989-94. Contbr. articles to profl. jours. Recipient Outstanding Svc. to Am. Embassy Cmty. award Am. Amb. to Pakistan. Recipient Outstanding Svc. award to Am. Embassy Cmty., Islamabad, Pakistan, 1993, 94. Mem. Mont. Druids, Gamma Sigma Delta, Sigma Xi, Xi Sigma Pi. Office: U Idaho Coll Natural Resources Range Scis Moscow ID 83844-0001

HATCH, GEORGE CLINTON, television executive; b. Erie, Pa., Dec. 16, 1919; s. Charles Milton and Blanche (Beecher) H.; m. Wilda Gene Glasmann, Dec. 24, 1940; children: Michael Gene Zbar, Diane Glasmann Orr, Jeffrey Beecher, Randall Clinton, Deepika Hatch Avanti. AB, Occidental Coll., 1940; MA in Econs., Claremont Coll., 1941; HHD (hon.), So. Utah U., 1988. Pres. Comms. Investment Corp., Salt Lake City, 1945-95; chmn. Double G Comm. Corp., Salt Lake City, 1956—; dir. Republic Pictures Corp., Los Angeles, 1971-94; pres. Sta. KVEL, Inc., 1978-94. Pres. Standard Corp., Ogden, 1993-98, Hatch Family LLC, 1998—; past mem. Salt Lake adv. bd. First Security Bank Utah; past chmn. Rocky Mountain Pub. Broadcasting Corp.; past chmn. bd. govs. Am. Info. Radio Network; past bd. govs. NBC-TV Affiliates. Past pres. Salt Lake Com. on Fgn. Relations; past mem. Utah Symphony Bd., Salt Lake City; past chmn. and mem. Utah State Bd. Regents, 1964-85. Recipient Svc. to Journalism award U. Utah, 1966, silver medal Salt Lake Advt. Club, 1969, Disting. Svc. award Utah Tech. U., 1984, Disting. Utahan Centennial Yr. award Margaret Thatcher U.K., Utah Festival, 1996. Mem. Nat. Assn. Broadcasters (past pres., radio bd. dirs., ambassador to Inter-Am. mtgs. in Latin Am. 1962), Utah Broadcasters Assn. (past pres., Mgmt. award 1964, Hall of Fame award 1981), Salt Lake City Advt. Club (silver medal 1969), Phi Beta Kappa, Phi Rho Pi (life). Democrat. Avocations: hiking, rock art. Office: Hatch Family LLC 1537 Chandler Dr Salt Lake City UT 84103-4220

HATCH, LYNDA SYLVIA, elementary and middle school education educator; b. Portland, Oreg., Feb. 19, 1950; d. Marley Elmo and Undine Sylvia (Crockard) Sims. BA, Wash. State U., 1972; MS, Portland State U., 1975; EdD, Oreg. State U., 1984. Cert. tchr., Oreg. Tchr. 5th grade, outdoor sch. specialist Clover Park Sch. Dist. 400, Tacoma, 1971-72; tchr. 6th grade, outdoor sch. specialist Hillsboro (Oreg.) elem. Dist. 7, 1972-78, Bend (Oreg.)-La Pine Sch. Dist., 1978-82, elem. curriculum specialist, 1983-85, tchr. 4th grade gifted and talented, 1985-90; grad. teaching asst. Oreg. State U., Corvallis, 1982-84; asst. prof., assoc. prof. No. Ariz. U., 1990-99, chair instnl. leadership, 1997-98; Boeing disting. prof. sci. edn. Wash. State U., Pullman, 1999—. Ednl. cons., tchr. workshops, 1973—; presenter workshop Soviet-Am. Joint Conf., Moscow State U., 1991, Meeting of Children's Culture Promoters, Guadalajara, Mex., 1994, Internat. Conf. Sci., Tech. and Math. Edn. for Human Devel., UNESCO, Panaji, India, 2001, and others; faculty Ariz. Journey Schs. for Math. and Sci. Tchg. Improvement; coord. Odyssey of the Mind, Bend, 1985-89, tchr.-mentor program for 1st-yr. tchrs., Beaverton, Oreg., 1982-83; presenter Social Edn. Assn. of Australia, 1997. Author: Pathways of America: Lewis and Clark, 1993, Pathways of America: The Oregon Trail, 1993, Pathways of America: The California Gold Rush Trail, 1994, Pathways of America: The Santa Fe Trail, 1995, Fifty States, 1997, U.S. Presidents, 1997, U.S. Map Skills, 1997, Human body, 1998, National Parks and Other Park Service Sites, 1999, Our National Parks, 1999, Pathways of America: The California Mission Trail, 2000, Circling the World: Festivals and Celebrations, 2000, Endangered Species, 2001; contbr. articles to profl. jours. Vol., leader, bd. dirs. Girl Scouts U.S., 1957—; elder First Presbyn. Ch., Bend, 1980—; vol. hist. interpretation High Desert Mus., Bend, 1987-91; docent Mus. No. Ariz.; pres. bd. dirs. The Arboretum at Flagstaff; sec. bd. dirs. Palouse Discovery Sci. Ctr., 2000—. Recipient Excellence in Teaching award Bend Found., 1985-86, 86-87; named Tchr. of Yr. Oreg. Dept. Edn., 1982; Celebration Teaching grantee Geraldine Rockefeller Dodge Found., 1989, 90, 91, 92, 93, 94, 95, EPA grantee, 1997-99, Eisenhower Math and Sci. Edn. Act grantee, 1997, 99, Grand Canyon Assn. grantee, 1996, 97, 98; commd. Ky. Col., 1993. Mem. NEA, Internat. Coun. Assns. Sci. Edn. (newsletter advisor), Nat. Coun. Tchrs. Math., NSTA (internat. com.), Nat. State Tchrs. of Yr. (nat. pres. 1988-90), Nat. Assn. Rsch. in Sci. Tchg., Oreg. Coun. Tchrs. Math. (bd. dirs. 1981-82), Oreg. Coun. Tchrs. English (bd. dirs. 1981-82), Ariz. Reading Assn. (bd. dirs.), Nat. Coun. for Social Studies, Coun. for Elem. Sci. Internat. (bd. dirs. 1995-98, 99—, chair informal edn. com.), Internat. Reading Assn., Oreg.-Calif. Trails Assn., Nat. Sci. Edn. Leadership Assn., Assn. for Edn. of Tchrs. in Sci., Nat. Assn. for Rsch. in Sci. Tchg., S.W. Oreg.-Calif. Trails Assn., Lewis and Clark Trail Heritage Found., Delta Kappa Gamma (1st v.p.), Phi Delta Kappa (found. rep. 1991-92, v.p. programs 1992-93, historian 1993-94, v.p. membership 1994-95), Golden Key Hon., Pi Lambda Theta, Phi Kappa Phi, Kappa Delta Pi (past chpt. counselor, mem. spkrs. bur.), others. Avocations: cross-country skiing, photography, hiking, researching immigrant trails, gardening. Home: 720 SE Pheasant Run Pullman WA 99163 E-mail: lhatch@wsu.edu

HATCH, ORRIN GRANT, senator; b. Homestead Park, Pa., Mar. 22, 1934; s. Jesse and Helen (Kamm) H.; m. Elaine Hansen, Aug. 28, 1957; children: Brent, Marcia, Scott, Kimberly, Alysa, Jess. B.S., Brigham Young U., 1959; J.D., U. Pitts., 1962; LLD (hon.), U. Md., 1981; MS (hon.), Def. Intelligence Coll., 1982; LLD (hon.), Pepperdine U., 1990, So. Utah State U., 1990. Bar: Pa. 1962, Utah 1962. Ptnr. firm Thomson, Rhodes & Grigsby, Pitts., 1962-69, Hatch & Plumb, Salt Lake City, 1976; senator from Utah U.S. Senate, 1977—, past chmn. labor and human resources com., chmn. Senate judiciary com., chmn. subcom. on taxation, mem. fin. com., senate Rep. policy com., com. on Indian affairs, fin. com., mem. select com. on intelligence, 1997—. Author ERA Myths and Realities, 1983; contbr. articles to newspapers and profl. jours. Recipient Outstanding Legislator award Nat. Assn. Rehab. Facilities, Legislator of Yr. award Am. Assn. Univ. Affiliated Programs, Legis. Leadership award Health Profl. Assn., many others. Mem. Am., Nat., Utah, Pa. bar assns., Am. Judicature Soc. Republican. Mormon. Avocations: golf, poetry, piano playing, composer lyrics.*

HATCHER, HERBERT JOHN, biochemist, microbiologist; b. Mpls., Dec. 18, 1926; s. Herbert Edmond and Florence Elizabeth (Larson) H.; m. Beverly J. Johnson, Mar. 28, 1953 (dec. July 1985); children: Dennis Michal, Steven Craig, Roger Dean, Mark Alan, Susan Diane, Laura Jean; m. Louise Fritsche Nelson, May 24, 1986; children: Carlos Howard Nelson, Kent Robert Nelson, Carolyn Louise Tyler. BA, U. Minn., 1953, MS, 1964, PhD, 1965. Bacteriologist VA Hosp., Wilmington, Del., 1956-57; microbiologist Smith, Kline, French, Phila., 1957-60, Clinton (Iowa) Corn Processing, 1966-67; microbiologist, biochemist Econs. Lab. Inc., St. Paul, 1967-84; biochemist EG&G Idaho Inc., Idaho Falls, 1984-90; co-owner B/CG Cons. Svcs., Idaho Falls, 1990—. Chmn. bd. edn. Cross of Christ Luth. Ch., Coon Rapids, Minn., 1974-76; pres. chpt. Aid Assn. Luths., Idaho Falls, 1986; pres.-elect St. Johns Luth. Ch., 1988, pres., 1989. With USNR, 1945-46. Avocations: skiing, hiking, camping, hunting, fishing.

HATELEY, J. MICHAEL, human resources executive; BA Psychology, U. Calif.-L.A. Mgr. human resourves Monogram Industries, ITT; v.p. pres. human resources Mil. Aircraft, Elec., Aircraft Northrop Grumman, Inc., L.A., 1976-99, corp. v.p. personnel, 1999; corp. v.p., chief human resourve Northrop Grumman Corp., L.A., 1999—. Office: Northrop Grumman Corp 1840 Century Park E Los Angeles CA 90067-2101

HATFIELD, ELAINE CATHERINE, psychology educator; b. Detroit, Oct. 22, 1937; d. Charles E. and Eileen (Kalahar) H.; m. Richard L. Rapson, June 15, 1982. BA, U. Mich., 1959; PhD, Stanford U., 1963. Asst. prof. U. Minn., Mpls., 1963-64, assoc. prof., 1964-66; asso. prof. U. Rochester, 1966-68, U. Wis., Madison, 1968-69, prof., 1969-81; now prof. U. Hawaii, Honolulu, chmn. dept. psychology, 1981-83. Author: Equity: Theory and Research, 1978, Mirror, Mirror: The Importance of Looks in Everyday Life, 1986, Psychology of Emotions, 1991, Love, Sex and Intimacy, 1993, Emotional Contagion, 1994, Love and Sex: Cross-cultural Perspectives, 1996, Rosie, 2000; contbr. articles to profl. jours. Recipient Disting. Scientist award Soc. Exptl. Social Psychology, 1993. Fellow APA; mem. Soc. Sci. Study of Sex (pres., Disting. Scientist award 1996, Alfred Kinsey award 1998). Home: 3334 Anoai Pl Honolulu HI 96822-1418 Office: U Hawaii 2430 Campus Rd Honolulu HI 96822-2216 E-mail: elaineh@Hawaii.edu

HATFIELD, MARK ODOM, former senator; b. Dallas, July 12, 1922; s. Charles Dolen and Dovie (Odom) H.; m. Antoinette Kuzmanich, July 8, 1958; children: Mark, Elizabeth, Theresa, Charles. AB, Willamette U., 1943; AM, Stanford U., 1948. Instr. Willamette U., 1949, dean students, assoc. prof. polit. sci., 1950-56; mem. Oreg. Ho. of Reps., 1951-55, Oreg. Senate, 1955-57; sec. State of Oreg., 1957-59, gov., 1959-67; U.S. senator from Oreg., 1967-97. Chmn. appropriations com., energy and natural resources com., rules and adminstrn. com., joint printing com., joint libr. com., select com. Indian Affairs, Republican Policy Com.; chmn. Appropriations subcom. on transp. & related agencies. Author: Not Quite So Simple, 1967, Conflict and Conscience, 1971, Between A Rock and A Hard Place, 1976; co-author: Amnesty: The Unsettled Question of Vietnam, 1976, Freeze! How You Can Help Prevent Nuclear War, 1982, The Causes of World Hunger, 1982; co-author: What About the Russians, 1984, Vice Presidents of the United States 1789-1993, 1997. Lt. (j.g.) USN, 1943-45, PTO. Recipient over 100 hon. degrees Republican. Baptist. Office: PO Box 8639 Portland OR 97207-8639*

HATHCOCK, BONITA CATHERINE, telecommunications company executive; b. Chambersburg, Pa., Oct. 30, 1948; d. John McGillis Gentry and Lola Vaneda (Showaker) Wood; m. Lindsay Levoy Hathcock, Apr. 14, 1984. BS in Bus., Shippensburg State U., 1971; MBA, Nova U., 1989. Instr. bus. Cen. Pa. Bus. Sch., Summerdale, 1972-75; with Xerox Corp., various locations, 1975-84, product planning mgr. Dallas, 1982-84; dir. mktg. edn. Datapoint Corp., San Antonio, 1984-85, sr. dir. corp. edn., 1985, sr. dir. worldwide edn., 1985-87; dir. corp. tng. Siemens/Tel Plus, Boca Raton, Fla., 1987—. Prin. bcG Enterprises (profl. awareness tng. co.) Dallas, 1982-84. Avocations: cooking, swimming, reading, walking, writing. Office: Rolm 4900 Old Ironsides Dr Santa Clara CA 95054-1811

HATLEN, JOEL S. electronics manufacturing executive; b. 1958; With Ernst & Young LLP; sr. tax acct., tax mgr., corp. contr., chief acctg. officer Data I/O Corp., Redmond, Wash., 1991, v.p. fin., CFO, 1998—. Office: PO Box 97046 10525 Willow Rd NE Redmond WA 98073-9746

HATTER, TERRY JULIUS, JR. federal judge; b. Chgo., Mar. 11, 1933; A.B., Wesleyan U., 1954; J.D., U. Chgo., 1960. Bar: Ill. 1960, Calif. 1965, U.S. Dist. Ct. 1960, U.S. Ct. Appeals 1960. Adjudicator, Chgo., 1960-61; assoc. Harold M. Calhoun, Chgo., 1961-62; asst. pub. defender Cook County Chgo., 1961-62; asst. U.S. atty. No. Dist. Calif., San Francisco, 1962-66; chief counsel San Francisco Neighborhood Legal Assistance Found., 1966-67; regional legal svcs. dir. Exec. Office Pres. OEO, San Francisco, 1967-70; exec. dir. Western Ctr. Law and Poverty, L.A., 1970-73; exec. asst. to mayor, dir. criminal justice planning L.A., 1974-75; spl. asst. to mayor, dir. urban devel., 1975-77; judge Superior Ct. Calif., L.A., 1977-80, U.S. Dist. Ct. (cen. dist.) Calif., L.A., 1979-98, chief judge, 1998—. Lectr. Police Acad., San Francisco Police Dept., 1963-66, U. Calif., San Diego, 1970-71, Colo. Jud. Conf., 1973; assoc. clin. prof. law U. So. Calif. Law Ctr., L.A., 1970-74, mem. bd. councilors; prof. law Loyola U. Sch. Law, L.A., 1973-75; mem. faculty Nat. Coll. State Judiciary, Reno, 1974. V.p. Northbay Halfway House, 1964-65; vice chmn. Los Angeles Regional Criminal Justice Planning Bd., 1975-76; mem. Los Angeles Mayor's Cabinet Com. Econ. Devel., 1976-77, Mayor's Policy Com., 1973-77, chmn. housing econ. and community devel. com., City Los Angeles, 1975-77, chmn. housing and community devel. tech. com., 1975-77; vice chmn. Young Dems. Cook County, 1961-62; chmn. bd. Real Estate Coop; bd. dirs. Bay Area Social Planning Con., Contra Costa, Black Law Center L.A., Nat. Fedn. Settlements & Neighborhood Ctrs., Edn. Fin. & Governance Reform Project, Mexican Am. Legal Def. & Ednl. Fund, Nat. Health Law Program, Nat. Sr. Citizens Law Ctr., Calif. Law Ctr., L.A. Regional Criminal Justice Planning Bd.; mem. exec. com. bd. dirs. Constl. Rights Found; trustee Wesleyan Univ. Meth. Ch.; mem. bd. visitors U. Chgo. Law Sch. Mem. NAACP (exec. com., bd. dirs. Richmond chpt.), Nat. Legal Aid & Defender Assn. (dir., vice chmn.), L.A. County Bar Assn. (exec. com.), Am. Judicature Soc., Charles Houston Law Club, Phi Delta Phi, Order Coif. Office: US Dist Ct 312 N Spring St Los Angeles CA 90012-4701

HAUGEN, MARY MARGARET, state legislator; b. Camano Island, Wash., Jan. 14, 1941; d. Melvin Harry and Alma Cora (Huntington) Olsen; m. Basil Badley; children: Mary Beth Fisher, Katherine Heitt, Richard, James. Mem. Wash. Ho. Reps., Olympia, 1982-1992, past mem. natural resources com., transp. com., mem. joint legis. com. on criminal justice system; mem. Wash. Senate, Dist. 10, Olympia, 1993—. Chmn. govt. ops. com., transp. com., natural resource com., law and justice com. Wash. State Senate. Mem. LWV, Stanwood Camano Soroptimists. Democrat. Methodist. Lodge: Order Ea. Star. Avocations: fishing, reading, collecting antique clothing. Office: Wash Senate John A Cherberg Bldg Rm 435 PO Box 40482 Olympia WA 98504-0482

HAUGHEY, JAMES MCCREA, lawyer, artist; b. Courtland, Kans., July 8, 1914; s. Leo Eugene and Elizabeth (Stephens) H.; m. Katherine Hurd, Sept. 8, 1938; children: Katherine (Mrs. Lester B. Loo), Bruce Stephens, John Caldwell. Student, Deep Springs Coll., 1930-31; LLB, U. Kans., 1939. Bar: Kans. 1939, Mont. 1943. Landman Carter Oil Co., 1939-43; practice in Billings, Mont., 1943-98; ptnr. Crowley, Haughey, Hanson, Toole & Dietrich, 1950-86, counsel, 1986-98; ret. dir. Mont.-Dakota Resources Group Inc., 1998. One-man shows include, U. Kans., U. Mont., Mont. State U., Concordia Coll., Nebr., C.M. Russell Mus., Great Falls, Mont., Boise Mus. Art, Mont. State Mus., Helena, Sandzen Gallery, Bethany Coll., Lindsborg, Kans., Yellowstone Art Mus., Billings, Mont., also numerous group shows. Pres. Rocky Mountain Mineral Law Found., 1957-58, trustee, 1955— ; pres. Mont. Inst. Arts Found., 1965-67; pres. Yellowstone Art Center Found., 1969-71, trustee, 1964-81; mem. Mont.

Ho. of Reps., 1960-64, Mont. Senate, 1966-70, senate minority leader, 1969-70. Recipient Gov.'s award for Arts, 1981 Fellow Mont. Inst. Arts (Permanent Collection award 1960), Am. Artists Profl. League; mem. ABA, Am. Coll. Real Estate Lawyers, Yellowstone County Bar Assn. (pres. 1960-61), U. Kans. Law Soc. (bd. govs. 1989-92), Am. Watercolor Soc. (Midwest v.p. 1978-82), N.W. Watercolor Soc. (life), Midwest Watercolor Soc., Kans. Watercolor Soc. (hon.), Mont. Watercolor Soc. (hon.), Phi Delta Theta, Phi Delta Phi. Republican. Episcopalian. Home: 2205 Tree Ln Billings MT 59102-2560 Office: Crowley Haughey Hanson Toole & Dietrich TransWestern Pla II 490 N 31st St Billings MT 59101-1256 E-mail: jhaughey@crowleylaw.com, jimhoy4@home.com

HAUGHTON, JAMES GRAY, medical facility administrator, municipal health department administrator, consultant, physician; b. Panama City, Republic of Panama, Mar. 30, 1925; came to U.S., 1942, naturalized, 1953; s. Johnathan Antonio and Alice Eugeney (Gray) H.; m. Vivian Bruna Sodini, July 10, 1982; children— James Gray, Paula Yvette B.A., Pacific Union Coll., 1947; M.D., Loma Linda U., 1950; M.P.H., Columbia U., 1962; D.Sc. (hon.), U. of Health Scis., Chgo. Med. Sch., 1971. diplomate Am. Bd. Preventive Medicine. Intern Unity Hosp., Bklyn., 1949-50, fellow in abdominal surgery, 1950-54; resident in preventive medicine N.Y.C. Health Dept., 1960-63, exec. med. dir., 1964-66; first dep. N.Y.C. Health Svcs. Adminstrn., 1966-70; exec. dir. Health and Hosps. Governing Commn. Cook County, Ill., 1970-79; v.p. Drew Postgrad. Med. Sch., Los Angeles, 1980-83; dir. Houston Dept. Health and Human Services, 1983-87; med. dir. Martin. Luther King Jr./Charles Drew Med. Ctr., L.A. Dept. Health Svcs., 1987-93; assoc. dean Drew U., 1989-93. Prof. medicine Charles Drew U., 1987—, UCLA, 1987—; cons. AID Costa Rica Mission, 1982; adj. prof. adminstrv. scis. U. Tex. Health Sci. Ctr., Houston, 1984-87; mem. health svcs. com. Houston Red Cross, 1984-87; mem. Houston Mayor's Task Force on Aids, 1984-87; bd. dirs. Alan Gutmacher Rsch. Inst., 1985-91; AIDS cons. Regional Ministry Pub. Health, Santiago de Compostela, Spain, 1986; sr. investigator Digestive Diseases Ctr., L.A., 1987-91; AIDS med. adv. com. L.A. County Dept. Health Svcs., 1988-91, chair com. on access to health svcs., 1988-91, sr. health svcs. policy advisor, 1993-96, med. dir. pub. health programs & svcs., 1996—; mem. substance abuse coverage study com. Inst. Medicine NAS, 1988-90, study com. environ. justice, 1996-99; mem. Commn. Future Structure of VA Med. Care, 1990-91; com. study co-adminstrn. svc./rsch. programs of Alcohol, Drug Abuse and Mental Health Adminstrn. HHS, 1990-91; mem. nat. adv. com. AIDS Svcs. Program, Robert Wood Johnson Found., 1986-91, AIDS Prevention Program, 1987-91; mem. personal health svcs. planning com. L.A. County Dept. of Health Svcs., 1991-93; mem. AIDS adv. com. Alcohol, Drug Abuse, Mental Health Adminstrn., U.S. Dept. Health and Human Svcs., 1991-93, mem. study com. ethics of the business aspects of Healthcare, 1995-97, study com. ethical considerations in managed care, 1997-99, Woodstock Theological Ctr., Georgetown; bd. dirs. Local Health Officers, 1993—, mem. health info. syss. com., 1993—, co-chair personal health svcs. com., 1996—; bd. dirs. Local Initiative Health Authority L.A. County, 1996-97, Preventive Med. Residence Adv. Com., State Calif. Preventive Med. Residency Prog.; hosp. surveyor Consolidated Accreditation and Licensure Survey Program, Calif. Med. Assn./Joint Com. Accreditation Healthcare Orgn., 1992-96. Mem. editl. bd. Jour. Cmty. Health, 1990—, Jour. Pub. Health Policy, 1999—. Mem. Houston Clean City Commn., 1985-87. Lt. comdr. USN, 1956-58. Recipient Merit award N.Y.C. Pub. Health Assn., 1964, Humanitarian award Nat. Assn. of Health Svc. Execs., 1972, cert. meritorious svc. Health and Hosp. Governing Commn. Cook County, Ill., 1979, Merit award March of Dimes, 1987, Sanville lectureship U.C.L.A. Sch. of Pub. Health, 1992. Fellow Am. Coll. Preventive Medicine (v.p. 1976-78), Am. Pub. Health Assn. (governing council 1965-70, medicine/pub. health initiative, chair com. on pub. health edn. in medicine residencies 1994—, managed care task force 1997—, Rosenhaus award 1974); mem. AMA, Inst. Medicine Nat. Acad. Scis., Tex. Med. Assn. (sexually transmitted diseases com. 1984-87), L.A. County Med. Assn., Calif. Med. Assn., Health Care Assn. So. Calif. (med. adv. com. 1995-99), L.A. Acad. Medicine. Democrat Avocations: music; photography; swimming. Home: 4259 Palmero Dr Los Angeles CA 90065-4220 Office: 313 N Figueroa St Ste 227 Los Angeles CA 90012-2602

HAUK, A. ANDREW, federal judge; b. Denver, Dec. 29, 1912; s. A.A. and Pearl (Woods) H.; m. Jean Nicolay, Aug. 30, 1941; 1 dau., Susan. AB magna cum laude, Regis Coll., 1935; LLB, Cath. U. Am., 1938; JSD (Sterling fellow), Yale U., 1942. Bar: Calif. 1942, Colo. 1939, D.C. 1938, U.S. Supreme Ct. 1953. Spl. asst. to atty. gen., counsel for govt. antitrust div. U.S. Dept Justice, Los Angeles, Pacific Coast, Denver, 1939-41; asst. U.S. atty., Los Angeles, 1941-42; with firm Adams, Duque & Hazeltine, Los Angeles, 1946-52; individual practice law Los Angeles, 1952-64; asst. counsel Union Oil Co., Los Angeles, 1952-64; judge Superior Ct., Los Angeles County, 1964-66; U.S. dist. judge Central Dist. Calif., 1966—, chief judge, 1980-82, now sr. judge, chief judge emeritus. Instr. Southwestern U. Law Sch., 1939-41; lectr. U. So. Calif. Law Sch., 1947-56; vice chmn. Calif. Olympic Com., 1954-61; ofcl. VIII Olympic Winter Games, Squaw Valley, 1960; Gov. Calif.'s del. IX Olympic Games, Innsbruck, Austria, 1964 Bd. dirs. So. Calif. Com. for Olympic Games. Served from lt. to lt. comdr., Naval Intelligence USNR, 1942-46. Recipient scroll Los Angeles County Bd. Suprs., 1965, 66, 75; Alumnus of Yr. Regis Coll., 1967; named to Nat. Ski Hall of Fame, 1975 Mem. Los Angeles County Bar Assn. (chmn. pleading and practice com. 1963-64, chmn. Law Day com. 1965-66), State Bar Calif. (corps. com., war work com. past vice-chmn.), ABA (com. criminal law sect.), Fed. Bar Assn., Lawyers Club Los Angeles, Am. Judicature Soc., Am. Legion, Navy League, U.S. Lawn Tennis Assn., Far West Ski Assn. (Nat. Sr. Giant Slalom champion 1954), Yale Law Sch. Assn. So. Calif. (dir., past pres.), Town Hall. Clubs: Yale of So. Calif. (dir. 1964-67), Newman; Valley Hunt (Pasadena); Jonathan (Los Angeles). Office: US Dist Ct US Courthouse 312 N Spring St Los Angeles CA 90012-4701

HAUN, HENRY LAMAR, protective services official; BS in Edn., U. Utah, 1959; postgrad., Patton State Mental Hosp., San Bernardino, Calif., 1960-61. Dir. Kiwanis, Salt Lake City, 1961-65; fed. probation and parole officer U.S. Cts., Utah, 1965-78, supr. fed. probation and parole, 1978-83, chief U.S. probation officer, 1983-89; chairperson Utah State Bd. Pardons, 1989-94, mem., 1994-97; exec. dir. Utah Corrections Dept., Murray, 1997—. Recipient J. A. Larson award State of Utah, citation Assn. of Parole Authorities Internat. Mem. U.S. Probational Alumni Assn., Utah State Corrections Assn., Commn. on Criminal and Juvenile Justice, Utah Sentencing Commn., Racial and Ethnic Commn. Office: State Utah 6100 Fashion Blvd Murray UT 84107-7378

HAUPT, RANDY LARRY, electrical engineering educator; b. Johnstown, Pa., Aug. 11, 1956; s. Howard and Anna Mae Haupt; m. Sue E. Slagle, Feb. 17, 1979; children: Bonny Ann, Amy Jean. BSEE, USAF Acad., 1978; MS in Engring. Mgmt., Western New Eng. Coll., 1981; MSEE, Northeastern U., 1983; PhD in Electrical Engring., U. Mich., 1987. Registered profl. engr., Colo. Commd. 2d lt. USAF, 1974, advanced through grades to lt. col., 1990, project engr. OTH-B Radar electronic systems divsn. Mass., 1978-80, rsch. engr. in microwave antennas Rome Air Devel. Ctr., 1980-84; instr., then asst. prof. elec. engring. USAF Acad., Colo., 1987-91; dir. rsch. dept. elec. engring. USAF, 1990-91, chief comm. div. dept. elec. engring., 1991—; assoc. prof. USAF Acad., 1991-94, prof., 1994-97, dept. for ops. dept. elec. engring., 1995-97; prof., chair dept. elec. engring. U. Nev., Reno, 1997—. Vis. rsch. engr. Los Alamos Nat. Lab., 1992; presenter numerous papers and tech. reports in field. Author: (with others) Practical Genetic Algorithms, 1998; contbr. numerous articles to engring. jours. Nordic ski team coach USAF Acad., 1992-93. Recipient USAF Rsch. and Devel. award, 1983, 87, Frank J. Seiler award for rsch. excellence, 1990, 92, Founder's Gold medal, 1993, 6 Rome Air Devel. Ctr. Sci. Achievement awards; named Outstanding Mil. Educator in Electrical Engring., 1992, USAF Mil. Engr. of Yr., 1993, Fed. Engr. of Yr., Nat. Soc. Profl. Engrs., 1993; rsch. grantee Rome Air Devel. Ctr., 1988-90, Frank J. Seiler Rsch. Lab., 1990—, Cray Rsch., Inc., 1991-92, Phillips Lab., 1992—. Mem. IEEE (sr., student br. counselor 1988-90, reviewer Transactions on Antennas and Propagation 1984—), Am. Soc. for Engring. Edn. (reviewer), Applied Computational Electromagnetics Soc., Tau Beta Pi. Achievements include research in electromagnetics, scattering, antennas, electro-optics, numerical methods, chaos theory, radar, systems engineering, communications systems. Office: U Nev Dept Elec Engring 260 Reno NV 89557-0001

HAUSER, RAY LOUIS, research engineer, entrepreneur; b. Litchfield, Ill., Apr. 16, 1927; s. A. Vernon and Grace (Gregg) H.; m. Consuelo Wright Minnich, Sept. 2, 1951; children: Beth, Cynthia, Dewi, Chris. BS, U. Ill., 1950; M in Engring., Yale U., 1952; PhD, U. Colo., 1957. Registered profl. engr., Colo., safety engr., Calif. Sr. project engr. Conn. Hard Rubber Co., New Haven, 1950-52; rsch. staff U. Colo., Boulder, 1954-57; material tech. staff Martin Co., Denver, 1957-61; owner, mgr. Hauser Labs., Boulder, 1961-89. Bd. dirs. Surface Solutions Inc., Boulder, ICAT Systems Inc., Phoenix; vis. lectr. U. Colo., Boulder, 1957-63. Pres. Boulder Civic Opera, 1971-72. Sgt. U.S. Army, 1952-54. Recipient U. Colo. medal, 1995. Fellow AAAS; mem. AIChE, Soc. Plastics Engrs. (bd. dirs. 1959-62), Assn. Cons. Chemists and Chem. Engrs. (bd. dirs. 1986), Am. Assn. Lab. Accreditation (bd. dirs. 1986-91), Rotary (bd. dirs. 1975-77). Home and Office: 5758 Rustic Knolls Dr Boulder CO 80301-3029 E-mail: ray@rayhauser.com

HAUSER, STEPHEN L. medical educator; Chair, prof. neurosurgery U. Calif., San Francisco. Office: U Calif San Francisco Dept Neurology PO Box 114 San Francisco CA 94143-0001

HAUSMAN, ARTHUR HERBERT, electronics company executive; b. Chgo., Nov. 24, 1923; s. Samuel Louis and Sarah (Elin) H.; m. Helen Mandelowitz, May 19, 1946; children: Susan Lois, Kenneth Louis, Catherine Ellen. B.S. in Elec. Engring, U. Tex., 1944; S.M., Harvard U., 1948. Electronics engr. Engring. Research Assos., St. Paul, 1946-47; supervisory electronics scientist U.S. Dept. Def., Washington, 1948-60; now advisor, v.p., dir. research Ampex Corp., Redwood City, Calif., 1960-63, v.p. ops., 1963-65, group v.p., 1965-67, exec. v.p., 1967-71, exec. v.p., pres., chief exec. officer, 1971-83, chmn. bd., 1981-87, chmn. bd. emeritus, 1987—. Chmn. tech. adv. com. computer peripherals Dept. Commerce, 1973-75; mem. Pres.'s Export Coun.; chmn. Subcom. on Export Adminstrn., 1984-88; bd. dirs. Drexler Tech. Inc., Vista Rsch. Inc., Calif.-Amplifier, Inc. Trustee United Bay Area Crusade.; mem. vis. com. dept. math. MIT; Bd. dirs. Bay Area Council. Served with USNR, 1944-54. Recipient Meritorious Civilian Service award Dept. Def. Mem. IEEE, Army Ordnance Assn. (dir. chpt. 1969-71), Am. Electronics Assn. (dir.) Clubs: Commonwealth of Calif.; Cosmos

HAVEKOST, DANIEL JOHN, architect; b. Fremont, Nebr., May 12, 1936; s. Alvin Deidrich and Magdalen (Osterman) H.; m. Patricia Jo Haney, June 6, 1959 (div. June 1983); children: Christopher, Karen; m. Sandra Schwendemann, Aug. 29, 1993 (div. Nov. 1999). Lic. architect, Colo., Calif., Tex., N.D.; cert. Nat. Council Archtl. Registration Bds. Designer Papachristou & Assoc., Denver, 1959-61; architect Anshen & Allen, San Francisco, 1961-62; assoc. Hornbein & White, Denver, 1962-63; ptnr. Papachristou & Havekost, Denver, 1963-64; prin. Havekost & Assocs., Denver, 1964-71; pres. HWH Assocs., Inc., Denver, 1971-91, Havekost & Lee Architects P.C., Denver, 1991-95, Havekost & Assoc., P.C., 1996—. Vis. lectr. U. Colo., Denver, 1969, 72, 82; sec., treas. Encore Devel. Corp., Denver, 1984-91. Prin. works include Encore Redevel. (AIA award 1985,86), Grant Street Mansion (Colo. Soc. Architects, AIA award 1979), Reverend's Ridge (Western Mountain Region AIA award 1973, Havekost Residence Western Mountain Region AIA award 1971). Bd. dirs. Denver Cmty. Design Ctr., 1968-72, Hist. Paramount Found., Denver, 1980-94, Hist. Denver, 1978-82; panel mem. Gen. Svcs. Adminstrn., Denver, 1978-79, mem. plan enforcement rev. and variation com., Denver, 1970-76. Served with USNR, 1954-62. Recipient Archtl. Excellence awards WOOD Inc., 1968-82, Honor award for Adaptive Re-use, Historic Denver, 1975, WOOD Design award Nat. Cattlemen's Hdqrs., 1982. Fellow AIA (pres. Denver chpt. 1978-81, chmn. Colo. chpt. govt. affairs com. 1984-91, pres. Colo. chpt. 1981-83, Colo. hist. preservation officer 1982—, recipient Fisher Traveling award of Colo. AIA Ednl. Fund 1988, excellence archtl. design award 1960). Avocations: skiing, tennis, drawing. Office: Havekost & Assocs PC 1121 Grant St Denver CO 80203-2301

HAVEL, RICHARD JOSEPH, physician, educator; b. Seattle, Feb. 20, 1925; s. Joseph and Anna (Fritz) H.; m. Virginia Johnson, June 28, 1947; children: Christopher, Timothy, Peter, Julianne. BA, Reed Coll., 1946; MS, MD, U. Oreg., 1949. Intern Cornell U. Med. Coll., N.Y.C., 1949-50, resident in medicine, 1950-53; clin. assoc. Nat. Heart Inst., NIH, 1953-54, research assoc., 1954-56; faculty Sch. Medicine, U. Calif., San Francisco, 1956—, prof. medicine, 1964—; assoc. dir. Cardiovascular Research Inst., 1961-73, dir., 1973-92. Chief metabolism sect., dept. medicine, 1967-97 ; dir. Arteriosclerosis Specialized Center of Research, 1971-96 ; mem. bd. sci. counselors Nat. Heart, Lung and Blood Inst., 1976-80; chmn. food and nutrition bd. NRC, 1987-90; pres. Lipid Rsch., Inc., 1999—. Contbr. chpts. to books, numerous articles to profl. jours.; editor: Jour. Lipid Research, 1972-75; mem. editorial bd.: Jour. Biol. Chemistry, 1981-85, Jour. Arteriosclerosis, 1980—. Established investigator Am. Heart Assn., 1956-61, chmn. coun. on arteriosclerosis, 1977-79. With USPHS, 1951-53. Recipient Disting. Achievement award Am. Heart Assn., 1993, Bristol-Myers award for nutrition rsch., 1989, gold medal Charles U., Prague, Czech Republic, 1996. Fellow AAS (Theobald Smith award 1960); mem. NAS, Inst. Medicine NAS, Am. Acad. Arts and Scis., Am. Soc. Clin. Nutrition (McCollum award 1993), Assn. Am. Physicians, Am. Soc. for Clin. Investigation, Am. Inst. Nutritional Sci., Western Soc. Clin. Investigation (Mayo Soley award 1997), Phi Beta Kappa, Alpha Omega Alpha. Office: U Calif San Francisco Cardiovascular Rsch In San Francisco CA 94143-0130

HAVEL, RICHARD W. lawyer; b. Fairmont, Minn., Sept. 20, 1946; s. Thomas Earl and Elizabeth (Shiltz) H.; m. Arlene Havel, July 6, 1968; children: Stephanie, Derek. BA, Notre Dame U., 1968; JD, UCLA, 1971. Bar: Calif., U.S. Dist. Ct. (no., ea., cen. and so. dists.) Calif., U.S. Ct. Appeals (9th cir.). Atty. Shutan & Trost, L.A., 1971-80, Sidley & Austin, L.A., 1980—. Instr. law U. Loyola, 1975-80; bd. govs. Fin. Lawyers Conf., 1991-94, 95-98, officer, 1998-2001; spkr., panelist Bankruptcy Litigation Inst., 1989-95, ALI-ABA, 1989, 90, 91; chmn. L.A. City Indsl. Devel. Authority, 1993-98, bd. dirs., 1998-2000. Contbr. articles to profl. jours. Trustee Jonsson/UCLA Cancer Ctr., 1998—. Fellow Am. Coll. Bankruptcy, 1997; mem. ABA, Calif. Bar Assn., L.A. County Bar Assn. (comml. law & bankruptcy sect. bankruptcy subcom. 1986-89, exec. com. 1987-90, lawyer assistance com. 1985—), UCLA Law Alumni Assn. (trustee 1996—). Office: Sidley & Austin 555 W 5th St 40th Fl Los Angeles CA 90013-1010 E-mail: RHavel@Sidley.com

HAVEMANN, MICHAEL R. legal administration; b. San Francisco, Aug. 31, 1944; BA in Polit. Sci., Brigham Young U., 1969, MPA, 1972. Coord. criminal justice planning City Mgr.'s Office City of Phoenix, 1972-74, asst. ct. adminstr. Mcpl. Ct., 1975-78, ct. adminstr., 1978-83; mgmt. asst. planning and rsch. bur. Phoenix Police Dept., 1974-75; ct. exec. State of Utah 4th Jud. Dist., 1983-92; ct. adminstr. Las Vegas Mcpl. Ct., 1992—. Mem. Ct. Exec. Devel. Program. Co-author: (study) Internal Audition in State Govt., 1972. Fellow Inst. Ct. Mgmt. (Nat. Ctr. State Cts.); mem. Nat. Assn. Ct. Mgmt. Office: Mcpl Ct City Las Vegas City Hall 400 Stewart Ave Las Vegas NV 89101-2927

HAVLICEK, MICHAEL, medical association administrator; Pres. ALS (Lou Gehrig's Disease) Assn. Office: ALS Lou Gehrigs Disease Assn 27001 Agoura Rd Ste 150 Agoura Hills CA 91301-5104

HAW, JAMES F. organic chemist; BS in Chemistry, Old Dominion U., 1977; MS, U. N.C., 1979; PhD in Chemistry, Va. Tech., 1982. Postdoctoral fellow Colo. State U., 1982-83; asst. prof. Tex. A&M U., 1984-89, assoc. prof., 1989-91, prof. chemistry, 1992—, dir. Lab. for Magnetic Resonance and Molecular Sci., 1993—; R.R. Irani CEO Occidental Petroleum, prof. chemistry U. So. Calif., L.A. Chair NMR Symposium, Rocky Mountain Conf., 1984-88; chair Tex. A&M local sect. Am. Chem. Soc., 1989-90. Contbr. articles to profl. jours. Recipient Yarwood medal Brit. Vacuum Coun., 1992, George A. Olah award in hydrocarbon or petroleum chemistry Am. Chem. Soc., 2000. Achievements include research in heterogeneous catalysis by zeolites, metal oxides and supported metals. Office: Dept Chemistry Univ So Calif Los Angeles CA 90089 Fax: 213-740-6679. E-mail: haw@methyl.usc.edu

HAWKE, BERNARD RAY, planetary scientist; b. Louisville, Oct. 22, 1946; s. Arvil Abner and Elizabeth Ellen (Brown) H. B.S. in Geology, U. Ky., 1970, M.S., 1974, Brown U., 1977, Ph.D. in Planetary Geology, 1978. Geologist U.S. Geol. Survey, 1967-68; researcher U. Ky., 1972-74, Brown U., 1974-78; planetary scientist Hawaii Inst. Geophysics, U. Hawaii, Honolulu, 1978—; dir. NASA Pacific Regional Planetary Data Ctr., 1981—; prin. investigator NASA grants. Assoc. dir. Hawaii Space Grant Coll. Author papers in field. Served with USAR, 1970-72. Decorated Bronze Star Mem. Geochem. Soc., Meteoritical Soc., Am. Geophys. Union, Am. Chem. Soc., Geol. Soc. Am., Sigma Xi, Sigma Gamma Epsilon, Alpha Tau Omega. Republican. Office: U Hawaii SOEST Hawaiian Inst Geophysics Honolulu HI 96822

HAWKE, ROBERT FRANCIS, dentist; b. Pasadena, Calif., Oct. 26, 1946; s. George Herbert and Mildred Estelle (Wood) H.; m. Emily Sue Wilkins, Aug. 17, 1973; 1 child, Kristen. BA, U. Ariz., 1969; DDS, Baylor U., Dallas, 1973. Assoc. B.J. Barber, Tucson, 1976-78; ptnr. Barber-Hawke, P.C., Tucson, 1978-87; pvt. practice Tucson, 1987—. Bd. dirs., pres. Delta Dental Ariz., Phoenix, 1985-91. Mem. Tucson Bus. Alliance, 1981—, pres., 1983, 94, Comty. Auto Immune Deficiency Syndrome Adv. Coun., Tucson, 1987-90, Auto Immune Deficiency Syndrome Edn. Project, Tucson, 1988-90. Maj. U.S. Army. Fellow Am. Coll. Dentists, Internat. Coll. Dentists; mem. ADA (alt. del. 1988-92, del. 1994-2000, 14th dist. chmn. ADPAC 1995-98), Ariz. State Dental Assn. (trustee 1988, v.p. 1991, pres.-elect 1992-93, pres. 1993-94, past pres. 1994-95), So. Ariz. Dental Soc. (bd. dirs. 1983-89, pres. 1987-88), Pierre Fauchard Acad., Rotary (Paul Harris fellow), Beta Beta Beta. Republican. Evangelical. Avocations: golf, jogging, tennis, racquetball, reading. Home: 6745 E Tivani Dr Tucson AZ 85715-3348 Office: 1575 N Swan Rd Ste 200 Tucson AZ 85712-4068 E-mail: robertfhawke@worldnet.att.net

HAWKINS, ALAN J. family life educator, researcher; b. Washington, July 8, 1955; s. Carl Stolworthy and Nelma Jean (Jones) H.; m. Lisa Anne Bolin, Feb. 18, 1977; children: Caitlin Anne, Brian Alan. BS, Brigham Young U., 1979, MS, 1984; PhD, Pa. State U., 1990. From personnel rsch. analyst to sr. compensation analyst BankAm. Corp., San Francisco, 1983-86; asst. prof. family scis. Brigham Young U., Provo, Utah, 1990—. Bd. dirs. Utah Coun. on Fam. Rels., 1992—. Assoc. editor Family Rels., 1992—, Family Perspective, 1990-93; reviewer Jour. Marriage & the Family, 1989—. Avocations: backpacking, basketball, racquetball. Office: Brigham Young U 1054 Kimball Tower Provo UT 84602

HAWKINS, JAMES VICTOR, former state official; b. Coeur d'Alene, Idaho, Sept. 28, 1936; s. William Stark and Agnes M. (Ramstedt) H.; m. Gail Ruth Guernsey, June 19, 1959; children— John William, Nancy Clare. BS, U. Idaho, 1959, D of Adminstrv. Sci., 1996; postgrad., Am. Savs. and Loan Inst., 1960-67, Pacific Coast Banking Sch., 1970—. Mgmt. trainee Gen. Telephone Co. of N.W., Coeur d'Alene, 1959-60; asst. mgr. First Fed. Savs. & Loan Assn., Coeur d'Alene, 1960-67; v.p., gen. mgr. Idaho S.W. Devel. Co., Boise, 1967-68; v.p., trust officer First Security Bank of Idaho, N.A., Boise, 1968-72; pres. Statewide Stores Inc., Boise, 1972-82; spl. projects adminstr. Lucky Stores Inc., 1982-84; pvt. practice fin. cons. Boise, 1984-87; dir. dept. commerce State of Idaho, Boise, 1987-96, ret., 1996; mng. ptnr. Hwy. 12 Ventures, 2000—. Bd. dirs. Blue Cross of Idaho, Early Childhood Devel., State of Idaho, Summit Securities, Old Standard Life, Old West Annuity and Life. Bd. dirs., chmn. adv. bd. Coll. Bus. and Econs. U. Idaho; bd. dirs. Idaho Total Quality Inst., Boise United Fund, Boise Art Assn.; pres. U. Idaho Found.; exec. bd. Coun. State Community Affairs Agys.; bd. dirs., pres. Nat. Assn. State Devel. Agys.; mem. Indsl. Devel. Rsch. Coun.; exec. com. Coun. State and Community Devel. Agys.; chmn. Idaho R.R. Adv. Coun. Named Outstanding Young Idahoan Idaho Jr. C. of C., 1967. Mem. Am. Inst. Banking, Boise C. of C., U. Idaho Alumni Assn. (mem. exec. bd.), Elks, Coeur d'Alene, Rotary, Crane Creek Country Club, Hayden Lake Country Club, Phi Gamma Delta. Episcopalian. Home: 163 E Ridgeline Dr Boise ID 83702-6517 E-mail: jim@highway12ventures.com

HAWKINS, JASPER STILLWELL, JR. architect; b. Orange, N.J., Nov. 10, 1932; s. Jasper Stillwell and Bernice (Ake) H.; m. Patricia A. Mordigan, Mar. 22, 1980; children: William Raymond, John Stillwell, Karen Ann, Jasper Stillwell III. B.Arch., U. So. Calif., 1955. Registered architect, Calif., Ariz., N.Mex. Founder, prin. Hawkins & Lindsey & Assocs., L.A., 1958-90, Hawkins Lindsey Wilson Assocs., L.A. and Phoenix, 1978-85; pres. Fletcher-Thompson Assocs., 1981-84; prin. Jasper Stillwell Hawkins, F.A.I.A., architect, Phoenix, 1990—. Bd. visitors Nat. Fire Acad., 1978-80; bd. dirs. Nat. Inst. Bldg. Scis., 1976-85, chmn. bd. dirs., 1981-83, consultative council, 1978— ; mem. com. protection of archives and records centers GSA, 1975-77; mem. archtl. adv. panel Calif. State Bldg. Standards Commn., 1964-70; mem. U.S. del. to UN Econ. Commn. for Europe Working Party on Bldg., 1978-84; mem. U.S. presdl. del. to Honduran Presdl. Elections, 1985; mem. com. standards and evaluation Nat. Conf. States on Bldg. Codes and Standards, 1971-74; mem. Am. Arbitration Assn., 1992—; trustee Underwriter's Labs., 1984—, mem. nat. coun. Archtl. Registration Bds., 1971—; participant and speaker numerous confs. Contbr. articles to profl. jours.; maj. works include Valley Music Theatre, L.A., Houston Music Theatre, Sundome Theatre and R.H. Johnson Ctr., Sun City West, Ariz., Bell Recreation Ctr., Sun City, U. Calif. at Irvine Student Housing, Oxnard (Calif.) Fin. Ctr., condominium devels. Lakes Club, Sun City. Mem. Nev. Gov.'s Commn. Fire Safety Codes, 1980-81, Pres. Reagan's Commn. on Housing, 1981-82, City of Phoenix ACDC Task Force, 1985-86, ACDC Aesthetics Commn., 1986-89, City of Phoenix Camelback East Village Planning Com., 1983-89; mem. fire rsch. panel Nat. Bur. Stds., 1978-81; chmn. NAS fire assessment rev. com., 1987-88, com. on analytical methods for designing bldgs. for fire safety, 1977-78; chmn. bldg. seismic safety coun. ind. rev. panel San Francisco

War Meml. Opera House, 1995. Recipient design awards from Ariz. Rock Products Assn., Theater Assn. Am., Nat. Food Facilities, House and Home Mag., Practical Builders Mag., Am. Builders Mag., Nat. Inst. of Bldg. Sci. Inst. award, 1995, others. Fellow AIA (mem. codes and stds. com. 1970—, chmn. 1970-73, nat. liaison commn. with Assoc. Gen. Contractors 1969-70, chmn. nat. fire safety task force 1972-74, chmn. Calif. coun. AIA state code com. 1964-68, chmn. nat. conf. industrialized constrn. 1969-70, nat. com. bldg. industry coordination 1969-70, nat. rep. to Internat. Conf. Bldg. Ofcls. 1969, state Calif. AIA codes com. 1960-70, chmn. 1965-70, nat. AIA codes and stds. com. 1970-80, chmn. 1970-74, nat. crisis adv. com. 1988-89), 1976—; mem. ASCE (task force bldg. codes 1971-74), ASTM, Nat. Fire Protection Assn. (com. bldg. heights and areas 1965-72, chmn. 1968-72, fire prevention code com. 1974-76, bd. dirs. 1985-93, chmn. nat. model codes coordinating com. 1983-86, stds. coun. 1996—, bldg. code task force 2000—), Nat. Fire Acad. (bd. regents 1980-83), Nat. Bur. Stds. Fire (rsch. adv. com. 1979-82), Nat. Acad. Forensic Engrs., Ariz. C. of C. (policy com. 1983-84), Ariz. Biltmore Village Estates Homeowners Assn. (pres. 1981-83), Phoenix C. of C. (chmn. Water task force 1982-83). Office: 1158 E Missouri Ave Ste 220 Phoenix AZ 85014-2720

HAWKINS, JAY L. electronics executive; BSBA, Boise State U. With test dept. Micron Tech., Inc., various positions, test prodn. control mgr., mgr. test dept., dir. mfg., 1991-96, v.p. ops., 1996—. Office: PO Box 6 Boise ID 83707-0006

HAWKINS, MICHAEL DALY, federal judge; b. Winslow, Ariz., Feb. 12, 1945; s. William Bert and Patricia Agnes (Daly) H.; m. Phyllis A. Lewis, June 4, 1966; children: Aaron, Adam. BA, Ariz. State U., 1967, JD cum laude, 1970; LLM, U. Va., 1998. Bar: Ariz. 1970, U.S. Ct. Mil. Appeals 1971, U.S. Supreme Ct. 1974. Pvt. practice law, 1973-77, 80-94; U.S. atty. Dept. Justice, Phoenix, 1977-80; judge U.S. Ct. Appeals (9th cir.), Phoenix, 1994—. Mem. Appellate Cts. Jud. Nominating Commn., 1985-89. Staff editor: Ariz. State U. Law Jour, 1968-70. Mem. Ariz. Lottery Commn., 1980-83, Commn. on Uniform State Laws, 1988-93. Capt. USMC, 1970-73. Recipient Alumni Achievement award Ariz. State U., 1995. Mem. ABA, Maricopa County Bar Assn. (bd. dirs. 1975-77, 81-89, pres. 1987-88), State Bar of Ariz., Ariz. Trial Lawyers Assn. (bd. dirs. 1976-77, state sec. 1976-77), Phoenix Trial Lawyers Assn., Adminstrv. Conf. U.S. (pub. mem. 1985-94), Nat. Assn. Former U.S. Attys. (pres. 1989-90).

HAWKINS, RICHARD, pharmaceutical and cosmetics company executive; CFO McKesson Corp., San Francisco. Office: McKesson Corp 1 Post St Ste 3275 San Francisco CA 94104-5292

HAWKINS, ROBERT B. think tank executive; PhD, U Wash. Chmn. Adv. Commn. on Intergovt. Rels., Washington, 1982-93; dir. Am. pub. policy program Woodrow Wilson Internat. Ctr. for Scholars, Washington; pres., CEO Inst. for Contemporary Studies, Oakland, Calif. Tv co-host, That's Politics, 1987-91; radio California Political Review; Books American Federalism: A New Partnership for the Republic, Self-government by District: Myth and Reality. Office: Inst Contemporary Studies Latham Sq 1611 Telegraph Ave Ste 406 Oakland CA 94612-2140

HAWKINS, ROBERT LEE, health facility administrator; b. Denver, Feb. 18, 1938; pr. 28, 1973; children: Robert, Jeanne, Julia, Rose. AA, Pueblo Jr. Coll., 1958; BS, So. Colo. State Coll., 1965; MSW, U. Denver, 1967. Psychiat. technician Colo. State Hosp., Pueblo, 1956-58, 62-63, occupl. therapist asst., 1964-65, clin. adminstr. psychiat. team, 1969-75, dir. cmty. svcs., 1975-92, supr. vol. svcs., mem. budget com., 1975—, asst. supt. clin. svcs., 1992—; supr. Colo. Mental Health Inst., Pueblo, 1996—. Part-time counseloer Family Svc. Agy., Pueblo, 1968-69, exec. dir., 1969-70; mem. faculty U. So. Colo., 1968-75; ptnr. Human Resource Devel., Inc., 1970-75; mem. Nat. Adv. Com. on Instnl. Quality and Integrity, U.S. Dept. Edn., Washington, 1993—. Mem. Pueblo Positive Action Com., 1970; chmn. adv. bd. Pueblo Sangre de Cristo Day Care Ctr., 1969-72; chmn. Gov.'s So. Area Adv. Coun. Employment Svc., 1975-76; chmn. Pueblo City CSC, 1976-77, Pueblo Cmty. Corrections, 1985-87, Pueblo CSC, 1988—; commr. Pueblo Housing Authority, 1986—; mem. Colo. Commn. Higher Edn., 1987—, USED Commn. for Ednl. Quality and Integrity, 1993—; mem. gov.'s adv. com. on mental health stds., 1981—; mem. Colo. Juvenile Parole Bd., 1977; bd. dirs. Pueblo United Fund, 1969-74, pres., 1973; bd. dirs. Pubelo Cmty. Orgn., 1974-76, Spanish Peaks Mental Health Ctr., 1976—, Neighborhood Health Ctr., 1977-79, Pueblo Neighborhood Housing Svcs., 2000, Puebloo Cmty. Corrections, 1983—, Pueblo Legal Svcs., 1983—, Girl Scouts USA, 1996—; mem. Pueblo 2010 Commn., 1994—; mem. adv. com. YWCA, 1994—, Healthy Pueblo 200 Task Force, 1993; bd. dirs. Posada Shelter for Homeless, 1990; bd. dirs. Boys and Girls Club, 1991—, ARC, 1994, pres., 1994—. With U.S. Army, 1958-62. Mem. NASW (nominating com. 1973-76), ACLU (bd. dirs. Pueblo chpt. 1980—), NAACP, Broadway Theatre Guild, Common Cause, Kiwanis. Democrat. Methodist. Home: 220 Melrose Ave Pueblo CO 81004-1053 Office: Colo State Hosp 1600 W 24th St Pueblo CO 81003-1411

HAWKINS, STAN, state legislator; b. St. Anthony, Idaho, Feb. 1, 1955; m. Linn Hawkins; children: Ryan, Tara, Katie, Dale, Chase. Student, Ricks Coll. In agribus.; elected rep. Idaho Ho. of Reps., Boise, 1984-90; mem. Idaho Senate, Dist. 28, Boise, 1990—. Mem. local govt. and tax., fin., and resources and environment coms. Republican. Office: State Capitol PO Box 83720 Boise ID 83720-3720

HAWKINS, TRIP, electronics company executive; Chmn. bd. dirs., CEO 3DO, Redwood City, Calif. Office: 3DO 600 Galveston Dr Redwood City CA 94063-4721

HAWKS, BILL, state legislator, oil company executive; b. Tulsa, Nov. 17, 1936; s. Jeff and Mary Blanche (Scrogham) H.; m. Jan G. Heibucher, Aug. 15, 1970; children: Brents, Christopher, James, Michael. BSBA, U. Denver, 1962. Cert. landman, airplane pilot. Landman Ozark Corp., Casper, Wyo., 1957-66; pvt. practice landman Casper, 1966-71; pres. Burton-Hawks Inc., Casper, from 1971; mem. Wyo. Senate, Dist. 29, Casper, 1994—. Mem. State of Wyo. Aero. Commn., 1987—. Bd. dirs. Natrona County Airport, Casper, 1980-85; mem. joint powers bd., Casper, 1984-85. Mem. Am. Assn. Petroleum Landmen, Wyo. Assn. Petroleum Landmen, Rocky Mountain Oil and Gas Assn., Aircraft Owners and Pilots Assn., Ind. Petroleum Assn. Am., Ind. Petroleum Assn. Mountain States, Petroleum Club (pres. Casper chpt. 1980-81). Clubs: Casper Country, Denver Country, PGA West (Palm Springs). Avocations: flying, fly tying and fishing, snow skiing, golf. Office: Burton Hawks Inc PO Box 359 Casper WY 82602-0359 Address: PO Box 1950 Casper WY 82602-1950

HAWLEY, GREG W. paper company executive; V.p., controller Willamette Industries, Portland, Oreg., 1996-99; exec. v.p., CFO, 1999—. Office: Willamette Industries 1300 SW 5th Ave Ste 3800 Portland OR 97201

HAWLEY, KIMRA, software company executive; BS in Psychology, Pitts. State U. Prin. MarketBound Assocs.; various mktg. mgmt. positions Amdahl Corp.; imaging mktg. dir. Action Point Software (formerly Cornerstone Imaging), 1992-96, gen. mgr. software divsn., 1996, now pres., CEO. Office: Actionpoint Software 1299 Parkmoor Ave San Jose CA 95126-3448

HAWLEY, PHILIP METSCHAN, retired retail executive, consultant; b. Portland, Oreg., July 29, 1925; s. Willard P. and Dorothy (Metschan) H.; m. Mary Catherine Follen, May 31, 1947; children: Diane (Mrs. Robert Bruce Johnson), Willard, Philip Metschan Jr., John, Victor, Edward, Erin (Mrs. Kevin Przybocki), George. BS, U. Calif., Berkeley, 1946; grad. advanced mgmt. program, Harvard U., 1967. With Carter Hawley Hale Stores, Inc., L.A., 1958-93, pres., 1972-83, chief exec. officer, 1977-93, chmn., 1983-93. Bd. dirs. Weyerhaeuser Co. Trustee Calif. Inst. Tech., U. Notre Dame; chmn. L.A. Energy Conservation Com., 1973-74. Decorated hon. comdr. Order Brit. Empire, knight comdr. Star Solidarity Republic Italy; recipient Award of Merit L.A. Jr. C. of C., 1974, Coro Pub. Affairs award, 1978, Medallion award Coll. William and Mary, 1983, Award of Excellence Sch. Bus. Adminstrn. U. So. Calif., 1987, Bus. Statesman of Yr. award Harvard Bus. Sch., 1989, 15th ann. Whitney M. Young Jr. award L.S. Urban League, 1988; named Calif. Industrialist of Yr. Calif. Mus. Sci. and Industry, 1975. Mem. Calif. Retailers Assn. (chmn. 1993-95, dir.), Beach Club, Calif. Club, L.A. Country Club, Bohemian Club, Pacific-Union Club, Newport Harbor Yacht Club, Multnomah Club, Links Club, Phi Beta Kappa, Beta Alpha Psi, Beta Gamma Sigma. Office: 400 S Hope St Ste 1900 Los Angeles CA 90071-2811

HAWTHORNE, MARION FREDERICK, chemistry educator; b. Ft. Scott, Kans., Aug. 24, 1928; s. Fred Elmer and Colleen (Webb) H.; m. Beverly Dawn Rempe, Oct. 30, 1951 (div. 1976); children: Cynthia Lee, Candace Lee; m. Diana Baker Razzaia, Aug. 14, 1977. BA, Pomona Coll., 1949; PhD (AEC fellow), U. Calif. at Los Angeles, 1953; DSc (hon.), Pomona Coll., 1974; PhD (hon.), Uppsala U., 1992. Rsch. assoc. Iowa State Coll., 1953-54; rsch. chemist Rohm & Haas Co., Huntsville, Ala., 1954-56, group leader, 1956-60, lab. head Phila., 1961; prof. chemistry U. Calif., Riverside, 1962-68, UCLA, 1968—, U. Calif., 1998—. Vis. lectr. Harvard U., 1960, Queen Mary Coll., U. London, 1963; vis. prof. U. Tex., Austin, 1974, Harvard, 1968; mem. sci. adv. bd. USAF, 1980-86, NRC Bd. Army Sci. and Tech., 1986-90; disting. vis. prof. Ohio State U., 1990; mem. dir.'s external adv. bd. divsn. M, Los Alamos (N.Mex.) Nat. Lab., 1991-94; lectr. in field. Editor-in-chief: Inorganic Chemistry, 1969-00. Decorated Meritorious Svc. medal USAF, 1986; recipient Chancellors Research award, 1968, Herbert Newby McCoy award, 1972, Am. Chem. Soc. award in Inorganic Chemistry, 1973, Glenn T. Seaborg medal, 1997, Tolman Medal award, 1986, Nebr. sect. Am. Chem. Soc. award, 1979, Disting. Service in the Advancement of Inorganic Chemistry award Am. Chem. Soc., 1988, Disting. Achievements in Boron Sci. award, 1988, Bailar medal, 1991, Polyhedron Medal and prize, 1993, Chem. Pioneer award Am. Inst. Chemists, 1994, Willard Gibbs medal Am. Chem. Soc., 1994, Internat. award in Polyhedral Borane Chemistry, Internat. Com. on Boron Chemistry, 1996, Basolo medal Am. Chem. Soc., 2001; named sr. scientist Alexander von Humboldt Found., Inst. Inorganic Chemistry U. Munich, 1990-96, Centenary lectr. Royal Soc. Chemistry, London, 1998; Sloan Found. fellow, 1963-65, Japan Soc. Promotion Sci. fellow, 1986; named Col. Confederate Air Force, 1984. Fellow AAAS; mem. U.S. Nat. Acad. Scis. (award in chem. scis. 1997), Am. Acad. Arts and Scis., Göttingen Acad. Scis. (corr. mem.), Aircraft Owners and Pilots Assn., Cosmos Club, The Internat. Soc. for Neutron Capture Therapy for Cancer (mem. exec. com. 1992-00, pres. 1996-98), Sigma Xi, Alpha Chi Sigma, Sigma Nu. Home: 3415 Green Vista Dr Encino CA 91436-4011 E-mail: mfh@chem.ucla.edu

HAY, DON, professional hockey coach; b. Feb. 13, 1954; m. Vicki; children: Darrell, Angela and Ashly (twins). Asst. coach Kamloops (BC) Blazers, 1985-92, head coach, 1992-95, Can. Nat. Jr. Team, 1995, Phoenix Coyotes, 1996-97; asst. coach NHL Mighty Ducks, Anaheim, Calif., 1996-97; head coach, gen. mgr. Tri-City Americans, 1998-99; head coach NHL Calgary Flames, 2000—. Named Coach of Yr., Exec. of Yr. Western Hockey League, 1998-99, Best All-Time Coach at 1999 Meml. Cup Canadian Hockey League, 1999. Achievements include leading Can. Nat. Jr. Team to gold medal during 1995 World Jr. Championships, leading Kamloop Blazers to 1994 and 1995 Meml. Cup championships and 2 Western Hockey League championships. Office: Canadien Airlines Saddledome PO Box 1540 Sta M c/o Calgary Flames Calgary AB T2P 3B9 Canada

HAY, HOWARD CLINTON, lawyer; b. Portland, Maine, Apr. 16, 1944; s. Willis and Ruth (Clark) H.; m. Carol Anne Newsome, Dec. 21, 1968; children: Mark, David, Scott. AB (with distinction), Duke U., 1966; JD magna cum laude, U. Mich., 1969. Bar: U.S. Supreme Ct. 1977, Calif. 1970. Law clerk U.S. Ct. Appeals, Boston, 1970; atty. NLRB; ptnr. Paul, Hastings, Janofsky & Walker, Costa Mesa, Calif., 1971—. Program chmn. Certificate in Employee Rels. Law; instr. U. S.C. Grad. Sch. Bus. Editor Mich. Law Review; contbr. articles to profl. jours. Mem. State Bar Calif. (exec. com. labor and employment sect.), Calif. Bar Assn. Office: Paul Hastings Janofsky & Walker 695 Town Center Dr Fl 17 Costa Mesa CA 92626-1924 E-mail: HCHAY@PHJW.com

HAY, RICHARD LAURENCE, theater set designer; b. Wichita, Kans., May 28, 1929; s. Laurence Charles and Ruth Mary (Rhoades) H. BA, Stanford U., 1952, MA, 1955. Tech. dir., designer Oreg. Shakespeare Festival, Ashland, 1953-55, prin. scenic designer, 1970—; instr. drama Stanford U., Palo Alto, Calif., 1957-62, assoc. prof., 1965-69; assoc. artistic dir. for design Denver Ctr. Theater Co., 1984-91. Freelance scenic designer Guthrie Theater, Mpls., Am. Conservatory Theater, San Francisco, Mo. Repertory Theater, Kansas City, Mark Taper Forum, Los Angeles, Old Globe Theater, San Diego, Berkekey (Calif.) Repertory Theater, Eisenhower Theatre, others; theatre designer: Source and Space Theatres, Denver Ctr. Theatre Co., New Old Globe Theatre and Festival Stage, Old Globe Theatre, San Diego, Intiman Theatre, Seattle, Black Swan, Angus Bowmer Theatre, Elizabethan Stage, Oreg. Shakespeare Festival. Author: (with others) A Space for Magic: Stage Settings by Richard L. Hay, 1979; exhibitor Prague Quadriennial, 1987, 99, U.S. Inst. Theatre Tech. Biennial Scenography Expn., 1984, 88, 90, Schneider Mus. of Art, 2001. Recipient Critics award Hollywood (Calif.) Drama-Logue, 1982, 85, 86, 89, Gov.'s award for the Arts State of Oreg., 1989; Fulbright grantee, 1955. Mem. United Scenic Artists, U.S. Inst. Theatre Tech. (bd. dirs. 1994-97, Disting. Achievement award in scenic design 1998), League Hist. Am. Theaters. Democrat. Congregationalist. Avocation: book collecting. Home: 707 Liberty St Ashland OR 97520-3140 Office: Oreg Shakespeare Festival PO Box 158 Ashland OR 97520-0158

HAY, WILLIAM CHARLES, professional hockey team executive; b. Saskatoon, Sask., Can., Dec. 9, 1935; s. Charles and Florence (Miller) H.; m. Nancy Ann Woodman, Aug. 24, 1957; children: Pam, Penny, Donald. B.S. in Geology, Colo. Coll., 1958. Profl. hockey player Chgo. Black Hawks, 1958-67; mgr. Sedco Drilling Co., Calgary, Alta., 1967-70, gen. mgr., from 1970, Hi-Tower Drilling Co., Calgary, from 1970; formerly pres., chief operating officer Hockey Can.; pres. Calgary Flames Hockey Club, NHL, 1991—; also alternate governor Calgary Flames; now planning advisor Canadian Hockey Association. Exec. dir. Champions in Hockey Endowment Fund; chmn., CEO Hockey Hall of Fame, Toronto. Office: Canadian Hockey Assoc 2424 University Dr Calgary AB Canada T2N 3Y9

HAYCOCK, KENNETH ROY, educator, consultant, administrator; b. Hamilton, Ont., Can., Feb. 15, 1948; s. Bruce Frederick T. and Doris Marion P. (Downham) H.; m. Sheila Tripp, Jan. 28, 1990. BA, U. Western Ont., 1968, diploma in edn., 1969; specialist cert., U. Toronto, Can., 1971; MEd, U. Ottawa, Can., 1973; AMLS, U. Mich., 1974; EdD, Brigham Young U., 1991. Tchr., dept. head Glebe Collegiate Inst., Ottawa, 1969-70, Col. By Secondary Sch., Ottawa, 1970-72; cons. Wellington County Bd. Edn., Guelph, Ont., 1972-76; coord. libr. svcs., supr. instrn. Vancouver (Can.) Sch. Bd., 1976-84, acting mgr., elem./secondary edn., 1984-85, dir. instrn., head program svcs., 1985-89, 91-92; prin. Waverley Elem. Sch., 1989-91; prof., dir. Sch. Libr., Archival and Info. Studies U. B.C., Vancouver, 1992—. Instr. univs. and colls.; pres. Ken Haycock and Assocs., Inc. Editor Tchr. Libr.; author various books; contbr. articles to profl. jours. Trustee Guelph Pub. Libr., 1975-76; trustee West Vancouver Sch. Bd., 1993-99, chair, 1994-97, councilor Dist. of West Vancouver, 1999—; trustee West Vancouver Pub. Libr., 1999-2001. Recipient award Beta Phi Mu, 1976, Queen Elizabeth Silver Jubilee medal, 1977. Fellow Can. Coll. Tchrs.; mem. ALA (coun. 1995-99, exec. bd., 1999—), ASCD (urban curriculum leaders 1985-92, internat. panel 1990-94), IFLA (Internatl. Federation of Libr. Assns. and Institutions, section on Edn. and Trng. 1997—, chair 1999—), Am. Assn. Sch. Librs. (pres. 1997-98, Baker and Taylor Disting. Svc. award 1996), Can. Sch. Libr. Assn. (pres. 1974-75, Margaret B. Scott award of merit 1979, rsch. award 1984, 95, Disting. Sch. Adminstr. award 1989), B.C. Sch. Libr. Assn. (Ken Haycock Profl. Devel. award named in his honor 1984, Disting. Svc. award 1989), Ont. Libr. Assn., Can. Libr. Assn. (pres. 1977-78, Outstanding Svc. award 1991), Assn. for Libr. and Info. Sci. Edn. (sec. coun. dean and dirs. 1993-96), B.C. Libr. Assn. (Ken Haycock Student Conf. award named in his honor 1999), Ont. Libr. Assn., Internat. Assn. Sch. Librarianship (dir. N.Am. chpt. 1993-95, exec. dir. 1995-2000, Ken Haycock Leadership Devel. award named in his honor 2001), Coun. for Can. Learning Resources (pres. 1995-98), Phi Delta Kappa (young leaders panel 1980). Home: 5118 Meadfeild Rd West Vancouver BC Canada V7W 3G2 Office: U BC Sch Libr Arch & Info 831-1956 Main Mall Vancouver BC Canada V6T 1Z1 E-mail: ken.haycock@ubc.ca

HAYDEN, CEDRIC L. state legislator, dentist; b. Eugene, Oreg., Aug. 4, 1934; s. Jesse and Gwendolen (Lampshire) H.; m. Marilyn Adele Jaekel, Dec. 27, 1961; children: Jonathan, Christopher, Matthew, Daniel, Cedric Ross, Kaminda. BS, U. Oreg., 1957; DMD, Washington U., St. Louis, 1960; MPH, Loma Linda U., 1979. Dentist Antioch (Calif.) Dental Group, 1963-65; missionary Seventh Day Adventist Ch., Port of Spain, Trinidad, 1965-69; dentist Hayden Family Dentistry Group, Eugene, Oreg., 1970—; legislator Oreg. Ho. of Reps., Salem, 1985-97, chmn. house com. on transp., house com. on gen. govt., 1991-95, asst. majority leader, asst. caucus leader, 1991-95, mem. ways and means com., 2001—. Lt. (s.g.) USN, 1960-63. Fellow Am. Dental Soc. Anesthesiology. Avocations: skiing, hiking, camping, horseback riding, travel. Home: 2645 Woodstone Pl Eugene OR 97405-1257 E-mail: hayden.rep@state.or.us

HAYDEN, JOHN OLIN, English literature educator, writer; b. Los Angeles, Dec. 18, 1932; s. John Ellsworth and Norah Elizabeth (Bussens) H.; m. Mary Kathleen Garland, Dec. 18, 1965; children— Michael, John, Mark, Ann BA, U. Calif.-Santa Barbara, 1958; MA, Columbia U., 1959, PhD, 1965. Asst. prof. U. Colo., Boulder, 1964-66; assoc. prof. English lit. U. Calif.-Davis, 1966-75, prof. English lit., 1975-94, prof. emeritus, 1994—. Author: Romantic Reviewers, 1969, Polestar of the Ancients, 1979, William Wordsworth and the Mind of Man, 1993, Why the Great Books are Great, 1998; editor: Sir Walter Scott, 1970, Wordsworth: The Poems, 1977, Wordsworth: The Prose, 1988, Wordsworth: Selected Poetry, 1994. Served with USAF, 1951-55 E. J. Noble Found. fellow Columbia U., N.Y.C., 1959-61; fellow NEH, 1971, Am. Council Learned Socs., 1984 Democrat. Roman Catholic Avocation: numismatics. Home: 25199 Carlsbad Ave Davis CA 95616-9434 Office: U Calif English Dept Davis CA 95616 E-mail: johayden@ucdavis.edu

HAYDEN, RON L. library director; b. San Pedro, Calif., Dec. 24, 1948; s. Larnie Alphonsis and Myrtie Louise (Pilcher) H.; m. Marilee Ann Brubaker, May 30, 1971 (dec. June 1978); m. Susan Ann Huffman, Jan. 1, 1982. AA, Golden West Coll., 1969; BA, Long Beach State U., 1972; MLS, Fullerton U., 1974. Reference sr. libr. Huntington Beach (Calif.) Libr., 1975-79, pub. svc. libr., 1979-86, libr. dir., 1986—. Liason Libr. Patrons Assn., Huntington Beach, 1986—. Author: Collection Development Library Journal, 1979. Recipient Award of Excellence Calif. S.W. Recreation Park Conf., 1990. Mem. ALA (Libr. in Media award, Best of Show award 1990), Calif. Libr. Assn., Friends Libr., So. Calif. Tennis Assn., Rotary (bd. dirs., vocat. chmn. 1988—). Avocations: tennis, running, reading. Office: Huntington Beach Libr 7111 Talbert Ave Huntington Beach CA 92648-1232

HAYDEN, TOM, retired state senator; b. Royal Oak, Mich., Dec. 11, 1939; m. Jane Fonda, Jan. 20, 1973 (div.); children: Troy, Vanessa; m. Barbara Williams, Aug. 8, 1993. Grad., U. Mich. Co-founder Students for a Democratic Soc., 1961, pres., 1962, 63; staff Student Non-violent Coordinating Com., 1963; co-founder Econ. Research and Action Project, 1964; leader Newark Community Union Project, 1964-67; founder Indochina Peace Campaign; candidate for U.S. Senate in Calif. Democratic Primary, 1976; founder, chmn. Calif. Campaign for Econ. Democracy, 1977—; chmn. SolarCal Council, State of Calif., 1978-82; mem. Calif. State Assembly, 1982-92; senator Calif. State Senate, 1993—2000. Chmn. higher edn. policy com. Calif. State Assembly, 1986-92; chmn. natural resources and wildlife polity com. Calif. State Senate, 1994—. Author: Port Huron Statement, 1962, Rebellion in Newark, 1967, Rebellion and Repression, 1969, Trial, 1970, The Love of Possession is a Disease with Them, 1972, The American Future, 1980, The Lost Gospel of the Earth, 1996; co-author: The Other Side, 1965, Reunion, 1988; contbr.: articles to periodicals including Washington Post, Los Angeles Times, N.Y. Times. Democrat.*

HAYDEN, WILLIAM ROBERT, lawyer; b. Chgo., May 22, 1947; s. Robert George and Dorothy (Honan) H.; m. Carol Ann Brock, Aug. 12, 1978; 1 child, Nathaniel. BA, Kans. State U., 1969; JD with honors, George Washington U., 1972. Bar: D.C. 1973, U.S. Dist. Ct. D.C. 1975, U.S. Ct. Appeals (D.C. cir.) 1975, Ariz. 1978, U.S. Dist. Ct. Ariz. 1978, U.S. Ct. Appeals (9th cir.) 1979, U.S. Ct. Appeals (10th cir.) 1997. Mem. gen. counsel's staff NLRB, Washington, 1973-75; assoc. O'Donoghue and O'Donoghue, Washington, 1975-78, Snell and Wilmer, Phoenix, 1978-82, ptnr., 1982—. Contbg. editor: Developing Labor Law, 1974, Employment Discrimination Law, 1989. Mem. ABA (labor and employment law sect.), Nat. Panel, Am. Arbitration Assn. (employment dispute resolution), Ariz. Bar Assn. (exec. com., past chmn. labor and employment law sect. 1984-89, employment civil jury instructions com.), Maricopa County Bar Assn., D.C. Bar Assn., Ariz. C. of C. (employee rels. subcom.). Avocations: tennis, softball, skiing. Office: Snell & Wilmer 1 Arizona Ctr Phoenix AZ 85004 E-mail: bhayden@swlaw.com

HAYES, ALICE BOURKE, academic administrator, biologist, educator; b. Chgo., Dec. 31, 1937; d. William Joseph and Mary Alice (Cawley) Bourke; m. John J. Hayes, Sept. 2, 1961 (dec. July 1981). BS, Mundelein Coll., Chgo., 1959; MS, U. Ill., 1960; PhD, Northwestern U., 1972; DSc (honoris causa), Loyola U., Chgo., 1994; HHD (honoris causa), Fontbonne Coll., 1994; LHD (honoris causa), Mount St. Mary Coll., 1998. Rschr. Mcpl. Tb San., Chgo., 1960-62; faculty Loyola U., Chgo., 1962-87, chmn. dept., 1968-77, dean natural scis. div., 1977-80, assoc. acad. v.p., 1980-87, v.p. acad. affairs, 1987-89; provost, exec. v.p. St. Louis U., 1989-95; pres. U. San Diego, 1995—. Mem. space biology program NASA, 1980-86; mem. adv. panel NSF, 1977-81, Parmly Hearing Inst., 1986-89; del. Bot. Del. to South Africa, 1984, to People's Republic China, 1988, to USSR, 1990; reviewer Coll. Bd. and Mellon Found. Nat. Hispanic Scholar Awards, 1985-86; bd. dirs. Pulitzer Pub. Co., The Globe Theatres, Loyola U. Chgo., Cath. Charities, San Diego Found., Jack-in-the-Box. Co-author books; contbr. articles to profl. publs. Campaign mem. Mental Health Assn. Ill., Chgo., 1973-89; trustee Chgo.-No. Ill. divsn. Nat. Multiple Sclerosis Soc., 1981-89, bd. dirs., 1980-88, com. chmn., sec. to bd. dirs., vice chmn.

bd. dirs.; trustee Regina Dominican Acad., 1984-89, Civitas Dei Found., 1987-92, Rockhurst Coll., Loyola U., Chgo., San Diego Found.; trustee St. Ignatius Coll. Prep. Sch., bd. dirs., 1984-89, sec., vice chmn.; bd. dirs. Urban League Met. St. Louis, St. Louis Sci. Ctr., 1991-95, Cath. Charities St. Louis, 1992-95, St. Louis County Hist. Soc., 1992-95, Cath. Charities San Diego, 1996—, San Diego Hist. Soc., 1996—, Old Globe Theater, 1996—, also trustee. Named to Teachers' Hall of Fame Blue Key Soc.; fellow in botany U. Ill., 1959-60; fellow in botany NSF, 1969-71; grantee Am. Orchid Soc., 1967; grantee HEW, 1969, 76; grantee NSF, 1975; grantee NASA, 1980-85. Mem. AAAS, AAUP (corp. rep. 1980-85), Am. Assn. for Higher Edn., Am. Assn. Univ. Adminstrs. (mem. program com. nat. meeting 1988), Am. Soc. Gravitational and Space Biology, Assn. Midwest Coll. Biology Teachers, Am. Soc. Plant Physiology, Bot. Soc. Am., Am. Inst. Biol. Scis. Acad., Chgo. Network, Soc. Ill. Microbiologists (edn. com. 1969-70, Pasteur award com. 1975, pub. rels. com. 1974, chair speakers' bur. 1974-79), Chgo. Assn. Tech. Socs. (acad. liaison 1982-85, awards com. 1984-89), Am. Coun. on Edn. (corp. rep. higher edn. panel), Ctr. Rsch. Librs. (nominating com. 1986), North Ctrl. Assn. Colls. and Schs. (cons., evaluator Commn. on Higher Edn. 1984-95, commr.-at-large 1988-94), Mo. Women's Forum Club, Sigma Xi, Delta Sigma Rho, Sigma Delta Epsilon, Phi Beta Kappa, Alpha Sigma Nu. Roman Catholic. Office: U San Diego 5998 Alcala Park San Diego CA 92110-2476

HAYES, EDWARD LEE, religious organization administrator; b. Modesto, Calif., Sept. 26, 1931; s. George Lester and Sylvia (Utzinger) H.; m. Marilyn Elizabeth Bjorklund, July 31, 1954; children: Carla Hayes Strickfaden, Darryl, Bryan. BA in Social Sci., Westmont Coll., 1953; ThM in Bibl. Studies, Dallas Theol. Sem., 1957; postgrad., Calif. State U., L.A., 1962-65, Iliff Theol. Sem., Denver, 1962-65; PhD in Higher Edn. Adminstrn., U. Denver, 1966. Ordained to ministry Bapt. Ch., 1957. Min. to youth Reinhardt Bible Ch., Dallas, 1954-57; asst. prof. ch. edn. Biola U., La Mirada, Calif., 1957-60; min. edn. First Bapt. Ch., Montebello, 1958-61; prof., acad. dean Denver Sem., 1960-79, pres., 1993-97, pres. emeritus, 1997—; exec. dir. Mt. Hermon (Calif.) Assn., 1979-92. Cons. Scripture Press Pub. Co., 1963-73; lectr. in field. Author: Words To Live By, 1968, The Focused Life, 1986, The Church, 1999. Pres. PTA, Littleton, Colo., 1975-77; trustee Westmont Coll., Santa Barbara, 1973—. Grantee Lilly Found., Assn. Theol. Schs., 1968, Rsch. grantee Assn. Theol. Schs., 1976. Mem. Evang. Theol. Soc., Assn. Governing Bds. Republican. Avocations: art, horticulture, music, travel. Office: Denver Sem PO Box 10000 Denver CO 80250-9099

HAYES, ISAAC, rhythm and blues singer, composer; b. Covington, Tenn., Aug. 20, 1942; Formerly singer rhythm and blues recs., Stax Records; albums recorded included Black Moses, Hot Buttered Soul, Enterprise: His Greatest Hits, Hotbed, Isaac Hayes Movement, ... To Be Continued, U-Turn, 1986, Love Attack, 1988, Greatest Hit Singles, (with Dionne Warwick) A Man and A Woman, Don't Let Go, And Once Again, Lifetime Thing, Back to Back (with Barry White), Branded, Raw and Refined; (with Donald Dunn and Al Jackson Jr.) Present; composer: musical score film Shaft (Grammy and Oscar awards); appeared on TV show Rockford Files; film appearances include: Escape from New York, Counterforce, I'm Gonna Git You Sucka!, Guilty As Charged, Robin Hood: Men in Tights, Out of Sync, It Could Happen To You; from 1962, wrote songs with David Porter. Office: c/o Ron Moss Management 2635 Griffith Park Blvd Los Angeles CA 90039-2519

HAYES, JANET GRAY, retired business manager, former mayor; b. Rushville, Ind., July 12, 1926; d. John Paul and Lucile (Gray) Frazee; m. Kenneth Hayes, Mar. 20, 1950; children: Lindy, John, Katherine, Megan. AB, Ind. U., 1948; MA magna cum laude, U. Chgo., 1950. Psychiat. caseworker Jewish Family Svc. Agy., Chgo., 1950-52; vol. Denver Crippled Children's Service, 1954-55, Adult and Child Guidance Clinic, San Jose, Calif., 1958-59; mem. San Jose City Coun., 1971-75, vice mayor, 1973-75, mayor, 1975-82; co-chmn. com. urban econs. U.S. Conf. Mayors, 1976-78, co-chmn. task force on aging, mem. sci. and teck task force, 1976-80, bd. trustees, 1977-82; bd. dirs. League Calif. Cities, 1976-82, mem. property tax reform task force, 1976-82; chmn. State of Calif. Urban Devel. Adv. Com., 1976-77; mem. Calif. Commn. Fair Jud. Practices, 1976-82; client-community relations dir. Q. Tech., Santa Clara, Calif., 1983-85; bus. mgr. Kenneth Hayes MD, Inc., 1985-88; CEO Hayes House, Book Distbr., 1998—. Mem. Dem. Nat. Campaign Com., 1976; mem. Calif. Dem. Commn. Nat. Platform and Policy, 1976; del. Dem. Nat. Conv., 1980; bd. dirs. South San Francisco Bay Dischargers Authority; chmn. Santa Clara County Sanitation Dist.; mem. San Jose/Santa Clara Treatment Plant Adv. Bd.; chmn. Santa Clara Valley Employment and Tng. Bd. (CETA), League to Save Lake Tahoe adv. bd., 2000—; past mem. EPA Aircraft/Airport Noise Task Group; bd. dirs. Calif. Center Rsch. and Edn. in Govt, Alexian Bros. Hosp., 1983-92; bd. dirs., chmn. adv. council Public Tech. Inc.; mem. bd. League to Save Lake Tahoe, 1984-2000; pres. bd. trustees San Jose Mus. Art, 1987-89; founder, adv. bd. Calif. Bus. Bank, 1982-85. AAUW Edn. Found. grantee. Mem. Assn. Bay Area Govts. (exec. com. 1971-74, regional housing subcom. 1973-74), LWC (pres. San Francisco Bay Area chpt. 1968-70, pres. local chpt. 1966-67), Mortar Bd., Phi Beta Kappa, Kappa Alpha Theta. E-mail: jghayes7@aol.com

HAYES, ROBERT MAYO, university dean, library and information science educator; b. N.Y.C., Dec. 3, 1926; s. Dudley Lyman and Myra Wilhelmina (Lane) H.; m. Alice Peters, Sept. 2, 1952; 1 son, Robert Dendrou. BA, UCLA, 1947, MA, 1949, PhD, 1952. Mathematician Nat. Bur. Standards, Washington and Los Angeles, 1949-52; mem. tech. staff Hughes Aircraft Co., 1952-54; head applications group Nat. Cash Register Co., 1954-55; head bus. systems group Magnavox Co., 1955- 60; pres. Advanced Information Systems, Inc., Los Angeles, 1960-64; v.p., sci. dir. Electrada Corp., Los Angeles, 1960-64; lectr. dept. math. UCLA, 1952-64, prof. library and info. sci., 1964-91, dean, 1974-89, dean emeritus, 1989—, dir. Inst. Libr. Rsch., 1965-70; prof. emeritus, 1991—. Vis. lectr. Am. Univ., 1959, U. Wash., 1960-62; Windsor lectr. U. Ill., 1970; vis. prof. U. NSW, 1979, 93, Tskuba U., 1987, Nankai U., 1987, Loughborough U., 1989, Keio U., Japan, 1994, Khazar U., Azerbaijan, 1995; mem. adv. com. White House conf. Libr. and Info. Svcs., 1979; v.p. Becker & Hayes, Inc., 1969-73, 93-96; cons. On Line Computer Libr. Ctr., 1990-94. Author: Strategic Management for Academic Libraries, 1993; co-author: Introduction to Information Storage and Retrieval: Tools, Elements, Theory, 1963, Handbook of Data Processing for Libraries, 2d edit., 1974, Strategic Management for Public Libraries, 1996; U.S. regional editor Problems in Info. Storage and Retrieval, 1959-63; editor Info. Scis. Series, 1963-75; mem. editorial bd. Libr. Info. Sci. Rsch., 1978—. Recipient Profl. Achievement award UCLA Alumni Assn., Beta Phi Mu award ALA, 1st Tezak award U. Zagreb, 1990. Mem. ALA (pres. info. sci. and automation div. 1969), Am. Soc. Info. Sci. (pres. 1962-63, nat. lectr. 1968, Award of Merit 1993), Am. Math. Soc., Assn. for Computing Machinery (assoc. editor jour. 1959-69, nat. lectr. 1969), Phi Beta Kappa, Sigma Xi. Club: Cosmos. Home: 3943 Woodfield Dr Sherman Oaks CA 91403-4239 Office: UCLA 405 Hilgard Ave Los Angeles CA 90095-9000

HAYFLICK, LEONARD, microbiologist, cell biologist, gerontologist, educator, writer; b. Phila., May 20, 1928; s. Nathan Albert and Edna (Silbert) H.; m. Ruth Louise Heckler, Oct. 3, 1954; children: Joel, Deborah, Susan, Rachel, Anne. BA in Microbiology and Chemistry, U. Pa., 1951, MS in Med. Microbiology, 1953, PhD in Med. Microbiology and Chemistry, 1956. McLaughlin rsch. fellow in infection and immunity, dept. microbiology U. Tex. Med. Br., Galveston, Tex., 1956-58; assoc. mem. Wistar Inst. Anatomy and Biology, Phila., 1958-68; asst. prof. rshc. medicine U. Pa., Phila., 1966-68; prof. med. microbiology Stanford (Calif.) U. Sch. Medicine, 1968-76, senator-at-large, Basic Med. Scis., 1970-73, chmn. gen. rsch. support grant com., 1972-74; sr. research cell biologist Children's Hosp., Oakland, Calif., 1976-81; prof. zoology, prof. microbiology and immunology U. Fla., Gainesville, 1981-87, dir. Ctr. for Gerontol. Studies, Coll. Liberal Arts and Scis., 1981-87; prof. anatomy, cell biology and aging sect. U. Calif. Sch. Medicine, San Francisco, 1988—. Mem. subcom. on mycoplasmataceae Internat. Com. Bacteriol. Nomenclature, 1965-78; mem. steering com. cell and devel. biology film program MIT, 1970-73; chmn. Calif. State Com. Health White Ho. Conf. Aging, 1971-72, Calif. state rep., 1972; Nat. Cancer Planning Com. Nat. Cancer Inst., NIH, 1972; chmn., adult devel. and aging rsch. and tng. com. Nat. Inst. Child Health and Human Devel., NIH, 1972-73; non-resident fellow Inst. Higher Studies, Santa Barbara, Calif., 1973—; mem. Argonne Nat. Lab. rev. com. biol. and med. rsch. div. Argonne Nat. Lab., 1973-76; mem. rsch. adv. com. Tchrs. Ins. and Annuity Assn. Am.-Coll. Retirement Equities Funds, N.Y.C., 1974-80; founding mem. Nat. Adv. Coun. on Aging, Nat. Inst. on Aging, NIH, Bethesda, Md., 1975; cons. Office of Dir. Nat. Cancer Inst., Bethesda, 1963-74; vis. scientist Ctr. for Aging Weizmann Inst. Sci., Rehovoth, Israel, 1980, 86; mem. adv. bd. Internat. Exchange Ctr. Gerontology, Fla. Univ. System, Tampa, 1982-86; mem. jury for Sandoz prize in gerontology and geriatrics, 1985-89; bd. dirs. Ctr. for Climacteric Studies, Inc., Gainesville, 1985-88; expert cons. various coms. U.S. Congress, vis. prof. Oita Med. U., Japan, 1991-95, U. Parma, Italy, 1991, Kurume U. Med. Sch., Japan; lectr. in field. Author: How and Why We Age, 1996; editor: Biology of the Mycoplasmas, 1969, Handbook of the Biology of Aging, 1977; sr. editor Biol. Scis. Microfiche Collection Info. on Gerontology and Geriatric Medicine Univ. Microfilms Internat., Ann Arbor, Mich., 1984-98; editor-in-chief Exptl. Gerontology, 1984-98; asst. editor In Vitro jour. Tissue Culture Assn., 1969-75; editor biol. scis. sect. Jour. Gerontology, 1975-80; assoc. editor Cancer Rsch., 1972-80; mem. editorial bd. Jour. Bacteriology, 1964-72, Jour. Virology, 1967-70, Infection and Immunity jour., 1968-78, Exec. Health Report, 1970—, Mechanisms of Aging and Devel., 1972—, Gerontology and Geriatrics Edn., 1980—, A Revista Portuguesa de Medicina Geriatrica, 1987—; mem. adv. com. Bergey's Manual of Determinative Bacteriology, 1965-78; bd. dirs., mem. editorial bd. Bollettino Dell Instituto Sieroterapico Milanese, Archivo de Microbiologia ed Immunologia, Milan, Italy, 1968—; contbr. numerous articles in field to profl. jours. Staff sgt. U.S. Army, 1946-48. Recipient Samuel Roberts Noble Found. Rsch. Recognition award, 1984; co-recipient Sandoz prize Internat. Assn. Gerontology, 1991, Biomed. Scis. & Aging award U. So. Calif., 1974, Rsch. Recognition award Samuel Roberts Noble Found., 1984; Karl-Forster lectr. Acad. Sci. and Lit., Mainz, Germany, 1983, Hoffman-LaRoche lectr. Waksman Inst. Microbiology Rutgers U., 1984, Wadworth Meml. Fund lectr. Rush-Presbyn.-St. Luke's Med. Ctr., Chgo., 1984, hon. lectr. Rosenfield Program Pub. Affairs Grinnell Coll., 1989, invited speaker Sandoz lectrs. in Gerontology, Basle, Switzerland, 1986, 92, numerous other lectureships U.S.A., Can. and Europe, 1970—, Career Devel. award Nat. Cancer Inst., NIH, 1962-70, Lifetime Achievement award Soc. In Vitro Biology, 1996, Van Wezel prize Euro. Soc. Animal Cell Technology, 1999, Lord Cohen of Birkinhead medal Brit. Soc. Rsch. on Aging, 1999. Fellow AAAS, Gerontol Soc. Am. (program and awards com. 1972-77, chmn., exec. com. biol. scis. sect. 1972-74, com. on internat. rels. 1980-82, pub. policy com. 1980-82, pres. 1982-83, ann. Robert W. Kleemeier award 1972, Brookdale award 1980); mem. Am. Soc. for Microbiology, Tissue Culture Assn. (hon., trustee 1966-68, program com. 1970, mem. coun. 1972-74, v.p. 1974-76, pres. Calif. chpt. 1971-73), Soc. for Exptl. Biology and Medicine (councillor 1984-88), Assn. for Advancement of Aging Rsch. (adv. coun. 1970-71), Am. Aging Assn., Am. Cancer Soc. (virology and cell biology study sect. 1974-76), Internat. Assn. Microbiol. Standardization (sec. cell culture com. 1963-73, chmn. 1985—, mem. coun. 1987-89), Internat. Orgn. for Mycoplasmology (Presdl. award 1984), Am. Gerontol. Soc. (v.p., coun. 1972-74, 81-83, program com. 1977-79, bd. dirs. 1981-83), Am. Fedn. Aging Rsch. (bd. dirs., exec. com., rsch. adv. com. 1981—, chmn. study sect. 1987—, v.p. 1988—, Leadership award 1983), Fedn. Am. Socs. for Exptl. Biology, Aging Prevention Rsch. Found. (sci. adv. bd. dirs.), Am. Assn. for Cancer Rsch., Am. Soc. Pathologists, Calif. Found. for Biomed. Rsch., Am. Longevity Assn. (sci. adv. bd. dirs. 1981—), Western Gerontology Assn. (coun. 1972-74, bd. dirs. 81-83), Internat. Assn. Gerontology (mem. Am. exec. com. 1972-75, treas., exec. com. 1985-89, co-recipient Sandoz award gerontology 1991), Found. on Gerontology (sci. adv. bd. 1985—), Soc. Medicine and Natural Sci., Ukrainian Acad. Med. Scis. (fgn., academician 1991), French Biol. Soc. (fgn.), Euro. Soc. Animal Cell Tech. (Van Wezel prize), Brit. Soc. Rsch. on Aging (Lord Cohen of Burkinhead medal). Office: U Calif 36991 Greencroft Close PO Box 89 The Sea Ranch CA 95497-0089

HAYNES, CALEB VANCE, JR. geology and archaeology educator; b. Spokane, Wash., Feb. 29, 1928; m. Elizabeth Hamilton, Jan. 11, 1954 (div. 1991); 1 child, Elizabeth Anne.. Student, Johns Hopkins U., 1947-49; degree in geol. engring., Colo. Sch. Mines, 1956; PhD, U. Ariz., 1965. Mining geology cons., 1958-60; sr. project engr. Am. Inst. Research, Golden, Colo., 1956-60; sr. engr. Martin Co., Denver, 1960-62; geologist Nev. State Mus. Tule Springs Expedition, 1962-63; research asst. U. Ariz., Tucson, 1963-64, asst. prof. geology, 1965-68, prof. geoscis., anthropology, 1974-99, Regents prof., 1991-99, Regents prof. emeritus, 1999; assoc. prof. So. Meth. U., Dallas, 1968-73, prof., 1973-74. Served with USAF, 1951-54. Guggenheim fellow 1980-81, Smithsonian sr. post doctoral fellow, 1987 ; grantee NSF, Nat. Geographic Soc., others. Fellow AAAS, Geol. Soc. Am. (Archeol. Geology award 1984); mem. Nat. Acad. Sci., Am. Quaternary Assn. (pres. 1976-78), Soc. Am. Archaeology (Fryxell award 1978), Sigma Xi. Office: U Ariz Dept Anthropology Tucson AZ 85721-0001

HAYNES, GARY ANTHONY, archaeologist; b. Long Beach, Calif., Sept. 30, 1948; s. Ellsworth Wallace and Martha Louise (Ryan) H. BA, U. Md., 1970; MA, Cath. U. Am., 1978, PhD, 1981. Vis. asst. prof. anthropology Cath. U. Am., Washington, 1981; assoc. prof. lectr. George Washington U., Washington, 1982; research assoc. anthropology dept. Smithsonian Inst., Washington, 1981-85; asst. prof. anthropology U. Nev., Reno, 1985-88, assoc. prof. anthropology, 1988-95, prof. anthropology, 1995—, chair dept., 1998—. Founder, vice-chmn. bd. Hwange Rsch. Trust, 1987—. Author: Mammoths, Mastodonts and Elephants, 1991; editor: Mammoths and the Mammoth Fauna, 2000; contbr. articles to profl. jours. Active Scientist Exchange Acad. Scis. U.S. Nat. Research Council, 1987. Smithsonian Inst. fellow, 1980; grantee Nat. Geog. Soc., 1981-88, 91, Leakey Found., 1990, 91, IREX, 1995; Fulbright sr. scholar Subsaharan Africa Rsch. Program, 1993. Mem. Soc. Am. Archaeology (Fryxell com. chmn. 1986-89), Am. Quarternary Assn., Soc. Vertebrate Paleontology, Zimbabwe Sci. Assn., Am. Geophys. Union. Office: U Nev Dept Anthropology Reno NV 89557-0001

HAYO, GEORGE EDWARD, management consultant; b. L.A., Nov. 2, 1934; s. George Edward Hayo Sr. and Esther Marie (Goodman) Arthur; m. Nixie Joanne Hunt, Aug. 4, 1956; children: Michael Edward, Kenneth Marvin, Michelle Virginia. BS in Applied Math., Calif. State U., 1960; MBA in Mgmt., U. Denver, 1968. Cert. mgmt. cons. Mathematician U.S. Naval Civil Engring. Lab., Port Hueneme, Calif., 1961-63; corp. systems planner No. Natural Gas Co., Omaha, 1963-66; asst. to pres. C.A. Norgren Co., Littleton, Colo., 1966-68; sr. staff cons. Emerson Electric, St. Louis, 1968-71; dir. adminstrn. Fisher Radio, N.Y.C., 1971-72; v.p., dir. The Emerson Cons., N.Y.C., 1973-87; pres. The Hayo Cons., Albuquerque, 1988—. Arbitrator Am. Arbitration Assn., N.Y., 1985—. Contbr. articles to profl. jours. Mem. Inst. Mgmt. Cons., Am. Inst. Plant Engrs., Am. Prodn. and Inventory Control Soc. Avocations: running, sailing, golf. Home and Office: The Hayo Cons 536 Stagecoach Rd SE Albuquerque NM 87123-4123 E-mail: hayocon@aol.com

HAY-ROE, VICTOR, plastic surgeon; b. Edmonton, Alta., Can., Dec. 23, 1930; s. Edmund Archer and Ruth Mildred (Maddison) Hay-Roe; m. Elizabeth Mae Davison, May 8, 1953 (div. 1978); children: Glenn Cameron, Elizabeth Diane, Scott Richard; m. Lynn Siu, Apr. 19, 1980. BSc, U. Alta., 1953, MD, 1955. Resident in surgery Queen's Hosp., Honolulu, 1956-59; resident in plastic surgery U. Pitts. Sch. Medicine, 1963-66; chief of plastic surgery Honolulu Med. Group, Inc., 1967—. Clin. assoc. prof. plastic surgery, U. Hawaii, Honolulu, 1973—; trip leader, Interplast plastic surgery team to Samoa, 1978, Jamaica, 1988, 90. Mem. Hawaii Plastic Surgery Soc. (pres. 1986-88), Northwest Soc. Plastic Surgeons, Am. Soc. Plastic and reconstructive Surgeons. Republican. Avocations: chess, needlepoint, cross-stitch, tennis, philately. Home: 2277 Halekoa Dr Honolulu HI 96821-1056 Office: Honolulu Med Group Inc 550 S Beretania St Honolulu HI 96813-2405

HAYS, GARRY D. academic administrator; Pres. U.S. Internat U., San Diego, 1992—. Office: US Internat U Office Pres 10455 Pomerado Rd San Diego CA 92131-1717

HAYS, MARGUERITE THOMPSON, nuclear medicine physician, educator; b. Bloomington, Ind., Apr. 15, 1930; d. Stith and Louise (Faust) Thompson; m. David G. Hays, Feb. 4, 1950 (div. 1975); children: Dorothy Adele, Warren Stith Thompson, Thomas Glenn. A.B. cum laude, Radcliffe Coll., 1951; postgrad., Harvard U. Med. Sch., 1954; M.D., UCLA, 1957; Sc.D. (hon.), Ind. U., 1979. Diplomate Am. Bd. Internal Medicine, Am. Bd. Nuclear Medicine. Intern UCLA Sch. Medicine, 1957-58, resident, 1958-59, 61-62, USPHS postdoctoral trainee, 1959-61, USPHS postdoctoral fellow, 1963-64, asst. prof. medicine, 1964-68, SUNY-Buffalo, 1968-70, asst. prof. biophys. sci., 1968-74, assoc. prof. medicine, 1970-76, clin. assoc. prof. nuclear medicine, 1973-77; asst. chief nuclear medicine VA Med. Ctr., Wadsworth, Calif., 1967-68; chief nuclear medicine Buffalo VA Med. Ctr., 1968-74, assoc. chief of staff for rsch., 1971-74; dir. med. rsch. svc. VA Central Office, Washington, 1974-79, asst. chief med. dir. for R&D, 1979-81; chief of staff Martinez VA Med. Ctr., Calif., 1981-83; prof. radiology Sch. Medicine U. Calif., Davis, 1981-93, prof. medicine and surgery, 1983-91, assoc. dean, 1981; clin. prof. diagnostic radiology and nuclear medicine Stanford U. Sch. Medicine, 1990—; assoc. chief of staff for rsch. Palo Alto VA Med. Ctr., Palo Alto, 1983-97, staff physician, 1997-99, cons., 1999—. Vis. rsch. scientist Euratom, Italy, 1962-63; chmn. radiopharm. adv. com. FDA, 1974-77; co-chmn. biomedicine com. Pres.'s Fed. Coun. on Sci., Engring. and Tech., 1979-81; mem. rsch. restructuring adv. com. Va. R&D Office, 1995-96, chair task group to restructure R&D Career Devel. Program, 1996-97; chmn. coop. studies evaluation com., Med. Rsch. Svc., VA, 1990-93; mem. sci. rev. and evaluation bd. Health Svcs. Rsch. and Devel. Svc., VA, 1988-91, chmn. career devel. com., 1991-99, chmn. career devel. com. Rehab. Rsch. and Devel. Svc., 1997—. Rsch. grantee VA, 1968—. NIH grantee, 1964-71; recipient Exceptional Svc. award Sec. Vets. Affairs, 2000. Fellow ACP; mem. Soc. Nuclear Medicine (chmn. publs. com., trustee, v.p. 1983-84), Am. Thyroid Assn. (bd. dirs. 1993-96), Endocrine Soc., Western Assn. Physicians, Western Soc. for Clin. Investigation. Home: 270 Campesino Ave Palo Alto CA 94306-2912 Office: 3801 Miranda Ave Palo Alto CA 94304-1207 E-mail: mhays19@home.com

HAYS, RONALD JACKSON, career officer; b. Urania, La., Aug. 19, 1928; s. George Henry and Fannie Elizabeth (McCartney) H.; m. Jane M. Hughes, Jan. 29, 1951; children: Dennis, Michael, Jacquelyn. Student, Northwestern U., 1945-46; B.S., U.S. Naval Acad., 1950. Commd. ensign U.S. Navy, 1950, advanced through grades to adm., 1983; destroyer officer Atlantic Fleet, 1950-51; attack pilot Pacific Fleet, 1953-56; exptl. test pilot Patuxent River, Md., 1956-59; exec. officer Attack Squadron 106, 1961-63; tng. officer Carrier Air Wing 4, 1963-65; comdr. All Weather Attack Squadron, Atlantic Fleet, 1965-67; air warfare officer 7th Fleet Staff, 1967-68; tactical aircraft plans officer Office Chief Naval Ops., 1969-71; comdg. officer Naval Sta., Roosevelt Roads, P.R., 1971-72; dir. Navy Planning and Programming, 1973-74; comdr. Carrier Group 4, Norfolk, Va., 1974-75; dir. Office of Program Appraisal, Sec. of Navy, Washington, 1975-78; dep. and chief staff, comdr. in chief U.S. Atlantic Fleet, Norfolk, Va., 1978-80; comdr. in chief U.S. Naval Force Europe, London, 1980-83; vice chief naval ops. Dept. Navy, Washington, 1983-85; comdr. in chief U.S. Pacific Command, Camp H.M. Smith, Hawaii, 1985-88; pres., chief exec. officer Pacific Internat. Ctr. for High Tech. Rsch., Honolulu, 1988-92; tech. cons., 1992—. Decorated D.S.M. with 3 gold stars, Silver Star with 2 gold stars, D.F.C. with silver star and gold star, Legion of Merit, Bronze Star with combat V, Air Medal with numeral 14 and gold numeral 3, Navy Commendation medal with gold star and combat V. Baptist. Home and Office: 869 Kamoi Pl Honolulu HI 96825-1318 E-mail: rjhayshawaii@msn.com

HAYTER, ROGER, geographer educator; BA, U. Newcastle Upon Tyne; MA, U. Alta.; PhD, U. Wash. Tchr. Meml. U., Newfoundland; prof. dept. geography Simon Fraser U., 1976—. Author: The Dynamics of Industrial Location: The Factory, the Firm and the Production System, 1997; contbr. articles to profl. jours. Mem. Can. Assn. Geographers (Scholarly Distinction award 1999). Achievements include research on industrial location, corporate strategy, foreign investment, technology policy, the employment implications of recession and restructuring, community development, international trade and industrial organization. Office: Simon Fraser Univ Dept Geography Burnaby BC Canada V5A 1S6

HAYUTIN, DAVID LIONEL, lawyer; b. Phoenix, Apr. 19, 1930; s. Henry and Eva (Gaines) H.; m. Lee June Rodgers, June 15, 1951 A.B., U. So. Calif., Los Angeles, 1952, J.D., 1958. Bar: Calif. 1958. Assoc. Pillsbury Winthrop LLP and predecessor firms., Los Angeles, 1958-67; ptnr. Pillsbury Madison & Sutro LLP and predecessor firms., Los Angeles, 1967—. Bd. dirs. Asahi Bank of Calif. Author: Distributing Foreign Products in the United States, 1988, revised edit., 2000; assoc. editor So. Calif. Law Rev.; contbr. legal articles to profl. jours. Served to lt. (j.g.) USN, 1952-55. Mem. ABA, Internat. Bar Assn., Calif. Bar Assn., Maritime Law Assn., Mountaingate Country Club. Republican. Avocations: opera, golf. Office: Pillsbury Winthrop LLP 725 S Figueroa St Los Angeles CA 90017-5524 E-mail: dhayutin@pillsburywinthrop.com

HAYWOOD, L. JULIAN, physician, educator; b. Reidsville, N.C., Apr. 13, 1927; s. Thomas Woodly and Louise Viola (Hayley) H.; m. Virginia Elizabeth Paige, Dec. 3, 1953; 1 child, Julian Anthony. BS, Hampton Inst., 1948; MD, Howard U., 1952. Intern St. Mary's Hosp., Rochester, N.Y., 1952-53; resident L.A. County Hosp., 1956-58; fellow cardiology White Meml. Hosp., 1959-61; traveling fellow U. Oxford, Eng., 1963; instr. medicine Loma Linda (Calif.) U., 1960-61, asst. prof., 1961-73, assoc. clin. prof., 1973-82, clin. prof., 1982—; asst. prof. medicine U. So. Calif., 1963-67, assoc. prof., 1967-76, prof., 1976—. Past dir. comprehensive sickle cell ctr. Los Angeles County/U. So. Calif. Med. Ctr., dir. ECG Dept., 1996—, past dir. coronary care unit, physicians tng. program (Regional Med. Programs), 1970-75; cons. Los Angeles County Coroner, Indsl. Accident Bd. Calif., Health Care Tech. Divsn., USPHS, Nat. Heart and Lung Inst.; past mem. cardiology adv. com. divsn. heart and vascular diseases; bd. dirs., pres. Sickle Cell Diseases Found.; mem. Armed Forces Epidemiol. Bd., 1996—; pres. U. So. Calif. Salerni Collegium, 1997-98; bd. dirs. Charles Drew U. Medicine and Scis., 1999—. Contbr. articles profl. jours.; Mem. editorial bds.: Jour. Nat. Med. Assn. Past pres., hon. mem., bd. dirs. Am. Heart Assn. Greater L.A., 1989—. With M.C. USNR, 1954-56. Recipient award of merit Los Angeles County Heart Assn., 1968, 69, 73, 75, Disting. Alumnus award Howard U., 1982, Louis B. Russel award Am. Heart Assn., 1988, Merit award, 1991, Heart of Gold award Am. Heart Assn./Greater L.A. Affiliate, 1989, Dedicated Svc. award, 1991,

93, award of Achievement in Rsch., 1994, 20th Anniversary Founder's award Assn. Black Cardiologists, 1994, Disting. Svc. award Howard U. Sch. Medicine, 1996; J.B. Johnson Meml. lectr., 1975, 88; honoree Internal Medicine sect. Nat. Med. Assn., 1988; named Alumnus of Yr.-at-Large, Hampton U., 1993. Fellow ACP, AAAS, L.A. Acad. Medicine, Am. Coll. Cardiology (Disting. Svc. award 2001), Am. Heart Assn. (coun. on clin. cardiology, coun. on atherosclerosis, exec. com. coun. on epidemiology, long range planning com., dir., past sec., v.p. Greater L.A. affiliate, pres.); mem. AMA, AAUP, Am. Fedn. Clin. Rsch., Western Soc. Clin. Investigation, Assn. Advancement Med. Instrumentation, Nat. Med. Assn. (Charles Drew Med. Soc.), N.Y. Acad. Scis., Hampton Inst. Alumni Assn. (past pres. L.A. chpt.), Med. Faculty Assn. U. So. Calif. Sch. Medicine (past pres.), Assn. Physicians L.A. County Hosp. (pres. 1991—), Western Assn. Physicians, Fedn. Am. Scientists, Assn. Black Cardiologists (Walter Booker Innovation award 1990), Assn. Acad. Minority Physicians (councilor, pres.-elect 1992-93, pres. 1993-94), Alpha Omega Alpha, Am. Coll. Physicians (Laureate award So. Calif. Region I 1997). Home: 3551 Lowry Rd Los Angeles CA 90027-1433 Office: LACTUSC Med Ctr Box 305 1200 N State St Los Angeles CA 90033-1029 Office Fax: 323-226-7458. E-mail: jhaywood@hsc.usc.edu

HAYWORTH, J(OHN) D(AVID), JR. congressman, former sportscaster; b. High Point, N.C., July 12, 1958; s. John David and Gladys Ethel (Hall) H.; m. Mary Denise Yancey, Feb. 25, 1989; children: Nicole Irene, Hannah Lynne, John Micah. BA in Speech and Polit. Sci., N.C. State U., 1980. Sports anchor, reporter Sta. WPTF-TV, Raleigh, N.C., 1980-81, Sta. WLWT-TV, Cin., 1986-87; sports anchor Sta. WYFF-TV (formerly Sta. WFBC-TV), Greenville, S.C., 1981-86, Sta. KTSP-TV, Phoenix, 1987-94; mem. U.S. Congress from 6th Ariz. dist., Washington, 1995—; mem. ways and means com., mem. resources com., asst. whip. Radio commentator; play-by-play broadcaster. Dist. committeeman Ariz. Rep. Com., Scottsdale, 1988-89; bd. dirs. Am. Humanics Found., Ariz. State U., Tempe, 1991-92; chmn. Scout-A-Rama, Theodore Roosevelt coun. Boy Scouts Am., 1991-92. Recipient honor roll award Atlantic Coast Conf., 1977, Young Am. award Unharrie coun. Boy Scouts Am., 1979, Friend of Edn. award Sch. Dist. Greenville County, 1985, Sch. Bell/Friend of Edn. award S.C. Dept. Edn., 1985. Mem. Rotary (bd. dirs. Phoenix 1989-90). Baptist. Avocations: reading, distance running, Bible study, public speaking, television trivia. Office: US House Reps 2434 Rayburn Ho Office Bldg Washington DC 20515-0306*

HAZARD, ROBERT CULVER, JR. hotel executive; b. Balt., Oct. 23, 1934; s. Robert Culver and Catherine B. H.; m. Mary Victoria Cranor, Jan. 2, 1981; children by previous marriage: Alicia W., Letitia A., Robert Culver, III, Thomas E.J., Anne. BA cum laude, Woodrow Wilson Sch., Princeton U., 1956; postgrad., Johns Hopkins U., U. Denver. Mktg. rep. IBM Corp., Denver, 1959-68; with Am. Express Co., 1968-74, v.p. exec. accounts, 1973-74; CEO Best Western Internat., 1974-80; CEO, retired chmn. Choice Hotels Internat., Silver Spring, Md., 1980-96; chmn. Creative Hotel Assocs., Phoenix, 1996—. Capt. USAF, 1956-59. Recipient Man of Yr. award Motel Brokers Assn. Am., 1976, Silver Plate award Hospitality mag., 1979, Albert E. Koehl award HSMA, 1992, Cecil B. Day Hospitality award AAHOA, 1993, Silver Plate award Lodging Hospitality Mag., 1995. Mem. Am. Hotel and Lodging Assn. Office: Creative Hotel Assocs LLC 5901 E Valley Vista Ln Paradise Valley AZ 85253 E-mail: bhazard@primenet.com

HAZELTON, PENNY ANN, law librarian, educator; b. Yakima, Wash., Sept. 24, 1947; d. Fred Robert and Margaret (McLeod) Pease; m. Norris J. Hazelton, Sept. 12, 1971; 1 child, Victoria MacLeod. BA cum laude, Linfield Coll., 1969; JD, Lewis and Clark Law Sch., 1975; M in Law Librarianship, U. Wash., 1976. Bar: Wash. 1976, U.S. Supreme Ct. 1982. Assoc. law libr., assoc. prof. U. Maine, 1976-78, law libr., assoc. prof., 1978-81; asst. libr. for rsch. svcs. U.S. Supreme Ct., Washington, 1981-85, law libr., 1985, U. Wash., Seattle, 1985—, prof. law. Tchr. legal rsch., law librarianship, Indian law; cons. Maine Adv. Com. on County Law Librs., Nat. U. Sch. Law, San Diego, 1985-88, Lawyers Cooperative Pub., 1993-94. Author: Computer Assisted Legal Research: The Basics, 1993; contbr. articles to legal jours. Recipient Disting. Alumni award U. Wash., 1992. Mem. ABA (sect. legal edn. and admissions to bar, chair com. on librs. 1993-94, vice chair 1992-93, 94-95, com. on law sch. facilities 1998—), Am. Assn. Law Schs. (com. law librs. 1991-94), Law Librs. New Eng. (sec. 1977-79, pres. 1979-81), Am. Assn. Law Librs. (program chmn. ann. meeting 1984, exec. bd. 1984-87, v.p. 1989-90, pres. 1990-91, program co-chair Insts. 1983, 95), Law Librs. Soc. Washington (exec. bd. 1983-84, v.p., pres. elect 1984-85), Law Librs. Puget Sound, Wash. State Bar Assn. (chair editl. adv. bd.), Wash. Adv. Coun. on Librs., Westpac. Office: U Wash Marian Gould Gallagher Law Libr 1100 NE Campus Pkwy Seattle WA 98105-6605

HAZEN, DON, communications executive; Exec. dir. AlterNet Independent Media Inst., San Francisco, 1994—. Office: AlterNet Independent Media Inst 77 Federal St San Francisco CA 94107-1414

HAZEN, PAUL MANDEVILLE, banker; b. Lansing, Mich., 1941; married. BA, U. Ariz., 1963; MBA, U. Calif., Berkeley, 1964. Asst. mgr Security Pacific Bank, 1964-66; v.p. Union Bank, 1966-70; chmn. Wells Fargo Realty Advisors, 1970-76, with, 1979—, exec. v.p., mgr. Real Estate Industries Group, 1979-80, mem. exec. office Real Estate Industry Group, 1980, vice-chmn. Real Estate Industries Group, 1980-84, pres., chief oper. officer Real Estate Industries Group, 1984—, also dir. Real Estate Industries Group, 1984—; pres., treas. Wells Fargo Mortgage & Equity Trust, San Francisco, 1977-84; with Wells Fargo & Co., San Francisco, 1978—, from exec. v.p. to vice-chmn., pres., chief operating officer, 1978-95, chmn, CEO, 1995-2000, chmn. bd. dirs. Trustee Wells Fargo Mortgage & Equity Trust; bd. dirs. Pacific Telesis Group. Office: Wells Fargo Bank NA 420 Montgomery St San Francisco CA 94104-1298

HAZEWINKEL, VAN, manufacturing executive; b. L.A., Oct. 2, 1943; s. Ben J. and Betty J. (Bishop) H.; m. Linda Bennett, Sept. 11, 1965; children: Van, Karey. BS, Calif. State U., Long Beach, 1967. With Daily Indsl. Tools Inc., Costa Mesa, Calif., 1959—, v.p., 1966-78, pres., 1978—. Founding mem. bd. dirs. Greater Irvine (Calif.) Indsl. League, 1970-73. Mem. Soc. Mfg. Engrs. Office: 3197 Airport Loop Dr Ste D Costa Mesa CA 92626-3424

HAZLETT, MARK A. lawyer; b. N.Y.C., Aug. 18, 1948; BA, Stanford U., 1970, JD, 1973. Bar: Hawaii 1973. Ptnr. Cades, Schutte, Fleming & Wright, Honolulu. Mem. adv. com. to Commr. of Fin. Insts., 1984-86; adj. prof. of law U. Hawaii Law Sch., 1995—. Co-editor: Hawaii Commercial Real Estate Manual, 1988; co-editor, co-author: Hawaii Real Estate Financing Manual, 1990, Hawaii Real Estate Law Manual, 1997. Mem. ABA, Hawaii State Bar Assn. (dir. fin. svcs. divsn. 1982-83, chmn. real property and fin. svcs. sect. 1984, bd. dirs. 1982-98). Office: Cades Schutte Fleming & Wright PO Box 939 1000 Bishop St Honolulu HI 96808

HAZZARD, WILLIAM RUSSELL, geriatrician, educator; b. Ann Arbor, Mich., Sept. 5, 1936; s. Albert Sidney and Florence Bernice (Woolsey) H.; m. Ellen Bennett Friedman, June 10, 1961; children: Susan Lovejoy Roque, Russell Holden, Rebecca Cornell Oliver, Daniel Bennett. AB, Cornell U., 1958, MD, 1962. Diplomate Am. Bd. Internal Med. Resident in internal medicine U. Wash. Sch. Med. and Affiliated Hosps., Seattle, 1966-67, fellow in endocrinology and metabolism, 1965-66, 67-69; from instr. to prof. medicine U. Wash., Seattle, 1969-82, dir. Northwest Lipid Rsch. Clinic, 1972-78; investigator Howard Hughes Med. Inst., U. Wash., Seattle, 1972-80; chief divsn. gerontology and geriatric medicine, 1978-82; prof. medicine, assoc. dir. dept. medicine Johns Hopkins Med. Instns., Balt., 1982-86, dir. ctr. on aging, 1983-86; prof., chmn. dept. internal med. Bowman Gray Sch. Medicine of Wake Forest U., Winston-Salem, N.C., 1986-98; dir. J. Paul Sticht Ctr. on Aging of Wake Forest U., Winston-Salem, 1987-97; sr. adv. J. Paul Ctr. On Aging of Wake Forest U., 1998—; prof. medicine U. Wash., Seattle, 1999—; dir. geriatrics and extended care VA Puget Sound Health Care Sys., 1999—. Editor: Principles of Geriatric Medicine and Gerontology, 1984, 89, 93, 99; contbr. over 100 articles to jours. in field. Lt. USNR, 1963-65. Fellow ACP; mem. Inst. Medicine of NAS, Am. Geriatrics Soc. (bd. dirs. 1988—, pres. 1993), Assn. Profs. Medicine, Gerontol. Soc. Am. (chmn. clin. med. sect. 1984), Am. Heart Assn. (Coun. on Arterosclerosis), Am. Fedn. Biomed. Rsch. (mem. emeritus), Am. Soc. Clin. Investigation (mem. emeritus), Assn. Am. Physicians, AM. Clin. and Climatol. Assn., Nat. Inst. on Aging (aging rev. com. 1990-94, Geriatric Medicine Acad. award 1980), Coun. on Aging (nat. advisor). Avocations: gardening, conservation and nature study, music, athletics. Home: 3515 E Conover Ct Seattle WA 98122-6426 Office: VA Puget Sound Health Care Sys Geriatric Extended Care 1660 S Columbian Way Seattle WA 98108-1532 E-mail: william.hazzard@med.va.gov

HEAD, IVAN LEIGH, law educator; b. Calgary, Alta., Can., July 28, 1930; s. Arthur Cecil and Birdie Hazel (Crockett) H.; m. Barbara Spence Eagle, June 23, 1952; children: Laurence Allan, Bryan Cameron, Catherine Spence, Cynthia Leigh; m. Ann Marie Price, Dec. 1, 1979. BA, U. Alta., 1951, LLB, 1952; LLM, Harvard U., 1960; LLD (hon.), U. Alta., 1987, U. West Indies, 1987, U. Western Ont., 1988, U. Ottawa, 1988, U. Calgary, 1989, Beijing U., 1990, St. Francis Xavier U., 1990, U. Man., 1991, U. Notre Dame, 1991, Carleton U., 1996. Bar: Alta. 1953; Queen's Counsel, Can. Practiced in, Calgary, 1953-59; partner Helman, Barron & Head, 1955-59; fgn. service officer Dept. External Affairs, Ottawa, Kuala Lumpur, 1960-63; prof. law U. Alta., 1963-67; assoc. counsel to Minister of Justice, Govt. of Can., 1967-68, spl. asst. to prime minister of Can., 1968-78; pres. Internat. Devel. Research Centre, Ottawa, 1978-91; prof. law, dir. Liu Centre for the study of global issues U. B.C., Vancouver, Can., 1991-99. Sr. fellow Salzburg Seminar; bd. dirs. Acad. Ednl. Devel.; adj. prof. Simon Fraser U., 2000—. Author: International Law, National Tribunals and the Rights of Aliens, 1971, On a Hinge of History, 1991, The Canadian Way, 1995; editor: This Fire Proof House, 1967, Conversation with Canadians, 1972; contbr. articles to profl. jours. Trustee Internat. Food Policy Rsch. Inst., 1979-88; mem. Ind. Commn. on Internat. Humanitarian Issues, 1983-87. Decorated officer Order of Can.; officer Grand Cross, Order of The Sun (Peru); Chief Justice's medallist U. Alta. Law Sch.; Frank Knox Meml. fellow Harvard Law Sch., 1959-60; named to Sports Wall of Fame U. Alta. Mem. Internat. Law Assn., Can. Council Internat. Law, Can. Inst. Internat. Affairs, Am. Soc. Internat. Law, Law Soc. Alta., Inter-Am. Dialogue. Anglican. Home: 2343 Bellevue Ave West Vancouver BC Canada V7V 1C9 Office: U BC Liu Ctr Study Global Issues Vancouver BC Canada V6T 1Z2 E-mail: ivanhead@home.com

HEADY, FERREL, retired political science educator; b. Ferrelview, Mo., Feb. 14, 1916; s. Chester Ferrel and Loren (Wightman) H.; m. Charlotte Audrey McDougall, Feb. 12, 1942; children— Judith Lillian, Richard Ferrel, Margaret Loren, Thomas McDougall. A.B., Washington U., St. Louis, 1937, A.M., 1938, Ph.D., 1940; hon. degrees, Park Coll., 1973, John F. Kennedy U., 1974, U. N.Mex., 1993. Jr. adminstrv. technician, also adminstrv. asst. Office Dir. Personnel, Dept. Agr., 1941-42; vis. lectr. polit. sci. U. Kansas City, 1946; faculty U. Mich., 1946-67, prof. polit. sci., 1957-67; dir. Inst. Pub. Adminstrn., 1960-67; acad. v.p. U. N.Mex., Albuquerque, 1967-68, pres., 1968-75, prof. pub. adminstrn. and polit. sci., 1975-81, prof. emeritus, 1981—. Asst. to commr. Com. Orgn. Exec. Br. of Govt., 1947-49; dir., chief adviser Inst. Pub. Adminstrn., U. Philippines, 1953-54; mem. U.S. del. Internat. Congress Adminstrn. Scis., Spain, 1956, 80, Germany, 1959, Austria, 1962, Poland, 1964, Mexico, 1974; exec. bd. Inter-Univ. Case Program, 1956-67; sr. specialist in residence East-West Center, U. Hawaii, 1965; mem. Conf. on Pub. Service, 1965-70; chmn. bd. Assoc. Western Univs., 1970-71; commr. Western Interstate Commn. Higher Edn., 1972-77; mem. commns. on bus. professions and water resources, mem. exec. com. Nat. Assn. State Univs. and Land Grant Colls., 1968-75 Author: Administrative Procedure Legislation in the States, 1952, (with Robert H. Pealy) The Michigan Department of Administration, 1956, (with Sybil L. Stokes) Comparative Public Administration: A Selective Annotated Bibliography, 1960, Papers in Comparative Public Administration, 1962, State Constitutions: The Structure of Administration, 1961, Public Administration: A Comparative Perspective, 1966, rev. edit., 1979, 6th edit., 2001, One Time Around, 1999; contbr. profl. jours. Chmn. state affairs com. Ann Arbor Citizens Coun., Mich., 1949-52; mem. exec. com. Mich. Meml.-Phoenix Project and Inst. Social Rsch., 1960-66; mem. Gov. Mich. Constl. Revision Study Commn., 1960-62; schs. and univs. adv. bd. Citizens Com. for Hoover Report, 1949-52, 54-58; cons. to Ford Found., 1962; chmn. Coun. on Grad. Edn. in Pub. Adminstrn., 1966; mem., vice chmn. N.Mex. Gov.'s Com. on Reorgn. of State Govt., 1967-70; mem. N.Mex. Am. Revolution Bicentennial Commn., 1970-73, N.Mex. Gov.'s Com. on Tech. Excellence, 1969-75, Nat. Acad. Pub. Adminstrn.; mem., vice chmn. N.Mex. Constl. Revision Commn., 1994-95. Served to lt. USNR, 1942-46. Recipient Faculty Disting. Achievement award U. Mich., 1964, N.Mex. Disting. Pub. service award, 1973, award of distinction U. N.Mex. Alumni Assn., 1975, Outstanding Grad. Tchr. award U. N.Mex., 1981-82, Fulbright sr. lectureship, Colombia, 1992, Waldo award for career contbns. to lit. and leadership of pub. adminstrn., 1994. Mem. Am. Polit. Sci. Assn., Am. Soc. Pub. Adminstrn. (pres. 1969-70), AAUP (chmn. com. T 1957-61), Am. Council Edn. (mem. commn. on fed. relations 1969-72), Phi Beta Kappa, Phi Kappa Phi. Presbyterian. Home: 2901 Cutler Ave NE Albuquerque NM 87106-1714

HEAFEY, EDWIN AUSTIN, JR. lawyer; b. Oakland, Calif., Nov. 1, 1930; s. Edwin Austin Sr. and Florence (Jochim) H.; married; children: Ryan, Matthew, Alison. AB, U. Santa Clara, 1952; LLB, Stanford U., 1955. Bar: Calif. 1955, U.S. Dist. Ct. (no. and cen. dists.) Calif. 1955, U.S. Supreme Ct. 1984. Sr. ptnr. Crosby, Heafey, Roach & May, Oakland, 1955—. Instr. law U. Calif., Berkeley, 1963-78; bd. fellows Georgetown Law Sch. Author: California Trial Objections, 1967, 8th edit., 2000. Trustee U. Santa Clara; bd. dirs. Georgetown U., 2000—. Fellow Am. Bd. Trial Advs. (life, sr., past pres.); mem. ATLA, Am. Bar Found., Am., Calif. Trial Lawyers Assn., Am. Coll. Trial Lawyers, Calif. Bar Assn., Alameda County Bar Assn., San Francisco Bar Assn., Internat. Soc. Barrister, Claremont Country Club, Pacific Union Club. Office: Crosby Heafey Roach & May Profl Corp PO Box 7936 4 Embarcadero Ctr 19th Fl San Francisco CA 94111-4106 also: 1999 Harrison St PO Box 2084 Oakland CA 94604-2084 also: 700 S Flower St Ste 2200 Los Angeles CA 90017-4209 also: 2049 Century Park E Ste 3870 Los Angeles CA 90067-3101 E-mail: eheafey@chrm.com

HEALY, ALICE FENVESSY, psychology educator, researcher; b. Chgo., June 26, 1946; d. Stanley John and Doris (Goodman) Fenvessy; m. James Bruce Healy, May 9, 1970; 1 dau., Charlotte Alexandra. AB summa cum laude, Vassar Coll., 1968; PhD, Rockefeller U., 1973. Asst. prof. psychology Yale U., New Haven, 1973-78, assoc. prof. psychology, 1978-81, U. Colo., Boulder, 1981-84, prof. psychology, 1984—. Rsch. assoc. Haskins Labs., New Haven, 1976-80; mem. com. NIMH, Washington, 1979-81; co-investigator rsch. contract USAF, U. Colo., 1985-86; prin. investigator rsch. contract U.S. Army Rsch. Inst., U. Colo., 1986—, Naval Tng. Systems Ctr., 1993-94; rsch. grant prin. investigator U.S. Army Rsch. Office, U. Colo., 1995—, NASA, 1999—. Co-author: Cognitive Processes, 2d edit., 1986; editor: Memory and Cognition, 1986-89, (with S.M. Kosslyn and R.M. Shiffrin) From Learning Theory to Connectionist Theory: Essays in Honor of William K. Estes, Vol. I, 1992, From Learning Processes to Cognitive Processes: Essays in Honor of William K. Estes, Vol. II, 1992, (with L.E. Bourne Jr.) Learning and Memory of Knowledge and Skills: Durability and Specificity, 1995, Foreign Language Learning: Psycholinguistic Studies on Training and Retention, 1998; assoc. editor Jour. Exptl. Psychology, 1982-84; contbr. more than 135 articles to profl. jours. and chpts. to books. Recipient Sabbatical award James McKeen Cattell Fund, 1987-88; NSF Rsch. grantee, 1977-86, Spencer Found. Rsch. grantee, 1978-80. Fellow APA (exec. com. divsn. 3 1989-92, 2001—, chair membership com. 1992-93), AAAS (nominating com. 1988-91, chair 1991, chair-elect psychology sect. 1994, chair psychology sect. 1995-96, retiring chair psychology sect. 1996-97), Soc. Exptl. Psychologists; mem. Psychonomic Soc. (governing bd. 1987-92, publs. com. 1989-93), Soc. Math. Psychology, Rocky Mountain Psychology Assn. (pres.-elect 1993-94, pres. 1994-95, past pres. 1995-96), Cognitive Sci. Soc., Soc. for Applied Rsch. in Memory and Cognition, Univ. Club, Phi Beta Kappa, Sigma Xi. Avocation: French pastries. Home: 840 Cypress Dr Boulder CO 80303-2820 Office: U Colo Dept Psychology PO Box 345 UCB Boulder CO 80309-0345 E-mail: ahealy@psych.colorado.edu

HEALY, CYNTHIA, pharmacologist, life scientist, researcher; BS in Chemistry, Coll. of White Plains; PhD in Pharmacology, N.Y. Med. Coll. Rschr. Roche Inst. Molecular Biology; mgr. drug discovery projects in inflammation CIBA-Geigy Corp.; dir. life sci. rsch. Kleiner, Perkins, Caufield & Byers, Menlo Park, Calif. Involved in beginning stage of privately held life scis. cos., inlcuidng Corixa, Georn, Pharmacopeia, and Signal Pharms.; bd. dirs. Argonaut Techs. Contbr. numerous articles on cellular immunology and inflammation to sci. jours. Office: Kleiner Perkins Caufield & Byers 2750 Sand Hill Rd Menlo Park CA 94025-7020 Fax: 650-233-0300

HEALY, JAMES BRUCE, cooking school administrator, writer; b. Paterson, N.J., Apr. 15, 1947; s. James Burn and Margaret Mercy (Patterson) H.; m. Alice Fenvessy, May 9, 1970; 1 child, Charlotte Alexandra. BA, Williams Coll., 1968; PhD, The Rockefeller U., 1973. Mem. faculty Inst. Advanced Study, Princeton, N.J., 1973-75; J.W. Gibbs instr. physics Yale U., New Haven, 1975-77, research affiliate, 1977-80; dir. Healy-Lucullus Sch. French Cooking, New Haven, 1978-80, Boulder, Colo., 1980—. Cons. Claudine's, Denver, 1985-86; vis. instr. Salem (Mass.) State Coll., 1984, and various culinary schs. Author: Mastering the Art of French Pastry, 1984, The French Cookie Book, 1994, The Art of the Cake, 1999; contbr. articles and revs. on restaurants and cooking to mags. and profl. jours. Mem. Internat. Assn. Cooking Profls. (cert.), Confederation Nationale des Patissiers, Glaciers, et Confiseurs de France. Methodist. Home and Office: Healy Lucullus Sch French Cooking 840 Cypress Dr Boulder CO 80303-2820 E-mail: hlucullus@earthlink.net

HEALY, SONYA AINSLIE, retired health facility administrator; b. Sudbury, Ont., Can., Apr. 7, 1937; came to U.S., 1949; d. Walter B. and Wilma A. Scott; m. Richard C. Healy, Jr., Dec. 16, 1961. Diploma, Good Samaritan Hosp., West Palm Beach, Fla., 1958; student, U. Mass., 1963-64, NYU, 1964-66; BS, Boston U., 1969, MS in Med.-Surg. Nursing, 1974. Various staff nursing, charge nurse positions, suprs., med.-surg. and obstet. nursing, 1958-69; chmn. jr.-sr. teaching team Sch. of Nursing Melrose (Mass.) Wakefield Hosp., 1969-73; asst. dir. nurses Boston State Hosp., 1973-74; asst. dir., DON Mt. Zion Hosp. and Med. Ctr., 1974-75; asst. dir. patient care svcs., DON St. Elizabeth's Hosp., Boston, 1975-80, St. Joseph's Hosp., Nashua, N.H., 1980-82; adminstr. U. Calif. Med. Ctr., San Diego, 1982-91, corp. chief nursing officer, 1991, assoc. dir. hosp. and clinics, dir. patient care svcs., 1982-93; exec. mgmt. cons. Noyes & Assocs. Ltd., Bainbridge Island, Wash., 1993—. Mem. acad. affairs com., bd. trustees U. San Diego; clin. assoc. Ul. San Diego, 1984—; mem. adj. faculty San Diego State U.; mem. clin. faculty UCLA Sch. of Nursing; presenter in field. Author: The 12-hour Shift: Is It Viable?-Nursing Outlook, 1984, (handbook) Human Resource Management Handbook, 1987, Human Resources Management Handbook, 1987, Nursing Economics, 1989; mem. editl. adv. bd. dirs. OR Nurse Today, 1989-96; editl. rev. Nursing Economics; contbr. articles to profl. jours. Mem. ASNSA (nominations com. 1978, cert.), Am. Orgn. of Nurse Execs. (bd. dirs. 1990-92, by laws com. 1990-92), Mass. Soc. of Nursing Svcs. Adminstrs. (pres. pres. 1977), Calif. Soc. of Nursing Svc. Adminstrs. (task force on orgns. program com. 1984-85, bd. dirs. 1985-87, mem. com. 1987-88, long range planning com.), San Diego Dirs. of Nurses (sec. 1982-83, pres. 1988-89), Sigma Theta Tau (Zeta Mu chpt.). Avocations: reading, golfing.

HEAPHY, JANIS D. newspaper executive; b. Kalamazoo, Oct. 10, 1951; d. Elvin Julius and Margaret Louise (Throndike) Olson; m. Douglas R. Dern, Aug. 15, 1980 (div. Nov. 1985); m. Robert Thomas Heaphy, Feb. 11, 1989; 1 child, Tanner. BS, Miami U., 1973, MEd, 1976. Tchr. Edgewood Jr. High Sch., Seven Mile, Ohio, 1973-75; acct. exec. L.A. Times, 1976-79, L.A. Mag., 1979-82; mgr. L.A. Omni Mag., 1982-86; sr. acct. exec. L.A. Times, 1986-87, ea. mag. mgr., 1987-89, nat. advt. mgr., 1989-92, retail advt. mgr., 1992—, sr. v.p., advt./mktg.; now pub. Sacramento Bee. Co-editor: Secrets of the Master Sellers, 1987. Mem. Advt. Club L.A. Avocations: home decorating, reading, swimming, music. Office: Sacramento Bee PO Box 15779 2100 Q St Sacramento CA 95852

HEARON, REED, chef; b. Austin, Tex., Oct. 4, 1957; Chef Rattlesnake Club, Denver, 1980, Coyote Cafe, Santa Fe, Corona Bar & Grill, San Francisco, Lulu, San Francisco, 1993, Cafe Marimba, 1993. Author: Salsa: Musica for your Mouth, La Prilla: The Mexica Grill, 1996, Bocaditos: The Little Bites of Mexico, 1997. Recipient James Beard award for Best New Restaurant, 1996; named Chef of the Yr. San Francisco Focus mag., 1996. Office: Nice Ventures 1606 Stockton St San Francisco CA 94133

HEARST, GARRISON (GERALD GARRISON HEARST), professional football player; b. Lincolnton, Ga., Jan. 4, 1971; Student, Ga. State U. Running back Phoenix Cardinals, 1993, Arizona Cardinals, Phoenix, 1994-95, Cin. Bengals, 1996, San Francisco 49ers, 1997—. Recipient Doak Walker award, 1992; named running back The Sporting News coll. All-Am. 1st team, 1992. Office: c/o San Francisco 49ers 4949 Centennial Blvd Santa Clara CA 95054-1229

HEARST, JOHN EUGENE, chemistry educator, researcher, consultant; b. Vienna, July 2, 1935; came to U.S., 1938; s. Alphonse Bernard and Lily (Roger) H.; m. Jean Carolyn Bankson, Aug. 30, 1958; children: David Paul, Leslie Jean. B.E., Yale U., 1957; Ph.D., Calif. Inst. Tech., 1961; D.Sc. (hon.), Lehigh U., 1992. Postdoctoral rschr. Dartmouth Coll., Hanover, N.H., 1961-62; prof. chemistry U. Calif., Berkeley, 1962-95, prof. emeritus, 1996—, Miller rsch. prof., 1970-71; founder, dir. HRI Rsch. Inc., 1978—; sr. rsch. scientist Lawrence Berkeley Lab., 1980-99, faculty chemist, 2000—, dir. divsn. chem. biodynamics, 1986-89; founder, sr. cons. Advanced Genetics Rsch., Inc., Oakland, Calif., 1981-84; founder, dir. Steritech Inc., Concord, 1992-96; founder, dir., v.p. new sci. opportunities Cerus Corp., Concord, 1992—. Disting. lectr. Purdue U., 1986; Merck Centennial lectr. Lehigh U., 1992, Robert A. Welch Found. lectr., 1992-93; adv. bd. Pharm. and Chem. Scis. Graduate Program Univ. of the Pacific, 2000—; cons. Codon, Inc., 1993-97. Author: Contemporary Chemistry, 1976. editor: General Chemistry, 1974; exec. editor Nucleic Acids Rsch., 1990-93; inventor, patentee in field. Bd. dirs. U. No. Calif., 1993-95, dir. Disability Policy and Planning Inst., Berkeley, 2000—. Recipient Sci. Profl. Devel. award NSF, 1977-78, The Berkeley citation, 1999, Mortimer Bortin award for outstanding rsch. in bone marrow transplant, 2000; John Simon Guggenheim fellow, 1968-69, European Molecular Orgn. sr. fellow, 1973-74. Mem. AAAS, Am. Chem. Soc.,

Biophys. Soc., Am. Soc. Biol. Chemists, Am. Soc. for Photobiology (coun., pres. elect 1990-91, pres. 1991-92, Rsch. award 1994), Am. Phys. Soc. Home: 101 Southampton Ave Berkeley CA 94707-2036 Office: Cerus Corp 2411 Stanwell Dr Concord CA 94520-4824

HEARST, WILLIAM RANDOLPH, III, newspaper publisher; b. Washington, June 18, 1949; s. William Randolph and Austine (McDonnell) H.; m. Margaret Kerr Crawford, Sept. 23, 1990; children: William, Adelaide, Caroline. A.B., Harvard U., 1972. Reporter, asst. city editor San Francisco Examiner, 1972-76, publisher, 1984-96; editor Outside Mag., 1976-78; asst. mng. editor Los Angeles Herald Examiner, 1978-80; mgr. devel. Hearst Corp., 1980-82; v.p. Hearst Cable Communications Div., 1982-84; now ptnr. Perkins, Coffield & Buyers, Menlo Park, Calif. Bd. dirs. Sun Microsystems; trustee Carnegie Inst. Washington. Office: Excite at home corp. 450 Broadway St Redwood City CA 94063

HEATH, GARY BRIAN, manufacturing firm executive, engineer; b. Pueblo, Colo., Nov. 5, 1954; s. William Sidney Heath and Eleanor Aileen (Mortimer) Svedman, (stepfather) Donald Svedman; m. Francine Marie Tamburelli, Apr. 28, 1990. BSME, U. So. Colo., 1979; MBA, U. Phoenix, 1984. Engr. ADR Ultrasound Corp., Tempe, Ariz., 1979-81; sr. engr. Technicare Ultrasound, Englewood, Colo., 1981-83; engring. mgr. COBE Labs., Inc., Lakewood, 1983-89; dir. mfg. Gambro BCT, Inc., Lakewood, 1989-96, v.p. mfg., 1996-2000, chief operating officer, 2000—. Patentee fluid flow transfer device, pressure diaphragm for fluid flow device. Mem. Soc. Mfg. Engrs., Soc. Plastics Engrs. Avocations: skiing, fishing, reading, weight training. Home: 6488 S Alkire St Apt #1837 Littleton CO 80127 Office: Gambro BCT Inc 10811 W Collins Ave Lakewood CO 80215-4409 E-mail: gary.heath@gambrobct.com

HEATH, GEORGE ROSS, oceanographer; b. Adelaide, Australia, Mar. 10, 1939; s. Frederick John and Eleanora (Blackmore) H.; m. Lorna Margaret Sommerville, Oct. 5, 1972; children: Amanda Jo, Alisa Jeanne. BSc, Adelaide U., 1960, BSc with honors, 1961; PhD, U. Calif., San Diego, 1968. Geologist S. Australian Geol. Survey, Adelaide, 1961-63; asst. prof. oceanography Oreg. State U., Corvallis, 1969-72, assoc. prof., 1972-75, prof., dean, 1978-84; assoc. prof. oceanography U. R.I., Narragansett, 1974-77, prof., 1977-78; dean U. Wash., Seattle, 1984-96, prof., 1984—, dean emeritus, 1996—; pres., exec. dir. Monterey Bay Aquarium Rsch. Inst., Moss Landing, Calif., 1996-97. Mem. bd. oceans and atmosphere Nat. Assn. State Univs. and Land Grant Colls., 1982-96, co-chmn. exec. com., 1992-93; chmn. legis. com. Commn. on Food, Environment and Renewable Resources, 1994-96; chmn. bd. ocean sci. and policy NRC, 1984-85, mem. bd. radioactive waste mgmt., 1982-90; bd. govs. Joint Oceanographic Instns., Inc., 1978-96, chmn., 1982-84; v.p. sci. com. on oceanic rsch. of Internat. Coun. of Sci. Unions, 1984-90; chmn. performance assessment peer rev. panel Waste Isolation Pilot Plant, 1987-98; bd. dirs. Monterey Bay Aquarium Rsch. Inst.; mem. found. com. Coll. Marine Sci. and Fisheries, Sultan Qaboos U., Muscat, Sultanate of Oman, 1994—; mem. adv. panel Odyssey, 1990—, mem. bd. govs., 1999-2000; environ. analyst Sta. KIRO-TV, Seattle, 1993; bd. govs. Consortium for Oceanographic Rsch. & Edn., 1994-98, chmn., 1996-98; bd. govs. Seattle Aquarium Soc., 1998—. Contbr. articles to profl. jours. Recipient Fulbright award, 1963. Fellow AAAS, Geol. Soc. Am., Am. Geophys. Union; mem. Oceanography Soc. Home: 3857 50th Ave NE Seattle WA 98105-5235 Office: U Wash Sch Oceanography PO Box 357940 Seattle WA 98195-7940 E-mail: rheath@u.washington.edu

HEATH, JAMES R. chemistry educator; Asst. prof. dept. chemistry UCLA. Packard fellow David and Lucile Packard Found., 1994. Office: U Calif Dept Chemistry 405 Hilgard Ave Los Angeles CA 90024-1301

HEATH, RICHARD RAYMOND, investment company executive, retired; b. La Junta, Colo., June 22, 1929; s. Perry Stanford and Genevieve Anabelle (Whitney) H.; m. Arlene Newbrow, Nov. 3, 1961. BA in Econs., U. Colo., 1951, LLB, 1954. Bar: Colo. 1954, Calif. 1957, Ark. 1973. Mem. firm Neyhart & Grodin, San Francisco, 1957-66; dep. Peace Corps dir. Ivory Coast, 1966-68; dir. Ivory Coast, 1968-69; Peace Corps dir. Mali, 1969-72; dir. Ark. Dept. Fin. and Adminstrn.; also chief fiscal officer, commr. revenues State of Ark., mem. gov.'s cabinet, 1972-77; dir. San Francisco Internat. Airport, 1977-81; v.p., dir. mktg. AIS, Inc., 1981-84; exec. v.p., CFO United Bank, San Francisco, 1984-85; chmn., CEO Nat. Bus. Resources Inc., 1985-87; ptnr. Hakman & Co., Investment Bankers, 1987-2000; chmn., CEO Podarok Internat., Inc., 1993-96; chmn., pres. Heath Mgmt. Svcs., 1994-2000; chmn. Laser Design Internat., LLC, 1996—. Chmn., CEO 1st Calif. Bus. and Indsl. Devel. Corp., United Bus. Ventures; bd. dirs. V-Ray Imaging, Inc.; vice chmn. Multi-State Tax Commn., 1973-74, chmn., 1976-77, mem. exec. com., 1974-77; del. Conf. State Bar Dels. Bd. dirs., treas. San Francisco Midsummer Mozart Festival, 1986-92, chmn., 1999-2000; mem. nat. bd. dirs. Coalition for a Dem. Majority, 1973-76; chmn. bd. dirs. FORUM; mem. conservative caucus nat. Tax Limitation Com., 1980—; mem. rep. presdl. task force Rep. nat. Com., 1980-91. Mem. State Bar Calif., San Francisco Bar Assn. (past chmn. indsl. accident com.), San Francisco Lawyers Club, Am., Calif. trial lawyers assns., San Francisco Planning and Urban Renewal Assn., Nat. Parks Assn., Calif. Applicants Attys. Assn. (v.p.) Clubs: Little Rock Racquet, San Francisco Tennis (gov.), Rotary Internat., World Trade. Home: One Treetops Lane #902 Little Rock AR 72202-1660

HEATHCOCK, CLAYTON HOWELL, chemistry educator, researcher; b. San Antonio, July 21, 1936; s. Clayton H. and Frances E. (Lay) H.; m. Mabel Ruth Sims, Sept. 6, 1957 (div. 1972); children: Cheryl Lynn, Barbara Sue, Steven Wayne, Rebecca Ann; m. Cheri R. Hadley, Nov. 28, 1980. BSc, Abilene Christian Coll., Tex., 1958; PhD, U. Colo., 1963. Supr. chem. analysis group Champion Paper and Fiber Co., Pasadena, Tex., 1958-60; asst. prof. chemistry U. Calif.-Berkeley, 1964-70, assoc. prof., 1970-75, prof., 1975—, chmn., 1986-89, dean Coll. of Chemistry, 1999—. Chmn. Medicinal Chemistry Study Sect., NIH, Washington, 1981-83; mem. sci. adv. coun. Abbott Labs., 1986-97. Author: Introduction to Organic Chemistry, 1976; editor-in chief Organic Syntheses, 1985-86, Jour. Organic Chemistry, 1989—; contbr. numerous articles to profl. jours. Recipient Alexander von Humboldt U.S. Scientist, 1978, Allan R. Day award, 1989, Prelog medal, 1991, Centenary medal Royal Soc. Chemistry, 1995. Mem. AAAS, Am. Acad. Arts and Scis., Am. Chem. Soc. (chmn. divsn. organic chemistry 1985, Ernest Guenther award 1986, award for creative work in synthetic organic chemistry 1990, A.C. Cope scholar 1990), Nat. Acad. Scis., Royal Soc. Chemistry (Centenary medal 1995), Am. Soc. Pharmacology. Home: 5235 Alhambra Valley Rd Martinez CA 94553-9765 Office: U Calif Dept Chemistry Berkeley CA 94720-0001 E-mail: heathcock@cchem.berkeley.edu

HEAVEY, MIKE, state legislator, lawyer; m. Connie Heavey; children: Michael James, Shana Marie, Christa Colleen. BA in Polit. Sci., U. Wash.; JD, U. Santa Clara. Pvt. practice, mem. Wash. Legislature, Olympia, 1995—, chair jud. com., mem. commerce, trade, housing and fin. instns. com., mem. transp. com. Mem. 34th Dist. Dems.; mem. Fauntleroy Cmty. Assn.; fundraiser West Seattle chpt. YMCA. 1st lt. U.S. Army, Vietnam. Decorated Bronze Star. Mem. Wash. State Bar Assn., Am. Legion (Post 160), Tyee Club (U. Wash.), Pres.'s Club (U. Wash.), Kiwanis, Quad Club, Phi Alpha Delta. Democrat. Office: 403 Legislative Bldg Olympia WA 98504-0001

HEBELER, HENRY KOESTER, retired aerospace and electronics executive; b. St. Louis, Aug. 12, 1933; s. Henry and Viola O. (Koester) H.; m. Mirriam Robb, Aug. 12, 1978; children by previous marriage: Linda Ruth, Laura Ann. BS in Aero. Engring., MS, MIT, 1956, MBA, 1970. Gen. mgr. rsch./engring. Boeing Aerospace Co., Seattle, 1970-72, pres., 1980-85; v.p. bus. devel. The Boeing Co., Seattle, 1973-74, exec. com. and corp. v.p. planning, 1988-89; pres. Boeing Engring. & Constrn. Co., Seattle, 1975-79, Boeing Electronics Co., Seattle, 1985-87. Bd. dirs. Microelectronics and Computer Tech. Corp.; mem. fusion panel Ho. of Reps., 1979-81, energy rsch. adv. bd. Dept. Energy, 1980-81, task force on internat. industry Def. Sci. Bd., 1982-84, adv. com. nat. strategic materials and minerals program U.S. Dept. Interior, 1986—. Patentee in field. Bd. govs. Sloan Sch., MIT, 1980-84; bd. visitors Def. Systems Mgmt. Coll., Ft. Belvoir, Va. Recipient Mead prize for aero. engrs., 1956; Kuljian humanities award, 1954; Sperry Gyroscope fellow, 1956; Sloan fellow M.I.T., 1970 Mem. AIAA, Nat. Aeros. Assn., Assn. of U.S. Army, Armed Forces Comm. and Electronics Assn. (bd. dirs.), Aviation Hall of Fame, Ala. Space and Rocket Ctr. (sci. and adv. com. 1980-85), Nat. Space (bd. govs. 1980-85), Meridian Valley Country Club. Home and Office: 24600 140th Ave SE Kent WA 98042-5160

HEBERT, GUY, professional hockey player; b. Troy, N.Y., Jan. 7, 1967; m. Sarah Szalach, 1995; 1 child, Madeline. Goalie St. Louis, 1991-93, Mighty Ducks, Anaheim, Calif., 1993-99, Phoenix (Ariz.) Coyotes, 1999—. Avocations: fly fishing, deep sea fishing, basketball, golf. Office: c/o Phoenix Coyotes Cellular One Ice Den 9375 E Bell Rd Scottsdale AZ 85260-1500

HEDGER, CECIL RAYMOND, lawyer; b. Tracy, Minn., Feb. 28, 1947; s. Raymond O. and Willie (Weems) H.; m. Jane E. Scott, June 6, 1970 (div. 1987); 1 child, Anne Kathryn. BA, U. S.D., 1969; JD, U. Nebr., 1972. Bar: Calif. 1972, U.S. Ct. Appeals (9th cir.) 1972, Nebr. 1973, U.S. Ct. Appeals (8th cir.) 1973, U.S. Ct. Appeals (5th cir.) 1973, Utah 1978, U.S. Dist. Ct. Utah 1978, U.S. Ct. Appeals (10th cir.) 1978, Colo. 1981, U.S. Dist. Ct. Colo. 1981. Assoc. Nelson & Harding, Lincoln, Nebr., 1972-74, ptnr., 1974-77, Salt Lake City, 1977-79, Denver, 1979-81, 84-88, Musick, Peeler & Garnett, L.A. and Denver, 1981-84, Harding & Ogborn (successor firm of Nelson & Harding), Denver, 1990-98; of counsel VanCott, Bagely, Cornwall & McCarthy, Salt Lake City, 1998—. Contbr. chpts. to legal book. Mem. ABA (practice and procedure under the nat. labor rels. act, labor law sect.). Avocations: golf, rocketry, hiking, reading. Office: VanCott Bagely Cornwall & McCarthy PO Box 45340 Salt Lake City UT 84145-0340

HEDRICK, BASIL CALVIN, state agency administrator, ethnohistorian, educator, museum and multicultural institutions consultant; b. Lewistown, Mo., Mar. 17, 1932; s. Truman Bloice and M. LaVeta (Stice) H.; m. Anne Kehoe, Jan. 19, 1957 (div. 1979); 1 dau., Anne Lanier Hedrick Caraker; m. Susan Elizabeth Pickel, Oct. 2, 1980. A.B., Augustana Coll., Rock Island, Ill., 1956; MA, U. Fla., 1957; PhD, Inter-Am. U., Mex., 1965; cert., U. Vienna, Strobl, Austria, 1956. Asst. prof., assoc. prof., prof. So. Ill. U., Carbondale, 1967-74, asst. dir. Univ. Mus., 1967-70, dir. Univ. Mus. and Art Galleries, 1970-77, dean internat. edn., 1972-74; asst. dir. Ill. Div. Mus., Springfield, 1977-80; prof. history U. Alaska, Fairbanks, 1980-88, dir. U. Alaska Mus., 1980-88, founder, dir. internat. affairs, 1985-87; founder, dir. Div. Mus., Archaeology and Publs. State of Mich., Lansing, 1988-91; multicultural cons., 1991—; dir. mktg., cons. Rosalie Whyel Mus. Doll Art, Bellevue, Wash., 1991—; cons. museums and cultural instns., 1995—. Fulbright sr. lectr., Brazil, 1972; mem. nat. register adv. panel, Ill., 1977-80; mem. Alaska Coun. on Arts, Anchorage, 1983-85; chmn. Fairbanks Hist. Preservation Commn., 1982-88; mem. Alaska Land Use Coun.; bd. dirs. Alaska Hist. Preservation Found., 1986-88; mem. Gov.'s Revitalization Task Force, Lansing, Mich., mem. ethnic coun., Mich., 1988-89; bd. dirs. East King County Visitors Bur., 1993-2000, officer, 1997-2000; officer, bd. dirs. Wash. Mus. Assn., 1993-2000. Author: (with others) A Bibliography of Nepal, 1973, (with Carroll L. Riley) The Journey of the Vaca Party, 1974, Documents Ancillary to the Vaca Journey, 1976, (with C.A. Letson) Once Was A Time, a Very Good Time: An Inquiry into the Folklore of the Bahamas, 1975, (with J.E. Stephens) In the Days of Yesterday and in the Days of Today: An Overview of Bahamian Folkmusic, 1976, It's A Natural Fact: Obeah in the Bahamas, 1977, Contemporary Practices in Obeah in the Bahamas, 1981; compilations and collections, 1959-69; editor: (with J. Charles Kelley and Riley) The Classic Southwest: Readings in Archaeology, Ethnohistory and Ethnography, 1973, (with J. Charles Kelley and Riley) The Mesoamerican Southwest: Readings in Archaelogy, Ethnohistory and Ethnology, 1974, (with Riley) Across the Chichimec Sea, 1978, (with others) New Frontiers in the Archaeology and Ethnohistory of the Greater Southwest, 1980, Trans. of Ill. Acad. Sci., 1979-81, (with Susan Pickel-Hedrick) Ethel Washington: The Life and Times of an Eskimo Dollmaker, The Role of the Steamboat in the Founding and Development of Fairbanks, Alaska, 1986, (with Susan Savage) Steamboats on the Chena, 1988; co-editor: Led Zeppelin live, 1993, 94, 97, Beautiful Children, 1996; author and editor of various other publications; contbr. articles to profl. jours. Chmn. Goals for Carbondale, 1972; active various local state, nat. polit. campaigns. Mem. NMA (bd. dirs. 1989-91), Am. Assn. Mus. (leader accreditation teams 1977-93, sr. examiner), Ill. Archaeol. Soc. (pres. 1973-74), Mus. Alaska, Assn. Sci. Mus. Dirs., Midwest Mus. Conf. (treas. 1977-80), Western Mus. Assn., Wash. Mus. Assn. (bd. dirs. 1994-99, v.p. 1995-97, pres. 1997-99), BD Arts (bd. dirs. 1995-96), Phi Kappa Phi. E-mail: djangob@aol.com

HEDRICK, JERRY LEO, biochemistry and biophysics educator; b. Knoxville, Iowa, Mar. 11, 1936; s. Harvard L. and Dorothy E. (Hardin) H.; m. Karel J. Harper, June 22, 1957; children: Michael L., Kerry L., Benjamin A., Kimberly L. B.S., Iowa State U., 1958; Ph.D., U. Wis., 1961, postgrad., 1961-62, U. Wash., 1962-65. Asst. prof. U. Calif.-Davis, 1965-68, assoc. prof., 1968-74, prof. biochemistry, 1974—, chmn. dept., 1982-84, assoc. dean grad. studies, 1998—. Sabbatical leave Hakkaido U., Sapporo, Japan, 1985-86, 89, 96; U. Calif. exch. scientist, Hokkaido U., 1989; vis. sr. scientist Mitsubishi-Kasei Inst. of Life Scis., Machida, Japan, 1989. Recipient Guggenheim Found. award; John Simon Guggenheim fellow, Cambridge U., Eng., 1971-72; grantee NIH, NSF, USDA, 1966—. Mem. AAAS, Am. Soc. Biol. Chemists, Am. Chem. Soc., Soc. Study Reprodn., Am. Soc. Cell Biology, Sigma Xi Home: 25280 Carlsbad Ave Davis CA 95616-9434 Office: U Calif Sect Molecular Cellular Bio 1 Shields Ave Davis CA 95616-5200

HEDRICK, WALLY BILL, artist; b. Pasadena, Calif., 1928; s. Walter Thomas and Velma Laurel (Thurman) H. Student, Otis Art Inst., Los Angeles, 1947, Calif. Coll. Arts and Crafts, , 1954; B.F.A., Calif. Sch. Fine Arts, 1955; MA, San Francisco State U., 1958. Instr. San Francisco State U., 1958-59, Calif. Sch. Fine Arts, 1960-64, Art Inst. San Francisco, 1964-70, San Francisco Acad. Art, 1971, San Jose State U., 1972-73, Indian Valley Coll., 1974—. Instr. summer session Art. Inst. San Francisco, 1978; instr. U. Calif., Davis, 1984, 86. One-man shows include Pasadena (Calif.) Arts Ctr., 1950, M.H. de Young Meml. Mus., San Francisco, 1955, Calif. Sch. Fine Arts, San Francisco, 1956, Oakland (Calif.) Mus., 1958, Isaacs Gallery, Toronto, Can., 1961, New Mission Gallery, San Francisco, 1963, San Francisco Art Inst., 1967, Sonoma Satte Coll., Calif., 1968, 63 Bluxome St., San Francisco, 1975, Gallery Paule Anglim, San Francisco, 1982, 84, 89, 90, Emanuel Walter Gallery, 1985, Atholl McBean Gallery, 1985, Natsoulas-Novelozo Gallery, Davis, Calif., 1989, Mills Coll. Art Gallery, 1994, Gallery Paule Anglim, 1994, Calif. Mus. of Art, 1999; group exhbns. include Pasadena Art Mus., L.A. County Mus. Art, 1953, San Francisco Mus. Modern Art, 1954, 57, 60, 66, Santa Barbara Mus. Modern Art, 1956, Mus. Modern Art, N.Y.C., 1959, 76, Calif. Palace Legion Honor., 1961, San Francisco Art Inst., 1962, San Francisco Mus. Art, 1962, 66, Norton Simon Mus. Art, Pasadena, 1962, Richmond (Calif.) Art Ctr., 1964, Calif. State U. Sonoma, Rhonert Park, 1968, Dallas Mus. Fine Arts, 1974, Wadsworth Antheneum, Hartford, Conn., 1975, San Francisco Mus. Modern Art, 1977, Gallery Paule Anglim, San Francisco, 1981, 83, 86, 92, South Market Cultural Ctr., 1982, Columbus (Ga.) Mus. Arts and Scis., 1984, Sheldon Meml. Art Gallery, U. Nebr., Licoln, 1984, Chgo. Internat. Arts Expo., 1984, Old Waterhouse Cabaret, Oakland, 1985, Arts Coun. San Mateo County, Belmont, Calif., 1985., Emanuel Walter Gallery, 1985, Atholl McBean Gallery, 1985, Newport Harbor Art Mus., Newport Beach., Calif., 1986, L.A. County Mus. Art, 1986-87, Mus. Contemporary Art, Chgo., 1986-87, Natsoulas Novelozo Gallery, 1990; group exhibitions include Gallery Paule Anglim, San Francisco, 1992, ACGI Gallery, Berkeley, Calif., 1993, The Crocker Mus., Sacramento, 1994, The Oakland Mus., Calif., 1994, San Francisco Art Inst., 1994, Richmond Art Ctr., Calif., 1995, San Francisco Women Artists Gallery, 1995, Whitney Mus. Am. Art, N.Y.C., 1995, Walker Art Ctr., Mpls., 1996, M.H. de Young Meml. Mus., 1996; represented in permanent collections, Aldrich Mus. Contemporary Art, Ridgefield, Conn., Mus. Modern Art, N.Y.C., Smithsonian Instn., San Francisco Mus. Modern Art, City and County San Francisco, L.A. County Mus. Art, Laguna (Calif.) Mus., Mus. Contemporary Art, Ridgefield, Conn., Oakland Mus., Calif. State U. Sonoma, U. Calif. San Francisco. San Francisco Art Commn., San Francisco Art Inst., San Francisco Internat. Airport, Univ. Art Mus., Berkeley, Calif., Mills Coll., Oakland; represented by Gallery Paule Anglim. Served with AUS, 1950-52. Recipient Adeline Kent award, 1985, Golden Bear award Calif. State Fair, 1990, merit award, 1991, award of excellence, 1996; grantee Nat. Endowment Arts, 1962, 82, 93, Marin Arts Coun.-Bucks Found., individual artist grantee San Francisco Found., 1985-86, Adolph and Esther Gottlieb Found. grantee, 1997, Pollack-Krasner Found. grantee, 1999. Office: PO Box 94 Bodega CA 94922-0094

HEEGER, ALAN JAY, physicist, educator; b. Sioux City, Iowa, Jan. 22, 1936; s. Peter J. and Alice (Minkin) H.; m. Ruthann Chudacoff, Aug. 11, 1957; children: Peter S., David J. BA, U. Nebr., 1957; PhD, U. Calif., Berkeley, 1961; hon. degree, U. Mons, Belgium, 1993; DTech (hon.), Linköping (Sweden) U., 1996; PhD (hon.), Abo Akademie, Turku, Finland, 1998; DHL (hon.), U. Mass., 1999; DSc (hon.), U. Nebr., 1999, So. China U. Tech., Japan Adv. Inst. Sci. & Tech., South China U. Tech. Asst. prof. U. Pa., Phila., 1962-64, assoc. prof., 1964-66, prof. physics, 1966-82, U. Calif., Santa Barbara, 1982—, dir. Inst. for Polymers and Organic Solids, 1983-2000; pres. UNIAX Corp., Santa Barbara, 1990-94, chmn. bd., 1990-99, chief tech. officer, 1999—. Dir. Lab. for Rsch. on Structure of Matter, U. Pa., 1974-81, acting vice provost for rsch., 1981-82; Morris Loeb lectr. Harvard U., 1973. Editor-in-chief Synthetic Metals jour., 1983-2000; contbr. sci. articles to profl. jours. Recipient John Scott medal City of Phila., 1989, Oliver P. Buckley prize Pres. medal for disting. achievement U. Pa., 2000; Alfred P. Sloan Found. fellow, Guggenheim fellow, Balzan prize for the sci. of new materials Balzan Found., Italy and Switzerland, 1995, Nobel Prize in Chemistry, 2000; govt. grantee. Fellow Am. Physics Soc. (Buckley prize for solid state physics 1983); mem. NAS, Korean Acad. Scis. (fgn.). Achievements include patents in field. Office: U Calif Dept Physics Santa Barbara CA 93103 also: UNIAX Corp 6780 Cortona Dr Santa Barbara CA 93117-3022 E-mail: ajh@physics.ucsb.edu

HEEN, WALTER MEHEULA, retired judge, political party executive; b. Honolulu, Apr. 17, 1928; s. Norma K. Tada; 1 child, Cameron K. BA in Econs., U. Hawaii, 1953; JD, Georgetown U., 1955. Bar: Hawaii 1955, U.S. Dist. Ct. Hawaii 1955. Dep. corp. counsel, Honolulu, 1957-58; territorial ho. of reps., 1958-59; mem. State Ho. Reps., 1959-64; state senator, 1966-68; mem. Honolulu City Coun., 1969-72, chair, 1972-74; state dist. ct. judge, 1972-74; state cir. ct. judge, 1974-78; U.S. atty. U.S. Dist. Hawaii, 1978-80, U.S. dist. ct. judge, 1981; assoc. judge State Intermediate Ct. Appeals, 1982-94; ret., 1994. Past pres. Honolulu Hawaiian Civic Club; precinct club pres. Dem. Party, 1956-72, now chmn.; vice chmn. Oahu Dem. County Com., 1956-62, chmn., 1962-64; del. State Dem. Party Conv., 1956-70. Recipient Lei Hulu Mamo award, 1992; named Outstanding Young Man of the Yr., 1962. Mem. Native Hawaiian Bar Assn. (dir. 1994—). Avocations: photography, fishing, surfing, golf, family activities. Office: 404 Ward Ave Ste 201 Honolulu HI 96814-3300

HEER, NICHOLAS LAWSON, Arabist and Islamist educator; b. Chapel Hill, N.C., Feb. 8, 1928; s. Clarence and Jean Douglas (MacAlpine) H. B.A., Yale U., 1949; Ph.D., Princeton U., 1955. Transl. analyst Arabian Am. Oil Co., Saudi Arabia, 1955-57; asst. prof. Stanford U., Calif., 1959-62; vis. lectr. Yale U., New Haven, 1962-63; asst. prof. Harvard U., Cambridge, Mass., 1963-65; assoc. prof. U. Wash., Seattle, 1965-76, prof. Near Eastern langs. and civilization, 1976-90, prof. emeritus, 1990—; chmn. dept. Near Eastern langs. and civilization U. Wash, 1982-87. Middle East curator Hoover Instn., Stanford, Calif., 1958-62 Editor: Tirmidhi: Bayan al-Farq, 1958, Jami: Al-Durrah al-Fakhirah, 1981, Islamic Law and Jurisprudence: Studies in Honor of Farhat J. Ziadeh, 1990; translator: Jami: The Precious Pearl, 1979. Mem. Am. Oriental Soc., Middle East Studies Assn., Am. Assn. Tchrs. of Arabic (treas. 1964-76, pres. 1981, dir. 1982-84) Home: 1821 10th Ave E Seattle WA 98102-4214 Office: U Wash Dept Near Ea Langs & Civ PO Box 353120 Seattle WA 98195-3120 E-mail: heer@eskimo.com, heer@u.washington.edu

HEERE, KAREN R. astrophysicist; b. Teaneck, N.J., Apr. 9, 1944; d. Peter N. and Alice E. (Hall) H. BA, U. Pa., 1965; MA, U. Calif., Berkeley, 1968; PhD, U. Calif., Santa Cruz, 1976. Rsch. assoc. NRC NASA Ames Rsch. Ctr., Moffett Field, Calif., 1977-79; rsch. astronomer U. Calif., Santa Cruz/NASA Ames Rsch. Ctr., 1979-86; assoc. prof. San Francisco State U., 1986-87; scientist Sci. Applications Internat. Corp., Los Altos, Calif., 1974-76, 87-93; rsch. specialist Sterling Software, Redwood City, 1993-98; sr. scientist Raytheon, Moffett Field, 1998—, mgr. space and earth sci., 2001—. Vis. scientist TATA Inst. for Fundamental Rsch., Bombay, India, 1984. Author numerous articles in field. Mem. Am. Astron. Soc. Avocations: hiking, birding, piano, adventure travel. Home: PO Box 2427 El Granada CA 94018-2427

HEERMANN, DALE FRANK, agricultural engineer; b. Scribner, Nebr., Mar. 2, 1937; s. Frank H. and Esther M. (Bock) H.; m. Betty Marie Tuchenhagen, July 21, 1957; children: Sara Heermann Buchleiter, Philip, Laura Heerman Langford. BS in Agrl. Engring., U. Nebr., 1959; MS in Agrl. Engring., Colo. State U., 1964, PhD, 1968. Instr. Colo. State U., 1965-68; engr. Agrl. Rsch. Svc., USDA, Ft. Collins, Colo., 1968-80, rsch. leader, 1980—. Cons. Rainbird, Glendora, Calif., 1973-75, Valmont Industries, Valley, Nebr., 1984-85. Contbr. articles to profl. jours. (Outstanding Paper awards 1968-85). Chmn. accountability com. Pourde Ri, Ft. Collins, 1981-85; bd. dirs. South Ft. Collins Sanitation Dist. Recipient Scribner Native Son award Scribner C. of C., 1996, Sr. Scientist award USDA-Agrl. Rsch. Svc., Outstanding No. Plains Area, 1996, Fed. Tech. Leadership award, 1997. Fellow Am. Soc. Agrl. Engrs. (bd. dirs. 1974-76, John Deere Gold medal 2000); mem. Irrigation Assn. (program com., Man of Yr. 1985), Colo. State Alumni Assn. (Alumnus Hon. award 1988, Fed. Energy and Mgmt. award 1994), Soil and Water Conservation Soc., Am. Soc. Agronomy, Soil Sci. Soc. Am., U.S. Com. Irrigation and Drainage. Lutheran. Home: 4780 Hogan Dr Fort Collins CO 80525-3732 Office: USDA ARS AERC Colo State U Fort Collins CO 85023

HEFFRON, WARREN A. medical educator, physician; b. St. Louis, Nov. 7, 1936; s. Willard Page H. and Alma Alberta Revington; m. Rosalee Bowdish, June 10, 1961; children: Kimberly, Wanda, Kara, Arthur. AB, U. Mo., 1958; MD, 1962. Diplomate Am. Bd. Family Practice (pres. 1998—). Rotating intern U. Calif., Orange, 1962-63; physician Hosp. Castaner

(P.R.), 1966-68; resident internal medicine U. N. Mex., Albuquerque, 1968-71, asst. prof., chief divsn., 1971-76; assoc. prof., asst. chair Family Committee and Emergency Medicine, Albuquerque, 1976-82, prof., chmn., 1982-93; chief med. staff U. N. Mex. Hosp., Albuquerque, 1993—. Bd. dirs. Am. Acad. Family Physicians, Am. Bd. Family Practice; dir. family Med. Residency Program, Albuquerque, 1971-82; vis. prof., cons. Dept. Cmty. Health, Punjab, India, Christian Med. Coll., Punjab U., Ludihiana; prof. Dept. Family and Cmty. Medicine, Albuquerque, 1993—; various internat. vis. professorships. Contbr. numerous articles to profl. jours. Mem. free clinic Albuquerque Rescue Mission. Lt. comdr. USPHS, 1964-66. Recipient Recognition award Am. Med. Assn. Physicians, 1971, 74, 77, 80, 83, 86, 89, 92, 95, 98, N. Mex. Family Physician of the Yr. award, 1990. Mem. N. Mex. Am. Acad. Family Physicians (pres. 1985, N. Mex. Family Dr. of Yr. award, chpt. svc. award 1988), Am. Bd. Family Practice (pres. 1998-99), N. Mex. Med. Soc. (pres. 1996-97, Robbins award Cmty. Svc. 1981), Soc. Tchrs. of Family Medicine (bd. dirs., treas. 1997, Smilkstein award for internat. family medicine edn. 1998), Christian Med. and Dental Soc. (bd. dirs. 1998-2001, pres. elect 2001), World Orgn. Family Drs. (v.p. for the Ams. 2000). Methodist. Home: 2406 Ada Pl NE Albuquerque NM 87106-2550 E-mail: wheffron@salud.unm.edu

HEFLEBOWER, CHARLES R. career officer; b. Washington, Sept. 18, 1945; s. Roy Cleveland and Barbara (Koenig) H.; m. Susan Ann McAvoy, Mar. 9, 1974; children: Jennifer, Michael. BS in Aeroengring., USAF Acad., 1967; MA in Internat. Rels., U. Ark., 1973; student, Nat. War Coll., 1984-85. Commd. 2d lt. USAF, 1967, advanced through grades to maj. gen., 1994, dep. comdr. ops. 31st tactical fighter wing Ill., 1985-86, dir. spl. programs hdqs. tactical air command Langley AFB, Va., 1986-87, vice comdr. 388th tactical fighter wing Hill AFB, Utah, 1987-88, comdr. 388th tactical fighter wing, 1988-90, dep. bases and units hdqs. Washington, 1990-91, dir. assignments hdqs. Air Force mil. pers. ctr. Randolph AFB, Tex., 1991-92, dir. pers. programs hdqs. Washington, 1992-94, dir. programs/evaluation hdqs., 1994-95; comdr. 17th Air Force and comdr. Interim Combined Air Ops. Ctr., Sembach Air Base, Germany, 1995-96; asst. chief of staff Ops. and Ligistics Divsn., Supreme HQ Allied Powers Europe, Casteau, Belgium, 1996-98; vice comdr. HQ Pacific Air Forces, Hickam AFB, Hawaii, 1998-99; dep. comdr.-in-chief UN Command, 1999—. Dep. comdr. U.S. Forces Korea, 1999—; comdr. Air Component Command, Republic of Korea and U.S. Combined Forces Command, 1999—, 7th Air Force, Pacific Air Forces, Osan Air Base, South Korea, 1999— Office: PACAF 25 E St Ste 6214 Hickam AFB HI 96853-5420 also: 17 AF/CC 09142 Sembach Air Base Germany APO AE

HEFLEY, JOEL M. congressman; b. Ardmore, Okla. s. J. Maurice and Etta A. (Anderson) H.; m. Lynn Christian, Aug. 25, 1961; children: jana, Lori, Juli. BA, Okla. Baptist U., 1957; MS, Okla. State U., 1963. Exec. dir. Community Planning and Research, Colorado Springs, Colo., 1966-86; mem. Colo. State Ho. of Reps., 1977-78, Colo. State Senate, 1979-86, U.S. Congress from 5th Colo. dist., 1987—; mem. armed svcs. com.; mem. natural resources com.; mem. small bus.-SBA com.; mem. nat. security com.; chmn. stds. of offcl. conduct com. Republican. Baptist. Clubs: Rotary, Colorado Springs Country Office: Ho of Reps 2230 Rayburn Ho Office Bldg Washington DC 20515-0001*

HEFNER, HUGH MARSTON, editor-in-chief; b. Chgo., Apr. 9, 1926; s. Glenn L. and Grace (Swanson) H.; m. Mildred M. Williams, June 25, 1949 (div.); children: Christie A., David P.; m. Kimberley Conrad, July 1, 1989 (div.); children: Marston G., Cooper B. BS, U. Ill., 1949. Subscription promotion writer Esquire mag., 1951; promotion mgr. Pubs. Devel. Corp., 1952; circulation mgr. Children's Activities mag., 1953; chmn. bd. HMH Pub. Co. Inc. (now Playboy Enterprises, Inc.), 1953-88; editor-in-chief Playboy mag., from 1953; pres. Playboy Clubs Internat., Inc., 1959-86; editor, pub. VIP mag., 1963-75, Oui mag., 1972-81. Occasional film appearances include History of the World, Part I, 1981, The Comeback Trail, 1982, Beverly Hills Cop II, 1987. Served with AUS, 1944-46. Recipient 1st Amendment Freedom award B'nai B'rith Anti-Defamation League, L.A., 1980, Internat. Pub. award Internat. Press Directory in London, 1997; ; named Man of Yr. Mag. Industry Newlsetter, 1967; named to Pub. Hall of Fame, 1989; honored with Hugh M. Hefner chair in study of Am. film U. So. Calif. Sch. Cinema/TV, 1996. Office: Playboy Enterprises Inc 9242 Beverly Blvd Beverly Hills CA 90210-3732

HEFNER, JOHN, principal; Principal Fruitvale Jr. H.S. Recipient Blue Ribbon award U.S. Dept. Edn., 1990-91. Office: Fruitvale Jr HS 2114 Calloway Dr Bakersfield CA 93312-2706

HEGARTY, CHRISTOPHER JOSEPH, management and financial consultant; b. Jersey City; s. Michael John and Catherine Mary (Morrissey) H.; children: Mahren, Cahlil, Michael. Student, Youngstown U., 1958-61; PhD in Mgmt. Edn., Creative Devel. Inst., 1977. Investors exec., zone mgr. Investors Diversified Svcs., Mpls., 1960-65; pres. Hegarty & Co., N.Y.C., 1965-67; founder, sr. v.p. Competitive Capital Corp., San Francisco, 1967-69; founder, pres. Charter St. Corp., San Francisco, 1969-71; pres. C.J. Hegarty & Co., Payson, Ariz., 1971—. Chmn. bd. dirs. Advanced Resources Mgmt.; faculty for continuing edn. U. So. Calif.; cons. SRI Internat.; prin. Inst. for Social Responsibility, 2001; founder, regent Coll. Fin. Planning; prin. Inst. Exceptional Performance, 1989; chmn. emeritus bd. govs. Nat. Ctr. for Fin. Edn.; spl. adv. Alternative Medicine.com., 1991—. Author: How To Manage Your Boss, 1980, Financial Planning for Chief Executives, 1983, Consistently Exceptional Leadership, 1989, Fiscal Fitness for Organizations, 1992, 7 Secrets of Exceptional Leadership, 1997, The Future Belongs to the Omnicompetent, 1997; co-author: Peak Performance for Executives and Professionals, 1983, Out of Harm's Way, 2001; contbg. editor Fin. Planning mag., 1973-77; mem. editl. bd. Health Consciousness mag., 1989, Future Medicine Pub., 1992, Alternative Medicine Mag., 1995. Adv. bd. Small Bus. Coun. Am., 1982—; active Calif. Gov.'s Task Force for Emergencies, 1981-83, Nat. Chaplains Corps, 1999; chmn., bd. govs. Digest Fin. Planning, 1983—; pres., CEO Internat. Ctr. Life Improvement, 1987. Recipient Judge U.S. C. of C. Blue Chip Enterprise award, 1991, Top Preview Spkr. of Yr. award Internat. Platform Assn., 1972, Spl. award Sci. Found., 1977, Leadership and Comm. award Toastmasters Internat., 1978-79, Innovative Mktg. award Sales and Mktg. Assn., 1979, Outstanding Spkr. award Am. Soc. Tng. and Devel., 1980, Spkr. of Decade award Internat. Comm. Congress, 1980, Legion of Honor award Nat. Chaplains Assn., 1981, Leadership award UN, 1981, Excellence award Am. Film Guild; named Spkr. of Yr., Young Pres.'s Orgn., 1982. Mem. Nat. Spkrs. Assn. (founding dir., Continuare Professos Articulatus Excellence award 1977, named to Spkrs. Hall of Fame 1998), Am. Inst. Mgmt. (pres. coun. 1981—), Sales and Mktg. Execs. Internat., Internat. Assn. Fin. Planners (founder, nat. adv. bd., Spokesman of Yr. 1974), Commonwealth Club. Office: CJ Hegarty & Co 1116 S Elk Ridge Dr Ste A Payson AZ 85541 E-mail: leaders@cutting-edge.com

HEGARTY, GEORGE JOHN, university president, English educator; b. Cape May, N.J., July 20, 1948; s. John Joseph and Gloria Anna (Bonelli) H.; m. Joy Elizabeth Schiller, June 9, 1979. Student, U. Fribourg, Switzerland, 1968-69; BA in English, LaSalle U., Phila., 1970; Cert., Coll. de la Pocatiere, Que., Can., 1970; postgrad., U. Dakar, Senegal, 1970, Case Western Res. U., , 1973-74, U. N.H., 1976; MA in English, Drake U., 1977; cert., U. Iowa, 1977; DA, Drake U., 1978; Cert., UCLA, 1979, U. Pa., 1981. Tchr. English, Peace Corps vol. College d'Enseignment General de Sedhiou, Senegal, 1970-71; tchr. English Belmore Boys' and Westfields High Schs., Sydney, Australia, 1972-73; teaching fellow in English Drake U., Des Moines, 1974-76; mem. faculty English Des Moines Area Community Coll., 1976-80; assoc. prof. Am. lit. U. Yaounde, Cameroon, 1980-83; prof. Am. lit. and civilization Nat. U. Cote D'Ivoire, Abidjan, 1986-88; dir. ctr. for internat. programs and svcs. Drake U., Des Moines, 1983-91; prof. grad. program intercultural mgmt. Sch. for Internat. Tng., The Experiment in Internat. Living, Brattleboro, Vt., 1991-93; provost, prof. English Teikyo Loretto Heights U., Denver, 1992-94; pres., prof. English, Teikyo Westmar U., Le Mars, Iowa, 1994-95; program dir. Am. degree program Taylor's Coll., Malaysia, 1996-97; v.p. academic affairs, prof. English Teikyo Loretto Heights U., Denver, 1997—. Acad. specialist USIA, 1983-84; workshop organizer/speaker Am. Field Svcs., 1986; cons. Coun. Internat. Ednl. Exch., 1986; evaluator Assn. des Univ. Partiellment Entierément de Langue Francais, 1987, Iowa Humanities Bd., 1990-91, USAID's Ctr. for Univ. Coop. and Devel., 1991; cons. in field. Book reviewer African Book Pub. Record, Oxford, Eng., 1981—, African Studies Rev., 1990—; host, creator TV show Global Perspectives, 1989-91; exhibitor of African art, 1989—; contbr. articles to profl. jours. Commr. Des Moines Sister City Commn., 1984-87, 91; bd. dirs. Iowa Sister State Com., 1988-91; pres. Chautauqua Park Nat. Hist. Dist. Neighborhood Assn., 1991; bd. dirs. Melton Found., 1994-95. Drake U. fellow, 1971-72, 74-76; Nat. Endowment for Humanities grantee, 1981; Fulbright grantee, USIA, 1980-83, 86-88. Mem. Am. Assn. Pres. Ind. Colls. and Univs., NAFSA: Assn. Internat. Educators (sectional chmn. region VI 1986-87, Vt. rep. 1992), Assn. Internat. Edn. Adminstrs., Inst. Internat. Edn. Avocations: collecting non-western art, travel, swimming, writing. E-mail: (home) (bus.). E-mail: ghegarty@aol.com, ghegarty@tlhv.edu

HEGYVARY, SUE THOMAS, nursing school dean; b. Dry Ridge, Ky., Nov. 28, 1943; BSN, U. Ky., 1965; MN, Emory U., 1966; PhD in Sociology, Vanderbilt U., 1974. Asst. prof. nursing and sociology Rush U., 1972-74, assoc. prof. med. nursing, chair dept., 1974-77; asst. prof. sociology Rush U. Med. Coll., 1977-80; prof. nursing, assoc. v.p., assoc. dean nursing Coll. Nursing, Rush U., Rush Presbyn.-St. Luke's Med. Ctr., 1977—; assoc. prof. sociology Med. Coll. Rush U., 1980-98, dean emeritus, prof., 1998-99; dean, prof. Sch. Nursing U. Wash., Seattle, 1986-98. Mem. health care adv. com. Rep. Jennifer Dunn, 1993-96; vis. com. Bd. 50 Emory U. Sch. Nursing, Atlanta, 1990-92; mem. adv. panel outcomes rsch. Nat. Ctr. Nursing Rsch. NIH, 1990-91; external mem. Five Yr. Review com. Coll. Nursing U. Ky., 1989-90; mem. govtl. affairs com. Am. Assn. Colls. Nursing, 1988-92; chair planning com. Wash. State Conf. Nursing Shortage, 1989; mem. Wash. State Commn. Nursing, 1989; mem. adv. com. Child Devel. & Mental Retardation Ctr. U. Wash., 1986—; mem. task force nursing shortage Seattle Area Hosp. Coun., 1987-88; vis. prof., ann. lectr. Sch. Nursing U. Va., Charlottesville, 1988; vis. prof. U. Oulu, Finland, 1985; site visitor accreditation schs. nursing Nat. League Nursing, 1977-80; cons. VA Hosp., Miami, Fla., 1968-69, Vanderbilt U., Nashville, 1971-72, Area Health Edn. Sys., Rockford, Ill., 1975, Western Interstate Commn. Higher Edn., Denver, 1975, Andrews U., Berrian Springs, Mich., 1976, dept. nursing studies Nat. Hosp. Inst., Utrecht, The Netherlands, 1976-80, Haukeland Sykehaus, Bergen, Norway, 1976-77, Sch. Nursing Marquette U., Milw., 1977, Wayne State U., Detroit, 1978, Cath. U. Leuven, Belgium, 1980, Walter Reed Army Med. Ctr., Washington, 1979-83, Dalhousie U. Sch. Nursing, Halifax, N.S., 1981, U. Minn., Mpls., 1988, U. Mo., Columbia, 1992. Editl. adv. bd. Nursing Policy Forum, 1995-96; editl. cons. Nursing Care Guide Pfizer Corp., 1993; editl. bd. Jour. Nursing & Health, 1993—, Nursing Adminstrn. Quarterly, 1988—, mem. manucscript review panel Jour. Nursing Quality Assurance, 1986—, Nursing Outlook, 1983—, Jour. Rsch. Nursing & Health, 1981—, Nursing Rsch., 1979-89; contbr. chpts. to books and articles to profl. jours. Mem. ANA, Am. Acad. Nursing, Sigma Theta Tau. Office: U Wash Sch Nursing BNHS PO Box 357266 Seattle WA 98195-7266

HEIDEMANN, ROBERT ALBERT, chemical engineering educator, researcher; b. St. Louis, Aug. 31, 1936; emigrated to Can., 1968; s. William Joseph and Gladys Emilie (Digman) H.; m. Linda Bea Szold, June 9, 1968; children: David, Douglas. B.Sc. in Chem. Engring., Washington U., St. Louis, 1958; Sc.D., Washington U., 1966. Asst. prof. chem. engring. Drexel Inst. Tech., Phila., 1963-68; assoc. prof. U. Calgary (Alta.), 1968-77, prof., 1977—, head dept. chem. and petroleum engring., 1981-92. Vis. prof. Tech. U. Denmark, 1986-87; cons., 1982— Co-author: (with A.A. Jeje and M.F. Mohtadi) Properties of Fluids and Solids, 1984; contbr. articles to profl. jours. Fellow Chem. Inst. Can.; mem. Canadian Soc. Chem. Engrs., Am. Inst. Chem. Engrs., Am. Chem. Soc., Am. Soc. Engring. Edn., Assn. Profl. Engrs., Geologists and Geophysicists of Alta., Tau Beta Pi Home: 63 Discovery Ridge Pt SW Calgary AB Canada T3H 4R1 Office: U Calgary 2500 University Dr NW Calgary AB Canada T2N 1N4 E-mail: heideman@ucalgary.ca

HEIDT, RAYMOND JOSEPH, insurance company executive; b. Bismarck, N.D., Feb. 28, 1933; s. Stephen Ralph and Elizabeth Ann (Hirschkorn) H.; BA, Calif. State U., San Jose, 1963, MA, 1968; PhD, U. Utah, 1977; m. Joyce Ann Aston, Jan. 14, 1956; children: Ruth Marie, Elizabeth Ann, Stephen Christian, Joseph Aston. Claims supr. Allstate Ins. Co., San Jose, Calif., 1963-65; claims mgr. Gen. Accident Group, San Francisco, 1965-69; owner, mgr. Ray Heidt & Assocs., Logan, Utah, 1969-76; v.p. claims Utah Home Fire Ins. Co., Salt Lake City, 1976—; with Utah State U., 1970-76; dir. Inst. for Study of Pacifism and Militarism; vice-chmn. Benton County Parks and Recreation Bd., 1987-90. Active Kennewick Hist. Preservation Commn., 1989-90, 1st chmn., 1989-90, Magna Area Coun., 1992, pres. 1993-94; bd. trustees, sec. treas. Utah Ethnic and Mining Mus., 1994—. With U.S. Army, 1952-57. Decorated Bronze Star. Mem. Southeastern Wash. Adjusters' Assn. (pres. 1988-90), Utah Claims Assn. (pres. 1977-78), nat. com. Preservation of Social Security and Medicare, Lions, Am. Legion. Mormon. Home: 1715 W Flamingo Ave Apt #50 Nampa ID 83651-1669

HEILBRON, DAVID M(ICHAEL), lawyer; b. San Francisco, Nov. 25, 1936; s. Louis H. and Delphine A. (Rosenblatt) H.; m. Nancy Ann Olsen, June 21, 1960; children: Lauren Ada, Sarah Ann, Ellen Selma. B.S. summa cum laude, U. Calif., Berkeley, 1958; A.B. first class, Oxford U., Eng., 1960; LL.B. magna cum laude, Harvard U., 1962. Bar: Calif. 1962, U.S. Dist. Ct. (no. dist.) Calif. 1963, U.S Ct. Appeals (9th cir.) 1963, U.S. Ct. Appeals (D.C. cir.) 1972, U.S. Ct. Appeals (8th cir.), 1985, U.S. Ct. Appeals (1st cir.) 1987, U.S. Ct. Appeals (10th cir.) 1988, U.S. Ct. Appeals (7th cir.) 1988, U.S. Ct. appeals (11th cir.) 1988, U.S. Dist. Ct. Nev. 1982, U.S. Dist. Ct. (cen. dist.) Calif. 1983, U.S. Supreme Ct. 1988, U.S. Ct. Appeals (3rd cir.) 1992, (6th cir.), 1995, U.S. Ct. Appeals (2d cir.) 1998, U.S. Ct. Appeals (5th cir.) 1998. Assoc. McCutchen, Doyle, Brown & Enersen, San Francisco, 1962-69, ptnr., 1969—, mng. ptnr., 1985-88. Vis. lectr. appellate advocacy U. Calif., Berkeley, 1981-82, 82-83. Bd. trustees Golden Gate U., 1993-97, vice chair, 1995-97; bd. dirs. San Francisco Jewish Cmty. Ctr., 1974—, Legal Aid Soc., 1974-78, Legal Assistance to Elderly, San Francisco, 1980, San Francisco Renaissance, 1982—; pres. San Francisco Sr. Ctr., 1972-75; co-chmn. San Francisco Lawyers' Com. for Urban Affairs, 1976. Rhodes scholar. Fellow Am. Bar Found.; mem. ABA, Am. Coll. Trial Lawyers, Am. Arbitration Assn. (bd. dirs. 1986—, adv. coun. No. Calif. chpt. 1982—, chmn. 1987, jud. coun. 1986-88, exec. bd. 1994—, instr. and panelist arbitrator tng. programs), Am. Acad. Appellate Lawyers, State Bar Calif. (chmn. com. cts. 1982-83. bd. govs. 1983-85, mem. commn. on discovery 1984-86, pres. 1985-86), Calif. Acad. Appellate Lawyers, Coll. Comml. Arbitrators, Bar Assn. San Francisco (chmn. conf. dels. 1975-76, pres. 1980). Democrat. Clubs: Calif. Tennis. Office: McCutchen Doyle Brown & Enersen 3 Embarcadero Ctr San Francisco CA 94111-4003

HEILES, CARL EUGENE, astronomer, educator; b. Toledo, Sept. 22, 1939; children: Tod Scott, Katrina Marie. B in Engring. Physics, Cornell U., 1962; PhD in Astronomy, Princeton U., 1966. Asst. prof., then assoc. prof. U. Calif., Berkeley, 1966-69, astronomy prof., 1970—; rsch. astronomer Arecibo (P.R.) Obs., 1969-70. Vis. fellow Joint Inst. for Lab. Astrophysics, Boulder, Colo., 1989-90. Recipient Dannie Heineman prize in astrophysics Am. Astron. Soc., 1989. Mem. NAS, Am. Acad. Scis., Calif. Acad. Scis. Office: U Calif Dept Astronomy Berkeley CA 94720-0001

HEIMANN, M.L. "DICK", auto dealership executive; Pres., COO Lithia Motors Inc., Medford, Oreg. Office: Lithia Motors Inc 360 E Jackson St Medford OR 97501

HEIMBUCH, BABETTE E. bank executive; b. 1948; Student, U. Calif., 1972. Audit mgr. Peat Marwick Mitchell & Co., 1973-81; corp. contr. Zoetrope Studios, 1981-82; CFO, exec. v.p., treas. First Fed. Bank Calif. (subs. First Fed. Fin. Corp.), Santa Monica, CFO, sr. exec. v.p., treas., pres. Office: First Fed Bank Calif 401 Wilshire Blvd Santa Monica CA 90401-1416

HEIN, LEONARD WILLIAM, accounting educator; b. Forest Park, Ill., Feb. 17, 1916; s. Harry Christian and Clara Antoinette (Klein) H.; m. Akemi Kishi, Feb. 28, 1981. B.S.C., Loyola U., Chgo., 1952; M.B.A., U. Chgo., 1954; Ph.D. (U. Calif. at Los Angeles Bus. Sch. Alumni Assn. fellow, Univ. fellow, Ford Found. fellow), U. Calif. at Los Angeles, 1962. C.P.A., Ill. With San. Dist. Chgo., 1941-56; asst. prof. accounting Calif. State U. at Los Angeles, 1956-59, asso. prof. accounting, 1959-65, prof. accounting, 1965—, coordinator program bus. info. systems, 1956-73, asst. dean grad. studies, 1963-72. Mem. nat. panel arbitrators Am. Arbitration Assn., 1972— Author: Introduction to Electronic Data Processing for Business, 1961, Quantitative Approach to Managerial Decisions, 1967, Contemporary Accounting and the Computer, 1969, The British Companies Acts and the Practice of Accountancy, 1844-1962, 1978; Contbr. articles to profl. jours. Served with USNR, 1942-45. Mem. Am. Inst. C.P.A.'s, Am. Accounting Assn., Calif. Soc. C.P.A.'s, Beta Gamma Sigma, Beta Alpha Psi, Alpha Kappa Psi, Phi Kappa Phi. Home: 1225 N Granada Ave Alhambra CA 91801-1154 Office: Calif State U 5151 State University Dr Los Angeles CA 90032-4226

HEINDL, CLIFFORD JOSEPH, physicist, researcher; b. Chgo., Feb. 4, 1926; s. Anton Thomas and Louise (Fiala) H. BS, Northwestern U., 1947, MS, 1948; AM, Columbia U., 1950, PhD, 1959. Sr. physicist Bendix Aviation Corp., Detroit, 1953-54; student rschr. Oak Ridge Nat. Lab., 1954-55; asst. sect. chief Babcock & Wilcox Co., Lynchburg, Va., 1956-58; research group supr. Jet Propulsion Lab., Pasadena, Calif., 1959-65, mgr. research and space sci., 1965—. Served with AUS, 1944-46. Mem. AIAA, Am. Nuclear Soc., Health Physics Soc., Planetary Soc., Am. Phys. Soc. Home: 179 Mockingbird Ln South Pasadena CA 91030-2047 Office: 4800 Oak Grove Dr Pasadena CA 91109-8001

HEINEMANN, STEPHEN F. molecular neurobiologist educator; BS, Calif. Inst. Tech., 1962; PhD, Harvard U., 1967; postgrad., MIT, Stanford U. Prof. molecular neurobiology lab. Salk Inst., dir. molecular neurobiology lab., 1989-95, chmn. of the faculty, 1992-93. Adj. prof. U. Calif. Med. Sch., San Diego. Section editor: Jour. Neurosci. Molecular Neurosci.; mem. assoc. editl. bd. Current Opinion in Neurobiology, Proceedings of the Royal Soc. series B, Hippocampus, Cellular and Molecular Neurobiology, Receptors and Channels, Neuron, 1987-91, Jour. Neurosci., 1987-91. Recipient Disting. Achievement in Neurosci. Rsch. award Bristol-Myers Squibb, 1995; named Schmidt. Lectr. U. Pa., Feigen Lectr. Stanford U., Cooper Lectr., Flynn Lectr. Yale U. Mem. NAS (vice-chair com. IBRO), Max-Planck Inst. (external mem.), Soc. Neurosci. (councilor 1992, Grass lectr.). Achievements include research in structure and function of brain receptors and their role in neurological disease and mental illness. Office: Salk Inst ML H PO Box 85800 San Diego CA 92186

HEINEN, NANCY R. computer company executive; AB in Psychology and English with honors, JD, U. Calif. Pvt. practice, San Francisco & Palo Alto; group counsel, asst. sec. Tandem Computers Inc.; v.p., gen. counsel, sec. NeXT Software, Inc.; sr. v.p., gen. counsel Apple Computer, Inc., Cupertino, Calif., 1997—. Office: Mail Stop 301-4GC 1 Infinite Loop Cupertino CA 95014-2083

HEINER, DENNIS GRANT, manufacturing company executive; b. Ogden, Utah, Aug. 18, 1943; s. Grant and Mary (Stoker) H.; m. Margo Proctor, Dec. 17, 1970; children: Shalayna, Bryce James, Jillian, Brittany. BA, Weber State Coll., 1969; MBA, Brigham Young U., 1971; M in Mktg., Northwestern U., 1983; cert. strategic mktg. mgmt., Harvard U., 1985. V.p. mktg., gen. mgr. Sportplay, Inc., Salt Lake City, 1971-72; dir. mktg. adminstrn. and fin. Sno-Jet, Inc., Burlington, Vt., 1972-74; v.p. fin. Glastron Boat Co., Austin, Tex., 1974-78, v.p. fin. and adminstrn., 1978-79; v.p. fin. Delmar Window Coverings, Westminster, Calif., 1979-81, pres., 1981-84; pres. window coverings div. Beatrice Cos., Inc., Westminster, 1984-85; group v.p. U.S. Household Products div. Black & Decker, Shelton, Conn., 1985-86, exec. v.p., pres., 1986-92, exec. v.p., pres. security hardware group Anaheim, Calif., 1992—. Bd. dirs. Raytech Corp., Trumbull, Conn. Bd. dirs. Jr. Achievement, Austin, 1978-79. Mem. Young Pres.' Orgn. (So. Calif. and Fairchester chpts.). Republican. Mormon. Avocations: sports, running, piano. Office: Black & Decker Corp 516 E Santa Ana St Anaheim CA 92805-4047

HEINER, DOUGLAS CRAGUN, pediatrician, educator, immunologist, allergist; b. Salt Lake City, July 27, 1925; s. Spencer and Eva Lillian (Cragun) H.; m. Joy Luana Wiest, Jan. 8, 1946; children: Susan, Craig, Joseph, Marianne, James, David, Andrew, Carolee, Pauli. BS, Idaho State U., 1946; MD, U. Pa., 1950; PhD, McGill U., 1969. Intern Hosp. U. Pa., Phila., 1950-51; resident, fellow Children's Med. Ctr., Boston, 1953-56; asst. prof. pediatrics U. Ark. Med. Ctr., Little Rock, 1956-60; assoc. prof. pediatrics U. Utah Med. Ctr., Salt Lake City, 1960-66; fellow in immunology McGill U., Montreal, 1966-69; prof. of pediatrics Harbor-UCLA Med. Ctr., Torrance, 1969-94; disting. prof. of pediatrics UCLA Sch. Medicine, 1985-94, prof. emeritus, 1994—; med. specialist Russia Latter Day Sts. Missions, 1997-99. Author: Allergies to Milk, 1980; mem. editl. bd. Jour. Allergy and Clin. Immunology, 1975-79, Allergy, 1981-88, Jour. Clin. Immunology, 1981-87, Pediat. Asthma, Allergy and Immunology, 1986-94; contbr. over 150 original articles to profl. jours. and chpts. to books. Scoutmaster Boy Scouts Am., Salt Lake City, 1963; com. chmn. Rancho Palos Verdes, 1979-81; high coun. mem. Mormon Ch., Rancho Palos Verdes, 1983-86. with U.S. Army, 1952-53, Korea. Recipient Disting. Alumni award Idaho State U., 1987. Fellow Am. Pediatric Soc., Am. Acad. Allergy and Clin. Immunology (food allergy com. 1981-94, Disting. fellow 1996), Am. Coll. Allergy Asthma and Immunology; mem. Soc. for Pediatric Rsch., Western Soc. for Pediatric Rsch. (Ross award 1961), Am. Assn. Immunologists, Clin. Immunology Soc., Am. Acad. Pediatrics. Republican. Avocations: gardening, tennis, fishing. E-mail: dougjoyh@cs.com

HEINKE, REX S. lawyer; b. Harrisburg, Ill., June 9, 1950; s. William Richard and Versa Lee Heinke; m. Margaret Ann Nagle, May 6, 1978; children: William Rex, Meghan Bradley. BA, U. Witwatersrand, Johannesburg, Republic of South Africa, 1971; JD, U. Columbia, 1975. Bar: Calif. 1975. Ptnr. Gibson, Dunn & Crutcher, L.A., 1983-99, Greines, Martin, Stein & Richland, Beverly Hills, Calif., 1999—. Office: 9601 Wilshire Blvd Ste 544 Beverly Hills CA 90210-5207 E-mail: rheinke@gmsr.com

HEINS, JOHN, publishing executive; Staff writer Forbes Mag., N.Y.C., L.A.; asst. to CEO Gruner & Jahr Internat., Paris; Pres., CEO Parents Mag., N.Y.C., 1994-2000, Gruner & Jahr USA Pub., N.Y.C., 1994-2000; v.p. sales and internat. ops. Netscape Comm., 2000—. Office: Netscape Comm 501 E Middlefield Rd Mountain View CA 94043-4042

HEIRD, JAMES C. agricultural studies educator; b. Blount County, Tenn. BS in Agr., U. Tenn., 1970, MS in Agr., 1971; PhD in Agr., Tex. Tech. U., 1978. Livestock and horse specialist N.C. State U., Raleigh, 1972-76; horse specialist Tex. Tech. U., Lubbock, 1976-86; tching. coord. equine sci. program Colo. State U., Fort Collins, 1986-89, acting dean, Coll. Agrl. Scis., 1991-92, interim dean, Coll. Bus., 1993-94, assoc. dean/dir. acad. programs, Coll. Agrl. Scis., 1989—. Office: Colo State U Coll Agrl Scis Fort Collins CO 80523-0001

HEISER, JAMES S. manufacturing company executive; b. 1956; BA in Econs., U. Va.; JD, Stanford U. With Ducommun Inc., L.A., 1985—, asst. gen. counsel, gen. counsel, treas., gen. counsel, treas., CFO, 1996—. Office: Ducommun Inc 111 W Ocean Blvd Ste 900 Long Beach CA 90802

HEITMAN, GREGORY ERWIN, state agency administrator; b. Lewiston, Idaho, June 7, 1947; s. Elmer William and Carmelita Rose Ann (Kinzer) H.; m. Phyllis Ann Pryor, Sept. 25, 1982. BS in Math., U. Idaho, 1969, MBA, 1971; student, Wash. State U., 1965-67. Student communications dir. Assoc. Students U. Idaho, Moscow, 1970-72, advisor, apt. mgr. dept. housing, 1971-72; traffic fatality analyst Idaho Dept. Transp., Boise, 1973-74; ops. mgr. Region IV Health & Welfare State of Idaho, Boise, 1974-78, supr. computer svcs., div. environ. in health and welfare, 1978-85; coord. field svcs., program dir. Idaho Bur. Vital Records and Health Stats., Boise, 1985—; acting dir. Idaho Ctr. for Health Stats., Boise, 1988-89, spl. asst. program and policy devel., 1989—. Mem. med. records adv. com. Boise State U., 1987—, cons., lectr. 1987—. Active various charitable orgns.; precinct committeeman Dem. of Latah County, 1972; election day coord. Ada County, 1986; vol. Am. Cancer Soc., 1990, Easter Seals, 1992, Arthritis Found., 1996. Mem. Idaho Pub. Health Assn., Assn. Vital Records and Health Statistics, Idaho Pub. Employees Assn., Assn. Govt. Employees. Roman Catholic. Avocations: bowling, card collecting. Home: 1762 E Summerridge Dr Meridian ID 83642-5586 Office: Idaho Vital Stats PO Box 83720 Boise ID 83720-3720

HELFORD, IRWIN, consumer products company executive; With Wilson-Jones, 1960, Reliable Stationary Co.; pres. Viking, 1983-, CEO, chmn.; vice-chmn. bd. Viking (part of Office Depot), 1999—, Office Depot; chmn. emeritus Viking Office Products. Office: Office Depot 950 W 190th St Torrance CA 90502

HELGELAND, BRIAN, film director, writer, producer; b. Providence, 1961; Writer (screeplays) A Nightmare on Elm Street 4: The Dream Master, 1988, 976-EVIL, 1988, Highway to Hell, 1992, Assassins, 1995, Conspiracy Theory, 1997, The Postman, 1997; writer, co-prodr. L.A. Confidential (N.Y. Film Critics Circle award 1997, Boston Soc. of Film Critics award 1997, Broadcast Film Critics Assn. award, 1997, Acad. award 1998, Fla. film Critics award 1998, Writers Guild of Am. award 1988); dir. Payback, 1999, Sin Eater, 1999. Address: DGA 7920 W Sunset Blvd Los Angeles CA 90046-3300

HELGERSON, RICHARD, English literature educator; b. Pasadena, Calif., Aug. 22, 1940; s. Donald Theodore and Viola Dolores (Huss) H.; m. Marie-Christine David, June 8, 1967; 1 child, Jessica. BA, U. Calif., Riverside, 1963; MA, Johns Hopkins U., 1964, PhD, 1970. Prof. English Coll. Notre-Dame d'Afrique, Atakpamé, Togo, 1964-66; asst. prof. English U. Calif., Santa Barbara, 1970-76, assoc. prof., 1976-82, chair dept. English, 1989-93, prof. English, 1982—. Vis. prof. Calif. Inst. Tech., Pasadena, 1987-88; chair Huntington (Calif.) Libr. Rsch. Rev., 1986-87; faculty rsch. lectr. U. Calif., Santa Barbara, 1998. Author: The Elizabethan Prodigals, 1976, Self-Crowned Laureates, 1983, Forms of Nationhood, 1992 (James Russell Lowell prize MLA, Brit. Coun. prize in humanities), Adulterous Alliances, 2000; contbr. numerous articles to profl. jours. Fellow Woodrow Wilson Found., 1963-64, NEH, 1979-80, Huntington Libr., 1984-85, Guggenheim Found., 1985-86, Folger-NEH, 1993-94, NEH, 1998-99, U. Calif. Pres.'s fellow, 1998-99. Mem. MLA (exec. com. English renaissance div. 1988-92), N.Am. Conf. on Brit. Studies, Renaissance Soc. Am., Spenser Soc. Am. (pres. 1988), Shakespeare Assn. Am., Western Humanities Conf. (exec. com. 1988-91). Democrat. Home: 334 E Arrellaga St Santa Barbara CA 93101-1106 Office: U Calif Dept English Santa Barbara CA 93106

HELGESON, DUANE MARCELLUS, retired librarian; b. Rothsay, Minn., July 2, 1930; s. Oscar Herbert and Selma Olivia (Sateren) H. BS, U. Minn., 1952. Libr. Chance-Vought Co., Dallas, 1956-59, Sys. Devel. Corp., Santa Monica, Calif., 1959-62, Lockheed Aircraft, Burbank, 1962-63, C.F. Braun Co., Alhambra, 1963-74; chief libr. Ralph M. Parsons Co., Pasadena, 1974-79; pres. Mark-Allen/Brokes-in-Info., L.A., 1976-80; phys. sci. libr. Calif. Inst. Tech., Pasadena, 1980-84; corp. libr. Montgomery Watson, Pasadena, 1985-94; ret., 1994. Mem. adv. bd. L.A. Trade Tech. Coll., 1974-79, U. So. Calif. Libr. Sch., 1974-79. Editor: (with Joe Ann Clifton) Computers in Library and Information Ctrs., 1973. With USAF, 1952-54. Mem. Spl. Librs. Assn. (chmn. nominating com. 1974). Home: 2706 Ivan Hill Ter Los Angeles CA 90039-2717

HELIN, ELEANOR FRANCIS, astronomer, geologist; b. Pasadena, Calif. Rsch. asst. meteorite statistics Jet Propulsion Lab., Calif. Inst. Tech., 1960-61, rsch. asst. meteorite analysis, 1961-68, assoc. sci. asteroid rsch. and survey, 1969-76, sr. sci. asteroid survey and planetary sci., 1976-79, mem. profl. staff, 1979-80, mem. tech. staff, 1980—. Mem. Am. Astron. Soc., Inst. Astron. Union, Meteorol. Soc. Office: Jet Propulsion Lab Calif Inst Tech 4800 Oak Grove Dr # 183501 Pasadena CA 91109-8001

HELINSKI, DONALD RAYMOND, biologist, educator; b. Balt., July 7, 1933; s. George L. and Marie M. (Naparstek) H.; m. Patricia G. Doherty, Mar. 4, 1962; children: Matthew T., Maureen G. BS, U. Md., 1954; PhD in Biochemistry, Western Res. U., 1960; postdoctoral fellow, Stanford U., 1960-62. Asst. prof. Princeton (N.J.) U., 1962-65; mem. faculty U. Calif., San Diego, 1965—, prof. biology, 1970—, chmn. dept., 1979-81, dir. Ctr. for Molecular Genetics, 1984-95, assoc. dean Natural Scis., 1994-97. Mem. com. guidelines for recombinant DNA research NIH, 1975-78 Author papers in field. Mem. Am. Soc. Biol. Chemists, Am. Soc. Microbiology, AAAS, Am. Acad. of Arts and Scis., Am. Acad. Microbiology, Nat. Acad. Scis., European Molecular Biology Orgn. (assoc.). Office: U Calif Ctr Molecular Gen 9500 Gilman Dr La Jolla CA 92093-5003 E-mail: dhelinski@ucsd.edu

HELLER, DEAN, state official; b. Castro Valley, Calif., May 10, 1960; m. Lynne Brombach, children: Hilary Anne, Harrison Clark, Andrew Dean. BS with honors, USC. Former mem. Ways & Means & Carson City Rep. Cent. Committee; former Rep. Assembly Caucus; former Nev. St. Assembly; former sr. cons. Bank of Amer.; former stockbroker, broker, trader Pac Stock Exchange; chief dep. Ofc. of St. Tex.; sec. of state State of Nev., Carson City, 1995—. Bd. dirs. Western Nev. Community Coll. Found, Boys & Girls Club. Natl. Assn. Sec. Dealers, Boy Scouts, Natl. Assn. Sec. [illegible] Carson City NV 89703 [illegible] Office: Sec State 101 N Carson St Ste 3 Carson City NV 89701-4786

HELLER, EDWARD P., III, lawyer; b. 1947; BS, Ill. Inst. Tech.; JD, Western State U. Bar: Calif. 1976. Patent counsel Seagate Technology, Inc., Scotts Valley, Calif. Office: Seagate Tech Inc 4585 Scotts Valley Dr Scotts Valley CA 95067 also: Seagate Tech Inc 920 Disc Dr PO Box Bldg 14 Scotts Valley CA 95067-0360

HELLER, H(EINZ) ROBERT, financial executive; b. Cologne, Germany, Jan. 8, 1940; s. Heinrich and Karoline (Hermann) H.; m. Emily Mitchell, Dec. 5, 1970; children: Kimberly, Christopher. MA in Econs., U. Minn., 1962; PhD, U. Calif., Berkeley, 1965. Instr. U. Calif., Berkeley, 1965; assoc. prof. econs. UCLA, 1965-71; prof. U. Hawaii, Honolulu, 1971-74; chief fin. studies div. Internat. Monetary Fund, Washington, 1974-78; sr. v.p., dir. internat. econ. rsch. Bank of Am., San Francisco, 1978-86; mem., bd. govs. Fed. Res. System, Washington, 1986-89; exec. v.p. VISA Internat., San Francisco, 1989-91; pres., CEO VISA, U.S.A., San Francisco, 1991-93; exec. v.p. Fair, Isaac and Co., San Rafael, Calif., 1994-2001, also bd. dirs. Bd. dirs. Fair, Isaac and Co., Plus Sys. Inc., Interlink, Merchant Bank Svcs. Corp., Bay Area Coun., San Francisco, Sonic Automotive, BMW of N.Am., Inc., mem. adv. bd.; vice-chmn. Fed. Fin. Instns. Examination Coun., 1988-89; mem. Nat. Adv. Coun. Internat. Monetary and Fin. Policies, 1987-89, U.S. Coun. Internat. Bus., N.Y.C., 1979—; trustee World Affairs Coun., 1990-96; mem. adv. bd. Nat. Ctr. Fin. Svcs., U.Calif., Berkeley, 1984-90, Ctr. Fin. Sys. Rsch., Ariz. State U., Tempe, 1989, Inst. Internat. Edn., San Francisco, 1989; mem. Bay Area Internat. Forum, 1989, Bay Area Coun., 1992; dir. Am. Inst. Contemporary German Studies, Johns Hopkins U., Washington, 1989; dir. Wharton Fin. Instns. Ctr., U. Pa., 1989—. Author: International Trade, 1968, rev. edit. 1973, International Monetary Economics, 1974, The Economic System, 1972, Japanese Investment in the U.S., 1974; mem. editorial bd. Jour. Money, Credit and Banking, 1975-83, Internat. Trade Jour., 1985-88. Dir. Marin Gen. Hosp., 2001— Mem. Bankers Club of San Francisco, Royal Econ. Soc., Am. Econ. Assn., Western Econo. Assn. (exec. bd. 1977-81), San Francisco Yacht Club, Tiburon Peninsula Club. Avocations: sailing, skiing. Office: 90 Gilmartin Dr Tiburon CA 94920 E-mail: hrobertheller@home.com

HELLER, JULES, artist, writer, educator; b. N.Y.C., Nov. 16, 1919; s. Jacob Kenneth and Goldie (Lassar) H.; m. Gloria Spiegel, June 11, 1947; children: Nancy Gale, Jill Kay. AB, Ariz. State Coll., 1939; AM, Columbia U., 1940; PhD, U. So. Calif., 1948; DLitt, York U., 1985. Spl. art instr. 8th St. Sch., Tempe, Ariz., 1938-39; dir. art and music Union Neighborhood House, Auburn, N.Y., 1940-41; prof. fine arts, head dept. U. So. Calif., 1946-61; vis. asso. prof. fine arts Pa. State U., summers 1955, 57; dir. Pa. State U. (Sch. Arts), 1961-63; founding dean Pa. State U. (Coll. Arts and Architecture), 1963-68; founding dean Faculty Fine Arts York U., Toronto, 1968-73; prof. fine arts Faculty of Fine Arts, York U., 1973-76; dean Coll. Fine Arts, Ariz. State U., Tempe, 1976-85, prof. art, 1985-90; prof. emeritus, dean emeritus, 1990—. Vis. prof. Silpakorn U., Bangkok, Thailand, 1974, Coll. Fine Arts, Colombo, Sri Lanka, 1974, U. Nacional de Tucumán, Argentina, 1990, U. Nacional de Cuyo, Mendoza, Argentina, 1990; lectr., art juror; Cons. Open Studio, 1975-76; mem. vis. com. on fine arts Fisk U., Nashville, 1974; co-curator Leopoldo Méndez exhbn. Ariz. State U., Tempe, 1999. Printmaker; exhibited one man shows, Gallery Pascal, Toronto, U. Alaska, Fairbanks, Alaskaland Bear Gallery, Visual Arts Center, Anchorage, Ariz. State U., Lisa Sette Gallery, 1990, Centro Cultural de Tucumán, San Miguel de Tucumán, 1990; retrospective exhbn. Ariz. State U., Tempe, 1999, Town Hall, Paradise Valley, Ariz., 1999-2000; exhibited numerous group shows including Canadian Printmaker's Showcase, Pollack Gallery, Toronto, Mazelow Gallery, Toronto, Santa Monica Art Gallery, L.A. County Mus., Phila. Print Club, Seattle Art Mus., Landau Gallery, Kennedy & Co. Gallery, Bklyn. Mus., Cin. Art Mus., Dallas Mus. Fine Arts, Butler Art Inst., Oakland Art Mus., Pa. Acad. Fine Arts, Santa Barbara Mus. Art, San Diego Gallery Fine Arts, Martha Jackson Gallery, N.Y.C., Yuma Fine Arts Assn., Ariz., Toronto Dominion Centre, Amerika Haus, Hannover, Fed. Rep. Germany, U. Md., Smith-Andersen Galleries, Palo Alto, Calif., Grunewald Ctr. Graphic Arts, L.A., Univ. So. Fla., Tampa, Sheldon Meml. Gallery, Lincoln, Nebr., Santa Cruz (Calif.) Mus., Drake U., Iowa, Bradley U., Ill., Del Bello Gallery, Toronto, Honolulu Acad. Fine Arts; represented in permanent collections, Nat. Mus. Am. Art Smithsonian Instn., Washington, Long Beach Mus. Art, Library of Congress, York U., Allan R. Hite Inst. of U. Louisville, Ariz. State U., Tamarind Inst., U. N.Mex., Zimmerli Mus. Rutgers U., N.J., Can. Council Visual Arts Bank, also pvt. collections; author: Problems in Art Judgment, 1946, Printmaking Today, 1958, revised, 1972, Papermaking, 1978, 79; co-editor: North American Women Artists of the Twentieth Century, 1995, Codex Méndez, 1999; contbg. artist: Prints by California Artists, 1954, Estampas de la Revolución Mexicana, 1948; illustrator: Canciónes de Mexico, 1948; author numerous articles. Adv. bd. Continental affairs com. Americas Soc., 1983-86. With USAAF, 1941-45. Can. Coun. grantee; Landsdowne scholar U. Victoria; Fulbright scholar, Argentina, 1990. Mem. Coll. Art Assn. (Disting. Teaching of Art award 1995), Authors Guild, Internat. Assn. Hand Papermakers (steering com. 1986—), Nat. Found. Advancement in the Arts (visual arts panelist 1986-90, panel chmn. 1989, 90), Internat. Assn. Paper Historians, Internat. Coun. Fine Arts Deans (pres. 1968-69), So. Graphics Coun. (printmaker emeritus 1999). Home: 8651 E Via de los Libros Scottsdale AZ 85258-3509 E-mail: jules.heller@asu.edu

HELLER, PAUL MICHAEL, film company executive, producer; b. N.Y.C., Sept. 25, 1927; s. Alex Gordon and Anna (Rappaport) H.; children: Michael Peter, Charles Paul. Student, Drexel Inst. Tech., 1944-45; BA, Hunter Coll., 1950. Freelance scenic designer, N.Y.C., 1952-61; film producer N.Y.C., 1961—; instr. NYU, N.Y.C., 1964-66; prodn. exec. Warner Bros., 1970-71; pres. Paul Heller Prodns. Inc., Beverly Hills, Calif., 1973—. Producer over 30 films including David and Lisa, 1962, Enter the Dragon, 1973, First Monday in October, 1981, Withnail and I, 1987, My Left Foot, 1989, The Lunatic, 1990, The Annihilation of Fish, 1999; mus. multi-media prodr. The Skirball Cultural Center Museum, 1997, The Hong Kong Museum of History, 2000. Founding mem. Com. 100, Am. Film Inst. Served with U.S. Army. Recipient spl. award Nat. Assn. Mental Health. Mem. Dirs. Guild Am., Screen Actors Guild, Actors Equity Assn., Acad. Motion Picture Arts and Scis., Brit. Acad. Film and TV Arts (bd. dirs.), Hearst Castle Preservation San Simeon (bd. dirs.), Lotos Club (N.Y.C.). Home and Office: 1666 N Beverly Dr Beverly Hills CA 90210-2316 E-mail: pheller@earthlink.net

HELLEWELL, PARLEY G. state legislator; b. Feb. 1, 1950; m. Marilyn Barlow. AA in Bus. Mgmt. and Mktg., Utah Valley C.C. Owner plumbing, heating, air and elec. svc. maintenance bus. PPM, Inc.; mem. Utah Senate, Dist. 15, Salt Lake City, 1998—; chair bus., labor and econ. devel. com; mem. judiciary com.; exec. office, criminal justice and legis. appropriation com. Republican. Home: 492 S 1000 W Orem UT 84058-5828 E-mail: parley@itsnet.com

HELLIWELL, THOMAS MCCAFFREE, physicist, educator; b. Minneapolis, Minn., June 8, 1936; s. George Plummer and Eleanor (McCaffree) H.; m. Bernadette Egan Busenberg, Aug. 9, 1997. BA, Pomona Coll., 1958; PhD, Calif. Inst. Tech., 1963. Asst. prof. physics Harvey Mudd Coll., Claremont, Calif., 1962-67, assoc. prof., 1967-73, prof., 1973—, chmn. dept. physics, 1981-89, chair of faculty, 1990-93, Burton Bettingen prof. physics, 1990—. Author: Introduction to Special Relativity, 1966; author papers in field of cosmology, gen. relativity and quantum theory. Sci. faculty fellow NSF, 1968. Mem. Am. Assn. Physics Tchrs., AAAS. Avocations: [illegible], hiking. Office: Harvey Mudd Coll Dept Physics 301 E 12th St Claremont CA 91711-5901

HELLMAN, SUSAN D. medical products manufacturing executive; b. 1958; Bachelors Degree, MD, U. Nev.; M in Epidemiology and Biostats., U. Calif., Berkeley. Bd. cert. internal medicine and med. oncology. Trainee U. Calif., San Francisco; assoc. dir. clin. cancer rsch., project team leader Taxol Bristol-Myers Squibb Pharm. Rsch. Inst.; clin. scientist Genentech, Inc., South San Francisco, 1995-96, sr. dir. clin. sci., 1996, v.p. med. affairs, chief med. officer, 1996, v.p. devel., 1997, sr. v.p. devel., 1997, exec. v.p. devel. and product ops., 1999. Vis. faculty Uganda Cancer Inst.; asst. prof. hematology-oncology U. Calif. San Francisco, adj. assoc. prof. epidemiology and biostats. Office: Genentech Inc One DNA Way South San Francisco CA 94080-4990 Office Fax: 650-225-6000

HELLON, MICHAEL THOMAS, tax consultant, political party official; b. Camden, N.J., June 24, 1942; s. James Bernard and Dena Louise (Blackburn) H.; m. (div.); 2 children. BS, Ariz. State U., 1972. Ins. investigator Equifax, Phoenix, 1968-69; exec. v.p. Phoenix Met. C. of C., 1969-76; exec. Londen Ins. Group, 1976-78; pres. Hellon and Assocs., Inc., 1978—. Small claims hearing officer Pima County Justice Ct., 1990—; mem. Pima County Bd. Adjustments, 1993-2000, Pima County Merit Commn., 2000—; nat. def. exec. res. U.S. Dept. of Commerce, 1986-97; bd. dirs. Equity Benefit Life Ins. Co., Modern Income Life Ins. Co. of Mo., First Equity Security Life Ins. Co., Tucson Classics. Mem. Ariz. Occupl. Safety and Health Adv. Coun., 1972-76, mem. Speaker's Select Com. Auto Emissions, 1976; Phoenix Urban League, 1972-73, Area Manpower Planning coun., 1971-72, Phoenix Civic Plaza Dedication Com., 1972, Phoenix Air Quality Maintenance Taks Force, 1976; pres. Vis. Nurse Svc., 1978-79; Rep. precinct capt., 1973—; state campaign dir. Arizonans for Reagan Com., 1980; alt. del. Rep. Nat. Conv., 1980, 84, 88; mem. staff Reagan-Bush Nat. Conv., 1984; campaign mgr. for various candidates, 1972-82; mem. exec. com. Ariz. Rep. Party, 1989-90, chmn., 1997-99; mem. Rep. Nat. Com., 1992—, mem. exec. com., 1997—; bd. dirs. ATMA Tng. Found., 1981-84. Served with USAF, 1964-68. Decorated Bronze Star medal, Purple Heart; Recipient George Washington Honor medal Freedom's Found., 1964; commendation Fed. Bar Assn., 1973. Mem. U.S. C. of C. (pub. affairs com. western divsn. 1974-76), Inst. of Property Taxation, Internat. Assn. Assessing Officers, U.S. Dept. Commerce Exec. Res., Ariz. C. of C. Mgrs. Assn. (bd. m em. 1974-76), Tucson C. of C., Trunk 'N Tusk Club, Catalina Soccer Club (bd. dirs. 1984-88). Home: 1261 W Hopbush Way Tucson AZ 85704-2647 Address: 6700 N Oracle Rd #110 Tucson AZ 85704

HELLON, TONI, state senator; 2 children. BA in Journalism, U. Ariz. Freelance writer, graphic artist; Rep. senator legis. dist. 12 Ariz. State Senate, Phoenix. Mem. appropriations, edn. and health coms. Ariz. State Senate, vice chmn. family svcs., mem. domestic rels. reform study subcom.; bd. dirs. Tucson Ariz. Boys Chorus; mem. pub. adv. bd. KUAT-TV, 2000—; mem. Pima County Trial Ct. Commn., 1992-2000; mem. gov.'s adv. bd. Ariz. Film Commn., 1997—; polit. cons. Former editor-in-chief Tombstone (Ariz.) Epitaph. Vol. 88-rime, 1988-97; dir. Alliance to Save the Poison Info. Ctr., U. Ariz., Coll. Pharmacy, 1993-94; del. II Congreso De Mujeres Empresarias and Profesionistas, Sonara, Ariz., 1995-96; mem. Hispanic Profl. Action Com., Ariz. Women's Polit. Caucus; chmn. Pima County Rep. Party, Tucson, 1997, past pres.; past pres. Cactus Wren Rep. Women, Phoenix; former chmn. Rep. Legis. Dist. 13. Mem. Am. Diabetes Assn. (Ariz. chpt. gala chmn. 1999). Office: Ariz State Senate State Capitol Rm 304 1700 W Washington Phoenix AZ 85007 E-mail: thellon@azleg.state.az.us

HELMBERGER, DONALD VINCENT, geophysical educator, researcher; b. Perham, Minn., Jan. 23, 1938; s. John David and Mary (Klein) H.; m. Florence Coles; 1 child, Genna; m. Annette Sellon; 1 child, Elliott. B in Geophysics, U. Minn., 1961; MS, U. Calif., San Diego, 1965, PhD, 1967; postdoctoral, MIT, 1968-69. Asst. prof. Princeton (N.J.) U., 1969-70, Calif. Inst. Tech., Pasadena, 1970-74, assoc. prof., 1974-79, prof. geophysics, 1979—. Fellow Am. Geophysical Union (Inge Lehmann medalist, 1997). Office: Calif Inst Tech Dept Geol & Planetary Sci Pasadena CA 91125-0001

HELMER, M(ARTHA) CHRISTIE, lawyer; b. Portland, Oreg., Oct. 8, 1949; d. Marvin Curtis and Inez Bahl (Corwin) H.; m. Joe D. Bailey, June 23, 1979; children: Tim Bailey, Bill Bailey, Kim Easton. BA in English magna cum laude, Wash. State U., 1970; JD cum laude, Lewis & Clark Coll., 1974; LLM in Internat. Law, Columbia U., 1998. Bar: Oreg. 1974. Assoc. Miller Nash, Portland, 1974-81, ptnr., 1981—. Adj. prof. Lewis & Clark Law Sch., 1999—; guest lectr. Xiamen U. Law, China, 1995; mem. Oreg. Bd. Bar Examiners, Portland, 1978-81; del. 9th Cir. Jud. Conf., 1984-87, mem. exec. com., 1987-90. Author: Arrest of Ships, 1985, Has China Adopted the UCC?, 1999. Mem. ABA, Oreg. Bar (mem. bd. govs. 1981-84, treas. 1983-84), Maritime Law Assn., Internat. Bar Assn., Pacific N.W. Internat. Trade Assn. (bd. dirs., mem. exec. com.), Multnomah Athletic Club, Phi Beta Kappa. Avocations: antiques, travel, fashion. Office: Miller Nash 111 SW 5th Ave Ste 3500 Portland OR 97204-3699 E-mail: helmer@millernash.com

HELMHOLZ, AUGUST CARL, physicist, educator emeritus; b. Evanston, Ill., May 24, 1915; s. Henry F. and Isabel G. (Lindsay) H.; m. Elizabeth J. Little, July 30, 1938; children: Charlotte C.K. Colby, George L., Frederic V., Edith H. Roth. A.B., Harvard Coll., 1936; student, Cambridge U., 1936-37; Ph.D., U. Calif., Berkeley, 1940; Sc.D. (hon.), U. Strathclyde, 1979. Instr. physics U. Calif.-Berkeley, 1940-43, asst. prof., 1943-48, assoc. prof., 1948-51, prof., 1951-80, emeritus, 1980—, chmn. dept., 1955-62; rsch. physicist Lawrence Berkeley Lab., 1940—. Mem. Vis. Scientist Program, 1966-71; governing bd. Am. Inst. Physics, 1964-67. Recipient Citation U. Calif., Berkeley, 1980; Berkeley fellow, 1988—, Guggenheim fellow, 1962-63. Fellow Am. Phys. Soc.; mem. AAAS, Am. Assn. Physics Tchrs., AAUP, Phi Beta Kappa, Sigma Xi. Home: 28 Crest Rd Lafayette CA 94549-3349 Office: U Calif Dept Physics Berkeley CA 94720-7300 E-mail: helmholz@socrates.berkeley.edu

HELMICK, D.O. protective services official; b. Tex. A.Police Sci., Yuba (Calif.) Coll.; BA, Golden Gate U.; grad., FBI Nat. Inst. State trooper Calif. Hwy. Patrol, Sacramento, 1969-75, liaison to legis., spl. rep., 1975-86, comdr. coastal divsn. San Luis Obispo, 1986-89, dep. commr. Sacramento, 1989-95, commr., 1995—. Office: Calif Highway Patrol PO Box 942898 Sacramento CA 94298-0001

HELMS, LUKE, bank executive; b. Lubbock, Tex. BA in History, U. Ariz., 1966; MBA, U. Santa Clara, 1968. Asst. v.p. corp. lending Bank of Calif., San Francisco, 1968-74; asst. v.p. nat. dept. Seafirst, 1974-76, v.p., 1976-79, mgr. U.S. dept., 1979-80, sr. v.p., mgr. nat. divsn., 1980-82, head internat. divsn., 1982-83, exec. v.p., mgr. world banking group, 1983-84, mgr. N.E. Pacific banking group, 1984-86, pres., 1987-93; vice chmn. BankAm. Corp., San Francisco, 1993-97; mng. ptnr. Sonata Capital Group Inc., Seattle, 2001—. Bd. dirs. ABM Industries Inc., San Francisco Mus. Modern Art, U. San Francisco, Oakland Children's Hosp., Wash. State U. Found., U. Wash. Found. Office: Sonata Capital Group Inc 1501 4th Ave #2600 Seattle WA 98101-1688

HELMUTH, PHILIP ALAN, tax consultant; b. Alhambra, Calif., Dec. 29, 1965; s. Melvin I. and Elsie (Borkholder) H. Student, MiraCosta Coll., 1985-89, Palomar Coll., 1989-90. Data entry operator Melco Bus. Svc., Vista, Calif., 1980-83, bookkeeper, 1983-91, ptnr., tax cons., 1992-95, owner, 1995—; bookkeeper Underwater Schs. of Am., Oceanside, 1985-86; owner, notary pub. Vista, 1987—; owner Melco Bus. Svcs., Vista, 1995—. Registered rep. H.D. Vest Fin. Svcs. Mem. Nat. Notary Assn.

(com. mem. editl. adv. com. 1990-93, pub. image com. 1990-93), Nat. Assn. Enrolled Agts., Calif. Soc. Enrolled Agts. (Palomar chpt. dir. 1995-96, 2d v.p. 1996-98), Escondido Grad. Spokesman Club (sec. 1991-92, pres. 1992-93, treas. 1993-95). Avocations: singing, collecting compact discs, reading history, science fiction. Office: Melco Bus Svc 410 S Santa Fe Ave Ste 102 Vista CA 92084-6163

HELPER, LEE, strategic business marketing and marketing communications consultant; Pres. Bender/Helper Impact, L.A. Office: Bender Helper Impact 11500 W Olympic Blvd Ste 655 Los Angeles CA 90064-1597

HELSELL, ROBERT M. construction executive; b. Seattle, Mar. 29, 1937; s. Frank P. and Ellen (Bringloe) H.; m. Linda M. Clark, Dec. 19, 1961; children— Kristina, Ingrid, Spencer, Alexa B.A., Dartmouth Coll., 1959, M.B.E., 1960. C.P.A., Wash. With Haskins & Sells, 1961-64; treas. Cascade Natural Gas Co., 1964-68; successively sec.-treas., exec. v.p., pres. and chief exec. officer Howard S. Wright Constrn. Co., Seattle, 1974-84; pres., chief exec. officer Wright Schuchart, Inc., 1980-84, Sprague Resources Corp., 1984-89; vice chmn. bd. Schuchart & Assocs., 1980-87; pres., chief exec. officer Wilder Constrn. Co., Bellingham, Wash., 1989—. Dir. Ranier Bancorp. and Security Pacific Bank, Seafirst Corp., 1992. Bd. dirs. Virginia Mason Hosp., 1984-89, Lakeside Sch., 1969-73, 93—, Seattle Children's Home, 1968-77, pres., 1972-75, Corp. Council for Arts, 1981—, pres., 1984, chmn., 1985, Washington Roundtable, 1988—; trustee Seattle Art Mus., 1973-88, Western Washington U., 1994—; mem. men's adv. com. Children's Orthopedic Hosp., 1980-89, Western Found., 1992. Lt. comdr. USCG, 1961-68. Mem. Assoc. Gen. Contractors. Republican. Episcopalian. Clubs: Univ., Rainier, Seattle Tennis, Seattle Yacht, Wash. Athletic (Seattle), Bellingham Yacht Club. Office: Wilder Constrn Co 1525 E Marine View Dr Everett WA 98201-1927

HELSLEY, CHARLES EVERETT, geologist, geophysicist; b. Oceanside, Calif., June 24, 1934; BS, Calif. Inst. Tech., 1956, MS, 1957; PhD in Geology, Princeton U., 1960. Asst. prof. geology Calif. Inst. Tech., 1960-62; asst. prof. Case Western Res. U., 1962-63; from asst. to assoc. prof. S.W. ctr. advancement studies U. Tex., Dallas, 1963-69, prof. geoscience, 1969-76, assoc. head geoscience divsn., 1971-72, head geoscience program, dir. inst. geoscience, 1972-75; prof. geology and geophysics U. Hawaii, Manoa, 1976—, dir. Hawaii inst. geophysics, 1976—. Adj. prof. So. Meth. U., 1963-76, marine sci. inst. U. Tex., Galveston, 1973-76. Mem. Geol. Soc. Am., Am. Geophys. Union. Achievements include research in rock magnetism and paleomagnetism and their implications regarding continental drift, marine geophysics, magnetostratigraphy, geothermal resource exploration. Office: U Hawaii Hawaii Inst Geophysics 2525 Correa Rd Honolulu HI 96822-2219

HELSTROM, CARL WILHELM, electrical engineering educator; b. Easton, Pa., Feb. 22, 1925; s. Carl Wilhelm H.; m. Barbro Elisabet Dahlbom, Oct. 13, 1956; children: Lars Vilhelm, Nils Stefan. BS in Engring Physics, Lehigh U., 1947; MS in Physics, Calif. Inst. Tech., 1949, PhD in Physics, 1951. Adv. mathematician Westinghouse Rsch. Labs, Pitts., 1951-66; prof. U. Calif.-San Diego, La Jolla, 1966-91, prof emeritus, 1991—. Author: Statistical Theory of Signal Detection, 1968, Quantum Detection and Estimation Theory, 1976, Probability and Stochastic Processes for Engineers, 1991, Elements of Signal Detection and Estimation, 1995. With USNR, 1944-46. Recipient Quantum Comm. award, 1996. Fellow IEEE (editor Trans. on Info. Theory jour. 1967-71, Centennial medal 1984, Third Millennium medal 2000), Optical Soc. Am.; mem. Phi Beta Kappa.

HELTON, TODD, professional baseball player; b. Knoxville, Tenn., Aug. 20, 1973; m. Kristi Helton, Jan. 29. Student, U. Tenn. With Colo. Rockies Maj. League Baseball, 1995—, first baseman, 1999—. Named Runner-up Rookie of Yr., 1999, Profl. Athlete of Yr. Tenn. Sports Hall of Fame, 1998. Office: Colo Rockies 2001 Blake St Denver CO 80205-2008

HELWICK, CHRISTINE, lawyer; b. Orange, Calif., Jan. 6, 1947; d. Edward Everett and Ruth Evelyn (Seymour) Hailwood; children: Ted C., Dana J. BA, Stanford U., 1968; MA, Northwestern U., 1969; JD, U. Calif., San Francisco, 1973. Bar: Calif., U.S. Supreme Ct. U. S. Ct. Appeals (9th cir.), U.S. Dist. Ct. (no., ctrl., so. and ea. dist.) Calif. Tchr. history New Trier Twp. High Sch., Winnetka, Ill., 1968-69; sec. to the producer Flip Wilson Show, Burbank, Calif., 1970; rsch. assoc. Bingham, Summers, Welsh & Spilman, Indpls., 1973; assoc. Crosby, Heafey, Roach & May, Oakland, Calif., 1973-78; asst. counsel litigation U. Calif., Oakland, 1978-84, mng. univ. counsel, 1984-94, counsel Berkeley campus, 1989-94; gen. counsel Calif. State U. Sys., 1994—. Lectr. in field. Mem. instnl. rev. bd. Devel. Studies Ctr., Oakland, 1990—; DECIDE project instr. Wildwood Elem. Sch., Piedmont, Calif., 1989-91; mem. Alameda County Fee Arbitration Panel. Mem. Nat. Assn. Coll. and Univ. Attys. (bd. dirs. 1995-98, 2nd v.p. 1999—), State Bar Calif. (exec. com. 1980-83, Leadership Calif. 1998), Alam eda County Bar Assn. (exec. com. trial practice sect. 1994, minority access program com. 1989, bd. dirs. 1977), Alameda County Bar Found. (adv. trustee 1988-90, bd. dirs. 1991), Order of Coif. Episcopalian. Office: Calif State U 401 Golden Shore 4th Fl Long Beach CA 90802-4275

HEMBREE, JAMES D. retired chemical company executive; b. Morris, Okla., Feb. 27, 1929; s. James D. and Mary Eleanor H.; m. Joyce Pickrell, Aug. 25, 1951; children: Victoria Lee Krivacs, Alex James, Kent Douglas. B.S.Ch.E., Okla. State U., 1951; M.S.Ch.E., U. Mich., 1952. Dir. mktg. inorganic chems. Dow Chem U.S.A., Midland, Mich., 1968-78, gen. mgr. designed products dept., 1976-78, v.p., 1978-80, group v.p., 1980-83; pres., chief exec. officer Dow Chem. Can., Sarnia, Ont., 1983-86; ret., 1986. Bd. dirs. Endless Youth Products Inc., Las Vegas. Home and Office: 4620 Jupiter Dr Salt Lake City UT 84124-3900 E-mail: jimhembree@compuserve.com

HEMION, DWIGHT ARLINGTON, television producer, director; b. New Haven, Mar. 14, 1926; s. Dwight Arlington and Bernice Ruby (Berquist) H.; m. Katherine Bridget Morrissy, Sept. 1, 1973; children— Katherine, Dwight Gustav. Student pub. schs., Verona, N.J. Asso. dir. ABC-TV, N.Y.C., 1946-49; TV dir. Tonight Show, NBC-TV, N.Y.C., 1950-60; dir. Perry Como TV show, N.Y.C., 1960-67; producer/dir. Yorkshire Prodns., N.Y.C., 1967-70; producer/dir. TV spls. in assn. with ATV, London; producer/dir. Smith-Hemion Prodns., Los Angeles, 1976-90, v.p., 1990—. Dir.: Frank Sinatra: A Man and His Music, 1965 (Emmy award TV Acad. Arts and Scis.); The Sound of Burt Bacharach, 1969, Singer Presents Burt Bacharacn, 1970, Barbra Streisand and Other Musical Instruments, 1973, Steve and Eydie-Our Love is Here to Stay, 1975, America Salutes Richard Rodgers: The Sound of His Music, 1976, Bette Midler-Ol' Red Hair is Back, 1977, Ben Vereen ... His Roots, 1977, Steve and Eydie Celebrate Irving Berlind, 1978, IBM Presents Baryshinikov on Broadway, 1979 (Emmy award), Goldie and Kids ... Listen to Us!, 1982 (Emmy award), Sheena Easton...Act I, 1983 (Emmy award), Anne Murray's Winter Carnival...From Quebec, 1984, 4 Emmy Award Shows, 15 Christmas in Wasington shows, 6 TV Acad. Hall of Fame shows, Neil Diamond Hello Again, opening cermemonies Liberty Weekend, Barbra Streisand One Voice, We The People Contitutional Gala, Julie Andrews the Sound of Christmas, All Star Salute to Our Troops, Barbra Streisand...The Concert, Disney's Young Musicians Symphony Orchestra, Disney's American Teachers Awards, 50th, 51st Presdl. Inaugural Galas, numerous other tv spls., events. Served in AC U.S. Army, 1944-46. Named Dir. of Year in TV Dirs. Guild Am., 1965 Mem. Purcival Country Club. Office: Smith Hemion Prodns Inc Box 15 1438 N Gower St Los Angeles CA 90028-8383

HEMMINGER, PAMELA LYNN, lawyer; b. Chgo., June 29, 1949; d. Paul Willis and Lenore Adelaide (Hennig) H.; m. Robert Alan Miller, May 14, 1979; children: Kimberly Anne, Jeffrey Ryan, Eric Douglas. BA, Pomona Coll., 1971; JD, Pepperdine U., 1976. Tchr. Etiwanda (Calif.) Sch. dist., 1971-74; law clerk Gibson Dunn & Crutcher, Newport Beach, Calif., 1974-76, assoc. L.A., 1976-84, ptnr., 1985—. Contbg. author Sexual Harassment, 1992, Employment Discrimination Law, 1993; contbr. articles to profl. jours. Mem. comparable worth task force Calif., Sacramento, 1984, Pepperdine U. Sch. of Law Bd. Visitors, 1990—, Calif. Law Revision Commn., 1998-99; mem., bd. dirs. Dispute Resolution Svcs., 1998—. Named alumnus of yr. Pepperdine Sch. Law, 1996; listed in Best Lawyers in Am., 1998-99. Mem. L.A. County Bar Assn. (chair, labor and employment sect. 1996-97), Calif. C. of C. (employment rels. com. 1984—). Republican. Lutheran. Office: Gibson Dunn & Crutcher 333 S Grand Ave Ste 4400 Los Angeles CA 90071-3197

HEMMINGS, FRED, state senator; b. Honolulu, Jan. 9, 1946; Owner Sports Enterprises, Inc., 1970—; Rep. rep. Hawaii Ho. of Reps., 1989-90; Rep. senator Hawaii State Senate, 2000—. Bd. dirs. Denver Broncos-NFL; Rep. floor leader Hawaii Ho. of Reps., 1989-90; mem. ways and means, water, land, energy and environ., transp., mil. affairs, govt. ops. and Hawaiian affairs coms. Hawaii State Senate. Author: The Soul of Surfing is Hawaiian, 1997, Surfing, Hawaii's Gift to the World, 1997; co-author: Illustrated Surfing Encyclopedia (in Japanese), 1979; weekly columnist Honolulu Star Bull., 1966; cons./test pilot first artificial wave machine, 1969; talent (commls.) United Airlines, 1966, Kellogg's Cereal, 1967, Eastman Kodak Co., 1970; prodr./host KITV Hawaii Sports Scene, 1972; commentator CBS Wide World of Sports, 1970-75, 78, NBC Sports World, 1979-83; talk show host KGU Radio, 1991-92. Oahu County chmn. Rep. Party Hawaii, 1975-76; founder, prodr. Triple Crown of Surfing, 1983-88; dir. Children's Adv., 1991; trustee Outrigger Duke Kahanamoku Found., 1990-91; mem. Gov.'s Millenium Commn., Hawaii, 2000 Named Athlete of Yr., Honolulu Quarterback Club, 1964; with Goodwill Tours with Duke Kahanamoku, Hawaii, 1966-67, vets. divsn. Nat. Super Stars Competition, 1976; recipient Duke Kahanamoku Sportsman award, 1969, Top Ten Businessmen's award Honolulu Jr. C. of C., 1969, Top Legislator award Small Bus. Hawaii, 1985-90; mem. championship teams Molokai to Oahu Canoe Race, 1967, 68, 75, Masters 1984; jr. divsn. Makaha Internat. Surfing Champion, 1962, 63, sr. divsn., 1964, 66; champion Peruvian Internat. Surfing, Peru, 1964, World Surfing, P.R., 1968; named to Internat. Surfing Hal of Fame, 1991, Punahou Sch. Athletic Hall of Fame, 1994, Hawaii-Sports Hall of Fame, 1999. Mem. Assn. Surfing Profls. (life dir.), U.S. Surfing Fedn. (hon. dir.-life 1987), Internat. Profl. Surfing (founder, pres. 1976-83). Avocations: sports (Honolulu Quarterback Club. Office: Hawaii State Senate Hawaii State Capitol Rm 208 415 S Beretania St Honolulu HI 96813 Fax: 808 587-7240. E-mail: senhemmings@Capitol.hawaii.gov

HEMMINGS, PETER WILLIAM, orchestra and opera administrator; b. London, Apr. 10, 1934; s. William and Rosalind (Jones) H.; m. Jane Frances Kearnes, May 19, 1962; children: William, Lucy, Emma, Rupert, Sophie. Grad., Gonville and Caius Coll., Cambridge, England, 1957; LLD (hon.), Strathclyude U., Glasgow, 1978; DFA, Calif. State U., 2000. Clk. Harold Holt Ltd., London, 1958-59; planning mgr. Sadlers Wells Opera, London, 1959-65, gen. adminstr. Scottish Opera, Glasgow, 1962-77; gen. mgr. Australian Opera, Sydney, 1977-79; gen. dir. L.A. Music Ctr. Opera, 1984-2000; gen. mgr. New Opera Co., London, 1956-65; dir. Royal Acad. Music. Gen. cons. Compton Verney Opera Project. Lt. Brit. Signal Corps, 1952-54. Decorated Order Brit. Empire. Fellow Royal Scottish Acad. Music, Royal Acad. Music (hon.); mem. Am. Friends of Sadlers Wells (pres. 1994-99), Opera Am. (bd. dirs.), Garrick Club (London), Royal Opera House Covent Garden (bd. dirs. 1999—). Anglican. Office: 51 Queens Gate Gardens London SW7 5NF England Fax: 0207 225 2476. E-mail: hemmings@mail.com

HEMMINGSEN, BARBARA BRUFF, microbiology educator; b. Whittier, Calif., Mar. 25, 1941; d. Stephen Cartland and Susanna Jane (Alexander) Bruff; m. Edvard Alfred Hemmingsen, Aug. 5, 1967; 1 child, Grete. BA, U. Calif., Berkeley, 1962, MA, 1964; PhD, U. Calif., San Diego, 1971. Lectr. San Diego State U., 1973-77, asst. prof., 1977-81, assoc. prof., 1981-88, prof., 1988—. Vis. asst. prof. Aarhus U. Denmark, 1971-72; cons. AMBIS, Inc., San Diego, 1984-85, Woodward-Clyde Cons., 1985, 87-91, Novatron, Inc., 2000—. Author: (with others) Microbial Ecology, 1972; contbr. articles to profl. jours. Mem. Planned Parenthood, San Diego. Mem. AAAS, Am. Soc. Microbiology, Am. Women in Sci., San Diego Assn. for Rational Inquiry (sec. 1998—), Sigma Xi, Phi Beta Kappa (past pres., corr. sec. Nu chpt. Calif. 1994—). Democrat. Office: San Diego State U Dept Biology San Diego CA 92182-4614

HEMOND, ROLAND A. professional baseball team executive; b. Central Falls, R.I., Oct. 26, 1929; m. Margaret Quinn, 1958; children— Susan, Tere, Robert, Jay, Ryan. Past dir. player personnel Chgo. White Sox, past exec. v.p., gen. mgr., spl. asst. to pres. and chmn., 1970-85; cons. commr. of Baseball, N.Y.C., 1986-87; formerly with Boston/Milw. Braves, Calif. Angels.; exec. v.p., gen. mgr. Baltimore Orioles, 1987-95; now sr. exec. vp baseball operations Arizona Diamondbacks, Phoenix, 1995-2000; exec. advisor to gen. mgr. Chgo. White Sox, 2000—. Served in USCG. Named The Sporting News Major League Exec. of Yr., 1972, 89, Major League Exec. of Yr. UPI, 1983, Am. League Exec. of Yr. UPI, 1989. Address: 1332 W Edgemont Ave Phoenix AZ 85007-1117

HEMP, RALPH CLYDE, retired reinsurance company executive, consultant, arbitrator, umpire; b. Fresno, Calif., Sept. 9, 1936; s. Ralph Edward and Mabel Alice (Knox) H.; m. Mary Ann Corley, Aug. 25, 1962; children— Ralph Kenneth, Laura Elizabeth B.A., San Diego State U., 1961; J.D., Western States U., Santa Ana, Calif., 1971. Office mgr. Crawford & Co., L.A., 1961-67; regional claims mgr. Olympic Ins. Co., L.A., 1967-68; sr. v.p. Leatherby Ins. Co., Fullerton, Calif., 1968-76; pres. North Am. Co., Greenwich, Conn., 1976-86; chmn. Mt. Eagle Cos., Whitefish, Mont., 1986—. Republican Avocations: hunting; fishing; golf; skiing. Home and Office: Mt Eagle Cos PO Box 1971 Whitefish MT 59937-1971

HEMRY, LARRY HAROLD, former federal agency official, writer, inventor; b. Seattle, Jan. 4, 1941; s. Harold Bernard and Florence Usborne (Achilles) H.; m. Nancy Kay Ballantyne, July 10, 1964 (div. Apr. 1976); children: Rachel Dalayne, Aaron Harold, Andrew LeRoy. BA, Seattle Pacific Coll., 1963; postgrad., Western Evang. Sem., Portland, Oreg., 1969, 70. Ordained to ministry Free Meth. Ch., 1968. Clergyman Free Meth. Ch., Vancouver, B.C., Can., 1963-64, Mt. Vernon, Wash., 1968-69, Colton (Oreg.) Community Ch., 1969-71; edit clk. Moody Bible Inst., Chgo., 1964-66; pres., founder Bethel Enterprises, Colton, 1969-71; immigration insp. U.S. Immigration and Naturalization Svc., Sumas, Wash., 1972-96. Author, historian: Some Northwest Pioneer Families, 1969, The Hemry Family History Book, 1985; author: An Earnest Plea to Earnest Christians, 1969; contbr. articles to profl. publs.; patentee mech. nut cracker. Chmn. com. to establish and endow the James A. Hemry meml. scholarship fund Seattle Pacific U., 1975. Fellow Seattle Pacific U. (Centurians Club); mem. The Nature Conservancy, The Sierra Club, The Audubon Soc. Avocations: camping, nature study, woodcarving. Home: PO Box 532 Sumas WA 98295-0532

HEMSLEY, SHERMAN, comedian, actor; b. Phila., Feb. 1, 1938; Student, Phila. Acad. Dramatic Arts; student acting, Lloyd Richards. Former postal worker; active advanced workshop Negro Ensemble Co., N.Y.C. Appeared in Purlie Victorious, other prodns., Theatre XIV, Phila., children's theater with Phoenix Prodns.; co-star local Phila. TV comedy series Black Book; off-Broadway debut in The People vs. Ranchman, 1968, also Alice in Wonderland, 1969; Broadway debut in Purlie, 1970; appeared with Toronto and San Francisco cos. Don't Bother Me, I Can't Cope; on stage in The Odd Couple, Dallas and Chgo., Norman is that You, Las Vegas, 1986, I'm Not Rappaport, Calgary, Alta., Can., 1987; TV series All in the Family, 1973-75, The Jeffersons, 1975-85, Amen, 1986-91; other TV appearances include Solid Gold, Dom De Luis Show, Twilight Zone, Love Boat, Fantasy Island, Star Search, 227, Alf, Fresh Prince of Bel Air, Hang'n with Mr. Cooper, Burkes Law, Thunder in Paradise, Designing Women, voice of Mr. Richfield for Dinosaurs, 1989-93, Up Up and Away, 2000; films Alice in Wonderland, 1985, Mr. Nanny, 1993, Senseless, 1998, Screwed, 2000; live appearances Caesar, 1988, Sands Hotel, 1989, Sahara, 1990, Dunes, 1991, command performance King of Morocco. Recipient Image award for The Jeffersons NAACP, 1982, 83, Amen, 1987, Hollywood Fgn. Press Assn. award; nominated Golden Globe award for The Jeffersons. Mem. AFTRA, Actors' Equity Assn., Screen Actors Guild. Office: c/o Kenny Johnston 15043 Valleyheart Dr Sherman Oaks CA 91403-1358

HEMSTREET, MARK S. hotel executive; b. Portland, Oreg., Mar. 15, 1950; Pres. Shilo Inns, Shilo Mgmt. Co., Portland, 1974—. Office: Shilo Inns 11600 SW Shilo Ln Portland OR 97225-5919

HENAGER, CHARLES HENRY, civil engineer; b. Spokane, Wash., July 11, 1927; s. William Franklin and Mary Agnes (Henry) H.; m. Dorothy Ruth Parker, May 6, 1950; children: Charles Henry, Jr., Donald E., Roberta R. BS in Civil Engring., Wash. State U., 1950. Registered profl. engr., Wash. Instrumentman Wash. State Dept. Hwys., Yakima, 1950-52; engr. Gen. Electric Co., Richland, Wash., 1952-62; shift supr., reactor GE, Richland, 1962-63, sr. engr., 1963-65; sr. devel. engr. Battelle Pacific N.W. Labs., Richland, 1965-68, sr. rsch. engr., 1968-90, ret., 1990. Contbr. articles to profl. jours.; patentee in field. With USN, 1945-46. Fellow Am. Concrete Inst. (tech. activities com. 1987-89, Del Bloem award 1986), ASTM (subcom. 1980-92), ASCE (pres. Columbia sect. 1961-62); mem. Kennewick Swim Club (pres. 1962-63), Village at Canyon Lakes Assn. (v.p. 1998, 2000-2001, bd. dirs. and mem. archtl. control com. 1996-98), Sigma Tau, Tau Beta Pi, Phi Kappa Phi. Republican. Methodist. Avocations: calligraphy, genealogy. Home: 3413 S Huntington Loop Kennewick WA 99337-2572

HENDEE, JOHN CLARE, university research educator; b. Duluth, Minn., Nov. 12, 1938; s. Clare Worden and Mary Myrtle (Parker) H.; m. Marilyn R. Riley; children: John Jr., James, Landon, Joy, Joni, Jared. BS in Forestry, Mich. State U., 1960; MF in Forestry Mgmt., Oreg. State U., 1962; PhD in Forestry, Econs. and Sociology, U. Wash., 1967. With USDA Forest Svc., 1961-85; with timber mgmt. dept. Waldport and Corvallis, Oreg., 1961-64; fire rsch. forester Pacific S.W. Forest Experiment Sta., Berkeley, Calif., 1964; recreation rsch. unit leader Pacific N.W. Forest Expt. Sta., Seattle, 1967-76; legis. affairs staff Washington, 1977-78; asst. sta. dir. Southeastern Forest Experiment Sta., Asheville, N.C., 1978-85; dean Coll. Forestry, Wildlife, and Range Sci. U. Idaho, Moscow, 1985-94, prof. forest resources and resource recreation and tourism, 1985, dir. wilderness rsch. ctr., 1994—; dir. Idaho Forest, Wildlife and Range Experiment Sta., 1985-94. Mem. affiliate faculty in forestry U. Wash., Seattle, 1968-76; vice chmn. for sci. 4th World Wilderness Congress, 1987. Co-author: Wildlife Management in Wilderness, 1978, Introduction to Forests and Renewable Resources, 6th edit., 1994; sr. co-author: Wilderness Management, 1978, rev. 2d edit., 1990; founding mng. editor Internat. Jour. of Wilderness, 1995; contbr. numerous articles to profl. jours. Bd. dirs. WILD Found.; active Boy Scouts Am. Recipient Spl. Merit award Keep Am. Beautiful, 1972, Nat. Conservation Achievement award Am. Motors, 1974, Spl. award for Wilderness Rsch. and Edn. Nat. Outdoor Leadership Sch., 1985, Merit award USDA-Forest Service, 1979, 80, 85, Lifetime Achievement award Am. Soc. Pub. Adminstrn., 1988; Fed. Congl. fellow, Washington, 1976-77. Mem. Nat. Assn. Profl. Forestry Schs. and Colls. (chmn. western div. 1987-89), Soc. Am. Foresters (edn. and communication working group chmn. 1986-89). Avocations: backpacking, hiking, hunting, fishing. Office: U Idaho Wilderness Research Ctr Moscow ID 83844-0001

HENDERSON, DOUGLAS JAMES, physicist, chemist, researcher; b. Calgary, Alta., Can., July 28, 1934; came to U.S., 1956; s. Donald Ross and Evelyn Louise (Scott) H.; m. Rose-Marie Steen-Nielssen, Jan. 21, 1960; children: Barbara, Dianne, Sharon. BA in Math., U. B.C., Vancouver, 1956; PhD in Physics, U. Utah, 1961. Instr. dept. math. U. Utah, Salt Lake City, 1960-61; asst. prof. physics U. Idaho, Moscow, 1961-62, Ariz. State U., Tempe, 1962-64, assoc. prof., 1964-67, prof. physics, 1967-69; assoc. prof. physics U. Waterloo, Can., 1964-67, prof. applied math. and physics Can., 1967-69; rsch. sci. IBM Almaden Rsch. Ctr., San Jose, Calif., 1969-90, IBM Corp., Salt Lake City, 1990-92, Utah Supercomputing Inst., U. Utah, Salt Lake City, 1990-95; prof. chemistry Brigham Young U., Salt Lake City, 1995—. Vis. sci. CSIRO Chem. Rsch. Labs., Melbourne, Australia, 1966-67, Inst. Phys. Chemistry, Polish Acad. Scis., 1973, Korea Advanced Inst. Sci., Seoul, 1974, Inst. Theoretical Physics, Ukrainian Acad. Scis., 1989; vis. prof. physics Nat. U. La Plata, Argentina, 1973; sabbatical visitor IBM Watson Rsch. Ctr., Yorktown Heights, N.Y., 1973-74; mem. evaluation panel Commn. Human Resources, NRC, 1976; vis. prof. chemistry U. Utah, 1976; Manuel Sandoval Vallarta Disting. vis. prof. physics Univ. Autonoma Met., Mex., 1985-86, 88; vis. prof. chem. physics U. Pisa, Italy, 1989; vis. prof. Scoula Normale Superiore, Pisa, Italy, 1989; adj. prof. applied math. and physics U. Waterloo, 1969-85; mem. adv. bd. Chem. Abstracts Svc., 1981-83; vis. prof. chemistry, math, and physics U. Guelph, Can., 1991; adj. prof. chemistry and math. U. Utah, 1990—; adj. prof. physics Utah State U., 1990-93; hon. prof. chemistry U. Hong Kong, 1992—; Juan de Oyarzabal prof. physics Univ. Autonoma Met., Mex., 1993-95; Henry Eyring lectr. U. Utah, 1994. Author: Statistical Mechanics and Dynamics, 1964, 2d rev. edit., 1982; editor: Physical Chemistry-An Advanced Treatise, Vols. 1-15, 1966-75, Theoretical Chemistry-Advances and Perspectives, Vols. 1-5, 1975-81, Fundamentals of Inhomogeneous Fluids, 1992; assoc. editor: Jour. Chem. Physics, 1974-76, mem. editl. bd., 1990-92; bd. editors Ultitas Mathematica, 1971-87, Jour. Phys. Chemistry, 1984-89, Jour. Chem. Phys., 1990-92; assoc. editor Electrochimica Acta, 1991—; contbr. over 375 articles to profl. jours. Missionary Ch. Jesus Christ Latter Day Saints, Africa, 1957-59; vol. Loma Prieta Vol. Fire Dept., Los Gatos, Calif., 1983-89. Fellow Corning Glass Found., 1959, Alfred P. Sloan Found., 1964, 66, Ian Potter Found., 1966, CSIRO Rsch., 1966, Guggenheim Found., 1997; Univ. Great War scholar, 1953, Daniel Buchanan scholar, 1955, Burbridge scholar, 1955; recipient Johnathan Rodgers award, 1954, NRC of Can. Bursary award, 1956, IBM Outstanding Rsch. Contbn. award, 1973, IBM Outstanding Innovation award, 1987, Catedra Patrimoniales de Excelencia, Mex., 1993-95. Fellow Inst. Physics, Am. Phys. Soc., Am. Inst. Chemists; mem. Can. Assn. Physicists, Am. Chem. Soc. (Joel Henry Hildebrand award 1999), Mex. Nat. Acad. Sci. (corr.), Math. Assn. Am., N.Y. Acad. Scis., Phi Kappa Phi, Sigma Xi, Sigma Pi

Sigma. Democrat. Achievements include statistical mechanics of liquids; co-developer first successful perturbation theory of liquids; intermolecular forces; phase changes; statis. mechanics of surfaces and solid-fluid and liquid-vapor interfaces; structure and electronic properties of amorphous solids; theory of electric double layer; theory of selectivity and transport of ions in biological membranes. Office: Brigham Young U Dept Chemistry Provo UT 84602

HENDERSON, JAI, museum director; Exec. dir. Calif. Afro-Am. Mus., L.A. Office: Calif Afro-Am Mus Expedition Park 600 State Dr Los Angeles CA 90037-1267

HENDERSON, JAMES, JR. former state legislator, political consultant; b. Ganado, Ariz., May 16, 1942; m. Deborah Henderson; children: Valencia, Clarissa, Jaime Jamesina, Marcus. Cert. in career counseling, Utah State U., 1962. Employment svcs. mgr. Ariz. Dept. Econ. Security-Employment Svcs., Phoenix, 1968-74; vocat. devel. specialist Bur. Indian Affairs, Ft. Defiance, Ariz., 1974-77; dir. divsn. resources The Navajo Tribe, 1977-84, dir. office legis. affairs, 1986-90; senator State of Ariz., 1990-98; cons., 1998—. With U.S. Army, 1966-68. Decorated Purple Heart; recipient Feed My People Internat. award, 1990, Outstanding Svc. award Navajo Nat. Coun. Resolution, 1990, Chief Manuelito Appreciation award Navajo Tribal Coun. Democrat. Presbyterian. Avocations: boxing, football, wildlife, travel. Office: PO Box 4588 Window Rock AZ 86515-4588

HENDERSON, JOHN DREWS, architect; b. St. Louis, July 30, 1933; s. Russell Dewey and Hazel Agnes (Drews) H.; m. Barbara Lee Beckman, June 25, 1955; children: Susan Lee, John Beckman. BArch, U. Ill., 1956. Registered architect, Calif. With Delawie, Macy & Henderson, San Diego, 1966-77, Macy, Henderson & Cole, AIA, San Diego, 1977-86; pres. John D. Henderson, FAIA, 1986—. Mem. San Diego Hist. Sites Bd., 1972-78, Gaslamp Quarter Task Force, 1976-78, Gaslamp Quarter Coun., 1984-86; mem. City Mgr.'s Com. for Seismic Retrofit for Older Bldgs., 1986-92; bd. dirs. Hist. Am. Bldgs. Survey Found., 1984-86; Calif. Hist. Bldgs. Code Safety Bd., 1976-96; apptd. by Gov. of Calif. to State Hist. Resources Commn., 1990-94, reapptd., 1994-98, 98-02, chmn. 1992-93, 2000-01, chmn. Calif. Heritage Fund com. 1993—; Calif. advisor Nat. Trust Hist. Preservation, 1975-78; chmn. adv. bd. Hist. Am. Bldgs. Survey, 1976-78; bd. dirs. Gaslamp Quarter Found., 1984-86. Lt. USN, 1956-59. Recipient Hist. Preservation awards from City San Diego, San Diego Hist. Soc., San Diego chpt. and Calif. Coun. AIA, La Jolla Women's Club, Am. Assn. State and Local History, Am. Inst. Planners, Save Our Heritage Orgn., Rancho Santa Fe Assn., Calif. Preservation Found., Ctrl. City Assn., Gaslmp Quarter Assn. Fellow AIA (officer, dir. local chpt. 1969-73, chpt. pres. 1972, editor guidebooks 1970, 76, state bd. dirs. 1971-73, nat. hist. resources com. 1974-76, 78, Calif. regional rep. 1976-78); mem. San Diego Archtl. Found. (bd. dirs. 1984-86, 89-91, emeritus 1999—), San Diego Hist. Soc. (officer, bd. dirs. 1975, pres. 1975), San Diego History Campaign (exec. com. 1981-86), Coronado Men's Golf Club, San Diego Host Golf Club. Republican. Presbyterian. Home and Office: John D Henderson FAIA 4879 Academy St San Diego CA 92109-3460 E-mail: jhende@tns.net

HENDERSON, KAREN SUE, psychologist; b. Bloomington, Ill., Mar. 25, 1946; d. Charles Lewis and Faye Lanore (Wantland) Henderson; m. David Thomas Biggs, Dec. 2, 1967 (div. 1972); m. Dean Eugene Dixon Jr., Jan. 13, 1973 (div. 1995); children: Christopher, Matthew; m. William Wayne Riggs, May 19, 1998. BA, U. Calif., Berkeley, 1966; MS, San Jose (Calif.) State Coll., 1971; PhD, Union Inst., 1991. Lic. clin. psychol., Alaska; cert. C.C. tchr.; registered play therapist and supr. Pvt. practice pvt. practice, Anchorage, 1980—; cons. Alaska Youth and Parent Found., Anchorage, 1989—, Kenai Peninsula Counseling Svcs., 1995-2000, Parents United, Anchorage, 1989; mental health cons. Rural Alaska Community Action Program, Anchorage, 1988; cons., mem. adolescent treatment team Charter North Hosp., Anchorage, 1985-88; cons. Infant Impaired Hearing Program, Anchorage, 1984-85, Parent Tng. Ctr., Anchorage, 1980-82; psychiat. social worker Langdon Psychiat. Clinic, Anchorage, 1976-80; instr. in psychology U. Alaska Community Coll., Anchorage, 1974-81; parole agt. narcotic outpatient program State Dept. Corrections, Oakland, Calif., 1972-74; group counselor II, caseworker Alameda County Probation Dept., Oakland, 1971-72; adj. prof. U. Alaska, Anchorage, 1999-2000. Adj. prof. U. Alaska, Anchorage, 1994-95; cons. psychologist Alviso (Calif.) Econ. Devel. Program, 1971-72; instr. psychology Coll. of Alameda, 1973; faculty adv. for coop. edn. U. Alaska C.C., 1975-76. Sec., liaison to bd. Susitna Sch. PTA, Anchorage, 1983-84; co-chmn. optional bd. Susitna Sch., 1984-85, chmn., 1985-86, vol. coord., 1988-89; mem. adv. bd. Steller Alt. Sch., 1992-95. Mem. APA, Alaska Psychol. Assn. Democrat. Avocations: running, reading, camping, travel, bridge. Office: 912 W 6th Ave Anchorage AK 99501-2024

HENDERSON, PAUL BARGAS, JR. economic development consultant, educator; b. McKees Rocks, Pa., Nov. 20, 1928; s. Paul Bargas and Viola Mae (Mullins) Henderson; m. Betty D. Langewisch, Aug. 25, 1951; children: Keith, Karen, Laura. B.S. in Mech. and Indsl. Engring., Washington U., St. Louis, 1948, M.S. in Bus. Adminstrn., 1950; Ph.D. in Indsl. Econs., MIT, 1960. Asst. for mgmt. U.S. Navy Bur. Ordnance, Washington, 1950-58; mgr. sys. tech. Westinghouse Electric Corp., Pitts., 1960-67; program mgr. United Aircraft Corp., Hartford, Conn., 1967-68; dir. data services Allis-Chalmers Corp., Milw., 1968-74; v.p. Fed. Res. Bank N.Y., N.Y.C., 1974-77, sr. v.p., 1977-82, sr. adviser, 1982-84; bank ops. cons. N.Y.C., 1984—; econ. devel. cons. in Russia, chmn. Sierra Caucasus Corp., 1990-2001; exec. dir. United Meth. Econ. Devel. Initiative in Kazakstan, 1996—; asst. prof. econs. Sierra Nevada Coll., Incline Village, Nev., 1997-2001. Bd. dirs. Direct Svcs., Inc., Found. for Ednl. Field Svcs. Author: (with E.M. Heigler) Library Automation, 1970, Electronic Funds Transfers and Payments: The Public Policy Issues, 1987; inventor in field. Bd. dirs. Cal-Nov conf. United Meth. Found.; mem. investment com., con. on fin. and adminstrn. United Meth. Ch. Office: 336 Cameron Station Blvd Alexandria VA 22304-8623

HENDERSON, RICKEY HENLEY, professional baseball player; b. Chgo., Dec. 25, 1958; With minor league baseball clubs, 1976-79; with Oakland Athletics, 1979-84, 89-93, 94-95, N.Y. Yankees, 1985-89, Toronto Blue Jays, 1993-94, San Diego Padres, 1996-98, New York Mets, 1998-2000, Seattle Mariners, 2000—. Winner Am. League Gold Glove, 1981; named Most Valuable Player, American League, 1990, Am. League All-Star team, 1980, 82-88, 90-91. Sporting News Am. League All-Star Team, 1981, 85, 90, Sporting News Am. League Silver Slugger Team, 1981, 85, 90, Sporting News Silver Shoe award, 1982, Sporting News Golden Shoe award, 1983, Am. Championship Series MVP, 1989. Achievements including holding a major league record for stolen bases in one season (130), 1982, for most stolen bases in career; player World Series 1989, 90, 93. Office: Seattle Mariners Safeco Field PO Box 4100 Seattle WA 98104

HENDERSON, ROGENE FAULKNER, toxicologist, researcher; b. [illegible] (Rogers) F.; m. Thomas Richard Henderson II, May 30, 1957; children: Thomas Richard III, Edith Jeanette, Laura Lee. BSBA, Tex. Christian U., 1955; PhD, U. Tex., 1960. Diplomate Am. Bd. Toxicology. Research assoc. U. Ark. Sch. Med., Little Rock, 1960-67; from scientist to sr. scientist and group supr. chemistry and toxicology Lovelace Inhalation Toxicology Research Inst., Albuquerque, 1967—; deputy dir. Nat. Environ. Respiratory Ctr. Lovelace Respiratory Rsch. Inst., Albuquerque, 1998—. Mem. adv. [illegible] Burroughs Wellcome Toxicology Scholar award 1987-89 NIH toxicology study sect., 1982-86, Nat. Inst. Environ. Health Scis. adv. coun., 1992-95, EPA scientific adv. bd. environ. health commn., 1991-95. Assoc. editor Toxicology Applied Pharmacology, 1989-95, Jour. Exposure Analysis and Environ. Epidemiology, 1991-95; contbr. articles to profl. jours. Named Woman on the Move YWCA, Albuquerque, 1985; grantee NIH, 1958-60, 1960-62, 1986—. Mem. AAAS, NAS (bd. on environ. studies and toxicology 1998—), Am. Chem. Soc. (chmn. ctrl. N.Mex. sect. 1981), Soc. Toxicology (pres. Mountain-West Regional chpt. 1985-86, pres. inhalation specialty sect. 1989—), N.Y. Acad. Scis., Nat. Acad. Scis. (com. toxicology 1985-98, chair 1992-98, com. epidemiology of air pollution 1983-85, com. biol. markers 1986—, com. on risk assessment methodology 1989-92, bd. environ. studies and toxicology 1998—). Presbyterian. Home: 5609 Don Felipe Ct SW Albuquerque NM 87105-6765 Office: Lovelace Inhalation Toxicology Rsch Inst PO Box 5890 Albuquerque NM 87185-5890 E-mail: rhenders@lrri.org

HENDERSON, THELTON EUGENE, federal judge; b. Shreveport, La., Nov. 28, 1933; s. Eugene M. and Wanzie (Roberts) H.; 1 son, Geoffrey A. B.A., U. Calif.-, Berkeley, 1956, J.D., 1962. Bar: Calif. 1962. Atty. U.S. Dept. Justice, 1962-63; assoc. firm FitzSimmons & Petris, 1964, assoc., 1964-66; directing atty. San Mateo County (Calif.) Legal Aid Soc., 1966-69; asst. dean Stanford (Calif.) U. Law Sch., 1968-76; ptnr. firm Rosen, Remcho & Henderson, San Francisco, 1977-80; judge U.S. Dist. Ct. (no. dist.) Calif., San Francisco, 1980-90, 98—, chief judge, 1990-97. Asso. prof. Sch. Law, Golden Gate U., San Francisco, 1978-80 Served with U.S. Army, 1956-58. Mem. ABA, Nat. Bar Assn., Charles Houston Law Assn. Office: US Dist Ct US Courthouse PO Box 36060 San Francisco CA 94102

HENDREN, ROBERT LEE, JR. academic administrator; b. Reno, Oct. 10, 1925; s. Robert Lee and Aleen (Hill) H.; m. Merlyn Churchill, June 14, 1947; children: Robert Lee IV, Anne Aleen. BA magna cum laude, LLD (hon.), Coll. Idaho; postgrad., Army Univ. Ctr., Oahu, Hawaii. Owner, pres. Hendren's Inc., 1947—; pres. Albertson Coll. Idaho, Caldwell, 1987—. Bd. dirs. 1st Interstate Bank Idaho. Trustee Boise (Idaho) Ind. Sch. Dist., chmn. bd. trustees, 1966; chmn. bd. trustees Coll. Idaho, 1980-84; bd. dirs. Mountain View coun. Boy Scouts Am., Boise Retail Merchants, Boise Valley Indsl. Found., Boise Redevel. Agy., Ada County Marriage Counseling, Ada County Planning and Zoning Com.; chmn. bd. Blue Cross Idaho. Recipient Silver and Gold award U. Idaho, Nat. award Sigma Chi. Mem. Boise C. of C. (pres., bd. dirs.), Idaho Sch. Trustees Assn., Masons, KT, Shriners, Rotary (Paul Harris fellow). Home: 3504 Hillcrest Dr Boise ID 83705-4503 Office: Albertson Coll Idaho 2112 Cleveland Blvd Caldwell ID 83605-4432

HENDRICK, HAL WILMANS, human factors educator; b. Dallas, Mar. 11, 1933; s. Harold Eugene and Audrey Sarah (Wilmans) H.; m. Mary Francis Boyle; children: Hal L., David A., John A. (dec.), Jennifer G. BA, Ohio Wesleyan U., 1955; MS, Purdue U., 1961, PhD, 1966. Cert. profl. ergonomist; bd. cert. forensic examiner. Asst. prof. U. So. Calif., L.A., assoc. prof., 1979-86; exec. dir. Inst. of Safety and Systems Mgmt., U. So. Calif., L.A., 1986-87; prof., dean Coll. of System Sci., U. Denver, 1987-90; prof. U. So. Calif., 1986-95, prof. emeritus, 1995—; prin. Hendrick and Assocs., 1996—. Pres. Bd. Cert. in Profl. Ergonomics, 1992-94. Author: Behavioral Research and Analysis, 1980, 2d edit., 1989, 3rd edit., 1990, Macroergonomics: An Introduction to Work System Design, 2001, Good Ergomomics is Good Economics, 1996; editor 10 books; contbr. articles to profl. jours. Lt. col. USAF, 1956-76. Fellow APA, Am. Psychol. Soc., Human Factors Ergonomics Soc. (pres. L.A. chpt. 1986-87, pres. Rocky Mountain chpt. 1989-90, 95-96); mem. Internat. Ergonomics Assn. (pres. Geneva 1990-94, immediate past pres. 1994-97, sec. gen. 1987-89, exec. com. 1984—, U.S. rep. 1981-87), Ergonomics Soc. (U.K.), Soc. for Indsl. and Orgnl. Psychology. Democrat. Avocations: travel, camping, hiking, reading, fishing. Home and Office: 7100 E Crestline Ave Englewood CO 80111-1600 E-mail: hhendrick@aol.com

HENDRICK, IRVING GUILFORD, education educator; b. L.A., Aug. 30, 1936; s. Guilford and Ingeborg Johanna (Eid) H.; m. Sandra Lee Scheer, Aug. 16, 1958 (dec. Aug. 1994); children: Julie Lynn, Maralene Ayn, Stephanie Lee; m. Linda DeSoucey Scott, 1996; stepchildren: Denise Levesque, Eve Scott. AB, Whittier Coll., 1958, MA, 1960; EdD with honors, UCLA, 1964. Asst. prof. edn. U. Mich., Flint, 1964-65, U. Calif., Riverside, 1965-69, assoc. prof. edn., 1969-75, prof. edn., 1975—, chair dept. edn., 1970-75, assoc. dean Sch. of Edn., 1975-83, dean Sch. of Edn., 1987-98, asst. vice chancellor of devel., 1998—, dean emeritus. Mem. com. on planning & budget U. Calif. Sys., 1985-87, vice-chair com. on planning & budget, 1986-87, chair subcom. on pvt. devel. activities, 1986-87, chair, 1987-88; mem. subject A com. U. Calif.-Riverside, 1966-68, vice-chair con. on ednl. policy, 1972-73, mem. com. on courses, 1969-71, chair, 1972-73, mem. com. on coms., 1973-74, mem. acad. planning com., 1973-75, chair acad. planning com., 1974-75, mem. budget com. resources sect., 1984-87, chair budget com. resources sect. 1984-87, mem. adv. com., 1974-75, 85-87, mem. highlander awards com., 1967-71, search com. for dean of grad. divsn., 1974, chair com. on faculty devel., 1977-78, learning handicapped credential programs, 1984—, chair exec. vice chancellor search com., 1985, acad. program planning rev. bd. sub-com. on organized rsch., 1986, pres.'s com. on profl. edn., 1988-89, pres.'s budget adv. com., 1987, chair adv. com. on instrnl. tech., 1994—; chancellor's rep. citizen's adv. com. Univ. Area Comty. Plan, Riverside, 1982-83; profl. day spkr. Internat. Sch. Theology, 1985; adv. com. assembly com. on econ. devel. and new techs. State of Calif., 1983-85; proposal reviewer intermediate sch. coll. readiness program Calif. State U., 1986; chair campaign com. to re-elect Dale Holmes County Supt. of Schs., Riverside County, 1990; cons. Riverside County Commn. on Future of Edn., 1993; mem. com. accreditation Calif. Commn. on Tchr. Credentialing, 1995-90, chair, co-chair, 1995-97; presenter papers at numerous profl. meetings. Author: Academic Revolution in California, 1968, Development of a School Integration Plan in Riverside, California: A Hisotry and Perspective, 1968, Public Policy Toward the Education of Non-white Minority Group Children in California, 1848-1970, 1975, The Education of Non-Whites in California, 1848-1970, 1977, California Educations, 1980; co-editor: (with Reginald L. Jones) Student Dissent in the Schools, 1972; contbr. articles to profl. jours.; contbr. book revs. to profl. jours. including History of Edn. Quar., Pacific Hist. Rev., Calif. History, So. Calif. Quar., Jour. Ednl. Adminstrn. and History. Mem. Am. Ednl. Rsch. Assn. (divsn. F editl. com. 1981-82, co-chair divsn. F program ann. program com. 1983-85, chair nominating com. divsn. F 1977, 79, sec. divsn. F 1976-78), Am. Hist. Assn. (Pacific Coast br.), Calif. Coun. on Edn. of Tchrs. (bd. dirs. 1989-93, chair programs com. fall 1991 conf.), Coun. for Exceptional Children (com. on history of individual differences 1985, cons. on oral history project, guest reviewer of manuscripts), History of Edn. Soc. (program com. 1986, nominating com. 1981-82), Nat. Soc. for Study of Edn. (com. on expansion of soc. activities 1972), Pacific Coast History of Edn. Soc. (program chair 1985), So. Assn. of Schs. and Colls. (sr. coll. [illegible] on-site visitation com. Walden U 1980), Western Assn. Schs. and Colls. (sr. coll. commn., on-site visitation com. mem. various univs.), Phi Delta Kappa (historian, mem. exec. com. Riverside chpt. 1976-78). Democrat. Lutheran. Achievements include research in history of education, specifically the history of teacher education and education of minority groups, as well as extension of public school's mission to include responsibility for education and training of learning disabled and mentally retarded children. Avocations: tennis, running. Office: U Calif Sch Edn Riverside CA 92521-0001

HENDRICK, JAMES T. lawyer; b. Fostoria, Ohio, Mar. 21, 1942; BA with honors and distinction in econs., U. Ill., 1963; JD, Harvard U., 1967. Bar: Ill. 1967, Calif. 1970. Ptnr. Thelen, Reid & Priest (formerly known as Thelen, Marrin, Johnson & Bridges), San Francisco, 1978—. Lt. USNR JAG, 1968-71. Mem. ABA. Office: Thelen Reid & Priest 101 2nd St Ste 1800 San Francisco CA 94105-3659

HENDRICK, RONALD LYNN, controller; b. Pontiac, Mich., Mar. 2, 1946; s. James B. and Iva L. (Bostic) H.; m. Terri L. Kellstrom, Nov. 28, 1970; children: Brad, Scott, Tyler. BA in Acctg., Mich. State U., 1969; MBA in Fin., U. Colo., Boulder, 1972. CPA, Colo. Staff acct. Arthur Young & Co., Detroit, 1969-71; controller, treas. Myers and Co./Coors Packaging Co., Boulder, 1972-76; group v.p., treas. Coors Distbg. Co., Denver, 1976-83; v.p., treas. Life Care Svcs., Inc., Boulder, 1983-84; pres. Advantage Health Systems, Golden, Colo., 1984-87; dir. treasury mgmt. Adolph Coors Co., Golden, 1987-89, v.p., corp. contr., asst. sec., 1989—. Bd. dirs. World Trade Ctr. Mem. investment, audit and ops. coms. U. Colo. Found., Boulder, 1989—. With U.S. Army Res., 1969-75. Mem. AICPA, Nat. Assn. Accts., Nat. Investor Rels. Inst., Fin. Execs. Inst. Office: Heska Corp 1613 Prospect Pkwy Fort Collins CO 80525

HENDRICKS, CHRIS, publishing executive; Pres., pub. Nando Media, Raleigh, N.C.; v.p., interactive media The McClatchy Co., Sacramento, 1999—. Office: The McClatchy Co 2100 Q St Sacramento CA 95816-6816

HENDRICKSON, ANITA ELIZABETH, biology educator; b. LaCross, Wis., Feb. 20, 1936; d. Walter V. and Alno (Larkin) Schnell; m. Morris N. Hendrickson, June 8, 1957; children: Lisa, Karin, Gordon. BA, Pacific Luth. Coll., 1957; PhD, U. Wash., Seattle, 1964. Instr. anatomy Northwestern Med. Sch., Chgo., 1964-65; rsch. assoc. Children's Meml. Hosp., Chgo., 1964-65; rsch. instr. dept. biol. structure U. Wash., Seattle, 1965-67, instr. dept. ophthalmology, 1967-69, asst. prof. dept. ophthalmology, 1969-73; affiliate/assoc. prof. dept. ophthalmology Reg. Primate Ctr./U. Wash., 1972—, 1973-81; affiliate Child Devel. & Mental Retardation Ctr., U. Wash., 1975; prof. dept. opthalmology U. Wash., 1981-97, prof. dept. biol. structure, 1984—, chair dept. biol. structure, 1994—, adj. prof. ophthalmology, 1997—. Vis. assoc. prof. neuropathology Harvard Med. Sch., Boston, 1975-76; adj. assoc. prof. dept. psychology U. Wash., 1975-78; mem. NIH VisB study section, 1976-80. Editorial bd. Jour. of Neurosci., 1982-88, Investigative Ophthalmology, 1977-82, Vision Research, 1990-95; contbr. articles to profl. jours. Dolly Green rsch. grantee, 1981; named Alumnus of the Yr., Pacific Luth. U., 1982. Mem. AAAS, Am. Assn. Anatomists, Soc. for Neurosci. (mem. nat. coun. 1982-86), Internat. Soc. for Eye Rsch., Assn. for Rsch. in Vision and Ophthalmology (prog. chmn. 1983-84, trustee 1993—), Cajal Club. Home: 1029C NE 120th St Seattle WA 98125-5003 Office: U Washington Dept Biol Structure Box 357420 Seattle WA 98195-7420

HENDRICKSON, THOMAS T. retail executive; b. 1955; V.p., contr. Millers Outpost Stores, 1987-93; v.p. fin. ops. Sportmart, 1993, CFO, 1993-95, sr. v.p., CFO, 1995-96, exec. v.p., CFO, 1996-98; exec. v.p., CFO, treas. Gart Sports Co., Denver, 1998—. Office: Gart Sports Co 1001 Lincoln Ave Denver CO 80203 Fax: 303-829-1511

HENDRICKX, ANDREW GEORGE, research physiologist; b. Butler, Minn., July 14, 1933; B.S. in Biology, Concordia Coll., Minn., 1959; M.S., Kans. State U., 1961, Ph.D. in Zoology, 1963. Head sect. embryology Southwest Found., San Antonio, 1964-68, assoc. scientist, chmn., 1969; assoc. research physiologist Calif. Primate Research Ctr., Davis, 1969-73, research physiologist, 1973— , assoc. dir., 1978-97, dir., 1987—; prof. Sch. Medicine, U. Calif.-Davis, 1971— ; adviser WHO, 1977— . Author: Embryology of the Baboon, 1971; numerous articles. Served with U.S. Army, 1953-55. NDEA scholar, 1959-62; recipient Disting. Alumni award Concordia Coll., 1977. Mem. Teratology Soc. (sec. 1979-83, pres. 1987), Am. Soc. Primatologists (pres. 1982-84), AAUP, Am. Assn. Anatomists, Internat. Soc. Primatologists, others. Office: U Calif Calif Primate Rsch Ctr Davis CA 95616

HENDRIX, LYNN PARKER, lawyer; b. McCook, Nebr., Apr. 24, 1951; s. Jack Hall and Betty Lee (Parker) H.; m. Theresa Louise Zabawa, June 19, 1976; children: Paige Ashley, Parker Jerome, Pierce Reid. BSEE, U. Nebr., 1973, JD with distinction, 1978. Bar: Nebr. 1978, U.S. Dist. Ct. Nebr. 1978, Colo. 1979, U.S. Dist. Ct. Colo. 1979, U.S. Ct. Appeals (10th cir.) 1993, Wyo. 1993, Mont. 1995, N.Y., 2000, U.S. Patent Office, 1994. Surveyor Nebr. Dept. Roads, McCook, 1973; constrn. adminstr. Commonwealth Electric Co., Lincoln, Nebr., 1974, cons. engr., 1975; instr. U. Nebr., Lincoln, 1974-75; law clk. Nebr. Atty.-Gen., Lincoln, 1976-77; assoc. Holme Robert & Owen, LLP, Denver, 1978-83; ptnr. Holme Robert & Owen, Denver, 1984—. Editor-in-chief Nebr. Law Rev., 1977-78, exec. editor, 1976-77; contbr. articles to profl. jours. Sec., bd. dirs. Girls Club Denver, 1984-90, Girls Inc. of Metro Denver, 1992-94; trustee Rocky Mountain Minn. Law Found. Mem. ABA, Colo. Bar Assn., Mont. Bar Assn., Nebr. Bar Assn., Wyo. Bar Assn., S.E. Law Club (pres. 1990-91), Meridian Golf Club, Tau Beta Pi, Sigma Tau (pres.), Eta Kappa Nu. Home: 8125 S Glencoe Ct Littleton CO 80122-3876 Office: Holme Roberts & Owen LLP 1700 Lincoln St Ste 4100 Denver CO 80203-4541

HENG, DONALD JAMES, JR. lawyer; b. Mpls., July 12, 1944; s. Donald James and Catharine Amelia (Strom) H.; m. Kathleen Ann Bailey, Sept. 2, 1967; 1 child, Francesca Remy BA cum laude, Yale U., 1967; JD magna cum laude, Minn., 1971. Bar: Calif. 1971, U.S. Dist. Ct. (no. dist.) Calif. 1971, U.S. Ct. Appeals (9th cir.) 1971. Assoc. Brobeck, Phleger & Harrison, San Francisco, 1971-73, ptnr., 1978-90; atty.-adviser Office Internat. Tax Counsel, Dept. Treasury, Washington, 1973-75; pvt. practice law San Francisco, 1990—. Lectr., writer on tax-related subjects Note and comment editor Minn. Law Rev., 1970-71 Co-recipient award for outstanding performance Am. Lawyer Mag., 1981; Fulbright scholar, Italy, 1967-68 Mem. ABA, Calif. Bar Assn., Oakland Mus. Assn. (pres. 1985-87, bd. dirs. 1983-89), Mus. Soc. San Francisco, Fine Arts Mus. (bd. dirs. 1989-90), Order Coif. Republican. Congregationalist Office: 388 Market St Ste 500 San Francisco CA 94111-5313

HENGSTLER, GARY ARDELL, publisher, editor, lawyer; b. Wapakoneta, Ohio, Mar. 23, 1947; s. Luther C. and N. Delphine (Sims) H.; m. Linda K. Spreen, Mar. 8, 1969 (div. Aug. 1986); children: Dylan A., Joel S.; m. Laura M. Williams, Dec. 15, 1986. BS, Ball State U., 1969; JD, Cleve. State U., 1983. Bar: Ohio 1984, U.S. Dist. Ct. (no. dist.) Ohio 1984. Assoc. Blaszak, Schilling, Coey & Bennett, Elyria, Ohio, 1984-85; editor The Tex. Lawyer, Austin, 1985-86; news editor ABA Jour., Chgo., 1986-89, editor, pub., 1989-2000; dir. Donald W. Reynolds Nat. Ctr. Cts. & Media, Reno, 2000—. Home: 5055 Carnoustie Dr Reno NV 89502-9724 Office: Donald W Reynolds Nat Ctr Cts & Media U Nev Jud Coll Bldg 358 Reno NV 89557-0001 Fax: 775 327 2160. E-mail: hengstler@judges.org

HENKEL, CATHY, newspaper sports editor; [illegible] 1120 John St Seattle WA 98109-5321

HENLEY, DALE C. grocery company executive; b. Mt. Vernon, Wash., 1946; V.p. Trillium Corp., Bellingham, Wash.; mng. ptnr. Metcalf, Hodges & Co., Bellingham; sr. v.p., CFO, Haggen Inc., Bellingham, 1984-96, pres., CEO, 1996—. Office: Haggen Inc 2211 Rimland Dr Bellingham WA 98226-5664 Fax: 360-650-8235

HENLEY, DON, singer, drummer, songwriter; b. Linden, Tex., 1948; m. Sharon Summerall, May 20, 1995. Drummer with band Eagles, L.A., performer in numerous albums including The Eagles, 1972, Desperado, 1973, On the Border, 1974, One These Nights, 1975, Hotel California, 1976, The Long Run, 1979, Hell Freezes Over, 1994; solo performer, singer, composer albums I Can't Stand Still, 1982, Building the Perfect Beast, 1985 (Grammy award for song The Boys of Summer), The End of Innocence, 1989, Actual Miles: Henley's Greatest Hits, 1995; songs include Dirty Laundry, 1982, Long Way Home, I Will Not Go Quietly, New York Minute, If Dirt Were Dollars, Little Tin God, The Heart of the Matter. Active So. Poverty Law Ctr., Walden Woods Project. Named to Songwriters' Hall of Fame, 2000. Office: c/o Lisa Barbaris Geffen Records 9130 W Sunset Blvd West Hollywood CA 90069-3110

HENLEY, ERNEST MARK, physics educator, university dean emeritus; b. Frankfurt, Germany, June 10, 1924; came to U.S., 1939, naturalized, 1944; s. Fred S. and Josy (Dreyfuss) H.; m. Elaine Dimitman, Aug. 21, 1948; children: M. Bradford, Karen M. B.E.E., CCNY, 1944; Ph.D., U. Calif. at Berkeley, 1952. Physicist Lawrence Radiation Lab., 1950-51; research assoc. physics dept. Stanford U., 1951-52; lectr. physics Columbia U., 1952-54; mem. faculty U. Wash., Seattle, 1954—, prof. physics, 1961-95; prof. emeritus, 1995—; chmn. dept. U. Wash., 1973-76, dean Coll. Arts and Scis., 1979-87, dir. Inst. for Nuclear Theory, 1990-91; assoc. dir. Inst. for Nuclear Theory U. Wash., 1991—. Rschr., author numerous publs. on symmetries, nuclear reactions, weak interactions and high energy particle interactions; chmn. Nuclear Sci. Adv. Com., 1986-89. Author: (with W. Thirring) Elementary Quantum Field Theory, 1962, (with H. Frauenfelder) Subatomic Physics, 1974, 2nd edit. 1991, Nuclear and Particle Physics, 1975. Bd. dirs. Pacific Sci. Ctr., 1984-87, Wash. Tech. Ctr., 1983-87; trustee Associated Univs., Inc., 1989—, chmn. bd., 1993-96. Recipient sr. Alexander von Humboldt award, 1984, T.W. Bonner prize Am. Physics Soc., 1989, Townsend Harris medal CCNY, 1989; F.B. Jewett fellow, 1952-53, NSF sr. fellow, 1958-59, Guggenheim fellow, 1967-68, NATO sr. fellow, 1976-77. Fellow AAAS (chmn. physics sect. 1989-90), Am. Phys. Soc. (chmn. div. nuclear physics 1979-80, pres. 1992), Am. Acad. Arts and Scis.; mem. NAS (chmn. physics sect. 1998-2001), Sigma Xi. Office: Univ Wash Physics Dept PO Box 351560 Seattle WA 98195-1560 E-mail: henley@phys.washington.edu

HENLEY, JEFFREY O. computer software company executive; b. Phoenix, Nov. 6, 1948; s. Justin Oniel and Jane Ellen (Rice) H.; children: Amy, Julie, Todd B.A., U. Calif.-Santa Barbara, 1966; M.B.A., UCLA, 1967. Cost acctg. supr. Hughes Aircraft Co., Culver City, CA, 1967-70; div. controller Tridair Industries, Redondo Beach, Calif., 1970-72, Fairchild Camera & Instrument, Mountain View, 1972-75; dir. fin. Memorex Corp., Santa Clara, 1975-79; v.p., controller Saga Corp, Menlo Park, 1979-86, exec. v.p., CFO, 1986-91, Pacific Holding Co., Menlo Park, Calif., 1986—; pres. Fast Service Restaurant Group, Menlo Park, from 1985; exec. v.p., CFO Oracle Corp., Redwood City, 1991—. Bd. dirs. Herbert Hoover Boys' & Girls' Club, Menlo Park, Calif., 1983, pres., 1984—. Mem. Fin. Exec. Inst., Sigma Phi Epsilon Republican. Presbyterian Avocations: golf, running. Home: 51 Monte Vista Ave Atherton CA 94027-5430 Office: Oracle Corp 500 Oracle Pkwy 5 Redwood City CA 94065-1675

HENN, MICHAEL, financial executive, home building company; BS in Fin., MBA in Fin., Northern Ill. U. Exec. v.p., CFO The Vons Cos., Inc., 1978; sr. v.p., CFO Kaufman & Broad Home Corp. Office: Kaufman & Broad Home 10990 Wilshire Blvd Fl 7 Los Angeles CA 90024-3913

HENNINGS, LAURY H. lawyer; b. 1946; BA, Willamette U.; JD, Northwestern U. Bar: Oreg. 1976. Office: US Bancorp 111 SW Fifth Ave Fl T2 Portland OR 97204

HENNION, REEVE LAWRENCE, communications executive; b. Ventura, Calif., Dec. 7, 1941; s. Tom Reeve and Evelyn Edna (Henry) H.; m. Carolyn Laird, Sept. 12, 1964; children: Jeffrey Reeve, Douglas Laird. B.A., Stanford U., 1963, M.A., 1965. Reporter Tulare (Calif.) Advance-Register, 1960-62; reporter UPI, San Francisco, 1963-66, mgr. Fresno, Calif., 1966-68, regional exec. Los Angeles, 1968-69, mgr. Honolulu, 1969-72, San Francisco, 1972-75, Calif. editor, 1975-77, gen. news editor, 1977-81, bus. mgr., 1981-83, v.p., gen. mgr. Pacific div., 1983-85; v.p., gen. mgr. Calif. Oreg. Broadcasting, Inc., 1985-86; pres. Viatech Inc., 1986-92, propr. Buncom Ranch; pres. Keypoint Svcs. Internat., Inc., Medford, Oreg., 1992—; interim exec. dir. Rogue Valley Coun. of Govts., 1998. Editor: The Modoc Country, 1971, Buncom: Crossroads Station, 1995. Chmn. Calif. Freedom of Info. Com., 1983-84; mem. Jackson County Planning Commn., Jackson County Roads Com.; mayor of Buncom, Oreg.; pres. Buncom Hist. Soc.; trustee So. Oreg. Hist. Soc. Mem. Am. Planning Assn. (exec. bd. Oreg. chpt.), Delta Kappa Epsilon. Home: 3232 Little Applegate Rd Jacksonville OR 97530-9303 Office: PO Box 4518 Medford OR 97501-0178

HENRIKSEN, MELVIN, mathematician, educator; b. N.Y.C., N.Y., Feb. 23, 1927; s. Kaj and Helen (Kahn) H.; m. Lillian Viola Hill, July 23, 1946 (div. 1964); children— Susan, Richard, Thomas; m. Louise Levitas, June 12, 1964 (dec. Oct. 1997). B.S., Coll. City N.Y., 1948; M.S., U. Wis., 1949, Ph.D. in Math, 1951. Asst. math., then instr. extension div. U. Wis., 1948-51; asst. prof. U. Ala., 1951-52; from instr. to prof. math. Purdue U., 1952-65; prof. math., head dept. Case Inst. Tech., 1965-68; research assoc. U. Calif. at Berkeley, 1968-69; prof., chmn. math. dept. Harvey Mudd Coll., 1969-72, prof., 1972-97, prof. emeritus, 1997—. Mem. Inst. Advanced Study, Princeton, 1956-57, 63-64; vis. prof. Wayne State U., 1960-61; rsch. assoc. U. Man., Winnipeg, Can., 1975-76; vis. prof. Wesleyan U., Middletown, Conn., 1978-79, 82-83, 86-87, 93-94. Author: (with Milton Lees) Single Variable Calculus, 1970; assoc. editor: Algebra Universalis, 1993—, Topology Atlas, 1996—, Topological Commentary, 1996—; author articles on algebra, rings of functions, gen. topology. Sloan fellow, 1956-58 Mem. Am. Math. Soc., Math. Assn. Am. (assoc. editor Am. Math. monthly 1988-91, assoc. editor Algebra Universalis 1993—). Office: Harvey Mudd Coll Math Dept Claremont CA 91711 E-mail: henriksen@hmc.edu

HENRIKSEN, THOMAS HOLLINGER, university official; b. Detroit, Nov. 16, 1939; s. Paul and Irene (Hollinger) H.; m. Margaret Mary Mueller, Sept. 9, 1968; children— Heather Anne, Damien Paul Hollinger B.A., Va. Mil. Inst., 1962; M.A., Mich. State U., 1966, Ph.D., 1969. Asst. prof. SUNY, Plattsburgh, 1969-73, assoc. prof., 1973-79, prof., 1979-80; Peace fellow Hoover Instn. on War, Revolution and Peace Stanford (Calif.) U., 1979-80, research fellow, 1980-82, sr. research fellow, 1982-86, sr. fellow, 1986—, assoc. dir., 1983—, exec. sec. nat. fellows program, 1984—, mem. Pres.'s Commn. on White House fellows, 1987-93. Mem. U.S. Army Sci. Bd., 1984-90. Author: Mozambique: A History, 1978, Revolutiona and Counterrevolution: Mozambique's War of Independence, 1964-74, 1983, The New World Order: War, Peace and Military Preparedness, 1992, Clinton's Foreign Policy in Somalia, Bosnia, Haiti, and North Korea, 1996, Using Power and Diplomacy to Deal With Rogue States, 1999; co-author: The Struggle for Zimbabwe: Battle in the Bush, 1981; contbg. author, editor: Soviet and Chinese Aid to African Nations, 1980; Communist Powers in Sub-Saharan Africa, 1981; assoc. editor Yearbook on Internat. Communist Affairs, 1982-91; contbg. author, editor: One Korea? Challenges and Prospects for Reunification, 1994. Trustee George C. Marshall Found., 1993—. Served to lt. U.S. Army, 1963-65 Home: 177 Lundy Ln Palo Alto CA 94306-4563 Office: Stanford U Hoover Instn Stanford CA 94305

HENRY, CHARLES L. (JERRY), manufacturing executive; b. Chattanooga, 1941; m. Kay Henry; 4 children. BS in Engring. Physics, U. Tenn., 1963. Process engr. DuPont Co., 1963, various positions, 1963-84, v.p. Del., 1984-86, group v.p., 1986-93, exec. v.p., CFO, 1993-96; chmn., pres., CEO Johns Manville Corp., Denver, 1996—. Office: Johns Manville Corp 717 17th St Denver CO 80202

HENRY, KAREN HAWLEY, lawyer; b. Whittier, Calif., Nov. 5, 1943; d. Ralph Hawley and Dorothy Ellen (Carr) Hawley; m. John Dunlap, 1968; m. Charles Gibbons Henry, Mar. 15, 1975; children: Scott, Alexander, Joshua; m. Don H. Phemister, June 21, 1991; children: Justin Phemister, Johnathan Phemister, Keith Phemister. BS in Social Scis., So. Oreg. Coll., 1965; MS in Labor Econs., Iowa State U., 1967; JD, U. Calif., Hastings, 1976. Instr. Medford (Oreg.) Sch. Dist., 1965-66; rsch. asst. dept. econs. Iowa State U., Ames, 1966-67; dir. rsch. program Calif. Nurses Assn., San Francisco, 1967-72; labor rels. coord. Affiliated Hosps. of San Francisco, 1972-79, labor counsel, 1979-88; ptnr. Littler, Mendelson, Fastiff & Tichy, San Francisco, 1979-86; mng. ptnr. labor and employment law Weissburg and Aronson, Inc., San Francisco, 1986-88; prin. Karen H. Henry, Inc., Auburn, Calif., 1991—. Author: Supervisors Guide to Labor Relations, 1981, Supervisor's Legal Guide, 1984, Nursing ADA: Ten Steps to Compliance, 1992, 6th edit., 2001; contbr. articles on employment issues to profl. jours. Mem. State Bar Calif., Thurston Soc., Order of Coif. Office: Karen H Henry Inc 1141 High St Auburn CA 95603-5132

HENRY, KEITH DOUGLAS, architect; b. Winnipeg, Man., Can., Oct. 25, 1957; s. Charles Eric and Ruth Elva (McDonald) H.; m. Elizabeth Anne McNulty, June 19, 1993. B of Environ. Studies, U. Man., Winnipeg, 1978, MArch, 1982. Ptnr. Friggstad Downing Henry Architects-Wilson Bailey Tech., Saskatoon, 1992—. Prin. works include John Paul II Collegiate (Award of Merit Sask. Assn. Architects 1991), Bedford Rd. Collegiate (City of Sask. Heritage award 1996), Can. Nat. Inst. Blind Svc. Ctr. (Award of Excellence Sask. Masonry Inst. 1993). Recipient Marion M. Graham Collegiate award Am. Assn. Sch. Adminstrs./AIA, 1985, Heritage award City of Saskatoon, 1996. Mem. Royal Archtl. Inst. Can., Sask. Assn. Architects (registered, mem. coun. 1993—, pres. 1995-96). Office: Friggstad Architects 2233 Avenue C North Saskatoon SK Canada S7L 5Z2

HENRY, PHILIP LAWRENCE, marketing professional; b. Los Angeles, Dec. 1, 1940; s. Lawrence Langworthy and Ella Hanna (Martens) H.; m. Claudia Antonia Huff, Aug. 9, 1965 (div. 1980); children: Carolyn Marie, Susan Michelle; m. Carrie Katherine Hoover, Aug. 23, 1985. BS in Marine Engring., Calif. Maritime Acad., 1961. Design engr. Pacific Telephone Co., San Diego, 1963-73; service engr. Worthington Service Corp., San Diego, 1973-78; pres. Realmart Corp., San Diego, 1978-81; dir. mktg. Orbit Inn Hotel and Casino, Las Vegas, 1981-84; pres. Comml. Consultants, Las Vegas, 1984—, Gray Electronics Co., Las Vegas, 1986—. Chmn. bd. dirs. Las Vegas Accomodations Unltd., 1997—; mng. mem. G/Tracker Techs., LLC, 1998, Strobe Detector Techs., LLC, 1998; bd. dirs. Silver State Classic Challenge, Inc. Inventor electronic detection devices, 1986—. Served to lt. (j.g.) USNR, 1961-67. Republican. Avocation: amateur radio, open road auto racing, storm chasing. E-mail: phenry@phenry.com

HENSON, JAMES BOND, veterinary pathologist; b. Colorado City, Tex., Nov. 13, 1933; s. John Lee Henson and Beatrice (Porter) Walls; m. Janet Christine Neol; children: Sarah, Ben, James. B.S. in Animal Sci., Tex. A&M U., 1956, DVM, 1958, MS, 1959; PhD, Wash. State U., Pullman, 1962. Diplomate Am. Coll. Vet. Pathologists. Assoc. prof. Wash. State U., Pullman, 1962-68, prof., chair vet. pathology, 1968-73; dir. rsch. grad. edn. Coll. Vet. Medicine, Pullman, 1973-74, dir. internat. program devel., prof. vet. pathology, 1978-98. Prof. exptl. animal medicine U. Wash., Seattle, 1968-74; dir. Internat. Lab. Research in Animal Diseases, Nairobi, Kenya, 1974-78; project dir. Western Sudan Agrl. Research Project, 1979-83; cons. U.S. AID, WHO, FAO, others, also various developing countries; mem. sci. and tech. adv. com. Spl. Program on Tropical Diseases, WHO, 1978-82; trustee Consortium Internat. Devel., 1982-84, 90-93; mem. exec. com. Small Ruminant Collaborative Research Support Project, 1981-84, 90-93, chair, 1993. Contbr. articles to profl. jours., chpts. to books. Recipient Outstanding Tchg. award Tex. A&M U., 1964, Mary K. Dunkle award Mich. State U., 1966; NIH fellow, 1965. Mem. Assn. Internat. Agrl. Rsch. and Devel. (pres.). Home: PO Box 2684 Pullman WA 99165-2684 Office: Wash State U 221 Hobart Hall Pullman WA 99164-0001

HENSON, RAY DAVID, law educator, consultant; b. Johnston City, Ill., July 24, 1924, s. Ray David and Lucile (Bell) Henson. B.S., U. Ill., 1947, J.D., 1949. Bar: Ill. 1950, U.S. Supreme Ct. 1960. Assoc. CNA Fin. Corp., Chgo., 1952-70; prof. law Wayne State U., 1970-75, Hastings Sch. Law, U. Calif., San Francisco, 1975—. Author: Landmarks of Law, 1960, Secured Transactions, 1973, 2d edit., 1979, Documents of Title, 1983, 2d edit., 1990, The Law of Sales, 1985; also various other books and numerous articles; editor: The Business Lawyer, 1967-68. Mem. legal adv. com. N.Y. Stock Exch., 1971-75. Served with USAAF, 1943-46. Mem. Am. Law Inst. (life), ABA (chmn. bus. law sect. 1969-70, adv. bd. jour. 1974-80), Ill. Bar Assn. (chmn. comml. banking and bankruptcy law sect. 1963-65), Chgo. Bar Assn. Club: Univ. (San Francisco). Home: 1400 Geary Blvd San Francisco CA 94109-6561 Office: U Calif Hastings Sch Law 200 Mcallister St San Francisco CA 94102-4707

HENTZ, VINCENT R. surgeon; b. Jacksonville, Fla., Aug. 29, 1942; MD, U. Fla., 1968. Intern Stanford (Calif.) Hosp., 1968-69, resident in plastic surgery, 1969-74; chief hand divsn. Stanford U. Sch. Medicine; fellow in hand surgery Roosevelt Hosp., N.Y.C., 1974-75; prof. functional restoration Stanford (Calif.) U. Office: Stanford U Sch Medicine 900 Welsh Rd # 15 Palo Alto CA 94305

HERALD, CHERRY LOU, research educator, research director; b. Beeville, Tex., Dec. 23, 1940; d. Edwin Sherley and Margaret Lucille (Caron) Bell; m. Delbert Leon Herald, Jr., July 31, 1964; children: Heather Amanda, Delbert Leon, III. BS, Ariz. State U., 1962, MS, 1965, PhD, 1968. Faculty rsch. assoc. Cancer Rsch. Inst. Ariz. State U., Tempe, 1973-74, sr. rsch. chemist Cancer Rsch. Inst., 1974-77, asst. to dir. and sr. rsch. chemist Cancer Rsch. Inst., 1977-83, asst. dir., assoc. rsch. prof. Cancer Rsch. Inst., 1984-88, assoc. dir., rsch. prof. Cancer Rsch. Inst., 1988—. Co-author: Biosynthetic Products for Cancer Chemotherapy, vols. 4, 5, & 6, 1984, 85, 87, Anticancer Drugs from Animals, Plants & Microorganisms, 1994, sci. jours. Mem. Am. Soc. Pharmacognosy, Am. Chem. Soc. Office: Ariz State U Cancer Rsch Inst Tempe AZ 85287-2404 E-mail: cherald@asu.edu

HERB, EDMUND MICHAEL, optometrist, educator; b. Zanesville, Ohio, Oct. 9, 1942; s. Edmund G. and Barbara R. (Michael) H.; divorced; children: Sara, Andrew; m. Jeri Heb. OD, Ohio State U., 1966. Pvt. practice optometry, Buena Vista, Colo., 1966—; past prof. Timberline campus Colo. Mountain Coll.; past clin. instr. Ohio State U. Sch. Optometry. Mem. Am. Optometric Assn., Colo. Optometric Assn. Home: 16395 Mt Princeton Rd Buena Vista CO 81211-9505 Office: 115 N Tabor St Buena Vista CO 81211 also: Leadville Colorado Med Ctr Leadville CO 80461

HERBERT, GAVIN SHEARER, health care products company executive; b. L.A., Mar. 26, 1932; s. Gavin and Josephine (D'Vitha) H.; children by previous marriage Cynthia, Lauri, Gavin, Pam; 2d. m. Ninetta Flanagan, Sept. 6, 1986. B.S., U. So. Calif., 1954. With Allergan, Inc., Irvine, Calif., 1950—, v.p., 1956-61, exec. v.p., pres., 1961-77, chmn. bd., CEO, 1977-91, chmn. bd., 1992-95, chmn. emeritus; pres. Eye and Skin Care Products Group Smith Kline Beckman Corp., 1981-89. Exec. v.p. Smith Kline Beckman Corp., 1986-89; bd. dirs. Beckman Instruments, Inc., Calif. Healthcare Inst. Mem. Rsch. to Prevent Blindness (bd. dirs.), Big Canyon Country Club, Newport Harbor Yacht Club, Pacific Club, Beta Theta Pi. Republican.

HERBIG, GEORGE HOWARD, astronomer, educator; b. Wheeling, W.Va., Jan. 2, 1920; s. George Albert and Glenna (Howard) H.; m. Delia Faye McMullin, Oct., 1943 (div. 1968); children: Marilyn, Lawrence, John, Robert; m. Hannelore Helene Tillmann, Sept. 3, 1968. AB, UCLA, 1943; PhD, U. Calif., Berkeley, 1948. From jr. astronomer to assoc. astronomer Lick Obs., U. Calif., Mt. Hamilton, 1948-60, astronomer, 1960-67; prof. astronomy U. Calif., Santa Cruz, 1967-87; astronomer Inst. for Astronomy, U. Hawaii, 1987—. Asst. dir. Lick Obs., 1960-63, acting dir., 1970-71. Editor: Non-Stable Stars, 1955, Spectroscopic Astrophysics, 1970; author over 230 sci. papers, articles, revs. Martin Kellogg fellow U. Calif., Berkeley, 1946-48, NRC fellow Pasadena and U. Chgo., 1948-49, Washington, 1948-49; recipient Medaille U. de Liège, Belgium, 1970, Catherine Wolfe Bruce Gold medal Astron. Soc. Pacific, 1980, Petrie prize and lecture Can. Astron. Soc., 1995. Fellow Am. Acad. Arts and Scis; mem. Nat. Acad. Scis., Internat. Astron. Union, Am. Astron. Soc. (Warner prize 1955, Henry Norris Russell lectr. 1975), Max Planck Inst. für Astronomie (fgn. sci. mem.), Soc. Royale des Scis. de Liège (corr.). Democrat. Office: U Hawaii Inst Astronomy 2680 Woodlawn Dr Honolulu HI 96822-1839

HERBOLD, ROBERT J. software company executive; m. Pat; 3 children. BS, U. Cin.; MS in Maths., PhD in Computer Sci., Case Western Reserve U. Sr. v.p. advtsg. and info. svcs. Procter & Gamble Co.; exec. v.p., COO Microsoft Corp., Redmond, Wash., 1994—. Bd. dirs. Browning-Ferris Industries, Inc., mem. advtsg. coun. Mem. Wash. Roundtable, James Madison Coun. Libr. Congress; bd. trustees Case We. Res. U., Seattle Found., Seattle Symphony, Overlake Hosp. Avocations: hiking, fishing. Office: Microsoft Corp One Microsoft Way Redmond WA 98052-6399

HERBST, DAVID W. lawyer; b. Pomona, Calif., June 17, 1952; BA magna cum laude, Pomona Coll., 1974; JD, Stanford U., 1977. Bar: Calif. 1977, U.S. Tax Ct. 1979. Ptnr. Manatt, Phelps & Phillips (formerly known as Wise & Shepard), Palo Alto, Calif., 1983—. Mem. ABA, State Bar Calif., Santa Clara County Bar Assn., Palo Alto Bar Assn. Office: Manatt Phelps & Phillips 1001 Page Mill Rd Bldg 2 Palo Alto CA 94304-1020

HERGER, WALLY W. congressman; b. Yuba City, Calif., May 20, 1945; Formerly mem. Calif. State Assembly; mem. U.S. Congress from 2d Calif. dist., 1987—; mem. ways and means com.; owner Herger Gas, Inc. Office: US Ho of Reps 2268 Rayburn Bldg Washington DC 20515-0502*

HERGOTT, ALAN, lawyer; Ptnr. Bloom Diemer Hergott & Cook, Beverly Hills, Calif. Office: Bloom Diemer Hergott & Cook 150 S Rodeo Dr Fl 3 Beverly Hills CA 90212-2410

HERLINGER, DANIEL ROBERT, hospital administrator; b. Boskovice, Czechoslovakia, Oct. 27, 1946; came to U.S., 1950, naturalized, 1956; s. Rudolf and Ingeborg (Gessler) H.; m. Susanne Reiter, June 1, 1969; children: Lisa, Rebecca, Joanna. BS, Loyola U., Chgo., 1968; MBA, George Washington U., 1971. Asst. adminstr. Michael Reese Hosp., Chgo., 1971-73; v.p. Mercy Hosp., Chgo., 1973-84; pres. St. John's Regional Med. Ctr., Oxnard, Calif., 1984-94, Mercy Healthcare Ventura County, 1994-96, CHW Ctrl. Coast, Santa Barbara, Calif., 1996—. Fellow Am. Coll. Hosp. Adminstrs.; mem. World Pres. Orgn., Rotary. Jewish. Home: 15 Camino Verde Santa Barbara CA 93103-2144 Office: CHW Ctrl Coast 511 Bath St Santa Barbara CA 93101-3403

HERMAN, DAVID JAY, orthodontist; b. Rome, Oct. 4, 1954; s. Maurice Joseph and Bettina S. (Stiener) H.; m. Mary Beth Appleberry, Apr. 11, 1976; children: Jeremiah D., Kellin A. BA in Biology, San Jose State U., 1976; DDS, Emory U., 1981; MS in Orthodontics, MPH, U. N.C., 1992. Comdr. USPHS, 1981-97; advanced gen. practice resident Gallup (N. Mex.) Indian Med. Ctr., 1983-84; Navajo area dental br. chief Window Rock, Ariz., 1986-89; mem. grad. residency com. U. N.C., Chapel Hill, 1990-91; Navajo area orthodontic specialist Shiprock, N. Mex., 1992-97; clin. dir. Nizhoni Smiles Inc., 1997-99; pvt. practice Farmington, N.Mex., 1998—; pres. Four Corners Orthodontics, Inc., 1998—. Mem. health adv. bd. Navajo Reservation Headstart, 1986-89; health promotion/disease prevention cons. USPHS-Indian Health Svc. Navajo Area, Window Rock, 1986-89; cons. Ariz. IHS Periodontal Health Task Force, 1986-90; bd. dirs. San Juan Regional Hosp. Corp. Asst. wrestling coach Winslow (Ariz.) H.S., 1984-86, Gallup High Sch., 1987-89, Chapel Hill H.S., 1991-92, Farmington H.S., 1992-2001, Aztec H.S., 1998-2000; mem. H.S. Youth Wrestling Program, 1992-2000; mem. corp. bd. San Juan Reg. Med. Ctr., 1996—. Recipient Healthy Mothers/Healthy Babies Disease Prevention award, 1988, USPHS Achievement medal, 1985, Headstart Achievement award, 1989, Ariz. Pub. Health Assn. Hon. award, 1989; Nat. Health Svc. Corp. scholar Emory U., 1977-81. Mem. ADA, Am. Assn. Orthodontists, Rocky Mountain Soc. Orthodontists, N.Mex. Soc. Orthodontists (pres. 1998-99), Northwestern N.Mex. Sco. Orthodontists (pres. 1999-00), Navajo Area Dental Soc. (pres. 1985), Am. Assn. Mil. Orthodontists (sec.reas. 1992, v.p. 1993-94, pres. 1995-97). Avocations: wrestling, weight lifting, jogging, skiing, backpacking.

HERMAN, GEORGE ADAM, retired writer; b. Norfolk, Va., Apr. 12, 1928; s. George Adam and Minerva Nevada (Thompson) H.; m. Patricia Lee Glazer, May 26, 1955 (div. 1989); children: Kurt, Erik, Karl, Lisa, Katherine, Christopher, Jena, Amanda; m. Patricia Jane Piper Dubay, Aug. 25, 1989; children: Lizette, Paul, Kirk, Victoria. PhB, Loyola Coll., 1950; MFA, Cath. U., 1954; cert. fine arts, Boston Coll., 1951,52,53. Asst. prof. Clarke Coll., Dubuque, Iowa, 1955-60, Villanova (Pa.) U., 1960-63; asst. prof., playwright in residence Coll. St. Benedict, St. Joseph, Minn., 1963-65; chmn. theatre dept. Coll. Great Falls, Mont., 1965-67; media specialist Hawaii State Dept. Edn., Honolulu, 1967-75, staff specialist, 1975-83; sr. drama critic Honolulu Advertiser, 1975-80; artistic dir. Commedia Repertory Theatre, Honolulu, 1978-80; freelance writer, lectr., composer Portland, Oreg., 1983—. Author: (plays) Company of Wayward Saints, 1963 (McKnight Humanities award 1964), Mr. Highpockets, 1968, A Stone for Either Hand, 1969, Tenebrae, 1984, (novels) Carnival of Saints, 1994 (finalist Oreg. Book Awards 1994), A Comedy of Murders, 1994, Tears of the Madonna, 1995, The Florentine Mourners, 1999; composer (ballets) The Dancing Princesses, Fraidy Cat. Pres. local chpt. Nat. Sch. Pub. Rels. Assn., Honolulu, 1981-83; bd. dirs. Honolulu Community Theatre, 1981-82, Hawaii State Theatre Coun., Honolulu, 1981. With U.S. Army, 1950-52. Recipient Hartke Playwrighting award Cath. U., 1954, Excellence award Am. Security Coun., 1967. Avocations: directing theatre, lecturing. E-mail: gadamo@aol.com

HERMAN, JOAN ELIZABETH, healthcare company executive; b. N.Y.C., June 2, 1953; d. Roland Barry and Grace Gales (Goldstein) H.; m. Richard M. Rasiej, July 16. 1977. AB, Barnard Coll., 1975; MS, Yale U., 1977. Actuarial student Met. Life Ins. Co., N.Y.C., 1978-82; asst. actuary Phoenix Mut. Life Ins. Co. (now Phoenix Home Life Mut. Ins.), Hartford, Conn., 1982-83; assoc. actuary, dir. underwriting research Phoenix Mut. Life Ins. Co., Hartford, 1983-84, 2d v.p., 1984-85, v.p., 1985-89, sr. v.p., 1989-98; pres. specialty businesses WellPoint Health Networks, Woodland Hills, Calif., 1998, group pres., 1999—. Bd. dirs. PM Holdings, Inc., Phoenix Group Holdings, Inc., Phoenix Am. Life Ins. Co., Emprendimiento Compartido, S.A., v.p., BC Life & Health Co., Profl. Claims Svcs Inc.,

Proserv., MEDIX. Contbr. articles to profl jours. Capt. fundraising team Greater Hartford Arts Coun., 1986; bd. dirs. Hadassah, Glastonbury, Conn., Temple Beth Hillel, South Windsor, Conn., 1983-84, Children's Fund Conn., 1992-98, My Sister's Place, Shelter, Hartford, 1989-94, Western Mass. Regional Nat. Conf. Conn., 1995-98, Greater Hartford Arts Coun., 1997-98; bd. dirs. Hartford Ballet, 1989-95, corporator, 1995-98; bd. dirs. Leadership Greater Hartford, 1989-94, chmn. bd. dirs., 1993-94; mem. bd. founders Am. Leadership Forum of Hartford, 1991-98; corporator Hartford Sem., 1994-98. Fellow Soc. Actuaries (chairperson health sect. coun. 1994-95); mem. Am. Acad. Actuaries (bd. dirs. 1994-97), Am. Leadership Forum, Home Office Life Underwriters Am. Jewish. Avocations: reading, swimming, bicycling, jogging, aerobic dancing, hiking. Office: Wellpoint Health Networks 1 Wellpoint Way Thousand Oaks CA 91362-3893 E-mail: joan.herman@wellpoint.com

HERMANN, ALLEN MAX, physics educator; b. New Orleans, July 17, 1938; s. Edward Frederick and Miriam (Davidson) H.; m. Leonora Christopher, May 19, 1979 ; children: Miriam, Mary, Neil, Scott. BS with honors in Physics, Loyola U., New Orleans, 1960; MS in Physics, U. Notre Dame, 1962; PhD in Physics, Tex. A&M U., 1965. Sr. research scientist Jet Propulsion Lab, Pasadena, Calif., 1965-67, tech. mgr., 1985-86; asst. prof. physics Tulane U., New Orleans, 1967-70, assoc. prof. physics, 1970-75, prof. physics, 1975-81; task mgr. Solar Energy Research Inst., Golden, Colo., 1980-85; prof., chmn. dept. physics U. Ark., Fayetteville, 1986-89, Disting. prof., 1989; prof. dept. physics U. Colo., Boulder, 1990—. Cons. Jet Propulsion Lab., 1978-81, 86-87, NASA-Lewis Rsch. Ctr., Cleve., 1978-80, Cardiac Pacemakers Inc., Mpls., 1976-79, Radiation Monitoring Devices, Newton, Mass., 1990-93, Superconducting Core Techs., Denver, 1989-95, Sumitomo Electric Industries, Osaka, Japan, 1991-98, MV Sys., Inc., Golden, 1999—. Founding co-editor Applied Physics Communication; editor Applied Physics Book Series; contbr. numerous articles to profl. jours. Bd. dirs. Colo. Assn. Retarded Citizens, Denver, 1983-85. Recipient NASA Outstanding Achievement award 1970, 72, Disting. Scientist award Am. Assn. Physics Tchrs., 1987; named Hero, State of Ark., Ark. Times mag.; named Person of the Yr., Superconductivity Week, 1989; elected to Acad. Disting. Grads., Coll. Sci., Tex. A&M U., 1999. Fellow Am. Phys. Soc.; mem. IEEE (sr.), Materials Rsch. Soc. Home: 2704 Lookout View Dr Golden CO 80401-2520 Office: U Colo PO Box 390 Boulder CO 80309-0390

HERMSEN, JAMES R. lawyer; b. Orange, Calif., Oct. 2, 1945; BA, U. Wash., 1967, JD, 1970. Bar: Wash. 1971. Mem. Bogle & Gates, PLLC, Seattle, Dorsey & Whitney, Seattle, 2000—. Mem. Bur. of Competition Fed. Trade Commn., 1971-73. Mem. ABA, Seattle-King County Bar Assn., Wash. State Bar Assn., Am. Bar Assn., Phi Beta Kappa, Omicron Delta Epsilon, Phi Delta Phi. Office: Dorsey & Whitney 1420 5th Ave Ste 3400 Seattle WA 98101-4010

HERNANDEZ, AILEEN C(LARKE), urban consultant; b. Bklyn., May 23, 1926; d. Charles Henry and Ethel Louise (Hall) Clarke; divorced. AB in Sociology and Polit. Sci. magna cum laude, Howard U., 1947; MA in Pub. Adminstrn. with honors, Calif. State U., L.A., 1961; LHD (hon.), So. Vt. Coll., 1979. From organizer to dir. edn. and pub. rels. Internat. Ladies' Garment Workers' Union, Calif., 1950-61; asst. chief Calif. div. Fair Employment Practices, 1962-65; appointed commr. U.S. EEOC, Washington, 1965-66; prin. Aileen C. Hernandez Assocs., San Francisco, 1966—. Rsch. asst. dept. govt. Howard U., 1948; specialist in labor edn., lectr. U.S. Dept. State, 1960; mem. internat. conf. on minorities and the metropolis Konrad Adenauer Found./U.S. Dept. State, 1975; mem. Nat. Commn. on Study of People's Republic of China, 1978, Nat. Commn. on Am. Fgn. Policy Towards South Africa, 1981; advisor BART impact study com. Nat. Acad. Engring.; commr. Bay Vision 2020, 1990-93; vice chair San Francisco 2000; lectr. polit. sci. UCB, UCLA, San Francisco State U. Columnist Washington Tribune, 1946-47; contbr. commn. report South Africa: Time Running Out, 1981. Coord. Senator Alan Cranston's campaign for State Controller of Calif., 1961; chair Working Assets Money Fund; co-chair Nat. Urban Coalition, bd. dirs. Death Penalty Focus; vice chair nat. adv. couns. ACLU; coord. San Francisco African Am. Agenda Coun.; mem. adv. bd. Program for Rsch. on Immigration Policy; mem. nat. adv. coun. Nat. Inst. for Women of Color; bd. dirs. Ctr. for Women Policy Studies; mem. Citizens Commn. on Civil Rights; treas. Eleanor R. Spikes Meml. Fund; active San Franciscans Seeking Consensus, 1982—; founding mem., chair Coalition for Econ. Equity; chair Sec's. Adv. Com. on Rights and Responsibilities of Women; officer, bd. dirs. Mt. Zion Hosp.; bd. dirs. Westside Community Mental Health Ctr.; chair Calif. Coun. Humanities; founding mem. Nat. Women's Polit. Caucus, Black Women Organized for Action, Bay Area Black Women United, Nat. Hook-Up of Black Women; bd. dirs., project dir. Nat. Com. Against Discrimination in Housing; mem. housing com. Assn. Bay Area Govts.; chmn. Ctr. Common Good, Calif. Women's Agenda (CANA); bd. dirs. Wellesley Ctrs. for Rsch.; chmn. bd. Ctr. Govtl. Studies. Named Woman of Yr., Community Rels. Conf. So. Calif. 1961, One of Ten Most Disting. Women in the San Francisco Bay Area, San Francisco Examiner, 1969, One of Ten Women Who Make a Difference, San Francisco LWV, 1985; recipient Disting. Postgrad. Achievement award Howard U., 1968, disting. svcs. to urban cmtys. award Nat. Urban Coalition, 1985, Bicentennial award Trinity Bapt. Ch., 1976, humanitarian svcs. award Glide Meml. United Meth. Ch., 1986, appreciation awards Nat. Inst. for Women of Color, 1987, Western Dist. Conf. of Nat. Assn. Negro Bus. & Profl. Women's Clubs, 1988, San Francisco Conv. and Visitors Bur., Parren J. Mitchell award San Francisco Black C. of C., 1985, Silver Spur award, Wise Woman award C.W.P.S., Women of Achievement, Vison and Excellence award. Mem. NAACP (life), NOW (past nat. pres.), Ms. Found. for Women (bd. dirs.), Bay Area Urban League (past bd. dirs.), Urban Inst. (life trustee), Gamma Phi Delta (hon.), Alpha Kappa Alpha. Office: Aileen C Hernandez Assocs 818 47th Ave San Francisco CA 94121-3208

HERNANDEZ, ANTONIA, lawyer; b. Torreon, Coahuila, Mexico, May 30, 1948; came to U.S., 1956; d. Manuel and Nicolasa (Martinez) H.; m. Michael Stern, Oct. 8, 1977; children: Benjamin, Marisa, Michael. BA, UCLA, 1971, JD, 1974. Bar: Calif. 1974, D.C. 1979. Staff atty. Los Angeles Ctr. Law and Justice, 1974-77; directing atty. Legal Aid Found., Lincoln Heights, Calif., 1977-78; staff counsel U.S. Senate Com. on the Judiciary, Washington, 1979-80; assoc. counsel Mexican Am. Legal Def. Ednl. Fund, Washington, 1981-83, employment program dir., 1983-84, exec. v.p., dep. gen. counsel Los Angeles, 1984-85, pres., gen. counsel, 1985—. Bd. dirs. Golden West Financial Corp., Automobile Club of So. Calif., Am. Charities. Contbr. articles to profl. jours. Active Inter-Am. Dialogue Aspen Inst., Nat. Com. Innovations in State and Local Govt., Nat. Endowment for Democracy, Pres.'s Commn. White House Fellowships. AAUW fellow, 1973-74. Mem. ABA, State Bar Calif., Washington D.C. Bar Assn., Mexican-Am. Roman Catholic. Avocations: gardening, outdoor sports. Office: Mexican Am Legal Def Ednl Fund 634 S Spring 11th Fl Los Angeles CA 90014-3921

HERNANDEZ, JO FARB, curator, consultant; b. Chgo., Nov. 20, 1952; BA in Polit. Sci. & French with honors, U. Wis., 1974; MA in Folklore and mythology, UCLA, 1975; postgrad., U. Calif., Davis, 1978, U. Calif., Berkeley, 1978-79, 81. Registration Mus. Cultural History UCLA, 1974-75; Rockefeller fellow Dallas Mus. Fine Arts, 1976-77; asst. to dir. Triton Mus. Art, Santa Clara, Calif., 1977-78, dir., 1978-85; adj. prof. mus. studies John F. Kennedy U., San Francisco, 1978; grad. advisor arts adminstrn. San Jose (Calif.) State U., 1979-80; dir. Monterey (Calif.) Peninsula Mus. Art, 1985-93, cons. curator, 1994—; prin. Curatorial and Mus. Mgmt. Svcs., Watsonville, Calif., 1993—. Cons.SPACES (Saving and Preserving Art and [illegible] Works Fund 2001, [illegible]

prof. gallery mgmt. art dept. U. Calif., Santa Cruz, 1999—; cons. Archives Am. Art., 1998—2000; dir. Thompson Gallery, San Jose State U., 2000—; lectr., panelist, juror, panelist in field USIA, Calif. Arts Coun., Calif. Confedn. for Arts, Am. Assn. Mus., Western Mus. Assn., Am. Folklore Soc., Calif. Folklore Soc., Internat. Coun. on Mus., others; vis. lectr. U. Wis., 1980, U. Chgo., 1981, Northwestern U., 1981, San Jose State U., 1985, UCLA, 1986, Am. Cultural Ctr., Jerusalem, 1989, Tel Aviv, 89, Binat Ctr., Lima, Peru, 1988, Daytona Beach Mus. Art, 1983, UCLA, 1986, Israel Mus., 1989, Mont. State U., 1991, Oakland Mus., 1996, High Mus. Art, Atlanta, 1997, Mus. Am. Folk Art, NY, 1998, San Francisco Mus. Modern Art, 1998, U. Calif., 1998, Grinnell Coll., Iowa, 1999, Arts Coun. Silicon Valley, 2000, U. Calif., Santa Cruz, 2000, ICOM, Barcelona, 2001; guest curator San Diego Mus. Art, 1995—98; guest on various TV and radio programs. Contbr. articles to profl. publs.; author: (mus. catalogs) The Day of the Dead: Tradition and Change in Contemporary Mexico, 1979, Three from the Northern Island: Contemporary Sculpture from Hokkaido, 1984, Crime and Punishment: Reflections of Violence in Contemporary Art, 1984, The Quiet Eye: Pottery of Shoji Hamada and Bernard Leach, 1990, Alan Shepp: The Language of Stone, 1991, Wonderful Colors: The Paintings of August Francois Gay, 1993, Jeannette Maxfield Lewis: A Centennial Celebration, 1994, Armin Hansen, 1994, Jeremy Anderson: The Critical Link/A Quiet Revolution, 1995, A.G. Rizzoli: Architect of Magnificent Visions, 1997 (one of 10 Best Books in field Amazon.com), Misch Kohn: Beyond the Tradition, 1998, Fire and Flux: An Undaunted Vision/The Art of Charles Strong, 1998, Mel Ramos: The Galatea Series, 2000, Holly Lane: Small Miracles, 2001. Bd. dirs. Bobbie Wynn and Co. of San Jose, 1981-85, Santa Clara Arts and Hist. Consortium, 1985, Non-Profit Gallery Assn., 1979-83, v.p., 1979-80; mem. nat. adv. bd. The Fund for Folk Culture, Santa Fe, 1995-98. Recipient Golden Eagle award, Coun. Internat. Non-theatrical Events, 1992, Leader of Decade award, Arts Leadership Monterey Peninsula, 1992, merit award, N.Y. Book Show, 1997; grantee Rsch., Calif. State U., 2001, Dean's grant, 2001. Mem.: Phi Beta Kappa, Am. Assn. Mus. (mus. assessment program surveyor 1990, mus. assessment program surveyor 1994, lectr. 1986, nat. program com. 1992—93), Calif. Assn. Mus. (chair ann. meeting 1990, chair nominating com. 1988, chair nominating com. 1990, chair nominating com. 1993, bd. dirs. 1985—94, v.p. 1987—91, pres. 1991—92), Art Table, Am. Folklore Soc., Western Mus. Conf. (bd. dir., exec. com. 1989—91, program chair 1990), Nat. Coun. for Edn. in Ceramic Arts, Alliance for Calif. Traditional Arts (mem. internat. editl. bd. for Raw Vision 2001—). Office: Curatorial Mus Mgmt Svcs 345 White Rd Watsonville CA 95076-0429 E-mail: jfh@cruzio.com

HERNANDEZ, LIVAN EISLER, professional baseball player; b. Villa Clara, Cuba, Feb. 20, 1975; Pitcher Fla. Marlins, 1996-99, San Francisco Giants, 1999—. Office: care San Francisco Giants 24 Willie Mays Plz San Francisco CA 94107-2134

HERNANDEZ, MIKE, city official; m. Sylvia Hernandez; children: Michelle, Emiliano. Past hon. mayor City of Highland Park; city councilman 1st dist. City of L.A., 1991—, chmn. adminstrv. svcs. com., mem. govt. efficiency & arts com., health & humanities com., chmn. cmty. & econ. devel. com., vice chair info. tech. gen. svcs. com., vice chmn. trans. com. Mem. Northeast Bus. Devel. Coun., Northeast L.A. Cmty. Planning Adv. Com. Mem. L.A. Jaycees, Highland Park Optimists, Kiwanis of Highland Park. Address: 200 N Main St Ste 413 Los Angeles CA 90012-4117

HERNANDEZ, ROBERT MICHAEL, state legislator, software engineer; b. Pueblo, Colo., Mar. 5, 1953; BS in Bus. Adminstrn., Regis U. Mem. Colo. Ho. of Reps., 1991-95, Colo. Senate, Dist. 34, Denver, 1995—; mem. agr., natural resources and energy com. Colo. State Senate, mem. bus. affairs and labor com., mem. joint legis. coun. Active Boulder County Com., 1971; treas. Denver Young Dems., 1984-85, pres., 1986-87. Mem. Comm. Workers Am. (area rep. 1973-81). Democrat. Home: 4600 W 36th Ave Denver CO 80212-2009 Office: State Capitol 200 E Colfax Ave Ste 274 Denver CO 80203-1716 Fax: 303-866-4543/303-624-2020

HERR, RICHARD, history educator; b. Guanajuato, Mexico, Apr. 7, 1922; s. Irving and Luella (Winship) H.; m. Elena Fernandez Mel, Mar. 2, 1946 (div. 1967); children: Charles Fernandez, Winship Richard; m. Valerie J. Jackson, Aug. 29, 1968; children: Sarah, Jane. A.B., Harvard U., 1943; Ph.D., U. Chgo., 1954. Instr. Yale U., 1952-57, asst. prof., 1957-59; assoc. prof. U. Calif., Berkeley, 1960-63, prof. history, 1963-91, prof. emeritus, 1991—, chancellor's fellow, 1987-90. Directeur d'études associé, sixième sect. Ecole Pratique des Hautes Etudes, Paris, 1973; dir. Madrid Study Ctr., U. Calif., 1975-77; chair Portuguese Studies Program, U. Calif., Berkeley, 1994-98; vis. life mem. Clare Hall, Cambridge, Eng., 1985—; vis. prof. U. Alcalá. Henares, Spain, 1991; bd. dirs. Internat. Inst. Found. in Spain, Boston, 1997—; fellow Ctr. for History of Freedom, Washington U., St. Louis, 1994. Author: The Eighteenth Century Revolution in Spain, 1958, Tocqueville and the Old Regime, 1962, Spain, 1971, Rural Change and Royal Finances in Spain at the End of the Old Regime, 1989 (Leo Gershoy award Am. Hist. Assn. 1990); co-author: An American Family in the Mexican Revolution, 1999; editor: Memorias del cura liberal don Juan Antonio Posse, 1984; co-editor, contbr.: Ideas in History, 1965, Iberian Identity, 1989; editor, contbr.: The New Portugal: Democracy and Europe, 1993, Themes in Rural History of the Western World, 1993; asst. editor: Jour. Modern History, 1949-50; mem. editl. bd. French Historical Studies, 1966-69, Revista de Historia Economica, 1983-91. With AUS, 1943-45. Decorated Comendador of the Orden de Isabel la Católica (Spain); recipient Bronze medal Collège de France, Paris, The Berkeley citation U. Calif., 1991; Social Sci. Rsch. Coun. grantee, 1963-64; Guggenheim fellow, 1959-60, 84-85; NEH sr. fellow, 1968-69. Fellow Am. Acad. Arts and Scis.; mem. Am. Philos. Soc., Real Academia de la Historia Madrid (corr.), Soc. for Spanish and Portuguese Hist. Studies. Office: U Calif Dept History Berkeley CA 94720-0001

HERRANEN, KATHY, artist, graphic designer; b. Zelienople, Pa., Dec. 22, 1943; d. John and Helen Elizabeth (Sayti) D'Biagio; m. John Warma Herranen, Dec. 31, 1974 (div. Feb. 1994); 1 child, Michael John. Student, Scottsdale (Ariz.) C.C., 1990—. Cert. tchr. art, State Bd. Dirs. for Cmty. Coll. of Ariz. Horseback riding instr. Black Saddle Riding Acad., Lancaster, Calif., early 1960's; tel. company supr. Bell Tel., Bishop, 1965; reporter, part-time photographer Ellwood City (Pa.) Ledger, 1967-70; back-country guide and cook Mammoth Lakes (Calif.) Pack Outfit, 1970; motel mgr. Mountain Property Mgmt., Mammoth Lakes, 1970-72; reporter, bookkeeper Hungry Horse (Mont.) News, 1973-74; pig farmer Columbia Falls, Mont., 1973-75; fine artist, illustrator, graphic designer Mont., Calif., and Ariz., 1980—; fine arts cons. Collector's Gallery, Galleri II, Yuma, Ariz., 1983-84; wind chime designer, creator Phoenix, 1995—; represented by Marcella's Ariz. Collection, Phoenix, 1995—, Backstreet Furniture and Art, Phoenix, 1995—, Hohn Gallery Fine Arts, Ltd., Scottsdale, 1997—. Guest lectr. Paradise Valley Tchrs Acad., Phoenix, 1993, Sr. Adult Edn. Program, Scottsdale (Ariz.) Cmty. Coll., 1994, pastel painting instr., 1996; guest demonstrator Binder's Art Ctr., Scottsdale, 1995, Backstreet Furniture and Art, Phoenix, 1995-96; guest lectr., demonstrator Summer Edn. Program Paradise Valley Sch. Dist., 1996, 99, 2000; guest demonstrator Phoenix Artists Guild, 2000, Paradise Valley Artists, 2000. Solo shows include Pinnacle, Phoenix, 1993, Villas of Sedona, Ariz., 1995. Sec. Young Dems., Ellwood City, late 1960's, Vistas Home Owners Assn., Phoenix, 1995—; troubleshooter Maricopa County Elections Dept., Phoenix, 1994-96, 2000. Recipient 1st place award Potpourri Artists, Yuma, Ariz., 1981, Subscriber award Butte (Mont.) Arts Coun., 1981, 2nd place award Desert Artists, Yuma, 1982, honorable mention Yuma County Fair, Yuma, 1983, Wildlife Painting Exhibit, Scottsdale, 1993, honorable mention Scottsdale Studio 13, 1991, 92, Fountain Festival Juried Competitive Exhbn. Fine Arts, 1993, Special award, 1993, Merit award, 1993, 94 (2). Mem. Nat. Assn. Sr. Friends Fine Artists (chair 1995—, honorable mention 1993, People's Choice award 1996, 1st place award, hon. mention, 2001), Women's Caucus for Art, Phoenix Artists Guild, Ariz. Pastel Artists Assn. (charter. membership chair 1995-96, 2d v.p., show chair 1996, guest demonstrator 1995, guest lectr. 1998, Merit award 1995), Ariz. Art Alliance (publicity chmn. 2000—), Artists and Craftsmen of Flathead Valley (founder, charter mem., pres. 1981-82), Phi Theta Kappa. Republican. Lutheran. Avocations: public speaking and acting, dancing, stamp collecting, photography, interior decorating. Office: 4114 E Union Hills Dr No 1011 Phoenix AZ 85050-3355 E-mail: kathyherranen@aol.com

HERRERA, JOHN, professional football team executive; married; 9 children. BA in History, U. Calif., Davis. Tng. camp asst. Oakland Raiders, 1963-68, pub. rels. asst., 1968, dir. pub. rels., 1978-80, sr. exec., 1985—; dir. player pers. B.C. Lions, 1981-82; gen. mgr. Sask. Roughriders, 1983-84; with scouting depts. Tampa Bay Buccaneers, 1975-76, Washington Redskins, 1977. Office: Oakland Raiders 1220 Harbor Bay Pkwy Alameda CA 94502-6570 E-mail: jherrera@raiders.com

HERRERA, SHIRLEY MAE, personnel and security executive; b. Lynn, Mass., Apr. 5, 1942; d. John Baptiste and Edith Mae Lagasse; m. Christian Yanez Herrera, Apr. 30, 1975; children: Karen, Gary, Ivan, Iwonne. AS in Bus., Burdette Bus. Coll., Lynn, 1960; student, Wright State U., 1975-78. Cert. facility security officer, med. asst. in pediatrics. Med. asst. Christian Y. Herrera, M.D., Stoneham, Mass., 1972-74; human resource adminstr. MTL Systems, Inc., Dayton, Ohio, 1976-79; dir. pers. and security Tracor GIE, Inc., Provo, Utah, 1979-95; health professions vol. PHS/IHS Hosp., Rosebud, S.D., 2001—. Cons. on family dynamics family enrichment program Hill AFB, Utah, 1980-82; cons. on health care memt. Guam 7th Day Adventist Clinic, 1983; cons. on basic life support and CPR, Projecto Corazon, Monterrey, Mex., 1987—; faculty mem. Inst. for Reality Therapy, 1991—. Contbg. editor Inside Tracor, 1991—. Chmn. women's aux. YMCA Counselling Svcs., Woburn, Mass., 1970; chmn. youth vols. ARC, Wright-Patterson AFB, Dayton, 1974-76; trustee Quail Valley Homeowner's Assn., Provo, 1988-89; rep. A Spl. Wish Found., Provo, 1989. Recipient James S. Cogswell award Def. Investigative Svc., Dept. Def., 1987. Mem. Inst. for Realty Therapy (cert.), Pers. Assn. Ctrl. Utah, Women in Mgmt. (coun. mem. 1991-95), Nat. Classification Mgmt. Soc. (chairperson Intermountain chpt. 1992-94). Republican. Avocations: writing, skiing, reading. Home: 3824 Little Rock Dr Provo UT 84604-5234

HERRES, PHILLIP BENJAMIN, computer software executive; b. Spokane, Wash., Nov. 5, 1941; s. Benjamin Jacob and Ollie Lee (Bell) H.; m. Lorelei Norma Munroe, June 15, 1963; children: Michele Marie, Anthony Phillip, Jason Randall. BSEE, Gonzaga U., 1963; MBA, U. Oreg., 1965. Registered profl. engr., Calif. Engr. Pacific N.W. Bell, Portland, Oreg., 1965-66; chief engr. Electronic Splty., Portland, 1966-71; dir. engring. Arcata Communications, Mountain View, Calif., 1971-73; engring. mgr. Clare-Pendar, Post Falls, Idaho, 1973-76; v.p. network systems Northern Telecom, Dallas, 1976-87; sr. v.p. engring. Avanti Communications, Newport, R.I., 1987-89; chief oper. officer Aldus Corp., Seattle, 1989-92; mgmt. cons. Mercer Island, Wash., 1993-94; pres. Evergreen Software Tools, Redmond, 1994-95; mgmt. cons. Herres Co., Mercer Island, 1995—; pres. ST Labs., Bellevue, 1997-98. 1st lt. U.S. Army, 1967-71. Mem. IEEE, Columbia Tower Club. Republican. Roman Catholic. Avocations: golf, scuba diving, target shooting, collections. Office: The Herres Co 8460 W Mercer Way Ste 244 Mercer Island WA 98040-5633 also: ST Labs 3535 128th Ave SE Bellevue WA 98006-1261

HERRICK, TRACY GRANT, fiduciary; b. Cleve., Dec. 30, 1933; s. Stanford Avery and Elizabeth Grant (Smith) H.; m. Maie Kaarsoo, Oct. 12, 1963; children: Sylvi Anne, Alan Kalev. BA, Columbia U., 1956, MA, 1958; postgrad., Yale U., 195-57, MA, Oxford U., England, 1960. Economist Fed. Res. Bank, Cleve., 1960-70; sr. economist Stanford Rsch. Inst., Menlo Park, Calif., 1970-73; v.p., sr. analyst Shuman, Agnew & Co., Inc., San Francisco, 1973-75; v.p. Bank of Am., San Francisco, 1975-81; pres. Tracy G. Herrick, Inc., 1981—. Lectr. Stonier Grad. Sch. Banking, Am. Bankers Assn., 1967-76; commencement speaker Memphis Banking Sch., 1974; bd. dirs. Jefferies Group, Inc., chmn. bd. audit com. 1989-96, chmn. bd. compensation com. 1991-96, dir. 1983-99; bd. dirs. Jefferies & Co., Inc.; dir. Com. Monetary Rsch. and Edn., Inc. Author: Bank Analyst's Handbook, 1978, Timing, 1981, Power and Wealth, 1988; contbr. articles to profl. jours. Mem. adv. bd. San Xavier Found., Monterey, Calif. Fellow Fin. Analysts Fedn.; mem. Assn. Investment Mgmt. Rsch., San Francisco Soc. Security Analysts. Republican. Congregationalist. Home: 1150 University Ave Palo Alto CA 94301-2238

HERRING, SUSAN WELLER, dental educator, oral anatomist; b. Pitts., Mar. 25, 1947; d. Sol W. and Miriam (Damick) Weller; m. Norman S. Wolf, May 27, 1995. BS in Zoology, U. Chgo., 1967, PhD in Anatomy, 1971. NIH postdoctoral fellow U. Ill., Chgo., 1971-72, from asst. prof. to prof. oral anatomy and anatomy, 1972-90; prof. orthodontics U. Wash., Seattle, 1990—. Vis. assoc. prof. biol. sci. U. Mich., Ann Arbor, 1981; cons. NIH study sect., Washington, D.C., 1987-89; sci. gov. Chgo. Acad. Sci., 1982-90; mem. pub. bd. Growth Pub. Inc., Bar Harbor, Maine, 1982—. Mem. editl. bd. Cells, Tissues, Organs, 1989—, Jour. Dental Rsch., 1995-98, Jour. Morphology, 1997—; contbr. articles to profl. jours. Predoctoral fellow NSF, 1967-71; rsch. grantee NIH, 1975-78, 81—, NSF, 1990-92, 94-95. Fellow AAAS; mem. Internat. Assn. Dental Rsch. (dir. craniofacial biology group 1994-95, v.p. 1995-96, pres.-elect 1996-97, pres. 1997-98, Craniofacial Biology Rsch. award 1999), Am. Soc. Zoologists (chmn. vertebrate zoology 1983-84, exec. com. 1986-88), Am. Soc. Biomechanics, Am. Assn. Anatomists (chmn. Basmajian com. 1988-90), Soc. Vertebrate Paleontology, Am. Soc. Mammalogists, Internat. Soc. Vertebrate morphology (convenor 4th congress 1994, pres. 1994-97), Sigma Xi. Avocation: semi-profl. violin. Office: U Wash Box 357446 Seattle WA 98195-7446 E-mail: herring@u.washington.edu

HERRING, WILLIAM CONYERS, physicist, emeritus educator; b. Scotia, N.Y., Nov. 15, 1914; s. William Conyers and Mary (Joy) H.; m. Louise C. Preusch, Nov. 30, 1946; children— Lois Mary, Alan John, Brian Charles, Gordon Robert. A.B., U. Kans., 1933; Ph.D., Princeton, 1937. NRC fellow Mass. Inst. Tech., 1937-39; instr. Princeton, 1939-40, U. Mo., 1940-41; mem. sci. staff Div. War Research, Columbia, 1941-45; prof. applied math. U. Tex., 1946; research physicist Bell Telephone Labs., Murray Hill, N.J., 1946-78; prof. applied physics Stanford (Calif.) U., 1978-81, prof. emeritus, 1981—. Mem. Inst. Advanced Study, 1952-53 Recipient Army-Navy Cert. of Appreciation, 1947; Distinguished Service citation U. Kans., 1973; J. Murray Luck award for excellence in sci. reviewing Nat. Acad. Scis., 1980; von Hippel award Materials Rsch. Soc., 1980, Wolf prize in Physics, 1985 Fellow Am. Phys. Soc. (Oliver E. Buckley solid state physics prize 1959), Am. Acad. Arts and Scis.; mem. AAAS, NAS, Am. Soc. Info. Scis. Home: 3945 Nelson Dr Palo Alto CA 94306-4524 Office: Stanford U Lab for Advanced Materials MS 4045 Stanford CA 94305-4045

HERRINGER, FRANK CASPER, diversified financial services company executive; b. N.Y.C., Nov. 12, 1942; s. Casper Frank and Alice Virginia (McMullen) H.; m. Maryellen B. Cattani; children: William, Sarah, Julia. AB magna cum laude, Dartmouth, 1964, MBA with highest distinction, 1965. Prin. Cresap, McCormick & Paget, Inc. (mgmt. cons.), N.Y.C., 1965-71; staff asst. to Pres., Washington, 1971-73; adminstr. U.S. Urban Mass Transp. Adminstrn., Washington, 1973-75; gen. mgr. San Francisco Bay Area Rapid Transit Dist., 1975-78; exec. v.p. Transam.

Corp., San Francisco, 1979-86, pres., dir., 1986-99, CEO, 1991-99, chmn., 1996—; mem. exec. bd. AEGON N.V., 1999-2000; chmn. AEGON USA, 1999-2000. Bd. dirs. Unocal Corp., Charles Schwab & Co., Mirapoint, Inc. Mem. Cypress Point Club, San Francisco Golf Club, Olympic Club, Pacific Union Club, Stock Farm Club, Phi Beta Kappa. Office: Transam Corp 600 Montgomery St San Francisco CA 94111-2702

HERRINGER, MARYELLEN CATTANI, lawyer; b. Bakersfield, Calif., Dec. 1, 1943; d. Arnold Theodore and Corinne Marilyn (Kovacevich) C.; m. Frank C. Herringer; children: Sarah, Julia. AB, Vassar Coll., Poughkeepsie, N.Y., 1965; JD, U. Calif. (Boalt Hall), 1968. Assoc. Davis Polk & Wardwell, N.Y.C., 1968-69, Orrick, Herrington & Sutcliffe, San Francisco, 1970-74, ptnr., 1975-81; v.p., gen. counsel Transamerica Corp., San Francisco, 1981-83, sr. v.p., gen. counsel, 1983-89; ptnr. Morrison & Foerster, San Francisco, 1989-91; sr. v.p. gen. counsel APL Ltd., Oakland, Calif., 1991-95, exec. v.p., gen. counsel, 1995-97; gen. counsel allied bus. Littler & Mendelson, San Francisco, 2000. Bd. dirs. Golden West Fin. Corp., World Savs. Bank, ABM Industries Inc. Author: Calif. Corp. Practice Guide, 1977, Corp. Counselors, 1982. Regent St. Mary's Coll., Moraga, Calif., 1986—, pres., 1990-92, trustee, 1990-99, chmn., 1993-95; trustee Vassar Coll., 1985-93, The Head-Royce Sch., 1993—, Mills Coll., 1999—, The Benilde Religious & Charitable Trust, 1999—, Alameda County Med. Ctr. Hosp. Authority, 1998—; bd. dirs. The Exploratorium, 1988-93. Mem. ABA, State Bar Calif. (chmn. bus. law sect. 1980-81), Bar Assn. San Francisco (co-chair com. on women 1989-91), Calif. Women Lawyers, San Francisco C. of C. (bd. dirs. 1987-91, gen. counsel 1990-91), Am. Corp. Counsel Assn. (bd. dirs. 1982-87), Women's Forum West (bd. dirs. 1984-87). Democrat. Roman Catholic. E-mail: mherringer@aol.com

HERRLINGER, STEPHEN PAUL, flight test engineer, air force officer, educator; b. Louisville, Nov. 23, 1959; s. John Howard and Josephine Doris (Martin) H.; m. Julie Louise Nelson, Feb. 4, 1989; children: Kyle H., Heidi K. BS in Chemistry, U. Akron, 1981; BS in Aero. Engring., USAF Inst. Tech., 1985; MS in Engring. Mgmt., Golden Gate U., 1989; M in Aero. Sci., Embry Riddle Aero. U., 1992. Registered Engr. in Tng., Ohio. Commd. 2d lt. USAF, 1981, advanced through grades to lt. col., 1998; rsch. chemist USAF Rocket Propulsion Lab., Edwards AFB, Calif., 1981-83; aerodynamic engr. advanced cruise missile 4200 Test and Evaluation Squadron USAF, Edwards AFB, 1985-86; chief advanced cruise missile aerodynamics sect. 31st Test and Evaluation Squadron USAF, Edwards AFB, 1986-87, chief advanced cruise missile performance, environ. sect., 1987-89; projct mgr E-9A surveillance aircraft program 4484th Test Squadron, Tyndall AFB, Fla., 1989-91, missile scoring flight test dir., 1991-92; dir. C-27A operational flight test 84th Test Squadron USAF, Tyndall AFB, 1992-94; chief of advanced testing ESC/ZJ USAF, Hanscom AFB, 1994-95, advanced sensor TBM program mgr., 1995-98, sys. program office dir. range threat sys. SM-ALC/LHR McClellan AFB, Calif., 1998—. Adj. instr. Gulf Coast C.C. U. West Fla., Embry Riddle Aero. U., 1991-99. Contbr. articles to Jour. Organic Chemistry, Soc. Flight Test Engrs. Jour., Jour. Aircraft. Leader youth group Calif. Luth. U. Chapel, Thousand Oaks, 1986-89; guitarist Luth. Ch. of the Savior, Bedford, Mass., 1995-97. Decorated USAF Meritorious Svc. medal with one oak leaf cluster, USAF Commendation medal, USAF Achievement medal with 1 oak leaf cluster, USAF Aerial Achievement medal, Spl. Achievement award Internat. Test and Evaluation Assn., 1994, Electronic Systems Ctr.'s Lt. Gen. O'Neill award for Acquisition Excellence, 1995. Achievements include U.S. patent for aerodynamic fairing /nose cone for M-130 chaff/flare dispenser design. Home: 3034 W 1300 N Clearfield UT 84015-7529

HERRMANN, GEORGE, mechanical engineering educator; b. USSR, Apr. 19, 1921; Diploma in Civil Engring., Swiss Fed. Inst. Tech., 1945, PhD in Mechanics, 1949. Asst., then asso. prof. civil engring. Columbia, 1950-62; prof. civil engring. Northwestern U., 1962-69; prof. applied mechanics Stanford, 1969-, prof. emeritus. Cons. SRI Internat., 1970-80 Contbr. 260 articles to profl. jours.; editl. bd. numerous jours. Fellow ASME (hon. mem. 1990, Centennial medal 1980); mem. ASCE (Th. v. Karman medal 1981), Nat. Acad. Engring., AIAA (emeritus). Office: Stanford U Divsn Mechanics Computation Durand Bldg 281 Stanford CA 94305-4040

HERSCHENSOHN, BRUCE, film director, writer; b. Milw., Sept. 10, 1932; Ed., Los Angeles. With art dept. RKO Pictures, 1953-55; dir., editor Gen. Dynamics Corp., 1955-56; dir., writer, editor Karma for Internat. Communications Found.; editor, co-dir. Friendship Seven for NASA; dir., editor Tall Man Five-Five for Gen. Dynamics Corp. and SAC; dir. motion picture and TV Service USIA, 1968-72, spl. cons. to dir., 1972—; staff asst. to Pres. U.S., 1972; dep. spl. asst. to Pres., 1973-74, mem. transition team, 1981; sr. fellow Claremont (Calif.) Inst., 1993; Rep. nominee U.S. Senate (Calif.), 1992. Tchr. U. Md., 1972; spl. cons. to Rep. Nat. Conv., 1972; polit. analyst KABC-TV and KABC radio, 1978-91. Directed and wrote films for USIA, including Bridges of the Barrios, The Five Cities of June, The President, John F. Kennedy: Years of Lightning, Day of Drums, Eulogy to 5:02; recipient Acad. award for Czechoslovakia 1968 as best documentary short 1969; author: The Gods of Antenna, 1976; contbg. editor: Conservative Digest. Bd. govs. Charles Edison Meml. Youth Fund; Rep. nom. U.S. Senate, Calif., 1992. Served with USAF, 1951-52. Recipient Arthur S. Flemming award as 1 of 10 outstanding young mem in fed. govt., 1969; Distinguished Service medal USIA, 1972; Ann. award Council Against Communist Aggression, 1972 Office: Claremont Inst 250 W 1st St Claremont CA 91711-4736

HERSCHER, PENNY, company executive; BA in Maths. with honors, Cambridge U., England. R&D engr. Tex. Instruments, England; mgr. Daisy Sys. Corp. ASIC Program; from v.p. mktg., gen. mgr. to dir. product mktg. Design Environ. Group Synopsys Inc.; pres., CEO Simplex Solutions Inc., 1996—. Office: Simplex Solutions Inc 521 Almanor Ave Sunnyvale CA 94085-3512 Fax: 408-774-0285. E-mail: info@simplex.com

HERSH, KRISTIN, vocalist, musician; b. Atlanta, 1965; Represented by 4AD, 1985-91, Sire Records, 1987—. Lead singer Throwing Muses, late 1970s—; solo vocalist, 1994—. Albums include Throwing Muses, 1986, The Fat Skier, 1987, House Tornado, 1988, Hunkpapa, 1989, The Real Ramonoa, 1991, Red Heaven, 1992, Hips and Makers, 1994, Strings, 1994, University, 1995, Sky Motel, 1999. Address: Summit Entertainment 1630 Stewart St Ste 120 Santa Monica CA 90404-4058

HERSHBERGER, ROBERT GLEN, architect, educator; b. Pocatello, Idaho, Apr. 4, 1936; s. Vernon Elver and Edna Syvilla (Kinsley) H.; m. Deanna Marlene Van Dyke, Mar. 25, 1961; children: Vernon, Andrew. AB, Stanford U., 1958; BArch, U. Utah, 1959; MArch, U. Pa., 1961, PhD, 1969. Registered architect, Idaho, Ariz. Project architect Spencer & Lee, Architects, San Francisco, 1961-63; project designer GBQC Architects, Phila., 1967-69; asst. prof. Idaho State U., Pocatello, 1963-65; adj. asst. prof. Drexel U., Phila., 1967-69; practicing architect Archtl. & Planning Cons., Tempe, Ariz., 1969-87; prof. Sch. of Architecture Ariz. State U., Tempe, 1969-87, acting dir. Sch. Architecture, 1986-87, assoc. dean Coll. of Architecture and Environ. Design, 1987; prof. U. Ariz. Coll. Arch., Tucson, 1988—, dean, 1988-96; ptnr. Hershberger and Nickels Archs./Planners, 1998—. Chmn. Environ. Design Rsch. Assoc., Washington, 1976-79, chair Archs. in Edn. Com. AIA, Washington, 1983-85; v.p. Arch. Rsch. Ctrs. Consortium, 1994-96; prin. Hershberger, Arch. and Planner, Tucson, 1997—. Prin. works include Covenant Bapt. Ch. (AIA Excellence award), Urban Renewal Plan Downtown Tempe (AIA Citation), Hershberger residence (AIA honor 1990); author: Architectural Programming and Predesign Manager, 1999. Bd. dirs. Rio Salado Found.; mem. Tempe Design Rev. Com., 1985-87, Tempe Elec. Adv. Com., 1982-85, Pocatello Planning Commn., 1962-65; mem. Tucson Planning Commn., 2000—; mem. pub. arts com. U. Ariz., 1988-96, chmn., 1994-96, mem. campus design rev. adv. com., 1990-96, chmn., 1990-93; chair staff parish com. Catalina United Meth. Ch., 1995; bd. dirs. Catalina Day Care Ctr., 1990-93, So. Ariz. chpt. Make-A-Wish Found., 1995-96; mem. fin. com. Christ Ch. United Meth., 2000—. Recipient Crescordia Environ. Excellence award Valley Forward Assn., 1986, Hon. Mention award Ariz. Hist. Mus. competition, 1985. Fellow AIA (pres. Rio Salado chpt. 1981, 74-88, bd. dirs. So. Ariz. chpt. 1988—, pres., 1993, Gold medal adv. bd. 1992-95). Democrat. Methodist. Avocations: fly fishing, skiing, hunting, tennis, golf, photography. Office: U Ariz PO Box 21-0075 Tucson AZ 85721-0075 E-mail: hershbergerfaia@qwest.net

HERSHEY, GERALD LEE, psychologist, educator; b. Detroit, Mar. 7, 1931; s Von Waltz and Clementine H.; m. Shirley Gauld, Oct. 2, 1954; children: Bruce, Dale, James. Student, UCLA, 1949-54; B.A. with honors, Mich. State U., 1957, M.A., 1958, Ph.D., 1961. Asst. instr., research assoc. Mich. State U., East Lansing, 1958-61; mem. faculty dept. psychology Fullerton Coll., Calif., 1961—, prof., 1965—, chmn. dept., 1980—; vis. prof. Chapman Coll., Calif., 1962-69. Co-author: Human Development (2d edit.), 1978, Living Psychology (3d edit.), 1981. Served to 1st lt. AUS, 1954-56. Mem. Am. Psychol. Assn., Assn. Humanistic Psychology, NEA Lodge: Lions. Office: Fullerton Coll 321 E Chapman Ave Fullerton CA 92832-2011

HERSHISER, OREL LEONARD, IV, professional baseball player; b. Buffalo, Sept. 16, 1958; s. Orel Leonard H. III and Millie H.; m. Jaimie (Byars) Hershiser, Feb. 7, 1981; 2 sons, Orel Leonard V, Jordan Douglass Student, Bowling Green State U. Pitcher minor league teams Clinton, Iowa, 1979, San Antonio, 1980-81, Albaqueque, 1982-83; with Los Angeles Dodgers, 1983-94, 99—, Cleve. Indians, 1995-97; pitcher San Francisco Giants, 1997-98, New York Mets, 1998-99. Mem. Nat. League All-Star Team, 1987, 88. Named Nat. League Cy Young award winner, 1988, Most Valuable Player 1988 World Series. NL Gold Glove, 1988, Major League Player of Yr. Sporting News, 1988, Nat. League Pitcher of Yr. Sporting News, 1988, Sporting News Nat. League All-Star Team, 1988, Sporting News Silver Slugger Team, 1993, All-Star Games, 1987-89. Achievements include playing in the World Series, 1988. Office: Los Angeles Dodgers 1000 Elysian Park Ave Los Angeles CA 90012-1199

HERSHMAN, LYNN LESTER, artist; b. Cleve. 1 dau., Dawn. B.S., Case-Western Res. U., 1963; M.A., San Francisco State U., 1972. Prof. U. Calif., Davis, 1984—. Vis. prof. art U. Calif., Berkeley, Calif. Coll. Arts and Crafts, San Jose State U., 1974-78; assoc. project dir. Christo's Running Fence, 1973-76; founder, dir. Floating Mus., 1975-79; ind. film/video producer and cons., 1979— Author works in field; one-man shows include Santa Barbara Mus. Art, 1970, Univ. Art Mus., Berkeley, Calif., 1972, Mills Coll., Oakland, Calif., 1973, William Sawyer Gallery, 1974, Nat. Galleries, Melbourne, Australia, 1976, Mandeville Art Gallery, U. Calif., San Diego, 1976, M.H. de Young Art Mus., 1978, Pallazo dei Diamonte, Ferrara, Italy, 1978, San Francisco Art Acad., 1980, Portland Center Visual Arts, 1980, New Mus., New Sch., N.Y.C., 1981, Inst. Contemporary Art, Phila., 1981, Anina Nosai Gallery, N.Y.C., 1981, Contemporary Art Center, Cin., 1982, Toronto, Los Angeles Contemporary Exhibits, 1986, Univ. Art Mus. Berkeley, 1987, Madison (Wis.) Art Ctr., 1987, Intersesction for the Arts, San Francisco, Pacific Film Archive, A. Space, "Guerilla Tactics" Toronto, Can., Venice Bienalle Global Village; group exhbns. include Cleve. Art Mus., 1968, St. Paul Art Ctr., 1969, Richmond (Calif.) Art Ctr., 1970, 73, Galeria del Sol, Santa Barbara, Calif., 1971, San Francisco Art Inst., 1972, Richard Demarco Art Gallery, Edinburgh, Scotland, 1973, Laguna Beach (Calif.) Art Mus., 1973, Univ. Art Mus., Univ. Calif., Berkeley, 1974, Bronx (N.Y.) Mus., 1975, Linda Ferris Gallery, Seattle, 1975, Madenville Art Gallery, San Diego, Contemporary Arts Mus., Houston, 1977, New Orleans, 1977, Ga. Mus. Art, Athens, 1977, New Mus., N.Y., 1981, Calif. Coll. Arts and Crafts, 1981, San Francisco Mus. Modern Art, 1979, 80, 90, Art-Beaubourg, Paris, 1980, Ars Electronica, 1989, Am. Film Inst., 1989, Mus. Moving Image Internat. Ctr. for Photography, 1989, Kitchen Ctr. for Video-Music, N.Y., 1990, Robert Koch Gallery, San Francsico, 1990, Inst. Contemporary Art, London, 1990, Frankfurt (Germany) Art Fair, 1990, Inst. Contemporary Art, Boston, 1991, Oakland (Calif.) Mus., 1991, La Cite des Arts et des Nouvelles Technologies, Montreal, 1991, Richard F. Brush Art Gallery, Canton, N.Y., 1992, Jack Tilton Gallery, N.Y., 1992, Southeastern Ctr. for Contemporary Art, Winston-Salem, N.C., 1992, Bonner Kunstverein, Bonn, Germany, 1992, Chgo. Ave. Armory, 1992, Retrospective, Tribute, 1994, Nelson Gallery, Paris, 1994, Hess Collection, 1994. Bd. dirs. San Francisco Art Acad., Spectrum Found., Motion a Performance Collective. Western States Regional fellow (film/video), 1990; grantee Nat. Endowment for the Arts, (2) Art Matters Inc., San Francisco Found., N.Y. State Coun. for the Arts, Zellerbach Family Fund, Inter Arts of Marin, Gerbode Found., The Women's Project; recipient Dirs. Choice award San Francisco Internat. Film Festival, 1987, tribute 1987 Mill Valley Video Festial, Exptl. Video award 1988, 1st prize Montbelliard, France, 1990, 2d prize, Vigo, Spain, 1992, 1993 Ars Electronica, Austria, WRO Poland, Nat. Film Theatre, London, Gerber award Seattle Art Mus., 1994, ZKM/Siemans award, 1995, Golden Nica, Ars Electronica, 1999, Flintridge award Lifetime Achievement in the Arts, 1999. Mem. Assn. Art Pubs. (dir., Annie Gerber award 1995). Office: 1201 California St San Francisco CA 94109-5001

HERSKOWITZ, IRA, educator, molecular geneticist; b. Bklyn., July 14, 1946; BS in Biology, Calif. Inst. Tech., 1967; PhD in Microbiology, MIT, 1971; PhD (hon.), St. Louis U., 1997. From asst. to full prof. biology U. Oreg., Eugene, 1972-81; assoc. Inst. Molecular Biology, U. Oreg., Eugene, 1972-81; prof. dept. biochemistry and biophysics U. Calif., San Francisco, 1981—, chmn. dept., 1990-95, head divsn. genetics, 1981—, co-dir. program in human genetics, 1997—, prof. dept. biopharm. scis., 2000—. Mem. genetics study sect. NIH, Bethesda, Md., 1986-90; mem. sci. rev. bd. in genetics Howard Hughes Med. Inst., Bethesda, 1986-94, mem. med. adv. bd., 1995-97; vis. prof. Coll. de France, Paris, 1992; sci. adv. bd. Tularik, Inc., 1992-96; mem. awards jury Albert Lasker Med. Rsch., 1994—; mem. sci. adv. com. Inst. Cancer Rsch., Fox Chase Cancer Ctr., 1995-99; bd. sci. counsellors Nat. Cancer Inst., 1996-2000; advisor Merck Genome Rsch. Inst., 1996—. Assoc. editor Virology, 1976-81, Genetics, 1982-87, Ann. Rev. Genetics, 1984-89; editor Jour. Molecular Biology, 1982-86, assoc. editor 1986-87; mem. editl. bd. Molecular Biology of the Cell, 1997—, Trends in Genetics, 1990—; mem. bd. reviewing editors Sci., 1991-96. Mem. vis. com. for dept. biology MIT, 1982—; mem. vis. com. divsn. biology Calif. Inst. Tech., 1999—; mem. coun. Am. Soc. Cell Biology, 1996-99; sci. adv. bd. Sandler Program in Asthma Rsch., 1999—. Recipient Eli Lilly award Am. Soc. Microbiology, 1983, Disting. Tchg. award U. Calif., San Francisco, 1984, medal Genetics Soc. Am., 1988, Howard Taylor Ricketts award, U. Chgo., 1992, Disting. Alumni award Calif. Inst. Tech., 1994; named Streisinger lectr. U. Oreg., 1984, Harvey Soc. lectr., 1986, Mendel lectr. Genetical Soc. Gt. Britain, 1991, Bateson lectr. John Innes Inst., Norwich, UK. Fellow AAAS, MacArthur Found., Am. Acad. Arts and Scis., Am. Soc. Microbiology; mem. Nat. Acad. Scis. (sci. reviewing award 1985), Genetics Soc. Am. (pres. 1985). Achievements include rsch. in control of gene expression in yeast, cell signalling and growth control, cell morphogenesis, drug action and drug resistance. Office: U Calif San Francisco Dept Biochem & Biophys 513 Parnassus Ave San Francisco CA 94143-0448

HERSMAN, MARION FRANK, professional administrator, lawyer; b. Huntington, W.Va., Nov. 12, 1932; s. Marion Rockefeller and Frances Mae (Peabody) H.; m. Carole Anne Birthright, Oct. 1960 (div.); 1 child, Frank Eric Birthright; m. Nina Claire Mohay, Dec. 24, 1976 (div.); 1 child, Alicia Claire; m. Eleonora Georgi Hivrina, April 11, 1995; children: Elizabeth Anne, Diana Frances. B.S. in Chemistry, Physics and Math, Ohio State U., 1953; Ph.D. in Chemistry (Victor Chem. fellow, Colgate Palmolive-Peet fellow, Univ. fellow), U. Ill., 1956; J.D., George Washington U., 1958, LL.M., 1960; M.A., New Sch. for Social Research, 1964. Bar: Va. 1958, N.Y. 1959, D.C. 1960, U.S. Supreme Ct. 1960, U.S. Ct. Appeals (D.C. cir.) 1960. Teaching fellow U. Ill.; patent examiner U.S. Patent Office, Washington, 1956-57; assoc. firm Burns Doane, Benedict & Irons, Washington, 1957-59, Arthur, Dry & Dole, N.Y.C., 1959-60, Fish, Richardson & Neave, N.Y.C., 1960-64; staff assoc. office sci. resources planning NSF, Washington, 1964-67, office of planning and policy studies, 1967-69, head office intergovtl. sci. programs, 1969-72, dir. office intergovtl. sci. and research utilization, 1972-75; exec. dir. Colo. Planning Coordinating Council, 1976; spl. asst., sci. and tech. advisor to Gov. Colo., 1976; sci. and tech. advisor Fedn. Rocky Mountain States, Denver, 1977; dir. Rocky Mountain Tech. Sharing Task Force, 1977; dir. Div. Water Resources Hillsborough County, Tampa, Fla., 1977, dir. Div. Pub. Utilities, 1977-78, dir. Office of Planning and Intergovtl. Relations, 1978-79; asst. county adminstr. Hillsborough County (Fla.) Div. Pub. Utilities, 1978-79; vice chmn. Hillsborough Intergovtl. Resource Recovery Mgmt. Com.; mem. Fla. Community Conservation Com., 1978-80, Urban Consortium, 1978-80; spl. asst. to pres. U. South Fla., 1979-80; atty. NSF, 1980-82; dir. com. on hazardous materials Fed. Emergency Mgmt. Agy., 1981-83; vis. disting. prof. Nova U., 1982, spl. asst. to pres. for program devel., 1982; asst. city mgr. for health and human services City of Austin, (Tex.), 1982-84; exec. v.p. Lawyers Title of Ky., 1983-85; ptnr. LTK Enterprises, 1983-85; exec. v.p., chief operating officer Automation Telecommunications and Management Inc., Austin, Tex., 1984-85; dir. research and state services The Council of State Govts., Lexington, Ky., 1985-87; town mgr. Town of Snow Hill, Md., 1988; county mgr. Nye County, Nev., 1988-90; dir. social svcs. Louis Berger Internat. Cons., Sasatov Oblast, Russia, 1996—98; pres. RH Mgmt. Assocs., 1990—; town mgr. Town of Pahrup, Nev., 2000—01. Spkr. in field; tchg. assoc. George Washington U., 1957-59; chmn., exec. dir. com. on intergovtl. sci. rels. Fed. Coun. Sci. and Tech., Exec. Office of Pres., 1979-83; mem. Agrl. Yearbook adv. bd. USDA, 1979, mem. tech. adv. bd. nat. rural cmtys. facilities assessment, 1978; chmn. com. on policy mgmt. and assistance U.S. Office Mgmt. and Budget, Washington, 1974-75; mem. com. on tech. sharing President's Office Sci. and Tech., 1972-74; chmn. So. Nev. Rural Health Fair, 1991; prof. urban engring. Nat. U. Mex., Mexico City, 1975; vis. faculty CSC, Kings Point, N.Y., 1975, Fed. Exec. Inst., Charlottesville, Va., 1977, Golden Gate U., 1979-80; vis. prof. U. Colo. Grad. Sch. Pub. Affairs, 1976-77, U. South Fla., 1978, Martin Sch., U. Ky., 1986-88; spl. asst. to dir. NSF, 1976-80; cons. Office Sci. and Tech., Exec. Office of Pres., 1976-80, Western Govs.' Task Force on Regional Policy Mgmt., 1976-77; cons. USDA, 1978; mem. Subcom. on Rsch. Itilization Transp. Rsch. Bd./NRC/NAS, 1981-82; adminstr. Pahrump Valley Med. Ctr., 1991-92; pres. Nev. Health and Med. Found., 1991-92; U.S. exec. advisor mayor and city coun. City of Narva, Estonia, 1994-96; U.S. exec. advisor City of Tartu, Estonia, 1994, Internat. Exec. Svcs. Corps, 1994; U.S. trade rep. City of Narva, Estonia, 1994—; exec. advisor Internat. Exec. Svc. Corps, City of Vladimir, Russia, 1995-96; dir. social svcs. Louis Berger Internat., Inc., 1996-98; exec. advisor Saratov, Russia, 1996-98. Contbg. author: Science and Technology Policies, 1973; bd. editors and consultants: Scholar and Educator, 1977; mem. editorial bd.: Jour. Edn. and Scholar, 1977-87; contbr. articles to profl. jours. Bd. dirs. Warwick Assn., 1980-81; chmn. consumers and bus. affairs com. D.C. Area Neighborhood Council; mem. Washington Mayor's Planning and Budget Adv. Com., 1980-82; vol. exec. Internat. Exec. Svcs. Corps., 1994—, Pahrump Arts Coun., 1994-96. Recipient Pub. Service award states of Ga., La., Ala., Pa., Okla., N.C., Pub. Service award So. Interstate Nuclear Bd., Pub. Service award Nat. Conf. State Legislatures; Picatinny Arsenal fellow, Victor Chem. fellow, Colgate Palmolive-Peet fellow, Ohio State Univ. fellow; U.S. Govt. grantee. Mem. Va., D.C., Fed. bar assns., Am. Chem. Soc., Am. Soc. Pub. Adminstrn. (chmn. sect. on intergovtl. adminstrn. and mgmt. 1977-79, Public Service award), AAAS, Sigma Xi, Phi Lambda Upsilon, Delta Theta Phi (chmn. scholarships), Alpha Chi Sigma, Kappa Sigma. Home and Office: PO Box 3434 2070 S Page St Pahrump NV 89041

HERTEL, JOHN R. state legislator, farmer, rancher; b. Lewistown, Mont., May 9, 1940; m. Dixie Hertel. BS, Rocky Mountain Coll., 1962. Tchr. high sch., 1962-73; farmer-rancher, 1973—; mem. Mont. State Senate, 1992—, chair bus./industry com., vice chair bills and jours. com., mem. edn. and cultural resources com., hwys. and transp. com. Bd. dirs. Moore Farmers Oil Co., Norwest Bank. Bd. dirs. Moccasin Experiment Sta.; mem. Moore Sch. Bd., 1972-92, chair 8 yrs. Mem. Mont. Stockgrowers, Fergus County Livestock Assn. (bd. dirs.), Fergus County Farm Bur. (bd. dirs.), Masons. Republican. Home: RR 1 Box 30 Moore MT 59464-9703

HERTZBERG, ABRAHAM, aeronautical engineering educator, university research scientist; b. N.Y.C., July 8, 1922; s. Rubin and Paulien (Kalif) H.; m. Ruth Cohen, Sept. 3, 1950 (dec.); children: Eleanor Ruth, Paul Elliot, Jean R. BS in Aero. Engring., Va. Poly. Inst., 1943; MS in Aero. Engring., Cornell U., 1949; postgrad., U. Buffalo, 1949-53. Engr. Cornell Aero. Lab., 1949-57, asst. head aerodynamics research, 1957-59, head aerodynamics research, 1959-65; dir. aerospace & energetic rsch. program U. Wash., 1966-93, prof. astronautics, 1966-93; prof. emeritus astronautics, 1993—. Prin. investigator numerous federal rsch. grants; cons. Aerospace Corp., past mem. sci. adv. bd. USAF, Olin-Rocket Rsch., STI Optronics; past mem. electro-optics panel SAB, mem. various ad hoc coms.; mem. space sys. and tech. adv. com., rsch. and tech. subcom., past mem. rsch. and tech. adv. coun. NASA; mem. plasma dynamics rev. panel NSF, U.S. Army; honored spkr. Laser Inst. Am., 1975, Citizens of Sendai, 1991; past mem. theory adv. com. Los Alamos Nat. Lab.; vis. lectr. Chinese Acad. Scis., Beijing, 1983, 88, 97; Paul Vieille lectr. 7th Internat. Shock Tube Symposium, 1969, 89, 17th Internat. Symposium on Shock Waves and Shock Tubes, 1989; Irvine I. Glass Meml. lectr. U. Toronto, 1996. Editor Physics of Fluids, 1968-70; contbr. numerous articles on modern gas dynamics, high powered lasers, controlled thermonuclear fusions processes, space laser solar energy concepts, space energy concepts and new ultra velocity propulsion concepts to profl. jours. Served with AUS, 1944-46. Honored speaker Laser Inst. Am. Fellow AIAA (Dryden lectr. 1977, Agard lectr. 1978, Plasmadynamics and Lasers award 1992), Internat. Acad. Astronautics; mem. AAAS, NAE, Am. Phys. Soc., Sigma Xi. Achievements include patents in field. Office: U Wash Aerospace & Energetics PO Box 352250 Seattle WA 98195-2250

HERTZBERG, ROBERT M. state legislator; m. Cynthia Telles; children: Daniel, David, Raymond. Graduated magna cum laude, U. Redlands, 1976; JD magna cum laude, U. Calif., 1979. Mem. Calif. State Assembly, 1996—, spkr., 2000—. Chmn. Calif. Assembly Rules Com., 1998—. Mem. L.A. County Quality and Productivity Commn., Calif. State Bd. Pharmacy, 1984-88; chmn. Calif. Adv. Commn. on Youth, 1978-79, dean's coun. Hebrew Union Coll., 1991-95, v.p. Am. Jewish Com.; bd. dirs. CORO Assocs., Chinatown Svc. Ctr., Mulholland Tomorrow.; mem. exec. com. Jewish Cmty. Rels. Com. of Valley Alliance, state issues com. Valley Industry and Commerce Assn., Sherman Oaks Town Coun. Commerce Assn. Recipient Paul Harris fellow Rotary Found. Rotary Internat, Joe

Farber Legis. award Peace Officers Rsch. Assn. Calif., Gold Key award L.A. Opportunities Industrialization ctr., PTA award 31st Dist. PTSA, Disting. Svc. award Planned Parenthood. Office: Calif State Assembly Van Nuys State Bldg 6150 Van Nuys Blvd Ste 350 Van Nuys CA 91401-3345 also: State Capitol Rm 219 Sacramento CA 95814

HERZ, LEONARD, financial consultant; b. Bronx, N.Y., June 25, 1931; s. Emanuel and Henrietta (Morris) H.; m. Sally Jampolsky, May 2, 1954 (dec. Apr. 1994); children: Michael, Hildee, Larry; m. Debra Brody, July 28, 1995. B.B.A., CCNY, 1952. C.P.A., N.Y. Auditor Lybrand Ross Bros., C.P.A.s, N.Y.C., 1954-60; asst. controller Merritt Chapman Scott, N.Y.C., 1960-66; treas. Baker Industries Inc., Parsippany, N.J., 1966-73; v.p. finance Del Labs. Inc., Farmingdale, N.Y., 1973-74; exec. v.p. Holmes Protection, Inc., N.Y.C., 1974-82; fin. cons. L. Herz, Denver, 1982-87. Dir. Oliver Exterminating Corp., Am. Med. Alert Corp.; bd. dirs. Ctrl. Sta. Electric Protective Assn. With AUS, 1952-54. Mem. N.Y. State Soc. C.P.A.s, Am. Inst. C.P.A.s, Exec. Assn. Greater N.Y. (bd. dirs. 1988-90). Home and Office: 254 Garfield St Denver CO 80206-5519

HERZ, MICHAEL JOSEPH, marine environmental scientist; b. St. Paul, Aug. 12, 1936; s. Malvin E. and Josephine (Daneman) H.; m. Joan Klein Levy, Feb. 3, 1962 (div. 1982); children: David M., Daniel J., Ann K.; m. Naomi Brodie Schalit, Aug. 21, 1984 (div. 1996); children: Nathaniel B., Hallie R.; m. Kate Pearson Josephs, Sept. 27, 1998. BA, Reed Coll., 1958; MA, San Francisco State U., 1962; PhD, U. So. Calif., 1966. Program coord. postdoctoral tng. program U. Calif., San Francisco, 1969-73, asst. prof., 1969-73, assoc. prof. in residence, 1973-74; exec. dir., dir. water quality tng. program San Francisco Bay. chpt. Oceanic Soc., 1974-77; exec. v.p., co-dir. rsch. and policy Oceanic Soc., San Francisco, 1977-84; sr. rsch. scientist San Francisco State U., 1984-88; exec. dir. and baykeeper San Francisco BayKeeper, 1989-95; pvt. cons. Alna, Maine, 1995—. Chmn. bd. govs. Tiburon Ctr. Environ. Studies, San Francisco State U., 1985-86; NRC com. mem. Effectiveness of Oil Spill Disperants, Washington, 1985-87, Risk Assessment Mgmt. Marine Systems, Washington, 1996-98; mem. com. on ocean disposal of radwaste Calif. Dept. Health, Sacramento, 1985-92; mem. tech. adv. com. Calif. Office of Oil Spill Prevention and Response, 1992-95; bd. dirs. Friends of the Earth, Washington, 1989—, chmn. bd. dirs., 1997-99; bd. dirs. Oceanic Soc., 1984-89; chmn. bd. dirs. Aquatic Habitat Inst.; mem. Alaska Oil Spill Commn., 1989-90; mem. NRC com. Risk Assessment and Mgmt. of Marine Systems, Washington, 1996—. Author, co-editor: (books) Memory Consolidation, 1972, Habituation I & II, 1973; contbr. reports to profl. publs. Chmn. community adv. bd. Sta. KQED (Pub. Broadcast System affiliate), 1979-85, San Francisco, citizens adv. com. San Francisco Bay Conservation and Devel. Commn., 1979—, chmn. 1984; mem. tech. adv. com. San Francisco Bay Regional Water Quality Control Bd., Oakland, Calif., 1979-82, Assn. Bay Area Govts., Oakland, 1983-84; mem. bay area adv. com. Sea Grant Marine Adv. Program, San Francisco, 1983-89; mem. com. Bur. Land Mgmt., Pacific States Regional Tech. Working Group, 1979-83; bd. dirs. Maine Initiatives, 1996—, Sheepscot Valley Conservation Assn. 1995—, pres. 1999—; bd. dirs. Citizens for a Better Environ., 1986-94, Oceanic Soc., 1984-89. Served with U.S. Army, 1958-59. Predoctoral fellow NIMH, U. So. Calif., 1963-64; postdoctoral fellow NIMH, UCLA Brain Research Inst, 1966-68. Mem. AAAS, Calif. Acad. Scis., San Francisco Bay and Estuarine Assn. E-mail: mherz@lincoln.midcoast.com

HERZBERGER, EUGENE E. retired neurosurgeon; b. Sotchi, USSR, June 7, 1920; came to U.S., 1957, naturalized, 1964; s. Eugene S. and Mary P. H.; married; children— Henry, Monica M.D., U. King Ferdinand I, Cluj, Rumania, 1947. Diplomate Am. Bd. Neurol. Surgery. Intern Univ. Hosp., Cluj, Rumania, 1946-47, resident in surgery Rumania, 1947-48; resident in neurosurgery Beilinson Hosp., Tel Aviv, 1949-53; chief neurosurgeon Tel Hashomer Govt. Hosp., Tel Aviv, 1953-57; research asst. Yale U., 1958-59; instr. neurosurgery Med. Coll. Ga., 1959-60; attending neurosurgeon St. Clare Hosp., Monroe, Wis., 1960-76, Mercy Hosp. and Finley Hosp., Dubuque, Iowa, 1976-94. Contbr. articles to med. jours. Mem. Am. Assn. Neurol. Surgeons, Iowa Midwest Neurosurg. Soc., Congress Neurol. Surgeons, Am. Acad. Neurology, Iowa State Med. Soc. Office: 15649 E El Lago Blvd Fountain Hills AZ 85268

HERZER, RICHARD KIMBALL, franchising company executive; b. Ogden, Utah, June 2, 1931; s. Arthur Vernon and Dorothy (Cortez) H.; m. Phyllis Ann McCullough, Mar. 29, 1958; children: Diane E., Mark V., Craig K. BS, UCLA, 1958. Vice-pres., contr. United Rent All, Inc., L.A., 1967-71; dir. fin. planning Internat. Industries Inc., North Hollywood, Calif., 1971-73, v.p., controller, 1973-75, v.p. fin., 1975-79, pres., 1979—, chmn. bd., CEO, 1983—; bd. dirs. IHOP Corp., 1979—. Trustee So. Calif. chpt. Multiple Sclerosis, 1984—. 1st lt. U.S. Army, 1953-56. Mem. Calif. Restaurant Assn. (dir. 1985-94), Phi Delta Theta. Republican. Home: 4411 Woodleigh Ln La Canada Flintridge CA 91011-3542 Office: IHOP Corp 525 N Brand Blvd Glendale CA 91203-1903

HERZLICH, HAROLD J. chemical engineer; b. Bklyn. m. Carol Ast; children: Amy, Adam. BSChemE, NYU, 1956; student, So. Conn. Coll., Quinnipiac Coll. Mem. prodn. squadron Goodyear Tire & Rubber Co., Akron, Ohio, 1956-57, mem. process devel., 1957-58; prodn. compounder Armstrong Rubber Co., New Haven, 1958-61, sr. compounder, 1961-62, divsn. compounder, 1962-65, mgr. pass tire comp. devel., 1965-66, mgr. auto tire comp. devel., 1966-68, mgr. pass car tire comp. devel., 1968-70, sr. rsch. chemist, 1970-73, mgr. compound rsch., 1973-75, mgr. compound devel., 1975-85, dir. tire engring., legal matters and product reliability, 1985-88, Pirelli Armstrong Tire Co., New Haven, 1988-90; consulting tire engr. Tire Engring., Chemistry and Safety, Las Vegas, 1990—. Pres. Elasphalt Corp.; chmn. Internat. Tire Conf.; speaker in field. Tech. editor Rubber and Plastics News. With USCG. Mem. ASTM (mem. E-40), Am. Chem. Soc. (chmn. rubber divsn. 1982—, chmn.-elect 1981, mem. membership com., mem. edn. com., mem. budget and fin. com., treas. rubber divsn. 1978-81, bus. mgr. rubber chemistry and tech., mem. divsn. chemistry and law, hon. life), Soc. Automotive Engrs., Acad. Forensics Sci. (engring. divsn.), Tire Soc., Conn. Rubber Group (edn. chmn., vice chmn., chmn. 1966, hon. life). Avocations: sports, community svc., travel. Home and Office: Tire Engring Chemistry & Safety 8908 Desert Mound Dr Las Vegas NV 89134-8801

HESS, CHARLES EDWARD, environmental horticulture educator; b. Paterson, N.J., Dec. 20, 1931; s. Cornelius W. M. and Alice (Debruyn) H.; children: Mary, Carol, Nancy, John, Peter; m. Eva G. Carroad, Feb. 14, 1981. BS, Rutgers U., 1953; MS, Cornell U., 1954, PhD, 1957; DAgr (hon.), Purdue U., 1983; DSc (hon.), Delaware Valley Coll., Doylestown, Pa., 1992. From asst. prof. to prof. Purdue U., West Lafayette, Ind., 1958-65; rsch. prof., dept. chmn. Rutgers U., New Brunswick, N.J., 1966, assoc. dean, dir. N.J. Agrl. Exptl. Sta., 1970, acting dean Coll. Agrl. and Environ. Sci., 1971, dean Cook Coll., 1972-75; assoc. dir. Calif. Agrl. Exptl. Sta., 1975-89; asst. sec. sci. and edn. USDA, Washington, 1989-91; dean Coll. Agrl. and Environ. Scis. U. Calif., Davis, 1975-89, prof. dept. environ. horticulture, 1975-94; prof. emeritus, 1994—; dir. internat. pro- [illegible] provost, 1994—. Cons. U.S. AID, 1965, Office Tech. Assessment, U.S. Congress, 1976-77; chmn. study team world food and nutrition study NAS, 1976; mem. Calif. State Bd. Food and Agr., 1984-89; mem. Nat. Sci. Bd., 1982-88, 92-98, vice-chmn., 1984-88; co-chmn. Joint Coun. USDA, 1987-91. Mem. West Lafayette Sch. Bd., Ind., 1963-65, sec., 1963, pres., 1964; mem. Gov.'s Commn. Blueprint for Agr., 1971-73; bd. dirs. Davis [illegible] The Netherlands, 1992-98, bd. chmn., 1995-96. Mem. U.S. EPA (mem. biotech. sci. adv. com. 1992-96), AAAS (chmn. agriculture sect. 1989-90), Am. Soc. Hort. Sci. (pres. 1973), Internat. Plant Propagators Soc. (pres. 1973), Agrl. Rsch. Inst., Phi Beta Kappa, Sigma Xi, Alpha Zeta, Phi Kappa Phi. Office: U Calif Coll Agrl Environ Scis Dept Environ Horticulture Davis CA 95616 E-mail: cehess@ucdavis.edu

HESS, JOHN WARREN, scientific institute administrator, educator; b. Lancaster, Pa., May 6, 1947; s. John Warren and Barbara Kathryn (Spencer) H.; m. Letitia Jean Schrantz, Mar. 20, 1971; children: Nathan James, Joshua Kyle. BS in Geol. Scis., Pa. State U., 1969, PhD in Geology, 1974. Asst. rsch. prof. water resources ctr. Desert Rsch. Inst., Las Vegas, Nev., 1974-78, assoc. rsch. prof., 1978-86, rsch. prof., 1986—, dir. environ. isotope lab., 1981-87, dep. dir., 1987-89, exec. dir., 1989-2000, interim v.p. rsch., 1994-95, v.p. acad. affairs, 1995—, congrl. fellow, 2000—. Chmn. bd. dirs. Karst Waters Inst., Charlestown, W.Va. Contbr. over 85 articles to profl. jours. Adult leader Boy Scouts Am., Las Vegas, 1978—. Hon. Rsch. fellow U. Glasgow, Scotland, 1980-81; Centennial fellow Coll. Earth and Mineral Scis., Pa. State U. Fellow Geol. Soc. Am. (2nd vice chmn. 1993-94, 1st vice chmn. 1994-95, chair 1995-96), Nat. Speleological Soc.; mem. AAAS, Am. Geophys. Union, Internat. Assn. Hydrogeologists, Geochem. Soc. Office: Desert Rsch Inst 755 E Flamingo Rd Las Vegas NV 89119-7363

HESS, RICHARD NEAL, plastic surgeon; b. Phila., June 16, 1957; MD, U. Ariz., 1983. Chmn. plastic surgery Northwest Hosp., Tucson. Office: 1050 E River Ste 200 Tucson AZ 85718

HESSE, MARTHA O. natural gas company executive; b. Hattiesburg, Miss., Aug. 14, 1942; d. John William and Geraldine Elaine (Ossian) H. B.S., U. Iowa, 1964; postgrad., Northwestern U., 1972-76; M.B.A., U. Chgo., 1979. Research analyst Blue Shield, 1964-66; dir. div. data mgmt. Am. Hosp. Assn., 1966-69; dir., chief operating officer SEI Info. Tech., Chgo., 1969-80; assoc. dep. sec. Dept. of Commerce, Washington, 1981-82; exec. dir. Pres.' Task Force on Mgmt. Reform, 1982; asst. sec. mgmt. and adminstrn. Dept. of Energy, Washington, 1982-86; chmn. FERC, Washington, 1986-89; sr. v.p. 1st Chgo. Corp., 1990; now pres. Hesse Gas, Houston. Bd. dirs. Pinnacle West Capital Corp., Ariz. Pub. Svc. Co., , Mut. Trust Life, Laidlaw, AMEC plc, The Beacon Coun. Office: Box 2160 Winnemucca NV 89446-2160

HESSELINK, LAMBERTUS, electrical engineering and physics educator; b. Enschede, The Netherlands, Dec. 4, 1948; came to U.S., 1971; s. Lambertus and Wilhelmina (ten Tye) H. BSME, Twente Inst. Tech., Enschede, 1970, BS in Applied Physics, 1971, postgrad., 1974; MSME, Calif. Inst. Tech., 1972, PhD in Applied Mechs., Physics, 1977. Rsch. fellow Calif. Inst. Tech., Pasadena, 1977-78, instr. applied physics, 1978-80, sr. rsch. fellow fluid mechs., 1979-80; asst. prof. aeros. and astronautics Stanford (Calif.) U., 1980-85, asst. prof., 1985—, assoc. prof. elec. engring., 1980-85, asst. prof., 1985-90, prof. electrical engring. and aeronautics/astonautics, 1990—. Cons. Hughes Aircraft Corp., Culver City, Calif., 1978-79, MCC Corp., 1986-92; invited scientist mem. image processing work group for Hubble Space Telescope, 1990; assoc. editor Jour. Applied Sci. and Applied Optics, 1990; founder Siros Technologies, Inc.; cons. to industry and govt.; mem. scientific adv. bd. USAF, 1995—; founder Senvid, Inc. Patentee in field. Recipient Stheeman prize Twente Inst. Tech., 1970; Fulbright fellow 1971-74; Josephine de Karman fellow, 1974-75. Fellow Optical Soc. Am.; mem. AIAA (Engr. of Yr. 1982), Soc. Photo-Optical Instrumentation Engrs. Optical Soc. Am., Am. Phys. Soc., Royal Dutch Acad. Arts and Scis. (corr.), Sigma Xi. Office: Stanford U Dept Electrical Engring Durand 353 Stanford CA 94305-4035 E-mail: bert@kaos.stanford.edu

HESSER, JAMES EDWARD, astronomy researcher; b. Wichita, Kans., June 23, 1941; arrived in Can., 1977; s. J. Edward and Ina (Lowe) H.; m. Betty Hinsdale, Aug. 24, 1963; children: Nadja Lynn, Rebecca Ximena, Diana Gillian. BA, U. Kans., 1963; MA, Princeton U., 1965, PhD, 1966. Rsch. assoc. Princeton (N.J.) U. Obs., 1966-68; from jr. astronomer to assoc. astronomer Cerro Tololo Inter-Am. Obs., La Serena, Chile, 1968-77; sr. rsch. officer Dominion Astrophys. Obs., NRC, Victoria, B.C., Can., 1977—; assoc. dir. Cerro Tololo Inter-Am. Obs., La Serena, Chile, 1974-76, Dominion Astrophys. Obs., NRC, Victoria, B.C., Can., 1984-86, dir. Can., 1986—. Editor: CTIO Facilities Manual, 1973, 2d rev. edit., 1978, Star Clusters, 1980; co-editor: Late Stages of Stellar Evolution, 1974; contbr. more than 200 articles to profl. and sci. jours. Mem. Am. Astron. Soc. (councilor 1985-88, v.p. 1991-94), Astron. Soc. Pacific (bd. dirs. 1981-84, v.p. 1985-86, pres. 1987-88), Can. Astron. Soc., Internat. Astron. Union, Royal Astron. Soc. Can. Avocations: reading, walking, cooking, gardening. Home: 1874 Ventura Way Victoria BC Canada V8N 1R3 Office: Dominion Astrophys Obs HIA NRC 5071 W Saanich Rd Victoria BC Canada V9E 2E7 E-mail: jim.hesser@nrc.ca

HESTER, NORMAN ERIC, chemical company technical executive, chemist; b. Niangua, Mo., Dec. 16, 1946; s Eric Ira and Norma Josephine (Wright) H.; m. Sylvie Jean Hunt, June 16, 1973; children: Jenay Aimee, Yvette Joy, Trinity Marie. AA, El Camino Coll., 1966; BS, Calif. State U., Long Beach, 1968; MS, U. Calif., Riverside, 1971, PhD, 1972. Postdoctoral rsch. chemist U. Calif. Air Pollution Ctr., Riverside, 1972-74; air quality chemist EPA, Las Vegas, Nev., 1974-77; program mgr. Rockwell Internat., Newbury Park, Calif., 1977-80; group head Occidental Petroleum Rsch. Ctr., Irvine, 1980-83; tech. dir. Truesdail Labs. Inc., Tustin, 1983—. Pvt. environ. cons., Mission Viejo, Calif., 1983. Contbr. articles to profl. jours. Mem. ASTM, Am. Chem. Soc., Assn. Hazardous Materials Profls. Republican. Avocations: growing hybrid roses, hiking, travel. Office: Truesdail Labs Inc 14201 Franklin Ave Tustin CA 92780-7008 E-mail: norman@truesdail.com

HESTER, RANDOLPH THOMPSON, JR. landscape architect, educator; b. Danville, Va., Dec. 12, 1944; s. Randolph Thompson and Virginia (Green) H.; m. Marcia Jeanne McNally, Mar. 17, 1983; 1 child, Nathaniel Christopher. BA, N.C. State U., 1969, BS in Landscape Architecture, 1968; M in Landscape Architecture, Harvard U., 1969. Registered landscape architect, N.C. Prof. Pa. State U., State Coll., 1969-70, N.C. State U., Raleigh, 1970-80, city univ. coord., 1972-75; prof. U. Calif., Berkeley, 1981—, chmn. dept. landscape architecture, 1987-92; assoc. dir. Ctr. Environ. Design Rsch., Berkeley, 1982-85. Designer community devel. sect., Cambridge, Mass., 1969-72; vis. scholar Kyoto (Japan) U., 2000-01. Author: Rural Housing Site Planning, 1974 (award 1975), Neighborhood Space, 1975, (Am. Soc. Landscape Archs. Merit award 1986), Community Goal Setting, 1982, Planning Neighborhood Space with People, 1984, The Meaning of Gardens, 1990, Community Design Primer, 1990, Living Landscape, 1999, Democratic Design in the Pacific Rim, 1999, A Theory for Community Building, 1999 (in Chinese); founder planning process Goals for Raleigh, 1972-76 (All Am. City award 1976); designer urban [illegible] 1986 (Am. Soc. Landscape Arch. Honor award 1987), Big Wild Park, Big Sky Gateway, 1990-95; mem. editl. bd. Places mag., 1985—. Chmn. Five Points Citizens Adv., Coun., Raleigh, 1973, Georgetown-Roanoke Neighborhood Assn., Raleigh, 1979; councilman City of Raleigh, 1975-77; commr. Parks and Recreation Bd., Berkeley, 1982-86; bd. dirs. Ctr. for Environ. Change, 1985—; trustee Small Town Inst., 1988—; founder Spoonbill Action Vol. Echo (SAVE), 1997. Recipi- [illegible] award City of Manteo, N.C., 1981. Mem. Am. Soc. Landscape Archs. (Nat. Merit award 1976, Nat. Honor award 1984, Honor award 1991, Coun. of Educators in Landscape Architecture, Nat. Outstanding Educator award 1995, numerous other awards). Democrat. Methodist. Avocations: water color painting, leaded glass, drawing, gardening. Office: U Calif Dept Landscape Architecture 202 Wurster Hall Berkeley CA 94720-2000

HESTON, CHARLTON (JOHN CHARLTON CARTER), actor; b. Evanston, Ill., Oct. 4, 1924; s. Russell Whitford and Lilla (Charlton) Carter; m. Lydia Marie Clarke, Mar. 17, 1944; children— Fraser Clarke, Holly Ann. Student, Northwestern U., 1941-43. Mem. Nat. Council on the Arts, 1967-72 Author: The Actor's Life, 1979, In the Arena, 1995; performances include: (stage) Antony and Cleopatra, 1947, Leaf and Bough, 1948, Design for a Stained Glass Window, 1949, The Tumbler, 1960; (TV appearances) Wuthering Heights, Macbeth, Taming of the Shrew, Of Human Bondage, Jane Eyre, The Nairobi Affair, 1984, The Proud Men, 1987, TNT, 1988, 90, 91, A Man For All Seasons (also dir.), 1988, Original Sin, 1989, Treasure Island, 1990, The Little Kidnappers, 1990, The Crucifer of Blood, Crash Landing: The Rescue of Flight 232, 1992, The Avenging Angel, 1995; (TV series) The Colbys, 1985-87, Chiefs (miniseries), 1983, (also writer) Charleton Heston Presents the Bible, 1993; (films) Dark City, Greatest Show on Earth, 1952, The Savage, 1952, Ruby Gentry, 1952, The President's Lady, 1952, Pony Express, 1983, Arrowhead, 1953, Bad for Each Other, 1954, Naked Jungle, 1954, The Secret of the Incas, 1954, The Far Horizons, 1955, Lucy Gallant, 1955, Private War of Major Benson, 1955, The Ten Commandments, 1956, Three Violent People, 1956, Touch of Evil, 1958, The Big Country, 1958, Ben Hur, 1959 (Acad. award for best actor), The Wreck of Mary Deare, 1959, El Cid, 1961, The Pigeon That Took Rome, 1962, 55 Days of Peking, 1963, Diamond Head, 1963, The Agony and The Ecstasy, 1963, The War Lord, 1965, The Greatest Story Ever Told, 1965, Khartoum, 1966, Planet of the Apes, 1967, Will Penny, 1968, Number One, 1969, Beneath The Planet of the Apes, 1969, Julius Caesar, 1970, The Hawaiians, 1970, The Omega Man, 1971, Antony and Cleopatra (also dir.), 1971, Skyjacked, 1972, Call of the Wild, 1972, Soylent Green, 1973, The Three Musketeers, 1973, Airport, 1974, The Four Musketeers, 1974, Earthquake, 1974, Midway, 1976, Two-Minute Warning, 1976, The Last Hard Men, 1976, The Prince and the Pauper, 1977, Gray Lady Down, 1977, Mountain Men, 1980, The Awakening, 1980, Mother Lode (also dir.), 1982, Solar Crisis, 1989, Almost An Angel, 1990 (cameo), Wayne's World 2 (cameo), Tombstone, 1993, True Lies, 1994, In the Mouth of Madness, 1995, Hamlet, 1996, Alaska, 1996, Ben Johnson: Third Cowboy On The Right, 1996, Hercules (voice), 1997, Illusion Infinity, 1998, Gideon's Webb, 1998, Armageddon (voice), 1998, Toscano, 1999, Any Given Sunday, 1999, Town & Country, 1999; TV movie Avenging Angel, 1995, I Am Your Child, 1997; dir. The Caine Mutiny Court-Martial (Beijing), 1988. Trustee Los Angeles Center Theatre Group, Am. Film Inst., 1971— , chmn., 1973; head President's Task Force on Arts and Humanities, 1981— ; led the Pledge of Allegiance at the Republican Conv., New Orleans, 1988. Served in USAAF, World War II. Recipient Jean Hersholt award as Humanitarian of Yr. Am. Acad. Motion Picture Arts and Scis., 1978, Citizenship medal VFW, 1982, Golden medal City of Vianna, 1995. Mem. Screen Actors Guild (pres. 1966-71), NRA (pres.) Office: care Jack Gilardi ICM 8942 Wilshire Blvd Beverly Hills CA 90211-1934 also: care NRA 11250 Waples Mill Rd Fairfax VA 22030-7400

HETT, JOAN MARGARET, civic administrator; b. Trail, B.C., Can., Sept. 8, 1936; d. Gordon Stanley and Violet Thora (Thors) Hett. BSc, U. Victoria, B.C., Can., 1964; MS, U. Wis., Madison, 1967; PhD, U. Wis., 1969. Ecologist Eastern Deciduous Forest Biome, Oak Ridge Nat. Lab., 1969-72; coord. sites dir. Coniferous Forest Biome, Oreg. State U. Corvallis and U. Wash., Seattle, 1972-77; ecol. cons. Seattle, 1978-84; plant ecologist Seattle City Light, 1986-91, vegetation mgmt. mgr., 1991-2000, ecol. cons., 2000—. Contbr. articles to profl. jours.; rsch. in plant population dynamics, land use planning, and forest succession. Mem. Ecol. Soc. Am.., Brit. Ecol. Soc., Am. Inst. Biol. Scis., Am. Forestry Assn., Sigma Xi.

HETZEL, FREDRICK WILLIAM, biophysicist, educator; b. Toronto, June 28, 1946; came to U.S., 1974; BS, U. Waterloo, Ont., Can., 1970, MS, 1971, PhD, 1974; JD, Wayne State U., 1994. Sr. CA rsch. scientist Radiation Med. Dept. Div. Radiology, Buffalo, 1976-78; asst. prof. Biophysics Dept. SUNY, Buffalo, 1977-78; rsch. prof. Grad. Div. Niagra (N.Y.) U., 1978; sr. radiation biologist Therapeutic Radiology, Henry Ford Hosp., Detroit, 1978-82; adjunct asst. prof. Biology Dept. Wayne State U., Detroit, 1979-85; clin. assoc. prof. Physics Dept. Oakland U., Rochester, Mich., 1982-85, assoc. prof., 1985-87; dir. radiobiology Neurology Dept. Henry Ford Hosp., Detroit, 1982-90; prof. Physics Oakland U., Rochester, Mich., 1987-93, dir. radiation oncology rsch., 1991-93; dir. R & D Presbyn./St. Luke's Med. Ctr., Denver, 1993-94; dir. R&D HealthOne, Denver, 1994-96, v.p., dir. rsch., 1996—. Co-organizer, guest faculty Hyperthermia and Cancer Therapy, Seattle, 1984, Madison, Wis., 1985, Durham, N.C., 1987; profl. cons. hyperthermia FDA Regulations, Protocol Design, 1986; mem. med. staff bylaws com. Henry Ford Hosp., 1989; mem. radiation study sect. DHHS/NIH/DRG, 1989-93. Assoc. editor: Radiation Rsch., 1987-91. Grantee NIH, 1979-88, 86-90 (2), 87-90, 92—. Mem. N.Am. Hyperthermia Group (memberhsip com. 1987-88, sec.-treas. 1989-91), Am. Assn. Physicians in Medicine (chmn. task group), Am. Soc. Clin. Oncology, Am. Coll. Med. Physics. Home: 201 Locust Ln Denver CO 80220-5973 Office: HealthOne Rsch 1850 High St Denver CO 80218-1308 E-mail: fwhetzel@aol.com

HEUSCH, CLEMENS AUGUST, physicist, educator; b. Aachen, Germany, Apr. 19, 1932; s. Hermann and Elisabeth (Pauli) H.; m. Karin von Gilgenheimb, July 6, 1968; children: Marina, Bettina. Student, Bowdoin Coll., 1951-52; Dipl. Phys., U. Aachen, 1955; postgrad., U. Paris, 1956; Dr. rer. nat., Tech. U. Munich, 1959. Rsch. asst. Tech. U., Munich, 1956-59; project leader rsch. div. AEG, Frankfurt, Germany, 1960-61; rsch. scientist DESY Accelerator Lab., Hamburg, Germany, 1961-63; from rsch. fellow to assoc. prof. Calif. Inst. Tech., Pasadena, 1963-69; prof., co-prin. investigator U. Calif., Santa Cruz, 1969—. Cons., referee Am. Inst. Physics, N.Y.C., European Orgn. for Nuclear Rsch., Geneva; cons. Nat. Acad. Scis.; mem. various internat. adv. coms., 1965—; founding dir. Santa Cruz Inst. for Particle Physics; lectr. musical criticism Porter Coll., U. Calif., vis. prof., RWTH Aachen, Germany, 1995—, U. Rome (Italy), La Sapienza, 1999. Free-lance music critic. Recipient Humboldt prize, 1990; Fulbright scholar, 1951; grantee Dept. Energy, NSF, 1963—. Roman Catholic. Office: U Calif Inst Particle Physics Dept Physics 1156 High St Santa Cruz CA 95064-1077

HEWETT, THOMAS AVERY, petroleum engineer, educator; b. Lansing, Mich., Apr. 23, 1944; s. Richard Eugene and Frances Marion (Perry) H.; m. Marilyn Roberta Lawley, July 11, 1970 (div. Mar. 1979); m. Evro Lynn Stylianides, Nov. 3, 1984 (div. Nov. 1992); m. Janet M. Bostrom, Mar. 17, 1994. BS, Mich. State U., 1966; MS, MIT, 1968, ME, 1969, PhD, 1970. Asst. prof. CUNY, 1970-75; rsch. scientist Union Carbide Corp., Tarrytown, N.Y., 1975-79; sr. engring. assoc. Chevron Oil Field Rsch. Co., Lahabra, Calif., 1979-91; prof. petroleum engring. dept. Stanford (Calif.) U., 1991—. Contbr. over 40 articles to profl. jours. Recipient Engring. Merit award Orange County Engring. Coun., 1991. Fellow Inst. for Advancement of Engring.; mem. AAAS, Soc. Petroleum Engrs. Achievements include two patents on solar heating; pioneering use of fractals in petroleum reservoir modeling. Office: Stanford U Dept Petroleum Engring Green Earth Scis Bldg Rm 096 Stanford CA 94305-2220

HEWITT, CONRAD W. bank executive; Supt. of banks State of Calif.; state commr. Calif. State Dept. Financial Inst.; bd. dirs. Point W. Capital Corp., San Francisco, 2000—. Office: Point W Capital Corp 1700 Montgomery St Ste 250 San Francisco CA 94111-5613

HEWITT, JENNIFER LOVE, actress, singer; b. Waco, Tex., Feb. 21, 1979; d. Danny and Pat. Appeared in films, including Munchies, 1992, Little Miss Millions, 1993, Sister Act 2: Back in the Habit, 1993, House Arrest, 1996, Trojan War, 1997, I Know What You Did Last Summer, 1997, Can't Hardly Wait, 1998, Telling You, 1998, I Still Know What You Did Last Summer, 1998, The Suburbans, 1999, Bunny, 2000, Breakers, 2000, Adventures of Tom Thumb and Thumbelina (voice), 2000; television appearances include Kids Inc., 1989-91, Shaky Ground, 1992, The Byrds of Paradise, 1994, McKenna, 1994, Party of Five, 1995-99, The Senior Prom, 1997, Time of Your Life, 1999—, The Audrey Hepburn Story, 2000; albums include Love Songs, 1992, Let's Go Bang, 1995, Jennifer Love Hewitt, 1996. Office: William Morris Agy 151 S El Camino Dr Beverly Hills CA 90212-2775

HEWITT, MIKE, state senator; m. Cory Hewitt; 2 children. Exec. dir. Walla Walla Valley C. of C.; Rep. senator dist. 16 Wash. State Senate, 2000—. Rep. asst. whip Wash. State Senate, mem. edn., human svcs. and corrections, ways and means coms. Mem. United Way, YMCA, State Penitentiary Citizen Adv. Coun.; former chmn. Walla Walla Planning Commn. Mem. Rotary, Elks. Office: PO Box 40416 115B Irving Newhouse Bldg Olympia WA 98504-0416 Fax: 360 786 7819. E-mail: hewitt_mi@leg.wa.gov

HEWITT, WILLIAM JAMES, municipal official; b. Apr. 29, 1944; m. Sharon Hewitt; 3 children. BS, Brandon (Can.) U.; cert. in adult edn., Red River C.C., Winnipeg, Can.; cert. in pub. adminstrn., Assiniboine Coll., Brandon; cert. in fire svc. mgmt., Internat. City Mgmt. Assn. cert. fire fighter, fire prevention officer, fire svc. instr., Can. Vol. fire fighter Virden Vol. Fire Dept., 1964-68; fire fighter City of Brandon Fire Dept., 1968-73; asst. fire commr. Office Manitoba Fire Commr., 1973-78, mgr. field svcs. sect., 1978-86; fire chief City of Saskatoon, Can., 1986—. Developer Manitoba Fire Coll., apptd. prin., 1978; past chair Manitoba Fire Svcs. Mobile Radio Comm. Com., Manitoba Fire Coll. Protection Tech. Adv. Com., Manitoba Pub. Fire Safety Edn. Com. Contbr. articles to profl. jours.; presenter confs. in Boston, Memphis, Cin., Toronto, Regina, Yellowknife, Winnipeg, Ottawa, others; speaker in field. Mem. Internat. Soc. Fire Svc. Instrs. (bd. dirs. 1976-92), Internat. City Mgmt. Assn. (instr. firesvc. adminstrn. program), Internat. Fire Svcs. Tng. Assn. (fire svc. instr. textbook and fire dept. ops. textbook coms. 1976-81), Internat. Assn. Fire Chiefs (1st v.p. Can. divsn.), Nat. Fire Protection Assn., Can. Fire Chief's Assn. (pres.), Sask. Fire Chief's Assn. (past pres.), Sask. Profl. Qualifications and Standards Bd. (chmn.), Sask. C. of C., N.D. State Fireman's Assn. (hon. life). Office: Fire Dept 125 Idylwyld Dr S Saskatoon SK Canada S7M 1L4

HEYLER, GROVER ROSS, retired lawyer; b. Manila, The Philippines, June 24, 1926; s. Grover Edwin and Esther Viola (Ross) H.; m. Caroline Yarbrough, Aug. 10, 1949; children: Richard Ross, Sue Louise, Randall Arthur BA, UCLA, 1949; LLB, U. Calif., Berkeley, 1952. Bar: Calif. 1953. Assoc. Latham & Watkins, L.A., 1952-60, ptnr., 1960-93, chmn., corp. securities dept., 1967-89. Bd. dirs. Nat. Alliance for Rsch. into Schizophrenia and Depression, N.Y.C.; bd. dirs. Mental Health Assn., L.A., 1992-99. Mem. Calif. Bar Assn. (com. on drafting Calif. corps. code 1971-75), Order of Coif, UCLA ALumni Assn. (bd. dirs. 1966-70, 1988-90), L.A. Country Club, Riviera Tennis Club. Home: 491 Homewood Rd Los Angeles CA 90049-2713

HEYMAN, MELVIN BERNARD, pediatric gastroenterologist; b. San Francisco, Mar. 24, 1950; s. Vernon Otto and Eve Elsie Heyman; m. Jody Ellen Switky, May 8, 1988. BA in Econs., U. Calif., Berkeley, 1972; MD, UCLA, 1976, MPH in Nutrition, 1981. Diplomate Am. Bd. Pediatrics (assoc. 1997—), Am. Bd. Pediatric Gastroenterology (assoc. 1997—). Intern, resident Los Angeles County-U. So. Calif. Med. Ctr., 1976-79; fellow UCLA, 1979-81; asst. prof. U. Calif., San Francisco, 1981-88, assoc. prof., 1988-94, prof., 1994—, chief pediatric gastroenterology, hepatology and nutrition, 1990—; dir. UCSF/Stanford Combined Tng. Program Pediatric Gastroenterology/Nutrition, 1998—. Assoc. dir. Pediatric Gastroenterology/Nutrition, San Francisco, 1986-89; mem. cons. staff San Francisco Gen. Hosp., Natividad Med. Ctr., Salinas, Calif., Scenic Gen. Hosp., Modesto, Calif.; assoc. dir. Pediatric IBD Consortium 2000—. Contbr. articles to profl. jours. Chmn. scientific adv. com. San Francisco chpt. Crohn's and Colitis Found. Am., 1987-94, bd. dirs., 1986—. Rsch. grantee Children's Liver Found., 1984-85, John Tung grantee Am. Cancer Soc., 1985-89. Mem. N.Am. Soc. Pediat. Gastro Nutrition (chair patient care com. 1997—), Am. Acad. Pediat. (com. on nutrition 1999—, exec. com. on pediat. gastroenterology and nutrition 1999—), Am. Inst. Nutrition, Am. Gastroenterol. Assn., Soc. Clin. Nutrition, Am. Soc. Parental Enteral Nutrition, Am. Bd. Pediatric Gastroenterology (chair sub-bd. 2000—). Avocations: skiing, swimming, hiking, tennis, biking. Office: U Calif Dept Pediat PO Box 0136 San Francisco CA 94143-0136

HEYMANN, STEPHEN, marketing management consultant; b. N.Y.C., Dec. 7, 1940; s. Harold Joseph and Estelle Olga H.; m. Elaine Puciat, June 24, 1962; children: Elizabeth Jill, Michael Carroll, Andrew Harold. BS, Wharton Sch., U. Pa., 1962. Div. mgr., mdse. mgr. Sears, Roebuck & Co., Phila., 1962-65; brand mgr. Household Products div. Procter & Gamble Co., Cin., 1965-69; pres., dir., mgmt. cons. Glendinning Assos., Westport, Conn., 1969-81; founder, pres. New Eng. Cons. Group, 1981-90, Tech. Transfer Assocs., Wilton, Conn., 1990-96; pres., COO Netalk, Internet Svcs., Los Gatos, Calif., 1996-97; pres., prin. Paladin Cons. Group, Los Altos, 1997—. Founder, pres. Paladin Consulting Group, 1992-98; dir. Penniman Chems. Inc., Glenco Enterprises Ltd., Glendinning Cos. Inc., Aficionado. Author: More People on Skis, 1972, Like, series of children's books, 1972-74. Mem. ASTM, Am. Mgmt. Assn., Am. Mktg. Assn., Young Pres. Orgn., Assn. Nat. Advertisers. Clubs: Stratton Mountain, Wharton, Lotos. Office: Paladin Cons Group 662 Arrowood Ct Los Altos CA 94024-4801

HEYNEMAN, DONALD, parasitology and tropical medicine educator; b. San Francisco, Feb. 18, 1925; s. Paul and Amy Josephine (KLauber) H.; m. Louise Davidson Ross, June 18, 1971; children: Amy J., Lucy A., Andrew P., Jennifer K., Claudia G. AB magna cum laude, Harvard U., 1950; MA, Rice U., 1952, PhD, 1954. Instr. zoology UCLA, 1954-56, asst. prof., 1956-60; head dept. parasitology U.S. Navy Med. Research unit, Cairo, also co-dir. Malakal, Sudan, 1960-62; assoc. research parasitologist Hooper Found. U. Calif., San Francisco, 1962-64, assoc. prof., 1966-68, prof., 1968-91, prof. emeritus, 1991—, asst. dir. Hooper found., 1970-74, acting chmn. dept. internat. health, 1976-78, assoc. dean Sch. Pub. Health Berkeley and San Francisco, 1987-91, assoc. dean emeritus, 1991—, chmn. joint med. program, 1987-91, chmn. emeritus, 1991—. Research coordinator U. Calif. Internat. Ctr. Med. Research and Tng., Kuala Lumpur, Malaysia, 1964-66; cons. physiol. processes sect. NSF, 1966-91; environ. biology div. NIH, 1968-91; mem. tropical medicine and parasitology study sect. NIAID-NIH, 1973-76; mem. adv. sci. bd. Gorgas Meml. Inst., 1967-90; cons. WHO, 1967, mem. sci. tech. rev. com. on Leishmaniases, 1984; cons. UN Devel. Program, 1978-91, US-AID, others; panel reviewer Internat. Nomenclature of Diseases, 1984—; Am. cons. and U.S. prin. investigator U. Linkage Project, Egypt-U.S., 1984—; mem. Calif. Health Adv. Com., 1983—. Author: (with R. Boolootian) An Illustrated Laboratory Text in Zoology, 1962, An Illustrated Laboratory Text in Zoology, A Brief Version, 1977, International Dictionary Medicine and Biology, (with R. Goldsmith) Textbook of Tropical Medicine and Parasitology, 1989;co-author, contbg. editor Phytolacca dodecandra: Endod, 1984, Endod II, 1987; contbr. articles to jours., chpts. to books.; editorial cons. Am. Jour. Tropical Medicine and Hygiene, Jour. Parasitology, Jour. Exptl. Parasitology, Sci., 1968—, other jours. Served with AUS, 1943-46. NIH grantee, 1966-85. Mem. Am. Soc. Parasitologists (council 1970-74, pres. 1982-83), Am. Micros. Soc. (exec. com. 1971-75), Am. Soc. Tropical Medicine and Hygiene (councilor 1981-84), So. Calif. Parasitol. Soc. (pres. 1957-58), No. Calif. Parasitologists (sec.- treas. 1969-72, pres. 1977-78), Phi Beta Kappa. Home: 1400 Lake St San Francisco CA 94118-1036 Office: U Calif Dept Epidemiology Biostat PO Box 560 San Francisco CA 94143-0001 E-mail: dheyneman@epi.ucsf.edu

HEYNES, AEDHMAR, public relations executive; Pres., regional dir. Text 100 Corp. N.Am. Office: Text 100 PR 30 Hotaling Pl Fl 2D San Francisco CA 94111-2201

HIATT, PETER, retired librarian studies educator; b. N.Y.C., Oct. 19, 1930; s. Amos and Elizabeth Hope (Derry) H.; m. Linda Rae Smith, Aug. 16, 1968; 1 child, Holly Virginia. B.A., Colgate U., 1952; M.L.S., Rutgers U., 1957, Ph.D., 1963. Libr. intern Elizabeth (N.J.) Pub. Libr., 1955-57; head Elmora Br. Libr., Elizabeth, 1957-59; instr. Grad. Sch. Libr. Service, Rutgers U., 1960-62; libr. cons. Ind. State Libr., Indpls., 1963-70; asst. prof. Grad. Libr. Sch., Ind. U., 1963-66, assoc. prof., 1966-70; dir. Ind. Libr. Studies, Bloomington, 1967-70; dir. continuing edn. program for library pers. Western Interstate Commn. for Higher Edn., Boulder, Colo., 1970-74; dir. Grad. Sch. Libr. and Info. Sci., U. Wash., Seattle, 1974-81, prof., 1974-98; prin. investigator Career Devel. and Assessment Ctr. for Librarians, 1979-83, 90-93; dir. library insts. at various colls. and univs.; adv. projects U.S. Office Edn.-ALA, 1977-80; prof. emeritus U. Wash., 1998—. Bd. dirs. King County Libr. Sys., 1989-97, pres., 1991, 95, sec., 1993, 94; prin. investigator Career Devel. and Assessment Ctrs. for Librs.: Phase II, 1990-93. Author: (with Donald Thompson) Monroe County in Public Library: Planning for the Future, 1966, The Public Library Needs of Delaware County, 1967, (with Henry Drennan) Public Library Services for the functionally Illiterate, 1967 (with Robert E. Lee and Lawrence A. Allen) A Plan for Developing a Regional Program of Continuing Education for Library Personnel, 1969, Public Library Branch Services for Adults of Low Education, 1964; dir., gen. editor: The Indiana Library Studies, 1970; author: Assessment Centers for Professional Library Leadership, 1993; mem. editorial bd. Coll. and Rsch. Librs., 1969-73; co-editor Leads: A Continuing Education Newsletter for Library Trustees, 1973-75, Octavio Noda; author chpts., articles on library continuing edn., staff devel. and libr. adult svcs. Dir. selection com. Jefferson County Pub. Libr., Washington, 2000—; sec. Port Townsend Pub. Libr. Found., 2000—; mem. Turtle Bluff Chamber Orch. soloist competition, 2000—, Jefferson Co., Washington, 2000—, Turtle Bluff Chamber Orch. bd., 2000—, mem. scholarship com., 2000—; bd. mem. Jefferson County, 2001—. Mem. ALA (officer), Pacific N.W. Libr. Assn., Assn. Libr. and Info. Sci. Educators (officer, Outstanding Svc. award 1979), ACLU. Home: 111 E Rhododendron Dr Port Townsend WA 98368-9414 E-mail: phiatt@waypt.com

HIBBARD, RICHARD PAUL, industrial ventilation consultant, educator; b. Defiance, Ohio, Nov. 1, 1923; s. Richard T. and Doris E. (Walkup) H.; m. Phyllis Ann Kirchoffer, Sept. 7, 1948; children: Barbara Rae, Marcia Kae, Rebecca Ann, Patricia Jan, John Ross. BS in Mech. Indsl. Engring., U. Toledo, 1949. Mech. engr. Oldsmobile divsn. GM, Lansing, Mich., 1950-56; design and sales engr. McConnell Sheet Metal, Inc., Lansing, 1956-60; chief heat and ventilation engr. Fansteel Metall. Corp., North Chicago, Ill., 1960-62; sr. facilities and ventilation engr. The Boeing Co., Seattle, 1962-63; ventilation engr. environ. health divsn. dept. preventive medicine U. Wash., Seattle, 1964-70, lectr. dept. environ. health, 1970-82, lectr. emeritus, 1983—. Prin. Indsl. Ventilation Cons. Svcs., 1983—; chmn. Western Indsl. Ventilation Conf., 1962, mem. com. indsl. ventilation Am. Conf. Govtl. Indsl. Hygienists, 1966—; mem. staff Indsl. Ventilation Conf., Mich. State U., 1955—. Contbr. articles on indsl. hygiene and ventilation to profl. jours. With USAAF, 1943-45; maj. C.E., USAR ret. Recipient Disting. Svc. award Indsl. Ventilation Conf., Mich. State U., 1975, 93. Mem. ASHRAE, Am. Soc. Safety Engrs. (R.M. Gillmore Meml. award Puget Sound chptc), Am. Inst. Plant Engrs., Am. Indsl. Hygiene Assn. (J.M. Dallevalle award 1977), Am. Foundryman's Soc., Elks, Masons. Home: 41 165th Ave SE Bellevue WA 98008-4721

HIBBS, LOYAL ROBERT, lawyer; b. Des Moines, Dec. 24, 1925; s. Loyal B. and Catharine (McClymond) H.; children: Timothy, Theodore, Howard, Dean. BA, U. Iowa, 1950, LLB, JD, 1952. Bar: Iowa 1952, Nev. 1958, U.S. Supreme Ct. 1971. Ptnr. Hibbs Law Offices, Reno, 1972—. Moderator radio, TV Town Hall Coffee Breaks, 1970-72; mem. Nev. State Bicycle Adv. Bd., 1996-2000, Reno Bicycle Coun., 1995-99; chmn. Reno Park Recreation Commn., 2001—. Fellow Am. Bar Found. (Nev. chmn. 1989-94); mem. ABA (standing com. Lawyer Referral Svc. 1978-79, steering com. state dels. 1979-82, consortium on legal svcs. and the pub. 1979-82, Nev. State Bar del. to Ho. of Dels. 1978-82, 89-90, bd. govs. 1982-85, mem. legal tech. adv. coun. 1985-86, standing com. on nat. conf. groups 1985-91, chmn. sr. lawyers divsn. Nev. 1988—), Nat. Conf. Bar Pres.'s Iowa Bar Assn., Nev. Bar Assn. (bd. govs. 1968-78, pres. 1977-78), Washoe County Bar Assn. (pres. 1966-67), Nat. Jud. Coll. (bd. dirs. 1986-92, sec. 1988-92), Assn. Def. Counsel No. Calif., Assn. Def. Counsel Nev., Assn. Ski Def. Attys., Aircraft Owners and Pilots Assn. (legal svcs. plan 1991—), Washoe County Legal Aid Soc. (co-founder), Lawyer-Pilots Bar Assn. (chmn. Nev.), Greater Reno C. of C. (bd. dirs. 1968-72), Phi Alpha Delta. Home: 1489 Foster Dr Reno NV 89509-1209 Office: 290 S Arlington Ave Ste 100 Reno NV 89501-1793 E-mail: loyalhibbs@aol.com

HICK, KENNETH WILLIAM, marketing company executive; b. New Westminster, B.C., Can, Oct. 17, 1946; s. Les Walter and Mary Isabelle (Warner) H. BA in Bus., Ea. Wash. State coll., 1971; MBA, U. Wash., 1973, PhD, 1975. Regional sales mgr. Hilti, Inc., San Leandro, Calif., 1976-79; gen. sales mgr. Moore Internat., Inc., Portland, 1979-80; v.p. sales and mktg. Phillips Corp., Anaheim, Calif., 1980-81; owner, pres., CEO K.C. Metals, San Jose, 1981-87, Losli Internat., Inc., Portland, 1987-89; pres. Resources N.W., Inc., Portland, 1989—. Communications cons. Asso. Pub. Safety Communication Officers, Inc., State of Oreg., 1975-93; numerous cons. assignments, also seminars, 1976-2000. Contbr. articles to numerous publs. Mem. Oreg. Gov.'s Tax Bd., 1975-76; pres. Portland chpt. Oreg. Jaycees, 1976; bd. fellows U. Santa Clara, 1983-90. With USAF, 1966-69. Decorated Commendation medal; U. Wash. fellow, 1973. Mem. Am. Mgmt. Assn., Am. Mktg. Assn., Assn. MBA Execs., Assn. Gen. Contractors, Soc. Advancement Mgmt., Home Builders Assn. Roman Catholic. Home: 25659 Cheryl Dr West Linn OR 97068-4589 Office: Resources NW Inc 19727 Highway 99E Hubbard OR 97032-9716

HICKEL, WALTER JOSEPH, investment firm executive, forum administrator; b. nr. Claflin, Kans., Aug. 18, 1919; s. Robert A. and Emma (Zecha) H.; m. Janice Cannon, Sept. 22, 1941 (dec. Aug. 1943); 1 child, Theodore; m. Ermalee Strutz, Nov. 22, 1945; children: Robert, Walter Jr., Jack, Joseph, Karl. Student pub. schs., Claflin; D.Eng. (hon.), Stevens Inst. Tech., 1970, Mich. Tech. U., 1973; LL.D. (hon.), St. Mary of Plains Coll., St. Martin's Coll., U. Md., Adelphi U., U. San Diego, Rensselaer Poly. Inst., 1973, U. Alaska, 1976, Alaska Pacific U., 1991; D.Pub. Adminstrn. (hon.), Willamette U. Founder Hickel Investment Co., Anchorage, 1947—; gov. State of Alaska, 1966-69, 90-94; sec. U.S. Dept. Interior, 1969-70; sec. gen. The Northern Forum, 1994—. Former mem. world adv. council Internat. Design Sci. Inst.; former mem. com. on sci. freedom and responsibility AAAS; nominated for pres. at 1968 Republican Nat. Convention; co-founder Yukon Pacific Corp.; founder Inst. of the North, 1996—. Author: Who Owns America?, 1971; contbr. articles to newspapers. Mem. Republican Nat. Com., 1954-64; bd. regents Gonzaga U.; bd. dirs. Salk Inst., 1972-79, NASA Adv. Coun. Exploration Task Force, 1989-91; mem. Governor's Econ. Com. on North Slope Natural Gas, Alaska, 1982. Named Alaskan of Year, 1969, Man of Yr. Ripon Soc., 1970; recipient DeSmet medal Gonzaga U., 1969, Horatio Alger award, 1972, Grand Cordon of the Order of Sacred Treasure award His Imperial Majesty the Emperor of Japan, 1988. Mem. Pioneers of Alaska, Alaska C. of C. (former chmn. econ. devel. com.), Equestrian Order Holy Sepulchre, Knights Malta, KC. Achievements include leading the first Alaska Chamber economic trade mission to Japan. Home: 1905 Loussac Dr Anchorage AK 99517-1225 Office: PO Box 101700 Anchorage AK 99510-1700

HICKERSON, GLENN LINDSEY, leasing company executive; b. Burbank, Calif., Aug. 22, 1937; s. Ralph M. and Sarah Lawson (Lindsey) H.; m. Jane Fortune Arthur, Feb. 24, 1973. BA in Bus. Adminstrn., Claremont Men's Coll., 1959; MBA, NYU, 1960. Exec. asst. Douglas Aircraft Co., Santa Monica, Calif., 1963; sec., treas. Douglas Fin. Corp., Long Beach, 1964-67, regional mgr. customer financing, 1967; exec. asst. to pres. Universal Airlines, Inc., Detroit, 1967-68, v.p., treas., asst. sec., 1968-69, pres., 1969-72; v.p., treas., asst. sec. Universal Aircraft Service, Inc., Detroit, 1968-69, chmn. bd., 1969-72; v.p., treas. Universal Airlines Co., Detroit, 1968-69, pres., 1969-72; group v.p. Marriott Hotels, Inc., Washington, 1972-76; dir. sales Far East and Australia Lockheed Calif. Co., 1976-78, dir. mktg. Americas, 1978-79, dir. mktg. Internat., 1979-81, v.p., internat. sales, 1981-83; v.p. comml. mktg. internat. Douglas Aircraft Co., McDonnell Douglas Corp., 1983-89; mng. dir. GPA Asia Pacific, El Segundo, Calif., 1989-90; exec. v.p. GATX Air Group, San Francisco, 1990-95, pres., 1995-98, chmn., dir. adv. bd., 1998—, GATX Capital Corp., San Francisco, 1998—; pres. Hickerson Assocs., 1998—. Chmn. Crown Aviation Techs., LLC; bd. dirs. Ayres Corp., Willis Lease Fin. Corp. Bd. govs. Keck Ctr. for Internat. Strategic Studies; mem. Calif. Export Adv. Council. Lt. (j.g.) USCGR, 1960-62. H.B. Earhart Found. fellow, 1962 0em. Internat. Assn. Charter Airlines (exec. com. 1971), Pacific Union Club, Saint Francis Yacht Club, St. Francis Yacht Club, Am. One. E-mail: ghickers@gatxcap.com

HICKEY, WINIFRED E(SPY), former state legislator, social worker; b. Rawlins, Wyo.; d. David P. and Eugenia (Blake) Espy; children: John David, Paul Joseph. BA, Loretto Heights Coll., 1933; postgrad. U. Utah, 1934, Sch. Social Service, U. Chgo., 1936; LLD (hon.) U. Wyo., 1991. Dir. Carbon County Welfare Dept., 1935-36; field rep. Wyo. Dept. Welfare, 1937-38; dir. Red Cross Club, Europe, 1942-45; commr. Laramie County, Wyo., 1973-80; mem. Wyo. Senate, 1980-90; dir. United Savs. & Loan, Cheyenne; active Joint Powers Bd. Laramie County and City of Cheyenne. Pub. Where the Deer and the Antelope Play, 1967. Pres., bd. dirs. U. Wyo. Found., 1986-87; pres. Meml. Hosp. of Laramie County, 1986-88, Wyo. Transp. Mus., 1990-92; chmn. adv. council div. community programs Wyo. Dept. Health and Social Services; pres. county and state mental health assn., 1959-63; trustee, U. Wyo., 1967-71, St. Mary's Cathedral, 1986—; active Nat. Council Cath. Women, Gov. Residence Found., 1991-93, Wyo. Transp. Mus., 1993—; chair Am. Heritage Assocs. of U. Wyo., 1992-96; com. chair Citizen of the Century State of Wyo., Am. Heritage Ctr., 1966—. Named Outstanding Alumna, Loretto Heights Coll., 1959, Woman of Yr. Commn. for Women, 1988, United Med. Ctr., Cheyenne, 1998, Legislator of Yr. Wyo. Psychologists Assn., 1988, Family of the Yr. U. Wyo., 1995, Person of Yr., United Med. Ctr., Cheyenne, Wyo., 1998. Mem. Altrusa Club (Cheyenne).

HICKLIN, RONALD LEE, music production company executive; b. Burlington, Wash., Dec. 4, 1937; s. Wendell C. and Theodora (Van Voorhis) H.; children: Jennifer Lynn, Mark Allan; m. Trudi Takamatsu, Oct. 23, 1994. Student, U. Wash., 1956-57. Pres. S.A.T.B. Inc., L.A., 1979-98, Killer Music, Inc., San Marino, Calif., 1982—, T.T. B.B., Inc., Hollywood, 1989-97. Ptnr. Killer Tracks, Primat Am., Hollywood, 1990-96. Lead tenor The Eligibles, 1958-62; vocal dir., singer Piece of Cake Inc., 1968-81; arranger, producer Calif. Raisin Adv. Bd., 1982 (recipient 2 Clios 1983); producer/co-writer Wheaties, 1983 (Clio award); producer/composer Gatorade, 1983; producer/performer Levi's 501 Blues, 1984. With USAF, 1959-65. Mem. NARAS (MVP award 1973, 75), AFTRA (nat. bd. dirs. 1970-85, local bd. dirs. 1968-85), Screen Actors Guild (nat. bd. dirs. 1975), Am. Fedn. Musicians, Hollywood C. of C. Avocations: golf, tennis, basketball. Home and Office: 30 Kewen Pl San Marino CA 91108-1104 E-mail: killermusic@earthlink.net

HICKMAN, BERT GEORGE, JR. economist, educator; b. Los Angeles, Oct. 6, 1924; s. Bert George and Caroline E. (Douglass) H.; m. Edythe Anne Warshauer, Feb. 9, 1947; children: Wendy Elizabeth, Paul Lawrence, Alison Diane. B.S., U. Calif.-Berkeley, 1947, Ph.D., 1951. Instr. Stanford U., 1949-51; research asso. Nat. Bur. Econ. Research, 1951-52; asst. prof. Northwestern, 1952-54; mem. sr. staff Council Econ. Advisers, 1954-56; research assoc. Brookings Instn., 1956-58, mem. sr. staff, 1958-66; prof. Stanford U., 1966-95, prof. emeritus, 1996—. Vis. prof. U. Calif. at Berkeley, 1960, London Grad. Sch. Bus Studies, 1972-73, , Inst. Advanced Studies, Vienna, Austria, 1974, 1975, Kyoto U., 1977; NSF fellow Netherlands Econometric Inst., Rotterdam, 1964-65; Ford Found. Faculty research fellow, 1968-69; mem. com. econ. stability Social Sci. Research Council, 1959-61, chmn., 1962-95; chmn. exec. com. Project Link, 1969—; hon. prof. U. Vienna, 1985—; chmn. Energy Modeling Forum working group on macroecon. impacts of energy shocks Stanford U., 1982-83; Am. coord. US-USSR program on econ.-math. macromodeling Am. Coun. Learned Socs., 1988-90. Author: Growth and Stability of the Postwar Economy, 1960, Investment Demand and U.S. Economic Growth, 1965, (with Robert M. Coen) An Annual Growth Model of the U.S. Economy, 1976; Editor: Quantitative Planning of Economic Policy, 1965, Econometric Models of Cyclical Behavior, 1972, Global International Economic Models, 1983, International Monetary Stabilization and the Foreign Debt Problem, 1984, International Productivity and Competitiveness, 1992; co-editor: Global Econometrics, 1983, Macroeconomic Impacts of Energy Shocks, 1987, Link Proceedings, 1991, 92, Studies in Applied Economics, Vol. 1, 1997; contbr. articles to profl. jours. Served with USNR, 1943-46. Vis. fellow Internat. Inst. Applied Systems Analysis, 1979, 80; resident fellow Rockefeller Found., 1989; named Hon. Prof. U. Vienna, Austria. Fellow Econometric Soc.; mem. Am. Econ. Assn. (chmn. census adv. com. 1968-71, tech. subcom. to rev. bus. cycle devels. 1962-68, nominating com. 1978-79, chmn. seminar on global modeling, conf. on econometrics and math. econs. 1975-83), Phi Beta Kappa, Phi Eta Sigma. Home: 904 Lathrop Pl Stanford CA 94305-1060 Office: Stanford U Dept Econs Stanford CA 94305

HICKMAN, JOHN WILLIAM, state legislator; m. DyAnn Davis. BS, So. Utah U. Banker; with Utah Ho. Reps., 1997-2000, Utah State Senate, 2001—. Active Dixie Med. Ctr. Bd. Affiliate. Mem. Western Ind. Bankers, Utah Bankers Assn., St. George Lions Club. Office: 214 N Emeraud Dr Saint George UT 84770 E-mail: jhickman@le.state.ut.us*

HICKS, BETHANY GRIBBEN, judge, commissioner, lawyer; b. N.Y., Sept. 8, 1951; d. Robert and DeSales Gribben; m. William A. Hicks III, May 21, 1982; children: Alexandra Elizabeth, Samantha Katherine. AB, Vassar Coll., 1973; MEd, Boston U., 1975; JD, Ariz. State U., 1984. Bar: Ariz. 1984. Pvt. practice, Scottsdale and Paradise Valley, Ariz., 1984-91; law clk. to Hon. Kenneth L. Fields Maricopa County Superior Ct. S.E. dist., Mesa, 1991-93; commr., judge pro tem domestic rels. and juvenile depts. Maricopa County Superior Ct. Ctrl. and S.E. Dists., Phoenix and Mesa, Ariz., 1993-99; magistrate Town of Paradise Valley, 1993-94; judge ctrl. dist. domestic rels. dept. Maricopa County Superior Ct., Phoenix,

1999-2000, presiding judge family ct. dept., 2000—. Mem. Jr. League of Phoenix, 1984-91; bd. dirs. Phoenix Children's Theatre, 1988-90; parliamentarian Girls Club of Scottsdale, Ariz., 1985-87, 89-90, bd. dirs., 1988-91; exec. bd., sec. All Saints' Episcopal Day Sch. Parents Assn., 1991-92, pres., 1993-94; active Nat. Charity League, 1995-99, Valley Leadership Class XIX, 1997-98; vol., Teach for Am., 1997—. Mem. ABA, State Bar Ariz., Ariz. State Bar Assn., Maricopa County Bar Assn., Ariz. Women Lawyers' Assn. (steering com. 1998—), Assn. Family Ct. Conciliators (bd. dirs. 2001—). Republican. Episcopalian. Office: 201 W Jefferson St Phoenix AZ 85003-2205 E-mail: whicks@swlaw.com, bhicks@superiorcourt.maricopa.gov

HICKS, DAVID EARL, writer, inventor; b. Indpls., Jan. 1, 1931; s. John Arthur and Marguerite (Barnes) H.; m. Shirlene Lavan Barlow, Jan. 22, 1958 (div. June 1973); children: Sharon Lynn, Brenda Kay; m. Margaret Leigh Payne, Feb. 17, 1977; children: David Bradley, Leslie Ann, Brian Patrick. Grad., Nat. Radio Inst., 1953; student, Purdue U., 1959-60, Miami-Dade Community Coll., 1971-72. Cert. advanced paramedic. Tech. writer, editor Howard W. Sams, Inc., Indpls., 1958-64; tech. writer Systems Engring. Labs, Inc., Ft. Lauderdale, Fla., 1964-67; publs. mgr. Novatronics, Inc., Pompano Beach, 1967-69; pres. Datatek, Inc., Ft. Lauderdale, 1969-71; tech. writer Systems Devel. Corp., Colorado Springs, Colo., 1973-74, Ford Aerospace Corp., Colorado Springs, 1974-76; pres. Nutronics Corp., Colorado Springs, 1982-87; tech. writer Digital Equipment Corp., Colorado Springs, 1978-88; pres. Innovation USA Mag., Colorado Springs, 1989; tech. cons., inventor pvt. practice, Colo. Springs, 1964-65, 75-92; novelist Colo. Springs, 1992—. Tech. cons. Japan Electronics, Tokyo, 1962-63, Nutronics Corp., Longmont, Colo., 1987, Gates Motor Corp., Kailua, Hawaii, 2000—. Author of eight tech. books (two made best seller list) including: Citizens Band Radio Handbook, 1961, Amateur Radio-VHF and Above, 1965, CB Radio Operating Procedures, 1976; contbr. articles to electronics jours.; inventor of new electric charging system, 1978, awarded U.S. patent, 1981; lectr. numerous sci. and invention seminars, 1978—. Communications officer CD, Indpls., 1962-63; judge sci. fair Pub. Sch. System, Colorado Springs, 1986-87. Served with USN, 1948. Recipient Red Cross Hall of Fame, Indpls., 1963; grantee U.S. Dept. of Energy, 1984; recipient Nat. Energy Resources Tech. Innovation award, 1989, Disting. Leadership award Am. Biog. Inst. 1990, cert. of merit Internat. Biog. Ctr., 1990 Mem. Soc. of Am. Inventors (bd. dirs., Pres. award 1989), Am. Radio Relay League, Author's Guild, Author's League of Am. Republican. Avocations: traveling, camping, hiking, photography. Office: PO Box 25053 Colorado Springs CO 80936-5053

HICKS, NORM, airport authority executive; b. 1941; BBA, Golden Gate U., 1964; postgrad., U.S. Naval Postgrad. Sch., 1971. Exec. dir., COO Mohave County Airport Authority, Bullhead City, Ariz. Office: Mohave County Airport Auth 2550 Laughlin Vw Bullhead City AZ 86429-5872

HICKS, R.B. astronomer, educator; BSc, U. Man., 1966, PhD, 1972. Postdoctoral fellow U. Calgary, Can., 1972-82, asst. prof., 1982-86, assoc. prof., 1986-2000, head dept. physics and astronomy, 2000—, mem. coms. Achievements include research on atmospheric acoustics which involves the use of active acoustic remote sensing devices to probe the turbulent structure of the atmospheric boundary layer; research on cosmic ray physics involving using the time variations of surface based cosmic ray detectors to determine aspects of cosmic rays propagation in the atmosphere and solar modulation of cosmic rays. Office: U Calgary Dept Physics/Astr 2500 University Dr NW Calgary AB Canada T2N 1N4 E-mail: hicks@phas.ucalgary.ca

HICKS, WILLIAM ALBERT, III, lawyer; b. Welland, Ont., Can., Apr. 6, 1942; s. William Albert and June Gwendolyn (Birrell) H.; m. Bethany G. Galvin, May 21, 1982; children: James Christopher, Scott Kelly, Alexandra Elizabeth, Samantha Katherine. AB, Princeton U., 1964; LLB, Cornell U., 1967. Bar: N.Y. 1967, Ariz. 1972, U.S. Dist. Ct. Ariz. 1972. Assoc. Seward & Kissel, N.Y.C., 1967-68, Snell & Wilmer LLP, Phoenix, 1972-75, ptnr., 1976—. Instr. Ariz. State U., 1974-75. Mem. U.S. Olympic Fencing Squad, 1964; mem. bd. advisors Casino USA, Inc., 1981-84; bd. dirs. Scottsdale Arts Ctr. Assn., 1984-88, v.p. devel,. 1985-87; bd. dirs. Valley Leadership, Inc., 1987-91, sec., 1988-89, sec.-treas., 1989-90; bd. dirs. Scottsdale Cultural Coun., 1988-97, vice chmn., 1992-95, chmn., 1995-96; active The Luke's Men, 1992—, bd. dirs., 1993-97, 99—, sec., 1993-94, v.p. 1995-96, pres., 1996-97; mem. adv. bd. Scottsdale Arts Ctr., 1988-91, chmn., 1988-90; bd. dirs., vice chmn. Ariz. Coun. on Econ. Edn., 1999-2000, chmn., 2000—. Capt. JAG Corps, USAF, 1968-72. Recipient DSM. Mem. ABA, N.Y. State Bar Assn., Nat. Assn. Bond Lawyers (vice chmn. on fin. health care facilities 1982-83, chmn. com. on fin. health care facilities 1983-86, securities law and disclosure com. 1994—), Assn. for Govtl. Leasing and Fin., Princeton U. Alumni Assn. Ariz. (pres. 1978-81, sec. 1981—), Paradise Valley (Ariz.) Country Club. Office: Snell & Wilmer LLP One Arizona Ctr Phoenix AZ 85004-2202 E-mail: whicks@swlaw.com

HICKSON, ERNEST CHARLES, financial executive; b. L.A., July 14, 1931; s. Russell Arthur and Marilyn Louise (Mambert) H.; m. Janice Beleal, Sept. 5, 1959; children: Arthur, Jennifer, Barton. BS, U. So. Calif., 1961; postgrad., UCLA Grad. Sch. of Bus. Admin., 1961-63. Lic. real estate broker, Calif., 1986. Credit supr. ARCO (Richfield Oil), L.A., 1955-60; asst. v.p. Union Bank L.A., 1960-64; v.p. County Nat. Bank (now Wells Fargo), Orange, Calif., 1964-67; v.p., sr. loan ofcr. City Bank, Honolulu, 1967-70; pres., CEO Shelter Corp., 1968-72; exec. v.p., dir. U.S. Fin., Inc. NYSE, San Diego, 1970-73, pres., CEO USF Investors, 1971-73; exec. v.p. Sonnenblick Goldman, L.A., 1973-76; pres., CEO First Hawaiian Devel., Honolulu, 1976-82; sr. ptnr. TMH Resources and affiliates, Laguna Niguel, Calif., 1982—. Expert witness in fin. Author: (novel) The Developers, 1978; editor: (monthly newsletter) Financial Marketing, 1978-83. Staff sgt. USAF, 1951-54. Recipient Exec. award Grad. Sch. of Credit and Fin. Mgmt., Stanford U., 1964, Assocs. award The Nat. Inst. of Credit, UCLA, 1959. Mem. U. So. Calif. Assocs., U. So. Calif. Pres.'s Circle, Urban Land Inst., Town Hall, Salt Creek Club (charter), Pacific Club (Honolulu), Outrigger Canoe Club (Honolulu), Phi Gamma Delta. Avocations: tennis, walking, writing. Fax: 948-495-9458. E-mail: ernesth541@aol.com

HICKSON, ROBIN JULIAN, mining company executive; b. Irby, Eng., Feb. 27, 1944; s. William Kellett and Doris Matilda (Martin) H.; m. P. Anne Winn, Mar. 28, 1964; children: Richard, Sharon, Nicholas, Steven. BS in Mining Engring. with honors, U. London, 1965; MBA, Tulane U., 1990. Chartered engr., U.K. and Europe. Mining engr. N.J. Zinc Co., Austinville, 1965-70, divisional mgr. Jefferson City, Tenn., 1970-71; spl. project engr. Kerr McGee Corp., Grants, N.Mex., 1971-72; gen. mgr. Asarco, Inc., Vanadium, N.Mex., 1972-78, Gold Fields Mining Corp., Ortiz, N.Mex., 1978-83, Mesquite, Calif., 1982-86; v.p. Freeport Mining Co., New Orleans, 1986-91, Freeport Indonesia Inc., Irian Jaya, 1991-92; pres. Freeport Rsch. and Engring. Co., New Orleans, 1992-93; sr. v.p. Cyprus Climas Metals Co., Tempe, Ariz., 1993-94; pres. Cyprus Amax Engring. and Project Devel. Co., Tempe, 1994-99; exec. officer Cyprus Amax Minerals Co., 1994-99; sr. v.p. engring. and project mgmt. Kvaerner Metals, San Ramon, Calif., 2000—. V.p. engring. and devel. exec. officer Cyprus Amax Minerals Co., 1994-99. Author: (with others) Interfacing Technologies in Solution Mining, 1981. Recipient Robert Earll McConnell [illegible] and Metallurgy, Mining and Metall. Soc., N.Mex. Mining Assn. (bd. dirs. Santa Fe, N.Mex. chpt. 1975-83), Calif. Mining Assn. (bd. dirs. Sacramento chpt. 1982-86), Beta Gamma Sigma. Episcopalian. Avocations: ornithology, travel. Home: 12246 S Honah Lee Ct Phoenix AZ 85044-3455 Office: 12657 Alcosta Blvd San Ramon CA 94583 E-mail: annerobin@worldnet.att.net, robin.Rickson@kvaerner.com

HIDDLESTON, RONAL EUGENE, drilling and pump company executive; b. Bristow, Okla., Mar. 21, 1939; s. C.L. and Iona D. (Martin) H.; m. Marvelene L. Hammond, Apr. 26, 1959; children: Michael Scott, Mark Shawn, Matthew Shane. Student, Idaho State U., 1957 58. With Roper's Clothing and Bishop Redi-Mix, Rupert, Idaho, 1960-61; pres., chmn. bd., gen. mgr. Hiddleston Drilling, Rupert, 1961-66, Mountain Home, Idaho, 1966—. Bd. dirs. Baker Mfg. Mem. Mountain Home Airport Adv. Bd., 1968—; hon. mem. Idaho Search and Rescue. Mem. Nat. Ground Water Assn. (past pres., life, Oliver award), Idaho Ground Water Assn. (hon. life, past pres.), Pacific N.W. Water Well Assn., N.W. Mining Assn., Nat. Fedn. Ind. Businessmen, Ground Water Inst. (bd. dirs.), Aircraft Owners and Pilots Assn., Ducks Unltd., Nat. 210 Owners Club, Nat. Sporting Clays Assn., Masons, Royal Arch, Scottish Rites, El Korzh Shrine. Home: 1730 E 8th N Mountain Home ID 83647-1726 Office: RR 3 Box 610D Mountain Home ID 83647-9206

HIERONYMUS, EDWARD WHITTLESEY, lawyer; b. Davenport, Iowa, June 13, 1943; B.A. cum laude, Knox Coll., 1965; J.D. with distinction, Duke U., 1968. Bar: Calif. 1969, Iowa 1968. Ptnr. O'Melveny & Myers, Los Angeles, 1974-96, of counsel, 1996—. Contbr. articles on law to profl. jours. Exec. sec. Los Angeles Com. Fgn. Relations, 1975-86. Served with Judge Adv. Gen. U.S. Army, 1965-74. Mem. ABA (award for profl. merit 1968), Calif. Bar Assn. (founding co-chair natural resources subsect., real property sect. 1986-88), Los Angeles County Bar Assn., Iowa Bar Assn. Office: O'Melveny & Myers 400 S Hope St Los Angeles CA 90071-2899

HIGDON, POLLY SUSANNE, federal judge; b. Goodland, Kans., May 1, 1942; d. William and Pauline Higdon; m. John P. Wilhardt (div. May 1988); 1 child, Liesl. BA, Vassar Coll., 1964; postgrad., Cornell U., 1967; JD, Washburn U., 1975; LLM, NYU, 1980. Bar: Kans. 1975, Oreg. 1980. Assoc. Corley & Assocs., Garden City, Kans., 1975-79, Kendrick M. Mercer Law Offices, Eugene, Oreg., 1980-82; pvt. practice law Eugene, 1983; judge U.S. Bankruptcy Ct., Eugene, 1983-95, Portland, Oreg., 1995-97, chief judge, 1997—. Active U.S. Peace Corps, Tanzania, East Africa, 1965-66. Mem. Am. Bankruptcy Inst., Nat. Conf. Bankruptcy Judges, Oreg. Women Lawyers. Office: US Bankruptcy Ct 1001 SW 5th Ave Fl 7 Portland OR 97204-1147

HIGGINS, ROBERT (WALTER), career officer, physician; b. Uniontown, Wash., Nov. 9, 1934; s. Nelson Leigh and Abbie Elizabeth (Rowe) H.; m. Barbara Jean Wright, Aug. 19, 1956; children: Fred, Colleen, Jay. BS in Pharmacy, Wash. State U., 1957; MD, U. Wash., 1965. Pharmacist Wenatchee (Wash.) Thrifty Drugs, 1957-59; owner Higgins Drug Store, Pullman, Wash., 1959-61; intern L.A. County Harbor Gen. Hosp., Torrance, 1965-66; commd. lt. USN, 1966; ships surgeon USS Tutuila, Vietnam, 1966-68; ptnr. Ludwick, Zook & Higgins Family Medicine, Wenatchee, 1968-72; commd. lt. comdr. USN, 1972, advanced through grades to rear adm., 1988; chmn. dept. family medicine Naval Hosp., Charleston, S.C., 1972-78, Camp Pendleton, Calif., 1978-80, Bremerton, Wash., 1980-86, comdg. officer Camp Pendleton, 1986-87; med. officer USMC Washington, 1987-89; dep. surgeon gen. USN, 1989-93. Specialty advisor surgeon gen. USN, Washington, 1973-86. Contbg. author: Behavioral Disorders, 1984, 90; contbr. articles to profl. jours. Scoutmaster Boy Scouts Am., Charleston, 1974-78, Camp Pendleton, 1978-80; trustee Family Health Found. Am., Wash. State U. Found., 1992-98; bd. visitors Wash. State U. Coll. Pharmacy, 1998—. Decorated Disting. Svc. medal, Legion of Merit, Meritorious Svc. medal, Navy Commendation medal; recipient Alumni Achievement award Wash. State. U., 1988, Disting. Alumnus award U. Wash. Sch. Medicine, 1996. Fellow Am. Acad. Family Physicians (pres. 1984-85, arl. del. to AMA 1985-91, del. 1992-2000), Philippine Acad. Family Physicians (hon. fellow 1999); mem. Uniformed Svcs. Acad. Family Physicians (pres. 1974-76), World Orgn. Family Medicine (v.p. 1986-95, pres. elect 1995-98, pres. 1998—), Masons. Avocations: bird watching, fly fishing, model airplanes, stamp collection, jogging. Home and Office: 2303 Highland Dr Anacortes WA 98221-3143 E-mail: rhigginsmd@aol.com

HIGGINS, RUTH ANN, social worker, family therapist; b. Rock Valley, Iowa, Sept. 23, 1944; d. Neal and Tillie (Feekes) Vonk; m. 1972 (div. Sept. 1986); children: Ashlie Kay, Steven Grant. BA, Northwestern Coll., 1966; MA, U. Colo., 1978; LCSW, U. Denver, 1983. Cert. profl. tchr., Colo., social worker, Colo. Tchr. Adams County Dist. 12, Northglenn, Colo., 1967-69, Dept. Def., Clark AFB, The Philippines, 1969-70, Jefferson County Schs., Lakewood, Colo., 1970-75; social worker Boulder (Colo.) County Mental Health Ctr., 1977, Boulder Community Counseling Ctr., 1979-81, Columbine Counseling Ctr., Broomfield, Colo., 1981—; sch. social worker Adams County Sch. Dist. 12, Northglenn, 1985—. Part time social worker Hospice of Metro Denver, 1984-85, Boulder Valley Pub. Schs., 1985, Lutheran Hospice Care, Wheatridge, Colo., 1985. Author, editor: Nothing Could Stop the Rain, 1976. Counselor trainer for Up With People (Worldsmart), 1998-2000. Recipient Hon. Mention Counselor of Yr. award Colo. Sch. Counselors Assn., 1994; named finalist Alteria M. Bryant award Met. Denver Baha'i Ctr., 1996. Mem. Nat. Assn. Social Workers. Democrat. Avocations: stained glass, hiking, reading, music.

HIGGINSON, JOHN, retired career officer; b. St. Louis, Oct. 24, 1932; s. John and Clara Elizabeth (Lindemann) H.; married; children: Robert, Mark, Patrick, Paul. BA, St. Mary's U., 1954; BS, Naval Postgrad. Sch., 1966; MS, George Washington U., 1968. Ensign USN, advanced through grades to Rear Adm., ret.; comdr. Helicopter Anti-submarine Squadron 2, 1973-74, Helicopter Anti-submarine Squadron 10, 1976-78, USS Inchon, 1979-80, Amphibious Squadron 7, 1981-83, Amphibious Group 3, 1985, Naval Surface Group, Long Beach, 1986, ret., 1990-92; pres. Long Beach C. of C. Prof. mgmt. Naval War Coll., Newport, R.I. Co-author: Sea and Air, The Marine Environment, 1968, 2nd. edit., 1973. Bd. dirs. United Way, L.A., Long Beach Symphony, Long Beach Youth Activities, DARE, Inc., USO, Leadership Long Beach, St. Mary's Med. Ctr., Meml. Med. Ctr. of Long Beach; trustee Long Beach City Coll. Found., Long Beach Civic Light Opera; mem. exec. bd. of Long Beach Boy Scouts of Am.; mem. exec. coun. Industry-Edn. Coun. of Calif.; former chmn. L.A. Combined Fed. Campaign; pres., CEO Am. Gold Star Manor Charitable Trust, 1993—. Mem. Navy Helicopter Assn. (former pres.), Fed. Exec. Bd. (former chmn.), Rotary (commr. Calif., mem. Vets. Meml. Commn.). Home: 5341 Las Lomas Park Estates Long Beach CA 90815 E-mail: jhigginson@mpicomputers.com

HIGGS, LLOYD ALBERT, astronomer, observatory administrator; b. Moncton, N.B., Can., June 21, 1937; s. Maxwell Lemert and Reta Mae (Jollimore) H.; m. Kathleen Mary Fletcher, Jan. 15, 1966; children: Kevin, Scott, Michelle. B.Sc., U. N.B., Fredericton, 1958; D.Phil., Oxford (Eng.) U., 1961. Rsch. officer NRC Can., Ottawa, Ont., 1961-81; dir. Dominion Radio Astrophys. Obs., Penticton, B.C., 1981-94, prin. rsch. officer, 1988-2001; ret., 2001. Research officer Leiden (Holland) U., 1964-65 Researcher numerous publs. in astronomy. Leader Boy Scouts Can., 1977-89. Beaverbrook scholar, 1954-58; Rhodes scholar, 1958-61 Fellow Royal Astron. Soc.; mem. Am. Astron. Soc., Can. Astron. Soc. (pres. 1992-94), Royal Astron. Soc. Can. (life mem., editor jour. 1976-80, Service award 1983, pres. 1988-90), Internat. Astron. Union. Office: Dominion Radio Astrophys Obs PO Box 248 Penticton BC Canada V2A 6K3

HIGH, STEVEN SAMUEL, art gallery official; b. Twin Falls, Idaho, June 17, 1956; s. Robert F. and Shirley H.; m. Lisa A. Lee, June 26, 1978; children: Jason S. Lee-High, Nicolas C. Lee-High. Student, U. Utah, 1974-75; BA in Art History, Antioch Coll., 1979; MA in Art History, Williams Coll., 1985; MBA, Va. Commonwealth U., 1995. Researcher San Francisco Mus. Modern Art, 1979-80; preparator, asst. curator MIT Mus., 1980-82; rsch. and teaching asst. Williams Coll., Williamstown, Mass., 1984-85; dir. Baxter Gallery, Portland (Maine) Sch. Art, 1985-88; instr. art history Portland Sch. Art, 1985-88; dir. Anderson Gallery, Richmond, Va., 1988—96; exec. dir. Nev. Museum of Art, Reno, 1996— Co-chmn. Artworks for Va., Richmond, 1988-96. Contbr. articles to profl. jours. Bd. dirs. Richmond Arts Coun., 1989-96. Exhbn. grantee NEA, 1988-, Va. Commn. for Arts, 1989, 90, numerous others. Mem. Am. Assn. Museums. Address: Nevada Museum of Art 160 W Liberty Reno NV 89501

HIGH, THOMAS W. energy services executive; b. Oakland, Calif., Dec. 7, 1947; s. William A. and Vera D. (Blumann) H.; m. Nancy J. Hughes, June 8, 1969. BA, U. Calif., Berkeley, 1968; grad. advanced mgmt. program, Harvard U., 1992. Rep. govt. and pub. affairs Pacific Gas and Electric Co., San Francisco, 1973-82, dir. legis. svcs., 1982-84, asst. sec., 1984-85, corp. sec., 1985-86, v.p., corp. sec., 1986-91, v.p., asst. to chmn., 1991-94, v.p., asst. to CEO, 1994-95, sr. v.p. corp. svcs., 1995-97; sr. v.p. adminstrn. and external rels. PG&E Corp., San Francisco, 1997—. Trustee Am. Conservatory Theatre, 1991—; mem. coun. Friends of the Bancroft Libr., 1993-95. Office: PG & E Corp Ste 2400 One Market Spear Tower San Francisco CA 94105

HIGHBERGER, WILLIAM FOSTER, lawyer; b. Suffern, N.Y., May 15, 1950; s. John Kistler and Helen Stewart (Foster) H.; m. Carolyn Barbara Kuhl, July 12, 1980; children: Helen Barbara, Anna Mary. AB, Princeton U.; JD, Columbia U. Bar: Calif. 1976, U.S. Dist. Ct. (cen. dist.) Calif. 1976, U.S. Ct. Appeals (2d cir.) 1976, U.S. Ct. Appeals (9th cir.) 1977, U.S. Dist. Ct. (so. and ea. dists.) Calif. 1979, U.S. Supreme Ct. 1980, D.C. 1981, U.S. Dist. Ct. (no. dist.) Calif. 1981, U.S. Dist. Ct. D.C. 1982, U.S. Ct. Appeals (D.C. cir.) 1982, U.S. Ct. Appeals (3d cir.) 1983, N.Y. 1984, U.S. Dist. Ct. (so. dist.) N.Y. 1984, U.S. Dist. Ct. (ea. dist.) N.Y. 1985. Law clk. to judge U.S. Ct. Appeals (2d cir.), Bridgeport, Conn., 1975-76; assoc. Gibson, Dunn & Crutcher, Washington and L.A., 1976-82, ptnr., 1983-98; with L.A. Superior Ct. Notes and comments editor Columbia U. Law Rev., 1974. Mem. Nature Conservatory, Calif., 1981—; active Pacific Palisades (Calif.) Presbhn. Ch., 1987—. James Kent scholar Columbia U., 1973. Mem. ABA (com. on individual rights and responsibilities in workplace, labor sect.), L.A. County Bar Assn., Indsl. Rels. Rsch. Assn., Am. Employment Law Coun., Univ. Cottage Club. Republican. Office: LA Superior Ct Criminal Cts Bldg Dept 112 210 W Temple St Los Angeles CA 90012

HIGHET, MAC, travel company executive; Exec. v.p. fin. & ops. Reed Travel Group, Secaucus, N.J., 1998; exec. v.p. corp. devel. Reed Elsevier, N.Y.C., 1996-98; pres., COO RezSolutions, 1998-99, CEO, 1999—2000. Office: REZsolutions 7500 N Dreamy Draw Dr Ste 120 Phoenix AZ 85020-4668

HIGHLANDER, RICHARD WILLIAM, communications executive; b. Beckley, W.Va., Feb. 17, 1940; s. Ronald William and Lucille Bernice (Bland) H.; m. Ida Mae Canterbury, June 26, 1965; one child, Alison Renee. BA, Rutgers U., 1963; MA, U. Ga., 1972. Commd. 2d lt. U.S. Army, 1963, advanced through grades to lt. col., 1979, ret., 1984; dir. communications, def. systems group FMC Corp., Santa Clara, Calif., 1984-94; v.p. comm. United Def. LP, San Jose, 1994-99; dir. pub. rels. Calpine, San Jose, 1999—. Contbr. articles to profl. jours., Freedom Found. award 1966, 81. Trustee San Jose Repertory Co., 1985, pres. bd., 1998-99. Decorated Legion of Merit with bronze oak leaf cluster, Bronze Star with two bronze oak leaf clusters, Purple Heart. Mem. PRSA (accredited), Assn. U.S. Army, Internat. Assn. Bus. Communicators, Calif. Mfrs. Assn. (bd. dirs. 1985, chmn. bd. 1993), Aerospace Industries Assn. (comm. coun.), Rotary, San Jose Met. C. of C. (bd. dirs.), Chi Psi. Republican. Methodist. Avocations: racquetball, golf. Home: 5906 Gleneagles Cir San Jose CA 95138-2370

HIGHT, B. BOYD, lawyer; b. Lumberton, N.C., Feb. 15, 1939; s. B. Boyd and Mary Lou (Lennon) H.; m. Mary Kay Sweeney, Mar. 31, 1962; children: Kathryn, Kevin. BA, Duke U., 1960; LLB, Yale U., 1966; diploma in comparative law, U. Stockholm, 1967. Assoc. O'Melveny & Myers, Los Angeles, 1967-74, ptnr., 1974-79, 81-84, 89—; dep. asst. sec. trans. and telecommunications U.S. Dept. State, Washington, 1979-81; exec. v.p., gen. counsel Sante Fe Internat. Corp., Alhambra, Calif., also bd. dirs. Bd. dirs. Planned Parenthood L.A., 1986-95, pres., 1992-94; mem. bd. overseers Rand Ctr. Russian and Eurasian Studies, 1987-2000, chair, 1994-2000; trustee Am. U. Cairo, 1987—; bd. dirs. Calif. Supreme Ct. Hist. Soc., 1993-2001; bd. overseers The Huntington, 1996—. Mem. Coun. Fgn. Rels., Pacific Coun. on Internat. Policy, Calif. Club, Los Angeles Country Club. Democrat. Office: O'Melveny & Myers 400 S Hope St Los Angeles CA 90071-2899 E-mail: bhight@omm.com

HIGHWATER, JAMAKE, author, lecturer; s. Jamie and Amana (Bonneville) H.; adopted by Alexander and Marcia Marks. Doctorate (hon.), Minn. Coll. Art. and Design, 1986. Lectr. primal and 20th century culture various univs. in, U.S. and Can., 1970—; grad. lectr. NYU Continuing Edn., 1979-83. Asst. adj. prof. Grad. Sch. Architecture, Columbia U., 1983-84, UCLA Film and Entertainment Ext., 1998—; cons. N.Y. State Council on the Arts, 1975-85; founding mem. Indian Art Found., Santa Fe, 1980-87, Cultural Council, Am. Indian Community House, N.Y.C., 1976, pres., 1976-78; mem. task force on individual artist N.Y. State Council on Arts, 1981, mem. lit. panel, 1982-83; mem. lit. panel N.Y. Found. of the Arts, 1989-90, Mass. Artists Fellowship, 1990-91; adj. faculty Inst. Am. Indian Art, Santa Fe, 1979—; lectr. UCLA Entertainment and Performing Arts Dept., 1999—; cons. Myth Quest, PBS, 2000—. Host, narrator and writer of: TV series Native Land, 1986, The Primal Mind, Public Broadcasting Svc. Network, 1986 (best film yr. Nat. Ednl. Film Festival, 1986, Ace award Discovery Channel 1991); Author: Indian America: A Cultural and Travel Guide, 1975, Song From the Earth: American Indian Painting, 1976 (Anisfield-Wolf award in race relations 1980), Ritual of the Wind: No. American Indian Ceremonies, Music and Dances, 1977, Many Smokes, Many Moons, 1978 (Jane Addams Peace Book award), Dance: Rituals of Experience, 1978, The Sweet Grass Lives On: 50 Contemporary North American Indian Artists, 1980, Masterpieces of American Indian Painting, 2 vols., 1978-80, The Primal Mind: Vision and Reality in Indian America, 1981 (Virginia McCormick Scully Lit. award 1982), Native Land (based on PBS program), 1986, Shadow Show: An Autobiographical Insinuation, 1987, Myth and Sexuality, 1990, The World of 1492, 1992, The Language of Vision, 1994, The Mythology of Transgression, 1997,; novels Anpao: An American Indian Odyssey (Newbery Honor award 1978), 1977 (Named Best Book for Young Adults, ALA 1978), Journey to the Sky: Stephens and Catherwood's Rediscovery of the Maya World, 1978, The Sun, He Dies: The End of the Aztec World, 1980 (named Best Book for Young Adults, Sch. Library Jour. 1980), Legend Days (Notable Book, ALA 1985), The Ceremony of Innocence, (Best book for Young Adults, ALA) 1986, I Wear the Morning Star, 1986, Eyes of Darkness, (Notable Book, ALA) 1985, I Took the Fire: A Memoir, 1988, Kill Hole, 1992, Dark Legend, 1994, Rama, 1994 (Best Books for Young Adults N.Y. Pub. Libr.), (poetry) Moonsong Lullaby, 1981, Songs for the Seasons, 1995; (as J. Marks) Rock and Other Four Letter Words, 1968, Mick Jagger: The Singer Not the Song, 1973; contbr. critiques to various lit. jours.; classical music editor: Soho Weekly News, 1975-79; sr. editor: Fodor Travel Guides, 1970-75; contbg. editor: N.Y. Arts Jours, 1978-84, Indian

Trader, 1977-80, Stereo Rev., 1972-79, Native Arts/West, 1980-81; nat. adv. bd. PEW Fellowships in the arts, 1991-92; mem. bd. Am. Poetry Ctr., 1991—; contbg. arts critic Christian Sci. Monitor, 1988-92; mem. adv. bd. Visions Mag., 1992—, The Highwater papers, N.Y. Pub. Libr. Mem. art task panel Pres.'s Commn. on Mental Health, 1977-78; gen. dir. S.W. Native Arts Festival, U.Tex., Houston, 1985-86; gen. dir. Festival Mythos, Phila., 1991; mem. adv. bd. Wheelwright Mus. Indian Art, 1980-82, Lame Deer Coll., 1981—; mem. nat. adv. bd. Native Am. Rights Fund, 1980-83; nat. adv. Joseph Campbell Libr./Archives, 1989—; creative adv. Griot: N.Y., Great Performances, PBS, Star Trek Voyager, Paramount Pictures, Brian Wilson Documentary, Don Was, BBC, Myth Quest, PBS, 13-part series. Named Hon. Citizen of Okla., 1977, New Mex., 1978. Mem. AFTRA, PEN (children's lit. com. Am. Ctr., 1990—, exec. bd. PEN Am. Ctr. 1983-86), Authors Guild, Dramatists Guild, Authors League. Office: Native Land Found 8491 W Sunset Blvd Los Angeles CA 90069-1911 E-mail: nativeland@earthlink.net

HILBERT, ROBERT S(AUL), optical engineer; b. Washington, Apr. 29, 1941; s. Philip G. and Bessie (Friend) H.; m. Angela Cinel Ferreira, June 19, 1966; children: David M., Daniel S. BS in Optics, U. Rochester, 1962, MS in Optics, 1964. Optical design engr. Itek Corp., Lexington, Mass., 1963-65, supr. lens design sect., 1965-67, asst. mgr. optical engr. dept., 1967-69, mgr. optical engring. dept., 1969-74, dir. optics, 1974-75; v.p. engring. Optical Rsch. Assocs., Pasadena, Calif., 1975-84, sr. v.p., 1985-91, pres., COO, 1991-2000, pres., CEO, 2000—, also bd. dirs. Lectr. Northeastern U., Burlington, Mass., 1967-69; mem. trustees vis. com. Sch. Engring. and Applied Sci., U. Rochester, 1995-97. Patentee in lens systems. Recipient Future Scientist of Am. award, 1957; Am. Optical Co. fellow U. Rochester, 1962. Fellow Soc. Photo-Optical Instrumentation Engrs. (chmn. fellows com.); mem. Optical Soc. Am. (engring. coun. 1990-92, mem. Fraunhofer award com. 1997-98), Lens Design Tech. Group (chmn. 1975-77). Jewish. Avocations: reading, the cinema. Home: 5055 Indianola Way La Canada Flintridge CA 91011-2657 Office: Optical Rsch Assocs 3280 E Foothill Blvd Pasadena CA 91107-3103 Business E-Mail: bob@opticalres.com

HILDEBRAND, CAROL ILENE, librarian; b. Presho, S.D., Feb. 15, 1943; d. Arnum Vance and Ethel Grace (Cole) Stoops; m. Duane D. Hildebrand, Mar. 21, 1970. BA, Dakota Wesleyan U., Mitchell, S.D., 1965; M in Librarianship, U. Wash., 1968. Tchr. Watertown (S.D.) H.S., 1965-67; libr. dir. Chippewa County Libr., Montevideo, Minn., 1968-70, The Dalles (Oreg.)-Wasco County Libr., 1970-72; libr. Salem (Oreg.) Pub. Libr., 1972-73; libr. dir. Lake Oswego (Oreg.) Pub. Libr., 1973-82; asst. city libr. Eugene (Oreg.) Pub. Libr., 1982-91, acting city libr., 1991-92, libr. dir., 1993-2000, libr. project mgr., 2000—. Cons., condr. workshops in field. Vice-chair LWV, Lane County, 1987; bd. dirs. People for Oreg. Librs. Polit. Action Com., 1986—; sec. Citizens for Lane County Libr., 1985-88. Named Woman of Yr., Lane County Coun. of Orgns., 1995, Oreg. Libr. of Yr., 1993. Mem. ALA (chpt. councilor 1990-94), AAUW (bd. dirs. 1986, sec. 1995-96), Pacific N.W. Libr. Assn. (pres. 1989-90), Oreg. Libr. Assn. (pres. 1976-77), Rotary, Phi Kappa Phi. Methodist. Avocations: reading murder mysteries, baking. Office: Eugene Pub Libr 100 W 13th Ave Eugene OR 97401-3433

HILDEBRAND, JOHN G(RANT), neurobiologist, educator; b. Boston, Mar. 26, 1942; s. John G. and Helen S. Hildebrand; m. Gail Deerin Burd, July 24, 1982. AB, Harvard U., 1964; PhD, Rockefeller U., 1969; Laurea Honoris Causa, U. Cagliari, Italy. Instr. neurobiology Harvard U. Med. Sch., Boston, 1970-72, asst. prof., 1972-77, assoc. prof., 1977-80, vis. prof., 1980-81; prof. biol. scis. Columbia U., N.Y.C., 1980-85; prof. neurobiol., biochemistry, molecular and cell biology, entomology U. Ariz., Tucson, 1985—, Regents prof., 1989—, dir. div. neurobiology, 1985—. Assoc. behavioral biology Harvard U. Mus. Comparative Zoology, Cambridge, Mass., 1980-97; trustee Marine Biol. Lab., Woods Hole, Mass., 1981-89, mem. exec. com., 1981-88; Jan de Wilde lectr. U. Wageningen, The Netherlands, 1992; King Solomon lectr., Hebrew U., Jerusalem, 1995; K.D. Roeder lectr. Tufts U., 1995; Felix Santschi lectr. U. Zurich, Switzerland, 1995. Co-editor: Chemistry of Synaptic Transmission, 1974, Receptors for Neurotransmitters, Hormones, and Pheromones in Insects, 1980, Molecular Insect Science, 1990; devel. neurosci. sect. editor Jour. Neurosci., 1983-88, co-editor Jour. Comparative Physiology A, 1990—; mem. editorial bd. various other jours. Trustee Rockefeller U., N.Y.C., 1970-73. Recipient Javits Neurosci. award Nat. Isnt. Neurol. and Communicative Disorders and Stroke, NIH, 1986-94, Merit award Nat. Inst. Allergy and Infectious Diseases, NIH, 1986-97, R.H. Wright award Simon Fraser U., B.C., Can., 1990, Max Planck Rsch. award Max Planck Gesellschaft and Alexander von Humboldt-Stiftung of Germany, 1990, Founder's Meml. award Entomol. Soc. Am., 1997, Humboldt rsch. award, 1997; Helen Hay Whitney Found. fellow, 1969-72, A.P. Sloan Found. fellow, 1973-77. Fellow: AAAS, Royal Entomol. Soc. UK; mem.: Am. Soc.Biochemistry and Molecular Biology, Assn. for Chemoreception Sci., Soc. for Neurosci. (treas. 1993—94), Internat. Soc. Neuroethology (pres. 1995—98), Soc. Integrative and Comparative Biology, Internat. Soc. Chem. Ecology (pres. 1998—99), Deutsche Akademie der Naturforscher Leopoldina, Norwegian Acad. Sci. and Letters, Acad. Arts and Sci. Avocations: music, lower brass instruments. Home: 629 N Olsen Ave Tucson AZ 85719-5136 Office: U Ariz ARL Div Neurobiology PO Box 210077 Tucson AZ 85721-0077

HILDEBRAND, VERNA LEE, human ecology educator; b. Dodge City, Kans., Aug. 17, 1924; d. Carrell E. and Florence (Smyth) Butcher; m. John R. Hildebrand, June 23, 1946; children: Carol Ann, Steve Allen. BS, Kans. State U., 1945, MS, 1957; PhD, Tex. Women's U., 1970. Tchr. home econs. Dickinson County H.S., Chapman, Kans., 1945-46; tchr. early childhood Albany (Calif.) Pub. Schs., 1946-47; grad. asst. Inst. Child Welfare U. Calif., Berkeley, 1947-48; tchr. kindergarten Albany Pub. Schs., 1948-49; dietitian commons and hosp. U. Chgo., 1952-53; instr. Kans. State U., Manhattan, 1953-54, 59, Okla. State U., Stillwater, 1955-56; asst. prof. Tex. Tech U., Lubbock, 1962-67; from asst. prof. to prof. Mich. State U., East Lansing, 1967-97, prof. emeritus, 1997—. Legis. clk. Kans. Ho. of Reps., Topeka, 1955. Author: Introduction to Early Childhood Education, 1971, 6th edit., 1997, Guiding Young Children, 1975, 6th edit., 1998, Parenting and Teaching Young Children, 1981, 90, Management of Child Development Centers, 1984, 4th edit., 1997, Parenting: Rewards and Responsibilities, 1994, 2d edit., 1997, 3d edit., 1999; co-author: China's Families: Experiment in Societal Change, 1985, Knowing and Serving Diverse Families, 1996, 2d edit., 1999. Mem. Nat. Assn. for the Edn. Young Children (task force 1975-77), Am. Home Econs. Assn. (bd. dirs., Leader award 1990), Women in Internat. Devel., Nat. Assn. Early Childhood Tchr. Edn. (award for meritorious and profl. leadership 1995). Home and Office: #904 4570 E Yale Ave Denver CO 80222

HILDEBRANDT, DARLENE MYERS, retired information scientist; b. Somerset, Pa., Dec. 18, 1944; d. Kenneth Geary and Julia (Klim) Myers; m. Peter Anton Hildebrandt, May 26, 1983; 1 child, Robin Adaire. BA, U. Calif., Riverside, 1969; MA, U. Wash., 1970. Info. specialist U. Wash. Acad. Computer Ctr., Seattle, 1970-73, library assoc., 1974-75, mgr. computing info. services adminstr., 1976-85, adminstr. computing info. services, 1986-91; head sci. librs. Wash. State U., Pullman, 1991-2000. Spl. librs. rep. Wash. State Adv. Coun. Librs., 1992-98; mem. Wash. State Librs. Database Selection Com., 1997—. Editor: (newsletter) Points Northwest (Elaine D. Kaskela award 1973, 75, Best ASIS 1974), Wash. State Tribal Librs. Info. Newsletter, 1998—; compiler and editor Computing Info. Directory, 1985-96. Recipient Civitan award, 1963. Mem. Am. Soc. for Info. Sci. (founding mem. Pacific Northwest chpt. 1971, chairperson 1975, 76, bd. dirs. 1980-83, chpt. award 1978). Office: Wash State U Owen Sci & Engring Libr Pullman WA 99164-0001

HILDNER, ERNEST GOTTHOLD, III, solar physicist, science administrator; b. Jacksonville, Ill., Jan. 23, 1940; s. Ernest Gotthold Hildner Jr. and Jean (Johnston) Duffield; m. Sandra Whitney Shellworth, June 29, 1968; children: Cynthia Whitney, Andrew Duffield. BA in Physics and Astronomy, Wesleyan U., 1961; MA in Physics and Astronomy, U. Colo., 1964, PhD in Physics and Astronomy, 1971. Experiment scientist High Altitude Obs., Nat. Ctr. Atmospheric Rsch., Boulder, Colo., 1972-80, vis. scientist, 1985-86; chief solar physics br. NASA Marshall Space Flight Ctr., Huntsville, Ala., 1980-85; dir. Space Environment Ctr. NOAA Oceanic and Atmospheric Rsch. and Nat. Ctrs. Environ., Boulder, 1986—. Mem. com. on solar and space physics NRC, Washington, 1986-90; chmn. Com. on Space Environment Forecasting, fed. coord. for meteorology, Washington, 1988-97; co-chmn. com. space weather Office of Fed. Coord. for Meteorology, 1998—. Contbr. rsch. papers in solar and interplanetary physics, 1971—; co-inventor spectral slicing X-ray telescope with variable magnification. Mem. AAAS, Am. Geophys. Union (assoc. editor Geophys. Rsch. Letters 1983-85), Am. Astron. Soc. (councillor solar physics div. 1979-80), Internat. Astron. Union, Sigma Xi. Achievements include patent for Spectral Slicing X-Ray Telescope with Variable Magnification. Office: NOAA Space Environment Ctr 325 Broadway St Boulder CO 80305-3337

HILGARD, ERNEST ROPIEQUET, psychologist; b. Belleville, Ill., July 25, 1904; s. George Engelmann and Laura (Ropiequet) H.; m. Josephine Rohrs, Sept. 19, 1931; children: Henry Rohrs, Elizabeth Ann Jecker. B.S., U. Ill., 1924; Ph.D., Yale, 1930; D.Sc., Kenyon Coll., 1964; LL.D., Centre Coll., 1974; D.Sc., Northwestern U., 1987, Colgate U., 1987; PhD (hon.), U. Oslo (Norway), 1994. Asst. instr. in psychology Yale U., 1928-29, instr., 1929-33; successively asst. prof., asso. prof., prof. psychology Stanford, 1933-69, emeritus prof., 1969—, exec. head dept., 1942-50, dean grad. div., 1951-55; Bd. dirs., pres. Ann. Reviews, Inc., 1948-73; With USDA, Washington, 1942, OWI, 1942-43, Office Civilian Requirements, WPB, 1943-44. Collaborator, div. child devel. and tchr. personnel Am. Council Edn., 1940-41; nat. adv. mental health council USPHS, 1952-56; fellow (Center Advanced Study Behavioral Scis.), 1956-57; Mem. U.S. Edn. Mission to Japan, 1946 Author: Theories of Learning, 1948, rev. edit., 1981, Introduction to Psychology, 1953, rev. edit., 1987, Hypnotic Susceptibility, 1965, Hypnosis in the Relief of Pain, 1975, rev. edit., 1983, Divided Consciousness, 1977, rev. edit., 1986, American Psychology in Historical Perspective, 1978, Psychology in America: A Historical Survey, 1987; editor: Fifty Years of Psychology, 1988. Bd. curators Stephens Coll., Mo., 1953-68. Recipient Warren medal in exptl. psychology, 1940; Wilbur Cross medal Yale U., 1971; Gold medal Am. Psychol. Found., 1978 Hon. fellow British Psychol. Assn.; mem. Am. Psychol. Assn. (pres. 1948-49, Outstanding Lifetime Achievement award 1994), Am. Acad. Arts and Scis., Nat. Acad. Edn., Soc. Psychol. Study Social Issues (chmn. 1944-45), AAAS, Nat. Acad. Scis. (sci. rev. award 1984), Am. Philos. Soc., Internat. Soc. Hypnosis (pres. 1973-76, Benjamin Franklin gold medal 1979), Sigma Xi. Home: 850 Webster St Apt 226 Palo Alto CA 94301-2857 Office: Stanford U Psychology Dept Bldg 420 Rm 206 Stanford CA 94305-2130

HILL, BONNIE GUITON, company executive; b. Springfield, Ill., Oct. 30, 1941; d. Henry Frank and Zola Elizabeth (Newman) Brazelton; m. Walter Hill Jr.; 1 child, Nichele Monique. BA, Mills Coll., 1974; MS, Calif. State U., Hayward, 1975; EdD, U. Calif., Berkeley, 1985. Adminstr. asst. to pres.'s spl. asst. Mills Coll., Oakland, Calif., 1970-71, adminstrv. asst. to asst. v.p., 1972-73, student svcs. counselor, adv. to resuming students, 1973-74, asst. dean of students, interim dir. ethnic studies, lectr., 1975-76; exec. dir. Marcus A. Foster Ednl. Inst., Oakland, 1976-79; adminstrv. mgr. Kaiser Aluminum & Chem. Corp., Oakland, 1979-80; v.p., gen. mgr. Kaiser CTR Inc., Oakland, 1980-84; vice chair Postal Rate Commn., Washington, 1985-87; asst. sec. for vocat. and adult edn. Dept. Edn., Washington, 1987-89; sec. State and Consumer Svcs. Agy. State of Calif.; spl. adv. to Pres. for Consumer Affairs, dir. U.S. Office Consumer Affairs, 1989-90; pres., CEO Earth Conservation Corps, Washington, 1990-91; sec. State and Consumer Svcs. Industry, State of Calif., 1991-92; dean McIntire Sch. Commerce U. Va., Charlottesville, 1992-97; v.p. The Times Mirror Co., 1997-2000; pres. B. Hill Enterprises, LLC, 2001—; COO Iconblue, Inc., LA Times, 1998—2001. Sr. v.p. comm. and pub. affairs L.A. Times, 1998—; pres., CEO The Times Mirror Found., 1997-2001; bd. dirs. The Home Depot Co., Niagara Mohawk Power Corp., Hershey Foods Corp., AK Steele Corp., Choice Point Inc. Office: Los Angeles Times 202 W 1st St Los Angeles CA 90012

HILL, BOYD H., JR. medieval history educator; b. Dunedin Isles, Fla., Feb. 21, 1931; s. Boyd Howard and Minnie Cauthen (Buchanan) H.; m. Alette Louise Olin, Jan. 26, 1956; children: Boyd Buchanan, Michael Howard. A.B., Duke U., 1953; M.A., U. N.C., 1957, Ph.D., 1963; postgrad., UCLA, 1957-58. Instr. La. State U., Baton Rouge, 1962-64; asst. prof. medieval history U. Colo., Boulder, 1964-66, assoc. prof., 1967-71, prof., 1971—, chmn. dept. history, 1981-85, chmn. dept. classics., 1986-87; scholarship dir. Coll. Arts and Sci., U. Colo., Boulder, 1992-96. Vis. asst. prof. UCLA, 1966-67 Author: Medieval Monarchy in Action, 1972; editor: The Rise of the First Reich, 1969, The Western World, 1974; contbr. articles to profl. jours. Town trustee Jamestown, Colo., 1990-92. With U.S. Army, 1953-55. Wellcome Hist. Med. Library fellow, 1962; Am. Philos. Soc. grantee, 1968; Council Research and Creative Work U. Colo. grantee, 1980 Mem. Am. Hist. Assn. (councillor Pacific Coast br. 1971-74), Medieval Acad. Am. (councillor 1973-76), Rocky Mountain Medieval and Renaissance Assn. (pres. 1983), Phi Kappa Psi Democrat. Presbyterian. Home: 1433 Tulip St Longmont CO 80501-2423 Office: U Colo Campus Dept History PO Box 234 Boulder CO 80309-0234

HILL, DAVID ALLAN, electrical engineer; b. Cleve., Apr. 21, 1942; s. Martin D. and Geraldine S. (Yoder) H.; m. Elaine C. Dempsey, July 9, 1971. BSEE, Ohio U., 1964, MSEE, 1966; PhD in Elect. Engring., Ohio State U., 1970. Vis. fellow Coop. Inst. for Rsch. Environ. Sci., Boulder, Colo., 1970-71; rsch engr. Inst. for Telecommunication Scis., Boulder, 1971-82; sr. scientist Nat. Inst. Standards and Tech., Boulder, 1982—. Adj. prof. U. Colo., Boulder, 1980—. Editor Geosci. and Remote Sensing Jour., 1980-84, Antennas and Propagation Jour., 1986-89; contbr. over 100 articles to profl. jours., chpts. to books. Recipient award for best paper Electromagnetic Compatability Jour., 1987. Fellow IEEE (chpt. chmn. 1975-76, editor 1986-89); mem. Electromagnetic Soc. (bd. dirs. 1980-86), Internat. Union Radio Sci. (nat. com. 1986-89), Colo. Mountain Club (Boulder), Sierra Club. Office: Nat Inst Standards & Tech 813-02 325 Broadway St Boulder CO 80305-3337 E-mail: dhill@boulder.nist.gov

HILL, GREG, newspaper bureau chief; San Francisco bur. chief Wall St. Jour. Office: Wall St Jour 201 California St Ste 1350 San Francisco CA 94111-5022

HILL, HARRY DAVID, city official, human resources professional; b. Whittier, Calif., Oct. 29, 1944; s. Harry Boreman and Winifred Nell (Purvis) Hill; m. Linda Mae Price, Nov. 8, 1969; 1 child, Jon Ryan. AA, Los Angeles Harbor Coll., Wilmington, Calif., 1964; BA in Polit. Sci., UCLA, 1966; M of Pub. Adminstrn. in Human Resources, U. So. Calif., 1972. Personnel aide City of Anaheim, Calif., 1966-67, personnel analyst, 1967-71, sr. personnel analyst, 1971-75, personnel services mgr., 1975-83, asst. human resources dir., 1983-88, asst. labor rels. dir., 1988-94, dir. human resources, 1994—. Chmn. supervisory com. Anaheim Area Credit Union, 1981-89, bd. dirs., 1989-95. Mem. So. Calif. Pub. Labor Coun. (treas. 1986-87, pres. 1988), Internat. Pers. Mgmt. Assn. (pres. western region 1983-84), So. Calif. Pers. Mgmt. Assn. (pres. 1978-79), Coop. Pers. Svcs. (bd. dirs. 1987—). Democrat. Office: City of Anaheim 200 S Anaheim Blvd Fl 3 Anaheim CA 92805-3820 E-mail: dhill@anaheim.net

HILL, HENRY ALLEN, physicist, educator; b. Port Arthur, Tex., Nov. 25, 1933; s. Douglas and Florence Hill. B.S., U. Houston, 1953; M.S., U. Minn., 1956, Ph.D., 1957; M.A. (hon.), Wesleyan U., 1966. Research asst. U. Houston, 1952-53; teaching asst. U. Minn., 1953-54, research asst., 1954-57; research assoc. Princeton U., 1957-58, instr., then asst. prof., 1958-64; assoc. prof. Wesleyan U., Middletown, Conn., 1964-66, prof. physics, 1966-74, chmn. dept., 1969-71; prof. physics U. Ariz., Tucson, 1966-95, prof. emeritus, 1995—. Chmn. bd. Zetetic Inst., 1992—; researcher on nuclear physics, relativity, astrophysics, and optics. Contbr. articles to profl. jours. Sloan fellow, 1966-68 Fellow Am. Phys. Soc.; mem. AAAS, Am. Astron. Soc., Optical Soc. Am., Am. Geophys. Union. Office: Zetetic Inst 1665 E 18th St Ste 206 Tucson AZ 85719-6809

HILL, JIM, state official; 1 child, Jennifer. BA in Econs., Mich. State U., 1969; MBA, Indiana U., 1971, JD, 1974. Asst. atty. gen. Oreg. Dept. of Justice, 1974-77; hearing referee Oreg. Dept. of Revenue, 1977-81; personnel specialist and cons. State Farm Ins., 1984-86; elected mem. Oreg. House of Reps., 1983-87, Oreg. State Sen., 1987-93; dir. mktg. PEN-NOR, Inc., Portland Gen. Contractors, 1986-88; corp. accts. mgr. for Latin Am. Mentor Graphics, 1988-93; state treas. State of Oreg., Salem, 1994—. Office: Oreg State Treasury 350 Winter St NE Ste 100 Salem OR 97301-3896

HILL, JOHN EARL, mechanical engineer; b. Ely, Nev., July 18, 1953; s. Earl M. and Florence Hill; m. Terry Lynn Biederman, Oct. 3, 1981; 1 child, Felicia Biederman. BA in Social Psychology, U. Nev., 1974, BSME, 1981. Cert. engr. in tng. Machinist B&J Machine and Tool, Sparks, Nev., 1977-78; designer, machinist Screen Printing Systems, Sparks, 1978, Machine Svcs., Sparks, 1978-81; computer programmer U. Nev., Reno, 1980-81; design engr. Ford Aerospace and Communications Corp., Palo Alto, Calif., 1981-82, 86-88; contract design engr. Westinghouse Electric Corp., Sunnyvale, 1982-83; contract project engr. Adcotech Corp., Milpitas, 1983-84; sr. engr. Domain Tech., Milpitas, 1984-85; project engr. Exclusive Design Co., San Mateo, Calif., 1985-86; automation mgr. Akashic Memories Corp., San Jose, 1988-94; ptnr. Automated Bus. Svcs., San Jose; dir. automation engring. Seagate Rec. Media, Fremont, Calif., 1994-97; mgr., equipment engr. FormFactor, Inc., Livermore, 1997—. Mem. Robotics Internat. of Soc. Mfg. Engrs., Tau Beta Pi, Pi Mu Epsilon, Phi Kappa Phi. Avocations: music, art, hang gliding. Home: 147 Wildwood Ave San Carlos CA 94070-4516 Office: Form Factor Inc 5666 La Ribera St Livermore CA 94550-9275

HILL, LOUIS ALLEN, JR. former university dean, consultant; b. Okemah, Okla., May 18, 1927; s. Louis Allen and Gladys Adelia (Dietrich) Hill Wise; m. Jeanne Rose Murray, June 14, 1951; children: Dawn, David, Dixon. B.A., Okla. State U., 1949, B.S.C.E., 1954, M.S.C.E., 1955; Ph.D., Case Inst. Tech., 1965. Registered profl. engr., Okla., Ariz. Engr. Lee Hendricks Engring., Tulsa, 1955-57, Hudgins, Thompson, Ball & Assocs., Oklahoma City, 1957-58; asst. prof. civil engring. Ariz. State U., 1958-66, assoc. prof., 1966-70, prof., 1970-74, chmn. dept. civil engring., 1974-81; dean Coll. Engring. U. Akron, 1981-88, assoc. v.p. rsch. and grad. studies, 1988. Chmn. Ohio Engring. Dean's Council, 1983-85; trustee Engring. Found. of Ohio, 1985-88; staff engr. Salt River Project, Ariz., 1962; cons. in field. Author: Fundamentals of Structures, 1975, Compendium of Structural Aids, 1975, Structured Programming in Fortran, 1981; contbr. numerous articles to profl. jours.; designer numerous bridges, hwys. Ch. leader-tchr. 1st Bapt. Ch., 1971-88, Scottsdale Presbyn. Ch., 1990—. Served to capt. C.E., U.S. Army, 1945-47, 51-53, The Philippines, Japan. Recipient Disting. award Akron Coun. Engring. and Sci. Socs., 1987, commendation Minorities in Mainstream Tech. Com., 1990, Disting. Svc. award U. Akron Coll. Engring., 1994; named Educator of Yr., Inroads N.E. Ohio, Inc., 1986; Louis A. Hill Jr. award established in his honor Qua Tech., 1987, Mayor Plusquellic proclaimed April 23, 1997 as Dr. Louis A. Hill Day in City of Akron; fellow Continental Oil Co., 1955, faculty fellow NSF, 1963. Fellow ASCE (life); mem. NSPE (sec., profl. engr. in edn. 1986-88), Am. Soc. Enging. Edn. (life, Western Electric Fund award 1967), Sigma Xi, Tau Beta Pi, Omicron Delta Kappa. Republican. Home and Office: 3208 N 81st Pl Scottsdale AZ 85251-5800

HILL, MICHAEL J. film editor; Works include TV movies Berlin Tunnel 21, 1981, Cagney & Lacey, 1981, The First Time, 1982, Baby Sister, 1983, Obsessive Love, 1984, Combat High, 1986, (films with Daniel P. Hanley): (also with Robert J. Kern) Night Shift, 1982, Splash, 1984, Cocoon, 1985, Gung Ho, 1986, (also with Gregory Prange) Armed and Dangerous, 1986, Willow, 1988, Parenthood, 1989, Pet Sematary, 1989, Problem Child, 1990, Backdraft, 1991, Far and Away, 1992, The Paper, 1994, Apollo 13, 1995 (Acad. award for best film editing 1996), Ransom, 1996, EdTV, 1999, How the Grinch Stole Christmas, 2000, A Beautiful Mind, 2001. Office: Broder Kurland Webb Uffner Agency 9242 Beverly Blvd Ste 200 Beverly Hills CA 90210-3731

HILL, RICHARD, egineering executive; B of Engring., U. Ill.; MBA, Syracuse U. With GE, Motorola, Hughes Aircraft; v.p. test & mgmt. croup, pres. Tektronix Components Corp., 1981-83; CEO, chmn. Novellus Systems, Inc., San Jose, Calif., 1993—; also bd. dirs. Office: 3970 N 1st St San Jose CA 95134-1501

HILL, RICK ALLAN, former congressman; b. Grand Rapids, Minn., Dec. 30, 1946; m. Betti Christie, June 10, 1983; children: Todd, Corey, Mike. BA in Econs. and Polit. Sci., St. Cloud State U., 1968. Surety bonding businessman, owner InsureWest, 1968-90; real estate and investment ptnr., 1983—; committeeman State Rep. Party, 1990-94; legis. liaison to Gov. Marc Racicot, Mont., 1993; mem. 105th-106th Congress from Mont. dist. U.S. Ho. Reps., Washington, 1997-2001, mem. banking and fin. svcs. com., mem. resources com., mem. small bus. com. Fin. chair State Rep. Party, 1989-91, state chair, 1991-92. Bd. dirs. Mont. Sci. and Tech. Alliance, 1992.*

HILL, WILLIAM U. state supreme court justice; Atty. gen., Cheyenne, Wyo., 1995-98; justice Wyo. Supreme Ct., Cheyenne, 1998—. Office: Wyoming Supreme Court 2301 Capitol Ave Cheyenne WY 82001-3656

HILLE, BERTIL, physiology educator; b. New Haven, Oct. 10, 1940; s. C. Einar and Kirsti (Ore) H.; m. Merrill Burr, Nov. 21, 1964; children: Erik D., J. Trygve. BS, Yale U., 1962; PhD, Rockefeller U., 1967. H.H. Whitney fellow Cambridge U., 1967-68; asst. prof. U. Wash., Seattle, 1968-71, assoc. prof., 1971-74, prof. physiology, 1974—. Vis. prof. U. Saarland, Hamburg, Germany, 1975-76. Author: Ion Channels of Excitable Membranes, 1984, 3d edit., 2001; mem. editl. bd. Jour. Gen. Physiology, 1971—, Am. Jour. Physiology, 1984-87, Jour. Neurosci., 1984-87, Neuron, 1987—, Curr. Opinion Neurobiol., 1990-99, Procs. of NAS, 1996-99; contbr. articles to profl. jours. Recipient Alexander von Humboldt Sr. Scientist award, 1975, Bristol-Myers Squibb award, 1990, (with Dr. Clay Armstrong) Louisa Gross Horowitz prize for biology or biochemistry

Columbia U., 1996, (with Drs. Clay Armstrong and Roderick MacKinnon) Albert Lasker Basic Med. Rsch. award, 1999; co-recipient Gairdner Found. 2001 Internat. award, 2001. Mem. NAS, Biophys. Soc. (K.S. Cole award 1975, 86). E-mial. Home: 10630 Lakeside Ave NE Seattle WA 98125-6934 Office: U Wash Box 357290 Seattle WA 98195-7290 E-mail: hille@u.washington.edu

HILLER, STANLEY, JR. financial company executive; b. San Francisco, Nov. 15, 1924; s. Stanley and Opal (Perkins) H.; student Atuzed Prep. Sch., U. Calif., 1943; m. Carolyn Balsdon, May 25, 1946; children: Jeffrey, Stephen. Pres. Hiller Aircraft divsn. Kaiser Cargo, Inc., Berkeley, Calif., 1944-45; organized Hiller Aircraft Corp. (formerly United Helicopters, Inc.), Palo Alto, Calif., 1945, became pres. and chief exec. officer, 1950-64 (co. bought by Fairchild Stratos 1964), mem. exec. com. Fairchild Hiller Corp., 1965; chmn. bd., chief exec. officer Reed Tool Co., Houston, Bekins, 1980, York Internat., 1985, Baker Internat. Corp., 1975; CEO Keytronic Corp., 1992—; ptnr. Hiller Investment Co.; dir. Boeing Co. Recipient Fawcett award, 1944; Distinguished Svc. award Nat. Def. Transp. Soc., 1958; named 1 of 10 Outstanding Young Men U.S., 1952. Hon. fellow Am. Helicopter Soc.; mem. Am. Inst. Aeros. and Astronautics, Am. Soc. of Pioneers, Phi Kappa Sigma. Office: Key Tronic Corp 4424 N Sullivan Rd Spokane WA 99214

HILLICKSON, MICHELE, national parks service administrator; CEO, supt. Petrified Forest Nat. Park, Ariz. Office: PO Box 2217 Petrified Forest Natl Park AZ 86028

HILLINGER, CHARLES, journalist, writer; b. Evanston, Ill., Apr. 1, 1926; s. William Agidious H. and Caroline Bruning; m. Arliene Otis, June 22, 1948; children: Brad, Tori. BS in Polit. Sci., UCLA, 1951; degree (hon.), Marymount Coll., Rancho Palos Verdes, 1997. Circulation mgr., columnist Park Ridge (Ill.) Advocate, 1938-41; copy boy, libr., feature writer Chgo. Tribune, 1941-43; reporter, feature writer, syndicated columnist L.A. Times, 1946-92, ret., 1992. Author: California Islands, 1957, Bel-Air Country Club, A Living Legend, 1993, Charles Hillinger's America, 1996, Charles Hillinger's Channel Islands, 1998, Hillinger's California, 1997, (audiobooks) Charles Hillinger's America, 1999, California Characters, 2001. Mem. adv. bd. Santa Cruz Is. Found., Santa Barbara, Calif., 1992—; treas. 8-Ball Welfare Found. Greater L.A. Press Club, 1992—. With USN, 1943-46. Mem. Greater L.A. Press Club (sec. 1978-88, v.p. 1988-90, pres. 1990-92), Dutch Treat Club W. Avocations: tennis, golf, hearts. Home: 3131 Dianora Dr Rancho Palos Verdes CA 90275 E-mail: chxlat@aol.com

HILLMAN, MARK D. state legislator; b. Burlington, Colo., May 24, 1967; Student, Colby C.C., Kans., 1985-86, Morgan C.C., Colo., 1991. Newspaper reporter, sports editor, 1986-94; freelance reporter, 1994—; farmer Dryland Wheat, 1994—; mem. Colo. Senate, Dist. 2, Denver, 1998—; mem. agr., natural resources and energy com.; vice-chair local govt. com.; mem. state, vets. and mil. affairs. Treas. Evang. Free Ch.; active Colo. Farm Bur., Heritage Found.; county chair Wayne Allard for Congress, 1990-94; vice-chair Kit Carson County Reps., 1993-94, chair, 1994-98; mem. Colo. Rep. Leadership Program, 1995-96. Republican. Office: State Capitol 200 E Colfax Ave Ste 346 Denver CO 80203-1716 E-mail: mhillman@sni.net

HILLS, AUSTIN EDWARD, vineyard executive; b. San Francisco, Oct. 13, 1934; s. Leslie William and Ethel (Lee) H.; m. Erika Michaela Brunar, May 20, 1978; children: Austin. AB, Stanford U., 1957; MBA, Columbia U., 1959. Chmn. bd. dirs. Hills Bros. Coffee, Inc., San Francisco, 1976, Grgich Hills Cellar, Rutherford, Calif., 1977—. Pres. Hills Vineyards, Inc., Rutherford, 1975-97; pres. Pacific Coast Coffee Assn., San Francisco, 1975-76, Hills Vineyard, Inc., 1999—. Pres. San Francisco Soc. for Prevention of Cruelty to Animals, 1972-78. No. Calif. Soc. for Prevention of Cruelty to Animals, 1972-78. With Air N.G. Mem. Am. Soc. Enologists. Libertarian. Office: 490 Post St Ste 1049 San Francisco CA 94102-1301 E-mail: hillsa@pacbell.net

HILLS, REGINA J. journalist; b. Sault Sainte Marie, Mich., Dec. 24, 1953; d. Marvin Dan and Ardithanne (Tilly) H.; m. Vincent C. Stricherz, Feb. 25, 1984 B.A., U. Nebr., 1976. Reporter UPI, Lincoln, Nebr., 1976-80, state editor, bur. mgr., 1981-82, New Orleans, 1982-84, Indpls., 1985-87; asst. city editor Seattle Post-Intelligencer, 1987-99, online prodr., 1999—, mng. prodr., 2001—. Panelist TV interview show Face Nebr., 1978-81; vis. lectr. U. Nebr., Lincoln, 1978, 79, 80; columnist weekly feature Capitol News, Nebr. Press Assn., 1981-82 Recipient Outstanding Coverage awards UPI, 1980, 82 Mem. U. Nebr. Alumni Assn., Zeta Tau Alpha. Office: Seattle Post Intelligencer 101 Elliott Ave W Ste 200 Seattle WA 98119-4295

HILLYARD, IRA WILLIAM, pharmacologist, educator; b. Richmond, Utah, Mar. 23, 1924; s. Neal Jacobsen and Lucille (Duce) H.; m. Venice Lenore Williams, July 10, 1945 (dec.); children: Christine, Kevin, Eric; m. Norma Larsen, May 1, 1970. B.S., Idaho State U., 1949; M.S., U. Nebr., 1951; Ph.D., St. Louis U., 1957. Pharmacologist Mead Johnson Co., Evansville, Ind., 1957-59; sr. pharmacologist, sect. leader Warner-Lambert Research Inst., Morris Plains, N.J., 1959-69; assoc. prof. pharmacology Idaho State U. Coll. Pharmacy, Pocatello, 1969-73, 77-79, dean, 1979-87, prof. pharmacology, 1979-91, prof. emeritus, 1991—. Dir. pharmacology and toxicology ICN Pharms., Irvine, Calif., 1973-77, cons., 1977-80; cons. Pennwalt Pharm. Co., Rochester, N.Y., 1978-83 Contbr. articles to profl. jours. Served with USN, 1943-45, 51-53. Decorated Purple Heart. Fellow Am. Found. Pharm. Edn.; mem. Western Pharmacology Soc., Am. Assn. Colls. Pharmacy, Am. Soc. Pharmacology and Exptl. Therapeutics, N.Y. Acad. Scis., Sigma Xi, Rho Chi, Phi Delta Chi. Lodge: Rotary. Home: 594 S 800 W Mapleton UT 84664-4313

HILLYARD, LYLE WILLIAM, state legislator, lawyer; b. Logan, Utah, Sept. 25, 1940; s. Alma Lowell and Lucille (Rosenbaum) H.; m. Alice Thorpe, June 24, 1964; children: Carrie, Lisa, Holly, Todd, Matthew. BS, Utah State U., 1965; JD, U. Utah, 1967. Bar: Utah 1967, U.S. Supreme Ct. 1977. Pres. Hillyard, Anderson & Olsen, Logan, 1967—; mem. Utah Senate, Dist. 25, Salt Lake City, 1985—. Rep. chmn. Cache County, Logan, 1970-76; Utah State Rep., 1981-84; pres. Cache County C. of C., 1977. Named one of Outstanding Young Men of Am., Utah Jaycees, 1972; recipient Disting. Svc. award, Logan Jaycees, 1972, Merit award Cache Valley coun. Boy Scouts Am., 1981. Mem. ABA, Utah State Bar Assn., Cache County Bar Assn., Assn. Trial Lawyers Am., Am. Bd. Trial Advocates. Mormon. Club: Big Blue (Logan). Lodge: Kiwanis. Office: Hillyard Anderson & Olsen 175 E 1st N Logan UT 84321-4601

HILPERT, EDWARD THEODORE, JR. [illegible] 29, 1928; s. Edward Theodore Sr. and Hulda Gertrude (Wilder) H.; m. Susan Hazelton, May 5, 1973. AB, U. Wash., 1954, JD, 1956. Bar: Wash. 1956, U.S. Dist. Ct. (we. dist.) Wash. 1956, U.S. Tax Ct. 1959, U.S. Ct. Appeals (9th cir.) 1959, U.S. Supreme Ct. 1970. Law clk. to Hon. George H. Boldt U.S. Dist. Ct. (we. dist.) Wash., Tacoma, 1956-58; assoc. Ferguson & Burdell, Seattle, 1958-63, ptnr., 1963-91; sr. ptnr. Schwabe, Williamson, Ferguson & Burdell, Seattle, 1992—. Exec. com. 9th cir. Jud. Conf., San Francisco, 1987-90. Judge pro tem Seattle Mcpl. Ct., 1971-80. Capt. USAR, 1946-49, 50-52, Korea. Mem. ABA, Mensa, Rainer Club, Seattle Tennis Club, Broadmoor Golf Club, Sea Pines Country Club. Republican. Lutheran. Home: 1434 Broadmoor Dr E Seattle WA 98112-3744 Office: Schwabe Williamson Ferguson & Burdell US Bank Ctr 1420 5th Ave Ste 3500 Seattle WA 98101-1397 E-mail: sshathhi@aol.com, kanderson@schwabe.com

HILTON, BARRON, hotel executive; b. Dallas, 1927; s. Conrad Hilton. Founder, pres. San Diego Chargers, Am. Football League, until 1966; v.p. Hilton Hotels Corp., Beverly Hills, Calif., 1954, pres., chief exec. officer, 1966—, chmn., 1979—, also dir.; chmn. Hilton Equipment Corp, Beverly Hills, Calif. Mem. gen. adminstrv. bd. Mfrs. Hanover Trust Co., N.Y.C. Office: Hilton Hotels Corp 9336 Civic Center Dr Beverly Hills CA 90210-3604

HILTZIK, MICHAEL, journalist; b. N.Y.C., Nov. 9, 1952; s. Harold & Bernice (Rothman) Hiltzik; m. Deborah Ibert, 2 children, Andrew, David. B.A. English, Colgate U., 1973; M.S. Journalism, Columbia U. Grad Sch Journalism, 1974. Journalist Buffalo Courier-Express, Buffalo, 1974-78, bureau chief, 1976-78; staff writer Providence Journal-Bulletin, Providence, 1979-81; finan. writer L.A. Times, 1981-83, N.Y. finan. correspondent, 1982-88, Nairobi bureau chief Nairobi, Kenya, 1988-93, Moscow correspondent Moscow, Russia, 1993-94, finan. staff writer/editor Los Angeles, 1994-. Author, non-fiction: A Death in Kenya, 1991, Dealers of Lightning: Xerox PARC and the Dawn of the Computer Age, 1999. Recipient Pulitzer prize for Beat Reporting, 1999. Office: c/o LA Times Bus Sect Times Mirror Sq Los Angeles CA 90053 E-mail: michael.hiltzik@latimes.com

HIMES, DIANE ADELE, buyer, fundraiser, actress, lobbyist; b. San Francisco, Aug. 11, 1942; d. L. John and Mary Louise (Young) H. BA, San Francisco State U., 1964. Rep. west coast home furnishings Allied Stores, nationwide; gift buyer Jordan Marsh, Miami; buyer The Broadway Stores; west coast sales mgr. Xmas divsn. Vincent-Lippe, L.A., midwest sales mgr. Chgo. Bd. dirs. L.A. Womens' Shakespeare Group, 1992-93. Actress Nine 'O Clock Players, 1995, short film The Traveling Companion, 1998. Co-chair Californians Against California Initiative No On #102, 1988; founding co-chair Life AIDS Lobby, 1985-88; Beverly Hills rent control bd., 1984; co-chair Californians Against Proposition # 64, 1986, co-chair mcpl. elections com., L.A. Named Woman of Yr. of L.A., ACLU, 1987, Christopher Street West, 1988. Avocations: acting, appearing in short films.

HINCHEY, BRUCE ALAN, environmental engineering company executive, state legislator; b. Kansas City, Mo., Jan. 24, 1949; s. Charles Emmet and Eddie Lee (Scott) H.; m. Karen Adele McLaughlin, Nov. 27, 1969 (div. Nov. 1983); children: Scott Alan, Traci Denise, Amanda Lee, Richard Austin; m. Karen Robitaille, Apr. 10, 1993. Student, U. Mo., Rolla, 1967-71. Source testing crew chief Ecology Audits, Inc., Dallas, 1971-76, lab. mgr. Casper, Wyo., 1976-78, mgr. ops. Dallas, 1978-79; v.p. Kumpe & Assoc. Engrs., Casper, 1979-81; pres. Western Environ. Svcs. and Testing, Inc., Casper, 1981—, Hawk Industries, Inc., 1993-2000; mem. Wyo. Senate, Dist. 27, Cheyenne, 1998-. Pres. Mining Assocs. Wyo., Cheyenne, 1986-87. Mem. Wyo. State Ho. of Reps., Cheyenne, 1989-99, spkr. of house, mgmt. coun., rules com., energy coun., select water com., sel. edn. com., active Natrona County Rep. precinct, Casper, 1986—, Am. Legis. Exch. Coun., 1989; chair Natrona County Rep. Party, 1988-89; mem. appropriations com. Wyo. Senate, 1999—. Mem. Am. Inst. Mining Engrs., Nat. Fedn. Ind. Bus. (Guardian award), Air Pollution Control Assn., Casper C. of C., Rotary, Shriners, Masons. Methodist. Office: Western Environ Svcs Testing Inc 913 N Foster Rd Casper WY 82601-1640

HINCKLEY, GORDON B. religious organization administrator; b. Salt Lake City, June 23, 1910; s. Bryant S. and Ada (Bitner) H.; m. Marjorie Pay, Apr. 29, 1937; children: Kathleen Hinckley Barnes, Richard G., Virginia Hinckley Pearce, Clark B., Jane Hinckley Dudley. Asst. Coun. of Twelve Apostles, LDS Ch., Salt Lake City, 1958-61, mem. Coun., 1961-81, counselor in 1st presidency, 1981-81, 2d counselor in 1st presidency, 1982-85, 1st counselor in 1st presidency, 1985-95, pres. of ch., 1995—. Office: First Presidency LDS Ch 47 E South Temple Salt Lake City UT 84150-9701

HIND, HARRY WILLIAM, pharmaceutical company executive; b. Berkeley, Calif., June 2, 1915; s. Harry Wyndham and B.J. (O'Connor) H.; m. Diana Vernon Miesse, Dec. 12, 1940; children: Leslie Vernon Hind Daniels, Gregory William. BS, U. Calif., Berkeley, 1939; LLD, U. Calif.-Berkeley, 1968; DSc (hon.), U. Scis. Phila., 1982. Founder Barnes-Hind Pharms., Inc., Sunnyvale, Calif., 1939—. Pres. Hind Health Care, Inc. Contbr. articles to profl. jours.; designer ph meter and developer of ophthalmic solutions. Mem. chancellor's assocs. U. Calif.; trustee emeritus U. Calif.-San Francisco Found. Recipient Ebert award for pharm. research, 1948, Eye Research Found. award, 1958, Helmholtz Ophthalmology award for research, 1968, Carbert award for sight conservation, 1973, Alumnus of Yr. award U. Calif. Sch. Pharmacy, 1965, Disting. Service award U. Calif. Proctor Found., 1985, Commendation by Resolution State of Calif., 1987, Pharmaceutical Achievements commendation State of Calif. Assembly, Hon. Recognition award Contact Lens Mfrs. Assn., 1990. Fellow AAAS; mem. Am. Pharm. Assn. (Man of Yr. Pharmacist's Planning Svc. 1987), Am. Optometric Assn. (Man of Yr. award, 1987), Contact Lens Soc. Am. (Hall of Fame 1989), Am. Assn. Pharm. Scientists, Am. Chem. Soc., Calif. Pharm. Assn., N.Y. Acad. Scis., Los Altos Country Club, Sigma Xi, Rho Chi, Phi Delta Chi.

HINDERY, LEO JOSEPH, JR. former media company executive, fiber optics executive; b. Springfield, Ill., Oct. 31, 1947; s. Leo Joseph and E. Marie (Whitener) H.; m. Deborah Diane Sale, Feb. 20, 1980; 1 child, Robin Cook. BA, Seattle U., 1969; MBA, Stanford U., 1971. Asst. treas. Utah Internat., San Francisco, 1971-80; treas. Natomas Co., San Francisco, 1980-82; exec. v.p. fin. Jefferies & Co., L.A., 1982-83; chief fin. officer A.G. Becker Paribas, N.Y.C., 1983-85; chief officer planning and fin. Chronicle Pub. Co., San Francisco, 1985-88; mng. gen. ptnr. InterMedia Ptnrs. (merged with ATT Broadband/Internet Svcs.), San Francisco, 1988-97; pres. Tele-Communications, Inc., 1997-2000; chmn., CEO Global Crossing Ltd., 2000—. Bd. dirs. DMX, Inc., NETCOM On-Line Comm. Svcs., Inc., Nat. Cable TV Assn., Cable Telecomms. Assn., C-Span. With U.S. Army, 1968-70. Mem. Calif. Golf Club. Avocation: golf. Office: Global Crossing Ltd 141 Caspian Ct Sunnyvale CA 94089-1013

HINERFELD, ROBERT ELLIOT, lawyer; b. N.Y.C., May 29, 1934; s. Benjamin B. and Anne (Blitz) H.; m. Susan Hope Slocum, June 27, 1957; children: Daniel Slocum, Matthew Ben. AB, Harvard U., 1956, JD, 1959. Bar: Calif. 1960. Asst. U.S. atty So. Dist. Calif., 1960-62; assoc. Leonard Horwin, Beverly Hills, Calif., 1962-66; mem. Simon, Sheridan, Murphy, Thornton & Hinerfeld, Los Angeles, 1967-74, Murphy, Thornton, Hinerfeld & Cahill, 1975-83, Murphy, Thornton, Hinerfeld & Elson, 1983-85, Manatt, Phelps & Phillips LLP, 1985-2000, sr. of counsel, 2000—; arbitrator bus. panel Los Angeles Superior Ct., 1979-82; assoc. ind. counsel [illegible] Judge pro tempore Beverly Hills Municipal Court, 1967-74; clin. lectr. U. So. Calif. Law Center, 1980-81, guest lectr., 1993-96; expert witness, 1987—, legal affairs on-air guest spkr. sta. KCRW-FM, Santa Monica, Calif., 1998-99. Contbr. articles to profl. jours. Trustee Westland Sch., Los Angeles, 1970-75, Pacific Hills Sch., 1971-72. Fellow Am. Bar Found. (life); mem. ABA, Fed. Bar Assn., Los Angeles County Bar Assn. (spl. com. jud. evaluation 1978-82, arbitration com. 1981-83, settlement officer 2d appellate dist. appellate case settlement project 1996—, spl. com. on appellate evaluation 1996—), Beverly Hills Bar Assn., State Bar Calif. (mem. com. on criminal law and procedure, chmn. spl. com. revision fed. criminal code, mem. disciplinary investigation panel dist. 7 1977-80, hearing referee State Bar Ct. 1981-83, referee rev. dept. 1984-87, exec. com. litigation sect. 1983-85, civil litigation adv. group 1985-88, mem. Jud. Nominees Evaluation Commn. 2000—), Am. Arbitration Assn. (arbitrator comml. panel 1966—), Calif. Acad. Appellate Lawyers (membership com. 1983-88, 2d v.p. 1985-87, 1st v.p. 1987-88, pres. 1988-89), Harvard Club So. Calif. (dir. 1974-73, sec. 1978-80, mem. prize book com. 1992-94), Harvard Club N.Y.C. Home and Office: 371 24th St Santa Monica CA 90402-2517

HINKLE, CHARLES FREDERICK, lawyer, clergyman, educator; b. Oregon City, Oreg., July 6, 1942; s. William Ralph and Ruth Barbara (Holcomb) H. BA, Stanford U., 1964; MDiv, Union Theol. Sem., N.Y.C., 1968; JD, Yale U., 1971. Bar: Oreg. 1971; ordained to ministry United Ch. of Christ, 1974. Instr. English, Morehouse Coll., Atlanta, 1966-67; assoc. Stoel Rives LLP (formerly Stoel, Rives, Boley, Jones & Grey), Portland, Oreg., 1971-77, ptnr., 1977—. Adj. prof. Lewis and Clark Law Sch., Portland, 1978—; bd. govs. Oreg. State Bar, 1992-95. Oreg. pres. ACLU, Portland, 1976-80, nat. bd. dirs., 1979-85; bd. dirs. Kendall Cmty. Ctr., 1987-93, Youth Progress Assn., 1994-98, Portland Baroque Orch., 1999-2000; mem. pub. affairs com. Am. Cancer Soc., 1994-99; mem. Oreg. Gov.'s Task Force on Youth Suicide, 1996. Recipient Elliott Human Rights award Oreg. Edn. Assn., 1984, E.B. MacNaughton award ACLU Oreg., 1987, Wayne Morse award Dem. Com. Oreg., 1994, Tom McCall Freedom of Info. award Women in Comm., 1996, Civil Rights award Met. Human Rights Commn., 1996, Pub. Svc. award Oreg. State Bar, 1997. Fellow Am. Bar Found.; mem. ABA (ho. of dels. 1998-2000), FBA, Multnomah County Bar Assn., City Club Portland (pres. 1987-88). Democrat. Home: 14079 SE Fairoaks Way Milwaukie OR 97267-1017 Office: Stoel Rives 900 SW 5th Ave Ste 2600 Portland OR 97204-1268 E-mail: cfhinkle@stoel.com

HINMAN, FRANK, JR. urologist, educator; b. San Francisco, Oct. 2, 1915; s. Frank and Mittie (Fitzpatrick) H.; m. Marion Modesta Eaves, Dec. 3, 1948. AB with great distinction, Stanford U., 1937; MD, Johns Hopkins U., 1941. Diplomate Am. Bd. Urology (trustee 1979-85). Intern Johns Hopkins Hosp., 1941-42; resident Cin. Gen. Hosp., 1942-44, U. Calif. Hosp., 1945-47; pvt. practice San Francisco, 1947-85; assoc. clin. prof. urology U. Calif., San Francisco, 1954-62, clin. prof., 1962—; urologist-in-chief Children's Hosp., 1957-85. Adv. council Nat. Inst. Arthritis, Diabetes, Digestive and Kidney Diseases, 1983-86 Lt. USNR, 1944-46. Named Disting. Alumnus, Johns Hopkins U., 1995. Fellow ACS (regent 1972-80, vice-chmn. 1978-79, v.p. 1982-83), Royal Coll. Surgeons (hon., Eng.); mem. Am. Urol. Assn. (hon.), Am. Assn. Genito-Urinary Surgeons (hon., pres. 1981, Keyes medalist 1998), Clin. Soc. Genito-Urinary Surgeons (pres. 1979), Internat. Soc. Urol. (pres. Am. sect. 1980-84), Am. Assn. Clin. Urologists, Am. Fedn. Clin. Research, Soc. Pediatric Urology (founding mem., pres. 1971), Soc. Univ. Urologists (founding mem., pres. 1973), Am. Acad. Pediatrics (pres. urology sect. 1986), Urodynamics Soc. (founding mem., pres. 1980-82), Genito Urinary Reconstructive Soc. (founding mem.), Pan Pacific Surg. Assn. (v.p. 1980-83), Internat. Continence Soc., Brit. Assn. Urologic Surgeons (hon.) (St. Paul Medalist 1991), Soc. Française d'Urologie, Australasian Soc. Urologic Surgeons (hon.), Phi Beta Kappa, Alpha Omega Alpha. Clubs: Bohemian, St. Francis Yacht, San Francisco Yacht. Home: 1000 Francisco St San Francisco CA 94109-1127 Office: U Calif Med Ctr San Francisco CA 94143-0738 E-mail: fhinman@urol.ucsf.edu

HINMAN, HARVEY DEFOREST, lawyer; b. Binghamton, N.Y., May 7, 1940; s. George Lyon and Barbara (Davidge) H.; m. Margaret Snyder, June 23, 1962; children: George, Sarah, Marguerite. BA, Brown U., 1962; JD, Cornell U., 1965. Bar: Calif. 1966. Assoc. Pillsbury, Madison & Sutro, San Francisco, 1965-72, ptnr., 1973-93, v.p., gen. counsel Chevron Corp., 1993—; bd. dirs. Legal Aid Soc., San Francisco. Bd. dirs., sec. Holbrook Palmer Park Found., 1977-86; bd. dirs. Phillips Brooks Sch., 1978-84, pres. 1983-84; trustee Castillija Sch., 1988-89; bd. govs. Filoli Ctr., 1988—, pres. 1994-95. Fellow Am. Bar Found.; mem. ABA, San Francisco Bar Assn. Office: Chevron Corporation 575 Market St San Francisco CA 94105-2856

HINSHAW, DAVID B., JR. radiologist; b. L.A., Dec. 28, 1945; s. David B. Sr. and Mildred H. (Benjamin) H.; m. Marcia M. Johns, Aug. 7, 1966; children: Amy, John. BA in German and Pre Medicine, Loma Linda U., Riverside, Calif., 1967; MD, Loma Linda U., 1971. Diplomate Am. Bd. Radiology in diagnostic radiology and neuroradiology. Intern Loma Linda U. Med. Ctr., 1971-72, resident diagnostic radiology, 1972-74; neuroradiologist 2d Gen. Army Hosp., Landstuhl, Fed. Republic Germany, 1975-77; asst. prof. Loma Linda U. Sch. Medicine, 1975-80, assoc. prof., 1981-85, prof., 1986—, vice chmn. dept. radiation scis., 1988-90, chmn. dept. radiology, 1990—; pres. med. staff Loma Linda U. Med. Ctr., 1994-95; vice chair faculty practice plan Loma Linda U., 1995—. Dir. sect. magnetic resonance imaging, Loma Linda, 1983—; cons. U.S. Army Med. command, Europe, 1976-77, Jerry L . Pettis Meml. VA Hosp., 1980— Contbr. numerous articles to profl. jours., book chpts. in field of radiology. Maj. U.S. Army, 1975-77. Recipient Pres's. award Loma Linda U., 1971, Donald E. Griggs award Internal Med. Fellow Am. Coll. Radiology, Walter E. McPherson Soc. (Outstanding Faculty Research award 1987); mem. AMA (Physicians Recognition award 1980-83, 84—), Am. Soc. Neuroradiology (sr., program com. 1989, chmn. pub. rels. com. 1989-90), Western Neuroradiol. Soc., Radiol. Soc. N.Am., Calif. Med. Assn., San Bernadino County Med. Assn., Inland Radiol. Soc. (pres. 1989-90), Calif. Radiol. Soc., Assn. Univ. Radiologists, Soc. Magnetic Resonance Imaging, Soc. Magnetic Resonance in Medicine, Fedn. Western Socs. Neurol. Scis., Am. Roentgen Ray Soc., Am. Soc. Head and Neck Radiology, L.A. Radiol. Soc., Soc. Chmn. Acad. Radiology Depts., Alpha Omega Alpha (pres. Epsilon chpt. 1987). Republican. Seventh-day Adventist. Avocations: traveling, electronics. Office: Loma Linda U Med Ctr Dept Radiology 11234 Anderson St MRI B 623 Loma Linda CA 92354-2804

HINSHAW, MARK LARSON, architect, urban planner; b. Glendale, Calif., Aug. 17, 1947; s. Lerner Brady and Alice Elaine (Larson) H.; m. Caryl Ann Kunsemuller, Dec. 21, 1968 (div. 1982); 1 child, Erica; m. Marilyn Kay Smith, June 18, 1983 (div. 1997); children: Lindsay, Christopher. BArch magna cum laude, U. Okla., 1970; M Urban Planning, CUNY, 1972. Registered architect, Wash. Sr. planner Planning Dept., Anchorage, 1976-77; project planner TRA, Seattle, 1977-82; urban designer City of Bellevue, Wash., 1982-90; ind. cons., 1991-97; dir. urban design Loschky Marquardt Nesholm Architects, Seattle, 1997—. Architect-in-the-sch. Seattle Sch. Dist., 1979. Columnist on architecture, urban design Seattle Times, 1993—; author: Citistate Seattle: Shaping a Modern Metropolis, 1999; contbr articles to profl. publs. and books. Mem. Urban Beautification Commn., Anchorage, 1975, Design Jury, Hemet (Calif.) Civic Ctr. Competition, Seattle Design Commn., 1990-91; mem. Downtown Seattle Design Rev. Bd. 1st lt. USAF, 1972-76. NEA grantee, 1975; recipient merit award for Hist. Preservation, City Seattle, 1983. Fellow [illegible] 1994-98); mem. Am. Planning Assn. (sec. Wash. chpt. 1982, v.p. 1983-85, pres. 1987-89). Office: 801 2nd Ave Fl 5 Seattle WA 98104-1576 E-mail: mhinshaw@imnarchitects.com

HINTON, JAMES H. healthcare services administrator; m. Carol Hinton; children: Rebecca, Robert. BA in Econs., U. N.Mex.; M in Healthcare Adminstrn., Ariz. State U. Pres., CEO Presbyn. Healthcare Svcs., Albuquerque.

HINZ, SHIRLEY SORENSEN, administrative secretary; b. Denver, Sept. 28, 1942; m. Dale Edward Hinz, Sept. 3, 1966; children: Andrew Christian, Tammy Lynn Dahl. Student, Ft. Lewis Coll., 1961, Barnes Bus. Coll., 1982; spl. publishing diploma, Inst. Children's Lit., 1994. Adminstrv. asst. USDA, Ft. Collins, Colo., 1989; divsn. sec. U.S. Dept. Energy, Golden, 1991; sect. sec. U.S. Dept. Interior, Ft. Collins, 1992—. Mem. labor mgmt. partnership coun. U.S. Dept. Interior, 1994-95. Author numerous poems and short stories; writer/songwriter. Active Ault (Colo.) Sr. Ctr., 1989—. Recipient Editor's Choice award Nat. Libr. Congress, Nat. Libr. Poetry, 1995-96, Accomplishment of Merit award Creative Arts & Sci. Enterprises, 1996, Nat. Merit Award cert. Larimer County Fed. Exec. Assn., 1996, awards Poetry Guild, 1996-97; named to Internat. Poetry Hall of Fame, Nat. Libr. Congress, 1997. Mem. Internat. Soc. Poets (disting.), Famous Poets Soc. (Diamond Homer award 1996), Acad. of Am. Poets. Lutheran. Avocations: gardening, studying and working in bonsai, song writing. Home: PO Box 1063 304 Cherry Ln Ault CO 80610 Office: US Dept Interior 4512 Mcmurry Ave Fort Collins CO 80525-3400

HIPP, KENNETH BYRON, lawyer; b. Charlotte, N.C., Aug. 4, 1945; s. Junius B. and Jeanne Carol (Gwaltney) H.; m. Ann Winfield Birmingham, Sept. 23, 1966; children: Kenneth Byron Jr., Andrew Clay. AB, Duke U., 1967; JD with high honors, U. N.C., Chapel Hill, 1971. Bar: N.C. 1971, Hawaii 1987, U.S. Dist. Ct. (no. dist.) Tex. 1978, U.S. Dist. Ct. Hawaii 1987, U.S. Ct. Appeals (2d, 4th and 5th cirs.) 1972, U.S. Ct. Appeals (9th cir.) 1976, U.S. Ct. Appeals (10th cir.) 1977, U.S. Supreme Ct. 1993. Assoc. Micronesian Claims Com., Saipan, Northern Mariana Islands, 1973-74; regional dir. Micronesian Claims Co., Palau, Western Caroline Islands, 1974-76; atty. enforcement litigation NLRB, Washington, 1971-73, 76-77, supr. atty. enforcement litigation, 1977, dep. asst. gen. counsel spl. litigation, 1977-78, dep. asst. gen. counsel appellate litigation, 1978-86, dep. asst. gen. counsel contempt litigation, 1986-87; ptnr. Goodsill Anderson Quinn & Stifel, Honolulu, 1987-95; mem. Nat. Mediation Bd., Washington, 1995-98, chmn., 1996-97; ptnr. Marr Hipp Jones & Pepper, Honolulu, 1998—. Bar examiner State of Hawaii, 1988-92; vis. assoc. prof. Law Sch., Boston Coll., 1983-84; adj. prof. Law Sch., Cath. U. Am., 1978-79, Law Ctr., Georgetown U., Washington, 1984-87; adj. prof. Grad. Sch. Bus. U. Hawaii, 1989-94. Mem. Hawaii State Bar Assn. (chair labor and employment law sect. 1990-91), Order of Coif. Presbyterian. Home: 314 Poipu Dr Honolulu HI 96825-2125 Office: Marr Hipp Jones Pepper Ste 1550 1001 Bishop St Pauahi Tower Honolulu HI 96813 E-mail: khipp@marrhipp.com

HIRANO, IRENE ANN YASUTAKE, museum director; b. L.A., Oct. 7, 1948; d. Michael S. and Jean F. (Ogino) Yasutake; 1 child, Jennifer. BS in Pub. Adminstrn., U. So. Calif., 1970, MPA in Pub. Adminstrn., 1972. Project adminstr. U. So. Calif., 1970-72; assoc. dir. Asian Women's Ctr., 1972-73; nat. project coord., Japanese site supr. Nat. Asian Am. Field Study, L.A., 1973-75; cons. U.S. Dept. Health, Edn. and Welfare, Adminstn. on Aging, San Francisco, 1975; exec. dir. T.H.E. Clinic for Women, Inc., L.A., 1975-88; exec. dir., pres. Japanese Am. Nat. Mus., L.A., 1988—. Lectr., spkr. in field. Mem. L.A. Ednl. Alliance for Restructuring Now, 1993—, Pres's. Com. on Arts & Humanities, 1994—, Commn. on Future of Smithsonian Inst., 1993—, L.A. Coalition, 1993—; trustee Malborough Sch., 1993—; co-founder Leadership Edn. for Asian Pacifics, 1983, pres. 1983-86, v.p. 1986-90; pres., bd. dirs. Asian Pacific Am. Support Group, U. So. Calif., 1984-88; bd. dirs. Liberty Hill Found., 1984-88, community funding bd., 1981-84, chairperson Calif. Commn. on the Status of Women, 1981-82, commn. mem., 1976-83, many others. Recipient Nat. Outstanding Asian/Pacific Islander award NEA, 1983, Outstanding Women of the '90's, Robinson's Corp., 1992, Outstanding Svc. award Nat. Women's Polit. Caucus, 1986, Nat. Inst. Women of Color, 1984, Outstanding Alumni award U. So. Calif., 1994, So. Calif. Hist. Soc. Cmty. award, 1995. Office: Japanese Am Nat Mus 369 E 1st St Los Angeles CA 90012-3901

HIRONO, MAZIE KEIKO, lieutenant governor; b. Fukushima, Japan, Nov. 3, 1947; came to U.S., 1955, naturalized, 1957; d. Laura Chie (Sato) H. BA, U. Hawaii, 1970; JD, Georgetown U., 1978. Dep. atty. gen., Honolulu, 1978-80; Shim, Tam, Kirimitsu & Naito, 1984-88; mem. Hawaii Ho. of Reps., Honolulu, 1980-94; elected lt. gov., 1994. Chair Hawaii Policy Group, Nat. Commn. on Tchg. and Ams. Future, Govs. Task Force on Sci. and Tech. Bd. dirs. Nuuanu YMCA, Honolulu, 1982-84, Moiliili Cmty. Ctr., Honolulu, 1984; dep. chair Dem. Nat. Com., 1997. Mem. U.S. Supreme Ct. Bar, Hawaii Bar Assn., Phi Beta Kappa. Democrat. Office: State Capitol Lt Govs Office PO Box 3226 Honolulu HI 96801-3226 E-mail: ltgov@exec.state.hi.us

HIROSE, AKIRA, physics educator, researcher; b. Kijimadaira, Nagano, Japan, Aug. 16, 1941; came to Can., 1971; s. Genji and Katsuyo (Yamada) H.; m. Kimiko Yamamoto, Feb. 4, 1969; children: Tadashi, Kyoko. B Engring., Yokohama (Japan) Nat. U., 1965, M Engring., 1967; PhD, U. Tenn., 1969; DSc, U. Sask., 1994. Mem. rsch. sect. Oak Ridge (Tenn.) Nat. Lab., 1969-71; rsch. scientist U. Sask., Saskatoon, Can., 1971-77, assoc. prof. Can., 1977-79, prof. physics Can., 1979—. Corr. Plasma Phys. Controlled Fusion, 1984—; chmn. Internat. Conf. on Plasma Sci., Saskatoon, 1986; vis. prof. FOM Inst. Plasmafysica, The Netherlands, 1989, Tokyo Met. Inst. Tech., 1996; disting. fgn. rschr. Japan Atomic Energy Rsch. Inst., 1995. Author: Introduction to Wave Phenomena, 1985; contbr. numerous articles to profl. jours. Recipient IEEE Merit award Nuclear and Plasma Scis. Soc., 1993, Disting. Rschr.'s award U. Sask., 1995, Plasma Sci. and Applications award IEEE Nuclear Plasma Sci. Soc., 1998, Can. Rsch. Chair, 2001; Fulbright scholar, 1967; Nat. Sci. Engring. Rsch. Coun. grantee, 1977; Japan Soc. Promotion Sci. rsch. fellow, 1984. Fellow IEEE (assoc. editor Trans. Plasma Sci. 1983—), Am. Phys. Soc., Acad. Sci.Royal Soc. Can.; mem. Can. Assn. Physicists (chmn. divsn. plasma physics 1981-82, 94-95, divsn. assoc. editor Phys. Rev. Letter 1999—). Home: 2914 East View Saskatoon SK Canada S7J 3H9 Office: U Sask Dept Physics & Engring Phys Saskatoon SK Canada S7N 5E2 E-mail: akira.hirose@usask.ca

HIRSCH, ANNE, dean, nursing educator; BSN, Wash. State U., 1974; MNin, U. Wash., 1978; DNS, U. Ind., 1983. Cert. family nurse practitioner. Nurse Ialdn Hosp., Anacortes, Providence Med. Ctr., Seattle, St. Luke's Hosp., Spokane; faculty Pacific Luth. U. Sch. Nursing, Tacoma, interim dean, assoc. dean for undergrad. nursing; assoc. dean for acad. affairs Wash. State U. Coll. of Nursing, 1998—. Lt. USN Nurse Corps. Res. Office: Wash State U Coll Nursing 2917 W Fort George Wright Dr Spokane WA 99224-5202

HIRSCH, ANTHONY TERRY, physician; b. N.Y.C., Jan. 29, 1940; s. Robert S. and Minna Hirsch; m. Barbara Hershan, July 8, 1961; children: Deborah, Kenneth, Steven. BS cum laude, Tufts U., 1961, MD, 1965. Diplomate Am. Bd. Pediatrics, Am. Bd. Allergy-Immunology. Pvt. practice pediatrics Children's Med. Group, L.A., 1973-84; chair dept. pediatrics, dir. residency tng. program in pediatrics White Meml. Med. Ctr., L.A., 1984—. Capt. USAF, 1969-71. Fellow Am. Acad. Pediatrics (chair access task force Calif. br., mem. nat. access task force, chair coun. on pediatric practice), Am. Acad. Allergy-Immunology. Avocation: sailing. Office: White Meml Med Ctr Dept Pediat 1701 Cesar Chavez Ave # 456 Los Angeles CA 90033-2410

HIRSCH, BARRY L. lawyer; b. Chgo., Nov. 11, 1933; Student, UCLA; LLB, U. So. Calif., 1957. Bar: Calif. 1957, N.Y. 1985. Ptnr. Armstrong, Hirsch, Jackoway, Tyerman & Wertheimer, L.A. Mem. State Bar Calif., L.A. County Bar Assn., Beverly Hills Bar Assn., L.A. Copyright Soc. Office: Armstrong Hirsch Jackoway Tyerman & Wertheimer 1888 Century Park E Los Angeles CA 90067-1702

HIRSCH, GILAH YELIN, artist, writer; b. Montreal, Quebec, Can., Aug. 24, 1944; came to U.S., 1963; d. Ezra and Shulamis (Borodensky) Y. BA, U. Calif., Berkeley, 1967; MFA, UCLA, 1970. Prof. of art Calif. State U., Dominguez Hills, L.A., 1973—. Adj. prof. Internat. Coll., Guild of Tutors, L.A., 1980-87, Union Grad. Sch., Cin., 1990. Founding mem. Santa Monica (Calif.) Art Bank, 1983-85; bd. dirs. Dorland Mountain Colony, Temecula, Calif., 1984-88. Recipient Disting. Artist award Calif. State U., 1985, Found. Rsch. award, 1988, 89, 97, 98; grantee Nat. Endowment for the Arts, 1985; Dorland Mountain Colony fellow, 1981-84, MacDowell Colony fellow, N.H., 1987, Banff Ctr. for the Arts fellow, Can., 1985; named artist-in-residence RIM Inst., Payson, Ariz., 1989-90, Tamarind Inst. of Lithography, Albuquerque, 1973, Rockefeller Bellagio Ctr., Italy, 1992, Tyrone Guthrie Ctr. for Arts, Annamahkerrig, Ireland, 1993, creative rsch. award Sally Canova Rsch. Scholarship and Creative Activities awards program, 1997, 98, 99. Office: Calif State Univ Dominguez Hills 1000 E Victoria St Carson CA 90747-0001 E-mail: gilah@linkline.com

HIRSCH, HORST EBERHARD, business consultant; b. Woelsendorf, Fed. Republic Germany, July 26, 1933; came to U.S., 1984; s. Albert and Emilie (Eberhardt) H.; m. Helga G. Gruber, May 2, 1961; children: Manon K., Fabiane M., Erin A. Diploma in chemistry, Tech. U. Karlsruhe, Fed. Republic Germany, 1959, D in Chem. Tech., 1961. Postdoctoral fellow NRC of Can., 1961-62; research and devel. engr., mgr. Cominco Ltd., Trail, B.C., Can., 1962-84; pres., chief exec. officer Cominco Electronic Materials Inc., Spokane, Wash., 1984-88; pres. Johnson Matthey Electronics N.Am., Spokane, 1989-91, MSM, 1991—; vis. exec. IESC, 1992, field assoc., 1993—; co-founder, CM, HT Metals LLC, 2001—. Mem. bd. mgmt. B.C. Rsch. Coun., Vancouver, 1980-84; senate U. B.C., Vancouver, 1981-85; mem. adv. com. Wash. Tech. Ctr., 1992-94. Contbr. articles on chemistry and metallurgy to profl. publs., chpts. to books; patentee in field. Recipient Excellence in Innovation award Fed. Govt. Can., 1985. Mem. Soc. German Mining and Metall. Engrs. Lutheran. Avocations: reading, skiing, swimming, golfing. E-mail: zollegeg@aol.com

HIRSCH, JUDD, actor; b. N.Y.C., Mar. 15, 1935; s. Joseph Sidney and Sally (Kitzis) H.; m. Bonni Chalkin, Dec. 24, 1992. BS in Physics, CCNY, 1960. Broadway appearances in Barefoot in the Park, 1966, Knock Knock, 1976 (Drama Desk award for best featured actor), Chapter Two, 1977-78, Talley's Folly, 1980, I'm Not Rappaport, 1985-86 (Tony award for best actor in play 1986, Outer Critics Circle award, 1986), Conversations with My Father, 1992 (Tony award for best actor in play 1992, Outer Critics Circle award, 1992), A Thousand Clowns, 1996, Art, 1998; off-Broadway appearances in On the Necessity of Being Polygamous, 1963, Scuba Duba, 1967-69, King of the United States, 1972, Mystery Play, 1972, Hot L Baltimore, 1973, Prodigal, 1973, Knock Knock, 1975, Talley's Folly, 1979 (Obie award), The Seagull, 1983, I'm Not Rappaport, 1985, Below the Belt, 1996; regional appearences include Theater for Living Arts, Phila., Line of Least Existence, Harry Noon and Night, The Recruiting Officer, Annenberg Ctr., Phila., 1969-70, Hough in Blazes, 1971, Conversations with My Father, Seattle Repertory, 1991, L.A., 1993, Scarborough, Eng., 1994, London, 1995, Death of a Salesman, Chapel Hill, N.C., 1994, Robbers, Long Wharf Theater, 1995, Death of a Salesman Manitoba Theatre Ctr., Winnipeg and Royal Alexandra Theatre, Toronto, 1997, Art, London, 1999, 2001; stock and tour appearances in A Thousand Clowns, Threepenny Opera, Fantastiks, Woodstock, N.Y., 1964, Peterpat, Houston and Ft. Worth, 1970, Harvey, Chgo., 1971, And Miss Reardon Drinks a Little, Palm Beach, Fla., 1972, I'm Not Rappaport, nat. tour, 1987, Art, nat. tour, 1999-2000; TV appearances include The Keegans, 1975, Medical Story, 1975, Delvecchio series, 1976-77, Rhoda, 1977, Taxi series, 1978-83 (Emmy award for best actor in a comedy series, 1981, 1983), Noel Edmunds Saturday Road Show, 1990 (Eng.), Dear John series (Golden Globe award 1988), 1988-92, George and Leo, 1997; TV movies include The Law, 1974, Fear on Trial, 1975, The Legend of Valentino, 1975, The Halloween That Almost Wasn't, 1979, Sooner or Later, 1979, Marriage Is Alive and Well, 1980, First Steps, 1985, Brotherly Love, 1985, The Great Escape-Untold Story, 1988, She Said No, 1990, Betrayal of Trust, 1993, Color of Justice, 1997, Rocky Marciano, 1999; films include King of the Gypsies, 1978, Ordinary People (nominated Acad. Award), 1980, Without a Trace, 1983, Teachers, 1984, The Goodbye People, 1984, Running on Empty, 1988, Independence Day, 1996, Man On the Moon, 1999, Beautiful Mind, 2001; dir. Squaring the Circle, 1962, Not Enough Rope, 1973, Talley's Folly, 1981, Art, 2000-01. Mem. Acad. Motion Picture Arts and Scis., Acad. TV Arts and Scis., Screen Actors Guild, Actors Equity Assn., AFTRA. Office: care J Wolfe Provident Fin Mgmt 10345 W Olympic Blvd Los Angeles CA 90064-2548

HIRSCH, STEVEN A. lawyer; b. Ariz., 1955; BA with distinction, U. Ariz., 1977, JD with high distinction, 1980. Bar: Ariz. 1980; cert. real estate specialist State Bar Ariz. Law clerk to Hon. James D. Hathaway Ariz. Ct. Appeals Divsn. 2, 1980-81; ptnr. Bryan Cave, Phoenix. Editorial bd. Ariz. Bar Jour., 1986-89. Fellow Ariz. Bar Found. (bd. dirs. 1989-97, pres. 1995); mem. ABA (del. and dist. rep. young lawyers divsn. assembly 1990-92), Maricopa County Bar Assn. (bd. dirs. 1987-88), Order of Coif. Office: Bryan Cave 2 N Central Ave Ste 2200 Phoenix AZ 85004-4406

HIRSCH, WALTER, economist, researcher; b. Phila., Apr. 21, 1917; s. Arnold Harry and Ann Belle (Feldstein) H.; m. Leanore Brod, Feb. 12, 1939 (dec. 1985); stepchild, Stephen M. Gold; children: Jeffrey A., Robert A.; m. June Freedman Gold Clark, Dec. 16, 1986. BS in Econs., U. Pa., 1938; LLD (hons.), Chapman Coll., 1968. Economist U.S. Bur. Stats., Washington and N.Y.C, 1946-50, Dept. USAF, Washington, 1950-51, Nat. Prodn. Auth., Washington, 1952-53; dir. indsl. mobilization Bur. Ordnance Dept. USN, Mechanicsburg, Pa., 1954-56, ops. rsch. analyst Bur. Supplies and Accts. Arlington, Va., 1956-58; economist, ops. rsch. analyst Internat. Security Affairs Office Sec. of Def., Arlington, 1958-61; chief ops., rsch. analyst Gen. Svcs. Adminstrn., Washington, 1961-63; ops. rsch. analyst Spl. Projects Office Sec. of Def., Arlington, 1963-67; dir. ednl. rsch. U.S. Office Edn., San Francisco, 1967-72; cons. on loan to Office of Dean Acad. Planning San Jose (Calif.) State U., 1972-74. Author: Unit Man-Hour Dynamics for Peace or War, 1957, Internal Study for Office Secretary of Defense: Sharing the Cost of International Security, 1961. Vol. De Young Mus., San Francisco, 1981-84, Calif. Palce of Legion of Honor, Phila. Mus. Art, 1984-86; pres. Met. Area Reform Temples, Washington, Nat. Fedn. Temple Brotherhoods; supporter Phila. Orch., San Francisco Symphony, San Francisco Conservatory Music, Curtis Inst. With USAAF, 1942-46. Recipient Meritorious Civilian Svc. award Navy Dept., 1956. Mem. Pa. Athletic Club, Commonwealth Club of Calif., World Affairs Council, Press Club of San Francisco, Phi Delta Kappa. Avocations: collecting art, music, chess, poetry.

HIRSCHFELD, GERALD JOSEPH, cinematographer; b. N.Y.C., Apr. 25, 1921; s. Ralph and Kate (Zirker) H.; m. Sarnell Ogus, June 5, 1945 (div. June 1972); children— Alec, Marc, Eric, Burt; m. Julia Warren Tucker, July 28, 1981. Student, Columbia U., 1938-40. Cinematic instr. New Inst. for Film, Bklyn., 1947-49; freelance dir. photography for TV and Film N.Y.C., 1949-54; dir. photography, v.p. MPO Videotronics, Inc., N.Y.C., 1954-72; free-lance dir. and cameraman, cinematographer, N.Y.C. and Hollywood, Calif., 1972—. Cinema instr. Am. Film Inst., L.A., 1980, Tahoe Film and Video Workshop, Lake Tahoe, Nev., 1984, Washington Film and Video Assn., 1987; staff mem. Internat. Film and Video Workshops, Rockport, Maine, 1996-99, cinema instr. So. Oreg. U., 1998—. Cinematographer for films including: Young Frankenstein, My Favorite Year, Diary of a Mad Housewife, The Neon Empire (ACE award nomination 1990); author: Image Control, 1992 (Kraszna-Krausz Internat. Book Award 1994). With Signal Corps, U.S. Army, 1941-45. Recipient Billy Bitzer award Internat. Photographers of the Motion Picture Industry, 1994. Mem. Internat. Photographer's Union, IATSE, Am. Soc. Cinematographers, Acad. Motion Picture Arts and Scis. Avocations: woodworker, miniaturist. Home and Office: 425 Ashland St Ashland OR 97520-3104 Fax: 541-488-8742. E-mail: gjhfilms@home.com

HIRSCHFELD, SUE ELLEN, geological sciences educator; b. Ossining, N.Y., Jan. 12, 1941; d. Ira Bertram and Helen Caroline (Rieser) H. BS, U. Fla., 1963, MS, 1965; PhD, U. Calif., Berkeley, 1971. Prof. Calif. State U., Hayward, 1971—, chair dept. geol. scis., 1988-94; ret., 2000. Co-author videotapes in field, 1985, 92, 95, 96; contbr. articles to profl. jours. Grantee Calif. State U., 1976, 78, 93, 95. Mem. AAAS, Geol. Soc. Am., Soc. for Sedimentary Geology, Assn. for Women Geoscientists (founder). Office: Calif State U Dept Geol Scis Hayward CA 94542

HIRSCHMAN, CHARLES, JR. sociologist, educator; b. Atlanta, Nov. 29, 1943; s. Charles Sr. and Mary Gertrude (Mullee) H.; m. Josephine Knight, Jan. 29, 1968; children: Andrew Charles, Sarah Lynn. BA, Miami U., Oxford, Ohio, 1965; MS, U. Wis., 1969, PhD, 1972. Vol. Peace Corps, Malaysia, 1965-67; prof. Duke U., Durham, N.C., 1972-81, Cornell U., Ithaca, N.Y., 1981-87, U. Wash., Seattle, 1987—, chair dept. sociology, 1995-98, Boeing internat. prof., 1999—. Cons. Ford Found., Malaysia, 1974-75; chair social scis. and population study sect. NIH, Washington, 1987-91; vis. scholar Russell Sage Found., 1998-99. Author: Ethnic and Social Stratification in Peninsula Malaysia, 1975; editor: The Handbook of International Migration: The American Experience, 1999; contbr. articles to profl. jours. Fellow Ctr. Advanced Study in the Bahavioral Scis., Stanford, Calif., 1993-94. Fellow AAAS; mem. Assn. for Asian Studies (bd. dirs. 1987-90), Population Assn Am. (bd. dirs. 1992-94, v.p. 1997). Office: U Wash Dept Sociology PO Box 353340 Seattle WA 98195-3340 E-mail: charles@u.washington.edu

HIRT, CYRIL WILLIAM, physicist; b. Flushing, N.Y., Dec. 20, 1936; s. Cyril W. and Margret E. (Plumb) H.; m. Virginia L. Warren, June 22, 1968; children: Heather, Amber. BS, U. Mich., 1958, MS, 1959, PhD, 1963. Staff scientist Los Alamos (N.Mex.) Nat. lab., 1963-72, group leader, 1973-80; chief scientist Sci. Applications Inc., La Jolla, Calif., 1972-73; founder, pres., chief scientist Flow Sci. Inc., Los Alamos, 1980—. Contbr. numerous articles to profl. jours. Avocations: cooking, reading, hiking, skiing. Office: Flow Sci Inc 1257 40th St Los Alamos NM 87544-1906

HIRUKI, CHUJI, plant virologist, science educator; b. Fukue, Nagasaki, Japan, June 16, 1931; arrived in Can., 1966; s. Chuichi and Mitsu (Kawamuko) H.; m. Yasuko Hijikata, Dec. 26, 1961; children: Tadaaki, Lisa. BSc, Kyushu U., Fukuoka, 1954, PhD, 1963. Plant pathologist Hatano Tobacco Expt. Sta., Hatano, Japan, 1954-65; asst. prof. U. Alberta, Edmonton, Can., 1966-70, assoc. prof. Can., 1970-76, prof. Can., 1976-91, univ. prof. Can., 1991-96, univ. prof. emeritus, 1996—. Vis. plant pathologist, U. Calif., Berkeley, 1963-64; vis. scientist INRA, Versailles, France, 1972; vis. prof. Agrl. U., Wageningen, The Netherlands, 1973; CSFP vis. prof. U. Queensland, Brisbane, Australia, 1984-85; hon. disting. scientist China Paulownia Rsch. Ctr., 1993-95; internat. cons. forest pathology FAO UN, 1993-95; hon. disting. prof. Yunnan Biotech. Rsch. Inst., Kunming, China, 2000—; chmn. Internat. Working Group Plant Viruses with Fungal Vectors, 1988-93, IUFRO Working Party on Virus and Mycoplasma Diseases, 1982—, Internet Orgn. of Mycoplasmology Subsect. on Phytoplasmas, 1992—. Editor: Tree Mycoplasmas and Mycoplasma Diseases, 1988; over 200 scientific rsch. papers, 300 rsch. paper presentations. Fellow U. Wis., 1964-66, The Netherlands Internat. Ctr., 1973; recipient rsch. award Disting. Fgn. Specialist Govt. Japan, 1991, J. Gordin Kaplan award U. Alberta, 1993; named Nat. Sci. Coun. lectr. Govt. Republic China, 1989. Fellow Royal Soc. Can., Am. Phytopathological Soc. (Pacific divsn., Lifetime Achievement award 1993), Can. Phytopathological Soc. (pres. 1990-91, award for outstanding rsch. 1996); mem. Internat. Soc. Plant Pathology (treas. 1998—), N.Y. Acad. Scis., Phytopathological Soc. Japan (award excellence in rsch. 1990), Internat. Orgn. for Mycoplasmology (mycoplasma recognition award 1998). Avocations: reading, classical music, swimming. Home: 152 Windermere Cres Edmonton AB Canada T6R 2H6 Office: U Alta Dept Agr Food and Nutrition Edmonton AB Canada T6G 2P5 E-mail: chiruki@ualberta.ca

HISAKA, ERIC TORU, plastic surgeon; b. Stockton, Calif., 1951; MD, U. Calif., Davis, 1977. Plastic surgeon Valley Care Hosp., Pleasanton, Calif.; also with Tri Valley Surgical Ctr., Pleasanton. Office: 5720 Stoneridge Mall Rd Ste 130 Pleasanton CA 94588-2829 Fax: 925-463-0748

HISE, MARK ALLEN, dentist; b. Chgo., Jan. 17, 1950; s. Clyde and Rose T. (Partipilo) H. AA, Mt. San Antonio Coll., Walnut, Calif., 1972, BA with highest honors, U. Calif., Riverside, 1974; MS, U. Utah, 1978; DDS, UCLA, 1983. Instr. sci. NW Acad., Houston, 1978-79; chmn. curriculum med. coll. prep program UCLA, 1980-85; instr. dentistry Coll. of Redwoods, Eureka, Calif., 1983; practice dentistry Arcata, 1983—. Participant numerous radio and TV appearances. Editor: Preparing for the MCAT, 1983-85; contbr. articles to profl. jours.; speaker in field. Recipient awards for underwater photography; Henry Carter scholar U. Calif., 1973, Calif. State scholar 1973, 74, Regents scholar U. Calif., 1973; Calif. State fellow, 1975, NIH fellow, 1975-79. Mem. AAAS, ADA, Calif. Dental Assn., Acad. Gen. Dentistry, Nat. Soc. for Med. Rsch., North Coast Scuba Club. Roman Catholic. Avocation: underwater photography. Home and Office: 1225 B St Arcata CA 95521-5936

HISERT, GEORGE A. lawyer; b. Schenectady, N.Y., Sept. 18, 1944; BS summa cum laude, MS, Brown U., 1966; JD cum laude, U. Chgo., 1970. Bar: Calif. 1971. Law clk. to Hon. Sterry R. Waterman U.S. Ct. Appeals (2nd cir.), 1970-71; ptnr. McCutchen, Doyle, Brown & Enersen, San Francisco, 1977-93; now ptnr. Brobeck, Phleger & Harrison. Mem. editl. bd. Chgo. Law Rev., 1969-70; ABA sect. on bus. law liaison to UCC Permanent Editl. Bd. Mem. ABA (subcom. letter of credit, subcom. secured trans. of uniform comml. code com. bus. law sect., subcom. on syndications and loan participations of comml fin. svc. com., bus. law sect.), Internat. Bar Assn. (banking law com., bus. law sect.), State Bar Calif. (uniform comml. code com. bus. law sect., vice-chair 1992-93, chair 1993-94), Am. Coll.Comml. Fin. Lawyers, Order of Coif, Sigma Xi. Office: Brobeck Phleger & Harrison Spear St Tower One Market Plz San Francisco CA 94105 E-mail: ghisert@brobeck.com

HISKEY, J. BRENT, metallurgical engineer, educator; b. Salina, Utah, Aug. 18, 1944; m. 1967; 2 children. BS, U. Utah, 1967, MS, 1971, PhD in Metallurgy, 1973. Rschr. Alcoa Labs, 1973-74; asst. prof. N. Mex. Inst. Mining & Tech., 1974-77; rsch. scientist US Steel Rsch. Labs, 1977-80; mgr. metallurgy rsch. Kennecott Copper Corp., 1980-84; dir. Ariz. Mining & Mineral Resources Rsch. Inst., 1985-96; prof. U. Ariz., 1984—, assoc. dean Coll. Engring. and Mines, 1999—; dir. Copper Rsch. Ctr., 1989-97. Lectr. Carnegie Mellon U., 1977-79; cons. E.I. du Pont de Nemours & Co., Inc., 1984—, Phelps Dodge, 1985—, Newcrest Gold Co., 1985-95, Kennecott Corp., 1985-96; chmn. Nat. Assn. Mineral Inst. Dirs., 1990-91, Cyrus AMAX Metals Corp., 1994—; bd. dirs. Am. Chemet Corp., 1993—. Recipient James Douglas Gold medal Am. Inst. Mech. Engrs., 1993. Mem. Nat. Acad. Engrs., Soc. Metallurgy Engrs. (Taggart award 1974), Soc. Mining Metallurgy & Exploration Inc. (chmn. mineral & metallurgy processing div. 1991-92), Sigma Xi. Home: 5540 E Silver Dust Pl Tucson AZ 85750-1083 Office: U Ariz Coll Engring Mines Dept Math Sci & Engring Tucson AZ 85721-0001 Fax: 520-621-8159. E-mail: jbh@bigdog.engr.arizona.edu

HISLOP, MERVYN WARREN, health advocate administrator, psychologist; b. Vancouver, B.C., Apr. 26, 1937; s. George and Freda (Wickenden) H.; m. Marilyn Gail Johnson, July 24, 1965; children: Lawren Nyall, Mylene Lorelle. B.A. with honors, U. B.C., 1965; M.A., McMaster U., 1967, Ph.D., 1970. Cert. health adminstr. Dir. behaviour mgmt. services Surrey Place Centre, Ministry of Health, Toronto, Ont., 1970-73; dir. psychol. services Woodlands Ministry of Human Resources, New Westminster, B.C., 1973-78; coordinator life edn. program New Westminster, 1975-77; exec. dir. Riverview Hosp., Port Coquitlam, B.C., 1978-85, Valleyview Hosp., Port Coquitlam, 1985-86; dir. legis. and regulatory affairs Mental Health Services Div., B.C. Ministry of Health, 1986-89; psychiat. adv. Govt. Alberta, Can., 1989—. Research proposal submission cons. Can. Council, 1973; mem. edn. adv. com. Douglas Coll., 1983-86 Demonstration model grantee Province Ont., 1971; province Ont. grad. fellow McMaster U., 1969; recipient David and Jean Bolocan Meml. prize U. B.C., 1965; Nat. Rsch. Coun. Can. scholar, 1965, 66, 67, 68. Mem. Can. Coll. Health Service Execs. (cert.), Can. Inst. Law and Medicine. Home: 17203-57 Ave Edmonton AB Canada T6M 1B8

HITCHCOCK, FRITZ, automotive company executive; CEO, owner Hitchcock Automotive Resources, City of Industry, CA, 1980—. Office: Hitchcock Automotive Resour 17340 Gale Ave La Puente CA 91748-1512

HITCHCOCK, VERNON THOMAS, farmer, lawyer; b. Selma, Ind., Feb. 21, 1919; s. Lucian Elmer and Loda Alice (King) H.; m. Betty Kathryn Orr, May 24, 1949; children: Brenda, Linda, Nancy, Debra, Randolph. BS in Agr., Purdue U., 1940; JD, Stanford U., 1953. Bar: Calif. 1954, U.S. Supreme Ct. 1961. Pilot Southwest Airways, San Francisco, 1946, TWA, Kansas City, Mo., 1947-51; pvt. practice Healdsburg, Calif., 1954-55; dep. atty. gen. State of Calif., Sacramento, 1956; dep. county counsel Sonoma County, Santa Rosa, Calif., 1957-65; exec. dir. Libyan Aviation Co., Tripoli, 1966-67; legal counsel Sonoma County Schs., 1967-82; farm mgr. Selma, Ind., 1975—. Originator Freedom Under Law program. Author: The Airline to Infinity, Diary of a Pilot, The Mildura March. Active Am. Security Council, 1965-95. Served to comdr. USNR, 1941-79. Mem. Res. Officers Assn., Naval Order U.S., Commonwealth Club San Francisco, Quiet Birdmen, Odd Fellows. Republican. Episcopalian. Avocations: music, amateur radio. $D.

HITLIN, DAVID GEORGE, physicist, educator; b. Bklyn., Apr. 15, 1942; s. Maxwell and Martha (Lipetz) H.; m. Joan R. Abramowitz, 1966 (div. 1981); m. Abigail R. Gumbiner, 1982 (div. 1998); m. Martha Mann Slagerman, 2000. BA, Columbia U., 1963, MA, 1965, PhD, 1968. Instr. Columbia U., N.Y.C., 1967-69; research assoc. Stanford (Calif.) Linear Accelerator Ctr., 1969-72, asst. prof., 1975-79, mem. program com., 1980-82; asst. prof. Stanford U., 1972-75; assoc. prof. physics Calif. Inst. Tech., Pasadena, 1979-85, prof., 1985—. Mem. adv. panel U.S. Dept. Energy Univ. Programs, 1983; mem. program com. Fermi Nat. Accelerator Lab., Batavia, Ill., 1983-87, Newman Lab., Cornell U., Ithaca, N.Y., 1986-88; mem. rev. com. U. Chgo., Argonne Nat. Lab., 1985-87; chmn. Stanford Linear Accelerator Ctr. Users Orgn., 1990-93; mem. program com. Brookhaven Nat. Lab., Upton, N.Y., 1992-95; spokesman BABAR Collaboration, 1994-2000; mem. high energy physics adv. panel, DOE/NSF, 2001—. Contbr. numerous articles to profl. jours. Fellow Am. Phys. Soc. Achievements include research in elementary particle physics. Office: Calif Inst Tech Dept Physics 356-48 Lauritsen Pasadena CA 91125-0001 E-mail: hitlin@hep.caltech.edu

HJORTSBERG, WILLIAM REINHOLD, writer; b. N.Y.C., Feb. 23, 1941; s. Helge Reinhold and Anna Ida (Welti) H.; m. Marian Souidee Renken, June 2, 1962 (div. 1982); children— Lorca Isabel, Max William.; m. Sharon Leroy, July 21, 1982 (div. 1985). BA, Dartmouth Coll., 1962; postgrad., Yale U., 1962-63, Stanford U., 1967-68. Ind. author, screenwriter, 1969—. Adj. prof. media and theatre arts Mont. State U., 1991—. Author: Alp, 1969, Gray Matters, 1971, Symbiography, 1973, Toro! Toro! Toro!, 1974, Falling Angel, 1978, Tales & Fables, 1985, Nevermore, 1994, films: Thunder and Lightning, 1977, Legend, 1986, Angel Heart, 1987; co-author TV film: Georgia Peaches, 1980; contbg. editor Rocky Mountain Mag., 1979; contbr. fiction to Realist, Playboy, Cornell Rev., Penthouse, Oui, Sports Illustrated; contbr. criticism to N.Y. Times Book Rev. Recipient Playboy Editorial award, 1971, 78; Wallace Stegner fellow, 1967-68; Nat. Endowment Arts grantee, 1976. Mem. Authors Guild, Writers Guild Am. Avocations: fly fishing, skiing, collecting modern first editions, art, antique toys. Home: 2586 Boulder Rd McLeod MT 59052 Office: care Harold Matson Co Ste 714 276 Fifth Ave New York NY 10001

HLATKY, MARK ANDREW, cardiologist, medical researcher; b. Windber, Pa., June 4, 1950; s. George Andrew and Rose Annette (Gonnella) H.; m. Donna Marie Alvarado, May 12, 1984; 1 child, Nicholas Michael. BS, MIT, 1972; MD, U. Pa., 1976. Diplomate Am. Bd. Internal Medicine, Am. Bd. Cardiovasc. Disease; lic. physician, Calif. Intern, resident U. Ariz., Tucson, 1976-79; Robert Wood Johnson clin. scholar U. Calif., San Francisco, 1979-81; fellow in cardiology Duke U., Durham, N.C., 1981-83, asst. prof. medicine, 1983-89; assoc. prof. health rsch. and policy, assoc. prof. medicine Stanford (Calif.) U., 1989-96, prof. health rsch. and policy, prof. medicine, 1996—. Attending physician, cardiovasc. medicine svc. Stanford U. Med. Ctr., 1989—; mem. Health Care Tech. Study sect. NIH, Rockville, Md., 1992-96. Contbr. more than 140 articles to profl. jours. Sloan scholar, 1972. Fellow Am. Coll. Cardiology; mem. Am. Heart Assn. (fellow coun. on clin. cardiology), Am. Fedn. Clin. Rsch., Internat. Soc. for Tech. Assessment in Health Care, Phi Beta Kappa. Achievements include research in outcomes after coronary surgery, coronary angioplasty, acute myocardial infarction, and cardiac arrhythmias. Home: 168 Rinconada Ave Palo Alto CA 94301-3725 Office: Stanford U Sch Medicine HRP Redwood Bldg Rm 150 Stanford CA 94305 E-mail: hlatky@stanford.edu

HLEDE, KORIE, professional basketball player; b. Mar. 29, 1975; BS in Psychology and Comm., Duquesne U. Guard Montig, Croatia, Detroit Shock, 1998-99, Utah Starzz, 1999—. Named 1995 Atlantic 10 Rookie of the Yr., 1997-98 Atlantic 10 Player of the Yr. Achievements include becoming first athlete in Duquesne history to have jersey number retired; ranks second in Atlantic 10 history in career points; Duquesne's all-time leading scorer, male or female, with 2,631 points. Avocations: tennis, travel, reading. Office: Utah Starzz 301 W South Temple Salt Lake City UT 84101-1216

HO, CHIH-MING, physicist, educator; b. Chung King, China, Aug. 16, 1945; came to U.S., 1968; s. Shao-Nan and I-Chu Ho; m. Shirley T.S. Ho, Mar. 4, 1972; 1 child, Dean. BSME, Nat. Taiwan U., 1967; PhD, Johns Hopkins U., 1974. Assoc. rsch. scientist Johns Hopkins U., Balt., 1974-75; asst. prof. U. So. Calif., L.A., 1976-81, assoc. prof., 1981-85, prof., 1985-91; assoc. vice-chancellor for rsch. UCLA, 2001—, prof., 1991—, Ben Rich-Lockheed Martin prof., 1996—. Assoc. dir. Ctr. for Micro Systems, 1993-2000; cons. Flow Industries, Kent, 1982, Dynamics Tech., Torrance, Calif., 1977, Rockwell Internat., Canoga Park, Calif., 1980-83. Contbr. articles to profl. jours.; patentee in field. Fellow AIAA, Am. Phys. [illegible] Achievements include research in micro-electro-mechanical systems, biomedical engineering, turbulence, aerodynamics, nois.

HO, REGINALD CHI SHING, medical educator; b. Hong Kong, Mar. 30, 1932; came to U.S., 1940; s. Chow and Elizabeth (Wong) Ho; m. Sharilyn Dang, Nov. 14, 1964; children: Mark, Reginald, Gianna Masca, Timothy. Student, St. Louis U., 1954, MD, 1959. Diplomate Nat. Bd. Med. [illegible] 1959-60, resident in internal medicine, 1960-62; fellow in hematology and oncology Barnes Hosp./Washington U., St. Louis, 1962-63; attending physician in oncology, hematology and internal medicine Queen's Med. Ctr., 1962—; instr. in medicine Sch. Medicine U. Hawaii, Honolulu, 1967-69, asst. clin. prof. medicine, 1969-72, assoc. clin. prof., 1972-77, clin. prof., 1977—; attending physician dept. hematology and oncology Straub Clinic and Hosp., Honolulu, 1973—. Mem. tech. rev. com. Regional Med. Program Hawaii, 1970-71, long range planning com. 1971; prin. investigator Hawaii Community Clin. Oncology Program, Honolulu, 1983-86; adj. prof. clin. sci. Cancer Rsch. Ctr. Hawaii, 1989—, mem. various coms. Contbr. articles to med. jours. Bd. dirs. Cath. Svcs. for Families, 1987-91. Mem. AMA, ACP, Am. Cancer Soc. (divsn. del. 1982-93, del. dir. 1983-92, exec. com. 1989—, chair med. and sci. exec. com. 1991-92, past officer dir. 1994—, v.p. 1991-92, pres. 1992-93, immediate past pres. 1993-94, Clin fellow 1962, bd. dirs. Hawaii divsn. 1968—, v.p. 1970-71, chmn. exec. com. 1971-73, v.p. 1973-75, pres. 1976-77, chmn. bd. dirs. 1977-78, hon. life mem. 1989—, bd. dirs. Honolulu chpt. 1980-86, bd. dirs. Oahu unit 1966-71, chair svc. and rehab. com. 1967-71), Hawaii Med. Assn. (Hawaii cancer commn. 1980-85, chair cancer com. 1981-90), Honolulu County Med. Assn. (del. to Hawaii Med. Assn. 1969-72, alt. del. 1972-74, bd. govs. 1972), Exptl. Med. Care Rev. Orgn. (exec. com., chair ambulatory care edn. audit com. 1972), Alpha Omega Alpha. Roman Catholic. Avocation: tennis. Office: Straub Clinic Hosp 888 S King St Honolulu HI 96813-3083

HO, STUART TSE KONG, investment company executive; b. Manila, Nov. 18, 1935; came to U.S., 1936; s. Chinn and Betty (Ching) H.; m. Mary Lois Lee, June 17, 1961; children: Peter, Cecily, Heather. BA, Claremont (Calif.) McKenna, 1957; JD, U. Mich., 1963. Bar: Hawaii. Asst. sec. to chmn. bd. Capital Investment of Hawaii, Honolulu, 1965—; chmn. bd. Gannett Pacific Corp., 1987—. Bd. dirs. Pacific Century Fin. Corp., Honolulu, Gannett Co., Inc., Rosslyn, Va., Aloha Airgroup, Inc., Honolulu. Representative Hawaii Ho. of Reps., Honolulu, 1966-70, majority fl. leader, 1968-70; del. Constnl. Conv. of 1968, Honolulu, 1968; regent U. Hawaii, Honolulu, 1971-74. 1st lt. U.S. Army, 1958-60, ETO. Democrat. Office: Capital Investment Hawaii 733 Bishop St Ste 1700 Honolulu HI 96813-4017

HOADLEY, WALTER EVANS, economist, financial executive, lay worker; b. San Francisco, Aug. 16, 1916; s. Walter Evans Sr. and Marie Howland (Preece) H.; m. Virginia Alm, May 20, 1939; children: Richard Alm, Jean Elizabeth (Mrs. Donald A. Peterson). AB, U. Calif., 1938, MA, 1940, PhD, 1946; D in Comml. Sci., Franklin and Marshall Coll., 1963; LLD (hon.), Golden Gate U., 1968, U. Pacific, 1979; hon. degree, El Instituto Technologico Autonomo de Mexico, 1974. Collaborator U.S. Bur. Agrl. Econs., 1938-39; rsch. economist Calif. Gov.'s Reemployment Commn., 1939, Calif. Gov.'s State Planning Bd., 1941; rsch. economist, teaching fellow U. Calif., 1938-41, supr. indsl. mgmt. war tng. office, 1941-42; econ. adviser U. Chgo. Civil Affairs Tng. Sch., 1945; sr. economist Fed. Res. Bank Chgo., 1942-49; economist Armstrong World Industries, Lancaster, Pa., 1949-54, treas., 1954-60, v.p., treas., 1960-66, dir., 1962-87; sr. v.p., chief economist, mem. mng. com. Bank of Am. NT & SA, San Francisco, 1966-68, exec. v.p., chief economist, mem. mng. com., mem. mgmt. adv. council, chmn. subs., 1968-81; ret., 1981; sr. research fellow Hoover Inst., Stanford U., 1981—. Dep. chmn. Fed. Res. Bank, Phila., 1960-61, chmn., 1962-66; chmn. Conf. Fed. Res. Chmn., 1966; faculty Sch. Banking U. Wis., 1945-49, 55, 58-66; adviser various U.S. Govt. Agys.; Wright Internat. Bd. Econ. and Investment Advisors, 1987—; spl. adviser U.S. Congl. Budget Office, 1975-87; mem. pub. adv. bd. U.S. Dept. Commerce, 1970-74; mem. White House Rev. Com. for Balance Payment Stats., 1963-65, Presdl. Task Force on Growth, 1969-70, Presdl. Task Force on Land Utilization, Presdl. Conf. on Inflation, 1974; gov. Com. on Developing Am. Capitalism, 1977—, chmn., 1987-88; dir. PLM Internat., 1989-97, Transisco Industries, Inc., 1981-95, Davis/Selected/Venture Advisors, 1981-96. Mem. Meth. Ch. Commn. on World Svc. and Fin. Phila. conf., 1957-64, chmn. investment com., 1964-66; bd. dirs., exec. com. Internat. Mgmt. and Devel. Inst., 1976-97; trustee Pacific Sch. Religion, 1968-89; adviser Nat. Commn. to Study Nursing and Nursing Edn., 1968-73; trustee Duke U., 1968-73, pres.'s assoc., 1973-80; trustee Golden Gate U., 1974-94, chmn. investment com., 1977-93; trustee World Wildlife U.S. Fund The Conservation Found., 1987-90; mem. periodic chmn. adminstrv. bd. Trinity United Meth. Ch., Berkeley, Calif., 1966-84; mem. adminstrv. bd., advisor Lafayette (Calif.) United Meth. Ch., 1984—; mem. bd. overseers vis. com. Harvard Coll. Econs., 1969-74; chmn. investment com. Calif.-Nev. Meth. Found., 1968-75, mem., 1976-91; mem. Calif. Gov.'s Coun. Econ. and Bus. Devel., 1978-82, chmn., 1980-82; co-chmn. San Francisco Mcpl. Adv. Com., 1996—, mem. 1981-96; trustee Hudson Inst., 1979-84; chmn. Bay Area Econ. Advisers, 1982—; spl. adviser Presdl. Cabinet Com. Innovation, 1978-79; mem. Calif. State Internat. Adv. Com., 1986-94; regent U. Calif., 1990-91; mem. adv. coun. Calif. Environ. Tech. Ptnrship., 1993-94; mem. econ. adv. coun. Calif. Inst. Fed. Policy Rsch., 1994—; trustee Internat. Ho. U. Calif., 1991—, Devel. Com., 1994—, chmn., 1995-97. Fellow Am. Statis. Assn. (v.p., bd. dirs. 1952-54, pres. 1958), Nat. Assn. Bus. Economists (San Francisco chpt. exec. com. 1989—), Am. Fin. Assn. (bd. dirs. 1955-56, pres. 1969); mem. Conf. Bus. Economists (chmn. 1962), Atlantic Coun. of U.S. (bd. dirs. 1985—), Internat. Acad. Mgmt., 1980—; U.S. Coun. for Internat. Bus. (sr. trustee 1992—), Commonwealth Club of Calif. (pres. 1987, chmn. pub. affairs-comm. com. 1995—), Am. Econ. Assn., Am. Mktg. Assn., Am. Bankers Assn. (chmn. urban and cmty. affairs com. 1972-73, mem. econ. adv. coun. 1976-78), Nat. Bur. Econ. Rsch. (bd. dirs. 1965-81), Western Econ. Assn. (bd. dirs., mem. steering com. 1966-94, 97—), U. Calif. Alumni Assn. (pres. 1989-91, pres. class of 1938 1988—, chmn. investment com. 1983-89, 94-96, Alumnus of Yr. 1993, Chancellor's Highest award 1999), U.S. Nat. Com. on Pacific Econ. Coop. (vice chmn. 1984-89, mem. exec. com. 1989-94), Caux Internat. Roundtable (chmn. steering com. 1993-97), St. Francis Yacht Club, Commonwealth Club, Pacific Union Club, Bankers Club, Silverado Country Club, Phi Beta Kappa Assocs. (bd. dirs. 1986-95), Kappa Alpha. Office: # 357-9 3201 Plumas St Reno NV 89509

HOAG, JOHN ARTHUR, retired bank executive; b. Freeport, N.Y., Sept. 29, 1932; s. John Hoag and Viola (Babcock) Hobson; m. Jeanette Makaio, Dec. 5, 1959; children: Steve, Vanessa, Kanani. BS, U. Mo., 1955; grad., Pacific Coast Banking Sch., Wash., 1970; MBA, U. Hawaii, 1977. Account exec. Walston & Co., N.Y.C., 1960; mgmt. trainee 1st Hawaiian Bank, Honolulu, 1960, br. mgr., Hilo, 1968, Island v.p., 1970-76, sr. v.p., mgr., 1976, exec. v.p. loan group, 1979, pres., 1989-94, also bd. dirs.; vice chmn. bd. dirs., 1994; retired 1st Hawaiian Bank, 1995; pres. 1st Hawaiian Inc., Honolulu, 1991-95, also bd. dirs.; vice chm. 1st Interstate Bank Hawaii, Honolulu, 1991—; vice chmn. of bd., 1994—; ret., 1995. Chmn. bd. Hawaii Reserves, Inc.; vice chmn. Pioneer Fed. Savs. Bank; bd. dirs. Castle Med. Ctr., BancWest Corp. Bd. regents Tokai Internat. Coll., 1992-95, U. Hawaii, 1995—; bd. dirs. Hawaii Med. Svc. Assn., 1981-93, Honolulu Polynesian Cultural Ctr, 1990-93, Kapiolani Med. Ctr. for Women and Children, Honolulu, 1989-95. Capt. USMC, 1955-60. Mem. Pres.' Club U. Hawaii, C. of C. of Hawaii (chmn. bd. 1992-93). Mem. LDS Ch. Office: PO [illegible] Box 3200 Honolulu HI 96847-0001

HOAG, PAUL STERLING, architect; b. Spokane, Aug. 7, 1913; s. Percival Doane and Emma Imogen (Rusk) H.; m. Nancy Jean Lawrence, Oct. 21, 1967. Student, Washington State Coll., Pullman, 1930-31, Stanford U., , 1932-33. Lic. architect, Calif., Colo., Tex., Wash. Gen. mgr. Hoag [illegible] Hunter and others, L.A., 1946-48; prin. Paul Sterling Hoag, L.A., 1948-87, Crane Island, Wash., 1987—. Intr. advanced design So. Calif. Inst. Architecture; entire body of archtl. design drawings placed in archives U. Calif. Art History Dept. Prin. works include Falcon Plastics Factory, Oxnard, Calif. (top plant of 1970 award Modern Mfg.), Old Ranch Country Club, Seal Beach, Calif., Huntington Harbor (Calif.) Beach Club, Happy Valley Sch., Ojai, Calif., Adobe Hotel, Yachats, Oreg., Sterling Holloway residence, Laguna Beach, Calif., Beatrice Wood studio and residence, Ojai; author: (novel) Life of Antonio Vivaldi, 1994-98; monthly columnist The Listener, L.A. Architect; contbr. articles to profl. jours. and newspapers. Architect mem. Bel-Air Archtl. Com., L.A., 1982-88, San Vicente Design Rev. Bd., 1980-86; design cons. San Juan County (Wash.) for Eastsound town redesign, 1990-94. Fellow AIA. Home and Office: 356 167th Ave NE Bellevue WA 98008-4534

HOAGLAND, ALBERT SMILEY, electrical engineer, researcher; b. Berkeley, Calif., Sept. 13, 1926; s. Dennis Robert and Jessie Agnes (Smiley) H.; m. Janine Maryse Simart, May 23, 1950; children: Catherine, Nicole, Richard. B.S., U. Calif.-Berkeley, 1947, M.S., 1948, Ph.D., 1954. Registered profl. engr., Calif. Asst. prof. elec. engring. U. Calif.-Berkeley, 1954-56; sr. engr. IBM, San Jose, Calif., 1956-59; mgr. engring sci. San Jose Research Lab., 1959-62; sr. tech. cons. IBM World Trade, The Hague, Holland, 1962-64; mgr. engring. sci. IBM Research Ctr., N.Y.C., 1964-68, dir. tech. planning Research Div., 1968-71; corporate program coordinator IBM, Boulder, Colo., 1971-76; mgr. exploratory magnetic rec. San Jose Research Lab., 1976-82; tech. adv. Gen. Products Div., 1982-84; acting dir. Ctr. for Magnetic Recording Research, U. Calif. San Diego, 1983-84; prof. elec. engring., dir. Inst. Info. Storage Tech. Santa Clara U., Calif., 1984—. Lectr. computer design U. Calif. Berkeley, 1948-54, 56-62; adj. prof. U. Calif. San Diego, 1986; cons. State Calif., 1955-56, IBM, 1954-56, also numerous cons. in data storage industry, 1984—; chmn. Nat. Computer Conf. Bd., 1976-78; adj. prof. Harvey Mudd Coll. Author: Digital Magnetic Recording, 1963, 2d edit., 1991, reprinted, 1998; contbr. articles on magnetic rec. and info. storage tech. to profl. publs.; patentee in field. Trustee Charles Babbage Inst.; regent Inst. Info. Mgmt., 1985-92; chmn. adv. com. TMRC, 1993—, Magnetic Disk Drive Heritage Ctr., 2001—. With USNR, 1943-46. Recipient outstanding paper award IEEE, 1957 Fellow IEEE (dir. 1974-77, Centennial medal 1984, 3d Millenium medal 2000), Am. Fedn. Info. Processing Socs. (dir. 1969-78, pres. 1978-80); mem. IEEE Computer Soc. (pres. 1971-73), Rsch. Soc. Am. (pres. Sequoia chpt. 1962-63), Phi Beta Kappa, Sigma Xi, Eta Kappa Nu, Tau Beta Pi. Club: Golden Bear. Home: 13834 Upper Hill Dr Saratoga CA 95070-5334 Office: Santa Clara U Inst Info Storage Tech Santa Clara CA 95053-0001

HOAGLAND, DONALD WRIGHT, lawyer; b. N.Y.C., Aug. 16, 1921; s. Webster Comley and Irene (Wright) H.; m. Mary Tiedeman, May 14, 1949; children— Peter M., Mary C., Sara H., Ann W. BA, Yale U., 1942; LLB, Columbia U., 1948. Bar: N.Y. 1948, Colo. 1951. Assoc. firm Winthrop, Stimson, Putnam & Roberts, N.Y.C., 1948-51; ptnr. Davis, Graham & Stubbs, Denver, 1951-63, 66-87, of counsel, 1987—; with AID, 1964-66, asst. adminstr. devel. finance and pvt. enterprise, 1965-66, cons. Indonesia, 1967-75. Lectr. U. Denver Sch. Law, 1971-75; chmn. bd. Bi-Nat. Devel. Corp., 1968-70; dir. Centennial Fund, Inc., 2d Centennial Fund, Inc., Gryphon Fund, Inc., 1959-63; mem. Colo. Supreme Ct. Grievance Com., 1992-98. Mem. Denver Planning Bd., 1955-61, 67-70, chmn., 1959-61; bd. dirs., vice pres. Denver Art Mus., 1959-63, 72-76, 79-82; bd. dirs. Colo. Urban League, 1960-63, 66-72, chmn. bd., 1968-72; adv. bd. Vols. Tech. Assistance vice chmn. bd. Denver chpt. ARC, 1959-61; bd. dirs. Legal Aid Soc. Colo., 1972-84, pres., 1975-79; trustee Phillips Exeter Acad., 1960-67, Colo. Rocky Mountain Sch., 1981-84, Am. U., Washington, 1982-85; chmn. bd. dirs. Legal Aid Found., Colo., 1983-87; chmn. Social Sci. Found. Denver U., 1995-2000; chmn. Colo. Health Data Commn., 1986-88; bd. dirs. Colo. Bus. Coalition for Health, 1988-89, Colo. Found. for Ednl. Excellence, 1998—; exec. dir. Ctr. for Health Ethics and Policy U. Colo., Denver, 1987-91; chmn. Gov. Romer's panel health advisors, 1992-94; pres. Colo. Found. Pub. Health and Environ., 1995-98; chmn. Caring for Colo. Found., 1993—, chmn., 1999-00; ethics com. Nat. Jewish Med. & Rsch. Ctr., 1999-2000. Served as dive bomber pilot USNR, 1943-45. Decorated Air medal with oak leaf cluster. Mem. ABA, Colo. Bar Assn., Denver Bar Assn. Home: 355 Garfield St Denver CO 80206-4509 Office: Davis Graham & Stubbs 1550 17th St Ste 500 Denver CO 80202 E-mail: Donald.Hoagland@DGSlaw.com

HOBBINS, WILLIAM T. career officer; BS in Bus. Fin., U. Col., 1969; grad., Squadron Officer Sch., Maxwell AFB, Ala., 1976; MA in Bus. Adminstr., Troy State U., 1977; grad., Armed Forces Staff Coll., Norfolk, Va., 1981, Air War Coll., Maxwell AFB, 1985; grad. Jt. Flag Officer Warfighting, Maxwell AFB, 1997; grad., Joint Force Air Cmdrs., 2000. Cert. command pilot. Commd. 2d. lt. USAF, 1969, advanced through grades to Lt. Gen., 2001; pilot trng. Laredo AFB, Tex., 1970-70; instr. pilot 3389th Pilot Training Squadron, Keesler AFB, Miss., 1970-73; instr. pilot, class commander 29th Flying Trng. Wing, Craig AFB, Ala., 1973-74; At-28 fight pilot/chief 1131st Spl. Activity Squadron, Udorn Royal Thai AFB, Thailand, 1974-75; chief 29th Flying Tng. Wing, Craig AFB, Ala., 1975-77; flight commaner, instr. pilot, opers. officer 7th Tactical Fighter Squadron, 49th Tactical Fighter Wing, Holloman AFB, N.Mex., 1977-80; program element monitor, chief Hdrs. USAF, Washington, 1981-84; chief wing inspections 33rd. Tactical Fighter Wing, Eglin AFB, Fla., 1985-87; dep. comdr. opers. 12th Flying Trng. Wing, Randolph AFB, Tex., 1987-88; vice commander, then commdr. Air Forces Iceland, Keflavik Naval Air Sta, Iceland, 1988-90; vice comdr., then comdr. 405th Tactical Tng. Wing, Luke AFB, Ariz., 1990-91; vice comdr. 58th Fighter Wing, Luke AFB, 1991-92; dir. plans, opers. Yokota Air Base, Japan, 1992-94; comdr. 18th Wing, Kadena Air Base, Japan, 1994-96; dir. plans and policy (J-5) U.S. Atlantic Command, Norfolk, Va., 1996-98; dir. ops. Hdqs. USAF in Europe, Ramstein Air Base, Germany, 1998-2000. Nat. security leadership course, Syracuse U., 2000. Decorated Disting. Svc. Medal, Def. Superior Svc. medal with oak leaf cluster, Legion of Merit, Meritorious Svc. medal with four oak leaf clusters, Joint Svc. Commendation medal Air Force Commendatin medal with oak leaf cluster, Ord. of the Rising Sun with Gold Rays; recipient Khmer Aviation citation, Air Force Assn. citation. Office: 12 Air Force Comdr 2915 S Twelfth Air Force Dr Ste 218 Davis Mountain AFB AZ 85707-4100

HOBBS, GREGORY JAMES, JR. state supreme court justice; b. Gainesville, Fla., Dec. 15, 1944; s. Gregory J. Hobbs and Mary Ann (Rhodes) Frakes; m. Barbara Louise Hay, June 17, 1967; children: Daniel Gregory, Emily Mary Hobbs Wright. BA, U. Notre Dame, 1966; JD, U. Calif., Berkeley, 1971. Bar: Colo. 1971, Calif. 1972. Law clk. to Judge William E. Doyle 10th U.S. Cir. Ct. Appeals, Denver, 1971-72; assoc. Cooper, White & Cooper, San Francisco, 1972-73; enforcement atty. U.S. EPA, Denver, 1973-75; asst. atty. gen. State of Colo. Atty. Gen.'s Office, Denver, 1975-79; ptnr. Davis, Graham & Stubbs, Denver, 1979-92; shareholder Hobbs, Trout & Raley, P.C., Denver, 1992-96; justice Colo. Supreme Ct., Denver, 1996—. Counsel No. Colo. Water Conservancy, [illegible] Corps-S.Am., Colombia, 1967-68; vice chair Colo. Air Quality Control Com., Denver, 1982-87; mem. ranch com. Philmont Scout Ranch, Boy Scouts Am., Cimarron, N.Mex., 1988-98; co-chair Eating Disorder Family Support Group, Denver, 1992—. Recipient award of merit Denver Area Coun. Boy Scouts, 1993, Pres. award Nat. Water Resources Assn., Washington, 1995. Fellow Am. Bar Found.; mem. ABA, Colo. Bar Assn., [illegible]

HOBBS, GUY STEPHEN, financial executive; b. Lynwood, Calif., Feb. 23, 1955; s. Franklin Dean and Bette Jane (Little) H.; m. Laura Elena Lopez, Jan. 6, 1984; 1 child, Mariah Amanda. BA, U. Calif., Santa Barbara, 1976; MBA, U. Nev., 1978. Sr. rsch. assoc. Ctr. for Bus. and Econ. Rsch., Las Vegas, Nev., 1978-80; pvt. practice mgmt. cons. Las Vegas, 1979-82; mgmt. analyst Clark County, Las Vegas, 1980-81, sr. mgmt. analyst, 1981-82, dir. budget and fin. planning, 1982-84, comptroller, dir. fin., chief fin. officer, 1984-96; pres. Hobbs, Ong & Assocs., Inc., 1996—. Lectr. in mgmt. Coll. Bus. and Econs., U. Nev., Las Vegas, 1977-88; pres. Pacific Blue Ent., 1991—; mem. Interim Legis. Com. Infrastructure Fin., 1993-94; mem. Interim Legis. Com. Studying Laws Relating to the Distbn. of Taxes in Nev., 1995-96, 97—; mem. fiscal rev. com. Henderson State Coll., 2001, County Mgrs.'s orgnl. rev. com., 2001. Author publs. in field. Mem. exec. bd. Miss Nevada USA and Miss NEVADA Teen USA, 1996—; instr. Las Vegas Baseball Acad., 1998—; head coach, Silver State Girls Soccer League, 1998—. Mem. Am. Soc. Pub. Adminstrn. (Pub. Adminstr. of Yr. 1987), Govt. Fin. Officers Assn. (Fin. Reporting Achievement award 1984-95, Disting. Budget Presentation, award 1993-96), Nev. Taxpayers Assn. Republican. Avocations: sports, photography, travel. Office: Hobbs Ong & Assocs Inc 3900 Paradise Rd Ste 152 Las Vegas NV 89109-0928

HOCH, ORION LINDEL, corporate executive; b. Canonsburg, Pa., Dec. 21, 1928; s. Orion L.F. and Ann Marie (McNulty) H.; m. Jane Lee Ogan, June 12, 1952 (dec. 1978); children: Andrea, Brenda, John; m. Catherine Nan Richardson, Sept. 12, 1980. BS, Carnegie Mellon U., 1952; MS, UCLA, 1954; PhD, Stanford U., 1957. With Hughes Aircraft Co., Culver City, Calif., 1952-54; with Stanford Electronics Labs., 1954-57; sr. engr., dept. mgr., divsn. v.p., divsn. pres. Litton Electron Devices div., San Carlos, Calif., 1957-68; group exec. Litton Components divsn., 1968-70; v.p. Litton Industries, Inc., Beverly Hills, Calif., 1970, sr. v.p., 1971-74, pres., 1982-88, chief exec. officer, 1986-93, chmn., 1988-94, chmn. emeritus, 1994—, also dir.; pres. Intersil, Inc., Cupertino, 1974-82; chmn. exec. com. Western Atlas, Inc., Beverly Hills, 1994-98. Bd. dirs. Litton Industries, Inc., Bessemer Trust Cos., Unova, Inc. Trustee Carnegie-Mellon U. Served with AUS, 1946-48. Mem. IEEE, Sigma Xi, Tau Beta Pi, Phi Kappa Phi. Office: Unova Inc 21 900 Burbank Blvd Woodland Hills CA 91367-7418

HOCHACHKA, PETER WILLIAM, biology educator; b. Therien, Alta., Can., Mar. 9, 1937; s. William and Pearl (Krainek) H.; m. Brenda Clayton, Dec. 12, 1970; children: Claire, Gail, Gareth William BSc with honors, U. Alta., Edmonton, Can., 1959; MSc, Dalhousie U., Halifax, N.S., Can., 1961; PhD, Duke U., 1965; DSc, St. F. Xavier, 1998. Rsch. asst. U. Alta., 1958-69; vis. investigator Woods Hole Oceanographic Inst., Mass., 1962; asst. prof. biology U. Toronto, Ont., Can., 1964-65; postdoctoral fellow Duke U., Durham, N.C., 1964-66; asst. prof. U. B.C., Vancouver, Can., 1966-70, assoc. prof., 1970-75, prof., 1975—. Rsch. scientist R-V Alpha Helix of NSF (U.S.) Amazon Expdn. and Bering Sea Expdn., 1967-68, R-V Alpha Helix Guade Lupe Expdn., 1970, Eklund Biol. Sta., McMurdo, Antarctica, 1976-77, 82-83, 93, Palmer Peninsula, 1986; sr. scientist Oceanic Inst., Hawaii, 1970-71, R-V Alpha Helix, Galapagos Expdn., 1970-71, Amazon Expdn., 1976; vis. investigator Inst. Arctic Biology, U. Alaska, 1971, Pacific Biomed. Rsch. Ctr., U. Hawaii, 1975, Nat. Marine Fisheries, Honolulu, 1976, 81, 82, 84, 89, Plymouth Marine Lab., Eng., 1978, Concord Field Sta., Harvard U., 1984; sr. research scientist R-V Alpha Helix Hawaii (Kona Coast) Expdn., 1973; vis. investigator dept. physiology U. Hawaii, 1973, vis. investigator dept. biochemistry, 1976; vis. prof. Friday Harbor Marine Lab., U. Wash., 1975, Harvard U. Med. Sch., 1976-77; mem. R-V Alpha Helix Expdn. to Philippines, 1979; mem. Kenya lungfish program, dept. physiology and biochemistry U. Nairobi, 1979-80; vis. sr. scientist Heron Island Biol. Research Sta., 1983; vis. Q.E. sr. fellow at 27 Australian sci. instns., 1983; mem. U.S. Antarctic Rsch. Program, 1982-83, R/V Polar Duke rsch. expdn., Palmer Peninsula, Antarctica, 1986, high-altitude biochem. adaptaion program, La Raya, Peru, 1982, 87. Author: Strategies of Biochemical Adaptation, 1973, Living Without Oxygen, 1980, Biochemical Adaptation, 1984, Metabolic Arrest and the Control of Biological Time, 1987; editor: The Mollusca, Vol. 1: Metabolic Biochemistry and Molecular Biomechanics, Vol. 2: Environmental Biochemistry and Physiology, 1983; mem. editl. bd. Molecular Physiology, Am. Jour. Physiology, Biochem. Systematics & Ecology, Functional Ecology; co-editor Comp. Biochem. Physiol.; contbr. more than 200 articles to profl. jours. Decorated officer Order of Can., 1999; recipient gold medal for natural scis. Sci. Coun. B.C., 1987, Killam rsch. prize U. B.C., 1988, 89, Killiam Meml. sci. award, 1993, gold medal Natural Scis. and Rsch. Coun., 1995, Acad. of Yr. award Can. U. Faculty Assns., 1995; Queen Elizabeth II sr. fellow, Australia, 1983; grantee NRC, 1976. Fellow AAAS, Royal Soc. Can. (v.p. Acad. Scis. 2000, Flavelle medal 1990); mem. Soc. Exptl. Biology, Can. Soc. Zoologists, Am. Soc. Biochem. and Molecular Biology, N.Y. Acad. Scis., Am. Physiol. Soc.,Soc. Integrative & Comparative Biology, Sigma Xi Home: 4211 Doncaster Way Vancouver BC Canada V6S 1W1 Office: Univ BC Dept Zoology Vancouver BC Canada V6T IZ4

HOCHSTATTER, HAROLD, state legislator; m. Paula Hochstatter; 5 children. BA, Wash. State U. Elec. contractor, land developer, Moses Lake, Wash.; mem. Wash. Senate, Dist. 13, Olympia, 1992—; mem. edn. com. Wash. Legislature, Olympia, mem. energy, tech. and telecom. com., mem. labor and workforce devel. com., mem. rules com., mem. select com. on water policy, mem. joint select com. on edn. restructuring, mem. joint com. on energy and utilities, mem. 911 excise tax task force. Bd. dirs. Inst. for Sci. and Soc., Wash. Family Coun.; mem. NFIB, Big Bend Econ. Devel. Coun.; past treas. Columbia Basin Constrn. Coun.; ch. assignment sec. Gideon's Internat. Mem. Kittitas County Cattleman's Assn. Republican. Office: 115B Irving Newhouse Ofc Olympia WA 98504-0001

HOCKMUTH, JOSEPH FRANK, physicist, psychotherapist; b. Buffalo, Mar. 6, 1942; s. Joseph Frank and Gertrude Marie (Merkley) H.; m. Sharon Louise Van Deusen Tiernan, June 30, 1965 (div.); children: Joseph Fess, Catherine Marie; m. Katherine Nancy Genco, June 1, 1991 (div.); m. Holly Lynn Knapp, Oct. 14, 2000. BS in Physics, Calif. State U., 1965; MA in Psychology, Norwich U., 1992. Cert. substance abuse counselor, Ariz. Bd. Behavioral Health Examiners; cert. coll. instr., Ariz. State Bd.; cert. profl. counselor. Rsch. engr. Westinghouse Astroelectronics, Newbury Park, Calif., 1965-66, Lockheed Missile & Space Co., Sunnyvale, 1966-69, sr. rsch. engr., 1972-78; radiation effects engr. IRT Corp., San Diego, 1969-72, staff scientist, 1984-87; addictions counselor Charter Hosp., Glendale, Ariz., 1992-93; prin. staff engr. Motorola Govt. Sys. & Tech. Group, Scottsdale, 1978-84; tech. staff engr. Motorola GSTG, Scottsdale, 1987—, divsn. cons. for radiation effects, 1987—; psychotherapist Fountain Hills, 1992—. Contbr. Awakenings mag., 1992—. Funds coord. United Way, Scottsdale, 1988-90; class sponsor Wounded Knee (Wyo.) Tribal Elem. Sch., 1992—. Sgt. Calif. NG, 1960-68. Fellow Am. Counseling Assn., Ariz. Counselors Assn., Noetic Scis. Inst.; mem. ASTM (com. 1985—), IEEE (ofcl. tech. paper reviewer 1993). Roman Catholic. Avocations: guitar, piano, fishing, camping, American Indian culture studies. Home: 15024 E Windyhill Rd Fountain Hills AZ 85268-1323 Office: Motorola GSTG 8201 E Mcdowell Rd # H2550 Scottsdale AZ 85257-3893

HOCKNEY, DAVID, artist; b. Bradford, Yorkshire, Eng., July 9, 1937; s. Kenneth and Laura H. Attended, Bradford Coll. Art, 1953-57, Royal Coll. Art, London, 1959-62; D (hon.), U. Aberdeen, 1988; hon. degree, Royal Coll. Art, London, 1992. Lectr. U. Iowa, 1964, U. Colo., 1965, U. Calif. Berkeley, 1967, UCLA, 1966, hon. chair of drawing, 1980. One-man shows include Kasmin Gallery, 1963-89, Mus. Modern Art, N.Y.C., 1964, 68, Stedelijk Mus., Amsterdam, Netherlands, 1966, Whitechapel Gallery, London, 1970, Andre Emmerich Gallery, N.Y.C., 1972-96, Musee des Arts Decoratifs, Paris, 1974, Museo Tamayo, Mexico City, 1984, L.A. Louver, Calif., 1986, 89—, Nishimura Gallery, Tokyo, 1986, 89, 90, 94, Met. Mus. Art, 1988, L.A. County Mus. Art, 1988, 96, Tate Gallery, London, 1988, 92, Royal Acad. Arts, London, 1995, Hamburger Kunsthalle, 1995, Nat. Mus. Am. Art, Washington, 1997, 98, Mus. Ludwig, Cologne, 1997, MFA, Boston, 1998, Centre Georges Pompidou, Paris, 1999, Mus. Contempary Art, L.A., 2001, Kunst-Und Ausstellung Halle, Bonne, 2001, La. Mus Mod. Art, Copenhagen, 2001, others; designer: Rake's Progress, Glyndebourne, Eng., 1975; sets for Magic Flute, Glyndebourne, 1978, Parade Triple Bill, Stravinsky Triple Bill, Met. Opera House, 1980-81, Tristan und Isolde, Los Angeles Music Ctr. Opera, 1987; Turandot Lyric Opera, Chgo., 1992—, San Francisco Opera, 1993, Die Frau Ohne Schatten, Covent Garden, London, 1992, L.A. Music Ctr.Opera, 1993; author: David Hockney by David Hockney, 1976, David Hockney: Travels with Pen, Pencil and Ink, 1978, Paper Pools, 1980, David Hockney Photographs, 1982, Cameraworks, 1983, David Hockney: A Retrospective, 1988, Hockney Paints the Stage, 1983, That's the Way I See It, 1993, David Hockney's Dog Days, 1998, Hockney on Art, 1999, Secret Knowledge: Rediscovering the Lost Techniques of the Old Masters, 2001; illustrator: Six Fairy Tales of the Brothers Grimm, 1969, The Blue Guitar, 1977, Hockney's Alphabet, 1991. Recipient Guinness award and 1st prize for etching, 1961, Gold medal Royal Coll. Art, 1962, Graphic prize Paris Biennale, 1963, 1st prize 8th Internat. Exhbn. Drawings Lugano, Italy, 1964, 1st prize John Moores Exhbn. Liverpool, Eng., 1967, German award of Excellence 1983, 1st prize Internat. Ctr. of Photography, N.Y., 1985, Kodak photography book award for Cameraworks, 1984, Praemium Imperiale Japan Art Assn., 1989, 5th Ann. Gov. Calif. Visual Arts award, 1994; named Companion of Honour, Her Majesty, the Queen of Eng., 1997. Office: 7508 Santa Monica Blvd Los Angeles CA 90046-6407

HODAL, MELANIE, public relations executive; Pres., CEO Dennis Davidson Assocs., Inc., L.A. Office: Dennis Davidson Assocs Inc US Divsn DDA Ltd London 5670 Wilshire Blvd Ste 700 Los Angeles CA 90036-5607

HODGE, PAUL WILLIAM, astronomer, educator; b. Seattle, Nov. 8, 1934; s. Paul Hartman and Frances H.; m. Ann Uran, June 14, 1962; children: Gordon, Erik, Sandra. BS, Yale U., 1956; PhD, Harvard U., 1960. Lectr. Harvard, 1960-61; asst. prof. astronomy U. Calif. at Berkeley, 1961-65; asso. prof. U. Wash., Seattle, 1965-69, prof. astronomy, 1969—, chmn. Astronomy dept., 1987-91; fellow Mt. Wilson, Palomar Obs., Calif. Inst. Tech., Pasadena, 1960-61; physicist Smithsonian Astrophys. Obs., Cambridge, Mass., 1956-74. Author: Solar System Astrophysics, 1964, Galaxies and Cosmology, 1966, The Large Magellanic Cloud, 1967, Concepts of the Universe, 1969, Galaxies, 1972, Concepts of Contemporary Astronomy, 1974, The Small Magellanic Cloud, 1977, An Atlas of the Andromeda Galaxy, 1981, Interplanetary Dust, 1982, The Universe of Galaxies, 1985, Galaxies, 1986, The Andromeda Galaxy, 1992, Meteorite Craters and Impact Structures of the World, 1994, An Atlas of Local Group Galaxies, 1999; editor: The Astron. Jour., 1984—. Mem. Am. Astron. Soc. (v.p. 1990-93), Internat. Astron. Union, Meteoritical Soc., AAAS (pres. sect. D 1978-79, 83-84), Astron. Soc. Pacific (v.p. 1974-75), Korean Astron. Soc., Euro-asian Astron. Soc. (hon.). Office: U Wash Dept Astronomy Box 351580 Seattle WA 98195-1580

HODGE, PHILIP GIBSON, JR. mechanical and aerospace engineering educator; b. New Haven, Nov. 9, 1920; s. Philip Gibson and Muriel (Miller) H.; m. Thea Drell, Jan. 3, 1943; children: Susan E., Philip T., Elizabeth M. AB, Antioch Coll., 1943; PhD, Brown U., 1949. Research asst. Brown U., 1947-49, asso., 1949; asst. prof. math. UCLA, 1949-53; assoc. prof. applied mechanics Poly. Inst. Bklyn., 1953-56, prof., 1956-57; prof. mechanics Ill. Inst. Tech., 1957-71, U. Minn., Mpls., 1971-91, prof. emeritus, 1991—. Russell Severance Springer vis. prof. U. Calif., 1976; vis. prof. emeritus Stanford U., 1993—; sec. U.S. nat. com. Theoretical and Applied Mechanics, 1982-2000. Author: 5 books, the most recent being Limit Analysis of Rotationally Symmetric Plates and Shells, 1963, Continuum Mechanics, 1971; also numerous rsch. articles in profl. jours.; tech. editor Jour. Applied Mechanics, 1971-76. Recipient Disting. Service award Am. Acad. Mechanics, 1984; Karman medal ASCE, 1985. NSF sr. postdoctoral fellow, 1963 Mem. NAE, ASME (hon., Worcester Reed Warner medal 1975, ASME medal 1987, Daniel C. Drucker medal 2000), Internat. Union Theoretical and Applied Mechanics (del. 1982-2000, asst. treas. 1984-92, mem. at large 2000—). Home: 580 Arastradero Rd Apt 701 Palo Alto CA 94306-3948 E-mail: phodge1@stanford.edu

HODGES, DAVID ALBERT, electrical engineering educator; b. Hackensack, N.J., Aug. 25, 1937; s. Albert R. and Katherine (Rogers) H.; m. Susan Spongberg, June 5, 1965; children: Jennifer, Alan. B.E.E., Cornell U., 1960; M.S., U. Calif., Berkeley, 1961, Ph.D. in Elec. Engring, 1966. Mem. tech. staff Bell Telephone Labs., Murray Hill, N.J., 1966-69, head system elements research dept. Holmdel, 1969-70; asso. prof. dept. elec. engring. and computer scis U. Calif., Berkeley, 1970-74, prof., 1974-98, chmn. dept., 1989-90, dean Coll. Engring., 1990-96, prof. Grad. Sch., 1998—. Contbr. articles to profl. jours.; patentee in field. Fellow AAAS, IEEE.; mem. NAE. Office: Univ Calif Coll Engring 516 Cory Hl Berkeley CA 94720-0001

HODGES, JOSEPH GILLULY, JR. lawyer; b. Denver, Dec. 7, 1942; s. Joseph Gilluly Sr. and Elaine (Chanute) H.; m. Jean Todd Creamer, Aug. 7, 1971; children: Ashley E., Wendy C., Elaine V. BA, Lake Forest Coll., 1965; JD, U. Colo., 1968. Bar: Colo. 1968, U.S. Dist. Ct. Colo. 1969, U.S. Ct. Mil. Appeals 1969. Assoc. Hodges, Kerwin, Otten & Weeks, Denver, 1969-73, Davis, Graham & Stubbs, Denver, 1973-76, ptnr., 1976-86; pvt. practice, Denver, 1986—. Bd. dirs. Arapahoe Colo. Nat. Bank, Littleton, Colo., 1971-90, Cherry Creek Improvement Assn., Denver, 1979-91; bd. trustees Lake Forest (Ill.) Coll., 1977-87; pres. Colo. Arlberg Club, Winter Park, Colo., 1984-85; treas. St. Johns Episcopal Cathedral, Denver, 1981-96; chmn. bd. Spalding Cmty. Found., 1995—. Capt. USAR, 1969-74. Named Best Lawyers in Am., Woodward/White, N.Y.C., 1994-95. Fellow Am. Coll. Trust and Estate Counsel (state chmn. 1991-96); mem. ABA (chmn. probate divsn. G-2 Tech. 1990-95, coun. mem. real property, probate and trust law sect. 1996—), Am. Judicature Soc., Colo. Bar Assn. (chair probate coun. 1981-82), Denver Bar Assn., Denver Estate Planning Coun., Colo. Planned Giving Roundtable (bd. 1991-94), Rotary Club Denver, Kappa Sigma, Phi Alpha Delta. Republican. Avocations: skiing, hiking, fishing, photography, computers. Office: 3300 E 1st Ave Ste 600 Denver CO 80206-5809

HODGES, ROBERT STANLEY, biochemist, educator, researcher in biotechnology; b. Saskatoon, Sask., Can., Dec. 30, 1943; s. Bert and Frances H.; children: Sherylynn June, Clinton Jeffrey; m. Phyllis Hodges. BS in Biochemistry with honors, U. Sask., 1965; PhD in Biochemistry, U. Alta., Edmonton, Can., 1971. Postdoctoral and rsch. assoc. Rockefeller U., N.Y.C., 1971-74; asst. prof. dept. biochemistry U. Alta., Edmonton, 1974-77, assoc. prof. dept. biochemistry, 1977-84, prof., 1984—. Mem. Med. Rsch. Coun. Group in Protein Structure and Function, Edmonton, 1974—; pres. Alta. Peptide Inst., 1985—, Synthetic Peptides Inc., 1986-94; network leader protein engring. network Ctr. Excellence, 1994—. Author: (with others) Calmodulin Antagonists and Cellular Physiology, 1985, HPLC of Biological Macromolecules: Methods and Applications, 1990, Computer-Assisted Method Development for High-Peformance Liquid Chromatography, 1990, HPLC of Proteins, Peptides and Polynucleotides, 1991, High Peformance Liquid Chromatography of Peptides and Proteins: Separation, Analysis and Conformation, 1991; editor Peptide Rsch., 1988—, Peptides: Chemistry Structure and Biology, 1994; editl. adv. bd. Protein and Peptides Letters, Jour. Peptide Sci., Biomed. Peptides, Proteins and Nucleic Acids; contbr. numerous articles to scholarly and profl. jours. Competitor in speed skating Winter Olympics, Grenoble, France, 1966, Sapporo, Japan, 1972; mgr. Can. speed skating team Winter Olympics, Lake Placaid, N.Y., 1980; vice chmn. competitive speed skating, Winter Olympics, Calgary, Alta., 1988. Recipient honors scholarship U. Sask., 1964, Med. Rsch. Coun. studentship, Edmonton, 1969-71, postdoctoral fellowship, N.Y.C., 1971-73, Spl. Recognition for Contbns. to Biotechnology, Govt. Alta., 1986, Disting. MRC Scientist award, 1995, Alberta Sci. and Tech. award, 1995. Fellow Royal Soc. Can.; mem. Can. Biochemical Soc. (Boehringer-Mannheim Can. prize 1995), Protein Soc., Am. Peptide Soc. (pres. elect), N.Y. Acad. Scis. Achievements include a patent for Synthetic Psuedomonas aeruginosa Pilin Peptide and Related Vaccines and Diagnostics; research in synthetic peptides and proteins, calcium regulation of muscle contractions, de novo design of proteins, high performance liquid chromatography of peptides and proteins, synthetic vaccines,m antibacterial peptides, kinesin-tubulin interactins, role of coded-coils in protein function and self assembly. Office: U Alta Dept Biochemsitry Edmonton AB Canada T6G 2H7

HODGKINS, FRANCIS IRVING (BUTCH HODGKINS), county official; BS with honors in Civil Engring., Calif. State U., Sacramento, 1972. Licensed civil engr. Mem. staff County of Sacramento, Calif., 1965-89, engr. tech., 1965-68; pvt. prac. Sacramento, 1972-74; chief engr. Sacramento Co. Sanitation Dist., 1974-89; Dep. dir. pub. works Sacramento County (Calif.), 1989-93; exec. dir. Flood Ctrl. Agy. Sacramento Area, 1993—. Mem. Calif. Flood Plain Mgrs. Assn. Office: Flood Ctrl Agy Sacramento Area 1007 7th St Fl 5 Sacramento CA 95814-3407

HOECKER, THOMAS RALPH, lawyer; b. Chicago Heights, Ill., Dec. 14, 1950; s. William H. and Norma M. (Wynkoop) H.; m. V. Sue Thornton, Aug. 28, 1971; children: Elizabeth T., Ellen T. BS, No. Ill. U., 1972; JD, U. Ill., 1975. Bar: Ill. 1975, Ariz. 1985. Assoc. Davis and Morgan, Peoria, Ill., 1975-80, ptnr., 1980-84; assoc. Snell and Wilmer, Phoenix, 1984-86, ptnr., 1987—. Mem. steering com. Western Pension Conf., Phoenix, 1986-92, pres., 1991-92. Fellow Am. Coll. Employee Benefits Coun. (charter), Ariz. Bar Found.; mem. ABA (vice chair tax sect. employee benefits com., co-chair legis. and administrv. subcom. of labor sect. employee benefits com. 1994-96), Ariz. Bar Assn., Ill. Bar Assn., Marciopa County Bar Assn., (mem. investment com. 1988-94). Avocation: fly fishing. Office: Snell Wilmer 1 Arizona Ctr Phoenix AZ 85004

HOEFFLIN, STEVEN M. plastic surgeon; b. Seattle, 1946; MD, UCLA, 1972. Plastic surgeon Santa Monica (Calif.) Hosp.; assoc. clin. prof. UCLA. Office: 1530 Arizona Ave Santa Monica CA 90404-1208

HOEHN, ROBERT J. plastic surgeon, educator; b. East St. Louis, Ill., 1929; children: Robert Anthony Till, Margaret Eve, David Ivan, Daniel Vincent; m. Nancy Ruth Vincent. MD, Washington U., St. Louis, 1956. Diplomate Am. Bd. Plastic Surgery. Intern Vancouver (B.C., Can.) Gen. Hosp., 1956-57; resident in internal medicine, 1957-58; resident McGill U., Montreal, Que., Can., 1960-61; resident in gen. surgery Boston City Hosp., 1961-62; fellow in orthopaedic surgery, 1962; fellow in transplantation immunology Westminster Hosp., London, 1962-63; resident in plastic surgery N.Y. Hosp.-Cornell, 1963-65; clin. prof. plastic surgery U. Colo., 1978—, with Aurora Presbyn. Hosp., 1978—, Aurora Regional Med. Ctr., 1978—, Denver Children's Hosp., 1978—, Porter Meml. Hosp., 1982—, Swedish Hosp., 1982—; pvt. practice. Fellow ACS; mem. AAPS, Am. Soc. Plastic Surgeons, Plastic Surgery Rsch. Coun. Home: 2601 S Quebec St Villa 3 Denver CO 80231-6039 Office: 3535 Cherry Cr N Dr # 306 Denver CO 80209

HOFERT, JACK, consulting company executive, lawyer; b. Phila., Apr. 6, 1930; s. David and Beatrice (Schatz) H.; m. Marilyn Tukeman, Sept. 4, 1960; children: Dina, Bruce. BS, UCLA, 1952, MBA, 1954, JD, 1957. Bar: Calif. 1957; CPA, Calif. Tax supr. Peat, Marwick Mitchell & Co., L.A., 1959-62, tax mgr., 1974-77; v.p. fin. Pacific Theaters Corp., L.A., 1962-68; freelance cons. L.A., 1969-74; tax mgr. Lewis Homes, Upland, Calif., 1977-80; pres. Di-Bru, Inc., L.A., 1981-87, Scolyn, Inc., L.A., 1988-95; bus. cons., 1995—. Dir. Valley Fed. Savs. and Loan Assn., 1989-92. Mem. UCLA Law Rev., 1956-57; contbr. articles to tax, fin. mags. Served with USN, 1948-49. Avocation: tennis. Home and Office: 2479 Roscomare Rd Los Angeles CA 90077-1812 E-mail: jhofert@usa.net

HOFF, MARCIAN EDWARD, JR. electronics engineer; b. Rochester, N.Y., Oct. 28, 1937; s. Marcian Edward and Mary Elizabeth (Fitzpatrick) H.; m. Judith Schless Rytand, May 19, 1977; children: Carolyn, Lisa, Jill. B.E.E., Rensselaer Poly. Inst., Troy, N.Y., 1958; M.S., Stanford U., 1959, Ph.D., 1962. Research asso. Stanford U., 1962-68; mgr. applications research Intel Corp., Santa Clara, Calif., 1968-83; v.p. research and devel. Atari Inc., Sunnyvale, 1983-84; Chief Technologist Teklicon Inc. Author articles on adaptive systems, microcomputers; patentee track circuits, electrochem. memory, digital filters, integrated circuits, invented microprocessor. NSF fellow, 1958-60; recipient Stuart Ballantine medal Franklin Inst., 1979 Mem. IEEE (Cledo Brunetti award 1980, Centennial Medal 1984), Sigma Xi, Eta Kappa Nu, Tau Beta Pi. Achievements include the development of the microprocessor. Home: 12226 Colina Dr Los Altos CA 94024-5299 Office: Teklicon Inc 3031 Tisch Way Ste 1010 San Jose CA 95128-2533*

HOFFENBERG, MARVIN, political science educator, consultant; b. Buffalo, July 7, 1914; s. Harry and Jennie Pearl (Weiss) H.; m. Betty Eising Stern, July 20, 1947; children— David A., Peter H. Student, St. Bonaventure Coll., 1934-35; B.Sc., Ohio State U., 1939, M.A., 1940, postgrad., 1941. Asst. chief div. interindustry econs. Bur. Labor Statistics, Dept. Labor, 1941-52; cons. U.S. Mut. Security Agy., Europe, 1952, Statistik Sentralbyra, Govt. of Norway, Oslo, 1955; dir. research, econ. cons. dept. deVegh & Co., 1956-58; economist RAND Corp., 1952-56; staff economist Com. Econ. Devel., 1958-60; project chmn. Johns Hopkins U., 1960-63; dir. cost analysis dept. Aerospace Corp., 1963-65; Research economist Inst. Govt. and Pub. Affairs, UCLA, 1965-67, prof.-in-residence polit. sci., 1967-85, prof. emeritus, 1985—; dir. M.P.A. program, co-chmn. Interdepartmental Program in Comprehensive Health Planning UCLA, 1974-76. Author: (with Kenneth J. Arrow) A Time Series Analysis of Inter-Industry Demand, 1959; editor: (with Levine, Hardt and Kaplan) Mathematics and Computers in Soviet Economics, 1967; contbr. articles to profl. jours., chpts. to books Mem. bd. advisers Sidney Stern Meml. Trust; bd. dirs. Vista del Mar Child Ctr., L.A. chpt. Am. Jewish Com., Reiss-Davis Child Study Ctr.; foreman L.A. County Grand Jury, 1990-91; commr. L.A. County Economy and Efficiency Commn., 1991-92. C.C. Stillman scholar; Littauer fellow Harvard U., 1946; recipient Disting. service award Coll. Adminstrv. Scis., Ohio State U., 1971 Fellow AAAS; mem. Am. Econ. Assn. Jewish Office: U Calif Dept Polit Sci 4289 Bunchesci Los Angeles CA 90095-0001 E-mail: hoffen@ucla.edu

HOFFLUND, PAUL, lawyer; b. San Diego, Mar. 27, 1928; s. John Leslie and Ethel Frances (Cline) H.; m. Anne Marie Thalman, Feb. 15, 1958; children: Mark, Sylvia. BA, Princeton (N.J.) U., 1950; JD, George Washington U., 1956. Bar: D.C. 1956, U.S. Dist. Ct. D.C. 1956, U.S. Ct. Appeals (D.C. cir.) 1956, Calif. 1957, U.S. Dist. Ct. (so. dist.) Calif. 1957, U.S. Ct. Mil. Appeals 1957, U.S. Ct. Claims 1958, U.S. Ct. Appeals (9th cir.) 1960, U.S. Supreme Ct. 1964, U.S. Tax Ct. 1989. Assoc. Wencke, Carlson & Kuykendall, San Diego, 1961-62; ptnr. Carlson, Kuykendall & Hofflund, San Diego, 1963-65, Carlson & Hofflund, San Diego, 1965-72; Christian Sci. practitioner San Diego, 1972-84; arbitrator Mcpl. Cts. and Superior Ct. of Calif., San Diego, 1984-99; pvt. practice San Diego, 1985—. Adj. prof. law Nat. U. Sch. Law, San Diego, 1985-94; judge pro tem Mcpl. Ct. South Bay Jud. Dist., 1990-99; disciplinary counsel to U.S. Tax Ct., 1989—; asst. U.S. atty. U.S. Dept. of Justice, L.A., 1959-60, asst. U.S. atty. in charge, San Diego, 1960-61, spl. hearing officer, San Diego, 1962-68; asst. corp. counsel Govt. of D.C., 1957-59. Author: (chpt. in book) Handbook on Criminal Procedure in the U.S. District Court, 1967; contbr. articles to profl. jours. Treas. Princeton Club of San Diego; v.p. Community Concert Assn., San Diego; pres. Sunland Home Found., San Diego, Trust for Christian Sci. Orgn., San Diego; chmn. bd. 8th Ch. of Christ, Scientist, San Diego. With USN, 1950-53, comdr. JAGC, USNR, 1953-72, ret. Mem. ABA, San Diego County Bar Assn., World Affairs Coun., Phi Delta Phi. Democrat. Avocations: theater, classical music, bridge, fine art, biblical study. Home and Office: 6146 Syracuse Ln San Diego CA 92122-3301

HOFFMAN, ALLAN SACHS, chemical engineer, educator; b. Chgo., Oct. 27, 1932; s. Saul A. and Frances E. (Sachs) H.; m. Susan Carol Freeman, July 29, 1962; children: David, Lisa. BSChemE, MIT, 1953, MSChemE, 1955, ScDChemE, 1957. Instr. chem. engring. MIT, Cambridge, 1954-56, asst. prof., 1958-60, assoc. prof., 1965-70; research engr. Calif. Research Corp., Richmond, 1960-63; asso. dir. research Amicon Corp., Cambridge, 1963-65; prof. bioengring. and chem. engring. U. Wash., Seattle, 1970—; asst. dir. Center for Bioengring., 1973-83. Cons. to various govtl., indsl. and acad. orgns., 1958—; UN adviser to Mexican govt., 1973-74. Author: (with W. Burlant) Block and Graft Copolymers, 1960; author numerous articles and book chpts. on chem. engring. and biomaterials; patentee in field. Kimberly Clark fellow, 1954-55, Visking fellow, 1955-56, Fulbright fellow, 1957-58, Battelle fellow, 1970-72; Festschrift in honor of 60th birthday 8 issues of Jour. Biomaterials Sci., Polymer Edn., 1993. 94. Mem. Am. Chem. Soc., Am. Inst. Chem. Engrs., Am. Soc. for Artificial Internal Organs, Internat. Soc. Artificial Internal Organs (trustee, bd. dirs. 1987-1990), Soc. for Biomaterials (pres. 1983-84, Clemson award for biomaterial sci. lit., 1985, Founder's award, 2000), Controlled Release Soc. (Excellence in Guiding Grad. Rsch. award 1989, 98), Japan Biomaterials Soc. (Biomaterials Sci. prize 1990. Home: 10616 Riviera Pl NE Seattle WA 98125-6938 Office: U Wash Mail Box 352255 Seattle WA 98195-2255 E-mail: hoffman@u.washington.edu

HOFFMAN, DANIEL STEVEN, lawyer, law educator; b. N.Y.C., May 4, 1931; s. Lawrence Hoffman and Juliette (Marbes) Ostrov; m. Beverly Mae Swenson, Dec. 4, 1954; children: Lisa Hoffman Ciancio, Tracy Hoffman Cockriel, Robin Hoffman Black. BA, U. Colo., 1951; LLB, U. Denver, 1958. Bar: Colo. 1958. Assoc., then ptnr. Fugate, Mitchem, Hoffman, Denver, 1951-55; mgr. of safety City and County of Denver, 1963-65; ptnr. Kripke, Hoffman, Carrigan, Denver, 1965-70, Hoffman, McDermott, Hoffman, Denver, 1970-78; of counsel Hoffman & McDermott, Denver, 1978-84; mem. Holme Roberts & Owen, LLC, Denver, 1984-94; dean Coll. Law, U. Denver, 1978-84, dean emeritus, prof. emeritus, 1984—; ptnr. McKenna & Cuneo LLP, Denver, 1994-2000, Hoffman Reilley Pozner & Williams LLP, 2000—. Chmn., mem. Merit Screening Com. for Bankruptcy Judges, Denver, 1979—84; chmn. subcom. Dist. Atty.'s Crime Adv. Commn., Denver, 1984—; chmn. Senator Wirth's jud. nomination rev. com., Cong. DeGette's jud. nomination rev. com. Contbr. chpts. to books Mem. Rocky Mountain region Anti-Defamation League, Denver, 1985; bd. dirs. Colo. chpt. Am. Jewish Com., 1985, Legal Ctr., Denver, 1985—; mem. adv. com. Samaritan Shelter, Denver, 1985; chmn. Rocky Flats Blue Ribbon Citizens Com., Denver, 1980-83; mem. bd. visitors J. Reuben Clark Law Sch. Brigham Young U., 1986-88. With USAF, 1951-55. Recipient Am. Jewish Com. Nat. Judge Learned Hand award, 1993, Humanitarian award Rocky Mountain chpt. Anti-Defamation League, 1984, Alumni of Yr. award U. Denver Coll. Law, 1997. Fellow: Am. Coll. Trial Lawyers (state chmn. 1975—76), Internat. Soc. Barristers, Colo. Bar. Found., Am. Bar Found.; mem.: Order of Coif (hon.), Colo. Bar. Assn. (pres. 1976—77, Young Lawyer of Yr. award 1965), Colo. Trial Lawyers Assn. (pres. 1961—62, Lifetime Achievement award), Assn. Trial Lawyers Am. (nat. com. mem. 1962—63), Am. Judicature Soc. (bd. dirs. 1977—81). Democrat. Jewish Avocation: platform tennis. Office: Hoffman Reilly Pozner & Williamson LLP Kittredge Bldg 511 16th St Ste 700 Denver CO 80202-4248 E-mail: dhoffman@hrpwlaw.com

HOFFMAN, DARLEANE CHRISTIAN, chemistry educator; b. Terril, Iowa, Nov. 8, 1926; d. Carl Benjamin and Elverna (Kuhlman) Christian; m. Marvin Morrison Hoffman, Dec. 26, 1951; children: Maureane R., Daryl K. BS in Chemistry, Iowa State U., 1948, PhD in Nuclear Chemistry, 1951. Chemist Oak Ridge (Tenn.) Nat. Lab., 1952-53; staff radiochemistry group Los Alamos (N.Mex.) Sci. Lab., 1953-71, assoc. leader chemistry-nuclear group, 1971-79, leader chem.-nuclear divsn., 1979-82, leader isotope and nuclear chem. divsn., 1982-84; prof. chemistry U. Calif., Berkeley, 1984-91, prof. emeritus, 1991-93, prof. grad. sch., 1993—; faculty sr. scientist Lawrence Berkeley (Calif.) Lab., 1984—; dir.'s fellow Los Alamos Nat. Lab., 1990—; dir. G.T. Seaborg Inst. for Transactinium Sci., 1991-96. Panel leader, speaker Los Alamos Women in Sci., 1975, 79, 82, 97; mem. subcom. on nuclear and radiochemistry NAS-NRC, 1978-81, chmn. subcom. on nuclear and radiochemistry, 1982-84; titular mem. commn. on radiochem. and nuclear techniques Internat. Union of Pure and Applied Chem., 1983-87, sec., 1985-87, chmn., 1987-91, assoc. mem. 1991-93; organizer symposium Pacifichem Confs., 1984, 89, 95; lectr. Japan Soc. Promotion Sci., 1987; com. mem. Internat. Symposium on Nuclear and Radiochemistry, 1988; organizing com. Actinides, 1993, 2001; mem. nat. adv. com. Actinides, 2001; mem. planning panel Workshop on Tng. Requirements for Chemists in Nuclear Medicine, Nuclear Industry, and Related Fields, 1988, radionuclide migration peer rev. com., Las Vegas, 1986-87, steering com. Advanced Steady State Neutron Source, 1986-90, steering com., panelist Workshop on Opportunities and Challenges in Rsch. with Transplutonium Elements, Washington, 1983; mem. energy rsch. adv. bd. cold fusion panel, Dept. Energy, 1989-90; mem. NAS separations subpanel of separations tech. and transmutation systems panel, 1992-94, NAS-NRC Bd. on Radioactive Waste Mgmt., 1994-99, mem. steeering com. for Accel. Transmutation Waste roadmapping study, 1999; DOE Nuclear Energy Rsch. Adv. Com., 2000-2001; Welch Found. lectr., 2001. Author: The Transuranium People, 2000; contbr. articles to profl. jours. Sr. fellow NSF, 1964-65, Guggenheim Found. fellow, 1978-79; recipient Alumni Citation of Merit Coll. Scis. and Humanities, Iowa State U., 1978, Disting. Achievement award Iowa State U., 1986, Inst. Phys. Rsch & Technology Disting. Lectr., 1998, Berkeley citation U. Calif., 1996, U.S. Nat. Medal Sci., 1997, Leonard A. Ford Lectureship Mankato State U., 1998, Soc. Cosmetic Chemists Frontiers Sci. award, 1998; named to Women in Tech. Internat. Hall of Fame, 2000. Fellow AAAS (mem. coun. 1995-97), Am. Inst. Chemists (pres. N.Mex. chpt. 1976-78), Am. Phys. Soc., Am. Acad. Arts and Scis.; mem. Am. Chem. Soc. (chmn. nuclear chemistry and tech. divsn. 1978-79, com. on sci. 1986-88, exec. com. divsn. nuclear chemistry and tech. 1987-90, organizer symposium on nuclear and chem. properties of heaviest elements 2000, John Dustin Clark award Ctrl. N.Mex. sect. 1976, Nuclear Chemistry award 1983, Francis P. Garvan-John M. Olin medal 1990, Priestley medal 2000, Mosher award Santa Clara Valley sect. 2001), Am. Nuclear Soc. (co-chmn. internat. conf. Methods and Applications of Radioanalytical Chemistry 1987), Norwegian Acad. Arts and Scis., Sigma Xi, Phi Kappa Phi, Iota Sigma Pi (nat. hon. [illegible] Home: 2277 Manzanita Dr Oakland CA 94611-1135 Office: Lawrence Berkeley Nat Lab MS70-319 NSD Berkeley CA 94720

HOFFMAN, DONALD DAVID, cognitive and computer science educator; b. San Antonio, Dec. 29, 1955; s. David Pollock and Loretta Virginia (Shoemaker) H.; m. Geralyn Mary Souza, Dec. 13, 1986; 1 child from previous marriage, Melissa Louise. BA, UCLA, 1978; PhD, MIT, 1983. MTS and project engr. Hughes Aircraft Co., El Segundo, Calif., 1978-83; rsch. scientist MIT Artificial Intelligence Lab, Cambridge, Mass., 1983; asst. prof. U. Calif., Irvine, 1983-86, assoc. prof., 1986-90, prof., 1990-97. Cons. Fairchild Lab. for Artificial Intelligence, Palo Alto, Calif., 1984; panelist MIT Corp. vis. com., Cambridge, 1985, NSF, Washington, 1988; conf. host IEEE Conf. on Visual Motion, Irvine, 1989; conf. host Office of Naval Rsch. Conf. on Vision, Laguna Beach, Calif., 1992; vis. prof. Zentrum für Interdisziplinäre Forschung, Bielefeld, Germany, 1995-96. Author: Visual Intelligence, 1998; co-author: Observer Mechanics, 1989; mem. editl. bd. Cognition, 1991—, Psychol. Rev., 1995-96; contbr. articles to profl. jours. Vol. tchr. Turtle Rock Elem. Sch., Irvine, 1988-90. Recipient Distinguished Scientific award, Am. Psychol. Assn., 1989, Troland Rsch. award U.S. Nat. Acad. Scis., 1994; grantee NSF, 1984, 87, 2001. Mem. Vision Sci. Soc. Avocations: running, swimming, racket sports, ice skating. Office: U Calif Dept Cognitive Sci Irvine CA 92697-0001

HOFFMAN, DONALD M. lawyer; b. Los Angeles, Aug. 27, 1935; s. Henry Maurice and Viola Gertrude (Rothe) H. B.S., UCLA, 1957, LL.B., 1960. Bar: Calif. 1961. Pvt. practice, L.A. County, 1961—; ptnr. firm Greenwald, Hoffman, Meyer & Montes, 1964—. Pres. L.A. Estate Planning Council. Served to 2d lt. U.S. Army. Mem. Am., Los Angeles County bar assns., Phi Alpha Delta, Beta Gamma Sigma. Club: Jonathan. Home: 3520 St Elizabeth Rd Glendale CA 91206-1226 Office: 500 N Brand Blvd Ste 920 Glendale CA 91203-1923

HOFFMAN, JOHN RALEIGH, physicist; b. Evansville, Ind., July 7, 1926; s. John Henry and Ruth Margaret (Bryant) H.; m. Phyllis Christine Reindel, July 5, 1950; children: John Russell, Gary Paul. BS, U. Richmond (Va.), 1949; MS, U. Fla., 1951, PhD, 1954. Research asst. U. Fla., 1950-54; research scientist Sandia Corp., Albuquerque, 1954-57; project supr. Kaman Nuclear Co., Colorado Springs, 1957-68; v.p. Kaman Scis. Corp., Colorado Springs, 1968-86, sr. v.p., 1986-90, exec. v.p., 1990-92; gen. mgr. Kaman Instrumentation Corp., 1989-90; ret. Kaman Scis Corp., 1992; tech. and mgmt. cons., 1992—. Bd. dirs. Red Spot Paint and Varnish Co., 1993—; mem. nominating commn. Colo. Supreme Ct., 1998—. Served with USNR, 1944-46. Mem. Am. Phys. Soc., IEEE. Republican. Presbyterian. Home and Office: 5020 Lyda Ln Colorado Springs CO 80904-1008 E-mail: JRaleighHo@aol.com

HOFFMAN, JULIEN IVOR ELLIS, pediatric cardiologist, educator; b. Salisbury, South Rhodesia, July 26, 1925; came to U.S., 1957, naturalized, 1967; s. Bernard Isaac and Minrose (Bermant) H.; m. Kathleen Lewis, 1986; children: Anna, Daniel. B.Sc., U. Witwaterstrand, Johannesburg, South Africa, 1944; B.Sc. Hons., 1945, M.B., B.Ch., 1949, M.D., 1970. Intern, resident internal medicine, South Africa and Eng., 1950-56; research asst., postgrad. Med. Sch., London, 1956-57; fellow pediatric cardiology Boston Children's Hosp., 1957-59; fellow Cardiovascular Research Inst., San Francisco, 1959-60; asst. prof. pediatrics, internal medicine Albert Einstein Coll., N.Y., 1962-66; assoc. prof. pediatrics U. Calif. at San Francisco, 1966-70, prof., 1970-94, prof. physiology, 1981-88, prof. emeritus, 1994. Sr. mem. Cardiovascular Research Inst., U. Calif. at San Francisco, 1966— ; mem. bd. examiners, sub-bd. pediatric cardiology Am. Bd. Pediatrics, 1973-78, subbd. pediatric intensive care, 1985-87; chmn. Louis Katz Award Com., Basic Sci. Council, Am. Heart Assn., 1973-74; George Brown Meml. lectr. Am. Heart Assn., 1977; George Alexander Gibson Meml. lectr. Royal Coll. Physicians (Edinburgh), 1978; Lilly lectr. Royal Coll. Physicians (London), 1981; Isaac Starr lectr. Cardiac Systems Dynamics Soc., Eng., 1982; John Keith lectr., 1985; Disting. Physiology lectr. Am. Coll. Chest Physicians, 1985; Nadas lectr. Am. Heart Assn., 1989; 1st Donald C. Fyler lectr. Children's Hosp., Boston, 1990. Recipient Bayer Cardiovascular Mentor award, 1989. Fellow Royal Coll. Physicians; mem. World Congress Pediatric Cardiology and Cardiac Surgery (hon. joint pres. Paris 1993), Am. Physiol. Soc., Am. Pediatric Soc., Soc. Pediatric Rsch. Achievements include extensive rsch. into congenital heart disease and coronary blood flow. Home: 925 Tiburon Blvd Belvedere Tiburon CA 94920-1525 Office: U Calif Med Ctr 1331 M Dept Pediats San Francisco CA 94143 E-mail: jhoffman@pedcard.ucsf.edu

HOFFMAN, LYMAN, state legislator; b. Bethel, Alaska, Feb. 13, 1950; m. Lillian Hoffman; children: Trina, Douglas. Student, U. Alaska, 1968-72, 73-74. City mgr., Bethel, 1977-85; dep. dir. Yukon-Kuskokwim Health Corp.; former owner North Star Gas; owner Bethel Drilling and Welding, Twilight Travel Agy.; mem. Alaska Ho. of Reps., 1986-92, Alaska Senate, Dist. T, Juneau, 1992—; mem. labor and commerce com., com. on legis. ethics; mem. cmty. and regional affairs com., legis. coun. Former chair, bd. dirs. Bethel Prematernal Home; former bd. mem. Bethel Native Corp., Bethel Family Clinic; former planning commr. City of Bethel. Democrat. Office: State Capitol 120 4th St Rm 7 Juneau AK 99801-1142 also: 716 W 4th Ave Ste 240B Anchorage AK 99501-2107 Fax: 907-465-4523/907-269-0270. E-mail: hoffman@legis.state.ak.us

HOFFMAN, MICHAEL JEROME, humanities educator, educator; b. Phila., Mar. 13, 1939; s. Nathan P. and Sara (Perlman) H.; m. Margaret Boegeman, Dec. 27, 1988; children by previous marriage: Cynthia, Matthew. BA, U. Pa., 1959, MA, 1960, PhD, 1963. Instr. Washington Coll., Chestertown, Md., 1962-64; asst. prof. U. Pa., Phila., 1964-67; from asst. prof. to prof. U. Calif., Davis, 1967—, asst. vice chancellor acad. affairs, 1976-83, chmn. English dept., 1984-89, dir. Davis Humanities Inst., 1987-91, coord. writing programs, 1991-94, undergrad. coord., 1994-95, grad. advisor, 1995-98, dir. honors program, 1992-99. Chmn. joint projects steering com. U. Calif.-Calif. State U., 1976-87; chmn. adv. bd. Calif. Acad. Partnership Program, 1985-87; dir. Calif. Humanities Project, 1985-91. Author: The Development of Abstractionism in the Writings of Gertrude Stein, 1965, The Buddy System, 1971, The Subversive Vision, 1972, Gertrude Stein, 1976, Critical Essays on Gertrude Stein, 1986, Essentials of the Theory of Fiction, 1988, rev. edit., 1996, Critical Essays on American Modernism, 1992. With USAR, 1957-61. Nat. Def. Edn. Act fellow U.S. Govt., 1959-62. Mem. Modern Lang. Assn. (Am. lit. group). Democrat. Jewish. Avocation: tennis. Home: 4417 San Marino Dr Davis CA 95616-5012 Office: U Calif Dept English Davis CA 95616

HOFFMAN, THOMAS EDWARD, dermatologist; b. L.A., Oct. 14, 1944; s. David Maurice and Ann (Corday) H.; m. Donna Madsen, 1973 (div. 1977); m. Linda L., Feb. 20, 1979; children: David, Jay. AB, U. So. Calif., 1966; MD, Tulane U., 1970. Intern U. So. Calif. USC Med. Ctr., 1970-71; residency dermatology Stanford (Calif.) U., 1973-76, fellow dermatopathology, 1973-74; dermatologist pvt. practice, Menlo Park, Calif., 1976—. Clin. assoc. prof. Stanford (Calif.) U., 1981-97, clin. prof. dermatology, 1997. With USPHS, 1971-73. Recipient Achievement award Tulane U., 1970. Fellow Am. Coll. Physicians, Am. Acad. Dermatology, Am. Soc. Dermatopathology, Am. Soc. Dermatologic Surgery, Am. Soc. Laser Medicine & Surgery, San Francisco Dermatologic Soc. (pres. 2000—). Avocations: tennis, skiing. Office: Menlo Dermatology Med Group 888 Oak Grove Ave Menlo Park CA 94025-4432

HOFFMAN, TREVOR WILLIAM, professional baseball player; b. Bellflower, Calif., Oct. 13, 1967; Student, U. Ariz. Pitcher San Diego [illegible] 1993—. Office: San Diego Padres PO Box 2000 San Diego CA 92112-2000

HOFFMAN, WAYNE MELVIN, retired airline official; b. Chgo., Mar. 9, 1923; s. Carl A. and Martha (Tamillo) H.; m. Laura Majewski, Jan. 26, 1946; children— Philip, Karen, Kristin. BA cum laude, U. Ill., 1943, J.D. with high honors, 1947. Bar: Ill. bar 1947, N.Y. bar 1958. Atty. I.C. R.R., 1948-52, with N.Y.C. R.R. Co., 1952-57, exec. asst. to pres., 1956-60, v.p. freight sales 1960-61, v.p. sales 1961-62, exec. v.p. 1962-67; chmn. bd. N.Y. Central Trans. Co., 1960-67, Flying Tiger Line, Inc. and Tiger Internat., Inc., 1967-86. Trustee McCallum Theatre, Palm Desert, Calif., Eisenhower Med. Ctr., Rancho Mirage, Calif. Served to capt. inf. AUS, World War II. Decorated Silver Star, Bronze Star with oak leaf cluster, Purple Heart with oak leaf cluster; Fourragere (Belgium). Mem. Bohemian Club (San Francisco), Vintage Club (Indian Wells), Phi Beta Kappa. Home: 74-435 Palo Verde Dr Indian Wells CA 92210-7367 Office: 2450 Montecito Rd Ramona CA 92065-1644

HOFFMANN, JON ARNOLD, aeronautical engineer, educator; b. Wausau, Wis., Jan. 13, 1942; s. Arnold D. and Rita J. (Haas) H.; m. Carol R. Frye. BSME, U. Wis., 1964, MSME, 1966. Register profl. engr., Calif. Research engr. Trane Co., 1966-68; prof. aeronautical engring. Calif. Poly. State U., San Luis Obispo, 1968—. Research engr. Stanford U. NSF Program, 1970; research fellow Ames Research Ctr. Ctr. NASA/ASEE, 1974-75; tech. cons. NASA/AMES Research Ctr., 1977; design engr. Cal/Poly ERDA contract, 1976-77; prin. investigator NASA-ARC Cooperative Agreement, 1983. Contbr. articles to profl. jours. Grantee NASA, NSF. Mem. ASME. Home: 1044 Via Chula Robles Arroyo Grande CA 93420-4915 Office: Calif Poly State U Dept Aero Engring San Luis Obispo CA 93407

HOFFMANN, KATHRYN ANN, humanities educator; b. Rockville Centre, N.Y., Oct. 26, 1954; d. Manfred and Catherine (Nanko) H.; m. Brook Ellis, Nov. 25, 1987. BA summa cum laude, SUNY Buffalo, 1975; MA, The Johns Hopkins U., 1979, PhD, 1981. Asst. prof. French lit. and lang. U. Wis., Madison, 1981-88, U. Hawaii-Manoa, Honolulu, 1992-97, assoc. prof., 1997—; mng. ptnr. Yuval Design Partnership, Chgo., 1988-92. Author: Society of Pleasures: Interdisciplinary Readings in Pleasure in Power during the Reign of Louis XIV, 1997 (Aldo and Jeanne Scaglione prize for French and Francophone Studies 1998); assoc. editor Substance, 1982-87; contbr. articles to profl. jours.; designer clothing accessories. Grantee NEH, 1993, 95; fellow Inst. Rsch. in Humanities, 1984-85, Am. Coun. Learned Socs., 1984-85, Camargo Found., 1998; recipient Aldo and Jeanne Scaglione prize for French and Francophone studies MLA, 1998, Regents' medal for excellence in tchg., 1998. Mem. MLA, Internat. Soc. for the Study of European Ideas, Am. Soc. for 18th Century Studies, Hawaii Assn. Lang. Tchrs., N.Am. Soc. for 17th Century French Lit., Soc. for Interdisciplinary French 17th Century Studies (exec. com. 1994-96), Soc. for Interdisciplinary Study Social Imagery, Phi Beta Kappa. Home: 3029 Lowrey Ave # K3203 Honolulu HI 96822-1800 Office: U Hawaii Manoa Langs & Lits Europe Ams 1890 East West Rd Rm 483 Honolulu HI 96822-2318

HOFFMANN, WILLIAM FREDERICK, astronomer; b. Manchester, N.H., Feb. 26, 1933; s. Maurice and Charlotte (Hibbs) H.; m. Silke Elisabeth Margaretha Schneider, June 5, 1965; children: Andrea Charlotte, Christopher James. AB in Physics, Bowdoin Coll., 1954; PhD in Physics, Princeton U., 1962. Instr. physics Princeton (N.J.) U., 1958-61; rsch. assoc. NASA-GISS, N.Y.C., 1962, staff astronomer, 1965-73; instr. physics Yale U., New Haven, 1963-64; adj. assoc. prof. Columbia U., N.Y.C., 1970-73; prof. astronomy U. Ariz., Tucson, 1973-98, prof. emeritus astronomy, 1998—. Editor: (with H.Y. Chiu) Gravitation & Relativity, 1964. Pres. Spuyten Duyvil Assn., N.Y.C., 1971. NSF fellow, 1954; Danforth fellow, 1954-58. Fellow AAAS, Am. Physics Soc.; mem. Am. Astron. Soc., Sigma Chi, Phi Beta Kappa. Home: 4225 E Kilmer St Tucson AZ 85711-2825 Office: U Ariz Steward Obs Tucson AZ 85721-0001

HOFMANN, ALAN FREDERICK, biomedical educator, researcher; b. Balt., May 17, 1931; s. Joseph Enoch and Nelda Rosina (Durr) H.; m. Marta Gertrud Pettersson, Aug. 15, 1969 (div. 1976); children: Anthea Karin, Cecilia Rae; m. Helga Katharina Aicher, Nov. 3, 1978. BA with honors, Johns Hopkins U., 1951, MD with honors, 1955; PhD, U. Lund, Sweden, 1965; MD honoris causis, U. Bologna, Italy, 1988; hon. fellow, Royal Coll. Physicians, 1996. Intern, then resident dept. medicine Columbia Presbyn. Med. Ctr., N.Y.C., 1955-57; clin. assoc. clin. ctr. Nat. Heart Inst., NIH, Bethesda, Md., 1957-59; postdoctoral fellow, dept. physiol. chemistry U. Lund, Sweden, 1959-62; asst. physician Hosp. of the Rockefeller U., N.Y.C., 1962-64; outpatient physician N.Y. Hosp., N.Y.C., 1963-64; assoc. physician Hosp. of Rockefeller U., N.Y.C., 1964-66; cons. in medicine, assoc. dir. gastroenterology unit Mayo Clinic, Rochester, Minn., 1966-77; prof. medicine, attending physician Med. Ctr. U. Calif., San Diego, 1977-98, emeritus prof., 1998—. Asst. prof. dept. medicine Rockefeller U., N.Y.C., 1964-66; assoc. prof. medicine and biochemistry U. Minn. Mayo Grad. Sch., 1966-69, assoc. prof. medicine and physiology, 1969-70, prof. medicine and physiology, 1970-73; prof. medicine and physiology Mayo Med. Sch., 1973-77; cons. physiology Mayo Clinic, Rochester, 1975-77; adj. prof. pharmacy, U. Cali, San Francisco, 1986-94; vis. prof. pharmacy U. Mich., Ann Arbor, 1980-85. Patentee solvent for direct dissolution of cholesterol gallstones, breath test for pancreatic exocrine function, bile acid replacement therapy; contbr. numerous articles to profl. jours., books, films. Recipient Travel award Wellcome Trust, 1961-63, Travel award NSF, 1964, Sr. Scientist award Humboldt Found., Fed. Republic of Germany, 1976, 91 (shared prize) Eppinger Prize, Falk Found., 1976, Disting. Achievement award Modern Medicine mag., 1978 Chancellor's Rsch. Excellence award U. Calif., 1986, Disting. Alumnus award Mayo Clinic, 2001; Nat. Found. fellow, 1959-61, USPHS fellow, 1962-63, Fogarty Internat. Sr. fellow NIH, 1986; Rockefeller Found. scholar, Bellagio, Italy, 1980. Fellow AAAS, Royal Soc. Medicine; mem. Am. Assn. Study of Liver Disease (numerous coms., pres. 1984, Disting. Achievement award 1997), Swedish Soc. for Gastroenterology (hon.), Soc. for Gastrointestinal Radiology (hon.), Gastroent. Soc. Australia (hon.), Chilean Soc. Gastroenterology (hon.), Brit. Soc. Gastroenterology (hon.), Royal Flemish Acad. for Medicine (hon., fgn. corr. mem.), German Soc. for Digestive and Metabolic Disease (hon. mem., Siegfried Thannhauser medal 1996), Serbian Soc. Medicine (hon.), Am. Soc. Clin. Investigation, Assn. Am. Physicians, Am. Liver Found. (chmn. sci. adv. bd. 1986-91), Am. Physiol. Soc. (Horace Davenport medal 1996), Am. Gastroent. Assn. (chmn. biliary diseases coun. 1991-92, Disting. Achievement award 1970, co-winner Beaumont prize 1979, Friedenwald medal 1994), Phi Beta Kappa, Sigma Xi, Alpha Omega Alpha, Omicron Delta Kappa. Home: 5870 Cactus Way La Jolla CA 92037-7069 E-mail: ahofmann@ucsd.edu, hofmannaf@cs.com

HOFMANN, JOHN RICHARD, JR. retired lawyer; b. Oakland, Calif., June 24, 1922; s. John Richard and Esther (Starkweather) H.; m. Mary Macdonough, Feb. 6, 1954; children: John Richard III, Gretchen Hofmann, Sarah Worthington Hack, John Macdonough Alexander. AB, U. Calif., Berkeley, 1943; JD, Harvard U., 1949. Bar: Calif. 1950. Assoc. Pillsbury, Madison & Sutro, San Francisco, 1949-58, ptnr., 1959-92, of counsel, 1992-96, ret., 1996—; exec. v.p. MPC Ins., Ltd., 1988-96. City atty. City of Belvedere (Calif.), 1957-58. Mem. Calif. Bar Assn. Office: Pillsbury Winthrop LLP PO Box 7880 San Francisco CA 94120-7880

HOFMANN, KEN, professional sports team executive; b. Oakland, Calif. m. Joan England; 2 children. Student, St. Mary's Coll.; grad., U.S. Merchant Marine Acad. Plastering contractor, 1948-51; home builder, [illegible] Oakland Athletics, 1995—. Regent emeritus, bd. trustees St. Mary's Coll.; fund-raiser Regional Theater for Arts in Walnut Creek, Mt. Diablo Med. Ctr. Master mariner, World War II. Named St. Mary's Alumnus of Yr., 1983. Mem. Nat. Assn. Home Builders, Local Bldg. Industry Assn. (pres., bd. dirs.), Alumni Assn. U.S. Merchant Marine Acad., Nat. Fish and Wildlife Found. (former dir.). Avocations: flying, golfing, hunting, fishing. Office: Oakland Athletics [illegible] Oakport St Ste [illegible] Oakland CA [illegible] 1933 Fax: 510-562-1633

HOFMANN, PAUL BERNARD, healthcare consultant; b. Portland, Oreg., July 6, 1941; s. Max and Consuelo Theresa (Bley) H.; m. Lois Bernstein, June 28, 1969; children: Julie, Jason. BS, U. Calif., Berkeley, 1963, MPH, 1965, DPH, 1994. Research assoc. in hosp. adminstrn. Lab. of Computer Sci., Mass. Gen. Hosp., Boston, 1966-68, asst. dir., 1968-69; asst. adminstr. San Antonio Community Hosp., Upland, Calif., 1969-70, assoc. adminstr., 1970-72; dep. dir. Stanford (Calif.) U. Hosp., 1972-74, dir., 1974-77; exec. dir. Emory U. Hosp., Atlanta, 1978-87; exec. v.p., chief ops. officer Alta Bates Corp., Emeryville, Calif., 1987-91, cons., 1991-92, Alexander & Alexander, San Francisco, 1992-94; disting. vis. scholar Stanford (Calif.) U. Ctr. for Biomed. Ethics, 1993-97; sr. fellow Stanford (Calif.) U. Hosp., 1993-94; sr. cons. strategic healthcare practice Alexander & Alexander Cons. Group, San Francisco, 1994-97; sr. v.p. strategic healthcare practice Aon Cons., San Francisco, 1997-99; pres. The Hofmann Healthcare Group, San Francisco, 2000-01; v.p. Provenance Health Ptnrs., Moraga, Calif., 2001—. Instr. computer applications Harvard U., 1968-69; lectr. hosp. adminstrn. UCLA, 1970-72, Stanford U. Med. Sch., 1972-77; assoc. prof. Emory U. Sch. Medicine, Atlanta, 1978-87. Author: The Development and Application of Ethical Criteria for Use in Making Programmatic Resource Allocation Decisions in Hospitals, 1994; co-editor: Managing Ethically: A Guide for Executives, 2001; contbr. articles to profl. jours. Served with U.S. Army, 1959. Fellow Am. Coll. Hosp. Adminstrs. (recipient Robert S. Hudgens meml. award 1976); mem. Am. Hosp. Assn., U. Calif. Alumni Assn.

HOGAN, CRAIG J. astronomer, educator; BA in Astronomy summa cum laude, Harvard Coll., 1976; PhD in Astronomy, U. Cambridge, 1980. Asst. prof., astronomer Steward Obs. U. Ariz., 1985-89, assoc. prof., astronomer, 1989-90; assoc. prof. astronomy and physics dept.s U. Wash., Seattle, 1990-93, prof. astronomy and physics dept., 1993—, chair astronomy dept., 1995-2000. Mem. ad hoc com. on funding of cosmology NSF, 1986, proposal rev. panel chair, 1998, com. of visitors divsn. astron. scis., 1999; mem. dark time telescope time allocation com. Kitt Peak Nat. Obs., 1992-95; sci. adv. com. Sloan Digital Sky Survey, 1994—, co-chair so. survey working group, 1994—, sci. dirs. adv. com., 1998—, adv. coun., 1998—, fundraising task force, 1998—; mem. program adv. com. Ctr. for Particle Astrophysics, 1995-2000; program organizer Inst. for Nuc. Theory, 1996; grad. program rev. com. physics dept. U. Calif. San Diego, 1996; mem. HDF archive panel Space Telescope Sci. Inst., 1996, cycle 7 TAC and panel chair, 1996; mem. proposal rev. panel NASA, 1998, mission definition team LISA, 1998—; bd. govs. Astrophys. Rsch. Consortium, 1998—; chair dean search com. UW Coll. Arts and Scis., 1998-99; panel on theory, computation and data exploration in astronomy and astrophysics Astronomy and Astrophysics Survey Com., NRC, 1999; lectr. in field; others. Recipient Humboldt Rsch. award Max Planck Inst. for Astrophysics, 1999—; Enrico Fermi fellow U. Chgo., 1980-81, NSF postdoctoral fellow, Cambridge, Eng., 1981-82, Bantrell prize fellow in theoretical astrophysics Calif. Inst. Tech., 1982-85, Alfred P. Sloan Found. fellow, 1986-91, vis. fellow Inst. Astronomy, Cambridge U., 1987, 89, 94; grantee NASA and NSF, 1987—, UW Royalty Rsch. Fund, 1992, Murdock Charitable Trust, 1996-98. Office: U Wash Dept Astronomy C319 Physics/Astronomy Box 351580 Seattle WA 98105 Office Fax: 206-685-0403. E-mail: hogan@astro.washington.edu

HOGAN, CURTIS JULE, union executive, industrial relations consultant; b. Greeley, Kans., July 25, 1926; s. Charles Leo and Anna Malene (Rousselo) H.; m. Lois Jean Ecord, Apr. 23, 1955; children: Christopher James, Michael Sean, Patrick Marshall, Kathleen Marie, Kerry Joseph. BS in Indsl. Rels., Rockhurst Coll., 1950; postgrad., Georgetown U., 1955, U. Tehran, Iran, 1955-57. With Gt. Lakes Pipeline Co., Kansas City, Mo., 1950-55; with Internat. Fedn. Petroleum and Chem. Workers, Denver, 1955-85, gen. sec., 1973-85; pres. Internat. Labor Rels. Svcs., Inc., 1976—. Cons. in field; lectr. Rockhurst Coll., Kansas City, 1951-52. Contbr. articles to profl. publs. Served with U.S. Army, 1945-46. Mem. Internat. Indsl. Rels. Assn., Indsl. Rels. Rsch. Assn., Oil Chem. and Atomic Workers Internat. Union. Office: Internat Fed Petroleum Chem Workers 435 S Newport Way Denver CO 80224-1321

HOGAN, MICHAEL R(OBERT), judge; b. Oregon City, Oreg., Sept. 24, 1946; married; 3 children. AB, U. Oreg. Honors Coll., 1968; JD, Georgetown U., 1971. Bar: Oreg. 1971, U.S. Ct. Appeals (9th cir.) 1971. Law clk. to chief judge U.S. Dist. Ct. Oreg., Portland, 1971-72; assoc. Miller, Anderson, Nash, Yerke and Wiener, Portland, 1972-73; magistrate judge U.S. Dist. Ct. Oreg., Eugene, 1973-91, dist. judge, 1991—, chief judge, 1995—; bankduptcy judge U.S. Dist. Oreg., Eugene, 1973-80. Mem. ABA, Oreg. State Bar Assn. Office: US Courthouse 211 E 7th Ave Eugene OR 97401-2773

HOGAN, STEVEN L. lawyer; b. Los Angeles, Aug. 31, 1953; s. Kenneth Carlton Hogan and Ninon Michelle Kingsley; m. Debra Karen Garshfield, June 27, 1975; children: Rebecca Sarah, Cheryl Lee. AB magna cum laude, UCLA, 1975; JD, U. So. Calif., 1978. Bar: Calif. 1978, U.S. Dist. Ct. (cen. dist.) Calif. 1979, U.S. Supreme Ct. 2000. Assoc. Anderson, McPharlin & Conners, L.A., 1978-80; ptnr. Bryan Cave, L.A., 1980-95; shareholder Lurie, Zepeda, Schmalz & Hogan, Beverly Hills, CA, 1995—. Mem. Los Angeles County Bar Assn., Order of Coif, Phi Beta Kappa, Phi Gamma Mu. Office: Lurie Zepeda Schmalz & Hogan 9107 Wilshire Blvd Ste 800 Beverly Hills CA 90210-5533 E-mail: shogan@lurie-zepeda.com

HOGANS, MACK L. paper company executive; BS in Forestry, U. Mich.; MS in Forest Resources, U. Wash. Forester, govt. affairs mgr. Weyerhaeuser Co., Tacoma, 1979-90, v.p. govt. affairs, 1990-95, sr. v.p. corp. affairs, 1995—. Chair Weyerhaeuser Co. Found.; bd. dirs. Wash. Coun. Internat. Trade. Bd. dirs. U. Puget Sound, Zion Preparatory Acad., Pub. Affairs Coun., Discovery Inst., Nature Conservancy. Office: Weyerhaeuser Co PO Box 9777 Federal Way WA 98063-9777

HOGARTY, CHARLES J. automotive executive; b. 1941; Pres. Keystone Automotive Industries, Inc., Pomona, Calif., 1987—, COO, 1987-97, CEO, 1997—, also bd. dirs. Mem. Aftermarket Body Parts Assn. (bd. dirs. 1984-93, pres. 1989, chmn. 1990). Office: Keystone Automotive Industry Inc 700 E Bonita Ave Pomona CA 91767

HOGGARTH, KAREN, lumber company executive; CFO, treas. Jeld-Wen, Inc., Klamath Falls, Oreg. Office: Jeld-Wen Inc 3303 Lakeport Blvd Klamath Falls OR 97601-1017 Fax: (541) 885-7425

HOGLUND, RICHARD FRANK, research and technical executive; b. Chgo., Mar. 22, 1933; s. Reuben Ture and Margaret Mabel (Thayer) H.; m. Arlene Diana Bieniasz, Jan. 7, 1956 (dec. Mar. 1986); children: Terrence, David, Mark; m. Susan Annette Vee, Feb. 10, 1987. Student, Valparaiso U., 1949-51; BS in Mech. Engring, Northwestern U., 1954, MS in Mech. Engring. (Gen. Electric fellow), 1955, PhD (Royal Cabell fellow), 1960. Dept. head Ford Aeronutronic, 1960-63; assoc. prof. aerospace engring., lab. dir. Purdue U., 1963-69; prof. aerospace engring. Ga. Inst. Tech., 1969; chief scientist Atlantic Research Corp., 1969-72; head ocean monitoring and control, chief advanced concepts tech. Def. Advanced Research Research Projects Agy., 1972-75; staff scientist Phys. Dynamics, Inc., Arlington, Va., 1975-77; v.p. Ops. Research, Inc., Silver Spring, Md., 1977; dep. asst. sec. of navy for research and advanced tech. and concepts Dept. Navy, Washington, 1977-80; sr. v.p. ORI, Inc., Silver Spring, Md., 1980-89; exec. v.p. Arete Assocs., Arlington, Va., 1989-90; staff v.p. undersea warfare Gen. Dynamics Corps., 1990-92; cons., 1993—. Contbr. articles to profl. jours.; editor: Energy Sources and Energy Conversion, 1967. Recipient Def. Meritorious Civilian Service medal Dept. Def., 1975 Home and Office: 32 Merill Dr Palm Desert CA 92260-0614

HOGNESS, JOHN RUSTEN, physician, academic administrator; b. Oakland, Calif., June 27, 1922; s. Thorfin R. and Phoebe (Swenson) H. Student, Haverford Coll., 1939-42, D.Sc. (hon.), 1973; B.S., U. Chgo., 1943, M.D., 1946; D.Sc. (hon.), Med. Coll. Ohio at Toledo, 1972; LL.D., George Washington U., 1973; D.Litt., Thomas Jefferson U., 1980. Diplomate: Am. Bd. Internal Medicine. Intern medicine Presbyn. Hosp., N.Y.C., 1946-47, asst. resident, 1949-50; chief resident King County Hosp., Seattle, 1950-51; asst. U. Wash. Sch. Medicine, 1950-52, Am. Heart Assn. research fellow, 1951-52, mem. faculty, 1954-71, prof. medicine, 1964-71, med. dir. univ. hosp., 1958-63, dean, chmn. bd. health scis., 1964-69, exec. v.p. univ., 1969-70; dir. Health Scis. Ctr., 1970-71; pres. Inst. Medicine, Nat. Acad. Scis., 1971-74; prof. medicine George Washington U., 1972-74; pres. U. Wash., Seattle, 1974-79, pres. emeritus, 1979—, prof. medicine, 1974-79; pres. Assn. Acad. Health Ctrs., 1979-88. Disting. professorial lectr. dept. medicine Georgetown U., 1983-88; prof. Sch. Pub. Health, U. Wash., 1989-92; provost Hahnemann U., 1992-93; mem. commr.'s adv. com. on exempt orgns. IRS, 1969-71; mem. adv. com. for environ. scis. NSF, 1970-71, adv. com. to dir. NIH, 1970-71; mem. Nat. Cancer Adv. Bd., 1972-76, Nat. Sci. Bd., 1976-82; trustee China Med. Bd., 1965-92; mem. selection com. for Rockefeller pub. service awards Princeton U., 1976-82; chmn. med. injury compensation study steering com. Inst. Medicine, NAS; mem. council for biol. scis. Pritzker Sch. Medicine, U. Chgo., 1977-89; chmn. adv. panel on cost-effectiveness of med. techs. Office Tech. Assessment, U.S. Congress, 1978-80, chmn. study sect. for health care tech. assessment Nat. Ctr. for Health Svcs. Rsch. and Health Care Tech. Assessment, 1985-88; pres. Sun Valley Forum on Nat. Health, 1986-94; dir. Inst. for Health Policy Edn. and Rsch., U. Tex. Health Sci. Ctr., Houston, 1988; mem. Council Health Care Tech., HEW; adv. panel for study fin. grad. med. edn. Dept. Health and Human Services, 1980-87; chmn. com. to evaluate the artificial heart, Inst. Medicine, NAS, 1990-91. Contbr. articles to profl. jours. Trustee Case Western Res. U., 1972-73. Served with AUS, 1947-49. Johns Hopkins U. Centennial scholar, 1976; recipient Disting. Service award Med. Alumni Assn. U. Chgo., 1966, Profl. Achievement award Alumni Assn. U. Chgo., 1973; Convocation medal Am. Coll. Cardiology, 1973; Cartwright medal Columbia U. Coll. Physicians and Surgeons, 1978; Carel C. Koch Meml. award Am. Acad. Optometry, Toronto, 1986. Master ACP (regent 1987-2000); fellow AAAS, Am. Acad. Arts and Scis.; mem. NAS, Inst. Medicine, Assn. Am. Physicians, Assn. Am. Med. Colls. (exec. council, chmn.-elect coun. of deans 1968-69), Alpha Omega Alpha. Office: 514 Lost River Rd Mazama WA 98833-9700

HOGUE, BOB, state senator; b. Whittier, Calif., Sept. 7, 1953; m. Elaine Hogue; children: Jessica, Becky, Jeff, Amanda. BS in Bus., U. So. Calif., 1975. CPA, Hawaii. Acct. Price Waterhouse and Co.; instr. U. Hawaii, U. No. Iowa, Columbia Sch. Broadcasting; Rep. senator dist. 24 Hawaii State Senate. Mem. commerce, consumer protection, housing, health and human svcs., edn. and agr. coms. Hawaii State Senate. Sportscaster KHON-TV, Honolulu, KCRA-TV, Sacramento, KWWL-TV, Waterloo, Iowa, KTIV-TV, Sioux City, KFBB-TV, Great Falls, Mont.; columnist MidWeek; play-by-play announcer U. Iowa, U. Hawaii, HPU. Coach Kailua Basketball Assn., Kailua Am. Little League; vol. Am. Heart Assn., Am. Cancer Soc., Hawaii Arthritic Found. Office: Hawaii State Senate State Capitol Rm 204 415 S Beretania St Honolulu HI 96813 Fax: 808 587-7220. E-mail: senhogue@Capitol.hawaii.gov

HOHNER, KENNETH DWAYNE, retired fodder company executive; b. St. John, Kans., June 24, 1934; s. Courtney Clinton and Mildred Lucile (Forrester) H.; m. Sherry Eloi Anice Edens, Feb. 14, 1961; children: Katrina, Melissa, Steven, Michael. BS in Geol. Engring., U. Kans., 1957. Geophysicist Mobil Oil Corp., New Orleans, Anchorage, Denver, 1957-72; sr. geophysicist Amerada Hess Corp., Houston, 1972-75, ARAMCO, London, 1975-79; far east area geophysicist Hamilton Bros., Denver, 1979-83; owner Hohner Poultry Farm, Erie, Colo., 1979-94; pres. Hohner Custom Feed, Inc., Erie, 1982-94. Mem. Soc. Exploration Geophysicists. Home: 1201 W Thornton Pkwy Lot 390 Denver CO 80260-5424

HOHNHORST, JOHN CHARLES, lawyer; b. Jerome, Idaho, Dec. 25, 1952; m. Raelene Casper; children: Jennifer, Rachel, John. BS in Polit. Sci./Pub. Adminstrn., U. Idaho, 1975, JD cum laude, 1978. Bar: Idaho 1978, U.S. Dist. Ct. Idaho 1978, U.S. Ct. Appeals (9th cir.) 1980, U.S. Ct. Claims 1983, U.S. Supreme Ct. 1987. Adminstrv. asst. to Sen. John M. Barker Idaho State Senate, 1975; ptnr. Hepworth, Lezamiz & Hohnhorst, Twin Falls, Idaho, 1978—. Contbr. articles to profl. jours. Mem. planning & zoning commn. City of Twin Falls, 1987-90. Mem. ABA, ATLA, Idaho State Bar (commr. 1990-93, pres. 1993), Idaho Trial Lawyers Assn. (regional dir. 1985-86), 5th Dist. Bar Assn. (treas. 1987-88, v.p. 1988-89, pres. 1989-90), Am. Acad. Appellate Lawyers, Greater Twin Falls C. of C. (chmn. magic valley leadership program 1988-89, bd. dirs. 1989-92), Phi Kappa Tau (Beta Gamma chpt., Phi award 1988). Office: Hepworth Lezamiz & Hohnhorst PO Box 389 133 Shoshone St N Twin Falls ID 83301-6150

HOI, SAMUEL CHUEN-TSUNG, art school president; b. Hong Kong, Mar. 25, 1958; came to U.S., 1975; AB, Columbia Coll., 1980; JD, Columbia Law Sch., 1983; AAS, Parsons Sch. Design, N.Y.C., 1986. Dir. AAS program Parsons Sch. Design, N.Y.C., 1987-88, dir. parsons Paris, 1988-91; dean Corcoran Sch. Art, Washington, 1991-2000; pres. Otic Coll. Art and Design, L.A., 2000—. Mem., bd. dirs. Leadership Washington, 1996. Mem. Assn. Ind. Colls. of Art and Design, Nat. Assn. Schs. Art and Design (bd. dirs.). Office: Otis Coll Art and Design 9045 Lincoln Blvd Los Angeles CA 90045-3505

HOLBEIN, JACK R. career officer; BA in Mktg. and Mgmt., St. Joseph's Coll., Rensselaer, Ind., 1971; Diploma, Squadron Officer Sch., 1977; MA in Mgmt., Webster U., 1981; Diploma, Air Command and Staff Coll., 1985, Nat. War Coll., 1992. Commd. 2d lt. USAF, 1971, advanced through ranks to brig. gen., 1997; various assignments to comdr. 16th Opers. Group, Hurlburt Field, Fla., 1993-94; dep. chief of staff U.S. Spl. Opers. Command, MacDill AFB, 1994-96; comdr. 314th Airlift Wing, Little Rock AFB, Ark., 1996-98, Spl. Opers. Command, Pacific, Camp H.M. Smith, Hawaii, 1998—. Decorated Def. Superior Svc. medal with oak leaf cluster, Legion of Merit, Meritorious Svc. medal with four oak leaf clusters, Air Force Commendation medal, Army Commendation medal, others. Office: SOCPAC/CC Camp HM Camp H M Smith HI 96861

HOLBROOK, DONALD BENSON, lawyer; b. Salt Lake City, Jan. 4, 1925; s. Robert Sweeten and Kinnie Benson H.; m. Bety J. Gilchrist, Apr. 23, 1947; children: Mark, Thomas, Gregory, Mary. Student, Colo. Coll., U. Utah; JD, U. Utah, 1952, PhD (hon.), 1990; PhD (hon.), HHD (hon.), Utah Valley C.C., 1990; DFA (hon.), 1990; DHL (hon.), Salt Lake City C.C. Bar: Utah 1953. Pres. Jones Waldo, Holbrook and McDonough, Salt Lake City, 1973-89; of counsel, 1995—. Exec. v.p., legal officer Am. Stores Co., 1990-95; bd. dirs. Blue Cross/Blue Shield Utah, The Regence Group; commr. Utah Bar, 1983-87; bd. advs. Mountain Bell, 1974-84. Editor in chief: Utah Law Rev., 1951-52. Bd. dirs. Utah Ass. UN, 1963-64; bd. dirs., exec. com. Utah Coop. Assn., 1962-83, vice chmn., 1970-73, chmn., 1974-82, 83-85; chmn. Utah Partnership for Ednl. and Econ. devel., 1987-95; pres. and chmn. bd. Ballet West, 1982-84; bd. dirs. Utah Dem. Party, exec. sec., 1955-65, exec. com., 1956-65; chmn. antitrust and monopoly subcom. Western States Dem. Conf., 1962-66; campaign mgr. Gov. Calvin L. Rampton, 1964-68; candidate for U.S. Senate, 1964; commr. Western Interstate Commn. on Higher Edn., 1978-83, chmn., 1982. Recipient Disting. Alumni award U. Utah, 1985, Resolution of Appreciation Utah Ste Bd. Regents, 1990, Light of Learning award Utah State Bd. Edn., 1994; named Lawyer of Yr. Utah State Bar, 1990. Fellow Internat. Acad. Trial Lawyers, Am. Bar Found.; mem. U. Utah Coll. Law Alumni Assn. (pres. 1957), ABA (gen. chmn. Rocky Mountain region 1962, Utha chmn., mem. com. sect. corp., banking, bus. law 1962-95), Utah Bar Assn. (bd. commrs. 1982-87, chmn. com. World Peace Through Law 1964, pres. 1964-65), Order of the Coif (award for contbns. to law, scholarship and cmty. svc. 1968), Salt Lake City Country Club, Beta Theta Phi, Phi Kappa Phi, Delta Theta Phi (disting. alumni award 1967). Home: 1752 Laurelhurst Dr Salt Lake City UT 84108-3310

HOLBROOK, MEGHAN ZANOLLI, fundraiser, public relations specialist, political organization chairman; BS in English and Edn., U. Tenn., 1971, postgrad., 1978-83. Dir. ancillary svcs. Ridgeview Psychiat. Hosp., Oak Ridge, Tenn., 1971-83; therapist The Children's Ctr., Salt Lake City, 1985-86; mgr. corp. contbns. Sundance Inst. and Film Festival, Salt Lake City, 1989-91; fund raising and pub. rels. cons. Salt Lake City, 1992—. Fundraiser congl. campaign Wayne Owens, 1986, bus. liaison, 1986-88; fin. dir. gubernatorial campaign Ted Wilson, 1988, mayoral campaign Deedee Corradini, 1991; campaign mgr. gubernatorial campaign Stewart Hanson, 1991-92; del. Dem. Nat. Conv., 1996; chair Utah State Dem. Party, 1996—; mem. bd. dirs. Sundance Inst., 1989—, Inst. at Deer Valley, 1995—; mem. Utah Air Travel Commn., 1996—; mem. pres.'s adv. com. on arts Kennedy Ctr., Washington, 1996—. Mem. Assn. State Dem. Chairs (exec. com. 1998—). Home: 775 Hilltop Rd Salt Lake City UT 84103-3311 Office: 455 S 300 E Ste 102 Salt Lake City UT 84111-3222

HOLDEN, FREDERICK DOUGLASS, JR. lawyer; b. Stockton, Calif., Nov. 21, 1949; s. Frederick Douglass and Sarah Frances (Young) H.; m. Patricia Brierton, June 25, 1988; children: Elizabeth, Andrew. BA, U. Calif., Santa Barbara, 1971; JD, U. Calif., Davis, 1974. Bar: Calif. 1974, U.S. Dist. Ct. (no., cen., ea. and so. dists.) Calif. 1974, U.S. Ct. Appeals (9th cir.) 1974, D.C. 1996, U.S. Dist. Ct. D.C. 1996, U.S. Supreme Ct. 2001. Assoc. Brobeck, Phleger & Harrison LLP, San Francisco, 1974-81; ptnr. Brobeck, Phleger & Harrison, San Francisco, 1981—. Mem. faculty Practising Law Inst., 1990; speaker Nat. Conf. Bankruptcy Judges, 1987, 91, Banking Law Inst., 1986, Calif. Continuing Legal Edn. of Bar, Calif., 1983-85, Calif. State Bar, 1993. Mng. editor U. Calif. Davis Law Rev., 1974. Fellow Am. Coll. Bankruptcy; mem. ABA (bus. bankruptcy com., spkr. 1991, 95), Calif. Bar Assn. (commendation 1983), San Francisco Bar Assn. (cert. appreciation 1985, 88, 90, 95), Turnaround Mgmt. Assn. (dir., sec. 1994-96), Am. Bankruptcy Inst., San Francisco Yacht Club, Sigma Pi (pres. 1970). Democrat. Avocations: triathlons, skiing, sailing. Home: 140 Bella Vista Ave Belvedere CA 94920-2466 Office: Brobeck Phleger & Harrison Spear St Tower 1 Market Plz Ste 341 San Francisco CA 94105-1420 E-mail: fholden@brobeck.com

HOLDEN, MICHAEL JOHN, lawyer; b. Sheboygan, Wis., Sept. 29, 1955; s. John Robert and Hilda H.; m. Mary Louise Turkovich, Apr. 9, 1983; children: John, Anne. AB, U. Mich., 1977; JD, Duke U., 1980. Bar: Ariz. 1980, U.S. Dist. Ct. Ariz. 1980, U.S. Ct. Appeals (9th cir.) 1980. Assoc. Lewis and Roca, Phoenix, 1980-85, ptnr., 1985-2000, Holden Walker PLC, Phoenix, 2000—. Mem. ABA, Am. Subcontractors Assn. Ariz. (bd. dirs. 1993), Associated Gen. Contractors Ariz. (assoc.), Ariz. State Bar (chmn. constrn. law sect. 1987-89). Office: Holden Walker PLC 2425 E Camelback Rd Ste 800 Phoenix AZ 85016-4208 E-mail: holden@holdenwalker.com

HOLDEN, RIC R. state legislator, farmer, rancher; b. Spokane, Wash., Aug. 31, 1961; m. Jan Holden; 3 children. BA, Mont. State U., 1984. Farmer, rancher; ins. rep.; mem. Mont. Senate, Dist. 1, Helena, 1994—. Active Dawson County 4-H Clubs, ABC Baseball. Mem. Mont. Stock Growers Assn., Mont. Wool Growers Assn., NRA, Mont. Farm Bur., Dawnson County Livestock Prodn. Assn. Republican. Lutheran. Home: 164 Road 253 Glendive MT 59330-9438

HOLDER, HAROLD D. public health administrator, communications specialist, educator; b. Raleigh, N.C., Aug. 9, 1939; AB in History and Journalism, Samford U., 1961; MA in Comm., Syracuse U., 1962, PhD, 1965. Dir. Comm. Rsch. Ctr., asst. prof. Dept. Journalism and Oral Comm. Baylor U., Tex., 1965-67; rsch. scientist divsn. rsch., dir. systems analysis and program evaluation N.C. Dept. Mental Health, Raleigh, 1967-69; assoc. prof., mem. grad. faculty dept. Sociology N.C. State U., Raleigh, 1967-75; site mgr. The Human Ecology Inst., Wellesley, Mass., 1973-75, sr. scientist Chapel Hill, N.C., 1977-87, dir., 1980-87; mgr. devel. City of Portsmouth, Va., 1975-76; lectr. dept. Health Adminstrn. Sch. Pub. Health U. N.C., Chapel Hill, 1980-86; dir. prevention rsch. ctr. Pacific Inst. Rsch. and Evaluation, Berkeley, Calif., 1987—; lectr. health edn. program Sch. Pub. Health U. Calif., Berkeley, 1987—. Vis. prof. Newhouse Comm. Ctr., 1966, U. N.C. Chapel Hill, 1979-80; guest lectr. Sch. Pub. Health U. Carolina, Chapel Hill, 1967-68, dept. Psychiatry, 1967-68; instr. advanced exec. systems N.C. Dept. Mental Health, 1967-69; program coord. John Ulmstead Disting. Lecture Series, 1970; ednl. evaluator Syracuse (N.Y.) Sch. Dist., 1971-73; trainer systems approaches and model bldg., dynamo computer simulation, United Meth. Ch., N.Y., 1972-73; sr. analyst Caseway, Inc., Brockton, Mass., 1977-78; mem. psycho-social internal review group Office Sci. Affairs Nat. Inst. Alcohol Abuse and Alcoholism, 1983-87, chmn. 1986-87; cons. Nat. Inst. Alcohol Abuse and Alcoholism, Washington, Tex. Ednl. Agy., Austin, Ctrl. Tex. Regional Edn. Ctr., James Connally Tech. Inst., Waco, Tex., Tech. Edn. Rsch. Ctr., Cambridge, Mass., U. N.C., Chapel Hill, N.C. Dept. Health, Child Advocacy Ctr., Durham, United Meth. Ch., N.Y.C., NIMH, Svcs. Integration Tech. Inst., Boston, Learning Inst. N.C; presenter, chairperson numerous confs. Editor: Advances in Substance Abuse: Behavioral and Biological Rsch., 1987; co-editor: Monitoring Child Service Agencies: A Guide for Child Advocacy Groups, 1974, Control Issues in Alcohol Prevention: State and Local Designs for the 80s, 1984, OSAP Prevention Monograph 4: Research, Action and the Community: Experiences in the Prevention of Alcohol and Other Drug Problems, 1990, Community Prevention Trials for Alcohol Problems: Methodological Issues, 1992; mem. editorial bd. Alcohol Health and Research World, 1990—; contbr. chpts. to books, articles to profl. jours. Bd. dirs. Ctrl. Tex. Rsch. Coun., 1965-67. Newhouse Rsch. fellow Syracuse U., 1961-65. Mem. APHA (alcohol and drug sect.), Am. Sociol. Assn., Am. Assn. Pub. Opinion Rsch.Nat. Soc. Study Comm., Nat. Assn. Pub. Health Policy (mem. alcohol policy com., sec./treas. 1985-86), Soc. Gen. Systems Rsch. (nat. coms. social systems, health systems), Rsch. Soc. Alcoholism (com. nat. advocacy), Soc. Health Svcs. Rsch. Office: Prevention Rsch Ctr Pacific Inst Rsch & Evaluation 2150 Shattuck Ave Ste 900 Berkeley CA 94704-1306

HOLDER, HAROLD DOUGLAS, SR. investor, industrialist, recreational executive; b. Anniston, Ala., June 25, 1931; s. William Chester and Lucile (Kadle) H.; m. Anna Maria Yaccarino, 1996; children: Debra Holder Carnaroli, Harold Douglas Jr. Student, Anniston Bus. Coll., 1949, Jacksonville State U., 1954-57, Druitt Sch. Speech, 1962. Dept. mgr. Sears, Roebuck & Co., Anniston, 1954-57, merchandising mgr. Atlanta, 1957-59, dir. coll. recruiting, 1959-61, dir. exec. devel. program, 1961, asst. personnel dir., 1962-63, store mgr. Cocoa, Fla., 1965-67, Ocala, 1963-65, asst. zone mgr. Atlanta, 1967-68, asst. gen. mgr. mdse., 1968-69, sales promotion mgr. So. area, 1968; pres., bd. dirs. Cunningham Drug Stores, Inc., Detroit, 1969-70; v.p. Interstate Stores, 1971; pres., bd. dirs. Rahall Communications Corp., 1971-73; chmn. bd., chief exec. officer, dir. Am. Agronomics Corp., 1973-86; pres. Harold Holder Leasing; mng. dir. The

Holder Group, Inc., 1987—. CEO, bd. dirs. Cutler Mfg. Corp., 1989-2000, Atlas Aircraft Corp., 1987-2000; mem. exec. com., bd. dirs. Coastland Corp., Fla., 1979-84; pres., bd. dirs. Golden Harvest, Inc., 1976-88; bd. dirs., treas. Dome Products, Inc., 1989-2000; CEO Casino Mgmt. Svcs. Internat., 1999—. Author: Don't Shoot, I'm Only a Trainee, 1975. Chmn., bd. dirs. Miracle, Inc., Brevard County; chmn. United Appeal, Ocala, Fla., 1964, Cocoa, Fla., 1966; bd. dirs. United Way Hillsborough County (Fla.); chmn. Heart Fund Drive, Ocala, 1964, Marion (Fla.) Com. of 100; bd. dirs. So. Coll. Placement Assn., Am. Acad. Achievement; bd. dirs. Marion chpt. ARC, Opera Arts Assn.; exec. com. Share, U. Fla.; bd. trustees U. Tampa; chmn. bd. trustees, trustee emeritus Eckerd Coll. With USMC, 1950-53. Endowed Harold D. Holder chair of mgmt. Eckerd Coll. Recipient Disting. Service award Marion County 4-H Club, 1965, Golden Plate award, 1983, Champion of Higher Edn. award, 1982, Fla. NAACP Humanitarian award, 1984 Mem. Chief Execs. Forum, C. of C. (chmn. beautification com., retail bus. com.), Young Pres. Orgn. (past chmn. Fla. chpt.), Univ. Club, Tampa Yacht and Country Club. Episcopalian. Office: Casino Mgmt Svcs Internat PO Box 10750 Reno NV 89510

HOLDING, R(OBERT) E(ARL), oil company executive; Pres. Sinclair Oil Corp., Salt Lake City, bd. dirs., now CEO. Office: Sinclair Oil Corp PO Box 30825 Salt Lake City UT 84130

HOLDSWORTH, RAY W. architectural firm executive; Pres., CEO Daniel Mann Johnson Mendenhall, L.A., 1989—. Office: Daniel Mann Johnson Mendenhall 3250 Wilshire Blvd Fl 4 Los Angeles CA 90010-1577

HOLDT, TERRY, computer company executive; CEO, pres., chmn. S3, Santa Clara, Calif. Office: S3 PO Box 58058 2841 Mission College Blvd Santa Clara CA 95052-8058

HOLL, WALTER JOHN, architect, interior designer; b. Richardton, N.D., May 14, 1922; s. John and Rose Mary Holl; m. Eleanor Mary Triervieler, Jan. 23, 1943; children: Mark Walter, Michael John, Randolph Gregory, Linda Michelle, Timothy James, John Walter. student, student in photography, Clarke Coll., 1981. Licensed arch., Calif., interior designer, Ill.; cert. Nat. Coun. for Interior Design Qualifications. Steel detailer, estimator E.J. Voggenthaler Co., Dubuque, Iowa, 1941-42; engr., also methods developer Marinship Corp., Sausalito, Calif., 1942-44; ptnr. Holl & Everly, Dubuque, Iowa, 1946-47; prin. Holl Designing Co., also W. Holl & Assocs., Dubuque, San Francisco, 1947-87, Walter J. Holl, Arch., Burlingame, Calif., 1987, 89, San Diego, 1989—. Cons. Clarke Coll. Art Students, Dubuque, 1953-61; commd. arch., interior designer, constructor renovations and hist. preservation Dubuque County Courthouse, 1978-85; mem. convoy USCG Ofcl. Presdl. Security Patrol, 1979; oral exam commr. Calif. Bd. Archtl. Examiners, 1994-96; cert. mem. Calif. State Office Emergency Svc.; participant The Brit. Coun.-Archs. Study Tour, Belfast, No. Ireland, 1995; juror Nat. Coun. for Interior Design Qualification, 1996, 98. Chmn. Dubuque Housing Rehab. Commn., 1976-77. With AUS, 1944-46, ETO. Decorated 2 bronze stars; recipient Nat. Bldg. Design awards, 1968, 69, 73, 94. Mem. AIA (bd. dirs. 1993-99, pres.-elect north county sect. San Diego chpt. 1995, pres. 1996, bldg. codes and stds. com. San Diego chpt. 1998-99), USCG Aux. (comdr. 1975-78), Am. Soc. Interior Designers (profl.), Am. Arbitration Assn. (panel arbitrators), Inst. Bus. Designers (profl. Chgo. chpt.), Dubuque Golf and Country Club (bldg. commn. 1953-54), Julien Dubuque Yacht Club (commodore 1974-75), Mchts. and Mfrs. Club (Chgo.). Roman Catholic. Achievements include patent for castered pallet. Home and Office: Walter J Holl Architect Penthouse 126 11255 Tierrasanta Blvd San Diego CA 92124-2890

HOLLADAY, SUSAN, publishing executive; V.p., CFO San Jose (Calif.) Mercury News. Office: San Jose Mercury News 750 Ridder Park Dr San Jose CA 95190-0001

HOLLAND, GARY NORMAN, ophthalmologist, educator; b. Long Beach, Calif., July 30, 1953; s. Richard L. and Edith (Hewson) H. MD, UCLA, 1979. Diplomate Am. Bd. Ophthalmology, Nat. Bd. Med. Examiners; lic. MD, Calif., Ga. Intern in internal medicine UCLA, 1979-80; resident in ophthalmology Jules Stein Eye Inst., L.A., 1980-83; fellowship in uveitis rsch. Proctor Found. U. Calif. San Francisco, 1983-84; cornea fellowship Emory U. Med. Sch., Atlanta, 1984-85; prof. ophthalmology Jules Stein Eye Inst. UCLA, 1985—. Assoc. editor Am. Jour. Ophthalmology, 1993—. Mem. Am. Uveitis Soc. Office: UCLA 100 Stein Plz Los Angeles CA 90095-7003

HOLLAND, H. RUSSEL, federal judge; b. 1936; m. Diane Holland; 3 children. BBA, U. Mich., 1958, LLB, 1961. With Alaska Ct. System, Anchorage, 1961, U.S. Atty.'s Office, Dept. Justice, Anchorage, 1963-65; assoc. Stevens & Savage, Anchorage, 1965-66; ptnr. Stevens, Savage, Holland, Erwin & Edwards, Anchorage, 1967-68; sole practice Anchorage, 1968-70; ptnr. Holland & Thornton, Anchorage, 1970-78, Holland, Thornton & Trefry, Anchorage, 1978, Holland & Trefry, Anchorage, 1978-84, Trefry & Brecht, Anchorage, 1984; judge U.S. Dist. Ct. Alaska, Anchorage, 1984—. Mem. ABA, Alaska Bar Assn., Anchorage Bar Assn. Office: US Dist Ct 222 W 7th Ave Unit 54 Anchorage AK 99513-7504

HOLLAND, MICHAEL JAMES, computer services administrator; b. N.Y.C., Nov. 20, 1950; s. Robert Frederick and Virginia June (Wilcox) H.; Anita Garay, Jan. 5, 1981 (Aug. 1989); 1 child, Melanie. BA in Comparative Lit., Bklyn. Coll., 1972. Enlisted USN, 1975, advanced to CPO, 1989; field med. technician 3rd Marine Divsn., Okinawa, Japan, 1976-77, 1st Marine Divsn., Camp Pendleton, Calif., 1978-79; clin. supr. Naval Hosp. Subic Bay, Philippines, 1979-81; dept. head Tng. Ctr. USMCR, Johnson City, Tenn., 1981-84; clin. supr. No. Tng. Area, Okinawa, 1984-85, 3rd Marine Air Wing, Camp Pendleton, 1985-88; cons. Naval Regional Med. Command, San Diego, 1988-90; system analyst Naval Med. Info. Mgmt. Ctr. Detachment, San Diego, 1990-92; computer svcs. adminstr. U.S. Naval Hosp., Guam, 1993-95; ret., 1995; svc. rep. Pacific Bell, 1997—. Mem. Fleet Res. Assn., Comm. Workers Am., Nat. City C. of C. (com. 1989-91).

HOLLANDER, DANIEL, gastroenterologist, medical educator; b. Mar. 3, 1939; Student, UCLA, to 1960; MD, Baylor U., 1964. Diplomate Am. Bd. Internal Medicine, Am. Bd. Gastroenterology. Intern Phila. Gen. Hosp., 1964-65; resident in internal medicine Med. Ctr., U. Kans., Kansas City, 1965-67; NIH rsch. fellow in gastroenterology U. Wash., Seattle, 1967-69; asst. prof. medicine Albany (N.Y.) Med. Coll., Union U., 1971-73, assoc. prof., 1973; assoc. prof. medicine, head div. gastroenterology Wayne State U., Detroit, 1973-77, prof. medicine, head div. gastroenterology, 1977-78, U. Calif., Irvine, 1978-94, prof. physiology and biophysics, 1981-94, assoc. dean for rsch. and program devel. Coll. Medicine, 1984-85, assoc. dean for acad. affairs, 1985-89, sr. assoc. dean for clin. affairs, 1989-91, chief gastroenterology Irvine Med. Ctr., 1979-94; exec. dean Sch. of Medicine U. Kans., Kansas City, 1994-95; chief med. officer Sierra Pacific Network, San Francisco, 1996-98; prof. medicine U. Calif., San Francisco, 1996-98; pres., CEO Harbor-UCLA, Rsch. and Edn. Inst., 1998-2001; prof. medicine UCLA, 1998—, dir. inflammatory bowel grants program, ELI and EDYTHE Broad Found., 2001—. Attending physician, attending gastroenterologist Albany Med. Ctr. Hosp., 1971-73; chief gastroenterology svc., attending physician Harper Hosp., Detroit, 1973-78; cons. in gastroenterology Children's, Detroit Gen. and VA hosps., 1973-78; chief gastroenterology VA Med. Ctr., Long Beach, Calif., 1978-80; chmn. Gastrointestinal Gerontology Rsch. Group, 1988-89; vis. scientist dept. molecular medicine U. Auckland, New Zealand, 1990-91; vis. prof., invited speaker numerous other univs., profl. meetings, confs. Author: (with G. Gitnick, H. Kaplowitz, I.M. Samloff, L.I. Schoenfield) Principles and Practice of Gastroenterology and Hepatology, 1988, (with A. Tarnawski) Gastic Cytoprotection—A Clinician's Guide, 1989, (with Porro G. Bianchi) Treatment of Digestive Disease with Sucralfate, 1989; mem. editl. bd., reviewer Can. Jour. Gastroenterology; contbr. numerous articles, revs. to profl. jours., book chpt. With USAF, 1969-71. Calif. Heart Assn. rsch. fellow, 1960; Fogarty Sr. Internat. fellow Oxford (Eng.) U., 1984-85; grantee NIH, Nat. Inst. on Aging, Nat. Insts. Arthritis, Metabolism and Digestive Diseases, Skillman Found., VA, Goldsmith Found., Internat. Pharm. Products. Mem. ACP (A. Blaine traveling scholar 1973), Am. Fedn. for Clin. Rsch. (pres. Midwestern sect. 1979-80), Am. Gastroent. Assn., Am. Physiol. Soc., Am. Soc. for Clin. Investigation, Orange County Gastroenterology Assn. (pres. 1986-87), Brit. Soc. Gastroenterology, European Assn. Gastroenterology, Western Assn. Physicians, Western Gut Club (pres. 1981-82), Alpha Omega Alpha. Office: The Broad Found 10900 Wilshire Blvd 12th Fl Los Angeles CA 90024

HOLLANDSWORTH, TODD MATHEW, professional baseball player; b. Dayton, Ohio, Apr. 20, 1973; Baseball player L.A. Dodgers, 1995—. Named Nat. League Rookie of the Yr. Baseball Writer's Assn. of Am., 1996.

HOLLENBECK, DOROTHY ROSE, special education educator; b. Yakima, Wash., May 8, 1941; d. George Milford and Blance Mary (McCarthy) Hollenbeck; m. Thomas M. Chambers, Aug. 14, 1971; adopted children: David, Monique, Christopher, George, Elizabeth. BS in Speech and Lang. Therapy, Marquette U., 1964; MA in Spl. Edn., San Francisco State U., 1969. Speech pathologist Mpls. Pub. Schs., 1964-65, Milbrae (Calif.) Sch. Dist., 1964-65; reading specialist Dept. Def., Landstuhl, Germany, 1970-71; tchr. children with extreme learning problems Portland (Oreg.) Public Schs., 1971-80, dept. chmn. spl. edn., 1980-84, program specialist program devel., 1984-86, diagnostic specialist assessment program spl. edn., 1986-94; speech and lang. pathologist, spl. edn. tchr. Chinacum, Washington Sch. Dist., 1995-2000, prin., 2000—. Cert. instr. develop. therapy U. Ga., 1982; instr. Portland State U., D.C.E., 1982, 83. Author: PEACHES (Pre-Sch. Ednl. Adaptation for Children Who Are Handicapped), 1978. HEW Dept. Rehab. fellow, 1969. Mem. Am. Speech and Hearing Assn. (cert. in clin. competence), Common Cause, Cousteau Soc., NEA, Oreg. Edn. Assn., Nat. Council Exceptional Children (presenter nat. conv. 1984). Democrat. Roman Catholic. Home: 505 Garfield St Port Townsend WA 98368-4405 Office: Chinacum Pub Schs PO Box 278 Chimacum WA 98325-0278

HOLLERAN, JOHN W. lawyer; b. Poughkeepsie, N.Y., June 17, 1954; BA, Gonzaga U., 1976, JD, 1979. Bar: Wash. 1979, Idaho, 1980, Calif. 1987. Counsel Boise (Idaho) Cascade Corp., 1979-83, assoc. gen. counsel, 1983-91, v.p., gen. counsel, 1991-96, sr. v.p., gen. counsel, 1996—. Chmn. Fibre Box Assn. Legal adv. com., 1989-91; bd. advisors Gonzaga U. Sch. Law, 1991—; mem. Idaho Vol. Lawyers Program Policy Coun., 1991—. Mem. ABA, Wash. State Bar Assn., Boise Bar Assn., Idaho State Bar, State Bar Calif., Am. Corp. Counsel Assn. Office: Boise Cascade Corp PO Box 50 1111 W Jefferson St Boise ID 83728-0071

HOLLIDAY, THOMAS EDGAR, lawyer; b. Ft. Hood, Tex., July 3, 1948; s. William Lamont and Eileen (Fiebig) H.; m. Linda Loudon, May 7, 1988; children: Devon M., Trey S. BA, Stanford U., 1971; JD, U. So. Calif., 1974. Bar: Calif. 1974. Assoc. Gibson, Dunn & Crutcher LLP, L.A., 1974-81; ptnr. Gibson, Dunn & Crutcher, L.A., 1981—. Editor: (book, desk edition) Antitrust and Trade Regulations. Trustee S.W. Mus., L.A., 1981-98, bd. pres., 1995-97; trustee Found. for People, L.A., 1985-90, Clarkson U., 2000—; mem. L.A. Police Dept. Meml. Found. Bd. Fellow Am. Coll. Trial Lawyers; mem. Fed. Bar Assn. (exec. com. L.A. chpt. 1990, pres. 1998). Avocation: collecting Southwestern art. Office: Gibson Dunn & Crutcher LLP 333 S Grand Ave Ste 4400 Los Angeles CA 90071-3197

HOLLIGER, FRED LEE, oil company executive; b. Kansas City, Mo., Feb. 4, 1948; s. Ronald and Margorie (Klein) H.; m. Susan Lynn Harris, Oct. 6, 1972; children: Meredith, Allison, Lauren. BS in Petroleum Engring., U. Mo., Rolla, 1970; postgrad., U. Mich., 1978. Petroleum engr. Transok Pipeline Co., Tulsa, 1971; reservoir engr. No. Natural Gas Co., Omaha, 1972-73, project mgr. Lyons, Kans., 1974-76, area mgr. Great Bend, 1977-79, gen. mgr. mktg. Omaha, 1980-83, v.p. gas supply, 1984-85, v.p. mktg., 1986, pres., COO, 1987-88; exec. v.p., COO Giant Industries, Scottsdale, Ariz., 1989—. Dir. Giant Industries. Mem. Nat. Petroleum Refining Assn. (dir. 1990—), Desert Highlands Golf Club. Office: Giant Industries 23733 N Scottsdale Rd Scottsdale AZ 85255-3410

HOLLINGER, MANNFRED ALAN, pharmacologist, educator, toxicologist; b. Chgo., June 28, 1939; BS, North Park Coll., Chgo., 1961; PhD, Loyola U., Chgo., 1967. Postdoctoral fellow Stanford U., Palo Alto, Calif., 1967-69; prof. U. Calif., Davis, 1969—, chmn. dept. med. pharmacology and toxicology, 1990—. Author: Respiratory Pharmacology and Toxicology, 1985, Yearbook of Pharmacology, 1990, 91, 92; asst. editor, field editor Jour. Pharm. Exptl. Therapy, 1978—; cons. editor CRC Press, Boca Raton, Fla., 1989—. Mem. Yolo County Grand Jury, Woodland, Calif.; bd. dirs. Davis Little League. Burroughs-Wellcome fellow Southampton U., U.K., 1986; Fogarty sr. fellow NIH, Heidelberg (Germany) U., 1988. Office: U Calif Sch Med Dept Med Pharm Toxicol 4453 Tupper Hall Davis CA 95616

HOLLINGER, WILLIAM R. controller home builder company; BS in Bus. Adminstrn. summa cum laude, Ca. (Northridge) State U. CPA. Auditor Pricewaterhouse, L.A., 1981-87; mgr. control eval., audit Kaufman & Broad Hom, 1987, v.p., contr. Mem. Am. Inst. CPA, Ca. Soc. CPA. Office: Kaufman & Broad Home 10990 Wilshire Blvd Fl 7 Los Angeles CA 90024-3913

HOLLINGSWORTH, BOBBY G. career officer; BS in Elec. Engring., La. State Univ. Flight line officer Marine Attack Squadron 331, Beaufort, S.C.; embarkation officer Marine Attack Squadron 223, Chu Lai, South Vietnam; landing signal officer Marine Aircraft Group 12, Chu Lai, South Vietnam; asst. divsn. air officer 3rd Marine Divsn., Phu Bai, South Vietnam; combat tactics instr. Marine Training Squadron 103, Yuma, Ariz.; asst. ops. officer Marine Fighter Squadron 112, Dallas; exec. officer Marine Aircraft Group 42, Alameda, Calif.; commander Marine Attack Squadron 133, Alameda; asst. chief of staff 4th Marine Aircraft Wing, New Orleans; chief of staff II Marine Expeditionary Brigade, Camp Lejeune, N.C.; commanding gen. Marine Corps Res. Support Command, Kans. City, Mo., Fourth Force Svc. Support Group, New Orleans; deputy commander Jt. Task Force, Saudi Arabia; vice commander Marine Forces Pacific, Camp Smith, Hawaii. Decorated Legion of Merit, Distinguished Flying Cross, Def. Meritorious Svc. medal, Air Medal with numeral 5, Combat Action Ribbon, Presdl. Unit Citation with Bronze Star, Meritorious Unit Commendation, Select Marine Corps. Res. medal with Silver Star, Nat. Def. Medal with Bronze star, Armed Forces Expiditionary medal, Vietnam Svc. medal with two Bronze Stars, Navy and Marine Corps Overseas Svc. Ribbon with two Bronze Stars, Armed Forces Res. medal with hourglass Device, Rep. of Vietnam Unit Citation, Rep. Vietnam Campaing medal with 1960 Deivce. Office: U S Marine Corps Forces Pacific Camp H M Smith HI 96861

HOLLOWAY, CHARLES ARTHUR, public and private management educator; b. Whittier, Calif., May 28, 1936; s. Heber H. and Theodosia S. (Stephens) H.; m. Christina Ahlm, July 11, 1959; children: Deborah, Susan, [illegible] with honors, U. Calif., Berkeley, [illegible]; MS, UCLA, [illegible]; PhD in Bus. Adminstrn. with distinction 1969. Sr. engr. Bechtel Corp. San Francisco, 1964-65; teaching fellow UCLA, 1965-66; asst. prof. to prof. Stanford (Calif.) U., 1968—, Herbert Hoover prof. pub. and pvt. mgmt., 1980-91, assoc. dean acad. affairs Grad. Sch. Bus., 1980-87, 90-91, Kleiner Perkins Caufield and Byers prof. mgt., 1991—; dir. Axicon, Escalate Corp. Bd. dirs. Axicon, Escalate Corp. Author: Decision Making Under Uncertainty: Models and Choices, 1979, Perpetual Enterprise Machine: Seven Keys to Corporate Renewal, 1994. Bd. dirs. League to Save Redwoods. Served with USN, 1959-63. Fellow Ford Found., 1966-68 Mem. Inst. Mgmt. Sci., Ops. Rsch. Soc. Am., Stanford Integrated Mfg. Assn. (co-chair 1991-95, co-chair Stanford Ctr. for Entrepreneurial Studies 1995—). Home: 730 Santa Maria Ave Palo Alto CA 94305-8438 Office: Stanford U Grad Sch Bus Stanford CA 94305 E-mail: holloway_chuck@gsb.stanford.edu

HOLLOWAY, DAVID JAMES, political science educator; b. Dublin, Ireland, Oct. 13, 1943; came to U.S., 1983; s. James Joseph and Gertrude Mary (Kennedy) H.; m. Arlene Jean Smith, June 12, 1976; children: James, Ivor. MA, PhD, Cambridge (Eng.) U., 1964. Asst. lectr. U. Lancaster, Eng., 1967-69; rsch. assoc. Inst. for Strategic Studies, London, 1969-70; lectr. U. Edinburgh, Scotland, 1970-84, reader Scotland, 1984-86; prof. Stanford (Calif.) U., 1986—, co-dir. Ctr. Internat. Security and Arms Control, 1991-97, Raymond A. Spruance prof. in internat. history, 1997—, assoc. dean humanities and scis., 1997-98, dir. Inst. for Internat. Studies, 1999—. Dir. internat. rels. program Stanford U., 1989-91. Author: The Soviet Union and the Arms Race, 1983, Stalin and the Bomb, 1994; co-author: (with S. Drell and P. Farley) The Reagan Strategic Defense Initiative, 1985. Bd. dirs. Ploughshares Found., San Francisco, 1989—. Mem. Am. Polit. Sci. Assn., Am. Assn. for the Advancement of Slavic Studies. Avocations: opera, reading. Home: 710 Torreya Ct Palo Alto CA 94303-4160 Office: Stanford U Inst Internat Studies Encina Hall Stanford CA 94305-6055

HOLM, VANJA ADELE, developmental pediatrician, educator; b. Kiruna, Sweden, Oct. 5, 1928; came to U.S, 1955. d. C.V. Hjalmar and Elma Adele (Nystrom) H.; m. Carl Holm, June 15, 1952; children: Ingrid Adele, Erik Carl Anders. Med. Kand., Karolinska Inst., Stockholm, 1950, MD, 1955. Intern Swedish Hosp., Seattle, 1955-56; resident in pediatrics U. Wash. Sch. Medicine, Seattle, 1956, 62-64, fellow in devel. pediatrics, 1964-65, instr. pediatrics, 1965-69, asst. prof. pediatrics, 1969-81, assoc. prof. pediatrics, 1981-96, prof. emeritus, 1996—. Attending pediatrician Children's Orthopedic Hosp., Univ. Hosp. Editor: Early Intervention: A Team Approach, 1978 (Am. Med. Writers award 1979), The Prader Willi Syndrome, 1981; contbr. some 60 articles to profl. jours. Fellow Am. Acad. Pediatrics, Am. Acad. Cerebral Palsy and Devel. Medicine, Am. Assn. Mental Retardation; mem. Soc. Devel. Pediatrics, Wash. State Med. Assn. (Aesculapius award 1979), Soc. Behavioral Pediatrics. Democrat. Office: U Wash CHDD PO Box 357920 Seattle WA 98195-7920

HOLMAN, BILL, composer; b. Calif. Student, U. Colo., 1944-45, UCLA, 1947, Westlake Coll. Music, 1948-50. Mem. Lighthouse All Stars, 1950-51, Conte Candoli, 1955, Shelley Manne, 1955, Shorty Rogers, 1957. Recs. include Kenton Presents: The Bill Holman Octet, 1954, The Fabulous Bill Holman, 1957, In a Jazz Orbit, 1958, Jive for five, 1958, Bill Holman's Great Big Band, 1960, The Bill Holman Band, 1988, A View From the Side (Grammy award for Best Instrumental Composition 1996), Brilliant Corners, 1997; composer for various artists including Count Basie, Louis Bellson, Natalie Cole, Maynard Ferguson, Woody Herman, Peggy Lee, Carmen McRae, Diane Schuur, Sarah Vaughn, Joe Williams, Doc Severinsen, others. Recipient Grammy award for Best Instrumental Arrangement, 1987, 97; named Best Arranger by Jazz Times Readers Poll, 1990, 95, 98, 99, Arranger of Yr. Downbeat Readers' Poll and Critics Poll, 1998.

HOLMAN, DONALD REID, lawyer; b. Astoria, Oreg., Jan. 30, 1930; s. Donald Reuben and Hattie Laveda (Card) H.; m. Susan Muncy Morris, Aug. 31, 1956; children: Donald Reid, Laura Morris Holman O'Brien, Douglas Edward. B.A., U. Wash.-Seattle, 1951, J.D., 1958; postgrad., U. Oreg.-Eugene, 1955-57. Bar: Oreg. Assoc. Miller Nash LLP, Portland, 1958-63, ptnr., 1963-93, mng. ptnr., 1987-90, sr. counsel, 1994-2001, ret., 2001. Bd. dirs. Byers Industries, Inc., Portland, Copeland Lumber Yards Inc., Portland, Huntair Inc., Portland. Lt. (j.g.) USN, 1951-55; capt. JAGC USNR, 1977-90, ret. Fellow Am. Bar Found.; mem. Oreg. State Bar Assn., Order of Coif, Multnomah Athletic club (trustee 1983-85, v.p. 1985-86), Waverley Country Club, Phi Delta Phi. Republican. Avocations: tennis, golf, squash. Home: 8040 SW Broadmoor Ter Portland OR 97225-2121 E-mail: holmor@aol.com

HOLMAN, HALSTED REID, medical educator, educator; b. Cleve., Jan. 17, 1925; s. Emile Frederic and Ann Peril (Purdy) H.; m. Barbara Marie Lucas, June 26, 1949 (div. July 9, 1982); children: Michael, Andrea, Alison; m. Diana Barbara Dutton, Aug. 10, 1985; 1 child, Geoffrey. Student, Stanford U., 1942-43, UCLA, 1943-44; MD, Yale U., 1949. Med. resident Montefiore Hosp., N.Y.C., 1952-55; staff physician Rockefeller Inst., N.Y.C., 1955-60; prof. medicine Stanford (Calif.) U., 1960—, chmn. dept. medicine, 1960-71, co-chief, divsn. family and community medicine, 1987-2001, dir. clin. scholar program, 1969-97, dir. Multipurpose Arthritis Ctr., 1977-97, co-chief, divsn. immunology and rheumatology, 1997-2000, dir. Stanford Program for Mgmt. of Chronic Disease, 1997—. Pres. Midpeninsula Health Svc., Palo Alto, Calif., 1975-80; mem. adv. bd. Calif Health Facilities Commn., Sacramento, 1978-81, Office Tech. Assessment, U.S. Congress, 1979-81, Inst. Advancement of Health, N.Y.C., 1982-90; Guggenheim prof. medicine, 1960—. Author 2 books; assoc. editor Arthritis and Rheumatism, 1995-2000; contbr. articles to profl. jours. Recipient Bauer Meml. award Arthritis and Rheumatism Found., N.Y., 1964, Vision award R.W. Johnson Found., 2001. Master Am. Coll. Rheumatology; fellow ACP (Laureate award no. Calif. chpt. 1994), AAAS (coun. 1974-79); mem. Assn. Am. Physicians, Am. Soc. Clin. Investigation (pres. 1970), Western Assn. Physicians (pres. 1966), Arthritis Found. (Hero Overcoming Arthritis 1998, Engalitcheff award 1999, McGuire Educator award 2000), Improving Chronic Illness Care-R.W. Johnson Found. (Vision award 2001). Democrat. Home: 747 Dolores St Stanford CA 94305-8427 Office: Stanford U Divsn Immunol and Rheumatol 1000 Welch Rd Ste 203 Palo Alto CA 94304-1808 E-mail: Holman@Stanford.edu

HOLMAN, J(OHN) LEONARD, retired manufacturing corporation executive; b. Moose Jaw, Sask., Can., Aug. 30, 1929; s. Charles Claude and Lillian Kathleen (Haw) H.; m. Julia Pauline Benfield, July 18, 1953; children: Nancy Jane, Sally Joan. B.S. in Civil Engring., U. Alta., 1953. Pres. Consolidated Concrete Ltd., Calgary, Alta., Can., 1969-72; dir., pres. BACM Industries Ltd., Calgary, 1972-76; exec. v.p. Genstar Corp., Calgary, 1976-79, San Francisco, 1980-87, dir. several subs. cos.; pres., chief exec. officer CBR Cement Corp., San Mateo, Calif., 1986-88, chmn. bd., 1988-89, ret., 1990. Bd. dirs., officer several nat. trade assns. Mem. Assn. Profl. Engr. Alta. (life), Calgary Exhbn. and Stampede (hon. life., dir.), Calgary Golf and Country Club, Bernardo Heights Country Club. Home: 111 Country Club Estates 111-5555 Elbow Dr SW Calgary AB Canada T2V 1H7 E-mail: johnlholman@home.com

HOLMAN, KERMIT LAYTON, chemical engineer; b. Morris, Minn., Nov. 16, 1935; s. Melvin Martinous and Jennie Ethel (Erickson) H.; m. Audrey Mae Redwing, Nov. 21, 1959; children: Erik, Jennifer, Peter. Student, St. Olaf Coll., 1953-54; B.S., U. N.D., 1957; M.S., U. Idaho, 1961; Ph.D., Iowa State U., 1964. Tape devel. engr. 3M Co., St. Paul, 1957-60; sr. chem. engr. Dow Chem. Co., Golden, Colo., 1964-65; mem. faculty dept. chem. engring. N.Mex. State U., Las Cruces, 1965-76, prof., [illegible], prof., chmn. dept. chem. engring. U. Idaho, Moscow, [illegible]; tech. assoc. Weyerhaeuser, Tacoma, 1981-85, sr. engring. specialist 1985-

97, engring. advisor, 1997-2001; ret., 2001. Chmn. Forest products Divsn., 1996-97; cons. in field. Mem. Am. Inst. Chem. Engrs., Sigma Xi, Tau Beta Pi. Independent. Lutheran. Home: 31619 37th Ave SW Federal Way WA 98023-4008 E-mail: holman_ka@msn.com, kermit.holman@weyerhaeuser.com

HOLMAN, PAUL DAVID, plastic surgeon; b. Waynesboro, Va., Mar. 13, 1943; s. Wallace D. and Rosalie S. Holman. BA, U. Va., 1965; MD, Jefferson Med. Coll., 1968. Intern, George Washington U. Hosp., Washington, 1968-69, resident in gen. surgery, 1969-70, 72-74; resident in plastic surgery Phoenix Plastic Surgery Residency, 1974-76; practice medicine specializing in plastic surgery, Phoenix, 1977—; mem. staff Good Samaritan Hosp., Phoenix, St. Joseph's Hosp., Phoenix, Phoenix Children's Hosp. Served to lt. comdr. USNR, 1970-72. Diplomate Am. Bd. Surgery, Am. Bd. Plastic Surgery. Mem. AMA, ACS, Am. Soc. Plastic and Reconstructive Surgeons, Phi Beta Kappa. Office: 2111 E Highland Ave Ste 105 Phoenix AZ 85016-4755

HOLME, RICHARD PHILLIPS, lawyer; b. Denver, Nov. 6, 1941; s. Peter Hagner Jr. and Lena (Phillips) H.; m. Barbara June Friel, July 17, 1944; children: Daniel Friel, Robert Muir. BA, Williams Coll., Williamstown, Mass., 1963; JD, U. Colo., 1966. Bar: Colo. 1966, U.S. Dist. Ct. Colo. 1966, U.S. Ct. Claims 1990, U.S. Ct. Appeals (10th cir.) 1966, U.S. Ct. Appeals (1st cir.) 1980, U.S. Dist. Ct. D.C. 1988, U.S. Ct. Appeals (D.C. cir.) 1988, U.S. Ct. Appeals (4th cir.) 1989, U.S. Ct. Appeals (fed. cir.) 1995, U.S. Supreme Ct. 1975. Assoc. Davis, Graham & Stubbs, Denver, 1966-68, ptnr., 1972-87, 91—, mng. ptnr., D.C. office Washington, 1987-91; dep. Denver Dist. Atty., 1969-71. Grievance com. Colo. Supreme Ct., Denver, 1979-85, civil rules com., 1994—, civil justice com., 1998—. Fellow Am. Bar Found., Am. Coll. Trial Lawyers (Colo. state chair 1994-96); mem. ABA, Colo. Bar Found., Colo. Bar Assn. (bd. govs. 1974-76, 85-87, 95-99, 2001—), Denver Bar Assn. (trustee 1977-80, 1st v.p. 1997-98), Pinehurst Country Club, Order of Coif. Republican. Presbyterian. Home: 3944 S Depew Way Denver CO 80235-3105

HOLMES, ALBERT WILLIAM, JR. physician; b. Chgo., Feb. 3, 1932; s. Albert William and Eleanor Muir H.; m. Lois Ann Geiger, Sept. 4, 1954; children: Nancy, William, Elizabeth, Robert. Student, U. Chgo., 1947-49; BA, Knox Coll., 1952; MD, Western Res. U., 1956. Diplomate Am. Bd. Internal Medicine. Intern Presbyn. Hosp., Chgo., 1956-57; resident Presbyn.-St. Luke's Hosp., Chgo., 1957-59, 61-62; instr. U. Ill., Chgo., 1961-62, asst. prof., 1963-65, assoc. prof., 1966-68, prof. medicine, 1968-70; prof. medicine and microbiology Rush Med. Coll., Chgo., 1971-75; dir. sect. hepatology Rush-Presbyn.-St. Luke's Med. Center, Chgo., 1966-75, asso. chmn. dept. medicine, 1972-75, acting v.p. research affairs, 1973-74; prof., chmn. dept. internal medicine Tex. Tech U., Lubbock, 1975-83, prof. medicine, 1983-85; prof., chmn. dept. medicine U. Ill., Peoria, 1985-89; prof. medicine U. Calif., San Francisco, 1990-96, prof. emeritus medicine, 1996—; chief medicine Valley Med. Ctr., 1990-96. Contbr. articles in field to profl. jours. Served with U.S. Army, 1959 61. Recipient Alumni Achievement award Knox Coll., 1976; NIH spl. fellow, 1963-66 Fellow ACP; mem. Am. Assn. Study Liver Diseases, Ctrl. Soc. Clin. Rsch., Alpha Omega Alpha. Presbyterian. Home: 1137 W Escalon Ave Fresno CA 93711-2018 Office: U Med Ctr Dept Med Fresno CA 93702 E-mail: bi2332@msn.com

HOLMES, EDWARD W. physician, educator; b. Winona, Miss., Jan. 25, 1941; s. Edward and Mary (Hart) H.; m. Judith L. Swain, Jan. 25, 1980. BS, Washington and Lee U., 1963; MD, U. Pa., 1967. Intern Hosp. of U. Pa., 1967-68; resident in medicine Duke U. Med. Ctr., Durham, N.C.; prof. medicine and biochemistry Duke U., Durham, 1974-91; investigator Howard Hughes Med. Inst., 1974-87; prof., chmn. dept. medicine U. Pa., Phila., 1991-97; assoc. dean for rsch. Stanford U. Sch. Medicine, 1997 2000; dean Duke U. Sch. Medicine, Durham; vice chancellor academic affairs Duke U. Med. Ctr., Durham; vice chancellor health scis., dean U. Calif. Sch. Medicine, La Jolla, 2000—. Reviewer in molecular medicine. With USPHS, 1968-70. Grantee NIH. Mem. Am. Soc. Clin. Investigation, Assn. Am. Physicians. Office: Univ Calif Sch Medicine Davidson Bldg Dean Suite Rm 125 9500 Gilman Dr MC 0602 La Jolla CA 92093-0602

HOLMES, GENTA HAWKINS, diplomat; b. Anadarko, Okla., Sept. 3, 1940; BA, U. So. Calif., 1962. Jr. officer U.S. Embassy, Abidjan, Ivory Coast, 1964-66; with office spl. assistance to Sec. of State for Refugee Affairs, 1966-68; spl. asst., youth officer U.S. Embassy, Paris, 1968-71; with N.Y. regional office OEO, 1972-73; with office devel. fin., econ. bur. U.S. Dept. State, 1973-74; chief econ. and commercial sect. U.S. Embassy, Bahamas, 1974-77; congl. fellow Am. Polit. Sci. Assn., 1977-78; with bur. congl. rels. U.S. Dept. State, 1978-79; asst. adminstr. legis. affairs AID, 1979-82; mem. 25th Exec. Seminar in Nat. and Internat. Affairs, 1982-83; mem. bd. examiners, 1983-84; dep. chief of mission U.S. Embassy, Lilongwe, Malawi, 1984-86, Port-au-Prince, Haiti, 1986-88, Pretoria, South Africa, 1988-90; U.S. amb. to Namibia, 1990-92; dir. gen. fgn. svc., dir. pers. U.S. Dept. State, Washington, 1992-95; diplomat in residence U. Calif., Davis, 1995-97; U.S. amb. to Australia, 1997—. Office: US Embassy 15106 Oak Meadow Rd Penn Valley CA 95946

HOLMES, GREGG, communications executive; B in advt., Texas Tech Univ. Various positions Times Mirror Cable Television, Ohio, 1981-86; v.p., gen. mgr. Cox Comm., Inc., Phoenix, 1986—. Bd. dirs. Greater Phoenix Econ. Coun. (pat chmn.), Valley of the Sun United Way, Met. Musical Theater; vice chmn. Phoenix Meml. Hosp.; mem. Phoenix Youth Edn. Commn. (past chmn.), United Way campaign cabinet. Mem. Greater Phoenix C. of C. (past chmn.), Greater Phoenix Leadership, Dean's Coun. 100 Ariz. State Univ. Office: Cox Comm 17602 N Black Canyon Hwy Phoenix AZ 85053-1997

HOLMES, IRVIN R., JR. marketing professional; V.p. mktg. Del Monte Foods, San Francisco, sr. v.p. mktg., 1999—. Office: Del Monte Foods 1 Market Plz San Francisco CA 94105-1420

HOLMES, JOHN RICHARD, physicist, educator; b. Chula Vista, Calif., Sept. 24, 1917; s. Robert and Mary Elizabeth (Burns) H.; m. Louise Murphy, 1951 (dec. Oct. 1989); children: Susan Diana, Ronald John, Sandra Kathleen. AB in Physics, U. Calif., Berkeley, 1938, MA, 1941, PhD, 1942. With radiation lab. U. Calif., 1942-45; mem. faculty physics U. So. Calif., Los Angeles, 1945-63, prof., 1954-63, chmn. dept. physics, 1956-62; prof. U. Hawaii, Honolulu, 1963—, chmn. physics dept., 1963-72, emeritus prof. physics, 1989—. Fulbright lectr. U. Madrid, 1962-63; cons. Autonetics Corp., Anaheim, Calif., Douglas Aircraft, Santa Monica, Calif., Electro-Optical Sys., Pasadena, Calif.; lectr. Edwards AFB, Loyola U., L.A.; UNESCO cons., Argentina, 1970 Mem. internat. adv. bd. Optica Pura y Aplicada, Madrid Whiting fellow in physics U. Calif., Berkeley, 1938. Fellow Am. Phys. Soc., Optical Soc. Am.; mem. AAAS. Home: 820 N Delaware St # 210 San Mateo CA 94401-1538

HOLMES, KING KENNARD, medical educator; b. St. Paul, Sept. 1, 1937; AB, Harvard Coll., 1959; MD, Cornell U., 1963; PhD in Microbiology, U. Hawaii, 1967. Diplomate Am. Bd. Internal Medicine, infectious diseases. Resident U. Wash., Seattle, 1967-68, chief resident, 1968-69, from instr. to assoc. prof. medicine, 1969-78, vice chmn. dept. medicine, 1984-89, prof. medicine, 1978—, dir. Ctr. AIDS and Sexually Transmitted Diseases, 1989—. Head divsn. pulmonary diseases USPHS Hosp., Seattle, 1969-70, asst. chief dept. medicine, 1969-83, head divsn. infectious diseases, 1970-83; dir. Sexually Transmitted Disease Clinic, Harborview Med. Ctr., 1972-79, chief med., 1984-89; mem. numerous adv. coms. Nat. Inst. Allergy & Infectious Diseases, NIH, USPHS, WHO, NAS; prin. investigator NIH, Nat. Cancer Inst., Nat. Inst. Allergy & Infectious Diseases, Nat. Inst. Child Health & Human Devel., Ctrs. Disease Control, 1983—. With USN, 1965-67. Recipient Squibb award Infectious Disease Soc. Am., 1978, Thomas Parran award Am. Veneral Disease Assn., 1983. Fellow ACP, Royal Coll. Physicians Eng.; mem. AMA, Inst. Medicine-NAS, Assn. Am. Physicians, Am. Epidemiol. Soc., Am. Fedn. Clin. Rsch. Office: U Wash Str AIDS & STDs Harborview Med Ctr 325 9th Ave MS# 359931 Seattle WA 98104-2420 Fax: 206-731-3694

HOLMES, MICHAEL GENE, lawyer; b. Longview, Wash., Jan. 14, 1937; s. Robert A. and Esther S. Holmes; children: Helen, Peyton Robert. AB in Econs., Stanford U., 1958, JD, 1960. Bar: Oreg. 1961, U.S. Dist. Ct. Oreg. 1961, U.S. Ct. Appeals (9th cir.) 1961, Temp. Emergency Ct. Appeals 1976, U.S. Supreme Ct. 1976. Assoc. Spears, Lubersky, Bledsoe, Anderson, Young & Hilliard, Portland, 1961-67, ptnr., 1967-90, Lane Powell Spears Lubersky, Portland, 1990-95, of counsel, 1995. Mem. Oreg. Joint Com. of Bar, Press & Broadcasters, 1982-85, sec., 1983-84, chmn. 1985. Author Survey of Oregon Defamation and Privacy Law, ann., 1982-95. Trustee Med. Rsch. Found. Oreg., Portland, 1985-94, exec. com., 1986-94; hon. trustee Oreg. Health Scis. Found., 1995—; trustee Portland Civic Theatre, 1962-66. Mem. Oreg. Bar Assn., Phi Beta Kappa.

HOLMES, MICHAEL L. career officer; m. Viola Holmes; children: Jared, Justin, Michael Jason. Diploma in Math., Pembroke State U., 1972. Commd. ensign USN, 1973, advanced through ranks to rear adm.; various assignments to aircraft comdr. Patrol Squadron 24, Jacksonville; comdr. Patrol Wings, U.S. Pacific Fleet, Pearl Harbor, Hawaii. Office: Box 64000 Marine Corp Base Hawaii Kaneohe HI 96863-4000

HOLMES, PAUL LUTHER, political scientist, educational consultant; b. Rock Island, Ill., Mar. 7, 1919; s. Bernt Gunnar and Amanda Sophia (Swenson) H.; m. Ardis Ann Grunditz, Nov. 1, 1946; children: Mary Ann, David Stephen. BA, U. Minn., 1940; MA, Stanford U., 1949, George Washington U., 1964; EdD, Stanford U., 1968. Career officer USN, 1941-64, ret. at capt.; adminstr. Laney Coll., Oakland, Calif., 1965-70; dean Contra Costa Coll., San Pablo, 1970-71; pres. Coll. Alameda (Calif.), 1971-75, prof. polit. sci., 1975-80; dir. doctoral studies program Nova U., No. Calif., 1975-80. Cons. higher edn. Gig Harbor, Wash., 1981—; regent Calif. Luth. U., 1973-76. Decorated with medals. Mem. Stanford U. Alumni Assn., Rotary, Phi Delta Kappa. Lutheran.

HOLMES, RANDALL KENT, microbiology educator, physician, university administrator; b. Muskegon, Mich., Nov. 7, 1940; s. Scott Travis and Helen Marie (Rosell) H.; m. Kathryn Louise Voelker, June 16, 1962; children: Rebecca Kathryn, Elisabeth Marie. AB, Harvard U., 1962; MD, PhD in Microbiology, NYU, 1968. Diplomate Am. Bd. Internal Medicine, Am. Bd. Infectious Diseases. Intern, then resident Beth Israel Hosp., Boston, 1968-70; research assoc. NIH, Bethesda, Md., 1970-72; instr. medicine U. Tex. Southwestern Med. Sch., Dallas, 1972-73, asst. prof., 1973-75, assoc. prof., 1975-76; prof., chmn. microbiology and immunology Uniformed Services U. Health Scis., Bethesda, 1976-95, assoc. dean for acad. affairs, 1984-93, acting chmn. biochemistry, 1993-95; prof., chmn. microbiology U. Colo. Sch. Medicine, Denver, 1995—. Mem. adv. com. vaccines and related biol. products Nat. Ctr. for Drugs and Biologics, Bethesda, 1983-87; mem. cholera panel NIH, 1987-92; mem. bacteriology and mycology 1 study sect. NIH, 1993-95, mem. microbiology and infectious disease rsch. com., 2000—; chair VA-DOD Rsch. Program on Mechs. of Emerging Pathogens Rev. Panel, 1997. Contbr. articles to profl. jours. Served to surgeon USPHS, 1968-70. Recipient Research Career Devel. award NIH, 1975-76. Fellow ACP, Infectious Diseases Soc. Am.; mem. Am. Acad. Microbiology (bd. govs. 1992-95, com. on awards 1995-2001), Am. Soc. for Clin. Investigation, Am. Soc. for Microbiology (editorial bd. Infection and Immunity 1978-86, Microbiol. Revs. 1983-88, mem. steering com. postdoctoral rsch. assoc. program Nat. Ctr. for Infectious Disease 1993-95, chmn. 1996—), Nat. Bd. Med. Examiners (mem. microbiology test com. 1984-86, chmn. 1987-93, mem. U.S. med. licensing exam. step I com. 1990-92, mem. U.S. med. licensing exam. composite com. 1992-95), Phi Beta Kappa, Alpha Omega Alpha. Republican. Avocations: reading, hiking, camping, swimming. Office: U Colo Health Scis Ctr Dept Microbiology PO Box B175 Denver CO 80262-0001

HOLMES, RICHARD ALBERT, software engineer, consultant; b. Santa Barbara, Calif., May 7, 1958; m. Janet M. Dunbar; children: Brian D., Kevin M. AA in Music summa cum laude, City Coll. San Francisco, 1987; BS in Computer Sci. summa cum laude, Nat. U., 1991; postgrad., Stanford U., 1993—. Ind. software cons., San Francisco, 1986-88; software quality assurance contractor Oxford & Assocs., Mountain View, Calif., 1988-89; microkernel diagnostics engr. Apple Computer, Cupertino, 1990-93, file system engr., 1994-96; operating sys. engr. Hewlett Packard, Cupertino, 1996-99; staff engr. Veritas, Mountain View, 1999—. CCSF tchr. & faculty scholar, 1986, 87, Alpha Gamma Sigma scholar, 1987. Mem. IEEE, Assn. for Computing Machinery, Alpha Gamma Sigma (treas. 1986-87). Avocations: playing classical guitar, gem & mineral collecting, computer music and sound generation, music improvisation and composition. Office: Hewlett Packard Co MS 47LA1 19447 Pruneridge Ave Cupertino CA 95014-0683

HOLMES, RICHARD BROOKS, mathematical physicist; b. Milw., Jan. 7, 1959; s. Emerson Brooks Holmes and Nancy Anne Schaffter; m. Sandra Lynn Wong, June 27, 1998. BS, Calif. Inst. Tech., 1981; MS, Stanford (Calif.) U., 1983. Sr. sys. analyst Comptek Rsch., Vallejo, Calif., 1982-83; staff scientist Western Rsch., Arlington, Va., 1983-85; sr. scientist AVCO Everett (Mass.) Rsch. Lab., 1985-88; prin. rsch. scientist North East Rsch. Assocs., Woburn, Mass., 1988-90; sr. mem. tech. staff Rocketdyne divsn. Rockwell Internat., Canoga Park, Calif., 1990-95; sr. staff scientist Lockheed Martin Rsch. Labs., Palo Alto, 1995-98; pres. Nutronics, Inc., Carson City, Nev., 1998—. Cons. North East Rsch. Assocs., 1990. Contbr. Matched Asymptotic Expansions, 1988; contbr. articles to Phys. Rev. Letters, Phys. Rev., Jour. of the Optical Soc. Am. and IEEE Jour. of Quantum Electronics. Mem. No. Calif. Scholarship Founds., Oakland, 1977; mem. Wilderness Soc., Washington, 1989. Stanford fellow Stanford U., 1982; fellow MIT, 1990; recipient Presdl. Medal of Merit, 1992. Mem. AAAS, SPIE (conf. organizer 1995—), Am. Phys. Soc., Optical Soc. Am. Achievements include patents for means for photonic communication, computation, and distortion compensation; discovery of spin-two phonons. Office: Nutronics Inc 1668 E Clearview Dr Carson City NV 89701-6572

HOLMES, ROBERT EUGENE, legislative staff member, journalist; b. Shelbyville, Ind., June 5, 1928; s. Eugene Lowell and Sarah Lucinda (Hughes) H.; m. Retha Carolyn Richey, June 27, 1955 (div. Sept. 1966); children: Enid Adair Offley, William Houstoun (dec.), Holly Ann Holmes. BA in Polit. Sci., DePauw U., 1950; MA in Journalism, Ind. U., 1953; MA in Communs. and Urban Affairs, Stanford U., 1976. Staff reporter Elkhart, Ind. Truth, 1954-57; city editor, investigative editor Press-Enterprise, Riverside, Calif., 1957-70; sr. cons. Calif. State Senate Dem. Caucus, Sacramento, 1971-74, dep. dir., 1978-79; press sec. Lt. Gov. of Calif., Sacramento, 1975-77; project dir. Border Area Devel. Study, U.S. Econ. Devel. Adminstrn., Sacramento, 1978; staff dep. dir. Calif. Senator Robert Presley, Sacramento, 1979-83; chief cons. Joint Legis. Ethics Com., Calif. Legislature, Sacramento, 1981-82; staff dir. Joint Com. on Prison Constrn. and Ops., Calif. Legislature, Sacramento, 1983-94. Rsch. cons. Calif. Rsch. Bur., Calif. State Libr., Sacramento, 1991-92; cons. Calif. Hist. State Capitol Commn., 1995-96. Author, editor rschr. legis. reports; contbg. editor creative writing quar. Noah's Hotel, Inverness, Calif., 1991—; editor/pub. sports newsletter weekly Big Red Ramblings, 1997-2001; contbr. articles to mags., short stories, 1961—. Pres., Golden Bear Dem. Club, Sacramento, 1972-74; media dir. Lt. Gov. Campaign, Sacramento and L.A., 1974. Sgt. USMC, 1951-53. Recipient Silver Gavel award ABA, 1969, 1st Place media award Calif. State Bar Assn., 1968, 1st Place award Calif. Newspaper Pubs. Best Series, 1969, 70, 71; Am. Polit. Sci. Assn. Ford Found. fellow Stanford U., 1970, Jack Anderson award for excellence in journalism Calif. Correctional Peace Officers Assn., 1993. Mem. NAACP, ACLU, Calif. Writers Club, Common Cause. Democrat. Avocations: bicycling, tennis, world travel, short story writing. Home: 416 Florin Rd Sacramento CA 95831-2007

HOLMGREN, JANET L, college president; b. Chgo., Dec. 1, 1948; d. Kenneth William and Virginia Ann (Rensink) H.; m. Gordon A. McKay, Sept. 7, 1968 (div. 1990); children: Elizabeth Jane, Ellen Katherine. BA in English summa cum laude, Oakland U., Rochester, Mich., 1968; MA in Linguistics, Princeton U., 1971, PhD in Linguistics, 1974. Asst. prof. English studies Federal City Coll. (now U. D.C.), Washington, 1972-76; asst. prof. English U. Md., College Park, 1976-82, asst. to chancellor, 1982-88; assoc. provost Princeton (N.J.) U., 1988-90, vice-provost, 1990-91; pres. Mills Coll., Oakland, Calif., 1991—. Mem. external adv. bd. English dept. Princeton U. Bay Area Biosci. Ctr. Author: (with Spencer Cosmos) The Story of English: Study Guide and Reader, 1986, Narration and Discourse in American Realistic Fiction, 1982; contbr. articles to profl. jours. Faculty rsch. grantee U. Md., 1978; fellow NEH, 1978, Princeton U., 1968-69, 70-72, NSF, 1969-70; recipient summer study aid Linguistic Soc. Am., Ohio State U., 1970. Mem. Assn. Ind. Caif. Colls. and Univs. (exec. com.), Nat. Assn. Ind. Colls. and Univs., Am. Coun. on Education (chair office of women in higher edn.), Calif. Acad. Sci. (coun.). Democrat. Episcopal. Avocations: traveling, swimming, reading. Office: Mills Coll Office Pres 5000 Macarthur Blvd Oakland CA 94613-1301

HOLMGREN, MIKE, professional football coach; b. San Francisco, June 15, 1948; m. Kathy Holmgren; children: Gretchen, Emily, Jenny and Calla (twins). BS in Bus. Fin., U. So. Calif., 1970. Coach Lincoln High Sch., San Francisco, 1971-72, Sacred Heart High Sch., 1972-74, Oakgrove High Sch., 1975-80; quarterbacks coach, offensive coord. San Francisco State U., 1981-82; quarterbacks coach Brigham Young U., 1982-85, San Francisco 49ers, 1985-89, offensive coord., 1989-92; head coach Green Bay Packers, 1992-98, Seattle Seahawks, 1999—. Office: Seattle Seahawks Kingdome 11220 NE 53rd St Kirkland WA 98033-7595

HOLO, SELMA REUBEN, museum director, educator; b. Chgo., May 21, 1943; d. Samuel and Ghita (Hurwitz) Reuben; children from previous marriage: Robert, Joshua; m. Fred Croton, June 18, 1989. BA, Northwestern U., 1965; MA, Hunter Coll., 1972; PhD, U. Calif., Santa Barbara, 1980; postgrad., Mus. Mgmt. Inst., 1985. Lectr. Art Ctr. Coll. of Design, Pasadena, Calif., 1973-77; curator of acquisitions Norton Simon Mus., Pasadena, 1977-81; dir. Fisher Gallery and mus. MA art history/mus. studies program U. So. Calif., L.A., 1981—. Guest curator, cons. Getty Mus., Malibu, Calif., 1975-76, 81, guest curator Isetan Mus., Tokyo, 1982, cons. Nat. Mus. for Women in Arts, Washington, 1984; reviewer grants Inst. Mus. Svcs., Washington, 1986-87, Getty Grant Program, 1988-90; panel chmn. Internat. Com. on Exhbn. Exch., Washington, 1984; panelist NEA, Washington, 1985, 91-93, Idaho Commn. on the Arts; admission panel mem. Mus. Mgmt. Inst., 1990; hon. curator Tokyo Fuji Mus.; lectr. museology IVAM, Valencia, Spain, 1994, Complutense U. Masters in Museology, 1994, U. Castilla La Mancha in Museology, 1995; presenter Museo/Mus. Conf., Barcelona, Spain, 1996, Bilbao (Spain) Mus. Fine Arts Conf. on Mus. Edn., 1996; co-author survey com. mus. studies programs, 1986. Author: (catalogues) Goya: Los Disparates, 1976; co-author: La Tauromaquia: Goya, Picasso and the Bullfight, 1986; editor: Keepers of the Flame, The Unofficial Artists of Leningrad, 1990; guest editor New Observations, 1990; contbr. articles to profl. jours. and mag. Fellow La Napoule Art Found., 1988, Fulbright Found., 1994; Kress Found. grantee, N.Y., 1979, Internationes Fed. Republic of Germany grantee, 1985, 92; recipient Fuj Fine Art award, 1990, Sr. Rsch. Fulbright fellowship to Spain, 1994, award from program for cooperation between the program for the Ministry of Culture of Spain and N.Am. Univ. Mem. Am. Assn. Mus., Art Table. Office: U So Calif Fisher Gallery 823 Exposition Blvd Los Angeles CA 90089-0001

HOLSTI, KALEVI JACQUE, political scientist, educator; b. Geneva, Apr. 25, 1935; s. Rudolf Woldemar and Liisa Anniki (Franssila) H.; children: Liisa, Matthew, Karina. B.A., Stanford U., 1956, M.A., 1958, Ph.D., 1961. Mem. faculty U. B.C., Vancouver, 1961—, U. Killam prof. polit. sci. Vis. prof. McGill U., Montreal, 1972-72, Kyoto (Japan) U., 1977, Hebrew U., Jerusalem, 1978, Internat. U. Japan, 1988, 92, 94; vis. fellow Australian Nat. U., 1983; cons. in field. Author: International Politics: A Framework for Analysis, 7th edit., 1994, Why Nations Realign, 1982, The Dividing Discipline: Hegemony and Pluralism in International Theory, 1985, Peace and War: International Order and Armed Conflict, 1648-1989, 1991, Change in the International System: Essays on the Theory and Practice of International Relations, 1991, The State, War, and the State of War, 1996; editor: Internat. Studies Quar., 1970-75; co-editor: Can. Jour. Polit. Sci., 1978-81. Recipient Killam Rsch. prize, 1992; Fulbright scholar, 1959-60; Can. Coun. leave fellow, 1967, 72, 78, Can. Coun. Killam Rsch. fellow, 1987-89; named Univ. Killiam Prof., 1997. Fellow Royal Soc. Can.; mem. Internat. Studies Assn. (pres. 1986-87), Can. Polit. Sci. Assn. (pres. 1984-85). Office: U BC Dept Polit Sci Vancouver BC Canada V6T 1Z1 E-mail: holsti@interchange.ubc.ca

HOLT, DENNIS F. media buying company executive; Student, U. So. Calif. Salesman RKO, L.A.; founder, pres., CEO, chmn. Western Internat. Media Corp., L.A.; chmn., CEO Patriot Comm., L.A. Office: Western Internat Media Corp 8544 W Sunset Blvd Los Angeles CA 90069-2310

HOLT, WILLIAM E. lawyer; b. Phila., Aug. 31, 1945; BBA, U. Iowa, 1967, JD with distinction, 1970. Bar: Iowa 1970, Wash. 1971. Law clk. to Hon. William T. Beeks U.S. Dist. Ct. (we. dist.) Wash., 1970-71; mem., chmn. Gordon, Thomas, Honeywell, Malanca, Peterson & Daheim, Tacoma, 1999, 2000. Adj. prof. U. Puget Sound Law Sch., 1974-75. Note editor Iowa Law Rev., 1969-70. Mem. ABA, Wash. State Bar Assn. (exec. com. real property, probate and trust sect. 1987-89), Phi Delta Phi. Office: Gordon Thomas Honeywell Malanca Peterson & Daheim PO Box 1157 Ste 2200 Tacoma WA 98401-1157 E-mail: holtw@gth-law.com

HOLTAN, RAMER B., JR. lawyer; b. Wilmington, Del., Oct. 20, 1944; AB, Harvard U., 1966; JD cum laude, U. Ill., 1972; postgrad., U. Freiburg, West Germany. Bar: Wash. 1973. Mem. Perkins Coie, Seattle. Articles editor U. Ill. Law Rev., 1971-72. Mem. Order of the Coif. Office: Perkins Coie 1201 3rd Ave Fl 40 Seattle WA 98101-3029

HOLTE, DEBRA LEAH, investment executive, financial analyst; b. Madison, Wis. d. Daniel Kennseth and Marian Anne Reitan. BA, Concordia Coll., Moorhead, Minn., 1973. Chartered Fin. Analyst, Cert. Divorce Planner. Capital markets specialist 1st Bank Mpls., 1981-83; v.p. Allison-Williams Co., Mpls., 1983-86; exec. v.p. Hamil & Holte Inc., Denver, 1986-93; pres. Holte & Assocs., Denver, Taos, N.Mex., 1993—. Active Denver Jr. League, Western Pension Com., 1986—; bd. dirs. Denver Children's Home, 1987—, treas., 1987-91, chmn. fin. com., 1987-91, v.p., 1990—, chmn. nominating com., 1991—, pres.-elect, 1994-95, bd. pres., 1995—; adv. bd. Luth. Social Svcs., 1987; co-chair U.S. Ski Team Fundraiser; bd. dirs. Minn. Vocat. Edn. Fin., Mpls., 1984-86; bd. dirs. Colo. Ballet, 1988-93, chair nominating com., 1991-93, v.p., 1992-93, chmn. bd., 1993; mem. Fin. Analyst Nat. Task Force in Bondholder Rights, 1988-90;

bd. dirs. Ctrl. City Opera Guild, 1994-95, Western Chamber Ballet, 1994-96, Taos Humane Soc., 1997—; social co-chmn. The Arapahoe Fox Hunt, 1993-94. Mem. Fin. Analysts Fedn., Denver Soc. Security Analysts (bd. dirs. 1990-97, chair ethics and bylaws com. 1987—, chair edn. com. 1988, chair membership com. 1989, rec. sec. 1990, sec. 1991, treas. 1992, program chair 1993, pres. 1994-95, dir. 1995-96). Died Jan. 30, 2001.

HOLTKAMP, JAMES ARNOLD, lawyer, educator; b. Albuquerque, Apr. 4, 1949; s. Clarence Jules and Karyl Irene (Roberts) H.; m. Marianne Coltrin, Dec. 28, 1973; children: Ariane, Brent William, Rachel, Allison, David Roberts. BA, Brigham Young U., 1972; JD, George Washington U., 1975. Bar: Utah 1976, U.S. Dist. Ct. Utah 1977, U.S. Ct. Appeals (10th cir.) 1979, Colo. 1995. Mem. staff U.S. Senate Watergate Com., Washington, 1974; atty.-advisor Dept. Transp., Washington, 1975; atty. Dept. Interior, Washington, 1975-77; assoc. Van Cott, Bagley, Cornwall & McCarthy, Salt Lake City, 1977-81, ptnr., 1981-89, Davis, Graham & Stubbs, Salt Lake City, 1989-92, Stoel Rives, Salt Lake City, 1992-97, LeBoeuf, Lamb, Greene & MacRae, Salt Lake City, 1997—. Adj. prof. Law Sch., Brigham Young U., Provo, Utah, 1979—, Coll. Law U. Utah, 1995—. Co-author: Utah Environmental and Land Use Permits and Approvals Manual, 1981; contbr. articles to legal jours. Missionary LDS Ch., 1968-70; active Gt. Salt Lake coun. Boy Scouts Am., 1977—; trustee Coalition for Utah's Future, 1996—. Mem. ABA (vice-chmn. air quality commn. 1985-89), Utah State Bar (chmn. energy and natural resources sect. 1984-85, chmn. pub. utilities law com. 1990-93, Lawyer of Yr. award 1981), Utah Mining Assn. (bd. dirs. 1999—), Rocky Mtn. Mineral Law Found. (trustee 1999—), Utah Petroleum Assn., George Washington Law Assn. (nat. bd. dirs. 1999—). Home: 7990 Deer Creek Rd Salt Lake City UT 84121-5752 Office: LeBoeuf Lamb Greene & MacRae 136 S Main St Ste 1000 Salt Lake City UT 84101-1685

HOLTON, EMILY, physicist; Pharmacologist Wallops Island; with Ames Rsch. Ctr. NASA, Moffett Field, Calif., 1973—, br. chief gravitational rsch. Avocations: landscaping, walking, listening to classical music, reading, attending plays. Office: NASA Ames Rsch Ctr Moffett Field CA 94035

HOLTZ, JOSEPH NORMAN, marketing executive; b. Matawan, N.J., Oct. 11, 1930; s. Joseph Antone and Catherine Martina (Crosby) H.; m. Irene Strano, July 15, 1951; children: Joseph Jr., Karl, Gary, Robert, Eric. AA, De Vry Tech. Inst., 1954; student, Monmouth Coll., 1955-56; BBA, Nat. U., 1988, MBA, 1989; grad., Realtor Inst. Lic. real estate broker Calif., Cert. Factoring Specialist designation Internat. Factoring Inst., Cert. Mortgage Investor designation Nat. Mortgage Investors Inst. Engr. Bendix Aviation, Red Bank, N.J., 1952-56, Hughes Aircraft Co., L.A., 1956-73; pres. Jo-Rene Assocs., Orange, Calif., 1973-86; asst. v.p. Builders Sales Corp., Santa Ana, 1986-87; exec. v.p. The Lehnert Group, Irvine, 1987-88; pres. J.N. Holtz Assocs., Orange, 1988—; CEO Holtz Funding Group, Orange, 1994—; v.p., corp. broker Mortgage Outlet Corp., 1992-94; corp. broker Shancie Real Estate Corp., Pomona, Calif., 1992-94; pres. CEO Sonoma Corp., Las Vegas, Nev., 1999—. Com. mem. United Way, Santa Ana, 1987-97. Mem. IEEE, Inst. Residential Mktg., Sales and Mktg. Coun., Nat. Assn. Factoring Profls., Nat. Real Estate and Mortgage Investors Assn., Phoenix Club, Am. Soc. for Quality Control. Republican. Avocations: computer programming, travel. Home: 5045-2 E Almond Ave Orange CA 92869-4245 Office: J N Holtz Assocs PO Box 10014 Santa Ana CA 92711-0014

HOLTZ, SARA, lawyer, consultant; b. L.A., Aug. 7, 1951; BA, Yale U., 1972; JD, Harvard U., 1975. Bar: D.C. 1975, Calif. 1982. Assoc. Brownstein, Zeidman & Schomer, Washington, 1975-77; dep. asst. dir. FTC, Washington, 1977-82; divsn. counsel Clorox Co., Oakland, Calif., 1982-90; v.p., dep. gen. counsel Nestle U.S.A., Inc., San Francisco, 1990-94; prin. Client Focus, 1996—. Mem. Am. Corp. Counsel Assn. (bd. dirs. 1986-95, chmn. 1994-95). Office: 5320 Olive Tree Ct Granite Bay CA 95746-9484

HOLTZMAN, ROBERT ARTHUR, lawyer; b. L.A., July 17, 1929; s. Ruben and Bertha (Dembowsky) H.; m. Barbara Polis, June 26, 1954 (dec. 1985); children: Melinda, Mark, Bradley; m. Liliane Gurwith Endlich, July 6, 1986. BA, UCLA, 1951; LLB, U. So. Calif., 1954. Bar: Calif. 1955, U.S. Dist. Ct. (cen. dist.) Calif. 1955, U.S. Ct. Appeals (9th cir.) 1958. Assoc. Gang, Tyre & Brown, L.A., 1954, Loeb and Loeb, L.A., 1956-63, ptnr., 1964-95; of counsel, 1996—. Judge pro tem Mcpl. Ct. L.A. Jud. Dist.; lectr. Calif. Continuing Edn. of Bar. Contbr. articles to legal publs. With U.S. Army, 1954-56. Mem. ABA (dispute resolution sect., vice-chmn. arbitration com.), Calif. Bar Assn. (chmn. com. on adminstrn. of justice 1984-85), L.A. County Bar Assn., Am. Arbitration Assn. (panel arbitrators 1974—, panel mediators 1992—, arbitrator large complex case program 1993—). Office: Loeb & Loeb LLP 1000 Wilshire Blvd Ste 1800 Los Angeles CA 90017-2475 E-mail: rholtzman@loeb.com

HOLZER, THOMAS E. physicist; PhD, U. Calif., San Diego, 1970. Sr. scientist High Altitude Obs., Nat. Ctr. for Atmospheric Rsch., Boulder, Colo., 1978—, dir., 1990-95. Fellow Am. Geophys. Union (James B. MacElwane award 1978); mem. Norwegian Acad. Sci. and Letters, Internat. Astron. Union, Am. Astron. Soc., Internat. Union of Radio Scis. Office: High Altitude Obs NCAR 3450 Mitchell Ln Boulder CO 80301-2260

HOLZMAN, D. KEITH, management consultant, record company executive, producer, arts consultant; b. N.Y.C., Mar. 22, 1936; s. Jacob Easton and Minnette Cathryn (Sternberger) H.; m. Jo Susan Handelman, Nov. 16, 1971; children: Susanne Carla, Lucas Jon, Rebecca Leigh. BA, Oberlin (Ohio) Coll., 1957; MFA, Boston U., 1959. Asst. to gen. mgr. and stage mgr. N.Y.C. Light Opera, 1959, 62-64; dir. prodn. Elektra Records, N.Y.C., 1964-70; v.p. prodn. and mfg. Elektra/Asylum/Nonesuch Records, Los Angeles, 1970-81, sr. v.p. prodn. and mfg., 1981-84; pres. ROM Records, 1987—; producer, arts cons. Treasure Trove, Inc., 1984—; mng. dir. Discovery Records, Santa Monica, Calif., 1991-98; prin. Keith Holzman Solutions Unltd., 1998—. Pres. Treasure Trove Inc.; dir. Nonesuch Records, 1980-84; music supr. Witches of Eastwick, Warner Bros., Los Angeles, 1986; bd. dirs. Plumstead Theatre Soc., Los Angeles, 1985—, Early Music Acad., Los Angeles, 1983-86, Assn. Classical Music, N.Y.C., 1983-86. Served with AUS, 1960-62. Mem. Audio Engring. Soc., Early Music Acad. (bd. dirs.) Nat. Acad. Rec. Arts and Scis., Assn. Classical Music (bd. dirs.), Plumstead Theatre Co. (bd. dirs.). Avocation: flying. E-mail: keith@holtzmansolutions.com

HOM, RICHARD YEE, research engineer; b. Phoenix, July 26, 1950; m. Kathleen Chien; 1 child, Matthew Richard Chien. BS in Engring. Sci. and Aero. and Aerospace Tech., Ariz. State U., 1973. Asst. engr. Sperry Flight System, Phoenix, 1973; sr. engr., composite tool engring. Boeing Comml. Airplane Co., Seattle, 1973-84, specialist engr., 1984-88; sr. specialist engr. R&D, metall. processing and advanced projects Boeing Aerospace Co., 1984-90, also automation tech.; with customer svcs. and airline support Boeing Comml. Airplace Group, 1990-91; prin. rsch. engr. metallics R&D Boeing Def. and Space Group, 1991—. Mem. AIAA, SMA, Air Force Assn., Soc. Mfg. Engrs., Aircraft Owners and Pilots Assn., ASM Internat. Home: 28704 15th Ave S Federal Way WA 98003-3161 Office: Boeing Mil Airplane & Missile Sys Group MS 06 14 PO Box 3999 Seattle WA 98124-2499 E-mail: richard.y.hom@boeing.com

HOMAN, RALPH WILLIAM, finance company executive; b. Wilkes-Barre, Pa., June 7, 1951; s. Norman Ryan and Adelaide Bernice (Sandy) H.; m. Donna Marie Webb, Jan. 25, 1975. BS in Acctg., Wheeling Coll., 1977; MBA in Mktg., Nat. U., 1986. Paymaster Dravo Corp., Pitts., 1974-75; tax preparer H&R Block, Wheeling, W.Va., 1977; fin. services exec. NCR Credit Corp., Sacramento, 1977-84; leasing exec. CSB Leasing, Sacramento, 1984-85; pres. Convergent Fin. Svcs., Colorado Springs, Colo., 1985—. Bd. dirs. Concord Coalition, Colorado Springs. Cons. Jr. Achievement, 1990—. Co-winner Name the Plane Contest Pacific Southwest Airlines, 1984; recipient Businessperson of Yr. award, Colo. Springs chpt. Future Bus. Leaders Am., 1995, 2000. Mem. The 30/40 Something Social Club (founder, pres. Sedona chpt.), Am. Assn. Boomers (pres. Pikes Peak chpt. 1992-93), Toastmasters (treas. Oak Creek chpt. 1988-89), Kiwanis (sec. 1988-89, founder, chmn. adult soccer league), Concord Coalition (bd. dirs., pres. Colorado Springs chpt.). Avocations: photography, camping, off-road motorcycling, woodworking. Home and Office: Convergent Fin Svcs 29 Mount Hope Dr Twin Lakes CO 81251-9705 E-mail: cfsleasing@aol.com

HOMER, BARRY WAYNE, lawyer; b. Junction City, Kans., Jan. 13, 1950; BA, U. Kans., 1972; JD, U. Chgo., 1975. Bar: Calif. 1975, U.S. Dist. Ct. (no. dist.) Calif. 1975, U.S. Tax Ct. 1980. Assoc. Brobeck, Phleger & Harrison, San Francisco, 1975-82, ptnr., 1982—. Co-author: Attorney's Guide to Pension and Profitsharing Plans, 1985, Compensating the Executive with Stock: Some Planning Possibilities and the Effect of the Parachute Provisions, 1986; contbr. articles to profl. jours. Mem. ABA (employee benefits com. tax sect. 1978—), Western Pension & Benefits Conf. Office: Brobeck Phleger & Harrison Spear St Tower 1 Market Plz Ste 341 San Francisco CA 94105-1420

HONDA, MICHAEL M. congressman; b. Calif. m. Jeanne; children: Mark, Michelle. BA in Biol. Sci., BA in Spanish, MA in Edn. Sci. tchr., Sunnyvale; prin. pub. sch.; elected to Calif. Assembly, 1996; mem. Congress, Calif. 15th dist., 2001—. Conducted ednl. rsch. at Stanford; apt. to San Jose City Plng. Com., 1971; mem. San Jose Unified sch. bd., 1981; served on Santa Clara County Bd. Supr.; elected Reg. Whip, vice chair Congressional Asian Pac. Am. Caucus, serves on House Budget com., Transportation com., Budget com. Congress, Calif. 15th dist. Served Peace Corps, 1965-67. Named High Tech Legislator Yr., Am. Electroics Assn. Mem. edn. com., Calif. Assembly. Office: 503 Cannon House Bldg Washington DC 20515*

HONEY, RICHARD CHURCHILL, retired electrical engineer; b. Portland, Oreg., Mar. 9, 1924; s. John Kohnen and Margaret Fargo (Larrison) H.; m. Helen Waugaman, June 8, 1952 (div. Feb. 1980; children: Leslie, Steven, Laura, Janine; m. Jo Anne Kipp, Jan. 11, 1993. BS, Calif. Inst. Tech., 1945; EE, Stanford U., 1950, PhD, 1953. Research asst. Stanford U., 1948-52; sr. research engr. microwave group Stanford Research Inst., 1952-60; tech. program coordinator Electromagnetic Techniques Lab., 1960-64, lab. dir., 1964-70, staff scientist, 1970-89, sr. prin. scientist, 1989-93. Dir. ILC Tech.; mem. Army Sci. Bd., 1978-84. Contbr. articles to books, encyc., profl. jours.; patentee in field. Served with USN, 1943-46. Fellow IEEE, Optical Soc. Am.; mem. Optical Soc. No. Calif., Coyote Point Yacht Club, Sigma Xi. Office: SRI Internat 333 Ravenswood Ave Menlo Park CA 94025-3453

HONEYCUTT, VAN B. computer services company executive; b. 1945; With Computer Scis. Corp., El Segundo, Calif., 1975—, v.p., pres. industry svcs. group, chmn., pres., CEO, 1996—. Office: Computer Scis Corp 2100 E Grand Ave El Segundo CA 90245-5024

HONEYFORD, JAMES D. state legislator; b. Ontario, Oreg. m. Jerri Honeyford; 4 children. BA in Edn. and Sociology, Ctrl. Wash. U., 1961, MEd in Instrl. Media, 1963. Policeman City of Ellensburg, 1960-66; tchr., coach, libr. Sunnyside Sch. Dist., 1966-95; farmer Sunnyside; mem. Wash. State Ho. Reps., Olympia, 1994-98, Wash. Senate, Dist. 15, Olympia, 1995—; mem. agr. and rural econ. devel. com. Wash. Senate, Olympia, mem. environ. quality and water resources com., mem. ways and means com. Trustee Wash. State Hist. Soc.; mem. Sunnyside City Coun.; bd. dirs. Habitat for Humanity; former coun. pres. Sunnyside Christian Reformed Ch.; mem. Wash. State Farm Bur.; founder, former pres. Wash. State Grape Soc. Mem. Wash. State Grape Soc., Sunnyside C. of C., Sunnyside Tennis Club (founder). Republican. Office: 204 Irving Newhouse Office Blvd Olympia WA 98504-0001 Fax: 360-786-1999. E-mail: honeyfor_ji@leg.wa.gov

HONEYSTEIN, KARL, lawyer, entertainment company executive; b. N.Y.C., Jan. 10, 1932; s. Herman and Claire (Rosen) H.; m. Buzz Halliday, Sept. 14, 1965 (div. Dec. 1978); 1 child, Gail; m. Shauna Wood Trabert, Jan. 24, 1995. BA, Yale U., 1953; JD, Columbia U., 1959. Bar: N.Y. 1959. Assoc. Greenbaum, Wolff & Ernst, N.Y.C., 1959-62; v.p. Ashley Famous Agy., N.Y.C., 1962-69, Internat. Famous Agy., N.Y.C., 1969-71; exec. v.p. The Sy Fischer Co., N.Y.C. and L.A., 1971-80; exec. v.p., chief operating officer The Taft Entertainment Co., Los Angeles, 1980-88; pres. K.H. Strategy Corp., Los Angeles, 1988—. Dir. Rhythm & Hues, Inc.; lectr. law Bklyn. Law Sch., N.Y.C., 1973-75 Served to lt. j.g. USNR, 1953-56 Fellow Internat. Coun. NATAS; mem. Friars Club, Regency Club.

HOOD, LEROY EDWARD, molecular biologist, educator; b. Missoula, Mont., Oct. 10, 1938; s. Thomas Edward and Myrtle Evylan (Wadsworth) H.; m. Valerie Anne Logan, Dec. 14, 1963; children: Eran William, Marqui Leigh Jennifer. B.S., Calif. Inst. Tech., 1960, Ph.D. in Biochemistry, 1968; M.D., Johns Hopkins U., 1964. Med. officer USPHS, 1967-70; staff scientist Pub. Health Svc., Bethesda, Md., 1967-70; sr. investigator Nat. Cancer Inst., 1967-70; asst. prof. biology Calif. Inst. Tech., Pasadena, 1970-73, assoc. prof., 1973-75, prof., 1975-92, Bowles prof. biology, 1977-92, chmn. div. biology, 1980-89; Gates prof. molecular biotech., chmn. bd. U. Wash. Sch. Medicine, Seattle, 1992—. Dir. NSF Sci. and Tech. Ctr. for Molecular Biotech., 1989—. Author: (with others) Biochemistry, a Problems Approach, 1974, Molecular Biology of Eukaryotic Cells, 1975, Immunology, 1978, Essential Concepts of Immunology, 1978, The Code of Codes: Scientific and Social Issues in the Human Genome Project, 1992; co-editor: Advances in Immunology, 1987, Genetics: From Genes to Genomics, 1999. Co-recipient, Albert Lasker Basic Medical Research Award, 1987, recipient Scientist of the Year Award, 1993, R&D Magazine. Mem. NAS, Am. Assn. Immunologists, Am. Assn. Sci., Am. Acad. Arts and Scis., Sigma Xi. Avocations: mountaineering, rockclimbing, photography. Office: U Washington Molecular Biotechnology Box 35 7730 Seattle WA 98195-7730

HOOD, WILLIAM BOYD, JR. cardiologist, educator; b. Sylacauga, Ala., Mar. 25, 1932; s. William Boyd and Katherine Elizabeth (Anderson) H.; m. Katherine Candace Todd, May 5, 1972; 1 son, Jefferson Boyce. B.S. summa cum laude, Davidson Coll., 1954; M.D., Harvard U., 1958. Intern Peter Bent Brigham Hosp., Boston, 1958-59, resident in internal medicine, 1959-60, 62-63; from asst. prof. to assoc. prof. medicine Harvard U., 1967-71; from assoc. prof. to prof. medicine Boston U., 1971-82; chief cardiology Boston City Hosp., 1973-82; prof. medicine U. Rochester (N.Y.), 1982-98; head cardiology unit Strong Meml. Hosp., Rochester, 1982-98; emeritus prof. medicine U. Rochester, 1998—. Cons. NIH, 1975—, NASA, 1994—; clin. prof. medicine U. Wash. Sch. Medicine, Seattle, 2000—. Mem. editorial bd. New Eng. Jour. Medicine, 1974-81, Circulation, 1980-83, Circulation Research, 1982-89, Jour. Clin. Investigation, 1984-89, Cochrane Collaboration Heart Group, 1997—. Contbr. articles, revs. and editorials on cardiovascular physiology to profl. jours. chpts. to books. Served to capt. USAF, 1963-65. Research grantee NIH, 1971-98; grantee Am. Heart Assn., 1971-76. Fellow ACP; mem. Am. Soc. Clin. Investigation, Assn. Am. Physicians, Am. Heart Assn., Am. Physiol. Soc., Assn. Profs. Cardiology (past pres.), N.Y. Cardiol. Soc. (past pres.), Phi Beta Kappa, Alpha Omega Alpha. Achievements include studies on experimental and clinical myocardial ischemia and infarction, and congestive heart failure.

HOOK, RALPH CLIFFORD, JR. business educator; b. Kansas City, Mo., May 2, 1923; s. Ralph Clifford and Ruby (Swanson) H.; m. Joyce Fink, Jan. 20, 1946; children— Ralph Clifford III, John Gregory. BA, U. Mo., 1947, MA, 1948; PhD, U. Tex., 1954. Instr. U. Mo., 1947-48; asst. prof. Tex. A&M U., 1948-51; lectr. U. Tex., 1951-52; co-owner, mgr. Hook Buick Co., also Hook Truck & Tractor Co., Lee's Summit, Mo., 1952-58; assoc. prof. U. Kansas City, 1953-58; dir. Bur. Bus. Research and Services, Ariz. State U., 1958-66, prof. mktg., 1960-68; dean Coll. Bus. Adminstrn., U. Hawaii, 1968-74; prof. mktg. U. Hawaii, 1974-96, prof. mktg. emeritus, 1996—. Vis. Disting. prof. N.E. La. U., 1979; dir. Hook Bros. Corp., Market City Ltd., M.L. Macademia Ptnrs., ltd. partnerships. Author: (with others) The Management Primer, 1972, Life Style Marketing, 1979, Marketing Service, 1983; contbr. (with others) monograph series Western Bus. Roundup; founder, moderator Western Bus. Roundup radio series, 1958-68. Bd. dirs. Samaritan Counseling Ctr. of Hawaii and Waikiki Health Ctr. 1st lt. F.A., AUS, 1943-46; col. Res. Recipient alumni citation of merit U. Mo. Coll. Bus. and Pub. Adminstrn., 1969; Distinguished Service award Nat. Def. Transp. Assn., 1977, God and Service award United Meth. Ch./Boy Scouts Am., 1986; named to Faculty Hall Fame Ariz. State U. Coll. Bus. Assn., 1977, Hawaii Transp. Hall of Fame, 1986; named Educator of Yr., Western Mktg. Educators' Assn., 1998, Hawaii Bus. Hall of Fame, 2000. Fellow Internat. Coun. for Sml. Bus. (pres. 1963); mem. Hawaii World Trade Assn. (pres. 1973-74), Am. Mktg. Assn. (v.p. 1965-67, pres. Cen. Ariz. chpt. 1960-61, pres. Honolulu chpt. 1991-92, Wayne A. Lemberg award for disting. svc. 1995), Western Assn. Collegiate Schs. Bus. (pres. 1972-73), Sales and Mktg. Execs. Internat. (life), Nat. Def. Transp. Assn. (Hawaii v.p. 1978-82), Newcomen Soc. N.Am. (Hawaii chmn.), Pi Sigma Epsilon (v.p. for edn. programs 1990-94), Mu Kappa Tau (pres. 1996-98), Beta Gamma Sigma, Omicron Delta Kappa, Beta Theta Pi, Delta Sigma Pi (gold coun.) United Methodist. Home: 311 Ohua Ave Apt 1104D Honolulu HI 96815-3636 Office: U Hawaii Coll Bus Adminstrn 2404 Maile Way Bldg C Honolulu HI 96822-2223

HOOKER, ELAINE NORTON, news executive; b. Rockville Center, N.Y., Dec. 4, 1944; d. Henry Gaither and Ann Lou (Allen) Norton; m. Ronald Wayne Johnson (div.); m. Kenneth Ward Hooker Jr. (div.); children: Alisa, Miranda, Nora, Emily. Student, Wilson Coll., 1962-64, U. Hartford, 1965, Trinity Coll., 1974, Andover Newton Theol. Sch., 1988-89. Reporter, editor The Hartford (Conn.) Courant, 1969-74; newswoman AP, Hartford, 1974-75, Conn. news editor, 1975-79, western Mass. corr. Springfield, Mass., 1979-80, Mass. day news supr. Boston, 1981-84, Mass. news editor, 1984, Conn. bur. chief Hartford, 1984-88, dep. dir. corp. comm. N.Y.C., 1990, gen. exec. newspaper membership, 1991-97, Oreg. bur. chief Portland, 1997—. Spkr. in field. Active various coms. at chs. in Concord, Mass., Hartford, Briarcliff, N.Y., Greenwich, Conn., N.Y.C. Recipient Sigma Delta Chi award, 1974. Mem. Soc. Profl. Journalists (mem. Freedom Info. coun. 1984-87), New Eng. Soc. Newspaper Editors (rep. Soviet journalists conf. 1985), Open Oreg. Home: 1005 SW Park Ave Apt 406 Portland OR 97205-2416 Office: AP 121 SW Salmon St Ste 1450 Portland OR 97204-2924

HOOLEY, DARLENE, congresswoman, former county commissioner; b. Williston, N.D., Apr. 4, 1939; d. Clarence Alvin and Alyce (Rogers) Olsen; m. John Hooley (div.); children: Chad, Erin. BS in Edn., Oreg. State U., 1961, postgrad., 1963-65, Portland State U., 1966-67. Tchr. Woodburn (Oreg.) & Gervais Sch., 1962-65, David Douglas Sch. Dist., Portland, Oreg., 1965-67, St. Mary's Acad., Portland, 1967-69; mem. West Linn (Oreg.) City Coun., 1976-80; state rep. Oreg. State Ho. of Reps., 1980-87; county commr. Clackamas County (Oreg.) Bd., 1987-96; mem. U.S. Congress from 5th dist. Oreg., 1996—; mem. budget com., fin. svcs. com. Vice-chair Oreg. Tourism Alliance, Portland, 1991—. bd. dirs. Pub. Employees Ret. Bd., Portland, 1989—, Cmty. Corrections Bd., Oregon City, 1990—, Providence Med. Ctr., Portland, 1989—; acting chair Oreg. Trail Found. Bd., Oregon City, 1991—; mem. Urban Growth Policy Adv. Com., Portland, 1991—. Named Legislator of the Year Oreg. Libr. Assn., 1985-86, Oreg. Solar Energy Assn., 1985; recipient Spl. Svc. award Clackamas City Coun. for Child Abuse Prevention, 1989. Mem. LWV, Oreg. Women's Polit. Caucus (Women of the Yr. 1988). Democrat. Office: 1130 Longworth Bldg Washington DC 20515-3705

HOOPER, EDWIN BICKFORD, physicist; b. Bremerton, Wash., June 18, 1937; s. E.B. and Elizabeth (Patrick) H.; m. Virginia Hooper, Dec. 28, 1963; children: Edwin, Sarah, William. SB, MIT, 1959, PhD, 1965. Asst. prof. applied sci. Yale U., New Haven, 1966-70; physicist, dep. program leader FE Lawrence Livermore (Calif.) Nat. Lab., 1970—. Contbr. articles to profl. jours. Pres. Danville (Calif.) Assn., 1982-84; pres. Friends Iron Horse Trail, 1984-86; v.p. San Ramon Valley Edn. Found., 1989-90; dir. Leadership, San Ramon Valley, 1990-92. Fellow Am. Phys. Soc. (bd. dirs. div. Plasma Physics 1990-91); mem. AIAA (sr.), AAAS. Office: Lawrence Livermore Nat Lab L-637 Livermore CA 94550-4436

HOOPER, ROGER FELLOWES, architect, retired; b. Southampton, N.Y., Aug. 18, 1917; s. Roger Fellowes and Justine Van Rensselaer (Barber) H.; m. Patricia Bentley, Aug. 10, 1946; children: Judith Bayard Teresi, Rachel Bentley Zingg, Roger Fellowes III. AB, Harvard U., 1939, MArch, 1948. Ptnr. Malone & Hooper, San Francisco, 1949-60; ptnr., pres. Hooper Olmsted & Emmons, San Francisco, 1964-79; chmn. Hooper Olmsted & Hrovat, San Francisco, 1980-94, retired, 1994. Bd. mgr. Marin YMCA, San Rafael, Calif.; bd. dirs., pres. Marin Conservation League, San Rafael. Lt. comdr. USNR, 1941-45, WWII. Mem. AIA.

HOOPES, FARREL G. secondary education educator; Tchr. Star Valley H.S., Afton, Wyo. Recipient Tchr. Excellence award Internat. Tech. Edn. Assn., 1992. Office: Star Valley HS PO Box 8000 Afton WY 83110-8000

HOOVER, GARY LYNN, banker; b. Tipton, Ind., Oct. 20, 1937; s. Carmel Wayne and Virginia Ruth (Mitchell) H.; m. Virginia Maxine James Monet, May 8, 1965 (div. Apr. 1976); m. Laura E. Grigg, June 25, 1988; children: Devin Page, Melissa Virginia. BS, Purdue U., 1959. Nat. bank examiner Internat. Comptroller of the Currency, Washington, 1962-71; v.p. Am. Fletcher Nat. Bank, Indpls., 1971-81; credit examiner Internat. Farm Credit Adminstrn., Washington, 1981-84; v.p. Nat. Bank for Cooperations, Englewood, Colo., 1984-95. Chmn. Hoover Farms, Inc., Tipton, Ind.; pres. Hoover Fin. Assn., LLC, Highlands Ranch, Colo., 1995—. With U.S. Army, 1961-66. Mem. Ind. Bankers Assn. Colo. Republican. Avocations: reading, travel. Home: 9057 S Bear Mountain Dr Hghlnds Ranch CO 80126-2269 Office: Hoover Fin Assocs PO Box 260826 Highlands Ranch CO 80163-0826 Fax: 303-791-0615. E-mail: glynhoo@aol.com

HOOVER, R. DAVID, manufacturing executive; Various positions Ball Corp., Broomfield, Colo., 1970-87, v.p., treas., 1988-92, sr. v.p., CFO, 1992—, exec. v.p., bd. dirs., 1996—, vice chmn., 1998—, pres., package ops., 2000—. Office: Ball Corp 9300 W 108th Cir Broomfield CO 80021-3682

HOOVER, RICHARD, set designer; Prodn. designer films including: It Takes Two, 1988, Feeling 109, 1988, Torch Song Trilogy, 1988, Bob Roberts, 1992, Storyville, 1992, Dream Lover, 1994, Panther, 1995, Dead Man Walking, 1995, The Blackout, 1997, Apt Pupil, 1998, The Cradle Will Rock, 1999, Payback, 1999; designer TV movies: Family of Spies, 1990, Heat Wave, 1990, Zooman, 1995, (TV series) Twin Peaks, 1990; art dir.: Somewhere Tomorrow, 1983, Checking Out, 1989, Cradle Will Rock, 1999; set decorator: Wisdom, 1986, In the Mood, 1987; visual cons. Ed Wood, 1994; set designer: Sweet Lorraine, 1987, Girl, Interrupted, 1999, Twilight: Los Angeles, 2000, Fail Safe, 2000. Winner 1999 Tony award for best set design for Not About Nightingales, Evening Standard award, London Critics' Cir. award, Drama Desk award, Outer Critics Cir. award. Office: c/o IATSE Local 847 13949 Ventura Blvd Ste 301 Sherman Oaks CA 91423-3570

HOOVER, ROBERT ALLAN, university president; b. Des Moines, May 9, 1941; s. Claude Edward and Anna Doris H.; m. Jeanne Mary Hoover, Feb. 22, 1968; children: Jennifer Jill Jacobs, Suzanne Elizabeth. BS, Ariz. State U., 1967, MA, 1969; PhD, U. Calif., Santa Barbara, 1973. Instr. polit. sci. Utah State U., Logan, 1971-73, asst. prof. polit. sci., 1973-79, assoc. prof. polit. sci., chair polit. sci. dept., 1979-84, prof. polit. sci., 1984-91, dean Coll. Humanities, Arts and Social Scis., 1984-91; v.p. for acad. affairs U. Nev., Reno, 1991-96; pres. U. Idaho, Moscow, 1996—. Author: The Politics of MX: A New Direction in Weapons Procurement?, 1982, The MX Controversy: A Guide to Issues and References, 1982, Arms Control: The Interwar Naval Limitation Agreements, 1980. Bd. dirs. United Way, Reno, 1994-96, Channel 5, Reno, 1991-95, St. Scholastica Acad., Canon City, Colo., 1991-96. Avocations: biking, jogging, camping. Office: Univ Idaho Adminstrn Bldg Rm 105 Moscow ID 83844-0001 E-mail: hoover@uidaho.edu

HOPFENBECK, GEORGE MARTIN, JR. lawyer; b. N.Y.C., Mar. 1, 1929; s. George Martin and Margaret Spencer (Felt) H.; m. Ruth Elizabeth Allen, June 27, 1953; children: Ann Elizabeth, James Allen. BA, Williams Coll., 1951; JD, Yale U., 1954. Bar: Colo., 1955. Assoc. Davis, Graham & Stubbs and predecessor Lewis, Grant & Davis, Denver, 1954-59, ptnr., 1959-92, of counsel, 1993—. Bd. dirs. Am. Cancer Soc. Inc., Colo. divsn., Denver, 1966-90, chmn., 1975-77; bd. dirs. Colo. Regional Cancer Ctr. Inc., Denver, 1974-81, pres., 1975-77; bd. dirs. Am. Cancer Soc. Inc., Atlanta, 1984-90, Denver Parks and Recreation Found., 1966-75; bd. dirs. Boys and Girls Clubs of Metro Denver, Inc., 1993—, chmn., 1998-2000; mem. Colo. State Pers. Bd., Denver, 1971-75, chmn., 1971-72; mem. Denver Bd. Parks & Recreation, 1961-69; trustee Kent Sch. for Girls, Denver, 1970-73; chmn. campaign com. for Gov. Love, Colo., 1966, campaign com. for McKevitt for Congress, Denver, 1970. Recipient St. George medal Am. Cancer Soc., 1982. Mem. ABA, Colo. Bar Assn., Denver Country Club (bd. dirs. 1967-70), University Club (Denver) (bd. dirs. 1973-82). Republican. Episcopalian. Home: 450 Race St Denver CO 80206-4121 Office: Davis Graham & Stubbs PO Box 185 1550 17th St Ste 500 Denver CO 80202-1500 also: 333 Logan St Ste 108 Denver CO 80203-4089

HOPKINS, CECILIA ANN, business educator; b. Havre, Mont., Feb. 17, 1922; d. Kost L. and Mary (Manaras) Sofos; m. Henry E. Hopkins, Sept. 7, 1944. BS, Mont. State Coll., 1944; MA, San Francisco State Coll., 1958; postgrad., Stanford U.; PhD, Calif. Western U., 1977. Bus. tchr. Havre (Mont.) H.S., Mateo, Calif., 1942-44; sec. George P. Gorham, Realtor, San Mateo, 1944-45; escrow sec. Fox & Cars, 1945-50; escrow officer Calif. Pacific Title Ins. Co., 1950-57; bus. tchr. Westmoor H.S., Daly City, Calif., 1958-59, Coll. of San Mateo, 1959-63, chmn. real estate-ins. dept., 1963-76, dir. divsn. bus., 1976-86, coord. real estate dept., 1986-91. Cons. to commr. Calif. Divsn. Real Estate, 1963-91, mem. periodic rev. exam. com.; chmn. C.C. Adv. Com., 1971-72, mem. com., 1975-91; projector direction Calif. State Chancellor's Career Awareness Consortium, mem. endowment fund adv. com., c.c. real estate edn. com., state c.c. adv. com.; mem. No. Calif. adv. bd. to Glendale Fed. Savs. and Loan Assn.; mem. bd. advisors San Mateo County Bd. Suprs., 1981-82; mem. real estate edn. and rsch. com. to Calif. Commr. Real Estate, 1983-90; mem. edn., membership, and profl. exch. coms. Am. chpt. Internat. Real Estate Fedn., 1985-92. Co-author: California Real Estate Principles; contbr. articles to profl. jours. Recipient Citizen of Day award KABL, Outstanding Contbns. award Redwood City-San Carlos-Belmont Bd. Realtors, Nat. Real Estate Educators Assn. award emeritus, 1993; named Woman of Achievement, San Mateo-Burlingame br. Soroptimist Internat., 1979. Mem. AAUW, Calif. Assn. Real Estate Tchrs. (state pres. 1964-65, life hon. dir. 1962—, Outstanding Real Estate Educator of Yr. 1978-79), Real Estate Cert. Inst. (Disting. Merit award 1982), Calif. Bus. Edn. Assn. (cert. of commendation 1979), San Francisco State Coll., Guidance and Counseling Alumni, Calif. Real Estate Educators' Assn. (dir. emeritus, hon. dir. 1990), Real Estate Nat. Educators Assn. (award emeritus for outstanding contbns. 1993), San Mateo-Burlingame Bd. Realtors (award emeritus Outstanding Contbrs. to Membership), Alpha Delta, Pi Lambda Theta, Delta Pi Epsilon (nat. dir. interchpt. rels. 1962-65, nat. historian 1966-67, nat. sec. 1968-69), Alpha Gamma Delta. Home: 504 Colgate Way San Mateo CA 94402-3206

HOPKINS, DONALD J. lawyer; b. Long Beach, Calif., Jan. 9, 1947; m. Ellen Colokathis, Aug. 29, 1970; children: Melanie J., Shannon R., Christopher S. AB, Stanford U., 1968; JD, Harvard U., 1971. Bar: Mass. 1971, Colo. 1974, U.S. Dist. Ct. Colo. 1974. Mem. firm Holme Roberts & Owen LLP, Denver, 1973—. Fellow Am. Coll. Trust and Estate Counsel. Office: Holme Roberts & Owen LLP 1700 Lincoln St Ste 4100 Denver CO 80203-4541

HOPKINS, HENRY TYLER, museum director, art educator; b. Idaho Falls, Idaho, Aug. 14, 1928; s. Talcott Thompson and Zoe (Erbe) H.; children— Victoria Anne, John Thomas, Christopher Tyler. BA, Sch. of Art Inst., Chgo., 1952, MA, 1955; postgrad., UCLA, 1957-60; PhD (hon.), Calif. Coll. Arts and Crafts, 1984, San Francisco Art Inst., 1986. Curator exhbns., publs. Los Angeles County Mus. of Art, 1960-68; dir. Fort Worth Art Mus., 1968-74; lectr. art history UCLA Ext., 1961-68; dir. San Francisco Mus. of Modern Art, 1974-86; chmn. art dept. UCLA, 1991-94, dir. F.S. Wight Gallery, 1991-95, dir. Armand Hammer Mus. Art and Cultural Ctr., 1994-99, prof. art, 1999—; lectr. art history UCLA Ext., 1994-99. Instr. Tex. Christian U., Ft. Worth, 1968-74; dir. U.S. representation Venice (Italy) Bienniel, 1970; dir. art presentation Festival of Two Worlds, Spoleto, Italy, 1970; co-commr. U.S. representation XVI Sao Paulo (Brazil) Biennale, 1981; cons. NEA, mem. mus. panel, 1979-84, chmn., 1981; cons., mem. mus. panel NEH, 1976. Contbr. numerous articles to profl. jours., also numerous mus. publs. Served with AUS, 1952-54. Decorated knight Order Leopold II, Belgium); recipient special internat. award, Art L.A., 1992. Mem. Assn. Art Mus. Dirs. (pres. 1985-86), Coll. Art Assn., Am. Assn. Museums, Western Assn. Art Museums (pres. 1977-78) Home: 939 1/2 Hilgard Ave Los Angeles CA 90024-3032 Office: UCLA Art Dept 405 Hilgard Ave Los Angeles CA 90095-9000

HOPKINSON, SHIRLEY LOIS, library and information science educator; b. Boone, Iowa, Aug 25, 1924; d. Arthur Perry and Zora (Smith) Hopkinson; student Coe Coll., 1942-43; AB cum laude (Phi Beta Kappa scholar 1944), U. Colo., 1945; BLS, U. Calif., 1949; MA (Honnold Honor scholar 1945-46), Claremont Grad. Sch., 1951; EdM, U. Okla., 1952, EdD, 1957 Tchr. pub. sch. Stigler, Okla., 1946-47, Palo Verde High Sch., Jr. Coll., Blythe, Calif., 1947-48; asst. librarian Modesto (Calif.) Jr. Coll., 1949-51; tchr., librarian Fresno, Calif., 1951-52, La Mesa, Cal., 1953-55; asst. prof. librarianship, instructional materials dir. Chaffey Coll., Ontario, Calif., 1955-59; asst. prof. librarian ship, San Jose (Calif.) State Coll., 1959-64; assoc. prof., 1964-69, prof., 1969—; bd. dirs. NDEA Inst. Sch. Librs., summer 1966; mem. Santa Clara County Civil Service Bd. Examiners. Recipient Master Gardner cert. Oreg. State U. Extension Svc. Book reviewer for jours. Mem. ALA, Calif. Library Assn., Audio-Visual Assn. Calif., NEA, AAUP, AAUW (dir. 1957-58), Bus. Profl. Women's Club, Sch. Librs. Assn. Calif. (com. mem., treas. No. sect. 1951-52), San Diego County Sch. Librs. Assn. (sec. 1945-55), Calif. Tchrs. Assn., LWV (bd. dirs. 1950-51, publs. chmn.), Phi Beta Kappa, Alpha Lambda Delta, Alpha Beta Alpha, Kappa Delta Pi, Phi Kappa Phi (disting. acad. achievement award 1981), Delta Kappa Gamma (sec. 1994-96, legis. liaison, 1996—). Author: Descriptive Cataloging of Library Materials; Instructional Materials for Teaching the Use of the Library. Contbr. to profl. publs. Editor: Calif. Sch. Libraries, 1963-64; asst. editor: Sch. Library Assn. of Calif. Bull., 1961-63; book reviewer profl. jours. Office: 1340 Pomeroy Ave Apt 408 Santa Clara CA 95051-3658

HOPP, RICHARD A. lawyer; b. Seattle, Dec. 11, 1946; BA, San Luis Rey Coll., 1969; JD, U. Wash., 1976. Bar: Wash. 1976. Mem. Stoel, Rives, Boley, Jones & Grey, Seattle; ptnr. Stoel Rives LLP, Seattle, 2000—. Chmn. Seattle Pension Roundtable, 1987—. Articles editor Washington Law Review, 1975-76. Mem. ABA, Wash. State Bar Assn. (bd. dirs. Seattle chpt., western pension conf. 1985-87, tax coun., taxation sect.), Seattle-King County. Office: Stoel Rives LLP 600 University St Ste 3600 Seattle WA 98101-4109

HOPP, TERRY A. computer company executive; BA in Bus. Adminstrn., Calif. State U., Fullerton. CPA, Calif. Audit ptnr. Earnst & Young LLP, 1981-98; v.p. fin. Western Digital Corp., Irvine, Calif., 1998, now sr. v.p., CFO. Mem. AICPA. Office: Western Digital Corp 8105 Irvine Center Dr Irvine CA 92618-2937

HOPPENSTEADT, FRANK CHARLES, educator, mathematician, university administrator; b. Oak Park, Ill., Apr. 29, 1938; s. Frank Carl and Margaret Hoppensteadt; children: Charles, Matthew, Sarah. BA, Butler U., 1960; MS, U. Wis., 1962, PhD, 1965. Instr. math. U. Wis., Madison, 1965; asst. prof. math. Mich. State U., East Lansing, 1965-68, dean Coll. Natural Sci., 1986-95; dir. sys. sci. engr. rsch., prof. math. and elec. engring. Ariz. State U., Tempe, 1995—; assoc. prof. NYU-Courant, N.Y.C., 1968-76; prof., 1976-79, U. Utah, Salt Lake City, 1977-86, chmn. dept. math., 1982-85. Author: Mathematical Methods in Population Biology, 1982, An Introduction to Mathematics of Neurons, 1986, 2d edit., 1997, Mathematics in Medicine and the Life Sciences, 1991, Analysis and Simulation of Chaotic Systems, 1993, Weakly Connected Neural Networks, 1997. Mem. Am. Math. Soc. (chmn. applied math. com. 1976-80), Soc. Indsl. and Applied Maths., Sigma Xi.

HOPPING, WILLIAM RUSSELL, hospitality industry consultant and appraiser; b. Balt., May 3, 1947; s. Russell Leroy and Janet Louise (Cloud) H.; m. Catherine Wilson; 1 child, William Alexander. BS in Hotel Adminstrn., Cornell U., 1969; MBA, U. Denver, 1978. Mgr. Sylvania (Ohio) Country Club, 1972-77; sr. cons. Pannell Kerr Forster, Denver, 1978-82; cons. Ginther Wycoff Grp., Denver, 1982-85; pres. W.R. Hopping & Co., Inc., Denver, 1985—. Mem. adv. bd. travel and tourism dept. Arapahoe C.C., 1998. Vol., Big Bros., Inc., Denver, 1990—; chmn. adv. bd. U. Denver Profl. Career Devel. Prog., 1987-88, chmn. task force, Career and Placement Ctr., 1989. 1st lt. U.S. Army, 1970-72. Mem. Appraisal Inst., Internat. Soc. Hospitality Cons. (pres. 1990-91, chmn. 1991-93, chmn. emeritus, 1993—), Cornell Soc. Hotelmen (pres. Rocky Mountain chpt. 1984-85), Counselors of Real Estate. Avocations: bicycling, skiing. Office: W R Hopping & Co Inc 6334 S Yates Ct Littleton CO 80123-6738

HOPSON, ANDY, public relations executive; Pres. Publicis (formerly Evans Group), Seattle. Office: Publicis 424 2nd Ave W Seattle WA 98119-4140

HORAK, JAN-CHRISTOPHER, film studies educator, curator; b. Bad Münstereifel, Fed. Republic Germany, May 1, 1951; came to U.S., 1951; s. Jerome V. and Giselle (Offermanns) H.; m. Martha F. Schirn, May 17, 1988; 1 child, Gianna. BA, U. Del., 1973; MS, Boston U., 1975; PhD, Westfälische Wilhelms-U., Münster, Germany, 1984. Intern Internat. Mus. Photography, Rochester, N.Y., 1975-76, assoc. curator George Eastman House, 1984-87, curator film, 1987-90, sr. curator, 1990-94; asst. prof. film studies U. Rochester, 1985-90, assoc. prof., 1990-93, prof., 1994; dir. Münchner Filmmuseum, Munich, Germany, 1994-98; prof. Hochschule f. Fernsehen u. Film, 1995-98; dir. Archives and Collections Universal Studios, L.A., 1998-00; prof. UCLA, 1999—; curator Hollywood Entertainment Mus., 2000—. Panelist, chmn. film panel N.Y. State Coun. of Arts, N.Y.C., 1986-89; cons. USIA, 1988-90; archivists adv. bd. The Film Found., N.Y.C., 1990-94; v.p., pres. Assn. Moving Image Archivists, 1991-93; exec. com. Internat. Fedn. Film Archives, 1993-95, Kuratorium Junger Deutscher Film, 1995-97. Author: Anti-Nazi Filme der Emigration, 1984, Fluchtpunkt Hollywood, 1986, The Dream Merchants, 1989, Lovers of Cinema: The First American Film Avant-Garde, 1995, Berge, Licht und Traum: Arnold Fanck und der deutsche Bergfilm, 1997, Making Images Move: Photography and Avant-Garde Cinema, 1997; editor: Film und Foto der 20er Jahre, 1979, Helmar Lerski, 1982; contbr. articles to profl. jours. Recipient Louis B. Mayer award Mayer Found., Am. Film Inst., 1975; Heinrich Herz Stiftung fellow, 1979-81. Mem. Soc. Cinema Studies, Assn. Moving Image Archivists (founding editor 2001), Soc. Exile Studies, Internat. Assn. Audio-Visual Media and History. Avocations: travel, skiing, swimming. Office: Universal Studios Inc 545 Sierra Vista Ave Pasadena CA 91107 E-mail: c.horak@hollywoodmuseum.com

HORAN, JOHN J. pharmaceutical company executive; b. S.I., N.Y., July 9, 1920; s. Michael T. and Alice (Kelly) H.; m. Julie Fitzgerald, Jan. 2, 1945; children: Mary Alice, Thomas, Jack, David. A.B., Manhattan Coll., 1940; LL.B., Columbia, 1946. Bar: N.Y. bar 1946. With firm Nims, Verdi & Martin, N.Y.C., 1946-52; atty. Merck & Co., Inc., 1952-55; counsel Merck & Co., Inc. (Merck Sharp & Dohme div.), 1955-57; dir. pub. relations Merck & Co., 1957-61, exec. dir. rsch. adminstrn., 1961-62, dir. corp. planning, 1962-63; exec. v.p. mktg. Merck Sharp & Dohme, 1963-67; exec. v.p., gen. mgr., 1967-69; pres., 1969-72; corp. sr. v.p., 1972-74; exec. v.p., 1974-75; pres., chief operating officer, 1975-76; chmn., chief exec. officer, 1976-85; vice chmn., 1985-86; also bd. dirs. Bd. dirs. Atrix Labs., Inc., Myriad Genetics, Inc., PathoGenesis Corp.; trustee Robert Wood Johnson Found. Ret. dir. Burlington Industries, GM, J.P. Morgan, Morgan Guaranty Trust, NCR Corp. Mem. Pharm. Mfrs. Assn. (chmn. bd. 1979-80). Office: Myriad Genetics Inc 320 Wakara Way Salt Lake City UT 84108

HORN, CHRISTIAN FRIEDRICH, venture capital company executive; b. Dresden, Germany, Dec. 23, 1927; came to U.S., 1954, naturalized, 1959; s. Otto Hugo and Elsa H.; m. Christa Winkler, Feb. 13, 1954; 1 child, Sabrina. MS, Technische Hochschule, Dresden, 1951; PhD, Technische Hochschule, Aachen, Germany, 1958. Rsch. scientist German Acad. Sci., Berlin, 1951-53, Farbwerke Hoechst, Germany, 1953-54; rsch. mgr. Union Carbide, N.Y.C., 1954-65; pres. Polymer Tech. Inc., N.Y.C., 1965-74; v.p. W.R. Grace & Co., N.Y.C., 1974-81, sr. v.p., 1981-95, also bd. dirs.; pres. Horn Venture Ptnrs. (formerly Grace Horn Ventures), Cupertino, Calif., 1983-2000, mng. ptnr., 1987-2000; pres. Horn Investment Corp., Saratoga, 1996-2000. Bd. dirs. Timothy's Coffees of the World. Patentee in field With German Army, 1944-45. Decorated Iron Cross. Lutheran. Office: Horn Venture Ptnrs 12930 Saratoga Ave Ste B9 Saratoga CA 95070-4661

HORN, JAMES A. state legislator; m. Joyce Horn; 2 children. BSME, U. Ill.; postgrad., So. Meth. U. Mgr. Def. and Space group Boeing Co.; mem. Wash. Senate, Dist. 41, Olympia, 1988—; spkr. pro tempore Wash. Legislature, Olympia, 1996, mem. state and local govt. com., mem. higher edn. com., mem. rules com., mem. transp. com., mem. joint legis. audit and rev. com., mem. joint legis. sys. com., mem. legis. transp. com., mem. organized crime adv. bd., mem. legis. evaluation and accountability program com., mem. legis. ethics bd., gov.'s ethics commn. Mem. Puget Sound Regional Coun., State Bldg. Code Coun.; Mcpl. Rsch. Coun., Pacific N.W. Econ. Regional Del. Coun.; past mayor Mercer Island, 1988-89; past mem. Mercer Island city Coun., King County Subregional Coun. and Puget Sound Coun. Govts.; bd. advisors Eastside Sexual Assault Ctr. for Children. Mem. VFW (past bd. trustees), Tech. Mktg. Soc. Am. (nat. v.p.), Kent Boeing Mgmt. Assn. (past chmn. civic affairs), Lions (Mercer Island). Republican. Office: 107 Irving Newhouse Ofc Olympia WA 98504-0001

HORN, STEPHEN, congressman, political science educator; b. San Juan Bautista, Calif., May 31, 1931; s. John Stephen and Isabelle (McCaffrey) H.; m. Nini Moore, Sept. 4, 1954; children: Marcia Karen, John Stephen. AB with great distinction, Stanford, 1953, postgrad., 1953-54, 55-56, PhD in Polit. Sci, 1958; M in Pub Adminstrn., Harvard, 1955. Congl. fellow, 1958-59; adminstrv. asst. to sec. labor James P. Mitchell Washington, 1959-60; legislative asst. to U.S. Senator Thomas H. Kuchel, 1960-66; sr. fellow The Brookings Instn., 1966-69; dean grad. studies and research Am. U., 1969-70; pres. Calif. State U., Long Beach, 1970-88, Trustee prof. polit. sci., 1988-93; mem. U.S. Congress from 38th Calif. dist., 1993—; mem. govt. reform com., transp. and infrastructure com. Sr. cons., host The Govt. Story on TV, The Election Game (radio series), 1967-69, vice chmn. U.S. Commn. on Civil Rights, 1969-80 (commr. 1980-82); chmn. Urban Studies Fellow Adv. Com., U.S. Dept. HUD, 1969-70; mem. Law Enforcement Ednl. Prog. Adv. Com., U.S. Dept Justice, 1969-70; adv. bd. Nat. Inst. Corrections, 1972-88 (chmn. 1984-87), Author: The Cabinet and Congress, 1960, Unused Power: The Work of the Senate Committee on Appropriations, 1970, (with Edmund Beard) Congressional Ethics: The View from the House, 1975. Active Pres.-elect Nixon's Task Force on Orgn. Exec. Br., 1968, Kutak Found.; vice chmn. Long Beach Area C. of C., 1984-88; co-founder Western U.S. Com. Arts and Scis. for Eisenhower, 1956; chmn. Am. Assn. State Colls. and Univs., 1985-86; mem. Calif. Ednl. Facilities Authority, 1984-93. USAR, 1954-62. Fellow John F. Kennedy Inst. Politics Harvard U., 1966-67. Fellow Nat. Acad. Pub. Adminstrn.; mem. Stanford Assocs., Stanford Alumni Assn. (pres. 1976-77), Phi Beta Kappa, Pi Sigma Alpha. Republican. Office: US Ho of Reps 2331 Rayburn Ho Office Bldg Washington DC 20515-0001

HORN, SUSAN DADAKIS, statistics educator; b. Cleve., Aug. 30, 1943; d. James Sophocles and Demeter (Zessis) Dadakis; m. Roger Alan Horn, July 24, 1965; children: Ceres, Corinne, Howard. BA, Cornell U., 1964; MS, Stanford U., 1966, PhD, 1968. Asst. prof. Johns Hopkins U., Balt., 1968-76, assoc. prof., 1976-86, prof. stats. and health svcs. rsch. methods, 1986-92, sr. scientist Intermountain Health Care, Salt Lake City, 1992-95; prof. dept. med. informatics Sch. Medicine U. Utah, Salt Lake City, 1992—; rsch. prof. U. Tex.-Houston Sch. Nursing, 1999—2001. Sr. scientist Inst. for Clin. Outcomes Rsch., Salt Lake City. Fellow Am. Statist. Assn., Assn. for Health Svcs. Rsch.; mem. APHA, Biometric Soc., Assn. for Health Svcs. Research, Sigma Xi, Phi Beta Kappa, Phi Kappa Phi. Presbyterian. Avocations: tennis, swimming. Home: 1793 Fort Douglas Cir Salt Lake City UT 84103-4451 Office: Inst Clin Outcomes Rsch 2681 Parleys Way Ste 201 Salt Lake City UT 84109-1630 E-mail: shorn@isisicor.com

HORNACEK, JEFFREY JOHN, professional basketball player; b. Elmhurst, Ill., May 3, 1963; Student, Iowa State. With Phoenix Suns, 1986-92, guard Phila. 76ers, 1992-94, Utah Jazz, 1994—. Named NBA All-Star, 1992. Office: Utah Jazz 301 W South Temple Salt Lake City UT 84101-1216

HORNADAY, ALINE GRANDIER, publisher, independent scholar; b. San Diego, Sept. 14, 1923; d. Frank and Lydia Landon (Weir) Grandier; m. Quinn Hornaday, Oct. 9, 1965. BA, Union of Experimenting Colls., San Diego, 1977; PhD, U. Calif., San Diego, 1984. Pub. San Diego Daily Transcript, 1952-72, columnist, 1972-74; dir. San Diego Ind. Scholars, 1985-87, 94-95; co-pub. Jour. Unconventional History, Cardiff, Calif., 1989-00. Vis. scholar U. Calif., San Diego, 1984—; speaker at profl. confs. Co-author: The Hornadays, Root and Branch; contbr. articles to profl. jours. and books. Commr. San Diego City Libr. Commn., 1964-70. Mem. San Diego Ind. Scholars, Nat. Coalition Ind. Scholars, Med. Assn. of Pacific, Am. Hist. Assn., Medieval Acad. Am., Nat. Soc. Colonial Dames of Am., Wed. Club (pres. 1964-65). Home and Office: 6435 Avenida Cresta La Jolla CA 92037-6514

HORNBEIN, THOMAS FREDERIC, anesthesiologist; b. St. Louis, Nov. 6, 1930; s. Leonard and Rosalie (Bernstein) H.; m. Gene Schwartz (div. 1968); children: Lia, Lynn, Cari, Andrea, Robert; m. Kathryn Mikesell, Dec. 24, 1971; 1 child, Melissa. BA, U. Colo.; MD, Wash. U. Diplomate Am. Bd. Anesthesiology. Intern King County Hosp., Seattle; resident in anesthesiology Wash. U., St. Louis, USPHS postdoctoral residency, instr. anesthesiology div., 1960-61; asst. prof. U. Wash., Seattle, 1963-67, assoc. prof., 1967-70, prof., 1970—. Vice chmn. Dept. Anesthesiology, U. Wash., Seattle, 1972-74, asst. chmn. research 1974-77, chmn. 1978-93, research affiliate Primate Ctr., 1980. Author: Everest the West Ridge, 1966. Mem. bd. trustees Little Sch., Bellevue, Wash., 1982-89. Served to lt. comdr. USN, 1961-63. Recipient George Norlin award U. Colo., Denver, 1970, Alumni Centennial Symposium award 1975, Disting. Teaching award U. Wash., 1982. Fellow AAAS; mem. Am. Physiol. Soc. (editor 1967-73), Am. Soc. Anesthesiologists (Rovenstine lectr. 1989), Assn. Univ. Anesthetists (treas. 1969-72, pres. 1974-75), Soc. Acad. Anesthesia Chairmen, Inst. of Medicine, Phi Beta Kappa, Alpha Omega Alpha. Avocation: mountaineering. Office: U Wash Sch Medicine Dept Anesthesiology PO Box 356540 Seattle WA 98195-6540 E-mail: hornbnt@u.washington.edu

HORNE, GRANT NELSON, public relations consultant; b. Salt Lake City, Jan. 14, 1931; s. Joseph Feramorz and Ida Verene (Nelson) H.; m. Georgia Henry, July 6, 1957 (div. Feb. 1977); 1 child, Mary Corneille. BA magna cum laude, Yale U., 1952; MA, U. Utah, 1954. Instr. Gunnery Sch., Washington, 1955-57, Great Books Found., N.Y.C., 1958-61; dir. pub. relations Edison Electric Inst., N.Y.C., 1961-72; sr. v.p. Underwood Jordan Assocs., N.Y.C., 1972-79; retired v.p. corp. comms. Pacific Gas and Electric Co., San Francisco, 1980-96. Past chmn. Pub. Rels. Seminar. Bd. dirs. Patrons the Vatican Mus.; bd. govs. San Francisco Symphony; active Knights of Malta. Mem. Arthur W. Page Soc. (Hall of Fame 1998), Yale Club (N.Y.C.), Villa Taverna Club (San Francisco). Roman Catholic. Avocations: chamber music, classical piano. Office: Pacific Gas & Electric Co 77 Beale St San Francisco CA 94105-1814 E-mail: granthorne@aol.com

HORNER, ALTHEA JANE, psychologist; b. Hartford, Conn., Jan. 13, 1926; d. Louis and Celia (Newmark) Greenwald; children: Martha Horner Hartley, Anne Horner Benck, David, Kenneth. BS in Psychology, U. Chgo., 1952; PhD in Clin. Psychology, U. So. Calif., 1965. Lic. psychologist, N.Y., Calif. Tchr. Pasadena (Calif.) City Coll., 1965-67; from asst. to assoc. prof. Los Angeles Coll. Optometry, 1967-70; supr. Psychology interns Pasadena Child Guidance Clinic, 1969-70; pvt. practice specializing in psychoanalysis and psychoanalytic psychotherapy, N.Y.C., 1970-83; supervising psychologist dept. psychiatry Beth Israel Med. Ctr., N.Y.C., 1972-

83, coordinator group therapy tng., 1976-82, clinician in charge Brief Adaptation-Oriented Psychotherapy Research Group, 1982-83; assoc. clin. prof. Mt. Sinai Sch. Medicine, N.Y.C., 1977-91, adj. assoc. prof., 1991—; mem. faculty Nat. Psychol. Assn. for Psychoanalysis, N.Y.C., 1982-83; sr. mem. faculty Wright Inst. Los Angeles Postgrad. Inst., 1983-85; pvt. practice L.A., 1983—; clin. prof. dept. Psychology UCLA, 1985-95. Author: (with others) Treating the Neurotic Patient in Brief Psychotherapy, 1985, Object Relations and the Developing Ego in Therapy, 1979, rev. edit., 1984, Little Big Girl, 1982, Being and Loving, 1978, 3d edit. 1990, Psychology for Living (with G. Forehand), 4th edit., 1977, The Wish for Power and the Fear of Having It, 1989, The Primacy of Structure, 1990, Psychoanalytic Object Relations Therapy, 1991, Working With the Core Relationship Problem in Psychotherapy, 1998, Chrysalis, 1999, Get Over It! Untie Your Relationship Knots and Move On, 2000; mem. editorial bd. Jour. of Humanistic Psychology, 1986—, Jour. of the Am. Acad. of Psychoanalysis; contbr. articles to profl. jours. Mem. AAAS, APA, Calif. State Psychol. Assn., Am. Acad. Psychoanalysis (sci. assoc.), So. Calif. Psychoanalytic Soc. and Inst. (hon.). Office: PMB 256 3579 E Foothill Blvd Pasadena CA 91107-3119

HORNER, ANTHONY ADAM, pediatrician, educator; b. N.Y.C., May 24, 1960; s. Harry and Joan Ruth (Frankel) H. BA in Biochemistry, U. Calif. San Diego, 1983; MD, St. Louis U., 1987. Diplomate Am. Bd. Pediatrics, Am. Bd. Allergy and Immunology. Resident in pediatrics UCLA Med. Ctr., 1990; fellow in pediatric immunology Boston Children's Hosp., 1994; asst. prof. pediatrics med. sch. U. Calif. San Diego, San Diego, 1994—. Co-principle investigator Children's Asthma Mgmt. Program, San Diego, 1994-99. Fellow Am. Acad. Pediatrics, Am. Acad. Allergy and Immunology. Avocations: skiing, music, entemology. Achievements include rsch. in the devel. of DNA-based vaccination strategies for the treatment of disease. Office: U Calif San Diego Med Sch 9500 Gilman Dr # Mc663 La Jolla CA 92093-5004

HORNER, JAMES, composer; b. 1953; Works include: composer (film scores) Battle Beyond the Stars, 1980, Humanoids from the Deep, 1980, Deadly Blessing, 1981, The Hand, 1981, The Pursuit of D.B. Cooper, 1981, Wolfen, 1981, Star Trek II: The Wrath of Khan, 1982, 48 Hours, 1982, Brainstorm, 1983, Gorky Park, 1983, Something Wicked This Way Comes, 1983, Space Raiders, 1983, Testament, 1983, Uncommon Valor, 1983, The Stone Boy, 1984, (with Chris Young) Barbarian Queen, 1985, Cocoon, 1985, Heaven Help Us, 1985, The Journey of Natty Gann, 1985, Volunteers, 1985, Wizard of the Lost Kingdom, 1985, In Her Own Time, 1985, An American Tail, 1986 (Grammy award nominee for best album of original instrumental score 1987), The Name of the Rose, 1986, Off Beat, 1986, Where the River Runs Black, 1986, *batteries not included, 1987, P.K. & the Kid, 1987, Project X, 1987, Cocoon: The Return, 1988, Red Heat, 1988, Vibes, 1988, Willow, 1988, The Land Before Time, 1988, Dad, 1989, Field of Dreams, 1989 (Acad. award nominee for best original score 1989), Glory, 1989 (Grammy award for best album of original instrumental score 1990), Honey, I Shrunk the Kids, 1989, In Country, 1989, I Love You to Death, 1990, Another 48 Hours, 1990, (with Ernest Troost) Andy Colby's Incredibly Awesome Adventure, 1990, Class Action, 1991, My Heroes Have Always Been Cowboys, 1991, Once Around, 1991, The Rocketeer, 1991, An American Tail: Fievel Goes West, 1991, Patriot Games, 1992, Sneakers, 1992, Thunderheart, 1992, Unlawful Entry, 1992, House of Cards, 1993, Jack the Bear, 1993, Swing Kids, 1993, A Far Off Place, 1993, Once Upon a Forest, 1993, Searching for Bobby Fischer, 1993, The Man Without a Face, 1993, Bopha!, 1993, We're Back!: A Dinosaur's Story, 1993, The Pelican Brief, 1993, The Pagemaster, 1994, Clear and Present Danger, 1994, Legends of the Fall, 1994, Apollo 13, 1995 (Acad. award nominee for best original dramatic score 1996), Braveheart, 1995 (Acad. award nominee for best original dramatic score 1996), Casper, 1995,The Devils' Own, 1997, Titanic, 1998 (Oscar & Grammy, 1998), Mighty Joe Young, 1998, The Mask of Zoro, 1998, Deep Impact, 1998; (film songs) (from An American Tail) Somewhere Out There, 1986 (Acad. award nominee for best original song 1986, Grammy awards for song of yr. and best song written for motion picture 1987), (from The Land Before Time) If We Hold on Together, 1988, (from An American Tail: Fievel Goes West) Way Out West, 1991, Dreams to Dream, 1991, The Girl I Left Behind, 1991; (film shorts scores) Tummy Trouble, 1989, (TV movie scores) Angel Dusted, 1981, A Few Days in Weasel Creek, 1981, Rascals and Robbers-The Secret Adventures of Tom Sawyer and Huck Finn, 1982, A Piano for Mrs. Cimino, 1982, Between Friends, 1983, Surviving, 1985, Extreme Close-Up, 1990; music adaptor, composer: (film score) The Lady in Red, 1979; music condr., composer: (film score) The Dresser, 1983; music designer, composer: (film score) Krull, 1983; music dir., composer: (film score) Star Trek III: The Search for Spock, 1984; music prodr., composer: (film score) Commando, 1985; music condr., arranger, composer: (film score) Aliens, 1986 (Acad. award nominee for best original score 1986, Grammy award nominee for best instrumental composition 1986). Office: Gorfaine Schwartz Agy 13245 Riverside Dr Ste 450 Sherman Oaks CA 91423-2172

HORNER, JOHN ROBERT, paleontologist, researcher; b. Shelby, Mont., June 15, 1946; s. John Henry and Miriam Whitted (Stith) H.; m. Virginia Lee Seacotte, Mar. 30, 1972 (div. 1982); 1 child, Jason James; m. Joann Katherine Raffelson, Oct. 3, 1986 (div. 1994); m. Celeste Claire Roach, Jan. 21, 1995. DSc (hon.), U. Mont., 1986. Rsch. asst. dept. geology Princeton (N.J.) U., 1975-82; curator paleontology Mus. of the Rockies, Mont. State U., Bozeman, 1982—. Adj. prof. biology and geology dept. geology Mont. State U., 1982—; rsch. scientist Am. Mus. Nat. History, N.Y.C., 1980-82. Co-author: Maia: A Dinosaur Grows up, 1985, Digging Dinosaurs, 1988 (N.Y. Acad. Sci. award 1989), Digging Up Tyrannosaurus Rex, 1993, The Complete T-Rex, 1993, Dinosaur Lives, 1997; contbr. articles to profl. jours. With USMC, 1966-68; Vietnam. MacArthur fellow, 1986. Achievements include discovery of a new genus of duckbilled dinosaur, Maiasaura; accomplishments include: the theory of endothermic metabolism in dinosaur development, of parental nurture of new-born hatchlings, that Tyrannosaurus rex was a scavenger; excavator of the Egg Mountain cache of dinosaur nests. Home: 310 Hoffman Dr Bozeman MT 59715-5724 Office: Mont State U Mus Of The Rockies Bozeman MT 59717-0001

HORNUNG, HANS GEORG, aeronautical engineering educator, science facility administrator; b. Jaffa, Israel, Dec. 26, 1934; came to U.S., 1987; s. Friedrich Gottlieb and Helene Wilhelmine (Wagner) H.; m. Gretl Charlotte Frank, Jan. 29, 1960; children: Ingrid, Karl, Lisa, Jenny. BMechE with honors, U. Melbourne, Australia, 1960, M in Engring. Sci. with honors, 1962; PhD in Aeros., U. London, 1965. Rsch. scientist Aero. Rsch. Labs., Melbourne, 1962-67; lectr., sr. lectr. then reader Australian Nat. U., Canberra, 1967-80; dir., mem. senate com. for sci. and tech. Inst. Exptl. Fluid Mechanics (DLR), Göttingen, Germany, 1980-87; dir. Grad. Aero. Labs. and Clarence Johnson prof. aero. Calif. Inst. Tech., Pasadena, 1987—. Mem. fluid dynamics panel Adv. Group. Aerospace R & D, 1983-88; mem. adv. com. Internat. Shock Tube Symposia, 1979-95; chmn. adv. com. von Kárman Inst. for Fluid Dynamics, 1984-85; mem. German del. Internat. Union Theoretical and Applied Mechanics, 1984-87; Lanchester Meml. lectr. Royal Aero. Soc., London, [illegible]; hon. prof. U. Göttingen; Prandtl mem. lectr. Ges. Angew. Math. and Mech., Vienna, 1988. Mem. editl. adv. bd. Zeitschrift für Flugwissenschaften und Weltraumforschung, 1984-96, Experiments in Fluids jour., 1987—, Physics of Fluids, 1988-91, Ing. Archiv, 1989-96; contbr. numerous articles to profl. jours. Recipient von Karman award and medal for internat. coop. in aero. Internat. Coun. Aero. Scis.; Humboldt fellow Tech. U., Darmstadt, Germany, 1974-75. Mem. Nat. Acad. of Engring.(fgn. assoc.), sci. mem. of bd. DLR [illegible], Australian Inst. Physics, Deutsche Gesellschaft für Luft- und Raumfahrt, Gesellschaft für angewandte Mathematik and Mechanik, Am. Phys. Soc., AIAA, Royal Swedish Acad. Engring. Scis., Ludwig Prandtl Ring German Soc. Aerospace Sci. Achievements include making important contbns. in hypersonic flow theory, exptl. methods and results in real-gas flows, Mach reflection and three-dimensional separation. Office: Calif Inst Tech 1201 E California Blvd Pasadena CA 91125-0001 E-mail: hans@galcit.caltech.edu

HOROVITZ, ADAM, recording artist; b. N.Y.C., Oct. 31, 1967; Founder, mem. Young and the Useless, 1981-83; mem. The Beastie Boys, 1983—. Owner Grand Royal, Grand Royal mag., 1984—. Albums include Licensed to Ill, 1986, Paul's Boutique, 1989, Check Your Head, 1992, 94, Ill Communication, 1994, Some Old Bullshit, 1994, In Sound from Way Out, 1996, Def & Dumb, 1996, (singles) Jimmy James, 1992, Gratitude, 1992, So What'cha Want, 1992, Sabotage, 1994, Hey Ladies, 1997, (extended play singles) Pollywog Stew, 1982, Cooky Puss, 1983, Rock Hard, 1984, Tour Shot, 1994, Sure Shot, 1994, Get It Together, 1994, Root Down, 1995, Aglio E Olio, 1995, (video) Skills to Pay the Bills, 1992, Hello Nasty, 1998, The Sounds of Science, 1999; rap artist Heart of Soul, 1988, Rap's Biggest Hits, 1990, Rap Rap Rap, 1996, Rap: Most Valuable Players, 1996; vocals Rap's Biggest Hits, 1990; prodr. Cb4, 1993, Rebirth of Cool (vol. 3), 1995, Music for Our Mother Ocean, 1996, Rap Rap Rap, 1996, Rap: Most Valuable Players, 1996. Office: care Grand Royal Capitol Records 1750 Vine St Los Angeles CA 90028-5209

HOROWITZ, BEN, health facility administrator; b. Bklyn., Mar. 19, 1914; s. Saul and Sonia (Meringoff) H.; m. Beverly Lichtman, Feb. 14, 1952; children: Zachary, Jody. BA, Bklyn. Coll., 1940; LLB, St. Lawrence U., 1940; postgrad., New Sch. Social Rsch., 1942. Bar: N.Y. 1941. Dir. N.Y. Fedn. Jewish Philanthropies, 1940-45; assoc., ea. regional dir. City of Hope, 1945-50, nat. exec. sec., 1950-53, exec. dir., 1953-85, gen. v.p., bd. dirs., 1985—, bd. dirs. nat. med. ctr., 1980—. Bd. dirs. Beckman Rsch. Inst., 1980—. Mem. Gov.'s Task Force on Flood Relief, 1969-74; bd. dirs., v.p. Hope for Hearing Found., UCLA, 1972-96; bd. dirs. Forte Found., 1987-92, Ch. Temple Housing Corp., 1988-93, Leo Baeck Temple, 1964-67, 86-89, Westwood Property Owners Assn., 1991—. Recipient Spirit of Life award, 1970, Gallery of Achievement award, 1974, Profl. of Yr. award So. Calif. chpt. Nat. Sco. Fundraisers, 1977; Ben Horowitz chair in rsch. established at City of Hope, 1981; city street named in his honor, 1986. Jewish. Formulated the role of City of Hope as pilot center in medicine, science and humanitarianism, 1959. Home: 221 Conway Ave Los Angeles CA 90024-2601 Office: City of Hope 11645 Wilshire Blvd Los Angeles CA 90025-1708

HOROWITZ, NORMAN HAROLD, biologist, emeritus educator; b. Pitts., Mar. 19, 1915; s. Joseph L. and Jeanette (Miller) H.; m. Pearl Shykin, June 16, 1939 (dec. Feb. 1985); children: Joel Lawrence, Elizabeth Anne. B.S., U. Pitts., 1936; Ph.D., Calif. Inst. Tech., 1939, research fellow biochemistry, 1940-42, sr. research fellow, 1946; NRC fellow, Stanford U., 1939-40, research assoc., 1942-46. Teaching fellow biology Calif. Inst. Tech., Pasadena, 1936-39, assoc. prof. biology, 1947-53, prof. biology, 1953-82, prof. emeritus, 1982—, chmn. dept., 1977-80; chief biol. sci. sect. Jet Propulsion Lab., Pasadena, 1965-70. Cons. NASA; mem., experimenter Viking Mars Biology Team, 1976-77 Editorial bd.: Jour. Biol. Chemistry, 1959-64; author: To Utopia and Back: The Search for Life in the Solar System, 1986; contbr. articles tech. jours. Fulbright and Guggenheim fellow U. Paris, 1954-55 Mem. Am. Soc. Biol. Chemists, Genetics Soc. Am., AAAS, Nat. Acad. Scis., Am. Acad. Arts and Scis., Phi Beta Kappa. Home: 2495 Brigden Rd Pasadena CA 91104-3428 Office: 156 29 Calif Inst Tech Pasadena CA 91125-0001 E-mail: nhorowit@itscaltech.edu

HORSEY, DAVID, editorial cartoonist; b. Evansville, Ind., Sept. 13, 1951; m. Nole Ann Ulery; children: Darielle Jean, Daniel Rayden. BA in Comms., U. Wash., 1976; MA in Internat. Rels., U. Kent, Canterbury, Eng., 1986. Formerly govt. reporter, polit. columnist Wash. State Capitol; polit. reporter, columnist, editl. cartoonist Daily Jour.-Am., Bellevue, Wash., 1976-79; editl. cartoonist, columnist, mem. editl. bd. Seattle Post-Intelligencer, 1979—. Syndicated Tribune Media Svcs., 1986-89, 2000—, King Features/N.Am. Syndicate, N.Y.C., 1988-2000; instr. Acad. Realist Art, Seattle, 1998; propr. Horsey--Words and Picturs, Seattle, 1993—. Author: Politics and Other Perversions, 1974, Horsey's Rude Awakenings, 1981, Horsey's Greatest Hits of the '80s, 1989, The Fall of Man, 1994, One Man Show, 1999; co-editor: (anthology) Cartooing AIDS Around the World, 1992; exhibited cartoons at Art Inst. Seattle, 1992, Michael Pierce Gallery, Seattle, 1997, Shoreline C.C., 1999, others. Asst. coach North Ctrl. Little League Baseball, 1992-94; youth coach Woodland Soccer Club, 1989-98; chmn. campaign for excellence St. Benedict Elem. and Mid. Sch., 1991-93, pres. sch. commn., 1993-95. Recipient 1st place Best of the West Journalism Competition, 1995, Environ. Media award, 1995, Global Media award Population Inst., 1991, Berryman award Nat. Press Found., 1998, Pulitzer prize for editl. cartooning, 1999, numerous others. Mem. Soc. Profl Journalists (12 1st place regional awards, Susan Hutchinson Bosch award 1999), Assn. Am. Editl. Cartoonists (pres.-elect 1999-2000, pres. 2000-01). Office: Seattle Post Intelligencer PO Box 1909 101 Elliott Ave W Ste 200 Seattle WA 98119-4295 E-mail: davidhorsey@seattle-pi.com

HORST, RANDY, museum director; Dir. Western Mont. Coll. Gallery Mus., Dillion. Office: Western Mont Coll Mus 710 S Atlantic St Dillon MT 59725-3511

HORTON, GARY BRUCE, transportation company executive; b. Vallejo, Calif., Aug. 27, 1943; s. John Vernon and Della Leona (Shock) H.; m. Janice DeLoach, Oct. 31, 1987; children: Cody Jacob, Dillon Edward, Rocky. Student, Ea. Ariz. Coll., 1964-65, Ariz. State U., 1965-68. Cost acct. Motorola, Inc., Mesa, Ariz., 1968-69; acct. supr. Arcoa, Phoenix, 1969-70, fin. acctg. mgr., 1970-77; fin. mgr. U-Haul Internat., Phoenix, 1977-82, v.p. fin., 1987-90; treas. Amerco, Reno, 1982-89, v.p. fin., 1989—; asst. treas. U-Haul Can., Ltd., Burlington, Ont., 1982—; pres., chmn. Sierra Entertainment, Ltd., Reno, 1993—. Bd. dirs. Amerco Lease, Las Vegas, Nationwide Comml. Co., Phoenix, Ponderosa Ins., U-Haul Real Estate Co. Pres. bd. trustees Nev. Mus. Art. Republican. Lutheran. Avocations: fishing, camping, golf, racquetball, waterskiing. Home: 3425 Meridian Ln Reno NV 89509-3883 Office: Amerco 1325 Airmotive Way Ste 100 Reno NV 89502-3294

HORTON, ROBERT CARLTON, geologist; b. Tonopah, Nev., July 25, 1926; s. Frank Elijah and Eathel Margaret (Miller) H.; m. Beverly Jean Burhans, Dec. 5, 1952; children: Debra, Robin, Cindy. B.S., U. Nev., 1949, D.Sc. (hon.), 1985, Geol. Engr., 1966. Assoc. dir. Nev. Bur. Mines, Reno, 1956-66; cons. Reno, 1966-76; dir. geology div. Bendix Field Engring Corp. (Grand Junction), Colo., 1976-81; dir. U.S. Bur. Mines, Washington, 1981-87; dir. strategic materials rsch. U. Nev., Reno, 1987-90, assoc. dean MacKay Sch. Mines, 1989-90, assoc. dean emeritus, 1990—. Mem. Nev. Gov.'s Mining Adv. Com., 1966-72. Author: Barite Deposits of Nevada, 1962, Fluorspar Deposits of Nevada, 1963, History of Nevada Mining, 1963. Republican candidate for Congress from Nev., 1958. Served to lt. USNR, 1944-46, 53-56, PTO. Kennecott scholar, 1948; named Engr. of Yr. Reno chpt., NSPE, 1967; recipient Outstanding Alumnus John Mackay [illegible] 1991. Mem. AIME (subsect. chmn. Reno 1962-63), Soc. Econ. Geologists, Mining and Metall. Soc. Am. Methodist.

HORTON, SHIRLEY A. mayor; BS in Acctg., San Diego State U. Pres. Grasser/Tate Real Estate Co., Calif.; planning commr. City of Chula Vista, 1985-91, elected councilwoman, 1991-94, elected mayor, 1994—. Past govt. svc. positions include: bd. del. San Diego Assn. Govts.; Met. Transit Devel. Bd. alternate, mem. Otay Valley (Calif.) Regional Park Policy com., mem. San Diego Interagy. Water Quality panel, mem. South County Econ. Devel. Coun., mem. Interagy. Water Task Force, mgm. Gang Issues com., mem. Bayfront subcom., mem. Appropriate Techs. subcom. Mem. San Diego County Assessment Appeals bd., 1982-86, pres. South San Diego Bay Cities Bd. Realtors, 1987, mem. Scripps Meml. Hosp. Cmty. Adv. Bd., 1990-91, mem. South Bay YMCA Support Campaign com., 1990. Mem. Calif. Assn. Realtors (regional v.p. 1989, dir. 1980-90), Chula Vista C. of C. (econ. devel. com. 1984-85). Office: Mayor Coun Office 276 4th Ave Chula Vista CA 91910-2631

HORTON, WILLIAM RUSSELL, retired utility company executive; b. Toronto, Ont., Can., Aug. 25, 1931; s. Russell Burton and Freda Catherine (Middleton) H.; m. Dorothy Viva Rye, Nov. 27, 1954; children: William Russell, Robert Freeman, Douglas Lloyd, Ronald Edward. BA Sci. in Mining Engring., U. Toronto, 1955. Engr. Imperial Oil Ltd., Calgary and Camrose, Alta., Can., 1955-56; engr., mgr. Black Sivalls & Bryson Ltd., Edmonton, 1956-65; v.p. Gamma Engring. Ltd., Edmonton, 1965-68; pres. Horton Engring. Ltd., Edmonton, 1968-2000, chmn., 2000—; mem. Alta Pub. Utilities Bd., Edmonton, 1973-76; chmn. Alta. Pub. Utilities Bd., Edmonton, 1976-83; exec. v.p. Can. Utilities Ltd., Edmonton, 1984-90. Bd. dirs. Can. Utilities Ltd., Atco Utilities Bus. Group; mem. Centre for Study Regulated Industries McGill U.; hon. mem. Can. Assn. Members Pub. Utility Tribunals. Mem. Assn. Profl. Engrs. Geologists and Geophysicists Alta. (life), Northwest Electric Light and Power Assn. (hon. life). Avocations: sports, music, reading. Home: 17490 Coral Beach Rd Winfield BC Canada V4V 1C1 Office: Can Utilities Ltd 1500-909 11th Ave SW Calgary AB Canada T2R 1N6 E-mail: wrhorton@cablelan.net

HORWITZ, BARBARA ANN, physiologist, educator, consultant; b. Chgo., Sept. 26, 1940; d. Martin Horwitz and Lillian Bloom; m. John M. Horowitz, Aug. 17, 1970. BS, U. Fla., 1961, MS, 1962; PhD, Emory U., 1966. Asst. rsch. physiologist U. Calif., Davis, 1968-72, asst. prof. physiology, 1972-75, assoc. prof., 1975-78, prof., 1978—, chair animal physiology, 1991-93, chmn. neurobiology, physiology and behavior dept., 1993-98, vice provost acad. personnel, 2001—. Cons. Am. Inst. Behavioral Rsch., Palo Alto, Calif., 1980, Am. Inst. Rsch., Washington, 1993-99, NSF, Washington, 1981-84, NIH, Washington, 1995-99. Contbr. articles to profl. jours. Recipient Disting. Tchg. award, 1982, Pres.'s award for Excellence in fostering Undergrad. Rsch., 1995; named Arthur C. Guyton Physiology Tchr. of Yr., 1996; USPHS postdoctoral fellow, 1966-68. Fellow AAAS; mem. Am. Physiology Soc. (edn. and program coms., coun. 1993-96, pres.-elect 2001—), Am. Soc. Zoologists, N.Y. Acad. Scis., N.Am. Assn. for Study of Obesity (exec. coun. 1988-92), Soc. Exptl. Biol. Medicine (exec. coun. 1990-94, pres.-elect 1999-2001, pres. 2001—), Phi Beta Kappa (pres. Davis chpt. 1991-92, 2000—), Sigma Xi (pres. Davis chpt. 1980-81), Phi Kappa Pi, Phi Sigma (v.p. Davis chpt. 1983—, nat. v.p. 1989—). Office: U Calif Dept Neurobiology Phys Davis CA 95616 E-mail: bahorwitz@ucdavis.edu

HORWITZ, DAVID A. physician, scientist, educator; BA, U. Mich., 1958; MD, U. Chgo., 1962. Intern, resident Michael Reese Hosp., Chgo., 1966; rheumatology fellow Southwestern Med. Sch. U. Tex., 1969, instr. internal medicine Southwestern Med. Sch., 1968-69; from asst. prof. to assoc. prof. medicine Sch. Medicine U. Va., Charlottesville, 1969-79, prof. medicine, 1979-80; prof. medicine and microbiology, chief divsn. rheumatology and immunology sect. Sch. Medicine U. So. Calif., L.A., 1980—. Vis. prof. Clin. Rsch. Ctr., Harrow, Eng., 1976-77; vis. investigator Inperial Cancer Rsch. Fund, London, 1988-89. Contbr. more than 100 articles to profl. jours. Achievements include research in elucidation of lymphocytes, cytokines and immunologic circuits involved in the regulation of antibody production, characterization of pathologic abnormalities in immune regulation in subjects with Systemic Lupus Erythematosus; use of novel strategies to treat patients with autoimmune disease. Office: U So Calif Divsn Rheumatology & Immunology 2011 Zonal Ave # 711 Los Angeles CA 90033-1034

HOSICK, HOWARD LAWRENCE, cell biology educator, academic administrator; b. Champaign, Ill., Nov. 1, 1943; s. Arthur Howard and Eunice Irma (Miller) H.; m. Cynthia Ann Jacobson, June 15, 1968; children: Steven Cameron, Anna Elise, Rachel Victoria. BA, U. Colo., 1965; PhD, U. Calif., Berkeley, 1970. Postdoctoral fellow Karolinska Inst., Stockholm, 1970-72; asst. research biochemist U. Calif., Berkeley, 1972-73; asst. prof. Wash. State U., Pullman, 1973-78, assoc. prof., 1978-83, prof. cell biology, 1983—, chmn. dept. zoology, 1983-87, chmn. dept. genetics and cell biology, 1987-91. Vis. scientist U. Reading, Eng., 1978; disting. scientist Aichi Cancer Ctr., Nagoya, Japan, 1986; vis. scholar Cambridge U., 1994; rsch. com. Am. Heart Assn., 1989; grant rev. com. Nat. Cancer Inst., 1993—. Rev. editor In Vitro Cellular and Molecular Biology, 1986—; contbr. articles to profl. jours. Bd. govs. Internat. Assn. Breast Cancer Rsch., 1993—. Recipient H.S. Boyce award, 1981, Shell Faculty Devel. award, 1984, Cancer Rsch. award Eagles Club, 1989, G. and L. Pfeiffer Rsch. Found. award, 1992; fellow NIH, NSF, Am. Cancer Soc., Damon Runyan-Walter Winchell Cancer Fund, Fogarty Internat. Ctr., 1968—; grantee NIH, NSF, Am. Cancer Soc., Am. Inst. Cancer Rsch., Pfeiffer Found., 1973—. U.S. Army. Mem. Am. Soc. Cell Biology, Tissue Culture Assn., Am. Assn. Cancer Research, Internat. Assn. Breast Cancer Research. Democrat. Buddhist. Lodge: Rotary. Avocations: running, woodworking, model aviation. Home: 1115 NE Lake St Pullman WA 99163-3869 Office: Wash State U Sch Biol Scis Wash State U Pullman WA 99164-4234

HOSOKAWA, KOICHI, engineering company executive; CFO Kingston Tech., Fountain Valley, Calif. Office: Kingston Technology 17600 Newhope St Fountain Valley CA 92708 Office Fax: (714) 435-2699

HOSTLER, CHARLES WARREN, former ambassador, international affairs consultant; b. Chgo., Dec. 12, 1919; s. Sidney Marvin and Catherine (Marshall) H.; 1 son, Charles Warren, Jr. B.A., U. Calif. at Los Angeles, L.A., 1942; M.A., Am. U., Beirut, Lebanon, 1955, Georgetown U., , 1950, Ph.D., 1956. Commd. 2d lt. U.S. Air Force, 1942, advanced through grades to col., 1955; ret., 1963; dir. internat. ops. McDonnell Douglas Corp., Middle East, N.Africa, Beirut, 1965-67, mgr. internat. ops. Paris, 1963-65, mgr. internat. mktg., missiles and space, 1967-69; pres. Hostler Investment Co., Newport Beach, Calif., 1969-74; chmn. bd. Irvine (Calif.) Nat. Bank, 1972-74; dir. Wynn's Internat., Inc., Fullerton, Calif., 1971-74; dep. asst. sec. for internat. commerce, dir. Bur. Internat. Commerce, U.S. Dept. Commerce, Washington, 1974-76; regional v.p. Mid-East and Africa, E-Systems Inc., Cairo, Egypt, 1976-77; pres. Pacific SW Capital Corp., San Diego, 1977-89, ambassador U.S. Govt., Bahrain, [illegible]; hon. consul gen. State of Bahrain, 1993—; adj. prof. Sch. Internat. Svc., Am. U., Washington, 1955-63, adj. prof. political sci., San Diego State U., 1999—. Author: Turkism and the Soviets, 1957, The Turks of Central Asia, 1993; contbr. articles to econ., comml. and mil. jours. Chmn. Calif. Contractors State Lic. Bd., 1973-79, San Diego County Local Agy. Formation Commn., 1979-80; chmn. Calif. State Park and Recreation Commn., 1983-89; pres. San Diego Consular Corps, 1996-98; chmn., bd. dirs. People-to-People

Internat. Decorated Legion of Merit; recipient Eisenhower Disting. Svc. award and decorations from 10 fgn. nations, Fgn. Affairs award for pub. svc. U.S. State Dept. Mem. Navy League (life), Middle East Inst. (bd. govs. 1962-80, 93—), VFW, Ret. Officers Assn., Coun. Am. Ambs., Vets. Office Strategic Svcs., Spl. Forces Club (London). Office: 1101 First St # 302 Coronado CA 92118-1474

HOSTON, GERMAINE ANNETTE, political science educator; b. Trenton, N.J. d. Walter Lee and Veretta Louise H. AB in Politics summa cum laude, Princeton U., 1975; MA in Govt., Harvard U., 1978, PhD in Govt., 1981. Rsch. asst. Princeton (N.J.) U., 1973-75; teaching asst. Harvard U., Cambridge, Mass., 1977-78; asst. prof. polit. sci. Johns Hopkins U., Balt., 1980-86, assoc. prof. polit. sci., 1986-92; prof. polit. sci. U. Calif., San Diego, 1992—, dir. Ctr. for Democratization and Econ. Devel., 1993-99; founder, pres. Inst. TransPacific Studies in Values, Culture and Politics, 1999—. Vis. prof. L'Ecole des Hautes Etudes en Scis. Sociales, Paris, 1986, Osaka City U., Japan, 1990, U. Tokyo, 1991; faculty advisor Chinese lang. program Johns Hopkins U., 1981-92, mem. undergrad. ethics bd., 1980-83, pub. interest investment adv. com., 1982-83, 84-85, undergrad. admissions com., 1983-84, 86-87, 88-89, pres.'s human climate task force, 1987, dir. undergrad. program, 1987, 88-89, mem. com. undergrad. studies, 1987-91, organizer comparative politics colloquium, 1987-89, dept. colloquium, 1987-89, 91-92; mem. Japanese studies program com. U. Calif., San Diego, 1992—, mem. Chinese studies program, 1994—, field coord. comparative politics, 1994—, dir. grad. studies comparative politics, 1997-98; bd. dirs. Inst. East-West Security Studies, N.Y.C., 1990-97; mem. Am. adv. com. The Japan Found., 1992—; mem. Edn. Abroad Program (EAP) com. U. Calif., 1996—; mem. adv. com. Calif. Ctr. Asia Soc.; mem. com. tech. comms. Inst. East West Security Studies, 1997—; participant numerous workshops and seminars; lectr. in field. Author: Marxism and the Crisis of Development in Prewar Japan: The Debate on Japanese Capitalism, 1986, The State, Identity, and the National Question in China and Japan, 1994, (with others) The Biographical Dictionary of Neo-Marxism, 1985, The Biographical Dictionary of Marxism, 1986, Culture and Identity: Japanese Intellectuals During the Interwar Years, 1990, The Routledge Dictionary of Twentieth-Century Political Thinkers, 1992; mem. editl. bd. Jour. Politics, 1997—; contbr. articles and book revs. to profl. jours.; pub. numerous papers. Active Md. Food Com., 1983-92, program concepts subcom. CROSS ROADS Com., Diocese of Md., 1987-88, outreach com. St. David's Episcopal Ch., Balt., standing commn. human affairs Gen. Conv. of the Episcopal Ch., 1991-97; chair peace and justice commn. Episcopal Diocese Md., 1984-87, co-chair companion diocese com., 1987-92, chair CROSS ROADS program bd., 1988-92; exec. bd. dirs. Balt. Clergy and Laity Concerned, 1985-86; alternate, regular lay del. 69th Gen. Conv. of The Episcopal Ch., Detroit, 1988; trustee Va. Theol. Sem., 1988—; lay del. 70th Gen. Conv. of The Episcopal Ch., Phoenix, Ariz., 1991; dep. Nat. Conv. Episcopal Ch., 1988-93. Am. Legion Aux. scholar, 1972, Am. Logistical Assn. scholar, 1972-76; fellow Harvard U., 1975-77, NSF, 1975-77; Lehman fellow Harvard U., 1978-79, Fgn. Lang. and Area Studies fellow, 1978-79; fellow Am. Assn. Univ. Women Edn. Found., 1979-80; Fgn. Rsch. scholar U. Tokyo, 1979, 82, 84, 85, 86, 91; Travel grantee Assn. Asian Studies, Japan-U.S. Friendship Commn., 1981; Internat. fellow Internat. Fedn. Univ. Women, 1982, 83; Postdoctoral grantee Social Sci. Rsch. Coun., 1983; fellow NEH, 1983; Kenan Endowment grantee Johns Hopkins U., 1984-85; fellow Rockefeller Found. Internat. Rels., 1985-88; Travel grantee Assn. Asian Studies, 1991; grantee Japan-U.S. Friendship Commn., 1997; rsch. grantee Acad. Senate Com. on Rsch., 1996. Mem. Asia Soc. (trustee 1994—), Am. Polit. Sci. Assn. (mem. coun. 1991-93, mem. com. on internat. polit. sci. 1997—, v.p. 1998—), Assn. Asian Studies (mem. N.E. Asia coun. 1992-95, vice-chair N.E. Asia coun. 1993—, nominated editor Jour. Asian Studies 1994—, mem. coun. on fgn. rels. 1990—), Internat. Platform Assn., Pacific Coun. on Internat. Policy, Women's Fgn. Policy Group. Democrat. Episcopalian. Avocations: reading, cooking, sailing, tennis, working out. Office: 2307B Central Dr Str 2-160 Bedford TX 76021 E-mail: ghoston@myesa.com

HOTCHKISS, HARLEY N. professional hockey team owner; b. Tillsonburg, Ont., Can. BS in Geology, Mich. State U. CEO, gov. Calgary Flames, owner, gov. Bd. dirs. Conwest Exploration Co. Ltd., Nova Corp., Mich. State U. Found., Telus Corp.; chmn. NHL Bd. Govs., 1995—. Past chmn. Foothills Hosp. Bd.; vice chmn. Foothills Hosp. Found.; co-chmn. Pntrs. in Health Campaign. Office: Calgary Flames PO Box 1540 Sta M Calgary AB Canada T2P 3B9

HOUGH, JOHN DENNIS, public relations executive; BA, Gonzaga U., 1968. Chief of staff Office of Gov. Cecil Andrus, Boise, Idaho, 1974-77; dir. field offices U.S. Dept. of Interior, 1977-80, regional mgr. ITT Corp., Seattle, 1980-84; exec. v.p. First Interstate Bank, 1984-90; co-pres. Rockey Co., Inc., Seattle, CEO, 1998—. Office: The Rockey Co Inc 2121 5th Ave Seattle WA 98121-2510

HOUK, KENDALL NEWCOMB, chemistry educator; b. Nashville, Feb. 27, 1943; s. Charles H. and Janet Houk; 1 child, Kendall M.; m. Robin L. Garrell. AB, Harvard U., 1964, MS, 1966, PhD, 1968. Asst. prof. chemistry La. State U., Baton Rouge, 1968-72, assoc. prof., 1972-75, prof., 1975-80, U. Pitts., 1980-86, UCLA, 1986-91, chmn. dept. chemistry and biochemistry, 1991-94. Dir. chemistry div. nat. Sci. Found., 1988-90. Contbr. numerous articles to profl. jours. Recipient Schrodinger medal World Assn. Theoretically Oriented Chemists, 1998. Fellow AAAS; mem. Am. Chem. Soc. (Cope Scholar award 1988, James Flack Norris award in physical organic chemistry 1991). Office: UCLA Dept Chemistry Biochemistry 405 Hilgard Ave Los Angeles CA 90095-9000

HOULIHAN, PATRICK THOMAS, museum director; b. New Haven, June 22, 1942; s. John T. and Irene (Rourke) H.; m. Betsy Eliason, June 19, 1965; children: Mark T. and Michael D. (twins). BS, Georgetown U., 1964; MA, U. Minn., 1969; PhD, U. Wis., Milw., 1971. Asst. commr. N.Y. State Mus., Albany, 1980-81; dir. Heard Mus., Phoenix, 1972-80, S.W. Mus., L.A., 1981-87, Millicent Rogers Mus., 1988-93; writer, rschr. Ugo Prodns., L.A., 1993—.

HOUSE, DAVID L. electronics components company executive; b. 1943; With Raytheon, 1965-69, Honeywell, 1969-72, Microdata, 1972-74; v.p., gen. mgr. Intel Corp., 1974-96; chmn., pres., CEO Bay Network Computers, Santa Clara, 1996; now sr. v.p. Intel Corp., 1996-98; pres. Nortel Network, Santa Clara, 1998-2000. Home: 25330 Via Pacifica Valencia CA 91355-2634

HOUSE, GEORGE MICHAEL, museum curator; b. Silver City, N.Mex., Apr. 2, 1955; s. William Winfrey House and Ruth Lestra (Williams) Billings; m. Maria Cedillo Enriquez, Dec. 24, 1983; children: Vanessa Yvette, Joshua Michael, Benjamin Alexander. BA in History and Social Sci., Western N.Mex. U., 1984, MA in History, 1985. With forest svc. USDA, Silver City, N.Mex., 1973, Kingston, 1976; museum curator N.Mex Mus. of Space History, Alamogordo, 1985—. Cons., instr., rschr., lectr. Space Ctr., Alamogordo, 1985—. Contbr. articles to publs. Sunday sch. tchr. Ch. of Christ, Bayard, N.Mex., 1976-85, Alamogordo, 1985—; juror Otero County Courthouse, Alamogordo, 1990. With USN, 1973-76. Dean Caulkins Meml. scholar Western N.Mex. U., 1983, Bd. of Regents scholar Western N.Mex., 1983. Mem. Pi Gamma Mu (Cert. of Merit 1984). Avocations: hunting, fishing, camping, sports, reading. Home: PO Box 382 Alamogordo NM 88311-0382 Office: NMex Mus Space History PO Box 5430 top NM Hwy 2001 Alamogordo NM 88311-5430 E-mail: curator@zianet.com

HOUSE, JOHN WILLIAM, otologist; b. L.A., July 12, 1941; s. Howard and Helen House; m. Barbara Breithaupt, Mar. 28, 1993; children: Hans, Chris, Kurt, Steven, Kevin. BS, U. So. Calif., 1964, MD, 1967. Intern L.A. County-U. So. Calif. Med. Ctr., 1967-68; resident Glendale (Calif.) Adventist Hosp., 1971-72, L.A. County Med. Ctr., 1972-74; fellow Otologic Med. Group, L.A., 1974, pvt. practice, 1975—; pres. House Ear Inst., L.A., 1987—. Mem. editorial bd. Am. J. Otology, 1986—; contbr. articles to jours. in field. Admissions com. interviewer, U. So. Calif. Sch. Medicine, Los Angeles, 1976—; mem. Los Angeles County Sheriff's Res. Med. Co. Capt. U.S. Army, 1969-71. Recipient Hocks Meml. award Am. Tinnitus Assn., 1988; named Tchr. of Yr., U. So. Calif. Family Practice Dept., 1987. Fellow Am. Acad. Otolaryngology/Head and Neck Surgery; mem. AMA, Am. Neurotology Soc. (program chmn. 1976—, pres. 1998-99), Am. Otol. Soc. (past pres.), Triologic Soc., Am. Soc. Mil. Otolaryngologists, Pan-Am. Assn. Otorhinolaryngology Broncho Esophagology, Jonathan Club (Los Angeles). Avocations: skiing, computers, running, swimming. Office: House Ear Clinic Inc 2100 W 3rd St Fl 1 Los Angeles CA 90057-1922

HOUSEL, JERRY WINTERS, lawyer; b. Cripple Creek, Colo., Aug. 9, 1912; s. James Robert and Emma (Winters) H.; m. Mary Elaine Bever, July 8, 1941; children: James Robert, Jerry Laine, John Ora, Peter Elliott. BA, U. Wyo., 1935, JD, 1936; PhD, Am. U., 1941; HD (hon.), U. Wyo., 1996. Bar: Wyo. 1936. Assoc. Arnold and Arnold, Laramie, 1936; teaching fellow Am. U. Grad. Sch., 1937; asst. to U.S. Senator Schwartz, 1937-40; atty. FTC, 1941, War Relocation Authority, 1942; practiced in Cody, Wyo., 1946—; past owner Cody Trading Co. and Bar TL Ranch. Past pres., mem. Wyo. Bd. Law Examiners, 1956-70; past chmn., dir. Key Bank formerly The Bank of Greeley, Colo.: past chmn. dir. Cmty. First Bank (formerly Key Bank-Cody); past dir. Key Bancshares Wyo. formerly 1st Wyo. Bancorp; chmn. Frosh LLC. Mem. Cody City Coun., 1950; past dem. nat. committeeman, Wyo. With USNR, 1943-46. Mem. ABA (ho. of dels. 1965-67, 76-94, bd. govs. 1989-92), Am. Judicature Soc. (bd. dirs. 1967), Wyo. State Bar (pres. 1964), Cody C. of C. (pres. 1953), Am. Legion (comdr. Cody post 1951, 1999 Disting. Alumnus). Office: 1100 Rumsey Ave Cody WY 82414-3606

HOUSEWORTH, RICHARD COURT, state agency administrator; b. Harveyville, Kans., Jan. 18, 1928; s. Court Henry and Mabel (Lynch) H.; m. Laura Louise Jennings, Nov. 1, 1952; children: Louise, Lucile, Court. B.S., U. Kans., 1950. Mgmt. trainee Lawrence Nat. Bank, Kans., 1951-52; pres. 1st Nat. Bank, Harveyville, 1952-55; exec. v.p. Ariz. Bank, Phoenix, 1955-87, cons., 1987-88; dir. Export-Import Bank of the US, Washington, 1988-91; alt. U.S. exec. dir. The Inter-American Devel. Bank, Washington, 1991-93; supt. of banks, Banking Dept. State of Ariz., 1993—. Past chmn. Conf. of State Bank Suprs., Washington. Past pres. Better Bus. Bur., Tucson; past chmn. bd. Pacific Coast Banking Sch. U. Wash.; past pres. Barrow Neurol. Inst. of St. Joseph's Hosp.; past chmn. Valley of the Sun Visitors and Conv. Bur. Served with U.S. Army, 1946-48. Recipient 1st Disting. Service award Scottsdale Jaycees, 1962 Mem. Ariz. C. of C. (1st pres., dir.), Tucson C. of C. (past pres.), Am. Inst. Banking (past pres. Maricopa chpt.), Ariz. Bankers Assn. (past pres.), Urban League of Phoenix (past chmn.), Paradise Valley Club, Mct. Club, Phi Delta Theta. Republican. Episcopalian. Home: 5434 E Lincoln Dr # 83 Paradise Vly AZ 85253-4118 Office: Supt of Banks 2910 N 44th St Ste 310 Phoenix AZ 85018-7270 E-mail: houseworth@azbanking.com

HOUSNER, GEORGE WILLIAM, retired civil engineering educator, consultant; b. Saginaw, Mich., Dec. 9, 1910; s. Charles and Sophie Ida (Schust) H. BSCE, U. Mich., 1933; PhD, Calif. Inst. Tech., 1941. Registered profl. engr., Calif. Engr. U.S. Corps Engrs., Los Angeles, 1941-42; ops. analyst 15th Air Force, Libya and Italy, 1943-45; prof. engring. Calif. Inst. Tech., Pasadena, 1945—, now prof. emeritus earthquake engring.; earthquake engring. cons. Pasadena, 1945—. Mem. Gov.'s Earthquake Coun., 1971-76, L.A. County Earthquake Commn., 1971-72; mem. adv. panel on Earthquake Hazard Nat. Acad. Scis., 1981-83; chmn. com. on earthquake engring. NRC, 1983-92, com. on internat. decade natural hazard reduction, 1986-88; chmn. seismic adv. bd. CALTRANS, 1990-94. Author 3 textbooks; contbr. articles to profl. jours. Recipient Disting. Civilian Svc. award U.S. War Dept., 1945, Bendix Rsch. award Am. Soc. Engring. Edn., 1967, Nat. medal Sci., 1988, The Washington award Western Soc. Engrs., 1995. Mem. NAE (Founders award 1991), NAS, Seismol. Soc. Am. (pres. 1977-78, medal 1981), ASCE (von Karman medal 1972, Newmark medal 1981), Internat. Assn. Earthquake Engring. (pres. 1969-73), Earthquake Engring. Rsch. Inst. (pres. 1954-65), Japan Acad. Office: Calif Inst Tech Dept Engring & Applied Sci 1200 E California Blvd Pasadena CA 91125-0001*

HOUSTON, ELIZABETH REECE MANASCO, correctional education consultant; b. Birmingham, Ala., June 19, 1935; d. Reuben Cleveland and Beulah Elizabeth (Reece) Manasco; m. Joseph Brantley Houston; 1 child, Joseph Brantley Houston III. BS, U. Tex., 1956; MEd, Boston Coll., 1969. Cert. elem. tchr., Calif., cert. spl. edn. tchr., Calif., cert. community coll. instr., Calif.; cert. adminstr., Calif. Tchr., elem. Ridgefield (Conn.) Schs., 1962-63; staff, spl. edn. Sudbury (Mass.) Schs., 1965-68; staff intern Wayland (Mass.) High Sch., 1972; tchr., home bound Northampton (Mass.) Schs., 1972-73; program dir. Jack Douglas Ctr., San Jose, Calif., 1974-76; tchr. specialist spl. edn., coord. classroom svcs., dir. alternative schs. Santa Clara County Office Edn., San Jose, 1976-94. Instr. San Jose State U., 1980-86, U. Calif., Santa Cruz, 1982-85, Santa Clara U., 1991-94; cons. Houston Rsch. Assocs., Saratoga, Calif., 1981—. Author: (manual) Behavior Management for School Bus Drivers, 1980, Classroom Management, 1984, Synergistic Learning, 1986, Learning Disabilities in Psychology for Correctional Education, 1992. Recipient President's award Soc. Photo-Optical Instrumentation Engrs., 1979, Classroom Mgmt. Program award Sch. Bds. Assn., 1984, Svc. to Youth award, Juvenile Ct. Sch. Adminstrs. of Calif., 1989-94; grantee Santa Clara County Office Edn. Tchr. Advisor Program U.S. Sec. Edn., 1983-84. Home: 12150 Country Squire Ln Saratoga CA 95070-3444

HOUSTON, IVAN JAMES, insurance company executive; b. Los Angeles, June 15, 1925; s. Norman Oliver and Doris Talbot (Young) H.; m. Philippa Elizabeth Jones, July 15, 1946; children— Pamela, Kathleen, Ivan Abbott. BS, U. Calif., Berkeley, 1948; postgrad., U. Man., 1948-49; LLD, U. La Verne, 1993. With Golden State Mut. Life Ins. Co., L.A., 1948—, v.p., actuary, 1962-66, sr. v.p., actuary, 1966-70, pres., CEO, 1970-77, chmn., pres., 1977-80, chmn., CEO, 1980-90, chmn., 1990—. Bd. dirs. First Interstate Bank Calif., Pacific Telesis Corp., Family Savs. Mem. L.A. World Affairs Coun., 1970—; chmn. ctrl. region United Way, Inc., L.A., 1973-75, mem. corp. bd. dirs., 1973-80, v.p., 1973-75; bd. dirs. M & M Assn., L.A. Urban League, pres., 1977—; bd. fellows Claremont U. Ctr., 1972-80; bd. regents Loyola Marymount U., 1972-75, 79-82; bd. visitors Anderson Grad. Sch. Mgmt., UCLA, 1990-93; pres. City of L.A. Human Rels. Commn., 1993-95, 99-2000. With Inf. AUS, 1944-45. Decorated Purple Heart, Bronze Star; knight comdr. Order St. Gregory the Great. Fellow Life Office Mgmt. Inst.; mem. Am. Acad. Actuaries, Am. Soc. Pension Actuaries, Internat. Actuarial Assn., Los Angeles Actuarial Club, Conf. Cons. Actuaries (assoc.), Am. Coun. Life Ins. (dir.), Life Office Mgmt. Assn. (dir., mem. exec. com. 1972-75, chmn. 1979), Calif. C. of C. (dir.), Los Angeles Area C. of C. (dir.), Town Hall, Calif. Club, Cosmos Club, Kappa Alpha Psi, Sigma Pi Phi. Roman Catholic. Home: 5111 S Holt Ave Los Angeles CA 90056-1117 Office: 1999 W Adams Blvd Los Angeles CA 90018-3500 E-mail: ihouston@aol.com

HOUSTON, JANE HUNT, retired educator; b. Upper Montclair, N.J., Dec. 22, 1919; d. MacLean and Mary Hunt (Young) H. BA, Duke U., 1941; MEd, U. Wyo., 1960. Cert. tchr., Wyo. Field worker Glendale (Calif.) coun. Girl Scouts U.S., 1941-45; exec. dir. Sacramento coun. Girl Scouts U.S., 1945-46, Cheyenne (Wyo.) coun. Girl Scouts U.S., 1946-56; tchr. Laramie County Sch. Dist. # 1, Cheyenne, 1956-79; ret., 1979. Co-author: Centennial, Wyoming 1876-1976-the Real Centennial. Bd. dirs. Carbon Power and Light Inc., Saratoga, Wyo., 1983-97; chmn. Centennial Water and Sewer Dist., 1988— Mem. LWV, Centennial Valley Hist. Assn. (sec. 1975—), Wyo. State Hist. Soc. (charter), Laramie County Ret. Tchrs. (com. chmn. 1980-95). Republican. Episcopalian. Avocations: outdoor activities, photography, history, reading, community service. Office: Centennial Valley Hist Assn PO Box 200 Centennial WY 82055-0130 E-mail: houmavrick@aol.com

HOUSTON, JOHN ALBERT, political science educator; b. Spokane, Dec. 24, 1914; s. John Alexander and Ethel (Robinson) H.; m. Marjorie Anne Robinson, Aug. 14, 1939 (dec. Sept. 1968); children: Alexandra Louise (Mrs. Lee Benham), John Alexander II (dec. Aug. 1979), Ann Celeste; m. Pollyanna Turner, Nov. 1, 1969. A.B. in Econs, Stanford, 1936, M.A. in Internat. Relations, 1947; Ph.D. in polit. sci, U. Mich., 1951. Ins. broker Johnson & Higgins, San Francisco, 1936-37; case aide Calif. Relief Adminstrn., 1938-40; asst., then asso. prof. polit. sci. U. Miss., 1949-54; faculty Knox Coll., Galesburg, Ill., 1954—, prof. polit. sci., 1957-80, prof. emeritus, 1980—, Philip Sydney Post disting. prof., 1961-80. Sec.-treas. Midwest Collegiate Athletic Conf., 1961-67. Author: Latin America in the United Nations, 1956, Book; rev. editor: Midwest Jour. Polit. Sci, 1962-65. Mem. Galesburg Planning Commn., 1956-57. Served to lt. comdr. USNR, 1941-45. Social Sci. Research Council fellow, 1956 Mem. Am. Polit. Sci. Assn., Midwest Conf. Polit. Scientists, Omicron Delta Kappa, Pi Sigma Alpha, Scabbard and Blade, Sigma Alpha Epsilon. Home: 565 Henley Way Ashland OR 97520-3119

HOUSTON, JOSEPH BRANTLEY, JR. optical instrument company executive; b. Birmingham, Ala., June 15, 1934; s. Joseph Brantley and Inez (Graben) H.; m. Elizabeth Reece Manasco; 1 child, J. Brantley III. AB in Astronomy, U. Tex., 1956; MS, Northeastern U., 1969. Commd. 2d lt. C.E., U.S. Army, 1956, advanced through grades to capt., 1968; optical engr. Perkin-Elmer, Wilton, Conn., 1961-64; mgr. massive optics, chief engr. underwater optical sys. Itek Corp., Lexington, Mass., 1964-71; asst. to pres. Kollmorgen E-O Divsn., Northampton, 1971-73; v.p. advanced devel. and spl. projects Itek Corp., Sunnyvale, Calif., 1973-81; founder Houston Rsch. Assocs., Saratoga, 1981—, Houston Tech. Internat., Inc., San Jose, 1991-97; founder, exec. dir. Forum for Mil. Applications of Directed Energy, Huntsville, Ala., 1989-96. Contbr. articles to profl. jours.; inventor. Recipient Outstanding Civilian Svc. medal U.S. Army, 1987. Fellow Internat. Soc. Optical Engring. (life; pres. 1977-78, advanced tech. advisor 1981—, Goddard award 1982); mem. Optical Soc. Am. (founder, chair Fabrication and Testing Tech. Group, editor Optical Workshop Notebook). Office: 12150 Country Squire Ln Saratoga CA 95070-3444

HOUTSMA, PETER C. lawyer; b. Denver, 1951; BA in Polit. Sci. and Econs. magna cum laude, U. Colo., 1973; JD magna cum laude, Cornell U., 1976. Bar: Colo. 1976. Mem. Holland & Hart, Denver, 1976—. Mem. Am. Arbitration Assn. (panel arbitrators), Order of Coif, Phi Beta Kappa. Office: Holland & Hart PO Box 8749 Denver CO 80201-8749

HOUZE, HERBERT GEORGE, writer; b. Brockville, Ont., Can., Apr. 18, 1947; s. McLean and Grace Lynham (Sayce) H.; m. Carolyn Pierce Johnson, July 8, 1972 (div. May 1990); children: Jennifer E., Alexander J. M., Andrew W.; m. Christine Mary Reinhard, Sept. 13, 1996. BA, McMaster U., Hamilton, Ont., 1969; MA, Vanderbilt U., 1971. Curator of mil. history Chgo. Hist. Soc., 1973-76; curator Winchester Mus. Buffalo Bill Hist. Ctr., Cody, Wyo., 1983-91. Advisor Royal Mil. Coll. Can. Mus., Kingston, Ont., 1979—; dir. John McLaren & Sons Distillers Ltd., London and Perth, 1990—. Author: (books) Knightly Musings, 1988, The Sumptuous Flaske, 1989, To the Dreams of Youth, 1992, Winchester History, 1994, Colt Rifles & Muskets, 1996, Winchester Model 52, 1997, Winchester Bolt Action Rifles, 1998, Winchester Model 1876 Centennial Rifle, 2001, Arming the West, 2001. Mem. Arms and Armour Soc. London, Armor & Arms Club N.Y., Les Amis du Musee de Liege.

HOVANESSIAN, SHAHEN ALEXANDER, electrical engineer, educator, consultant; b. Tehran, Iran, Sept. 6, 1931; came to U.S., 1949; s. Alexander and Jenik (Thadeus) H.; m. Mary Mashourian, Sept. 17, 1960; children: Linda Larsen and Christina Tchaparian (twins). BSEE, UCLA, 1954, MSME, 1955, PhDEE, 1958. Registered profl. engr., Calif. Research scientist Chevron Research Corp., La Habra, Calif., 1958-63; sr. scientist Hughes Aircraft Co., El Segundo, 1963-86; sr. tech. specialist Aerospace Corp., El Segundo, 1986-96; lectr. UCLA, 1962—; cons. engr. L.A., 1996—. Mem. adv. group for aerospace R & D NATO, 1985-87. Author: (with Louis A. Pipes) Matrix—Computer Methods in Engineering, 1969; Digital—Computer Methods in Engineering, 1969; Radar, Detection and Tracking Systems, 1973; Computational Mathematics in Engineering, 1976; Synthetic Array and Imaging Radars, 1980; Radar System Design and Analysis, 1984; Introduction to Sensor Systems, 1988; (with Khalil Seyrafi) Introduction to Electro-Optical Imaging and Tracking Systems, 1993; editor Computers and Elec. Engring., 1973-76. Inventor radar computer Fellow IEEE (U.S. del. Moscow 1973, disting. lectr.); mem. ASME, Sigma Xi, Tau Beta Pi. Democrat. Roman Catholic. Avocations: investments, real estate. Home: 3039 Greentree Ct Los Angeles CA 90077-2020 E-mail: shovaness@aol.com

HOVANNISIAN, RICHARD G. Armenian and Near East history educator; b. Tulare, Calif., Nov. 9, 1932; s. Kaspar and Siroon (Nalbandian) H.; m. Vartiter Kotcholosian, Mar. 2, 1957; children: Raffi, Armen, Ani, Garo. BA in History, U. Calif., Berkeley, 1954, MA in History, 1958; cert. in Armenian, Coll. Arménien, Beirut, 1956; PhD in History, UCLA, 1966; hon. doctorate, Erevan State U., Armenia, 1994, Artsakh State U., 1997. cert. tchr., Calif. Tchr. Fresno (Calif.) City Schs., 1958-62; lectr. Armenian UCLA, 1962-69, prof. Armenian and Near Ea. history, 1969—; chair modern Armenian history Armenian Ednl. Found., 1987—; assoc. dir. G.E. von Grunebaum Ctr. Near Ea. Studies UCLA, 1979-95. Assoc. prof. history Mt. St. Mary's Coll., L.A., 1965-69; advisor Calif. Bd. Edn., Sacramento, 1984-85, 86-88; cons. on multicultural edn.; lectr. to univ. and cmty. groups and profl. confs. worldwide; mem. U.S.-USSR commns. Am. Coun. Learned Socs., 1985-91, U.S. project coord. for study contemporary ethnic processes in U.S. and USSR. Author: Armenia on the Road to Independence, 1967, 4th edit., 1984, The Republic of Armenia, vol. I, 1971, vol. II, 1982, vols. III-IV, 1996, The Armenian Holocaust, 1980, The Armenian Genocide in Perspective, 1986, The Armenian Genocide: History, Politics, Ethics, 1992, The Armenian People form Ancient to Modern Times, vol. I, The Dynastic Periods: From Antiquity to the Fourteenth Century, vol. II, Foreign Dominion to Statehood: The Fifteenth to Twentieth Century, 1997, Remembrance and Denial: The Case of the Armenian Genocide, 1998, Armenian Van Vaspurakan, 2000; author: (with others) Transcaucasia: Nationalism and Social Change, 1983, Le Crime de Silence: Le Génocide des Arméniens, 1984, A Crime of Silence, 1985, Toward the Understanding and Prevention of Genocide, 1984, Genocide: A Critical Bibliographic Review, 1988, Embracing the Other: Philosophical, Psychological, and Historical Perspectives on Altruism, 1992, Diasporas in World Politics, 1993, Genocide and Human Rights, 1993, Genocide: Conceptual and Historical Dimensions, 1994, The Legacy of History in Russia and the New States of Eurasia, 1994; editor: The Armenian Image in History and Literature, 1981, Islam's Understanding of Itself, 1983, Ethics in Islam, 1985, Poetry and Mysticism in Islam: The Heritage of Rumi, 1994, The

Thousand and One Nights in Arabic Literature and Society, 1997, The Persian Presence in Islam, 1998, Religion and Culture in Medieval Islam, 1999, Enlightenment and Diaspora: The Armenian and Jewish Cases, 1999; chmn. editorial bd. Armenian Rev., Ararat, Haigazian Armenological Rev., Mitk, Human Rights Rev.: Jour. of Soc. for Armenian Studies; contbr. numerous articles to profl. jours. Calif. rep. Western Interstate Commn. for Higher Edn., 1978-94; bd. dirs. Facing History and Ourselves Found., Internat. Alert, Found. for Rsch. on Armenian Architecture, Internat. Inst. Holocaust and Genocide Studies, Armenian Nat. Inst., Ctr. for Comparative Genocide Studies, Sydney, Australia, Armenian Ctr. for Nat. and Internat. Studies, Armenia. Recipient Nat. Svc. award Armenian Nat. Com. of Am., 1978, Man of Yr. award Armenian Profl. soc., 1980, Citizen of Yr. award Armenian Am. Citizens League, 1981, Citizen of Yr. award United Armenian Cultural Assn. of Chgo., 1981, Recognition award Armenian Cultural Assn., Fresno, Calif., 1982, Man of Yr. award Rep. Assembly Armenian Ch. Am., 1983, Recognition award Armenian Ednl. Found., 1984, Mesrop Mashdots medal and citation Catholicos of Cilicia, Lebanon, 1984, Person of Yr. award Armenian Cultural Assns. Western U.S., 1985, Disting. Scholar award and medal Armenian Cultural Assns. U.S. and Can., 1986, Recognition Program award Armenian Assembly and Hamazkaine, Nor Seroont and Tekeyan Cultural Assns., 1987, Humanity award Facing History and Ourselves Found., 1988, Dadian award for advancement of Armenian culture Armenian Students Assn. Am., 1990, Disting. Svc. award Armenian Nat. Com. Western U.S., 1996, Disting. Achievement award Internat. Soc. for Traumatic Stress Studies, 1998, Movses Khorenatsi award and medal Republic Armenia, 1998, Pan-Kharpert Assn., 2000, also other citations and recognitions; grantee NEH, 1981-82, Calif. Coun. Humanities, 1985-86; Humanities Inst. fellow, 1972, Guggenheim fellow, 1974-75. Fellow Middle East Studies Assn. (mem. editorial bd.), Am. Assn. Advancement of Slavic Studies; mem. Armenian Acad. Sci. (academician), Am. Hist. Assn., Soc. for Armenian Studies (founder, pres. 1974-75, 90-92, book rev. editor jour., mem. editorial bd.), Oral History Assn., Nat. Assn. Armenian Studies (hon.), Armenian Ednl. Found. (hon.). Armenian Apostolic. Office: UCLA Dept History PO Box 951473 Los Angeles CA 90095-1473

HOVIN, ARNE WILLIAM, agronomist, educator; b. Norway, Dec. 30, 1922; came to U.S., 1952, naturalized, 1957; s. Einar Lauritz and Aslaug Hovind; m. Carol Helen Frink, Oct. 24, 1953; children: Randi Ann, Leif Erik. B.S., Agrl. U. of Norway, 1949; Ph.D., UCLA, 1957. Research geneticist USDA Regional Pasture Research Lab., University Park, Pa., 1958-64; investigation leader Forage Br., Beltsville, Md., 1964-69; prof. agronomy and plant genetics U. Minn., St. Paul, 1969-81; assoc. dir. Mont. Agrl. Expt. Sta., Bozeman, 1981-87; prof. emeritus agronomy Mont. State U., Bozeman, 1987—. Chmn. Nat. Grass Variety Rev. Bd., 1968-69; sec. Grass Breeders Work Planning Conf., 1973-75, v.p., 1975-77, pres., 1977-79; sec., chmn. Regional Tech. Coms. on Forage Crop Breeding. Contbr.: chpts. to Turfgrass Science, 1969, Hybridization of Crop Plants, 1980; sci. articles to profl. jours. Served with Norwegian N.G., 1943-46. Mellon-King travel grantee Australia, 1970; Fulbright-Hays sr. research scholar Norway, 1978 Mem. Am. Forage and Grassland Council (Merit cert. 1975), Am. Soc. Agronomy, Crop Sci. Soc. Am., Alpha Zeta, Gamma Sigma Delta. Office: Mont State U Dept Plant Sci/Plant Path Bozeman MT 59717-0001 E-mail: ussah@gemini.oscs.montana.edu

HOVIND, DAVID J. manufacturing company executive; b. 1940; BA, U. Wash., 1964; postgrad., Stanford U., 1984. With PACCAR Inc., Bellevue, Wash., 1964—, sr. v.p., 1986-87, exec. v.p., 1987-93, now pres., 1993—. Office: PACCAR Inc PO Box 1518 777 106th Ave NE Ste B Bellevue WA 98004-5017

HOWARD, BRADFORD REUEL, travel company executive; b. Honolulu, Aug. 6, 1957; s. Joseph DeSylva and Marguerite Evangeline (Barker) H.; m. Marcia Andresen, June 23, 1985; children: Evan DeSilva Andresen, Blair Marguerite. BS in Bus., U. Calif., Berkeley, 1979. Owner, operator Howard Janitorial Svcs., Oakland, Calif., 1970-80; prodn. mgr. Oakland Symphony Orch., 1976-80; brand mgr. The Clorox Co., Oakland, 1980-85; gen. mgr., corp. sec. Howard Tours, Inc./Howard Enterprises, Oakland, 1985—. Co-owner Howard Mktg. Cons., Oakland, 1985—; cons. Marcus Foster Found., Oakland, 1984-85; pres., gen. mgr. Piedmont (Calif.) Community Theater, 1976-92. Mem. Calif. Alumni Assn. (bd. dirs. 1991-95), U. Calif. Bus. Alumni Assn. (v.p. 1986-88, pres. 1988-89, Bay Area chpt. 1983-84), U. Calif. Devel. Coun., Oakland-Sunrise Rotary (sec. 1985-87, pres. 1987-88, gov. Dist. 5170, 2002—), Lake Merrit Breakfast Club. Avocations: theater, athletics, wine appreciation. Office: Howard Tours Inc 516 Grand Ave Oakland CA 94610-3515

HOWARD, CAROLE MARGARET MUNROE, retired public relations executive; b. Halifax, N.S., Can., Mar. 5, 1945; came to the U.S., 1965; d. Frederick Craig and Dorothy Margaret (Crimes) Munroe; m. Robert William Howard, May 15, 1965. BA, U. Calif., Berkeley, 1967; MS, Pace U., 1978. Reporter Vancouver (Can.) Sun, 1965; editl. assoc. Pacific N.W. Bell, Seattle, 1967-70, employee info. supr., 1970-72, advt. supr., 1972, project mgr. EEO, 1972-73, mktg. mgr., 1973, info. mgr., 1974-75; dist. mgr. media rels. AT&T, N.Y.C., 1975-77, dist. mgr. planning, 1977-78, dist. mgr. advt., 1978-80; media rels. mgr. Western Electric, N.Y.C., 1980-83; divsn. mgr. regional pub. rels. AT&T Info. Sys., Morristown, N.J., 1983-85; v.p., pub. rels. and comm. policy The Reader's Digest Assn., Inc., Pleasantville, N.Y., 1985-95; ret., 1995. Faculty profl. pub. course Stanford U., summer, 1993-95; bd. dirs. Andrew Corp. Author: On Deadline: Managing Media Relations, 1985, 2d edit., 1994, 3rd edit., 2000; contbg. author: Communicators' Guide to Marketing, 1987, Experts in Action: Inside Public Relations, 2d edit., 1988, Travel Industry Marketing, 1990, The Business Speakers Almanac, 1994, Majoring in the Rest of your Life, 2000; newsletter editor Wash. State Rep. Ctrl. Com., 1973-74; contbg. editor Pub. Rels. Quar.; pres. The Reader's Digest Found.; adv. bd. Pub. Rels. News, Pub. Rels. Rev., Jour. Employee Comm. Mgmt., Ragan Pub. Rels. Jour. Corp. adv. bd. Caramoor Ctr. for Music and the Arts; bd. dirs. The Hundred Club of Westchester, Inc., The Lila Acheson Wallace Fund for Met. Mus. of Art, Madison Square Boy's and Girl's Club of N.Y.C. Mem. Women in Comm. (bd. dirs. Wash. state 1973), Internat. Assn. Bus. Communicators, Pub. Rels. Soc. Am., Nat. Press Women, Wash. Press Women (bd. dirs. 1972), Issues Mgmt. Assn., Pub. Rels. Seminar, Am. Cancer Soc., Arthur Page Soc., Wisemen, The Aspen Club, La Paloma Country Club, Gray Wolf Ski Club, San Juan Outdoor Club, Pagosa Springs Arts Coun., Pi Beta Phi. Anglican. Home and Office: PO Box 5499 Pagosa Springs CO 81147-5499

HOWARD, CHRISTOPHER PHILIP, business consultant; b. N.Y.C., Aug. 6, 1947; s. Murray and Hope (McGurn) H.; m. Danina Mary Hill, June 29, 1987; children: Sean, Stephen, Coby, Katherine, Sara. BA in Econs., Stanford U., 1968; MBA, Santa Clara U., 1970. Cert. mgmt. cons.; cert. profl. cons. to mgmt; cert. mgmt. acct.; cert. bus. counselor. Cons. Ernst & Ernst, CPAs, Phoenix, 1972-74; ops. mgr. Jensen Tools & Alloys [illegible] 1974-77, CEO [illegible] Industries Inc., Phoenix, 1977-80; sr. v.p. Health-Tech Mgmt., Inc., Phoenix, 1980-84; mng. prin. Howard and Assocs., Inc., Phoenix, 1984-87; consulting mgr. Grant Thornton, CPAs, Reno, 1987-89; mng. dir. Howard Consulting Group, Inc., Reno, 1989—; faculty mem. U. Nev., Reno, 1991—. 1st lt. USAF, 1970-72. Mem. Inst. Cert. Mgmt. Accts., Nat. Bur. Cert. Cons., Inst. Cert. Mgmt. Cons., Inst. Bus. Appraisers, Inst. Mgmt. Cons., Inst. Cert. Bus. Counselors, Stanford U. [illegible] Office: Howard Consulting Group 605 Sierra Rose Dr Reno NV 89511 E-mail: chris@hcgconsulting.com

HOWARD, DAVID E. artist; b. N.Y.C., Jan. 25, 1952; s. John C. and Florence (Martino) H. Student, Ohio U., 1969-71; MFA, San Francisco Art Inst., 1974. Comml. photographer, Athens, Ohio, 1969-71; tchr. photography San Francisco Ctr. for Visual Studies, 1971-74, visual artist in photography, 1975—, dir., 1975—. Vis. instr. City Coll. San Francisco; grad. isntr. San Francisco Art Inst. Author: Photography for Visual Communicators, Objective Reality, 1972, monographs Realities, 1976, Perspectives, 1978, American Artist, 1990, Illusionistic Perceptions; photography numerous periodicals including Village Voice, N.Y.C., San Francisco Chronicle, Artweek, N.Y. Art Revs., 1990, L.A. Reader, Tribal Arts, 1998, Filipinas, 1998, monograph The Last Filipino Head Hunters, 2000, TV Documentary series; one-man shows include G. Ray Hawkins Gallery, Images Gallery N.Y.C., U. Calif. Extension, John Bolles Gallery, San Francisco, Hirshhorn Mus., Smithsonian Instn., Washington, San Francisco Art Inst., Ohio U., Athens, Thomas J. Crowe Gallery, L.A., Madison (Wis.) Art Ctr., Lehigh U., Pa., Fourth Street Gallery, N.Y.C., Intersection Gallery, San Francisco, Third Eye Gallery, N.Y.C., Ctr. for Visual Studies, San Francisco, Hutchinson Community Coll., Kans., Hank Baum Gallery, San Francisco, Martin Webber Gallery, 1986, Marc Richards Gallery, L.A., 1987, E.Z.T.V., L.A., 1987, 88, G. Ray Hawkins Gallery, L.A., 1988, Fine Arts Mus. L.I., 1989, Phila. Mus. Art, 1990, San Jose, Calif., 2000; numerous group shows including Art Commn. Gallery, San Francisco, DeYoung Mus., San Francisco, Oakland (Calif.) Mus., Palace of Fine Arts, San Francisco, Camera Work, L.A., Erie (Pa.) Art Ctr., Vorpal Gallery, 1985, Cal. State U., 1988, San Francisco Pub. Libr., 1987, Video Refuses, 1986, Hadley Martin Gallery, San Francisco, 1987, Fine Art Mus. L.I., 1989, Chandler Gallery, Seattle, 1991; represented in collections Mus. Modern Art, N.Y.C., Oakland (Calif.) Mus., San Francisco Mus. Modern Art, City of San Francisco, De Saisset Art Gallery, Santa Clara, Calif., Whitney Mus. Am. Art, Hirshhorn Mus., Smithsonian Instn., Art Ctr., Waco, Tex., Memphis Brooks Mus., Memphis, Akron (Ohio) Art Mus., Am. Mus. Natural History, N.Y.C.; pvt. collections; prodr. videotape New York's East Village Art Scene, 1985, California's Art Scene, 1986, others; prodr. exptl. films: Analysis of Realities, 1974, Levels of Consciousness, 1976, Levels of Reality; prodr., dir. Art Seen, TV comml. documentary series on contemporary art televised in N.Y.C., L.A., San Francisco, Miami, Fla., Portland, Oreg., New Orleans, San Francisco, aired PBS, 1994, T.V. show Keith Haring: Artist at Work, selected segments shown Whitney Mus., Hirschhorn-Smithsonian Instn.; internat. exhbns. 10th and 13th Internat. Exhbns. Contemporay Art, Royan, France, 34thand 41st Internat. Salons of Japan, Tokyo, and 5 cities, Mex. Exhbn., Ex Convento de Carman, Guadalajara, 31st Cork Film Festival, 1986, Chgo. Film Festival, 1986, 42nd San Francisco Internatl. Film Fest., 1999, Presidio Earth Days Fest., 1999; other mus., galleries, univs. in U.S. and Europe; produced and directed films New York's East Village Art Scene, 1985, California's Art Scen, Parts 1 & 2, Levels of consciousness, Levels of Reality; presenter weekly cable TV series; Blackstar syndicated photographer, N.Y.C. Recipient San Francisco Art Festival award. Home and Office: Visual Studies 49 Rivoli St San Francisco CA 94117-4306 E-mail: artseen@sirius.com

HOWARD, H. TAYLOR, electrical engineer, educator; BS, Stanford U. Prof. dept. elec. engring. Stanford U., 1967—, prof. emeritus dept. elec. engring. Leader radio sci. team on NASA Galileo mission to Jupiter; chief scientist Chaparral Comm. Contbr. articles to profl. jours. Recipient medal for exceptional sci. achievement NASA, 1973. Fellow IEEE (life); mem. NAE, AAS, AGU, URSI, Satellite and Broadcasting and Comm. Assn. (chmn.). Achievements include research in radar astronomy, development of instrumentation and experimental techniques for planetary exploration, antennas, transmitters, and satellite communication. Office: 350 Serra Mall # 309 David Packard EE Bldg Stanford U Stanford CA 94305-9515 Fax: 650-723-9251. E-mail: hthoward@stanford.edu

HOWARD, J. ANTHONY (TONY), industrial engineering consultant; b. Montreal, Can. BSc in Engring., McGill U., 1964; MBA, Stanford U., 1966. Jr. engr. Montreal Engring., 1966; site commissioning engr. Sask. Power Corp.; dir. mktg., v.p. energy supply sys. TransAlta Utilities, 1982; mktg. and bus. profl. Monenco AGRA, 1990; joined Stantec Consulting, 1997, mgr. indsl. Mem. Assn. Profl. Engrs., Geologists and Geophysicists Alta. (conv. planning com. 1981-85, councillor 1987-90, enforcement rev. com. 1988-92, exec. com. 1992-94, self-governance coording com. 1992-93, first v.p. 1992-93, pres. 1993-94, nominating com., dir. edn. found, L.C. Charlesworth Profl. Svc. award 2000). Office: Stantec Consulting 1122 4 St SW Ste 400 Calgary AB Canada T2R 1M1

HOWARD, JAMES WEBB, investment banker, lawyer, engineer; b. Evansville, Ind., Sept. 17, 1925; s. Joseph R. and Velma (Cobb) H.; m. Phyllis Jean Brandt, Dec. 27, 1948; children: Sheila Rae, Sharon Kae. BS in Mech. Engring, Purdue U., 1949; postgrad., Akron (Ohio) Law Sch., 1950-51, Cleve. Marshall Law Sch., 1951-52; MBA, Case Western Res. U., 1962; J.D., Western State Coll. Law, 1976. Registered profl. engr., Ind., Ohio. Jr. project engr. Firestone Tire & Rubber Co., Akron, 1949-50; gen. foreman Cadillac Motor Car div. GM, 1950-53; mgmt. cons. M.K. Sheppard & Co., Cleve., 1953-56; plant mgr. Lewis Welding & Engring. Corp., Ohio, 1956-58; underwriter The Ohio Co., Columbus, 1959; chmn. Growth Capital, Inc., Chgo., 1960-98; pvt. practice law San Diego, 1979-85. Pres. Meister Brau, Inc., Chgo., 1965-73, The Home Mart, San Diego, 1974-82; mng. agt., fin. instn. specialist FDIC/RTC, 1985-90; specialist in charge Office of FDIC-DOL, Portland, Oreg., 1986-87. Developer of "Lite" beer. Co-chmn. Chgo. com. Ill. Sesquicentennial Com., 1968. Served with AUS, 1943-46. Decorated Bronze Star, Parachutist badge, Combat Inf. badge. Mem. ASME, Nat. Assn. Small Bus. Investment Cos. (past pres.), State Bar Calif., Grad. Bus. Alumni Assn. Western Res. U. (past gov.), Masons, Tau Kappa Epsilon, Pi Tau Sigma, Beta Gamma Sigma. Methodist.

HOWARD, MARILYN, school system administrator; BA in Edn., U. Idaho, 1960, MSc in Edn., 1965; EdD, Brigham Young U., 1986; postgrad., Idaho State U. adj. faculty Idaho State U., U. Idaho. Supt. pub. instrn. Idaho State Dept. Edn., Boise, Idaho, 1998—. Past state pres. Internat. Reading Assn., nat. rsch. and studies com; bd. dirs. State Bd. Edn., State Land Bd., Northwest Regional Edn. Lab. Office: Idaho State Dept Edn PO Box 83720 Boise ID 83720-3720 E-mail: mhoward@sde.state.id.us

HOWARD, MARK J. hospital administrator; BS in Health Scis., Brigham Young U.; MS in Hosp. Adminstrn., UCLA. Asst. adminstr. Utah Valley Hosp., Provo; adminstr. Am. Fork (Utah) Hosp.; exec. dir. Utah Valley Regional Med. Ctr., Orem Cmty. Hosp., Provo; adminstr. Utah Valley Regional Med. Ctr.; CEO IHC Hosps., Utah County, Ctrl. Utah, MountainView Hosp., Las Vegas. Adj. faculty Brigham Young U., Provo, U. Minn., Mpls. Active Boy Scouts Am., chmn. Bighorn dist. Named Citizen of Month Las Vegas. Fellow Am. Coll. of Heathcare Execs. (chmn. 1999—, bd. govs. 1991-95, regent for Utah 1986-91); mem. Utah Hosp. Assn. (past chair), Am. Hosp. Assn. (ho. of dels.), E-mail: mark.howard@columbia.net

HOWARD, NANCY E. lawyer; b. Ft. Wayne, Ind., Aug. 13, 1951; BA, Stanford U., 1973, JD, 1977. Bar: Calif. 1977. Mem. Tuttle & Taylor, L.A., 1977—. Contbr. articles to profl. jours. Mem. Order of Coif., Phi Beta Kappa. Office: Tuttle & Taylor [illegible] 90071-1560

HOWARD, ROBERT FRANKLIN, observatory administrator, astronomer; b. Delaware, Ohio, Dec. 30, 1932; s. David Dale and Clarine Edna (Morehouse) H.; m. Margaret Teresa Farnon, Oct. 4, 1958; children: Thomas Colin, Alan Robert, Moira Catharine. BA, Ohio Wesleyan U., 1954; PhD, Princeton U., 1957. Carnegie fellow Mt. Wilson and Palomar Obs., Pasadena, Calif., 1957-59, staff mem., 1961-81; asst. prof. U. Mass., Amherst, 1959-61; asst. dir. for Mt. Wilson Mt. Wilson & Las Campanas Obs., Pasadena, 1981-84; dir. Nat. Solar Obs., Tucson, 1984-88, astronomer, 1988-98, astronomer emeritus, 1998—. Editor: Solar Magnetic Fields, 1971; editor: (jour.) Solar Physics, 1987-98; contbr. articles to profl. jours. Mem. Am. Astron. Soc., Internat. Astron. Union Office: Nat Solar Obs PO Box 26732 950 N Cherry Ave Tucson AZ 85719-4933

HOWARD, ROBERT STAPLES, newspaper publisher; b. Wheaton, Minn., Oct. 23, 1924; s. Earl Eaton and Helen Elizabeth (Staples) H.; m. Lillian Irene Crabtree, Sept. 2, 1945; children: Thomas, Andrea, William, David. Student, U. Minn., 1942, 45. Pub. various daily, weekly newspapers, 1946-55; pub. Chester, Pa. Times, 1955-61; Pres. Howard Publs. (18 daily newspapers), 1961—. With AUS, 1942-43; 2d lt. USAAF, 1944-45. Home: PO Box 1337 Rancho Santa Fe CA 92067-1337 Office: PO Box 570 Oceanside CA 92049-0570

HOWARD, RONALD A. systems engineer, educator; DSc in Elec. Engring., MIT, 1958. Prof. dept. engring.-econ. sys./ops. rsch. Stanford U., 1965—. Founder, dir. Strategic Decisions Group; dir. Decisions and Ethics Ctr. Author: Dynamic Programming and Markov Processes, 1960, Dynamic Probabilistic Systems, 1971, Readings in Decision Analysis, 1977, READINGS on The Principles and Applications of Decision Analysis, 1984, Decision Analysis, 1996; contbr. numerous articles to profl. jours. Fellow IEEE; mem. NAE, TIMS, Operational Rsch. Soc. (U.K., Frank P. Ramsey medal for disting. contbns. in decision analysis 1986). Office: Dept Engring-Econ Sys/Ops Rsch Terman Engring Ctr Rm 324 Stanford U Stanford CA 94305-4023 E-mail: rhoward@leland.stanford.edu

HOWARD, WILLIAM GATES, JR. electronics company executive; b. Boston, Nov. 6, 1941; s. William Gates and Mary Louise (Creager) H.; m. Kathleen Louretta Shipp, June 4, 1983. B.E.E. with distinction, Cornell U., 1964, M.S., 1965; Ph.D., U. Calif.-Berkeley, 1967. Asst. prof. dept. elec. engring. and computer scis. U. Calif.-Berkeley, 1967-69; group ops. mgr. Motorola Semicondr. Group, Mesa, Ariz., 1969-76; v.p., dir. tech. and planning Motorola Semicondr. Sector, Phoenix, 1976-83; v.p., dir. R&D Motorola Inc., Schaumburg, Ill., 1983-87; sr. fellow Nat. Acad. Engring., Washington, 1987-91; chmn. bd. Credence Sys. Corp. Dir. Arete Assocs., Biometric Identification, Inc., BEI Techs., Inc., Ramtron Internat Corp., Thunderbird Techs., Inc., Xilinx, Inc., Sandia Corp.; chmn. semicondr. tech. adv. com. U.S. Dept. Commerce, 1978-83; chmn. adv. group on electron devices Dept. Def., 1982-99, mem. def. sci. bd., 1996—; mem. study com. on tech. and implications of VLSI, NAS, 1980; chmn. vis. com. on advanced tech. Nat. Inst. Stds. and Tech., 1988-92; chmn. Def. Sci. Bd. Task Force on Microelectronics Rsch. Facilities, 1991-92; mem. Sandia Pres. Adv. Coun.; chmn. bd. dirs. Credence Sys., Inc. Author: (with D.J. Hamilton) Basic Integrated Circuit Engineering, 1976, (with B. Guile) Profiting from Innovation, 1992; patentee (with J.B. Cecil) improved reference current source, ladder termination circuit, three terminal zener diode. Fellow AAAS, IEEE (vice chmn. circuits and systems soc. 1976-78); mem. Nat. Acad. of Engring., Sigma Xi, Phi Kappa Phi, Eta Kappa Nu, Tau Beta Pi. Office: 10642 E San Salvador Dr Scottsdale AZ 85258-6114

HOWARD, WILLIAM MATTHEW, arbitrator, writer, lawyer; b. Oak Park, Ill., Dec. 16, 1934; s. William and Martha Geraldine (Herlock) H.; children: Matthew William, Stephanie Sue. BSBA, U. Mo., 1956, JD, 1958; postgrad., U. Nice, France, 1976, U. London, , 1977; PhD, Ariz. State U., 1995. Bar: Mo. 1958, U.S. Supreme Ct. 1986; cert. mediator and arbitrator, Fla. Supreme Ct. Jr. ptnr. Bryan Cave, St. Louis, 1958-66; asst. to pres. Granite City (Ill.) Steel Co., 1966-69; pres. Thomson Internat. Co., Thibodaux, La., 1969-70; founder, pres., chmn. bd. The Catalyst Group, Phoenix, 1970-97; dean, ctr. adminstr. The Union Inst., San Diego, 1997-99; pres. Dispute Solutions, Inc., Scottsdale, Ariz., 1999—. Mem. adj. faculty U. Mo., Columbia, 1956-58, St. Louis U., 1958-61, Ariz. State U., 1994-96, Ottawa U., 1994-96, Nova Southeastern U., 1996-97; chmn. unauthorized practice law com. Mo. Bar, St. Louis, 1964-65; chmn. bd. N.V. Vulcaansoord, Terborg, The Netherlands, 1975-78, E. Chalmers Holdings, Ltd., Glasgow, Scotland, 1977-78; exec. com. Chem. Bank, Irvine, Calif., 1985-90; vis. lectr. UCLA, 1987; arbitrator Am. Arbitration Assn., N.Y.C., 1987—, N.Y. Stock Exch., 1987—, Nt. Assn. Securities Dealers, Chgo., 1987—, Nat. Futures Assn., Chgo., 1988—, Am. Stock Exch., N.Y.C., 1988; hearing officer Mo. Dept. Natural Resources, Jefferson City, 1987-89, Internat. Ct. Arbitration, 1993—, Inter-Am. Comml. Arbitration Commn., 1993—; mem. Fla. Automobile Arbitration Bd., 1997-98; bd. dirs. Xeric Corp., Denver, Phoenix. Editor newsletter Extras, 1970—; exec. producer: (motion picture) Twice a Woman, 1979; contbr. numerous articles and revs. to various jours. Bd. dirs. U. Mo. Alumni Assn., 1986, Breckenridge (Colo.) Film Festival, 1989, Actors Theatre Phoenix, 1990; mem. club adv. bd. Phoenix Art Mus., 1990; dir. Scottsdale Cultural Coun., 1991. Mem. Am. Arbitration Assn. (regional adv. com.), Soc. Profls. in Dispute Resolution, Fla. Acad. Mediators, Nat. Inst. Dispute Resolution, Mensa, Order of Coif. Avocations: literature, travel, theatre, visual arts, skiing. Office: Dispute Solutions Inc PO Box 9159 Scottsdale AZ 85252-9159 Fax: 480-990-8970. E-mail: howardbill@msn.com

HOWATT, SISTER HELEN CLARE, former human services director, former college library director; b. San Francisco, Apr. 5, 1927; d. Edward Bell and Helen Margaret (Kenney) H. BA, Holy Names Coll., 1949; MS in Libr. Sci., U. So. Calif., 1972; cert. advanced studies, Our Lady of Lake U., 1966. Joined Order Sisters of the Holy Names, Roman Cath. Ch., 1945. Life tchg. credential, life spl. svcs. credential, prin. St. Monica Sch., Santa Monica, Calif., 1957-60, St. Mary Sch., L.A., 1960-63; tchr. jr. high sch. St. Augustine Sch., Oakland, Calif., 1964-69; tchr. jr. high math St. Monica Sch., San Francisco, 1969-71, St. Cecilia Sch., San Francisco, 1971-77; libr. dir. Holy Names Coll., Oakland, Calif., 1977-94; Spanish instr. Collins Ctr. Sr. Svcs., 1994-99; acct. St. Monica Sch., San Francisco, 1999—. Contbr. math. curriculum San Francisco Unified Sch. Dist., Cum Notis Varioru m, publ. Music Libr., U. Calif., Berkeley. Contbr. articles to profl. jours. Recipient NSF grantee, 1966, NDEA grantee, 1966. Mem. Cath. Libr. Assn. (chmn. No. Calif. elem. schs. 1971-72). Home and Office: 5920 Geary Blvd San Francisco CA 94121-2007

HOWE, ART (ARTHUR HENRY HOWE JR.), professional baseball manager; b. Pitts., Dec. 15, 1946; m. Elizabeth Louise Falconio, Aug. 16, 1969; children: Stephanie Lynn, Gretchen Leigh, Matthew Louis. BS, BA, U. Wyoming, 1969. Computer programmer Westinghouse Corp., 1969-70; player Carolina League, Salem, 1971, International League, Charleston, WV, 1972-75, Pittsburg Pirates, Pittsburg, PA, 1974, 75, International League, Memphis, 1976, Houston Astros, Houston, 1976-83, St. Louis Cardinals, St. Louis, 1984-85; coach Texas Rangers, Arlington, TX, 1985-88; mgr. Houston Astros, Houston, 1988-93, Puerto Rican League, Bayamon, PR, winters 1979, 80, 82, Ponce, PR, winter 1985, Oakland Athletics, 1996—; hitting coach Colo. Rockies, 1995. Named Mgr. of Yr. P.R. League, 1980, Dominican Rep. La Romana, 1994-95. Office: Oakland Athletics 7677 Oakport St Ste 2002D Oakland CA 94621-1929

HOWE, CON EDWARD, city manager; b. St. Louis, Oct. 23, 1949; BA, Yale U., 1972; MA in City Planning, MIT, 1975. Exec. dir. Mass. Land Bank; with Gov.'s Office Mass.; dir. Manhattan Office N.Y. City Planning Dept., 1982-87, exec. dir., 1987-91; dir. planning City of L.A., 1992—. Mem. Am. Planning Assn., Urban Land Inst. Office: Planning Dept 200 N Spring St Rm 525 Los Angeles CA 90012 E-mail: [illegible]

HOWE, DRAYTON FORD, JR. lawyer; b. Seattle, Nov. 17, 1931; s. Drayton Ford and Virginia (Wester) H.; m. Joyce Arnold, June 21, 1952; 1 son, James Drayton. AB, U. Calif., Berkeley, 1953; LLB, U. Calif., San Francisco, 1957. Bar: Calif. 1958. CPA Calif. Atty. IRS, 1958-61; tax dept. supr. Ernst & Ernst, San Francisco, 1962-67; ptnr. Bishop, Barry, Howe, Haney & Ryder, San Francisco, 1968—. Lectr. on tax matters U. Calif. extension, 1966-76. Mem. Calif. Bar Assn., San Francisco Bar Assn. (chmn. client relations com. 1977), Calif. Soc. CPA's. Office: Bishop Barry Howe Haney & Ryder 2000 Powell St Ste 1425 Emeryville CA 94608-1861 E-mail: dhowe@bbhhr.com

HOWE, RICHARD CUDDY, state supreme court chief justice; b. South Cottonwood, Utah, Jan. 20, 1924; s. Edward E. and Mildred (Cuddy) H.; m. Juanita Lyon, Aug. 30, 1949; children: Christine Howe Schultz, Andrea Howe Reynolds, Bryant, Valerie Howe Winegar, Jeffrey, Craig. BS, U. Utah, 1945, JD, 1948. Bar: Utah. Law clk. to Justice James H. Wolfe, Utah Supreme Ct., 1949-50; judge city ct. Murray, Utah, 1951; individual practice law Murray, 1952-80; assoc. justice Utah Supreme Ct., Salt Lake City, 1980—, justice, chief justice. Mem. Utah Constnl. Revision Commn., 1976-85. Chmn., original mem. Salt Lake County Merit Coun.; mem. Utah Ho. of Reps., 1951-58, 69-72, Utah Senate, 1973-78. Named Outstanding Legislator Citizens' Conf. State Legislatures, 1972 Mem. ABA, Utah Bar Assn., Sons of Utah Pioneers. Mem. LDS Ch. Office: Utah Supreme Ct 450 S State St PO Box 140210 Salt Lake City UT 84114-0210

HOWE, WARREN BILLINGS, physician; b. Jackson Heights, N.Y., Oct. 25, 1940; s. John Hanna and Francelia (Rose) H.; m. Hedwig Neslanik, Aug. 7, 1971; children: Elizabeth Rose, Sarah Billings. BA, U. Rochester, 1962; MD, Washington U., St. Louis, 1965. Diplomate Am. Bd. Family Practice with CAQ in Sports Medicine, Nat. Bd. Med. Examiners. Intern Phila. Gen. Hosp., 1965-66; resident physician Highland Hosp./U. Rochester, 1969-71; family physician Family Medicine Clinic of Oak Harbor (Wash.), Inc., PS, 1971-92; student health physician, univ. team physician We. Wash. U., Bellingham, 1992—. Team physician Oak Harbor High Sch., 1972-92; head tournament physician Wash. State High Sch. Wrestling Championships, Tacoma, 1989—; attending physician Seattle Goodwill Games, 1990; clin. asst. prof. U. Wash. Sch. Medicine, 1975-82. Contbr. articles to profl. jours. and chpts. to books; editl. bd. The Physician and Sports Medicine Jour., 1984—. Bd. dirs. Oak Harbor Sch. Dist. #201, 1975-87; chmn. Oak Harbor Citizen's Com. for Sch. Support, 1988-90. Lt. comdr. USN, 1966-69, Vietnam. Recipient Disting. Svc. award City of Oak Harbor, 1984; Paul Harris fellowship Oak Harbor Rotary Club. Fellow Am. Coll. Sports Medicine (chair membership com. 1986-95), Am. Acad. Family Physicians; mem. Wash. State Med. Assn., Am. Med. Soc. for Sports Medicine, Am. Coll. Health Assn. Presbyterian. Home: 4222 Northridge Way Bellingham WA 98226-7804 Office: WWU Student Health Ctr 25 High St Bellingham WA 98225-5942

HOWELL, FRANCIS CLARK, anthropologist, educator; b. Kansas City, Mo., Nov. 27, 1925; s. Edward Ray and Myrtle Marie (Clark) H.; m. Betty Ann Tomsen, June 17, 1955; children: Brian David, Jennifer Clare PhB, U. Chgo., 1949, MA, 1951, PhD, 1953. Instr. anatomy Washington U., St. Louis, 1953-55; asst. prof. to prof. anthropology U. Chgo., 1955-70; prof. anthropology U. Calif.-Berkeley, 1970-91, emeritus prof., 1991—. Contbr. numerous articles on human biol. and cultural evolution to profl. jours. Trustee L.S.B. Leakey Found., 1969—. Served with USN, 1944-46 Recipient Franklin L. Burr prize, Nat. Geographic Soc., 1993, Leakey prize L.S.B. Learey Fedn., 1998, Charles Robert Darwin Lifetime Achievement award Am. Assn. Phys. Anthropology, 1998. Fellow Am. Acad. Arts and Scis.; mem. Nat. Acad. Scis., Am. Philos. Soc., AAAS, Calif. Acad. Sci. (trustee 1975—, Fellows medal 1990), Acad. des Scis., Inst. de France. Home: 1994 San Antonio Ave Berkeley CA 94707-1620 Office: U Calif Mus Vertebrate Zoology Berkeley CA 94720-0001

HOWELL, JAMES EDWIN, economist, educator; b. Sterling, Colo., Mar. 6, 1928; s. James William, Jr. and Lois (Brown) H.; m. Linda Leinbach, 1965; children: Kenneth E., William J., Jan E., Caitlyn B. BA, Fresno State Coll., 1950; MA, U. Ill., 1951, Yale U., 1953, PhD, 1955. Instr. econs. and stats. Yale U., 1954-56; mem. staff Ford Found., 1956-58, 62, cons., 1958-72; Theodore J. Kreps prof. econs. Stanford U., 1958—, asso. dean Grad. Sch. Bus., 1965-70; vis. prof. econs. London Bus. Sch., 1992. Dir. gen. Internat. Inst. Mgmt. and Adminstrn., Berlin, 1970-72; dir. Stanford-Insead Advanced Mgmt. Program, European Inst. Bus. Adminstrn., France, 1979-81; sometime prof., lectr. U. Hawaii, U. Calif.-Berkeley, Stanford in Vienna, U. Pa., Nat. U. Singapore, London Bus. Sch.; vis. prof. Humboldt U., Berlin, 1995; cons. U.S. and Europe; dir., v.p. Ann. Revs. Inc. Author/co-author: Higher Education for Business, 1959, European Economics-East and West, 1967, Mathematical Analysis for Business Decisions, 1963, 2d edit., 1971, (with G. L. Bach) Economics, 11th edit., 1987. Served with AUS, 1946-47. Ford Found. faculty fellow Harvard U., 1959-60; NSF sr. postdoctoral fellow London Sch. Econs., 1963-64; recipient Davis award for lifetime achievement Stanford U., 1996. Club: University (N.Y.C.). Home: 96 Serrano Dr Atherton CA 94027-3934 Office: Stanford U Grad Sch Bus Stanford CA 94305

HOWELL, KEVIN L. hotel executive; V.p. Nat. 9 Inns, Salt Lake City, 1987—. Office: Nat 9 Inns 2285 S Main St Ste 9 Salt Lake City UT 84115-2626

HOWELL, R. SCOTT, industry executive; CEO Nicholson Industries, Seattle. Office: Nicholson Industries 3670 E Marginal Way S Seattle WA 98134-1130

HOWELL, SCOTT NEWELL, computer company executive, state legislator; b. Provo, Utah, Sept. 28, 1953; s. Varon L. and Kathryn (Tuttle) H.; m. Linda Skanchy, Sept. 8, 1978; children: Bryan, Bradley, Jason, Jeffrey. BA, U. Utah, 1978. With sales IBM Corp., mgr., global policy exec.; chair., Utah State Judicial Conduct Review Comm., 1990-; mem. Utah Senate, Salt Lake City, 1990-, minority leader, 1993-; mem. Nat. Conference State Legislators, 1992-. Mem. Utah info. tech. com. Utah Senate, transportation & environ. quality appropriations subcom., mem. state & local affairs standing com.; chmn. Nat. Acad. Fin., Salt Lake City, 1991-93. Bd. dirs. Utah Chpt. Nat. Children's Protection of Child Abuse, Salt Lake City, 1992-93, visually handicapped divsn. United Way, Salt Lake City, 1992-93; trustee Utah Symphony, 1994—. Mem., Nat. Academy of Finance (chair. 1990-92); Utah Info. Tech. Assoc., Intermountain Healthcare, State Legis. Leaders Found., Dem. Leadership Coun., Harvard Policy Group. Democrat. Mormon. Home: 9711 S 3725 E Sandy UT 84092-6047 Address: 319 State Capitol Salt Lake City UT 84114

HOWELLS, R. TIM, professional sports team executive; m. Patty Howells; four children. Grad., U. Utah, 1968. With Howells, Inc., Salt Lake City, 1968-82, v.p., co-owner, pvt. investor, from 1982; gen. mgr. Utah Jazz NBA, 1989—. Office: Utah Jazz 301 W South Temple Salt Lake City UT 84101-1216

HOWES, GLORIA, state legislator; b. Gallup, N. Mex., 1931; BA, West Tex. U.; MA, U. N.Mex. County mgr. McKinley County, N.Mex., county comr.; mem. N. Mex. Senate, 4th dist., Santa Fe, 1988-. Democrat. Address: 1515 Monterey Dr Gallup NM 87301-5637 Office: NM State Senate State Capitol Rm 302 Santa Fe NM 87503

HOWLEY, PETER ANTHONY, communications executive; b. Phila., Mar. 5, 1940; s. Frank Leo and Edith Jenkins (Cadwallader) H.; m. M. Mavin Renz, June 25, 1966; children: Tara Noel, Christina Maeve, Sean-Francis Cadwallader. B in Indsl. Engring., NYU, 1962, MBA in Mktg., 1970. Mem. mgmt. staff AT&T, White Plains, N.Y., 1965-73, MCI, Inc., N.Y.C., 1973-76; v.p., gen. mgr. Citizens Utilities Co., Kingman, Ariz., 1976-85; chmn., pres., CEO Centex Telemgmt., Inc., San Francisco, 1985-94; founder, chmn., pres., CEO, Air Power Comm., Inc., San Francisco, 1995-96; chmn. Western Ventures, San Francisco, 1994-98; co-founder, chmn., pres., CEO IPWireless, Inc., San Bruno, Calif., 1998—. Former bd. dirs. NetMoves, Inc.; bd. dirs. Woodbridge, N.J., Exodus Comm., Inc., Santa Clara, Calif., Worldport Comms., Inc., Houston; mem. adv. bd. NASDAQ Corp., 1992-94. Contbr. to numerous profl. publs. Dir. The Ind. Inst.; founder Am. Bus. Conf. Found. Capt. USAF, 1962-65, 68-69. Recipient Outstanding Achievement award USAF. Mem. Am. Bus. Conf. Roman Catholic. Avocations: skiing, tennis, running, sailing. Home: 25 Cornwall St Mill Valley CA 94941-1730 Office: IP Wireless Inc 1250 Bayhill Dr Ste 113 San Bruno CA 94066 E-mail: pahowley@aol.com, phowley@ipwireless.com

HOWROYD, JANICE BRYANT, personnel placement executive; b. Tarboro, N.C. Pres., CEO, prin. ACT 1 Pers. Svcs., Torrance, Calif., 1978—. Lectr. in field. Mem. Minority Bus. Opportunity Day trade fair, LA, Jr. Achievement of Ctrl. Ariz. Inc., 1992-93, Project Life; bd. dirs. L.A. Urban League, St. Anne's Maternity Home, Internat. Visitors coun. for city of L.A., L.A. Urban League. Recipient Minority Enterprise Devel. Week Achievement award U.S. Dept. of Commerce, Ceert. of Achievement award No. Calif. Regional Purchasing coun., 1992, Entertainment and Bus. Cmty Achievement award NAACP Legal Def. Fund. 1992, Distinguished Svc. award Joint Conf., Inc., 1993, Nat. Minority Supplier of the Year award Nat. Minority Supplier Devel. coun., 1993, Black Women of Achievement AT & T Entrepreneur of the Year, 1994. Mem. Nat. Assn. of Women Bus. Owners; bd. dirs. Greater L.A. African Am. C. of C.; adv. bd. mem. Northrop-Rice Aviation Inst. of Technol. Office: ACT 1 Pers Svc 5334 Torrance Blvd Torrance CA 90503-4012

HOWRY, JOE, newspaper editor; Mng. editor Ventura (Calif.) County Star, 1992—. Address: 5250 Ralston St Ventura CA 93003-7318

HOXIE, JOEL P. lawyer; b. Waterloo, Iowa, Dec. 4, 1948; s. Wirt Pierce and Jeanne (Ogle) H.; m. Cynthia Ann Mast, Aug. 12, 1978; children: Robert Lewis, Laura Ann. AB, Princeton U., 1971; JD, U. Iowa, 1978. Atty. Snell & Wilmer, Phoenix, 1978—. Trustee Heard Mus., Phoenix, 1990—, v.p., 1990-95, pres., 1995-97, pres. bd. trustees; pres. Princeton Alumni Assn. No. Ariz., Phoenix, 1990—. Lt. USN, 1971-75. Mem. Nat. Bar Assn., Ariz. State Bar Assn., County Bar Assn., Securities Industry Assn. (legal and compliance divsn. 1992—), Phoenix Country Club (bd. dirs. 2001—). Methodist. Avocations: golf, tennis, swimming, hiking. Home: 5301 E Mariposa St Phoenix AZ 85018-3029 Office: Snell & Wilmer 1 Arizona Ctr Phoenix AZ 85004 E-mail: jhoxie@swlaw.com

HOY, WILLIAM, film editor; Prin. works include films The Philadelphia Experiment, 1984, No Way Out, 1986, Silent Assassins, 1986, Best of the Best, 1988, Dances with Wolves, 1990, Star Trek VI: The Undiscovered Country, 1992, Patriot Games, 1992, Sliver, 1993, Judicial Consent, 1994, Outbreak, 1995, Seven, 1995, The Eighteenth Angel, 1996, Man in the Iron Mask, 1998, The Bone Collector, 1999, (TV) Houdini, 1998. Office: Broder Kurland Webb & Uffner 9242 Beverly Blvd Ste 200 Beverly Hills CA 90210-3731

HSI, DAVID CHING HENG, plant pathologist and geneticist, educator; b. Shanghai, China, May 17, 1928; came to U.S., 1948, naturalized, 1961; s. Yulin and Sue Jean (King) H.; m. Kathy S.W. Chiang, 1952; children: Andrew C., Steven D. BSA, St. John's U., Shanghai, 1948; MS, U. Ga., 1949; PhD, U. Minn., 1951. Grad. teaching asst. U. Minn., St. Paul, 1950; postdoctoral fellow U.S. Cotton Field Sta., Sacaton, Ariz., 1951-52; mem. faculty N.Mex. State U., Las Cruces, 1952—, prof. plant pathology and genetics, 1968-92, prof. emeritus, 1992—. Cons. AID, Pakistan, 1970; coord. external evaluation panel Peanut Collaborative Rsch. Support Program, U.S.A., West Africa, S.E. Asia, 1993-95; acad. exch. People's Republic China, 1978, 84, 85, Republic China, 1979, 81, 82, Brazil and Argentina, 1980, Australia, 1983, South Africa, 1981; judge sr. botany N.Mex. Sci. and Engring. Fair, 1979—; adj. prof. biology U. N.Mex., 1986—. Author rsch. papers in field; co-developer new crop cultivars. Past bd. dirs., treas. Carver Pub. Libr., Clovis, N.Am.; elder 1st Presbyn. Ch., Albuquerque, workship com. chmn., 1981-82, adult edn. com. chmn., 1988-91, pers. com., 1995-98; mem. nat. adv. coun. discipleship and worship Gen. Assembly United Presbyn. Ch. U.S.A., 1978-81, mem. nat. theol. reflections working group, 1980-81, mem. ednl. and congl. nurture unit, 1991-93, N.Mex. Child Abuse Neglect Prevention Implementation Task Force, 1993-97; mem. bd. edn. Albuquerque Pub. Schs., 1982, sec. bd. edn., 1983, v.p., 1984; bd. dirs. Mid. Rio Grande Coun. Govts., 1983, 84; chair Albuquerque Sisters Cities Bd., 1986-88; 1st v.p. Albuquerque Sister Cities Found., 1995-96, pres., 1996-98; mem. com. higher edn. Gen. Assembly The Presbyn. Ch. (U.S.A.), 1991-93, preparation ministry com., Presbytery Santa Fe, 1993-98, chair, 1996-97; co-chair N.Mex. Advocates for Children and Families, 1993-95, vice chair, 1995-98; bd. dirs. Greater Albuquerque Vol. Adminstrs., 1992-95, 97-99, Project Change, 1994-98, v.p., 1996-98; v.p. Albuquerque Edn. Retirees, 1995-96, pres., 1996-98; v.p. Edn. Success Alliance, 1996-98; trustee All Faiths Receiv. Home, 1997—; trustee, bd. dirs. Sandia Prep Sch., 2001—, Explora Sci. Ctr. and Children Mus. Albuquerque, 1998—; v.p. The Friendship Force of N.Mex., 2001—, Recipient Disting. Rsch. award Coll. Agr. and Home Econs. N.Mex. State U., 1971, Disting. Svc. award, 1985; inducted into Sr. Citizen's Hall of Fame, 1993. Fellow AAAS (hon., coun. mem. 1998—, Southwestern and Rocky Mountain divsn., exec. com. 1993-95, pres.-elect 1995-96, pres. 96-97); mem. Internat. Soc. Plant Pathology, Am. Phytopath. Soc. (judge Internat. Sci. and Engring. Fair 1983), Nat. Sweet Potato Collaborators Group (chmn. sprout prodn. and root piece propagation com. 1982-84), Nat. Geog. Soc., Am. Peanut Rsch. and Edn. Soc. (chmn. site selection com. 1981, award com., pres.-elect 1981, pres. 1982), N.Mex. Acad. Sci. (chmn. com. 1980, pres. 1981, 82, treas. 1984-92, dist. scientist award 1984), Nat. Assn. Acad. Sci. (pres.-elect 1992-93, pres. 1993-94), N.Mex. Chinese Assn. (pres. 1983-84, 92-93, treas. 1985-86, past bd. dirs.), Chinese Am. Citizens Alliance (v.p. Albuquerque lodge 1988-92), Albuquerque Coun. for Internat. Visitors (v.p. 1988, pres. 1989-91), Sigma Xi (life, N.Mex. coord. centennial celebration), Kiwanis Internat. (past pres. Clovis, past chmn. spl. program com., past bd. dirs. Albuquerque). Home and Office: 2504 Griegos Pl NW Albuquerque NM 87107-2874 E-mail: Davidnkathyhsi@aol.com

HSU, CHIEH SU, applied mechanics engineering educator, researcher; b. Soochow, Kiangsu, China, May 27, 1922; came to U.S., 1947, s. Chung yu and Yong Feng (Wu) H.; m. Helen Yung-Feng Tse, Mar. 28, 1953; children: Raymond Hwa-Chi, Katherine Hwa-Ling. BS, Nat. Inst. Tech., Chungking, China, 1945; MS, Stanford U., 1948, PhD, 1950. Project engr. IBM Corp., Poughkeepsie, N.Y., 1951-55; assoc. prof. U. Toledo, 1955-58, Univ Calif.-Berkeley, 1958-64, prof., 1964—, chmn. div. applied mechanics, 1969-70. Mem. sci. adv. bd. Alexander von Humboldt Found. of Fed. Republic Germany, Bonn, 1985—; mem. U.S. nat. com. theoretical and applied mechanics U.S. Nat. Acad. Sics., 1985-90. Author: Cell-to-Cell Mapping, 1987; contbg. author: Thin-Shell Structures, 1974, Advances in Applied Mechanics, vol. 17, 1977; tech. editor Jour. Applied Mechanics, N.Y.C., 1976-82; assoc. editor profl. jours.; author of over 106 tech. papers. Recipient Alexander von Humboldt award Fed. Republic Germany, 1986; Guggenheim Found. fellow, 1964-65; Miller research prof., U. Calif.-Berkeley, 1973-74. Fellow ASME (Centennial award 1980, N.O. Myklestad award 1995) Am. Acad. Mechanics; mem. Acoustical Soc. Am., Soc. Indsl. and Applied Math., U. S. Nat. Acad. Engring., Acad. Sinica, Sigma Xi. Office: U Calif Dept Mech Engring Berkeley CA 94720-1740

HSU, GERALD C. electrical company executive; Chmn., pres., CEO Avant!, Freemont, Calif. Office: Avant! Corp 46871 Bayside Pkwy Fremont CA 94538-6572

HSU, IMMANUEL CHUNG YUEH, history educator; b. Shanghai, China, May 6, 1923; came to U.S., 1949, naturalized, 1962; s. Thomas K.S. and Mary (Loh) H.; m. Dolores Menstell, Apr. 14, 1962; 1 child, Vadim Menstell. B.A., Yenching U., China, 1946; M.A., U. Minn., 1950; Ph.D. (Harvard-Yenching fellow), Harvard U., 1954. Postdoctoral research fellow Harvard U., 1955-58; vis. asso. prof. history, vis. prof. Harvard Summer Sch., 1961, 64, 68, 75; asst. prof. history U. Calif. at Santa Barbara, 1959-60, asso. prof., 1960-65, prof., 1965-91, chmn. history dept., 1970-72. Faculty rsch. lectr., 1971; mem. del. to Chinese Acad. Scis., Beijing, spring 1979, 80; vis. prof. Hamburg U., Germany, spring 1973, Stockholm U., 1990, Leningrad (St. Petersburg) U., 1991; Fulbright lectr., 1973; vis. Wei Lun prof. The Chinese U. Hong Kong, 1998. Author: Intellectual Trends in the Ch'ing Period, 1959, China's Entrance into the Family of Nations, 1960, The Ili Crisis: A Study of Sino-Russian Diplomacy, 1871-1881, 1965, The Rise of Modern China, 1970, 2d edit., 1975, internat. edit., 1975-76, 3d edit., 1983, 4th edit., 1990, 5th edit., 1995 (Commonwealth Lit. priz of Calif. 1971), 6th edit., 2000; editor: Readings in Modern Chinese History, 1971, Late Ch'ing Foreign Relations, 1866-1905, in The Cambridge History of China, Vol. 11, 1980, China Without Mao, 1983, 2d edit., 1990. Guggenheim fellow, 1962-63; Nat. Acad. Scis. disting. scholar to China, spring 1983 Mem. Am., Pacific hist. assns., Assn. Asian Studies, Assn. Ch'ing Studies. Office: U Calif Dept History Santa Barbara CA 93106 E-mail: lhsu@silcom.com

HU, CHENMING, electrical engineering educator; b. Beijing, China, July 12, 1947; came to U.S., 1969; m. Margaret Hu, Feb. 14, 1972; children: Raymond, Jason. BS, Nat. Taiwan U., Taipei, 1968; MS, U. Calif., Berkeley, 1970, PhD, 1973. Asst. prof. MIT, 1973-76; prof. U. Calif., Berkeley, 1976—, Chancellor's prof., 1998-2000, Taiwan Semicondr. Mfg. Corp. Disting. prof. microelectronics, 2000—. Mgr. nonvolatile memory devel. Nat. Semicondr., Santa Clara, 1980-81; hon. prof. Beijing U., 1988, Tsing Hwa U., 1991, Chinese Acad. Sci., 1991; dir. Joint Svcs. Electronics Program, 1989-92, Indsl. Liaison Program, 1992-95; founder, chmn. BTA Tech. Inc., 1995—. Co-author: Solar Cells, 1983, Advanced MOS Device Physics, 1989, Nonvolatile Semiconductor Memory, 1991, MOSFET Modeling, 1999; patentee solid state devices and tech.; contbr. over 500 articles to profl. jours. Chmn. bd. East Bay Chinese Sch., Oakland, Calif., 1989-91. Recipient Design News Excellence in Design award, 1991, Semiconductor Rsch. Corp. Tech. Excellence award, 1992, Outstanding Inventor award, 1993, R&D 100 award, 1996, Monic Ferst award Sigma Xi, 1998, W.Y. Pang Found. award for rsch. excellence, 1999. Fellow IEEE (editl. bd. Trans. on Electronic Devices 1986-88, Jack Morton award 1997), NAE., Inst. Physics. Office: U Calif Dept Elec Engring Computer Sci Berkeley CA 94720-0001

HU, EVELYN LYNN, electrical and computer engineering educator; b. N.Y.C., May 15, 1947; d. David Hosheng and Carolyn Jui-chen (Hsu) H. BA in Physics, Barnard Coll., 1969; MA in Physics, Columbia U., 1971, PhD in Physics, 1975. Mem. tech. staff AT&T Bell Labs., Holmdel, N.J., 1975-81, supr. Murray Hill, 1981-84; prof. elec. and computer engring. U. Calif., Santa Barbara, 1985—; assoc. dir. Ctr. Robotic Systems in Microelectronics, 1985—. Mem. MIT vis. com. EECS, 1983—; mem. program com. Nat. Research and Resource Facility for Submicron Structures; mem. steering com. Internat. Symposium on Electron, Ion and Photon Beams; chmn. Gordon Conf. on Chemistry and Physics of Microstructures, 1986. Contbr. articles to profl. jours.; patentee in field. Mem. IEEE, Am. Phys. Soc., Am. Vacuum Soc., Phi Beta Kappa, Sigma Xi. Office: U Calif Ctr Quantized Elec Structures Santa Barbara CA 93106

HUANG, LINDA CHEN, plastic surgeon; b. Ithaca, N.Y., July 24, 1952; MD, Stanford U., 1979. Chmn. plastic surgery St. Joseph Hosp., Denver. Office: 1578 Humboldt St Denver CO 80218-1638

HUANG, PAN MING, soil science educator; b. Pu-tse, Taiwan, Sept. 2, 1934; arrived in Can., 1965; s. Rong Yi and Koh (Chiu) H.; m. Yun Yin Lin, Dec. 26, 1964; children: Daniel Chian Yuan, Crystal Ling Hui. BSA, Nat. Chung Hsing U., Taichung, Taiwan, 1957; MSc, U. Man., Winnipeg, Can., 1962; PhD, U. Wis., Madison, 1966. Cert. prof. agrologist. Asst. prof. soil sci. U. Sask., Saskatoon, Can., 1965-71, assoc. prof. Can., 1971-78, prof. Can., 1978—. Nat. vis. prof., head dept. soil sci. Nat. Chung Hsing U., 1975-76; mem. agr. adv. bd. Lewis Pubs., 1991—; hon. prof. Huazhong Agr. U., 1992—, Guanxi Agrl U., 1993—, Henan Agrl. U., 1996—, Langzhou U., 1999—; acad. advisor Chinese Acad. Scis., 1996—. Author: Soil Chemistry, 1991; mem. editl. bd. Chemosphere, 1987-97, Pedosphere, 1990—, Trends in Agr. Sci., 1991-95, Advances in Environ. Sci., 1993—, Geodema, 1994—, Soil Sci. Plant Nutrition, 1998—, Water, Air, and Soil Pollution, 1998—, Humic Substances in the Environment, 1998—; editor 10 books; spl. editor, mem. editl. bd. Water Pollution Rsch. Jour. Can., 1983-89, 91-93, Agro's Ann. Rev. Crop Ecology, 1995—; mem. editl. adv. bd. Trends in Soil Sci., 1995—; contbr. over 250 articles to profl. jours., chpts. to books. Bd. dirs. Saskatoon Chinese Mandarin Sch., 1977-79, Saskatoon Soc. for Study Chinese Culture, 1983—. 2d lt. Taiwan Mil. Tng. Corps, 1957-59. Recipient Disting. Rschr. award U. Sask., 1997; grantee The UN Environment Programme, Nat. Scis. and Engring. Rsch. Coun. Can. and numerous other agys., 1965—. Fellow AAAS, Can. Soc. Soil Sci., Soil Sci. Soc. Am. (rep. Clay Minerals Soc. 1979-83, chmn. divsn. S-9, 1983-84, bd. dirs. 1983-84, assoc. editor 1987-92, editor spl. publ. 1986, 98, rep. to Internat. Union Pure and Applied Chemistry 1990—, Internat. Soil Sci. award com. 1986-87, Marion L. and Christie M. Jackson Soil Sci. award com. 1990—, fellow com. 1992—, chmn.-elect divsn. S-2, 1993-94, chmn. 1994-95,, past chmn. 1995-96, bd. dirs. 1995-96, spl. awards com. 1995-96, chair nominations com. divsn. s-2 1995-96), Am. Soc. Agronomy; mem. Internat. Soc. Soil Sci. (chmn. working group MO 1990—), Am. Chem. Soc., N.Y. Acad. Scis., Internat. Union Pure and Applied Chemistry (assoc., commn. environ. analytical chemistry 1993-95, titular mem. comm. fundamental environ. chemistry 1995-97, 99—), Internat. Assn. Study Clays (treas. 1993—), Internat. Human Substances Soc. (leader Can. nat. chpt. 1992—), Can. Network Toxicology (team on metal speciation 1993-96), Sigma Xi. Avocations: music, reading. Home: 130 Mount Allison Cres Saskatoon SK Canada S7H 4A5 Office: U Sask Dept Soil Sci Campus Dr 51 Saskatoon SK Canada S7N 5A8 E-mail: Huangp@sask.usask.ca

HUANG, ROBERT, electronics manufacturing executive; BS, Kyushu U., Japan; MS, U. Rochester; MBA, MIT. Sales mgr. Advanced Micro Devices; founder Compac Microelectronics, 1980; founder, pres., CEO Synnex (formerly Compac Microelectronics), Fremont, Calif., 1992—. Office: Synnex Info Tech Inc 3797 Spinnaker Ct Fremont CA 94538

HUBBARD, ARTHUR THORNTON, chemistry educator, electrosurface chemist; b. Alameda, Calif., Sept. 17, 1941; s. John White and Ruth Frances (Gapen) H.; children: David A., Lynne F. BA, Westmont Coll., 1963; PhD, Calif. Inst. Tech., 1967. Prof. chemistry U. Hawaii, Honolulu, 1967-76, U. Calif., Santa Barbara, 1976-86; Ohio eminent scholar and prof. chemistry U. Cin., 1986-99, dir. Surface Ctr., 1986-99; dir. Santa Barbara

Sci. Project, 1999—. Chmn. Ohio Sci. and Engring. Roundtable, 1990-95. Co-editor Jour. Colloid and Interface Sci., 1993—; series editor Surfactant Science Series; editor: Encyclopedia of Surface and Colloid Science. Mem. Am. Chem. Soc. (assoc. editor jour. Langmuir 1984-90, vice chair surface and colloid div. 1999, chair-elect 2000, chair 2001, Kendall award 1989), Electrochem. Soc. (David C. Grahame award 1993), Am. Phys. Soc. Office: Santa Barbara Sci Project PO Box 42530 Santa Barbara CA 93140-2530

HUBBARD, HAROLD MEAD, independent consultant; b. Beloit, Kans., Apr. 16, 1924; s. Clarence Richard and Elizabeth (Mead) H.; m. Doreen J. Wallace, Aug. 13, 1948 (div. 1975); children: Stuart W., David D.; m. Barbara Bell Czarnecki, May 9, 1976 (div. 1987), remarried Sept. 9, 1999. BS, U. Kans., 1948, PhD, 1951; DSc (hon.), Regis U., 1984. Instr. chemistry U. Kans., Lawrence, 1949-51; rsch. chemist, rsch. mgr., lab. mgr. E. I. DuPont de Nemours & Co., Inc., Wilmington, Del., 1951-69; dir. phys. sci. Midwest Rsch. Inst., Kansas City, Mo., 1970-75, v.p. rsch., 1976-78, sr. v.p. ops., 1979-82, exec. v.p., 1983-90; dir. Solar Energy Rsch. Inst., 1982-90; Spark M. Matsunaga disting. fellow in energy and environ. U. Hawaii at Manoa, 1991-96; pres., CEO Pacific Internat. Ctr. for High Tech. Rsch., Honolulu, 1992-95. Vis. sr. fellow Resources for the Future, 1990-91; bd. dirs. Guaranty State Bank; chmn. Nat. Rsch. Coun. bd. on energy and environ. sys., 1991-96. With U.S. Army, 1942-45. Mem. Mo. Acad. Sci. (councillor at large 1977-80), Tech. Transfer Soc. (v.p. 1978-79), Am. Chem. Soc., AAAS, N.Y. Acad. Scis., Am. Solar Energy Soc., Colo. Renewable Energy Soc. (pres. 1996-97), Sigma Xi, Delta Upsilon, Cosmos Club. Home: 3938 SW Linden Ct Lees Summit MO 64082-4643 E-mail: hubbet@aol.com

HUBBARD, JOHN RANDOLPH, university president emeritus, history educator, diplomat; b. Belton, Tex., Dec. 3, 1918; s. Louis Herman and Bertha (Altizer) H.; m. Lucille Luckett, Jan. 29, 1947 (div. Dec. 1983); children: Elisa, Melisse, Kristin. A.B., U. Tex., 1938, A.M., 1939, Ph.D., 1950; L.H.D., Hebrew Union Coll., Los Angeles, 1971, Westminster Coll., Fulton, Mo., 1977; LL.D., Sch. of Ozarks, 1973, U. So. Calif., 1980. Pvt. sec. to ICC commr., 1939-41; teaching fellow U. Tex., 1946-48; vis. asst. prof. Brit. history La. State U., 1948; asst. prof. European history Tulane U., 1949-52, asso. prof., 1953-58, prof., 1958-65; dean Newcomb Coll., 1953-65; vis. asst. prof. European history Yale, 1952-53; chief edn. adviser U.S. AID, India, 1965-69; v.p. for acad. affairs, provost U. So. Calif., Los Angeles, 1969-70, pres., 1970-80, pres. emeritus, 1980—, John R. Hubbard Chair Brit. history, 1980—; U.S. amb. to India, 1988-89. Co-chmn. Indo-U.S. Subcommn. on Edn. and Culture, 1982—. Contbr.: articles and revs. to Jour. Modern History; other ednl. jours. Mem. bd. Tulane-Lyceum Assn., 1953-65, Isidore Newman Sch., 1953-65; mem. Region 12 selection com. Woodrow Wilson Fellowship Program, also chmn., 1955-65; mem. bd. U.S. Edn. Found., India; mem. Indian adv. bd. Women's Coll. Faculty Exchange program; pres. bd. Am. Internat. Sch., New Delhi; mem. So. Calif. adv. bd. Inst. Internat. Edn.; trustee Scholarships for Children of Am. Mil. Personnel; bd. dirs. Community TV So. Calif., Los Angeles. Served as an aviator in USN, 1941-46; flight instr. and patrol plane comdr. Atlantic and Pacific fleets; lt. comdr. Res. Decorated D.F.C., Air medals (4); chevalier des Palmes Académiques; Stella della Solidarietá Italiana Italy; Order of Taj 3d degree Iran; recipient Disting. Services to Higher Edn. in U.S. award Tulane U., New Orleans, 1976; Air U. award, 1976; Disting. Alumnus award U. Tex., Austin, 1978, Alben W. Barkley medal for disitng. svc., 1989. Mem. Am., Miss. Valley hist. assns., So. Hist. Soc. (exec. council 1954-56), Anglo-Am. Hist. Soc., Assn. Ind. Calif. Colls. and Univs. (trustee), Am. Council Edn. (commn. on fed. relations 1975-77), Assn. Am. Univs. (council on fed. relations 1975-79), Orgn. Am. Historians, Conf. Brit. Studies, Am. Council Learned Socs., Phi Beta Kappa, Phi Delta Kappa, Alpha Kappa Psi, Delta Kappa Epsilon, Omicron Delta Kappa. Clubs: Royal Aero (London), Athenaeum (London); Los Angeles Country; California (Los Angeles); University (N.Y.C.); Cosmos (Washington). Office: U So Calif Dept History Los Angeles CA 90089-0001

HUBBARD, WILLIAM BOGEL, planetary sciences educator; b. Liberty, Tex., Nov. 14, 1940; s. William Bogel and Marie Hubbard; m. Jean North Gilliland, June 8, 1963; children: Lynne Marie, Laurie North. BA, Rice U., Houston, 1962; PhD, U. Calif., Berkeley, 1967. Rsch. fellow Calif. Inst. Tech., Pasadena, 1967-68; asst. prof. astronomy U. Tex., Austin, 1968-72; assoc. prof. planetary scis. U. Ariz., Tucson, 1972-75, dir. Lunar and Planetary Lab., 1977-81, prof., 1975—. Cons. Lawrence Livermore (Calif.) Nat. Lab., 1972-86, NASA, 1994—; prin. investigator NASA, 1974—, NSF, 1970, 79, 83, 86-93; exch. scientist USSR Nat. Acad. Sci., 1973, mem. com. div. for planetary scis., 1985-88. Contbr. articles to profl. jours.; assoc. editor: Icarus, 1980—. Fellow Japan Soc. for Promotion of Sci., Am. Geophys. Union; mem. AAAS, Am. Astron. Soc., Internat. Astron. Union, Am. Hereford Assn., Nat. Cattlemen's Beef Assn., Sigma Xi. Democrat. Episcopalian. Home: 2618 E Devon St Tucson AZ 85716-5506 Office: U Ariz Lunar & Planetary Lab Tucson AZ 85721-0001

HUBBELL, FLOYD ALLAN, physician, educator; b. Waco, Tex., Nov. 13, 1948; s. F.E. and Margaret (Fraser) H.; m. Nancy Cooper, May 23, 1975; 1 child, Andrew Allan. BA, Baylor U., 1971, MD, 1974; MS in Pub. Health, UCLA, 1983. Diplomate Am. Bd. Internal Medicine. Intern, then resident Long Beach med. program U. Calif., Irvine, 1975-78, asst. prof. medicine, 1981-89, assoc. prof. medicine and social ecology, 1989-97; prof. medicine and social ecology, 1997—; dir. primary care internal medicine residency U. Calif., Irvine, 1992-97, chief divsn. gen. internal medicine and primary care, 1992—, dir. Ctr. for Health Policy and Rsch., 1993—. Contbr. articles to profl. jours. Recipient Outstanding Tchr. award U. Calif., Irvine, 1985, 89. Fellow ACP; mem. APHA, Soc. Gen. Internal Medicine, Physicians for Social Responsibility. Democrat. Avocations: reading, skiing, water sports. Office: U Calif Health Policy Rsch 100 Theory # 110 Irvine CA 92697-5800 E-mail: fahubbel@uci.edu

HUBBELL, LINDA, publishing executive; Pub. Calif. Lawyer, San Francisco. Address: San Francisco Daily Journal 1145 Market St Fl 8 San Francisco CA 94103-1546

HUBBS, DONALD HARVEY, foundation executive; b. Kingman, Ariz., Jan. 3, 1918; s. Wayne and Grace Lillian (Hoose) H.; m. Flora Vincent, June 14, 1945; children: Donald Jr., Susan Tyner, Diane Schultz, Wayne, David, Adrienne Busk. BA in Edn., Ariz. State U., 1940; JD, Southwestern U., 1956. Bar: Calif., 1956; CPA. Acct. Wright and Hubbs, L.A., 1945-67; pvt. practice atty. L.A., 1956-81; pres., dir. Conrad N. Hilton Found., L.A., 1981-98, chmn. bd., CEO, 1998—. Bd. dirs. Trans World Airlines, 1977, Vita Palet Citrus Products Co.; regent Mt. St. Mary's Coll., 1983-98; bd. councilors U. So. Calif. Law Sch., 1992-99. Hon. chief of the tribes, Oku Ghana, West Africa. 1st lt. (inf.) U.S. Army. Decorated Purple Heart. Mem. State Bar of Calif., So. Calif. Assn. for Philanthropy (pres. 1985-86), Riviera Country Club, L.A. Country Club. Avocations: cattle ranching, hunting, fishing, golfing. Home: 1658 San Onofre Dr Pacific Palisades CA 90272-2735 Office: Conrad N Hilton Found Ste 1000 10100 Santa Monica Blvd Los Angeles CA 90067-4100 E-mail: floradon@aol.com

HUBERT, HELEN BETTY, epidemiologist; b. N.Y.C., Jan. 22, 1950; d. Leo and Ruth (Rosenbaum) H.; m. Carlos Barbaro Arostegui, Sept. 11, 1976 (div. May 1987); 1 child, Joshua Daniel Hubert. BA magna cum laude, Barnard Coll., 1970; MPH, Yale U., 1973, MPhil, 1976, PhD, 1978. Rsch. assoc. Yale U., New Haven, 1977-78; rsch. epidemiologist Nat. Heart, Lung and Blood Inst., Bethesda, Md., 1978-84; rsch. dir. Gen. [illegible] 1988—. Peer rev. Am. Jour. Epidemiology, Am. Jour. Pub. Health, Chest, Jour. AMA (JAMA), Archives Internal Medicine; contbr. articles to profl. jours., chpts. to books. NIH grantee, 1997—. Mem. Am. Coll. Epidemiology, Soc. Epidemiol. Rsch., Assn. Rheumatology Health Profls., Phi Beta Kappa, Sigma Xi (grant-in-aid for rsch. 1978). Avocations: swimming, hiking. Office: Stanford Univ Med Ctr 701 Welch Rd Ste 3305 Palo Alto CA 94304-1701

HUCK, LARRY RALPH, manufacturing executive, sales consultant; b. Yakima, Wash., Aug. 10, 1942; s. Frank Joseph and Helen Barbara (Swalley) H.; m. Peggy L. Huck; 1 child, Larry Ralph II. Student, Wash. Tech. Inst., 1965-66, Edmonds Coll., 1966-67, U. Wash., 1967-69, Seattle C.C., 1969-70. Salesman Kirby Co., Seattle, 1964-68, sales mgr., 1968-69; salesman Sanico Chem. Co., Seattle, 1968-69, Synkoloid Co., Seattle, 1970-71; tech. sales rep. Vis. Queen divsn. Ethyl Corp., Seattle, 1971-75; western sales mgr. B & K Films, Inc., Belmont, Calif., 1975-77; pres. N.W. Mfrs. Assocs., Inc., Bellevue, Wash., 1977-86, pres. combined sales group, 1984, 86-96; nat. sales mgr. Gazelle Inc., Tomah, Wis., 1979-81; dir. sales J.M.J. Mktg. E.Z. Frame divsn., 1984-85; nat. accounts mgr. Upnorth Plastics, St. Paul, 1984-87; gen. mgr. Otool Co., 1996-98; N.W. sales mgr. Roberts Consol. divsn. Q.E.P. Inc., 1998-2000; area sales mgr. State Indsl. Products, Cleve., 2000—. V.p. Bellevue Nat. Little League; basketball corrd. Cath. Youth Orgn., Sacred Heart Ch.; head baseball coach Pierce Coll., Tacoma. With USMC, 1959-66. Mem. Nat. Coun. Salesmen's Orgns., Mfrs. Agts. Nat. Assn., Am. Hardware Mfrs. Assn., N.W. Mfrs. Assn. (pres.), Hardware Affiliated Reps., Inc., Door and Hardware Inst., Internat. Conf. Bldg. Ofcls., Am. Baseball Coaches Assn., Marine Corps Assn., 1st Marine Divsn. Assn., 3d Marine Divsn. Assn. (life, v.p.). Roman Catholic. Office: 521 Elma Ave NE Renton WA 98058

HUCKESTEIN, DIETER H. hotel company executive; Mgmt. Hilton Internat., Americana Hotels, Intercontinental Hotels; exec. v.p., pres. hotel ops. Hilton Hotels Corp., Beverly Hills, Calif., 1999—. Mem. USA Nat. Tourism Orgn. (bd. dirs.), Am. Hotel & Motel Assn. Ednl. Inst. (bd. dirs.), Travel Bus. Roundtable, World Tourism Orgn. Office: Hilton Hotels Corp 9336 Civic Center Dr Beverly Hills CA 90210-3604

HUDNER, PHILIP, lawyer, rancher; b. San Jose, Calif., Feb. 24, 1931; s. Paul Joseph and Mary E. (Dooling) H.; m. Carla Raven, Aug. 6, 1966; children: Paul Theodor, Mary Carla. B.A. with great distinction, Stanford U., 1952, LL.B., 1955. Bar: Calif. 1955. Lawyer Pillsbury, Madison & Sutro, San Francisco, 1958—, ptnr., 1970-99, Botto Law Group, San Francisco, 1999—; rancher San Benito County, Calif., 1970—. Asst. editor: Stanford Law Rev., 1954-55; author articles on estate and trust law. Pres. Soc. Calif. Pioneers, 1976-78;trustee, sec. Louise M. Davies Found., 1974—; pres. Drum Found., 1985—. Served with U.S. Army, 1956-58. Fellow Am. Bar Found.; mem. Internat. Acad. Estate and Trust Law (steering com. 1974-75, exec. coun. 1980-85), San Benito County Saddle Horse Assn., Order of Malta, Phi Beta Kappa, Pacific Union Club, Lagunitas Country Club, Frontier Boys, Bohemian Club, Rancheros Visitadores. Democrat. Roman Catholic. Office: Botto Law Group 180 Montgomery St Fl 16 San Francisco CA 94104-3104 Fax: 415-364-0075. E-mail: phudner@bottolaw.com

HUDSON, EDWARD VOYLE, linen supply company executive; b. Seymour, Mo., Apr. 3, 1915; s. Marion A. and Alma (Von Gonten) H.; m. Margaret Carolyn Greely, Dec. 24, 1939; children: Edward G., Carolyn K. Student, Bellingham Normal Coll., 1933-36, U. Wash., 1938. Asst. to mgr. Natural Hard Metal Co., Bellingham, 1935-37; ptnr. Met. Laundry Co., Tacoma, 1938-39; propr., mgr. Peerless Laundry & Linen Supply Co., Tacoma, 1939—. Propr. Ind. Laundry & Everett Linden Supply Co., 1946-74, 99 Cleaners and Launderers Co., Tacoma, 1957-59; chmn. Tacoma Pub. Utilities, 1959-60; trustee United Mut. Savs. Bank; bd. dirs. Tacoma Better Bus. Bur., 1977—. Pres. Wash. Conf. on Unemployment Compensation, 1975-76; pres. Tacoma Boys' Club, 1970; v.p. Puget Sound USO, 1972-91; elder Emmanuel Presbyn. Ch., 1974—; past campaign mgr., pres. Tacoma-Pierce County United Good Neighbors. Recipient Disting. Citizen's cert. USAF Mil. Airlift Com., 1977; U.S. Dept. Def. medal for outstanding pub. svc., 1978. Mem. Tacoma Sales and Mktg. Execs. (pres. 1957-58), Pacific NW Laundry, Dry Clearning and Linen Supply Assn. (pres. 1959, treas. 1965-75), Internat. Fabricare Inst. (dir. dist. 7, treas. 1979, pres. 1982), Am. Security Coun. Bd., Tacoma C. of C. (pres. 1965), Air Force Assn. (pres. Tacoma chpt. 1976-77, v.p. Wash. state 1983-84, pres. 1985-86), Navy League, Puget Sound Indsl. Devel. Coun. (chmn. 1967), Tacoma-Ft. Lewis Olympia Army Assn. (past pres.), Elks Club (vice chmn. bd. trustees 1984, chmn. 1985-86), Shriners (potentate 1979), Masons, Scottish Rite, Tacoma Club, Tacoma Country and Golf Club, Jesters Club, Rotary (pres. Tacoma chpt. 1967-68), Tacoma Knife and Fork Club (pres. 1964). Republican. Home: 3901 N 37th St Tacoma WA 98407-5636 Office: Peerless Laundry & Linen Supply Co 2902 S 12th St Tacoma WA 98405-2598

HUDSON, JEFFREY REID, lawyer; b. Santa Monica, Calif., Mar. 15, 1952; s. Caswell Hadden and Donna Rita (Mazzulla) H.; children: Joan Louise, Reid Adams. BA, Claremont McKenna Coll., 1974; JD, Harvard U., 1978. Bar: Calif. 1978. Assoc. Gibson, Dunn & Crutcher, L.A., 1978-85, ptnr., 1986—. Office: Gibson Dunn & Crutcher 333 S Grand Ave Ste 4400 Los Angeles CA 90071-3197

HUDSON, JERRY E. foundation administrator; b. Chattanooga, Mar. 3, 1938; s. Clarence E. and Laura (Campbell) H.; m. Myra Ann Jared, June 11, 1957; children: Judith, Laura, Janet, Angela. B.A., David Lipscomb Coll., 1959; M.A., Tulane U., 1961, Ph.D., 1965; LL.D. (hon.), Pepperdine U., 1983; D of Comm. (hon.), Tokyo Internat. U., 1997; LHD (hon.), U. Portland, 1997, Willamette U., 1997. Systems engr. IBM, Atlanta, 1961; prof. Coll. Arts and Scis., Pepperdine U., 1962-75; provost, dean Coll. Arts and Scis., Malibu Campus, Pepperdine U., 1971-75; pres. Hamline U., St. Paul, 1975-80, Willamette U., Salem, Oreg., 1980-97; exec. v.p. Collins Found., Portland, 1997—. Dir. Portland Gen. Co., E.I.I.A. Bd. dirs. PGE/Enron Found. Mem. Nat. Assn. Ind. Colls. (bd. dirs.), Phi Alpha Theta. Office: Collins Found 1618 SW 1st Ave Portland OR 97201-5752 E-mail: jhudson@collinsfoundation.org

HUDSON, JOHN IRVIN, retired career officer; b. Louisville, Oct. 12, 1932; s. Irvin Hudson and Elizabeth (Reid) Hudson Hornbeck; m. Zetta Ann Yates, June 27, 1954; children: Reid Irvin, Lori Ann, John Yates, Clark Ray BS in Bus. Mgmt., Murray State U., 1971. Commd. 2nd lt. USMC, 1954, advanced through grades to lt. gen., 1987; comdg. officer Marine Fighter Attack Squadron 115, Vietnam, 1968, Marine Corps Air Sta., Yuma, Ariz., 1977-80; asst. wing comdr. 2nd Marine Air Wing, Cherry Point, N.C., 1980-81; comdg. gen. Landing Force Tng. Command/At.,4th Marine Amphibious Brigade, Norfolk, Va., 1981-83, 3rd Marine Aircraft Wing, El Toro, Calif., 1985-87, First Marine Amphibious Force, Campen, 1986-87; dep. chief staff for manpower Hdqrs. USMC, Washington, 1987-89; dir. U.S. Marine Corps Edn. Ctr., Quantico, Va., 1983-85; ret. active duty Hdqrs. USMC, Washington, 1989. Apptd. to Ariz. State Transp. Bd., 1994-2000, chmn. 1999; apptd. commr. Ariz. Power Authority, 2000—; apptd. bd. dirs. Greater Yuma Port Authority, chmn., 2000—; operating bd. dirs. Yuma Regional Med. Ctr., 2001—. Decorated DFC, DSM, Bronze Star, Air medals, Silver Hawk; flew 308 combat missions in Vietnam in F-4 Phantom; inductee Early and Pioneer Naval Aviators' Assn., 1998. Mem. VFW, Golden Eagles, Marine Corps Aviation Assn. (life), Marine Corps Assn., Marine Corps Hist. Soc., Order of Daedalians (life). Avocations: [illegible] 85367-7366

HUDSON, LEONARD DEAN, physician; b. Everett, Wash., May 7, 1938; s. Marshall W. and Blanche V. (Morgan) H.; children: Sean Marshall, Margaret Kahle, Sherry Elizabeth, Kevin Arthur. BS, Wash. State U., Pullman, 1960; MD, U. Wash., Seattle, 1964. Diplomate: Am. Bd. Internal Medicine (pulmonary disease). Intern Bellevue Hosp. Ctr., N.Y.C., 1964-65; resident in internal medicine N.Y. Hosp., 1965-66, U. Wash. Hosps., 1968-69; chief resident Harborview Med. Ctr., Seattle; also instr. U. Wash. Med. Sch., 1967-70; Am. Thoracic Soc. fellow in pulmonary diseases U. Colo. Med. Ctr., 1970-71, instr., then asst. prof. medicine, 1971-73; mem. faculty U. Wash. Med. Ctr., 1973—, assoc. prof. medicine, 1976-82, prof., 1982—, head pulmonary critical care medicine divsn., 1985—; endowed chair in pulmonary disease rsch. U. Wash. Hosps., 1999—; chief pulmonary critical care medicine divsn., med. dir. MICU, Harborview Med. Ctr., 1976-86. Chmn. Tb adv. com. Wash. Dept. Social and Health Svcs. Author papers, revs. in field. With USPHS, 1966-68. Named Outstanding Resident, Harborview Med. Ctr. Fellow ACP, Am. Coll. Chest Physicians (state gov. 1980-87); mem. Am. Fedn. Clin. Rsch., Am. Thoracic Soc. (sec.-treas. 1983-84, v.p. 1993-94, pres.-elect 1994-95, pres. 1995-96), Western Soc. Clin. Rsch., Assn. Am. Physicians, Wash. Lung. Assn. (dir., Vol. Hall of Fame 1977), Wash. Thoracic Soc., Seattle Flounders Soc., Phi Beta Kappa. Democrat. Office: Harborview Med Ctr Mailbox 359762 325 9th Ave Seattle WA 98104-2420

HUDSON, MARK WOODBRIDGE, lawyer; b. Pasadena, Calif., May 14, 1940; s. Victor Stuart and Mary Charlotte (Woodbridge) H.; m. Marsha Fae Alderson, Dec. 20, 1969; children: Peter, Ashley, Holly. BA, U. Calif., Berkeley, 1961; JD, U. Calif., San Francisco, 1967. Bar: Calif., 1968, U.S. Dist. Ct. 1968, U.S. Ct. Appeals (9th cir.) 1968. Atty. Dunn, Hart & McDonald, San Francisco, 1968-73; assoc. Sedgwick, Detert, Moran & Arnold, San Francisco, 1973-78, of counsel, 1979—. 1st lt. U.S. Army, 1961-63. Mem. Calif. Bar Assn., Assn. Def. Counsel, San Francisco Bar Assn. Democrat. Home: 15 Robertson Ter Mill Valley CA 94941-3358 Office: Sedgwick Detert Moran & Arnold 1 Embarcadero Ctr Ste 1600 San Francisco CA 94111-3716

HUDSON, PATRICK A. plastic surgeon; b. Blickling, Eng., July 4, 1948; came to U.S., 1974; MD, London U., 1972. Diplomate Am. Bd. Plastic Surgery. Intern St. Stephens-Hillingdon, London, 1972-73; resident Danbury Hosp., 1973-74, U. N.Mex. Hosp., Albuquerque, 1974-78, fellow in hand surgery, 1978; with Presbyn. Hosp., St. Joseph Hosp., Albuquerque; pvt. practice. Preceptor U. N.Mex. Author: Esthetics: Comprehensive Online Information About Cosmetic Plastic Surgery, 1996. Fellow ACS; mem. BMA, NMMS, Am. Assn. Hand Surgery, Am. Soc. Plastic and Reconstructive Surgeons. Office: 1101 Med Arts Ave Bldg 3 Ste 300 Albuquerque NM 87102 Fax: 505-242-0060. E-mail: doctor@phudson.com

HUERTA, DOLORES FERNANDEZ, labor union administrator; b. Dawson, N. Mex., Apr. 10, 1930; d. Juan and Alicia Fernandez; children: Celeste, Lori, Fidel, Emilio, Vincent, Alicia, Angela, Juanita, Maria, Elena, Ricky, Camilla. Co-founder, first v.p. United Farm Workers of Am., Keene, Calif., 1962—. Co-founder, first v.p., bd. mem. Fund for the Feminist Majority. Recipient Martin Luther King award NAACP, Roger Baldwin award ACLU, Labor award Eugene V. Debs Found., Trumpeters award Consumers Union, Women First award YWCA, 1993; inductee Nat. Women's Hall of Fame, 1993.

HUFF, C(LARENCE) RONALD, public policy and criminology educator; b. Covington, Ky., Nov. 10, 1945; s. Nathaniel Warren G. and Irene Opal (Mills) H.; m. Patricia Ann Plankenhorn, June 15, 1968; children: Tamara Lynn, Tiffany Dawn. BA, Capital U., 1968; MSW, U. Mich., 1970; PhD, Ohio State U., 1974. Social worker Franklin County Children's Svcs., Columbus, Ohio, 1968; social work intern Pontiac (Mich.) State Hosp. and Family Svc. Met. Detroit, 1969-70; dir. psychiat. social work Lima (Ohio) State Hosp., 1970-71; chief psychiat. social worker N.W. Cmty. Mental Health Ctr., Lima, 1971-72; grad. tchg. assoc. sociology Ohio State U., 1972-74; asst. prof. social ecology U. Calif., Irvine, 1974-76; asst. prof. sociology Purdue U., 1976-79; assoc. prof. pub. policy/mgmt. Ohio State U., Columbus, 1979-87, dir. Criminal Justice Rsch. Ctr., 1979-99, prof., 1987-99, prof. emeritus, 1999—, dir. Sch. Pub. Policy and Mgmt., 1994-99; dean Sch. Social Ecology U. Calif., Irvine, 1999—, prof. criminology, law and society, 1999—. Vis. prof. U. Hawaii, 1995; cons. Bur. Justice Stats., Nat. Inst. Justice, Nat. Inst. Corrections, Nat. Inst. Juvenile Justice and Delinquency Prevention, U.S. Senate Jud. Com., NSF, FBI, others; expert witness fed. and state cts. Author: Youth Violence: Prevention, Intervention, and Social Policy, 1999, Convicted But Innocent: Wrongful Conviction and Public Policy, 1996, (Outstanding Acad. Book award Choice Mag., 1996), The Gang Intervention Handbook, 1993, Gangs in America, 1990, 2d edit., 1996, 3rd edit., 2002, House Arrest and Correctional Policy: Doing Time at Home, 1988, The Mad, The Bad, and The Different: Essays in Honor of Simon Dinitz, 1981, Attorneys as Activists: Evaluating the American Bar Association's BASICS Program, 1979, Contemporary Corrections: Social Control and Conflict, 1977, Planning Correctional Reform, 1975, and others; mem. editl. bd. various jours.; contbr. articles to profl. jours., chpts. to books. Recipient Nat. Security award Mershon Found., 1980, prize New Eng. Sch. Law, 1981, Outstanding Tchg. award, 1985, Donald R. Cressey award Nat. Coun. on Crime and Delinquency, 1992, Paul Tappan award Western Soc. Criminology, 1993, Herbert Bloch award Am. Soc. Criminology, 1994; grantee ABA, 1974-77, Purdue U., 1978, Dept. Justice, 1978-79, 85-88, 91-95, Ohio Dept. Mental Health, 1982-83, 84-85, 85-87, Gov.'s Office Criminal Justice, 1985-88, 92-95, 98, Ohio Dept. Youth Svcs., 1989-90, Ohio State U./Ohio Bd. Regents, 1990-92. Fellow Western Soc. Criminology; mem. Acad. Criminal Justice Scis., Am. Soc. Criminology (exec. bd., pres.-elect 1999-2000, pres. 2000-01, Herbert Bloch award 1994),Nat. Coun. on Crime and Delinquency, Phi Kappa Phi, Phi Beta Delta. Office: U Calif Irvine Sch Social Ecology 300 Social Ecology I Irvine CA 92697-7050 E-mail: rhuff@uci.edu

HUFF, DALE EUGENE, retired environmental services executive; b. Windsor, Colo., Nov. 1, 1930; s. Floyd Eugene and Katherine Oleva (Parsons) H.; m. Flossie Leone Moses, Nov. 18, 1951; children: Clifford Allen, Herbert Eugene, Dalene Faye, Linda Reneé. BA, Pacific Union Coll., 1963, MA, 1968. Tchr. Pleasant Hill (Calif.) Jr. Acad., 1963-66; prin. Ukiah (Calif.) Jr. Acad., 1966-71; tchr. Paradise (Calif.) Adventist Acad., 1971-80; acct. Loma Linda (Calif.) U., 1980-86, environ. svcs. exec., 1986-96; ret., 1996. With U.S. Army, 1946-49. Mem. Nat. Exec. Housekeeping Assn. (exec. bd. 1987-90). Republican. Avocation: camping. Home: 1175 La Moree Rd # 41 San Marcos CA 92078-4517

HUFF, GARY D. lawyer; b. Seattle, May 9, 1950; BA cum laude, U. Wash., 1972, JD, 1975. Bar: Wash. 1975. Lawyer Karr Tuttle Campbell, Seattle, 1986—. Mem. ABA, Wash. State Bar Assn., Seattle-King County Bar Assn., Phi Beta Kappa. Office: Karr Tuttle & Campbell 1201 3rd Ave Ste 2900 Seattle WA 98101-3028

HUFF, MARILYN L. federal judge; b. 1951; BA, Calvin Coll., Grand Rapids, Mich., 1973; JD, U. Mich., 1976. Assoc. Gray Cary Ames & Frye, 1976-83, ptnr., 1983-91; judge U.S. Dist. Ct. (so. dist.) Calif., San Diego, 1991-98, chief judge, 1998—. Contbr. articles to profl. jours. Mem. adv. coun. Calif. LWV, 1987—, Am. Lung Assn.; bd. dirs. San Diego and Imperial Counties, 1989—; mem. LaJolla Presbyn. Ch. Named Legal Profl. of Yr. San Diego City Club and Jr. C. of C., 1990; recipient Superior Ct. Valuable Svc. award, 1982. Mem. ABA, San Diego Bar Found., San Diego [illegible] award to legal profession, 1989, Lawyer of Yr. 1990), Calif. State Bar

Assn., Calif. Women Lawyers, Am. Bd. Trial Advs., Libel Def. Resource Ctr., Am. Inns of Ct. (master 1987—, exec. com. 1989—), Lawyers' Club San Diego (adv. bd. 1989-90, Belva Lockwood Svc. award 1987), Univ. Club, Aardvarks Lt. Office: US Dist Ct Courtroom 1 940 Front St San Diego CA 92101-8994

HUFFMAN, EDGAR JOSEPH, oil company executive; b. Hartford City, Ind., Aug. 24, 1939; s. Floyd Edgar and Elizabeth Jean (Rawlings) H.; m. Margaret Mary Brenet, May 3, 1980; children: Donovan L. Walker, Maryanne Ramirez. BBA, Ind. Cen. U., 1961; MA, NYU, 1968. V.p. corp. profitability Valley Nat. Bank, Phoenix, 1978-82, v.p. corp. planning, 1982-85; v.p., chief exec. officer Visa Industries Ariz., Phoenix, 1985—. Chmn. bd. dirs. Montessori Day Schs., Inc., Phoenix, 1981; bd. dirs. Basic Earth Scis., Calpcco III, Denver. Home: 1710 E Cinnabar Ave Phoenix AZ 85020-1915 E-mail: ehuffman@mdpsc.org

HUFFMAN, JAMES THOMAS WILLIAM, oil exploration company executive; b. Norman, Okla., Mar. 27, 1947; s. Thomas William and Dorlese M. (Hicks) H.; children: Laura Anne, Christopher James. BBA, Baylor U., 1970. CPA. Mgr. Arthur Andersen & Co., Houston, 1970-76; sr. mgr. Price, Waterhouse & Co., Denver, 1976-79; v.p. Credo Petroleum Corp., 1978-80, pres., 1980-81, chmn., chief exec. officer, 1981—, also dir. Dir. Huffman Heat Exchangers Inc.; dir. XF&R, Inc.; pres., dir. SECO Energy Corp.; pres., dir. United Oil Corp. Mem. AICPA, Tex., Colo. socs. CPAs, Petroleum Landman, Ind. Petroleum Assn. Am., Ind. Petroleum Assn. Mountain State, Petroleum Accts. Soc.

HUFFMAN, NONA GAY, financial consultant, retirement planning specialist; b. Albuquerque, June 22, 1942; d. William Abraham and Opal Irene (Leaton) Crisp; m. Donald Clyde Williams, Oct. 20, 1961; children: Debra Gaylene, James Donald. Student pub. schs., Lawndale, Calif. Lic. ins. and securities dealer, N.Mex. Sec. City of L.A., 1960, L.A. City Schs., 1960-62, Aerospace Corp., El Segundo, Calif., 1962-64, Albuquerque Pub. Schs., 1972-73, Pub. Svc. Co. N.Mex., Albuquerque, 1973; rep., fin. planner Waddell & Reed, Inc., Albuquerque, 1979-84; broker Rauscher Pierce Refsnes, Inc., 1984-85; rep., investment and retirement specialist Fin. Network Investment Corp., 1985-89, John Hancock Fin. Svcs., 1989-90; account exec. Eppler, Guerin & Turner, Inc., 1990-91, Fin. Network Investment Corp., Albuquerque, 1991-98; fin. cons. retirement and estate planning Nat. Planning Corp., 1998-99; fin. cons. Linsco Pvt. Ledger Fin. Svcs., 1999—. Instr. on-site corp. tng. of fin. strategies for retirement Philips Semi Conductors, Honeywell & Gulton Industries. Office: Linsco Pvt Ledger 6020 Academy Rd NE Ste 202 Albuquerque NM 87109

HUFSTEDLER, SETH MARTIN, lawyer; b. Dewar, Okla., Sept. 20, 1922; s. Seth Martin and Myrtle (Younts) H.; m. Shirley Ann Mount, Aug. 16, 1949; 1 child, Steven. B.A. magna cum laude, U. So. Calif., 1944; LL.B., Stanford U., 1949. Bar: Calif. 1950. Pvt. practice, L.A.; assoc. Lillick, Geary & McHose, 1950-51; with Charles E. Beardsley, 1951-53; ptnr. Beardsley, Hufstedler & Kemble, 1953-81, Hufstedler, Miller, Carlson & Beardsley, 1981-88, Hufstedler, Kaus & Ettinger, L.A., 1988-94; Hufstedler & Kaus, 1994-95; sr. of counsel Morrison & Foerster LLP, 1995—. Mem. Calif. Jud. Coun., 1977-78. Legis. editor Stanford U. Law Rev., 1948-49. Sec. regional planning coun. United Way, 1971-75; co-chmn. Pub. Commn. County Govt., L.A., 1975-76, 89-92; trustee AEFC Pension Fund, 1978-82; mem. Calif Citizens Commn. on Tort Reform, 1976-77; bd. visitors Stanford Law Sch., chmn., 1972-73. Lt. (j.g.) USNR, 1943-46. Mem. ABA (chmn. action commn. to reduce ct costs and delay 1979-81, mem. action commn. sr. bar div. 1986-89, chmn. 1987-88), Los Angeles County Bar Assn. (trustee 1963-65, 66-70, pres. 1969-70, Shattuck Price award 1976), State Bar Calif. (bd. govs. 1971-74, pres. 1973-74), Am. Judicature Soc., Am. Law Inst., Am. Coll. Trial Lawyers, Am. Bar Found. (bd. govs. 1975-86, pres. 1982-84), Chancery Club (pres. 1974-75), Order of Coif, Phi Beta Kappa, Phi Kappa Phi, Delta Tau Delta. Democrat. Office: Morrison & Foerster 555 W 5th St Ste 3500 Los Angeles CA 90013-1024

HUFSTEDLER, SHIRLEY MOUNT (MRS. SETH M. HUFSTEDLER), lawyer, former federal judge; b. Denver, Aug. 24, 1925; d. Earl Stanley and Eva (Von Behren) Mount; m. Seth Martin Hufstedler, Aug. 16, 1949; 1 son, Steven Mark. BBA, U. N.Mex., 1945, LLD (hon.), 1972; LLB, Stanford U., 1949; LLD (hon.), U. Wyo., 1970, Gonzaga U., 1970, Occidental Coll., 1971, Tufts U., 1974, U. So. Calif., 1976, Georgetown U., 1976, U. Pa., 1976, Columbia U., 1977, U. Mich., 1979, Yale U., 1981, Rutgers U., 1981, Claremont U. Ctr., 1981, Smith Coll., 1982, Syracuse U., 1983, Mt. Holyoke Coll., 1985; PHH (hon.), Hood Coll., 1981, Hebrew Union Coll., 1986, Tulane U., 1988. Bar: Calif. 1950. Mem. firm Beardsley, Hufstedler & Kemble, L.A., 1951-61; practiced in L.A., 1961; judge Superior Ct., County L.A., 1961-66; justice Ct. Appeals 2d dist., 1966-68; circuit judge U.S. Ct. Appeals 9th cir., 1968-79; sec. U.S. Dept. Edn., 1979-81; ptnr. Hufstedler & Kaus, L.A., 1981-95; sr. of counsel Morrison & Foerster LLP, L.A., 1995—. Emeritus dir. Hewlett Packard Co., US West, Inc.; bd. dirs. Harman Internat. Industries. Mem. staff Stanford Law Rev, 1947-49; articles and book rev. editor, 1948-49. Trustee Calif. Inst. Tech., Occidental Coll., 1972-89, Aspen Inst., Colonial Williamsburg Found., 1976-93, Constl. Rights Found., 1978-80, Nat. Resources Def. Coun., 1983-85, Carnegie Endowment for Internat. Peace, 1983-94; bd. dirs. John T. and Catherine MacArthur Found., 1983—; chair U.S. Commn. on Immigration Reform, 1996-97. Named Woman of Yr. Ladies Home Jour., 1976; recipient UCLA medal, 1981. Fellow Am. Acad. Arts and Scis.; mem. ABA (medal 1995), L.A. Bar Assn., Town Hall, Am. Law Inst. (coun. 1974-84), Am. Bar Found., Women Lawyers Assn. (pres. 1957-58), Am. Judicature Soc., Assn. of the Bar of City of N.Y., Coun. on Fgn. Rels. (emeritus), Order of Coif. Office: Morrison & Foerster LLP 555 W 5th St Ste 3500 Los Angeles CA 90013-1024

HUG, PROCTER RALPH, JR. federal judge; b. Reno, Mar. 11, 1931; s. Procter Ralph and Margaret (Beverly) H.; m. Barbara Van Meter, Apr. 4, 1954; children: Cheryl Ann English, Procter James, Elyse Marie Pasha. BS, U. Nev., 1953; LLB, JD, Stanford U., 1958. Bar: Nev. 1958. Mem. Springer, McKissick & Hug, 1958-63, Woodburn, Wedge, Blakey, Folsom & Hug, Reno, 1963-77; U.S. judge 9th Circuit Ct. Appeals, Reno, 1977—, U.S. chief judge, 1996-2000. Dep. atty. gen. State of Nev.; v.p. dir. Nev. Tel. & Tel. Co., 1958-77. Mem. bd. regents U. Nev., 1962-71, chmn., 1969-71; bd. visitors Stanford Law Sch.; mem. Nev. Humanities Commn., 1988-94; vol. civilian aid sect. U.S. Army, 1977. Lt. USNR, 1953-55. Recipient Outstanding Alumnus award U. Nev., 1967, Disting. Nevadan citation, 1982; named Alumnus of Yr. U. Nev., 1988. Mem. ABA (bd. govs. 1976-78), Am. Judicare Soc. (bd. dirs. 1975-77), Nat. Judicial Coll. (bd. dirs. 1977-78, 2001—), Nat. Assn. Coll. and Univ. Attys. (past mem. exec. bd.), U. Nev. Alumni Assn. (past pres.), Stanford Law Soc. Nev. (pres.) Office: US Ct Appeals 9th Cir US Courthouse Fed Bldg 400 S Virginia St Ste 708 Reno NV 89501-2181

HUGGETT, MONICA, performing company executive; Artistic dir. Portland Baroque Orch., Oreg. Office: Portland Baroque Orch 1425 SW 20th Ave Ste 102 Portland OR 97201-2485

HUGHES, EDWARD JOHN, artist; b. North Vancouver, B.C., Feb. 17, 1913; s. Edward Samuel Daniell and Katherine Mary (McLean) H.; m. Fern Rosabell Irvine Smith, Feb. 10, 1940 (dec. 1974). Grad., Vancouver Sch. Art, 1933; D Fine Art (hon.), U. Victoria, 1995; DLL (hon.), Emily Carr Inst. Art & Design, Vancouver, B.C., 1997, Malaspina Univ.-Coll., Nanaimbo, B.C., 2000. Exhbns. include retrospective, Vancouver Art Gallery, 1967, Surrey Art Gallery, Art Gallery of Greater Victoria, Edmonton Art Gallery, Calgary Glenbow Gallery, 1983-85, Nat. Gallery Can., Beaverbrook Gallery, Fredericton, 1983-85; represented in permanent collections, Nat. Gallery Can., Ottawa, Art Gallery Ont., Toronto, Vancouver Art Gallery, Montreal Mus. Fine Art, Greater Victoria Art Gallery; ofcl. Army war artist, 1942-46. Served with Can. Army, 1939-46. Recipient Can. Council grants, 1958, 63, 67, 70 Mem. Royal Can. Acad. Arts. Presbyterian. Address: 2449 Heather St Duncan BC Canada V9L 2Z6

HUGHES, GETHIN B. bishop; Bishop Episcopal Diocese of San Diego, 1992—. Office: Episcopal Diocese San Diego 2728 6th Ave San Diego CA 92103-6301

HUGHES, JOHN W. film producer, screenwriter, film director; b. Mich., Feb. 18, 1950; m. Nancy Ludwig; children: John III, James. With Needham Harper & Steers, Chgo.; copywriter, creative dir. Leo Burnett Co.; editor National Lampoon; founder, pres. Hughes Entertainment, 1985—. Screenwriter: National Lampoon's Class Reunion, 1982, National Lampoon's Vacation, 1983, Mr. Mom, 1983, Nate and Hayes, 1983, National Lampoon's European Vacation, 1985, (as Edmond Dantes) Beethoven, 1992, 101 Dalmations, 1996; screenwriter, prodr.: Pretty in Pink, 1986, Some Kind of Wonderful, 1987, The Great Outdoors, 1988, National Lampoon's Christmas Vacation, 1989, Home Alone, 1990, Career Opportunities, 1990, Dutch, 1991, Home Alone 2: Lost in New York, 1992, Dennis the Menace, 1993, Baby's Day Out, 1994, Miracle on 34th Street, 1994, 101 Dalmations, 1996, Flubber, 1997, Home Alone 3, 1997, Reach the Rock, 1998; screenwriter, dir.: Sixteen Candles, 1984, Weird Science, 1985; screenwriter, dir., prodr.: The Breakfast Club, 1985, Ferris Bueller's Day Off, 1986, Planes, Trains and Automobiles, 1987, She's Having a Baby, 1988, Uncle Buck, 1989, Curly Sue, 1991; prodr.: Only the Lonely, 1991. Recipient Commitment to Chgo. award, 1990; named NATO/ShoWest Prodr. of Yr., 1990. Office: c/o Jacob Bloom Bloom Hergot DeKom & Cook 150 S Rodeo Dr Beverly Hills CA 90212-2408 also: Hughes Entertainment 10201 W Pico Blvd Los Angeles CA 90064-2606 also: c/o Jack Rapke CAA 9830 Wilshire Blvd Beverly Hills CA 90212-1804

HUGHES, LINDA J. newspaper publisher; b. Princeton, B.C., Can., Sept. 27, 1950; d. Edward Rees and Madge Preston (Bryan) H.; m. George Fredrick Ward, Dec. 16, 1978; children: Sean Ward, Kate Ward. BA, U. Victoria (B.C.), 1972; LittD (hon.), Athabasca U., 1997; hon. diploma in journalism, Grant MacEwan C.C., Edmonton, Alta., Can., 1999. With Edmonton Jour., Alta., Can., 1976—, from reporter to asst. mng. editor Can., 1984-87, editor Can., 1987-92, pub. Can., 1992—. Southam fellow U. Toronto, Ont., Can., 1977-78; recipient Disting. Citizen award Grant MacEwan C.C., 1999. Office: Edmonton Journal 10006 101st St PO Box 2421 Edmonton AB Canada T5J 2S6

HUGHES, MARGARET EILEEN, law educator, former dean; b. Saskatoon, Sask., Can., Jan. 22, 1943; d. E. Duncan and Eileen (Shaver) Farmer; m. James Roscoe Hughes, May 21, 1966; children: Shannon Margaret, Krista Lynn. BA, U. Sask., 1965, LLB, 1966; LLM, MSW, U. Mich., 1968. Asst. prof. law U. Windsor, Ont., Can., 1968-71, assoc. prof. law Can., 1971-75; exec. interchange Dept. Justice, Ottawa, 1975-77, counsel, 1977-78; prof. law U. Sask., 1978-84; dean law U. Calgary, Alta., Can., 1984-89, prof. Can., 1989—. Faculty sr. univ. adminstrs.'s course Centre Higher Edn., R & D, Banff, Can., 1990-2000; bd. dirs. Indsl. Rels. Rsch. Group; co-chair Annual Labour Arbitration Conf., 1990-2000. Contbr. articles to profl. jours. and chpts. to books. William Cooke fellow U. Mich. Faculty Law, 1966-68. Mem. Law Soc. Alta., Law Soc. Sask., Legal Edn. Soc. Alta. (bd. dirs. 1984-89), Law Soc. Alta. (legal edn. com. 1984-89), Can. Assn. Law Tchrs., Council Can. Law Deans (sec. 1986-87, chmn. 1987-88), Can. Inst. Resources Law (exec. com. 1984-89, bd. dirs. 1984-89), Can. Research Inst. for Law and Family (exec. com. 1986-88, bd. dirs. 1986-89, 97-2001). Avocations: swimming, skiing. Office: U Calgary Faculty Law 2500 University Dr NW Calgary AB Canada T2N 1N4

HUGHES, MARVALENE, academic administrator; Student, Tuskegee U., NYU, Columbia U.; PhD in Counseling and Adminstrn., Fla. State U.; postgrad., Harvard U., U. Calif., San Diego. Dir. counseling and career devel. Eckerd Coll., Fla.; dir. counseling svcs. and placement, prof. and adminstr. San Diego State U.; assoc. v.p. student affairs Ariz. State U.; v.p. student affairs, prof. counseling and human svcs. U. Toledo; v.p. student affairs, vice provost, prof. ednl. psychology U. Minn.; pres. Calif. State U., Stanislaus, 1994—. Nat., internat. keynote spkr. Contbr. chpts. to books and articles to profl. jours. Keynoter Pres.-to-Pres. Address, Internat. Conf. Pres. and Chancellors, Puerto Rico, 1999; chmn. Women Pres. and Chancellors Am. Assn. State Colls. and Univs., 1999—, prof. devel. com.; adv. bd. 1st Nat. Women's Mus.; mem. divsn. II pres. coun. NCAA, mem. divsn. II budget and fin. com., liason pres. coun. divsn. II student athlete adv. com.; mem. evaluation com. Accrediting Commn. Sr. Colls. and Univs., We. Assn. Schs. and Colls.; mem. Lt. Gov.'s Commn One Calif., 1999. Mem. Leadership Calif. Office: 801 W Monte Vista Ave Turlock CA 95382-0256

HUGHES, MICHAEL PATRICK, artist; b. Chgo., Dec. 25, 1950; s. William George and Patricia Ann (Guilfoil) H.; m. Dorothea Sofia Savage, May 11, 1977 (div. June 1987); 1 stepchild, Stefani Savage; m. Deborah Kay Horewitz, Aug. 5, 1991 (div. June 1997). AA in Fine Arts, L.A. Valley Coll., 1975; BFA in Painting, Otis Art Inst., 1977; MFA in Art & Design, Calif. Inst. Arts, 1980. One-man shows include Calif. Inst. Arts, 1979, 80, West Colo. Gallery, Pasadena, Calif., 1980, The Art Dock, L.A., 1985, Orlando Gallery, Sherman Oaks, Calif., 1986, 87, Jose Drudis-Biada Art Gallery, L.A., 1990; group shows include Calif. Inst. Arts, 1980, 81, Lehigh U. Art Gallery, Bethlehem, Pa., 1983, Calif. State U. Art Gallery, San Bernardino, 1982, Future Perfect Gallery, L.A., 1984, Tortue Gallery, Santa Monica, Calif., 1987, Downey Mus. Art, 1988, The Tanzmann Assocs., L.A., 1989, Boritzer/Gray Gallery, Santa Monica, 1991, 98, Touchstone Ctr. Arts, Pitts., 1992, Brand Libr. Art Galleries, Glendale, Calif., 1992, Mt. San Antonio Coll. Art Gallery, Walnut, Calif., 1993, Downtown Arts Devel. Assn., L.A., 1994, 93, others; represented in permanent collections at Lee & Paulette Arnone, Culver City, Calif., Steve Sharpe, Somis, Calif., Joseph A. Hardy Sr., Farmington, Pa., Ellie Blankfort, L.A., Chaim Ben Basat, Sepulveda, Calif., Mr. & Mrs. Murray Horewitz, Connellsville, Pa., Downey Mus. Art, Rudy & Chris Andl, Thousand Oaks, Calif., Miki Warner, Malibu, Calif., Carl Schlossberg, Encino, Calif., Jack Sullivan, San Gabriel, Calif., Mr. & Mrs. Robert Taylor, L.A., Ben Tunnel, L.A., William Bingham, Encino, Calif., Richard Godfrey, L.A., others. Avocations: cooking, golf.

HUGHES, SARAH, figure skater; b. Great Neck, N.Y., 02 May; Mem. U.S. Olympic Team, Sydney, 2000. Competitive history includes: 3d place North Atlantic Novice, 1996, 1st place North Atlantic Novice, 1997, 1st place North Atlantic Novice, 1998, 2d place Mexico Cup, 1998, 1st place Eastern Jr., 1998, 1st place U.S. Championships Jr., 1998, 2d place Hungarian Trophy, 1998, 4th place U.S. Championships, 1999, 7th place World Championships, 1999, 1st place World Jr. Team Selection Competition, 2d place World Jr. Championships, 1999, 2d place ISU Jr. Grand Prix, 2d place Hershey's Kisses (Team USA), 1999, 1st place Vienna Cup, 1999, 4th place Skate America, 1st place Keri Lotion vs. The World (Team USA-1st place), 1999, 5th place World Championships, 2000, 3d place Trophee Lalique, 1999, 3d place U.S. Championships, 2000, 2d place Internat. Figure Skating Challenge (Team USA-2d place), 2000. Avocations: reading, tennis, violin. Office: USFSA 20 1st St Colorado Springs CO 80906-3624

HUGHES, TERESA P. state legislator; b. N.Y.C., Oct. 3, 1932; m. Frank E. Staggers; children: Vincent, Deidre. BA, Hunter Coll.; MA, NYU; PhD, Claremont Grad. Sch. Prof. edn. Calif. State U., L.A.; social worker; mem. Calif. Assembly, 1975-92, Calif. State Senate, Sacramento, 1993—. Bd. trustees L.A. County H.S. for Arts and Edn. Coun. Music Ctr., Calif. Founder Aware Women. Mem. Nat. Coalition 100 Black Women, Calif. State Employees Assn., Calif. Tchrs. Assn., Coalition Labor Union Women. Democrat. Office: Calif Senate 5114 State Capitol Rm 5050 Sacramento CA 95814 also: 1 W Manchester Blvd Ste 600 Inglewood CA 90301-1750

HUGHES, THOMAS J.R. mechanical engineering educator, consultant; b. Bklyn., Aug. 3, 1943; s. Joseph Anthony and Mae (Bland) H.; m. Susan Elizabeth Weh, July 1, 1972; children: Emily Susan, Ian Thomas, Elizabeth Claire. B.M.E., Pratt Inst., Bklyn., 1965; M.M.E., Pratt Inst., 1967; M.A. in Math., Ph.D. in Engring. Sci., U. Calif.-Berkeley, 1974. Mech. design engr. Grumman Aerospace, Bethpage, N.Y., 1965-66; mgr. R & D Gen. Dynamics, Groton, Conn., 1967-69; lectr., asst. rsch. engr. U. Calif., Berkeley, 1975-76; assoc. prof. structural mechanics Calif. Inst. Tech., Pasadena, 1976-80; assoc. prof. mech. engring. Stanford U., Calif., 1980-82, prof., 1983—, chmn. divsn. applied mechanics, 1984-88, 94—, chmn. dept. mech. engring., 1988-89; founder, chmn. CENTRIC Engring. Sys., Inc., 1990-99. Galileo vis. prof. Scuola Normale Superiore, Pisa, Italy, 1999; Eshbach vis. prof. Northwestern U., 2000; cons. in field. Author: A Short Course in Fluid Mechanics, 1976, Mathematical Foundations of Elasticity, 1983, The Finite Element Method: Linear Static and Dynamic Finite Element Analysis, 1987, Computational Inelasticity, 1998; editor: Nonlinear Finite Element Analysis of Plate and Shells, 1981, Computational Methods in Transient Analysis, 1983; editor Jour. of Computer Methods in Applied Mechanics and Engring., 1980—; contbr. numerous articles to profl. jours. Recipient Computational Mechanics prize Japan Soc. Mech. Engrs., 1993. Fellow AAAS, ASME (Melville medal 1979, Worcester Reed Warner medal 1998), AIAA (assoc.), Am. Acad. Mechanics, U.S. Assn. Computational Mechanics (pres. 1990-92, von Neumann medal 1997), Nat. Acad. Engring; mem. ASCE (Huber prize 1978), Internat. Assn. Computational Mechanics (pres. 1998—, Gauss-Newton medal), Sigma Xi, Phi Beta Kappa. Office: Stanford U Dept Mech Engring Durand Bldg Stanford CA 94305

HUGHS, MARY GERALDINE, accountant, social service specialist; b. Marshalltown, Iowa, Nov. 28, 1929; d. Don Harold Sr. and Alice Dorothy (Keister) Shaw; m. Charles G. Hughs, Jan. 31, 1949; children: Mark George, Deborah Kay, Juli Ann, Grant Wesley. AA, Highline C.C., 1970; BA, U. Wash., 1972. Asst. contr. Moduline Internat., Inc., Chehalis, Wash., 1972-73; contr. Data Recall Corp., El Segundo, Calif., 1973-74; fin. adminstr., acct. Saturn Mfg. Corp., Torrance, 1974-77; sr. acct., adminstrv. asst. Van Camp Ins., San Pedro, 1977-78; asst. adminstr. Harbor Regional Ctr., Torrance, 1979-87; active bookkeeping svc., 1978—. Instr. math. and acctg. South Bay Bus. Coll., 1976-77; treas., bd. dirs., Harbor Fed. Credit Union. Author: Iowa Auto Dealers Assn. Title System, 1955, Harbor Regional Center Affirmative Action Plan, 1980, Harbor Regional Ctr. Financial Format, 1978, Provider Audit System, 1978, Handling Client Funds, 1983. Sec. Pacific N.W. Mycol. Soc., 1966-67. Recipient award Am. Mgmt. Assn., 1979. Mem. Beta Alpha Psi. Republican. Mem. Ch. of Christ. Home and Office: 32724 Coastsite Dr Unit 107 Palos Verdes Estates CA 90275 E-mail: mghughs@earthlink.net

HULBERT, STEPHEN THOMPSON, academic administrator; BS in Edn., Worcester (Mass.) State Coll., 1966; MEd, U. Mass., Amherst, 1968; DEd, SUNY, Albany, 1972. Dir. student activities and residence life Western New England Coll., Springfield, Mass., 1968-70; cons. Univ. Assocs. Inc., Washington, 1971-72; exec. asst. to the pres. Mansfield (Pa.) U., 1972-77; v.p. for fin. and adminstrn. Slippery Rock (Pa.) U., 1977-88; v.p. adminstrv. svcs., treas. bd. trustees U. Northern Colo., Greeley, 1988-91, interim pres., 1991, sr. v.p., 1992-94, provost, v.p. for acad. affairs, 1994-96; commr. higher edn., CEO R.I. Bd. of Govs. for Higher Edn., Providence, 1996-99; chancellor U. Montana-Western, Dillon, 1999—. Govs. cabinet State of R.I. and Providence Plantations; mem. R.I. Juvenile Justice Oversight Commn. Mcpl. coun. Grove City, Pa., 1986-88; adv. bd. Franklin Regional Hosp., Franklin, Pa., 1985-88; exec. bd. Longs Peak Coun. of Boy Scouts Am., 1991-96, disting. citizen com. chair, 1992, others; mayor's adv. task force City of Greeley, 1992-96, U. No. Colo. Found., Inc., 1991-96, R.I. Children's Crusade for Higher Edn., 1996-99, U. of No. Colo. Rsch. Corp., Inc., 1988-96, chair 1994-96, vice chair 1992-94, corp. treas. 1988-92; steering com. Edn. Commn., 1988—99, bd. govs. Colo. Alliance for Sci., 1995-96. Mem. Am. Assn. for Higher Edn., Nat. Assn. Intercollegiate Athletics (coun. pres.), Frontier Athletic Cons. (chair coun. pres. 2000), Phi Delta Kappa. Home: 602 E Poindexter St Dillon MT 59725 Office: Univ Mont Western 710 S Atlantic St Dillon MT 59725-3511 Fax: 401-222-2545. E-mail: s_Hulbert@umwestern.edu

HULET, ERVIN KENNETH, retired nuclear chemist; b. Baker, Oreg., May 7, 1926; s. Frank E. and Marjorie (Suiter) H.; m. Betty Jo Gardner, Sept. 10, 1949 (dec. Jan. 1992); children: Carri, Randall Gardner. B.S., Stanford U., 1949; Ph.D., U. Calif. at Berkeley, 1953. AEC grad. student U. Calif. Radiation Lab., Berkeley, 1949-53; research chemist nuclear chemistry div. Lawrence Livermore Nat. Lab., Livermore, Calif., 1953-66, group leader, 1966-91, ret., active emeritus, 1991—. Achievements include discovery of divalent oxidation state in actinide elements; co-discovery of symmetric fission in actinides. Served with USNR, 1944-46. Fulbright scholar Norway; Welch Found. lectr., 1990; recipient Am. Chem. Soc. award for Nuc. Chemistry, 1994. Fellow AAAS, Am. Inst. Chemists (chmn. Golden Gate chpt. 1992); mem. Am. Chem. Soc. (chmn. divsn. nuclear chemistry and tech. 1987, award in nuclear chemistry 1994), Am. Phys. Soc. Achievements include co-discovery of Element 106; discovery of bimodel fission. Office: U Calif Lawrence Livermore Nat Lab PO Box 808 Livermore CA 94551-0808 E-mail: ekhulet@csi.com

HULING, MORRIS, protective services official; b. Albuquerque, June 2, 1955; Fire fighter City of Albuquerque, 1978-97, fire chief, 1997—. Office: Fire Dept PO Box 2086 Albuquerque NM 87103-2086

HULL, CORDELL WILLIAM, business executive; b. Dayton, Ohio, Sept. 12, 1933; s. Murel George and Julia (Barto) H.; m. Susan G. Ruder, May 10, 1958; children: Bradford W., Pamela H., Andrew R. B.E., U. Dayton, 1956; M.S., MIT, 1957; J.D., Harvard U., 1962. Bar: Ohio 1962; Registered profl. engr., Mass. Atty. Taft, Stettinius & Hollister, Cin., 1962-64, C & I Girdler, Cin., 1964-66; gen. counsel, treas., pres. C&I Girdler, Internat., Brussels, 1966-70; v.p. Bechtel Overseas Corp., San Francisco, 1970-73, pres., dir. Am. Express Mcht. Bank, London, 1973-75, v.p., treas. Bechtel Corp. and Bechtel Power, San Francisco, 1975-80; pres. Bechtel Fin. Services, San Francisco, 1975-82; v.p., chief fin. officer Bechtel Group Inc., 1980-85; pres. Bechtel Power Corp., 1987-89, dir.; chmn. Bechtel Enterprises, 1990-95. Bd. dirs., mem. exec. com. Sequoia Ventures, Inc., Fremont Group, Inc., Bechtel Group, Inc.; chmn. C. Hull Enterprises; bd. dirs. Darby Overseas Ltd.; chmn. Infrastructure World.com Trustee U. Dayton. Mem. Bankers Club, Knickerbocker Club, Pacific Union Club, Links, Menlo Country Club, Am. Soc. Macro Engrs. Office: Bechtel Group Inc 50 Beale St San Francisco CA 94105-1813 also: Infrastructure Worldcom Ste 112 400 Oyster Point Blvd South San Francisco CA 94080

HULL, JANE DEE, governor, former state legislator; b. Kansas City, Mo., Aug. 8, 1935; d. Justin D. and Mildred (Swenson) Bowersock; m. Terrance Ward Hull, Feb. 12, 1954; children: Jeannette Shipley, Robin Hillebrand, Jeff, Mike. BS, U. Kans., 1957; postgrad., U. Ariz., 1972-78. Spkr. pro tem Ariz. Ho. of Reps., Phoenix, 1993, chmn. ethics com., chmn. econ. devel.,

1993, mem. legis. coun., 1993, mem. gov.'s internat. trade and tourism adv. bd., 1993, mem. gov.'s strategic partnership for econ. devel., 1993, mem. gov.'s office of employement implementation task force, 1993, spkr. of house, 1989-93, house majority whip, 1987-88; sec. of state State of Arizona, Phoenix; gov. State of Ariz., Phoenix, 1997—. Bd. dirs. Morrison Inst. for Pub. Policy, Beatitudes D.O.A.R., 1992, Ariz. Town Hall, Ariz. Econs. Coun.; mem. dean's coun. Ariz. State U., 1989-92; assoc. mem. Heard Mus. Guild, Cactus Wren Rep. Women, ; mem. Maricopa Med. Aux., Ariz. State Med. Aux., Freedom Found., Valley Citizens League, Charter 100, North Phoenix Rep. Women, 1970, Trunk 'N Tusk Legis. Liaison Ariz. Rep. Party, 1993; Rep. candidate sec. of state, 1994. Recipient Econ. Devel. award Ariz. Innovation Network, 1993. Mem. Nat. Orgn. of Women Legislators, Am. Legis. Exch. Coun., Nat. Rep. Legislators Assn. (Nat. Legislator of Yr. award 1989), Soroptimists (hon.). Republican. Roman Catholic. Address: Office Gov State Capitol 1700 W Washington St Phoenix AZ 85007-2812*

HULL, JOSEPH L. state legislator; b. Ogden, Utah, Dec. 18, 1945; m. Sandra Glanville. BA, Weber State Coll.; MEd, Utah State U. Educator Utah State U.; mem. Utah State Senate, 1992—, asst. minority whip, 1995-96; mem. Utah Ho. of Reps., 1986-92; educator Sanders Jr. High Sch. Mem. various coms. including edn. and human svcs. Democrat. Office: 5250 W 4000 S Hooper UT 84315-9613

HULL, MCALLISTER HOBART, JR. retired university administrator; b. Birmingham, Ala., Sept. 1, 1923; s. McAllister Hobart and Grace (Johnson) H.; m. Mary Muska, Mar. 23, 1946; children: John McAllister, Wendy Ann. BS with highest honors, Yale, 1948, PhD in Physics, 1951. Tech. asst. Los Alamos Lab., 1944-46; From instr. to asso. prof. physics Yale U., 1951-66; prof. physics, chmn. dept. Oreg. State U., 1966-69, State U. N.Y. at Buffalo, 1969-72, dean Grad. Sch., 1972-74, dean. grad. and profl. edn., 1974-77; provost U. N.Mex., 1977-85, counselor to pres., 1985-88, prof. emeritus physics, 1988—. Adviser to supt. schs., Hamden, Conn., 1958-65 Author papers, books, chpts. in books, articles in encys. Bd. dirs. Western N.Y. Reactor Facility, 1970-72; trustee N.E. Radio Obs. Corp., 1971-77; pres. Western Regional Sci. Labs., 1977; chmn. tech. adv. com. N.Mex. Energy Research Inst., 1981-83, mem., 1983-88; co-chmn. Nat. Task Force on Ednl. Tech., 1984-86. Served with AUS, 1943-46. Faculty fellow Yale U., 1964-65 Fellow Am. Phys. Soc.; mem. Am. Assn. Physics Tchrs. (chmn. Oreg. sect. 1967-68) E-mail: machull@unm.edu

HULL, SUZANNE WHITE, writer, retired administrator; b. Orange, N.J., Aug. 24, 1921; d. Gordon Stowe and Lillian (Siegling) White; m. George I. Hull, Feb. 20, 1943 (dec. Mar. 1990); children: George Gordon, James Rutledge, Anne Elizabeth Hull Sheldon. BA with honors, Swarthmore Coll., 1943; MSLS, U. So. Calif., 1967. Mem. staff Huntington Libr., Art Gallery and Bot. Gardens, San Marino, Calif., 1969-86, dir. adminstrn. and pub. svcs., 1972-86, also prin. officer. Cons. Women Writers Project, Brown U., 1989-2001. Author: Chaste, Silent and Obedient, English Books for Women, 1475-1640, 1982, 88, Women According to Men: The World of Tudor-Stuart Women, 1996; editor: State of the Art in Women's Studies, 1986. Charter pres. Portola Jr. H.S. PTA, L.A., 1960-62; pres. Children's Svc. League, 1963-64, YWCA, L.A., 1967-69; mem. alumni coun. Swarthmore Coll., 1959-62, 83-86, mem.-at-large, 1986-89; mem. adv. bd. Hagley Mus. and Libr., Wilmington, Del., 1983-86, Betty Friedan Think Tank, U. So. Calif., 1985-93; hon. life mem. Calif. Congress Parents and Tchrs.; bd. dirs. Pasadena Planned Parenthood Assn., 1978-83, mem. adv. com., 1983—; founder-chmn. Swarthmore-L.A. Connection, 1984-85, bd. dirs., 1985-92; founder Huntington Women's Studies Seminar, 1984, mem. steering com., 1984-91, mem. adv. bd., 1991-96; mem. organizing com. Soc. for Study of Early Modern Women, 1993-94; adv. bd. the Early Modern Englishwoman: A Facsimile Libr. of Essential Works, 1995—. Mem. Monumental Brass Soc. (U.K.), Renaissance Soc., Brit. Studies Conf., Western Assn. Women Historians, Soc. Study of Early Modern Women, Authors Guild, Beta Phi Mu (chpt. dir. 1981-84). Home: 211 S Wilson Ave Pasadena CA 91106 Office: 1151 Oxford Rd San Marino CA 91108-1218 E-mail: suehull@compuserve.com

HUME, FREDERICK RAYMOND, electronics company executive; b. Los Angeles, Feb. 23, 1943; s. Laurence Frederick and Willetta Fredericka (Balderson) H.; m. Betty Ruth Dudley, Mar. 30, 1963; children: Joy Anne Sprague, Frederick William III. Student, Calif. State U., Long Beach, 1960-61, Biola Coll., , 1961-62. Test engr. Autoretics div. Rockwell, Anaheim, Calif., 1964-67, research engr., 1967-72; mgr. new products John Fluke Mfg. Co. Inc., Everett, Wash., 1972-76, div. gen. mgr., 1976-80, v.p., 1980-88; v.p., gen. mgr. Keithley Investments, Cleve., 1988—. Bd. dirs. Artech Corp., Seattle, 1985—. Author: Transactions of IEEE, 1973. Inventor radio frequency power testing equipment, broadband spectral intensity measurement system. Chmn. Wash. High Tech. Coordinating Bd., Seattle, 1983-87; co. chmn. Jr. Achievement, Seattle, 1984. Mem. Higher Edn. Fin. Assn. (bd. dirs. 1987—), Am. Electronics Assn. (bd. dirs. 1982-86), Nat. Acad. Sci. (panel mem. 1986—), Electronics Edn. Found. (bd. dirs. 1985—), Soc. Mfg. Engrs. (sr. mem. 1983—), Precision Measurements Assn. (pres. 1978-79). Avocation: literature. Home: 11415 176th Pl NE Redmond WA 98052-2806

HUME, JAMES BORDEN, corporate professional, foundation executive; b. Halifax, N.S., Can., Nov. 6, 1950; s. Thomas White and Elizabeth Mae (Spears) H.; m. Penelope Ann Morris, June 3, 1972; children: Kathryn Ann, David Stuart. BA, U. Calgary, Alta., Can., 1972. Chartered acct. V.p. TIW Industries Ltd., Ottawa, Ont., Can., 1978-80; pres. Hume Mgmt. Cons. Ltd., Calgary, 1980-85, Kanesco Holdings Ltd., Calgary, 1985—, The Kahanoff Found., Calgary, 1984—, also bd. dirs. Bd. dirs. Southern Alberta Inst. Tech. Mem. Can. Inst. Chartered Accts. Office: Kahanoff Found 400 Third Ave SW Ste 4206 Calgary AB Canada T2P 4H2 E-mail: jbhume@kanesco.com

HUME, WYATT, university administrator; Exec. vice chmn. UCLA. Office: UCLA Care Mail Svcs PO Box 951361 Los Angeles CA 90095-1361

HUMMEL, JOSEPH WILLIAM, retired hospital administrator; b. Vinton, Iowa, Dec. 7, 1940; married. BA, Calif. State U., 1965; M Health Adminstrn., U Calif., 1966. Adminstrv. instr. Merrithew Meml. Hosp., Martinez, Calif., 1965; adminstrv. res. Mt. Zion Hosp. and Med. Ctr., San Francisco, 1966-67, adminstrv. pat. care, 1967-68, adminstrv. asst., 1968-70; assoc. adminstr. Valley Med. Ctr., Fresno, Calif., 1970-74; CEO Kern Med. Ctr., Bakersfield, 1974-86; adminstr. Kaiser Found. Hosp., L.A., 1987-99, sr. v.p. area mng., 1987-99. Mem. Calif. Hosp. Assn. (bd. dirs. 1983-89).

HUMPHREYS, ROBERT LEE, advertising executive; b. Burbank, Calif., Dec. 30, 1924; s. Robert E. and Nancy Lucille (Gum) H.; m. Marie Dorthea Wilkinson, May 10, 1951; children: Dina Lizette, Gia Monique Thompson. BS in Mktg., UCLA, 1947. Merchandising rep. Life mag., L.A., 1947-48; promotion mgr. Fortune mag., N.Y.C., 1948-49; copy writer BBDO, L.A., 1950-51; account exec. KNBC-TV, L.A., 1951-52; v.p., account group mgr. Foote, Cone & Belding, L.A., 1952-62; CEO, chmn. emeritus Western divsn. Grey Advt., Inc., L.A., 1962-2000, dir., 1963-92; pres. Humphreys Seminars, L.A., 2000—. Dir. William O'Neil Fund, Beverly Hills, Calif. Featured guest on Corp. Viewpoint, PBS, 1978. Founding pres. UCLA Chancellor's Assocs., 1967—; founding chmn. [illegible] 1967—; mem. president's circle Los Angeles County Mus. Art, 1983—; bd. dirs. Advt. Industry Emergency Fund, Banning Park Mus., 1991-96. Mem. Am. Advt. Fedn. (bd. dirs. 1982-92), World Affairs Coun., Hollywood Radio and TV Soc. (bd. dirs. 1976-82), L.A. Advt. Club (bd. dirs. 1974-76), Sierra Club (life), Bel Air Bay Club, Phi Gamma Delta. Home and Office: 12830 Parkyns St Los Angeles CA 90049-2630

HUMPHREYS, ROY, construction executive; Pres., CEO Shea Homes, Walnut, Calif., 19776. Office: PO Box 489 Walnut CA 91788-0489

HUNDLEY, NORRIS CECIL, JR. history educator; b. Houston, Oct. 26, 1935; s. Norris Cecil and Helen Marie (Mundine) H.; m. Carol Marie Beckquist, June 8, 1957; children: Wendy Michelle Hundley Harris, Jacqueline Marie Hundley Reid. A.A., Mt. San Antonio Coll., 1956; A.B., Whittier Coll., 1958; Ph.D. (Univ. fellow), UCLA, 1963. Instr. U. Houston, 1963-64; asst. prof. Am. history UCLA, 1964-69, assoc. prof., 1969-73, prof., 1973-94, prof. emeritus, 1994—, chmn. exec. com. Inst. Am. Cultures, 1976-93, chmn. univ. program on Mex., 1981-94, acting dir. Latin Am. Ctr., 1989-90, dir. Latin Am. Ctr., 1990-94. Mem. exec. com. U. Calif. Consortium on Mex. and the U.S., 1981-86; mem. adv. com. Calif. water atlas project Calif. Office Planning and Research, 1977-79 Author: Dividing the Waters: A Century of Controversy Between the United States and Mexico, 1966, Water and the West: The Colorado River Compact and the Politics of Water in the American West, 1975, The Great Thirst: Californians and Water 1770s-1990s, 1992, Las aquas divididas: Un siglo de controversia entre México y Estados Unidos, 2000, The Great Thirst: Californians and Water-A History, 2001; co-author: The Calif. Water Atlas, 1979, California: History of a Remarkable State, 1982; editor: The American Indian, 1974, The Chicano, 1975, The Asian American, 1976; co-editor: The American West: Frontier and Region, 1969, Golden State Series, 1978—; mng. editor Pacific Hist. Rev., 1968-97; mem. bd. editors Jour. San Diego History, 1970—; mem. editorial bd. cons. Calif. Hist. Soc., 1980-89; contbr. articles to profl. jours. Bd. dirs. John and LaRee Caughey Found., 1983—, Henry J. Bruman Ednl. Found., 1983—, Forest History Soc., 1987-93. Recipient award of merit Calif. Hist. Soc., 1979; Am. Philos. Soc. grantee, 1964, 71, Ford Found. grantee, 1968-69, U. Calif. Water Resources Ctr. grantee, 1969-72, 91, 2000, Sourisseau Acad. grantee, 1972, NEH grantee, 1983-89, Hewlett Found. grantee, 1986-89, U. Calif. Regents faculty fellow in humanities, 1975, Guggenheim fellow, 1978-79, Hist. Soc. So. Calif. fellow, 1996—; Whitsett lectr., 2000. Mem. Am. Hist. Assn. (exec. coun. Pacific Coast br. 1968-97, v.p. 1993-94, pres. 1994-95), Western History Assn. (coun. 1985-88, 93-97, pres. 1994-95, Winther award 1973, 79), Orgn. Am. Historians. Office: UCLA Dept History Los Angeles CA 90095-1473 E-mail: hundley@history.ucla.edu

HUNDLEY, TODD RANDOLPH, professional baseball player; b. Martinsville, Va., May 27, 1969; s. Randy Hundley. Student, William Rainey Harper Coll., Ill. Selected 2d round free-agt. draft N.Y. Mets, 1987, catcher, 1991-98, L.A. Dodgers, 1998—. Selected to Nat. League All-Star Team, 1996. Office: LA Dodgers Shea Stadium 1000 Elysian Park Ave Los Angeles CA 90012-1112

HUNING, DEVON GRAY, actress, dancer, audiologist, veterinary technician, photographer, video producer and editor; b. Evanston, Ill., Aug. 23, 1950; d. Hans Karl Otto and Angenette Dudley (Willard) H.; divorced; 1 child, Bree Alyeska. BS, No. Ill. U., 1981, MA, 1983; AAS in Vet. Tech. with honors, Colo. Mountain Coll., 2000. Actress, soloist, dancer, dir. various univ. and community theater depts., Bklyn., Chgo. and Cranbrook, B.C., Can., 1967—; ski instr. Winter Park (Colo.) Recreation Assn., 1975-79; house photographer C Lazy U Ranch, Granby, Colo., 1979; audiologist, ednl. programming cons. East Kootenay Ministry of Health, Cranbrook, 1985-89; ind. video prodn./asst., 1991—; owner Maxaroma Espresso and Incredible Edibles, 1993-95; pres. Sound Comms., 1989—; writer, prodr., editor Sta. KTVZ, Bend, Oreg., 1996-97. Master of ceremonies East Kootenay Talent Showcase, EXPO '86, Vancouver B.C., Can., 1986; creator, workshop leader: A Hearing Impaired Child in the Classroom, 1986. Producer, writer, dir., editor (video) Down With Decibels, 1992; author: Living Well With Hearing Loss: A Guide for the Hearing-Impaired and Their Families, 1992. Sec., treas. Women for Wildlife, Cranbrook, 1985-86; assoc. mem. adv. bd. Grand County Community Coll., Winter Park, Colo., 1975-77; assoc. mem. bd. dirs. Boys and Girls Club of Can., Cranbrook, 1985. Mem. Phi Theta Kappa. Avocations: snow and water skiing, scuba diving, dancing, marine animals, studying animal behavior. E-mail: dev11@earthlink.net

HUNSBERGER, CHARLES WESLEY, library director; b. Elkhart, Ind., Sept. 25, 1929; s. Charles August and Emma Edna (Zimmerman) H.; m. Hilda Carol Showalter, July 3, 1949 (div.); children: Jonathan Wesley, Jerald Wayne, Jane Wannette. BA, Bethel Coll., Mishawaka, Ind., 1952; MLS, Ind. U., 1967. Mem. Ft. Wayne (Ind.) Libr. Staff, 1960-62; dir. Columbia (Ind.) City Libr., 1962-64, Monroe County Libr., Bloomington, Ind., 1964-71, Clark County Libr. Dist., Las Vegas, Nev., 1971-93. Owner Las Vegas Libr. Cons. Svcs., 1993—, Las Vegas, Nev. cons. sch., pub. librs., 1968-70; lectr. libr. schs. Ind. U., 1970-71, U. Ariz., 1974, U. Nev., Reno, 1976; mem. Nev. Coun. on Librs., 1973-81, chmn., 1980-81. Mem. Calif. Libr. Assn., Ala., Nev. Libr. Assn. (named Libr. of Yr. 1988), Internat. Assn. of Met. City Librs. (sec./treas., 1992-95), Rotary (pres. 1979-80, Las Vegas-Paradise chpt.). Democrat. Home: 52 Crestview Dr Las Vegas NV 89124-9155

HUNSUCKER, WAYNE (CARL WAYNE HUNSUCKER), architectural firm executive, educator; b. Morganton, N.C., Feb. 16, 1945; s. Earnest Howard and Reba (Laughridge) H.; m. Edith Mabel Whittaker Guisto, May 23, 1990; children: Wendy Edith Guisto, Bret Thomas Guisto. Student, Old Dominion Coll.; BFA, Coll. William and Mary, 1968; BArch with Distinction, U. Ariz., 1975. Lic. architect, Calif., Nev., Idaho, Oreg., Wash., Ariz.; cert. Nat. Coun. Archtl. Registration Bds. Archtl. draftsman Woodmoor Corp., Colorado Springs, Colo., 1971-72; architect-in-training James Gresham & Assocs., Tuscon, 1975-76; prin., pres. Hummel Hunsucker Archs., Boise, Idaho, 1976—, prin.-in-charge office ops. Spokane, Wash., 1998—. Part-time draftsperson Forrest Coile & Assocs., Newport News, Va., 1959-63; asst. instr. U. Ariz. Prin. works include U.S. Courthouse and Fed. Office Bldg., Boise, Idaho, Earl F. Chandler Bldg., Boise, Benton County Jud. Facility, San Francisco, Orchard Pl. Office Complex, Boise, 1st Security Bank addition and remodel, Nampa Main Br., Blue Cross Idaho, Idaho N.G. Armory Annex, Boise, various bldgs. Mt. Home AFB (Citation and Design awards Dept. Air Force), Mountain Home Twn Jr. High Sch. addition; co-author: (text books) Architectural Drafting, 1976, Neighborhood Planning - Case Study of the Sam Hughes Neighborhood. Bd. dirs. Ada County Hist. Soc., 1989-90, Boise; mem. Lincoln Day Banquet Com., Boise, 1984-86; mem. licensing bd. Idaho Outfitters and Guides, 1996—; bd. mem. Bldg. Owners and Mgrs. Assn., Boise chpt., 1998. 1st lt. U.S. Army, 1969-71, Vietnam. Recipient Citation award USAF, Best Stand Alone Bldg. award TAC Air Force, 1984, Henry Adams Fund for Excellence award. Mem. AIA (state pres. 1990, pres. ctrl. sect. Idaho chpt. 1988, Silver medal 1976), Nat. Coun. Archtl. Registration Bds. Avocations: bird hunting, fishing, boating. Office: Hummel Hunsucker Archs PA 802 W Bannock St Ste 700 Boise ID 83702-5844

HUNT, BRIAN L. program manager; MA, Cambridge U.; ScM, PhD, Brown U. Acting program mgr. Northrop Grumman Corp., Hawthorne, Calif., England, 1967-79; tech. mgr. Northrop Corp., 1979-90, 92-97; chmn. aerospace engring. U. Md., 1990-92; program mgr. F/A 18A/B/C/D Northrop Grumman Corp., 1997-98, v.p. engring. and tech. air combat sys. Calif., 1998-2000. Recipient AIAA Aircraft Design award, 1996. Office: Northrop Grumman Corp [illegible] Northrop Ave Hawthorne CA 90250-3236

HUNT, DENNIS, public relations executive; BA in English, Notre Dame U.; MA in Edn. Adv. mgr., contbg. editor San Francisco Bus. Mag.; exec. v.p., gen. mgr. Deaver & Hannaford; mng. ptnr. Hunt/Marmillion Assocs., 1983-88; exec. v.p., gen. mgr. Ogilvy Adams &Rinehart, 1988-92; pres. Stoorza, Ziegaus, Metzger & Hunt, Sacramento, 1992-99, sr. cons., 1999-2000; ptnr. Pacific Visions, L.A., 2000—. Adj. instr. Santa Monica (Calif.) Coll. Office: Pacific Visions 900 W Sunset Blvd Los Angeles CA 90012-2133

HUNT, GORDON, lawyer; b. L.A., Oct. 26, 1934; s. Howard Wilson and Esther Nita (Dempsey) H. BA in Polit. Sci, UCLA, 1956; JD, U. So. Calif., 1959. Bar: Calif. 1960. Law clk. Appellate Dept., Superior Ct. L.A. County, 1959-60; mem. firm Behymer & Hoffman, Los Angeles, 1960-65; partner firm Behymer, Hoffman & Hunt, Los Angeles, 1965-68; ptnr. firm Munns, Kofford, Hoffman, Hunt & Throckmorton, Pasadena, 1969-90, Hunt, Ortman, Blasco, Palffy & Rossell, Pasadena, 1990-95; mem. Hunt, Ortman, Blasco, Palffy & Rossell Inc., 1995—. Lectr. UCLA, various yrs.; chmn. legal adv. com. Assoc. Gen. Contractors Calif., 1985; arbitrator L.A. Superior Ct., State of Calif. Author: Construction Surety and Bonding Handbook; co-author: California Construction Law, 16th edit.; contbr. numerous articles to legal jours. Mem. ABA, Calif. Bar Assn. (del. Conv. 1964-69), L.A. County Bar Assn. (real property com. 1965-66, exec. com. 1970-72, sec. 1972-73, vice chmn. 1972-75, chmn. real property sect. 1975-76, co-chmn. continuing edn. bar com. 1969-71), Am. Arbitration Assn. (arbitrator, mediator). Office: 301 N Lake Ave Fl 7 Pasadena CA 91101-4108 E-mail: goff@hober.com

HUNT, H(AROLD) KEITH, business management educator, marketing consultant; b. Apr. 16, 1938; married; 8 children. BS in Mktg. and Mgmt., U. Utah, 1961, MBA, 1962; PhD in Mktg., Northwestern U., 1972. Instr. Imperial Valley Coll., El Centro, Calif., 1962-64; teaching asst. Northwestern U., 1964-66, instr., 1966-67; asst. prof. bus. adminstrn. and journalism U. Iowa, 1967-73; cons., staff mem. Office Policy Planning and Evaluation, FTC, Washington, 1973-74; assoc. prof. bus. adminstrn. U. Wyo., Laramie, 1974-75; assoc. prof. bus. mgmt. Brigham Young U., Provo, Utah, 1975-78, prof., 1978—. Participant, chmn. various workshops, seminars, meetings; research expert, cons., expert witness on consumer research FTC, 1974-81; cons., expert witness div. drug advt. FDA, 1975-82; cons., adv. on consumer research Consumer and Corp. Affairs Can., 1978-82. Editor: Advances in Consumer Research, vol. 5, 1977; co-editor conf. proc. (with Francees Magrabi) Interdisciplinary Consumer Research, 1980, (with Ralph Day) Consumer Satisfaction/Dissatisfaction and Complaining Behavior, 8 vols., 1975-85, Jour. 1988—. Elected to Orem City Coun., Utah, 1986-93. Recipient Maeser Research award Brigham Young U., 1981; scholar-in-residence adv. dept. U. Ill., 1979; vis. research scholar Coll. Home Econs., U. Ala., 1980; vis. research scholar dept. mktg. and transp. U. Tenn., 1981; NSF grantee, 1975-77 Mem. Assn. Consumer Research (pres. 1979, exec. sec. 1983-2000, 1st Disting. Svc. award 1989), Am. Acad. Advt. (pres. 1982-83, exec. sec. 1983-86, elected fellow 1987), Am. Mktg. Assn., Soc. Consumer Psychology, Am. Council on Consumer Interests, Beta Gamma Sigma, Kappa Tau Alpha, Omicron Delta Epsilon, Phi Kappa Phi E-mial. Home: 835 High Country Dr Orem UT 84097-2370 Office: Brigham Young U Grad Sch Mgmt 632 TNRB Provo UT 84602-1133 E-mail: hkhunt@byu.edu

HUNT, JAMES L. lawyer; b. Chgo., Oct. 20, 1942; BA magna cum laude, DePauw U., 1964; JD, Northwestern U., 1967. Bar: Calif. 1967. Atty. McCuthen, Doyle, Brown & Enersen, San Francisco. Atty. rep. 9th Cir. Jud. Conf., 1991-94; bd. dirs. The Lurie Co.; trustee The Lurie Found. Assoc. editor: Northwestern U. Law Rev., 1966-67. Bd. dirs. San Francisco Giants; bd. visitors Northwestern U. Law Sch., 1989—. Mem. Am. Coll. Trial Lawyers, Phi Beta Kappa, Order of the Coif. Office: McCutchen Doyle Brown & Enersen 3 Embarcadero Ctr Ste 18000 San Francisco CA 94111-4003

HUNT, LORRAINE T. lieutenant governor; m. Charles Hunt; 3 children. Former pres., CEO Perri Inc.; founder, also bd. dirs. Continental Nat. Bank; lt. gov. State of Nev., 1998—, pres. Senate, 1999—. Bd. dirs. First Security Bank Nev.; chmn. bd. trustees Las Vegas Convention and Visitors Authority; former commr. and vice chair Nev. Commn. on Tourism; dir. Nev. Hotel/Motel Assn.; vice chmn. Nev. Motion Picture Found., Nev. Motion Picture Commn. Commr. Clark county Commn., 1995-99. Office: 101 N Carson St Ste 2 Carson City NV 89701-4786 also: 555 E Washington Ave Ste 5500 Las Vegas NV 89101-1081

HUNT, ROGER LEE, judge; b. Overton, Nev., Apr. 29, 1942; s. Ferlin Hansen and Verda (Peterson) H.; m. Mauna Sue Hawkes, July 20, 1965; children: Roger Todd (dec.), Rachelle, Kristina, Tyler, Melanee, Ryan. Student, Coll. So. Utah, 1960-61; BA, Brigham Young U., 1966; JD, George Washington U., 1970. Bar: Nev. 1970, U.S. Dist. Ct. Nev. 1970, U.S. Supreme Ct. 1977, U.S. Ct. Appeals 1980. Dep. dist. atty. Clark County Dist. Atty.'s Office, Las Vegas, Nev., 1971; assoc. Rose & Norwood, Las Vegas, 1971-73; sr. ptnr. Edwards, Hunt, Hale & Hansen, Las Vegas, 1973-92; magistrate judge U.S. Dist. Ct. Nev., Las Vegas, 1992, judge, 2000—. Office: US Dist Ct 333 Las Vegas Blvd Ste 6018 Las Vegas NV 89101-5814

HUNT, WILLIAM E., SR. state supreme court justice; b. 1923; BA, LLB, U. Mont., JD, 1955. Bar: 1955. Judge State Workers' Compensation Ct., 1975-81; justice Mont. Supreme Ct., Helena, 1984—. Office: Mont Supreme Ct Justice Bldg Rm 434 215 N Sanders St Helena MT 59601-4522

HUNTEN, DONALD MOUNT, planetary scientist, educator; b. Montreal, Mar. 1, 1925; came to U.S., 1963, naturalized, 1979; s. Kenneth William and Winnifred Binnmore (Mount) H.; m. Isobel Ann Rubenstein, Dec. 28, 1949 (div. Apr. 1995); children: Keith Atherton, Mark Ross; m. Ann Louise Sprague, May 21, 1995. B.Sc., U. Western Ont., 1946; Ph.D., McGill U., 1950. From research asso. to prof. physics U. Sask. (Can.), Saskatoon, 1950-63; physicist Kitt Peak Nat. Obs., Tucson, 1963-77; sci. adv. to asso. adminstr. for space sci. NASA, Washington, 1976-77; prof. planetary scis. U. Ariz., Tucson, 1977-88, Regents prof., 1988—. Cons. NASA, 1964—. Author: Introduction to Electronics, 1964; (with J.W. Chamberlain) Theory of Planetary Atmospheres, 1987; contbr. articles to profl. jours. Recipient Pub. Svc. medal NASA, 1977, 85,96, medal for exceptional sci. achievement, 1980, Space Sci. award Com. on Space Rsch., 2000. Mem. Am. Phys. Soc., Can. Assn. Physicists (editor 1961-63), Am. Geophys. Union (John Adam Fleming medal 1998), Am. Astron. Soc. (chmn. div. planetary scis. 1977), Internat. Astron. Union, Internat. Union Geodesy and Geophysics, Internat. Assn. Geomagnetism and Aeronomy, AAAS, Nat. Acad. Scis., Explorers Club. Club: Cosmos (Washington). Home: 3445 W Foxes Den Dr Tucson AZ 85745-5102 Office: U Ariz Dept Planetary Scis Tucson AZ 85721-0001

HUNTER, DUNCAN LEE, congressman; b. Riverside, Calif., May 31, 1948; m. Lynne Layh, 1973; children: Robert Samuel, Duncan Duane. JD, Western State U., 1976. Bar: Calif. 1976. Pvt. practice, San Diego; mem. U.S. Congress from 52nd Calif. dist., 1981—; mem. armed svcs. com. With [illegible] Navy League. Republican. Baptist.*

HUNTER, LARRY DEAN, lawyer; b. Leon, Iowa, Apr. 10, 1950; s. Doyle J. and Dorothy B. (Grey) H.; m. Rita K. Barker, Jan. 24, 1971; children: Nathan (dec.), Allison. BS with high distinction, U. Iowa, 1971; AM, JD magna cum laude, U. Mich., 1974, CPhil in Econs., 1975. Bar: Va. 1975, Mich. 1978, Calif. 1992. Assoc. McGuire Woods & Battle, Richmond, Va., 1975-77; asst. counsel, internat. counsel Clark Equipment Co., Buchanan, Mich., 1977-80; ptnr. Honigman, Miller, Schwartz and Cohn, Detroit, 1980-93; asst. gen. counsel Hughes Electronics Corp., L.A., 1993-98, corp. v.p., 1998—; sr. v.p., gen. counsel DIRECTV, Inc., El Segundo, Calif., 1996-98; chmn. pres. DIRECTV Japan Mgmt., Inc., Tokyo, 1998-2000. Mem. faculty Wayne State U. Law Sch., Detroit, 1987-89. Mem. Order of Coif. Home: 1101-B S Catalina Ave Redondo Beach CA 90277 Office: Hughes Electronics Corp 200 N Sepulveda El Segundo CA 90245 E-mail: larry.hunter@hughes.com

HUNTER, TONY (ANTHONY REX HUNTER), molecular biologist, educator; b. Ashford, Kent, Eng., Aug. 23, 1943; came to U.S., 1971; s. Ranulph Rex and Nellie Ruby Elsie (Hitchcock) H.; m. Philippa Charlotte Marrack, July 19, 1969 (div. 1974); m. Jennifer Ann Maureen Price, June 8, 1992; children: Sean Alexander Brocas, James Samuel Alan. BA, U. Cambridge, Eng., 1965, MA, 1966, PhD, 1969. Rsch. fellow Christ's Coll., U. Cambridge, 1968-71, 73-75; rsch. assoc. Salk Inst., San Diego, 1971-73, asst. prof., 1975-78, assoc. prof., 1978-82, prof., 1982—, Am. Cancer Soc. Rsch. Prof., 1992—. Adj. prof. biology U. Calif. San Diego, La Jolla, 1982—. Contbr. articles to sci. jours. Recipient award Am. Bus. Found. for Cancer Rsch., 1988, Katharine Berkan Judd award Meml. Sloan-Kettering Cancer Ctr., 1992, Internat. award Gairdner Found., 1994, Hopkins Meml. award Biochem. Soc., 1994, Mott prize GM Cancer Rsch. Found., 1994, Feodor Lynen medal, 1999, J. Allyn Taylor Internat. prize in medicine John P. Roberts Rsch. Inst. and C. H. Stiller Meml. Found., 2000. Fellow Am. Acad. Arts and Scis., Royal Soc. London, Royal Soc. for Arts, Mfrs. and Commerce; mem. NAS (fgn. assoc.), European Molecular Biology Orgn. (assoc.). Avocations: white water rafting, desert camping. Home: 4578 Vista de la Patria Del Mar CA 92014-4150 Office: Salk Inst Biol Studies Molecular-Cell Biology Lab 10010 N Torrey Pines Rd La Jolla CA 92037-1099 E-mail: hunter@salk.edu

HUNTER, WILLIAM DENNIS, lawyer; b. Boise, Idaho, June 26, 1943; s. William Gregory and Lorene (Persilla) H.; m. Jane Emily Porter, Apr. 30, 1966; children: Keith Alan, Elise Aubrey. BA, Stanford U., 1965; JD, U. Calif., San Francisco, 1973. Bar: Calif. 1973, U.S. Dist. Ct. (no. dist.) Calif. 1974, U.S. Ct. Appeals (9th cir.) 1974, U.S. Supreme Ct. 1996. Assoc. Pettit & Martin, San Francisco, 1973-79, ptnr., 1980-92, counsel, 1993-95, Collette & Erickson LLP, San Francisco, 1995-2000; regional counsel The Nature Conservancy, San Francisco, 2000—. Bd. dirs. City Celebration, Inc., San Francisco, 1984-91, pres., 1989-91. Recipient Service award Calif. Nature Conservancy, 1987. Mem. ABA, Calif. State Bar Assn., San Francisco Bar Assn., Nat. Assn. Installation Devel. (regional dir. 1993-2000), Order of coif. Democrat. Office: The Nature Conservancy 201 Mission St 4th Fl San Francisco CA 94105

HUNTHAUSEN, RAYMOND GERHARDT, archbishop; b. Anaconda, Mont., Aug. 21, 1921; s. Anthony Gerhardt and Edna (Tuchacherer) H. A.B., Carroll Coll., 1943, St. Edward's Sem., 1946; M.S., Notre Dame U., 1953; LL.D., DePaul U., 1960; postgrad. summers, St. Louis U., Cath. U., Fordham U. Ordained priest Roman Cath. Ch., 1946. Instr. chemistry Carroll Coll., 1946-57, football, basketball coach, 1953-57, pres., 1957-62; bishop Helena Diocese, Mont., 1962-75; archbishop of Seattle, 1975-91. Recipient Martin Luther King Jr. award Fellowship of Reconciliation, 1987. Mem. Am. Chem. Soc. Office: Chancery Office 910 Marion St Seattle WA 98104-1274

HUNTLEY, JAMES ROBERT, government official, international affairs scholar and consultant; b. Tacoma, July 27, 1923; s. Wells and Laura H.; m. Colleen Grounds Smith, May 27, 1967; children by previous marriage: Mark, David, Virginia, Jean. BA magna cum laude in Econs., Sociology, U. Wash., 1948, postgrad. sociology and internat. relations (Carnegie fellow), 1951; MA in Internat. Relations, Harvard U., 1956. Cons. Wash. Parks Recreation Commn., Olympia, 1949-51; exchange of persons officer U.S. Fgn. Service, Frankfurt, Nuremberg, Germany, 1952-54; dir. cultural center USIA, Hof/Saale, Germany, 1954-55; USIA postgrad. scholar Harvard U., 1955-56; asst. to Pres.'s coordinator for Hungarian relief Washington, 1956; European regional affairs officer USIA, Washington, 1956-58; dep. pub. affairs officer U.S. Mission to European Communities, Brussels, 1958-60; mem. U.S. Delegation to Atlantic Congress, London, 1959; sec. organizing com. Atlantic Inst., Brussels and Milan, 1960, exec. officer and co-founder Paris, 1960-63; dir. Atlantic Inst. (N.Am. Office), Washington, 1963-65; founder, sec. Com. Atlantic Studies, 1963-65; sec. edn. com. NATO Parliamentarians Conf., Brussels, 1960-64; program asso., internat. affairs div. Ford Found., N.Y.C., 1965-67; sec. gen. Council Atlantic Colls., London, 1967-68; ind. writer, cons., lectr., internat. affairs Guildford, Eng., 1968-74; founder, sec. Assn. Mid-Atlantic Clubs, 1970-74; founder, sec. gen. Standing Conf. Atlantic Orgns., 1972-74; rsch. fellow, sr. advisor to pres. on internat. affairs Battelle Meml. Inst., Seattle, 1974-83; pres., chief exec. officer Atlantic Council of U.S., Washington, 1983-85; ind. cons., author internat. affairs, 1985—. European corr., environ. affairs Saturday Rev./World, 1972-74; Corrs. World Wide, London, 1970-74; European corr. Non-Profit Report, 1970-74 Author: The NATO Story, 1965, (with W.R. Burgess) Europe and America - The Next Ten Years, 1970, Man's Environment and the Atlantic Alliance, 1972, Uniting the Democracies, 1980, Pax Democratica—A Strategy for the 21st Century, 1998, 2d edit., 2001; contbr. articles to profl. jours. Bd. dirs. Internat. Standing Conf. Phlanthropy, 1969-74, Assn. to Unite Democracies, 1976-94, Seattle Com. Fgn. Rels., 1975-78, World Affairs Coun. Seattle, 1975-83, adv. bd. 1986—, Bainbridge Island Land Trust, 1994-97; founding chmn. Coms. for a Cmty. of Democracies, 1979-92; co-founder 21st Century Found., 1987-91; mem. adv. bd. 21st Century Trust, London, 1988—; co-founder Next Century Initiative, 1992-95, New Century Initiative, 1996-99, pres. 1996-98; co-founder, v.p. Coun. for Cmty. of Democracies, 1999—. Recipient Disting. Eagle Scout award 1995; named Kappa Sigma Man of Yr., 1999. Mem. Rainier Club (Seattle), DACOR (Washington). E-mial. Home and Office: 1213 Towne Rd Sequim WA 98382-8849 E-mail: huntleypax@aol.com

HUNTSMAN, JON MEADE, chemical company executive; b. 1937; BS, U. Pa., 1959; MBA, U. So. Calif., 1970. With Olson Bros, Inc., North Hollywood, Calif., from 1961; assoc. adminstr. HEW, spl. asst. to the pres., 1971-72; with Huntsman Container Corp., Salt Lake City, 1972-83, Huntsman Chem. Corp, Salt Lake City, 1982—; CEO Huntsman Corp., Salt Lake City, 1996-2000, chmn., 2000—. Pres. mission LDS Ch., Washington, 1980-83. Office: Huntsman Corp 500 Huntsman Way Salt Lake City UT 84108-1235

HUNTSMAN, LEE, university provost, academic administrator; Provost, v.p. acad. affairs U. Wash., Seattle. Office: U Wash Seattle WA 98195-1237

HUNTSMAN, PETER R. chemicals executive; Started as truck driver Huntsman Corp., Salt Lake City, 1993—, various mgmt. positions in several of co.'s gobal divsns., v.p. Polymers, sr. v.p. purchasing and logistics, pres. Huntsman Petrochemical Corp., pres., COO, CEO, 2000—. Office: Huntsman Corp 500 Huntsman Way Salt Lake City UT 84108

HUNTWORK, JAMES RODEN, lawyer; b. Milw., May 6, 1948; s. Daniel Lawrence and Gladys (Roden) H.; m. Patience Tipton Huntwork, July 7, 1972; children: Andrew Stuart, Sarah Noel. BA with distinction, Shimer Coll., 1968; JD, Yale U., 1972, MA Econs., 1973. Bar: Ariz. 1977. Atty. Sullivan & Worcester, Boston, 1972-77, Jennings, Strouss & Salmon, Phoenix, 1977-91, Fennemore Craig, Phoenix, 1992-98, Salmon, Lewis & Weldon, Phoenix, 1998—. Dir. exec. com. Phoenix Econ. Growth Corp., 1987-91; state ballot security chmn. Ariz. Rep. Party, Phoenix, 1992—; originator The Comml. Law Project for Ukraine, 1991—. Co-recipient Judge Learned Hand Human Rels. award Am. Jewish Com., 1992. Mem. ABA, Ariz. Bar Assn., Maricopa County Bar Assn., Phoenix C. of C. (N.Am. Free Trade Task Force 1991-95). Republican. Office: Salmon Lewis & Weldon 4444 N 32nd St Ste 200 Phoenix AZ 85018-3975 E-mail: jrh@huntwork.net, jrh@slwplc.com

HUPP, HARRY L. federal judge; b. L.A., Apr. 5, 1929; s. Earl L. and Dorothy (Goodspeed) H.; m. Patricia Hupp, Sept. 13, 1953; children: Virginia, Karen, Keith, Brian. AB, Stanford U., 1953, LLB, 1955. Bar: Calif. 1956, U.S. Dist. Ct. (cen. dist.) Calif. 1956, U.S. Supreme Ct. Pvt. practice law Beardsley, Hufstedler and Kemble, L.A., 1955-72; judge Superior Ct. of Los Angeles, 1972-84; appointed fed. dist. judge U.S. Dist. Ct. (cen. dist.) Calif., L.A., 1984-97, sr. judge, 1997—. Served with U.S. Army, 1950-52. Mem. Calif. Bar Assn., Los Angeles County Bar Assn. (Trial Judge of Yr. 1983), Order of Coif, Phi Alpha Delta. Office: US Dist Ct 312 N Spring St Ste 218P Los Angeles CA 90012-4704

HUPPENTHAL, JOHN, state senator, planning analyst; b. Michigan City, Ind., Mar. 3, 1954; m. Jennifer Huppenthal. BS, North Ariz. U.; MS, Ariz. State U. Sr. planning analyst SRP, 1977—; mem. Chandler City Coun., 1984-92, Ariz. State Senate, 1992—, mem. appropriations com., chmn. edn. com., mem. health com., vice-chmn. govt. and environ. stewardship com. Active Friends of the Libr., Chandler Hist. Soc. Mem. Chandler C. of C. Republican. Office: State Capitol Bldg 1700 W Washington St Ofc 308 Phoenix AZ 85007-2812 also: 8 N Bullmoose Cir Chandler AZ 85224-4120 Fax: 602-542-3429; 480-963-0844. E-mail: jhuppent@azleg.state.az.us

HURD, GALE ANNE, film producer; b. L.A., Oct. 25, 1955; d. Frank E. and Lolita (Espiau) H. Degree in econs. and communications, Stanford U., 1977. Dir. mktg. and publicity, co-producer New World Pictures, L.A., 1977-82; pres., producer Pacific Western Prodns., L.A., 1982—. Producer: (films) The Terminator, 1984 (Grand Prix Avoiriaz Film Festival award), Aliens 1986 (nominated for 7 Acad. awards, recipient Best Sound Effects Editing award, Best Visual Effects award Acad. Picture Arts & Scis.), Alien Nation (Saturn award for best sci. fiction film), The Abyss, 1989 (nominated for 4 Acad. awards, Best Visual Effects award), The Waterdance, 1991 (2 IFP Spirit awards, 2 Sundance Film Festival awards), Cast a Deadly Spell, 1991 (Emmy award), Raising Cain, 1992, No Escape, 1994, Safe Passage (Beatrice Wood award for Creative Achievement), 1994, The Ghost and the Darkness, 1996, The Relic, 1996, Going West in America, 1996, Dante's Peak, 1997, Virus, 1997, Dead Man on Campus, 1997, Armageddon, 1998, Dick, 1998; exec. producer: (films) Switchback, 1997, Tremors, 1990, Downtown, 1990, Terminator 2, 1991 (winner 3 Acad. awards), Witch Hunt, 1994, Sugartime, 1995; creative cons. (TV program) Alien Nation, 1989-90. Juror Focus Student Film Awards, 1989, 90; chmn. Nicholl Fellowship Acad. Motion Picture Arts & Scis., 1989—; mem. Show Coalition, 1988—; mem. Hollywood (Calif.) Women's Polit. Com., 1987—; mem. U.S. Film Festival Juror; bd. dirs. IFP/West, Artists Rights Found.; trustee Am. Film Inst.; bd. dirs. L.A. Internat. Film Festival, Coral Reef Rsch. Found., Ams. for a Safe Future; mentor Peter Stark Motion Picture Producing Program, Sch. of Cinema-TV, U. of So. Calif., Women in Film Mentor Program. Recipient Spl. Merit award Nat. Assn. Theater Owners, 1986, Stanford-La Entrepreneur of Yr. award Bus. Sch. Alumni L.A., 1990, Fla. Film Festival award, 1994. Mem. AMPAS (prodr.'s br. exec. com. 1990—, festival grants com.), Am. Film Inst. (trustee 1989—), Americans for a Safe Future (bd. dirs. 1993—), Prodr.'s Guild Am. (bd. dirs.), Women in Film (bd. dirs. 1989-90), Inst. for Rsch. on Women and Gender (nat. adv. panel 1997—), Feminist Majority, Internat. Seakeepers Soc., Mulholland Tomorrow, The Trusteeship, Phi Beta Kappa. Avocations: scuba diving, Paso Fino horses. Office: Pacific Western Prodns 270 N Canon Dr Ste 1195 Beverly Hills CA 90210-5323

HURLBERT, ROGER WILLIAM, information service industry executive; b. San Francisco, Feb. 18, 1941; s. William G. and Mary (Greene) H.; m. Karen C. Haslag, Nov. 6, 1982; children: Sage, Mica, Chula, Monk, Morris, Cassie. BS in Community Devel., So. Ill. U., 1965. Newspaper editor and reporter various, San Francisco Bay Area, 1958-62; pvt. practice investigation Ill., 1963-65; advisor San Francisco Planning Urban Rsch. Assn., 1969-87; pres. Sage Info. Svcs., Glen Ellen, Calif., 1988—. Compiler U.S. Land Data Base, 1972—. Pres. Haight-Ashbury Neighborhood Coun., San Francisco, 1959-61. With U.S. Army, 1966-68, Vietnam. Recipient Cert. of Merit, San Francisco Coun. Dist. Mchts. Assn., 1972. Mem. Real Estate Info. Profls. Assn. (sec. 1998—), Direct Mktg. Assn., Mail Advt. Svc. Assn. Internat., League of Men Voters (v.p. 1959—). Democrat. Office: Sage Info Svcs 13606 Arnold Dr PO Box 1832 Glen Ellen CA 95442-1832

HURLEY, BRUCE PALMER, artist; b. Tacoma, May 9, 1944; s. Gerald Baynton and Donna Ray (Whealey) H.; m. Ivy Jane Partridge; 1 child, Paul George. BS in Edn., Oreg. Coll. Edn., 1968. Cert. secondary edn. tchr. One-man shows include Goldberg's, 1966, Hillsboro Pub. Libr., 1969, 71, Valley Art Assn., Forest Grove, 1971, 74; group shows include Portland Art Mus., 1970, Northwest Artist Workshop, 1979, Sun Bird Gallery, 1986, Sunriver Juried Show, 1986, 92 (hon. mention), Beaverton Arts Showcase, 1990, 91, 92, 93, 94, 96, 97, 98 (1st Place watercolor); represented in permanent collections Oreg. Coll., Oriental Medicine, David Wheeler, D.C., Libr. of Am. Psychiat. Assn., D.C., Schools Med. Plz., Tigard, Oreg., Atty. Mark Olson, N.Y.C., Nicholas S. Law, Cambridge, Eng., Washington County Pub. Svc. Bldg., Hillsboro, Portland (Oreg.) Ctr., others; author: Planet Ploob Vacation, 1992, Divine Soliloquy, 1994; inventor: numerous paintings, drawings and sculptures. Mem. Portland Art Mus. Recipient Cmty. Svc. award Beaverton Arts Commn., 1993, Royal Patronage award Hutt River, Australia, 1995. Mem. Theosophical Soc. Avocations: musicology, camping, raw foods, naturopathy, mysticism. Home: 251 NW Bailey St Hillsboro OR 97124-2903

HURLEY, ELIZABETH, actress, model; b. Hampshire, Eng., June 10, 1965; m. Hugh Grant. Student, London Studio Ctr. Head devel. Simian Films, London and L.A., 1994—; model, cosmetic rep. Estee Lauder. Actress appearing in TV programs and movies including (films) Die Tote Stadt, 1987, Rowing with the Wind, 1988, Bloody Atlantic, 1991, The Orchid House, 1991, Passenger 57, 1992, El Largo Invierno, 1992, Beyond Bedlam, 1993, Goldeneye, 1995, Mad Dogs and Englishmen, Austin Powers: International Man of Mystery, 1997, (TV movies) The Shamrock Conspiracy, 1995, Samson and Delilah, 1996, Permanent Midnight, 1998, Edtv, 1999, My Favorite Martian, 1999, Austin Powers: The Spy Who Shagged Me, 1999, The Weight of Water, 2000, Bedazzled, 2000, (TV series) Cristabel, 1989, Rumpole and the Barrow boy, 1989, Sharpe II, 1995; host (TV spl.) The World of James Bond, 1995; prodr. Mickey Blue Eyes, 1999. Office: CAA 9830 Wilshire Blvd Beverly Hills CA 90212-1804

HURLEY, FRANCIS T. archbishop; b. San Francisco, Jan. 12, 1927; Ed., St. Patrick Sem., Menlo Park, Calif., Catholic U. Am. Ordained priest Roman Cath. Ch., 1951; with Nat. Cath. Welfare Conf., Washington, asst. sec., 1958-68; assoc. sec. Nat. Cath. Welfare Conf., now U.S. Cath. Conf., 1968-70; consecrated bishop, 1970; titular bishop Daimlaig and aux. bishop Diocese of Juneau, Alaska, 1970-71; bishop of Juneau, 1971-76; archbishop of Anchorage, 1976—. Office: Archdiocese Anchorage 225 Cordova St Anchorage AK 99501-2409

HURLEY, MARK JOSEPH, bishop; b. San Francisco, Dec. 13, 1919; s. Mark J. and Josephine (Keohane) H. Student, St. Joseph's Coll., Mountain VIew, Calif., 1939, St. Patrick's Sem., Menlo Park, Calif., 1944; postgrad., U. Calif., Berkeley, 1943-45; PhD, Cath. U. Am., 1947; JCB, Lateran U., Rome, 1963; LLD, U. Portland, 1971. Ordained to priest Roman Cath. Ch., 1944. Asst. supt. schs. Archdiocese, San Francisco, 1944-51; tchr. Serra High Sch., San Mateo, Calif., 1944; prin. Bishop O'Dowd High Sch., Oakland, 1951-58, Marin Cath. High Sch., Marin County, 1959-61; supt. schs. Diocese, Stockton, 1962-65, chancellor, diocesan counsultor, 1962-65; asst. chancellor Arcdiocese, San Francisco, 1965-67, vicar gen., 1967-69; titular bishop Thunusuda, aux. bishop, 1967-69; bishop Santa Rosa, Cal., 1969—; pastor St. Francis Assisi Ch., San Francisco, 1967—. Prof. grad. schs. Loyola U., Balt., 1946, U. San Francisco, 1948, San Francisco Coll. Women, 1949, Dominican Coll., San Rafael, Calif., 1949, Cath. U. Am., 1954; prof. theology Beda Coll. Rome, 1987—, Angelicum U., Rome, 1989—; Del. Conf. Psychiatry and Religion, San Francisco, 1957; mem. bd. Calif. Com. on Study Edn., 1955-60; cons. Congregation for Cath. Edn., 1986—; del.-at-large Cal., White House Conf. on Youth, 1960; Cath. del., observer Nat. Council Chs., Columbus, Ohio, 1964; del. edn. conf. German and Am. educators, Nat. Cath. Edn. Assn., Munich, Germany, 1960; mem. commns. sems., univs. and schs. II Vatican Council, Rome, 1962-65; mem. commn. Christian formation U.S. Cath. Conf. Bishops, 1968; asst. archdiocesan coordinator Campaign on Taxation Schs. Calif., 1958, Rosary Crusade, 1961; adminstr. Cath. Sch. Purchasing Div., 1948-51, St. Eugene's Ch., Santa Rosa, Calif., 1959, St. John's Ch., San Francisco, 1961; mem. U.S. Bishops' Press Panel, Vatican Council, 1964-65, U.S. Bishops' Com. on Laity, 1964, U.S. Bishops' Com. Cath.-Jewish Relationships, 1965— , U.S. Bishops' Com. on Ecumenical and Interreligious Affairs, 1970, Conf. Maj. Superiors of Men, 1970; chmn. citizens Com. for San Francisco State Coll., 1968— ; mem. adminstrn. bd. Nat. Council Cath. Bishops, 1970, mem. nominating com., 1971; mem. Internat. Secretariat for Non-Believers, Vatican, 1973; chmn. Secretariat for Human Values, Nat. Conf. Cath. Bishops, Washington, 1975; mem. Secretariat for Non-Believers, Vatican, 1986—; Vatican del. World Intellectual Properties Orgn., Washington, 1990; adj. prof. philosophy Grad. Theol. Union, Berkeley, Calif., 1994; prof. theology U. San Francisco, 1994-97; radio commentator AM 1400, San Francisco, 1994-99, Sta. KPL SAM, Orange, Calif. Syndicated columnist San Francisco Monitor, Sacramento Herald, Oakland Voice, Yakima (Wash.) Our Times, Guam Diocesan Press, 1949-66, TV speaker and panelist, 1956-67; author: Church State Relationships in Education in California, 1948, Commentary on Declaration on Christian Education in Vatican II, 1966, Report on Education in Peru, 1965, The Church and Science, 1982, Blood on the Shamrock, 1989, The Unholy Ghost, 1992, Vatican Star, Star of David, 1996. Trustee N.Am. Coll., Rome, 1970, Cath. U. Am., 1978— , Cath. Relief Services, 1979; cons. Congregation for Edn.; mem. Secretariat for Non-Belief, Vatican City; bd. dirs. Overseas Blind Found., Ctr. for Theology and Natural Sci., Berkeley, FlaxTrust Corp., Belfast, Christians and Israel, Berkeley. Address: 273 Ulloa St San Francisco CA 94127-1226

HURLEY, MORRIS ELMER, JR. management consultant; b. Berkeley, Calif., Mar. 26, 1920; s. Morris Elmer Sr. and Alice Grace (Johnson) H.; m. Jeanne Marie Bassett, Jan. 31, 1943; children: Morris Elmer III, James, Richard, Steven, Robert. A.B., Harvard, 1941, M.B.A., 1943; Ph.D., Syracuse U., 1956. Asst. dean Coll. Bus. Adminstrn., Syracuse (N.Y.) U., 1946-53, acting dean, 1953-54, dean, 1954-58, instr. mgmt., 1946-48, asst. prof., 1948-53, assoc. prof., 1953-57, prof., 1957-60, Istituto Direzionale ENI, San Donato Milanese, Italy, 1958, IPSOA Istituto Post-Universitairo Torino, Italy, 1959-61; dir. mgmt. edn. programs U. Berkeley, Berkley, 1961—. Assoc. economist N.Y. Dept. Commerce, 1948; rsch. aide Study for Ford Found., 1949; cons. prof. IBM Exec. Sch. Blaricum, Holland, 1960-61; mem. San Francisco C.C. Faculty, 1974-91, pres. acad. senate, 1979-81; bd. dirs. WIZ Corp., Empire Casting Co. Author: Elements of Business Administration, 1953, Economic Development Regionalism, 1956, Business Administration, 2d edit., 1960, Managing Human Endeavor, 1975, Supervision and Management, 1980, Business Management, 1991, Supervision, 1992, Presentation of Reports, 1993, Sexual Harassment, 1993, Training the Trainer, 1994. Mem. Syracuse city planning commn., 1957-58; bd. dirs. Portsmouth (Va.) Community Chest, 1944-46, Frank S. Hiscock Legal Aid Soc., Syracuse, 1951 54; mem. Piedmont Charter Rev. Commn., 1981-82. Served from ensign to lt. USNR, 1943-46; mem. Res. Mem. ASTD, Am. Econ. Assn., Acad. Mgmt., Acad. Polit. and Social Sci., George F. Baker Scholars, Phi Beta Kappa, Beta Gamma Sigma, Pi Eta, Sigma Iota Epsilon, Alpha Kappa Psi. Home and Office: 36 Greenbank Ave Piedmont CA 94611-4334

HURST, DEBORAH, pediatric hematologist; b. Washington, May 9, 1946; d. Willard and Frances (Wilson) H.; m. Stephen Mershon Senter, June 14, 1970; children: Carlin, Daniel. BA, Harvard U., 1968; MD, Med. Coll. Pa., 1974. Diplomate Nat. Bd. Med. Examiners, Am. Bd. Pediatrics, Am. Bd. Pediatric Hematology-Oncology. Intern Bellevue Hosp., NYU Hosp., N.Y.C., 1974-75, resident in pediatrics, 1975-76; ambulatory pediatric fellow Bellevue Hosp., N.Y.C., 1976-77; hematology, oncology fellow Bellevue Hosp., Columbia U., N.Y.C., 1977-80; assoc. hematologist Childrens Hosp. Oakland, Calif., 1980-92; asst. clin. prof. U. Calif. San Francisco Med. Ctr., 1992—; med. dir. Bayer Corp., Berkeley, Calif., 1992-98; dir. clin. devel. Chiron Corp., Emeryville, 1998—. Hematology cons. Assn. Asian/Pacific Community Health Orgns., Oakland; dir. Satellite Hematology Clinic/Valley Childrens Hosp., Fresno, Calif., 1984-92; cons. state dept. epidemiology Calif. State Dept. Health, Berkeley, 1992; chelation cons. lead poisoning program Childrens Hosp., Oakland, 1986-92. Contbr. articles to profl. jours. Vol. cons. lead poisoning State Dept. Epidemiology and Toxicology, Berkeley, 1986-92. Fellow Am. Acad. Pediatrics; mem. Am. Soc. Hematology, Am. Soc. Gene Therapy, Am. Soc. Clin. Oncology, Am. Soc. Pediat. Hematology/Oncology, Nat. Hemophilia Found., Internat. Soc. Thrombosis and Hemostasis. Office: Chiron Corp 4560 Horton St MS120 Emeryville CA 94608-2900

HURT, ALLEN V. state senator; Physician; Rep. senator dist. 2 N.Mex. State Senate. Mem. corps. and transp., pub. affairs coms. N.Mex. State Senate. Home: Box 639 Waterflow NM 87421 Office: NMex State Senate State Capitol Rm 415 Santa Fe NM 87503 E-mail: hurt@cybernet.com

HURT, WILLIAM HOLMAN, investment management company executive; b. L.A., Mar. 29, 1927; s. Holman G. and Mary E. (Ortloff) H.; m. Sheridan Ann Stephens, Aug. 10, 1950 (div. May. 1970); children: Kelley Anne Hurt Purnell, Kathleen Constance, Courtney Diana Hurt MacMillan; m. Sarah Sherman, May 28, 1970. BS magna cum laude, U. So. Calif., 1949; MBA, Harvard U., 1951. With Dean Witter & Co., Los Angeles, 1951-71, prin., 1959, sr. v.p., 1968-70, exec. v.p., dir., mem. exec. com., dir. mktg. and rsch., 1969-71; vice chmn. bd., chmn. exec. com. Capital Rsch. Co., 1972-77; chief exec. office Capital Group, Inc., L.A., 1978-82; chmn. Capital Strategy Rsch., Inc., 1982—. Mem. adv. com. Coldwell Banker Funds, 1978-99. Mem. bd. councilors Grad. Sch. Bus., U. So. Calif., L.A., 1978-88, vis. com., 1990—; bd. dirs. L.A. Children's Hosp., 1985— . Served with USNR, 1945-46. Mem. Calif. Club, L.A. Athletic Club, N.Y. Athletic Club, Phi Kappa Phi, Beta Gamma Sigma, Kappa Alpha. Republican. Office: 333 S Hope St Los Angeles CA 90071-1406

HURWITZ, LAWRENCE NEAL, investment banking company executive; b. Austin, Tex., Mar. 21, 1939; s. John and Sarah Ruth (Blumenthal) H.; m. Kathleen O'Day, Feb., 1977 (div. Dec. 1985); 1 child, Kimberlee Colleen; m. Mynette Lee, Nov., 1989 (div. Jan. 1996); 1 child, Jonathan Lee. Student, U. Tex., 1957-59; MBA with distinction, Harvard U., 1961. With rsch. dept. Harvard U., 1961-62; asst. to v.p. Atlantic Rsch. Corp., 1962-65; comptr. TelAutograph Corp., 1965; dir. Gen. Artists Corp., 1965-69; pres. Sprayregen & Co., N.Y.C., 1969-83; chmn. Country Junction, Inc., 1969-82; mktg. dir. Beneflex, Inc., 1985-86; v.p. Tech. Liberation Capital, Inc., Houston, 1986-89, Amex Systems, Houston, 1986-89; v.p., chief fin. officer Intile Designs, Inc., Houston, 1989-94; pres. Lawrence Fin. Ptnrs., L.A., 1990—; dir. Kings Rd Entertain Pacific Coast Apparel Max Studios. Vice chmn., mem. exec. com. Empire Life Ins. Co. Am.; dir., mem. exec. com. Old Town Corp., Stratton Group Ltd., Sayre & Fisher Co., Tech. Tape, Inc., DFI Communications Inc., Columbia Gen. Corp., Cal. Data Systems Corp.; bd. dirs. Leon Max Inc., Pacific Coast Apparel, Air Motive Holdings Inc., Indsl. Electronic Hardware Corp., Bloomfield Bldg. Industries, Inc., Apollo Industries, Inc., Aberdeen Petroleum Corp., Investors Book Club, Inc., Ling Fund, Am. Land Co., Terrific Nutrient & Chem. Corp., N. Lake Corp., Datatronics, Inc., Merada Industries, Inc., AK Electric Corp., Aerocon, Inc., Hallmark Communications, Inc., Detroit Gray Iron & Steel Foundries, Inc., Fin. Tech., Inc., Wid's Films & Film Folks, Investors Preferred Life Ins. Co., Langdon Group, Inc., Essex Systems Corp., Chelsea Nat. Bank, Newport Chem. Industries, Inc. Editor: How to Invest in Letter Stock, 1970, Spin-Offs and Shells, 1970. Mem. Harvard Bus. Sch. Club, Comml. Fin. Assn., Am. Cash Flow Assn. (pres. L.A. chpt.), Harvard Club (v.p. Orange County). Jewish. Home: 701 Teakwood Rd Los Angeles CA 90049-1327 Office: 11661 San Vicente Blvd Ste 408 Los Angeles CA 90049-5112

HUSBAND, JOHN MICHAEL, lawyer; b. Elyria, Ohio, Apr. 7, 1952; s. Clint F. and Emma H.; m. Jan Lee Umbenhour, Sept. 15, 1975; children: Heather, John. BS, Ohio State U., 1974; JD, U. Toledo, 1977. Law clk. U.S. Ct. Appeals (10th cir.), Denver, 1977-78; ptnr. Holland & Hart, Denver, 1978—, chair labor and employment law dept., 1991—; counsel Western Gov.'s Office, Denver, 1984, Vols. of Am., Denver, 1984. Editor, The Colorado Lawyer, Employment and Labor Rev., 1984—; co-editor Colo. Employment Law Letter; contbr. articles to profl. jours. Bd. dirs. Colo. Safety Assn., 1984—, Denver Four Mile House, Town of Bow Mar, 1987-90, 1984; mem. Denver Leadership Assn.; sec., treas. Colo. Safety Assn., 1988—; bd. govs. U. Toledo Coll. Law. Inductee Elyria Sports Hall of Fame, 1997. Mem. ABA (labor law sect., individual rights and responsibilities com., co-chair pub. subcom. individual rights and responsibilities com.), Assn. Trial Lawyers Am., Nat. Inst. Trial Advocate, Ohio Bar Assn., Colo. Bar Assn. (labor sect.), Denver Bar Assn., Colo. Safety Assn. (exec. com. sec. treas. 1987—). Republican. Lutheran. Home: 5280 Ridge Trl Littleton CO 80123-1410 Office: Holland & Hart LLP PO Box 8749 555 17th St Ste 2900 Denver CO 80202-3979

HUSKEY, HARRY DOUGLAS, information and computer science educator; b. Whittier, N.C., Jan. 19, 1916; s. Cornelius and Myrtle (Cunningham) H.; m. Velma Elizabeth Roeth, Jan. 2, 1939 (dec. Jan. 1991); children: Carolyn, Roxanne, Harry Douglas, Linda; m. Nancy Grindstaff, Sept. 10, 1994. BS, U. Idaho, 1937; student, Ohio U., 1937-38; MA, Ohio State U., 1940, PhD, 1943. Temp. prin. sci. officer Nat. Phys. Labs., Eng., 1947; head machine devel. lab. Nat. Bur. Standards, 1948; asst. dir. Inst. Numerical Analysis, 1948-54; asso. dir. computation lab. Wayne U., Detroit, 1952-53; asso. prof. U. Calif., Berkeley, 1954-58, prof., 1958-68, vice chmn. elec. engring., 1965-66, prof. info. and computer sci. Santa Cruz, 1968-85, prof. emeritus, 1985—; dir. Computer Center, 1968-77, chmn. bd. info. sci., 1976-79, 82-83. Vis. prof. Indian Inst. Tech., Kanpur; (Indo-Am. program), 1963-64, 71, Delhi U., 1971; cons. computer div. Bendix, 1954-63; vis. prof. M.I.T., 1966; mem. computer sci. panel NSF, Naval Research Adv. Com.; cons. on computers for developing countries UN, 1969-71; chmn. com. to advise Brazil on computer sci. edn. NAS, 1970-72; project coord. UNESCO/Burma contract, 1973-79; mem. adv. com. on use microcomputers in developing countries NRC, 1983-85. Co-editor: Computer Handbook, 1962. Recipient Disting. Alumni award Idaho State U., 1978, Pioneer award Nat. Computer Conf., 1978, IEEE Computer Soc., 1982; U.S. sr.scientist awardee Fulbright-Alexander von Humboldt Found., Mathematisches Institut der Tech. U. Munich, 1974-75, 25th Ann. medal ENIAC; inducted into U. Idaho Alumni Hall of Fame, 1989. Fellow AAAS, ACM, IEEE (edit. bd., editor-in-chief computer group 1965-71, Centennial award 1984), Brit. Computer Soc.; mem. Am. Math. Soc., Math. Assn. Am., Assn. Computing Machinery (pres. 1960-62), Am. Fedn. Info. Processing Socs. (governing bd. 1961-63), Sigma Xi. Achievements include designing SWAC computer, Bendix G-15 and G-20 computers. Home: 10 Devant Ln Bluffton SC 29910-4534 Office: U Calif Computer & Info Sci Santa Cruz CA 95064 E-mail: hhuskey@davtv.com

HUSKEY, ROBERT LEON (BUTCH HUSKEY), professional baseball player; b. Anadarko, Okla., Nov. 10, 1971; Outfield/first baseman New York Mets, N.Y.C., 1989-98; outfielder Seattle Mariners, 1999, Boston Red Sox, 1999-00, Minn. Twins, 2000, Colo. Rockies, Denver, 2000—. Named Internat. League Most Valuable Player, 1995. Office: c/o Colo Rockies Coors Field 2001 Blake St Denver CO 80205

HUSTON, JOHN CHARLES, law educator; b. Chgo., Mar. 21, 1927; s. Albert Allison and Lillian Helen (Sullivan) H.; m. Joan Frances Mooney, Aug. 1, 1954; children: Mark Allison, Philip John, Paul Francis James; m. Inger Margareta Westerman, May 4, 1979. AB, U. Wash., Seattle, 1950; JD, U. Wash., 1952; LLM, NYU, 1955. Bar: Wash. 1952, N.Y. 1964, U.S. Dist. Ct. (we. dist.) Wash. 1953, U.S. Ct. Appeals (9th cir.) 1953, U.S. Tax Ct. 1977, U.S. Supreme Ct. 1993. Assoc. Kahin, Carmody & Horswill, Seattle, 1952-53; teaching fellow NYU Law Sch., 1953-54; asst. co-dir. U. Ankara Legal Research Inst., Turkey, 1954-55; asst. prof. NYU, 1953-57, Syracuse U., N.Y., 1957-60, assoc. prof., 1960-65, prof., 1960-67; prof., assoc. dean U. Wash., Seattle, 1967-73, prof. law, 1973-96, prof. emeritus, 1996—. Of counsel Carney, Badley, Smith & Spellman, Seattle, 1967—73; vis. prof. U. Stockholm, 1986, U. Bergen, 1989, Bond U., Australia, 1991. Author: (with Redden) The Mining Law of Turkey, 1956, The Petroleum Law of Turkey, 1956, (with Mucklestone and Cross) Community Property: General Considerations, 1971, (with Price and Treacy) 4th edit., 1994, (with Sullivan and others) Administration of Criminal Justice, 166, 2d edit., 1969, (with Miyatake and Way) Japanese International Taxation, 1983, supplements through 1997, (with Cross and Shields) Community Property Desk Book, 1989, supplement, 1997, (with Williams) Permanent Establishment, 1993. With USNR, 1945-46; capt. USAFR. Mem. ABA, Am. Coll. Trust and Estate Coun., Wash. State Bar Assn. (chmn. tax sect. 1984-85), King County bar Assn., Japanese Am. Soc. Legal Studies, Internat. Fiscal Assn. (past regional v.p., past mem. coun.). Office: 2200 Bank of America Tower 701 Fifth Ave Seattle WA 98104-7091 Fax: 206-525-1758. E-mail: huston@u.washington.edu

HUTCHENS, TYRA THORNTON, physician, educator; b. Newberg, Oreg., Nov. 29, 1921; s. Fred George and Bessie (Adams) H.; m. Betty Lou Gardner, June 7, 1942; children: Tyra Richard, Robert Jay, Rebecca (Mrs. Mark Pearsall). BS, U. Oreg., 1943, MD, 1945. Diplomate: Am. Bd. Pathology, Am. Bd. Nuclear Medicine. Intern Minn. Gen. Hosp., Mpls., 1945-46; AEC postdoctoral research fellow Reed Coll., Med. Sch. U. Oreg., 1948-50; NIH postdoctoral research fellow Med. Sch. U. Oreg., 1951-53; mem. faculty Oreg. Health Scis. U., 1953—, prof., chmn. dept. clin. pathology, 1962-87, prof. emeritus, 1987—, prof. radiotherapy, 1963-71, allied health edn. coordinator, 1969-77. Vis. lectr. radiobiology Reed Coll., 1955, 56 Mem. adv. bd. Oreg. Regional Med. Program, 1968-75; mem. statuatory radiation adv. com. Oreg. Bd. Health, 1957-69, chmn., 1967-69; founding trustee Am. Bd. Nuclear Medicine, 1971-77, 82-84, sec., 1973-75, 84-85 ; voting rep. Am. Bd. Med. Specialties, 1973-78, chmn. com. long range planning, 1976-78; mem. sci. adv. bd. Armed Forces Inst. Pathology, 1978-83; chmn. Portland Com. on Fgn. Affairs, 1990-91. Lt. (j.g.) M.C., USNR, 1946-48. Charter mem. Acad. Clin. Lab. Physicians and Scientists, Soc. Nuclear Medicine (de Hevesey Nuclear Medicine Pioneer award 1995), Am. Coll. Nuclear Physicians; mem. Oreg. Pathologists Assn. (pres. 1968), Pacific N.W. Soc. Nuclear Medicine (pres. 1958), AMA, Coll. Am. Pathologists (bd. govs. 1967-74, pres. 1977-79, chmn. commn. on internat. affairs 1979-83, chmn. planning com. 1987 World Congress Pathology), Am. Soc. Clin. Pathologists (bd. registry med. technologists 1967-71), World Assn. of Socs. of Pathology (bur. of pathology 1981-87, 89-93, v.p. 1985-87, pres. 1989-91, chmn. commn. on world stds. 1981-86, Gold Headed Cane award 1995), World Pathology Found. (pres. 1987-89, trustee 1989-91), Assn. Clin. Pathologists (hon.), Italian Soc. Lab. Medicine (hon.), Phi Beta Kappa, Sigma Xi, Alpha Omega Alpha. Achievements include research and publications on radioactive carbon tracer studies of lipid metabolism, clinical radioisotope techniques. Home: 15385 SW Petrel Ln Beaverton OR 97007-8182 Office: Oreg Health Scis U 3181 SW Sam Jackson Park Rd Portland OR 97201-3011 E-mail: tyrahutchens@msn.com

HUTCHESON, J(AMES) STERLING, lawyer; b. Nanking, China, Oct. 17, 1919; s. Allen Carrington and Strausie (McCaslin) H.; m. Marilyn Brown, Dec. 26, 1944; children— James Sterling, Holly Hutcheson Jasperson, Joanne Hutcheson Denton, Scott Brown, Allen McCaslin. B.A., Princeton U., 1941; LL.B., Stanford U., 1949. Bar: Calif. 1949, U.S. Dist. Ct. (no. dist.) Calif. 1949, U.S. Ct. Apls. (9th cir.) 1949, U.S. Dist. Ct. (so. dist.) Calif. 1950, U.S. Ct. Mil. Appeals 1955, Clk. jud. com. Calif. State Assembly, 1949; assoc., then ptnr. Gray, Cary, Ames & Frye, San Diego, 1950-93; ptnr. emeritus Gray, Cary Ware & Freidenrich, 1994—. Mem. San Diego City Traffic Commn.; bd. dirs. San Diego County Hosp. and Health Facility Planning Commn.; trustee Francis Parker Sch., San Diego, 1956-59, pres. bd., 1957-58; trustee La Jolla (Calif.) Country Day Sch., 1956-59. Served to comdr. USNR, 1941-45. Mem. Internat. Assn. Def. Counsel (state editor 1958, 61-63, 66-67, chmn. legal malpractice subcom. 1962, exec. com. 1976-79), State Bar Calif. (lectr. continuing edn. bar 1960, 63, mem. disciplinary bd. 1973-77, referee rev. bd. 1979-83, client security fund 1977-78), San Diego County Barristers, San Diego County Bar Assn. (sec. 1963-64, v.p. 1964-65, chmn. med. legal com. 1961-62), Am. Bd. Trial Advs., Assn. So. Calif. Def. Counsel (dir. 1974-76), Southwestern Legal Found. (lectr. 1963), Am. Coll. Trial Lawyers, Def. Research Inst. (regional v.p. Pacific 1971-74), Navy League, Phi Alpha Delta. Republican. Presbyterian. Club: Princeton of San Diego (pres. 1955-71). Home: 7784 Hillside Dr La Jolla CA 92037-3944 Office: Gray Cary Ware & Freidenrich 401 B St Ste 1700 San Diego CA 92101-4297

HUTCHESON, JERRY DEE, manufacturing company executive; b. Hammon, Okla., Oct. 31, 1932; s. Radford Andrew and Ethel Mae (Boulware) H.; B.S. in Physics, Eastern N. Mex. U., 1959; postgrad. Temple U., 1961-62, U. N.Mex., 1964-65; m. Lynda Lou Weber, Mar. 6, 1953; children— Gerald Dan, Lisa Marie, Vicki Lynn. Research engr. RCA, 1959-62; sect. head Motorola, 1962-63; research physicist Dikewood Corp., 1963-66; sr. mem. tech. staff Signetics Corp., 1966-69; engring. mgr. Litton Systems, Sunnyvale, Calif., 1969-70; engring. mgr. Fairchild Semiconductor, Mountain View, Calif., 1971; equipment engr., group mgr. Teledyne Semiconductor, Mountain View, 1971-74; dir. engring. DCA Reliability Labs., Sunnyvale, 1974-75; founder, prin. Tech. Ventures, San Jose, Calif., 1975— ; chief exec. officer VLSI Research, Inc., 1981— . Democratic precinct committeeman, Albuquerque, 1964-66. Served with USAF, 1951-55. Registered profl. engr., Calif. Mem. Nat. Soc. Profl. Engrs., Profl. Engrs. Pvt. Practice, Calif. Soc. Profl. Engrs., Semiconductor Equipment and Materials Inst., Soc. Photo-Optical Instrumentation Engrs., Am. Soc. Test Engrs., Presbyterian. Club: Masons. Contbr. articles to profl. jours. Home: 5950 Vista Loop San Jose CA 95124-6562 Office: VSLI Rsch 1754 Technology Dr Ste 117 San Jose CA 95110-1320

HUTCHESON, MARK ANDREW, lawyer; b. Phila., Mar. 29, 1942; s. John R. and Mary Helen (Willis) H.; m. Julie A. Olander, June 13, 1964; children: Kirsten Elizabeth, Mark Andrew II, Megan Ann. BA, U. Puget Sound, 1964; LLB, U. Wash., 1967. Bar: Wash. 1967, U.S. Dist. Ct. (we. and ea. dists.) Wash., U.S. Ct. Appeals (9th cir.), U.S. Supreme Ct. Staff counsel Com. on Commerce U.S. Senate, Washington, 1967-68; assoc. Davis Wright Tremaine, Seattle, 1968-72; ptnr. Davis, Wright Tremaine, Seattle, 1973—; mng. ptnr., chief exec. officer Davis Wright Tremaine, Seattle, 1989-94; chmn. Davis, Wright Tremaine, Seattle, 1994—. Mem., co-founder labor law com. Nat. Banking Industry, 1984—. Co-author: Employer's Guide to Strike Planning and Prevention, 1986; contbr. articles to profl. jours. Chmn., trustee Virginia Mason Hosp., Seattle, 1980—, Overlake Sch., Redmond, Wash., 1984-89, Epiphany Sch., Seattle, 1982-84, Legal Aid for Wash. Fund, 1991—; bd. dirs. Vis. Nurse Svcs., Seattle-King County, 1985-88; trustee Pacific N.W. Ballet, 1991-99, Pacific N.W. Assn. Ind. Schs., 1996-98. Nelson T. Hartson scholar U. Wash., 1966; Deerfield fellow Heritage Found., Deerfield, Mass., 1963. Mem. ABA (health care forum, employment law sect.), Seattle-King County Bar Assn. (employment law sect.), Am. Acad. Hosp. Attys., Am. Hosp. Assn. (labor rels. adv. com. 1978—), Coll. Labor and Employment Lawyers, Greater Seattle C. of C. (bd. dirs. 1991-94), Rainier Club, Seattle Tennis Club, Univ. Club, Order of Coif. Episcopalian. Avocations: sailing, tennis, skiing, reading, travel. Office: Davis Wright Tremaine 2600 Century Sq 1501 4th Ave Seattle WA 98101-1688 E-mail: markhutcheson@dwt.com

HUTCHINGS, JOHN BARRIE, astronomer, researcher; b. Johannesburg, Republic of South Africa, July 18, 1941; arrived in Can., 1967; BSc, Witwatersrand U., Johannesburg, 1962; MSc, Witwatersrand U., 1964; PhD, U. Cambridge, Eng., 1967. Rsch. scientist Dominion Astrophys. Obs., Nat. Rsch. Coun. Can., Victoria, B.C., 1967—. Author numerous rsch. papers and revs., 1964—. Recipient Gold medal Sci. Coun. B.C., 1983. Fellow Royal Soc. Can.; mem. Internat. Astron. Union, Am. Astron. Soc., Can. Astron. Soc. (Beals award 1982). Office: Dominion Astrophys Obs 5071 W Saanich Rd Victoria BC Canada V9E 2E7

HUTCHINSON, DONALD WILSON, state commissioner; b. Seattle, Dec. 29, 1936; BS in Bus. and Edn., Mont. State U., 1960; Grad. Degree in Banking, Pacific Coast Banking Sch., Seattle, 1979. With First Nat. Bank, Bozeman, Mont., 1963-69, Owatonna, Minn., 1969-71, First Security Bank, Livingston, Mont., 1971-82; v.p. Bank of Sheridan, 1983-84; gen. mgr., cons. Pryor Creek Devel. Co., Billings, 1984-85; chief lending officer Valley Bank of Belgrade, 1986-90; state commr. fin. institutions State of Mont. Divsn. Banking and Fin. Instns., Helena, 1990-2000. Dir. Livingston (Mont.) Meml. Hosp., Livingston Alcohol & Drug Abuse Ctr., Gallatin County (Mont.) Big Bros. and Big Sisters; mem. Belgrade City/County Planning Bd.; treas., bd. trustees, Paul Clark Home/McDonald's Family Place, Butte, Mont. Mem. Livingston Rotary Club (past pres.). Office: Divsn Banking & Fin Instns PO Box 200546 Helena MT 59620-0546

HUTCHISON, JAMES E. chemistry educator; Prof. dept. chemistry U. Oreg., Eugene. Chemistry grantee Camille and Henry Dreyfus Found., 1994. Office: U Oreg Dept Chemistry Eugene OR 97403

HUTTON, FIONA S. communications executive; Strategic planning coun. Gov. Pete Wilson, 1994-96; with Stoorza, Ziegaus and Metzger; v.p. corp. comm. Cadiz, Inc., Santa Monica, Calif. Mem. Pub. Rels. Soc. Am. Office: Cadiz Inc 100 Wilshire Blvd Ste 1600 Santa Monica CA 90401-1115

HUTTON, PAUL ANDREW, history educator, writer; b. Frankfurt, Germany, Oct. 23, 1949; naturalized citizen; s. Paul Andrew and Louise Katherine (Johnson) H.; m. Vicki Lynne Bauer, 1972 (div. 1985); 1 child, Laura; m. Lynn Terri Brittner, Dec. 31, 1988 (div. 1996); children: Lorena, Paul. BA, Ind. U., 1972, MA, 1974, PhD, 1981. Editorial asst. Jour. Am. History, Bloomington, Ind., 1973-77; instr. history Utah State U., Logan, 1977-80, asst. prof., 1980-84, U. N.Mex., Albuquerque, 1984-86, assoc. prof., 1986-96; prof. U. N. Mex., Albuquerque, 1996—. Author: Phil Sheridan and His Army, 1985; editor: Ten Days on the Plains, 1985, Soldiers West, 1987, The Custer Reader, 1992, (series) Eyewitness to the Civil War, 1991-93, Frontier and Region, 1997; assoc. editor Western Hist. Quar., 1977-84; editor N.Mex. Hist. Rev., 1985-91. Mem. Little Bighorn Battlefield Indian Meml. Adv. Com., Nat. Park Svc., 1994—. Recipient Evans Biography award Brigham Young U., 1986, Paladin award Mont. Hist. Soc., 1991, Western Heritage award Nat. Cowboy Hall of Fame, 1996, 99; named Mead Disting. Rsch. fellow Huntington Libr., 1988. Mem. Orgn. Am. Historians (Ray A. Billington award 1986), Western Hist. Assn. (exec. dir. 1990—), Soc. for Mil. History, Western Writers Am. (exec. bd. 1997-99, Spur award 1985, Pres. award 1998), Writers Guild Am. West. Office: U NMex Dept History Albuquerque NM 87131-0001 E-mail: wha@unm.edu

HUVANE, KEVIN, talent agent; Talent agt. Creative Artists Agy., Beverly Hills, Calif. Office: Creative Artists Agy 9830 Wilshire Blvd Beverly Hills CA 90212-1825

HUYER, ADRIANA, oceanographer, educator; b. Giessendam, The Netherlands, May 19, 1945; arrived in Can., 1950; came to U.S., 1975; d. Jacob Catharinus and Sophia (Van Loon) H.; m. Robert Lloyd Smith. BS, U. Toronto, 1967; MS, Oreg. State U., 1971, PhD, 1974. Scientific officer Marine Scis. Branch, Ottawa, Can., 1967-73; rsch. scientist Marine Environ. Data Svc., Ottawa, Can., 1974-75; rsch. assoc. Oreg. State U., Corvallis, 1975-76, rsch. asst. prof., 1976-79, asst. prof., 1979-80, assoc. prof., 1980-85, prof., 1985—. Vis. scientist Csiro Marine Labs, Hobart, Australia, 1988. Contbr. articles to profl. jours. Mem. AAAS, Am. Meterol. Soc., Am. Geophys. Union, Can. Meterol. and Oceanographic Soc., Am. Soc. Limnology and Oceanography. Office: Oreg State U Coll Oceanic Atmospher Scis 104 Ocean Adminstrn Bldg Corvallis OR 97331

HWANG, JOHN DZEN, information systems educator; b. Shanghai, China, Sept. 8, 1941; came to U.S., 1956; s. John Ding and Sylvia H.; m. Gloria Hoi-Hoon Lum, June 17, 1967; children: John Dar, Andrew Cherng, Audrey Ming. BSEE, U. Calif., Berkeley, 1964; MA, Oreg. State U., 1966, PhD, 1968. Ops. rschr. Army Weapons Command, Rock Island, Ill., 1970-71; program mgr. Army Air Mobility R&D Lab., Moffett Field, Calif., 1971-75; divsn. chief Def. Comm. Agy., Arlington, Va., 1975-82; assoc. dir. Fed. Emergency Mgmt. Agy., Washington, 1982-96; gen. mgr. Info. Tech. Agy. City of L.A., 1996-99; prof. dept. info. sys. Calif. State U., Long Beach, 1999—. Editor: Analytical Concepts of Command and Control, 1976. Capt. U.S. Army, 1968-70. Univ. fellow Dept. Def., Harvard Bus. Sch., Boston, 1981. Home: 2157 Moreno Dr Los Angeles CA 90039-3061 E-mail: jdhwang@csulb.edu

HYATT, JAMES ARMSTRONG, university administrator; b. Chilliwack, B.C., Can., May 28, 1949; s. Delbert Harold and Agnes (Barr) H.; m. Sandra Allard, May 23, 1981; children: Kathryn Barr, John Allard. BA, U. Wash., 1972, MBA, 1976. Mgmt. analyst Dept. Social and Health Svcs., Olympia, Wash., 1976-77; planning analyst U. Wash., Seattle, 1977-79; dir. fin. mgmt. ctr. Nat. Assn. Coll. and Univ. Bus. Officers, Washington, 1979-86, exec. v.p., 1986-87; asst. vice chancellor U. Md., College Park, 1987-91; assoc. chancellor U. Calif., Berkeley, 1991-98, vice chancellor, CFO, 1998—. Bd. dirs., mem. exec. com. Nat. Ctr. for Higher Edn. Mgmt. Sys., Bolder, Colo., 1984-86; cons. U. Mass., Amherst, 1982, Am. U., Washington, 1988-89, U. Md. Sys., College Park, 1994; primary rep. Coun. on Govtl. Rels., 1994—; mem. nat. higher edn. adv. panel Nat. Ctr. on Ednl. Stats., 1983-86; mem. nat. planning com. project to develop Integrated Post-Secondary Edn. Data Sys., U.S. Dept. Edn., 1983-86; mem. nat. task force econs. of rsch. librs. project Coun. on Libr. Resources, 1983-86. Author: Reallocation: Strategies for Effective Resource Management, 1984, University Libraries in Transition, 1986, Financial Management of Colleges and Universities, 1986, Presentation and Analysis of Financial Management Information, 1989. Avocations: writing, sketching, bicycling. Office: U Calif 200 California Hall Berkeley CA 94720-1500 E-mail: jahyatt@uclink4.berkeley.edu

HYBL, WILLIAM JOSEPH, lawyer, foundation executive; b. Des Moines, July 16, 1942; s. Joseph A. and Geraldine (Evans) H.; m. Kathleen Horrigan, June 6, 1967; children: William J. Jr., Kyle Horrigan. BA, Colo. Coll., 1964; JD, U. Colo., 1967. Bar: Colo. 1967. Asst. dist. atty. 4th Jud. Dist. El Paso and Teller Counties, 1970-72; pres., dir. Garden City Co., 1973—; dir. Broadmoor Hotel, Inc., 1973—, also vice-chmn., 1987—; chmn., CEO, trustee El Pomar Found., Colorado Springs, Colo., 1973—; pres. U.S. Olympic Com., 1991-92,96-2000. Vice chair USAA, San Antonio; dir. Kinder Morgan Inc., Houston, FirstBank Holding Co. of Colo., Lakewood; mem. Colo. Ho. Reps., 1972-73; spl. counsel The White House, Washington, 1981. Pres. Air Force Acad. Found.; sec., dir. Nat. Jr. Achievement; vice chmn. bd. U.S. Adv. Commn. on Pub. Diplomacy, 1990-97; civilian aide to sec. of army, 1986—. Capt. U.S. Army, 1967-69. Republican.

HYMAN, MILTON BERNARD, lawyer; b. L.A., Nov. 19, 1941; s. Herbert and Lillian (Rakowitz) Hyman; m. Sheila Goldman, July 4, 1965; children: Lauren Davida, Micah Howard. BA in Econs. with highest honors, UCLA, 1963; JD magna cum laude, Harvard U., 1966. Bar: Calif. 1967. Assoc. Irell & Manella LLP, L.A., 1970-73, ptnr., 1973—. Co-author: Partnerships and Associations: A Policy Critique of the Morrisey Regulations, 1976, Consolidated Returns: Summary of Tax Considerations in Acquisition of Common Parent of Subsidiary Member of Affiliated Group, 1980, Tax Aspects of Corporate Debt Exchanges, Recapitalization and Discharges, 1982, Tax Strategies for Leveraged Buyouts and Other Corporate Acquisitions, 1986, Preservation and Use of Net Operating Losses and Other Tax Attributes in a Consolidated Return Context, rev. edit., 1992, Collier on Bankruptcy Taxation, 1992, Real Estate Workouts and Bankruptcies, 1993, Current Corporate Bankruptcy Tax Issues, 1993, Tax Strategies for Corporate Acquisitions, Dispositions, Financing, Joint Ventures, Reorganizations, and Restructurings, 1995; author: A Transactional Encounter with the Partnership Rules of Subchapter K: The Effects of the Tax Reform Act of 1984, 1984, Net Operating Losses and Other Tax Attributed of Corporate Clients, 1987. Past pres., bd. dirs. Sinai Temple, West Los Angeles, Calif. Capt. JAGC, U.S. Army, 1967-70. Sheldon traveling fellow Harvard U., 1966-67. Mem. ABA (chmn. com. affiliated and related corps. 1981-83, chmn. corp. tax com. 1999-2000), Calif. State Bar Assn., Am. Law Inst. (fed. income tax project tax adv. group 1976—), Masons, Phi Beta Kappa. Jewish. Office: Irell & Manella LLP Ste 900 1800 Avenue Of The Stars Los Angeles CA 90067-4276

HYNE, JAMES BISSETT, chemistry educator, industrial scientist, consultant; b. Dundee, Scotland, Nov. 23, 1929; emigrated to Can., 1954, naturalized, 1969; s. William Simpson and Winifred Moore (Bissett) H.; m. Ada Leah Jacobson, Sept. 3, 1958. B.Sc., St. Andrews U., Scotland, 1951, Ph.D., 1954. Instr. Yale U., 1956-59; asst. prof. Dartmouth U., 1959-60; prof., head dept. chemistry U. Alta., Calgary, 1960-90, prof. emeritus, 1990—; dean grad. studies, prof. chemistry U. Calgary, 1966-89; pres. Hyjay R & D Ltd., Calgary, 1978—. Dir. rsch. Alta. Sulphur Rsch., Ltd., 1964-94; owenr HJ Ranches, 1963—; cons. oil, gas and sulphur/sulphur fertilizer industries in Can. U.S. and Gt. Britain; pres. Can. Assn. Grad.

Schs., 1969-70. Author articles on sulphur chemistry and tech. and sulphur in agr. Served with Can. Cameron Highlanders of Ottawa, 1954-58. Recipient Can. Centennial medal, 1967, R.S. Jane Meml. award for exceptional achievement in chem. engring. and indsl. chemistry, 1977, Queen Elizabeth II Jubilee medal, 1977, Alta. Achievement Excellence award, 1980, Bell Forum award for corp.-univ. cooperation in rsch., 1990; NRC fellow, 1954-56; Arthur B. Purvis Meml. lectr. Soc. Chem. Industry, 1991. Mem. Am. Chem. Soc., Chem. Soc., Chem. Inst. Can., Assn. Chem. Profession of Alta. (founding). Office: 312 Superior Ave SW Calgary AB Canada T3C 2J2 Fax: 403-229-2760

IACOCCA, LEE (LIDO ANTHONY IACOCCA), former automotive manufacturing executive, venture capitalist; b. Allentown, Pa., Oct. 15, 1924; s. Nicola and Antoinette (Perrotto) I.; m. Mary McCleary, Sept. 29, 1956 (dec.); m. Darrien Earle, March 30, 1991; children— Kathryn Lisa Hentz, Lia Antoinette Nagy. BS, Lehigh U., 1945; ME, Princeton U., 1946. With Ford Motor Co., Dearborn, Mich., 1946-78, successively mem. field sales staff, various merchandising and tng. activities, asst. dirs. sales mgr. Phila., dist. sales mgr. Washington, 1946-56, truck mktg. mgr. div. office, 1956-57, car mktg. mgr., 1957-60, vehicle market mgr., 1960, v.p.; gen. mgr. Ford Motor Co. (Ford div.), 1960-65, v.p. car and truck group, 1965-69, exec. v.p. of co., 1967-69, pres., 1970-78, Ford N.Am. automobile ops.; pres., chief operating officer Chrysler Corp., Highland Park, Mich., 1978-79, chmn. bd., chief exec. officer, 1979-93; prin. Iacocca Ptnrs., 1994—; pres. Iacoccca Assocs., L.A.; founder EV Global Motors. Bd. dirs. Chrysler Fin. Corp. Author: Iacocca: An Autobiography, 1984, Talking Straight, 1988. Past chmn. Statue of Liberty-Ellis Island Centennial Commn. Wallace Meml. fellow Princeton U. Mem. NAE, 1986—, Tau Beta Pi. Club: Detroit Athletic. Office: EV Global Motors 10900 Wilshire Blvd Ste 310 Los Angeles CA 90024-6533

IACONO, JAMES MICHAEL, research center administrator, nutrition educator; b. Chgo., Dec. 11, 1925; s. Joseph and Angelina (Cutaia) I.; children: Lynn, Joseph, Michael, Rosemary. BS, Loyola U., Chgo., 1950; MS, U. Ill., 1952, PhD, 1954. Chief Lipid Nutrition Lab. Nutrition Inst. Agrl. Rsch. Svc. USDA, Beltsville, Md., 1970-75, dep. asst. adminstr. nat. program Washington, 1975-77, assoc. adminstr. office human nutrition, 1978-82, dir. Western Human Nutrition Rsch. Ctr. San Francisco, 1982-94. Adj. prof. nutrition Sch. Pub. Health UCLA, 1987—. Author over 100 rsch./tech. publs. and chpts. in books relating to nutrition and biochemistry and lipids. With U.S. Army, 1944-46. Recipient Rsch. Career Devel. award NIH, 1964-70. Fellow Am Heart Assn. (coun. on arteriosclerosis and thrombosis), Am. Inst. Chemists; mem. Am. Inst. Nutrition, Am. Soc. Clin. Nutrition, Am. Oil Chemists Soc. E-mail: JIacono25@aol.com

IAMELE, RICHARD THOMAS, law librarian; b. Newark, Jan. 29, 1942; s. Armando Anthony and Evelyn Iamele; m. Marilyn Ann Berutto, Aug. 21, 1965; children: Thomas, Ann Marie. BA, Loyola U., L.A., 1963; MSLS, U. So. Calif., 1967; JD, Southwestern U., L.A., 1976. Bar: Calif. 1977. Cataloger U. So. Calif., L.A., 1967-71; asst. cataloger L.A. County Law Libr., 1971-77, asst. ref. libr., 1977-78, asst. libr., 1978-80, libr. dir., 1980—. Law librarian; b. Newark, Jan. 29, 1942; s. Armando Anthony and Evelyn Iamele; m. Marilyn Ann Berutto, Aug. 21, 1965; children: Thomas, Ann Marie. BA, Loyola U., L.A., 1963; MSLS, U. So. Calif., 1967; JD, Southwestern U., L.A., 1976. Bar: Calif. 1977. Cataloger U. So. Calif., L.A., 1967-71; asst. cataloger L.A. County Law Libr., 1971-77, asst. ref. libr., 1977-78, asst. libr., 1978-80, libr. dir., 1980—. Mem. ABA, Am. Assn. Law Librs., Calif. Libr. Assn., So. Calif. Assn. Law Librs., Coun. Calif. County Law Librs. (pres. 1981-82, 88-90). Office: LA County Law Libr 301 W 1st St Los Angeles CA 90012-3140 E-mail: richard@lalaw.lib.ca.us

IANNOLI, JOSEPH JOHN, JR. university development executive; b. Worcester, Mass., Oct. 28, 1939; s. Joseph John and Alice Bernadette (Moore) I.; m. Gail V. Cummings, Oct. 21, 1972; children: Juliet, Christopher. AB, Franklin and Marshall Coll., 1962; MA, Syracuse U., 1967. Devel. officer Franklin & Marshall Coll., Lancaster, Pa., 1965-68; assoc. dir. med. devel. U. Miami, 1968-70; adminstr. Children's Hearing and Speech Ctr., 1970-73; asst. dir., cons. Am. Bankers Assn., Washington, 1973-74, Marts & Lundy, Inc., N.Y.C., 1974-78; dir. capital support and planned giving U. Hartford, Conn., 1978-82; v.p. devel. Ripon (Wis.) Coll., 1982-90; chief devel. officer Am. Inst. Physics, Washington, 1990-92; pres., CEO M&I Advancement Group, Annapolis, Md., 1992-96; v.p. Mid-Atlantic region First Counsel, Inc., Annapolis, 1996-99; sr. counsel Nat. Cmty. Devel. Svcs., Inc., 1999—. Sr. cons. J.M. Lord & Assocs.; lectr. in field. Bd. dirs. Wau-Bun coun. Girl Scouts USA. Mem. Nat. Soc. Fund Raising Execs. (cert.), Coun. for Advancement and Support of Edn., Fund Raising Inst., Bushnell Meml. Steering Com., 1980-82, Ripon Area C. of C. (bd. dirs. 1985-89). Office: PO Box 62 Logan UT 84323

IAPALUCCI, SAMUEL H. financial executive; b. Cresson, Pa., July 19, 1952; s. Anthony F. and Dorthy (Quartz) I.; m. Berniece Reichert, June 5, 1976; children: Amanda Berniece, Cara Elizabeth. BS, St. Francis Coll., Loretto, Pa., 1974; MBA, Duquesne U., 1980. CPA, Pa. Audit sr. Coopers & Lybrand, Pitts., 1974-76; asst. v.p. Equibank, N.A., Pitts., 1976-78; with Allegheny Internat., Inc., Pitts., 1978-91, v.p., treas., 1987-90, v.p., CFO, 1990, cons., 1990-91; v.p., CFO OHM Corp., Findlay, Ohio, 1991—; CFO CH2M Hill Companies, Greenwood Village, CO, sr. v.p., CFO, sec. Mem. AICPA, Pa. Inst. CPAs, Fin. Execs. Inst., Findlay Country Club. Avocations: golf, tennis, reading. Office: CH2M Hill Companies 6060 South Willow Drive Englewood CO 80111

IBARRA, JOSE, city council; BA in Mexican-Am. studies, U. Ariz., 1994. Campaign mgr. Mayor George Miller, 1991; with Border Vol. Corps., 1991-94; aide County Supv. Raul Grijalva, 1994; city coun. Tucson, 1995—; vice-mayor Tucson. Office: 940 W Alameda St Tucson AZ 85745-2932

ICE, RICHARD EUGENE, retired minister, retirement housing company executive; b. Ft. Lewis, Wash., Sept. 25, 1930; s. Shirley and Nellie Rebecca (Pedersen) I.; m. Pearl Lucille Daniels, July 17, 1955 (dec. June 1992); children: Lorinda Susan, Diana Laurene, Julianne Adele. AA, Centralia Coll., 1950; BA, Linfield Coll., 1952, LHD (hon.), 1978; MA, Berkeley Bapt. Div. Sch., 1959, DD (hon.), 1995; grad. advanced mgmt. program, Harvard U., 1971. Ordained to ministry, Am. Bapt. Ch., 1954. Pastor Ridgecrest Cmty. Bapt. Ch., Seattle, 1955-59; dir. ch. extension Wash. Bapt. Conv., 1959-61; dir. loans Am. Bapt. Extension Corp., Valley Forge, Pa., 1961-64; assoc. exec. min. Am. Bapt. Chs. West, Oakland, Calif., 1964-67; dep. exec. sec., treas. Am. Bapt. Home Mission Socs., Valley Forge, 1967-72; pres. Am. Bapt. Homes of the West, Oakland, 1972-95, pres. emeritus, 1995—. Dir. Min.'s Life Ins. Co., Mpls., 1975-87, chmn. bd. dirs., 1986-87; bd. dirs. Bapt. Life Assn., Buffalo; pres. Am. Bapt. Homes and Hosps. Assn., 1978-81; v.p. Am. Bapt. Chs. U.S.A., 1990-91; mins. & missionaries Benefit Bd., 1982-89; mem. Bapt. Joint Com. Pub. Affairs; trustee Linfield Coll., 1972—, chmn. bd. trustees, 1994—; trustee Calif./Nev. Methodist Homes, Bacone Coll., 1968-77, Grad. Theol. Union, Berkeley, Calif., 1982—; trustee Am. Bapt. Sem. of West, Berkeley, 1975—, chmn. bd. trustees, 1987-95, exec. bd. adv. Sch. Econ. and Bus., St. Mary's Coll., Calif. Recipient Disting. Baconian award Bacone Coll., 1977, Disting. Alumnus award Centralia Coll., 19841, Meritorious Svc. award Am. Assn. Homes Aging, 1982, Merit citation Am. Bapt. Homes and Hosps. Assn., 1985, award of Honor Calif. Assn. Homes Aging, 1988. Mem. U.S. Assn. UN, Am. Assn. Homes and Svcs. Aging (award Honor 1994), Calif. Assn. Homes Aging, The Oakland 100, Harvard Club San Francisco, Pi Gamma Mu. Democrat. Office: Am Baptist Homes of West Stone Ridge Corp Plz V 6120 Stoneridge Mall Rd Pleasanton CA 94588-3296

ICE-T, (TRACY MARROW), rap singer, actor; b. Newark; m. Darlene Oritz; 1 child. Album: Rhyme Pays, 1987, The Iceberg/Freedom of Speech, Just Watch What You Say, 1989, O.G. Original Gangster, 1991, (with King Tee) Havin' a "T" Party, 1991, Body Count, 1992, Home Invasion, 1993, The Classic Collection, 1993, (with Body Count) Born Dead, 1994, 7th Deadly Sin, 1999; actor: Breakin', 1984, New Jack City, 1991, Ricochet, 1991, Trespass, 1992, Surviving the Game, 1994, Tank Girl, 1995, Johnny Mnemonic, 1995, Final Voyage, 1999, Corrupt, 1999, Leprechcun 5, 2000; author: The Ice Opinion, 1994. Office: Priority Records 6430 W Sunset Blvd Los Angeles CA 90028-7901

IDLE, ERIC, actor, screenwriter, producer, songwriter; b. South Shields, Eng., Mar. 29, 1943; Pres. The Cambridge Footlights, 1964-65. TV shows include The Frost Report, Monty Python's Flying Circus, 1969-74, Rutland Weekend TV, 1975, Suddenly Susan, 1999-2000; films include And Now For Something Completely Different, 1971, Monty Python and the Holy Grail, 1975, The Rutles, 1978, Monty Python's Life of Brian, 1979, Monty Python Live at the Hollywood Bowl, 1982, Monty Python's The Meaning of Life, 1983, Yellowbeard, 1983, National Lampoon's European Vacation, 1985, Transformers: The Movie, 1986, The Adventures of Baron Munchausen, 1988, Nuns on the Run, 1990, Too Much Sun, 1991, Mom and Dad Save the World, 1993, Splitting Heirs, 1993, Casper, 1995, The Wind in the Willows, 1996, Burn Hollywood Burn, 1998, Dudley Do-Right, 1999, South Park: Bigger, Longer and Uncut (voice), 1999. Office: Grant & Tani Inc 9100 Wilshire Blvd Ste 1000 Beverly Hills CA 90212-3415 also: William Morris 151 S El Camino Dr Beverly Hills CA 90212-2704

IERARDI, STEPHEN JOHN, physician; b. Honolulu, July 5, 1960; s. Ernest John and Robert Ann (Hackett) I.; m. Erica Ewing, May 28, 1989; children: Daphne Alexandra, Weston Eric. BA in Biology, Williams Coll., 1982; MD, U. Rochester, 1986. Diplomate Am. Bd. Family Physicians. Intern U. Calif. at Irvine Med. Ctr., Orange, 1986-87, resident, 1987-89, chief resident, 1988-89; physician Laguna Hills, Calif., 1989—; med. dir. Lake Forest Nursing Ctr., 1993-96. Chief of medicine Saddleback Meml. Med. Ctr., Laguna Hills, 1996, chmn. family practice, 1994-96. Recipient UCI Care awards Univ. Calif. at Irvine Med. Ctr., 1986-89. Fellow Am. Acad. Family Physicians, AMA (Physician Recognition award 1996); mem. Am. Acad. Family Physicians, Calif. Acad. Family Physicians. Avocations: surfing, sailing, windsurfing, skiing, travel. Home: 13 Pacifico Laguna Niguel CA 92677-4242 Office: Saddleback Family Medicine 24411 Health Center Dr Laguna Hills CA 92653-3633

IGE, DAVID Y. state legislator; b. Jan. 15, 1957; m. Dawn Ige; children: Lauren, Amy, Matthew. BSEE, U. Hawaii, 1979, MBA in Decision Scis., 1985. Sr. adminstr. Hawaiian Telephone Co.; electronics engr., analyst Pacific Analyst Corp.; mem. Hawaii Ho. of Reps., Honolulu, 1986-93, Hawaii Senate, Dist. 17, Honolulu, 1994—; chair edn. and tech. com., mem. ways and means com. Hawaii Senate, Honolulu, mem. transp. and intergovtl. affairs com. Mem. Pearl City Cmty. Assn., Newtown Estates Cmty. Assn. Mem. IEEE. Democrat. Office: State Capitol 415 S Beretania St Honolulu HI 96813-2407

IGE, MARSHALL, state legislator; b. Honolulu, Sept. 10, 1954; Student, Windward C.C., Kaneohe, 1974; B in Edn., U. Hawaii, Manoa, 1978. Mem. Hawaii Ho. of Reps., Honolulu, 1978-96, asst. majority floor leader, chair youth and elderly affairs com., 1982, vice spkr. of house, liaison to spkr., mem. house fin. com., 1984, asst. majority floor leader, 1986, 88, 90; mem. Hawaii Senate, Honolulu, 1996—, co-chair com. on govt. ops. and housing, 1996, mem. ways and means com., mem. edn. com., 1996, vice chair com. on labor and environ., 1998, mem. econ. devel. com., mem. ways and means com., 1998. Office: State Capitol 415 S Beretania St Honolulu HI 96813-2407

IGLESIAS, JULIO (JULIO JOSE IGLESIAS DE LA CUEVA), singer, songwriter; b. Madrid, Sept. 23, 1943; s. Julio Iglesias Puga and Maria del Rosario de la Cueva (Perignat) I.; m. Isabel Preisler, Jan. 20, 1971 (div.); children: Julio Jose, Enrique, Chaveli. Profl. singer, songwriter, 1968—. Ltd. ptnr. Miami Heat Basketball Team. Participant internat. music festivals including: Benidorm Song Festival, Spain; Vina del Mar Festival, Chile; Eurovision Festival, The Netherlands; songs written include: La Vida sigue igual, 1968, No llores, Mi amor, Yo Canto, Lagrimas tienc al camino, Alguien en algun lugar, Guendoline; albums include: Como el Alamo al camino, 1972, Julio Iglesias, 1972, Soy, 1973, A Mexico, 1975, El Amor, 1975, America, 1976, A mis 33 anos, 1977, Emociones, 1978, De nina a mujer, 1981, Hoy, 1980, El Disco de Oro, 1981, Momentos, 1982, 1100 Bel Air Place, 1984, Un Hombre Solo, 1987, Nonstop, 1988, Starry Night, 1990, (with Dolly Parton) Crazy, 1994, Tango, 1996, My Life: The Greatest Hits, 1998, Noche de Cuatro Lunas, 2000; Author: (autobiography) Entre el cielo y el infierno, 1981; has sold more than 100 million albums. Rep. to UNICEF in performing arts. Recipient Medaille de Vermeil de la Ville de Paris, 1983, Diamond Disc award Guiness Book of World Records, 1983, Grammy award for best Latin pop performance, 1987 Office: c/o Rogers & Cowan 1888 Century Park E Ste 500 Los Angeles CA 90067-1709 also: Columbia Records 550 Madison Ave New York NY 10022-3211

IGNARRO, LOUIS J. pharmacology educator; b. Bklyn., May 31, 1941; BA in Pharmacy, Columbia U., 1962; PhD in Pharmacology, U. Minn., 1966. Prof. dept. molecular and med. pharmacology UCLA Sch. Medicine. Contbr. articles to profl. jours. Postdoctoral fellow NIH, 1966-68; recipient Rsch. Career Devel. award USPHS, 1975-80, Nobel prize in Medicine, 1998. Mem. NAS, Alpha Omega Alpha (hon.). Achievements include research in the biochemical, physiological, and pathophysioilogical roles of nitric oxide and cyclic GMP in mammalian cell function; the transcriptional, translational and catalytic regulation of constitutive and inducible nitric oxide synthases; the role of other biochemical pathways in the regulation of biosynthesis and metabolism of nitric oxide; the biochemical and chemical mechanisms by which nitric oxide elicits cytotoxic effects on invading target cells and microorganisms; the role of nitric oxide as a neurotransmitter in non-adrenergic non-cholinergic neurons innervating various issues. Office: UCLA Sch Medicine Dept Molecular & Med Pharmacology 23-315 Chs 10833 Leconte Ave Los Angeles CA 90095-0001

IHARA, LES, JR. state legislator; b. Honolulu, Apr. 19, 1951; BA in Liberal Studies, U. Hawaii. Comms. dir. cmty. devel. orgn.; mem. Hawaii Ho. of Reps., 1986-94, Hawaii Senate, Dist. 10, 1994—; mem. judiciary com., commerce and consumer protection com. Hawaii Senate; mem. labor and environment com. Hawaii State Senate. Chmn. Oahu Dem. Party, 1982-84, 90-94; del. Hawaii State Constl. Conv., 1978; mem. Ala Wai Moiliili McCully Neighbors; mem. Ala Wai Watershed Cmty. Network, Conv. Ctr. Cmty. Network, Waikiki Mgrs. Against Crime, Waikiki Residents Assn. Mem. Kaimuki Bus. and Profl. Assn., Kapahulu Bus. Assn., Kaimuki Lions Club. Democrat. Office: Hawaii State Capitol 415 S Beretania St Rm 214 Honolulu HI 96813-2407

IHRIG, JUDSON LA MOURE, chemist; b. Santa Maria, Calif., Nov. 5, 1925; s. Harry Karl and Luella (LaMoure) I.; m. Gwendolyn Adele Montz, July 22, 1950; children— Kristin, Neil Marshall. B.S., Haverford Coll., 1949; M.A., Princeton U., 1951, Ph.D., 1952. Asst. prof. chemistry U. Hawaii, 1952-58, assoc. prof., 1958-72, prof., 1972-94, dir. honors program, 1958-64, 87-95, dir. liberal studies program, 1973-79, chmn. chemistry dept., 1981-86; prof. emeritus, 1994—. Cons. chemistry local firms. Author publs. in field. Served with AUS, 1945-46. Mem. Am. Chem. Soc., Phi Beta Kappa, Sigma Xi. Home: 386 Wailupe Cir Honolulu HI 96821-1525 Office: U Hawaii 2545 The Mall Honolulu HI 96822-2233

IKEDA, CLYDE JUNICHI, plastic and reconstructive surgeon; b. Kobe, Japan, 1951; s. Paul Tamotsu and Kazu Ikeda. BA, SUNY, Binghamton, 1973; MD, N.Y. Med. Coll., Valhalla, 1979. Resident Vincent Hosp., N.Y.C., 1979-83, Francis Meml. Hosp., San Francisco, 1983-86; med. dir. Burn Ctr. St. Francis Meml. Hosp., San Francisco, 1992—, med. examiner, 1993—, med. dir. Wound Healing Ctr., 1994—. Asst. clin. prof. plastic surgery U. Calif., San Francisco, 1998—. Fellow Am. Coll. Surgeons. Office: 1199 Bush St Ste 640 San Francisco CA 94109-5977

ILETT, FRANK, JR. trucking company executive, educator; b. Ontario, Oreg., June 21, 1940; s. Frank Kent and Lela Alice (Siver) I.; m. Donna L. Andlovec, Apr. 3, 1971; children: James Frank, Jordan Lee. BA, U. Wash., 1962; MBA, U. Chgo., 1969. CPA, Idaho, Ill., Wash. Acct. Ernst & Young, Boise, Cleve., Spokane, 1962-69, mgr. Boise, 1970-72, regional mgr. San Francisco, 1972-73; treas. Interstate Mack, Inc., Boise, 1973-81, pres., CEO, 1981-82; pres. Interstate NationLease, Inc., Boise, 1975-81, Contract Carriers, Inc., Boise, 1983-89, Ilett Transp. Co., Boise, 1985-90; chmn. Carriers/West, Inc., Salem, Oreg., 1986-89; CFO, White GMC Trucks, 1988-92; v.p., CFO, May Trucking Co., Payette, Idaho, 1992-94; acct., mng. ptnr. Frank Ilett, Jr., CPA, Boise, 1994—. Spl. lectr. Boise State U., 1964-67, 94—, St. Mary's Grad. Sch., Moraga, Calif., 1989-92 ; v.p. I.D.E.A.L., Inc., Nampa, Idaho, 1997—; cons. Calif. Hosp. Commn., 1973, Idaho Hosp. Assn., 1974; chmn. Mack Truck Western Region Distbr. Coun., 1979-82; mem. nat. distbr. adv. com. Mack Trucks, Inc., 1980-82; dir. stds. enforcement Idaho State Bd. Accountancy, 1983-84. Contbr. articles to profl. jours. Named Arthur Andersen Outstanding Acctg. Prof., 1996, 2001. Mem. AICPA, Gen. Soc. Mayflower Descs., SAR, Crane Creek Country Club, Masons, Shriners, Alpha Kappa Psi (Outstanding Bus. Prof. award 1997). Episcopalian. Home: 1701 Harrison Blvd Boise ID 83702-1015 Office: 1910 University Dr Boise ID 83725 E-mail: ilett@micron.net

ILIFF, WARREN JOLIDON, zoo administrator; b. Madison, Wis., Nov. 5, 1936; s. Warren Jolidon and Wilma Marie (Lowenstein) I.; m. Ghislaine de Brouchoven de Bergeyck, Feb. 13, 1970. A.B., Harvard U., 1958. Helicopter pilot, crop duster, Central Am., 1962-66; dir. planning Air Transport Assn., Washington, 1966-67; spl. asst. to dir. Nat. Zoo, Washington, 1967-71; exec. dir. Friends of Nat. Zoo, 1971-73; asst. dir. Nat. Zoo, 1973-75; dir. Washington Park Zoo, Portland, Oreg., 1975-84, Dallas Zoo, 1984-91, Phoenix Zoo, 1991; pres., chief exec. ofcr. Long Beach Aquarium of the Pacific, Long Beach, Calif. Bd. dirs. Wildlife Preservation Trust Internat., 1985— , Jane Goodall Inst., 1985—. Served with USMC, 1958-62. Mem. Am. Assn. Zool. Parks and Aquariums (past pres.), Internat. Union Dirs. Zool. Gardens. Office: Long Beach Aquarium of the Pacific Admin Ofc 310 Golden Shore St Ste 300 Long Beach CA 90802-4240

ILLSTON, SUSAN Y. judge; b. 1948; BA, Duke U., 1970; JD, Stanford U., 1973. Ptnr. Cotchett, Illston & Pitre, San Francisco, 1973-95; judge U.S. Dist. Ct. (no. dist.) Calif., San Francisco, 1995—. Author: Insurance Coverage in a Toxic Tort Case, A Guide to Toxic Torts, 1987, California Complex Litigation Manual, 1990. Active Legal Aid Soc. San Mateo County, Svc. League San Mateo County. Recipient Appreciation for Vol. Svcs. cert. No. Dist. Calif. Fed. Practice Program, 1989, Svc. and Appreciation cert. 1992. Mem. ABA, ATLA, Assn. Bus. Trial Lawyers, San Mateo County Bar Assn. (Eleanor Falvey award 1994), State Bar Calif. (mem. jud. coun., mem. ethics com. 1975-79, mem. com. on women in law 1985-87, mem. jud. nominees evaluation commn. 1988, mem. exec. com. on litigation 1990-93), Calif. Women Lawyers, Calif. Trial Lawyers Assn., Trial Lawyers for Pub. Justice. Office: US Dist Ct No Dist Calif PO Box 36060 450 Golden Gate Ave San Francisco CA 94102-3661

IMBER, RICHARD JOSEPH, physician, dermatologist; b. Darby, Pa., Apr. 9, 1944; s. Joseph and Geraldine (Frances) I.; m. Helen Lee Stick, Nov. 18, 1971. BS, U. Dayton, 1966; MD, Temple U., 1970. Diplomate Am. Bd. Dermatology. Intern Denver Presbyn. Med. Ctr., 1970-71; resident dept. dermatology U. Colo. Health Sci. Ctr., 1971 74; chief of dermatology USAF Acad., Colorado Springs, 1974-76; sr. staff dermatologist Colo. Permanente Med. Group, Denver, 1976-83; dermatologist Denver Skin Clinic, 1983—. Asst. clin. prof. dermatology U. Colo. Med. Sch., Denver, 1974—. Contbr. articles to profl. jours. Maj. USAF, 1974 76. Fellow Am. Acad. Dermatology; mem. Pacific Dermatologic Assn., Colo. Med. Soc., Denver Med. Soc., Colo. Dermatologic Soc. (sec.-treas. 1980, v.p. 1981, pres. 1982). Avocation: scuba diving. Home: 4020 S Bellaire St Englewood CO 80110-5028 Office: Denver Skin Clinic 2200 E 18th Ave Denver CO 80206-1205

IMBROGNO, CYNTHIA, magistrate judge; b. 1948; BA, Indiana U. Pa., 1970; JD cum laude, Gonzaga U., 1979. Law clk. to Hon. Justin L. Quackenbush U.S. Dist. Ct. (Wash. ea. dist.), 9th circuit, 1980-83; law clk. Wash. State Ct. of Appeals, 1984; civil rights staff atty. Ea. Dist. of Wash., 1984-85, complex litigation staff atty., 1986-88; with Preston, Thorgrimson, Shidler, Gates & Ellis, 1988-90, Perkins Coie, 1990-91; magistrate judge U.S. Dist. Ct. (Wash. ea. dist.), 9th circuit, Spokane, 1991—. Office: 740 US Courthouse 920 W Riverside Ave Spokane WA 99201-1010

IMHOFF, WALTER FRANCIS, investment banker; b. Denver, Aug. 7, 1931; s. Walter Peter and Frances Marie (Barkhausen) I.; m. Georgia Ruth Stewart, June 16, 1973; children: Stacy, Randy, Theresa, Michael, Robert. BSBA, Regis U., Denver, 1955; D Pub. Svc. (hon.), Regis U., 1991. Asst. v.p. Coughlin & Co., Denver, 1955-60; pres., chief exec. officer Hanifen, Imhoff Inc., Denver, 1960-2000; mng. dir. Stifel, Nicolaus & Co., 2000—. Guest lectr. U. Colo., 1976 Trustee Regis Coll., 1975-95, treas., 1976-79, vice chmn., 1981, chmn., 1982-89, life trustee, 1998—; bd. dirs. NCCJ, 1980-89, chmn. 1986-89, life trustee 1998—; bd. dirs. Arapahoe Libr. Found., 1990-94, Channel 6 Ednl. TV, treas. 1996-97, vice chmn., 1997-98, chmn., 1998-99; bd. dirs. Highland Hills Found., 1993—; bd. dirs. Denver Area coun. Boy Scouts Am., 1986—, v.p., 1989—; bd. dirs. St. Joseph's Hosp., mem. exec. com., 1991, vice chmn., 1994, chmn., 1995-98; bd. dirs. Kempe Children's Found., 1992, chmn., 1994-97; bd. dirs. 9 Who Cares, 1998—, Caring for Colo., 2001—; chmn. Colo. Concern, 1988—, St. Joseph Hosp. Found., 2000—; mem. exec. com. 2% Club, 2000—; trustee Irish Cmty. Ctr., 2001. Named Outstanding Alumnus Regis Coll., 1970 Mem. Bond Club Denver (pres. 1965), Colo. Mcpl. Bond Dealers Assn. (pres. 1973), Mid-Continent Securities Industry Assn. (dir. 1972-75), Securities Industry Assn. (chmn. S.W. region 1991-95, dir. 1993-96), Nat. Assn. Security Dealers, Pub. Securities Assn. (dir. 1972-75), Denver C. of C. (bd. dirs. 1986-91, treas. 1989-91), Rose Hosp. Found., Centennial C. of C. (vice chmn.), NAACP, Alpha Kappa Psi, Alpha Sigma Nu. Republican. Roman Catholic. Club: Denver (pres. 1981-82). Home: 10432 E Ida Pl Greenwood Village CO 80111-3753 Office: 1125 17th St Ste 1600 Denver CO 80202-2024

IMLE, JOHN F., JR. oil company executive; b. San Antonio; Degrees in mech. and petroleum engring., Tex. A&M, 1963. Registered petroleum engr., Calif. and Alaska. Engr. trainee Unocal, Houston, 1963-65, various positions Alaska, 1968-72, with divsn. internat. oil and gas West Africa and N. Sea, 1972-77, project mgr. Heather field Eng., 1974, dist. mgr. ops. Scotland, 1977, resident mgr. Netherland's ops., 1980, pres. internat. divsn.

internat. oil and gas, 1983, sr. v.p. energy resources, 1988; also bd. dirs. Unocal Corp., exec. v.p. energy resources, 1992, pres., 1994—; asst. Nev. Beech. Served mil., 1965-68. Mem. Am. Assn., Petroleum Geologists, Independent Petroleum Assn., Soc. Petroleum Engrs. Office: Unocal Corp 2141 Rosecrans Ave Ste 4000 El Segundo CA 90245-4746

IMWINKELRIED, EDWARD JOHN, law educator; b. San Francisco, Sept. 19, 1946; s. John Joseph and Enes Rose (Gianelli) I.; m. Cynthia Marie Clark, Dec. 30, 1978; children— Marie Elise, Kenneth West B.A., U. San Francisco, 1967, J.D., 1969. Bar: Calif. 1970, Mo. 1984, U.S. Supreme Ct. 1974. Prof. law U. San Diego, 1974-79; prof. law Washington U., St. Louis, 1979-85, U. Calif.-Davis, 1985—. Disting. faculty mem. Nat. Coll. Dist. Attys., Houston, 1978— Author: Evidentiary Foundations, 1980, 4th rev. edit., 1998, Uncharged Misconduct Evidence, 1984, rev. edit., 1999; co-author: McCormick, Evidence, 5th edit., 1999, Materials for Study of Evidence, 1983, 4th edit., 1997, Scientific Evidence, 1986, 3d edit., 1999, Pretrial Discovery: Strategy and Tactics, 1986, Courtroom Criminal Evidence, 1987, 3d edit., 1998, California Evidentiary Foundations, 1988, 3d edit., 2000, Dynamics of Trial Practice, 1989, 2d edit., 1995, Exculpatory Evidence, 1990, 2d edit., 1996, Florida Evidentiary Foundations, 1991, 2d edit., 1997, Illinois Evidentiary Foundations, 1991, 2d edit., 1997, Texas Evidentiary Foundations, 1992, 2d edit., 1998, New York Evidentiary Foundations, 1993, 2d edit., 1997, Evidentiary Distinctions, 1993, Colorado Evidentiary Foundations, 1997; contbg. editor Champion pub. Assn. Criminal Def. Lawyers, 1983, Courtroom Law Bull. Mem. Am. Acad. Forensic Sci., ABA (continuing edn. com. 1983-84), Am. Assn. Law Schs. (chmn. evidence sect. 1983) Democrat. Roman Catholic Avocation: jogging. Home: 2204 Shenandoah Pl Davis CA 95616-6603 Office: U Calif Law Sch Davis CA 95616

INA, KYOKO, professional figure skater; b. Tokyo, Oct. 11, 1972; Competitive history includes placing 11th at Nat. Sr., 1997, 4th, 1995, 1st place Ea. Sr., 1995, 2d place World Univ. Games, 1993, 10th place Nat. Sr., 1993, 1st place North Atlantic Sr., 1993, others; winner Nat. Jr. Title, Japan, 1987; three-time Silver medallist in skating pairs with ptnr. Jason Dungjen. 2 time Nat. Pairs Champion. Avocations: horseback riding, tennis, car racing. Office: 20 1st St Colorado Springs CO 80906-3624

INAN, UMRAN SAVAS, electrical engineering educator, researcher; b. Erzincan, Turkey, Dec. 28, 1950; came to U.S., 1973; s. Mustafa and Ayse Hayriye (Basgoze) I.; m. Elif Basgoze, Sept. 3, 1973; children: Ayse, Ali. BSEE, Mid. East Tech. U., Ankara, Turkey, 1972, MSEE, 1973; PhD in Elec. Engring., Stanford, 1977. Rsch. affiliate Stanford (Calif.) U. Elec. Engring. Dept., 1977-78, acting asst. prof., 1978-80, 81-82, asst. prof., 1982-85, assoc. prof., 1985-91, prof., 1991—; acting asst. prof. Bogazici U. Elec. Engring. Dept., Istanbul, Turkey, 1980-81. Cons. Lockheed Palo Alto (Calif.) Rsch. Lab., 1989—. Contbr. over 95 articles to profl. jours. Mem. IEEE, Internat. Union Radio Sci., Am. Geophys. Union, The Electromagnetics Soc., Sigma Xi. Achievements include development of the first quantitative model of energetic electron precipitation induced by electromagnetic waves from lightning; discovery of ionospheric heating and ionization by lightning radiation; research includes ionospheric effects of lightning discharges, remote sensing, wave particle interaction. Home: 935 Mears Ct Palo Alto CA 94305-1041 Office: Star Lab Elec Engring Dept Packard Bldg # 355 Stanford CA 94305-9515

INCAUDO, JOSEPH AUGUST, engineering company executive; b. 1940; MA, UCLA, 1961; MBA, Harvard U., 1964. CPA, Calif. Cons., auditor Touche Ross & Co., L.A., 1964-68; contr. Bullocks, L.A., 1969-76; v.p. ops. May Co., L.A., 1976-78; v.p. fin. Tobias Kotzin Corp., L.A., 1978-80; v.p., CFO Vinnell Corp., Alhambra, Calif., 1980-83; exec. v.p., CFO Aecom Tech. Corp., L.A., 1983—. Bd. dirs. Resource Scis. of Arabia Ltd., Inst. of Social and Econ. Policy in the Middle East, John F. Kennedy Sch. Govt., Harvard U. Office: Aecom Tech Corp 3250 Wilshire Blvd Los Angeles CA 90010

INDIEK, VICTOR HENRY, finance corporation executive; b. Spearville, Kans., Nov. 15, 1937; s. Ben W. and Helen Ann (Schreck) I.; m. Marlene Gould, June 2, 1962; children: Kathy, Kevin. Student, U. Nebr., 1955-57; BS in Bus., U. Kans., 1959. CPA, Kans. Audit mgr. Arthur Andersen & Co., Kansas City, Mo., 1961-70; pres., chief exec. officer Fed. Home Loan Mortgage Corp., Washington, 1970-77; pres., dir. Builders Capital Corp., Los Angeles, 1977-84; chief fin. officer, exec. v.p. Fin. Corp. of Am., Irvine, Calif., 1984-88; pres., chief exec. officer FarWest Savs. and Loan Assn., Newport Beach, 1988—; with Kennedy Wilson, 1989-98; pvt. practice in real estate, 1998—. V.p. and pres. regional Assn. Small Businesses Investment Cos., 1979-81, bd. govs. nat. assn., 1982. Mem. Selective Service Bd., Santa Monica, Calif., 1978; capt. United Fund, Kansas City, 1968. Served with USN, 1959-61. Republican. Roman Catholic. Avocations: boating, skiing. Office: 50 Hillsdale Dr Newport Beach CA 92660-4234

INFANTE, EDWARD A. federal judge; b. 1940; AB, Boston Coll., 1962; JD, Boston U., 1965. Law clk. to Hon. Edward McEntree 1st cir. U.S. Ct. Appeals; fed. pub. defender so. dist. U.S. Dist. Ct. Calif., 1970; bus. litigation and white collar criminal def. Pedersen, Flowers & Infante, San Diego, 1971-72; ptnr. bus. litigation Schall, Boudreau & Gore, San Diego, 1986-88; apptd. magistrate judge no. dist. U.S. Dist. Ct. Calif., 1990. Adj. prof. Santa Clara U. Sch. Law, 1990—. With USN, 1966-69, USNR, 1980-90. Mem. Nat. Magistrate Judges Assn. (treas. 1979, v.p. 1980, pres. 1981). Office: 4198 US Courthouse 280 S 1st St San Jose CA 95113-3002

INGALLS, ROBERT LYNN, physicist, educator; b. Spokane, Wash., June 15, 1934; s. Keith Irving and Ruth Louise (Strauss) I.; m. Liisa Vasama, Jan. 28, 1961 (div. Apr. 1993); children: Karen Liisa, Johanna Louise, David Robert. B.S., U. Wash., 1956; M.S., Carnegie Inst. Tech., 1960, Ph.D., 1962. Instr. physics Carnegie Inst. Tech., 1961-63; research asso. U. Ill., 1963-65, research asso. prof., 1965-66; asst. prof. U. Wash., Seattle, 1966-69, asso. prof., 1969-74, prof. physics, 1974-2000, prof. emeritus, 2001—. Vis. scholar State U. Groningen, Netherlands, 1972-73 Bassoonist, Seattle Symphony Orch., 1952-57; contbr. articles on solid state and high pressure physics, Mossbauer effect X-ray absorption and quasicrystal tilings to profl. jours., books and encys.; pioneer in electric quadruple splitting theory in ferrous compounds, X-ray absorption fine structure studies of materials at high pressure. AEC contract, 1967-77; NSF grantee, 1976-83; Dept. Energy grantee, 1983— Mem. AAAS, Am. Phys. Soc., Fedn. Am. Scientists, Sigma Xi, Sigma Phi Epsilon, Zeta Mu Tau. Office: U Wash Dept Physics Seattle WA 98195-0001 E-mail: ingalls@phys.washington.edu

INGELS, MARTY, theatrical agent, television and motion picture production executive; b. Bklyn., Mar. 9, 1936; s. Jacob and Minnie (Crown) Ingerman; m. Jean Maire Frassinelli, Aug. 3, 1960 (div. 1969); m. Shirley Jones, 1977. Ed., Erasmus High Sch., 1951-53, Forest Hills High Sch., 1953-55. Founder Ingels Inc., 1975—; formed Stoneypoint Prodns., 1981; TV and motion picture producer U.S. and abroad. Star: Dickens and Fenster series, ABC-TV, 1964; co-star: Pruitts of Southampton, 1968-69; films include Armored Command, 1962, Horizontal Lieutenant, 1965, Busy Body, 1967, Ladies Man, 1966, If It's Tuesday This Must Be Belgium, 1970, Wild and Wonderful, 1965, Guide for a Married Man, 1968; numerous TV appearances. Active various charity drives. Achievements include Owning the world's largest celebrity brokerage service, 1974; widely noted as the Henry Kissinger of Madison Avenue. Office: 701 N Oakhurst Dr Ste 1 Beverly Hills CA 90210-3532

INGERSOLL, ANDREW PERRY, planetary science educator; b. Chgo., Jan. 2, 1940; s. Jeremiah Crary and Minneola (Perry) I.; m. Sarah Morin, Aug. 27, 1961; children: Jeremiah, Ruth Ingersoll Wood, Marion Ingersoll Quinones, Minneola, George. BA, Amherst Coll., 1960; PhD, Harvard U., 1965. Rsch. fellow Harvard U., Cambridge, Mass., 1965-66; asst. prof. planetary sci. Calif. Inst. Tech., Pasadena, 1966-71, assoc. prof., 1971-76, prof., 1976—. Mem. staff summer study program Woods Hole (Mass.) Oceanopgraphic Inst., 1965, 70-73, 76, 80, 92; prin. investigator Pioneer Saturn Infrared Radiometer Team, NASA; mem. Voyager Imaging Team, NASA, Cassini Imaging Team, interdisciplinary scientist, Mars Global Surveyor Project, Galileo Project, NASA. Bd. trustees Poly. Sch., Pasadena. Fellow AAAS, Am. Geophys. Union, Am. Acad. Arts and Scis.; mem. Am. Astron. Soc. (vice-chmn. div. planetary sci. 1988-89, chmn. 1989-90). Office: Calif Inst Tech Dept Planetary Sci 150 21 Pasadena CA 91125-0001

INGLE, CRESS STUART, state legislator; b. Clovis, N.Mex., Dec. 27, 1947; BS, Okla. State U. Mem. N.Mex. Senate, Dist. 27, Santa Fe, 1984—; chair Rep. caucus N.Mex. Senate, Santa Fe, mem. fin. com., mem. pub. affairs com. Republican. Office: Minority Whip 2106 W University Dr Portales NM 88130-9352

INGLE, JAMES CHESNEY, JR. geology educator; b. Los Angeles, Nov. 6, 1935; s. James Chesney and Florence Adelaide (Geldart) I.; m. Fredricka Ann Bornholdt, June 14, 1958; 1 child, Douglas James B.S. in Geology, U. So. Calif., 1959, M.S. in Geology, 1962, Ph.D. in Geology, 1966. Registered geologist, Calif. Research assoc. Univ. So. Calif., 1961-65; vis. scholar Tohoku U., Sendai, Japan, 1966-67; asst., assoc. to full prof. Stanford U., Calif., 1968—, W.M. Keck prof. earth scis., 1984—, chmn. dept. geology, 1982-86. Co-chief scientist Leg 31 Deep Sea Drilling Project, 1973, co-chief scientist Leg 128 Ocean Drilling Program, 1989; geologist U.S. Geol. Survey W.A.E, 1978-81 Author: Movement of Beach Sand, 1966; contbr. articles to profl. jours. Recipient W.A. Tarr award Sigma Gamma Epsilon, 1958; named Disting. lectr. Am. Assn. Petroleum Geologists, 1986-87, Joint Oceanographic Institutions, 1991; A.I. Leverson award Am. Assn. Petroleum Geologists, 1988. Fellow Geol. Soc. Am., Calif. Acad. Scis.; mem. Cushman Found. (bd. dirs. 1984-91), Soc. Profl. Paleontologists and Mineralogists (Pacific sect. 1958—, pres. 1993-94), Am. Geophys. Union. E-mail: ingle@pangea.stanford.edu

INGLE, ROBERT D. newspaper editor, newspaper executive; b. Sioux City, Iowa, Apr. 29, 1939; s. Walter J. and Thelma L (McCoy) I.; m. Martha N. Nelson, Sept. 12, 1964 (div. 1984); 1 child, Julia L.; m. Sandra R. Reed, Mar. 2, 1985 B.A. in Journalism and Polit. Sci., U. Iowa, 1962. Various positions Miami Herald, 1962-75, asst. mng. editor, 1975-77, mng. editor, 1977-81; exec. editor San Jose (Calif.) Mercury News, 1981-93, pres., exec. editor, 1993-95; v.p. Knight-Ridder Inc., San Jose, Calif., 1995-99; pres. Knight-Ridder Ventures, San Jose, 1999—. Pres. Calif. First Amendment Coalition, 1990-92. Mem. AP Mng. Editors Assn., Am. Soc. Newspaper Editors Office: Knight Ridder New Media 50 W San Fernando St Ste 1200 San Jose CA 95113-2436

INGRAM, CECIL D. accountant, state legislator; b. Blackfoot, Idaho, Dec. 27, 1932; s. Orval Otto and Mary Marjorie (Evans) I.; m. Lois Ann Glenn, Dec. 28, 1952; children: Cynthia, William, Christopher. BBA, U. Oreg., 1962. Contr. transp. & distbn. divsn. Boise (Idaho) Cascade Corp., 1962-91; mem. Idaho Senate, Dist. 16, Boise, 1993—. Capt. U.S. Army, 1953-58, Korea. Mem. Masons, Mountain States Tumor Inst., Golf for Charity, Morrison Ctr., W Idaho Fair Bd., Salvation Army, United Way, Recreation Unlimited, Junior Achievement, Idaho Education Alliance for Science. Republican. Baptist. Home: 7025 El Caballo Dr Boise ID 83704-7320 Office: State Capitol PO Box 83720 Boise ID 83720-3720

INGRAM, WILLIAM AUSTIN, federal judge; b. Jeffersonville, Ind., July 6, 1924; s. William Austin and Marion (Lane) I.; m. Barbara Brown Lender, Sept. 18, 1947; children: Mary Ingram Mac Calla, Claudia, Betsy Ingram Friebel. Student, Stanford U., 1947; LL.B., U. Louisville, 1950; LLD honoris causas, Santa Clara U., 1994. Assoc., Littler, Coakley, Lauritzen & Ferdon, San Francisco, 1951-55; dep. dist. atty. Santa Clara (Calif.) County, 1955-57; mem. firm Rankin, O'Neal, Luckhardt & Center, San Jose, Calif., 1957-69; judge Mcpl. Ct., Palo Alto-Mountain View, 1969-71, Calif. Superior Ct., 1971-76, U.S. Dist. Ct. (no. dist.) Calif., San Jose, 1976-88, chief judge, 1988-90; sr. judge, 1990—. Served with USMCR, 1943-46. Fellow Am. Coll. Trial Lawyers. Republican. Episcopalian. Office: US Dist Ct 280 S 1st St Rm 5198 San Jose CA 95113-3002

INKELES, ALEX, sociology educator; b. Bklyn., Mar. 4, 1920; s. Meyer and Ray (Gewer) K.; m. Bernadette Mary Kane, Jan. 31, 1942; 1 child, Ann Elizabeth BA, Cornell U., 1941, MA, 1946; postgrad., Washington Sch. Psychiatry, 1943-46; PhD, Columbia U., 1949; student, Boston Psychoanalytic Inst., 1957-59; A.M. (hon.), Harvard U., 1957; prof. honoris causa, Faculdade Candido Mendez, Rio de Janerio, 1969. Social sci. research analyst Dept. State and OSS, 1942-46; cons. program evaluation br., internat. broadcasting div. Dept. State, 1949-51; instr. social relations Harvard U., Cambridge, Mass., 1948, lectr., 1948-57, prof. sociology, 1957-71, dir. studies social relations Russian Research Ctr., dir. studies social aspects econ. devel. Ctr. Internat. Affairs, 1963-71, research assoc., 1971-79; Margaret Jacks prof. edn., prof. sociology Stanford U., Calif., 1971-78, prof. sociology, 1978-90; sr. fellow Hoover Inst., 1978—; prof. emeritus, 1990—. Mem. exec. com. behavioral sci. div. NRC, 1968-75; lectr. Nihon U., Japan, 1985. Author: Public Opinion in Soviet Russia, 1950 (Kappa Tau Alpha award 1950, Grant Squires prize Columbia 1955); with R. Bauer, C. Kluckhohn) How the Soviet System Works, 1956, (with R. Bauer) The Soviet Citizen, 1959, Soviet Society (edited with H.K. Geiger), 1961, What is Sociology?, 1964, Readings on Modern Sociology, 1965, Social Change in Soviet Russia, 1968, (with D.H. Smith) Becoming Modern, 1974 (Hadley Cantril award 1974), Exploring Individual Modernity, 1983; editor: (with Masamichi Sasaki) Comparing Nations and Cultures, 1996, National Character: A Psychosocial Perspective, 1997, One World Emerging? Convergence and Divergence in Industrial Societies, 1998; editor-in-chief Ann. Rev. Sociology, 1971-79; editl. cons. Internat. Rev. Cross Cultural Studies; editl. bd. Ethos, Jour. Soc. Psychol. Anthropology, 1978; editor Founds. Modern Sociology Series; adv. editor in sociology to Little, Brown & Co.; contbr. articles to profl. jours. Recipient Cooley Mead award for Disting. Contbn. in Social Psychology, 1982; fellow Ctr. Advanced Study Behavioral Sci., 1955, Founds. Fund Research Psychiatry, 1957-60, Social Scis. Research Council, 1959, Russell Sage Found., 1966, 85, Fulbright Found., 1977, Guggenheim Found., 1978, Bernard van Leer Jerusalem Found., 1979, Rockefeller Found., 1982, Eisenhower Exch., Taiwan, 1984; NAS Disting. Scholar Exchange, China, 1983; grantee Internat. Rsch. and Exchs. Bd., 1989, NSF, 1989. Fellow AAAS (co-chmn. western ctr. 1984-87, chmn. Talcott Parsons award com. 1988-93), Am. Philos. Soc., APA; mem. NIMH, Nat. Inst. Aging (monitoring com. health retirement survey 1990—), Nat. Acad. Scis. (corr. human rights com. 1986-88, mem. com. on scholarly comms. with People's Republic of China, chmn. panel on social sci. and humanities, NRC panel on issues in democratization 1991-92), Am. Sociol. Soc. (coun. 1961-664, v.p. 1975-76), Ea. Sociol. Soc. (pres. 1961-62), World Assn. Pub. Opinion Rsch., Am. Assn. Pub. Opinion Rsch., Inter-Am. Soc. Psychology, Sociol. Rsch. Assn. (exec. com. 1975-79, pres. 1979), Soc. for Study Social Problems. Home: 1001 Hamilton Ave Palo Alto CA 94301-2215 Office: Stanford U Hoover Instn Stanford CA 94305 E-mail: inkeles@hoover.stanford.edu

INMAN, JAMES RUSSELL, claims consultant; b. Tucson, May 24, 1936; s. Claude Colbert and Myra Eugenia (Langdon) I.; m. Charleen M. Bowman, Feb. 22, 1964 (div. 1977); m. Margaret Williams Kendrick, Apr. 26, 1996. Student, Pomona Coll., Claremont, Calif., 1954-60. Supr. res. dept. Honnold Libr. Claremont Coll., 1959-60; supr. casualty claims CNA Ins., L.A., 1961-70; asst. mgr., asbestos specialist, head entertainment claims Firemen's Fund, L.A., Beverly Hills, 1970-83; pres. Wilnor Corp., L.A., 1982—. Claims auditor dirs. and officers claims Harbor/Continental Ins., L.A., 1984-86; claims mgr. Advent Mgmt., L.A., 1987, Completion Bond Co., Century City, Calif., 1988; asst. to pres., claims specialist Am. Multiline Corp., L.A., 1988-92; sr. claims specialist Reliance Ins. Co., Glendale, Calif., 1992-94; expert witness in field. Mem. First Century Families: Calif.; mem. com. Baldwin Hills Dam Disaster, 1968-72; pres. Alcohol Info. Ctr., L.A., 1983-85. Mem. L.A. Athletic Club, Wilshire Country Club. Avocations: Classic cars, American and English silver. Home: 623 S Arden Blvd Los Angeles CA 90005-3814

INMAN, WILLIAM PETER, lawyer; b. Cleve., June 29, 1936; s. James B. and Lillian (Frances) I.; m. Judith A. Clay, Feb. 5, 1994; children: William Peter, Elizabeth, David. Student, Miami U., 1954-55; B.A., Ohio State U., 1958; J.D., Case Western Res. U., 1960, M.B.A., 1966. Bar: Ohio 1960, Tex. 1985. Tax accountant U.S. Steel Corp., Cleve., 1960-63; asso. trust counsel Central Nat. Bank of Cleve., 1963-66; atty. Sherwin-Williams Co., Cleve., 1966-67, tax counsel, 1967, mgr. tax dept., 1967-68, corporate dir. taxes, 1968-69, asst. sec., dir. taxes, 1969-71, sec., dir. taxes, 1971-75, v.p., sec., asst. treas., 1975-78, v.p., treas., chief fin. officer, 1978-80; v.p. fin., chief fin. officer RTE Corp., Waukesha, Wis., 1980-83; fin. cons. Houston, 1983-85; corp. sec., gen. counsel Mera Bank, Phoenix, 1985-88; gen. counsel CADTEL Sys. Inc., Phoenix, 1988-95, Ariz. Bus. Assocs., L.L.C., Phoenix, 1995—. Mem. Greater Cleve. Growth Assn., 1969-80; Trustee Ohio Pub. Expenditure Council, 1969-80, v.p., 1970-73, pres., 1973-75, chmn. bd., 1975-77. Mem. Am. Soc. Corp. Secs., Fin. Execs. Inst., Cleve. Treasurers Club, N.A.M., Ohio Mfrs. Assn., Am., Ohio, Greater Cleve., Tex., Maricopa County, Ariz. bar assns., Estate Planning Council of Cleve., Phi Delta Phi, Beta Gamma Sigma, Beta Alpha Psi. Home: 10333 E Pine Valley Dr Scottsdale AZ 85259-8300 Office: 5364 E Juniper Ave # 175 Scottsdale AZ 85254-1152

INOCENCIO, E. BING, college president; came to U.S., 1979; Grad. journalism, Ateneo De Manila U.; MS in Mktg. and Advt., U. Ill.; MA in Bus. and Applied Econs., PhD in Econs. and Comm., U. Pa. Assoc. dean bus., math. and tech. C.C. of Balt.; instructional dean humanities and social scis. Inst. at Montgomery Coll., Takoma Park, Md.; dean instrn. and acad. svcs. Cumberland County Coll., Vineland, N.J.; assoc. provost acad. adminstrn. N.Y.C. Tech. Coll. CUNY; pres. L.A. Pierce Coll., 1996-99, Am. Intercontinental U., L.A., 1999—. Fulbright scholar U. Ill.; fellowship Ford Found. Wharton Sch., Harvard Bus. Sch, Kellogg fellow, 1991; named One of Rising Stars in cmty. leadership League for Innovation in the C.C., 1993. Office: 12655 W Jefferson Blvd Los Angeles CA 90066-7008

INOUYE, DANIEL KEN, senator; b. Honolulu, Sept. 7, 1924; s. Hyotaro I. and Kame Imanaga; m. Margaret Shinobu Awamura, June 12, 1949; 1 child, Daniel Ken. A.B., U. Hawaii, 1950; J.D., George Washington U., 1952. Bar: Hawaii 1953. Asst. pub. prosecutor, Honolulu, 1953-54; pvt. practice Honolulu, 1954—; majority leader Territorial Ho. of Reps., 1954-58, Senate, 1958-59; mem. 86th-87th U.S. Congresses from Hawaii; senator from Hawaii U.S. Senate (now 106th Congress), 1962—; sec. Senate Dem. Conf., 1978-88; chmn. Dem. Steering Com., Senate Com. on Appropriations; chmn. subcom. def., mem. Commerce Com.; chmn. subcom. on communications Select Com. on Intelligence, 1976-77, ranking mem. subcom. budget authorizations, 1979-84; former chmn. Select Com. Indian Affairs; mem. Select Com. on Presdl. Campaign Activities, 1973-74; chmn. Sen. select com. Secret Mil. Assistance to Iran and Nicaraguan Opposition, 1987. Ranking minority mem. Appropriations subcom. on defense, Commerce, Sci., & Transp. subcom on surface transp. & merchant marine; mem. Indian Affairs Com., Rules & Adminstrn. Com. Joint Com. on the Libr. & Congl. Intern Program, Dem. Steering & Coordination Com., Joint Com. on Printing. Author: Journey to Washington. Active YMCA, Boy Scouts Am. Keynoter; temporary chmn. Dem. Nat. Conv., 1968, rules com. chmn., 1980, co-chmn. conv., 1984. Pvt. to capt. AUS, 1943-47. Decorated D.S.C., Bronze Star, Purple Heart with cluster; named 1 of 10 Outstanding Young Men of Yr. U.S. Jr. C. of C., 1960; recipient Splendid Am. award Thomas A. Dooley Found., 1967 Golden Plate award Am. Acad. Achievement, 1968 Mem. DAV (past comdr. Hawaii), Honolulu C. of C., Am. Legion (Nat. Comdr.'s award 1973) Methodist. Clubs: Lion. (Hawaii), 442d Veterans (Hawaii). Home: 469 Ena Rd Honolulu HI 96815-1749 Office: US Senate 722 Hart Senate Bldg Washington DC 20510-0001*

INOUYE, LORRAINE R. state legislator; b. Hilo, HI, June 22, 1940; m. Vernon Inouye; children: Ronald Jitchaku, Jay Kitchaku, Marcia Johansen. Mgr. Orchid Island Hotel, 1967-75; sales mgr. Hilo Hawaiian Hotel, Hilo and Kona Lagoon Hotels, 1975-86; pres. Aloha Blooms, Inc., 1998—; mem. Hawaii Senate, Dist. 1, Honolulu, 1998—; chair econ. devel. com. Hawaii Senate, Honolulu, mem. commerce and consumer protection com., mem. transp. and intergovtl. affairs com. Mayor County of Hawaii, 1990-92; mem. Hawaii County Coun., 1984-90, Hawaii County Planning Commn., 1974-79; dir. Girl Scout Coun. Hawaii, 1995X; charter mem. Ho'okumu, North Hawaii Cmty. Hosp., 1991X. Mem. Rotary Club of Hilo. Democrat. Office: State Capitol 415 S Beretania St Rm 201 Honolulu HI 96813-2407

INOUYE, MICHAEL K. medical products company executive; BS, U. Calif., Davis; MBA, Calif. State Poly. U. With Am. Home Products; to sr. dir. mktg. planning, sr. regional dir. field sales Merch and Co., Inc., 1980-94; v.p. sales and mktg. InSite Vision, 1991-95; v.p. sales and mgr. Gilead Scis., Inc., Foster City, Calif., 1995-2000, sr. v.p. sales and mktg., 2000. Office: Gilead Scis Inc 333 Lakeside Dr Foster City CA 94404-1146 Fax: (650) 573-4800

INSLEE, JAY R. congressman; b. Seattle, Feb. 9, 1951; s. Frank and Adele Inslee; m. Trudi Anne Inslee, Aug. 27, 1972; children: Jack, Connor, Joe. BA in Econs., U. Wash., 1973; JD magna cum laude, Willamette U., 1976. Atty. Peters, Fowler & Inslee, Selah, Wash., 1976-92; mem. from 14th dist. Wash. State Ho. of Reps., 1988-92; mem. from the 4th Dist. State of Wash. U.S. Congress, 1993-95; atty. Gordon, Thomas, Honeywell, Malanca, Peterson and Daheim, Seattle, 1995-96; regional dir., region 10 U.S. Dept. Health & Human Svcs., Seattle, 1997-98; mem. U.S. Congress from 1st Wash. dist., 1999—; resources com., fin. svcs. com.; banking and fin. svcs. com. U.S. Ho. Reps., 1999—. Adv. mem. Bainbridge Island Boys and Girls Club 1998—; charter mem. Hoopaholics1988—. Democrat. Office: US Ho Reps 308 Cannon Ho Office Bldg Washington DC 20515-4701 Fax: 202-226-1606*

INTRIERE, ANTHONY DONALD, retired internist, gastroenterologist; b. Greenwich, Conn., May 9, 1920; s. Rocco and Angelina (Belcastro) I.; m. Carol A. Yarmey, Aug. 1, 1945; children: Sherry Shoemaker, Michael, Nancy M., Lisa A. MD, U. Mich., 1944. Intern New Rochelle (NY.) Hosp., 1944-45; pvt. practice Greenwich, 1947-53, Olney, Ill., 1956-61, Granite City, 1961-74, San Diego, 1975—; fellow in internal medicine Cleve. Clinic, 1953-55; fellow in gastroenterology Lahey Clinic, Boston, 1955-56; ret., 1974. Capt. M.C., U.S. Army, 1945-47. Fellow Am. Coll. Gastroenterology (assoc.); mem. AMA, ACP (assoc.), Am. Soc. Internal Medicine, 50 Yr. Club Ill. Med. Soc. Home: 9981 Caminito Chirimolla San Diego CA 92131-2001 E-mail: tintriere@aol.com

INTRILIGATOR, DEVRIE SHAPIRO, physicist; b. N.Y.C. d. Carl and Lillian Shapiro; m. Michael Intriligator; children: Kenneth, James, William, Robert. BS in Physics, MIT, 1962, MS, 1964; PhD in Planetary and Space Physics, UCLA, 1967. NRC-NASA rsch. assoc. NASA, Ames, Calif., 1967-69; rsch. fellow in physics Calif. Inst. Tech., Pasadena, 1969-72, vis. assoc., 1972-73; asst. prof. U. So. Calif., 1972-80; mem. Space Scis. Ctr., 1978-83; sr. rsch. physicist Carmel Rsch. Ctr., Santa Monica, Calif., 1979—; dir. Space Plasma Lab., 1980—. Cons. NASA, NOAA, Jet Propulsion Lab.; chmn. NAS-NRC com. on solar-terrestrial rsch., 1983-86, exec. com. bd. atmospheric sci. and climate, 1983-86, geophysics study com., 1983-86; U.S. nat. rep. Sci. Com. on Solar-Terrestrial Physics, 1983-86; mem. adv. com. NSF Divsn. Atmospheric Sci. Co-editor: Exploration of the Outer Solar System, 1976; contbr. articles to profl. jours. Recipient 3 Achievement awards NASA, Calif. Resolution of Commendation, 1982. Mem. AAAS, Am. Phys. Soc., Am. Geophys. Union, Cosmos Club. Achievements include being a participant Pioneer 10/11 missions to outer planets; Pioneer Venus Orbiter, Pioneers 6, 7, 8 and 9 heliocentric missions. Home: 140 Foxtail Dr Santa Monica CA 90402-2048 Office: Carmel Rsch Ctr PO Box 1732 Santa Monica CA 90406-1732

INTRILIGATOR, MICHAEL DAVID, economist, educator; b. N.Y.C., Feb. 5, 1938; s. Allan and Sally Intriligator; m. Devrie Shapiro; children: Kenneth, James, William, Robert. SB in Econs., MIT, 1959; MA, Yale U., 1960; PhD, MIT, 1963. Asst. prof. econs. UCLA, 1963-66, assoc. prof., 1966-72, prof., 1972—, prof. dept. polit. sci., 1981—, prof. dept. policy studies, 1994—, dir. Ctr. Internat. and Strategic Affairs, 1982-92; dir. Jacob Marschak Interdisciplinary Coll., 1977—; dir. Burkle Ctr. Internat. Rels. Cons. Inst. Def. Analysis, 1974-77, ACDA, 1968, Rand Corp., 1962-65. Author: Mathematical Optimization and Economic Theory, 1971, also Taiwanese, Spanish and Russian edits., Econometric Models, Techniques and Applications, 1978, also Greek and Spanish edits., 2d edit. (with Ronald Bodkin and Cheng Hsiao), 1996, (with others) A Forecasting and Policy Simulation Model of the Health Care Sector, 1979; mem. adv. editorial bd. Math. Social Scis., 1983—; assoc. editor Jour. Optimization Theory and Applications, 1979-91, Conflict Mgmt. and Peace Sci., 1980—; co-editor: (series) Handbooks in Economics, 1980—, Advanced Textbooks in Economics, 1972—; editor: (with Kenneth J. Arrow) Handbook of Mathematical Economics, 3 vols., 1981-85; (with Zvi Griliches) Handbook of Econometrics, 3 vols., 1983-86, (with B. Brodie and R. Kolkowicz) National Security and International Stability, 1983, (with H.A. Jacobsen) East-West Conflict: Elite Perceptions and Political Opinions, 1988, numerous others; contbr. articles to profl. jours. Woodrow Wilson fellow, 1959-60; MIT fellow, 1960-61; recipient Disting. Teaching award UCLA, 1966; Ford fellow, 1967-68; Warren C. Scoville disting. teaching award UCLA, 1976, 79, 82, 84 Fellow Econometric Soc.; mem. Internat. Inst. Strategic Studies, Council Fgn. Relations, others. Office: UCLA Dept Econs Los Angeles CA 90095-0001

INVERSO, MARLENE JOY, optometrist; b. Los Angeles, May 10, 1942; d. Elmer Encel Wood and Sally Marie (Sample) Hirons; m. John S. Inverso, Dec. 16, 1962; 1 child, Christopher Edward. BA, Calif. State U., Northridge, 1964; MS, SUNY, Potsdam, 1975; OD, Pacific U., 1981. Cert. doctor optometry, Wash., Oreg. English tchr. Chatsworth (Calif.) High Sch., 1964-68, Nelson A. Boylen Second Sch., Toronto, Ont., Can., 1968-70, Gouverneur (N.Y.) Jr.-Sr. High Sch., 1970-74, 76-77; reading resource room tchr. Parishville (N.Y.) Hopkinton Sch., 1974-75; optometrist and vision therapist Am. Family Vision Clinics, Olympia, Wash., 1982—. Coord. Lng. Disability Clin. SUNY, summers, 1975-77; mem. adv. com. Sunshine House St. Peter Hosp., Olympia, 1984-86, Pacific U. Coll. Optometry, Forest Grove, Oreg. 1986. Contbr. articles to profl. jours. Mem. Altrusa Svc. Club, Olympia, 1982-86; tchr. Ch. Living Water, Olympia, 1983-88, Olympia-Lacey Ch. of God, 1989—, sec. women's bd., 1990; bd. advisors Crisis Pregnancy Ctr., Olympia, 1987-89; den mother Cub Scouts Am. Pack 202, Lacey, Wash., 1987-88; vol. World Vision Countertop ptnr., 1986-97. Fellow Coll. Optometrists in Optometric Devel.; mem. Am. Optometric Assn. (sec. 1983-84), Assn. Children and Adults with Learning Disabilities, Optometric Extension Program, Sigma Xi, Beta Sigma Kappa. Avocations: bible study, professional speaking, training, and teaching. Home: 4336 Libby Rd NE Olympia WA 98506-2555

IONA, MARIO, retired physics educator; b. Berlin, June 17, 1917; came to U.S., 1941, naturalized, 1948; s. Mario G.V. and Dorothee (Berendes) I.; m. Nancy Mossman, Aug. 31, 1949; children: Steven, Ann. PhD, U. Vienna, Austria, 1939; postgrad., U. Uppsala, Sweden, 1939-41. Research asst., instr. U. Chgo., 1941-46; from asst. prof. to prof. physics U. Denver, 1946-85, prof. emeritus, 1985—; coord. High Altitude Labs., Mt. Evans and Echo Lake, Colo., 1946-82; cons. pvt. practice Denver, 1985—. Cons. Denver Schs., 1962-65, 84, Jefferson County Schs., Golden, Colo., 1973, Adams County Sch. Dist. 12, Northglenn, Colo., 1985, Internat. Orgn. for Standardization, tech. adv. group, 1990—; vis. prof. U. No. Colo., summer 1971; specialist U. Saugar, India, summer, 1966; cons. various manuscript revs., 1975—. Assoc. editor: Physics Tchr., 1962-65, column editor, 1970-2000. Treas., sec., pres. Group Health Assn., Denver, 1952-66. Fellow AAAS; mem. ASTM, Am. Phys. Soc., Am. Assn. Physics Tchrs. (chmn. com. on SI units and metric edn. 1987-91, Disting. Svc. citation 1971, Millikan Lecture award 1986), Colo.-Wyo. Acad. Sci. (pres. 1974-75), Nat. Sci. Tchrs. Assn., AAUP. Home: 2333 S Columbine St Denver CO 80210-5421 Office: U Denver Dept Physics & Astronomy Denver CO 80208-2238

IONTA, ROBERT W. federal judge, lawyer; Part-time magistrate judge for N.Mex., U.S. Magistrate Ct., Gallup, 1985—. Office: 300 W Hill Ave Gallup NM 87301-6364

IOVINE, JIMMY, recording industry executive; b. Bklyn., 1953; s. Jimmy Iovine Sr. Former engineer The Record Plant, New York, N.Y.; ind. prodr., co-head of Interscope Records, 1991—. Office: c/o Interscope Comm 10900 Wilshire Blvd Ste 1230 Los Angeles CA 90024-6532

IPSEN, GRANT RUEL, state legislator, insurance and investments professional; b. Malad, Idaho, Nov. 6, 1932; s. Nephi Ruel and Ada (Hughes) I.; m. Edna Wayne Hughes, July 27, 1956; children: Edna Gaye, LeAnn, Garin Grant, Shawna Lee, Wayne Ruel. BA, Brigham Young U., 1961. CPA, CLU, ChFC. Acct. Ernst & Ernst, Boise, Idaho, 1961-64; with sales dept. Mut. of N.Y., Boise, 1964-73; mem. Idaho Senate, Dist. 17, Boise, 1992—. Active Boy Scouts Am., 1945—; co-convener Boise Religious Freedom Com., 1991-94. With U.S. Army, 1956-58. Named Agt. of Yr., Boise Assn. Life Underwriters, 1978, Man of Yr., Mut. of N.Y., 1982. Mem. Million Dollar Round Table (life), Brigham Young Univ. Alumni (bd. dirs. 1987-93). Republican. LDS. Avocations: reading, outdoor recreation, hiking, travel. E-mail: gipsen@senate.state.id.us

IRANI, RAY R. oil, gas and chemical company executive; b. Beirut, Lebanon, Jan. 15, 1935; came to U.S., 1953, naturalized, 1956; s. Rida and Naz I.; children: Glenn R., Lillian M., Martin R. BS in Chemistry, Am. U. Beirut, 1953; PhD in Phys. Chemistry, U. So. Calif., 1957. Rsch. scientist, then sr. rsch. scientist Monsanto Co., 1957-67; assoc. dir. new products, then dir. research Diamond Shamrock Corp., 1967-73; with Olin Corp., 1973-83, pres. chems. group, 1978-80, corp. pres., dir. Conn., 1980-83, COO, 1981-83; chmn. Occidental Petroleum Corp. subs. Occidental Chem. Corp., Dallas, 1983-94; CEO Occidental Petroleum Corp., subs. Occidental Chem. Corp., Dallas, 1983-91; chmn. Can. Occidental Petroleum Corp. Ltd., Calgary, 1987-99; exec. v.p. Occidental Petroleum Corp., L.A., 1983-84, pres., COO, 1984-91, pres., 1991-96, chmn., CEO, 1991—, also bd. dirs. Bd. dirs. Am. Petroleum Inst., Oxy Oil and Gas USA Inc., Occidental Oil and Gas Corp., Occidental Petroleum Investment Corp., Cedars Bank, Kaufman and Broad Home Corp., Jonsson Cancer Ctr. Found./UCLA. Author: Particle Size; also author papers in field; numerous patents in field. Vice chmn. Am. U. Beirut; trustee U. So. Calif., St. John's Hosp. and Health Ctr. Found., Natural History Mus. Los Angeles County; bd. govs. Los Angeles Town Hall, Los Angeles World Affairs Coun. Mem. Nat. Petroleum Coun., Am. Inst. Chemists, Am. Chem. Soc., Sci. Rsch. Soc. Am., Indsl. Rsch. Inst., The Conf. Bd., The CEO Roundtable, Nat. Assn. Mfrs. (bd. dirs.), Am. Petroleum Inst. (bd. dirs.), U.S.-Russia Bus. Coun. Office: 10889 Wilshire Blvd Los Angeles CA 90024-4201

IRELAND, FAITH, state supreme court justice; b. Seattle, 1942; d. Carl and Janice Enyeart; m. Chuck Norem. BA, U. Wash.; JD, Willamette U., 1969; M in Taxation with honors, Golden Gate U. Past assoc. McCune, Godfrey and Emerick, Seattle; pvt. practice Pioneer Square, Wash., 1974; judge King County Superior Ct., 1984-98; justice Wash. Supreme Ct., 1998. Past dean Washington Jud. Coll., past mem. Bd. Ct. Edn. Served on numerous civic and charitable bds.; past pro-bono atty. Georgetown Dental Clin.; past bd. dirs. Puget Sound Big Sisters, Inc.; founding mem. Wing Luke Asian Mus., 1967—, past pres., past bd. dirs.; bd. dirs. Youth and Fitness Found., 1998. Recipient Disting. Svc. award Nat. Leadership Inst. Jud. Edn., 1998; named Judge of Yr. Washington State Trial Lawyer's Assn., Man of Yr. for efforts in founding Wing Luke Asian Mus. Mem. Washington Women Lawyer's (founding mem., Pres.'s award, Vanguard award), Wash. State Trial Lawyer's Assn. (past chair bd. dirs), Superior Ct. Judges Assn. (past bd. dirs., pres. 1996-97, vice chair bd. dirs. jud. adminstrn. 1996-98), Rainer Valley Hist. Soc. (founding mem., life), Rotary (bd. dirs. Seattle No. 4 1998). Office: Washington Supreme Ct Temple Justice PO Box 41174 Olympia WA 98504-1174

IRIBE, P. CHRISMAN, utilities executive; BA in Econs., postgrad., George Washington U. Energy economist, policy analyst Exec. Office of the President; various positions predecessor agys. U.S. Dept. Energy; officer Am. Gas Assn.; sr. v.p. ANR Pipeline Co. Coastal Corp.; sr. v.p. PG&E Corp., U.S. Gen., 1998—. Office: PG&E Generating Co One Market Plz Spear Tower 32400 San Francisco CA 94105

IRISH, THOMAS JUDSON, plastic surgeon; b. Forest City, Iowa, May 23, 1936; m. Sandra Rudolph. BS, Iowa State Coll., 1958; MD, State U. of Iowa, 1962. Intern King County Hosp. (now Harborview Hosp.), Seattle, 1962-63; pvt. practice Forest City, Iowa, 1963-66; resident in gen. surgery U. Colo. Med. Ctr., Denver, 1966-70; resident in plastic surgery Norfolk Gen. Hosp. & Kings Daughters Children's Hosp., Va., 1970-72; pvt. practice Plastic Surgeons NW, Tacoma, 1972—; med. dir. Franciscan Wound Care Ctr. Fellow in plastic surgery Canniesburn Hosp., Glasgow, Scotland, 1971. Fellow ACS; mem. Am. Soc. Plastic and Reconstructive Surgery, Alpha Omega Alpha. Office: 1802 S Yakima Ave Ste 202 Tacoma WA 98405-5304

IRWIN, JAY R. federal judge; Apptd. part-time magistrate judge U.S. Dist. Ct. Ariz. Office: 888 W 16th St Yuma AZ 85364-4542

IRWIN, PHILIP DONNAN, lawyer; b. Madison, Wis., Sept. 6, 1933; s. Constant Louis and Isabel Dorothy (Elfving) I.; divorced; m. Sandra L. McMahan, Sept. 14, 1985; children: Jane Donnan, James Haycraft, Victoria Wisnom, Philip Donnan Jr. BA, U. Wyo., 1954; LLB, Stanford U., 1957. Bar: Wyo. 1957, Calif. 1958. Assoc. O'Melveny & Myers, L.A., 1957-65, ptnr., 1965-2000, of counsel, 2000—. Mem. planning com. Inst. Fed. Taxation of U. So. Calif. Law Ctr., 1976—, chairperson, 1995-98; spkr. legal seminars. Contbr. articles legal jours. Trustee Mackenzie Found., Los Angeles, 1969— . Republican. Episcopalian. Club: California (Los Angeles). Office: O'Melveny & Myers 400 S Hope St Rm 1853 Los Angeles CA 90071-2899 E-mail: pirwin@omm.com

IRWIN, R. ROBERT, lawyer; b. Denver, July 27, 1933; s. Royal Robert and Mildred Mary (Wilson) I.; m. Sue Ann Scott, Dec. 16, 1956; children: Lori, Stacy, Kristi, Amy. Student, U. Colo., 1951-54; BS in Law, U. Denver, 1955, LLB, 1957. Bar: Colo. 1957, Wyo. 1967. Asst. atty. gen. State of Colo., 1958-66; asst. divsn. atty. Mobil Oil Corp., Casper, Wyo., 1966-70; prin. atty. No. Natural Gas Co., Omaha, 1970-72; sr. atty., asst. sec. Coastal Oil & Gas Corp., Denver, 1972-83; ptnr. Baker & Hostetler, 1983-87; pvt. practice, 1987—. Mem. Colo. Bar Assn., Arapahoe County Bar Assn., Rocky Mountain Oil and Gas Assn., Los Verdes Golf Club, Petroleum Club, Denver Law Club. Republican. Office: 650 S Alton Way Apt 4D Denver CO 80231-1669

IRWIN, WILLIAM RANKIN, retired lawyer; b. Springfield, Ill., Feb. 26, 1940; s. William Ross and Helen Katherine (O'Brien) I.; m. Alyce-Kaye Moffett, Oct. 1969 (div.); children: Elizabeth, Stephanie; m. Brenda L. Reinertson, Oct. 1, 1983; children: Matthew, Cydney. BA with honors, U. Ill., 1962; LLB with honors, U. Calif., Berkeley, 1965. Bar: Calif. 1966. Asst. Adminstrv. Office of the Cts., San Francisco, 1965-66; assoc. atty., ptnr. Brobeck, Phleger & Harrison, San Francisco, 1966-99. Mem. ABA (litigation sect., com. on ins. coverage), Calif. Bar Assn., Bar Assn. of San Francisco, Order of Coif, Phi Delta Phi. Avocations: sailing, travel, reading. Office: Brobeck Phleger & Harrison Spear St Tower 1 Market St San Francisco CA 94105-1420

IRWIN-HENTSCHEL, NOËL, travel company executive; b. Fresno, Calif. m. Gordon Hentschel; 7 children. Co-founder, chmn., CEO Am. Tours Internat., L.A., 1977—. Bd. regents Loyola Marymount U.; rep. Gov.'s Crime Summit; speaker Gov.'s Conf. Women; bd. dirs. Travel Industry Assn., C. of C. Candidate Lt. Gov. Calif.; co-chair Nat. Policy Forum's Coun. Econ. Growth and Workplace Opportunities; active Gov. Pete Wilson's team. Recipient Entrepreneur of Yr. award Calif. Travel Industry, 1995, Woman Bus. Owner of Yr. award Nat. Assn. Women Bus. Owners, 1996; named Humanitarian of Yr. Calif. Mothers Assn., 1998, Top 100 Entrepreneurs Success Mag. Mem. L.A. World Affairs Coun., L.A. Libr. Found. Office: American Tours Internat LA Internat Airport 6053 W Century Blvd Los Angeles CA 90045-6430 Fax: 310-216-5807

ISAACSON, MICHAEL, civil engineering educator; BA in Engring. with distinction, U. Cambridge, 1971, MA, PhD, U. Cambridge, 1975. Profl. engr., B.C., Can., chartered engr., Great Britain. With civil engring. dept. U. B.C., Vancouver, 1976—, prof., head civil engring. dept., dean faculty applied sci. Mem. code design offshore prodn. structures tech. com. Can. Stds. Assn.; mem. com. environ. forces Internat. Ship and Offshore Structures Congress; cons. in field. Co-author: Mechanics of Wave Forces on Offshore Structures, 1981; assoc. editor Can. Jour. Civil Engring., Internat. Jour. Offshore and Polar Engring. Recipient R.A. McLachlan award Assn. Profl. Engrs. and Geoscientists B.C., 1992. Mem. ASCE, Can. Soc. Civil Engring. (chair engring. mechanics divsn., bd. dirs., Camille A. Dagenais award 1992, T.C. Keefer Medal 1996), Engring. Inst. Can., Royal Instn. Naval Architects, Internat. Assn. Hydraulic Rsch., Internat. Soc. Offshore and Polar Engrs. (PACOMS award 1992). Achievements include research in coastal and ocean engineering. Office: U BC Faculty Applied Scis 2006-2324 Main Mall Vancouver BC Canada V6T 1Z4

ISAKI, LUCY POWER SLYNGSTAD, lawyer; b. Jersey City, Oct. 21, 1945; d. Charles Edward and Ann Mary (Power) Slyngstad; m. Paul S. Isaki, Aug. 26, 1967. BA summa cum laude, Seattle U., 1973; JD cum laude, U. Puget Sound, 1977. Bar: Wash. 1977. Case worker San Joaquin County Welfare, Stockton, Calif., 1968-70, Alameda County Welfare, Oakland, 1971-73; legal intern King County Prosecutor's Office, 1976-77; law clk. to hon. Justice Hamilton Wash. Supreme Ct., 1977-78; ptrn. Bogle & Gates, Seattle, 1978-99, mem. exec. com., 1990-94; sr. asst. atty. gen. State of Wash., 1999—. Cons. Region X, HHS, 1975; chair Atty. Gen. Gregoire's Task Force on Alternative Dispute Resolution, 1993-94. Bd. dirs. King County Family Svcs., Seattle, 1982-84, Wash. State Coun. Crime and Delinquency, 1981; treas. Mother's Against Violence in America, 1994; trustee U. Puget Sound, 1985—, Seattle Youth Symphony, 1995, Ea. Wash. U., 1998-99; chmn. law sch. bd. visitors Seattle U., 1984-96; trustee Legal Found., Wash., 1992-95, sec. bd. dirs. 1993, v.p. bd. dirs. 1994, pres. 1995. Dean's scholar U. Puget Sound, 1976-77; recipient Disting. Law Grad. award U. Puget Sound, 1984, Majis award Seattle U., 1997. Mem. Wash. Women Lawyers (pres. Seattle-King County chpt. 1982), ABA (del. ABA Ho. Delegates, 1995-97), Wash. State Bar Assn. (bd. govs. 2000—), King County Bar Assn. (sec. 1986-87, trustee 1987-90, treas. 1995-97, 1st v.p. 1998, pres. 1999-2000), Wash. Women Lawyers (v.p. 1984), King County Bar Found. (trustee 1987-90), U. Puget Sound Law Alumni Soc. (pres. 1979). Democrat. Home: 1001 2d Ave W # 203 Seattle WA 98119 Office: Atty Gens Office 900 4th Ave Ste 2000 Seattle WA 98164-1076 E-mail: lucyi@atg.wa.gov

ISBELL, HAROLD M(AX), writer, investor; b. Maquoketa, Iowa, Sept. 20, 1936; s. H. Max and Marcella E. Isbell; m. Mary Carolyn Cosgriff, June 15, 1963; children: Walter Harold, Susan Elizabeth, David Harold, Alice Kathleen. BA cum laude, Loras Coll., 1959; MA, U. Notre Dame, 1962; grad., U. Mich., 1982. Instr. U. Notre Dame, South Bend, Ind., 1963-64; asst. prof. San Francisco Coll. for Women, 1964-69; assoc. prof. St. Mary's Coll., 1969-72; with Continental Bank & Trust Co., Salt Lake City, 1972-83, v.p., 1977-83, comml. credit officer, 1978-83, also bd. dirs. Editor, translator: The Last Poets of Imperial Rome, 1971, Ovid: Heroides, 1990; contbr. to publs. in field of classical Latin lit. and contemporary Am. lit. Trustee Judge Meml. Cath. H.S., Salt Lake City, 1977-84; mem. Utah Coun. for Handicapped and Developmentally Disabled Persons, 1980-81; bd. dirs. Ballet West, 1983-90, emeritus, 1990—, Story Line Press, 1994-99, Smuin Ballets, San Francisco, 1994-99; founder Cath. Found. Utah, pres., 1984-86, trustee, 1984-89. Mem. AAAS, MLA, Medieval Acad. Am., Alta Club. Democrat. Roman Catholic.

ISENBERG, JON IRWIN, gastroenterologist, educator; b. Chgo., Mar. 21, 1937; s. Lucien and Roselle (Moss) I.; children: Nancy Beth, Noah William, Rebecca Moss. BS with honors, U. Ill., 1959; MD, U. Ill., Chgo., 1963. Diplomate Am. Bd. Internal Medicine, Am. Bd. Gastroenterology. Assoc. prof. in residence UCLA, 1973-78, prof. medicine in residence, 1978-79; key investigator Ctr. for Ulcer Rsch. and Edn./UCLA, 1979—; prof. medicine U. Calif., San Diego, 1979—, divsn. head, 1979-92. Vis. scientist Karolinska Hosp. and Inst., Stockholm, 1982-83, U. Uppsala Biomed. Inst., Sweden, 1991-92; sci. com. mem. 5th Internat. Conf. on Peptic Ulcer, Boston, 1985; mem. study sect. GMA-2, NIH, 1988-92. Author: Physicians Guide to Computers and Computing, 1985; editor: Peptic Ulcer Disease: Clinics in Gastroenterology, 1984. Served to maj. U.S. Army, 1968-70. NIH grantee, 1984—. Fellow ACP; mem. Western Assn. Physicians (counselor 1981-85, pres. 1989-90), So. Calif. Soc. Gastroenterology (pres. 1978-79), Am. Gastroenterology Assn. (councilor 1993-96, v.p. 1999-2000, pres.-elect 2000—), Assn. Am. Physicians, Am. Soc. Clin. Investigation. Democrat. Jewish. Avocation: photography. Home: 1131 W Muirlands Dr La Jolla CA 92037-5505 Office: U Calif Med Ctr Divsn Gastroenterology 200 W Arbor Dr San Diego CA 92103-9000

ISENBERG, WALTER L. recreational facility executive; Grad., Cornell U. Exec. v.p. ops., founder Sage Hospitality Resources, L.P., Denver; exec. v.p., COO, founder Sage Hospitality Resources LLC, Denver. Office: Sage Hospitality Resources LLC 1512 Larimer St Ste 800 Denver CO 80202-1623

ISH, DANIEL RUSSELL, law educator, academic administrator; b. Loon Lake, Sask., Can., Aug. 28, 1946; s. Leme Jay and Obeline Delia (Sicotte) I.; m. Diane Maureen Cote, Sept. 2, 1967 (div. 1970); m. Bonnie Jeanne Bolger, Dec. 22, 1970; children: Jason Bolger, Rachel Bolger. LLB, BA, U. Sask., 1970; LLM, Osgoode Hall Law Sch., Toronto, Ont., Can., 1974. Bar: Alta. 1971, Sask. 1979; called to Queen's Counsel, 1991. Lawyer H. Lloyd MacKay, Banff, Alta., 1970-71; asst. prof. law McGill U., Montreal, Que., Can., 1972-75; assoc. prof. U. Sask., Saskatoon, 1975-80, prof. law, 1980—, asst. dean law, 1977-78, dean, 1982-88, 96-97; dir. Ctr. for Study of Cooperatives, 1989-95; Fulbright fellow Stanford U., 1995-96. Author: The Taxation of Canadian Co-operatives, 1975, The Law of Canadian Co-operatives, 1981, Co-operatives in Principle and Practice, 1992, Legal Responsibilities of Directors and Officers in Canadian Cooperation, 1996. Pres. Univ. Credit Union, Saskatoon, 1979-80. Mem. Law Found. Sask. (bencher 1982-88), Law Soc. Sask. (trustee 1982-88). Avocations: skiing, running. Office: U Sask Coll Law Saskatoon SK Canada S7N 0W0

ISHAM, MARK, composer, jazz musician; b. N.Y.C., Sept. 7, 1951; s. Howard Fuller and Patricia (Hammond) I.; m. Donna Linson, Feb. 24, 1990. Film scores include Never Cry Wolf, 1983, Mrs. Soffel, 1984, The Times of Harvey Milk, 1984, Country, 1984, Trouble in Mind, 1985, The Hitcher, 1986, Made in Heaven, 1987, The Moderns, 1988, The Beast, 1988, Everybody Wins, 1990, Love at Large, 1990, Reversal of Fortune, 1990, Mortal Thoughts, 1991, Crooked Hearts, 1991, Point Break, 1991, Little Man Tate, 1991, Billy Bathgate, 1991, Cool World, 1992, A Midnight Clear, 1992, Of Mice and Men, 1992, The Public Eye, 1992, A River Runs Through It, 1992 (Academy award nomination best original score 1992), Sketch Artist, 1992, Nowhere to Run, 1993, Fire in the Sky, 1993, Made in America, 1993, Short Cuts, 1993, Hidden Hawaii, 1994, Romeo is Bleeding, 1994, The Getaway, 1994, Quiz Show, 1994, Mrs. Parker and the Vicious Circle, 1994, Nell, 1994, Losing Isiah, 1995, The Net, 1995, Home for The Holidays, 1995, Last Dance, 1996, Gotti, 1996, Fly Away Home, 1996, Night Falls on Manhattan, 1997, Afterglow, 1997, The Education of Little Tree, 1997, Kiss The Girls, 1997, Blade, 1998, The Gingerbread Man, 1998, At First Sight, 1999, Free Money, 1999, October Sky, 1999, Body Shots, 1999, Galapagos, 1999, Varsity Blues, 1999, Rules of Engagement, 2000; TV themes include Chicago Hope, EZ Streets; recs. include (solo) Vapor Drawings, 1983, Castalia, 1988, Tibet, 1989, Mark Isham, 1991, (Grammy award), Blue Sun, 1995, (with Charles Jankel) Charles Jankel, (with Tom Fogerty) Deal It Out, (with America) View From the Ground, (with Van Morrison) Live at the Belfast Opera House, Into the Music, Inarticulate Speech of the Heart, Common One, Beautiful Vision, (with Art Lande) Story of Baku, Eccentricities of Earl Dant, Rubisa Patrol, Desert Marauders, We Begin, (with Group 87) Group 87, A Career in Dada Processing, (with the Rolling Stones) Voodoo Lounge, (with Bruce Springsteen) Human Touch, (with Willie Nelson) Across The Borderline, (with Toots Thielmans) Toots, Film Music. Office: Earle Tones Music Inc 23679 Calabasas Rd. #522 Calabasas CA 91302

ISHII, ANTHONY W. judge; PharmD, U. of the Pacific, 1970; JD, U. Calif., Berkeley, 1973. Judge U.S. Dist. Ct. (ea. dist.) Calif., 1997—. Office: 1130 O St Fresno CA 93721-2201

ISHII, CLYDE HIDEO, plastic surgeon; b. Lihue, Hawaii, Mar. 29, 1952; MD, Jefferson Med. Coll., 1978. Diplomate Am. Bd. Surgery, Am. Bd. Plastic Surgery. Past chief plastic surgery Queens Med. Ctr., Honolulu, asst. chief of surgery; chief plastic surgery Shriners Hosp., Honolulu, 1993—. Office: 1329 Lusitana St Ste 502 Honolulu HI 96813-2412

ISHIMARU, AKIRA, electrical engineering educator; b. Fukuoka, Japan, Mar. 16, 1928; came to U.S., 1952; s. Shigezo and Yumi I.; m. Yuko Kaneda, Nov. 21, 1956; children: John, Jane, James, Joyce. BSEE, U. Tokyo, 1951; PhD, U. Wash., 1958. Registered profl. engr., Wash. Engr. Electro-Tech. Lab, Tokyo, 1951-52; tech. staff Bell Telephone Lab,

Holmdel, N.J., 1956; asst. prof. U. Wash., Seattle, 1958-61, assoc. prof., 1961-65, prof. elec. engring., 1965-98, prof. emeritus, 1998—. Vis. assoc. prof. U. Calif., Berkeley, 1963-64; cons. Jet Propulsion Lab., Pasadena, Calif., 1964—, The Boeing Co., Seattle, 1984—. Author: Wave Propagation & Scattering in Random Media, 1978, Electromagnetic Wave Propagation, Radiation and Scattering, 1991; editor: Radio Science, 1982; founding editor Waves in Random Media, U.K., 1990. Recipient Faculty Achievement award Burlington Resources, 1990; Boeing Martin professorship, 1993. Fellow IEEE (editl. bd., Region VI Achievement award 1968, Centennial medal 1984, Antennas and Propagation Disting. Achievement award 1995, Heinrich Hertz medal 1999), IEEE Geosci. and Remote Sensing (Disting. Achievement award 1998, Third Millennium medal 2000), Acoustical Soc. Am., Optical Soc. Am. (assoc. editor jour. 1983), Inst. Physics U.K. (chartered physicist); mem. NAE, Internat. Union Radio Sci. (chmn. commn. B, John Howard Dellinger Gold medal 1999). Home: 2913 165th Pl NE Bellevue WA 98008-2137 Office: U Wash Dept Elec Engring PO Box 352500 Seattle WA 98195-2500 E-mail: ishimaru@ee.washington.edu

ISLAMBOULY, HAGAR ABDEL-HAMID, consul general; b. Cairo, Jan. 5, 1947; d. Abdel Hamid and Souad (ElSherif) I.; m. Mohamed Adel Ezzat, Jan. 22, 1970. Diploma, Am. Coll. Girls, Cairo, 1964; BSc in Polit. Sci., Cairo U., 1969. With state info. svc. Ministry Information, Cario, 1970-74; with the cabinet of the ofcl. spokesman Ministry Fgn. Affairs Diplomatic Inst., Cairo, 1974; mem. internal. orgn. dept. Ministry Fgn. Affairs, Cairo, 1975-76; second sec. Embassy of Egypt, Madrid, 1976-80; with cabinet of the asst. minister of fgn. affairs for legal internat. orgns. affairs Ministry Fgn. Affairs, Cairo, 1980-81, mem. cabinet of the head of Egyptian mechanism for negotiation with Israel, 1981-84; counselor Egyptian Embassy, Bonn, Germany, 1984-88; dep. dir. Israeli affairs dept. Ministry Fgn. Affairs, Cairo, 1988-90, dep. dir. internat. orgns. dept., 1990-91, dir. environ. affairs dept., 1991-93, dir. internat. environ. affairs dept., 1991-95, dir. internat. economic affairs dept., 1993-95; consul gen., chief of mission Egyptian Consulate, San Francisco, 1995—. Attended UN Conf. for Environ. and Devel., Rio De Janeiro, 1992, Middle East/North Africa Economic Summit, UN Gen. Assembly, UN Agencies and UN Environ. Programs, UN Conf. Trade and Devel., UN Conf. on Population and Devel., 1991-95; attended Morocco Conf. Internat. Trade for Gen. Agreements of Tarrifs and Trade, Uruguay, 1994; mem. Egyptian Gen. Com. assigned to prepare for the Peace Conf. in the Middle East, Ministry Fgn. Affairs, 1990-95; head of the Egyptian delegation to the working group of environ.-multi lateral track of the Peace Conf. in the Middle East, Ministry Fgn. Affairs, 1991-95. Contbr. articles to profl. jours. Active environ. groups in Egypt; mem. regional organization and related com., summits Islamic Conf. Orgn., Arab League, Orgn. African Unity, 1993-95. Recipient The Order of Civil Merit, King of Spain, 1980, Order of Civil Merit, Pres. Germany, 1988. Mem. World State Forum (coord. Middle East affairs 1996—), World Trade Club, UN, San Francisco Consular Corps., World Affairs Coun., San Francisco Ladies of Consular Corps, Commonwealth Club. Islamic. Avocations: reading, classical music, jogging. Office: Egyptian Consulate 3001 Pacific Ave San Francisco CA 94115-1099 Fax: 415-346-9480

ISRAEL, ALLEN D. lawyer; b. Seattle, Nov. 28, 1946; m. Nettie Israel. BSME, U. Wash., 1968, MBA, 1971, JD, 1978. Bar: Wash. 1978. Ptnr. Foster Pepper & Shefelman PLLC, Seattle, 1978—. Office: Foster Pepper & Shefelman PLLC 1111 3rd Ave Ste 3400 Seattle WA 98101-3299

ISRAEL, DAVID, journalist, screenwriter, producer; b. N.Y.C., Mar. 17, 1951; s. Hyman and Edith Oringer I.; m. Lindy De Koven, Aug. 8, 1987. B.S. in Journalism, Northwestern U., 1973. Reporter Chgo. Daily News, 1973-75; columnist Washington Star, 1975-78, Chgo. Tribune, 1978-81, Los Angeles Herald Examiner, 1981-84; chmn., pres. Big Prodns., Inc., Los Angeles; producer, writer OCC Prodns., Los Angeles, 1985-88; exec. prodr., writer Lorimar Television, L.A., 1988-92, Paramount Pictures, Hollywood, 1992-93; writer, exec. prodr. Stephen J. Cannell Prodns., Inc., Hollywood, 1993-95. Dir. office of Pres., Los Angeles Olympic Organizing Com., 1984; exec. prodr. House of Frankenstein, NBC, Universal, 1997, exec. prodr. Mutiny, NBC, 1999, Y2K, NBC, 1999. Supervising prodr., writer: A Comedy Salute to Baseball, NBC, 1985; supervising prodr., writer: Fast Copy, NBC, 1985-86; co-creator, supervising prodr.: Crimes of the Century, 1987-88; co-exec. prodr., writer: Midnight Caller, NBC, Lorimar TV, 1988-91, The Untouchables, Paramount TV, 1992-93; exec. prodr., writer: Jake Lassiter: Justice on the Bayou, NBC, Stephen J. Cannell Prodns., 1995; exec. prodr., writer: Pandora's Clock, NBC, Citadel Entertainment, 1996; consulting prodr., writer, Turks, CBS Studios, U.S.A., 1998-99; coord. prodr. Monday Night Football, ABC Sports, 2000-01. Mem. AFTRA, Writers Guild Am., Chgo. Athletic Assn. Office: c/o Jared Levine Nelson Guggenheim Felker & Levine 10880 Wilshire Blvd Ste 2070 Los Angeles CA 90024

ISRAEL, JOAN, social worker; b. Bklyn., July 19, 1943; d. Joseph Israel and Irene (Solon) Kansey; m. Ronald Jerome Janesh, June 28, 1980 (div. Feb. 1985); 1 child, Ariel Naomi. BA, Bklyn. Coll., 1965; MSW, U. Mich., 1974. Lic. clin. social worker, Nev. Social worker Alameda County Welfare Dept., Oakland, Calif., 1965-72; group therapist Pacific Ctr. for Human Growth, Berkeley, 1975-77; individual and group therapist, bd. dir. Bi-Ctr., San Francisco, 1976-78; clin. social worker, supr. Audrey L. Smith Devel. Ctr., San Francisco, 1977-78; psychiat. social worker South Nev. Adult Mental Health Dept., Las Vegas, 1978-84, part-time clin. social worker, 1988—; pvt. practice clin. social worker Las Vegas, 1984—. Contbr. articles to profl. publs. Organizer Drug/Alcohol Abuse Task Force, Las Vegas, 1983-84, Task Force on AIDS, Las Vegas, 1985-86. Mem. NASW (chair nominating com. 1978-80, 82-84, sec. 1984-86, chair com. on inquiry 1988—, legis. chair 1982-84, diplomate clin. social work), Sierra Club. Democrat. Jewish. Avocations: hiking, singing, opera, science fiction, dance. E-mail: israeljoan@wgbtv. Office: Ste 120 7200 Cathedral Rock Dr Las Vegas NV 89128

ISRAEL, RICHARD STANLEY, investment banker; b. Oakland, Calif., Sept. 27, 1931; s. Sybil Noble, July 29, 1962; children: Richard Lee, Lynne, Lawrence. BA, MA, U. Calif., 1953. Copy editor San Francisco Chronicle, 1953-59; publicist CBS TV Network, L.A., 1959-62; sr. v.p. Rogers & Cowan, Beverly Hills, Calif., 1962-69; v.p. Cantor, Fitzgerald, Beverly Hills, 1969-73; pres. Sponsored Cons. Svcs., L.A., 1973—. Bd. dirs. Hurst Labeling Systems. Pres. North Beverly Dr. Homeowners Assn., Beverly Hills, 1986-88; v.p. Temple Emanuel, Beverly Hills, 1988-93, L.A. chpt. Juvenile Diabetes Found. Internat, 1987—. With U.S. Army, 1956-58. Recipient Alumni citation U. Calif. Alumni Assn., Berkeley, 1984. Mem. L.A. Venture Assn. (pres. 1987), Assn. for Corp. Growth (pres. bd. dirs. L.A. chpt.). Democrat. Avocations: volleyball, travel. Office: Dick Israel & Ptnrs 8929 Wilshire Blvd Ste 214 Beverly Hills CA 90211-1951 E-mail: r.lnay@aol.com

ISRAEL, WERNER, physics educator; b. Berlin, Oct. 4, 1931; s. Arthur and Marie (Kappauf) I.; m. Inge Margulies, Jan. 26, 1958; children: Mark Abraham, Pia Lee B.Sc., U. Cape Town, 1951, M.Sc., 1954; Ph.D., Trinity Coll., Dublin, 1960; D.Sc. (hon.), Queen's U., Kingston, Ont., 1987; Docteur honoris causa, U. Francois Rabelais, France, 1994; DSc (hon.), U. Victoria, B.C., Can., 1999. Asst. prof. physics U. Alta., 1958-68, prof., 1968-85, Univ. prof., 1985-96; adj. prof. dept. physics and astronomy U. Victoria, B.C., Can., 1996—; hon. prof. dept. physics and astronomy U. B.C. Sherman Fairchild disting. scholar Calif. Inst. Tech., 1974-75; vis. prof. Dublin Inst. Advanced Studies, 1966-68, U. Cambridge, 1975-76, [illegible] fellow Gonville and Caius Coll., Cambridge, 1985; fellow Can. Inst. for Advanced Rsch., 1986—. Editor: Relativity, Astrophysics and Cosmology, 1973; co-editor: General Relativity, An Einstein Centenary Survey, 1979, 300 Years of Gravitation, 1987 Decorated officer Order of Can.; recipient Izaak Walton Killiam meml. prize, 1984, Joint medal in math. physics Ctr. de Recherche Math./Can. Assn. Physicists, 1995, Tomalla Found. for Gravitational Rsch. prize, 1996. Fellow Royal Soc. Can., Royal Soc. (London); mem. Can. Assn. Physicists (medal of Achievement in Physics 1981), Internat. Soc. Gen. Relativity and Gravitation (pres. 1997-01). Jewish. Office: U Victoria Dept Physics Astronomy Victoria BC Canada V8W 3P6 E-mail: israel@uvic.ca

ISSA, DARRELL E. congressman; b. Cleveland, Ohio; m. Kathy; 1 child: William. Grad., Siena Heights U. Founder Directed Electronics, Vista, Calif.; mem. Congress, Calif., 48th dist. Mem. House com. on Internat. Rels., House Judiciary com., House com. on Small Bus. Co-chair Calif. Civic Rights Initiative, 1996; served in Army. Recipient Inc. Magazine's Entreprenuer Yr. award, 1994, Ellis Island Medal of Honor. Past chmn. Consumer Electronics Assn., former govr. Electronic Indus. Alliance; dir. Bus.-Industry Political Action com., San Diego Econ. Devel. Assn., Greater San Diego County Chamber of Commerce; past pres. Am. Task Force for Lebanon; served bd. trustees Siena Heights U. Office: 1725 Longworth House Office Bldg Washington DC 20515*

ISSARI, M(OHAMMAD) ALI, film producer, writer, consultant; b. Esfahan, Iran; s. Abbas Bek and Qamar (Soltan) I.; m. Joan Gura Aamodt, 1958; children: Scheherezade, Katayoun, Roxana. BA, U. Tehran, Iran, 1963; MA, U. So. Calif., 1968; PhD, 1979. Films officer Brit. Embassy, Brit. Council Joint Film Div., Tehran, 1944-50; asst. motion picture officer USIS, Tehran, 1950-65; cons. to various Iranian Govt. ministries on film and TV devels., 1950-77; liaison officer Am. and Iranian govt. ofcls., 1950-65; prof. cinema Coll. Communication Arts and Scis. Mich. State U., East Lansing, 1969-81, also dir. instructional film and multimedia prodn., 1969-78; mass media cons., 1981—; pres. Multimedia Prodn. Svcs., Thousand Oaks, Calif., 1989—. Film, public relations adviser to Iranian Oil Operating Cos. in, Iran, 1963-65; spl. cons. on edn. and instructional TV Saudi Arabian Ministry of Info., 1972; tchr. Persian lang. Iran-Am. Soc., Tehran, 1949-59; introduced audio-visual edn. in Iran, 1951; established first film festivals in Iran, 1949. Producer, dir. over 1000 instructional and documentary films, 1956-78; freelance film reporter: Telenews, UPI, CBS Iran, 1959-61; project dir., exec. producer: Ancient Iran Film Series, 1974-78; dir. film prodn. workshops, Cranbrook Inst., Detroit, 1973-74; author: A Picture of Persia, 1977, (with Doris A. Paul) What is Cinema Vérité?, 1979, Cinema in Iran, 1900-1979, 1989; contbr. articles on ednl. comm. and audio-visual instrn. to periodicals and profl. jours. Founder, exec. sec. Youth Orgn. of Iran, 1951-52; v.p. Rugby Football Fedn., Iran, 1952-53, pres., 1954-55. Decorated Order of Magnum Cap Ord: S.F. Danaie M. Sigillum (Denmark), Order of Cavalieres (Italy), Order of Oranje Nassau (The Netherlands), Orders of Kooshesh and Pas (Iran), Order of Esteghlal (Jordan), Order of Ordinis Sancti Silvestri Papae (Pope John 23d); recipient Meritorious Honor award USIA, 1965, Golden Eagle award Couns. for Internat. Non-Theatrical Events, 1975. Mem. Anglo-Iranian Dramatic Soc. (bd. dirs. 1943-50), Mich. Film Assn. (co-founder 1972, bd. dirs. 1972-73), Mid. East Studies Assn., N.Am. Soc. Motion Picture and TV Engrs. (life), Ancient Studies Inst. Inc. (co-founder, pres. 1991, 97-98), House of Iran, Inc. (co-founder, pres. 1990—), Delta Kappa Alpha (v.p. 1967). Fax: 805-498-0550

ISSEL, DANIEL PAUL, sports team executive, former professional basketball coach; b. Batavia, IL, Oct. 25, 1948; m. Cheri Issel; children: Sheridan, Scott. Student, U. Ky. Basketball player Ky. Cols., 1970-75, Denver Nuggets, 1975-85; broadcast analyst U. Ky., 1987-88; color analyst, mgr. player edn. and career enhancement programs Denver Nuggets, 1988-92, head coach, 1992-94, gen. mgr., 1998-99, pres., head coach, 1999—. Prin. Courtland Farms Horse Racing. Office: Denver Nuggets 1000 Chopper Cir Denver CO 80204-5809

ISTEL, JACQUES ANDRE, mayor; b. Paris, Jan. 28, 1929; came to U.S., 1940, naturalized, 1951; s. Andre and Yvonne Mathilde Cremieux I.; m. Felicia Juliana Lee, June 14, 1973; 1 dau. by previous marriage, Claudia Yvonne. A.B., Princeton, 1949. Stock analyst Andre Istel & Co., N.Y.C., 1950, 55; pres. Parachutes Inc., Orange, Mass., 1957-87, Intramgmt. Inc., N.Y.C., 1962-80; chmn. Pilot Knob Corp., 1982—; mayor Town of Felicity, Calif., 1986—; curator Ctrl. Point for Memories, 1992—. Pres. VI World Parachuting Championships, 1962; capt. U.S. Parachuting team, 1956, capt., team leader, 1958; chmn. Mass. Parachuting Commn., 1961-62; lifetime hon. pres. Internat. Parachuting Commn., Fedn. Aero. Internat., 1965— ; chmn. Hall of Fame of Parachuting, 1973—; chmn. Imp. Co. water commn. 1997—; founder Nat. Collegiate Parachuting League, 1957; founder World Commemorative Ctr., 1993. Author: Coe the Good Dragon at the Center of the World, 1985, Coe le Bon Dragon au Centre du Monde, 1985; contbr. articles to encys., profl. publs; patentee in field. Trustee Inst. for Man and Sci., 1975-82; bd. dirs. Marine Corps Scholarship Found., 1975-85. Served with USMC, 1952-54; lt. col. Res. Recipient Leo Stevens award, 1958, Diplome Paul Tissandier, 1969 Mem. Nat. Aero. Assn. (bd. dirs. 1965-68), Fedn. Internat. des Centres (pres. 1990—), Cercle de l'Union Interalliée (Paris), Marine Corps Res. Officers Assn., DAV (life), Racquet and Tennis Club (N.Y.C.), Princeton Club (N.Y.C.). Achievements include being a holder for the world record, parachuting, 1961; co-leader Nat. Geog. Soc. Vilcabamba Expdn., 1964. Home: Northview Felicity CA 92283 also: 10 rue Galilée 75116 Paris France Office: 1 Center Of The World Plz Felicity CA 92283-7777 E-mail: ctrworld@aol.com

ITABASHI, HIDEO HENRY, neuropathologist; b. Los Angeles, July 7, 1926; s. Masakichi and Mitsuko (Kobayashi) I.; m. Yoko Osawa, Feb. 3, 1952; children: Mark Masa, Helen Yoko. A.B., Boston U., 1949; postgrad., Yale U., 1949-50; M.D., Boston U., 1954. Diplomate: in neuropathology Am. Bd. Pathology. Intern U. Mich. Hosp., Ann Arbor, 1954-55, resident in neurology, 1955-58; assoc. rsch. neurologist U. Calif., San Francisco, 1958-60, asst. clin. prof., 1964-65; asst. neuropathologist Langley Porter Neuropsychiat. Inst., San Francisco, 1960-65; cons. Neuropathologist San Francisco Gen. Hosp., 1964-65; assoc. prof. neurology, pathology U. Mich. Med. Sch., Ann Arbor, 1968-71; prof.-in-residence pathology and neurology UCLA, 1975-93, prof. emeritus, 1993—, acting vice chair dept. pathology Sch. Medicine; acting chair pathology Harbor-UCLA Med. Ctr., 1990-91; cons. neuropathology dept., chief med. examiner-coroner Los Angeles County, L.A., 1977—. Cons. VA Hosp., Sepulveda, Calif., 1977-92; spl. fellow in neuropathology Nat. Inst. Neurol. Diseases and Blindness, 1958-60. Contbr. numerous articles on neurol. disorders to med jours. Mem. Am. Assn. Neuropathologists, Am. Acad. Forensic Scis., Nat. Assn. Med. Examiners, Am. Acad. Neurology. Office: County LA Dept Coroner 1104 N Mission Rd Los Angeles CA 90033

ITANO, HARVEY AKIO, biochemistry educator; b. Sacramento, Nov. 3, 1920; s. Masao and Sumako (Nakahara) I.; m. Rose Nakako Sakemi, Nov. 5, 1949; children: Wayne Masao, Glenn Harvey, David George. BS, U. Calif., Berkeley, 1942; MD, St. Louis U., 1945; PhD, Calif. Inst. Tech., 1950; DSc (hon.), St. Louis U., 1987. Intern City of Detroit Receiving Hosp., 1945-46; commd. officer USPHS, Bethesda, Md., 1950-70, advanced through grades to chief, sect. on chem. genetics, Nat. Inst. Arthritis and Metabolic Diseases, NIH, 1962-70, mem. hematology study sect., NIH, 1959-63, research fellow then sr. research fellow, Calif. Inst. Tech. Pasadena, 1950-54; prof. Dept. Pathology U. Calif. San Diego, La Jolla, 1970-88, prof. emeritus, 1988—. Vis. prof. Osaka (Japan) U., 1961-62, U. Chgo., 1965, U. Calif., San Francsico, 1967; cons. sickle cell anemia, mem. [illegible] 1970-81, NIH, Bethesda. Editor: (with Linus Pauling) Molecular Structure and Biological Specificity, 1957; contbr. articles to profl. jours. George Minot lectr., AMA, 1955; Japan Soc. for Promotion of Sci. fellow, Okayama U., 1983-84. Mem. AAAS, NAS, Am. Acad. Arts and Scis., Am. Chem. Soc. (Eli Lilly award in Biol. Chemistry 1954), Am. Soc. Biochemistry and Molecular Biology, Am. Soc. Hematology, Internat. Soc. Hematology, Phi Beta Kappa, Sigma Xi, Alpha Omega Alpha. Office: U Calif Dept Pathology La Jolla CA 92093-0506

ITO, HIROSHI, research chemist; Rsch. scientist Almaden Rsch. Ctr. IBM, San Jose, Calif. Recipient award Coop. Rsch. in Polymer Sci. and Engring., Am. Chem. Soc., 1992, award Soc. of Polymer Sci. (Japan), 1990, Photopolymer Sci. and Tech. award Tech. Assn. Photopolymer Japan, 1997, Kosar Meml. award Soc. Imaging Sci. Tech., 1999. Office: IBM Almaden Rsch Ctr 650 Harry Rd San Jose CA 95120-6099

ITO, LANCE ALLAN, judge; b. L.A., Aug. 2, 1950; s. Jim and Toshi I.; m. Margaret York. BA cum laude, UCLA, 1972; JD, U. Calif., Berkeley, 1975. Bar: Calif. 1976. Civil atty., 1975-77; dep. dist. atty. gang unit, complaints divsn., organized crime unit L.A. County Dist. Attys. Office, 1977-87; judge L.A. County Mcpl. Ct., 1987-89, Superior Ct. Calif., L.A. County, 1989—. Vice chair Calif. Task Force on Youth Gang Violence, 1986, 89, Calif. Task Force on Victims Rights, 1988. Named Trial Judge of Yr. L.A. County Bar Assn., 1992. Mem. Calif. Judges Assn. (bd. dirs., mem. Calif. coun. on criminal justice), L.A. County Bar Assn., Japanese-Am. Bar Assn. Democrat. Office: Criminal Cts Bldg 210 W Temple St Los Angeles CA 90012-3210

ITOH, TATSUO, engineering educator; b. Tokyo, May 5, 1940; s. Yohnosuke and Kimi (Okamoto) I.; m. Seiko Fukumori, June 16, 1969; children: Akihiro, Eiko. B.S., Yokohama Nat. U., Japan, 1964, M.S., 1966; Ph.D., U. Ill., 1969. Registered prof. engr., Tex. Research assoc. U. Ill., Urbana, 1969-71, research asst. prof., 1971-76; sr. research engr. Stanford Research Inst., Menlo Park, Calif., 1976-77; assoc. prof. U. Ky., Lexington, 1977-78, U. Tex., Austin, 1978-81, prof., 1981-90, Hayden Head prof., 1983-90; prof.and TRW endowed chair UCLA, 1991—. Guest rschr. AEG-Telefunken, Ulm, Fed. Republic of Germany, 1979; vis. prof. Def. Acad. Japan, 1991, U. Leeds, Eng., 1994—; hon. vis. prof. Nanjing Inst. Tech., China; hon. prof. Beijing Aeronautical and Astron. U., China, 1995—; adj. rsch. officer Comms. Rsch. Lab., Ministry of Post and Telecom., Japan, 1994; cons. Tex. Instruments, Dallas, 1979, Hughes Aircraft. Guest editor: Transactions, 1981; inventor millimeter-wave line, 1975, quasi-optical mixer, 1982, non-contact TD, 1995, high-power photo detector, 1995. Recipient Engring. Found. faculty awards, 1980-81, Billy and Claude Hocott Disting. Rsch. award, 1988, Disting. Alumnus award U. Ill., 1990, Shida award Min. of Post and Telecom., Japan, 1998, Japan Microwave prize Asia-Pacific Microwave Conf., 1998. Fellow IEEE (Millennium medal 2000, MTT Disting. Microwave Educator award 2000); mem. Microwave Theory and Techniques Soc. (hon. life; editor 1983-85, pres. 1990, jour. editor Microwave and Guided Wave Letters 1991-94), Internat. Sci. Radio Union (chmn. USNC commn. D 1988-90, chmn. commn. D 1993-96, long range planning com. 1996—), Inst. Electronics and Comm. Engrs. Home: 919 Levering Ave Apt 405 Los Angeles CA 90024-6617 Office: UCLA Dept Elec Engring Los Angeles CA 90095-0001 E-mail: itoh@ee.ucla.edu

IVERSON, PAUL, government agency administrator; BS in edn., So. Utah State Coll., 1970; MS in Ednl. Adminstrn., U. Nev., Las Vegas, 1976. Tchr. 5th grade Clark County Sch. Dist., 1970-75, sci. curriculum coord., 1975-80; adminstr. conservation and planning Nev. Dept. Energy, 1980-83; dep. dir. Nev. Dept. Minerals, 1983-95; adminstr. Nev. Dept. Agr., 1995—. Spkr. in field. Office: Nev Dept Agr 350 Capitol Hill Ave Reno NV 89502-2923

IVERSON, PETER JAMES, historian, educator; b. Whittier, Calif., Apr. 4, 1944; s. William James and Adelaide Veronica (Schmitt) I.; m. Kaaren Teresa Gonsoulin, Mar. 7, 1983; children: Erika, Jens, Tim, Scott. BA in History, Carleton Coll., 1967; MA in History, U. Wis., 1969, PhD in History, 1975. Vis. asst. prof. Ariz. State U., Tempe, 1975-76; from asst. prof to prof. U. Wyo., Laramie, 1976-86; coordinator div. social and behavioral scis. Ariz. State U., Phoenix, 1986-88, prof. history Tempe, 1988—, regents prof. history, 2000—; vis. prof. Carleton Coll., 1991. Panelist, reviewer Nat. Endowment Humanities, Washington, 1986—. Author: The Navajos: A Critical Bibliography, 1976, The Navajo Nation, 1981, Carlos Montezuma, 1982, The Navajos, 1990, When Indians Became Cowboys: Native Peoples and Cattle Ranching in the American West, 1994, Barry Goldwater: Native Arizonan, 1997, We Are Still Here: American Indians in the 20th Century, 1998, Riders of the West: Portraits From Indian Rodeo, 1999; co-editor: Indians in American History, 1998; editor: The Plains Indians of the 20th Century, 1985; co-editor: Major Problems in American Indian History, 1994, 2d edit., 2001; assoc. editor The Historian, 1990-95; editl. bd. Pacific Hist. Rev., 1986-88, Jour. Ariz. History, 1987-89, Social Sci. Jour., 1988-96, Montana: The Magazine of Western History, 1993—. Acting dir. McNickle Ctr. for History of Am. Indian, Newberry Libr., 1994-95, mem. adv. bd., 1993—; bd. dirs. Ariz. Humanities Coun., 1993-99; chmn. Wyo. Coun. Humanities, 1981-82; mem. Heard Mus., Phoenix, 1986—, Desert Bot. Garden, Phoenix, 1986—. Recipient Chief Manuelito Appreciation award Navajo Nation, 1984, Disting. Achievement award Carleton Coll. Alumni Assn., 1992, Lifetime Achievement award Am. Indian Hist. Assn., 1999; Newberry Libr. fellow, Chgo., 1973-74, Nat. Endowment Humanities fellow, 1982-83, Leadership fellow Kellogg Found., Battle Creek, Mich., 1982-85, NEH fellow, 1999-2000, Guggenheim Found. fellow, 1999-2000; Disting. Pub. scholar, Ariz. Humanities Coun., 1999. Mem. Am. Soc. Ethnohistory (coun. 1991-93, chmn. program com. 1994, chmn. prize com. 1987), Western Social Sci. Assn. (pres. 1988-89), Orgn. Am. Historians, Western History Assn. (chmn. prize com. 1991, co-chmn. program com. 1995, coun. 1995-98). Office: Ariz State U Dept History Tempe AZ 85287-2501 E-mail: peter.iverson@asu.edu

IVERSON, WAYNE DAHL, landscape architect, consultant; b. Mt. Horeb, Wis., Oct. 27, 1931; s. Inman Oliver and Anna Mathilda (Dahl) I.; m. Barbara Ruth Lusk, May 17, 1958; children: David, Ann, Caroline. BS, U. Wis., 1955, MS, 1956. Landscape architect Nat. Pk. Svc., San Francisco, 1956-58, Inyo Nat. Forest, Bishop, Calif., 1958-66; regional landscape architect, So. region U.S. Forest Svc., Atlanta, 1966-67, Calif. region, 1967-86; prin. Scenic Resource Mgmt., Sedona, Ariz., 1987—. Author: (handbook) National Forest Landscape Management, (with others) Landscape Assessment, 1975, (with others) American Landscape Architecture, 1989. Co-founder No. Ariz. Trust Lands, Sedona, 1988 mem. bd. adjustment City of Sedona, 1989; mem. pks. and recreation com. Coconino County, Flagstaff, Ariz., 1989-97; bd. dirs. Keep Sedona Beautiful, Inc., 1988-97. Cpl. U.S. Army, 1952-54, Korea. Recipient 1st Alumni award Landscape Architecture dept., U. Wis., Madison, 1981, Award of Excellence, Nat. Soc. for Pk. Resources, 1982, Presdl. Design award Nat. Endowment for Arts, 1984, 1st Arthur Hawthorne Carhart award U.S. Forest Svc., 1992. Fellow Am. Soc. Landscape Architects. Avocations: hiking, travel, photography, nature study, genealogy. Office: Scenic Resources Mgmt 115 Highland Rd Sedona AZ 86336-6152 E-mail: wiversrm@sedona.net

IVESTER, (RICHARD) GAVIN, industrial designer; b. San Jose, Calif., May 28, 1963; BS in Indsl. Design, San Jose State U., 1987; postgrad., Domus Acad., Milan, 1989. Materials clk., project coord., product designer Apple Computer, Cupertino, Calif., 1981-87, indsl. designer, 1987-92; [illegible] Inc., Beaverton, Oreg., 1997—. Guest lectr. Stanford (Calif.) U., 1991—;

indsl. designer for Apple Computer, Silicon Graphics, Sun Microsys., Bell Sports, Sony Microsys., Hewlett-Packard, Samsung, Digidesign, Nike. Co-inventor PowerBook; patentee in field. Recipient Ann. Design Rev. awards ID, 1988, 90, 91, 92, Industrie Forum Hannover Top Ten Design award for Macintosh Power Books, Germany, 1992, 93, Top Ten Design award for Newton, 1994, Gold award for Macintosh PowerBooks, Indsl. Designers Soc. Am., 1992, 93. Avocations: playing bass in a rock band, painting, bicycling. Office: Nike Inc One Bowerman Dr MJ-4 Beaverton OR 97005-6453

IVRY, RICHARD, psychology educator; b. May 22, 1958; BA in Psychology, Brown U., 1981; MS in Psychology, U. Oreg., Eugene, 1983, PhD in Psychology, 1986. Rsch. assoc. U. Oreg. and Good Samaritan Hosp., Portland, 1987-88; asst. prof. psychology U. Calif., Santa Barbara, 1987-90, Berkeley, 1990-93, assoc. prof., prof., 1993—. Mem. human perception and cognition panel NSF; ad hoc reviewer Behavioral Neurosci., Biol. Psychology, Cognitive Neuropsychology, Cognitive Neurosci., Cognitive Psychology, Jour. Exptl. Psychology, NIH, Nature, Perception, Procs. NAS, Psychol. Rsch., Psychol. Rev., also others. Mem. editl. bd. Jour. Motor Behavior; cons. editor Jour. Expt. Psychology: Human Perception and Performance; contbr. numerous articles and revs. to sci. jours., including Perception and Psychophysics, Acta Psychologia, Jour. Motor Behavior, Computer Vision, Graphics and Image Processing, Contemporary Psychology, Exptl. Brain Rsch., Jour. Exptl. Psychology, Brain, Jour. Cognitive Neurosci., Psychol. Rsch., Brain and Behavioral Scis., Current Opinion in Neurobiology, Can. Jour. Neurol. Sci., Psychol. Sci., Neuropsychology, Neuropsychologia, also chpts. to books. Recipient Troland rsch. award NAS, 1997; Alfred P. Sloan rsch. fellow in neurosci., 1990-93, Internat. Ctr. Etudiants et Stagiaires rsch. fellow, 1995; rsch. grantee Office Naval Rsch., 1987-90, Nat. Inst. for Neurol. Diseases and Stroke, 1991-98. Whitehall Found., 1994-97, NSF, 1994-97, NIMH, 1994-99. Mem. APA, Psychonomic Soc., Soc. for Cognitive Neurosci., Soc. for Neurosci. Office: U Calif 3210 Tolman Hall Dept Psychology Berkeley CA 94720

IWAN, WILFRED DEAN, mechanical engineer, educator; b. Pasadena, Calif., May 21, 1935; s. Wilfred August and Dorothy Anna Sarah (Glass) I.; m. Alta Joan Gish, Sept. 13, 1957; children: William Douglas, Robert Dean, Stephen Bruce. B.S., Calif. Inst. Tech., 1957, M.S., 1958, Ph.D., 1961. Asst. and assoc. prof. mechanics U.S. Air Force Acad., 1961-64; asst., assoc. and prof. applied mechanics Calif. Inst. Tech., 1964—; dir. Earthquake Engring. Rsch. Lab., 1993—, 1993—; pres. Calif. Univs. for Rsch. in Earthquake Engring., 1988-91. Chmn. Calif. Seismic Safety Commn., 1986-88, 92-94; cons. to industry; prin. investigator on various federally sponsored rsch. projects; mem. NRC Bd. on Natural Disasters, 1992—, chmn., 1996—, mem. com. on hazard mitigation engring., 1992-95, chmn., 1992-95. Assoc. editor Jour. Applied Mechanics, ASME, 1982-89; mem. editorial bd. Internat. Jour. Soil Dynamics and Earthquake Engring., 1981-93, Internat. Jour. Probabilistic Engring. Mechanics, 1985—; contbg. editor Internat. Jour. Nonlinear Mechanics, 1996—; contbr. articles to profl. jours. Active Lake Ave Congregational Ch., Pasadena. Capt. USAF, 1961-64. Fellow ASME; mem. ASCE (Nathan M. Newmark medal 1997), Earthquake Engring. Rsch. Inst. Rsch. in vibration dynamics, earthquake engring. Office: Calif Inst Tech Mail Code 104 # 44 Pasadena CA 91125-0001

IWASE, RANDALL YOSHIO, former state legislator; b. Honolulu, Dec. 1, 1947; s. Bruce S. and Ruby N. (Hamasaki) Hamada; m. Jan W. Amemiya, Jan. 8, 1977; 3 children. BA, U. Fla., 1971; JD, U. San Francisco, 1974. Dep. atty. gen. Dept. of Atty. Gen., Honolulu, 1974-85; city coun. mem. Honolulu City Coun., 1986-88; exec. dir. Aloha Tower Devel. Corp., Honolulu, 1988-90; state senator Hawaii St. Senate, Honolulu, 1990-2000; atty. Dwyer, Imanaka, Schraff, Honolulu, 1991—. Mem. Japanese Am. Citizens League, Honolulu, 1990—; bd. dirs. Nanakuli (Hawaii) Neighborhood Housing Svc., 1990—, West Oahu YMCA, Mililani, Hawaii, 1990—. Mem. Hawaii State Bar Assn., Phi Beta Kappa, Phi Kappa Phi. Democrat. Avocations: reading, tennis. Office: Hawaii State Senate 415 S Beretania St Rm 222 Honolulu HI 96813-2407

IZATT, REED M. chemistry researcher; b. Logan, Utah, Oct. 10, 1926; s. Alexander Spowart Jr. and Marian (McNeil) I.; m. Helen Felix, Aug. 10, 1949 (dec. July 1998); children: Susan Marie Foster, Linda Jean, Neil Ernest, Ted Alexander, Steven Reed, Anne Marie; m. Virginia Bills Christensen, Oct. 24, 1998. BS, Utah State U., 1951; PhD, Pa. State U., 1954; postgrad., Carnegie Mellon U., 1954-56. Dir. grad. and undergrad. student rsch. Brigham Young U., Provo, Utah, 1956—. Vis. prof. U. Utah, Salt Lake City, 1972, U. Calif., San Diego, 1977. Contbr. articles to profl. jours. and books. Recipient Karl G. Maeser Rsch. and Creative Arts award, 1967, NIH Career Devel. award, 1967-72, Huffman award, 1983, Utah Gov.'s medal for Sci., 1990. Fellow AAAS; mem. Am. Chem. Soc. (chmn. Salt Lake sect. 1965, councilor Salt Lake and ctrl. Utah sects. 1966-72, mem. local sect. activities com. 1966-72, Separations Sci. and Tech. award 1996, Utah award 1971), Utah Acad. Scis., Arts and Letters (Gardner prize 1983), Calorimetry Conf. (bd. dirs. 1973-76), Internat. Symposium on Macrocyclic Chemistry (chmn. internat. adv. com.), Sigma Xi (pres. Brigham Young U chpt. 1980-82), Phi Kappa Phi. Office: Brigham Young U Dept Chem & Biochem C100 Benson Sci Bldg Provo UT 84602-5700

JABBARI, AHMAD, publishing executive; b. Tehran, Iran, Feb. 28, 1945; BA, Pa. State U., 1967, MA, 1969, Washington U., St. Louis, 1974; PhD, Washington U., 1978. Assoc. prof. econs. and mgmt. Centre Coll. of Ky., 1976-78; editor, chief Mazda Publishers, Costa Mesa, Calif., 1978—. Office: Mazda Publishers PO Box 2603 Costa Mesa CA 92628-2603

JABLONS, DAVID M. surgeon, educator; BA in Lit., Yale U., 1979; MD, Albany Med. Coll., 1984. Resident Tufts-New England Med. Ctr., Boston; surg. oncology fellow Nat. Cancer Inst., NIH, Bethesda, Md.; fellow cardiothoracic surgery Cornell Med. Ctr., Meml.-Sloan Kettering Med. Ctr., N.Y.C.; head divsn. thoracic surgery Naval Med. Ctr., Oakland, Calif., 1993—; asst. clin. prof. surgery U. Calif. San Francisco Med. Ctr., 1994-95; asst. prof. surgery U. Calif. San Francisco/Mt. Zion Med. Ctr., 1995—, chief-sect. thoracic surgery, 1997—. Contbr. articles to profl. jours. Mem. ACS, Soc. Thoracic Surgeons, Am. Assn. for Cancer Rsch., Soc. Surg. Oncology. Office: UCSF Mt Zion Med Ctr San Francisco CA 94143-0001 also: 2330 Post St Ste 420 San Francisco CA 94115-3466 Fax: 415-353-9525. E-mail: jablonsd@surgery.ucsf.edu

JABS, REINY, state legislator, farmer, rancher; b. Hardin, Mont., May 4, 1929; m. Monte Lee Jabs. BS in Agr./Edn., Mont. State U., 1951. Tchr. pub. schs., 1954-65; farmer, rancher, 1956-96; mem. Mont. State Senate, 1994—, chair agr., livestock and irrigation com.; mem. judiciary com., mem. hwys. and transp. com. Past bd. dirs. Big Horn County FHA; mem. Hardin Sch. Bd., 1972-78; trustee Big Horn County Electric Coop.; bd. dirs. REA, 1980-94. Served with USAF, 1951-53. Mem. Luth. Laymen's League, C. of C., Soil Conservation Assn. Republican. Home: HC 36 Hardin MT 59034-9802

JACKMAN, ROBERT ALAN, retail executive; b. N.Y.C., Mar. 22, 1939; s. Joseph and Kate Queenie (Silverman) J.; m. Lois Wiederschall, June 10, 1962; children: Jennifer Sharon, Deborah Lynn. BS, U. Bridgeport, 1961. Dir. sales Mattel Inc., Hawthorne, Calif., 1963-75; sr. v.p. mktg. and sales Tyco Industries Inc., Moorestown, N.J., 1975-78; gen. mgr. Aurora Products Inc., Stamford, Conn., 1978-80; ptnr. Scott Lancaster Jackman Mills Atha, Westport, 1980-83; pres., chief exec. officer Leisure Dynamics Inc. div. Coleco Industries, Westport, 1983-86; with Oak Tree Publs., San Diego, 1983-87; exec. v.p. Coleco Industries Inc., West Hartford, Conn., 1986-88; gen. mgr. Tomy Am., Inc., Southport, 1988-90, also bd. dirs.; owner Yes I Can, 1990—. Cons. Harvard U. Bus. Sch. Club, N.Y.C., 1984. Patentee in field. With USAR, 1961-62. Recipient Disting. Alumni award U. Bridgeport (Conn.), 1986. Mem. U. Bridgeport Mktg. Coun., Mission Hills Country Club (Rancho Mirage, Calif.). Avocations: tennis, music, reading. Home: 8 Via Elegante Rancho Mirage CA 92270-1969 Office: 35 325 Date Palm Dr Ste 131 Cathedral City CA 92234-7031

JACKSON, ALLEN KEITH, museum administrator; b. Rocky Ford, Colo., July 22, 1932; s. Monford L. and Leliah Jean (Hipp) J.; m. Barbara May Hollard, June 13, 1954; children: Cary Vincent, Deborah Kay and Edward Keith (twins), Fredrick James. B.A., U. Denver, 1954; postgrad., Cambridge (Eng.) U., 1955; Th.M. (Elizabeth Iliff Warren fellow), Iliff Sch. Theology, 1958; Ph.D., Emory U., 1960. Meth. student minister, Erie, Colo., 1955-58; ordained elder Meth. Ch., 1958; instr. sociology Emory U., 1958-60; chaplain, asst. prof. religion and sociology Morningside Coll., Sioux City, Iowa, 1960-62, dean coll., 1962-67; pres. Huntingdon Coll., Montgomery, Ala., 1968-93; exec. dir. natural heritage Idaho Mus. Natural History, Idaho State U., Pocatello, 1993—. Contbr. articles to profl. jours. Past pres. Montgomery Area United Appeal. Fulbright scholar Cambridge U., 1955; honor fellow Emory U., 1960. Mem. Ala. Assn. Ind. Colls. and Univs. (pres. 1969-71), Ala. Council Advancement Pvt. Colls. (pres. 1975-81), Phi Beta Kappa, Omicron Delta Kappa, Beta Theta Pi, Phi Kappa Phi. Club: Rotarian. Home: 633 W Mcnabb Rd Inkom ID 83245-1502 Office: Idaho State Univ PO Box 8040 Pocatello ID 83209-0001

JACKSON, BEVERLEY JOY JACOBSON, columnist, lecturer; b. L.A., Nov. 20, 1928; d. Phillip and Dorothy Jacobson; m. Robert David Jackson (div. Aug. 1964); 1 child, Tracey Dee. Student, U. So. Calif. , UCLA, UCLA. Daily columnist Santa Barbara (Calif.) News Press, 1968-92, Santa Barbara Independent, 1992-2001; internat. lectr., 2001—. Nat. lectr. Santa Barbara History, History of China Recreated, Chinese Footbinding, Shoes for Bound Feet, China Today; free lance writer, fgn. corr. Author: Dolls and Doll Houses of Spain, 1970, (with others) I'm Just Wild About Harry, 1979, Spendid Slippers: A Thousand Years of an Erotic Tradition, 1997, Ladder to the Clouds-Intrigues and Traditions of Chinese Rank, 1999, King Fisher Blue, 2001. Bd. dirs. Santa Barbara br. Am. Cancer Soc., 1963-92; mem. art mus. coun. L.A. Mus. Art, 1959-96, mem. costume coun., 1983-92; docent L.A. Mus. Art, 1962-64; mem. exec. bd. Channel City Club (formerly Channel City Women's Forum), 1969-2000; mem. adv. bd. Santa Barbara Hist. Soc. Mus., Coun. of Christmas Cheer, Women's Shelter Bldg., Direct Relief Internat., Nat. Coun. Drug and Alcohol Abuse, Am. Oceans Campaign; mem. adv. bd. Hospice of Santa Barbara, 1981-92, Stop AIDS Coun., Arthritis Found.; bd. dirs. So. Calif. Com. for Shakespear's Globe Theatre, Friends of UCSB Libr.; chmn. Santa Barbara Com. for Visit Queen Elizabeth II, 1982—; founder costume guild Santa Barbara Hist. Soc.; curator Chinese collections Santa Barbara Hist. Mus.; adv. bd. Santa Barbara Choral Soc.; hon. bd. Santa Barbara Salvation Army, Ensemble Theatre Santa Barbara; adv. bd. Storyteller Sch. Homeless Children. Mem. Commanderie Bordeaux de San Francisco. Home: PO Box 5118 Santa Barbara CA 93150-5118 E-mail: bevjack@silcom.com

JACKSON, CYNTHIA L. lawyer; b. Houston, May 6, 1954; BA, Stanford U., 1976; JD, U. Tex., 1979. Bar: Tex. 1979, Calif. 1980. Mem. Heller, Ehrman, White & McAuliffe, Palo Alto, Calif., 1983—, Baker & McKenzie, Palo Alto, 2000—. Mem. ABA. Office: Baker & McKenzie 660 Hansen Way Palo Alto CA 94304-1044

JACKSON, DAVID ROBERT, school system administrator; b. Long Beach, Calif., Jan. 15, 1945; s. Harlan Leroy and Helen Louise (Worthen) J.; m. Stacey Ann Bryan, Nov. 13, 1971; children: David, Daniel, Chad, Loren, Darcy. Student, Fullerton Coll., 1963-64, Brigham Young U., 1965-67, Santa Ana Coll., 1977, Orange Coast Coll., 1977-78. Mgr. trainee Carl Karcher Enterprizes, Fullerton, Calif., 1964; asst. mgr. Household Fin. Co., Santa Ana., 1964-65; mgr. Chateau Apres Lodge, Park City, Utah, 1965-69; pres. Aero Wash Co., Santa Ana., Calif., 1970-79; pres., exec. dir. Fairmont Schs. Inc., Anaheim, 1979—. Former leader Boy Scouts Am.; bishop LDS Ch., Corona, 1990-96; chmn. Orange County 2000, Calif., 1991-93, also bd. dirs. Mem. Nat. Ind. Pvt. Sch. Assn. (bd. dirs. 1981—, founding mem., pres. 1993-98), Calif. Assn. Nationally Recognized Schs. (founder, pres. 1992-93), Orange County Pvt. Sch. Assn. (pres. 1990-93, founder). Republican. Avocations: snow skiing, geneology, private pilot. Office: Fairmont Sch 1575 W Marble St Anaheim CA 92802

JACKSON, DILLON EDWARD, lawyer; b. Washington, Apr. 18, 1945; s. Paul David and Virginia (Dillon) J.; children: David I., Anne E.; m. Misha Halvarsson, Aug. 19, 1989. BA, Middlebury (Vt.) Coll., 1967; JD, U. Wash., 1970. Bar: Wash. 1970, U.S. Dist. Ct. (we. and ea. dists.) Wash. 1970, U.S. Ct. Appeals (9th cir.) 1970, U.S. Dist. Ct. Ariz. 1991. Assoc. Kleist & Helmick, Seattle, 1971-73, Powell Livengood & Silvernale, Kirkland, Wash., 1973-75; ptnr. Keller Jacobsen Jackson & Snodgrass, Bellevue, 1975-85, Hatch & Leslie, Seattle, 1985-91, Foster Pepper & Shefelman, Seattle, 1991—. Chairperson creditor rights and bankruptcy dept. Am. Bankruptcy Bd. Cert.; bd. mem. Consumer Credit Counseling, Seattle, 1975-79; chmn. publs. com. Am. Bankruptcy Inst., bd. mem., 1999—. Co-author: Commercial Law Desk Book, 1995; contbg. author: Advance Chapter 11 Bankruptcy Practice, 1989-95. Pres. Dox Coop., Seattle, 1989-91. Fellow Am. Coll. Bankruptcy (co-founder, mem. copyright com.); mem. ABA, Wash. State Trial Lawyers Assn., Wash. State Bar Assn. (creditor-debtitor sect., chairperson 1984-88), Continuing Legal Edn. Bd. (chairperson 1991-92). Office: Foster Pepper & Shefelman PLLC 1111 3rd Ave Ste 3400 Seattle WA 98101-3299

JACKSON, HANNA BETH, state legislator; BA, Scripps Coll.; JD, Boston U. Atty. Santa Barbara (Calif.) County Dist. Atty. Office; pvt. practice; assembly mem. Calif. State, Santa Barbara. Chair State Commn. Status of Women; appointee Blue Ribbon Commn. Child Support Devel. and Enforcement; task force Family Equity, State Senate. Office: Calif State Assembly 101 W Anapamu St Ste A Santa Barbara CA 93101-3140 Fax: 805-564-1651. E-mail: assemblymember.Jackson@assembly.ca.gov

JACKSON, JACK C. state legislator, rancher, educator; b. Leupp, Ariz., Sept. 14, 1933; m. Eloise Jackson. Student, No. Ariz. U. Rancher; educator; mem. Ariz. Ho. of Reps., 1985-98, Ariz. Senate, Dist. 3, Phoenix, 1998—. Active Window Rock (Ariz.) Sch. Bd.; past pres. N.A.C. of Navajoland. With Nat. Guard. Mem. All Indian Rodeo Cowboy Assn. (past pres.). Democrat. Office: State Capitol Bldg 1700 W Washington St # 313 Phoenix AZ 85007-2812 also: PO Box 4 Window Rock AZ 86515-0004 E-mail: jjackson@azleg.state.az.us

JACKSON, JAMES F. nuclear engineer, educator; b. Ogden, Utah, Aug. 15, 1939; s. Allyn Boyd and Virginia (Dixon) J.; m. Joan Borger, Aug. 25, 1960; children: James D., Bret A., Tracy L., Wendy L. BS, U. Utah, 1961; MS, MIT, 1962; PhD, UCLA, 1969. Rsch. engr. Atomics Internat., L.A., 1962006; nuclear engr. Argonne Nat. Lab., Idaho Falls, Idaho, 1969-72, group leader Argonne, Ill., 1972-74; assoc. prof. Brigham Young U., Provo, Utah, 1974-76, adj. prof., 1998—; cons. Los Alamos (N.Mex.) Nat. Lab., 1974-76, group/div. leader, 1976-82, dep. assoc. dir., 1979-81, div. leader, 1983-84, assoc. dir., 1984-86, dep. dir., 1986-98, staff mem., 1998-99. Contbr. articles to jours. in field. Mem. exec. bd. Community Devel. Com., Los Alamos, 1989-93; bd. dirs. Los Alamos Citizens Against Substance Abuse, 1989-93. Recipient E.O. Lawrence award Dept. Energy, Washington, 1983. Mem. NAE, Am. Nuclear Soc. (safety div. 1967—, exec. com. 1977-80), Tau Beta Pi. Republican. Mem. LDS Ch. Avocations: history, motorsports, photography. Home: 536 Sheffield Dr Provo UT 84604-5666 Office: Los Alamos Nat Lab Ofc Deputy Dir Los Alamos NM 87545-0001 E-mail: jackson538@home.com, jackson-james-f@lanl.gov

JACKSON, JAMES T. career officer; b. Ft. Knox, Ky. BS in Aerospace Engring., Kent State U.; MA in Personnel Mgmt. and Adminstrn., Ctrl. Mich. U.; grad., Army Command Gen. Staff Coll., Army War Coll. Commd. 2d lt. U.S. Army, advanced through grades to brig. gen., early assignments include co. comdr., asst. divsn. comdr., S-3 (air) 2d bn., S-3 (ops.) 1st bn.; ops. officer, then asst. chief of staff 1st corps support command; S-4 logistics, S-3 ops., then exec. officer 3d brigade, 82d airborne divsn.; G-3 ops. 7th Infantry divsn.; strategic planner U.S. Spl. Ops. Command, exec. officer to comdr.-in-chief; asst. divsn. comdr. 7th Infantry divsn., U.S. Army. Decorated Legion of Merit with oak leaf custer, bronze star, Def. Meritorious Svc. medal with oak leaf cluster, Meritorious Svc. medal with 3 oak leaf clusters, others. Achievements include being a master parachutist.

JACKSON, JANET DAMITA, singer, dancer; b. Gary, Ind., June 16, 1966; d. Joseph and Katherine J.; m. James DeBarge, 1984 (div. 1985). Albums include Janet Jackson, Dream Street, 1984, Control, 1986, Rhythm Nation 1814, 1991, janet, 1993, Design of a Decade, The Velvet Rope, 1997; actress (TV series) Good Times, 1977, A New Kind of Family, Diff'rent Strokes, Fame; (films) Poetic Justice, 1993 (Academy award nomination Best Original Song 1993), Nutty Professor II, 2000. Recipient 6 Am. Music awards, 1987, 1988, 1991, 5 Grammy nominations, MTV Video Vanguard award, 1990, Grammy award, Best R&B song 1994 for "That's the Way Love Goes" with Terry Lewis and James Harris III; MTV Best Female Video for "If". Office: Creative Artists Agency 9830 Wilshire Blvd Beverly Hills CA 90212-1825

JACKSON, JEANNE PELLEGREN, apparel executive; b. Denver, Aug. 10, 1951; d. John James and Barbara (Grove) Pellegren; m. Douglas Emmett Jackson, Nov. 23, 1984; children: Lindsay, Craig. BS in Fin., U. Colo., 1974; MBA, Harvard Bus. Sch., 1978. Buyer, mgr. Bullocks Dept. Stores, L.A., 1978-85; v.p. merchandise mgr. to sr. v.p. direct mail pvt. brands Saks Fifth Ave., N.Y.C., 1985-89; sr. v.p. merchandising Walt Disney Attractions, Orlando, 1989-92; exec. v.p. merchandising Victoria's Secret, Columbus, Ohio, 1992-95; CEO Banana Republic, 1996-2000, Wal-Mart.com, 2000—. Instr. mktg. U. So. Calif., L.A., 1979-81; adv. bd. Navy Exch., Norfolk, Va., 1991—. Bd. dirs. Orlando Mus. Art, 1990-92. Republican. Avocations: skiing, tennis. Office: Walmartcom 135 Constitution Dr Menlo Park CA 94025

JACKSON, JOHN JAY, clergyman; b. Chula Vista, Calif., July 13, 1961; s. E. Marvin and Mildred L. Jackson; m. Pamela Harrison, Aug. 18, 1979; children: Jennifer, Dena, Rachel, Joshua. BA in Religion, Chapman U., 1981; MA in Theology, Fuller Theol. Sem., 1983; MA in Ednl. Adminstrn., U. Calif., Santa Barbara, 1984, PhD in Ednl. Adminstrn., 1986. Youth dir. First Bapt. Ch., Buena Park, Calif., 1979-81; min. of youth Oxnard (Calif.) First Bapt., 1981-83, min. of edn., 1983-84, assoc. pastor, 1984-87, sr. pastor, 1988-92; exec. min. Am.-Bapt. Chs. Pacific S.W., Covina, Calif., 1993-97; pastor Carson Valley Christian Ctr., Minden, Nev., 1997—. Bd. dirs. Am. Bapt. Homes of the West, Oakland, Calif., 1993-97, Atherton Bapt. Homes, 1993-97; chair integration adv. com. Oxnard Sch. Dist., 1990-92. Recipient Disting. Svc. award Oxnard Sch. Dist., 1992. Mem. Christian Mgmt. Assn., Oxnard C. of C. (leadership com. 1991, chair edn. com. 1988-90). Office: Carson Valley Christian Ctr PO Box 892 Minden NV 89423-0892

JACKSON, KENNETH ARTHUR, physicist, researcher; b. Connaught, Ont., Can., Oct. 23, 1930; s. Arthur and Susanna (Vatcher) J.; m. Jacqueline Della Olyan, June 20, 1952 (div.); children: Stacy Margaret, Meredith Suzanne, Stuart Keith; m. Camilla M. Maruszewski, June 21, 1980 (div.). BS, U. Toronto, 1952, MS, 1953; PhD, Harvard U., 1956. Postdoctoral fellow Harvard U., Cambridge, Mass., 1956-58, asst. prof. metallurgy, 1958-62; mem. tech. staff Bell Labs., Murray Hill, N.J., 1962-67, head material physics research dept., 1967-81, head optical materials research dept., 1981-89; prof. materials sci. and engring. U. Ariz., 1989—. Lectr. Welch. Found., 1970, 85; mem. research adv. panel Air Force Office Sci. Research, 1976-82, space application bd. Nat. Acad. Sci., 1974-82. Editor-in-chief Optical Materials, 1999—; contbr. articles to profl. jours.; patentee in field. Recipient Mathewson Gold medal AIME, 1966, Crystal growth award AACG, 1993. Fellow AAAS, The Metall. Soc.-AIME, Am. Phys. Soc.; mem. Internat. Orgn. Crystal Growth (treas. 1978-86, Frank prize 1998), Am. Assn. Crystal Growth (pres. 1968 75, coun., award 1993), Materials Rsch. Soc. (v.p. 1975-77, pres. 1977-78, coun.), Am. Soc. Metals, Engring. Coun. for Profl. Devel. (mem. coun.), Fedn. Materials Soc. (trustee). Office: U Ariz 4715 E Ft Lowell Rd Tucson AZ 85712-1201 E-mail: kaj@aml.arizona.edu

JACKSON, KINGSBURY TEMPLE, educational contract consultant; b. Newton, Mass., May 15, 1917; s. Ralph Temple and Elizabeth Mesarole (Rhodes) J.; m. June Stewart Cooper, July 29, 1950 (dec. Feb. 1976). B.S., MIT, 1940; postgrad., NYU, 1949-51; M.S., U. Ala., 1964, U. So. Calif., 1969, Pepperdine U., 1975. Registered profl. engr., Calif., Ala. Commd. 2d lt. U.S. Army, 1940, advanced through grades to lt. col., 1961, ret., 1965; comdr. U.S. Army Depot, also Camp Mercer, Korea, 1957-58; project officer, indsl. project dir. U.S. Army Saturn Space Vehicle Program and Pershing Missile System, 1959-61; dir. U.S. Army Missile Command Engring. Documentation Ctr., Redstone Arsenal, Ala., 1962-63; program coordinator NATO-Hawk Missile System, 1963-65; prin. contracting officer, chief European procurement U.S. Army Ordnance, 1964-65; lectr. mgmt. and engring. Grad. Sch., U. So. Calif., L.A., 1965-69; contractual relations supr. L.A. Bd. Edn., 1969-82; pres. Contract Consultants, L.A., 1982—, K.T. Jackson, Gen. Contractors, L.A., 1991—. Author: Engineering documentation Systems Development: Department of Defense and NASA, 1963, Aerospace Propellants and Chemicals: The Manager's Approach, 1968 Vice pres., mem. bd. dirs. Kingsbury Properties Ltd.; corp. sec., bd. dirs. The Concert Singers, Inc. Mem. Am. Soc. Indsl. Engrs., Am. Soc. Mil. Comptrs., Am. Ordnance Assn. (mem. exec. bd. prodn. technique divsn., Army rep. to engring. documentation sect. 1962-65), Soc. Automotive Engrs. (rep. to aerospace gen. stds. divsn. 1962-65), Ret. Officers Assn. (life), Calif. Assn. Sch. Bus. Ofcls., Internat. Assn. Sch. Bus. Ofcls. (emeritus), Aircraft Owners and Pilots Assn., The Concert Singers, Inc., The Planetary Soc., Nat. Space Soc., MIT Club (So. Calif.), A&E Flying Club. Clubs: Mass. Inst. Tech. (So. Calif.); A & E Flying Office: Contract Consultants PO Box 91161 Los Angeles CA 90009-1161 E-mail: kingtemp@aol.com

JACKSON, MELBOURNE LESLIE, chemical engineering educator and administrator, consultant; b. Wisdom, Mont., Sept. 27, 1915; s. James R. and Adeline (Mallon) J.; m. Elizabeth Clara Ford, Apr. 2, 1944; children: Gary Leslie, Linda Mary, Laurie Elizabeth, Nancy Ruth. BSChemE, Mont. State U., 1941, D in Engring. (hon.), 1980; PhDChemE, U. Minn., 1948. Registered profl. engr., Wash., Idaho. Instr. chem. engring. U. Minn., Mpls., 1944-48; from asst. prof. to assoc. prof. U. Colo., Boulder, 1948-50; head process devel. U.S. Naval Ordnance Test Sta., China Lake, Calif., 1950-53; prof. U. Idaho, Moscow, 1953-65, 70-80, head dept. chem. engring., 1953-65, dean grad. sch., 1965-70, dean Coll. Engring., 1973, 78-80, 83. Cons. numerous corps. including James River Corp.; pres. U. Idaho Fed. Credit Union, Moscow, 1972-74. Patentee aeration/flotation devices, 1978,

80; contbr. articles to profl. jours. Chmn. Idaho Air Pollution Control Commn., Boise, 1959-72; chmn., trustee Moscow Sch. Dist., 1957-63. Fellow Am. Inst. Chem. Engrs; mem. Am. Chem. Soc., Am. Soc. Engring. Edn., Sigma Xi. Methodist. Avocations: boating, photography. Address: 532 Eisenhower Moscow ID 83843-9596 E-mail: mlj@uidaho.edu

JACKSON, PHILIP DOUGLAS, professional basketball coach; b. Deer Lodge, Mont., Sept. 17, 1945; m. June; 5 children. Grad., North Dakota, 1967. Basketball player N.Y. Knicks, 1967-78, N.J. Nets, 1978-80, asst. coach, 1980-82; head coach Albany Patrons (Cen. Basketball Assn.), 1982-87; asst. coach Chicago Bulls, 1987-89, head coach, 1989-98, Los Angeles Lakers, Los Angeles, 1999-. Mem. NBA Championship Team, 1970, 73; coach NBA championship team, 1991, 92, 93,96; named Coach of Yr., NBA, 1996. Office: Los Angeles Lakers PO Box 10 3900 W Manchester Blvd Inglewood CA 90306

JACKSON, PHILLIP ELLIS, marketing executive, writer; b. Kansas City, Mo., June 4, 1952; s. Phillip Anthony and Lois Irene (Seward) J.; m. Dawn Mutolo Jackson, Aug. 9, 1975; 1 child, Emily Mutolo. AA, Mohawk Valley C.C., 1972; BA magna cum laude in Liberal Arts, SUNY, Albany, 1974; MA in Internat. Rels., SUNY, 1975; PhD in Polit. Sci., U. Chgo., 1981. Speech writer; speech writer, issue com. chmn. Steve Bartlett Congl. Campaign, 1982; sr. v.p. pub. affairs Greater Dallas C. of C., 1982-93; exec. dir. Dallas United, 1984-93; dir. Tex. office Cassidy & Assocs., Dallas, 1993-95; v.p. Signal Sites, Dallas, 1995—. Author fiction. Cons. Dallas Charter Rev. Com., 1989; dir. City of Dallas, Dallas C. of C. N.Am. Free Trade Agreement Labor Secretariat Task Force, 1991-93. Recipient Citizens award Chgo. Police Dept., 1978, Presdl. citations Pvt. Sector Initiatives, 1985, 86, 89. Home: 3901 Morningside Dr Plano TX 75093-7902 Office: 3068 E Sunset Rd Ste 1 Las Vegas NV 89120 E-mail: pejackson@earthlink.net

JACKSON, RICHARD BROOKE, judge; b. Bozeman, Mont., Mar. 5, 1947; s. William T. and Myra (McHugh) J.; m. Elizabeth Ciner, Sept. 19, 1971; children: Jeffrey, Brett, Jennifer. AB magna cum laude, Dartmouth Coll., 1969; JD cum laude, Harvard U., 1972. Bar: Colo. 1972, U.S. Dist. Ct. Colo. 1972, D.C. 1980, U.S. Dist. Ct. D.C. 1980,U.S. Ct. Appeals (10th cir.) 1972, U.S. Ct. Appeals (D.C. cir.) 1980, U.S. Supreme Ct. 1980. Assoc. Holland & Hart, Denver, 1972-78, ptnr. Denver and Washington, 1978-98; dist. ct. judge Jefferson County, Golden, Colo., 1998—. Instr. in trial practice U. Colo. Law Sch., Boulder, 1984-85, 87, 88, 89, 91, 98, Nat. Inst. Trial Advocacy, 1986, 87, 90, 91, 98. Co-author: Manual for Complex Insurance Coverage Litigation, 1993; editor: A Better New Hampshire, 1968; contbr. articles to profl. jours. Fellow Am. Coll. Trial Lawyers; mem. ABA (former co-chair ins. coverage com. sect. of litigation), Colo. Bar Assn., Denver Bar Assn. Democrat. Avocations: running, golf, reading, travel, Spanish. Home: 5355 Yellowstone St Bow Mar CO 80123-1423 Office: Dist Ct Jefferson Cty 100 Jefferson County Pkwy Golden CO 80401-6000 E-mail: rbrooke.jackson@judicial.state.co.us

JACKSON, STU, professional sports team executive, former university basketball coach; b. Reading, Pa., Dec. 11, 1955; m. Dr. Janet Taylor; four daughters. BA, business administration and management, Seattle U., 1978. Grad. asst. coach U. Oregon, 1981-82, asst. coach, 1982-83, Wash. State U., 1983-85; assoc. coach Providence Coll., 1985-87; asst. coach N.Y. Knicks, 1987-89, head coach, 1989-91; dir. basketball ops. NBA, N.Y.C., 1991-92; head coach Univ. Wisc., Madison, 1992-94; pres., gen. mgr. basketball ops. NBA Vancouver expansion team, B.C., Canada, 1994—. NBA Coach of the Month for December, 1989. Office: Vancouver Grizzlies 800 Griffiths Way Vancouver BC Canada V6B 6G1

JACKSON, THIRSTON HENRY, JR. retired adult education educator; b. Camden, N.J., Mar. 28, 1913; s. Thirston Henry and Elizabeth Loraine (Keck) J.; m. Grace Roberta Ballard, Sept. 26, 1934 (dec. Dec. 1993); 1 child, Diane Jackson Bove. BSEE, Duke U., 1934; MA in Edn., Calif. Luth. U., 1984. Registered profl. engr., Calif.; registered tchr., Calif. Physicist Hughes Aircraft, Hawthorne, Calif., 1932-40; radio engr. Northrop Aviation, Hawthorne, 1940-50; electronic engr. N.Am. Aviation, Inglewood, Calif., 1950-60, sr. design engr. Downey, 1960-72; asst. chief engr. Marquardt Aircraft, Van Nuys, 1972-79; exec. v.p. 21st Century Tech., L.A., 1979-82; tchr. electronics Simi Adult Sch., Simi Valley, Calif., 1982-90; ret., 1990. Patentee automatic navigation device; developer missile navigation heat seeker. Scoutmaster Boy Scouts Am., N.J., 1929-32, N.C., 1932-33, L.A., 1933-54. Mem. Nat. Eagle Scout Assn. (sr.). Avocation: model railroading. Home: 6694 Tremont Cir Simi Valley CA 93063-3945

JACOB, DIANNE, county official; m. Paul, 1961; 1 son, Tom. Tchr. East County; mem. Jamul/Dulzura Sch. Bd.; supr. dist. 2 San Diego County Bd. Suprs., 1992—. Bd. dirs. East County Econ. Devel. Coun.; co-chmn. Criminal Justice Coun.; past mem. San Diego County Planning Commn.; mem., past chmn. Local Agy. Formation Commn. and numerous others; pres. Calif. Sch. Bds. Assn., 1987. Recipient Alumna of Yr. award San Diego State U. Coll. Edn., 1993, Women Who Mean Bus. award San Diego Bus. Jour., 1995, Legislator of Yr. award Indsl. Environ. Assn., 1995, Most Accessible Politician award Forum Publs., award of excellence Endangered Habitats League, 1999, Legislator of Yr. award Calif. Narcotics Assn., 1998, Legislator of Yr. award Border Solution Task Force, 1998, Legislator of Yr. award San Diego Mchts. Assn., 2000, Ofcl. of Yr., San Diego Domestic Violence Coun., 2000. Avocation: golfing. Office: Office County Supr County Adminstrn Ctr 1600 Pacific Hwy Ste 335 San Diego CA 92101-2470

JACOB, STANLEY WALLACE, surgeon, educator; b. Phila., 1924; s. Abraham and Belle (Shulman) J.; m. Marilyn Peters; 1 son, Stephen; m. Beverly Swarts; children: Jeffrey, Darren, Robert; m. Gail Brandis; 1 dau., Elyse. M.D. cum laude, Ohio State U., 1948. Diplomate: Am. Bd. Surgery. Intern Beth Israel Hosp., Boston, 1948-49, resident surgery, 1949-52, 54-56; chief resident surg. service Harvard Med. Sch., 1956-57, instr., 1958-59; asso. vis. surgeon Boston City Hosp., 1958-59; Kemper Found. research scholar A.C.S., 1957-60; asst. prof. surgery U. Oreg. Med. Sch., Portland, 1959-66, asso. prof., 1966—; Gerlinger prof. surgery Oreg. Health Scis. U., 1981—. Author: Structure and Function in Man, 5th edit, 1982, Laboratory Guide for Structure and Function in Man, 1982, Dimethyl Sulfoxide Basic Concepts, 1971, Biological Actions of DMSO, 1975, Elements of Anatomy and Physiology, 1989; contbr. to: Ency. Brit. Served to capt. M.C. AUS, 1952-54; col. Res. ret. Recipient Gov.'s award Outstanding N.W. Scientist, 1965; 1st pl. German Sci. award, 1965; Markle scholar med. scis., 1960 Mem. Phi Beta Kappa, Sigma Xi, Alpha Omega Alpha. Achievements include co-discovery of therapeutic usefulness of dimethyl sulfoxide and MSM. Home: 1055 SW Westwood Ct Portland OR 97201 2708 Office: Oreg Health Scis U Dept Surgery 3181 SW Sam Jackson Park Rd Portland OR 97201-3011 E-mail: jacobs@ohsu.edu

JACOBS, CHARLOTTE DE CROES, medical educator, oncologist; b. Oak Ridge, Tenn., Jan. 27, 1946; BA, U. Rochester, 1968; MD, Washington U., St. Louis, 1972. Diplomate Am. Bd. Internat. Medicine, Am. Bd. Med. Oncology, Nat. Bd. Med. Examiners. Acting asst. prof. oncology Stanford (Calif.) U. Med. Sch., 1977-80, asst. prof. medicine and oncology, 1980-86, assoc. prof. clin. medicine, 1986-92, assoc. prof. medicine and oncology, 1992-96, prof., 1996—, sr. assoc. dean. edn. and student affairs, 1990-97, acting dir. Clin. Cancer Ctr., 1994-97; dir. Oncology Day Care Ctr. Stanford Med. Ctr., 1977-90, dir. Clin. Cancer Ctr., 1997—. Bd. dirs. Nat. Comprehensive Cancer Network, Rockledge, Pa., 1994—. Recipient presdl. citation Am. Soc. for Head and Neck Surgery, 1990, Aphrodite Hofsomner award Washington U., 1993. Mem. AMA, Am. Soc. Clin. Oncology (bd. dirs. 1992-95), Am. Assn. for Cancer Rsch. Office: Clin Cancer Ctr 300 Pasteur Dr H-3249 Stanford CA 94305-5225

JACOBS, DONALD PAUL, architect; b. Cleve., Aug. 8, 1942; s. Joseph W. and Minnie Mae (Grieger) J.; m. Sharon Daugherty, Apr. 14, 1963 (dec. Feb. 1992); m. Julie Brinkerhoff, Apr. 24, 1993. BS, U. Cin., 1967. Registered architect, Calif., Tex., Ariz., Nev., Ga., Fla., Colo. Draftsman, intern Skidmore, Owings & Merrill, San Francisco, 1967-70; pvt. practice architecture Sea Ranch, 1970-86, chmn. design com., 1975-79; prin. Dorius Archs., Corona del Mar, Calif., 1986-94; pres. JBZ Arch. & Planning, Newport Beach, 1994—. Bd. dirs. Homeaid Am. Prin. works represented to numerous newspapers and magazines. Co-chair Project Playhouse, Homeaid, 1993-95. Mem. AIA (chmn. nat. housing com. 1996, awards 1973-74, 77-78, Bay Area Honor Design Excellence award 1974, Homes for Better Living Merit award 1976, Housing Merit award 1978), Sr. Housing Coun. (bd. dirs. Orange County chpt. 1993-94). Democrat. Avocations: tennis, skiing, hiking. Home: 309 Poppy Ave Corona Del Mar CA 92625-3024 Office: JBZ Arch & Planning 5010 Campus Dr Ste 100 Newport Beach CA 92660-2178 E-mail: djacobs@jbzarchitects.com

JACOBS, IRWIN MARK, communications executive; b. New Bedford, Mass., Oct. 18, 1933; B in Elec. Engring., Cornell U., 1956; MS, MIT, 1957, ScD, 1959. Rsch. asst. in elec. engring. MIT, Cambridge, Mass., 1958-59, from asst. to assoc. prof., 1959-66; from assoc. to prof. info. and computer sci. U. Calif., San Diego, 1966-72; pres. Linkabit Corp., 1968-85; chmn. & CEO Qualcomm Inc., San Diego, 1985—. Cons. Applied Rsch. Lab. Sylvania Elect. Products, Inc., 1959—, Lincoln Lab. MIT, 1961-62, Indsl. Tchg. Mpls. Honeywell, Inc., 1963, Bolt Beranek & Newman, Inc., 1965; NASA resident rsch. fellow Jet Propulsion Lab., 1964-65; chmn. sci. adv. group Def. Comm. Agy. and Engring. Adv. Coun. U. Calif. Recipient Biann award, 1980, Excel award Am. Electronics Assn., 1989, Nat. Tech. medal U.S. Dept. Commerce Tech. Adminstrn., 1994. Fellow IEEE; mem. NAE, Assn. Computing Machinery, Sigma Xi. Office: Qualcomm Inc 5775 Morehouse Dr San Diego CA 92121-1714 also: 10185 Mckellar Ct San Diego CA 92121-4233

JACOBS, JOSEPH JOHN, engineering company executive; b. June 13, 1916; s. Joseph and Afiffie (Forzley) J.; m. Violet Jabara, June 14, 1942; children: Margaret, Linda, Valerie. B.S. in Chem. Engring, Poly. Inst. N.Y., Bklyn., 1937, M.S., 1939, Ph.D., 1942. Registered profl. engr., N.Y., N.J., La., Calif. Chem. engr. Autoxygen, Inc., N.Y.C., 1939-42; sr. chem. engr. Merck & Co., Rahway, N.J., 1942-44; v.p., tech. dir. Chemurgic Corp., Richmond, Calif., 1944-47; pres. Jacobs Engring. Co., Pasadena, 1947-74; chmn. bd., CEO Jacobs Engring. Group Inc., Pasadena, 1974-92, chmn. bd., 1992—. Prin. ptnr. Calif. Tech. Ptnrs.; bd. dirs. Cedars Bank. Contbr. tech. articles to profl. jours. Trustee Poly. U. N.Y., Harvey Mudd Coll.; mem. Assocs. Calif. Inst. Tech.; bd. dirs. Inst. Contemporary Studies, Calif.; bd. visitors Anderson Sch., UCLA. Recipient Herbert Hoover medal United Engring. Socs., 1983 Fellow AIChE, Am. Inst. Chemists, Inst. for Advancement Engring.; mem. AAAS, Nat. Acad. Engring., Am. Chem. Soc., L.A. C. of C., Pasadena C. of C., Annandale Golf Club, Sigma Xi, Phi Lambda Upsilon. Office: Jacobs Engring Group Inc 1111 S Arroyo Pkwy Pasadena CA 91105-3254

JACOBS, KENT FREDERICK, dermatologist; b. El Paso, Tex., Feb. 13, 1938; s. Carl Frederick and Mercedes D. (Johns) J.; m. Sallie Ritter, Apr. 13, 1971. BS, N.Mex. State U., 1960; MD, Northwestern U., 1964; postgrad., U. Colo., 1967-70. Dir. service unit USPHS, Laguna, N.Mex., 1966-67; pvt. practice specializing in dermatology Las Cruces, 1970—. Cons. U.S. Army, San Francisco, 1968-70, cons. NIH, Washington, 1983, Holloman AFB, 1972-77; research assoc. VA Hosp., Denver, 1969-70; preceptor U. Tex., Galveston, 1976-77; mem. clin. staff Tex. Tech U., Lubbock, 1977—; asst. clin. prof. U. N.Mex., Albuquerque, 1972—; bd. dirs. First Security Corp. of N.Mex. Author: Breckkan, 1996; contbr. articles to profl. jours. and popular mags. Trustee Mus. N.Mex. Found., 1987-99, mem. bd. regents, 1987-99, pres., 1989-91, 95-99; bd. dirs. Dona Ana Arts Coun., 1992-93, Border Book Festival, 1996—, N.Mex. State U. Found., 1993—. Invitational scholar Oreg. Primate Ctr., 1968; Acad. Dermatology Found. fellow, 1969; named Disting. Alumnus N.Mex. State U., 1985. Fellow Am. Acad. Dermatology, Royal Soc. Medicine, Soc. Investigative Dermatology; mem. AMA, Fedn. State Med. Bds. (bd. dirs. 1984-86), N.Mex. Med. Soc., N.Mex. Bd. Med. Examiners (pres. 1983-84, N.Mex. State U. Alumni Assn. (bd. dirs. 1975-79), Mil Gracias Club (pres. 1972-74) Pres.'s Assocs., Univ. Ambs., Rotary, Phi Beta Kappa, Beta Beta Beta. Democrat. Presbyterian. Home: 3610 Southwind Rd Las Cruces NM 88005-5556

JACOBS, MARIAN, advertising agency owner; b. Stockton, Calif., Sept. 11, 1927; d. Paul and Rose (Sallah) J. AA, Stockton Coll. With Bottarini Advt., Stockton, 1948-50; pvt. practice Stockton, 1950-64; with Olympius Advt., Stockton, 1964-78; pvt. practice Stockton, 1978—. Pres. Stockton Advt. Club, 1954, Venture Club, Stockton, 1955; founder Stockton Advt. and Mktg. Club, 1981. Founder Stockton Arts Comms., 1976, Sunflower Entertainment for Institutionalized, 1976, Women Execs., Stockton, 1978; founding dir. Pixie Woods, Stockton; bd. dir. Goodwill Industries, St. Mary's Dining Room, Alan Short Gallery; mem. Calif. Coun. for the Humanities, 1994-95. Paul Harris fellow Rotary Club, 1994; recipient Woman of Achievement award San Joaquin County Women's Coun., Stockton, 1976, Achievement award San Joaquin Delta Coll., Stockton, 1978, Friend of Edn. award Calif. Tchrs. Assn., Stockton, 1988, Stanley McCaffrey Disting. Svc. award, U. of the Pacific, Stockton, 1988, Athena award for Businesswoman of Yr. Greater Stockton C. of C., 1989, Role Model award Tierra del Oro Girl Scouts U.S., 1989, Heart of Gold award Dameron Hosp. Found., 2000; named Stocktonian of the Yr. Stockton Bd. of Realtors, 1978, Outstanding Citizen Calif. State Senate & Assembly, 1978; the Marian Jacobs Writers & Poets Symposium was established in her honor. Republican. Roman Catholic. Avocations: art, photography. Home and Office: 4350 Mallard Creek Cir Stockton CA 95207-5205

JACOBS, PAUL ALAN, lawyer; b. Boston, June 5, 1940; s. Samuel and Sarah (Rodman) J.; m. Carole Ruth Greenstein, Aug. 28, 1962; children: Steven N., Cheryl R., David F., Craig A. BA in Econs. magna cum laude, Tufts U., 1960; JD magna cum laude, U. Denver, 1968. Bar: Colo. 1968, U.S. Dist. Ct. Colo. 1968. Personnel officer First Nat. Bank Denver, 1964-68; assoc. Holme Roberts & Owen, Denver, 1968-73, sr. ptnr., 1973-93; exec. v.p., gen. counsel Colo. Rockies profl. baseball orgn., Denver, 1991-95; ptnr. Jacobs Chase Frick Kleinkopf & Kelley, Denver, 1995—. Bd. dirs. Anti-Defamation League B'nai B'rith, Denver, 1987-95, Colo. Sports Hall of Fame, 2000—. Served to 1st lt. USAF, 1960-63. Mem. ABA, Denver Bar Assn., Colo. Bar Assn. Jewish. Avocations: skiing, racquetball. Home: 4041 S Narcissus Way Denver CO 80237-2025 Office: Independence Plz 1050 17th St Ste 1500 Denver CO 80265-2078 E-mail: pjacobs@jcfkk.com

JACOBS, RALPH, JR. artist; b. El Centro, Calif., May 22, 1940; s. Ralph and Julia Vahe (Kirkorian) J. Paintings appeared in: Prize Winning Art (3 awards), 1964, 65, 66, and New Woman Mag., 1975; one man shows and exhbns. Villa Montalvo, Calif., Stanford Rsch. Inst., Calif., Fresno Art Ctr., Calif., de Young Meml. Mus., Calif., Rosicrucian Mus., Calif., Cunningham Meml. Gallery, Calif., 40th Ann. Nat. Art Exhibit, Utah, Nat. Exhbn. Coun. of Am. Artists Socs., N.Y.C., Am. Artists Profl. League Show, Armenian Allied Arts, Calif., Monterey Peninsula Mus. Art, Calif. Recipient 1st place award Statewide Ann. Santa Cruz Art League Gallery, 1963, 64; 2nd place award Soc. Western Artists Ann. M.H. de Young Mus., 1964; A.E. Klumpkey Meml. award, 1965. Address: PO Box 5906 Carmel CA 93921-5906

JACOBS, ROBERT COOPER, political scientist, consultant; b. N.Y.C., Jan. 23, 1939; s. Max and Paula (Glotzer) J.; m. Barbara Linda Lax (div.); children: Michael, Deborah; m. Mollie Jenks Edson (div.); children: Elliot, Madeleine, Eleanor. AB, CCNY, 1959; AM, Columbia U., 1961, PhD, 1970. Instr. Colby Coll., Waterville, Maine, 1965-68, asst. prof., 1968-70; from asst. prof. to prof. Cen. Wash. U., Ellensburg, 1970—, dir. law and justice, 1974-88, prof., 1982—. Vis. prof. criminal justice Temple U., 1988-89. Contbr. articles to profl. jours. and encyclopedias. Mem. Kittitas County Juvenile Accountability Bd., Ellensburg, 1975-79; trustee Ellensburg Pub. Libr., 1994—, chmn., 1996, 2000. N.Y. State Regents scholar, 1955-59; State of N.Y. teaching fellow, 1962-63. Mem. Am. Polit. Sci. Assn., Wash. Assn. Criminal Justice Educators (past pres.), Supreme Ct. Hist. Soc. Democrat. Avocations: computers, hiking, target shooting. Home: 707 E 7th Ave Ellensburg WA 98926-3214 Office: Ctrl Wash U Dept Polit Sci Ellensburg WA 98926 E-mail: jacobsr@cwu.edu

JACOBS, RODNEY L. retired bank executive; Vice chmn., CFO Wells Fargo & Co., San Francisco, 1998-99. Office: Wells Fargo and Co 420 Montgomery St San Francisco CA 94104-1205

JACOBSEN, JEFFREY SCOTT, environmental scientist; BS in Soil Sci., Calif. Polytech. State U., San Luis Obispo, 1979; MS in Agronomy, Colo. State U., 1982; PhD in Soil Sci. Fertility and Plant Nutrition, Okla. State U., 1985. Rsch asst. dept. agronomy Colo. State U., Fort Collins, 1979-82, technician dept. agronomy, 1982; tchg. asst. dept. agronomy Okla. State U., Stillwater, 1982-86; from asst. prof. to assoc. prof, soil scientist Mont. State U., Bozeman, 1986—, interim head dept. plant, soil and environ. scis., 1994-98, dept. head land resources environ. sci., 1998—. Recipient CIBA-GEIGY award in Agronomy Am. Soc. of Agronomy, 1994. Fellow Am. Soc. Agronomy. Office: Montana State U Land Resource Environ Scis Bozeman MT 59717-0001

JACOBSEN, KENNETH G. state legislator; b. Dannebrog, Nebr. m. Rachel Jacobsen; children: Sonja, Kiri. Grad., U. Wash. & Tchrs. Coll., New Zealand. Mem. Wash. Senate, Dist. 46, Olympia, 1997—; chair natural resources, parks and recreation com. Wash. Legislature, Olympia, mem. environ. quality and water resources com., mem. higher edn. com., mem. transp. com., mem. joint pension and policy com., majority caucus vice chmn., 1999. Mem. Citizens Scholarship Found., Dollars for Scholars, Friends of the U. Wash. Libr., Am. Indian Endowment Com., Ravenna and Thornton Creek Alliances, Bring the Purple Martin Back to Seattle Com.; sponsor annual Raoul Wallenberg Dinner. Mem. Aubudon Soc. Democrat. Avocations: birding, hummingbird and butterfly gardening. Office: 427 John Cherberg Bldg Olympia WA 98054-0482

JACOBSEN, LAREN, programmer, analyst; b. Salt Lake City, June 15, 1937; s. Joseph Smith and Marian (Thomas) J.; m. Audrey Bartlett, July 29, 1970 (div.); children: Andrea, Cecily, Julian. BS, U. Utah, 1963. Programmer IBM, 1963-70; sys. programmer Xerox Computer Svcs., 1970-79; pres. Prescient Investment Co., 1975-82; sr. sys. analyst Quotron Sys., L.A., 1979-86; programmer, analyst Gt. Western Bank, 1987-92; word processing adminstr. Intex Svcs, Inc. , Montebello, Calif., 1993-99; data processing specialist ACC Info. Svcs., L.A., 2000—. Cons. / trainer Mt. San Antonio Coll. and Co. of Los Angeles, Dept. of Public Social Services, 2001. With USAR, 1961. Mem. Am. Build Organists (dean San Jose chpt. 1967), Mensa. Home: PO Box 91174 Los Angeles CA 90009-1174 E-mail: larenj@mediaone.net

JACOBSEN, LAWRENCE E. state legislator; b. Gardnerville, Nev., July 1, 1921; m. Betty Lundergreen; children: Bruce, Gary, Susan, Tim. Mem. Nev. Assembly, 1963-77, spkr. pro tempore, 1969; mem. Nev. Senate, Western Nev., Carson City, 1978—; pres. pro tempore Nev. Senate, 1987-90, 93-95, mem. fin. com., mem. transp. com., vice chair natural resources com. Mem. Legis. Commn., 1963-93. With USN. Mem. Am. Legion (comdr. Carson Valley Post 110, Minden Rotary Club, Douglas County Engine Co., C. of C., Gardnerville Gun Club, Douglas County Emergency Response Commn., Sierra Front Wildlife Cooperators, Nev. State Rep. Ctrl. Com., DouglasCounty Edn. Found., State 4-H Camp Adv. Coun., Navy League, Douglas County Rep. Ctrl. Com. Republican. Office: PO Box 367 Minden NV 89423-0367 also: Nev State Legis Bldg 401 S Carson St Rm 114A Carson City NV 89701-4747 Fax: 702-687-8206

JACOBSEN, RICHARD T. mechanical engineering educator; b. Pocatello, Idaho, Nov. 12, 1941; s. Thorleif (dec.), and Edith Emily (Gladwin) J. dec.); m. Vicki Belle Hopkins, July 16, 1959 (div. Mar. 1973); children: Pamela Sue, Richard T, Eric Ernest; m. Bonnie Lee Stewart, Oct. 19, 1973; 1 child, Jay Michael; stepchild: Erik David Lustig. BSME, U. Idaho, 1963, MSME, 1965; PhD in Engring. Sci., Wash. State U., 1972. Registered profl. engr., Idaho. Instr. U. Idaho, 1964-66, asst. prof. mech. engring., 1966-72, assoc. prof., 1972-77, prof., 1977—, chmn. dept. mech. engring., 1980-85, assoc. dean engring., 1985-90, assoc. dir. Ctr. for Applied Thermodynamic Studies, 1975-86, dir., 1986-99, dean engring., 1990-99; dep. lab. dir., chief scientist Idaho Nat. Engring. Environ. Lab. Bechtel BWXT Idaho LLC, Idaho Falls, 1999-2001, assoc. lab. dir. strategic mgmt., chief scientist, 2001—. Guest rschr. Nat. Inst. Standards Tech., 1979, 86, 99; mem. annex 18 thermophys. properties environ. acceptable refrigerants com. Internat. Energy Agy., 1991-98. Author: International Union of Pure and Applied Chemistry, Nitrogen-International Thermodynamic Tables of the Fluid State-6, 1979; Oxygen-International Thermodynamic Tables of the Fluid State-9, 1987, Ethylene-International Thermodynamic Tables of the Fluid State-10, 1988, ASHRAE Thermodynamic Properties of Refrigerants (2 vols.), 1986, (monograph series) Thermodynamic Properties of Cryogenic Fluids, 1997; numerous reports on thermodynamic properties of fluids, 1971— ; contbr. articles to profl. jours. NSF sci. faculty fellow, 1968-69; NSF rsch. and travel grantee, 1976-83; Nat. Inst. Standards and Tech. grantee, 1974-91, 95-98, Gas Rsch. Inst. grantee, 1986-91, 1992-98, Dept. Energy grantee, 1991-95. Fellow ASME (faculty advisor 1972-75, 78-84, chmn. region VIII dept. heads com. 1983-85, honors and awards chmn. 1985-91, K-7 tech. com. thermophys. properties 1985—, chmn. 1986-89, 92-95, 2001—, rsch. tech. com. on water and steam in thermal power systems, 1988—, gen. awards com. 1985-91, chmn. 1988-91, com. on honors 1988-99, vice chmn. 1995-99, mem. bd. on profl. practice and ethics, 1991—, v.p. profl. practice 1998-2001, Inland Empire Sect. Engr. of Yr. award 1999), N.W. Coll. and Univ. Assn. for Sci. (bd. dirs. 1990-93), Idaho Rsch. Found. (bd. dirs. 1991-99, 2000—), Soc. Automotive Engrs. (Ralph R. Teetor Edn. award, Detroit 1968), ASHRAE (co-recipient Best Tech. Paper award 1984), Sigma Xi, Tau Beta Pi, Phi Kappa Phi (Disting. Faculty award 1989). Office: Idaho Nat Engring Environ Lab Bechtel BWXT Idaho LLC PO Box 1625 Idaho Falls ID 83415-0001 E-mail: jacor@inel.gov

JACOBSON, CRAIG, lawyer; Ptnr. Hansen Jacobson & Teller, Beverly Hills, Calif. Office: Hansen Jacobson & Teller 450 N Roxbury Dr Fl 8 Beverly Hills CA 90210-4222

JACOBSON, EDWARD (JULIAN EDWARD JACOBSON), lawyer; b. Chgo., Mar. 18, 1922; s. Lewis Frederick and Pearl (Hoffman) J. BA magna cum laude, Carleton Coll., 1942; Baker Scholar with Distinction, Harvard Bus. Sch., 1943; JD with honors, U. Ariz., 1946; DHL (hon.), Carleton Coll., 1994, Ariz. State U., 1995. Bar: Ariz. 1947, U.S. Dist. Ct. Ariz. 1947, U.S. Ct. Appeals (9th cir.) 1956, U.S. Supreme Ct. 1963. Law clk. to presiding justice Ariz. Supreme Ct., Phoenix, 1947-48; asst. atty. gen. Ariz. Atty. Gen.'s Office, Phoenix, 1948-50; ptnr. Snell and Wilmer, Phoenix, 1950-89, of counsel, 1990—. Author: The Art of Turned Wood Bowls, 1985. Pres. Civic Ctr. Mgmt. Bd., 1960-90, Phoenix Art Mus., 1974-76, Heard Mus., 1962-64, Phoenix Cmty. Coun., 1960-62, Family Svc. Phoenix; mem. Ariz. Commn. on Arts, 1979-88; bd. visitors Coll. Law U. Ariz., Tucson, 1978-80. Recipient Man of Yr. award Phoenix Advt. Club, 1974, Disting. Achievement award Ariz. State U. Law Sch., 1976, Disting. Achievement award Ariz. State U. Coll. Fine Arts, 1982, Gov.'s Arts award State of Ariz., 1983, Centennial Presdl. medal Ariz. State U., 1985, Visionary award Valley Leadership Alumni Assn., 1990, Historymaker award The Hist. League of Ariz. Hist. Soc., 1993. Fellow Ariz. Bar Found. (founding bd. mem. 1980, Walter E. Craig award 1995); mem. ABA, Ariz. Bar Assn., Maricopa County Bar Assn., Law Soc. Ariz. State U. (pres. 1974-75), Am. Judicare Soc., University Club, Phoenix Country Club. Home: 2201 N Central Ave Phoenix AZ 85004-1417 Office: Snell & Wilmer One Arizona Ctr Phoenix AZ 85004-0001 E-mail: bjacobson@swlaw.com

JACOBSON, EDWIN JAMES, medical educator; b. Chgo., June 27, 1947; s. Edwin Julius and Rose Josephine (Jirinec) J.; m. Martha Shanks; 1 child, Emily. BA, U. So. Calif., 1969; MD, UCLA, 1976. Diplomate Nat. Bd. Med. Examiners, Am. Bd. Internal Medicine; lic. physician, Calif. Intern in medicine UCLA Hosp., 1976-77, resident in medicine, 1977-79, fellow in nephrology, 1979-81, chief resident in medicine, 1979-81; asst. clin. prof. of medicine UCLA, 1981-88, assoc. clin. prof. medicine, 1988-94, clin. prof. medicine, 1994—. Adj. asst. prof. medicine, UCLA, 1980-81; mem. med. sch. admissions com. UCLA, 1981—, med. staff credentials com., 1984—, med.staff exec. com., 1990-94, med. staff/hosp. adminstrn. liaison com. 1991-94, hosp./med. sch. faculty rels. com., 1991—, nat. kidney found., 1991—, med. adv. bd., 1991—; prin. investigator A/M Group Grant, UCLA Med. Ctr., 1993, Peter Langer Meml. Fund Award, 1993; lectr. in field. Author: Medical Diagnosis: An Algorithmic Approach, 1989, rev. edit., 2000; co-author: (with P. Healy) Il Proceso Decisionale nella Diagnosi Medica, 1992; manuscript rev. bd.: Bone Marrow Transplantation, 1988—, Jour. Am. Geriatrics Soc., 1989—; editor: Clin. Controverics; mem. editl. bd. Jour. Drugs; editor for symposia in field; contbr. articles to profl. jours.; editor book chpts. Recipient Upjohn Achievement award, 1977. Mem. ACP, Alpha Omega Alpha. Office: UCLA 100 Ucla Medical Plz Ste 690 Los Angeles CA 90024-6992

JACOBSON, EUGENE DONALD, educator, administrator, researcher; b. Bridgeport, Conn., Feb. 19, 1930; s. Morris and Mary (Mendelsohn) J.; m. Laura Kathryn Osborn, June 9, 1973; children from previous marriage: Laura Ellen, Susan Ruth, Morris David, Daniel Frederick, Miriam Louise. B.A., Wesleyan U., 1951; M.D., U. Vt., 1955; M.S., SUNY-Syracuse, 1960; DrMed (hon.), Jagiellonian U., 1996. Assoc. prof. UCLA Sch. Medicine, 1965-66; prof., chmn. U. Okla. Sch. Medicine, Okla. City, 1966-71, U. Tex. Med. Sch., Houston, 1971-77; vice dean Coll. Medicine U. Cin., 1977-85; dean Sch. Medicine, U. Kans., Kansas City, 1985-88; dean Sch. Medicine, U. Colo., Denver, 1988-90, prof., 1990-99, acting head divsn. gastroenterology, 1994, prof. emeritus, 1999—. Cons. NIH, Bethesda, Md., 1968-72, mem. nat. digestive adv. bd., 1985-87; chmn. Nat. Commn., U.S. Congress, Washington, 1977-79; cons. Upjohn Co., Kalamazoo, 1970-87, G. D. Searle and Co., Chgo., 1984-85 Contbr. 320 articles to profl. jours. Served to maj. U.S. Army, 1956-64 NIH Rsch. grantee, 1967-97. Fellow ACP; mem. AMA (ho. of dels. 1991—), Am. Soc. Clin. Investigation, Assn. Am. Physicians, Am. Physiol. Soc., Am. Gastroenterol. Assn. (pres. 1989-90, Friedenwald medal 1998), Am. Digestive Health Found. (bd. dirs. vice chair 1995-98).

JACOBSON, FRANK JOEL, cultural organization administrator; b. Phila., Sept. 14, 1948; s. Leonard and June Anette (Groff) J.; m. Stephanie Lou Savage, July 5, 1970; children: Aaron Jeffery, Adam Michael, Ashley Celeste. BA, U. Wis., 1970; MFA, Boston U., 1973. Mng. dir. Mont. Repertory Theater, Missoula, Mo., 1973-75; asst. prof. drama U. Mont., Missoula, 1973-75; program dir. Western States Arts Found., Denver, 1975-77, dir. programs, 1977-78, gen. mgr. budget/planning, 1978-79; exec. dir. Arvada (Colo.) Ctr. for the Arts & Humanities, 1979-85; dir. theatres and arenas City & County of Denver, 1985-87; pres., CEO Scottsdale (Ariz.) Cultural Coun., 1987—. Bd. dirs. Met. Denver Arts Alliance, pres., 1979-85, Rocky Mountain Arts Consortium, pres., 1979-80. Contbr. articles to profl. jours. Mem. panel theater program Nat. Endowment for the Arts, Washington, 1990-92; bd. dirs. Scottsdale Focus, 1988-93, 93-97, Arizonans for Cultural Devel., 1992-97; bd. dirs. Scottsdale Edn. Found., 1994-99, chmn., 1994-96; bd. dirs. Scottsdale Convention and Visitors Bur., 2001—. Mem. Am. Theatre Assn. (bd. dirs. 1976-78), Mont. State Theatre Assn. (bd. dirs., pres. 1974-75), Rocky Mountain Theatre Assn. (bd. dirs., pres. 1976-78), Assn. for Performing Arts Presenters (bd. dirs. 1984-87), Scottsdale C. of C. Office: Scottsdale Cultural Council 7380 E 2nd St Scottsdale AZ 85251-5604

JACOBSON, PHILLIP LEE, architect, educator; b. Santa Monica, Calif., Aug. 27, 1928; s. Allen Wilhelm and Greta Percy (Rohde) J.; m. Effie Laurel Galbraith, Nov. 6, 1954; children: Rolf Wilhelm, Christina Lee, Erik Mackenzie. B. Archtl. Engring. with honors, Wash. State U., 1952; postgrad. (Fulbright scholar), U. Liverpool, Eng., 1952-53; M.Arch., Finnish Inst. Tech., Helsinki, 1969. Field supr. Gerald C. Field Architect, 1950; designer, draftsman John Maloney Architect, 1951, 53-55; designer, project mgr. Young, Richardson, Carleton & Detlie Architects, 1955-56; designer, project architect John Carl Warnecke Architect, San Francisco, 1956-58; ptnr., design dir. TRA, Seattle, 1958-92; prof. architecture/urban design and planning U. Wash., Seattle, 1962—. Author: Housing and Industrialization in Finland, 1969, The Evolving Architectural Design Process, 1969; contbr. articles to profl. jours.; major archtl. works include Aerospace Research Lab., U. Wash., Seattle, 1969, McCarty Residence Hall, 1960, Highway Adminstrn. Bldg., Olympia, Wash., 1970, Sea-Tac Internat. Airport, 1972, Issaquah (Wash.) High Sch., 1962, State Office Bldg. 2, Olympia, 1976, Sealaska Corporate Hdqrs. Bldg., Juneau, Alaska, 1977, Group Health Hosp., Seattle, 1973, Metro Shelter Program, Seattle, 1977, N.W. Trek Wildlife Preserve, 1976, Rocky Reach/Rock Island Recreation Plan, 1974, master plan mouth of Columbia River, 1976, U. Wash. Biol. Sci. Bldg., 1981, Wegner Hall, Wash. State U., 1982, Wash. Conv. Ctr., 1988, King County Aquatics Ctr., 1990, Albuquerque Airport, 1989, U. Wash. Health Scis. H Wing, 1993. Mem. Seattle Planning and Redevel. Council, 1959-69, v.p., 1966-67; mem. Seattle Landmark Preservation Bd., 1976-81; trustee Pilchuck Sch., 1982—, Northwest Trek Found., 1987-94, AIA/Seattle Archtl. Found., 1986-92. With U.S. Army, 1946-47. Fulbright-Hays Sr. Rsch. fellow Finland, 1968-69; named to Order of White Rose Govt. of Finland, 1985; recipient Silver plaque Finnish Soc. Architects, 1992; recipient numerous design awards. Fellow AIA (pres. Wash. state Council 1965, dir. Seattle chpt. 1970-73, sr. council 1970—, Seattle chpt. medal 1994); mem. Am. Inst. Cert. Planners, Phi Kappa Phi, Tau Beta Pi, Tau Sigma Delta, Scarab, Sigma Tau (outstanding alumnus 1967). Home: 3935 51st Ave NE Seattle WA 98105-5243 Office: U Wash PO Box 355720 Seattle WA 98195-5720 E-mail: plj54@msn.com

JACOBSON, RAYMOND EARL, electronics company entrepreneur and executive; b. St. Paul, May 25, 1922; s. Albert H. and Gertrude W. (Anderson) J.; m. Margaret Maxine Meadows, Dec. 22, 1959 (div. 1986); children: Michael David, Karl Raymond, Christopher Eric. BE with high honors, prize for excellence in mech. engring., Yale U., 1944; MBA with distinction, Harvard U., 1948; BA (Rhodes Scholar), Oxford U., 1950, MA, 1954. Asst. to gen. mgr. PRD Electronics, Inc., Bklyn., 1951-55; sales mgr. Curtiss-Wright Electronics Divsn., Carlstadt, N.J., 1955-57; dir. mktg. TRW Computers Co., L.A., 1957-60; v.p. ops. Electro-Sci. Investors, Dallas, 1960-63; pres. Whitehall Electronics, Inc., Dallas, 1961-63, dir., 1961-63; chmn. bd. Gen. Electronic Control, Inc., Mpls., 1961-63, Staco, Inc., Dayton, Ohio, 1961-63; pres. Maxson Electronics Corp., Gt. River, N.Y., 1963-64, Jacobson Assocs., San Jose, Calif., 1964-67; co-founder, pres., chmn., CEO Anderson Jacobson, Inc., San Jose, 1967-88. Chmn. Anderson Jacobson, SA, Paris, 1974-88, Anderson Jacobson, Ltd., London, 1975-85, Anderson Jacobson Can., Ltd./Ltée, Toronto, 1975-85, Anderson Jacobson, GmbH, Cologne, 1978-83, CXR Corp., San Jose, 1988-94; bd. dirs. Tamar Electronics, Inc., L.A., Rawco Instruments, Inc., Dallas, 1960-63, Micro Radionics, Inc., L.A., 1964-67, ComputerMan USA, Inc., Reno, 1997—; lectr. engring., UCLA, 1958-60, lectr. bus. adminstrn. U. Calif. Berkeley, 1965-66; mem. underwriting Lloyd's London, 1975-96. Eagle Scout Boy Scouts Am., 1935, committeeman, 1968-80. Lt. (j.g.) USNR, 1943-46. Mem. Assn. Am. Rhodes Scholars, Harvard Bus. Sch. Assn., Oxford Soc., Yale Club, Brasenose Soc., Courtside Tennis Club, Seascape Swim and Racquet Club, Sigma Xi, Tau Beta Pi. Republican. Lutheran. Home: 1247 Montcourse Ln San Jose CA 95131-2420

JACOBSON, SIDNEY, editor; b. N.Y.C., Oct. 20, 1929; s. Reuben and Beatrice (Edelman) J.; m. Ruth Allison, July 4, 1957 (div. Feb. 1975); children: Seth, Kathy Battat; m. Maggi Silverstein, Feb. 26, 1975. BA, NYU, 1950. Exec. editor Harvey Comics, N.Y.C., 1952-83, Marvel Comics, N.Y.C., 1983-89; v.p., editor in chief Harvey Comics Entertainment, L.A., 1989—. Author: Streets of Gold, 1985, Another Time, 1989; writer (comic books) Captain Israel, 1972, The Black Comic Book, 1973, (TV animation series) Johnny Cypher in Dimension Zero, 1975, (TV series) Felix the Cat, 1982, (monthly) You Can't Do That in Comics, 1986; lyricist various popular songs. Mem. Am. Soc. Composers, Authors and Pubs., Am. Guild Authors and Composers, Authors Guild. Home: 11636 Montana Ave Los Angeles CA 90049-4900 Office: Harvey Comics Entertainment 11835 W Olympic Blvd Los Angeles CA 90064-5001

JACOBSON, SVERRE THEODORE, retired minister; b. Loreburn, Sask., Can., Sept. 20, 1922; s. Sverre and Aline Tomina (Joel) J.; m. Phyllis Lorraine Sylte, Sept. 14, 1948; children— Katherine Ann, Paul Theodore. BA, U. Sask., 1946; BD, Luther Theol. Sem., Sask., 1947; postgrad., Luther Theol. Sem., St. Paul, Minn., 1952-53; ThD, Princeton Theol. Sem., 1959. Ordained to ministry Evang. Luth. Ch., 1947. Pastor, Lomond, Alta., 1947-53; lectr. Luther Theol. Sem., Saskatoon, Sask., 1956-57; pastor Torquay, 1958-63; asst. to pres. Evang. Luth. Ch. Can., Saskatoon, 1963-70, pres., 1970-85. Interim parish pastor Calgary, Alta., Saskatoon, Weyburn, Elbow and Loreburn, Sask., 1987-98; lectr. Luth. Theol. Sem., Saskatoon, 1987-88. Home: 53 Moxon Crescent Saskatoon SK Canada S7H 3B8

JACOBUS, ARTHUR, dance company administrator; BBA, Columbia Coll.; Artist's diploma, Accademia di Musica, Italy; M in Arts Adminstrn., MBA, Golden Gate U.; M in Human Resources Mgmt., Pepperdine U.; grad. exec. mgmt. program, U. Wash.; grad. strategic perspectives program, Harvard U. Founder, dir. NATO Internat. Band, Naples, 1973-79; pres., gen. mgr. Oakland Symphony, 1979-84; pres., chief exec. officer Pacific N.W. Ballet, Seattle, 1984-93; exec. dir. San Francisco Ballet, 1993—. Mem. Dance/USA. Office: San Francisco Ballet 455 Franklin St San Francisco CA 94102-4471

JACOBY, IRVING, physician; b. N.Y.C., Sept. 30, 1947; s. Philip Aaron and Sylvia Jacoby; m. Sara Kay Vartanian; children: James Tyler, Kathryn Aaryn. BS magna cum laude, U. Miami, Coral Gables, Fla., 1969; MD, Johns Hopkins U., 1973. Diplomate Am. Bd. Internal Medicine, Am. Bd. Infectious Diseases, Am. Bd. Emergency Medicine, Am. Bd. Preventive Medicine (undersea and hyperbaric medicine). Intern Boston City Hosp., 1973-74, resident in medicine, 1974-75, chief resident, 1978-79; resident in medicine Peter Bent Brigham Hosp., Boston, 1975-76, fellow in infectious diseases, 1976-78; asst. dir. emergency med. svcs. U. Mass. Med. Ctr., Worcester, 1979-84; asst. dir. dept. emergency med. U. Calif. Med. Ctr., San Diego, 1984—, assoc. prof. med. surgery, 1988-94; prof. med. surgery, 1994—. Disaster control officer, assoc. dir. Hyperbaric Med. Ctr., 1985—; vis. physician, cons. infectious diseases Soroka Med. Ctr., Ben Gurion U., Beer-Sheva, Israel, 1980; flight physician New Eng. Life Flight, Worcester, 1982-84, Life Flight Aeromed. Program U. Calif., 1984-87. Sect. editor for disaster medicine Jour. Emergency Medicine; assoc. editor Undersea and Hyperbaric Medicine, 1996—. Comdr. Disaster Med. Assistance Team CA-4, 1991—. Fellow ACP, Am. Coll. Emergency Physicians; mem. Am. Soc. Microbiology, Infectious Diseases Soc. Am., Nat. Assn. Disaster Med. Assistance Teams (vice chair 1999,, chmn. 2000-01), Soc. Acad. Emergency Medicine, Undersea and Hyperbaric Med. Soc., World Assn. for Disaster and Emergency Medicine, Disaster Emergency Response Assn., Johns Hopkins Med. and Surg. Assn., Iron Arrow Leadership Soc., Omicron Delta Kappa, Phi Kappa Phi, Alpha Epsilon Delta, Phi Eta Sigma. Office: U Calif Med Ctr 200 W Arbor Dr San Diego CA 92103-8676

JADVAR, HOSSEIN, nuclear medicine physician, biomedical engineer; b. Tehran, Iran, Apr. 6, 1961; came to U.S., 1978, naturalized, 1995; s. Ramezan Ali and Fatemeh (Afzal) J.; m. Mojgan Maher, 1995. BS, Iowa State U., Ames, 1982; MS, U. Wis., Madison, 1984, U. Mich., Ann Arbor, 1986, PhD, 1988; MD, U. Chgo., 1993. Diplomate Am. Bd. Nuclear Medicine, Cert. Bd. Nuc. Cardiology. Rsch. asst. dept. human oncology U. Wis., Madison, 1983-84; rsch. asst. dept. elec. engring. U. Mich., Ann Arbor, 1984-88; sr. rsch. engr. Arzco Med. Electronics, Inc., Chgo., 1988-89; sr. rsch. assoc. Pritzker Inst., Ill. Inst. Tech., Chgo., 1989-92; med. intern U. Calif., San Francisco, 1993-94; resident in radiology Stanford (Calif.) U., 1994-96, resident in nuclear medicine, 1996-98, chief resident in nucelar medicine, 1997-98; fellow in nuclear medicine (positron emission tomography) Harvard Med. Sch., Boston, 1998-99; asst. prof. radiology and biomed. engring. U. So. Calif., L.A., 1999—. Reviewer study sect. small bus. innovative rsch. program NIH, 1989; session chmn. IEEE/EMBS Ann. Conf., Seattle, 1989; vis. assoc. in bioengring. Calif. Inst. Tech., Pasadena, 2001—. Contbr. articles to profl. jours., chpts. to books. Recipient Resident Rsch. award NIH, 1994. Mem. IEEE, Am. Roetgeon Ray Soc., Am. Coll. Radiology, Am. Coll. Nuclear Physicians (Resident Rsch. award 1998), Radiol. Soc. N.Am. (Resident Rsch. award 1997), Am. Coll. Nuclear Medicine (mem. faculty New Orleans 2000, Tampa 2001), Aerospace Med. Assn., Am. Soc. Nuclear Cardiology, Soc. Nuclear Medicine (Tetalman Young Investigator award 2000), Acad. Molecular Imaging, Computers in Cardiology (local organizing com. 1990), Tau Beta Pi, Sigma Xi, Eta Kappa Nu. Achievements include patents for esophgeal catheters and method and apparatus for detection of posterior ischemia. Home: 1125 Medford Rd Pasadena CA 91107-1703 Office: U So Calif Divsn Nuc Medicine Keck Sch Medicine 1200 N State St GNH 5250 Los Angeles CA 90033 E-mail: jadvar@hsc.usc.edu

JAFEK, BRUCE WILLIAM, otolaryngologist, educator; b. Berwyn, Ill., Mar. 4, 1941; s. Robert William and Viola Mabel (Newstrom) J.; m. Mary Bell Kirkpatrick, Sept. 1, 1962; children: Lynette A., Robert K., Timothy B., Britta C., Kayla E., Kristen M. BS, Coe Coll., 1962; postgrad., U. Omaha, 1962; MD, UCLA, 1966. Instr. dept. otology/laryngology Johns Hopkins Sch. Medicine, Balt., 1971-73; asst. prof. dept. otolaryngology U. Pa. Med. Sch., Phila., 1973-76; prof., dept. chmn. dept. otolaryngology/head and neck surgery U. Colo. Med. Sch., Denver, 1976-98, prof., 1998—. Served with USPHS, 1971-73. Recipient Fowler award Triologic Soc., 1983. Mem. Triologic Soc. (west region v.p. 1999), Am. Acad. Otolaryngology/Head and Neck Surgery. Republican. Mem. LDS Ch. Office: U Colo Health Sci Ctr 4200 E 9th Ave # B-205 Denver CO 80220-3706 E-mail: bruce.jafek@uchsc.edu

JAFFE, CHARLES J. allergist; b. Phila., Feb. 3, 1946; MD, Duke U., 1971, PhD, 1972. Allergist Scripps Meml. Hosp., Encinitas, Calif. Prof. allergy and immunology U. Calif., San Diego. Mem. Am. Coll. Allergy Asthma and Immunology (chair computer sect.), Am. Acad. Allergy Asthma and Immunology (chair med. informatics), Am. Med. Informatics Assn. (chmn. clin. info. syss.). Office: 477 N El Camino Real Ste A308 Encinitas CA 92024-1350

JAFFE, EDWARD A. lawyer; b. Chgo., Sept. 17, 1945; s. Julius C. and Esther R. (Cohen) J.; m. Marlene E. Epstein, June 16, 1968; children: Kimberly A., Jonathan S. BA, Drake Univ., 1967; JD cum laude, Northwestern Univ., 1970. Bar: Ill. 1970, Hawaii 1971, U.s. Dist. Ct. Hawaii 1971, U.S. Ct. Appeals (9th cir.) 1972, (2d cir.) 1979, U.S. Supreme Ct. 1984. Assoc. Cades, Schutte, Fleming & Wright, Honolulu, 1970-75, ptnr., 1976-88; sr. ptnr. Torkildson, Katz, Fonseca, Jaffe, Moore & Hetherington, Honolulu, 1988—. Facualty Nat. Inst. Trail Advocacy, Honolulu, 1985—, Univ. Hawaii Col. Continuing Edn., Honolulu, 1973—; arbitrator Am. Arbitration Assn., Honolulu, 1973—, Ct. Annexed Arbitration Program, Honolulu, 1987—. Pres. Temple Emanu-El, Honolulu, 1989-91, bd. trustees, 1980-93. Office: Torkildson Katz Fonseca Jaffe Moore Hetherington Amfac Bldg 700 Bishop St Fl 15 Honolulu HI 96813-4187

JAFFE, F. FILMORE, lawyer, retired judge; b. Chgo., May 4, 1918; s. Jacob Isadore and Goldie (Rabinowitz) J.; m. Mary Main, Nov. 7, 1942; children: Jo Anne, Jay. Student, Southwestern U., 1936-39; J.D., Pacific Coast U., 1940. Bar: Calif. 1945, U.S. Supreme Ct. 1964. Practiced law, Los Angeles, 1945-91; ptnr. Bernard & Jaffe, Los Angeles, 1947-74, Jaffe & Jaffe, Los Angeles, 1975-91; apptd. referee Superior Ct. of Los Angeles County, 1991-97, apptd. judge pro tem, 1991-97; ret., 1997; atty. in pvt. practice L.A., 1997—. Mem. L.A. Traffic Commn., 1947-48; arbitrator Am. Arbitration Assn., 1968-91; chmn. pro bono com. Superior Ct. Calif., County of Los Angeles, 1980-86; lectr. on paternity; chair family law indigent paternity panel L.A. County Supr. Ct., 2001—. Served to capt. inf. AUS, 1942-45. Decorated Purple Heart, Croix de Guerre with Silver Star, Bronze Star with oak leaf cluster; honored Human Rights Commn. Los Angeles, Los Angeles County Bd. Suprs.; recipient Pro Bono award State Bar Calif., commendation State Bar Calif., 1983. Mem. ABA, Los Angeles County Bar (honored by family law sect. 1983), Los Angeles Criminal Ct. Bar Assn. (charter mem.), U.S. Supreme Ct. Bar Assn., Masons, Shriners Office: 433 N Camden Dr Ste 400 Beverly Hills CA 90210-4408 E-mail: filmorejaffe@earthlink.net

JAFFE, ROBERT BENTON, obstetrician, gynecologist, reproductive endocrinologist; b. Detroit, Feb. 18, 1933; s. Jacob and Shirley (Robins) J.; m. Evelyn Grossman, Aug. 29, 1954; children: Glenn, Terri. M.S., U. Colo., 1966; M.D., U. Mich., 1957. Intern U. Colo. Med. Ctr., Denver, 1957-58, resident, 1959-63; asst. prof. Ob-Gyn. U. Mich. Med. Ctr., 1964-68, assoc. prof., 1968-72, prof., 1972-74, dir. steroid rsch. unit, 1964-74; prof. U. Calif., San Francisco, 1974—, chmn. dept. ob-gyn and reproductive scis., 1974-96, dir. reproductive endocrinology ctr., ctr. reproductive scis., 1977-2000. Mem. nat. adv. council, mem. human embryology and devel. and reproductive biology study sect. Nat. Inst. Child Health and Human Devel.; bd. dirs. Population Resource Center. Author: Reproductive Endocrinology: Physiology, Pathophysiology and Clinical Management, 1978, 4th edit., 1999, Prolactin, 1981, The Peripartal Period, 1985; contbr. numerous articles to profl. jours.; mem. editorial bd. Jour. Clin. Endocrinology and Metabolism, 1971-75, Fertility and Sterility, 1972-78; editor-in-chief Obstetric and Gynecologic Survey, 1991—. Josiah Macy Found. faculty fellow, 1967-70, 81; USPHS postdoctoral fellow, 1958-59, 63-64; Rockefeller Found. grantee, 1974-78 ; Andrew Mellon Found. grantee, 1978-81 Mem. Endocrine Soc. (coun. 1985-86, sec.-treas. 1994-99), Soc. Gynecologic Investigation (pres. 1975-76, Pres.'s Disting. Scientist award 1993, Pres.'s Mentorship award 2000), Perinatal Rsch. Soc. (pres. 1973-74), Am. Coll. Obstetricians and Gynecologists (awards), Assn. Am. Physicians, Inst. Medicine Nat. Acad. Scis., Royal Coll. Obstetricians and Gynaecologists, The Hormone Found. (pres. 1999—). Democrat. Jewish. Home: 90 Mt Tiburon Rd Belvedere Tiburon CA 94920-1512 Office: U Calif Med Sch OB Gyn & Reproductive Sci San Francisco CA 94143-0556

JAFFE, ROBERT STANLEY, lawyer; b. Walla Walla, Wash., May 16, 1946; BA, U. Wash., 1968, JD, 1972. Bar: Wash. 1972. Ptnr. Preston Gates & Ellis, L.L.P., Seattle, 1986—. Mem. ABA (mem. corp., banking and bus. law sect., mem. small bus. com. 1982-92), Order of Coif. Office: Preston Gates & Ellis LLP Bank Am Tower 701 5th Ave Ste 5000 Seattle WA 98104-7078

JAFFE, SIGMUND, chemist, educator; b. New Haven, Mar. 1, 1921; s. Morris and Rose (Blosveren) J.; m. Elaine Leventhal, Aug. 25, 1946; children— Matthew Lee, Paul Jonathan. A.B. with high distinction in Chemistry, Wesleyan U., Middletown, Conn., 1949; Ph.D., Iowa State U., 1953. Research in rare earths Ames (Iowa) Lab., 1949-53; research in carbides, metal and high temperature inorganic reactions, research labs. Air Reduction Corp., 1953-58; prof. chemistry Calif. State U. at Los Angeles, 1958-86, prof. emeritus, 1986—, chmn. dept., 1958-64, part-time prof., 1986—. Vis. prof. Queen Mary Coll., U. London, 1978-79; Research solid propellant fuel systems, 1958-60; photochemistry and gas phase kinetics Jet Propulsion Lab., Calif. Inst. Tech., Pasadena, Calif., 1960-64; NIH fellow Wiezmann Inst. Sci., Israel, 1964-65, vis. prof., 1971-72 Contbr. articles to profl. jours. Served with USNR, 1942-46. Named Outstanding prof. Calif. State U. at Los Angeles, 1973-74 Mem. Am. Chem. Soc., Sigma Xi, Phi Beta Kappa, Phi Lambda Upsilon, Phi Kappa Phi. Home: 14107 Village 14 Camarillo CA 93012-7013 Office: Calif State U Dept Chemistry Los Angeles CA 90032

JAFFER, ADRIAN MICHAEL, physician; b. Cape Town, S. Africa, Aug. 24, 1943; came to U.S., 1969; s. George Daniel Jaffer and Theresa (Kourie) Binsted; children: Brendan, Terence. MBchB, U. Cape Town Med. Sch., 1966. Diplomate Am. Coll. Physicians. Intern Loyola Univ. Hosp., Maywood, Ill., 1969-70; resident Northwestern U., Chgo., 1970-72; fellow Harvard U., Boston, 1972-73, Scapps Clinic & Rsch., LaJolla, Calif., 1973-75, Northwestern U., Chgo., 1975-76; pvt. practice LaJolla, 1976—. Assoc. clin. prof. U. Calif. San Diego, LaJolla, 1976—. Contbr. articles to profl. jours. Mem. AMA, Am. Coll. Rheumotology, Am. Acad. Allergy. Office: 9850 Genesee Ave Ste 860 La Jolla CA 92037-1233

JAGER, MERLE LEROY, aerospace engineer; b. Eugene, Oreg., Sept. 22, 1942; s. Earl Christian and Alma Marie (Jensen) J.; m. Shannon Kay Jacobsen, Mar. 18, 1967; children: Holly, Peter, Melanie, Marissa BS in Mech. Engring., Oreg. State U., 1965; MS in Aeronautical Engring., U. So. Calif., 1967. Aerodynamicist Lockheed-Calif. Co., Burbank, 1965-68; rsch. engr. The Boeing Co., Seattle, 1968-70; aerodynamics engr. Gates Learjet Corp., Torrance, Calif., 1970; project engr. Irvin Industries, Inc., Gardena, 1971-73; aerodynamics mgr. Northrop Corp., Hawthorne, 1973-91, mgr. flight mechanics Pico Rivera, 1991-95; aerodynamics mgr. McDonnell Douglas Corp., Long Beach, 1995—. Patentee in field. Treas.

Goldenwest Assn., Westminster, Calif., 1976-78; tribal chief YMCA Indian Princesses Program, Huntington Beach, Calif., 1986-87; bishopric counselor Mormon Ch., Westminster, 1986-95. Mem. AIAA, Tau Beta Pi, Pi Tau Sigma, Sigma Tau. Republican. Home: 6771 Findley Cir Huntington Beach CA 92648-3075 Office: McDonnell Douglas Corp Long Beach CA 90810

JAGLOM, HENRY DAVID, actor, director, writer; b. London, Jan. 26, 1941; s. Simon M. and Marie (Stadthagen) J.; m. Victoria Foyt, 1991. Pres. Rainbow Film Co., Los Angeles, Jagfilms, Inc., Los Angeles, Rainbow Releasing, Los Angeles. Writer, dir. (films) A Safe Place, 1971 (selected for N.Y. Film Festival 1971), Tracks (selected for Cannes Film Festival 1976), Sitting Ducks, 1980 (selected for Cannes Film Festival), Can She Bake a Cherry Pie?, 1983 (selected for Berlin Film Festival 1983); actor, writer, dir. (films) Always (But Not Forever), 1985, Someone to Love, 1987 (selected for Cannes Film Festival), New Year's Day, 1989 (selected for Venice Film Festival 1989), Eating (selected for Deauville Film Festival 1990), Venice/Venice, 1991 (selected for AFI/L.A. Film Festival), Baby Fever, 1993, Last Summer in The Hamptons, 1995 (selected for London Film Festival, AFI/L.A. Film Festival), Déjà Vu, 1997, Festival, 2000; presenter Hearts and Minds, 1973 (Acad. award best documentary 1973). Office: Rainbow Film Co 9165 W Sunset Blvd West Hollywood CA 90069-3129 E-mail: rainbow@rainbowfilms.com

JAKUBOWSKY, FRANK RAYMOND, religious writer; b. Belfield, N.D., Oct. 11, 1931; s. William and Catherine (O'bach) J. Student, U. N.D., 1950-52. Chemist Sherwin-Williams Paint Co., Emeryville, Calif., 1958-85; pres. Bold Books, Oakland, 1978—. Editor Spiritfest, Berkeley, Calif., 1997—. Author: Creation, 1978, Jesus Was a Leo, 1979, The Psychological Patterns of Jesus Christ, 1982, The Creative Theory of the Universe, 1983, Caldecott, 1985, Frank on a Farm, 1988, Lake Merritt, 1988, Thank God, I Am Alive, 1989, Whitman Revisted, 1989, Spiritual Symbols for the Astrology of the Soul, 1990, This New World; Birth: Sept. 8, 1958, 1990, Perceptive Types, 1993, Father Figure Frank's Stories, 1996, Inspiration Stories, 1998, Universal Mind, 1998, Big Bang Goes Puff, 1999. Pfc. U.S. Army, 1952-54. Mem. Urantia Fellowship, Inst. Noetic Scis., Nat. Coun. Geocosmic Rsch. Roman Catholic. Avocations: writing songs for children on fraimba. Home: 1565 Madison St Apt 308 Oakland CA 94612-4511

JALALI, BEHNAZ, psychiatrist, educator; b. Mashad, Iran, Jan. 26, 1944; came to U.S., 1968; d. Badiolah and Bahieh (Shahidi) Samimy; m. Mehrdad Jalali, Sept. 18, 1968. MD, Tehran (Iran) U., 1968. Rotating intern Burlington County Meml. Hosp., Mt. Holly, N.J., 1968-69; resident in psychiatry U. Md. Hosp., Balt., 1970-73; asst. prof. psychiatry dept. psychiatry Sch. Medicine Rutgers U., Piscataway, N.J., 1973-76, Yale U., New Haven, 1976-81, assoc. clin. prof. psychiatry, 1981-85; assoc. clin. prof. psychiatry dept. psychiatry UCLA, 1985-94, clin. prof. psychiatry dept. psychiatry Sch. Medicine, 1994—. Dir. psychotherapy Sch. Medicine Rutgers U., Piscataway, 1973-76; dir. family therapy unit dept. psychiatry Yale U., New Haven, 1976-85; chief clin. med. svcs. Mental Health Clinic, 1987-96; coord. med. student edn. in psychiatry West L.A. VA Hosp., 1985—; dir. family therapy clinic W.Va. VA Hosp., 1991—, co-leader Schozophrenia Clinic, Mental Health Clinic, West Los Angeles VA Med. Ctr., 1996—. Author: (with others) Ethnicity and Family Therapy, 1982, Clinical Guidlines in Cross-Cultural Mental Health, 1988; contbr. articles to profl. jours. Fellow Am. Psychiatric Assn., Am. Orthopsychiatry Assn., Am. Assn. Social Psychiatry; mem. Am. Family Therapy Assn., So. Calif. Psychiatric Assn. (chair com. for women 1992), World Fedn. Mental Health. Avocations: photography, hiking, cinema, painting. Home: 1203 Roberto Ln Los Angeles CA 90077-2304 Office: UCLA Dept Psychiatry West LA VA Med Ctr B116aa Los Angeles CA 90073-1003

JAMES, CHARLES E., JR. lawyer; b. Pontiac, Mich., Sept. 19, 1948; BA, Occidental Coll., 1970; JD with highest distinction, U. Ariz. Bar: Ariz. 1973. Ptnr. Snell & Wilmer, Phoenix, 1990-99, Squires, Sanders and Dempsey, Phoenix, 1999—. Mem. ABA, Nat. Assn. Bond Lawyers. Office: Squires Sanders Dempsey 1 Arizona Ctr 40 N Central Ave Ste 2700 Phoenix AZ 85004-2223

JAMES, HELEN ANN, plastic surgeon; b. Palmerston North, New Zealand, May 5, 1940; came to U.S., 1977; d. George Headley and Betty Beatrice (McDonald) J.; married (dec. Apr. 1993). MB, ChB, U. Otago, Dunedin, New Zealand, 1964; Fellow, Royal Coll. Surgeons, London, England, 1972. Diplomate Am. Bd. Plastic Surgery. Internship Palmerston North Hosp., New Zealand, 1965-66; residency plastic surgery Brdg Earn Hosp., Perthshire, England, 1973-74, St. Lukes Hosp., Bradford, England, 1975-77; fellow plastic surgery Mount Sinai Med. Ctr., Miami Beach, 1977-79; residency plastic surgery N.C. Meml. Med. Ctr., Chapel Hill, 1979-81; St. Joseph Hosp., Bellingham, Wash.; pvt. practice Bellingham. Mem. AMA, Am. Soc. Plastic and Reconstructive Surgeons, Wash. State Med. Assn. Avocations: tennis, birding, cycling. Office: 3001 Squalicum Pkwy Ste 5 Bellingham WA 98225-1950

JAMES, JEANNETTE ADELINE, state legislator, accountant; b. Maquoketa, Iowa, Nov. 19, 1929; d. Forest Claude and Winona Adeline (Meyers) Nims; m. James Arthur James, Feb. 16, 1948; children: James Arthur Jr., Jeannette, Alice Marie. Student, Merritt Davis Sch. Commerce, Salem, Oreg., 1956-57. Payroll supr. Gen. Foods Corp., Woodburn, Oreg., 1956-66; cost acctg., inventory control clk. Pacific Fence & Wire Co., Portland, 1966-67, office mgr., 1968-69; substitute rural carrier U.S. Post Office, Woodburn, 1967-68; owner, mgr., acct. and tax preparer James Bus. Svc., Goldendale, Wash., 1969-75, Anchorage, 1975-77, Fairbanks, Alaska, 1977-94; co-owner, mgr. Jolly Acres Motel, North Pole, Alaska, 1987—; mem. Alaska Ho. of Reps., Juneau, 1993—; chmn. House State Affairs, 1995-2000; jud. com., 1998-99; vice chmn. Legis. Coun., 1995-96; chmn. joint com. Adminstrv. Regulation Rev., 1997-98, ho. majority leader, 2000-01. Cert. workshop and seminar leader, 1989-91; instr. workshop Comm. Dynamics, 1988. Vice chmn. Klickitat County Dems., Goldendale, 1970-74; bd. dirs. Mus. and Art Inst., Anchorage, 1976-80; pres. Anchorage Internat. Art Inst., 1976-78; chmn. platting bd. Fairbanks North Star Borough, 1980-84, mem. Planning Commn., 1984-87; treas., vice chmn. 18th Dist. Reps., North Pole, Alaska, 1984-92; mem. City of North Pole Econ. Devel. Com., 1992-93. Named Legislator of Yr., Alaska Farm Bur., 1994, Alaska Outdoor Coun., 2000, Alacha Outdoor Coun., 2000, Guardian of Small Bus., Nat. Fedn. Ind. Bus., 1998; recipient Defender of Freedom award NRA, 1994, Courage in Preserving Equal Access award Alaska chpg. Safari Club Internat., 2000. Mem. Internat. Tgn. in Comm. (Alaska State winner speech contest 1981, 86), North Pole C. of C., Emblem Club, Rotary (treas. North Pole 1990), Eagles, Women of Moose. Presbyterian. Avocations: bowling, dolls, children. Home: 3068 Badger Rd North Pole AK 99705-6117 also: Alaska Ho of Reps 3340 Badger Rd North Pole AK 99705-6129 E-mail: usual@ptialaska.net

JAMES, MARIA-ELENA, federal judge; b. 1953; BA, U. Calif., Irvine, 1975; JD, U. San Francisco, 1978. Dir. consumer fraud unit Office of Dist. Atty., San Francisco, 1978-80; dep. pub. defender San Francisco, 1980-84; dep. city atty. San Francisco, 1984-88; commr. Calif. Superior Ct., 1988-94; apptd. magistrate judge no. dist. U.S. Dist. Ct. Calif., 1994. Office: 450 Golden Gate Ave San Francisco CA 94102-3661 Fax: 415-522-2140

JAMES, MARION RAY, magazine founder, editor; b. Bellmont, Ill., Dec. 6, 1940; s. Francis Miller and Lorraine A. (Wylie) J.; m. Janet Sue Tennis, June 16, 1960; children: Jeffrey Glenn, David Ray, Daniel Scott, Cheryl Lynne BS, Oakland City Coll., Ind., 1964; MS, St. Francis Coll., Fort Wayne, Ind., 1978. Sports and city editor Daily Clarion, Princeton, Ind., 1963-65; English tchr. Jac-Cen-Del H.S., Osgood, 1965-66; indsl. editor Whirlpool Corp., Evansville and LaPorte, 1966-68, Magnavox Govt. and Indsl. Electronics Co., Fort Wayne, 1968-79; editor, pub., founder Bowhunter mag., Fort Wayne, Ind., 1971-88, editor-in-chief Kalispell, Mont., 1989-2001, editor emeritus, 2001—. Instr. Purdue U., Ft. Wayne, Ind., 1980-88. Author: Bowhunting for Whitetail and Mule Deer, 1975, Successful Bowhunting, 1985, My Place, 1991, The Bowhunter's Handbook, 1997; editor: Pope and Young Book of Bowhunting Records, 1975, 93, 99, Bowhunting Adventures, 1977. Recipient Best Editorial award United Community Svc. Publs., 1970-72; named Alumnus of Yr., Oakland City Coll., 1982, to Hall of Fame, Mt. Carmel High Sch., Ill., 1983 Mem. Outdoor Writers Assn. Am. (Excellence in Craft Lifetime Achievement award 1999), Ft. Wayne Assn. Bus. Editors (pres. 1975-76, Ft. Wayne Bus. Editor of Yr. award 1969), Toastmasters (Able Toastmaster award), Alpha Phi Gamma, Alpha Psi Omega, Mu Tau Kappa Home: PO Box 1509 2011 Ridgecrest Dr Whitefish MT 59937-1509 E-mail: mrjames@cyberport.net

JAMES, MARK A. state legislator, lawyer; b. Eugene, Oreg., Oct. 9, 1959; m. Lori M. James; children: Anne A., John S. BS, Lewis and Clark Coll.; JD, U. Ariz. Bar: U.S. Dist. Ct. Nev., U.S. Dist. Ct. (so. dist.) Tex., U.S. Ct. Appeals (9th and 5th cirs.). Senate judiciary intern Senator Paul Laxalt, Nev., 1981; mem. Nev. Senate, Dist. 8, Carson City, 1992—. Articles editor Ariz. Law Rev. Active Clark County Pub. Edn. Found., Boys and Girls Clubs; mem. statewide adv. coun. Water Resources Rsch. of the Desert; bd. dirs. Aquavision, chair water law forum, 1992. Mem. ABA, State Bar Nev., State Bar Tex., Nev. Water Resources Assn. Republican. Office: 3773 Howard Hughes Pkwy Las Vegas NV 89109-0949 also: Nev State Legis Bldg 401 S Carson St Rm 240 Carson City NV 89701-4747 Fax: 702-791-1912; 702-687-8206. E-mail: mjames@sen.state.nv.us

JAMES, THOMAS LARRY, chemistry educator; b. North Platte, Nebr., Sept. 8, 1944; s. James Jennings and Guinevere (Richards) J.; m. Olga Schmidlin; children: Marc, Tristan. BS, U. N.M., 1965; PhD, U. Wis., 1969. Research chemist Celanese Chem. Co., Corpus Christi, Tex., 1969-71; NIH post-doctorate fellow U. Pa., Phila., 1971-73; prof. chem., pharmaceutical chemistry and radiology U. Calif., San Francisco, 1973—, chair dept. pharm. chemistry, 1995—, dir. Magnetic Resonance Lab., 1975. Author: NMR in Biochemistry, 1975; editor: Biomedical NMR, 1984, Methods in Enzymology, 1989, 94, 95, 2001; mem. editl. bd. Jour. Magnetic Resonance, FEBS Letters, Jour. Biomolecular NMR, Magnetic Resonance Imaging; contbr. numerous articles to profl. jours. Mem. Internat. Soc. Magnetic Resonance, Am. Biophys. Soc., Am. Chem. Soc., Am. Biochem. Soc., Soc. Magnetic Resonance in Medicine, Phi Beta Kappa, Phi Kappa Phi, Kappa Mu Epsilon. Reorganized Ch. of Jesus Christ of Latter-day Saints. Avocations: skiing, kayaking, travel, photography. Office: U Calif # 926-s San Francisco CA 94143-0001 E-mail: james@pollack.ucsf.edu

JAMES, WAYNE EDWARD, electronic engineer; b. Racine, Wis., Apr. 2, 1950; s. Ronald Dean James and Arlene Joyce (Mickelsen) Dawson; m. Edith Yvonne Cone, Apr. 6, 1997; children: Terry Scott, Kevin Arthur. BS in Electronic Engring. Tech., U. So. Colo., 1976; MS in Computer Sci., Colo. U., 1996. Electronic technician Lawrence Livermore (Calif.) Nat. Lab., 1976-80, Inmos Corp., Colorado Springs, Colo., 1980-86, CAD engr., 1986-87, United Techs. Microelectronics Ctr., Colorado Springs, 1988-97, ASIC engr., 1997—. Sec.-treas. Stratmoor Hills Vol. Fire Dept., Colorado Springs, 1983, 84, lt., 1985, capt., 1986. Served with USN, 1968-72. Named Fireman of Yr., Stratmoor Hills Vol. Fire Dept., 1983. Lutheran. Office: Aeroflex UTMC 4350 Centennial Blvd Colorado Springs CO 80907-3778

JAMES, WILLIAM J. lawyer; AB, Occidental Coll., Los Angeles, 1966; JD, U. Calif., San Francisco, 1974; LLM in Taxation, N.Y.U., 1975. Bar: Calif. 1974, U.S. Dist. Ct. (ctrl. dist.) Calif. 1976, U.S. Dist. Ct. (no. dist.) Calif. 1992, U.S. Dist. Ct. (ea. dist.) Wis. 1997, U.S. Ct. Appeals (9th cir.) 1976, U.S. Tax Ct. 1979. Asst. U.S. atty. U.S. Atty's Office, L.A., 1976-86; ptnr. Graham & James, LLP, L.A., 1986-2000, Squire, Sanders and Dempsey, LLP, L.A., 2000—. Sr. adjunct prof. Golden Gate U., L.A., 1978—. Mem. Fed. Bar Assn. (pres. L.A. chpt. 1991-92), L.A. County Bar Assn. Office: Squire Sanders & Dempsey LLP 801 S Figueroa St Fl 14 Los Angeles CA 90017-2573

JAMESON, ANTONY, aerospace engineering educator; b. Gillingham, Kent, Eng., 1934; BA, Cambridge (Eng.) U., MA in Engring. with honors, 1958, PhD, 1963. Rsch. fellow Trinity Hall, Cambridge, Eng., 1960-63; economist Trades Union Congress, London, 1964-65; chief mathematician missile divsn. Hawker Siddeley Dynamics, Coventry, Eng., 1965-66; staff engr. Grumman Aerospace Corp., Bethpage, N.Y., 1966-72; sr. rsch. scientist Courant Inst. Math. Scis., NYU, N.Y.C., 1972-74, prof. computer sci., 1974-80; prof. mech. & aerospace engring. Princeton (N.J.) U., 1980-82, James S. McDonnell Disting. U. prof. aerospace engring., 1982-96, prof. emeritus, 1996—, dir. program in applied and computational math., 1986-88; prof. aeronautics Stanford (Calif.) U., 1997—. Contbr. articles to profl. jours., chpts. to books. 2nd lt. British Army, 1953-55. Open scholar Trinity Hall, Cambridge, 1955, Hon. fellow, 1990; Alfred P. Sloan Fgn. Post-Doctoral fellow MIT, 1962; named Hon. Prof., Northwestern Polytech. U., Xian, China, 1986, W.R. Sears Disting. lectr. Cornell U., 1992; recipient NASA medal Exceptional Sci. Achievement, 1980, Gold medal Brit. Royal Aero. Soc., 1988, Spirit of St. Louis medal ASME, 1995. Fellow AIAA (Fluid Dynamics award 1993), Royal Soc. London. Office: Stanford U Astronautic Durand Stanford CA 94305-1928

JAMIESON, JAMES BRADSHAW, foundation administrator; b. L.A., June 10, 1931; s. Charles Cameron and Ruth (Bradshaw) J.; m. Perry McNaughton, Dec. 27, 1959; children: Jeffrey McNaughton, Dalton Charles. AA, Citrus Coll., 1950; BA, Claremont Men's Coll., 1955; MA, Claremont Grad. Sch., 1958; PhD, Brown U., 1966. Assoc. prof. polit. studies Pitzer Coll. and Claremont Grad. Sch., 1968-75; rsch. polit. scientist UCLA, 1972-73; v.p. for devel. Pitzer Coll., 1968-72, v.p., 1973-78, prof. polit. studies, 1975-83, exec. v.p., 1979-83, acting pres., 1978-79; prof. govt. Claremont Grad. Sch., 1975-87; v.p. for rsch. Claremont McKenna Coll., 1983-87; exec. dir. Found. for Performing Art Ctr., San Luis Obispo, Calif., 1987-96; pres. SLO Capers, San Luis Obispo, 1997—. Commr. Calif. Postsecondary Edn. Commn., Sacramento, 1987-92; dir. Global Village, Seattle, 1989-95; resident cons. Centennial Celebration Calif. Politech. State U., Obispo, Calif., 2000—. Contbr. articles to profl. jours. Staff, sec. Ctrl. Coast Performing Arts Ctr. Commn., San Luis Obispo, 1993-95. Sgt. USAF, 1950-52. Fellow Brown U., 1960, 63, tchg. fellow, 1962, fellow Resources for the Future, 1964; rsch. grantee U.S. Dept. Interior, 1972-73; recipient Cal. Poly U. Pres.' Arts award, 1999. Mem. Santa Lucia Flyfishers (bd. dirs. 1988—), Trout Unltd. (bd. dirs. Calif. coun. 1989-94, bd. dirs. nat. bd. 1986-90), Marine's Meml. Club. Avocations: flyfishing, tennis, restoring vintage automobiles. Office: SLO Capers PO Box 12843 San Luis Obispo CA 93406-2843

JAMIESON, STUART WILLIAM, surgeon, educator; b. Bulawayo, Rhodesia, July 30, 1947; came to U.S., 1977; MB, BS, U. London, 1971. Intern St. Mary's Hosp., London, 1971; resident St. Mary's Hosp., Northwick Park Hosp., Brompton Hosp., London, 1972-77; asst. prof. Stanford U., Calif., 1980-83, assoc. prof., 1983-86; prof., head cardiac surgery U. Minn., Mpls., 1986-89, U. Calif., San Diego, 1989—. Dir. Minn. Heart and Lung Inst., Mpls., 1986-89; pres. Calif. Heart and Lung Inst., San Diego, 1991-95. Co-author: Heart and Heart-Lung Transplantation, 1989; editor: Heart Surgery, 1987; contbr. over 500 papers to med. jours. Recipient Brit. Heart Found. Fellowship award, 1978, Irvine H. Page award Am. Heart Found., 1979, Silver medal Danish Surg. Soc., 1986. Fellow ACS, Royal Coll. Surgeons, Royal Soc. Medicine, Am. Coll. Chest Physicians, Am. Coll. Cardiology; mem. Royal Coll. Physicians (licentiate), Internat. Soc. for Heart Transplantation (pres. 1986-88), Calif. Heart and Lung Inst. (pres. 1991—). Office: U Calif Divsn Cardiothoracic Surgery 200 W Arbor Dr San Diego CA 92103-1911

JAMIN, MATTHEW DANIEL, lawyer, magistrate judge; b. New Brunswick, N.J., Nov. 29, 1947; s. Matthew Bernard and Frances Marie (Newburg) J.; m. Christine Frances Bjorkman, June 28, 1969; children: Rebecca, Erica. BA, Colgate U., 1969; JD, Harvard U., 1974. Bar: Alaska 1974, U.S. Dist. Ct. Alaska 1974, U.S. Ct. Appeals (9th cir.) 1980. Staff atty. Alaska Legal Svcs., Anchorage, 1974-75, supervising atty. Kodiak, Alaska, 1975-81; contract atty. Pub. Defender's Office State of Alaska, Kodiak, 1976-82; prin. Matthew D. Jamin, Atty., Kodiak, 1982; ptnr. Jamin & Bolger, Kodiak, 1982-85, Jamin, Ebell, Bolger & Gentry, Kodiak, 1985-97; part-time magistrate judge U.S. Cts., Kodiak, 1984—; shareholder Jamin, Ebell, Schmitt & Mason, Kodiak, 1998—. Part-time instr. U. Alaska Kodiak Coll., 1975—; active Theshold Svcs., Inc., Kodiak, 1985—, pres., 1985-92, 95-96, 99-2000. Mem. Alaska Bar Assn. (Professionalism award 1988), Kodiak Bar Assn. Office: US Dist Ct 323 Carolyn Ave Kodiak AK 99615-6348 E-mail: matt@jesmkod.com

JAMISON, DEAN TECUMSEH, economist; b. Springfield, Mo., Oct. 10, 1943; s. Marshall Verdine and Mary Dell (Temple) J.; m. Joanne Leslie, Sept. 14, 1971 (div. 1995); children: Julian C., Eliot A., Leslie S.; m. Kin Bing Wu, Jan. 19, 1997. AB in Philosophy, Stanford U., 1966, MS in Engring. Sci., 1967; PhD in Econs., Harvard U., 1970. Asst. prof. grad. sch. bus. Stanford U., Palo Alto, Calif., 1970-73; economist World Bank, Washington, 1976-88, dir., 1992-93, advisor, 1993-98; dir. Ctr. for Pacific Rim Studies UCLA, 1993-2000, prof. Sch. Pub. Health, Grad. Sch. Edn. and Info. Studies, 1988—; dir. econs. adv. svc. WHO, Geneva, 1998-2000. Chmn. ad hoc com. on health R&D for developing countries WHO, Geneva, 1996-97; bd. trustees Drug Strategies, 1994—; chmn. bd. on global health Inst. Medicine NAS, 2000—; mem. adv. bd. Inst. Human Virology, 2001—. Author (with L. J. Lau): Farmer Education and Farm Efficiency, 1982, Disease Control Priorities in Developing Countries, 1993, World Bank World Development Report 1993: Investing in Health, 1993, WHO World Health Report 1999: Making a Difference, 1999; cons. editor AERA Ency. Rsch., 6th edit., 1992. Fellow Woodrow Wilson Found., 1967, NSF, 1968, Bill and Melinda Gates Found. fellow, 2001—. Mem. Inst. Medicine Nat. Acad. Scis. Avocation: tennis. Office: UCLA Internat Studies and Overseas Programs 11-292 Bunche Hl Los Angeles CA 90095-0001 Fax: (310) 206-4018. E-mail: djamisond@isop.ucla.edu

JAMISON, HARRISON CLYDE, former oil company executive, petroleum exploration consultant; b. St. Louis, Jan. 15, 1925; s. William Clyde and Katherine Maurice (Fitzgerald) J.; m. Beverly Joy Johnson, June 26, 1946; children: Susan, David, Leslie, Daniel, Dale, Nancy, Sara BA cum laude, UCLA. Geologist Richfield Oil Corp., Bakersfield, Calif., 1950-52, Olympia, Wash., 1952-55, L.A., 1955-60, regional exploration supr., 1961-65; Alaska dist. mgr. Atlantic Richfield Co., Anchorage, 1966-69, Alaska coord. Dallas, 1969-70; mgr. govt. rels. Alyeska Pipeline Svc. Co., 1971-72; chief geologist ARCO Oil & Gas Co., Dallas, 1973-80, v.p. dist. mgr. Denver, 1981; pres. ARCO Exploration Co., Dallas, 1981-85; sr. v.p. Atlantic Richfield Co., L.A., 1981-85. Contbr. articles to profl. jours. Former bd. dirs. Tex. Rsch. League, Austin, Dallas Citizens Coun., Mex. Am. Legal Def. and Edn. Fund, Resolution Seismic Svcs. Inc., Wilmington, Del., ARCO Alaska Inc., Thomas Wilson Dibblee Jr. Geol. Found., Hospice of Bend. Fellow Geol. Soc. Am. (former chmn. bd. dirs., trustees GSA Found. 1986-88); mem. Am. Assn. Petroleum Geologists, N.W. Energy Assn. Home and Office: 37615 S Stoney Cliff Ct Tucson AZ 85739-1412

JAMISON, REX LINDSAY, medical educator; b. Des Moines, July 8, 1933; s. Orin Lindsay and Helen Belle (Buck) J.; m. Dorothy Tufts Lockwood, Mar. 3, 1962; children: Richard Lindsay, John Lockwood. AB, U. Iowa, 1955; BA, U. Oxford, Eng., 1957, MA, 1961; MD, Harvard U., 1960. Intern Mass. Gen. Hosp., Boston, 1960-61, asst. resident in medicine, 1961-62; sr. asst. resident in medicine Columbia-Presbyn. Med. Ctr., N.Y.C., 1962-63; clin. assoc. Lab. Kidney and Electrolyte Metabolism, NIH, Bethesda, Md., 1963-66; instr. in medicine Washington U. Sch. Medicine, St. Louis, 1966-67, asst. prof. medicine, 1967-71, asst. prof. physiology and biophysics, 1968-71; assoc. prof. medicine Stanford (Calif.) U. Sch. Medicine, 1971-82, co-head div. nephrology, 1971-80, chief div., 1980-87, prof. medicine and physiology, 1982-87, acting chmn. dept. medicine, acting physician-in-chief, 1984-86, prof. medicine, 1992—; Charles A. Dewey prof. medicine, chmn. dept. medicine U. Rochester (N.Y.) Sch. Medicine and Dentistry, 1987-90, prof. medicine and physiology, 1990-92. Physician-in-chief Strong Meml. Hosp., Rochester, 1987-90; chief renal div. Jewish Hosp. St. Louis, 1966-71, div. nephrology Stanford U. Hosp., 1971-87; vis. prof. Laboratoire de Physiologie Physico-Chimique Centre d'Etudes, Nucleaires de Saclay, Gif-sur-Yvette, France, 1977-78; mem. external monitoring com. modification of diet in renal disease study Nat. Inst. Arthritis, Diabetes and Digestive and Kidney Diseases, 1989-90; med. adv. bd. Nat. Kidney Found. Upstate N.Y., 1987-91, No. Calif., 1992—; mem. Intersoc. Coun., 1988-92; cons. pharm. and biotech. cos., 1993—; William C. Smith lectr. UCLA St. Mary Hosp. Author: (with Wilhelm Kriz) Urinary Concentrating Mechanism: Structure and Function, 1982; author, editor: Transplantation in the 1980s: Recent Advances, 1984, (with Serge Jard) Vasopressin, 1991, Nephrology (with Robert Wilkinson), 1997; editor Nephrology Rounds; contbr. numerous articles to profl. jours. Mem. Rhodes Scholar Selection Coms. Vt., Md., Mo., Calif. Dist. V. Rhodes scholar, Markle scholar; John S. Guggenheim Found. fellow; Rsch. Career Devel. grantee USPHS, 1963-66, grantee Calif. Acad. Medicine, Rochester Acad. Medicine; recipient Champion of Hope award Nat. Kidney Found., No. Calif. Fellow ACP, Royal Coll. Physicians (hon.); mem. Am. Heart Assn. (vice chmn. coun. on cardiovascular disease and the kidney 1986-88, chmn. 1988-92), Am. Physiol. Soc., Am. Soc. Clin. Investigation , Am. Soc. Nephrology (chmn. program com. 1984), Assn. Am. Physicians, Assn. Profs. Medicine, Western Assn. Physicians, Western Soc. Clin. Investigation (councilor 1974-77), Peruvian Soc. Nephrology (hon.), Internat. Soc. Nephrology Commn. on Devel. Countries, Phi Beta Kappa. Episcopalian. Avocations: music, golf. Home: 850 Cedro Way Palo Alto CA 94305-1003 E-mail: rjamison@leland.stanford.edu

JAMPLIS, ROBERT WARREN, surgeon, medical foundation executive; b. Chgo., Apr. 1, 1920; s. Mark and Janet (McKenna) J.; m. Roberta Cecelia Prior, Sept. 5, 1947; children: Mark Prior, Elizabeth Ann Jamplis Bluestone. BS, U. Chgo., 1941, MD, 1944; MS, U. Minn., 1951. Diplomate Am. Bd. Surgery, Am. Bd. Thoracic Surgery. Asst. resident in surgery U. Chgo., 1946-47; fellow in thoracic surgery Mayo Clinic, Rochester, Minn., 1947-52; chief thoracic surgery Palo Alto (Calif.) Med. Clinic, 1958-81, exec. dir., 1965-81; clin. prof. surgery Stanford U. Sch. Medicine, 1958—. Mem. coun. SRI Internat.; chmn. bd. TakeCare Corp.; charter mem., bd. regents Am. Coll. Physician Execs.; mem. staff Stanford Univ. Hosp., Santa Clara Valley Med. Ctr., San Jose, VA Hosp., Palo Alto, Sequoia Hosp., Redwood City, Calif., El Camino Hosp., Mountain View, Calif., Harold D. Chope Cmty. Hosp., San Mateo, Calif.; pres., CEO Palo Alto Med. Found., 1965—; past chmn. Fedn. Am. Clinics; dir. Blue Cross Calif.; varsity football team physician Stanford U. Author: (with G.A. Lillington) A

Diagnostic Approach to Chest Diseases, 1965, 2d edit., 1979; contbr. numerous articles to profl. jours. Trustee Santa Barbara Med. Found. Clinic; past pres. Calif. div. Am. Cancer Soc.; past chmn. bd. Group Practice Polit. Action Com.; past mem. athletic bd. Stanford U.; past mem. cabinet U. Chgo.; bd. dirs. Herbert Hoover Boys' Club; past trustee No. Calif. Cancer Program; past bd. dirs. Core Communications in Health, Community Blood Res., others. Served to lt. USNR, 1944-46, 52-54. Recipient Alumni citation U. Chgo., 1968, Nat. Divsn. award Am. Cancer Soc., 1979, Med. Exec. award Am. Coll. Med. Group Adminstrs., 1981, Russel V. Lee award lectr. Am. Group Practice Assn., 1982, Mayo Disting. Alumnus award, 1991. Mem. Inst. Medicine of Nat. Acad. Scis., ACS, Am. Assn. Thoracic Surgery, Am. Surg. Assn., Soc. Thoracic Surgeons (past pres.), Western Thoracic Surg. Assn. (past pres.), Western Surg. Assn., Pacific Coast Surg. Assn., San Francisco Surg. Soc. (past pres.), Portland Surg. Soc. (hon.), Doctors Mayo Soc., Am. Coll. Chest Physicians (bd. govs.), Calif. Acad. Medicine, Am. Fedn. Clin. Research, Am. Group Practice Assn. (past pres.), AMA, Calif. Med. Assn., Santa Clara County Med. Assn., Sigma Xi Republican. Roman Catholic. Clubs: Bohemian, Pacific Union, Commonwealth of California (San Francisco); Menlo Country (Woodside, (Calif.); Menlo Circus (Atherton, Calif.); Stanford (Calif.) Golf; Rancheros Visitadores (Santa Barbara, Calif.). Office: Palo Alto Med Foundation 795 El Camino Rd Palo Alto CA 94301-2726

JANCZAK, MARTIN E. career officer; Commd. ensign USN, 1969, advanced through ranks to rear adm.; various assignments to comdr. U.S. Naval Forces, Marianas; dep. chief of staff Shore Installation Mgmt. U.S. Pacific Fleet, 1998—. Office: 250 Makalapa Dr Pearl Harbor HI 96860-3131

JANDA, KIM D. chemist, educator; b. Cleve., Aug. 23, 1958; married; children: Nikole, Christopher. BS, U. Southern Fla., 1980; MS, U. Ariz., 1983, PhD, 1984. Adj. asst. mem. dept. molecular biology Rsch. Inst. Scripps Clinic, La Jolla, Calif., 1987-88, asst. prof. dept. molecular biology, 1989-90, assoc. prof. dept. molecular biology and chem., 1991-92, assoc. prof., 1993—. Cons. Procter and Gamble, Unilever Rsch., Inc.; sci. adv. bd. mem. Catalytic Antibodies, Inc., Found. CombiChem.; lectr. in field. Contbr. numerous articles to profl. jours. Named Scholar Athlete of Yr. U. South Fla., 1979-80; recipient Alfred P. Sloan fellowship, 1993-95, NIH First award, 1990-95, Carl S. Marvel fellowship U. Ariz., 1984; numerous other grants. Fellow Am. Inst. Chemists; mem. Am. Chem. Soc. (Arhtur C. Cope Scholar Award, 1999), Themis Honor Soc., Sigma Phi Epsilon. Office: The Scripps Rsch Inst 10550 N Torrey Pines Rd La Jolla CA 92037-1000

JANES, ROBERT ROY, museum executive, archaeologist, museum consultant; b. Rochester, Minn., Apr. 23, 1948; m. Priscilla Bickel; children: Erica Helen, Peter Bickel. Student, Lawrence U., 1966-68, BA in Anthropology cum laude, 1970; student, U. of the Ams., Mexico City, 1968, U. Calif., Berkeley, 1968-69; PhD in Archaeology, U. Calgary, Alta., Can., 1976. Postdoctoral fellow Arctic Inst. N.Am., U. Calgary, 1981-82; founding dir. Prince of Wales No. Heritage Centre, Yellowknife, N.W.T., 1976-86, project dir. Dealy Island Archaeol. and Conservation Project, 1977-82; founding exec. dir. Sci. Inst. of N.W.T.; sci. advisor Govt. of N.W.T., Yellowknife, 1986-89; exec. dir., pres., CEO Glenbow Mus. Art Gallery Libr. and Archives, Calgary, 1989-2000; fellow Glenbow-Alta. Inst., 2000—. Mus./heritage cons., 2000—; adj. prof. archaeology U. Calgary, 1990—. Author: Preserving Diversity-Ethnoarchaeological Perspectives on Culture Change in the Western Canadian Subarctic, 1991, Museums and the Paradox of Change, 1995, 2d edit., 1997; author: (with others) The Arctic Institute of North America Technical Paper No. 28, 1983; author manuscripts, monographs; contbr. articles to profl. jours. Mem. First Nations/CMA Task Force on Mus. and First Peoples, 1989-92, Banff, Kootenay and Yoho Nat. Pks. Devel. Adv. Bd.; bd. dirs. Yoho Burgess Shale Found.; mem. nat. adv. bd. Ctr. for Cultural Mgmt., U. Waterloo; bd. dirs. Friends of Banff Nat. Park. Recipient Nat. Parks Centennial award Environ. Can., 1985, Can. Studies Writing award Assn. Can. Studies, 1989, Disting. Alumni award Alumni Assn. of U. Calgary, 1989, L.R. Briggs Disting. Achievement award Lawrence U., 1991; Can. Coun. doctoral fellow, 1973-76; rsch. grantee Govt. of Can., 1974, Social Scis. and Humanities Rsch. Coun. Can., 1988-89. Fellow Arctic Inst. N.Am. (bd. dirs. 1983-90, vice chmn. bd. 1985-89, hon. rsch. assoc. 1983-84, chmn. priorities and planning com. 1983-84, exec. com. 1984-86, assoc. editor Arctic jour. 1987-97), Am. Anthrop. Assn. (fgn. fellow); mem. Can. Archaeol. Assn. (v.p. 1980-82, pres. 1984-86, co-chmn. fed. heritage policy com. 1986-88), Current Anthropology (assoc.), Can. Mus. Assn. (hon. life mem., cert accreditation 1982, Outstanding award in Mus. Mgmt., Outstanding Achievement award for publ. 1996), Internat. Coun. Mus., Can. Art Mus. Dirs. Orgn. (mem.-at-large bd. dirs.), Can. Mus. Assn. (bd. dirs., v.p. 1999), Alta. Mus. Assn. (moderator seminars 1990, Merit award 1992, Merit award for Museums and the Paradox of Change 1996), Assn. Cultural Execs. (bd. dirs. 1999-2000, ACE award for Can. Cultural Mgmt. 1998), Sigma Xi. Home: 104 Prendergast Pl Canmore AB Canada T1W 2N5 E-mail: janes@telusplanet.net

JANEWAY, BARBARA, public relations executive; Coord. pub. rels. Ralph's Grocery, Compton, Calif., 1987—. Office: Ralphs Grocery 1100 W Artesia Blvd Compton CA 90220-5186

JANKURA, DONALD EUGENE, hotel executive, educator; b. Bridgeport, Conn., Dec. 20, 1929; s. Stephen and Susan (Dirga) J.; m. Elizabeth Deborah Joynt, June 20, 1952; children: Donald Eugene Jr., Stephen J., Daria E., Diane E., Lynn M. BA in Hotel Adminstrn., Mich. State U., 1951. Asst. sales mgr. Pick Fort Shelby Hotel, Detroit, 1951-53; steward Dearborn Inn and Colonial Homes, Dearborn, Mich., 1953-54, sales mgr., 1954-60, resident mgr., 1960-62; gen. mgr. Stouffer's Northland Inn, Southfield, 1962-64; staff adviser Stouffer Motor Inns, Cleve., 1964-66, v.p., 1966-68, Assoc. Inns & Restaurants Co. Am., Denver, 1968-76, exec. v.p., 1976-81, sr. v.p., 1981-91; pres. Waverly Hospitality Assocs., Parker, Colo., 1991-94. Dir. Sch. Hotel and Restaurant Mgmt. U. Denver, 1988-91; disting. spl. lectr. hospitality U. New Haven, Conn.; pres. Am. Hotel Assn. Directory Corp., 1986; guest lectr. Mich. State U., 1964, Fla. Internat. U., 1968, Cornell U., 1983, Denver U., 1986-87; mem. industry adv. bd. U. Denver, Mich. State U.; mem. adv. bd. Acad. Travel and Tourism-Nat. Acad. found., Denver, 1991-99, chmn. 1998; commr. Accreditation Commn. Programs in Hospitality Adminstrn., 1995-99. Commr. Commn. on Accreditation for Hospitality Mgmt., 1994—; pres. Evergreen Homeowner's Assn., 1994-99; mem. USAF Innkeeper Evaluation Team, 1993, 95. Named to Hall of Fame Colo. Hotel and Lodging Assn., 1992, Mich. State U. Sch. Hospitality Bus., 1995, Wall of Fame, 1995; named Alumnus of Yr., Mich. State U. Hotel Sch., 1986. Mem. Am. Hotel and Motel Assn. (dir. 1978-80, vice chmn. industry adv. coun. 1980-81, sec.-treas. 1985, v.p. 1986, pres. 1987—, chmn. host com. 1994, Ednl. Inst. Emeritus award 1995), Colo./Wyo. Hotel and Motel Assn. (dir., bd. dirs. 1984—, Disting. Svc. award 1983), Pres.'s Club, Masons, Phi Kappa Tau. Episcopalian. Avocations: gardening, sailing, cooking, woodworking. Home and Office: 7445 E Windlawn Way Parker CO 80134-5941

JANSEN, ALLAN W. lawyer; b. Oak Park, Ill., July 22, 1948; BS in Aerospace Engring., U. Ill., 1971; JD, John Marshall Law Sch., 1978. Bar: Calif. 1978, U.S. Dist. Ct. (cen. dist.) Calif. 1978, U.S. Ct. Appeals (9th cir.) 1978, U.S. Patent Office, U.S. Ct. Appeals (fed. cir.) 1986. Ptnr. Lyon & Lyon, L.A., 1986—. Mem. editorial bd. John Marshall Jour. Practice & Procedure, 1977-78. Mem. ABA, Am. Intellectual Property Law Assn., State Bar Calif., L.A. County Bar Assn., L.A. Intellectual Property Law Assn., Phi Delta Phi. Office: Lyon & Lyon 1900 Main St Fl 6 Irvine CA 92614-7317

JANSEN, ROBERT BRUCE, consulting civil engineer; b. Spokane, Wash., Dec. 14, 1922; s. George Martin and Pearl Margaret (Kent) J.; m. Barbara Mae Courtney, Sept. 18, 1943. BSCE, U. Denver, 1949; MSCE, U. So. Calif., 1955. Registered profl. engr., Calif., Colo., Wash. Chief Calif. Div. Dam Safety, Sacramento, 1965-68; chief of ops. Calif. Dept. Water Resources, Sacramento, 1968-71, dep. dir., 1971-75, chief design and constrn., 1975-77; asst. commr. U.S. Bur. Reclamation, Denver, 1977-80; cons. civil engr., 1980—. Cons. TVA, Chattanooga, 1981—, So. Calif. Edison Co., Rosemead, 1982—, Pacific Gas and Electric, San Francisco, 1982-93, Hydro-Quebec, Montreal, 1986-98, Ala. Power Co., Birmingham, 1986-98, Ga. Power Co., 1989-94. Author: Dams and Public Safety, 1983; editor: Safety of Existing Dams, 1983; co-author: Development of Dam Engineering in the United States, 1988; editor and co-author: Advanced Dam Engineering for Design, Construction, and Rehabilitation, 1988. Mem. U.S. Com. on Large Dams (chmn.1979-81), ASCE, NAE (elected). Home and Office: 509 Briar Rd Bellingham WA 98225-7811

JANSON, RICHARD ANTHONY, plastic surgeon; b. Passaic, N.J., Nov. 30, 1945; m. Mary Ann Janson, 1971; children: Sarah, Matthew. BA, Rice U., 1967; MD, Med. Coll. Wis., 1971. Diplomate Am. Bd. Plastic Surgery. Intern St. Joseph Hosp., Denver, 1971-72, resident in gen. surgery, 1972-76; resident in plastic surgery U. Tex. Med. Branch, Galveston, 1976-79; pvt. practice Grand Junction, Colo., 1979—. Fellow ACS, Am. Soc. Plastic & Reconstructive Surgeons; mem. Colo. Soc. Plastic & Reconstructive Surgeons. Office: 1120 Wellington Ave Grand Junction CO 81501-6129

JANTZEN, J(OHN) MARC, retired education educator; b. Hillsboro, Kans., July 30, 1908; s. John D. and Louise (Janzen) J.; m. Ruth Patton, June 9, 1935; children: John Marc, Myron Patton, Karen Louise. A.B., Bethel Coll., Newton, Kans., 1934; A.M., U. Kans., 1937, Ph.D., 1940. Elementary sch. tchr., Marion County, Kans., 1927-30, Hillsboro, Kan., 1930-31; high sch. tchr., 1934-36; instr. sch. edn. U. Kans., 1936-40; asst. prof. Sch. Edn., U. of Pacific, Stockton, Calif., 1940-42, assoc. prof., 1942-44, prof., 1944-78, prof. emeritus, 1978—, also dean sch. edn., 1944-74, emeritus, 1974—, dir. summer sessions, 1940-72. Condr. overseas seminars; mem., chmn. commn. equal opportunities in edn. Calif. Dept. Edn., 1959-69; mem., chmn. Commn. Tchr. Edn. Calif. Tchrs. Assn., 1956-62; mem. Nat. Coun. for Accreditation Tchr. Edn., 1969-72. Bd. dirs. Ednl. Travel Inst., 1965-89. Recipient hon. svd. award Calif. Congress Parents and Tchrs., 1982, McCaffrey disting. Svc. award in recognition of leadership in higher edn., cmty. relationships and internat. svc. San Joaquin Delta Coll., 1996. Mem. NEA, Am. Edn. Rsch. Assn., Calif. Edn. Rsch. Assn. (past pres. 1954-55), Calif. Coun. for Edn. Tchrs., Calif. Assn. of Colls. for Tchr. Edn. (sec., treas. 1975-85), Rotary (Outstanding Rotarian of Yr. award North Stockton 1990, Paul Harris fellow 1980), Stockton Coun. PTA Found., Phi Delta Kappa. Methodist. Home: 117 W Euclid Ave Stockton CA 95204-3122

JAOUEN, RICHARD MATTHIE, plastic surgeon; MD, U. Autonoma de Guadalajara, Jalisco, Mexico, 1975. Intern St. Joseph Hosp., Denver, 1976-77, surgeon, 1977-81; plastic surgeon Ind. U. Med. Sch., Indpls., 1981-83, North Colo. Med. Ctr., Greeley, Colo., 1983—. Office: 1640 25th Ave Greeley CO 80634-4959

JAPHA, BARBARA, financial executive; BBA, U. Colo.; JD, U. Denver. Acct.; assoc. Holme, Roberts & Owen; asst. v.p., legal counsel Columbia Savs.; v.p. law and human resources, assoc. gen. counsel US West, Inc., Englewood, Colo., v.p. bus. devel., CFO; pres. Marsico Capital Mgmt., Denver. Mem. Order St. Ives, Beta Gamma Sigma, Beta Alpha Psi.

JARC, FRANK ROBERT, printing company executive; b. Waukegan, Ill., Apr. 4, 1942; s. Frank Joseph and Edith Gertrude (Cankar) J.; m. MeRandy Jarc, 1 dau., Jennifer. BS in Indsl. Engring, U. Mich., 1964; MBA, Harvard U., 1967. Mgmt. trainee Mich. Bell Telephone Co., 1964; with regulatory proceedings dept. United Airlines, Chgo., 1966; fin. analyst Ford Motor Co., Dearborn, Mich., 1967, Freeport Minerals Co., N.Y.C., 1972-73; Fin. analyst Esmark, Inc., Chgo., 1973; controller subs. Swift Grocery Products Co., Chgo., 1973-75; fin. v.p. subs. Estech, Inc., Chgo., 1975-77; v.p. consumer products subs. Estech Gen. Chem. Co., Agrl. Chems. Corp., Chgo., 1977-80; exec. v.p., chief fin. officer Wilson Foods, Oklahoma City, 1980-87; sr. v.p., chief fin. officer United Airlines, Chgo., 1987; exec. v.p., chief fin. officer R.R. Donnelley Co., Chgo., 1987-95; exec. v.p., CFO Viking Office Products, L.A., 1996-99; sr. v.p. corp. devel. Office Depot, 1999—. Chmn. audit com. Brady Corp., 2000—. Bd. mgrs. YMCA. Capt. USAF, 1967-71. Mem. Evans Scholarship Alumni Assn., Chgo. Club, Execs. Club Chgo., Chgo. Commonwealth Club, Econ. Club. Home: 501 Oakwood # 3E Lake Forest IL 60045 Office: Office Depot 950 W 190th St Torrance CA 90502-1001

JARDETZKY, OLEG, medical educator, researcher; b. Yugoslavia, Feb. 11, 1929; came to U.S., 1949, naturalized, 1955; s. Wenceslas Sigismund and Tatiana (Taranovsky) J.; m. Erika Albensberg, July 21, 1975; children by previous marriage: Alexander, Theodore, Paul. B.A., Macalester Coll., 1950, D.Sc. (hon.), 1974; M.D., U. Minn., 1954, Ph.D. (Am. Heart Assn. fellow), 1956; postgrad., U. Cambridge, Eng., 1965-66; LL.D. (hon.), Calif. Western U., 1978; M.D. (hon.), U. Graz, Austria, 1994; Doctorate (hon.), U. Aix-Marseille II, 1998. Research fellow U. Minn., 1954-56; NRC fellow Calif. Inst. Tech., 1956-57; asso. Harvard U., 1957-59, asst. prof. pharmacology, 1959-66; dir. biophysics and pharmacology Merck & Co., 1966-68, exec. dir., 1968-69; prof. Stanford U., 1969—, dir. Stanford Magnetic Resonance Lab., 1975-97, dir. NMR Center, Sch. Medicine, 1983-84; dir. emeritus Stanford Magnetic Resonance Lab., 1998—. Vis. fellow Merton Coll., Oxford (Eng.) U., 1976; cons., vis. prof., lectr. in field; chmn. Internat. Coun. on Magnetic Resonance in Biology, 1972-74; dir. Internat Sch. on Magnetic Resonance in Biology, Ettore Majorana Ctr., Sicily, 1993—; chmn. biotech. panel World Fedn. Scientists, 1998—. Contbr. articles to profl. jours.; mem. editorial bd. Jour. Theoretical Biology, 1961-88, Molecular Pharmacology, 1965-75, Jour. Medicinal Chemsitry, 1970-78, Biochimica Biophypica Acta, 1970-86, Revs. on Bioenergetics, 1972-89, Biomembrane Revs., 1972-80, Jour. Magnetic Resonance in Biology and Medicine, 1986—, Jour. Magnetic Resonance, 1993—. Recipient career devel. award USPHS, 1959-66, Kaiser award, 1973, Von Humboldt award, 1977, Pauling medal, 1984, Grand Gold Honor insignia (Austria), 1993, Founder's gold medal Internat. Coun. Magnetic Resonance in Biology, 1994, Prix Marianne Dessewffy Internat. Conf. of Genealogy and Heraldry, 1998; grantee NSF, 1957—, NIH, 1957—; travel fellow Am. Physiol. Soc., 1959. Fellow AAAS; mem. Am. Chem. Soc., Am. Soc. Biol. Chemistry and Molecular Biology, Biophys Soc., Assn. Advanced Tech. in Biomed. Scis. (pres. 1981-88), Internat. Soc. Magnetic Resonance (chmn. divns. of biology and Medicine 1986-89), Phi Beta Kappa, Sigma Xi, Alpha Omega Alpha. Home: 950 Casanueva Pl Stanford CA 94305-1068 Office: Stanford U CCSR 269 Campus Dr Rm 3155-B Stanford CA 94305-5174 E-mail: jardetzky@stanford.edu

JARMIE, NELSON, physicist, consultant; b. Santa Monica, Calif., Mar. 24, 1928; s. Louis and Ruth (Wydman) J. BS, Calif. Inst. Tech., 1948; PhD, U. Calif., Berkeley, 1953. Staff mem. Los Alamos Sci. Lab., 1953-97. Co-founder Pajarito Ski Area, 1957; Los Alamos Sci. Lab. cons. for Dept. Energy regulatory compliance; vis. prof. U. Calif., Santa Barbara, 1960; adj. prof. U. N.Mex., 1957-71; mem. adv. coun. Los Alamos Grad. Ctr., 1958-88; participant Vis. Scientist Program, 1965-71; field mycologist Nat. Park Svc., 1991-98; rsch. on nuclear and particle physics, astrophysics and mycology; cons. for conduct of ops. and quality assurance fed. regulations; taxonomist of macromycetes cons., 1997—. Contbr. numerous articles to sci. jours. and mags.; rsch. in nuclear and particle physics, astrophysics and taxonomic mycology. Mem. Econ. Devel. Council Los Alamos County, N.Mex., 1968. Recipient Disting. Performance award Los Alamos Nat. Lab., 1986. Fellow AAAS, Am. Phys. Soc.; mem. Mycol. Soc. Am., N.Am. Mycol. Soc., Am. Assn. Physics Tchrs., Sigma Xi, Tau Beta Pi. Achievements include research in light-nuclei energy levels; 3-body breakup, nucleon-nucleus scattering, astrophysical reactions; kinematic codes, straggling calculations and infrared laser diagnostics; fundamental properties of antimatter; field surveys of macromycetes.

JAROS, DEAN, university official; b. Racine, Wis., Aug. 23, 1938; s. Joseph and Emma (Kotas) J. B.A., Lawrence Coll., Appleton, Wis., 1960; M.A., Vanderbilt U., 1962, Ph.D., 1966. Asst. prof. polit. sci. Wayne State U., Detroit, 1963-66; from asst. prof. to prof. polit. sci. U. Ky., 1966-78, assoc. dean Grad. Sch., 1978-80; dean Grad. Sch. No. Ill. U., DeKalb, 1980-84, Colo. State U., Ft. Collins, 1984-91, assoc. provost, 1991—; dir. Soc. Sr. Scholars. Author: Socialization to Politics, 1973, Political Behavior: Choices and Perspectives, 1974, Heroes Without Legacy, 1993, also articles.; Mem. editorial bds. profl. jours. Mem. Exptl. Aircraft Assn. Office: Colo State U Grad Sch Fort Collins CO 80523-0001

JARRELL, LEEANN, investment company executive; CFO, human resources officer Capital Group Cos., L.A. Office: Capital Group Companies 333 S Hope St Los Angeles CA 90071 Office Fax: (213) 486-9217

JARRETT, KEITH, pianist, composer; b. Allentown, Pa., May 8, 1945; Student, Berklee Sch. Music, 1963. Pianist with groups led by Art Blakey, 1965, Charles Lloyd, 1966-69, Miles Davis, 1970-71; rec. with group led by Art Blakey: Buttercorn Lady, 1966; recs. with groups led by Charles Lloyd: Dreamweaver, Forest Flower, In Europe, The Flowering, 1966, Love In (Live at Fillmore), Journey Within, Live in the Soviet Union, 1967, Soundtrack, 1968; recs. with groups led by Miles Davis: Miles Davis at Fillmore, Live—, Evil, Get Up With It, Directions, 1970; soloist, leader of own groups, 1969—; recs. as leader of own groups or as solo artist: Life Between The Exit Signs, 1967, Restoration Ruin, Somewhere Before, 1968, Gary Burton/Keith Jarrett, 1971, Mourning of a Star, Birth, El Juicio, Ruta and Daitya, Expectations, Facing You, 1971, Fort Yawuh, In The Light, Solo Concerts Bremen & Lausanne, 1973, Treasure Island, Belonging, Luminessence, Death and the Flower, Backhand, 1974, The Koln Concert, Mysteries, Shades, Bob-Be, Byablue, Arbour Zena, 1975, Survivors' Suite, Eyes of The Heart, Staircase, Hymns/Spheres, Sun Bear Concerts, 1976, My Song, 1977, Personal Mountains, Nude Ants, Moth and The Flame, 1979, The Celestial Hawk, Sacred Hymns, Invocations, 1980, Concerts Bregenz and Munich, 1981, Standards Volumes 1 & 2, Changes, 1983, Spirits, Standards Live, 1985, Still Live, Book of Ways, 1986, Dark Intervals, Changeless, 1987, Paris Concert, 1988, Tribute, 1989, Standards In Norway, 1989, The Cure, 1990, Vienna Concert, Bye Bye Black Bird, 1991, At the Dear Head Inn, 1992, Bridge of Light, 1993, At The Blue Note (6 CD set, 1994), La Scala, 1995, Tokyo '96; also recorded with Airto, Freddie Hubbard, Marion Williams, Kenny Wheeler, Gary Peacock, Charlie Haden, Paul Motian; classical recs. include J. S. Bach—Well Tempered Clavier Book 1 (piano), 1987, Book 2 (harpsichord), 1991, Goldberg Variations (harpsichord), 1989, French Suites (harpsicord), 1991, Handel Keyboard Suites, 1993, (with Michala Petri) Handel—Sonatas for Recorder and Continuo, 1990, Bach— Sonatas for Flute and Harpsicord, 1992, (with Dennis Russell Davies/Stuggart Chamber Orch.) Mozart Piano Concerto No. 21, 23, 27, Lou Harrison—Piano Concerto and Suite for violin, piano and orch., 1988, Alan Hohvaness—Lousadzak, 1989, (with Gidon Kremer) Arvo Part—Fratres, 1983, Shostakovich—24 Preludes and Fugues, Opus 87, 1991; (with Kim Kashkashian) Bach Sonatas for Viola da Gamba, 1991; concert soloist with San Francisco Symphony, Phila. Orch., Boston Symphony Orch., Am. Composers Orch., St. Paul and English Chamber Orch., Rochester and Bklyn. Philharm.; subject of biography: Keith Jarrett: The Man and His Music (Ian Carr), 1991. Decorated officier de L'Ordre des Arts et des Lettres (France); recipient Guggenheim award, 1972, Grand Prix du Disque, Govt. of France, 1972, Prix du Pres. de la Republique (France), 1991; recs. nominated for Grammy award, 1974, 86, 88, 92, 98; recs. named Record of Yr., Time mag., Downbeat mag., Stereo Rev., 1974, N.Y. Times, 1975, 92, Rolling Stone mag., 1976, CD Rev., 1992, Downbeat, 1996; named Pianist/Artist of Yr., Downbeat mag., 1974, 75, 94, 96, 97, 98, Keyboard mag., 1976, 82, 91, Swing Jour. (Japan), 1980, 86, 87, 89, 91, 93, 94, 95, 96; 1st improvising musician to perform Met. Opera, N.Y.C., 1978, Vienna State Opera, 1991, La Scala, Milan, 1995. Mem. Royal Swedish Acad. Music.

JARVEY, PAULETTE SUE, publishing executive; b. Camp LeJuene, N.C., Aug. 10, 1945; d. Charles O. and Reva Wanda (Shirley) McCord; m. John M. Jarvey, Aug. 22, 1964; children: Shawn M., J. Adam. Student, Portland Community Coll., Oreg., 1973. Teller new accounts Bank of Am., Anaheim, Calif., 1964-68; owner The Dough Nut, Canby, Oreg., 1971-85, P.J. Promotions, Canby, 1972-85; pres. Hot Off the Press, Inc., Canby, 1980—. Founder N.W. Assn. Book Pubs., Portland, 1983. Author: You Can Dough It, 1980, Let's Dough It Again, 1982, Dough Art Lumpies, 1983, Dough It For Christmas, 1983, Decorative Dough, 1984. Mem. Soc. Craft Designers. Democrat. Avocations: white water rafting, reading. Office: Hot Off Press Inc 1250 NW 3rd Ave Canby OR 97013-3499

JARVIK, GAIL PAIRITZ, medical geneticist; b. Evanston, Ill., Feb. 8, 1959; d. Lawrence Alan and Lenore Mae P.; m. Jeffrey Gil Jarvik, Aug. 22, 1992. PhD in Human Genetics, U. Mich., 1986; MD, U. Iowa, 1987. Sr. rsch. fellow U. Wash., Seattle, 1992-95, asst. prof. medicine, divsn. med. genetics, 1995-2000, assoc. prof., 2000—. Affiliate mem. Fred Hutchinson Cancer Rsch. Ctr., Seattle, 1994—. Contbr. to profl. jours. Howard Hughes Rsch. fellow, 1992-95; Pew scholar, 1997—. Mem. Am. Soc. Human Genetics, Internat. Genetic Epidemiology Soc.

JARVIS, DONALD BERTRAM, judge; b. Newark, Dec. 14, 1928; s. Benjamin and Esther (Golden) J.; m. Rosalind C. Chodorcove, June 13, 1954; children: Nancie, Brian, Joanne. BA, Rutgers U., 1949; JD, Stanford U., 1952. Bar: Calif. 1953. Law clk. to justice John W. Shenk Calif. Supreme Ct., 1953-54; assoc. Erskine, Erskine & Tulley, 1955, Aaron N. Cohen, 1955-56; law clk. Dist. Ct. Appeal, 1956; assoc. Carl Hoppe, 1956-57; adminstrv. law judge Calif. Pub. Utilities Commn., San Francisco, 1957-91, U.S. Dept. of Labor, San Francisco, 1992—. Mem. exec. com. Nat. Conf. Adminstrv. Law Judges, 1986-88, sec. 1988-89, vice-chair, 1990-91, chair-elect, 1991-92, chair 1992-93; pres. Calif. Adminstrv. Law Judges Coun., 1978-84; mem. faculty Nat. Jud. Coll., U. Nev., 1977, 78, 80; mem. U.S. Bd. of Alien Labor Cert. Appeals, 1995—. Chmn. pack Boy Scouts Am., 1967-69, chmn. troop 1972; class chmn. Stanford Law Sch. Fund, 1959, mem. nat. com., 1963-65; dir. Forest Hill Assn., 1970-71; patron San Francisco Opera. Served to col. USAF Res., 1949-79. Decorated Legion of Merit. Mem. ABA (mem. ho. of dels. 1993-99, vice chair jud. divsn. 1997-98, chair elect 1998-99, chair 1999-2000), State Bar Calif., Bar Assn. San Francisco, Calif. Conf. Pub. Utility Counsel (pres. 1980-81), Air Force Assn., Res. Officers Assn., Ret. Officers Assn., San Francisco Gem and Mineral Soc., Stanford Alumni Assn., Rutgers Alumni Assn., Phi Beta Kappa (pres. No. Calif. 1973-74), Tau Kappa Alpha, Pi Alpha Theta, Phi Alpha Delta. Home: 530 Dewey Blvd San Francisco CA 94116-1427 Office: 50 Fremont St San Francisco CA 94105-2230

JARVIS, MARY G. principal; Prin. Smoky Hill High Sch., Aurora, Colo., 1988—. Recipient Blue Ribbon Sch. award, 1990-91. Office: Smoky Hill High Sch 16100 E Smoky Hill Rd Aurora CO 80015-1751

JARVIS, PETER R. lawyer; b. N.Y.C., July 19, 1950; BA in Econs. magna cum laude, Harvard U., 1972; MA in Econs., JD, Yale U., 1976. Bar: Oreg. 1976, U.S. Dist. Ct. Oreg. 1976, U.S. Ct. Appeals (9th cir.) 1977, Wash. 1983, U.S. Dist. Ct. (we. dist.) Wash. 1983, U.S. Dist. Ct. (ea. dist.) Wash. 1985, U.S. Tax Ct. 1991. Mem. Stoel Rives LLP, Portland, Oreg. Author: (with others) Oregon Rules of Professional Responsibility (updated annually); editor, author: (with others) The Ethical Oregon Lawyer, 1991, 98; ethics columnists: The Multnomah Lawyer; spkr. on legal ethics issues. Mem. ALI (Harrison Tweed Spl. Merit award 1993), Oreg. State Bar (former mem. legal ethics com., Pres.'s Membership Svcs. award 1991), Wash. State Bar (mem. profl. conduct com.), Phi Beta Kappa. Office: Stoel Rives LLP 900 SW 5th Ave Ste 2600 Portland OR 97204-1268

JARVIS, RICHARD S. academic administrator; b. Nottingham, Eng., Feb. 13, 1949; came to U.S., 1974; s. John Leslie and Mary Margaret (Dodman) J.; m. Marilou Thompson, Nov. 7, 1986; stepchildren: Kimberly Nipko, Christopher Healey. BA in Geography, Cambridge (Eng.) U., 1970, MA, 1974, PhD in Geography, 1975. Lectr. Durham (Eng.) U., 1973-74; assoc. prof. SUNY, Buffalo, 1975-87, asst. to pres., 1986-87, v.p. acad. Fredonia, 1987-90, prof. geoscis., 1987-90; vice provost SUNY Sys., Albany, 1990-94; chancellor Univ. and C.C. Sys. Nev., Reno and Las Vegas, 1994-99, U.S. Open U., Aurora, Colo., 1999—. Mem. adv. bd. Bechtel Nev., Las Vegas, 1995-97, NTS Devel. Corp., Las Vegas, 1997, INC, Las Vegas, 1997. Editor: River Networks, 1983; contbr. articles to profl. jours. Trustee United Way, Reno, 1996-99, EDAWN, Reno, 1996-99. Office: US Open Univ Chancellors Office Ste 212 9125 Lowry Pl Bldg 905 Denver CO 80230-6011 E-mail: r.s.jarvis@open.edu

JASTROW, ROBERT, physicist, educator; b. N.Y.C., Sept. 7, 1925; s. Abraham and Marie (Greenfield) J. A.B., Columbia, 1944, M.A., 1945, Ph.D., 1948; post-doctoral fellow, Leiden U., 1948-49, Princeton Inst. Advanced Study, 1949-50, 53, U. Calif. at Berkeley, 1950-53; D.Sc. (hon.), Manhattan Coll., 1980, N.J. Inst. Tech., 1987. Asst. prof. Yale, 1953-54; cons. nuclear physics U.S. Naval Research Lab., Washington, 1958-62; head theoretical div. Goddard Space Flight Center NASA, 1958-61, chmn. lunar exploration com., 1959-60, mem. com., 1960-62; dir. Goddard Inst. Space Studies, N.Y.C., 1961-81; adj. prof. geology Columbia, 1961-81, dir. Summer Inst. Space Physics, 1962-70; adj. prof. astronomy Columbia (Summer Inst. Space Physics), 1977-82; adj. prof. earth sci. Dartmouth, 1973-92; pres. G.C. Marshall Inst., 1985—; dir. Mt. Wilson Inst., 1991—. Author: The Evolution of Stars, Planets and Life, 1967, Astronomy: Fundamentals and Frontiers, 1972, Until the Sun Dies, 1977, God and the Astronomers, 1978, 2d edit., 1992, Red Giants-White Dwarfs, 1991, The Enchanted Loom, 1981, How To Make Nuclear Weapons Obsolete, 1985, Journey to the Stars, 1989; editor: Exploration of Space, 1960; co-editor: Jour. Atmospheric Scis., 1962-74, The Origin of the Solar System, 1963, The Venus Atmosphere, 1969. Recipient Medal of Excellence Columbia, 1962, Grad. Faculties Alumni award, 1967; Arthur S. Flemming award, 1965; medal for exceptional sci. achievement NASA, 1968 Fellow Am. Geophys. Union, A.A.A.S., Am. Phys. Soc.; mem. Internat. Acad. Astronautics, Council Fgn. Relations, Leakey Found., Nat. Space Soc. (bd. govs.) Clubs: Cosmos, Explorers, Century. Office: Mt Wilson Observatory Hale Solar Lab 740 Holladay Rd Pasadena CA 91106-4115 E-mail: jastrow@mtwilson.edu

JEANLOZ, RAYMOND, geophysicist, educator; b. Winchester, Mass., Aug. 18, 1952; BA, Amherst Coll, 1975; PhD in Geology and Geophysics, Calif. Inst. Tech., 1979. Asst. prof. Harvard U., 1979-81; from asst. prof. to assoc. prof. U. Calif., Berkeley, 1982-85, prof., 1985—. Exec. dir. Miller Inst. for Basic Rsch. in Sci., 1998—; chair bd. on earth scis. and resources NRC, 1999—. Editor Ann. Rev. Earth and Planetary Sci., 1996—. Recipient Mineral. Soc. Am. award, 1988, life fellow, 1988; MacArthur grantee, 1988. Fellow AAAS, Am. Geophysics Union (J.B. Macelwane award 1984); mem. Am. Acad. Arts and Scis. Office: U Calif Dept Earth & Planetary Sci Berkeley CA 94720-0001

JEANNES, CHARLES A. lawyer; b. Henderson, Nev., Sept. 26, 1958; s. Charles and Irene (Staviski) J.; m. Elizabeth S. Gray, June 5, 1982; children: Matthew A., Scott C. BA in Polit. Sci., U. Nev.; JD, U. Ariz. Bar: Nev. 1983, U.S. Dist. Ct. Nev. 1983, Ariz. 1984. Assoc. Woodburn, Wedge, Blakely & Jeppson, Reno, 1983—. Mem. cen. com. Washoe County Rep. Party, Reno, 1983—. Mem. State Bar Nev., State Bar Ariz., Rocky Mountain Mineral Law Found. Office: Glamis Gold Ltd 5190 Neil Rd Ste 310 Reno NV 89502

JEFFERS, DONALD E. retired insurance executive, consultant; b. Louisville, Aug. 21, 1925; s. Byron V. and Alice B. (Burgess) J.; m. Marion D. Benna, Aug. 14, 1948 (dec.); 1 son, Derek; m. Janice C. Smith, Apr. 21, 1979 (dec.). B.S. in Accountancy, U. Ill., 1948. C.P.A., Ill., D.C. Sr. acct. Coopers & Lybrand, CPAs, N.Y.C. and Chgo., 1948-56; asst. v.p. Continental Casualty Co., Chgo., 1956-64; dep. comptr. First Nat. Bank Boston, 1965-67; exec. v.p., treas. Interstate Nat. Corp., Chgo., 1967-74, pres., chief exec. officer, 1974-85, also dir.; chmn., dir. Interstate Ins. Group and Geo. F. Brown & Sons Inc.; chmn. Jeffers & Assocs., Inc., San Diego, 1985—. Former sec., dir. Ill. Ins. Info. Service; underwriting mem. Lloyd's London, 1977—. Served with inf. AUS, 1943-45. Decorated Purple Heart. Mem. AICPA. Home: 3405 Florida St Apt 308 San Diego CA 92104

JEFFERS, MICHAEL BOGUE, lawyer; b. Wenatchee, Wash., July 10, 1940; s. Richard G. and Betty (Ball) J. BA, U. Wash., 1962, LLB, 1964; LLM in Taxation, NYU, 1970. Bar: Wash. 1964, N.Y. 1970, Calif. 1988. Ptnr. Hughes & Jeffers, Wenatchee, 1964-65, 68, Hill, Betts & Nash, N.Y.C., 1970-72, Battle Fowler, N.Y.C., 1973-88, Buchalter, Nemer, Fields & Younger, Newport Beach, Calif., 1988-89, Riordan & McKinzie, Costa Mesa, 1989-90, Phillips, Haglund, Haddan & Jeffers, Newport Beach, 1991-93, Jeffers, Shaff & Falk, LLP, Newport Beach, Calif., 1994—. Sec. Thornburg Mortgage Inc. Alumni trustee U. Wash., 1970-73; pres. Ballet Pacifica. Mem. ABA, Calif. Bar Assn., Orange County Bar Assn., Wash. State Bar Assn., U. Wash. Alumni Assn. (pres. Greater N.Y. chpt. 1972-88), Pacific Club, Nat. Wild Turkey Fedn., Explorers Club, Phi Gamma Delta. Office: Jeffers Shaff & Falk LLP 18881 Von Karman Ave Ste 1400 Irvine CA 92612-1562 E-mail: mjeffers@jsfllp.com

JEFFREY, JOHN ORVAL, lawyer; b. Portsmouth, Va., Aug. 6, 1963; s. Orval L. and Mary L. (Coakley) J. BA, U. Dayton (Ohio), 1985; diploma internat. legal studies, U. San Diego, Paris, 1987; JD, Southwestern U., L.A., 1988. Bar: Calif. 1988, U.S. Dist. Ct. (cen. dist.) Calif. 1988. Assoc. Shield & Smith, L.A., 1989-90, Hewitt, Kaldor & Prout, L.A., 1990-93; mgr. bus. and legal affairs fx subs. Fox TV; v.p. bus. and legal affairs AND Interactive; sr. counsel, dir. legal affairs Discovery Comms.; now exec. v.p. corp. strategy and gen. counsel Live365.com. Campaign worker John Glenn Campaign for Pres., N.H., 1984; vol. Amnesty Internat. Mem. ABA (internat. law sect., litigation sect., entertainment/sports law sect.), Internat. Bar Assn., Los Angeles County Bar Assn. (mem. evaluation profl. standards com., mem. legis. activity com., mem. artists and the law com.), Phi Alpha Delta, Alpha Nu Omega. Democrat. Avocations: tennis, long distance running, French reading proficiency. Office: [illegible] 1801 E Hillsdale Blvd Ste 225 Foster City CA 94404

JEFFRIES, ROBIN, computer engineer; BA in Math. summa cum laude, U. Iowa, 1969; MA in Quantitative Psychology, U. Colo., 1977, PhD in Quantitative Psychology, 1978. Rsch. assoc. U. Colo., Boulder, Carnegie-Mellon U., 1983-93; mem. tech. staff Hewlett Packard Labs.; disting. engr. Sun Microsystems, Palo Alto, Calif., 1993—. Office: Sun Microsystems 901 San Antonio Rd Palo Alto CA 94303-4900

JEFFRIES, RUSSELL MORDEN, communications company official; b. Carmel, Calif., July 15, 1935; s. Herman M. and Louise (Morden) J.; m. Barbara Jean Borcovich, Nov. 24, 1962; 1 child, Lynne Louise. AA, Hartnell Coll., 1971. Sr. communications technician AT&T, Salinas, Calif., 1955-91. Mayor City of Salinas, 1987-91. Pres. El Gabilan Sch. PTA, Salinas, 1971-74, Salinas Valley Council PTA, 1975-76; mem. Salinas City Sch. Bd., 1975-81; mem. Salinas City Council, 1981-87; bd. dirs. Community Hosp. Salinas Found., 1987—, Salinas-Kushikino Sister City, 1987—, pres. 1992-93, John Steinbeck Ctr. Found., 1987-96, Food Bank for Monterey County, 1992-96; hon. bd. dirs. Monterey Film Festival, 1987-96, Calif. Rodeo Assn., 1987; mem. ctrl. bd. Calif. Regional Water Quality, 1992—; commr. Moss Landing Harbor, 1996. Recipient hon. service award PTA, Salinas, 1976; cert. of appreciation Calif. Dept. Edn., 1980, Salinas City Sch. Dist., 1981, Calif. Sch. Bds. Assn., 1981, Steinbeck Kiwanis, Salinas, 1987; named hon. mem. Filipino community Salinas Valley, 1988. Mem. Salinas C. of C., Native Sons Golden West, K.C., Rotary, Moose. Republican. Roman Catholic. Avocations: fishing, hunting, bowling, golf. Home: 204 E Curtis St Salinas CA 93906-2804

JEKOWSKY, BARRY, conductor, music director; b. N.Y. MusB and MusM, Juilliard Sch. Founder, music dir. Calif. Symphony Orch. Assoc. condr. Nat. Symphony Orch., Washington, 1994—. Numerous orch. appearances throughout N.Am. and Europe including London Phila. Orch., Halle Orch. Recipient Leopold Stokowski Conducting prize. Achievements include creation of the Young American Composer-in-Residence Program, 1991, unique in its orchestra-laboratory forum. Office: Calif Symphony Orch 1603 Oak Park Blvd Pleasant Hill CA 94523-4487

JELLEN, EDWARD D. federal bankruptcy judge; b. 1946; BA, U. Calif., Berkeley, 1967; JD, U. Calif., 1971. With legal dept. Bank of Am., 1972-78; with Jellen & Holman, 1978-82, Jellen & Assocs., 1982-87; apptd. bankruptcy judge no. dist. U.S. Dist. Ct. Calif., 1987, apptd. chief judge, 1997. Office: 1300 Clay St Rm 215 Oakland CA 94612-1425

JELLIFFE, ROGER WOODHAM, cardiologist, clinical pharmacologist; b. Cleve., Feb. 18, 1929; s. Russell Wesley and Rowena (Woodham) J.; m. Joyce Miller, June 12, 1954; children: Susan, Amy, Elizabeth, Peter. BA, Harvard U., 1950; MD, Columbia U., 1954. Diplomate Am. Bd. Internal Medicine, Am. Bd. Cardiovascular Disease. Intern Univ. Hosps., Cleve., 1954-56; also jr. asst. resident in medicine; Nat. Found. Infantile Paralysis exptl. medicine fellow Case Western Res. U., Cleve., 1956-58; staff physician in medicine VA Hosp., Cleve., 1958-60, resident in medicine, 1960-61; instr. medicine U. So. Calif. Sch. Medicine, L.A., 1961-63, asst. prof., 1963-67, assoc. prof., 1967-76, prof. medicine, 1976—. Developer Lab. Applied Pharmacokinetics, 1973—, The USC*PACK Computer Programs, 1973—; cons. Dynamic Scis., Inc., Van Nuys, Calif., 1976-93, Simes S.P.A., Milan, 1979-97, IVAC Corp., San Diego, 1983-88, Bionica, Sydney, Australia, 1987-94. Author: Fundamentals of Electrocardiography, 1990; cons. editor Am. Jour. Medicine, 1972-78, Current Prescribing, 1974-79, Am. Jour. Physiology, 1984-91, Computers in Biology amd Medicine, 1994—, Therapeutic Drug Monitoring, 1995—; contbr. articles to profl. jours.; patentee in field. Advanced Rsch. fellow L.A. County Heart Assn., 1961-64; recipient Rsch. Achievement award Clin. Scis. Am. Assn. Pharm. Scis., 1997. Fellow ACP, Am. Coll. Med. Informatics, Am. Coll. Clin. Pharmacology, Am. Heart Assn. Coun. on Clin. Cardiology; mem. Am. Soc. Clin. Pharmacology and Therapeutics (chmn. pharmacometric sect. 1995-97), Am. Fedn. Clin. Rsch., Am. Med. Informatics Assn. Achievements include research on optimal mgmt. of drug therapy; development of computer programs for optimal mgmt. of drug therapy; population pharmacokinetic modeling; development of intelligent infusion devices; supercomputer resources for parametric and nonparametric population modeling; software for "multiple model" design of drug dosage regimens. Office: U So Calif Sch Medicine CSC 134-B 2250 Alcazar St Los Angeles CA 90033-1004 E-mail: jelliffe@hsc.usc.edu

JELLINEK, ROGER, editor; b. Mexico City, Jan. 16, 1938; came to U.S., 1961; s. Frank Louis Mark and Marguerite Lilla Donne (Lewis) J.; m. Margherita DiCenzo, Dec. 22, 1963 (div. 1984); children: Andrew Mark, Claire; m. Eden-Lee Murray, 1984; 1 child, Everett Peter Murray. Student, Bryanston Sch., Dorset, Eng., 1951-56; MA, Cambridge U., Eng., 1961. Assoc. editor Random House, 1963-64; editor Walker & Co., 1964-65, N.Y. Times Book Rev., 1966-70, dep. editor, 1970-73; editor in chief Times Books, Quadrangle/N.Y. Times Book Co., 1974-78, sr. editor, 1978-81, editor Lamont newsletter and yearbook, 1981-91; pres. Clairemark, Ltd., 1981—. Jellinek & Murray Lit. Agy.; editl. dir. Inner Ocean Pub., Honolulu, 2000—. Editor Atlantic Realm Project, 1983-93; editl. dir. Inner Ocean Pub., 2000—; pub. Hawaii map series. Pres. ArtMaps Ltd., 1996—. With Royal Marines, 1956-57; 2d lt. Brit. Intelligence Corps, 1957-58. Mellon fellow Yale U., 1961-63. Home and Office: 3623 Kumu St Honolulu HI 96822-1102

JEMELIAN, JOHN NAZAR, management consultant; b. N.Y.C., May 10, 1933; s. Nazar and Angel (Jizmejian) J.; m. Rose Melkonian, Nov. 22, 1958; children: Sheri, Lori, Brian, Joni. BS, U. So. Calif., 1956. CPA, Calif., 1961. Mgr. audit staff Price Waterhouse & Co., Los Angeles, 1958-64; treas. The Akron, Los Angeles, 1964-82, v.p. fin., 1976, exec. v.p., 1977-82; v.p., gen. mgr., dir. Acromil Corp., City of Industry, Calif., 1982-85; sr. v.p. fin. and adminstrn., chief fin. officer, sec., treas. World Vision Inc., 1985-98; pres. Claremont Facilities Corp., 1990—, Pasadena Resources Corp., 1990-94. Dir. D.L. Engring., Inc.; fin. adviser African Enterprises, 1966-68 Bd. dirs. Pasadena Christian Sch., 1965-67, 69-70, treas., 1965-67; deacon Lake Ave. Congregrational Ch., 1964-68, trustee, 1970-73, chmn. bd. trustees, 1972-73, chmn. ch. com. 1974; bd. dirs. Forest Home Christian Conf. Ctr., 1972-75, 78-81, 84-88, 1992-95, 2000—; chmn. bd. Media Ministries, Inc., 1975-95, Donor Automation, 1975-2001; trustee Haigazian Coll., Beirut, 1974-78, Narramore Christian Found., 1976-93, Met. Ministries, 1979-80; chmn. Christian Bus. Men's Com., 1979-81, 86-87, Sahag Mesrob Armenian Christian Sch., 1980-85; deacon, elder Ch. on the Way, 1980-95; bd. dirs. Armenian Gospel Mission, 1999—. With F.A., U.S. Army, 1956-58. Named Boss of Year Beverly Hills chpt. Nat. Secs. Assn., 1970 Mem. Am. Inst. C.P.A.s, Calif. Soc. C.P.A.s, Retail Controllers Assn. (dir. 1973-74), Delta Sigma Pi, Beta Alpha Psi, Beta Gamma Sigma. Clubs: Los Angeles Athletic, Toastmasters-Windjammers (Los Angeles) (pres. 1963). Home: 261 Sharon Rd Arcadia CA 91007-8044 Office: PO Box 5051 Monrovia CA 91016-3198 Fax: 626-301-1128. E-mail: jjemelia@worldvision.org

JENDEN, DONALD JAMES, pharmacologist, educator; b. Horsham, Sussex, Eng., Sept. 1, 1926; came to U.S., 1950, naturalized, 1958; s. William Herbert and Kathleen Mary (Harris) J.; m. Jean Ickeringill, Nov. 18, 1950; children: Tricia Jenden Billes, Peter Donald, Beverly Jean Jenden Riedlinger. BSc in Physiology with 1st class honours, Kings Coll. London, 1947; MB, BS with honours, U. London, 1950; PhD in Pharm. Chemistry (hon.), U. Uppsala, Sweden, 1980. Demonstrator pharmacology U. London, 1948-49; lectr. pharmacology U. Calif.-San Francisco, 1950-51, asst. prof. pharmacology, 1952-53; mem. faculty UCLA, 1953, assoc. prof., [illegible] prof. pharmacology and biomath. 1967—, chmn. dept. pharmacology, 1968-89. Wellcome vis. prof. U. Ala., Birmingham, 1984; mem. brain research inst. UCLA, 1961—. Contbr. articles in field. Served to lt. comdr. M.C., USNR, 1954-58. USPHS Postdoctoral fellow, 1951-53, NSF Sr. Postdoctoral fellow; hon. research assoc. Univ. Coll., London, 1961-62; Fulbright Short-Term Sr. Scholar award, Australia, 1983; recipient Univ. Gold medal U. London, 1950. Fellow Am. Coll. Neuropsychopharmacology, West Coast Coll. Biol. Psychology (charter); mem. AAAS, Am. Soc. Pharmacology and Exptl. Therapeutics, Am. Physiol. Soc., Physiol. Soc. (London), Soc. Neurosci., Am. Chem. Soc., Western Pharmacology Soc. (pres. 1970), Assn. for Med. Sch. Pharmacology, Am. Soc. Neurochemistry, Internat. Union Pharmacology. Home: 3814 Castlerock Rd Malibu CA 90265-5625 E-mail: jenden@ucla.edu

JENES, THEODORE GEORGE, JR. retired career officer; b. Portland, Oreg., Feb. 21, 1930; s. Theodore George and Mabel Marie (Moon) J.; m. Beverly Lorraine Knutson, Jan. 29, 1953; children— Ted, Mark BS, U. Ga., 1956; MS, Auburn U., 1969; grad., Army Command and Gen. Staff Coll., Armed Forces Staff Coll., Air War Coll.; LLD (hon.), U. Akron, 1986. Enlisted U.S. Army, 1951, commd. 2d lt., 1953, advanced through grades to lt. gen., 1984, various assignments, 1953-75; comdr. 3d Brigade, 2d Inf. Div., Republic of Korea, 1975-76, 172d Inf. Brigade, Ft. Richardson, Alaska, 1978-81; dep. commdg. gen. U.S. Army Tng. Ctr., Ft. Dix, N.J., 1976-78; comdr. 4th Inf. Div., Ft. Carson, Colo., 1982-84; dep. commdg. gen. U.S. Army Combined Arms Combat Devel. Activity, Ft. Leavenworth, Kans., 1981-82; comdg. gen. 3d U.S. Army, Ft. McPherson, Ga., 1984-87; commander U.S. Army Forces Ctrl. Command, Ft. McPherson, 1984-87; dep. comdg. gen. hdqrs. U.S. Army Forces Command, Ft. McPherson, 1984-87, ret., 1987; cons. Burdeshaw and Assocs., 1987-88; gen. mgr. Seattle Tennis Club, 1988-94. Decorated D.S.M., Legion of Merit, Bronze Star, Meritorious Service medal, Air medal, Army Commendation medal, Vietnamese Cross of Gallantry with Silver Star. Mem. Assn. of U.S. Army, Rotary. United Methodist. Avocations: reading military history; cycling; skiing, golf. Home: 809 169th Pl SW Lynnwood WA 98037-3307 Fax: 425-745-8068

JENKINS, BRUCE, sportswriter; b. Oct. 4, 1948; s. Gordon Jenkins; m. Martha Jane Stanton; 2 children. Degree in Journalism, U. Calif., Berkeley, 1971. With San Francisco Chronicle, 1973—, sports columnist, 1989—. Author: Life After Saberhagen, 1986, North Shore Chronicles, 1990. Recipient nat. awards AP, UPI, Basketball Writers Assn.; nominated Pulitzer Prize for columns Barcelona Olympics, 1992. Office: San Francisco Chronicle 901 Mission St San Francisco CA 94103-2905

JENKINS, BRUCE STERLING, federal judge; b. Salt Lake City, May 27, 1927; s. Joseph and Bessie Pearl (Iverson) J.; m. Margaret Watkins, Sept. 19, 1952; children— Judith Margaret, David Bruce, Michael Glen, Carol Alice. BA with high honors, U. Utah, 1949, LLB, JD, U. Utah, 1952. Bar: Utah 1952, U.S. Dist. Ct. 1952, U.S. Supreme Ct. 1962, U.S. Circuit Ct. Appeals 1962. Pvt. practice, Salt Lake City, 1952-59; assoc. firm George McMillan, 1959-65; asst. atty. gen. State of Utah, 1952; dep. county atty. Salt Lake County, 1954-58; bankruptcy judge U.S. Dist. Ct., Utah, 1965-78, judge, 1978—, chief judge, 1984-93. Adj. prof. U. Utah, 1987-88, 96—. Research, publs. in field; contbr. essays to Law jours.; bd. editors: Utah Law Rev, 1951-52. Mem. Utah Senate, 1959-65, minority leader, 1963, pres. senate, 1965, vice chmn. commn. on orgn. exec. br. of Utah Govt., 1965-66; Mem. adv. com. Utah Tech. Coll., 1967-72; mem. instl. council Utah State U., 1976. Served with USN, 1945-46. Named Alumnus of Yr. award Coll. Law Univ. Utah, 1985; recipient Admiration and Appreciation award Utah State Bar, 1995, Emeritus Merit of Honor award U. Utah Alumni Assn., 1997. Fellow Am. Bar Found.; mem. ABA, Am. Inn Ct., Utah State Bar Assn. (Judge of Yr. 1993), Salt Lake County Bar Assn., Fed. Bar Assn. (Disting. Jud. Svc. awrd Utah chpt. 1993), Order of Coif, Phi Beta Kappa, Phi Kappa Phi, Phi Eta Sigma, Phi Sigma Alpha, Tau Kappa Alpha. Democrat. Mormon. Office: US Dist Ct 462 US Courthouse 350 S Main St Salt Lake City UT 84101-2106

JENKINS, DONALD JOHN, museum administrator; b. Longview, Wash., May 3, 1931; s. John Peter and Louise Hazel (Pederson) J.; m. Mary Ella Bemis, June 29, 1956; children— Jennifer, Rebecca B.A., U. Chgo., 1951, M.A., 1970. Mus. asst. Portland (Oreg.) Art Mus., 1954-56, asst. curator, 1960-69, curator, 1974-75, dir., 1975-87, curator Asian art, 1987—, chief curator, 1998-2001; assoc. curator oriental art Art Inst. Chgo., 1969-74. Mem. gallery adv. com. Asia House Gallery, N.Y.C., 1977-91; application reviewer NEH, Washington, 1984-86; lectr. various museums and art orgns., 1969—. Author: (exhbn. catalogues) Ukiyo-e Prints and Paints, 1971, The Ledoux Heritage, 1973, Masterworks in Wood/China and Japan, 1976, Images of Changing World, 1983, The Floating World Revisited, 1993. Mem. Pittock Mansion Adv. Com., Portland, 1975-87, chmn., 1983-84; chmn. NW Regional China Coun., Portland, 1980-89; mem. art selection com. Performing Arts Ctr., Portland, 1983-89; bd. dirs. Classical Chinese Garden, Portland, 2000—. Recipient Uchiyama Susumu Meml. award Japan Ukiyo-e Soc., 1993, Order of Rising Sun with gold rays and rosette Japanese Govt., 1994, Flying Horse Cmty. Svc. award N.W. China Coun., 1996. Mem. Am. Assn. Mus., Soc. for Japanese Arts, Assn. Asian Studies, Japan-Am. Soc. Oreg. (chmn. cultural affairs com. 1987-98), The Internat. House of Japan. Home: 16418 NW Rock Creek Rd Portland OR 97231-2406 Office: Portland Art Mus 1219 SW Park Ave Portland OR 97205-2486 E-mail: donald.jenkins@pam.org

JENKINS, GEORGE, stage designer, film art director; b. Balt., Nov. 19, 1908; s. Benjamin Wheeler and Jane (Clarke) J.; m. Phyllis Adams, May 6, 1955; 1 dau by previous marriage, Jane Jenkins Dumais; 1 stepdau., Alexandra Kirkland Marsh (dec.). Student architecture, U. Pa., 1931. Cons. theatre U. Pa., Anenberg Theatre. Vis. prof. motion picture design UCLA, 1985-87, 88. Set designer Broadway prodns. including I Remember Mamma, 1944, Dark of the Moon, 1945, Lost in the Stars, 1949, Bell, Book and Candle, 1950, The Bad Seed, 1954, Happiest Millionaire, 1956, Miracle Worker, 1959, Wait Until Dark, 1966, Only Game in Town, 1968, Night Watch, 1972, Sly Fox, 1976; art dir. films including Best Years of Our Lives, 1946, Secret Life of Walter Mitty, 1948, Mickey One, 1965, Up the Down Staircase, 1966, Wait Until Dark, 1967, No Way to Treat a Lady, 1967, Subject Was Roses, 1968, Klute, 1970, 1776, 1971, The Paper Chase, 1972, Parallax View, 1973, Funny Lady, 1974, All the President's Men, 1977, Comes A Horseman, 1978, China Syndrome, 1978, Starting Over, 1979, The Postman Always Rings Twice, 1980, Roll Over, 1981, Sophie's Choice, 1982, Dream Lover, 1984, Orphans, 1987, See You in the Morning, 1989, Presumed Innocent, 1990; TV programs including Annie Get Your Gun, NBC TV, 1957, The Dollmaker, ABC-TV, 1983; art dir. in charge color, CBS-TV, 1953-54. Recipient Donaldson award for I Remember Mama, Billboard Publs., 1946, Acad. award for All the President's Men, 1977, nominated for Acad. award for China Syndrome, 1978. Mem. Delta Phi. Office: 740 Kingman Ave Santa Monica CA 90402-1336

JENKINS, JAMES C. lawyer; b. Logan, Utah, July 16, 1948; BA in Fin., U. Utah, 1972; JD, Gonzaga U., 1976. Bar: Utah 1976, U.S. Dist. Ct. Utah 1976, U.S. Ct. Appeals (10th cir.) 1992, U.S. Tax Ct. 1985, U.S. Supreme Ct. 1981. Ptnr. Olson & Hoggan, P.C., Logan, Utah; Rich county atty., 1978-81; Cache county dep. atty., 1981-95; gen. counsel Bear Lake Spl. Svcs. Dist., Rich County, Utah, 1978-2001. Instr. Utah State U., 1976; trustee Utah Bankruptcy Ct., 1977-80. Chair jud. conduct commn. Utah Jud. Coun., 1996-97, mem. jud. performance and evaluation com., mem. adv. bd. Utah State Crime Lab. Mem. ABA (trial practice com., litig. sect.

1986-95), Utah State Bar Assn. (pres.-elect 1997-98, pres. 1998-99, law benefit com. 1978-80, law day com. 1989-90, ethics and discipline com. 1992-93, exec. com., litig. com. 1993-95, bd. commrs. 1993-96), Utah Statewide Assn. Pros., Cache County Bar Assn. (sec.-treas. 1978-81) Office: Olson & Hoggan PC PO Box 525 88 W Center St Logan UT 84323-0525

JENKINS, KEVIN J. technology and industrial company executive; b. Edmonton, Alta., Can. m. Helen Jenkins; 3 children. Law degree, U. Alta.; MBA, Harvard U. Ptnr. law firm Can Airlines, Edmonton, Alta., 1980s; with fin. dept. Can. Airlines, Calgary, 1985, various positions including CFO; pres. Wardair, 1986-91; pres., CEO Can. Airlines, Calgary, Alta., 1991-96, The Westaim Corp., Calgary, 1996—; also bd. dirs. Bd. dirs. Neyen Inc.; mem. Corp. of World Vision Canada. Mem. bus. adv. coun. Faculty of Bus., U. Alta.; mem. Young Pres.'s Orgn.; bd. dirs. Young Life of Can. Office: The Westaim Corp 144 4th Ave SW Ste 1010 Calgary AB Canada T2P 3N4

JENKINS, MAYNARD, automotive executive; With Orchard Supply Hardware, pres., CEO, 1986-97; chmn., CEO CSK Auto Corp., Phoenix, 1997—. Office: CSK Auto Corp 645 E Missouri Ave Ste 400 Phoenix AZ 85012

JENKINS, SCOTT K. state legislator; b. Ogden, Utah, Apr. 13, 1950; m. Rebecca, 5 children. AA, Weber State Coll., 1974. Sales Mountain State Supply, 1977-82, Hojaca Corp., 1982-87; owner Great Western Supply, Inc., 1987—; mem. Utah State Senate, Sale Lake City, 2001—. Mayor City of Plain, Utah, 1990-94, mem. city coun., 1980-88, planning com., 1978-79. With Utah NG, 1972-79. Office: 4385 W 1975 N Plain City UT 84404*

JENKINS, SPEIGHT, opera company executive, writer; b. Dallas, Jan. 31, 1937; s. Speight and Sara (Baird) J.; m. Linda Ann Sands, Sept. 6, 1966; children: Linda Leonie, Speight. B.A., U. Tex.-Austin, 1957; LL.B., Columbia U., 1961; DMus (hon.), U. Puget Sound, 1992; HHD, Seattle U., 1992. News and reports editor Opera News, N.Y.C., 1967-73; music critic N.Y. Post, N.Y.C., 1973-81; TV host Live from the Met, Met. Opera, N.Y.C., 1981-83; gen. dir. Seattle Opera, 1983—. Classical music editor Record World, N.Y.C., 1973-81; contbg. editor Ovation Mag., N.Y.C., 1980— , Opera Quar., Los Angeles, 1982— Served to capt. U.S. Army, 1961-66. Recipient Emmy award for Met. Opera telecast La Boheme TV Acad. Arts and Scis., 1982 Mem. Phi Beta Kappa Assocs. Presbyterian. Home: 903 Harvard Ave E Seattle WA 98102-4561 Office: Seattle Opera PO Box 9248 Seattle WA 98109-0248

JENNER, MIKE, newspaper editor; Reporter, photographer Hattiesburg (Miss.) Am.; editing positions The Phila. Inquirer, Columbia (Mo.) Tribune, Coffeyville (Kans.) Jour.; asst. mng. editor Hartford (Conn.) Courant, mng. editor; ind. newspaper cons.; mng. editor The Bakersfield Californian, 1993-98, exec. editor, 1998—. Office: The Bakersfield Californian 1707 Eye St Bakersfield CA 93301-5299

JENNERICH, EDWARD JOHN, university official and dean; b. Bklyn., Oct. 22, 1945; s. William James and Anna Johanna (Whicker) J.; m. Elaine Zaremba, May 27, 1972; children— Ethan Edward, Emily Elaine B.A., Trenton State Coll., 1967; M.S.L.S., Drexel U., 1970; Ph.D., U. Pitts., 1974. Cert. tchr., learning resources specialist. Tchr. U.S. history Rahway High Sch., N.J., 1967-70; librarian Westinghouse High Sch., Pitts. Pub. Sch., 1970-74; adminstrv. intern U. Pitts, 1973; chmn. dept. library sci. Baylor U., Waco, Tex., 1974-83; dean Sch. Library Sci. So. Conn. State U., New Haven, 1983-84; v.p. acad. affairs Va. Intermont Coll., Bristol, 1984-87; grad. dean Seattle U., 1987-89; assoc. provost for acad. adminstrn., dean Grad. Sch., 1989-97; pres. Knowledge N.W. Inc., 1997—. Mem. rev. panel Fulbright Adminstrv. Exch., 1983-86. Co-author: University Administration in Great Britain, 1983, The Reference Interview as a Creative Art, 1987, 2d edit., 1997; contbr. articles to profl. jours. Bd. dirs. Waco Girls Club, Tex., 1977-83 Mem. ALA (coun. for libr. pers. resources 1980-82), Am. Assn. Univ. Adminstrs. (bd. dirs. 1980-82, 83-86, 89-93, 94—, v.p. 1996—, exec. com. 1982-87, chmn. overseas liaison com. 1982-87, Eileen Tosney Adminstrv. Excellence award 1985), Assn. for Coll. and Rsch. Librs. (exec. bd. dirs. 1984-88), Phi Delta Kappa. Republican. Episcopalian. Avocations: collecting and painting military miniatures, reading, travel, outdoor sports, sailing. Home: 6935 NE 164th St Kenmore WA 98028-4282 Office: Seattle U Seattle WA 98122

JENNETT, SHIRLEY SHIMMICK, home care management executive, nurse; b. Jennings, Kans., May 1, 1937; d. William and Mabel C. (Mowry) Shimmick; m. Nelson K. Jennett, Aug. 20, 1960 (div. 1972); children: Jon W., Cheryl L.; m. Albert J. Kukral, Apr. 16, 1977 (div. 1990) Diploma, Rsch. Hosp. Sch. Nursing, Kansas City, Mo., 1958. RN, Mo., Colo., Tex., Ill. Staff nurse, head nurse Rsch. Hosp., 1958-60; head nurse Penrose Hosp., Colorado Springs, Colo., 1960-62, Hotel Dieu Hosp., El Paso, Tex., 1962-63; staff nurse Oak Park (Ill.) Hosp., 1963-64, NcNeal Hosp., Berwyn, Ill., 1964-65, St. Anthony Hosp., Denver, 1968-69; staff nurse, head nurse, nurse recruiter Luth. Hosp., Wheat Ridge, Colo., 1969-79; owner, mgr. Med. Placement Svcs., Lakewood, 1980-84; vol., primary care nurse, admissions coord., team mgr. Hospice of Metro Denver, 1984-88, dir. patient and family svcs., 1988, exec. dir., 1988-94; pres. Care Mgmt. & Resources, Inc., Denver, 1996—. Mem. NAFE, Nat. Women Bus. Owners Assn., Nat. Hospice Orgn. (bd. dirs. 1992-95, coun. former bd. mems. 1995—), Nat. Orgn. Profl. Geriatric Care Mgrs., Denver Bus. Women's Network. Mem. Ch. of Religious Sci. Avocations: reading, walking, golf. Office: Care Mgmt & Resources Inc 2055 S Oneida St Ste 150 Denver CO 80224-2435 E-mail: caremgt@earthnet.net

JENNICHES, F. SUZANNE, engineering executive; BS in Biology, Clarion State Coll., 1970; MS in Environ. Engring., Johns Hopkins U., 1978. Postgrad. with def. decision making internat. affairs Cath. U. Am.; v.p., gen. mgr. Automation and Info. Sys. Northrop Grumman Corp., L.A. Bd. dirs. Tech. Coun. Greater Balt. Com., 1990—; active Nat. Acad. Engring. Task Force on Celebration of Women in Engring., 1997—. Fellow Soc. Women Engrs. (life, pres. Balt. Washington sect. 1978-80, rep. Balt. Washington sect. 1981-83, Disting. New Engr. award 1983, co-chair internat. conf. on women in engring. and sci. 1984, regional dir. mid-atlantic area 1984-85, nat. v.p. student svcs. 1985-86, nat. sec. 1986-87, nat. pres.-elect 1987-88, nat. pres. 1988-89); mem. Am. Assn. Engring. Socs. (bd. govs. 1988-89). Office: Northrop Grumman Corp 1840 Century Park E Los Angeles CA 90067-2101

JENNINGS, JACKIE, construction executive, contractor; Pres. Johnson & Jennings Gen. Contracing, San Diego, 1979—. Chair San Diego Regional Econ. Task Force. Bd. mem. St. Vincent de Paul, San Diego. Recipient Woman-Owned Small Bus. Yr. award, 1998. Office: Johnson & Jennings 6165 Greenwich Dr Ste 180 San Diego CA 92122-5910 Fax: 619-612-1108. E-mail: info@johnsonandjennings.com

JENNINGS, MARCELLA GRADY, rancher, investor; b. Springfield, Ill., Mar. 4, 1920; d. William Francis and Magdalene Mary (Spies) Grady; student pub. schs.; m. Leo J. Jennings, Dec. 16, 1950 (dec.). Pub. relations Econolite Corp., Los Angeles, 1958-61; v.p., asst. mgr. LJ Quarter Circle Ranch, Inc., Polson, Mont., 1961-73, pres., gen. mgr., owner, 1973— ; dir. Giselle's Travel Inc., Sacramento; fin. advisor to Allentown, Inc., Charlo, Mont.; sales cons. to Amie's Jumpin' Jacks and Jills, Garland, Tex. Investor. Mem. Internat. Charolais Assn., Los Angeles County Apt. Assn. Republican. Roman Catholic. Home and Office: 509 Mount Holyoke Ave Pacific Palisades CA 90272-4328

JENNINGS, MARIANNE MOODY, lawyer, educator; b. Sept. 11, 1953; d. James L. and Jennie (Ure) Moody; m. Terry H. Jennings, Nov. 5, 1976; children: Sarah Anne, Claire Elizabeth. BS in Fin., Brigham Young U., 1974, JD, 1977. Bar: Ariz. 1977, U.S. Dist. Ct. Ariz. 1977. Law clk. Fed. Pub. Defender, Las Vegas, 1975; U.S. atty. Las Vegas, 1976, Udall, Shumway, Bentley, Allen & Lyons, Mesa, Ariz., 1976; from asst. prof. bus. law to assoc. prof. Ariz. State U., Tempe, 1977-83, prof., 1983—, assoc. dean, 1986-88. Columnist Tribune newspapers. Author: Business Strategy for the Political Arena, 1984, Real Estate Law, 6th edit., 2000, Business: Its Legal, Ethical and Global Environment, 5th edit., 2000, Avoiding and Surviving Lawsuits: An Executive Guide to Legal Strategy, 1988, N.Y. Times MBA Pocket Scenes: Corporate Boards, 2000. Bd. dirs. Ariz. Pub. Svc., Inc., 1987-2000. Named Outstanding Undergrad. Bus. Prof., Ariz. State U., 1980, 85, 2000; recipient Burlington No. Found. Tchg. Excellence award, 1986; Dean's Coun. of 100 scholar, 1996—. Mem. Ariz. Bar Assn., Am. Bus. Law Assn., Pacific S.W. Bus. Law Assn. Mormon. Office: Ariz State U c/o M Jennings Coll Bus Tempe AZ 85287 E-mail: marianne.jennings@asu.edu

JENNINGS, PAUL CHRISTIAN, civil engineering educator, academic administrator; b. Brigham City, Utah, May 21, 1936; s. Robert Webb and Elva S. (Simonsen) J.; m. Millicent Marie Bachman, Aug. 28, 1981; m. Barbara Elaine Morgan, Sept. 3, 1960 (div. 1981); children: Kathryn Diane, Margaret Ann. BSCE, Colo. State U., 1958; MSCE, Calif. Inst. Tech., 1960, PhD, 1963. Prof. civil engring., applied mechanics Calif. Inst. Tech., Pasadena, 1966—, chmn. divsn. engring., 1985-89, v.p., provost, 1989-95, acting v.p. for bus. and fin., 1995, 98-99. Mem. faculty bd. Calif. Tech. Inst., 1974-76, steering com., 1974-76, chmn. nominating com., 1975, grad. studies com., 1978-80; cons. in field. Author: (with others) Earthquake Design Criteria. Contbr. numerous articles to profl. jours. 1st lt. USAF, 1963-66. Recipient Honor Alumnus award Colo. State U., 1992, Achievement in Academia award Coll. Engring., 1992; Erskine fellow U. Canterbury, New Zealand, 1970, 85. Fellow AAAS, New Zealand Soc. Earthquake Engring.; mem. ASCE (Walter Huber award 1973, Newmark medal 1992), Seismol. Soc. Am. (pres. 1980), Earthquake Engring. Rsch. Inst. (pres. 1981-83), Athenaeum Club. Avocations: fly fishing, running. Home: 640 S Grand Ave Pasadena CA 91105-2423 Office: Calif Inst Tech Mail Code 104-44 Pasadena CA 91125-0001 E-mail: pcjenn@caltech.edu

JENNINGS, TIMOTHY ZEPH, rancher, state legislator; b. Roswell, N.Mex., Sept. 4, 1950; s. James Traynor and Frances Mitchell (Schultz) J. Student, N.Mex. State U., 1968-69; BSBA, Creighton U., 1972. With Bill Deane Goodyear, San Jose, Calif., 1973; operator Penasco River Ranch, Roswell, 1973—. V.p. First Roswell Co.; mem. N.Mex. Senate, 1978— , mem. conservation com., edn. com., legis. fin. com., legis. coun., majority whip. Mem. Chaves County Bd. Commrs., 1974-78; mem. N.Mex. Standards and Goals Com. for Juvenile Justice, 1974-76. Mem. Elks. Democrat. Roman Catholic. Address: PO Box 1797 Rm 120 Roswell NM 88202-1797 Office: N Mex Senate State Capitol Rm 120 Santa Fe NM 87503-0001

JENSEN, ARTHUR ROBERT, psychology educator; b. San Diego, Aug. 24, 1923; s. Arthur Alfred and Linda (Schachtmayer) J.; m. Barbara Jane DeLarme, May 6, 1960; 1 child, Roberta Ann. BA, U. Calif., Berkeley, 1945; PhD, Columbia U., 1956. Asst. med. psychology U. Md., 1955-56; research fellowInst. Psychiatry U. London, 1956-58; prof. ednl. psychology U. Calif., Berkeley, 1958-94; prof. emeritus, 1994—. Author: Genetics and Education, 1972, Educability and Group Differences, 1973, Educational Differences, 1973, Bias in Mental Testing, 1979, Straight Talk about Mental Tests, 1981, The g Factor, 1998; contbr. to profl. jours., books. Guggenheim fellow, 1964-65, fellow Ctr. Advanced Study Behavioral Scis., 1966-67 Fellow AAAS, Am. Psychol. Assn., The Glaton Inst., Am. Psychol. Soc.; mem. Psychonomic Soc., Am. Soc. Human Genetics, Soc. for Social Biology, Behavior Genetics Assn., Psychometric Soc., Sigma Xi. Office: U Calif Sch Edn Berkeley CA 94720-0001

JENSEN, D. LOWELL, federal judge, lawyer, government official; b. Brigham, Utah, June 3, 1928; s. Wendell and Elnora (Hatch) J.; m. Barbara Cowin, Apr. 20, 1951; children: Peter, Marcia, Thomas. A.B. in Econs, U. Calif.-Berkeley, 1949, LL.B., 1952. Bar: Calif. 1952. Dep. dist. atty., Alameda County, 1955-66; asst. dist. atty. Alameda County, 1966-69; dist. atty. Alameda County, 1969-81; asst. atty. gen. criminal div. Dept. Justice, Washington, 1981-83, assoc. atty. gen., 1983-85, dep. atty. gen., 1985-86; judge U.S. Dist. Ct. (no. dist.) Calif., Oakland, 1986—. Mem. Calif. Council on Criminal Justice, 1974-81; past pres. Calif. Dist. Atty.'s Assn. Served with U.S. Army, 1952-54. Fellow Am. Coll. Trial Lawyers; mem. Nat. Dist. Atty.'s Assn. (victim/witness commn. 1974-81), Boalt Hall Alumni Assn. (past pres.) Office: US Dist Ct 1301 Clay St Rm 490C Oakland CA 94612-5217

JENSEN, EDMUND PAUL, retired bank holding company executive; b. Oakland, Calif., Apr. 13, 1937; s. Edmund and Olive E. (Kessell) J.; m. Marilyn Norris, Nov. 14, 1959; children: Juliana L., Annika M. BA, U. Wash., 1959; postgrad., U. Santa Clara, Stanford U., 1981. Lic. real estate broker, Oreg., Calif. Mgr. fin. plan and evaluation Technicolor, Inc., Los Angeles, 1967-69; group v.p. Nat. Industries & Subs, Louisville, 1969-72; v.p. fin. Wedgewood Homes, Portland, 1972-74; various mgmt. positions U.S. Bancorp, Portland, 1974-83; pres., COO U.S. Bancorp, Inc., Portland, 1983-93; vice chmn., COO U.S. Bancorp, Inc., Portland, 1993-94; pres., CEO Visa Internat., 1994-99; ret., 1999. Bd. dirs. U.S. Nat. Bank of Oreg., U.S. Bank Washington. Chmn. United Way, 1986, N.W. Bus. Coalition, 1987; bd. dirs. Saturday Acad., Portland, 1984—, Visa U.S.A., Visa Internat., Marylhurst Coll., Oreg. Bus. Coun., Oreg. Downtown Devel. Assn., Oreg. Ind. Coll. Found., 1983—, treas., 1986—, chmn., 1988—; bd. dirs. Portland Art Mus., 1983—, vice chmn., 1989—. Mem. Portland C. of C. (bd. dirs. 1981—, chmn. 1987), Assn. Res. City Bankers, Assn. for Portland Progress (pres. 1988), Waverly Country Club, Multnomah Athletic Club, Arlington Club, Olympis Club.

JENSEN, HANNE MARGRETE, pathology educator; b. Copenhagen, Dec. 9, 1935; came to U.S., 1957; d. Niels Peter Evald and Else Signe Agnete (Rasmussen) Damgaard; m. July 21, 1957 (div. Apr. 1987); children: Peter Albert, Dorte Marie, Gordon Kristian, Sabrina Elisabeth. Student, U. Copenhagen, 1954-57; MD, U. Wash., 1961. Resident and fellow in pathology U. Wash., Seattle, 1963-68; asst. prof. dept. pathology U. Calif. Sch. Medicine, Davis, 1969-79, assoc. prof., 1979—, dir. transfusion svc., 1973—. McFarlane prof. exptl. medicine U. Glasgow, Scotland, 1983. Mem. No. Calif. Soc. for Electron Microscopy, U.S. and Can. Acad. of Pathology, Am. Cancer Soc., Am. SOc. Clin. Pathologists, Am. Assn. for Advancement of Sci., Am. Assn. of Blood Banks, Calif. Blood Bank System, People to People Internat., Internat. Platform Assn; fellow Pacific Coast Obstetrician and Gynecol. Soc., Coll. of Am. Pathologists. Office: U Calif Sch Medicine Dept Pathology Davis CA 95616

JENSEN, JACK MICHAEL, publishing executive; b. Salt Lake City, June 5, 1951; s. W. Donald and Catherine Ann (Hearley) J.; m. Cathleen Ann O'Brien, Sept. 15, 1985; children: Grace Ann, Ned Michael. BA, Ft. Wright Coll. of the Holy Names, 1974. Bookseller Dayton Hudson, 1972-76; salesman Chronicle Books, San Francisco, 1976-82, mktg. dir., 1983-86, gen. mgr., 1987-89, pub., 1989—, pres., 1996—. Mem. faculty Stanford Pub. Course, 1988-89.

JENSEN, RICHARD DENNIS, librarian; b. Payson, Utah, Oct. 20, 1944; s. Ruel Whiting and Ethel Josepha (Otte) J.; m. Maxine Swasey, Apr. 21, 1966; children: Shaun, Craig, Todd, Jana, Brad, Kristine, April, Lynne. BS in Zoology, Brigham Young U., 1971, MLS, 1976. Asst. sci. libr. Brigham Young U., Provo, Utah, 1971-76, life sci. libr., 1976-84, dept. chair sci. and tech. libr., 1985—. Co-author: Agricultural and Animal Sciences Journals and Serials: An Analytical Guide, 1986, (indexes) Great Basin Naturalist, 50 Year Index, 1991, BYU Geology Studies, Cumulative Index, vol. 1-37, 1954-1991, 1992. Mormon. Avocations: farming, sports, camping. Office: Brigham Young U Libr Sci & Maps Dept 2324 HBLL Provo UT 84602-2734 E-mail: Richard_Jensen@byu.edu

JENSEN, ROBERT TRYGVE, retired lawyer; b. Chgo., Sept. 16, 1922; s. James T. and Else (Uhlich) J.; m. Marjorie Rae Montgomery, Oct. 3, 1959 (div. June 1973); children: Robert Trygve, James Thomas, John Michael; m. Barbara Mae Wilson, Aug. 5, 1974. Student, U. N.C., 1943; LL.B., J.D., B.S., Northwestern U., 1949; LL.M., U. So. Calif., 1955. Bar: Calif. 1950. Asst. counsel Douglas Aircraft Co., Inc., 1950-52, 58-60, counsel El Segundo div., 1952-58; gen. counsel Aerospace Corp., El Segundo, 1960-84, asst. sec., 1961-67, sec., 1967-85. Founding mem. World Assn. Lawyers of World Peace Through Law Center. Served with AUS, 1942-46, PTO. Mem. Alpha Delta Phi, Phi Delta Phi. Fax: (310) 475-0445. E-mail: rtjsr@aol.com

JENSEN, RODNEY H. hotel executive; V.p. Nat. 9 Inns, Salt Lake City, 1985—. Office: National 9 Inns 2285 S Main St Ste 9 Salt Lake City UT 84115-2626

JENSON, TIMOTHY N. computer software and services executive; V.p. corp. banking Bank of Am.; v.p. Citicorp N.Am., Inc.; treas., v.p. Merisel Inc., El Segundo, Calif., 1993—. Office: Merisel Inc 200 Continental Blvd El Segundo CA 90245-0948

JERGESON, GREG, state legislator; b. Havre, Mont., Dec. 29, 1950; m. Barb Jergeson; 2 children. BA in Polit. Sci., U. Mont., 1974. Farmer, rancher, 1969-95; fundraiser, grant writer, 1995—; mem. Mont. Senate, Dist. 46, Helena, 1974-80, 86—; asst. minority leader Mont. Senate, 1979-80, majority leader, 1993-94; mem. joint appropriations subcom. on edn./cultural resources; mem. agr., livestock and irrigation com.; mem. hwys. and transp. com., mem. fin. and claims com. Mem. Mont. Bd. Investments, 1981-85; mem. Blaine County Planning Bd., 1983—; Blaine County Dem. State Committeeman, 1972-74; chair Mont. delegation Dem. Nat. Conv., 1984. Mem. Mont. Farmers Union, North Ctrl. Stockgrowers Assn., Chinook Lions Swim Team, Chinook Men's Bowling League, Eagles. Democrat. Roman Catholic. Home: PO Box 1568 Chinook MT 59523-1568

JERMOLUK, THOMAS A. computer company executive; BS in Computer Sci., MS in Computer Sci., Va. Tech. With Hewlett Packard, Bell Labs.; pres., COO Silicon Graphics, Inc.; chmn., pres., CEO Home Network, Redwood City, Calif. Office: EXCITE AT Home CORP 450 BROADWAY ST Redwood City CA 94063

JERRITTS, STEPHEN G. management consultant; b. New Brunswick, N.J., Sept. 14, 1925; s. Steve and Anna (Kovacs) J.; m. Audrey Virginia Smith, June 1948; children: Marsha Carol, Robert Stephen, Linda Ann; m. 2d, Ewa Elizabet Rydell-Vejlens, Nov. 5, 1966; 1 son, Carl Stephen. Student, Union Coll., 1943-44; B.M.E., Rensselaer Poly. Inst., 1947, M.S. Mgmt., 1948. With IBM, various locations, 1949-58, IBM World Trade, N.Y.C., 1958-67, Bull Gen. Electric divsn. Gen. Electric, France, 1967-70, merged into Honeywell Bull, 1970-74; v.p., mng. dir. Honeywell Info. Systems Ltd., London, 1974-76; group v.p. Honeywell U.S. Info. Systems, Boston, 1977-80; pres., COO Honeywell Info. Systems, 1980-82; pres., CEO Lee Data Corp., 1983-85; with Storage Tech. Corp., 1985-88, pres., COO, 1985-87, vice-chmn., 1988; pres., CEO NBI Corp., 1988-92; cons., advisor Price Waterhouse and Wang Labs Creditors Comm., 1992-93; corp. sr. v.p., pres. Latin Am., bd. dirs. Wang Labs. Inc., 1994-98; corp. sr. v.p., pres. Latin Am. Price Waterhouse and Wang Labs Creditors Comm., 1994-98; bd. dirs. Pub Netics, 1995-99. Interim CEO Zapotec Inc., 1999. Bd. dirs. Guthrie Theatre, 1980-83, Charles Babbage Inst., 1980-92, Minn. Orch., 1980-85; trustee Rensselaer Poly. Inst., 1980-85, mem. adv. bd. Lally Sch. Mgmt., 1994—, Rensselaer Poly. Inst. With USN, 1943-46, lt. USNR, 1946-57. Mem. Computer Bus. Equipment Mfrs. (dir. exec. com. 1979-82), Assoc. Industries Mass. (dir. 1978-80). Home and Office: 650 College Ave Boulder CO 80302-7136 Fax: 303-541-0646

JERRYTONE, SAMUEL JOSEPH, trade school executive; b. Pittston, Pa., Mar. 21, 1947; s. Sebastian and Susan Teresa (Chiampi) J.; children: Sandra, Cheryl, Samuel, Sebastian. Assoc. in Bus., Scranton (Pa.) Lackawanna Jr. Coll., 1966. Mgr. House of Jerrytone Beauty Salon, West Pittston, Pa., 1967-68; regional sales dir. United Republic Life Ins., Harrisburg, 1970-76; night instr. Wilkes-Barre (Pa.) Vo-Tech High Sch., 1976-78; spl. sales agt. Franklin Life Ins. Co., Wilkes-Barre, 1978-80; instr. Jerrytone Beauty Sch., Pittston, Pa., 1968-69, supr., 1969-95; fin. broker Exec. Bus. Mgmt. and Property Svcs., 2001—. Prof. sch. evaluator Nat. Accrediting Com. Arts and Scis., 1974-95; mem. adv. craft com. Wilkes-Barre Vo-Tech H.S., 1988—. Mem. com. Rep. Presdl. Task Force, Washington, 1984, mem. parish coun. Guardian Angel Cathedral, Las Vegas, 1997. Mem. Pa. Hairdressers Assn., Nat. Accrediting Com. Cosmetology, Am. Coun. Cosmetology Educators, Masons (3d degree award 1983, 32d degree award Lodge Coun. chpt. consistory 1984), Shriners (Irem temple). Roman Catholic. Avocations: reading, golf, bowling, music, video filming. E-mail: s.jerrytone@att.net

JERVIS, JANE LISE, college official, science historian; b. Newark, June 14, 1938; d. Ernest Robert and Helen Jenny (Roland) J.; m. Kenneth Albert Pruett, June 20, 1959 (div. 1974); children: Holly Jane Pruett, Cynthia Lorraine Pruett; m. Norman Joseph Chonacky, Dec. 26, 1981; children: Philip Joseph Chonacky, Joseph Norman Chonacky. AB, Radcliffe Coll., 1959; MA, Yale U., 1974, MPhil, 1975, PhD in History of Sci., 1978. Freelance sci. editor and writer, 1962-72; lectr. in history Rensselaer Poly. Inst., 1977-78; dean Davenport Coll., lectr. in history of sci. Yale U., 1978-82; dean students., assoc. prof. history Hamilton Coll., 1982-87; dean coll., lectr. in history Bowdoin Coll., 1988-92; pres. Evergreen State Coll., Olympia, Wash., 1992-2000. Author: Cometary Theory in 15th Century

Europe; contbr. articles to profl. jours.; book reviewer; presenter in field. Trustee Maine Hist. Assn., 1991-92, Stonehill Coll., 1996—, Providence St. Peter's Hosp., 1997-2000; chair Maine selection com. Rhodes Scholarship Trust, 1990-92, chair N.W. selection com., 1992-93; commr. N.W. Assn. Schs. and Colls. Commn. on Colls., 1994-99. E-mail: jervisj@earthlink.net

JESSOR, RICHARD, psychologist, educator; b. Bklyn., Nov. 24, 1924; s. Thomas and Clara (Merkin) J.; m. Shirley Glasser, Sept. 27, 1948 (div. 1982); children: Kim, Tom; m. Jane Ava Menken, Nov. 13, 1992. Student, CCNY, 1941-43; BA, Yale U., 1946; MA, Columbia U., 1947; PhD, Ohio State U., 1951. Intern, clin. psychology trainee VA/Ohio State U., Columbus, 1947-50; asst. prof. psychology U. Colo., Boulder, 1951-56, assoc. prof., 1956-61, prof., 1961—, dir. rsch. program problem behavior Inst. Behavioral Sci., 1966-97, dir. Inst. Behavioral Sci., 1980—. Dir. MacArthur Found. Rsch. Network on Successful Adolescent Devel. Among Youth in High Risk Settings, 1987-96; cons. Nat. Inst. on Drug Abuse, 1975-76, Nat. Inst. on Alcohol Abuse and Alcoholism, 1976-80, WHO, Geneva, 1976-80; cons. in field. Author: (with T.D. Graves, R.C. Hanson & S.L. Jessor) Society, Personality, and Deviant Behavior: A Study of a Tri-Ethnic Community, 1968, (with S.L. Jessor) Problem Behavior and Psychosocial Development: A Longitudinal Study of Youth, 1977, (with J.E. Donovan and F. Costa) Beyond Adolescence: Problem Behavior and Young Adult Development, 1991; co-editor: Contemporary Approaches to Cognition, 1957, Cognition, Personality and Clinical Psychology, 1967, Perspectives on Behavioral Science: the Colorado Lectures, 1991, Ethnography and Human Development: Context and Meaning in Social Inquiry, 1996; editor: New Perspectives on Adolescent Risk Behavior, 1998; cons. editor Jour. Cons. and Clin. Psychology, 1975-77, Cmty. Mental Health Jour., 1974-78, Alcohol Health and Rsch. World, 1981-90, Alcohol, Drugs and Driving, 1985-92, Adolescent Medicine: State of the Art Revs., 1989—; mem. editl. bd. Prevention Sci., 1999—; cons. editor Sociometry, 1964-66, assoc. editor, 1966-69; contbr. articles to profl. jours. Served with USMC, 1943-46, PTO. Decorated Purple Heart; Social Sci. Rsch. Coun. pre-doctoral fellow Ohio State and Yale U., 1950-51; Social Sci. Rsch. Coun. fellow Ohio State U., 1954, Social Sci. Rsch. Coun. postdoctoral fellow U. Calif.-Berkeley, 1956-57, NIMH spl. rsch. fellow Harvard-Florence Rsch. Project, Italy, 1965-66, Ctr. for Advanced Study in the Behavioral Scis. fellow Stanford U., 1995-96; recipient Faculty Rsch. Lectureship award U. Colo., 1981-82; Gallagher lectr. Soc. Adolescent Medicine, 1987. Fellow APA, Am. Psychol. Soc. (charter fellow); mem. Soc. for Psychol. Study of Social Issues, Soc. for Study of Social Problems. Avocations: mountain climbing, running marathons. Home: 1303 Marshall St Boulder CO 80302-5803 Office: U Colo Inst Behavioral Sci Cb 483 Boulder CO 80309-0001 E-mail: jessor@colorado.edu

JETT, JAMES, professional football player; b. Charleston, W.Va., Dec. 28, 1970; Student, W.Va. U. Wide receiver Oakland (Calif.) Raiders, 1993—. Office: Oakland Raiders 1220 Harbor Bay Pkwy Alameda CA 94502-6570

JETT, STEPHEN CLINTON, geography and textiles educator, researcher; b. Cleve., Oct. 12, 1938; s. Richard Scudder Jett and Miriam Ida (Horn) Greene; m. Mary Frances Manak, Aug. 7, 1971 (div. 1977); 1 child, Jennifer Frances; m. Lisa Sue Roberts, June 17, 1995. AB, Princeton U., 1960; postgrad., U. Ariz., 1962-63; PhD, Johns Hopkins U., 1964. Instr. geography Ohio State U., Columbus, 1963-64; asst. prof. geography U. Calif., Davis, 1964-72, assoc. prof., 1972-79, prof., 1979-1996, prof. textiles, 1996-2000, prof. geography and textile clothing, 2000—, chmn., 1978-82, 87-89. Author: Navajo Wildlands, 1967 (1 of 50 Books of Yr., Am. Inst. Graphic Arts 1967, 1 of 20 Merit Award Books, Western Book Pubs. Assn. 1969), House of Three Turkeys, 1977, Navajo Architecture, 1981 (1 of Outstanding Acad. Books, Choice mag. ALA 1981), Navajo Placenames and Trails of the Canyon de Chelly System, Arizona, 2001; (monograph) Tourism in the Navajo Country, 1966; editor jour. Pre-Columbiana; contbr. numerous articles to profl. jours. and chpts. to books. Mem. Hist. and Landmarks Commn., Davis, 1969-73; vice chmn. Gen. Plan Noise Element Study Com., Davis, 1974-76, chmn. ad hoc citizens noise com., 1997-98; mem. exec. coun. Univ. Farms Unit Number 1 Neighborhood Assn., Davis, 1987-90. Fellow Am. Geog. Soc., Explorers Club; mem. AAAS, Assn. Am. Geographers (chair Am. Indian splty. group 1989-91), Soc. Am. Archaeology, Epigraphic Soc. (bd. dirs. 1996—), Inst. for Study of Am. Cultures (bd. dirs. 1996—). Avocations: travel, photography, textiles and other ethnographic arts, French language and culture. Office: U Calif Davis Divsn Textiles Clothing 1 Shields Ave Davis CA 95616-5270 E-mail: ljett@dcn.davis.ca.us

JEUB, MICHAEL LEONARD, financial consultant; b. Mpls., Mar. 2, 1943; s. Leonard M. and Florence J.; m. Alice Ann Linden (div. 1980); children: Christopher Michael, Annette Michelle; m. Julia Jean Stephenson, Feb. 4, 1983; children: Michael Leonard Jr., Robert. BS in Acctg., Calif. State Poly. U., 1966. CPA, Tex., Calif. Staff acct. Ernst & Whinney, L.A., 1966-70; CFO Internat. Clin. Lab., Inc., Nashville, 1970-85, pres. east, 1985-88; pres. August Enterprises, 1988-91; pres., COO, CFO MICA, San Diego, 1991-93; exec. v.p., CFO, treas. Nat. Health Labs., Inc., 1993-94; sr. v.p., CFO Jenny Craig Internat., 1994-2000; fin. cons. La Jolla, Calif., 2000—. Fin. executive; b. Mpls., Mar. 2, 1943; s. Leonard M. and Florence J.; m. Alice Ann Linden (div. 1980); children: Christopher Michael, Annette Michelle; m. Julia Jean Stephenson, Feb. 4, 1983; children: Michael Leonard Jr., Robert. BS in Acctg. Calif. State Poly. U., 1966. CPA, Tex., Calif. Staff acct. Ernst & Whinney, L.A., 1966-70; CFO Internat. Clin. Lab., Inc., Nashville, 1970-85, pres. east, 1985-88; pres. August Enterprises, 1988-91; pres., COO, CFO MICA, San Diego, 1991-93; exec. v.p., CFO, treas. Nat. Health Labs., Inc., 1993-94. Office: 11355 N Torrey Pines Rd La Jolla CA 92037-1013 E-mail: MikeJeub@aol.com

JEWELL, WILLIAM SYLVESTER, engineering educator; b. Detroit, July 2, 1932; s. Loyd Vernon and Marion (Sylvester) J.; m. Elizabeth Gordon Wilson, July 7, 1956; children— Sarah, Thomas, Miriam, William Timothy. B of Engring. Physics, Cornell U., 1954; MSEE, MIT, 1955, DSc, 1958. Assoc. dir. mgmt. scis. div. Broadview Research Corp., Burlingame, Calif., 1958-60; asst. prof. dept. indsl. engring. and operations research U. Calif.-Berkeley, 1960-63, assoc. prof., 1963-67, prof., 1967—, chmn. dept., 1967-69, 76-80. Dir. O.R. Ctr., U. Calif., 1985-87, Engring. Systems Rsch. Ctr. U. Calif., 1987-88, 91-92; dir. Teknekron Industries, Inc., Incline Village, Nev., 1968-86, Creance Capital, Inc., Oakland, Calif., 1993—; cons. ops. rsch. problems, 1960—; guest prof. Eidgenössiches Technische Hochschule, Zurich, 1980-81. Contbr. articles to profl. jours. Trustee New Coll., Berkeley, 1992-94. Recipient Halmstead prize, 1982; Fulbright research scholar France, 1965; research scholar Internat. Inst. Applied Systems Analysis, Austria, 1974-75 Mem. Informs, Assn. Swiss Actuaries, Internat. Actuarial Assn., Rotary Internat., Triangle, Sigma Xi. Home: 67 Loma Vista Dr Orinda CA 94563-2236 Office: U Calif Dept Indsl Engring Ops Rsch Berkeley CA 94720-0001

JEWETT, GEORGE FREDERICK, JR. forest products company executive; b. Spokane, Wash., Apr. 10, 1927; s. George Frederick and Mary Pelton (Cooper) J.; m. Lucille Winifred McIntyre, July 11, 1953; children: Mary Elizabeth, George Frederick III. BA, Dartmouth Coll., 1950; MBA, Harvard U., 1952. Asst. sec., asst. treas. Potlatch Corp., 1955-62, v.p. adminstrn., 1962-68, corp. v.p. adminstrn., 1968-71, sr. v.p., 1972-77, vice chmn. bd. adminstrn., 1977-78, vice chmn., 1979-99, retired, 1999. Dir. Potlatch Corp., 2000—. Trustee Calif. Pacific Med. Found. Clubs: St. Francis Yacht, N.Y. Yacht, Bohemian, Pacific Union, San Diego Yacht. Home: 2990 Broadway St San Francisco CA 94115-1062 Office: 1 Maritime Plz Ste 1640 San Francisco CA 94111-3506

JIMENEZ, LUIS ALFONSO, JR. sculptor; b. El Paso, Tex., July 30, 1940; s. Luis Alfonso and Alicia (Franco) J.; m. Susan Brockman; children: Elisa Victoria, Luis Adan, Juan Orion, Sarah Alicia Xochil. B.S. in Art and Architecture, U. Tex., Austin, 1964, postgrad., Ciudad U., Mexico City, 1964. Exhibited in one-man shows, including, Graham Gallery, N.Y.C., 1969-70, O.K. Harris Works of Art, N.Y.C., 1972-75, Contemporary Arts Mus., Houston, 1974, Mus. of N.Mex., Santa Fe, 1980, Frumkin Struve, Chgo., 1981, Adeliza's Candy Store Gallery, Folsom, Calif., 1983, Phyllis Kind Gallery, N.Y.C., 1984, Moody Gallery, Houston, 1987, 95, Scottsdale Cultural Arts Ctr., Nat. Mus. Am. Art, Washington, 1994, Marsha Mateyka Gallery, Washington, 1994, Adair Margo Gallery, El Paso, Tex., 1995, A.C.A. Galleries, N.Y.C., 1998, Working Class Heroes: Images from the Popular Culture, traveling retrospective, opened Dallas, Dallas Mus. Art 1997, Palm Springs Mus. Art, 1998, Blaffier Mus., Tex., Mex. Fine Arts Ctr. Mus., 2000, 2 Albuquerque Mus. Art; exhibited in group shows, including, Human Concern Personal Torment, Whitney Mus., N.Y., 1969, Nat. Mus. Am. Art, Washington, 1980, Albuquerque Mus., 1980, Edinburgh (Scotland) Festival, 1980, Walker Art Center, Mpls., 1980, U. Minn., Mpls., 1981, Roswell Mus. and Art Ctr., N. Mex., 1984, Albright-Knox Art Mus., Buffalo, N.Y., Hirshhorn Mus. and Sculpture Garden, Smithsonian Instn., Washington, Hispanic Art in the U.S., 1988, Hispanic Arts in the U.S. traveling show, 1987-89, Latin Am. Spirit in the U.S., 1989, Committed To Print, Mus. Modern Art, N.Y.C., 1989, Whitney Biennial, N.Y.C., 1991, New Mus., N.Y.C., Art of the Other Mex. traveling exhibit, 1993, 20 Yrs. of Landfall Prints, Whitney Mus., 1997, Arte Latino, traveling Smithsonian Inst. exhibit, 2000—; represented in permanent collections, Nat. Mus. Am. Art, Anderson Mus. Contemporary Art, Roswell N.M., Witte Mus., San Antonio, Long Beach (Calif.) Mus., New Orleans Mus. Art, Roswell (N. Mex.) Mus. and Art Center, Sheldon Meml. Gallery, Lincoln, Nebr., Art Inst. Chgo., Met. Mus. Art, N.Y.C., Smithsonian Instn., Mus. Modern Art, Albuquerque Mus. Art, Fed. Reserve Bank, Dallas, Fine Arts Mus., Santa Fe, U. Texas, San Antonio, U. New Mex., Albuquerque, others, also pvt. collections; works include Vaquero Sculpture, Moody Park, Houston, 1977; Nat. Endowment for Arts and City Housing Authority commn. Sodbuster sculpture, Fargo, N.D., 1977; Southwest Pietà, Nat. Endowment for Arts commn. Art in Pub. Places, City of Albuquerque, 1981; Steel Worker, Nat. Endowment for Arts, La Salle Sta., Buffalo, N.Y.; Niagara Frontier, Transp. Authority Commn., VA Hosp., 1982; Flag Raising, Oklahoma City Sculpture Commn.; Howl, Wichita State U., Kans., 1983; Border Crossing, Otis Art Inst. of Parsons Sch. Design, Los Angeles, 1984; Fiesta Dancers, Gen. Services Adminstrn., Otay Mesa, Calif., 1986; sculpture commn. NEA and City of El Paso, 1986, Plaza de los Lagartos, Omni Hotel, San Diego, 1986, City of Las Vegas, 1989, New Denver Airport, 1991, City of N.Y. Cultural Affairs, Hunt's Point Market, Bronx, N.Y., Firefighter, Cleve., 1996, sculpture commn. U. OK, Norman, OK, 1998. Recipient Steuben Glass award 1972, Hassam Fund award Am. Acad. Arts and Letters, 1977, Awards in Visual Arts, 1985, Greenburger Found. award, 1987, Showhegan sculpture award, 1989, Gov.'s award State of N.Mex., 1993, Award of Distinction Nat. Coun. of Art Adminstrs., 1995; named goodwill amb. City of Houston, 1993, 98, Tex. Artist of Yr., Houston Art League, 1998, Distinguished Alumni, Univ. Tex. and Austin; fellow Nat. Endowment Arts, 1987, 88, Am. Acad. in Rome, 1979, La Napoule Art Found. and Nat. Endowment Arts residency fellow, 1990; sculpture designated U.S. Nat. Treasure, 1999; grantee Fund for Am. Culture, 1999.

JIRAUCH, CHARLES W. lawyer; b. St. Louis, Apr. 27, 1944; s. Mary K. (Horan) J.; m. Sally J. Costello, June 1, 1968 (div. Mar. 1977); m. Dana K. Bowen; children: Melissa, Mathew, Kathleen. BSEE, Washington U., 1966; JD, Georgetown U., 1970. Bar: Ill. 1971, Ariz. 1975, Nev. 1991, , Calif. 1993, Colo. 1993, U.S. Patent Office 1970, U.S. Supreme Ct. 1978. Atty. Leydig, Voit & Mayer, Chgo., 1970-71, McDermott, Will & Emery, Chgo., 1971-75, Streich Lang, Phoenix, 1975-2000, Quarles & Brady Streich Lang, Phoenix, 2000—. Bd. dirs. Valley Big Bros./Big Sisters, 1980-86, pres. bd. dirs., 1985-86, pres.; bd. dirs. Valley Big Bros./Big Sisters Found., 1988-92; bd. advisors to dean Ariz. State U. Sch. Engring., 1998—. Mem. ABA, Ariz. Bar Found., Maricopa County Bar Found., Am. Judicature Soc., Am. Intellectual Property Law Assn., Ariz. Dem. Coun., Ariz. Civil Liberties Union, Ariz. Software and Internet Assn. (bd. dirs. 2000—), Am. Electronic Assn. (exec. com. Ariz. chpt. 1999—). Democrat. Roman Catholic. Office: Quarles & Brady Streich Lang 2 N Central Ave Fl 2 Phoenix AZ 85004-2345 E-mail: cjirauch@quarles.com

JOB, RAE LYNN, state legislator; b. Rock Springs, Wyo., May 2, 1948; BA, MS in Speech Lang. Pathology, U. Wyo. Dir. special project academic facilitor Sweetwater Sch. Dist #1; mem. Wyo. Senate, Dist. 12, Cheyenne, 1996—; mem. edn. com. Wyo. Senate, Cheyenne, mem. corp., elections and polit. com., mem. transp. and hwys. com. Mem. Western Interstate Compact on Higher Edn., Am. Cancer Soc. Mem. Wyo. Edn. Assn., Sweetwater Edn. Assn., Phi Delta Kappa. Democrat. Office: 1344 Moran St Rock Springs WY 82901-7319 also: Wyo Senate State Capitol Cheyenne WY 82002-0001 E-mail: rjob@senate.wyoming.com

JOBS, STEVEN PAUL, computer corporation executive; b. Feb. 24, 1955; adopted s. Paul J. and Clara J. (Jobs); m. Laurene Powell, Mar. 18, 1991. Student, Reed Coll. With Hewlett-Packard, Palo Alto, Calif.; designer video games Atari Inc., 1974; co-founder Apple Computer Inc., Cupertino, Calif., chmn. bd., 1975-85, former dir.; pres. NeXT, Inc., Redwood City, 1985-96; chief exec. officer NeXT, Inc. (bought by Apple, 1996), Redwood City; interim CEO Apple Computer, Cupertino, Calif., 1997—, now CEO, chmn. Chmn., chief exec. officer Pixar Animation Studios, 1986-. Co-designer: (with Stephan Wozniak) Apple I Computer, 1976. Recipient Nat. Medal Tech. presented by Pres. Ronald Reagan, Entrepreneur of the Decade award, Inc. Mag., Jefferson award for Pub. Svc. Office: Pixar Animation Studios 1001 W Cutting Blvd Richmond CA 94804-2028

JOCHIM, MICHAEL ALLAN, archaeologist; b. St. Louis, May 31, 1945; s. Kenneth Erwin and Jean MacKenzie (Keith) J.; m. Amy Martha Waugh, Aug. 12, 1967; children: Michael Waugh, Katherine Elizabeth. BS, U. Mich., 1967, MA, 1971, PhD, 1975. Lectr. anthropology U. Calif., Santa Barbara, 1975-77, asst. prof., 1979-81, assoc. prof., 1981-87, prof., 1987—, dept. chmn., 1987-92; asst. prof. Queens Coll. CUNY, Flushing, 1977-79. Mem. archaeology rev. panel NSF, Washington, 1988-90. Author: Hunter-Gatherer Subsistence and Settlement, 1976, Strategies for Survival, 1981, A Hunter-Gatherer Landscape, 1998; editor (series) Interdisciplinary Contributions to Archaeology, 1987—. Chmn. Community Adv. Com. for Spl. Edn., Santa Barbara County, 1980-82. Grantee NEH, 1976, NSF, 1980, 81, 83, 89, 91, 94, Nat. Geog. Soc., 1987, 97, Wenner-Gren, 1999. Fellow Am. Anthrop. Assn.; mem. Soc. for Am. Archaeology, Sigma Xi. Office: U Calif Dept Anthropology Santa Barbara CA 93106 E-mail: jochim@sscf.ucsb.edu

JOFFE, BARBARA LYNNE, computer management professional, computer artist; b. Bklyn., Apr. 12, 1951; d. Lester L. and Julia (Schuelke) J.; 1 child, Nichole. BA, U. Oreg., 1975; MFA, U. Mont., 1982. Cert. project mgr. IBM; cert. project mgmt. profl. Project Mgmt. Inst. Applications engr., software developer So. Pacific Transp., San Francisco, 1986-93; computer fine artist Barbara Joffe Assocs., San Francisco, Englewood, Colo., 1988—; instr. computer graphics Ohlone Coll., Fremont, Calif., 1990-91; adv. programmer, proj. mgr.-client/server Integrated Sys. Solutions Corp./IBM Global Svcs. So. Pacific/Union Pacific Railroads, Denver, 1994-97; applications sys. mgr. IBM Global Svcs./CoBank, Greenwood Village, Colo., 1997-99; exec. project mgr. IBM/GM Web Hosting, 2000—. Artwork included in exhibits at Calif. Crafts XIII, Crocker Art Mus., Sacramento, 1983, Rara Avis Gallery, Sacramento, 1984, Redding (Calif.) Mus. and Art Ctr., 1985, Euphrat Gallery, Cupertino, Calif., 1988, Computer Mus., Boston, 1989, Siggraph Traveling Art Shown, Europe and Australia, 1990, 91, 4th and 7th Nat. Computer Art Invitational, Cheney, Wash., 1991, 94, Visual Arts Mus., N.Y.C., 1994, 96, IBM Golden Circle, 1996. Recipient IBM Project Mgmt. Excellence award, 1998. Mem. Assn. Computing Machinery, Project Mgmt. Inst. (cert.). Avocations: art, gardening, hiking.

JOHANNESSEN, MAURICE, state senator; b. Oslo, Norway; came to U.S., 1952; m. Marianne Johannessen; 4 children. In real estate profession; established own real estate firm, Redding, Calif.; mem. Calif. State Senate, 1993—, chmn. vets. affairs com., vice chair bus./professions com., mem. fin., investment and internat. trade com., mem. agr. and water resources com., mem. natural resources and wildlife com. Mem. Redding City Coun., mayor of Redding, 1988-89; mem. Shasta County Bd. Suprs., 1990, chmn., 1992; res. dep. sheriff. Republican. Office: State Capitol Rm 5061 Sacramento CA 95814 also: 410 Hemsted Dr Ste 200 Redding CA 96002-0164

JOHANSEN, JUDITH A. lawyer; b. Colo. Springs, Colo., June 17, 1958; d. John Carlo and Joan Elizabeth (Bischof) B.; m. Kirk Johansen, May 16, 1992. BA in Polit. Sci., Colo. State U., 1980; JD, Lewis & Clark Law Sch., 1983. Bar: Oreg. 1983, Washington 1986, U.S. Dist. Ct. Oreg. 1989, U.S. Ct. Appeals (9th cir. 1983). Staff counsel Pub. Power Coun., Portland, Oreg., 1983-86; assoc. Gordon, Thames, Honeywell, Tacoma, 1986-89, ptnr. Seattle, 1989-91; sr. policy advisor U.S. Dept. Energy, Bonneville Power Admin., Portland, Oreg., 1992-93, dir. fish and wildlife, 1993-94, v.p. generation supply, 1994-96; v.p. bus. devel. Avista Energy, WA Water Power, 1996-98; adminstr. and CEO Bonneville Power Adminstr., Dept. of Energy, Portland, OR, 1998—. Mem. editorial bd. Nat. Resource & Environ. Mag., 1992—. Contbr. articles to profl. jours. Mem. ABA, (vice chair 1989-91, chair 1992—). Democrat. Avocations: skiing, gardening, cooking, traveling, fishing. Office: Bonneville Power Adminstrn Dept Energy PO Box 3621 Portland OR 97208-3621

JOHANSON, DONALD CARL, physical anthropologist; b. Chgo., June 28, 1943; s. Carl Torsten and Sally Eugenia (Johnson) J. ; m. Lenora Carey, 1988; 1 child, Tesfaye Meles. BA, U. Ill., 1966; MA, U. Chgo., 1970, PhD, 1974; DSc (hon.), John Carroll U., 1979; D.Sc. (hon.), Coll. of Wooster, 1985. Mem. dept. phys. anthropology Cleve. Mus. Natural History, 1972-81, curator, 1974-81; pres. Inst. Human Origins, Berkeley, Calif., 1981-97, dir. Tempe, Ariz., 1997—. Prof. anthropology Stanford U., 1983-89, Ariz. State U., 1997, Virginia M. Ullman chair human origins, 2000; adj. prof. Case Western Res. U., 1978-81, Kent State U., 1978-81. Co-author: (with M.A. Edey) Lucy: The Beginnings of Humankind, 1981 (Am. Book award 1982), Blueprints: Solving the Mystery of Evolution, 1989, (with James Shreeve) Lucy's Child: Discovering a Human Ancestor, 1989, (with Kevin O'Farrell) Journey from the Dawn: Life with the World's First Family, 1990, (with Lenora Johanson and Blake Edgar) Ancestors: In Search of Human Origins, 1994, (with Blake Edgar) From Lucy to Language, 1997, (with Giancarlo Ligabue) Ecce Homo, 1999; host PBS Natures Series; prodr. (film) Lucy in Disguise, 1982; host, narrator NOVA series In Search of Human Origins, 1994 (Emmy nomination 1995); contbr. numerous articles to profl. jours. Recipient Jared Potter Kirtland award for outstanding sci. achievement Cleve. Mus. Natural History, 1979, Profl. Achievement award U. Chgo., 1980, Gold Mercury Internat. ad personem award Ethiopia, 1982, Humanist Laureate award Acad. of Humanism, 1983, Disting. Svc. award Am. Humanist Assn., 1983, San Francisco Exploratorium award, 1986, Internat. Premio Fregene award, 1987, Alumni Achievement award U. Ill., 1995, Anthropology Media award Am. Anthropol. Assn., 1999; named Endowed Chair Virginia Ullman Chair in Human Origins; grantee Wenner-Gren Found., NSF, Nat. Geog. Soc., L.S.B. Leakey Found., Cleve. Found., George Gund Found., Roush Found. Fellow AAAS, Calif. Acad. Scis., Rochester (N.Y.) Mus., Royal Geog. Soc.; mem. Am. Assn. Phys. Anthropologists, Internat. Assn. Dental Research, Internat. Assn. Human Biologists, Am. Assn. Africanist Archaeologists, Soc. Vertebrate Paleontology, Soc. Study of Human Biology, Societe de l'Anthropologie de Paris, Centro Studi Ricerche Ligabue (Venice), Founders' Coun., Chgo. Field Mus. Natural History (hon.), Assn. Internationale pour l'etude de Paleontologie Humaine, Mus. Nat. d'Histoire Naturelle de Paris (corr.), Explorers Club (hon. dir.), Nat. Ctr. Sci. Edn. (supporting scientist). Office: Inst Human Origins Ariz State U PO Box 874101 Tempe AZ 85287-4101

JOHN ROBERT, BRUCE, healthcare company executive; Student, Tex. Christian U. Sales, mktg. dir., v.p. sales Blue Cross Blue Shield, 1971-88; v.p. sales Occupl. Urgent Care Health Sys., Inc., Sacramento, 1988-89; sr. sales exec. Blue Shield of Calif., San Francisco, 1989-90; dir. group plans Found. Health Plans, Sacramento, 1990-91; dir. sales & mktg. PCA Health Plan, Sacramento, 1991-92; exec. dir. Health Net Sacramento, 1992-94, Qualmed Plans for Health Colo., Inc., Pueblo, 1994-96; pres. Qualmed Plans for Health, Inc., Phila., 1996-98; pres. ctrl. divsn. Found. Health Sys., Inc., Woodland Hills, Calif., 1998—. Served in U.S. Army, Vietnam. Office: FHS Inc 21600 Oxnard St Woodland Hills CA 91367-4976

JOHNS, MICHAEL A. prosecutor; 1st asst. U.S. atty. State of Ariz., Phoenix. Office: US Courthouse Fed Bldg 230 N 1st Ave Phoenix AZ 85025-0230

JOHNSEN, EUGENE CARLYLE, mathematician and educator; b. Mpls., Jan. 27, 1932; s. Bernhardt Thorwald and Esther Elvira (Eklund) J.; m. Marjorie Marie Wacklin, Aug. 31, 1957. BChem, U. Minn., 1954; PhD, Ohio State U., 1961. NAS/NRC Rsch. Assoc. Nat. Bur. Stds., Washington, 1962-63; lectr. math. U. Calif., Santa Barbara, 1963-64, asst. prof., 1964-68, assoc. prof., 1968-74, prof., 1974-94, prof. emeritus, 1994—, dir. summer sessions, 1981-94, 94-97. Vis. lectr. in math. U. Mich., Ann Arbor, 1968-69; vis. scholar in sociology Harvard U., Cambridge, Mass., 1984-85; mathematician Sperry Rand, St. Paul, 1956, 57; instr. chem. and math. U. Minn., 1956-57; instr. math. Ohio State U., Columbus, 1962. Contbr. numerous articles to profl. jours.; mem. editl. bd. Jour. Math. Sociology. Mem. Los Angeles County Mus. Art, 1985—, L.A. Music Ctr. Opera League, 1986—; mem. Santa Barbara C. of C./U. Calif. Santa Barbara Bus. Adv. Com., 1979-84. Grantee USAFOSR, NSF, Dept. Edn.; Fulbright fellow U. Tübingen, 1969; fellow NSF, 1959. Mem. AAAS, AAUP, Am. Math. Soc., Math. Assn. Am., Am. Statis. Assn., Soc. Indsl. and Applied Math., Internat. Network for Social Network Analysis, Am. Sociol. Assn. (acting chairperson, then chairperson math. sociology sect. 1995-97), U. Calif. Santa Barbara Faculty Club, Channel City Club, Am.-Scandinavian Found., Sons of Norway (pres. Ivar Aasen Lodge 1999-2001), Phi Beta Kappa, Sigma Xi, Phi Lambda Upsilon, Pi Mu Epsilon, Alpha Chi Sigma. Avocations: music, opera, tennis, travel. Home: 1603 Paterna Rd Santa Barbara CA 93103-1826 Office: U Calif Dept Math Santa Barbara CA 93106

JOHNSEN, KEN C. steel products company executive; b. 1958; BA in Fin., Utah State U.; JD, Yale U. Assoc. Parr Waddoups Brown Gee & Loveless, 1986-91; mgr. spl. projects Geneva Steel Holdings Corp., Vineyard, Utah, 1991, v.p., gen. counsel, 1991-97, sec., 1992—, exec. v.p., gen. counsel, 1997—, also bd. dirs. Mem. AISI (com. mem.). Office: Geneva Steel Holdings Corp 10 S Geneva Rd Vineyard UT 84058 Office Fax: 801-227-9090

JOHNSON, ALAN BOND, federal judge; b. 1939; BA, Vanderbilt U., 1961; JD, U. Wyo., 1964. Pvt. practice law, Cheyenne, Wyo., 1968-71; assoc. Hanes, Carmichael, Johnson, Gage & Speight P.C., Cheyenne, 1971-74; judge Wyo. Dist. Ct., 1974-85, U.S. Dist. Ct. Wyo., 1986-92, chief judge, 1992—. Part-time fed. magistrate U.S. Dist. Ct. Wyo., 1971-74; substitute judge Mcpl. Ct., Cheyenne, 1973-74. Served to capt. USAF, 1964-67, to col. Wyo. Air N.G., 1973-90. Mem. ABA, Wyo. State Bar, Laramie County Bar Assn. (sec.-treas. 1968-70), Wyo. Jud. Conf. (sec. 1977-78, chmn. 1979), Wyo. Jud. Council. Office: US Dist Ct O'Mahoney Fed Ctr 2120 Capitol Ave Ste 2242 Cheyenne WY 82001-3666

JOHNSON, ALEXANDER CHARLES, lawyer, electrical engineer; b. Richmond, Va., Aug. 1, 1948; BSEE, The Citadel, 1970; MSEE, Purdue U., 1974; JD cum laude, Brigham Young U., 1978. Bar: Oreg. 1978, U.S. Patent and Trademark Office 1979, U.S. Ct. Appeals (8th, 9th and Fed. cirs.) 1984. From assoc. to ptnr. Klarquist, Sparkman, Campbell, Leigh & Whinston, Portland, Oreg., 1978-86; prin. Marger, Johnson, & McCollom, P.C., Portland, 1986—. Author: IP Protection in Semiconductor Industry, 1989. Capt. USAF, 1975, USAFR, 1975-83. Mem. ABA (intellectual property sect.), Am. Intellectual Property Law Assn., Oreg. Bar Assn., Order of Barristers, Tau Beta Pi. Office: Marger Johnson & McCollom PC 1030 SW Morrison St Portland OR 97205-2626

JOHNSON, ARTHUR WILLIAM, JR. planetarium executive; b. Steubenville, Ohio, Jan. 8, 1949; s. Arthur William and Carol (Gilcrest) J. BMus, U. So. Calif., 1973. Lectr. Griffith Obs. and Planetarium, 1969-73; planetarium writer, lectr. Mt. San Antonio Coll. Planetarium, Walnut, Calif., 1970-73; dir. Fleischmann Planetarium U. Nev., Reno, 1973-2001. Apptd. Nev. state coord. NSTA/NASA Space Sci. Student Involvement Program, 1994. Writer, prodr. films (with Donald G. Potter) Beautiful Nevada, 1978, Riches: The Story of Nevada Mining, 1984. Organist, choirmaster Trinity Episcopal Ch., Reno, 1980—; bd. dirs. Reno Chamber Orch. Assn., 1981-87, 1st v.p., 1984-85. Nev. Humanities Com., Inc. grantee, 1979-83. Mem. Am. Guild Organists (dean No. Nev. chpt. 1984-85, 96-99), Internat. Planetarium Soc., Cinema 360 (treas. 1985-90, pres. 1990-98), Pacific Planetarium Assn. (pres. 1980), Lions (pres. Reno Host Club 1991-92), Large Format Cinema Assn. (v.p. 1996-99). Republican. Episcopalian. Office: U Nev Fleischmann Planetarium Mail Stop 272 Reno NV 89557-0001

JOHNSON, AUSTON GILBERT, III, auditor; m. Mary Bosworth; 3 children. BS, Utah State U., 1976. CPA, Utah. Auditor State of Utah, Salt Lake City, 1996—. Acctg. adv. bd. U. Utah Sch. Acctg., 1993; sch. accountancy adv. coun. Utah State U., 1994—. With USN, 1969-73. Mem. AICPA (Outstanding Discussion Leader 1993), Utah Assn. CPAs (vice-chmn. state and local govt. com. 1987-88). Office: Office Utah State Auditor 211 State Capitol Building Salt Lake City UT 84114-1202 E-mail: ajohnson@sao.state.ut.us

JOHNSON, BRUCE EDWARD HUMBLE, lawyer; b. Columbus, Ohio, Jan. 22, 1950; s. Hugo Edward and M. Alice (Humble) J.; m. Paige Robinson Miller, June 28, 1980; children: Marta Noble, Winslow Collins, Russell Scott. AB, Harvard U., 1972; JD, Yale U., 1977; MA, U. Cambridge, Eng., 1978. Bar: Wash. 1977, Calif. 1992. Atty. Davis Wright Tremaine LLP, Seattle, 1977—. King County Gov. Access Channel Oversight com., 1996—. Bd. dirs. Seattle Repertory Theatre, 1993—, pres., 1999-01. Mem. ABA (tort and ins. practice sect., media law and defamation torts com. chair 1999-2000). Home: 711 W Kinnear Pl Seattle WA 98119-3621 Office: Davis Wright Tremaine LLP 2600 Century Sq 1501 4th Ave Seattle WA 98101-1688

JOHNSON, BYRON JERALD, retired state supreme court judge; b. Boise, Idaho, Aug. 2, 1937; s. Arlie Johnson and V. Bronell (Dunten) J.; children: Matthew, Ethan, Elaine, Laura; m. Paticia G. Young, 1984. AB, Harvard U., 1959, LLB, 1962. Bar: Idaho, 1962. Justice Idaho Supreme Ct., Boise, 1988-98; ret., 1998.

JOHNSON, CAGE SAUL, hematologist, educator; b. New Orleans, Mar. 31, 1941; s. Cage Spooner and Esther Georgianna (Saul) J.; m. Shirley Lee O'Neal, Feb. 22, 1968; children: Stephanie, Michelle. Student, Creighton U., 1958-61, MD, 1965. Intern U. Calif., 1965-66, resident, 1966-67, U. So. Calif., 1969-71, instr., 1971-74, asst. prof., 1974-80, assoc. prof., 1980-88, dir. Comprehensive Sickle Cell Ctr., 1991—, prof., 1988—. Chmn. adv. com. Calif. Dept. Health Svcs., Sacramento, 1977—; dir. Hemoglobinopathy Lab., L.A., 1976—; bd. dirs. Sicke Cell Self-Help Assn., L.A., 1982-86. Contbr. numerous articles to profl. jours. Dir. Sickle Cell Disease Rsch. Found., L.A., 1986-94; active Nat. Med. Fellowships, Inc., Chgo., 1979—; chmn. rev. com. NIH, Washington, 1986-91; chmn. adv. com., 1995-97, mem. adv. coun., 1997—. Major U.S. Army, 1967-69, Vietnam. Fellow N.Y. Acad. Scis., Am. Coll. Angiology; mem. Am. Soc. Hematology, Am. Fedn. Clin. Rsch., Western Soc. Clin. Investigation, Internat. Soc. Biorheology, E.E. Just Soc. (sec.-treas. 1985-93, pres. 1994-95, sec. 1996—). Avocation: restoring antique automobiles. Office: U So Calif 2025 Zonal Ave Los Angeles CA 90033-1034

JOHNSON, CAMILLE, media executive; BA in Journalism, U. Oreg. With Chiat/Day Advt., San Francisco, 1980-90; sr. v.p., media dir. GMO/Hill Holliday, San Francisco, 1990—. Office: GMO/Hill Holliday 600 Battery St San Francisco CA 94111-1802

JOHNSON, CANDICE ELAINE BROWN, pediatrics educator; b. Cin., Mar. 21, 1946; d. Paul Preston and Naomi Elizabeth Brown; m. Thomas Raymond Johnson, June 30, 1973; children: Andrea Eleanor, Erik Albert. BS, U. Mich., 1968; PhD Microbiology, Case Western Reserve U., 1973, MD, 1976. Diplomate Am. Bd. Pediat., 1981. Intern, resident in pediat. Rainbow Babies and Children's Hosp./Met. Gen. Hosp., Cleve., 1976-78; fellow in ambulatory pediatrics Met. Gen. Hosp., 1978-79; asst prof. pediat. Case Western Res. U., Cleve., 1980-90, assoc. prof., 1990-97; prof. pediat. U. Colo., Denver, 1997—; pediatrician Children's Hosp., Denver, 1997—. Mem. rev. panel NIH, Washington, 1993; faculty sen. Case Western Res. U., 1988-91. Contbr. articles profl. jours. Mem. Am. Acad. Pediat., Ambulatory Pediatric Assn., Soc. for Pediatric Rsch., So. Utah Wilderness Alliance, Sierra Club. Home: 2290 Locust St Denver CO 80207-3943 Office: Child Health Clinic B032 1056 E 19th Ave Denver CO 80218-1007 E-mail: johnson.candice@tchden.org

JOHNSON, CAROL ANN, editor; b. Seattle, Aug. 19, 1941; d. Jack Rutherford and Marian Frances (Cole) Schisler; m. Gary L. Johnson, Sept. 8, 1962; children: Deborah Carol Johnson Erickson, Barbara Ann Johnson Lilland. Grad., Bethany Coll. of Missions, Mpls., 1962. Typesetter Bethany Printing Div., Mpls., 1960-69; librarian Bethany Coll. of Missions, Mpls., 1969-79; editl. dir. Bethany House Pubs., Mpls., 1980-98, v.p. editl., 1998—. Avocations: reading, sewing, tennis, bicycling, cooking, hiking. E-mail: carol.johnson@bethanyhouse.com

JOHNSON, CHARLES BARTLETT, mutual fund executive; b. Montclair, N.J., Jan. 6, 1933; s. Rupert Harris and Florence (Endler) J.; m. Ann Demarest Lutes, Mar. 26, 1955; children: Charles E., Holly, Sarah, Gregory, William, Jennifer, Mary (dec.). BA, Yale U., 1954. With R.H. Johnson & Co., N.Y.C., 1954-55; pres. Franklin Distbrs., Inc., 1957-97; chmn., CEO, Franklin Resources, Inc., 1969—. Bd. dirs. various Franklin and Templeton Mut. Funds; bd. govs. Investment Co. Inst., 1973-88. Trustee Crystal Springs Uplands Sch., 1984-92; bd. dirs. Peninsula Cmty. Found., 1986-96, San Francisco Symphony, 1984—; bd. overseers Hoover Instn., 1993—. Mem. Nat. Assn. Securities Dirs. (bd. govs. 1990-92, 96-98, chmn. 1992), Burlingame Country Club, Pacific Union Club (San Francisco), Commonwealth Club of Calif. (bd. dirs. 1995-97). Office: Franklin Resources Inc PO Box 7777 San Mateo CA 94403-7777

JOHNSON, CHARLES M. former banker; b. 1941; married. BS, Ohio State U., 1963; MA, Stanford U., 1978. With Wells Fargo Bank, San Francisco, 1967—, personnel officer, 1969-70, internat. banking officer, 1970-71, asst. v.p., Nicaragua rep., 1971-74, asst. v.p., Hong Kong rep., 1974-75, v.p. real estate indsl. group, 1975-78, v.p., mgr. constrn. loan dept., 1978-79, sr. v.p. retail banking group, dep. head group, 1979-80, sr. v.p. comml. banking group, 1980-83, exec. v.p., 1983—; group head for comml. banking group, 1985—; corp. banking group, 1991-92; vice chmn. Wells Fargo Bank, 1992-99; ret., 1999. Office: Wells Fargo Bank 420 Montgomery St San Francisco CA 94104-1298

JOHNSON, CHARLES N. elementary education educator; Tchr., vice prin. Morgan (Utah) Middle Sch.; prin. Clinton (Utah) Elem., 1997-99, Burton Elem., Kaysville, Utah, 1999—. Recipient Tchr. Excellence award Internat. Tech. Edn. Assn., 1992. Office: Burton Elem 827 E 200 S Kaysville UT 84037-2299

JOHNSON, CHARLES WILLIAM, state supreme court justice; b. Tacoma, Mar. 16, 1951; BA in Econs., U. Wash., 1973; JD, U. Puget Sound, 1976. Bar: Wash. 1977. Justice Wash. Supreme Ct., 1991—. Co-chair Wash. State Minority and Justice Commn. Mem. bd. dirs. Wash. Assn. Children and Parents; mem. vis. com. U. Wash. Sch. Social Work; bd. visitors Seattle U. Sch. Law; liaison ltd. practice bd., co-chair BJA subcom. on juc. svcs.; mem. Am. Inns of Ct., World Affairs Coun. Pierce County. Mem. Wash. State Bar Assn., Tacoma-Pierce County Bar Assn. (Liberty Bell award young lawyers sect. 1994). Avocations: sailing, downhill skiing, cycling. Office: Wash State Supreme Ct Temple of Justice PO Box 40929 Olympia WA 98504-0929

JOHNSON, CONOR DEANE, mechanical engineer; b. Charlottesville, Va., Apr. 20, 1943; s. Randolph Holaday and Louise Anna (Deane) J.; m. Laura Teague Rogers, Dec. 20, 1966; children: William Drake, Catherine Teague. BS in Engring. Mechanics, Va. Poly. Inst., 1965; MS, Clemson U., 1967, PhD in Engring. Mechanics, 1969. Registered profl. engr., Calif. With Anamet Labs., Inc., 1973-82, sr. structural analyst Ohio, 1973-75, prin. engr. San Carlos, Calif., 1975-81, v.p., 1981-82; program mgr. Aerospace Structures Info. and Analysis Ctr., 1975-82; co-founder, pres. CSA Engring., Inc., Mountain View, Calif., 1982—. Tech. dir. damping conf., exec. com. N.Am. Conf. on Smart Materials and Structures. Contbr. articles to profl. jours. Capt. USAF, 1969-73 Mem. AIAA (structural dynamics tech. com.), ASME (adaptive structures tech. com., structures and materials award 1981), N.Am. Smart Structures and Materials Conf. (mem. exec. com., tech. chmn. Damping confs. 1991, 93, 95, 96), Gourmet Cooking Club, Sigma Xi. Methodist. Home: 3408 Beresford Ave Belmont CA 94002-1302 Office: CSA Engring Inc 2565 Leghorn St Mountain View CA 94043-1613

JOHNSON, DANIEL LLOYD, entomologist, biogeographer, educator; b. Yankton, S.D., Sept. 30, 1953; children: Sam, Eric, Meg. BSc in Biology with high honours, U. Sask., Can., 1978; MSc in Insect Biology, U. B.C., 1980, PhD in Plant Sci., 1983. Rsch. scientist Agr. Can. Rsch. Sta., Lethbridge, Alta., 1983—. Adj. assoc. prof. biogeography dept. geography U. Lethbridge, Alta., Can.; project monitor for locust rsch. Can. Internat. Devel. Agy. Contbr. articles to profl. jours. Postgrad. scholar Natural Scis. and Engring. Rsch. Coun., 1981, 82. Achievements include research in ecology and control of grasshoppers attacking grassland, cereals and oilseed crops. Office: U Lethbridge Dept Geography PO Box 3000 Lethbridge AB Canada T1J 4B1 also: Agr Can Rsch Sta Dept Geography 4401 University Dr Lethbridge AB Canada T1K 3M4

JOHNSON, DANIEL M. provost; b. Springfield, Ohio, June 10, 1940; m. Elaine Clark Johnson; children: Brent, Darin. BA, Tex. Christian U., 1963, MA, 1965; PhD, U. Mo., 1973. Instr. dept. sociology Blackburn Coll., Carlinville, Ill., 1965-67, chmn. dept. sociology, chmn. divsn. social scis., 1970-73; instr. dept. sociology Christian Coll., Columbia, Mo., 1967-69; asst. prof. sociology, dir. sociology honors program Wichita (Kans.) State U., 1969-70; assoc. prof. sociology and pub. affairs Sangamon State U., Springfield, Ill., 1973-78, dir. Ctr. for Study and Pub. Affairs, 1975-79, prof. sociology and pub. affairs, 1978-79; assoc. prof. sociology, co-dir. Va. Commonwealth U., Richmond, 1979-80, chmn. dept. sociology and anthropology, 1980-83, prof. sociology, 1980-91, interim assoc. dean Coll. of Humanities and Scis., 1987-88; dean Sch. of Cmty. Svc., prof. sociology U. North Tex., Denton, 1991-97; provost U. of Alaska, Anchorage, 1997—. Vis. asst. prof. sociology Lincoln U., Jefferson City, Mo., 1968, 69, 70; founder, dir. Survey Rsch. Lab., Va. Commonwealth U., Richmond, 1983-88; spkr. in field.; cons. in field. Author: (with others) Metropolitan Universities: An Emerging Model in Higher Education, 1995, Black Migration in America: A Social Demographic History, 1981, The Middle Size Cities of Illinois: Their People, Politics and Quality of Life, 1980, Churches in Transitional Neighborhoods: Options for Local Congregations, 1992, Cities and Sickness: Health Care in Urban America, 1983; contbr. numerous articles to profl. jours. Fellowship NSF, 1971; recipient numerous grants. Mem. Met. Univs. Coalition, Coun. for the Arts and Scis. in Urban Univs., Am. Sociol. Assn., Population Assn. of Am., Phi Kappa Phi. Home: 7321 E Chester Heights Cir Anchorage AK 99504-3565 Office: U Alaska Anchorage Office Acad Affairs 3211 Providence Dr Anchorage AK 99508-4614

JOHNSON, DAVEY (DAVID ALLEN JOHNSON), professional baseball team manager; b. Orlando, Fla., Jan. 30, 1943; children: Dave Jr., Dawn, Andrea. Student, Johns Hopkins U.; B.S., Trinity U. Baseball player Balt. Orioles, 1965-72; baseball player Atlanta Braves, 1973-75, Phila. Phillies, 1977-78, Chgo. Cubs, 1978; mgr. Inter-Am. League, Miami, 1979, Jackson League, Tex., 1981, Tidewater, Internat. League, 1983, N.Y. Mets, N.Y.C., 1984-90, Cin. Reds, 1993-96, Balt. Orioles, 1996-97, L.A. Dodgers, 1999—. Recipient Am. Gold Glove, 1969-71; mem. Am. League All-Star Team, 1968, 70, Nat. League All-Star Team, 1973; mgr. Nat. League All-Star Team, 1986, World Series championship team, 1986. Co-holder single season record most home runs by second baseman (42), 1973. Office: Los Angeles Dodgers 1000 Elysian Park Ave Los Angeles CA 90012-1199

JOHNSON, DAVID J. educational center administrator; b. 1946; Pres., CEO Cal Gas Corp., 1984-87; pres., COO, dir. Dillingham Holdings, San Francisco, 1986-88; gen. ptnr. Hellman & Friedman, San Francisco, 1989-91; pres., CEO, chmn. bd. Red Lion Hotels, 1991-96; CEO, chmn. bd. KinderCare Learning Ctrs., Inc., Portland, 1997—. Office: Kindercare Learning Centers Inc 650 NE Holladay St #1400 Portland OR 97232

JOHNSON, DOUG, advertising and public relations executive; b. Watertown, N.Y., Aug. 16, 1919; s. H. Douglas and Clare (Lane) J.; m. Geraldine Evans, Aug. 11, 1943; children: Andrew (dec.), Molly E., Faith D. Student pub. schs. Pres. Doug Johnson Assos. (pub. relations), Syracuse, N.Y., 1949-61, Barlow/Johnson, Inc. (advt. and pub. relations), Syracuse, 1961-80, Johnlow Corp., Fayetteville; chmn. bd. Nowak Barlow Johnson, Fayetteville, 1980-82; v.p. mktg. Edward Joy Co., Inc., Syracuse, 1982-84. Playwright, pres. 10 Co. Mktg.; dir. Agway Indemnity Ins. Co., Dewitt, N.Y., Key Bank of Central N.Y., Syracuse, Syracuse Baseball Club, Inc.; chmn. exec. com. Agway Ins. Co., Dewitt Home sec. to congressman, 1949-65; bd. dirs., v.p. Community Gen. Hosp. Syracuse, N.Y. State Coll. Forestry Found.; bd. dirs., past pres. Syracuse Boys Club ; v.p. N.Y.C. Assoc. Artists; pres. L.W. Artists Assn., 1997-98. Served with AUS, 1941-45. Decorated Purple Heart with 3 oak leaf clusters, Bronze Star, Combat Infantry Badge with Silver Star. Mem. Pub. Rels. Soc. Am. (cert. bus. communicator), Syracuse C. of C. (pres. 1968-69) Club: Century (gov.) Home and Office: 1444 Leisure World Mesa AZ 85206-2304 E-mail: dougjohnse@aol.com

JOHNSON, E. ERIC, insurance executive; b. Chgo., Feb. 7, 1927; s. Edwin Eric and Xenia Alice (Waisanen) J.; m. Elizabeth Dewar Brass, Sept. 3, 1949; children: Christal L. Johnson Neal, Craig R. BA, Stanford U., 1948. Dir. group annuities Equitable Life Assurance Soc., San Francisco, 1950-54, div. mgr. L.A., 1955-59; v.p. Johnson & Higgins of Calif., L.A., 1960-67, dir., 1968-87, chmn., 1986-87, TBG Fin., L.A., 1988—. Bd. dirs. Am. Mutual Fund; exec. v.p. Johnson & Higgins, N.Y.C., 1984-87, Law Environ. Group, Showscan Corp. Bd. dirs. Sta. KCET, pub. TV, L.A., 1977-95, chmn., 1992-94; mem. adv. bd. UCLA Med. Ctr., 1983—, chmn. 1995-97; bd. dirs. Jonsson Comprehensive Cancer Ctr., UCLA, 1985—, Stanford U. Grad Sch. Bus., 1986-91; trustee Nuclear Decommissioning Trust, Rosemead, Calif., 1986-94, Calif. State Dept. Mental Hygiene, Calif. Coun. for Econ. Edn. Mem. Calif. Club, L.A. Country Club, Vintage Club, Riviera Tennis Club, Links Club N.Y.C., Beach Club, So. Calif. Tennis Assn. (v.p.), Tehama Golf Club. Avocations: golf, tennis, contemporary art, spectator sports. Office: TBG Fin 2029 Century Park E Los Angeles CA 90067-2901

JOHNSON, EARVIN See JOHNSON, MAGIC

JOHNSON, EDWARD ARNOLD, ecologist, educator; b. Long Branch, N.J., Aug. 24, 1943; s. Arnold Alfred and Dorthy (Grunander) J.; m. Susan Jean Bagley (div. 1988); 1 child, Joanne Sonia; m. Kiyoko Miyanishi, 1994. BSc, U. Wis., 1968; MSc, U. N.H., 1972; PhD, U. Saskatchewan, 1977. Asst. prof., biol. scis. U. Calgary, Alta., Can., 1979-87, assoc. prof., biol. scis. Can., 1987-93, prof. biol. scis. Can., 1993—, dir. Kananaskis Field Stations, Can., 1992—. Mem. editorial bd. Jour. Vegetation Sci., 1990-97; editor Ecology, 1993-96; assoc. editor Can. Jour. Forest Rsch., 1992—; contbr. articles to profl. jours. Mem. Internat. Assn. for Vegetation Sci. (sec. N.Am. sect. 1988-90), British Ecol. Soc., Ecol. Soc. Am. (William S. Cooper award 1986), Wis. Acad. Sci., Arts and Letters, Sigma Xi. Achievements include research on plant population dynamics, on forest fire behavior and ecological effects, on ecological mechanics, aerodynamics and small particle dispersal models and on ecological effects of natural disturbances. Office: U Calgary Dept Biol Scis Calgary AB Canada T2N 1N4

JOHNSON, GARY EARL, governor; b. Minot, N.D., Jan. 1, 1953; s. Earl W. and Lorraine B. (Bostow) J.; m. Dee Simms, Nov. 27, 1976; children: Seah, Erik. BA in Polit. Sch., U. N.Mex., 1975. Pres., CEO Big J Enterprises, Albuquerque, 1976—; gov. State of N.Mex., 1995-98, 98—. Bd. dirs. Entrepreneurship Studies at U. N.Mex., 1993-95. Named to list of Big 50 Remodelers in the USA, 1987; named Entrepreneur of Yr., 1995. Mem. LWV, C. of C. Albuquerque (bd. dirs. 1993-95). Republican. Lutheran. Avocations: rock-climbing, mountain climbing, skiing, pilot, triathlete. Office: Office of Gov State Capitol Rm 400 Santa Fe NM 87503*

JOHNSON, GOODYEAR See O'CONNOR, KARL WILLIAM

JOHNSON, GORDON JAMES, artistic director, conductor; b. St. Paul, 1949; BS, Bemidji State U., 1971; MS, Northwestern U., 1977; D in Mus. Arts, U. Oreg.; studied with Leonard Bernstein, Erich Leinsdorf, Herbert Blomstedt. Music dir., condr. Great Falls (Mont.) Symphony Assn., 1981—, Glacier Orch. and Chorale, Mont., 1982-97; artistic dir., condr. Flathead Music Festival, 1987-96; music dir., condr. Mesa (Ariz.) Symphony Orch., 1997—. Grad. teaching fellow U. Oreg., 1979-81; artist in residence Condr's Guild Inst., W.Va. U., condr. orch., 1984; condr. Spokane Symphony at The Festival at Sandpoint; guest condr. St. Paul Chamber Orch., 1971, Spokane Symphony, 1983, 86, Dubuque (Iowa) Symphony, 1985, Charlotte (N.C.) Symphony, 1985, Lethbridge (Alberta, Can.) Symphony, 1986, Cheyenne (Wyo.) Symphony, 1986, West Shore (Mich.) Symphony, 1988, Bozeman (Mont.) Symphony, 1989, Kumamoto Symphony (Kyshu, Japan), 1991, Kankakee (Ill.) Symphony, 1993, Toulon (France) Symphonies, 1994, Guam Symphony, 1995, Tokyo Lumiere Orch., 1995, Fort Collins (Colo.) Symphony, 1995, Wilmslow (Eng.) Symphony Orch., 1997; guest ballet condr. Alberta Ballet, 1986, Oakland (Calif.) Ballet, 1988, Eugene (Oreg.) Ballet, 1993, David Taylor Ballet, Colo., 1994, St. Petersburg (Russia) Ballet, 1995, Western Ballet Theater, Oreg., 1996; spkr. regional conf. Am. Symphony Orch. League, 1987, nat. conf., 1988; mem. adj. faculty U. Great Falls, 1981—, U. Mont., 1996—; lectr. U. Guam, 1995; condr. seminars L.A. Philharmonic Inst., 1983, Condr.'s Guild Inst., 1984, Festival at Sandpoint, Condr.'s Program, 1986, Am. Symphony Orch. League's Am. Condr.'s Program, N.Y. Philharmonic, 1987, Condr.'s Guild "Bruckner Seminar", Chgo. Symphony Orch., 1989, Carnegie Hall Tng. Program for Condrs., Cleve. Orch., 1993. Philharmonic Condr.'s scholar St. Paul Chamber Orch., 1971; L.A. Philharmonic Inst. fellow, 1983; named to Highland Park High Sch. Hall of Fame, St. Paul, 1997. Mem. ASCAP. Office: Great Falls Symphony Assn PO Box 1078 Great Falls MT 59403-1078 E-mail: gjohnson@mcn.net

JOHNSON, JAMES ARNOLD, business consultant, venture capitalist; b. Detroit, June 15, 1939; s. Waylon Z. and Elsie Jean (Peuser) J.; 1 child, Stephanie Louise. BA, Stanford U., 1961; MBA, U. Chgo., 1968. CPA, Calif. Asst. cashier internat. banking First Nat. Bank of Chgo., 1965-68; ptnr.-in-charge mgmt. cons. Peat, Marwick, Mitchell & Co., Honolulu, 1968-79, ptnr.-in-charge small bsu. svcs., 1977-80; pres. Johnson Internat., Inc., Incline Village, Nev., 1980—, BioEngring. Applications, Inc., Honolulu, 1981-90; gen. ptnr. numerous investment partnerships; CFO TransData Internat., Inc., 1995-2000, Ad Express Can. Inc., 1996-99, pres., CFO Board Vantage, Inc., 2001—. Bd. dirs. TransData Internat. Inc. Served to lt. USNR, 1962-65. Mem. AICPA, Calif. Soc. CPAs. Home: 685 Wilson Way Incline Village NV 89450-5131 Office: PO Box 6898 Incline Village NV 89450-6898 E-mail: tahoejj@aol.com

JOHNSON, JOHN J. historian, educator; b. White Swan, Wash., Mar. 26, 1912; s. George E. and Mary (Whitford) J.; m. Maurine Amstutz, June 8, 1942; 1 son, Michael G. B.A., Central Wash. Coll., 1940; M.A., U. Calif.-Berkeley, 1943, Ph.D., 1947; postgrad., U. Chgo., 1943-44, U. Chile, 1946. Tchr. pub. schs., Wash., 1935-39; mem. faculty Stanford U., 1946-78, prof. history, 1958-78, emeritus prof., 1977—; chmn. com. Latin Am. studies, 1966-72; prof. U. N.Mex., Albuquerque, 1980-85. Acting chief S. Am. br., div. research Am. Republic, State Dept., 1952-53; lectr. U. Ariz. Summer Sch., Guadalajara, Mex., 1955, 58, 61; cons. to industry and govt., 1959— ; Fulbright lectr. U. Auckland, New Zealand, 1974; vis. prof. U. N.Mex., 1977, 79, Ariz. State U., 1980 Mng. editor Hispanic Am. Hist. Rev., 1980-85. Author: Pioneer Telegraphy in Chile, 1948, Political

Change in Latin America; The Emergence of the Middle Sectors, 1958, The Military and Society in Latin America, 1964, Simon Bolivar and Spanish American Independence: 1783-1830, 1967, 2d edit., 1992, Latin America in Caricature, 1980, 2d edit., 1993, A Hemisphere Apart: The Foundations of United States Policy Toward Latin America, 1990; editor, contbr.: Role of the Military in Underdeveloped World, Continuity & Change in Latin America, 1964. Recipient Bolton prize Conf. Latin Am. History, 1959, Disting. Alumnus award Cen. Wash. U., 1977, Disting. Service award Conf. Latin Am. History, 1987; fellow Nat. Humanities Ctr., 1985-86. Mem. Am. Hist. Assn. (mem. council 1976-79, chmn. conf. Latin Am. history 1961), Latin Am. Studies Assn. (pres. 1970, 1st Kalman Silvert Pres.'s prize 1983) Home: 2602 Kings Forest Dr Kingwood TX 77339

JOHNSON, JOHN PHILIP, geneticist, researcher; b. Wabash, Ind., June 6, 1949; s. Melvin Leroy and Cleo Pauline (Aldrich) J.; m. Sheryl Kay Kennedy, June 3, 1978; children: Craig Eric, Lindsay Sara. BS, U. Mich., 1971, MD, 1975. Diplomate Am. Bd. Pediatrics, Am. Bd. Med. Genetics. Intern, 2d-yr. resident Children's Hosp. Los Angeles, 1975-77; 3d yr. resident in pediatrics U. Utah, Salt Lake City, 1977-78, fellow in genetics, 1980-82, asst. prof. pediatrics, 1982-85; pediatrician Family Health Program, Salt Lake City, 1978-80; assoc. dir. med. genetics, attending/active staff physician Children's Hosp. Oakland, Calif., 1985-92; dir. med. genetics, attending/active staff physician Children's Hosp., Oakland, 1992-94; dir. med. genetics Shodair Children's Hosp., Helena, Mont., 1994—, active mem. staff, 1995—. Clinic physician Utah State Tng. Sch., American Fork, 1982-85; attending and staff physician Primary Children's Med. Ctr., Salt Lake City, 1978-80. Assoc. editor Am. Jour. Med. Genetics, 1995-97; contbr. articles to med. jours. Recipient William J. Branstrom award U. Mich., 1967. Fellow Am. Acad. Pediatrics; mem. Am. Soc. Human Genetics, Soc. for Pediatric Rsch., Alpha Omega Alpha. Avocations: skiing, hiking, camping, piano, jazz. Home: 2604 Gold Rush Ave Helena MT 59601-5625 Office: Shodair Childrens Hosp PO Box 5539 Helena MT 59604-5539

JOHNSON, JON L. advertising executive; Chmn., CEO, dir. Publicis, Salt Lake City. Office: Publicis 110 Social Hall Ave Salt Lake City UT 84111-1504

JOHNSON, JONATHAN EDWIN, II, lawyer; b. Whittier, Calif., May 1, 1936; s. Roger Edwin and Louise (Thompson) J.; m. Clare Hardy, June 23, 1963 (dec. 1995); children: Jonathan III, Hardy, Benjamin, Adam, Rufus, Bradford, Roger, Ralph; m. Garnet Mantor, June 17, 2000. BChemE, Cornell U., 1959, MBA, 1960; JD with honors, George Washington U., 1963. Bar: Calif. 1964; cert. specialist family law, Calif. Assoc. Tuttle & Taylor, L.A., 1963-65; pvt. practice L.A., 1965-67; ptnr. Johnson & Jarvis, L.A., 1967-68, Johnson, Poulson, Coons & Slater, L.A., 1968—. Instr. paralegal probate U. West L.A. Sch. Law, 1974; mem. clergy adv. com. to supt. edn., City of L.A., 1978-81. Fellow Am. Acad. Matrimonial Lawyers (counsel So. Calif. chpt. 1998-99); mem. Calif. State Bar Assn. (legis. com. family law sect. 1978-88, chmn. 1980), Beverly Hills Bar Assn. (exec. com. family law sect. 1977-82, 86-88, 91—), Inter-stake Bus. and Profl. Assn. L.A. (pres. 1974), Cornell Club of So. Calif. (pres. 1966-68), Order of Coif, Sigma Chi, Phi Delta Phi. Mem. LDS Ch. Home: 1094 Acanto Pl Los Angeles CA 90049-1604 Office: Johnson Poulson Coons 10880 Wilshire Blvd Ste 1100 Los Angeles CA 90024-4112

JOHNSON, KENNETH BJORN, botany and plant pathology educator; BS in Plant Health Tech. with high distinction, U. Minn., 1979, PhD in Plant Pathology, 1986; MS in Plant Pathology, Oreg. State U., 1986. Extension intern Plant Disease Clinic dept. plant pathology U. Minn., St. Paul, 1979, lab., field rsch. asst. dept. plant pathology, 1979-80, grad. rsch. asst. dept. plant pathology, 1983-86, rsch. assoc. dept. plant pathology, 1986-88, lectr. dept. plant pathology, 1987-88; grad. rsch. asst. dept. botany and plant pathology Oreg. State U., Corvallis, 1980-83, asst. prof. dept. botany and plant pathology, 1988-93, assoc. prof., 1993—, instr. plant disease mgmt., 1992, 96. Mem. Am. Phytopathol. Soc. (disease losses com. 1988-92, chair 1990-91, epidemiology com. 1988-93, chair 1991-92, adhoc com. plant pathology 2000: directions for plant pathology in the next century, 1993, Ciba Geigy award 1996), Internat. Soc. for Plant Pathology (epidemiology com. 1989-94, chair epidemiology symposium 1998 congress), Phi Kappa Phi, Gamma Sigma Delta, Sigma Xi. Office: Oreg State U Dept Botany & Plant Pathol 2082 Cordley Hall Corvallis OR 97331-8530

JOHNSON, KENNETH F. lawyer; b. Ft. Bragg, Calif., June 10, 1938; s. Frank W. and Gertrude Johnson; m. Jane Perry Drennan, June 11, 1961; children: Erik Allan, Mark. BSCE, U. Calif., Berkeley, 1962; JD, U. Calif., Hastings, 1969. Bar: Calif. 1970. V.p., shareholder Crosby, Heafey, Roach & May, Oakland, Calif., 1969—. Note and comment editor: Hastings Law Jour., 1968-69. With USNR, 1962-66. Scholar U. Calif. Hastings, 1967-68, 68-69. Mem. ABA, ATLA, Calif. Bar Assn., Alameda County Bar Assn., Contra Costa County Bar Assn., Bar Assn. San Francisco, Calif. Bus. Trial Lawyers Assn., Assn. Def. Counsel, Order of Coif. Office: Crosby Heafey Roach & May 1999 Harrison St Fl 26 Oakland CA 94612-3520

JOHNSON, KEVIN MAURICE, professional basketball player; b. Sacramento, Mar. 4, 1966; Student, U. Calif., 1987. Basketball player Cleveland Cavaliers, 1987-88, Phoenix Suns, 1988—. Named to Dream Team II, 1994, NBA Most Improved Player, 1989, All-NBA Second Team, 1989-91, 94, All-NBA Third Team, 1992. Office: care Phoenix Suns 201 E Jefferson St Phoenix AZ 85004-2412

JOHNSON, LAWRENCE M. banker; b. 1940; Student, U. Hawaii. With Bank of Hawaii, Honolulu, 1963-2000, exec. v.p., 1980-84, vice chmn., 1984-89, pres., 1989-2000, now chmn. bd., CEO, until 2000, ret., 2000. Pres. Pacific Century Fin. Corp. Office: Bancorp Hawaii Inc Ste # 230 130 Merchant St Honolulu HI 96813 also: Pacific Century Fin Corp Fin Plz Pacific 130 Merchant St Honolulu HI 96813-4405

JOHNSON, MAGIC (EARVIN JOHNSON), professional sports team executive, former professional basketball coach; b. Lansing, Mich., Aug. 14, 1959; s. Earvin and Christine Johnson; m. Cookie Kelly; 1 son, Earvin. Student, Mich. State U., 1976-79. Basketball player L.A. Lakers, 1979-91, 95-96; sportscaster NBC-TV, 1993-94; chmn. Johnson Devel. Corp., 1993—; head coach L.A. Lakers, 1994, v.p., co-owner, 1994—; chmn. Magic Johnson Entertainment, 1997—; talk show host The Magic Hour, 1998—. Gold medalist, U.S. Olympic Basketball Team, 1992. Author: (autobiography) Magic, 1983; (autobiography, with Roy S. Johnson) Magic's Touch, 1989; What You Can Do to Avoid AIDS, 1992; My Life, 1992. Recipient Citizenship award, 1992, All-Around Contbns. to Team Success award IBM, 1984; mem. NCAA Championship Team, 1979, NBA All-Star Team, 1980, 82-92, MVP NBA All-Star Game, 1990, 92, NBA Championship Team, 1980, 82, 85, 87, 88; named MVP NBA Playoffs, 1980, 82, 87, NBA, 1987, 89, 90, All Star Game, 1990, 92, Player of the Year, Sporting News, 1987; recipient Schick Pivotal Player award, 1984; named to All-NBA first team, 1983-91, second team, 1982, NBA All-Rookie Team, 1980. Achievements include being a holder of NBA playoff record most assists (2320); NBA Finals single-series record highest assists-per-game avg. (14), 1985, highest assists per game, rookie (8.7), 1980, NBA Finals single game record most points by rookie (42), 1980, NBA Finals single game recored most assists one quarter (8), NBA single game record most assists (22). Office: Magic Johnson Found 1600 Corporate Pointe Ste 1080 Culver City CA 90230 also: Johnson Devel Corp 9100 Wilshire Blvd Beverly Hills CA 90212-3415 also: TA Networks Inc 1440 S Sepulveda Blvd Los Angeles CA 90025-3458

JOHNSON, MARIAN ILENE, education educator; b. Hawarden, Iowa, Oct. 3, 1929; d. Henry Richard and Wilhelmina Anna (Schmidt) Stoltenberg; m. Paul Irving Jones, June 14, 1958 (dec. Feb. 1985); m. William Andrew Johnson, Oct. 3, 1991. BA, U. La Verne, 1959; MA, Claremont Grad. Sch., 1962; PhD, Ariz. State U., 1971. Cert. tchr., Iowa, Calif. Elem. tchr. Cherokee (Iowa) Sch. Dist., 1949-52, Sioux City (Iowa) Sch. Dist., 1952-56, Ontario (Calif.) Pub. Schs., 1956-61, Reed Union Sch. Dist., Belvedere-Tiburon, Calif., 1962-65, Columbia (Calif.) Union Sch. Dist., 1965-68; prof. edn. Calif. State U., Chico, 1972-91. Avocation: travel. Home: 26437 S Lakewood Dr Sun Lakes AZ 85248-7246

JOHNSON, MARK ANDREW, lawyer; b. Plainville, Kans., Feb. 27, 1959; s. Delton Lee and Margaret Ellen (McCracken) J. BA in Chemistry, Reed Coll., 1982; JD, U. Calif., Berkeley, 1987. Bar: Oreg. 1987, U.S. Supreme Ct. 1991. Jud. clk. U.S. Dist. Ct. Oreg., Portland, 1987-88, Oreg. Ct. of Appeals, Salem, 1988-89; assoc. Gevurtz, Menashe, Larson, Kurshner & Yates, PC, Portland, 1989-93; ptnr. Findling & Johnson LLP, Portland, 1993-99; of counsel Bennett Morris & Kaplan, LLP and predecessor, Portland, 1999—. Mem. ABA, Nat. Gay and Lesbian Law Assn. (co-chmn. 1994-95), Oreg. Gay and Lesbian Law Assn. (co-chair 1990-92), Oreg. State Bar (pres. 1998-99). Office: Hartman Morris & Kaplan LLP 851 SW 6th Ave Ste 1600 Portland OR 97204-1307 E-mail: johnsonm@bennetthartman.com

JOHNSON, MARK BERNARR, preventive medicine physician; b. Addis Ababa, Ethiopia, June 10, 1953; MD, Loma Linda U., 1980. Diplomate Am. Bd. Preventive Medicine. Intern (rotation) White Meml. Med. Ctr., L.A., 1980-81; resident in preventive medicine Johns Hopkins U., Balt., 1984-86; clin. assoc. prof. U. Colo., Boulder, 1986-99. Fellow Am. Coll. Preventive Medicine; mem. AMA, APHA. Office: Jefferson County Dept Health & Environment 1801 19th St Dept Health& Golden CO 80401-1709 E-mail: mjohnson@co.jefferson.co.us, mbjohnsonmd@aoo.com

JOHNSON, MARTIN WAYNE, lawyer; b. Portland, Oreg., Nov. 9, 1946; s. David S. and Elsie Jane (Kalmen) Johnson; m. Kathleen Umrein, Mar. 27, 1977; children: Jessica, Brian, Douglas. BA, Lewis & Clark Coll., 1968; JD, U. Calif., 1974. Bar: Calif. 1974. Assoc. Wilson, Elser, Moskowitz, Edelman & Dicker, San Francisco, 1982-86, ptnr., 1987—. Assoc. editor Calif. Law Review, U. Calif., 1972-74. Dir. Sleepy Hollow Homes Assn., San Anselmo, Calif., 1991-93. Lt. (j.g.) USNR, 1968-71. Mem. Order of Coif. Democrat. Presbyterian. Avocations: backpacking, fishing, gardening. Office: Wilson Elser Moskowitz Edelman & Dicker 650 California St Ste 1400 San Francisco CA 94108-2718

JOHNSON, MARY, museum director; Acting dir. Dept. Libr. and Pub. Records, Phoenix, now dep. dir. Office: Dept Libr Archives Pub Records 1700 W Washington St Ste 200 Phoenix AZ 85007-2812

JOHNSON, MAURICE VERNER, JR. agricultural research and development executive; b. Duluth, Minn., Sept. 13, 1925; s. Maurice Verner Sr. and Elvira Marie (Westberg) J.; m. Darlene Ruth Durand, June 23, 1944; children: Susan Kay, Steven Dale. BS, U. Calif., 1953. Registered profl. engr. From research engr. to dir. research and devel. Sunkist Growers, Ontario, Calif., 1953-84, v.p. research and devel., 1984-90, ret., 1990—. V.p., dir. Calif. Citrus Quality Council, Claremont. Contbr. articles to profl. pubs.; patentee in field. Sgt. U.S. Army, 1944-46, ETO. Fellow Am. Soc. Agrl. Engrs. (dir. 1969-70); mem. ASME, Am. Inst. Indsl. Engrs., Am. Assn. Advancement Sci., Nat. Soc. Profl. Engrs., Tau Beta Pi. Republican. Avocation: golf.

JOHNSON, MIKKEL BORLAUG, physicist; b. Waynesboro, Va., Jan. 2, 1943; s. Wallace A. and Anne D. (Davies) J.; m. Lynne McFadden, June 14, 1966; children: Kara Marit, Krista Lynne. BS, Va. Poly. Inst., 1966; MS, Carnegie Mellon U., 1968, PhD, 1970. Rsch. assoc. Cornell U., Ithaca, N.Y., 1970-72; staff mem., fellow Los Alamos (N.Mex.) Nat. Lab., 1972—. Vis. prof. SUNY, Stony Brook, 1981-82, Carnegie Mellon U., 1997-98. Editor: Relativistic Dynamics and Quark-Nuclear Physics, 1986, Nuclear and Particle Physics on the Light Cone, 1989, LAMPF Workshop on (Pi,K) Physics, 1991; assoc. editor Nuclear Physics, 1975-97. Lab. fellow Los Alamos Nat. Lab, 1991; recipient Humboldt award for Sr. U.S. Scientist, Humboldt Found., 1986. Fellow Am. Phys. Soc. Home: 118 Piedra Loop Los Alamos NM 87544-3828 Office: Los Alamos Nat Lab P divsn Ms H846 Los Alamos NM 87545-0001 E-mail: mbjohnson@lanl.gov

JOHNSON, NED KEITH, ornithologist, educator; b. Reno, Nov. 3, 1932; BS, U. Nev., 1954; PhD in Zoology, U. Calif., 1961. From asst. to assoc. prof. U. Calif., Berkeley, 1962-74, prof. zoology, 1974—, vice chmn. dept. zoology, 1968—, asst. curator birds mus. vertebrate zoology, 1962-63, curator birds, 1963—, acting dir., 1981. Rsch. grantee NSF, 1965—. Mem. Am. Soc. Zoology, Am. Ornithologists' Union (William Brewster Meml. award 1992), Am. Soc. Naturalists, Cooper Ornithol. Soc., Soc. Study Evolution, Soc. Systematic Biology. Achievements include research in biosystematics, distribution and ecology of New World birds. Office: U Calif Mus Vertebrate Zoology 3101 Valley Life Sciences Berkeley CA 94720-3160

JOHNSON, NOBLE MARSHALL, research scientist; b. San Francisco, Feb. 23, 1945; BSE cum laude, U. Calif., Davis, 1967, MSE, 1970; PhD, Princeton U., 1974. Mem. rsch. staff SRI Internat., Menlo Park, Calif., 1974-76, Xerox Palo Alto (Calif.) Rsch. Ctr., 1976-85, prin. scientist Electronic Materials Lab., 1987—; mgr. Blue laser Diode Area, 1999—. Vis. lectr. Princeton (N.J.) U., 1986, U. Erlangen-Nürnberg, Germany, 1987. Co-editor: 4 books; contbr. more than 275 articles to profl. jours.; patentee in field. Recipient Disting. Sr. U.S. Scientist award, Alexander von Humboldt Found., Germany, 1987; Nat. Def. Grad. fellow, Princeton U., 1969-72. Fellow Am. Phys. Soc.; mem. IEEE (sr.), Materials Rsch. Soc. (coun. 1986-88), Sigma Xi. Office: Xerox Palo Alto Rsch Ctr Electronic Materials Lab 3333 Coyote Hill Rd Palo Alto CA 94304-1314

JOHNSON, NOEL LARS, biomedical engineer; b. Palo Alto, Calif., Nov. 11, 1957; s. LeRoy Franklin and Margaret Louise (Lindsley) J.; m. Elise Lynnette Moore, May 17, 1986; children: Margaret Elizabeth, Kent Daniel. BSEE, U. Calif., Berkeley, 1979; ME, U. Va., 1982, PhD, 1990. Mgr. R&D Hosp. Products divsn. Abbott Labs., Mountain View, Calif., 1986-99; COO HealtheTech., Inc., 1999—. Contbr. articles to profl. jours. Fellowship NIH 1980-85; rsch. grantee Abbott Labs. 1989. Mem. IEEE, Biomed. Engring. Soc., Sigma Xi, Delta Chi (founder, 1st pres. chpt. U. Calif. at Berkeley). Achievements include invention of respiratory monitor, patented automated drug delivery system, pharmacokinetic drug infusion, and critical care disposables. Home: 14586 Aloha Ave Saratoga CA 95070-6004 E-mail: njohnson@healthetech.com

JOHNSON, PAM, newspaper editor; Mng. editor Ariz. Republic, Phoenix, 1993-96, sr. v.p. news, exec. editor, 1996—. Office: Ariz Republic PO Box 1950 Phoenix AZ 85001-1950

JOHNSON, PAUL E. astronomer, educator; BS in Physics, Davidson Coll., 1973; MS in Astronomy, U. Wash., 1977, PhD in Astronomy, 1979. NASA-NRC resident rsch. assoc. Jet Propulsion Lab., Pasadena, Calif., 1979-80; sr. rsch. fellow U.K. Infrared Telescope Project Royal Obs., Edinburgh, Scotland, 1980-81; asst. prof. dept. physics and astronomy U. Wyo., Laramie, 1981-86, assoc. prof. dept. physics and astronomy, 1986-93, prof., [illegible] U. Paul Sabatier Toulouse France, 1994; assoc. dir. rsch. CNRS Obs. Midi-Pyrénées, Toulouse, 1994; dir. Wyo. Infrared Obs., 1999—. Contbr. articles to profl. jours. Grantee NASA, NSF, USAF, U.S. Dept. Edn., 1981—. Achievements include research on detection of individual selected bacteria with a CCD flow cytometer; management of the design and fabrication of CCD cameras using 7 different visible CCDS and 1 infrared CCD; design and fabrication of 2 optical and 2 infrared polarimeters, large-beam mid-infrared photometer, 2 high-throughput visible CCD spectrophotometers. Office: Dept Physics and Astronomy U Wyo Laramie WY 82071-3905 E-mail: pjohnson@uwyo.edu

JOHNSON, RANDY (RANDALL DAVID JOHNSON), professional baseball player; b. Walnut Creek, Calif., Sept. 10, 1963; Student, U. So. Calif. With Montreal (Can.) Expos, 1985-89; pitcher Seattle Mariners, 1989-98, Houston Astros, 1998-99, Ariz. Diamondbacks, 1999—. Named to All-Star Team, 1990, 93-95; recipient Cy Young award, 1995; named Pitcher of Yr. Sporting News, 1995; Am. League strikeout leader, 1995. Achievements include leadingin Am. League Strikeouts., 1992. Office: c/o Ariz Diamondbacks BankOne Ballpark 401 E Jefferson St Phoenix AZ 85004-2438

JOHNSON, REVERDY, lawyer; b. N.Y.C., Aug. 24, 1937; s. Reverdy and Reva (Payne) J.; m. Pamela Forbes, Mar. 10, 1961 (div.); m. Marta Schneebeli, Apr. 4, 1970 (div.); children: Deborah Ghiselin, Reverdy Payne; m. Robbie M. Williams, Feb. 20, 1994. AB cum laude, Harvard U., 1960, LLB, 1963. Bar: Fla. 1963, Calif. 1964, N.Mex. 1997. Assoc. Brobeck, Phleger & Harrison, San Francisco, 1963-66; from assoc. to ptnr. Pettit & Martin, San Francisco, 1966-95; of counsel Steinhart & Falconer LLP, San Francisco, 1995-97, Scheuer Yost & Patterson, Sante Fe, NMex., 1996—, Fenwick and West, LLP, Palo Alto, Calif., 1999—. Co-owner Johnson Turnbull Vineyards, Napa Valley, Calif., 1977-93; tech. adv. com., com. open space lands Calif. Joint Legislature, 1968-69, chmn., 1969-70. Bd. dirs. Planning and Conservation League, 1966-72, League to Save Lake Tahoe, 1972-77, Found. for San Francisco's Archtl. Heritage, 1975-84, San Francisco Devel. Fund, 1986-96, Shakespeare in Santa Fe, 2001—. Mem. Urban Land Inst. (vice chmn. recreational devel. council 1975-78, comml. and retail devel. council 1980-99), Napa Valley Vintners Assn. (bd. dirs. 1985-88, v.p. 1987, pres. 1988), Am. Coll. Real Estate Lawyers, Lambda Alpha. also: Scheuer Yost & Patterson 125 Lincoln Ave Ste 223 Santa Fe NM 87501-2053 E-mail: reverdyj@santafelawyers.com

JOHNSON, RICHARD KARL, hospitality company executive; b. Gaylord, Minn., May 27, 1947; s. Karl S. and Mildred (Tollefson) J.; m. Eva Margaret Wick, Oct. 12, 1973; children: Michelle, Richard, Ryan. BA, Gustavus Adolphus U., St. Peter, Minn., 1969. Gen. mgr. Green Giant Restaurants, Inc., Mpls., 1969-71, Mpls. Elks Club, Mpls., 1971-73; dir. concept devel. Internat. Multifoods, Mpls., 1972-75; v.p. concept devel. A&WFood Svcs. Can., North Vancouver, B.C., 1975-81; dir. food and beverages Ramada, Reno, 1981-82; pres., owner R.K. Johnson & Assoc., Reno, 1981—; owner D.J. Mgmt., 1990—. Asst. gen. mgr. Gold Dust West Casino, Reno, 1983-85; gen. mgr. P&M Corp., Reno, 1985-86; v.p. ops. C.P.S.W. Inc., Reno and Tempe, Ariz., 1986-87, Lincoln Fairview, Reno, 1987-89; v.p. corp. affairs Prudential Realty, Nev., 1991—. Mem. Aircraft Owners and Pilots Assn., Nat. Restaurant Assn., Nev. Realtor, Elks Club. Lutheran. Avocations: flying, scuba diving. Home and Office: RK Johnson & Assoc 825 Meadow Springs Dr Reno NV 89509-5913

JOHNSON, ROBERT BRUCE, company director; b. 1944; MS, U. Ariz., 1980, BS, 1968. Hydrologist W.S. Gookin & Assocs., Scottsdale, Ariz., 1972-75; hydrologist II City of Tucson, 1975-78, chief hydrologist, 1978-97, lead adminstr., 1997-98, asst. dir., 1998—. Office: City Tucson PO Box 27210 Tucson AZ 85726-7210

JOHNSON, ROBERT D. aerospace transportation executive; Various positions GE Aircraft Engines; v.p., gen. mgr. aerospace svcs. Allied Signal Inc., 1994, pres. electronic and avionics sys., pres. aerospace mktg., sales and svc.; pres., CEO AlliedSignal Aerospace. Office: 1944 E Sky Harbor Cir NW Phoenix AZ 85034-3442

JOHNSON, ROBERT HERSEL, journalist; b. Colorado City, Tex., May 28, 1923; s. Robert Hersel and Leah (Sikes) J.; m. Luise Putcamp, Jr., Feb. 24, 1945; children: Robert Hersel, III, Luise Robin, Jan Leah, Stephanie Neale, Jennifer Anne, Ann Tapia. B.S. in Journalism, So. Methodist U., 1947. Reporter Phoenix Gazette, 1940-42; asst. sports editor Ariz. Republic, Phoenix, 1942-43; newscast writer Sta. KOY, Phoenix, 1943; reporter Dallas Times-Herald, 1946; with AP, 1946-88, Utah-Idaho bur. chief, 1954-59, Ind. bur. chief, 1959-62, Tex. bur. chief, 1962-69, gen. sports editor, 1969-73, mng. editor, 1973-77, asst. gen. mgr., spl. asst. to pres., 1977-84, N.Mex. bureau chief, 1984-88; prof. journalism N.Mex. State U., Las Cruces, 1988, U. N.Mex., Albuquerque, 1989; exec. dir. N.Mex. Found. for Open Govt., Albuquerque, 1989—. Mem. Newspaper Readership Coun., 1977-82. Mem. N. Mex. Hist. Records Adv. Bd., 1993—. Capt. USMCR, 1943-46, 51-52. Home: 2740 Tramway Cir NE Albuquerque NM 87122-1205 E-mail: nmfoe@aol.com

JOHNSON, ROSS, state legislator; b. Sept. 28, 1939; m. Diane Morris; 2 children. BA in History, Calif. State U., Fullerton; JD, Western State U. Mem. Calif. Assembly, 1978-95, Republican leader, 1988-91; mem. Calif. State Senate, 1995—, mem. appropriations com., edn. com., ins. com., mem. fin., investment and internat. trade com. Mem. Republican State Ctrl. Com.; former chair Orange County Citizens for Law and Order. Served with USN. Republican. Office: State Capitol Rm 305 Sacramento CA 95814 also: 18552 Macarthur Blvd Ste 395 Irvine CA 92612-1226

JOHNSON, ROY RAGNAR, electrical engineer, researcher; b. Chgo., Jan. 23, 1932; s. Ragnar Anders and Ann Viktoria (Lundquist) J.; m. Martha Ann Mattson, June 21, 1963; children: Linnea Marit, Kaisa Ann. BSEE, U. Minn., 1954, MS, 1956, PhD, 1959. Rsch. fellow U. Minn., 1957-59; from rsch. engr. to sr. basic rsch. scientist Boeing Sci. Research Labs., Seattle, 1959-72; prin. scientist KMS Fusion, Inc., Ann Arbor, Mich., 1972-74, dir. fusion expts., 1974-78, tech. dir., 1978-91, dept. head for fusion and plasmas, 1985-88; tech. dir. Innovation Assocs., Inc., Ann Arbor, 1992; inertial confinement fusion classification/records mgr. Lawrence Livermore Nat. Lab., 1992—. Vis. lectr. U. Wash., Seattle, 1959-60; vis. scientist Royal Inst. Tech., Stockholm, 1963-64; cons. Dept. Edn., Washington, 1995, 98, 2000. Author: Nonlinear Effects in Plasmas, 1969, Plasma Physics, 1977, Research Trends in Physics, 1992; contbr. articles to profl. publs.; patentee in field. Bd. advisors Rose-Hulman Inst. Tech., 1982— . Decorated chevalier Order of St. George; comdr. Order of Holy Cross of Jerusalem. Fellow Am. Phys. Soc.; mem. AAAS, AIAA, IEEE (life), Nuclear Plasma Scis. Soc. of IEEE (exec. com. 1972-75), N.Y. Acad. Scis., Am. Def. Preparedness Assn., Assn. of Old Crows, Vasa Order Am. (past chmn. Svea lodge), Am. Swedish Inst., Torpar Riddar Orden, Swedish Coun. Am., Detroit Swedish Coun., Swedish Club of Detroit, Swedish Am. Hist. Soc., Commonwealth Club San Francisco, Eta Kappa Nu, Gamma Alpha. Lutheran. Home: 1141 Concannon Blvd Livermore CA 94550-6451 Office: Livermore Nat Lab PO Box 808 Livermore CA 94551-0808

JOHNSON, ROYAL C. state senator; b. Hettwoger, N.C., May 2, 1925; m. Norma Johnson. BA, U. Mont., 1950; postgrad., Northwestern U. Owner Royal C. Johnson Investment Mgmt., 1988—; Rep. rep. dist. 10 Mont. Ho. of Reps., 1991-2000; Rep. senator dist. 5 Mont. State Senate, 2000—. Mem. Mont. State Adv. Com. Dept. Family Svcs., Mont. State [illegible] Task Force on Workers Compensation Interim Com. on Sch. Funding; mem. joint appropriations subcom. on edn.

and cultural resources Mont. State Senate, chair appropriations. Mem. United Way of Yellowstone County, Billings Preservation Soc., Billings Libr. Found. Bd.; councilman City of Billings, 1971-81. With USAF, WWII. Mem. Rotary, Masons. Office: 2915 Illinois St Billings MT 59102-0814 also: Mont State Senate Capitol Station Helena MT 59620 Fax: 406 259-7531

JOHNSON, RUPERT HARRIS, JR. finance company executive; BA, Washington and Lee U., 1962. With Franklin Resources, Inc., San Mateo, Calif., 1965—, exec. v.p., chief investment officer, dir.; sr. v.p., asst. sec. Franklin Templeton Distbrs., Inc.; pres. Franklin Advisers, Inc.; now v.p. Traiting Portfolio. Mem. exec. com., bd. govs. Investment Co. Inst.; trustee Santa Clara U., Washington and Lee U.; chmn. bd. dirs. Franklin Mgmt., Inc.; exec. v.p., sr. investment officer Franklin Trust Co.; dir. various Franklin Templeton funds; portfolio mgr. Franklin DynaTech Fund. With USMC, 1962-65. Mem. Nat. Assn. Securities Dealers (dist. conduct com.). Office: Franklin Resources Inc Templeton Group 777 Mariners Island Blvd San Mateo CA 94404-1585

JOHNSON, STEPHEN CHARLES, exercise physiology and sport science educator; b. Vancouver, Wash., Sept. 15, 1950; s. Russell Cahrles and Jeanne (Stephens) J.; m. Marianne Griffith, Dec. 27, 1971 (div. 1978); m. Kristine McTavish, June 26, 1994. BS in Biology, U. Utah, 1976, PhD in Exercise Physiology, 1985. Vis. asst. prof. dept. exercise and sport sci. U. Utah, Salt Lake City, 1985-87, asst. prof. dept. exercise and sport sci., 1987-91, assoc. prof., 1991—, adj. assoc. prof. dept. bioengring., 1996—. Adj. assoc. prof. dept. bioengring. U. Utah, 1996—; adj. asst. prof. div. foods and nutrition U. Utah, 1987-98, dir. Human Performance Rsch. Lab., 1987—; dir. physiology U.S. Ski Team, Park City, Utah, 1987-90; dir. sport sci. U.S. Skiing, 1991-97; cons. to Health Rider, Inc., Salt Lake City, 1995—, Vetta Sports, Inc., Park City, 1995-96, Orthopedic Splty. Hosp., Salt Lake City, 1994—, Utah Sports Found., 1988-91; cons. cardiac rehab. Holy Cross Hosp., Salt Lake City, 1985-90; dir. project triad U.S.a. Cycling, 1998—; dir. rsch. and edn. Orthop. Specialty Hosp., 1998—. Author: Coaches Guide to Diet and Weight Control, 1990; contbr. over 100 articles and abstracts to profl. jours. Mem. Utah Gov.'s Coun. on Health and Phys. Fitness, Salt Lake City, 1986-88, chmn. sport medicine, 1988; mem. Mayor's Bicycle Com., Salt Lake City, 1986-89. Grantee Purdue Frederick Co., 1988, U.S. Olympic Com., 1990, 98, HealthRider, Inc., 1994, 95, Nat. Operating Com. on Stds. in Athletic Equipment 1994-95, U.S. Ski Team Found., 1992, 93, 94, others; named U.S. Cycling Fedn. Masters Athlete of Yr., 1989; recipient Outstanding Contbn. to Fitness award Utah Gov. Coun. on Phys. Fitness, 1988. Mem. Am. Coll. Sports Medicine, AAHPERD (chmn. sports medicine S.W. dist.), AAAS, AAUP. Democrat. Avocations: biking, alpine and back-country skiing, mountain biking, hiking. Home: 12258 Mount Baldy Dr Colorado Springs CO 80921-3669 Office: U Utah Dept Exercise & Sport Sci 230 Hper Salt Lake City UT 84112-1184

JOHNSON, STEPHEN L. state legislator, lawyer; m. Lynn Johnson; children: Jennifer Johnson Smith, Tom. BA, Whitman Coll.; JD, U. Wash. Pvt. practice; mem. Wash. Senate, Dist. 47, Olympia, 1994—; mem. health and long-term care com. Wash. Senate, Olympia, mem. jud. com., mem. rules com., mem. transp. com., mem. joint select com. on edn. restructuring, mem. joint legis. edn. fiscal study com., mem. adv. com. Office Pub. Def. Mem. Kent Sch. Bd.; mem. Green River Coll. Found., Kent Libr. Bd. Mem. Kiwanis (Kent). Republican. Office: 401B Legislative Bldg Olympia WA 98504-0001 Fax: 360-786-1999. E-mail: johnson_st@leg.wa.gov

JOHNSON, THOMAS FLOYD, former college president, educator; b. Detroit, June 1, 1943; s. Edward Eugene and Adella Madeline (Norton) J.; m. Michele Elizabeth Myers, Mar. 26, 1965; children: Jason, Amy, Sarah. BPh, Wayne State U., 1965; BD, Fuller Theol. Sem., 1968; ThM, Princeton Sem., 1969; PhD, Duke U., 1979. Pastor Presbyn. Ch. U.S.A., Pa., Mich., 1969-76; asst. prof. U. Sioux Falls, S.D., 1978-83; acad. dean Sioux Falls (S.D.) Coll., 1981-83, pres., 1988-97; prof. N.Am. Baptist Sem., Sioux Falls, 1983-88; dean, prof. biblical theology George Fox Evangelical Sem., Newberg, Oreg., 1997—; interim pres. George Fox U., Newberg, 1997-98. Contbr. 9 articles to Internat. Standard Bible Ency., 1988; author: 1, 2, and 3 John New International Biblical Commentary, 1993. Bd. dirs. Children's Home Soc. S.D., Sioux Falls, 1980-86, S.D. Symphony Orch., 1988-92, Carroll Inst., 1989-93, Coalition Christian Colls. and Univs., 1992-97. Mem. Am. Bapt. Assn. Colls. and Univs. (pres. 1992-94), Soc. Bibl. Lit., Sioux Falls C. of C. (bd. dirs. 1992-95), Rotary (bd. dirs. Downtown Club 1991-95, pres. 1993-94). Office: George Fox Univ 12753 SW 68th Ave Portland OR 97223-8305 E-mail: tjohnson@georgefox.edu

JOHNSON, THOMAS WEBBER, JR. lawyer; b. Indpls., Oct. 18, 1941; s. Thomas W. and Mary Lucinda (Webber) J.; m. Sandra Kay McMahon, Aug. 15, 1964 (div. 1986); m. Deborah Joan Collins, May 17, 1987 (div. 1990); m. Barbara Joyce Walter, Mar. 13, 1992. BS in Edn., Ind. U., 1963, JD summa cum laude, 1969. Bar: Ind. 1969, Calif. 1970. Law clk. Ind. Supreme Ct., Indpls., 1968-69; assoc. Irell & Manella, L.A., 1969-76, ptnr., 1976-84, Irell & Manella , Newport Beach, Calif., 1984—99; atty. Irell & Manella, of counsel, 2000—. Chair Com. on Group Ins. Programs for State Bar of Calif., San Francisco, 1978-79; adj. prof. law UCLA, 1996—; lectr. for Practicing Law Inst., Calif. Continuing Edn. of the Bar, Calif. Judges Assn., seminars on ins. and bus. litigation. Editor-in-chief: Ind. Law Review, 1968-69; contbr. articles to profl. jours. With USNR, 1959-65. Named Outstanding Grad. Province XII, Phi Delta Phi legal fraternity, 1969. Mem. ABA (lectr. chair ins. coverage litigation com., tort and ins. practice sec. 1995-96), Calif. Bar Assn., Orange County Bar Assn., Masons, Newport Beach Country Club. Republican. Mem. Christian Ch. Office: Irell & Manella 840 Newport Center Dr Ste 400 Newport Beach CA 92660-6323

JOHNSON, VAN R. health facility administrator; b. Idaho; BS, Brigham Young U.; MS, U. Minn. Past sr. mgr. Intermountain Healthcare Corp., Salt Lake City; past sr. v.p., COO Sutter Health, Sacramento, now pres., CEO. Bd. dirs. Boy Scouts Am. Golden Empire Coun. Recipient award of distinction Hosp. Coun. No. and Ctrl. Calif., 1996. Office: Sutter Health 1 Capitol Mall Sacramento CA 95814-3229

JOHNSON, WAYNE EATON, writer, editor, former drama critic; b. Phoenix, May 9, 1930; s. Roscoe and Marion (Eaton) J.; children: Katherine, Jeffrey. BA, U. Colo., 1952; postgrad., Duke U., 1952-53; postgrad. (KLM polit. reporting fellow 1957), U. Vienna, Austria, 1955-56; MA, UCLA, 1957. Reporter Internat. News Service, Des Moines, 1958, Wheat Ridge (Colo.) Advocate, 1957, Pueblo (Colo.) Chieftain, 1959, Denver Post, 1960, editl. writer, music critic, 1961-65; arts and entertainment editor Seattle Times, 1965-82, drama critic, 1980-92. Instr. journalism Colo. Woman's Coll., 1962 Author: Show: A Concert Program for Actor and Orchestra, 1971, America! A Concert of American Images, Words and Music, 1973, From Where the Sun Now Stands: The Indian Experience, 1973, Let's Go On: Pacific Northwest Ballet at 25, 1997; editor, co-pub.: Secrets of Warmth, 1992, Footprints on the Peaks, 1995, The Burgess Book of Lies, 1995. With CIC AUS, 1953-55, Korea. Home: 11303 Durland Pl NE Seattle WA 98125-5926 E-mail: waynojvay@msn.com

JOHNSON, WAYNE HAROLD, librarian, county official; b. El Paso, Tex., May 2, 1942; s. Earl Harold and Cathryn Louise (Greeno) J.; m. Patricia Ann Froedge, June 15, 1973; children: Meredith Jessica (dec.), Alexandra Noëlle Victoria. BS, Utah State U., 1968; MPA, U. Colo., 1970; MLS, U. Okla., 1972. Circulation libr. Utah State U., Logan, 1968, adminstrv. asst. libr., 1969; with rsch. dept. Okla. Mgmt. and Engring. Cons., Norman, 1972; chief adminstrv. svcs. Wyo. State Libr., Cheyenne, 1973-76, chief bus. officer libr. archives and hist. dept., 1976-78, state libr., 1978-89; county grants mgr. Laramie County, Wyo., 1989-2001. Trustee Bibliog. Ctr. for Rsch., Denver, pres., 1983, 84; mem. Cheyenne dist. Longs Park coun. Boy Scouts Am., 1982-86; active Cheyenne Frontier Days, 1975—; mem. admissions and allocation com. United Way, 1991-94; mem. Ho. of Reps., Wyo. Legislature, 1993—; chmn. Transp. Hwys. Com., 1999—. Served with USCG, 1960-64. Mem. Aircraft Owners and Pilots Assn., Cheyenne C. of C. (chmn. transp. com. 1982, 83, military affairs com. 1994—), Am. Legion. Republican. Presbyterian. Club: No. Colo. Yacht. Lodges: Masons, Kiwanis (bd. dirs. 1986, 87).

JOHNSON, WENDY S. women's healthcare company executive; BS in Microbiology, U. Md.; MS in Clin. Microbiology, Hahnemann Med. Sch.; MBA, Loyola U., Balt. Asst. dir. Ctr. for Devices and Radiol. Health, FDA, 1976-86; internat. affairs adminstr. Coralab Rsch., 1986-88; mgr. bus. devel. Synbiotics Corp., 1988-90; v.p. bus. devel. and regulatory affairs Cytel Corp., 1990-94; v.p. corp. devel. and ops. Prizm Pharms. (now Selective Genetics Inc.), 1994-98; v.p. bus. devel. Women First Health-Care, Inc., San Diego, 1998—. Office: Women First HealthCare Inc 12220 El Camino Real Ste 400 San Diego CA 92130-2091 Fax: 619-509-1353

JOHNSON, WILLIAM LEWIS, materials science educator; b. Bowling Green, Ohio, July 26, 1948; s. Melvin Carl and Martha Maxine (Roller) J.; m. Rachel Marie Newman, Jan. 21, 1984. BA, Hamilton Coll., 1970; PhD, Calif. Inst. Tech., 1974. Mem. staff IBM Watson Rsch. Ctr., Yorktown Heights, N.Y., 1975-77; asst. prof. materials sci. Calif. Inst. Tech., Pasadena, 1977-80, assoc. prof., 1980-84, prof., 1984—, R.F. Mettler Prof. materials sci., 1989—. Cons., GM Rsch., Warren, Mich., 1983— , Amorphous Techs. Internat., Laguna,Calif., 1992—. Co-author: Glassy Metals I, 1981, Properties of Amorphous Metals, 1983, Physical Metallurgy, 1983, ASM Metals Handbook-Metallic Glasses, 1990. U.S. Steel fellow, 1971; Alexander von Humboldt fellow, 1988; recipient William-Hume-Rothery award Metals Soc., 1996. Mem. AAAS, Metals Soc. AIME, Am. Phys. Soc., Meterials Rsch. Soc. (Medal award 1998), Nat. Acad. Engring. (elected), Phi Beta Kappa, Sigma Xi. Lutheran. Home: 3546 Mountain View Ave Pasadena CA 91107-4616 Office: Calif Inst Tech Divsn Engring & Applied Scis Mail Code 138-78 Pasadena CA 91125-0001

JOHNSON, WILLIAM POTTER, newspaper publisher; b. Peoria, Ill., May 4, 1935; s. William Zweigle and Helen Marr (Potter) J.; m. Pauline Ruth Rowe, May 18, 1968; children: Darragh Elizabeth, William Potter. AB, U. Mich., 19957. Gen. mgr. Bureau County Rep., Inc., Princeton, Ill., 1961-72; pres. Johnson Newspapers, Inc., Sebastopol, Calif., 1972-75, Evergreen, Colo., 1974-86, Canyon Commons Investment, Evergreen, 1974—, Johnson Media, Inc., Granby, Colo., 1987—. Author: How the Michigan Betas Built a $1,000,000 Chapter House in the '80s. Alt. del. Rep. Nat. Conv., 1968. Lt. USNR, 1958-61. Mem. Colo. Press Assn., Nat. Newspaper Assn., Maple Bluff Country Club, Madison Club, Bishops Bay Country Club, Beta Theta Pi. Home: 5302 Lighthouse Bay Dr Madison WI 53704-1114 Office: PO Box 409 Granby CO 80446-0409

JOHNSON, WILLIAM STANLEY, metal distribution company executive; b. Elmhurst, Ill., May 11, 1957; s. Raymond J. and Nancy A. (Zinns) J.; m. Lisa Ann Grundy, July 14, 1990; 1 child, William Chase. BS in Bus. and Acctg., Ind. U., 1979; MBA in Fin., Mercer U., 1986. CPA, Calif.; CFP. Auditor, sr. auditor Ernst & Young, CPA's, Indpls., 1979-80; various fin. and acctg. positions Am. Hosp. Supply Co., Evanston, Ill., 1980-86; v.p. fin., dir. acctg. Abbey Med./Beaverbrook Group, Costa Mesa, Calif., 1987-91; corp. fin. mgr. Severin Group, Ivrine, 1991-94; corp. contr., CFO, Earle M. Jorgensen Co., Brea, 1994—. Mem. adj. faculty U. Phoenix, Fountain Valley, Calif., 1998—. Mem. FEI, AICPA, Calif. Soc. CPA's. Home: 116 Via Yella Newport Beach CA 92663-5537

JOHNSTON, BERNARD FOX, foundation executive, writer; b. Taft, Calif., Nov. 19, 1934; s. Bernard Lowe and Georgia Victoria (Fox) J.; m. Audrey Rhoades, June 9, 1956 (div. Sept. 1963); 1 child, Sheldon Bernard. BA in Creative Arts, San Francisco State U., 1957, MA in World Lit., 1958. Lectr. philosophy Coll. of Marin, Kentfield, Calif., 1957-58; lectr. humanities San Francisco State U., 1957-58, 67-68; instr. English Contra Costa Coll., San Pablo, Calif., 1958-63; Knowles Found. philosophy fellow, 1962; fellow Syracuse (N.Y.) U., 1964-66; freelance writer Piedmont, Calif., 1968-77; pres. Cinema Repertory, Inc., Point Richmond, 1978-89; pres., exec. dir. Athena Found., Tiburon, 1990—, Incline Village, Nev., 1990—. Exec. prodr. (TV series) The Heroes of Time, (TV documentary) The Shudder of Awe; CEO The Athena Found., Inc., 1997, Mahler Festival, U. Colo., Boulder, 1998. Author: (screenplay) Point Exeter, 1979, Ascent Allowed, 1988 (award); author, editor: Issues in Education: An Anthology of Controversy, 1964, The Literature of Learning, 1971; festival pianist Lake Tahoe Internat. Film Festival, 1998; resident pianist Tahoe-Chrysler Corp., 1998; pianist (CD) Time Remembered; musical dir., featured pianist Lake Tahoe Summer Music Series, 2000, piano soloist Sierra Nevada Coll. Presdl. Dinner, 2000; featured pianist Lake Tahoe Hebrew Assn. Concert, 2001. Arts grantee Silicon Valley Cmty. Found., 1998; recipient T.V. Arts award Krisch Found., 2001. Mem. Dirs. Guild Am., Writers Guild Am., Coun. for Basic Edn., Wilson Ctr. Assocs., Assn. Lit. Scholars and Critics, Smithsonian Instn., Donner Land Trust, Nat. Assn. Scholars, Calif. Assn. Scholars, San Francisco State Alumni Assn., Commonwealth Club of Calif. Avocations: classical and jazz piano, backpacking, softball. Office: 845 Southwood Blvd Ste 50 Incline Village NV 89451-9463 E-mail: athenaprods@powernet.net

JOHNSTON, BRUCE FOSTER, economics educator; b. Lincoln, Nebr., Sept. 24, 1919; s. Homer Klotz and Ethel Matilda (Hockett) J.; m. Harriet L. Pollins, Mar. 31, 1944; children— Bruce C., Patricia C. B.A., Cornell U., 1941; M.A., Stanford U., 1950, Ph.D., 1953. Agrl. mktg. adminstr. Dept. Agr., 1941-42; chief food br. econ. and sci. sect. SCAP, Tokyo, 1945-48; agrl. economist Food and Agr. div. U.S. Mission to NATO and European Regional Orgn., Paris, 1952-54; assoc. prof. econs., assoc. economist Food Research Inst., Stanford U., Calif., 1954-59, prof. econs., economist, 1959—. Cons. World Bank, FAO, others Author: (with Tomich and Kilby) Transforming Agrarian Economies: Opportunities Seized, Opportunities Missed, 1995, (with Clark) Redesigning Rural Development: A Strategic Perspective, 1982, (with Anthony, Jones and Uchendu) Agricultural Change in Tropical Africa, 1979, (with Kilby) Agriculture and Structural Transformation: Economic Strategies in Late-Developing Countries, 1975; co-editor:, contbr.: (with Ohkawa and Kaneda) Agriculture and Economic Growth: Japan's Experience, 1969. Guggenheim fellow, 1962, Internat. Inst. Applied Systems Analysis fellow, 1978-79, Adminstr.'s fellow AID, 1991. Fellow Am. Agrl. Econs. Assn.; mem. Am. Econ. Assn., African Studies Assn., Phi Beta Kappa, Phi Kappa Phi Home: 613 Walnut St Pacific Grove CA 93950-3932 Office: Stanford U Food Rsch Inst Stanford CA 94305 E-mail: bfjohn@stanford.edu

JOHNSTON, CHARLES, protective services official; BA in Law Enforcement Adminstrn., San Jose State U.; MPA, U. No. Colo.; grad., Nat. Acad. FBI; attended, Harvard U., Northwestern U., U. Denver, U. Colo. Police officer Salinas (Calif.) Police Dept., Lakewood (Calif.) Police Dept., 1970-80, acting chief of police, 1980-81, chief of police, 1981—. Active Colo. Peace Officer Stds. and Tng. Bd., Justice Assistance Act Adv. Bd. Mem. Jefferson County coun. ARC; chmn. steering com. Law Enforcement Torch Run; active Colo. Spl. Olympics. Decorated Bronze star (4), Purple Heart, Army Air medal; recipient Man of Yr. award Lakewood Sentinel, 1984, Hall of Fame award Lakewood/South Jefferson County C. of C., 1989; named Vol. of Yr., Colo. Spl. Olympics Hall of Fame, 1990. Office: Lakewood Police Dept 445 S Allison Pkwy Lakewood CO 80226-3106

JOHNSTON, CHARLES H., JR. career officer; married; two children. Grad., Aviation Officer Candidate, Program, 1973; MS in Aeronaut. Systems, U. W. Fla. Commd. USN, 1973; various to aerospace engring. duty officer USS Forrestal, 1981-86; project dir. Ordnance Br. head, chief test pilot Naval Air Test Ctr., 1986-89; exec. officer to commanding officer NAVPRO, Melbourne, Australia, 1989-92; officer F/A-18 Program Office/Tactical Aircraft Program, 1989-96; program mgr. convential strike weapons PEO TAC, 1996-99; rear adm. USN, 1999—; comdr. Weapons Divsn. Naval Air Warfare Ctr., 1999—. Decorated Navy Meritorious Svc. medal, Navy Commendation medal, Navy Achievement medal, others.

JOHNSTON, GERALD E. manufacturing company executive; V.p., gen. mgr. Kingsford Products; v.p. corp. devel. and planning Procter and Gamble; with Clorox Co., Oakland, Calif., 1981—, pres., COO, 1999—. Office: Clorox Co 1221 Broadway Oakland CA 94612-1888

JOHNSTON, GWINAVERE ADAMS, public relations consultant; b. Casper, Wyo., Jan. 6, 1943; d. Donald Milton Adams and Gwinavere Marie (Newell) Quillen; m. H.R. Johnston, Sept. 26, 1963 (div. 1973); children: Gwinavere G., Gabrielle Suzanne; m. Donald Charles Cannalte, Apr. 4, 1981. BS in Journalism, U. Wyo., 1966; postgrad., Denver U., 1968-69. Editor, reporter Laramie (Wyo.) Daily Boomerang, 1965-66; account exec. William Kostka Assocs., Denver, 1966-71, v.p., 1969-71; exec. v.p. Slottow, McKinlay & Johnston, Denver, 1971-74; pres. The Johnston Group, Denver, 1974-92; chair, CEO JohnstonWells Pub. Rels., Denver, 1992—. Adj. faculty U. Colo. Sch. Journalism, 1988-90. Bd. dirs. Leadership Denver Assn., 1975-77, 83-86, Mile High United Way, 1989-95, Denver's 2% Club, chair, 1996—; bd. dirs. Spring Inst., 1997—, Lower Downtown Denver, Inc.; bd. dirs. Colo. Jud. Inst., 1991—, Inst. for Internat. Edn., 1998-99, U. Wyo. Found., 2000—. Recipient Athena award Colo. C. of C., 1999. Fellow Am. Pub. Rels. Soc. (pres. Colo. chpt. 1978-79, bd. dirs. 1975-80, 83-86, nat. exec. com. Counselor's Acad. 1988-93, sec.-treas. 1994, pres.-elect 1995, pres. 1996, profl. award Disting. Svc. award 1992); mem. Colo. Women's Forum, Rocky Mountain Pub. Rels. Group (founder), Denver Athletic Club, Denver Press Club. Republican. Home: 717 Monaco Pky Denver CO 80220-6040 Office: JohnstonWells Pub Rels 1512 Larimer St Ste 720 Denver CO 80202-1610

JOHNSTON, HAROLD S(LEDGE), chemistry educator; b. Woodstock, Ga., Oct. 11, 1920; s. Smith L. and Florine (Dial) J.; m. Mary Ella Stay, Dec. 29, 1948; children: Shirley Louise, Linda Marie, David Finley, Barbara Dial. AB, Emory U., 1941, ScD (hon.), 1965; PhD, Calif. Inst. Tech., 1948. Instr. to assoc. prof. chemistry Stanford (Calif.) U., 1947-56; assoc. prof. Calif. Inst. Tech., Pasadena, 1956-57; prof. U. Calif., Berkeley, 1957-91, dean, coll. chemistry, 1966-70, prof. emeritus, 1991—. Vis. prof. U. Rome, 1964; adv. com. Calif. Statewide Air Pollution Rsch.Ctr., 1969-73, Nat. Ctr. Atmospheric Rsch., 1975-78, FAA High Altitude Polution Program; vis. adv. com. Brookhaven Nat. Lab., 1970-73; faculty rsch. lectr. U. Calif., Berkeley, 1989. Author: Gas Phase Reaction Rate Theory, 1966, Gas Phase Reaction Kinetics of Neutral Oxygen Species, 1968, Reduction of Stratospheric Ozone by Nitrogen Oxide Catalysts from Supersonic Transport Exhaust, 1971; contbr. articles to profl. jours. Recipient Tyler prize Environ. Achievement, 1983, Disting. Alumni award Calif. Inst. Tech., 1985, NAS award for Chemistry in Service to Society Nat. Acad. of Sciences, 1993, Nat. Medal of Scis., 1997; grantee Materials and Molecular Rsch. divsn. Lawrence Berkeley Lab., 1966—. Fellow AAAS, Am. Chem. Soc. (Gold Medal award Calif. sect. 1956, Pollution Control award 1974, award in the Chemistry of Contemporary Technol. Problems 1985), Am. Phys. Soc., Am. Geophys. Union (Roger Revelle medal 1998), Nat. Acad. Scis. (adv. panel to Nat. Bur. Standards, 1965-67, com. Motor Vehicle Emissions, 1971-75, Svc. to Soc. award in chemistry 1993), Am. Assn. Arts and Scis., Sigma Xi (nat. lectr. 1973). Home: 132 Highland Blvd Berkeley CA 94708-1023 Office: U Calif Dept Chemistry Berkeley CA 94720-0001*

JOHNSTON, KRISTEN, television personality; b. Washington, Sept. 20, 1967; BFA, N.Y. Univ. Mem. Atlantic Theatre Co., Chelsea, N.Y.; actress CBS Television, L.A. Appeared in numerous stage productions; guest appearances on television include Chicago Hope, Heart's Afire, The Five Mrs. Buchanans; TV series Third Rock from the Sun; movies include Austin Powers: The Spy Who Shagged Me, 1999. Office: 3rd Rock from the Sun c/o Carsey Werner Prods 4024 Radford Ave Bldg 3 Studio City CA 91604-2101

JOHNSTON, NORMAN JOHN, architecture educator, department chairman; b. Seattle, Dec. 3, 1918; s. Jay and Helen May (Shultis) J.; m. Lois Jane Hastings, Nov. 22, 1969. B.A., U. Wash.-Seattle, 1942; B.Arch., U. Oreg., 1949; M. in Urban Planning, U. Pa.-Phila., 1959, Ph.D., 1964. Registered architect, Wash. City planner Seattle City Planning Commn., 1951-55; asst. prof. arch. U. Oreg.-Eugene, 1956-58; assoc. prof. architecture and urban planning U. Wash.-Seattle, 1960-64, prof., 1964-85, prof. emeritus, 1985—, assoc. dean, 1964-76, 79-84, chmn. dept. architecture, 1984-85. Mem. nat. exams. com. Nat. Coun. Archtl. Registration Bds., Washington, 1970-81, 88-99; vis. prof. Tokyo Inst. Tech., 1991, 98; mem. Wash. State Archtl. Registration Bd., 1998-2000, chmn., 1992, 99. Author: Cities in the Round, 1983, Washington's Audacious State Capitol and its Builders, 1988 (Gov.'s Book award 1984, 89), The College of Architecture and Urban Planning, 75 Years at the University of Washington: A Personal View, 1991, The Fountain and the Mountain - The University of Washington Campus, 1895-1995, 1995, National Guide Series: The University of Washington, 2001; editor: NCARB Architectural Registration Handbook, 1980; contbr. articles to profl. jours. Mem. King County Policy Devel. Commn., Seattle, 1970-76; mem. Capitol campus design adv. com. State of Wash., Olympia, 1982-2000, chmn., 1980-88, 96; trustee Mus. History and Industry, 1997—. Recipient Wash. Disting. Citizen award, 1987. Fellow AIA (pres. Seattle chpt. 1981, AIA medal Seattle chpt. 1991, Washington Coun. medal 1997); mem. Phi Beta Kappa, Sigma Chi, Tau Sigma Delta. Presbyterian. Home: 900 University St Apt Au Seattle WA 98101-1778 Office: U Wash C Architecture & Urban Planning PO Box 355726 Seattle WA 98195-5726 E-mail: njjo@u.washington.edu

JOHNSTON, OLIVER MARTIN, JR. animator; b. Palo Alto, Calif., Oct. 31, 1912; s. Oliver Martin and Arclissa Florence (Boggs) J.; m. Marie Estelle Worthey, Jan. 23, 1943; children: Richard Oliver, Kenneth Andrew. Student, Stanford U., 1931-34, U. Calif., Berkeley, 1932, Chouinard Art Inst., , 1934-35. Directing animator Walt Disney Co., Burbank, Calif., 1935-78. Lectr., spkr. in field. Asst. animator Snow White and the Seven Dwarfs, 1937; animation supr. Fantasia, 1940, Bambi, 1942; animator Pinnochio, 1940, The Fox and the Hound, 1981, Victory Through Air Power, 1943, The Three Caballeros, 1945, Make Mine Music, 1946; directing animator Song of the South, 1946, Melody Time, 1948, The Adventures of Ichabod and Mr. Toad, 1949, Cinderella, 1950, Alice in Wonderland, 1951, Peter Pan, 1953, Lady and the Tramp, 1955, Sleeping Beauty, 1959, 101 Dalmatians, 1961, Sword in the Stone, 1963, Mary Poppins, 1964, The Jungle Book, 1967, The Aristocats, 1970, Robin Hood, 1973, Rescuers, 1977, also shorts and TV cartoons; author: Disney Animation -- The Illusion of Life, 1981, Too Funny For Words, 1987, Bambi-the Story and the Film, 1990, Jungle Book Portfolio, 1992, The Disney Villain, English edit., 1993, French edit., 1995; contbg. editor sketch book series; subject of documentary Frank and Ollie; drawings exhibited in Whitney Mus., N.Y.C., 1981. Guest spkr. Russian Govt. and Soyuzmultifilm, 1976, other East European Countries, U.S. Info. Agy. Cultural Exch. Program, 1986. Recipient Pioneer in Film award Delta Kappa Allpha, 1978, honor award Mus. Modern Art, 1978, Annie award Internat. Animated Film Soc., 1980, Disney Legend award, 1989, Grand Prix of the Ams., 1995. Avocations: trains, reading, studying, sports. Address: 748 Flintridge Ave Flintridge CA 91011-4027

JOHNSTON, PATRICK, state senator; b. San Francisco, Sept. 3, 1946; m. Margaret Mary Nevin. BA in Philosophy, St. Patrick's Coll. Mem. Calif. State Assembly, 1981-90, Calif. State Senate, 1991-, chair appropriations com., 1991-, mem. natural resources and wildlife com., 1991, mem. energy, utilities and comms. com., mem. ins. com., mem. agr. and water resources com., mem. local govt. com. Democrat. Office: State Capitol Rm 5066 Sacramento CA 95814 also: 1020 N St Ste 504 Sacramento CA 95814-5624 also: 31 E Channel St Ste 440 Stockton CA 95202-2314 E-mail: Senator.Johnston@sen.ca.gov

JOHNSTON, RICHARD BOLES, JR. pediatrician, educator, biomedical researcher; b. Atlanta, Aug. 23, 1935; s. Richard Boles and Jane (Dillon) J.; m. Mary Anne Claiborne, Aug. 13, 1960; children: Richard B. III, S. Claiborne, Kristin M. BA, Vanderbilt U., 1957, MD, 1961; MS (hon.), U. Pa., 1986. Diplomate Am. Bd. Pediatrics, Am. Bd. Pediatric Infectious Disease. Resident in pediat. Vanderbilt U., 1961-63, Harvard U., 1963-64, fellow pediat. immunology, 1967-70; asst. prof., assoc. prof. depts. pediat. and microbiology U. Ala. Med. Ctr., Birmingham, 1970-76; vis. assoc. prof. Rockefeller U., N.Y.C., 1976-77, vis. prof., 1983-84; prof. pediat. U. Colo. Sch. Medicine, Denver, 1977-86; chmn. dept. pediat. Nat. Jewish Ctr. Immunology and Respiratory Medicine, Denver, 1977-86, U. Pa. Sch. Medicine, Phila., 1986-90, Wm. H. Bennett prof. pediat., 1986-92; med. dir. March of Dimes Birth Defects Found., White Plains, N.Y., 1992-98. Adj. prof. pediat, chief sec. pediat. immunology Yale U. Sch. Medicine, 1992-98; prof. pediatrics Sch. Medicine U. Colo., Denver, 1999—; bd. trustees Internat. Pediatric Rsch. Found., 1983-87, 95-98, chmn. 1984-87, 97-98; chmn. adv. bd. for vaccines and related biols. FDA, Bethesda, Md., 1990-93; chmn. com. vaccine safety, Inst. Medicine, 1992-93, chmn. com new rsch. in vaccines, 1993-94, chmn. forum vaccine safety, 1995-98, chmn. com. asthma and indoor air, 1998-99, mem bd. health promotion disease prevention, 1994—, chmn. com. rsch. in multiple sclerosis, 1999-2001. Mem. editl. bd. 7 profl. jours., 1978—; contbr. 250 articles to profl. jours.; editor Current Opinion in Pediatrics, 1997—. Capt. M.C., U.S. Army, 1964-66. Faculty scholar Josiah Macy Jr. Found., 1976-77; recipient Commr. citation and Wiley medal FDA, 1994. Fellow AAAS; mem. Inst. Medicine NAS, Am. Soc. Clin. Investigation, Am. Pediat. Soc. (pres. 1996-97), Assn. Am. Physicians, Soc. Pediat. Rsch. (pres. 1980-81). Office: Nat Jewish Med and Rsch Ctr 1400 Jackson St Denver CO 80206-2761 E-mail: johnstonr@njc.org

JOHNSTON, RICHARD C. newspaper editor; BS, Portland State U., 1965. Reporter The Oregonian, Portland, 1965-66, asst. city editor, 1966-79, Washington corr., 1979-82, asst. mng. editor, 1982-94, asst. to the editor, 1994—. Office: The Oregonian 1320 SW Broadway Portland OR 97201-3499

JOHNSTON, ROBERT JAKE, federal magistrate judge; b. Denver, Sept. 30, 1947; m. Julie Ann Black; children: Jennifer, Robert, Jr., Michelle. BS, Brigham Young U., 1973; JD, U. Pacific, 1977. Bar: Nev. 1977, U.S. Dist. Ct. Nev. 1978, U.S. Ct. Appeals (9th cir.) 1984. Law clk. to Hon. Merlyn Hoyt Nev. 7th Judicial Dist., Ely, 1977-78; dist. atty. White Pine County, Ely, 1979-82; pvt. practice Johnston & Fairman, Ely, 1979-82; deputy dist. atty. Office Clark County Dist. Atty., Las Vegas, Nev., 1983-84; asst. U.S. atty. Office U.S. Atty., Las Vegas, 1984-87, chief civil div., 1986-87; U.S. magistrate judge U.S. Dist. Ct., Las Vegas, 1987—. Dir. Boy Scouts Am. Boulder Dam Area Coun., Las Vegas. With U.S. Army, 1967-70. Mem. Nev. Bar Assn., Clark County Bar Assn., Fed. Magistrate Judicial Assn. (dir. 1990-92), Las Vegas Track Club, 9th Jud. Cir. Hist. Soc., Southwest Oral History Soc. Office: US Dist Ct Ste 3005 333 Las Vegas Blvd S Las Vegas NV 89101

JOHNSTON, ROY G. consulting structural engineer; b. Chgo., Jan. 7, 1914; s. Karl Gunnar and Esther M. (Youngberg) J.; m. Naomi Harmon, July 30, 1936 (dec.); children: Judith R., Robert K.; m. Lucille Peterson, Dec. 28, 1991. B.S.C.E., U. So. Calif., 1935. Cert. civil and structural engr., Calif. Plan checker County of Los Angeles, 1935; structural designer C. Devel., Los Angeles, 1936-44; structural engr. Lummis Co., Los Angeles, 1944-45, Brandow & Johnston, Los Angeles, 1945-64; v.p., structural engr. Brandow & Johnston Assocs., Los Angeles, 1964—. Mem. structural safety com. VA, 1973-91; mem. Calif. Bd. Registration Engrs., 1971-78, pres., 1975-76; past chmn. Bldg. Seismic Safety Coun., Washington, 1982-85; mem. State Bldg. Stds. Commn., Calif., 1985-94; mem. steering com. 8th World Conf. Earthquake Engring., 1984; cons. U.S.-Japan Seismic Rsch. Program, 1980-87; lectr. earthquake engring. seminars. Contbr. articles to profl. jours. Trustee Westmont Coll., 1964—, chmn., 1972-88. Recipient Disting. Alumni award U. So. Calif., 1972, 82, George Washington award Inst. Advancement Engring., L.A., 1985; named Constrn. Man Yr., Constrn. Industry so. Calif., 1981, Engr. of Yr. SEOSC, 1990, Pres. award Tall Bldg. Coun., 1994, SEAOSC S.B. Barnes Lifetime Achievement award, 2000. Fellow ASCE, Am. Concrete Inst.; mem. NAE, Earthquake Engring. Rsch. Inst. (bd. dirs., v.p.), Structurals Engr. Assn. (Calif. pres.), Structurals Engrs. So. Calif. (pres., engr. of Yr. 1990), Nat. Acad. Engrs. Republican Avocations: travelling; golf. Office: Brandow & Johnston Assocs 1660 W 3rd St Los Angeles CA 90017-1138

JOHNSTON, VIRGINIA EVELYN, editor; b. Spokane, Wash., Apr. 26, 1933; d. Edwin and Emma Lucile (Munroe) Rowe; m. Alan Paul Beckley, Dec. 26, 1974; children: Chris, Denise, Rex. Student, Portland C.C., 1964, Portland State U., 1966, 78-79. Proofreader the Oregonian, Portland, 1960-62, teletypesetter operator, 1962-66, operator Photon 200, 1966-68, copy editor, asst. women's editor, 1968-80, spl. sects. editor (UPDATE), 1981-83, editor FOODay, 1982—. Pres. Matrix Assos., Inc., Portland, 1975—, chmn. bd., 1979—; past pres. Bones & Brew Inc., now chmn. bd. dirs. Editor Principles of Computer Systems for Newspaper Mgmt., 1975-76. Cons. Dem. Party Oreg., 1969, Portland Sch. Dist. No. 1, 1978. Mem. Assn. of Food Journalists, Internat. Assn. of Cooking Profls., Portland Culinary Alliance, Eating and Drinking Soc. Oreg. (past pres.), We. Culinary Inst. (mem. adv. bd.), Internat. Food Media Conf. (past mem. adv. bd.). Democrat. Home: 4140 NE 137th Ave Portland OR 97230-2624 Office: Oregonian Pub Co 1320 SW Broadway Portland OR 97201-3499 E-mail: gingerjohnston@news.oregonian.com

JOHNSTON, WILLIAM FREDERICK, emergency services administrator; b. Oakridge, Tenn., Mar. 4, 1945; s. Leonard E. and Helene C. (Spicker) J.; m. Kathleen Jo Hotaling, Nov. 17, 1988; 1 child, Lindsey Anne. BS, U. Wash., 1969, MS, 1971, MD, 1974, MBA, 1998. Diplomate Am. Bd. Emergency Medicine. Med. intern U. Wash. Affiliated Hosps., Seattle, 1971-75; emergency medicine resident Valley Med. Ctr. Fresno/U. Calif. San Francisco, Fresno, 1975-77; pres., CEO N.W. Emergency Physicians, Seattle, 1977-81; med. dir. emergency svcs. N.W. Hosp., Seattle, 1977—. Bd. dirs. First Choice Health Plan, Inc., First Choice Health Network, Inc., Washington Casualty Co., N.W. Healthcare Ins. Svcs. Contbr. articles to med. jours. Fellow Am. Coll. Emergency Physicians. Avocations: skiing, hiking, kayaking. Home: 4731 Beach Dr SW Seattle WA 98116-4340 Office: N W Hosp 1550 N 115th St Seattle WA 98133-8498 E-mail: billj@nwlink.com

JOLLES, BERNARD, lawyer; b. N.Y.C., Oct. 5, 1928; s. Harry and Dora (Hirschorn) J.; m. Lenore Madison Jolles, Oct. 11, 1953 (div. Jan. 1984); children: Abbe, Jacqueline, Caroline. BA, N.Y.U., 1951; LLB, Lewis & Clark Coll., 1961. Bar: Oreg. 1963, U.S. Dist. Ct. Oreg. 1964, U.S. Dist. Ct. (no. dist.) Miss. 1968, U.S. Ct. Appeals (9th cir.) 1965, U.S. Supreme Ct. 1979. Assoc. Anderson Franklin Jones & Olsen, Portland, Oreg., 1963-68; ptnr. Franklin Olsen Bennett & Desbarsay, Portland, 1968-79, Jolles Bernstein & Garone and predecessor firms Jolles Sokol & Bernstein, Portland, 1979—. Editor: Damages, 1974. Bd. dirs. ACLU, Portland, Oreg., 1975—. Fellow Am. Coll. Trial Lawyers; mem. Oreg. State Bar Assn. (pres. 1986-87), Am. Inns of Ct. (sr. barrister 1985—). Avocations: cooking, reading. Office: Jolles Bernstein & Garone 721 SW Oak St Fl 2 Portland OR 97205-3712

JOLLEY, R. GARDNER, lawyer; b. Salt Lake City, May 12, 1944; s. Reuben G. and Varno J.; m. Sharon Lea Thomas, Aug. 21, 1965; children—Christopher Gardner and Jennifer Lea. B.S. in Econs., U. Utah, 1966; J.D., U. Calif.-Berkeley, 1969. Bar: Calif. 1970, Nev. 1970, U.S. Dist. Ct. Nev. 1970. Law clk. to presiding justice Nev. Supreme Ct., 1969-70; assoc. Wiener, Goldwater and Galatz, Las Vegas, 1970-73; ptnr. Jolley, Urga, Wirth & Woodbury, Las Vegas, Nev., 1974— ; lectr. new law clks. for Nev. judges, 1973-74; instr. Clark County Community Coll., 1975-77; instr. Nev. Continuing Legal Edn., 1983. Bd. dirs. Catholic Community Services, 1973-80; bd. govs. Easter Seal Soc., 1977-78. Mem. Nev. State Bar Assn. (bd. govs. 1976-86, pres. 1985-86), ABA (Nev. rep. to Ho. Dels. 1986-88), Assn. Trial Lawyers Am., Nev. Trial Lawyers Assn.

JONAITIS, ALDONA CLAIRE, museum administrator, art historian; b. N.Y.C., Nov. 27, 1948; d. Thomas and Demie (Genaitis) J. BA, SUNY, Stony Brook, 1969; MA, Columbia U., 1972, PhD, 1977. Chair art dept. SUNY, Stony Brook, 1983-85, assoc. provost, 1985-86, vice provost undergrad. studies, 1986-89; v.p. for pub. programs Am. Mus. Natural History, N.Y.C., 1989-93; dir. U. Alaska Mus., Fairbanks, 1993—. Author: From the Land of the Totem Poles, 1988; editor, author: Chiefly Feasts: The Enduring Kwakiutl Potlatch, 1991; editor: A Wealth of Thought: Franz Boas on Native American Art History, 1995, Looking North: Art from the University of Alaska Museum, 1998, The Yuquot Whaler's Shrine, 1999. Mem. Am. Assn. Mus. (bd. dirs. 1999-2002), Am. Assn. Mus./ICOM (bd. dirs. 2000-2003), Native Am. Art Studies Assn. (bd. dirs. 1985-95). Office: U Alaska Mus 907 Yukon Dr Fairbanks AK 99775 E-mail: ffaj@naf.edu

JONAS, TONY, television executive; Dir. dramatic series Aaron Spelling Prodns.; v.p. dramatic series and long form programming MGM/UA TV Group; sr. exec. in charge of devel. Winkler/Rich Prodns., Paramount; v.p. devel. Disney TV; sr. v.p. drama devel. Warner Bros. TV (previously Lorimar TV), 1989-91, exec. v.p. creative affairs, 1991-95, pres., 1995-98, Tony Jonas Prodns., Burbank, Calif., 1999—. Office: Tony Jonas Prodns Bldg 34 Rm 100 4000 Warner Blvd Burbank CA 91522-0001

JONASSEN, JAMES O. architect; b. Aberdeen, Wash., July 23, 1940; s. James E. and Marjorie E. (Smith) J.; m. Patricia E. Glen, June 9, 1958 (div. Oct. 1975); m. Marilyn Joan Kampa, June 11, 1977; children: Christian A., Steven E. BArch, U. Wash., 1964; MS in Architecture, Columbia U., 1965. Registered architect Ala., Alaska, Ariz., Calif., Colo., Fla., Ga., Idaho, Ill., Kans., La., Minn., Mo., Mont., Nebr., Nev., N.Mex., N.C., N.C., Ohio, Okla., Oreg., S.D., Tex. Wash., Utah., Wis., D.C., Del. Mass. Miss., N.H., N.Y., R.I., Vt., P.R., British Columbia, Can. Designer NBBJ Group, Seattle, 1965-70, ptnr., 1970—; CEO NBBJ West, 1983-96, mng. ptnr., 1997—. Bd. dirs. Health Insights Found. Prin works include Bettelle Meml. Lab., Richland, Wash., 1965 (lab of yr. award 1968), Heath Profl. Bldg., 1970, Children's Orthopedic Hosp., Seattle, 1972 (AIA Honor award 1976), St. Mary's Hosp., Surg. Pavilion, Rochester, Minn., 1982, St. Vincent Med. Office Bldg., Portland, Oreg., 1983, Scottsdale Meml. Hosp. N., Ariz., 1984, Seattle VA Hosp., 1985, Stanford U. Hosp., 1986, St. Joseph Host. Med. Ctr., 1988, Providence Med./ Ctr., Seattle, 1990 (AIA Merit award), David Grant Med. Ctr., Fairfield, Calif., 1986 (USAF Honor award 1989, Spl. citation DOD 1988, Type i Honor award USAF 1989, Excellence in Design award DOD 1991), Alaska Native Med. Ctr., 1997, Kangbuk Med. Ctr., Seoul, Korea, 1998, Capital Coast Health Med. Ctr., Wellington, New Zealand, 2000. Bd. dirs. Health Facilities Rsch. and Edn. Project, 1991-98, Swedish Med. Ctr. Found., 1993—, Sch. Zone Inst., 1990—; pres. bd. Architecture and Children project, 1990-92. Recipient Seattle Newsmaker Tomorrow award Time Mag., 1978, Modern Health Care awards Swedish Med. Ctr., 1997-2000; Naramore Found. fellow, 1969; Columbia U. scholar, 1964. Fellow AIA (chmn. steering com. 1983-85, nat. com. architecture for health, mem. Nat. Life Cycle Task Force 1977, bd. dirs. Seattle chpt. 1985-87, Modern Healthcare award 1998); mem. Sr. Coun. Archs. (pres. 1999, 2000), Wash. Athletic Club, Colunbia Tower Club, Rotary. Office: NBBJ 111 S Jackson St Seattle WA 98104-2881

JONES, A. DURAND, park administrator; Chief supt. Rocky Mountain Nat. Park, Estes Park, Colo. Office: Rocky Mountain Nat Park Estes Park CO 80517

JONES, BILL, state official, rancher; b. Coalinga, Calif., Dec. 20, 1949; s. C.W. and Cora Jones; m. Maurine Abramson, Aug. 29, 1971; children: Wendy, Andrea. BS in Agribus. and Plant Sci., Calif. State U., Fresno, 1971. Ptnr. ranch, nr. Firebaugh, Calif.; mem. Calif. Assembly, Sacramento, 1983—, Rep. leader, 1991—; Sec. of State State of California, 1994—. Former chmn. Fresno County Rep. Cen. Com. Named Outstanding Young Farmer, Fresno C. of C. Mem. Fresno County and City C. of C. (past bd. dirs.). Methodist. Avocations: horseback riding, golf, flying, travel. Home: 2254 W Dovewood Ln Fresno CA 93711-2810 Office: Office Sec State 1500 11th St Ste 600 Sacramento CA 95814

JONES, CHARLES E. state supreme court justice; BA, Brigham Young U., 1959; JD, Stanford U., 1962. Bar: Calif. 1963, U.S. Dist. Ct. Ariz. 1964, U.S. Ct. Appeals (9th cir.) 1963, Ariz. 1964, U.S. Ct. Appeals (10th cir.) 1974, U.S. Supreme Ct. 1979. Law clk. to Hon. Richard H. Chambers U.S. Ct. Appeals (9th cir.), 1962-63; assoc., ptnr. Jennings, Strouss & Salmon, Phoenix, 1963-96; apptd. justice Ariz. Supreme Ct., Phoenix, 1996, vice chief justice, 1997—. Bd. visitors Brigham Young U. Law Sch., 1973-81, chmn., 1978-81. Named Avocat du Consulat-Gen. de France, 1981—; Alumni Dist. Svc. award Brigham Young U., 1982; recipient Aaron Feuerstein award U. Ariz., 1998. Mem. ABA, State Bar Ariz., Fed. Bar Assn. (pres. Ariz. chpt. 1971-73), J. Reuben Clark Law Soc. (nat. chmn. 1994-97), Maricopa County Bar Assn., Am. Coll. Labor & Employment Lawyers, Pi Sigma Alpha. Office: Ariz Supreme Court 1501 W Washington St Phoenix AZ 85007-3222

JONES, CHARLES IRVING, bishop; b. El Paso, Tex., Sept. 13, 1943; s. Charles I. Jr. and Helen A. (Heyward) J.; m. Ashby MacArthur, June 18, 1966; children: Charles I. IV, Courtney M., Frederic M., Keith A. BS, The Citadel, 1965; MBA, U. N.C., 1966; MDiv, U. of the South, 1977, DD, 1989. CPA. Pub. acctg. D.E. Gatewood and Co., Winston-Salem, N.C., 1966-72; dir. devel. Chatham (Va.) Hall, 1972-74; instr. acctg. U. of the South, Sewanee, Tenn., 1974-77; coll. chaplain Western Ky. U., Bowling Green, 1977-81; vicar Trinity Episcopal Ch., Russelville, Ky., 1977-85; archdeacon Diocese of Ky., Louisville, 1981-86; bishop Episcopal Diocese of Mont., Helena, 1986-2001. Bd. dirs. New Directions Ministries, Inc., N.Y.C.; mem. standing com. Joint Commn. on Chs. in Small Communities, 1988-91, Program, Budget and Fin., 1991-94; v.p. province VI Episcopal Ch., 1991-94, mem. Presiding Bishop's Coun. Advice, 1991-94. Author: Mission Strategy in the 21st Century, 1989, Total Ministry: A Practical Approach, 1993; bd. editors Grass Roots, Luling, Tex., 1985-90; contbr. articles to profl. jours. Founder Concerned Citizens for Children, Russelville, 1981; bd. dirs. St. Peter's Hosp., Helena, 1986-2001; bd. dirs. Christian Ministry in Nat. Parks, 1992—. With USMCR, 1961-65. Mem. Aircraft Owners and Pilots Assn. Avocations: running, flying, writing, skiing. Office: Diocese Mont 515 N Park Ave Helena MT 59601-2703 E-mail: bpci@aol.com

JONES, CHARLIE, television sports announcer; b. Ft. Smith, Ark. m. Ann; children: Chuck, Julie. JD, U. Ark., 1953. Play-by-play broadcaster Am. Football League, ABC-TV, 1960-64, NFL, NBC, 1965-98, Cin. Reds TV Network, 1973-74, USC Basketball, 1974-75, Seattle Seahawks preseason football, Sta. KING-TV, 1985-89; commentator for Wide World of Sports ABC, 1961-64; sports dir. Sta. WFAA-TV, Dallas, 1962-65, Sta. WMAQ-TV, Chgo., 1974; sports commentator NBC-TV, 1965-98; play-by-play broadcaster Colo. Rockies TV Network, 1993-95. Author: What Makes Winners Win (N.Y. Times Bestseller); Television broadcasting firsts include Super Bowl I, first Am. Football League Championship game, first Am. Football League nationally televised game, first NBC SportsWorld, first World Cup Gymnastics, first World Cup Marathon, first World Championships of Track and Field , Helsinki, 1983, first World Indoor Championships of Track and Field, Indpls., 1987, first Sr. Skins Game, Hawaii, 1988; hosted TV shows: Seahawks Insider, Almost Anything Goes, Pro-Fan; appeared in TV series: Ironside, McMillan and Wife, Columbo, The Dick Van Dyke Show, Rich Man, Poor Man; appeared in several Movies of the Week and motion pictures Personal Best, Without Limits, Return of the Killer Tomatoes, and Killer Tomatoes Strike Back. Recipient Emmy award for documentary Is Winning the Name of the Game, 1982, Outstanding Achievement award Freedoms Found. of Valley Forge, 1982, Bronze medal for co-producing, co-hosting, co-writing The American Frontier, PBS-TV, Internat. TV Festival of N.Y., 1982, Headliner of Yr. award for outstanding contbns. in field of TV San Diego Press Club, 1986, Disting. Alumnus award U. Ark., 1989; inductee Pro Football Hall of Fame, 1997, Aks. Sports Hall of Fame, 2000. Mem. Confrerie des Chevaliers du Tastevin. Office: 8080 El Paseo Grande La Jolla CA 92037-3284

JONES, CLARIS EUGENE, JR. botanist, educator; b. Columbus, Ohio, Dec. 15, 1942; s. Claris Eugene and Clara Elizabeth (Elliott) J.; m. Teresa Diane Wagner, June 26, 1966; children: Douglas Eugene, Philip Charles, Elizabeth Lynne. B.S., Ohio U., 1964; Ph.D., Ind. U., 1969. Asst. prof. botany Calif. State U., Fullerton, 1969-73, assoc. prof., 1973-77, prof. botany, 1977—, chmn. dept. biol. sci., 1989—, dir. Fullerton Arboretum, 1970-80, dir. Faye MacFadden Herbarium, 1969—; disting. faculty mem. Sch. Natural Sci. and Math., 1999—. Adj. instr. Marshall Coll. Natural Sci. and Math., 2000. Author: A Dictionary of Botany, 1980; editor: Handbook of Experimental Pollination Biology, 1983; contbr. articles to profl. jours. Mem. Am. Inst. Biol. Sci., AAAS, Bot. Soc. Am., Internat. Assn. Plant Taxonomy, Am. Soc. Plant Taxonomists, Soc. Study Evolution, Systematics Assn., Ecol. Soc. Am., Calif. Bot. Soc., Sigma Xi Methodist. Office: 800 N State College Blvd Fullerton CA 92834-6850

JONES, CLEON BOYD, research engineer; b. Norwalk, Calif., Nov. 9, 1961; s. Cleon Earl and Marjorie Helen (McDade) J. BS in Math., Biola U., 1983. Rsch. libr. Christian Rsch. Inst., San Juan Capistrano, Calif., 1981-84; flight control engr. Leading Systems, Inc., Irvine, 1984-90; sr. staff engr. Dynamic Rsch., Inc., Torrance, 1990-98; sr. flight dynamics engr. Frontier Systems, Inc., Irvine, 1998—. Recipient NASA Group Achievement award Pilot Project Team, 1994. Republican. Avocations: reading, soccer, music, theology, aviation. Home: 720 N Markwood St Orange CA 92867-7214

JONES, CRAIG ROBERT, financial executive; b. Long Branch, N.J., Apr. 5, 1946; s. Donald Robert and Ruth Budd (Thompson) J.; m. Tamara Edith Jamet, May 25, 1982; children: Alex, Nick. BA, Rutgers U., 1974. CPA. Sr. mgr. Price Waterhouse, Phila., 1974-83; contr. Ultrasystems, Inc., Irvine, Calif., 1983-85; dir. corp. acctg. Fluor Corp., Irvine, 1985-86; v.p., chief fin. officer Hollywood Park Cos., Inglewood, 1986-89, Electro Rent Corp., Van Nuys, 1989—. With USN, 1968-72, Viet Nam. Mem. AICPA, Fin. Execs. Inst., Assn. Corp. Growth. Avocations: sailing, skiing, chess, travel. Home: 2021 Jamestown Way Oxnard CA 93035-3747

JONES, D. MICHAEL, banker; b. Tacoma, June 25, 1942; s. Delbert Edward and Marilyn Maurine (Myers) J.; m. Linda R. Lavigne, June 7, 1964; 1 child, Karee Michele. BA in Econs., Wash. State U., 1964. CPA, Wash. Acct. Deloitte Haskins & Sells, Seattle, 1964-68, princ., 1968-72; treas. Old Nat. Bancorp., Spokane, Wash., 1973-76, exec. v.p., 1976-81, pres., 1982-87, Moore Fin. Group Inc. (now West One Bancorp), Boise, ID, 1987-1996; pres., ceo Source Capitol Corp., Spokane, Wa, 1996. Bd. dirs. Columbia Paint Co., Spokane. Bd. dirs. Spokane City Libraries, 1974-78, Leadership Spokane, 1982-84; sec. treas., bd. dirs. Spokane Unltd., 1980-86. Recipient Outstanding Alumnus award, Wash. State U., 1986. Mem. Am. Inst. CPA's, Wash. Soc. CPA's, Spokane C. of C. (sec. treas. 1985-86). Episcopalian. Clubs: Spokane (pres. 1984-85); Hayden Lake (Idaho) Country (pres. 1982-83). Office: Source Capitol Corp 1825 N Hutchinson Rd Spokane WA 99212-2444

JONES, DAVID MILTON, economist, educator; b. Newton, Iowa, June 22, 1938; s. Charles Raymond and Mary Evelyn (Corrough) J.; m. Becky Ann Jones Strait, Aug. 4, 1962; children: David, Jennifer, Stephen. BA with honors, Coe Coll., 1960; MA, U. Pa., 1961, PhD, 1969. Economist Fed. Res. Bank N.Y., N.Y.C., 1963-68; v.p., fin. economist Irving Trust Co., N.Y.C., 1968-72; vice-chmn., chief economist, bd. dirs. Aubrey G. Lanston & Co., Inc., N.Y.C., 1972-2000; owner DMJ Advisors LLC, $D, 2000—, Crystal Lake Resort, Pine, Colo. Advisor panel Fed. Res. Bank N.Y., 1982-93, cons. bd. govs., 1996—; mem. econ. adv. bd. Columbia U., 1982-87; former dir. pub. interest Suffolk County Savs. and Loan, Centerreach, N.Y.; bd. dirs. Aubrey G. Lanston & Co., Inc., Coe Coll., Union Theol. Sem.; cons., chmn. bd. dirs. Aglanston & Co., Inc., N.Y.C., 2000—. Author: Fed Watching and Interest Rate Projections: A Practical Guide, 1986, The Politics of Money: The Fed under Alan Greenspan, 1991, The Buck Starts Here: How the Federal Reserve Can Make or Break Your Financial Future, 1995. Chmn. fin. and investment com. United Ch. Bd. for World Ministries, N.Y.C., 1975-86; mem. bond com. Twp. of Montclair, 1982-83. Woodrow Wilson Found. fellow, 1960; NDEA fellow, 1960 Mem. Nat. Assn. Bus. Economists, Econ. Club of N.Y., Nat. Econ. Club (bd. dirs.). Home: 483 E Gulf Dr Sanibel FL 33957-7219 Office: PO Box 529 Pine CO 80470

JONES, DAVID ROBERT, zoology educator; b. Bristol, Eng., Jan. 28, 1941; came to Can., 1969; s. William Arnold and Gladys Margery (Parker) J.; m. Valerie Iris Gibson, Sept. 15, 1962; children: Melanie Ann, Vivienne Samantha B.Sc., Southampton U., 1962; Ph.D., U. East Anglia, Norwich, Eng., 1965. Rsch. fellow U. East Anglia, Eng., 1965-66; lectr. zoology U. Bristol, Eng., 1966-69; prof. zoology U. B.C., Vancouver, B.C., Can., 1969—. Contbr. numerous articles to profl. jours. Fellow Killam Found. Can., 1973, 89; recipient Killam Rsch. prize, 1993. Fellow Royal Soc. Can. (Flavelle medal 2000); mem. Soc. Exptl. Biology, Am. Physiol. Soc., Can. Zool. Soc. (Fry medal 1992). Office: U BC 6270 University Blvd Vancouver BC V6T 1Z4 Canada V6T 1Z4 also: U BC 6270 University Blvd Vancouver BC Canada V6T 1Z4 E-mail: jones@zoology.ubc.ca

JONES, DONNA MARILYN, state agency administrator, former legislator; b. Brush, Colo., Jan. 14, 1939; d. Virgil Dale and Margaret Elizabeth (McDaniel) Wolfe; m. Donald Eugene Jones, June 9, 1956; children: Dawn Richter, Lisa Shira, Stuart. Student, Treasure Valley Community Coll., 1981-82; grad., Realtors Inst. Cert. residential specialist. Co-owner Parts, Inc., Payette, Idaho, 1967-79; dept. mgr., buyer Lloyd's Dept. Store, Payette, 1979-80; sales assoc. Idaho-Oreg. Realty, Payette, 1981-82; mem. dist. 13 Idaho Ho. of Reps., Boise, 1987-90, mem. dist. 10, 1990-94, mem. dist. 9, 1995-98; assoc. broker Classic Properties Inc., Payette, 1983-91; owner, broker ERA Preferred Properities Inc., 1991-98; mem. dist. 9 Idaho Ho. of Reps., 1992-98. Co-chmn. Apple Blossom Parade, 1982; mem. Payette Civic League, 1968-84, pres. 1972; mem. Payette County Planning and Zoning Commn., 1985-88, vice-chmn. 1987; field coordinator Idaho Rep. Party Second Congl. Dist., 1986; mem. Payette County Rep. Cen. Com. 1978—; precinct II com. person, 1978-79, state committeewoman, 1980-84, chmn. 1984-87; outstanding county chmn. region III Idaho Rep. Party Regional Hall of Fame, 1985-86; mem. Payette County Rep. Women's Fedn., 1988—, bd. dirs., 1990-92; mem. Idaho Hispanic Commn., 1989-92, Idaho State Permanent Bldg. Adv. Coun., 1990-98; bd. dirs. Payette Edn. Found., 1993-96, Western Treasure Valley Cultural Ctr., 1993-96; nat. bd. dirs. Am. Legis. Exchange Coun., 1993-98; mem. legis. adv. coun. Idaho Housing Agy., 1992-97; committeperson Payette County Cen.; chmn. Ways and Means Idaho House of Reps., 1993-97, House Revenue & Taxation Com., 1997-98; mem. Multi-State Tax Compact, 1997-98; Idaho chmn. Am. Legis. Exchange Coun., 1991-95; exec. dir. Idaho Real Estate Commn., 1998—. Recipient White Rose award Idaho March of Dimes, 1988; named Payette/Washington County Realtor of Yr., 1987. Mem. Idaho Assn. Realtors (legis. com. 1984-87, chmn. 1986, realtors active in politics com. 1982-98, polit. action com. 1986, polit. affairs com. 1986-88, chmn. 1987, bd. dirs. 1984-88), Payette/Washington County Bd. Realtors (v.p. 1981, state dir. 1984-88, bd. dirs 1983-88, sec. 1983), Bus. and Profl. Women (Woman of Progress award 1988, 90, treas. 1988), Payette C. of C., Fruitland C. of C., Wiesr C. of C.. Republican. Avocations: reading, interior decoration. Home: 1911 1st Ave S Payette ID 83661-3003 Office: Idaho Real Estate Commn 633 N 4th St Boise ID 83720-0001

JONES, DOUGLAS RAYMOND, farming executive, state legislator; b. Twin Falls, Idaho, Mar. 24, 1949; s. Leslie Raymond and Charlotte Jones; m. Mary Elizabeth Morris, June 11, 1972; children: Jennifer, Heather, Douglas Jr. BS in Agr., U. Idaho, 1972. V.p. Leslie R. Jones, Inc., Twin Falls, 1972-86, pres., 1986—; rep. Idaho Ho. of Reps., Boise, 1985—, chmn. agrl. affairs com., 1997—. Chmn. edn. com. Nat. Conf. State Legislators, 1994-95, mem. exec. com., 1995-98. Mem. Gov.'s Task Force on Agr., Boise, 1979-80; mem. exec. com. Agrl. Cons. Coun., U. Idaho, Moscow, 1984-96; pres. Twin Falls County Farm Bur., 1980-82; bd. dirs. young farmers Idaho Farm Bur., Boise, 1978-80; troop fin. chmn. Boy Scouts Am., Twin Falls, 1972-94; v.p. Twin Falls Zoning and Planning Bd., 1984-85; mem. Nat. Edn. Goals Panel, 1994—; mem. adv. bd. for standards for excellence in edn. project Coun. for Basic Edn., 1995-97. Recipient Golden Apple award Idaho Edn. Assn., 1988, Terry Reilly Dedication to Young Children with Disabilities award Assn. for Early Childhood Learning, 1989, Friends of Coops. award, Idaho Coop. Coun., 1992. Mem. Twin Falls C. of C. (chmn. agrl. com. 1982-85), Rotary (Blue Lakes chpt.), Alpha Zeta. Republican. Avocation: private pilot. Office: Leslie R Jones Inc 3653 Highway 93 Twin Falls ID 83301-0237

JONES, EDWARD GEORGE, neuroscience professor; b. Upper Hutt, Wellington, N.Z., Mar. 26, 1939; came to U.S., 1972; s. Frank Ian and Theresa Agnes (Riordan) J.; m. Elizabeth Suzanne Oldham, Apr. 27, 1963; children: Philippa Emilie, Christopher Edward. MD, U. Otago, Dunedin, N.Z., 1962; PhD, U. of Oxford, Eng., 1968. Med. and surg. intern Tauranga Hosp., New Zealand, 1963; demonstrator to assoc. prof. dept. anatomy U. Otago Med. Sch., Dunedin, New Zealand, 1964-72; Nuffield Dominions demonstrator and lectr. Balliol Coll., U. of Oxford, Eng., 1964-72; assoc. prof. to prof., dept. anatomy and neurobiology Washington U. Sch. Medicine, St. Louis, 1972-84, George H. and Ethel Ronzini Bishop scholar, 1981-84, dir. div. exptl. neurology, 1981-84; prof. and chmn. dept. anatomy and neurobiology U. Calif., Irvine, 1984-98, dir. Ctr. Neurosci. Davis, 1998—. Cons. NIH, 1972—; dir. Neural Systems Lab., Frontier Rsch. Program in Neural Mechanisms of Mind and Behavior, Riken, Japan, 1988-96; vis. sr. rsch. fellow St. John's Coll. at U. Oxford, Eng., 1989-90. Author: The Thalamus, 1984; co-author: Thalamus, 1997, The Thalamus and Basal Telencephalon, 1982; co-editor: (book series) Cerebral Cortex, 1984—; author, reviewer numerous sci. and hist. articles, chpts. in books, 1964—. Mem. Pres.'s Adv. Bd. Calif. State U., Long Beach, 1986-90. Recipient Rolleston Meml. prize U. Oxford, 1970; rsch. grantee NIH, 1971—, named one of 1000 most cited biol. scientists, Sci. Citation Index, 1982. Mem. Soc. for Neurosci. (com. chair 1978-81, 88-89, pres.-elect 1997-98, pres. 1998-99), Am. Assn. Anatomists (Cajal medal 1989, Henry Gray award 2001), AAAS, Anat. Soc. Great Britain and Ireland (Symington Meml. prize 1968) Democrat. Avocations: reading, writing, carpentry. Office: U Calif Ctr Neurosci 1544 Newton Ct Davis CA 95616-4859

JONES, EDWARD LOUIS, historian, educator; b. Georgetown, Tex., Jan. 15, 1922; s. Henry Horace and Elizabeth (Steen) J.; m. Dorothy M. Showers, Mar. 1, 1952 (div. Sept. 1963); children: Cynthia, Frances, Edward Lawrence; Lynne Ann McGreevy, Oct. 7, 1963; children Christopher Louis, Teresa Lynne. BA in Philosophy, BA in Far East, U. Wash., 1952, BA in Speech, 1955, postgrad., 1952-54; JD, Gonzaga U., 1967. Social worker Los Angeles Pub. Assistance, 1956-57; producer, dir. Little Theatre, Hollywood, Calif. and Seattle, 1956-60; research analyst, cons. to Office of Atty. Gen., Olympia and Seattle, Wash., 1963-66; coordinator of counseling SOIC, Seattle, 1966-68; lectr., advisor, asst. to dean U. Wash., Seattle, 1968—. Instr. Gonzaga U., Spokane, Wash., 1961-62, Seattle Community Coll., 1967-68; dir. drama workshop, Driftwood Players, Edmonds, Wash., 1975-76. Author: The Black Diaspora: Colonization of Colored People, 1988, Tutankhamon: Son of the Sun, King of Upper and Lower Egypt, 1978, Black Orators' Workbook, 1982, Black Zeus, 1972, Profiles in African Heritage, 1972, From Rulers of the World to Slavery, 1990, President Zachary Taylor and Senator Hamlin: Union or Death, 1991, Why Colored Americans Need an Abraham Lincoln in 1992, Forty Acres and a Mule: The Rape of Colored Americans, 1994, Mister Moon Goes to Japan, A children's story, 2001; editor pub. NACADA Jour. Nat. Acad. Advising Assn., more. V.p. Wash. Com. on Consumer Interests, Seattle, 1966-68. Served to 2d lt. Fr. Army, 1940-45. Recipient Outstanding Teaching award U. Wash., 1986, Tyee Inst. Yr. U. Wash., 1987, appreciation award Office Minority Affairs, 1987, acad. excellence award Nat. Soc. Black Engrs., 1987, Appreciation award Fla. chpt. Nat. Bar Assn., 1990; Frederick Douglass scholar Nat. Coun. Black Studies, 1985, 86. Mem. Nat. Assn. Student Personnel Adminstrs., Smithsonian Inst. (assoc.), Am. Acad. Polit. and Social Sci., Nat. Acad. Advising Assn. (bd. dirs. 1979-82, Cert. of Appreciation 1982, editor Jour. 1981—, award for Excellence 1985), Western Polit. Sci. Assn. Democrat. Baptist. Avocations: travel, research, chess. Office: U Wash Ethnic Cultural Ctr Seattle WA 98195-0001

JONES, FLETCHER, JR. automotive company executive; CEO Fletcher Jones Mgmt., Las Vegas, Nev., pres. Office: Fletcher Jones Mgmt 175 E Reno Ave Ste C-6 Las Vegas NV 89119-1102

JONES, FREDERICK RANDAL, mathematician, educator; b. Gisborne, New Zealand, Dec. 31, 1952; BSc, U. Auckland, New Zealand, 1972, MSc with first class honors, 1973; DSc in Math., Ecoles Mathematiques, Geneva; DSc (hon.), U. Auckland, 1992, U. Wales, 1993. Asst. lectr. U. Auckland; with Ecole de Physique, Geneva, 1974-76, Ecoles Mathematiques, Geneva, 1976; E.R. Hedrick asst. prof. math. UCLA, 1980-81; asst. prof. U. Pa., 1981-84, assoc. prof., 1984-85; prof. math. U. Calif., Berkeley, 1985—. Recipient F W W Rhodes Meml. Scholarship, Swiss Govt. Scholarship, 1973, Guggenhein fellowship, 1986, Fields medal Internat. Congress, Kyoto, Japan, 1990, New Eng. Govt. Sci. medal, 1991. Fellow Royal Soc.; mem. Am. Acad. Arts and Scis. Achievements include index theorem for von Neumann algebras; discovery of a new polynomial invariant for knots which led to surprising connections between apparently quite different areas of mathematics. Office: U Calif Berkeley Dept Math 970 Evans Hall Berkeley CA 94720-3841

JONES, GEOFFREY MELVILL, physiology research educator; b. Cambridge, Eng., Jan. 14, 1923; s. Benett and Dorothy Laxton (Jotham) J.; m. Jenny Marigold Burnaby, June 21, 1953; children: Katharine, Francis, Andrew, Dorothy. BA, Cambridge U., 1944, MA, 1947, MB, BCh, 1949. House surgeon Middlesex Hosp., London, 1949-50; sr. house surgeon Addenbrookes Hosp., Cambridge, Eng., 1950-51; sci. med. officer Royal Air Force Inst. Aviation Medicine, Farnborough, Eng., 1951-55; sci. officer Med. Rsch. Coun., Eng., 1955-61; assoc. prof. physiology, dir. aviation med. rsch. unit McGill U., Montreal, Que., Can., 1961-68, prof., dir. Can., 1968-88, Hosmer rsch. prof. Can., 1978-91, emeritus prof. physiology, 1991—. Rsch. prof. clin. neuroscis. U. Calgary, Alta., Can., 1991—, Coll. France, 1979, 95; vis. prof. Stanford U., 1971-72. Author: (with another) mammalian Vestibular Physiology, 1979; editor: (with another) Adaptive Mechanisms in Gaze Control, 1985; contbr. numerous articles to profl. jours. Served to squadron leader Royal Air Force, 1951-55 Sr. rsch. assoc. Nat. Acad. Sci., 1971-72; recipient Skylab Achievement award NASA, 1974, 1st recipient Dohlman medal Dohlman Soc. Toronto U., 1987, Quinquennial Gold medal Barany Soc. Internat., 1988, Ashton Graybiel award U.S. Naval Aerospace Labs., 1989, Wilbur Franks Annual award Can. Soc. Aerospace Medicine, Buchanan-Barbour award Royal Aeronautical Soc., 1991, Mc Laughlin Medal, 1991, Royal Soc. Can. Fellow Can. Aeronautics and Space Inst., Aerospace Med. Assn. (Harry Armstrong award 1968, Arnold D. Tuttle award 1971), Royal Soc. Can. (McLaughlin medal 1991), Royal Soc. London, Royal Aeronautical Soc. London (Stewart Meml. award 1989, Buchanan Barbour award 1990); mem. U.K. Physiol. Soc., Can. Physiol. Soc., Can. Soc. Aerospace Med. Soc., Internat. Collegium Otolaryngology, Soc. Neurosci. Avocations: tennis, sailing, outdoor activities, reading, choral singing. Office: U Calgary Dept Clin Neuroscis 3330 Hospital Dr NW Calgary AB Canada T2N 4N1

JONES, GEORGIA ANN, publisher; b. Ogden, Utah, July 6, 1946; d. Sam Oliveto and Edythe June Murphy; m. Lowell David Jones; children: Lowell Scott, Curtis Todd. Sculptor, 1964-78; journalist, 1968-80; appraiser real property Profl. Real Estate Appraisal, San Carlos, Calif., 1980-95; online columnist, 1995-97; owner, pub. Ladybug Press, San Carlos, 1996—. Leader workshops for writers, 1994—. Author: A Garden of Weedin', 1997, Write What You Know: A Writer's Adventure, 1998, In Line at the Lost and Found, 2000, The Real Dirt on the American Dream: Home Ownership and Democracy, 2000; patentee Scruples-tag, 1980; editor, pub. Women on a Wire, 1996, vol. 2, 2001; author, playwright, A Stitch in Time, 1995, The Usual Suspects, 1995. Spkr. Jubillenium Interfaith Conf. for World Peace, 1999. Mem. Internat. Friends of Lit. and Culture (bd. dirs., U.S. chpt., Pave Peace keynote spkr. internat. congress 1999). Avocations: drawing, designing and building homes, landscape gardening. Office: Ladybug Press 751 Laurel St Ste 223 San Carlos CA 94070-3113

JONES, GLENN ROBERT, cable systems executive; b. Jackson Center, Pa., Mar. 2, 1930; BS in Econs., Allegheny Coll.; JD, U. Colo.; diploma exec. program, Stanford U.; LHD (hon.), Allegheny Coll. CEO, chmn. Jones Intercable Inc., Englewood, Colo. Author: (poetry) Briefcase Poetry of Yankee Jones, vol. I, 1978, vol. II, 1981, vol. III, 1985, Jones: Dictionary of Cable Television Terminology, 1973, 2d edit., 1976, 3d edit., 1987. Mem. World Future Soc., Nat. Cable TV Assn. Office: Jones Internat Ltd 9697 E Mineral Ave Englewood CO 80112-3408

JONES, GRANT RICHARD, landscape architect, planner; b. Seattle, Aug. 29, 1938; s. Victor Noble and Iona Bell (Thomas) J.; m. Ilze Grinbergs, 1965 (div. 1983); 1 child, Kaija. Student, Colo. Coll., 1956-58; BArch, U. Wash., 1962; M in Landscape Arch., Harvard U., 1966, postgrad. (Frederick Sheldon fellow), 1967-68. Draftsman Jones Lovegren Helms & Jones, Seattle, 1958-59; assoc. Richard Haag Assos., Seattle, 1961-65; rsch. assoc. landscape architecture rsch. office Harvard U., 1966-67; state conservation planner Eckbo Dean Austin & Williams, Honolulu, 1968-69; prin. Jones & Jones, Seattle, 1969—. Lectr. and spkr. in field; chmn. landscape archtl. registration bd., State of Wash., 1974-79; mem. coun. Harvard U. Grad. Sch. Design, 1978-82, 91-96; vis. com. Harvard U. Grad. Sch., 1993—, U. Wash. Coll. Architecture, 1990—; bd. dirs. Scenic Am., Waterfront Ctr., Arcade Mag. Author: The Nooksack Plan: An Approach to the Investigation and Evaluation of a River System, 1973; (with B. Gray and J. Burnham) A Method for the Quantification of Aesthetic Values for Environmental Decision Making, 1975, Design as Ecogram, 1975; (with J. Coe and D. Paulson) Woodland Park Zoo: Long Range Plan, Development Guidelines and Exhibit Scenarios, 1976, Landscape Assessment. . .Where Logic and Feelings Meet, 1978, Design Principles for Presentation of Animals and Nature, 1982, What Are Zoos?, 1984, An Arboretum on a Landfill, 1984, Beyond Landscape Immersion to Cultural Resonance, 1989, Some Thoughts on Power and Influence, 1993; prin. works include Nooksack River Plan, Bellingham, Wash.; Yakima (Wash.) River Regional Greenway, Union Bay Teaching and Research Arboretum, U. Wash., Seattle, Newhalem Campground, North Cascades Nat. Park, Woodland Park Zool. Gardens, Seattle, Washington Park Arboretum, U. Wash., Seattle, zoo master plans for Kansas City, Roanoke, Va., Detroit and Honolulu, Dallas Arboretum and Bot. Garden, Toledo Zoo African Savannah Complex, Thai Elephant Forest at Woodland Park Zoo, Singapore Bot. Gardens, Paris Pike Hist. Hwy, Denver Commons, others. Recipient Nat. award Am. Assn. Zoos and Pub. Aquaria, 1981-84. Fellow Am. Soc. Landscape Architects (chmn. Wash. chpt. 1972-73, trustee 1979—, v.p., 1988-90, Merit award in community design 1972, Honor award in regional planning 1974, Merit award in regional planning 1977, Merit award in park planning 1977, Merit award in instnl. planning 1977, Pres.'s award of excellence 1980, merit awards in landscape planning), Nature Conservancy, Am. Hort. Soc., Am. Assn. Bot. Gardens and Arboreta, Wash. Environ. Council, Phi Gamma Delta. Office: Jones & Jones 4th Fl 105 S Main St Ste 400 Seattle WA 98104-2578

JONES, H(AROLD) GILBERT, JR. lawyer; b. Fargo, N.D., Nov. 2, 1927; s. Harold Gilbert and Charlotte Viola (Chambers) J.; m. Julie Squier, Feb. 15, 1964; children: Lenna Lettice Mills Jones Carroll, Thomas Squier, Christopher Lee. B of Engring., Yale U., 1947; postgrad., Mich. U., 1948-49; JD, UCLA, 1956. Bar: Calif. 1957. Mem., ptnr. Overton, Lyman & Prince, L.A., 1956-61; founding ptnr. Bonne, Jones, Bridges, Mueller & O'Keefe, L.A., 1961-89, of counsel, 1990-92, Lewis, D'Amato, Brisbois & Bisgaard, 1992—. Bd. dirs. Wilshire YMCA, 1969-75. With U.S. Army, 1950-52. Fellow Am. Coll. Trial Lawyers, Am. Bd. Trial Advs. (nat. pres. 1988-89, nat. exec. com. 1990, 92, 96, nat. bd. dirs. 1977—, pres. L.A. chpt. 1980, Calif. Trial Lawyer of Yr. 1999), Internat. Acad. Trial Lawyers: mem. ABA, Calif. Bar Assn., Los Angeles County Bar Assn. (past. chmn. legal-med. rels. com.), Orange County Bar Assn., So. Calif. Assn. Def. Counsel, Jonathan Club, Transpacific Yacht Club (commodore 1996-98), Newport Harbor Yac ht Club (commodore 1998), Cruising Club Am., L.A. Yacht Club, Univ. Athletic Club, Ctr. Club. Home: 818 Harbor Island Dr Newport Beach CA 92660-7228 Office: 650 Town Center Dr Ste 1400 Costa Mesa CA 92626-7020 E-mail: hg5150@aol.com, gjones@ldbb.com

JONES, J. SORTON, lawyer; b. Llandudno, Wales, 1941; BSc, U. St. Andrews, Scotland, 1964; JD, U. Calif., Berkeley, 1973. Bar: Calif. 1973, N.Y. 1975; Registered Civil Engr. Calif. 1969. Mem. Carroll, Burdick & McDonough, San Francisco, 1994—; ptnr. Squires, Sanders & Dempsey LLP, San Francisco. Fellow Chartered Inst. of Arbitrators London; mem. ABA (internat. law sect.), Corp. Counsel Com., Am. Arbitration Assn., Inst. Civil Engrs. London (assoc.). Office: Squires Sanders & Dempsey LLP 1 Maritime Plz Ste 300 San Francisco CA 94111-3406

JONES, JAN LAVERTY, mayor; B degree, Stanford U. Dir. human resources S.M.C. Restaurants, Menlo Park, Calif., 1972-74; dir. R & D Thriftmart Corp., 1976-85; CEO Jan-Mar Corp., 1985-89; mayor City of Las Vegas, 1991-99. Former pres. Fletcher Jones Mgmt. Group; bd. dirs. Bank of Am., Nev., Desert Springs Hosp., Pub. Edn. Found. Founder, chair Mayor's Com. for a Better Cmty.; adv. bd. U. Nev. Las Vegas Law Sch., Nathan Adelson Hospice, Lied Discovery Mus., Shade Tree Shelter for Homeless Women and Children. E-mail: mayor-jjjones@ci.las-vegas.nv.us

JONES, JERVE MALDWYN, construction company executive; b. L.A., Sept. 21, 1918; s. Oliver Cromwell and Zola (Hill) J.; m. Alice Castle Holcomb, Apr. 12, 1942; children— Jay Gregory, Janey Lee Matt, Joel Kevin B.S. in Civil Engring., U. So. Calif., 1939. Registered profl. engr., Calif. Stress analyst Northrop Aircraft, L.A., 1940-43; ptnr. Jones Bros. Constrn. Co., Beverly Hills, Calif., 1946-56; pres., chief exec. officer Peck/Jones Constrn. Corp. (formerly Jones Bros. Constrn. Co.), Beverly Hills, 1956—. Cons. Jerve M. Jones Assocs., Beverly Hills, 1970— ; chmn. exec. com. Jones Constrn. Mgmt., Beverly Hills, 1983— Bd. dirs. Huntington Library, San Marino, Calif., 1984— , Pepperdine U., Malibu, Calif., Boy Scouts Am., L.A., Santa Monica Hosp. Found., YMCA Met. L.A.; chmn. L.A. Music Ctr., United Fund Campaign; life mem. Town Hall Calif., L.A., adv. bd. UCLA Med. Ctr.; mem. State Calif. Strong Motion Instrumentation Program, Dept. Mines and Geology. With USNR, 1943-46, PTO Recipient Civil Engring. Alumnus of Yr. award U. So. Calif., 1985, Bronze Hat award United Contractors Assn., 1985, Disting. Scout award, 1989. Mem. Constrn. Mgmt. Assn. Am. (nat. pres. 1984, Founders award 1985), Archtl. Guild, Archimedes Circle, Constrn. Industry Commn. (chmn. 1980-84), Assoc. Gen. Contractors Am., Los Angeles Area C. of C. (dir.) Republican. Episcopalian. Clubs: Los Angeles Country, California. Lodge: Rotary (dir. 1962-68) Avocations: yachting; skiing; fly fishing. Office: Peck Jones Constrn Corp 10866 Wilshire Blvd Fl 7 Los Angeles CA 90024-4300

JONES, JEWEL, social services administrator; b. Oklahoma City, Dec. 7, 1941; d. Joseph Samuel and Jewell (Hathyel) Fisher; m. Maurice Jones, July 17, 1976; children: Anthony, Carmen. BA in Sociology, Langston (Okla.) U., 1962; MA in Pub. Adminstrn., U. Alaska, Anchorage, 1974. Tchr. Seidman Sch., L.A., 1962; correctional offcer State of Calif. Dept. Corrections, Corona, 1963-65; probation officer County of San Bernardino, Calif., 1965-67; dep. exec. dir. Cmty. Action Agy., Anchorage, 1967-70; social svcs. dir. City of Anchorage, 1970-87; social svcs. mgr. Municipality of Anchorage, 1987-2000, dir. health & human svcs., 2000—. Chmn. bd. Alaska Housing Fin. Corp., Anchorage, 1995—; pres. Anchorage KidsPlace Project, 1994-95; chair Alaskan of the Yr. Scholarship Com., 1985—; chmn. bd. Janet Helen Tolan Gamble and Toby Gamble Ednl. Trust, 1998—. Mem. adv. bd. Salvation Army, Anchorage, 1982-87, Alaska R.R., Anchorage, 1990—;m trustee United Way of Anchorage, 1990-97; bd. dirs Alaska Ctr. for Performing Arts, 1987-97. Recipient Pres.'s award Alaska Black Caucus, 1984, Employment of Handicapped award Mayor of Anchorage, 1979, Execs. in Profile award Region X Blacks in Govt. award, 1998. Mem. NAACP (Harambe award 1973), Alaska Black Leadership Conf. (Cmty. Svc. award 1979-80), Links Inc., Quota Club Intenrat., Valli Vue Homeowners Assn. (v.p.), Zeta Phi Beta. Democrat. Avocations: cooking, reading, gardening. Office: Municipality Anchorage PO Box 196650 Anchorage AK 99519-6650

JONES, JOEL MACKEY, academic administrator; b. Millersburg, Ohio, Aug. 11, 1937; s. Theodore R.a nd Edna Mae (Mackey) Jones; children: Carolyn Mae, Jocelyn Corinne. BA, Yale U., 1960; MA, Miami U., Oxford, Ohio, 1962; PhD, U. N.Mex., 1966. Dir. Am. studies U. Md., Balt., 1966-69; chmn. Am. studies U. N.Mex., Albuquerque, 1969-73, asst. v.p. acad. affairs, 1973-77, dean faculties, assoc. provost, prof. Am. studies, 1977-85, v.p. adminstrn., 1985-88; pres. Ft. Lewis Coll., Durango, Colo., 1988-99; interim supr. of schs. Durango Pub. Schs., 1999. Bd. dirs. 1st Nat. Bank. Contbr. numerous essays, articles and chpts. to books. Founder Rio Grande Nature Preserve Soc., Albuquerque, 1974—; bd. dirs., mem. exec. com. United Way, Albuquerque, 1980-83; na. bd. cons. NEH, 1978—; bd. dirs. Mercy Hosp., 1990-94; mem. ACE Commn. on Leadership. Farwell scholar Yale U., New Haven, 1960; sr. fellow NEH, 1972; adminstrv. fellow Am. Coun. Edn., Washington, 1972-73. Mem. Am. Studies Assn., Am. Assn. Higher Edn., Am. Assn. State Colls. and Univs. (chair com. on cultural diversity, Colo. state rep. 1994—). Home: PO Box 428 Durango CO 81302-0428 Office: Ft Lewis Coll 214 Reed Libr Durango CO 81301-3999

JONES, JOHN STANLEY, urban development executive; b. Scranton, Pa., Mar. 25, 1947; BA, SUNY, Stony Brook, 1968; MS, U. Ariz., 1977. Prin. planner Pima County, Tucson, 1979-84; planning cons. pvt. practice, Tucson, 1984-89; dir. devel. svcs. ctr. City of Tucson, 1989-90, dir. devel. svcs. dept., 1990-93, acting water dir., 1993-94, dir. spl. projects, 1995-99; dir. Rio Nuevo, 1999—. Recipient Local Official award, Nat. Assn. Homebuilders, 1995. Mem. Am. Planning Assn., Am. Inst. Cert. Planners. Office: City Tucson PO Box 27210 Tucson AZ 85726-7210 E-mail: jjones1@ci.tucson.az.us

JONES, JOHN WESLEY, entrepreneur; b. Wenatchee, Wash., Nov. 15, 1942; s. Richard F. and Hazel F. (Hendrix) J.; m. Melissa L. Meyer, June 22, 1968 (div. 1982); children: John E., Jennifer L.; m. Deborah G. Matthews, Apr. 24, 1993. BA in Bus./Econs., Western Wash. U., Bellingham, 1966. Trainee Jones Bldg., Seattle, 1967-69, mgr., 1969-78; owner/mgr. N.W. Inboards, Bellevue, Wash., 1974-78, Jones Bldg., Seattle, 1978-86; pvt. investor Bellevue, 1987—; owner/mgr. J. Jones Enterprises, 1994—. Trustee BOMA Health & Welfare Trust, 1982-86, chmn. 1986; mem. Seattle Fire Code Adv. Bd., 1979-86. With USMCR, 1966-72. Mem. Seattle Bldg. Owners and Mgrs. Assn. (trustee 1979-86), Bldg. Owners and Mgrs. Internat., N.W. Marine Trade Assn., Am. Assn. Individual Investors, Composite Fabricators Assn., Soc. Naval Architects and Marine Engrs., Boat U.S., Seattle Yacht Club, NRA, Internat. Show Car Assn., Nat. Street Rod Assn., Specialty Equipment Mktg. Assn. Republican. Avocations: boating, water skiing, snow skiing, automobiles, photography. Home: 61 Skagit Key Bellevue WA 98006-1021 Office: PO Box 52745 Bellevue WA 98015-2745

JONES, JOIE PIERCE, entrepreneur, acoustician, educator, writer, scientist; b. Brownwood, Tex., Mar. 4, 1941; s. Aubrey M. and Mildred K. (Pierce) J.; m. Kay Becknell, June 12, 1965. BA (Jr. fellow 1961-63), U. Tex., Austin, 1963, MA, 1965; PhD, Brown U., 1970. Sr. scientist Bolt Beranek & Newman, Inc., Cambridge, Mass., 1970-75; assoc. prof., dir. ultrasonics research lab. Case Western Res. U. Sch. Medicine, Cleve., 1975-77; prof., chief med. imaging, dir. grad. studies, dept. radiol. scis. U. Calif., Irvine, 1977—. Cons. acoustics; pres. Computer Sci. Systems, 1978—; founding gen. ptnr. Of Food and Wine, 1982—, Meditherm Assocs., Ltd., 1983-85, Spar Techs., 1987-90, Surgisonics Inc., 1991—; proposal reviewer NSF/NIH, 1974—; appointee sci. and tech. adv. com. Pres. Carter, 1977-81. Author 3 books; mem. editorial bd. Ultrasound in Medicine and Biology, 1976—; contbr. over 300 articles to profl. jours.; 25 patents in field. Active vol. local govt. Fellow Am. Inst. Ultrasound in

Medicine, IEEE, Acoustical Soc. Am., Am. Phys. Soc.; mem. AAAS, Am. Assn. Physicists in Medicine, Calif. Wine and Food Soc., Phi Beta Kappa. Democrat. Home: 2094 San Remo Dr Laguna Beach CA 92651-2628 Office: U Calif Dept Radiol Sci Irvine CA 92697-5000 E-mail: jpjones@ucl.edu

JONES, L. Q. See MCQUEEN, JUSTICE ELLIS

JONES, LEONADE DIANE, media publishing company executive; b. Bethesda, Md., Nov. 27, 1947; d. Leon Adger and Landonia Randolph (Madden) J. BA with distinction, Simmons Coll., 1969; JD, MBA, Stanford U., 1973. Bar: Calif. 1973, D.C. 1979. Summer assoc. Davis Polk & Wardwell, N.Y.C., summer 1972; securities analyst Capital Rsch. Co., L.A., 1973-75; asst. treas. Washington Post Co., 1975-79, 86-87, treas., 1987-96; dir. fin. services Post-Newsweek Stas., Inc., Washington, 1979-84, v.p. bus. affairs, 1984-86; ind. mgmt. cons., pvt. equity investor, 1997-99; CFO, sec. VentureThink, LLC, 1999-2001; exec. v.p., CFO Versura, Inc., 2000-01. Bd. dirs. Am. Balanced Fund, Inc., Income Fund Am., Inc., Fundamental Investors, Growth Fund Am., Inc., The New Economy Fund, Smallcap World Fund, Inc.; mem. investment mgmt. subcom. of benefit plans com. Am. Stores Co., 1992-99; mem. investment adv. com. N.Y. State Tchrs.' Retirement Sys., 1999—; mem. investment mgmt. sub-com. Albertson's Inc., 1999—. Treas., bd. dirs. Big Sisters Washington Met. Area, 1984-85; bd. dirs. D.C. Contemporary Dance Theatre, 1987-89, Washington Performing Arts Soc., 1990-94, treas., 1992-94; mem. adv. coun. Charlin Jazz Soc., 1988-92; mem. adv. bd. Sta. WHMM-TV, 1989-93; asst. chmn. budget and audit D.C. chpt. Met. Washington, Edges Group, Inc., 1989-93; mem. adv. coun. Bus. Sch., Stanford U., 1991-98, bd. visitors Law Sch., 1982-84, 93-98; trustee Am. Inst. Mng. Diversity, Inc., 1991-96; mem. corp. Simmons Coll., 1992-96; bd. dirs. Yerba Buena Ctr. for Arts, 1999—. Recipient Candace award for bus., 1992, Serwa award, 1993; named to D.C. Women's Hall of Fame, 1992. Mem. ABA, Calif. Bar Assn., D.C. Bar Assn., Stanford U. Bus. Sch. Alumni Assn. (bd. dirs. 1986-88, pres. Washington-Balt. chpts. 1984-85). Avocations: tennis, travel.

JONES, LORIN V. state senator; b. St. George, Utah, Jan. 28, 1929; m. Ferral Leavitt. Student, Dixie Coll.; BEE, San Bernardino Valley Coll. Formerly oper. engr. and mgr. electric utility; mem. Utah State Senate, 1996—, chair edn. com., mem. energy, natural resources and agr. com., co-chair commerce and revenue appropriations com. Bd. dirs. Rural Water Assn. Utah; dir. tng. Western Sys. Coordinating Coun. Mem. Nat. Assn. Power Engrs., Am. Power Dispatchers Assn., St. George Rotary Club. Republican. Home: 177 E Center St Veyo UT 84782-4040

JONES, M. DOUGLAS, JR. pediatrics educator; b. San Antonio, Apr. 22, 1943; BA, Rice U., 1964; MD, U. Tex., 1968. Diplomate Am. Bd. Pediat. Intern U. Colo. Sch. Medicine, Denver, 1968-69, resident, 1969-71, fellow neonatal-perinatal medicine, 1973-75; pediatrician-in-chief Children's Hosp., U. Hosp., Denver; prof., chmn. pediatrics U. Colo. Sch. Medicine. Mem. Am. Bd. Pediat., Am. Acad. Pediat., Am. Pediat. Soc., Soc. for Pediat. Rsch. Office: Childrens Hosp 1056 E 19th Ave Denver CO 80218-1088

JONES, MARK LOGAN, educational association executive, educator; b. Provo, Utah, Dec. 16, 1950; s. Edward Evans and Doris (Logan) J.; m. Catherine A. Bailey. BS, Ea. Mont. Coll., 1975; postgrad. in labor rels., Cornell U.; postgrad., SUNY, Buffalo. Narcotics detective Yellowstone County Sheriff's Dept., Billings, Mont., 1972-74; math tchr. Billings (Mont.) Pub. Schs., 1975-87; rep. Nat. Edn. Assn. of N.Y., Buffalo, Jamestown, 1987-91, Nat. Edn. Assn. Alaska, Anchorage, 1991—. Mem. Alaska Tchr. Licensure Task Force, Tchr. Edn. Adv. Coun., Adv. Com. on Tchr. Stds., Alaska Partnership Tchr. Enhancement; bd. mem. Alaska staff Devel. Network; mem. various coms. Alaska Dept. Edn. Photographs featured in 1991 N.Y. Art Rev. and Am. Artist. Committeeman Yellowstone Dem. Party, Billings, 1984-87; exec. com. Dem. Cen. Com., Billings, 1985-87; bd. dirs. Billings Community Ctr., 1975-87; concert chmn. Billings Community Concert Assn., 1980-87; bd. dirs. Chautauqua County Arts Coun.; bd. dirs. Big Brothers and Big Sisters Anchorage. With U.S. Army, 1970-72. Recipient Distinguished Svc. award, Billings Edn. Assn., 1985, Mont. Edn. Assn., 1987. Mem. ACLU, Billings Edn. Assn. (bd. dirs. 1980-82, negotiator 1981-87, pres. 1982-87), Mont. Edn. Assn. (bd. dirs. 1982-87), Ea. Mont. Coll. Tchr. Edn. Project, Accreditation Reviewer Team Mont. Office Pub. Edn., Big Sky Orchard, Masonic, Scottish Rite. Avocations: Bonsai, photography, reading, classical and jazz music, hunting, fishing. Home: PO Box 102904 Anchorage AK 99510-2904 Office: Nat Edn Assn Alaska 1840 S Bragaw St Ste 103 Anchorage AK 99508-3463

JONES, MICHAEL T. real estate development executive; Exec. v.p. ops., Pres. Hawaii divsn. Schuler Homes Inc., Honolulu, 1998—. Office: Schuler Homes Inc 828 4th St Mall Fl 4 Honolulu HI 96813-4321

JONES, MILTON BENNION, retired agronomist, educator; b. Cedar City, Utah, Jan. 15, 1926; s. William Lunt and Claire (Bennion) J.; m. Grace Elaine Guymon, Sept. 8, 1951; children: Milton B. Jr., Richard W., Jo Layne, Tamera, Sherilee, Karolyn. BS, Utah State U., 1951; PhD, Ohio State U., 1955. Successively jr. agronomist, asst. agronomist, assoc. agronomist, agronomist, lectr. U. Calif., Hopland, Davis, 1955-91. Cons. IRI Rsch. Inst., Campinas, Brazil, 1963-65, CSIRO, Australia, 1974, BLM, Ukiah, Calif., 1970-77, Sulphur Inst., Washington, 1967-88, AID U. Evora, Portugal, 1984, Basque Govt., Bilbao, Spain, 1987, MAF, Invermay, New Zealand, 1990. Contbr. articles to profl. jours. Mem. Sch. bd. Ukiah Elem. Sch. Dist., 1962-63; scout leader local chpt. Boy Scouts Am., Ukiah, 1962-70. With USN, 1944-47. Fellow Agronomy Soc., Soil Sci. Soc. Home: 3501 Leland Ln Ukiah CA 95482-6911 Office: U Calif 4070 University Rd Hopland CA 95449-9717 E-mail: mbjggj@juno.com

JONES, MILTON WAKEFIELD, publisher; b. Burbank, Calif., Apr. 18, 1930; s. Franklin M. and Lydia (Sinclair) J.; m. Rita Strong, May 4, 1959; 1 son, Franklin Wayne. Student, Santa Monica City Coll., 1948-50; AA, U. So. Calif., 1950-52. V.p. mktg. Sav-Ink Co., Newport Beach, Calif., 1956-58; account exec. KDES-Radio, Palm Springs, 1958-60; pres. Milton W. Jones Advt. & Pub. Rels. Agy., Palm Springs, 1960—, Desert Publs., Inc., Palm Springs, 1965—, Riverside Color Press, Inc., Palm Springs, Olman Travel Svc., Palm Springs, 1979-84. Pres. Franklin Comms. (Sta. KPSL-Radio), 1987-98, Airport Displays Ltd., 1972—; vice chmn. Palm Springs Savings Bank, 1981-96; bd. dirs., treas. Canyon Nat. Bank. Pub. Palm Springs Life Mag., 1965—, Wheeler Bus. Letter, Palm Springs, 1969-77, San Francisco mag., 1973-79, Guest Life, Orange County, N.Mex., Carmel/Monterey, St. Petersburg/Clearwater, Vancouver, Can., El Paso, Houston, 1978—, Orange County mag., 1987-89, McCallum Theatre Program, 1989—, Ofcl. Guide to Houston, 1993, El Paso Guest Life, 1993, Pub. Record newspaper, 1996, Ofcl. Guide to Ontario, 2001. Mem. Desert Press Club (pres. 1965). Home: 422 N Farrell Dr Palm Springs CA 92262-6559 also: 206 Abalone Ave Balboa Island CA 92662-1304 Office: 303 N Indian Canyon Dr Palm Springs CA 92262-6015 E-mail: milt@palmspringslife.com

JONES, NAPOLEON A., JR. judge; b. 1940; BA, San Diego State U., 1962, MSW, 1967; JD, U. San Diego, 1971. Legal intern, staff atty. Calif. Rural Legal Assistance, Modesto, Calif., 1971-73; staff atty. Defenders, Inc., San Diego, 1973-75; ptnr. Jones, Cazares, Adler & Lopez, San Diego, 1975-77; judge San Diego Mcpl. Ct., 1977-82, San Diego Superior Ct., 1982-94; U.S. Dist. Ct. (so. dist.) Calif., San Diego, 1994—. Mem. San Diego County Indigent Def. Policy Bd. Bd. visitors Sch. Social Work San Diego State U.; active Valencia Park Elem. Sch. Mem. San Diego County Bar Assn., Earl B. Gilliam Bar Assn., San Diego Bar Found., Nat. Bar Assn., Calif. Bar Assn., Calif. Black Attys. Assn., Nat. Assn. Women Judges, Masons, Sigma Pi Phi, Kappa Alpha Psi. Office: US Dist Ct So Dist Calif US Courthouse 940 Front St Ste 2125 San Diego CA 92101-8912

JONES, NATHANIEL B., JR. bishop; Bishop Ch. of God in Christ, Barstow, Calif. Founder, adminstr., prin. Barstow Ch. of God in Christ Christian Day Sch. Office: Ch God in Christ 1375 Sage Dr Barstow CA 92311-2446

JONES, NEIL FORD, surgeon, educator; b. Merthyr Tydvil, Wales, Nov. 30, 1947; s. John Robert and Kathleen Mary (Ford) J.; m. Barbara Rose Unterman, Feb. 18, 1978; 1 child, Nicholas Huw. B of Medicine, B of Surgery, MA, Oxford (Eng.) U., 1975. Registrar N.E. Thames Regional Plastic Surgery Centre, Billericay, Eng., 1982; fellow in hand surgery and microsurgery Mass. Gen. Hosp. Harvard U., Boston, 1983; asst. prof. surgery U. Pitts., 1984-89, assoc. prof. surgery, 1989-93, dir. hand and microsurgery, 1987-93; prof., chief hand surgery UCLA Sch. Medicine, 1993—. Contbr. articles to profl. jours. Fellow ACS, Royal Coll. Surgeons Eng.; mem. Am. Assn. Plastic Surgeons, Am. Soc. Surgery of Hand (mem. coun. 2000—), Am. Soc. Reconstructive Microsurgery (sec. 1999-2001), Internat. Soc. Reconstructive Microsurgery. Avocation: travel. Home: 532 N Bonhill Rd Los Angeles CA 90049-2326 Office: 200 UCLA Med Ctr Medical Plz 140 Los Angeles CA 90095-8344 E-mail: njones@mednet.ucla.edu

JONES, ORLO DOW, lawyer, drug store executive; b. Logan, Utah, June 10, 1938; s. Orlo Elijah and Joyce (Lewis) J.; m. Ilarene Balls, July 9, 1958; children— Monica, Orlo Courtney. B.S., Utah State U., 1960; LL.B., U. Calif., Berkeley, 1963. Bar: Calif. bar 1964. Atty. Carlson, Collins & Bold, Richmond, Calif., 1968-69, A.T. and T., San Francisco, 1969-71, Longs Drug Stores, Inc., Walnut Creek, Calif., 1971-76, sec., gen. counsel, 1976—, v.p., 1979-87, sr. v.p., 1987—. Lectr. comml. leases Continuing Edn. of Bar Univ. Extension U. Calif., Berkeley Served to capt. JAGC AUS, 1964-68. Republican. Mormon. Home: 156 Santiago Dr Danville CA 94526-1941 Office: Longs Drug Stores Corp 141 N Civic Dr Walnut Creek CA 94596-3858

JONES, PAMELA S. real estate development executive; Sr. v.p. fin., CFO, bd. dirs. Schuler Homes Inc., Honolulu, 1996—. Office: Schuler Homes Inc 828 4th St Mall Fl 4 Honolulu HI 96813-4321

JONES, PETER ANTHONY, medical research administrator; b. Cape Town, South Africa, Jan. 21, 1947; naturalized citizen U.S. married; 3 children. BSc with 1st class honors, U. Coll. Rhodesia, 1969; PhD, U. London, 1973. NIH tng. fellow divsn. hematology-oncology Children's Hosp. of L.A., 1973-75; dir. basic rsch. and dir. Urol. Cancer Lab. U. So. Calif., L.A., 1984-93, assoc. dean for acad. and sci. affairs Sch. Medicine, 1991-94, interim chmn. dept. molecular microbiology and immunology, dir. Comprehensive Cancer Ctr., 1993—. Mem. integration panel breast cancer program U.S. Army Med. Rsch. and Devel. Command to date; mem. cancer5 ctr. support rev. com. Nat. Cancer Inst., 1988-92; mem. Bladder Cancer Working Group of the Organ Sys. Program, 1986-89; mem. cellular biology and physiology study sect. NIH, 1984-87, mem. chem. pathology, spl. study sect., 1985, ad hoc mem. cellular physiology rev. group, 1983, ad hoc mem. pathology B study sect., 1981, mem. spl. study sect. tumor promoters, 1982. Assoc. editor Cancer Rsch., 1983—, Molecular Carcinogenesis, 1987—, Carcinogenesis, 1990-93, Invasion and Metastasis, 1982—. Cancer Assn. Rhodesia Jr. Rsch. fellow, 1969-70, U. Rhodesia Postgrad. fellow, 1971; rsch. grantee Am. Cancer Soc., 1977-78, 78-79, 79-82, Nat. Cancer Assn. South Africa, Nat. Inst. Gen. Med. Scis., 1982-85, Nat. Cancer Inst., 1978-89, 82-89, 89—. Mem. AAAS, Am. Soc. Biochemistry and Molecular Biology, Am. Assn. for Cancer Rsch. (pubs. com., bd. dirs. 1989-92, program com. 1988, chmn. biology sect. 1989, chmn. local arrangements com. ann. meeting 1986), Am. Urol. Assn. (affiliate), DNA Methylation Soc., Soc. for Basic Urol. Rsch. Achievements include research in DNA methylation and cell differentiation; molecular biology of cancer. Office: U Southern Calif Norris Comprehen Cancer Ctr 1441 Eastlake Ave Los Angeles CA 90033-1048

JONES, PETER F. lawyer; b. Hanover, N.H., Jan. 3, 1944; s. J. Franklin Jr. and Elizabeth Anne (Dunning) J.; m. Anne Meyer, Apr. 17, 1971; children: David, Philip. BA, Ripon Coll., 1967; JD, U. Denver, 1970. Bar: Colo. 1971, U.S. Dist. Ct. Colo. 1971. Assoc. Duane O. Littell, Denver, 1971-76, Hall & Evans, Denver, 1976-78, ptnr., 1978—. Office: Hall & Evans 1200 17th St Ste 1700 Denver CO 80202-5817

JONES, POPEYE, professional basketball player; b. Dresden, Tenn., June 17, 1970; m. Amy Jones; children: Justic, Seth, Caleb. Student, Murray State Coll., 1992. Center Dallas Mavericks, 1993-96, Toronto Raptors, 1996-97, Boston Celtics, 1997-99; forward Denver Nuggets, 1999—. Avocations: video games, auto racing. Office: Denver Nuggets Pepsi Ctr 1635 Clay St Denver CO 80204

JONES, QUINCY, producer, composer, arranger, conductor, trumpeter; b. Chgo., Mar. 14, 1933; s. Quincy Delight and Sarah J.; children: Kidada, Rashida, Jolie, Martina-Lisa, Quincy III, Rachelle, Kenya. Student, Seattle U., Berklee Coll. Music; pvt. study with, Nadia Boulanger; student, Boston Conservatory; hon. degree, Berklee Coll. Music, 1983, Howard U., 1985, Seattle U., 1990, Wesleyan U., 1991, Loyola U., 1992, Brandeis U., 1992, Clark U., 1993. Trumpeter, arranger Lionel Hampton Orch., 1950-53; arranger for orchs., singers including Frank Sinatra, Dinah Washington, Count Basie, Sarah Vaughan, Peggy Lee, USA For Africa; organizer, trumpeter Dizzy Gillespie Orch. for Dept. of State tour of Near East, Mid. East, S.Am., 1956; music dir. Barchlay Disques, Paris; leader own orch. European tour, concerts, TV, radio, 1960; music dir., Mercury Records, 1961, v.p., 1964; composer: background scores The Boy in the Tree, 1964; condr. (film music) The Pawnbroker, Mirage, The Slender Thread, 1965, Walk Don't Run, Made in Paris, 1966, Banning (Acad. awd. nom. best song 1967), The Deadly Affair, Enter Laughing, In Cold Blood (Acad. awd. nom. best score 1967), In the Heat of the Night, 1967, For the Love of Ivy (Acad. awd. nom. best song 1968), The Split, Mirage, A Dandy in Aspic, The Hell with Heroes, Jigsaw, 1968, Bob and Carol and Ted and Alice, Cactus Flower, John and Mary, The Italian Job, The Lost Man, MacKenna's Gold, 1969, Eggs, Of Men and Demons, The Out-Of-Towners, Up Your Teddy Bear, The Last of the Mobile Hotshots, They Call Me Mr. Tibbs, 1970, The Anderson Tapes, Brother John, Honky, $, 1971, Come Back Charleston Blue, The Hot Rock, 1972, The New Centurions, 1972, The Getaway, 1972, Mother, Jugs, and Speed, 1976, The Wiz, 1978, (also co-producer) The Color Purple (Acad. awd. noms., best picture, best song 1985), Fever Pitch, (exec. music producer) The Slugger's Wife, 1985, Listen Up: The Lives of Quincy Jones, 1990; composer, actor (film) Blues for Trumpet and Koto, Life Goes On; rec. artist numerous platinum albums including Body Heat, 1974, Mellow Madness, 1975, I Heard That, 1976, The Dude, 1981, Back on the Block, 1989, Snackwater Jack, 1991; producer videotape Portrait of An Album: Frank Sinatra with Quincy Jones and Orchestra, 1986 (platinum); producer recordings Michael Jackson's Off the Wall, 1980, Thriller, 1982 (world's best selling record), Bad; producer (with Steven Spielberg) The E.T. Storybook, (TV series) Fresh Prince of Bel Air, 1990—; composer (television) Hey Landlord, 1966-67, Ironside, 1967-75, The Bill Cosby Show, 1969-71, The New Bill Cosby Show, 1972-73, Sanford and Son, 1972-77, Sanford Arms, 1977, The Cosby Show, 1984-92, The Oprah Winfrey Show, 1989, (mini series Roots (Emmy awd., best music composition, 1977), 1977; founder Vibe Magazine, 1992, exec. prodr. A Call for Reunion concert Lincoln Meml. for Clinton Inauguration, 1993. Recipient 76 Grammy nominations, 26 Grammy awards, numerous Readers Poll awards Downbeat Mag., Trendsetters awards Billboard Mag., Golden Note award ASCAP, 1982, Image award NAACP, 1974, 80, 81, 83, 90, 91, Hollywood Walk of Fame, 1980, Man of the Yr. award City of Hope, 1982, Whitney Young Jr. award Urban League, 1986, Humanitarian of Yr. award T.J. Martell Found., 1986, Lifetime Achievement award Nat. Acad. Songwriters, 1989, Grammy Living Legend award, 1990, Grammy award for Best Jazz instrumental, individual or group 1994 for "Miles and Quincy Live ath Montreux", Scopus award Hebrew U., 1991, Spirit of Liberty award People for the Am. Way, 1992; named Entrepreneur of the Yr. USA Today/Fin. News Network, 1991; film biography: Listen Up: The Lives of Quincy Jones, 1990. Office: Eliot Sekuler Publicist Rogers & Cowan 3800 Barham Blvd Ste 503 Los Angeles CA 90068-1042

JONES, RICHARD MICHAEL, lawyer; b. Chgo., Jan. 16, 1952; s. Richard Anthony and Shirley Mae (Wilhelm) J.; m. Catherine Leona Ford, May 25, 1974. BS, U. Ill., 1974; JD, Harvard U., 1977. Bar: Colo. 1977, U.S. Dist. Ct. Colo. 1977. Assoc. Davis, Graham & Stubbs, Denver, 1977-81; corp. counsel Tosco Corp., Denver, 1981-82; asst. gen. counsel Anschutz Corp., Denver, 1982-88, gen. counsel, v.p., 1989—. Mem. ABA, Colo. Bar Assn., Denver Bar Assn. Office: Anschutz Corp 555 17th St Ste 2400 Denver CO 80202-3987

JONES, ROBERT EDWARD, federal judge; b. Portland, Oreg., July 5, 1927; s. Howard C. and Leita (Hendricks) J.; m. Pearl F. Jensen, May 29, 1948; children— Jeffrey Scott, Julie Lynn BA, U. Hawaii, 1949; JD, Lewis and Clark Coll., 1953, LHD (hon.), 1995; LLD (hon.), City U., Seattle, 1984, Lewis and Clark Coll., , 1995. Bar: Oreg. Trial atty., Portland, Oreg., 1953-63; judge Oreg. Circuit Ct., Portland, 1963-83; justice Oreg. Supreme Ct., Salem, 1983-90; judge U.S. Dist. Ct. Oreg., Portland, 1990—. Mem. faculty Nat. Jud. Coll., Am. Acad. Jud. Edn., ABA Appellate Judges Seminars; former mem. Oreg. Evidence Revision Commn., Oreg. Ho. of Reps.; former chmn. Oreg. Commn. Prison Terms and Parole Stds.; adj. prof. Northwestern Sch. Law, Lewis and Clark Coll., 1963—, Willamette Law Sch., 1988—. Author: Rutter Group Practice Guide Federal Civil Trials and Evidence, 1999. Mem. bd. overseers Lewis and Clark Coll., mem. bd. visitors to Northwestern Sch. Law. Served to capt. JAGC, USNR. Recipient merit award Multnomah Bar Assn., 1979; Citizen award NCCJ, Legal Citizen of the Yr. award Law Related Edn. Project, 1988; Service to Mankind award Sertoma Club Oreg.; James Madison award Sigma Delta Chi; named Disting. Grad., Northwestern Sch. Law; Outstanding Profl. Achievement Alumnus award, U.S. Merchant Marine Acad., 1998; Judge Robert E. Jones Oreg. Justice award, Am. Judicature Soc., 1999. Mem. Am. Judicature Soc. (bd. dirs. 1997—), State Bar Oreg. (past chmn. Continuing Legal Edn.), Oregon Circuit Judges Assn. (pres. 1967—), Oreg. Trial Lawyers Assn. (pres. 1959, chair 9th cir. edn. com. 1996-97). E-mail: robert. Office: US Dist Ct House 1000 SW 3rd Ave Ste 1407 Portland OR 97204-2944 E-mail: jones@ord.uscourts.gov

JONES, ROGER WAYNE, electronics executive; b. Riverside, Calif., Nov. 21, 1939; s. Virgil Elsworth and Beulah (Mills) J.; m. Sherill Lee Bottjer, Dec. 28, 1975; children: Jerrod Wayne, Jordan Anthony. BS in Engring., San Diego State U., 1962. Br. sales mgr. Bourns, Inc., Riverside, 1962-68; sales and mktg. mgr. Spectrol Electronics, Industry, Calif., 1968-77, v.p. mktg., 1979-81; mng. dir. Spectrol Reliance, Ltd., Swindon, England, 1977-79; sr. v.p. S.W. group Kierulff Electronics Corp., L.A., 1981-83; v.p. sales and mktg. worldwide electronic techs. div. Beckman Instruments, Fullerton, Calif., 1983-86; pres., ptnr. Jones & McGeoy Sales, Inc., Newport Beach, 1986—. Author: The History of Villa Rockledge, A National Treasure in Laguna Beach, 1991, California From the Conquistadores to the Legends of Laguna, 1997. Republican. Office: 5100 Campus Dr Newport Beach CA 92660-2101

JONES, RONALD H. computer information systems executive; b. San Diego, Feb. 11, 1938; s. Henry G. and Geneva H. (Hodges) J.; m. Carol Sue Carmichael, Dec. 9, 1967. BS, San Diego State Coll., 1959, MS, 1961. Project mgr. UNIVAC, San Diego, 1961-67, Computer Scis. Corp., San Diego, 1967-75; v.p. Interactive, Inc., San Diego, 1975-92; owner Consulting Co., San Diego, 1992—; ind. cons., programmer various mfg. & distbg. cos., San Diego, 1992—. Contbr. articles to profl. jours; tech. advisor to Internat. Spectrum Mag. Advisor San Diego State Univ.; Rep. nat. committeeman, 1979—. Mem. AARP, Am. Prodn. and Inventory Control Soc., Assn. for Computing Machinery, Calpirg and Ucan. Presbyterian. Avocations: golf, tennis, fishing, collecting. Home and Office: 2484 Pine St San Diego CA 92103-1042 also: Ron Jones Cons PO Box 370083 San Diego CA 92137-0083

JONES, SAMUEL LEANDER, conductor; b. Inverness, Miss., June 2, 1935; s. Samuel Leander and Ella Mae (Spencer) J.; m. Nancy Ruth Peacock, Jan. 29, 1957 (div.); children: Rachel Ann, Alison Frances; m. Kristin Barbara Schutte, Dec. 22, 1975. BA, Millsaps Coll., 1957; MA, U. Rochester, 1958, PhD, 1960; D (hon.), Millsaps Coll., 2000. Dir. instrumental music Alma (Mich.) Coll., 1960-62, instr., 1960-61, asst. prof., 1961-62; music dir. Saginaw Symphony Orch., 1962-65; asst. condr. Rochester Philharm. Orch., N.Y., 1965-67, assoc. condr., 1967-69, resident condr., 1969-70, condr., 1970-72; dean Shepherd Sch. of Music Rice U., Houston, 1973-79, prof. of conducting and composition, Shepherd Sch. Music, 1973-97, prof. emeritus, 1997—; prof. of conducting and composition, dir. orchestral studies Carnegie-Mellon U., Pitts., 1988-89. Assoc. dir. Am. Symphony Orch. League Inst. of Orchestral Studies, Orkney Springs, Va., 1966-76; mus. advisor Flint Symphony Orch., 1974-76; guest condr. Pitts. Symphony, Detroit Symphony, Houston Symphony, Buffalo Philharm., Prague Symphony; composer-in-residence Seattle Symphony Orch., 1997—. Founder Alma Symphony, 1961; condr., Saginaw (Mich.) Symphony, 1962-65, also, dir., Saginaw Choral Soc., composer-in-residence, Delta Coll., Univ. Ctr., Mich., 1964-65; founder, conductor: Festival Orch, Univ. Ctr., 1964-65; guest condr., Pitts. Symphony, Buffalo Philharmonic, Shenandoah Valley Music Festival, Naumberg, Iceland symphonies, others.; Composer: Symphony 1, 1960, In Retrospect, 1959, Overture for a City, 1964, Festival Fanfare (commd. Am. Symphony Orch. League), 1964, Elegy in Memory of John Fitzgerald Kennedy, 1917-63, 1963, Let Us Now Praise Famous Men (commd. Shenandoah County Bicentennial Commn.), 1972, Spaces, 1974, Contours of Time, 1975, Fanfare and Celebration (commd. Houston Symphony), 1980, A Symphonic Requiem (commd. Sioux City Symphony), 1983, The Trumpet of the Swan (commd. Millsaps Coll.), 1985, Listen Now, My Children (commd. Midland-Odessa Symphony), 1985, (opera) A Christmas Memory, 1982, Canticles of Time, Symphony No. 2 (commd. Millsaps Coll.), 1990, Symphony No. 3 (commd. Amarillo Symphony), 1991, The Seas of God (commd. Greensboro Choral Soc.), 1992, (oratorio) The Temptation of Jesus (commd. 2d Presbyn. Ch. Richmond), 1995, Cello Sonata, 1997, Janus (commd. Seattle Symphony), 1998, (commd. Amarillo Symphony) Roundings, 1999-2000; orchestral works, 1958—, solos, songs, chamber works, 1958—; writer/narrator: ednl. TV series for N.Y. State Dept. Edn. The World of Music. Recipient Founders medal Millsaps Coll., 1957, rec. publ. award Ford Found., 1976; Woodrow Wilson fellow, 1958; Martha Baird Rockefeller Found. grantee, 1973; music award Miss. Inst. Arts and Letters, 1986, 91; Internat. Angel award, 1997; named to Miss. Musicians Hall of Fame, 2000. Mem. ASCAP, Houston Profl. Musicians Assn., Am. Music Ctr., Condrs. Guild (pres. 1987-89), Nat. Assn. Humanities Edn., Tex. Composers Forum (adv. bd.). Meet the

Composer, Am. Symphony Orch. League, Coll. Music Soc., Omicron Delta Kappa, Lambda Chi Alpha. Methodist. Avocations: birding, reading. Home: 35247 34th Ave S Auburn WA 98001-9034 Office: Seattle Symphony Orch Benaraya Hall PO Box 21906 200 University St Seattle WA 98111-3906 E-mail: campanile@earthlink.net

JONES, THORNTON KEITH, research chemist; b. Brawley, Calif., Dec. 17, 1923; s. Alfred George and Madge Jones; m. Evalee Vestal, July 4, 1965; children: Brian Keith, Donna Eileen. BS, U. Calif., Berkeley, 1949, postgrad., 1951-52. Research chemist Griffin Chem. Co., Richmond, Calif., 1949-55; western product devel. and improvement mgr. Nopco Chem. Co., Richmond, 1955; research chemist Chevron Research Co., Richmond, 1956-65, research chemist in spl. products research and devel., 1965-1982; product quality mgr. Chevron USA, Inc., San Francisco, 1982-87, ret. Patentee in field. Vol. fireman and officer, Terra Linda, Calif., 1957-64; mem. adv. com. Terra Linda Dixie Elem. Sch. Dist., 1960-64. Served with Signal Corps, U.S. Army, 1943-46. Mem. Am. Chem. Soc., Forest Products Research Soc., Am. Wood Preservers Assn., Alpha Chi Sigma. Republican. Presbyterian. Avocations: music, gardening, wine and food.

JONES, TOM, singer; b. Pontypridd, Wales, June 7, 1940; s. Thomas and Freda (Jones) Woodward; m. Melinda Trenchard, 1956; 1 son, Mark. Attended Treforrest Secondary Modern Sch. Bricklayer, factory and constrn. laborer. Pub. singing debut at age 3 in village stores of Wales; sang in local pubs; changed name to Tom Jones, 1963; organized backup group the Playboys to sing in London clubs; first hit record was It's Not Unusual, 1964; appeared on Brit. radio and TV; toured U.S. in 1965, 68; appeared on Ed Sullivan Show; star of TV show This is Tom Jones, 1969-71; regular appearances in nightclubs, concert halls and on TV; songs recorded include What's New Pussycat, 1965, Thunderball, 1965, Green Green Grass of Home, 1966, Delilah, 1968, Love Me Tonight, 1969, Can't Stop Loving You, 1970, She's A Lady, 1971, Letter to Lucille, 1973, Say You'll Stay Until Tomorrow, 1976; albums Darlin, 1981, Move Closer, 1989, Carrying A Torch, 1990 (includes collaborations with Van Morrison); sang score for mus. play Matador; hit single A Boy From Nowhere, 1987, Kiss (in collaboration with Art of Noise), 1988, The Complete Tom Jones, 1993, Reload, 1999 (multi-platinum worldwide), Best of Tom Jones, 2000; film Mars Attacks, 1996, Agnes Brown, 1999, The Emperor's New Groove, 2000; TV appearances include Here, There and Everywhere: a Concert for Linda, 1999, Jerry Springer on Sunday, 1999, An Audience with Tom Jones, 2000, TV series The Morecambe & Wise Show, The Sonny and Cher Show, (voice) The Simpsons, The Fresh Prince of Bel-Air, Russell Gilbert Live, The Panel. Recipient Grammy award as Best New Artist, 1965. Office: c/o Tom Jones Enterprises 10100 Santa Monica Blvd Ste 225 Los Angeles CA 90067-4100

JONES, VERNON QUENTIN, surveyor; b. Sioux City, Iowa, May 6, 1930; s. Vernon Boyd and Winnifred Rhoda Jones; m. Rebeca Buckovecz, Oct. 1981; children: Steven Vernon, Gregory Richard, Stanley Alan, Lynn Sue. Student, UCLA, 1948-50. Draftsman III, city engr. City of Pasadena, Calif., 1950-53; sr. civil engring. asst. L.A. County Engrs., L.A., 1953-55; v.p. Treadwell Engring. Corp., Arcadia, Calif., 1955-61, pres., 1961-64, Hillcrest Engring. Corp., Arcadia, 1961-64; dep. county surveyor Ventura County, Calif., 1964-78; propr. Vernon Jones Land Surveyor, Bullhead City, Ariz., 1978—; city engr. City of Needles, Calif., 1980-87. Instr. Mohave Community Coll., 1987-90. Chmn. graphic tech. com. Ventura Unified Sch. Dist., 1972-78, mem. career adv. com., 1972-74; mem. engring. adv. com. Pierce Coll., 1973; pres. Mgmt. Employees of Ventura County, 1974; v.p. Young Reps. of Ventura County, 1965; pres. Marina Pacifica Homeowners Assn., 1973. Mem. League Calif. Surveying Orgns. (pres. 1975), Am. Congress on Surveying and Mapping (chair so. Calif. sect. 1976), Am. Soc. Photogrammetry, Am. Pub. Works Assn., County Engrs. Assn. Calif. Home: PO Box 20761 Bullhead City AZ 86439-0761

JONES, WALTER HARRISON, chemist, educator; b. Griffin, Sask., Can., Sept. 21, 1922; s. Arthur Frederick and Mildred Tracy (Walter) J.; m. Marion Claire Twomey, Oct. 25, 1959 (dec. Jan. 1976); m. Dorothy-Lynne Byrne, 1979 (div. 1981, remarried 1994, div. 1997). BS with honors, UCLA, 1944, PhD in Chemistry, 1948. Rsch. chemist Dept. Agr., 1948-51, Los Alamos Sci. Lab., 1951-54; sr. rsch. engr. N.Am. Aviation, 1954-56; mgr. chemistry dept. Ford Motor Co., 1956-60, sr. staff and program mgr., chmn. JANAF-ARPA-NASA Thermochem. panel Inst. Def. Analyses, 1960-63; head propulsion dept. Aerospace Corp., 1963-64; sr. scientist, head advanced tech. Hughes Aircraft Co., 1964-68; prof. aero. systems, dir. Corpus Christi Ctr. U. West Fla., Pensacola, 1969-75, prof. chemistry, 1975-95; vis. rsch. chemist UCLA, 1994—. Vis. prof. U. Toronto, 1979, 92, U. Queensland 1998; cons. pvt., fed. and state agys. Author: (fiction) Prisms in the Pentagon, 1971; contbr. numerous articles to tech. jours., chpts. to books; patentee in field. Mem. Gov.'s Task Force on Energy, Regional Energy Action Com., Fla. State Energy Office, adv. com. Tampa Bay Regional Planning Coun.; judge regional and state sci. fairs. Fed. and state grantee; rsch. corp. grantee. Fellow ASEE/ONR, NATO, Am. Inst. Chemists; mem. AIAA, AAUP, AAAS, Am. Astron. Soc. (propulsion com.), Am. Chem. Soc. (chmn. Pensacola sect.), N.Y. Acad. Scis., Am. Phys. Soc., Internat. Solar Energy Soc., Combustion Inst. World Assn. Theoretical Organic Chemists, Am. Ordnance Assn., Air Force Assn., Philos. Soc. Washington, Pensacola C. of C., Milurophile, Phi Beta Kappa, Sigma Xi (pres. local chpt.), Pi Mu Epsilon, Phi Lambda Upsilon (sec. local chpt.), Alpha Mu Gamma, Alpha Chi Sigma (pres. local chpt.). E-mail: ailurophile. Home and Office: 355 Calle Loma Norte Santa Fe NM 87501-1256

JONES, WILLIAM ALLEN, lawyer, entertainment company executive; b. Phila., Dec. 13, 1941; s. Roland Emmett and Gloria (Miller) J.; m. Margaret Smith, Sept. 24, 1965 (div. 1972); m. Dorothea S. Whitson, June 15, 1973; children— Darlene, Rebecca, Gloria, David. BA, Temple U., 1967; MBA, JD, Harvard U., 1972. Bar: Calif. 1974. Atty. Walt Disney Prodns., Burbank, Calif., 1973-77, treas., 1977-81; atty. Wyman Bautzer et al, L.A., 1981-83, MGM/UA Entertainment Co., Culver City, 1983, v.p., gen. counsel, 1983-86; sr. v.p., corp. gen. counsel, sec. MGM/UA Communications Co., Culver City, Calif., 1986-91; exec. v.p., gen. counsel, sec. Metro-Goldwyn-Mayer Inc., Santa Monica, 1991-95, exec. v.p. corp. affairs, 1995-97, sr. exec. v.p., 1997—. Bus. mgr. L.A. Bar Jour., 1974-75; bd. dirs. The Nostalgia Network Inc.; mem. bd. of govs. Inst. for Corp. Counsel, 1990-93. Charter mem. L.A. Philharm. Men's Com., 1974-80; trustee Marlborough Sch., 1988-93, Flintridge Preparatory Sch., 1993-96. With USAF, 1960-64. President's scholar Temple U., 1972 Mem. Harvard Bus. Sch. Assn. So. Calif. (bd. dirs. 1985-88). Home: 1557 Colina Dr Glendale CA 91208-2412 Office: Metro Goldwyn Mayer Inc 2500 Broadway Santa Monica CA 90404-3065

JONGEWARD, GEORGE RONALD, retired systems analyst; b. Yakima, Wash., Aug. 9, 1934; s. George Ira and Dorothy Marie (Cronk) J.; m. Janet Jeanne Williams, July 15, 1955; children: Mary Jeanne, Dona Lee, Karen Anne. BA, Whitworth Coll., 1957; postgrad., Utah State U., 1961. Sr. systems analyst Computer Scis. Corp., Honolulu, 1969-71; cons. in field Honolulu, 1972-76; prin. The Hobby Co., Honolulu, 1977-81; sr. systems analyst Computer Systems Internat., Honolulu, 1981-96, asst. v.p., 1994-96, ret. instr. EDP Hawaii Pacific U., Honolulu, 1982-90. Mem. car show com. Easter Seal Soc., Honolulu. 1977-82; active Variety Club, Honolulu, 1978-81. Mem. Mensa (Hawaii pres. 1967-69), Triple-9. Presbyterian. Avocations: piano, community theatre, golf, sports-car rallies. Home: 4108 Avalanche Ave Yakima WA 98908-2915

JONSEN, ALBERT R(UPERT), retired medical ethics educator; b. San Francisco, Apr. 4, 1931; s. Albert R. and Helen (Sweigert) J. BA, Gonzaga U., 1955, MA, 1956; STM, U. Santa Clara, 1963; PhD, Yale U., 1967. Mem. S.J., 1949-76; ordained priest Roman Cath. Ch.; instr. philosophy Loyola U., L.A., 1956-59; asst. in instrn. Yale Div. Sch., 1966-67; asst. prof. theology and philosophy U. San Francisco, 1967-72, pres., 1969-72; prof. med. ethics Sch. Medicine, U. Calif.-San Francisco, 1972-87; adj. assoc. prof. dept. community medicine and internat. health Sch. Medicine, Georgetown U., 1977; prof. med. ethics, chmn. dept. med. history and ethics Sch. Medicine U. Wash., Seattle, 1987-99; prof. emeritus. Vis. prof. Yale U., 1999-2000; mem. artificial heart assessment panel Nat. Heart and Lung Inst., 1972-73, 84-86; mem. Am. Bd. Med. Spltys., 1978-81; cons. Am. Bd. Internal Medicine, 1978-82, ACOG, 1983-88; mem. Pres.'s Commn. for Study of Ethical Problems in Medicine, 1979-82, Nat. Commn. for Protection Human Subjects of Biomed. and Behavioral Rsch., HEW, 1974-78; mem. Nat. Bd. Med. Examiners, 1985-87; mem. Commn. on AIDS Rsch., NRC, 1986-92, Panel on Social Impact of AIDS (chmn.), 1989-91; chmn. nat. adv. bd. Ethics and Reprodn., 1991-96; mem. ethics adv. bd. GERON Corp., 2000—. Author: Responsibility in Modern Religious Ethics, 1968, Patterns of Moral Responsibility, 1969, Christian Decision and Action, 1970, Ethics of Newborn Intensive Care, 1976, Clinical Ethics, 1982, The Abuse of Casuistry: A History of Moral Reasoning, 1987, The New Medicine and the Old Ethics, 1990, The Social Impact of AIDS in the United States, 1993, Bioethics, 1997, The Birth of Bioethics, 1998, A Short History of Medical Ethics, 2000; mem. editl. bd. Jour. Philosophy and Medicine, Jour. Clin. Ethics. Trustee Inst. Ednl. Mgmt., Harvard U., 1971-74, Ploughshares Found., 1980-84; mem. San Francisco Crime Com., 1969-71; bd. dirs. Found. Critical Care Medicine, 1983-86, Sierra Health Found., 1987—. Guggenheim fellow, 1995-96. Fellow Inst. for Soc., Ethics and Life Scis.; mem. Soc. Health and Human Values (pres. 1986-87), Am. Soc. Law and Medicine (bd. dirs. 1986-88), Soc. Christian Ethics, Inst. Medicine of NAS (com. human values 1973, coun. 1983-85, 90-92), Instituto de Bioetica (Madrid), Blue Cross and Blue Shield Assn. (med. adv. panel, tech. assessment program 1985—). Home: 1383 Jones St # 502 San Francisco CA 94109 Office: U Wash Med History Ethics PO Box 357120 Seattle WA 98195-7120

JOPPA, ROBERT GLENN, aeronautics educator; b. Orchard, Colo., Aug. 25, 1922; s. Martin and Beatrice Virginia (Winkelseth) J.; m. Dorris Eileen Campbell, Mar. 3, 1944; children— Paul Douglas, Susan Elise. B.S., U. Wash., 1945, M.S., 1951; M.A., Princeton U., 1962, Ph.D., 1972. Wind tunnel operator U. Wash., Seattle, 1942-49, instr., 1949-53, asst. prof., 1953, assoc. prof., 1956, prof. aeronautics, 1970-88, dir. advising Coll. Engring., 1987, prof. emeritus, 1988—. Vis. prof. Nat. U. Singapore, 1989-90, 91-92; NSF faculty fellow Princeton U., 1960-62; with Boeing Co., Seattle, summers, 1955, 61; mem. com. NAE, 1984-85; aircraft accident analyst cons. and expert witness in field. Contbr. articles in field to profl. jours.; patentee in field of gliding anchor. Fellow AIAA (assoc.); mem. Soc. Flight Test Engrs., Sigma Xi. Unitarian. Office: U Wash Dept Aero & Astronautics PO Box 352400 Seattle WA 98195-2400 E-mail: Joppa@u.washington.edu

JORDAN, AMOS AZARIAH, JR. foreign affairs educator, retired army officer; b. Twin Falls, Idaho, Feb. 11, 1922; s. Amos Azariah and Olive (Fisher) J.; m. MarDeane Carver, June 5, 1946; children: Peggy Jordan Hughes, Diana Jordan Paxton, Keith, David, Linda Jordan Mabey, Kent. BS, U.S. Mil. Acad., 1946; BA, Oxford U., Eng., 1950, MA, 1955; PhD, Columbia U., 1961. Commd. 2d lt. U.S. Army, 1946, advanced through grades to brig. gen., 1972; instr. U.S. Mil. Acad., 1950-53, prof. social scis., 1955-72; arty. battery comdr. U.S. Army, Korea, 1954-55; asst. S-3 7th Divsn. Arty. Korea, 1955; adviser econ. and fiscal policy U.S. Econ. Mission to Korea, 1955; ret. U.S. Army, 1972; dir. Aspen Inst., 1972-74; prin. dep. asst. sec. for internat. security affairs Dept. Def., Washington, 1974-76; dep. undersec. and acting undersec. for security assistance Dept. State, Washington, 1976-77; with Ctr. for Strategic and Internat. Studies, Washington, 1977-94, pres, chief exec. officer, 1983-88, vice chmn., 1988-94, pres. Pacific Forum Honolulu, 1990-94; sr. adviser CSIS, 1994—; counselor Pacific Forum, 1994—. Mem. staff Pres.'s Com. to Study Fgn. Assistance Program, 1959; staff dir. Adv. Com. to Sec. Def. on Non-Mil. Instrn., 1962; spl. polit. advisor to U.S. amb. to India, 1963-64; cons. NSC, 1979; mem. Nat. Com. on Security and Econ. Assistance, 1983; Henry Kissinger rsch. chair in nat. security policy CSIS, 1988-92; mem. Pres.'s Intelligence Oversight Bd., 1989-93; internat. co-chmn. Coun. on Sec. Coop. in the Asia Pacific, 1993-96, chmn. U.S. com., 1993-98; co-chmn. Korean-Am. Wisemen Coun., 1991-98; Asia area adminstr. Latter Day Saint Charities, 1998-99; mem. bd. dirs. Pacific Forum, Ctr. for Strategic and Internat. Studies. Author: Foreign Aid and the Defense of Southeast Asia, 1962, Issues of National Security in the 1970's, 1967; co-author: American National Security Policy and Process, 1981, 5th edit., 1999; contbr. chpts. to books and articles to profl. jours. Asia area adminstr. Latter Day Saints Charities, 1998-99. Decorated D.S.M., Legion of Merit with oak leaf cluster, Disting. Civilian Svc. medal Dept. Def. Mem. Coun. Fgn. Rels., Assn. Am. Rhodes Scholars, Pacific Coun. Internat. Policy, Bretton Woods Com. Office: Pacific Forum CSIS Pauahi Tower 1001 Bishop St Ste 1150 Honolulu HI 96813-3407 E-mail: jordanaamc@sisna.com

JORDAN, GLENN, director; b. San Antonio, Apr. 5, 1936; BA, Harvard U., 1957; postgrad., Yale U. Drama Sch., 1957-58. Dir. regional and stock theatre, including Cafe La Mama, late 1950s; N.Y. directorial debut with Another Evening With Harry Stoones, 1961; other plays include A Taste of Honey, 1968; Rosencrantz and Guildenstern Are Dead, 1969, A Streetcar Named Desire at Cin. Playhouse in the Park, 1973, All My Sons at Huntington Hartford Theatre, 1975; founder, N.Y. TV Theater, 1965, dir. various plays, including Paradise Lost and Hogan's Goat; dir. mini-series Benjamin Franklin, CBS, 1974 (Emmy award 1975, Peabody award); Family, ABC-TV series, 1976-77, including segment Rights of Friendship (Dirs. Guild Am. award); numerous TV plays for public TV, including Eccentricities of a Nightingale, 1976; The Displaced Person, 1976; TV movies including Shell Game, 1975, One Of My Wives Is Missing, 1975, Delta County U.S.A, 1977, In The Matter of Karen Ann Quinlan, 1977, Sunshine Christmas, 1977, Les Miserables, 1978, Son-Rise, A Miracle of Love, 1979, The Family Man, 1979, The Women's Room, 1980, Lois Gibbs and the Love Canal, 1982, Heartsounds, 1984 (Peabody award), Toughlove, 1985, Dress Gray, 1986, Something in Common, 1986, Promise, 1986 (2 Emmy awards for producing, directing, Peabody award, Golden Globe award), Echoes in the Darkness, 1987, Jesse, 1988, Home Fires Burning, 1988, Challenger, 1989, The Boys, 1990, Sarah Plain and Tall, 1990, Aftermath, 1990, O Pioneers!, 1991, Barbarians at the Gate, 1992 (Emmy award Outstanding Made for TV Movie, 1993, Golden Globe award, Best Mini-series or movie made for TV, 1994), To Dance with the White Dog, 1994, Jane's House, 1994, My Brother's Keeper, 1994, A Streetcar Named Desire, 1995, Jake's Women (Neil Simon), 1996, After Jimmy, 1996, Mary and Tim, 1996, A Christmas Memory, 1997, The Long Way Home, 1998, Legalese, 1998, Night Ride Home, 1999, Winter's End: Sarah Plain & Tall III, 1999, Midwives, 2000; dir: feature film Only When I Laugh (Neil Simon), 1981, The Buddy System, 1983, Mass Appeal, 1984. Recipient Emmy awards for N.Y. TV Theater Plays, 1970, Actors Choice, 1970. Office: Creative Artists Agy 9830 Wilshire Blvd Beverly Hills CA 90212-1825 also: 9401 Wilshire Blvd Ste 700 Beverly Hills CA 90212-2920

JORDAN, JEFFREY GUY, marketing and marketing research consultant; b. Oshkosh, Wis., May 21, 1950; s. Berwin Russell and Delores Suzanne (Tomlitz) J. BS, U. Wis., Oshkosh, 1973; postgrad., UCLA, 1978. Analyst corp. planning and rsch. May Co. Dept. Store, L.A., 1973-77; dir. mktg. svcs. DJMC Advt., L.A., 1977-80; dir. mktg. Wienerschnitzel, Internat., Newport Beach, Calif., 1980-84, York Steakhouse Restaurants (Gen. Mills), Columbus, Ohio, 1984-85, Paragon Restaurant Group, San Diego, 1985-87; v.p. mktg. Paragon Steakhouse Restaurants, Inc., San Diego, 1987-94; owner, pres. 1-on-One Mktg. Assocs., 1994—. Cons., presenter U.S. Internat. U., San Diego, 1989. Mem. Conv. and Visitors Bur., San Diego; vol. Boys' Club of Am., Oshkosh, 1973-74; fundraising coord. Am. Cancer Soc., L.A., 1976. Mem. Am. Mktg. Assn. (treas., bd. dirs. 1996-97), Multi Unit Foodservice Operators Assn., San Diego Advt. Assn. (creative exec. 1986-88), San Diego C. of C. Republican. Lutheran. Avocations: sports, travel, photography.

JORDAN, MICHELLE HENRIETTA, public relations company executive; b. Sussex, Eng., Sept. 19, 1948; came to U.S., 1975; d. Raymond Cameron and Liliane (Ambar) J.; m. Billy Owens, 1994. Student, Sorbonne, 1966-67. With Coordinated Mktg. Services Ltd., London, 1967-71; dir. Spectrum Public Relations, London, 1971-74; with Rowland Co., N.Y.C., 1975-87, exec. v.p.; sr. v.p., mng. dir. mktg. svcs. div. Hill and Knowlton, N.Y.C., 1987-91; prin. The Dilenschneider Group, N.Y.C., 1991-94; v.p. Digital Pictures, San Mateo, Calif., 1994-96; pres. The GCI Group, L.A., 1996-98; owner Jordan LLC, 1998—. Mem. Mayor N.Y.C. Commn. Status Women, 1980-86; bd. dirs. New Dramatists, Religion in Am. Life, 1992-94, Working Wardrobes, 1999—. Recipient Matrix award N.Y. Women in Communications, 1990. Office: Jordan LLC 18101 Von Karman Ave Ste 1280 Irvine CA 92612-0168

JORDAN, RICHARD CHARLES, engineering executive; b. Mpls., Apr. 16, 1909; s. A.C. and Estelle R. (Martin) J.; m. Freda M. Laudon, Aug. 10, 1935; children: Mary Ann, Carol Lynn, Linda Lee. B. Aero. Engring., U. Minn., 1931, M.S., 1933, Ph.D., 1940. In charge air conditioning div. Mpls. br. Am. Radiator & Standard San. Corp., 1933-36; instr. petroleum engring. U. Tulsa, 1936-37; instr. engring. expt. sta. U. Minn., Mpls., 1937-41, asst. dir., 1941-44, assoc. prof., 1944-45, prof., asst. head mech. engring. dept., 1946-49, prof., head dept. mech. engring., 1950-77, prof., head Sch. Mech. and Aero. Engring., 1966-77, acting assoc. dean Inst. Tech., 1977-78, assoc. dean, 1978-85; pres. Jordan Assocs., 1985—. Dir. Onan Corp. of McGraw-Edison; cons. various refrigeration and air conditioning cos., 1937—; cons. NSF, U.S. Dept. State, Control Data Corp., others.; Mem. engring. sci. adv. panel NSF, 1954-57, chmn., 1957; mem. div. engring. and indsl. research NRC, mem. exec. com., 1957-69, chmn., 1962-65; del. OAS Conf. on Strategy for Tech. Devel. Latin Am., Chile, 1969; chmn. U.S.-Brazil Sci. Coop. Program Com. on Indsl. Research, Rio de Janeiro, 1967, Washington, 1967, Belo Horizonte, 1968, Houston, 1968; del. World Power Conf., Melbourne, 1962; v.p. sci. council Internat. Institut du Froid, 1967-71; cons. to World Bank on alternative energy for Northeastern Brazil, 1976 Author: (with Priester) Refrigeration and Air Conditioning, 1948, rev. edit., 1956, also more than 300 publs. on mech. engring., environ. control, solar energy, energy resources, engring. edn., tech. transfer.; Contbr. Mech. Engring. Recipient F. Paul Anderson medal ASHRAE, 1966, E.K. Campbell award, 1966, Outstanding Publs. Golden Key award, 1994, Outstanding Achievement award U. Minn., 1979; elected to Solar Energy Hall of Fame, 1980; Richard C. Jordan disting. prof. in mech. engring. established in his honor, 1994. Fellow ASME, AAAS, ASHRAE (presdl. mem.); mem. Nat. Acad. Engring., Assn. Applied Solar Energy (adv. council 1958-61), Am. Soc. Refrigerating Engrs. (1st v.p. 1952, pres. 1953, dir., council mem. 1946-53), Am. Soc. Engring. Edn., AAAS, Nat., Minn. (Engr. of Yr. award 1972), socs. profl. engrs., Internat. Inst. Refrigeration (hon. mem., del. NRC to exec. com. 1957-76, v.p. exec. com. 1959-63, v.p. sci. council 1963-71), Engr. Council Profl. Devel. (chmn. regional edn. and accreditation com.), Sigma Xi, Tau Beta Pi, Pi Tau Sigma, Sigma Chi. Club: Campus. Home and Office: 18418 E Horseshoe Cir Rio Verde AZ 85263-7036

JORDAN, ROBERT LEON, lawyer, educator; b. Reading, Pa., Feb. 27, 1928; s. Anthony and Carmela (Votto) J.; m. Evelyn Allen Willard, Feb. 15, 1958 (dec. Nov. 1996); children: John Willard, David Anthony BA, Pa. State U., 1948; LLB, Harvard U., 1951. Bar: N.Y. 1952. Assoc. White & Case, N.Y.C., 1953-59; prof. law UCLA, 1959-70, 75-91, prof. law emeritus, 1991—, assoc. dean Sch. Law, 1968-69. Vis. prof. law Cornell U., Ithaca, N.Y., 1962-63; co-reporter Uniform Consumer Credit Code, 1964-70, Uniform Comml. Code Articles 3, 4, 4A, 1985-90; Fulbright lectr. U. Pisa, Italy, 1967-68 Co-author: (with W.D. Warren) Commercial Law, 1983, 5th edit., 2000, Bankruptcy, 1985, 5th edit., 1999. Lt. USAF, 1951-53. Office: UCLA Sch Law 405 Hilgard Ave Los Angeles CA 90095-9000

JORDAN, STEPHEN M. university president; m. Ruth Kinnie; 3 children. BA in Polit. Sci., U. No. Colo., 1971; MPA in Fin. Adminstrn., U. Colo., Denver, 1979, PhD in Pub. Adminstrn./Policy Analysis, 1990. Vice chancellor for budgets and facilities U. Colo. Health Scis. Ctr., 1985—, asst. sec. bd. regents, 1985—; dep. exec. dir. fin. and planning, Bd. Regents Ariz. State U., 1989—; exec. dir. Kans. Bd. Regents, 1994—; pres. Eastern Wash. U., Cheney, 1998—. Mem. Spokane Valley High Tech. Coun.; mem. bd. Spokane Symphony, 2000, Wash. Tech. Ctr., 2000. Mem. Spokane Area C. of C. (bd. dirs. 2000). Office: Eastern Wash U Showalter Hall Rm 214 Cheney WA 99004-2444

JORDAN, THOMAS HILLMAN, geophysicist, educator; b. Coco Solo, C.Z., Republic of Panama, Oct. 8, 1948; s. Clarence Eugene and Beulah (Greer) J.; m. Margaret Jordan; 1 child, Alexandra Elyse. BS, Calif. Inst. Tech., 1969, MS in Geophysics, 1970, PhD in Geophysics and Applied Math., 1972. Asst. prof. Princeton (N.J.) U., 1972-75, Scripps Instn. of Oceanography, U. Calif. San Diego, La Jolla, 1975-77, assoc. prof., 1977-82, prof., 1982-84, MIT, Cambridge, 1984-85, U. So. Calif., L.A., 2000—. Contbr. over 120 articles to sci. publs. Fellow AAAS, Am. Geophys. Union (James B. Macelwane award 1983, George P. Woolard award 1998); mem. NAS. Office: U So Calif Dept Earth Scis Los Angeles CA 90089-0740 E-mail: tjordan@usc.edu

JORGENSEN, ERIK HOLGER, lawyer; b. Copenhagen, July 19, 1916; s. Holger and Karla (Andersen) J.; children: Jette Friis, Lone Olssen, John, Jean Ann. JD, San Francisco Law Sch., 1960. Bar: Calif. 1961. Atty. pvt. practice, 1961-70; ptnr. Hersh, Hadfield, Jorgensen & Fried, San Francisco, 1970-76, Hadfield & Jorgensen, San Francisco, 1976-88. Author: Master Forms Agreements, Successful Real Estate Sales Agreements, 1991; contbr. articles on law and real estate to profl. jours. Pres. Aldersley, Danish Retirement Home, San Rafael, Calif., 1974-77, REbild Park Soc. Bay Area chpt., 1974-77. Fellow Scandinavian Am. Found. (hon.); mem. ABA, Calif. Assn. Realtors Assn. (hon. life bd. dirs.), San Francisco Lawyers Club, Bar Assn. San Francisco.

JORGENSEN, GORDON DAVID, retired engineering company executive; b. Chgo., Apr. 29, 1921; s. Jacob and Marie (Jensen) J.; m. Nadina Anita Peters, Dec. 17, 1948 (div. Aug. 1971); children: Karen Ann, David William, Susan Marie; m. Barbara Noel, Feb. 10, 1972 (div. July 1976); m. Ruth Barnes Chalmers, June 15, 1990. BSEE, U. Wash., 1948, postgrad. in bus. and mgmt., 1956-59. Registered profl. engr., Alaska, Ariz., Calif., Colo., Nev., N.Mex., N.D., Utah, Wash., Wyo. With R.W. Beck & Assocs., Cons. Engrs., Phoenix, 1948—, ptnr., 1954-86; pres. Beck Internat., Phoenix, 1971—; ret. Project mgr. for mgmt., operation studies and reorgn. study Honduras power sys., 1969-70. Served to lt. (j.g.) U.S. Maritime Svc., 1942-45. Recipient Outstanding Svc. award Phoenix Tennis Assn., 1967, Commendation, Govt. Honduras, 1970. Mem. IEEE (chmn. Wash.-Alaska sect. 1959-60), NSPE, Am. Soc. Appraisers (sr. mem.), Ariz. Cons.

Engrs. Assn., Ariz. Soc. Profl. Engrs., Internat. Assn. Assessing Officers, Southwestern Tennis Assn. (past pres.), U.S. Tennis Assn. (pres. 1987-88, chmn. U.S. Open com.), chmn. U.S. Davis Cup com., chmn. Internat. Tennis Fed., Davis Cup com.). Presbyterian (elder). Home: 74-574 Palo Verde Dr Indian Wells CA 92210-7314

JORGENSEN, LOU ANN BIRKBECK, social worker; b. Park City, Utah, May 14, 1931; d. Robert John and Lillian Pearl (Langford) Birkbeck; m. Howard Arnold Jorgenson, June 9, 1954; children: Gregory Arnold, Blake John, Paul Clayton. Student, Westminster Coll., 1949-51; BS, U. Utah, 1953, MSW, 1972, DSW, 1979; grad., Harvard Inst. Ednl. Mgmt., 1983. Social work adminstr. nursing home demonstration project, dept. family and cmty. medicine U. Utah Med. Ctr., Salt Lake City, 1972-74; mental health ednl. specialist Grad. Sch. Social Work U. Utah, Salt Lake City, 1974-77, 77-80, asst. prof., 1974-80, assoc. prof., 1980-94, prof., 1994-97, prof. emeritus, 1997—, dir. doctoral program, 1984-89, 94-97, assoc. dean, 1986-94. Regional mental health cons. Author: Explorations in Living, 1978, Social Work in Business and Industry, 1979, Handbook of the Social Services, 1981, (with others) Women as They Are, 2d edit., 2001; editl. bd. Jour. of Women and Aging; contbr. articles to profl. jours. Bd. dirs. Info. and Referral Ctr., 1975-82, United Way of Utah, 1976-82, Pioneer Trail Parks, 1977-83, Rowland Hall-St. Mark's Sch., 1980-86, Salt Lake County Housing commr., 1980-86, Utah State Health Facilities Bd., 1991-2001, chmn., 1994-95, 97-98; pres. Human Svcs. Conf. for Utah, 1979-80; bd. dirs. Alzheimer's Assn., Utah chpt., 1990-97, Salt Lake County Coalition Bus. and Human Svcs., 1990-94; mem. Valley Mental Health Bd., 1990-2000; bd. dirs. Ballet West, 2000—; bd. dirs., chair Norman S. Anderson MD Mental Health Award, 1999-2000. Mem. NASW (pres. Utah chpt. 1978-79), Coun. on Social Work Edn., Commn. Women in Higher Edn. Adminstrs. Pub. Agys. Assn., Human Svcs. Assn. Utah, Jr. League Salt Lake City, Town Club (pres. bd. dirs. 2000—), Phi Kappa Phi. Republican. Episcopalian. Home and Office: 1458 Kristianna Cir Salt Lake City UT 84103-4221 E-mail: ljorgensen@uofu.com

JORGENSEN, PAUL J. research company executive; b. Midway, Utah, Sept. 1, 1930; s. Joseph and Alice P. Jorgensen; m. Ardelle M. Bloom, Sept. 11, 1959; children: Paula, Mark, Janet, LaDell, Brett, Scott. Student, U. Utah, 1948-50, PhD, 1960; BS, Brigham Young U., 1954. Scientist Gen. Electric Co., Schenectady, N.Y., 1960-68; mgr. ceramics group Stanford Research Inst., Menlo Park, Calif., 1968-74, dir. materials research ctr., 1974-76; exec. dir. phys. sci. div. SRI Internat., Menlo Park, 1976-77, v.p. phys. and life sci. div., 1977-80, sr. v.p. scis. group, 1980-88, exec. v.p., COO, 1988-94, also bd. dirs., exec. v.p., 1994—. Cons. GTE, 1971-82; mem. com. high temperature chemistry NRC, 1972-75, nat. materials adv. bd., 1982-85; mem. Internat. Panel of Advisors on Tech., Singapore Inst. Stds. & Indsl. Rsch. Contbr. articles to profl. jours.; patentee in field. Served with U.S. Army, 1954-56. Recipient IR-100, Indsl. Research Mag., 1967. Fellow Am. Ceramic Soc. (chmn. basic sci. div. 1975). Republican. Mormon. Office: SRI Internat 333 Ravenswood Ave Menlo Park CA 94025-3453 E-mail: paul.jorgensen@sri.com

JOSELYN, JO ANN, space scientist; b. St. Francis, Kans., Oct. 5, 1943; d. James Jacob and Josephine Felzien (Firkins) Cram. BS in Applied Math., U. Colo., 1965, MS in Astro Geophysics, 1967, Ph.D. in Astro Geophysics, 1978. Research asst. NASA-Manned Space Ctr., Houston, 1966; physicist NOAA-Space Environ. Lab., Boulder, Colo., 1967-78; space scientist NOAA-Space Environ. Ctr., Boulder, 1978-99; chief Geospace Branch, 1992-95; sec.-gen. Internat. Union Geodesy and Geophysics, 1999—. U.S. del. study group 6 Consultive Com. for Ionospheric Radio, 1981, 83; mem. com. on data mgmt. and computation NASA Space Sci. Bd., 1988. Mem. U. Colo. Grad. Sch. Alumni Coun., 1986-90, U. Colo. Engring. Devel. Coun., 1991-99, U. Colo. Adv. Coun. for the Women in Engring. Program, 1992-98, Grad. Sch. Adv. Coun. Recipient unit citation NOAA, 1971, 80, 85, 86, sustained superior performance award 1985, 87-90, 92, 94; group achievement award NASA, 1983, Disting. Engring. Alumnus award U. Colo., 1987, Dir.'s award Space Environ. Lab., 1991, 95, Pacesetter award Boulder County, 1994, Sec. Commerce award for Customer Svc. Excellence, 1994, George Norlin award U. Colo. Alumni Assn., 2000; elected to U. Colo. Disting. Alumni Gallery, 1995; named Woman of Achievement, Zonta Club, Boulder, 1996; fellow Sci. and Tech. Agy. Japan, 1990-91. Mem. AAAS, AAUW, PEO, Am. Women in Sci., Am. Geophys. Union, Union Radio Sci. Internat. (commns. G and H, membership chair of commn. H 1993-96), Internat. Assn. Geomagnetism and Aeronomy (co-chair Divsn. V on observatories, instruments, indices and data 1991-95, sec.-gen. 1995-99), Internat. Astron. Union (commns. 10 and 49), Rotary Internat., Ikebana Internat., Sigma Xi, Tau Beta Pi, Sigma Tau. Republican. Methodist. Office: Univ Colo CIRES Campus Box 216 Boulder CO 80309-0216 E-mail: jjoselyn@cires.colorado.edu

JOSEPH, ALLAN JAY, lawyer; b. Chgo., Feb. 4, 1938; s. George S. and Emily (Miller) Cohen; m. Phyllis L. Freedman, Sept. 1, 1958; children—Elizabeth, Susan, Katherine. B.B.A., U. Wis., Madison, 1959; J.D. cum laude, 1962. Bar: Wis. bar 1962, Calif. bar 1964. Ptnr. Pettit & Martin, San Francisco, 1965-80, Rogers, Joseph, O'Donnell & Quinn, San Francisco, 1981—. Served to capt. JACG AUS, 1962-65. Am. Bar Found. fellow, 1978— Mem.ABA (nat. chmn. pub. contract law sect. 1977-78, ho. of dels. 1980-84, bd. govs. 1995-98, chair fin. com. 1997-98), FBA, Am. Bar Retirement Assn. (trustee 1984-92, pres. 1989-90), State Bar Calif., Nat. Contract Mgmt. Assn., Order of Coif. Home: 2461 Washington St San Francisco CA 94115-1816 Office: 311 California St Fl 10 San Francisco CA 94104-2614

JOSEPH, EZEKIEL (ED JOSEPH), manufacturing company executive; b. Rangoon, Burma, June 24, 1938; s. Joe E. Joseph and Rachel Levi; m. Sheila G. Rabinovitch, Feb. 17, 1963; children: Renah, Heather, Jerald. Mktg. mgr. Gen. Electric Corp., Waynesboro, Va., 1968-75; dir. Actron div. McDonnell Douglas Corp., Monrovia, Calif., 1975-78; pres. Joseph Machinery Inc., Huntington Beach, 1978-84, Xtalite Display Systems Inc.), Huntington Beach, 1985-88, Secure Optical Systems Inc., Anaheim, Calif., 1992-98, Peak Machinery Sales, Inc., Irvine, 1998-99, Select Machine Tool Group, Huntington Beach, 1999; gen. mgr. Yamage Tech. Inc., Compton, Calif., 1999—. Democrat. Avocations: antique cars, sailing. Home: 19092 Redford Dr Huntington Beach CA 92648 Office: Yamage Tech Inc 825 W Walnut St Compton CA 90220-5100

JOSEPH, MICHAEL THOMAS, broadcast consultant; b. Youngstown, Ohio, Nov. 23, 1927; s. Thomas A. and Martha (McCarius) J.; m. Eva Ursula Boerger, June 21, 1952. BA, Case Western Res. U., 1949. Program dir. Fetzer Broadcasting, Grand Rapids, Mich., 1952-55; nat. program dir. Founders Corp., N.Y.C., 1955-57; program cons. to ABC, CBS, NBC, Capital Cities, Infinity, Cox, Gannett, Greater Media, N.Y. Times, 1958—; v.p. radio Capital Cities, N.Y.C., 1959-60; v.p. owned radio stas. NBC, N.Y.C., 1963-65. Mem. Internat. Radio and TV Soc., Nat. Assn. Broadcasters Roman Catholic.

JOSEPHSON, NANCY, talent agent; d. Marvin J.; m. David Stern; 3 children. Grad., Brown U., 1980, Harvard Law Sch., 1982. Atty., 1982-86, Internat. Creative Mgmt., Beverly Hills, 1986, head N.Y. TV dept.; various positions as an agent, 1979-87; head TV lit. dept. Internat. Creative Mgmt., Beverly Hills, 1987-95, exec. v.p. of TV, 1995—, co-pres., 1998—. Developer (TV shows) Friends, Nash Bridges, Caroline in the City, The Simpsons. Named one of top twenty-five most important women in entertainment Hollywood's Reporter. Office: Internat Creative Mgmt 8942 [illegible]

JOSEPHSON, RICHARD CARL, lawyer; b. Washington, Nov. 20, 1947; s. Horace Richard and Margaret Louise (Loeffler) J.; m. Jean Carol Attridge, Aug. 1, 1970; children: Lee Margaret, Amy Dorothy. AB, Case Western Res. U., 1969; JD, Coll. of William and Mary, 1972. Bar: Oreg. 1973. Law clk. Hon. John D. Butzner, Jr., U.S. Ct. Appeals, 4th Cir., Richmond, Va., 1972-73; mem. Stoel Rives LLP, Portland, Oreg., 1973—. Bd. dirs. Tucker-Maxon Oral Sch., Portland, 1987—, Vis. Nurse Assn., Portland, 1978-89, Healthlink, Portland, 1984-89, St. Mary's Acad., Portland, 1998-2001. 1st lt. U.S. Army, 1973-79. Fellow Am. Coll. Bankruptcy, Am. Coll. Comml. Fin. Lawyers; mem. ABA, Am. Bankruptcy Inst., Oreg. Bar Assn. (chmn. debtor-creditor sect. 1980-81). Presbyterian. Avocations: skiing, white water rafting, running, cycling, theatre. Office: Stoel Rives LLP 900 SW 5th Ave Ste 2300 Portland OR 97204-1229 E-mail: rcjosephson@stoel.com

JOSHI, CHANDRASHEKHAR JANARDAN, physics educator; b. Wai, India, July 22, 1953; came to U.S., 1981; s. Janardan Digambar and Ramabai (Kirpekar) J.; m. Asha Bhatt, Jan. 18, 1982. BS, London U., 1974; PhD, Hull U., U.K., 1978. Research assoc. Nat. Research Council, Can., 1978-81; research engr. UCLA, 1981-83, adj. assoc. prof., 1983-86, assoc. prof.-in-residence, 1986-87, assoc. prof., 1987-88, prof. elec. engring., 1988—. Cons. Lawrence Livermore (Calif.) Nat. Lab., 1984, Los Alamos (N.Mex.) Nat. Lab., 1985—. Editor: Laser Acceleration of Particles, 1985, Advanced Acceleration Concepts, 1989; contbr. articles ot profl. jours. Grantee NSF, U.S. Dept. Energy; recipient Queen Mary Prize, Inst. Nuclear Engring., 1974. Mem. AAAS, IEEE, Am. Phys. Soc. (award for excellence in plasma rsch. 1996), N.Y. Acad. Scis. Avocation: traveling. Office: UCLA 405 Hilgard Ave Los Angeles CA 90095-9000

JOURNEL, ANDRÉ G. petroleum engineering educator; BS in Mining Engring., Ecole Nat. Superieure Mines, Nancy, France, 1967; DSc in Econ. Geology, U. Nancy, 1974, DSc in Applied Math., 1977. Mining project engr. Ctr. Morphologie Math., 1969-73; maitre rsch. Ctr. Geostatisque Paris Sch. Mines, 1973-78; vis. assoc. prof. applied earth scis. Stanford (Calif.) U., 1978-79, assoc. prof. applied earth scis., 1979-86, chmn. applied earth scis., 1986-92, prof. applied earth scis., 1987-92, Donald and Donald M. Steel prof. earth scis., 1994, prof. petroleum engring. and geol. and environ. scis., 1992—, dir. Ctr. for Reservoir Forecasting, 1986—. Cons., spkr. in field; mem. sci. com. Geostats. Congress, 1980—. Assoc. editor Math. Geology, 1989-95. Recipient Krumbein medal Math. Geology, 1989, Anthony F. Lucas Gold medal Soc. Profl. Engrs., 1998. Mem. N.Am. Coun. on Geostats. (founder), NAE. Achievements include research in modeling of spatially heterogeneous media accounting for information of diverse sources, scales and accuracies. Avocations: postry, running. Office: Stanford U Dept Petroleum Engring Green Earth Scis Bldg 098 Stanford CA 94305-2220

JOY, BILL, computer company executive; BSEE, U. Mich., 1975, MSEE and Computer Sci., 1982. Co-founder, v.p. rsch. Sun Microsyss. Inc., Mountain View, Calif., founder, chief scientist, 1998—. Prin. designer U. Calif. (Berkeley) version of UNIX operating sys.; co-designer SPARC microprocessor architecture. Mem. NAE. Office: Sun Microsyss Inc 901 San Antonio Rd Palo Alto CA 94303-4900

JOY, EDWARD BENNETT, electrical engineer, educator; b. Troy, N.Y., Nov. 15, 1941; s. Herman Johnson and Elizbeth (Bennett) J.; m. Patricia Marie Huddleston, Aug. 27, 1966; children: Frederick Huddleston, Rebecca Elizabeth. BEE, Ga. Inst. Tech., 1963, MSEE, 1967, PhDEE, 1970. Asst. prof. elec. engring. Ga. Inst. Tech., Atlanta, 1970-75, assoc. prof., 1975-80, prof., 1980-98, prof. emeritus, 1998—; pres. Joy Engring. Co., Boulder, Colo., 1981—. Cons. to cos., govtl. agys., orgns. Patentee in field; contbr. to profl. publs. Lt. USN, 1963-65, Vietnam. Fellow IEEE; mem. Antenna Measurements Techniques Assn. (past vice-chmn., tech. coord., disting. achievement award). Republican. Presbyterian. Avocations: amateur radio, electronics, jogging. Home and Office: 1450 Rembrandt Rd Boulder CO 80302-9478 E-mail: ed.joy@ece.gatech.edu

JOYCE, GERALD FRANCIS, biochemist, educator; b. Manhattan, Kans., Nov. 28, 1956; BA, U. Chgo., 1978; MD, PhD, U. Calif., San Diego, 1984. Postdoctoral fellow The Salk Inst., 1985-88, sr. rsch. assoc., 1988-89; clin. instr. dept. neuroscis. U. Calif., San Diego, 1987—; asst. prof. dept. chemistry and molecular biology The Scripps Rsch. Inst., La Jolla, Calif., 1989-92, faculty grad. program in macromolecular and cellular structure and chemistry, 1989—, faculty grad. program in chemistry, 1990—, assoc. prof. dept. chemistry and molecular biology, 1992-96, prof. depts. chemistry & molecular biology, 1996—. Mem. exobiology discipline working group NASA, 1990—; investigator NASA Specialized Ctr. for Rsch. and Tng. in Exobiology, 1992—; sci. adv. bd. Ribozyme Pharms., Inc., Boulder, Colo., 1991—; admissions com. grad. program in chemistry The Scripps Rsch. Inst., 1991—, admissions com. grad. program in macromolecular and cellular structure and chemistry, 1994—; lectr. in field. Assoc. editor: Chemistry & Biology; contbr. articles to profl. jours. Recipient Pfizer award in Enzyme Chemistry Am. Chem. Soc., 1995, NAS award in Molecular Biology, 1994; Merck, Sharp & Dohme fellow Life Scis. Rsch. Found., 1985-88. Office: The Scripps Rsch Inst 10550 N Torrey Pines Rd La Jolla CA 92037-1000

JOYCE, ROSEMARY ALEXANDRIA, anthropology educator; b. Lackawanna, N.Y., Apr. 7, 1956; d. Thomas Robert and Joanne Hannah (Poth) J.; m. Russell Nicholas Sheptak, Jan. 7, 1984. BA, Cornell U., 1978; PhD, U. Ill., 1985. Instr. Jackson (Mich.) Community Coll., 1983; lectr. U. Ill., Urbana, 1984-85; asst. curator Peabody Mus., Harvard U., Cambridge, Mass., 1985-86, asst. dir., 1986-89; asst. prof. anthropology Harvard U., Cambridge, 1989-91, assoc. prof. anthropology, 1991-94, U. Calif., Berkeley, 1994—. Author: Cerro Palenque, 1991, Encounters with the Americas, 1995, Gender in Prehispanic Mesoamenica, 2001; editor: Maya History, 1993, Women in Prehistory, 1997, Social Patterns in Preclassic Mesoamerica, 1999, Beyond Kinship, 2000; contbr. articles to profl. jours. NEH grantee, 1985, 86, NSF grantee, 1989, 98, Famsi grantee, 1996, Heinz Found., Wenner-Gren Found. grantee, 1997; Fulbright fellow, 1981-82. Mem. Soc. for Am. Archaeology, Am. Anthropol. Assn. Office: U Calif Anthropology Dept 232 Kroeber Hall # 3710 Berkeley CA 94720-3710 E-mail: rajoyce@uclink.berkeley.edu

JOYCE, STEPHEN MICHAEL, lawyer; b. Los Angeles, Mar. 19, 1945; s. John Rowland and Elizabeth Rose (Rahe) J.; m. Bernadette Anne Novey, Aug. 18, 1973; children: Natalie Elizabeth, Vanessa Anne. BS, Calif. State U., Los Angeles, 1970; JD, U. LaVerne, 1976. Bar: Calif. 1976, U.S. Dist. Ct. (cen. dist.) Calif. 1977, U.S. Ct. Claims 1981. Pvt. practice, Beverly Hills, Calif., 1976-93; ptnr. Gold & Joyce, Beverly Hills, 1982-84. Personal atty. to Stevie Wonder and various other celebrities, 1977—. Contbr. articles to profl. jours. Served to pvt. USAR, 1963-69. Mem. ABA, Calif. Bar Assn., Los Angeles County Bar Assn., Beverly Hills Bar Assn., Los Angeles Trial Lawyers Assn., San Fernando Valley Bar Assn., Calabasas Athletic Club. Democrat. Roman Catholic. Avocation: long distance running. Home: 4724 Barcelona Ct Calabasas CA 91302-1403 Office: 15260 Ventura Blvd Ste 640 Sherman Oaks CA 91403-5340 E-mail: enjoyce2@aol.com

JU, JIANN-WEN, mechanics educator, researcher; b. Taiwan, 1958; s. Jiang and Kwai J.; m. Mali J., 1985; children: Derek, Tiffany. BS, Nat. (Taipei) Taiwan U., 1980; MS, U. Calif., Berkeley, 1983, PhD, 1986. Teaching asst. U. Calif., Berkeley, 1983-84, rsch. asst., 1984-86, lectr., 1986, postdoctoral rsch. engr., 1986-87; asst. prof. Princeton (N.J.) U., [illegible] prof. UCLA, [illegible] prof., [illegible] chmn., [illegible]

Cons. Air Force Engring. and Svcs. Ctr., Panama City, Fla., 1990—, Titan R&T, Chatsworth, Calif., Kasdan and Simonets, Irvine, Calif.; mem. rev. panel NSF, Washington, 1991—; chmn., organizer Symposiums; invited lectr. 90 univs. and profl. socs. Author, editor: Damage Mechanics in Engineering Materials, 1990, Recent Advances in Damage Mechanics and Plasticity, 1992, Damage Mechanics and Localization, 1992, Homogenization and Constitutive Modeling, 1993, Micromechanics and Inelasticity of Metal Matrix Composites, 1994, Damage Mechanics in Composites, 1994, Numerical Methods in Structural Mechanics, 1995, Damage Mechanics in Engineering Materials, 1998, T.H. Lin 90th Birthday Symposium on Mechanics and Materials, 2001; mem. editl. bd. Internat. Jour. Damage Mechanics, 1992; assoc. tech. editor ASME Jour. of Engring. Materials and Technology, ASME Jour. of Applied Mechanics; contbr. articles to profl. jours.; author conf. procs. Fed. and indsl. rsch. grantee U.S. Govt., U.S. cos., Japanese cos., 1987—; recipient Presdl. Young Investigator award NSF, 1991. Fellow ASME (com. mem. 1989—, assoc. editor Jour. Engring. Materials Tech., Jour. Applied Mechanics 1995—); mem. ASCE (control group 1989-93, Walter L. Huber Civil Engring. Rsch. prize 1997), U.S. Assn. Computational Mechanics, Am. Acad. Mechanics, Am. Concrete Inst., Soc. Engring. Sci., Internat. Assn. for Computational Mechanics. Office: UCLA Dept Civil Engring Los Angeles CA 90095-0001 E-mail: juj@ucla.edu

JUBERG, RICHARD KENT, mathematician, educator; b. Cooperstown, N.D., May 14, 1929; s. Palmer and Hattie Noreen (Nelson) J.; m. Janet Elisabeth Witchell, Mar. 17, 1956 (div.); children: Alison K., Kevin A., Hilary N., Ian C.T.; m. Sandra Jean Vakerics, July 8, 1989. BS, U. Minn., 1952, PhD, 1958. Asst. prof. U. Minn., Mpls., 1958-65; sci. faculty fellow Universita di Pisa, Italy, 1965-66; assoc. prof. U. Calif., Irvine, 1966-72, U. Sussex, Eng., 1972-73; prof. U. Calif., Irvine, 1974-91, prof. emeritus, 1991—. Vis. prof. U. Goteborg, Sweden, 1981; mem. Courant Inst. Math. Scis., NYU, 1957-58. Contbr. articles to profl. jours. With USN, 1946-48, Guam. NSF Faculty fellow, Univ. Pisa, Italy, 1965-66. Mem. Am. Math. Soc., Tau Beta Pi. Democrat. Avocation: bird watching. Office: U Calif Math Dept Irvine CA 92717

JUDD, BRUCE DIVEN, architect; b. Pasadena, Calif., Sept. 28, 1947; s. David Lockhart and Martha Leah (Brown) J.; m. Diane Reinbolt, Feb. 4, 1976 (div. Oct. 1985); 1 child, Ian David. BArch, U. Calif., Berkeley, 1970, MArch, 1971. Registered arch., Calif., Nev.; cert. Nat. Coun. Archtl. Registration Bds. Designer Ribera and Sue Landscape Archs., Oakland, Calif., 1968-70, Page Clowdsley & Baleix, San Francisco, 1971-75; v.p. Charles Hall Page Assocs., San Francisco, 1975-80; prin. Archtl. Resources Group, San Francisco, 1980—. Mem. adv. bd. fed. rehab. guidelines program Nat. Inst. Bldg. Scis., HUD, 1979-80; mem. city-wide survey planning com. City of Oakland, Calif., 1979-80; cons. Nat. Main St. Program, Washington. Bd. dirs., co-founder Oakland Heritage Alliance, 1980-85; mem. Calif. Hist. Resources Commn., 1982-86, chmn., 1983-85; bd. dirs. Preservation Action, Washington, 1982-85, 90—, Friends of Terra Cotta, 1981-86, Berkeley Archtl. Heritage Assn., 1993—; mem. bd. advisors Nat. Trust for Hist. Preservation, Washington, 1981-90, advisor emeritus, 1990—; bd. trustees Calif. Preservation Found., San Francisco, 1985—, v.p., 1990-92, trustee, 1990—; active Calif. State Hist. Bldg. Safety Bd., 1991-93, also others. Recipient Excellence Honor award State of Calif., Excellence award in archtl. conservation, Spl. Restoration award Sunset Mag.; named Preservationist of Yr., Calif. Preservation Found., 1993. Fellow AIA (preservation officer No. Calif. chpt. 1978-81, hist. resources com. Calif. coun. 1979-80, nat. hist. resources com. 1981—, chmn. 1981-82); mem. Internat. Assn. for Preservation Tech. (bd. dirs. 1983-85), Park Hills Homes Assn. (chmn. archtl. com. 1992—), U.S./Internat. Coun. Monuments and Sites. Office: Archtl Resources Group Pier 9 The Embarcadero San Francisco CA 94111

JUDD, JAMES THURSTON, savings and loan executive; b. Hurricane, Utah, Dec. 13, 1938; s. Finley MacFarland and Bessie (Thurston) J.; m. Janis Anderson, July 15, 1960; children: Juliet, Brian. BS, Utah State U., 1961; postgrad., Los Angeles State U., 1962-63, U. Detroit, 1963-64. Cert. flight instr. Fin. analyst automotive assembly div. Ford Motor Co., Detroit, 1961-64; sales mgr. Xerox Corp., Rocester, N.Y., 1966-75; loan mgr. Golden West Fin. Corp. Savs. and Loan, Oakland, Calif., 1975—, now sr. exec. v.p.; pres. World Savings and Loan Co. (formerly Golden West Fin. Corp. Savings and Loan), Oakland. Pres. Judd Ranch. Chmn. northbay Bringing Entertainment To The Elderly, Saratoga, Calif., 1972—; chmn. Beef for the Poor, Oakland, 1983-87. Mem. Nat. Assn. Real Estate Appraisers, Calif. Assn. Real Estate, Exptl. Aircraft Assn., Simga Nu. Republican. Mormon. Avocations: fly fishing, skiing, golfing. Home: 3284 Blackhawk Meadow Dr Danville CA 94506-5804 Office: World Savings Loan 1901 Harrison St Fl 17 Oakland CA 94612-3588

JUDD, LEWIS LUND, psychiatrist, educator; b. L.A., Feb. 10, 1930; s. George E. and Emmeline (Lund) J.; B.S., U. Utah, 1954; M.D. cum laude, UCLA, 1956; m. Patricia Ann Hoffman, Jan. 26, 1974; children by previous marriage: Allison Clark, Catherine Anne, Stephanie. Intern, UCLA Sch. Medicine, 1958-59, resident in psychiatry, 1959-60, 62-64, fellow in child psychiatry, 1964-65, asst. prof. depts. psychiatry and psychology, 1965-70, dir. edn., child and adolescent psychiatry dept. psychiatry, 1968; asso. prof. psychiatry U. Calif. at San Diego, La Jolla, 1970, vice chmn., dir. clin. programs dept. psychiatry, 1970-73, dir. drug abuse programs, 1970-73, prof., from 1973, acting chmn. dept., 1974, co-chmn., 1975-77, chmn., 1977—; dir. NIMH, 1988—; chief psychiat. service San Diego VA Hosp., La Jolla, 1972-77; chief psychiat. service U. Calif. Med. Center, San Diego, from 1982, pres. med. staff, chmn. exec. com., from 1982; mem. adv. com. on evaluation drug abuse programs County of San Diego, 1970-73; chmn. clin. projects rev. com. NIMH, 1975-79; guest faculty San Diego Psychoanalytic Inst. Served to capt., M.C., USAF, 1960-62. Fellow Am. Psychiat. Assn.; mem. Soc. Neurosics., Psychiat. Research Soc., Assn. Acad. Psychiatry, Soc. Research in Child Devel., Am. Coll. Neuropsychopharmacology, So. Calif., San Diego psychiat. socs., Am. Assn. Chmn. Depts. Psychiatry, Alpha Omega Alpha. Contbr. articles to med. jours. Home: 1367 Via Alta Del Mar CA 92014-2546 Office: Univ Calif San Diego 9500 Gilman Dr La Jolla CA 92093-5004

JUDD, O'DEAN P. physicist; b. Austin, Minn., May 26, 1937; MS in Physics, UCLA, 1961, PhD in Physics, 1968. Staff physicist and project dir. Hughes Rsch. Lab., Malibu, Calif., 1959-67; postdoctoral fellow UCLA Dept. Physics, 1968-69; researcher Hughes Rsch. Lab., Malibu, Calif., 1969-72; researcher, group leader Los Alamos Nat. Lab., 1972-82, chief scientist for def. rsch. and applications, 1981-87; chief scientist Strategic Def. Initiative Orgn., Washington, 1987-90; energy and environ. chief scientist, lab. fellow Los Alamos (N.Mex.) Nat. Lab., 1990-93; nat. intelligence officer for sci. and tech. Nat. Intelligence Coun., Washington, 1993-94; tech. advisor and cons. Los Alamos, 1994-95; ind. tech. advisor, cons. Los Alamos, 1995—. Mem. numerous govt. coms. related to sci. and tech., def. and nat. security policy adv. com. to SDIO, 1990-93; adj. prof. of physics U. N.Mex., Albuquerque. Patentee in sci. and tech.; contbr. numerous articles to sci. and def.-related jours. Fellow IEEE, AAAS, Inst. Advanced Engring.; mem. Am. Phys. Soc. Office: Los Alamos Nat Lab MS F650 Los Alamos NM 87544-2648

JUDD, THOMAS ELI, electrical engineer; b. Salt Lake City, Apr. 12, 1927; s. Henry Eli Judd and Jennie Meibos; m. Mary Lu Edman, June 21, 1948; children: Shauna, Kirk E., Blake E., Lisa. BSEE, U. Utah, 1950. Registered profl. engr., Utah. Mech. engr. Utah Power & Light Co., Salt Lake City, 1950-55; chief engr. Electronic Motor Car Corp., Salt Lake City, 1955-56, Equi Tech Corp., Salt Lake City, 1978-79; hydraulic devel. engr.

Galigher Co., Salt Lake City, 1956-58; pres. Toran Corp., Salt Lake City, 1958-71, T M Industries, Salt Lake City, 1971-78; chief exec. officer, mgr. Ramos Corp., Salt Lake City, 1979—. Project cons. Eimco Corp., Salt Lake City, 1966; design cons. to tech. cos. Patentee in field in U.S. and fgn. countries; contbr. editor U.S. Rail News, 1982—. Cons. Nat. Fedn. Ind. Bus., 1983—. With USNR, 1945-46, PTO. Mem. Tau Beta Pi. Republican. Mormon. Avocation: flying. Office: Ramos Corp 956 Elm Ave Salt Lake City UT 84106-2330

JUDGE, MIKE, animator; b. Guayaquil, Ecuador, Oct. 17, 1962; m. Francesca Morocco, 1989; 2 children. BA in Phys. Sci., U. Calif., San Diego, 1985. Creator (TV series) Beavis and Butt-head, 1993—; (film) Beavis and Butt-head Do America, 1996; co-prodr. (TV series) King of the Hill, 1997—. Office: King of the Hill Watt Plaza 1875 Century Park E Fl 4 Los Angeles CA 90067-2501

JUDSON, C(HARLES) JAMES (JIM JUDSON), lawyer; b. Oregon City, Oreg., Oct. 24, 1944; s. Charles James and Barbara (Busch) J.; m. Diana L. Gerlach, Sept. 7, 1965; children: Kevin, Nicole. BA cum laude, Stanford U., 1966, LLB with honors, 1969. Bar: Wash. 1969, U.S. Tax Ct. 1970, D.C. 1981. Ptnr. Davis Wright Tremaine, Seattle, 1969—; v.p. Eagle River, Inc. Speaker various convs. and seminars. Author: State Taxation of Fin. Instns., 1981; contbr. articles to profl. jours. Chmn. Bus. Tax Coalition, Seattle, 1987; chmn. lawyers div. United Way, Seattle, 1986, 87, commerce and industry div., 1989-91; trustee Wash. State Internat. Trade Fair, Seattle, 1981-86; bd. dirs. Seattle Prep. Sch., 1986-88; bd. dirs. Olympic Park Inst., 1988—, Yosemite Nat. Insts., 1993—; mem. Assn. Wash. Bus. Tax Com., 1978—; tax advisor Wash. State House Reps. Dem. Caucus; advisor Wash. State Dept. Revenue on Tax and Legis. Matters; mem. Seattle Tax Group, 1983—. Fellow Am. Coll Tax Counsel; mem. ABA (chmn. com. on fin. orgns. tax sect. 1978-82, subcom chmn. state and local tax com. tax sect. 1979—, chmn. excise tax com. 1983-90, interorgn. coordination com. 1985—, chmn. environ. tax com. 1991—), Wash. State Bar Assn. (chmn. tax sect. 1984-86, chmn. western region IRS/bar liaison com. 1987-88, mem. rules com. 1991—), Seattle-King County Bar Assn. (mem. tax sect. 1973-86), Seattle C. of C. (tax com. 1982—), Wash. Athletic Club (Seattle), Broadmoor Golf Club (Seattle), Bear Creek Golf Club (Redmond). Avocations: skiing, golf, basketball, wood working, hiking. Office: Davis Wright Tremaine 2600 Century Sq 1501 4th Ave Seattle WA 98101-1688

JULANDER, PAULA FOIL, health care and political consultant, state legislator; b. Charlotte, N.C., Jan. 21, 1939; d. Paul Baxter and Esther Irene (Earnhardt) Foil; m. Roydon Odell Julander, Dec. 21, 1985; 1 child, Julie McMahan Shipman. Diploma, Presbyn. Hosp. Sch. Nursing, Charlotte, N.C., 1960; BS magna cum laude, U. Utah, 1984; MS in Nursing Adminstrn., Brigham Young U., 1990. RN, Utah. Nurse various positions, Fla. and S.C., 1960-66; co-founder, office mgr. Am. Laser Corp., 1970-79; gen. staff nurse, oper. rm. Salt Lake Surg. Ctr., 1976-79; self employed Salt Lake City; tchg. asst. U. Utah, Salt Lake City; mem. Utah Ho. of Reps., Salt Lake City, 1989-92; Dem. nominee lt. gov. State of Utah, 1992; mem., minority whip Utah Senate, Dist. 1, Salt Lake City, 1998—; health care/polit. cons. Salt Lake City, 1998—. Mem. adj. faculty Brigham Young U. Coll. Nursing, 1987—, clin. asst. prof. of nursing, 1996—; bd. dirs. Block Fin. Svcs.; mem. Utah state exec. bd. U.S. West Comm., 1993-96; bd. regents Calif. Luth. U., 1994. Co-author: (cookbook) Utah State Fare, 1995. Pres. Utah Nurses Found., 1986-88; mem. Statewide Task Force on Child Sexual Abuse, 1989-90, Utah Nursing Resource Study, 1985-96, State Feasibility Task Force for Nurses, 1985-96, Women's Polit. Caucus, Statewide Abortion Task Force, 1990; bd. dirs. Cmty. Nursing Svc. Home Health Plus, 1992-94, Planned Parenthood Assn. Utah, 1994—, Utahns for Choice, 1995—; trustee Westminster Coll., 1994—, HCA-St. Mark's Hosp., 1994-95; elected sen. State of Utah, 1999—. Mem. ANA (del. conv. 1986-90), LWV, Utah Nurses Assn. (legis. rep. 1987-88, pres., Lifetime Achievement award), Nat. Orgn. Women Legislators, Sigma Theta Tau, Phi Kappa Phi (Susan Young Gates award 1991). Office: Utah Nurses Assn 455 E 400 S Ste 40 Salt Lake City UT 84111-3017

JULIEN, ROBERT MICHAEL, anesthesiologist, writer; b. Port Townsend, Wash., Mar. 24, 1942; s. Frank Felton and Mary Grace (Powers) J.; m. Judith Dianne DeChenne, Feb. 26, 1963; children: Robert Michael, Scott M. BS in Pharmacy, U. Wash., 1965, MS in Pharmacology, 1968, PhD, 1970; MD, U. Calif.-Irvine, 1977. Intern Good Samaritan Hosp., Portland, Oreg., 1977-78; resident Oreg. Health Scis. U., 1978-80; asst. prof. pharmacology U. Calif.-Irvine, 1970-74, asst. clin. prof., 1974-77; assoc. prof. anesthesiology and pharmacology U. Oreg., Portland, 1980-83; staff anesthesiologist St. Vincent Hosp., Portland, 1983—. Author: Primer of Drug Action, 1975, 9th edit., 2000, Understanding Anesthesiology, 1984, Drugs and the Body, 1987. Recipient Svc. award Am. Epilepsy Soc., 1975. Mem. Am. Soc. Anesthesiologists, Am. Assn. Pharmacology and Exptl. Therapeutics, Soc. Neurosci., Oreg. Med. Assn., Western Pharmacology Soc. Roman Catholic. Home: 1212 SW Hessler Dr Portland OR 97201-2807 Office: St Vincent Hosp Dept Anesthesia 9205 SW Barnes Rd Portland OR 97225-6603

JUMONVILLE, FELIX JOSEPH, JR. physical education educator, realtor; b. Crowley, La., Nov. 20, 1920; s. Felix Joseph and Mabel (Rogers) J.; m. Mary Louise Hoke, Jan. 11, 1952; children: Carol, Susan. BS, La. State U., 1942; MS, U. So. Calif., 1948, EdD, 1952. Assoc. prof. phys. edn. Los Angeles State Coll., 1948-60; prof. phys. edn. Calif. State U., Northridge, 1960-87, emeritus prof. phys. edn., 1987—. Owner Felix Jumonville Realty, Northridge, 1974-82, Big Valley Realty, Inc., 1982-83, Century 21 Lamb Realtors, 1983-86, Cardinal Realtors, 1986-87; varsity track and cross-country head coach L.A. State Coll., 1952-60, Calif. State U., Northridge, 1960-71. Served with USCGR, 1942-46. Mem. Assn. Calif. State Univ. Profs., AAHPER, Pi Tau Pi, Phi Epsilon Kappa. Home: Unit N98 2001 E Camino Parocela Palm Springs CA 92264-8283

JUNE, ROY ETHIEL, lawyer; b. Forsyth, Mont., Aug. 12, 1922; s. Charles E. and Elizabeth F. (Newnes) J.; m. Laura Brautigam, June 20, 1949; children: Patricia June, Richard Tyler. BA, U. Mont., 1948, BA in Law, 1951, LLB, 1952. Bar: Mont. 1952, Calif. 1961. Sole practice, Billings, Mont., 1952-57; atty. Sanders and June, 1953-57; real estate developer Orange County, Calif., 1957-61; ptnr. Dugan, Tobias, Tornay & June, Costa Mesa, 1961-62; city prosecutor Costa Mesa, 1962-63; asst. city atty. Costa Mesa, 1963-67; city atty. Costa Mesa, 1967-78; sole practice Costa Mesa, 1962—. Atty., founder, dir. Citizens Bank of Costa Mesa, 1972-92; atty. Costa Mesa Hist. Soc., Costa Mesa Playhouse Patron's Assn., Red Barons Orange County, Costa Mesa Meml. Hosp. Aux., Harbor Key, Child Guidance Ctr. Orange County, Fairview State Hosp. Therapeutic Pool Vols., Inc. Active Eagle Scout evaluation team Harbor Area Boy Scouts Am., YMCA; atty. United Fund/Cmty. Chest Costa Mesa and Newport Beach; bd. dirs. Boys' Club Harbor Area, Mardan Ctr. Ednl. Therapy, United Cerebral Palsy Found., Orange County; docent Palm Springs Mus., 1996—. With USAF, WWII. Decorated Air medal with oak leaf cluster, DFC. Mem. Calif. Bar Assn., Costa Mesa C. of C. (bd. dirs.), Masons, Scottish Rite, Shriners, Santa Ana Country, Amigos Viejos, Los Fiestadores, Palm Springs Calif. Air Mus. (docent). E-mail: RoyJune@cs.com

JUNG, CHARLENE, city treasurer; b. Maoui, Hawaii; BA, Univ. S.C., 1977; postgrad., Calif. State Univ. City treas., Anaheim, Calif., 1992—. Office: City Hall 200 S Anaheim Blvd Anaheim CA 92805-3820

JUNG, DAVID JOSEPH, law educator; b. St. Louis, Aug. 19, 1953; s. Joseph Henry and Leona Louise Jung; m. Jennifer Beryl Hammett, Oct. 15, 1951; children: David O'Grady Hammett, Brennan Joseph Hammett. BA, Harvard U., 1975; JD, U Calif., Berkeley, 1980. Lectr. in law U. Calif., Berkeley, 1980-82, from asst prof. to assoc. prof. Hastings Coll. Law San Francisco, 1982-88, prof., 1988—. Vis. prof. U. Hamburg, Germany, 1992, U. Iowa, Iowa City, 1993—; dir. Pub. Law Rsch. Inst., 1994—. Co-author: Remedies: Public and Private, 2d edit., 1996; contbr. articles to profl. jours. Bd. dirs. San Francisco Neighborhood Legal Aid, 1983, North of Market Child Car Ctr., 1984-86; sec. El Cerrito Youth Baseball, 1997-99, pres., 1999-2000. Recipient U.S. Law Week award U.S. Law Week, 1980, 1066 Found. award 1066 Found., 1986. Mem. Am. Assn. Law Schs. (remedies section, exec. com. 1991-92). Office: U Calif Hastings Coll Law 200 Mcallister St San Francisco CA 94102-4707

JUNG, MICHAEL ERNEST, chemistry educator; b. New Orleans, May 14, 1947; s. Albert J. and Helen N. Jung; m. Alice M. Smith. BA, Rice U., 1969; PhD, Columbia U., 1973. Postdoctoral assoc. Eidgenossische Tech. Hochschule, Zurich, 1973-74; mem. faculty UCLA, L.A., 1974—, prof. chemistry, 1983—. Contbr. acticles to profl. jours. Recipient Disting. Reaching award UCLA, 1978, Gold Shield Faculty prize, 1986—; ARthur C. Cope scholar Am. Chem. Soc., 1995, Fulbright-Hays rsch. scholar, Paris, 1980-81; Tchr.-Scholar grantee Camille and Henry Dreyfus Found., 1978-83; rsch. fellow Alfred p. Sloan Found., 1979-81. Mem. Am. Chem. Soc., Royal Chem. Soc.; mem. AAAS, UCLA Cancer Ctr. Office: UCLA Dept Chemistry & Biochemistry 405 Hilgard Ave Los Angeles CA 90095-9000

JUNG, TIMOTHY TAE KUN, otolaryngologist; b. Seoul, Korea, Dec. 1, 1943; came to U.S., 1969; s. Yoon Yong and Helen Chung-Hyuk (Im) J.; m. Lucy Moon Young, Sept. 10, 1972; children: David, Michael, Karen. BS, Seoul Nat. U., 1966, Loma Linda U., 1971, MD, 1974; PhD, U. Minn., 1980. Diplomate, Am. Bd. Otolaryngology. Med. intern Loma Linda (Calif.) U. Med. Ctr., 1974-75; resident in surgery U. Minn. Med. Sch., Mpls., 1975-76, resident in otolaryngology, 1976-80, asst. prof. otolaryngology, 1980-84, clin. asst. prof., dir. prostaglandin lab., 1984-85; assoc. prof., dir. otolaryngology rsch. Loma Linda U., 1985-90, prof., dir. otolaryngology rsch., 1990-92, clin. prof., dir. otolaryngology rsch., 1992—. Mem. deafness and communications disroders rev. com. Nat. Inst. Deafness and Communications, NIH, 1989-92. Mem. bd. editors Annals of Otology, Rhinology & Laryngology, 1994—; mem. internat. bd. editors Acta Otolaryngologica, 1999—; contbr. numerous chpts. to med. books, over 100 articles and abstracts to med. jours. Sgt. Korean army, 1966-69. Recipient Edmund Price Fowler award. Fellow ACS, Triological Soc., Am. Acad. Otolaryngology (honor award 1990); mem. AMA, Am. Otol. Soc., Am. Neurotol. Soc., Soc. Univ. Otolaryngologists, Assn. Rsch. in Otolaryngology, Centurions, Collegium Otorhinolaryngogicum Amicetiae Sacrum, N.Am. Skull Base Soc., Alpha Omega Alpha. Seventh-day Adventist. Avocations: horticulture, photography, hiking. Home: 11790 Pecan Way Loma Linda CA 92354-3452 Office: 3975 Jackson St Ste 202 Riverside CA 92503-3947 E-mail: tjung1790@aol.com

JUNGERMAN, JOHN ALBERT, physics educator; b. Modesto, Calif., Dec. 28, 1921; s. Albert Augustus and Freda (Durst) J.; m. Nancy Lee Kidwell, Oct. 23, 1948; children: Mark, Eric, Roger, Anne. AB, U. Calif., Berkeley, 1943, PhD, 1949. Research physicist Manhattan Project, Oak Ridge, Tenn. and Berkeley, 1944-45, Los Alamos, N.Mex., 1945-46, Lawrence Berkeley Lab., Berkeley, 1946-49, 50-51; asst. prof. physics U. Calif., Davis, 1951, prof. physics, 1960-91, prof. emeritus, 1991, founding dir. Crocker Nuclear Lab., 1965-80, chmn. physics dept., 1981-82, 83-87; assoc. mem. faculty Starr King Sch. for Ministry, Berkeley, Calif., 1992-93. Vis. prof. U. Grenoble, France, 1972; prin. investigator nuclear physics Atomic Energy Commn., U. Calif., Davis, 1956-71; cons. OAS U. Chile, Santiago, 1982, OAS, 1971, Internat. Atomic Energy Agy., 1982. Author: Nuclear Arms Race: Technology and Society, 1986, 2d edit., 1990, World in Process, 2000. Organizer, instr. Davis Summer Insts. on Nuclear Age Edn. for Secondary Sch. Instrs., 1986-93. NSF Nuclear Physics grantee, 1971-73, NSF Sci. Edn. grantee, 1990-93. Fellow Am. Physical Soc.; mem. Am. Solar Soc., Sigma Xi. Democrat. Avocations: piano, sailing, bicycling, painting. Office: U Calif Dept Physics Davis CA 95616 E-mail: jajungerman@ucdavis.edu

JUNGERS, FRANCIS, oil consultant; b. July 12, 1926; s. Frank Nicholas and Elizabeth (Becker) J.; children— Gary M., Randall O. BSME, U. Wash., 1947; student, Advanced Mgmt. Program, Harvard U., 1967. With Arabian Am. Oil Co., 1947-78, chmn. bd., chief exec. officer, 1973-78. Bd. dirs. Donaldson Lufkin & Jenrette, Thermo Electron, The AES Corp., Esco, Thermo Ekotek Corp., Statia. Trustee Am. U., Cairo; bd. overseers Oreg. Health Scis. With USN, 1944-46. Mem. Waverly Golf Club, Multnomah Athletic Club, Athletic Club of Bend. Republican. Roman Catholic. Office: 822 NW Murray Blvd Ste 242 Portland OR 97229-5868

JUNGKIND, WALTER, design educator, writer, consultant; b. Zurich, Switzerland, Mar. 9, 1923; came to Can., 1968; s. Oskar and Frieda (Leuthold) J.; m. Jenny Voskamp, 1953; children— Christine, Stefan, Brigit Nat diploma, Kunstgewerbeschule, Zurich, 1943; nat diploma, Regent Street Poly tech., London, 1953. Freelance designer, London, 1955-68; lectr. London Coll. Printing and Graphic Arts, 1960-65, sr. lectr., 1965-68; assoc. prof. dept. art and design U. Alta., Edmonton, Can., 1968-72, prof. Can., 1972-90, prof. emeritus Can., 1990—. Design cons. pub. works Province of Alta., 1972-75; chmn. Canadian Adv. Com. Standards Council Can., 1978— Initiator and curator internat. exhbn. Graphic Design for Pub. Service, 1972, Language Made Visible, 1973. Recipient Design Can. award Nat. Design Council Can., 1979, 1984; Chmns. award Nat. Design Council Can., 1982 Fellow Soc. Chartered Designers Gt. Britain, Soc. Graphic Designers Can. (pres. 1978-82); mem. Internat Coun. Graphic Design Assns. (pres. 1974-76, Design for Edn. award 1972.). Home: 6304 109th Ave Edmonton AB Canada T6A 1S2

JURY, MEREDITH A. federal judge; Apptd. bankruptcy judge cen. dist. U.S. Dist. Ct. Calif., 1997. Office: 3420 12th St Riverside CA 92501-3801

JUVET, RICHARD SPALDING, JR. chemistry educator; b. L.A., Aug. 8, 1930; s. Richard Spalding and Marion Elizabeth (Dalton) J.; m. Martha Joy Myers, Jan. 29, 1955 (div. Nov. 1978); children: Victoria, David, Stephen, Richard P.; m. Evelyn Raeburn Elthon, July 1, 1984. BS, UCLA, 1952, PhD, 1955. Research chemist Dupont, 1955; instr. U. Ill., 1955-57, asst. prof., 1957-61, assoc. prof., 1961-70; prof. analytical chemistry Ariz. State U., Tempe, 1970-95, prof. emeritus, 1995—. Vis. prof. UCLA, 1960, U. Cambridge, Eng., 1964-65, Nat. Taiwan U., 1968, Ecole Polytechnique, France, 1976-77, U. Vienna, Austria, 1989-90; mem. air pollution chemistry and physics adv. com. EPA, HEW, 1969-72; mem. adv. panel on advanced chem. alarm tech., devel. and engring. directorate, def. sys. divsn. Edgewood Arsenal, 1975; mem. adv. panel on postdoctoral associateships NAS-NRC, 1991-94; mem. George C. Marshall Inst., 1998—. Author: Gas-Liquid Chromatography, Theory and Practice, 1962, Russian edit., 1966; editl. advisor Jour. Chromatographic Sci., 1969-85, Jour. Gas Chromatography, 1963-68, Analytica Chimica Acta, 1972-74, Analytical Chemistry, 1974-77; biennial reviewer for gas chromatography lit. Analytical Chemistry, 1962-76. Deacon Presbyn. Ch., 1960—, ruling elder, 1972—, commr. Grand Canyon Presbytery, 1974-76; moderator, communion com. Valley Presbyn. Ch., Scottsdale, Ariz., 1999-2001. NSF sr. postdoctoral fellow, 1964-65; recipient Sci. Exch. Agreement award to Czechoslovakia, Hungary, Romania and Yugoslavia, 1977. Fellow Am. Inst. Chemists; mem. AAAS, Am. Chem. Soc. (nat. chmn. divsn. analytical chemistry 1972-73, nat. sec.-treas. 1969-71, divsn. com. on chem. edn., subcom. on grad. edn. 1988—, councilor 1978-89, coun. com. analytical reagents 1985-95, co-author Reagent Chemicals, 7th edit. 1986, 8th edit. 1993, 9th edit. 2000, chmn. U. Ill. sect. 1968-69, sec. 1962-63, directorate divsn. officers' caucus 1987-90), Internat. Union Pure and Applied Chemistry, Internat. Platform Assn., Am. Radio Relay League (Amateur-Extra lic.), Sigma Xi, Phi Lambda Upsilon, Alpha Chi Sigma (faculty adv. U. Ill. 1958-64, Ariz. State U. 1975-95, profl. rep.-at-large 1989-94, chmn. expansion com. 1990-92, nat. v.p. grand collegiate alchemist 1994-96). Achievements include rsch. on gas and liquid chromatography, instrumental analysis, computer interfacing, plasma desorption mass spectroscopy. Home: 4821 E Calle Tuberia Phoenix AZ 85018-2932 Office: Ariz State U Dept Chem and Biochem Tempe AZ 85287-1604 E-mail: rsjuvet@juno.com, rsjuvet@imap3.asu.edu

KABACK, MICHAEL, medical educator; b. Phila., Sept. 1, 1938; MD, U. Pa., 1963. Diplomate Am. Bd. Med. Genetics, Am. Bd. Pediatrics. Intern Johns Hopkins Hosp., Balt., 1963-64, resident pediatrics, 1966-68; fellow molecular biology and genetics NIH, Bethesda, Md., 1964-66; mem. staff Children's Hosp., San Diego; prof. pediatrics and reproductive medicine U. Calif., San Diego. Recipient William Allan Meml. award Am. Soc. Human Genetics, 1993, Harland Sanders award March of Dimes, 2000. Fellow AAAS; mem. AMA, NAS, Inst. Medicine, Am. Acad. Pediatrics, Am. Pediatric Soc., Am. Coll. Med. Genetics, Am. Soc. Human Genetics, Soc. for Pediatric Rsch. Office: Childrens Hosp San Diego 8110 Birmingham Way San Diego CA 92123-2758 E-mail: mKaback@ucsd.edu

KABEL, STEVE, home construction company executive; m. Kathleen Kabel; 2 children. Grad., Ca. Polytechnic U., U. So. Ca. Lic. building contractor, Ca. Regional pres. WL Homes, Inc., 1998—. Office: WL Homes Inc 19600 Fairchild Ste 150 Irvine CA 92612-2516

KADISH, SANFORD HAROLD, law educator; b. N.Y.C., Sept. 7, 1921; s. Samuel J. and Frances R. (Klein) K.; m. June Kurtin, Sept. 29, 1942; children: Joshua, Peter. B Social Scis, CCNY, 1942; LLB, Columbia U., 1948; JD (hon.), U. Cologne, 1983; LLD (hon.), CUNY, 1985, Southwestern U., 1993. Bar: N.Y. 1948, Utah 1954. Pvt. practice law, N.Y.C., 1948-51; prof. law U. Utah, 1951-60, U. Mich., 1961-64, U. Calif., Berkeley, 1964-91, dean Law Sch., 1975-82, Morrison prof., 1973-91, prof. emeritus, 1991—. Fulbright lectr. Melbourne (Australia) U., 1956; vis. prof. Harvard U., 1960-61, Freiburg U., 1967; lectr. Salzburg Seminar Am. Studies, 1965; Fulbright vis. lectr. Kyoto (Japan) U., 1975; vis. fellow Inst. Criminology, Cambridge (Eng.) U., 1968. Author: (with M.R. Kadish) Discretion to Disobey— A Study of Lawful Departures from Legal Rules, 1973, (with Schulhofer) Criminal Law and Its Processes, 6th edit., 1995, Blame and Punishment—Essays in the Criminal Law, 1987; editor-in-chief Ency. Crime and Justice, 1983; contbr. articles to profl. jours. Reporter Calif. Legis. Penal Code Project, 1964-68; pub. mem. Wage Stblzn. Bd., region XII, 1951-53; cons. Pres.'s Commn. Adminstrn. of Justice, 1966; mem. Calif. Coun. Criminal Justice, 1968-69. Lt. USNR, 1943-46. Fellow Ctr. Advanced Study Behavioral Scis., 1967-68; Guggenheim fellow Oxford U., 1974-75; vis. fellow All Souls Coll. Oxford U. Fellow AAAS (v.p. 1984-86), Brit. Acad. (corr.); mem. AAUP (nat. pres. 1970-72), Am. Assn. Law Schs. (exec. com. 1960, pres. 1982), Order of Coif (exec. com. 1966-67, 74-75), Phi Beta Kappa. Home: 774 Hilldale Ave Berkeley CA 94708-1318 E-mail: shk@law.berkeley.edu

KADNER, CARL GEORGE, biology educator emeritus; b. Oakland, Calif., May 23, 1911; s. Adolph L. and Otilia (Pecht) K.; m. Mary Elizabeth Moran, June 24, 1939; children: Robert, Grace Wickersham, Carl L. BS, U. San Francisco, 1933; MS, U. Calif., Berkeley, 1936, PhD, 1941. Prof. biology Loyola Marymount U., Los Angeles, 1936-78, prof. emeritus, 1978—. Trustee Loyola U., Los Angeles, 1970-73. Served to maj. U.S. Army, 1943-46. Mem. Entomol. Soc. Am. (emeritus), Sigma Xi, Alpha Sigma Nu. Republican. Roman Catholic. Avocation: insect photography. Home: 8100 Loyola Blvd Los Angeles CA 90045-2639

KADO, CLARENCE ISAO, molecular biologist; b. Santa Rosa, Calif., June 10, 1936; s. James Y. and Chiyoko K.; m. Barbara M. Kawahara, June 30, 1963; children: Deborah, Diana M. B.Sc., U. Calif., Berkeley, 1959, Ph.D., 1964. Rsch. asst. Virus Lab., U. Calif., Berkeley, 1960-64, NIH postdoctoral fellow, 1964-67, asst. rsch. biochemist, 1967-68; asst. prof. plant pathology U. Calif., Davis, 1968-72, assoc. prof., 1972-76, prof., 1976—. Dir. Fallen Leaf Lake Confs., 1985—. Author: (novels) Principles and Techniques in Plant Virology, 1972; editor Molecular Mechanisms of Bacterial Virulence, 1994, Horizontal Gene Transfer, 1998; editor: (assoc. editor) Virology, 1970—73, (Jours.) Jour. Bacteriology, 1987—93, Molecular Microbiology, 1989—. Recipient Bronze medal for virus rsch., WHO, 1968; fellow Sr. fellow, NATO, 1974—75; grantee, NIH, 1968—, Am. Cancer Soc., 1969—73, %, 1980—82, SEA, 1979—85, CRGO, 1985—. Fellow: Am. Phytopath. Soc., Am. Acad. Microbiology; mem.: Fly Fishers, Fly Fishers Davis (dir, past pres.), Sigma Xi, AAAS, N.Y. Acad. Scis., Am. Soc. Microbiology, Am. Soc. Biochemistry and Molecular Biology, Internat. Soc. Molecular Plant-Microbe Interactions. Office: U Calif Davis Crown Gall Group One Shields Ave Davis CA 95616

KADONAGA, JAMES TAKURO, biochemist; b. Ft. Bragg, N.C., Aug. 24, 1958; s. Tadashi and Alice Ayako K.; m. Anne Kadonaga, Sept. 15, 1984; children: William, Natalie. SB, MIT, 1980; AM, Harvard U., 1982, PhD, 1984. Fellow U. Calif., Berkeley, 1984-88, asst. prof. molecular biology San Diego, 1988-92, assoc. prof., 1992-94, prof., 1994—, vice chmn., 2000—. Mem. editl. bd. Molecular Cell Jour., 1997—, Genes and Devel. Jour., 1994—, Molecular and Cellular Biology, 1993—, Protein Expression and Purification, 1990—, Bio Protocol, 2000—; mem. adv. bd. Ency. of Transcription, 2001—; contbr. articles to profl. jours. Recipient Biochemistry award Eli Lilly, 1989-91, Am. Inst. of Chemists/MIT award, 1980, prize Alpha Chi Sigma/MIT, 1980; named to Hall of Fame, East Side Union H.S. Dist., San Jose, Calif., 1991; DuPont fellow Harvard U., 1983-84, Miller fellow, 1984-86, sr. fellow Am. Cancer Soc. (Calif. div.), 1986-87, Presdl. Faculty fellow Pres. George Bush, 1992-97; Lucille P. Markey scholar, 1987-93. Fellow AAAS, Am. Acad. Microbiology; mem. Am. Chem. Soc., Am. Soc. Microbiology, Am. Soc. Biochemistry and Molecular Biology. Office: U Calif San Diego 9500 Gilman Dr La Jolla CA 92093-5004

KADUSHIN, KAREN DONNA, law school dean; b. L.A., Sept. 3, 1943; BA, UCLA, 1964; JD, Golden Gate U., 1977. Bar: Calif. 1977, U.S. Dist. Ct. (no. dist.) Calif. 1977. Mem. adj. faculty law Golden Gate U. and U. San Francisco, 1977-84; assoc. Law Offices Diana Richmond, San Francisco, 1978-80; ptnr. Richmond & Kadushin, San Francisco, 1981-83; prin. Kadushin Law Offices, San Francisco, 1983-88; ptnr. Kadushin-Fancher-Wickland, San Francisco, 1989-94; dean Monterey (Calif.) Coll. Law, Monterey, Calif., 1995—. Judge pro tem settlement confs. dept. domestic rels. San Francisco Superior Ct., 1985-95; bd. dirs. Lawyers Mut. Ins. Co. Author: California Practice Guide: Law Practice Management, 1992—. Bd. dirs. Legal Assistance for Elderly, San Francisco, 1983, San Francisco Neighborhood Legal Assistance Found., 1984. Mem. Calif. Women Lawyers, Bar Assn. San Francisco (bd. dirs. 1985-86, pres. 1993, Merit award 1980, 90), Barristers Club (pres. 1982), Monterey County Women Lawyers (treas. 1999-2000, pres. 2001). Office: Monterey Coll Law 404 W Franklin St Monterey CA 93940-2303 Fax: 831-373-0143. E-mail: kdkdean@montereylaw.edu

KAEMPEN, CHARLES EDWARD, manufacturing company executive; b. Quincy, Ill., Mar. 10, 1927; s. Charles Herman and Margo (Gochicoa) K.; m. Inger Margareta Nystrom, Aug. 5, 1951; children: Charles Robert, Donald Michael, Annette Earline, Laura Inger. BS in Aeron. Engring., U. Ill., Urbana, 1950; DSc in Astronautics, Internat. Acad. Astronautics, Paris, 1964. Registered profl. engr., Calif., Conn. Sr. designer Saab Aircraft Co., Linkôping, Sweden, 1950-52; design analyst Sikorsky Helicopter United Aircraft, Stratford, Conn., 1952-56; space mission analyst Missle div. N.Am. Rockwell, Downey, Calif., 1957-60; staff scientist Hughes Aircraft, Fullerton, 1961-63; lunar systems analyst Northrop Space Lab., Hawthorne, 1963-64; pres. Am. Space Transport Co., Tustin, 1964-66; transport systems analyst Dashaveyor Co., Venice, 1966-67; pres. Kaempen & Assocs., Orange, 1967-68; sr. rsch. engr. Baker Oil Tools Inc., L.A., 1968-69; pres. Kaempen Industries, Inc., Santa Ana, Calif., 1969-82, Kaempen & Assocs., 1982—; pres., CEO Kaempen Composite Products, Inc., 1996-2000; pres. Kaempen Corp., Inc., 2000-. Author papers on fiberglass composites and filament winding; patentee in field. With U.S. Army, 1944-47. Reciepient Cert. of Merit Pictionary of Internat. Biography, London, 1965, Fellow AIAA; mem. ASME, ASTM, Soc. Aerospace Materials and Process Engring., Soc. of Plastics Industry, Nat. Soc. Profl. Engrs., Mason. Republican. Lutheran. Home: 3202 E Larkstone Dr Orange CA 92869-5546 Office: Kaempen Composite Products Inc 681 S Tustin St Ste 110 Orange CA 92866-3345

KAESZ, HERBERT DAVID, chemistry educator; b. Alexandria, Egypt, Jan. 4, 1933; BA, NYU, 1954; MA, Harvard U., 1956, PhD, 1959. Prof. inorganic chemistry UCLA, L.A. Mem. Am. Chem. Soc. Office: UCLA Chem & Biochem Dept 1505 B Molecular Sci Bldg Los Angeles CA 90095-0001

KAFADAR, CHARLES BELL, mechanical engineer, engineering executive; b. Evanston, Ill., Oct. 13, 1945; s. Ahmed Dogan and Maryanna (Bell) K.; m. Ursula Lutz, Nov. 27, 1964; children: Kimberly, Paul. BS, MS, Purdue U., 1966, PhD in Aerospace and Mech. Sci., 1970. Rsch. fellow, lectr. Princeton (N.J.) U., 1970-73; mem. tech. staff TRW Systems Group, Redondo Beach, Calif., 1973-76; pres., chief oper. officer OEA, Inc., Denver, 1976—. Co-author: Continuum Physics, Vol. II, 1975, Vol. III, 1976; contbr. articles to profl. jours. Mem. vis. com. to math. dept. Colo. Sch. Mines, Golden, 1989—. NSF fellow, 1968-69; Phillips fellow, 1966-67. Mem. Sigma Pi Sigma, Tau Beta Pi, Sigma Gamma Tau. Achievements include expansion of everyday use of high-reliability pyrotechnic items for commercial and government applications. Office: OEA Inc PO Box 100488 34501 Quincy Ave Denver CO 80250

KAFENTZIS, JOHN CHARLES, journalist, educator; b. Butte, Mont., Aug. 18, 1953; s. Christian and Betty Ann (Gaston) K.; m. Teresa Marie Nokleby, June 5, 1976; children: Kathryn Anne, Christian John. BA in Journalism, U. Mont., 1975. Reporter The Missoulian, Missoula, Mont., 1974-76, The Hardin (Mont.) Herald, 1976, The Spokesman-Rev., Spokane, Wash., 1976-80, copy editor, 1980-83, chief copy desk, 1983-89, news editor, 1989-94, news designer, 1994—. Adj. faculty Ea. Wash. U., Cheney, 1982—, Whitworth Coll., 1998. Greek Orthodox. Avocation: competitive swimming. Office: The Spokesman Rev 999 W Riverside Ave Spokane WA 99201-1098

KAGAN, ROBERT ALLEN, law educator; b. Newark, June 13, 1938; s. George and Sylvia K. AB, Harvard U., 1959; LLB, Columbia U., 1962; PhD, Yale U., 1974. Now prof. polit. sci. and law U. Calif., Berkeley. Office: U Calif Sch Law Boalt Hall Berkeley CA 94720

KAGAN, STEPHEN BRUCE (SANDY KAGAN), network marketing executive; b. Elizabeth, N.J., Apr. 27, 1944; s. Herman and Ida (Nadel) K.; m. Susan D. Kaltman, July 3, 1966; children: Sheryl, Rachel BS in Econs., U. Pa., 1966; MBA in Fin., Bernard Baruch Coll., 1969. Chartered fin. analyst. Security analyst Merrill Lynch Pierce Fenner & Smith, N.Y.C., 1966-68; dir. rsch. Deutschmann & Co., N.Y.C., 1968-70; v.p. Equity Sponsors, Inc., N.Y.C., 1970-72; v.p., investment counselor Daniel H. Renberg & Assocs., Inc., Los Angeles, 1972-78; regional v.p. Carlson Travel Network, Van Nuys, Calif., 1978-95; rep. Excel Telecomms., Van Nuys, 1995—; CFO, ptnr. Tatum, 2000—. Vice pres. bd. Temple Beth Hillel, North Hollywood, Calif., 1976-83 Mem. Inst. Cert. Fin. Analysts, Beta Gamma Sigma Avocations: golf; skiing; poker; travel. Home and Office: 13952 Weddington St Van Nuys CA 91401-5751

KÅGE, JONAS, ballet company artistic director; b. Stockholm; m. Deborah Dobson; 1 child, Isabelle. Student, Royal Swedish Ballet Sch. Mem. Royal Swedish Ballet, Am. Ballet Theatre, 1971-75, soloist, 1972-75, prin. dancer, 1973-75, Stuttgart (Germany) Ballet, 1975-76, Geneva (Switzerland) Ballet, 1976-78, Zürich (Switzerland) Ballet, 1978-88; artistic dir. Malmo (Sweden) Opera Ballet, 1988-95; freelance guest artist, master tchr., 1995-97; artistic dir. Ballet West, Salt Lake City, 1997—. Guest artist Am. Ballet Theatre, 1977—, Frankfort (Germany) Ballet, Basel (Switzerland) Ballet, Royal Swedish Ballet, 1980-81, Deutsche Opera Berlin, 1982, Pitts. Ballet, 1984-85, Nat. Ballet of Can., 1984-85, 85-86, Milw. Ballet, 1984-85, NAPAC Dance Co., 1985-86, Munich Opera Ballet, 1985-86, Nat. Ballet of Portugal, 1986-87, Ariz. Ballet, 1987-88, Prin. dancer Swan Lake, Coppélia, La Bayadere, Tales of Hoffmann, Lander's Etudes, Shadowplay, Leaves are Fading, Balanchine's Theme and Variations, Gemini, Some Times, Intermezzo, Les Noces, Am. Ballet Theatre, 1971-75, Swan Lake, Don Quixote, Sphinx, Voluntaries, 1977; prin. dancer The Taming of the Shrew, Romeo & Juliet, Onegin, Gemini, La Sacre de Printemps, Greening, Stuttgart Ballet, 1975-76, Apollo, The Four Temperaments, Agon Symphony in C, Who Cares?, Geneva Ballet, 1976-77, Romeo & Juliet, The Sleeping Beauty, Sphinx, Rosalinda, London Festival Ballet (now English Nat. Ballet), 1977, La Sylphide, Cinderella, Swan Lake, Giselle, Romeo & Juliet, 1982-83; prin. dancer Swan Lake, Frankfort Ballet, Giselle, Basel Ballet, Don Quixote, Vienna Ballet, The Taming of the Shrew, Manon, Royal Swedish Ballet, 1980-81, La Sylphide, Deutsche Opera Berlin, 1982, Coppélia, Giselle, Greening, Apollo, Spoleto and Naples, 1982, Swan Lake, Pitts. Ballet Theatre, 1984-85, Romeo & Juliet, Nat. Ballet of Can., 1984-85, Swan Lake, 1985-86; prin. dancer The Merry Widow, Milw. Ballet, 1984-85, Apollo, NAPAC Dance Co., 1985-86, Romeo & Juliet, Munich Opera Ballet, 1985-86, Apollo, Nat. Ballet of Portugal, 1986-87, The Nutcracker, Ariz. Ballet, 1987-88; creator prin. role Chopin Pas de Deux, Malmo Opera Ballet, 1993-94; choreographer Swedish TV, 1983, Simple Symphony, Zurich Ballet, 1984, Baroque Variations, Malmo Opera Ballet, 1988, Swan Lake, 1992-93 (Thalia prize 1993); master of ceremonies dance competition, Swedish TV, 1997. Bd. dirs. Swedish Dance U., Stockholm, Dalhalla amphitheater, Rattvik, Sweden. Recipient Carina Ari Found. for Dance medal, 1994. Avocations: photography, skiing, mountain climbing, horseback riding, wilderness guide training.

KAGIWADA, REYNOLD SHIGERU, advanced technology manager; b. L.A., July 8, 1938; s. Harry Yoshifusa and Helen Kinue (Imura) K.; children: Julia, Conan. BS in Physics, UCLA, 1960, MS in Physics, 1962, PhD in Physics, 1966. Asst. prof. in residence physics UCLA, 1966-69; asst. prof. physics U. So. Calif., 1969-72; mem. tech. staff TRW, Redondo Beach, Calif., 1972-75, scientist, sect. head, 1975-77, sr. scientist, dept. mgr., 1977-83, lab. mgr., 1984-87, project mgr., 1987-88, MIMIC chief scientist, 1988-89, asst. program mgr., 1989-90, advanced technology mgr., 1990—. Presenter papers at numerous profl. meetings, contbr. over 40 articles to profl. jours.; patentee 9 solid state devices. Recipient Gold Medal award TRW, 1985, Ramo Tech. award, 1985, Transfer award, IEEE MTT-S N. Walter Cox award, 1997. Fellow IEEE (v.p. IEEE MTT-S adminstrn. com. 1991, pres. 1992, Disting. Svc. award 2001); mem. Assn. Old Crows, Sigma Xi, Sigma Pi Sigma. Home: 3117 Malcolm Ave Los Angeles CA 90034-3406 Office: TRW SEG Bldg R6 Rm 2509 One Space Park Bldg Redondo Beach CA 90278 E-mail: reynold.kagiwada@trw.com

KAHLE, BREWSTER, communications executive; m. Mary Austin; 1 child, Caslon. Grad., MIT. Founder Wide Area Info. Servers Inc., 1996—; pres. Internet Achives, San Francisco, 1996—; CEO Alexa Internet, San Francisco, 1996—. Office: Internet Archives PO Box 29141 San Francisco CA 94129-0141

KAHN, EDWIN SAM, lawyer; b. N.Y.C., Jan. 22, 1938; m. Cynthia Chutter, May 30, 1966; children: David, Jonathan, Jennifer. BA, U. Colo., 1958; JD, Harvard U., 1965. Bar: Colo. 1965, U.S. Dist. Ct. (Colo.) 1965, U.S. Ct. Appeals (10th cir.) 1965, U.S. Supreme Ct. 1968. Assoc. Holland & Hart, Denver, 1965-70, ptnr., 1970-77; ptnr., shareholder Kelly, Haglund, Garnsey & Kahn, LLC, Denver, 1978—. 1st lt. USAF, 1959-62. Fellow Am. Coll. Trial Lawyers; mem. Denver Bar Assn. (pres. 1984-85). Home: 2345 Leyden St Denver CO 80207-3441 Office: Kelly Haglund Garnsey & Kahn LLC 1441 18th St Ste 300 Denver CO 80202-1255 E-mail: edkahn@qwest.com

KAHN, FREDRICK HENRY, internist; b. L.A., Aug. 26, 1925; s. Julius and Josephine Leone (Langdon) K.; m. Barbara Ruth Visscher, Feb. 14, 1952; children: Susan, Kathryn, William. AB, Stanford U., 1947, MD, 1951. Diplomate Am. Bd. Internal Medicine. Rotating intern San Francisco Gen. Hosp., 1950-51, fellow pathology, 1951-52; resident medicine Los Angeles VA Hosp., 1954-57, sr. resident, 1956-57; asst. clin. prof. medicine UCLA Sch. Medicine, 1957—; attending physician Cedars Sinai Med. Ctr., L.A., 1957-96, attending physician emeritus, 1996—; attending physician UCLA, 1957-95. Med. advisor Vis. Nurse Assn., Los Angeles, 1957-87. Contbr. articles to med. jours.; inventor blow-through high altitude chamber; promoter iodine method of personal water disinfection for travelers and hikers. Served with USNR, 1943-46; lt. (M.C.), USNR, 1952-54. Fellow ACP; mem. AMA, Am. Handel So, Sierra Club. Avocations: hiking, collecting and listening to baroque music. Home: 3309 Corinth Ave Los Angeles CA 90066-1312

KAHN, IRWIN WILLIAM, industrial engineer; b. N.Y.C., Feb. 3, 1923; s. Milton and Clara (Clark) K.; BS, U. Calif.-Berkeley, 1949; student Cath. U., 1943-44; m. Mildred Cross, May 14, 1946 (dec. May 1966); children: Steven Edward, Michael William, Evelyn Ruth, Joanne Susan; m. 2d, Marajayne Smith, Oct. 9, 1979. Chief indsl. engr. Malsbary Mfg. Co., Oakland, Calif., 1953-57, Yale & Towne Mfg. Co., San Leandro, Calif., 1957-60; sr. indsl. engr. Eitel McCulloch, San Carlos, Calif., 1961-62, Lockheed, Sunnyvale, Calif., 1962-69; v.p. Performance Investors, Inc., Palo Alto, 1969-74; with Kaiser-Permanente Svcs., Oakland, 1974-76; nat. mgr. material handling Cutter Labs., Berkeley, Calif., 1976-83; sr. mgmt. engr. Children's Hosp. Med. Ctr., Oakland, 1983; sr. indsl. engr. Naval Air Rework Facility, Alameda, Calif., 1983-85, Naval Supply Ctr., Oakland, 1985-88; vis. lectr. U. Calif., Berkeley, 1986; tchr. indsl. engring. Laney Coll., Oakland, 1967—, Chabot Coll., Hayward, Calif.; pres. East Bay Table Pad Co., 1990. Chmn. Alameda County Libr. Adv. Commn., 1965—. Served with AUS, 1943-46. Registered profl. engr., Calif. Mem. Am. Inst. Indsl. Engrs. (chpt. pres. 1963-64, chmn. conf. 1967 nat. publ. dir. aerospace div. 1968-69), Calif. Soc. Profl. Engrs. (pres. chpt.). Club: Toastmasters (dist. gov. 1960-61).

KAHN, STEVEN EMANUEL, medical educator; b. Durban, South Africa, July 28, 1955; m. Stephanie Berk; 2 children. MB, ChB, U. Cape Town, South Africa, 1978. Diplomate Am. Bd. Internal Medicine. Intern depts. ob./gyn. and medicine Somerset Hosp., Cape Town, South Africa, 1979; resident dept. ob./gyn. 2 Mil. Hosp., Wynberg, South Africa, 1980, resident and coord. dept. ob./gyn. South Africa, 1981; resident dept. medicine divsn. endocrinology Groote Schuur Hosp., Cape Town, 1982; rsch. fellow diabetes and endocrine rsch. group U. Cape Town, 1983; resident dept. medicine Albert Einstein Med. Ctr., Phila., 1983-86; sr. rsch. fellow divsn. metabolism, endocrinology and nutrition Dept. Medicine U. Wash. Sch. of Medicine, VA Med. Ctr., Seattle, 1986-88; assoc. investigator, staff physician divsn. endocrinology and metabolism Dept. Medicine VA Med. Ctr., Seattle, 1988-91, rsch. assoc., staff physician divsn. endocrinology and metabolism Dept. Medicine, 1991-95; acting instr. divsn. metabolism, endocrinology and nutrition Dept. Medicine U. Wash. Sch. of Medicine, Seattle, 1988-92, asst. prof. divsn. metabolism, endocrinology and nutrition Dept. Medicine, 1992-95, assoc. prof. divsn. metabolism, endocrinology and nutrition Dept. Medicine, 1995-2001, prof. divsn. metabolism, endocrinology and nutrition, 2001—; dir. R&D VA Puget Sound Health Care Sys., 2001—. Prizer vis. prof. Case Western Res. U., 1999. Mem. editl. bd. Jour. Clin. Endocrinology and Metabolism, 1995-98, Diabetes Care, 1997-99; contbr. articles to profl. jours. Amelia Schenkman scholar, 1973-75; named Assoc. Investigator, Dept. VA, 1988, Rsch. Assoc., 1991; recipient Career Devel. award Juvenile Diabetes Found., 1988, NIH, 1999, Feasibility award Dana Found., 1989, Clin. Investigator award NIH, 1991, New Investigator award Diabetes Rsch. Coun., 1992-94, rsch. award NIH, 1997, Novartis Young Investigator award in diabetes rsch., 2001. Mem. ACP, Am. Diabetes Assn. (bd. dirs. Wash. affiliate 1993-94, exec. bd. dirs. 1994-98, rsch. grant rev. panel 1994-97, rsch. award 1996, mentor award 1999), Am. Fedn. Clin. Rsch. (chair program com. for metabolism 1994, 96, councillor western sect. 1994-96, pres.-elect western sect. 1996, pres. western sect. 1997, nat. councillor 1996), Am. Soc. for Clin. Investigation, Endocrine Soc., Western Soc. Clin. Investigation (councillor 1998—), Gen. Med. Coun. (U.K.). Office: VA Puget Sound Health Cr Dept Medicine 151 1660 S Columbian Way Seattle WA 98108-1532

KAHN, STEVEN MICHAEL, astrophysicist, educator; b. N.Y., Nov. 23, 1954; s. George Arthur and Muriel Vera (Gross) K.; m. Susan Marlene Sacks, July 16, 1978; 1 child, Isaac Alden. AB, Columbia U, 1975; PhD, U. Calif., Berkeley, 1980. Postdoctoral fellow Smithsonian Astrophys. Obs., Cambridge, Mass., 1980-82; asst. prof. physics Columbia U., N.Y., 1982-84; from asst. prof. to assoc. prof. physics U. Calif., Berkeley, 1984-90, assoc. prof. astronomy, 1989-90, prof. physics and astronomy, 1990—. Assoc. dir. Space Scis. Lab., U. Calif., Berkeley, 1986—. Contbr. articles to profl. jours. Recipient Earl C. Anthony fellowship, U. Calif., Berkeley, 1976, Andrew R. Michelson award, Columbia U., 1975. Office: U Calif Physics Dept Berkeley CA 94720-0001

KAHN, TIMOTHY F. food products company executive; b. 1954; grad., MBA, Dartmouth Coll. With PepsiCo., Inc., sr. v.p., fin. and devel. restaurant svcs. group; v.p. fin. and administrn., CFO Dreyer's Grand Ice Cream, Inc., Oakland, Calif., 1998—. Office: Dreyer's Grand Ice Cream Inc 5929 College Ave Oakland CA 94618

KAHNE, STEPHEN JAMES, systems engineer, educator, academic administrator, engineering executive; b. N.Y.C., Apr. 5, 1937; s. Arnold W. and Janet (Weatherlow) K.; m. Irena Nowacka, Dec. 11, 1970; children: Christopher, Kasia. BEE, Cornell U., 1960; MS, U. Ill., 1961, PhD, 1963. Asst. prof. elec. engring. U. Minn., Mpls., 1966-69, assoc. prof., 1969-76; dir. Hybrid Computer Lab., 1968-76; founder, dir., cons. InterDesign Inc., Mpls., 1968-76; prof. dept. sys. engring. Case Western Res. U., Cleve., 1976-83, chmn. dept., 1976-80; dir. divsn. elec., computer and sys. engring. NSF, Washington, 1980-82; prof. Poly Inst. N.Y., 1983-85, dean engring., 1983-84; pres. Oreg. Grad. Ctr., Beaverton, 1985-86, prof. dept. applied physics and elec. engring., 1985-89; chief engr. civil systems divsn. MITRE Corp., McLean, Va., 1989-90, chief scientist Washington Group, 1990-91, cons. engr. Ctr. for Advanced Aviation Sys. Devel., 1991-94; exec. dir., CEO Triangle Coalition for Sci. and Tech. Edn., 1994; chancellor, v.p. Embry-Riddle Aeronautical U., Prescott, Ariz., 1995-97, prof. engring., 1995—. Cons. in field; exchange scientist NAS, 1968, 75. Editor: IEEE Transactions on Automatic Control, 1975-79; hon. editor: Internat. Fedn. of Automatic Control, 1975-81, dep. chmn. mng. bd. publs., 1976-87, chmn., 1999—, v.p., 1987-90, pres.-elect, 1990-93, pres., 1993-96, advisor, 1999—; assoc. editor: Automatica, dep. chmn. editl. bd., 1976-82; mem. editl. bd. IEEE Spectrum, 1979-82; contbr. articles to sci. jours. Active Mpls. Citizens League, 1968-75; regent L.I. Coll. Hosp., Bklyn., 1984-85; trustee Yavapai Regional Med. Ctr., 1999—; chmn. Beaverton Sister Cities Found., 1986-89. Served with USAF, 1963-66. Recipient Amicus Poloniae award POLAND Mag., 1975, John A. Curtis award Am. Soc. Engring. Edn., Outstanding Svc. award Internat. Fedn. Automatic Control, 1990; Case Centennial scholar, 1980 Fellow AAAS, IEEE (pres. Control Sys. Soc. 1981, bd. dirs. 1982-86, v.p. tech. activities 1984-85, Centennial medal 1984, Disting. Mem. award 1983, Richard Emberson award 1991, Disting. Lectr. 1998—), Am. Soc. Engring. Edn., Air Traffic Control Assn., Eta Kappa Nu. Office: Embry Riddle Aero U 3200 Willow Creek Rd Prescott AZ 86301-3721 E-mail: kahne@pr.erau.edu

KAIDA, TAMARRA, art and photography educator; b. Lienz, Austria, July 6, 1946; came to U.S., 1950; d. Ivan and Matrona (Bratasuk) K.; m. Paul S. Knapp; 1 child, Krister. BA, Goddard Coll., 1974; MFA, SUNY, Buffalo, 1979. Tutor photography Empire State Coll., 1977-79; asst. dir. dept. edn. Internat. Mus. Photography, George Eastman House, 1976-79; vis. lectr. Ariz. State U., Tempe, 1979-80, asst. prof., 1980-85, assoc. prof., 1985-92, prof., 1992—; represented by Etherton Gallery, Tucson, Califia Books, San Francisco. Mem. faculty Internat. Sommerakademie fur Bildende Kunst, Salzburg, Austria, 1985, Friends of Photography Summer Workshop, Carmel, Calif., 1989, vis. photographers program R.I. Sch. Design, 1989, guest artist lecture and lazer print transfer demonstration Photography Studies in France, Paris, 1991; panelist NEA S.W. Regional Photography Task Force, 1980; juror nat. photography competition Calif. Inst. Arts, Valencia, 1981; curator, lectr., cons. in field. Author: (with Rita Dove) The Other Side of the House, 1988; Tremors from the Faultline, 1989; contbr. articles to profl. jours.; author short stories; many one-woman shows including Scottsdale (Ariz.) Ctr. Arts, 1987, Fine Arts Gallery RISD, 1989, OPSIS Found. Gallery, N.Y.C., 1990, Fyerweather Gallery U. Va., Charlottesville, 1991, Photography Gallery, Fine Art Ctr., U. R.I., Kingston, R.I., 1992, Kharkov (Ukraine) Regional Mus. Art, 1993, Sky Harbor Airport, Phoenix, Ariz., 1994; numerous nat. and internat. group shows including Coconino Ctr. Arts, Flagstaff, Ariz., 1985, Frankfurt Art Soc., Germany, 1985, Mus. Art and Trade, Hamburg, Germany, 1985, Boulder (Colo.) Ctr. Visual Arts, 1985, Art Inst. Chgo., Mpls. Coll. Art & Design, 1986, Hood Mus. Art Dartmouth Coll., Hanover, N.H., 1987, Lawrence (Kans.) Art Ctr., 1987, Miller's Studio, Zurich, Switzerland, 1987, Palazzo Braschi, Rome, 1987, Sante Fe Ctr. Photography, 1987, Dinnerware Gallery, Tucson, 1987, Sante Fe Ctr. Arts (purchase award), 1987, Rockwell Mus., Corning, N.Y., 1987, Grand Canyon Coll., Phoenix, 1987, Tucson Mus. Art, 1988, Halsey Gallery Coll. of Charleston, S.C., 1988, Long Beach (Calif.) Coll. Fine Arts, 1988, Atrium Gallery U. Conn. Storrs, 1988, Gallery of Kans. City (Mo.) Artists Coalition (1st prize, fellowship award) 1989, Lieberman and Saul Gallery, N.Y.C., 1989, Downey (Calif.) Mus. Art, 1989, Anderson Ranch Arts Ctr., Aspen, Colo., 1989, San Francisco Camerawork, 1990, Phoenix Mus. Art, 1990, Ctr. for Photography, Cin., 1991, Mus. Art U. Okla., 1991, Rockford (Ill.) Coll., 1991, Ctr. for Creative Photography, Tucson, 1991-92; Huntington Gallery, Mass. Coll. Art, Boston, 1992, Ariz. State Capital, Phoenix, 1992, Barbara Zusman Art and Antiques Gallery, Santa Fe, N.Mex., 1992; internat. traveling exhbns.; represented in permanent collections Union Russian Art Photography, Moscow, U. Calif. Santa Cruz, Kennedy Ctr. Performing Arts, Washington, L.A. County Mus. Art, Internat. Mus. Photography George Eastman House, Rochester, N.Y., N.Y. Pub. Libr., SUNY Buffalo, Libr. Congress, Polaroid Corp., Cambridge, Mass., Sante Fe Mus. Fine Arts, Scottsdale Ctr. Art, Snell and Wilmer, Phoenix, Valley Nat. Bank, Phoenix, others; photographs featured various works. Judge spring art show Scottsdale C.C., 1980; organizer Artist Against Hunger money and food drive Ariz. State U. Sch. Art, 1984; juror New Times Newspaper, 1985, Tempe Fine Arts Ctr., 1989, Yavapai Coll., Prescott, Ariz., 1989. Recipient Faculty Grant-in-Aid, 1982, 85, 93, Current Works 1989 Excellence award Soc. Contemporary Photography, Visual Artists fellowship grant Nat. Endowment for Arts, 1986, rsch. grant Coll. Fine Arts, 1987, 93, grant Arts/Social Svcs./Humanities, 1989, Sch. Art Assistance to Faculty, 1990, Visual Arts fellowship grant Ariz. Commn. Arts, 1989-90, Inst. for Studies in Arts, 1992, materials grant Polaroid Corp., 1992, Gov.'s Arts award, 1992, Women's Studies Summer Rsch. award., 1992. Mem. Coll. Arts Assn., Soc. Photographic Edn. (co-chair, organizer West/S.W. Regional Conf. 1983), Friends of Photography (Ferguson award 1983). Democrat. Russian Orthodox. Home: 534 N Orange Mesa AZ 85201-5609

KAILATH, THOMAS, electrical engineer, educator; b. Poona, India, June 7, 1935; came to U.S., 1957, naturalized, 1976; s. Mamman and Kunjamma (George) K.; m. Sarah Jacob, June 11, 1962; children: Ann, Paul, Priya, Ryan. BE, U. Poona, 1956; SM, MIT, 1959, ScD, 1961; Dr. Tek (hon.), Linkoping U., Sweden, 1990; D hon. causa, Strathclyde U., Scotland, 1992; hon. degree, U. Carlos III, Madrid, 1999. Comm. rschr. Jet Propulsion Labs., Pasadena, Calif., 1961-62; faculty Stanford (Calif.) U., 1963—, prof. elec. engring., 1968—, Hitachi Am. prof. engring., 1988—; dir. Info. Systems Lab., 1971-81, assoc. chmn. dept., 1981-87. Vis. prof., cons. univs., industry, govt. Author: Linear Systems, 1980, Least-Squares Estimation, 2d edit, 1981, State-Space Estimation Theory, 1999; edit. bd. various jours.; contbr. articles to profl. jours. Recipient Edn. award Am. Control Coun., 1986, Tech. Achievement and Soc. awards Signal Processing Soc. IEEE, 1989, 91, Donald G. Fink Prize award, 1996, Shannon award, 2000; Sr. Vinton Hayes fellow MIT, 1992, Guggenheim fellow, 1970, Churchill fellow, 1977, Michael fellow Weizmann Inst., Israel, 1984, Royal Soc. guest rsch. fellow, 1989. Fellow IEEE (Edn. medal 1995), Inst. Math. Stats., Am. Acad. Arts and Scis.; mem. NAS, Indian Nat. Acad. Engring., Nat. Acad. Engring., Am. Math. Soc., Soc. Indsl. and Applied Math., Third World Acad. Scis., Sigma Xi. Home: 1024 Cathcart Way Palo Alto CA 94305-1047 Office: Stanford U Dept Elec Engring Stanford CA 94305-9510 E-mail: kailath@stanford.edu

KAISCH, KENNETH BURTON, psychologist, priest; b. Detroit, Aug. 29, 1948; s. Kenneth R. Kaisch and Marjorie F. (Howe) Bourke; m. Suzanne Carol LePrevost, Aug. 31, 1969; 1 child, Samuel. BA, San Francisco State U., 1972; MDiv, Ch. Divinity Sch. Pacific, 1976; MS, Utah State U., 1983, PhD in Clin. Psychology, 1986. Ordained deacon Episcopal Ch., 1976, priest, 1977; lic. clin. psychologist, Calif.; diplomate Nat. Inst. Sports Psychologists. Intern local parish, 1973-76; ordinand tng. program Ch. of the Good Shepherd, Ogden, Utah, 1976-77; pastor St. Francis' Episc. Ch., Moab, 1977-80, St. John's Episc. Ch., Logan, 1980-84; psychol. asst. Peter Ebersole, Ph.D., Fullerton, Calif., 1984-86; intern in clin. psychology Patton State Hosp., 1985-86; psychol. asst. Ronald Wong Jue, Ph.D., Fullerton and Newport Beach, 1986-88; pvt. practice clin. psychologist, 1988—; clin. dir. Anxiety Clinic, Fullerton, 1993—. Exec. dir. Contemplative Congress, Fullerton, 1988-91, Inner Peace Conf., 1995-97; founder, pres. OneHeart, 1986-98, Contemplative Visions, Fullerton, 1990-2000; supply priest Episc. Diocese of L.A.; invited lectr. Acad. Sch. Profl. Psychology, Moscow, 1992, 93, Moscow Med. Acad., 1998. Co-author: Fundamentals of Psychotherapy, 1984, Developing Your Feel for Golf, 1998; author: Finding God: A Handbook of Christian Mediation, 1994, The Mental Golf Inventory, 1998, Hit it With Your Best Shot: How to Play Golf in the Zone, 2000; co-editor: God in Russia: The Challange of Freedom, 1999, Turning the Heart to God, 2001; contbr. numerous articles to profl. jours. Mem. St. Andrew's Episc. Ch., Fullerton. Mem. APA, Calif. Psychol. Assn., Anxiety Disorders Assn. Am., Nat. Register of Health Svc. Providers in Psychology, Phi Kappa Phi, Rotary (past bd. dirs., past officer). Episcopalian. Office: 2555 E Chapman Ave Ste 617 Fullerton CA 92831-3621 E-mail: kenkaisch@home.com

KAISER, GLEN DAVID, construction company executive; s. David and Margaret Jane (Frye) K.; m. Pamela Blyo Barris, Sept. 7, 1972 (div. 1974); m. Pamela Blyo Barris, Nov. 7, 1976; children: Barris David, Katrina Tara. BS in Civil Engring., Stanford U., 1974, MS in Constrn. Mgmt., 1975. Registered profl. engr., Nev., Calif. Constrn. engr. Kaiser Engrs., Oakland, Calif., 1975-79; project coord. Corrao Constrn., Reno, 1979-81; chief estimator Marnell Corrao Assocs., Las Vegas, Nev., 1981-82, exec. v.p., 1982-91, pres., 1991—. Bd. dirs. Pop Warner, Las Vegas, 1991-93, Las Vegas Symphony, 1992-93. Mem. Associated Gen. Contractors (2d v.p. 1992, sec.-treas. 1993), United Builders and Contractors (v.p. 1998, pres. 2001), Appaloosa Horse Club, Sigma Chi Alumni Assn., Stanford U. Alumni Assn. Roman Catholic. Avocations: snow skiing, horseback riding, golf. Office: Marnell Corrao Assocs 4495 S Polaris Ave Las Vegas NV 89103-4119 E-mail: gkaiser@marnellcorrao.com

KAISER, NICHOLAS, physicist, educator; b. Sept. 15, 1954; BSc in Physics, Leeds U., 1978; Pt III maths tripos, Cambridge U., 1981, PhD in Astronomy, 1982. Lindemann fellow U. Calif., Berkeley, 1983, postdoctoral fellow Santa Barbara, 1984, Berkeley, 1984, U. Cambridge, 1985-86, SERC advanced fellow, 1986-88; SERC sr. visitor U. Sussex, 1985; assoc. prof. CITA, 1988-90, prof., 1990-97; prof. astronomy Inst. Astronomy U. Hawaii, Honolulu, 1997—. Recipient Helen Warner prize Am. Astron. Soc., 1989, Gerhard Herzberg medal Can. Assn. Physicists, 1993, Rutherford Meml. medal in physics Royal Soc. Canada, 1997; grantee NSERC, 1988, 91, 93; Ontario fellow CIAR Cosmology Program, 1988—, Steacie fellow, 1991-92. Achievements include research in observational cosmology, galaxy formation, large-scale structure, bulk flows, gravitational lensing. Home: 1633A Paula Dr Honolulu HI 96816-4315 Office: U Hawaii Inst Astronomy 2688 Woodlawn Dr Honolulu HI 96822-1839

KALABA, ROBERT EDWIN, applied mathematician; b. Mt. Vernon, N.Y., Sept. 21, 1926; s. Edwin Albert and Leona Margaret (Winkler) K.; m. Wilma Joy Becker, Dec. 23, 1950; children: Robert John, Darlene Day, Kathy Lynn, Richard William. B.A., NYU, 1948, Ph.D., 1958. Mathematician Rand Corp., Santa Monica, Calif., 1951-70; prof. econs., elec. and biomed. engring U. So. Calif., Los Angeles, 1969—. Author: Invariant Imbedding and Radiative Transfer in Slabs of Finite Thickness, 1963, Quasilinearization and Nonlinear Boundary-Value Problems, 1965, Dynamic Programming and Modern Control Theory, 1965, Imbedding Methods in Applied Mathematics, 1973, Integral Equations via Embedding Methods, 1974, Control, Identification and Input Optimization, 1982, Numerical Derivatives and Nonlinear Analysis, 1986, A New Analytical Dynamics, 1995; founding editor Jour. Applied Math. and Computation, 1975; contbr. articles to profl. jours. Served with USN, 1945-46. Mem. IEEE (life), Assn. Computing Machinery, Math. Assn. Am., Riviera Country Club, Am. Econ. Assn., Phi Beta Kappa. Home: 370 Aderno Way Pacific Palisades CA 90272-3344 Office: U So Calif Los Angeles CA 90089-0251

KALINA, ROBERT EDWARD, opthalmologist, educator; b. New Prague, Minn., Nov. 13, 1936; s. Edward Robert and Grace Susan (Hess) K.; m. Janet Jessie Larsen, July 18, 1959; children: Paul Edward, Lynne Janet. B.A. magna cum laude, U. Minn., 1957, B.S., M.D., U. Minn., 1960. Diplomate Am. Bd. Ophthalmology (dir. 1981-89). Intern U. Oreg. Med. Sch. Hosp., Portland, 1960-61, resident in ophthalmology, 1961-62, 63-66; asst. in retina surgery Children's Hosp., San Francisco, 1966-67; Nat. Inst. Neurol. Diseases and Blindness Spl. fellow Mass. Eye and Ear Infirmary, Boston, 1967; instr. ophthalmology U. Wash., 1967-69, asst. prof., 1969-71, acting chmn. dept. ophthalmology, 1970-71, asso. prof., 1971-72, chmn. dept. ophthalmology, 1971-96, prof., 1972—. Mem. staffs Univ. Hosp., Harborview Hosp., Children's Hosp., Seattle; cons. VA Hosp., Seattle, Madigan Hosp., Tacoma; assoc. head divsn. ophthalmology dept. surgery Children's Hosp., Seattle, 1975-86; pres. U. Wash. Physicians, 1990-93. Contbr. author: Introduction to Clinical Pediatrics, 1972, Ophthalmology Study Guide for Medical Students, 1975; contbr. numerous articles to profl. publs. Served to capt., M.C. USAF, 1962-63. Fellow ACS, Am. Acad. Ophthalmology (Sr. Honor award 1989); mem., Assn. Univ. P rofs. Ophthalmology (pres. 1983-84, exec. v.p. 1989-94), Assn. Rsch. in Vision and Ophthalmology, Pacific Coast Oto Ophthalmol. Soc. (councilor 1972-74), King County Med. Soc., Wash. State Acad. Ophthalmology, Phi Beta Kappa. Home: 2627 96th Ave NE Bellevue WA 98004-2107 Office: U Wash Dept Ophthalmology Box 356485 1959 NE Pacific St Seattle WA 98195-0001

KALINSKE, THOMAS J. education, video game and toy company executive; b. 1944; married. BS, U. Wisconsin, 1966; MBA, U. Arizona, 1968. Acct. rep. Strauss Broadcasting Co., 1966-68, J. Walter Thompson, 1968, sr. acct. rep., 1969; sr. acct. rep., acct. supr. Case & Krone Inc., 1970-72; product mgr. Mattel Toys Mattel Inc., 1972-73, dir. product planning, 1973-77, dir. mktg., 1977-78, v.p. mktg., 1978-79, sr. v.p. mktg., 1979-82, sr. v.p. domestic, worldwide mktg., 1982-83, sr. v.p., gen. mgr. mktg., 1983-84, pres. Mattel USA, 1984-85, pres., CEO, 1985-87; pres., chief oper. officer Universal Matchbox Group, N.Y.C., 1987-90; pres., CEO Sega of Am., Redwood City, Calif., 1990-96; ceo Knowledge Universe, Menlo Park, Calif, 1996—. Office: Knowledge Universe 3351 El Camino Ste 200 Menlo Park CA 94027

KALKHOVEN, KEVIN N. electronics company executive; Pres., CEO Uniphase, San Jose, Calif. Office: JDS UNIPHASE CORP 163 Baypointe Pkwy San Jose CA 95134

KALLAHER, MICHAEL JOSEPH, mathematics educator; b. Cin., Sept. 4, 1940; s. Martin Henry and Lou Will (Huff) K.; m. Donalyn May Laraway, Aug. 17, 1963; children: Jay, Michael, Christopher, Daniel, Raymond. BS, Xavier U., 1961; MS, Syracuse U., 1963, PhD, 1967. Postdoctoral fellow U. Man., Winnipeg, Can., 1967-69; from asst. prof. prof. math. Wash. State U., Pullman, 1969—, assoc. dean scis., 1979-84, acting dean scis., 1982, chmn. math dept., 1984-92; vis. prof. Auckland U., New Zealand, 1988. Author: Affine Planes with Transitive Collineation Groups; contbg. editor Finite Geometries, 1982; contbr. articles to profl. jours. Grantee NSF; Fulbright Research scholar, Kaiserslautern, Fed. Republic Germany, 1975-76. Fellow Inst. Combinatories and Its Application (founding); mem. Am. Math. Soc., Math. Assn. Am., N.Y. Acad. of Scis., Assn. of Research Profs. (pres. 1986-87), Sigma Xi. Home: 235 NW Joe St Pullman WA 99163-3410 Office: Wash State U Dept Of Math Pullman WA 99163

KALLAY, MICHAEL FRANK, II, medical devices company official; b. Painesville, Ohio, Aug. 24, 1944; s. Michael Frank and Marie Francis (Sage) K.; m. Irma Yolanda Corona, Aug. 30, 1975; 1 son, William Albert. BBA, Ohio U., 1967. Salesman Howmedica, Inc., Rutherford, N.J., 1972-75, Biochem Procedures/Metpath, North Hollywood, Calif., 1975-76; surg. specialist USCI divsn. C.R. Bard, Inc., Billerica, Mass., 1976-78; western and ctrl. regional mgr. ARCO Med. Products Co., Phila., 1978-80; midwest reigonal mgr. Intermedics, Inc., Freeport, Tex., 1980-82; western U.S. mgr. Renal Systems, Inc., Mpls., 1982—. Pres. Kall-Med, Inc., Anaheim Hills, Calif., 1982—. Mem. Am. Mgmt. Assn., Phi Kappa Sigma. Home and Office: 7539 E Bridgewood Dr Anaheim CA 92808-1407

KALLENBERG, JOHN KENNETH, librarian; b. Anderson, Ind., June 10, 1942; s. Herbert A. and Helen S. K.; m. Ruth Barrett, Aug. 19, 1965; children: Jennifer Anne, Gregory John. A.B., Ind. U., 1964, M.L.S., 1969. With Fresno County Library, Fresno, Calif., 1965-70, dir., 1976—; librarian Fig Garden Pub. Library br., 1968-70; asst. dir. Santa Barbara (Calif.) Pub. Library, 1970-76. Mem. Calif. Libr. Svcs. bd., 1990-99, v.p., 1992-95, pres., 1996-98, Libr. of Calif. Bd., 1999—; Beth Ann Harnish lectr. com., 1988-91, chmn., 1989-90; adv. bd. Pacific Southwest Regional Med. Libr., 1999—. Mem. Calif. Libr. Assn. (councilor 1976-77, v.p., pres. 1987), Calif. County Librs. Assn. (pres. 1977), Calif. Libr. Authority for Sys. and Svcs. (chmn. authority adv. coun. 1978-80), Kiwanis (pres. Fresno 1981-82, lt. gov. divsn. 5 1991-92, co-editor Cal-Nev-Ha News 1993-94, 95-96, bd. dirs. 1999-2001). Presbyterian. Office: Fresno County Free Libr 2420 Mariposa St Fresno CA 93721-2204 E-mail: jkallenb@sjvls.lib.ca.us

KALLET, JUDITH S. publishing executive; Sr. v.p., chief info. officer L.A. Times. Office: LA Times Times Mirror Sq Los Angeles CA 90053

KALLGREN, EDWARD EUGENE, lawyer; b. San Francisco, May 22, 1928; s. Edward H. and Florence E. (Campbell) K.; m. Joyce Elaine Kislitzin, Feb. 8, 1953; children: Virginia K. Pegley, Charles Edward. AB, U. Calif., Berkeley, 1951, JD, 1954. Bar: Calif. Assoc., ptnr. Brobeck, Phleger & Harrison, San Francisco, 1954-93, of counsel, 1993—. Bd. dirs. Olivet Meml. Park, Colma, Calif., 1970-98, pres., 1991-98; chair, pres. Five Bridges Found., 1998—; mem. Berkeley City Council, 1971-75; bd. dirs., v.p./treas. Planned Parenthood Alameda/San Francisco, 1984-89. Served to sgt. USMC, 1945-48. Mem. ABA (ho. of dels. 1985-2000, state del. 1997-98, coun. sr. law divsn. 1996-2001, chair 1999-2000), State Bar of Calif. (bd. govs. 1989-92, v.p 1991-92), Found. of State Bar Calif. (bd. dirs. 1993-98, v.p., 1994-96, chair fellows soc. 1996-98), Bar Assn. San Francisco (pres. 1988, bd. dirs.), San Francisco Lawyers Com. Urban Affairs (co-chair 1983-85), Lawyers Com. Civil Rights Under Law (trustee 1985—), The TenBroek Soc. (chair bd. dirs. 1992-95). Democrat. Office: Brobeck Phleger & Harrison Spear St Tower 1 Market Plz San Francisco CA 94105-1100 E-mail: ekallgren@brobeck.com

KALLMAN, BURTON JAY, foods association director; b. N.Y.C., Nov. 1, 1927; s. Leo Melville and Muriel Kallman; m. Ellis Katherine Hachikian, Dec. 12, 1958; children: Lisa, David. BS, Bethany Coll., 1947; MS, U. So. Calif., 1951, PhD, 1958. Research biochemist U.S. Govt., Denver, Los Angeles, 1959-67; mem. profl. staff TRW Systems, Redondo Beach, Calif., 1967-76; sr. scientist Sci. Applications Inc., La Jolla, 1976-80; prin. Interdisciplinary Sci. Assocs., Torrance, 1980-82; lab. dir. Applied Biol. Scis., Glendale, 1982-85; dir. sci. and tech. Nat. Nutritional Foods Assn., Newport Beach, 1985-96, cons. Cons. Children's Asthma Research Inst., Denver, 1961-63, Behavioral Health Services, Redondo Beach, 1973-77, Centinela Child Guidance, Inglewood, Calif., 1984-86. Mem. editl. bd. Jour. Applied Nutrition, 1991-99, Jour. Optimal Nutrition, 1992-96; reviewer sci. books and films, 1978—; contbr. articles to profl. jours. Bd. dirs. Drum Barracks Civil War Mus., Wilmington, Calif., 2000—. Recipient Merit award NASA, 1976, Burton Kallman Scientific Achievement award, Nat. Nutritional Foods Assn., 1997. Mem. Am. Chem. Soc., Sigma Xi. Democrat. Jewish. Home: 23214 Robert Rd Torrance CA 90505-3244 Office: Nat Nutritional Foods Assn 3931 Macarthur Blvd Ste 101 Newport Beach CA 92660-3013 E-mail: Kallman2@aol.com

KALLOSH, RENATA, physics educator; BS, Moscow State U., 1966; PhD, Lebedev Physical Inst., Moscow, 1968. Prof. Lebedev Physical Inst., Moscow, 1981-89; sci. assoc. CERN, Switzerland, 1989-90; prof. physics Stanford U., Calif., 1990—. Avocations: gardening, biking, hiking, swimming, travelling. Achievements include research in unified theories of fundamental interactions including gravity, different aspects of supersymmetry, supergravity, and superstring theory, gen. theory of quantization, manifestly supersymmetric quantization of superparticle and superstring theory, quantum theory of black holes and gravitational waves in supersymmetric theories. Office: Stanford U Varian 342 Stanford CA 94305 Fax: 650-725-6544. E-mail: kallosh@physics.stanford.edu

KALLSHIAN, JAN, electronics manufacturing company executive; b. 1955; CPA. With Coopers & Lybrand; cons., CFO Datamarine Internat., Inc., Mountlake, Wash., 1995, CFO, 1997—. Office: 7030 220th SW Mountlake Terrace WA 98043

KALRA, YASH PAL, soil chemist; b. Gunjial, Punjab, India, Oct. 28, 1940; arrived in Can., 1963; s. Amir Chand and Hemo Devi (Sapra) K.; children: Maneesh, Navita. BSc in Agr., Agra U., Kanpur, Uttar Pradesh, India, 1961, MSc in Agrl. Chemistry, 1963; MSc in Soil Sci., U. Man., Winnipeg, Can., 1967. Head soil and plant analysis Can. Forestry Svc., Edmonton, Alta., Can., 1967—. Mem. safety com. No. Forestry Ctr., 1970-72, 94—; chmn. registration com. Environ. Soil Sci. Conf., Can. Land Reclamation Assn.-Can. Soc. Soil Sci., 1992; mem. biol. svcs. and environ. scis. adv. com. No. Alta. Inst. Tech., Edmonton, 1993-94; mem. environ. conservation and reclamation adv. com. Lakeland Coll., Vermilion, Alta., 1993-97; mem., chemistry exec. Profl. Inst. Pub. Svc. Can., 1984-2000, exec. Edmonton br., 1991—; panelist in field. Author: (methods manual) Information Report, 1991; referee for several sci. publs.; mem. editl. bd. Comms. in Soil Sci. and Plant Analysis; contbr. articles to profl. jours. Grantee Prime Min. India, 1963, Nat. Rsch. Coun. Can., 1964-66; rsch. fellow Indian Coun. Agrl. Rsch., 1961-63, U. Man., 1963-64; recipient J.B. Jones award Soil and Plant Analysis Coun., Lincoln, Nebr., 1993. Fellow Can. Soc. Soil Sci. (sec. 1993-95, pres. 1996-97), Indian Soc. Soil Sci., Assn. Ofcl. Analytical Chemists Internat. (co-chmn. soil and environ. workshop 1992-93, chmn. 1994—, chair methods com. on environ. quality 1997-2000, office methods bd. 1997-2000); mem. Internat. Soc. Soil Sci. (treas. workshop working group MO 1992), Soil Sci. Soc. Am. (assoc. referee method validation for pH measurement in soil with AOAC), Am. Soc. Agronomy, Soc. Ind. Foresters, Western Enviro-Agrl. Lab. Assn. (co-founder, sec.-treas. 1981-82, 85-86, vice chmn. 1982-83, 86-87, chmn. 1983-84, 87-88, first check sample program 1979-81), Group Analytical Labs. (founder, chmn. 1990-92), Soil Sci. Soc. Pakistan, Soil Sci. Soc. Bangladesh, Soil and Plant Analysis Coun. (bd. dirs. 1993-2000, pres. 2000—), Pacific Regional Soc. Soil Sci., Potash Rsch. Inst. Office: Can Forest Svc 5320 122 St Edmonton AB Canada T6H 3S5 E-mail: ykalra@nrcan.gc.ca

KALTENBACH, C(ARL) COLIN, dean, educator; b. Buffalo, Mar. 22, 1939; s. Carl H. and Mary Colleen (McKeag) K.; m. Ruth Helene Johnson, Aug. 22, 1964; children: James Earl, John Edward. BSc, U. Wyo., 1961; MSc, U. Nebr., 1963; PhD, U. Ill., 1967. Postdoctoral fellow U. Melbourne, Australia, 1967-69; from asst. prof. to prof. U. Wyo., Laramie, 1969-89, assoc. dean, dir. Agrl. Expt. Sta., 1980-89; vice dean, dir. Agrl. Expt. Sta. U. Ariz., Tucson, 1989—. Contbr. 200 articles to profl. publs. Named Outstanding Alumnus Coll. Agriculture U. Wyo., 1991. Mem. Nat. Assn. State Univs. and Land Grant Colls. (chmn. expt. sta. sect. 1997), Soc. for Study Reprodn. (treas. 1979-82), Am. Soc. Animal Sci., Civitan (officer 1972-85), Agrl. Experiment State Dirs. (chair 1996-97). Office: U Ariz Coll Agriculture Tucson AZ 85721-0001 E-mail: kltnbch@ag.arizona.edu

KAMEMOTO, FRED ISAMU, zoologist, educator; b. Honolulu, Mar. 8, 1928; s. Shuichi and Matsu (Murase) K.; m. Alice Takeyo Asayama, July 20, 1963; children: Kenneth, Garett, Janice. Student, U. Hawaii, 1946-48; A.B., George Washington U., 1950, M.S., 1951; Ph.D., Purdue U., 1954. Research assoc., acting instr. Wash. State U., 1957-59; asst. prof. zoology U. Mo., 1959-62; asst. prof. U. Hawaii, Honolulu, 1962-64, assoc. prof., 1964-69, prof. zoology, 1969-94, prof. emeritus, 1995—, chmn. dept., 1964-65, 71-80, 81-90, dir. biology program, 1992-94. Vis. rsch. scholar Ocean Rsch. Inst., U. Tokyo, Biol. Lab., Fukuoka U., 1968-69; vis. prof. Coll. Agr. and Vet. Medicine, Nihon U., Tokyo, summer 1973, 1979; vis. scholar dept. biology Conn. Wesleyan U., 1975-76; sr. scientist dept. fisheries Nihon U., Tokyo, 1986; vis. fgn. rschr. Tropical Biosphere Rsch. Ctr. U. of Ryukyus Okinawa, Japan, 1994. Contbr. articles to profl. jours. Chmn. Hawaii State Natural Areas Reserve System Commn., 1985-88. Served with AUS, 1954-57. NSF grantee, 1960-79; National Oceanic and Atmospheric Administration grantee, 1985-89. Fellow AAAS; mem. Sigma Xi. Buddhist. Home: 3664 Waaloa Way Honolulu HI 96822-1151 Office: U Hawaii Dept Zoology Honolulu HI 96822

KAMEMOTO, GARETT HIROSHI, reporter; b. Honolulu, Oct. 30, 1966; s. Fred I. and Alice T. (Asayama) K. BA, U. Hawaii, 1989. Reporter Sta. KHVH, Honolulu, 1989-92, 93-94; Sta. KGMB-TV, Honolulu, 1992-93, 94—. Home: 3664 Waaloa Way Honolulu HI 96822-1151 Office: Sta KGMB TV 1534 Kapiolani Blvd Honolulu HI 96814-3715 E-mail: gkamemoto@netscape.com

KAMEMOTO, HARUYUKI, horticulture educator; b. Honolulu, Jan. 19, 1922; s. Shuichi and Matsu (Murase) K.; m. Ethel Hideko Kono, June 7, 1952; children— David Yukio, Mark Toshio, Claire Naomi. B.S., U. Hawaii, 1944, M.S., 1947; Ph.D., Cornell U., 1950. Asst. in horticulture U. Hawaii, Honolulu, 1944-47, asst. prof. horticulture, 1950-54, assoc. prof., 1954-58, prof., 1958—, chmn. dept., 1969-75. Horticulture adviser Kasetsart U., Bangkok, Thailand, U. Hawaii AID contract, 1962-65; UNFAO hort. cons. to, India, 1971, 80 Author: (with R. Sagarik) Beautiful Thai Orchid Species, 1975; contbr. articles to profl. jours. Recipient Gold medal Malayan Orchid Soc., 1964; Norman Jay Coleman award Am. Assn. Nurserymen, 1977, Norman F. Childers award Am. Soc. for Hort. Sci., 1984, Scientist of Yr. award ARCS Found., 1990; Fulbright rsch. fellow Kyoto U., Japan, 1956-57. Fellow AAAS, Am. Soc. Hort. Sci.; hon. mem. Am. Orchid Soc. (Gold medal 1990), Soc. Am. Florists (Alex Laurie award 1982, inducted into Floriculture Hall of Fame 1991), Japan Orchid Soc., Orchid Soc. Thailand (award of honor 1978), Orchid Soc. S.E. Asia; mem. Am. Genetic Assn., Am. Hort. Soc., Bot. Soc. Am., Internat. Soc. Hort., Internat. Assn. Plant Taxonomy, Soc. Advancement Breeding Rsch. in Asia and Oceania, Phi Kappa Phi. Home: 3246 Lower Rd Honolulu HI 96822-1457 Office: U Hawaii 3190 Maile Way Honolulu HI 96822-2232

KAMEN, MARTIN DAVID, physical biochemist; b. Toronto, Aug. 27, 1913; BS with honors, U. Chgo., 1933, PhD, 1936, ScD (hon.), 1969; PhD (hon.), U. Paris, 1969; ScD (hon.), Washington U., St. Louis, 1977, U. Ill., Chgo., 1978, U. Freiburg, Germany, 1979, Weizmann Inst., Rehovot, Israel, 1987, Brandeis U., , 1988. Fellow nuc. chemistry Radiation Lab. U. Calif., 1937-39, rsch. assoc., 1939-41; marine test engr. Kaiser Cargo., Calif., 1944-45; assoc. prof. biochemistry Wash. U., 1945-46, assoc. prof. chemistry and chemist Mallinckrodt Inst., 1945-57; prof. biochemistry Brandeis U., 1957-61; prof. chemistry U. Calif., San Diego, 1961-74, chmn. dept., 1971-73, prof. biol. scis., 1974-78, prof. emeritus biol. scis., 1978—; prof. emeritus chem. scis. U. So. Calif., Los Angeles, 1978—. NSF sr. fellow, 1956, Guggenheim fellow, 1956, 72; recipient C.F. Kettering Award Am. Soc. Plant Physiologists, 1969. Fellow Am. Inst. Chemists, Am. Philos. Soc.; mem. Nat. Acad. Sci., Am. Chem. Soc. (award 1963), Am. Soc. Biol. Chemists (Merck award 1982), Am. Acad. Arts and Scis. (John Scott award Phila., 1989, Einstein award, Fermi award 1996).

KAMER, LARRY, public relations executive; MA, Northwestern U. Prin. GCI Kamer Singer, San Francisco, 1990—. Mem. Pub. Rels. Soc. Am. Office: GCI Kamer Singer 74 New Montgomery St Ste 450 San Francisco CA 94105-3442

KAMIL, ELAINE SCHEINER, pediatrician, educator; b. Cleve., Jan. 26, 1947; d. James Frank and Maud Lily (Severn) Scheiner; m. Ivan Jeffery Kamil, Aug. 29, 1970; children: Jeremy, Adam, Megan. BS magna cum laude, U. Pitts., 1969, MD, 1973. Diplomate Am. Bd. Pediats., Am. Bd. Pediat. Nephrology. Intern in pediats. Children's Hosp. Pitts., 1973-74, resident in pediats., 1974-76; clin. fellow in pediat. nephrology Sch. Medicine, UCLA, 1976-79, acting asst. prof. pediats., 1979-80; rsch. fellow in nephrology Harbor-UCLA Med. Ctr., Torrance, Calif., 1980-82; med. dir. The Children's Clinic of Long Beach, 1984-87; med. dir. pediat. nurse practitioner program Calif. State U., Long Beach, 1984 87; asst. clin. prof. pediats. Sch. Medicine, UCLA, 1988-91, assoc. clin. prof. pediats., 1991-97; assoc. dir. pediat. nephrology and transplant immunology Cedars-Sinai Med. Ctr., L.A., 1990—; clin. prof. pediats. Sch. Medicine, UCLA, 1997—. Adj. asst. prof. pediats. Harbor-UCLA, Torrance, Calif., 1983-87, UCLA, 1987-88; cons. in pediat. nephrology Hawthorne (Calif.) Cmty. Med. Group, 1981-2000. Author chpts. to books; contbr. articles to profl. jours. Pres.-elect med. adv. bd. Nat. Kidney Found. So. Calif., 2000—. Recipient Vol. Svc. award Nat. Kidney Found., 1998. Mem. AAUW, Am. Soc. Nephrology, Am. Soc. Pediat. Nephrology, Am. Fedn. Clin. Rsch., Internat. Soc. Nephrology, Internat. Soc. Pediat. Nephrology, Internat. Soc. Peritoneal Dialysis, Renal Pathology Soc., So. Calif. Pediat. Nephrology Assn. (chair steering com. 1998—), Nat. Kidney Found. So. Calif. (med. adv. bd. 1987-96, rsch. com. 1987-90, chmn. pub. info. med. adv. bd. 1988-92, handbook com. 1988, co-chair med. adv. bd. cmty. svcs. com. 1992-93, chair-elect patience svcs. and cmty. edn. com. 1993-94, chair patients svcs. and cmty. edn. com. 1994-95, kidney camp summer vol. physician 1988-91, 93, 94, 97, 99, 2000, Arthur Gordon award 1991, Exceptional Svc. award 1992, Exceptional Leadership and Support award 1995, bd. dirs. 1995-96), Alpha Omega Alpha, Phi Beta Kappa. Office: Cedars Sinai Med Ctr 8700 Beverly Blvd Los Angeles CA 90048-1865 E-mail: elaine.kamil@cshs.org

KAMINS, PHILIP E. diversified manufacturing company executive; b. 1936; Salesman H. Muehlstein, 1957-62; founder Kamco Plastics Inc., Sun Valley, Calif., 1965-71; pres., CEO PMC Inc., Sun Valley, 1971—, also bd. dirs. Office: PMC Inc 12243 Branford St Sun Valley CA 91352-1010

KAMINSKI, JANUSZ, cinematographer; b. Ziembice, Poland, June 27, 1959; came to U.S., 1981; s. Marian Kaminski and Jadwiga Celner; m. Holly Hunter, May 20, 1995. BA in Film, Columbia Coll., 1987. Dir. photography film Lisa, 1988 (Line Eagel award Ill. Film Festival), Absence, 1988, Selling Short, 1988, Grim Prairie Tales, 1989, All The Love in The World, 1989, Rain Killer, 1990, The Terror Within II, 1991, The Adventures of Huck Finn, 1992, Cool As Ice, 1992, Mad Dog Coll, 1992, Trouble Bound, 1993, Schindler's List, 1993 (Academy Award, Best Cinematography), How to Make an American Quilt, 1995, Jerry Maguire, 1996, Lost World, 1997, Amistad, 1997, Saving Private Ryan, 1998 (Academy Award, Best Cinematography), A.I.-2001 Minority Report, 2001; dir. Lost Souls, 2000. Office: 1223 Wilshire Blvd # 645 Santa Monica CA 90403-5400

KAMINSKY, GLENN FRANCIS, retired protective services official, business owner, teacher; b. Passaic, N.J., Apr. 29, 1934; s. Francis Gustave and Leona Regina (Tubach) K.; m. Janet Lindesay Strachan (div. June 1985); childrenn: Lindesay Anne, Jon Francis; m. Melanie Sue Rhamey, Mar. 11, 1989. BS in Police Sci., San Jose (Calif.) State Coll., 1958; MS in Adminstrn., San Jose State U., 1975. Cert. tchr., Alaska, N.Y., Calif., Colo., Fla., N.Mex., Oreg., Wyo., Va., Oreg., also others. Police officer San Jose Police Dept., 1957-65, sgt., 1965-75, lt., 1975-81; dep. chief Boulder (Colo.) Police Dept., 1981-92; ret. Pres. Kaminsky & Assocs., Inc., Longmont, Colo. 1981—. Author, editor: (textbook) The Field Training Concept in Criminal Justice Agencies, 2000; contbr. articles to profl. jours. Exec. dir. Nat. Assn. Field Tng. Officers Assn., 1993-2000. Sgt. U.S. Army, 1957-61, Korea. Recipinet Lifetime Achievement award Am. Soc. L.E. Trainers, 2000. Mem. Police Mgmt. Assn. (sec. 1983-88), Calif. Assn. Police Tng. Officers, Internat. Assn. Women Police, Calif. Assn. Adminstrn. of Justice Educators, Internat. Assn. Chiefs of Police (use of deadly force com.). Republican. Episcopalian. Avocations: bowling, softball, art collecting. Home and Office: 8965 Sage Valley Rd Longmont CO 80503-8885 E-mail: kaminskygf@msn.com

KAMINSKYJ, SUSAN GAIL WILLETS, fungal research biologist; BSc in Zoology and Botany, U. Toronto, 1978, MSc in Botany, 1982; PhD in Biology, York U., 1994. Rsch. tech. U. Toronto, 1977-79; rsch. assoc. U. Western Ontario, 1982-84, York U., 1984, rsch. tech., 1984-89; rsch. biologist Purdue U., W. Lafayette, Ind., 1994-2000; assoc. prof. dept. biology U. Sask., Saskatoon, Can., 2000—. Contbr. articles to profl. jours., numerous presentations. Recipient Alice Wilson award Royal Soc. Can., 1995. Office: U Sask Dept Biology 112 Science Pl Saskatoon SK Canada S7N 5E2 E-mail: Susan.Kaminskyj@usask.ca

KAMM, BARBARA B. bank executive; BA in Comm., Stanford U.; M of Internat. Mgmt., Am. Grad. Sch. Internat. Mgmt. Exec. v.p., group mgr. So. Calif. Tech. and Life Scis. teams and Entertainment; chief adminstrv. officer Silicon Valley Bank, Santa Clara, Calif., 1996-98, exec. v.p., strategic products & svcs., 1998—. Chmn. adv. bd. UCI ACCELERATE Tech. SBDC. Bd. dirs. So. Calif. Entrepreneurship Acad., Orange County United Way. Office: Silicon Valley Bank Corp Hdqrs 3003 Tasman Dr Santa Clara CA 95054-1191

KAMM, HERBERT, journalist; b. Long Branch, N.J., Apr. 1, 1917; s. Louis and Rose (Cohen) K.; m. Phyllis I. Silberblatt, Dec. 6, 1936; children: Laurence R., Lewis R., Robert H. Reporter, sports editor Asbury Park (N.J.) Press, 1935-42; with AP, 1942-43, N.Y. World-Telegram and Sun, 1943-66, successively rewrite man, picture editor, asst. city editor, feature editor, mag. editor, 1943-63, asst. mng. editor, 1963, mng. editor, 1963-66; exec. editor N.Y. World Jour. Tribune, 1966-67; editorial cons. Scripps Howard Newspapers, 1967-69; assoc. editor Cleve. Press, 1969-80, editor, 1980-82, editor emeritus, 1982; edit. dir. Sta. WJW-TV, Cleve., 1982-85. Instr. journalism Case Western Res. U., 1972-75, Calif. Poly., San Luis Obispo, 1991—. Radio and TV news commentator and panelist, 1950-85, TV talk show host, 1974-85; freelance writer, 1985—; author: A Candle for Popsy, 1953; editor: Junior Illustrated Encyclopedia of Sports, 1960. Bd. overseers Case Western Res. U., 1974-78. Two Herb Kamm scholarships in journalism established Kent State U., 1983, Calif. Poly., 1995; inducted Cleve. Journalism Hall of Fame, 1986. Mem. AFTRA, Soc. Profl. Journalists (pres. Calif. Missions chpt. 1986-87), Calif. Ambassadors for Higher Edn. Clubs: City of Cleve. (pres. 1982), Silurians Home: 147 River View Dr Avila Beach CA 93424-2307 E-mail: hkamm@calpoly.edu, hkace@charter.net

KAN, YUET WAI, hematologist, educator; b. Hong Kong, June 11, 1936; came to U.S., 1960; s. Tong-Po and Lai-Wai (Li) K.; m. Alvera Lorraine Limauro, May 10, 1964; children: Susan Jennifer, Deborah Ann BS, MB, U. Hong Kong, 1958, DSc, 1980, DSc (hon.), 1987, Chinese U., Hong Kong, 1981; MD (hon.), U. Cagliari, Sardinia, Italy, 1981. Investigator Howard Hughes Med. Inst., San Francisco, 1976—; prof. lab. medicine U. Calif., San Francisco, 1977—, Louis K. Diamond prof. hematology, 1991—. Mem. NIDDK adv. coun. NIH, 1991-95; trustee Croucher Found., Hong Kong, 1992—, chmn., 1997—. Contbr. over 250 articles to med. jours., chpts. to books. Recipient Dameshek award Am. Soc. Hematology, 1980, George Thorn award Howard Hughes Med. Inst., 1980, Gairdner Found. Internat. award, 1984, Allan award Am. Soc. Human Genetics, 1984, Lita Annenberg Hazen award for Excellence in Clin. Rsch., 1984, Waterford award, 1987, ACP's award, 1988, Genetic Rsch. award Sanremo Internat., 1989, Warren Alpert Found. prize, 1989, Albert Lasker Clin. Med. Rsch. award, 1991, Christopher Columbus Discovery award, 1992, City of Medicine award, 1992, Excellence 2000 award, 1993, Helmut Horten Rsch. award, 1995. Fellow Royal Coll. Physicians (London), Royal Soc. (London), Third World Acad. Scis., AAAS, Am. Acad. Arts and Scis.; mem. Nat. Acad. Scis. USA, Acad. Sinica (Taiwan), Chinese Acad. Scis. (fgn. mem.), Assn. Am. Physicians, Am. Soc. Hematology (pres. 1990), Soc. Chinese Bioscientists in Am. (pres. 1998-99). Avocations: tennis, skiing. Office: U Calif 3D Parnassus Ave # U426 San Francisco CA 94143-0001 E-mail: kanyuet@labmed2.ucsf.edu

KANAMORI, HIROO, geophysics educator; b. Tokyo, Oct. 17, 1936; Prof. Tokyo U., 1970-72, Calif. Inst. Tech., Pasadena, 1972-89, John E. and Hazel S. prof., 1989—, dir. Seismological Lab. 1990—. Recipient Arthur L. Day prize and lectureship NAS, 1993; California Scientist of the Year, Calif. Museum of Science and Industry, 1993. Fellow Am. Geophys. Union (Walter H. Bucher medal 1996); mem. Seismol. Soc. Am., Seimol. Soc. Japan. Office: Calif Inst Tech Seismology Lab 1201 E California Blvd Pasadena CA 91125-0001

KANDELL, HOWARD NOEL, pediatrician; BS, U. Miami, 1956; MD, Tulane U., 1959. Diplomate Am. Bd. Pediatrics. Intern Phila. Gen. Hosp., 1959-60; resident N.Y. Hosp. Cornell Med. Ctr., N.Y.C., 1960-62; pediatrician Phoenix, 1965-2001; retired Phoenix, 2001. Chief pediatrics Health Maintenance Assocs., Ltd., Phoenix, 1977-82; assoc. chmn. dept. pediatrics, Maricopa County Hosp., Phoenix, 1965-71, svc. chief dept. pediatrics, 1972-77; assoc. in pediatrics U. Ariz. Coll. Medicine, 1970-82, clin. instr. 1982-83; asst. prof., 1983-87; chmn. pediatric dept. CIGNA Healthplan of Ariz., Phoenix, 1984-87; adj. faculty mem. Ariz. State U. Coll. Nursing, 1986-95; med. dir. INA Healthplan (CIGNA) South Fla., 1982-83. Capt. MC USAF, 1962-64. Recipient Tchr. of Yr. award dept. pediatrics Maricopa County Gen. Hosp., 1972. Fellow Am. Acad. Pediatrics (Ariz. chpt. treas., exec. com. 1970-76, Phoenix chpt. v.p. 1970-72); mem. Am. Coll. Phys. Exec. Home: 7257 E Echo Ln Scottsdale AZ 85258-2768

KANE, ALAN HENRY, lawyer; b. Seattle, Nov. 7, 1940; s. Henry and Alice (Harbak) K.; m. Martha Dressler, June 25, 1966; children: Karen, Graham, AMy. BA in Law, U. Wash., 1963, JD, 1965. Bar: Wash. 1965. Ptnr. Sax & Maciver, Seattle, 1966-84, Preston Gales & Ellis, LLP, Seattle, 1985—. Fellow Am. Coll. Trusts and Estates Counsel (Wash. State chair 1985-88). Avocations: boating, water and snow skiing, fishing. Office: Preston Gates & Ellis LLP 701 5th Ave Ste 5000 Seattle WA 98104-7078 E-mail: alank@prestongates.com

KANE, CHRISTOPHER, lawyer; b. L.A., Aug. 4, 1944; s. William Jerome and Mary Katherine Kane; m. Kathryn Ann Lalley, June 27, 1970; children: Kevin Jerome, Ryan Robert, Matthew Christopher, Molly Kathryn. BA in Polit. Sci., Seattle U., 1966; JD, Georgetown U., 1969. Bar: Wash. 1969, U.S. Ct. Mil. Appeals 1969, U.S. Dist. Ct. (we. dist.) Wash. 1973, U.S. Dist. Ct. (ea. dist.) Wash. 1975, U.S. Ct. Appeals (9th cir.) 1976, U.S. Ct. Appeals (10th cir.) 1977; cert. internat. arbitrator. Legis. aide to Henry M. Jackson U.S. Senate, Washington, 1968-69; assoc. Ferguson & Burdell, Seattle, 1973-79, ptnr., 1979-95; prin. Law Offices Christopher Kane, Seattle, 1995-96; chmn. bd., pres. Lawyer Selection Advisors, Seattle, 1996-97; of counsel Foster, Pepper & Shelfelman, Seattle, 1998-2000, orgnl. devel. cons. Reid & Assocs., Inc. and Baldwin Resource Group, Seattle and Bellevue, Wash., 2001—. Adj. prof. European single market law and bus. Seattle U., 1994-95; instr. law and civil procedure Edmonds (Wash.) C.C., 2001—. Contbr. articles to profl. jours. Capt. USAR, 1969-73. Mem. ABA (sects. of corp. law, internat. law and practice, antitrust), Wash. State Bar Assn. (chmn. antitrust sect. 1986-87), Rotary (vice chmn. internat. students com. 1992), Seattle Tennis Club. Roman Catholic. Avocations: skiing, tennis, jogging, writing. Office: Foster Pepper & Shefelman 1111 Third Ave Bldg Ste 3400 Seattle WA 98101 E-mail: kanelaw@home.com

KANE, JOHN LAWRENCE, JR. federal judge; b. Tucumcari, N.Mex., Feb. 14, 1937; s. John Lawrence and Dorothy Helen (Bottler) K.; m. Stephanie Jane Shafer, Oct. 5, 1993; children: Molly Francis, Meghan, Sally, John Pattison. B.A., U. Colo., 1958; J.D., U. Denver, 1961, LL.D. (hon), 1997. Bar: Colo. 1961. Dep. dist. atty., Adams County, Colo., 1961-62; assoc. firm Gaunt, Byrne & Dirrim, 1961-63; ptnr. firm Andrews and Kane, Denver, 1964; pub. defender Adams County, 1965-67; dep. dir. eastern region of India Peace Corps, 1967-69; with firm Holme Roberts & Owen, 1970-77, ptnr., 1972-77; judge U.S. Dist. Ct. Colo., Denver, 1978-88, U.S. sr. dist. judge, 1988—. Adj. prof. law U. Denver, U. Colo., 1996—; vis. lectr. Trinity Coll., Dublin, Ireland, winter 1989; adj. prof. U. Colo., 1996. Contbr. articles to profl. jours. Recipient St. Thomas More award Cath. Lawyers Guild, 1983, U.S. Info. Agy. Outstanding Svc. award, 1985, Outstanding Alumnus award U. Denver, 1987, Lifetime Jud. Achievement award Nat. Assn. Criminal Def. Lawyers, 1987, Civil Rights award B'nai B'rith, 1988, Justice Gerald Le Dain award Drug Policy Found., 2000. Fellow Internat. Acad. Trial Lawyers, Am. Bd. Trial Advs. (hon.). Roman Catholic. Office: US Dist Ct C-428 US Courthouse 1929 Stout St Denver CO 80294-1929 E-mail: john_L_Kane@cod.uscourts.gov

KANE, MARY KAY, dean, law educator; b. Detroit, Nov. 14, 1946; d. John Francis and Frances (Roberts) K.; m. Ronan Eugene Degnan, Feb. 3, 1987 (dec. Oct. 1987). BA cum laude, U. Mich., 1968, JD cum laude, 1971. Bar: Mich., N.Y., Calif. Rsch. assoc., co-dir. NSF project on privacy, confidentiality and social sci. rsch. data sch. law U. Mich., 1971-72, Harvard U., 1972-74; asst. prof. law SUNY, Buffalo, 1974-77; mem. faculty Hastings Coll. Law U. Calif., San Francisco, 1977—, prof. law, 1979—, assoc. acad. dean, 1981-83, acting acad. dean, 1987-88, acad. dean., 1990-93, dean, 1993—; chancellor U. Calif., San Francisco, 2001—. Vis. prof. law U. Mich., 1981, U. Utah, 1983, U. Calif., Berkeley, 1983-84, sch. law U. Tex., 1989; cons. Mead Data Control, Inc., 1971, 74, Inst. on Consumer Justice, U. Mich. Sch. Law, 1972, U.S. Privacy Protection Study Commn., 1975-76; lectr. pretrial mgmt. devices U.S. magistrates for 6th and 11th cirs. Fed. Jud. Ctr., 1983; Siebenthaler lectr. Samuel P. Chase Coll. Law, U. North Ky., 1987; reporter ad hoc com. on asbestos litigation U.S. Jud. Conf., 1990-91, mem. standing com. on practice and procedure, 2001—; mem. 9th Cir. Adv. Com. on Rules Practice and Internal Oper. Procedures, 1993-96; spkr. in field. Author: Civil Procedure in a Nutshell, 1979, 4th edit., 1996, Sum and Substance on Remedies, 1981; co-author: (with C. Wright and A. Miller) Pocket Supplements to Federal Practice and Procedure, 1975—, Federal Practice and Procedure, vols. vol. 7, 3d edit., 2001, 10, 10A and 10B, 3d edit., 1998, vols. 7-7C, 2d edit., 1986, vols. 6-6A, 2d edit., 1990, vols. 11-11A, 2d edit., 1995, (with J. Friedenthal and A. Miller) Hornbook on Civil Procedure, 3d edit., 1999, (with D. Levine) Civil Procedure in California, 6th edit., 1998; mem. law sch. divsn. West. Adv. Editl. Bd., 1986—; contbr. articles to profl. jours. Mem. ABA (mem. bar admissions com. 1995—), Assn. Am. Law Schs. (com. on prelegal edn. statement 1982, chair sect. remedies 1982, panelist sect. on prelegal edn. 1983, exec. com. sect. on civil procedure 1983, 86, panelist sect. on tchg. methods 1984, spkr. new tchrs. conf. 1986, 89, 90, chair sect. on civil procedure 1987, spkr. sects. civil procedure and conflicts 1987, 91, chair planning com. for 1988 Tchg. Conf. in Civil Procedure 1987-88, nominating com. 1988, profl. devel. com. 1988-91, planning com. for workshop in conflicts 1988, planning com. for 1990 Conf. on Clin. Legal Edn. 1989, chair profl. devel. com. 1989-91, exec. com. 1991-93, 2000-02, pres.-elect 2000, pres. 2001), Am. Law Inst. (assoc. reporter complex litigation project 1988-93, coun. 1998—), ABA/Assn. Am. Law Schs. Commn. on Financing Legal Edn., State Bar Mich. Home: 8 Admiral Dr Ste 421 Emeryville CA 94608-1567 Office: U Calif Hastings Coll Law 200 Mcallister St San Francisco CA 94102-4707

KANE, THOMAS JAY, III, orthopaedic surgeon, educator; b. Merced, Calif., Sept. 2, 1951; s. Thomas J. Jr. and Kathryn (Hassler) K.; m. Marie Rose Van Emmerik, Oct. 10, 1987; children: Thomas Keola, Travis Reid, Samantha Marie. BA in History, U. Santa Clara, 1973; MD, U. Calif., Davis, 1977. Diplomate Am. Bd. Orthopaedic Surgery. Intern U. Calif. Davis Sacramento Med. Ctr., 1977-78, resident in surgery, 1978-81; resident in orthopaedic surgery U. Hawaii, 1987-91; fellowship adult joint reconstruction Rancho Los Amigos Med. Ctr., 1991-92; ptnr. Orthop. Assocs. of Hawaii, Inc., Honolulu, 1992—; asst. prof. surgery U. Hawaii, Honolulu, 1993—, chief divsn. implant surgery, 1993—. Contbr. articles to profl. jours. Mem. AMA, Am. Assn. Hip and Knee Surgeons, Hawaii Med. Assn., Hawaii Orthop. Assn., Am. Acad. Orthop. Surgery, Western Orthopedic Assn., Alpha Omega Alpha, Phi Kappa Phi. Avocations: tennis, golf, skiing, music, surfing. Office: Orthopaedic Svcs Co LLP 1380 Lusitana St Ste 608 Honolulu HI 96813-2442

KANE, THOMAS REIF, engineering educator; b. Vienna, Austria, Mar. 23, 1924; came to U.S., 1938, naturalized, 1943; Ernest Kanitz and Gertrude (Reif) K.; m. Ann Elizabeth Andrews, June 4, 1951; children: Linda Ann, Jeffrey Thomas. BS, Columbia U., 1950, MS, 1952, PhD, 1953; D Tech. Scis. (hon.), Tech. U. Vienna, Austria, 1990. Asst. prof., assoc. prof. U. Pa., Phila., 1953-61; prof. Sch. Engring. Stanford U., Calif., 1961-93, prof. emeritus, 1993—. Cons. NASA, Harley-Davidson Motor Co., AMF, Lockheed Missiles and Space Co., Vertol Aircraft Corp., Martin Marietta Co., Kellet Aircraft Co. Author: (vol. 1) Analytical Elements of Mechanics, 1959, (vol. 2), 1961, Dynamics, 1972, Spacecraft Dynamics, 1983; Dynamics: Theory and Applications, 1985; contbr. over 150 articles to profl. jours. Served with U.S. Army, 1943-45, PTO. Recipient Alexander von Humboldt prize, 1988. Fellow Am. Astron. Soc. (Dirk Brouwer award 1983); mem. ASME (hon.), Sigma Xi, Tau Beta Pi. Office: Stanford University Dept Mechanical Engring Stanford CA 94305

KANES, WILLIAM HENRY, geology educator, research center administrator; b. N.Y.C., Oct. 15, 1934; married. BS in Geol. Engring., CCNY, 1956; MS in Geology, W.Va. U., 1958, PhD in Geology, 1965. Sr. rsch. geologist Esso Prodn. Co., Houston Rsch. Co., 1964-65; sr. exploration geologist, head New Concepts Group Esso Stds., Libya, 1966-67, frontier exploration geologist, administr. Frontier Area Group Libya, 1967-69; asst. prof. geology W.Va. U., Morgantown, 1970-71; assoc. prof. geology U. S.C., Columbia, 1971-74, prof. geology, dir. Earth Scis. and Resources Inst., 1975-95, Disting. prof. earth resources, chair Rsch. and Devel. Found., 1984-97, disting. prof. emeritus, 1998; prof. civil amd environ. engring. U. Utah, 1994-96, dir. Earth Scis. and Resources Inst., 1994-96, dir. Energy and Geoscis. Inst., rsch. prof., civil and environ. engr., 1996-99; pres. W.H. Kanes & Assocs., 2000—. NSF Resident Rsch. prof. Acad. Sci. Rsch. and Tech., Cairo, 1976-77; hon. professorial fellow Univ. Coll. Aberystyth U. Wales, 1979-83, Univ. Coll. Swansea U. Wales, 1983-88, U. Bristol, U.K., 1986-89; hon. mem. Acad. Engring., Republic of Kazakhstan, 1994; academician Internat. Acad. Mineral Resources, Russia; vis. professorial fellow Univ. Coll. Swansea, 1977-83; vis. prof. Postgrad. Rsch. Inst. Sedimentology, U. Reading, U.K., 1989-92; co-dir. Earth Resources Inst. Univ. Coll. Swansea, U. Wales, U.K., 1980-86; advisor Atomic Energy Establishment, Egypt, 1974-77, Nat. Oil Co., Libya, 1975-78, U.S. Pres., exec. br. Energy Problems and Controls, 1977-78, Nuclear Materials Corp., Egypt, 1977-81, mem. tech. adv. task force Fed.

Power Commn. Contbr. numerous articles, papers to profl. publs. 1st lt. C.E., U.S. Army, 1955, 58-59. Recipient Disting. Svc. award U.S.C. Ednl. Found., 1985; grantee NSF, 1971-81, U.S. Dept. Interior, 1972-74, others. Fellow AAAS, Geol. Soc. Am.; mem. Am. Assn. Petroleum Geologists (cert., chmn. rsch. symposium 1976, acad. affairs com. 1973-76, acad. liaison com. 1976—, rsch. com. on pub. affairs 1975—), Am. Geophys. Union, Sigma Xi.

KANNER, EDWIN BENJAMIN, electrical manufacturing company executive; b. N.Y.C., July 2, 1922; s. Charles and Grace (Edelson) K.; m. S. Barbara Penenberg, Aug. 3, 1944; children: Jaimie Sue, Richard, Keith. BBA, CCNY, 1943; MBA, Harvard U., 1947. Asst. West Coast mgr. Fairchild Publs., N.Y.C. and L.A., 1948-50; gen. mgr. Dible Enterprises, L.A., 1951-53; sales mgr., gen. mgr., prs. Western Insulated Wire Co. div. Teledyne, L.A., 1954-68; pres. Carol Cable Co. West div. Avnet, L.A., 1969-79; exec. v.p., COO Avnet Inc., N.Y.C., 1980-83; pres. Pacific Electricord and Am. Ins. Wire Co., L.A., also Providence, 1948—. Lt. comdr. USNR, 1943-47, PTO. Office: Pacific Electricord 747 W Redondo Beach Blvd Gardena CA 90247-4203

KANNO, BRIAN M. state legislator, volunteer worker; b. Honolulu, Oct. 23, 1961; s. Toshio and Kimiko (Takahashi) K. BA in Econs., Yale U., 1983. Group asst. N.W. Ayer, N.Y.C., 1983-84; adminstrv. asst. Benton & Bowles, N.Y.C., 1984-85; account exec. Ogilvy & Mather Hawaii, Honolulu, 1985-87, Starr Seigle McCombs, Honolulu, 1987; campaign office mgr. Patsy T. Mink campaign com., Honolulu, 1988, 90; legis. asst. Rep. Patsy T. Mink, U.S. Ho. of Reps., Washington, 1990-91; advt. mgr. Servco Pacific Inc., Honolulu, 1988-90; youth vol. coord. Boys & Girls Club Waianae, 1991-92; mem. Hawaii Senate, Dist. 20, Honolulu, 1992-. Mem. steering com. Sandy Beach Coalition, 1987—. Mem. Yale Club of Hawaii (treas. 1987-90, bd. dirs. 1987—). Office: Hawaii State Capitol 415 S Beretania St Rm 202 Honolulu HI 96813-2407

KANTER, STEPHEN, law educator, dean; b. Cin., June 30, 1946; s. Aaron J. and Edythe (Kasfir) K.; m. Dory Jean Poduska, June 24, 1972; children: Jordan Alexander, Laura Elizabeth. BS in Math., MIT, 1968; JD, Yale U., 1971. Spl. asst. Portland (Oreg.) City Commr., 1971-72; from staff atty. to asst. dir. Met. Pub. Defender, Portland, 1972-77; prof. law Lewis and Clark Coll., Portland, 1977—, assoc. dean, 1980-81, acting dean, 1981-82, dean, 1986-94. Fulbright prof. law Nanjing (China) U., 1984-85, U. Athens (Greece) Faculty of Law, 1993; bd. dirs. Northwest Regional China Coun., 1996—, pres.- elect, 1997-98, pres., 1998-99; exec. com. Owen M. Panner Am. Inns of Ct., pres., 1994-95; mem. judicial selection com. U.S. Dist. Ct. Oreg., 1993; cons. on drafting and implementation of Kazakhstan Constn., 1992, 94. Contbr. articles to profl. jours. Mem. bd. overseers World Affairs Coun. Oreg., Portland, 1986-89; mem. Oreg. Criminal Justice Coun., Salem, 1987-92, Oreg. Bicentennial Commn., Portland, 1986-89. Named One of 10 Gt. Portlanders, Willamette Week newspaper, 1980; recipient E.B. MacNaughton Civil Liberties award, 1991. Fellow Am. Bar Found.; mem. ACLU (bd. dirs. Oreg. chpt. 1976-82, pres. 1979-81, lawyers com. 1976—), Oreg. State Bar Assn., Am. Law Inst. (ex-officio 1986-94), Fulbright Assn. (bd. dirs. 1987-93, exec. com. 1989-93). Home: 3142 SW Fairview Blvd Portland OR 97201-1831 Office: Lewis & Clark Coll Northwestern Sch Law 10015 SW Terwilliger Blvd Portland OR 97219-7768

KANTOR, IGO, film and television producer; b. Vienna, Austria, Aug. 18, 1930; came to U.S., 1947; s. Samuel and Miriam (Sommerfreund) K.; m. Enid Lois Dershewitz, June 24, 1962; children: Loren, Mark, Lisa. AA, UCLA, 1950, BS, 1952, MS in Polit. Sci., 1954. Fgn. corr. Portuguese Mag. Flama, L.A., 1949-57; music supr., editor Screen Gems, Columbia, L.A., 1954-63; post-prodn. supr. various ind. cos. L.A., 1963-64; music supr.-editor Universal-MCA, L.A., 1964-66; pres., film editor Synchrofilm, Inc., L.A., 1966-74; pres., producer Duque Films, Inc., L.A., 1971-78; ind. producer Jerry Lewis Films, Film Ventures, L.A., 1979-84; pres., producer Laurelwood Prodns. Inc., L.A., 1984-87, Major Arts Corp., L.A., 1987—. Pres. Jubilee Holding Co., L.A., 1988—. Producer Legends of the West with Jack Palance (TV spl. series), 1992, United We Stand, 1988, Act of Piracy, 1987, The Golden Eagle Awards, 1986, It's A Wonderful World, 1986, The Grand Tour, 1985, Shaker Run, 1984, From Hawaii with Love, 1983, Night Shadows, 1983, Kill and Kill Again, 1981, Hardly Working, 1980, Good Luck, Miss Wyckoff, 1979, Holiday Classic Cartoons, 1994, Mom USA, 1996; writer, prodr., dir. Scope, 1999—. Named Emmy nominee, 1967, 68, 69, 70. Mem. Acad. Motion Picture Arts & Scis. (exec. sound bd. 1969-71), Dirs. Guild Am. (assoc. dir.). Democrat. Jewish. Avocations: swimming, chess, ping-pong, philately, collecting movie classics. Office: Major Arts Corp 11501 Duque Dr North Hollywood CA 91604-4279 Address: PO Box 1340 Studio City CA 91614-0340 E-mail: igo.kantor@gte.net

KAO, CHENG CHI, electronics executive; b. Taipei, Taiwan, Republic of China, Aug. 3, 1941; s. Chin Wu and Su Chin (Wu) K.; m. Susan Lin, July 4, 1970; children: Antonia Hueilan, Albert Chengwei, Helen Siaolan. BS, Taiwan U., 1963; AM, Harvard U., 1965, PhD, 1969. Research fellow Harvard U., Cambridge, Mass., 1969-70; scientist Xerox Corp., Webster, N.Y., 1970-75; mgr. Internat. Materials Research, Inc., Santa Clara, Calif., 1976-78; exec. v.p. President Enterprises Corp., Tainan, Taiwan, 1979-85; pres. Kolyn Internat., Los Altos, Calif., 1979—. Contbr. articles to profl. jours. Bd. dirs. Taipei Am. Sch., 1980-82. Mem. IEEE, Chinese Inst. Elec. Engring. (bd. dirs. 1982-85), Sigma Xi. Club: Am. in China (Taipei), Palo Alto Hills Golf and Country. Avocations: jogging, golf. Office: Kolyn Internat 4962 El Camino Real Ste 119 Los Altos CA 94022-1410 E-mail: kolyn@kolyn.com

KAPCSANDY, LOUIS ENDRE, building construction and manufacturing executive, chemical engineering consultant; b. Budapest, Hungary, June 5, 1936; came to U.S., 1957; s. Lajos Endre and Margit (Toth) K.; m. Roberta Marie Henson, Jan. 25, 1964; 1 son, Louis. B.S. in Chem. Engring., Tech. U. Hungary, 1956; postgrad. in law, U. San Francisco, 1963-64; M.S. in Petroleum Tech., U. Calif.-Berkeley, 1969. Freedom fighter Hungarian Revolution, Budapest, 1956; profl. football player San Diego Chargers, 1963-65; western regional mgr. Norton Co., San Francisco, 1965-72; product mgr. Koch Industries, Wichita, Kans., 1972-74; v.p., gen. mgr. Flow Systems, Inc., Seattle, 1974-78; pres. Fentron Bldg. Products, Inc., Seattle, 1978-85; CEO Baugh Enterprises Inc., Seattle, 1985—. Chem. engring. cons. HK Assocs., Seattle, 1974— Contbr. articles to profl. jours.; patentee vacuum fraction of crude oil, purification of hydrogen. Bd. dirs. Boy Scouts Chief Seattle, Seattle C. of C., Virginia Mason Med. Ctr.; active United for Wash., Seattle, 1982. With U.S. Army, 1959-62. Fellow AIChE; mem. Constrn. Specifications Inst., TAPPI, Columbia Tower Club, Rainier Club, Newcastle Golf Club, Seattle Rotary Lodge, PGA West. Republican. Roman Catholic.

KAPLAN, ALVIN IRVING, lawyer, adjudicator, investigator; b. Providence, Apr. 19, 1925; s. David J. and Pauline (Rosenberg) K., m. Eleanor Ruth Apt, Apr. 7, 1957; 1 son, Laurence J. A.B., Cornell U., 1948; LL.B., N.Y. U., 1963. Bar: N.Y. bar 1964, U.S. Supreme Ct 1970. Internat. rep., staff engr. Internat. Ladies Garment Workers Union, AFL-CIO, St. Louis and N.Y.C., 1950-56; asst. personnel dir. Lightolier, Inc., Jersey City, 1956-59; dir. indsl. relations Climatic, Inc., Yonkers, N.Y., 1959-67; mgr. indsl. relations Koracorp Industries Inc., San Francisco, 1967-70, dir. indsl. relations, asst. sec., 1971-74, sec., 1974—, v.p., 1978-79; v.p. legal affairs, indsl. relations Diversified Apparel Enterprises, Inc., 1979-80; asst. gen. counsel Levi Strauss & Co., 1980-83; asst. v.p., sr. trust officer Cen. Banking Systems, Inc., Walnut Creek, Calif., 1984-90; asylum officer polit. asylum unit, Immigration and Naturalization Svc. U.S. Dept. Justice, San

Francisco, 1992—; equal opportunity specialist Office of Fair Housing HUD, San Francisco, 1993-95; compliance officer U.S. Dept. of Labor, 1995-97; ind. cons. civil rights investigations, 1997—. Mem. wage bd. 1 Calif. Indsl. Welfare Commn., 1976, 79; cons. Bank Trust Svcs., 1990-91. Trustee Homewood Terrace, San Francisco, 1971-73, Internat. Ladies Garment Workers Nat. Retirement Fund, Nat. Retirement Fund United Hatters, Cap and Millinery Workers Union. Served with C.E. AUS, 1943-46. Mem. ABA, N.Y. State Bar Assn., Fed. Bar Assn., Indsl. Relations Research Assn., Am. Arbitration Assn. (mem. comml. panel arbitrators), Internat. Soc. Labor Law and Social Security, Am. Soc. Corp. Secs. Democrat. Jewish. Club: Cornell No. Calif. Office: AZK Assocs 151 Edgewood Ave San Francisco CA 94117-3712 E-mail: kaplan.ace@worldnet.att.net

KAPLAN, BARRY MARTIN, lawyer; b. N.Y.C., Nov. 9, 1950; s. Stanley Seymour and Lillian (Schner) K.; m. Erica Green, July 26, 1981; children: Matthew Aaron, Elizabeth Rose, Andrew Nathan. BA, Colgate U., 1973; JD cum laude, U. Mich., 1976. Bar: Mich. 1976, Wash., 1978, U.S. Dist. (ea. dist.) Mich. 1976, U.S. Dist. Ct. (we. dist.) Wash. 1978, U.S. Dist. Ct. (ea. dist.) Wash. 1986, U.S. Tax Ct. 1983, U.S. Ct. Appeals (9th cir.) 1990. Law clk. to Hon. Charles W. Joiner U.S. Dist. Ct. (ea. dist.) Mich., Detroit, 1976-78; assoc. Perkins Coie, Seattle, 1978-85, ptnr., 1985—. Spkr. in field. Author: Washington Corporate Law, Corporations and LLCs, 2000; contbr. articles to legal jours. and procs. Mem. ABA (litigation sect., securities litigation com., bus. law sect., bus. and corp. litigation com., subcom. chmn. on control transactions 1993), Wash. State Bar Assn. (CLE spkr., bus. law sect., securities com., subcom. chair on dir.'s liability 1993), Wash. Athletic Club. Office: Perkins Coie 1201 3rd Ave Fl 40 Seattle WA 98101-3029 E-mail: kaplb@perkinscoie.com

KAPLAN, GEORGE WILLARD, urologist; b. Brownsville, Tex., Aug. 24, 1935; s. Hyman J. and Lillian (Bennett) K.; m. Susan Gail Solof, Dec. 17, 1961; children: Paula, Elizabeth, Julie, Alan. BA, U. Tex., 1955; MD, Northwestern U., 1959, MS, 1966. Diplomate Am. Bd. Urology. Intern Charity Hosp. of La. at New Orleans, 1959-60; resident Northwestern U., 1963-68, instr. Med. Sch., 1968-69; clin. prof., chief pediatric urology Sch. Medicine U. Calif., San Diego, 1970—. Trustee Children's Hosp. and Health Ctr., San Diego, 1978-90, Am. Bd. Urology, Bingham Farms, Mich., 1991-96; del. Am. Bd. Med. Specialties, Evanston, Ill., 1992-96. Author: Genitourinary Problems in Pediatrics; asst. editor Jour. Urology, Balt., 1982-89, 98—; assoc. editor Child Nephrology and Urology, Milan, Italy, 1988—; contbr. articles to profl. publs. Pres. med. staff Children's Hosp., San Diego, 1980-82. Lt. USN, 1960-63. Recipient Joseph Capps prize Inst. of Medicine, 1967. Fellow ACS (pres. San Diego chpt. 1980-82), Am. Acad. Pediatrics (chmn. sect. on urology 1986); mem. AMA, Soc. for Pediatric Urology (pres. 1993), Am. Urol. Assn., Soc. Internat. Urologie, Soc. Univ. Urologists, Am. Assn. Genito-Urol. Surgery. Republican. Jewish. Avocations: history of medicine, rare books. Office: Pediatric Urology Assocs 7930 Frost St Ste 407 San Diego CA 92123-4286

KAPLAN, ISAAC RAYMOND, chemistry educator, corporate executive; b. Baranowicze, Poland, July 10, 1929; came to U.S., 1957; s. Morris and Anny (Chait) K.; m. Helen Fagot, Sept. 4, 1955; children: Debora, David Joel. BS, Canterbury U., Christchurch, New Zealand, 1951, MS, 1953; PhD, U. So. Calif., 1961. Rsch. scientist Commonwealth Sci. and Indsl. Rsch. Orgn., Sydney, Australia, 1953-57; postdoctoral fellow Calif. Inst. Tech., Pasadena, 1961-62; guest lectr. Hebrew U., Jerusalem, 1962-65; assoc. prof. UCLA, 1965-69, prof., 1969-93, prof. emeritus, 1993—. Pres. Global Geochemistry Corp., Northridge, Calif., 1977—; cons. city, county, state and fed. regulatory agys., L.A. Contbr. and co-contbr. over 300 sci. rsch. articles to profl. jours. Guggenheim Found. fellow, Sydney, 1970-71. Fellow AAAS, Am. Inst. Chemists, Geol. Soc. Am.; mem. Russian Acad. Natural Sci. (fgn., Kapitsa medal 1998), Am. Chem. Soc., Geophys. Union, Geochem. Soc. (Alfred Treibs medal for organic geochm. 1993). Office: U Calif ESS Dept Plaza Circle Dr Los Angeles CA 90024

KAPLAN, JERRY (S. JERROLD KAPLAN), electronics company executive; B in History and Philosophy of Sci., U. Chgo.; D in Computer and Info. Sci., U. Pa. Prin. technologist Lotus Devel. Corp.; co-founder, chmn. GO Corp.; co-founder, CEO ONSALE, Inc., Menlo Park, Calif., 1994-2000; now CEO Egghead.com (merged with ONSALE, Inc.), Menlo Park, 2000—. Author: Startup-A Silicon Valley Adventure, 1995. Office: Egghead.com 1350 Willow Rd Menlo Park CA 94025-1516

KAPLAN, ROBERT MALCOLM, health researcher, educator; b. San Diego, Oct. 26, 1947; s. Oscar Joel and Rose (Zankan) K.; m. Catherine J. Atkins; children— Cameron Maxwell, Seth William AB in Psychology, San Diego State U., 1969; MA, U. Calif., Riverside, 1970, PhD, 1972. Lic. psychologist, Calif. Teaching asst. U. Calif., Riverside, 1969-72, vis. assoc. prof. psychology, 1977-78, asst. prof. in residence San Diego, 1973, asst. research psychologist and cons. dept. community medicine div. health policy, assoc. adj. prof., 1980-86, prof., 1986—, chief div. health care scis., 1989-96, chair dept. family and preventive medicine, 1997—; sr. rsch. assoc. Am. Inst. for Rsch., Palo Alto, Calif., 1972-73; from asst. prof. to prof. psychology San Diego State U., 1974-88, dir. Ctr. for Behavioral Medicine. Bd. dirs. NATO Advanced Rsch. Workshop on Behavioral Epidemiology and Disease Prevention; mem. health svcs. rsch. study sect. Nat. Ctr. Health Svcs. Rsch., 1981-85, 88-92, VA Sci. Rev. and Evaluations Bd. for Health Svcs., 1989-91 (chair 1991-92); cons., lectr. in field. Faculty fellow San Diego State U., 1977; epidemiology fellow Am. Heart Assn., 1983; recipient Career Rsch. Devel. award NIH, 1981-86, Alumni and Assocs. Disting. Faculty award San Diego State U., 1982, Exceptional Merit service award San Diego State U., 1984 Fellow APA (bd. dirs., Outstanding Sci. Achievement award health psychology divsn. 1987, 2001, pres. 1992-93); mem. AAAS (exec. com. Pacific divsn. 1978-82), Soc. Behavioral Medicine (bd. dirs., pres. 1996-97, pres. elect 2001—, editor-in-chief Annals of Behavioral Medicine, 2000—) Office: U Calif Sch Medicine Dept Family Preventive Medicine La Jolla CA 92093-0628 E-mail: RKaplan@ucsd.edu

KAPLAN, SAMUEL, pediatric cardiologist; b. Johannesburg, South Africa, Mar. 28, 1922; came to U.S., 1950, naturalized, 1958; s. Aron Leib and Tema K.; m. Molly Eileen McKenzie, Oct. 17, 1952. MB, BcH., U. Witwatersrand, Johannesburg, 1944, MD, 1949. Diplomate: Am. Bd. Pediatrics. Intern, Johannesburg, 1945; registrar in medicine, 1946; lectr. physiology and medicine U. Witwatersrand, 1946-49; registrar in medicine U. London, 1949-50; fellow in cardiology, research assoc. U. Cin., 1950-54, asst. prof. pediatrics, 1954-61, assoc. prof. pediatrics, 1961-66, prof. pediatrics, 1967-87, asst. prof. medicine, 1954-67, assoc. prof. medicine, 1967-82, prof. medicine, 1982-87; prof. pediatrics UCLA, 1987-98, emeritus prof. pediat., 1998—. Cons. NIH; hon. prof. U. Santa Tomas, Manila. Mem. editl. bd. Circulation, 1974-80, Am. Jour. Cardiology, 1976-81, Am. Heart Jour., 1981-96, Jour. Electrocardiology, 1977-94, Clin. Cardiology, 1979—, Jour. Am. Coll. Cardiology, 1983-87, Progress Pediat. Cardiology, 1990—. Cecil John Adams fellow, 1949-50; grantee Heart, Lung and Blood Inst. of NIH, 1960-2000. Mem. Am. Pediatric Soc., Am. Soc. Pediatric Rsch., Am. Heart Assn. (med. adv. bd. sect. circulation), Am. Fedn. Clin. Rsch., Am. Coll. Cardiology, Internat. Carviovascular Soc., Am. Acad. Pediatrics, Midwest Soc. Pediatric Rsch. (past pres.), Sigma Xi. Alpha Omega Alpha; hon. mem. Peruvian Soc. Cardiology, Peruvian Soc. Angiology, Chilean Soc. Cardiology, Burma MEd. Assn. Achievements include research and publications on cardiovascular physiology, diagnostic methods, cardiovascular complications of pediatric AIDS and heart disease in infants, children and adolescents. Office: UCLA Sch Medicine Dept Pediatric Cardiology Los Angeles CA 90095-0001

KAPLAN, SELNA L. medical educator; Prof. pediatrics U. Calif., San Francisco, chief divsn. of pediatric endocrinology. Mem. Lawson Wilkins Pediatric Endocrine Soc. (past pres.), Endocine Soc. (Koch award, Ayerst Svc. award). Office: U Calif San Francisco Cardiothoracic Surg 505 Parnassus Ave Rm M593 San Francisco CA 94143-0001 Fax: 415-476-9678

KAPLAN, SHEILA, academic administrator; b. Bklyn. BA in European History, PhD in Modern European History, CUNY; MA, Johns Hopkins U. Instr. history CUNY System; dir. spl. baccalaureate program CUNY; v.p. acad. affairs Winona (Minn.) State U.; vice-chancellor for acad. affairs Minn. State U. System; chancellor U. Wis.-Parkside, Kenosha, 1986-93; pres. Met State Coll., Denver, 1993—. Bd. dirs. Kenosha Area Devel. Corp., Racine County Econ. Devel. Corp.; chmn. bd. Council for Adult and Experiential Learning. Office: Metropolitan State Coll Office of President PO Box 173362 Campus Box 1 Denver CO 80217-3362

KAPLANSKY, IRVING, mathematician, educator, research institute director; b. Toronto, Ont., Can., Mar. 22, 1917; came to U.S., 1940, naturalized, 1955; s. Samuel and Anna (Zuckerman) K.; m. Rachelle Brenner, Mar. 16, 1951; children— Steven, Daniel, Lucille. B.A., U. Toronto, 1938, M.A., 1939; Ph.D., Harvard, 1941; LL.D. (hon.), Queen's U., 1969. Instr. math. Harvard, 1941-44; mem. faculty U. Chgo., 1945-84, prof. math., 1956-84, chmn. dept., 1962-67, George Herbert Mead Distinguished Service prof. math., 1969-84; dir. Math. Scis. Research Inst., Berkeley, Calif., 1984-92; dir. emeritus, 1992. Mem. exec. com. div. math. NRC, 1959-62 Author books, tech. papers. Mem. Nat. Acad. Scis., Am. Math. Soc. (pres. 1985-86) Office: Math Scis Rsch Inst 1000 Centennial Dr Berkeley CA 94720-5070 E-mail: kap@mahi.org

KAPLOWITZ, KAREN (JILL), lawyer, business consultant; b. New Haven, Nov. 27, 1946; d. Charles Cohen and Estelle (Gerber) K.; m. Alan George Cohen, Aug. 17, 1980; children: Benjamin, Elizabeth. BA cum laude, Barnard Coll., 1968; JD, U. Chgo., 1971. Bar: Calif. 1971, U.S. Dist. Ct. (Cen. Dist.) Calif. 1971. Assoc. O'Melveny & Myers, L.A., 1971-74; ptnr. Bardeen, Bersch & Kaplowitz, L.A., 1974-80, Alschuler, Grossman & Pines, L.A., 1980-96, of counsel, 1997—. Contbr. articles to profl. jours. Mem. vis. com. U. Chgo. Law Sch., 1990-93. Mem. ABA (chmn. employer-employee rels. com. of tors and ins. practice sect.), Assn. Bus. Trial Lawyers (pres.), Calif. Women Lawyers (Fay Stender award 1982), Women Lawyers Assn. L.A. Home: 1 Woodside Ln New Hope PA 18938-9281 Office: 2049 Century Park E # 39 Los Angeles CA 90067-3101

KAPLOWITZ, NEIL, physician, educator; b. N.Y.C., Mar. 16, 1943; s. Louis and Henrietta (Schall) K.; m. Fattaneh E. Enayat; children: Hillary C., Gregory D. BS, NYU, 1964, MD, 1967. Dipl. Nat. Bd. Med. Examiners, 1968; bd. qualified, Am. Bd. Internal Med., 1970, Cert. Int. Med., 1975, Cert. Gastroenterology, 1975, Lic. Calif. 1975—. Intern, resident Bellevue Hosp., 1967-69; resident Albert Einstein Med. Ctr., 1969-70; asst. res. phys. Rockefeller Univ. Hosp., 1970-71; fellowship Cornell U. Coll. Medicine, 1970-72; guest investigator Rockefeller U., N.Y.C., 1970-71; instr. in med. Cornell Univ. Med. Coll., 1971-72; asst. prof. Cornell U. Med. Coll., N.Y.C., 1972-73, UCLA Sch. Medicine, 1975-77; chief hepatology Wadsworth VA Hosp., Los Angeles, 1975-79; dir. UCLA Wadsworth Gastroenterology/Hepatology Fellshp. Tng. Prog., 1980-84; chief gastroenterology/hepatology section Wadsworth VA Hosp., Los Angeles, 1980-89; assoc. prof. UCLA Sch. Medicine, 1977 82, prof., 1982-90, U. So. Calif. Sch. Medicine, L.A., 1990—, chief div. gastrointestinal and liver diseases, 1990—; chief gastroenterology Wadsworth VA Hosp., L.A., 1980-90; prof. molecular pharmacology & toxicology USC Sch. of Pharmacy, 1992—; prof. physiology USC Sch. Med., 1993—; dir. USC Liver Diseases Rsch. Ctr. (NIDDK Digestive Disease Core Ctr. Grant), 1994—. Affiliated investigator, Ctr. for Ulcer rsch., 1978-89, coord. for liver disease, UCLA affiliated hosps., 1975-89, coord. gastroenterology/hepatology, UCLA Sch. Med., 1981-84, mem. Search Com., Nephrology, Wadsworth, 1985-86, Search Com., Cardiology, Wadsworth, 1986—, chmn. Search Com. for Chief of Psych., Wadsworth 1986-87, chmn. R&D Com., VAOPC 1990—. Search Com., chair dept. Physiology, USC Sch. Med., 1992, Planning Com. Transplantation Biol. Rsch. Bldg., USC Sch. of Med., 1992, subcom. Academic Senate, 1992, chmn. Res. Review Com., VAOPC, 1992—, mem. Rsch. Design Team, subcom. on criteria for rsch. space allocation, USC, 1995, Dept. Med. Steering Com. for Productivity Criteria, 1995, mem. steering com. Gastroenterology Rsch. Grp., 1981-85, 90-94, NIH Reviewers Reserve (NRR), 1990-94, NIH, GMA-1 Special Study Section, 1992, 91, 92, AGA/Industry Rsch. Scholar Awd. Com. 1993-96, Special Review Grp., NIDDK Core Ctr. Grants, 1995, Councilor, AASLD, 1993-96 (pres. elect, 1997, pres. 1998), vice chair for rsch., bd. dirs., chmn., scientific advisory council, Am. Liver Found., 1994-96, DDW Council, 1996—. Editor: Liver and Biliary Diseases, 1992; assoc. editor: Hepatology, 1985-90, Am. Jour. Physiology, 1991—; contbr. over 100 articles to profl. publs. Lt. comdr. USN, 1973-75. Recipient Western Gastroenterology Rsch. prize Western Gut Club, 1986, Tchr. of Yr., Wadsworth VA, 1977-78, NIH Merit awd. 1992, William S. Middleton awd., 1993, Solomon A. Berson Med. Alumni Achievement awd. in clin. sci., NYU Sch. Med., 1994. Mem. Am. Asns. Physicians, Am. Soc. Clin. Investigation, Western Soc. Clin. Investigation (pres. 1985-86), Am. Fedn. for Clin. Rsch., Am. Assn. for Study of Liver Disease, Southern Calif. Gastroenterology Soc., Southern Calif. Liver Rsch. Forum (founder), Am. Gastroenterology Soc., Am. Soc. for Pharmacology and Experimental Therapeutics, Internat. Biliary Assn., Internat. Assn. for Study of Liver Disease, Soc. for Experimental Biol. and Med., 1983, Am. Physiological Soc., Western Assn. of Phys., Rsch. Soc. on Alcoholism, European Assn. for Study of Liver, Am. Coll. of Gastroenterology (fellow), Phi Beta Kappa, Alpha Omega Alpha. Achievements include research in regulation and role of hepatic glutathione in detoxification; transport of glutathione and organic anions; identification and characterization of cytosol proteins in liver which bind and transport bile acids, organic anions and tocopherol. Office: U So Calif Sch Medicine Dept Med AHC 127 1355 San Pablo St Los Angeles CA 90033-1034

KAPTEYN, HENRY CORNELIUS, physics and engineering educator; b. Oak Lawn, Ill., Jan. 21, 1963; m. Margaret Mary Murnane, 1988. BS, Harvey Mudd Coll., 1982; MA, Princeton U., 1984; PhD, U. Calif., Berkeley, 1989. Rsch. asst. U. Calif., 1985-89, postdoctoral rschr., 1989-90; asst. prof. physics Wash. State U., Pullman, 1990-95, assoc. prof., 1995, U. Mich., Ann Arbor, 1996-99; prof. JILA, U. Colo., Boulder, 1999—. Contbr. articles to profl. jours. Regents fellow U. Calif., 1985, Sloan rsch. fellow, 1995. Fellow Optical Soc. Am. (Adolph Lomb medal 1993); mem. Am. Phys. Soc., Soc. Photo-Optical Instrumentation Engrs. (scholar 1988). Office: JILA Univ Colo Boulder CO 80309-0001 E-mail: kapteyn@jila.colorado.edu

KAPUR, KAILASH CHANDER, industrial engineering educator; b. Rawalpindi, Pakistan, Aug. 17, 1941; s. Gobind Ram and Vidya Vanti (Khanna) K.; m. Geraldine Palmer, May 15, 1969; children: Anjali Joy, Jay Palmer. BS, Delhi U., India, 1963; M of Tech., Indian Inst. Tech., Kharagpur, 1965; MS, U. Calif., Berkeley, 1968, PhD, 1969. Registered profl. engr., Mich. Sr. rsch. engr. Gen. Motors Rsch. Labs., Mich., 1969-70; sr. reliability engr. TACOM, U.S. Army, 1978-79; mem. faculty Wayne State U., Detroit, 1970-89, assoc. prof. indsl. engring. and ops., 1973-79, prof., 1979-89; prof., dir. Sch. Indsl. Engring. U. Okla., Norman, 1989-92; dir., indsl. engring. U. Wash., Seattle, 1992—. Vis. prof. U. Waterloo, Can., 1977-78; vis. scholar Ford Motor Co., Mich., summer 1973. Author: Reliability in Engineering Design, 1977; contbr. articles to profl. jours. Grantee GM, 1974-77, U.S. Army, 1978-79, U.S. Dept. Transp., 1980-82. Fellow Am. Soc. Quality Control; mem. Ops. Rsch. Soc. Am. (sr.), Inst. Indsl. Engrs. (assoc. editor 1980—). Home: 4484 E Mercer Way Mercer Island WA 98040-3828 Office: U Wash PO Box 352650 Seattle WA 98195-2650 E-mail: kkapur@home.com, kkapur@u.washington.edu

KARADY, GEORGE GYORGY, electrical engineering educator, consultant; b. Budapest, Hungary, Aug. 17, 1930; came to U.S., 1976; s. Gyozo and Anna (Szamek) K.; 1 child, Gyuri. MSEE, Tech. U. Budapest, 1952, DEng, 1960, D (hon.), 1996. Registered profl. engr., N.Y., N.J., Que. From instr. to assoc. prof., docent Tech. U. Budapest, Hungary, 1952-66; lectr. U. Baghdad, Iraq, 1966-68, U. Salford, Eng., 1968-69; program mgr. Hydro Quebec Inst. of Rsch., Can., 1969-76; chief elec. cons. engr. Ebasco Svcs., N.Y.C., 1976-86; Salt River Project Chair prof. Ariz. State U., Tempe, 1986—. Adj. prof. McGill U., Montreal, 1972-76, Poly. Inst. N.Y., 1980-86; lectr. (part time) U. Montreal, 1970-76. Author: Operation of Electric Appliances and Network (in Hungarian), 1964; (with others) Advances in Electronics and Electron Physics, 1976; co-author: Electric Power Systems, Vol. V (in Hungarian), 1963, Electrical Power Systems and Networks (in Hungarian), 1964; contbr. more than 150 papers to tech. jours. Fellow IEEE (paper award 1982, working group achievement award 1986); mem. U.S. Nat. Com. of Internat. Conf. of Large Elec. Network (sec.-treas. 1978-94), Princeton Ski Club (bd. dirs. 1977-86). Avocations: skiing, sailing, tennis, opera. Home: 11836 N 134th Way Scottsdale AZ 85259-3642 Office: Ariz State U Coll Engring Applied Sci Dept Elec Engring Tempe AZ 85287-5706

KARALIS, JOHN PETER, computer company executive, lawyer; b. Mpls., July 6, 1938; s. Peter John and Vivian Karalis; m. Mary Curtis, Sept. 7, 1963; children: Amy Curtis, Theodore Curtis. BA, U. Minn., 1960, JD, 1963. Bar: Minn. 1963, Mass. 1972, Ariz. 1983, N.Y. 1986, Pa. 1986. Pvt. practice, Mpls., 1963-70; assoc. gen. counsel Honeywell Inc., Mpls., 1970-83, v.p., 1982-83; pvt. practice Phoenix, 1983-85; sr. v.p., gen. counsel Sperry Corp., N.Y.C., 1985-87; v.p. gen. counsel Apple Computer Inc., Cupertino, Calif., 1987-89; of counsel Brown and Bain, Phoenix, 1989-92; sr. v.p. corp. devel. Tektronix, Inc., Portland, 1992-98. Mem. bd. advisors Ctr. for Study of Law, Sci. and Tech., Ariz. State U. Coll. Law, Tempe, 1983-89, 2000—, adj. prof., 1990-91. Author: International Joint Ventures, A Practical Guide, 1992. Recipient Disting. Achievement award Ariz. State U., Tempe, 1985. Mem. Met. Club (N.Y.C.), Gainey Ranch Golf Club.

KARATZ, BRUCE E. business executive; b. Chgo., Oct. 10, 1945; s. Robert Harry and Naomi Rae (Goldstein) K.; children: Elizabeth, Matthew, Theodore. BA, Boston U., 1967; JD, U. So. Calif., 1970. Bar: Calif. 1971. Assoc. Keatinge & Sterling, Los Angeles, 1970-72; assoc. corp. counsel Kaufman and Broad, Inc., Los Angeles, 1972-73, dir. forward planning Irvine, Calif., 1973-74; pres. Kaufman and Broad Provence, Aix-en-Provence, France, 1974-76, Kaufman and Broad France, Paris, 1976-80, Kaufman and Broad Devel. Group, Los Angeles, 1980-86; chmn., pres., CEO KB Home (formerly Kaufman and Broad Home Corp.), Los Angeles, 1985—; also bd. dirs. Kaufman and Broad Home Corp., Los Angeles, also chmn. bd. dirs., 1993. Bd. dirs. Nat. Golf Properties, Inc., Honeywell Internat., Inc., Kroger Co.; trustee RAND Corp. Founder Mus. Contemporary Art, L.A., 1981; trustee Pitzer Coll., Claremont, Calif., 1983—; bd. councilors U. So. Calif. Law Ctr. Mem. Calif. Bus. Roundtable (chmn.), Coun. on Fgn. Rels., Pacific Coun. on Internat. Policy, L.A. World Affairs Coun. (chmn.). Democrat. Avocations: modern art, skiing, travel, golf. Office: KB Home 10990 Wilshire Blvd Fl 7 Los Angeles CA 90024-3913

KARENTTE, BETTY, state legislator; b. Paducah, Ky., Sept. 13, 1931; m. Richard; 1 child, Mary. BA, MA, Calif. State U. Tchr. L.A. Unified Sch. Dist., 1961-92, cons., substitute tchr., 1994-96; mem. Calif. State Senate, Sacramento, 1996—. Office: 3711 Long Beach Blvd Ste 81 Long Beach CA 90807 Fax: 562-997-0799. E-mail: senator.karnette@sen.ca.gov*

KARGES, WILLIAM A., III, food company executive; b. Newport Beach, Calif., Feb. 11, 1963; divorced; one child. AA, Marymount Palos Verdes Coll.; restaurant mgmt. courses, UCLA. Co-founder Jones Hollywood, 1994; ptnr. Johnnie's N.Y. Cafe Pizzeria, 1984, Rix, Santa Monica, 1997; owner Blueberry, 1999; founder Voda, Santa Monica. Conceived food and decor concepts for Johnnie's N.Y., Rix. Blueberry and Voda restaurants; food and operating sys. design; former ptnr. in Jones Hollywood. Recipient Best Pizza in L.A. award, 1995, Top Bang for the Buck for Johnnie's, Zagat Survey, 1996-98; Coming Into Focus award, Buzz mag., 1997. Office: Progressive Pizza Trends Inc 10350 Santa Monica Blvd Ste 160 Los Angeles CA 90025

KARI, DAVEN MICHAEL, religious studies educator; b. Hot Springs, S.D., Sept. 24, 1953; s. John Nelson and Corinna Nicolls (Morse) K.; m. Priya Perianayakam, Apr. 4, 1988; children: David Prem, Daniel Michael, Dante Gabriel. BA in English, Bibl. Studies, History, Fresno Pacific Coll., 1975, BA in Music, 1977; MA in English, Baylor U., 1983; MA, PhD in English, Purdue U., 1985, 86; MDiv, PhD, So. Bapt. Theol. Sem., 1988, 91. Lic. to ministry So. Bapt. Ch., 1971, ordained to ministry, 1996. Photography studio technician Johnson's Studio, Manteca, Calif., 1975-77; grad. teaching asst. Baylor U., Waco, Tex., 1978-79; minister of music Calvary Bapt. Ch., West Lafayette, Ind., 1984-85; grad. teaching asst. Purdue U., West Lafayette, 1979-85; lectr. in English Jefferson C.C., Louisville, 1987-90, Spalding U., Louisville, 1986-90, U. Louisville, 1986-90; asst. prof. English Mo. Bapt. Coll., St. Louis, 1991; assoc. prof. English Calif. Bapt. Coll., Riverside, 1991-93, assoc. prof. English, dir., Christian Ministry and Fine Arts, 1993-98; prof. Christian Studies and English Calif. Baptist U., 1998; acad. dean Washington Bible Coll., Lanham, Md., 1998-2000; adminstr., min. Bapt. Christian Sch., Hemet, Calif., 2000—. Author: T. S. Eliot's Dramatic Pilgrimage, 1990, Bibliography of Sources in Christianity and the Arts, 1995; co-editor: Baptist Reflections on Christianity and the Arts: Learning from Beauty, 1997, Contemporary Authors, 1997. Founder, co-dir. local Boys Brigade, Linden, Calif., 1969-71; asst. pastor Linden (Calif.) First Bapt. Ch., 1971; chair transp. com. Calvary Bapt. Ch., West Lafayette, 1982-83, dir. singles ministry, 1983-85; moderator Scholar's Bowl Quiz Contest, Riverside, 1993-94; min. First Bapt. Ch. Hemet, 2000—. Recipient Lit. Criticism award Purdue U., 1983; named to Outstanding Young Men Am., 1985; named Faculty Mem. of Yr., Calif. Bapt. Coll., 1993; named to Contemporary Authors, 1997. Mem. Am. Acad. Religion, Conf. on Christianity and Lit., Evang. Theol. Soc. Democrat. Baptist. Avocations: poetry, stained glass windows, sculpture, photography, painting, composing music. Home: 23878 Bouquet-Cyn Pl Moreno Valley CA 92557-3538

KARI, ROSS, banking executive; BA in Math., U. Oreg., 1980, MBA in Fin., 1983. Analyst in fin. Wells Fargo, 1983, v.p., 1987, sr. v.p. fin. and planning, gen. auditor, exec. v.p., 1995, head fin., mgr. controller's divsn./corp. tax., 1997, CFO, 1998—. Office: Wells Fargo Bank 420 Montgomery St San Francisco CA 94163

KARIN, SIDNEY, computer science and engineering educator; b. Balt., July 8, 1943; BSME, CCNY, 1966; MS in Nuclear Engring., U. Mich., 1967, PhD in Nuclear Engring., 1973. Registered profl. engr., Mich. Computer programmer, nuc. engr. ESZ Assocs., Inc., Ann Arbor, Mich., 1968-72; sr. engr., sect. leader Gen. Atomics (formerly GA Techs., Inc.), San Diego, 1973-75, mgr. fusion divsn. Computer Ctr., 1975-82, dir. info. sys. divsn., 1982-85; dir. San Diego Supercomputer Ctr., 1985-2001, Nat. Partnership for Advanced Computational Infrastructure, 1997-98. Bd. dirs. Corp. for Ednl. Network Initiatives in Calif.; prof. computer sci. and engrng., 1986—; chair Fed. Networking Adv. Com., 1991-97; mem. adv. com. CISE Directorate, NSF. Contbr. articles to profl. jours. NDEA fellow, AEC fellow. Fellow AAAS; mem. Assn. for Computing Machinery, IEEE Computer Soc., Computing Rsch. Assn. (bd. dirs. 1998—). Avocations: flying, technical rock climbing, motorcycle riding, alpine skiing, reading. Home: 748 Avocado Ct Del Mar CA 92014-3911 Office: U Calif San Diego Supercomputer Ctr 9500 Gilman Dr La Jolla CA 92093-5003 E-mail: skarin@ucsd.edu

KARIYA, PAUL, professional hockey player; b. Vancouver, Oct. 16, 1974; Forward/hockey player Anaheim (Calif.) Mighty Ducks, 1994—. Winner Lady Byng Meml. Trophy for sportsmanship and gentlemanly conduct, 1995-96; mem. silver-medal-winning Can. Olympic team, 1994. Office: Anaheim Mighty Ducks PO Box 61077 2695 E Katella Ave Anaheim CA 92803-6177

KARKOSCHKA, ERICH, planetary science researcher, writer; b. Stuttgart, Federal Republic of Germany, Nov. 6, 1955; came to U.S., 1983; s. Erhard Karkoschka and Rothraut Leiter. Diploma in math., U. Stuttgart, 1981; PhD, U. Ariz., 1990. Wissenschaftlicher Mitarbeiter U. Stuttgart, 1982; rsch. assoc. U. Ariz., Tucson, 1992—. Group leader Internat. Workshop Astronomy, Europe, 1981-89. Author: The Observer's Sky Atlas, 1990, German edit., 1988, Japanese edit., 1991, Czech edit., 1995, Drehbare Welt-Sternkarte, 1990; co-author: Das Himmelsjahr, 1982—. Recipient 2d European prize European Philips Contest for Young Scientists and Inventors, 1973. Mem. Am. Meteorol. Soc. Avocations: playing violin in symphony orchestra, playing organ, amateur astronomy, worldwide travel. Office: Univ Ariz Lunar & Planetary Lab Tucson AZ 85721-0001 E-mail: erich@lpl.arizona.edu

KARLEN, PETER HURD, lawyer, writer; b. N.Y.C., Feb. 22, 1949; s. S. H. and Jean Karlen; m. Lynette Ann Thwaites, Dec. 22, 1978. BA in History, U. Calif., Berkeley, 1971; JD, U. Calif., Hastings, 1974; MS in Law and Soc., U. Denver, 1976. Bar: Calif. 1974, Hawaii 1989, Colo. 1991, U.S. Dist. Ct. (so. dist.) Calif. 1976, U.S. Dist. Ct. (no. dist.) Calif. 1983, U.S. Dist. Ct. (Hawaii) 1989, U.S. Supreme Ct. 1990. Assoc. Sankary & Sankary, San Diego, 1976; teaching fellow Coll. of Law U. Denver, 1974-75; lectr. Sch. of Law U. Warwick, United Kingdom, 1976-78; pvt. practice La Jolla, Calif., 1979-86; prin. Peter H. Karlen, P.C., La Jolla, 1986—. Adj. prof. U. San Diego Sch. of Law, 1979-84; mem. adj. faculty Western State U. Coll. of Law, San Diego, 1976, 79-80, 88, 92. Contbg. editor Artweek, 1979-95, Art Calendar, 1989-96, Art Cellar Exch. mag., 1989-92; mem. editl. bd. Copyright World, 1988—, IP World, 1997—; contbr. numerous articles to profl. jours. Mem. Am. Soc. for Aesthetics, Brit. Soc. Aesthetics. Office: 1205 Prospect St Ste 400 La Jolla CA 92037-3613

KARLIN, JOEL MARVIN, allergist; b. N.Y.C., Oct. 5, 1944; s. Louis and Frances (Weisenberg) K.; m. Caroline McInerney, July 7, 1977; children: Scott, Bradley, Bethany, Becky. BA, NYU, 1964; MD, Washington U., St. Louis, 1968; MS, U. Colo. Med. Sch., 1972. Bd. Cert. Am. Bd. Pediatrics and Am. Bd. Allergy and Immunology. Intern, residency pediatric Cornell U. Med. Ctr., N.Y.C., 1968-70; fellow pediatric allergy and immunology Nat. Jewish Hosp., Denver, 1970-72. Bd. dirs. Colo. Physicians' Network; clin. prof. medicine and pediatrics U. Colo. Sch. Medicine; chmn. bd. HealthInsuranceSelect. Maj. USAF, 1970-72. Fellow Am. Acad. Allergy and Immunology, Am. Coll. Allergy and Immunology; mem. AMA (chair coun. on legislation 2000-2001), Colo. Med. Soc. (pres. 1995-96), Phi Beta Kappa. Avocations: golf, skiing. Office: 8805 W 14th Ave Lakewood CO 80215-4848

KARLIN, SAMUEL, mathematics educator, researcher; b. Yonova, Poland, June 8, 1924; s. Morris K.; m. Elsie (div.); children: Kenneth, Manuel, Anna B.S. in Math., Ill. Inst. Tech., 1944; Ph.D. in Math., Princeton U., 1947; D.Sc. (hon.), Technion-Israel Inst. Tech., Haifa, 1985. Instr. math. Calif. Inst. Tech., Pasadena, 1948-49, asst. prof., 1949-52, assoc. prof., 1952-55, prof., 1955-56; vis. asst. prof. Princeton U., N.J., 1950-51; prof. Stanford U., Calif., 1956—. Wald lectr., 1957; Andrew D. White prof.-at-large Cornell U., 1975-81; Wilks lectr. Princeton U., 1977; pres. Inst. Math. Stats., 1978-79; Commonwealth lectr. U. Mass., 1980; 1st Mahalanobis meml. lectr. Indian Statis. Inst., 1983, prin. invited speaker XII Internat. Biometrics Meeting, Japan; prin. lectr. Que. Math. Soc., 1984; adv. dean math. dept. Weizmann Inst. Sci., Israel, 1970-77; Britton lectr. McMaster U., Hamilton, Ont., Can., 1990; Cockerham lectr. N.C. State U., 1996. Author: Mathematical Methods and Theory in Games, Programming, Economics, Vol. I: Matrix Games, Programming and Mathematical Economics, 1959, Mathematical Methods and Theory in Games, Programming, Economics, Vol. II: The Theory of Infinite Games, 1959, A First Course in Stochastic Processes, 1966, Total Positivity Vol. I, 1968; (with K. Arrow and H. Scarf) Studies in the Mathematical Theory of Inventory and Production, 1958; (with W.J. Sudden) Tchebycheff Systems: With Applications in Analysis and Statistics, 1966; (with H. Taylor) A First Course in Stochastic Processes, 2d edit., 1975, A Second Course in Stochastic Processes, 1980, An Introduction to Stochastic Modeling, 1984; (with C.A. Micchelli, A. Pinkus, I.I. Schoenberg) Studies in Spline Functions and Approximation Theory, 1976; editor: (with E. Nevo) Population Genetics and Ecology, 1976; (with T. Amemiya and L.A. Goodman) Studies in Econometric, Time Series, and Multivariate Statistics, 1983; (with K. Arrow and P. Suppes) Contributions to Mathematical Methods in the Social Sciences, 1960; (with K. Arrow and H. Scarf) Studies in Applied Probability and Management Sciences, 1962; (with S. Lessard) Theoretical Studies on Sex Ratio Evolution, 1986; editor: (with E. Nevo) Evolutionary Processes and Theory, 1986; sr. editor Theoretical Population Biology, Jour. D'Analyse; assoc. editor Jour. Math. Analysis, Lecture Notes in Biomath., Jour. Applied Probability, Jour. Multivariate Analysis, Jour. Approximation Theory, SIAM Jour. Math. Analysis, Jour. Linear Algebra, Computers and Math. with Applications, Ency. of Math. and Its Applications, Advanced in Applied Math.; contbr. articles to profl. jours. Proctor fellow, 1945, Bateman Rsch., 1947-48, Guggenheim Found., 1959-60, NSF, 1960-61; recipient Lester R. Ford award Am. Math. Monthly, 1973, Robert Grimmett Chair Math., Stanford U., 1978, The John Von Neumann Theory prize, 1987, U.S. Nat. Medal Sci., 1989; The Karlin Prize in Math. Biology named in honor Stanford U. Dept. Biol. Scis., 1992. Fellow AAAS, Internat. Statis. Inst., Inst. Math. Stats.; mem. NAS (award in applied math. 1973), Am. Math. Soc., Am. Acad. Arts and Scis., Am. Soc. Human Genetics, Genetics Soc. Am., Am. Naturalist Soc., Human Genome Orgn., London Math. Soc. (hon.), Am. Philos. Soc. Office: Stanford U Bldg 380 Stanford CA 94305-2125 E-mail: karlin@math.stanford.edu

KARLINSKY, SIMON, language educator, writer; b. Harbin, Manchuria, Sept. 22, 1924; came to U.S., 1938, naturalized, 1944; s. Aron and Sophie (Levitin) K. BA, U. Calif., Berkeley, 1960, PhD, 1964; MA, Harvard U., 1961. Conf. interpreter, music student, Europe, 1947-57; teaching fellow Harvard U., Cambridge, Mass., 1960-61; asst. prof. Slavic langs. and lits. U. Calif., Berkeley, 1963-65, prof., 1967-91, prof. emeritus, 1991—, chmn. dept., 1967-69. Vis. asso. prof. Harvard, 1966 Author: Marina Cvetaeva: Her Life and Her Art, 1966, The Sexual Labyrinth of Nikolai Gogol, 1976, 2d edit., 1992, Russian Drama from Its Beginnings to the Age of Pushkin, 1985, Marina Tsvetaeva: The Woman, Her World and Her Poetry, 1986, 2nd edit., 1988, Italian edit., 1989, Spanish edit., 1990, Japanese edit., 1991; editor: The Bitter Air of Exile, 1977; editor, annotator: Anton Chekhov's Life and Thought, 1974, 2d edit. 1997, The Nabokov-Wilson Letters, 1979, 2nd edit., 2001, French edit., 1988, German edit., 1995; co-editor: Language, Literature, Linguistics, 1987, O RUS! Studia literaria slavica in honorem Hugh McLean, 1995; contbr. articles to nat. and profl. jours. Served with AUS, 1944-46. Woodrow Wilson fellow, 1960-61; Guggenheim fellow, 1969-70, 77-78 Mem. Phi Beta Kappa. Office: U Calif Dept Slavic Lang & Lit Berkeley CA 94720-0001

KARLSBERG, PAUL, neurosurgeon; b. Springfield, Mass., July 2, 1933; s. Isador Joseph and Ciel (Robinovitz) K.; m. Helen Fay Pugach, June 23, 1959 (div. Aug. 1995); children: Elizabeth V., Peter L., Sharon D.; m. Norine Carol Dotseth, Sept. 2, 1995. AB, Harvard U., 1954; MD, Boston U., 1958. Diplomate Am. Bd. Neurologic Surgery. Intern New Eng. Med. Ctr., 1958-59; resident U. Calif., San Francisco, 1959-63; chief surgery St. Johns Hosp., Oxnard, Calif., 1978, Cmty. Meml. Hosp., Ventura, 1978-88, ret., 1990. Cons. dept. biology and philosophy U. Calif., Santa Barbara, 1993—. Contbr. articles to profl. jours. Pres. Temple Beth Torah, Ventura, Calif., 1976, 78-80. Col. USAR, 1983-93. Fellow Internat. Coll. Surgeons, Am. Bd. Neurological Surgery, Am. Coll. Surgeons; mem. AMA (Calif. chpt.), AAAS, Am. Assn. Neurol. Surgeons, Congress Neurol. Surgeons, N.Y. Acad. Sci. Avocations: music, boating. Office: Neurosurgical Associates 168 N Brent St Ste 408 Ventura CA 93003-2824

KARLSTROM, PAUL JOHNSON, art historian; b. Seattle, Jan. 22, 1941; s. Paul Isadore and Eleanor (Johnson) K.; m. Ann Heath, Dec. 29, 1964; 1 dau., Clea Heath. BA in English Lit, Stanford U., 1964; MA, UCLA, 1969, PhD (Samuel H. Kress fellow), 1973. Asst. curator Grunwald Center for Graphic Arts, UCLA, 1967-70; Samuel H. Kress fellow Nat. Gallery Art, Washington, 1970-71; instr. Calif. State U., Northridge, 1972-73; West Coast regional dir. Archives Am. Art, Smithsonian Instn. at De Young Mus., San Francisco, 1973-91, Huntington Libr., San Marino, Calif., 1991—. Guest curator Hirshhorn Mus., Washington, 1977. Author: Louis M. Eilshemius, 1978, Los Angeles in the 1940s Post Modernism and the Visual Arts, 1987, The Visionary Art of James M. Washington, Jr., 1989, Turning the Tide: Early Los Angeles Modernists, 1920-56, 1990; editor: On the Edge of America: California Modernist Art, 1900-1950, 1996, (with others) Diego Rivera: Art and Revolution, 1999, (with others) Reading California, 2000, (with others) , Over the Line: The Art and Life of Jacob Lawrence, 2000, Eros in the Studio in Poetics of Memory: Vision, Voice, Performance, 2001; video prodr. David Hockney, 1984, 93, George Tsutakawa in Japan, 1988, Richard Shaw, 1998; prin. advisor, editor Calif. Asian Am. Artist Biog. Dir.; contbr. articles to profl. jours. Mem. adv. bd. Humanities West, Jacob Lawrence Catalogue Raisonné Project; former bd. dirs. S.W. Art History Coun., Bay Area Video Coalition; sec. Va. Steele Scott Found; v.p. Noah Purifoy Found. Office: Archives Am Art Huntington Libr 1151 Oxford Rd San Marino CA 91108-1218 E-mail: pkarlstrom@earthlink.net

KARLTON, LAWRENCE K. federal judge; b. Bklyn., May 28, 1935; s. Aaron Katz and Sylvia (Meltzer) K.; m. Mychelle Stiebel, Sept. 7, 1958 (dec.); m. Sue Gouge, May 22, 1999. Student, Washington Sq. Coll., 1952-54; LL.B., Columbia U., 1958. Bar: Fla. 1958, Calif. 1962. Acting legal officer Sacramento Army Depot, Dept. Army, Sacramento, 1958-60, civilian legal officer, 1960-62; individual practice law Sacramento, 1962-64; mem. firm Abbott, Karlton & White, 1964, Karlton & Blease, 1964-71, Karlton, Blease & Vanderlaan, 1971-76; judge Calif. Superior Ct. for Sacramento County, 1976-79, U.S. Dist. Ct. (ea. dist.) Calif., Sacramento, 1979-83; formerly chief judge U.S. Dist. Ct., Sacramento, 1983-90, chief judge emeritus, 1990-2000, sr. judge, 2000—. Co-chmn. Central Calif. council B'nai B'rith Anit-Defamation League Commn., 1964-65; treas. Sacramento Jewish Community Relations Council, chmn., 1967-68; chmn. Vol. Lawyers Commn. Sacramento Valley ACLU, 1964-76. Mem. Am. Bar Assn., Sacramento County Bar Assn., Calif. Bar Assn., Fed. Bar Assn., Fed. Judges Assn., 9th Cir. Judges Assn. Club: B'nai B'rith (past pres.). Office: US Dist Ct 501 I St Sacramento CA 95814-7300

KARNI, SHLOMO, retired engineering and religious studies educator; b. Lódz, Poland, June 23, 1932; came to U.S., 1950; BSEE cum laude, Technion, Israel, 1956; MEngring., Yale U., 1957; PhD, U. Ill., 1960. Asst. prof. U. Ill., Urbana, 1960-61; assoc. prof. U. N.Mex., Albuquerque, 1961-64, prof., 1967-99, emeritus, 1999—, the Gardner-Zemke prof., 1993—. Vis. prof. U. Hawaii, 1969, Tel Aviv U., 1970, Technion, 1977; cons. Dept. Energy, Westinghouse Corp., USAF, Los Alamos Nat. Labs., Burnell Electronics, DOE, major pub. houses, 1962—; vis. mem. Acad. Hebrew Lang., Jerusalem, 1970-71. Author 7 engrng. and Hebrew lang. textbooks, more than 90 papers in profl. jours.; editor or assoc. editor several IEEE publs. Fellow IEEE (life). Office: U New Mex Dept Elect & Computer Engrin Albuquerque NM 87131-0001

KARP, NATHAN, political activist; b. Bklyn., Apr. 25, 1915; s. Daniel and Sarah (Goldenzweig) K.; m. Anne Werthamer, June 19, 1937; children: Alan, Diane, Stanley. Student pub. schs., Vineland, N.J. Garment worker; mem. nat. exec. subcom. Socialist Labor Party, 1943-63, asst. to nat. sec., 1964-68, nat. sec., 1969-80, fin. sec., 1980-82, mem. hdqrts. staff, 1963-74, Palo Alto, Calif., 1974-85. Author: Unionism, Fraudulent or Genuine, 1958, Crises in America: A Revolution Overdue, 1970; contbr. numerous articles to Weekly People (ofcl. jour. Socialist Labor Party). Candidate for lt. gov. State of N.Y., 1946, 50, U.S. senator from N.Y., 1952, mayor City of N.Y., 1953, for gov. State of N.Y., 1954. Home: 2250 Homestead Ct Apt 308 Los Altos CA 94024-7332 Office: 156 E Dana St Mountain View CA 94041-1508

KARP, RICHARD MANNING, computer sciences educator; b. Boston, Jan. 3, 1935; s. Abraham Louis and Rose (Nanes) K.; m. Diana Leigh Grand; 1 child, Jeremy Alexander. AB, Harvard U., 1955, SM, 1956, PhD in Applied Math., 1959; DSc (hon.), U. Pa., 1986, Technion, 1989, U. Mass., 1990, Georgetown U., 1992. Rsch. staff mem. IBM Watson Rsch. Ctr., Yorktown Heights, N.Y., 1959-68; visiting assoc. prof. elec. engring. U. Mich., Ann Arbor, 1964-65; prof. computer sci., indsl. engring., ops. rsch. U. Calif., Berkeley, 1968-96, assoc. chmn. elec. engring., computer sci., 1973-75, prof. math., 1980-96; co-chmn. program in computational complexity Math. Sci. Rsch. Inst., Berkeley, 1985-86; rsch. scientist Internat. Computer Sci. Inst., Berkeley, 1988-96; prof. computer sci. U. Wash., Seattle, 1996-2000, adj. prof. molecular biotech., 1996-2000; univ. prof. U. Calif., Berkeley, 2000—; Hewlett-Packard vis. prof. Math Sci. Rsch. Inst., Berkeley, 1999-2000. Bd. govs. Weizmann Inst. Soc.; adv. bd. Computer Professions for Social Responsibility; faculty rsch. lectr. Berkeley, 1981-82; Miller rsch. prof., Berkeley, 1980-81. Contbr. articles to profl. jours. Recipient Einstein fellowship, Lady Davis fellowship, Technion, Haifa, Israel, 1983, Fulkerson Prize in Discrete Math., 1979, Lanchester Prize in Ops. Rsch., 1977, ORSA/TIMS von Neumann Theory prize, 1990, ACM Turing award, 1985, Babbage prize, 1995, Nat. Medal of Sci. award NSF, 1996, Harvey prize, 1998. Fellow ACM, Inst. Combinatorics and Applications; mem. NAE, NAS, Am. Acad. Arts and Scis., Am. Philos. Soc. Office: U Calif Computer Sci Divsn 387 Soda Hall # 1776 Berkeley CA 94720 E-mail: karp@icsi.berkeley.edu

KARPELES, DAVID, museum director; b. Santa Barbara, Calif., Jan. 26, 1936; s. Leon and Betty (Friedman) K.; m. Marsha Mirsky, June 29, 1958; children: Mark, Leslie, Cheryl, Jason. BS, U. Minn., 1956, postgrad., 1956-59; MA, San Diego State U., 1962; postgrad., U. Calif., Santa Barbara, 1965-69. Founder Karpeles Manuscript Libr. Mus., Montecito, Calif., 1983—, dir., founder Santa Barbara, 1988—, N.Y.C., 1990—, Tacoma, 1991—, Jacksonville, Fla., 1992—, Duluth, Minn., 1993—, Charleston, S.C., 1995—, Buffalo, 1995—, Newburgh, 1999—, Wichita, 2001—. Founder, dir. 102 mini-museums throughout U.S. and Can.; established the 1st cultural literacy program, presented to schs. by respective mus. staffs, 1993—. Creator program to provide ownership of homes to low-income families, 1981. Recipient Affordable Housing Competition award Gov. Edmund G. Brown Jr., State of Calif., Dept. Housing and Community Devel., 1981; invited to present Commencement Address to graduating class, U. Minn., Duluth, 1996, also recipient Disting. Alulmni award. Jewish. Home: 465 Hot Springs Rd Santa Barbara CA 93108-2029

KARPF, MICHAEL, health facility administrator; grad., MD, U. Pa. Intern Johns Hopkins Hosp.; rsch. assoc. immunology lab. NIH; resident U. Pa., fellow, chief resident; with divsn. gen. internal medicine VA Hosp, Miami, 1978-79, U. Pitts., 1979-1985, Falk Chair in gen. medicine, vice chair dept. medicine, 1985-94; sr. v.p. clin. affairs Allegheny Gen. Hosp. Allegheny Health Systems, 1994-95; sr. v.p. clin. affairs Allegheny Integrated Health Group, 1994-95; vice provost hosp. systems UCLA Med. Ctr., 1995—. Bd. dirs. So. Calif. Organ Procurement Ctr. Contbr., reviewer numerous jours. in field. Chmn. Statewide Healthcare Coord. Com., Pa., 1993; mem. gov.'s task force evaluating managed care, Calif., 1997-98. Mem. Hosp. Assn. So. Calif. (bd. dirs.), AMA (bd. dirs.). Office: UCLA Med Ctr 10833 Leconte Ave Los Angeles CA 90024

KARPLUS, PAUL ANDREW, biochemistry educator; b. Oakland, Calif., Sept. 25, 1957; s. Robert and Elizabeth Jane (Frazier) K.; m. Karen Elisabeth Andersen, July 26, 1980; children: Elisabeth Marie, Christina Jane, Timothy Robert. Student, U. Calif., Berkeley, 1974-76; BS in Biochemistry with highest honors, U. Calif., Davis, 1978; PhD in Biochemistry, U. Wash., 1984. Postdoctoral rsch. assoc. Inst. Organic Chemistry and Biochemistry, U. Freiburg, Federal Republic of Germany, 1984-88; asst. prof. biochemistry, molecular and cell biology Cornell U., Ithaca, N.Y., 1988-93; assoc. prof. biochemistry, molecular and cell biology, 1993-98. Assoc. prof. dept. biochemistry and biophysics Oreg. State U., Corvallis, 1998-99, prof., 1999—. Recipient Nat. Rsch. Svc. award NIH-NIGMS, 1979, Pfizer award in enzyme chemistry Am. Chem. Soc., 1996; Alexander von Humboldt fellow, 1984-85, 90, Guggenheim fellow, 1996-97. Mem. Phi Kappa Phi. Office: Oreg State U Dept Biochem and Biophysics 2011 ALS Bldg Corvallis OR 97331 E-mail: karplus@ucs.orst.edu

KARPLUS, WALTER J. engineering educator; b. Vienna, Austria, Apr. 23, 1927; came to U.S., 1938; s. Robert and Garda K.; m. Takako Kohda, Feb. 8, 1969; children— Maya, Anthony. B.E.E., Cornell U., 1949; M.S., U. Calif. at Berkeley, 1951; Ph.D., U. Calif. at Los Angeles, 1955. Field engr. Sun Oil Co., 1949-50; research engr. Internat. Geophysics, Inc., Los Angeles, 1951-52; prof. engrng. and applied sci. UCLA, 1955—, chmn. computer sci. dept., 1972-79, 94-95, dean Sch. Engring., 2001—. Co-founder, chmn. bd. Torr Labs., Inc. Author or co-author: Analog Simulation, 1958, Analog Methods, 1959, High-Speed Analog Computers, 1961, On-Line Computing, 1967, Solution Des Equations Differentielles, 1968, Hybrid Computation, 1968, Digital Computer Treatment of Partial Differential Equations, 1981, The Heavens are Falling: The Scientific Prediction of Catastrophes in our Time, 1992; contbr. articles to profl. jours.; patentee in field. Served with USNR, 1945-46. Fulbright research fellow, 1961-62; Guggenheim fellow, 1968-69 Fellow IEEE; mem. Assn. Computing Machinery, Soc. Computer Simulation, Sigma Xi. Home: PO Box 24673 Los Angeles CA 90024-0673 Office: U Calif 3732 Boelter Hall Los Angeles CA 90095-1596 E-mail: karplus@cs.ucla.edu

KARPMAN, HAROLD LEW, cardiologist, educator, writer; b. Belvedere, Calif., Aug. 23, 1927; s. Samuel and Dora (Kastleman) K.; m. Molinda Karpman. Student, UCLA, 1945-46; BA, U. Calif., Berkeley, 1950; MD, U. Calif., San Francisco, 1954. Diplomate Am. Bd. Internal Medicine. Rotating intern L.A. County Gen. Hosp., L.A., 1954-55; cardiovascular trainee Nat. Heart Inst., L.A., 1957-58; asst. resident Beth Israel Hosp., Boston, 1955-57; fellow Wyley Winsor Rsch. Found., L.A., 1958-59; pvt. practice Beverly Hills, Calif., 1958—; clin. instr. medicine U. So. Calif., L.A., 1958-64, asst. clin. prof., 1964-71, assoc. clin. prof., 1971-72; assoc. clin. prof. medicine UCLA Sch. Medicine, 1972-92, clin. prof. medicine, 1992—. Attending physician, bd. govs. Cedars-Sinai Med. Ctr., L.A.; attending physician UCLA Med. Ctr., Westside Hosp., L.A., Brotman Med. Ctr., Culver City, Calif.; examiner in cardiovascular diseases Calif. Indsl. Accident Commn., Calif. Dept. Vocat. Rehab.; founder, bd. dirs., chmn. bd. Cardio-Dynamics Labs., Inc., 1969-82; gen. ptnr. Camden Med. Bldg., L.A., 1970-86; bd. dirs. Mcht. Bank Calif.; bd. dirs. med. rsch. Faberge, Inc., N.Y.C., 1980-84; cardiovascular cons. Delta Air Lines, 1992-94; founder, bd. dirs., chmn. bd., chief med. officer CORDA Med. Care, Inc., 1995-2000; chmn., founder, dir. Integrated Diagnostice Ctrs., Inc., 2000—. Author: Your Second Life, 1979, Preventing Silent Heart Disease, 1989; assoc. editor Internat. Medicine Alert, 1992—; contbr. numerous articles to med. jours. Fellow ACP, Am. Coll. Cardiology, Am. Coll. Chest Physicians, Internat. Cardiovascular Soc., Am. Coll. Angiology, Internat. Coll. Angiology, Am. Thermographic Soc. (charter, pres. 1971-72), Am. Acad. Thermology; mem. AMA, Calif. Med. Assn., L.A. Med. Assn., Nat. Cardiovascular Network (exec. com., bd. dirs. 1994-98), Western Cardiovascular Network (chmn., med. dir. 1993-96), Am. Soc. Internal Medicine, Am. Heart Assn., Calif. Heart Assn., L.A. County Heart Assn. Office: 414 N Camden Dr #1100 Beverly Hills CA 90210-4532

KARR, JAMES RICHARD, ecologist, educator, research director; b. Shelby, Ohio, Dec. 26, 1943; s. Rodney Joll and Marjorie Ladonna (Copeland) K.; m. Kathleen Ann Reynolds, Mar. 23, 1963 (div. Nov. 1982); children: Elizabeth Ann, Eric Leigh; m. Helen Marie Herbst Serrano, Dec. 22, 1984. BS, Iowa State U., 1965; MS, U. Ill., 1967, PhD, 1970. Fellow in biology Princeton (N.J.) U., 1970-71, Smithsonian Tropical Rsch. Inst., Balboa, Panama, 1971-72, dep. dir. Panama, 1984-87, acting dir., 1987-88; asst. prof. biology Purdue U., Lafayette, Ind., 1972-75; assoc. prof. U. Ill., Urbana, 1975-80, prof., 1980-84; Harold H. Bailey prof. biology Va. Poly. Inst. and State U., Blacksburg, 1988-91; prof. zoology, fisheries, environ. health, civil engrng. and pub. affairs U. Wash., Seattle, 1991—, dir. Inst. Environ. Studies, 1991-95. Cons. on water resources EPA, 1978—, OAS, Washington, 1980, South Fla. Water Mgmt. Dist., West Palm Beach, 1989—. Grantee EPA, 1972-85, 93-2000, U.S. Forest Svc., 1980-81, 90-91, U.S. Fish and Wildlife Svc., 1979-82, NSF, 1982-84, 1997-2000, TVA, 1990-93, Dept. Energy, 1995—. Fellow AAAS, Am. Ornithologists Union. Achievements include development of Index of Biotic Integrity, now used in North and South America, Asia, Australia, and Europe to assess directly the quality of water resources. Office: U Wash PO Box 355020 Seattle WA 98195-5020

KARROS, ERIC PETER, professional baseball player; b. Hackensack, N.J., Nov. 4, 1967; BA in Econs., UCLA, 1993. 1st baseman L.A. Dodgers, 1988—. Named Nat. League Rookie of the Year, 1992, The Sporting News, N.L. Silva Slugger Team, 1995. Office: Dodger Stadium 1000 Elysian Park Ave Los Angeles CA 90012-1199

KARSH, PHILIP HOWARD, advertising executive; b. Salt Lake City, Sept. 19, 1935; s. Sol and Ruth (Marks) K.; m. Carol Hyman, July 3, 1962 (div. Sept. 1973); children: Michael David, Jill Ann; m. Linda Love, Sept. 7, 1984. BA, U. Colo., 1957. Account exec. Ted Levy/Richard Lane & Co., Denver, 1957-59; v.p. Jerome/Philip Advt., Denver, 1959-62, pres., 1962-65; v.p. Frye Sills Advt., Denver, 1966-77; pres. Karsh & Hagan Advt. Inc., Denver, 1977-85, chmn., 1985-97. Trustee Nat. Jewish Ctr. Immunology and Respiratory Medicine, Denver, 1963—, chmn. 1991-95, Kern Rsch. Found., Denver, 1984—, Mile High United Way, Denver, 1986-92; mem. Denver Metro Conv. and Visitors Bur., 1994—, chmn., 1997. Mem.

Worldwide Ptnrs. (internat. chmn. 1986-87), Denver Advt. Fedn. (bd. dirs. 1968-69, 87-88), Rotary (pres. S.E. Denver club 1989-90). Republican. Jewish. Avocations: skiing, traveling, reading. Home: 6235 S Iola Ct Englewood CO 80111-6825 Office: Karsh & Hagan Comm Inc 707 17th St Denver CO 80202-3404 E-mail: philkarsh@aol.com

KARSH, YOUSUF, photographer; b. Mardin, Armenia, Dec. 23, 1908; emigrated to Can., 1924; s. Amsih and Bahia K.; m. Estrellita Nachbar, Aug. 28, 1962. Pupil, John H. Garo; numerous hon. degrees including; LL.D., Queen's U., Kingston, Ont., Carleton U.; D.H.L., Dartmouth Coll., Ohio U., Mt. Allison U.; D.C.L., Bishop's U., Lennoxville, Que.; D.H.L., Emerson Coll.; B in Profl. Arts, Brooks Inst.; D.F.A., U. Mass., 1979; DFA, U. Hartford, 1980; MFA, Tufts U., 1981, Dawson Coll., Montreal, Can., 1981; DFA (hon. degree), Syracuse U., 1986, Yeshiva U., N.Y.C., 1989, Columbia Coll., Chgo., 1990, U. Victoria, B.C., Can., 1990, U. B.C., Can., 1991, Salisbury Coll., , 1998. Opened photog. studio, Ottawa, Ont., Can., 1932. Vis. prof. photography Ohio U., Emerson Coll.; lectr in field Author: Faces of Destiny, 1946, Portraits of Greatness, 1959, This is the Mass, 1958, This is Rome, 1959, This Is the Holy Land, 1960, These are the Sacraments, 1962, In Search of Greatness (autobiography), 1962, The Warren Court, 1965, Karsh Portfolio, 1967, Faces of Our Time, 1971, Karsh Portraits, 1976, Karsh Canadians, 1978, Karsh: A Fifty Year Retrospective, 1983, paperback edit. 1986, Karsh: American legends, 1992, Karsh: A Sixty-Year Retrospective, 1996; portrait photographer leading nat. and internat. statesmen, corp. execs., polit. and govtl. ofcls., religious leaders including royal families of Eng., Monaco, Norway, Greece, Pope John Paul II, also leading intellectual and entertainment figures; first one-man show Nat. Gallery Can., 1959, one man shows Men Who Make Our World, Expo 67, Internat. Ctr. Photography, N.Y.C., 1983, Mus. Photography, Bradford, Eng., 1983, Nat. Portrait Gallery, London, 1984, Edinburgh, Scotland, 1984, People's Republic China, 1985, Helsinki, 1985, Muscarelle Mus. Art, 1987, William and Mary Coll., Williamsburg, Va., 1987, Barbican Ctr., London, 1988, Palais de Tokyo, Paris, 1988, Geneva Inst. Photography, Mus. für Gestanlung, Zürich, 1988, Huntington Libr. and Art Gallery, San Marino, Calif., 1988—, Frankfurter Kunstverein, Frankfurt, 1989, Internat. Ctr. Photography, 1992, Nat. Gallery, Copenhagen, Buda Castle Palace, Budapest, Hungary, Gulbenkian Found., Lisbon, Portugal; retrospective Nat. Gallery, Ottawa, Karsh: The Art of the Portrait, 1989; one-man retrospective exhbn. Vancouver (B.C.) Art Gallery, 1990, Glenbow Mus., Calgary,1990, Art Gallery N.C., 1992, Montreal Mus. Fine Arts, 1992, Halifax, Nova Scotia, 1992, Toronto, Ont., Can., 1992; exhbn. gift of portraits Nat. Portrait Gallery, London, 1991, one man retrospective Nat. Gallery, Nova Scotia, 1992, Montreal Mus. Fine Arts, 1992, McMichael Mus., Toronto, 1992, exhbn. Am. Legends Internat. Ctr. Photography, 1992, Corcoran Gallery, Washington, 1993, Mint Mus. Charlotte, 1993, 10th anniversary inaugural retrospective, 85th birthday tribute exhbn. Mus. Photography Film and TV, Bradford, Eng., 1993, Art Gallery Can. Embassy, Washington, 1994, Mus. Fine Arts, Boston, 1996, Mus. Fine Arts, Montgomery, Ala., 1996, Detroit Art Inst., 1996—, Tower Gallery, Yokahama, Japan, 1997, Canada, Ho., London, 1998, Charlottetown (Can.) Festival, June-Sept. 1998, Nat. PortraitGallery Australia, Canberra, 1999, Boston/Nagoya (Japan) Mus. Fine Arts, 2000, BankBoston Internat. Hdqs., São Paulo, Brazil, 2000, Sherbrook (Que., Can.) Mus., 2000, Deutsche Historisches Mus., Berlin, 2000—; exhibited throughout Can., U.S., Europe, Australia, TV appearances, Canadian Cultural Ctr., Rio de Janeiro, 2001; works represented in permanent collections: Mus. Modern Art, N.Y.C., Met. Mus. Art, N.Y.C., Detroit Inst. Arts; Internat. Ctr. Photography, N.Y., Montgomery Mus. Art, Art Inst. Chgo., St. Louis Art Mus., George Eastman House, Rochester, N.Y., Nat. Portrait Gallery, London, Nat. Gallery Can., Mus. Fine Arts, Boston, Can. House, London, numerous others; photographer ann. psoetr child: Muscular Dystrophy Assn. Am.; 25 photographs used on postage stamps in 15 countries. Decorated Order of Can., Companion of Can., 1990; recipient Centennial medal, Can. Council medal, U.S. Presdl. citation for service to handicapped, 1971, Achievement in Life award Ency. Brit., Silver Shingle award Boston U. Sch. Law, 1983, America's Soc. medal, 1989, Creative Edge award Time Inc. and NYU, 1989, 90, Gold medal of merit Nat. Soc. Arts and Letters, 1991, Jerusalem prize in the arts, Bezalel Acad., Israel, 1997, Fox Talbot award, Eng., 1998, Key to City of Ottawa, Can., 2000; named Master Photog. Arts Profl. Photographers Assn. Can. (Infinity award), Master Photographer Internat. Ctr. Photography, Person of the Week, World News Tonight-ABC, 1997, 60 Minutes update on 1977 segment, 1999-2000, documentary film The Searching Eye, 1983, In Search of Greatness, 2000; annual Karsh Lectureship, Karsh prize in photography established Sch. of the Mus. Fine Arts, Boston, 1998; portraits of med. and scientific luminaries gift Harvard Med. Sch., 1998; established Karsh Med. fellowship Brigham & Women's Hosp., Boston, 1998, Mary Fay Essence of Nursing fellowship, 1999, Gift of Artists Portraits Bretholtz Family Ctr., 2000 Fellow Royal Photog. Soc. Gt. Britain; mem. Royal Can. Acad. Arts, Dutch Treast Club (N.Y.C.), Century Club (N.Y.C.), Rideau Club (Ottawa). Office: c/o Jerry Fielder PO Box 430 Monterey CA 93942-0430 E-mail: karshphoto@aol.com

KARSON, BURTON LEWIS, musician, educator; b. Los Angeles, Nov. 10, 1934; s. Harry L. and Cecilia K. B.A., U. So. Calif., 1956, M.A., 1959, D.M.A., 1964. Instr. music Univ. Coll., U. So. Calif., Los Angeles, 1958-59, univ. chapel organist, 1960-61; instr. music Glendale (Calif.) Coll., 1960-65; asst. prof. music Calif. State U., Fullerton, 1965-69, assoc. prof., 1969-74, prof., 1974-97, prof. emeritus, 1997—; writer, critic Los Angeles Times, 1966-71. Founder, condr., artistic dir., Baroque Music Festival, Corona del Mar, Calif., 1980— ; concert preview lectr. Los Angeles Philharm. Orch., Carmel Bach Festival, Pacific Symphony and Pacific Chorale, Orange County Phil. Soc., others; editor: Festival Essays for Pauline Alderman, Brigham Young Univ. Press, 1976; contbr. articles to profl. jours. including Mus. Quar. Pianist, harpsichordist, organist, choirmaster St. Joachim Ch., Costa Mesa, Calif., 1974-82, St. Michael and All Angels Episc. Ch., Corona del Mar, Calif., 1982-2000, organist, choirmaster emeritus, 2000—; choral condr. Luth. Chorale L.A., 1979-83. Mem. Am. Musicol. Soc., Am. Guild Organists, Phi Mu Alpha Sinfonia (province gov. 1976-81, chair nat. com.), Pi Kappa Lambda. Achievements include profl. rsch. on music history and criticism in early Calif., German, Czech and English Baroque, cantatas and concertos; conductor first American performances. Home: 404 De Sola Terr Corona Del Mar CA 92625-2650 Office: Calif State U Dept Music PO Box 6850 Fullerton CA 92834-6850

KARST, KENNETH LESLIE, law educator; b. Los Angeles, June 26, 1929; s. Harry Everett and Sydnie Pauline (Bush) K.; m. Smiley Cook, Aug. 12, 1950; children— Kenneth Robert, Richard Eugene, Leslie Jeanne, Laura Smiley A.B., UCLA, 1950; LL.B., Harvard U., 1953. Bar: Calif. 1954, U.S. Dist. Ct. (cen. dist.) Calif. 1954, U.S. Ct. Appeals (9th cir.) 1954, U.S. Supreme Ct. 1970. Assoc. Latham & Watkins, Los Angeles, 1954, 56-57; teaching fellow law Harvard U. Law Sch., 1957-58; asst. prof. Ohio State U. Coll. Law, Columbus, 1958-60, assoc. prof., 1960-62, prof., 1962-65; prof. law UCLA, 1965-90, David G. Price and Dallas P. Price prof. law, 1990—. Author: (with Harold W. Horowitz) Law, Lawyers and Social Change, 1969, (with Keith S. Rosenn) Law and Development in Latin America, 1975, Belonging to America: Equal Citizenship and the Constitution, 1989, Law's Promise, Law's Expression: Visions of Power in the Politics of Gender, Race, and Religion, 1993; assoc. editor Ency. of Am. Constn., 1986, co-editor-in-chief, 2d edit., 2000; contbr. articles to profl. jours. Served to 1st lt. JAGC, USAF, 1954-56 Law faculty fellow Ford Found., 1962-63 Fellow Am. Acad. Arts and Scis.; mem. State Bar Calif. Office: UCLA Law Sch PO Box 951476 Los Angeles CA 90095-1476 E-mail: karst@law.ucla.edu

KARSTAEDT, ARTHUR R., III, lawyer; b. Madison, Wis., Sept. 15, 1951; BA, U. Wis., 1972; JD, U. Denver, 1975. Bar: Colo. 1976. Formerly lawyer Hall & Evans, Denver; ptnr. Harris, Karstaedt, Jamison & Powers, P.C., Englewood, Colo., 1995—. Office: Harris Karstaedt Jamison & Powers PC 383 Inverness Dr S Ste 400 Englewood CO 80112-5864

KARTHA, KUTTY KRISHNAN, plant pathologist; b. Shertallai, India, Aug. 9, 1941; married, 1972; 2 children. BSc, Saugar U., India, 1962; MSc, Jawaharal Nehru Agrl. U., India, 1965; PhD in Plant Pathology, India Agrl. Rsch. Inst., 1969. Fellow Nat. Inst. Agrl. Rsch., France, 1970-72; vis. scientist Prairie Regional Lab., Nat. Rsch. Coun., Saskatoon, Can., 1973-74; asst. rsch. officer Plant Biotechnology Inst., 1974-76, assoc. rsch. officer, 1976-81, head cell tech. sect., 1985-87; sr. rsch. officer Plant Biotech. Inst., Nat. Rsch. Coun., Saskatoon, 1981, group leader cereal biotech., 1985-93, acting rsch. dir., 1993-95, dir. gen., 1995—. Adj. prof. U. Sask., Saskatoon, 1987—; mem. Can. Agrl. Rsch. Coun., 1990-94. Editor Jour. Plant Physiology, 1987, Cyropreservation Plant Cells and Organs, 1985. Recipient George M. Darrow award Am. Soc. Horicultural Sci., 1981, C.J. Bishop award Can. Soc. Horticultural Sci., 1992, Excellence in Rsch. award Treasury Bd. Can., 1992, Commemorative medal for 125th anniversary of Confedn. Can., 1992. Mem. Internat. Assn. Plant Tissue Culture (nat. corr. 1982-86), Can. Soc. Plant Physiologists, Can. Phytopathol. Soc. Achievements include research in plant biotechnology, cryopreservation of plant cells and organs, plant tissue culture. E-mial. Office: Plant Biotech Inst 110 Gymnasium Pl Saskatoon SK Canada S7N OW9 E-mail: kutty.kartha@nrc.ca

KASANIN, MARK OWEN, lawyer; b. Boston, June 28, 1929; s. Jacob Sergei and Elizabeth Owen (Knight) K.; m. Anne Camilla Wimbish, Dec. 18, 1960; children: Marc S., James W. B.A., Stanford U., 1951; LL.B., Yale U., 1954. Bar: Calif. Assoc. McCutchen, Doyle, Brown & Enersen, San Francisco, 1957-62, 63-67, ptnr., 1967—. Mem. planning commn. City of Belvedere, Calif., 1974-76. Served with USNR, 1955-57 Named among Best Lawyers in Am., 1997-2000. Fellow Am. Coll. Trial Lawyers; mem. Maritime Law Assn. U.S. (exec. com. 1984-87), Product Liability Adv. Coun. Found. (trustee 1990—), Jud. Conf. U.S. (mem. fed. civil rules adv. com. 1992—). Home: PO Box 698 Belvedere Tiburon CA 94920-0698 Office: McCutchen Doyle Brown & Enersen 3 Embarcadero Ctr San Francisco CA 94111-4003 Fax: 415-393-2286

KASHNOW, RICHARD A. executive; m. Marcia, 2 children. B of Physics, Worcester polytech Inst., 1963; D, Tufts U., 1968. Physicist GE Co., 1970-83, gen. mgr. quartz & chem. products bus., 1983; v.p., gen. mgr. Manville Corp., until 1991; pres. Schuller, Denver, 1991-95; CEO, pres. Raychem Corp, Menlo Park, Calif., 1995-99; pres. Tyco Ventures, Menlo Park, 2000—. With U.S. Army. NASA fellow, 1968. Office: 300 Constitution Dr Menlo Park CA 94025-1140

KASSON, JAMES MATTHEWS, electronics executive; b. Muncie, Ind., Mar. 19, 1943; s. Robert Edwin and Mary Louise K.; m. Betty Roseman, Aug. 14, 1976. B.S.E.E., Stanford U., 1964; M.S.E.E., U. Ill., 1965. Engring. mgr. Santa Rita Tech., Santa Clara, Calif., 1963-69; engring. sect. mgr. Hewlett-Packard, Palo Alto, 1969-73; v.p. research and devel. ROLM Corp., Santa Clara, 1973-88; fellow IBM Corp., San Jose, Calif., 1988-95; v.p. engring. Echelon Corp., Palo Alto, 1995-98, CIO, 1998-2000. Patentee in field. Trustee Choate Rosemary Hall, Wallingford, Conn., 1990-96, Ctr. Photographic Art, Carmel, Calif., 2001—. Mem. IEEE (citation for contbn. 1981). Home: 33732 E Carmel Valley Rd Carmel Valley CA 93924 E-mail: jimk@echelon.com, jim@kasson.com

KASTAMA, JIM, state senator; b. Bellingham, Wash., Oct. 5, 1959; m. Barbara Kastama; children: Isaac, Anna Laura, Michael, Sarah, Rachael. BA, U. Calif., Berkeley. Sales cons. MCI, Giant Bicycle Mfg.; Dem. rep. dist. 25 Wash. Ho. of Reps., 1996-99; Dem. senator dist. 25 Wash. State Senate, 2000—. Asst. Dem. leader Wash. Ho. of Reps., 1999-2000; Dem. asst. whip Wash. State Senate, 2001, edn., human svcs. and corrections, judiciary and transp. coms. Mem. Puyallup Main St. Assn., Children's Rights Coun.; former vol. VISTA; former bd. dirs. Pike Market Child Care Ctr.; founding mem. S.H.A.R.P. Mem. Ea. Pierce County C. of C. Office: PO Box 40425 406 John A Cherberg Bldg Olympia WA 98504-0425 also: 110 W Meeker Puyallup WA 98371 Fax: 360 786-1999. E-mail: kastama_ja@leg.wa.gov

KASTEN, KARL ALBERT, painter, printmaker, educator; b. San Francisco, Mar. 5, 1916; s. Ferdin and Barbara Anna Kasten; m. Georgette Gautier, Mar. 29, 1958; children: Ross, Lee, Beatrix, Joellen, Cho-An. MA, U. Calif., 1939; postgrad., U. Iowa, 1949; student, Hans Hofmann Sch. Fine Arts, 1951. Instr. Calif. Sch. Fine Arts, 1941, U. Mich., 1946-47; asst. prof. art San Francisco State U., 1947-50; prof. U. Calif., Berkeley, 1950-83. Bibliography appears in Etching (Edmondson), 1973, Collage and Assemblage (Meilach and Ten Hoor), 1973, Modern Woodcut Techniques (Kuroski), 1977, California Style (McClelland and Last), 1985, Art in the San Francisco Bay Area (Albright), 1985, Breaking Type: The Art of Karl Kasten (Landauer), 1999; group shows include San Francisco Mus. Art, 1939, Chgo. Art Inst., 1946, Whitney Mus., 1952, Sao Paolo Internat. Biennials, 1955, 61, Achenbach Found., 1976, World Print III Traveling Exhbn., 1980-83, Gallery Sho, Tokyo, 1994, Inst. Franco-Americain, Rennes, 1995, Calif. Heritage Gallery, 1999; patentee etching press. Capt. U.S. Army, 1942-46. Decorated 4 battle stars; fellow Creative Arts Inst., 1964, 71, Tamarind Lithography Artist Fellowship, 1968, Regents Humanities, 1977. Mem. Berkeley Art Ctr. Assn. (bd. dirs. 1987-92), Calif. Soc. Printmakers (Disting. Artist award 1997), Univ. Faculty Club, Univ. Arts Club. Home: 1884 San Lorenzo Ave Berkeley CA 94707-1841 Office: Univ Calif Berkeley Art Dept Berkeley CA 94720-0001

KASTENBERG, WILLIAM EDWARD, nuclear engineering and applied science educator; b. N.Y.C., June 25, 1939; s. Murray and Lillian Kastenberg; m. Berna R. Miller, Aug. 18, 1963; children: Andrew, Joshua, Lillian; m. Gloria Hauser, May 3, 1992. BS, UCLA, 1962, MS, 1963; PhD, U. Calif., Berkeley, 1966. Asst. prof. Sch. Engring. and Applied Sci. UCLA, 1966-71, assoc. prof. Sch. Engring. and Applied Sci., 1971-75; guest scientist Karlsruhe (Fed. Republic Germany) Nuclear Rsch., 1972-73; sr. fellow U.S. NRC, Washington, 1979-80; assoc. dean Sch. Engring. and Applied Sci. UCLA, 1981-85, chmn. mech. aerospace and nuclear engring., 1985-88, prof. mech., aerospace and nuclear engring. dept., 1975-94; prof. nuclear engring. dept. U. Calif., Berkeley, 1995—, chmn. nuclear engring. dept., 1995-2000, Daniel Tellep disting. prof. engring., 1999—. Chmn. nuclear reactor safety Am. Nuclear Soc., 1984-85; chmn. peer rev. com. USNRC, Washington, 1987-88; mem. Nat. Rsch. Com. on Reactor Safety, 1985-86, mem. adv. com. nuclear facility safet DOE, 1988-92; mem. adv. com. Diablo Canyon Nuclear Power Plant, 1990-2000; dir. Risk and Sys. Analysis Control Toxics Program, UCLA, 1989-95; chmn. Ctr. for Clean Tech., UCLA, 1992-94; project dir. Ctr. for Nuclear and Toxic Waste Mgmt., U. Calif., Berkeley, 1995—. Contbr. articles to Jour. Hazardous Materials, Nuclear Sci. & Engring., Am. Jour. Pub. Health, Nuclear Engring. and Design, Jour. for Risk Analysis, Nuclear Tech. Recipient Disting. Teaching award Am. Soc. Engring. Edn., 1973. Fellow AAAS, Am. Nuclear Soc. (Arthur Holly Compton award); mem. NAE (elected). Office: Univ Calif Nuclear Engring Dept 4155 Etcheverry Hall Berkeley CA 94720-1731*

KATAYAMA, ARTHUR SHOJI, lawyer; b. Los Angeles, June 10, 1927; s. Asaji and Teru (Mori) K.; m. Mie Nakamura, Dec. 23, 1976. A.B., Morningside Coll., 1951; LL.B., Pacific Coast U., 1956. Bar: Calif. 1959, U.S. Dist. Ct. (cen. dist.) Calif. 1959, U.S. Ct. Appeals (9th cir.) 1959, U.S. Tax Ct. 1971, U.S. Supreme Ct. 1971. With intelligence div. U.S. Treasury Dept., Los Angeles, 1953-58; with N. Am. Aviation, Los Angeles, 1958-59; practiced in Los Angeles, 1959-60; mem. firm Mori & Katayama, Los Angeles, 1960-77; prin. Nagata, Masuda & Katayama, 1980-83, Katayama & Nagata, 1983-84; pvt. practice Arthur S. Katayama, P.C., Newport Beach, Calif., 1984—. Mem. adv. bd. Sumitomo Bank of Calif., Los Angeles.; Mem. Calif. Democratic State Ctrl. Com., 1958-60 Served with AUS, 1945-47. Mem. ABA, Los Angeles County, Orange County bar assns. Clubs: Mesa Verde/Costa Mesa Country; Big Canyon Country (Newport Beach) Home: 32 Canyon Fairway Dr Newport Beach CA 92160 Office: 4400 Macarthur Blvd Ste 700 Newport Beach CA 92660-2038

KATAYAMA, ROBERT NOBUICHI, lawyer; b. Honolulu, Oct. 11, 1924; s. Sanji K.; married; children: Alyce A. Katayama Jenkins, Robert Nobuichi, Kent J., Susan H. Ono, Carole Y. Kaneshiro, Wendy L. Lee. BA, U. Hawaii, 1950; LLB, Yale U., 1955; grad., Command and Gen. Staff Coll., 1964; LLM, George Washington U., 1967; grad., Indsl. Coll. Armed Forces, 1971. Bar: Calif. 1956, Ill. 1973, Hawaii 1989. Commd. 1st lt. JAGC U.S. Army, 1958, advanced through grades to col., 1973, ret., 1973; gen. counsel Overseas Mdse. Inspection Co., San Francisco, 1956-58, Army Contract Adjustment Bd., Washington, 1964-68; prof. law JAG Sch. U. Va., 1968-70; from assoc. to ptnr. Baker & McKenzie, Chgo., Tokyo and San Francisco, 1973-85; ptnr. Seki & Jarvis, San Francisco and San Jose, 1985-86, Nutter, McClennen & Fish, San Francisco, 1986-88; spl. counsel, sr. advisor Crosby, Heafey, Roach & May, Oakland, Calif., 1988; ptnr. Carlsmith Ball, Honolulu, 1988-95, counsel, 1995—. Bd. dirs. BIC Bridal Hawaii Inc., Honolulu; chmn., CEO Kapolei People's Inc. dba Kapolei Golf Course, Honolulu, 1996-2000; pres. Kapolei Holding Corp. Trustee Nat. Japanese Am. Meml. Found., 1995-97, gov., 1997—; bd. dirs. Japanese Cultural Ctr. Hawaii, 1997-98, bd. govs., 1998— Named Real Dean U. Hawaii, Honolulu, 1950; Community Chest scholar Honolulu Community Chest, 1950. Mem. ABA, Calif. Bar Assn., Hawaii Bar Assn., Japan Am. Soc. Hawaii, Nat. Japanese Am. Hist. Soc. (legal officer 1984-89), Japanese Am. Soc. Legal Studies, Ret. Officers Assn., 442d Regimental Combat Team Found. (trustee 1993—, pres. 1999—), 442d Vets. Club (legal advisor 1994-95, 2000—, pres.-elect 1996, pres. 1997-98), Japanese C. of C. of No. Calif. (bd. dirs. 1987-89), Oahu AJA Vets. Coun. (pres. 1997). Democrat. Buddhist. Office: Carlsmith Ball 1001 Bishop St Ste 2200 Honolulu HI 96813-3676

KATHER, GERHARD, retired federal administrator; b. Allenstein, Germany, Jan. 30, 1939; came to the U.S., 1952, naturalized, 1959; s. Ernst and Maria (Kempa) K.; m. Carol Anne Knutsen, Aug. 18, 1962; children: Scott T., Cynthia M., Tracey S., Chris A.; m. Mary Elsie Frank, Oct. 25, 1980. BA in Govt., U. Ariz., 1964; MPA, U. So. Calif., 1971; cert. in pers. adminstrn., U. N.Mex., 1987. Tchr. social studies, Covina, Calif., 1965-67; tng. officer Civil Pers., Ft. MacArthur, 1967-70; chief employee tng. and devel. Corps Engrs., L.A., 1970-72, Frankfurt Area Army Pers. Office, 1972-73; chief employee rels. and tng. brs. Corps Engrs., L.A., 1973-74; chief employee devel. and tng. Kirtland AFB, N.Mex., 1974-87; labor rels. officer Kirtland AFB and detachments in 13 U.S. cities, 1987-90; project coord., adv. Protection and Advocacy Sys., 1991-96; ret., 1996. Mem. adv. com. Albuquerque Tech.-Vocat. Inst., 1982-92, U. N.Mex. Valencia Campus, 1985-92; mem. Coalition for Disability Rights, 1988-96; chmn. Comprehensive Accessibility Network, 1990-96; adv. coun. N.Mex. Disability Prevention, 1992-96; rec. sec. N.Mex. Commn. Blind State Rehab. Adv. Coun., 1993-96. With USAF, 1958-64. Named Prominent Tng. and Devel. Profl., H. Whitney McMillan Co., 1984. Mem. ASTD (treas. chpt. 1984-85), Paralyzed Vets. Am. (bd. dirs. 1986-87, pres. local chpt. 1986-87, 90-92), Toastmasters Internat. (chpt. treas., v.p., pres. 1967-70), Vietnam Vets. Am. (chpt. newsletter editor 1994-95), Phi Delta Kappa. Democrat. Roman Catholic.

KATHKA, DAVID ARLIN, director educational services; b. Columbus, Nebr. s. Arlin Arthur and Edith Ferne (Wilcox) K.; m. Anne Condon Butler, Aug. 15, 1965. BA, Wayne (Nebr.) State Coll., 1964, MA, 1966; PhD in History, U. Mo., 1976. Tchr. Ravenna (Nebr.) Pub. Schs., 1964-65; instr. Midwestern Coll., Denison, Iowa, 1966-68; prof. history Western Wyo. Coll., Rock Springs, 1972-87, dean acad. affairs, 1980-84, interim pres., 1984-85, v.p. acad. affairs, 1985-87; dir. State Pks. and Cultural Resources Divsn., State of Wyo., Cheyenne, 1987-94, Sweetwater Bd. Coop. Ednl. Svcs., Wyo., 1994—. Adj. prof. U. Wyo., Laramie, 1976—, adj. prof. history Western Wyo. Coll., 1996—; vis. instr. U. Mo., St. Louis, 1971-72; cons. various Wyo. govt. agys.; mem. gov.'s Blue ribbon Task Force on Cultural Resources, Wyo. Trails adv. com. Author hist. papers; contbr. hist. articles to mags. Bd. dirs. Sweetwater Mus. Found., Wyo. Territorial Park, 1987-94, Tracks Across Wyo., Wyo. Hist. Found., Rock Springs Area Cmty. Found.; mem. Wyo. Centennial Commn., 1986-87, Rock Springs Libr. Bd.,1 984-87, Gov.'s Com. on Hist. Preservation, 1982; v.p. Rocky Mountain Region Kidney Found., Denver, 1976-77. Recipient Wyo. Humanities award for exemplary svc., 1990. Mem. Wyo. State Hist. Soc. (pres. 1984-85), Wyo. Assn. Profl. Historians (v.p. 1994-96, pres. 1996-97). Democrat. Office: Sweetwater Bd Coop Ednl Svcs PO Box 428 Rock Springs WY 82902-0428

KATINSKY, STEVEN, communications company executive; b. Phila., Feb. 6, 1959; BS, Rutgers Coll., 1981. CEO, pres. Supertuner.com, Santa Monica, Calif.; co-founder, former CEO Hollywood Online, Santa Monica. Office: Supertuner.com 3015 Main St Ste 400 Santa Monica CA 90405-5361

KATO, BRUCE, curator; Chief curator Alaska State Mus., Juneau, 1987—. Office: Alaska State Mus 395 Whittier St Juneau AK 99801-1718

KATZ, ALAN ROY, public health educator; b. Pitts., Aug. 21, 1954; s. Leon B. and Bernice Sonia (Glass) K.; m. Donna Marie Crandall, Jan. 19, 1986; 1 child, Sarah Elizabeth. BA, U. Calif., San Diego, 1976; MD, U. Calif., Irvine, 1980; MPH, U. Hawaii, 1987; postgrad., U. So. Calif., 1980-81, U. Hawaii, 1982-83. Staff physician emergency medicine L.A. County U. So. Calif. Med. Ctr., 1981-82; staff physician, med. dir. Waikiki Health Ctr., Honolulu, 1983-87; dir. AIDS/STD prevention program Hawaii State Dept. of Health, Honolulu, 1987-88; asst. prof. dept. pub. health scis. U. Hawaii, Honolulu, 1988-94, assoc. prof., 1994—. Dir. preventive medicine residency program U. Hawaii, Honolulu, 1994-99; com. mem. Chlamydia control workgroup USPHS, 1985-87, sci. adv. bd. Hawaii AIDS Clin. Trials Rsch. Program; staff physician, lab. dir. Diamond Head STD Clinic, Hawaii State Dept. Health, 1998—. Contbr. articles to profl. jours. Leptospirosis ad hoc com. Hawaii State Dept. Health, Honolulu, 1988—; mem. com. human subjects U. Hawaii, 1989—. USPHS Chlamydia Prevalence Survey grantee, Hawaii, 1986, Tuberculosis Survey grantee U. Hawaii, 1991; recipient presdl. citation for meritorious teaching, U. Hawaii, 1989, Regents medal excellence in teaching, 1992. Fellow Am. Coll. Preventive Medicine; mem. Am. Pub. Health Assn., Soc. Epidemiologic Rsch., Delta Omega. Office: U Hawaii Sch Pub Health Dept Pub Health Sci 1960 E West Rd Honolulu HI 96822-2319 E-mail: katz@hawaii.edu

KATZ, BRUCE R. company executive; b. Newton, Mass., Feb. 17, 1947; s. Saul T. and Dorothy (Golden) K. Student, Cornell U., 1965-69. Founder, chief exec. officer Rockport Shoe Co., Marlboro, Mass., 1970-86, Rosewood Stone Group, San Francisco, 1986—, chmn., 1986—. Trustee, Pacific Crest Outward Bound Sch. Recipient Cross-Cultural award EdVenture Holdings, Inc., 1989. Mem. Social Venture Network, Global Bus. Network. Office: 2320 Marine Shipway Sausalito CA 94965-1966

KATZ, CHARLES J., JR. lawyer; b. San Antonio, Mar. 25, 1948; AB, Stanford U., 1969; MA, N.Y.U., 1973; JD, U. Tex., 1976. Book review editor Tex. Law Review, 1975-76; mem. Perkins Coie, Seattle, 1982. Mem. Order of the Coif. Office: Perkins Coie 1201 3rd Ave Fl 40 Seattle WA 98101-3029

KATZ, LEW, advertising executive; Dir. finance Team One Advertising, El Segundo, Calif. Office: Team One Advertising 1960 E Grand Ave Ste 700 El Segundo CA 90245-5059

KATZ, RANDY H. electrical engineering, computer sciences educator; AB, Cornell U., 1976; MS, U. Calif., Berkeley, 1978, PhD, 1980. With U. Wis., Madison; program mgr. Computing Sys. Tech. Office Def. Advanced Rsch. Projects Agy., office dep. dir.; with U. Calif., Berkeley, 1983-93, 94—, prof., chairperson dept. elec. engring. and computer sci., 1996—. Participant U.S. V.p. Al Gore's Nat. Performance Rev.; presenter sci. confs. Author: Contemporary Logic Design, 1993; contbr. articles to profl. publs. Mem. NAE. Office: Univ Calif Adminstrv Office Cory Hall 1770 Rm 231 Berkeley CA 94720-0001 also: Univ Calif Rsch Office Soda Hall 1776 Rm 637 Berkeley CA 94720-0001

KATZ, ROGER, pediatrician, educator; b. Menominee, Mich., Feb. 23, 1938; s. Peter W. and Mae C. (Chudacoff) K.; m. Barbara Morguelan, Feb. 6, 1966; children: Carl, Gary, Robyn. BS, U. Wis., 1960; MD, U. Louisville, 1965. Diplomate Am. Bd. Allergy and Immunology, Am. Bd. Pediatric Allergy, Am. Bd. Pediatrics. Clin. prof. pediatrics UCLA, 1978—. Spkr. in field; expert legal evaluator. Author and editor sci. books and manuscripts. Maj. U.S. Army, 1970-72. Named 1 of Best Drs. in Am., 1996, 97. Fellow Am. Acad. Allergy, Asthma and Immunology, Am. Coll. Allergy, Asthma and Immunology (bd. regents 1990-93), Am. Acad. Pediat., Am. Coll. Chest Physicians, Joint Coun. Allergy, Asthma and Immunology (pres. 1986-90). Office: UCLA Med Ctr 1304 15th St # 102 Santa Monica CA 90404-1810

KATZ, RONALD LEWIS, physician, educator; b. Bklyn., Apr. 22, 1932; s. Joseph and Belle (Charnis) K.; children: Richard Ian, Laura Susan, Margaret Karen. B.A., U. Wis.-Madison, 1952; M.D., Boston U., 1956; postgrad. in Pharmacology (NIH fellow), Coll. Physicians and Surgeons, Columbia U., 1959-60; postgrad. (John Simon Guggenheim fellow), Royal Postgrad. Med. Sch., U. London, 1968-69. Intern USPHS Hosp., S.I., 1956-57; resident Columbia-Presbyn. Med. Center, 1957-60; asst. prof. anesthesiology Coll. Physicians and Surgeons, Columbia U., 1960-66, assoc. prof., 1966-70, prof., 1970-73; prof., chmn. dept. anesthesiology UCLA, 1973-90, prof. anesthesiology, 1990-94, chief staff Med. Ctr., 1984-86; prof., chmn. dept. anesthesiology U. So. Calif., L.A., 1995—. Cons. NIH, FDA, numerous state agys. Author, editor: Muscle Relaxants, 1975; Contbr. numerous articles to profl. jours.; Mem. editorial bd.: Handbook of Anesthesiology, 1972—, Progress in Anesthesiology, 1973—; editor in chief Seminars in Anesthesia, 1982—. Mem. Am. Soc. Anesthesiologists, Am. Physiol. Soc., Am. Soc. Pharmacology and Exptl. Therapeutics, N.Y. Acad. Medicine; Faculty Anaesthetists of Royal Coll. Surgeons of Eng. Achievements include inventor peripheral nerve stimulator. E-mail: merit.hsc.usc.edu. Home: 2910 Neilson Way Apt 407 Santa Monica CA 90405-5323 Office: U So Calif Dept Anesthesiology Health Sci Campus 1200 N State St Rm 14901 Los Angeles CA 90033-1029

KATZ, TONNIE, newspaper editor; BA, Barnard Coll., 1966; MSc, Columbia U., 1967. Editor, reporter newspapers including The Quincy Patriot Ledger, Boston Herald Am., Boston Globe; Sunday/projects editor Newsday; mng. editor Balt. News Am., 1983-86, The Sun, San Bernardino, Calif., 1986-88; asst. mng. editor for news The Orange County Register, Santa Ana, 1988-89, mng. editor, 1989-92, editor, v.p., 1992-98, editor, sr. v.p., 1998—. Office: Orange County Register 625 N Grand Ave Santa Ana CA 92701-4347

KATZ, VERA, mayor, former college administrator, state legislator; b. Dusseldorf, Germany, Aug. 3, 1933; came to U.S., 1940; d. Lazar Pistrak and Raissa Goodman; m. Mel Katz (div. 1985); 1 child, Jesse. BA, Bklyn. Coll., 1955, postgrad., 1955-57. Market research analyst TIMEX, B.T. Babbitt, N.Y.C., 1957-62; mem. Oreg. Ho. of Reps., Salem; former dir. devel. Portland Community Coll., from 1982; mayor City of Portland, Oreg., 1993—. Mem. Gov.'s Council on Alcohol and Drug Abuse Programs, Oreg. Legis., Salem, 1985—; mem. adv. com. Gov.'s Council on Health, Fitness and Sports, Oreg. Legis., 1985—; mem. Gov.'s Commn. on Sch. Funding Reform; mem. Carnegie task Force on Teaching as Profession, Washington, 1985-87; vice-chair assembly Nat. Conf. State Legis., Denver, 1986—. Recipient Abigail Scott Duniway award Women in Communications, Inc., Portland, 1985, Jeanette Rankin First Woman award Oreg. Women's Polit. Caucus, Portland, 1985, Leadership award The Neighborhood newspaper Portland, 1985, Woman of Achievement award Commn. for Women, 1985, Outstanding Legis. Advocacy award Oreg. Primary Care Assn., 1985, Service to Portland Pub. Sch. Children award Portland Pub. Schs., 1985. Fellow Am. Leadership Forum (founder Oreg. chpt.); mem. Dem. Legis. Leaders Assn., Nat. Bd. for Profl. Teaching Standards. Democrat. Jewish Avocations: camping, jogging, dancing. Office: Office of the Mayor City Hall 1221 SW 4th Ave Rm 340 Portland OR 97204-1900

KATZEN, MOLLIE, writer, artist; b. Rochester, N.Y., Oct. 13, 1950; d. Leon and Betty (Heller) K.; m. Jeffrey David Black, June 26, 1983 (div. Oct. 1985); 1 child, Samuel Katzen Black; m. Carl Shames, Dec. 12, 1986. BFA, San Francisco Art Inst., 1972. Author, illustrator: Mossewood Cookbook, 1977, Enchanted Broccoli Forest, 1982, Still Life with Menu, 1988, Molly Katzen's Still Life Sampler, 1993, Pretend Soup & Other Real Recipes: A Cookbook for Preschoolers & Up, 1994, Enchanted Broccoli Forest, 1995, Moosewood Cookbook Classics: Miniature Edition, 1996. Recipient Graphic Arts award Arnot Art Gallery, 1976, Cert. of Commendation, Calif. State Assembly, 1989. Jewish. Avocations: classical pianist, painter. Office: care Ten Speed Press PO Box 7123 Berkeley CA 94707-0123

KATZENBERG, JEFFREY, motion picture studio executive; b. 1950; m. Marilyn Siegel; children: Laura, David. Asst. to chmn., chief exec. officer Paramount Pictures, N.Y.C, 1975-77, exec. dir. mktg., 1977; then v.p. programming Paramount TV, Calif., 1977-78; v.p., feature prodn. Paramount Pictures, 1978-80, sr. v.p., prodn. motion picture div., 1980-82, pres. prodn., motion pictures & TV, 1982-94; chmn. Walt Disney Studios, [illegible] 1994. Office: Dreamworks SKG 100 Flower St Glendale CA 91201

KATZIN, CAROLYN FERNANDA, nutritionist, consultant; b. London, July 21, 1946; came to U.S., 1983; d. John Mourier and Shelagh B. A. (Tighe) Lade; m. Anthony Arthur Speelman, Mar. 18, 1968 (div. Dec. 1984); 1 child, Zara Jane; m. David Brandeis Katzin (div. Mar. 1999). BS with honors, U. London, 1983; MS in Pub. Health, UCLA, 1988. Nutritionist L.A., 1986—. Chair dean's adv. bd. UCLA Sch. Pub. Health 1997—; mem. profl. adv. bd. The Wellness Community, L.A., 1998—; pres. Am. Cancer Soc., L.A., Coastal Cities U., 1999—. Author: (books) The Advanced Enegy Guide, 1994, The Good Eating Guide and Cookbook, 1996, The Cancer Nutrition Ctr. Handbook, 2001. Democrat. Jewish. Office: 12011 San Vicente Blvd Ste 402 Los Angeles CA 90049-4946 E-mail: cfk@aol.com

KATZMAN, ROBERT, medical educator, neurologist; b. Denver, Nov. 29, 1925; s. Maurice and Leah K. (Schnitt) K.; m. Nancy Bernstein, Sept. 2, 1947; children: David Jonathan, Daniel Mark. BS, U. Chgo., 1949, MS, 1951; MD cum laude, Harvard U., 1953. Diplomate Am. Bd. Psychiatry and Neurology. Intern Boston City Hosp., 1953-54; chief resident Neurol. Inst. Columbia Presbyn. Hosp., N.Y.C., 1956-57; faculty mem. Albert Einstein Coll. Medicine, N.Y.C., 1957-84, prof., chmn. neurology dept., 1964-84, dir. Resnick Gerontology Ctr., 1979-84; chmn. dept. neuroscis. U. Calif., San Diego, 1984-90, Florence Riford prof. neuroscis. and rsch. in Alzheimer's disease, 1984-94, rsch. prof. neuroscis., 1994—. Mem. clin. rsch. adv. com. Nat. Found. March of Dimes, 1975-76; mem. adv. coun. Nat. Inst. on Aging, 1982-85; chmn. med. and sci. bd. Alzheimer Disease and Related Disorders Assn., Chgo., 1979-85; mem. adv. panel on Alzheimer's disease HHS, 1987-93. Co-author: Brain Electrolytes and Fluid Metabolism, 1973, Neurology of Aging, 1983, Alzheimer Disease: The Changing View, 2000; co-editor: Basic Neurochemistry, 1972-81, Principles of Geriatric Neurology, 1992, Alzheimer Disease, 1994, Alzheimers Disease, 2d edit., 1999. With USN, 1944-46, PTO. Recipient Humanitarian Award Alzheimer's Disease and Related Disorders Assn., 1985, Disting. Svc. award, 1989, Allied Achievement in Aging award Allied Signal Corp., 1985, Henderson Meml. award Am. Geriatric Soc., 1986, 7th Ann. Chgo. Rita Hayworth Gala award recipient, Alzheimer's Assn., 1994, Pioneer in Alzheimer's Disease Rsch. award, 1998. Fellow Am. Acad. Neurology (S. Weir Mitchell award 1960, George W. Jacoby award 1989, co-recipient Potamkin prize for Alzheimer's disease rsch. 1992); mem. Assn. for Rsch. in Nervous and Mental Disorders (pres. 1977), Am. Physiol. Soc. (cons.) Inst. Medicine, Am. Neurol. Assn. (pres. 1985-86), Internat. Soc. for Alzheimer's Disease Rsch. (pres. 1996—), Alpha Omega Alpha. Office: U Calif San Diego Sch Medicine 9500 Gilman Dr Dept 949 La Jolla CA 92093-0949 E-mail: rkatzman@ucsd.edu

KATZUNG, BERTRAM GEORGE, pharmacologist; b. Mineola, N.Y., June 11, 1932; m. Alice V. Camp; children: Katharine Blanche, Brian Lee. BA, Syracuse U., 1953; MD, SUNY, Syracuse, 1957; PhD, U. Calif., San Francisco, 1962. Prof. U. Calif., San Francisco, 1958—. Author: Drug Therapy, 1991, Pharmacology, Examination and Board Review, 2001, Basic and Clinical Pharmacology, 2000; contbr. to profl. jours. Markle scholar. Mem. AAAS, AAUP, Am. Soc. Pharmacology and Exptl. Therapeutics, Biophysical Soc., Fed. Am. Scientists, Internat. Soc. Heart Rsch., Soc. Gen. Physiologists, Western Pharmacology Soc., N.Y. Acad. Sci., Astron. Soc. of Pacific, Internat. Dark-Sky Assn., Nat. Deep Sky Observers Soc., Planetary Soc., Royal Astron. Soc. of Canada, San Francisco Amateur Astronomers Soc., Sonoma County Astron. Soc., Phi Beta Kappa, Alpha Omega Alpha, Golden Gate Computer Soc. Office: U Calif San Francisco Dept Cellular/Molec Pharm PO Box 450 San Francisco CA 94143-0450

KAUFFMAN, GEORGE BERNARD, chemistry educator; b. Phila., Sept. 4, 1930; s. Philip Joseph and Laura (Fisher) K.; m. Ingeborg Salomon, June 5, 1952 (div. Dec. 1969); children: Ruth Deborah (Mrs. Martin H. Bryskier), Judith Miriam (Mrs. Mario L. Reposo); m. Laurie Marks Papazian, Dec. 21, 1969; stepchildren: Stanley Robert Papazian, Teresa Lynn Papazian Baron, Mary Ellen Papazian. BA with honors, U. Pa., 1951; PhD, U. Fla., 1956. Grad. asst. U. Fla., 1951-55; rsch. participant Oak Ridge Nat. Lab., 1955; instr. U. Tex., Austin, 1955-56; rsch. chemist Humble Oil & Refining Co., Baytown, Tex., 1956, GE, Cin., 1957, 59; asst. prof. chemistry Calif. State U., Fresno, 1956-61, assoc. prof., 1961-66, prof., 1966—. Guest lectr. coop. lecture tours Am. Chem. Soc., 1971; vis. scholar U. Calif., Berkeley, 1976, U. Puget Sound, 1978; dir. undergrad. rsch. participation program NSF, 1972. Author: Alfred Werner— Founder of Coordination Chemistry, 1966, Classics in Coordination Chemistry, Part I, 1968, Part II, 1976, Part III, 1978, Werner Centennial, 1967, Teaching the History of Chemistry, 1971, Coordination Chemistry: Its History through the Time of Werner, 1977, Inorganic Coordination Compounds, 1981, The Central Science: Essays on the Uses of Chemistry, 1984, Frederick Soddy (1877-1956): Early Pioneer in Radiochemistry, 1986, Aleksandr Porfirevich Borodin: A Chemist's Biography, 1988, Coordination Chemistry: A Century of Progress, 1994, Classics in Coordination Chemistry, 1995, Metal and Nonmetal Biguanide Complexes, 1999; contbr. articles to profl. jours.; contbg. editor: Jour. Coll. Sci. Tchg., 1973—, The Hexagon, 1980—, Polyhedron, 1983-85, Industrial Chemist, 1985-88, Jour. Chem. Edn., 1987—, Today's Chemist, 1989-91, The Chemical Intelligencer, 1994-2000, Today's Chemist at Work, 1995—, Chemical Heritage, 1996—, The Chemical Educator, 1998—, Chem. 13 News, 1998—; guest editor: Coodination Chemistry Centennial Symposium (C3S) issue, Polyhedron, 1994; editor tape lecture series: Am. Chem. Soc, 1975-81. Named Outstanding Prof., Calif. State U. and Colls. Sys., 1973; recipient Exceptional Merit Svc. award, 1984, Meritorious Performance and Profl. Promise award, 1986-87, 88-89, Coll. Chemistry Tchr. Excellence award Mfg. Chemists Assn., 1976, Chugaev medal, 1976, Kurnakov medal, 1990, Chernyaev medal, 1991, USSR Acad. Sci., George C. Pimentel award in chem. edn. Am. Chem. Soc., 1993, Dexter award in history of chemistry, 1978, Marc-Auguste Pictet medal Soc. Physique et Histoire Naturelle de Genéve, 1992, Pres.'s medal of Distinction, Calif. State U., Fresno, 1994, Rsch. award at an Undergraduate Instn., Am. Chem. Soc., 2000, Laudatory Decree Inst. History of Sci. and Tech. Russian Acad. Sci., 2000; Rsch. Corp. grantee, 1956-57, 57-59, 59-61, Am. Chem. Soc. Petroleum Rsch. Fund grantee, 1963-64, 69-70, NSF grantee, 1960-61, 63-64, 67-69, 76-77, NEH grantee, 1982-83; John Simon Guggenheim Meml. Found. fellow, 1972-73, grantee, 1975; Strindberg fellow Swedish Inst., Stockholm, 1983. Mem. AAAS, AAUP, Assn. Univ. Pa. Chemists, History of Sci. Soc., Soc. History Alchemy and Chemistry, Am. Chem. Soc. (chmn. divsn. history of chemistry 1969, mem. exec. com. 1970, councilor 1976-78, George C. Pimentel award in Chem. Edn., 1993), Mensa, Sigma Xi, Phi Lambda Upsilon, Phi Kappa Phi, Alpha Chi Sigma, Gamma Sigma Epsilon. Home: 1609 E Quincy Ave Fresno CA 93720-2309 Office: Calif State U Dept Chemistry Fresno CA 93740-0001 E-mail: georgek@csufresno.edu

KAUFMAN, ALBERT I. lawyer; b. N.Y.C., Oct. 2, 1936; s. Israel and Pauline (Pardes) K.; m. Ruth Feldman, Jan. 25, 1959; 1 son, Michael Paul. AA, L.A. City Coll., 1957; BA, U. San Fernando Valley, 1964, JD, 1966. Bar: Calif. 1967, U.S. Ct. Appeals (9th cir.) 1968, U.S. Supreme Ct. 1971, U.S. Dist. Ct. (cen. dist.) Calif. 1967, U.S. Tax Ct. 1971, U.S. Ct. Internat. Trade 1981. Sole practice, Encino, Calif., 1967—; judge pro tem L.A. Mcpl. Ct., 1980—, L.A. Superior Ct., 1991—; family law mediator L.A. Superior Ct., 1980—. Mem. Pacific S.W. regional bd. Anti-Defamation league of B'nai B'rith, 1970-91. Served with USAF, 1959-65, to col. CAP, 1956—. Recipient Disting. Svc. award B'nai B'rith, 1969; Exceptional Svc. award CAP, 1977, 95. Mem. ABA, L.A. County Bar Assn., San Fernando Valley Bar Assn., Consumer Atty. of Calif., Consumer Atty. Assn. [illegible] 1117 ([illegible] 1969), B'nai B'rith (pres. 1971-72), Santa Monica Yacht (judge adv.) Office: 17609 Ventura Blvd Ste 201 Encino CA 91316-3825

KAUFMAN, CHRISTOPHER LEE, lawyer; b. Chgo., Mar. 17, 1945; s. Charles R. and Violet-Page (Koteen) K.; m. Carlyn A. Clement, Jan. 25, 1986; children: Charles Alexander, Caroline Clement. BA, Amherst Coll., 1967; JD, Harvard U., 1970. Bar: Ill. 1970, Calif. 1972. Law clk. to judge U.S. Ct. Appeals (2d cir.), N.Y.C., 1970-71; from assoc. to ptnr. Heller Ehrman, White and McAuliffe, San Francisco, Palo Alto, Calif., 1974-90; ptnr. Latham & Watkins, Menlo Park, 1990—. Editor: Harvard Law Review., 1968-70. Mem. ABA (com. on negotiated acquisitions, com. on fed. regulation of securities). Office: Latham & Watkins 135 Commonwealth Dr Menlo Park CA 94025-1105 E-mail: christopher.kaufman@lw.com

KAUFMAN, DAVID GRAHAM, construction company executive; b. North Canton, Ohio, Mar. 20, 1937; s. DeVere and Josephine Grace (Graham) K.; m. Carol Jean Monzione, Oct. 5, 1957 (div. Aug. 1980); children: Gregory Allan, Christopher Patrick. Student, Kent State U., 1956; grad., Internat. Corr. Schs., 1965, N.Y. Inst. Photography, 1983; postgrad., Calif. Coast U. Cert. constrn. insp., constrn. project mgr., asbestos insp., lead insp., lead risk assessor, asbestos project designer, lock-out/tag-out, environ. inspl., environ. specialist, environ. mgr.; EPA cert. lead insp. and risk assessor. Machinist apprentice Hoover Co., North Canton, Ohio, 1955-57; draftsman-designer Goodyear Aircraft Corp., Akron, 1957-60, Boeing Co., Seattle, 1960-61; designer Berger Industries, Seattle, 1961-62, Puget Sound Bridge & Drydock, Seattle, 1963, C.M. Lovsted, Seattle, 1963-64, Tracy, Brunstrom & Dudley, Seattle, 1964, Rubens & Pratt Engrs., Seattle, 1965-66; founder, owner Profl. Drafting Svcs., Seattle, 1965, Profl. Take-Off Svcs., Seattle, 1966, Profl. Representation Svcs., Seattle, 1967; pres. Kaufman Inc., Seattle, 1967-83, Kaufman-Alaska Inc., Juneau, 1975-83, Kaufman-Alaska Constructors, Inc., Juneau, 1975-83; constrn. mgr. U. Alaska, 1979-84; constrn. cons. Alaskan native and Eskimo village corps., 1984—; prin. Kaufman S.W. Assocs., N.Mex., 1984—, Graham Internat., 1992—, Parsons-Brinckernoff, 2000—. Trustee, advisor Kaufman Internat., The Kaufman Group, Kaufman Enterprises. Mem. Constrn. Specifications Inst., Assn. Constrn. Insps., Associated Gen. Contractors Seattle Constrn. Coun., Producers Coun. Oreg., Wash., Idaho, Hawaii, Alaska, Portland C. of C., Nat. Eagle Scout Assn., Toastmasters (past gov.), Lions. Republican. Roman Catholic. Home: PO Box 1781 Santa Fe NM 87504-1781 Office: PO Box 458 Haines AK 99827-0458 also: # 409 505 Oppenheimer Los Alamos NM 87544 also: 505 Oppenheimer Dr #409 Los Alamos NM 87544

KAUFMAN, HAROLD RICHARD, mechanical engineer and physics educator; b. Audubon, Iowa, Nov. 24, 1926; s. Walter Richard and Hazel (Steere) K.; m. Elinor Mae Wheat, June 25, 1948; children: Brian, Karin, Bruce, Cynthia. Student, Evanston Community Coll., 1947-49; B.S.M.E., Northwestern U., 1951; Ph.D., Colo. State U., 1971. Researcher in aerospace propulsion NACA, Cleve., 1951-58; mgr. space propulsion research NASA, Cleve., 1958-74; prof. physics and mech. engring. Colo. State U., Ft. Collins, 1974-84, prof. emeritus, 1984—, chmn. dept. physics, 1979-84; pres. Front Range Research, Ft. Collins, 1984—; v.p. R&D Commonwealth Sci. Corp., Alexandria, Va., 1984-96. Pioneer in field of electron bombardment ion thruster, 1960; cons. ion source design and applications. Contbr. over 140 publs. and 30 patents in field. Served with USNR, 1944-46. Recipient NASA medal for exceptional sci. achievement, 1971. Fellow Am. Vacuum Soc. (Albert Nerken award 1991), AIAA (assoc. fellow, James H. Wyld Propulsion award 1969); mem. Tau Beta Pi, Pi Tau Sigma. Office: Front Range Rsch 1306 Blue Spruce Dr Ste 2A Fort Collins CO 80524-2067

KAUFMAN, HERBERT MARK, finance educator; b. Bronx, N.Y., Nov. 1, 1946; s. Henry and Betty (Fried) K.; m. Helen Laurie Fox, July 23, 1967; 1 child, Jonathan Hart. BA, SUNY, Binghamton, 1967; PhD, Pa. State U., 1972. Economist Fed. Nat. Mortgage Assn., Washington, 1972-73; asst. prof. Ariz. State U., Tempe, 1973-76, econs. prof., 1980-88, fin. prof., 1988—, chair dept. fin., 1991—, exec. dir. Ctr. for Fin. System, 1988—. Cons. World Bank, Washington, 1985-86, Gen. Acctg. Office, Washington, 1985, Congl. Budget Office, Washington, 1980, N.Y. Stock Exch., 1995—. Author: Financial Markets, Financial Institutions and Money, 1983, (with others) The Political Economy of Policy Making, 1979, Money and Banking, 1991; contbr. articles to profl. jours. Mem. Am. Econ. Assn., Am. Fin. Assn., Nat. Assn. of Bus. Economists. Avocations: tennis, piano. Home: 1847 E Calle De Caballos Tempe AZ 85284-2505 Office: Ariz State U Dept Fin Tempe AZ 85287 Business E-Mail: herbert.kaufman@asu.edu

KAUFMAN, IRVING, retired engineering educator; b. Geinsheim, Germany, Jan. 11, 1925; came to US., 1938, naturalized, 1945; s. Albert and Hedwig Kaufmann; m. Ruby Lee Dordek, Sept. 10, 1950; children— Eve Deborah, Sharon Anne, Julie Ellen. BE, Vanderbilt U., 1945; MS, U. Ill., 1949, PhD, 1957. Engr. RCA Victor, Indpls., Ind. and Camden, N.J., 1945-48; instr., research assoc. U. Ill., Urbana, 1949-56; sr. mem. tech. staff Ramo-Wooldridge & Space Tech. Labs., Calif., 1957-64; prof. engring. Ariz. State U., 1965-94, ret., 1994; founder, dir. Solid State Research Lab., 1968-78. Collaborator Los Alamos Nat. Lab., 1989, 91; vis. scientist Consiglio Nazionale delle Ricerche, Italy, 1973-74; vis. prof. U. Auckland, N.Z., 1974; liaison scientist U.S. Office Naval Rsch., London, 1978-80; lectr. and cons. elec. engring. Contbr. articles to profl. jours. and encys.; patentee in field. Recipient Disting. Research award Ariz. State U. Grad. Coll., 1986-87; Sr. Fulbright research fellow Italy, 1964-65, 73-74, Am. Soc. for Engring. Edn./Naval Rsch. Lab. fellow, 1988. Fellow IEEE (life, Phoenix sect. leadership award 1994); mem. Electromagnetics Acad., Gold Key (hon.), Sigma Xi, Tau Beta Pi, Eta Kappa Nu, Pi Mu Epsilon. Jewish. Office: Ariz State U Dept Elec Engring Tempe AZ 85287-5706 E-mail: rubyirv@earthlink.net

KAUFMAN, JULIAN MORTIMER, broadcasting company executive, consultant; b. Detroit, Apr. 3, 1918; s. Anton and Fannie (Newman) K.; m. Katherine LaVerne Likins, May 6, 1942; children: Nikki, Keith Anthony. Grad. high sch., Newark. Pub. Elizabeth (N.J.) Sunday Sun, Inc., 1937-39; account exec. Tolle Advt. Agy., San Diego, 1947-49; pub. Tucson Shopper, 1948-50; account exec. ABC, San Francisco, 1949-50; mgr. Sta. KPHO-TV, Phoenix, 1950-52; gen. mgr., v.p. Bay City TV Corp., San Diego, 1952-95; v.p. Jai Alai Films, Inc., San Diego, 1961—; TV cons. Julian Kaufman, Inc., San Diego, 1985—. Dir. Spanish Internat. Broadcasting, Inc., L.A.; chmn. bd. dirs. Bay City TV Inc. Contbr. articles to profl. jours.; producer (TV show) Pick a Winner. Mem. Gov.'s adv. bd., Mental Health Assn., 1958—; bd. dirs. Francis Parker Sch., San Diego Better Bus. Bur., 1979-84, San Diego Conv. and Visitors Bur., World Affairs Coun., Pala Indian Mission. Served with USAAF, 1942-46. Recipient Peabody award, 1975, Emmy award, 1980. Mem. San Diego C. of C., Advt. and Sales Club, Sigma Delta Chi. Republican. Clubs: San Diego Press, University (San Diego). Home: 3125 Montesano Rd Escondido CA 92029-7302 Office: 7677 Ronson Rd Ste 210 San Diego CA 92111-1538

KAUFMAN, ROGER WAYNE, judge; b. Elizabeth, N.J., Aug. 27, 1938; s. Albert Henry and Selma Bernice (Cloner) K.; m. Lou Jan Erwin, Apr. 20, 1968; children: David Michael, Erin Anne. BA, Cornell U., 1960; JD, Harvard U., 1963. Bar: Ariz. 1964, U.S. Dist. Ct. Ariz. 1964, U.S. Ct. Appeals (9th cir.) 1965, U.S. Supreme Ct. 1971. Assoc. Lewis and Roca, Phoenix, 1963-68, ptnr., 1968-93; judge pro tem Superior Ct. State of Ariz. for Maricopa County, Phoenix, 1977-80; judge Maricopa County Superior Ct., Phoenix, 1993—; [illegible] 1993-95, presiding judge Civil Dept., 1995-98, presiding judge Criminal Dept., 1998-2000. Chmn. Civil Jury Instrns. Com., 1993-96, Com. on Superior Ct.; mem. Ariz. Jud. Coun. Author: Arizona Courtroom Handbook, 1967, 70, Consent Manual, 1979. Mem. bd. visitors Ariz. State U. Law Sch., Tempe, 1979-85; bd. dirs. Bapt. Hosp. Found., Phoenix, 1980-83, Am. Cancer Soc., Phoenix, 1985-90. Mem. ABA, Ariz. Bar Assn. (bd. govs. 1979-81), Am. Judicature Soc., Ariz. Judges Assn. (sec., v.p., pres. 1995-96). Democrat. Home: 6112 N 31st Pl Phoenix AZ 85016-2322

KAUFMAN, SANFORD PAUL, lawyer; b. N.Y.C., Jan. 4, 1928; s. Max and Rose (Kornitzky) K.; m. Bernice R. Sulkis, June 17, 1956; children—Leslie Keith, Brad Leigh, Rona Sheryl, Jeffrey Scott, Adam Ira. B.B.A. in Accounting, Coll. City N.Y., 1948; LL.B., N.Y. U., 1952, LL.M. in Taxation, 1957. Bar: N.Y. bar 1953, Calif. bar 1962. With firm Garey & Garey, N.Y.C., 1953-55; asst. gen. counsel Olympic Radio & TV, L.I. City, 1961-63; sec., gen. counsel Tel-Autograph Corp., L.A., 1961-63; asst. gen. counsel Nat. Gen. Corp., L.A., 1963-74; sec., gen. counsel Familian Corp., L.A., 1974-77; pvt. practice Torrance, Calif., 1977—. Bd. dirs. Temple Ner Tamid, S. Bay, Calif. Mem. Am. Soc. Corporate Secs., Los Angeles County Bar Assn., Beverly Hills Bus. Men's Assn. Club: K.P. (past chancellor). Home: 28412 Golden Meadow Dr Palos Verdes Peninsula CA 90275-2926 Office: 23505 Crenshaw Blvd Ste 246 Torrance CA 90505-5223

KAUPINS, GUNDARS EGONS, education educator; b. Mpls., Dec. 29, 1956; s. Alfreds and Skaidrite Kaupins; m. Debra Ann Queen, Mar. 27, 1998; children: Amanda, Kyle. BA, Wartburg Coll., 1979; MBA, U. No. Iowa, 1981; PhD, U. Iowa, 1986. Sr. prof. in human resources. Grad. asst. U. No. Iowa, Cedar Falls, 1979-81; employee rels. asst. Norand Corp., Cedar Rapids, 1983; grad. asst. Univ. Iowa, Iowa City, 1981-86; prof. Boise (Idaho) State U., 1986—. Cons. in field. Contbr. articles to profl. jours. Recipient rsch. grants Boise State U., 1987-2001, Ponder scholarship U. Iowa, 1983-85; named Adv. of the Yr., Boise State U., 1989. Mem. Soc. for Human Resource Mgmt. (faculty advisor 1986—), Assn. for Advancement of Baltic Studies, Acad. of Mgmt. Avocations: racewalking, golf, racquetball, tennis, skiing. Home: 8475 W Beachside Ct Boise ID 83703-6022 Office: Boise State U Dept Mgmt Boise ID 83725-0001

KAUVAR, ABRAHAM J. gastroenterologist, medical administrator; b. Denver, May 8, 1915; s. Charles Hillel and Belle Gertrude (Bluestone) K.; m. Jean Bayer, Aug. 22, 1943; children: Kenneth B., Jane Kauvar Athens, Lawrence, David. B.A., U. Denver, 1935; M.D., U. Chgo., 1939; Sc.D. (hon.), Hawthorne Coll., 1981; DHL (hon.), U. Denver, 2000. Diplomate: Am. Bd. Internal Medicine. Intern Billings Hosp., U. Chgo., 1939-40; resident Peter Bent Brigham Hosp., Boston, 1940-41, Mayo Clinic, Rochester, Minn., 1941-42; practice medicine specializing in gastroenterology Denver, 1946-74; mgr., chief exec. officer Health and Hosps. Agy., City and County of Denver, 1974-80; pres. Health and Hosp. Corp., N.Y.C., 1980-81. Spl. cons. med. Care and Rsch. Found., Denver; Goodstein Disting. prof. emeritus medicine and geriatrics U. Colo. Med. Sch.; adj. prof. Health Policy Univ. Colo. at Denver; health cons. govts., Ireland, Israel; mem. Social Security Appeals Coun., Dept. Health and Human Svcs.; pres. med. staffs Colo. Gen. Hosp., 1954-55, Rose Meml. Hosp., 1955-56; dir. Nat. Jewish Hosp., 1957—; pres. Tchrs. Award Found., 1957. Contbr. articles to profl. jours.; lectr.: hypoglycemia Am. Lecture Series, 1954. Bd. dirs. Salvation Army, 1957— . Served to maj. U.S. Army, 1942-46. Recipient Disting. award Denver Med. Soc., 1975, Disting. Humanitarian award U. Chgo. Alumni Assn., 1981, Disting. Svc. award U. Colo., 1987, award for profl. achievement U. Denver, 1994, Lifetime Achievement award Denver Med. Soc., 1996. Mem. Am. Fedn. Clin. Research, ACP, Am. Gastroent. Assn., Am. Endoscopic Soc., Am. Geriatric Soc., Soc. Med. Adminstrs., Am. Coll. Gastroenterology (v.p. 1976-77) Jewish. Clubs: Denver, Denver Tennis, Rotary. Home and Office: 70 S Ash St Denver CO 80246-1004

KAVANAUGH, MICHAEL C. environmental engineer; V.p. Malcolm Pirnie, Inc., Oakland, Calif., 1997—. Mem. NAE. Office: Malcolm Pirnie Inc 180 Grand Ave Ste 1000 Oakland CA 94612

KAVLI, FRED, manufacturing executive; b. Norway, Aug. 20, 1927; came to U.S., 1956; Grad., Norwegian Inst. Tech., 1955. Founder, CEO automotive and aerospace sensor engrng.-mfg. Kavlico Corp., 1958—. Bd. dirs. Surg. Eye Expdns. Internat., The Found. for Santa Barbara City Coll., U. Calif., Santa Barbara. Avocations: tennis, skiing, travel. Office: Kavlico Corp 14501 E Los Angeles Ave Moorpark CA 93021-9775

KAWACHIKA, JAMES AKIO, lawyer; b. Honolulu, Dec. 5, 1947; s. Shinichi and Tsuyuko (Murashige) K.; m. Karen Keiko Takahashi, Sept. 1, 1973; 1 child, Robyn Mari. BA, U. Hawaii, Honolulu, 1969; JD, U. Calif., Berkeley, 1973. Bar: Hawaii 1973, U.S. Dist. Ct. Hawaii 1973, U.S. Ct. Appeals (9th cir.) 1974, U.S. Supreme Ct. 1992. Dep. atty. gen. Office of Atty. Gen. State of Hawaii, Honolulu, 1973-74; assoc. Padgett, Greeley & Marumoto, Honolulu, 1974-75, Law Office of Frank D. Padgett, Honolulu, 1975-77, Kobayashi, Watanabe, Sugita & Kawashima, Honolulu, 1977-82; ptnr. Carlsmith, Wichman, Case, Mukai & Ichiki, Honolulu, 1982-86, Bays, Deaver, Hiatt, Kawachika & Lezak, Honolulu, 1986-95; propr. Law Offices of James A. Kawachika, Honolulu, 1996—. Mem. Hawaii Bd. of Bar Examiners, Honolulu; arbitrator Cir. Ct. Arbitration Program State of Hawaii, Honolulu, 1986—. Chmn. Disciplinary Bd. Hawaii Supreme Ct., 1991-97; mem. U.S. dist. Ct. Adv. Com. on the Civil Justice Reform Act of 1990, 1991—. Mem. ABA, ATLA, Am. Judicature Soc., Hawaii Bar Assn. (bd. dirs. Honolulu chpt. 1975-76, young lawyers sect. 1983-84, 92-93, treas. 1987-88, v.p./pres.-elect 1997-98, pres. 1998-99), 9th Cir. Jud. Conf. (lawyer rep. Honolulu chpt. 1988-90). Avocations: running, tennis, skiing. Office: Pacific Guardian Ctr Mauka Tower 737 Bishop St Ste 2750 Honolulu HI 96813-3216

KAWAMOTO, CALVIN KAZUO, state legislator; b. Pepeekeo, Hawaii, Apr. 14, 1940; m. Carolyn Kawamoto; children: Walter, Nina. BA, U. Hawaii, 1963; postgrad., No. Mich. U. Mem. Hawaii Senate, Dist. 19, Honolulu, 1994—; co-chair transp. and mil. affairs, govt. ops. Hawaii Senate, Honolulu, 1996-98, mem. ways and means com., mem. tourism and econ. devel. com., 1994-98, sen. mil. liaison, 1994-98, mem. edn. com., agrl. com., labor com. Exec. dir. Waipahu Cmty. Found.; dir. Waipahu Bus. Assn., Wahiawa Hosp. Bd., Rural Oahu Family Bd., Waianae Coast Comprehensive Ctr., Am. Box Car Racing Internat.; mem. Pearl City H.S., Manana Elem. PTA, Kanoelani Elem. PTA, Aiea/Pearl City Bus. Assn., Waipahu H.S.; mem. mgmt. coun. Waipahu H.S. Budget Com.; exec. dir. Waipahu Cmty. Adult Day Health Ctr. and Youth Ctr. With USAF. Recipient award Waipahu Pride; decorated Disting. Flying Cross, thirteen air medals. Mem. VFW. Democrat. Office: State Capitol 415 S Beretania St Honolulu HI 96813-2407

KAWAMOTO, HENRY K. plastic surgeon; b. Long Beach, Calif., 1937; Intern U. Calif. Hosp., L.A., 1965; resident gen. surgery Columbia Presbyn. Med. Ctr., N.Y., 1969-71; resident plastic surgery NYU, 1971-73; fellow crano-facial surgery Dr. Paul Tessier, Paris, 1973-74; clin. prof. plastic surgery U. Calif., L.A. Mem. Am. Assn. Plastic Surgery, Am. Soc. Plastic Surgery, ASMS, AOA. Office: 1301 20th St Ste 460 Santa Monica CA 90404-2054

KAWESKI, SUSAN, plastic surgeon, naval officer; b. Oil City, Pa., Jan. 27, 1955; d. Richard Francis and Lottie Ann (Malek) K.; m. Henry Nicholas Ernecoff, Aug. 7, 1983. BA, Washington and Jefferson Coll., 1976; MA, SUNY, Buffalo, 1979; MD, Pa. State U., 1983. Diplomate Am. Bd. Surgery, Am. Bd. Plastic Surgery. Commd. lt. USN, 1983, advanced through grades to capt., 1993; intern Naval Hosp., San Diego, 1983-84; head med. dept. USN, 1984-85; resident in gen. surgery Naval Hosp., San Diego, 1985-89; resident in plastic surgery Pa. State U., Hershey, 1989-91; staff plastic surgeon Naval Med. Ctr., San Diego, 1991-95; head divsn. plastic surgery, surgeon gen. advisor USN, 1994-95; craniofacial fellow Dr. Ian T. Jackson, Mich., 1995-96; head cleft palate/craniofacial team Naval Med. Ctr., 1996-98; resigned, 1998; pvt. practice, San Diego, 1998—. Chmn. Cleft Palate/Craniofacial Bd., San Diego; plastic surgery advisor to surgeon gen. USN, 1994-95; presenter in field. Author chpt. to book. Recipient Ernest Witebsky Meml. award for proficiency in microbiology SUNY at Buffalo, 1978. Fellow ACS (assoc., 1st Place Rsch. award 1991); mem. Am. Assn. Plastic and Reconstructive Surgeons, Am. Cleft Palate Assn., Am. Assn. Women Surgeons, Am. Med. Women's Assn., Assn. Mil. Surgeons U.S., Univ. Club. Republican. Roman Catholic. Avocations: skiing, tennis, swimming, oil painting, playing piano. Home: 1158 Barcelona Dr San Diego CA 92107-4151 Office: Craniofacial Reconstructive 3444 Kearny Villa Rd Ste 401 San Diego CA 92123-1964 E-mail: skaweski@pacbell.net

KAY, ALAN, computer scientist; b. 1940; BS in Math., Molecular Biology, U. Colo., 1966; PhD, U. Utah, 1969. Fellow Xerox Palo Alto (Calif.) Rsch. Ctr.; chief scientist Atari; fellow Apple Computer, Brentwood, Calif., 1984-96, Walt Disney Co., 1996—, v.p., Disney fellow. Fellow AAAS, NAE, Royal Soc. Arts. Office: Walt Disney Imagineering 1401 Flower St Glendale CA 91221-2421

KAY, ALAN COOKE, federal judge; b. 1932; s. Harold Thomas and Ann (Cooke) K. BA, Princeton U., 1957; LLB, U. Calif., Berkeley, 1960. Assoc. Case, Kay & Lynch, Honolulu, 1960-64, ptnr., 1965-86; judge U.S. Dist. Ct. Hawaii, Honolulu, 1986-92, chief judge, 1992—, sr. dist. judge. Bd. regents Internat. Coll. and Grad. Sch., 1994—. Mem. steering com. Fuller Theol. Sem. Hawaii, 1985-86; pres., trustee Hawaii Mission Children's Soc., Honolulu, 1980-86; bd. dirs. Good News Mission, 1980-86, Econ. Devel. Corp. Honolulu, 1985-86, Legal Aid Soc., Honolulu, 1968-71. Mem. ABA, Hawaii Bar Assn. (exec. com. 1972-73, bd. dirs. real estate sect. 1983-86), Fed. Judges Assn. (9th cir. jud. coun. 1994—, 9th cir. Pacific Islands com. 1994—), Am. Inns of Ct. (counselor Aloha Inn 1987—). Republican. Office: US Dist Ct C-415 Kuhio Federal Bldg 300 Ala Moana Blvd Rm Honolulu HI 96850-4971

KAY, CYRIL MAX, biochemist, educator; b. Calgary, Alta., Can., Oct. 3, 1931; s. Louis and Fanny (Pearlmutter) K.; m. Faye Bloomenthal, Dec. 30, 1953; children: Lewis Edward, Lisa Franci. B.Sc. in Biochemistry with honors (J.W. McConnell Meml. scholar), McGill U., 1952; Ph.D. in Biochemistry (Life Ins. Med. Research Fund fellow), Harvard U., 1956; postgrad., Cambridge (Eng.) U., 1956-57. Phys. biochemist Eli Lilly & Co., Indpls., 1957-58; asst. prof. biochemistry U. Alta., Edmonton, 1958-61, assoc. prof., 1961-67, prof., 1967—, co-dir. Med. Rsch. Coun. Group on Protein Structure and Function, 1974-95, mem. protein engring. network Centre of Excellence, 1990—; v.p. rsch. Alta Cancer Bd., 1999—. Med. Rsch. Coun. vis. scientist in biophysics Weizmann Inst., Israel, 1969-70, summer vis. prof. biophysics, 1975, summer vis. prof. chem. physics, 1977, 80; mem. biochemistry grants com. Med. Research Council, 1970-73; mem. Med. Rsch. Coun. Can., 1982-88; Can. rep. Pan Am. Assn. Biochem. Socs., 1971-76; mem. exec. planning com. XI Internat. Congress Biochemistry, Toronto, Ont., Can., 1979; mem. med. adv. bd. Gairdner Found. for Internat. awards in Med. Sci., 1980-89. Contbr. numerous articles to profl. publs.; assoc. editor Can. Jour. Biochemistry, 1968-82; editor-in-chief Pan Am. Assn. Biochem. Socs. Revista, 1971-76. Decorated Order of Can.; recipient Ayerst award in biochemistry Can. Biochem. Soc., 1970, Disting. Scientist award U. Alta. Med. Sch., 1988. Fellow N.Y. Acad. Scis., Royal Soc. Can.; mem. Order of Can., Can. Biochem. Soc. (coun. 1971—, v.p. 1976-77, pres. 1978-79). Home: 9408-143d St Edmonton AB Canada T5R 0P7 Office: U Alta Dept Biochemistry Med Scis Bldg Edmonton AB Canada T6G 2H7 E-mail: ckay@gpu.srv.ualberta.ca

KAY, ELIZABETH ALISON, zoology educator; b. Kauai, Hawaii, Sept. 27, 1928; d. Robert Buttercase and Jessie Dowie (McConnachie) K. BA, Mills Coll., 1950, Cambridge U., Eng., 1952, MA, 1956; PhD, U. Hawaii, 1957. From asst. prof. to prof. zoology U. Hawaii, Honolulu, 1957-62, assoc. prof., 1962-67, prof., 1967-98, prof. emeritus, 1998—. Research assoc. Bishop Mus., Honolulu, 1968—. Author: Hawaiian Marine Mollusks, 1979, Shells of Hawaii, 1991; editor: A Natural History of the Hawaiian Islands, 1972, 94. Chmn. Animal Species Adv. Commn., Honolulu, 1983-87; v.p. Save Diamond Head Assn., Honolulu, 1968-87, pres., 1987—; trustee B.P. Bishop Mus., Honolulu, 1983-88. Fellow Linnean Soc., AAAS; mem. Marine Biol. Assn. (Eng.), Australian Malacol. Soc. Episcopalian. Office: U Hawaii Manoa Dept Zoology 2538 The Mall Honolulu HI 96822-2200

KAY, HERMA HILL, education educator; b. Orangeburg, S.C., Aug. 18, 1934; d. Charles Esdorn and Herma Lee (Crawford) Hill. BA, So. Meth. U., 1956; JD, U. Chgo., 1959. Bar: Calif. 1960, U.S. Supreme Ct. 1978. Law clk. to Hon. Roger Traynor Calif. Supreme Ct., 1959-60; asst. prof. law U. Calif., Berkeley, 1960-62, assoc. prof., 1962, prof., 1963, dir. family law project, 1964-67, Jennings prof., 1987-96, dean, 1992-2000, Armstrong prof., 1996—; co-reporter uniform marriage and div. act Nat. Conf. Commrs. on Uniform State Laws, 1968-70. Vis. prof. U. Manchester, Eng., 1972, Harvard U., 1976; mem. Gov.'s Commn. on Family, 1966. Author: (with Martha S. West) Text Cases and Materials on Sex-based Discrimination, 4th edit., 1996, supplement, 1999; (with D. Currie and L. Kramer) Conflict of Laws: Cases, Comments, Questions, 6th edit., 2001; contbr. articles to profl. jours. Trustee Russell Sage Found., N.Y., 1972-87, chmn. bd., 1980-84; trustee, bd. dirs. Equal Rights Advs. Calif., 1976-99, chmn., 1976-83; pres. bd. dirs. Rosenberg Found., Calif., 1987-88, bd. dirs. 1978—. Recipient Rsch. award Am. Bar Found., 1990, Margaret Brent award ABA Commn. Women in Profession, 1992, Marshall-Wythe medal, 1995; fellow Ctr. Advanced Study in Behavioral Sci., Palo Alto, Calif., 1963. Mem. ABA (sect. on legal edn. and admissions to the bar coun. 1992-99, sec. 1999-2001), Calif. Bar Assn., Bar U.S. Supreme Ct., Calif. Women Lawyers (bd. govs. 1975-77), Am. Law Inst. (mem. coun. 1985-), Assn. Am. Law Schs. (exec. com. 1986-87, pres.-elect 1988, pres. 1989, past pres. 1990), Am. Acad. Arts and Scis., Am. Philosophical Soc., Order of Coif (nat. pres. 1983-85). Democrat. Office: U Calif Law Sch Boalt Hall Berkeley CA 94720-7200 E-mail: kayh@law.berkeley.edu

KAY, KENNETH JEFFREY, food products company executive; b. L.A., Apr. 2, 1955; s. Morton M. and Beverly J. Kay; m. Lisa Ellen, July 24, 1982. BS in Acctg., U. So. Calif., 1978, MBA in Fin., 1980. CPA, Calif. Staff acct. in charge Price Waterhouse and Co. (now PriceWaterhouse Coopers LLP), Century City, Calif., 1980-82; mgr. acctg. TRW-Fujitsu Co., L.A., 1982-83; corp. controller Ameron, Internat., Pasadena, Calif., 1983-88; sr. v.p. fin. and adminstrn., CFO Ameron, Inc., Pasadena, 1990-92, group v.p., 1992-94; pres., CEO, dir. Bishop, Inc., Westlake Village, 1988-90; sr. v.p. fin. and adminstrn., CFO Systemed, Inc., Torrance, 1994-96; sr. v.p., CFO Playmates Inc., Costa Mesa, 1997; exec. v.p., CFO Universal Studios Consumer Products Group, Universal City, 1998-99; v.p., CFO, Dole Food Co., Inc., Westlake Village, 2000—. Chmn. supervisory com. Ameron Fed. Credit Union, South Gate, Calif., 1986. Bd. govs. Cedars-Sinai Med. Ctr.; mem. exec. com. Friends for Life, L.A.; mem. bus. coun. Paralysis Project. Mem. AICPA, Am. Mgmt. Assn., Calif. Soc. CPAs, Assn. for Strategic Planning, Fin. Execs. Inst., USC Marshall Sch. Alumni. Office: Dole Food Co Inc One Dole Dr Westlake Village CA 91362-7300 E-mail: kenneth_kay@na.dole.com

KAY, PAUL DE YOUNG, linguist; b. N.Y.C., Nov. 7, 1934; s. William de Young and Alice Sarah Kay; m. Patricia Boehm, Feb. 13, 1934; children: Yvette, Suzanne de Young. BA in Econs., Tulane U., 1955; PhD in Anthropology, Harvard U., 1963. Asst. prof. MIT, Cambridge, Mass., 1964-65; asst prof., prof. dept. anthropology U. Calif., Berkeley, 1966-83, prof. dept. linguistics, 1983—, chmn. dept., 1986-91. Author: Words and the Grammar of Context, 1997; editor: Explorations in Mathematical Anthropology, 1971; co-author: Basic Color Terms, 1969; contbr. articles to Language, Linguistic Inquiry, Foundations of Language, Linguistics and Philosophy, Language and Society, Am. Anthropologist, Current Anthropology, Jour. of Linguistic Anthrop. Fellow Ctr. Advanced Study in Behavioral Scis., Stanford, Calif., 1965-66, Guggenheim Found., U. Hawaii, Oahu, 1972-73. Mem. NAS, Linguistic Soc. Am., Am. Anthrop. Assn., Soc. for Linguistic Anthropology (pres. 1988-89). Office: U Calif Dept Linguistics Berkeley CA 94720-0001 E-mail: kay@cogsi.berkeley.edu

KAYE, CAROLE, museum director and curator; b. Somerville, N.J., Apr. 24, 1933; d. Harry and Grace (Schwartz) Golison; m. Paul Littman, June 29, 1952 (dec. Apr. 1960); children: Fern, Alan; m. Barry Kaye; children: Howard. Student, Syracuse U., 1951. With Barry Kaye Assocs., L.A.; owner, curator Carole and Barry Kaye Mus. Miniatures, L.A.; v.p. Barry Kaye Assocs. Mus., 1994—. Past pres. Hadassah, Beverly Hills, Calif.; founder Music Ctr., Cedars-Sinai Hosp., L.A.; mem. Jewish Fedn. Mem. Friends of Ben Gurion U. Office: Carole & Barry Kaye Mus Miniatures 5900 Wilshire Blvd Los Angeles CA 90036-5013

KAYE, JHANI, radio station manager, owner production company; b. Maywood, Calif., June 18, 1949; s. Jimmie Eccak and Betty Jo (Holland) Kazaroff. BA, UCLA, 1971. Lic. 1st class radio. Music dir. Sta. KFXM, San Bernardino, Calif., 1969-73; announcer Stas. KUTE-FM/KKDJ-FM, L.A., 1972-74; asst. program dir. Sta. KROQ, L.A., 1973-74, Sta. WCFL, Chgo., 1980-82, Sta. KFI, L.A., 1982; program dir. Sta. KINT-FM, El Paso, Tex., 1975-80; sta. mgr., program dir. Sta. KOST-FM, L.A., 1982-99; program dir. Sta. KBIG-FM, Glendale, Calif, 1999—. Dir. adult contemporary programming Clear Channel Radio, 1999—; sta. mgr. KIG/KOST, 2001—; owner Los Feliz Post Prodn. Video Svcs. Appeared in TV series Falcon Crest, 1985, Drew Carey Show, 1998; dir. TV commls., 1986—; voice-over motion picture The Couch Trip, 1987; dir., video editor Dick Clark TV Commls. Recipient Marconi Radio awards Nat. Assn. Broadcasters, 1990, 91. Avocation: video production. Office: Sta KBIG-FM 330 N Brand Blvd Ste 800 Glendale CA 91203-2318

KAYE, PETER FREDERIC, newspaper columnist; b. Chgo., Mar. 8, 1928; s. Ralph A. and Sara Corson (Philipson) K.; m. Martha Louise Wood, Mar. 20, 1955; children: Loren, Terry, Adam. BA in Govt., Pomona Coll., 1949. Reporter Alhambra (Calif.) Post-Advocate, 1950-53; reporter, editorial writer, polit. writer The San Diego Union, 1953-68; news and pub. affairs dir. KPBS-TV, San Diego State Coll., 1968-72; corr., producer Nat. Pub. Affairs Ctr. for TV, Washington, 1972-74; comm. dir. So. Calif. First Nat. Bank, San Diego, 1974-75; press sec. The Pres. Ford Com., Washington, 1975-76; mgr. Copley Videotex, San Diego, 1982-84; assoc. editor The San Diego Union, 1976-94; editl. dir. KNSD, San Diego, 1996-99. Freelance TV producer programs KPBS, PBS, BBC; San Diego corr. Newsweek, 1968-71, McGraw-Hill, 1959-67; lectr. comm. U. Calif., San Diego, 1971; copywriter Washburn-Justice Advt., San Diego, 1959-70. Producer 10 TV programs including including Jacob Bronowski: Life and Legacy, Twenty-Five Years of Presidency, The Presidency, The Press and the People. Press asst. Eisenhower-Nixon Campaign, L.A., 1952; asst. press sec. Richard Nixon Presdl. Campaign, Washington, 1960; dir. Pete Wilson for Mayor Campaign, San Diego, 1971; comm. dir. Flournoy for Gov. Campaign, Beverly Hills, Calif., 1974. With U.S. Mcht. Marines, 1945, U.S. Army, 1950-52. Jefferson fellow East-West Ctr., Honolulu, 1987; recipient Golden Mike awards So. Calif. TV News Dirs. Assn., 1969, 70, 71, Best Pub. Affairs Program award Nat. Edni. TV, 1970, Best Local TV Series award Radio-TV Mirror, 1971, Nat. Emmy award Spl. Events Reporter, Watergate Coverage, 1973-74, Best Editorial awards Copley Newspapers Ring of Truth, 1979, Sigma Delta Chi, 1985, Calif. Newspaper Pubs. Assn., 1985; San Diego Emmy awards, 1985, 87, 91. Mem. NATAS, State Bar Calif. (bd. govs. 1991-97, v.p. 1993-94, 96-97), Sigma Delta Chi. Republican. Home: 240 Ocean View Ave Del Mar CA 92014-3322

KAYLAN, HOWARD LAWRENCE, musical entertainer, composer; b. N.Y.C., June 22, 1947; s. Sidney and Sally Joyce (Berlin) K.; m. Mary Melita Pepper, June 10, 1967 (div. Sept. 1971); 1 child, Emily Anne; m. Susan Karen Olsen, Apr. 18, 1982 (div. June 1996); 1 child, Alexandra Leigh. Student, UCLA; PhD in Philosophy, Am. Coll. Metaphys. Theology, St. Paul, Minn., 2000. Lead singer and founder rock group The Turtles, Los Angeles, 1965—; lead singer rock group Mothers of Invention, Los Angeles, 1970-72, Flo and Eddie, 1972-83; radio, TV, recording entertainer various broadcast organizations, Los Angeles, 1972—; screenwriter Larry Gelbart, Carl Gotleib prodns., Los Angeles, 1979-85; producer children's records Kidstuff Records, Hollywood, Fla., 1980-83; singer, producer rock band Flo and Eddie, Los Angeles, 1976-83; singer, producer The Turtles (reunion of original band), Los Angeles, 1980—; actor, TV and film Screen Actors Guild, Los Angeles, 1983—. Background vocalist various albums for numerous performers; syndicated talk show host Unistar Radio Network, 1989—; radio personality Sta. WXRK-FM, N.Y.C., 1990-91, KLOU, St. Louis, 1993, WGRR, Cin., 1995-97. Author: Hi Bob, 1995, The Energy Pals, 1995; contbr. articles to Creem mag., L.A. Free Press, Rockit mag., Phonograph Record; screenwriter: (film) Death Masque, 1985, My Dinner With Jimi, 2000; actor: (film) 200 Motels, 1971, Get Crazy, 1985, General Hospital, Suddenly Susan, 1999; performed at the White House, 1970; exec. producer: (radio) Down Eerie Street, 1998. Recipient 10 Gold and Platinum LP album awards while lead singer, 1965—, Fine Arts award, Bank of Am., L.A., 1965, Spl. Billboard Mag. award, 1992; recorded numerous top ten hit songs with Turtles, Bruce Springsteen, The Ramones, Duran Duran, T. Rex, John Lennon and others; recipient numerous for commls. including Chevrolet, Pepsi, Burger King and the NFL, 1970—. Mem. AFTRA, Screen Actors Guild, Am. Fedn. Musicians, AGVA.

KAYS, WILLIAM MORROW, university administrator, mechanical engineer; b. Norfolk, Va., July 29, 1920; s. Herbert Emery and Margaret (Fechteler) K.; m. Alma Campbell, Sept. 14, 1947 (dec. June 1982); children: Nancy, Leslie, Margaret, Elizabeth; m. Judith Scholtz, July 17, 1983. A.B., Stanford U., 1942, M.S., 1947, Ph.D. in Mech. Engring., 1951. Asst. prof. mech. engring. Stanford U., 1951-54, assoc. prof., 1954-57, prof., 1957-90, prof. emeritus, 1990—, chmn. dept. mech. engring, 1961-72, dean engring., 1972-84. Dir. Acurex Corp., Alcohol Energy Systems; cons. to numerous firms. Author: Compact Heat Exchangers, 1964, 93, Convective Heat and Mass Transfer, 1966, 80. Hon. editorial adv. bd.: Internat. Jour. Heat and Mass Transfer. Served with U.S. Army, 1942-46. Fulbright fellow, 1959-60; NSF sr. postdoctoral fellow, 1966-67 Fellow ASME (Heat Transfer Divsn. Meml. award 1965, Max Jacob award 1992); mem. Am. Soc. Engring. Edn., Nat. Acad. Engring. Office: Stanford U Dept Mech Engring Stanford CA 94305

KAYTON, MYRON, engineering company executive; b. N.Y.C., Apr. 26, 1934; s. Albert Louis and Rae (Danoff) K.; m. Paula Erde, Sept. 5, 1954; children: Elizabeth Kayton Kerns, Susan Kayton Barclay. BS, The Cooper Union, 1955; MS, Harvard U., 1956; PhD, MIT, 1960. Registered engr., Calif. Sect. head Litton Industries, Woodland Hills, Calif., 1960-65; dep. mgr. NASA, Houston, 1965-69; mem. sr. staff TRW, Inc., Redondo Beach, Calif., 1969-81; pres. Kayton Engring. Co., Inc., Santa Monica, 1981—. Chmn. bd. dirs. WINCON Conf., L.A., 1985-92; founding dir. Caltech-MIT Enterprise Forum, Pasadena, Calif., 1984—; dir. Electronic Convs., Inc., 2000-01; tchr. tech. courses UCLA Extension, 1969-88. Author: Avionic Navigation Systems, 1966, 2d edit., 1997, Navigation: Land, Sea, Air and Space, 1990; contbr. numerous articles on engring., econs. and other profl. subjects. Founding dir. UCLA Friends of Humanities, 1971-75; West coast chmn. Cooper Union Fund Campaign, 1989-93. Fellow NSF, Washington, 1956-57, 58-60; recipient Gano Dunn medal The Cooper Union, N.Y.C., 1975. Fellow IEEE (nominating com. 1999—, corp. bd. dirs. 1996-97, pres. aerospace 1993-94, exec. v.p. aerospace 1991-92, v.p. tech. ops. 1988-90, nat. bd. govs. 1983—, vice-chmn. L.A. coun. 1983-84,

M.B. Carlton award 1988, Disting. lectr., Millennium medal 2000); mem. ASME, Harvard Grad. Soc. (coun. mem. chmn. nominating com. 1988-91, Inst. Navigation, Soc. Automotive Engr., Harvard Club So. Calif. (pres. 1979-80), MIT Club (L.A.). Avocations: tennis, history, languages, flying, running. Office: Kayton Engring Co PO Box 802 Santa Monica CA 90406-0802

KAZANJIAN, PHILLIP CARL, lawyer, business executive; b. Visalia, Calif., May 15, 1945; s. John Casey and Sat-ten Arlene K.; m. Wendy Coffelt, Feb. 5, 1972; 1 child, John. BA with honors, U. So. Calif., 1967; JD with honors, Lincoln U., 1973. Bar: Calif. 1979, U.S. Dist. Ct. (ctrl. dist.) Calif. 1980, U.S. Tax Ct. 1980, U.S. Ct. Appeals (9th cir.) 1980, U.S. Mil. Ct. Appeals 1980, U.S. Supreme ct. 1983. Ptnr. Brakefield & Kazanjian, Glendale, Calif., 1981-87; sr. ptnr. Kazanjian & Martinetti, Glendale, 1987—. Judge pro tem L.A. County Superior Ct., 1993—; instr. U.S. Naval Acad., Annapolis, Md., 1981; adj. prof. Glendale C.C., 1997—. Author: The Circuit Governor, 1972; editor-in-chief Lincoln Law Rev., 1973. Mem. Calif. Atty. Gen.'s Adv. Commn. on Cmty.-Police Rels., 1973; bd. dirs. L.A. County Naval Meml. Found., Inc,. 1981-85; pres., bd. trustees Glendale C.C. Dist., 1981-97, L.A. World Affairs Coun., Town Hall Calif., Rep. Assocs. (dir.), Rep. Lincoln Club; vice chmn. bd. govs. Calif. Maritime Acad., 1986-94. Capt. USNR, 1969-99. Decorated Navy Commendation medal, Navy Achievement medal, knight Order of Knights Templar, 1990; recipient Patrick Henry medal Am. Legion, 1963, Congl. Record tribute U.S. Ho. of Reps., 1974, Centurion award Chief of Naval Ops., 1978; commendatory resolutions Mayor of L.A., L.A. City Coun., L.A. County Bd. Suprs., Calif. State Assembly and Senate, and Govt. of Calif., 1982, Justice award Calif. Law Student Assn., 1973. Mem. ABA (Gold Key 1972), Calif. Bar Assn., L.A. County Bar Assn., Am. Judicature Soc., ATLA, Glendale C. of C. (bd. dirs., Patriot Yr. 1986), Res. Officers Assn. (nat. judge adv., award 1981), Naval Res. Assn. (nat. adv. com.), U.S. Naval Inst., Interallied Confedn. Res. Officers (internat. chmn. 1987-94), Explorers Club, Commonwealth of Calif. Club. Republican. Episcopalian. Office: Kazanjian & Martinetti 520 E Wilson Ave Ste 250 Glendale CA 91206-4346

KAZEMI, HOSSEIN, petroleum engineer; BS in Petroleum Engring., U. Tex., 1961, PhD in Petroleum Engring., 1963. Rsch. scientist Sinclair Oil Corp./Atlantic Richfield Co., Tulsa, Dallas, 1963-69; adv. rsch. scientist Petroleum Tech. Ctr., Marathon, Littleton, Colo., 1969-74, sr. rsch. scientist, 1974-79, sr. tech. cons., 1979-81, mgr. engring., 1981-86, mgr. reservoir mgmt., 1986-88, assoc. dir., 1988-94, mgr. product tech., 1994-96, mgr. reservoir tech., 1997-99, exec. tech. fellow, 1999—. Adj. prof. Colo. Sch. Mines, Golden, 1981—; lectr., speaker in field. Contbr. articles to profl. jours. Mem. Soc. Petroleum Engrs. AIME (hon., disting., Henry Mattson tech. svc. award 1980, John Franklin Carll award 1987, Disting. Svc. award 1991, DeGolyer Disting. Svc. award 1995), Nat. Acad. Engring. Office: Petroleum Tech Ctr Marathon PO Box 269 Littleton CO 80160-0269

KEARNEY, JOSEPH LAURENCE, retired athletic conference administrator; b. Pitts., Apr. 28, 1927; s. Joseph L. and Iva M. (Nikirk) K.; m. Dorothea Hurst, May 13, 1950; children: Jan Marie, Kevin Robert, Erin Lynn, Shawn Alane, Robin James. B.A., Seattle Pacific U., 1952, LL.D., 1979; M.A., San Jose State U., 1964; Ed.D., U. Wash., 1970. Tchr., coach Paradise (Calif.) High Sch., 1952-53; asst. basketball coach U. Wash., 1953-54; coach, tchr. Sunnyside (Wash.) High Sch., 1954-57; prin. high sch., coach Onalaska (Wash.) High Sch., 1957-61; prin. Tumwater (Wash.) High Sch., 1961-63; asst. dir. Wash. High Sch. Activities Assn., 1963-64; athletic dir., assoc. dir. U. Wash., 1964-76; athletic dir. intercollegiate athletics Mich. State U., East Lansing, 1976-80, Ariz. State U., Tempe, 1980; commr. Western Athletic Conf., Denver, 1980-95. Hon. chmn. Holiday Bowl, 1994, commr. emeritus, 1994. Pres. Cmty. Devel. Assn., 1957-61; bd. dirs. U.S. Olympic Com., 1985-94, chmn. games preparation com., 1985-2001. Recipient Disting. Service award Mich. Assn. Professions, 1979, Citation for Disting. Svc., Colo. Sports Hall of Fame, U.S. Olympic Com. Order of Olympic Shield, 1996. Mem. Nat. Football Found. (ct. of honors com., Western Regional Leadership award 1999), Nat. Collegiate Athletic Assn., Nat. Assn. Collegiate Dirs. Athletics (Corbett award 1991, Adminstr. Excellence award), Collegiate Commrs. Assn. (pres., award of Merit 1998), Am. Football Assn. (Commrs. award 1996, Athletic Dir.'s award 1998). Home: 2810 W Magee Rd Tucson AZ 85742-1500 E-mail: jlkearney@qwest.net

KEARNS, DAVID RICHARD, chemistry educator; b. Urbana, Ill., Mar. 20, 1935; s. Clyde W. and Camille V. (French) K.; m. Alice Chen, July 5, 1958; children: Jennifer, Michael. BS in Chem. Engring., U. Ill., 1956; PhD., U. Calif., Berkeley, 1960. USAF doctoral fellow U. Chgo., 1960-61, MIT, Cambridge, 1961-62; asst. prof. chemistry U. Calif., Riverside, 1962-63, assoc. prof., 1964-67, prof., 1968-75, San Diego, 1975—. Assoc. editor Molecular Photochemistry, 1969-75, Photochemistry and Photobiology, 1971-75, Chem. Revs., 1974; assoc. editor Biopolymers, 1975-78, editorial bd., 1978—. Sloan Found. fellow, 1965-67; Guggenheim fellow, 1969-70. Mem. Am. Chem. Soc. (Calif. sect. award 1973), Am. Phys. Soc., Am. Soc. Photobiology. Home: 8422 Sugarman Dr La Jolla CA 92037-2225 Office: U Calif San Diego Dept Chemistry La Jolla CA 92093

KEATING, DAVID, photographer; b. Rye, N.Y., Sept. 5, 1962; BA in Philosophy, Yale U., 1985; MA in Studio Art with distinction, U. N.Mex., 1991; student, Calif. Inst. Arts, Santa Clarita, 1992; MFA in Studio Art with distinction, U. N.Mex., 1994. Solo exhbns. include U. N.Mex., 1990 (traveled to Pace U., N.Y.C., Nat. Coun. Alcoholism Conf. of Affiliates, Nashville), 91, Calif. Inst. Arts, 1992, Graham Gallery, Albuquerque, 1994, Univ. Art Mus. Downtown, Albuquerque, 1995-96, George Eastman House, Rochester, N.Y., 1997, others; group exhbns. include Raw Space Gallery, Albuquerque, 1990, Betty Rymer Gallery, Sch. Art Inst. Chgo., 1991, 92, Randolph St. Gallery, Chgo., 1992, Atlanta Gallery Photography, 1992, San Jose (Calif.) Inst. Contemporary Art, 1992, Univ. Art Mus., Albuquerque, 1993, Ctr. African Am. History and Culture, Smithsonian Instn., Washington, 1994-95, Mus. Photographic Arts, San Diego, 1996-97, SF Camerawork, San Francisco, 1993, 98, others; represented in pub. collections, including Univ. Art Mus., Albuquerque; subject of various articles and catalogs, 1992—. NEA Visual Artists fellow in photography, 1994, Van Deren Coke fellow, U. N.Mex., 1991; recipient award Photographers and Friends United Against AIDS/Art Matters Inc., 1992. Home: 1410 Central Ave SW Apt 38 Albuquerque NM 87104-1166

KEATING, EUGENE KNEELAND, animal scientist, educator; b. Liberal, Kans., Feb. 15, 1928; s. Arthur Hitch and Nilie Charlotte (Kneeland) K.; m. Iris Louise Myers, Aug. 12, 1951; children— Denise Keating Schnagl, Kimberly Alan. BS, Kans. State U., 1953, MS, 1954; PhD, U. Ariz., 1964. Owner, mgr. ranch, Kans., 1954-57; instr., farm mgr. Midwestern U., Wichita Falls, Tex., 1957-60; rsch. asst. U. Ariz., Tucson, 1960-64; prof. animal sci. Calif. State Poly. U., Pomona, 1964-98, prof. emeritus, 1998—, chmn. dept., 1971-78. Contbr. articles to profl. jours. Bd. dirs. Los Angeles County Jr. Livestock Fair, 1971-79, chmn., 1975. With USAAF, 1946-49. Recipient Farm Bur. Century award, 2000. Fellow Am. Inst. Chemists; mem. NRA (benefactor), NRA Whittington Ctr. Founder's Club, Nat. Intercollegiate Rodeo Assn. (West Coast regional faculty dir. 1972-76), Coun. for Agrl. Sci. and Tech., Calif. Rifle and Pistol Assn. (Gold Eagle), Am. Soc. Animal Sci., Am. Soc. Lab. Animal Sci., Brit. Soc. Animal Prodn., Rep. Nat. Com. (life), Am. Legion, Block and Bridle Club, Ind. Order Foresters, Santa Fe Trail and Gun Club (life), Western Heritage Ctr., Sigma Xi, Phi Lambda Upsilon, Gamma Sigma Delta, Alpha Zeta. Presbyterian. Home: 149 W Loretto Ct Claremont CA 91711-1739 Office: 3801 W Temple Ave Pomona CA 91768-2667

KEATING, THOMAS FRANCIS, state legislator; b. Langdon, N.D., Nov. 26, 1928; s. Thomas Delbert and Olive Mary (Bear) K.; m. Anna Louise Walsh, Aug. 22, 1953; children: Thomas J., Patrick, Michael, Kathryn, Terence. Student, Eastern Mont. Coll., 1951; BA in Bus. Adminstrn., U. Portland, 1953. Landman Mobil Oil Corp., Billings, Mont., 1954-61, Okla. City, 1961-66, Burlington No. R.R., Billings, 1966-67; Mont., landman Billings, 1967-81; mem. Mont. Senate, 1981—. Served with USAF, 1946-49. Mem. Am. Assn. Petroleum Landmen (pres. dir. 1971 73, Mont. chpt. pres. 1969), Ind. Petroleum Assn., Billings C. of C. Republican. Roman Catholic. Home: PO Box 20522 Billings MT 59104-0522

KEATOR, CAROL LYNNE, library director; b. Annapolis, Md., Aug. 9, 1945; d. Lyle H. and Juanita F (Waits) K. BA, Syracuse U., 1967; MS, Simmons Coll., 1968. Librarian Bristol (Conn.) Pub. Sch.s, 1968-69, MIT, Cambridge, 1969-72, Santa Barbara (Calif.) Pub. Library, 1972-77, br. supr., 1977-81, prin. librarian, 1981-88, library dir., 1988—. Mem. ALA, Calif. Libr. Assn., Pub. Libr. Assn. Unitarian. Office: Santa Barbara Pub Libr 40 E Anapamu St Santa Barbara CA 93101-2722

KEDES, LAURENCE H. biochemistry educator, physician, researcher; b. Hartford, Conn., July 19, 1937; s. Sammuel Ely and Rosalyn (Epstein) K.; m. Shirley Beck, June 15, 1958; children: Dean Hamilton, Maureen Jennifer, Todd Russell. Student, Wesleyan U., 1955-58; BS with distinction, Stanford U., 1961, MD, 1962. Intern Presbyn. U. Hosp., Pitts., 1962-63, asst. resident, 1963-64; rsch. assoc. lab. biochemistry Nat. Cancer Inst. Peterson, 1964-66; sr. asst. med. resident Peter Bent Brigham Hosp., Boston, 1966-67; surgeon USPHS, 1964-66; postdoctoral fellow dept. biology MIT, 1967-68; jr. assoc. in medicine and hematology assoc. Peter Bent Brigham Hosp., Boston, 1967-69; rsch. trainee in embryology Marine Biol. Lab., Woods Hole, Mass., 1969; instr. biology MIT, Boston, 1969-70; asst., assoc. then prof. medicine Stanford U., 1970-89, dir. admissions med. sch., 1978-81; William M. Keck prof. biochemistry and medicine, chair biochemistry, dir. Inst. Genetic Medicine U. So. Calif. Keck Sch. Medicine, L.A., 1989—. Staff physician VA, 1970-92; vis. scientist Lab. Molecular Embryology, Naples, Italy, 1969-70, Dept. Animal Genetics, U. Edinburgh, 1970, Imperial Cancer Rsch. Fund, London, 1976-77; instr. embryology Marine Biol. Lab., Woods Hole, 1976; investigator Howard Hughes Med. Inst., 1974-82; founder, dir. IntelliCorp., Mountain View, Calif., 1980-90, chmn., 1982-86. Mem. editorial bd. Jour. Biol. Chemistry, 1982-88, Molecular and Cellular Biology, 1982-89, Jour. Applied Molecular Biology, 1982-85, Oxford Surveys on Eukaryotic Genes, 1983-94, Trends in Genetics, 1984-88; assoc. editor Jour. Molecular Evolution, 1982-90; cons. editor Circulation Rsch., 1994-99. Mem. fellowship award com. Am. Cancer Soc., 1978-81; co-principle investigator BIONET, 1984-89; mem. rsch. com. Am. Heart Assn., 1987; mem. sci. adv. bd. Muscular Dystrophy Assn., 1988-93. Fellow Med. Found. Boston, 1967-69, John Simon Guggenheim Found. fellow, 1976-77; Leukemia Soc. Am. scholar, 1969-74. Mem. Western Soc. for Clin. Rsch., Am. Soc. Clin. Investigation, Assn. Am. Psysicians, Am. Soc. Microbiology, Am. Soc. Biochemistry and Molecular Biology, Internat. Soc. Devel. Biology, Alpha Omega Alpha. Office: U So Calif 2250 Alcazar St Ste 240 Los Angeles CA 90033-1004 E-mail: KEDES@HSC.USC.EDU

KEEGAN, JOHN E. lawyer; b. Spokane, Wash., Apr. 29, 1943; BA, Gonzaga U., 1965; LLB, Harvard U., 1968. Bar: Wash. 1968, U.S. Ct. Appeals (9th cir.) 1976, U.S. Supreme Ct. Gen. counsel Dept. Housing and Urban Devel., Washington, 1968-70; instr. in bus. sch. and inst. environ. studies U. Wash., 1973-76, instr. land use and environ. law, 1976-78; now ptnr. Davis, Wright & Tremaine, Seattle. Office: Davis Wright Tremaine 2600 Century Sq 1501 4th Ave Seattle WA 98101-1688

KEEGAN, LISA GRAHAM, state agency administrator; m. John Keegan; 5 children. BS in Linguistics, Stanford U.; MS in Comm. Disorders, Ariz. State U. Mem. Ariz. Ho. of Reps., 1991-95, chair edn. com., joint legis. budget com., 1993-94; state supt. of pub. instrn. Dept. of Edn., State of Ariz., Phoenix, 1994—. Founder Edn. Leaders Coun. Office: Edn Dept Supt of Pub Instrn 1535 W Jefferson St Phoenix AZ 85007-3209

KEELING, CHARLES DAVID, oceanography educator; b. Scranton, Pa., Apr. 20, 1928; s. Ralph Franklin and Grace Noerr (Sherburne) K.; m. Louise Barthold; children: Andrew, Ralph, Emily, Eric, Paul. BA, U. Ill., 1949; PhD, Northwestern U., 1954. Research fellow Calif. Inst. Tech., Pasadena, 1953-56; asst. research chemist Scripps Instn. Oceanography U. Calif., San Diego, 1956-60, assoc. research chemist, 1960-64, assoc. prof. oceanography, 1964-68, prof. oceanography, 1968—. Recipient Half Century award Am. Meteorol. Soc., 1981, Spl. Achievement award v.p. U.S., 1997; fellow J.S. Guggenheim Found., 1962. Fellow AAAS, Am. Geophys. Union (Ewing medal 1991), Blue Planet Prize, Asahi Glass Foundation, 1993, Am. Acad. Arts and Scis.; mem. NAS, Sigma Xi. Avocations: musical performance, off-road walking. Office: U Calif Scripps Inst Oceanography 8602 La Jolla Shores Dr La Jolla CA 92037-1508 E-mail: cdkeeling@ucsd.edu

KEEN, NOEL THOMAS, plant pathology educator; b. Marshalltown, Iowa, Aug. 13, 1940; s. Walter Thomas and Evelyn Mae (Mayo) K.; m. Diane I. Keen, Nov. 15, 1986. BS, Iowa State U., 1963, MS, 1965; PhD, U. Wis., 1968. Asst. prof. plant pathology U. Calif., Riverside, 1968-72, assoc. prof., 1972-78, prof., 1978—, chmn. dept. plant pathology, 1983-89, chmn. dept. genetics, 1994-97. Faculty rsch. lectr. U. Calif., Riverside, 1995-96. Recipient Ruth Allen award, Am. Phytopathological Soc., 1995, Superior Svc. award USDA, 1996. Fellow AAAS, Am. Phytopathol. Soc. (v.p. 1999-2000, pres.-elect 2000-01), Am. Acad. Microbiology; mem. NAS, Internat. Soc. Plant Molecular Biology, Am. Soc. Microbiology, Am. Soc. Plant Biology. Office: U Calif Dept Plant Pathology Riverside CA 92521-0001 E-mail: Keen@ucrac1.ucr.edu

KEENAN, BOB, state legislator; b. Salem, Mass., Mar. 11, 1952; m. Suzie Keenan. Grad., U. Mass. Owner Bigfork Inn; ptnr. Internat. Newspaper Network; self-employed entrepreneur; mem. Mont. Ho. of Reps., 1995-98, Mont. Senate, Dist. 38, 1998—; mem. fin. and claims com., labor and employment rels. com.; mem. joint appropriations subcom. on health and human svcs.; mem. edn. and cultural resources com. Trustee Bigfork Cmty. Fund, Bigfork Lighting Dist.; mem. Mont. Food Code Task Force; mem. adv. coun. Swan River Correctional Tng. Ctr., Mont. Dept. Corrections. Mem. Bigfork C. of C. (bd. dirs.). Republican. Home: PO Box 697 Bigfork MT 59911-0697 E-mail: inn1@digisys.net

KEENAN, NANCY A. state agency administrator; BA in Elem. and Spl. Edn., Mont. Coll., 1974. Tchr. Yellowstone Boys' Ranch, 1974-75; tchr. spl. edn. Anaconda, Mont., 1975-88; mem. Mont. Ho. of Reps., 1982-88; supt. of pub. instrn. State of Mont., 1988—. Mem. taxation, edn., local govt. and revenue oversight coms., 1982-84; chmn. ho. human svcs. and aging com.; asst. Dem. whip. Active Anaconda Local Devel. Corp.; past pres. A.W.A.R.E.; bd. dirs. Deer Lodge County Hospice; mem. Mont. Coun. for Exceptional Children. Recipient Pub. Svc. award Mont. Coun. for Exceptional Children, 1981. Mem. AAUW. Office: Public Instruction Office State Capitol Rm 106 PO Box 20251 Helena MT 59620

KEEP, JUDITH N. federal judge; b. Omaha, Mar. 24, 1944; B.A., Scripps Coll., 1966; J.D., U. San Diego, 1970. Bar: Calif. 1971. Atty. Defenders Inc., San Diego, 1971-73; pvt. practice law, 1973-76; asst. U.S. atty. U.S. Dept. Justice, 1976; judge Mcpl. Ct., San Diego, 1976-80, U.S. Dist. Ct. (so. dist.) Calif., San Diego, 1980—, chief judge, 1991-98; judge U.S. Office: US Dist Ct Ct Rm 16 940 Front St Ste 5190 San Diego CA 92101-8917

KEEVIL, NORMAN BELL, mining executive; b. Cambridge, Mass., Feb. 28, 1938; s. Norman Bell and Verna Ruth (Bond) K.; m. Joan E. Macdonald, Dec. 1990; children: Scott, Laura, Jill, Norman Bell III. BA in Sci., U. Toronto, Ont., Can., 1959; PhD, U. Calif., Berkeley, 1964; LLD (hon.), U. B.C., 1993. Registered profl. engr., Ont. V.p. exploration Teck Corp., Vancouver, B.C., Can., 1962-68, exec. v.p., 1968-81, pres., CEO, 1981-89, chmn., pres., CEO, 1989-94, pres., CEO, 1994-2000, chmn., CEO, 2000—; chmn. Cominco Ltd., Vancouver, 1986—. Named Mining Man of Yr. No. Miner, 1979. Mem. Can. Inst. Mining and Metallurgy (Selwyn G. Blaylock medal 1990, Inco medal 1999), Prospectors and Developers Assn. (Disting. Svc. award 1990, Viola R. MacMillan Developer's award 1997), Soc. Exploration Geophysicists, Vancouver Club, Shaughnessy Golf and Country Club (Vancouver). Office: Teck Corp 200 Burrard St # 700 Vancouver BC Canada V6C 3L9

KEGLEY, JACQUELYN ANN, philosophy educator; b. Conneaut, Ohio, July 18, 1938; d. Steven Paul and Gertrude Evelyn (Frank) Kovacevic; m. Charles William Kegley, June 12, 1964; children: Jacquelyn Ann, Stephen Lincoln Luther. BA cum laude, Allegheny Coll., 1960; MA summa cum laude, Rice U., 1964; PhD, Columbia U., 1971. Asst. prof. philosophy Calif. State U., Bakersfield, 1973-77, assoc. prof., 1977-81, prof., 1981—. Vis. prof. U. Philippines, Quezon City, 1966-68; grant project dir. Calif. Council Humanities, 1977, project dir. 1980, 82; mem. work group on ethics Am. Colls. of Nursing, Washington, 1984-86; mem. Am. Bd. Forensic Examiners; chair acad. senate Calif. State U., 2000—. Author: Introduction to Logic, 1978, Genuine Individuals and Genuine Communities, 1997; editor: Humanistic Delivery of Services to Families, 1982, Education for the Handicaped, 1981, Genetic Knowledge, 1998; mem. editl. bd. Jour. Philosophy in Lit., 1979-84; contbr. articles to profl. jours. Bd. dirs. Bakersfield Mental Health Assn., 1982-84, Citizens for Betterment of Community. Recipinet Outstanding Leadership award Calif. State U., 1997-98, Outstanding Prof. award Calif. State U., 1989-90, Golden Roadrunner award Bakersfield Community, 1991, Wang Family Excellence award, 2000. Mem. Philosophy of Sci. Assn., Soc. Advancement Am. Phil. soc. (chmn. Pacific div. 1979-83, nat. exec. com. 1974-79), Philosophy Soc., Soc. Interdisciplinary Study of Mind, Am. Philosophical Assn. (bd. mem. 1999—, chair com. on tchg.), Dorian Soc., Phi Beta Kappa. Democrat. Lutheran. Avocations: music, tennis. Home: 7312 Kroll Way Bakersfield CA 93309-2336 Office: Calif State U Dept Philosophy Bakersfield CA 93311

KEHOE, VINCENT JEFFRÉ-ROUX, photographer, author, cosmetic company executive; b. Bklyn., Sept. 12, 1921; s. John James and Bertha Florence (Roux) K.; m. Gena Irene Marino, Nov. 2, 1966. Student, MIT, 1940-41, Lowell Technol. Inst., 1941-42, Boston U., 1942; BFA in Motion Picture and TV Prodn., Columbia U., 1957. Dir. make-up dept. CBS-TV, N.Y.C., 1948-49, NBC Hallmark Hall of Fame series, 1951-53; make-up artist in charge of make-up numerous film, tv and stage prodns., 1942—; dir. make-up Turner Hall Corp., 1959-61, Internat. Beauty Show, 1962-66. Pres., dir. rsch. Rsch. Coun. Make-Up Artists, Inc., 1963—; chief press officer Spanish Pavilion N.Y. World's Fair, 1965; free-lance photographer, 1956—. Author: The Technique of Film and Television Make-Up for Color, 1970, The Make-Up Artist in the Beauty Salon, 1969, We Were There: April 19, 1775, 1974, A Military Guide, 1974, 2nd rev. edit., 1993, 3rd rev. edit., 1998-99, The Re-Created Officer's Guide, 5 vols., 1996-98, The Technique of the Professional Make-Up Artist, 1985, 2nd edit., 1995, Special Make-Up Effects, 1991, The British Story of the Battles of Lexington and Concord, 2000; author, photographer: (bullfighting book) Aficionado! (N.Y. Art Dirs. Club award 1960), Wine Women and Toros! (N.Y. Art Dirs. award 1962); prodr.: (documentary color film) Matador de Toros, 1959; contbr. photographs to numerous mags. including Time, Life, Sports Illustrated, Argosy, Popular Photography. Served with U.S. Army, WWII, ETO. Decorated Purple Heart, Bronze Star, CIB; recipient Torch award Coun. of 13 Original States, 1979. Fellow Co. Mil. Historians; mem. Tenth Foot Royal Lincolnshire Regimental Assn. (life; Hon. Col. 1968), Soc. Motion Picture and TV Engrs. (life), Acad. TV Arts and Scis., Soc. Army Hist. Rsch. (Eng., life), Brit. Officers Club New Eng. (life), Army Hist. Found. (life), 10th Mountain Divsn. Assn. (life), NRA (life), 70th Divsn. (life), DAV (life), Eagle Scout Assn. (life), Naval Club (London). Home and Office: PO Box 850 Somis CA 93066-0850

KEIL, KLAUS, geology educator, consultant; b. Hamburg, Germany, Nov. 15, 1934; s. Walter and Elsbeth K.; m. Rosemarie, Mar. 30, 1961; children: Kathrin R., Mark K.; m. Linde, Jan. 28, 1984. M.S., Schiller U., Jena, Germany, 1958; Ph.D., Gutenberg U., Mainz, Fed. Republic Germany, 1961. Rsch. assoc. Mineral. Inst., Jena, 1958-60, Max Planck-Inst. Chemistry, Mainz, 1961, U. Calif., San Diego, 1961-63; rsch. scientist Ames Rsch. Ctr. NASA, Moffett Field, Calif., 1963-68; prof. geology, dir. Inst. Meteoritics, U. N.Mex., Albuquerque, 1968-90; pres., prof. U. N.Mex., 1985-90, chmn. dept. of geology, 1986-89; prof. geology U. Hawaii, Honolulu, 1990—, rsch. prof., head planetary geoscis. div., 1990-93, dir. Hawaii Inst. Geophysics and Planetology, 1994—; cons. Sandia Labs., others. Contbr. over 600 articles to sci. jours. Recipient Apollo Achievement award NASA, 1970; recipient George P. Merrill medal Nat. Acad. Scis., 1970, Exceptional Sci. Achievement medal NASA, 1977, Regents Meritorious Service medal U. N.Mex., 1983, Leonard medal Meteoritical Soc., 1988, Zimmerman award U. N.Mex., 1988, numerous others Fellow Meteoritical Soc., AAAS, Mineral. Soc. Am., Am. Geophys. Union, German Mineral. Soc., others. Office: U Hawaii at Manoa Hawaii Inst Geophys & Planetology Honolulu HI 96822

KEIL, STEPHEN LESLEY, astrophysicist; b. Billings, Mont., Feb. 21, 1947; s. Nolan F. and Billy Lou (Benjamin) K.; m. Alice Ann Orient, June 18, 1972; children: Pamela Lynn, Wesley Forrester. BS in Physics, Univ. Calif., Berkeley, 1969; PhD in Astronomy, Boston U., 1975. Teaching fellow Boston (Mass.) Univ., 1969-74; postdoctoral fellow Univ. Colo., Sunspot, N.Mex., 1975-76; rsch. fellow, applied math. dept. Univ. Sydney, Australia, 1976-78; NRC fellow Sacramento Peak Obs., Sunspot, 1978-80, rsch. scientist, 1980-83; chief, solar rsch. USAF Solar Rsch. Br., Sunspot, 1983-99; dir. Nat. Solar Observatory, Sunspot, 1999—. Mem. Nat. Solar Obs. adv. com., Tucson, 1983-89, NSF Astronomy Survey com., Washington, 1990-91; prin. investigator USAF Solar Mass Ejection Imager, 1996-99; project dir. Advanced Tech. Solar Telescope, 2000—. Editor: (workshop proceedings) Small-Scale Dynamical Processes in Quiet Stellar Atmospheres, 1984; co-editor: (workshop proceedings) Solar Drivers of Interplanetary and Terrestrial Disturbances. Mayor Sacramento Peak Community, Sunspot, 1990-91, treas., 1981-87. Maj. USAF, 1980-85. Named Company Grade Officer of Yr., USAF, 1984, Officer of the Yr., Geophysics Lab., Boston, 1983. Mem. Internat. Astron. Union, Am. Astron. Soc., Am. Phys. Soc., Calif. Scholarship Fedn. (life). Achievements include first to make an accurate determination of the height variation of convective penetration in the solar atmosphere. Home: 3015 Corona Loop Sunspot NM 88349 Office: National Solar Observatory 1 Corona Loop Sunspot NM 88349 E-mail: skeil@sunspot.noao.edu

KEIM, MICHAEL RAY, dentist; b. Sabetha, Kans., June 8, 1951; s. Milton Leroy and Dorothy Juanita (Stover) K.; m. Christine Anne Lorenzen, Nov. 20, 1971; children: Michael Scott, Dawn Marie, Erik Alan. Student, U. Utah, 1969-72; DDS, Creighton U., 1976. Pvt. practice, Casper, Wyo., 1976—. Vertical math. com. mem. Natrona County Sch. Dist., 1997-2000. Mem. organizing bd. dirs. Ctrl. Wyo. Soccer Assn., 1976-77; mem. Casper Mountain Ski Patrol, Nat. Ski Patrol Sys., 1980-2000, Big Horn Ski Patrol, 2001—, avalanche and ski mountaineering advisor No. Divsn. Region III, 1992-96, outdoor emergency care instr. trainer, 1996-99, 1st asst. patrol dir., 1996-98, patrol dir., 1998-99; bd. dirs., dep. commr. for fast pitch Wyo. Amateur Softball Assn., 1980-84; bd. dirs. Ctrl. Wyo. Softball Assn., 1980-84; pres. Wyo. Spl. Smiles Found., 1995-96; mem. organizing com. Prevent Abuse & Neglect thru Dental Awareness Coalition, Wyo., 1996; mem. adv. com. Natrona County Headstart, 1985—. Recipient Purple Merit Star for Saving a Life, 1992. Fellow Acad. Gen. Dentistry; mem. ADA, Acad. Computerized Dentistry, Fedn. Dentaire Internat., Pierre Fauchard Acad., Wyo. Acad. Gen. Dentristry (sec.-treas. 1980-82, pres. 1982-87), Wyo. Dental Assn. (bd. dirs. 1992-97, chmn. conv. 1999—, ADA alt. del. 1994-95, v.p. 1993-94, pres.-elect 1994-95, pres. 1995-96, editor 1997—), Wyo. Dental Polit. Action Com. (sec.-treas. 1985-97), Ctrl. Wyo. Dental Assn. (sec.-treas. 1981-82, pres. 1982-83), Wyo. Dental Hist. Assn. (bd. dirs. 1989-95), Wyo. Donated Dental Svcs. (organizing bd. dirs. 1994, pres. 1995-96), Kiwanis (v.p. Casper club 1988-89, bd. dirs. 1986-96, pres.-elect 1989-90, pres. 1990-91, internat. del. 1989-91, chmn. internat. rels. com. 1992-99, Rocky Mountain dist. lt. gov.-elect divsn. 1 1997-98, lt. gov. divsn. I 1998-99), Creighton Club (pres. 1982-84). Methodist. Avocations: hunting, skiing, sports, woodworking, photography. Home: 58 Jonquil St Casper WY 82604-3863 Office: 1749 S Boxelder St Casper WY 82604-3538

KEIM, WAYNE FRANKLIN, retired genetics educator, plant geneticist; b. Ithaca, N.Y., May 14, 1923; s. Franklin David and Alice Mary (Voigt) K.; m. Ellen Joyce Neumann, Sept. 6, 1947; children: Kathryn Louise Keim Logsdon, David Wayne, Julie Anne Keim Hughes. BS with distinction, U. Nebr., 1947; MS, Cornell U., 1949, PhD, 1952. Instr., then asst. prof. Iowa State U., Ames, 1952-56; from asst. prof. to prof. Purdue U., West Lafayette, Ind., 1956-75; vis. prof., NSF sci. faculty fellow U. Lund, (Sweden), 1962-63; vis. prof. Colo. State U., Fort Collins, 1971-72, prof. dept. agronomy, 1975-92, chmn. dept., 1975-85. Recipient Best Tchr. award Sch. Agr., Purdue U., 1965, 68 Fellow AAAS, Am. Soc. Agronomy (Agronomic Edn. award 1971, Agronomic Svc. award 1991), Crop Sci. Soc. Am. (pres. 1983-84); mem. Am. Inst. Biol. Sci., Agronomic Sci. Found. (trustee). Home: 1441 Meeker Dr Fort Collins CO 80524-4311 Office: Colo State U Dept Soil Crop Scis Fort Collins CO 80523-0001

KEIR, GERALD JANES, banker; b. Ludlow, Mass., Aug. 22, 1943; s. Alexander J. and Evelyn M. (Buckley) K.; m. Karen Mary Devine, July 22, 1972; children: Matthew J., Katherine B., Megan E. BA, Mich. State U., 1964, MA, 1966. Reporter Honolulu Advertiser, 1968-74, city editor, 1974-86, mng. editor, 1986-89, editor, 1989-95; exec. v.p. corp. comms. First Hawaiian Bank, Honolulu, 1995—. Co-author text: Advanced Reporting: Beyond News Events, 1985, Advanced Reporting: Discovering Patterns in News Events, 1997. Bd. govs. Hawaii Cmty. Found.; mem. adv. bd. Salvation Army Honolulu. Recipient Nat. Reporting award Am. Polit. Sci. Assn., 1971, Benjamin Fine Nat. award Am. Assn. Secondary Sch. Prins., 1981; John Ben Snow fellow, 1983, NEH fellow, 1973. Mem. Social Sci. Assn., Am. Bankers Assn. (comm. coun.), Pub. Rels. Soc. Am., Honolulu Cmty.-Media Coun., Fin. Svcs. Roundtable Pub. Affairs Coun. Office: First Hawaiian Bank PO Box 3200 Honolulu HI 96847-0001 E-mail: gerry.keir@fhwn.com

KEITH, BRUCE EDGAR, political analyst, genealogist; b. Curtis, Nebr., Feb. 17, 1918; s. Edgar L. and Corinne E. (Marsteller) K.; m. Evelyn E. Johnston, Oct. 29, 1944; children: Mona Louise, Kent Marsteller, Melanie Ann. AB with high distinction, Nebr. Wesleyan U., 1940; MA, Stanford U., 1952; grad. Command and Staff, Marine Corps Schs., 1958, Sr. Resident Sch., Naval War Coll., 1962; PhD, U. Calif.-Berkeley, 1982. Commd. 2d lt. U.S. Marine Corps, 1942, advanced through grades to col., 1962, ret., 1971, OinC Marine Corps Nat. Media, N.Y.C., 1946-49, support arms coord. 1st Marines, Seoul, Chosin, Korea, 1950, comdg. officer 3d Bn., 11th Marines, 1958-59, ops. officer, Pres. Dwight D. Eisenhower visit to Okinawa, 1960, G-3 ops. officer Fleet Marine Force, Pacific, Cuban Missile Crisis, 1962, mem. U.S. del. SEATO, Planning Conf., Bangkok, Thailand, 1964, G-3, Fleet Marine Force, Pacific, 1964-65, head Strategic Planning Study Dept., Naval War Coll., 1966-68, genealogist, 1967—, exec. officer Hdqrs. Marine Corps programs, Washington, 1968-71; election analyst Inst. Govtl. Studies, U. Calif.-Berkeley, 1974-86, polit. analyst, 1986—; teaching asst. U. Calif.-Berkeley, 1973-74. Bd. dirs., Bay Area Funeral Soc., 1980-83, v.p., 1981-83. Decorated Bronze Star, Navy Commendation medal, Presdl. Unit citation with 3 bronze stars. Recipient Phi Kappa Phi Silver medal Nebr. Wesleyan U., 1940, Alumni award, 1964. Mem. Am. Polit. Sci. Assn., Acad. Polit. Sci., Am. Acad. Polit. and Social Sci., World Affairs Coun. No. Calif., Marine Corps Assn., Ret. Officers Assn. Phi Kappa Phi, Pi Gamma Mu. Republican. Unitarian. Clubs: Commonwealth of Calif. (San Francisco), Marines' Meml. (San Francisco). Lodge: Masons. Contbg. author: The Descendants of Daniel and Elizabeth (Disbrow) Keith, 1979-81; History of Curtis, Nebraska-The First Hundred Years, 1984; author: A Comparison of the House Armed Services Coms. in the 91st and 94th Congresses: How They Differed and Why, 1982; The Johnstons of Morning Sun, 1979; The Marstellers of Arrellton, 1978; The Morris Family of Brookville, 1977; Japan-the Key to America's Future in the Far East, 1962; A United States General Staff: A Must or a Monster?, 1950; co-author: California Votes, 1960-72, 1974; The Myth of the Independent Voter, 1992; Further Evidence on the Partisan Affinities of Independent " Leaners," 1983. Address: PO Box 2368 Walnut Creek CA 94595-0368

KELEN, JOYCE ARLENE, social worker; b. N.Y.C., Dec. 5, 1949; d. Samuel and Rebecca (Rochman) Green; m. Leslie George Kelen, Jan. 31, 1971; children: David, Jonathan. BA, Lehman Coll., 1970; MSW, Univ. Utah, 1974, DSW, 1980. Recreation dir. N.Y.C. Housing Authority, Bronx, 1970-72; cottage supr. Kennedy Home, Bronx, 1974; sch. social worker Davis County Sch. Dist., Farmington, Utah, 1976-86; clin. asst. prof. U. Utah., Salt Lake City, 1976—; sch. social worker Salt Lake City Sch. Dist., 1986—. Cons. in field, Salt Lake City, 1981—. Editor: To Whom Are We Beautiful As We Go?, 1979; contbr. articles to profl. jours. Utah Coll. of Nursing grantee, 1985. Mem. Nat. Assn. Social Workers (chairperson Gerontology Council, 1983-84, Utah Sch. Social Worker of Yr., 1977), NEA, Utah Edn. Assn., Davis Edn. Assn. Democrat. Jewish. Avocations: tennis, camping, guitar. Home: 128 M St Salt Lake City UT 84103-3854 Office: Rose Park Elem Sch 1105 W 10th North St Salt Lake City UT 84116

KELLEHER, RICHARD CORNELIUS, marketing and communications executive; b. Buffalo, Nov. 21, 1949; s. Cornelius and Lucile Norma (White) K.; m. Sherri Fae Anderson, Mar. 17, 1981 (div. 1991); children: Erin Marie, Shawn Michael. BA, U. New Mex., 1975; MBA, U. Phoenix, 1984. Reporter, photographer Daily Lobo, Albuquerque, 1973-75; mgn. editor News Bulletin, Belen, New Mex., 1975-77; various corp. mktg. titles AT&T Mountain Bell, Denver, 1978-84; exec. editor Dairy Mag., Denver, 1984-86; communications dir. Am. Heart Assn., Phoenix, 1987-90; cons. Kelleher Communications & Mktg., Phoenix, 1990—. Spl. writer Denver Post, 1977-82, Denver Corr. Billboard Mag., 1977-82. Mem. Gov.'s Roundtable on Employee Productivity, Gov. of Ariz., 1990-91; vol. communications Am. Cancer Soc., 1990-92. Recipient Harvey Communications Study award, 1986. Mem. Pub. Rels. Soc. Am., Toastmasters.

KELLEHER, ROBERT JOSEPH, federal judge; b. N.Y.C., Mar. 5, 1913; s. Frank and Mary (Donovan) K.; m. Gracyn W. Wheeler, Aug. 14, 1940; children: R. Jeffrey, Karen Kathleen Kelleher King. A.B., Williams Coll., 1935; LL.B., Harvard U., 1938. Bar: N.Y. 1939, Calif. 1942, U.S. Supreme Ct 1954. Atty. War Dept., 1941-42; asst. U.S. atty. So. Dist. Calif., 1948-50; pvt. practice Beverly Hills, 1951-71; U.S. dist. judge, 1971-83; sr. judge U.S. Dist. Ct. 9th Cir., 1983—. Mem. So. Calif. Com. Olympic Games, 1964; capt. U.S. Davis Cup Team, 1962-63; treas. Youth Tennis Found. So. Calif., 1961-64. Served to lt. USNR, 1942-45. Recipient Bicentennial Medal award Williams Coll., 2001; enshrined in Internat. Tennis Hall of Fame, 2000. Mem. So. Calif. Tennis Assn. (v.p. 1958-64, pres. 1983-85), U.S. Lawn Tennis Assn. (pres. 1967-68), Internat. Lawn Tennis Club U.S.A., Gt. Britain, France, Can., Mex., Australia, India, Israel, Japan, All Eng. Lawn Tennis and Croquet (Wimbledon), Harvard Club (N.Y./So. Calif.), Williams Club (N.Y.), L.A. Country Club, Delta Kappa Epsilon. Home: 15 St Malo Bch Oceanside CA 92054-5854 Office: US Dist Ct 255 E Temple St Ste 830 Los Angeles CA 90012-3334

KELLER, EDWARD LOWELL, electrical engineer, educator; b. Rapid City, S.D., Mar. 6, 1939; s. Earl Lowell and E. Blanche (Oldfield) K.; m. Carole Lynne Craig, Sept. 1, 1963; children: Edward Lowell, Craig, Morgan. BS, U.S. Naval Acad., 1961; PhD, Johns Hopkins U., 1971. Mem. faculty U. Calif., Berkeley, 1971—, assoc. prof. elec. engring., 1977-79, prof., 1979-94, prof. emeritus, 1994—; assoc. dir. Smith Kettlewell Eye Rsch. Inst., San Francisco, 1998—; chmn. bioengring. program U. Calif., Berkeley and San Francisco, 1989; chmn. engring. sci. program Coll. of Engring. U. C., Berkeley, 1991-94. Contbr. articles to sci. jours. Served with USN, 1961-65. Sr. Von Humboldt fellow, 1977-78 Fellow IEEE; mem. AAAS, Assn. for Rsch. in Vision and Ophthalmology, Soc. for Neurosci., Internat. Neural Network Soc. Achievements include rsch. on oculomotor system and math. modelling of nervous system. Office: Smith-Kettlewell Eye Rsch Inst 2318 Fillmore St San Francisco CA 94115-1813 E-mail: elk@ski.org

KELLER, GLEN ELVEN, JR. lawyer; b. Longmont, Colo., Dec. 21, 1938; s. Glenn Elven and Elsie Mildred (Hogsett) K.; m. Elizabeth Ann Kauffman, Aug. 14, 1960; children: Patricia Carol, Michael Ashby. BS in Bus., U. Colo., 1960; JD, U. Denver, 1964. Bar: Colo. 1964, U.S. Dist. Ct. Colo. 1964, U.S. Ct. Appeals (10th cir.) 1982. Assoc. Phelps, Hall & Keller and predecessor, Denver, 1964-67, ptnr., 1967-73; asst. atty. gen. State of Colo., Denver, 1973-74; judge U.S. Bankruptcy Ct., Dist. Colo., 1974-82; ptnr. Davis, Graham & Stubbs LLP, Denver, 1982—. Lectr. law U. Denver, 1977-87; adj. prof., 1987-98, Frank E. Rickston Jr. adj. prof. law, 1998—; mem. ct. adminstrn. com. Jud. Conf. U.S.; dir., mem. fin. com. sch. constrn. Colo. Lawyers' Com., 1997-2000, dir., mem. exec. com., 1999-2000, chmn. task force on sch. discipline, 1999-2000; bd. dirs. Western Stock Show Assoc. Mem. Colo. Bd. Health, 1968-74, pres., 1970-74; pres., dir. The Westernaires, Golden, Colo., Jefferson County R-1 Sch. Bd., 1984-89. Named Colo. Horse Person of Yr., Colo. Horse Coun., 1999. Fellow Am. Coll. Bankruptcy; mem ABA, Colo. Bar Assn., Denver Bar Assn., Nat. Conf. Bankruptcy Judges, Law Club. Republican. Office: Davis Graham & Stubbs LLP 1550 17th St Ste 500 Denver CO 80202-1202

KELLER, HERBERT BISHOP, mathematics educator; b. Paterson, N.J., June 19, 1925; BEE, Ga. Inst. Tech., 1945; MA, NYU, 1948, PhD in Math., 1954. Instr. physics & math. Ga. Inst. Tech., 1946-47; rsch. scientist divsn. electromagnetic rsch. Inst. Math Sci., NYU, 1948-53; head dept. math. Sarah Lawrence Coll., 1951-53; lectr. math. Washington Sq. Coll., 1957-59; assoc. prof. NYU, 1959-61; prof. applied math. Courant Inst., 1961-67, assoc. dir. AEC Computer & Appl. Math. Ctr., 1964-67; prof. appl. math. Calif. Inst. Tech., 1967—. Vis. prof. Calif. Inst. Tech., 1965-66; mem. math. divsn. Nat. Rsch. Coun., 1969-72; mem. coun. Conf. Bd. Math. Sci., 1971-73; dist. vis. fellow Christ's Coll., Cambridge, 1993-94; cons. various industry & govt. concerns. Assoc. editor: (jour.) Jour. Appl. Math., Soc. Indsl. & Appl. Math., 1961-66, Jour. Computer & Systems Science, 1971-74; editor: Jour. Computer & Systems Science, 1974—, Japan Jour. Appl. Math., 1984—, Monogr. Ser. Assn. Computing Machinery, 1963-65, Jour. Numerical Analysis, 1964-71, Jour. Numerical Math., 1981—. Recipient, Theodore von Kármán Prize, Soc. of Industrial and Applied Mathematics, 1994; Guggenheim fellow, 1979-80. Fellow AAAS; mem. Am. Math. Soc., Math. Assn. Am., Soc. Indsl. & Applied Math. (pres. 1975-76), Assn. Computing Machinery. Office: Calif Inst Tech Dept Applied Math 1201 E California Blvd Pasadena CA 91125-0001 E-mail: hbk@caltech.edu

KELLER, JACK, agricultural engineering educator, consultant; b. Roanoke, Va., Jan. 5, 1928; s. Eugene and Clara (Lauber) K.; m. Sara Altick, June 4, 1954; children: Andrew A., Jeffery S., Judith. BSCE, U. Colo., 1953; MS in Irrigation Engring., Colo. State U., 1955; PhD in Agrl. Engring., Utah State U., 1967. Registered profl. engr., Utah, Calif. Work unit engr. USDA Soil Conservation Svc., Victor, Colo., 1953; sales engr. So. Irrigation Co., Memphis, 1955-56; chief irrigation engr. W.R. Ames Co., San Jose, Calif., 1956-60; prof. Utah State U., Logan, 1960-88, dept. chmn., 1979-85, project mgr., 1978-88; pres., founder Keller-Bliesner Engring. Co., Logan, 1962—, CEO, 1989—. Co-dir. U.S. AID Water Mgmt. Synthesis Project, Logan, 1978-88, team leader tech. assistance teams, worldwide, 1980-98; chmn. Conservation Verification Cons. for the IID/MWD Conservation Agreement, Imperial, Calif., 1992—; sr. policy advisor to Egyptian Ministry Pub. Works and Water Resources for U.S. AID's WRSR Activity, 1995-98; sr. rsch. assoc. Internat. Water Mgmt. Inst., 1995-2000; sr. adv. agrl. water use efficiency program CAL FED, 1999—; sr. irrigation policy advisor, bd. dirs. Internat. Devel. Enterprises, 2000—. Co-author: Trickle Irrigation Design, 1974, Sprinkle and Trickle Irrigation, 1990; contbr. articles to profl. jours.; patentee in field. NRC Com. Soil and Water Rsch. Priorities for Devel. Countries, Washington, 1990-91; Water Resources Rsch., Washington, 1988; chmn. Red River Chloride Control Panel, Tulsa, 1988. With USN, 1945-47, PTO; sgt. USAF, 1951-53. Named Engr. of Yr. Utah Joint Engring. Coun., Salt Lake City, 1988. Fellow ASCE, Am. Soc. Agrl. Engrs.; mem. NAE, Internat. Commn. Irrigation and Drainage, The Irrigation Assn. (Man of Yr. 1972). Mem. Bahai Ch. Avocations: bicycling, hiking, gardening, fishing. Home: 35 River Park Dr Logan UT 84321-4345 Office: Keller-Bliesner Engring 78 E Center St Logan UT 84321-4619

KELLER, JOHN FRANCIS, retired wine company executive, mayor; b. Mt. Horeb, Wis., Feb. 5, 1925; s. Frank S. and Elizabeth K. (Meier) K.; m. Barbara D. Mabbott, Feb. 18, 1950; children: Thomas, Patricia, Daniel, David, John. BBA in Acctg., U. Wis., 1949; MBA, U. Chgo., 1963; grad., Stanford U., 1978. CPA, Wis., Ill. Acct. Bank of Am., 1949-51; mgr. statis. control and gen. accounting Miller Brewing Co., Milw., 1952-58; contr. Maremont Corp., 1958-68; with Heublein, Inc., 1968-84; v.p. fin. Hamm's Brewing Co., 1968-70; v.p. fin., dir. United Vintners, Inc., San Francisco, 1970-80, chmn. bd., CEO, dir., 1980-84; group v.p. Heublein Wines Group, 1980-84; pres. ISC Wines of Calif., 1983-85; adminstrv. dir. Winegrowers of Calif. (a Calif. state mktg. order for wineries and grape growers), 1985-87; mgmt. cons. J.F. Keller & Assocs., 1988-2000. Lectr., assoc. prof. Calif. State U./Hayward Grad. Sch. Bus. and Econs., 1978-82; adj. prof. Golden Gate U. Grad. Sch. Bus., 1983-86, lectr., instr. Coll. San Mateo, 1990; bd. dirs. Servicor, Inc., Duckhorn Vineyards, Fife and Horn Vineyards. Councilman City of Hillsborough, Calif., 1982-91, mayor, 1988-90; active Boy Scouts Am., 1952-58, Cmty. Chest; mem. parish coun. St. Lamberts Cath. Ch., 1966-68; pres. parish coun. St. Bartholomew Cath. Ch., 1980; dir. Serra H.S. Bd., 1979-82; bd. dirs. U. Wis. Found., 1986-92, Seton Health Scis. Found., 1988—, chmn., 1994-96; bd. dirs. Seton Med. Ctr., 1989-94, sec.-treas., 1992-94; Cath. Health Care West, 1995—, fin. and investment com.; bd. dirs., pres. Alemany Scholarship Found., 1983-95; bd. dirs. Peace and Justice Task Force Commn., 1986-92; mem. Pastoral Planning Commn., 1994-95; trustee St. Patrick's Sem., 1994—, investment advisor, 1990—, Archdiocese of San Francisco; dir. St. Vincent de Paul-San Mateo County, 1997—; bd. dirs. Big Bros., San Francisco, 1971-75, Hill High St., St. Paul, 1969-70, Lesley Found., 1983-85, St. Vincent de Paul Soc., San Mateo County, Cath. Healthcare West, San Francisco Bay area, Seton Health Sererive Found., Daly City, Calif., St. Patrick's Seminary, Menlo Park, Calif.,; vol. exec. Internat. Exec. Svc. Corp., 1995-2000. 2d lt. 82d Airborne divsn. AUS, 1944-46, ETO; with USAR, 1946-52. Named to Equestrian Order of the Holy Sepulchre of Jerusalem, 1990, Knight of Grand Cross, Knight of Magistral Grace, 1989; recipient Disting. Bus. Alumnus award U. Wis. Sch. Bus., 1990. Mem. AICPA, Fin. Execs. Inst., Wis. Soc. CPAs, Calif. Soc. CPAs, Nat. Assn. Accts., VFW, American Legion, JUnipero Serra Internat. (pres. 1992-94), Commonwealth Club, World Trade Club, Peninsula Golf and Country Club, Phi Kappa Alpha (past treas., bd. dirs.). Home and Office: 785 Tournament Dr Hillsborough CA 94010-7423 E-mail: jfkeller785@msn.com

KELLER, JOSEPH BISHOP, mathematician, educator; b. Paterson, N.J., July 31, 1923; s. Isaac and Sally (Bishop) K.; m. Evelyn Fox, Aug. 29, 1963 (div. Nov. 17, 1976); children— Jeffrey M., Sarah N. BA, NYU, 1943, MS, 1946, PhD, 1948. Prof. math. Courant Inst. Math. Scis., NYU, 1948-79; chmn. dept. math. Univ. Coll. Arts and Scis. and Grad. Sch. Engring. and Sci., 1967-73; prof. math. and mech. engring. Stanford U., 1979—. Hon. prof. math. scis. Cambridge U., 1990—; rsch. assoc. Woods Hole Oceanographic Instn., 1965—; Gibbs lectr. Am. Math. Soc., 1977; von Neumann lectr. Soc. Indsl. and Applied Math., 1983; Rouse Ball lectr. U. Cambridge, Eng., 1993. Contbr. articles to profl. jours. Recipient von Karman prize Soc. Indsl. and Applied Math., 1979, Eringen medal Soc. Engring. Scis., 1981, Timoshenko medal ASME, 1984, U.S. Nat. Medal of Sci., 1988, NAS award in Applied Mathematics and Numerical Analysis, 1995, Frederic Esser Nemmers prize in math. Northwestern U., Evanston, Ill., 1996, Wolf prize, Israel, 1997. Mem. NAS, Royal Soc. (fgn.), Am. Acad. Arts and Scis., Am. Math. Soc., Am. Phys. Soc., Soc. Indsl. and Applied Math. Home: 820 Sonoma Ter Stanford CA 94305-1072 Office: Stanford U Dept Math Stanford CA 94305-2125

KELLER, LARRY ALAN, water transportation executive; b. San Pedro, Calif., Mar. 2, 1945; married; 3 children. BA in Anthropology, San Francisco State U. Various mgmt. positions Maersk Inc; COO Port of L.A., 1996-97, exec. dir., 1997—. Bd. dirs. Alameda Corridor Transp. Authority. Mem. Am. Assn. Port Authorities (bd. dirs.), Calif. Assn. Port Authorities (pres., 2001-02, bd. dirs.), Steamship Assn. So. Calif. (past sec.-treas., v.p., pres., chmn.), L.A. Area C. of C. (bd. dirs.), Alameda Corridor Transp. Authority (bd. dirs.), Danish-Am. C. of C., Internat. Assn. Ports and Harbors (bd. dirs.), Harbor Assn. Industry and Commerce (bd. dirs.). Office: Harbor Dept Port of Los Angeles 425 S Palos Verdes St San Pedro CA 90731-3309

KELLER, MICHAEL ALAN, librarian, educator, musicologist; b. Sterling, Colo., Apr. 5, 1945; s. Ephraim Richard and Mary Patricia (Warren) K.; m. Constance A. Kyle, Sept. 3, 1967 (div. Aug. 1979); children: Kristen J., Paul B.; m. Carol Lawrence, Oct. 6, 1979; children: Laura W., Martha M. BA, Hamilton Coll., 1967; MA, SUNY, Buffalo, 1970, postgrad., 1970-91; MLS, SUNY, Geneseo, 1972. Asst. libr. for reference and cataloging SUNY Music Libr., Buffalo, 1970-73; acting undergrad. libr. Cornell U., Ithaca, N.Y., 1976, music libr., sr. lectr., 1973-81; head music libr. U. Calif., Berkeley, 1981-86; assoc. univ. libr. for collection devel. Yale U., 1986-93; director Stanford (Calif.) U. Librs., 1993-94, univ. libr., dir. acad. info. resources, 1994—; pub. HighWire Press, Stanford, 1995—, Stanford U. Press, 2000—. Cons. numerous orgs.; mem. Nat. Digital Libr. Fedn., 1993—, Bibliog Commn., Repertoire Internat. de la Presse Mus. de XIXve Siecle, 1981—84; chmn. music program com. Rsch. Librs. Group, 1982—86; reviewer NEH, 1982—88, panelist, 1979—95; chmn. Assoc. Music Librs. Group, Joint Com. Retrospective Conversion in Music, 1989—93; mem. collection mgmt. devel. com. Rsch. Librs. Group, 1986—91, chmn., 1989—91, mem. program adv. com., 1991—93; dir. Berkeley Italian Renaissance Project, 1985—95, Digital Libr. Fedn., 1994—; mem. bd. overseers Stanford U., 1997—; mem. gov. com. Stanford-Japan Ctr. Rsch.; mem. adv. bd. Ebrary, Inc., 1999—; bd. dirs. Alibris Inc., 1999—; mem. adv. bd. 4Digital Books, AG, 2001—; mem. bd. trustees Hamilton Coll., 2001—; mem. info. tech. adv. group New Libr. of Alexandria, Egypt, 2001—. Author: MSS on Microfilm in Music Libr. at SUNYAB, 1971, (with Duckles) Music Reference and Rsch. Materials; an annotated bibliography, 1988, 94; contbr. articles to profl. jours. Firefighter, rescue squad mem. Cuyuga Heights Vol. Fire Co., N.Y., 1980-81; bd. dirs. Long Now Found., 1998—; bd. trustees, Hamilton Coll., 2001—. Recipient spl. commendation Nat. Music Clubs, 1978, Berkeley Bronze medal U. Calif.-Berkeley, 1983, Deems Taylor award ASCAP, 1988; NDEA Title IV fellow SUNY-Buffalo, 1967-70, Pierson Coll., Yale U., Stanford U., 1994-95, World Econ. Forum, 2000; Cornell Coll. Arts and Scis. rsch. grantee, 1973-81, U. Calif.-Berkeley humanities rsch. grantee, 1983-84, Coun. on Libr. Resources grantee, 1984, 93-99, Libr. Assn. U. Calif. grantee, 1985-86, NEH grantee, 1986; recipient various grants NSF, 1999—, State Libr. Calif., Mellon Found. Mem. ALA, AAUP, Music Libr. Assn. (bd. dirs. 1975-77, mem. fin. com. 1982-83, mem. editl. com. index and bibliography series 1981-85), Internat. Assn. Music Librs., Am. Musicol. Soc. (mem. com. on automated bibliography 1982-83, mem. coun. 1986-88), Conn. Acad. Arts and Scis. (bd. dirs.), Ctr. Rsch. Librs. (mem. adv. com. 1988-90), Conn. Ctr. for Books (bd. dirs.), Book Club of Calif., Roxburghe Club of San Francisco, Bohemian Club, San Francisco. Home: 809 San Francisco Ter Stanford CA 94305-1070 Office: Stanford U Cecil Green Libr Stanford CA 94305-6004 E-mail: michael.keller@stanford.edu

KELLER, PETER CHARLES, museum director, mineralogist; b. Allentown, Pa., Aug. 16, 1947; s. Charles Donald and Barbara Jean (Miller) K.; children: Bret Charles, Elizabeth Austin. BA, George Washington U., 1972; MA, U. Tex., 1974, PhD, 1977. Grad. gemologist, 1980. Curator mineralogy L.A. County Mus., Los Angeles, 1976-80; dir. edn. Gemological Inst. Am., Santa Monica, Calif., 1980-84; lectr. geology U. So. Calif., L.A., 1980-87; assoc. dirs. L.A. County Mus. Natural History, 1987-91; exec. dir. Bowers Mus. of Cultural Art, Santa Ana, Calif., 1991—. Assoc. editor: Gems and Gemology, 1980-91; contbr. articles in field to profl. jours. Trustee, Natural History Mus. Found., 1980-84; treas. Mineral Mus. Adv. Council, 1984. Fellow Leakey Found., Explorers Club; mem. Internat. Commn. Mus., Am. Assn. Mus., Mineral. Soc. Am., Gemol. Assn. Gt. Britain, Internat. Mineral. Assn. (U.S. rep. for mus.), Geol. Soc. Am., Mineral. Soc. Gt. Britain, Sigma Xi, Phi Kappa Phi. Office: Bowers Mus Cultural Art 2002 N Main St Santa Ana CA 92706-2731

KELLER, RICHARD ALLEN, chemist; b. Pitts., Nov. 28, 1934; BS, Allegheny Coll., 1956; PhD in Phys. Chemistry, U. Calif., Berkeley, 1961. Asst. prof. chemistry U. Oreg., Eugene, 1959-63; staff mem. Divsn. Phys. Chemistry Nat. Bur. Stds., 1963-76; staff mem. chemistry Los Alamos (N.Mex.) Nat. Labs., 1976—, fellow, 1983—. Recipient Lester W. Strock award Soc. for Applied Spectroscopy, 1996, ACS divsn. of analytical chemistry award for Spectrochemical Analysis, 1993. Mem. Am. Chem. Soc., Soc. of Flourescence. Office: Los Alamos Nat Lab Biosci Divsn Ms M888 Los Alamos NM 87545-0001

KELLER, WILLIAM D. federal judge; b. 1934; BS, U. Calif., Berkeley, 1956; LLB, UCLA, 1960. Asst. U.S. atty. U.S. Dist. Ct. (so. dist.) Calif., 1961-64; assoc. Dryden, Harrington, Horgan & Swartz, Calif., 1964-72; U.S. atty. U.S. Dist. Ct. (cen. dist.) Calif., Los Angeles, 1972-77; ptnr. Rosenfeld, Meyer & Susman, 1977-78; solo practice, 1978-81; ptnr. Mahm & Cazier, 1981-84; judge U.S. Dist. Ct. (cen. dist.) Calif., Los Angeles, 1984—; sr. judge L.A., 1999—; ptnr. Rosenfeld, Meyer & Susman, Calif., 1977-78; pvt. practice law, 1978-81; ptnr. Hahn & Cazier, 1981-84. Office: US Dist Ct 312 N Spring St Ste 1653 Los Angeles CA 90012-4718

KELLEY, DAVID E. producer, writer; b. 1956; m. Michelle Pfeiffer, 1993; 2 children. BA, Princeton U., 1979; JD, Boston U., 1983. CEO David E. Kelley Prodns., Inc., L.A. Writer (film) From the Hip, 1987; writer, prodr. (film) To Gillian on Her 37th Birthday, 1996; writer, prodr. (film) Lake Placid, 1999, Mystery, Alaska, 1999; writer, story editor, exec. story editor, supervising prodr., exec. prodr. L.A. Law (Emmy award for Outstanding Drama Series 1989, 90, Emmy award for outstanding writing in a dram series 1990); writer, exec. prodr. Picket Fences (Emmy award for outstanding drama series 1993, 94), Chicago Hope, 1994-2000, The Practice, 1997— (Golden Globe award for best tv drama 1998, Emmy award for outstanding drama series, 1998, 99), Ally McBeal, 1997— (Golden Globe winner, Emmy award for best tv series-musical or comedy 1997, 98, Emmy award for outstanding comedy series 1999), Snoops, 1999-2000, Boston Public, 2000—. Office: David E Kelly Prodns care 20th Century Fox 10201 W Pico Blvd Bldg 80 Los Angeles CA 90064-2606

KELLEY, DAVID G. state senator; b. Riverside County, Calif. m. Brigitte Kelley; 4 children. Grad., Calif. State Poly. U., San Luis Obispo. Served with USAF, Korea. With Peace Corps, India, 1968, 70-71; citrus rancher Hemet area, Calif.; mem. Calif. Assembly, 1978-92, Calif. State Senate, 1992—, vice chmn. agr. and water resources com., chmn. select com. on So. Claif. Water Dists. Active Riverside County Farm Bur., 1955—, pat v.p. and pres.; bd. dirs. Calif. Farm Bur. Fedn.; bd. dirs. Hemet-San Jacinto Basin Resource Conservation Dist. Mem. Western Growers Assn., Farm Bur., Century Club of Riverside County (past pres.), Hemet-San Jacinto Noon Exch. Club, Lincoln Club of Coachella Valley. Republican. Lutheran. Office: State Capitol Rm 3082 Sacramento CA 95814 also: 11440 W Bernardo Ct Ste 104 San Diego CA 92127-1642

KELLEY, DAVID M. mechanical engineer, educator; BS in Elec. Engring., Carnegie Mellon U., 1973; MS in Product Design, Stanford U., 1978. Elec. engring. Boeing, Nat. Cash Register; assoc. prof. mech. engring. Stanford (Calif.) U., 1978—; founder IDEO Product Devel., Palo Alto, Calif., 1978—, Onset, 1984—. Named one of 100 Most Powerful Men in Silicon Valley, San Jose Mercury News, one of 21 Most Important People of the 21st Century, Esquire mag. Mem. ASME, IEEE, NAE, Indsl. Designers Soc. Am. Office: Stanford U Dept Mech Engring Bldg 530 Stanford CA 94305-3030 E-mail: dkelley@ideo.com

KELLEY, HAROLD HARDING, psychology educator; b. Boise, Idaho, Feb. 16, 1921; s. Harry H. and Maude M. Kelley; m. Dorothy J. Drumm, Jan. 4, 1942; children: Ann R., Harold S., Laura Megan. AB, U. Calif., Berkeley, 1942, MA, 1943; PhD, MIT, 1948. Study dir. in group dynamics U. Mich., Ann Arbor, 1948-50; asst. prof. psychology Yale U., New Haven, 1950-55; asso. prof., then prof. U. Minn., Mpls., 1955-61; prof. psychology UCLA, 1961-91, prof. emeritus, 1991—. Author: (with C.I. Hovland & I.L. Janis) Communication and Persuasion, 1953, (with J.W. Thibaut) The Social Psychology of Groups, 1959, Interpersonal Relations, 1978, (with others) Attribution: Perceiving the Causes of Behavior, 1972, Personal Relationships, 1979, (with others) Close Relationships, 1983. Served with USAAF, 1943-46. Center for Advanced Study in Behavioral Sci. fellow, 1956-57; Am. Psychol. Soc. William James fellow. Fellow Nat. Acad. Scis., Am. Acad. Arts and Scis., APA (pres. personality and social psychology div. 1965-66, Disting. Sci. Contbn. award 1971, Kurt Lewin Meml. award 1990), Am. Sociol. Assn. (Cooley-Mead award 1999). Home: 21634 Rambla Vis Malibu CA 90265-5126 Office: U Calif Dept Psychology Los Angeles CA 90095-0001 E-mail: hal@ucla.edu

KELLEY, JOHN F. airline executive; Chmn., pres., CEO Alaska Air Group, Seattle. Office: Alaska Air Group PO Box 68900 Seattle WA 98168-0900

KELLEY, LEE, publishing executive; V.p., exec. pub. Motor Trend, L.A. Office: McMullen-Argus Pub Inc Ste 1100 2400 E Katella Ave Anaheim CA 92806 also: Automobile Mag k-111 Mags Publication 575 Lexington Ave 24th Fl New York NY 10022

KELLEY, LUCILLE MARIE KINDELY, dean, psychosocial nurse; b. Bridgeport, Conn., May 18, 1944; m. Robert Kelley, 1968; children: Ryan Patrick, Megan Maura. Diploma, St. Vincent Hosp., Bridgeport, 1965; BSN, U. Conn., 1969; MNursing, U. Wash., 1973, PhD, 1990. Assoc. prof., RNB program dir. Seattle Pacific U., 1985-99, dean Sch. Health Scis., 1998—. Sr. cons. healthcare The Effectiveness Inst., Redmond, Wash., 1984-99. Pres. Nat. Coun. Cmty. Mental Health Ctrs., 1983-84. Recipient Disting. Svc. award Eastside Mental Health, 1987, Tchg. award Burlington No., 1993. Mem. Sigma Theta Tau. Home: 14115 SE 46th St Bellevue WA 98006-3045 Office: Seattle Pacific U Sch Health Scis Marston Hall Rm 335 3307 3rd Ave W Seattle WA 98119-1940

KELLEY, MICHAEL JOHN, newspaper editor; b. Kansas City, Mo., July 5, 1942; s. Robert Francis and Grace Lauretta (Schofield) K.; 1 child, Anne Schofield BA, Rockhurst Coll., 1964. Reporter, polit. writer Kansas City Star & Times, 1960-69; asst. Sen. Thomas F. Eagleton, Washington, 1969-76; pres. Swensen's Midwest, Inc., Kansas City, 1976-80; exec. asst. Cen. States Pension Fund, Chgo., 1981-83, 85-87; asst. mng. editor Kansas City Times, 1984; editor The Daily Southtown, Chgo., 1987-97; mng. editor Las Vegas (Nev.) Sun, 1997—. Office: Las Vegas Sun 2275 Corporate Cir Dr Henderson NV 89074

KELLEY, RICHARD ROY, hotel executive; b. Honolulu, Dec. 28, 1933; s. Roy Cecil and Estelle Louise (Foote) K.; m. Jane Zieber, June 21, 1955 (dec. 1978); children: Elizabeth, Kathryn, Charles, Linda J., Mary Colleen; m. Linda Van Gilder, June 23, 1979; children: Christopher Van Gilder, Anne Marie. BA, Stanford U., 1955; MD, Harvard U., 1960. Pathologist Queen's Med. Ctr., Honolulu, 1962-70, Kapiolani Maternity Hosp., Honolulu, 1961-70; asst. prof. pathology John A. Burns Med. Sch., U. Hawaii, Honolulu, 1968-70; chmn. bd. Outrigger Enterprises, Honolulu. Bd. dirs. First Hawaiian Bank, Outrigger Internat. Travel, Inc. Former trustee, past chmn. Punahou Sch.; dean's adv. bd. Travel Industry Mgmt. Sch., U. Hawaii; former vice-dean Ednl. Inst. AH & MA Pres.'s Acad. Bd. Regents; former chmn. bd. councilors Hawaii Pacific divsn. Am. Cancer Soc., past chmn. commn. on performance stds. State of Hawaii; trustee Kent-Denver Sch., Craig Hosp., Denver. Named Marketer of Yr., Am. Mktg. Assn., 1985, Communicator of Yr., Internat. Bus. Communicators, 1987, Salesperson of Yr., Sales & Mktg. Execs. Honolulu, 1995; named to Hawaii Bus. Hall of Fame, 1993; recipient Hope award Multiple Sclerosis Soc., 1995, Ihe award Hawwaii Army Mus. Soc., 2000. Mem. Hawaii Visitors Bur. (bd. dirs., chmn. 1991-92), Waikiki Oahu Visitors Assn., Waikiki Improvement Assn., Chief Execs. Orgn., Japan Assn. Travel Agts., Japan Hawaii Econ. Coun., Pacific Asia Travel Assn., World Pres.'s Orgn., World Travel and Tourism Coun. E-mial. Office: Outrigger Hotels & Resorts 2375 Kuhio Ave Honolulu HI 96815-0000 E-mail: richard.kelley@outrigger.com

KELLEY, ROBERT OTIS, medical science educator; b. Santa Monica, Calif., Apr. 30, 1944; s. David Otis and Onetia May (Nettles) K.; m. Marcia Jean Bell; children: Jennifer Leigh, Karin Michelle, Matthew Philip, Sarah Ann. BS, Abilene Christian U., 1965; MA, U. Calif., Berkeley, 1966, PhD, 1969. Asst. prof. U. N.Mex. Sch. of Medicine, Albuquerque, 1969-74, assoc. prof., 1974-79, prof., 1979—; chmn. dept. anatomy U. N.Mex. Sch. Medicine, Albuquerque, 1981-97; assoc. vice chancellor rsch., exec. dean grad. coll. U. Ill., Chgo., 1997-99; dean Coll. Health Sics., U. Wyo., 1999—. Vis. scientist Okazaki (Japan) Nat. Labs., 1984-85; mem. study sect. NIH, Bethesda, Md., 1982-86, U.S. Med. Licensing Exam. Step 1, 1995—; anatomy com. Nat. Bd. mex. Examiners, Phila., 1992—. Author: Basic Histology, 1989; editor Cell and Tissue Rsch., 1970—, Anat. Record, 1970-97; contbr. articles to profl. jours. Patroller Nat. Ski Patrol, 1970—. Recipient Rsch. Career Devel. award NIH, 1972-77, Kaiser award U. Calif., Irvine, 1976; Internat. Exch. Scholar NSF; NIH grantee, 1970— Mem. Fedn. Am. Socs. for Exptl. Biology (pub. affairs exec. com. 1993—), Am. Soc. Cell Biology, Soc. for Devel. Biology, Electron Microscopy Soc. Am. (bd. dirs. 1987—), Am. Assn. Anatomists (exec. com. 1988—), Assn. Am. Med. Colls. (exec. coun. 1995—, chair assembly 1997-99), Nat. Caucus of Basic Biomed. Sci. Chairs, Nat. Bd. Med. Examiners. Democrat. Protestant. Avocations: sailing, skiing, soaring, SCUBA diving, backpacking. Address: 1162 Granito Dr Laramie WY 82072-5027 Office: U Wyo PO Box 3432 Laramie WY 82071-3432

KELLISON, CRAIG M. federal judge; b. 1950; BS, U. Nev., 1972; JD, Gonzaga U., 1976. Law clk. to Hon. Bruce Thompson U.S. Dist. Ct. Nev., 1976; with Office of U.S. Atty., Nev., 1976-78; apptd. magistrate judge ea. dist. U.S. Dist. Ct. Calif., 1988. Instr. law Lassen Coll., 1988-94. Mem. Calif. State Bar, Nev. State Bar, Oreg. State Bar, Lassen County Bar Assn., Washoe County Bar Assn. Office: PO Box 1238 Susanville CA 96130-1238 Fax: 916-257-2021

KELLMAN, BARNET KRAMER, film, stage and television director; b. N.Y.C., Nov. 9, 1947; s. Joseph A.G. and Verona D. (Kramer) K.; m. Nancy Mette, 1982; children: Katherine Mette, Eliza Mette, Michael Mette. BA, Colgate U., 1969; postgrad., Yale U., 1970; PhD, Union Grad. Sch., 1972. Dir. plays, TV and film prodns. Tchr., guest dir. N.C. Sch. Arts, 1973-80, CCNY, 1975-76, grad. film div. Columbia U., 1984-87. Dir.: (feature films) Key Exchange, 1985, Straight Talk, 1992, Stinkers, 1997, Mary and Rhoda, 2000; dir. 6 seasons Eugene O'Neill Theatre Ctr.; assoc. artistic dir. Williamstown Theatre Festival, 1974, 75; dir.: (off-Broadway plays) Key Exchange, 1981, Breakfast with Les and Bess, 1982, The Good Parts, 1982, Danny and the Deep Blue Sea, 1984, The Loman Family Picnic, 1989, Defiled, 2000; dir. (TV series) Gemini Showtime, 1981, All is Forgiven, 1986, My Sister Sam, 1987, Designing Women, 1987, E.R., 1996; prodr., dir.: (TV series) Murphy Brown, 1989-92 (Dir.'s Guild award 1990, Outstanding Dir. in Comedy Series Emmy award 1992); co-exec. prodr., dir.: (TV series) Mad About You, 1992-93, Good Advice, 1992-93, (TV pilot) The Second Half, 1993, Thunder Alley, 1994; exec. prodr., dir.: (TV series) Something Wilder, 1994, (TV pilots) Hope and Gloria, 1995, Bless This House, 1995, If Not For You, 1995, Suddenly Susan, 1996, Life with Roger, 1996, For Your Love, 1998, Felicity, 1999, Once and Again, 2000, Ally McBeal, 2000. Danforth fellow, 1969-72; Thomas J. Watson fellow, 1969-71 Mem. AEA, SAG, Dirs. Guild Am., Soc. Stage Dirs. and Choreographers (bd. dirs. 1984-86), New Dramatists (bd. dirs.). Jewish. Office: care Marty Adelstein The Endeavor Agy 9701 Wilshire Blvd Fl 10 Beverly Hills CA 90212-2010

KELLNER, JAMIE, broadcasting executive; With CBS, 1969; former v.p. first-run programming, devel., sales Viacom Enterprises; pres. Orion Entertainment Group, 1979-86; pres., CEO Fox Broadcasting Co., L.A., 1986-93; CEO, pres. WBTV Network, Burbank, Calif. Office: WBTV Network 4000 Warner Blvd Bldg 34R Burbank CA 91522-0001

KELLOGG, KENYON P. lawyer; b. Dubuque, Iowa, Aug. 5, 1946; s. Kenyon P. and Maleta (Fleege) K.; m. Carolyn Jo Dick, July 18, 1970; children: Andrew P., Kenyon P., Jonathan P. BSBA summa cum laude, Creighton U., 1968; JD cum laude, U. Mich., 1971. Bar: U.S. Dist. Ct. (we. dist.) Wash. 1971, U.S. Tax Ct. 1980; CPA, Wash. With Arthur Andersen & Co., Omaha and Detroit, 1968-71; assoc. Lane Powell Spears Lubersky, Seattle, 1971-78, ptnr., 1978—. Bd. regents Seattle U., 1989—, dean's coun. Alber's Sch. Bus. and Econs., 1992—; mem. nat. alumni bd. Creighton U., 1995—; trustee Naval Undersea Mus. Found., 1995—; mem. FALES com. USN Acad., 1995—. Capt. USAR, 1968-77. Mem. AICPAs, Wash. Soc. CPAs, Seattle Rotary, Seattle Yacht Club (trustee), Cruising Club of Am., Naval Acad. Sailing Squadron. Avocations: sailing, skiing. Office: Lane Powell Spears Lubersky 1420 5th Ave Ste 4100 Seattle WA 98101-2338

KELLY, ALAN, public relations executive; BA in Pub. Rels., U. So. Calif.; M in Comm. Rsch., Stanford U. V.p. client svcs. Cunningham Comm.; v.p. Jennings & Co. (now GCI/SF); sr. v.p. Hi-Tech Comm. (now Golin/Harris); founder, pres., CEO Applied Comm. Pub. quarterly column MC Magazine. Office: Applied Comm Corp 185 Berry St Ste 6500 San Francisco CA 94107-1728

KELLY, ARTHUR PAUL, physician; b. Asheville, N.C., Nov. 23, 1938; s. Joseph Paul and Amanda Lee (Walker) K.; m. Beverly Gayle Baker, June 25, 1966; children: Traci Allyce, Kara Gisele. BA, Brown U., 1960; MD, Howard U., 1965. Intern Harper Hosp., Detroit, 1965-66; resident in dermatology Henry Ford Hosp., Detroit, 1968-71; instr. in dermatology Brown U., Providence, 1971-73; asst. prof. internal medicine Charles R. Drew U. Medicine and Sci., Los Angeles, 1973-77, prof. L.A., 1983; chief div. dermatology King.-Drew Med. Ctr., L.A., 1976—, interim chmn. dept. internal medicine, 1985-86, vice chmn., 1987-91, chmn., 1992-95; assoc. prof. medicine U. So. Calif., L.A., 1977-80; prof. UCLA, 1995—. Contbr. numerous articles to profl. jours., chpts. to books. Served to capt. U.S. Army, 1966-68, Vietnam. Recipient Act So award NAACP, 1983. Fellow Am. Acad. Dermatology; mem. Met. L.A. Dermatology Soc. (v.p. 1986-87, pres. 1987-88), Nat. Med. Assn. (chmn. sect. on dermatology 1978-80, Outstanding Minority Dermatology fellow 1972), Assn. of Profs. of Dermatology (pres.-elect 1996-98, pres. 1998-2000), Am. Dermatology Assn. (v.p. 1997-98, pres. 1998-99). Democrat. Avocations: travel, tennis. Office: King/Drew Med Ctr 12021 S Wilmington Ave Los Angeles CA 90059-3019 E-mail: apkelly@cdrewu.edu

KELLY, CAROLYN SUE, newspaper executive; b. Pasco, Wash., Oct. 25, 1952; d. Jerald Davin and Margaret Helen (Nibler) K. BBA, Gonzaga U., 1974; MBA, Seattle U., 1985. CPA, Wash. Acct. Brajcich & Loeffler, Spokane, Wash., 1972-74; auditor Peat, Marwick, Mitchell & Co., Seattle, 1974-77; fin. analyst Seattle Times, 1977-81, asst. circulation mgr., 1981-83, spl. project advt. mgr., 1983-86, dir. mktg. and new bus., 1986-89, v.p., chief fin. officer, 1989-97, sr. v.p. and gen. mgr., 1997—. Bd. dirs. Econ. Devel. Coun., Seattle, 1992, Campfire, Artists Unltd. Mem. Fin. Execs. Avocation: running. Office: Seattle Times PO Box 70 Seattle WA 98111-0070

KELLY, DANIEL GRADY, JR. lawyer; b. Yonkers, N.Y., July 15, 1951; s. Daniel Grady and Helene (Coyne) K.; m. Annette Susan Wheeler, May 8, 1976; children— Elizabeth Anne, Brigid Claire, Cynthia Logan. Grad., Choate Sch., Wallingford, Conn., 1969; BA magna cum laude, Yale U., 1973; JD, Columbia U., 1976. Bar: N.Y. 1977, U.S. Dist. Ct. (so. and ea. dists.) N.Y. 1977, Calif. 1986, U.S. Dist. Ct. (cen. dist.) Calif. 1987. Law clk. to judge U.S. Ct. Appeals (2d cir.), N.Y.C., 1976-77; assoc. Davis Polk & Wardwell, N.Y.C., 1977-83; sr. v.p. Lehman Bros., N.Y.C., 1983-85; sr. v.p., gen. counsel Kaufman & Broad, Inc., L.A., 1985-87; ptnr. Manatt, Phelps, Rothenberg & Phillips, L.A., 1987-90, Sidley & Austin, L.A. and N.Y., 1990-99, Davis Polk & Wardwell, N.Y.C. and Menlo Park, Calif., 1999—. Mem. editl. bd. Columbia Law Rev., 1975-76. Office: Davis Polk & Wardwell 1600 El Camino Real Menlo Park CA 94025-4119 E-mail: dankelly@dpw.com

KELLY, HENRY ANSGAR, English language educator; b. Fonda, Iowa, June 6, 1934; s. Harry Francis and Inez Ingeborg (Anderson) K.; m. Marea Tancred, June 18, 1968; children— Sarah Marea, Dominic Tancred. A.B., St. Louis U., 1959, A.M., Ph.L., St. Louis U., 1961; Ph.D., Harvard U., 1965. Asst. prof. English UCLA, 1967-69, assoc. prof. English, 1969-72, prof. English, 1972—, dir. Ctr. for Medieval and Renaissance Studies, 1998—. Author: The Devil, Demonology and Witchcraft, 1968, 74, Divine Providence in the England of Shakespeare's Histories, 1970, Love and Marriage in the Age of Chaucer, 1975, The Matrimonial Trials of Henry VIII, 1976, Canon Law and the Archpriest of Hita, 1984, The Devil at Baptism, 1985, Chaucer and the Cult of St. Valentine, 1986, Tragedy and Comedy from Dante to Pseudo-Dante, 1989, Ideas and Forms of Tragedy from Aristotle to the Middle Ages, 1993, Chaucerian Tragedy, 1997, Inquisitions and Other Trial Procedures in the Medieval West, 2001; co-editor Viator 1970-90. Guggenheim felow, 1971-72, Nat. Endowment Humanities fellow, 1980-81, 96-97. Fellow Medieval Acad. Am.; mem. Medieval Assn. of Pacific (pres. 1988-90). Roman Catholic. Home: 1123 Kagawa St Pacific Palisades CA 90272-3838 Office: UCLA Dept English 405 Hilgard Ave Los Angeles CA 90095-9000

KELLY, J. MICHAEL, lawyer; b. Hattiesburg, Miss., Dec. 5, 1943; BA, Emory U., 1966; LLB, U. Va., 1969. Bar: Ga. 1969, U.S. Supreme Ct. 1978, D.C. 1980, Utah 1982, Calif. 1988. Law clerk to Judge Griffin B. Bell (5th cir.) U.S. Ct. Appeals, Atlanta, 1969-70; ptnr. Alston & Bird (formerly Alston, Miller & Gaines), Atlanta, 1970-77, 81-82; counselor to atty. gen. U.S. Dept. Justice, Washington, 1977-79; counselor to sec. U.S. Dept. Energy, Washington, 1979-81; ptnr., shareholder, dir. Ray, Quinney & Nebeker, Salt Lake City, 1982-87; ptnr. Cooley Godward LLP, San Francisco, 1987—. Mem. Omicron Delta Kappa, Phi Alpha Delta. Office: Cooley Godward LLP 1 Maritime Plz Fl 20 San Francisco CA 94111-3510

KELLY, JAMES J. dean, social work educator; BS, Edinboro State U., 1970; MSW, U. Tenn., 1972; PhD, Brandeis U., 1975. Lic. clin. social worker. Clin. fellow in psychiatry UCLA, 1979; instr. San Diego State U., U. Hawaii; dir. dept. social work, prof. Calif. State U., Long Beach, dean Sch. Health and Human Svcs., prof. social work L.A., 1997—. Mem. cmty. adv. bd. coun. County Dept. Children's Svcs.; mem. bd. govs. Sr. Care Action Network Health Plan. Named U.S. Social Worker of the Yr. NASW; recipient Merit award, 1981. Mem. Nat. Assn. Deans and Dirs. Schs. Social Work (pres.), Calif. Assn. Deans and Dirs. Schs. Social Work (pres.). Office: Calif State U 5151 State University Dr Los Angeles CA 90032-4226 Fax: 323-343-5598. E-mail: jkelly@calstatela.edu

KELLY, JAMES S. personal care industry executive; BBA in Acctg., U. San Diego. CPA. Audit mgr. KPMG Peat Marwick LLP; contr. Jenny Craig Internat., 1989—, v.p., 1992—, CFO, 1999—, treas. Office: Jenny Craig Internat 11355 N Torrey Pines Rd La Jolla CA 92037 Fax: 858-812-2718; 858-812-2713

KELLY, JOHN F. air transportation executive; b. Tacoma; Degree in bus. adminstrn., U. Puget Sound. Various positions Continental Airliens, Seattle, Houston, L.A.; asst. v.p. sales Alaska Airlines, 1976-78; staff v.p. sales, 1978; v.p. mktg., 1981-87; COO; pres., CEO, 1995—, Horizon Air Industries Inc. subs. Alaska Air Group, 1987-94; chmn.; chmn., pres., CEO Alaska Air Group, Seattle, 1995—. Bd. trustees Seattle Repertory Theatre; mem. bus. adv. com. Northwestern U. Transp. Ctr.; bd. dirs. Wash. Roundtable; chmn. bd. vis. Sch. Bus. U. Puget Sound, mentor bus. leadership program. Office: Alaska Air Group 19300 Pacific Hwy S Seattle WA 98188

KELLY, JOHN J. former prosecutor; U.S. atty. for N.Mex. U.S. Dept. Justice, Albuquerque, 1993-99. Office: US Atty Dist NMex PO Box 607 Albuquerque NM 87103-0607

KELLY, KEVIN, editor; b. Penn State, Pa., Apr. 27, 1952; s. Joseph John and Patricia Kelly; m. Gia-Minn Fuh, Jan. 2, 1987; children: Kaileen, Ting, Tywen. Freelance photographer, 1971-80; editor, pub. Walking! Jour., Athens, Ga., 1982-84, Whole Earth Rev., Sausalito, Calif., 1984-90; exec. editor Wired Mag., San Francisco, 1992-98; pres. All Species Inventory, 2001—. Bd. dirs. Well, Inc., Sausalito; pres. All Species Inventory, 2001. Editor: Signal, 1988; author: Out of Control, 1994, New Rules for the New Economy, 1998. Recipient Gen. Excellence Nat. Mag. Award, 1993, 96. Avocation; beekeeping. Home: 149 Amapola Ave Pacifica CA 94044-3102 Office: Wired 520 3rd St San Francisco CA 94107-1814 E-mail: kk@well.com

KELLY, KEVIN FRANCIS, lawyer; b. New Orleans, Apr. 27, 1949; s. Frank J. and Dorothy P. (Paige) K.; m. Jean A. Friedhoff, Dec. 27, 1969; children: Bryan F., Eric W. BA, Gonzaga U., 1970; JD, U. Calif. Berkeley, 1973. Bar: Wash. 1973. Law clk. to Hon. Eugene A. Wright U.S. Ct. Appeals, 9th Cir., Seattle, 1973-74; assoc. Davis, Wright, Todd, Riese & Jones, Seattle, 1974-76; ptnr. Wickwire, Goldmark & Schorr, Seattle, 1976-88, Heller, Ehrman, White & McAuliffe, Seattle, 1988—. Bd. dirs. Big Bros. King County, Seattle, 1985-95, v.p., 1991, pres., 1992; bd. trustees Legal Found. Wash., Seattle, 1994-97, pres., 1997. Mem. Wash. Biotechnology and Biomedical Assn. (bd. dirs. 1996—), Wash. Soc. Hosp. Lawyers, Order of Coif. Avocation: cycling. Home: 4040 55th Ave NE Seattle WA 98105-4957

KELLY, PAUL JOSEPH, JR. judge; b. Freeport, N.Y., Dec. 6, 1940; s. Paul J. and Jacqueline M. (Nolan) Kelly; m. Ruth Ellen Dowling, June 27, 1964; children: Johanna, Paul Edwin, Thomas Martin, Christopher Mark, Heather Marie. BBA, U. Notre Dame, 1963; JD, Fordham U., 1967. Bar: N.Mex. 1967. Law clk. Cravath, Swaine & Moore, N.Y.C., 1964—67; assoc. firm Hinkle, Cox, Eaton, Coffied & Hensley, Roswell, N.Mex., 1967—71, ptnr., 1971—92; judge U.S. Ct. Appeals (10th cir.), Santa Fe, 1992—. Mem. N.Mex. Bd. Bar Examiners, 1982—85, N.Mex. Ho. of Reps., 1976—81, chmn. consumer and pub. affairs com., mem. judiciary com.; mem. N.Mex. Pub. Defender Bd. Bd. visitors Fordham U. Sch. Law, 1992—; pres. Oliver Seth Inn of Ct., 1993—, Roswell Drug Abuse Com, 1970—71; mem. Appellate Judges Nominating Commn., 1989—92, Eastern N.Mex. State Fair Bd., 1978—83; pres. Chaves County Young Reps., 1971—72; vice chmn. N.Mex. Young Reps., 1969—71, treas., 1968—69; pres. parish coun. Roman Cath. Ch., 1971—76; bd. dirs. Zia coun. Girl Scouts Am., Roswell Girls Club; bd. dirs.. Chaves County Mental Health Assn., 1974—77; bd. dirs. Santa Fe Orch., 1992—93, Roswell Symphony Orch. Soc., 1969—82, treas., 1970—73, pres., 1973—75. Mem.: KC, ABA, Fed. Bar Assn., State Bar N.Mex. (v.p. young lawyers sect. 1969, co-chmn. ins. sub-com. 1972—73, mem. continuing legal edn. com. 1970—73). Office: US Court Appeals 10th Circuit Federal Courthouse PO Box 10113 Santa Fe NM 87504-6113

KELLY, PETE, state legislator; b. Fairbanks, Alaska, June 3, 1956; m. Perri Brechan; children: Devin, Katlin, Dominic. Student, U. Alaska; BS Bus. Adminstrn. and Mgmt., Liberty U. Va. Mem. Alaska Ho. of Reps., 1994-98, Alaska Senate, Dist. P, Juneau, 1998—, vice-chair health, edn. and social svcs. com., mem. fin. com., resources com., adminstrv. regulation rev. com., co-chair fin. com. Co-chair Com. to Prevent Base Closures;

mem. Gov.'s Conf. on Youth and Justice. Active Immaculate Conception Parish; bd. dirs. Vols. in Policing; vol. youth sports. Republican. Avocations: scenic photography, outdoor sports, American history. Office: State Capitol 120 4th St Rm 510 Juneau AK 99801-1142 also: 119 N Cushman St Ste 201 Fairbanks AK 99701-2879 Fax: 907-465-5241/907-465-9293. E-mail: kelly@legis.state.ak.us

KELLY, REGIS BAKER, biochemistry educator, biophysics educator; b. Edinburgh, Scotland, May 26, 1940; m. Rae L. Burke, 1992; children: Gordon, Alison, Colin. BSc, U. Edinburgh, 1961; PhD, Calif. Inst. Tech., 1967. Instr. neurobiology Harvard Med. Sch., Boston, 1969-71; from asst. prof. to prof. biochem. and biophysics U. Calif., San Francisco, 1971—, chair dept. biochemistry and biophysics, 1995—. Dir. cell biology program U. Calif., 1988-95, dir. Hormone Rsch. Inst., 1992—; adv. panelist Nat. Engring. Inst.; mem. study sect. NIH; vis. prof. MIT, Cambridge, 1986—. Helen Hay Whitney Found. fellow, 1967-70, Multiple Sclerosis Soc. fellow, 1970-71. Mem. Soc. Neurosci., Am. Soc. Biol. Chem., Am. Soc. Cell Biology. Office: Univ Calif Dept Biochem & Biophysics PO Box 534 San Francisco CA 94143-0001

KELLY, THOMAS J. sports association executive; b. Madison, Wis. m. Carole Duh. BA in Journalism, U. Wis., 1974. Photographer Madison's daily newspapers; sports editor weekly newspaper; pub. rels. dir. midwestern ski resort, 1977; asst. nat. nordic dir. U.S. Ski Assn., 1988-95; dir. comms. U.S. Skiing, 1988—, dir. ops., 1995-96; v.p. pub. rels. U.S. Ski and Snowboard Assn. (formerly U.S. Skiing), 1996—. Mem. bd. dirs. Ski Utah. Mem. Rotary. Office: US Ski Snowboard Assn PO Box 100 Park City UT 84060-0100

KELLY, TIMOTHY DONAHUE, state legislator; b. Sacramento, Aug. 15, 1944; m. Lisa B. Nelson, Jan. 1, 1994; children: Ingrid Brose, Theodore Ambrose. Former legis. aide to Calif. and Nev. Legislatures; mortgage banker; mem. Alaska Ho. of Reps., 1976-78, Alaska Senate, 1978—, senate pres., 1989-90. With USMCR, Alaska Air NG. Office: State Capitol Juneau AK 99801-1182

KELLY, WILLIAM M. former computer company executive; BA in History, JD, Columbia Coll. With Shearman & Sterling, N.Y., ptnr., 1987; v.p. bus. devel. Silicon Graphics, Inc., 1994-96; sr. v.p., gen. counsel, sec. Silicon Interactive Group; sr. v.p. corp. ops. Silicon Graphics, Inc., 1996-99. Bd. editors Columbia Law Rev. Address: PO Box 7311 Mountain View CA 94039-7311 Office: Silicon Graphics Inc 2011 N Shoreline Blvd Mountain View CA 94043-1389

KELTON, ARTHUR MARVIN, JR. real estate developer; b. Bennington, Vt., Sept. 12, 1939; s. Arthur Marvin and Lorraine (Millington) K.; m. Elaine White, Nov. 1, 1986; 1 child, Ashley. BA, Dartmouth Coll., 1961; postgrad., U. Vt., 1963. Ptnr. Kelton and Assocs., Vail, Colo., 1966-77; pres. Kelton, Garton and Assocs. Inc., Vail, 1977-84, Kelton, Garton, Kendall, Vail, 1984-93, Christopher, Denton, Kelton, Kendall, Vail, 1993—. Head agt. Dartmouth Alumni Fund, Hanover, N.H., 1985-90, class pres., 1990-96; Dartmouth Alumni Coun., 1996—; pres. Vail Valley Med. Ctr. Found., 1991—. Republican. Congregationalist. Avocations: skiing, golf, wingshooting. Home: 1034 Homestake Cir Vail CO 81657-5111 Office: Christopher Denton Kelton & Kendall Ste 200 225 Wall St Vail CO 81657-3615 Fax: 970-476-7994. E-mail: akjr@vail.net

KEMMERLY, JACK DALE, retired state official, aviation consultant; b. El Dorado, Kans., Sept. 17, 1936; s. Arthur Allen and Eythel Louise (Throckmorton) K.; m. Frances Cecile Gregorio, June 22, 1958; children: Jack Dale Jr., Kathleen Frances, Grant Lee. BA, San Jose State U., 1962; cert. in real estate, UCLA, 1970; MPA, Golden Gate U., 1973; cert. labor-mgmt. rels., U. Calif., Davis, 1978; cert. orgnl. change, Stanford U., 1985. Right of way agt. Calif. Div. Hwys., Marysville, 1962-71; adminstrv. officer Calif. Dept. Transp., Sacramento, 1971-82, dist. dir. Redding, 1982-83, chief aeros. Sacramento, 1984-94; mgmt. cons. U.S. Dept. Transp., Riyadh, Saudi Arabia, 1983-84. Mem. tech. adv. com. on aeronautics Calif. Transp. Commn. Bd. dirs. Yuba-Sutter Campfire Girls, 1972-73. With USN, 1954-57. Recipient superior accomplishment award Calif. Dept. Transp., 1981. Mem. Nat. Assn. State Aviation Ofcls. (nat. pres. 1989—), Am. Assn. State Hwy. and Transp. Ofcls. (aviation com. 1985-94), Calif. Assn. Aerospace Educators (adv. bd. 1984—), Calif. Assn. Airport Execs., Calif. Aviation Coun., Aircraft Owners and Pilots Assn. (Western regional rep.), Elks (exalted ruler Marysville, Calif. 1974-75). Republican. Roman Catholic. Avocations: non-partisan political activities, reading, flying. Office: 1285 Charlotte Ave Yuba City CA 95991-2803 E-mail: jdkemm@jps.net

KEMMIS, DANIEL ORRA, cultural organization administrator, author; b. Fairview, Mont., Dec. 5, 1945; s. Orra Raymond and Lilly Samantha (Shidler) K.; children: Abraham, Samuel, Deva, John. BA, Harvard U., 1968; JD, U. Mont., 1978. Bar: Mont. 1978. State rep. Mont. Ho. of Reps., Helena, 1975-84, minority leader, 1981-82, Speaker of House, 1983-84; ptnr. Morrison, Jonkel, Kemmis & Rossbach, Missoula, 1978-80, Jonkel & Kemmis, 1981-84; mayor City of Missoula, Mont., 1990-96; dir. Ctr. Rocky Mountain West Univ. Mont., Missoula, 1996—. Cons. No. Lights Inst., Missoula, Mont., 1985-89; Kennedy fellow Inst. Politics Harvard U., 1998. Author: Community and the Politics of Place, 1990, The Good City and the Good life, 1995, This Sovereign Land, 2001; contbr. articles to profl. jours. Candidate for chief justice Mont. Supreme Ct.; former mem. adv. bd. and bd. dirs. Nat. Civic League, 1990-93; mem. adv. bd. Pew Partnership for Civic Change, 1991-97, Brookings Instn. Ctr. Urban and Met. Policy, Snake River Inst.; chmn. leadership tng. coun. Nat. League Cities, 1992-94; bd. dirs. Charles F. Kettering Found., N.W. Area Found., Inst. for Environ. and Natural Resources U. Wyo., Bolle Ctr. for People and Forests, U. Mont., Redefining Progress Am. Planning Assn. Growing Smart Initiative; fellow Dallas Inst. for Humanities and Culture 1991-98; presdl. appt. Am. Heritage Rivers Commn., 1998. Inst. Politics fellow Kennedy Sch. Govt., Harvard LU., 1998; named Disting. Young Alumnus U. Mont., 1981, 100 Visionaries, Utne Reader, 1995; recipient Charles Frankel prize NEH, 1997, Disting. Achievement award, Soc. for Conservation Biology, 1997, Wallace Stegner award, Ctr. Am. West, 1998. Democrat. Home: 521 Hartman St Apt 10 Missoula MT 59802-4771 Office: U Mont Milw Sta 2nd Fl OConnor Ctr Rocky Mountain W Missoula MT 59812-3096 E-mail: kemmis@crmw.org

KEMP, ALSON REMINGTON, JR. lawyer, former law educator; b. Rossville, Ga., July 3, 1941; s. Alson R. Dorothy (Walters) K.; m. Martha Gudenrath, Aug. 7, 1967; children— Alson Remington, Colin T. B.S., U. Tenn., 1962; J.D., U. Cin., 1965. Bar: Tenn. 1965, Ohio 1965, Calif. 1970, U.S. Dist. Ct. (no. and cen. dists.) Calif. 1971, U.S. Ct. Appeals (9th cir.) 1971, U.S. Ct. Appeals (D.C. cir.) 1982. Asst. prof. Hancock Coll., Santa Maria, Calif., 1966-68; asst. prof. U. Tenn., Chattanooga, 1969; mem. Morgan & Garner, Chattanooga, 1968-70, Pillsbury, Madison & Sutro, San Francisco, 1970-75, ptnr., 1975-99; pvt. practice Healdsburg, Calif., 1999—. Served to capt. USAF, 1965-68 Benwood Found. grantee, 1962-65 Fellow Am. Coll. Trial Lawyers; mem. ABA, Calif. Bar Assn. Republican. Office: 22190 Puccioni Rd Healdsburg CA 95448

KEMP, JOHN DANIEL, biochemist, educator; b. Mpls., Jan. 20, 1940; s. Dean Dudley and Catherine Georgie (Treleven) K.; children: Todd, Christine, Laura. B.A. in chemistry, UCLA, 1962, Ph.D, 1965. NIH postdoctoral fellow U. Wash., Seattle, 1965-68; prof. plant pathology U. Wis., Madison, 1968-81; assoc. dir. Agrigenetics Advanced Research Labs., Madison, 1981-85; prof., dir. plant genetic engring. lab. N.Mex. State U., Las Cruces, 1985—. Author papers on plant molecular genetics. Grantee NSF; grantee Dept. Agr. Mem. Sigma Xi Office: N Mex State U Plant Genetic Engring Lab PO Box 3GL Las Cruces NM 88004-0003

KEMPTHORNE, DIRK ARTHUR, governor; b. San Diego, Oct. 29, 1951; s. James Henry and Maxine Jesse (Gustason) K.; m. Patricia Jean Merrill, Sept. 18, 1977; children: Heather Patricia, Jeffrey Dirk. BS in Polit. Sci., U. Idaho, 1975. Exec. asst. to dir. Idaho Dept. Lands, Boise, 1975-78; exec. v.p. Idaho Home Builders Assn., Boise, 1978-81; campaign mgr. Batt for Gov., Boise, 1981-82; lic. securities rep. Swanson Investments, Boise, 1983; Idaho pub. affairs mgr. FMC Corp., Boise, 1983-86; mayor Boise, 1986-93; U.S. Senator from Idaho, 1993-98; gov. State of Idaho, 1999—. 1st v.p. Assn. of Idaho Cities, 1990-93; chmn. U.S. Conf. of Mayors Standing Com. on Energy and Environment, 1991-93, mem. adv. bd., 1991-93 ; sec. Nat. Conf. of Rep. Mayors and Mcpl. Elected Officials, 1991-93; mem. Senate Armed Svcs. Com., 1993—, Senate Small Bus. Com., 1993—, Senate Environ. and Pub. Works Com., 1993—, Nat. Rep. Senatorial Com., 1993—; chmn. Senate Drinking Water, Fisheries and Wildlife Subcommittee, 1995—, mem. advisory commn. on Intergovernmental Rels., 1995-96; chmn. Armed Svcs Personnel Subcommittee, 1996—. Pres. Associated Students U. Idaho, Moscow, 1975; chmn. bd. dirs. Wesleyan Presch., Boise, 1982-85; mem. magistrate commn. 4th Jud. Dist., Boise, 1986-93; mem. task force Nat. League of Cities Election, 1988; bd. dirs. Parents and Youth Against Drug Abuse, 1987—; mem. bd. vis. USAF Acad., 1994—; chmn. Idaho Working Ptnrs. Ltd., 1993—; hon. chmn. Idaho Congressional Award, 1994—. Named Idaho Citizen of Yr. The Idaho Statesman, 1988, Legislator of the Year Nat. Assn. Counties, 1995, State Legislator of the Year Nat. Assn. of Towns and Townships, 1995; recipient U.S. Conference of Mayor's Nat. Legis. Leadership award, 1994, Disting. Svc. award Nat. Conf. State Legislatures, 1995, Disting. Congressional award Nat. League of Cities, 1995, Guardian of Freedom award Council of State Governments, 1995. Republican. Methodist. Office: Office of Governor PO Box 83720 Boise ID 83720-0034*

KENDALL, JOHN WALKER, JR. medical educator, researcher, university dean; b. Bellingham, Wash., Mar. 19, 1929; s. John Walker and Mathilda (Hansen) K.; m. Elizabeth Helen Meece, Mar. 19, 1954; children: John, Katherine, Victoria. BA, Yale Coll., 1952; MD, U. Wash., 1956. Intern, resident in internal medicine Vanderbilt U. Hosp., Nashville, 1956-59, fellow in endocrinology, 1959-60, U. Oreg. Med. Sch., Portland, 1960-62; asst. prof. medicine Oreg. Health Scis. U., Portland, 1962-66, assoc. prof. medicine, 1966-71, prof. medicine, 1971—, head divsn. metabolism, 1971-80, dean Sch. Medicine, 1983-92, dean emeritus Sch. Medicine, 1992—; assoc. chief staff-rsch. VA Med. Ctr., Portland, 1971-83, dep. chief of staff, 1993, VA disting. physician, 1993-96, acad. affiliates officer, 1997—. Cons. Med. Rsch. Found. Oreg., Portland, 1975-83; sec. Oreg. Found. Med. Excellence, Portland, 1984-89, pres., 1989-91; grad. med. edn. adv. com. Dept. Vets. Affairs, 2001—. Lt. comdr. M.C., USN, 1962 64 Recipient Outstanding Physician award Found. Med. Excellence, 1995. Mem. AMA (governing coun. med. sch. sect. 1989-93, chair 1991-92, alt. del. 1992-93, Oreg. del. 1994-98, rep. Coun. Grad. Med. Edn. 1993-94), Assn. Am. Physicians, Am. Soc. Clin. Investigation, Am. Fedn. Clin. Rsch., We. Soc. Clin. Rsch. (councillor 1972-75), Endocrine Soc., Multnomah County Med. Soc. (treas. 1989, pres. 1991), Med. Rsch. Found. (Mentor award 1992), Royal Soc. Medicine (endocrinology sect. coun. 1999—). Presbyterian. Home: 3131 SW Evergreen Ln Portland OR 97201-1816 Office: Oreg Health Scis U Sch Medicine 3181 SW Sam Jackson Park Rd Portland OR 97201-3011

KENDIG, JOAN JOHNSTON, neurobiology educator; b. Derby, Conn., May 1, 1939; d. Frank and Agnes (Kerr) Johnston; children: Scott Johnston Kendig, Leslie Anne Kendig. BA, Smith Coll., 1960; PhD, Stanford U., 1966. Rsch. assoc. Stanford U. Med. Sch., 1968-71, asst. prof. biology in anesthesia, 1971-76, assoc. prof., 1976-86, prof., 1986--. Mem. physiology study sect. NIH, 1981-85, mem. surgery, anesthesia and trauma study sect., 1996-2000. NIH neurosci. grantee, 1973—; Javits neurosci. investigator, 1988-95. Mem. Soc. for Neurosci., Assn. U. Anesthesiologists, Am. Pain Soc., Internat. Assn. for Study of Pain. Office: Stanford U Med Sch Dept Anesthesia Stanford CA 94305 E-mail: kendig@stanford.edu

KENDLER, HOWARD H(ARVARD), psychologist, educator; b. N.Y.C., June 9, 1919; s. Harry H. and Sylvia (Rosenberg) K.; m. Tracy Seedman, Sept. 20, 1941; children— Joel Harlan, Kenneth Seedman. A.B., Bklyn. Coll., 1940; M.A., U. Iowa, 1941, Ph.D., 1943. Instr. U. Iowa, 1943; research psychologist OSRD, 1944; asst. prof. U. Colo., 1946-48; assoc. prof. NYU, 1948-51, prof., 1951-63; chmn. dept. Univ. Coll., 1951-61; prof. U. Calif., Santa Barbara, 1963-89, prof. emeritus, 1989—, chmn. dept. psychology, 1965-66. Project dir. Office Naval Rsch., 1950-68; prin. investigator NSF, 1953-65, USAAF, 1951-53; mem. adv. panel psychobiology NSF, 1960-62; tng. com. Nat. Inst. Child Health and Human Devel., 1963-66; cons. Dept. Def., Smithsonian Instn., 1959-60, Human Resources Rsch. Office, George Washington U., 1960; vis. prof. U. Calif., Berkeley, 1960-61, Hebrew U., Jerusalem, 1974-75, Tel Aviv U., 1990; chief clin. psychologist Walter Reed Gen. Hosp., 1945-46. Author: Basic Psychology, 1963, 2d edit., 1968, 3d edit., 1974, Basic Psychology: Brief Version, 1977, Psychology: A Science in Conflict, 1981, Historical Foundations of Modern Psychology, 1987, Amoral Thoughts About Morality: The Intersection of Science, Psychology, and Ethics, 2000; co-author: Basic Psychology: Brief Edition, 1970; co-editor: Essays in Neobehaviorism: A Memorial Volume to Kenneth W. Spence; assoc. editor: Jour. Exptl. Psychology, 1963-65; contbr. to profl. jours., books. Served as 1st lt. AUS. Fellow Center for Advanced Studies in Behaviorial Scis., Stanford, Calif., 1969-70; NSF grantee, 1954-76 Mem. Am. Psychol. Assn. (pres. div. exptl. psychology 1964-65, pres. div. gen. psychology 1967-68), Western Psychol. Assn. (pres. 1970-71), Soc. Exptl. Psychologists (exec. com. 1971-73), Psychonomic Soc. (governing bd. 1963-69, chmn. 1968-69), Sigma Xi. Home and Office: 4596 Camino Molinero Santa Barbara CA 93110-1040 E-mail: tkendler@psych.ucsb.edu

KENDRICK, BUDD LEROY, psychologist; b. Pocatello, Idaho, Apr. 19, 1944; s. Oscar Fredrick Kendrick and Miriam Stuart (Thorn) Stewart; m. Sue Lorraine Allen, Nov. 11, 1966; children: Aaron Matthew and Edgar Seth; m. Beverly Ann Dockter, Dec. 26, 1978; children: Cassandra Rachelle, Angela Priscilla. BA, Idaho State U., 1967, MEd, 1969, EdD, 1974. Lic. psychologist, lic. counselor, Idaho; lic. clin. profl. counselor Mont.; cert. health svc. provider in psychology, nat. cert. counselor; cert. clin. mental health counselor; nat. bd. cert. diplomate hypnotherapist; cert. profl. qualification in psychology. Tchr. psychology Pocatello High Sch., 1967-69; dir. counseling services Midwestern Coll., Denison, Iowa, 1969-70; rehab. counselor Idaho Div. of Vocat. Rehab., Pocatello, 1970-73; counselor (doctoral internship) Counseling Ctr., Idaho State U., Pocatello, 1973-74; rehab. counselor Idaho Div. of Vocat. Rehab., Pocatello, 1974-75; chief of psychology Adult and Child Devel. Ctr., Boise, 1975—; pvt. practice psychology Boise, Idaho, 1977—. Vice-chmn. Idaho State Counselor Licensing Bd., 1982-84, chmn. 1984-85, sec. 1985-86; bd. dirs. Nat. Bd. Cert. Counselors Inc., Alexandria, Va., 1986-93, sec., treas., 1987-89; licensure com. Idaho Personnel and Guidance Assn., 1975-78, chmn. 1977-78, rep. Am. Personnel and Guidance Assn. Licensure Network, 1977-78; allied clin. staff Intermountain Hosp., Boise, 1983-93, Northwest Passages Adolescent Hosp., Boise, 1986-93, Saint Alphonsus Regional Med. Ctr., Boise, 1986-93; designated examiner and dispositioner involuntary commitments and guardianships State of Idaho, 1981—; cons. Idaho Personnel Commn., 1982—; grad. sch. lectr. Idaho State U., 1975; grad. sch. faculty affiliate, Coll. of Idaho, Caldwell, 1981-86; presenter concerning counselor credentialing issues, 1981-86; treas. Idaho Mental Health Assn., 1980-81; mem. Idaho Psychology, Social Work reclassification task force, 1990-91; mem. Idaho Assn. Counseling and Devel. Legis. Task Force for Third Party Benefits for Lic. Profl. Counselors, 1990. Editor: Directory of the Idaho Psychol. Assn., 1983; author numerous articles on hypnosis, counseling and profl. credentialing. Mem. adv. bd. Trio (Upward Bound, Talent Search, Head Start), Idaho State U., 1975-76; mem. Human Rights Com., Idaho State Sch. and Hosp., 1977. Recipient Disting. Svc. award Idaho Pers. & Guidance Assn., 1978, Profl. Achievement award Idaho State U., 1987, Spl. Recognition award Idaho Assn. for Counseling and Devel., 1989, Lawrence Schumacher Meml. Employee of Yr. award State of Idaho, 1995, Friend of Rsch. and Assessment for Counseling, Inc. Fellow Am. Coll. Advanced Practice Psychologists (founding mem. Idaho chpt.), Idaho Psychol. Assn. (sec. 1982-84); mem. Idaho Mental Health Counselors Assn. (charter), Idaho Counseling Assn. (leadership coun. 1977-78), Am. Counseling Assn. (pub. policy and legis. com., mem.-at-large 1992-94, chairperson nat. licensure subcom. 1992-94), Am. Mental Health Counselors Assn., Am. Psychol. Assn. (divsn. 17 counseling psychology, div. 30 psychol. hypnosis), Sons of Confederate Vets., Chi Sigma Iota Internat. Profl. Counseling and Acad. Honor Soc., Friends of Rsch. and Assessment for Counseling, Inc., Idaho Hist. Soc. (cert. Idaho pioneer descendant), Stuart-Mosby Hist. Soc. Avocations: sword collecting, genealogy, collecting limited edits. Civil War pewter sculptures, War Between the States history, collecting autographed celebrity photographs.

KENDRICK, RONALD H. banker; b. San Diego, Sept. 17, 1941; s. Wesley Samuel and Ruth Helen (Hunter) K.; m. Cheryl Donofrio Ayers, June 10, 1989; 1 child by previous marriage, Kirsten Dawn; stepchildren: Joshua Ayers, Benjamin Ayers. AB in Econs., San Diego State U., 1964, MBA in Fin., 1975; grad. investment mgmt. workshop, Harvard U., 1974, grad. strategic mktg. mgmt., 1993; grad., Pacific Coast Banking Sch. U. Wash., 1981. Chartered fin. analyst. Exec. v.p. Union Bank, San Diego, 1959—. Lectr. San Diego State U., 1975-81; faculty Pacific Coast Banking Sch., Seattle, 1983-85; regent Fin. Analysts Seminar, Rockford, Ill., 1975-78; bd. dirs. Union Bank Found., Union Bank PAC, Old Globe, Pacific Bankers Mgmt. Inst.; bus. and econ. devel. counsel to Mayor of San Diego, 1995; chmn. bd. dirs. San Diego State U. Coll. Bus., 2000—. Treas. Boy Scouts Am. San Diego coun., 1984-85, bd. dirs. 1977-94; mem. adv. com. North County Campus San Diego State U., 1984-89; mem. adv. com. Calif. State U., San Marcos, 1989-93; trustee Hall Sci. and Reuben H. Fleet Space Theater, San Diego, 1984-91, pres., 1988-90; bd. dirs. ARC, SanDiego, 1983-90, chmn., 1985-87; bd. dirs. Symphony Assn., San Diego, 1983-86, San Diegan's Inc., San Diego, 1984-89, United Way San Diego, 1988-94, chmn. United Way San Diego campaign, 1995-96, San Diego County YMCA, 1992-2000, Old Globe Theatre, 1995-2000; bd. dirs. Lead, Inc., 1985-86, 87-93, pres., 1990-91; bd dirs. Children's Hosp. Found., 1988-98, chmn., 1992-93; bd. dirs. Children's Hosp., 1998—; mem. task force to study indsl. element San Diego gen. plan, 1977; mem. bus. and econ. devel. coun. Mayor of San Diego, 1995. Recipient Disting. Alumnus award Coll. Bus. San Diego State U.,1984, Silver Beaver award, Humanitarian of Yr. Boy Scouts Am., 1991, Disting. Eagle award Boy Scouts Am., 1993; named Alumnus of Yr., Lead Inc., 1992. Mem. Fin. Analysts Soc. (pres. 1978-79), Calif. Bankers Assn. (bd. dirs.), Greater San Diego C. of C. (exec. com. 1989), Zool. Soc. San Francisco, Indian Wells C. of C., La Jolla Country Club (bd. dirs. 1997—), Century Club (bd. dirs. 1996-2000), Rotary. Republican. Avocations: tennis; golf; woodworking; skiing. Home: 3620 Curtis St San Diego CA 92106-1202 Office: Union Bank 530 B St San Diego CA 92101-4407

KENDRICK, WILLIAM BRYCE, biology educator, writer, publisher; b. Liverpool, Lancashire, Eng., Dec. 3, 1933; arrived in Can., 1958; s. William and Lillian Maud (Latham) K.; m. Laureen Anne Carscadden, Dec. 14, 1978; children: Clinton, Kelly. BSc with honors, U. Liverpool, 1955, PhD, 1958, DSc, 1980. Postdoctoral fellow NRC, Ottawa, Ont., Can., 1958-59; rsch. scientist Agr. Can., Ottawa, 1959-65; asst. prof. U. Waterloo, Ont., 1965-66, assoc. prof., 1966-71, prof., 1971-94, disting. prof. emeritus, 1994—, assoc. dean, 1985-93. Adj. prof. U. Victoria, B.C., 1994—; propr. Mycologue Pub. Author: The Fifth Kingdom, 1985, 2d rev. and enlarged edit., 1991, 3rd edit., 2001, CD Rom version 2.6, 2001, A Young Person's Guide To The Fungi, 1986; co-author: Genera of Hyphomycetes, 1980, An Evolutionary Survey of Fungi, Algae and Plants, 1992, editor: Taxonomy of Fungi Imperfecti, The Whole Fungus, Biology of Conidial Fungi; contbr. articles to profl. jours. Guggenheim fellow, 1979-80. Fellow Royal Soc. Can.; mem. Acad. Sci. (hon. sec. 1984-91), Mycological Soc. Am. (Disting. Mycologist award 1995), Br. Mycol. Soc. (centenary fellow 1996), Can. Botan. Assn. (Lawson medal 2001). Mem. Green Party. Avocations: reading, music, walking, photography, rowing. Home and Office: 8727 Lochside Dr Sidney BC Canada V8L 1M8 E-mail: bryce@mycolog.com

KENISON, LYNN T. chemist; b. Provo, Utah, Feb. 20, 1943; s. John Silves and Grace (Thacker) K.; m. Daralyn Wold, June 10, 1969; children: Marlene, Mark, Evan, Guy, Amy, Suzanne. BS in Chemistry, Brigham Young U., 1968, MS in Chemistry, 1971. Tchr. Weber County Sch. Dist., Ogden, Utah, 1968-69; bench chemist (drugs) Salt Lake City/County Health Dept., 1971-74; chemist U.S. Dept. Labor, OSHA Salt Lake Tech. Ctr., 1974—, bench chemist, 1974-77, supr., br. chief, 1977-84, sr. chemist, 1984—. Tech. writer OSHA. Editor: Review Methods and Analytical Papers Before Publication, 1984—; tech. writer, 1984—. Councilman West Bountiful City, Utah, 1980-83, 85-89; scouting coord. Boy Scouts Am., cubmaster local pack, 1990-94, unit commr. scouting, 1995—; full-time missionary LDS Ch., Ark., Mo., Ill., 1962-64; vol. spkr. in local pub. schs., 1988—. Mem. Am. Indsl. Hygiene Assn., Fed. Exec. Assn. (Disting. Svc. award, Jr. Award for Outstanding Fed. and Cmty. Svc. 1980), Toastmasters Internat. (treas. Salt Lake City chpt. 1987-91). Avocations: woodworking, church activities, Boy Scout activities. Home: 1745 N 600 W West Bountiful UT 84087-1150 Office: US Dept of Labor OSHA Salt Lake Tech Ctr 1781 S 300 W Salt Lake City UT 84115-1802

KENNA, MICHAEL, photographer; b. Widnes, Cheshire, Eng., Nov. 20, 1953; Student, Banbury Sch. Art, Oxfordshire, Eng., 1972-73; HND with distinction, Coll. Printing, London, 1976. Tchr. Friends of Photography, San Francisco. One-man shows Fox Talbot Mus., Lacock, Wiltshire, Eng., 1983, Bampton Arts Ctr., Oxfordshire, 1984, Madison (Wis.) Art Ctr., 1985, Gallery Min, Tokyo, 1987, Fuerte Gallery, Tokyo, 1990, Palace of the Legion of Honor, San Francisco, 1991, Cleve. Art Mus., 1992, Internat. Ctr. for Photography, N.Y., 1993, Galerie Zur Stockeregg, Zurich, 1994, Detroit Inst. of Arts, 1995, Nicephore Niepce Mus., France, 1996; exhibited in group show Georges Pompidou Ctr., Paris, 1982; represented in permanent collections Australian Nat. Gallery, Canberra, Bibliotheque Nationale, Paris, San Francisco Mus. Modern Art, Fox Talbot Mus., Milw. Art Mus., Victoria and Albert Mus., London. Recipient award Friends of Imogene Cunningham, 1981, KQED/Zellerbach award, 1981. Office: care Weston Gallery PO Box 655 Carmel CA 93921-0655

KENNARD, JOYCE L. state supreme court justice; Former judge L.A. Mcpl. Ct., Superior Ct., Ct. Appeal, Calif.; assoc. justice Calif. Supreme Ct., San Francisco, 1989—. Office: Calif Supreme Ct 350 Mcallister St San Francisco CA 94102-4712

KENNARD, LYDIA H. airport terminal executive; BA, Stanford U.; MS, MIT; JD, Harvard U. Former pres./prin.-in-charge KDG Devel. Constrn. Consulting, L.A.; former mem. L.A. Planning Commn.; dep. exec. dir. design and constrn. L.A. World Airports, 1994-99, interim exec. dir., 1999-2000, exec. dir., 2000—. Lawyer in real estate and constrn. law. Active UniHealth Found. Bd.; past mem. Calif. Med. Ctr. Found. Bd., Equal Opportunity Adv. Coun. So. Calif. Edison. Named Woman of Yr. L.A. chpt. Women's Trans. Seminar, 1995, Civic Leader of Yr. Nat. Assn. Women Bus. Owners-L.A., 2000. Office: LA World Airports PO Box 92216 Los Angeles CA 90009-2216

KENNEDY, CORTEZ, professional football player; b. Osceola, Ark., Aug. 23, 1968; Student, Northwest Miss. Jr. Coll.; BA, criminal justice, U. Miami, Fla. Defensive tackle Seattle Seahawks, 1990—. Named All-America team defensive tackle, The Sporting News, 1989; AP Defensive Player of Yr., 1992; named to Pro Bowl, 1991-93, NFL All-Pro team defensive tackle, The Sporting News, 1992, 93. Office: Seattle Seahawks 11220 NE 53rd St Kirkland WA 98033-7595

KENNEDY, D. J. LAURIE, civil engineering educator; Prof. emeritus civil engring. U. Alberta, Edmonton, Can. Recipient A.B. Sanderson award, 1989, Sir. Casimir Gzowski medal Can. Soc. Civil Engring., 1980, 92, Le Prix P.L. Pratley award, 1992, Shortridge Hardesty award ASCE, 1994, John Jenkins award Can. Stds. Assn., 1995. Office: Univ Alberta Dept Civil Engring Edmonton AB Canada T6G 2G7

KENNEDY, DAVID MICHAEL, historian, educator; b. Seattle, July 22, 1941; s. Albert John and Mary Ellen (Caufield) K.; m. Judith Ann Osborne, Mar. 14, 1970; children: Ben Caufield, Elizabeth Margaret, Thomas Osborne. BA, Stanford U., 1963; MA, Yale U., 1964, Oxford U., 1995; PhD, Yale U., 1968. Asst. prof. history Stanford (Calif.) U., 1967-72, assoc. prof., 1972-80, prof., 1980—, chmn. program in internat. relations, 1977-80, assoc. dean Sch. Humanities and Scis., 1981-85, William Robertson Coe prof. history and Am. studies, 1987-93, Donald J. McLachlan prof. history, 1993—, chair, history dept., 1990-94. Vis. prof. U. Florence, Italy, 1976-77; lectr. Internat. Communications Agy., Denmark, Finland, Turkey, Italy, 1976-77, Ireland, 1980; Harmsworth prof. Am. history Oxford U., 1995-96. Author: Birth Control in America: The Career of Margaret Sanger, 1970, Over Here: The First World War and American Society, 1980, (with Thomas A. Bailey and Lizabeth Cohen) The American Pageant: A History of the Republic, 11th edit., 1998, Power and Responsibility: Case Studies in American Leadership, 1986, Freedom From Fear: The American People in Depression & War, 1929-1945, 1999; mem. adv. bd. (TV program) The American Experience, Sta. WGBH, 1986—. Mem. nat. planning group Am. Issues Forum, 1974-75; bd. dirs. CORO Found., 1981-87, Environ. Traveling Companions, 1986—, Stanford U. Bookstore, 1994—. Recipient Bancroft prize, 1971, John Gilmary Shea prize, 1970, Richard W. Lyman award Stanford U. Alumni Assn., 1989, Pulitzer prize 2000, Frances Parkman prize 2000, Ambs. Book prize, 2000, Calif. Book award 2000; fellow Am. Council Learned Socs., 1971-72, John Simon Guggenheim Meml. Found., 75-76, Ctr. for Advanced Study in Behavioral Scis., 1986-87, Stanford Humanities Ctr., 1989-90. Fellow Am. Acad. Arts and Scis., Am. Philos. Soc.; mem. Am. Hist. Assn., Orgn. Am. Historians, Soc. Am. Historians. Democrat. Roman Catholic. Office: Stanford U Dept History Stanford CA 94305 E-mail: dmk@stanford.edu

KENNEDY, DEBRA JOYCE, marketing professional; b. Covina, Calif., July 9, 1955; d. John Nathan and Drea Hannah (Lancaster) Ward; m. John William Kennedy, Sept. 3, 1977 (div.); children: Drea, Noelle. BS in Communications, Calif. State Poly. U., 1977. Pub. rels. coord. Whittier (Calif.) Hosp., 1978-79, pub. relations mgr., 1980; pub. rels. dir. San Clemente (Calif.) Hosp., 1979-80; dir. pub. rels. Garfield Med. Ctr., Monterey Park, Calif., 1980-82; dir. mktg. and community rels. Charter Oak Hosp., Covina, 1983-85; mktg. dir. CPC Horizon Hosp., Pomona, 1985-89; dir. mktg. Sierra Royale Hosp., Azusa, 1989-90; mktg. rep. PacifiCare, Cypress, 1990-92; regional medicare mgr. Health Net, Woodland Hills, Calif., 1992-95; dist. sales mgr. Kaiser Permante Health Plan, Pasadena, Calif., 1995—. Mem. Am. Soc. Hosp. Pub. Rels., Healthcare Mktg. Assn., Healthcare Pub. Rels. and Mktg. Assn., Covina and Covina West C. of C., West Covina Jaycees. Republican. Methodist. Club: Soroptimists. Contbr. articles to profl. jours.

KENNEDY, DENNIS L. lawyer; b. Tacoma, Oct. 28, 1950; BA, U. Wash., 1972, JD, 1975. Bar: Nev. 1975. Ptnr. Lionel Sawyer & Collins, Las Vegas, Nev., 1979—. Bd. editors Washington Law Review, 1974-75. Fellow Am. Coll. Trial Lawyers; mem. ABA (administrv. law sect., antitrust law sect., forum com. health law 1980—), Am. Acad. Hosp. Attys., Am. Soc. Law and Medicine, Internat. Assn. Gaming Attys., Nat. Health Lawyers Assn., State Bar Nev. (mem. disciplinary comm. 1988—), Office: Lionel Sawyer & Collins Bank Am Plz 300 S 4th St Ste 1700 Las Vegas NV 89101-6053

KENNEDY, DONALD, editor, environmental science educator, former academic administrator; b. N.Y.C., Aug. 18, 1931; s. William Dorsey and Barbara (Bean) K.; children: Laura Page, Julia Hale; m. Robin Beth Wiseman, Nov. 27, 1987; stepchildren: Cameron Rachel, Jamie Christopher. AB, Harvard U., 1952, AM, 1954, PhD, 1956; DSc (hon.), Columbia U., Williams Coll., U. Mich., U. Ariz., U. Rochester, Reed Coll., Whitman Coll. Mem. faculty Stanford (Calif.) U., 1960-77, prof. biol. scis., 1965-77, chmn. dept., 1965-72, sr. cons. sci. and tech. policy Exec. Office of Pres., 1976, commr. FDA, 1977-79, provost, 1979-80, pres., 1980-92; prof. emeritus, Bing prof. environ. sci. Stanford U., 1992—. Bd. overseers Harvard U., 1970-76; bd. dirs. Health Effects Inst., Nat. Commn. on Pub. Svc., Carnegie Commn. on Sci., Tech. and Govt. Author: Academic Duty, 1997; mem. editl. bd. Jour. Neurophysiology, 1969-75, Science, 1973-77, editor-in-chief, 2000—; contbr. articles to profl. jours. Bd. dirs. Carnegie Endowment for Internat. Peace. Fellow AAAS, Am. Acad. Arts and Scis.; mem. NAS, Am. Philos. Soc. Office: Stanford U Inst for Internat Studies Encina Hall 401 Stanford CA 94305-6055 E-mail: kennedyd@stanford.edu

KENNEDY, DONALD PARKER, title insurance company executive; b. San Jacinto, Calif., Oct. 16, 1918; s. Louis Rex and Elsie (Parker) K.; AB, Stanford U., 1940; LLB, U. So. Calif., 1948; m. Dorothy Alice Suppiger, Dec. 20, 1946; children: Parker Steven, Elizabeth Ann, Amy Frances. Bar: Calif.; asso. counsel Orange County Title Co., 1948-58; exec. v.p. 1st Am. Title Ins. Co., Santa Ana, Calif., 1958-63, pres. , 1963-89, chmn., 1989—, also bd. dirs.; pres. 1st Am. Fin. Corp., Santa Ana, 1963— , also dir., chm.; founder, dir. Pacific View Meml. Park, Newport Beach, Calif., Premier Savs. & Loan Assn., Orange, Calif.; dir. Western Pacific Fin. Corp., Newport Beach, Christiana Oil Corp., Huntington Harbour, Calif., Mission Bank, El Toro, Calif., Mission Savs. & Loan Assn., Santa Ana, Los Alamitos (Calif.) Race Course, 1st Am. Title Ins. Co. Ariz., Phoenix, 1st Am. Title Ins. Co. N.Y., Garden City, 1st Am. Title Ins. Co. Oreg., Portland, Mass. Title Ins. Co., Boston, Title Guaranty Co. Wyo., Casper, Butler Housing Corp., Irvine, Calif. Chmn. pres.'s council Chapman Coll.; pres. Santa Ana-Tustin Community Chest; mem. Santa Ana Bd. Edn., 1953; Orange County chmn. U.S. Savs. Bond Program; bd. dirs. Santa Ana YMCA, World Affairs Council Orange County, Emphysema Found. Am., [illegible] Riverside Found., 1990—; trustee St. Joseph's Found., 1970—, So. Coast Repertory, 1990—, Chapman Coll, 1989—; bd. dirs. Festival of Learning and Performing, 1988—, Orange County Bus. Commn. for the Arts, 1989—. Served to lt. Office Intelligence, USNR, 1942-46. Named to Hall of Fame, Calif. Bldg. Industry, 1989. Mem. Calif. Land Title Assn. (pres. 1960), Am. Land Title Assn. (chmn. fin. com., pres. 1983-84, chmn. govt. affairs com.), [illegible] Calif. C. of C. (So. Calif. council exec. com.) U. So. Calif. Presdl. Assn.,

So. Calif. Golf Assn. Club: Orange County Press (Headliner of Yr. in Bus. 1969). Republican. Clubs: Santa Ana Country, LaQuinta (Calif.) Country, California, Pacific, Center, Eldorado Country, Lake Arrowhead Country. Office: First Am Title Ins Co PO Box 267 114 E 5th St Santa Ana CA 92701-4642

KENNEDY, GEORGE HUNT, chemistry educator; b. Seattle, Apr. 24, 1936; s. George Francis and Frances (Huse) K.; m. Kay Rife, Sept. 1, 1961; children: Joseph, Jill. BS in Chemistry, U. Oreg., 1959; MS in Chemistry, Oreg. State U., 1962, PhD in Phys. Chemistry, 1966. Chemist Borden Chem. Co., Springfield, Oreg., 1957-58; rsch. chemist Chevron Rsch. Corp., Richmond, Calif., 1961-62; prof. chemistry Colo. Sch. Mines, Golden, 1965—. Pres. faculty senate Colo. Sch. Mines, 1992-93. Contbr. articles to profl. jours. With USNR, 1954-62. Recipient Outstanding Tchr. award Amoco Found., 1992. Mem. Am. Chem. Soc., Internat. Oceanographic Found., Sigma Xi, Phi Lambda Upsilon. Democrat. Avocations: fishing, hunting, mountaineering, travel. Office: Colo Sch Mines Dept Chemistry Golden CO 80401

KENNEDY, GEORGE WENDELL, prosecutor; b. Altadena, Calif., Aug. 5, 1945; s. Ernest Campbell Kennedy and Mildred (Onstott) Stuckey; m. Janet Lynn Stites, Aug. 3, 1978; children: Campbell, Britton. BA, Claremont Men's Coll., 1968; postgrad., Monterey Inst. Fgn. Studies, 1968; JD, U. So. Calif., 1971; postgrad., Nat. Coll. Dist. Attys., 1974, F.B.I. Nat. Law Inst., 1989. Bar: Calif. 1972, U.S. Dist. Ct. (no. dist.) Calif. 1972, U.S. Ct. Appeals (9th cir.) 1972. Dep. dist. atty. Santa Clara County, San Jose, Calif., 1972-87, asst. dist. atty., 1987-88, chief asst. dist. atty., 1988-90, dist. atty., 1990—. Author: California Criminal Law Practice and Procedure, 1986. Active NAACP, 1989—, police chiefs' assn. Santa Clara County, San Jose, 1990—; chair domestic violence coun. Santa Clara County, San Jose, 1990-92; bd. dirs. Salvation Army, 1993. Recipient commendation Child Advocates of Santa Clara & San Mateo Counties, 1991, Santa Clara County Bd. Suprs., 1992, Valley Med. Ctr. Found., 1992, 93; elected Ofcl. of Yr. award Am. Electronics Assn., 1998. Mem. Nat. Dist. Attys. Assn. (bd. dirs.), Calif. Dist. Attys. Assn. (bd. dirs. 1988-90, officer 1993-97, pres. 1997-98), Santa Clara County Bar Assn., Rotary Club. Avocation: sailing. Office: 70 W Hedding St 5th Flr West Wing San Jose CA 95110

KENNEDY, JACK LELAND, lawyer; b. Portland, Oreg., Jan. 30, 1924; s. Ernest E. and Lera M. (Talley) K.; m. Clara C. Hagans, June 5, 1948; children: James M., John C. Student, U.S. Maritime Commn. Acad., Southwestern U., L.A.; JD, Lewis and Clark Coll., 1951. Bar: Oreg. 1951. Pvt. practice, Portland; ptnr. Kennedy & King, Portland, 1971-77, Kennedy, King & McClurg, Portland, 1977-82, Kennedy, King & Zimmer, Portland, 1982-98, Kennedy, Watts, Arellano & Ricks L.L.P., Portland, 1998—. Trustee Northwestern Coll. Law, Portland; dir. Profl. Liability Fund, 1979-82. Contbr. articles to legal jours. Mem. bd. visitors Lewis and Clark Coll. With USNR, 1942-46. Recipient Disting. Grad. award Lewis and Clark Coll., 1983. Fellow Am. Coll. Trial Lawyers, Am. Bar Found. (life), Oreg. Bar Found. (charter); mem. ABA (ho. of dels. 1984-88), Oreg. State Bar (bd. govs. 1976-79, pres. 1978-79), Multnomah Bar Assn., City Club, Columbia River Yacht Club. Republican. Office: Kennedy Watts Arellano & Ricks LLP 2850 Pacwest Ctr 1211 SW 5th Ave Portland OR 97204-3713

KENNEDY, JAMES WAITE, management consultant, writer; b. Belding, Mich., Sept. 23, 1937; s. Lloyd Weston and Lois (Waite) K.; m. Anna Everest; children: David, Sarah, Polly, Leif, Damian. B.A., Stanford U., 1959; P.M.D., Harvard Bus. Sch., 1969. With Foote, Cone & Belding, San Francisco and Chgo., 1959-66, Gen. Foods Corp., White Plains, N.Y., 1966-79; dir. human resources J. Walter Thompson Co., N.Y.C., 1979-83; pres. Mgmt. Team Cons., Inc., San Rafael, Calif., 1983—. Author: Getting Behind the Resume, Interviewing Today's Candidates, 1987. Mem. Instrnl. Sys. Assn., Theta Delta Chi. Office: Mgmt Team Cons Inc 1010 B St Ste 403 San Rafael CA 94901-2921

KENNEDY, JOHN EDWARD, art dealer, appraiser, curator; b. Glens Falls, N.Y., Apr. 21, 1930; s. John Edward and Veronica Irene (Young) K.; m. Katherine Joan Donovan, July 14, 1956 (div. June 1973); m. Blake Hale Whitney, Dec. 24, 1995. AB with hons., Boston Coll., 1951; JD, Harvard U., 1956; grad., U.S. Army Command and Gen. Staff Coll., 1964. Bar: Mass. 1956. Asst. counsel New England Mut. Life Ins., Boston, 1956-64; counsel Pa. Life Ins. Co., Beverly Hills, Calif., 1964-68; investment banker Smith Barney and Co., L.A. and N.Y.C., 1968-70; real estate developer Calif. and Hawaii, 1970-80; v.p. Galerie De Tours, Carmel, Calif., 1980-88; curator Gallery Americana, Carmel, 1988-92. Patron Monterey Peninsula Mus. of Art., 1988—, Carmel Art Assn., 1985—. Trustee Harrison Meml. Libr., Carmel, 1986-88; commr. Planning comm., Carmel, 1988-94, chmn., 1992-94. With U.S. Army, 1952-53, Korea, Lt. Col., U.S. Army Res., 1969. Decorated Bronze Star for Valor, Purple Heart with cluster; recipient Disting. Mil. Svc. medal Republic of Korea, 1953. Mem. Am. Soc. of Appraisers (cert.), New England Appraisers Assn. (cert.), Am. Planning Assn., Marines Meml. Club. Republican. Episcopalian. Avocation: golf. Home: PO Box 222162 Carmel CA 93922-2162 Office: New Masters Gallery Dolores 7th Carmel CA 93921

KENNEDY, MARJORIE ELLEN, librarian; b. Dauphin, Man., Can., Sept. 14, 1946; d. Stanley Harrison and Ivy Marietta (Stevens) May; m. Michael P.J. Kennedy, Apr. 3, 1980. BA, U. Sask., Regina, 1972; BLS, U. Alta., Edmonton, 1974; BEd, U. Regina, 1981. Profl. A cert. edn., Sask. Elem. sch. tchr. Indian Head (Sask) Pub. Sch., 1965-66, Elgin Sch., Weyburn, Sask., 1967-68; tchr., libr. Ctrl. Sch., Prince Albert, 1970-71; elem. sch. tchr. Vincent Massey Sch., Prince Albert, 1969-70, 72-73; children's libr. J.S. Wood br. Saskatoon (Sask.) Pub. Libr., 1974-77, asst. coord. children's svcs., 1977-79; programme head, instr. libr. tech. Kelsey Inst., Saskatoon, 1979—; head libr. and info. tech. SIAST-Kelsey Campus, Saskatoon. Presenter workshops on reference materials for elem. sch. librs., storytelling and libr. programming for children, 1980—; vol. dir. Children's Lit. Workshops, Sask. Libr. Assn., 1979-80; mem. organizing com. Sask. Libr. Week, Saskatoon, 1988. Mem. Vanscoy (Sask.) and Dist. Agr. Soc., 1983-95. Named to Libr. Edn. Honor Roll ALA, 1987. Mem. Can. Libr. Assn. (instl. rep. 1984—), Sask. Libr. Assn. (insl. rep. 1984—, mem. children's sect. 1982-83), Sask. Assn. Libr. Techs. (instl. rep. 1984—), Can. Club (bd. mem. 1981-84). Mem. United Ch. Can. Avocations: antique doll restoration, porcelain doll making, antiques, pottery, gardening. Office: Kelsey Inst Box 1520 Libr Info Tech Program Saskatoon SK Canada S7K 3R5 E-mail: Kennedy@siast.sk.ca

KENNEDY, PARKER S. finance company executive; b. Orange, Calif. m. Sherry Kennedy; children: Donald, Katie. AB in Econs., U. So. Calif., L.A., 1970; JD, U. Calif., San Francisco, 1973. Assoc. Levinson & Lieberman, Beverly Hills, Calif.; joined First Am., 1977, various positions including v.p.-nat. sales dir.; exec. v.p. First Am. Title, 1984-89, pres., 1989—; exec. v.p. First Am. Fin. Corp., 1986-93, pres., 1993—, also bd. dirs. Mem. Calif. Bar Assn. Office: First Am Corp One First American Way Santa Ana CA 92707

KENNEDY, RAOUL DION, lawyer; b. San Jose, Calif., Feb. 6, 1944; s. Ralph Craig and Maxine Thelma (Schoemake) K.; m. Patricia Ann Bilbrey. BA, U. Pacific, 1964; JD, U. Calif., Berkeley, 1967. Bar: Calif. 1967, U.S. Supreme Ct. 1970. Assoc. Hagar, Crosby Heafey, Roach & May, Oakland, Calif., 1969-96, Morrison & Foerster, San Francisco, 1996-99; ptnr. [illegible] Co-author: California Expert Witness Guide, 1983, 2d edit., 1991. Fellow Am. Coll. Trial Lawyers, Internat. Soc. of Barristers; mem. Am. Bd. Trial Advocates, Internat. Acad. of Trial Lawyers, Am. Acad. Appellate Lawyers, Calif. Acad. Appellate Lawyers (pres. 1983-84). Republican. Home: 1701 Gough St San Francisco CA 94109-4419 Office: Skadden Arps Slate Meagher & Flom LLP Four Embarcadero Ctr San Francisco CA 94111

KENNEDY, RICHARD JEROME, writer; b. Jefferson City, Mo., Dec. 23, 1932; s. Donald and Mary Louise (O'Keefe) K.; m. Lillian Elsie Nance, Aug. 3, 1960; children: Joseph Troy, Matthew Cook. BS, Portland State U., 1958. Author: (novel) Amy's Eye, 1985 (Internat. Rattenfanger Lit. prize, Fed. Republic Germany 1988), also 18 children's books including Richard Kennedy: Collected Stories, 1988 and 3 musicals, including adaptation of H.C. Andersen's The Snow Queen; inclusion of stories in: The Oxford Book of Modern Fairy Tales, 1993, The Oxford Book of Children's Stories, 1993. With USAF, 1951-54. Home and Office: 415 W Olive St Newport OR 97365-3716

KENNEDY, ROGER GEORGE, museum director, park service executive; b. St. Paul, Aug. 3, 1926; s. Walter J. and Elisabeth (Dean) K.; m. Frances Hefren, Aug. 23, 1958; 1 dau., Ruth. Grad., St. Paul Acad., 1944; B.A., Yale, 1949; LL.B., U. Minn., 1952. Bar: Minn. 1952, D.C. 1953. Atty. Justice Dept., 1953; corr. NBC, 1954-57; dir. Dallas Council World Affairs, 1958; spl. asst. to sec. Dept. Labor, 1959; successively asst. v.p., v.p., chmn. exec. com., dir. Northwestern Nat. Bank St. Paul, 1959-69; v.p. finance, exec. dir. Univ. Found., Minn., 1969-70; v.p. financial affairs Ford Found., N.Y.C., 1970-78, v.p. arts, 1978-79; dir. Nat. Mus. Am. History Smithsonian Instn., Washington, 1979-92, dir. emeritus, 1993—; dir. Nat. Park Svc., Washington, 1993-97. Spl. asst. to sec. HEW, 1957, cons. to sec., 1969 Author: Minnesota Houses, 1967, Men on a Moving Frontier, 1969, American Churches, 1982, Architecture, Men, Women and Money, 1985, Orders from France, 1989, Greek Revival America, 1989; editl. dir.: Smithsonian Guide to Historic America, 12 vols., 1989-90, Rediscovering America, 1990, Mission 1993, Hidden Cities, 1993, Burr, Jefferson, and Hamilton, 1999; appearances on NBC radio and TV Today, also others, 1954-57; contbr. articles to mags. and profl. jours. Served with USNR, 1944-46. Office: 855 El Caminito St Santa Fe NM 87505-2842 E-mail: rkennedy@attglobal.net

KENNEDY, THOMAS J. lawyer; b. Milw., July 29, 1947; s. Frank Philip and June Marian (Smith) K.; m. Cathy Ann Cohen, Nov. 24, 1978; children: Abby, Sarah. BA, U. Wisc., 1969, JD cum laude, 1972. Bar: Wis. 1972, U.S. Dist. Ct. (ea. and we. dists.) Wis. 1972, Ariz. 1981, U.S. Dist. Ct. Ariz. 1981, U.S. Ct. Appeals (7th cir.) 1980, U.S. Ct. Appeals (9th cir.) 1981, U.S. Ct. Appeals (D.C. cir.) 1983, U.S. Supreme Ct. 1984, U.S. Ct. Appeals (11th cir.) 1986. Assoc. Goldberg, Previant, Milw., 1972-79, Brynelson, Herrick, Madison, Wisc., 1979-81; ptnr. Snell & Wilmer, Phoenix, 1981-93, Lewis and Roca, Phoenix, 1993-96, Ryley, Carlock and Applewhite, Phoenix, 1996-99, Gallagher & Kennedy, 1999—. Contbg. editor The Developing Labor Laws, 2d, 3d edits., The Fair Labor Standards Act. Mem. ABA, Ariz. State Bar, State Bar Wisc., Maricopa County Bar Assn. Avocations: tennis, reading, hiking.

KENNEDY-MINOTT, RODNEY, international relations educator, former ambassador; b. Portland, Oreg. s. Joseph Albert and Gainor (Baird) Minott; children: Katharine Pardow, Rodney Glisan, Polly Berry AB, Stanford U., 1953, MA, 1956, PhD, 1960. Instr. history Stanford U., 1960-61, asst. prof., asst. dir. history of western civilization program, 1961-62, asst. dir. summer session, 1962-63, dir. summer session, 1963-65; mem. staff Congresswoman Edith Green, 1965; assoc. prof. Portland State U., 1965-66; assoc. prof., assoc. dean instrn. Calif. State U., Hayward, 1966-67, prof., 1967-77, head div. humanities, 1967-69; ambassador to Sweden and chmn. Swedish Fulbright Com., 1977-80; adj. prof. Monterey Inst. Internat. Studies, Calif., 1981; exec. v.p. Direction Internat., Washington, 1982-83; sr. research fellow Hoover Instn., 1981-82, 85—; chmn. Alpha Internat., Washington, 1983-85. Sr. fellow Ctr. Internat. Rels., UCLA, 1986-90; prof. nat. security affairs tng., U.S. Naval Postgrad. Sch., Monterey, Calif., 1990—, acad. assoc. for area studies, 1995-97, asst. provost for external affairs, 1995—; dir. environ. security program U.S. Naval Postgrad. Sch., 1999—. Author: Peerless Patriots: The Organized Veterans and the Spirit of Americanism, 1962, The Fortress That Never Was: The Myth of Hitler's Bavarian Stronghold, 1964, The Sinking of the Lollipop: Shirley Temple v. Pete McCloskey, 1968, Regional Force Application: The Maritime Strategy and Its Affect on Nordic Stability, 1988, Tension in the North: Sweden and Nordic Security, 1989, Lonely Path to Follow: Non-aligned Sweden, United States/NATO, and the U.S.S.R., 1990, (with Ciro E. Zoppo) Nordic Security at the Turn of the 21st Century, 1992. Mem. adv. bd. Ctr. for the Pacific Rim U. San Francisco, 1988-93. With U.S. Army, 1946-48, USAR, 1948-53. Mem. VFW, World Affairs Coun., Am. Fgn. Svc. Assn. (assoc.), Marines Meml. Assn. (San Francisco), US Naval Inst., Am. Legion, Stanford U. Faculty Club, Officer Clubs Mil. Dist. Washington D.C. Office: Dept Nat Security Affairs US Naval Postgrad Sch Monterey CA 93943

KENNEL, CHARLES FREDERICK, physics educator, government official, academic administrator; b. Cambridge, Mass., Aug. 20, 1939; s. Archie Clarence and Elizabeth Ann (Fitzpatrick) K.; m. Ellen Lehman; children: Matthew Bochner, Sarah Alexandra. AB (Nat. scholar), Harvard U., 1959; Ph.D. in Astrophys. Scis. (W.C. Peyton Advanced fellow 1962-63), Princeton U., 1964. Prin. rsch. scientist Avco-Everett Rsch. Lab., Mass., 1960-61, 64-67; vis. scientist Internat. Center Theoretical Physics, Trieste, Italy, 1965; faculty UCLA, 1967-71, prof. physics, 1971-98, chmn. dept., 1983-86; mem. Inst. Geophysics and Planetary Physics, 1972-98, acting assoc. dir. inst., 1976-77; space sci. bd. NRC, 1977-80, chmn. com. space physics, 1977-80; Fairchild prof. Calif. Inst. Tech., 1987; assoc. adminstr. NASA, Washington, 1994-96; exec. vice-chancellor UCLA, 1996-98; dir., vice-chancellor Scripps Inst. Oceanography U. Calif.-San Diego, La Jolla, 1998—. Space and earth scis. adv. com. NASA, 1986-89, adv. coun., 1998, chmn., 2001—; mem. NRC Bd. Physics and Astronomy, 1987-94, chmn., 1992-94; chmn. fusion sci. adv. com. NRC, 1998-2001, chmn. NRC com. on global change rsch., 1999—; chmn. Partnership for the Observation of the Global Oceans, 1999—; chmn. plasma sci. NRC, DOE fusion policy adv. com., 1990; Fulbright lectr., Brazil; visitor U.S.-USSR Acads. Exch., 1988-90; disting. vis. prof. U. Alaska, 1988-93; Pew Oceans Commn., 2000—; cons. in field. Co-author: Matter in Motion, The Spirit and Evolution of Physics, 1977; co-editor: Solar System Plasma Physics, 1978. Bd. dirs. L.A. Jr. Ballet Co., 1977-83, pres., 1979-80; bd. dirs. Inst. for Theoretical Physics, Santa Barbara, Calif., 1986-90, San Diego Nat. History Mus., 1998—. NSF postdoctoral fellow, 1965-66, Sloan fellow, 1968-70, Fulbright scholar, 1985, Guggenheim fellow, 1987; recipient Aurelio Peccei prize Acad. Lincei, 1995, Hannes Alfven prize European Geophys. Soc., 1998, NASA Disting. Svc. medal, 1996. Fellow Am. Geophys. Union, Am. Phys. Soc. (pres. div. plasma physics 1989, James Clerk Maxwell prize 1997), AAAS; mem. NAS, Am. Acad. Arts and Scis., Internat. Acad. Astronautics, Calif. Coun. on Sci. and Tech.

KENNEY, BELINDA JILL FORSEMAN, technology company executive; b. Oak Ridge, Tenn., Dec. 18, 1955; d. Jack Woodrow and Betty Jean Forseman; m. Ronald Gene Kenney, Feb. 23, 1985; 1 child, Brandon. BS, U. Tenn., 1977, postgrad., 1977-78; MBA, Emory U., 2000. Sales rep. Xerox Corp., Nashville, 1978-82, maj. account sales mgr., 1982-83, region [illegible] 1987-89, dist. mgr. San Antonio, 1989-95, v.p. Houston, 1995-97, v.p., region gen. mgr. Bus. Svcs. Atlanta, 1998-99, sr. v.p. region mgr. NASG, 2000-2001; corp. v.p. worldwide mktg. and corp. strategy Storage Tech. Corp., Superior, Colo., 2001—. Mem. Emory Univ. Rehab. Golf Bd. Patron, M.D. Anderson Cancer Ctr. Mem. Mensa USA. Lutheran. Avocations: jogging, reading, tennis, health and fitness. Office: StorageTek One StorageTek Dr Louisville CO 80027

KENNEY, RICHARD LAURENCE, poet, English language educator; b. Glens Falls, N.Y., Aug. 10, 1948; s. Laurence Augustine and Martha (Clare) K.; m. Mary Frances Hedberg, July 4, 1982; children: Hollis, Will. BA, Dartmouth Coll., 1970. Poet, 1970—; prof. U. Wash., Seattle, 1986—. Author: (poetry) The Evolution of the Flightless Bird, 1984, Orrery, 1985, The Invention of the Zero, 1993. Recipient Yale Series of Younger Poets prize Yale U. Press, 1983, Rome prize Am. Acad. and Inst. Arts and Letters, 1986, Lannan Literary award, 1994; Guggenheim Found. fellow, 1984; John D. and Catherine MacArthur Found. fellow, 1987-92. Office: U Wash Dept English Seattle WA 98195-0001

KENNEY, THOMAS FREDERICK, broadcasting executive; b. Dearborn, Mich., Sept. 25, 1941; s. Charles B. and Grace M. (Wilson) K.; m. Beth H. Rockwood, Aug. 22, 1964; children: Sean, Blair. B.S., Mich. State U., 1964. Program mgr. Sta. WMBD-TV, Peoria, Ill., 1969-71; exec. producer Sta. WJZ-TV, Balt., 1971-73; program mgr. Sta. KFMB-TV, San Diego, 1973-75; program mgr., then dir. broadcasting ops. Sta. KHOU-TV, Houston, 1975-79; v.p., gen. mgr. KHOU-TV, 1979-84, Sta. WROC-TV, Rochester, N.Y., 1984-90; owner Santa Fe Wireless, Inc., Gainesville, Fla., 1990—. Freelance TV cons., Houston, 1984. Home and Office: 1858 E Campbell Ave Gilbert AZ 85234-8228

KENNEY, WILLIAM JOHN, JR. real estate development executive; b. Huntington Park, Calif., Mar. 9, 1949; s. William John Sr. and Dorothy Marie (Smith) K.; m. Susan Louise Wattson, Sept. 26, 1987. BS in Econs., Calif. State U., Fullerton, 1970, BBA, 1971. Lic. real estate broker, Calif.; cert. leasing specialist, Ariz. Leasing agt. John S. Griffith, Irvine, Calif., 1972-78, dir. leasing, 1978-84; v.p. leasing John S. Griffith (now Donahue Schriber), Newport Beach, Calif., 1984-85, sr. v.p., 1986-91, sr. v.p. devel., 1991-95; founder The Kenney Co., 1995—. Speaker numerous orgns. Bd. dirs. Riverside YMCA, 1989-92. Recipient Certs. Appreciation Hemet C. of C., Riverside (Calif.) Bd. Realtors, Hemet Valley Kiwanis, Riverside Kiwanis. Mem. Calif. Bus. Properties Assn. (chmn. 1988-89, dir. 1976-96), Internat. Coun. Shopping Ctrs. (assoc., chair govt. affairs com. 1994-98), Newport Harbor Bd. Realtors (cert. appreciation), Frank Miller Club (life). Avocations: surfing, fishing, skiing. Office: The Kenney Co 824 Harbor Island Dr Newport Beach CA 92660-7228

KENT, FRANCO J. broadcasting executive; Pres., chief editl. exec. Internat. News Broadcasting Co., Tarzana, CA, 1989—. Office: Internat News Broadcasting Co 19528 Ventura Blvd Ste 140 Tarzana CA 91356-2917

KENT, JEFFREY FRANKLIN, professional baseball player; b. Bellflower, Calif., Mar. 7, 1968; Grad., Edison H.S., Calif. Played 2d base Toronto Blue Jays, 1992; 2d baseman N.Y. Mets, 1992-96, San Francisco Giants, 1996—. Office: San Francisco Giants 24 Willie Mays Plz San Francisco CA 94107-2199

KENT, SUSAN, library director, consultant; b. N.Y.C., Mar. 18, 1944; d. Elias and Minnie (Barnett) Solomon; m. Eric Goldberg, Mar. 27, 1966 (div. Mar. 1991); children: Evan, Jessica, Joanna; m. Rolly Kent, Dec. 20, 1991. BA in English Lit. with honors, SUNY, 1965; MS, Columbia U., 1966. Libr., sr. libr. N.Y. Pub. Libr., 1965-67, br. mgr. Donnell Art Libr., 1967-68; reference libr. Paedergaat br. Bklyn. Pub. Libr., 1971-72; reference libr. Finkelstein Meml. Libr., Spring Valley, N.Y., 1974-76; coord. adult and young adult svcs. Tucson Pub. Libr., 1977-80, acting libr. dir., 1982, dep. libr. dir., 1980-87; mng. dir. Ariz. Theatre Co., Tucson and Phoenix, 1987-89; dir. Mpls. Pub. Libr. and Info. Ctr., 1990-95; city libr. L.A. Pub. Libr., 1995—. Tchr. Pima C.C., Tucson, 1978, grad. libr. sch. U. Ariz., Tucson, 1978, 79; panelist Ariz. Commn. Arts, 1981-85; reviewer pub. programs NEH, 1985, 89, panelist challenge grants, 1986-89, panelist state programs, 1988; cons. to librs. and nonprofit instns., 1989-90, 92—; mem. bd. devel. and fundraising Child's Play, Phoenix, 1983; bd. dirs., mem. organizing devel. and fundraising com. Flagstaff (Ariz.) Symphony Orch., 1988; cons., presenter workshops Young Adult Svcs. divsn. ALA, 1986-88; bd. advisors UCLA Grad. Sch. Edn. and Info. Scis., 1998-2001; presenter in field. Contbr. articles to profl. jours. Chair arts and culture com. Tucson Tomorrow, 1981-85; bd. dirs., v.p. Ariz. Dance Theatre, 1984-86; bd. dirs. women's studies adv. coun. U. Ariz., 1985-90, Arizonans for Cultural Devel., 1987-89, YWCA Mpls., 1991-92; commr. Ariz. Commn. on Arts, 1983-87; participant Leadership Mpls., 1990-91. Fellow Sch. Libr. Sci., Columbia U., 1965-66. Mem. ALA (membership com. S.W. regional chair 1983-86, com. on appts. 1986-87, planning and budget assembly del. 1991-93, gov. coun. 1990-98, chair conf. com. 1996-97), Pub. Libr. Assn. (nominating com. 1980-82, v.p. 1986-87, pres. 1987-88, chair publs. assembly 1988-89, chair nat. conf. 1994, chair legis. com. 1994-95), Calif. Libr. Assn., Urban Librs. Coun. (exec. bd. 1994-2001, treas. 1996-98, vice chair/chair elect 1998, 99, chair 1999-2000), Libr. Adminstrn. and Mgmt. Assn. (John Cotton Dana Award com. 1994-95), Coun. Libr. and Info. Resources (bd. dirs. 2000—). Office: LA Pub Libr 630 W 5th St Los Angeles CA 90071-2002 E-mail: skent@lapl.org

KENYON, CARLETON WELLER, librarian; b. Lafayette, N.Y., Oct. 7, 1923; s. Herbert Abram and Esther Elizabeth (Weller) K.; m. Dora Marie Kallander, May 21, 1948; children: Garnet Eileen, Harmon Clark, Kay Adelle. A.B., Yankton Coll., 1947; M.A., J.D., U. S.D., 1950; A.M. in L.S, U. Mich., 1951. Bar: S.D. 1950. Asst. law librarian, head catalog librarian U. Nebr., 1951-52; asst. reference librarian Los Angeles County Law Library, 1952-54, head catalog librarian, 1954-60; law librarian State of Calif., Sacramento, 1960-69; became cons. Library of Congress, Washington, 1963, asso. law librarian, 1969-71, law librarian, 1971-89. Cons. county law libraries; lectr. legal bibliography and research. Author: California County Law Library Basic List Handbook and Information of New Materials, 1967; compiler: Calif. Library Laws; assisted in compiling checklists of basic: Am. publs. and subject headings; contbr. articles and book revs. to law revs., library jours. Served with USAAC, 1943-46. Mem. ABA, State Bar S.D., Am. Assn. Law Librarians (chmn. com. on cataloging and classification 1969-71, mem. staff Law Library Inst. 1969, 71), Law Librarians Soc. Washington. Home: 4239 44th Ct NE Salem OR 97305-2117

KEOGH, HEIDI HELEN DAKE, advocate; b. Saratoga, N.Y., July 12, 1950; d. Charles Starks and Phyllis Sylvia (Edmunds) Dake; m. Randall Frank Keogh, Nov. 3, 1973; children: Tyler Cameron, Kelly Dake. Student, U. Colo., 1972. Reception, promotions Sta. KLAK, KJAE, Lakewood, Colo., 1972-73; acct. exec. Mixed Media Advt. Agy., Denver, 1973-75; writer, mktg. Jr. League Cookbook Devel., Denver, 1986-88; chmn., coord. Colorado Cache & Creme de Colorado Cookbooks, 1988-90. Speakers bur. Mile High Transplant Bank, Denver, 1983-84, Writer's Inst., U. Denver, 1988; bd. dirs. Stewart's Ice Cream Co., Inc., Jr. League, Denver. Contbr. articles to profl. jours. Fiscal officer, bd. dirs. Mile High Transplant Bank; blockworker Heart Fund and Am. Cancer Soc., Littleton, Colo., 1978—, Littleton Rep. Com., 1980-84; fundraising vol. Littleton Pub. Schs., 1980—; vol. Gathering Place, bd. dirs., 1996—, chmn. Brown Bag benefit, 1996; vol. Hearts for Life, 1991—, Oneday, 1992, Denver Ballet Guild, 1992—, Denver Ctr. Alliance, 1993—, Newborn Hope, 1980—, Girls, Inc., 1995—, Girls Hope, VOA Guild, 1996—, Le Bal de Ballet, 1998—, The Denver Social Register and Record, 1999, 00. Mem. Jr. League Denver (pub. rels. bd., v.p. ways and means 1989-90, planning coun./ad hoc 1990-92, sustainer spl. events 1993-94), Community Emergency Fund (chair 1991-92), Jon D. Williams Cotillion at Columbine (chmn. 1991-93), Columbine Country Club, Gamma Alpha Chi, Pi Beta Phi Alumnae Club (pres. Denver chpt. 1984-85, 93-94, nat. conv. chmn. Denver 2001), Pi Beta Phi. Episcopalian. Avocations: traveling, skiing, golf, family activities. Home: 63 Fairway Ln Littleton CO 80123-6648

KEOGH, KEITH, food company executive; b. Sanford, Fla., Dec. 24, 1952; married; two children. Apprentice, Disney Sch. of Culinary Arts. Chef Walt Disney World Co.; mgr. Culinary Team USA, 1992-96; exec. v.p., COO CCA, 1996, pres., CEO. Recipient Prestigious World Medal, World Assn. Cooks Socs., 1996, three world championships Culinary Team USA; named First Am. Pres. World Assn. Cooks Socs., 1992-96. Office: California Culinary Acad 625 Polk St San Francisco CA 94102-3336

KEOUGH, SHAWN, state legislator; b. Pompton Plains, N.J., Dec. 30, 1959; m. Mike Keough; children: Bryan, Daniel. Student, North Idaho Coll.; student in bus. mgmt., Lewis Clark State Coll. In pub. rels.; mem. Idaho Senate, Dist. 1, Boise, 1996—. Vice chair transp. com., mem. agrl. affairs, commerce and human resources, and edn. coms. Mem. Idaho Women in Timber, Greater Sandpoint (Idaho) C. of C. Republican. Protestant. Office: State Capitol PO Box 83720 Boise ID 83720-3720

KERBS, WAYNE ALLAN, transportation executive; b. Hoisington, Kans., Mar. 21, 1930; s. Emanuel and Mattie (Brack) K.; m. Patricia Ann Aitchison, Dec. 5, 1953; children: Jacqueline Lee Kerbs Kepler, Robert Wayne. BSEE, U. Kans., 1952; MSEE, Ohio State U., 1960; M Engring., UCLA, 1968; postgrad., Calif. State U., Long Beach, 2000—. Test engr. Mpls.-Honeywell, 1952-54; sr. engr. Booz Allen & Hamilton, Dayton, Ohio, 1957-60; program mgr. Hughes Aircraft Co., L.A., 1960-74; pres., bd. dirs. Kerbs Industries, Inc., Los Alamitos, Calif., 1975—. Developer spacecraft devel. surveyor, 1960's, transit plan, 1996; patentee in field. Vol. PTA, Boy Scouts Am., Meth. Ch., 1952—; organizer Am. Mature Vols., L.a., 1994—; active Orange County Transp. Authority, 1994—. Lt. USN, 1954-57. Fellow Inst. for the Advancement of Engring.; mem. Soc. Automotive Engrs. (bd. dirs.), Inst. of Transp. Engrs., Elec. Automobile Assn., Advanced Transit Assn., Transp. Rsch. Bd., Am. Legion, Sigma Tau, Eta Kappa Nu, Kappa Eta Kappa. Republican. Avocations: sports, building, inventing, writing, investing. E-mail: kkerbs@socal.rr.com

KERKORIAN, KIRK, motion picture company executive, consultant; b. Fresno, Calif., June 6, 1917; s. Ahron and Lily K.; m. Hilda Schmidt, Jan. 24, 1942 (div. 1951); m. Jane Maree Hardy, Dec. 5, 1954; children: Tracy, Linda. Student pub. schs., L.A. Comml. airline pilot, from 1940; founder L.A. Air Svc. (later Trans Internat. Airlines Corp.), 1948, Internat. Leisure Corp., 1968; controlling stockholder Western Airlines, 1970; chief exec. officer Metro-Goldwyn-Mayer, Inc., Culver City, Calif., 1973-74, chmn. exec. com., vice-chmn. bd., 1974-79; controlling stockholder MGM/UA Communications Co.; cons., 1979—. Served as capt. Transport Command RAF, 1942-44. Office: Tracinda 4835 Koval Ln Las Vegas NV 89109-7308

KERMAN, JOSEPH WILFRED, musicologist, critic; b. London, Apr. 3, 1924; U.S. citizen; married, 1946; 3 children. PhD in Music, Princeton U., 1951. Instr. music Princeton U., 1948-49; dir. grad. studies Westminster Choir Coll., 1949-51, from asst. prof. to assoc. prof., 1951-60, chmn. dept., 1961-64, 91-93; prof. music U. Calif., Berkeley, 1960-94, Jerry and Evelyn Hemmings Chambers prof. music, 1985-87, prof. emeritus, 1994—; C.E. Norton prof. poetry Harvard U., 1997. Heather prof. music Oxford U., 1972-74; Valentine prof. music Amherst Coll., 1988, Phi Beta Kappa, scholar, 1993. Author: Opera as Drama, 1956, rev. edit., 1989, The Elizabethan Madrigal, 1962, The Beethoven, Quartets, 1967, The Masses and Motets of William Byrd, 1981, Contemplating Music, 1985, Write All These Down, 1994, Concerto Conversations, 1999; (with others) History of Art and Music, 1968, Listen, 1972, 7th edit., 1999, The New Grove Beethoven, 1983; editor: Beethoven: Autograph Miscellany, 1970, Music at the Turn of the Century, 1970; co-editor Jour. 19th Century Music U. Calif., 1977-88. Recipient Nat. Inst. Arts and Letters award, 1956, Kinkeldey award Am. Musicol. Soc., 1970, 81, Deems Taylor award ASCAP, 1981, 95; Guggenheim fellow, 1960, Fulbright fellow, 1967, NEH fellow, 1982. Fellow Am. Acad. Arts and Scis., Brit. Acad. (corr.), Royal Musical Assn. (hon. fgn.), Am. Musicol. Soc. (hon.). Office: U Calif Berkeley Dept Music Berkeley CA 94720-0001 E-mail: jokerm@socrates.berkeley.edu

KERN, DONALD MICHAEL, internist; b. Belleville, Ill., Nov. 21, 1951; s. Donald Milton and Dolores Olivia (Rust) K. BS in Biology, Tulane U., 1973; MD magna cum laude, U. Brussels, 1983. ECFMG cert.; lic. Calif., Fla. Intern in surgery Berkshire Med. Ctr., Pittsfield, Mass., 1983-84; intern in psychiatry Tufts New England Med. Ctr., Boston, 1984-85; resident in internal medicine Kaiser Found. Hosp., San Francisco, 1985-87; with assoc. staff internal medicine Kaiser Permanente Med. Group, Inc., San Francisco, 1987-89; assoc. investigator AIDS Clin. Trial Unit Kaiser Permanente Med. Ctr., Stanford U., Nat. Inst. Allergy & Infectious Disease, San Francisco, 1988-90; mem. staff internal medicine Kaiser Permanente Med. Group, South San Francisco, 1989-96; mem. staff Desert Med. Group, Palm Springs, Calif., 1996—. Democrat. Roman Catholic. Avocations: theatre, ballet, traveling, 17th and 18th century French antiques. Office: Desert Medical Group 275 N El Cielo Rd Palm Springs CA 92262

KERN, IRVING JOHN, retired food company executive; b. N.Y.C., Feb. 10, 1914; s. John and Min (Weitzner) Kleinberger; m. Beatrice Rubenfeld, June 22, 1941; children— John A., Arthur H., Robert M. BS, NYU, 1934, student Grad. Sch. Art and Sci., 1960-65; DHL, Mercy Coll., Dobbs Ferry, N.Y., 1980. Asst. buyer Bloomingdale's Dept. Store, N.Y.C., 1934-40; with Dellwood Foods, Inc., Yonkers, N.Y., 1945-82, pres., 1966-77, chmn. and chief exec. officer, 1977-82. Dir. Scarsdale Nat. Bank; adj. prof. polit. sci., San Diego State U., 1989-95. Mem. County Mental Health Svcs. Bd. of Westchester County, 1954-59; mem. bd. dirs., sec. Westchester County Assn., 1950-57, 76-80; exec. bd. Westchester County Better Bus. Bur., 1970-73; bd. dirs. Westchester Coalition, 1972-80, Westchester Minority Bus. Assistance Orgn., 1973-75, Milk Industry Found., 1976-82, Nat. Dairy Coun., 1979-81; bd. dirs., vice chmn. Westchester Pvt. Industry Coun., 1979-82; mil. adv. coun. Ctr. for Def. Info., 1986-97. Lt. col. AUS, 1940-45. Decorated Bronze Star. Mem. N.Y. Milk Bottlers Fedn. (pres., dir.), Met. Dairy Inst. (exec. v.p., dir.), Phi Beta Kappa, Tau Epsilon Phi.

KERN, JOHN MCDOUGALL, lawyer; b. Omaha, Nov. 28, 1946; m. Susan McDougall Kern, Oct. 15, 1977. BA, Creighton U., 1970; JD cum laude, George Washington U., 1973. Bar: D.C. 1973, Calif. 1980, U.S. Dist. Ct. D.C. 1974, U.S. Dist Ct. (no. dist.) Calif. 1980, U.S. Dist. Ct. (ctrl. dist.) Calif. 1996, U.S. Ct. Appeals (D.C. cir.) 1974, U.S. Ct. Appeals (9th cir.) 1978; bd. cert. specialist in civil trial advocacy, Nat. Bd. Trial Advocacy. Asst. U.S. atty. criminal divsn. Office of U.S. Atty. D.C., Washington, 1973-78; asst. U.S. atty. civil divsn. Office U.S. Atty. No. Dist. Calif., San Francisco, 1978-82; v.p., dir. Crosby, Heafey, Roach & May P.C., San Francisco, Oakland, L.A., 1981—. Faculty Nat. Inst. Trial Advocacy, 1987—; spkr. numerous programs, confs.; lectr. in field. Contbr. abstracts, book chpt., articles to profl. jours. Mem. Am. Bd. Trial Advocates (advocate), Am. Inn of Ct., Assn. Bus. Trial Lawyers, Nat. Inst. Trial Advocacy. Office: Crosby Heafey Roach & May PC 2 Embarcadero Ctr Ste 2000 San Francisco CA 94111-3922 E-mail: jkern@chrm.com

KERNS, JOANNA DE VARONA, actress, writer, director; b. San Francisco, Feb. 12, 1953; d. David Thomas and Martha Louise (Smith) de V.; m. Richard Martin Kerns, Dec. 11, 1976 (div. Dec. 1986); 1 child, Ashley Cooper. Student, NYU, 1970-71. TV series include The Four Seasons, 1984, Growing Pains; TV includes A Wedding On Waltons Mountain, 1982, V, 1983, Stormin' Home, 1985, The Return of Marcus Welby, M.D., 1984, The Rape of Richard Beck, 1985, Mother's Day On Waltons Mountain, 1982, A Bunny's Tale, 1985, Robin Cook's Mortal Fear, 1994, Whose Daughter is She?, 1995, No One Could Protect Her, 1995, See Jane Run, 1995, Terror In the Family, 1996; movies include Cross My Heart, 1986, Mother Knows Best, 1997, Sisters and Other Strangers, 1997, Emma's Wish, 1998, Girl Interrupted, 1999. Democrat. Office: CAA 9830 Wilshire Blvd Beverly Hills CA 90212-1804

KERR, ANDREW W. aerodynamics researcher; b. N.Y.C., Feb. 15, 1941; BSE in Aero. Engring., Princeton U., 1962; MSAE, U. So. Calif., 1965. With Lockheed-Calif. Co., 1963-75, group engr. rotary-wing aero/propulsion, acting mgr., rotary-wing flight scis.; chief Advanced Sys. Rsch. Office U.S. Army Aviation and Troop Command, Moffett Field, Calif., dir. aeroflightdynamics directorate, 1986—. Contbr. articles to profl. jours. Fellow Am. Helicopter Soc. (hon., mem. aerodynamics and handling qualities tech. com.); mem. Am. Inst. Aero. and Astronaut. (sr., V/STOL com.) Office: US Army Aviation Missile Command Aeroflightdynamics Directorate MS 219-3 Ames Rsch Ctr Moffett Field CA 94035-1000

KERR, CLARK, academic administrator emeritus; b. Stony Creek, Pa., May 17, 1911; s. Samuel William and Caroline (Clark) K.; m. Catherine Spaulding, Dec. 25, 1934; children: Clark E., Alexander W., Caroline M. BA, Swarthmore Coll., 1932, LLD, 1952; MA, Stanford U., 1933; postgrad., London Sch. Econs., 1936, 39; PhD, U. Calif., 1939; LLD, Harvard U., 1958, Princeton U., 1959, others. Traveling fellow Am. Friends Svc. Com., 1935-36; instr. econs. Antioch Coll., 1936-37; tchg. fellow U. Calif., 1937-38; Newton Booth fellow, 1938-39; acting asst. prof. labor econs. Stanford, 1939-40; asst., later assoc. prof. U. Wash., 1940-45; assoc. prof., prof., prof. emeritus, dir. Inst. Indsl. Rels., U. Calif., Berkeley, 1945-52, chancellor, 1952-58, pres., 1958-67, pres. emeritus, 1974—. Chmn. Carnegie Commn. on Higher Edn., 1967-73, Carnegie Coun. Policy Studies in Higher Edn., 1974-79; vice chmn. divsns. War Labor Bd., 1943-45; nat. arbitrator Armour Co. and United Packing House Workers, 1945-52; impartial chmn. Waterfront Employers, Pacific Coast and Internat. Longshoremen's and Warehousemen's Union, 1946-47; pub. mem. Nat. WSB, 1950-51; various arbitrations in pub. utilities, newspaper, aircraft, canning, oil, local transport and other industries, 1942— ; mem. adv. panel Soc. Sci. Rsch., NSF, 1953-57; chmn. Armour Automation Com., 1959-79; chmn. bd. arbitrators U.S. Postal Svc. and Nat. Assn. Letter Carriers (AFL-CIO) and Am. Postal Workers Union (AFL-CIO), 1984 Author: (with E. Wight Bakke) Unions, Management and the Public, rev. edit., 1960, 67, (with Dunlop, Harbison, Myers) Industrialism and Industrial Man, rev. edit., 1964, 73, The Uses of the University, rev. edit., 1972, 82, 95, 2001, Labor and Management in Industrial Society, 1964, Marshall, Marx and Modern Times, 1969, Labor Markets and Wage Determination: The Balkanization of Labor Markets and Other Essays, 1977, Education and National Development: Reflections from an American Perspective during a Period of Global Reassessment, 1979, The Future of Industrial Societies, 1983, (with Marian L. Gade) The Many Lives of Academic Presidents, 1986; editor: (with Paul D. Staudohar) Industrial Relations in a New Age, 1986, Economics of Labor in Industrial Society, 1986, (with Dunlop, Lester, Reynolds; editor Bruce E. Kaufman) How Labor Markets Work: Reflections on Theory and Practice, 1988, (with Marian L. Gade) The Guardians: Boards of Trustees of American Colleges and Universities, 1989, The Great Transformation in Higher Education, 1960-80, 1991, Troubled Times for American Higher Education: The 1990s and Beyond, 1994, Higher Education Cannot Escape History: Issues for the Twenty-First Century, 1994, (with Paul D. Staudohar) Labor Economics and Industrial Relations: Markets and Institutions, 1994, The Gold and the Blue, Vol. 1: Academic Triumphs, 2001. Trustee Rockefeller Found., 1960-76; mem. bd. mgrs. Swarthmore Coll., 1969-80, life mem., 1981. Recipient Harold W. McGraw Jr. prize in Edn., 1990; named Hon. fellow London Sch. Econs. Mem. Am. Econ. Assn., Royal Econ. Assn., Am. Acad. Arts and Scis., Indsl. Rels. Rsch. Assn., Nat. Acad. Arbitrators, Phi Beta Kappa, Kappa Sigma. Mem. Soc. of Friends. Home: 8300 Buckingham Dr El Cerrito CA 94530-2530 Office: U Calif Inst Indsl Rels 2521 Channing Way # 5555 Berkeley CA 94720-5556

KERR, FREDERICK HOHMANN, retired health care company executive; b. Pitts., July 11, 1936; s. Nathan Frederick and Laura Marie (Hohmann) K.; m. Ethyl Nylene Bashline, 1960 (div. 1969); m. Phyllis Jensen, Aug. 21, 1970, 1 child, Linda Jean. BA, Pa. State U., 1958; MPA, U. Pitts., 1961; LLD (hon.), Luth. Coll. Health Professions, Ft. Wayne, Ind., 1996. Exec. sec. Pa. Economy League Fayette County Br., Uniontown, Pa., 1959, Armstrong County Br., Kittanning, 1959-62; exec. sec. Woodbury Tax Rsch. Conf., Sioux City, Iowa, 1962-65; pub. svc. dir. City of Sioux City, 1965-66; from asst. administr. to assoc. administr. St. Luke's Regional Med. Ctr., Sioux City, 1966-71; administr., CEO, Meml. Hosp. of Michigan City, Inc., Ind., 1971-75; pres., CEO, St. Luke's Hosp., Maumee, Ohio, 1975-86, Luth. Hosp. Ind., Luth. Coll. Health Professions, Ft. Wayne, 1986-95; v.p. for devel. Quorum Health Resources, Inc., Brentwood, Tenn., 1995-2001. Dir. Ohio Hosp. Ins. Co., Columbus, treas. 1981-84. Trustee Ohio Hosp. Assn., Columbus, 1983-85; dir. Siouxland United Way, 1968-71, Ft. Wayne Pub. TV, 1990-94, United Way Allen County, Ft. Wayne, 1990-94; mem. Iowa Intergovtl. Rels. Com., Des Moines, 1964-67. 2nd lt. U.S. Army, 1958-59. Mem. Am. Protestant Health Assn. (vice chmn. 1988-90), Am. Hosp. Assn. (ho. dels. 1991—), ASPA (life, nat. coun. 1966-69), Avocations: wine appreciation, golf.

KERRICK, DAVID ELLSWORTH, lawyer; b. Caldwell, Idaho, Jan. 15, 1951; s. Charles Ellsworth and Patria (Olesen) K.; m. Juneal Casper, May 24, 1980; children: Peter Ellsworth, Beth Anne, George Ellis, Katherine Leigh. Student, Coll. of Idaho, 1969-71; BA, U. Wash., 1972; JD, U. Idaho, 1980. Bar: Idaho 1980, U.S. Dist. Ct. Idaho 1980, U.S. Ct. Appeals (9th cir.) 1981. Mem. Idaho Senate, 1990-96, majority caucus chmn., 1992-94, majority leader, 1994-96. Mem. S.W. Idaho Estate Planning Coun. Mem. ABA, Assn. Trial Lawyers Am., Idaho Bar Assn. (3d dist. pres. 1985-86), Idaho Trial Lawyers Assn., Canyon County Lawyers Assn. (pres. 1985). Republican. Presbyterian. Lodge: Elks. Avocations: skiing, photography. Office: PO Box 44 Caldwell ID 83606-0044

KERSCHNER, LEE R(ONALD), academic administrator, political science educator; b. May 31, 1931; m. Helga Koller, June 22, 1958; children: David, Gabriel, Riza. B.A. in Polit. Sci. (Univ. fellow), Rutgers U., 1953; M.A. in Internat. Relations (Univ. fellow), Johns Hopkins U., 1958; Ph.D. in Polit. Sci. (Univ. fellow), Georgetown U., 1964. From instr. to prof. polit. sci. Calif. State U., Fullerton, 1961-69, prof., 1988—; state univ. dean Calif. State Univs. and Colls. Hdqrs., Long Beach, 1969-71, asst. exec. vice chancellor, 1971-76, vice chancellor for adminstrv. affairs, 1976-77, vice chancellor acad. affairs, 1987-92; exec. dir. Colo. Commn. on Higher Edn., Denver, 1977-83, Nat. Assn. Trade and Tech. Schs., 1983-85, Calif. Commn. on Master Plan for Higher Edn., 1985-87; interim pres. Calif. State U., Stanislaus, 1992-94, spl. asst. to the chancellor, 1994-97; exec. vice chancellor Minn. State Colls. and Univs., St. Paul, 1996-97; vice chancellor emeritus Calif. State U., 1997—. Mem. Calif. Student Aid Commn., 1993-96; cons. in field. Mem. exec. com. Am. Jewish Com., Denver, 1978-83; internat. bd. dirs. Amigos de las Americas, 1982-88 (chmn. 1985-87). Served with USAF, 1954-58; col. Res., ret. Home: PO Box 748 Weimar CA 95736-0748

KERTH, LEROY T. physics educator; b. Visalia, Calif., Nov. 23, 1928; s. Lewis John and Frances (Niccolls) K.; m. Ruth Lorraine Littlefield, Nov. 19, 1950; children: Norman Lewis, Randall Thomas, Christine Jane, Bradley Niccolls. A.B. in Physics, U. Calif., Berkeley, 1950, Ph.D., 1957. Mem. staff Lawrence Berkeley Lab, U. Calif., Berkeley, 1950-59, sr. scientist, 1959-61; assoc. prof. physics U. Calif., Berkeley, 1961-65, prof., 1965-93, prof. emeritus, 1993—, assoc. dean Coll. Letters and Scis., 1966-70, spl. asst. to chancellor, 1970-71, assoc. dir. for info. and computing scis. div., 1983-87, assoc. lab. dir. for gen. scis., Lawrence Berkeley Lab., 1987-89, assoc. lab. dir. sci. and tech. resources, Lawrence Berkeley Lab., 1990-92. Fellow Am. Phys. Soc. Home: 5 Los Conejos Orinda CA 94563-2214 Office: U Calif Lawrence Berkeley Lab Berkeley CA 94720-0001 E-mail: ltkerth@lbl.gov

KERTTULA, BETH, state legislator; b. Guthrie, Okla., Jan. 8, 1956; d. Jan and Joyce Kerttula; m. Jim Powell. BA, Stanford U., 1978; JD, U. Santa Clara, 1981. Pub. defender, Alaska, 1982-86; atty. pvt. practice, 1986-96; rep. Alaska Ho. Reps., Anchorage, 1998—. Counsel Alaska State Senate Judiciary Com., 1988; pro bono program Alaska Legal Svcs. Active Alaska Native Sisterhood, Big Bros./Big Sisters Juneau, past pres. Mem. Alaska Bar Assn. (past pres., bd. govs.), Coastal State Orgn. (past chair legal coun.), Juneau Nordic Ski Club. Democrat. Office: Alaska Ho Reps State Capitol Rm 430 Juneau AK 99801-1182 E-mail: representative_beth_kertula@legis.state.ak.us

KERTZ, MARSHA HELENE, accountant, educator; b. Palo Alto, Calif., May 29, 1946; d. Joe and Ruth (Lazear) K. BSBA in Acctg., San Jose State U., 1976, MBA, 1977. CPA, Calif., cert. tax profl. Staff acct. Steven Kroff & Co., CPA's, Palo Alto, 1968-71, 73-74; contr. Rand Teleprocessing Corp., San Francisco, 1972; auditor, sr. acct. Ben F. Priest Accountancy Corp., Mountain View, Calif., 1974-83; tchr. San Jose Unified Regional Occupation Program, San Jose, 1977; pvt. practice accounting San Jose, 1977-2000; lectr. San Jose State U., 1977—. Bd. dirs. San Jose State U. Coll. of Bus. Alumni Assn. Mem. AICPA, Nat. Soc. of Tax Profls., Am. Inst. Tax Studies, Am. Acctg. Assn., Calif. Soc. CPAs, San Jose State U. Coll. Bus. Alumni Assn. (bd. dirs.), Beta Alpha Psi, Beta Gamma Sigma. Democrat. Jewish. Avocations: piano, travel, art history. Home: 4544 Strawberry Park Dr San Jose CA 95129-2213 Office: San Jose State U Acctg & Fin Dept San Jose CA 95192-0066 E-mail: kertz_m@cob.sjsu.edu, MarshaHK@aol.com

KERTZMAN, MITCHELL E. software company executive; LHD (hon.), U. Mass., Lowell. Founder Computer Solutions, 1974; founder, CEO Powersoft Corp., 1993; chmn. bd. dirs., CEO Sybase, Inc., Emeryville, Calif., 1995-98; pres., CEO Liberate Techs., Redwood Shores, 1998—. Bd. dirs. Sybase, Inc., Shiva Corp., CNET, Interconnect Syss., Inc.; pres. Mass. Software Coun., 1994-96. Founder, chmn. Mass. Inst. New Commonwealth; mem. N.Y. State Comm. Indsl. Competitiveness, chair task force indsl. policy. Recipient Inc. Mag. and Ernst & Young's New England Entrepreneur of Yr. award, 1993, Disting. Achievement award Tech. Unit New England B'nai B'rith, 1993. Office: Liberate Techs 2 Circle Star Way San Carlos CA 94070-6200

KERWIN, WILLIAM JAMES, electrical engineering educator, consultant; b. Portage, Wis., Sept. 27, 1922; s. James William and Nina Elizabeth (Haight) K.; m. Madolyn Lee Lyons, Aug. 31, 1947; children: Dorothy E., Deborah K., David W. B.S., U Redlands, 1948; M.S., Stanford U., 1954, Ph.D., 1967. Aero. research scientist NACA, Moffett Field, Calif., 1948-59; chief measurements research br. NASA, Moffett Field, 1959-62, chief space tech. br., 1962-64, chief electronics research br., 1964-70; head electronics dept. Stanford Linear Accelerator Ctr., 1962; prof. elec. engrng. U. Ariz., Tucson, 1969-85, prof. emeritus, 1986—. Cons. Power Electronics, 1980—. Author: (with others) Active Filters, 1970, Handbook Measurement Science, 1982, Instrumentation and Control, 1990, Handbook of Electrical Engineering, 1993, 97; contbr. articles to profl. jours.; patentee in field. Served to capt. USAAF, 1942-46. Recipient Invention NASA, 1969, 70; recipient fellow NASA, 1966-67 Fellow IEEE (Centennial medal 1984) Home: 1981 W Shalimar Way Tucson AZ 85704-1250 Office: U Ariz Dept Elec And Computer Engri Tucson AZ 85721-0001

KESEY, KEN, writer; b. La Hunta, Colo., Sept. 17, 1935; s. Fred and Geneva (Smith) K.; m. Norma Faye Haxby, May 20, 1956; children: Shannon, Zane, Jed (dec. 1984) Sunshine. BS, U. Oreg., 1957; postgrad., Stanford U., 1958-60. Pres. Intrepid Trips, Inc., 1964; editor, pub. mag. Spit in the Ocean, 1974—. Author: One Flew Over the Cuckoo's Nest, 1962, Sometimes a Great Notion, 1964, Garage Sale, 1973, Demon Box, 1986, Little Tricker the Squirrel Meets Big Double the Bear, 1988; co-author: Caverns, 1989, The Further Inquiry, 1990, The Sea Lion, 1991, Sailor Song, 1992; (with Ken Babbs) Last Go Round: a Real Western, 1994; author, prodr.: (play) Twister, 1995; (video and script) Twister, 1998, (video movie) Intrepid Traveler and His Merry Band of Pranksters Look for a Cool Place, Episode One, 2000. E-mail: intrepidtrips.com. Address: 85829 Ridgeway Rd Pleasant Hill OR 97455-9627 E-mail: kenk@efn.org

KESSEL, BRINA, ornithologist, educator; b. Ithaca, N.Y., Nov. 20, 1925; d. Marcel and Quinta (Cattell) K.; m. Raymond B. Roof, June 19, 1957 (dec. 1968). BS (Albert R. Brand Bird Song Found. scholar), Cornell U., 1947, PhD, 1951; MS (Wis. Alumni Research Found. fellow), U. Wis.-Madison, 1949. Student asst. Patuxent Research Refuge, 1946; student teaching asst. Cornell U., 1945-47, grad. asst., 1947-48, 49-51; instr. biol. sci. U. Alaska, summer 1951, asst. prof. biol. sci., 1951-54, assoc. prof. zoology, 1954-59, prof. zoology, 1959-96, head dept. biol. scis., 1957-66; dean U. Alaska (Coll. Biol. Scis. and Renewable Resources), 1961-72, curator terrestrial vertebrate mus. collections, 1972-90, curator ornithology collection, 1990-95, adminstrv. assoc. for acad. programs, grad. and undergrad., dir. acad. advising, office of chancellor, 1973-80; sr. scientist U. Alaska, 1996-99, prof. emeritus, dean emeritus, curator emeritus, 1999—. Project dir. U. Alaska ecol. investigation for AEC Project Chariot, 1959-63; ornithol. investigations NW Alaska pipeline, 1976-81, Susitna Hydroelectric Project, 1980-83 Author books, monographs; contbr. articles to profl. jours. Fellow AAAS, Am. Ornithologists' Union (v.p. 1977, pres.-elect 1990-92, pres. 1992-94), Arctic Inst. N.Am.; mem. Wilson, Cooper ornith. socs., Soc. for Northwestern Vertebrate Biology, Pacific Seabird Group, Assn. Field Ornithologists, Sigma Xi (pres. U. Alaska 1957), Phi Kappa Phi, Sigma Delta Epsilon. Office: U Alaska Mus PO Box 80211 Fairbanks AK 99708-0211 E-mail: ffbxk@uaf.edu

KESSELHAUT, ARTHUR MELVYN, financial consultant; b. Newark, May 18, 1935; s. Harry and Rela (Wolk) K.; m. Nancy Slater, June 17, 1956; children— Stuart Lee, Amy Beth. B.S. in Bus. Adminstrn, Syracuse (N.Y.) U., 1958; postgrad., NYU. With Coopers & Lybrand, N.Y.C., 1958-64; treas., chief fin. officer and sr. v.p. Anchor Group, Elizabeth, N.J., 1964-79; treas., sr. v.p. also Anchor Capital Fund, Anchor Daily Income Fund, Inc., Anchor Growth Fund, Inc., Anchor Income Fund, Inc., Anchor Spectrum Fund, Inc., Fundamental Investors, Inc., Westminster Fund, Washington Nat. Fund, Inc., Anchor Pension Mgmt. Co.; sr. v.p. corp. [illegible] USLIFE Corp., N.Y.C., 1979-82, exec. v.p., chief operating officer, 1982-86; pres., chief exec. officer, dir. USLIFE Equity Sales Corp, 1985-86; exec. v.p. Pacific Mut. Life Ins. Co., Newport Beach, Calif., 1986-92; chmn., CEO, bd. dirs. Pacific Equities Network, Newport Beach, 1992-93; chmn., CEO Resource Network, San Juan Capistrano, 1993—. Bd. dirs. Mut. Svc. Corp., United Planners Group, So. Calif. Entrepreneurship Acad. Commr. econ. devel., City of Dana Point, Calif. With U.S. [illegible] 92629

KESSELMAN, JONATHAN RHYS, economics educator, public policy researcher; b. Columbus, Ohio, Mar. 17, 1946; s. Louis C. and Jennie K.; m. Sheila Kaplan, Mar. 12, 1973; 1 child, Maresa. BA with honors, Oberlin Coll., 1968; PhD in Econs., MIT, 1972. Asst. prof. econs. U. B.C., Vancouver, Can., 1972-76, assoc. prof. Can., 1976-81, prof. Can., 1981—, dir. Ctr. for Rsch. on Econ. and Social Policy Can., 1992—. Rsch. assoc. Inst. for Rsch. on Poverty, Madison, Wis., 1974-75; vis. scholar Delhi Sch. Econs., New Delhi, 1978-79; cons. econs., 1973—; prin. investigator Equality, Security and Community Rsch. Project, 1998—. Author: Financing Canadian Unemployment Insurance, 1983, Rate Structure and Personal Taxation, 1990, General Payroll Taxes, 1997; editorial bd.: Can. Pub. Policy, 1997—, Can. Tax Jour., 1999—; contbr. numerous articles on taxation, income security, employment policy to profl. jours. Bd. dirs. Tibetan Refugee Aid Soc., Vancouver, 1980-82; mem. adv. panel Can. Ministry Employment and Immigration, Ottawa, Ont., 1982-83; mem. B.C. Econ. Policy Inst., 1983-86; trustee pension plan U. B.C., 1988-90; chmn. Musqueam Indian Band Taxation Adv. Coun., 1992-96, mem., 1996-98; mem. B.C. Premier's Forum on New Opportunities for Working and Living, 1994-95; mem. compliance adv. com. Revenue Can. Taxation, 1997-99. Sr. scholar Oberlin Coll., 1967-68; NSF fellow, 1968-70; grantee U.S. Dept. Labor, 1971-72; leave fellow Can. Coun., (locat.) New Delhi, 1978-79; grantee Social Sci. and Humanities Rsch. Coun. Can., 1983-84, 90—; vis. fellow Australian Nat. U., Canberra, 1985; professorial fellow in econ. policy Res. Bank of Australia, 1985; recipient Doug Purvis award, Can. Econ. Assn., 1998. Mem. Am. Econ. Assn., Can. Econs. Assn., Can. Tax Found. Home: 4273 Musqueam Dr Vancouver BC Canada V6N 3R8 Office: U BC Dept Econs 997-1873 E Mall Vancouver BC Canada V6T 1Z1 E-mail: kessel@econ.ubc.ca

KESSLER, A. D. business, financial, investment and real estate advisor, consultant, educator, lecturer, author, broadcaster, producer; b. N.Y.C., May 1, 1923; s. Morris William and Belle Miriam (Pastor) K.; m. Ruth Schwartz, Nov. 20, 1944 (div. 1974); children: Brian Lloyd, Judd Stuart, Earl Vaughn; m. Jaclyn Jeanne Sprague. Student U. Newark, 1940-41, Rutgers U., 1941-42, 46, Albright Coll., 1942, Newark Coll. Engring., 1946; PhD in Pub. Adminstrn. U. Fla., 1972; MBA, Kensington U., 1976, PhD in Mgmt. and Behavioral Psychology, 1977. Sr. cert. rev. appraiser; cert. bus. counselor; cert. exchanger; registered mortgage underwriter; registered investment advisor. Pvt. practice real estate, ins. and bus. brokerage, N.J., Pa., Fla., N.Y., Nev., Calif., Hong Kong, 1946—; pres. Armor Corp., 1947-68; pres. Folding Carton Corp., Am., N.Y.C., 1958-68; exec. v.p. Henry Schindall Assocs., N.Y.C., 1966-67; tax rep. Calif. State Bd. Equalization, 1968-69; aviation cons. transp. div. Calif., Dept. Aeros., also pub. info. officer; 1969-71; FAA Gen. Aviation Safety Counselor; broker, mgr. La Costa (Calif.) Sales Corp., 1971-75; chmn. bd. Profl. Ednl. Found., 1975—, Timeshare Resorts Internat., 1975—, Interex, Leucadia, Calif., 1975-82, The Kessler Orgn., Rancho Santa Fe, Calif., 1975—, The Kessler Fin. Group, Fin. Ind. Inst., 1977—; pres. Ednl. Video Inst., 1978—, Fin. Planning Inst., 1975—, Rancho Santa Fe Real Estate & Land, Inc., 1975—; treas., exec. bd. dirs. Nat. Challenge Com. on Disability, 1983-90; dir. Practice Mgmt. Cons. Abacus Data Systems, 1984—; broker mgr. Rancho Sante Fe Acreage & Homes, Inc., 1987-89; mktg. dir. Commercial Real Estate Services, Rancho Santa Fe, 1987—; cons. broker Glenct. Properties Ptnrs., 1989-90; dir. U.S. Advisors, 1989—; founder Creative Real Estate Movement, 1946—; pub., editor in chief Creative Real Estate Mag., 1975—; pub. Creative Real Estate Mag. of Australia and New Zealand; founder, editor Moderator of Tape of the Month Club; founder, producer, chmn. Internat. Real Estate Expo; chmn. bd. The Brain Trust, Rancho Santa Fe, Calif., 1977—; fin. lectr. for Internat. Cruise Ships, Cunard Line, Norwegian Am. Cruises, P&O, Princess, others; lectr. life enrichment and stress mgmt. Internat. Cruise Ships; Calif. adj. faculty, prof. fin. Clayton U., St. Louis; developer, operator Barnegat Baywood Seaplane Base, Barnegat Bay, N.J.; owner, operator Skyline Airport, Hunterdon County, N.J. Scoutmaster Orange Mountain coun. Boy Scouts Am., 1955-62; harbor master N.J. Marine Patrol, 1958-67; dep. sheriff, Essex County, N.J., 1951-65; mem. pres.' adv. bd. Seton Hall U., 1961-64; chmn. Stop Smoking, 1990, Quick Study, 1990; feature broadcaster/producer Kalaidascope Radio Mag., Am. Radio Network, 1990—. Served with USAF, 1942-45. Decorated D.F.C., Air medal, Purple Heart; named to French Legion of Honor, Order of Lafayette; named a flying col, a.d.c., Gov. of Ga., 1957. Mem. Am. Soc. Editors and Pubs., Author's Guild, Internat. Platform Assn., Nat. Speakers Assn., Nat. Press Photographers Assn., Guild Assn. Airport Execs., Aviation and Space Writers Assn., Nat. Assn. of Real Estate Editors, Internat. Exchangors Assn. (founder), Air Force Assn. (dep. comdr. N.J. chpt. 1955-57). Clubs: Nat. Press, Overseas Press, La Costa Country, Cuyamaca, Rancho Santa Fe Country, Passport. Lodges: Masons, Shriners. Author: A Fortune At Your Feet, 1981, How You Can Get Rich, Stay Rich and Enjoy Being Rich, 1981, Financial Independence, 1987, The Profit, 1987, A Fortune at Your Feet in the '90s, 1994, The Midas Touch, Turning Paper Into Gold, 1994; author, instr. Your Key to Success seminar, 1988, Your Key to Creative Real Estate Success tng. program, 1996; The A to Z of Lease Purchase and 11 Other Options Training Prog.; editor: The Real Estate News Observer, 1975—; fin. editor API, 1978—; fin. columnist Money Matters, 1986—; syndicated columnist, radio and TV host of "Money Making Ideas," 1977—; songwriter: Only You, 1939, If I'm Not Home For Christmas, 1940, Franny, 1940, Flajaloppa, 1940, They've Nothing More Dear Only They've Got It Here, 1941, The Summer of Life, 1956; producer (movies) The Flight of the Cobra, Rena, We Have Your Daughters, Music Row; speaker for radio and TV as The Real Estate Answerman, 1975—; host (radio and TV show) Ask Mr. Money; conceptualist, exec. prodr. (TV show) The Trading Game, 1994; exec. prodr., moderator (TV show) A.D. Kessler's Real Estate Roundtable, 1993—. Inventor swivel seat, siptop, inflatumbrella. Home: PO Box 1144 Rancho Santa Fe CA 92067-1144

KESSLER, JOHN OTTO, physicist, educator; b. Vienna, Austria, Nov. 26, 1928; came to U.S., 1940, naturalized, 1946; s. Jacques and Alice Blanca (Neuhut) K.; m. Eva M. Bondy, Sept. 9, 1950; children: Helen J., Steven J. A.B., Columbia U., 1949, Ph.D., 1953. With RCA Corp., Princeton, N.J., 1952-66, sr. mem. tech. staff, 1964-66, mgr. grad. recruiting, 1964-66; prof. physics U. Ariz., Tucson, 1966-93, prof. emeritus, 1994—. Vis. research asso. Princeton, 1962-64; sr. vis. fellow, vis. prof. physics U. Leeds, Eng., 1972-73, sr. vis. fellow, 1990-91; vis. prof. Technische Hogeschool Delft, Netherlands, spring 1979; Fulbright fellow dept. applied math. and theoretical physics Cambridge U., Eng., 1983-84 Contbr. articles to profl. jours. Fellow AAAS; mem. Am. Phys. Soc. Achievements include patentee in field; research in low Reynolds number fluid mechanics; mechanisms of bacterial propulsion, interaction and formation of coherent swarms, leading to microturbulence; bioconvection and consumption patterns of micro-organism populations; measurement of probability densities for swimming velocity of algae and bacteria. Home: 2740 E Camino La Zorrela Tucson AZ 85718-3126 Office: U Ariz Physics Dept Bldg 81 Tucson AZ 85721-0001 E-mail: kessler@physics.arizona.edu

KESSLER, LYNN ELIZABETH, state legislator; b. Seattle, Feb. 26, 1941; d. John Mathew and Kathryn Eisen; m. Keith L. Kessler, Dec. 24, 1960; children: William John Moore, Christopher Scott Moore, Dudley Jerome Moore, Jamie. Attended, Seattle U., 1958-59. Mem. Wash. Ho. of Reps., 1993—. Co-majority leader rules com., appropriations com. Exec. dir. United Way Grays Harbor, 1984-92; mem. adv. coun. Head Start, 1986-89, Cervical Cancer Awareness Task Force, 1990-91, vocat. adv. coun. Hoquiam High Sch., 1991—, strategic planning com. Grays Harbor Community Hosp., 1991-92, Grays Harbor Food Bank Com., 1991-92, [illegible] lines Mgmt. Bd., 1988-90; chair Disability Awareness Com., 1988-90, Youth 2000 Com., 1990-91; pres. Teenage Pregnancy, Parenting and Prevention Adv. Coun., 1989-91; v.p. Grays Harbor Econ. Devel. Coun., 1990-92; trustee Grays Harbor Coll., 1991—, Aberdeen YMCA, 1991—. Mem. Aberdeen Rotary (pres. 1993-94). Home: 62 Kessler Ln Hoquiam WA 98550-9742 Office: Wash Ho of Reps Legislative Bldg Rm 409 Olympia WA 98504-0001

KESSLER, ROBERT ALLEN, data processing executive; b. N.Y.C., Feb. 2, 1940; s. Henry and Caroline Catherine (Axinger) K.; m. Marie Therese Anton, Mar. 17, 1967; children: Susanne, Mark. BA in Math., CUNY, 1961; postgrad., UCLA, 1963-64. EDP analyst Boeing Aircraft, Seattle, 1961-62; computer specialist System Devel. Corp., Santa Monica, Calif., 1962-66; mem. tech. staff Computer Scis. Corp., El Segundo, 1966-67, sr. mem. tech. staff, 1971-72, computer scientist, 1974-81; systems mgr. Xerox Data Systems, L.A., 1967-71; prin. scientist Digital Resources, Algiers, Algeria, 1972-74; sr. systems cons. Atlantic Richfield, L.A., 1981-94; computer cons., 1994—. Mem. Big. Bros. L.A., 1962-66; precinct capt. Goldwater for Pres., Santa Monica, 1964; mem. L.A. Conservancy, 1987. Mem. Assn. Computing Machinery. Avocations: racquetball, theatre, gourmet dining. Home: 6138 W 75th Pl Los Angeles CA 90045-1634 Office: Pfizer Health Solutions 2400 Broadway Santa Monica CA 90404-3030 E-mail: kesslbi@pfizer.com

KESTER, RANDALL BLAIR, lawyer; b. Vale, Oreg., Oct. 20, 1916; s. Bruce R. and Mabel M. (Judd) K.; m. Rachael L. Woodhouse, Oct. 20, 1940; children: Laura, Sylvia, Lynne. A.B., Willamette U., 1937; J.D., Columbia U., 1940. Bar: Oreg. 1940, U.S. Dist. Ct. Oreg. 1940, U.S. Ct. Appeals (9th cir.) 1941, U.S. Supreme Ct. 1960. Assoc., then partner firm Maguire, Shields, Morrison & Bailey, Portland, 1940-57; justice Oreg. Supreme Ct., Salem, 1957-58; partner Maguire, Shields, Morrison, Bailey & Kester, 1958-66, Maguire, Kester & Cosgrave, 1966-71, Cosgrave & Kester, Portland, 1972-78, Cosgrave, Kester, Crowe, Gidley & Lagesen, Portland, 1978-89, Cosgrave, Vergeer & Kester, Portland, 1989—. Instr. Northwestern Coll. Law, 1947-56; gen. solicitor northwestern dist. U.P. R.R., 1958-79; sr. counsel UPRR Co., 1979-81 Co-author: The First Duty: History of the U.S. District Court of Oregon, 1993; contbr. articles to profl. jours. Past v.p. Portland area council Boy Scouts of Am.; past pres. Mountain Rescue and Safety Council Oreg.; past trustee Willamette U.; past bd. dirs. Oreg. Symphony Soc., Oreg. Mus. Sci. and Industry. Recipient Silver Beaver award Boy Scouts Am., 1956, alumni citation Willamette U., 1987. Fellow Am. Acad. Appellate Lawyers; mem. ABA, Am. Bar Found. (life), Multnomah Bar Assn. (past pres. 1956, Professionalism award 1991), Oreg. State Bar (treas. 1965-66, Disting. Svc. award pub. utility sect. 1991), Am. Law Inst. (life), Nat. Ski Patrol, Mt. Hood Ski Patrol (past pres.), Mazamas (past pres., climbing chmn.), Wy'east Climbers, Portland C. of C. (pres. 1973, chmn. bd. 1974), U.S. Dist. Ct. Oreg. Hist. Soc. (past pres, bd. dirs.) Oreg. Ethics Commons (co-founder, sec.), Phi Delta Phi, Beta Theta Pi, Tau Kappa Alpha. Republican. Unitarian. Clubs: Arlington (Portland), City (Portland) (v.p. 1978-80, pres. 1986-87), University (Portland), Multnomah Athletic (Portland). Home: 10075 SW Hawthorne Ln Portland OR 97225-4322 Office: Cosgrave Vergeer & Kester 121 SW Morrison St Ste 1300 Portland OR 97204-3143 E-mail: rkester@cuk-law.com

KETCHUM, ROBERT GLENN, photographer, print maker; b. L.A., Dec. 1, 1947; s. Jack Burson and Virginia (Moorhead) K. BA. cum laude, UCLA, 1970; MFA, Calif. Inst. Arts, 1974; MS (hon.), Brooks Inst. Photography, 1995. Founder, tchr. photography workshops Sun Valley Center for Arts and Humanities, 1971-73; tchr. photography Calif. Inst. Arts, 1975; curator photography Nat. Park Found., Washington, 1979-95. Trustee L.A. Ctr. Photog. Studies, 1975-81, pres., 1979-81, v.p., 1981, 96—, bd. dirs.; bd. of councillors Am. Land Conservancy, 1993—; bd. trustees Alaska Conservation Found., 1994—, bd. dirs. Advocacy Arts Found., 1996—; bd. dirs. Earth Comm. Office, 1997—, Internat. Photography Coun.; co-chair west coast coun. Aperture Found., 1996—. Author: The Hudson River and the Highlands; The Photographs of Robert Glenn Ketchum, 1985, The Tongass: Alaska's Vanishing Rain Forest, 1987, Overlooked in America: The Success and Failure of Federal Land Management, 1991, The Legacy of Wildness: A 25 Year Retrospective, 1994, Northwest Passage, 1996; author and contbg. photographer: American Photographers and the National Parks, 1981; project dir. and contbg. photographer Presidio Gateways, 1994, Threads of Light: Chinese Embroidery From Suzhou and the Photography of Robert Glenn Ketchum, Rivers of Life: Southwest Alaska, The Last Great Salmon Fishery; one-man shows include Akron Art Mus., Ohio, 1985, 89, Santa Barbara Mus. Art, Calif., 1985, Chrysler Mus., Va., 1986, N.Y. Hist. Soc., 1987, The Hudson River Mus., N.Y., 1987, Pentax Forum Gallery, Tokyo, 1988, Fine Art Mus. of the South, Fla., 1990, Nat. Mus. Brazil, Rio de Janeiro, 1992, Am. House, Heidelburg, Germany, 1992, The Huntington Libr. and Art Collections, 1993, The Nat. Acad. Sci., 1994, Cleve. Mus. Art, 1996, Ga. Mus. Art, 1996-97, George Eastman House/Internat. Mus. Photography, 1997, Internat. Photography Hall of Fame Mus., 1997; group shows include Mpls. Inst. of Arts, 1978, White House, Washington, 1979, Friends of Photography, Calif., 1980, Nat. Mus. Am. Art, Washington, 1986, Internat. Photokina, Fed. Republic of Germany, 1986, San Francisco Mus. Art, 1987, Nat. Mus. Am. Art, 1991-94, Honolulu Acad. of the Arts, 1994, Stanford U. Art Mus., 1996, Amon Carter Mus., Ft. Worth, 1997, UCLA Fowler Mus., 1999. Recipient Ansel Adams award for conservation photography Sierra Club, 1989, UN award for outstanding environ. achievement, 1991, award of excellence for profl. achievement UCLA Alumni Assn., 1993, Chevron-Times Mirror Mag. Conservation award, 1994, Frank and Josephine Duveneck Humanitarian award, 2000, Photographer of Yr., 2001; rsch. grantee Ciba-Geigy, 1979, Nat. Park Found., 1978, 79, grantee Lila Acheson Wallace Fund, 1983, 85, 86, McIntosh Found., 1986-87, Akron Art Mus., 1987. Fellow The Explorer's Club; mem. Jonathan Club (resident artist), Phi Delta Theta. Home and Office: 696 Stone Canyon Rd Los Angeles CA 90077-2925 E-mail: peace2rth@aol.com

KETTELL, RUSSELL WILLARD, banker; b. Boston, Feb. 2, 1944; s. Prescott Lowell and Wilhelmina (Schurrman) K.; m. Carol Bailey, Oct. 27, 1973; 1 son, Alexander. B.A. in Econs., Middlebury Coll.; M.B.A., U. Chgo. Sr. v.p., treas. World Savs. and Loan Corp., Oakland, Calif. Office: Golden W Fin Corp 1901 Harrison St Fl 6 Oakland CA 94612-3588

KETTEMBOROUGH, CLIFFORD RUSSELL, computer scientist, consultant, manager; b. Pitesti, Arges, Romania, June 8, 1953; came to U.S., 1983; s. Petre and Constanta (Dascalu) I. MS in Math., U. Bucharest, Romania, 1976; MS in Computer Sci., West Coast U., L.A., 1985; MS in Mgmt. Info. System, West Coast U., Los Angeles, 1986; PhD in Computer and Info. Sci., Pacific We. U., 1988; MBA, U. LaVerne, 1992; PhD in Bus. Adminstrn., U. Santa Barbara, 1996; EdD in Computer Tech. in Edn., Nova Southeastern U., 1998. Lic. mathematician. Mathematician, programmer Nat. Dept. Chemistry, Bucharest, 1976-80; sr. programmer, analyst Nat. Dept. Metallurgy, Bucharest, 1980-82; sr. software engr. Xerox Corp., El Segundo, Calif., 1983-88; task mgr. Rockwell Internat., Canoga Park, 1989-91, cons., 1991-93; mgr. micro devel. Transam. Corp., L.A., 1993-95; MIS dir. Maxicare Health Plans, L.A., 1995-96; computer and info scientist Jet Propulsion Lab.-NASA, Pasadena, Calif., 1988-89, project mgr., 1996—. Adj., asst. prof. W. Coast U., Chapman U., U. Redlands, Nat. U., U. Phoenix, Union Inst., Pepperdine U., UCLA Ext., Keller Grad. Sch., 1991—. Contbr. articles to profl. jours. Sec. Romanian Nat. Body Bldg. Com., Bucharest, 1980-82; pres., chmn. Bucharest Mcpl. Body Bldg. Com., 1978-82. Served to lt. Romanian Army, 1978. Mem. IEEE, Assn. for Computing Machinery [illegible] traveling. Home: 6004 N Walnut Grove Ave San Gabriel CA 91775-2530

KEY, MARY RITCHIE (MRS. AUDLEY E. PATTON), linguist, writer, educator; b. San Diego, Mar. 19, 1924; d. George Lawrence and Iris (Lyons) Ritchie; children: Mary Helen Key Ellis, Harold Hayden Key (dec.), Thomas George Key. Student, U. Chgo., summer 1954, U. Mich., 1959; M.A., U. Tex., 1960, Ph.D., 1963; postgrad., UCLA, 1966. Asst. prof. linguistics Chapman Coll., Orange, Calif., 1963-66; asst. prof. linguistics U. Calif., Irvine, 1966-71, assoc. prof., 1971-78, prof., 1978—, chmn. program linguistics, 1969-71, 75-77, 87—. Cons. Am. Indian langs., Spanish, in Mexico, 1946-55, S.Am., 1955-62, English dialects, 1968-74, Easter Island, 1975, Calif. Dept. Edn., 1966, 70-75, Center Applied Linguistics, Washington, 1967, 69; lectr. in field. Author: Comparative Tacanan Phonology, 1968, Male/Female Language, 1975, 2d edit., 1996, Paralanguage and Kinesics, 1975, Nonverbal Communication, 1977, The Grouping of South American Indian Languages, 1979, The Relationship of Verbal and Nonverbal Communication, 1980, Catherine the Great's Linguistic Contribution, 1980, Polynesian and American Linguistic Connections, 1984, Comparative Linguistics of South American Indian Languages, 1987, General and Amerindian Ethnolinguistics, 1989, Language Change in South American Indian Languages, 1991; founder, editor: newsletter Nonverbal Components of Communication, 1972-76; mem. editoral bd. Forum Linguisticum, 1976—, Lang. Scis., 1978—, La Linguistique, 1979—, Multilingua, 1987—; contbr. articles to profl. jours. Recipient Friends of Libr. Book award, 1976, hon. mention, Rolex awards for Enterprise, project Computerizing the Languages of the World, 1990; U. Calif. Regent's grantee, 1974, Fulbright-Hays grantee, 1975; faculty rsch. fellow, 1984-85. Mem. Linguistic Soc. Am., Am. Dialect Soc. (exec. council; regional sec. 1974-83), Internat. Reading Assn. (dir. 1968-72), Delta Kappa Gamma (local pres. 1974-76). Office: U Calif-Irvine Dept Linguistics Irvine CA 92697-0001

KEYT, DAVID, philosophy and classics educator; b. Indpls., Feb. 22, 1930; s. Herbert Coe and Hazel Marguerite (Sissman) K.; m. Christine Harwood Mullikin, June 25, 1975; children by previous marriage: Sarah, Aaron. A.B., Kenyon Coll., 1951; M.A., Cornell U., 1953, Ph.D., 1955. Instr. dept. philosophy U. Wash., 1957-60, asst. prof., 1960-64, assoc. prof., 1964-69, prof., 1969—, adj. prof. classics, 1977-79, acting chmn. dept. philosophy, 1967-68, 70, 86, winter, spring, 94, chmn. dept. philosophy, 1971-78. Vis. asst. prof. dept. philosophy UCLA, 1962-63; vis. assoc. prof. Cornell U., 1968-69; vis. prof. U. Hong Kong, autumn 1987, Princeton U., autumn 1988, U. Calif., Irvine, autumn 1990; vis. scholar Social Philosophy and Policy Ctr., Bowling Green State U., 2001. Co-editor: (with Fred D. Miller Jr.) A Companion to Aristotle's Politics, 1991; Author: Aristotle Politics, Books V, VI, 1999; contbr. articles in field to profl. jours. Served with U.S. Army, 1955-57. Inst. for Rsch. in the Humanities fellow U. Wis., 1966-67; Ctr. for Hellenic Studies fellow, 1974-75; mem. Inst. for Advanced Study, 1983-84. Mem. Am. Philos. Assn., Soc. Ancient Greek Philosophy. Home: 12032 36th Ave NE Seattle WA 98125-5637 Office: U Wash Box 353350 Dept Philosophy Seattle WA 98195-3350 E-mail: keyt@u.washington.edu

KHAN, AHMED MOHIUDDIN, finance, insurance executive; b. Hyderabad, Andhra Pradesh, India, Nov. 14, 1955; s. Mohammad Mominuddin and Mehar-Unnisa Begum Hyderabad; m. Marjorie L. Klein-Khan, Mar. 31, 1983; 1 child, Yosef F. MBA, U. Palm Beach, 1975; PhD in Bus. Adminstrn., Northwestern U., 2000. Inventory auditor RGIS, Inc., Chgo., 1975-78; staff acct. Sommerset, Inc., Chgo., 1978-85; fin. cons. Provident Mutual Fin. Svc., Inc., Phoenix, 1985-92; pres. Khan and Assocs., Fin./Ins. Svcs., Phoenix, 1992—. Author: Financial-Insurance Services in the New Millenium, 2000. Named Hon. Mem. Exec. Hall of Fame, 2000, named one of Outstanding Scholars of 20th Century; recipient Nat. Sales Achievement award, 2000, Nat. Quality award, 2000. Mem. Assn. MBA Execs., Nat. Assn. Ins. Fin. Advisors, Millon Dollar Round Table. Democrat. Islam. Avocations: golf, traveling, classical music. Home and Office: 4643 E Grandview Rd Phoenix AZ 85032-3416 E-mail: amkhan_2001@yahoo.com

KHANG, CHULSOON, economics educator; b. Kaesong City, South Korea, May 10, 1935; s. Woon-sung and Ji-chung (Lim) K.; m. Yee Yu Lau, Sept. 15, 1959; children— Kenneth, Maurice B.A. in Econs., Mich. State U., 1959; M.A. in Econs., U. Minn.-Mpls., 1962, Ph.D. in Econs., 1965. Asst. prof. econs. San Diego State U., 1963-66; asst. prof. econs. U. Oreg., Eugene, 1966-69, assoc. prof., 1969-73, prof., 1973-97, prof. emeritus, 1997. Vis. prof., research grantee U. New South Wales, Australia, 1972-73; vis. prof., Fulbright fellow Hanguk U. Fgn. Studies, Seoul, Korea, 1979; vis. prof. U. Hawaii, Honolulu, 1989. Referee, Am. Econ. Rev., Jour. Internat. Econs., Rev. Econ. Studies, Jour. Fin., Jour. Polit. Econs., Jour. Banking and Fin., Jour. Econs. and Bus., Internat. Econ. Rev. Contbr. articles to profl. jours. Mem. Eugene Area Korean Assn. (past pres.), Am. Econ. Assn. Republican Home: 224 Edgewood Dr Port Ludlow WA 98365-9225 Office: U Oreg Dept Econs Eugene OR 97403

KHANNA, FAQIR CHAND, physics educator; b. India, Jan. 23, 1935; came to U.S., 1958; s. Ram S. D. Khanna and Ram Ditti Malhotra; m. Swaraj Mukul, Jan. 16, 1966; children: Shrawan F., Varun F. BSc with honors, Panjab U., 1955, MSc with honors, 1956; PhD, Fla. State U., 1962. Sr. rsch. officer Chalk River Nuclear Labs., 1966-84; prof. physics U. Alta., Edmonton, Alta., Can., 1984—. Fellow Am. Phys. Soc. Achievements include research in subatomic physics; nuclear and particle physics; many-body physics. Office: U Alta Theoretical Physics Inst Edmonton AB Canada T6G 2J1

KHERDIAN, DAVID, writer; b. Racine, Wis., Dec. 17, 1931; s. Melkon and Veron (Dumehjian) K.; m. Kato Rozeboom, 1968 (div. 1970); m. Nonny Hogrogian, Mar. 17, 1971. BS in Philosophy, U. Wis., 1960. Lit. cons. Northwestern U., 1965; founder/editor Giligia Press, 1966-72; rarebook cons. Fresno State Coll., Calif., 1968-69, lectr., 1969-70; ofcl. poet-in-the-schs. State of N.H., 1971; editor Ararat mag., 1971-72; dir. Two Rivers Press, Aurora, Oreg., 1978-86. Poetry judge, lectr., reader of own poetry; founder, editor (with Nonny Hogrogian) The Press at Butternut Creek, 1987-88. Author: On The Death of My Father and Other Poems, 1970, Homage to Adana, 1970, Looking Over Hills, 1972, The Nonny Poems, 1974, Any Day of Your Life, 1975, Country, Cat: City, Cat, 1978, I Remember Root River, 1978, The Road From Home: The Story of an Armenian Girl (Lewis Carroll Shelf award, Boston Globe/Horn Book award, Newbery Honor Book award, Jane Addams Peace award, Banta award), 1979, The Farm, 1979, It Started With Old Man Bean, 1980, Finding Home, 1981, Taking the Soundings on Third Avenue, 1981, The Farm: Book Two, 1981, Beyond Two Rivers, 1981 (Friends of Am. Writers award), The Song in the Walnut Grove, 1982, Place of Birth, 1983, Right Now, 1983, The Mystery of the Diamond in the Wood, 1983, Root River Run, 1984, The Animal, 1984, Threads of Light: The Farm Poems Books III and IV, 1985, Bridger: The Story of a Mountain Man, 1987, Poems to an Essence Friend, 1987, A Song for Uncle Harry, 1989, the Cat's Midsummer Jamboree, 1990, The Dividing River/The Meeting Shore, 1990, On a Spaceship with Beelzebub: By a Grandson of Gurdjieff, 1990, The Great Fishing Contest, 1991, Friends: A Memoir, 1993, Juna's Journey, 1993, Asking the River, 1993, By Myself, 1993, My Racine, 1994, Lullaby for Emily, 1995, Seven Poems for Mikey, 1997, The Rose's Smile, 1997, I Called It Home, 1997, The Golden Bracelet, 1998, Chippecotton: Root River Tales of Racine, 1998, The Neighborhood Years, 2000, The Revelations of alvin Tolliuer, 2001, Seeds of Light: Poems From a Gurdjieff Community, 2001; also bibliographies.; editor: Visions of America by the Poets of Our Time, 1973, Settling America: The Ethnic Expression of 14 Contemporary Poets, 1974, Poems Here and Now, 1976, Traveling America with Today's Poets, 1976, The Dog Writes on the Window with His Nose and Other Poems, 1977, If Dragon Flies Made Honey, 1977, I Sing the Song of Myself, 1978, Beat Voices: An Anthology of Beat Poetry, 1995; co-editor: Down at the Santa Fe Depot: 20 Fresno Poets, 1970; translator: The Pearl: Hymn of the Robe of Glory, 1979, Pigs Never See the Stars: Armenian Proverbs, 1982, Monkey: A Journey to the West, 1992, Feathers and Tails: Animal Fables From Around the World. Served with AUS, 1952-54. Office: 600 W 12th St Mcminnville OR 97128 E-mail: tavit@earthlink.net

KHOSLA, VED MITTER, oral and maxillofacial surgeon, educator; b. Nairobi, Kenya, Jan. 13, 1926; s. Jagdish Rai and Tara V. K.; m. Santosh Ved Chabra, Oct. 11, 1952; children: Ashok M., Siddarth M. Student, U. Cambridge, 1945; L.D.S., Edinburgh Dental Hosp. and Sch., 1950, Coll. Dental Surgeons, Sask., Can., 1962. Prof. emeritus, dir. postdoctoral studies in oral surgery Sch. Dentistry U. Calif., San Francisco, 1968—; chief oral surgery San Francisco Gen. Hosp. Lectr. oral surgery U. of Pacific, VA Hosp.; vis. cons. Fresno County Hosp. Dental Clinic.; Mem. planning com., exec. med. com. San Francisco Gen. Hosp. Contbr. articles to profl. jours. Examiner in photography and gardening Boy Scouts Am., 1971-73, Guatemala Clinic, 1972. Granted personal coat of arms by H.M. Queen Elizabeth II, 1959 Fellow Royal Coll. Surgeons (Edinburgh), Internat. Assn. Oral Surgeons, Internat. Coll. Applied Nutrition, Internat. Coll. Dentists, Royal Soc. Health, AAAS, Am. Coll. Dentists; mem. Brit. Assn. Oral Surgeons, Am. Soc. Oral Surgeons, Am. Dental Soc. Anesthesiology, Am. Acad. Dental Radiology, Omicron Kappa Upsilon. Club: Masons. Home: 1525 Lakeview Dr Hillsborough CA 94010-7330 Office: U Calif Sch Dentistry Oral Surgery Div 3D Parnassus Ave San Francisco CA 94117-4342

KIDD, DON, state legislator, bank executive; b. Crowell, Tex., Oct. 10, 1937; m. Sarrah D. Kidd; children: Vickye Faulk, Rena Shuller, Dion Kidd-Johnson. Student, San Angelo State Coll., 1961-63, So. Meth. U., 1972. Pres., CEO Western Commerce Bank, Carlsbad, N.Mex., 1973—; mem. N.Mex. Senate, Dist. 34, Santa Fe, 1992—. Pres., CEO Western Bank Alamogordo, Western Bank Clovis; pres. Western Bancshares of Carlsbad, Inc., Western Commerce Bancshares of Clovis, Inc., Western Data Svcs., Inc.; bd. dirs. Bank of the S.W. N.Mex. state sen. dist. 34, 1993—; bd. dirs. N.Mex. Ednl. Assistance Found., Carlsbad Literacy Program; bd. dirs., past pres. Carlsbad Dept. Devel.; bd. dirs., past chmn. Western States Sch. Banking, U. N.Mex., 1978-84, Guadalupe Med. Ctr., 1988-91; mem., past pres. Eddy County Sheriff's Posse; past pres. Eddy County United Way, N.Mex. State U. Bd. Regents, 1985-91. Mem. Am. Bankers Assn., N.Mex. Bankers Assn. (past pres.), Carlsbad C. of C. (bd. dirs. 1979-83, past pres.). Republican. Avocation: reading. Office: Western Commerce Bank PO Box 1358 Carlsbad NM 88221-1358 also: N Mex Senate State Capitol Rm 423 Santa Fe NM 87503-0001

KIDD, JASON, professional basketball player; b. San Francisco, Mar. 23, 1973; Guard Dallas Mavericks, 1994-96, Phoenix Suns, 1996—. Active West Dallas Cmty. Ctr., formed Jason Kidd Found., Jason Kidd Basketball Scholarship Fund. Named Pac-10 Player of the Year, 1993-94; named nat. freshman of the yr. by The Sporting News and USA Today, 1993-94; voted Shick Rookie of the Year (with Grant Hill), 1994-95; tied for fourth on all time NBA rookie impact list, 1994-95. Avocations: R&B music, movies, baseball. Office: Phoenix Suns 201 E Jefferson St Phoenix AZ 85004-2412

KIDDER, RAY EDWARD, physicist, consultant; b. N.Y.C., Nov. 12, 1923; s. Harry Alvin and Laura Augusta (Wagner) K.; m. Marcia Loring Sprague, June 12, 1947 (div. Aug. 1975); children: Sandra Laura, David Ray, Matthew Sprague. BS, Ohio State U., 1947, MS, 1948, PhD, 1950. Physicist Calif. Rsch. Corp., La Habra, 1950-56, Lawrence Livermore Nat. Lab., Livermore, Calif., 1956—. Mem. adv. bd. Inst. for Quantum Optics, Garching, Germany, 1976-90; bd. editors Nuc. Fusion IAEA, Vienna, 1979-84; cons. Sci. Applications Internat. Corp., San Diego, 1991-94; mem. hon. adv. bd. Inst. for Advanced Physics Studies, La Jolla, Calif., 1991—. Contbr. chpts. to books. With USN, 1944-46. Recipient Humboldt award Alexander von Humboldt Found., 1988. Fellow Am. Phys. Soc. (Szilard award 1993); mem. AAAS, Sigma Xi. Achievements include research in physics of nuclear weapons, inertial confinement fusion, megagauss magnetic fields, laser isotope enrichment, containment of low-yield nuclear explosions. Home: 637 E Angela St Pleasanton CA 94566-7413 Office: Lawrence Livermore Nat Lab PO Box 808 Livermore CA 94551-0808

KIDDOO, ROBERT JAMES, engineering service company executive; b. Kansas City, Mo., July 8, 1936; s. Robert Leroy and Margaret Ella (Wolford) K.; m. Patricia Anne Wakefield, Apr. 17, 1957; children: Robert Michael, Stacey Margaret Kiddoo-Lee. BSBA, UCLA, 1960; MSBA, Calif. State U., Northridge, 1969; MBA, U. So. Calif., 1972, D of Bus. Adminstrn., 1978. Cert. mgmt. acct. Asst. v.p., nat. div. loan officer Crocker-Citizen's Nat. Bank, L.A., 1958-69; v.p., chief fin. officer, dir. corp. sec. Kirk-Mayer, Inc., L.A., 1969-87; prof. acctg. and MIS Calif. State U., Northridge, 1970—; region adminstr. mgr. CDI Corp.-West, Chatsworth, Calif., 1990; exec. v.p. Kirk-Mayer, Inc., L.A., 1990-92; pres. Creative Software Designs, Inc., Northridge, Calif., 1995—. Asst. v.p. financial affairs, univ. controller Calif. State U., Northridge, 1997-2000. With U.S. Army, 1955-56. Mem. Mensa, Ltd., Beta Gamma Sigma, Beta Alpha Psi. Office: Calif State Univ Acctg And Mis Northridge CA 91330-8372

KIDERA, GEORGE JEROME, former physician; b. Chgo., Apr. 29, 1913; s. Edward J. and Marie (Nadherny) K.; m. Marie A. Cuchna, Aug., 1938 (dec. Feb., 1973); children: George Peter, Kristina Alice; m. Jean Allen, Aug. 16, 1975. Student, Northwestern U., 1930-31, Crane Jr. Coll., 1931-33; BS, U. Ill., 1935, MD, 1937; postgrad., Sch. Aviation Medicine, 1942; student postgrad. sch., Cook County Hosp., 1948. Diplomate Am. Bd. Preventive Medicine. Intern West Suburban Hosp., Oak Park, Ill., 1937-38, then mem. surg. staff; regional med. dir. United Air Lines, Chgo., 1938, 46-51, med. dir., 1951-72, v.p. med. svcs., 1972-78, cons. to chmn., 1978-83. Cons. Dart Industries, 1979-80; avaiation med. cons. Dart-Kraft, 1980-86, Kraft, Inc., 1986—, Premark, Internat., 1986—; cons. life scis. com. NASA, 1970—; pres. West Suburban Hosp. Interns Alumni Assn., 1949-51. Contbr. articles to profl. jours. Lt. col., flight surgeon USAAF, 1942-46. Fellow Aerospace Med. Assn. (pres. 1960, mem. exec. coun. 1963, Howard D. Edwards award 1960, Theodore C. Lyster award 1970), Am. Coll. Preventive Medicine; mem. AMA, Airline Med. Dirs. Assn. (mem. exec. coun. 1950-51, pres. 1955, award 1972), Ill. Med. Soc., Chgo. Med. Soc., Des Plaines Med. Soc., Am. Assn. Indsl. Physicians and Surgeons, Am. Med Writers Assn., Internat. Air Transport Assn., Internat. Acad. Aviation and Space Medicine (chancellor 1972-77, 1st v.p. 1977). Home and Office: 1432 Bel Aire Rd San Mateo CA 94402-3618

KIDWELL, WAYNE L. state supreme court justice; b. Council, Idaho, 1938; m. Shari Linn; children: Vaughn, Blair. BA, JD, U. Idaho. Bar: Idaho 1964, Hawaii, former U.S. Trust Territories. Past atty. law firms, Idaho and Hawaii; past pvt. practice Idaho and Hawaii; past atty. gen. State of Idaho; past majority leader Idaho Senate; past prosecuting atty. Ada County, Idaho; past assoc. dep. atty. gen. Pres. Reagan adminstrn., past liason Dept. Justice U.S. Govt.; past atty. gen. Republic of Marshall Islands; judge Idaho Supreme Ct. Photographer pvt. shows; one-man shows include galleries in Hawaii. Active numerous civic and profl. orgns. Served USMCR, U.S. Army Mil. Police Corps. Office: Idaho Supreme Ct Supreme Ct Bldg PO Box 83720 Boise ID 83720-3720

KIEHN, MOGENS HANS, aviation engineer, consultant; b. Copenhagen, July 30, 1918; came to U.S., 1957; s. Hans-Christian and Lydia-Thea-Constans (Theill) K.; children: Marianne, Hans. BS, ME, PE, Tech. Engring., Copenhagen, 1940; MS, Copenhagen, 1942; degree in Army Intelligence, Def. Indsl. Security Inst., 1972. Registered profl. engr., Ariz., also chemical engineer. Pres. Hamo Engring., Copenhagen, 1939-47, Evanston, Ill., 1958-78; engr. Sundstrand, Rockford, 1957-58; pres., owner Kiehn Internat. Engring. Co., Phoenix, 1978—; chmn., pres. ETO Internat. Engring., Phoenix, 1978—. Tech. engring. cons. Scandinavian Airlines, Sundstrand Engring., McDonnell Douglas, Ford, GM, Chrysler, Honeywell, Motorola, Gen. Electric, Hughes Aircraft; chmn. bd. Internat. Tech. Engring. Recipient 32 patents including rehab. hosp. lighting for highmast, drafting machine, tooling machinery, parts for aircraft, garbage and pollution machine, optical coupler, also others. With Finnish Army, 1939, Danish Underground, 1940-45, Morocco French Fgn. Legion, 1948-54, Vietnam. Mem. AIII, NSPE, Soc. Illuminating Engrs., Nat. Geog. Soc., Am. Fedn. Police, East Africa Wildlife Soc., Interpol Intelligence and Organized Crime Orgn., Adventures Club Denmarkk, Honors Club, Am. Inst. of Aeronautics and Astronautics., St. Joseph's Legacy Club., St. Joseph's Indian Sch. Office: Kiehn Internat Tech Engring PO Box 1561 Scottsdale AZ 85252-1561

KIEKHOFER, WILLIAM HENRY, lawyer; b. Madison, Wis., June 19, 1952; s. William and Emily (Graham) K.; m. Leslie A. Cohen., Jan. 27, 1956; children: Allison Laura, Phoebe Leigh, Rachel Elizabeth. BA, U. Wis., 1976; JD, U. So. Calif., 1980. Assoc. Sidley & Austin, L.A., 1980-82, Fried & King, L.A., 1982-83, McKenna Conner & Cuneo, L.A., 1983-90; ptnr. Kelley Drye & Warren LLP, L.A., 1990—. Office: Kelley Drye & Warren 777 S Figueroa St Ste 2700 Los Angeles CA 90017-5825

KIELAROWSKI, HENRY EDWARD, marketing executive; b. Pitts., Dec. 29, 1946; s. Henry Andrew Kielarowski and Evelyn Marie Kline Boileau; m. Lynda Blair Powell, Aug. 1971 (div. 1976); children: Amorette, Blair. BA, Duquesne U., Pitts., 1969; MA, PhD, Duquesne U., 1974. Pres. Communicators, Inc., Pitts., 1974-76; mktg. specialist McGraw-Hill, Inc., N.Y.C., 1976-81; mktg. dir. Fidelity S.A., Allison Park, Pa., 1981-86; exec. v.p. ARC Systems, Inc., Pitts., 1986-88; v.p. mktg. Providian Financial Corp., San Francisco, 1988-98; pres. La Playa Cons., Inc., San Francisco, 1999—. Author: Microcomputer Consulting in the CPA Environment, 1987; contbr. articles to profl. jours. Mem. Am. Mktg. Assn. (mktg. excellence award 1988), Direct Mktg. Assn. Democrat. Avocations: fiction writing, music, dance, travel, film making. Home: 1496 La Playa St San Francisco CA 94122-2813 E-mail: bonerinc@aol.com

KIENITZ, LADONNA TRAPP, librarian, city official; b. Bay City, Mich. d. Orlin D. and Mary (Stanford) Trapp; m. John Kienitz, Feb. 9, 1951 (div. Dec. 1974); children: John, Jim, Rebecca, Mary, Timothy, David. BA, Westmar Coll., 1951; MA in Libr. Sci., Dominican U., River Forest, Ill., 1970; M Mgmt., Northwestern U., 1984; JD, Western State U., Fullerton, Calif., 1995. Head libr. Woodlands Acad., Lake Forest, Ill., 1973-77; project officer North Suburban Libr. Sys., Wheeling, 1977-78; libr. dir. Lincolnwood (Ill.) Pub. Libr. Dist., 1978-86; city libr. City of Newport Beach, Calif., 1987—, dir. cmty. svcs., 1994—. Mem. ALA, ABA, Pub. Libr. Assn. (pres. 1995-96), Calif. Bar Assn., Calif. Libr. Assn., Calif. Parks and Recreation Soc., Nat. Assn. Parks and Recreation, State Bar of Calif. Avocation: law. Office: City of Newport Beach PO Box 1768 3300 Newport Blvd Newport Beach CA 92658-8915

KIESLER, CHARLES ADOLPHUS, psychologist, academic administrator; b. St. Louis, Aug. 14, 1934; m. Teru Morton, Feb. 28, 1987; 1 child, Hugo; children from previous marriage: Tina, Thomas, Eric, Kevin. BA, Mich. State U., 1958, MA, 1960; PhD (NIMH fellow), Stanford U., 1963; D (hon.), Lucian Blaga U., Romania, 1995. Asst. prof. psychology Ohio State U., Columbus, 1963-64, Yale U., New Haven, 1964-66, assoc. prof., 1966-70; prof., chmn. psychology U. Kans., Lawrence, 1970-75; exec. officer Am. Psychol. Assn., Washington, 1975-79; Walter Van Dyke Bingham prof. psychology Carnegie Mellon U., Pitts., 1979-85, head psychology, 1980-83, acting dean, 1981-82, dean Coll. Humanities and Social Scis., 1983-85; provost Vanderbilt U., 1985-92; chancellor U. Mo., Columbia, 1992-96, Weil Disting. prof. health svcs. mgmt., 1996-98; prof., sr. advisor San Diego State U., 1998-99. Pres., CEO, Virtual Univ. Internat., 1996-97. Author: (with B.E. Collins and N. Miller) Attitude Change: A Critical Analysis of Theoretical Approaches, 1969, (with S.B. Kiesler) Conformity, 1969, The Psychology of Commitment: Experiments Linking Behavior to Belief, 1971, (with N. Cummings and G. VandenBos) Psychology and National Health Insurance: A Sourcebook, 1979, (with A.E. Sibulkin) Mental Hospitalization: Myths and Facts About a National Crisis, 1987, (with C. Simpkins) The Unnoticed Majority: Psychiatric inpatient care in general hospitals, 1993. Served with Security Service USAF, 1952-56. Recipient Disting. Alumnus award Mich. State U., 1987, Gunnar Myrdal award for Evaluation Practice Am. Evaluation Assn., 1989. Fellow AAAS, APA (Distng. Contbr. to Rsch. in Pub. Policy award 1989), Am. Psychol. Soc. (founding past pres. 1988-90); mem. AAUP, Inst. of Medicine of Nat. Acad. Scis., Sigma Xi, Psi Chi, Phi Kappa Phi. Home and Office: 3427 Mount Laurence Dr San Diego CA 92117-5649 E-mail: ckiesler@san.rr.com

KIKUCHI, RYOICHI, physics educator; b. Osaka, Japan, Dec. 25, 1919; came to U.S., 1950; m. Toshiko Sono; children: John M., Ann K. Snyder. BS, Tokyo U., 1942, PhD, 1951. Research assoc. MIT, Cambridge, 1951-53; asst. prof. U. Chgo., 1953-55; rsch. physicist Armour Rsch. Found., Chgo., 1955-56; assoc. prof. Wayne State U., Detroit, 1956-58; sr. scientist Hughes Rsch. Labs., Malibu, Calif., 1958-85; rsch. prof. U. Wash., Seattle, 1985-89; adj. prof. UCLA, 1975-86, 89-96; vis. scholar U. Calif., Berkeley, 1996—. Vis. prof. Purdue U., West Lafayette, Ind., 1977-93, Tohoku U., Sendai, Japan, 1982, Technische Hugeschool, Delft, The Netherlands, 1980, 81, Swiss Fed. Inst. Tech., Zurich, 1998, U. Sao Paolo, 2000. Contbr. articles to profl. jours. Recipient A. Von Humboldt Sr. U.S. Scientist award, Bonn, Germany, 1985. Fellow Minerals, Metals, & Materials Soc. (hon., Hume-Rothery award 1998); mem. Am. Phys. Soc., Phys. Soc. Japan, Japan Inst. Metals (hon.). Home: 1702 Comstock Dr Walnut Creek CA 94595-2469 Office: U Calif Dept Materials Sci Berkeley CA 94720-1760 E-mail: klogw@uclink4.berkeley.edu

KILBOURN, LEE FERRIS, architect, specifications writer; b. L.A., Mar. 9, 1936; s. Lewis Whitman and Kathryn Mae (Lee) K.; m. Joan Priscilla Payne, June 11, 1961; children: Laurie Jane, Ellen Mae. BS in Gen. Sci., Oreg. State U., 1963; BS in Architecture, U. Oreg., 1965. Registered architect, Oreg. Specifier Wolff Zimmer Assocs., Portland, Oreg., 1965-75; specifier, assoc. Wolff Zimmer Gunsul Frasca, Portland, 1975-77, Zimmer Gunsul Frasca Partnership, Portland, 1977-81, specifier, assoc. ptnr., 1981—. Jr. warden, then sr. warden St. Stephen's Episcopal Parish, Portland. With U.S. Army, 1959-60. Fellow AIA (mem. master spec. rev. com. 1976-78, mem. documents com. 1981-89), Constrn. Specifications Inst. (mem. participating tech. documents com. 1976-78, cert. com. 1980-82, Al Hansen Meml. award Portland chpt. 1987, Frank Stanton Meml. award N.W. region 1987, chpt. pres. 1979-80); mem. Internat. Conf. Bldg. Ofcls. Home: 3178 SW Fairmount Blvd Portland OR 97201-1468 Office: Zimmer Gunsul Frasca Partnership 320 SW Oak St Ste 500 Portland OR 97204-2737

KILGORE, EUGENE STERLING, JR. former surgeon; b. San Francisco, Feb. 3, 1920; s. Eugene Sterling and Mary (Kirkpatrick) K.; m. Marilynn Wines; children: Eugene Sterling, Marilynn Ann. BS, U. Calif., Berkeley, 1941; MD, U. Calif., San Francisco, 1949. Intern in medicine Harvard service Boston City Hosp., 1949-50; intern in surgery Roosevelt

Hosp., N.Y.C., 1950-51, resident gen. surgery, reconstructive hand surgery, 1951-55; practice medicine specializing in reconstructive hand surgery San Francisco, 1955—; asso. clin. prof. surgery U. Calif.-San Francisco, 1955-75, clin. prof., 1975-91, prof. emeritus, 1991—; chief hand surgery dept. surgery U. Calif. Hosp., also San Francisco Gen. Hosp., 1965-91; chief hand service Ft. Miley Vets. Hosp., San Francisco, 1965-91, Martinez (Calif.) Vets. Hosp., 1970-91, Livermore (Calif.) Vets. Hosp., 1965-70; chief hand service plastic surgery tng. service St. Francis Meml. Hosp., 1965-91, chief of surgery, 1979—, chief surgery emeritus, 1984-99; ret., 1999. Cons. hand surgery numerous pvt. hosps., San Francisco, 1955— Author numerous publs. in field. Served to lt. col., inf. AUS, 1941-45. Decorated Bronze Star; recipient Gold Headed Cane, AOA medal; Kaiser award for excellence in teaching U. Calif.-San Francisco Sch. Medicine, 1976, Charlotte Baer Meml. Clin. Faculty award U. Calif., 1993, Alumnus of Yr. award U. Calif. Med. Sch., 1998. Mem. AMA, ACS, Am. Assn. Surgery of Trauma, Am. Trauma Soc., Am. Soc. Surgery of Hand, Carribean Hand Soc., San Francisco Surg. Soc. (pres. 1979-80), Pacific Coast Surg. Assn., City Club. Clubs: Rotary; Bohemian (San Francisco). Office: 3910 Paradise Dr Tiburon CA 94920-1119 Fax: (415) 435-6742

KILKENNY, JOSEPH DAVID, physics researcher; b. Eng., July 7, 1947; BS, Imp Coll., London, 1968, MS, 1970, PhD in Physics, 1972. Rsch. scientist Lawrence Livermore (Calif.) Nat. Lab., 1983—. Recipient Excellence in Plasma Physics award Am. Phys. Soc., 1995. Office: Lawrence Livermore Nat Lab PO Box 808 Livermore CA 94551-0808

KILLACKY, JOHN R. museum administrator, educator, writer, filmmaker; BA, Hunter Coll. Past mng. dir. Trisha Brown Dance Co., Inc.; past dir. Laura Dean Dancers and Musicians; past curator performing arts Walker Art Ctr., Mpls.; exec. dir. Yerba Buena Ctr. Arts., San Francisco, 1996—. Gen. mgr. PepsiCo Summerfare, 1986; past program officer Pew Charitable Trusts; adj. prof. U. Minn., 1991-96; cons. in field; lectr. in field. Author, dir. several short films and videos; contbr. articles to profl. jours. Recipient 1st Bank Sally Ordway Irvine award for artistic vision, 1995, William Dawson award for programming excellence Assn. Performing Arts Presenters, 1995. Office: Yerba Buena Ctr Arts 701 Mission St San Francisco CA 94103-3138

KILLEEN, MICHAEL JOHN, lawyer; b. Washington, Oct. 5, 1949; s. James Robert and Georgia Winston (Hartwell) K.; m. Therese Ann Goeden, Oct. 6, 1984; children: John Patrick, Katherine Therese, Mary Clare, James Philip. BA, Gonzaga U., 1971, JD magna cum laude, 1977. Bar: Wash. 1977, U.S. Dist. Ct. (we. dist.) Wash. 1979, U.S. Ct. Appeals (9th cir.) 1984, U.S. Supreme Ct. 1990. Jud. clk. Wash. State Ct. Appeals, Tacoma, 1977-79; assoc. Davis Wright Tremaine, Seattle, 1979-85, ptnr., 1985—. Dir. Seattle Goodwill Bd., 1987—, sec., 1998—. Author: Guide to Strike Planning, 1985, Newsroom Legal Guidebook, 1996, Employment in Washington, 1984—. Active Gonzaga Law Bd. Advisors, Spokane, Wash., pres., 1992-96. Recipient Freedom's Light award Washington Newspaper Pub. Assn., 1999. Mem. ABA, Wash. State Bar Assn., King County Bar Assn. (treas. 1987-89, pres. award 1989). Democrat. Roman Catholic. E-mail: mikekilleen@dwt.com

KILLIAN, GEORGE ERNEST, educational association administrator; b. Valley Stream, N.Y., Apr. 6, 1924; s. George and Reina (Moeller) K.; m. Janice E. Bachert, May 26, 1951 (dec.); children: Susan E., Sandra J.; m. Marilyn R. Killian, Sept. 1, 1984 BS in Edn., Ohio No. U., 1949; EdM, U. Buffalo, 1954; PhD in Phys. Scis., Ohio Northern U., 1989; PhD (hon.), U.S. Sports Acad., 1998. Tchr.-coach Wharton (Ohio) High Sch., 1949-51; insp. USN, Buffalo, 1951-54; dir. athletics Erie County (N.Y.) Tech. Inst., Buffalo, 1954-69, asst. prof. health, phys. edn., recreation, 1954-60, asso. prof., 1960-62, prof., 1962-69; exec. dir. Nat. Jr. Coll. Athletic Assn., Colorado Springs, Colo., 1969—. Editor: Juco Rev., 1960— . Served with AUS, 1943-45. Recipient Bd. Trustees award Hudson Valley C. of C., 1969, Erie County Tech. Inst., 1969, Service award Ohio No. U. Alumni, 1972, Service award Lysle Rishel Post, Am. Legion, 1982; named to Ohio No. U. Hall of Fame, 1979, Olympic Order, IOC, 1996, Women's Basketball Hall of Fame, 2000. Mem. U.S. Olympic Com. (dir.), Internat. Olympic Com., Am. Legion, Internat. Basketball Fedn. (pres. 1990-98), Internat. U. Sports Fedn. (1st v.p. 1995, pres. 2000), Phi Delta Kappa, Delta Sigma Phi. Clubs: Masons, Rotary. Home: 325 Rangely Dr Colorado Springs CO 80921-2655 Office: Nat Jr Coll Athletic Assn PO Box 7305 Colorado Springs CO 80933-7305 E-mail: gkillian@njcaa.org

KILLIAN, RICHARD M. library director; b. Buffalo, Jan. 13, 1942; m. Nancy Killian; children from previous marriage: Tessa, Lee Ann. BA, SUNY, Buffalo, 1964; MA, Western Mich. U., 1965; grad. advanced mgmt. library adminstrn., Miami U., Oxford, Ohio, 1981; grad. library adminstrn. devel. program, U. Md., 1985. Various positions Buffalo and Erie County Pub. Libraries, 1963-74, asst. dep. dir., personnel officer, 1979-80; dir. Town of Tonawanda (N.Y.) Pub. Library, 1974-78; asst. city librarian, dir. pub. svcs. Denver Pub. Library, 1978-79; exec. dir. Nioga Library System, Buffalo, 1980-87; library dir. Sacramento (Calif.) Pub. Library, 1987—. Mem. ALA, Calif. Library Assn., Rotary. Home: 3501 H St Sacramento CA 95816-4501 Office: Sacramento Pub Libr Adminstrn Ctr 828 I St Sacramento CA 95814-2589

KILLINGER, KERRY KENT, bank executive; b. Des Moines, June 6, 1949; m. Debbie Roush. BBA, U. Iowa, 1970, MBA, 1971. Exec. v.p. Murphey Favre, Inc., Spokane, 1976-82; exec. v.p. fin. mgmt., investor rels., corp. mktg. Wash. Mutual, Seattle, 1983-86; sr. exec. v.p., 1986-88; pres., dir. Wash. Mutual Savs. Bank, Seattle, 1988—, CEO, 1990—, chmn. bd., 1991—. Bd. dirs. Wash. Savs. League; mem. Thrift Inst. Adv. Coun. to Fed. Res. Bd., 1992-94; speaker in field. Bd. dirs. Fed. Home Loan Bank of Seattle, 1995—, Seattle Repertory Theatre, 1990—, Washington Roundtable, 1990—, Downtown Seattle Assn., 1991, Leadership Tomorrow, Seattle Found., 1992—; mem. Alliance for Edn., 1992—, chair, 1994-96, co-chmn. AIDS Walk-a-thon, Seattle, 1990; chair Partnership for Learning, 1997. Fellow Life Mgmt. Inst.; mem. Soc. Fin. Analysts, Greater Seattle C. of C. (bd. dirs. 1992—), Rotary. Office: Wash Mutual Bank 1201 3rd Ave Seattle WA 98101

KILLMAR, LAWRENCE E. animal park curator; BSBA, Calif. Coast Univ., 1995, postgrad., 1996—. directed transp. four So. White Rhino from San Diego Zoo and Wild Animal Park to Can., 1974, to Europe, 1977; participant Gian Eland capture, Senegal, West Afirca, 1979; accompanied four Asiatic Lions to Jerusalem Zoo, 1984, others; facilitator Feline Immunodeficiency Viruses Workshop for Cheetahs, Escondido, 1995, others. Park keeper to curatorial field supr. San Diego (Calif.) Wild Animal Park, 1970-80, curator of mammals, 1982-91, gen. curator/mammal and bird collections, 1991-92, gen. curator/mammal, bird and reptile collections, 1992—. Contbr. articles to profl. jours. Fellow Am. Assn. Zoos, Parks, Aquariums; mem. Wildlife Conservation Mgmt. Com./Am. Zool. Assn., Am. Zoo and Aquarium Assn. (bd. regents 1996). Office: San Diego Wild Animal Park 15500 San Pasqual Valley Rd Escondido CA 92027-7017

KIM, DONNA MERCADO, state senator; b. Honolulu; BA, Wash. State U., 1974. Recreation dir.; small bus. exec. dir.; comm. sales rep.; hotel catering sales rep.; pub. rels. dir. KUMU Radio; Dem. senator dist. 15 Hawaii State Senate. Past mem. Pres.'s Nat. Com. on Transp.; past mem. steering com. Nat. League Cities, Econ. Devel.; bd. dirs. Bank of Am. Hawaii; trained facilitator The Pacific Inst. Active Aliamanu unit Boys and Girls Club Honolulu, Hawaii's Jr. Miss, Inc., Planned Parenthood, YMCA Century Club, mem. Hawaii Korean Millenium Commn; bd. trustees Palama Settlement. Named one of Three Outstanding Young Persons, Hawaii Jaycees, 1988; recipient Outstanding Alumni award Farrington H.S., 1997. Mem. ASPA (Outstanding City and County Adminstr. award 1997), Asian Pacific Am. Mcpl. Ofcls., Kaliki Bus. Assn., Hawaii Korean C. of C. (hon.), Filipino C. of C. Office: Hawaii State Senate State Capitol Rm 218 415 S Beretania St Honolulu HI 96813 Fax: 808 587-7205. E-mail: senkim@Capitol.hawaii.gov

KIM, EDWARD WILLIAM, ophthalmic surgeon; b. Seoul, Korea, Nov. 25, 1949; came to U.S., 1957; s. Shoon Kul and Pok Chu (Kim) K.; m. Carole Sachi Takemoto, July 24, 1976; children: Brian, Ashley. BA, Occidental Coll., Los Angeles, 1971; postgrad., Calif. Inst. Tech., 1971; MD, U. Calif., San Francisco, 1975; MPH, U. Calif., Berkeley, 1975. Diplomate Nat. Bd. Med. Examiners, Am. Bd. Ophthalmology. Resident in ophthalmology Harvard U.-Mass. Eye and Ear Infirmary, Boston, 1977-79; clin. fellow in ophthalmology Harvard U., 1977-79, clin. fellow in retina, 1980; practice medicine in ophthalmic surgery Laguna Hills, San Clemente, Calif., 1980—. Vol. ophthalmologist Eye Care Inc., Ecole St. Vincent's, Haiti, 1980, Liga, Mex., 1989, Tonga, 1997; chief staff, South Coast Med. Ctr., 1988-89; assoc. clin. prof. dept. ophthalmology, U. Calif., Irvine. Founding mem. Orange County Ctr. for Performing Arts, Calif., 1982, dir. at large, 1991; pres. Laguna Beach Summer Music Festival, Calif., 1984. Reinhart scholar U. Calif.-San Francisco, 1972-73; R. Taussig scholar, 1974-75. Fellow ACS, Am. Acad. Ophthalmology, Internat. Coll. Surgeons; mem. Calif. Med. Assn., Keratorefractive Soc., Orange County Med. Assn., Mensa, Expts. in Art and Tech. Office: Harvard Eye Assocs 665 Camino De Los Mares Ste 102 San Clemente CA 92673-2840

KIM, JEONG-HAN, researcher; b. Korea, July 20, 1962; BS in Physics, Yonsei U., Seoul, Korea, 1985, MS in Math. Physics, 1987; PhD in Math., Rutgers U., 1993. Sr. tech. staff Info. Scis. Rsch. Ctr., AT&T Labs.-Rsch., 1993-97, prin. tech. staff, 1997; assoc. prof. math. Carnegie Mellon U., 1996-97; rschr. Mocrosoft Rsch., 1997—. Contbr. articles to profl. jours. Mem. Am. Math. Soc. Office: Microsoft Rsch 1 Microsoft Way Redmond WA 98052-8300

KIM, MOON HYUN, endocrinologist, educator; b. Seoul, Korea, Nov. 30, 1934; s. Jae Hang and Kum Chu (Choi) K.; m. Yong Cha Pak, June 20, 1964; children: Peter, Edward. M.D., Yonsei U., 1960. Diplomate: Am. Bd. Ob-Gyn. (examiner 1979-98). Sr. instr. Ob-Gyn Yonsei U., Seoul, 1967-68; intern Md. Gen. Hosp., Balt., 1961-62; resident in Ob-Gyn Cleve. Met. Gen. Hosp., 1962-66; fellow in reproductive endocrinology U. Wash., Seattle, 1966-67, U. Toronto, Ont., Can., 1968-70; asst. prof. Ob-Gyn, also chief endocrinology and infertility U. Chgo., 1970-74; asso. prof. Ob-Gyn Ohio State U., Columbus, 1974-78, prof., 1978-92, chief div. reproductive endocrinology, 1974-92, vice chmn. dept. ob-gyn, 1982-96. Richard L. Meiling chair in ob-gyn., Ohio State U., 1987-98; prof. U. Calif., Irvine, 1998—. Contbg. author books; contbr. articles to profl. jours. Recipient McClintock award U. Chgo., 1975; named Prof. of Yr. Ohio State U., 1976; recipient Clin. Teaching award, 1980 Fellow Am. Coll. Ob-Gyn; mem. Am. Gynecol. and Obstetric Soc., Am. Fertility Soc., Chgo. Gynecol. Soc., Endocrine Soc., Soc. Study Reprodn., Soc. Gynecol. Investigation. Home: 24 Whistler Ct Irvine CA 92612-4069 Office: Univ Calif Irvine Med Ctr 101 The City Dr S Bldg 22A Orange CA 92868-3201

KIM, SANG KOO, pastor, educator; b. Joongwon, Choongbuk, Korea, July 22, 1938; came to U.S., 1978; s. Seyong and Sun (Shin) K.; m. Sunok Lee, Oct. 3, 1969; children: James Han, Grace Jong. BA, Korea U., Seoul, 1964; MDiv, Presbyn. Theol. Sem., Seoul, 1966; D Ministry, San Francisco Theol. Sem., 1981. Ordained to ministry 33th Daejon Presbytery Presbyn. Ch., 1968. Sr. pastor Seattle Korean Presbyn. Ch., 1980-88, Dong Shin Presbyn. Ch., Fullerton, Calif., 1988—. Moderator Western Presbytery in U.S.A., La., 1983-84; prof. Faith Evang. Sem., Federalway, Wash., 1983-88, K.P.C.A. Presbyn. Sem., L.A., 1988—; vice moderator K.P.C.A., 1995; moderator Korean Presbyn. Ch. in Am., 1995-96. Author: The Core Theory of Salvation, 1993. Democrat. Home: 5777 Los Arcos Way Buena Park CA 90620-2724 Office: Dong Shin Presbyn Ch 2121 E Wilshire Ave Fullerton CA 92831-4159 E-mail: kimsangkoo@yahoo.com

KIM, SUNG WAN, educator; b. Pusan, South Korea, Aug. 21, 1940; came to U.S., 1966; BS, MS, Seoul U.; PhD, U. Utah. Asst. rsch. prof. U. Utah Salt Lake City, 1971-73, asst. prof., 1974-76, assoc. prof., 1977-79, prof., 1980—, dir. Ctr. Controlled Chemical Delivery, 1986—. Mem. study section SGYB, NIH, Bethesda, Md., 1985-89, 95—. Editor numerous books; patentee in field; contbr. articles to profl. jours. Recipient Founders award CRS, 1995, Clemson Basic Rsch. award Biomaterials Soc., 1987, Gov.'s medal for sci., State of Utah, 1989, Inst. Soc. Blood Purification award, 1995. Fellow Am. Assn. Pharm. Sci., Am. Inst. Med. Bioengring, Biomaterials Soc. Home: 1711 Devonshire Dr Salt Lake City UT 84108-2562 Office: U Utah Ctr Controlled Chem Delivery Biomedical Polymers Rsch Bldg Rm 205 Salt Lake City UT 84112

KIM, WAN HEE, electrical engineering educator, business executive; b. Osan, Korea, May 24, 1926; came to U.S., 1953, naturalized, 1962; s. Sang Chul and Duck Hyung (Chong) K.; m. Chung Sook Noh, Jan. 23, 1960; children: Millie, Richard K. B.E., Seoul Nat. U., 1950; M.S. in Elec. Engring, U. Utah, 1954, Ph.D., 1956. Research asst. U. Ill., Urbana, 1955-56; research staff IBM Research Ctr., Poughkeepsie, N.Y., 1956-57; asst. prof. Columbia U., N.Y.C., 1957-59, assoc. prof., 1959-63, prof. elec. engring., 1963-78; chmn., CEO Tech. Assessment Corp. Internat., 1991—. Chmn. Tech. Cons., Inc., N.Y.C., 1962-69; chmn. KOMKOR Am., Inc., N.Y.C., 1970-72; spl. advisor to the pres. and govt. Republic of Korea, 1967-79; advisor Korea Advanced Inst. Sci., Seoul, 1971-73; chmn. Korea Inst. Electronics Tech., 1977-81; mem. bd. Korea Telecommunication Electric Rsch. Inst., 1977-81; pres. WHK Engring. Corp. Am., 1982-84, WHK Electronics Inc., 1982-84; chmn., chief exec. officer Industries Assn. Electronic Korea, 1978-81; chmn. WHK Industries Inc., 1984-88, AEA Corp., WHK-FJF&M Assocs., 1988-89; pres. Asian Electronics Union, 1979-83; pub. Electronic Times of Korea, 1982-83, Dr. Kim Report on Korea, 1988—; cons. The World Bank, Washington, other indsl. orgns.; chmn., CEO Tech. Assessment Corp. Internat. (TACI), 1991—; bd. dirs., chmn. exec. com. Xentex Techs., Inc., 2000—. Author (with R.T. Chien): Topological Analysis and Synthesis of Communication Networks, 1962; author: (with H.E. Meadows) Modern Network Analysis, 1970; author: (Auto Biography) Embracing Two Suns, 1999, numerous articles, —. U.S. rep. on U.S.-Japan Scientists Coop. Program.; trustee U.S.-Asia Inst., Washington, 1984-88. Served with Korean Army, 1950-53. Decorated Bronze Star; recipient Achievement medal U.S.-Asia Inst., Industry medal Republic of Korea, 1989; Guggenheim grantee, 1964, NSF rsch. grantee, 1958-78. Fellow IEEE, Union Radio Scientifique Internat. (mem. U.S. nat. com. Commn. Band C 1963-78), Sigma Xi, Tau Beta Pi. Achievements include being honorarily named the father of Korean electronics industry for his contbrn. to promotion of industry. Home: PO Box 778 Palo Alto CA 94302-0778 Office: 1250 Oakmead Pkwy Ste 210 Sunnyvale CA 94085-4036 E-mail: whkim@xentex.com

KIMBALL, BRUCE ARNOLD, soil scientist; b. Aitkin, Minn., Sept. 27, 1941; s. Robert Clinton and Rica (Barneveld) K.; m. Laurel Sue Hanway, Aug. 20, 1966; children: Britt, Rica, Megan. BS, U. Minn., 1963; MS, Iowa State U., 1965; PhD, Cornell U., 1970. Soil scientist USDA-Agrl. Rsch. Svc. U.S. Water Conservation Lab., Phoenix, 1969-90, rsch. leader Environ. and Plant Dynamics Rsch. Group, 1990—. Editor: Impact of Carbon Dioxide, Trace Gases and Climate Change on Global Agriculture, 1990; co-editor: Carbon Dioxide Enrichment of Greenhouse Crops, 1986; contbr. articles to profl. jours. Fellow Am. Soc. Agronomy (chmn. program div. A3 1988, assoc. editor 1977-83, bd. dirs. 1994-97, assoc. editor Global Change Biology); mem. AAAS. Avocations: computers, biking. Office: US Water Conservation Lab 4331 E Broadway Rd Phoenix AZ 85040-8832

KIMBLE, WILLIAM EARL, lawyer; b. Denver, May 4, 1926; s. George Wilbur and Grace (Fick) K.; m. Jean M. Cayia, Dec. 27, 1950; children: Mark, Cary, Timothy, Stephen, Philip, Peter, Michael. LL.B., U. Ariz., 1951. Bar: Ariz. 1951. Spl. agt. FBI, 1951-52; pvt. practice Bisbee, 1952-60, Tucson, 1962—; judge Superior Ct. Ariz., 1960-62; ptnr. Kimble, Nelson, Audilett, McDonough & Molla, 1962—. Commr. Ariz. Oil and Gas Commn., 1958-60; adj. prof. law U. Ariz. Coll. Law, 1962-86. Author: The Consumer Product Safety Act, 1973, Products Liability, 1977; sr. editor Consumer Products Alert newsletter, 1980-81; editor, pub. In Def. of Elec. Accidents newsletter, 1993—. Founder Naval War Coll. Found.; Rep. nominee Ariz. atty. gen., 1956; Rep. nominee Ariz. U.S. Congress, 1964. Served with USNR, 1944-46. Fellow Am. Coll. Trial Lawyers; mem. Sigma Chi, Phi Alpha Delta. Home: 95 N Camino Miramonte Tucson AZ 85716-4945 Office: Kimble Nelson Audilett McDonough & Molla 335 N Wilmot Rd Ste 500 Tucson AZ 85711-2636 E-mail: idea2@mindspring.com

KIMMICH, JON BRADFORD, computer science program executive; b. Lancaster, Pa., Aug. 8, 1964; s. John Howard and Alice (Ingram) K. BS in Computer Sci., Ind. U. Pa., 1986; MS in Computer Sci., Ohio State U., 1988; MBA, Seattle U., 1993. Developer Microsoft, Redmond, Wash., 1988-93, lead program mgr., sr. producer, 1993-97, lead product planner, 1997—. Dir. PKT Found. Contbr. articles to profl. jours. Trustee PKT Found. Mem. IEEE (Computer Soc.), Assn. for Computing Machinery, Acad. Interactive Arts and Scis., Internat. Interactive Comms. Soc., Am. Film Inst. Achievements include 7 patents pending. Home: 1442 W Lake Sammamish Pkwy SE Bellevue WA 98008-5218 Office: Microsoft Corp 1 Microsoft Way Redmond WA 98052-8300

KIMMITT, ROBERT MICHAEL, executive, banker, diplomat; b. Logan, Utah, Dec. 19, 1947; s. Joseph Stanley and Eunice L. (Wegener) K.; m. Holly Sutherland, May 19, 1979; children: Kathleen, Robert, William, Thomas, Margaret. BS, U.S. Mil. Acad., 1969; JD, Georgetown U., 1977. Bar: D.C. 1977. Commd. 2d lt. U.S. Army, 1969, advanced through grades to maj., 1982, served in Vietnam, 1970-71; maj. gen. USAR, 1999—; law clk. U.S. Ct. Appeals, Washington, 1977-78; sr. staff mem. NSC, Washington, 1978-83, dep. asst. to Pres. for nat. security affairs and exec. sec. and gen. counsel, 1983-85; gen. counsel U.S. Dept. Treasury, Washington, 1985-87; ptnr. Sidley & Austin, Washington, 1987-89; undersec. for polit. affairs Dept. State, Washington, 1989-91, ambassador to Germany, 1991-93; mng. dir. Lehman Bros., Washington, N.Y.C., 1993-97; sr. ptnr. Wilmer, Cutler & Pickering, Washington, 1997-00; vice-chmn., pres. Commerce One, Pleasanton, Calif., 2000-01; exec. v.p. AOL Time Warner, Washington, 2001—. U.S. mem. panel of arbitrators Ctr. Settlement of Investment Internat. Disputes, 1988—89. Bd. dirs. Commerce One, Inc., Siemens AG, Allianz Life Ins. Co. N.Am., United Def. Industries, Xign Corp., German Marshall Fund, Atlantic Coun., Mike Mansfield Found., Am. Coun. Germany, Am. Inst. Contemproray German Studies. Decorated Bronze star (3), Purple Heart, Air medal, Vietnamese Cross of Gallantry, German Svc. Cross, German Army Cross in Gold; recipient Arthur Flemming award Downtown Jaycees, 1987, Alexander Hamilton award U.S. Dept. Treasury, 1987, Presdl. Citizens medal, 1991, Def. Disting. Civilian Svc. medal, 1993. Mem. Am. Acad. Diplomacy, Assn. Grads. U.S. Mil. Acad. (trustee 1976-82), Coun. Fgn. Rels. Roman Catholic. Office: AOL Time Warner Ste 800 800 Connecticut Ave NW Washington DC 20006

KIMNACH, MYRON WILLIAM, botanist, horticulturist, consultant; b. Los Angeles, Dec. 26, 1922; s. Elmer Edward and Ida (Johnson) K.; m. Maria Jaeger, Nov. 17, 1961. Grad. h.s. Asst. mgr. U. Calif. Botanic Garden, Berkeley, 1951-62; curator Huntington Bot. Gardens, San Marino, 1962-88; now book-dealer Monrovia, Calif. Contbr. articles profl. jours. Pres., bd. dirs. Palm Soc., 1976-78. With USCG, 1943-46. Fellow Cactus and Succulent Soc. Am. (pres. 1970-71, bd. dirs. 1968-74, editor jour. 1993—). Home and Office: 509 Bradbury Rd Monrovia CA 91016-3704 E-mail: mkimnach@aol.com

KIMPORT, DAVID LLOYD, lawyer; b. Hot Springs, S.D., Nov. 28, 1945; s. Ralph E. and Ruth N. (Hutchinson) K.; m. Barbara H. Buggert, Apr. 2, 1976; children: Katrina Elizabeth, Rebecca Helen, Susanna Ruth. AB summa cum laude, Bowdoin Coll., 1968; postgrad., Imperial Coll., U. London, 1970-71; JD, Stanford U., 1975. Bar: Calif. 1975, U.S. Supreme Ct. 1978. Assoc. Baker & McKenzie, San Francisco, 1975-82, ptnr., 1982-90, Nossaman, Guthner, Knox & Elliot, 1990—. Active San Francisco Planning and Urban Rsch., 1978—, The Family, 1987—. Served with U.S. Army, 1968-70. Mem. ABA, San Francisco Bar Assn., Commonwealth Club of Calif., Phi Beta Kappa. Democrat. Episcopalian. Office: Nossaman Guthner Knox & Elliott 50 California St Fl 34 San Francisco CA 94111-4624

KIMPTON, BILL, hotel executive; b. Kansas City, Mo. BS in Econs., Northwestern U.; grad., U. Chgo. Chmn. Kimpton Hotel and Restaurant Group, Inc., San Francisco, 1981—. Office: Kimpton Hotel Restaurant Group Inc 222 Kearny St Ste 200 San Francisco CA 94108-4510

KIMURA, DOREEN, psychology educator, researcher; b. Winnipeg, Man., Can. 1 child, Charlotte Vanderwolf. BA, McGill U., Montreal, Que., Can., 1956, MA, 1957, PhD, 1961; LLD (hon.), Simon Fraser U., 1993, Queen's U., 1999. Lectr. Sir George Williams U. (now Concordia U.), Montreal, 1960-61; rsch. assoc. otol. rsch. lab. UCLA Med. Ctr., 1962-63; rsch. assoc. Coll. Medicine, McMaster U., Hamilton, Ont., 1964-67; assoc. prof. psychology U. Western Ont., London, 1967-74, prof., 1974-98, coord. clin. neuropsychology program, 1983-97. Supr. clin. neuropsychology Univ. Hosp., London, 1975-83; vis. prof. psychology Simon Fraser U., 1998—. Author: Neuromotor Mechanisms in Human Communication, 1993, Sex and Cognition, 1999; contbr. numerous articles to profl. jours. Recipient Outstanding Sci. Achievement award Can. Assn. Women in Sci., 1986, John Dewan award Ont. Mental Health Found., 1992; fellow Montreal Neurol. Inst., 1960-61, Geigy fellow Kantonsspital, Zürich, Switzerland, 1963-64. Fellow Royal Soc. Can., Can. Psychol. Assn. (Disting. Contbns. to Sci. award 1985); mem. Soc. Acad. Freedom & Scholarships (founding pres. 1992-93, 98-2000). Office: Simon Fraser U Dept Psychology Burnaby BC Canada V5A 1S6 E-mail: dkimura@sfu.ca

KIND, KENNETH WAYNE, lawyer, real estate broker; b. Missoula, Mont., Apr. 1, 1948; s. Joseph Bruce and Elinor Joy (Smith) K.; m. Diane Lucille Jozaitis, Aug. 28, 1971; children: Kirstin Amber, Kenneth Warner. BA, Calif. State U., Northridge, 1973; JD, Calif. Western U., 1976. Bar: Calif. 1976, U.S. Dist. Ct. (ea., so., no. dists.) Calif., 1976, U.S. Cir. Ct. Appeals (9th cir.); lic. NASCAR driver, 1987. Mem. celebrity security staff Brownstone Am., Beverly Hills, Calif., 1970-76; tchr. Army and Navy Acad., Carlsbad, 1975-76; real estate broker Bakersfield, 1978—; sole practice Bakersfield, 1976—. Lectr. mechanic's lien laws, Calif., 1983—. Staff writer Calif. Western Law Jour., 1975. Sgt. U.S. Army, 1967-70. Mem. ABA, VFW, Nat. Order Barristers, Rancheros Visitadores. Libertarian. Office: 4042 Patton Way Bakersfield CA 93308-5030

KINDEL, JAMES HORACE, JR. lawyer; b. L.A., Nov. 8, 1913; s. James Horace and Philipina (Butte) K.; children: William, Mary, Robert, John. AB, UCLA, 1934; LLB, Loyola U., Los Angeles, 1940. Bar: Calif. 1941; CPA, Calif. Pvt. practice law Kindel & Anderson, L.A., Calif., 1945-96; of counsel McKenna & Cuneo, L.A., 1997—. Ret. ptnr. Coopers-Lybrand; co-owner sand and gravel and poultry bus., Guatemala; co-owner Sunnymead Poultry Ranch, Calif. Trustee UCLA Found. Mem. ABA, L.A. Bar Assn., Orange County Bar Assn., State Bar Calif., AICPA, Chancery Club, Calif. Club, Phi Delta Phi, Theta Xi. Home: 800 W 1st St Apt 2405 Los Angeles CA 90012-2432 Office: 444 S Flower St Fl 7 Los Angeles CA 90071-2901

KINDERWATER, DIANE, state official; BA in Broadcast Journalism, U. Wis. Promotions and mktg. dir., prodr., nat. sales mgr.; media advisor, press sec. N.Mex. Legislature; press sec. Office Gov. Gary Johnson, Santa Fe, 1994—. Office: Office Gov State Capitol Bldg Rm 400 Santa Fe NM 87503-0001 Fax: 505-986-4364

KINDERWATER, JOSEPH C. (JACK KINDERWATER), publishing company executive; b. Milw., Aug. 5, 1922; s. Joseph Charles and Ida (Noll) K.; m. Jacqueline Shirley Marsh, 1948; children— Mark, Mary Jo, Nancy, Scott, Diane B.A., U. Minn., 1948. Advt. copywriter C. Derosier Inc., St. Paul, 1948-50; account exec. David Advt. Agy., St. Paul, 1950-53; advt. rep. The Webb Pub. Co., St. Paul, 1953-63, advt. sales mgr., 1963-68, advt. dir., 1968-78, v.p., pub., 1979-87, exec. v.p., 1987-88, chmn., pres., 1988-89; pub. cons., 1990—; v.p. Midwest Unit Farm Publs., 1979-84, pres., 1985-88. Bd. dirs. Nat. Audit Bur. Circulation, 1985-89, Better Bus. Bur. Minn., St. Paul, 1985-89; fund vol. Am. Heart Assn., St. Paul, 1983-85, Children's Hosp., St. Paul, 1975; instr. Jr. Achievement, St. Paul, 1970-75; bus. exec. rsch. com. U. Minn., 1966. With USAAF, 1943-46; ETO Mem. Northwest Farm Equipment Assn. (pres. 1984-87), Nat. Agr. Mktg. Assn. (v.p. 1976-77), State Farm Mag. Pubs. Assn. (dir. 1980-89), Agr. Pub. Assn. (bd. dirs. 1981-89), St. Paul Advt. Club (pres. 1974-76), Am. Advt. Fedn. (Cleo award 1965, dist. gov. 1965-69) Roman Catholic. Clubs: Minn. Press, Midland Hills Country, St. Paul Athletic, Minn. Advt. Home: 2680 Oxford St N Saint Paul MN 55113-2089 Office: 13013 Panorama Dr Ste 101 Fountain Hills AZ 85268

KING, ALONZO, artistic director, choreographer; Student, Sch. Am. Ballet, Am. ballet theatre Sch., Harkness House Ballet Arts. Art dir. Lines Ballet, San Francisco, 1982—. Master tchr. working with Les Ballets de Monte-Carlo, London's Ballet Rambert, Nat. Ballet of Can., N.C. Sch. of Arts, San Francisco Ballet; inaugurator San Francisco Inst. Choreography, 1982; performer Bella Lewitzsky Dance Co., DTH. Commd. to create and stage ballets for The Joffrey Ballet, Dance Theatre of Harlem; ballets in repertoires of Frankfurt Ballet, Dresden Ballet, BalletMet, Washington Ballet, Hong Kong Ballet; choreographer for Les Ballets de Monte-Carlo; choreogrpaher for prima ballerine Natalia Makarova, Patrick Swazye; original works choreographed include Who Dressed You Like a Foreigner, 1998 (2 Isadora Duncan awards for best costumes and mus. composition), Ocean (3 Isadora Duncan Dance award 1994 for outstanding achievement in choreography, original score and co. performance)), Rock, 1995, others. Mem. panels Nat. Endowment for Arts, Calif. Arts Coun., City of Columbus Arts Coun., Lila Wallace-Reader's Digest Arts Ptnrs. Program; former art commr. City and County of San Francisco. Nat. Endowment for Arts Chroeographer's fellow. Office: Lines Ballet 50 Oak St Fl 4 San Francisco CA 94102-6011

KING, ARTHUR R., JR. education educator, researcher; b. Portland, Oreg., Dec. 17, 1921; BA, U. Wash., 1943; MA, Stanford U., 1951, EdD, 1955. Tchr., counselor Punahou Sch., Honolulu, 1946-49; rsch. assoc. Stanford (Calif.) U., 1949-51; dir. curricular svcs. Sonoma County Schs., Calif., 1951-55; assoc. prof. edn. Claremont Grad. Sch., Claremont, 1955-65; prof. edn. U. Hawaii, Honolulu, 1965—, dir. Curriculum Rsch. & Devel. Group, 1966—, rschr. Edn. Rsch. and Devel. Ctr., 1966-74. Prin. investigator, editor courses Hawaii State Dept. Edn.; head Ocean Project, 1979-90; co-founder Pacific Cir. Consortium. Author: (with John A. Brownell) The Curriculum and the Disciplines of Knowledge: A Theory of Curriculum Practice, 1966; contbr. articles to profl. jours. Served USN, WWII; capt., USNR, ret. Office: U Hawaii at Manoa Curriculum Rsch & Devel Group 1776 University Ave Honolulu HI 96822-2463 E-mail: aking@hawaii.edu, kinga002@hawaii.vv.com

KING, C. JUDSON, academic administrator; B in Chem. Engring., MIT, 1956, SM, ScD in Chem. Engring., MIT. Asst. prof. U. Calif., Berkeley, 1963—66, assoc. prof., 1966—69, prof. chem. engring., 1969—, chmn. dept. chem. engring., 1972-81, dean Coll. Chemistry, 1981-87, provost profl. schs. and colls., 1987-94, provost, sr. v.p. academic affairs, 1996—, vice provost rsch. systemwide, 1995—96. Dir. chem. engring. program divsn. nuclear chemistry Lawrence Berkeley Lab.; with coun. for chem. rsch. Gov.'s Task Force on Toxics, Waste and Tech. Recipient Clarence G. Gerhold award, Warren K. Lewis award, Mac Pruitt award for Excellence in Drying Rsch. Internat. Drying Symposium. Fellow AIChE; mem. AAAS, AICE (William H. Walker award, Centennial medallion), NSF, NAE, Am. Soc. Engring. Edn. (George Westinghouse award), Am. Chem. Soc. (internat. com. solvent extraction), Nat. Rsch. Coun. (com. separation sci. and tech.), Nat. Bur. Stds. Programs (bd. assessment), Nat. Acad. Engring. (chair com. alternatives). Office: U Calif Office Pres & Regents 1111 Franklin St Oakland CA 96460-0520

KING, CARY JUDSON, III, chemical engineer, educator, university official; b. Ft. Monmouth, N.J., Sept. 27, 1934; s. Cary Judson and Mary Margaret (Forbes) K., Jr.; m. Jeanne Antoinette Yorke, June 22, 1957; children: Mary Elizabeth, Cary Judson IV, Catherine Jeanne. B. Engring., Yale, 1956; S.M., Mass. Inst. Tech., 1958, Sc.D., 1960. Asst. prof. chem. engring. MIT, Cambridge, 1959-63; dir. Bayway Sta. Sch. Chem. Engring. Practice, Linden, N.J., 1959-61; asst. prof. chem. engring. U. Calif., Berkeley, 1963-66, assoc. prof., 1966-69, prof., 1969—, vice chmn. dept. chem. engring., 1967-72, chmn., 1972-81, dean Coll. Chemistry, 1981-87, provost profl. schs. and colls., 1987-94; vice provost for rsch. U. Calif. Sys., Oakland, 1994-96, interim provost, sr. v.p. acad. affairs, 1995-96, provost, sr. v.p. acad. affairs, 1996—. Cons. Procter & Gamble Co., 1969-87; bd. dirs. Coun. for Chem. Rsch., chmn., 1989, Am. U. of Armenia Corp., chmn., 1995—, Calif. Assn. for Rsch. in Astronomy, 2001—. Author: Separation Processes, 1971, 80, Freeze Drying of Foods, 1971; contbr. numerous articles to profl. jours.; patentee in field. Active Boy Scouts Am., 1947-86; pres. Kensington Community Council, 1972-73, dir., 1970-73. Recipient Malcolm E. Pruitt award Coun. for Chem. Rsch., 1990. Mem. AIChE (Inst. lectr. 1973, Food, Pharm. and Bioengring Divsn. award 1975, William H. Walker award 1976, Warren K. Lewis award 1990, bd. dirs. 1987-89, Clarence G. Gerhold award 1992); mem. AAAS, Nat. Acad. Engring., Am. Soc. Engring. Edn. (George Westinghouse award 1978), Am. Chem. Soc. (Separations Sci. and Tech. award 1997). Home: 7 Kensington Ct Kensington CA 94707-1009 Office: U Calif Office of Pres 1111 Franklin St Fl 12 Oakland CA 94607-5201

KING, DUANE HAROLD, museum administrator; b. Bristol, Tenn., May 18, 1947; BA, U. Tenn., 1969; MA, U. Ga., 1972, PhD, 1975. Dir. Mus. Cherokee (N.C.) Nation, 1975-82; exec. dir. Cherokee Nat. Hist. Soc., Tahlequah, Okla., 1982-87, Mid. Oreg. Indian Hist. Soc., Warm Springs, 1987-90; asst. dir. George Gustav Heye Ctr. Nat. Mus. Am. Indian, N.Y.C., 1990-95; exec. dir. Southwest Mus., L.A., 1995—. Chmn. adv. com. Trail of Tears Nat. Hist. Trail Nat. Park Svc., 1991—; bd. trustees mem. Inst. Am. Indian and Alaska Native Culture and Arts Devel., Santa Fe, 1988—; exec. dir. Friends of Sequoyah Found. of Ea. Band Cherokee Indians, 1989-90; periodic cons. Cherokee Nation of Okla., 1989-94, Mus. Cherokee Indian, 1985—, Walt Disney Imagineering, Glendale, Calif., 1994; hist. advisor KUSA-TV, Denver, 1994-95; Sequoyah prof. We. Carolina U., Cullowhee, N.C., 1995, adj. asst. prof. dept. sociology and anthropology, 1976-82; adj. prof. divsn. arts and humanities Northeastern State U., Tahlequah, 1986-87; vis. asst. prof. dept. anthropology U. Tenn., Knoxville, 1974-82; asst. prof. dept. sociology and anthropology U. Tenn., Chattanooga, 1974-76. Contbr. video documentaries and articles to profl. jours. Recipient Spl. Achievement and Exceptional Svc. awards (6) Smithsonian Instn., 1992-95, Gold award Nat. Park Svc., 1995, Svc. award Confederated Tribes Warm Springs, 1990, Performance award Cherokee Nation Okla., 1985, Mayor's Merit award for exceptional achievements City of Knoxville, 1983, Disting. Svc. award Ea. Band Cherokee Indians, 1982, Vol. Svc. award Save the Children Found., 1982. Home: 311 Santa Rosa Rd Arcadia CA 91007-3040 Office: Southwest Museum PO Box 41558 Los Angeles CA 90041-0558 Fax: 213 224-8223

KING, EDWARD LOUIS, retired chemistry educator; b. Grand Forks, N.D., Mar. 15, 1920; s. Edward Louis and Beatrice (Nicholson) K.; m. Joy Kerler, Dec. 20, 1952; children: Paul, Marcia (dec.). Student, Long Beach (Calif.) Jr. Coll., 1938-41; B.S., U. Calif., Berkeley, 1942, Ph.D., 1945. Research chemist Manhattan Project, U. Cal., Berkeley, 1942-46; mem. chemistry faculty Harvard, 1946-48, U. Wis., 1948-62, U. Colo., Boulder, 1963-90, chmn. dept. chemistry, 1970-72. Author: How Chemical Reactions Occur, 1963, Chemistry, 1979; Editor: Inorganic Chemistry, 1964-68. Guggenheim fellow, 1957-58 Mem. Am. Chem. Soc., Phi Beta Kappa, Sigma Xi. Office: U Colo Dept Chemistry PO Box 215 Boulder CO 80309-0215

KING, FELTON, bishop; Bishop Ch. of God in Christ, Phoenix. Office: Emmanuel Ch God in Christ 1537 W Buckeye Rd Phoenix AZ 85007-3516

KING, GEORGE H. judge; AB, UCLA, 1971; JD, U. So. Calif., L.A., 1974. Judge U.S. Dist. Ct. (cen. dist.) Calif., 1995—. Office: 255 E Temple St Los Angeles CA 90012-3332

KING, GUNDAR JULIAN, retired university dean; b. Riga, Latvia, Apr. 19, 1926; came to U.S., 1950, naturalized, 1954; s. Attis K. and Austra (Dale) Kenins: m. Valda K. Andersons, Sept. 18, 1954; children: John T., Marita A. Student, J.W. Goethe U., Frankfurt, Germany, 1946-48; BBA, U. Oreg., 1956; MBA, Stanford U., 1958, PhD, 1964; DSc (hon.), Riga Tech. U., 1991; D Habil. Oecon., Latvian Sci. Coun., 1992. Asst. field supr. Internat. Refugee Orgn., Frankfurt, 1948-50; br. office mfr. Williams Form Engring. Corp., Portland, Oreg., 1952-54; project mgr. Market Rsch. Assocs., Palo Alto, Calif., 1958-60; asst. prof., assoc. prof. Pacific Luth. U., 1960-66, prof., 1966—, dean Sch. Bus. Adminstrn., 1970-90. Vis. prof. mgmt. U.S. Naval Postgrad. Sch., 1971-72, San Francisco State U., 1980, 1987-88; internat. econ. mem. Latvian Acad. Scis., 1990—; regent Estonian Bus. Sch., 1991-99; vis. prof. Riga Tech. U., 1993-97; dir. Baltic Studies fund, 1995—. Author: Economic Policies in Occupied Latvia, 1965, additional books on business; contbr. articles to profl. publs. Mem. Gov.'s Com. on Reorgn. Wash. State Govt., 1965-88; mem. study group on pricing U.S. Commn. Govt. Procurement, 1971-72; pres. N.W. Univs. Bus. Adminstrn. Conf., 1965-66. With AUS, 1950-52. Spidola prize Latvian Culture Found., 1999; Fulbright-Hayes scholar, Thailand, 1988, Fulbright scholar, Latvia, 1993-94. Mem. AAUP (past chpt. pres.), Am. Mktg. Assn. (past chpt. pres.), Assn. Advancement Baltic Studies (pres. 1970), Western Assn. Collegiate Schs. Bus. (pres. 1971), Latvian Acad. Scis., Alpha Kappa Psi, Beta Gamma Sigma. Home: PO Box 44401 Tacoma WA 98444-0401 Office: Pacific Lutheran U Tacoma WA 98447-0003 E-mail: KinggJ@plu.edu

KING, HELEN EMORI, dean; b. Stockton, Calif., Apr. 10, 1936; d. Susumu and Sumi Emori; m. William King, Aug. 5, 1973; children: Bill, Brian, Donna, Debbie. BS, Loma Linda U., 1959, MS, 1965; PhD, Boston U., 1973. Asst. prof. Boston U., 1973-75; dept. chmn., prof. Atlantic Union Coll., South Lancaster, Mass., 1978-81; dean sch. nursing Loma Linda (Calif.) U., 1981—. Mem. Nat. League Nursing, Sigma Theta Tau. Office: Loma Linda U Sch Nursing Loma Linda CA 92350-0001 E-mail: hKing@sn.llu.edu

KING, INDLE GIFFORD, industrial designer, educator; b. Seattle, Oct. 23, 1934; s. Indle Frank and Phyllis (Kenney) K.; m. Rosalie Rosso, Sept. 10, 1960; children: Indle Gifford Jr., Paige Phyllis. BA, U. Wash., 1960, MA, 1968. Indsl. designer Hewlett-Packard, Palo Alto, Calif., 1961-63; mgr. indsl. design Sanborn Co., Boston, 1963-65; mgr. corp. design Fluke Corp., Everett, Wash., 1965-97; prof. indsl. design Western Wash. U., Bellingham, 1985—; pres., CEO Teaque Inc., 1998—. Judge nat. and internat. competitions; cons. in field. Contbr. articles to profl. jours.; designer patents in field. Coach Mercer Island (Wash.) Boys' Soccer Assn., 1972-77; pres. Mercer Island PTA, 1973; advisor Jr. Achievement, Seattle, 1975-78. Recognized as leading one of Am.'s Top 40 Design Driven Cos., ID Jour., 1999. Mem. Idsl. Design Soc. Am. (Alcoa award 1965, v.p. Seattle chpt. 1986-88), Mercer Island Country Club. Office: 14727 NE 87th St Redmond WA 98052-6500

KING, IVAN ROBERT, astronomy educator; b. Far Rockaway, N.Y., June 25, 1927; s. Myram and Anne (Franzblau) K.; m. Alice Greene, Nov. 21, 1952 (div. 1982); children: David, Lucy, Adam, Jane. AB, Hamilton Coll., 1946; AM, Harvard U., 1947, PhD, 1952. Instr. astronomy Harvard U., 1951-52; mathematician Perkin-Elmer Corp., Norwalk, Conn., 1951-52; methods analyst U.S. Dept. Def., Washington, 1954-56; with U. Ill., 1956-64; assoc. prof. astronomy U. Calif., Berkeley, 1964-66, prof., 1966-93, chmn. astronomy dept., 1967-70, prof. emeritus, 1993—. Mem. faint object camera team Hubble Space Telescope. Contbr. numerous articles to sci. jours. Served with USNR, 1952-54. Fellow AAAS (chmn. astronomy sect. 1974), NAS, Am. Acad. Arts & Scis., Am. Astron. Soc. (councillor 1963-66, chmn. div. dynamical astronomy 1972-73, pres. 1978-80), Internat. Astron. Union. Achievements include rsch. study of stellar systems. Office: U Calif Dept Astronomy Berkeley CA 94720-3411

KING, JAMES NEDWED, construction company executive, lawyer; b. Chgo., July 9, 1947; s. Ralph C. and Marie (Nedwed) K.; m. Ellen Josephine Carpenter, Jan. 29, 1977; children: Cynthia Marie, Michelle Ellen BBA, U. Notre Dame, 1969; JD, U. N.Mex., 1972. Bar: N.Mex. 1972. Pres. Bradbury & Stamm Constrn. Co., Albuquerque, 1972—. Bd. dirs. Albuquerque Econ. Devel. Corp. Mem. N.Mex. Amigos. Home: 13731 Apache Plume Pl NE Albuquerque NM 87111-8090 Office: Bradbury & Stamm Constrn Co PO Box 10850 Albuquerque NM 87184-0850 E-mail: jking@bradburystamm.com

KING, JANET CARLSON, nutrition educator, researcher; b. Red Oak, Iowa, Oct. 3, 1941; d. Paul Emil and Norma Carolina (Anderson) Carlson; m. Charles Talmadge King, Dec. 25, 1967; children: Matthew, Samuel. BS, Iowa State U., 1963; PhD, U. Calif., Berkeley, 1972. Dietitian Fitzsimmons Gen. Hosp., Denver, 1964-67; NIH postdoctoral fellow dept. nutrition sci. U. Calif., Berkeley, 1972-73, asst. prof. nutrition dept. nutrition sci., 1973-78, assoc. prof. nutrition dept. nutrition sci., 1978-83, prof. nutrition dept. nutrition sci., 1983—, chair dept. nutrition sci., 1988-94; dir. USDA Western Human Nutrition Rsch.Ctr., San Francisco, 1995—. Frances E. Fischer Meml. nutrition lectr. Am. Dietetic Assn. Found., 1985, Lotte Arnrich Nutrition lectr. Iowa State U., 1985; Massee lectr. N.D., 1991, Lydia J. Roberts lectr. U. Chgo., 1995, Virginia A. Beal lectr. U. Mass., 1998; vis. prof. U. Calif., Davis, 1998—. Contbr. articles to Jour. Am. Diet. Assn., Am. Jour. Clin. Nutrition, Jour. Nutrition, Nutrition Rsch., Obstetrics and Gynecology, Brit. Jour. Obstetrics and Gynaecology. Recipient Lederle Labs. award in human nutrition Am. Inst. Nutrition, 1989, Internat. award in human nutrition, 1996. Mem. AAAS, Nat. Acad. Scis. Inst. Medicine, Am. Dietetic Assn., Am. Inst. Nutrition, Am. Soc. Clin. Nutrition. Office: USDA Western Human Nutrition Rsch Ctr Univ Calif Davis CA 95616

KING, JOHN G. health service administrator; BA, Dartmouth Coll.; MHA, U. Minn. Various positions Fairview Sys., Mpls.; pres. Holy Cross Health Sys., Evang. Health Sys., 1980-91; pres., CEO Legacy Health Sys., Portland, Oreg. Bd. dirs. Blue Cross Blue Shield Oreg., Premier, Health-East, Minn. Bd. dirs. United Way, Columbia-Willamette. Mem Am. Hosp. Assn. (trustee), Portland C. of C. Office: Legacy Health Sys 1919 NW Lovejoy St Portland OR 97209-1599

KING, LOWELL RESTELL, pediatric urologist; b. Salem, Ohio, Feb. 28, 1932; s. Lowell Waldo and Vesta Ethylwin (Snyder) K.; m. Mary Elizabeth Hill, July 9, 1960; children: Andrew Restell, Erika Lillie. BA, Johns Hopkins U., 1953, MD, 1956. Intern Johns Hopkins Hosp., Balt., 1956-57, resident in urology, 1957-62; asst. prof. urology Johns Hopkins U., 1962-63, Northwestern U., 1963-67, assoc. prof., 1967-70, prof., 1970-81, prof. urology and surgery, 1974-81; prof. urology and pediatrics Duke U., Durham, N.C., 1981-97, prof. emeritus, 1997; prof. surgery/urology U. N.Mex., Albuquerque, 1997—. Prof., chmn. dept. urology Presbyn.-St. Luke's Hosp., 1968-70; surgeon-in-chief Children's Meml. Hosp., Chgo., 1974-80 Author: (with P.P. Kelalis) Clinical Pediatric Urology, 1976, 3d edit., 1992; (with A.B. Belman) 4th edit., 2001, Bladder Replacement and Continent Urology Diversion, 1986, 2d edit., 1991, Urologic Surgery in the Neonate and Young Infant, 1992, Reconstructive Urology, 1992, Urologic Surgery in Infants and Children, 1997; cons. editor Urology; editor profl. jours.; contbr. articles to profl. jours. Vestryman, sr. warden Ch. of Our Savior, 1974-80; bd. dirs. Gads Hill Settlement House, 1969-73. Recipient Gold medal All India Urologic Congress, 1996, Gold medal Mex. Coll. Urology, 1991. Mem. AMA, Am. Urol. Assn. (career achievement award 1996), Am. Acad. Pediats. (chmn. sect. urology 1969-72, sec. 1972-76, pres. 1977-78, Urology medal 1992), Soc. Pediat. Urology (pres. 1983), Soc. U. Urologists, Am. Assn. Genitourinary Surgeons, Clin. Soc. Genitourinary Surgeons (pres. 1996). Republican. Episcopalian. Home: 2012 Dietz Pl NW Albuquerque NM 87107-3220 Office: U NMex Health Scis Ctr Sch Medicine Dept Surgery Divsn Urology 2211 Lomas Blvd NE Albuquerque NM 87106-2745

KING, MARY-CLAIRE, geneticist, educator; b. Evanston, Ill., Feb. 27, 1946; m. 1973; 1 child, Emily King Colwell. BA in Math., Carleton Coll., 1966; PhD in Genetics, U. Calif., Berkeley, 1973. Am. Cancer Soc. prof. medicine and genetics U. Wash., Seattle, 1995—. Mem. bd. sci. counselors Nat. Cancer Inst.; cons. Com. for Investigation of Disappearance of Persons, Govt. Argentina, Buenos Aires, 1984—. Contbr. more than 150 articles to profl. jours. Recipient Alumni Achievement award Carleton Coll., Basic Rsch. award Susan G. Komen Breast Cancer Found., 1999. Mem. AAAS, Am. Soc. Human Genetics, Soc. Epidemiologic Research, Inst. Medicine, Phi Beta Kappa, Sigma Xi. Office: U Wash 1959 NE Pacific St # 357720 Seattle WA 98195-0001

KING, MICHAEL, syndicated programs distributing company executive, s. Charles King. BA in Mktg., Fairleigh Dickinson U., 1971. Advt. salesman Sta. WORC, Worcester, Mass.; from sales mgr. to part owner Sta. WAAF-FM, Worcester; pres., CEO, King World Prodns., N.Y.C., 1977—. Office: 12400 Wilshire Blvd Ste 1200 Los Angeles CA 90025 1058

KING, PETER D. psychiatrist, educator, real estate developer; b. Chgo., Feb. 20, 1927; s. Ralph DeWitt and Jane Munn (Spear) K.; m. Harriet Virginia Morse, Dec. 16, 1950 (div. Sept. 1968); children: Katherine V. Wangsgard, Dana Hutchins, Kevin Allison; m. Patricia Hopson, Jan. 1, 1969 (div. Apr. 1972); m. Simone Misook Cho, Oct. 25, 1974; 1 child, Carol Denise. BA with spl. honors, U. Chgo., 1950, BS, MD, U. Chgo., 1954; PhD, So. Calif. Psychoanal. Inst., 1967. Diplomate psychiatry Am. Bd. Psychiatry and Neurology. Rsch. assoc. hematology U. Chgo. (Ill.) Clinics, 1951-54; resident in psychiatry Warren (Pa.) State Hosp., 1955-58; clin. dir., dir. rsch. Madison (Ind.) State Hosp., 1958-59; USPHS fellow in child psychiatry Reiss-Davis Child Ctr., L.A., 1959-61; asst. prof. psychiatry and behavioral sci. UCLA Med. Ctr., L.A., 1961-67; clin. prof. psychiatry and behavioral sci. U. So. Calif. Sch. Medicine, L.A., Calif., 1967—; pres. King Devel. Corp., Encino, 1978-98; pvt. practice psychiatry Encino, 1962-96, Sherman Oaks, Calif., 1996—; staff psychiatrist Calif. Dept. Corrections, 1996—. Founder Coagulation Lab., U. Chgo. (Ill.) Clinics, 1952-54; founder Mental Health Clinic, Altoona, Pa., 1958; med. dir. Madre de Vida Inst., Tarzana, Calif., 1962; cons. on immunology Euvita/Eudyna, L.A., 1994-95, founder Formula 2001, 1994-95. Author: The Principle of Truth, 1960, Studies on Early Infantile Autism, 1973, Collected Poetry, 1975; contbr. chpts. to books and articles to profl. jours. Cpl. USAAF, 1945-47. Shurtleff scholar U. Chgo. (Ill.) Sch. Medicine, 1951-54; recipient Spl. award Citizens of Altoona, 1958, 3d pl. award Nat. Libr. Poetry, 1997. Fellow Am. Psychiat. Assn., Am. Acad. Psychoanalysis, Am. Group Psychotherapy Assn.; mem. ACLU, NOW, So. Calif. Psychoanalytic Inst. (chair faculty selection 1993-96, Franz Alexander prize), Coun. for a Livable World. Achievements include research on the study of sleep; hypnosis theory of schizophrenia; effects of therapy, drugs and electroshock on schizophrenia; autism; and others. Avocations: civil rights, computers, body building, triathlon, writing. Home and Office: 3757 Crownridge Dr Sherman Oaks CA 91403-4820

KING, RAY JOHN, electrical engineer, educator; b. Montrose, Colo., Jan. 1, 1933; s. John Frank and Grace (Rankin) K.; m. Diane M. Henney, June 20, 1964; children: Karl V., Kristin J. BS in Electronic Engring., Ind. Inst. Tech., 1956, BS in Elec. Engring., 1957; MS, U. Colo., 1960, PhD, 1965. Instr. Ind. Inst. Tech., 1956-58, asst. prof., 1960-62, acting chmn. dept. electronics, 1960-62; research asso. U. Colo., 1962-65; research assoc. U. Ill., 1965; assoc. prof. elec. engring. U. Wis., Madison, 1965-69, prof., 1969-82, assoc. dept. chmn. for research and grad. affairs, 1977-79; staff rsch. engr. Lawrence Livermore Nat. Lab. (Calif.), 1982-90, sr. scientist high power microwaves program, 1989-90; co-founder KDC Tech. Corp., 1983, v.p., 1990—, cons. Vis. Erskine fellow U. Canterbury, N.Z., 1977; guest prof., Fulbright scholar Tech. U. Denmark, 1973-74 Author: Microwave Homodyne Systems, 1978; contbr. articles to profl. jours.; patentee in field; guest editor spl. issue Subsurface Sensing Techs. and Applications jour., 2000. NSF Faculty fellow, 1962-65 Fellow IEEE (life); mem. IEEE Soc. on Antennas and Propagation (adminstrv. com. 1989-91, chmn. wave propagation stds. com. 1986-89, gen. chmn. symposium 1989), IEEE Soc. Microwave Theory and Techniques, IEEE Soc. Instrumentation and Measurements, Forest Products Soc., Electromagnetics Acad., Internat. Sci. Radio Union (commns. A, B, F), Sigma Xi, Iota Tau Kappa, Sigma Phi Delta. Home: 2595 Raven Rd Pleasanton CA 94566-4605 Office: KDC Tech Corp 2011 Research Dr Livermore CA 94550-3803 E-mail: kdc@ant-s.com, raydiking@earthlink.net

KING, ROBERT, retail company executive; COO, pres. Corp. Express Inc., Broomfield, Colo., pres., CEO. Office: Corp Express Inc One Environmental Way Broomfield CO 80021-3416

KING, ROBERT WILSON, public relations specialist; b. Newport, R.I., Sept. 25, 1954; BA in Lit., Boston U., 1977. With Sta. WBUR-FM, Boston, 1976-77; pub. affairs dir. Sta. KDLG-AM, Dillingham, Alaska, 1978-79, news dir., 1979-94; comm. dir. Knowles for Gov. Campaign, 1994; press sec. Office Gov. Tony Knowles, Juneau, Alaska, 1994. Bd. dirs. Juneau Symphony, Alaska Hist. Soc. Home: 419 Kennedy St Juneau AK 99801-1054 Office: Office of Gov PO Box 110001 Juneau AK 99811-0001 E-mail: Bob_King@gov.state.ak.us

KING, SAMUEL PAILTHORPE, federal judge; b. Hankow, China, Apr. 13, 1916; s. Samuel W. and Pauline (Evans) K.; m. Anne Van Patten Grilk, July 8, 1944; children— Samuel Pailthorpe, Louise Van Patten, Charlotte Lelepoki. B.S., Yale, 1937, LL.B., 1940. Bar: D.C., Hawaii bars 1940. Practiced law, Honolulu, 1941-42, 46-61, 70-72, Washington, 1942; atty. King & McGregor, 1947-53, King & Myhre, 1957-61; judge 1st Circuit Ct. Hawaii, 1961-70, Family Ct., 1966-70; sr. judge U.S. Dist. Ct. for Hawaii, 1972—, chief judge, 1974-84. Faculty Nat. Coll. State Judiciary, 1968-73, Nat. Inst. Trial Advocacy, 1976, U. Hawaii Law Sch., 1980-84 Co-translator, co-editor: (O. Korschelt) The Theory and Practice of Go, 1965. Served with USNR, 1941-46; capt. Res. ret. Fellow Am. Bar Found.; mem. ABA, Hawaii Bar Assn. (pres. 1953), Order of Coif. Republican (chmn. Hawaii central com. 1953-55, nat. com. 1971-72). Episcopalian. Home: 1717 Mott-smith Dr Apt 2814 Honolulu HI 96822-2850 Office: US Dist Ct 300 Ala Moana Blr Rm C461 Honolulu HI 96850-0461

KING, SHARON MARIE, consulting company executive; b. Clarksville, Ark., Sept. 16, 1946; d. Argie L. and Vida M. K.; m. Robert W. Warnke, Feb. 14, 1983; children: Michael R., Jenna L. AA, Coll. of Ozarks, Clarksville, 1966; BA summa cum laude, Calif. State U., Dominguez Hills, 1979. Sr. exec. asst. Computer Sci. Corp., El Segundo, Calif., 1973-79; office mgr., bookkeeper Internal Charter Brokers, Manhattan Beach, 1979-80; office mgr. Metal Box Can, Torrance, 1980-81; sec. to pres. Filtrol, L.A., 1981-82; owner, mgr. Select Secretarial Svc., Manhattan Beach, 1982-89; pres., CEO Chipton-Ross, Inc., El Segundo, Calif., 1989—. Mem. Calif. C. of C. Presbyterian. Office: Chipton-Ross Inc 343 Main St El Segundo CA 90245 E-mail: sking@chiptonross.com

KING-BARRUTIA, ROBBIE L. state senator; b. Waco, Tex., Jan. 10, 1959; m. Kevin Barrutia; children: Kandace, Kenzie. Student, Coll. So. Idaho. Legis. attache; Rep. rep. dist. 20 Idaho Ho. of Reps., 1992-96; Rep. senator dist. 20 Idaho State Senate, 1996—. Mem. commerce and human resources, health and welfare, judiciary and rules coms. Idaho State Senate. Mem. Owyhee County Cowbelles; mem. Mountain Home Mil. Affairs Com., Region IV Infant and Toddler Com., Idaho Rural Devel. Coun. With Idaho Air N.G. Mem. South Ctrl. Idaho Recreation and Tourism Devel. Assn., Owyhee County Cattlemens Assn., Mountain Home C. o C., Glenns Ferry C. of C. Roman Catholic. Office: PO Box 28 Glenns Ferry ID 83623 also: Idaho State Senate State Capitol PO Box 83720 Boise ID 83720-0081 E-mail: infocntr@lso.state.id.us

KINGERY, WILLIAM DAVID, ceramics and anthropology educator; b. N.Y.C., July 7, 1926; s. Lisle Byron and Margaret (Reynolds) K.; children: William, Rebekah, Andrew. SB, MIT, 1948, ScD, 1950; PhD (hon.), Tokyo Inst. Tech.; ScD (hon.), Ecole Poly. Federale de Lausanne. From instr. to assoc. prof. MIT, Cambridge, Mass., 1951-62, prof., 1962—, Kyocera prof. ceramics, 1984-88; prof. materials sci. and anthropology U. Ariz., Tucson, 1988—, Regents prof., 1992—. Vis. prof. Imperial Coll. Sci. and Tech., London, 1995—. Author: (text) Introduction to Ceramics, 1960, 2d edit., 1976 (translated into 3 langs.), Ceramic Masterpieces, 1986 (Hon. Mention, Pub. Inst.), others; editor: Ceramic Fabrication Processes, Property Measurements at High Temperatures, Kinetics of High Temperature Processes, Ceramics and Civilization I: Ancient Technology to Modern Science, 1985, Ceramics and Civilization II: Technology and Style, 1986, Ceramics and Civilization III: High Tech Ceramics-Past, Present and Future, 1987, Ceramics and Civilization, 1990, Technolo-gical Innovation, 1991, (with S. Lubar) History from Things, 1993, Learning from Things, 1995; editor-in-chief Ceramics Internat. Chmn. bd. trustees Acad. Ceramics, 1989—. Named Wagener lectr. Tokyo Inst. Tech., 1976, Kurtz lectr. Technion, Haifa, Israel, 1978, Nelson W. Taylor lectr. Pa. State U., 1982; recipient Albert V. Bleininger award, 1977, F.H. Norton award, 1977 recipient of the Pomerance award, Am. Inst. of Archaeology, 1996; Regents fellow Smithsonian Instn., Washington, 1988, Van Horn lectr. Case Western Reserve U., 1995. Fellow Am. Acad. Arts and Scis.; mem. NAE, Am. Ceramic Soc. (life, disting., Ross coffin Purdy award, John Jeppson award 1958, Robert Sosman Meml. Lecture award 1973, Hobart M. Kraner award 1985 outstanding Edn. award, 1992), Cosmos Club, Blue Water Sailing Club, Royal Hamilton Amateur Dinghy Club, Naval Club. Office: U Ariz 338 Mines Bldg Tucson AZ 85721-0001

KING-NING, TU, materials science and engineering educator; b. Canton, China, Dec. 30, 1937; came to U.S., 1962; s. Ying-Chiang Tu and Sau-Yuk Chen; m. Ching Chiao, Sept. 25, 1964; children: Olivia, Stephen. BSc, Nat. Taiwan U., 1960; MSc, Brown U., 1964; PhD, Harvard U., 1968. Rsch. staff mem. IBM Watson Rsch. Ctr., Yorktown Heights, N.Y., 1968-93, sr. mgr. thin film sci. dept., 1978-85, sr. mgr. materials sci. dept., 1985-87; prof. dept. materials sci. & engring. UCLA, 1993—. Co-author: (textbook) Electronic Thin Film Science, 1992. Recipient Acta/Scripta Metallurgica Lecturer, 1990; grantee Alexander von Humboldt, 1996. Fellow Am. Phys. Soc., The Metall. Soc. (Applications to Practice award 1988), Churchill Coll. (U.K.). Achievements include 8 patents on thin film technology for microelectronics. Office: UCLA Boelter Hall 6532 B Los Angeles CA 90095-0001 E-mail: kntu@ucla.edu

KINGSLEY, PATRICIA, public relations executive; b. Gastonia, N.C., May 7, 1932; d. Robert Henry and Marjorie (Norment) Ratchford; m. Walter Kingsley, Apr. 1, 1966 (div. 1978); 1 child, Janis Susan. Student, Winthrop Coll., 1950-51. Publicist Fountainebleau Hotel, Miami Beach, Fla., 1952; exec. asst. ZIV TV, N.Y.C., 1953-58; publicist Rogers & Cowan, L.A. and N.Y.C., 1960-71; ptnr. Pickwick Pub. Rels., L.A., 1971-80, PMK Pub. Rels., L.A., 1980—. Adv. com. Women's Action for Nuclear Disarmament, Arlington, Mass., 1983—. Democrat. Office: PMK Pub Rels Inc 8500 Wilshire Blvd Beverly Hills CA 90211

KINGSOLVER, BARBARA ELLEN, writer; b. Annapolis, Md., Apr. 8, 1955; d. Wendell and Virginia (Henry) K.; m. Steven Hopp; 2 children. BA, DePauw U., 1977; MS, U. Ariz., 1981; LittD (hon.), DePauw U., 1994. Sci. writer U. Ariz., Tucson, 1981-85; free-lance journalist Tucson, 1985-87; novelist Tucson, 1987—. Book reviewer N.Y. Times, 1988—, L.A. Times, 1989—. Author: The Bean Trees, 1988 (ALA award 1988), Homeland and Other Stories, 1969 (ALA award 1990), Holding the Line: Women in the Great Arizona Mine Strike of 1983, 89, Animal Dreams, 1990 (PEN West Fiction award 1991, Edward Abbey Ecofiction award 1991), Another America, 1992, Pigs in Heaven, 1993 (L.A. Times Fiction prize 1993, Mountains and Plains Fiction award 1993, Western Heritage award 1993, ABBY Honor Book 1994), Essays, High Tide in Tucson, 1995, The Poisonwood Bible, 1998 (ABBY Honor Book 2000, PEN/Faulkner honoree 1999, Pulitzer runner-up 1999, Orange Prize short list 1999). Recipient Feature-writing award Ariz. Press Club, 1986; citation of accomplishment UN Nat. Coun. of Women, 1989; Woodrow Wilson Found./Lila Wallace fellow, 1992-93. Mem. PEN Ctr. USA West, Nat. Writers Union, Phi Beta Kappa. Avocations: human rights, environmental conservation, gardening, natural history. Office: PO Box 31870 Tucson AZ 85751-1870 also: care Harper Collins 10 E 53rd St New York NY 10022-5244

KINGSTON, MAXINE HONG, writer, educator; b. Stockton, Calif., Oct. 27, 1940; d. Tom and Ying Lan (Chew) Hong; m. Earll Kingston, Nov. 23, 1962; 1 child, Joseph Lawrence. BA, U. Calif., Berkeley, 1962; D degree (hon.), Ea. Mich. U., 1988, Colby Coll., 1990, Brandeis U., 1991, U. Mass., 1991. Tchr. English, Sunset High Sch., Hayward, Calif., 1965-66, Kahuku (Hawaii) High Sch., 1967, Kahaluu (Hawaii) Drop-In Sch., 1968, Kailua (Hawaii) High Sch., 1969, Honolulu Bus. Coll., 1969, Mid-Pacific Inst., Honolulu, 1970-77; prof. English, vis. writer U. Hawaii, Honolulu, 1977; Thelma McCandless Disting. Prof. Eastern Mich. U., Ypsilanti, 1986, Chancellor's Disting. Prof. U. Calif., Berkeley, 1990—. Author: The Woman Warrior: Memoirs of a Girlhood Among Ghosts, 1976 (Nat. Book Critics Cir. award for non-fiction; cited by Time mag., N.Y. Times Book Rev. and Asian Mail as one of best books of yr. and decade), China Men, 1981 (Nat. Book award; runner-up for Pulitzer prize, Nat. Book Critics Cir. award nominee 1988), Hawai' One Summer, 1987 (Western Books Exhbn. Book award, Book Builders West Book award), Tripmaster Monkey-His Fake Book, 1989 (PEN USA West award in Fiction), Through the Black Curtain, 1988; editor: The Literature of California, 2001, (Commonwealth Club Book award 2001); contbr. short stories, articles and poems to mags. and jours., including Iowa Rev., The New Yorker, Am. Heritage, Redbook, Mother Jones, Caliban, Mich. Quarterly, Ms., The Hungry Mind Rev., N.Y. Times, L.A. Times, Zyzzyva; prodr. The Woman Warrior, Berkeley Repertory Co., 1994, The Huntington Theater, Boston, 1994, The Mark Taper Forum, L.A., 1995; host: (TV series) Journey to the West, 1994; subject of documentaries Talking Story, Stories My Country Told Me, Writers and Places; interviews on Dick Cavett, Bill Moyers, Ken Burns' The West, The News Hour with Jim Lehrer. Guggenheim fellow, 1981; recipient Nat. Endowment for the Arts Writers award, 1980, 82, Mademoiselle mag. award, 1977, Anisfield Wolf Book award, 1978, Calif. Arts Commn. award, 1981, Hawaii award for lit., 1982, Calif. Gov.'s award art, 1989, Major Book Collection award Brandeis U. Nat. Women's Com., 1990, award lit. Am. Acad. & Inst. Arts & Letters, 1990, Lila Wallace Reader's Digest Writing award, 1992, Spl. Achievement Oakland Bus. Arts award, 1994; named Living Treasure Hawaii, 1980, Woman of Yr. Asian Pacific Women's Network, 1981, Cyril Magnin award for Outstanding Achievement in the Arts, 1996, Disting. Artists award The Music Ctr. of L.A. County, 1996, Nat. Humanities medal NEH, 1997, Fred Cody Lifetime Achievement award, 1998, John Dos Passos prize for lit., 1998, Ka Palapola Po'okela award 1999, Profiles of Courage honor Swords to Plowshares, 1999, Alumna of Yr. award U. Calif.-Berkeley, 2000. Mem. Am. Acad. Arts and Scis. Office: Univ Calif Dept English 322 Wheeler Hall Berkeley CA 94720-1030

KINNEY, LISA FRANCES, lawyer; b. Laramie, Wyo., Mar. 13, 1951; d. Irvin Wayne and Phyllis (Poe) K.; m. Rodney Philip Lang, Feb. 5, 1971; children: Cambria Helen, Shelby Robert, Eli Wayne. BA, U. Wyo., 1973, JD, 1986; MLS, U. Oreg., 1975. Reference libr. U. Wyo. Sci. Libr., Laramie, 1975-76; outreach dir. Albany County Libr., Laramie, 1975-76, dir., 1977-83; mem. Wyo. State Senate, Laramie, 1984-94, minority leader, 1992-94; with documentation office Am. Heritage Ctr. U. Wyo., 1991-94; assoc. Corthell & King, 1994-96, shareholder, 1996-99; owner Summit Bar Rev., 1987—. Author: (with Rodney Lang) Civil Rights of the Developmentally Disabled, 1986; (with Rodney Lang and Phyllis Kinney) Manual For Families with Emotionally Disturbed and Mentally Ill Relatives, 1988, rev. 1991, 99, Lobby For Your Library, Know What Works, 1992; contbr. articles to profl. jours.; editor, compiler pub. rels. directory of ALA, 1982. Bd. dirs. Big Bros./Big Sisters, Laramie, 1980-83, Children's Mus., 1993-97; bd. dirs. Am. Heritage Ctr., 1993-97, Citizen of the Century, 1997-99, govt. chmn. 1997-99. Recipient Beginning Young Prof. award Mt. Plains Libr. Assn., 1980; named Outstanding Wyo. Libr. Assn., 1977, Outstanding Young Woman State of Wyo., 1980, Arts and Scis. Disting. Alumni award U. Wyo., 1997, Making Democracy Work award Wyo. LWV, 2000. Mem. ABA, Nat. Confs. of State Legislatures (various coms. 1985-90), Laramie Area C. of C. (bd. dirs. 1996—, pres. 1999, Top Hand award 1997), Zonta. Democrat. Avocations: photography, dance, reading, travel, languages. Home: 1415 Baker St Laramie WY 82072 Office: PO Box 1710 Laramie WY 82073-1710 E-mail: lfkl@aol.com

KINNEY, ROBERT BRUCE, mechanical engineering educator; b. Joplin, Mo., July 20, 1937; s. William Marion and Olive Frances (Smith) K.; m. Carol Stewart, Jan. 29, 1961; children— Rodney, David, Linda B.S., U. Calif.-Berkeley, 1959, M.S., 1961; Ph.D., U. Minn., 1965. Sr. research engr. United Aircraft Research Labs., East Hartford, Conn., 1965-68; assoc. prof. mech. engring. U. Ariz., Tucson, 1968-78, prof., 1978-87, assoc. dept. head, 1980-83, prof. emeritus, 1987—. Alexander von Humboldt grantee, 1976-77 Mem. Tau Beta Pi, Phi Kappa Phi. Office: U Ariz Dept Mech Engring Tucson AZ 85721-0001

KINNISON, ROBERT WHEELOCK, retired accountant; b. Des Moines, Sept. 17, 1914; s. Virgil R. and Sopha J. (Jackson) K.; m. Randi Hjelle, Oct. 28, 1971; children: Paul F., Hazel Jo Lewis. BS in Acctg., U. Wyo., 1940. CPA, Wyo., Colo. Ptnr. 24 hour auto service, Laramie, Wyo., 1945-59; pvt. practice acctg. Laramie, 1963-71, Las Vegas, Nev., 1972-74, Westminster, Colo., 1974-76, Ft. Collins, 1976-97; ret. Ft. Collins, 1997. Served with U.S. Army, 1941-45, PTO. Mem. Wyo. Soc. CPAs, Am. Legion (past comdr.), Laramie Soc. CPAs (pres. 1966), VFW, Laramie Optimist Club (pres. 1950), Sertoma Club. Home: PO Box 168 Fort Collins CO 80522-0168

KINNISON, THOMAS, state legislator; b. Buffalo, Aug. 30, 1947; m. Sharon Kinnison. BA in Bus. and Econs. with honors, Rocky Mountain Coll.; postgrad., U. Wyo., 1985-86. Mem. Wyo. Ho. Reps., Cheyenne, Wyo. Senate, Dist. 21, Cheyenne, 1984—; chair appropriations com. Wyo. Senate, Cheyenne. Past mem. Sheridan City Coun. Mem. Elks, Masons, Shriners, Lions. Republican. Office: 307 W Burkitt St Sheridan WY 82801-4109 also: Wyo Senate State Capitol Cheyenne WY 82002-0001 Fax: 307-672-8838. E-mail: kinnison@mailhost.cyberhighway.net

KINNUNE, WILLIAM P. forest products executive; b. 1939; Grad., U. Wash., 1961. With Willamette Industries, Inc., Portland, Oreg., 1961—, various sales and mgmt. positions, 1961-75, v.p., 1975-77, sr. v.p., from 1977, now exec. v.p. Office: Willamette Industries Inc Wells Fargo Ctr Portland OR 97201

KINO, GORDON STANLEY, electrical engineering educator; b. Melbourne, Australia, June 15, 1928; came to U.S., 1951, naturalized, 1967; s. William Hector and Sybil (Cohen) K.; m. Dorothy Beryl Lovelace, Oct. 30, 1955; 1 child, Carol Ann. B.Sc. with 1st class honours in Math, London (Eng.) U., 1948, M.Sc. in Math, 1950; Ph.D. in Elec. Engring, Stanford U., 1955. Jr. scientist Mullard Research Lab., Salford, Surrey, Eng., 1947-51; research asst., then research assoc. Stanford U., 1951-55, research assoc., 1957-61, mem. faculty, 1961—, prof. elec. engring., 1965—, assoc. dean facilities and planning Sch. Engring., 1986-92, assoc. chmn. elec. engring., 1984-88, W.M. Keck Found. chair engring., 1992-97, W.M. Keck Found. chair engring. emeritus, 1997—; dir. Ginzton Lab., 1994-96. Mem. tech. staff Bell Telephone Labs., 1955-57; cons. to industry, 1957— Author: (with Kirstein, Waters) Space Charge Flow, 1968, Acoustic Devices, 1987, (with Corle) Confocal Scanning Optical Microscopy and Related Imaging Systems, 1996; also numerous papers on microwave tubes; electron optics, plasma physics, bulk effects in semiconductors, acoustic surface waves, acoustic imaging, optical microscopy, fiber optics, non-destructive testing, optical storage. Guggenheim fellow, 1967-68; recipient Applied Research Achievement award Am. Soc. Non-destructive Testing, 1986. Fellow IEEE (Centennial medal, Sonics and Ultrasonics Group Achievement award 1984), Am. Phys. Soc., AAAS; mem. Nat. Acad. Engring. Inventor Kino electron gun, 1959; co-inventor real-time scanning optical microscope, 1987, solid immersion lens, 1989, microfabricated miniature microscope, 1995. Home: 867 Cedro Way Stanford CA 94305-1002 E-mail: kino@stanford.edu

KINSELLA, WILLIAM PATRICK, writer, educator; b. Edmonton, Alta., Can., May 25, 1935; s. John Matthew and Olive Mary (Elliott) K.; m. Mildred Irene Clay, Sept. 10, 1965 (div. 1978); children: Shannon, Lyndsey, Erin; m. Ann Ilene Knight, Dec. 30, 1978 (div. 1997); m. Barbara L. Turner, Mar. 2, 1999. BA, U. Victoria, B.C., Can., 1974; MFA, U. Iowa, 1978; DLitt, Laurentian U., Sudbury, Ont., Can., 1990, U. Victoria, , 1991. Prof. U. Calgary, Alta., Can., 1978-83; freelance author Chilliwack, B.C., Can., 1983—. Author: Dance Me Outside, 1977, Scars, 1978, Shoeless Joe Jackson Comes to Iowa, 1980, Born Indian, 1981, Shoeless Joe, 1982, Mocassin Telegraph, 1983, The Thrill of Grass, 1984, The Alligator Report, 1985, The Iowa Baseball Confederacy, 1986, The Fencepost Chronicles, 1986, Five Stories, 1987, Red Wolf, Red Wolf, 1987, The Further Adventures of Slugger McBatt, 1988 (reissued as Go The Distance, 1995), The Miss Hobbema Pageant, 1989, Two Spirits Soar: The Art of Allen Sapp, 1990, Box Socials, 1991; co-author: (poetry with Ann Knight) The Rainbow Warehouse, 1989, Even At This Distance, 1994, The Dixon Cornbelt League, 1993, Brother Frank's Gospel Hour, 1994, The Winter Helen Dropped By, 1995, If Wishes Were Horses, 1996, The Secret of the Northern Lights, 1998, Magic Time, 1998, Japanese Baseball, 2000. Houghton Mifflin Lit. fellow, 1982; recipient Fiction award Can. Authors Assn., 1982, Vancouver Writing award, 1987, Stephen Leacock medal, 1987; decorated Order of Can., 1994; named Author of Yr., Can. Libr. Assn., 1987. Mem. Enoch Emery Soc. Office: 9442 Nowell Chilliwack BC Canada V2P 4X7 Address: PO Box 3067 Sumas WA 98295-3067

KINSLEY, MICHAEL E. magazine editor; b. Detroit, Mar. 9, 1951; s. George and Lillian (Margolis) K. AB, Harvard U., 1972, JD, 1977; postgrad., Magdalen Coll., Oxford U., Eng., 1972-74. Bar: D.C. Mng. editor The Washington Monthly, 1975, The New Republic, Washington, 1976-79, editor, 1979-81, 85-89, sr. editor, 1989-95; editor Harper's Mag., N.Y.C., 1981-83; Am. Survey editor The Economist, London, Eng., 1988-89; contbg. writer Time mag., 1987—. Co-host CNN Crossfire, 1989-95. Editor Slate Mag., 1996—. Office: Slate Magazine One Microsoft Way Redmond WA 98052

KINTSCH, WALTER, psychology educator, director; b. Temesvar, Romania, May 30, 1932; came to U.S., 1955; s. Christof and Irene (Hollerbach) K.; m. Eileen Hoover, June 27, 1959; children: Anja, Julia. PhD, U. Kans., 1960. Prof. U. Colo., Boulder, 1968—. Editor: Psychol. Rev., 1989-94; author books. Office: U Colo Dept Psychology Institute Cognitive Scis Boulder CO 80309-0344

KINTZELE, JOHN ALFRED, lawyer; b. Denver, Aug. 16, 1936; s. Louis Richard and Adele H. Kintzele; children: John A., Marcia A., Elizabeth A.; m. Suzanne Hinsberger; stepchildren: William Karp III, Christopher Karp. BS in Bus., U. Colo., 1958, LLB, 1961. Bar: Colo. bar 1961. Assoc. James B. Radetsky, Denver, 1962-63; pvt. practice law Denver, 1963—. Corp. officer, dir. Kintzele, Inc.; rep. 10th cir. U.S. Ct. of Claims Bar. Chmn. Colo. Lawyer Referral Service, 1978-83, Election commr., Denver, 1975-79, 83-86. Mem. ABA, Colo. Bar Assn., Denver Bar Assn., Am. Judicature Soc. Democrat. Roman Catholic. Home: 10604 E Powers Dr Englewood CO 80111-3957 Office: 1317 Delaware St Denver CO 80204-2704 E-mail: kintzeles@aol.com, jkintlaw@aol.com

KIPKE, MICHELE DIANE, education and social services administrator, former hospital director; b. Glendale, Calif., Mar. 4, 1962; d. Arthur Harold and Anne Stuart (Mills) K. BA, NYU, 1984; PhD, Yeshiva U., 1989. Rsch. asst. Montefiore Med. Ctr., Bronx, N.Y., 1984-86; psychology intern Albert Einstein Coll. Medicine, Bronx, 1986-87; dir. AIDS prevention Montefiore Med. Ctr., Bronx, 1987-89; coord. substance abuse program Childrens Hosp. L.A., Calif., 1990-92, assoc. dir. rsch. and evaluation, 1992-98; dir. bd. children, youth & families Nat. Res. Council, Washington, 1998—. Cons. HHS, SAMSA, HRSA, Washington, 1990—; coun. rep. elect Homeless Caucus, APHA, 1992-93; peer reviewer NIH, Washington, 1993—; cons. WHO/Mentor Found., Geneva, 1994—; spl. advisor Primary Health Care Initiative, Office of Treatment Improvement, Alcohol, Drug Abuse and Mental Health Adminstrn.; presenter in field. Reviewer AIDS Edn. and Prevention: An Interdisciplinary Jour., Jour. Adolescent Health Care; contbr. articles to profl. jours. Grantee Ctrs. for Disease Control (AIDS Evaluation of Street Outreach Project), 1992-95, Universitywide AIDS Rsch. Program (HIV Prevention Intervention Study with Seropositive Youth, 1993-95, Nat. Inst. on Drug Abuse (Investigation of Drug Use and HIV-Risk Sexual Behaviors Among Homeless Youth, 1993—, Substance Abuse and Mental Health Svc. Adminstrn./Ctr. for Substance Abuse Treatment, 1993—, Health Resources and Svcs. Adminstrn./Bur. Health Cre and Delivery and Assistance, 1993—, others. Mem. APA, Soc. Adolescent Medicine (ad hoc com. on health needs of homeless youth). Office: Childrens Hosp LA Mail Stop #2 PO Box 54700 Los Angeles CA 90054-0700

KIPPUR, MERRIE MARGOLIN, lawyer; b. Denver, July 24, 1962; d. Morton Leonard and Bonnie (Seldin) Margolin; m. Bruce R. Kippur, Sept. 7, 1986. BA, Colo. Coll., 1983; JD, U. Colo., 1986. Bar: Colo. 1986, U.S. Dist. Ct. Colo. 1986, U.S. Ct. Appeals (10th cir.) 1987. Assoc. Sterling & Miller, Denver, 1985-88, McKenna & Cuneo, Denver, 1989-94; sr. v.p., gen. counsel, dir. First United Bank, Denver, 1994-96; prin. Merrie Margolin Kippur Assocs., PC, Denver, 1997—. Lectr. in field. Author: Student Improvement in the 1980's, 1984; (with others) Ethical Considerations in Bankruptcy, 1985, Partnership Bankruptcy, 1986, Colorado Methods of Practise, 1988. Pres.-elect Jr. League Denver, 2001—; bd. mgrs. Met. Mayors and Commrs. Youth Award. Mem. ABA, Nat. Network Estate Planning Attys., Colo. Bar Assn., Denver Bar Assn., Gamma Phi Beta, Phi Delta Phi, Pi Gamma Mu. Democrat. Avocations: reading, scuba diving, wine collecting. E-mail: mmkassocs@aol.com

KIRCH, PATRICK VINTON, anthropology educator, archaeologist; b. Honolulu, July 7, 1950; s. Harold William and Barbara Ver (MacGarvin) K.; m. Debra Connelly, Mar. 3, 1979 (div. 1990); m. Therese Babineau, Feb. 6, 1994. BA, U. Pa., 1971; MPhil, Yale U., 1974, PhD, 1975. Assoc. anthropologist Bishop Mus., Honolulu, 1975-76, anthropologist, 1976-82, head archaeology div., 1982-84, asst. chmn. anthropology, 1983-84; dir., assoc. prof. Burke Mus. U. Wash., Seattle, 1984-87, prof., 1987-89, U. Calif., Berkeley, 1989—, prof. anthropology, endowed chair, 1994—; curator Hearst Mus. Anthropology, 1989—, dir., 1999—. Adj. faculty U. Hawaii, Honolulu, 1979-84; mem. lasting legacy com. Wash. State Centennial Commn., 1986-88; pres. Soc. Hawaiian Archaeology, 1980-81. Author: The Anthropology of History in the Kingdom of Hawaii, 1992, Feathered Gods and Fishhooks, 1985, Evolution of the Polynesian Chiefdoms, 1984, The Wet and the Dry, 1994, The Lapita Peoples, 1996, Legacy of the Landscape, 1996, On the Road of the Winds, 2000, Hawaiki, Ancestral Polynesia, 2001; editor: Island Societies, 1986, Historical Ecology in the Pacific Islands, 1997; contbr. articles to profl. pubs. Trustee Berkeley Art Mus. and Pacific Film Archives, 1999—. Recipient J.I. Staley prize in anthropology Sch. Am. Rsch., 1998; grantee NSF, 1974, 76, 77, 82, 87, 88, 89, 93, 96, 98, NEA, 1985, NEH, 1988, Hawaii Com. for Humanities, 1981, rsch. grantee Nat. Geog. Soc., 1986, 89, 96, Wenner-Gren Found. for Anthropol. Rsch., 1998; fellow Ctr. for Advanced Study in Behavioral Scis., 1997-98. Fellow AAAS, NAS (John J. Carty medal for the advancement of sci. 1997), Am. Acad. Arts and Scis., Am. Anthrop.

Assn., Am. Philos. Soc., Calif. Acad. Scis. (trustee 1999—); mem. Assn. Field Archaeology, Polynesian Soc., Sigma Xi. Democrat. Avocations: cross-country skiing, gardening. Office: U Calif Dept Anthropology 232 Kroeber Hall Berkeley CA 94720-3710

KIRCHER, MATT, retail executive; Mng. ptnr. Terranomics Retail Svcs., Inc., San Francisco, 1999—. Office: Terranomics Retail Svcs Inc 126 Post St 5th Fl San Francisco CA 94108

KIRCHHEIMER, ARTHUR E(DWARD), lawyer, business executive; b. N.Y.C., June 26, 1931; s. Arthur and Lena K.; m. Esther A. Jordan, Sept. 11, 1965. B.A., Syracuse U., 1952, LL.B., 19S4. Bar: N.Y. 1954, Calif. 1973. Ptnr. Block, Kirchheimer, Lemax & Failmezger, Syracuse, N.Y., 1954-70; corp. counsel Norwich Pharmacal Co., 1970-72; sr. v.p., gen. counsel Wickes Cos., Inc., San Diego, 1972-84; prin. Arthur E. Kirchheimer, Inc., P.C., San Diego, 1984-90; writer, cons. in bus. matters La Jolla, Calif., 1990—. Sec., dir. Corp. Fin. Council San Diego, 1975 Pres. Mental Health Assn. Onondaga County, 1970; chmn. Manlius (N.Y.) Planning Commn., 1969-72; mem. Alternatives to Litigation Spl. Panel, 1984—; mem. San Diego County Grand Jury, 1991-92. Mem. ABA, Calif. Bar Assn. Home and Office: 2876 Palomino Cir La Jolla CA 92037-7066

KIRK, CASSIUS LAMB, JR. retired lawyer, investor; b. Bozeman, Mont., June 8, 1929; s. Cassius Lamb and Gertrude Violet (McCarthy) K. AB, Stanford U., 1951; JD, U. Calif., Berkeley, 1954. Bar: Calif. 1955. Assoc. Cooley, Godward, Castro, Huddleson & Tatum, San Francisco, 1956-60; staff counsel for bus. affairs Stanford U., 1960-78; chief bus. officer, staff counsel Menlo Sch. and Coll., Atherton, Calif., 1978-81; chmn. Eberli-Kirk Properties, Inc. (dba Just Closets), Menlo Park, 1981-94. Faculty Coll. Bus. Adminstrn. U. Calif., Santa Barbara, summers 1967-73; past adv. bd. Allied Arts Guild, Menlo Park; past nat. vice-chmn. Stanford U. Annual Fund. Past v.p. Palo Alto C. of C., pres. Menlo Towers Assn., 2000-. With U.S. Army, 1954-56. Mem. VFW, Stanford Faculty Club, Order of Coif, Menlo Towers Assn. (pres. 2000-01), Phi Alpha Delta. Republican. Home and Office: 1330 University Dr Apt 52 Menlo Park CA 94025-4241

KIRK, DONALD EVAN, electrical engineering educator, dean; b. Balt., Apr. 4, 1937; m. Judith Ann Sand, Sept. 4, 1962; children: Kara Diane, Valerie Susan, Dana Elizabeth. BSEE, Worcester Poly. Inst., 1959; MSEE, Naval Postgrad. Sch., Monterey, Calif., 1961; PhD in Elec. Engring., U. Ill., 1965. From asst. to full prof. Naval Postgrad. Sch., Monterey, Calif., 1965-87; assoc. dean engring. San Jose (Calif.) State U., 1987-90, prof. elec. engring., 1990-93, dean engring., 1994—. Vis. scientist MIT Lincoln Lab., Lexington, Mass., 1981-82; program officer NSF, Arlington, Va., 1993-94. Author: Optimal Control Theory: An Introduction, 1970; co-author: First Principles of Discrete Systems and Digital Signal Processing, 1988, Contemporary Linear Systems, 1994. Bd. dirs. Carmel (Calif.) Sanitary Dist., 1973-77. Fellow IEEE, ASEE; mem. Sigma Xi, Tau Beta Pi, Eta Kappa Nu. Office: San Jose State Univ Coll Engring San Jose CA 95192-0001

KIRK, GERALD ARTHUR, nuclear radiologist; b. L.A., Jan. 20, 1940; s. Arthur H. and Aural (Roderick) K.; m. Cherie J. Hutson, Dec. 27, 1965; children: Shannon Richard, Joel Daryn. BA in Physics, La Sierra Coll., 1962; MD, Loma Linda U., 1967. Intern Deaconess Hosp., Spokane, Wash., 1967-68; staff physician Empress Zandith Meml. Hosp., Addis Ababa, Ethiopia, 1968-69; pvt. practice Simi Valley, Calif., 1969-70; resident in radiology Loma Linda (Calif.) Med. Ctr., 1972-75, dir. sect. nuclear radiology, 1975—. Maj. USPHS, 1970-72. Home: 1341 Pine Knolls Cres Redlands CA 92373-6545 Office: Loma Linda U Dept Nuc Radiology 11234 Anderson St Dept Nuclear Loma Linda CA 92354-2870

KIRK, HENRY PORT, academic administrator; b. Clearfield, Pa., Dec. 20, 1935; s. Henry P. and Ann (H.) K.; m. Mattie F., Feb. 11, 1956 (dec. July 1996); children: Mary Ann, Rebecca; m. Jenny Sheldon, Dec. 13, 1997. BA, Geneva Coll., 1958; MA, U. Denver, 1963; EdD, U. Southern Calif., 1973. Counselor, ednl. Columbia Coll., Columbia, Mo., 1963-65; dean Huron (S.D.) Coll., 1965-66; assoc. dean Calif. State U., L.A., 1966-70; dean El Camino Coll., Torrance, Calif., 1970-81; v.p. Pasadena (Calif.) City Coll., 1981-86; pres. Centralia (Wash.) Coll., 1986—. Contbr. articles to profl. jours. Mem. hist. commn., City Chehalis, 1990, pres. econ. devel. coun., 1992; campaign chmn., United Way, Centralia, 1989-90. Recipient PTK Bennett Disting. Pres. award, 1990, Exemplary Contbn. to Resource Devel. award Nat. Coun. Resource Devel., 1993, Earl Norman Leadership award, 2000. Mem. Wash. Assn. Community Colls. (pres. 1998-99), C. of C. (pres. 1998) Torrance Rotary Club (pres. 1977-78), Centralia Rotary Club (pres. 1990-91), Phi Theta Kappa, Phi Delta Kappa. Presbyterian. Avocation: antique restoration. Office: Centralia Coll 600 W Locust St Centralia WA 98531-4035 E-mail: hkirk@centralia.ctc.edu

KIRKHAM, JOHN SPENCER, lawyer, director; b. Salt Lake City, Aug. 29, 1944; s. Elbert C. and Emma Kirkham; m. Janet L. Eatough, Sept. 16, 1966; children: Darcy, Jeff, Kristie. BA with honors, U. Utah, 1968, JD, 1971. Bar: Utah 1971, U.S. Dist. Ct. Utah 1971, U.S. Ct. Appeals (10th cir.) 1990, U.S. Supreme Ct. 1991. Assoc. Senior & Senior, Salt Lake City, 1971-73; ptnr. VanCott, Bagley, Cornwall & McCarthy, Salt Lake City, 1973-92, Stoel Rives LLP, Salt Lake City. Mem. exec. bd. Great Salt Lake coun. Boy Scouts Am., 1987—; mem. Utah Statewide Resource Adv. Coun., 1995-97. Mem. Utah Bar Assn., Utah Mining Assn. (bd. dirs. Salt Lake City chpt. 1987—), Rocky Mountain Mineral Law Found. (trustee 1989-92). Republican. Mormon. Office: Stoel Rives LLP 201 S Main St Ste 1100 Salt Lake City UT 84111-4904 E-mail: jskirkham@stoel.com

KIRKORIAN, DONALD GEORGE, retired college official, management consultant; b. San Mateo, Calif., Nov. 30, 1938; s. George and Alice (Sergius) K. BA, San Jose State U., 1961, MA, 1966, postgrad., 1968, Stanford U., 1961, U. So. Calif., 1966; PhD, Northwestern U., 1972. Producer Sta. KNTV, San Jose, Calif., 1961; tchr. L.A. City Schs., 1963; instrnl. TV coord. Fremont Union High Sch. Dist., Sunnyvale, Calif., 1963-73; assoc. dean instrn. learning resources Solano C.C., Suisun City, 1973-85, dean instrnl. services, 1985-89, dean learning resources and staff devel., 1989-99; exec. dir. Learning Resources Assn. of Calif. Cmty. Colls., 1976—. Owner, CEO The Cruise Doctor travel agy., 1999—; owner, pres. Kirkorian and Assocs., Suisun City; field cons. Nat. Assn. Edn. Broadcasters, 1966-68; adj. faculty San Jose State U., 1968-69, U. Calif., Santa Cruz, 1970-73, U. Calif., Davis, 1973-76; chmn. Bay Area TV Consortium, 1976-77, 86-87; mem. adv. panel Speech Comm. Assn./Am. Theater Assn. tchr. preparation in speech., comm., theater and media, N.Y.C., 1973-77. Author: Staffing Information Handbook, 1990, National Learning Resources Directory, 1991, 93; editor: Media Memo, 1973-80, Intercom: The Newsletter for Calif. Community Coll. Librs., 1974-75, Update, 1980-90, Exploring the Benicia State Recreation Area, 1977, California History Resource Materials, 1977, Time Management, 1980; contbr. articles to profl. jours. Chmn. Solano County Media Adv. Com., 1974-76; bd. dirs. Napa-Solano United Way, 1980-82; mem. adv. bd. Calif. Youth Authority, 1986-93. Mem. Nat. Assn. Ednl. Broadcasters, Assn. for Edn. Comm. and Tech., Broadcast Edn. Assn., Calif. Assn. Ednl. Media and Tech. (treas.), Western Ednl. Soc. for Telecomm. (bd. dirs. 1973-75, pres. 1976-77, State Chancellor's com. on Telecomm. 1982-86), Learning Resources Assn. Calif. Comm. Colls. (sec.-treas., pres.), Assn. Calif. C.C. Adminstrs. (bd. dirs. 1985-91), Cmty. Coll. Instrnl. Network. Home: 1655 Rockville Rd Suisun City CA 94585-1373 Office: PO Box 298 Fairfield CA 94533-0029

KIRKPATRICK, BRUCE CHARLES, plant pathology educator; b. Davis, Calif., Aug. 20, 1949; two children. BS in Biol. Scis., U. Calif., Irvine, 1980; MS in Plant Pathology, U. Calif., Berkeley, 1983, PhD in Plant Pathology, 1986. Asst. prof. plant pathology U. Calif., Davis, 1986-92, assoc. prof., 1992-98, prof., 1999—. Mem. Am. Phytopathol. Soc. (Ruth Allen award 1996), Internat. Orgn. for Mycoplasmology, Am. Soc. Microbiology, Sigma Xi. Office: U Calif Davis Dept Plant Pathology Davis CA 95616

KIRKPATRICK, CHARLES HARVEY, physician, immunology researcher; b. Topeka, Nov. 5, 1931; s. Hazen Leon and Clarice Opal (Privott) K.; m. Janice Faye Fosha, July 11, 1959; children: Heather, Michael, Brian. BA, U. Kans., 1954; MD, U. Kans., Kansas City, 1958. Diplomate Am. Bd. Internal Medicine, Am. Bd. Allergy and Immunology. Asst. prof. U. Kans., Kansas City, 1965-68, assoc. prof., 1967; sr. investigator Nat. Inst. Allergy and Infectious Diseases, NIH, Bethesda, Md., 1968-79; dir. allergy and clin. immunology Nat. Jewish Ctr., Denver, 1979-93; prof. U. Colo., Denver, 1979—; dir. rsch. Innovative Therapeutics, Inc., 1993-96; pres. Cytokine Sci., Inc., Denver, 1996-99. Active NIH study sects., Bethesda. Editor: 4 books; contbr. numerous articles to profl. jours. NIH research grantee, 1981-86. Fellow ACP, Am. Acad. Allergy and Immunology, Molecular Med. Soc.; mem. Am. Soc. Clin. Investigation, Am. Assn. Immunologists. Episcopalian. Avocations: enology, antique corkscrews, antique automobiles. Home: 295 Leyden St Denver CO 80220-5951 Office: U Colo Health Sci Ctr 1899 Gaylord St Denver CO 80206-1210 E-mail: ckirkpat@eri.uchsc.edu

KIRKPATRICK, WILLIS F. retired state agency administrator; b. Caldwell, Idaho; m. Phyllis Galloway; 3 children. Grad., Coll. Idaho, 1957; postgrad., U. Oreg., 1957-59. Dist. mgr. Chrysler Corp., Dodge Divsn., Spokane, Wash.; staff Walston & Co. Investment Brokers, Spokane; examiner State of Alaska Divsn. Banking, Securities and Corps., Juneau, 1969-73, dir., 1973, 81-99; mgr. Juneau offices Alaska Fed. Savings and Loan, 1974-81; retired, 1999. Apptd. acting commr. dept. commerce and econ. devel., State of Alaska, during 3 gov. transitions, 1981—. Past pres. Juneau Children's Receiving Home, Southeast Alaska Coun. Boy Scouts Am. Mem. Juneau Downtown Rotary Club (pres. 1978-79, cmty. svc. chmn. Alaska-Whitehorse dist.). Office: State Alaska Dept Cmty Econ Devel Divsn Banking Securities PO Box 110807 Juneau AK 99811-0807

KIRKWOOD, ROBERT KEITH, applied physicist; b. Santa Monica, Calif., Mar. 10, 1961; s. Robert Lord and Patricia Cathrine (Keith) K.; m. Kimberly DeNeve Saunders, May 2, 1991; children: Rebekah Marie, Rachel Kathryn. BS, UCLA, 1982, MS, 1984; PhD, MIT, 1989. Rsch. asst. dept. elec. engring. UCLA, 1982-84; mem. tech. staff TRW Space and Tech. Group, Redondo Beach, Calif., 1984-85; rsch. asst. MIT, Cambridge, 1985-89, vis. scientist Plasma Fusion Ctr., 1992-94; postdoctoral fellow Calif. Inst. Tech., Pasadena, 1989-91; rsch. assoc. geophysics div. Air Force Phillips Lab., Hanscom AFB, Mass., 1991-92, physicist, 1992-94, Lawrence Livermore (Calif.) Lab., 1994—. Contbr. articles to Nuclear Fusion, Physics of Plasmas, Rev. Sci. Instruments, Physics Letters A, Physical Review Letters. Recipient Rsch. Associateship award NRC, 1991; postdoctoral fellow Dept. Energy, 1989; doctoral fellow TRW Space and Tech. Group, 1985. Mem. Am. Phys. Soc. (Simon Ramo award in plasma physics 1991), Am. Geophys. Union. Achievements include development of wave transmission diagnostics for plasmas and demonstration of the interaction between multiple laser beams in plasmas. Office: Lawrence Livermore Lab L-473 PO Box 808 Livermore CA 94551-0808

KIRMAN, CHARLES GARY, photojournalist; b. Chgo., Feb. 2, 1949; s. Irving A. and Sylvia Lea K.; m. Heidemarie Mocker, Nov. 15, 1976 (div.); children: Christian, Courtney. BS in Profl. Photography, Rochester (N.Y.) Inst. Tech., 1972. Staff photographer Chgo. Sun-Times, 1972-81; pres. European Beauty Culture Coll., Phoenix, 1982-86; owner Phoenician Grill, Phoenix, 1987-88; admissions dir. Al Collins Graphic Design Sch., Tempe, Ariz., 1988-92; staff photographer Ventura County (Calif.) Newspapers, 1992—. With USNR, 1966-68. Recipient Nat. Headliner award for spot news photography, 1977; named Ill. Press Photographer of Year, 1975, Chgo. Press Photographer of Year, 1974 Mem. Ill. Press Photographers Assn., Chgo. Press Photographers Assn., Nat. Headliner Club. Home: 1505 Visalia St Oxnard CA 93035-3462 Office: 5250 Ralston St Ventura CA 93003-7318

KIRSCHNER, RICHARD MICHAEL, naturopathic physician, speaker, writer; b. Cin., Sept. 27, 1949; s. Alan George and Lois (Dickey) K.; 1 child, Aden Netanya; m. Lindea Bowe. BS in Human Biology, Kans. Newman Coll., 1979; D in Naturopathic Medicine, Nat. Coll. Naturopathic Medicine, 198l. Vice pres. D. Kirschner & Son, Inc., Newport, Ky., 1974-77; co-owner, mgr. Sunshine Ranch Arabian Horses, Melbourne, 1975-77; pvt. practice Portland, Oreg., 198l-83, Ashland, 1983—. Seminar leader, trainer Inst. for Meta-Linguistics, Portland, 1981-84; cons. Nat. Elec. Contractors Assn., So. Oreg., 1985-86, United Telephone N.W., 1986; spkr. Ford Motor Co., Blue Cross-Blue Shield, Balfour Corp., NEA, AT&T, Triad Sys., Supercuts, 1986-89, Hewlett-Packard, Pepsi Co., George Bush Co., 1990-91, Goodwill Industries Am., Motorola, 1992, The Homestead T.V.A., Federated Ambulatory Surg. Assn., V.H.A. Satellite Broadcast, 1993, Oreg. Dept. Edn., Anaheim Meml. Hosp., 1994, Inc. 500 Conf., U.S. C. of C., Inst. Indsl. Engrs., 1995, EDS, ASFSA, Safeco Ins., Fairfax County, Va.; spkr., trainer Careertrack Seminars, Boulder, Colo., 1986-93; owner, spkr., trainer R & R Prodns., Ashland, Oreg., 1984—. Co-author: audio tape seminar How to Deal with Difficult People, 1987, video tape seminar, 1988, interactive CD-Rom The Leadership Series: Difficult People, 1997, others; author: (audio tape seminar) How to Find and Keep a Mate, 1988, (videotape seminar) How to Find a Mate, 1990, The Happiness of Pursuit, 1994, (videotape seminar) How to Deal with Difficult People, Vol. II, 1992, (book) Dealing With People You Can't Stand, 1994, Digital Publishing on e World, Discussions of Problem People and Happiness, 1995, (7 vol. video series) Telecare: Exceptional Service on the Phone, 1998, (book) Life By Design, 1999. Spokesman Rogue Valley PBS, 1986, 87. Mem. Am. Assn. Naturopathic Physicians (bd. dirs., chmn. pub. affairs 1989-93, bd. dirs. 1995-2000, Webmaster, 1996-2000), Wilderness Soc., Internat. Platform Assn. Republican. Office: Talknatural.com PO Box 896 Ashland OR 97520-0030

KIRSHBAUM, HOWARD M. retired judge, arbiter; b. Oberlin, Ohio, Sept. 19, 1938; s. Joseph and Gertrude (Morris) K.; m. Priscilla Joy Parmakian, Aug. 15, 1964; children— Audra Lee, Andrew William B.A., Yale U., 1960; A.B., Cambridge U., 1962, M.A., 1966; LL.B., Harvard U., 1965. Ptnr. Zarlengo and Kirshbaum, Denver, 1969-75; judge Denver Dist. Ct., Denver, 1975-80, Colo. Ct. Appeals, Denver, 1980-83; justice Colo. Supreme Ct., Denver, 1983-97; arbiter Jud. Arbiter Group, Inc., Denver, 1997—, sr. judge, 1997—; adj. prof. law U. Denver, 1970—. Dir. Am. Law Inst. Phila., Am. Judicature Soc., Chgo., Colo. Jud. Inst. Denver, 1979-89; pres. Colo. Legal Care Soc., Denver, 1974-75 Bd. dirs. Young Artists Orch., Denver, 1976-85; pres. Community Arts Symphony, Englewood, Colo., 1972-74; dir. Denver Opportunity, Inc., Denver, 1972-74; vice-chmn. Denver Council on Arts and Humanities, 1969 Mem.: ABA (standing com. pub. edn. 1996—2001), Colo. Bar Assn., Denver Bar Assn. (trustee 1981—83), Soc. Profls. in Dispute Resolution. Avocations: music performance; tennis. Office: Jud Arbiter Group Inc 1601 Blake St Ste 400 Denver CO 80202-1328

KIRST, MICHAEL WEILE, education educator, researcher; b. Westreading, Pa., Aug. 1, 1939; s. Russell and Marian (Weile) K.; m. Wdndy Burdsall, Sept. 6, 1975; children: Michael, Anne. AB summa cum laude, Dartmouth Coll., 1961; MPA, Harvard U., 1963, PhD, 1964. Budget examiner U.S. Bur. Budgets, Office of Edn., Washington, 1964-64; assoc. dir. President's comsn. on White House fellows Nat. Adv. Coun. on Edn. Disadvantaged Children, Washington, 1966; dir. program planning and evaluation Bur. Elem. and Secondary Edn., U.S. Office Edn., Washington, 1967; staff dir. U.S. Senate Subcommittee Manpower, Employment and Poverty, Washington, 1968-69; with Ca. State Bd. Edn., Sacramento, 1975-77, pres., 1977-81; prof. edn. Stanford (Calif.) U., 1969—. Prin. investigator Policy Analysis for Calif. Edn., Berkeley, 1984—, Ctr. Policy Rsch. in Edn., Rutgers U., Stanford U., Mich. State U., 1984—, Reform Up Close, 1988-92; chmn. bd. comparative studies in edn. U.S. Nat. Acad. Scis., 1994—. Author: Government Without Passing Laws, 1969, (with Frederick Wirt) The Political Web of American Schools, 1972, revised, 1975, republished as Political and Social Foundations of Education, (with Joel Berke) Federal Aid to Education: Who Governs, Who Benefits, 1972, (with W. Garms) Revising School Finance in Florida, 1973, (with others) State School Finance Alternatives, 1975, (with others) Contemporary Issues in Education: perspectives from Australia and U.S.A., 1983, (with others) Who Controls Our Schools: American Values in Conflict, 1984, (with Frederick Wirt) Schools in Conflict: Political Turbulence in American Education, 1982, 3d edit., 1992, Political Dynamic of American Education, 1997; editor: The Politics of Education at the Local, State, and Federal Levels, 1970, State, School and Politics, 1972; author numerous monographs; contbr. numerous articles to profl. jours., newspapers and mags. Pres. Calif. State Bd. Edn., Sacramento, 1977-80. Mem. NAS (chmn. bd. international comparative studies in edn.), Nat. Acad. Edn., Am. Edn. Rsch. Assn. (v.p.), Internat. Acad. Edn., Phi Beta Kappa. Office: Stanford U Sch Edn MC 3096 Stanford CA 94305

KIRVEN, TIMOTHY J. lawyer; b. Buffalo, May 26, 1949; s. William J. and Ellen F. (Farrell) K.; m. Elizabeth J. Adams, Oct. 31, 1970; 1 child, Kristen B. BA in English, U. Notre Dame, 1971; JD, U. Wyo., 1974. Bar: Wyo. 1974. Ptnr. Kirven & Kirven, PC, Buffalo, 1974—. Author Rocky Mountain Mineral Law, 1982. Mem. Johnson County Libr. Br., Buffalo. Mem. ABA, Wyo. State Bar (pres. 1998-99), Johnson County Bar Assn., KC (grand knight, treas. 1992-96), Western States Bar Conf. (pres. 1998-99), Rotary (pres. Buffalo club 1988-89, youth exch. program chmn. 1993-98). Home: PO Box C Buffalo WY 82834-0060 Office: Kirven & Kirven PC PO Box 640 Buffalo WY 82834-0640

KIRWAN, R. DEWITT, lawyer; b. Albany, Calif., Aug. 30, 1942; s. Patrick William and Lucille Anne (Vartanian) K.; m. Betty-Jane Elias, June 29, 1969 (div. 1982); children: Katherine DeWitt, Andrew Elias; m. Nancy Jane Evers, Oct. 27, 1984; 1 child, Fletcher Evers. BA, U. Calif., Berkeley, 1966; JD, U. San Francisco, 1969. Bar: Calif. 1971, U.S. Dist. Ct. (ctrl. dist.) Calif. 1971, U.S. Ct. Appeals (9th cir.) 1971. Assoc. Schell & Delamer, L.A., 1971-73; ptnr. Lillick & McHose, L.A., 1973-90, Pillsbury Madison & Sutro, L.A., 1990-98, Akin, Gump, Strauss, Hauer & Feld, L.A., 1998—. Chmn., exec. bd. dirs. U. Calif., Berkeley, 1988-97, trustee U. Calif. Berkeley Found., 1995-98; bd. dirs., trustee Pacific Crest Outward Bound Sch., 1993-99; bd. dirs. L.A. Philharm. Assn., 1985-89, pres., 1986-88, mem. bus. and profl. com.; bd. dirs. Pasadena (Calif.) Symphony Assn., 1978-82; adv. bd. Opus Alliance Com., 1999—. Capt. USAR, 1966-71. Mem. ABA, Am. Bd. Trial Advs., Calif. Club. Democrat. Roman Catholic. Avocations: fly fishing, mountaineering, hunting, skiing. Office: Akin Gump Strauss Hauer & Feld Ste 2400 2029 Century Park E Los Angeles CA 90067-3012

KISER, ROBERTA KATHERINE, medical records administrator, education educator; b. Alton, Ill., Aug. 13, 1938; d. Stephen Robert and Virginia Elizabeth (Lasher) Golden; m. James Robert Crisman, sept. 6, 1958 (div. May 1971); 1 child, Robert Glenn; m. James Earl Kiser, Dec. 19, 1971; 1 child, James Jacob. BEd, So. Ill. U., 1960. Cert. tchr., Ill., Calif. Librarian Oaklawn (Ill.) Elem. Sch., 1960 62, Alsip (Ill.) Elem. Sch., 1966-69; tchr. Desert Sands Unified Sch. Dist., Indio, Calif., 1969-79; prin. Mothercare Infant Sch., Rancho Mirage, 1980-89; substitute tchr. Greater Coachella Valley Sch., 1989-91; med. acct. Desert Health Care, Bermuda Dunes, 1990-92; mentor tchr., computing, typing skils Wilde Woode Children's Ctr., Palm Springs, 1990-92; chiropractic asst. Rapp Chiropractic Health Ctr., Palm Desert, 1992-93; sr. med. records clerk Eisenhower Med. Ctr., Rancho Mirage, 1993-2000, transcription coord., 2000—. V.p. Palm Desert (Calif.) Community Ch. Montessori Sch. Bd., 1982-85; mem. choir Cmty. Ch. of Joy. Republican. Home: 39-575 Keenan Dr Rancho Mirage CA 92270 3610 Office: Eisenhower Med Ctr 39000 Bob Hope Dr Rancho Mirage CA 92270-3221 E-mail: Rkgkiser@aol.com

KISPERT, JOHN H. tool manufacturing executive; b. 1964; B of Polit. Sci., Grinnell Coll., MBA, UCLA. Various mgmt. positions IBM, contr. instrument's wafer, reticle and SEMspec insp. divsn. KLA-Tencor, San Jose, Calif., 1995, v.p. corp. fin., 1999, CFO, 2000—. Office: 160 Rio Robles San Jose CA 95134 Office Fax: 408-875-3030

KISSINGER, KAREN G. energy executive; V.p., contr. UniSource Energy Corp., Tucson, 1997—. Office: UniSource Energy Corp 220 W 6th St Tucson AZ 85701-1014

KISSNER, CHARLES D. electrical company executive; Chmn., pres., CEO Digital Microwave, San Jose, Calif. Office: Digital Microwave 170 Rose Orchard Way San Jose CA 95134-1396

KITANIDIS, PETER K. engineering educator; Prof. civil and environ. engring. Stanford (Calif.) U. Recipient Walter L. Huber Civil Engring. Rsch. prize ASCE, 1994. Office: Stanford U Dept Civil Engring Stanford CA 94305 E-mail: peterk@stanford.edu

KITCHEN, JOHN MARTIN, historian, educator; b. Nottingham, Eng., Dec. 21, 1936; s. John Sutherland and Margaret Helen (Pearson) K. BA with honors, U. London, 1963, PhD, 1966. Mem. Cambridge Group Population Studies, Eng., 1965-66; mem. faculty Simon Fraser U., Burnaby, B.C., Can., 1966—. Author: The German Officer Corps 1890-1914, 1968, A Military History of Germany, 1975, Fascism, 1976, The Silent Dictatorship, 1976, The Political Economy of Germany 1815-1914, 1979, The Coming of Austrian Fascism, 1980, Germany in the Age of Total War, 1981, British Policy Towards the Soviet Union During the Second World War, 1986, The Origins of the Cold War in Comparative Perspective, 1988, Europe Between the Wars, 1988, A World in Flames, 1990, Empire and After: A Short History of the British Empire and Commonwealth, 1994, Nazi Germany at War, 1994, The Cambridge Illustrated History of Germany, 1996, Empire and Commonwealth, 1996, Kaspar House, 2001, The German Offensives of 1918, 2001. Fellow Royal Hist. Soc., Royal Soc. Can. Home: 24B-6128 Patterson Ave Burnaby BC Canada V5H 4P3 Office: Simon Fraser U Dept History Burnaby BC Canada V5A 1S6 E-mail: kitchen@sfu.ca

KITE, MARILYN S. state supreme court justice, lawyer; b. Laramie, Wyo., Oct. 2, 1947; BA with honors, U. Wyo., 1970, JD with honors, 1974. Bar: Wyo. 1974. Mem. Holland & Hart, Jackson, Wyo.; justice Wyo. Supreme Ct., 2000—. Contbr. articles to profl. jours. Mem. ABA (nat. resources sect., litigation sect.), Wyo. State Bar. Address: Wyo Supreme Ct Temple of Justice PO Box 40929 Olympia WA 98504-0929

KITTEL, CHARLES, physicist, educator emeritus; b. N.Y.C., July 18, 1916; s. George Paul and Helen Kittel; m. Muriel Agnes Lister, June 23, 1938; children: Ruth, Peter, Timothy. BA, Cambridge (Eng.) U., 1938, MA, 1993; PhD, U. Wis., 1941. Research physicist Bur. Ordnance, head USN team attached to Brit. Admiralty, Helensburgh, Scotland, 1940-42; supr.

Submarine Ops. Research Grp. USN, Washington, 1943-45; research assoc. MIT, Cambridge, 1945-47; research physicist Bell Labs., Murray Hill, N.J., 1947-51; prof. physics U. Calif., Berkeley, 1951-78, prof. emeritus, 1978—. Cons. E.I. Du Pont & Co., RCA, Westinghouse Corp., Hughes Aircraft Co., Chevron Corp., numerous others. Author: Introduction to Solid State Physics, 7th edit., 1996, (with H. Kroemer) Thermal Physics, 2d edit., 1980, Quantum Theory of Solids, rev. edit., 1987. Guggenheim fellow, 1947, 57, 64, Miller fellow, U. Calif., 1959, 60; recipient Disting. Tchrs. award, U. Calif. Berkeley, 1972. Fellow Am. Acad. Arts and Scis., Am. Phys. Soc. (Oliver Buckley Solid State Physics prize 1957, coun. 1958-62); mem. NAS, Am. Assn. Physics Tchrs. (Oersted medal 1978), Am. Inst. Physics (bd. govs. 1954-58). Office: U Calif Dept Physics Berkeley CA 94720-0001 E-mail: kittel@uclink4.berkeley.edu

KITTEL, PETER, research scientist; b. Fairfax, Va., Mar. 23, 1945; s. Charles and Muriel K.; m. Mary Ellen, Aug. 12, 1972; 1 child, Katherine. BS, U. Calif., Berkeley, 1967; MS, U. Calif., La Jolla, 1969; PhD, Oxford U., 1974. Rsch. asst. U. Calif., La Jolla, 1967-69, Oxford (Eng.) U., 1969-74; rsch. assoc., adj. assoc. prof. U. Oreg., Eugene, 1974-78; rsch. assoc. Stanford (Calif.) U., 1978; rsch. assoc. Nat. Rsch. Coun. Ames Rsch. Ctr. NASA, Moffett Field, Calif., 1978-80, rsch. scientist, 1980—. Dir. Internat. Cryogenic Engring. Conf., 1998—, Cryogenic Engring. Conf., 1983-89, 92—, internat. CryoCooler conf., 1996—; co-chmn. Internat. CryoCooler conf., 1996-98. Adv. editor: Cryogenics, 1987—; editor: Advances in Cryogenic Engineering, 1992-98; contbr. articles to profl. jours. Fellow Oxford U., 1972-74, Nat. Rsch. Coun., 1978-80; recipient medal for Exceptional Engring. Achievement NASA, 1990, Space Act award NASA, 1989, 91. Mem. Am. Phys. Soc., AAAS. Home: 3132 Morris Dr Palo Alto CA 94303-4037 Office: NASA 244-10 Ames Research Ctr Moffett Field CA 94035-1000 E-mail: pkittel@mail.arc.nasa.gov

KITTO, FRANKLIN CURTIS, computer systems specialist; b. Salt Lake City, Nov. 18, 1954; s. Curtis Eugene and Margaret (Ipson) K.; m. Collette Madsen, Sept. 16, 1982; children: Melissa Erin, Heather Elise, Stephen Curtis. BA, Brigham Young U., 1978, MA, 1980. Tv sta. operator Sta. KBYU-TV, Provo, Utah, 1973-78; grad. teaching asst. Brigham Young Univ., 1978-80; cable TV system operator Instructional Media U. Utah, Salt Lake City, 1980-82, data processing mgr., 1982-83, media supr., 1983-85, bus. mgr., 1985-87; dir. computer systems tng. MegaWest Systems, Inc., Salt Lake City, 1987-90, dir. new product devel., 1990-91, mgr. tng. and installation, 1991-93, mgr. rsch. and devel., 1993; tng. and installation mgr. Total Solutions, American Fork, Utah, 1993-95, tng., support and installation mgr., 1995; EDI programmer Megawest Systems, Inc., Salt Lake City, 1996; EDI supervisor Companion Technologies (formerly Megawest Systems, Inc.), Midvale, Utah, 1996-99; software developer Nuskin Internat., Provo, 1999—. Recipient Kiwanis Freedom Leadership award, Salt Lake City, 1970, Golden Microphone award Brigham Young U., 1978. Mem. Assn. Ednl. Communications and Tech., Utah Pick Users Group (sec. 1983-87, pres. 1987-89, treas. 1989-90), Am. Soc. Tng. and Devel., Assn. for Computer Tng. and Support, Phi Eta Sigma, Kappa Tau Alpha. Mormon. Home: 10931 S Avila Dr Sandy UT 84094-5965 Office: NuSkin Internat IT Dept 75 W Center St Provo UT 84601-4432 E-mail: fckitto@nuskin.net, fkitto@iname.com

KITTREDGE, WILLIAM ALFRED, humanities educator; b. Portland, Oreg., Aug. 14, 1932; s. Franklin Oscar and Josephine (Miessner) K.; m. Janet O'Connor, Dec. 8, 1952 (div. 1968); children: Karen, Bradley. BS, Oreg. State U., 1953; MFA in Creative Writing, U. Iowa, 1969. Rancher Warner Valley Livestock, Adel, Oreg., 1957-67; prof. U. Mont., Missoula, 1969—, now Regents Prof. emeritus. Author: We Are Not In This Together, 1984, Owning It All, 1987, Hole in the Sky, 1992, Who Owns the West, 1996, The Portable Western Reader, 1997, Taking Care, 1999, Balancing Water, 2000, The Nature of Generosity, 2000. With USAF, 1954-57. Recipient award for lit. Gov. of Mont., 1988, Charles Frankel prize in Humanities, NEH, 1994; named Mont. Humanist of Yr., 1989. Home: 143 S 5th St E Missoula MT 59801-2719

KITZHABER, JOHN ALBERT, governor, physician, former state senator; b. Colfax, Wash., Mar. 5, 1947; s. Albert Raymond and Annabel Reed (Wetzel) K. BA, Dartmouth Coll., 1969; MD, U. Oreg., 1973. Intern Gen. Rose Meml. Hosp., Denver, 1976-77; Emergency physician Mercy Hosp., Roseburg, Oreg., 1974-75; mem. Oreg. Ho. of Reps., 1979-81, Oreg. Senate, 1981-95, pres., 1985, 87, 89, 91; gov. State of Oregon, 1995—. Assoc. prof. Oreg. Health Sci. U., 1986—. Mem. Am. Coll. Emergency Physicians, Douglas County Med. Soc., Physicians for Social Responsibility, Am. Council Young Polit. Leaders, Oreg. Trout. Democrat Office: Office of Gov 254 State Capitol 900 Court St NE Salem OR 97301-4047*

KIVELSON, DANIEL, chemistry educator; b. N.Y.C, July 11, 1929; AB, Harvard U., 1949, MA, 1950, PhD, 1953. Instr. physics MIT, Cambridge, Mass., 1953-55; from asst. prof. to prof. chemistry U. Calif., 1955—; sr. postdoct. fellow NSF, 1965-66. Guggenheim fellow, 1959, Sloan fellow, 1961-65, Fulbright fellow, 1983; recipient award Calif. sect. Am. Chem. Soc., 1967, Irving Langmuir prize, 1999. Fellow Am. Phys. Soc., Japan Soc. Promotion Sci. Office: U Calif Dept Chem & Biochem Los Angeles CA 90095-0001 E-mail: kivelson@chem.ucla.edu

KIVELSON, MARGARET GALLAND, physicist; b. N.Y.C., Oct. 21, 1928; d. Walter Isaac and Madeleine (Wiener) Galland; m. Daniel Kivelson, Aug. 15, 1949; children: Steven Allan, Valerie Ann. AB, Radcliffe Coll., 1950, AM, 1951, PhD, 1957. Cons. Rand Corp., Santa Monica, Calif., 1956-69; asst. to geophysicist UCLA, 1967-83, prof., 1983—, also chmn. dept. earth and space scis., 1984-87; prin. investigator of magnetometer, Galileo Mission, Jet Propulsion Lab., Pasadena, Calif., 1977—. Overseer Harvard Coll., 1977-83; mem. adv. coun. NASA, 1987-93; chair atmospheric adv. com. NSF, 1986-89, Com. Solar and Space Physics, 1977-86, com. planetary exploration, 1986-87, com. solar terrestial phys., 1989-92; mem. adv. com. geoscis. NSF. Editor: The Solar System: Observations and Interpretations, 1986; co-editor: Introduction to Space Physics, 1995; contbr. artilcels to profl. jours. Named Woman of Yr., L.A. Mus. Sci. and Industry, 1979, Woman of Sci., UCLA, 1984; recipient Grad. Soc. medal Radcliffe Coll., 1983, 350th Anniversary Alumni medal Harvard U. Fellow AAAS, NAS, Am. Geophysics Union, Am. Acad. Arts and Scis.; mem. Am. Phys. Soc., Am. Astron. Soc., Internat. Inst. Astronautics. Office: UCLA Dept Earth & Space Scis 6847 Slichter Los Angeles CA 90095-0001

KIZZIAR, JANET WRIGHT, psychologist, writer, lecturer; b. Independence, Kans. d. John L. and Thelma (Rooks) Wright; m. Mark Kizziar. BA, U. Tulsa, 1961, MA, 1964, EdD, 1969. Sch. psychologist Tulsa Pub. Schs.; pvt. practice psychology Tulsa, 1969-78, Bartlesville, Okla., 1978-88. Lectr. univs., corps., health spas, 1989—. Co-host: Psychologists' Corner program, Sta. KOTV, Tulsa.; author: (with Judy W. Hagedorn) Gemini: The Psychology and Phenomena of Twins, 1975, Search for Acceptance: The Adolescent and Self Esteem, 1979. Sponsor Youth Crisis Intervention Telephone Center, 1972-74; bd. dirs. March of Dimes, Child Protection Team, Women and Children in Crisis, United Fund, YMCA Fund, Mental Health of Washington County, Alternative H.S.; edn. dir. appt. Gov.'s Commn. on Violence Against Women, Pub. Awarness Com., 1996, Women's Found. Fresh Start Women's Found., 1995. Named Disting. Alumni U. Tulsa, Outstanding Young Woman of Okla. Mem. APA, NOW, Internat. Twins Assn. (pres. 1976-77) Home: 9427 N 87th Way Scottsdale AZ 85258-1919 Office: PO Box 5997 Scottsdale AZ 85261-5997

KLAFTER, CARY IRA, lawyer; b. Chgo., Sept. 15, 1948; s. Herman Nicholas and Bernice Rose (Maremont) K.; m. Kathleen Ann Kerr, July 21, 1974; children: Anastasia, Benjamin, Eileen. BA, Mich. State U., 1968, MS, 1971; JD, U. Chgo., 1972. Bar: Calif. 1972. Assoc. Morrison & Foerster, San Francisco, 1972-79, ptnr., 1979-96; dir. corp. affairs legal dept. Intel Corp., 1996—. Lectr. law Stanford Law Sch., 1990-99. Capt. USAR, 1971-78. Mem. Am. Soc. Corp. Secs. (bd. dirs.).

KLAKEG, CLAYTON HAROLD, cardiologist; b. Big Woods, Minn., Mar. 31, 1920; s. Knute O. and Agnes (Folvik) K.; student Concordia Coll., Moorhead, Minn., 1938-40; BS, N.D. State U., 1942; BS in Medicine, N.D. U., 1943; M.D., Temple U., 1945; MS in Medicine and Physiology, U. Minn.-Mayo Found., 1954; children: Julie Ann, Robert Clayton, Richard Scott. Intern, Med. Ctr., Jersey City, 1945-46; mem. staff VA Hosp., Fargo, N.D., 1948-51; fellow in medicine and cardiology Mayo Found., Rochester, Minn., 1951-55; internist, cardiologist Sansum Med. Clinic Inc., Santa Barbara, Calif., 1955—; mem. staff Cottage Hosp., St. Francis Hosp. Bd. dirs. Sansum Med. Rsch. Found., pres., 1990. Served to capt. M.C., USAF, 1946-48. Diplomate Am. Bd. Internal Medicine. Fellow ACP, Am. Coll. Cardiology, Am. Coll. Chest Physicians, Am. Heart Assn. (mem. council on clin. cardiology); mem. Calif. Heart Assn. (pres. 1971-72, Meritorious Service award 1968, Disting. Service award 1972, Disting. Achievement award 1975), Santa Barbara County Heart Assn. (pres. 1959-60, Disting. Service award 1958, Disting. Achievement award 1971), Calif. Med. Assn., Los Angeles Acad. Medicine, Santa Barbara County Med. Assn., Mayo Clinic Alumni Assn., Santa Barbara Soc. Internal Medicine (pres. 1963), Sigma Xi, Phi Beta Pi. Republican. Lutheran. Club: Channel City. Contbr. articles to profl. jours. Home: 5956 Trudi Dr Santa Barbara CA 93117-2175 Office: Sansum Med Clinic Inc PO Box 1239 Santa Barbara CA 93102-1239

KLASSEN, PETER JAMES, academic administrator, history educator; b. Crowfoot, Alta., Can., Dec. 18, 1930; came to U.S., 1955; s. John C. and Elizabeth (Martens) K.; m. Nancy Jo Cooprider, Aug. 1, 1959; children: Kenton, Kevin, Bryan. BA, also cert., U. B.C., Can., 1955; MA, U. So. Calif., 1958, PhD, 1962. Cert. secondary tchr. Lectr. U. So. Calif., Los Angeles, 1957-62; prof. history Fresno (Calif.) Pacific Coll., 1962-66, Calif. State U., Fresno, 1966—, dean sch. social scis., 1979-97, dir. internat. programs, 1992—. Author: The Economics of Anabaptism, 1964, Europe in the Reformation, 1979, Reformation: Change and Stability, 1980, A Homeland for Strangers, 1989; contbr. articles to jours. Pres. West Fresno Home Improvement Assn., 1966-70, Fresno Sister Cities Coun., 1987-90; mem. Calif. Coun. for Humanities, 1987-92. Research grantee Deutscher Akademischer Austauschdienst, 1975. Mem. Am. Hist. Assn., Am. Soc. Ch. History, Fresno City and County Hist. Soc. (pres. 1983-85), Soc. Reformation Rsch., German Studies Assn., Sixteenth Century Studies Assn., Assn. Advancement Slavic Studies, Golden Key, Phi Alpha Theta, Phi Kappa Phi, Phi Beta Delta. Home: 1838 S Bundy Dr Fresno CA 93727-6201 Office: Internat Program Calif State U Fresno CA 93740-0001 E-mail: peterk@csufresno.edu

KLAUSE, KLAUS J. aircraft company executive; b. Berlin, Germany, Sept. 29, 1942; came to U.S., 1956; s. Kurt and Susan (Decker) K.; m. Betty C. DeVore, July 31, 1964; children: Gregory, Thomas, William. BS, Allegheny Coll., 1964; MBA, Golden Gate U., 1979; D in Aerospace Warfare, USAF Fighter Weapons Sch., 1982. Enlisted USAF, 1965, advanced through grades to col., cmdr. 21st Fighter Squadron Calif., 1984-86, chief Europe/NATO divsn. Arlington, Va., 1986-88, cmdr. 37th Ops. Group Las Vegas, 1988-91, chief forces Hampton, Va., 1991-94, ret., 1994; F-117 program mgr. Boeing Aerospace Ops., Alamogordo, N.Mex., 1994—. Soccer coach Hi Desert Soccer Club, Apple Valley, Calif., 1982-86, Las Vegas Soccer Club, 1972, 76-79. Mem. Air Force Assn., River Rats Fighter Pilot Assn., Phi Gamma Delta, Order of Daedalion. Republican. Lutheran. Avocations: golf, skiing, camping, fishing. Office: Boeing 744 Delaware Ave Holloman Air Force Base NM 88330-8014

KLAUSNER, JACK DANIEL, lawyer; b. N.Y.C., July 31, 1945; s. Burt and Marjory (Brown) K.; m. Dale Arlene Kreis, July 1, 1968; children: Andrew Russell, Mark Raymond. BS in Bus., Miami U., Oxford, Ohio, 1967; JD, U. Fla., 1969. Bar: N.Y. 1971, Ariz. 1975, U.S. Dist. Ct. Ariz. 1975, U.S. Ct. Appeals (9th cir.) 1975, U.S. Supreme Ct. 1975. Assoc. counsel John P. McGuire & Co., Inc., N.Y.C., 1970-71; assoc. atty. Hahn & Hessen, N.Y.C., 1971-72; gen. counsel Equilease Corp., N.Y.C., 1972-74; assoc. Burch & Cracchiolo, Phoenix, 1974-78, ptnr., 1978-98; judge pro tem Maricopa County Superior Ct., 1990—, Ariz. Ct. Appeals, 1992—; ptnr. Warner Angle Roper & Hallam, Phoenix, 1998—. Bd. dirs. Hunter Contracting Co. Bd. dirs. Santos Soccer Club, Phoenix, 1989-90; bd. dirs., pres. south Bank Soccer Club, Tempe, 1987-88. Home: 9146 N Crimson Canyon Fountain Hills AZ 85268 Office: Warner Angel Roper & Hallam 3550 N Central Ave Ste 1500 Phoenix AZ 85012-2112

KLAWITTER, RONALD F. computer company executive; b. 1952; V.p. fin. Baker Hughes Tubular Svc., 1987-92; v.p. fin., treas. Key Tronic Corp., Spokane, Wash., 1992-95, acting sec., 1994-95, v.p. fin., sec., treas., 1995-97, exec. v.p. adminstrn., CFO, treas., sec., 1997—. Office: Key Tronic Corp N 4424 Sullivan Rd Spokane WA 99216 Fax: 509-927-5248

KLEBANOFF, SEYMOUR JOSEPH, medical educator; b. Toronto, Ont., Can., Feb. 3, 1927; s. Eli Samuel and Ann Klebanoff; m. Evelyn Norma Silver, June 3, 1951; children: Carolyn, Mark. MD, U. Toronto, 1951; PhD in Biochemistry, U. London, 1954. Intern Toronto Gen. Hosp., 1951-52; postdoctoral fellow dept. path. chemistry U. Toronto, 1954-57; postdoctoral fellow Rockefeller U., N.Y.C., 1957-59, asst. prof., 1959-62, N.Y.C., 1959-62; assoc. prof. medicine U. Washington, Seattle, 1962-68, prof., 1968-2000, prof. emeritus, 2000—. Mem. adv. coun. Nat. Inst. Allergy and Infectious Diseases, NIH, 1987-90. Author: The Neutrophil, 1978; contbr. over 200 articles to profl. jours. Recipient Merit award NIH, 1988, Mayo Soley award Western Soc. for Clin. Investigation, 1991, Bristol-Myers Squibb award for Disting. Achievement in Infectious Disease Rsch., 1995. Fellow AAAS; mem. NAS, Am. Soc. Clin. Investigation, Am. Soc. Biol. Chemists, Assn. Am. Physicians, Infectious Diseases Soc. Am. (Bristol award 1993), Endocrine Soc., Soc. for Leukocyte Biology (Marie T. Bonazinga rsch. award 1985), Inst. of Medicine, Am. Acad. Arts and Scis. Home: 509 Mcgilvra Blvd E Seattle WA 98112-5047 Office: U Wash Dept Medicine Div Al & Infectious Disease PO Box 357185 Seattle WA 98195-7185

KLEE, VICTOR LA RUE, mathematician, educator; b. San Francisco, Sept. 18, 1925; s. Victor La Rue and Mildred (Muller) K.; m. Elizabeth Bliss; children: Wendy Pamela, Barbara Christine, Susan Lisette, Heidi Elizabeth; m. Joann Polack, Mar. 17, 1985 BA, Pomona Coll., 1945, DSc (hon.), 1965; PhD, U. Va., 1949; Dr. honoris causa, U. Liège, Belgium, 1984, U. Trier, Germany, 1995. Asst. prof. U. Va., 1949-53; NRC fellow Inst. for Advanced Study, 1951-52; asst. prof. U. Wash., Seattle, 1953-54, assoc. prof., 1954-57, prof. math., 1957-97, adj. prof. computer sci., 1974—, prof. applied math., 1976-84; prof. emeritus, 1998—. Vis. asso. prof. UCLA, 1955-56; vis. prof. U. Colo., 1971, U. Victoria, 1975, U. Western Australia, 1979; cons. IBM Watson Research Center, 1972; cons. to industry; mem. Math. Scis. Research Inst., 1985-86; sr. fellow Inst. for Math. and its Applications, 1987. Co-author: Combinatorial Geometry in the Plane, 1963, Old and New Unsolved Problems in Plane Geometry and Number Theory, 1991; contbr. more than 200 articles to profl. jours. Recipient Rsch. prize U. Va., 1952, Vollum award for disting. accomplishment in sci. and tech. Reed Coll., 1982, David Prescott Burrows Outstanding Disting. Achievement award Pomona Coll., 1988, Max Planck rsch. prize, 1990, NSF postdoctoral fellow, Sloan Found. fellow U. Copenhagen, 1958-60, fellow Ctr. Advanced Study in Behavioral Scis., 1975-76, Guggenheim fellow, Humboldt award U. Erlangen-Nürnberg, 1980-81, Fulbright fellow U. Trier, 1992. Fellow AAAS (chmn. sect. A 1975), Am. Acad. Arts and Scis.; mem. Am. Math. Soc. (assoc. sec. 1955-58, mem. exec. com. 1969-70), Math. Assn. Am. (pres. 1971-73, L.R. Ford award 1972, Disting. Svc. award 1977, C.B. Allendoerfer award 1980, 99), Soc. Indsl. and Applied Math. (mem. coun. 1966-68), Assn. Computing Machinery, Informs, Math. Programming Soc., Internat. Linear Algebra Soc., Phi Beta Kappa, Sigma Xi (nat. lectr. 1969). Home: 13706 39th Ave NE Seattle WA 98125-3810 Office: U Wash Dept Math PO Box 354350 Seattle WA 98195-4350 E-mail: klee@math.washington.edu

KLEEMAN, CHARLES RICHARD, medical educator, nephrologist, researcher; b. L.A., Aug. 19, 1923; m. 1945; 3 children. BS, U. Calif., 1944, MD, 1947. Rotating intern San Francisco City Hosp., 1947-48; asst. resident pathology Mallory Inst.-Boston City Hosp., 1948-49; resident in medicine Newington VA Hosp., 1949-51; from instr. to asst. prof. metabolism Yale U. Sch. Medicine, 1953-56; from assoc. clin. prof. to assoc. prof. UCLA Sch. Medicine, L.A., 1956-64, prof., dir. divsn. medicine Cedars-Sinai Med Ctr., 1964-74, prof. divsn. nephrology, 1975-94, prof. emeritus, 1994—. Nephrologist VA Med. Ctr., West L.A., 1993—; prof. medicine, dept. chief Hadassah Med. Sch.-Hebrew U., Israel, 1972-75; vis. prof. Beilinson Hosp.-Tel Aviv U., 1968, St. Francis Hosp., Honolulu, 1968, U. Queensland, 1966; chief metabolic sect. VA Hosp., L.A. 1956-60, cons., 1962—. Upjohn-Endocrine Soc. scholar U. London, 1960-61. Mem. AMA, Am. Physiol. Soc., Inst. Medicine-NAS, Am. Soc. Clin. Investigation, Endocrine Soc., Am. Assn. Physicians. Office: VAMC West LA Dept Med Divsn Nephr W111L Wilshire and Sawtelee Blvds Los Angeles CA 90073 E-mail: ckleeman@ucla.edu

KLEEMAN, MICHAEL JEFFREY, business strategist and environmentalist; b. Santa Monica, Calif., July 13, 1949; s. Eugene Stanley and Sylvia (Liebman) K.; m. Janet Louise Depree, Jan. 1, 1977 (div. June 1981); m. Veronica K. Napoles, May 5, 1985; 1 child, Samuel Andres. AB in Psychology, Syracuse U., 1970; MA in Psychology, Claremont Grad. Sch., 1975, postgrad., 1975-78. Asst. v.p. Fairleigh Dickinson U., Rutherford, N.J., 1970-71; research dir., back unit Casa Colina Hosp., Pomona, Calif., 1973-75; assoc. researcher U. Calif., San Francisco, 1975-77; project dir. Teknekron Inc., Berkeley, Calif. and Washington, 1977-80; tech. mgr. 3 Mile Island Class Action Berger & Montague, Phila., 1980-81; mgr.-systems Systems Applications Inc., San Rafael, Calif., 1981-82; mgr.-overseas Sprint (Internat.), Burlingame, 1982-83; dir. planning Med. Retirement Communities, Larkspur, 1984-85; dir. telecommunications Arthur D. Little Inc., San Francisco, 1985-89; dir. Comms. Planning, Kentfield, Calif., 1990-94; v.p. Hill Arts & Entertainment, Emeryville, 1990-93; founder, bd. dirs. San Francisco-Moslow Teleport/SFMT, Inc. (now Global Telesys. Group, Inc.), 1987-92; dir. MCGI, San Rafael, Calif., 1992-94; v.p. Boston Consulting Group, San Francisco, 1994-99; co-founder, v.p., chief tech. officer Aerie Networks, Inc., Denver, San Francisco, 1999—. Sr. fellow U. Calif., Berkeley, 1999—. Author: PC LAN Primer, 1987; contbg. editor Adminstrv. Mgmt. Mag., 1985-90; contbr. articles to profl. jours.; patentee in field. Cons. United Way of Bay Area, San Francisco, 1977-79; mem. adv. bd. Found. for Arts of Peace, Berkeley, 1984-89; cons., advisor Inst. for Global Comm., San Francisco, 1986-89, Ark Found., Bolinas, Calif., 1985-86; tech. lead Project Calif., Calif. Coun. on Sci. and Tech., 1992-93; bd. dirs. eTrust, 1997-99; bd. govs. strategy com. ARC, Washington, 1998—; bd. dirs. marine Mammal Ctr., 1999—. Mem. AAAS, IEEE, Assn. Computing Machinery, Am. Psychol. Assn.. West Point Inn Assn (bd. dirs.). Jewish. Avocations: rowing, photography, poetry. Office: 1400 Glenarm Pl Denver CO 80202-5034 E-mail: mkleeman@aerienetworks.com

KLEESE, WILLIAM CARL, genealogy research consultant, financial services representative; b. Williamsport, Pa., Jan. 20, 1940; s. Donald Raymond and Helen Alice (Mulberger) K.; m. Vivian Ann Yeager, June 12, 1958; children: Scott, Jolene, Mark, Troy, Brett, Kecia, Lance. BS in Wildlife Biology, U. Ariz., 1975, MS in Animal Physiology, 1979, PhD in Animal Physiology, 1981. Sales rep. Terminix Co., Tucson, 1971-72; pest control operator, 1973-75; fire fighter Douglas Ranger Dist. Coronado Nat. Forest U.S. Forest Svc., 1975, biol. technician Santa Catalina ranger dist., 1975-76; lab. technician dept. animal scis. U. Ariz., 1977-78, rsch. technician dept. pharmacology and toxicology, 1978, rsch. asst. dept. biochemistry, 1979-81, rsch. specialist muscle biology group, 1981-91; genealogy rsch. cons. Tucson, 1988—; fin. svcs. rep. World Fin. Group, Tucson, 1999—. Author: Introduction to Genealogy, 1988, Introduction to Genealogical Research, 1989, The Genealogical Researcher, Neophyte to Graduate, 1992, Genealogical Research in the British Isles, 1991; contbr. numerous articles to profl. jours. Chaplain Ariz. State Prisons, Tucson, 1988—. Mem. Ariz. Geneaolgy Adv. Bd. (com. chmn. 1990-92), Herpetologists League, Lycoming County Geneal. Soc., Nat. Geneal. Soc., Nat. Wildlife Fedn., Pa. Geneal. Soc., Soc. for the Study of Amphibians and Reptiles, Soc. of Vertebrate Paleontology, Ariz. State Geneal. Soc. (pres. 1990-93). Republican. Mem. LDS Ch. Avocation: photography. Home: 6521 E Fayette St Tucson AZ 85730-2220 Office: 6121 E Broadway Blvd Ste143 Tucson AZ 85711-4020 E-mail: wmkleese@familyhistoryland.com

KLEIN, ARNOLD WILLIAM, dermatologist; b. Mt. Clemens, Mich., Feb. 27, 1945; s. David Klein; m. Malvina Kraemer. BA, U. Pa., 1967, MD, 1971. Intern Cedars-Sinai Med. Ctr., Los Angeles, 1971-72; resident in dermatology Hosp. U. Pa., Phila., 1972-73, U. Calif., Los Angeles, 1973-75; pvt. practice dermatology Beverly Hills, Calif., 1975—. Prof. dermatology/medicine U. Calif. Ctr. for Health Scis; mem. med. staff Cedars-Sinai Med. Ctr.; asst. clin. prof. dermatology Stanford U., 1982-89; asst. clin. prof. to prof. dermatology/medicine, UCLA; mem. Calif. State Adv. Com. on Malpractice, 1983-89; med. adv. bd. Skin Cancer Found., Lupus Found. Am., Botox adv. bd., Allergan; presenter seminars in field. Assoc. editor Jour. Dermatologic Surgery and Oncology; reviewer Jour. Sexually Transmitted Diseases, Jour. Am. Acad. Dermatology; mem. editorial bd. Men's Fitness mag., Shape mag., Archives of Dermatology; contbr. numerous articles to med. jours. Founder R. Tarlow/Dr. Arnold Klein Fund for Breast Cancer Treatment. Mem. AMA, Calif. Med. Assn., Am. Soc. Dermatologic Surgery, Internat. Soc. Dermatologic Surgery, Am. Assn. Cosmetic Surgeons, Assn. Sci. Advisors, Los Angeles Med. Assn., Am. Coll. Chemosurgery, Met. Dermatology Soc., Am. Acad. Dermatology, Dermatology Found., Scleroderma Found., Internat. Psoriasis Rsch. Inst., Lupus Found., Discovery Fund for Eye Rsch. (dir.), Hereditary Disease Found. (dir.), Jennifer Jones Simon Found. (trustee), Am. Venereal Disease Assn., Soc. Cosmetic Chemists, AFTRA, Los Angeles Mus. Contemporary Art (founder), Dance Gallery Los Angeles (founder), Am. Found. AIDS Research (founder, dir.), Children's Mus. L.A. (founder), Friars Club, Phi Beta Kappa, Sigma Tau Sigma, Delphos. Office: 435 N Roxbury Dr Ste 204 Beverly Hills CA 90210-5004 E-mail: awkleinmd1@aol.com

KLEIN, BENJAMIN, economics educator, consultant; b. N.Y.C., Jan. 29, 1943; s. Hyman and Beartha (Kristel) K.; m. Lynne Schneider; children: Franz, Emily, Amanda. ABA in Philosophy, Bklyn. Coll., 1964; MA in Econs., U. Chgo., 1967, PhD in Econs., 1970. Asst. prof. UCLA, 1968-72, assoc. prof., 1973-78, prof. econs., 1978—; faculty research fellow Nat. Bur. Econs., N.Y.C., 1971-72, research assoc., 1976-77; pres. Econ. Analysis Corp., Los Angeles, 1980—. Vis. prof. U. Wash., Seattle, 1978; cons. FTC, Washington, 1976-86, bd. govs. FRS, Washington, 1973-75. Contbr. articles to profl. jours. Ford Found. fellow, 1967-68, Scaiffe Found.

fellow, 1975-76, Law and Econs. fellow U. Chgo. Law Sch., 1979; grantee Sloan Found., 1981-87; recipient ann. prize for disting. scholarship in law and econs. U. Miami Law and Econ. Ctr., 1978-79. ann. award for best articles Western Econ. Assn., 1979. Mem. Am. Econs. Assn. Office: UCLA Dept Econs 405 Hilgard Ave Los Angeles CA 90095-9000

KLEIN, CHRISTOPHER M. federal judge; b. Seattle, 1946; BA, MA, Brown U., 1969; JD, MBA, U. Chgo., 1976. Trial atty. U.S. Dept. Justice, 1978-80; with Cleary, Gottlieb, Steen & Hamilton, 1980-83; dep. gen. counsel Nat. Rd. Passenger Corp., 1983-87; apptd. bankruptcy judge ea. dist. U.S. Dist. Ct. Calif., 1988. Mem. U.S. Bankruptcy Appellate Panel of 9th Cir., 1998. Lt. col. USMCR, 1969-79. Office: 3-200 US Courthouse 501 I St Sacramento CA 95814-7300

KLEIN, HAROLD PAUL, microbiologist; b. N.Y.C., Apr. 1, 1921; Alexander and and Lillyan (Pal) K.; m. Gloria Nancy Dolgov, Nov. 14, 1942; children: Susan Ann, Judith Ellen. B.A., Bklyn. Coll., 1942; Ph.D., U. Calif., Berkeley, 1950. Am. Cancer Soc. fellow Mass. Gen. Hosp., Boston, 1950-51; instr. microbiology U. Wash., Seattle, 1951-54, asst. prof., 1954-55; asst. prof. biology Brandeis U., Waltham, Mass., 1955-56, assoc. prof., 1956-60, prof., 1960-63, chmn. dept. biology, 1956-63; vis. prof. bacteriology U. Calif., Berkeley, 1960-61; div. chief exobiology, dir. life scis. Ames Research Center, NASA, Mountain View, Calif., 1963-84; scientist-in-residence Santa Clara U., Calif., 1984-95; sr. rsch. scientist SETI Inst., Mountain View, Calif., 1984—. Mem. U.S.-USSSR Working Group in Space Biology and Medicine, 1971-84; investigator US/USSR Cosmos 936 flight, 1975, Cosmos 1129 flight, 1979; leader biology team Viking Mars Mission, 1976; mem. space sci. bd. NAS, 1984-89; participating scientist USSR Mars 1996 flight. Mem. editorial bd. Origins of Life, 1970-89. Served with U.S. Army, 1943-46. NSF Sr. Postdoctoral fellow, 1963; grantee NIH, 1955-63; NSF, 1957-63; named to Hall of Fame NASA, 2000. Mem. Internat. Soc. Study Origin of Life, Am. Soc. Biol. Chemists, Internat. Astronautical Fedn., Phi Beta Kappa. Home: 1022 N California Ave Palo Alto CA 94303-3123 Office: SETI Inst Mountain View CA 94043 E-mail: hpklein@seti.org

KLEIN, HENRY, architect; b. Cham, Germany, Sept. 6, 1920; came to U.S., 1939; s. Fred and Hedwig (Weiskopf) K.; m. Phyllis Harvey, Dec. 27, 1952; children: Vincent, Paul, David. Student, Inst. Rauch, Lausanne, Switzerland, 1936-38; BArch, Cornell U., 1943. Registered architect, Oreg., Wash. Designer Office of Pietro Belluschi, Architect, Portland, Oreg., 1948-51; architect Henry Klein Partnership, Architects, Mt. Vernon, Wash., 1952—. Bd. dirs. Wash. Pks. Found., Seattle, 1977-92, Mus. N.W. Art, 1988-95. With U.S. Army, 1943-46. Recipient Louis Sullivan award Internat. Union Bricklayers and Allied Craftsmen, 1981; Presdl. Design award Nat. Endowment Arts, 1988; George A. and Eliza Howard Found. fellow. Fellow AIA (Seattle chpt. medal 1995). Jewish. Home: 21625 Little Mountain Rd Mount Vernon WA 98274-8003 Office: Henry Klein Partnership 314 Pine St Mount Vernon WA 98273-3852

KLEIN, HERBERT GEORGE, newspaper editor; b. L.A., Apr. 1, 1918; s. George and Amy (Cordes) K.; m. Marjorie Galbraith, Nov. 1, 1941; children: Joanne L. (Mrs. Robert Mayne), Patricia A. (Mrs. John Root). AB, U. So. Calif., 1940; Hon. Doctorate, U. San Diego, 1989. Reporter Alhambra (Calif.) Post-Advocate, 1940-42, news editor, 1946-50; spl. corr. Copley Newspapers, 1946-50, Washington corr., 1950; with San Diego Union, 1950-68, editl. writer, 1950-52, editl. page editor, 1952-56, assoc. editor, 1956-57, exec. editor, 1957-58, editor, 1959-68; mgr. communications Nixon for Pres. Campaign, 1968-69, dir. comm. Exec. Br., U.S. Govt., 1969-73; v.p. corp. rels. Metromedia, Inc., 1973-77; media cons., 1977-80; editor-in-chief, v.p. Copley Newspapers, Inc., San Diego, 1980—. Publicity dir. Eisenhower-Nixon campaign in Calif., 1952; asst. press. sec. V.P. Nixon campaign, 1956; press sec. Nixon campaign, 1958; spl. asst., press sec. to Nixon, 1959-61; press sec. Nixon Gov. campaign, 1962; dir. comm. Nixon presdl. campaign, 1968; mem. Advt. Coun., N.Y. Author: Making It Perfectly Clear, 1980. Trustee U. So. Calif.; past chmn. Holiday Bowl; bd. dirs. Greater San Diego Internat. Sports Coun.; mem. com. Super Bowls XXII, XXIII, and XXXVII; chair internat. com. Scripps Health and Sci. Found.; active Olympic Tng. Site Com.; trustee U. So. Calif.; trustee U. Calif. San Diego Found; bd. dirs. San Diego Econ. Devel. Com. With USNR, 1942-46; comdr. Res. Recipient Fourth Estate award U. So. Calif., 1947, Alumnus of Yr. award U. So. Calif., 1971, Gen. Alumni Merit award, 1977, Spl. Svc. to Journalism award, 1969, Headliner of Yr. award L.A. Press Club, 1971, San Diego State U. First Fourth Estate award, 1986, Golden Man award Boys and Girls Club, 1994, Newspaper Exec. of Yr. award Calif. Press Assn., 1994; named Community Champion, Hall of Champions, 1993, Mr. San Diego, 2001. Mem. Am. Soc. Newspaper Editors (past dir.), Calif. Press Assn., Pub. Rels. Seminar, Gen. Alumni U. So. Calif. (past pres.), Alhambra Jr. C. of C. (past pres.), Greater San Diego C. of C. (mem. exec. com.), Bohemian Club, Fairbanks Country Club, Kiwanis, Rotary (hon.), Sigma Delta Chi (chmn. nat. com., chmn. gen. activities nat. conv. 1958), Scripps Inst. (chair internat com.), Delta Chi. Presbyterian. Home: 5110 Saddlery Sq PO Box 8935 Rancho Santa Fe CA 92067-8935 Office: Copley Press Inc 350 Camino De La Reina San Diego CA 92108-3003

KLEIN, JAMES MIKEL, music educator, associate dean; b. Greenville, S.C., Aug. 27, 1953; s. Rubin Harry Klein and Billie (Mikel) Newton. BM, U. Tex., 1975, MM, 1977; MusD, U. Cincinnati, 1981. Prin. trombone player Austin (Tex.) Symphony Orch., 1973-77; conducting asst. U. Tex., Austin, 1975-77, U. Cin., 1977-78; dir. instrumental music Valparaiso (Ind.) U., 1978-84; prof. music Calif. State U. Stanislaus, Turlock, 1984-99, spkr. of faculty, 1997-98; assoc. dean Coll. Arts, Letters, and Scis., 1999—. Mem. faculty Nat. Luth. Music Camp, Lincoln, Nebr., 1985-86, 95-97; guest conductor, clinician, adjudicator various states, internationally, 1978—; trombone player Modesto (Calif.) Symphony Orch., 1984—; conductor Stanislaus Youth Symphony, Modesto, 1985; music dir. Modesto Symphony Youth Orch., 1986—; site adminstr. Nat. Honors Orch., Anaheim, Calif., 1986, Indpls., 1988, Cin., 1992, asst. condr., Kansas City, 1996, Phoenix, 1998; faculty, coord. instrumental music Calif. State Summer Sch. of Arts, 1987-88. Pres. Turlock Arts Fund for Youth, 1986-88; mem. internat. Friendship Com., subcom., City of Modesto, 1990-92; vol. Big Bros. Am. Recipient Meritorious Prof. award Calif. State U., Stanislaus, 1988, Outstanding Young Man of Am. award, 1990, Orch. Dir. of Yr. award, Calif., 1994, Outstanding Arts Educator award, Stanislaus County, Calif., 2000. Mem. Music Educators Nat. Assn., Nat. Sch. Orch. Assn. (pub. rels. chair 1994-96), Am. Fedn. Musicians (local 1), Condrs. Guild, Am. Symphony Orch. League, Calif. Orch. Dir.'s Assn. (pres.-elect 1988-90, pres. 1990-92, Orch. Dir. of the Year, 1994). Avocations: sailing, racquetball, reading, skiing. Home: 565 N Daubenberger Rd Turlock CA 95380-9144 Office: Calif State U Coll of ALS 801 W Monte Vista Ave Turlock CA 95382-0256 Business E-Mail: jklein@stan.csustan.edu

KLEIN, JEFFREY S. lawyer, media executive; b. Los Angeles, Apr. 15, 1953; s. Norman and Shirlee Klein; m. Karyn Kitson, Sept. 29, 1984; 3 children. BA suma cum laude, Claremont Mens Coll., 1975; M in Journalism, Columbia U., 1978; JD, Stanford U., 1980. Assoc. Kaplan, Livingston, Goodwin, Berkowitz & Selvin, Beverly Hills, Calif., 1980-81, Garey, Mason & Sloane, Santa Monica, 1981-83; weekly contbr. UPI-Radio, L.A., 1983-84; sr. staff counsel Times Mirror, 1983-87, asst. to pres., 1987-90; asst. to pub. L.A. Times, 1989-91; pres. L.A. Times Valley and Ventura County edits., 1991-96; v.p. L.A. Times, 1991-96, sr. v.p. consumer mktg., 1996-97, sr. v.p., gen. mgr. news, 1997-98; pres. COO 101communications LLC, 1999—. Pres., CEO Calif. Cmty. News Corp., 1995-97; adj. prof. journalism U. So. Calif., 1985-87; adv. Gov. Bruce Babbitt, Phoenix, 1980. Author weekly column Legal View, L.A. Times, 1985-93, various book revs., contrb. Online Journalism Review 1999, Columbia Journalism Rev., 2000. Bd. dirs. Found. for Am. Commn., Gould Ctr. for Humanities, Claremont McKenna Coll. Recipient Angel award Vol. League of San Fernando Valley, Disting. Cmty. Svc. award Anti-Defamation League, 1994, Visionary award United Way North Angeles Region, 1995, Premiere Parents award March of Dimes, 1996. Mem. Calif. Bar Assn. Office: 101 Comm 9121 Oakdale Ave Ste 101 Chatsworth CA 91311-6517 E-mail: jklein@101com.com

KLEIN, JIM, company executive; Pres. Oakwood Corp. Housing, L.A., 1996—. Office: Oakwood Corp Housing 2222 Corinth Ave Los Angeles CA 90064-1602

KLEIN, MARC S. newspaper editor and publisher; b. Feb. 16, 1949; married; 2 children. BA in Journalism, Pa. State U., 1970. Bur. chief Courier-Post, Camden, N.J., 1970-75; asst. mng. editor Phila. Bull., 1975-81; editor Jewish Exponent, Phila., 1981-83; editor, pub. Jewish Bull. of No. Calif., San Francisco, 1984—. Publ. Jewish Cmty. Online. Past pres. Temple Israel, Alameda; former bd. dirs. Oakland-Piedmont Jewish Community Ctr. Recipient 1st place awards Phila. Press Assn., 1973, 1st place award N.J. Press Assn., 1973; Wall St. Jour. Newspaper Fund intern, fellow, 1969. Mem. Am. Jewish Press Assn. (pres.), Soc. Profl. Journalists (past bd. dirs.). Office: 225 Bush St Ste 1480 San Francisco CA 94104-4216

KLEIN, OTTO GEORGE, III, lawyer; b. Berkeley, Calif., Dec. 7, 1950; BA, U. Wash., 1973; JD, Yale U., 1976. Bar: Wash. 1976. Atty. Perkins Coie, 1976-81; ptnr. Syndal, Danelo, Klein, Myne & Watts, 1981-88, Heller Ehreman, 1988-97; mem. Summit Law Group, Seattle, 1997—. Office: Summit Law Group 1505 Westlake Ave N Ste 300 Seattle WA 98109-6211

KLEIN, R. KENT, lawyer; b. Richmond, Mo., Feb. 11, 1944; BA with distinction, U. Ariz., 1965, JD, 1968. Bar: Ariz. 1968. Atty. State Compensation Fund Ariz., 1968-74, Lewis & Roca, Phoenix, 1974—. Mem. State Bar Ariz. Office: Lewis & Roca Renaisance 2 40 N Central Ave Phoenix AZ 85004-4424

KLEIN, ROBERT GORDON, former state supreme court justice; b. Honolulu, Nov. 11, 1947; s. Gordon Ernest Klein and Clara (Cutter) Elliot; m. Aleta Elizabeth Webb, July 27, 1986; children: Kurt William, Erik Robert. BA, Stanford U., 1969; JD, U. Oreg., 1972. Dep. atty. gen. State of Hawaii, 1973, with state campaign spening commn., 1974, with state dept regulatory agys., 1975-78; judge State Dist. Ct. Hawaii, 1978-84; judge cir. ct. State of Hawaii, 1984-92, supreme ct. justice, 1992—2000. Office: Supreme Ct 417 S King St Honolulu HI 96813-2902

KLEINBERG, DAVID LEWIS, education administrator; b. San Francisco, Feb. 28, 1943; s. Moe and Lilyan (Abrams) K.; m. Gay Buros, Mar. 21, 1970 (div. 1983); children— Leah, Rebecca; m. Patrice Ellen Greenwood, Apr. 29, 1984; stepchildren: Aaron, Brian, Jesse. B.A., San Francisco State U., 1970. Prodr. Sta. KTVU TV, Oakland, Calif., 1978-79, 89-90; writer, editor San Francisco Chronicle, 1960-80, editor Sunday Datebook, 1980-94; co-dir. Bay Area Classic Learning, San Francisco, 1994—. Served with U.S. Army, 1965-67, Vietnam Decorated Bronze Star Jewish Avocation: basketball, post card collecting, stand-up comic, producer of comedy. Home and Office: 287 Sussex St San Francisco CA 94131-2936

KLEINBERG, JAMES P. lawyer; b. Pitts., Mar. 28, 1943; BA, U. Pitts., 1964; JD, U. Mich., 1967. Bar: Calif. 1968. Trial atty. antitrust divsn. Dept. Justice, 1967-68; ptnr. McCutchen, Doyle, Brown & Enersen, Palo Alto, Calif. Atty. rep. 9th Cir. Jud. Conf. No. Dist. Calif., 1984-84, mem. exec. com., 1984-87; mem. adv. group No. Dist. Calif., 1990—; mem. civil trial advocacy consulting group Bd. Legal Specialization, 1979-90, mem. com. adminstrn. justice, 1984-87; panelist Ann. Fed. Practice Insts., 1992—. Mem. visitors com. U. Mich. Law Sch., 1985—. Fellow Am. Bar Found. Office: McCutchen Doyle Brown & Enersen 3150 Poster Dr Palo Alto CA 94304-1212

KLEINBERG, MARVIN H. lawyer; b. N.Y.C., Aug. 17, 1927; s. Herman and Lillian (Grossman) K.; m. Irene Aertker, July 7, 1962; children— Sarah Elizabeth, Ethan Chaim, Joel Victor. BA in Physics, UCLA, 1949; JD, U. Calif., Berkeley, 1953. Bar: Calif. 1954, also U.S. Patent Office, U.S. Supreme Ct. 1954. Dep. pub. defender, Los Angeles County, 1954; patent atty. RCA, Camden, N.J., 1955-57, Litton Industries, Inc., Beverly Hills, Calif., 1957-61; patent counsel Modal Systems Inc., La Jolla, 1961-63; mem. firm Golove & Kleinberg, Los Angeles, 1963-70, Golove, Kleinberg & Morganstern, Los Angeles, 1970-72, Kleinberg, Morganstern & Scholnick, Los Angeles, 1973-76, Kleinberg, Morganstern, Scholnick & Mann, Beverly Hills, 1976-79; sole practice Marvin H. Kleinberg, Inc., Beverly Hills, 1979-84; ptnr. Arant, Kleinberg & Lerner, 1985-93, Arant, Kleinberg, Lerner & Ram, 1993-95, Arant, Kleinberg, Lerner & Ram, LLP, L.A., 1996-97, Kleinberg & Lerner, LLP, 1998—. Adj. lectr. patent law, mem. Innovation Clinic Adv. Council Franklin Pierce Law Center, Concord, N.H., 1975— ; adv. council PTC Research Found., 1981; dir., sec. Digem, Inc., Los Angeles. Active YMCA Indian Guides, 1974-79; pres. Opportunity Houses Inc., Riverside, Calif., 1973-76, UCLA Class of '49, 1979-84; co-chairperson Sholem Ednl. Inst., Los Angeles, 1974-75; chief referee Region 58, Am. Youth Soccer Orgn., 1976-84; dir. Dental Med. Diagnostic Sys., Inc,. 1996—. Sgt. AUS, 1946-47. Mem. ABA, Los Angeles Intellectual Property Law Assn., Los Angeles County Bar Assn., Am. Intellectual Property Law Assn., Zeta Beta Tau. Home: 3901 Cody Rd Sherman Oaks CA 91403-5022 Office: Kleinberg & Lerner LLP 2049 Century Park E Ste 1080 Los Angeles CA 90067-3112 E-mail: mhk@kl-iplaw.com, mhk@bbs-la.com

KLEINER, ARNOLD JOEL, television station executive; b. N.Y.C., Apr. 7, 1943; s. Leo and Hannah K.; m. Carol Dunn, Aug. 15, 1965; children: Kim, Kerri, Keith. BBA, Pace Coll., 1967. Acct. exec. KDKA Radio, Pitts., 1968-69, WJZ-TV, Balt., 1969-71; sales mgr. TVAR (Group W), N.Y.C., 1974-75; acct. exec. TVAR, Chgo., 1971-72; sales mgr. WBZ-TV, Boston, 1972-74; gen. sales mgr. WJZ-TV, Balt., 1975-78; dir. sales WPVI-TV, Phila., 1978-81; v.p., gen. mgr. WMAR-TV, Balt., 1981-96; pres., gen. mgr. KABC-TV, L.A., 1996—. Chmn. media rels. com. United Way Ctrl. Md., Balt., 1982-84; co-chmn. Md. reg. NCCJ, 1986-90, sr. co-chair, 1990-91; bd. dirs. Levindale, Balt., 1982-84; mem. adv. bd. Md. Fedn. Parents for Drug Free Use, Balt., 1986—, William Donald Schaefer Ctr. for Pub. Policy, Balt., 1986—; chmn. edn. com. Greater Balt. Com., 1986—, bd. dirs., 1989—, pres. chamber divsn., 1991—, Coll. of Notre Dame, Md., 1989—; mem. Mayor's Coord. Com. on Criminal Justice, Balt., 1983-88, Variety Club of Md., 1984, Johns Hopkins Children Ctr.'s Devel. Com., 1984—; bd. dirs. Balt. Reads, Inc., Greater Balt. Com.; chmn. adv. com. Mayor's Office Internat. Programs; bd. dirs. Alvin Ailey Dance Theater Found. of Md., Inc., 1990—. Recipient Victorine Q. Adams Humanitarian award, Am. Men's ORT Cmty. Achievement award, 1986. Mem. Md./D.C. Broadcasters Assn. (dir. 1984), TV Bur. Advt. (sales adv. com. 1975-78), Advt. Assn. of Balt., Advt. Club of Balt., Balt. Jewish Coun. (bd. dirs., mem. exec. com. 1985—), Nat. Assn. Broadcasters. Office: Sta KABC-TV 4151 Prospect Ave Los Angeles CA 90027-4524

KLEINFELD, ANDREW J. federal judge; b. 1945; BA magna cum laude, Wesleyan U., 1966; JD cum laude, Harvard U., 1969. Law clk. Alaska Supreme Ct., 1969-71; U.S. magistrate U.S. Dist. Ct. Alaska, Fairbanks, 1971-74; pvt. practice law Fairbanks, 1971-86; judge U.S. Dist. Ct. Alaska, Anchorage, 1986-91, U.S. Ct. Appeals (9th cir.), San Francisco, 1991—. Contbr. articles to profl. jours. Mem. Alaska Bar Assn. (pres. 1982-83, bd. govs. 1981-84), Tanana Valley Bar Assn. (pres. 1974-75), Phi Beta Kappa. Republican. Office: US Ct Appeals 9th Cir Courthouse Sq 250 Cushman St Ste 3-a Fairbanks AK 99701-4665

KLEINGARTNER, ARCHIE, founding dean, educator; b. Gackle, N.D., Aug. 10, 1936; s. Emanuel and Ottile (Kuhn) K.; m. Dorothy Jean Hanselmann, Sept. 21, 1957; children: Elizabeth, Thomas. BA, U. Minn., 1959; MS, U. Oreg., 1961; PhD, U. Wis., 1965. Asst. and assoc. prof. UCLA, 1964-69, assoc. dean, chmn., 1969-71, prof., 1971-75, 83—, dir. entertainment mgmt. program, 1988—, founding dean Sch. Pub. Policy and Social Rsch., 1994—; v.p. U. Calif. Sys., Berkeley, 1975-83. Cons. in field, 1967—; arbitrator in field, 1971—; chmn. Global Window Ptnrs., Inc., 1998—. Mem. labor mgmt. disputes panel City of L.A., 1978—. With U.S. Army, 1954-56. Mem. London Sch. Econs., Alpha Kappa Psi. Republican. Methodist. Avocations: tennis, biking, gardening. Home: 13014 Brentwood Ter Los Angeles CA 90049-4807 Office: UCLA Sch Pub Policy Social Rsch PO Box 951656 Los Angeles CA 90095-1656 E-mail: archie.kleingartner@anderson.ucla.edu

KLEINROCK, LEONARD, computer scientist; b. N.Y.C., June 13, 1934; s. Bernard and Anne (Schoenfeld) K.; m. Stella Schuler, Dec. 1, 1967; children: Nancy S., Martin C. BEE, CCNY, 1957; MS, MIT, 1959, PhD, 1963; DS (hon.), CCNY, 1997. Asst. elec. engr. Photobell Co. Inc., 1951-57; rsch. engr. Lincoln Labs., MIT, 1957-63; mem. faculty UCLA, 1963—, prof. computer sci., 1970—, chairperson dept., 1991-94, co-chairperson dept., 1994-95; co-founder Linkabit Corp., 1968-69, pres.; CEO, chmn. Tech. Transfer Inst., 1976—; founder, chmn. Nomadix Inc., 1998—. Cons. in field, prin. investigator govt. contracts; Disting. lectr. UCLA, 1994; chair Realizing the Info. Future: The Internet and Beyond, 1994. Author: Queueing Systems, Vol. I, 1975, Vol. II, 1976, Communication Nets: Stochastic Message Flow and Delay, 1964, Solutions Manual for Queueing Systems, Vol. I, 1982, Vol. II, 1986, Queueing Systems: Problems and Solutions, 1996; also articles. Recipient Paper award ICC, 1978, Leonard G. Abraham paper award Communications Soc., 1975, Outstanding Faculty Mem. award UCLA Engring. Grad. Students Assn., 1966, Townsend Harris medal CCNY, 1982, L.M. Ericsson Prize Sweden, 1982, 12th Marconi award, 1986, Monie A. Ferst award Sigma Xi, 1997; Guggenheim fellow, 1971-72. Fellow IEEE (Disting. lectr. 1973, 76), Internat. Engring. Consortium; mem. NAE, Ops. Rsch. Soc. Am. (Lancaster prize 1976), Assn. Computing Machinery (SIG com. award 1990), Internat. Fedn. Info. Processes Sys. (Harry H. Goode award 1996), Amateur Athletic Union. Jewish. Avocations: karate, hiking, jogging, swimming. Home: 318 N Rockingham Ave Los Angeles CA 90049-2636 Office: UCLA Dept Computer Sci 405 Hilgard Ave 3732 Boelter Hall Los Angeles CA 90095-1596

KLEINSMITH, BRUCE JOHN See NUTZLE, FUTZIE

KLEPPE, JOHN ARTHUR, electrical engineering educator, business executive; b. Oakland, Calif., Feb. 21, 1939; s. Arthur William and Musa (Anderson) K.; m. Julianna Marie Galli, Aug. 12, 1961; children: John Frederick, Johanna Beth, Judith Anne. BSEE, U. Nev., 1961, MSEE, 1967; PhD, U. Calif., Davis, 1970. Registered profl. engr., Nev., Calif. Prof. elec. engring. U. Nev., Reno, 1970—, dir. Engring. Research and Devel., 1976-88; pres., research cons. Sci. Engring. Instruments, Inc., Reno, 1968-97; pres. Klepco, Inc., 1976—. Cons.; chief engr. NSF weather expdn. to Antarctica, 1977; del. White House Conf. Small Bus., 1980 Author: (textbook) Engineering Applications of Acoustics, 1989; contbr. articles, papers to publs. and confs. around the world. Served to lt. C.E. USN, 1961-65. Recipient Outstanding Engring. Achievement award for Nev., 1981, 84; Inventor of Yr. award, 1985 Mem. IEEE, Nev. Innovation and Tech. Coun. (pres. 1981-93, pres. 1996-97), Sigma Xi, Tau Beta Pi. Home: 2776 Spinnaker Dr Reno NV 89509 Office: U Nev Dept Elec Engring MS 260 Reno NV 89557-0153 E-mail: kleppe@ee.unr.edu

KLEPPER, ELIZABETH LEE, physiologist; b. Memphis, Mar. 8, 1936; d. George Madden and Margaret Elizabeth (Lee) K. BA, Vanderbilt U., 1958; MA, Duke U., 1963, PhD, 1966. Research scientist Commonwealth Sci. and Indsl. Research Orgn., Griffith, Australia, 1966-68, Battelle Northwest Lab., Richland, Wash., 1972-76; asst. prof. Auburn (Ala.) U., 1968-72; Plant physiologist USDA Agrl. Research Service, Pendleton, Oreg., 1976-85, research leader, 1985-96. Assoc. editor Crop Sci., 1977-80, 88-90, tech. editor, 1990-92, editor, 1992-95; mem. editl. bd. Plant Physiology, 1977-92, Irrigation Sci., 1987-92; mem. editl. adv. bd. Field Crops Rsch., 1983-91; contbr. articles to profl. jours., chpts. to books. Marshall scholar British Govt., 1958-59; NSF fellow, 1964-66. Fellow AAAS, Crop Sci. Soc. Am. (fellows com. 1989-91, pres.-elect 1995-96, pres. 1996-97, past pres. 1997-98), Soil Sci. Soc. Am. (fellows com. 1986-88), Am. Soc. Agronomy (monograph com. 1983-90, bd. dirs. 1995-98); mem. Agronomic Sci. Found. (bd. dirs. 1993-99), Sigma Xi. Home: 1454 SW 45th Pendleton OR 97801 Office: USDA Agrl Rsch Svc PO Box 370 Pendleton OR 97801-0370 E-mail: klepperb@ucinet.com

KLEWENO, GILBERT H. lawyer; b. Endicott, Wash., Mar. 21, 1933; s. Melvin Lawrence and Anna (Lust) K.; m. Virginia Symms, Dec. 28, 1958; children: Stanley, Douglas, Phillip. BA, U. Wash., 1955; LLR, U. Idaho, 1959. Bar: Wash. 1960. Assoc. Read & Church, Vancouver, Wash., 1960-68, Boettcher, LaLonde & Kleweno, Vancouver, 1968-99; sole practitioner Vancouver, 1999—. Part-time U.S. Magistrate Judge, 1979. Chmn. Bd. Adjustors, Vancouver, Civil Svc. Commn., Vancouver. Mem. Wash. State Bar Assn., Elks, Gyro Club. Office: 610 Esther St # 225 Vancouver WA 98660

KLINE, ADAM, state legislator, lawyer; s. Laura Gene Middaugh; 1 child, Genevieve. BS, Johns Hopkins U., 1968; JD, U. Md., 1972. Pvt. practice; mem. Wash. Senate, Dist. 37, Olympia, 1997—; vice chair jud. com. Wash. Senate, Olympia, mem. labor and workforce devel. com.; mem. state and local govt. com. Wash. State Senate, Olympia, mem. ways and means com. Coop. atty. ACLU; former co-chair Wash. Conservation Voters; former chair Nat. Abortion Rights Action League PAC of Wash.; former legis. dir. MADD. Democrat. Office: 431 John Cherberg Bldg Olympia WA 98504-0001 Fax: 360-786-1999. E-mail: kline_ad@leg.wa.gov

KLINE, FRANK MENEFEE, psychiatrist; b. Cumberland, Md., May 14, 1928; s. Frank Huber and Margaret (Menefee) K.; m. Shirley Steinmetz, June 27, 1953; children: Frank F., Margaret L. BS, U. Md., 1950, MD, 1952; PhD, So. Calif. Psychoanalytic Ins., 1977. Diplomate Am. Bd. Psychiatry and Neurology (examiner 1970—). Intern Cin. Gen. Hosp., 1952-53; resident Brentwood VA Med. Ctr., West L.A., 1955-58; Regional chief West Cen. Mental Svc., L.A. County Dept. Mental Health, L.A., 1967-68; assoc. dir. adult psychiatry out-patient dept. L.A. County, U. So. Calif. Med. Ctr., 1968-77, acting dir. adult psychiatric dept., 1977; chief psychiatry VA Med. Ctr., Long Beach, Calif., 1977-91. Assoc. prof. U. So. Calif., clin. prof., prof. emeritus, 1992—; clin. prof., vice-chair U. Calif., Irvine, 1978-91, prof. emeritus, 1995—; clin. prof. Drew King, 1992—, MS; reviewer Hosp. Comty. Psychiatry, 1978—, Am. Jour. Psychiatry, 1978—, Readings, 1995—. Editor: A Handbook of Group Psychotherapy, 1983. 1st lt. M.C., U.S. Army, 1953-55. Office: 24 Sorrel Ln Rllng Hls Est CA 90274-4226 Fax: 310-325-3941

KLINE, HOWARD JAY, cardiologist, educator; b. White Plains, N.Y., Nov. 5, 1932; s. Raymond Kline and Rose Plane; divorced; children: Michael, Ethan; m. Ellen Sawamura, June 13, 1987; 1 child, Christopher. BS, Dickinson Coll., 1954; MD, N.Y. Med. Coll., 1958. Intern San Francisco Gen. Hosp., 1958-59; resident Mt. Sinai Hosp., N.Y.C., 1959-61; sr. resident U. Calif. Med. Ctr., San Francisco, 1961-62; cardiology fellow Mt. Sinai Hosp., N.Y.C., 1962-64; dir. cardiology training program St. Mary's Hosp., San Francisco, 1970-90, Calif. Pacific Med. Ctr., San Francisco, 1992—. Clin. prof. medicine and cardiology U. Calif. Med. Ctr., San Francisco, 1984—; vis. prof. Nihon U., Tokyo, 1986. Editor (jours.) Hosp. Practice, Cardiology, 1992—; contbr. articles to cardiology jours. Lt. col. U.S. Med. Corps, 1967-69. Fellow ACP, Am. Heart Assn., Am. Coll. Cardiology, Am. Coll. Chest Physicians; mem. Burkes Tennis Club. Avocations: painting, reading, running, skiing, tennis. Office: 2100 Webster St Ste 516 San Francisco CA 94115-2382

KLINE, JOHN ANTHONY, justice; b. N.Y.C., Aug. 17, 1938; s. Harry and Bertha (Shapiro) K.; m. Fiona Fleming, Dec. 7, 1968 (div. 1977); m. Susan Sward, Nov. 25, 1982 (div.); children: Nicholas Sward, Timothy Sward. BA, Johns Hopkins U., 1960; MA, Cornell U., 1962; LLB, Yale U., 1965. Bar: Calif. 1966, N.Y. 1967, U.S. Supreme Ct. 1971. Assoc. atty. Davis Polk & Wardwell, N.Y.C., 1966-69; staff atty. legal svcs. program OEO, Berkeley, Calif., 1969-70; mng. atty. Pub. Advocates Inc., San Francisco, 1970-75; legal affairs sec. to gov. Calif. Sacramento, 1975-80; judge Superior Ct., San Francisco, 1980-82; presiding justice 1st appelate dist. div. two Calif. Ct. Appeal, 1982—. Mem. Calif. Commn. on Jud. Appointments, 1995—; mem. Calif. Jud. Coun. Adv. Commn. Juvenile Law, 1997—. Bd. dirs. San Francisco Lawyers Commn. Urban Affairs, 1972-74, San Francisco Pvt. Industry Coun., 1981-89, Am. Jewish Congress of No. Calif., 1981-85, Youth Svc. Am., 1987-90; chmn. bd. dirs. Golden Gate Kindergarten Assn., 1992—, Youth Guidance Ctr. Improvement Com., 1982-90, San Francisco Conservation Corps, 1984—, Environ. Action Ctr., 1980—. Alfred P. Sloan fellow Cornell U., 1960-62; recipient Ambrose Gherini prize and Sutherland Cup Yale U., 1965. Mem. Calif. Judges Assn. Democrat. Jewish. Office: 350 Mcallister St San Francisco CA 94102-4712 E-mail: justice.Kline@jud.ca.gov

KLINE, LEE B. retired architect; b. Renton, Wash., Feb. 2, 1914; s. Abraham McCubbin and Pearl (Davidson) K.; m. Martha Myers, Aug. 29, 1936 (div. Oct. 1995); children— Patricia, Joanne Louise Kline Kresse; m. Marilyn Gibson, May 7, 1997. B.Arch., U. So. Calif., 1937. Draftsman, designer, 1937-43; pvt. archtl. practice Los Angeles, 1943-2001; ret., 2001. Instr. engring. extension U. Calif., 1947-53; mem. panel arbitrators Am. Arbitration Assn., 1964— Pres. LaCanada Irrigation Dist., 1966-96, dir., 1963-96; bd. dirs. Foothill Mcpl. Water Dist., 1980-96, LaCanada br. ARC, 1959-81. Recipient Disting. Service citation Calif. council AIA, 1960, honor awards AIA, 1957, 59, Sch. of Month awards Nation's Schools, 1964, 71 Fellow AIA (pres. Pasadena chpt. 1957, pres. Calif. council 1959) Home: 526 W Huntington Dr Unit F Arcadia CA 91007-3443 Office: Kline Enterprises Inc 969 Colorado Blvd Los Angeles CA 90041-1773

KLINE, RICHARD STEPHEN, public relations executive; b. Brookline, Mass., June 20, 1948; s. Paul and Helen (Chartoff) K.; m. Carroll Potter, (dec. Apr. 1984); m. Sharon Tate, June 16, 1985; stepchildren: Allison, Kevin. BA, U. Mass., 1970. Reporter, photographer Worcester (Mass.) Telegram & Gazette, 1970-71; account exec. Wenger-Michael Advt., L.A., 1971; pub. rels. dir. Oakland (Calif.) Symphony Orch., 1972; asst. v.p., dir. promotions Gt. Western Savs. and Loan, Beverly Hills, Calif., 1972-75; v.p., dir. mktg. Union Fed. Savs. and Loan, L.A., 1975-78; chmn. bd. dirs. Berkhemer & Kline, L.A., 1978-88, Berkhemer Kline Golin/Harris, L.A., 1988-93; COO Golin/Harris Comm., Chgo., 1992-95; pres. Shandwick U.S.A., N.Y.C., N.Y., 1995-96, Kline Consulting Group, L.A., 1997; exec. v.p., sr. ptnr. Fleishman-Hillard, Inc., L.A., 1997—. Former instr. Am. Savs. and Loan Inst.; bd. dirs. Golin/Harris Communications; exec. com. Santa Barbara Old Spanish Days Fiesta Rodeo, 1992. Past pres., mem. exec. com. Big Bros. L.A.; bd. dirs. Am. Cancer Soc., L.A., Solvang (Calif.) TheatreFest; mem. Town Hall Forum, L.A.; commr. Parks and Recreation, City of Oakland, 1973-74; bd. dirs. United Way, 1988-93, TheaterFest, 1990-94.. Recipient Pres.'s Club award Big Bros. Greater L.A., 1987, 88, Best in West Pub. Svc. award Am. Advt. Fedn., San Francisco, 1975, Commitment to Youth award Big Bros. Greater L.A., 2001. Mem. Nat. Investor Rels. Inst., Pub. Rels. Soc. Am. (Disting. Cmty. Svc. award 1987), Internat. Assn. Bus. Communicators, Motor Press Guild, Newcomen Soc., Nat. Cattlemen's Assn., Arthur W. Page Soc., Calif. Cattlemen's Assn., Am. Quarter Horse Assn., Rancheros Visitadores, Vaqueros de Los Ranchos, Publicity Club L.A., Jonathan Club. Avocation: horseback riding, fishing. Office: Fleishman-Hillard Inc 515 S Flower St Ste 700 Los Angeles CA 90071-2209

KLINGER, ALLEN, engineering and applied science educator; b. N.Y.C., Apr. 2, 1937; s. Benjamin and Evelyne Klinger; m. Judith Theresa Flesch, Aug. 31, 1958 (div. Dec. 1980); children: Deborah, Richard; m. Dorothy Joy Fisher, Feb. 14, 1988; stepchildren: Elisa, Laura, Kevin. BEE, The Cooper Union, 1957; MS, Calif. Inst. Tech., 1958; PhD, U. Calif., Berkeley, 1966. Mem. tech. staff Hughes Aircraft Co., Culver City, Calif., 1957; teaching asst. Calif. Inst. Tech., Pasadena, 1957-58; electronics engr. ITT Labs., Nutley, N.J., 1958-59; electronics system engr. System Devel. Corp., Santa Monica, Calif., 1959-62; rsch. asst. U. Calif. Electronics Rsch. Lab., Berkeley, 1962-64; sr. rsch. engr. Jet Propulsion Lab., Pasadena, Calif., 1964-65; researcher Rand Corp., Santa Monica, 1965-67; prof. UCLA, 1967—. Mem. L.A. County Data Processing and Telecom. Adv. Com., 1994-95; cons. in pattern recognition, image analysis, computer systems and math. modeling; expert witness, 1990—. Author: Data Structures, in Ency. Phys. Sci. and Tech., 1987, 92, 2001; editor: Soviet Image Pattern Recognition Research, 1989, Human Machine Interactive Systems, 1991; co-editor: Data Structures, Pattern Recognition and Computer Graphics, 1977 Structured Computer Vision, 1980; contbr. 11 chpts. to books; contbr. articles to profl. jours. Fulbright fellow India, 1990. Fellow IEEE (Disting vis. 1975-76, 88-90), Tau Beta Pi (nat. dist. dir. 2001—). Office: UCLA Computer Sci Dept 3531-h Boelter Hl Los Angeles CA 90095-1596 E-mail: klinger@cs.ucla.edu

KLINGER, MARILYN SYDNEY, lawyer; b. N.Y.C., Aug. 14, 1953; d. Victor and Lillyan Judith (Hollinger) K. BS, U. Santa Clara, 1975; JD, U. Calif., Hastings, 1978. Bar: Calif. 1978. Assoc. Chickering & Gregory, San Francisco, 1978-81, Steefel, Levitt & Weiss, San Francisco, 1981-82, Sedgwick, Detert, Moran & Arnold, San Francisco and L.A., 1982-87, ptnr. San Francisco, 1988-98, L.A., 1998—. Guest lectr. Stanford U. Sch. Engring. Vol. atty. Lawyers Commn. on Urban Affairs, San Francisco, 1978-80. Mem. ABA (tort and ins. practice sect., surety and fidelity com., constrn. forum, pub. contracts sect.), Internat. Assn. Def. Counsel (chmn. fidelity and surety com. 1996-98), Nat. Assn. Bond Claims (spkr.), Surety Claims Inst. (spkr.), No. Calif. Surety Underwriters Assn., No. Calif. Surety Claims Assn. (lectr., pres. 1989-90), Surety Assn. L.A. (spkr.). Avocations: reading, hiking, golf. Home: 939 15th St # 10 Santa Monica CA 90403-3146 Office: Sedgwick Detert Moran & Arnold 801 S Figueroa St Fl 18 Los Angeles CA 90017-2573 E-mail: msk939@aol.com, Marilyn.S.Klinger@sdma.com

KLINMAN, JUDITH POLLOCK, biochemist, educator; b. Phila., Apr. 17, 1941; d. Edward and Sylvia (Fitterman) Pollock; m. Norman R. Klinman, July 3, 1963 (div. 1978); children: Andrew, Douglas. BA, U. Pa., 1962; PhD, 1966; PhD (hon.), U. Uppsala, Sweden, 2000. Postdoct. fellow Weizmann Inst. Sci., Rehovoth, Israel, 1966-67; postdoct. assoc. Inst. Cancer Rsch., Phila., 1968-70; rsch. assoc., 1970-72; asst. mem., 1972-77; assoc. mem., 1977-78; asst. prof. biophysics U. Pa., Phila., 1974-78; assoc. profl. chemistry U. Calif., Berkeley, 1978-82; prof., 1982—; chair dept., 2000—. Mem. ad hoc biochemistry and phys. biochemistry study sects. NIH, 1977-84, phys. biochemistry study sect., 1984-88. Mem. editl. bd. Jour. Biol. Chemistry, 1979-84, Biofactors, 1991-98, European Jour. Biochemistry, 1991-95, Biochemistry, 1993—, Ann. Rev. of Biochemistry, 1996-2000; contbr. articles to profl. jours. Fellow NSF, 1964, NIH, 1964-66, Guggenheim fellow, 1988-89. Mem. Am. Chmn. Soc. (exec. coun. biol. dvisn. 1982-85, chmn. nominating com. 1987-88, program chair 1991-92, Repligen award 1994), NAS, Am. Acad. Arts and Scis., Am. Soc. Biochemistry and Molecular Biology (membership com. 1984-86, pub. affairs com. 1987-94, program com. 1995, pres.-elect 1997, pres. 1998, past pres. 1999), Am. Philosoph. Soc., Sigma Xi. Office: U Calif Dept Chemistry Berkeley CA 94720-0001

KLITTEN, MARTIN R. oil industry executive; b. L.A., Aug. 1944; B in Fin., U. Calif., Berkeley, 1966; MBA, U. So. Calif., 1968. Fin. analyst comptr. devel. program Chevron U.S.A., Inc., 1970-85, comptr., 1985-87; pres. Chevron Info. Tech. Co., 1987-89; v.p. fin., CFO Chevron Corp., 1989—, exec. v.p. handling, refining and mktg. Mem. profl. acctg. program adv. bd. Walter A. Haas Sch. Bus., U. Calif., Berkeley. Former mem. bd. dirs., exec. com. and fin. com. United Way of the Bay Area. 1st lt. U.S. Army, Vietnam. Mem. Am. Petroleum Inst. (mem. fin. com., chmn. exec. com.), Fgn. Affairs Coun., World Affairs Coun., Fin. Execs. Inst., Bay Area CFO Forum, Commonwealth Club. Office: Chevron Corp 575 Market St San Francisco CA 94105-2856

KLOBE, TOM, art gallery director; b. Mpls., Nov. 26, 1940; s. Charles S. and Lorna (Effertz) K.; m. Delmarie Pauline Motta, June 21, 1975. BFA, U. Hawaii, 1964, MFA, 1968; postgrad., UCLA, 1972-73. Vol. peace corps, Alang, Iran, 1964-66; tchr. Calif. State U., Fullerton, 1969-72, Santa Ana (Calif.) Coll., 1972-77, Orange Coast Coll., Costa Mesa, Calif., 1974-77, Golden West Coll., Huntington Beach, 1976-77; art gallery dir. U. Hawaii, Honolulu, 1977—. Acting dir. Downey (Calif.) Mus. Art, 1976; exhibit design cons. Honolulu Acad. Arts, 1998-2001; exhibit designer John Young Mus., U. Hawaii, 1998; cons. Judiciary History Mus., Honolulu, 1982-96, Maui (Hawaii) Arts and Cultural Ctr., 1984-94, curator Keia Wai Ola: This Living Water, 1994; exhibit designer Inst. for Astronomy, Honolulu, 1983-86; exhibit design cons. Japanese Cultural Ctr. Hawaii, 1993—; juror Print Casebooks; project coord. Crossings '97: France/Hawaii, Crossings 2003: Korea/Hawaii. Recipient Best in Exhbn. Design award Print Casebooks, 1984, 86, 88, Vol. Svc. award City of Downey, 1977, Chevalier l'Ordre des Arts et des Letters, France, 2000; Exhbn. grantee NEA, 1979-93, State Found. Culture and the Arts, 1977—. Mem. Hawaii Mus. Assn., Nat. Assn. Mus. Exhbn. Roman Catholic. Office: U Hawaii Art Gallery 2535 The Mall Honolulu HI 96822-2233 E-mail: gallery@hawaii.edu

KLOOSTER, JUDSON, academic administrator, dentistry educator; b. La Combe, Alta., Can., Dec. 24, 1925; s. Henry J. and Evelyn Mae (Eglin) K.; m. Arlene Jean Madsen, Nov. 28, 1948; children: Cherylin Klooster Peach, Lynette Carol Tibbetts, Terrill Ann Klooster McClanahan Hannum. Student, Andrews U., 1942-43, Pacific Union Coll., 1943-44; DDS, U. Pacific, 1947; MMS, Tulane U., 1968. Pvt. practice dentistry, San Francisco, 1947-49, Escondido, Calif., 1949-67; part-time mem. faculty Loma Linda (Calif.) U. Sch. Dentistry, 1956-67, full-time prof. restorative dentistry, 1967—, dir. continuing edn., 1968-72, dean, 1971-94, dean emeritus, 1994—, emeritus prof. dentistry, 1997—. Mem. faculty U. Pacific Sch. Dentistry, 1947-49; cons. USPHS, VA. Treas. Am. Fund for Dental Health, 1987-89, v.p. 1990-91, pres., 1992-93. Lt. Dental Corps USNR, 1953-55. Fellow Am. Coll. Dentists, Internat. Coll. Dentists (councillor); mem. ADA, Calif. Dental Assn. (chmn. coun. dental edn. 1972-75), Tri-County Dental Soc. (ex officio dir. 1971-94, pres.-elect 1978-79, pres. 1979-80), Rotary (pres. San Bernardino S. club 1977-78), Xi Psi Phi. Republican. Mem. Seventh Day Adventist Ch. (elder 1969—). Home: 25131 Crestview Dr Loma Linda CA 92354-3508 Office: Loma Linda U Sch Dentistry Ctr Dental Rsch Loma Linda CA 92350-0001

KLOR DE ALVA, JORGE, academic administrator; JD, U. Calif., Berkeley; PhD in History/Anthropology, U. Calif., Santa Cruz. Prof. anthropology Princeton (N.J.) U., 1989-94; prof. ethnic studies and anthropology U. Calif., Berkeley, 1994-96; v.p. bus. devel. Apollo Group Inc., 1996-98; pres. U. Phoenix, 1988-2000; chmn., CEO Apollo Internat., Inc., 2000—. Bd. dirs. Apollo Group Inc., 1991—, U. Phoenix, 1991—. Co-editor: Interethnic Encounters: Discourse and Practice in the New World, 1993, Interethnic Images: Discourse and Practice in the New World, 1993. Office: Apollo Internat Inc 4635 E Elwood St Phoenix AZ 85040-1958

KLOWDEN, MICHAEL LOUIS, lawyer; b. Chgo., Apr. 7, 1945; s. Roy and Esther (Siegel) K.; m. Patricia A. Doede, June 15, 1968; children: Kevin B., Deborah C. AB, U. Chgo., 1967; JD, Harvard U., 1970. Bar: Calif. 1971. From assoc. to ptnr. Mitchell, Silberberg & Knupp, L.A., 1970-78; mng. ptnr. Morgan, Lewis & Bockius, L.A., 1978-95; vice chmn. Jefferies Group, Inc. and Jefferies Co., Inc., L.A., 1995-96, pres., COO, 1996-2000, vice chmn., 2000—. Bd. dirs. Jefferies Group, Inc., L.A. Trustee U. Chgo., 1986—. Office: Jefferies Group Inc 11100 Santa Monica Blvd Los Angeles CA 90025-3384 E-mail: mklowden@jefco.com

KLUG, JOHN JOSEPH, secondary education educator, director of dramatics; b. Denver, Apr. 27, 1948; s. John Joseph Sr. and Dorthea Virginia (Feely) Carlyle. BA in English, U. N.C., 1974; MA in Theatre, U. Colo., 1984. Tchr. Carmody Jr. High Sch., Lakewood, Colo., 1976-78, Golden (Colo.) High Sch., 1978—, dir. of dramatics, 1978—; producer, dir. Children's Theatre Tours, 1978—. Theatrical cons., 1983—; improvisational workshop leader, 1983—. Playwright, editor: Children's Theatre scripts, 1982—; producer, dir. Denver Theatre Sports, 1993—. Recipient Bravo/TCI Theatre award, 1995. Home: 4565 King St Denver CO 80211-1357 Office: Golden HS 701 24th St Golden CO 80401-2379

KLUGER, RUTH, German language educator, editor; b. Vienna, Austria, Oct. 30, 1931; came to U.S., 1947, naturalized, 1952; d. Viktor and Alma (Gredinger) Kluger Hirschel; m. Werner T. Angress, Mar. 1952 (div. 1962); children: Percy, Dan. BA, Hunter Coll., 1950; MA, U. Calif.-Berkeley, 1952, PhD, 1967. Asst. prof. German lang. and lit. Case Western Res. U., 1966-70; assoc. prof. U. Kans., Lawrence, 1970-73, U. Va., Charlottesville, 1973-75, prof., 1975-76, U. Calif.-Irvine, 1976-80, 86-88, dir. Göttingen Study Ctr., Edn. Abroad Program, 1988-90, prof. emeritus; prof. Princeton U., 1980-86; editor German Quar., 1977-84. Author: The Early German Epigram: A Study in Baroque Poetry, 1971, Weiter leben Eine Jugend, 1992, Katastrophen, Uber Deutsche Literatur, 1994, Frauen lesen anders, 1996; corr. editor Simon Wiesenthal Ctr. Ann., 1987; contbr. articles to profl. jous. Recipient Rauriser Literaturpreis, 1993, Grimmelshausen-Preis, 1993, Niedersachsen Preis, 1993, Marie-Louise-Kaschnitz preis, 1994, Heine-Preis, 1997, Thomas-Mann-Preis, 1999; ACLS fellow, 1978. Mem. MLA (exec. coun. 1978-82), Am. Assn. Tchrs. German (exec. coun. 1976-81), Deutsche Akademie für Sprache und Dichtung, Lessing Soc. (pres. 1977-79), PEN Club. Democrat. Jewish. Home: 62 Whitman Ct Irvine CA 92612-4066 Office: U Calif Dept German Irvine CA 92697-0001 E-mail: rkluger@uci.edu

KLUMP, RON, food products executive; V.p. fin. Leprino Foods Co., Denver. Office: Leprino Foods Co 1830 W 38th Ave Denver CO 80211 Office Fax: (303) 480-2605

KNAPP, CHARLES LINCOLN, law educator; b. Zanesville, Ohio, Oct. 22, 1935; s. James Lincoln and Laura Alma (Richardson) K.; m. Beverley Earle Trott, Aug. 23, 1958 (dec. 1995); children: Jennifer Lynn, Liza Beth. BA, Denison U., 1956; JD, NYU, 1960. Bar: N.Y. 1961. Assoc. Paul, Weiss, Rifkind, Wharton & Garrison, N.Y.C., 1960-64; asst. prof. law NYU Law Sch., N.Y.C., 1964-67, assoc. prof., 1967-70, prof. law, 1970-88, Max E. Greenberg prof. contract law, 1988-98, Max E. Greenberg prof. emeritus contract law, 1998—, assoc. dean, 1977-82. Vis. prof. law U. Ariz. Law Sch., Tucson, 1973, Harvard U. Law Sch., Cambridge, Mass., 1974-75; vis. prof. law Hastings Coll. Law, San Francisco, 1996-97, disting. prof. law, 1998-2000, Joseph W. Cotchett Disting. prof. law, 2000—. Author: Problems in Contract Law, 1976, (with N. Crystal and H. Prince) 4th edit., 1999; editor-in-chief: Commercial Damages, 1986. Mem. Am. Law Inst., Order Coif, Phi Beta Kappa. Office: Hastings Coll Law 200 Mcallister St San Francisco CA 94102-4707 E-mail: knappch@uchasting.edu

KNAPP, CLEON TALBOYS, business executive; b. Los Angeles, Apr. 28, 1937; s. Cleon T. and Sally (Brasfield) K.; m. Elizabeth Ann Wood, Mar. 17, 1979; children: Jeffrey James, Brian Patrick, Aaron Bradley, Laura Ann. Student, UCLA, 1955-58. With John C. Brasfield Pub. Corp. (purchased co. in 1965, changed name to Knapp Comm Corp. 1977, sold to Condé Nast Publs. in 1993); pres. Talwood Corp., Knapp Found., L.A. Bd. visitors John E. Anderson Grad. Sch. of Mgmt., UCLA; chmn. bd. trustees Art Ctr. Coll. Design. Mem. Bel Air Country Club, Regency Club, Country Club of the Rockies, Eagle Springs Golf Club. Office: Talwood Corp 10100 Santa Monica Blvd Los Angeles CA 90067-4003

KNAPP, EDWARD ALAN, retired government agency administrator, scientist; b. Salem, Oreg., Mar. 7, 1932; s. Gardner and Lucille (Moore) K.; m. Jean Elaine Hartwell, June 27, 1954; children: Sandra, David, Robert, Mary. A.B., Pomona Coll., 1954; Ph.D., U. Calif., Berkeley, 1958; D.Sc. (hon.), Pomona Coll., 1984, Bucknell U., 1984. With Los Alamos Sci. Lab., U. Calif., 1958-82, dir. accelerator tech. div., 1977-82; asst. dir., then dir. NSF, Washington, 1982-84; sr. fellow Los Alamos Nat. Lab., 1984; pres. Univs. Rsch. Assn., Washington, 1985-89; sr. fellow Los Alamos Nat. Lab., 1990, dir. Los Alamos meson physics facility, 1990-91; pres. Santa Fe Inst., 1991-96, prof., 1996. Bd. trustee Coll. Santa Fe; bd. dirs. K/P Corp.; cons. in field Contbr. articles to profl. jours. Fellow AAAS, Am. Phys. Soc.; mem. IEEE, Sigma Xi. Methodist. Office: Santa Fe Inst 1399 Hyde Park Rd Santa Fe NM 87501-8943

KNAPP, EVAN, construction executive; Sr. v.p. ops. Western Pacific Housing, El Segundo, Calif., 1994—. Office: Western Pacific Housing 300 Continental Blvd Ste 390 El Segundo CA 90245

KNAUS, TIM, political organization administrator; Chmn. Jefferson County Dem. Com., Colo. State Dem. Party, 1999—. Office: Colo Dem Party 5200 E Colfax Ave Denver CO 80220-1304

KNAUSS, WOLFGANG GUSTAV, engineering educator; Prof. aeronautics and applied sci. Calif. Inst. Tech., Pasadena. Editor: (with I. Emri) Mechanics of Time-Dependent Materials. Fellow ASME, Soc. Exptl. Mechanics (Murray medal 1995, Lazan award 1999), Am. Acad. Mechanics, Inst. for the Advancement of Engring.; mem. AIAA, Nat. Acad. Engring., Russian Acad. Natural Scis. (fgn., Kapitsa medal), Internat. (Russian Acad. Engring. (corr.), The Adhesion Soc., Soc. Rheology, Soc. for the Advancement Sci., Sigma Xi. Office: Calif Inst of Tech Div Engring & Applied Sci Mail Code 105 50 Pasadena CA 91125-0001

KNEBEL, JACK GILLEN, lawyer; b. Washington, Jan. 28, 1939; s. Fletcher and Amalia Eleanor (Rauppius) K.; m. Linda Karin Ropertz, Feb. 22, 1963; children: Hollis Anne (dec.), Lauren Beth. BA, Yale Coll., 1960; LLB, Harvard U., 1966. Bar: Calif. 1966, U.S. Dist. Ct. (no. dist.) Calif. 1966, U.S. Ct. Appeals (9th cir.) 1966. Assoc. McCutchen, Doyle, Brown & Enersen, San Francisco, 1966-74, ptnr., 1974-94, of counsel, 1994-99; owner Artema, 1999—; lectr. in law Stanford Law Sch., 1998-2001, Harvard U. Sch. Law, 2002—. Mem. exec. com. San Francisco Lawyers Com. for Urban Affairs, 1991-93; mem. adv. coun. Hastings Coll. Trial Advocacy, San Francisco, 1981-91, chair, 1990-91; mediator, arbitrator Am. Arbitration Assn., 1989—. Bd. dirs., pres. Orinda (Calif.) Assn., 1972-74, Sea Ranch (Calif.) Assn., 1978-79; co-chmn. Citizens to Preserve Orinda, 1983-85. Lt. (j.g.) USN, 1960-66. Fellow Am. Coll. Trial Lawyers (mem. com. on fed. rules civ. pro 1990-93); mem. ABA, Maritime Law Assn. of U.S. Democrat. Home: PO Box 1133 Gualala CA 95445 Office: McCutchen Doyle Brown & Enersen Three Embarcadero Ctr Ste 1800 San Francisco CA 94111 E-mail: jknebel@mdbe.com, knebeljack@juno.com

KNECHT, JAMES HERBERT, lawyer; b. Los Angeles, Aug. 5, 1925; s. James Herbert and Gertrude Martha (Morris) K.; m. Margaret Paton Vreeland, Jan. 3, 1953 (dec. 1994); children— Susan, Thomas Paton, Carol. BS, UCLA, 1947; LLB, U. So. Calif., 1957. Bar: Calif. bar 1957, U.S. Supreme Ct. bar 1969. Mem. firm Forster, Gemmill & Farmer, Los Angeles, 1957-84; sole practice, 1985—. Chmn. bd. Templeton (Calif.) Nat. Bank, 1992-95. Fellow Am. Bar Found. (life); mem. ABA, San Luis Obispo County Bar Assn., Legion Lex, Caltech Assocs., L.A. Area C. of C. (dir. 1979-83), Beta Theta Pi. Home: 5030 Vineyard Dr Paso Robles CA 93446-9682 Office: PO Box 2280 Paso Robles CA 93447-2280 E-mail: jknecht@ccaccess.org

KNIGHT, GARY J. transportation executive; Pres. Knight Transp., Inc., Phoenix, 1990—. Office: Knight Transp Inc 5601 W Buckeye Rd Phoenix AZ 85043-4698

KNIGHT, KEVIN P. transportation executive; CEO Knight Transp., Inc., Phoenix, 1990—. Office: Knight Transp Inc 5601 W Buckeye Rd Phoenix AZ 85043-4698

KNIGHT, PATRICIA MARIE, optics researcher; b. Schnectady, N.Y., Jan. 25, 1952; d. Donald Orlin and Mary Ann K. BS in Engring. Sci., Ariz. State U., 1974, MSChemE, 1976; PhD in Biomed. Engring., U. Utah, 1983. Teaching and rsch. asst. Ariz. State U., Tempe, 1974-76; product devel. engr. Am. Med. Optics, Irvine, Calif., 1976-79, mgr. materials rsch., 1983-87; rsch. asst. U. Utah, Salt Lake City, 1979-83; dir. materials rsch. Allergan Surg. Products, Irvine, 1987-88, dir. rsch., 1988-91, v.p. rsch., devel. and engring., 1991—. Contbr. articles to profl. jours. Mem. Soc. Biomaterials, Am. Chem. Soc., Soc. Women Engrs., Assn. Rsch. in Vision and Opthalmology, Biomed. Engring. Soc. Avocations: photography, skiing, golf. Office: Allergan Inc PO Box 19534 Irvine CA 92623-9534

KNIGHT, PHILIP H(AMPSON), shoe manufacturing company executive; b. Portland, Oreg., Feb. 24, 1938; s. William W. and Lota (Hatfield) K.; m. Penelope Parks, Sept. 13, 1968; children: Matthew, Travis. B.B.A., U. Oreg.; M.B.A., Stanford U. C.P.A., Oreg. Chmn., CEO, past pres. Nike, Inc., Beaverton, Oreg., 1967—. Bd. dirs. U.S.-Asian Bus. Coun., Washington, 1st lt. AUS, 1959-60. Named Oreg. Businessman of Yr., 1982, One of 1988's Best Mgrs., Bus. Week Magazine. Mem. AICPA. Republican. Episcopalian. Office: Nike Inc One Bowerman Dr Beaverton OR 97005

KNIGHT, ROBERT EDWARD, banker; b. Alliance, Nebr., Nov. 27, 1941; s. Edward McKean and Ruth (McDuffee) K.; m. Eva Sophia Youngstom, Aug. 12, 1966. BA, Yale U., 1963; MA, Harvard U., 1965, PhD, 1968. Asst. prof. U.S. Naval Acad., Annapolis, Md., 1966-68; lectr. U. Md., 1967-68; fin. economist Fed. Res. Bank of Kansas City (Mo.), 1968-70, rsch. officer, economist, 1971-76, asst. v.p., sec., 1977, v.p., sec., 1978-79; pres. Alliance (Nebr.) Nat. Bank, 1979-94, also chmn., 1983-94;

pres. Robert Knight Assocs., banking and econ. cons., Cheyenne, 1979—. Chmn. Eldred Found., 1985—; vis. prof., chair banking and fin. East Tenn. State U., Johnson City, 1988; mem. faculty Stonier Grad. Sch. Banking, 1972—, Colo. Grad. Sch. Banking, 1975-82, Am. Inst. Banking, U. Mo., Kansas City, 1971-79, Prochnow Grad. Sch. Banking, U. Wis., 1980-84; mem. extended learning faculty Park Coll., 1996—; mem. Coun. for Excellence for Bur. Bus. Rsch. U. Nebr., Lincoln, 1991-94, mem. Grad. Sch. Arts and Scis. Coun., Harvard, 1994—; chmn. Taxable Mcpl. Bondholders Protective Com., 1991-94. Contbr. articles to profl. jours. Bd. dirs. People of Faith (Royal Oaks) Found., 2000—, Stonier Grad. Sch. Banking, 1979-82, Nebr. Com. for Humanities, 1986-90; trustee Knox Presbyn. Ch., Overland Park, Kans., 1965-69; bd. regents Nat. Comml. Lending Sch., 1980-83; mem. Downtown Improvement Com., Alliance, 1981-94; trustee U. Nebr. Found., 1982-94; mem. fin. com. United Meth. Ch. Alliance, 1982-85, trustee, 1990-93; mem. Box Butte County Indsl. Devel. Bd., 1987-94. Woodrow Wilson fellow, 1963-64. Mem. Am. Econ. Assn., Am. Fin. Assn., So. Econ. Assn., Nebr. Bankers Assn. (com. state legis. 1980-81, com. comml. loans and investments 1986-87), Am. Inst. Banking (state com. for Nebr. 1980-83), Am. Bankers Assn. (econ. adv. com. 1980-83, cmty. bank leadership coun.), Western Econ. Assn., Econometric Soc., Rotary, Masons. Home and Office: 429 W 5th Ave Cheyenne WY 82001-1249

KNIGHT, WILLIAM J. (PETE KNIGHT), state legislator, retired air force officer; b. Noblesville, Ind., Nov. 18, 1929; s. William T. and Mary Emma (Illyes) K.; m. Helena A Stone, June 7, 1958; children: William Peter, David, Stephen; m. Gail A. Johnson, Sept. 3, 1983. BS, Air Force Inst. Tech., 1958; student, Indsl. Coll. Armed Forces, 1973-74. Commd. 2d lt. USAF, 1953, advanced through grades to col., 1971; fighter pilot Kinross AFB, Mich., 1953-56; exptl. test pilot Edwards AFB, Calif., 1958-69; exptl. test pilot, Viet Nam, 1969-70; dir. test and deployment F-15 program, 1976; dir. Flight Attack System Program Office, 1977-79; vice comdr. Air Force Flight Test Ctr. Edwards AFB, 1979-82; ret. USAF, 1982; mayor City of Palmdale, Calif., 1988-92; mem. Calif. Assembly, Sacramento, 1992-96, Calif. Senate, Sacramento, 1996—. V.p. Eidetics Internat., Torrance, Calif., 1988-92. Decorated D.F.C. with 2 oak leaf clusters, Legion of Merit with 2 oak leaf clusters, Air medal with 11 oak leaf clusters, Astronauts Wings; recipient Octave Chanute award, 1968, Harmon Internat. trophy, 1968, citation of honor Air Force Assn., 1969 winner Allison Jet Trophy Race, 1954; named to Nat. Aviation Hall of Fame, 1988, Lancaster Aerospace Walk of Honor, 1990, Internat. Space Hall of Fame, 1998. Fellow AIAA (assoc.), Soc. Exptl. Test Pilots (past pres.); mem. Air Force Assn., Internat. Order of Characters, Aerospace Primus Club, Daedalians, Elks, Shriners. Holder world's speed record for winged aircraft, 4520 m.p.h., 1967. Home: 220 Eagle Ln Palmdale CA 93551-3613 Office: 2196 State Capital Sacramento CA 95814

KNOBLOCH, FERDINAND J. psychiatrist, educator; b. Prague, Czechoslovakia, Aug. 15, 1916; emigrated to Can., 1970; s. Ferdin and Marie (Verunac) K.; m. Susana Hartman (dec. 1944 victim of Holocaust); m. Jirina Skorkovska, Sept. 5, 1947; children: Katerina, Yohana. Maturity degree, Realgymnasium, Prague, 1927-35; student med. sch., Charles U., Prague, 1935-46; psychoanalytic tng., 1945-53. Successively lectr., asst. prof., assoc. prof. psychiatry Charles U., 1946-70; mem. faculty U. B.C., Vancouver, Can., 1970 , prof. psychiatry, 1971-83, prof. emeritus, 1983—; clin. dir. Day House Univ. Hosp., 1972-90. Vis. prof. U. Havana, 1963, U. Ill., Chgo., 1968-69, Columbia U., 1969-70, Albert Einstein Med. Coll., 1970; pres. European seminar mental health and family WHO, 1961, 3d Internat. Congress Psychodrama, 1968; co-chmn. Internat. Symposium Non-Verbal Aspects and Techniques of Psychotherapy, 1974; hon. dir. psychodrama Moreno Inst., N.Y.C., 1974. Author: (with Jirina Knobloch) Forensic Psychiatry, 1967 (award Czechoslovak Med. Soc. 1968), Psychotherapy, 1968, Neurosis and You, 1962, 63, 68, Integrated Psychotherapy, 1979 (transl. into German 1983, Japanese 1984, Czech 1993, Chinese, 1995), Integrated Psychotherapy in Action, 1999; contbr. articles on psychotherapy integration, psychology of music and evolutionary psychology to profl. jours. Political prisoner of Gestapo, 1943-45. Mem. Czechoslovak Soc. Advancement Psychoanalysis and Integration of Psychotherapy (pres. 1968-72), Am. Acad. Psychoanalysis, Polish Psychiat. Assn. (corr.), Am. Psychiat. Assn., Can. Psychiat. Assn., Am. Group Psychotherapy Assn., Can. Soc. for Integrated Psychotherapy and Psychoanalysis (pres. 1972—), World Psychiat. Assn. (co-chmn. sect. psychotherapy 1983-93, chmn. 1993-96). Home and Office: 4137 W 12th Ave Vancouver BC Canada V6R 2P5

KNOELKER, MICHAEL, science observatory director; b. Feb. 9, 1953; Diploma in Physics, U. Göttingen, Germany, 1978; PhD in Physics, U. (Germany) Freiburg, 1983. Asst. prof. U. Göttingen, 1983-87, 88-90; astronomer Kiepenheuer-Instut Sonnenphysik, Freiburg, 1990—; affiliate scientist High Altitude Obs. Nat. Ctr. Atmospheric Rsch., Boulder, Colo., 1994-95, sr. scientist, dir. High Altitude Obs., 1995—. Vis. scientist High Altitude Obs. Nat. Ctr. Atmospheric Rsch., Boulder, 1987-88. Office: NCAR PO Box 3000 High Altitude Observatory 3450 Mitchell Ln Boulder CO 80301-2260

KNOLL, JAMES LEWIS, lawyer; b. Chgo., Oct. 5, 1942; AB, Brown U., 1964; JD, U. Chgo., 1967. Bar: Ill. 1967, Oreg. 1971, Wash. 1984, Alaska 1993. Mediator, arbitrator, Portland, Oreg. Adj. prof. law Northwestern Sc. Law, Lewis and Clark Coll., 1982-91. Mem. ABA (mem. TIPS coun. 1989-92, chair property ins. com. 1984-85, mem. fidelity surety com., chair comml. tort com. 1985-86), Oreg. State Bar (editor 2 vol. text on ins. 1983, 96), Wash. State Bar, Oreg. Assn. Def. Coun. (pres. 1984). Office: 1500 SW Taylor St Portland OR 97205-1819 E-mail: jim@hamiltonmediation.com

KNOLLER, GUY DAVID, lawyer; b. N.Y.C., July 23, 1946; s. Charles and Odette Knoller; children: Jennifer Judy, Geoffrey David. BA cum laude, Bloomfield (N.J.) Coll., 1968; JD cum laude, Ariz. State U., 1971. Bar: Ariz. 1971, U.S. Dist. Ct. Ariz. 1971, U.S. Supreme Ct. 1976. Trial atty. atty. gen.'s hons. program Dept. Justice, 1971-72; atty., adv. NLRB, 1972-73, field atty. region 28, 1972-74; assoc. Powers, Ehrenreich, Boutell & Kurn, Phoenix, 1974-79; ptnr. Froimson & Knoller, Phoenix, 1979-81; sole practice Phoenix, 1985—; of counsel Burns & Burns. Mem. bd. visitors Ariz. State U. Coll. Law, 1975-76; pres. Ariz. Theatre Guild, 1990, 91. Fellow Ariz. Bar Found.; mem. ABA, State Bar Ariz. (chmn. labor rels. sect. 1977-78), Ariz. State U. Coll. Law Alumni Assn. (pres. 1977). Office: 2828 N Central Ave Ste 1110 Phoenix AZ 85004-1028

KNOOP, VERN THOMAS, civil engineer, consultant; b. Paola, Kans., Nov. 19, 1932; s. Vernon Thomas and Nancy Alice (Christian) K. Student, Kans. U., 1953-54; BSCE, Kans. State U., 1959. Registered profl. engr., Calif. Surveyor James L. Bell, Surveyors and Engrs., Overland Park, Kans., 1954; engr. asst. to county engr. Miami County Hwy. Dept., Paola, 1955; engr. State of Calif. Dept. Water Resources, L.A., 1959-85, sr. engr., 1986-88, chief, water supply evaluations sect. L.A., Glendale, 1989—. Hydrology tchr. State of Calif. Dept. Water Resources, L.A., 1984; mem. Interagency Drought Task Force, Sacramento, 1988-91. Mem. Jefferson Ednl. Found., Washington, 1988-91, Heritage Found., Washington, 1988—, Nat. Rep. Senatorial Com., Washington, 1990—, Rep. Presdl. Task Force, Washington, 1990-91. With U.S. Army, 1956-57. Decorated Good Conduct medal U.S. Army, Germany, 1957. Mem. ASCE (life, dir. L.A. sect. hydraulics/water resources mgmt. tech. group 1985-86, chmn. 1984-85), Profl. Engrs. Calif. Govt. (dist. suprs. rep. 1986—), Am. Assn. Individual Investors (life), L.A. World Affairs Coun., Singles Internat. Baptist. Home: 116 N Berendo St Los Angeles CA 90004-4711 Office: State Calif Dept Water Resources 770 Fairmont Ave Glendale CA 91203-1035 E-mail: vernk@msn.com

KNOPF, KENYON ALFRED, economist, educator; b. Cleve., Nov. 24, 1921; s. Harold C. and Emma A. (Underwood) K.; m. Madelyn Lee Siddy Trebilcock, Mar. 28, 1953 (dec. June 1999); children— Kristin Lee, Mary George. A.B. magna cum laude with high honors in Econs., Kenyon Coll., 1942; M.A. in Econs.; Ph.D., Harvard U., 1949; LLD (hon.), Kenyon Coll., 1993. Mem. faculty Grinnell Coll., 1949-67, prof. econs., 1960-67, Jentzen prof., 1961-67, chmn. dept., 1958-60, chmn. div. social studies, 1962-64, chmn. faculty, 1964-67; dean coll. Whitman Coll., Walla Walla, Wash., 1967-70, prof. econs., 1967-89, Hollon Parker prof. econs., 1985-89, prof. emeritus, 1989—, provost, 1970-81, dean faculty, 1970-78, acting pres., 1974-75; pub. interest dir. Fed. Home Loan Bank, Seattle, 1976-83. Mem. council undergrad. assessment program Ednl. Testing Service, 1977-80 Author: (with Robert H. Haveman) The Market System, 4th edit, 1981; A Lexicon of Economics, 1991; editor: Introduction to Economics Series (9 vols.), 1966, 2d edit., 1970-71; co-editor: (with James H. Strauss) The Teaching of Elementary Economics, 1960. Mem. youth coun. City of Grinnell, 1957-59; bd. dirs. Walla Walla United Fund, 1968-76, pres. 1973; mem. Walla Walla County Mental Health bd., 1968-75; mem. Walla Walla Civil Svc. Comm., 1978-84, chmn., 1981-84, councilman City of Grinnell, 1964-67; pres. Walla Walla County Human Svcs. Adminstrv. Bd., 1975-77; mem. Iowa adv. coun. SBA; tax aide AARP/IRS Tax Counseling for Elderly, 1987-98, local coord., 1990-91, assoc. dist. coord. S.E. Wash., 1991-94, assoc. dist. coord. tng., 1994-98; bd. dirs. Shelter Bay Cmty., Inc., 1995—, v.p. 1995-97, pres., 1997—; bd. dirs. La Conner Cmty. Scholarship Found., 1997—, La Conner Boys and Girls Club, 1999—. With U.S. Army Air Force, 1942-46, PTO. Social Sci. Rsch. Coun. grantee, 1951-52. Mem. Am. Conf. Acad. Deans (exec. com. 1970-77, chmn. 1975), Am. Econ. Assn., Am. Assn. Ret. Persons, Kiwanis, Phi Beta Kappa, Delta Tau Delta. Office: 223 Skagit Way La Conner WA 98257-9602

KNOPOFF, LEON, geophysics educator; b. L.A., July 1, 1925; s. Max and Ray (Singer) K.; m. Joanne Van Cleef, Apr. 9, 1961; children— Katherine Alexandra, Rachel Anne, Michael Van Cleef. Student, Los Angeles City Coll., 1941-42; B.S. in Elec Engring, Calif. Inst. Tech., 1944, M.S. in Physics, 1946, Ph.D. in Physics, 1949. Asst., then assoc. prof. physics Miami U., Oxford, Ohio, 1948-50; mem. faculty UCLA, 1950—, prof. physics, 1961—, prof. geophysics, 1959—, rsch. musicologist, 1963—; assoc. dir. Inst. Geophysics and Planetary Physics, 1972-86; prof. geophysics Calif. Inst. Tech., 1962-63, research assoc. seismology, 1963-64; vis. prof. Technische Hochschule, Karlsruhe, Germany, 1966, Harvard U., 1972, U. Chile, Santiago, 1973. Chmn. U.S. Nat. Upper Mantle Com., 1963-71; sec. Internat. Upper Mantle Com., 1963-71; chmn. com. math. geophysics Internat. Union Geodesy and Geophysics, 1971-75; mem. Internat. Union Geodesy and Geophysics (U.S. nat. com.), 1973-75; vis. prof. U. Trieste, 1984. Recipient Wiechert medal German Geophys. Soc., 1978; Gold medal Royal Astron. Soc., 1979; NSF sr. postdoctoral fellow Cambridge (Eng.) U., 1960-61; Guggenheim Found. fellow, 1976-77; Selwyn Coll. Cambridge U. fellow. Fellow AAAS, Am. Acad. Arts and Scis., Royal Astron. Soc. (Jeffreys lectr.), Am. Geophys. Union (Gutenberg lectr. 1992), Nat. Acad. Scis., Seismol. Soc. Am. (hon., medal 1990); mem. Am. Phys. Soc., Am. Philosophical Soc., Phi Beta Kappa (hon.). Office: U Calif Dept Physics Los Angeles CA 90095-0001

KNOSPE, WILLIAM HERBERT, medical educator; b. Oak Park, Ill., May 26, 1929; s. Herbert Henry and Dora Isabel (Spruce) K.; m. Adris M. Nelson, June 19, 1954. B.A., U. Ill., Chgo. and Urbana, 1951; B.S., U. Ill., 1952; M.D., U. Ill., Chgo., 1954; M.S. in Radiation Biology, U. Rochester, 1962. Diplomate Am. Bd. Internal Medicine and Subspecialty Bd. on Hematology. Rotating intern Upstate Med. Ctr. Hosps-SUNY-Syracuse, 1954-55; resident in medicine Ill. Central Hosp., Chgo., 1955-56, VA Research Hosp-Northwestern U. Med. Sch., Chgo., 1956-58; investigator radiation biology Walter Reed Army Inst. Research, Washington, 1962-64, investigator hematology, asst. chief dept. hematology, 1964-66; attending physician med. service Walter Reed Gen. Hosp., Washington, 1963-64, fellow in hematology, 1964-65; asst. chief hematology service, chief hematology clinic Walter Reed Army Inst. of Rsch., Washington, 1964-66; asst. attending staff physician Presbyn. St. Luke's Hosp., Chgo., 1967-68, asst. dir. hematology radiohematology lab., 1967-74, assoc. attending staff physician, 1968-74, sr. attending staff physician, 1974—; asst. prof. medicine U. Ill.-Chgo., 1967-69, assoc. prof., 1969-72; assoc. prof. medicine Rush Med. Coll., Chgo., 1971-74, prof. medicine, 1974—; dir. sect. hematology Rush-Presbyn.-St. Luke's Med. Ctr., Chgo., 1974-93; Elodia Kehm prof. hematology Rush-Med. Coll., Chgo., 1986-94, prof. emeritus, 1994—; prof. medicine U. N.Mex., Albuquerque, 1994—. Speaker at profl. confs. U.S. and abroad; vis. prof. medicine dept. hematology U. Basel, Switzerland, 1980-81, Cancer Ctr., U. N.Mex., 1992-93. Contbr. numerous articles to profl. publs. Trustee Ill. chpt. Leukemia Soc. Am., 1977-88, v.p., 1979-80; trustee Bishop Anderson House (Rush-Presbyn.-St. Luke's Med. Ctr.), 1980-94. Served to capt. M.C., USAR, 1958-61, to lt. col., U.S. Army, 1961-66. Fellow ACP; mem. Am. Fedn. Clin. Research, AMA, Am. Soc. Hematology, Am. Soc. Clin. Oncology, Central Soc. Clin. Research, Chgo. Med. Soc., Inst. Medicine Chgo., Internat. Soc. Exptl. Hematology, Radiation Research Soc., Southeastern Cancer Study Group, Polycythemia Vera Study Group, Eastern Coop. Oncology Group, Ill. State Med. Soc., Assn. Hematology-Oncology Program Dirs., Sigma Xi. Club: Chgo. Literary. Office: 310 Big Horn Ridge Dr NE Albuquerque NM 87122-1455

KNOTT, DOUGLAS RONALD, college dean, agricultural sciences educator, researcher; b. Fraser Mills, B.C., Can., Nov. 10, 1927; s. Ronald David and Florence Emily (Keeping) K.; m. Joan Madeline Hollinshead, Sept. 2, 1950 (dec.); children: Holly Ann, Heather Lynn, Ronald Kenneth, Douglas James (dec.). BSA, U. B.C., 1948; MS, U. Wis., 1949, PhD, 1952. Asst. prof. U. Sask., Saskatoon, 1952-56, assoc. prof., 1956-65, prof., 1965-93, head dept. crop sci., 1965-75, assoc. dean rsch. Coll. Agr., 1988-93; prof. emeritus, 1993—. Author: The Wheat Rusts—Breeding for Resistance, 1989; also numerous papers. Named to Saskatchewan Agr. Hall of Fame. Fellow Am. Soc. Agronomy, Agrl. Inst. Can.; mem. Can. Soc. Agronomy, Genetics Soc. Can., Order of Can. Mem. United Ch. of Can. Avocations: squash, tennis. Office: U Sask Dept Plant Scis 51 Campus Dr Saskatoon SK Canada S7N 5A8 E-mail: knott@sask.usask.ca

KNOTT, WILLIAM ALAN, library director, manager and building consultant; b. Muscatine, Iowa, Oct. 4, 1942; s. Edward Marlan and Dorothy Mae (Holzhauer) K.; m. Mary Farrell, Aug. 23, 1969; children: Andrew Jerome, Sarah Louise. BA in English, U. Iowa, 1967, MA in L.S., 1968. Asst. dir. Ottumwa (Iowa) Pub. Libr., 1968-69; libr. cons. Iowa State Libr., Des Moines, 1968-69; dir. Hutchinson (Kans.) Pub. Libr., S. Cen. Kans. Libr. Sys., 1969-71, Jefferson County Pub. Libr., Lakewood, Colo., 1971—. With USAR, 1965—67. Mem.: ALA, Colo. Libr. Assn., Urban Libs Coun. Office: Jefferson County Pub Libr 10200 W 20th Ave Lakewood CO 80215-1402 E-mail: wknott@jefferson.lib.co.us

KNOWLES, JAMES KENYON, applied mechanics educator; b. Cleve., Apr. 14, 1931; s. Newton Talbot and Allyan (Gray) K.; m. Jacqueline De Bolt, Nov. 26, 1952; children: John Kenyon, Jeffrey Gray, James Talbot. SB in Math., MIT, 1952, PhD, 1957; DSc (hon.), Nat. U. Ireland, 1985. Instr. math. MIT, Cambridge, 1957-58; asst. prof. applied mechanics Calif. Inst. Tech., Pasadena, 1958-61, assoc. prof., 1961-65, prof. applied mechanics, 1965—, William R. Kenan Jr. prof., 1991—, William R. Kenan Jr. prof. emeritus, 1996—. Vis. prof. MIT, 1993-94; cons. in field. Contbr. articles to profl. jours. Recipient Eringen medal Soc. Engring. Sci., 1991. Fellow ASME, AAAS, Am. Acad. Mechanics. Home: 522 Michillinda Way Sierra Madre CA 91024-1066 Office: Calif Inst Tech Divsn Engring & Applied Sci 104-44 1201 E California Pasadena CA 91125-0001 E-mail: knowles@caltech.edu

KNOWLES, MARIE L. transportation executive; Sr. fin. analyst Arco Transp. Co., Long Beach, Calif., 1972-1986; asst. treas. for banking, 1986-1988; v.p. of fin., planning and control ARCO Internat. Oil and Gas Co., 1988-90; v.p. and controller ARCO, 1990-93; sr. v.p. and pres. ARCO Transp. Co., 1993-96, exec. v.p., CFO, 1996—. Office: Atlantic Richfield 515 S Flower St Ste 3700 Los Angeles CA 90071-2201

KNOWLES, TONY, governor; b. Tulsa, Jan. 1, 1943; m. Susan Morris; children: Devon, Lucas, Sara. BA in Econs., Yale U., 1968. Owner, mgr. The Works, Anchorage, 1968—, Downtown Deli, Anchorage, 1978—; mayor Municipality of Anchorage, 1981-87; gov. State of Alaska, 1994—. Mem. citizen's com. to develop comprehensive plan for growth and devel., Anchorage, 1972; mem. Borough Assembly, Anchorage, 1975-79; bd. dirs. Fairview Cmty. Ctr., March of Dimes, Pub. TV Sta. KAKM, numerous sports facilities coms. Served with U.S. Army, 1961-65, Vietnam. Named Child Advocate of the Yr., Child Welfare League Am., 1999. Mem. Anchorage C. of C. (bd. dirs.). Office: Office Gov PO Box 110001 Juneau AK 99811-0001*

KNOWLES, WILLIAM LEROY (BILL KNOWLES), television news producer, journalism educator; b. L.A., June 23, 1935; s. Leroy Edwin and Thelma Mabel (Armstrong) K.; children from previous marriage: Frank, Irene, Daniel, Joseph, Ted; m. Sharon Weaver, Dec. 28, 1990. B.A. in Journalism, San Jose State Coll., 1959; postgrad., U. So. Calif., 1962-63. Reporter, photographer, producer KSL-TV, Salt Lake City, 1963-65; producer, editor, writer WLS-TV, Chgo., 1965-70; news writer ABC News, Washington, 1970-71, asso. producer, 1971-75, ops. producer, 1975-77, So. bur. chief, 1977-81, Washington bur. chief, 1981-82, West Coast bur. chief, 1982-85; prof. U. Mont., Missoula, 1986—; jazz writer and historian; chair radio-TV dept. U. Mon., 2000—. Advisor U. Mont. Student Documentary Unit. Served with U.S. Army, 1959-62. Decorated Commendation medal; Gannett fellow Ind. U., 1987; Media Mgmt. fellow Poynter Inst. Media Studies, 1988. Mem. Assn. for Edn. in Journalism (head radio-TV divsn. 1995-96). Office: U Mont Radio-TV Dept Missoula MT 59812-6480 E-mail: knowles@selway.umt.edu

KNOWLTON, NANCY, biologist; b. Evanston, Ill., May 30, 1949; d. Archa Osborn and Aline (Mahnken) K.; m. Jeremy Bradford Cook Jackson; 1 child, Rebecca Knowlton. AB, Harvard U., 1971; PhD, U. Calif., Berkeley, 1978. Asst. prof. biology Yale U., New Haven, 1979-84, assoc. prof., 1984; biologist Smithsonian Tropical Rsch. Inst., Panama, Republic of Panama, 1985—; prof. Scripps Instn. Oceanography U. Calif., San Diego, 1997—. Panelist animal learning and behavior NSF, Washington, 1989-92; vis. scholar Wolfson Coll., Oxford (Eng.) U., 1990-91, Zoology Inst., U. Basel, Switzerland, 1996-97. Editor Am. Scientist, 1981-90, Evolution, 1995-97. NATO postdoctoral fellow NSF, Liverpool, Cambridge, Eng., 1978-79; Aldo Leopold Leadership fellow, 1999. Mem. AAAS (coun. del. sect. on biol. scis., com. on coun. affairs), Ecol. Soc. Am., Soc. Study Evolution. Office: U Calif San Diego La Jolla CA 92093

KNOX, VENERRIA L. city official; BS in Journalism, Northwestern U., 1978; M in Adminstrn., Willamette U., 1980. Asst. to dep. treas. Treasury Dept. State of Oreg., Salem, 1979-80; fin. analyst Pacific Power, Portland, Oreg., 1980-83; fin. officer Security Pacific Bank, Seattle, 1983-85; legis. analyst City of Seattle, 1985-87, mgr. fin. and govt. ops., 1987-91, dep. dir., program support divsn. dir. Dept. Housing and Human Svcs., 1991-93, dir. Dept. Housing and Human Svcs., 1994-99, dir. human svcs. dept., 1999—. Mem. U.S. Conf. City Human Svc. Ofcls., Nat. Cmty. Devel. Assn., Nat. Forum Black Pub. Adminstrs. Office: Human Svcs Dept Dept Housing & Human Svcs 618 2nd Ave Fl 6 Seattle WA 98104-2289

KNUDSON, PETER C. state legislator, orthodontist; b. Brigham City, Utah, Oct. 26, 1937; m. Georgianna W. Knudson; 4 children. Student, U. Utah, 1955-60; AS, Weber State U., 1962; DDS, U. Pacific, 1966; MS, postgrad., Loyola U., 1969. Diplomate Am. Bd. Orthodontics. Practice dentistry specializing in orthodontics, to 1994; mem. Utah Ho. of Reps., 1994-98, Utah Senate, Dist. 24, 1998—; mem. bus., labor and econ. devel. com.; mem. transp. and pub. safety com.; co-chair transp. and environ. quality appropriations com. Mayor of Brigham City, 1978-90; mem. City Coun., Brigham City, 1974-78; chmn. State Job Tng. Coordinating Coun.; mem. Utah Seismic Safety Commn., 1994—. Named Most Outstanding Elected Pub. Ofcl., Utaha League of Cities and Towns. Fellow Internat. Coll. Dentists; mem. ADA, Am. Assn. Orthodontists, Pierre Fauchard Acad., Utah Dental Assn., Utah Assn. Orthodontists. Republican. Home: 1209 Michelle Dr Brigham City UT 84302-3179

KNUDSON, THOMAS JEFFERY, journalist; b. Manning, Iowa, July 6, 1953; s. Melvin Jake and Coreen Rose (Nickum) K. B.A. in Journalism, Iowa State U., 1980. Reporter/intern Wall Street Jour., Chgo., summer 1979; staff writer Des Moines Register, 1980-99; sr. writer Sacramento (Calif.) Bee, 1999—. Office: Sacramento Bee PO Box 15779 Sacramento CA 95852-0779

KNUTH, DONALD ERVIN, computer sciences educator; b. Milw., Jan. 10, 1938; s. Ervin Henry and Louise Marie (Bohning) K.; m. Jill Carter, June 24, 1961; children: John Martin, Jennifer Sierra. BS, MS, Case Inst. Tech., 1960; PhD, Calif. Inst. Tech., 1963; DSc (hon.), Case Western Res. U., 1980, Luther Coll., Decorah, Iowa, 1985, Lawrence U., , 1985, Muhlenberg Coll., 1986, U. Pa., 1986, U. Rochester, 1986, SUNY, Stony Brook, 1987, Valparaiso U., , 1988, Oxford (Eng.) U., 1988, Brown U., 1988, Grinnell Coll., 1989, Dartmouth Coll., 1990, Concordia U., Montréal, 1991, Adelphi U., , 1993, Masaryk U., Brno, 1996, Duke U., , 1998, St. Andrews U., 1998, Williams Coll., 2000; Docteur, Docteur, U. Paris-Sud, 1986, Marne-la-Vallée, 1993; D Tech., Royal Inst. Tech., Stockholm, 1991; Pochetnogo Doktora, St. Petersburg U., Russia, 1992; DLitt (hon.), U. Waterloo, 2000, Athens U. Econ. and Bus. , 2001. Asst. prof. Calif. Inst. Tech., Pasadena, 1963-66, assoc. prof., 1966-68; prof. Stanford (Calif.) U., 1968-92, prof. emeritus, 1993—. Cons. Burroughs Corp., Pasadena, 1960-68. Author: The Art of Computer Programming, 1968 (Steele prize 1987), Computers and Typesetting, 1986. Guggenheim Found. fellow, 1972-73; recipient Nat. medal of Sci., Pres. James Carter, 1979, Disting. Alumni award Calif. Inst. Tech., 1978, Priestly award Dickinson Coll., 1981, Franklin medal, 1988, J.D. Warnier prize, 1989, Adelsköld medal Swedish Acad. Scis., 1994, Harvey prize Israel Institute of Technology, 1995, Kyoto prize Inamori Found., 1996. Fellow Am. Acad. Arts and Scis.; mem. IEEE (hon., McDowell award 1980, Computer Pioneer award 1982, von Neumann medal 1995), NAS, Nat. Acad. Engring., Assn. for Computing Machinery (Grace Murray Hopper award 1971, Alan M. Turing award 1974, Computer Sci. Edn. award 1986, Software Sys. award 1986), Acad. Sci. (fgn. assoc. Paris, Oslo and Munich). Fellow, The Computer Mus. Lutheran. Avocation: playing pipe organ. Office: Stanford Univ Computer Scis Dept Stanford CA 94305-9045

KNUTH, ELDON LUVERNE, engineering educator; b. Luana, Iowa, May 10, 1925; s. Alvin W. and Amanda M. (Becker) K.; m. Marie O. Parrat, Sept. 10, 1954 (div. 1973); children: Stephen B., Dale L., Margot O., Lynette M.; m. Margaret I. Nicholson, Dec. 30, 1973. B.S., Purdue U., 1949, M.S., 1950; Ph.D. (Guggenheim fellow), Calif. Inst. Tech., 1953. Aerothermodynamics group leader Aerophysics Devel. Corp., 1953-56; asso. research engr. dept. engring. UCLA, 1956-59, asso. prof. engring., 1960-65, prof. engring. and applied sci., 1965-91, prof. emeritus, 1991—, head chem., nuclear thermal div. dept. engring., 1963-65, chmn. energy kinetics dept., 1969-75, head molecular-beam lab., 1961-88. Gen. chmn. Heat Transfer and Fluid Mechanics Inst., 1959; vis. scientist, von Humboldt fellow Max-Planck Inst. für Strömungsforschung, Göttingen, Fed.

Republic Germany, 1975-76; mem. Internat. Adv. Com. Internat. Symposium Rarefied Gas Dynamics., 2000—. Author: Introduction to Statistical Thermodynamics, 1966; also numerous articles; patentee radial-flow molecular pump. Served with AUS, 1943-45. Mem. AIAA, Am. Soc. Engring. Edn., Am. Inst. Chem. Engrs., Combustion Inst., Soc. Engring. Sci., AAAS, Am. Phys. Soc., Am. Vacuum Soc., Sigma Xi, Tau Beta Pi, Gamma Alpha Rho, Pi Tau Sigma, Sigma Delta Chi, Pi Kappa Phi. Club: Gimlet (Lafayette, Ind.). Home: 18085 Boris Dr Encino CA 91316-4350

KNUTZEN, MARTHA LORRAINE, lawyer; b. Bellingham, Wash., Aug. 28, 1956; BA in Polit. Sci., Scripps Coll., 1978; MA in Polit. Sci, Practical Politics, JD, U. San Francisco, 1981. Bar: Calif. Lawyer, mgr. legal computer support svcs., San Francisco, 1981—. Mem. San Francisco Citizens' Adv. Com. on Elections, 1994—; 3d vice chair Dem. Party, San Francisco, 1996—; chair San Francisco Human Rights Commn., 1996—; cmty. organizer. Recipient Civil Rights Leadership award, 1996. Home: 109 Bartlett St Apt 301 San Francisco CA 94110-3087 Office: Office Atty Gen 50 Fremont St San Francisco CA 94105-2230

KOBAYASHI, ALBERT SATOSHI, mechanical engineering educator; b. Chgo., Dec. 9, 1924; s. Toshiyuki and Taka (Torii) K.; m. Elizabeth Midori Oba, Sept. 24, 1953; children: Dori Kobayashi Ogami, Tina, Laura. BS in Engring., U. Tokyo, 1947; MSME, U. Wash., 1952; PhD, Ill. Inst. Tech., 1958. Position II engr. Konishiroku Photo Industry, Tokyo, 1947-50; design engr. Ill. Tools Works, Chgo., 1953-55; rsch. engr. Armour Rsch. Found., Ill. Inst. Tech., Chgo., 1955-58; from asst. prof. to assoc. prof. dept. mech. engring. U. Wash., Seattle, 1958-64, prof., 1964-97, Boeing Pennell prof. structural mechanics, 1988-95, prof. emeritus, 1997—. Coll. faculty assoc. The Boeing Co., Seattle, 1958-76; cons. Math. Sci. Northwest, Bellevue, Wash., 1962-82, UN Development Program, N.Y., 1984; vis. scholar U. Tokyo, 1969, 77; program dir. mech., structural and materials engring. div. NSF, 1987-88; consulting prof. Northwestern Poly. U., Xi'an, China, 1999—. Contbr. over 450 papers to Fracture Mechanics, Exptl. Mechanics Biomechanics and numerical analysis. Recipient F. G. Tatnell award Soc. Exptl. Stress Analysis, 1973, B.J. Lazan award, 1981, R. E. Peterson award, 1983, William Murray Lecture medal, 1983, Burlington Resources Found. Faculty Achievement award, 1992, M. M. Frocht award, 1995, G. E. Sr. Rsch. award Am. Soc. Engring. Edn., 1995, Disting. Alumni award Univ. Student Club (UW), 1997; decorated Order of Rising Sun, gold rays with neck ribbons Emperor of Japan, 1997. Fellow ASME, Soc. Exptl. Mechanics (hon. life mem., pres. 1989-90); mem. NAE, Am. Ceramic Soc. Home: 15420 62nd Pl NE Kenmore WA 98028-4312 Office: U Wash Dept Mech Enging Box 352600 Seattle WA 98195-2600 E-mail: ask@u.washington.edu

KOBLIK, STEVEN S. academic administrator; Pres. Reed Coll., Portland, Oreg., 1992—. Office: Reed Coll Office Pres 3203 SE Woodstock Blvd Portland OR 97202-8199

KOBLUK, MICHAEL DANIEL, retired municipal official; b. Trail, B.C., Can., Dec. 10, 1937; came to U.S., 1956; BA, Gonzaga U., 1969. Owner Am. Theater Prodns., N.Y.C., 1965-69; dir. opera house and convention ctr. City of Spokane (Wash.), 1974-79; dir. entertainment facilities, 1979-2000; retired, 2000—. Dir. performing and visual arts Expo 74, Spokane, Wash., 1971-74. Entertainer The Chad Mitchell Trio, 1958-69; recs. include: An Evening with the Chad Mitchell Trio—Live at the Birchmere, The Chad Mitchell Trio, The Best of the Chad Mitchell Trio—The Mercury Years, Blowin' in the Wind, The Chad Mitchell Trio at the Bitter End, Mighty Day on Campus, The Very Best of the Chad Mitchell Trio, The Chad Mitchell Trio Collection—The Original Kapp Recordings; (with John Denver) Mighty Day—The Chad Mitchell Trio Reunion, The Chad Mitchell Trio Reunion...Part 2. Alumni dir. Gonzaga U., 1970-71. Recipient Disting. Svc. award State of Wash., 1974, Disting. Alumni award Gonzaga U., 1999; inductee Hall of Fame, Trail, 1999; named Profl. of Yr., Spokane Conv. and Visitors Bur., 1999, one of 80 Most Important and Influential People of Century for Spokane, spl. millenium edit. Inlander, 1999. Mem. Internat. Assn. Assembly Mgrs. (pres. 1990-91). Home: 5908 S Martin St Spokane WA 99223-6836

KOCH, RICHARD, pediatrician, educator; b. N.D., Nov. 24, 1921; s. Valentine and Barbara (Fischer) K.; m. Kathryn Jean Holt, Oct. 2, 1943; children: Jill, Thomas, Christine, Martin, Leslie. B.A., U. Calif. at Berkeley, 1958; M.D., U. Rochester, 1951. Mem. staff Children's Hosp., Los Angeles, 1952-75, 77-98, dir. child devel. div., 1955-75; dep. dir. Calif. Dept. Health, 1975-76; prof. pediatrics U. So. Calif., 1955-75, 77—; prof. clin. pediatrics U. So. Calif. Sch. of Medicine, L.A., 1958—; co-dir. Phenylketonuria Collaborative Study, 1966-82; med. dir. Spastic Children's Found., Los Angeles, 1980-85. Mem. Project Hope, Trujillo, Peru, 1970; dir. Regional Center for Developmentally Disabled at Children's Hosp., Los Angeles, 1966-75; mem. research adv. bd. Nat. Assn. Retarded Citizens, 1974-76; mem. Gov.'s Council on Devel. Disabilities, 1981-83; bd. dirs. Down's Syndrome Congress, 1974-76; prin. investigator Maternal Phenylketonuria Project Nat. Inst. Child Health and Human Devel., Washington, 1985—. Author: (with James Dobson) The Mentally Retarded Child and his Family, 1971, (with Kathryn J. Koch) Understanding the Mentally Retarded Child, 1974, (with Felix de la Cruz) Downs Syndrome, 1975; contbr. articles to profl. jours. Recipient Albert L. Anderson award for outstanding health care profl., 1997, Homer Smith Rsch. award, 1998; Carrie D. Jones scholar, U. Calif., Berkeley, 1941. Mem. Am. Assn. on Mental Deficiency (pres. 1968-69), Am. Acad. Pediatrics, Western Soc. Pediatric Research, Soc. for Study Inborn Errors Metabolism, Soc. Inborn Metabolic Disorders, Sierra Club (treas. Mineral King task force 1972). Achievements include research in mental retardation, phenylketonuria and relation to pediatrics. Home: 2125 Ames St Los Angeles CA 90027-2902 Office: Children's Hosp of LA MPKU # 73 4650 Sunset Blvd Los Angeles CA 90027-6062 E-mail: rkoch8@earthlink.net

KOCH, TAD HARBISON, chemistry educator, researcher; b. Mount Vernon, Ohio, Jan. 1, 1943; s. Justin Louis and Mary Fosdick (Grove) K.; m. Carol Ann Kuban, May 28, 1976 B.S., Ohio State U., 1964; Ph.D., Iowa State U., 1968. Asst. prof. chemistry U. Colo., Boulder, 1968-74, assoc. prof., 1974-82, prof., 1982—, chmn. dept. chemistry and biochemistry, 1983-86; mem. U. Colo. Cancer Ctr., 1997—; mem. grad. sch. faculty Sch. Pharmacy, U. Colo. Health Scis. Ctr., 1999—. Contbr. numerous articles to profl. jours.; patentee in field With U.S. Army Med. Comd., 1998, 2001. Grantee NSF, 1985, 89, 92, NIH, 1985, 87, 93, 98, 2001, Coun. Tobacco Rsch., 1992, 96, Petroleum Rsch. Fund, 1997, Am. Cancer Soc., 1997. Mem. AAAS, Am. Chem. Soc., Am. Assn. Cancer Rsch., Am. Soc. Photobiology. Office: U Colo PO Box 215 Boulder CO 80309-0215 E-mail: tad.koch@colorado.edu

KOEGEN, ROY JEROME, lawyer; b. Spokane, Wash., Mar. 1, 1949; s. Frank J. and Jeanne (Bardsley) K.; m. Ann Martinelli, Aug. 28, 1970; children: Jennifer, Christopher. BA, Gonzaga U., 1971; JD, U. Calif., San Francisco, 1974. Bar: Calif. 1974, Wash. 1979, U.S. Supreme Ct. 1982. Assoc. Wilson, Jones, Morton & Lynch, San Mateo, Calif., 1974-78, Blair & Koegen, Spokane, 1978-80; ptnr. Preston, Thorgrimson, Ellis & Holman, Spokane, 1980-90, Perkins Coie LLP, Seattle, Spokane, 1990—. Author: Washington Municipal Financing Deskbook, 1992. Chmn. exec. com. Community Alcohol Ctr., Spokane, 1982-84, Century II Park Dist., Spokane, 1982-84; bd. dirs. Nature Conservancy. Mem. ABA, Wash. Bar Assn., Calif. Bar Assn., Nat. Assn. Bond Lawyers, The Nature Conservancy (bd. dirs.). Roman Catholic. Office: Perkins Coie LLP 221 N Wall St [illegible]

KOEHLER, JOHN EDGET, entrepreneur; b. Olympia, Wash., June 8, 1941; s. Herman Richard and Frances (Schwartz) K.; divorced; 1 child, Andrew C.; m. Susan m. Fiske, Apr. 27, 1991, children: Matthew J., Margaret S. Student, MIT, 1963-64; BA, Yale U., 1963, MA, 1965, PhD, 1968. Economist, assoc. dept. head Rand Corp., Santa Monica, Calif., 1967-75; asst. dir. Congl. Budget Office, Washington, 1975-78; dep. to dir. cen. intelligence Intelligence Community Staff, Washington, 1978-81, dir., 1981-82; dir. resources planning space and communications group Hughes Aircraft Co., El Segundo, Calif., 1982-84; exec. v.p. Hughes Communications, Inc., El Segundo, 1984-86, pres., chief exec. officer, 1986-87; v.p. internat. Hughes Aircraft Co., L.A., 1987-88, v.p. telecomm. and space sector, 1988-92; pres., CEO Hughes Asia/Pacific, 1992-95; exec. v.p., COO Titan Corp., San Diego, 1995; pres. J. Koehler & Co., Inc., Del Mar, Calif., 1995—; sr. advisor RAND, Santa Monica, 1995—; pres., CEO, founder Tachyon, Inc., San Diego, 1997-2000; exec. chmn. La Volla Networks, San Diego, 2001—. Co-author: The Matrix of Policy in the Philippines, 1971; contbr. articles on internat. econs. and nat. security issues to profl. jours. Recipient Nat. Intelligence Disting. Svc. medal Nat. Fgn. Intelligence Bd., 1981. Mem. Coun. Fgn. Rels., Pacific Coun. Internat. Policy, Internat. Inst. for Strategic Studies. Democrat. Episcopalian. Avocations: tennis, skiing. Home: 2982 Camino Serbal La Costa CA 92009 Office: 6224 Nancy Ridge Dr Ste 101 San Diego CA 92121-2244 E-mail: jekoehler@lunets.com

KOEHLER, REGINALD STAFFORD, III, lawyer; b. Bellevue, Pa., Dec. 29, 1932; s. Reginald S. and Esther (Hawken) K.; m. Ann Ellsworth Rowland, June 15, 1956; children: Victoria Elizabeth, Cynthia Rowland, Robert Steven. B.A., Yale U., 1956; J.D., Harvard U., 1959. Bar: N.Y. 1960, Calif., Fla., D.C. 1979, Wash. 1984, Oreg. 1985, Alaska 1985, U.S. Supreme Ct. 1973. Assoc. Davis Polk & Wardwell, N.Y.C., 1959-68; ptnr. Donovan Leisure Newton & Irvine, N.Y.C., 1968-84, Perkins Coie, Seattle, 1984—. Author: The Planning and Administration of a Large Estate, 1982, 5th edit. 1986. Chmn. bd. trustees Fred Hutchinson Cancer Rsch. Ctr. With U.S. Army, 1952-54. Fellow Am. Coll. Trust and Estate Counsel; mem. N.Y. State Bar Assn., Calif. Bar Assn., D.C. Bar Assn., Wash. Bar Assn., Oreg. Bar Assn., Alaska Bar Assn., Rainier Club, Chi Psi. Episcopalian. Office: Perkins Coie 1201 3rd Ave Fl 40 Seattle WA 98101-3029

KOELZER, GEORGE JOSEPH, lawyer; b. Orange, N.J., Mar. 21, 1938; s. George Joseph and Albertina Florence (Graul) K.; m. Patricia Ann Kilian, Apr. 8, 1967; 1 son, James Patrick. AB, Rutgers U., 1962, LLB, 1964. Bar: N.J. 1964, D.C. 1978, N.Y. 1980, Calif. 1993; registered fgn. lawyer, U.K., 2001. Assoc. Louis R. Lombardino, Livingston, N.J., 1964-66, Lum Biunno & Tompkins, Newark, 1971-73, Giordano, Halleran & McOmber, Middletown, N.J., 1973-74; asst. U.S. atty. for N.J. U.S. Dept. Justice, 1966-71; ptnr. Evans, Koelzer, Osborne & Kreizman, N.Y.C. and Red Bank, N.J., 1974-86, Ober, Kaler, Grimes & Shriver, N.Y.C., 1986-92, Lane Powell Spears Lubersky, L.A., 1993-97, Hancock, Rothert & Bunshoft, L.A., 1997-2000, Coudert Bros., L.A., London, 2000—. Adj. prof. Seton Hall U. Sch. Law, 1989-92; mem. lawyers adv. com. U.S. Ct. Appeals (3d cir.) 1985-87, vice chmn., 1986, chmn., 1987; mem. lawyers adv. com. U.S. Dist. Ct. N.J., 1984-92; permanent mem. Jud. Conf. of U.S. Ct. Appeals for 3d cir.; del. jud. conf. U.S. Ct. Appeals for 2d cir., 1987, 88, 89. Recipient Atty. Gen.'s award, 1970. Fellow Am. Bar Found.; mem. ABA (sect. litigation, co-chmn. com. on admirality and maritime litigation 1979-82, 89-90, mem. coun. sect. litigation 1985-88, chmn. 9th ann. meeting sect. litigation 1984, dir. divsn. IV procedural coms. 1982-85, dir. divsn. I adminstrn. 1988-89, mem. nominating com. 1982, 84, 87, advisor standing com. lawyer competence 1986—), Maritime Law Assn. U.S. (ABA relations com., fed. procedure com., vice chmn. com. on maritime fraud and crime 1989-94, chmn. 1994-98, bd. dirs. 1998-2001), State Bar Calif., N.Y. State Bar Assn. (chmn. admiralty com., comml. and fed. litigation sect. 1989-92), Assn. of Bar of City of N.Y. (admirality com. 1987-90), D.C. Bar Assn., Fed. Bar Assn. (mem. fed. practice com. 1994—), Fed. Bar Council, Comml. Bar Assn. (London), Assn. Average Adjustrs Gt. Britain, Assn. Average Adjusters U.S., Assn. Bus. and Trial Lawyers, L.A. World Affairs Coun.; Clubs: Mid-Ocean (Bermuda), Jonathan Club (L.A.). Roman Catholic. Republican. Home: 521 S Orange Grove Blvd 100 Pasadena CA 91105-3504

KOEPPEL, JOHN A. lawyer; b. Jersey City, Aug. 9, 1947; s. A.J. and Florence (McDonald) K.; m. Susan Lynn Rothstein, Nov. 12, 1972; children: Adam, Leah. BA in Govt. cum laude, U. Notre Dame, 1969; MA in Internat. Law, Tufts U., 1970; JD, U. Calif., San Francisco, 1976. Bar: Calif. 1976, D.C. 1980, U.S. Dist. Ct. (no. dist.) Calif. 1976, U.S. Supreme Ct. 1980. Assoc. Barfield, Barfield, Dryden & Ruane, San Francisco, 1976-80; from assoc. to shareholder Ropers, Majeski, Kohn & Bentley, San Francisco, 1980—; resident dir. Ropers, Majeski, Kohn, Bentley, Wagner & Kane, San Francisco, 1992-95, 97-99. Arbitrator San Francisco Superior Ct., 1979—; legal counsel San Francisco Jaycees, 1980-81, Amigos de los Americas, San Francisco, 1982-84, St. Francis Homes Assn., 1987-89, treas.; instr. Hastings Coll. Advocacy, San Francisco, 1988-91; lectr. U. Calif., San Francisco, 1990-95; sec. San Francisco Casualty Claims Assn., 1993-95. Active youth sports coaching San Francisco Sch., bd. dirs., 1997-2000. Mem. Nat. Bd. Trial Advocacy, Am. Bd. Profl. Liability Attys., Calif. State Bar (certificate of recognition for pro bono legal work, 1989), D.C. Bar, San Francisco Bar Assn. Avocations: running, skiing, hiking, camping, travel. Office: Ropers Majeski Kohn & Bentley 333 Market St Ste 3150 San Francisco CA 94105-2132 E-mail: jkoeppel@ropers.com, johna1k@aol.com

KOESTEL, MARK ALFRED, geologist, photographer; b. Cleve., Jan. 1, 1951; s. Alfred and Lucille (Kemeny) K.; life ptnr. Jennifer E. Budzak; children: Jennifer Rose, Bonnie Leigh. BS, U. Ariz., 1978. Registered profl. geologist Wyo., Alaska, Ind.; registered environ. assessor, Calif. Sr. geologist Union Oil Co. of Calif., Tucson and Denver, 1978-86; mgr. geology Harmsworth Assocs., Laguna Hills, Calif., 1986-88; sr. project mgr. Applied GeoSystems, Irvine, 1988-90; cons. geologist, photographer Adventures in Geology/Outdoor Images, Chino, 1990—. Contbr. articles and photographs to profl. jours. and mags. N.Mex. state rep. Minerals Exploration Coalition, Tucson and Denver, 1982. Sci. Found. scholarship No. Ariz. U., 1969, Acad. Achievement scholarship, 1970, Disting. Scholastic Achievement scholarship, 1971. Mem. Am. Inst. of Profl. Geologists (cert.), Soc. of Mining Engrs., Aircraft Owners and Pilots Assn., Geol. Soc. of Am., Nat. Geographic Soc. Avocations: woodworking, skeet and trap shooting, backpacking, travel, scuba. Home and Office: 13214 Breton Ave Chino CA 91710-5952 E-mail: makjeb@juno.com

KOESTER, BERTHOLD KARL, lawyer, law educator, retired honorary German consul; b. Aachen, Germany, June 30, 1931; s. Wilhelm P. and Margarethe A. (Witteler) K.; m. Hildegard Maria Buettner, June 30, 1961; children: Georg W., Wolfgang J., Reinhard B. JD, U. Muenster, Fed. Republic Germany, 1957. Cert. Real Estate Broker, Ariz. Asst. prof. civil and internat. law U. Muenster, 1957-60; atty. Cts. of Duesseldorf, Fed. Republic Germany, 1960-82; v.p. Bank J. H. Vogeler & Co., Duesseldorf, 1960-64, pres. Bremer Tank-u, Kuchlschiffahrtsges.m.b.H., 1964-72; atty., trustee internat. corps. Duesseldorf and Phoenix, 1983—; of counsel Tancer Law Offices, Phoenix, 1978-86; prof. internat. bus. law Am. Grad. Sch. Internat. Mgmt., Glendale, Ariz., [illegible] Phoenix, 1979—; ptnr. Applewhite, Laflin & Lewis, Real Estate Investments, Scottsdale, Ariz., 1981-88; chief exec. officer, chmn. bd. German Consultants in Real Estate Investments, Phoenix, 1988—; prof. internat. bus. law, chmn. dept. Western Internat. U., Phoenix, 1996—. Bd. dirs. Ariz. Partnership for Air Transp., 1988-92; chmn. Finvest Corp., Phoenix, 1990—; hon. German consul for Ariz., 1982-92. Author: The Refinancing of the Banking System, 1963, Longterm Finance, 1968, International Joint [illegible], 1974, History and Economy of the Middle East, 1975, Bauhaus and the Expressionism, 1983; contbr. articles to profl. jours. Pres. Parents Assn. Humboldt Gymnasium, Duesseldorf, 1971-78; active German Red Cross, from 1977. Mem. Duesseldorf Chamber of Lawyers, Bochum (Fed. Republic Germany) Assn. Tax Lawyers, Bonn German-Saudi Arabian Assn. (pres. 1976-79), Bonn German-Korean Assn., Assn. for German-Korean Econ. Devel. (pres. 1974-78), Ariz. Consular Corps (sec., treas. 1988-89), Nat. Soc. Arts and Letters (Greater Ariz. chpt., bd. dirs. 1997—), German-Am. C. of C., Phoenix Met. C. of C., Rotary (Scottsdale, Ariz.). Home: 6201 E Cactus Rd Scottsdale AZ 85254-4409 Office: PO Box 15674 Phoenix AZ 85060-5674

KOFFEL, MARTIN M. engineering company executive; b. 1939; MS, MBA, Stanford U., 1971. With Homestake Mining Co., 1974-81, Cooper Labs., Inc., 1981-84, Gilette Corp., 1984-86, Cooper Vision Inc., 1986-88; chmn. bd., pres., CEO URS Corp., San Francisco, 1989—. Adv. coun. McLaren Sch. Bus., U. San Francisco; trustee Am. Enterprise Inst. Pub. Policy, Washington; bd. dirs. McKesson HBOC, San Francisco, James Hardie Industries Ltd., Sydney, Australia. Office: URS Corp 100 California St San Francisco CA 94111-4510

KOFFLER, HERBERT, health plan administrator, educator; b. Columbus, Ohio, July 7, 1940; s. Joseph and Esther Koffler; m. Michelle Ann Rudman, Dec. 29, 1965; children: evan Douglas, Joshua Adam. BS in Zoology, U. Cin., 1962, MD, 1966; postgrad., Ariz. State U., 1989-91; MS in Adminstrv. Medicine, U. Wis., 1993. Diplomate Am. Bd. Pediatrics, Am. Bd. Neonatology. Instr. in pediatrics U. Cin., 1969-70, 72-74, U. Calif., Davis, 1971-72; assoc. prof. pediatrics U. N.Mex., Albuquerque, 1974-78, dir. newborn svcs. divsn. neonatology, 1976-88, assoc. prof. pediatrics and ob-gyn., 1978-88, prof. pediatrics and ob-gyn., 1988-95, prof. emeritus, 1995, clin. prof. family and cmty. medicine, 1995-97; asst. dir. managed care svcs. U. N.Mex. Hosp., Albuquerque, 1992-95; med. dir. Prudential HealthCare, Albuquerque, 1995-97, Presbyn. Salud, Albuquerque, 1997-99; assoc. chief med. officer Paradigm Health Corp., Concord, Calif., 1999—. Mem. cons. staff pediatrics Presbyn. Hosp., Albuquerque, 1974-95, Lovelace Hosp., Albuquerque, 1974-95. Author: (with R. Coen) Primary Care of the Newborn, 1987. Bd. dirs. Chaparral Home and Adoption Svcs., Family and Children Svcs., Albuquerque, 1984, Ronald McDonald Charities, Albuquerque, 1987—. Maj. USAF, 1970-72. Herb Koffler Day proclaimed in his honor State of N.Mex. and U. N.Mex., 1995. Mem. Am. Acad. Pediatrics, Am. Coll. Physician Execs., Western Soc. for Pediatrics Rsch., Greater Albuquerque Med. Assn. (alternate del., del. 1992—), Phi Delta Epsilon. Home: 41 Agua Sarca Rd Placitas NM 87043-9405 Office: Paradigm Health Corp 1001 Galaxy Way Ste 300 Concord CA 94520-5754 E-mail: hkofflee@paradigmhealth.com

KOFRANEK, ANTON MILES, floriculturist, educator; b. Chgo., Feb. 5, 1921; s. Antonin J. and Emma (Rehorek) K.; children— Nancy, John A. B.S., U. Minn., 1947; M.S., Cornell U., 1949, Ph.D., 1950. Asst. prof. to prof. U. Calif., Los Angeles, 1950-68, prof. hort. dept. Davis, 1968-87, ret. prof. emeritus, 1987. Vis. prof. U. Wageningen, Netherlands, 1958, Cornell U., 1966, Hebrew U., Rehovot, Israel, 1972-73, Lady Davis fellow, 1980; vis. prof. Glasshouse Crops Research Inst., Littlehampton, U.K., 1980, AID, Egypt, 1978-82, FAO-UN, India, 1985 Co-author: (with Hartmann, Rubatzky and Flocker) Plant Science— Growth, Development and Utilization of Cultivated Plants, 2d edit., 1981; co-editor: (with R. A. Larson) U. Calif. Azalea Manual, 1975; contbr. articles to profl. jours. Served with AUS, 1942-45, ETO; Served with AUS, PTO. Recipient rsch. awards of merit Calif. State Florist Assn., 1966, Garland award 1974; named Young Man of Yr. Westwood Jr. C. of C., 1956; recipient rsch. and tchng. award Soc. Am. Florists, 1993. Fellow Am. Soc. Hort. Sci (dir., sectional chmn. 1973-74); mem. Sigma Xi, Pi Alpha Xi. Office: U Calif Dept Environ Hort Davis CA 95616

KOGA, ROKUTARO (ROCKY) (ROCKY KOGA), physicist; b. Nagoya, Japan, Aug. 18, 1942; came to U.S., 1961, naturalized, 1966; s. Toyoki and Emiko (Shinra) K.; m. Cordula Rosow, May 5, 1981; children: Evan A., Nicole A. BA, U. Calif., Berkeley, 1966; PhD, U. Calif., Riverside, 1974. Rsch. fellow U. Calif., Riverside, 1974-75; rsch. physicist Case Western Res. U., Cleve., 1975-79, asst. prof., 1979-81; physicist Aerospace Corp., L.A., 1981-96, sr. scientist, 1996-2000, dsting. scientist, 2000—. Contbr. articles to profl. confs. Mem. IEEE, Am. Phys. Soc., Am. Geophys. Union, N.Y. Acad. Scis., Sigma Xi. Achievements include research on gamma-ray astronomy, solar neutron observation, space sciences, charged particles in space and the effect of cosmic rays on microcircuits in space. Home: 7325 Ogelsby Ave Los Angeles CA 90045-1356 Office: Aerospace Corp Space Scis Lab Los Angeles CA 90009 E-mail: rocky.koga@aero.org

KOHAN, DENNIS LYNN, international trade educator, consultant; b. Kankakee, Ill., Nov. 22, 1945; s. Leon Stanley and Nellie (Foster) K.; m. Julianne Johnson, Feb. 14, 1976 (dec. Sept. 1985); children: Toni, Bart, Elyse; m. Betsy Burns, Mar. 8, 1986; 1 child, David. BA, Ill. Wesleyan U., 1967; MPA, Gov.'s State U., 1975; postgrad., John. Marshall Law Sch., 1971-74. Police officer Kankakee County, 1967-75; loan counselor, security officer Kankakee Fed. Savs. & Loan, Kankakee, 1975-76; mgr. Bank Western, Denver, 1976-85; mgr. real estate lending dept. Cen. Savs., San Diego, 1985-87; maj. loan work-out officer Imperial Savs., San Diego, 1987-88; cons. Equity Assurance Holding Corp., Newport Beach, Calif., 1987-88; compliance officer Am. Real Estate Group and New West Fed. Savs. and Loan, Irvine, 1988-90; co-founder Consortium-Real Estate Asset Cons., Costa Mesa, 1990-91; investigator, criminal coord. Resolution Trust Corp., Newport Beach, 1991-94; instr. for Internat. Trade Anhui Inst. Fin. and Trade, Bengbu, People's Republic of China, 1994-95; instr. Guangzhou Inst. Fgn. Trade, People's Republic of China, 1995—; owner Kohan Internat. Bus. Forensics, 1995—; investigator Office Inspector Gen. L.A. Unified Sch. Dist., 2000—. Instr. U. No. Colo. Coll. Bus., Greeley, 1981-85; chmn. bd. North Colo. Med. Ctr., Greeley, 1983-85; pres. bd. Normedco, Greeley, 1984-85; part-time prof. bus. pub. adminstrn. So. Calif. Internat. Coll., 1998—. Vol. cons., chmn. ARC, Colo., 1979-85; campaign mgr. Donley Senatorial campaign, Colo., 1982, Kinkade City Coun. campaign, Colo., 1983; chmn. Weld County Housing Authority, 1981. Staff sgt. U.S. Army, 1969-71, Vietnam. Mem. Nat. Assn. Realtors, Shriners, Kiwanis. E-mail: dkohan@earthlink.net

KOHLER, PETER OGDEN, physician, educator, university president; b. Bklyn., July 18, 1938; s. Dayton McCue and Jean Stewart (Ogden) K.; m. Judy Lynn Baker, Dec. 26, 1959; children: Brooke Culp, Stephen Edwin, Todd Randolph, Adam Stewart. BA, U. Va., 1959; MD, Duke U., 1963. Diplomate Am. Bd. Internal Medicine and Endocrinology. Intern Duke U. Hosp., Durham, N.C., 1963-64, fellow, 1964-65; clin. assoc. Nat Cancer Inst., Nat Inst. Child Health and Human Devel., NIH, Bethesda, Md., 1965-67, sr. investigator, 1968-73, head endocrinology service, 1972-73; resident in medicine Georgetown U. Hosp., Washington, 1969-70; prof. medicine and cell biology, chief endocrinology divsn. Baylor Coll. Medicine, Houston, 1973-77; prof., chmn. dept. medicine U. Ark., 1977-86, interim dean, 1985-86; chmn. Hosp. Med. Bd., 1980-82, chmn. council dept. chmn., 1979-80; prof., dean Sch. Medicine, U. Tex., San Antonio, [illegible] Cons. endocrinology merit rev. bd. VA, 1985-86; mem. endocrinology study sect. NIH, 1981-85, chmn., 1984-85; mem. bd. sci. counselors NICHD, 1987-92, chair, 1990-92; mem. Nat. Adv. Rsch. Resources Coun., NIH, 1998—; chair task force on health care delivery AAHC, 1991-92; Inst. Medicine bd. dirs. Stds. Ins. Co., Assn. Acad. Health Ctrs., (chair 1998-99), OHSU bd. Northwest Health Found., 1997-2001; mem. adv. bd. Loaves and Fishes, 1989; mem. Gov.'s adv. com. Commn. on Tech. Edn., 1989-92; chair Oreg. Health Coun., 1993-95; mem. bd. govs. Am. Bd. Internal Medicine,

1987-93, mem. endocrinology bd., 1983-91, chmn., 1987-91, 97. Editor: Current Opinion in Endocrinology and Diabetes, 1994-97, Diagnosis and Treatment of Pituitary Tumors, (with G. T. Ross), 1973, Clinical Endocrinology, 1986; assoc. editor: Internal Medicine, 1983, 87, 90, 94, 98; contbr. articles to profl. jours. Mem. campaign cabinet United Way, 1999—; bd. dirs. Portland C. of C., 1997—. With USPHS, 1965-68. NIH grantee, 1973—; Howard Hughes Med. Investigator, 1976-77; recipient NIH Quality awrds, 1969, 71, Disting. Alumnus award Duke Med. Sch., 1992, MRF Mentor award, Med. Rsch. Found., 1994, Humanitarian award Am. Lung Assn., 1996, Jewish Nat. Fund Tree of Life award, 1998. Fellow ACP; mem. AMA (William Beaumont award 1988), Inst. Medicine, Am. Soc. Clin. Investigation, Am. Fedn. Clin. Rsch. (nat. coun. 1977-78, pres. so. sect. 1976), So. Soc. Clin. Investigation (coun. 1979-82, pres. 1983, Founder's medal 1987), Am. Soc. Cell Biology, Assn. Am. Physicians, Am. Diabetes Assn., Endocrine Soc. (coun. 1990-93), Raven Soc., Phi Beta Kappa, Sigma Xi, Alpha Omega Alpha, Omicron Delta Kappa, Phi Eta Sigma. Methodist. Office: Oreg Health Scis U Office of Pres 3181 SW Sam Jackson Park Rd Portland OR 97201-3011

KOHLOSS, FREDERICK HENRY, consulting engineer; b. Ft. Sam Houston, Tex., Dec. 4, 1922; s. Fabius Henry and Rowena May (Smith) K.; m. Margaret Mary Grunwell, Sept. 9, 1944; children: Margaret Ralston, Charlotte Todesco, Eleanor. B.S. in Mech. Engring, U. Md., 1943; M.Mech. Engring., U. Del., 1951; J.D., George Washington U., 1949. Engring. faculty George Washington U., Washington, 1946-50; devel. and standards engr. Dept. Def., 1950-51; chief engr. for mech. contractors Washington, 1951-54, Cleve., 1954-55; chief engr. for mech. contractor Honolulu, 1955-56; cons. engr. Honolulu, 1956-61; pres. Frederick H. Kohloss & Assocs., Inc., Cons. Engrs., Honolulu, 1961-91; chmn. Lincolne, Scott & Kohloss Inc, Cons. Engrs., Honolulu, 1991-97, sr. cons., 1997-2001, cons. engr., 2001—. Contbr. articles to profl. jours. Served with AUS, 1943-46. Fellow ASME, ASHRAE, Chartered Inst. Bldg. Svcs. Engrs., Instn. Engrs. Australia, Australian Inst. Refrigeration, Air Conditioning, Heating, Soc. Mil. Engrs.; mem. IEEE (sr.), NSPE. Clubs: Oahu Country (Honolulu). Home and Office: 1645 Ala Wai Blvd Penthouse 1 Honolulu HI 96815

KOHL-WELLES, JEANNE ELIZABETH, state legislator, sociologist, educator; b. Madison, Wis., Oct. 19, 1942; d. Lloyd Jr. and Elizabeth Anne (Sinness) K.; m. Kenneth D. Jenkins, Apr. 15, 1973; children: Randall Hill, Brennan Hill, Terra Jenkins, Kyle Jenkins, Devon Jenkins; m. Alexander Sumner Welles, Nov. 10, 1985. BA in Edn., Calif. State U., Northridge, 1965, MA in Edn., 1970; MA in Sociology, UCLA, 1973, PhD, 1974. Tchr. L.A. Sch. Dist., 1965-70; lectr. Calif. State U., Long Beach, 1973-85; vis. asst. prof. U. Calif., Irvine, 1974-77; So. Calif. mgr. Project Equity/U.S. Dept. Edn., 1978-84; asst. dean, coord. women's programs U. Calif., Irvine, 1979-82; lectr. Calif. State U., Fullerton, 1982-85, U. Wash., Seattle, 1985—; asst. prof. Pacific Luth. U., Tacoma, 1986-88; mem. 36th dist. Wash. Ho. Reps., Olympia, 1992-94, majority whip, 1993-94; mem. Wash. Senate, Dist. 36, Olympia, 1994—. Chair Wash. State Senate Higher Edn. Com., 1999—; Flemming fellow Ctr. Policy Alternatives, 1999; mem. women's legislature network bd. Nat. Conf. State Legislatures, 1997—, vice chair assembly state issues edn. com., 2000—; Fannie Mae Found fellow Kennedy Sch. Govt. Sr. Execs. in State and Local Gov., Harvard U., 2001; mem. study tour U.S.-Japan Women Legislators; mem. U.S.-Brazil Women Legis. Exch., 2001; Fgn. Policy Inst. fellow Ctr. for Women Policy Studies, 2001. Author: Growing Up Equal, 1979, Explorations in Social Research, 1993, Student Study Guide-Marriage and the Family, 1993, 94, 95, 97, 98, 99, 2001; contbr. articles to profl. jours. Bd. dirs. Com. for Children, Seattle, 1986-91, Queen Anne Cmty. Coun., Seattle, 1988-93, Stop Youth Violence, Wash., 1993—, Queen Anne Helpline, Seattle, 1992—, Youth Care, 1996—; mem. Wash. State Sentencing Guidelines Commn., 1995—, Wash. State Child Care Coord. Com., 1995—; mem. Gov.'s Task Force on Higher Edn., 1995-96; mem. Gov.'s Fire Protection Task Force, 1998. Grantee U.S. Dept. Edn., 1988-89, 90-91. Fellow Foreign Policy Inst. Ctr. Women Policy Studies, Fanny Mae Found., Sr. Execs. in State and Local Govt., The Kennedy Sch. Harvard Univ. Home: 301 W Kinnear Pl Seattle WA 98119-3732 Office: Wash State Senate PO Box 40436 Olympia WA 98504-0436 also: 521 2d Ave W Seattle WA 98119 E-mail: kohl_je@leg.wa.gov

KOHN, ALAN J. zoology educator; b. New Haven, July 15, 1931; s. Curtis and Harriet M. (Jacobs) K.; m. Marian S. Adachi, Aug. 29, 1959; children: Lizabeth, Nancy, Diane, Stephen. AB. in Biology, Princeton U., 1953; PhD in Zoology, Yale U., 1957. Asst. prof. zoology Fla. State U., Tallahassee, 1958-61, U. Wash., Seattle, 1961-63, assoc. prof. zoology, 1963-67, prof., 1976-98, prof. emeritus, 1998—. Bd. dirs. Coun. Internat. Exchange Scholars, Wash., 1986-90. Author: A Chronological Taxonomy of Conus, 1758-1840, 1992, (with F.E. Perron) Life History and Biogeography: Patterns in Conus, 1994, (with D. Röckel and W. Korn) Manual of the Living Conidae, 1995, (with others) The Natural History of Enewetak Atoll, 1987; editor: (with F.W. Harrison) Microscopic Anatomy of Invertebrates, vol. 5, Mollusca I, 1994, vol. 6 II, 1997; mem. editl. bd. Am. Zoologist, 1973-77, Am. Naturalist, 1976-78, Malacologia, 1974—, Jour. Exptl. Marine Biology and Ecology, 1981-84, Coral Reefs, 1981-87, Am. Malacological Bull., 1983—; assoc. editor Am. Zoologist, 1999—; contbr. articles to profl. jours. Sr. postdoctoral fellow Smithsonian Inst., 1990, John Simon Guggenheim fellow, 1974-75, Nat. Rsch. Coun. fellow, 1967; numerous rsch. grants NSF, 1960-94. Fellow AAAS, Linnean Soc. London; mem. Internat. Soc. Reef Studies, Soc. for Integrative and Comparative Biology (treas. 1971-74, pres. 1997-98), Am. Malacol. Union (pres. 1982-83), Marine Biol. Assn. India, Marine Biol. Assn. U.K., Malacol. Soc. London, Malacol. Soc. Japan, Pacific Sci. Assn., Am. Microscopical Soc., Sigma Xi (pres. U. Wash. chpt. 1971-72). Home: 18300 Ridgefield Rd NW Shoreline WA 98177-3224 Office: U Wash Dept Zoology Seattle WA 98195-0001 E-mail: kohn@u.washington.edu

KOHN, ROGER ALAN, surgeon; b. Chgo., May 1, 1946; s. Arthur Jerome and Sylvia Lee (Karlen) K.; m. Barbara Helene, Mar. 30, 1974; children: Bradley, Allison. BA, U. Ill., 1967; MD, Northwestern U., 1971. Diplomate Am. Bd. Ophthalmology. Internship UCLA, 1971-72; residency Northwestern U., Chgo., 1972-75; fellowship U. Ala., Birmingham, 1975, Harvard Med. Sch., Boston, 1975-76; chmn. dept. ophthalmology Kern Med. Ctr., Bakersfield, Calif., 1978-87; asst. prof. UCLA Med. Sch., 1978-82, assoc. prof., 1982-86, prof., 1986—. Author: Textbook of Ophthalmic Plastic and Reconstructive Surgery, 1988; contbr. numerous articles to profl. jours.; author chpts. in 16 additional textbooks; patentee in field. Bd. dirs. Santa Barbara (Calif.) Symphony, 1990—. Capt. USAR, 1971-77. Name applied to med. syndrome Kohn-Romano Syndrome. Mem. Am. Soc. Ophthalmic Plastic and Reconstructive Surgery (cert.), Am. Acad. Ophthalmology (Honor award 1995), Santa Barbara Ophthalmologic Soc. (pres. 1998), Pacific Coast Ophthal. Soc. (bd. dirs. 1986—, 1st v.p. 1990). Jewish. Avocations: guitar, tennis. Office: 525 E Micheltorena St Ste 201 Santa Barbara CA 93103-4212

KOHN, WALTER, educator, physicist; b. Vienna, Austria, Mar. 9, 1923; m. Mara Schiff; children: J. Marilyn , Ingrid E. Kohn Katz, E. Rosalind. BA, U. Toronto, Ont., Can., 1945, MA, 1946, LLD (hon.), 1967; PhD in Physics, Harvard U., 1948; DSc (hon.), U. Paris, 1980; PhD (hon.), Brandeis U., 1981, Hebrew U. Jerusalem, 1981; DSc (hon.), Queens U., Kingston, Can., 1986, Fed. Inst. of Tech., Zurich, 1994, U. Wuerzburg, , 1995, Tech. U. Vienna, 1996; PhD (hon.), Weizmann Inst., Israel, 1997. Indsl. physicist Sutton Horsley Co., Can., 1941-43; geophysicist Koulomzine, Que., Can., 1944-46; instr. physics Harvard U., Cambridge, Mass., 1948-50; asst. prof. physics Carnegie Mellon U., Pitts., 1950-60, assoc. prof. physics, 1953-57; prof. physics U. Calif., San Diego, 1960-79, chmn. dept. physics, 1961-63; dir. Inst. for Theoretical Physics, U. Calif., Santa Barbara, 1979-84; prof. dept. physics U. Calif., Santa Barbara, 1984-91, prof. of physics emeritus, rsch. prof. of physics, 1991—; rsch. physicist Ctr. for Quantized Electronic Structures, U. Calif., Santa Barbara, 1991—. Vis. scholar U. Pa., U. Mich., U. Wash., U. Paris, U. Copenhagen, U. Jerusalem, Imperial Coll., London, ETH, Zurich, Switzerland; cons. Gen. Atomic, 1960-72, Westinghouse Rsch. Lab., 1953-57, Bell Telephone Labs., 1953-66, IBM, 1978; mem. or chmn. rev. coms. Brookhaven Nat. Labs., Argonne Nat. Labs., Oak Ridge Nat. Labs., Ames Lab., Tel Aviv U. (physics dept.), Brown U., Harvard U., U. Mich., Simon Frazer U., Tulane U., Reactor Divsn. NIST, Gaithersburg, Md.; chmn. S.D. divsn. Acad. Senate, 1968-69; dir. NSF Inst. Theoretical Physics, U. Calif. Santa Barbara, 1979-84; mem. senate rev. com. U. Calif. Management Nat. Labs., 1986-89; adv. bd. Statewide Inst. Global Conflict and Cooperation, 1982-92; mem. bd. govs. Weizmann Inst. of Sci., 1997—. Contbr. over 200 sci. articles and revs. to profl. jours. With inf., Can. Army, 1944-45. Recipient Buckley prize, 1960, Davisson-Germer prize, 1977, Nat. Medal of Sci., 1988, Feenberg medal, 1991, Niels Bohr/UNESCO Gold Medal, 1998, Nobel prize in chemistry, 1998; Lehman fellow Harvard U., 1946-46, fellow Nat. Rsch. Coun., 1950-51, sr. fellow NSF, 1958, Guggenheim fellow, 1963, sr. postdoctoral fellow NSF, 1967. Fellow AAAS, Am. Phys. Soc. (counselor-at-large 1968-72), Am. Acad. Arts and Scis.; mem. NAS, Internat. Acad. Quantum Molecular Scis., Am. Philos. Soc. Achievements include research on electron theory of solids and solid surfaces. Office: U Calif Dept Physics Santa Barbara CA 93106

KOIDE, FRANK TAKAYUKI, electrical engineering educator; b. Honolulu, Dec. 25, 1935; s. Sukeichi and Hideko (Dai) K.; children: Julie Anne M., Cheryl Lynne K. BSEE, U. Ill., 1958; MEE, Clarkson U., Potsdam, N.Y., 1961; PhD (NIH predoctoral fellow), U. Iowa, 1966. Publs. engr. to electronics engr. Collins Radio Co., Cedar Rapids, Iowa, 1958-61; tchr. Cedar Rapids Adult Edn. Sch., 1960-61; lab. instr. U. Iowa Coll. Medicine, 1963-64; asst. prof. Iowa State U., 1966-69; prin. biomed. engr. Tech., Inc., San Antonio, 1968-69; mem. faculty U. Hawaii, 1969—, prof. elec. engring. and physiology, 1974—. Cons. in field. Author papers, reports in field. NASA-Am. Soc. Engring. Edn. Space systems Design Inst. fellow, 1967; NSF Digital and Analogue Electronics Inst. fellow U. Ill., 1972 Mem. IEEE. Office: U Hawaii Dept Electrical Engring 2540 Dole St Honolulu HI 96822-2303

KOKALJ, JAMES EDWARD, retired aerospace administrator; b. Chgo., Oct. 29, 1933; s. John and Antoinette (Zabukovec) K. AA in Engring., El Camino Coll., Torrance, Calif., 1953. Dynomometer lab. technician U.S. Electric Motors, L.A., 1953-54; devel. lab. technician AiResearch divsn. Garrett, L.A., 1956-59; tech. rep. McCulloch, L.A., 1959-65; dist. mgr. Yamaha Internat., Montebello, Calif., 1965-67; salesman Vasek Polak BMW, Manhattan Beach, 1967-68; sr. svc. rep. Stratos-We. div. Fairchild, Manhattan Beach, 1968-70; asst. regional mgr. we. states J.B.E. Olson div. Grumman, L.A., 1970-71, gen. mgr. Internat. Kart Fedn., Glendora, Calif., 1971-73; logistics support data specialist Mil. Aircraft divsn. Northrop Grumman, Hawthorne, 1974-95; ret., 1995. Author: Technical Inspection Handbook, 1972; contbr. articles to profl. jours. With USN, 1954-56. Mem. U.S. Naval Inst., Internat. Naval Rsch. Orgn., Nat. Maritime Hist. Soc., So. Calif. Hist. Aircraft Found., Found. L.A. Maritime Mus. Republican. Roman Catholic. Avocations: woodworking, ship modeling, maritime history, auto and aircraft restoration. Home: 805 Bayview Dr Hermosa Beach CA 90254-4147 E-mail: jekokalj@netzero.net

KOKOTOVIC, PETAR V. electrical and computer engineer, educator; b. Mar. 18, 1934; Dipl.Eng., U. Belgrade, Yugoslavia, 1958, Magistar (Elec. Engring.), 1963; Candidate of Tech. Scis., Russian Acad. Scis., Moscow, 1965. Prof. elec. engring. U. Ill., Urbana, 1966-91, Grainger prof. emeritus, 1991—; prof. elec. and computer engring. U. Calif., 1991—; dir. Ctr. for Control Engring. and Computation. Recipient Quazza medal Internat. Fedn. Automatic Control, 1990, IEEE Control Sys. Field award, 1995. Fellow IEEE (Engring., Outstanding AC Transactions Paper award 1982-83, Axelby Outstanding Paper award 1991-92, H. Bode Prize lecture 1991); mem. NAE. Office: U Calif Electrical & Comp Eng Dept Santa Barbara CA 93106

KOKUBUN, RUSSELL, state senator; Senator dist. 3 Hawaii State Senate, 2000—. Mem. Hawaiian affairs, judiciary, health and human svcs., agr., water, land, energy and environ. coms. Hawaiian State Senate. E-mail: Sen.Kokubun. Office: Hawaii State Senate State Capitol Rm 207 415 S Beretania St Honolulu HI 96813 Fax: 808 586-6689

KOLAROV, KRASIMIR DOBROMIROV, computer scientist, researcher; b. Sofia, Bulgaria, Oct. 16, 1961; came to the U.S., 1987; s. Dobromir Krastev and Margarita Georgieva (Kurukafova) K.; m. Janet Louise Barba, July 4, 1990; children: April, Kathryn, Sonia, Elena. BS in Math. with honors, U. Sofia, Bulgaria, 1981, MS in Ops. Rsch. with honors, MA in English, U. Sofia, 1982; MS in Mech. Engring., Stanford U., 1990, PhD in Mech. Engring., 1993. Rschr. Bulgarian Acad. Scis., Sofia, 1982-83; rsch. assoc., vis. prof. Inst. Mechanics and Biomechanics, Bulgarian Acad. Scis., Sofia, 1983-87; tchg. asst. Stanford (Calif.) U., 1988-92; mem. rsch. staff Interval Rsch. Corp., Palo Alto, Calif., 1992-2000; CEO, pres., founder Droplet Tech., Mtn. View, 2000—. Vis. prof. Inst. for Civil Engring., Sofia, 1983-86; lectr. H.S. U., Sofia, 1985; reviewer Jour. Robotic Sys., Palo Alto, 1991—, others. Contbr. articles to profl. jours. Mem. IEEE, Assn. for Computing Machinery, Soc. for Indsl. and Applied Math. Avocations: bridge, travel, skiing, bicycling, flying. Office: Droplet Tech Inc 2628 Bayshore Pkwy Mountain View CA 94043 E-mail: kolarov@stanfordalumni.org

KOLB, JAMES A. science association director, writer; b. Berkeley, Calif., May 31, 1947; s. James DeBruler and Evelyn (Thomas) K.; m. Mary Catherine Eames; children: Thomas, Catherine Mary. BA in Zoology, BA in Biol. Sci., Ecology, U. Calif., 1970, MS in Wildland Resource Sci., 1972. Rsch. asst. Sagehen Creek Rsch. Sta. U. Calif., Berkeley, 1970, teaching asst. dept. wildlife & fisheries, 1970-71, rsch. assoc. air pollution resource ctr. Berkeley, Riverside, 1971; tchr. secondary sci. Hayward (Calif.) Unified Sch. Dist., 1972-77; dir. Marine Sci. Ctr., Poulsbo, Wash., 1981-92; exec. dir. Marine Sci. Soc. Pacific Northwest, Poulsbo, 1992-95, For Sea Inst. Marine Sci., Indianola, 1995—. Project dir. Marine Sci. Project FOR SEA, Poulsbo, 1978-81; mem. Wash. State Environ. Edn. Task Force, Olympia, 1986—, Puget Sound Water Quality Authority Edn. & Pub. Involvement, Olympia, 1987-91, Marine Plastics Debris Task Force, Olympia, 1987; cons./tchr., trainer Hood Canal Wetlands Project, Hoodsport, Wash., 1990. Author: Marine Science Activities, 1979 (NSTA award 1986), Marine Biology and Oceanography, 1979, 80, 81 (NSTA award 1985, 86), Marine Science Career Awareness, 1984 (NSTA award 1985), The Changing Sound, 1990, Puget Soundbook, 1991, Life in the Tidal Zone, 1995, The Sea Around Us, 1995, Life in the Estuary, Begining in the Watershed, 1995, Life With Pagoo, 1995, Investigating the Ocean Planet, 1995, Ocean Studies, Ocean Issues, 1995, Marine Biology and Oceanography, 1995, Marine Explorations CD-ROM, 1997, The Tuna/Dolphin Controversy CD-ROM, 1998, Marine Science Clip Art Portfolio CD-ROM, 1998, Marine Biology and Oceanography CD-ROM, 2000, Ocean Studies, Ocean Issues CD-ROM, 2001; co-author: A Salmon in the Sound, 1991, Discovering Puget Sound, 1991. Mem. NSTA, ASCD, Internat. Reading Assn., Nat. Marine Educators Assn. (Marine Edn. award 1997), Northwest Assn. Marine Educators (past pres.), Wildlife Soc., People for Puget Sound (v.p.).

KOLB, KEITH ROBERT, architect, educator; b. Billings, Mont., Feb. 9, 1922; s. Percy Fletcher and Josephine (Randolph) K.; m. Jacqueline Cecile Jump, June 18, 1947; children: Brooks Robin, Bliss Richards. Grad. basic engring., US Army Specialized Training Rutgers U., 1944; BArch cum laude, U. Wash., 1947; MArch, Harvard U., 1950. Registered architect, Wash., Mont., Idaho, Calif., Oreg., Nat. Council Archtl. Registration Bds. Draftsman, designer various archtl. firms, Seattle, 1946-54; draftsman, designer Walter Gropius and Architects Collaborative, Cambridge, Mass., 1950-52; prin. Keith R. Kolb, Architect, Seattle, 1954-64, Keith R. Kolb Architect & Assocs., Seattle, 1964-66; ptnr. Decker, Kolb & Stansfield, Seattle, 1966-71, Kolb & Stansfield AIA Architects, Seattle, 1971-89; pvt. practice Keith R. Kolb FAIA Architects, Seattle, 1989—. Instr. Mont. State Coll., Bozeman, 1947-49; asst. prof. arch. U. Wash., Seattle, 1952-60, assoc. prof., 1960-82, prof., 1982-90, prof. emeritus, 1990—. Design architect Dist. II Hdqrs. and Comm. Ctr., Wash. State Patrol, Bellevue, 1970 (Exhbn. award Seattle chpt. AIA), Hampson residence, 1970 (nat. AIA 1st honor 1973, citation Seattle chpt. AIA 1980), Acute Gen. Stevens Meml. Hosp., 1973, Redmond Pub. Libr., 1975 (jury selection Wash. coun. AIA 1980), Tolstedt residence, Helena, Mont., 1976, Herbert L. Eastlick Biol. Scis. Lab. bldg. Wash. State U., 1977, Redmond Svc. Ctr., Puget Sound Power and Light Co., 1979, Computer and Mgmt. Svcs. Ctr., Paccar Inc., 1981 (curatorial team selection Mus. History and Industry exhbn. 100th anniversary of AIA 1994), Seattle Town House, 1960 (curatorial team selection Mus. History and Industry exhbn. 100th anniversary of AIA 1994), Comm. Tower, Pacific N.W. Bell, 1981 (nat. J.F. Lincoln bronze), Forks br. Seattle 1st Nat. Bank, 1981 (commendation award Seattle chpt. AIA 1981, nat. jury selection Am. Architecture, The State of the Art in the '80's 1985, regional citation Am. Wood Coun. 1981), Reg. ops. Control Ctr. Sacramento Dist. Corps Engrs. McChord AFB, Wash., 1982, Puget Sound Blood Ctr., 1983-88, expansion vis./dining/recreation facilities Wash. State Reformatory, Monroe, 1983, Univ. Sta. P.O., U.S. Postal Svc., Seattle, 1983, Guard Towers, McNeil Island Corrections Ctr. Wash., 1983, Magnolia Queen Anne Carrier Annex, U.S. Postal Svc., Seattle, 1986, Tolstedt residence, Seattle, 1987, Maxim residence, Camano Island, Wash., 1991, Carmean residence alterations/additions, Seattle, 1995, 96, 97, 2001, Susanna Burney and Bliss Kolb residence, Seattle, 2001. Pres. Laurelhurst Community Club, Seattle, 1966. Served with U.S. Army, 1943-45, ETO. Decorated Bronze Star medal ETO; recipient Alpha Rho Chi medal; selected Am. Architects, Facts on File, inc., 1989. Fellow AIA (dir. Seattle chpt. 1970-71, sec. Seattle chpt. 1972, Wash. state coun. 1973, pres. sr. coun. Seattle chpt. 1994-96, trustee Seattle Archtl. Found. 1994-96, Citation award Seattle chpt. for a Seattle 1960 Town House, 1990); mem. U. Wash. Archtl. Alumni Assn. (pres. 1958-59), Phi Beta Kappa, Tau Sigma Delta. Home and Office: 3379 47th Ave NE Seattle WA 98105-5326

KOLB, KEN LLOYD, writer; b. Portland, Oreg., July 14, 1926; s. Frederick Von and Ella May (Bay) K.; m. Emma LaVada Sanford, June 7, 1952; children: Kevin, Lauren, Kimrie. BA in English with honors, U. Calif., Berkeley, 1950; MA with honors, San Francisco State U., 1953. Cert. jr. coll. English tchr. Freelance fiction writer various nat. mags., N.Y.C., 1951-56; freelance screenwriter various film and TV studios, Los Angeles, 1956-81; freelance novelist Chilton, Random House, Playboy Press, N.Y.C., 1967—. Instr. creative writing Feather River Coll., Quincy Calif., 1969; minister Universal Life Ch. Author: (teleplay) She Walks in Beauty, 1956 (Writers Guild award 1956), (feature films) Seventh Voyage of Sinbad, 1957, Snow Job, 1972, (novels) Getting Straight, 1967 (made into feature film), The Couch Trip, 1970 (made into feature film), Night Crossing, 1974; contbr. fiction and humor to nat. mags. and anthologies. Foreman Plumas County Grand Jury, Quincy, 1970; chmn. Region C Criminal Justice Planning commn., Oroville, Calif., 1975-77; film commr. Plumas County, 1986-87. Served with USNR, 1944-46. Establishment Ken Kolb Collection (Boston U. Library 1969). Mem. Writers Guild Am. West, Authors Guild, Mensa, Phi Beta Kappa, Theta Chi. Democrat. Club: Plumas Ski (pres. 1977-78). Avocations: skiing, tennis, traveling. Home and Office: PO Box 30022 Cromberg CA 96103-3022

KOLBE, JAMES THOMAS, congressman; b. Evanston, Ill., June 28, 1942; s. Walter William and Helen (Reed) K. BA in Polit. Sci., Northwestern U., 1965; MBA in Econs., Stanford U., 1967. Asst. to coordinating architect Ill. Bldg. Authority, Chgo., 1970-72; spl. asst. to Gov. Richard Ogilvie Chgo., 1972-73; v.p. Wood Canyon Corp., Tucson, 1973-80; mem. Ariz. State Senate, 1977-83, majority whip, 1979-80; mem. U.S. Congress from 5th dist. Ariz., 1987—; mem. appropriations com.; chmn. appropriations subcom. treasury, postal svc., gen. gov. Trustee Embry-Riddle Aero. U., Daytona Beach, Fla.; bd. dirs. Community Food Bank, Tucson; Republican precinct committeeman, Tucson, 1974—. Served as lt. USNR, 1968-69, Vietnam. Republican. Methodist Office: US Ho of Reps 2266 Rayburn Ho Office Bldg Washington DC 20515-0001

KOLDE, BERT, professional basketball team executive; Vice chmn. Portland Trail Blazers. Office: Portland Trail Blazers One Center Ct Ste 200 Portland OR 97227

KOLKEY, DANIEL MILES, judge; b. Chgo., Apr. 21, 1952; s. Eugene Louis and Gilda Penelope (Cowan) K.; m. Donna Lynn Christie, May 15, 1982; children: Eugene, William, Christopher, Jonathan. BA, Stanford U., 1974; JD, Harvard U., 1977. Bar: Calif. 1977, U.S. Dist. Ct. (ea. dist.) Calif. 1978, U.S. Dist. Ct. (cen. dist.) Calif. 1979, U.S. Ct. Appeals (9th cir.) 1979, U.S. Dist. Ct. (no. dist.) Calif. 1980, U.S. Supreme Ct. 1983, U.S. Dist. Ct. Ariz. 1992, U.S. Dist. Ct. (so. dist.) Calif. 1994. Law clk. U.S. Dist. Ct. judge, N.Y.C., 1977-78; assoc. Gibson Dunn & Crutcher, L.A., 1978-84, ptnr., 1985-94; counsel to Gov., legal affairs sec. to Calif. Gov. Pete Wilson, 1995-98; assoc. justice Calif. Ct. Appeal, 3rd Appellate Dist., Sacramento, 1998—. Arbitrator bi-nat. panel for U.S.-Can. Free Trade Agreement, 1990—94; commr. Calif. Law Revision Commn., 1992—94, vice chair, 1993—94, chair, 1994; mem. Blue Ribbon Commn. on Jury Sys. Improvement, 1996; adj. prof. McGeorge Sch. Law, 2001—. Contbr. articles to profl. jours. Co-chmn. internat. rels. sect. Town Hall Calif., L.A., 1985—90; chmn. internat. trade legis. subcom., internat. commerce steering com. L.A. Area C. of C., 1983—91, law and justice com., 1993—94; adv. coun., exec. com. Asia Pacific Ctr. for Resolution of Internat. Bus. Disputes, 1991—94; mem. L.A. Com. on Fgn. Rels., 1983—95, Pacific Coun. Internat. Policy, 1999—; gen. counsel Citizens Rsch. Found., 1990—94; assoc. mem. ctrl. com. Calif. Rep. Party, 1983—94, mem. ctrl. com., 1995—98; dep. gen. coun. credentials com. Rep. Nat. Conv., 1992, alt. Calif. Delegation, 1992, Calif. del., 1996; bd. dirs. L.A. Ctr. for Internat. Comml. Arbitration, 1986—94, treas., 1986—88, v.p., 1988—90, pres., 1990—94. Master Anthony Kennedy Inns. of Ct., 1996-99. Mem. Am. Arbitration Assn. (panel of arbitrators, arbitrator large complex case dispute resolution program 1993-94), Chartered Inst. Arbitrators, London (assoc. 1986-94), Friends of Wilton Park So. Calif. (chmn. exec. com. 1986-94, exec. com. 1986—). Jewish. Office: Calif Ct of Appeal 3d Appellate Dist 914 Capitol Mall Sacramento CA 95814-4802

KOLLER, LOREN D. veterinary medicine educator; b. Pomeroy, Wash., June 16, 1940; s. Edwin C. and Doris K. (Shelton) K.; m. Kathleen Noel Ringness, Sept. 7, 1963; children: Susan E., Michael D., Christopher L. DVM, Wash. State U., 1965; MS, U. Wis., 1969, PhD, 1971. Head diagnostic and comparative pathology Nat. Inst. Environ. Health Scis., Research Triangle Park, N.C., 1971-72; rsch. assoc. dept. vet. medicine Oreg. State U., Corvallis, 1972-76, assoc. prof., 1976-78, prof., 1995—, dean Coll. Vet. Medicine, 1985-95; assoc. prof., asst. dean Dept. Vet. Medicine, U. Idaho, Moscow, 1978-81, assoc. prof., assoc. dean, 1981-82, prof., assoc. dean, 1982-85. Research asst. Dept. Vet. Sci. U. Wis., Madison, 1968-71; assoc. veterinarian Blue Cross Vet. Clinic, Corvallis,

1965-66; mem. Nat. Adv. Com. to establish Acute Exposure Guidelines for hazardous substances commn. Contbr. articles to profl. jours., chpts. to books. Served to capt. M.C., U.S. Army, 1966-68. Grantee NIH, USDA, Dow Chem. Co., EPA, WHO, FDA, Merck Sharp & Dohme, Warner-Lambert, Pew Found. Fellow Acad. Toxicol. Sci.; mem. AVMA, NAS (mem. com. toxicology and Inst. of Medicine, Ctrs. E-mail: loren.koller@orst.edu

KOLLMAN, PETER A. chemistry educator; b. Iowa City, July 24, 1944; m. 1970; 2 children. BA, Grinnell Coll., 1966; PhD in Chemistry, Princeton U., 1970. Fellow theoretical chemistry Cambridge U., 1970-71; asst. prof. U. Calif., San Francisco, 1971-76, assoc. prof., 1976-80, prof. chemistry and pharmaceutical chemistry, 1980—. Recipient Career Devel. award Nat. Inst. Gen. Med. Sci., 1974, Am. Chem. Soc. award for Computers in Chemistry, 1995. Mem. Am. Chem. Soc. (Computers in Chemistry award 1995), Am. Phys. Soc., Sigma Xi. Research includes application of quantum mechanics and molecular mechanics to intermolecular interactions and to structure activity relationships in biological systems. Office: U Calif Med Sch Dept Pharmacy 513 Parnassus Ave San Francisco CA 94122-2722

KOLODNER, RICHARD DAVID, biochemist, educator; b. Morristown, N.J., Apr. 3, 1951; s. Ignace Izack and Ethel (Zelnick) K.; m. Karin Ann Gregory, Aug. 6, 1983 (div. May 1991). BS, U. Calif., Irvine, 1971, PhD, 1975; MS (hon.), Harvard U., 1988. Rsch. fellow Harvard U. Med. Sch., Boston, 1975-78; asst. prof. Dana Farber Cancer Inst. and Harvard U. Med. Sch., Boston, 1978-83, assoc. prof., 1983-88, prof. biochemistry, 1988-97; chmn. divsn. cellular molecular biology Dana-Farber Cancer Inst., Boston, 1991-94, head x-ray crystallography lab., 1991-97, chmn. divsn. of human cancer genetics, 1995-97; prof. medicine, mem. Cancer Ctr. U. Calif. Med. Sch., San Diego, 1997—; mem. Ludwig Inst. for Cancer Rsch., San Diego, 1997—. Editor PLASMID jour., 1986-95; assoc. editor Cancer Rsch., 1995-2000; mem. editl. bd. Cell, 1996—, Molecular Cellular Biology, 1999—, Jour. Biol. Chemistry, 2000—; contbr. articles to sci. jours. Recipient Jr. Faculty Rsch. award Am. Cancer Soc., 1981, Faculty Rsch. award, 1984, Merit award NIH, 1993, Charles S. Mott prize GM Cancer Rsch. Found., 1996; rsch. grantee Am. Cancer Soc., 1980-82, grantee NIH, 1978—. Fellow Am. Acad. Microbiology; mem. Am. Soc. for Biochemistry and Molecular Biology, Am. Soc. for Microbiology, Genetics Soc. Am., Am. Assn. Cancer Rsch., Nat. Acad. Scis. Home: 13468 Kibbings Rd San Diego CA 92130-1231 Office: Ludwig Inst for Cancer Rsch CMME 3080 9500 Gilman Dr La Jolla CA 92093-5004 E-mail: rkolodner@ucsd.edu

KOLSRUD, HENRY GERALD, dentist; b. Minnewaukan, N.D., Aug. 12, 1923; s. Henry G. and Anna Naomi (Moen) K.; m. Loretta Dorothy Cooper, Sept. 3, 1945; children: Gerald Roger, Charles Cooper. Student, Concordia Coll., 1941-44; DDS, U. Minn., 1947. Gen. practice dentistry, Spokane, Wash., 1953—. Bd. dirs. Spokane County Rep. Com., United Crusade, Spokane; at-large-del. Rep. Planning Com.; mem. Rep. Presdl. Task Force. Capt. USAF, 1950-52. Recipient Employer of the Yr. award Lilac City Bus. and Profl. Women, 1994. Mem. ADA, Wash. State Dental Assn., Spokane Dist. Dental Soc., Spokane Country Club, Masons, Shriners. Home: 2107 W Waikiki Rd Spokane WA 99218-2780 Office: 3718 N Monroe St Spokane WA 99205-2850

KOLVE, V. A. English literature educator; b. Taylor, Wis., Jan. 18, 1934; s. Amos and Gunda (Lien) K. BA, U. Wis., 1955; BA with honors, Oxford U., 1957, MA, D Philosophy, Oxford U., 1962. From asst. prof. to assoc. prof. English Stanford (Calif.) U., 1962-69; prof. English U. Va., Charlottesville, Va., 1969-78, Commonwealth prof. English, 1979-86, chmn. dept. English, 1979-81; Found. prof. English UCLA, 1986—. Guggenheim Found. ednl. adv. bd., 1988—; The Alexander Lectures, U. Toronto, 1993, The Clark Lectures, Cambridge U., 1994. Author: The Play Called Corpus Christi, 1966, Chaucer and The Imagery of Narrative, 1984; author, editor: (with Glending Olson) Norton Critical Edition: Chaucer: The Canterbury Tales, 1989. 1st lt. U.S. Army, 1959. Recipient Brit. Coun. Humanities prize, 1985, Harbison Teaching award Danforth Found., 1972, UCLA Disting. Teaching award, 1995, Disting. Faculty award, 1999; Jenkins Rsch. fellow Oxford U., 1958-62, Guggenheim fellow, 1968, Sr. fellow Ctr. Advanced Studies in Visual Arts, Nat. Gallery, 1984, fellow Ctr. Advanced Study in Behavioral Scis., Stanford U., 1985; Rhodes scholar, 1955-58. Fellow Medieval Acad. Am. (pres. 1992), Am. Acad. Arts and Scis.; mem. MLA (chair exec. com. Chaucer divsn. 1973-77, 86-90, James Russell Lowell prize 1985), New Chaucer Soc. (trustee 1988-92, pres. 1994-96), Early English Text Soc., AAUP, Phi Beta Kappa. Democrat. Home: 2034 Outpost Dr Los Angeles CA 90068-3726 Office: UCLA Dept English Los Angeles CA 90024

KOMADINA, STEVE, state senator; Physician; Rep. senator dist. 9 N.Mex. State Senate. Mem. judiciary and pub. affairs com. N.Mex. State Senate. Home: Box 2085 Corrales NM 87048 Office: NMex State Senate State Capitol Mail Rm Dept Santa Fe NM 87503 E-mail: senate@state.nm.us

KOMEN, RICHARD B. food service executive; Founder Restaurants Unlimited, Inc., Seattle. Office: Restaurants Unlimited Inc 1818 N Northlake Way Seattle WA 98103-9036

KOMENICH, KIM, photographer; b. Laramie, Wyo., Oct. 15, 1956; s. Milo and Juanita Mary (Beggs) K. BA in Journalism, San Jose State U., 1979. Reporter/photographer Manteca (Calif.) Bull., 1976-77; staff photographer Contra Costa Times, Walnut Creek, Calif., 1979-82, San Francisco Examiner, 1982—. Lectr. San Francisco Acad. Art; vis. lectr. Mo. Sch. Journalism, 1998—. John S. Knight fellow Stanford U., 1993-94; recipient 1st Pl. award UPI, 1982, 85, Nat. Headliner award, 1983, 88, 87 1st Pl. award World Press Photo Awards, 1983, 1st Pl. award AP, 1985, 87, Disting. Svc. award Sigma Delta Xi, 1986, Pulitzer prize, 1987, others. Office: San Francisco Examiner 110 5th St San Francisco CA 94103-2918

KONECNY-COSTA, JENNIFER, computer company executive; B in Political Sci., M in Counseling Psychology, Santa Clara U. Various mgmt. positions Hewlett-Packard; campus min. U. Santa Clara; v.p. human resources Silicon Graphics, Wilson Sonsini Goodrich & Rosati; sr. v.p. human resources Novell, Inc., Provo, Utah, 1996—. Active HR Consortium, Calif. Leadership Coun., Bay Area Human Resources Exec. Com., Am. Electronics Assn. Human Resource Com.; del. to Russia Soc. Human Resource Mgmt., 1991, 92; bd. trustees Santa Clara U.; exec. com. mem. Tech. Mus. Innovation Bd. Dirs.; bd. dirs. San Jose Repertory Theater. Office: Novell Inc 122 E 1700 S Provo UT 84606-6194 Fax: 801-228-7077

KONING, HENDRIK, architect; came to the U.S., 1979; BArch, U. Melbourne, Australia, 1978; MArch II, UCLA, 1981. Lic. architect Calif., 1982, contractor, 1984; registered architect, Australia; cert. Nat. Coun. Archtl. Registration Bds. Prin. in charge of tech., code, and prodn. issues Koning Eizenberg Architecture, 1981—, v.p. Calif., 1990—. Instr. UCLA, U. B.C., Harvard U., MIT; lectr. in field. Exhbns. incl. "House Rules" Wexner Ctr., 1991, "The Architect's Dream Houses for the Next Millennium", The Contemporary Arts Ctr., 1993, " Angels & Franciscans", Gagosian Gallery, 1992, "Conceptual Drawings by Architects", Bannatyne Gallery, 1991, Koning and Eizenberg Projects Grad. Sch. Architecture & Urban Planning UCLA, 1990, others; prin. works include Digital Domain renovation and screening rm., Santa Monica, Lightstorm Entertainment offices and THX theater, Santa Monica, Gilmore Bank addition and remodel, L.A., 1548-1550 Studios, Santa Monica, (with RTA) Materials Rsch. Lab. U. Calif., Santa Barbara, Ken Edwards Ctr. Cmty. Svcs., Santa Monica, Peck Park Cmty. Ctr. Gymnasium, San Pedro, Calif., Sepulveda Recreation Ctr. Gymnasium, L.A., (Nat. Concrete /Masonry award 1996, AIA Calif. Coun. Honor award 1996, AIA L.A. Chpt. Merit Award, 1997, L.A. Bus. Coun. Beautification awrd 1996, AIA/SFV Design award 1995), PS# 1 Elem. Sch., Santa Monica, Famers Market additions and master plan, L.A. (Westside Urban Forum prize 1991), Stage Deli, L.A., Simone Hotel, L.A. (Nat. Honor award AIA 1994), Boyd Hotel, L.A. Cmty. Corp. Santa Monica Housing Projects, 5th St. Family Housing, Santa Monica, St. John's Hosp. Replacement Housing Program, Santa Monica, Liffman Ho., Santa Monica, (with Glenn Erikson) Electric Artblock, Venice (Beautification award L.A. Bus. Coun. 1993), 6th St. Condominiums, Santa Monica, Hollywood Duplex, Hollywood Hills (Record Houses Archtl. Record 1988), Calif. Ave. Duplex, Santa Monica, Tarzana Ho. (Merit award L.A. chpt. AIA 1991, Merit Award AIA Calif. Coun., 1998, Sunset Western Home awards 1993-94), 909 Ho., Santa Monica (Merit award L.A. chpt. AIA 1991), 31st St. Ho., Santa Monica (Honor award AIACC 1994, Record House 1995, Nat. AIA Honor award 1996), others. Recipient 1st award Progressive Architecture, 1987; named one of Domino's Top 30 Architects, 1989. Fellow AIA (juror San Diego design awards 1992, panelist honor awards 1994, Calif. coun. spl. awards 1997, nat. interior design awards 1997), Royal Australian Inst. Archs.; mem. Nat. Trust for Hist. Preservation, So. Calif. Assn. Non-Profit Housing, L.A. Conservancy. Office: Koning Eizenberg Architecture 1454 25th St Santa Monica CA 90404-3008

KONISHI, MASAKAZU, neurobiologist, educator; b. Kyoto, Japan, Feb. 17, 1933; BS, Hokkaido U., Japan, 1956, MS, 1958, LLD (hon.), 1991; PhD in Zoology, U. Calif., Berkeley, 1963. Postdoctoral Alexander von Humboldt Found. fellow, 1963-64; Internat. Brain Rsch. Orgn. and UNESCO fellow, 1964-65; asst. prof. zoology U. Wis., 1965-66; asst. prof. to assoc. prof. biology Princeton (N.J.) U., 1970-75; prof. biology Calif. Inst. Tech., Pasadena, 1975-79, Bing Prof. behavioral biology, 1979—. Mem. Salk Inst., 1991—. Assoc. editor Jour. Neurosci., 1980-89, sect. editor, 1990-93; mem. editorial adv. bd. Jour. Comparative Physiology. Recipient Elliot Coues award Am. Ornithologists Union, 1983, F.O. Schmitt prize, 1987, Internat. prize for biology Japan Soc. for Promotion Sci., 1990, honoris causa Hokkaide Univ., 1991, Fondation Ipsen prize, 1999. Recipient David Sparks award in Integrative Neurophysiology U. Ala., 1992, Charles A. Dana award for Pioneering Achievements in Health and Edn., 1992, Sci. Writing prize Acoustical Soc. Am., 1994. Office: Calif Inst Tech Divsn Biology 1200 E California Blvd Pasadena CA 91125-0001

KONNYU, ERNEST LESLIE, former congressman; b. Tamasi, Hungary, May 17, 1937; came to U.S., 1949; s. Leslie and Elizabeth Konnyu; m. Lillian Muenks, Nov. 25, 1959; children: Carol, Renata, Lisa, Victoria. Student, U. Md., 1960-62; BS in Acctg., Ohio State U., 1965. Mem. Calif. Assembly, Sacramento, 1980-86, 100th Congress from 12th Calif. dist., 1987-89; owner Premier Printing, San Jose, Calif., 1990—; CEO Konnyu Fins. and Taxes, Inc. Chmn. Assembly Rep. Policy Com. of State Assembly, Sacramento, 1985-86; vice chmn. Assembly Human Svcs., Sacramento, 1980-86; vice chmn. Policy Rsch. Com., Sacramento, 1985-86. Mem. Rep. State Cen. Com., Calif., 1977-88, Rep. Cen. Com., Santa Clara County, Calif., 1980-88; mem. adv. bd. El Camino Hosp., Mountain View, Calif., 1987-89. Served to maj. USAF, 1959-69. Recipient Nat. Def. Medal, 1968, Disting. Service award U.S. Jaycees, 1969, Nat. Security award Am. Security Council Found., 1987; named lifetime senator U.S. Jaycees, 1977. Mem. Am.- Hungarian C. of C. (v.p. 1995-97). Republican. Roman Catholic. Avocations: politics, golf. E-mail: premcolor@msn.com

KONOWIECKI, JOSEPH S. lawyer, healthcare organization executive; BA in Polit. Sci. magna cum laude, UCLA; JD, U. Calif., 1978. Bar: Calif., D.C. Gen. counsel, asst. sec. PacifiCare Health Sys., Inc., Santa Anna, Calif., 1988—; founding ptnr. Konowiecki & Rank. Rep. non-profit and proprietary hosps., Preferred Provider Orgns., full-svc. and specialty HMOs, various med. groups. Founding editor: Hastings Comms. and Entertainment Law Jour.; contbr. articles to Practicing Law Inst., chair, participant; contbr. articles to law jours. Office: 3120 W Lake Center Dr Santa Ana CA 92704-6917

KOOGLE, TIMOTHY K. communications executive; MS in Engr., Stanford U. Pres. Intermec Corp.; corp. v.p. Western Atlas Inc.; with Motorola Inc.; chmn., CEO Yahoo! Corp., Santa Clara, Calif., 1999—. Chmn. bd. dirs. AIM. Office: Yahoo! Corp 3400 Central Expy Santa Clara CA 95051-0703

KOOL, ERIC T. chemist, educator; b. 1960; BS, Miami U., Ohio, 1982; PhD, Columbia U., 1988. Prof. dept. chemistry Stanford (Calif.) U. Contbr. articles to profl. jours. Recipient faculty awad Am. Cyanamid, 1994, Pfizer award Am. Chem. Soc., 2000; named Young Investigator, Office Naval Rsch., 1992, Young Investigator, Beckman Found., 1992, Young Investigator, Army Rsch. Office, 1993; Dreyfus Found. Tchr.-scholar, 1993, Arthur C. Cope scholar Am. Chem. Soc., 2000; Alfred P. Sloan Found. fellow, 1994. Achievements include research on design, synthesis and study of molecules that mimic complex biological functions such as replication. Office: Stanford U Dept Chemistry Stauffer I Rm 103 Stanford CA 94305-5080 E-mail: kool@leland.stanford.edu

KOONIN, STEVEN ELLIOT, physicist, educator, academic administrator; b. Bklyn., Dec. 12, 1951; BS, Calif. Inst. Tech., 1972; PhD, MIT, 1975. Asst. prof. Calif. Inst. Tech., Pasadena, Calif., 1975-78, assoc. prof., 1978-81, prof., 1981—, v.p., provost, 1995—. Cons. Inst. for Def. Analysis, MITRE Corp., Lawrence Livermore Nat. Lab., Oak Ridge Nat. Lab. Author: Computational Physics, 1985, Computational Nuclear Physics, vol. 1, 1991, vol. 2, 1993. Recipient Green Prize for Creative Scholarship, Calif. Inst. Tech., 1972, Assoc. Students Teaching award Calif. Inst. Tech., 1975-76, Sr. U.S. Scientist award Humboldt Found., 1985-86, Fusion Power Assocs. Leadership award, 1994, E.O. Lawrence award U.S. Dept. Energy, 1998; Alfred P. Sloan fellow, 1977-81. Fellow AAAS, Am. Acad. Arts and Scis., Am. Phys. Soc. (chmn. APS divsn. nuclear physics 1988-89, exec. bd. dirs. 1994-96), Calif. Coun. on Sci. and Tech. Office: Calif Inst Tech Office Of Provost 206 31 Pasadena CA 91125-0001 E-mail: koonin@caltech.edu

KOPP, EUGENE HOWARD, electrical engineer; b. N.Y.C., Oct. 1, 1929; s. Jacob and Fanny (Lipschitz) K.; m. Claire Bernstein, Aug. 31, 1950; children: Carolyn, Michael, Paul. B.E.E., CCNY, 1950, M.E.E., 1953; Ph.D. in Engring, UCLA, 1965. Registered profl. engr., Calif. Project engr. Polarad Electronics Corp., Long Island City, N.Y., 1950-53, Kaye Halbert Corp., Culver City, Calif., 1953-55; chief engr. Precision Radiation Instruments, Inc., Los Angeles, 1955-58; mem. faculty sch. engring. Calif. State U., Los Angeles, 1958-74, assoc. prof., 1962-66, prof., 1966-74, dean engring. Sch., 1967-73; v.p. acad. affairs West Coast U., Los Angeles, 1973-79; sr. scientist Hughes Aircraft Co., 1980-85, mgr. research and devel., 1985-93, dir. advanced programs, 1994-95; v.p. mobile satellites Boeing Satellite Systems, 1996-97, chief scientist comml. satellites, 1998—. Lectr. evening divsn. CCNY, N.Y.C., 1950-53; lectr. UCLA, 1979-91. Vis. research fellow U. Leeds, Eng., 1966-67. Mem. IEEE, AIAA, Tau Beta Pi, Eta Kappa Nu, Pi Tau Sigma. Office: Boeing Satellite Systems PO Box 1351 South Pasadena CA 91031-1351

KORAN, DENNIS HOWARD, publisher; b. L.A., May 21, 1947; s. Aaron Baer and Shirley Mildred (Kassan) K.; m. Roslynn Ruth Cohen, Apr. 6, 1979; 1 child, Michael; stepchildren: Jeff, Beth, Judy. Student, U. Leeds, Eng., 1966-67, UCLA, , 1979-80; BA, U. Calif., Berkeley, 1980; postgrad., Loyola U., L.A., 1982-84, 86-89. Co-founder, co-editor Cloud Marauder Press, Berkeley, 1969-72, Panjandrum/Aris Books, San Francisco, 1973-81; founder, editor Panjandrum Books, San Francisco, 1971—, Panjandrum Press, Inc., San Francisco, 1971—. Substitute tchr. L.A. Unified Sch. Dist., 1997—; co-dir. poetry reading series Panjandrum Books, 1972-76. Author: (book of poetry) Vacancies, 1975, After All, 1993; (with Mike Koran) Refrigerator Poems: Variations on 24, 48 & 120 Words, 1998, Love & Space, 2000; editor Panjandrum Poetry Jour., 1971—, Noumenal Books, 1998—; co-editor Cloud Marauder, 1969-72; author poetry pub. various jours. Liaison between U.S. Govt. and Seminole Indians VISTA, Sasakwa, Okla., 1969-70. Nat. Endowment for Arts Lit. Pub. grantee, 1974, 76, 79, 81, 82, 84, Coord. Coun. for Lit. Mags., 1971-80, grantee Lit. Pub. Calif. Arts Coun., 1985-86, L.A. Cultural Arts Found., 1986. Mem. Lovers of the Stinking Rose, Poets and Writers. Avocations: rare book collecting, travel, athletics, stamp and coin collecting. Office: Panjandrum Books 6156 Wilkinson Ave North Hollywood CA 91606-4518

KORB, LAWRENCE JOHN, metallurgist; b. Warren, Pa., Apr. 28, 1930; s. Stanley Curtis and Dagna (Pedersen) K.; m. Janet Davis, Mar. 30, 1957; children: James, William, Jeanine. B in Chem. Engring., Rensselaer Poly. Inst., Troy, N.Y., 1952. Registered profl. engr., Calif. Sales engr. Alcoa, Buffalo, 1955-59; metall. engr. N.Am. Rockwell Co., Downey, Calif., 1959-62; engring. supr. metallurgy Apollo program Rockwell Internat. Co., Downey, 1962-66, engring. supr. advanced materials, 1966-72, engring. supr. metals and ceramics space shuttle program, 1972-88; cons., 1988—. Mem. tech. adv. com. metallurgy Cerritos Coll., 1969-74. Contbr. chpts. to books and articles to profl. jours. Served with USNR, 1952-55. Fellow Am. Soc. Metals (chmn. aerospace activity com. 1971-76, judge materials application competition 1969, handbook com. 1978-83, chmn. handbook com. 1983, chmn. publs. coun. 1984). Republican. Home: 251 S Violet Ln Orange CA 92869-3740

KORC, MURRAY, endocrinologist; b. Gunsburg, Fed. Republic of Germany, Apr. 3, 1947; came to U.S., 1960; m. Antoinette Korc. BA, Bklyn. Coll., 1968; MD, Albany (N.Y.) Med. Coll., 1974. Intern, then resident Albany Med. Ctr. Hosp., 1974-77; endocrinology fellow U. Calif., San Francisco, 1977-79, from prof. to chief divsn. endocrinology, diabetes and metab Irvine, 1989—. Office: U Calif Div Endocrinology Med Sci I # C240 Irvine CA 92697-0001

KORG, JACOB, English literature educator; b. N.Y.C., Nov. 21, 1922; s. Reuben and Mary (Lehrman) K.; m. Cynthia Stewart, Jan. 21, 1952; 1 dau., Nora Francis. B.A., CCNY, 1943; M.A., Columbia U., 1947, Ph.D., 1952. Instr. English Bard Coll., 1947-49, CCNY, 1950-55; from asst. prof. to prof. U. Wash., Seattle, 1955-68, prof. English, 1970-91, prof. emeritus, 1991—; prof. English U. Md., 1968-70. Vis. prof. Nat. Taiwan U., 1960. Author: George Gissing, A Critical Biography, 1963, Dylan Thomas, 1965, Language in Modern Literature, 1979, rev. edit., 1992, Browning and Italy, 1983, Ritual and Experiment in Modern Poetry, 1995, also articles, revs.; editor: London in Dickens' Day, 1960, George Gissing's Commonplace Book, 1962, The Force of Few Words, 1966, Twentieth Century Views of Bleak House, 1968, Poetry of Robert Browning, 1971; co-editor: George Gissing on Fiction, 1978; mem. editl. bd. Victorian Poetry, 1979—, Nineteenth-Century Lit., 1983-95, Rivista di Studi Vittoriani. Served with AUS, 1943-46. Mem. MLA, Assn. Literary Scholars and Critics. Home: 6530 51st Ave NE Seattle WA 98115-7741 Office: Univ Wash Dept English Seattle WA 98195-0001 E-mail: korg@u.washington.edu

KORMAN, LEO, wholesale distribution executive; CFO Core-Mark Internat., San Francisco. Office: Core-Mark Internat 395 Oyster Point Blvd Ste 415 South San Francisco CA 94080

KORMONDY, EDWARD JOHN, retired university chancellor, biology educator; b. Beacon, N.Y., June 10, 1926; s. Anthony and Frances (Glover) K.; m. Peggy Virginia Hedrick, June 5, 1950 (div. 1989); children: Lynn Ellen, Eric Paul, Mark Hedrick. BA in Biology summa cum laude, Tusculum Coll., 1950, DSc (hon.), 1997; MS in Zoology, U. Mich., 1951, PhD in Zoology, 1955. Tchg. fellow U. Mich., 1952-55; instr. zoology, curator insects Mus. Zoology, 1955-57; asst. prof. Oberlin (Ohio) Coll., 1957-63, assoc. prof., 1963-67, prof., 1967-69, acting assoc. dean, 1966-67; dir. Commn. Undergrad. Edn. in Biol. Scis., Washington, 1968-72; dir. Office Biol. Edn., Am. Inst. Biol. Scis., Washington, 1968-71; mem. faculty Evergreen State Coll., Olympia, Wash., 1971-79, interim acting dean, 1972-73, v.p., provost, 1973-78; sr. profl. assoc., directorate sci. edn. NSF, 1979; provost, prof. biology U. So. Maine, Portland, 1979-82; v.p. acad. affairs, prof. biology Calif. State U., Los Angeles, 1982-86; sr. v.p., chancellor, prof. biology U. Hawaii, Hilo/West Oahu, 1986-93; pres. U. West L.A., 1995-97; chancellor emeritus U. Hawaii, Hilo, 2000—; special asst. to the pres. Pacific Oaks Coll., 2001—. Spl. asst. to pres. Pacific Oaks Coll. Author: Concepts of Ecology, 1969, 76, 83, 96, General Biology: The Integrity and Natural History of Organisms, 1977, Handbook of Contemporary World Developments in Ecology, 1981, International Handbook of Pollution Control, 1989, (textbook) Biology, 1984, 88, Fundamentals of Human Ecology, 1998, University of Hawaii-Hilo: A University in the Making, 2001; contbr. articles to profl. jours. Served with USN, 1944-46. U. Ga. postdoctoral fellow radiation ecology, 1963-64; vis. research fellow Center for Bioethics, Georgetown U., 1978-79; research grantee Nat. Acad. Scis., Am. Philos. Soc., NSF, Sigma Xi. Fellow AAAS; mem. Ecol. Soc. Am. (sec. 1976-78), Nat. Assn. Biology Tchrs. (pres. 1981), So. Calif. Acad. Scis. (bd. dirs. 1985-86, 93-97, v.p. 1995-96), Sigma Xi. E-mail: ekor@aol.com

KORN, LESTER BERNARD, business executive, diplomat; b. N.Y.C., Jan. 11, 1936; BS with honors, UCLA, 1959, MBA, 1960; postgrad., Harvard Bus. Sch., 1961. Mgmt. cons. Peat, Marwick, Mitchell & Co., L.A., 1961-66, ptnr., 1966-69; founder, CEO Korn/Ferry Internat., L.A., 1969-91, chmn. emeritus, 1991—; U.S. amb. and U.S. rep. Econ. and Social Coun. UN, 1987-88; chmn., founder Korn Tuttle Capital Group, Inc., 1991; alt. rep. 42d and 43d UN Gen. Assembly. Chmn., CEO Korn Tuttle Capital Group, Inc., 1991; bd. dirs. Continental Am. Properties, Coun. Am. Ambs., Music Ctr. Operating Co. L.A., Performing Arts Ctr., L.A., Tenet Healthcare Corp., RAND-Ctr. for Russian and Eurasian Studies; mem. U.S. Presdl. Del. to Observe Elections in Bosnia, 1996. Author: The Success Profile, 1989. Trustee UCLA Found.; bd. overseers and bd. visitors Anderson Grad. Sch. Mgmt., UCLA; trustee, founding mem. Dean's Coun. UCLA, Performing Arts Cen. L.A., 1999—; mem. adv. coun. Am. Heart Assn.; spl. advisor, del. UNESCO Inter-gov. Conf. on Edn. for Internat. Understanding, Coop., Peace, 1983; adv. bd. Women in Film Found., 1983-84; chmn. Commn. on Citizen Participation in Govt., State of Calif., 1979-82; bd. dirs. John Douglas French Found. for Alzheimer's Disease; mem. Republican Nat. Exec. Fin. Com., 1985, Pres.'s Commn. White House Fellowships, Republican Eagles; hon. chairperson 50th Am. Presdl. Inaugural, 1985; co-chmn. So. Calif. region NCCJ, mem. U.S. Presdl. Del. to observe elections in Bosnia, 1996. Recipient Alumni Profl. Achievement award UCLA, 1984, Superior Honor award U.S. Dept. State, 1988, Neil H. Jacoby Internat. award, 1990, Internat. Citizen of Yr. award Internat. Visitors Coun., 1991; Korn Convocation Hall at UCLA dedicated in his honor, 1995. Mem. AICPAs, Calif. Soc. CPAs, Am. Bus. Conf. (founding mem.), Coun. Am. Ambs., Prodrs. Guild of Am., Hillcrest Country Club, Rockefeller Ctr. Club. Office: Korn Tuttle Capital Grp 468 N Camden Dr Beverly Hills CA 90210-4507

KORNBERG, ARTHUR, biochemist, educator; b. N.Y.C., N.Y., Mar. 3, 1918; s. Joseph and Lena (Katz) K.; m. Sylvy R. Levy, Nov. 21, 1943 (dec. 1986); children: Roger, Thomas Bill, Kenneth Andrew; m. Charlene Walsh Levering, 1988 (dec. 1995); m. Carolyn Frey Dixon, 1998. BS, CCNY, 1937, LLD (hon.), 1960; MD, U. Rochester, 1941, DSc (hon.), 1962, U. Pa., U. Notre Dame, 1965, Washington U., 1968, Princeton U., 1970, Colby Coll., 1970; LHD (hon.), Yeshiva U., 1963; MD honoris causa, U. Barcelona, Spain, 1970. Intern in medicine Strong Meml. Hosp., Rochester, N.Y., 1941-42; commd. officer USPHS, 1942, advanced through grades to med. dir., 1951; mem. staff NIH, Bethesda, Md., 1942-52, nutrition sect., div. physiology, 1942-45; chief sect. enzymes and metabolism Nat. Inst. Arthritis and Metabolic Diseases, 1947-52; guest research worker depts. chemistry and pharmacology coll. medicine NYU, 1946; dept. biol. chemistry med. sch. Washington U., 1947; dept. plant biochemistry U. Calif., 1951; prof., head dept. microbiology, med. sch. Washington U., St. Louis, 1953-59; prof. biochemistry Stanford U. Sch. Medicine, 1959—, chmn. dept., 1959-69, prof. emeritus dept. biochemistry, 1988—. Mem. sci. adv. bd. Mass. Gen. Hosp., 1964-67; bd. govs. Weizmann Inst., Israel. Author: For the Love of Enzymes, 1989; contbr. sci. articles to profl. jours. Served lt. (j.g.), med. officer USCGR, 1942. Recipient Paul-Lewis award in enzyme chemistry, 1951; co-recipient Nobel prize in medicine, 1959; recipient Max Berg award prolonging human life, 1968, Sci. Achievement award AMA, 1968, Lucy Wortham James award James Ewing Soc., 1968, Borden award Am. Assn. Med. Colls., 1968, Nat. medal of sci., 1979, Gairdner Found. Internat. Awards, 1995; Arthur Kornberg Med. Rsch. Bldg. at U. Rochester named in his honor, 1999. Mem. Am. Soc. Biol. Chemists (pres. 1965), Am. Chem. Soc., Harvey Soc., Am. Acad. Arts and Scis., Royal Soc., Nat. Acad. Scis. (mem. council 1963-66), Am. Philos. Soc., Phi Beta Kappa, Sigma Xi, Alpha Omega Alpha. Office: Stanford U Sch of Med Dept Biochemistry Beckman Ctr Rm B400 Stanford CA 94305-5307 E-mail: akornberg@cmgm.stanford.edu

KORNBERG, ROGER DAVID, biochemist, structural biologist; b. St. Louis, Apr. 24, 1947; s. Arthur and Sylvy Ruth (Levy) K.; m. Yahli Deborah Lorch, Sept. 18, 1984; children: Guy Joseph, Maya Lorch, Gil Lorch.adr BS, Harvard U., 1967; PhD, Stanford U., 1972. Mem. sci. staff MRC Lab. Molecular Biology, Cambridge, Eng., 1974-75; asst. prof. biol. chemistry Harvard Med. Sch., Cambridge, Mass., 1976-77; prof. cell/structural biology Stanford (Calif.) U., 1978—, chmn. dept., 1984-92. Contbr. articles to profl. jours. Recipient Eli Lilly award, 1981, Passano award, 1982, Ciba-Drew award, 1990, Harvey prize Technion, 1997, Gairdner Internat. award, 2000, Welch award in chemistry, 2001. Mem. NAS. Office: Stanford U Dept Structural Biology Fairchild Bldg D-123 Stanford CA 94305-5400 E-mail: kornberg@stanford.edu

KORNFIELD, JULIA ANN, chemical engineering educator; b. Oakland, Calif., July 2, 1962; BA, Calif. Inst. Tech., 1983; MS, Stanford U., 1984, PhD in Chemical Engring., 1988. Rsch. asst. Calif. Inst. Tech., 1983-84, asst. prof. chemical engring., 1990—; rsch. asst. chem. engring. Stanford U., 1984-88, tchg. asst. appl. math., 1986, 87. NSF/NATO fellow chem. engring. Max-Planck Inst., 1989. Mem. AIChE, Am. Phys. Soc. (John H. Dillon medal Rsch. in Polymer Physics 1996), Am. Chem. Soc., Soc. Rheology. Office: Calif Inst Tech Dept Chem Engring 206-41 1201 E California Blvd Pasadena CA 91125-0001

KORNSTEIN, DON ROBERT, gaming industry executive; b. N.Y.C., Feb. 9, 1952; s. Sol and Faye (Manheim) K.; m. Leslie Gayle Harris, May 18, 1975; children: Eric Chad, Rachel Blair. BA, U. Pa., 1973; MBA, Columbia U., 1975. Rsch. analyst Citibank, NA, N.Y.C., 1975-77; sr. mng. dir. investment banking dept. Bear, Stearns & Co. Inc., N.Y.C., 1977-94; pres., CEO Jackpot Enterprises, Inc., Las Vegas, Nev., 1994—. Office: Jackpot Enterprises, Inc 1110 Palms Airport Dr Las Vegas NV 89119-3730

KORSCH, BARBARA M. pediatrician; b. Jena, Germany, Mar. 30, 1921; came to U.S., 1937; widowed; 1 child. BA, Smith Coll., 1941; MD, Johns Hopkins U., 1944. Cert. Am. Bd. Pediats. Asst. resident Bellevue Hosp., 1945, Mary Imogene Basset Hosp., 1946, N.Y. Hosp., 1947, fellow Inst. Child Devel., 1948-49; asst. pediats. Med. Coll. Cornell U., 1949-50, from instr. to assoc. prof., 1950-61; assoc. clin. prof. preventive medicine Sch. Medicine UCLA, 1961-64; assoc. prof. U. So. Calif., L.A., 1964-69, prof. pediats. Sch. Medicine, 1969—. George Armstrong lectr. Ambulatory Pediat. Assn., 1973; Katherine D. McCormick Disting. lectr. Stanford U., 1977; Kathy Newman Meml. lectr. Tulane U., 1987; asst. outpatient pediatrician N.Y. Hosps., 1949-50, asst. attending pediatrician, 1950-55, clin. dir. pediat. outpatient dept., 1950-61, assoc. attending pediatrician, 1955-61; pediat. cons. Dept. Health, N.Y., 1949-51, Hosp. Spl. Surgery, 1955-61, Gen. Pediat. Childrens Hosp., L.A., 1961-65, Med. Ctr., U. So. Calif., 1969-74; coord. pediat. rehab. program Nat. Found. Infantile Paralysis, 1953-61; pediat. dir. Obs. Clinic Children L.A., 1961-64; assoc. attending pediatrician Cedars Lebanon Hosp., 1961—; vis. prof. numerous U.S. and fgn. univs., 1973-89; hon. staff mem. dept. pediats. Cedars-Sinai Med. Ctr., 1976—. Author: Intelligent Patients Guide to the Doctor-Patient Relationship, 1997; contbr. articles to profl. jours. Chmn. coun. Bayer Inst. for Health Comm., 1989-98. Recipient Disting. Career award Ambulatory Pediat. Assn., 1991. Mem. Inst. Medicine-NAS, Am. Acad. Pediats. (C. Anderson Aldrich award 1988, Genesis award for med. ethics 1998), Am. Pediat. Soc., Soc. Behavioral Pediats. (pres. 1985), Soc. Pediat. Rsch., Sigma Xi. Office: Childrens Hosp Divsn Gen Pediats MB # 76 4650 W Sunset Blvd Los Angeles CA 90027-6062 E-mail: bkorsch@chla.usc.edu

KOSHALEK, RICHARD, former museum director, consultant; b. Wausau, Wis., Sept. 20, 1941; s. H. Martin and Ethel A. (Hochtritt) K.; m. Elizabeth J. Briar, July 1, 1967; 1 child, Anne Elizabeth. Student, U. Wis., 1960-61, MA, 1965-67; BA, U. Minn., 1965. Curator Walker Art Ctr., Mpls., 1967-72; asst. dir. NEA, Washington, 1972-74; dir. Ft. Worth Art Mus., 1974-76, Hudson River Mus., Westchester, N.Y., 1976-80, Mus. Contemporary Art, L.A., 1980-99, Pasadena Design Ctr. Mem. Pres.' Coun. on Arts, Yale U., New Haven, Conn., 1989-94; mem. internat. bd. Biennale di Venezia, Italy, 1992-93; mem. internat. adv. bd. Wexner Ctr., Ohio State U., Columbus, 1990—; mem. com. of assesors The Tate Gallery of Art, London; mem. internat. jury Philip Morris Art award, 1996; commr. Kwangju Biennale, 1997; mem. screening com. Osaka Triennale, 1997; selection com. Museo de Art Contemporaneo de Monterrey prize, 1997-98; panel chair Phila. Exhbns. Initiative, 1998, fed. adv. com. for internat. exhbns. Nat. Endowment for the Arts, 1997; cons. in field. Co-curator (exhibitions and books) Panza Collection, 1986, Ad Reinhardt, 1991, Arata Isozaki, 1991, Louis I. Kahn, 1992, Robert Irwin, 1993, At the End of the Century: One Hundred Years of Architecture, 1998, Richard Serra, 1998. Mem. Chase Manhattan Bank Art Com., N.Y.C., 1986—; chmn. architect selection Walt Disney Concert Hall, L.A., 1988-90; mem. adv. Neighborhood Revitalization Bd. for Pres. Clinton, Little Rock, Ark., 1993; bd. dirs. Am. Ctr. in Paris, 1993—. Recipient Parkinson Spirit of Urbanism award U. So. Calif. Archtl. Guild, 1996; NEA fellow, 1972, Durfee Found. fellow, 1992, Design fellow IBM, 1984. Mem. Am. Assn. Mus. Dirs.

KOSHLAND, DANIEL EDWARD, JR. biochemist, educator; b. N.Y.C., Mar. 30, 1920; s. Daniel Edward and Eleanor (Haas) K.; m. Marian Elliott, May 25, 1945 (dec. 1997); children: Ellen, Phyllis, James, Gail, Douglas; m. Yvonne Cyr, Aus. 27, 2000. BS, U. Calif., Berkeley, 1941; PhD, U. Chgo., 1949; PhD (hon.), Weizmann Inst. Sci., 1984; ScD (hon.), Carnegie Mellon U., 1985; LLD (hon.), Simon Fraser U., 1986; LHD (hon.), Mt. Sinai U.; LLD (hon.), U. Chgo., 1992; PhD (hon.), U. Mass., 1992, Ohio State U., 1995, Brandeis U., 2000. Chemist Shell Chem. Co., Martinez, 1941-42; research asso. Manhattan Dist. U. Chgo., 1942-44; group leader Oak Ridge Nat. Labs., 1944-46; postdoctoral fellow Harvard, 1949-51; staff Brookhaven Nat. Lab., Upton, N.Y., 1951-65; affiliate Rockefeller Inst., N.Y.C., 1958-65; prof. biochemistry U. Calif., Berkeley, 1965-97, prof. molecular biology, 1997—, chmn. dept., 1973-78. Fellow All Souls, Oxford U., 1972; Phi Beta Kappa lectr., 1976; John Edsall lectr. Harvard U., 1980, William H. Stein lectr. Rockefeller U., 1985; Robert Woodward vis. prof. Harvard U., 1986; G. N. Lewis lectr. U. Calif., Berkeley. Author: Bacterial Chemotaxis as a Model Behavioral System, 1980; mem. editl. bd. jours. Accounts Chem. Rsch., Jour. Chemistry, Jour. Biochemistry; editor jour. Procs. NAS, 1980-85; editor Sci. mag., 1985-95. Recipient T. Duckett Jones award Helen Hay Whitney Found., 1977, Nat. Medal of Sci. NSF, 1990, Merck award Am. Soc. Biochemistry and Molecular Biology, 1991; Guggenheim fellow, 1972; recipient Clark Kerr award U. Calif., 1994, Lasker Found. award, 1998. Mem. NAS, Am. Chem. Soc. (Edgar Fahs Smith award 1979, Pauling award 1979, Rosentiel award 1984, Waterford prize 1984, Sealong medal 2000), Am. Philos. Soc., Am. Soc. Biol. Chemists (pres.), Am. Acad. Arts and Scis. (coun.), Acad. Forum (chmn.), Japanese Biochem. Soc. (hon.), Royal Swedish Acad. Scis. (hon.), Alpha Omega Alpha (hon.). Home: 3991 Happy Valley Rd Lafayette CA 94549-2423 Office: U Calif Dept Molecular Cell Biology 329 Stanley Hl # 3206 Berkeley CA 94720-0001 E-mail: dek@uclinic4.berkeley.edu

KOSSEL, CLIFFORD GEORGE, retired philosophy educator, clergyman; b. Omro, Wis., Apr. 22, 1916; s. George C. and Sarah (Haigh) K. A.B., Gonzaga U., 1940, M.A., 1941; Ph.D., U. Toronto, 1945; Th.L., Alma Coll., 1949. Assoc. prof. Gonzaga U., Spokane, 1950-63, prof. philosophy, 1963-87, emeritus, 1988, chmn. dept. philosophy, 1966-69, dean Sch. Philosophy and Letters, 1958-71; sabbatical leave to Oxford, Eng. and Florence, Italy, 1969-70. Bd. editors Communio: Internat. Cath. Rev., 1974-93; contbr. profl. jours. Mem. Am. Cath. Philos. Assn., Jesuit Philos. Assn. (past pres.) Office: Gonzaga U Philosophy Dept Spokane WA 99258-0001

KOSTOULAS, IOANNIS GEORGIOU, physicist; b. Petra, Pierias, Greece, Sept. 12, 1936; came to the U.S., 1965, naturalized, 1984; s. Georgios Ioannou and Panagiota (Zarogiannis) K.; m. Katina Sioras Kay, June 23, 1979; 1 child, Alexandra. Diploma in physics, U. Thessoloniki, Greece, 1963; MA, U. Rochester, 1969, PhD, 1972; MS, U. Ala., 1977. Instr. U. Thessaloniki, 1963-65; tchg. asst. U. Ala., 1966-67, U. Rochester, 1967-68; guest jr. rsch. assoc. Brookhaven Nat. Lab., Upton, N.Y., 1968-72; rsch. physicist, lectr. UCLA, U. Calif.-San Diego, 1972-76; sr. rsch. assoc. Mich. State U., East Lansing, 1976-78, Fermi Nat. Accelerator Lab., Batavia, iLL., 1976-78; rsch. staff mem. MIT, Cambridge, 1978-80; sr. sys. engr., physicist Hughes Aircraft Co., El Segundo, Calif., 1980-86; sr. physisict electro-optics and space sensors Rockwell Internat. Corp., Downey, 1986-96, Boeing Corp., Downey, 1996-98; scientist Raytheon Sys. Co., El Segundo, Calif., 1998-2000; engring. specialist Aerojet, Azusa, 2000—. Contbr. articles to profl. jours. With Greek Army, 1961-63. Rsch. grantee U. Rochester, 1968-72. Mem. Am. Phys. Soc., N.Y. Acad. Scis., Internat. Soc. Optical Engring., Pan Macedonian Assn., Sigma Pi Sigma, Hellenic U. Club, Ahepa Lodge. Home: 2404 Marshallfield Ln # B Redondo Beach CA 90278-4406 Office: Aerojet Bldg 59 Dept 8510 1100 W Hollyvale St Azusa CA 91702-3305 E-mail: katinakay@earthlink.net

KOTCHIAN, SARAH BRUFF, municipal official; MEd, Harvard U., 1977; MPH, U. Wash., 1985. Dir. dept. environ. health City of Albuquerque, 1982—. Office: City of Albuquerque Environ Health Dept PO Box 1293 Albuquerque NM 87103-1293

KOTLER, RICHARD LEE, lawyer; b. L.A., Apr. 13, 1952; s. Allen S. Kotler and Marcella (Fromberg) Swartz; m. Cindy Jasik, Dec. 9, 1990; children: Kelsey Elizabeth, Charles Max. BA, Sonoma State Coll., 1976; JD, Southwestern U., 1979. Bar: Calif. 1980, U.S. Dist. Ct. (cen. dist.) Cal. 1980; cert. family law specialist. Sole practice, Newhall, Calif., 1980-83, 88—; sr. ptnr. Kotler & Hann, Newhall, 1983-88; pvt. practice Law Offices of Richard L. Kotler, Newhall, 1984-86. Judge pro temp Municipal Ct., 1981-84, Superior Ct., 1985—. Chmn. Santa Clarita Valley Battered Women's Assn., Newhall, 1983-87; bd. dirs. Santa Clarita Valley Hotline, Newhall, 1981-83. Recipient Commendation award L.A. County, 1983; named SCV Paintball champion. Mem. Santa Clarita Valley Bar Assn. (v.p. 1985—), L.A. Assn. Cert. Family Law Specialtists, Los Angeles Astronomy Soc., Newhall Astronomy Club. Avocations: astronomy, classic cars, collecting stamps, precious metals, trout fishing. Office: B Penthouse 23900 Lyons Ave Santa Clarita CA 91321-2440

KOURLIS, REBECCA LOVE, state supreme court justice; b. Colorado Springs, Colo., Nov. 11, 1952; d. John Arthur and Ann (Daniels) Love; m. Thomas Aristithis Kourlis, July 15, 1978; children: Stacy Ann, Katherine Love, Aristithis Thomas. BA with distinction in English, Stanford U., 1973, JD, 1976; LLD (hon.), U. Denver, 1997. Bar: Colo. 1976, D.C. 1979, U.S. Dist. Ct. Colo. 1976, U.S. Ct. Appeals (10th cir.) 1976, Colo. Supreme Ct., U.S. Ct. Appeals (D.C. cir.), U.S. Claims Ct., U.S. Supreme Ct. Assoc. Davis, Graham & Stubbs, Denver, 1976-78; sole practice Craig, Colo., 1978-87; judge 14th Jud. Dist. Ct., Craig, 1987-94; arbiter Jud. Arbiter Group, Inc., 1994-95; justice Colo. Supreme Ct., 1995—. Water judge divsn. 6, 1987-94; lectr. to profl. groups. Contbr. articles to profl. jours. Chmn. Moffat County Arts and Humanities, Craig, 1979; mem. Colo. Commn. on Higher Edn., Denver, 1980-81; mem. adv. bd. Colo. Divsn. Youth Svcs., 1988-91; mem. com. civil jury instructions, 1990-95, standing com. gender & justice, 1994-97, chair jud. adv. coun., 1997—, chair com. on jury reform, 1996—; co-chair com. on atty. grievance reform, 1997—; mem. long range planning com. Moffat County Sch., 1990; bd. visitors Stanford U., 1989-94, Law Sch. U. Denver, 1997—; bd. trustees Kent Denver Sch., 1996—. Named N.W. Colo. Daily Press Woman of Yr., 1993; recipient Trailblazer award AAUW, 1998, Mary Lathrop award, 2001. Fellow Am. Bar Found., Colo. Bar Found.; mem. Am. Law Inst., Rocky Mountain Mineral Found., Colo. Bar Assn. (bd. govs. 1983-85, mineral law sect. bd. dirs. 1985, sr. v.p. 1987-88), Dist. Ct. Judges' Assn. (pres. 1993-94), N.W. Colo. Bar Assn. (Cmty. Svc. award 1993-94). Office: State Jud Bldg 2 E 14th Ave Denver CO 80203-2115

KOURLIS, THOMAS A. state commissioner; m. Rebecca Kourlis; 3 children. BS in Fin., U. Denver. Owner, operator cattle and sheep ranch, Craig, Colo., 1973—; commr. Colo. Dept. Agr., Lakewood, 1994-99. Mem. Colo. Sheep and Wool Bd.; mem. N.W. Coordinated Resource Mgmt. Steering Com.; mem. Colo. Rangeland Reform Working Group; a founder Habitat Partnership Program. Mem. Soc. Range Mgmt. (award for excellence in grazing mgmt.), Colo. Woolgrowers Assn. (pasat v.p.), Am. sheep Industry Assn. (past bd. dirs.). Office: Colo Dept Agr 5310 Nassau Cir E Englewood CO 80110-5142

KOUSSER, J(OSEPH) MORGAN, history educator; b. Lewisburg, Tenn., Oct. 7, 1943; s. Joseph Maximillian and Alice Holt (Morgan) K.; m. Sally Ann Ward, June 1, 1968; children: Rachel Meredith, Thaddeus Benjamin. AB, Princeton U., 1965; M.Phil., Yale U., 1968, PhD, 1971; MA, Oxford U., Eng., 1984. Instr. Calif. Inst. Tech., Pasadena, 1969-71, assoc. prof. Padadena, 1975-79, prof., 1979—. Vis. prof. U. Mich., Ann Arbor, 1980, Harvard U., Cambridge, Mass., 1981-82, Oxford U., 1984-85, Claremont Grad. Sch., 1993; expert witness Minority Voting Rights Cases; researcher. Author: Shaping of Southern Politics, 1974, Colorblind Injustice: Minority Voting Rights and the Undoing of the Second Reconstruction, 1999. Recipient Lillian Smith award So. Regional Coun., 1999, Ralph J. Bunche award Am. Polit. Sci. Assn., 2000; Guggenheim Found. fellow, 1984-85, Woodrow Wilson Ctr. fellow, 1984-85; grantee NEH, 1974, 82. Mem. Orgn. Am. Historians, Am. Hist. Assn., Social Scis. History Assn., So. Hist. Assn. Democrat. Avocation: running. Office: Calif Inst Tech 228-77 Caltech Pasadena CA 91125-0001 E-mail: kousser@hss.caltech.edu

KOVACEVICH, RICHARD M. bank executive; BA, Stanford U., 1965, MBA, 1967. Exec. v.p. Kenner div. Gen. Mills, Inc., Mpls., 1967-72; prin. Venture Capital, 1972-75; v.p. consumer services Norwest Corp., Mpls., from 1975, then sr. v.p. N.Y.C. banking group, then exec. v.p., mgr. N.Y.C. bank div., then exec. v.p.. mem. policy com., vice-chmn., chief operating officer banking group, from 1986, now pres., chief oper. officer, vice chmn., also dir., chmn., CEO, 1996—, now chmn., CEO; pres., CEO Wells Frargo & Co. (merged with Norwest Corp.), San Francisco, 1999—. Office: Wells Fargo & Co 420 Montgomery St San Francisco CA 94163-1205*

KOVACH, ROBERT LOUIS, geophysics educator; b. L.A., Feb. 15, 1934; s. Nicholas Arthur and Stefania Teresa (Rüssler) K.; m. Linda Elly Heyn, Dec. 23, 1960; children: Denise Lynn, Dianne Yvonne, John Robert, Robert John. Geophysical Engring Degree, Colo. Sch. Mines, 1955; MA, Columbia U., 1959; PhD, Calif. Inst. Tech., 1962. Registered geophysicist, Calif. Sr. scientist Jet Propulsion Lab., Pasadena, Calif., 1961-63; asst. prof. Calif. Inst. Tech., Pasadena, 1963-65, Stanford (Calif.) U., 1965-66, assoc. prof., 1966-70, prof. geophysics, 1970—. Prin. investigator Apollo Moon Seismic Expts., 1996-76; cons. DOE, 1996-97. Author: Earth's Fury, 1995, Conflict with the Earth, 1997. Lt. U.S. Army, 1956-58. Fellow John Simon Guggenheim Found., 1971; recipient Exceptional Sci. Achievement award NASA, 1973. Fellow Geol. Soc. Am.; mem. Am. Geophysical Union (pres. seismology sect. 1976-78), Can. Well Logging Soc., Seismol. Soc. Am., Soc. Exploration Geophysicists. Office: Dept Geophysics Stanford University Stanford CA 94305 E-mail: kov@pangea.stanford.edu

KOVACHY, EDWARD MIKLOS, JR. psychiatrist, consultant; b. Cleve., Dec. 3, 1946; s. Edward Miklos and Evelyn Amelia (Palenscar) K.; m. Susan Eileen Light, June 21, 1981; children: Timothy Light, Benjamin Light. BA, Harvard U., 1968, JD, MBA, Harvard U., 1972; MD, Case Western Reserve U., 1977. Diplomate Nat. Bd. Med. Examiners. Resident in psychiatry Stanford U. Med. Ctr., Stanford, Calif., 1977-81; pvt. practice psychiatry, mediation, exec. coaching Menlo Park, 1981—. Presenter ann. meeting Am. Psychol. Assn., 1998, Calif. Assn. Marriage and Family Therapists, 1999. Columnist The Peninsula Times Tribune, 1983-85. Trustee Mid-Peninsula H.S., Palo Alto, Calif., 1990-2001; mem. gift com. Harvard Coll. Class of 1968, 25th reunion chmn. participation, San Francisco, 1993, 30th reunion chmn. participation, West Coast, 1998, nat. co-chmn. participation, 1999—. Recipient Albert H. Gordon award Harvard U., 2000. Mem. Am. Psychiat. Assn. (presenter annual meetings 1984, 98), Physicians for Social Responsibility, Assn. Family and Conciliation Cts., No. Calif. Psychiat. Soc. Presbyterian. Avocations: personal activism, musical comedy, athletics. Office: 1187 University Dr Menlo Park CA 94025-4423

KOVACS, LASZLO, cinematographer; b. Hungary, May 14, 1933; came to U.S., 1957, naturalized, 1963; s. Imre and Julia K. M.A., Acad. Drama and Motion Picture Arts of Budapest, Hungary, 1956. Lectr. at univs., film schs. Dir. photography for numerous motion pictures including Hell's Angels on Wheels, 1967, A Man Called Dagger, 1968, Psych-Out, 1968, The Savage Seven, 1968, Single Room Furnished, 1968, Targets, 1968, That Cold Day in the Park, 1969, Easy Rider, 1969, Alex in Wonderland, 1970, Getting Straight, 1970, Five Easy Pieces, 1970, The Last Movie, 1971, The Marriage of a Young Stockbroker, 1971, The King of Marvin Gardens, 1972, Pocket Money, 1972, Slither, 1972, Steelyard Blues, 1972, What's Up Doc?, 1972, Huckleberry Finn, 1973, Paper Moon, 1973, A Reflection of Fear, 1973, Freebie and the Bean, 1974, For Pete's Sake, 1974, At Long Last Love, 1975, Shampoo, 1975, Harry and Walter Go to New York, 1976, Baby Blue Marine, 1976, Nickelodeon, 1976, New York, New York, 1977, The Last Waltz, 1978, Paradise Alley, 1978, F.I.S.T., 1978, Heart Beat, 1979, The Runner Stumbles, 1979, Butch and Sundance: The Early Days, 1979, Inside Moves, 1980, The Legend of the Lone Ranger, 1981, Frances, 1982, The Toy, 1982, Crackers, 1982,, Ghostbusters, 1983, Mask, 1985, Legal Eagles, 1986, Little Nikita, 1988, Say Anything, 1989, Shattered, 1991, Radio Flyer, 1992, Ruby Cairo, 1992, The Next Karate Kid, 1993, The Scout,, 1993, Free Willy 2, 1994, Copycat, 1994, Multiplicity, 1995, My Best Friends Wedding, 1996, Jack Frost, 1998, Return To Me, 2000, Miss Congeniality, 2000; freelance cinematographer for motion pictures and TV commls. Mem. Acad. Motion Picture Arts and Scis., Am. Soc. Cinematographers. Office: Mirisch Agency 1801 Century Park E Ste 1801 Los Angeles CA 90067-2320

KOVAL, DON O. electrical engineering educator; b. Pickle Crow, Ont., Can., Mar. 20, 1942; s. Peter and Katherine Koval. BE, U. Sask., Saskatoon, 1965, MSc, 1969, PhD, 1978. Distbn. subtransmission design engr. Sask. Power Corp., Regina, 1965-66; distbn. spl. studies engr. B.C. Hydro & Power Authority, Vancouver, 1967-79; prof. elec. engring. U. Alta., Edmonton, 1980—. IEEE IAS disting. lectr., 2000-01. IEEE IAS Disting. lectr., 2000-2001. Fellow IEEE (chmn. Gold Book 1991—, Ralph H. Lee prize paper 1991, IEEE Disting. Lectr. 2000-01), Am. Biog. Inst. (life, commemorative medal of honor 1991), Internat. Biog. Assn. (life); mem. Internat. Assn. Sci. and Tech. for Devel. (Zurich, bd. dirs. 1990—), Assn. Profl. Engrs. (B.C.), Assn. Profl. Engrs. and Geologists of Province Alta., Internat. Inst. for Advanced Studies in Systems Rsch. and Cybernetics (Baden-Baden, Fed. Republic Germany, bd. dirs. 1990—). Home: 155 Marion Dr Sherwood Park AB Canada T8A 2G9 Office: U Alta Dept Elec Engring Edmonton AB Canada T6G 2G7

KOVTYNOVICH, DAN, civil engineer; b. Eugene, Oreg., May 17, 1952; s. John and Elva Lano (Robie) K. BCE, Oreg. State U., 1975, BBA, 1976. Registered profl. engr., Calif., Oreg. V.p. Kovtynovich, Inc., Contractors and Engrs., Eugene, 1976-80, pres., chief exec. officer, 1980—. Apptd. to State of Oreg. Bldg. Codes and Structures Bd., 1996—. Fellow ASCE; mem. Am. Arbitration Assn. (arbitrator 1979—), N.W. China Coun., Navy League of U.S., Eugene Asian Coun. Republican. Avocations: flying, skiing, fishing, hunting. Office: Kovtynovich Inc PO Box 898 Lake Oswego OR 97034-0143

KOWALSKI, KAZIMIERZ, computer science educator, researcher; b. Turek, Poland, Nov. 7, 1946; came to U.S., 1986; naturalized, 1994; s. Waclaw and Helena (Wisniewska) K.; m. Eugenia Zajaczkowska, Aug. 5, 1972. MSc, Wroclaw (Poland) U. Tech., 1970, PhD, 1974. Asst. prof. Wroclaw U. Tech., 1970-76, assoc. prof., 1976-86, Pan Am. U., Edinburg, Tex., 1987-88; prof. computer sci. Calif. State U.-Dominguez Hills, Carson, 1988—, chmn. computer sci. dept., 1998—. Lectr. U. Basrah, Iraq, 1981-85; cons. XXCal, Inc., L.A., 1987-91; conf. presenter in field; rsch. fellow Power Inst. Moscow, USSR, 1978; info. sys. tng. UNESCO, Paris, 1978; cons. Tex. Instruments, Inc., 1999—. Co-author: Principles of Computer Science, 1975, Organization and Programming of Computers, 1976; also articles. Recipient Bronze Merit Cross, Govt. of Poland, 1980, Knights' Cross of the Order of Merit Republic of Poland, 1997. Mem. IEEE Computer Soc., Assn. for Computing Machinery, Assn. for Advancement of Computing in Edn., Am. Assn. for Artificial Intelligence, Mensa, Sigma Xi. Avocations: travel, puzzles. Home: 3836 Weston Pl Long Beach CA 90807-3317 Office: Calif State U 1000 E Victoria St Carson CA 90747-0001 E-mail: kowalski@csudh.edu

KOZINSKI, ALEX, federal judge; b. Bucharest, Romania, July 23, 1950; came to U.S., 1962; s. Moses and Sabine (Zapler) K.; m. Marcy J. Tiffany, July 9, 1977; children: Yale Tiffany, Wyatt Tiffany, Clayton Tiffany. AB in Econs. cum laude, UCLA, 1972, JD, 1975. Bar: Calif. 1975, D.C., 1978. Law clk. to Hon. Anthony M. Kennedy U.S. Ct. Appeals (9th cir.), 1975-76; law clk. to Chief Justice Warren E. Burger U.S. Supreme Ct.,

1976-77; assoc. Covington & Burling, Washington, 1979-81; asst. counsel Office of Counsel to Pres., White House, Washington, 1981; spl. counsel Merit Systems Protection Bd., Washington, 1981-82; chief judge U.S. Claims Ct., Washington, 1982-85; judge U.S. Ct. Appeals (9th cir.), 1985—. Lectr. law U. So. Calif., 1992. Office: US Ct Appeals 125 S Grand Ave Ste 200 Pasadena CA 91105*

KOZIOL, CHRISTOPHER J. communications executive; Grad., U. Ariz., Harvard Bus. Sch. Former pres. Pinacor; exec. v.p. sales MicroAge Technology Svcs., Inc., Tempe, Ariz., 1985-99, pres., 1999—. Office: MicroAge Tech Svcs 2400 S MicroAge Way Tempe AZ 85282-1890

KOZLOFF, BENETT, food products executive; CEO Coast to Coast Seafood, Inc. Office: Coast To Coast Inc 10613 NE 38th Pl Kirkland WA 98033-7927

KOZLOFF, LLOYD M. university dean, educator, scientist; b. Chgo., Oct. 15, 1923; s. Joseph and Rose (Hollobow) K.; m. Judith Bonnie Friedman, June 16, 1947; children— James, Daniel, Joseph, Sarah B.S., U. Chgo., 1943, Ph.D., 1948. Asst., then assoc. prof. biochemistry U. Chgo., 1949-61, prof., 1961-64; prof. microbiology U. Colo., Denver, 1964-80, chmn. dept. microbiology, 1966-76, assoc. dean, prof., 1976-80; dean, prof. U. Calif., San Francisco, 1981-91, prof., dean emeritus, 1991—. Career investigator USPHS, U. Chgo., 1962 Founding editor Jour. Virology, 1966-76; contbr. articles to profl. jours., chpts. to books. Chmn. bd. dirs. Proctor Fund., 1981-91; v.p. San Francisco Alliance for Mental Illness, 1993-96; pres. emeritus U. Calif. San Francisco Faculty Assn., 1996-2000. With USN, 1944-46. Commonwealth Fund fellow, 1953, Lederle Found. fellow, 1954 Fellow AAAS, Am. Acad. Microbiol. (hon.); mem. Am. Soc. Biol. Chemistry, Am. Soc. Microbiology (head virology sect. 1974-76), Am. Chem. Soc., N.Y. Acad. Sci. Home: 43000 Lyndon Ave Fort Bragg CA 95437 Office: U Calif Grad Divsn San Francisco CA 94114-2732

KOZOLCHYK, BORIS, law educator, consultant; b. Havana, Cuba, Cuba, Dec. 6, 1934; came to U.S., 1956; s. Abram and Chana (Brewda) D.; m. Elaine Billie Herman, Mar. 5, 1967; children: Abbie Simcha, Raphael Adam, Shaun Marcie. DCL, U. Havana, 1956; Diplome, Faculte Internat. de Droit, Luxembourg, 1958; LLB, U. Miami, 1959; LLM, U. Mich., 1960, SJD, 1966. Teaching asst. Sch. of Law U. Miami, Fla., 1957-59; asst. prof. law Sch. of Law So. Meth. U., Dallas, 1960-64; resident cons. The Rand Corp., Santa Monica, Calif., 1964-67; dir. Law Reform Project USAID, San Jose, Costa Rica, 1967-69; prof. law Coll. of Law U. Ariz., 1969—. Teaching asst. Faculte Internat. de Droit Campare, 1958; vis. prof. law Nat. U. of Mex., 1961; vis. exch. prof. law Nat. U. of Chile, Santiago, 1962; guest lectr. Latin Am. Law seminar Stanford (Calif.) U., 1964; guest lectr. extension grad. seminar on Latin Am. law UCLA, 1965; Bailey vis. prof., Tucker lectr. La. State U., 1979; vis. prof. U. Aix en Provence, France, 1985; cons. on legal system U.S. Agy. Internat. Devel., 1974-77; legal cons. Overseas Pvt. Investment Corp., 1974; cons. uniformity of comml. laws Orgn. of Am. States and U.S. State Dept., 1974-77; expert witness on banking and comml. law and custom issues; advisor Libr. Congress Law div.; Joseph Bernfeld Meml. lectr. L.A. Bankruptcy Forum, 1989; magisterial lectr. Nat. U. Mex. Sch. Law, 1989; advisor Project Lao, 1991; lectr. in field. Author of books; bd. mem. Am. Jour. of Comparative Law; mem. editorial bd. Internat. Banking Law Jour.; founder, faculty advisor Ariz. Jour. of Internat. and Comparative Law, 1982-86; reporter Ency. Comparative Law, 1989; contbr. articles to profl. jours. and publs. Selected Nat. U. Mex. rep. First Mexican congress Comml. Law, 1974; pres. Ariz. Friends of Music, 1975-76; hon. chmn. community rels. com. Jewish Fedn. So. Ariz.; mem. adv. com. Ariz.-Mex. Commn. Govs.; legal advisor Ariz.-Mex. Banking com.; del U.S. Coun. on Internat. Banking to ICC; adv. mem. U.S. del. to UNCITRAL Internal. Contract Law, 1989-95; dir., pres., bd. dirs. Nat. Law Ctr. for InterAm. Free Trade, 1992—. NSF rsch. grantee, 1973-75; recipient Extraordinary Teaching and Rsch. Merit award Coll. Law, U. Costa Rica, 1969, Community Svc. award Tucson Jewish Community Coun., 1979, Man of Yr. award, 1982, Commendation award U.S. Dept. Justice, 1979, Disting. Svc. award Law Coll. Alumni Assn., 1990, Commendation award U.S. Dept. State, 1990; named to Hall of Fame of Profs. of Comml. Law, Nat. U., Mex., 1987; named One of Most Influential Hispanics, Hispanic Bus. Mag., 1991, Man of Yr., Hispanic Profl. Sch. Com., 1995, others. Mem. ABA (task force for the revision of UCC article 5), State of Ariz. Bar (Honoree at 100 Women and Minority Lawyers Dinner), Inter-ABA (co-chmn. comml. law and procedure sec. 1973-78, Best Book award 1973), Am. Soc. of Internat. Law, Internat. Acad. Comml. and Comsumer Law (pres. 1988-90), Am. Acad. Fgn. Law (founding), Am. Law Inst. (consultative com. to UCC articles 3, 4, 4a and 5), Nat. Mexican Notarial Bar Assn. (hon. life 1982), Internat. Acad. Comml. and Consumer Law (elected pres. 1988), Sonora Bar Assn. (1st Disting. Svc. award 1989). Home: 7401 N Skyline Dr Tucson AZ 85718-1166 Office: U Ariz Coll Of Law Tucson AZ 85721-0001 E-mail: b.kozolchyk@worldnet.att.net

KRAEMER, KENNETH LEO, architect, urban planner, educator; b. Plain, Wis., Oct. 29, 1936; s. Leo Adam and Lucy Rose (Bauer) K.; m. Norine Florence, June 13, 1959; children: Kurt Randall, Kim Rene. BArch, U. Notre Dame, 1959; MS in City and Regional Planning, U. So. Calif., 1964, M of Pub. Adminstrn., 1965, PhD, 1967. From instr. to asst. prof. U. So. Calif., Los Angeles, 1965-67; asst. prof. U. Calif., Irvine, 1967-71, assoc. prof., 1971-78, prof., 1978—, dir. Pub. Policy Research Orgn., 1974-92, dir. Ctr. for Rsch. on Info. Tech. and Orgns., 1992—. Cons. Office of Tech. Assessment, Washington, 1980, 84-85; pres. Irvine Research Corp., 1978—. Author: Management of Information Systems, 1980, Computers and Politics, 1982, Dynamics of Computing, 1983, People and Computers, 1985, Modeling as Negotiating, 1986, Data Wars, 1987, Wired Cities, 1987, Managing Information Systems, 1989, Asia's Computer Challenge, 1998. Mem. Blue Ribbon Data Processing Com., Orange County, Calif., 1973, 79-80, Telecomm. Adv. Bd., Sacramento, 1987-92. Mem. Am. Soc. for Pub. Adminstrn. (Disting. Research award 1985), Internat. Conf. on Info. Systems, Am. Planning Assn., Assn. for Computing Machinery. Democrat. Roman Catholic. Club: Notre Dame. Office: U Calif Ctr Rsch Info Tech & Orgns Berkley Pl N Ste 3200 Irvine CA 92697-0001 E-mail: kkraemer@uci.edu

KRAFT, DONALD BOWMAN, advertising agency executive; b. Seattle, Mar. 20, 1927; s. Warren E. and Beulah (Bowman) K.; m. Mary Jo Erickson, Dec. 20, 1973; children: Daniel, Karen Kraft VanderHoek, Berkeley, Erika. BA, U. Wash., 1948. Pres. Kraft Advt., Seattle, 1948-54; v.p. Honig Cooper, Seattle, 1954-59; pres., chief exec. officer Kraft Smith Advt., Seattle, 1959-84, Evans, Kraft Advt., Seattle, 1984-87; chmn. emeritus EvansGroup, Publics, Seattle, 1998—. Chmn. Evans Group, Inc., Salt Lake City, 1989—. Bd. dirs. KCTS Assn., Public TV, Seattle, 1982-90. Served with USN, 1945-46. Recipient Man and Boy award Boys Club Am., 1960; named Young Man of Yr., Seattle Jaycees, 1962 Mem. Am. Assn. Advt. Agys. (chmn. we. region 1962-64, nat. sec.-treas. 1970-71, mem. nat. govt. relations com. 1983-86), Affiliated Advt. Agys. Internat. (internat. pres. 1967-68, Albert Emery Mgmt. Excellence award 1984, 92), Young Pres.'s Orgn Alumni (chmn. Pacific NW chpt. 1980-81), Greater Seattle C. of C. (bd. dirs.). Republican. Methodist. Clubs: Wash. Athletic (pres. 1987-88), Rainier (pres. 1990-91), Seattle Tennis, Broadmoor Golf, Rotary Seattle (pres. 1973-74, Paul Harris fellow 1974). Home: 6530 NE Windermere Rd Seattle WA 98105-2058 Office: Evans Group Inc 424 2nd [illegible]

KRAFT, GEORGE HOWARD, physician, educator; b. Columbus, Ohio, Sept. 27, 1936; s. Glen Homer and Helen Winner (Howard) K.; children: Jonathan Ashbrook, Susannah Mary. AB, Harvard U., 1958; MD, Ohio State U., 1963, MS, 1967. Diplomate Am. Bd. Phys. Medicine and Rehab., Am. Bd. Electrodiagnostic Medicine. Intern U. Calif. Hosp., San Francisco, 1963-64, resident in phys. medicine and rehab., 1964-65, Ohio State U., Columbus, 1965-67; assoc. U. Pa. Med. Sch., Phila., 1968-69; asst. prof. U. Wash., Seattle, 1969-72, assoc. prof., 1972-76, prof., 1976—; chief of staff U. Wash. Med. Ctr., Seattle, 1993-95. Dir. electrodiagnostic medicine U. Wash. Hosp., 1987—, dir. Multiple Sclerosis Ctr., 1982—; co-dir. Muscular Dystrophy Clinic, 1974—; assoc. dir. rehab. medicine Overlake Hosp., Bellevue, Wash., 1989—; bd. dirs. Am. Bd. Electrodiagnostic Medicine, 1993-2000, chmn., 1996-2000. Co-author: Chronic Disease and Disability, 1994, Living with Multiple Sclerosis: A Wellness Approach, 2000; cons. editor: Phys. Medicine and Rehab. Clinics, 1990—, EEG and Clin. Neurophysiology, 1992-96; assoc. editor Jour. Neurol. Rehab. and Neurol. Repair, 1988-2000, Muscle and Nerve, 1998-2000; contbr. articles to profl. jours. Sci. peer rev. com. C Nat. Multiple Sclerosis Soc., N.Y.C., 1990-96, chmn., 1993-96, med. adv. bd., 1991—; bd. sponsors Wash. Physicians for Social Responsibility, Seattle, 1986—. Rsch. grantee Rehab. Svcs. Adminstrn., 1976-81, Nat. Inst. Handicapped Rsch., 1984-88, Nat. Multiple Sclerosis Soc., 1990-92, 94-95, Nat. Inst. Disability and REhab. Rsch., 1998—. Fellow Am. Acad. Phys. Medicine and Rehab. (pres. 1984-85, Zeiter award 1991); mem. Am. Assn. Electrodiagnostic Medicine (pres. 1982-83), Assn. Acad. Physiatrists (pres. 1980-81), Am. Acad. Clin. Neurophysiology (pres. 1995-97), Am. Acad. Neurology, Internat. Rehab. Medicine Assn., Alpha Omega Alpha. Episcopalian. E-mail: ghkraft@uwashington.edu

KRAFT, RICHARD LEE, lawyer; b. Lassa, Nigeria, Oct. 14, 1958; m. Tanya Kraft, July 14, 1984; children: Devin, Kelsey. BA in Fgn. Svc., Baylor U., 1980, JD, 1982. Bar: N.Mex. 1982, U.S. Dist. Ct. N.Mex., U.S. Ct. Appeals, U.S. Supreme Ct. Assoc. Sanders, Bruin & Baldock, Roswell, N.Mex., 1982-87, ptnr., 1987-98, Kraft & Stone, LLP, Roswell, 1998-2000; owner The Kraft Law Firm, 2000—. Vol. lawyer Ea. N.Mex. U. Roswell, 1984-98; bd. dirs. Roswell YMCA, 1983-87, Crimestopper, 1991-94; pres. Roswell Mens Ch. Basketball League; participant Roswell Mens Ch. Softball League; asst. chair legal div. United Way Drive, 1990. Recipient Outstanding Contribution award N.Mex. State Bar, 1987. Mem. ABA, N.Mex. Trial Lawyers Assn., N.Mex. Bar Assn. (bd. dirs. young lawyers div. 1983-91, pres. 1986-87, chmn. membership com., bar commr. 1986-87, 91—, pres. 1998-99, Outstanding Young Lawyer award 1990), Chaves County Bar Assn. (chair law day activities, chair ann. summer picnic com., rep. bench and bar com.), Roswell Legal Secs. Assn. (hon.), Roswell C. of C. (participant and pres. Leadership Roswell, exec. dir., bd. dirs. 1991-97), Sertoma (bd. dirs. Roswell club 1989-91). Baptist. Office: The Kraft Law Firm 400 N Pennsylvania Ave Ste 1250 Roswell NM 88201-4783

KRAFT, ROBERT PAUL, astronomer, educator; b. Seattle, June 16, 1927; s. Victor Paul and Viola Eunice (Ellis) K.; m. Rosalie Ann Reichmuth, Aug. 28, 1949; children: Kenneth, Kevin. B.S., U. Wash., 1947, M.S., 1949; Ph.D., U. Calif.-Berkeley, 1955; DSc (hon.), Ind. U., 1995. Postdoctoral fellow Mt. Wilson Obs., Carnegie Inst., Pasadena, Calif., 1955-56; asst. prof. astronomy Ind. U., Bloomington, 1956-58, Yerkes Obs., U. Chgo., Williams Bay, Wis., 1958-59; staff Hale Obs., Pasadena, 1960-67; prof., astronomer Lick Obs., U. Calif., Santa Cruz, 1967-92; astronomer, prof. emeritus, 1992—. Acting dir. Lick Obs., 1968-70, 71-73, dir., 1981-91; dir. U. Calif. Observatories, 1988-91; chmn. Fachbeirat, Max-Planck-Inst., Munich, Fed. Republic Germany, 1978-88; bd. dirs. Cara corp. (Keck Obs.), Pasadena, 1985-91; bd. dirs. AURA, 1989-92. Contbr. articles to profl. jours. Jila vis. fellow U. Colo., Nat. Bur. Stds., Boulder, 1970; Fairchild scholar Calif. Inst. Tech., Pasadena, 1980, Tinsley prof. U. Tex., 1991-92; Henry Norris Russell lectr. Am. Astron. Soc., 1995; recipient Disting. Alumnus award Coll. Arts and Scis., U. Wash., 1995. Mem. Nat. Acad. Sci., Am. Acad. of Arts and Scis., Am. Astron. Soc. (pres. 1974-76, Warner prize 1962, Russell prize lectr. 1995), Internat. Astron. Union (v.p. 1982-88, pres.-elect 1994-97, pres. 1997-2000), Astron. Soc. Pacific (bd. dirs. 1981-87), Royal Astron. Soc. (fgn. assoc.). Democrat. Unitarian Avocations: contract bridge, art appreciation, classical music, opera, eonology. Office: U Calif Lick Observatory Santa Cruz CA 95064 E-mail: kraft@ucolick.org

KRAFT, SCOTT COREY, correspondent; b. Kansas City, Mo., Mar. 31, 1955; s. Marvin Emanuel and Patricia (Kirk) K.; m. Elizabeth Brown, May 1, 1982; children: Kate, Kevin. BS, Kans. State U., 1977. Staff writer AP, Jefferson City, Mo., 1976-77, Kansas City, 1977-79, corr. Wichita, Kans., 1979-80, nat. writer N.Y.C., 1980-84; nat. corr. L.A. Times, Chgo., 1984-86, bur. chief Nairobi, Kenya, 1986-88, Johannesburg, South Africa, 1988-93, Paris, 1993-96, dep. fgn. editor, 1996-97, nat. editor, 1997—. Recipient Disting. Reporting in a Specialized Field award Soc. of the Silurians, 1982, Peter Lisagor award Headline Club Chgo., 1985, Feature Writing finalist Pulitzer Prize Bd., 1985, Sigma Delta Chi award, 1993. Office: LA Times Nat Editor Times Mirror Square Los Angeles CA 90053

KRAG, OLGA, interior designer; b. St. Louis, Nov. 27, 1937; d. Jovica Todor and Milka (Slijpecevic) Golubovic. AA, U. Mo., 1958; cert. interior design, UCLA, 1979. Interior designer William L. Pereira Assocs., L.A., 1977-80; aassoc. Reel/Grobman Assocs., L.A., 1980-81; project mgr. Kaneko/Laff Assocs., L.A., 1982, Stuart Laff Assocs., L.A., 1983-85; restaurateur The Edge, St. Lois, 1983-84; pvt. practice comml. interior design, L.A., 1981—. Mem. invitation and ticket com. Calif. Chamber Symphony Soc., 1980-81; vol. Westside Rep. Coun., Proposition 1, 1971; asst. inaugural presentation Mus. of Childhood, L.A., 1985. Recipient Carole Eichen design award U. Calif., 1979. Mem. Am. Soc. Interior Designers, Inst. Bus. Designers, Phi Chi Theta, Beta Sigma Phi. Republican. Serbian Orthodox. Home and Office: 700 Levering Ave Apt 10 Los Angeles CA 90024-2797

KRAICHNAN, ROBERT HARRY, theoretical physicist, consultant; b. Phila., Jan. 15, 1928; s. Robert Maxwell and Anna (Maximon) K.; m. Carol Gebhardt, May 22, 1954 (div. 1988); 1 child, John; m.Judy Ellen Moore, June 30, 1989. BS in Physics, MIT, 1947, PhD in Theoretical Physics, 1949. Mem., asst. to Albert Einstein Inst. Advanced Study, Princeton, N.J., 1949-50; mem. tech. staff Bell Telephone Labs., 1950-52; rsch. assoc. Columbia U., N.Y.C., 1952-56; rsch. assoc. Courant Inst. NYU, 1956-58, sr. rsch. scientist Courant Inst., 1958-62; pvt. practice physicist, 1962-80; pres., prin. Robert H. Kraichnan, Inc., Santa Fe, 1980—. Adj. assoc. prof. dept. grad. physicis NYU, 1956-57; assoc. in physics Woods Hole (Mass.) Oceanographic Inst., 1960-70; rsch. affiliate meteorology MIT, 1963—; contractor Office Naval Rsch., 1962-80, NASA, 1967-69; cons. Naval Rsch. Lab., 1957-59, Inst. for Space Studies, NASA, 1961-69, Inst. fro Def. Analyses, 1967-70, Los Alamos Nat. Lab., 1979—, Princeton U., 1987—. Contbr. over 100 articles to sci. jours. Recipient ADION medal Observatoire de Nice; grantee NSF, 1970—. Fellow AAAS, Am. Phys. Soc. (Otto Laporte award 1993, Lars Onsager Meml. prize 1997); mem. NAS. Avocations: mountain hiking, violin, carpentry.

KRALLINGER, JOSEPH CHARLES, entrepreneur, business advisor, author; b. Lancaster, Pa., May 29, 1931; s. Ferdinand and Mathilde (Meyer) K.; m. Hilde Eisenhauer, Oct. 1, 1955; children— Joanne, Diane, Robert BS in Econs. cum laude, Franklin and Marshall Coll., 1953. C.P.A. Auditor GAO, Denver, 1953; auditor Army Audit Agy., 1953-55; ptnr. Arthur Andersen & Co., Phila., 1955-76; v.p. strategic planning and acquisitions, chief fin. officer Berwind Corp., Phila., 1976-88; cons. Palm Desert, Calif., 1988—. Dir., bus. advisor and investor various indsl., health care, mining, oil and gas cos., 1976—; [illegible] in field. Author: An Auditor's Approach to Statistical Sampling, 5 vols., 1967-72, Strategic Planning Workbook, 1989, 2d edit., 1993, How to Acquire the Perfect Business for Your Company, 1991; Planeacion Estrategica Practica, 1991; Mergers and Acquisitions: Managing the Transactions, 1997, Chinese and Spanish edits., 2000; contbr. articles to profl. jours. Bd. dirs. alumni coun. Franklin and Marshall Coll., Lancaster, 1969-75; pres., tchr. religious edn. St. Genevieve Cath. Ch., Flourtown, Pa., 1971-76; bd. dirs. Whitemarsh Twp. Citizens Coun., Plymouth Meeting, Pa., 1972-75; hon. life mem., past chmn. bd. dirs. Phila. chpt. Am. Cancer Soc. Recipient Nat. Vol. award Am. Cancer Soc., 1985, Crusade award Am. Cancer Soc., 1985, Teaching award St. Genevieve Ch., 1985, Cert. Merit Inst. Mgmt. Accts., 1998. Mem. AICPA (statis. sampling com.), Pa. Inst. CPAs, Nat. Assn. Accts. (past pres. Phila. chpt.), Planning Forum (past pres. Phila. chpt.), Soc. Children's Book Writers and Illustrators, Ironwood Country Club (bd. dirs. 1991-93). Avocations: golf, racquet sports, writing, reading. Home and Office: 48-120 Alder Ln Palm Desert CA 92260-6652

KRAMER, DONOVAN MERSHON, SR. newspaper publisher; b. Galesburg, Ill., Oct. 24, 1925; s. Verle V. and Sybil (Mershon) K.; m. Ruth A. Heins, Apr. 3, 1949; children: Donovan M. Jr., Diana Sue, Kara J. Kramer Cooper, Eric H. BS in Journalism, Pub. Mgmt., U. Ill., 1948. Editor, publisher, ptnr. Fairbury (Ill.) Blade, 1948-63, Forrest (Ill.) News, 1953-63; ptnr. Gibson City (Ill.) Courier, 1952-63; pres., publisher, editor Casa Grande (Ariz.) Valley Newspapers, Inc., 1963—; mng. ptnr. White Mt. Pub. Co., Show Low, Ariz., 1978—. Wrote, edited numerous articles and newspaper stories. Many award-winners including Sweepstakes award in Ill. and Ariz. Mem., chmn. Econ. Planning and Devel. Bd. State of Ariz., Phoenix, 1976-81; mem. Ctrl. Ariz. Coll. Found. Bd.; pres. Indsl. Devel. Authority of Casa Grande, 1977—; founding pres. Greater Casa Grande Econ. Devel. Found., exec. bd. dirs., 1982-2001 (Lifetime Achievement award 1994); gov. apptd. bd. mem. Ariz. Dept. Transp., 1992-97, chmn., 1997; adv. bd. dept. journalism U. Ariz.; mem. Ctrl. Ariz. Coll. Found. Bd.; bd. mem. Ctrl. Ariz. Found. With USAAF, WWII, PTO. Recipient Econ. Devel. plaque City of Casa Grande, 1982. Mem. Ariz. Newspapers Assn. (pres. 1980, Master Editor-Pub. 1977, Hall of Fame, 1998), Cmty. Newspapers Ariz. (pres. 1970-71), Inland Newspapers Assn., Newspapers Assn. Am., Ctrl. Ariz. Project Assn., Nat. Newspapers Assn., Greater Casa Grande C. of C. (pres. 1981-82, Hall of Fame 1991), Soc. Profl. Journalists. Republican. Lutheran. Avocations: hiking, fishing, nature studies, travel, health awareness, econ. devel., military history.

KRAMER, EDWARD JOHN, materials science and engineering educator; b. Wilmington, Del., Aug. 5, 1939; s. Edward Noble and Irma (Nemetz) K.; m. Gail Allen Woodford, Aug. 24, 1963; children: Eric Woodford, Jeanne Noble. BChemE, Cornell U., 1962; PhD, Carnegie-Mellon U., 1967. Asst. prof. dept. materials sci. and engring. Cornell U., Ithaca, N.Y., 1967-72, assoc. prof., 1972-79, prof., 1979-88, Samuel B. Eckert prof. materials sci. and engring., 1988-97; prof. dept. materials & chem. engring. U. Calif., Santa Barbara, 1997—. Vis. scientist Argonne (Ill.) Nat. Lab., 1974-75; vis. prof. Akademie der Wissenschaften Inst. Metallphysik, Göttingen, Germany, 1979, Ecole Poly. Federale de Lausanne, Switzerland, 1982, Johannes Gutenberg U., Mainz, Germany, 1987-88. Contbr. over 300 articles to sci. jours. Recipient U.S. Sr. Scientist award Alexander von Humboldt Stiftung, 1987-88, Swinburne award Inst. Materials, U.K., 1996; NATO fellow, 1966-67, John Simon Guggenheim Found. fellow, N.Y.C., 1988. Fellow AAAS, Am. Phys. Soc. (High Polymer Physics prize 1985); mem. NAE, Materials Rsch. Soc., Am. Chem. Soc., Böhmische Phys. Soc. Avocation: masters swimming. Office: Univ Calif Materials Dept Engring II Santa Barbara CA 93106

KRAMER, GORDON, mechanical engineer; b. Bklyn., Aug. 1937; s. Joseph and Etta (Grossberg) K.; m. Ruth Ellen Harter, Mar. 5, 1967 (div. June 1986); children: Samuel Maurice, Leah Marie; m. Eve Burstein, Dec. 17, 1988. BS, Cooper Union, 1959; MS, Calif. Inst. Tech., 1960. With Hughes Aircraft Co., Malibu, Calif., 1959-63; sr. scientist Avco Corp., Norman, Okla., 1963-64; asst. divsn. head Batelle Meml. Inst., Columbus, Ohio, 1964-67; sr. scientist Aerojet Electrosystems, Azusa, Calif., 1967-75; chief engr. Beckman Instrument Co., Fullerton, 1975-82; prin. scientist McDonnell Douglas Microelectronics Co., 1982-83, Kramer and Assocs., 1983-85; program mgr. Hughes Aircraft Co., 1985-96, ret., 1996; personal fin. advisor Am. Express, 1999—. Cons. Korea Inst. Tech. NSF fellow, 1959-60. Mem. IEEE. Democrat. Jewish. Home: 153 Lake Shore Dr Rancho Mirage CA 92270-4055 E-mail: gordeve@aol.com, gordon.x.kramer@aexp.com

KRAMER, GORDON EDWARD, manufacturing executive; b. San Mateo, Calif., June 22, 1946; s. Roy Charles and Bernice Jeanne (Rones) K.; m. Christina Hodges, Feb. 14, 1970; children: Roy Charles, Charlena. BS in Aero. Engring., San Jose State Coll., 1970. Purchasing agt. Am. Racing Equipment, Brisbane, Calif., 1970-71, asst. to v.p. mktg., 1971-72; founder, pres. Safety Direct, Inc., Sparks, Nev., 1972—. Manufacturing executive; b. San Mateo, Calif., June 22, 1946; s. Roy Charles and Bernice Jeanne (Rones) K.; BS in Aero. Engring., San Jose State Coll., 1970; m. Christina Hodges, Feb. 14, 1970; children: Roy Charles, Charlena. Purchasing agent Am. Racing Equipment, Brisbane, Calif., 1970-71, asst. to v.p. mktg., 1971-72; founder, pres. Safety Direct Inc., hearing protection equipment, Sparks, Nev., 1972—; dir. Hodges Transp., Condor Inc.; mem. adv. bd. to pres. Truckee Meadows Community Coll., 1991—. Named Nev. Small Businessperson of Yr., Nev. Small Bus. Adminstrn., 1987, Bus. Person of Yr. Sparks Community C. of C., 1987. Mem. Am. Soc. Safety Engrs., Safety Equipment Distributors Assn., Indsl. Safety Equipment Assn., Nat. Assn. Sporting Goods Wholesalers, Nat. Sporting Goods Assn., Nev. State Amature Trapshooting Assn. (dir. 1978-79), Pacific Internat. Trapshooting Assn. (Nev. pres. 1979-80, 80-81), Nev. Mfrs. Assn. (dir. 1992—), Advanced Soccer Club (pres.1985-86). Republican. Methodist. Rotary Club (pres. Spark Club 1988-89). Named Nev. Small Businessperson of Yr., Nev. Small Bus. Adminstrn., 1987, Bus. Person of Yr., Sparks Cmty. C. of C., 1987. Mem. Am. Soc. Safety Engrs., Safety Equipment Distributors Assn., Indsl. Safety Equipment Assn., Nat. Assn. Sporting Goods Wholesalers, Nat. Sporting Goods Assn., Nev. State Amature Trapshooting Assn. (dir. 1978-79), Pacific Internat. Trapshooting Assn. (pres. Nev. chpt. 1979-81), Nev. Mfrs. Assn. (dir. 1992—), Advanced Soccer Club (pres. 1985-86), Rotary (pres. Spark Club 1988-89). Republican. Methodist. Office: Safety Direct Inc 56 Coney Island Dr Sparks NV 89431-6335 E-mail: gordonkramer@worldnet.att.net

KRAMER, LAWRENCE STEPHEN, journalist; b. Hackensack, N.J., Apr. 24, 1950; s. Abraham and Ann Eve (Glasser) K.; m. Myla F. Lerner, Sept. 3, 1978; children: Matthew Lerner, Erika. B.S. in Journalism, Syracuse U., 1972; M.B.A., Harvard U., 1974. Reporter San Francisco Examiner, 1974-77; reporter Washington Post, 1977-80; exec. editor Trenton Times, N.J., 1980-82; asst. to exec. editor Washington Post, 1982, asst. mng. editor, 1982-86; exec. editor San Francisco Examiner, 1986-91; pres. Datasport Inc., San Mateo, Calif., 1991-94; v.p. Data Broadcasting Corp., San Mateo, 1994-97; pres., CEO CBS.Marketwatch.com., San [illegible] 1971-72, Gerald Loeb award 1977. Mem. Soc. Profl. Journalists Home: 8 Auburn Ct Belvedere Tiburon CA 94920-1349

KRAMER, LORNE C. protective services official; BA in Pub. Mgmt., U. Redlands, 1977; MPA with honors, U. So. Calif., 1979; Advanced Exec. Cert., Calif. Law Enforcement Coll., 1987; grad., Nat. Exec. Inst., 1993. Comdr. L.A. Police Dept., 1965-91, chief police Colorado Springs (Colo.) Police Dept., 1991—. Cons. instr. drugs and gangs Nat. Inst. Justice Office

Juvenile Justice U.S. Dept. Justice. Active Colo. State DARE Adv. Bd.; bd. dirs. Ctr. Prevention Domestic Violence, Pikes Peak Mental Health. Mem. Colo. Assn. Chiefs Police (bd. dirs., major cities rep.), Internat. Assn. Chiefs Police (juvenile justice com.), Police Exec. Rsch. Forum. Office: PO Box 2169 Colorado Springs CO 80901-2169

KRAMER, REMI THOMAS, film director; b. L.A., Mar. 7, 1935; s. Justina Magdelene Kramer; m. Agnes Marie Gallagher, Feb. 1, 1969; children: Matthew, Christiana, Timothy, Ian, Vincent, Brigitte, Danika. BA, UCLA, 1956; MA, Calif. State U., L.A., 1963. Art dir. Doyle, Dane, Bernbach Advt., L.A., 1965-66, N.W. Ayer Advt., N.Y.C., 1966-67; dir. John Urie & Assocs. Haboush Co., Hollywood, Calif., 1967-69, Columbia-Screen Gems, Hollywood, 1969-76, 79-81, 1st Asian Films, Hollywood and Manila, 1976-77, Peterson Co., Hollywood, 1977-79; freelance film dir. Hollywood, 1981-85; founder Oz Enterprises, Inc., Sandpoint, Idaho, 1985—. Author: The Legend of Lonestar Bear Series, 1988—, How Lonestar Got His Name, 1988, Soaring with Eagles, 1989, The Mystery of the Walking Cactus, 1990 (The 100 Best Products of the Yr. 1990, Best Illustration: Creativity 90, 1990); author, illustrator: Klondike Ike, 1992; writer, dir. film High Velocity, 1976; patentee children's pacifier toy; designer Lonestar Bear plush animal collection. With U.S. Army, 1958-60. Recipient Clio award, 1971, 1st Internat. Broadcast awards, 1973, Cine Golden Eagle award, 1976, The Golden Teddy award, 1990, 91. Mem. Dirs. Guild Am., Writers Guild Am. Roman Catholic. Avocations: oil painting, inventing. Office: PO Box 637 Sandpoint ID 83864-0637

KRAMER, RICHARD JAY, gastroenterologist; b. Morristown, N.J., Mar. 31, 1947; s. Bernard and Estelle (Mishkin) K.; m. Leslie Fay Davis, June 28, 1970; children: Bryan Jeffrey, Erik Seth Davis. Student, UCLA, 1965-68; MD, U. Calif., Irvine, 1972. Diplomate Am. Bd. Internat. Med., Am. Bd. Gastroenterology. Intern Los Angeles County Harbor Gen. Hosp., Torrance, Calif., 1972-73; resident Santa Clara Valley Med. Ctr., San Jose, 1973-76; fellow gastroent. Stanford (Calif.) U. Hosp., 1976-78; pvt. practice, San Jose, 1978—. Clin. assoc. prof. of medicine Stanford (Calif.) U., 1984—; chmn. med. dept. Good Samaritan Hosp., San Jose, 1988-90. Pres. Jewish Family Service Bd., San Jose, 1974. Recipient Regents scholarship U. Calif., 1965, 68, Mosby Book award, Mosby Books, Inc., Irvine, Calif., 1972. Mem. Am. Coll. Physicians, Calif. Med. Soc., Santa Clara County Med. Soc., No. Calif. Soc. Clin. Gastroenterologists, Internat. Brotherhood Magicians, Mystic 13 (pres. 1986-87, San Jose), Masons, Alpha Omega Alpha. Democrat. Jewish. Avocations: magic, piano, tennis, traveling. Office: 2505 Samaritan Dr Ste 401 San Jose CA 95124-4013

KRAMER, STEVEN G. ophthalmologist, educator; b. Chgo., Feb. 28, 1941; s. Paul and Maria Kramer; m. Anne Crystal Kramer, Dec. 26, 1961 (div.); children: Janice Lynn, Kenneth David; m. Bernadette E. Coatar, June 30, 1974 (div.); children: Daniel Steven, Susan Mary; m. Susan E. Garrett, Jan. 17, 1997. BA in Biology, U. Chgo., 1967; MD, Case Western Res. U., 1965; PhD, U. Chgo., 1971. Cert. assoc. examiner Am. Bd. Ophthalmology; lic. ophthalmologist, Calif., Wash. Instr. ophthalmology U. Chgo., 1968-71; chief of ophthalmology Madigan Army Med. Ctr., Tacoma, 1971-73; chief of ophathlmology VA Med. Ctr., San Francisco, 1973-75; prof. ophthalmology, chmn. U. Calif., San Francisco, 1975—, dir. Beckman Vision Ctr., 1988—. Mem. various coms. VA Hosp., San Francisco, 1973—; mem. exec. med. bd. sch. medicine U. Calif., 1975—, mem./chmn. various coms., 1975—, mem. clin. dept. chmn. group, 1975—, mem. governing bd. continuing med. edn. program, 1984-85, mem. clin. rev. working group, 1985-86, pres.-elect med. staff, 1985, pres., 1986-88, mem. chancellor's governance group, 1986—, mem. adv. group devel. spine svcs., 1992—; v.p. That Man May See, Inc., 1975—, bd. trustees, 1975—, campaign cabinet mem. for Vision Rsch. Ctr., 1983—; sec., bd. govs. Francis Proctor Found. for Rsch. in Opthalmology, 1975—; mem. Rsch. to Prevent Blindness, Inc., N.Y., 1976—, ad hoc adv. com., 1976-77; NIH mem. vision rsch. program com. NEI, 1978-82, chmn., 1980-82; site visit chmn. U. Wash., Seattle, 1979, Mass. Eye and Ear Infirmary, Boston, 1980, dept. neurobiology Harvard Med. Sch., Boston, 1980; mem. joint program and planning bd. sch. medicine U. Calif./Mt. Zion, 1985-88; mem. courtesy staff San Francisco Gen. Hosp.; lectr. in field. Editor, editl. bd. therapeutics rev. sect. Survey of Ophthalmology, 1977-84, diagnostic and surg. techniques sect., 1984—; sci. referee Am. Jour. Ophthalmology, 1967-81, editl. bd., 1981—; editl. bd. Ophthalmic Soc., sci. referee Life Scis., editor CMA Ophthalmology Epitomes, Western Jour. Medicine, 1976-77; med. adv. bd. Nat. Soc. to Prevent Blindness, 1979—; editor sect. cornea and sclera Yearbook of Ophthalmology, 1982. Mem. legis. com. for State of Calif., 1977; bd. dirs. Found. for Glaucoma Rsch., 1980—. Maj. U.S. Army, 1971-73. USPHS Spl. fellow in ophthalmologic rsch., 1970; VA Hosp. Rsch. Program grantee; NIH grantee, That Man May See grantee. Mem. AMA, ACS, Am. Acad. Ophthalmology, Am. Intra-Ocular Implant Soc., Assn. for Rsch. in Vision and Ophthalmology, Pacific Coast Oto-Ophthalmology Soc., Frederick C. Cordes Eye Soc., Calif. Med. Assn. (sci. adv. panel 1974—, adv. panel on ophthalmology subcom. for accreditation 1976-77, 78), Calif. Assn. Ophthalmology (adv. cons.), Assn. Univ. Profs. Ophthalmology (chmn. resident placement svc. com., mem. ophthalmology resident and fellowship edn. com.), No. Calif. Soc. To Prevent Blindness (med. adv. bd.), Pan Am. Assn. Ophthalmology, Am. Congress, San Francisco Ophthal. Round Table, Rsch. to Prevent Blindness, Retinitis Pigmentosa Internat. Soc. (founding mem., sci. adv. bd.), Castroviejo Corneal Soc., Internat. Cornea Soc., Internat. Soc. Refractive Keratoplasty, Calif. Cornea Club, Ophthalmologic Hon. Soc. of Am. Ophthal. Soc., Phi Beta Kappa, Sigma Xi, Alpha Omega Alpha. Achievements include patents on surgical instrument tray; multi-compartmentalized bottle; instrument for cataract extraction through small incision; bottle closure; reminder closure; surg. instrument; internally sterile pulsatile irrigator, others. Office: U Calif Beckman Vision Ctr 10 Koret Way Ste K-301 San Francisco CA 94143-0001

KRANTZ, JUDITH TARCHER, novelist; b. N.Y.C., Jan. 9, 1928; d. Jack David and Mary (Brager) Tarcher; m. Stephen Falk Krantz, Feb. 19, 1954; children: Nicholas, Anthony. BA, Wellesley Coll., 1948. Fashion publicist, Paris, 1948-49; fashion editor Good Housekeeping mag., N.Y.C., 1949-56; contbg. writer McCalls, 1956-59, Ladies Home Jour., 1959-71; contbg. west coast editor Cosmopolitan mag., 1971-79. Author: Scruples, 1978, Princess Daisy, 1980, Mistral's Daughter, 1982, I'll Take Manhattan, 1986, Till We Meet Again, 1988, Dazzle, 1990, Scruples Two, 1992, Lovers, 1994, Spring Collection, 1996, The Jewels of Tessa Kent, 1998, Sex & Shopping: Confessions of a Nice Jewish Girl, 2000.

KRATOCHVIL, BYRON GEORGE, chemistry educator, researcher; b. Osmond, Nebr., Sept. 15, 1932; came to Can., 1967; s. Frank James and Mabel Louise (Schneider) K.; m. Marianne Spain; children: Susan, Daniel, Jean, John. BS, Iowa State U., 1957, MS, 1959, PhD, 1961. Asst. prof. chemistry U. Wis.-Madison, 1961-67; assoc. prof. chemistry U. Alta., Edmonton, Can., 1967-71, prof. chemistry Can., 1971-98, prof. emeritus, 1998—, dept. chmn. Can., 1989-95, assoc. v.p. rsch. Can., 1996-98, sr. advisor, v.p. rsch., 1998-2001. Co-author: (with W.E. Harris) Chemical Analysis, 1969, Chemical Separations and Measurements, 1974, Introduction to Chemical Analysis, 1981; analytical editor Can. Jour. Chemistry, Ottawa, Ont., 1985-88, sr. editor, 1988-93; contbr. numerous articles to sci. jours. Recipient merit award Iowa State U. Alumni, 1990. Fellow AAAS, Chem. Inst. Can. (bd. dirs. 1977-80, Fisher Lectr. award 1990); mem. Am. Chem. Soc. Office: U Alta Dept Chemistry Chemistry Centre Edmonton AB Canada T6G 2G2 E-mail: ron.kratochvil@ualberta.ca

KRAUS, PANSY DAEGLING, gemology consultant, editor, writer; b. Santa Paula, Calif., Sept. 21, 1916; d. Arthur David and Elsie (Pardee) Daegling; m. Charles Frederick Kraus, Mar. 1, 1941 (div. Nov. 1961). AA, San Bernardino Valley Jr. Coll., 1938; student, Longmeyer's Bus. Coll., 1940; grad. gemologist diploma, Gemol. Inst. Gt. Britain, 1960, Gemol. Inst. Am., 1966. Clk. Convair, San Diego, 1943-48, San Diego County Schs. Publs., 1948-57; mgr. Rogers and Boblet Art-Craft, San Diego, 1958-64; part-time editl. asst. Lapidary Jour., San Diego, 1963-64, assoc. editor, 1964-69, editor, 1970-94, sr. editor, 1984-85; pvt. practice cons. San Diego, 1985—. Lectr. gems, gemology local gem, mineral groups; gem & mineral club bull. editor groups. Author: Introduction to Lapidary, 1987; editor, layout dir.: Gem. Cutting Shop Helps, 1964, The Fundamentals of Gemstone Carving, 1967, Appalachian Mineral and Gem Trails, 1968, Practical Gem Knowledge for the Amateur, 1969, Southwest Mineral and Gem Trails, 1972, Introduction to Lapidary, 1987; revision editor Gemcraft (Quick and Leiper), 1977; contbr. articles to Lapidary jour., Keystone Mktg. catalog. Mem. San Diego Mineral and Gem. Soc., Gemol. Soc. San Diego, Gemol. Assn. Gt. Britain, Mineral. Soc. Am., Gemol. Inst. Am., Epsilon Sigma Alpha. Home and Office: 6127 Mohler St San Diego CA 92120-3515

KRAUSE, KEITH WINSTON, quality engineer executive; b. Houston, Aug. 22, 1957; s. Leeland Stanford Jr. and Kay Marjorie (Keller) K.; m. Debbie Ann Richardson, Sept. 4, 1984 (div. Oct. 1988); m. Angeles Arquisola, July 3, 1991; 1 child, Kaylin Dominique; stepchildren: Michelle Economos, Steven Economos. BS in Indsl. Tech., Tex. So. U., 1980. Draftsman B-1 divsn. Rockwell Internat., L.A., 1977-78, draftsman Rocketdyne divsn. Canoga Park, Calif., 1978; draftsman Schlumberger Well Svcs., Houston, 1979; pipe design quality mgr. Hughes Aircraft Co., El Segundo, Calif., 1980-97; quality mgr. Irvin Aerospace Co., Santa Ana, 1997; sr. quality project engr. Fairchild Aerospace Co., Torrance, 1997-2000; mgr. quality engring. Krause, Keith, Winston; dir. quality engring. Hydroform USA, Carson, Calif., 2001—. Author: Electronics Workmanship Criteria Manual, 1996. Indsl. Tech. scholar Tex. So. U., 1977. Mem. C. of C., Phi Beta Sigma (life, v.p. 1978-79). Avocations: karate, sports, landscaping, interior decorating and design, electronics.

KRAUSKOPF, KONRAD BATES, geology educator; b. Madison, Wis., Nov. 30, 1910; s. Francis Craig and Maude Luvan (Bates) K.; m. Kathryn Isabel McCune, Jan. 1, 1936; children— Karen Hyde, Frances Conley, Karl, Marion Foerster A.B. in Chemistry, U. Wis., 1931; Ph.D. in Chemistry, U. Calif.-Berkeley, 1934; Ph.D. in Geology, Stanford U., 1939; Ph.D. (hon.), U. Wis., 1972. Instr. chemistry U. Calif., Berkeley, 1934-35; asst. to full prof. geology Stanford U., Calif., 1939-76, chmn. geology dept., 1972-76; geologist U.S. Geol. Survey, Menlo Park, Calif., 1943-88; chief geog. sect. U.S. Army F.E.C., Tokyo, 1947-48; prof. geology emeritus Stanford U., 1976—. Cons. Woodward-Clyde, Arthur D. Little, Aerospace Corp, Phillips Petroleum, EPA, NRC, Dept. Energy 1954— Author: Introduction to Geochemistry, 1967—, The Third Planet, 1974, Radioactive Waste Disposal and Geology, 1988; co-author: (with A. Beiser) Fundamentals of Physical Science, 1941-74, The Physical Universe, 1960—. Recipient Ian Campbell medal Am. Geol. Inst., 1984 Fellow Geol. Soc. Am. (pres. 1967, Day medal 1961); mem. NAS, Geochem. Soc. (pres. 1970, Goldschmidt medal 1982), Soc. Econ. Geologists, Am. Geophys. Union, Am. Philos. Soc., Am. Inst. Profl. Geologists (hon.). Democrat. Home: Stanford U 13 Pearce Mitchell Pl Stanford CA 94305-8518 Office: Stanford U Dept Geology & Environ Scis Stanford CA 94305-2115 E-mail: konrad@pangea.stanford.edu

KRAUSS, GEORGE, metallurgist; b. Phila., May 14, 1933; s. George and Berta (Reichelt) K.; m. Ruth A. Oeste, Sept. 10, 1960; children: Matthew, Jonathan, Benjamin, Thomas. B.S. in Metall. Engring., Lehigh U., 1955; M.S., MIT, 1958, Sc.D., 1961. Registered profl. engr., Colo., Pa. Devel. metallurgist Superior Tube Co., Collegeville, Pa., 1955-56; prof. Lehigh U., Bethlehem, 1963-75, Colo. Sch. Mines, Golden, 1975—; dir. Advanced Steel Processing and Products Research Ctr., 1984-93; Amax Found. prof., 1975-90; prof. dept. metall. engring. Colo. Sch. Mines, Golden, 1990-92, John Henry Moore prof., 1992-97, Univ. prof. emeritus, metallurg. cons., 1997—. Author: Principles of Heat Treatment of Steel, 1980, Steels: Heat Treatment and Processing Principles, 1990, Tool Steels, 5th edit., 1998; editor: Deformation Processing and Structure, 1984,, Carburizing: Processing and Performance, 1989; editor Jour. Heat Treating, 1978-82; co-editor Fundamentals of Microalloying Forging Steels, 1987; contbr. articles profl. jours. NSF fellow Max Planck Inst. fur Eisenforschung, 1962-63; recipient Adolf Martens medal, Wiesbaden, 1990, Disting. Alumni award Lehigh U., 1993, George R. Brown gold medal, 1998; named Outstanding Educator, Colo. Sch. Mines, 1990. Fellow ASM, Japan Soc. Promotion Sci.; mem. AIME, Iron and Steel Soc.-AIME (disting. mem. 1993), Iron and Steel Inst. Japan (hon.), Am. Soc. Materials Internat. (trustee 1991-94, v.p. 1995-96, pres. 1996-97, C.S. Barrett silver medal 1998, Bodeen Heat Treating Achievement award 1999, A.E. White Disting. Tchr. award 1999), Internat. Fedn. Heat Treatment (pres. 1989-91). Home: 3807 S Ridge Rd Evergreen CO 80439-8517 Office: Colo Sch Mines Dept Metall Engring Golden CO 80401 E-mail: gkrauss@mines.edu

KRAUSS, MICHAEL EDWARD, linguist; b. Cleve., Aug. 15, 1934; s. Lester William and Ethel (Sklarsky) K.; m. Jane Lowell, Feb. 16, 1962; children: Marcus Feder, Stephen Feder, Ethan, Alexandra, Isaac. Bacc. Phil. Islandicae, U. Iceland; BA, U. Chgo., 1953, Western Res. U., 1954; MA, Columbia U., 1955; Cert. d'études supérieures, U. Paris, 1956; PhD, Harvard U., 1959. Postdoctoral fellow U. Iceland, Reykjavik, 1958-60; rsch. fellow Dublin Inst. Advanced Studies, Ireland, 1956-57; vis. prof. MIT, Cambridge, 1969-70; prof. linguistics Alaska Native Lang. Ctr., U. Alaska, Fairbanks, 1960—, dir., 1972-2000, head Alaska native lang. program, 1972-2000; prof. emeritus linguistics U. Alaska, Fairbanks, 2000—. Panel mem. linguistics NSF. Author: Eyak Dictionary, 1970, Eyak Texts, 1970, Alaska Native Languages: Past, Present and Future, 1980; editor: In Honor of Eyak: The Art of Anna Nelson Harry, 1982, Yupik Eskimo Prosodic Systems, 1985; mem. editorial bd.: Internat. Jour. Am. Linguistics, Arctic Anthropology; edited dictionaries and books in Alaska Eskimo and Indian langs. Halldor Kiljan Laxness fellow Scandinavian-Am. Found., Iceland, 1958-60, Fulbright fellow Leningrad, USSR, 1990; Fulbright study grantee Iceland, 1958-60; grantee NSF, 1961—, NEH, 1967; named Humanities Forum, 1981; recipient Athabaskan and Eyak rsch. award NSF, 1961—. Mem. Linguistics Soc. Am. (chair com. endangered langs. and preservation 1991-95), Am. Anthropol. Assn., Soc. Study Indigenous Langs. of the Ams. (pres. 1991). Jewish. Office: U Alaska Fairbanks Alaska Native Lang Ctr Fairbanks AK 99775

KRAVITZ, LENNY, singer, guitarist; b. May 26, 1964; 1 child: Zoe. Albums: Let Love Rule, 1989, Mama Said, 1991, Are You Gonna Go My Way, 1993 (2 Grammy nominations), Circus, 1995, Five, 1998 (Grammy); Soundtrack Cutting Edge, 1998, Waterboy, 1998, Twice Upon a Yesteryear, 1999, Austin Powers, The Spy Who Shagged Me, 1999; appeared in films: Lennon: A Tribute, 1991, Lenny Kravitz: Video Retrospective, 1992, Rugrats: The Movie (voice), 1999. Recipient Grammy award, 1999. Office: care CAA 9830 Wilshire Blvd Beverly Hills CA 90212-1804 also: Virgin Records 550 Madison Ave New York NY 10022-3211 also: 2100 Columbia Ave Santa Monica CA 90404

KREBS, EDWIN GERHARD, biochemistry educator; b. Lansing, Iowa, June 6, 1918; s. William Carl and Louise Helena (Stegeman) K.; m. Virginia Frech, Mar. 10, 1945; children: Sally, Robert, Martha. AB in Chemistry, U. Ill., 1940; MD, Washington U., St. Louis, 1943, DSc (hon.), 1995; DSc honoris causa, U. Geneva, 1979; hon. degree, Med. Coll. Ohio, 1993; DSc (hon.), U. Ind., 1993, U. Ill., 1995; D honoris causa, U. Nat. De Cuyo, 1993. Intern, asst. resident Barnes Hosp., St. Louis, 1944-45; rsch. fellow biol. chemistry Wash. U., St. Louis, 1946-48; prof., chmn. dept. biol. chemistry Sch. Medicine U. Calif., Davis, 1968-76; from asst. prof. to prof. biochemistry U. Wash., Seattle, 1948-66, prof., chmn. dept. pharmacology, 1977-83, prof. biochemistry and pharmacology, 1984-91; investigator, sr. investigator Howard Hughes Med. Inst., Seattle, 1983-90, sr. investigator emeritus, 1991—. Mem. Phys. Chemistry Study Sect. NIH, 1963-68, Biochemistry Test Com. Nat. Bd. Med. Examiners, 1968-71, rsch. com. Am. Heart Assn., 1970-74, bd. sci. counselors Nat. Inst. Arthritis, Metabolism and Digestive Diseases, NIH, 1979-84, Internat. Bd. Rev., Alberta Heritage Found. for Med. Rsch., 1986, external adv. com. Weis Ctr. for Rsch., 1987-91; mem. subgroup interconvertible enzymes IUB Spl. Interest Group Metabolic Regulation; internat. adv. bd. Advances in Second Messenger Phosphoprotein Rsch.; external adv. com. Cell Therapeutics Inc., Seattle; adv. bd. Kinetek, Vancouver, B.C. Mem. editorial bd. Jour. Biol. Chemistry, 1965-70; mem. editorial adv. bd. Biochemistry, 1971-76; mem. editorial and adv. bd. Molecular Pharmacology, 1972-77; assoc. editor Jour. Biol. Chemistry, 1971-93; mem. internat. adv. bd. Advances in Cyclic Nucleotide Rsch., 1972—; editorial advisor Molecular and Cellular Biochemistry, 1987—. Recipient Nobel Prize in Medicine or Physiology, 1992, Gairdner Found. award, Toronto, 1978, J.J. Berzelius lectureship, Karolinska Institutet, 1982, George W. Thorn award for sci. excellence, 1983, Sir Frederick Hopkins Meml. lectureship, London, 1984, Rsch. Achievement award Am. Heart Assn., Anaheim, Calif., 1987, 3M Life Scis. award FASEB, New Orleans, 1989, Albert Lasker Basic Med. Rsch. award, 1989, CIBA-GEIGY-Drew award Drew U., 1991, Steven C. Beering award, Ind. U., 1991, Welch award in chemistry Welch Found., 1991, Louisa Gross Horwitz award Columbia U., 1989, Alumni Achievement award Coll. Liberal Arts and Scis. U. Ill., 1992, Kaul Found. award for excellence, 1996; John Simon Guggenheim fellow, 1959, 66. Mem. NAS, Am. Soc. Biol. Chemists (pres. 1986, ednl. affairs com. 1965-68, councillor 1975-78), Am. Acad. Arts and Scis., Am. Soc. Pharmacology and Exptl. Therapeutics. Achievements include life-long study of the protein phosphorylation process. Office: U Wash J-681F Health Sci Bldg PO Box 357370 Seattle WA 98195-7370*

KREGER, BRIAN FREDERICK, lawyer; b. Saginaw, Mich., Jan. 17, 1947; s. Walter L. and June R. (Schultz) K.; m. Peggy J. Martin, July 10, 1971. BA, Concordia Coll., Ft. Wayne, Ind., 1969; MA, U. Nebr., 1971, JD, 1974. Bar: Nebr. 1974, U.S. Dist. Ct. (no. dist.) Nebr. 1974, Wash. 1980, U.S. Dist. Ct. (we. dist.) Wash. 1980. Legis. com. counsel Nebr. State Legis., Lincoln, 1974-79; pvt. practice Lincoln, 1974-79; atty. Safeco Ins. Co., Seattle, 1979-85; assoc. Waitt Johnson & Martens, Seattle, 1985-87; gen. counsel, sec. Empire Ins. Co., Seattle, 1987-97; of counsel Ryan Swanson and Cleveland, Seattle, 1997—. Gen. counsel WM Ins. Co. Vol. atty. Nebr. Civil Liberties Union, Lincoln, 1974-79; dist. rep. Ravenna-Bryant Community Assn., Seattle, 1985—; elder Messiah Luth. Ch., Seattle, 1986—; bd. dirs. Compass Ctr., Seattle Internat. Children's Festival. Mem. Coll. Club (Seattle).

KREGER, MELVIN JOSEPH, lawyer; b. Buffalo, Feb. 21, 1937; s. Philip and Bernice (Gerstman) K.; m. Patricia Anderson, July 1, 1955 (div. 1963); children: Beth Barbour, Arlene Roux; m. Renate Hochleitner, Aug. 15, 1975. JD, Mid-valley Coll. Law, 1978; LLM in Taxation, U. San Diego, 1988. Bar: Calif. 1978, U.S. Dist. Ct. (cen. dist.) Calif. 1979, U.S. Tax Ct. 1979, U.S. Supreme Ct. 1995; cert. specialist in probate law, trust law and estate planning law, taxation law, Calif. Life underwriter Met. Life Ins. Co., Buffalo, 1958-63; bus. mgr. M. Kreger Bus. Mgmt., Sherman Oaks, Calif., 1963-78, enrolled agt., 1971—; pvt. practice North Hollywood, 1978—. Mem. Nat. Assn. Enrolled Agts., Calif. Soc. Enrolled Agts., State Bar Calif., L.A. Bar Assn., San Fernando Valley Bar Assn. (probate sect., tax sect.). Jewish. Avocations: computers, travel. Office: 11424 Burbank Blvd North Hollywood CA 91601-2301 E-mail: mel@meltaxlaw.com

KREISMAN, ARTHUR, higher education consultant, humanities educator emeritus; b. Cambridge, Mass., June 7, 1918; s. Louis and Rose (Shechtell) K.; m. B. Evelyn Goulston, Apr. 20, 1940 (dec. July 1992); children: Peter Jon, Steven Alan, Richard Curt, James Bruce; m. Mamie Jewel Liles Tribble, July 17, 1994. AB, Brigham Young U., 1942; student, Harvard U., 1939; AM, Boston U., 1943, PhD, 1952; LittD (hon.), City U., 1988. Grad. asst. in English Boston U., 1942-43, instr. U.S. Armed Forces Inst., 1945; with Signal Corps. U.S. Army, 1943-45, with Signal Corps. overseas, 1944-45; instr. So. Oreg. U., Ashland, 1946, asst. prof., 1947-51, assoc. prof., 1951-55, prof., 1955-81, chmn. dept. English, 1951-63, chmn. humanities div., 1955-69, dir. gen. studies, 1959-66, dean arts and scis., 1966-77, dir. curricular affairs, 1978-80, prof. emeritus, 1981—, appt. ofcl. univ. historian, 1985; co-founder with Evelyn Kreisman Edukon, Inc., 1982—. TV lectr. Network Ednl. TV, 1955-58; dir. Block Teaching Project, U.S. Office Edn., 1957-59, Nat. Def. Edn. Act Inst. for Advanced Study in English, 1966; cons. Fedn. Regional Accrediting Commns. in Higher Edn., 1974-75, Council on Postsecondary Accreditation, 1975-79, Chico (Calif.) State U., 1973-76, City U. Seattle, 1975—, Lincoln Meml. U., 1976, Marylhurst Edn. Center, 1976, Oreg. Inst. Tech., 1977-79, Sheldon Jackson Coll., 1979-83, Council on Chiropractic Edn., 1982, 83, Griffin Coll., 1990-91; mem. Gov.'s Adv. Com. on Arts and Humanities, 1966-69, 71-76; mem. task force human services Oreg. Ednl. Coordinating Council, 1972; mem. steering com. Oreg. Joint Com. for Humanities, 1972-74; chmn. Seminar Coll. Evaluators NW Assn. Schs. and Colls., U. Wash., 1977-84; mem. nat. adv. bd. on quality assurance in experiental learning Council on Advancement Experiental Learning, 1978-80; team leader Danforth Found. Workshop on Liberal Arts Edn., Colo. Coll., 1972. Author: Correspondence Courses for State System, American Literature, 1955, World Literature, 1956, Contemporary Literature, 1961, Reader's Guide to the Classics, 1961; Editor: Oregon Centennial Anthology, 1959; Contbr. poetry and articles to periodicals. Mem. Ashland City Coun., 1950-54; co-founder Rogue Valley Unitarian Fellowship, 1953; bd. dirs. Comty. Chest, Inst. Renaissance Studies, 1956-64, Friends of Libr., 1991-96, pres., 1994-96; mem. steering com. Learning in Retirement Program, 1993-94; chmn. bd. trustees Ashland Comty. Hosp., 1960-64; bd. dirs. So. Calif. U. for Profl. Studies, 1997-99; chmn. bd. dirs. North Ctrl. U., 1998-99. With U.S. Army, 1943-45. Recipient Bicentennial anniversary prize in humanities Columbia U., 1954, disting. svc. award Ashland Cmty. Hosp. Found., 1998; prize for excellence in teaching, 1966, Outstanding Service award Indsl. Coll. Armed Forces, 1976, Disting. Service award Alumni Assn., 1977; Ford Found. fellow in Oriental philosophy and religion Harvard, 1954 Mem. AAUP (past pres. Oreg. coun.), Nat. Coun. Tchrs. English (past pres. Oreg. coun.), Commn. of Pacific Assn. of Schs. and Colls. (elected 1994-95), N.W. Assn. Schs. and Colls. (examiner 1958—, trustee 1976-80, mem. comm. colls. 1972-80), Am. Legion (past post comdr.), Lambda Iota Tau, Phi Kappa Phi, Tau Kappa Alpha. Office: 1880 Green Meadows Way Ashland OR 97520-3683

KREISSMAN, STARRETT, librarian; b. N.Y.C., Jan. 4, 1946; d. Bernard and Shirley (Relis) K.; m. David Dolan, Apr. 13, 1985; 1 child, Sonya. BA, Grinnell Coll., 1967; MLS, Columbia U., 1968. Asst. circulation libr. Columbia U., N.Y.C., 1968-70; sci. libr. N.Y. Pub. Libr., N.Y.C., 1970-71; outreach libr. Stanislaus County Free Libr., Modesto, Calif., 1971-73, Oakdale libr., 1974-79, acquisitions libr., 1979-85, br. supr., 1985-92, county libr., 1992—. Writer book revs. Stanislaus County Commn. on Women. Mem. ALA, Pub. Libr. Assn., Calif. Libr. Assn. (legis. com. 1993-95), Rotary. Office: Stanislaus County Free Libr 1500 I St Modesto CA 95354-1120

KREITH, FRANK, research engineer, consultant; b. Vienna, Austria, Dec. 15, 1922; s. Fritz and Elsa (Klug) K.; m. Marion Finkels, Sept. 21, 1951; children: Michael, Marcia, Judith. BSME, U. Calif., Berkeley, 1945; MS in Engring., UCLA, 1946; DSc, U. Paris, 1964. Registered profl. engr., Calif., Colo. Rsch. engr. Jet Propulsion Lab. Calif. Inst. Tech., 1945-49; asst. prof. U. Calif., Berkeley, 1951-53; assoc. prof. mech. engring. Lehigh U., Bethlehem, Pa., 1953-59; prof. engring. U. Colo., 1959-77; chief solar thermal rsch. Solar Energy Rsch. Inst., Golden, Colo., 1977-87; sr. fellow Nat. Conf. State Legis., 1987—; pres. Environ. Cons. Svcs., 1974-77; cons. NATO, 1980-85, Nat. Renewable Energy Lab, 1990-98. Author: Principles of Heat Transfer, 1958, 2d edit., 1965, 3d edit., 1973, (with C. B. Wrenn) Nuclear Impact, 1975, (with J. F. Kreider) Principles of Solar Engineering, 1980; editor-in-chief Handbook of Energy Efficiency, 1996, Handbook of Mechanical Engineering, 1997, Handbook of Thermal Engineering, 2000. Mem. Human Rels. Commn., 1963-65, Energy Adv. Com., 1979-82. Guggenheim fellow, 1950; recipient medal ASME, 1998. Mem. ASME (heat transfer meml. award 1972, Edwin F. Church medal 2001), Internat. Solar Energy Soc., Sigma Xi (nat. lectr. 1980-81), Phi Tau Sigma. Office: NCSL ASME Legislative Fellow 1560 Broadway Ste 700 Denver CO 80202-5140

KREITZBERG, FRED CHARLES, construction management company executive; b. Paterson, N.J., June 1, 1934; s. William and Ella (Bohen) K.; m. Barbara Braun, June 9, 1957; children: Kim, Caroline, Allison, Bruce, Catherine. BSCE, Norwich U., 1957, DS in Bus. Adminstrn. (hon.), 1994. Registered profl. engr., Ala., Alaska, Ariz., Ark., Calif., Colo., Del., D.C., Fla., Ga., Idaho, Ill., Ind., Iowa, Kans., Ky., Md., Mass., Minn., Miss., Mo., Nebr., Nev., N.H., N.J., N.Mex., N.Y., Ohio, Okla., Oreg., S.C., S.D., Tenn., Va., Vt., Wash., W.Va., Wis., Wyo. Asst. supt. Turner Constrn. Co., N.Y.C., 1957; project mgr. Project Mercury RCA, N.J., 1958-63; schedule cost mgr. Catalytic Constrn. Co., Pa., 1963-65, 65—; cons. Meridien Engring., 1965-68; prin. MDC Systems Corp., 1968-72; chmn., CEO O'Brien-Kreitzberg Inc., San Francisco, 1972—. Lectr. Stanford (Calif.) U., U. Calif., Berkeley. Author: Crit. Path Method Scheduling for Contractor's Mgmt. Handbook, 1971; tech. editor Constrn. Inspection Handbook, 1972; contbr. articles to profl. jours. Bd. dirs. Partridge Soc.; chmn. bd. trustees Norwich U. 2d lt. C.E., U.S. Army, 1957-58. Recipient Disting. Alumnus award Norwich U., 1987, Crystal Vision award Nat. Assn. Women in Constrn., 1997; named Boss of Yr., Nat. Assn. Women in Constrn., 1987; Kreitzberg Amphitheatre named in his honor, 1987, also Kreitzberg Libr. at Norwich U., 1992; Bay Area Discovery Mus.-Birthday Room, State of Vt. Gov. Proclamation Day, 1992, San Francisco Mayor Willie Brown Proclamation Day, 2000, and Snack Bar named in honor of Kreitzberg family, 1989. Fellow ASCE (Constrn. Mgr. of Yr. 1982); mem. Am. Arbitration Assn., Constrn. Mgmt. Assn. Am. (founding, bd. dirs.), Soc. Am. Value Engrs., Community Field Assn., Ross Hist. Soc., N.J. Soc. Civil Engrs., N.J. Soc. Profl. Planners, Project Mgmt. Inst., Constrn. Industry Pres. Forum. Avocations: running, bicycling, tropical fish. Home: PO Box 1200 Ross CA 94957-1200 Office: O'Brien Kreitzberg Inc 50 Fremont St Fl 24 San Francisco CA 94105-2236

KREJCI, ROBERT HARRY, non-profit organizations development consultant; b. Chgo., June 4, 1913; s. John and Johanna (Tischer) K.; m. Marian Hallock, Mar. 28, 1941 (dec. Aug. 1986); 1 child, Susan Ann Krejci Stevens. BS in Forestry with honors, Mich. State U., 1940. Dist. exec. Boy Scouts Am., Chgo., 1940-48, asst. scout exec., 1948-50, scout exec. Herrin, Ill., Huntington, W.Va., 1950-65; devel. cons. The Cumerford Corp., Kansas City, 1965-73, dir. western divsn. Ft. Lauderdale, Fla., 1974-78; devel. cons. in pvt. practice, San Diego, 1978-90. Co-founder, pres. Philanthropy Coun., San Diego, 1987-93; dir. World War II Farm Labor Camp, State of Ill., 1942, 43. Author: How to Succeed in Fund Raising For Your Non-Profit Organization, 1989. Vol. organizer United Way, various cities, Ill., 1955, 56. Recipient George Washington medal Freedoms Found. at Valley Forge, 1953; named Vol. of Yr. Philanthropy Coun., 1996, Exemplar, Rancho Bernardo Rotary Found., 1995. Mem. Rotary Internat. (Paul Harris fellow). Avocations: travel, gardening, writing, collecting humor. Home: 16566 Casero Rd San Diego CA 92128-2743

KREJCI, ROBERT HENRY, aerospace engineer; b. Shenandoah, Iowa, Nov. 15, 1943; s. Henry and Marie Josephine (Kubicek) K.; m. Carolyn R. Meyer, Aug. 21, 1967; children: Christopher S., Ryan D. BS with honors in Aerospace Engring., Iowa State U., 1967, M Aerospace Engring., 1971. Commd. 2d lt. USAF, 1968, advanced thoru grades to capt., 1978; lt. col. USAFR; served with Sys. Command Space Launch Vehicles Sys. Program Office; advanced ICBM program officer Space Launch Vehicles Sys. Program Office; U.S. Dept. Energy rsch. assoc. Lawrence Livermore Lab.; dept. mgr. advanced tech. programs statregic divsn. Thiokol Corp., Brigham City, Utah, 1978-84, mgr. space programs, 1984-85, mgr. Navy advanced programs, 1986—. Fellow AIAA (assoc.). Home: 885 North 300 East Brigham City UT 84302-1310 Office: ATC Thiokol Propulsion PO Box 707 Brigham City UT 84302-0707

KRENDL, CATHY STRICKLIN, lawyer; b. Paris, Mar. 14, 1945; d. Louis and Margaret Helen (Young) S.; m. James R. Krendl, July 5, 1969; children: Peggy, Susan, Anne. BA summa cum laude, North Tex. State U., 1967; JD cum laude, Harvard U., 1970. Bar: Alaska 1970, Colo. 1972. Atty. Hughes, Thorsness, Lowe Gantz & Clark, Anchorage, 1970-71; adj. prof. U. Colo. Denver Ctr., 1972-73; from asst. prof. to prof. law, dir. bus planning program U. Denver, 1973-83; ptnr. Krendl, Krendl, Sachnoff & Way, Denver, 1983—. Author: Business Organizations, 1999, Colorado Business Corporation Act Deskbook, 1999; editor: Colorado Methods of Practice, 8 vols. 1983-99, Closely Held Corporations in Colorado, vols. 1-3, 1981; contbr. articles to profl. jours. Named Disting. Alumna North Tex. State U., 1985. Mem. Colo. Bar Assn. (bd. govs. 1982-86, 88-91, chmn. securities subsect. 1986, bus. law sect. 1988-89, Professionalism award), Denver Bar Assn. (pres. 1989-90). Avocation: reading. Home: 1551 Larimer St Apt 1101 Denver CO 80202-1630 E-mail: csk@krendl.com

KRENER, ARTHUR J. systems engineering educator; b. Bklyn., Oct. 8, 1942; BS, Holy Cross Coll., 1964, MS, 1967; PhD, U. Calif., Berkeley, 1971. Prof. math. U. Calif., 1943—. Fellow IEEE. Office: U Calif-Davis Dept Maths 660 Kerr Hall Davis CA 95616

KREPS, DAVID MARC, economist, educator; b. N.Y.C., Oct. 18, 1950; s. Saul Ian and Sarah (Kaskin) Kreps; m. Anat Ruth Admati, Jan. 4, 1984; children: Tamar, Oren, Avner. AB, Dartmouth Coll., 1972; MA, PhD, Stanford U., 1975. Asst. prof. Stanford U., 1975-78, assoc. prof., 1978-80, prof., 1980-84, Holden prof., 1984—. Rsch. officer U. Cambridge, Eng., 1978-79, fellow commoner Churchill Coll., Cambridge, 1978-79; vis. prof. Yale U., New Haven, 1982, Harvard U., Cambridge, Mass., 1983, U. Paris, 1985; vis. prof. U. Tel Aviv, 1989-90, sr. prof. by spl. apppintment, 1991—. Author: Notes on the Theory of Choice, 1988, A Course in Microeconomic Theory, 1990, Game Theory and Economic Modelling, 1990; co-author: Strategic Human Resources, 1999; co-editor Econometrica, 1984-88. Alfred P. Sloan Found. fellow, 1983, John S. Guggenheim fellow, 1988. Fellow Econometric Soc.; mem. Am. Econ. Assn. (J.B. Clark medal 1989), Am. Acad. Arts and Scis., Nat. Acad. Scis. Office: Stanford U Grad Sch of Bus Stanford CA 94305-5015

KRESA, KENT, aerospace executive; b. N.Y.C., Mar. 24, 1938; s. Helmy and Marjorie (Boutelle) K.; m. Joyce Anne McBride, Nov. 4, 1961; 1 child, Kiren BSAA, MIT, 1959, MSAA, 1961, EAA, 1966. Sr. scientist rsch. and advanced devel. divsn. AVCO, Wilmington, Mass., 1959-61; staff mem. MIT Lincoln Lab., Lexington, 1961-68; dep. dir. strategic tech. office Def. [illegible] office Def. Advanced Rsch. Project Agy., Washington, 1973-75; v.p., mgr. Rsch. & Tech. Ctr. Northrop Corp., Hawthorne, Calif., 1975-76, v.p., gen. mgr. Ventura divsn. Newbury Park, 1976-82, group v.p. Aircraft Group L.A., 1982-86, sr. v.p. tech. devel. and planning, 1986-87, pres., COO, 1987-90; chmn. bd., pres., CEO Northrop Grumman Corp., L.A., 1990—. Bd. dirs. John Tracy Clinic; mem. Chief of Naval Ops. exec. panel Washington, Def. Sci. Bd., Washington, DNA New Alternatives Working Group, L.A., Dept. Aeronautics and Astronautics Corp. Vis. Com. MIT. Bd. dirs. John Tracy Clinic for the Hearing-Impaired, W.M. Keck Found., L.A. World Affairs Coun.; bd. govs. L.A. Music Ctr. Recipient Henry Webb Salsbury award MIT, 1959, Arthur D. Flemming award, 1975, Calif. Industrialist of Yr. Calif. Mus. of Sci. and Industry and the Calif. Mus. Found., 1996, Bob Hope Disting. Citizen award Nat. Security Indsl. Assn., 1996; Sec. of Def. Meritorious Civilian Svc. medal, 1975, USN Meritorious Pub. Svc. citation, 1975, Exceptional Civilian Svc. award USAF, 1987. Fellow AIAA; mem. Aerospace Industries Assn. (past bd. govs.), Naval Aviation Mus. Found., Navy League U.S., Soc. Flight Test Engrs., Assn. U.S. Army, Nat. Space Club, Am. Def. Preparedness Assn., L.A. Country Club, NAE. Office: Northrop Grumman Corp 1840 Century Park E Los Angeles CA 90067-2101

KRESTA, SUZANNE M. chemical engineering educator; BSc in Chem. Engring., U. N.B., Can., 1986; MSc in Chem. Engring., U. Leeds, Eng., 1987; PhD in Chem. Engring., McMaster U., 1992. Prof. chem. and materials engring. U. Alta., Edmonton, Can., 1992—, assoc. chair chem. engring. program Can. Mem. 9th European Conf. on Mixing; presenter in field. Contbr. articles to profl. publs. Recipient Young Engr. Achievement award Can. Coun. Profl. Engrs., 1998; NSERC grantee. Mem. APEGGA (Early Accomplishment award 1998). Office: U Alta Dept Chem Engring 536 Chem/Mineral Engring Edmonton AB Canada T6G 2G6 E-mail: suzanne.kresta@ualberta.ca

KREUTZBERG, DAVID W. lawyer; b. Edwardsville, Ill., May 20, 1953; BA summa cum laude, Ariz. State U., 1975, JD magna cum laude, 1978. Bar: Ariz. 1978, U.S. Dist. Ct. (Ariz. dist.) 1978. Law clk. to Hon. William E. Eubank Ariz. Ct. Appeals, Phoenix, 1978-79; ptnr. Squire, Sanders & Dempsey LLP, Phoenix, 1989. Mem. ABA (mem. bus. law sect.), State Bar Ariz., Maricopa County Bar Assn., Phi Beta Kappa. Office: Squire Sanders & Dempsey LLP Two Renaissance Sq 40 N Central Ave Ste 2700 Phoenix AZ 85004-4498

KREVANS, JULIUS RICHARD, university administrator, physician; b. N.Y.C., May 1, 1924; s. Sol and Anita Krevans; m. Patricia N. Abrams, May 28, 1950; children: Nita, Julius R., Rachel, Sarah, Nora Kate. B.S. Arts and Scis, N.Y. U., 1943, M.D., 1946. Diplomate: Am. Bd. Internal Med. Intern, then resident Johns Hopkins Med. Sch. Hosp., mem. faculty, until 1970, dean acad. affairs, 1969-70; physician in chief Balt. City Hosp., 1963-69; prof. medicine U. Calif., San Francisco, 1970—, dean Sch. Medicine, 1971-82, chancellor, 1982-93, chancellor emeritus, 1993—. Contbr. articles on hematology, internal med. profl. jours. Served with M.C. AUS, 1948-50. Mem. ACP, Assn. Am. Physicians. Office: U Calif San Francisco Sch Medicine San Francisco CA 94143-0001

KRIDER, E. PHILIP, atmospheric scientist, educator; b. Chgo., Mar. 22, 1940; s. Edmund Arthur and Ruth (Abbott) K.; m. Barbara A. Reed, June 13, 1964 (div. Mar. 1983); children: Ruth Ellen, Philip Reed; m. Patricia L. MacCorquodale, Aug. 14, 1999. BA in Physics, Carleton Coll., 1962; MS in Physics, U. Ariz., 1964, PhD in Physics, 1969. Resident rsch. assoc. NASA Manned Spacecraft Ctr. NAS, Houston, 1969-71; asst. rsch. prof. Inst. Atmospheric Physics U. Ariz., Tucson, 1971-75, asst. prof. dept. atmospheric scis., 1973-75, assoc. prof. dept. atmospheric scis., Inst. Atmos. Physics, 1975-80; exec. v.p., part-time chmn. Lightning Location and Protection, Inc., Tucson, 1976-83; adj. prof. dept. elec. engring. U. Fla., Gainesville, 1988—; prof. dept. atmospheric scis. Inst. Atmospheric Physics U. Ariz., 1980—, dir. Inst. Atmospheric Physics, head dept. atmospheric scis., 1986-95. Pres. Internat. Commn. Atmospheric Electricity, 1992-99; co-chmn. panel Earth's elec. environment geophysis study com. NAS, 1982-86; mem. panel weather support for space ops. NAS, 1987-88, geostationary platform sci. steering com. NASA, 1987—; mems. rep. Univ. Corp. for Atmospheric Rsch., 1986-95; mem. U.S. nat. com. Internat. Sci. Radio Union; mem. aerospace corp. adv. team USAF Launch Vehicle Lightning/Atmospheric Elec. Constraints, Post Atlas/Centaur 67 Incident, 1987-89; sci. advisor Air Force Geophys. Lab., 1988; mem. lightning adv. com. U.S. Army Missile Command, 1986-87; lectr. in field. Author: (with others) Thunderstorms, 1983, Lightning Electromagnetics, 1990, Benjamin Franklin des Lumieres á nos Jours., 1991; contbr. numerous articles to profl. jours.; co-chief editor Jour. of Atmospheric Scis., 1990-92, editor, 1992-93; assoc. editor Jour. Geophys. Rsch., 1977-79; referee Jour. Geophys. Rsch., Geophys. Rsch. Letters, Jour. of Atmospheric Scis., Planetary and Space Sci. Fellow Am. Meteorol. Soc. (Outstanding Contbn. to Advance Applied Meteorology award 1985), Am. Geophys. Union (Smith medal selection com. 1994, com. on atmospheric and space electricity 1990-98); mem. IEEE (Transactions Prize Paper award EMC Soc. 1982), Am. Assn. Physics Tchrs., Sigma Xi, Sigma Pi Sigma. Achievements include patents for All-Sky camera apparatus for time-resolved lightning photography, photoelectric lightning detector apparatus, transient event data acquisition apparatus for use with radar systems and the like, lightning detection system utilizing triangulation and field amplitude comparison techniques, thunderstorm sensor and method of identifying and locating thunderstorms. Office: U Ariz Dept Atmospheric Scis PO Box 210081 Tucson AZ 85721-0081

KRIEGER, MARCIA SMITH, judge; b. Denver, Mar. 3, 1954; d. Donald P. Jr. and Marjorie Craig (Gearhart) Smith; m. Michael S. Krieger, Aug. 26, 1976 (div. July 1988); children: Miriam Anna, Matthias Edward; m. Frank H. Roberts, Jr., Mar. 9, 1991; stepchildren: Melissa Noel Roberts, Kelly Suzanne Roberts, Heidi Marie Roberts. BA, Lewis & Clark Coll., 1975; postgrad., U. Munich, 1975-76; JD, U. Colo., 1979. Bar: Colo. 1979, U.S. Dist. Ct. Colo. 1979, U.S. Ct. Appeals (10th cir.) 1979. Assoc. Mason, Reuler & Peek, P.C., Denver, 1976-83, Smart, DeFurio Brooks, Eklund & McClure, Denver, 1983-84; ptnr. Brooks & Krieger, P.C., Denver, 1984-88, Wood, Ris & Hames, P.C., Denver, 1988-90; pvt. practice U.S. Bankruptcy Court, 10th Circuit, Denver, 1990-94; judge U.S. Bankruptcy Ct., 10th Circuit, Denver, 1994-2000; chief judge U.S. Bankruptcy Ct., Denver, 2000—. Lectr. U. Denver Grad. Tax Program, 1987—, Colo. Soc. CPA's, Denver, 1984-87, Colo. Continuing Legal Edn., Denver, 1980—, Colo. Trial Lawyers Assn., Denver, 1987—. Contbr. articles to profl. publs. Vestry person Good Shepherd Episcopal Ch., Englewood, 1986—, judge and coach for H.S. mock trial. Mem. Colo. Bar Assn., Arapahoe Bar Assn., Arraj Inn of Ct. (v.p.), Nat. Conf. Bankruptcy Judges, Littleton Adv. Coun. for Gifted and Talented education. Republican. Avocations: international relations, travel, marksmanship. Office: US Custom House 721 19th St Fl 5 Denver CO 80202-2500

KRIENS, SCOTT G. information technology executive; BA, Calif. State U., Hayward. CEO Juniper Networks, Inc., Mountain View, Calif., 1996—. Office: Juniper Networks Inc 1194 N Mathilda Ave Sunnyvale CA 94089-1206

KRIETOR, DAVID, airport authority executive; B in Fin., M in Pub. Adminstrn., Syracuse U. Former dir. Cmty. and Econ. Devel. Dept. City of Phoenix (Ariz.), dir. Aviation Dept., 2000—. Office: City of Phoenix [illegible]

KRIKEN, JOHN LUND, architect; b. Calif., July 5, 1938; s. John Erik Nord and Ragnhild (Lund) K.; m. Anne Girard (div.); m. Katherine Koelsch, Aug. 8, 1988. BArch, U. Calif., Berkeley, 1961; MArch, Harvard U., 1968. Ptnr. Skidmore, Owings and Merrill, San Francisco, 1970—. Tchr. Washington U., St. Louis, 1968, U. Calif., Berkeley, 1972, Rice U., Houston, 1979; design advisor, chief architect Ho Chi Minh City, Vietnam, 1994—; mem. design rev. bd. Port San Francisco, 1995—. Mem. Bay Conservation and Devel. Commn., Calif., 1984—; mem. Arts Commn. City and County of San Francisco, 1989-95; mem. design rev. bd. Berkeley campus U. Calif., 1986-92; bd. dirs. San Francisco Planning and Rsch., 1995—; vice chair, Eng. and Des. Advisory Panel (EDAP) for the rebuilding pf San Francisco Bay Bridge, 1997—; mem. GSD's alumni coun. Harvard U, 2000—; CED's dean's adv. coun. U. Calif., Berkeley, 2000—. Fellow AIA; mem. Am. Inst. Cert. Planners, Sunday Afternoon Watercolor Soc. (founding mem.), Lambda Alpha Internat. Office: Skimore Owings & Merrill 1 Front St San Francisco CA 94111-5303

KRIPKE, KENNETH NORMAN, retired lawyer; b. Toledo, Feb. 16, 1920; s. Maurice and Celia (Vine) K.; m. Derril Kanter, Nov. 4, 1945; children: Teri Schwartz, Marcie K. Gaon. Student, Ohio State U., 1937-41; LL.B., U. Colo., 1948. Bar: Colo. 1949, U.S. Ct. Appeals (10th cir.) 1954, U.S. Ct. Appeals (5th cir.) 1965, U.S. Supreme Ct. 1967, U.S. Ct. Appeals (8th cir.) 1974. Mem. firm Kripke & McLean, 1953-58, Kripke, Hoffman & Carrigan (and successors), 1965-73; pvt. practice law Denver, 1991-95; ptnr. Kripke, Epstein & Lawrence (P.C.), Denver, 1980-90. Mem. nominating com. 9th Jud. Cir., 1976-78, standing com. on rules civil procedure Colo. Supreme Ct., 1978-93; guest speaker Internat. Congress Hosp. Laws, Tel Aviv, 1985. Treas. Denver Allied Jewish Fedn., 1978-84; chmn. Denver civil rights com. Anti-Defamation League B'nai Brith, 1976-82; mem. nat. law com. Anti-Defamation League, 1980—, chair mountain state region, 1990-92; commr. Denver Pub. Safety Rev. Commn., 1992-95; mem. San Diego Citizens' Rev. Bd. on Police Practices, 1996-97. With USAAF, 1942-46. Recipient Kenneth Norman Kripke Ann. award for Lifetime Achievement Colo. Trial Lawyers Assn., 1996. Fellow Internat. Soc. Barristers (emeritus); mem. ABA (discovery subcom. litigation sect. 1982-93), Colo. Bar Assn. (bd. dirs. lend-a-lawyer program 1990-92), Assn. Trial Lawyers Am. (past bd. govs., past exec. adv. com., chmn. conv. 1962, 69), Western Trial Lawyers Assn. (sec. 1971-72, v.p. 1973, pres. 1974-75), Colo. Trial Lawyers Assn. (pres. 1958), Pub. Justice Found. (pres. 1986-89). Office: 5310 Renaissance Ave San Diego CA 92122-5632 E-mail: krpk@aol.com

KRISTOF, KATHY M. journalist; b. Burbank, Calif., Feb. 4, 1960; d. Joseph E. and Frances S. Kristof; m. Richard R. Magnuson, Jr., Jan. 4, 1986; 2 children. BA, U. So. Calif., L.A., 1983. Reporter L.A. Bus. Jour., 1984-88, Daily News, Woodland Hills, Calif., 1988-89, L.A. Times, 1989—; syndicated columnist L.A. Times Syndicate, 1991—. Author: Kathy Kristof's Complete Book of Dollars and Sense, 1997, Investing 101, 2000; contbr. articles to mags. and profl. jours. Recipient John Hancock Fin. Svcs. award, 1992, Personal Fin. Writing award ICI/Am. U., 1994, Consumer Adv. of Yr., Calif. Alliance for Consumer Edn., 1998. Mem. Soc. Bus. Editors and Writers, Calif. Newspapers Pubs. Assn. (2nd pl. Bus. and Fin. Story award 1999). Office: Los Angeles Times Times Mirror Sq Los Angeles CA 90053 E-mail: kathy.kristof@latimes.com

KRISTOF, LADIS KRIS DONABED, political scientist, writer; b. Cernauti, Romania, Nov. 26, 1918; came to U.S., 1952, naturalized, 1957; s. Witold and Maria (Zawadzki) Krzysztofowicz; m. Jane McWilliams, Dec. 29, 1956; 1 son, Nicholas. Student, U. Poznan, Poland, 1937-39; BA, Reed Coll., Portland, Oreg., 1955; MA, U. Chgo., 1956, PhD, 1969. Regional exec. dir., Sovromlemn, Romania, 1948; sales mgr. Centre du Livre Suisse, Paris, France, 1951-52; lectr. U. Chgo., 1958-59; assoc. dir. Inter-Univ. Project History Menshevism, N.Y.C., 1959-62; mem. faculty dept. polit. sci. Temple U., 1962-64; research fellow Hoover Instn., Stanford U., 1964-67; faculty polit. sci. U. Santa Clara, 1967-68; asso. Studies Communist System, Stanford, 1968-69; mem. faculty polit. sci. U. Waterloo, Ont., Can., 1969-71; prof. polit. sci. Portland (Oreg.) State U., 1971-89, prof. emeritus, 1990—. Vis. prof. U. Wroclaw, Poland, 1990, U. Iasi, Romania, 1991, U. Punjab, India, 1992. Author: The Nature of Frontiers and Boundaries, 1959, The Origins and Evolution of Geopolitics, 1960, The Russian Image of Russia, 1967, The Geopolitical Contours of the Post-Cold War World, 1992; also articles in Romania; co-author, co-editor: Revolution and Politics in Russia, 1972. Active Internat. YMCA Center, Paris, 1950-52, NAACP, Chgo., 1957-59, Amnesty Internat., Portland, 1975— . Served with Corps Engrs. Romanian Army, 1940-43. Fulbright scholar Romania, 1971, 84 Mem. Am. Polit. Sci. Assn., Assn. Am. Geographers, Am. Assn. for Advancement of Slavic Studies, Internat. Polit. Sci. Assn., Western Slavic Assn. (pres. 1988-90), Am.-Romanian Acad. Arts and Scis. (v.p. 1995—). Home: 23050 NW Roosevelt Dr Yamhill OR 97148-8336 Office: Portland State Univ Dept Polit Sci Portland OR 97207 E-mail: kristofj@pdx.edu

KROCHALIS, RICHARD F. municipal government official; BS in Environ. Sys. Engring., Cornell U.; M in City and Regional Planning, Harvard U. Dir. dept. constrn. and land use City of Seattle, Seattle, 1992-99, dir. dept. design, constrn. and land use, 1999—. Examiner Wash. State Quality Award Bd., 1995-96. Pres. bd. dirs. Sustainable Seattle; active Cornell U. Alumni Affairs; mem. coun. Cornell U., 1991-98. Mem. Urban Land Inst., Am. Planning Assn., Am. Inst. Cert. Planners, Wash. State City Planning Dir.'s Assn. (pres.). Office: City of Seattle Key Tower 700 5th Ave Ste 2000 Seattle WA 98104-5070 E-mail: rick.krochalis@ci.seattle.wa.us

KROEMER, HERBERT, electrical engineering educator; b. Weimar, Ger., Germany, Aug. 25, 1928; Diplom-Physiker, Gottingen U., Ger., 1951, Dr. rer. nat., 1952; Doctorate (hon.) (hon.) , Tech. U. Aachen (Ger.), 1985, U. Lund, 1998, , 2001. Prof. elec., computer engring. U. Calif., Santa Barbara; Faculty Rsch Lecturer U. Calif, 1985—; Donald W. Whittier Chair in Electrical Engineering U. Calif., 1986—. J.J. Ebers Award of the Electron Devices Group of the IEEE, 1973, Heinrich Welker Medal of the Internat. Symposium on GaAs and related compounds, 1982, Nat. Lecturer, IEEE Electron Devices Soc., 1983, Jack Morton Award of the IEEE, 1986, Alexander von Humboldt Rsch. Award, 1994, Nat. Acad. of Engineering, 1997, Nobel Prize, 2000. Mem. NAE (fgn. assoc.), IEEE (J.J. Ebers award 1973, Jack Morton award 1986), Am. Phys. Soc. Office: U Calif Elec-Computer Engring Dept Santa Barbara CA 93106

KROENKE, E. STANLEY, professional sports team executive, sports association administrator; b. Cole Camp, Mo. m. Ann Kroenke; children: Whitney, Josh. degree, grad. degree, U. Mo. Chmn., owner The Kroenke Group, Columbia, Mo.; vice chmn., owner St. Louis Rams; owner Denver Nuggets, 2000—, Colo. Avalanche, 2000—. Bd. dirs. Wal-Mart Stores, Inc., Cmty. Investment Partnership I and II, St. Louis, Boone County Nat. Bank, Columbia, Ctrl. Bancompany, Jefferson City, Mo. Trustee Coll. of the Ozarks; mem. strategic devel. bd. U. Mo. Sch. Bus.; trustee Mo. Basketball Hall of Fame. Address: c/o Denver Nuggets 1635 Clay St Denver CO 80204-1743 also: St Louis Rams 1 Rams Way Earth City MO 63045-1525

KROLICKI, BRIAN KEITH, state official; b. Providence, Dec. 31, 1960; s. Thadeus James Krolicki and Gail Carolyn (Gourdeau) Jacus; m. Kelly Lea DiGiusto, May 21, 1994. BA in Polit. Sci., Stanford U., 1983. Cert. gov. fin. mgr.; lic. securities dealer. Assoc. banker Bankers Trust Co., N.Y.C., 1984-85; sr. acct. exec. First Commodity Boston, Zephyr Cove, Nev., 1985-86; acct. exec. Smith Barney, San Francisco, 1986-87, investment banker Manama, Bahrain, 1987-89; pres. Inter Am. Mktg. Corp., [illegible]

Nev., Carson City, 1991-99, state treas., 1999—. Sec. Nev. Master Lease Corp., Carson City, 1992—. Mem. Rep. State Ctrl. Com., Nev., 1990—; vice-chmn. planning commn. Douglas County, Minden, Nev., 1991—; chmn. support svcs. Am. Cancer Soc., Nev., 1993-96, bd. dirs. Southwestern U.S. divsn.; bd. dirs. found. Lake Tahoe (Calif.) C.C., 1996—. Mem. Nev. Govt. Fin. Officer Assn. (pres. 1997—). Avocations: guitar, outdoors. Home: PO Box 7033 Stateline NV 89449-7033 Office: State Treasurers Office Capitol Complex Carson City NV 89701

KRONE, RAY BEYERS, civil and environmental engineering educator, consultant; b. Long Beach, Calif., June 7, 1922; s. Ray Bell and Vera Harriet (Beyers) K.; m. Charlotte Jane Baldrige, June 18, 1946 (dec. June 1999); children: Charlotte Ann Krone Nelson, Ray Baldrige. BS in Soil Sci., U. Calif., Berkeley, 1950, MS in Sanitary Engring., 1957, PhD in Sanitary Engring., 1962. Soil scientist, staff sanitary engr., assoc. rsch. engr. U. Calif., Berkeley, 1950-64, assoc. prof. Davis, 1964-72, prof., 1972-88, prof. emeritus, 1988—, assoc. dean engring., 1972-88. Cons. Ray B. Krone & Assoc., Davis, 1981—; cons. to com. tidal hydraulics U.S. Army Corps Engrs., Vicksburg, Miss., 1975—; mem. bd. cons. Phila. Dist. USACE, 1972-74. 1st lt. USAAC, 1943-45. Fellow AAAS; mem. ASCE (life, Einstein award 1991, Moffatt-Nichol award 1991), NAE, Am. Geophys. Union, Estuarine Rsch. Fedn. Avocations: flying, photography. Office: U Calif Dept Civil Environ Engring Davis CA 95616

KROTKI, KAROL JOZEF, sociology educator, demographer; b. Cieszyn, Poland, May 15, 1922; emigrated to Can., 1964; s. Karol Stanislaw and Anna Elzbieta (Skrzywanek) K.; m. Joanna Patkowski, July 12, 1947; children— Karol Peter, Jan Jozef, Filip Karol. BA (hons.), Cambridge (Eng.) U., 1948, MA, 1952, Princeton U., 1959, PhD, 1960. Civil ser., Eng., 1948-49; dep. dir. stats. Sudan, 1949-58; vis. fellow Princeton U., 1958-60; rsch. adviser Pakistan Inst. Devel. Econs., 1960-64; asst. dir. census rsch. Dominion Bur. Stats., Can., 1964-68; prof. sociology U. Alta., 1968-83, prof., 1983-91, prof. emeritus, 1991—. Vis. prof. U. Calif., Berkeley, 1967, U. N.C., 1970-73, U. Mich., 1975, U. Costa Rica, 1993; coord. program socio-econ. rsch. Province Alta., 1969-71; cons. in field. Author 14 books; contbr. articles to profl. jours. Served with Polish, French and Brit. Armed Forces, 1939-46. Decorated 10 wartime medals; recipient Achievement award Province of Alta, 1970, Commemorative medal for 125th Ann. of Can., 1992; hon. citizen Gizalki, Poland, 1994; grantee in field. Fellow Am. Statis Assn., Royal Soc. Can. (v.p. 1986-88), Acad. Humanities and Social Scis. (v.p. 1984-86, pres. 1986-88); mem. Fedn. Can. Demographers (v.p. 1977-82, pres. 1982-84), Can. Population Soc., Assn. des Demographes du Que., Soc. Edmonton Demographers (founder, pres. 1990-96, hon. advisor), Ctrl. and E. European Studies Soc. (pres. 1986-88), Population Assn. Am., Internat. Union Sci. Study Population, Assn. Internat. des Demographes de Langue Francaise, Internat. Statis. Inst., Royal Statis. Soc., Polish Culture Soc. (hon. mem.), Polish Soc. Arts & Scis. (London). Roman Catholic. Home: 10137 Clifton Pl Edmonton AB Canada T5N 3H9 Office: U Alta Dept Sociology Edmonton AB Canada T6G 2H4 E-mail: kkrotki@alberta.ca

KRUBITZER, LEAH, psychology educator, neuroscientist; b. Wilkes-Barre, Pa., 1961; BS, Pa. State U., 1983; PhD, Vanderbilt U., 1989. Asst. prof. psychology U. Calif., Davis, 1995—, tchr. Ctr. for Neurosci. Presenter in field. Contbr. articles to profl. jours. MacArthur fellow John D. and Catherine T. MacArthur Found., 1998. Achievements include cross-species comparative studies to show the relationship between brain organization and brain function, providing new insights into the cerebral cortex development and the evolutionary forces responsible for brain adaptation. Office: U Calif Ctr Neurosci One Shields Ave Davis CA 95616

KRUCKEBERG, ARTHUR RICE, botanist, educator; b. L.A., Mar. 21, 1920; s. Arthur Woodbury and Ella Muriel K.; m. Mareen Schultz, Mar. 21, 1953, children— Arthur Leo, Enid Johanna, children by previous marriage— Janet Muriel, Patricia Elayne, Caroline. BA, Occidental Coll., Los Angeles, 1941; postgrad., Stanford U., 1941-42; PhD, U. Calif.-Berkeley, 1950. Instr. biology Occidental Coll., 1946; teaching asst. U. Calif.-Berkeley, 1946-50; mem. faculty U. Wash., Seattle, 1950—, prof. botany, 1964-88, emeritus, 1988—, chmn. dept., 1971-77. Cons. in field. Co-founder Wash. Natural Area Preserves system, 1966. Served with USNR, 1942-46. Mem. Wash. Native Plant Soc. (founder 1976), Calif. Bot. Soc. Rsch. edaphics of serpentines, flowering plants. Home: 20312 15th Ave NW Shoreline WA 98177-2166 Office: U Wash PO Box 351330 Seattle WA 98195-1330 E-mail: ark@u.washington.edu

KRUEGER, ANNE O. economics educator; b. Endicott, N.Y. BA, Oberlin (Ohio) Coll., 1953; MS, U. Wis., 1956, PhD, 1958, Georgetown U., 1992; PhD (hon.), Hacettepe U., Ankara, Turkey, 1990, Monash U., , 1995. Asst. prof. econs. U. Minn., Mpls., 1959-63, assoc. prof. econs., 1963-66, prof. econs., 1966-82; v.p. econs. and rsch. The World Bank, Washington, 1982-86; art and scis. prof. econs. Duke U., Durham, N.C., 1987-93; Herald and Caroline L. Ritch prof arts and scis. in econs. Stanford (Calif.) U., 1993—, dir. Ctr. Rsch. Econ. Devel. and Policy Reform, 1996-2001; 1st dep. mng. dir. IMF, 2001—. Bd. dirs. Nordson Corp., Westlake, Ohio; mem. vis. com. Econs. Dept. Harvard U., 1990-98; sr. non-resident fellow Brookings Inst.; rsch. assoc. Nat. Bur. Econ. Rsch. Author: Trade Policies and Developing Nations, 1995, Economic Policies at Cross Purposes, 1993, Economic Policy Reform in Developing Countries, 1992, The Political Economy of Agricultural Pricing Policy, Vol. 5: A Synthesis of the Political Economy in Developing Countries, 1992, Economic Policy Reform: The Second Stage, 2000; co-author (with O. Aktan): Swimming Against the Tide: Turkish Trade Reform in the 1980s, 1992; editor: (with R.H. Bates) Political and Economic Interactions in Economic Policy Reform, 1993, The World Trade Orgnaization as an International Institution, 1998. Mem. N.Y. State Regents Commn. on Higher Edn., 1992-93. Recipient Robertson prize NAS, 1984, Bernhard Harms prize Inst. for World Economy, Kiel, 1990, Enterprise award Kenan Inst., 1990, Seidman prize, 1994. Fellow AAAS, Econometric Soc. (award 1984); mem. NAS, Am. Econ. Assn. (disting. fellow, chmn. com. rsch. 1988-92, chmn. commn. on grad. edn. in econs. 1989-90, v.p. 1977, pres.-elect 1995, pres. 1996, rep. to Internat. Econ. Assn. and mem. IEA exec. com. 1992-98, v.p. Internat. Econ. Assn. 1994-98). Office: Stanford U Dept Econs Stanford CA 94305

KRUEGER, EUGENE REX, academic program consultant; b. Grand Island, Nebr., Mar. 30, 1935; s. Rudolph F. and Alma K.; m. Karin Schubert, June 9, 1957; children: Eugene Eric, Richard Kevin, Kristina. Student, Kans. State U., 1952-53; B.S. in Physics, Rensselaer Poly. Inst., 1957, M.S. in Math, 1960, Ph.D. in Applied Math, 1962. Research physicist IBM, 1957-58; research fellow Army Math. Research Center, U. Wis., 1962-63; prof. U. Colo., Boulder, 1965-74; vice chancellor, prof. Oreg. State System of Higher Edn., Eugene, 1974-82; exec. cons. Control Data Corp., 1982-85, v.p., 1985-89; exec. dir. tech.-based engring. edn. consortium William C. Norris Inst., 1989-96, v.p., 1996-97. Adj. prof. computer sci. U. Minn., 1989-94; chmn. seminar for dirs. of acad. computing facilities, 1969-82; pres. Krueger & Assocs., 1989—; cons. on computer graphics computing facility mgmt.; dir. various research grants and contracts; U.S. acad. cons. African Virtual U./World Bank, 1995—; interim pres. Christian Heritage Coll., 1998. Contbr. research papers in field to publs. Mem. Sigma Xi, Phi Kappa Phi. E-mail: rex@bendcable.com

KRUEGER, KENNETH JOHN, corporate executive, nutritionist, educator; b. L.A., Jan. 29, 1946; s. Charles Herbert and Adelaide Marie K.; m. Ellen Santucci, June 16, 1979 (div. 1989); children: Kenneth, Michael, Scott, David. BA in Humanities, U. So. Calif., 1968; MS in Edn. (Psychology), Mt. St. Mary's Coll., 1972. English tchr. Corcoran (Calif.) High Sch., 1968, Charter Oak High Sch., Covina, Calif., 1969-90; nutrition and exercise instr. Mt. San Antonio Coll., Walnut, 1974-90; pres. Mega Group, Ltd., 1990, The Krueger Group, Malibu, Calif., 1991—; exec. Overnite Express, L.A., 1993, Calif. Parcel Express, Encino, 1994-95; nutritionist Swiss Nat. Team, 1995-99; phys. edn. tchr. Hiram Johnson H.S., Sacramento, 1995-96. Adj. prof. phys. edn. Sierra Coll., Rocklin, Calif., 1996; health instr. L.A. City Coll., 1996-97, West L.A. Coll., 1998; swim coach Mt. San Antonio Coll., Walnut, Calif., 1974-77; coach, v.p. Trojan Swim Club, Newport Beach, Calif., 1978-90; bd. dirs. Nutrition and Exercise Cons., Tustin, Calif.; nutrition and exercise dir. Health Am., 1987-90; chmn., nutrition and fitness com. Internat. Eating Disorders Com., 1988; U.S. nat. team nutritionist for (FINA) World Cup 1988 Champions; recruiter Club Med, Paris, 1976-78; program coord. Pacific Am. Inst., San Francisco, 1983; asst. coach Vevey Natation, Switzerland, 1972-73; asst. swim coach Swiss Nat. Team, 1968, 85; chief marshall U.S. Olympic Swim Trials, Irvine, 1980, linguistics chmn. protocol U. So. Calif. Venue, L.A. Olympic Com., 1983-84; mem.-at-large long distance com. U.S. Swimming, Colorado Springs, 1987-91, coach So. Calif. Long Distance Swimming, 1987-89; del. chief, coach and swimmer So. Calif. Swimming for Internat. Crossing of Lake Geneva, sponsored by Internat. Olympic Com., Switzerland, 1987; meet dir. U.S. 25K Long Distance Swimming Championships/FINA World Cup Trials, Long Beach, Calif., 1988, U.S. 25K Swim Championships, Long Beach, 1989. Author: Reflections and Refractions, 1973; contbr. articles to internat. profl. nutrition and sport jours. Bd. dirs. U.S.A. Athletes Hall of Fame, 1991-92. Recipient NCAA All Am. award U. So. Calif., 1966, NCAA Nat. Champ award, 1966, U.S. Masters Swimming Champion, 1972 and annually 1974-81, Internat. Sr. Olympics Champion, 1972 and annually 1974-85; recipient commendations U.S. Congress, Calif. Senate, L.A. County Bd. Suprs; inducted into U.S.A. Athletes Hall of Fame. Mem. KC. Republican. Roman Catholic. Avocations: sports, reading. E-mail: k2krueger@hotmail.com

KRUEGER, ROBERT WILLIAM, management consultant; b. Phila., Nov. 16, 1916; s. Robert Henry and Frieda (Lehmann) K.; m. Marjorie Evelyn Jones, July 26, 1941; children: Arlene R. Krueger Pappan, Diane L. Krueger Lane. PhD in Physics, UCLA, 1942. Research engr. Douglas Aircraft Co., Santa Monica, Calif., 1942-46; asst. chief missiles div. RAND Corp., Santa Monica, 1946-53; missle systems cons. L.A., 1953-54; pres. Planning Research Corp., L.A., 1954-73, Profl. Services Internat., 1973—. Founder Profl. Svcs. Coun., 1970, bd. dirs. Chmn. 59th Dist. Republican Central Com., 1960-61; pres. 59th Dist. Rep. Assembly, 1960-61; mem. Calif. Rep. Central Com., 1962-66; Trustee U. Calif. Los Angeles Found. Mem. Am. Phys. Soc. Home and Office: 1016 Moraga Dr Los Angeles CA 90049-1621

KRUGER, CHARLES HERMAN, JR. mechanical engineering educator; b. Oklahoma City, Oct. 4, 1934; s. Charles H. and Flora K.; m. Nora Nininger, Sept. 10, 1977; children— Sarah, Charles III, Elizabeth, Ellen. S.B., M.I.T., 1956, Ph.D., 1960; D.I.C., Imperial Coll., London, 1957. Asst. prof. MIT, Cambridge, 1960; research scientist Lockheed Research Labs., 1960-62; prof. mech. engring. Stanford (Calif.) U., 1962—, chmn. dept. mech. engring., 1982-88, sr. assoc. dean engring., 1988-93, vice provost, dean rsch. and grad. policy, 1993—. Vis. prof. Harvard U., 1968-69, Princeton U., 1979-80; mem. Environ. Studies Bd. NAS, 1981-83; mem. hearing bd. Bay Area Air Quality Mgmt. Dist., 1969-83 Co-author: Physical Gas Dynamics, 1965, Partially Ionized Gases, 1973, On the Prevention of Significant Deterioration of Air Quality, 1981; asso. editor: AIAA Jour, 1968-71; contbr. numerous articles to profl. jours. NSF sr. postodoctoral fellow, 1968-69 Fellow AAAS; mem. AIAA (medal, award 1979), ASME, Am. Phys. Soc., N.Y. Acad. Scis. Office: Stanford U Bldg 10 Stanford CA 94305-2061

KRUGER, KENNETH CHARLES, retired architect; b. Santa Barbara, Calif., Aug. 19, 1930; s. Thomas Albin and Chleople (Gaines) K.; m. Patricia Kathryn Rasey, Aug. 21, 1955; children: David, Eric. B.Arch., U. So. Calif., 1953. Registered architect, Calif. Pres. Kruger Bensen Ziemer, Santa Barbara, 1960-90; part-time instr. architecture dept. Calif. Poly., San Luis Obispo, 1993-95; part-time architect, 1993—. Regent Calif. Archtl. Found., 1997—. Bd. dirs. United Boys and Girls Club. Fellow AIA; mem. Archtl. Found. Santa Barbara (pres. 1987-89). Democrat. Home: 1255 Ferrelo Rd Santa Barbara CA 93103 2101

KRUGGEL, JOHN LOUIS, plastic surgeon, b. Lake Mills, Iowa, Jan. 27, 1931; s. August and Elizabeth (Gleitz) K.; m. Kathleen Ann Lawson, June 1958 (div. 1972); children: Deborah, Natalie, Victoria, Pamela, Michael; m. Donna Marie Koerner, Mar. 2, 1978; 1 child, Matthew. AS, Waldorf Coll., 1951; MD, U. Iowa, 1957. Diplomate Am. Bd. Plastic Surgery, Am. Bd. Surgery. Intern Mercy Hosp., San Diego; resident Orange Meml. Hosp., Orlando, Fla., Mercy Hosp., San Diego, U. Calif., San Francisco; pvt. practice in plastic surgery San Diego, 1966—. Capt. USAF, 1959-61. Mem. Am. Soc. Plastic and Reconstructive Surgery, Calif. Soc. Plastic and Reconstructive Surgery, Calif. Med. Soc., San Diego County Med. Soc. (del. to Calif. Med. Assn.). Avocations: snow skiing, water skiing, hiking, pilot. Office: 4060 4th Ave Ste 120 San Diego CA 92103-2120

KRUGMAN, RICHARD DAVID, pediatrician, university administrator, educator; b. N.Y.C., Nov. 28, 1942; s. Saul and Sylvia (Stern) K.; m. Mary Elizabeth Kerber, July 9, 1966; children: Scott, Joshua, Todd, Jordan. AB, Princeton U., 1963; MD, NYU, 1968. Resident U. Colo. Sch. Medicine, Denver, 1968-71; staff assoc. Nat. Inst. Health, Bethesda, Md., 1971-73; asst. prof. U. Colo. Sch. Medicine, 1973-78, assoc. prof., 1978-87, prof. of pediatrics, 1988—, dean, 1992—. Author: The Battered Child, 5th edit., 1997; editor: (jour.) Child Abuse/Neglect, 1986—. Chmn. U.S. Adv. Bd. Child Abuse and Neglect, Washington, 1989-91; dir. Kempe Nat. Ctr. for Prevention and Treatment of Child Abuse and Neglect, Denver, 1981-92; trustee Princeton U., 2001—. Recipient C. Henry Kempe award Nat. Conf. on Child Abuse, 1989, St. Geme award U. Colo. Sch. Medicine, 1992, 98; Paul Harris fellow Rotary Internat., Sydney, Australia, 1992. Mem. Internat. Soc. Prevention of Child Abuse and Neglect (pres. 1992-94), Am. Acad. Pediatrics (Ray Helfer award 1995, Brandt Steele award 1996), Am. Pediatric Soc. Office: U Colo Sch Medicine 4200 E 9th Ave Denver CO 80262-0001

KRUGMAN, STANLEY LEE, international management consultant; b. N.Y.C., Mar. 2, 1925; s. Harry and Leah (Greenberg) K.; m. Helen Schorr, June 14, 1947; children: Vicky Lee, Thomas Paul; m. Carolyn Schambra, Sept. 17, 1966; children: David Andrew, Wendy Carol; m. Gail Jennings, Mar. 17, 1974. B Chem. Engring., Rensselaer Poly. Inst., 1947; postgrad., Poly. Inst. Bklyn., Columbia U., 1947-51. Process devel. engr. Merck & Co., Rahway, N.J., 1947-51; sr. process and project engr. C.F. Braun & Co., Alhambra, Calif., 1951-55; with Jacobs Engring. Co., Pasadena, 1955-76; from chief engr. to v.p. engring. and constrn. to v.p. gen. mgr. to exec. v.p. to pres., and dir.; exec. v.p., dir. Jacobs Engring. Group Inc., Pasadena, Calif., 1974-82; pres., dir. Jacobs Constructors of P.R., San Juan, 1970-82; pres. Jacobs Internat. Inc., 1971-82, Jacobs Internat. Ltd., Inc., Dublin, Ireland, 1974-82; dep. chmn. Jacobs LTA Engring., Ltd., Johannesburg, South Africa, 1981-82; pres. Krugman Assocs., 1982—; internat. mgmt. cons. Patentee in field. Served to lt. (j.g.) USNR, 1944-46, PTO. Mem. Am. Inst. Chem. Engrs., Am. Chem. Soc. Presbyterian. Home and Office: 24452 Portola Rd Carmel CA 93923-9327

KRULAK, VICTOR HAROLD, newspaper executive; b. Denver, Jan. 7, 1913; s. Morris and Besse M. (Ball) K.; m. Amy Chandler, June 1, 1936; children: Victor Harold Jr., William Morris, Charles Chandler. B.S., U.S. Naval Acad., 1934; LL.D., U. San Diego. Commd. 2d lt. USMC, 1934; advanced through grades to lt. gen.; service in China, at sea, with USMC (Fleet Marine Forces), 1935-39; staff officer, also bn. regimental and divsn. comdr. World War II, World War II; chief staff (1st Marine Div. Korea); formerly comdg. gen. (Marine Corps Recruit Depot), San Diego; formerly spl asst. to dir., joint staff counterinsurgency and spl. activities (Office Joint Chiefs Staff); comdg. gen. Fleet Marine Force Pacific, Pacific, 1964-68; ret., 1968; v.p. Copley Newspaper Corp., 1968-79; pres. Words Ltd. Corp., San Diego. Trustee Zool. Soc. San Diego. Decorated D.S.M., Navy Cross, Legion of Merit with 3 oak leaf clusters, Bronze Star, Air medal, Purple Heart (2) U.S.; Cross of Gallantry; Medal of Merit Vietnam; Distinguished Service medal (Korea), Order of Cloud and Banner, Republic of China. Mem. U.S. Naval Inst., U.S. Marine Corps Assn., Am. Soc. Newspaper Editors, InterAm. Press Assn., U.S. Strategic Inst. (chmn.). Home: # 307 2404 Loring St San Diego CA 92109 Office: Words Ltd 2404 Lorima St San Diego CA 92110-4827

KRULL, KATHLEEN, juvenile fiction and nonfiction writer; b. Ft. Leonard Wood, Mo., July 29, 1952; d. Kenneth Owen and Helen (Folliard) K.; m. Loyal D. Cowles, Dec. 14, 1974 (div. May 1982); m. Paul W. Brewer, Oct. 31, 1989; stepchildren: Jacqui, Melanie. BA in English magna cum laude, Lawrence U., 1974. Editl. asst. Harper & Row, Evanston, Ill., 1973-74; assoc. editor Western Pub./Golden Books, Racine, Wis., 1974-79; mng. (acquiring) editor Raintree Pubs., Milw., 1979-82; sr. editor Harcourt Brace Jovanovich, San Diego, 1982-84; freelance writer and reviewer children's books, 1984—. Frequent speaker at confs., workshops and univs. Author: Golden Everything Workbook Series, 1979, Beginning To Learn (24 books transl. into 5 langs. 1979-82), Sometimes My Mom Drinks Too Much, 1980 (Outstanding Social Studies Trade Book award 1980), Trixie Belden and the Hudson River Mystery, 1979, Twelve Keys to Writing Books That Sell, 1989, Songs of Praise, 1989, Alex Fitzgerald, TV Star, 1990, Alex Fitzgerald's Cure for Nightmares, 1991, Gonna Sing My Head Off; American Folk Songs for Children, 1992, World of My Own (4 books 1994, 95), Lives of the Musicians: Good Times, Bad Times...And What the Neighbors Thought, 1993, Maria Molina and the Days of the Dead, 1994, Lives of the Writers: Comedies, Tragedies (And What the Neighbors Thought), 1995, V is for Victory: America Remembers World War II, 1995, Lives of the Artists, 1995, Wilma Unlimited, 1996, Wish You Were Here, 1997, Lives of the Athletes, 1997, Lives of the Presidents, 1998, Lives of the Musicians: Good Times, Bad Times: (And What the Neighbors Thought), 1998, Alex Fitzgerald's Cure for Nightmares, 1999, Gonna Sing My Head Off!: American Folk Songs for Children, 1999; also articles and revs. Recipient Celebrate Literacy award Greater San Diego Reading Assn., 1994, also numerous awards for writing, including Boston Globe/Horn Book honor award, PEN West children's lit. award, 1994, nonfiction award So. Calif. Coun. on Lit. for Children and Young People, ALA Notable Book awards, Tchrs.' Choice award Internat. Reading Assn., Best Book of 1993 award Pubs. Weekly. Mem. Soc. Children's Book Writers and Illustrators (bd. dirs. 1995—, Golden Kite honor award for nonfiction). Avocations: quilting, gardening, singing, playing piano, travel. Office: c/o Harcourt Brace & Co Childrens Books 525 B St Ste 1900 San Diego CA 92101-4495

KRUMBOLTZ, JOHN DWIGHT, psychologist, educator; b. Cedar Rapids, Iowa, Oct. 21, 1928; s. Dwight John and Margaret (Jones) K.; m. Helen Brandhorst, Aug. 22, 1954 (div. Aug. 1986); children: Ann, Jennifer; m. Betty Lee Foster, Nov. 8, 1987. BA, Coe Coll., Cedar Rapids, 1950; MA, Columbia Tchrs. Coll., 1951; PhD, U. Minn., 1955; PhD (hon.), Pacific Grad. Sch. Psychology, 1991. Counselor, tchr. W. Waterloo (Iowa) H.S., 1951-53; from teaching asst. to instr. U. Minn., 1953-55; from asst. prof. ednl. psychology to assoc. prof. Mich. State U., 1957-61; faculty Stanford U. Sch. Edn., 1961-66, prof. edn. and psychology, 1966—. Vis. sr. research psychologist Ednl. Testing Service, 1972-73; fellow Ctr. for Advanced Study in Behavioral Scis., 1975-76, Advanced Study Ctr., Nat. Ctr. for Research in Vocat. Edn., Ohio State U., 1980-81; vis. colleague dept. psychology Inst. Psychiatry, U. London, 1983-84 Author: (with others) Learning to Study, 1960; (with Helen B. Krumboltz) Changing Children's Behavior, 1972; editor: Learning and the Educational Process, 1965, Revolution in Counseling, 1966; (with Carl E. Thoresen) Behavioral Counseling: Cases and Techniques, 1969, Counseling Methods, 1976; (with Anita M. Mitchell and G. Brian Jones) Social Learning and Career Decision Making, 1979; (with Daniel A. Hamel) Assessing Career Development, 1982; contbr. articles to profl. jours. With USAF, 1955-57. Recipient Eminent Career award Nat. Career Devel. Assn., 1994; Guggenheim fellow, 1967-68. Mem. Am. Psychol. Assn. (pres. div. counseling psychology 1974-75), Am. Ednl. Research Assn. (v.p. div. E. 1966-68), Am. Personnel and Guidance Assn. (Outstanding Research award 1959, 66, 68, Disting. Profl. Services award 1974, Leona Tyler award 1990). Home: 933 Valdez Pl Stanford CA 94305-1008

KRUMM, CHARLES FERDINAND, electrical engineer; b. Macomb, Ill., Aug. 3, 1941; s. Harold F. and Jean Dunlap (Burns) K.; m. Patricia L. Kosanke, Dec. 9, 1967; children: Jennifer, Frederick. AS, Grand Rapids Jr. Coll., 1961; BSEE, U. Mich., 1963, MSEE, 1965, PhD, 1970. Sr. scientist Raytheon Co., Waltham, Mass., 1969-76; mem. tech. staff Hughes Rsch. Labs., Malibu, Calif., 1976-77, sect. head, 1977-79, asst. dept. mgr., 1979-81, dept. mgr., 1981-86, lab. mgr., 1986-89; program mgr. Hughes Radar and Comm. Sys., El Segundo, 1989-96; product line mgr. Hughes GaAs Operation, Torrance, 1996; divsn. mgr. Hughes Microelectronics Divsn., Newport Beach, 1996-98; v.p., dep. mgr. ctrs. excellence and strategic components, sensors, and elec. sys. segment Raytheon Sys. Co., 1998-99; gen. mgr. Raytheon RF Components, Andover, Mass., 1999-2000; progrm dir. GAAS Tech., Conexant Sys., Inc., Newbury Park, Calif., 2000—. Home: 3223 Monte Carlo Dr Thousand Oaks CA 91362-4604

KRUPP, CLARENCE WILLIAM, lawyer, personnel and hospital administrator; b. Cleve., June 20, 1929; s. William Frederick and Mary Mae (Volchko) K.; m. Janice Margaret Heckman, June 28, 1952; children: Bruce, Carolyn. B.B.A. cum laude, Cleve. State U., 1958, LL.B., 1959, LL.M., 1963; LL.D. (hon.), 1974. Bar: Wis. 1972. Dir. indsl. relations and indsl. engring. Buxbaum Co., Canton, Ohio, 1963-66; mgr. indsl. relations Trane Co., La Crosse, Wis., 1966-73; dir. personnel-labor relations environ. products div. ITT, Phila., 1973; v.p. indsl. relations, gen. counsel G. Heileman Brewing Co., La Crosse, 1973-76; atty., v.p. human resources-risk control, sec. Good Samaritan Hosp., Dayton, Ohio, 1976-80; mgr. compensation and benefits State of Ariz., Phoenix, 1980-83; personnel adminstr., land mgmt. agt. Salt River Project, 1983-94; Indian and sch. land specialist, 1992—; chmn., pres. C.W. Krupp P.C., 1986—. Cons. on labor relations, 1969, 81-83, 88—. Contbr. articles to profl. jours. Mcpl. arbitrator, La Crosse, 1976; pres., mem. La Crosse Bd. Edn., 1969-72; mem. Wis. Gov.'s Task Force on Edn., 1972-73, Ohio Little White House library del.; mem. Ariz. Spinal Injury Panel, 1984-2000. Served with U.S. Army, 1951-53. Named Outstanding Ariz. State Profl. Employee, 1982, Employee of Quarter, 1990, 91. Mem. Am. Bar Assn. (forum hosp. on law, labor law sect.), Am. Corp. Counsel Assn., Nat. Notary Assn., Wis Bar Assn. (Continuing Edn. award 1972), Am. Assn. Hosp. Attys., Ariz. Assn. Industries (healthcare com. 1983-97, chmn. legis. subcom. 1983-97), Am. Soc. Law and Medicine, Dayton C. of C., Electric League of Ariz. (ins. advisor 1985-97), Internat. Right of Way Assn. (regional cons. Native Am. land rights 1998—). Democrat. Roman Catholic. Club: Rotary. Home and Office: 8701 E Via De La Gente Scottsdale AZ 85258-4040 E-mail: ckrupp@coqui.net

KRUPP, EDWIN CHARLES, astronomer; b. Chgo., Nov. 18, 1944; s. Edwin Frederick and Florence Ann (Olander) K.; m. Robin Suzanne Rector, Dec. 31, 1968; 1 son, Ethan Hembree. BA, Pomona Coll., 1966; MA, UCLA, 1968, PhD (NDEA fellow, 1970-71), 1972. Astronomer Griffith Obs., Los Angeles Dept. Recreation and Parks, 1972—, dir., 1976—. Mem. faculty El Camino Coll., U. So. Calif., extension divs. U. Calif.; cons. in ednl. TV C.C. Consortium; host teleseries Project: Universe. Author: Echoes of the Ancient Skies, 1983, The Comet and You, 1986 (Best Sci. Writing award Am. Inst. Physics 1986), The Big Dipper and You, 1989, Beyond the Blue Horizon, 1991, The Moon and You, 1993, Skywatchers, Shamans & Kings, 1996, The Rainbow and You, 2000; editor, co-author: In Search of Ancient Astronomies, 1978 (Am. Inst. Physics-U.S. Steel Found. award for best sci. writing 1978), Archaeoastronomy and the Roots of Science; editor-in-chief Griffith Obs., 1984—; contbg. editor Sky & Telescope, 1993—. Mem. Am. Astron. Soc. (past chmn. hist. astronomy divsn.), Astron. Soc. Pacific (past dir., Klumpke-Roberts Outstanding Contbns. to the Public Understanding and Appreciation of Astronomy award 1989, G. Bruce Blair medal for contbns. to pub. astronomy 1996), Internat. Astron. Union, Explorers Club, Sigma Xi. Office: Griffith Observatory 2800 E Observatory Rd Los Angeles CA 90027-1255

KRYDER, ANDREW, lawyer; b. 1952; BCom, JD, Santa Clara U. Bar: Calif., 1977. Gen. counsel Quantum Corp., Milpitas, Calif. Mem. ABA. Office: Quantum Corp 500 McCarthy Blvd Milpitas CA 95035

KUBAS, GREGORY JOSEPH, research chemist; b. Cleve., Mar. 12, 1945; s. Joseph Arthur and Esther Kubas; m. Chrystal Henry, Dec. 22, 1973; children: Kelly Richmond (dec. 1997), Sherry Lopez. BS, Case Inst. Tech., 1966; PhD, Northwestern U., 1970. Postdoctoral fellow Princeton (N.J.) U., 1971-72, Los Alamos (N.Mex.) Nat. Lab., 1972-74, mem. staff, 1974—; lab. fellow, 1987—. Author: Metal Dihydrogen And Sigma Complexes, 2001; contbr. articles to profl. jours. Recipient E.O. Lawrence Meml. award US Dept. Energy, 1994. Mem. Am. Chem. Soc. (Inorganic Chemistry award 1993, E.O. Lawrence award 1994). Home: 29 Camino Cielo Santa Fe NM 87501-8614 Office: Los Alamos Nat Lab # Ms-j514 Los Alamos NM 87545-0001

KUBIC, CHARLES RICHARD, naval officer; b. Greensburg, Pa., Dec. 7, 1950; s. William Louis and Josephine Roberta (Mologne) K.; m. Anne Renee Sheroda, July 29, 1972; children: Charles Brian, Kathryn Anne, Andrew William. BSCE, Lehigh U., 1972; MSCE, 1978. Registered profl. engr., Pa., Va. Commd. ensign CEC U.S. Navy, 1972, advanced through grades to rear admiral, 1998; asst. head constrn. dept. OICC, Thailand, Bangkok, 1973-75; co-comdr. NMCE Four, Port Hueneme, Calif., 1975-77; assignment officer Naval Mil. Pers. Command, Washington, 1978-80; asst. pub. works officer Nat. Naval Med. Ctr., Bethesda, Md., 1980-82; AOICC for design OICC Mediterranean, Madrid, 1982-85; White House fellow White House Office Policy Devel., 1985-86; dir. Strategic Programs Office Naval Facilities Engring. Command, Alexandria, Va., 1986-89; comdg. officer NMCB Three, San Francisco, 1989-91; prodn. officer Navy Pub. Works Ctr., Norfolk, Va., 1991-94; vice comdr. Atlantic Divsn. Navfacengcom, Norfolk, 1994-97; com 22NCR Norfolk, 1997-98; vice comdr. Navfacengcom, 1998-99; comdr. Third Naval Constrn. Brigade and PACNAVFACENGCOM, 1999—. Contbr. articles to profl. jours. Scoutmaster Boy Scouts Am., Bangkok, 1973-75, cubmaster, Madrid, 1984, Va., 1985-87, 92-94. Decorated 2 Legion of Merit medals, 4 Meritorious Service medals; CNO scholar, 1977-78. Mem. NSPE, Soc. Am. Mil. Engrs., U.S. Naval Inst., Phi Beta Kappa, Tau Beta Pi, Sigma Phi Epsilon. Republican. Roman Catholic. Avocations: golf, skiing, scuba diving, running. Office: Third Naval Constrn Brigade 258 Makalapa Dr Pearl Harbor HI 96860-3134 E-mail: kubicfam@worldnet.att.net

KUBOTA, GAYLORD, museum director; Exec. dir. Alexander & Baldwin Sugar Mus., Puunene, Hawaii, 1983—. Office: Alexander & Baldwin Sugar Mus PO Box 125 Puunene HI 96784-0125

KUBOTA, MITSURU, chemistry educator; b. Eleele, Hawaii, Sept. 25, 1932; s. Giichi and Kiyono (Naskashima) K.; m. Jane Kinue Taketa, June 30, 1956; children: Lynne K., Keith N. BA, U. Hawaii, 1954; MS, U. Ill., 1957, PhD, 1960. Prof. chemistry Harvey Mudd Coll., Claremont, Calif., 1959-2000. Vis. prof. U. Venice, Italy, 1988, Cambridge (Eng.) U., 1989. 1st lt. U.S. Army, 1954-56. Faculty fellow NSF, 1966, career devel. award, 1981; Fulbright advanced rsch. fellow, Sussex, Eng., 1973, Spl. fellow NIH, 1974. Fellow Royal Soc. Chemistry, AAAS, Am. Chem. Soc. (rsch. award 1992); mem. Sigma Xi. Office: Harvey Mudd Coll 301 E 12th St Claremont CA 91711-5901 E-mail: kubota@hmc.edu

KUC, JOSEPH A. education educator, consultant; b. N.Y.C., Nov. 24, 1929; s. Peter and Helen (Dubec) K.; m. Karola Ingrid Maywald, July 17, 1991; children: Paul D., Rebecca R., Miriam A. BS, Purdue U., 1951, MS, 1953, PhD, 1955. Asst. prof. Purdue U., West Lafayette, Ind., 1955-59, assoc. prof., 1959-63, prof., 1963-74, U. Ky., Lexington, 1974-95, prof. emeritus, 1995—. Contbr. numerous articles to profl. jours. Pres. Cen. Ky. ACLU, Lexington, 1977-79. Mem. Am. Chem. Soc., Am. Phytopathol. Soc., Am. Soc. Plant Physiologists, Am. Soc. for Biochemistry and Molecular Biology, N.Y. Acad. Sci., Phytochem. Soc., Ky. Acad. Sci., Sigma Xi. Avocations: hiking, gardening, conversation. Home and Office: 5502 Lorna St Torrance CA 90503

KUCHAR, THEODORE, conductor, academic administrator, musician; b. N.Y.C. Music dir., condr. Boulder (Colo.) Philharm. Orch., 1987—. Prin. violist leading orchs. Cleve. and Helsinki, Finland; soloist, chamber musician Australia, Europe, New Zealand, U.S., Russia, festivals including Blossom, Edinburgh, Kuhmo, Tanglewood, others; dir. orchestral studies U. Colo., 1996—; artistic dir., prin. condr. Nat. Symphony Orch. Ukraine; artistic dir. Australian Festival Chamber Music, 1990—; past music dir. Queensland Philharm. Orch., Brisbane, Australia, W. Australian Ballet, Perth. Muscian Penderecki's String Trio, N.Y.C., 1994; music dir., condr. recordings with Nat. Symphony Orch. and Ukrainian Chamber Orch. including Lyatoshynsky's Symphonies Nos. 2 and 3 (Best Internat. Recording of Yr. 1994), others; music dir., condr. worldwide tours. Paul Fromm fellow, 1980; recipient bronze medal for his work in promoting that country's music Finnish Govt., 1989. Office: Boulder Philharm Orch 2590 Walnut St Ste 6 Boulder CO 80302-5700

KUCHEMAN, CLARK ARTHUR, philosophy and religious studies educator; b. Akron, Ohio, Feb. 7, 1931; s. Merlin Carlyle and Lucile (Clark) K.; m. Melody Elaine Frazer, Nov. 15, 1986. BA, U. Akron, 1952; BD, Meadville Theol. Sch., 1955; MA in Econs., U. Chgo., 1959, PhD, 1965. Instr., then asst. prof. U. Chgo., 1961-67; prof. Claremont (Calif.) McKenna Coll., 1967—, Claremont Grad. Sch., 1967—. Co-author: Belief and Ethics, 1978, Creative Interchange, 1982, Economic Life, 1988; contbg. editor: The Life of Choice, 1978; contbr. articles to profl. jours. 1st lt. USAF, 1955-57. Mem. Am. Acad. Religion, Hegel Soc. Am., N.Am. Soc. for Social Philosophy. Democrat. Home: 10160 60th St Riverside CA 92509-4745 Office: Claremont McKenna Coll Dept Philosophy Religon Pitzer Hall 850 Columbia Ave Claremont CA 91711-6420 E-mail: clark.kucheman@claremontmckenna.edu

KUECHLE, JOHN MERRILL, lawyer; b. Mpls., Dec. 18, 1951; s. Harry Bronson and Virginia (McClure) K.; m. Nancy Anderson, June 20, 1976; 1 child, David Michael. AB magna cum laude, Occidental Coll., 1974; JD cum laude, Harvard U., 1977. Bar: Calif. 1977. Assoc. Mitchell, Silberberg & Knupp, L.A., 1977-83, ptnr., 1983-2000, of counsel, 2001—. Mem. Phi Beta Kappa. Republican. Episcopalian. Avocations: masters track and field, orienteering, rock climbing. Home: 10733 Ranch Rd Culver City CA 90230-5458 Office: Mitchell Silberberg & Knupp 11377 W Olympic Blvd Los Angeles CA 90064-1625 E-mail: jmk@post.harvard.edu

KUEHL, HANS HENRY, electrical engineering educator; b. Detroit, Mar. 16, 1933; s. Henry Martin and Hilde (Schrader) K.; m. Anna Meidinger, July 25, 1965; children: Susan, Michael. BS, Princeton U., 1955; MS, Calif. Inst. Tech., 1956, PhD, 1959. Asst. prof. elec. engring. U. So. Calif., 1960-63, assoc. prof., 1963-72, prof., 1972—, chmn. dept. elec. engring., electrophysics, 1987-98. Cons. Deutsch Co., L.A., 1973, Hughes Aircraft Co., Culver City, Calif., 1975. Contbr. articles to profl. jours. Recipient U. So. Calif. Teaching Excellence award, 1964, Haliburton award U. So. Calif., 1980; Outstanding Faculty award Eta Kappa Nu, Los Angeles, 1977 Fellow IEEE; mem. Am. Phys. Soc., Internat. Sci. Radio Union Avocations: tennis; racquetball. Office: U So Calif Elec Engring Dept Phe 622 Mc 0271 Los Angeles CA 90089-0271 E-mail: kuehl@usc.edu

KUEHL, SHEILA JAMES, state legislator; b. Tulsa, Feb. 9, 1941; d. Arthur Joseph and Lillian Ruth (Krasner) K. BA, UCLA, 1962; JD, Harvard U., 1978. Bar: Calif. 1978. Actress, 1950-65; assoc. dean of students UCLA, 1969-75; pvt. practice L.A., 1978-85; law prof. Loyola U. of L.A., 1985-89; mng. atty. Calif. Women's Law Ctr., L.A., 1989-93; mem. Calif. State Assembly, Sacramento, 1995-2000, spkr. pro tem, 1997-99, chair jud. com., 1999-2000; mem. Calif. State Senate, 2001—, chmn. natural resource com., 2001—. Appeared in TV series Broadside, 1964-65, as Zelda Gilroy in Dobie Gillis, 1959-63, as Jackie Erwin in Trouble with Father, 1950-56. Mem. gender bias adv. com. Calif. Supreme Ct., 1985-91; bd. overseers Harvard U., 1997—. Named One of 20 Most Fascinating Women in Politics, George Mag., 1996, Alumni of Yr. State Bar of Calif.'s Conf. of Dels., 1998, One of 100 Most Influential Attys. in Calif., Calif. Law Bus., 1998; recipient Barry Goldwater Human Rights award, 1998, Legislator of Yr., Calif. Fedn. Bus. and Profl. Women, 1999, Legislator of Yr., Calif. Pks. and Recreation Soc., 1999, Pub. Svc. award UCLA Alumni Assn., 2000. Mem. Women Lawyers' Assn. of L.A. (pres. 1986-87). Office: State Capitol Sacramento CA 95814-4906

KUEHLER, JACK DWYER, engineering consultant; b. Grand Island, N.B., Aug. 29, 1932; married. BS, Santa Clara U., 1954, MS, 1974; DSc, Clarkson U., 1989. Assoc. engr. San Jose rsch. lab IBM Corp., 1958-67, dir. Raleigh (N.C.) comm. lab, 1967-70, dir. San Jose and Menlo Park devel. labs, 1970-72, v.p. gen. prodn. divsn., 1972-74, v.p. devel., 1974-77, pres. system prodn. divsn., 1978-70, v.p., pres. gen. tech. divsn., 1980-81, sr. v.p., 1982, group exec., tech. group, 1982-88, vice-chmn. bd., 1988-89, pres., 1989-93; ret., 1993; ind. cons., 1993—. Asst. group exec. systems devel. Data Processing Prodn. Group, 1977-78, info. systems and tech. group exec., 1981, mem. corp. mgmt. bd., 1985, bd. dirs., 1986, exec. v.p., 1987; bd. dirs. Olin Corp., Nat. Assn. Mfrs., Aetna, Inc. Fellow IEEE, Am. Acad. Arts and Sci.; mem. NAE. Office: PO Box 11130 Telluride CO 81435

KUH, ERNEST SHIU-JEN, electrical engineering educator; b. Peking, China, Oct. 2, 1928; came to U.S., 1948, naturalized, 1960; s. Zone Shung and Tsia (Chu) K.; m. Bettine Chow, Aug. 4, 1957; children: Anthony, Theodore. BS, U. Mich., 1949; MS, MIT, 1950; PhD, Stanford U., 1952; DEng (hon.), Hong Kong U. Sci. and Tech., 1997; D Eng. (hon.), Nat. Chiao Tung U., Taiwan, 1999. Mem. tech. staff Bell Tel. Labs., Murray Hill, N.J., 1952-56; assoc. prof. elec. engring. U. Calif., Berkeley, 1956-62, prof., 1962—, Miller rsch. prof., 1965-66, William S. Floyd Jr. prof. engring., 1990—, William S. Floyd Jr. prof. engring. emeritus, 1993—, chmn. dept. elec. engring. and computer sci., 1968-72, dean Coll. Engring., 1973-80. Cons. IBM Rsch. Lab., San Jose, Calif., 1957-62, NSF, 1975-84; mem. panel Nat. Bur. Stds., 1975-80; vis. com. Gen. Motors Inst., 1975-79, dept. elec. engring. and computer scis. MIT, 1986-91; mem. adv. coun. elec. engring. dept. Princeton (N.J.) U., 1986—; mem. bd. councilors sch. engring. U. So. Calif., 1986-91; mem. sci. adv. bd. Mills Coll., 1976-80. Co-author: Principles of Circuit Synthesis, 1959, Basic Circuit Theory, 1967, Theory of Linear Active Network, 1967; Linear and Nonlinear Circuits, 1987 Recipient Alexander von Humboldt award, 1980, Lamme medal Am. Soc. Endring. Edn., 1981, U. Mich. Disting. Alumnus award, 1970, Berkeley citation, 1993, C & C prize Japanese Found. for Computers and Comm. Promotion, 1996, 1998 EDAC, Phil Kaufman award; Brit. Soc. Engring. and Rsch. fellow, 1982. Fellow IEEE (Edn. medal 1981, Centennial medal 1984, Circuits and Systems Soc. award. 1988), AAAS; mem. NAE, Acad. Sinica, Chinese Acad. Scis. (fgn. mem.), Sigma Xi, Phi Kappa Phi. Office: U Calif Elec Engring & Computer Sci Berkeley CA 94720-0001

KUHL, PATRICIA K. science educator, educator; b. Mitchell, S.D., Nov. 5, 1946; d. Joseph John and Susan Mary (Schaeffer) K.; m. Andrew N. Meltzoff, Sept. 28, 1985; 1 child, Katherine. BA, St. Cloud (Minn.) State U., 1967; MA, U. Minn., 1971, PhD, 1973. Postdoctoral research assoc. Cen. Inst. for Deaf, St. Louis, 1973-76; research assoc. U. Wash., Seattle, 1976-77, asst. prof., 1977-79, assoc. prof., 1979-82, prof. speech, language, hearing, 1982—, William P. and Ruth Gerberding univ. prof., 1997—, dept. chair, 1994—, dir. Ctr. for Mind, Brain and Learning, 2000—. Gov. bd. Am. Inst. Physics, 1994-96; trustee Neurosci. Rsch. Found., 1994—; bd. dirs. Wash. Tech. Ctr., U. Wash., 1994-96; invited presenter White House Conf. on Early Learning and the Brain, 1997, Early Childhood Cognitive Devel., 2001. Editor Jour. Neurosci., 1989-96. Recipient Women in Research citation Kennedy Council, 1978, Virginia Merrill Bloedel Scholar award, 1992-94. Fellow AAAS, Am. Psychol. Soc., Acoustical Soc. Am. (assoc. editor Jour. 1988-92, chair medals and awards, 1992-94, v.p. 1997, Silver medal 1997, pres. 1999—); mem. Am. Acad. Arts and Scis. Office: Ctr for Mind Brain and Learning Dept Speech & Hearing Sciences # 357988 Seattle WA 98105-6247

KUHL, PAUL BEACH, lawyer; b. Elizabeth, N.J., July 15, 1935; s. Paul Edmund and Charlotte (Hetche) K.; m. Janey Mae Stadheim, June 24, 1967; children: Alison Lyn, Todd Beach. BA, Cornell U., 1957; LLB, Stanford U., 1960. Assoc. Law Offices of Walter C. Kohn, San Francisco, 1961-63, Sedgwick, Detert, Moran & Arnold, San Francisco, 1963-73, ptnr., 1973-99, of counsel, 2000—. Pro tem judge, arbitrator San Francisco Superior Ct., 1989—. Served to lt. USCG, 1961. Mem. ABA, Am. Coll. Trial Lawyers, Am. Bd. Trial Advocates, Def. Rsch. Inst., No. Calif. Assn. Def., Am. Arbitration Assn. (mem. arbitration panel), Mediation Soc., Tahoe Tavern Property Owners Assn. (sec. 1979-81, pres. 1981-83), Lagunitas Country Club (v.p. 1995-97). Avocations: tennis, reading. Home: PO Box 1434 Ross CA 94957-1434 Office: Sedgwick Detert Moran & Arnold 1 Embarcadero Ctr Ste 1600 San Francisco CA 94111-3716 E-mail: beachp.kuhl@sdma.com

KUHLMAN, WALTER EGEL, artist, educator; b. St. Paul, Nov. 16, 1918; s. Peter and Marie (Jensen) K.; m. Nora McCants; 1 son, Christopher; m. Tulip Chestman, April 9, 1979. Student, St. Paul Sch. Art; BS, U. Minn., 1941; postgrad., Tulane U., Academié de la Grand Chaumierè, Paris, Calif. Sch. Fine Arts. Mem. faculty Calif. Sch. Fine Arts Stanford, U. Mich., Santa Clara (Calif.) U., U. N. Mex., Sonoma State U., Calif., (prof. emeritus, 1988—). One person shows include U. N.Mex., Walker Art Center, Mpls., The Berkshire Museum, Mass., La Jolla Museum of Contemporary Art, Calif., Santa Barbara Mus. of Art, Calif., San Francisco Mus. of Modern Art, 1958, New Arts Gallery, Houston, 1959-61, Roswell Mus. Calif. Palace of the Legion of Honor, 1956, 64, De Saisset Gallery, Santa Clara U. 20-Year Retrospective, Jonson Gallery, U. N.Mex., 1963, 64, 65, Charles Campbell Gallery, San Francisco, 1981, 83, 85, The Carlson Gallery, San Francisco, Gump's Gallery, San Francisco, 1976, 1992, University Gallery, Sonoma State U. 40 Year Retrospective, Calif. Natsoulis Gallery, Davis, Calif., Albuquerque Mus. Fine Arts, George Krevsky Fine Arts, San Francisco, 1994, 96, 99, Robert Green Gallery, Mill Valley, Calif.; group shows include N.Y. World's Fair, St. Paul Gallery, WPA Exhibition, Lawson Galleries, San Francisco, A 1948 Portfolio: 16 Lithographs (Diebenkorn, Lobdell, Hultberg), All Annual Invitational Exhibitions, San Francisco Mus. Modern Art, 1948-58, Petit Palais Mus., Paris, San Francisco Mus. Modern Art, III Biennial of Sao Paulo, Museo de Arte Moderna, Brazil, L.A. County Mus., Mus. Modern Art, Rio de Janiero, San Francisco Mus. Modern Art, 1955, 57, 66, 76, 96, Graham Found., Chgo, L.A. County Mus., Calif. Palace of the Legion of Honor, Virginia Mus. Fine Arts, Richmond, Stanford U., Gallery, Roswell Mus., 1961, 62, Univ. Art Mus., Austin, Texas Santa Fe Mus. Fine Arts, NM, Ca. Palace of Legion of Honor, Richard L. Nelson Gallery, UC Davis, Natsoulis Gallery, Northern California Figuration Expositions Art USA, 1992, 93, 94, George Krevsky Fine Art, San Francisco, Art Mus. Santa Cruz, Calif., 1993, Pasquale Ianetti Art Galleries, San Francisco, 1994, Robert Green Fine Arts, Mill Valley, Calif. 1994, 95, Am. Acad. Arts and Letters, N.Y. 1995, Dark Avenue Armory Annual Internat. Fine Print Exhbn., N.Y., Va. Mus. Modern Art Am. Paintings, Petit Palais Mus., Paris, Mus. of Modern Art, Sao Paulo British Mus., London, Nat. Mus. Am. Art, Phillip Meml. Gallery, Washington, DC, Oakland Mus. Art, Calif., Laguna Mus. of Art, Calif., 1998, The Menil Collection, Houston, Cleve. Mus. Art, Mus. Modern Art, San Francisco Mus. Modern Art, Salander O'Reilly Gallery, N.Y.; permanent collections include: The Phillips Collection, Washington, Nat. Gallery Am. Art, Washington, Walker Art Ctr., Washington, San Francisco Mus. Modern Art, Brit. Mus., Met. Mus. Art, NAD, N.Y., others. Recipient Maestro award Calif. Arts Coun.; Outstanding Calif. Working Artist and Tchr. grantee; fellow Tiffany Found., Graham Found., Chgo., Cummington Found. Mem. Nat. Acad. Design N.Y. Studio: Indsl Ctr Bldg Studio 335 480 Gate 5 Rd Sausalito CA 94965-1461

KUHN, DONALD MARSHALL, marketing professional; b. Miami, Fla., Nov. 2, 1922; s. Paul Carlton Kuhn and Helen (Merrick) Bond; m. Jane Emma Williams, Dec. 24, 1948 (dec. 1988); children: Marshall Merrick, Richard Williams, Diane Joan, Paul Willard; m. Kay Bardsley, Feb. 25, 1990. BA in Journalism and Drama, U. Miami, 1949. Cert. fundraising executive. Advt. copywriter Sears Roebuck and Co., Chgo., 1949-50; dir. pub. relations Tb Inst. Chgo. and Cook County, 1950-54; dir. fundraising Dade County Tb Assn., Miami, 1955-59, Minn. Tb and Health Assn., St. Paul, 1959-60, Mich. Lung Assn., Lansing, 1960-68, Am. Lung Assn., N.Y.C., 1968-78; nat. founder, dir. regional fin. program Rep. Nat. Com., Washington, 1978-79; exec. v.p., dir. fundraising div. Walter Karl, Inc., Armonk, N.Y., 1979-90, cons., 1990-93, May Devel. Svcs., Greenwich, Conn., 1993—. Mem. direct mktg. task force Am. Red Cross, Washington, 1983-84; mem. direct mail task force Am. Heart Assn., Dallas, 1982. Editor: Non-profit Council Info. Exchange, 1987-90; contbr. articles to Fundraising Mgmt. Mag. and other publs. Bd. dirs. Isadora Duncan Internat. Inst., N.Y.C., 1987—. Mem. Assn. Fundraising Profls. (bd. dirs. 1978-80), Direct Mktg. Assn. (mem. operating com., non-profit coun. 1987-90, recipient non-profit coun. fundraising achievement award 1991). Republican. Congregational. Avocations: personal computers, croquet. Home and Office: 6305 S Geneva Cir Englewood CO 80111-5437 E-mail: d.m.kuhn@worldnet.att.net

KUHN, ROBERT LAWRENCE, investment banker, corporate financier, strategist, author, educator; b. N.Y.C., Nov. 6, 1944; s. Louis and Lee (Kahn) K.; m. Dora Elana Serviarian, June 23, 1967; children: Aaron, Adam, Daniella. AB in Human Biology, Johns Hopkins U., 1964; PhD in Brain Sci., UCLA, 1968; MS in Mgmt., MIT, 1980. Investment banker, fin. adv. representing various firms, N.Y.C., L.A., Beijing, Tokyo, 1980—; pres. The Geneva Cos., Irvine, Calif., 1991—. Cons. copr. strategy and fin., N.Y.C., L.A., Beijing, Tokyo, 1980—; adj. prof. Grad. Sch. Bus. Adminstrn. NYU, 1981-89; exec.-in-residence U. So. Calif., 1990; bd. advisors U. So. Calif. Sch. Bus., 1992—; internat. adviser in fin. and high tech. to govts. U.S., Israel, Fed. Republic Germany, China, 1984—; vice chmn. bd. dirs. Data Software and Sys.; bd. dirs. Tower Semiconductor, N.Y.C.; sr. rsch. fellow in creatove amd innovative mgmt. IC2 Inst. U. Tex., Austin, 1986—; cons. and lectr. in field. Author: Mid-Sized Firms: Success Strategies and Methodology, 1982, Creativity and Strategy in Mid-Sized Firms, 1988, (with George Geis) The Firm Bond: Linking Meaning and Mission in Business and Religion, 1984, Micromanaging: Transforming Business Leaders with Personal Computers, 1987, To Flourish Among Giants: Creative Management for Mid-Sized Firms, 1985, Japanese translation, 1986, (Macmillan Book Club main selection), (with Arie Lavie) Industrial Research and Development in Israel, 1986, Dealmaker: All the Negotiating Skills and Secrets You Need, 1988, Investment Banking: the Art and Science of High-Stakes Dealmaking, 1989, Japanese translation, 1990, Chinese translation, 1995, (with Don Gamache The Creativity Infustion, 1989; editor: Commercializing Defense-Related Technology, 1984, (wht RAymond Smilor) corporate Creativity: Robust Companies and the Entrepreneurial spirit, 1984, (with Margaret Maxey) Reglatory Reform: Private Enterprise and Risk Assessment, 1985, (with Eugene Konecci) Technology Venturing: American Innovation Management, 1985, (with Yuji Ijiri) New Directions in Creative and Innovative Management, 1988, Medical Strategic Defense Technologist, 1986, Commercializing SDI Technologies, (with Stewart Nozette 1987); editor-in-chief: Handbook for Creative and Innovative Managers, 1987, Libr. of Investmen Banking, 7 vols., 1990; contbg. editor, columnist Jour. Bus. Strategy, 1984-90. Sloan fellow MIT, Cambridge, 1979. Mem. Phi Beta Kappa. Avocations: weightlifting, table tennis, chess, classical music. Office: The Geneva Coms 5 Park Plz Irvine CA 92614-5995

KUHNS, CRAIG SHAFFER, business educator; b. Spokane, Wash., Apr. 14, 1928; s. Theodore Lewis and Audrey Grace (Shaffer) K. BS, U. Calif., Berkeley, 1950, BA, 1954, MBA, 1955. Analyst Standard Oil Co. of Calif., San Francisco, 1955-57; bus. educator U. Calif./San Jose State U., 1958-63, City Coll. of San Francisco, 1963—. Adj. faculty U. San Francisco, 1977-90. 1st lt. U.S. Army, 1951-52, col. Mil. Intelligence USAR, 1953-80, col. AUS, ret. Mem. Calif. Alumni Assn., U.S. Army War Coll. Alumni Assn., Res. Officers Assn,. Japan Soc. Republican. Avocation: travel. Home: 8 Locksley Ave Apt 8A San Francisco CA 94122-3850 Office: City Coll San Francisco 50 Phelan Ave San Francisco CA 94112-1821 E-mail: croco_dile123@msn.com

KUHRAU, EDWARD W. lawyer; b. Caney, Kans., Apr. 19, 1935; s. Edward and Dolores (Hardman) K.; m. Janiece Christal (div. 1983); children: quentin, Clayton; m. Sandy Shreve. BA, U. Tex., 1960; JD, U. So. Calif., 1965. Bar: Calif. 1966, Wash. 1968, Alaska 1977. With Perkins Coie (and predecessor firms), Seattle, 1968—, ptnr., 1973—. Editor-in-chief Wash. Real Property Deskbook; contbr. articles to profl. jours. With USAF, 1955-58. Mem. ABA, Wash. Bar Assn., Am. Coll. Real Estate Lawyers, Pacific Real Estate Inst. (pres., founding trustee), Order of Coif, Seattle Yacht Club, Wing Point Golf and Country Club, Poulsbo Yacht Club. Office: Perkins Coie 1201 3rd Ave Fl 40 Seattle WA 98101-3029 E-mail: kuhre@perkinscoie.com

KULLAS, ALBERT JOHN, management and systems engineering consultant; b. Webster, Mass., May 5, 1917; s. Albert J. and Mary (Piechowiak) K.; m. Joyce M. Gladue, Jan. 31, 1942; children: Michael, Daniel, Mark, James. B.S. in Civil Engring., Worcester Poly. Inst., 1938; grad., Am. Mgmt. Assn. 1956; M.S. in Civil Engring., NYU, 1940; grad., Sloan Sch.

Mgmt. Sr. Execs., MIT, 1973. With Martin Marietta Corp., 1940-82, structures mgr., 1955-57, chief engr., 1957, design engring. mgr., 1957-59, tech. devel. mgr., 1959-60, Dyna Soar and Gemini Launch vehicle tech. dir., 1960-62, research and engring. dir., 1962-65, dir. tech. ops., 1965-66, dir. space sci., research, adv. tech., 1966-67, dir. Voyager program, 1967-68, dir. Planetary Systems, 1968, dir. Viking project, div. v.p., 1969-72, div. v.p. ops. rev., 1972-73, v.p. data systems, 1973-82; mgmt. and systems engring. cons. Littleton, Colo., 1982-98; pres. Albert J. Kullas, Inc. Rsch. and tech. panel space vehicles NASA, 1968-78; chmn. bd. Biax Corp., 1987-90; 1st v.p. The Highlands, Inc., 1999-2001. Contbr. articles to profl. jours. Mem. rsch. adv. coun. Colo. State U., 1971—; treas. Porter Hosp. Found., 1980-85, 1st v.p., 1986-88, pres., 1988-90, v.p., 1990-93, active, 1993—; bd. dirs. Colo. Jud. Inst., 1980-91, chmn., 1984-86; mem. exec. com. Rocky Mountain Sci. Coun., 1964-65; bd. dirs. MIT Alumni Colo., 1990—. Recipient Robert H. Goddard award Worcester Poly. Inst., 1962 Fellow AIAA (award 1967); Asso. fellow (chmn. honors and awards com. 1973-81); mem. ASCE, Sigma Xi, Tau Beta Pi. Office: 5088 W Maplewood Ave Littleton CO 80123-6729

KULONGOSKI, THEODORE RALPH, state supreme court justice; b. Nov. 5, 1940; married; 3 children. BA, U. Mo., 1967, JD, 1970. Bar: Oreg., Mo., U.S. Dist. Ct. Oreg., U.S. Ct. Appeals (9th cir.). Legal counsel Oreg. State Ho. of Reps., 1973-74; founding and sr. ptnr. Kulongoski, Durham, Drummonds & Colombo, Oreg., 1974-87; deputy dist. atty. Mulnomah County, 1992—; atty. gen. State of Oreg., 1993-97; justice Oreg. Supreme Ct, 1997—. State rep. Lane County (Oreg.), 1974-77, state senator, 1977-83; chmn. Juvenile Justice Task Force, 1994, Gov.'s Commn. Organized Crime; mem. Criminal Justice Coun.; exec. dir. Met. Family Svc., 1992; dir. Oreg. Dept. Ins. and Fin., 1987-91. Mem. Oreg State Bar Assn., Mo. Bar Assn. E-mail: moberstWhevanet.com. Office: Oreg Supreme Ct PO Box 399 Portland OR 97207 Error in get_biog_sketch x2461700ORA-20101: in exception ORA-06502: PL/SQL: numeric or value error: character string buffer too small

KUMAR, RAJENDRA, electrical engineering educator; b. Amroha, India, Aug. 22, 1948; came to U.S., 1980; s. Satya Pal Agarwal and Kailash Vati Agarwal; m. Pushpa Agarwal, Feb. 16, 1971; children: Anshu, Shipra. BS in Math. and Sci., Meerut Coll., 1964; BEE, Indian Inst. Tech., Kanpur, 1969, MEE, 1977; PhD in Electrical Engring., U. New Castle, NSW, Australia, 1981. Mem. tech. staff Electronis and Radar Devel., Bangalore, India, 1969-72; rsch. engr. Indian Inst. Tech., Kanpur, 1972-77; asst. prof. Calif. State U., Fullerton, 1981-83, Brown U., Providence, 1980-81; prof. Calif. State U., Long Beach, 1983—. Cons. Jet Propulsion Lab., Pasadena, Calif., 1984-91, Aerospace Corp., El Segundo, Calif., 1995—. Contbr. numerous articles to profl. jours.; patentee; efficient detection and signal parameter estimation with applications to high dynamic GPS receivers; multistage estimation of received carrier signal parameters under very high dynamic conditions of the receiver; fast frequency acquisition via adaptive least squares algorithms, Kalman filter ionospheric delay estimator, others. Recipient Best Paper award Internat. Telemetering Conf., Las Vegas, 1986, 10 New Technology awards NASA, Washington, 1987-91. Mem. IEEE (sr.), NEA, AAUP, Calif. Faculty Assn., Auto Club So. Calif. (Cerritos), Sigma Xi, Eta Kappa Nu, Tau Beta Pi (eminent mem.). Avocations: gardening, walking, hiking, reading. Home: 13910 Rose St Cerritos CA 90703-9043 Office: Calif State U 1250 N Bellflower Blvd Long Beach CA 90840-0001

KUMMER, GLENN F. manufactured housing executive; b. Park City, Utah, 1933; B.S., U. Utah, 1961. Sr. acct. Ernst & Ernst, 1961-65; trainee Fleetwood Enterprises Inc., Riverside, Calif., 1965-67, purchasing mgr., 1967-68, plant mgr., 1968-70, gen. mgr. recreational vehicle div., 1970-71, asst. v.p. ops., 1971-72, sr. v.p. ops., 1972-77, exec. v.p. ops., 1977-82, pres., 1982-98, dir., 1983—, chmn., CEO, 1998—. Office: Fleetwood Enterprises Inc PO Box 7638 3125 Myers St Riverside CA 92503-5544

KUMMER, WOLFGANG H. freelance/self-employed electrical engineer; b. Stuttgart, Germany, Oct. 10, 1925; BS, U. Calif., Berkeley, 1946, MS, 1947, PhD, 1954. Self-employed elec. engr. Mem. U.S. Comms. B & F, Internat. Sci. Radio Union; mem. evaluation panel NBS, Nat. Acad. Scis., 1975-81. Fellow IEEE (activities editor AP-S newsletter 1964-68, gen. chmn. AP-S internat. conv. 1971, chmn. antenna stds. subcom. 2.11 1971-77, adcom mem. AP-S 1972-79); mem. Antennas and Propagation Soc. (pres. 1975, chmn. 1985-86), Phi Beta Kappa, Tau Beta Pi, Eta Kappa Nu, Sigma Xi, Alpha Mu Gamma. Office: 1310 Sunset Ave Santa Monica CA 90405-5843

KUMPFER, KAROL LINDA, research psychologist; b. Neptune, N.J., July 30, 1943; d. Beverly Donald and Mary Belle (Campbell) K.; m. Henry Overton Whiteside, Mar. 6, 1978; 1 child, Jane H. BA, Colo. Women's Coll., 1966; MA, U. Utah, 1970, PhD, 1972; postdoctoral, U. Minn., 1975. Lic. psychologist, Utah. Asst. prof. psychology Oberlin (Ohio) Coll., 1971-73; research assoc. Inst. Child Devel. U. Minn., Mpls., 1975-76; asst. prof. Colo. Women's Coll., Denver, 1976-78; psychologist Salt Lake County Mental Health Dept., 1979-80; dep. dir. State Div. Alcoholism and Drugs, Salt Lake City, 1980-84; vis. assoc. prof. Grad. Sch. Social Work U. Utah, Salt Lake City, 1984—, asst. prof. pyschiatry, 1986—; dir. Ctr. Substance Abuse & Prevention. Editor/author: Childhood and Chemical Abuse: Prevention and Intervention, 1986, Social Facts: Utah in Perspective, 1986. Bd. dirs. Repetory Dance Theatre, Salt Lake City, 1983—, Western Assn. Concerned Adoptive Parents, Salt Lake City, 1985—, Utah Alliance for Mentally Ill, Salt Lake City, 1979-80; pres. U. Utah. Faculty Women's Club, 1974-75. Grantee Utah Dept. Social Services, Salt Lake City, 1984—; grantee Dept. Justice Office Juvenile Justice and Juvenile Delinquency Prevention, 1987—. Mem. Utah Psychologists in Pvt. Practice Assn. (pres. 1985—), Am. Psychol. Assn., Am. Pub. Health Assn., AAAS, Nat. Council Social Work Edn., Utah Psychol. Assn. (bd. dirs. 1985—), Am. Acad. Child Psychiatry (spl. task force 1986—), Nat. Inst. Drug Abuse (spl. task force 1985—, grantee 1982-86), Nat. Inst. Alcoholism and Alcohol Abuse (spl. task force 1985—, grantee 1980), Council on Social Work Edn., Evaluation Research Soc., Utah Mental Health Assn., Sigma Xi. Democrat. Unitarian. Avocations: skiing, sailing, travelling. Office: Health Promotion Edn U Utah 250 S 1850 East Salt Lake City UT 84112-0920 Address: Ctr Substance Abuse Treatment Rockwall II Bldg 5515 Security Ln # 900 Rockville MD 20857-0001

KUNG, FRANK F. biotechnology and life sciences investor, venture capitalist; b. 1948; BS, Nat. Tsing Hwa U., Taiwan, 1970; MBA, U. Calif., Berkeley, 1983, PhD in Molecular Biology, 1976. Post doctoral rsch. scientist Univ. Calif., Berkeley, 1976-77; rsch. dir. Clin. Bio-Rsch., Emeryville, Calif., 1977-79; scientist, asst. to pres. Cetus Corp., Berkeley, 1979-81; dir. Cetus Immune Corp. (subs. of Cetus Corp.), Palo Alto, 1980-84; pres., CEO Genelabs Techs., Inc., Redwood City, 1984-95, chmn., 1984-96, BioAsia Investments, Palo Alto, 1996—. Office: BioAsia Investments 575 High St Ste 201 Palo Alto CA 94301-1648 E-mail: fkung@bioasia.wm

KUNKEL, RICHARD LESTER, public radio executive; b. Syracuse, N.Y., Nov. 12, 1944; s. Lester DeLong Kunkel and Margaret Fanny Ralph; m. Mary Joan Goldsworthy, Aug. 10, 1968; children: Richard J., Charles J., Joseph B. BS, Syracuse U., 1967, MS, 1969. Lic. real estate broker, N.C. Program dir. Sta. WNBI, Northland Broadcasting, Park Falls, Wis., 1969-72; instr., prodn. dir. Sta. WMKY, Morehead (Ky.) State U., 1972-77; radio mgr. Maine Pub. Broadcasting Network, Orono, 1977-78; instr., sta. mgr. Sta. KNTU, U. North Tex., Denton, 1978-84; v.p., dean Southeastern Ctr. for Arts, Atlanta, 1985-88; pres., gen. mgr. Spokane (Wash.) Pub. Radio Inc., 1988—. Cons., 1978—. With Army N.g., 1968-74. Recipient Addy award 1975. Avocations: photography, computers. Home: 18212 N Atlantic Rd Colbert WA 99005-9608 Office: KPBX/KIBX and KSFC Spokane Pub Radio 2319 N Monroe St Spokane WA 99205-4586 E-mail: rkunkel@kpbx.org

KUNZ, APRIL BRIMMER, state legislator, lawyer; b. Denver, Apr. 1, 1954; divorced. AA, Stephens Coll., 1974; BS, U. So. Calif., 1976; JD, U. Wyo., 1979. Bar: Wyo. Pres. K and R Enterprises; mem. Wyo. Ho. Reps., Cheyenne, 1985-86, 90-92, Wyo. Senate, Cheyenne, 1992—, chair jud. com. Mem. Women's Civic League; mem. Laramie County Rep. Women's Club. Mem. ABA, Wyo. State Bar Assn, Laramie County Bar Assn. Republican. Office: PO Box 285 Cheyenne WY 82003-0285 also: Wyo Senate State Capitol Cheyenne WY 82002-0001

KUNZ, HEIDI, retail store executive; Grad., Georgetown U., 1977; MBA, Columbia U. Dir. overseas financing, asst. treas., then treas. GM Can.; treas. GM, White Plains, N.Y., 1993-95; exec. v.p., CFO ITT, 1995-99, Gap Inc., 1999—. Office: Gap Inc One Harrison St San Francisco CA 94105

KUNZ, PHILLIP RAY, sociologist, educator; b. Bern, Idaho, July 19, 1936; s. Parley P. and Hilda Irene (Stoor) K.; m. Joyce Sheffield, Mar. 18, 1960; children: Jay, Jenifer, Jody, Johnathan, Jana. BS, Brigham Young U., 1961, MS cum laude, 1962; PhD (fellow), U. Mich., 1967. Instr. Eastern Mich. U., Ypsilanti, 1964, U. Mich., Ann Arbor, 1965-67; asst. prof. sociology U. Wyo., Laramie, 1967-68; prof. sociology Brigham Young U., Provo, Utah, 1968—, acting dept. chmn., 1973; dir. Inst. Geneal. Studies, 1972-74; cons. various ednl. and rsch. instns., 1968—. Missionary Ch. Jesus Christ LDS, Ga. and S.C., 1956-58, mem. high coun., 1969-70, bishop; mission pres. La. Baton Rouge Mission, 1990-93. Author: 10 Critical Keys for Highly Effective Families, other books; contbr. articles on social orgn., family rels. and deviant behavior to profl. jours. Housing commr. City of Provo, 1984— . Served with AUS, 1954-56. Recipient Karl G. Maeser rsch. award, 1977 Mem. Am. Sociol. Assn., Rocky Mountain Social Sci. Assn., Am. Coun. Family Rels., Rural Sociol. Soc., Am. Soc. Criminology, Soc. Sci. Study of Religion, Religious Rsch. Assn., Sigma Xi, Phi Kappa Phi, Alpha Kappa Delta (Alcuin award 1997). Democrat. Home: 3040 Navajo Ln Provo UT 84604-4820 Office: Brigham Young Univ Dept Sociology Provo UT 84602

KUO, FRANKLIN F. computer scientist, electrical engineer; b. Apr. 22, 1934; came to U.S., 1950, naturalized, 1961; s. Steven C. and Grace C. (Huang) K.; m. Dora Lee, Aug. 30, 1958; children: Jennifer, Douglas. BS, U. Ill., 1955, MS, 1956, PhD, 1958. Asst. prof. dept. elec. engring. Poly. Inst. Bklyn., 1958-60; mem. tech. staff Bell Telephone Labs., Murray Hill, N.J., 1960-66; prof. elec. engring. U. Hawaii, Honolulu, 1966-82; exec. dir. SRI Internat., Menlo Park, Calif., 1982-94; founder, v.p. GWcom, 1994-98; sr. advisor W Channel Sys., 1998-2000. Dir. info. systems Office Sec. of Def., 1976-77; liason scientist U.S. Office Naval Research, London, 1971-72; cons. prof. elec. engring. Stanford U., Calif., 1982—; vis. prof. U. Mannheim, Germany, 1995-96; mem. exec. panel Chief of Naval Ops., 1980-85. Author: Network Analysis and Synthesis, 1962, (2d edit.), 1966, Linear Circuits and Computations, 1973; co-author: System Analysis by Digital Computer, 1966, Computer Oriented Circuit Design, 1969, Computer Communications Networks, 1973, Protocols and Techniques in Data Communication Networks, 1981, Multimedia Communications, 1997; cons. editor, Prentice Hall Inc., 1967— ; mem. editorial bd. Future Generations Computer Systems; contbr. articles to profl. jours.; developer Alohanet packet broadcast radio network Mem. Pres. coun. U. Ill.; adv. bd. Beckman Inst. Recipient Alexander von Humboldt Found. Rsch. award, 1994. Fellow IEEE; mem. The Internet Soc., Tau Beta Pi, Eta Kappa Nu Home: 824 La Mesa Dr Portola Valley CA 94028 E-mail: fkuo@ix.netcom.com

KUO, PING-CHIA, historian, educator; b. Yangshe, Kiangsu, China, Nov. 27, 1908; s. Chu-sen and Hsiao-kuan (Hsu) K.; m. Anita H. Bradley, Aug. 8, 1946. A.M., Harvard U., 1930, Ph.D., 1933. Prof. modern history and Far Eastern internat. relations Nat. Wuhan U., Wuchang, China, 1933-38; editor China Forum, Hankow and Chungking, 1938-40; counsellor Nat. Mil. Council, Chungking, China, 1940-46, Ministry Fgn. Affairs, 1943-46; participated in Cairo Conf. as spl. polit. asst. to Generalissimo Chiang Kai-shek, 1943; during war yrs. in Chungking, also served Chinese Govt. concurrently in following capacities: mem. fgn. affairs com. Nat. Supreme Def. Council, 1939-46; chief, editorial and pubs. dept. Ministry Information, 1940-42, mem. central planning bd., 1941-45; tech. expert to Chinese delegation San Francisco Conf., 1945; chief trusteeship sect. secretariat UN, London; (exec. com. prep. commn. and gen. assembly), 1945-46; top-ranking dir. Dept. Security Council Affairs, UN, 1946-48; vis. prof. Chinese history San Francisco State Coll., summers 1954, 58; assoc. prof. history So. Ill. U., 1959-63, prof. history, 1963-72, chmn. dept. history, 1967-71, prof. emeritus, 1972—. Sr. fellow Nat. Endowment for Humanities, 1973-74; Pres. Midwest Conf. Asian Studies, 1964 Author: A Critical Study of the First Anglo-Chinese War, with Documents, 1935, Modern Far Eastern Diplomatic History (in Chinese), 1937, China: New Age and New Outlook, 1960, China, in the Modern World Series, 1970; Contbr. to Am. hist. pubs. and various mags. in China and Ency. Brit. Decorated Kwang Hua medal A-1 grade Nat. Mil. Council, Chungking, 1941; Auspicious Star medal Nat. Govt., Chungking, 1944; Victory medal, 1945 Mem. Am. Hist. Assn., Assn. Asian Studies. Club: Commonwealth (San Francisco). Home: 8661 Don Carol Dr El Cerrito CA 94530-2752

KUPCHAK, MITCHELL, professional sports team executive; b. Hicksville, N.Y., May 24, 1954; m. Claire Kupchak. MBA, UCLA, 1987. Basketball player Washington Bullets, 1976-81, L.A. Lakers, 1981-85, asst. gen. mgr., 1986-94, gen. mgr., 1994—. Mem. U.S. basketball team World Univ. Games, 1973, Olympics, 1976. One of 20 players in NBA history to win a championship with 2 different clubs; recipient Gold medal World Univ. Games, 1973, Olympics, 1976. Office: LA Lakers PO Box 10 3900 W Manchester Blvd Inglewood CA 90306

KUPEL, FREDERICK JOHN, business executive; b. Burbank, Calif., Apr. 22, 1929; s. Martin Charles and Lorene (Murray) K.; m. Nancy Kathryn Eubank, 1952 (div. 1979); children: James Frederick, Douglas Edward; m. Karen J. Jensen, 1980 (div. 1992); 1 stepchild, John Robert Jensen, Jr. Student, Claremont Men's Coll., 1948-50; B.A., U. Calif., Berkeley, 1951; M.A. in Psychology, Sonoma State U., 1980. Lic. profl. counselor. Acctg., fin. and mgmt. positions, 1951-66; acctg. and ops. exec. Evans Products Co., Portland, Oreg., 1967-71; v.p. fin. Columbia Corp., Portland, 1971-77, Plantronics, Inc., Santa Cruz, Calif., 1977-78; counselor Yellow Brick Rd. Program, Portland, 1975-76; cons., 1978-84; dir. bus. devel. and acquisitions ITT Communication Services, Inc., 1985-87; v.p. fin., chief fin. officer Bohemia, Inc., Eugene, Oreg., 1987-89; pres. Bus. Devel. Corp., Lake Oswego, 1989-93; pvt. practice as counselor, 1990-2000; bus. owner, 1994—; CEO, Kupel & Co., Portland, 2000—. With AUS, 1946-47. Mem. Portland Indsl. Rotary (pres. 1999-2000). E-mial. Office: 3735 SE Ogden St Portland OR 97202 E-mail: fred@kupel.com

KUPERMAN, ROBERT IAN, advertising agency executive; b. Bklyn., Dec. 31, 1941; s. Morris and Gertrude Kuperman; m. Ellen Rose, June 6, 1973; children: Jason, Molly. BFA, Pratt Inst., 1963. Vice pres., sr. art dir. Doyle Dane Bernbach, N.Y.C., 1963-71; v.p., creative dir. Della Femina Travisano & Ptnrs., N.Y.C., 1971-73; sr. v.p., creative dir. Wells, Rich & Greene, N.Y.C. and Los Angeles, 1973-80, BBDO/West, Los Angeles, 1980-82; exec. v.p., exec. creative dir. Doyle Dane Bernbach/West, Los Angeles, 1982-87; exec. v.p., creative dir. chiat/Day, Los Angeles, 1987-98, pres., CEO, 1998—. Instr. Sch. Visual Arts, N.Y.C., 1968-74, Pratt Inst., Bklyn., 1966-68, Art Ctr., Los Angeles, 1975-79. Art dir. TV comml. 1949 Auto Show, 1970 (Clio Hall of Fame award 1979), Volkswagen advertisements, (now in Smithsonian Mus. Art), other TV commls. Recipient Gold medals N.Y. Art Dirs. Show, 1969, 71, Andy award Advt. Club N.Y., 1970, Clio awards for excellence in worldwide advt., 1970, 72, 74, 78, 83. Mem. Los Angeles Creative Club (co-founder, chmn. bd. dirs.), Los Angeles Advt. Club (bd. dirs. 1979). Office: TBWA Chiat/Day LA 5353 Grosvenor Playa Del Rey CA 90296

KUPIETZKY, MOSHE J. lawyer; b. N.Y.C., May 17, 1944; s. Jacob Harry and Fanny (Dresner) K.; m. Arlene Debra Usdan, June 22, 1966; children: Jay, Jeff, Jacob. BBA cum laude, CCNY, 1965; LLB, JD magna cum laude, Harvard U., 1968. Bar: N.Y. 1969, Calif. 1970. Law clerk to Hon. William B. Herlands U.S. Dist. Ct., N.Y.C., 1968-69; assoc. Mitchell Silberberg & Knupp, L.A., Calif., 1969-74, ptnr., 1974-80; ptnr., prin. Hayutin Rubinroit Praw & Kupietzky, L.A., 1980-87; ptnr. Sidley, Austin, Brown & Wood, L.A., 1987—. Bd. dirs. Nat. Inst. Jewish Hospice, Beverly Hills, Calif., 1986-98, L.A. Econ. Devel. Corp.; bd. advisors Graziadio Sch. Bus. and Mgmt. Pepperdine U., L.A., 1996-98. Mem. ABA, Beverly Hills Bar Assn., L.A. County Bar Assn. Office: Sidley Austin Brown & Wood 555 W 5th St Ste 4000 Los Angeles CA 90013-3000 E-mail: mkupietzky@sidley.com

KUPSCH, WALTER OSCAR, geologist; b. Amsterdam, Netherlands, Mar. 2, 1919; emigrated to Can., 1950, naturalized, 1956; s. Richard Leopold and Elizabeth (Heuser) K.; m. Emmy Helene de Jong, Oct. 2, 1945; children— Helen Elizabeth, Yvonne Irene, Richard Christopher. M. Cand, U. Amsterdam, 1943; M.Sc., U. Mich., 1948, Ph.D., 1950, LLD (hon.), 1997. Asst. prof. geology U. Sask., Saskatoon, Can., 1950-56, assoc. prof., 1956-64, prof., 1964-86, emeritus prof., 1986—. Dir. Inst. North Studies, 1965-73, Churchill River Study, 1973-76, Sask. Heritage Assocs. Ltd., 1973-76; bd. govs. Arctic Inst. N.Am., 1969-74, chmn., 1973-74; mem. Sci. Coun. Can., 1976-82; vice chmn. sci. adv. bd. N.W. Terrs., 1976-85; exec. dir. adv. com. Devel. of Govt. in N.W. Terrs., 1965-66; petroleum advisor to Govt. N.W. Terrs., 1980-85; mem. North Devel. adv. coun. to Govt. Sask., 1985-88; mem. BHP Diamond Mine Environ. Rev. Panel, N.W. Terrs., 1994-96. Contbr. articles to profl. jours. Served with Netherlands Army, 1939-40. Recipient Pub. Svc. award Commr. N.W.T., 1992; named mem. Order of Can., 1996. Fellow Royal Soc. Can., Geol. Soc. Am., Royal Can. Geographic Soc., Geol. Assn. Can., Arctic Inst. N.Am.; mem. Am. Assn. Petroleum Geologists, Sask. Geol. Soc. Home: 319 Bate Cr Saskatoon SK Canada S7H 3A6 Office: U Sask Dept Geol Sci Saskatoon SK Canada S7N 5E2 E-mail: walter.kupsch@usask.ca

KURLAND, STANFORD L. financial lending company executive; Sr. v.p. Countryside Credit Industries, Calabasas, Calif., 1979-83, CFO, 1983-88, mng. dir., 1988-89, sr. mng. dir., 1989-95, pres., COO, 1995-99, pres., CEO, 1999—, also bd. dirs. Office: Countrywide Credit Industries Inc 4500 Park Granada Calabasas CA 91302-1613

KURN, NEAL, lawyer; b. Springfield, Mass., July 19, 1934; s. Samuel and Jane Etta (Freeman) K.; m. Barbara Agron, June 9, 1957; children: Jeffrey Howard, Sharon Ilene, Jennifer Rose. BSBA with high honors, U. Ariz., 1956, JD with honors, 1963. Bar: Ariz. 1963; cert. specialist tax, estate and trust law, Ariz.; CPA, Ariz. Staff mem. Price Waterhouse & Co., San Francisco, L.A. and Phoenix, 1956, 58-60; assoc., ptnr. Moore, Romley, Kaplan, Robbins & Green, Phoenix, 1963-71; ptnr. Powers, Ehrenreich, Boutell & Kurn, Phoenix, 1971-82; ptnr., also bd. dirs. Fennemore Craig, Phoenix, 1982—. Adj. prof. law Ariz. State U., 1980-82. Editor-in-chief Ariz. Law Rev., 1962-63. Past chmn. tax adv. commn. Ariz. State Bd. Legal Specialization; bd. dirs. Ariz. Cmty. Found., 1986—, chmn. 1994-96; bd. dirs. Ariz. Bar Found., 1983-89, chmn., 1988; bd. dirs. Jewish Fedn. Greater Phoenix, pres., 1977-79; bd. dirs. U. Ariz. Found., 1998—; bd. visitors U. Ariz. Law Sch.; v.p. coun. Jewish Fedn., 1988-90; chmn. Jewish Cmty. Found. Greater Phoenix, 1998-2001; bd. dirs. Trust for Jewish Philanthropy, 2000—; chmn. adv. bd. Leave a Legacy, State of Ariz, 2001. With U.S. Army, 1956-58. Fellow Am. Coll. Tax Counsel, Am. Bar Found., Am. Coll. Trusts and Estates Counsel; mem. ABA, State Bar Ariz. (past chmn. taxation sect., bd. govs. 1991-93), Maricopa County Bar Assn., Phi Kappa Phi, Beta Gamma Sigma. Democrat. Jewish. Office: Fennemore Craig 3003 N Central Ave Ste 2600 Phoenix AZ 85012-2913 E-mail: nkurn@fclaw.com

KURODA, YASUMASA, political science educator, researcher; b. Tokyo, Apr. 28, 1931; came to U.S., 1951; s. Shohei and Take (Ishii) K.; m. Alice Kassis, Mar. 21, 1961 (dīv. Mar. 1995); children: Kamilla, Kamil; m. Miyoko Otaguro, Aug. 14, 1998. Student, Waseda U., 1951; BA, U. Oreg., 1956, MA, 1958, PhD, 1962. From instr. to asst. prof. polit. sci. Mont. State U., Bozeman, 1960-64; asst. prof. polit. sci. U. So. Calif., L.A., 1964-66; from assoc. to prof. polit. sci. U. Hawaii-Manoa, Honolulu, 1966-69; assoc. program officer advanced projects East-West Ctr., Honolulu, 1967-69; lectr. Japan-Am. Inst. Mgmt. Sci., Honolulu, 1973-90; pres. Election Svcs. Hawaii, Inc., 1996—. V.p. Minerva Rsch., Inc., Honolulu, 1981-96. Author: Reed Town, Japan, 1974, Chiho Toshi no Kenryokukozo, 1976, (with others) Palestinians Without Palestine, 1978; co-editor: Studies in Political Socialization in the Arab States, 1987, Japan in a New World Order: Contributing to the Arab-Israeli Peace Process, 1994, Japanese Culture in Comparative Perspective, 1997. Bd. of govs. Japanese Cultural Ctr. Hawaii, Honolulu, 1988—, program com., 1988—. Recipient Disting. Vis. Lectr. award SUNY, 1994; Rockefeller Found. grantee, 1963-64, Social Sci. Rsch. Coun. grantee, 1966-67, Toyota Found. grantee, 1984-87, 87-90; vis. rsch. fellow Harry S. Truman Rsch. Inst. of the Advancement of Peace, Hebrew U., 1992, Inst. Legal Studies, Kansai U., 1994. Mem. Am. Polit. Sci. Assn., Internat. Polit. Sci. Assn., Internat. Assn. Middle Ea. States (coll. of fellows 1986—). Democrat. Avocation: stamp collecting. Office: U Hawaii Dept Polit Sci Honolulu HI 96822 E-mail: ykuroda@hawaii.edu

KURREN, BARRY M. federal judge; BA with highest honors, U. Hawaii, 1973, JD, 1977. Law clk. to Hon. Martin Pence U.S. Dist. Ct. Hawaii, 1977-78; with Goodsill Anderson & Quinn, 1978-80, Burke, Sakai, McPheeters, Bordner & Gilardy, 1980-91; judge Dist. Ct. (1st cir.) Hawaii, 1991; apptd. magistrate judge U.S. Dist. Ct. Hawaii, 1992. Adj. prof. law William S. Richardson Sch. of Law, Hawaii, 1994—; arbitrator Ct. Annexed Arbitration Program, 1st Jud. Cir., Hawaii, 1986-91. Mem. ABA, Am. Judicature Soc., Am. Arbitration Assn. (panel of arbitrators 1989-91), Fed. Magistrate Judges' Assn., Fed./State Jud. Coun., Am. Inn of Ct. (bencher), Hawaii State Bar Assn., Aloha Inn, Honolulu County Med. Soc. (med. practices com. 1987-90). Office: C-229 US Courthouse 300 Ala Moana Blvd Honolulu HI 96850-0001 Fax: 808-541-3500. E-mail: Barry_Kurren@hid.uscourts.gov

KURSEWICZ, LEE Z. marketing consultant; b. Chgo., Oct. 26, 1916; s. Antoni and Henryka (Sulkowska) K.; ed. Chgo. and Bata ind. schs.; m. Ruth Elizabeth Venzke, Jan. 31, 1940; 1 son, Dennis. With Bata Shoe Co., Inc., 1936-78, plant mgr., Salem, Ind., 1963-65, v.p., mng. dir., Batawa, Ont., Can., 1965-71; v.p., dir. Bata Industries, Batawa, 1965-71, plant mgr., Salem, 1971-76; pres. Bata Shoe Co., Inc., Belcamp, Md., 1976-77, sr. v.p., dir., 1977-79; gen. mgr. Harford Insulated Panel Systems div. Hazleton Industries, 1981-82. City mgr. City of Batawa, 1965-71; vice chmn. Trenton (Ont.) Meml. Hosp., 1970-71; pres. Priestford Hills Community Assn., 1979-80; chmn. adv. bd. Phoenix Festival Theatre, Hartford County Community Coll., 81; vice chmn. Harford County chpt. ARC, 1980-81, chmn., 1982-83; chmn. Harford County Econ. Devel. Adv. Bd., 1983-85; mem. Susquehanna Region Pvt. Industry Council, 1983-85. Mem. Am. Mgmt. Assn. Clubs: Rotary, Bush River Yacht (commodore 1956), Bush River Power Squadron (comdr. 1957), Western Hills Country of Salem (pres. 1975), Trenton Country (pres. 1968-69), Md. Country. Home and Office: 31382 Abanita Way Laguna Niguel CA 92677-2725

KURTZ, LARRY, corporate communications executive; m. Melissa Kurtz. AB in Econs., Princeton U.; postgrad., U. Mo. V.p., tech. group mgr. Burson-Marsteller, N.Y.C., Chgo., San Francisco and Houston, 1974-84; asst. dir. corp. comm. Crown Zellerbach Corp., San Francisco, 1984-86; dir. corp. comm. Chiron Corp., 1988-92, past v.p. corp. comm.; v.p. corp. comm. and investor rels. McKesson HBOC, Inc., San Francisco, 1997—. Office: McKesson HBOC Inc 1 Post St Ste 3275 San Francisco CA 94104-5236

KURTZIG, SANDRA L. software company executive; b. Chgo., Oct. 21, 1946; d. Barney and Marian (Boruck) Brody; children: Andrew Paul, Kenneth Alan; BS in Math., UCLA, 1968; MS in aeronaut. engring., Stanford U., 1968. Math analyst TRW Systems, 1967-68; mktg. rep., Gen. Electric Co., 1969-72; chmn. bd., CEO, pres. ASK Computer Systems, Mountain View, Calif., 1972-85, chmn. bd., 1986-89; founder The ASK Group, 1972—, chmn., pres., CEO, 1989-93; chmn. emeritus, 1993—, chmn. E-Benefits, 1996—. bd. dirs. Hoover Instn., Harvard Bus. Sch., Stanford Sch. of Engring., UCLA Anderson Grad. Sch. Mgmt. Author: CEO: Building a $400 Million Company from the Ground Up, 1991, 94. Cited one of 50 most influential bus. people in Am., Bus. Week, 1985. Office: 2420 Sand Hill Rd Ste 201 Menlo Park CA 94025-6942

KURZ, MORDECAI, economics educator; b. Natanya, Israel, Nov. 29, 1934; came to U.S., 1957, naturalized, 1973; s. Moshe and Sarah (Kraus) K.; m. Lillian Rivlin, Aug. 4, 1963 (div. Mar. 1967); m 2d Linda Alice Cahn, Dec. 2, 1979. BA in Econs. and Polit. Sci., Hebrew U., Jerusalem, 1957; MA in Econs., Yale U., 1958, PhD in Econs., 1962; MS in Stats., Stanford U., 1960. Asst. prof. econs. Stanford U., 1962-63, assoc. prof., 1966-68, prof., 1969—, Joan Kenney prof. econs., 1997—, dir. econs. sect. Inst. for Math. Studies, 1971-89; sr. lectr. in econs. Hebrew U., 1963-66. Cons. econs. SRI Internat., Menlo Park, Calif., 1963-78; spl. econ. advisor Can. health and Welfare Ministry, Ottawa, Ont., 1976-78; spl. econ. advisor Pres.'s Commn. on Pension, Washington, 1979-81; rsch. assoc. Nat. Bur. Econ. Rsch., 1979-82; Lady Davis vis. prof. Hebrew U., Jerusalem, 1993; prin. investigator Smith Richardson Found., 2001. Author: (with Kenneth J. Arrow) Public Investment, The Rate of Return and Optimal Fiscal Policy,1970, Endogenous Economic Fluctuations: Studies in the Theory of Rational Beliefs, 1997; co-editor Econ. Theory, 1997—. Bd. dirs. Ben-Gurion U. of the Negev, Israel, 1998—. Ford Found. faculty fellow Stanford U., 1973; Guggenheim Found. fellow Stanford U., Harvard U., Jerusalem, 1977-78; Inst. Advanced Studies fellow Hebrew U., Mt. Scopus, Jerusalem, 1979-80; prin. investigator NSF, 1969-93, Smith-Richardson Found., 2001—. Fellow Econometric Soc. (assoc. editor Jour. Econ. Theory 1976-90); mem. Am. Econ. Assn. Democrat. Jewish. Office: Stanford U Econs Dept Serra St at Galvez Stanford CA 94305-6702 E-mail: mordecai@leland.stanford.edu

KUSAKA, MARYANNE WINONA, mayor; b. Kamuela, Hawaii, Sept. 11, 1935; BA in Elem. Edn., U. No. Colo. Mayor City of Lihue, Hawaii, 1994—. Office: County of Kauai Mo ikeha Bldg 4444 Rice St Ste 235 Lihue HI 96766-1340

KUSHNER, TODD ROGER, computer scientist, software engineer; b. Bethesda, Md., June 18, 1956; s. Harvey David and Rose Molly (Rehert) K.; m. Lea Louise Friedman, Nov. 11, 1990; children: Joshua Philip, Daniel Stuart. BS in Life Scis., MIT, 1976; MS in Computer Sci., U. Md., 1980, PhD in Computer Sci., 1982. Rsch. technician NIH, Bethesda, 1976-77; programmer Tech. Mgmt. Inc., Washington, 1977-78, GTE-Telenet, McLean, Va., 1978-79; grad. rsch. asst. U. Md., College Park, 1980-82, mem. rsch. staff, 1985-88; computer scientist SRI Internat., Menlo Park, Calif., 1982-83; sr. software engr. Vicom Sys. Inc., San Jose, 1983-85; sr. engr. Stanford Telecoms., Reston, Va., 1988-89; adv. programmer IBM Corp., Gaithersburg, Md., 1989-93; sr. scientist CTA Inc., Rockville, 1993-96; mem. sr. software staff Lockheed Martin Fed. Systems, Denver, 1996-99; mem. tech. staff Lucent Techs., Denver, 1999—. Adj. lectr. U. Santa Clara, Calif., 1983, U. Md., Gaithersburg, 1989-90, Johns Hopkins U., Gaithersburg, 1989-93; participant Software Process Interchange Network, McLean, Va., 1993—. Contbr. articles to profl. publs. Grad. fellow Air Force Office Sci. Rsch., 1980. Mem. IEEE Computer Soc., Assn. Computer Machinery. Democrat. Jewish. Avocations: swimming, racquetball, skiing, golf. Office: Lucent Techs 1999 Broadway Ste 1800 Denver CO 80202-5718

KUSHNER, TONY, playwright; Student, Columbia U., NYU. Assoc. artistic dir. N.Y. Theatre Workshop, 1987; adj. faculty dramatic writing program NYU. Author: (plays) A Bright Room Called Day, 1990, Angels in America: A Gay Fantasia on National Themes Part I "Millenium Approaches," 1992 (Pulitzer Prize for drama 1993, Tony award Best Play 1993), Part II "Perestroika," 1993 (Tony award Best Play 1994), Slavs!, 1994; adaptor: The Illusion (Pierre Corneille), 1988; writer, dir.: Yes Yes No No: The Solice of Solstice, Apogee/Perigee, Bestial/Celestial Holiday Show, 1985, In Great Eliza's Golden Time, 1986. Recipient Writers award Whiting Found., 1990, AAAL award, 1994; NEA grantee 1985, 87, 93.

KUSTER, ROBERT KENNETH, former scientist; b. Los Angeles, July 11, 1932; s. Arthur Rollo Kuster and Ermine Rosebud (Prittchett) Woodward. AS, Gavilan Coll., 1974, AA in Humanities, 1981; student, San Jose State U., 1955, 1974-76, UCLA, 1977. Installer Western Electric Co., Inc., Corpus Christi, Tex., 1951-52, 1955, San Jose, Calif., 1957-58, 1960-83; ptnr., scientist, cons. WE-Woodward's Enterprises, Morgan Hill, 1975—; technician Lucent Tech., Inc., San Jose, 1983-85, ret., 1985. Scientist pvt. practice, Gilroy, 1978—. Served to sgt. U.S. Army Corps Engrs., 1952-54. Mem. AAAS, Astron. Soc. Pacific, Calif. Acad. Scis., N.Y. Acad. Scis., Am. Legion, VFW. Baptist. Lodge: Elks. Avocations: photography, golf, camping, hiking, music. Home: 17506 Hoot Owl Way Morgan Hill CA 95037-6524

KUSTIN, KENNETH, chemist; b. Bronx, N.Y., Jan. 6, 1934; s. Alex and Mae (Marvisch) K.; m. Myrna May Jacobson, June 24, 1956; children: Brenda Jayne, Franklin Daniel, Michael Thorpe. B.Sc., Queens Coll., Flushing, N.Y., 1955; Ph.D., U. Minn., 1959. Postdoctoral fellow Max Planck Inst. for Phys. Chemistry, Göttingen, Germany, 1959-61; asst. prof. chemistry Brandeis U., Waltham, Mass., 1961-66, assoc. prof., 1966-72, prof., 1972-97, prof. emeritus, 1997—, chmn. dept. chemistry, 1974-77. Vis. prof. pharmacology Harvard U. Med. Sch., 1977-78; Fulbright-Hays lectr., 1978; program dir. NSF, 1985-86; adj. rsch. scientist U.S. Army, Natick RD&E Ctr., 1991—. Editor: Fast Reactions, vol. 16 of Methods in Enzymology, 1969; bd. editors Internat. Jour. Chem. Kinetics, 1983-90, Inorganic Chemistry, 1993-95; rsch. and publs. in field. Mem. AAAS, Am. Chem. Soc. (councilor 1983-85), Phi Beta Kappa.

KUWABARA, DENNIS MATSUICHI, optometrist; b. Honolulu, July 20, 1945; s. Robert Tokuichi and Toshiko (Nakashima) K.; m. Judith Naomi Tokumaru, June 28, 1970; children: Jennifer Tomiko, Susan Kazuko. BS, So. Calif. Coll. Optometry, 1968, OD cum laude, 1970. Pvt. practice optometry Waipahu, Honolulu, Hawaii, 1972—. Pres. 1st Study Club for Optometrists, Honolulu, 1982-83; chmn. Bd. Examiners in Optometry, Honolulu, 1982-90, state dir. Optometric Extension Found., Honolulu, 1980-88. Served to lt. Med. Service Corps, USN, 1970-72. Named Outstanding Young Person of Hawaii, Hawaii State Jaycees, 1979, Disting. Practitioner, Nat. Acads. of Practice, 1999. Fellow Am. Acad. Optometry (diplomate cornea and contact lens sect. 1991); mem. Hawaii Optometric Assn. (pres. 1979-80, Man of Yr. award 1976, Optometrist of Yr. 1983), Am. Optometric Assn., Armed Forces Optometric Soc. Home: 94-447 Holaniku St Mililani HI 96789-1710 Office: 94-748 Hikimoe St Waipahu HI 96797-3350 also: 1441 Kapiolani Blvd Ste 1520 Honolulu HI 96814-4407

KUZMA, GEORGE MARTIN, bishop; b. Windber, Pa., July 24, 1925; s. Ambrose and Anne (Marton) K. Student, Benedictine Coll., Lisle, Ill.; BA, postgrad., Duquesne U., U. Mich.; grad., SS Cyril and Methodius Byzantine Cath. Sem. Ordained priest Byzantine Cath. Ch., 1955. Asst. pastor SS Peter and Paul Ch., Braddock, Pa., 1955-57; pastor Holy Ghost Ch., Charleroi, 1957-65, St. Michael Ch., Flint, Mich., 1965-70, St. Eugene Ch., Bedford, Ohio, 1970-72, Annunciation Ch., Anaheim, Calif., 1970-86; rev. monsignor Byzantine Cath. Ch., 1984, titular bishop, 1986, consecrated bishop, 1987; aux. bishop Byzantine Cath. Diocese of Passaic, N.J., 1987-90; bishop Van Nuys, Calif., 1991—. Judge matrimonial tribunal, mem. religious edn. commn., mem. commn. orthodox rels. Diocese of Pitts., 1955-69; judge matrimonial tribunal, vicar for religious Diocese of Parma, 1969-82; treas., bd. dirs., chmn. liturgical commn., mem. clergy & seminarian rev. bd., liaison to ea. Cath. dirs. religious edn., bd. dirs. diocesan credit union, chmn. diocesan heritage bd., chmn. diocesan ecumenical commn. Diocese of Van Nuys, 1982-86; vicar gen. Diocese of Passaic; episcopal vicar for Ea. Pa.; chmn. Diocesan Retirement Plan Bd.; pres. Father Walter Cizsek Prayer League; chaplain Byzantine Carmelite Monastery, Sugarloaf, Pa. Assoc. editor Byzantine Cath. World; editor The Apostle. With USN, 1943-46, PTO. Office: Byzantine Cath Eparchy of Van Nuys 8131 N 16th St Phoenix AZ 85020-3901

KVAMME, MARK D. marketing professional; BA in French, Econs. and Lit., U. Calif., Berkeley. Programmer Apple Computer; founding mem., then internat. product mgr. in U.S. Apple France; founder, pres., CEO Internat. Solutions, 1984-86; dir. internat. mktg. Wyse Tech., 1986-89; ptnr. CKS Group, Cupertino, Calif., 1989-91, chair, CEO, 1991-98; chair USWEB/CKS, Cupertino, 1998—; ptnr. Sequoia Capital, Menlo Park, 1999—. Office: Sequoia Capital 3000 Sand Hill Rd Bldg 4 Menlo Park CA 94025-7113

KWAN, KAREN, professional figure skater; b. Torrance, Calif., June 1, 1978; Student, Boston U. Competitive history includes 7th place at Nat. Sr., 1997, 7th place Lalique trophy, 1996, 4th place Vienna Cup, 1996, 3rd place Nebelhorn trophy, 1996, 5th place World Jr. Selections Competition, 1997, 5th place Nat. Sr., 1996, 4th place Pacific Coast Sr., 1996, 4th place World Jr. Selections Competition, 1996, others. Avocations: photography, modeling, music. Office: 20 1st St Colorado Springs CO 80906-3624

KWAN, MICHELLE, professional figure skater; b. Torrance, Calif., 07 July; Grad. H.S. Nat. spokesperson Children's Miracle Network, co-chair ProKids program. Recipient Skating Mag. Readers' Choice award for figure skater of the year, 1993-94, 95-96, Dial award, 1997; named 1996 Female Athlete of Yr., U.S. Olympic Com. Achievements include being the youngest World Champion in U.S. history; third youngest World Champion; victories include: World Junior Championships, 1994, 96, Hershey's Kisses Internat. Challenge, 1995, 96, 97, Skate Am., 1995, Skate Can., 1995, Nations cup, 1995, U.S. Postal Svc. Challenge, 1995, State Farm U.S. Championships, 1996, Champions Series Final, 1996, Japan Open, 1997, 99, Thrifty Car Rental Skate Am., 1997, 1997 Skate Can., 1997, U.S. Championships, 1998, 99, World Championships, 1998, 99, Goodwill Games, 1998, 1998 Ultimate Four, 1998, Grand Slam Figure Skating, 1998, U.S. Pro Classic, 1998, 1998 Keri Lotion Figure Skating Classic, 1998, 1998 Masters Figure Skating, World Profl. Championships, 1998, others. Avocations: swimming, bowling, riding four wheeler, biking. Office: USFSA 20 1st St Colorado Springs CO 80906-3624

KWIRAM, ALVIN L. physical chemistry educator, university official; b. Riverhills, Man., Can., Apr. 28, 1937; came to U.S., 1954; s. Rudolf and Wilhelmina A. (Bilske) K.; m. Verla Rae Michel, Aug. 9, 1964; children: Andrew Brandt, Sidney Marguerite. BS in Chemistry, BA in Physics, Walla Walla (Wash.) Coll., 1958; PhD in Chemistry, Calif. Inst. Tech., 1963; DS (hon.), Andrews U., 1995. Alfred A. Noyes instr. Calif. Inst. Tech., Pasadena, 1962-63; research asso. physics dept. Stanford (Calif.) U., 1963-64; instr. chemistry Harvard U., Cambridge, Mass., 1964-67, lectr., 1967-70; asso. prof. chemistry U. Wash., Seattle, 1970-75, prof., 1975—, chmn. dept. chemistry, 1977-87, vice provost, 1987-88, sr. vice provost, 1988-90, vice provost for rsch., 1990—. Bd. dirs. Seattle Biomed. Rsch. Inst., 1992—; mem. divsn. rev. com. Pacific N.W. Nat. Lab., Environ. and Health Scis. Divsn., 1998—; mem. adv. bd. for univ. connections U. Hawaii, 1999-2001; mem. adv. com. Pacific N.W. Nat. Lab., 2000—. Contbr. numerous articles to sci. jours. Bd. dirs. Seattle Econ. Devel. Commn., 1988-92, Wash. Rsch. Found., 1989-94, Seattle-King County Econ. Devel. Coun., 1989-98, Helen R. Whiteley Found., 1997—; mem. vis. com. divsn. chemistry and chem. engring. Calif. Inst. Tech., 1991-96; chmn. adv. bd. Sch. Engring., Walla Walla Coll., 1992—. Recipient Eastman-Kodak Sci. award, U.-Industry Relations award Council for Chem. Research, 1986; Woodrow Wilson fellow, 1958; Alfred P. Sloan fellow, 1968-70; Guggenheim Meml. Found. fellow, 1977-78 Fellow AAAS (chmn.-elect, chmn., past chmn. sect. on chemistry 1991-94, mem. program com. 1994-98), Am. Phys. Soc.; mem. NASULGC (mem. exec. com. 1999—, mem. coun. rsch. policy and grad. edn., chmn.-elect 2000-01, chmn., 2001—), Am. Chem. Soc. (sec.-treas. div. phys. chemistry 1976-86, divsn. councilor 1986—; mem. com. on sci., chmn. subcom. on fed. funding for rsch. 1990-94, mem. adv. bd. for grad. edn. 2000—), Coun. Chem. Rsch. (bd. dirs. 1980-84, chmn. 1982-83), Sigma Xi. Office: Univ Wash Office Provost 312 Gerberding Hl Seattle WA 98195-1237

KWOCK, ROYAL, architect; b. San Bernardino, Calif., Sept. 29, 1947; s. Eddie Sing and Jeanie K.; m. Irene L. Leau, June 26, 1983. BArch, Calif. Poly. U., 1972. Registered architect, Calif.; Cert. Nat. Coun. Archtl. Registration Bds. Draftsman Martinskis & Prodis, San Jose, Calif., 1973-74; intern architect, staff architect, assoc. Hawley, Stowers & Assoc., San Jose, 1974-83; project architect Winston & May, Santa Clara, Calif., 1983-86; prin. May & Kwock, Santa Clara, 1986-98, Ahearn & Kwock Archs., San Jose, 1998—. Bd. dirs. Youth Sci. Inst. Santa Clara Valley, 1985-95; mem. Nat. Trust Hist. Preservation, San Jose, 1984. Corp. mem. AIA (corr. mem. Interiors Commn. 1982-83), Kiwanis Club of West San Jose (bd. dirs. 1993, 98). Office: Ahearn & Kwock Archs 600 N 3rd St San Jose CA 95112-5119

KYBETT, BRIAN DAVID, chemist; b. Oxford, U.K., May 10, 1938; arrived in Can., 1965; s. Henry and Gwenllian (Williams) K.; m. Gaynor Margaret Davies, Aug. 31, 1963, children: Gareth, Spencer. BSc, U. Coll. Wales, 1960; PhD, U. Wales, 1963. Post-doctoral Rice U., Houston, 1963-65; prof. U. Regina, Sask., Can., 1965—; dir. Energy Rsch. Unit, Regina, 1987—. Author over 200 papers and reports on chemistry, fossil fuel and renewable energy sources. Office: U Regina Energy Rsch Unit Regina SK Canada S4S 0A2

KYL, JON L. senator; b. Oakland, Nebr., Apr. 25, 1942; s. John and Arlene (Griffith) K.; m. Caryll Louise Collins, June 5, 1964; children: Kristine Kyl Gavin, John Jeffry. BA U. Ariz., 1964, LLB, 1966. Atty. Jennings, Strouss & Salmon, Phoenix, 1966-86; mem. U.S. Ho. Reps. 100th-103rd Congresses from 4th Ariz. dist., 1987-94, senator from Ariz U.S. Senate, Ariz., 1994—. Mem. Appropriations Com., Jud. Com., Select Com. on Intelligence. Past chmn. Phoenix C. of C.; founding dir. Crime Victim Found., Phoenix Econ. Growth Corp.; past bd. dirs. Ariz. Acad.; past chmn. Young Rep.; gen. coun. Ariz. Rep. Party. Mem. Ariz. State Bar Assn. Office: US Senate 730 Hart Senate Bldg Washington DC 20515-0001*

KYSAR, RAYMOND L. state legislator; b. Hays, Kans., Jan. 21, 1931; BS, N.Mex. State U. Mem. N.Mex. Legislature, Santa Fe, 1988—, mem. rules com., mem. corps. and transp. com. Republican. Office: 300 W Arrington St Ste 100 Farmington NM 87401-8432

LABA, MARVIN, management consultant; b. Newark, Mar. 17, 1928; s. Joseph Abraham and Jean Cecil (Saunders) L.; m. Sandra Seltzer, Apr. 16, 1961 (div. May 1974); children: Stuart Michael, Jonathan Todd; m. Elizabeth Luger, June 11, 1974 (div. 1979). BBA, Ind. U., 1951. Buyer Bamberger's (Macy's N.J.), Newark, 1951-67; v.p., mdse. adminstr. Macy's N.Y., 1967-73; v.p., gen. mdse. mgr. Howland/Steinback, White Plains, N.Y., 1973-75, Pomeroy's, Levittown, Pa., 1975-76; v.p., gen. mdse. mgr., sr. v.p., exec. v.p. May Co. Calif., North Hollywood, 1976-79; pres., chief exec. officer G. Fox & Co. (div. of the May dept. stores), Hartford, Conn., 1979-82; pres. Richard Theobald & Asocs., L.A., 1983; pres., chief exec. officer Marvin Laba & Assocs., L.A., 1983—. With U.S. Army, 1946-48. Avocations: coins, tennis, theatre, travel. Office: Marvin Laba & Assoc 16030 Ventura Blvd Ste 660 Encino CA 91436

LABBE, ARMAND JOSEPH, curator, anthropologist; b. Lawrence, Mass., June 13, 1944; s. Armand Henri and Gertrude Marie (Martineau) L.; m. Denise Marie Scott, Jan. 17, 1969 (div. 1972). BA in Anthropology, Univ. Mass., 1969; MA in Anthropology, Calif. State U., 1986; lifetime instr. credential in anthropology, State Calif. Curator collections Bowers Mus., Santa Ana, Calif., 1978-79, curator anthropology, 1979-86, chief curator, 1986—, dir. rsch. and collections, 1991—. Instr. prof. Santa Ana Coll., 1981-86, U. Calif., Irvine, 1983, 87, 91, 93, Calif. State U., Fullerton, 1982, 83, 88, 97, 98, 99, part-time faculty, appt. rsch. assoc. dept. anthropology, 1997—, Calif. State U., Fullerton; trustee Balboa Arts Conservation Ctr., San Diego, 1989-97, Ams. Found., Greenfield, Mass., 1985-94, Quintcentenary Festival Discovery, Orange County, Calif., 1990-91, Mingei Internat. Mus., La Jolla, Calif., 1993—, treas. bd. dirs. 1996—; inaugural guest lectr. Friends of Ethnic Art, San Francisco, 1988; hon. bd. dirs., Ethnic Arts Coun., L.A.; mem. Orange County 46th Congressional Dist. Art Bd., 1997—. Author: Man and Cosmos, 1982, Ban Chiang, 1985, Colombia Before Columbus, 1986 (1st prize 1987), Leigh Wiener: Portraits, 1987, Colombia Antes de Colón, 1988 (honored at Gold Mus. Bogotá, Colombia, 1988), Images of Power: Master Works of the Bowers Museum of Cultural Art, 1992; co-author Tribute to The Gods: Treasures of the Museo del Oro, Bogotá, 1992, Guardians of the Life Stream: Shamans, Art and Power In Prehispanic Central Panama, 1995, Shamans, Gods, and Mythic Beasts: Colombian Gold and Ceramics in Antiquity, 1998; contbg. author: What Is A Shaman: Shamans and Medicine Men From A Western Point of View, 1999. Hon. bd. dirs. Ethnic Arts Coun. L.A.; cons. Orange County Coun. on History and Art, Santa Ana, 1981-85; mem. Task Force on County Cultural Resources, Orange County, 1979; cons., interviewer TV prodn. The Human Journey, Fullerton, 1986-89; treas., bd. trustees Mingei Internat. Mus., San Diego, 1996—; mem. art bd. Orange County 46th Congl. Dist., 1997—. With USAF, 1963-67. Recipient cert. of Recognition Orange County Bd. Suprs., 1982, award for outstanding scholarship Colombian Community, 1987, Distinguished Citizens for the Arts award NAACP, 1999, cert. of recognition Calif. State Senate, 1999; honored for authorship Friends of Libr., 1987, 88; grantee Nat. Endowment for Arts, 1994, NEH, 2000. Fellow Am. Anthrop. Assn.; mem. AAAS, Am. Assn. Mus., N.Y. Acad. Scis., S.W. Anthrop. Assn. Avocations: photography, travel. Home: 2854 Royal Palm Dr Apt C Costa Mesa CA 92626-3828 E-mail: labbe@bowers.org

LABELLE, PATTI, singer; b. Phila., Oct. 4, 1944; d. Henry Holte; m. Armstead Edwards; children: Zuri, Stanley, Dodd. Singer Patti LaBelle and the Bluebelles, 1962-70; lead singer musical group LaBelle, 1970-76; solo performer, 1977—. Albums include Over the Rainbow, 1967, La Belle, 1971, Moon Shadows, 1972, Pressure Cookin', 1974, Chameleon, 1976, Patti LaBelle, 1977, Live at the Apollo, 1980, Gonna Take A Miracle-The Spirit's in It, 1982, I'm in Love Again, 1984, Winner in You, 1986, The Best of Patti LaBelle, Patti, Be Yourself, Burnin', 1991, Live (Apollo Theater), 1993, Gems, 1994, Live! One Night Only (Grammy, 1999); appeared in films A Soldier's Story, 1985, Beverly Hills Cop, 1985; appeared in TV movie Unnatural Causes, 1986, TV series A Different World, Out All Night, 1992. Recipient award of Merit, Phila. Art Alliance, 1987.Recipient Grammy award: best Rhythm & Blues vocal for "Burnin'", 1991, Grammy nomination (Best Rhythm & Blues Female Vocal, 1994) for "All Right Now". Home: 8730 W Sunset Blvd Ph W Los Angeles CA 90069-2210 Office: c/o MCA Records Inc 2220 Colorado Ave Santa Monica CA 90404

LABELLE, THOMAS JEFFREY, academic administrator; b. Owen, Wis., Sept. 21, 1941; s. Wendell Allen and Katherine (Dolan) LaB.; m. Nancy Reik, June 16, 1966 (dec. 1981); children: Katherine Anne, Jeanette Marie AA, Pierce Coll., Woodland Hills, Calif., 1962; BA, Calif. State U., Northridge, 1964; MA, U. N.Mex., Albuquerque, 1967, PhD, 1969. Prof. UCLA, 1969-86, asst. dean edn., 1971-79, assoc. dean grad. div., 1980-86; prof. comparative and internat. edn. U. Pitts., 1986-90, dean Sch. Edn., 1986-90; v.p. acad. programs, provost Ga. State U., Atlanta, 1990-93; provost, v.p. acad. affairs and rsch. W.Va. U., Morgantown, 1993-96; provost v.p. acad. affairs San Francisco State U., 1996—. Cons. InterAm. Found., U.S. AID, Ford Found., CBS, Acad. Ednl. Devel., Juarez and Assocs. Author: Education and Development in Latin America, 1972, Nonformal Education in Latin America and the Caribbean, 1986, Stability, Reform or Revolution, 1986, Education and Intergroup Relations, 1985, Multiculturalism and Education, 1994, Ethnic Studies and Multiculturalism, 1996. Vol. Peace Corps, Colombia, 1964-66. Grantee Fulbright Found., 1983, 96, InterAm. Found., Latin America, 1984; recipient Andres Bello award 1st Class, Venezuela, 1987. Fellow Soc. Applied Anthropology; mem. Comparative and Internat. Edn. Soc. (pres. 1981), Coun. on Anthropology and Edn. (bd. dirs. 1977), Inter-Am. Found. (chmn. learning fellowship on social change), Golden Key, Omicron Delta Kappa, Phi Kappa Phi. Democrat Office: San Francisco State U Acad Affairs 1600 Holloway Ave San Francisco CA 94132-1722

LABONTÉ, C(LARENCE) JOSEPH, financial and marketing executive; b. Salem, Mass. children: Linda, Joseph. BS, AME, Northeastern U.; MBA with distinction (Baker scholar), Harvard U. With H.P. Hood & Sons, Boston; project engr., mktg. coordinator Market Forge Co., Everett, Mass.; with ARA Services, Inc., Phila., exec. asst. to pres., v.p., exec. v.p.; pres. Western Co., Los Angeles; pres., chief operating officer, dir. Twentieth Century-Fox Film Corp., Beverly Hills, Calif.; chmn., chief exec. officer The Vantage Group Inc.; pres., chief operating officer Reebok Internat. Ltd., Canton, Mass.; also bd. dirs. Reebok Internat., Stoughton; chmn., CEO, Vantage Group, Inc., Palos Verdes, Calif.; pres., CEO, Jenny Craig, Internat., La Jolla, also bd. dirs., mem. exec. com. Del Mar. Bd. dirs. several cos.; founder Am. Bus. Initiative for Free South Africa; bd. dirs. U.S.-SALEP, Washington; mem. com. for econ. devel., Washington. Founding dir. South African Free Elections Fund; nat. bd. dirs. Big Bros. Am., 1970-74, pres.; bd. dirs. L.A. Philharm. Assn., 1990-94, pres., CEO, chmn. bd. dirs., trustee Northeastern U.; mem. Harvard U. Bus. Sch. Fund;

trustee Orthop. Hosp., L.A. Mem. Harvard U. Bus. Sch. Assn., Husky Assocs. Northeatern U., Huntington Soc., Human Rights Watch (Calif. exec. com.), Phila. Country Club Down Town Club, Vesper Club, Bankers Club San Francisco, 100 Club L.A. Office: The Vantage Group Inc PO Box 9488 Rancho Santa Fe CA 92067-4488 E-mail: vantagegroup@home.com

LABOVITZ, EARL A. allergist; b. Cleveland, Miss., June 12, 1949; MD, U Miss, 1975. Allergist Desert Samaritan Hosp., Mesa, Ariz. Office: Mesa-Tempe Allergy & Asthma Clinic 2451 E Baseline Rd Ste B-300 Gilbert AZ 85234-2471

LA CAGNINA, VICTOR S. company executive; V.p. Grubb & Ellis, Encino, Calif., 1997—. Office: Grubb & Ellis 16027 Ventura Blvd Ste 300 Encino CA 91436

LACHENBRUCH, ARTHUR HEROLD geophysicist, researcher; b. New Rochelle, N.Y., Dec. 7, 1925; s. Milton Cleveland and Leah (Herold) L.; m. Edith Bennett, Sept. 7, 1950; children: Roger, Charles, Barbara. BA, Johns Hopkins U., 1950; MA, Harvard U., 1954, PhD, 1958. Registered geophysicist and geologist, Calif. Research geophysicist U.S. Geol. Survey, 1951—. Vis. prof. Dartmouth Coll., 1963; mem. numerous adv. coms. and panels. Contbr. articles to sci. jours. Mem. Los Altos Hills (Calif.) Planning Commn., 1966-86. Served with USAAF, 1943-46. Recipient Spl. Act award U.S. Geol. Survey, 1970, Meritorious Service award, 1972, Disting. Service award U.S. Dept. Interior, 1978. Fellow AAAS, Am. Geophys. Union (Walter H. Bucher medal 1989), Royal Astron. Soc., Geol. Soc. Am. (Kirk Bryan award 1963), Arctic Inst. N.Am.; mem. Nat. Acad. Sci. Achievements include current work: solid-earth geophysics, terrestial heat flow, tectonophysics, permafrost; subspecialties: tectonics, geophysics. Office: US Geol Survey 345 Middlefield Rd Menlo Park CA 94025-3591

LACITIS, ERIK, journalist; b. Buenos Aires, Argentina, Dec. 10, 1949; came to U.S., 1960, naturalized, 1965; s. Erik and Irene Z. L.; m. Malorie Nelson, Aug. 30, 1976. Student, Coll. Forest Resources, U. Wash., 1967-71. Editor U. Wash. Daily, 1970; pub. New Times Jour., 1970-71; reporter, pop-music cons. Seattle Post Intelligencer, 1972—; reporter, columnist Seattle Times, 1974—; v.p., treas. Malorie Nelson, Inc., 1980—. Recipient numerous awards from Wash. State chpt. Sigma Delta Chi; Nat. Headliners Club award, 1978; winner gen. interest competition Nat. Soc. Newspaper Columnists, 1987, Best of the West Journalism contest, 2000. Lutheran. Office: The Seattle Times PO Box 7070 Fairview Ave N & John St Seattle WA 98111-0070

LACKLAND, JOHN, lawyer; b. Parma, Idaho, Aug. 29, 1939; A.B., Stanford U., 1962; J.D., U. Wash., 1964; master gardener, Colo. State U., 1996. Bar: Wash. 1965, U.S. Dist. Ct. (we. dist.) Wash. 1965, (ea. dist.) Wash. 1973, U.S. Ct. Appeals (9th cir.) 1965, Conn. 1981, U.S. Dist. Ct. Conn. 1983, U.S. Supreme Ct. 1973, U.S. Dist. Ct. (so. dist.) N.Y. 1988. Assoc. firm Lane Powell Moss & Miller, Seattle, 1965-69; asst. atty. gen. State of Wash., Seattle, 1969-72; asst. chief State of Wash. (U. Wash. div.), 1969-72; v.p., sec., gen. counsel Western Farmers Assn., Seattle, 1972-76, Fotomat Corp., Stamford, Conn., 1976-80; ptnr. Leepson & Lackland, 1981-88, Lackland and Nalewaik, 1988-92; pvt. practices Westport, Conn., 1992-94; prin. Lackland Assocs., Grand Junction, Colo., 1994—. Bd. dirs. Mercer Island (Wash.) Congl. Ch., 1967-70, pres. bd. dirs., 1970; mem. land use plan steering com. City of Mercer Island, 1970-72; bd. dirs. Mercer Island Sch. Dist., 1970-73, v.p. bd. dirs., 1972, pres. 1973; trustee Mid-Fairfield Child Guidance Ctr., 1982-84, Norfield Congl. Ch., 1982-84; bd. dirs. Grand Junction Symphony Orch., 1995-99.

LACOVARA, MICHAEL, lawyer; b. Bklyn., Oct. 21, 1963; s. Philip Allen and Madeline Estelle (Papio) L.; m. Carla J. Foran, Sept. 9, 1989; children: Claire Elizabeth, Edward Christopher. BA, U. Pa., 1984; MPhil, Cambridge (U.K.) U., 1985; JD, Harvard U., 1988. Law clk. Hon. Stephen Reinhardt, L.A., 1988-89; assoc. Sullivan & Cromwell, N.Y.C., 1989-96, ptnr., 1997-2000, Palo Alto, Calif., 2000—. Bd. dirs. Lower Manhattan Cultural Coun., N.Y.C., 1995—, chair, 1998; trustee Cambridge U. in Am. Thouron Found. fellow, 1984. Mem. ABA, Assn. of Bar of City of N.Y., Phi Beta Kappa. Democrat. Roman Catholic. Home: 2740 Divisadero St San Francisco CA 94123 Office: Sullivan & Cromwell 1870 Embarcadero Rd Palo Alto CA 94303 E-mail: lacovaram@sullcrom.com

LACROIX, PIERRE, professional sports team professional; m. Colombe Lacroix; children: Martin, Eric. Agt. NHL; gen. mgr. Colo. Avalanche, Denver, 1994—. Recipient 1996 Stanley Cup Championship, Denver Avalanche; named 1996 NHL Exec. of Yr., The Hockey News.

LACROSSE, PATRICK, retired museum administrator; CEO, pres. Oreg. Mus. of Sci. & Industry, Portland, Oreg. Office: Oreg Mus Sci Industry 1945 SE Water Ave Portland OR 97214-3356

LACY, ELSIE, state legislator; b. Las Animas, Colo., May 22, 1947; m. Duane Lacy. Mem. Colo. State Senate, 1992—, chair appropriations com., chair joint budge com. Fund raising coord. YMCA; pres. PTO; dist. chair Cancer Crusade; mem. Aurora City Coun., 1983-87, 89-92; mayor pro tem Aurora, 1991; active Denver Regional Coun. Govts., Transp. Fin. Task Force; vice-chair Aurora Econ. Devel. Coun. Mem. Aurora C. of C. Republican. Home: 11637 E Mexico Ave Aurora CO 80012-5213 Office: State Capitol 200 E Colfax Ave Ste 346 Denver CO 80203-1716

LACY, JOHN R. lawyer; b. Dallas, Dec. 15, 1942; BS, San Diego State U., 1966; MS, U. So. Calif., 1971; JD, U. Calif., 1973. Bar: Calif. 1973, Hawaii 1974. Atty. Goodsill Anderson Quinn & Stifel, Honolulu. Arbitrator Ct. Annexed Arbitration Program, 1986—. Comment editor Hastings Law Jour., 1972-73. Mem. ABA, Hawaii Bar Assn., State Bar Calif., Am. Bd. Trial Advs., Maritime Law Assn. U.S., Thurston Soc., Order of Coif. Office: Goodsill Anderson Quinn & Stifel PO Box 3196 1800 Alii Pl 1099 Alakea St Honolulu HI 96813-4511 E-mail: jlacy@goodsill.com

LADANYI, BRANKA MARIA, chemist, educator; b. Zagreb, Croatia, Sept. 7, 1947; came to U.S., 1969; d. Branko and Nevenka (Zilic) L.; m. Marshall Fixman, Dec. 7, 1974. BSc, McGill U., Montreal, Can., 1969; M in Philosophy, Yale U., 1971, PhD, 1973. Vis. prof. of chemistry U. Ill., 1974; postdoctoral research assoc. Yale U., 1974-77, research assoc., 1977-79; asst. prof. chemistry Colo. State U., Ft. Collins, 1979-84, assoc. prof. chemistry, 1985-87, prof. chemistry, 1987—. Vis. fellow Joint Inst. for Lab. Astrophysics, 1993-94. Assoc. editor Jour. Chem. Physics, 1994—; referee and contbr. articles to profl. jours. Fellow Sloan Found., 1982-84, Dreyfus Found., 1983-87; grantee NSF, NATO, 1983-89. Fellow Am. Phys. Soc.; mem. AAAS, Am. Chem. Soc. (PRF grantee 1979-82, 1989-91, 95-98), Sigma Xi. Office: Colo State U Dept Chemistry Fort Collins CO 80523-0001 E-mail: bl@lamar.colostate.edu

LADAR, JERROLD MORTON, lawyer; b. San Francisco, Aug. 2, 1933; AB, U. Wash., 1956; LLB, U. Calif., Berkeley, 1960. Bar: Calif. 1961, U.S. Supreme Ct. 1967. Law clk. to judge U.S. Dist. Ct. (no. dist.) Calif., 1960-61; asst. U.S. atty. San Francisco, 1961-70; chief criminal div., 1968-70; mem. firm MacInnis & Donner, San Francisco, 1970-72; prof. criminal law and procedure U. San Francisco Law Sch., 1962-83; pvt. practice San Francisco., 1970—; ptnr. Ladar & Ladar, San Francisco, 1994—. Lectr. Hastings Coll. Law, Civil and Criminal Advocacy Programs, 1985—; chair pvt. defender panel U.S. Dist. Ct. (no. dist.) Calif., 1980-90; ct. apptd. chair stats. and tech. subcom. Fed. Civil Justice Reform Act Com. (no. dist.) Calif., 1990-95; ct. apptd. mem. Fed. Ct. Civil Local Rules Revision Com. (no. dist.) Calif., 1994—; ct. apptd. chmn. Criminal Local Rules Revision Com. (no. dist.) Calif., 1991-99; mem. continuing edn. of bar criminal law adv. com. U. Calif., Berkeley, 1978-83, 89-2001; panelist, mem. nat. planning com. ABA Nat. Ann. White Collar Crime Inst., 1996—; ct. apptd. mem. Local Disciplinary Rule Draft com., 1998-99 Author: (with others) Selected Trial Motions, Grand Jury Practice, Asset Forfeiture, California Criminal Law and Procedure Practice, 5th edit., 2000, Direct Examination-Tips and Techniques, 1982, Collateral Effects of Federal Convictions, 1997, Insult Added to Injury: The Fallout From Tax Conviction, 1997, Give Me A Break-Finding Federal Misdemeanors, 1998, The Court: We're Here to Seek the Truth; Defense Counsel: Excuse Me, That's Not My Job, 1999, A Day At The Grand Jury, 2000, Daubert at the Gates: Use A Trojan Horse, 2001. Trustee Tamalpais Union High Sch. Dist., 1968-77, chmn. bd., 1973-74; mem. adv. com. Nat. PTA Assn., 1972-78; apptd. mem. criminal justice act com. U.S. Ct. Appeals (9th cir). Fellow Am. Bd. Criminal Lawyers; mem. ABA, San Francisco Bar Assn. (editor in Re 1974-76), State Bar Calif. (pro-tem disciplinary referee 1976-78, vice chmn. pub. interest and edn. com. criminal law sect., mem. exec. com. criminal law sect. 1980-87, editor Criminal Law Sect. News 1981-87, chmn. exec. com. 1983-84), Am. Inns. of Ct. (exec. com. 1994-97), Fed. Bar Assn. (panelist), Nat. Sentencing Inst. (contbr.) Office: 507 Polk St Ste 310 San Francisco CA 94102-3339

LADD, JAMES ROGER, international business executive and consultant; b. San Diego, Mar. 5, 1943; s. Robert Dwinell and Virginia Ruth (Dole) L.; m. Sharon Patricia Smith, Aug. 22, 1964; children— Brian Andrew, Jennifer Louise, Casey James AB, Duke U., 1964. CPA, CMC. With Deloitte Haskins & Sells, Seattle, 1964-79, mng. ptnr. Tokyo, 1979-84, dir. human resources N.Y.C., 1984-86, area mng. ptnr. Seattle, 1986-89; mng. dir. Deloitte & Touche, Seattle, 1989-92; pres. Ladd Pacific Cons., Seattle, 1992-97; pres., CEO EnCompass Globalization Inc., Kirkland, Wash., 1997—. Pres. Seattle Children's Home, 1979; bd. dirs., treas. Seattle Found., 1988-97; trustee Duke U., 1991-93; chair internat. bus. adv. coun. U. Wash., 1995-97. Mem. AICPA, Japan Am. Soc. State Wash. (pres. 1996-98), Wash. Soc. CPAs, Duke Alumni Assn. (nat. pres. 1991-92), Inst. Mgmt. Cons., Rainier Club. Office: Ste 205 4040 Lake Washington Blvd NE Kirkland WA 98033-7874

LADEHOFF, ROBERT LOUIS, bishop; b. Feb. 19, 1932; m. Jean Arthur Burcham (dec. Feb. 1992); 1 child, Robert Louis Jr. Grad., Duke U., 1954, Gen. Theol. Sem., 1957, Va. Theol. Sem., 1980. Ordained deacon, priest The Episcopal Ch., 1957. Priest in charge N.C. parishes, 1957-60; rector St. Christopher's Ch., Charlotte, N.C., 1960-74, St. John's Ch., Fayetteville, 1974-85; bishop, co-adjutor of Oreg., 1985; bishop, 1986—. Office: Diocese of Oreg PO Box 467 Lake Oswego OR 97034-0467

LADNER, THOMAS E. lawyer; b. Vancouver, B.C., Can., Dec. 8, 1916; B.A., U. B.C., 1937; LLB, Osgoode Hall. Bar: B.C. bar 1940. Ret. partner firm Borden Ladner Gervais LLP (formerly Ladner Downs), Vancouver, Can. Mem. Canadian, Vancouver bar assns., Law Soc. B.C. Office: PO Box 48600 1200-200 Burrard St Vancouver BC Canada V7X 1T2

LA FORCE, JAMES CLAYBURN, JR. economist, educator; b. San Diego, Dec. 28, 1928; s. James Clayburn and Beatrice Maureen (Boyd) La F.; m. Barbara Lea Latham, Sept. 23, 1952; children: Jessica, Allison, Joseph. BA, San Diego State Coll., 1951; MA, UCLA, 1958, PhD, 1962. Asst. prof. econs. UCLA, 1962-66, assoc. prof., 1967-70, prof., 1971-93, prof. emeritus, 1993—, chmn. dept. econs., 1969-78, dean Anderson Sch. Mgmt., 1978-93; acting dean Hong Kong U. Sci. & Tech., 1991-93. Bd. dirs. Jacobs Engring. Group Inc., The Timken Co., The Black Rock Funds, Payden & Rygel Investment Trust, Providence Investment Coun. Mut. Funds, Motor Cargo Industries, Trust Investment Mgrs.; chmn. adv. com. Calif. Workmen's Compensation. Author: The Development of the Spanish Textile Industry 1750-1800, 1965, (with Warren C. Scoville) The Economic Development of Western Europe, vols. 1-5, 1969-70. Bd. dirs. Nat. Bur. Econ. Rsch., 1975-88, Found. Francisco Marroquin, Lynde and Harry Bradley Found., Pacific Legal Found., 1981-86; trustee Found. for Rsch. in Econs. and Edn., 1970—, chmn., 1977—; mem. bd. overseers Hoover Inst. on War, Revolution and Peace, 1979-85, 86-93; mem. nat. coun. on humanities NEH, 1981-88; chmn. Pres.'s Task Force on Food Assistance, 1983-84. Social Sci. Research Council research tng. fellow, 1958-60; Fulbright sr. research grantee, 1965-66; Am. Philos. Soc. grantee, 1965-66 Mem. Econ. History Assn., Mont Pelerin Soc., Phi Beta Kappa Office: UCLA Anderson Grad Sch Mgmt 405 Hilgard Ave Los Angeles CA 90095-9000

LAGADIN, JOHN, engineering consultant; BS in Geol. Engring., Mich. Tech. U. Founder, devloper Energy Exch., Inc.; pres., CEO Direct Energy Mktg. Ltd., GeoScope Exploration Techs., Inc., Calgary, Alta., Can. Bd. dirs. Cabre Exploration Ltd., PetroReef Resources Ltd., Alliance Pipeline, Autumn Industries, Ltd., Redmond Capital Corp., Dynamic Oil and Gas, Inc. Recipient Centennial Leadership award Assn. Profl. Engrs., Geologists and Geophysicists Alta., 2000. Office: Airport Exec Pk 10711 Cambie Rd Ste 205 Richmond BC Canada V6X 3G5

LAGORIA, GEORGIANNA MARIE, curator, writer, editor, visual art consultant; b. Oakland, Calif., Nov. 3, 1953; d. Charles Wilson and Margaret Claire (Vella) L.; m. David Joseph de la Torre, May 15, 1982; 1 child, Mateo Joseph. BA in Philosophy, Santa Clara U., 1975; MA in Museology, U. San Francisco, 1978. Exhbn. coord. Allrich Gallery, San Francisco, 1977-78; asst. registrar Fine Arts Mus., San Francisco, 1978-79; gallery coord. de Saisset Mus., Santa Clara, Calif., 1979-80, asst. dir., 1980-83, dir., 1983-86, Palo Alto (Calif.) Cultural Ctr., 1986-91; ind. writer, editor and cons. mus. and visual arts orgns., Hawaii, 1991-95; dir. The Contemporary Mus., Honolulu, 1995—. V.p. Non-Profit Gallery Assn., San Francisco, 1980-82; bd. dirs. Fiberworks, Berkeley, Calif., 1981-85; field grant reviewer Inst. Mus. Svcs., Washington, 1984, 85, 97, 98; adv. bd. Hearst Art Gallery, Moraga, Calif., 1986-89, Womens Caucus for Art, San Francisco, 1987—; mem. adv. bd. Weigand Art Gallery, Notre Dame Coll., Belmont, Calif. Curator exhbns. The Candy Store Gallery, 1980, Fiber '81, 1981; curator, author exhbn. catalogue Contemporary Hand Colored Photographs, 1981, Northern Calif. Art of the Sixties, 1982, The Artist and the Machine: 1910-1940, 1986; author catalogue, guide Persis Collection of Contemporary Art at Honolulu Advertiser, 1993; co-author: The Little Hawaiian Cookbook, 1994; coord. exhbn. selections Laila and Thurston Twigg-Smith Collection and Toshiko Takaezu ceramics for Hui No'eau Visual Arts Ctr., Maui, 1993; editor Nuhou (newsletter Hawaii State Mus. Assn.), 1991-94; spl. exhbn. coord. Honolulu Acad. Arts, 1995; dir. The Contemporary Mus., Honolulu, 1995—. Mem. Arts Adv. Alliance, Santa Clara County, 1985-86; grant panelist Santa Clara County Arts Coun., 1987; mem. art adv. bd. Kapiolani C.C., 1994—. Exhbn. grantee Ahmanson Found., 1981, NEA, 1984, Calif. Arts Coun., 1985-89 Mem. Am. Assn. Mus., ArtTable, 1983—, Calif. Assn. Mus. (bd. dirs. 1987-89), Assn. Art Mus. Dirs., Hawaiian Craftsmen (bd. dirs. 1994-95), Honolulu Jr. League, Key Project (bd. dirs. 1993-94). Democrat. Roman Catholic. Avocations: dance, fiction writing. Home and Office: 47-665 Mapele Rd Kaneohe HI 96744-4918

LAI, LIWEN, molecular geneticist, educator; b. Taipei, Taiwan, 1957; d. Kwan-Long Lai. BS, Nat. Taiwan U., 1980; MS, U. Calif., San Francisco, 1983; PhD, U. Tex., Dallas, 1987. Diplomate Am. Coll. Med. Genetics. Postdoctoral fellow NIH, Bethesda, Md., 1987-89; asst. rsch. sci. U. Ariz., Tuscon, 1990-94, asst. dir. Molecular Diagnostic Lab., 1992—, rsch. asst. prof., 1995-97; rsch. assoc. prof., 1997—. Rsch. grantee Elks, 1994-96, Dialysis Clinic Inc., 1994-96, So. Ariz. Found., 1996—, NIH, 1997—. Mem. Am. Soc. Human Genetics, Am. Soc. Gene Therapy. Office: U Ariz Dept Medicine 1501 N Campbell Ave Tucson AZ 85724-0001

LAIDLAW, VICTOR D. construction executive; b. 1946; Officer Moran Cons., Alhambra, Calif., 1972-88; pres. Koll Cons., 1988-2000; ptnr. Focus Real Estate L.P., Irvine, Calif. Office: Focus Real Estate LP 16485 Laguna Canyon Rd Irvine CA 92618-3837 E-mail: vlaidlaw@focusrelp.com

LAING-MALCOLMSON, SALLY ANNE, enrolled tax agent, tax consultant; b. Seattle, Sept. 25, 1957; d. Ian Laing-Malcolmson and Frances Rutherford (Arold) Cook; children: Rhiannon Ethel Quandt, Peter Eugene Stone, Benjamin Elliott Stone. AS in Bus., SUNY, 1989. With accounts payable dept. King County Airport, Seattle, 1984-86; bookkeeper Driftmeir Architects, P.S., Kirkland, Wash., 1986; pvt. practice tax cons. Bellevue, 1987—; tax specialist Puget Sound Nat. Bank, Tacoma, 1990-92; bookkeeper Papillon, Inc.; tax specialist Barbara Pulley CPA, 1995, Energy Relcon, 1996—. Sec. Washington State Tax Cons., Bellevue, 1991—, tax specialist Barbara Pulley, CPA, Missoula, Mont; bookkeeper/sec. Energy Re/con, Inc., Stevensville, Mont. Newsletter editor PTA, 1991-93. Mem. Pentecostal Ch. Avocations: reading, sewing, swimming, tennis, camping. Home and Office: 3170 Kinsler Ln Stevensville MT 59870-6967 E-mail: donking@montana.com

LAIRD, DAVID, humanities educator emeritus; b. Marshfield, Wis., Oct. 17, 1927; s. Melvin Robert and Helen Melissa (Connor) L.; m. Helen Astrid Lauritzen, Sept. 10, 1955; 1 child, Vanessa Ann. PhB, U. Chgo., 1947; BA with highest honor, U. Wis., 1950, MA, 1951, PhD, 1955; postgrad., Courtauld Inst., 1953. Instr. to asst. prof. Oberlin Coll., 1955-58; mem. faculty Calif. State U., L.A., 1958—, chmn. dept. English, 1969-73, chmn. dept. Am. studies, 1977-79. Nat. Humanities Inst. fellow U. Chgo., 1978-79; sr. Fulbright lectr. U. Tunis, Tunisia, 1979-80; fellow Folger Shakespeare Libr., 1982; Fulbright lectr. Odense U. (Denmark), 1983-84; vis. prof. U. Ottawa, 1984-85; cons. to Choice. Mem. editorial bd. Jour. Forest History; contbr. articles on Shakespeare, Am. lit. and cultural history to profl. jours. Mem. Western Shakespeare Seminar, Friends of Huntington Libr. Recipient Outstanding Prof. award Calif. State U., 1987, Nat. Endowment for the Humanities Summer Seminar award Northwestern U., 1989; Uhrig Found. grantee, 1964-65; Fulbright fellow, 1953-54. Mem. MLA, Malone Soc., Am. Studies Assn., Phi Beta Kappa. Home: 208 S Cherry Ave Marshfield WI 54449-3732 Office: Calif State U Humanities Dept Los Angeles CA 90032

LAIRD, JERE DON, news reporter; b. Topeka, Aug. 8, 1933; s. Gerald Howard and Vivian Gertrude (Webb) L.; m. Alexandra Berezowsky, Aug. 4, 1957; children: Lee, Jennifer, Christopher. BA in Journalism, U. Nev., 1960. Disc jockey Sta. KHBC Radio, Hilo, Hawaii, 1949-50; announcer, chief engr. Sta. KOLO Radio, Reno, 1951-58; program dir. Sta. KOLO-TV, Reno, 1958-60; news reporter Sta. KCRA Radio and TV, Sacramento, 1960-61, Sta. KRLA Radio, L.A., 1962-63; news reporter, editor Sta. KNXT-TV, L.A., 1964-68; news reporter, fin. editor Sta. KNX-CBS Radio, L.A., 1968—; fin. reporter Sta. KCBS-TV, L.A., 1990—. Lectr. U. So. Calif., L.A., 1984-85; instr. Calif. State U., Northridge, 1978-79. Cpl. U.S. Army, 1953-55. Recipient Emmy award, L.A., 1964, Peabody award, U. Ga., 1984, Best Bus. News award, L.A. Press Club, 1983, 84, 86, 87, 88, 89, Martin K. Gainsburgh award, Fiscal Policy Coun., Fla., 1978. Mem. Radio TV News Assn. (bd. dirs. 1966-68, Golden Mike award 1984), Sigma Delta Chi. Avocation: sailing. Office: Sta KNX-CBS 6121 W Sunset Blvd Los Angeles CA 90028-6423

LAIRD, WILBUR DAVID, JR. bookseller, editor; b. Kansas City, Mo., Mar. 15, 1937; s. Wilbur David and Alma Blanche (Turner) L.; children: Wendy, Cynthia, Brian Andrew, David Alexander; m. Helen M. Ingram, July 12, 1984. Student, U. Wichita, 1959-60; BA, UCLA, 1965, MLS, 1966. Reference libr. U. Calif., Davis, 1966-67; acquisitions libr. U. Utah, 1967-70, asst. dir. for tech. svcs., 1970-71, assoc. dir., 1971-72; univ. libr. U. Ariz., Tucson, 1972-90; pres. Books West S.W., Tucson, 1990—. Author: Hopi Bibliography, 1977; editor: Books of the Southwest, 1977-97. Bd. dirs. Westerners Internat., 1974-87, Tucson Civic Ballet, 1975-76, S.W. Pks. and Mon. Assn., 1993—. With USN, 1955-59. Mem. ALA, Ariz. State Libr. Assn. (pres. 1978-79), Western History Assn., Western Lit. Assn., Guild Ariz. Antiquarian Booksellers. Office: Books West Southwest Inc 4749 E San Francisco St Tucson AZ 85712 E-mail: wdlbks@home.com

LAITIN, DAVID DENNIS, political science educator; b. Bklyn., June 4, 1945; s. Daniel and Frances (Blumenkranz) L.; m. Delia Fortune; children: Marc Oliver, Anna Elizabeth. BA, Swarthmore Coll., 1967; PhD, U. Calif., Berkeley, 1974. Instr. Nat. Tchr. Edn. Ctr., Afgoy, Somalia, 1969; master Grenada Boys' Secondary Sch., West Indies, 1970-71; asst. prof. dept. polit. sci. U. Calif.-San Diego, La Jolla, 1975-79, prof., 1984-87, chmn., 1986-87; reader dept. polit. sci. U. Ife, Nigeria, 1979-80; prof. polit. sci., dir. Wilder House Ctr. for Study Politics, History and Culture U. Chgo., 1987-99, William R. Kenan, Jr. prof., 1992-99; prof. polit. sci. Stanford (Calif.) U., 1999—. Expert witness fgn. affairs subcom. U.S. Ho. Reps., 1981; resident Rockefeller Found., Bellagio Ctr., Sept. 1996. Author: Politics, Language and Thought: The Somali Experieince, 1977, Hegemony and Culture: Politics and Religious Change Among the Yoruba, 1986, Somalia: A Nation in Search of a State, 1987, Language Repertoires and State Construction in Africa, 1992, Identity in Formation: The Russian-Speaking Populations of the Near Abroad, 1998. Fellow NEH, 1979-80, Howard Found., 1984-85, German Marshall Fund, 1984-85, John Simon Guggenheim Found., 1995-96, Harry F. Guggenheim Found., 1997—, Ctr. for Advanced Study in Behavioral Scis., 19989-2000; co-prin. investigator award NSF, 1993-95; recipient award Am. Assn. for the Advancement of Slavic Studies, Dogan award Soc. for Comparative Rsch.; co-prin. investigator award Carnegie Found., 2000-01. Mem. Am. Polit. Sci. Assn. (2 awards), Am. Acad. Arts and Scis., Coun. Am. Polit. Sci. Assn. Office: Stanford U Dept Polit Sci Stanford CA 94305 E-mail: dlaitin@stanford.edu

LAKE, BRUCE MENO, applied physicist; b. L.A., Nov. 22, 1941; s. Meno Truman and Jean Ivy (Hancock)_ L. BS in Engring., Princeton U., 1963; MS, Calif. Inst. Tech., 1965, PhD, 1969. Mem. tech. staff advanced instrumentation dept. TRW Corp., Redondo Beach, Calif., 1969-73, head exptl. hydrodynamics sect., 1973-81, asst. mgr. dept. fluid mechanics, 1977-81, mgr. dept. fluid mechanics, 1981-96, mgr. computational physics bus. area, 1996-2000. Contbr. articles to profl. jours. and books. Ford Found. fellow, 1964-65, TRW tech. fellow. Mem. Am. Phys. Soc., Nat. Acad. Engring. Office: 41650 Calle Pino Murietta CA 92562

LAKE, WILLIAM J. career officer; BS in Mktg., U. Tenn., 1970; MS in Internat. Rels., Troy State U., 1976; Diploma, Squadron Officer Sch., 1975, Air Command and Staff Coll., 1980, Air War Coll., 1986, Royal Coll. of Def. Studies, London, 1990; postgrad., U. Pitts., Harvard U., 1994, 98. Commd. 2d lt. USAF, 1971, advanced through ranks to brig. gen., 1997; various assignments to dep. chief of staff U.S. Cen. Command, MacDill AFB, Fla., 1994-96; comdr. 3rd Wing, Elmendorf AFB, Alaska, 1996-98, 49th Fighter Wing, Holloman AFB, N.Mex., 1998—. Decorated Def.

Superior Svc. medal, Legion of Merit with oak leaf cluster, Meritorious Svc. medal with four oak leaf clusters, Air medal, Aerial Achievement medal, Air Force Commendation medal with two oak leaf clusters, U.S. Air Force Aviator's Valor award, Anthony C. Shine Fighter Pilot award, others. Office: 49 FW/CC 490 1st St Ste 1700 Holloman Air Force Base NM 88330-8277

LAL, DEVENDRA, nuclear geophysics educator; b. Varanasi, India, Feb. 14, 1929; s. Radhe Krishna and Sita Devi L.; m. Aruna Damany, May 17, 1955 (dec. July 1993). BS, Banaras Hindu U., Varanasi, 1947, MS, 1949, DSc (hon. causa), 1984; PhD, Bombay U., 1960. Research student Tata Inst. of Fundamental Research, Bombay, 1949-60, research fellow, fellow, assoc. prof., 1960-63, prof., 1963-70, sr. prof., 1970-72; dir. Phys. Research Lab., Ahmedabad, India, 1972-83, sr. prof., 1983-89; vis. prof. UCLA, 1965-66, 83-84; prof. Scripps Instn. Oceanography, La Jolla, Calif., 1967—. Editor: Early Solar System Processes and the Present Solar System, 1980, Biogeochemistry of the Arabian Sea, 1995. Recipient K.S. Krishnan Gold medal Indian Geophys. Union, 1965, S.S. Bhatnagar award for Physics, Govt. of India, 1971, award for Excellence in Sci. and Tech., Gedn. of Indian Chamber Com., 1974, Pandit Jawaharlal Nehru award for Scis., 1986, Group Achievement award NASA, 1986, Raman Birth Centenary award, 1996, V.M. Goldschmidt medal, 1997. Fellow AAAS, Royal Soc. London, Indian Nat. Sci. Acad., Indian Acad. Scis., Geol. Soc. India (hon.), Phys. Rsch. Lab. Ahmedabad, Tata Inst. Fundamental Rsch., Geochem. Soc. USA; mem. NAS U.S.A. (fgn. assoc.), Third World Acad. Scis. (founding mem.), Indian Geophys. Union, NAS India, Royal Astron. Soc. (assoc.), Internat. Acad. Aeronautics, Internat. Union of Geodesy and Geophysics (pres. 1984-87), Am. Acad. Arts and Scis. (fgn., hon. mem.), Internat. Assn. Phys. Sci. of Ocean (hon. mem., pres. 1979-83). Hindu. Avocations: chess, photography, painting, math. puzzles. Office: U Calif Scripps Inst Oceanography GRD-0244 La Jolla CA 92093-0244 Fax: (858) 822-3310. E-mail: dlal@ucsd.edu

LALLY, VINCENT EDWARD, atmospheric scientist; b. Brookline, Mass., Oct. 13, 1922; s. Michael James and Ellen Teresa (Dolan) L.; m. Marguerite Mary Tibert, June 5, 1949; children: Dennis V., Marianne Baugh, Stephen J. BS in Meteorology, U. Chgo., 1944; BSEE, MIT, 1948, MS in Engring. Adminstrn., 1949. Engr. Bendix-Friez, Balt., 1949-51; chief metall. equip. devel. Air Force Cambridge Rsch. Labs., Bedford, Mass., 1951-58; rsch. dir. Teledynamics, Phila., 1958-61; dir. Nat. Sci. Balloon Facility Nat. Ctr. for Atmospheric Rsch., Boulder, Colo., 1961-66, sr. scientist, 1966-91, sr. scientist emeritus, 1991—. Contbr. articles to sci. jours., chpt. to handbook in field. 1st lt. USAAC, 1942-46. Fellow Am. Meteorol. Soc. (Cleveland Abbe award 1990); mem. Inst. Navigation, Sigma Xi. Achievements include 7 patents for space inflatables, superpressure balloons, rocket instruments, communications techniques; made first balloon flight around the world, longest balloon flight; pioneered technology in measurements from radiosondes, aircraft and rockets. Avocations: running, golf, application of Monte Carlo techniques to gaming. Home: 4875 Sioux Dr Apt 304 Boulder CO 80303-3765 Office: Nat Ctr Atmospheric Rsch PO Box 3000 Boulder CO 80307-3000

LA MAINA, FRANCIS C. performing company executive; Formerly exec. v.p. dick clark prodns., inc., Burbank, Calif.; now pres., chief operating officer Dick Clark Prodns., inc., Burbank. Office: Dick Clark Prodns inc 3003 W Olive Ave Burbank CA 91505-7811

LAMB, ISABELLE SMITH, manufacturing company executive; b. Charteris, Que., Can., Dec. 14, 1922; came to U.S., 1948; d. Gordon R. and Beatrice L. (Dale) Smith; married, Oct. 2, 1948 (dec.); 1 child, David E. Student, Gowling Bus. Coll., Ottawa, Ont., 1939, Carleton U., 1940-42. Sec. Gatineau Power, Ottawa, 1942; sec. to city treas. Ottawa, 1943; sec. Can. Internat. Paper, Gatineau, Que., 1943-48; adminstrv. asst. to C/B Enterprises Internat., Inc., Hoquiam, Wash., 1948-84, pres., 1984—. Bd. dirs. U.S. Bank Washington, Seattle, Export Assistance Ctr. Wash., Seattle, N.W. Burn Found., Seattle, Wash. Coun. for Econ. Edn., Seattle, Ind. Colls. of Wash., Seattle. Participant spl. gifts United Way, Aberdeen, Wash., 1988—; active scholarships and philanthropic causes E.K. and Lillian Bishop Found., Seattle, 1985—. Avocation: reading, horseback riding. Office: Enterprises Internat Inc Blaine And Firman St Hoquiam WA 98550

LAMB, PHILIP, museum administrator; Pres. Pacific Northwest Mus. of Natural History, Ashland, Oreg. Office: Pacific Northwest Mus Natural History 1500 E Main St Ashland OR 97520-1312

LAMB, WILLIS EUGENE, JR. physicist, educator; b. L.A., July 12, 1913; s. Willis Eugene and Marie Helen (Metcalf) L.; m. Ursula Schaefer, June 5, 1939 (dec. Aug. 1996); m. Bruria Kaufman, Nov. 29, 1996. BS, U. Calif., 1934, PhD, 1938; DSc (hon.), U. Pa., 1953, Gustavus Adolphus Coll., 1975, Columbia U., 1990; MA, Oxford (Eng.) U., 1956; MA (hon.), Yale, 1961; LHD (hon.), Yeshiva U., 1965; Dr.rer.nat (hon.), U. Ulm., Germany, 1997. Mem. faculty Columbia U., 1938-52, prof. physics, 1948-52, Stanford U., 1951-56; Wykeham prof. physics and fellow New Coll., Oxford U., 1956-62; Henry Ford 2d prof. physics Yale U., 1962-72, J. Willard Gibbs prof. physics, 1972-74; prof. physics and optical scis. U. Ariz., Tucson, 1974—, Regents prof., 1990—. Morris Loeb lectr. Harvard U., 1953-54; Gordon Shrum lectr. Simon Fraser U., 1972; cons. Philips Labs., Bell Telephone Labs., Perkin-Elmer, NASA; vis. com. Brookhaven Nat. Lab. Recipient (with P. Kusch) Nobel prize in physics, 1955, Rumford premium Am. Acad. Arts and Scis., 1953, Nat. medal of Sci., 2000; award Rsch. Corp., 1954, Yeshiva award, 1962; Guggenheim fellow, 1960-61, sr. Alexander von Humboldt fellow, 1992-94. Fellow Am. Phys. Soc., Optical Soc. Am., N.Y. Acad. Scis.; hon. fellow Inst. Physics and Phys. Soc. (Guthrie lectr. 1958), Royal Soc. Edinburgh (fgn. mem.); mem. Nat. Acad. Scis., Phi Beta Kappa, Sigma Xi. Office: U Ariz Optical Scis Ctr PO Box 210094 Tucson AZ 85721-0094

LAMBERSON, JOHN ROGER, insurance company executive; b. Aurora, Mo., Aug. 16, 1933; s. John Oral Lamberson and Golda May (Caldwell) Tidwell; m. Virginia Lee, Aug. 10, 1957; 1 child, John Clinton. BA, U. Calif., Berkeley, 1954. Coach, tchr. Thousand Palms (Calif.) Sch., 1954-55; underwriter trainee Fireman's Fund Ins. Co., San Francisco, 1955; surety mgr. Safeco Ins. Co. (formerly Gen. Ins. Co.), San Francisco and Sacramento, Calif., 1957-61; pres., COO Willis Corroon Corp., N.Y.C., 1966-92, also bd. dirs., chmn. constrn. industry div., mem. exec. com., aquisition com.; pres., chmn., CEO Lamberson Consulting LLC, San Francisco, 1992—. Bd. dirs. Willis Cornoon Group PLC, London, Consumers Benefit Life Ins. Co., Constrn. Inst. Mem. ASCE (bd. dirs. Construction Institute), Nat. Assn. Heavy Engring. Constructors (bd. dirs. 1985—, Golden Beavers award for outstanding svc. to industry), Constrn. Fin. Mgmt. Assn. (bd. dirs. 1987-91, exec. com.), Assoc. Gen. Contractors Am. (membership devel. com., past chmn. bd. dirs., nat. assoc. mems. coun.), Assoc. Gen. Contractors Calif. (bd. dirs. 1976), Nat. Assn. Surety Bond Prodrs. (past nat. pres., regional v.p.), Am. Inst. Contractors, Soc. Am. Mil. Engrs., The Moles-Heavy Engring. Constrn. Soc., Young Pres. Orgn. (sem. leader), Bankers Club, Sharon Heights Golf and Country Club, Bermuda Dunes Country Club, Rockaway Hunting Club, Villa Taverna Club, Bldg. Futures Coun. Home: 85 Greenoaks Dr Atherton CA 94027-2160 Office: Lamberson Consulting LLC 580 California St Ste 500 San Francisco CA 94104-1000

LAMBERT, FREDERICK WILLIAM, lawyer, educator; b. Millburn, N.J., Feb. 12, 1943; m. Barbara E. Fogell, Aug. 13, 1965; children: Elisabeth, Mark. BA, U. Mich., 1965, JD, 1969. Bar: Ohio 1969, Fla. 1973, Calif. 1973, U.S. Supreme Ct. 1975. Law clk. to Stanley N. Barnes, U.S. Cir. Judge U.S. Cir. Ct., L.A., 1969-70; atty. advisor Office Legal Counsel U.S. Dept. Justice, Washington, 1970-71; law clk. to Justice William H. Rehnquist U.S. Supreme Ct., Washington, 1971-72; pvt. practice L.A., 1973-90; acting gen. counsel Itel Corp., San Francisco, 1981-82; ptnr. Adams, Duque & Hazeltine, L.A., 1985-90, chmn. bus. law dept., 1989-90; assoc. prof. Hastings Coll. Law, U. Calif., San Francisco, 1993-99, prof. law, 1999—. Vis. prof. U. Mich. Law Sch., Ann Arbor, 1990-91, Duke Law Sch., Durham, N.C., 1992-93. Mem. Am. Law Inst., Am. Law and Econs. Assn., Econ. Round Table of L.A., Calif. State Bar Assn., Half Moon Bay Yacht Club. Home: 1100 Pilarcitos Ave Half Moon Bay CA 94019-1459

LAMBERT, JAMES L. data storage systems company executive; b. 1954; BS in Civil and Environ. Engring., MS in Civil and Environ. Engring., U. Wis. Various positions CALMA divsn. GE Co., 1979-81, v.p. R&D, 1981-84; pres., CEO, dir. Artecon, 1984; co-CEO, COO, pres., dir. Dot Hill Sys. Corp., Carlsbad, Calif., 1999, pres., CEO, 2000—. Dir. Nordic Group of Cos., Snow Valley, Inc. Office: 6305 El Camino Real Carlsbad CA 92009

LAMBERT, NADINE MURPHY, psychologist, educator; b. Ephraim, Utah; m. Robert E. Lambert, 1956; children— Laura Allan, Jeffrey. Ph.D. in Psychology, U. So. Calif., 1965. Diplomate Am. Bd. Profl. Psychology, Am. Bd. Sch. Psychology. Sch. psychologist Los Nietos Sch. Dist., Whittier, Calif., 1952-53, Bellflower (Calif.) Unified Sch. Dist., 1953-58; research cons. Calif. Dept. Edn., Los Angeles, 1958-64; dir. sch. psychology tng. program U. Calif., Berkeley, 1964—, asst. prof. edn., 1964-70, asso. prof., 1970-76, prof., 1976—, assoc. dean for student svcs., 1988-94. Mem. Joint Com. Mental Health of Children, 1967-68; cons. state depts. edn., Calif., Ga., Fla.; cons. Calif. Dept. Justice; mem. panel on testing handicapped people Nat. Acad. Scis., 1978-81. Author: School Version of the AAMD Adaptive Behavior Scale, 3d edit., 1993; co-author: (with Wilcox and Gleason) Educationally Retarded Child: Comprehensive Assessment and Planning for the EMR and Slow-Learning Child, 1974, (with Hartsough and Bower) Process for Assessment of Effective Functioning, 1981, (with Windmiller and Turiel) Moral Development and Socialization -- Three Perspectives, 1979; assoc. editor Am. Jour. Orthopsychiatry, 1975-81, Am. Jour. Mental Deficiency, 1977-80, (with McCombs) How Students Learn-Reforming Schools Through Learner-Centered Education, 1998, others. With Hartsough and Sandoval Children's Attention and Adjustment Survey, 1990. Recipient Dorothy Hughes award for outstanding contbn. to edni. and sch. psychology NYU, 1990, Tobacco Disease Related Rsch. award U. Calif., 1990-94, NIDA, 1994-2001; grantee NIMH, 1965-87, Calif. State Dept. Edn., 1-72, 76-78, NHSTE Dept. Transportation, 1995. Fellow APA (coun. reps. divsn. sch. psychologists, bd. dirs. 1984-87, mem. bd. profl. affairs 1981-83, bd. ednl. affairs 1991-94, chmn. 1992-94, exec. com. divsn. sch. psychology 1994-96, mem. commn. for recognition of specialities and professions in psychology 1993-97, Disting. Svc. award 1980, award for disting. profl. contbns. 1986, award for disting. career contbns. of applications of psychology to edn. and tng. 1999), Nat. Assn. of Sch. Psychologists (hon., Legend in Sch. Psychology 1998), Am. Orthopsychiat. Assn.; mem. NEA, Calif. Assn. Sch. Psychologists (pres. 1962-63, Sandra Goff award 1985). Office: U Calif Dept Education Berkeley CA 94720-0001 E-mail: nlambert@socrates.berkeley.edu

LAMBERT, SHIRLEY ANNE, marketing professional, publisher; b. Dayton, Ohio, Sept. 28, 1945; d. Norman Frank and Muriel Noreen (Atkinson) Best; m. Joseph Calvin Lambert, Apr. 27, 1968 (div. 1986); children: Joseph Calvin III, James Edward, Kristin Carole. BA in Polit. Sci., Wellesley Coll., 1967; degree in French, Universite de Paris, 1966; MLS, Simmons Coll., 1980. Mktg. asst. G.K. Hall and Co., Boston, 1969-73; cons. Info. Dynamics Corp., Reading, Mass., 1973-75, Pergamon Press, Elmsford, N.Y., 1979-82; computer lab. coordinator Cherry Creek Schs., Aurora, Colo., 1983-85; mktg. dir. Libraries Unltd., Littleton, 1985—. Author: Clip Art and Dynamic Designs for Libraries and Media Centers, vol. 1; reviewer Am. Reference Books Ann., 1987-88, Library and Info. Sci. Ann., 1986-88. Host parent Am. Field Service, N.Y., 1986-87; selection chmn. Ams. Abroad; Returnee, 1962. Mem. ALA, Rocky Mountain (Colo.) Dressage Assn. (local chpt. sec. 1984-85), Colo. Hunter/Jumper Assn., Phi Beta Kappa, Beta Phi Mu. Republican. Congregationalist. Avocations: horse breeder, duplicate bridge. Office: Librs Unltd PO Box 3988 Englewood CO 80155-3988

LAMBERT, THOMAS P. lawyer; b. Kankakee, Ill., Oct. 14, 1946; BA, Loyola U., L.A., 1968; JD, UCLA, 1971. Bar: Calif. 1971. Atty. Mitchell, Silberberg & Knupp, L.A., 1971—. Note and comment editor UCLA Law Rev., 1970-71. Mem. ABA (antitrust law sect., litigation sect.), State Bar Calif., Beverly Hills Bar Assn., L.A. County Bar Assn. Office: Mitchell Silberberg & Knupp 11377 W Olympic Blvd Los Angeles CA 90064-1625

LAMBORN, DOUGLAS L. state legislator; b. May 24, 1954; m. Jeanie Lamborn; children: Luke, Eve, Will, Nathan, Mark. Grad., U. Kans., 1978, JD, 1985. Pvt. practice, Colo. Springs, 1987—; mem. Colo. Ho. of Reps., 1994-96, Rep. whip, 1997; pres. pro tem Colo. Senate, Dist. 9, Denver, 1997—. Mem. appropriations com., fin. com., state, veterans and mil. affairs com., 1999. Active mem. Antelope Trails Elem. Sch. Prins. Adv. Coun., former mem. Pike's Peak Area Coun. of Govs. Citizen's Adv. Com. Republican. Office: 259 Colo State Capitol Denver CO 80203 also: 200 E Colfax Ave Ste 259 Denver CO 80203-1716

LAMENDOLA, WALTER FRANKLIN, technology educator, business executive; b. Donora, Pa., Jan. 29, 1943; BA in English, St. Vincent Coll., 1964; MSWin Community Orgn., U. Pitts., 1966; diploma in Sociology and Social Welfare, U. Stockholm, 1970; PhD in Social Work, U. Minn., 1976. Cmty. svcs. dir. Ariz. tng. programs State Dept. Mental Retardation, Tucson, 1970-73; assoc. prof. social welfare adminstrn. Fla. State U., 1976-77; pres., CEO, Minn. Rsch. and Tech., Inc., 1977-81; assoc. prof., dir. Allied Health Computer Lab. East Carolina U., 1981-84; prof., dir. info. tech. ctr. Grad. Sch. Social Work U. Denver, 1984-87, 99—; cons. info. tech., rsch. human svcs., 1987-90; v.p. rsch. Colo. Trust, Denver, 1990-93, info. tech. and rsch. cons., 1993—. Cons. European Network Info. Tech. & Human Svcs.; mem. rebldg. communities initiative PODER project Casey Found., 1996-97; mem. adv. bd. ctr. Computers in Tchg. Initiative, U. Southampton, Brit. Rsch. Coun. Univs., Human Svc. Info. Tech. Applications, CREON Found., The Netherlands; lectr. conf., symposia, univs. U.S., Europe; mem. nat. adv. bd. Native Elder Health Resource Ctr., 1994-96; co-founder Denver Free Net, 1993; adj. prof. U. Colo. Health Scis. Ctr., 1996—; dir. tech. GSSU, U. Denver, 1998—; info. tech. cons. Healthy Nations Program Robert Wood Johnson Found, 1993-96; evaluator Nat. Libr. Rsch. Program, Access Colo. grant, 1994, Nat. Info. Infrastructure grant Colo. State Libr.; cons. set up on the Internet for U.S. Cts.-Ct. for Mental Health Svcs., NIH, Frontier Mental Health Svcs. Network grant; collaborating investigator SBIR award Computerized Advance Directives, tech. plan San Mateo County and Seattle Dist. Cts.; keynote spkr. conf. Human Svc. Info. Tech. Applications, Finland, 1996; adj. prof. U. Colo., 1997-98; dir. tech., adj. prof. U. Denver, 1997-98; adj. prof. informatics U. Colo. Health Scis. Ctr., 1998; mem. nat. adv. coun. Ctr. Substance Abuse Prevention Dept. Health & Human Svcs., 1998, co-chair prevention decision support sys. steering group, 1999; pres. ActiveGuide, L.L.C.; mem. nat. design team Decision Support Sys., U.S. Dept. Health & Human Svcs., 1998—, mem. nat. adv. bd. Data Coord. Ctr., 1999—; prin. investigator bridge project Cmty. Tech. Ctr., U.S. Dept. Edn., 2000—; prin. investigator The Bridge Cmty. Tech. Ctr. Dept. Edn., 2000-03. Co-author: Choices for Colorado's Future, 1993, The Integrity of Intelligence: A Bill of Rights for the Information Age, 1992, Choices for Colorado's Future: Executive Summary, 1991, Choices for Colorado's Future: Regional Summaries, 1991; co-editor: A Casebook of Computer Applications in Health and Social Services, 1989; contbr. numerous articles to profl. jours. Capt. U.S. Army, 1966-69. Recipient Innovative Computer Application award Internat. Fedn. Info. Processing Socs., 1979; Nat. Lib. Rsch. Evaluator grantee, Colo., 1994—, Nat. Info. Infrastructure grantee Dept. Edn., State Libr. and Adult Literacy, 1994-95; Funds & Couns. Tng. scholar United Way Am., 1964-66, Donaldson Fund scholar, 1965-66, NIMH scholar, 1964-66, 73-76, St. Vincent Coll. Benedictine Soc. scholar, 1963-64; vis. fellow U. Southampton, 1992-95. Office: GSSW Univ Denver 2148 South High St Denver CO 80208 also: ActiveGuide LLC PO Box 351 Wheat Ridge CO 80034-0351 E-mail: wlamendola@du.edu

LAMONT, SANDERS HICKEY, journalist; b. Atlanta, Nov. 9, 1940; s. Louis Earnest and Dorothy Rebecca (Strickland) LaM.; m. Patricia Jean Taylor, Aug. 5, 1966; children— Patricia Ruth, Zachary Taylor. A.A., Marion Mil. Inst., Ala., 1960; B.A. in Journalism, U. Ala., 1962; postgrad. U. Mich., 1977-78. Reporter, bur. chief Gannett News Service, various locations, 1961-74; mng. editor Ft. Myers News Press, Fla., 1974-77; exec. editor Marietta Times, Ohio, 1978-80, Modesto Bee, Calif., 1980-98; ombudsman Sacramento Bee, Calif., 1998—; chmn. AP News Execs. Council, Calif., 1984-85. NEH journalism fellow, U. Mich., 1977-78; Pulitzer prize juror, 1984-85. Served to 1st lt. U.S. Army, 1963-65. Mem. Am. Soc. Newspaper Editors, AP Mng. Editors, Soc. Profl. Journalists . Methodist. Office: The Sacramento Bee PO Box 15779 Sacramento CA 95852-0779

LAMPERT, ELEANOR VERNA, retired human resources specialist; b. Porterville, Calif., 23 Mar. d. Ernest Samuel and Violet Edna (Watkins) Wilson; m. Robert Mathew Lampert, Aug. 23, 1935; chidren: Sally Lu Winton, Lary Lampert, Carol R. John. Student in bus. fin., Porterville Jr. Coll., 1977-78; grad., Anthony Real Estate Sch., 1971; student, Laguna Sch. of Art., 1972, U. Calif., Santa Cruz, 1981. Bookkeeper Porterville (Calif.) Hos., 1956-71; real estate sales staff Ray Realty, Porterville, 1973; sec. Employment Devel. Dept. State of Calif., Porterville, 1973-83; orientation and tng specialist CETA employees, 1976-80. Sec. Employer Adv. Group, 1973-80, 81—. Author: Black Bloomers and Han-Ga-Ber, 1986. Mem. U.S. Senatorial Business Adv. Bd., 1981-84, Rep. Nat. congl. Com., 1982-88, Sierra View Hosp. Vol. League, 1988-89 (pres.); charter mem. Presdl. Republican Task Force, 1981—, Republican National Committee; vol. Calif Hosp. Assn., 1983-89, Calif. Spl. Olympics Spirit Team, Sonora Community Hospital Oak Plus League, Special Olympics Northern Calif. partner. Recipient Merit Cert., Gov. Pat Brown, State of Calif., 1968. Mem. Lindsay Olive Growers, Sunkist Orange Growers, Am. Kennel Club, Internat. Assn. Personnel in Employment Security, Calif. State Employes Assn. (emeritus Nat. Wildlife Fedn., NRA, Friends of Porterville Library, Heritage Found., DAR (Kaweah chpt. rec. sec. 1988—), Internat. Platform Assn., Dist. Fedn. Women's Clubs (recording sec. Calif. chpt. 1988—), Ky. Hist. Soc., Women's Club of Calif. (pres. Porterville chpt. 1988-89, dist. rec. sec. 1987-89), Mo. Rep. Women of Taney County, Internat. Sporting and Leisure Club. Ladies Aux, VFW (No. 5168 Forsyth,Mo.), Ozark Walkers League, Women of the Moose Lodge, Humane Soc. U.S. Republican.

LAMPORT, LESLIE B. computer scientist; b. N.Y.C., Feb. 7, 1941; s. Benjamin and Hannah (Lasser) L.; m. Carol Dahl Crum, Oct. 31, 1968 (div. Feb. 1978); 1 child, Jason Christopher. BS, MIT, 1960; MA, Brandeis U., 1963, PhD, 1972. Mem. faculty Marlboro (Vt.) Coll., 1965-69; systems analyst Mass. Computer Assocs., Wakefield, 1970-77; sr. computer scientist SRI Internat., Menlo Park, Calif., 1977-85; sr. cons. engr. Digital Equipment Corp., Palo Alto, 1985-98, Compaq, Palo Alto, 1998—. Patentee in field. Mem. NAE. Office: Compaq Systems Rsch Ctr 130 Lytton Ave Palo Alto CA 94301-1044 E-mail: lamport@pa.dec.com

LANAHAN, DANIEL JOSEPH, lawyer; b. Bklyn., Jan. 13, 1940; Attended, L.I. U., Temple U.; JD, San Francisco Law Sch., 1969. Bar: Calif. 1970. Dir. Ropers, Majeski, Kohn & Bentley, P.C., Santa Rosa, Calif., 1970-96; mng. ptnr. Lanahan & Reilley L.L.P., Santa Rosa, 1997—. Mem. State Bar Calif., Sonoma County Bar Assn., Internat. Assn. Def. Counsel, Assn. Def. Counsel. Office: Lanahan & Reilley LLP 3558 Round Barn Blvd Ste 300 Santa Rosa CA 95403-0992 E-mail: dlanahan@lanahan.com

LANCE, ALAN GEORGE, state attorney general; b. McComb, Ohio, Apr. 27, 1949; s. Cloyce Lowell and Clara Rose (Wilhelm) L.; m. Sheryl C. Holden, May 31, 1969; children: Lisa, Alan Jr., Luke. BA, S.D. State U., 1971; JD, U. Toledo, 1973. Bar: Ohio 1974, U.S. Dist. Ct. (no. dist.) Ohio 1974, U.S. Ct. Mil. Appeals 1974, Idaho 1978, U.S. Supreme Ct. 1996. Asst. pros. atty. Fulton County, Wauseon, Ohio, 1973-74; ptnr. Foley and Lance, Chartered, Meridian, Idaho, 1978-90; prin. Alan G. Lance, Meridian, 1990-94; rep. Idaho Ho. of Reps., Boise, 1990-94, majority caucus chmn., 1992-94; atty. gen. State of Idaho, 1995—. Capt. AUS, 1974-78. Mem. Nat. Assn. Attys. Gen. (vice chair conf. western attys. gen. 1998, chmn. 1999), Ohio Bar Assn., Idaho Bar Assn., Idaho Trial Lawyers Assn., Meridian C. of C. (pres. 1983), Am. Legion (judge adv. 1981-90, state comdr. 1988-89, alt. nat. exec. com. 1992-94, nat. exec. com. 1994-96, chmn. nat. fgn. rels. commn. 1996-97, ex-officio mem. nat. POW/MIA com. 1996—, nat. comdr. 1999-2000, chair nat. adv. com. 2000-01), Elks. Republican. Avocation: fishing. Home: 1370 Eggers Pl Meridian ID 83642-6528 Office: PO Box 83720 Boise ID 83720-3720

LANCE, SEAN P. pharmaceutical executive; Formerly with Noristan Group of Cos. Ltd.; from various positions to exec. chmn. Boots Co. Pty Ltd., South Africa, 1982-85; from various mgmt. positions to COO internat. ops., chief exec. designate Glaxo Wellcome Plc, Europe, Asia, Africa, Australia, 1985-97; pres., CEO Chiron Corp., Emeryville, Calif., 1998—, chmn. bd. dirs., 1999—. Office: Chiron Corp 4560 Horton St Emeryville CA 94608-2900 Fax: 510 655-9910

LAND, GEORGE A. philosopher, writer, educator, consultant; b. Hot Springs, Ark., Feb. 27, 1933; s. George Thomas Lock and Mary Elizabeth Land; m. Jo A. Gunn, 1957 (dec. 1969); children— Robert E., Thomas G., Patrick A.; m. Beth Smith Jarman, 1987. Student, Millsaps Coll., 1952-54, U. Veracruz, Mexico, 1957-59; numerous hon. degrees U.S. and abroad. Program dir. Woodall TV Stas. of Ga., Columbus, 1951-52; ops. mgr. Lamar Broadcasting, Jackson, Miss., 1952-54; anthrop. research Cora, Huichole and Yaqui tribes, Latin Am. Mexico, 1955-60; dir. gen. Television del Norte (NBC), Mexico, 1960-62; v.p. Roman Corp., St. Louis, 1962-64; chmn. Transolve Inc., Cambridge, Mass., and St. Petersburg, Fla., 1964-68; chief exec., chmn. Innotek Corp., N.Y.C.; also pres. Hal Roach Studios, Los Angeles and N.Y.C., 1969-71; chmn. emeritus Turtle Bay Inst., N.Y.C., 1971-80; vice chmn. Wilson Learning Corp., Mpls., 1980-86; chmn., CEO Leadership 2000 (subs. Sci. Applications Internat. Corp.), Phoenix, 1986—; chmn., CEO, chief scientist Sci. Applications Internat. Corp., 2000—; pres. Inst. Transformational Research, Honolulu and Buffalo, 1980—; prof. Mankato State U., 1972-74; sr. fellow U. Minn., 1987—. Cons.-in-residence Synplex Inc., N.Y.C., AT&T, Forest Hosp., Des Plaines, Social Systems Inc., Chapel Hill, N.C., Children's Hosp., Nat. Med. Ctr., Washington, Herman Miller Inc., Arthur Anderson & Co., strategy cons. Intermedics Orthopedics; mem. Nat. Action Com. on Drug Edn., 1974-75, sr. exec. svc. U.S. Govt. 2000-2001, Assn. Non-profit mgmt., 1999, The Congerence Bd. 1999, 2000, Ctr.; co-chmn. Syncon Conf., So. Ill. U., 1972-74; keynoter Emerging Trends in Edn. Conf., Minn., 1974, 75, Bicentennial Conf. on Limits to Growth, So. Ill. U., 1976, No. States Power

Conf., 1975, U.S. Office Edn., Nat. Conf. Improvements in Edn., 1979, World Conf. on Gifted, 1977, S.W. Conf. on Arts, 1977, World Symposium on Humanity, 1979, Internat. Conf. Internal Auditors, 1977, Four Corners Conf. on Arts, 1977, Chautaugua Inst., 1977, 78, Conf. Am. Art Tchrs. Assn., 1979, Internat. Conf. on Gifted, 1982, Japan Mgmt. Assn., Nat. Conf. Art Curators, Chgo., 1985, others; keynoter, Nat. Conf. on Econ. Devel., Mex., 1988, Credit Union Roundtable, Tampa, Fla., 1988, Internat. Bihai Conf., Princeton, N.J., 1982, co-chmn. com. on society World Conf. Peace and Poverty, St. Joseph's U., Phila., 1968, Internat. Bahai Conf. Princeton U., 1987, Gov.'s Trade Corridor Conf., Phoenix, 1994, Cath. Hosp. Assn., Phila, 1994, Am. Assn. Adminstrs., 1994, Inst. Pub. Execs., 1994, Fed. Conf. Quality, Washington, 1994, MAC IS Nat. Conf., Ont., 1994, Innovative Thinking Conf., 1994, Ventana Groupware Conf., 1994, Assn. Non-Profit Orgs., 1998, The Conf. Bd., 1999, 2000, Strategic Innovation Conf., 1999, Tng. Dirs. Forum, 1999, Young Pres.' Orgn., Cannes, 1993, Assn. Convn. and Visitors Bureau, Phoenix, 1993, Profession Conv. Mgmt. Assn., Atlanta, Internat. Assn. Law Enforcement, 1995, Cath. Health Assn., 1995, Excellence in Govt. Fellows, 1996, many others; mem. Nat. Security Sem., U.S. Dept. Def., 1975; cons. keynoter corp. policy strategic sems. The Bell System, AT&T, 1978—; mem. faculty Edison Electric Grad. Mgmt. Inst., 1972-78; lectr., seminarian in transformation theory, strategic planning and interdisciplinary rsch. Menninger Found., U. Ga., Emory U., Waterloo (Can.), Office of Sec. HEW, Jamestown (N.Y.) Coll., Hofstra U., U.S. Office Edn., Calif. Dept. Edn., St. Louis U., Coll. William and Mary, Webster Coll., St. Louis, Wash. State Dept. Edn., U. Ky., So. Ill. U., St. John's U., Harvard U., U. South Fla., MIT, U. Veracruz, Children's Hosp. D.C., Gov.'s Sch. N.C., Scottsdale (Ariz.) Ctr. Arts, Humbolt U., East Berlin, AAAS, others; advanced faculty Creative Problem SolvingInst., SUNY, 1965—, S, Conn. Coll.; disting. lectr. Northwestern State U., La., SUNY, Coll. of the Lakes, Ill.; cons. govt., industry and instns. in U.S. and abroad including AT&T, IBM, Dow Chem, Dow Corning, DuPont, Hughes, TRW, 3Mm OAS, Fed. Quality Inst., U.S. Dept. Commerce, Office Patent & Trademarks, U.S. Gen. Svc. Adminstrn., Gen Mills, GM, Moore Corp., Branch Corp., Credit Union Nat. Assn., USDA, Excellence in Govt. Fed. Quality Cons. Group, U.S. Dept. Energy, Lockheed Martin, Dept. Housing and Urban Devel., Wescorp, Petnotes Mexicanas, Petnotes de Venezuela, Am. Medicas Sys., Def. Evaluation and Rsch. Agy (U.K.)., others. Author: Innovation Systems, 1967, Innovation Technology, 1968, Four Faces of Poverty, 1968, (as George T.L. Land) Grow or Die: The Unifying Principle of Transformation, 1973, Creative Alternatives and Decision Making, 1974, The Opportunity Book, 1980, (with Vaune E. Ainsworth), Breakpoint and Beyond, 1994, (with Beth Jarman) New Paradigm in Business, 1994, Community Building in Business, 1995, Forward to Basics; contbr. to profl. jours. and gen. mags. Sr. fellow U. Mich. Fellow N.Y. Acad. Scis., World Bus. Acad.; mem. Soc. Gen. Systems Rsch., Soc. Study Gen. Process (founding dir.), Am. Soc. Cybernetics (past v.p.), Creative Edn. Found. (trustee, Lifetime Achievement award 1993, New Paradigm in Bus. award 1994, colleague), Soc. Am. Value Engrs. (past dir.), World Future Soc., Com. for Future (colleague), Authors Guild, Authors League Am. Achievements include research on interdisciplinary unification, orginated transformation theory. Inventor computer-assisted group creative thinking processes, "The Innovator," "CoNexus," "TeamWare" and others. Home: 7470 E San Miguel Ave Scottsdale AZ 85250-6446 Office: Leadership 2000 3333 N 44th St Phoenix AZ 85018-6481

LAND, KENNETH DEAN, test and balance agency executive, energy and environmental consultant; b. Central City, Nebr., Oct. 5, 1931; s. Adrew Kenneth Land and Marie Eveline (Weaver) Gehrke. Grad., El Camino Coll., Gardena, Calif., 1954-56; student, Long Beach City Coll., 1958, Calif. State Coll., Long Beach, 1959. Cert. quality assurance inspector for smoke removal and life safety systems; cert. test & balance engr. for bldg., environ. sys. Gen. mgr. Air Heat Engrs., Inc., Santa Fe Springs, Calif., 1956-61; sales and estimating engr. Thermodyne Corp., Los Alamitos, 1962-64; pres., founder Air Check Co., Inc., Santa Ana, 1964-69; chief engring. technician Nat. Air Balance Co., Los Angeles, 1969-73; gen. mgr. B&M Air Balance Co., South El Monte, Calif., 1973-78; chief exec. officer, founder Land Air Balance Tech. (LABTECH), Las Vegas, Nev., 1978—. Founder, bd. dirs. Energy Resources and Mgmt., Inc., San-I-Pac, Internat., Inc., Energy Equities Group, Inc., Utility Connection, 1990—. Active Las Vegas Founders Club-Las Vegas Invitational PGA Tournament, 1983—, player, 1992; former trustee Assoc. Air Balance Coun.-Sheet Metal Workers Internat. Apprenticeship Tng. Fund; mem. Citizens Against Govt. Waste, 1990—, YNOT Night for YMCA, 1987—; co-founder The GOF Com., operators charity golf tournament for Am. Cancer Soc., 1990, 91, Am. Diabetes Assn., 1992, Nev. Child Seekers, 1992— . With USN, 1951-54, journalist. Mem. ASHRAE (pres. so. Nev. chpt. 1983-84, editor chpt. bull. 1979-89, Citizen of Yr. 1989), CSI (co-founder Las Vegas chpt., pres. 1989-90, editor, founder chpt. bull. 1987-90, S.W. regional mem. chmn. 1990-91), Assn. Energy Engrs., Am. Soc. Profl. Cons., Associated Air Balance Coun. (cert. test and balance engr. 1966—, internat. pres. 1988-89, bd. dirs. 1982-90, mem. numerous coms.), Sheet Metal Workers Internat. Tng. Fund, Internat. Conf. Bldg. Officials, Internat. Assn. Plumbing and Mech. Officials, Nat. Fedn. Ind. Businessmen, Rotary (So. El Monte Calif. Club 1977-78, Las Vegas S.W. Nev. Club 1978-94, bd. dirs. 1983-85, 88-90, photographer 1987-90, chmn. internat. svc., 4 Paul Harris fellowships, charter mem. Las Vegas West Club, Nev., 1994—), Citizens for Pvt. Enterprise, Nev. Taxpayers Assn., UNLV Golf Found., UNLV Presdl. Assocs. Group, Nev. Devel. Assn., Nev. Nuclear Waste Study Com. adv. coun., Sheet Metal and Air Conditioning Contractors Assn. (nat. and so. Nev. chpt. bd. dirs.), Associated Gen. Contractors (nat. and Las Vegas chpt.), Nat. Energy Mgmt. Inst. (cert., co-chmn. Nev. adv. coun., instr. Energy Mgmt. Tng. 1991), Las Vegas C. of C., Nat. Inst. Bldg. Scis., Nev. Assn. Ind. Businessman, Nat. Fire Protection Assn., Am. Soc. Hosp. Engrs., Nev. Profl. Facility Mgrs. Assn., 1992—, Las Vegas Country Club. Avocations: golf, dancing, racquetball, collecting jazz, swing and big band music. Fax: 702-382-3299. E-mail: Labtech7@juno.com

LANDAHL, HERBERT DANIEL, biophysicist, mathematical biologist, researcher, consultant; b. Fancheng, China, Apr. 23, 1913; (parents Am. citizens); s. Carl W. and Alice (Holmberg) L.; m. Evelyn Christine Blomberg, Aug. 23, 1940; children: Carl David, Carol Ann Landahl Kubai, Linda C. Landahl Shidner. Student, U. Minn., 1931-32; AB, St. Olaf Coll., Northfield, Minn., 1934; SM, U. Chgo., 1936, PhD, 1941. Rsch. asst. psychometric lab. U. Chgo., 1937-39, rsch. asst. math. biophysics, 1938-41, instr., 1942-45, asst. prof. com. on math. biology, 1945-48, assoc. prof., 1949-56, prof., 1956-68, acting. chmn., 1965-67; prof. biophysics and math. U. Calif., San Francisco, 1968-80, prof. emeritus, 1980—. Cons. Respiratory Project, U. Chgo., 1944-46, toxicity lab. U. Chgo., 1947-51, USAF radiation lab., U. Chgo., 1951-67, dept. biomath. U. Tex., Houston, 1968-89; mem. NIH com. on epidemiology and biometry, Bethesda, Md., 1960-64. Co-author: Mathematical Biophysics of Central Nervous System, 1945; contbr. approximately 190 sci. papers to various jours.; chief editor Bull. Math. Biology, 1973-80; mem. editl. Computers in Biology and Medicine, 1971-90. Recipient Career Devel. award NIH, 1962-67, Career Achievement award Soc. Toxicology, 1987; grantee NIH, 1963-67. Fellow AAAS; mem. Biophys. Soc., Biometric Soc. (charter), Bioengring. Soc. (charter), Latin Am. Biomath. Soc. (charter), Soc. for Math. Biology (founding, pres. 1981-83). Home: 472 Lansdale Ave San Francisco CA 94127-1617 Office: U Calif PO Box 970 San Francisco CA 94143-0001

LANDAU, ELLIS, gaming company executive; b. Phila., Feb. 24, 1944; s. Manfred and Ruth (Fischer) L.; m. Kathy Suzanne Thomas, May 19, 1968 (div.); children: Rachel, David; m. Yvette Ehr Cohen, Nov. 1, 1992. BA in Econs., Brandeis U., 1965; MBA, Columbia U., 1967. Fin. analyst SEC, Washington, 1968-69; asst. treas. U-Haul Internat., Phoenix, 1969-71; v.p., treas. Ramada, Inc., Phoenix, 1971-90; CFO Boyd Gaming Corp., Las Vegas, Nev., 1990—. Home: 7571 Silver Meadow Ct Las Vegas NV 89117-2986 Office: Boyd Gaming Corp 2950 Industrial Rd Las Vegas NV 89109-1100 E-mail: ellislandau@boydgaming.com

LANDAU, MARTIN, political science educator; b. N.Y.C., July 12, 1921; s. User Noah and Clara (Markowitz) L.; m. Bernice Feldman, July 11, 1943; children— Madeline, Claudia. A.B., Bklyn. Coll., 1947; M.A. in Pub. Adminstrn, N.Y. U., 1948; Ph.D., 1952; Docteur Honoris Causa, U. Paris, Dauphine, 1993. Vis. research prof. U. Calif. at Berkeley, 1969-71, prof. polit. sci., 1972—; Distinguished prof. City U. N.Y., Bklyn., 1970-72; lectr. orgn. and decision theory Fgn. Service Inst., U.S. Dept. State, Washington, 1969-72. Cons. in field; chancellor Grad. Sch. Pub. Adminstrn., U. P.R., San Juan, 1970-71; Berkeley Exch. prof., Peking U., 1985; Phi Beta Kappa Nat. Lectr., 1984; dir. Berkeley-Hong Kong Project, 1984—. Author: Political Theory and Political Science; Studies in the Methodology of Political Inquiry, 1972; Chmn. editorial bd.: Polit. Sci, 1971— ; mem. editorial bd.: Jour. Comparative Adminstrv. Studies, 1969— , Comparative Politics, 1970—, Jour. Theoretical Politics, 1988—, Jour. Behavioral Decision Making, 1988—. Served with Signal Corps AUS, 1941-45. Recipient Distinguished Teaching award Bklyn. Coll., 1963, E. Harris Harbison award gifted teaching Danforth Found., 1969-70, William E. Mosher award distinguished scholarship Soc. Pub. Adminstrn., 1970, 79; John Simon Guggenheim fellow, 1976-77; fellow Center Advanced Study in Behavioral Sci., 1976-77 Fellow Nat. Acad. Public Adminstrn.; mem. Am. Polit. Sci. Assn., Philosophy of Sci. Assn. Home: 1410 Summit Rd Berkeley CA 94708-2215 Office: U Calif Dept Polit Sci Berkeley CA 94720-0001

LANDE, JAMES AVRA, lawyer; b. Chgo., Oct. 2, 1930; s. Theodore and Helen C. (Hamburger) L.; m. Ann Mari Gustavsson, Feb. 21, 1959; children: Rebecca Susanne, Sylvia Diane. BA, Swarthmore Coll., 1952; JD, Columbia U., 1955. Bar: N.Y. 1958, Calif. 1967. Assoc. Rein, Mound & Cotton, N.Y.C., 1957-59; atty. VA, Seattle, 1959-61, Weyerhaeuser Co., Tacoma, 1961-63, Lande Assocs., San Francisco, 1963-67, NASA, Ames Rsch. Ctr., Moffett Field, Calif., 1967-70; house counsel Syntex Corp., Palo Alto, 1970-73; dir. contracts dept. Electric Power Rsch. Inst., Palo Alto, 1973-81; corp. atty., dir. contracts Lurgi Corp., Belmont, 1981-82; contracts mgr. Bechtel Corp., San Francisco, 1982-92; sr. contract mgr. Bay Area Rapid Transit Dist., Millbrae, Calif., 1992—. Adj. prof. U. San Francisco Sch. Law, 1972-73; lectr. law U. Santa Clara Sch. Law, 1968-82; pres. Syntex Fed. Credit Union, 1971-72. Served with U.S. Army, 1955-57. Mem. Calif. Bar Assn., Nat. Contract Mgmt. Assn. (past pres., dir. Golden Gate chpt.), Lawyers Club San Francisco. Home: 1330 33rd Ave San Francisco CA 94122-1305 Office: Bay Area Rapid Transit Dist 979 Broadway Millbrae CA 94030-1912

LANDECKER, TOM L. research center director; Dir. Dominion Radio Astrophys. Observatory Nat. Rsch. Coun., Penticton, B.C., Can. Office: NRC Dominion Radio Astrophys Observatory PO Box 248 Penticton BC Canada V2A 6K3

LANDERS, TERESA PRICE, librarian; b. N.Y.C., Dec. 28, 1954; d. Stanley and June Ethel (Novick) Price; m. Gary David Landers, Sept. 2, 1979; children: Joshua Price, Alisha Rose. BA in History cum laude, Williams Coll., 1976; MA in LS, U. Denver, 1978; postgrad., Ctrl. Wash. U., 1980; MA in Orgnl. Mgmt., U. Phoenix, 1999. Libr., asst. analyst Earl Combs, Inc., Mercer Island, Wash., 1979; reference libr. Yakima (Wash.) Valley Regional Libr., 1981-83, coord. youth svcs., 1983-84; libr. Tempe (Ariz.) Pub. Libr., 1984-85; supervisory libr. Mesa (Ariz.) Pub. Libr., 1985-90; head telephone reference Phoenix Pub. Libr., 1990-91, head bus. and scis., 1991-95, info. svcs. mgr., 1995-99; dep. dir. Corvallis-Benton County Pub. libr., 1999—. Cons. Fed. Dept. Corrections, Phoenix, 1993. Mem. ALA, Oreg. Libr. Assn., Nat. Wildlife Fedn. (life), Altrusa, Beta Phi Mu. Democrat. Unitarian. Avocations: cooking, camping. Office: Corvallis-Benton County Pub Libr 645 NW Monroe Ave Corvallis OR 97330-4722 E-mail: teresa.landers@ci.corvallis.or.us

LANDING, BENJAMIN HARRISON, pathologist, educator; b. Buffalo, Sept. 11, 1920; s. Benjamin Harrison Sr. and Margaret Catherine (Crohen) L.; m. Dorothy Jean Hallas; children: Benjamin H., Susan L. Phillips, William M., David A. AB, Harvard U., 1942, MD, 1945. Diplomate Am. Bd. Pathology (anatomic pathology and pediatric pathology). Intern pathology Children's Hosp., Boston, 1945-46, asst. resident, then resident pathology, 1948-49; resident pathology Boston Lying-in Hosp., 1949, Free Hosp. for Women, Brookline, Mass., 1949; pathologist Children's Med. Ctr., Boston, 1950-53, Cin., 1953-61; pathologist-in-chief Children's Hosp., L.A., 1961-88, rsch. pathologist, 1988—. Asst. pathologist Harvard U. Med. Sch., Boston, 1950-53; from asst. prof. to assoc. prof. U. Cin. Coll. Medicine, 1953-61; prof. pathology and pediatrics U. So. Calif. Sch. Medicine, L.A., 1961-91, prof. emeritus, 1991—. Author: Butterfly Color/Behavior Patterns, 1984; author chpts. in books; contbr. articles to profl. jours. Chmn. Pacific S.W. Dist. Unitarian-Universalist Assn., 1968-70; pres. Burbank (Calif.) Unitarian Fellowship, 1964-66. Capt. Med. Corps AUS, 1946-48. Mem. Soc. for Pediatric Pathology (pres. 1973-74), Internat. Pediatric Pathology Soc. (pres. 1980). Democrat. Unitarian-Universalist. Home: 4513 Deanwood Dr Woodland Hills CA 91364-5622 Office: Childrens Hosp LA Box 103 4650 W Sunset Blvd Los Angeles CA 90027-6062

LANDIS, RICHARD GORDON, retired food company executive; b. Davenport, Okla., Apr. 5, 1920; s. John William and Venna Marie (Perrin) L.; m. Beth Throne, Nov. 6, 1943; children: Gary Perrin, Dennis, Michael, Kay Ellen. BA, U. LaVerne, 1942; postgrad., Claremont Grad. Sch., 1947; LLD (hon.), U. LaVerne, 1981. Mgmt. Delmonte Corp, San Francisco, 1942-83, pres., 1971-77, pres. & chief exec. officer, 1977-78, chmn. & chief exec. officer, 1978-81; pres. Pacific div. R.J. Reynolds, Inc., San Francisco, 1981-83; former chancellor U. LaVerne, Calif. Bd. dirs. Stanford Rsch. Internat., Menlo Park, Calif. Mem. Commn. of Calif., 1984-90; chmn. Pacific Basin Econ. Coun., 1975-83; officer Boy Scouts Am., 1946—, Invest in Am.; Lt. USAF, 1942-46. Mem. Pacific Union Club, Bohemian Club, Peachtree C. of C. Republican. Avocations: golf, edn. activities, youth programs. Office: 120 Montgomery St Ste 1880 San Francisco CA 94104-4321

LANDON, SUSAN MELINDA, petroleum geologist; b. Mattoon, Ill., July 2, 1950; d. Albert Leroy and Nancy (Wallace) L.; m. Richard D. Dietz, Jan. 24, 1993. BA, Knox Coll., 1972; MA, SUNY, Binghamton, 1975. Cert. profl. geologist; cert. petroleum geologist. Petroleum geologist Amoco Prodn. Co., Denver, 1974-87; mgr. exploration tng. Amoco, Houston, 1987-89; ind. petroleum geologist Denver, 1990—. Instr. petroleum geology & exploration Bur. of Land Mgmt., U.S. Forest Svc., Nat. Park Svc., 1978-86. Editor: Interior Rift Basins, 1993. Mem., chmn. Colo. Geol. Survey Adv. Com., Denver, 1991-98; mem. Bd. on Earth Sci. and Resources-NRC, 1992-97, chair com. on earth resources, 1998—; mem. Nat. Coop. Geologic Mapping Program Fed. Adv. Com., 1997—. Recipient Disting. Alumni award Knox Coll., 1986, Disting. Svc. award Rocky Mountain Assn. Geologists, 1986, Disting. Pub. Svc. to Earth Sci. award Rocky Mountain Assn. Geologists, 1998. Mem. Am. Assn. Petroleum Geologists (hon., treas., Disting. Svc. award 1995), Am. Inst. Profl. Geologists (pres. 1990, Martin Van Couvering award 1991), Am. Geol. Inst. (pres. 1998), Rocky Mtn. Assn. Geologists (pres. elect 2000). Achievements include frontier exploration for hydrocarbons in U.S. Home: 780 Ballantine Rd Golden CO 80401-9503 Office: Thomasson Ptnr Assocs 1410 High St Denver CO 80218-2609 E-mail: susanlandon@att.net

LANDRE, DEBRA ANN, mathematics educator; b. Quantico, Va., Sept. 15, 1955; d. Thomas F. and Joy L. (Carstens) L. BA in French and Math., Bradley U., 1976, MS in Edn., 1977; MS in Math., Ill. State U., 1979. Math. instr. Bradley U., Peoria, Ill., 1977-79, Ill. Valley Community Coll., Peru, 1980, Ill. Wesleyan U., Bloomington, 1981; computer sci. instr. Lincoln Coll., Bloomington, 1981-85; math. instr. Ill. State U., Normal, 1979-85; pres. Quality Input Inc., Normal, 1983-85; dir. acad. computing San Joaquin Delta Coll., Stockton, Calif., 1985-88, prof. math., 1988—. Author: Explorations in Elementary Algebra, 1992, Explorations in Intermediate Algebra, 1992, Explorations in College Algebra, 1992, Explorations in Statistics and Probability, 1992, Amusements in Algebra, 1994; co-author: Mathematics: Theory into Practice, 1980, Microprocessor-Based Operations: Systems Software, 1985, Data Acquisition, 1985; contbr. articles to profl. jours. Treas. Acad. Senate Calif. C.C., 1996-97, mem. exec. com., 1999—, dir. legis. and govtl. affairs, 1999—; mem. chancellor's consultation com. Calif. C.C., 1997-99. Mem. Am. Statis. Assn., Calif. Assn. Dirs. Acad. Computing (pres. 1988-90), Calif. Ednl. Computer Consortium (bd. dirs. 1987-90, editor 1988-90), No. Calif. C.C. Computer Consortium (sec./editor 1986-91), Calif. Math. Coun. C.C. (editor exec. bd. 1990—, pres. elect 1991-93, pres. 1994-95, past pres. 1995-97, mem. found. 1995-97), Am. Math. Assn. of Two Yr. Colls. (del. 1993-97, editor 1994-97), Calif. Tchrs. Assn. (pres.-elect 1994-95, pres. 1995-96), Calif. Assn. Women in Edn. and Rsch., C.C. Assn. (dist. dir. 1995-97, pres. 1997-99). Avocations: international travel, horses. Office: San Joaquin Delta Coll 5151 Pacific Ave Stockton CA 95207-6304

LANDRETH, KATHRYN E. prosecutor; U.S. atty. Dept. Justice, Las Vegas, 1993—. Office: US Attys Office 701 E Bridger Ave Ste 600 Las Vegas NV 89101-5554

LANDRY, RICHARD, publishing executive; Pub. New Media Mag., San Mateo, Calif.; chmn., CEO New Media mag., San Mateo. Office: New Media Mag Ste 365 901 Mariners Island Blvd San Mateo CA 94404-1592

LAND-WEBER, ELLEN, photography educator; b. Rochester, N.Y., Mar. 16, 1943; d. David and Florence Epstein; 1 child, Julia. BA, U. Iowa, 1965, MFA, 1968. Faculty mem. UCLA Extension, 1970-74, Orange Coast Coll., Costa Mesa, Calif., 1973, U. Nebr., Lincoln, 1974; asst. prof. photography Humboldt State U., Arcata, Calif., 1974-79, assoc. prof., 1979-83, prof., 1983—. Photographer Seagram's Bicentennial Courthouse Project, 1976-77, Nat. Trust for Hist. Preservation/Soc. Photographic Edn., 1987. Author: The Passionate Collector, 1980, To Save a Life: Stories of Holocaust Rescue, 2000; contbr. sects. to books; photographs pub. in numerous books and jours. Nat. Endowment for Arts fellow, 1974, 79, 82; Artist's support grantee Unicolor Corp., 1982, Polaroid 20X24 Artist's support grantee, 1990, 91, 93, 94; Fulbright sr. fellow, 1993-94. Mem. Soc. for Photog. Edn. (exec. bd. 1979-82, treas. 1979-81, sec. 1981-83) Avocation: weaving. Office: Humboldt State U Art Dept Arcata CA 95521

LANE, ALFRED THOMAS, medical educator; b. Dayton, Ohio, July 17, 1947; BS, U. Dayton, 1969; MD, Ohio State U., 1973. Diplomate Am. Bd. Pediatrics, Am. Bd. Dermatology; lic. physician, Calif. Intern, resident pediatrics Children's Hosp. L.A., 1973-76; pvt. practice Pleasant Valley Pediatric Med. Group, Camarillo, Calif., 1976-79; resident dermatology U. Colo. Sch. Medicine, Denver, 1979-82; asst. prof. dermatology and pediatrics U. Rochester (N.Y.) Med. Ctr., 1982-88; attending physician Strong Meml. Hosp., 1982-90; staff dermatologist Rochester Gen. Hosp., 1985-90; dir. Dermatology Clinic VA, Rochester, 1985-90; assoc. prof. dermatology and pediatrics U. Rochester Med. Ctr., 1988-90; staff physician in dermatology and pediatrics Stanford (Calif.) U. Med. Ctr., Stanford Children's Hosp., 1990—, dir. pediatric dermatology, 1990—; assoc. prof. dermatology and pediatrics Stanford U. Med. Ctr., 1990-96; prof. dermatology Stanford (Calif.) U. Med. Ctr., 1996—; acting chmn. dept. dermatology Stanford U. Med. Ctr., 1995-96, chmn. dermatology, 1996—; chief dermatology svc. Stanford U. Med. Ctr., Stanford Health Svcs., 1995—. Author: with W.L. Weston) Color Textbook of Pediatric Dermatology, 1991; (with W.L. Weston and J.G. Morelli) Color Textbook of Pediatric Dermatology, 1995; contbr. articles to profl. jours. Recipient Buswell fellowship U. Rochester, 1982-83, Clin. Investigator award NIH, 1983-88. Fellow Am. Acad. Pediatrics, Am. Acad. Dermatology (mem. task force on pediatric dermatology 1987-92, mem. adv. coun. 1988-90, mem. Presdl. Commn. on Melanoma/Skin Cancer 1988-92, mem. task force on youth edn. 1989-94)); mem. Soc. Pediatric Dermatology (bd. dirs. 1986-93, pres. elect 1990-91, pres. 1991-92), Soc. Investigative Dermatology (com. on pub. rels. 1990-94, com. on govt. and pub. rels. 1992-94), Soc. Pediatric Rsch., Am. Dermatol. Assn., Am. Soc. Laser Medicine and Surgery. Office: Stanford U Med Ctr Dept Dermatology 900 Blake Wilbur Dr Dept W71 Palo Alto CA 94304-2201

LANE, ERIC JAY, retail executive; BA in Econs., U. Calif., Santa Barbara. With Macy's, The Men's Wearhouse, Inc., Fremont, Calif., 1988—, v.p. store ops., 1990-93, sr. v.p. merchandising, 1993-97, COO, 1997-2000, pres., COO, 2001—. 1st lt. USAR, 1982. Office: The Mens Wearhouse Inc 40650 Encyclopedia Cir Fremont CA 94538

LANE, FIELDING H. lawyer; b. Kansas City, Mo., May 6, 1926; s. Ralph Fielding and Nancy Lee (Greene) L.; m. Patricia Cecil Parkhurst, Jan. 25, 1980 B.S. in Bus. Adminstrn., U. Mo.-Columbia, 1948; LL.B. cum laude, Harvard U., 1951. Bar: Mo. 1951, Calif. 1956. Assoc. Watson Ess Marshall & Enggas, Kansas City, Mo., 1951-55; assoc. Thelen Marrin Johnson & Bridges, San Francisco, 1955-66, ptnr., 1967-95, of counsel, 1996—. Served with USN, 1944-46; PTO; lt. comdr. Res. (ret.) Club: Olympic (San Francisco) Home: PO Box 1495 Aptos CA 95001-1495 Office: Thelen Reid & Priest LLP 101 2d St Ste 1800 San Francisco CA 94105 E-mail: fhlane@thelenreid.com

LANE, LARRY K. air industry service executive; b. 1948; BS in Social Scis., Oreg. Coll. Edn., 1974. With Evergreen Aviation Ground Logistics, 1967-78, 1984—, now chmn.; regional sales rep. Skyline Mobile Home Mfr., McMinnville, Oreg., 1978-84; pres. Evergreen Internat. Airlines, Inc., 1992—. Bd. dirs. Evergreen Internat. Aviation. With USAR, 1969-75. Office: Evergreen Internat Airlines Inc 3850 NE Three Mile Ln Mcminnville OR 97128-9402

LANE, LAURENCE WILLIAM, JR. retired ambassador, publisher; b. Des Moines, Nov. 7, 1919; s. Laurence William and Ruth (Bell) L.; m. Donna Jean Gimbel, Apr. 16, 1955; children: Sharon Louise, Robert Laurence, Brenda Ruth. Student, Pomona Coll., 1938-40, LLD (hon.), 1976; BJ, Stanford U., 1942; DHL (hon.), Hawaii Loa Coll., 1991. Chmn. bd. Lane Pub. Co.; pub. Sunset Mag., Sunset Books and Sunset Films; U.S. amb. to Australia and Nauru, 1985-89; ret., 1990. Bd. dirs. Calif. Water Svc. Co., Crown Zellerbach Corp., Pacific Gas and Electric Co.; bd. dirs. Time Inc.; bd. dirs. Oreg. Coast Aquarium, Internat. Bd. Advice, ANZ Bank; U.S. amb. and commr. Gen. Worlds Fair, Japan, 1975-76; hon. fellow Coll. Notre Dame, 1974. Former mem. adv. bd. Sec. Interior's Bd. Nat. Parks; mem. adv. coun. Grad. Sch. Bus., Stanford U., SRI; mem. Pres.'s Nat. Productivity Adv. Com.; mem. Pacific Basin Econ. Coun.; former bd. dirs. Pacific Forum, CSI, Nat. Parks Found.; vol. The Nat. Ctr.; mem. bd. overseers Hoover Instn. War, Revolution and Peace; mem. exec. com. Ctr. for Australian Studies, U. Tex., Austin. Lt. USNR, World War II,

PTO. Decorated officer Order of Australia; recipient Conservation Svc. award Sec. Interior; Theodore and Conrad Wirth award NPF, 1994; Wiliam Penn Mott Jr. Conservationist of Yr. award NPCA, 1995; named hon. prof. journalism Stanford U. Mem. Newcomen Soc. N.Am., Pacific Asia Travel Assn. (life mem., chmn. 1980-81), Coun. of Am. Ambs., Los Rancheros Vistadores, Advt. Club San Francisco, No. Calif. Alumni Assn., Bohemian Club, Pacific Union, Men's Garden Club L.A., Alpha Delta Sigma. Republican. Presbyterian. Office: 3000 Sand Hill Rd Bldg 215 Menlo Park CA 94025-7113

LANE, RAYMOND J. software systems consulting company executive; b. 1947; Various product and mktg. positions IBM, until 1977; divsn. v.p. Electronic Data Sys. Corp., 1977-80; prin. inf. sys. practice in western U.S., Booz-Allen & Hamilton, 1980-83, mng. ptnr. S.W. region, 1983-86, sr. v.p., mng. ptnr. worldwide info. svcs. group, 1986-92, mem. exec. com., 1986-92, bd. dirs., 1985-88, 91-92; sr. v.p. Oracle USA, Redwood City, Calif., 1992-96; exec. v.p. Oracle Corp., Redwood City, 1996—, pres. world ops., 1996-98; pres., COO, Oracle Sys. Corp., Redwood City, 1998—. Office: Oracle Sys Corp 500 Oracle Pky Redwood City CA 94065-1677

LANE, SYLVIA, economist, educator; b. N.Y.C. m. Benjamin Lane, Sept. 2, 1939; children: Leonard, Reese, Nancy. AB, U. Calif., Berkeley, 1934, MA, 1936; postgrad., Columbia U., 1937; PhD, U. So. Calif., 1957. Lectr., asst. prof. U. So. Calif., Los Angeles, 1947-60; assoc. prof. econs. San Diego State U., 1961-65; assoc. prof. finance, assoc. dir. Ctr. for Econ. Edn. Calif. State U., Fullerton, 1965-69, chmn. dept. fin., 1967-69; prof. agrl. econs. U. Calif., Davis, 1969-82, prof. emerita, 1982—; prof. emerita and economist Giannini Found., U. Calif.-Berkeley, 1982—; vis. scholar Stanford U., 1975-76. Cons. Calif. Adv. Commn. Tax Reform, 1963, Adv. Office Consumer Affairs, Exec. Office of Pres., 1972-77, FAO, UN, 1983. Author: (with E. Bryant Phillips) Personal Finance, 1963, rev. edit., 1979, The Insurance Tax, 1965, California's Income Tax Conformity and Withholding, 1968, (with Irma Adelman) The Balance Between Industry and Agriculture in Economic Development, 1989; editl. bd. Agrl. Econs., 1986-92; also articles, reports in field. Project economist Los Angeles County Welfare Planning Coun., 1956-59; del. White House Conf. on Food and Nutrition, 1969, Pres.'s Summit Con. on Inflation, 1974; mem. adv. com. Ctr. for Bldg. Tech., Nat. Bur. Stds., 1975-79; bd. dirs. Am. Coun. Consumer Interests, 1972-74; exec. bd. Am. Agr. Econ. Assn. 1976-79. Ford Found. fellow UCLA, 1963; Ford Found. fellow U. Chgo., 1965; fellow U. Chgo., 1968 Fellow Am. Agrl. Econ. Assn. (life, Sylvia Lane Fellowship Fund 1993); mem. Am. Econ. Assn., Am. Coun. Consumer Interests, Omicron Delta Epsilon (pres. 1973-75, trustee 1975-83, chmn. bd. trustees 1982-84). Home and Office: 2231 Caminito Preciosa N La Jolla CA 92037-7231

LANEY, MICHAEL L. manufacturing executive; b. Los Angeles, Sept. 10, 1945; s. Roy and Wanda Laney; m. Marti Miller, Dec. 31, 1964; children: Tynna, Kristen. BS with honors, Calif. State U., Northridge, 1967; MBA, UCLA, 1969. CPA, Calif. Sr. tax acct. Haskins-Sells, Los Angeles, 1967-69; asst. prof. acctg. Calif. State U., Northridge, 1969-72; tax prin. M. Klaiman Acctg. Corp., Beverly Hills, Calif., 1972-75; pvt. practice Beverly Hills, 1975-80; v.p., controller Ducommun, Inc., Los Angeles, 1980-87; sr. v.p., fin. and adminstrn. Monarch Mirror Door Co. Inc., Chatsworth, Calif., 1987-92; v.p. ops. feature animation Walt Disney Pictures and TV (part of The Walt Disney Co.), Glendale, 1992-93; sr. v.p. ops. Warner Bros., Glendale, 1994-96; pres. Children's Wonderland, Agoura, 1996-97; CFO Dacor, Pasadena, 1997-2001; pres., CEO Cool Roof of Calif., Inc., Calabasas, 2001—. Mem. Fin. Execs. Inst., Tax Execs. Inst., Am. Inst. CPA's, Calif. Soc. CPA's. Office: Laney & Assocs PO Box 8993 Calabasas CA 91372-8993 E-mail: MLaney@Cool-Roof.com, Mlaneyassoc.@yahoo.com

LANG, GEORGE FRANK, insurance executive, consultant, lawyer; b. Orange, N.J., Aug. 21, 1937; s. Frank W. and Hilda I. (Pierson) L.; m. Grace B. Preisler, Jan. 30, 1960; children: Christine, Gregg, Cynthia; m. Valerie J. Hanson, Nov. 24, 1978. BS, Ill. Wesleyan U., 1960; JD, Ill. Inst. Tech., 1968. Account exec. Scarborough & Co., Chgo., 1960-67; dir. fin. inst. George F. Brown & Sons, Chgo., 1967-69; v.p., dir. Fin. Ins. Svc., Schaumburg, Ill., 1969-79; pres. City Ins. Svc., Elizabeth, N.J., 1980-84; mng. dir. Res. Fin. Mgmt., Miami, Fla., 1984-85; v.p. Beneficial Ins. Group, Newport Beach, Calif., 1985-86, Ask Ins. Svc., Irvine, 1986-89, cons. product ctr. sales, 1989; cons. Nat. Dealer Ins. Systems, 1989, New Liberty Adminstrn., 1990—, Home Crest Ins., 1991—, Great Western Ins. Agy., 1992—, Dana Harbor Ins. Svcs., Inc., 1995—. Cons. in field. Bd. dirs. Woodview Civic Assn., Mt. Prospect, Ill., 1964-70, pres., bd. dirs., 1969; bd. dirs. Chippendale Assn., Barrington, Ill., 1972-76, v.p., bd. dirs., 1976. Avocations: boating, fishing, traveling. Home: 173 Ave del Poniente San Clemente CA 92672-4647 Office: 34512 Embarcadero Pl Dana Point CA 92629-2910 E-mail: Danaharbo@AOL.com

LANG, K. D. (KATHERINE DAWN LANG), country music singer, composer; b. Consort, Alta., Can., Feb. 11, 1961; d. Adam and Audrey L. Lang. Mem. Tex. swing fiddle band, 1982—; formed band The Reclines. Albums include A Truly Western Experience, 1984, Angel with a Lariat, 1986, Shadowland, 1988, Absolute Torch and Twang, 1990 (Can. Country Music Awards album of the yr.), Ingenue, 1992, Even Cowgirls Get the Blues (soundtrack), 1993, Drag, 1997, Australian Tour, 1997; (with others) All You Can Eat, 1995; actress (film) Salmonberries, 1991; Teresa's Tattoo, 1994, The Last Don, 1997, TV guest appearance Ellen, 1997, Eye of The Beholder, 1999. Recipient Can. Country Music awards, including Entertainer of Yr., 1989, Grammy award, 1990, 1993, Best Pop Female Vocal for Constant Craving, Grammy nomination Best Pop Female Vocal for Miss Chatelaine, 1994, William Harold Moon award Soc. of Composers, Authors and Music Publishers of Can., 1994. Office: Warner Bros Records Inc 3300 Warner Blvd Burbank CA 91505-4694

LANG, LAURIE, entertainment company executive; 1 child. BA in Theater Arts and Polit. Sci., Wash. U.; MBA, Columbia U. V.p., account supr. DDB Needham Advt., N.Y.C.; sr. v.p. strategic mktg. Walt Disney Co., Burbank, Calif., 1988-98, head Learning Initiative, 1998—. Office: Walt Disney Co 500 S Buena Vista St Burbank CA 91521-0006

LANG, MARGO TERZIAN, artist; b. Fresno, Calif. d. Nishan and Araxie (Kazarosian) Terzian; m. Nov. 29, 1942; children: Sandra J. (Mrs. Ronald L. Carr), Roger Mark, Timothy Scott. Student, Fresno State U., 1939-42, Stanford U., 1948-50, Prado Mus., Madrid, 1957-59, Ariz. State U., , 1960-61; workshops with, Dong Kingman, Ed Whitney, Rex Brandt, Millard Sheets, George Post. Maj. exhbns. include, Guadalajara, Mex., Brussels, N.Y.C., San Francisco, Chgo., Phoenix, Corcoran Gallery Art, Washington, internat. watercolor exhbn., Los Angeles, Bicentennial shows, Hammer Galleries, N.Y.C., spl. exhbn. aboard, S.S. France, others, over 80 paintings in various Am. embassies throughout world; represented in permanent collections, Nat. Collection Fine Arts Mus., Smithsonian Instn., lectr., juror art shows; condr. workshops.; interviews and broadcasts on Radio Liberty, Voice of Am. Bd. dirs. Phoenix Symphony Assn., 1965-69, Phoenix Musical Theater, 1965-69. Recipient award for spl. achievements Symphony Assn., 1966, 67, 68, 72, spl. awards State of Ariz., silver medal of excellence Internat. Platform Assn., 1971; honoree U.S. Dept. State celebration of 25 yrs. of exhbn. of paintings in embassies worldwide, 1989. Mem. Internat. Platform Assn., Ariz. Watercolor Assn., Nat. Soc. Arts and Letters (nat. dir. 1971-72, nat. art chmn. 1971-76), Nat. Soc. Lit. and Arts,

Phoenix Art Mus., Friends of Mexican Art, Am. Artists Profl. League, English-Speaking Union, Musical Theater Guild, Ariz. Costume Inst., Phoenix Art Mus., Scottsdale Art Ctr., Ariz. Arts Commn. (fine arts panel 1990-91), Friends of Art and Preservation in Embassies. Home: 6127 E Calle Del Paisano Scottsdale AZ 85251-4212

LANG, THOMPSON HUGHES, publishing company executive; b. Albuquerque, Dec. 12, 1946; s. Cornelius Thompson and Margaret Miller (Hughes) L. Student, U. N.Mex., 1965-68, U. Americas, Mexico City, 1968-69. Advt. salesman Albuquerque Pub. Co., 1969-70, pres., 1971—; pub., pres., treas., dir. Jour. Pub. Co., 1971—; pres., dir. Masthead, Internat., 1971—; pres. Magnum Systems, Inc., 1973—; pres., treas., dir. Jour. Ctr. Corp., 1979—; chmn. bd., dir. Starline Printing, Inc., 1985—. Chmn. bd. dirs. Corp. Security and Investigation, Inc., 1986—; pres., bd. dirs. Eagle Systems, Inc., 1986—. Mem. HOW Orgn., Sigma Delta Chi. Home: 8643 Rio Grande Blvd NW Albuquerque NM 87114-1301 Office: Albuquerque Pub Co PO Drawer JT 87103 7777 Jefferson St NE Albuquerque NM 87109-4343

LANGACKER, RONALD WAYNE, linguistics educator; b. Fond du Lac, Wis., Dec. 27, 1942; s. George Rollo and Florence (Hinesley) L.; m. Margaret G. Fullick, June 5, 1966 (dec.); m. Sheila M. Pickwell, Mar. 28, 1998. A.B. in French, U. Ill., 1963, A.M. in Linguistics, 1964, Ph.D., 1966. Asst. prof. U. Calif. at San Diego, La Jolla, 1966-70, asso. prof., 1970-75, prof. linguistics, 1975—. Author: Language and its Structure, 1968, Fundamentals of Linguistic Analysis, 1972, Non-Distinct Arguments in Uto-Aztecan, 1976, An Overview of Uto-Aztecan Grammar, 1977, Foundations of Cognitive Grammar I, 1987, Concept, Image and Symbol, 1990, Foundations of Cognitive Grammar II, 1991, Grammar and Conceptualization, 1999; assoc. editor: Lang, 1971-77, Cognitive Linguistics, 1989—; contbr. articles in field to profl. jours. Guggenheim fellow, 1978 Mem. Linguistic Soc. Am., Cognitive Sci. Soc., Soc. for Study Indigenous Langs. of Ams., Internat. Cognitive Linguistics Assn. (pres. 1997-99), AAUP, ACLU. Home: 7381 Rue Michael La Jolla CA 92037-3915 Office: U Calif San Diego Dept Linguistics 0108 La Jolla CA 92093 E-mail: rlangacker@ucsd.edu

LANGDON, FRANK CORRISTON, political science educator, researcher; b. LaGrange, Ill., June 3, 1919; s. Ernest Warren and Julia Ida (Mondeng) L.; m. Virginia Irene Osborne, Nov. 11, 1922; children: Peter John, Marc Christopher. A.B., Harvard U., 1941, A.M., 1949; Ph.D., U. Calif.-Berkeley, 1953. Japanese Lang. Sch. intelligence officer U.S. Navy, Stillwater, Okla., 1945-46; econ. analyst Hdqrs. SCAP, Fgn. Trade div., Tokyo, 1946-47; instr. polit. sci. U. Calif. Far East Program, Korea, Japan, Guam, 1953-55; sr. lectr. Canberra U. Coll., Australia, 1955-58; prof. polit. sci. Univ. B.C., Vancouver, 1958-84, emeritus prof., 1984—, sr. research assoc. Inst. Internat. Rels., 1984—. Author: Politics in Japan, 1967, Japan's Foreign Policy, 1973, Politics of Canadian-Japanese Economic Relations, 1952-83, 83; co-editor, co-author: Japan in the Post Hegomonic World, 1993; co-editor, contbr.: Superpower Maritime Strategy in the Pacific, 1990; contbr. articles to profl. jours. Served to lt. comdr. USNR, 1941-45. Mem. Internat. House Japan, Internat. Studies Assn., Can. Consortium on Asia Pacific Security, Vancouver Mokuyokai Soc., Japan Studies Assn. of Can. Democrat. Presbyterian. Club: Mokuyokai (Vancouver). Home: 4736 W 4th Ave Vancouver BC Canada V6T 1C2 Office: U BC Inst Intl Rels Dept Pol Sci Buchanan C472 1866 Main Mal Vancouver BC Canada V6T 1Z1

LANGDON, GLEN GEORGE, JR. electrical engineer; b. Morristown, N.J., June 30, 1936; s. Glen George and Mildred (Miller) L.; m. Marian Elizabeth Jacobsen, Aug. 10, 1963; 1 child, Karen Joan. BSEE, Wash. State U., 1957; MSEE, U. Pitts., 1963; PhD, Syracuse U., 1968. Elec. engr. Westinghouse Electric Co., East Pittsburgh, Pa., 1960-62; applications programmer Churchill Boro, 1962-63; engr. IBM Corp., Endicott, N.Y., 1963-73; rsch. staff mem. San Jose, Calif., 1974-87; prof. computer engring. U. Calif., Santa Cruz, 1987—. Vis. prof. U. São Paulo, Brazil, 1971-72; lectr. U. Santa Clara, 1975-78, Stanford U., 1984; U. Calif. affiliate lectr. Los Alamos Nat. Lab., 2001. Author: Logic Design: A Review of Theory and Practice, 1974, (with Edson Fregni) Projecto de Computadores Digitals, 1974, Computer Design, 1982; patentee in field. Lt. Signal Corps., U.S. Army, 1958-59. Recipient Armed Svcs. Comm. award Wash. State U., 1957, Outstanding Innovation award IBM, 1980, 91; Erskine fellow U. Canterbury, 1993, 99. Fellow IEEE, Computer Soc. IEEE (stds. com. 1969-70, 74-81, sec. 1982, edn. bd. 1983-86, pub. bd. 1984-85, 87-90, bd. govs. 1984-87, v.p. edn. 1986, Compcon gen. chair 1986, Hot Chips IV Symposium gen. chair 1992, cons. data compression patent disputes 1993—, mem. joint steering com. hot chips and hot interconnects 1999—); mem. Assn. Computing Machinery (vice chmn. So. Tier chpt. 1973), Soc. Photog. Instrumentation Engrs., Soc. Motion Picture and TV Engrs., Sigma Xi. Home: 220 Horizon Way Aptos CA 95003-2739 Office: U Calif Dept Computer Engring Santa Cruz CA 95064

LANGE, CLIFFORD E. librarian; b. Fond du Lac, Wis., Dec. 29, 1935; s. Elmer H. and Dorothy Brick (Smithers) L.; m. Janet M. LeMieux, June 6, 1959; children: Paul, Laura, Ruth. Student, St. Norbert Coll., 1954-57; B.S., Wis. State U., 1959; M.S.L.S. (Library Services Act scholar), U. Wis., 1960, Ph.D. (Higher Edn. Act fellow), 1972. Head extension dept. Oshkosh (Wis.) Public Library, 1960-62, head reference dept., 1962-63; asst. dir. Jervis Library, Rome, 1962; dir. Eau Claire (Wis.) Public Library, 1963-66; asst. dir. Lake County Public Library, Griffith, Ind., 1966-68; asst. prof. Sch. Library Sci., U. Iowa, 1971-73; dir. Wauwatosa (Wis.) Public Library, 1973-75; asst. prof. U. So. Calif., 1975-78; state librarian N.Mex. State Library, Santa Fe, 1978-82; dir. Carlsbad City Library, Calif., 1982—. Served with U.S. Army, 1958. Mem. ALA, Calif. Libr. Assn. Home: 3575 Ridge Rd Oceanside CA 92056-4952 Office: 1775 Dove Ln Carlsbad CA 92009-4048 E-mail: clang@ci.carlsbad.ca.us

LANGE, FREDERICK F. materials engineer, educator; BS in Ceramics, Rutgers U., 1961; PhD in Solid State Tech., Pa. State U., 1965. Sr. scientist, fellow sci. dept. materials Westinghouse Rsch. Labs., 1967-76; mgr., prin. scientist structural ceramics group Rockwell Internat. Sci. Ctr., 1976-86; prof. dept. materials and chem. engring. U. Calif., Santa Barbara, 1986—. Adj. prof. UCLA, 1979-86. Contbr. articles to profl. jours. Humboldt Sr. fellow German govt., 1996; recipient Centennial Fellow award Pa. State U., Max Planck Rsch. award, Max Planck Soc., Germany, 1997; named Jubilee prof. Chalmers U., Sweden, 1983, Disting. Dow lectr., Northwe. U., 1992. Fellow Am. Ceramic Soc. (Ross Coffin Purdy award 1982, Richard M. Fulrath award 1982, Sosman Meml. lecture 1987, John Jeppson award 1988, Kraner award 1989); mem. NAE, Acad. Ceramics. Achievements include research in interrelations between processing, phase relations, microstructure and properties leading to either new or improved structural ceramics and their composites; processing of ceramic microstructure that produce higher crack growth resistance, and colloidal powder. Office: U Calif Dept Materials Santa Barbara CA 93106-5050 E-mail: flange@engineering.uscb.edu

LANGE, LESTER HENRY, mathematics educator; b. Concordia, Mo., Jan. 2, 1924; s. Henry William Christopher and [illegible] L.; m. Anne Marie Pelikan, Aug. 17, 1947 (div. Oct. 1960); children: Christopher, Nicholas, Philip, Alexander; m. Beverly Jane Brown, Feb. 4, 1962; 1 son, Andrew. Student, U. Calif., Berkeley, 1943-44; B.A. in Math, Valparaiso U., 1948; M.S. in Math, Stanford, 1950; Ph.D. in Math, U. Notre Dame, 1960. Instr., then asst. prof. math. Valparaiso U., 1950-56; instr. math. U. Notre Dame, 1956-57, 59-60. Mem. faculty San Jose State U., Calif., 1960—, prof. math., head dept., 1961-70, dean Sch. Natural Scis. and Math., 1970-[illegible], dean Sch. Sci., 1972-88, emeritus prof. math., emeritus

dean, 1988—; founder Soc. Archimedes at San Jose State U., 1982; now spl. asst. to dir. Moss Landing (Calif.) Marine Labs.; founding bd. dirs. Friends of MLML, Inc. Author text on linear algebra; sr. editor Calif. Math, 1981-84; contbr. to profl. jours. Served with inf. AUS, 1943-46, ETO. Decorated Combat Infantryman's Badge and Bronze Star; Danforth fellow, 1957-58; NSF faculty fellow, 1958-59. Fellow Calif. Acad. Scis.; mem. Math. Assn. Am. (bd. govs., L.R. Ford Sr. award 1972, George Polya award 1993), Calif. Math. Coun., London Math. Soc., Fibonacci Assn. (bd. dirs. 1987-97), Nat. Coun. Tchrs. Home: 308 Escalona Dr Capitola CA 95010-3419 Office: Moss Landing Marine Labs Moss Landing CA 95039 E-mail: lange@cruzio.com

LANGE, TIM, newspaper publishing executive; Exec. editor L.A. Times Syndicate, 1999—. Office: Los Angeles Times Syndicate Times Mirror Sq 145 S Spring St Los Angeles CA 90012-3601

LANGENDOEN, DONALD TERENCE, linguistics educator; b. Paterson, N.J., June 7, 1939; s. Gerrit and Wilhelmina (Van Dyk) L.; m. Sally Wicklund, Aug. 16, 1964 (div. Mar. 1982); 1 child, David; m. Nancy Susan Kelly, July 28, 1984. BS, MIT, 1961, PhD, 1964. Asst. prof. Ohio State U., Columbus, 1964-68; vis. assoc. prof. Rockefeller U., N.Y.C., 1968-69; prof. Bklyn. C. and Grad. Ctr., CUNY, N.Y.C., 1969-88, U. Ariz., Tucson, 1988—. Exec. officer grad. linguistics program, CUNY, N.Y.C., 1971-78; head dept. linguistics, U. Ariz., Tucson, 1988-97; vis. prof. City U. Hong Kong, 1998; vis. scientist IBM T.J. Watson Research Ctr., Yorktown Heights, N.Y., 1986-87; sr. lectr. Fulbright, Utrecht, Holland, 1977. Author: The London School of Linguistics, 1968; co-author: The Vastness of Natural Languages, 1984; editor: Linguistics Abstracts, 1997—; co-editor: Optimality Theory: An Overview, 1997; mem. editl. bd. Linguist List, 2001—. Fellow N.Y. Acad. of Scis., N.Y.C., 1977; named Ptnr. in Edn., Bd. of Edn., N.Y.C., 1982. Mem. AAAS (chair sect. Z 1999), Linguistic Soc. Am. (sec., treas. 1984-88, pres. 1998), Assn. for Computational Linguistics, Assn. for Linguistic and Lit. Computing. Office: U Ariz Dept Linguistics Box 210028 Tucson AZ 85721-0028

LANGENHEIM, JEAN HARMON, biology educator; b. Homer, La., Sept. 5, 1925; d. Vergil Wilson and Jeanette (Smith) H.; m. Ralph Louis Langenheim, Dec. 1946 (div. Mar. 1961). BS, U. Tulsa, 1946; MS, U. Minn., 1949, PhD, 1953. Rsch. assoc. botany U. Calif., Berkeley, 1954-59, U. Ill., Urbana, 1959-61; rsch. fellow biology Harvard U., Cambridge, Mass., 1962-66; asst. prof. biology U. Calif., Santa Cruz, 1966-68, assoc. prof. biology, 1968-73, prof. biology, 1973-93, prof. biology emerita, 1993—. Academic v.p. Orgn. Tropical Studies, San Jose, Costa Rica, 1975-78; mem. sci.adv. bd. EPA, Washington, 1977-81; chmn. com. on humid tropics U.S. Nat. Acad. Nat. Research Council, 1975-77; mem. com. floral inventory Amazon NSF, Washington, 1975-87. Author: Botany-Plant Biology in Relation to Human Affairs.; contbr. articles to profl. jours. Grantee NSF, 1966-88; recipient Disting. Alumni award U. Tulsa, 1979. Fellow AAAS, AAUW, Calif. Acad. Scis., Bunting Inst.; mem. Bot. Soc. Am., Ecol. Soc. Am. (pres. 1986-87), Internat. Soc. Chem. Ecology (pres. 1986-87), Assn. for Tropical Biology (pres. 1985-86), Soc. for Econ. Botany (pres. 1993-94). Home: 191 Palo Verde Ter Santa Cruz CA 95060-3214 Office: U Calif Sinsheimer Labs Dept Biol Santa Cruz CA 95064 E-mail: lang@darwin.ucsc.edu

LANGER, JAMES STEPHEN, physicist, educator; b. Pitts., Sept. 21, 1934; s. Bernard F. and Liviette (Roth) L.; m. Elinor Goldmark Aaron, Dec. 21, 1958; children: Ruth, Stephen, David. B.S., Carnegie Inst. Tech., 1955; Ph.D., U. Birmingham, Eng., 1958. Prof. physics Carnegie-Mellon U., Pitts., 1958-82, assoc. dean, 1971-74; prof. physics U. Calif., Santa Barbara, 1982—, dir. Inst. for Theoretical Physics, 1989-95. Contbr. articles to profl. jours. Guggenheim fellow, 1974-75; Marshall scholar, 1955-57 Fellow AAAS, Am. Acad. Arts and Scis., Am. Phys. Soc. (chair divsn. condensed matter physics 1997-98, pres.-elect 1999, pres. 2000, Oliver E. Buckley Condensed-Matter Physics prize 1997); mem. NAS (v.p. 2001—). Democrat. Jewish. Home: 1130 Las Canoas Ln Santa Barbara CA 93105-2331 Office: U Calif Dept Physics Santa Barbara CA 93106 E-mail: langer@physics.ucsb.edu

LANGONI, RICHARD ALLEN, civil engineer; b. Trinidad, Colo., Aug. 7, 1945; s. Domenic and Josephine (Maria) L.; m. Pamela Jill Stansberry, Aug. 19, 1972; children: Kristi, Kerri. A of Applied Sci., Trinidad State Jr. Coll., 1966; BSCE, Colo. State U., 1968; MA, U. No. Colo., 1978. Registered profl. engr., Colo. Civil engr. Dow Chm. Co., Golden, Colo., 1968-71; city engr., dir. pub. works City of Trinidad, 1971-74; civil engr. Clement Bros. Constrn. Co., 1974-75; instr. Trinidad State Jr. Coll., 1975-78; city engr., dir. pub. works City of Durango, Colo., 1978-82; traffic engr. Colo. Dept. Transp., Durango, 1982—. Civil engineer; b. Trinidad, Colo., Aug. 7, 1945; s. Domenic and Josephine (Maria) L.; A of Applied Sci., Trinidad State Jr. Coll., 1966; BSCE Colo. State U., 1968; MA, U. No. Colo., 1978; m. Pamela Jill Stansberry, Aug. 19, 1972; children: Kristi, Kerri. Registered profl. engr. Colo., N.Mex. Civil engr. Dow Chem. Co., Golden, Colo., 1968-71; city engr., dir. public works City of Trinidad, 1971-74; civil engr. Clement Bros. Constrn. Co., 1974-75; instr. Trinidad State Jr. Coll., 1975-78; city engr., dir. public works City of Durango (Colo.), 1978-82; traffic engr. Colo. Dept. Transp., Durango, 1982—. Recipient Meritorious Svc. award City of Durango. Mem. Nat. Soc. Profl. Engrs., ASCE, Am. Public Works Assn., Water Pollution Control Fedn., Profl. Engrs. Colo., Durango C. of C., Nat. Ski Patrol (Purgatory and Wolf Creek), Phi Theta Kappa, Chi Epsilon. Recipient Meritorious Svc. award City of Durango. Mem. ASCE, Nat. Soc. Profl. Engrs., Am. Pub. Works Assn., Water Pollution Control Fedn., Profl. Engrs. Colo., Durange C. of C., Nat. Ski Patrol (Purgatory and Wolf Creek), Phi Theta Kappa, Chi Epsilon. Home: 30 Moenkopi Dr Durango CO 81301-8599 E-mail: Richard.Langoni@dot.state.co.us

LANGWORTHY, WILLIAM CLAYTON, college official; b. Watertown, N.Y., Sept. 3, 1936; s. Harold Greene and Carolyn (Peach) L.; m. Margaret Joan Amos, Sept. 6, 1958; children: Kenneth, Geneva. B.S. magna cum laude, Tufts U., 1958; Ph.D., U. Calif.-Berkeley, 1962. Asst. prof. Alaska Meth. U., Anchorage, 1962-65; asst. prof. chemistry Calif. State U.-Fullerton, 1965-67, assoc. prof., 1967-72, prof., 1972-73, assoc. dean Sch. Letters Arts and Scis., 1970-73; prof. chemistry Calif. Poly. State U., San Luis Obispo, 1973-76, head dept. chemistry, 1973-76; dean Sch. Sci. and Math Calif. Poly State U., San Luis Obispo, 1976-83; v.p. acad. affairs Ft. Lewis Coll., Durango, Colo., 1983-95, prof., 1995-2000. Author: monograph Environmental Education, 1971; contbr. articles to profl. jours. Treas. Coun. Concerned Citizens, Inc., Arroyo Grande, Calif., 1976-83; mem. Clean Air Coalition, San Luis Obispo, 1978-83; active Mozart Festival, 1981-82; bd. dirs. Durango Choral Soc., 1984-93; bd. dirs. San Juan Symphony League, pres., 1997-2000; bd. dirs. Durango Repertory Theatre Co., 1990-96, pres., 1992-94. Mem. AAAS, AAHE, Am. Chem. Soc., Coun. Colls. Arts and Scis. (bd. dirs. 1982), Sierra Club, Phi Beta Kappa, Sigma Xi, Kappa Mu Epsilon, Phi Kappa Phi. E-mail: wclngwor@frontier.net

L'ANNUNZIATA, MICHAEL FRANK, chemist, consultant; b. Springfield, Mass., Oct. 11, 1943; s. Michael Peter and Irene M. L'Annunziata; m. Maria del Carmen Elena Monge, Mar. 3, 1973; children: Michael O., Helen, Frank E. BS, St. Edward's U., Austin, Tex., 1965; MS, U. Ariz., 1967, PhD, 1970. Rsch. chemist Amchem Products, Inc., Ambler, Pa., 1971-72; rsch. assoc. U. Ariz., Tucson, 1972-73; prof., sect. head U. Chapingo, Mexico, Mexico, 1973-75; rsch. scientist Nat. Inst. Nuclear Rsch., Mexico City, 1975-77; assoc. officer IAEA, Vienna, Austria, 1977-80; [illegible] Austria, 1983-86, sr. officer, head fellowships and tng. sect. Austria,

1986-91; mng. dir. LMS Internat. Tech. Svcs., Ltd., Coronado, Calif., 1992-95; dir. WorldTech Internat. Tech. Svcs., Oceanside, 1995-99; pres. The Montague Group, 1999—. Bd. dirs. internat. sci. programs Uppsala (Sweden) U.; internat. IAEA cons.; cons., lectr. Forestry Rsch. Inst., Ibadan, Nigeria, 1994, 95, Ministry Edn., Jakarta, Indonesia, 1995, Internat. Sales, Mktg., and Tng., Packard Instrument Co., Meriden, Conn., 1995-2001, Egypt Atomic Energy Authority, Cairo, 1995, 96, Gezira Rsch. Sta., Wad Medani, Sudan, 1995, Ethopian Sci. and Tech. Commn., Addis Ababa, 1996, Nat. Radiation Commsn., Arusha, Tanzania, 1996; vis. lectr. Advanced Sch. Tropical Agriculture, Cardenas, Mexico, 1973, Atomic Energy Commn. of Ecuador, Quito, 1978, Timiryazev Agrl. Acad., Moscow, 1980, 81, Nuc. Rsch. Inst. in Vet. Medicine, Lalahan, Turkey, 1981, IAEA Seilbersdorf Labs., Seibersdorf, Austria, 1978-82, U. Guanajuato, Mex., 1981, Coll. Montecillo, Chapingo, Mex., 1989, Korea Atomic Energy Rsch. Inst., Seoul, 1991, Nat. Atomic Energy Agy., Jakarta, 1991-94, Zhejiang Agrl. U., Hangzhou, China, 1992, Ctrl. Nuc. "La Reina", Santiago, Chile, 1992, Internat. Atomic Energy Agy., Vienna, 1993, Mt. Makulu Ctrl. Rsch. Sta., Lusaka, Zambia, 1994, Office Atomic Energy Peace, Bangkok, 1995, Swedish Radiation Protection Inst., Stockholm, 1996, CIEMAT, Madrid, 1996, Laguna Verde Nuc. Power Plant, Vera Cruz, Mex., 1996, Oak Ridge (Tenn.) Nat. Labs., 1998, Min. Water and Irrigation, Amman, Jordan, 1998, Wyeth-Ayerst, Pearl River, N.Y., 1998, Chem. Industry Inst. Toxicology, Rsch. Triangle Park, N.C., 1998, Los Alamos Nat. Labs., N.Mex., 2000, U.S. Dept. Energy Idaho Nat. Engring. and Environ. Labs., Idaho Falls, 2000; hon. prof. Zhejiang Agrl. U., 1992. Author: (textbooks) Radiotracers in Agricultural Chemistry, 1979, Radionuclide Tracers, Their Detection and Measurement, 1987; author, editor (with J.O. Legg) Isotopes and Radiation in Agricultural Sciences, Vol. 1, 1984, Vol. 2, 1984, Handbook of Radioactivity Analysis, 1998; contbr. articles to profl. jours. Recipient hon. tchg. diploma, silver plaque Ctrl. U., Ecuador, Quito, 1978. Mem. AAAS, N.Y. Acad. Scis., Am. Nuc. Soc., Sigma Xi, Phi Lambda Upsilon, Gamma Sigma Delta. Roman Catholic. Achievements include discovery of molecular D-chiro-inositol phosphate in soil/plant systems; determination of the biochemical mechanism and pathway involved in the formation of soil chiro-inositol phosphate; discovered microbial epimerization as origin of inosital phosphate isomers in soil; elucidated mechanisms of soil organic phosphorus fixation; separation of the radioactive nuclides Sr-90 from soil surfaces after nuclear fallout; first separation of radioactive nuclides Sr-90 and Y-90 by electrophoresis; execution of over 80 fact-finding, planning, and implementation missions to over 60 countries of Asia, Africa, Europe, Latin America, North America, and the Middle East for United Nations, International Atomic Energy Agy. from 1978 to the present; development of several chemical and instrumental techniques for the analysis of radioactive nuclides. Office: The Montague Group PO Box 1471 Oceanside CA 92051-1471 E-mail: montaguegroup@cs.com

LANSING, SHERRY LEE, motion picture production executive; b. Chgo., July 31, 1944; d. Norton and Margo L.; m. William Friedkin. BS summa cum laude in Theatre, Northwestern U., 1966. Tchr. math. public high schs., Los Angeles, 1966-69; model TV commls. Max Factor Co., 1969-70, Alberto-Culver Co., 1969-70; story editor Wagner Internat. Prodn. Co., 1972-74, dir. west coast devel., 1974-75; story editor MGM. 1975-77, v.p. creative affairs, 1977; v.p. prodn. Columbia Pictures, 1977-80; pres. 20th Century Fox Prodns., 1980-82; founder Jaffee-Lansing Prodns., 1982—; chmn. Paramount Motion Pictures Group, L.A. Chmn. Paramount Pictures' Motion Picture Group, 1992—. Appeared in movies Loving, 1970, Rio Lobo, 1970; exec. story editor movies, Wagner Internat., 1970-73; v.p. prodn., Heyday Prodns., Universal City, Calif., 1973-75; exec. story editor, then v.p. creative affairs, MGM Studios, Culver City, Calif., 1975-77; sr. v.p. prodn., Columbia Pictures, Burbank, Calif., 1977-80, pres., 20th Century-Fox Prodns., Beverly Hills, Calif., 1980-83; ind. producer., Jaffe-Lansing Prodns., Los Angeles, 1983-91; producer Racing With the Moon, 1984,Firstborn, 1984, Fatal Attraction, 1987, The Accused, 1988, Black Rain, 1989, School Ties, 1992, Indecent Proposal, 1993; TV exec. producer When the Time Comes,1987, Mistress, 1992. Office: Paramount Pictures Corp 5555 Melrose Ave Los Angeles CA 90038-3197

LANTER, SEAN KEITH, software engineer; b. Los Alamos, N.Mex., May 8, 1953; s. Robert Jackson and Norma Esther (Jonas) L.; m. Lauri Jane Willand, July 16, 1977; children: Tully Erik, Sarah Elizabeth, Rachel Erin. BA in Physics, U. Utah, 1974, MSME, 1977; MS in Computer Sci., LaSalle U., 1998. Registered profl. engr., Wash. Sr. engr. Boeing Comml. Airplane Co., Seattle, 1977-82; systems analyst Internat. Submarine Tech. Ltd., Redmond, Wash., 1982-83; engr. software Advanced Tech. Labs., Bellevue, 1983-84; engr. contract Rho Co., Redmond, 1984-85; sr. tech. staff Cedar Software Inc., Redmond, 1985-87; pres. Connexions Engring. and Software, Woodinville, Wash., 1987-88; pres., chief engr. Connexions Engring., Inc., Woodinville, 1990-95; sys. engr. Microrim Software, Inc., Bellevue, Wash., 1998-99. Cons., contract programmer, 1990—. Contbr. articles to profl. jours. Mem. Assn. Computing Machinery, NSPE. Lutheran. Avocations: chamber music, reading, history, baseball. Office: Connexions Engring PO Box 3007 Woodinville WA 98072-3007

LANTOS, THOMAS PETER, congressman; b. Budapest, Hungary, Feb. 1, 1928; m. Annette Tillemann; children: Annette, Katrina. BA, U. Washington, 1949, MA, 1950; PhD, U. Calif., Berkeley, 1953. Faculty U. Wash., San Francisco State U., 1950-83; TV news analyst, commentator; sr. econ. and fgn. policy adviser to several U.S. senators; mem. Presdl. Task Force on Def. and Fgn. Policy, U.S. Congresses from 12th Calif dist., 1981—; ranking minority mem., internat. rels. subcomm., mem. govt. reform com. Founder study abroad program Calif. State U. and Coll. System. Mem. Millbrae Bd. Edn., 1950-66. Democrat. Office: US Ho of Reps 2217 Rayburn Ho Office Bldg Washington DC 20515-0001*

LANTZ, KENNETH EUGENE, consulting firm executive; b. Altoona, Pa., Mar. 9, 1934; s. William Martin and Alice Lucretia (Glass) L.; m. D. Arlene Yocum, Nov. 28, 1959; children: Antonia Marie, Theresa Antoinette. BS cum laude, Fordham U., 1956. Cons. Sutherland Co., 1960-62; spl. rep. IBM, L.A., 1962-67; dir. info. svcs. Loyola-Marymount U., L.A., 1967-70; pres. CBIS, L.A., 1970-72; mgr. fin. sys. Occidental Life Ins., L.A., 1973-77; pres. Kenneth Lantz Assocs., L.A., 1977-82; dir. sys. Sayre & Toso, L.A., 1982-83; prin. Atwater, Lantz, Hunter & Co., L.A., 1983—. Lectr. computing topics Technology Transfer Inst., 1987-88. Author: The Prototyping Methodology, 1984; contbr. articles to profl. jours. 1st lt. USAF, 1957-60. Mem. Future of Automation Roundtable (dir. 1983—), Ins. Acctg. and Sys. Assn. (nat. Merit award 1984). Republican. Roman Catholic. Office: Atwater Lantz Hunter & Co PO Box 572366 Tarzana CA 91357-2366 E-mail: kel@manageknowledge.com

LAO, LANG LI, nuclear fusion research physicist; b. Hai Duong, Vietnam, Jan. 28, 1954; came to U.S., 1972; s. Thich Cuong and Boi Phan (Loi) L.; m. Ngan Hua, Dec. 22, 1979; children: Bert J., Brian J. BS, MS, Calif. Inst. Tech., 1976; MS, U. Wis., 1977, PhD, 1979. Staff scientist Oak Ridge (Tenn.) Nat. Lab., 1979-81, TRW, Redondo Beach, Calif., 1981-82; sr. staff scientist Gen. Atomics, San Diego, 1982—. Contbr. articles to sci. jours. Recipient award for Excellence in Plasma Physics Research Am. Physical Society, 1994 Fellow Am. Phys. Soc. (co-recipient excellence in plasma physics rsch. award 1994). Achievements include being world leader in equilibrium analysis of magnetic fusion plasma physics experiments; developed a widely used computer code essential for successful operation and interpretation of tokamak fusion experiments. Office: General Atomics 3550 General Atomics Ct San Diego CA 92121-1194

LAPEYRE, GERALD J. physics educator, researcher; b. Riverton, Wyo., Jan. 3, 1934; BS in Physics, U. Notre Dame, 1956; MS in Physics, U. Mo., 1958, PhD in Physics, 1962. Prof. physics Mont. State U., Bozeman. Dir. Ctr. Rsch. in Surface Sci.; coord. Materials Rsch. Group; interim dir. Ctr. Advanced Materials; R&D engr. Convair Astronautics, San Diego, 1957, RadioCorp. of Am., Camden, N.J., 1959; vis. prof. Stanford U., Calif., 1963, Lawrence Radiation Lab., Livermore, Calif., 1969; vis. rsch. physicist Brookhaven Nat. Lab. NSLS, 1984; mem. program com. Physics of Compound Semiconductor Interfaces, 1984, planning com. 1985—, chmn., 1988-89; local chmn. 41st Annual Conf. on Phys. Electronics, 1981; spkr. in field. Mem. internat. adv. com. Vibrations at Surfaces, 1989—, Atomically Controlled Surfaces & Interfaces, 1991—; contbr. 158 articles to scientific jours. Vis. fellow Sci. and Engring. Rsch. Coun. Cardiff Coll. U. Wales, 1991; recipient Sr. Humboldt Rsch. award Fritz-Haber, Berlin and KFA, 1992. Fellow Am. Phys. Soc. (solid state divsn.); mem. Am. Assn. Physics Tchr., Am Vacuum Soc. (sec., treas. surface sci. divsn. 1989, chmn. 1990, bd. dirs. 1991-93, mem. electronic materials and processing divsn. coun. 1994-96, Langmuir award 1996), Wis. Synchrotron Radiation Ctr. User Adv. Coun. (chmn. 1986, 93—), Materials Rsch. Soc. Achievements include contribution to the development of photoemission spectroscopy with synchrotron radiation. Office: Montana State U Dept Physics Bozeman MT 59717-0001

LAPIROFF, JERRY, secondary school educator; b. Bklyn., Feb. 11, 1947; s. Harry and Betty (Klein) L.; m. Helen Chu, July 24, 1988; children: Harris, Mariah. Tchr. John F. Kennedy High Sch., 1971—. Fulbright exch. tchr., 1992-93; coord. Virtual H.S. Project. Named Spl. Recognition advisor Journalism, 1989, Disting. advisor Dow Jones Newspaper Fund, 1992. Office: 39999 Blacow Rd Fremont CA 94538-1913

LAPONCE, JEAN ANTOINE, political scientist, educator; b. Decize, France, Nov. 1925; s. Fernand and Fernande (Ramond) L.; m. Joyce Price, July, 1950; children: Jean-Antoine, Marc, Patrice; m. Iza Fiszhaut, Apr. 10, 1972; 1 child, Danielle. Diploma, Inst. d'études politiques, Paris, 1947; Ph.D., UCLA, 1955. Instr. U. Santa Clara, 1956; asst. prof. polit. sci. U. B.C., Can., Vancouver, 1956-61, assoc. prof., 1961-66, prof., 1966—; dir. Inst. Interethnic Rels. U. Ottawa, 1993-2001. Mem. grad. faculty Aichi Shukutoku U., 1994-97. Author: The Protection of Minorities, 1961, The government of France under the Fifth Republic, 1962, People vs Politics, 1970, Left and Right, 1981, Langue et territoire, 1984, Languages and Their Territories, 1987. Fellow Royal Soc. Can. (pres. Acad. Humanities and Social Scis. 1988-91); mem. Can. Polit. Sci. Assn. (pres. 1972-73), Am. Polit. Sci. Assn., French Polit. Sci. Assn., Internat. Polit. Sci. Assn. (pres. 1973-76) Office: U BC Dept Polit Sci Vancouver BC Canada V6T 1Z1

LAPORTA, SCOTT A. recreation facility executive; V.p. corp. fin. Host Marriott Corp., treas., 1995. Office: Park Place Entertainment Corp 4th Fl 3930 Howard Huges Hwy Las Vegas NV 89109

LAPPEN, CHESTER I. lawyer; b. Des Moines, May 4, 1919; s. Robert C. and Anna (Sideman) L.; m. Jon Tyroler Irmas, June 29, 1941; children—Jonathan Bailey, Timothy, Andrea L., Sally Morris. A.B. with highest honors in Econs, U. Calif., 1940; LL.B. magna cum laude (Faye diploma), Harvard, 1943. Bar: Calif. bar 1943. Practice in, Los Angeles, 1946—; sr. partner firm Mitchell, Silberberg & Knupp, 1949—; advisory bd. Bank Am., 1962-65; chmn. bd., dir. Zenith Nat. Ins. Corp., 1975-77. Bd. dirs. Arden Group, Inc. (chmn. exec. com. 1978), 1963-91, Data Products Corp. (chmn. fin. com.), 1965-93, City Nat. Bank Corp., 1967-92; trustee, pres. Citinat, Devel. Trust; bd. dirs., chmn. bd. Pacific Rim Holding Corp., 1987-94. Editor-in-chief: Harvard Law Rev, 1942-43. Chmn. bd. trustees Immaculate Heart Coll., 1981-88; trustee UCLA Found.; v.p., dir. Ctr. for Childhood. Served as spl. agt. CIA AUS, 1943-46. Mem. ABA, Los Angeles Bar Assn. (dir. 1953), Los Angeles Jr. Bar Assn. (pres. 1953), Beverly Hills (Calif.) Bar Assn., Harvard Law Sch. Alumni Assn. So. Calif. (pres. 1973-82). Republican. Office: Mitchell Silberberg & Knupp 11377 W Olympic Blvd Los Angeles CA 90064-1625

LARA, ADAIR, columnist, writer; b. San Francisco, Jan. 3, 1952; d. Eugene Thomas and Lee Louise (Hanley) Daly; m. James Lee Heig, June 18, 1976 (div. 1989); children: Morgan, Patrick; m. William Murdock LeBlond, Nov. 2, 1991. BA in English, San Francisco State U., 1976. Reader Coll. of Marin, Kentfield, Calif., 1976-83; freelance editor, 1983-86; mng. editor San Francisco Focus mag., 1986-89; exec. editor San Francisco mag., 1988-89; columnist San Francisco Chronicle, 1989—. Author: History of Petaluma: A California River Town, 1982, Welcome to Earth, Mom, 1992, Slowing Down in a Speeded-up World, 1994, At Adair's House, More Columns by America's Funniest Formerly Single Man, 1995; contbr. articles to profl. publs. Recipient Best Calif. Columnist award AP, 1990. Democrat. Avocations: reading, photography, travel, softball, biking. Office: San Francisco Chronicle 901 Mission St San Francisco CA 94103-2905

LARKIN, THOMAS ERNEST, JR. investment management company executive; b. Wilkes-Barre, Pa., Sept. 29, 1939; s. Thomas Ernest and Margaret (Gorman) L.; m. Margaret Giban, Nov. 2, 1979; 1 child, Thomas Ernest III. BA in Econs., U. Notre Dame, 1961; postgrad., Grad. Sch. Bus., NYU, 1962-66. New bus. rep. Mfrs. Hanover Trust Co., 1963-66; mgr. pension dept. Eastman Dillon, Union Securities, 1966-69; v.p. Shearson Hayden Stone, Inc., N.Y.C., 1969-75; sr. v.p. Bernstein Macaulay Inc., N.Y.C., 1969-75, Crocker Investment Mgmt. Corp., San Francisco, 1975-77, Trust Co. of the West, L.A., 1977, mng. dir., 1982—, pres., COO, 1989-2000; vice chmn. The TCW Group, Inc., 2000—. Trustee U. Notre Dame, Loyola Marymount U., Mt. St. Mary's Coll., Harvard Westlake Sch., Childrens Hosp. L.A., Performing Arts Ctr. of Los Angeles County, L.A. Orthopaedic Hosp. Found. Served with U.S. Army, 1961-63. Mem. Assn. Investment Mgmt. Sales Execs., Internat. Fedn. Employee Benefit Plans, Investment Counsel Assn. Am., Calif. Club, Jonathan Club, Wilshire Country Club, Bel Air Bay Club, Regency Club, L.A., Tennis Club, Olympic Club, N.Y. Athletic Club, Westchester Country Club, L.A. Country Club. Republican. Roman Catholic. Office: TCW Group 865 S Figueroa St Ste 1800 Los Angeles CA 90017-2593

LAROCK, BRUCE EDWARD, civil engineering educator; b. Berkeley, Calif., Dec. 24, 1940; s. Ralph W. and Hazel M. L.; m. Susan E. Gardner, June 17, 1968; children: Lynne M., Jean E. BS in Civil Engring., Stanford U., 1962, MS in Civil Engring., 1963, PhD, 1966. Registered profl. engr., Calif. Asst. prof. U. Calif., Davis, 1966-72, assoc. prof., 1972-79, prof., 1979—. Sr. vis. fellow U. Wales, Swansea, 1972-73; U.S. sr. scientist Tech. U., Aachen, Germany, 1986-87. Author: (with D. Newnan) Engineer-in-Training Examination Review, 3d edit., 1991, (with R. Jeppson and G. Watters) Hydraulics of Pipeline Systems, 1999; contbr. over 80 tech. articles to profl. jours. Mem. ASCE, Sigma Xi, Tau Beta Pi. Lutheran. Avocation: duplicate bridge. E-mail: ucdavis.edu. Office: Dept Civil Environ Engring U Calif Davis CA 95616-5294

LARPENTEUR, JAMES ALBERT, JR. lawyer; b. Seattle, Aug. 6, 1935; s. James Albert and Mary Louise (Coffey) L.; m. Hazel Marie Arntson, Apr. 23, 1965 (div. 1983); children: Eric James, Jason Clifford; 1 adopted child, Brenda Mon Fong; m. Katherine Annette Bingham, Nov. 8, 1986. BS in Bus., U. Oreg., 1957, LLB, 1961. Bar: Oreg. 1961, U.S. Dist. Ct. Oreg. 1961, U.S. Tax Ct. 1962, U.S. Ct. Appeals (9th cir.) 1962, U.S. Supreme Ct. 1965. Assoc. Schwabe Williamson & Wyatt, Portland, Oreg., 1961-69, ptnr., 1969-82, sr. ptnr., 1982—, mem. exec. com., 1989-92. Dir. exec. com. Portland Rose Festival Assn., 1975—, pres., 1987; ex-officio dir. Portland Visitors Assn., 1981—; bd. dirs., mem. exec. com. Providence Child Ctr. Found., 1983-94, chmn. exec. com., 1986-87; bd. dirs. Willamette Light Brigade, 1987—, Cath. Charities Portland, 1989-92; bd. dirs. Albertina Kerr Ctrs., 1996—, Japanese Garden Soc., 2000—. Mem. Oreg. Bar Assn. (editor, writer, speaker numerous continuing legal edn. programs, chmn. bus. law sect. 1986-87, real estate, estate planning, securities regulation sects.), Multnomah Athletic Club (pres. 1984), Univ. Club of Portland, Waverley Country Club, Astoria Golf and Country Club, City Club of Portland, Thunderbird Country Club of Rancho Mirage. Avocation: golf. Office: Schwabe Williamson & Wyatt 1211 SW 5th Ave Ste 1800 Portland OR 97204-3713 E-mail: jlarpenteur@schwabe.com

LARRABEE, WAYNE FOX, JR. plastic surgeon; b. Ft. Benning, Ga., May 10, 1945; s. Wayne Fox and Ruth (Truex) L.; children: Shane, Sascha, Kai, Gregory. BS in Math., Midland Coll., 1967; postgrad., U. Edinburgh, 1965-66; MD, MPH in Epidemiology, Tulan U., 1971. Diplomate Am. Bd. Otolaryngology; lic. MD, Wash. Intern Letterman Gen. Hosp., San Francisco, 1971-72; resident in surgery Tulane U. Svc. Charity Hosp., New Orleans, 1975-76, resident in otolaryngology and maxillofacial surgery, 1976-79; head sect. reconstructive and aesthetic plastic surgery Va. Mason Med. Ctr., Seattle, 1986-88, head sect. otolaryngology, 1985-88. Instr. dept. surgery Tulane Med. Sch., 1975-79, instr. dept. otolaryngology, 1976-79; clin. prof. U. Wash., 1979-88; clin. prof., U. Wash., 1988-2001; pres. med. bd. Va. Mason Hosp., 1984-85, Va. Mason Rsch. Ctr., 1985-88; observations fellowship Moorfields Eye Hosp., London, 1988; presenter in field; pres. Am. Bd. Facial Plastic Surgery, 2000-01). Books: Surgical Anatomy of the Face, 1993, Principles of Facial Reconstruction, 1995; editl. bd., Jour. AMA, 1999—; editor, Archives of Facial Plastic Surgery, 1999—. Maj. U.S. Army Med. Corps, 1972-75, Panama Canal Zone. Fellow Am. Coll. Surgeons, Am. Acad. Facial Plastic and Reconstructive Surgery (pres. 1996), Am. Soc. Head and Neck Surgery, Triological Soc., Am. Bd. Otolaryngology (bd. dirs.); mem. King County Med. Soc., Am. Acad. Otolaryngology-Head and Neck Surgery, Northwest Acad. Otolaryngology-Head and Neck Surgery (program chmn. 1984-86, sec./treas. 1984-86, pres. 1988—). Avocations: photography, poetry. Office: Ctr for Facial Plastic Surgery 600 Broadway # 280 Seattle WA 98122 E-mail: larrabee@u.washington.edu

LARRICK, JAMES WILLIAM, science administrator; b. Englewood, Colo., Jan. 4, 1950; s. William Franklin and Louise (Scatman) L. BA in Chemistry magna cum laude, Colo. Coll., 1972; MD, PhD, Duke U., 1980. Research fellow Marie Stauffer Sigall Found., Stanford U., Palo Alto, Calif., 1981-82; staff physician Kaiser Permanente Hosp., Santa Clara, 1982-88; sci. project leader Human Monoclonal Antibodies Cetus Immune Research Labs, Palo Alto, 1982-87; research scientist Cetus Immune Research Labs., Palo Alto, Calif., 1982-85, sr. research scientist, 1985, dir. research, 1985-87; dir. exploratory research Genelabs, Inc., Redwood City, 1988-91; founder, sci. dir. Palo Alto Inst. for Molecular Medicine, Mountain View, Calif., 1991—. Contbr. numerous articles to profl. jours.; chpts. to books. Staff Young Lords Free Health Clinic, Chgo., 1972-73; staff Edgemont Health Clinic, Durham, N.C., 1975-76, mem. curriculum com. Duke U. Sch. Medicine, 1974-75; active Bay Area Physicians for Social Responsibility, 1982-88; vol. physician Haight-Ashbury Free Health Clinic, San Francisco, 1983-88; bd. dirs. Emergency Relief Fund Internat., San Francisco, 1985-88. Mem. AAAS, Am. Fedn. Clin. Research, Am. Assn. Immunologists, Am. Assn. Phys. Anthropology, Calif. Acad. Scis., N.Y. Acad. Scis., Phi Beta Kappa. Avocations: cross country skiing, bicycling, scuba diving, mountaineering, sailing. Home: Star Rte Box 48 Woodside CA 94062 Office: Palo Alto Inst Medicine 2462 Wyandotte St Mountain View CA 94043-2313 E-mail: jwlarrick@aol.com

LARSEN, DAVID COBURN, lawyer, educator; b. Honolulu, Mar. 20, 1944; s. Harold Samuel and Eugenia Bowen (Coburn) L.; m. Pamela Ann Magee, Aug. 1, 1970; 1 child, Jennifer M. BA with honors, U. Va., 1965, MA, 1966; JD, UCLA, 1974. Bar: Calif. 1974, Hawaii 1975. Assoc. Cades Schutte, Honolulu, 1974-80, ptnr., 1980—. Tchr. U. Hawaii Law Sch., Honolulu, 1975-79, U. Hawaii Cont. Edn., 1980—. Author: Who Gets It When You Go, 1982, 2d edit. 1987, You Can't Take It With You, 1986. Lt. USN, 1967-70. Ford Found. fellow 1966. Office: Cades Schutte PO Box 939 1000 Bishop St Honolulu HI 96808

LARSEN, GARY LOY, physician, researcher; b. Wahoo, Nebr., Jan. 10, 1945; s. Allan Edward and Dorothy Mae (Hengen) L.; m. Letitia Leah Hoyt, Dec. 22, 1967; children: Kari Lyn, Amy Marie. BS, U. Nebr., 1967; MD, Columbia U., 1971. Diplomate Am. Bd. Pediatrics, Am. Bd. Pediatric Pulmonology (chmn. 1990-92)/. Pediatric pulmonologist Nat. Jewish Med. and Rsch. Ctr., Denver, 1978—; mem. faculty U. Colo. Sch. Medicine, Denver, 1978—, dir. sect. of pediatric pulmonary medicine, 1987—, prof. pediatrics, 1990—. Contbr. articles to prof. jours. Mem. sci. adv. panel Nat. Urban Air Toxics Rsch. Ctr., 1998—. Maj. M.C., U.S. Army, 1974-76. NIH med. rsch. grantee NIH, 1981—. Mem. AM. Thoracic Soc. (chmn. pediatric assembly 1987-88), Soc. Pediatric Rsch., Phi Beta Kappa, Alpha Omega Alpha, N.Y. Acad. Scis., Chilean Respiratory Soc. (hon.). Lutheran. Office: Nat Jewish Med & Rsch Ctr 1400 Jackson St Denver CO 80206-2761 E-mail: larseng@njc.org

LARSEN, RICHARD LEE, former mayor and city manager, business, municipal and labor relations consultant, arbitrator; b. Jackson, Miss., Apr. 16, 1934; s. Homer Thorsten and Mae Cordelia (Amidon) L.; m. Virginia Fay Alley, June 25, 1955; children: Karla, Daniel, Thomas (dec.), Krista, Lisa. BS in Econs. and Bus. Adminstrn, Westminster Coll., Fulton, Mo., 1959; postgrad., U. Kans., 1959-61. Fin. dir. Village of Northbrook, Ill., 1961-63; city mgr. Munising, Mich., 1963-66, Sault Ste. Marie, 1966-72, Ogden, Utah, 1972-77, Billings, Mont., 1977-79; mcpl. cons., 1979—; pub./pvt. sector labor rels. cons., arbitrator, 1979—. Mayor City of Billings, Mont., 1990-95; dep. gen. chmn. Greater Mich. Found., 1968. Bd. dirs. Ctrl. Weber Sewer Dist., 1972-77; chmn. labor com. Utah League Cities and Towns, 1973-77, Mont. League Cities and Towns, 1977-79; bd. dirs., coach Ogden Hockey Assn., 1972-77, Weber Sheltered Workshop, 1974-77, Billings YMCA, 1980-86, Rimrock Found., 1980-86; chmn. cmty. rels. coun. Weber Basin Job Corps Ctr., 1973-77; bishop LDS Ch. With USCG, 1953-57. Recipient Cmty. Devel. Disting. Achievement awards Munising, 1964, Cmty. Devel. Disting. Achievement awards Sault Ste. Marie, 1966-70, Citizen award Dept. of Interior, 1977, Alumni Achievement award Westminster Coll., 1990, Dist. award of merit Boy Scouts Am., 1993, Silver Beaver award Boy Scouts Am., 1994; named Utah Adminstr. of Yr., 1976. Mem. Internat. City Mgmt. Assn. (L.P. Cookingham career devel. award 1974, Clarence Ridley in-service tng. award 1979), Utah City Mgrs. Assn. (pres. 1972-74), Greater Ogden C. of C. (dir.), Rotary (pres. Billings 1997-98), Phi Gamma Delta. Home and Office: 1733 Parkhill Dr Billings MT 59102-2358 E-mail: rlarsen@wtp.net

LARSEN, WELDON, company executive; Exec. v.p., COO devel. and ops. Trizec Hahn Devel. Corp., San Diego, 1997—.

LARSON, BRENT T. broadcasting executive; b. Ogden, Utah, Sept. 23, 1942; s. George Theodore and Doris (Peterson) L.; m. Tracy Ann Taylor; children: Michelle, Brent Todd, Lindsey. Student, pub. schs., Los Angeles; diploma in radio operational engring., Burbank, Calif., 1962. Owner, mgr. Sta. KAIN, Boise, Idaho, 1969-77; owner, operator Sta. KXA Radio, Seattle, 1975-83, Sta. KYYX Radio, Seattle, 1980-83, Sta. KGA Radio, Spokane, Wash., 1978-84, Sta. KUUZ Radio, Boise, 1976-82, Sta. KOOS Radio, North Bend, Oreg., 1980-81, Sta. KODL Radio, The Dalles, 1974-80, Sta. KKWZ Radio, Richfield, Utah, 1980-94, Sta. KSVC Radio, Richfield, 1980-94; v.p. Casey Larson Fast Food Co., Oreg. and Idaho, 1976-94, Imperial Broadcasting Corp., Idaho, 1970—, KSOS Am & KLZX

FM, 1983—; pres. First Nat. Broadcasting Corp., 1970—; v.p. Larson-Wynn Corp., 1974—, Brentwood Properties, Ogden, 1977—; pres. Sta. KSIT Broadcasting, Rock Springs, Wyo., 1980-90, Gold Coast Communications Corp., Oreg., 1980-81, Sevier Valley Broadcasting Co., Inc., Utah, 1980-94, Brent Larson Group Stas., Western U.S., 1969—; v.p. mktg. Internat. Foods Corp., Boise, 1969-81; ptnr. Larson Tours and Travel, Burley, Idaho, 1977-87; v.p. Harrison Square Inc., 1995—. Bd. dirs. Casey-Larson Foods Co., La Grande, Oreg., Studio City Entertainment (Nev. L.C.), 1996—. Bd. dirs. Met. Sch., 1981-93, Children's Aid Soc., 1991-94; chmn. bd. ZLX Limited Libility Co., 1995—. Mem. Am. Advt. Fedn., Nat. Assn. Broadcasters, Nat. Radio Broadcasters Assn., Wash. Broadcasters Assn., Oreg. Broadcasters Assn., Idaho Broadcasters Assn., Utah Broadcasters Assn., Citizens for Responsible Broadcasting (bd. dirs.) Republican. Mem. LDS Ch. Home: 5777 S 3550 W Roy UT 84067-8131 Office: First Nat Broadcasting Corp 4455 S 5500 W Ogden UT 84315-9650

LARSON, GRANT C. state legislator; b. Provo, Utah, June 2, 1933; married. BS, U. Utah. Mem. Wyo. Senate, Dist. 17, Cheyenne, 1994—; chair appropriations com., v.p. Wyo. Senate, Cheyenne. Bd. dirs., past pres. Jackson State Bank. Chair Teton County Rep. Party; mem. Wyo. Hwy. Commn., bd. dirs. Jackson Hole Airport. Mem. Am. Legion, Jackson C. of C., U.S. Ski Assn. (past dir.), Rotary (past pres.). Republican. Office: PO Box 3490 Jackson WY 83001-3490 also: Wyo Senate State Capitol Cheyenne WY 82002-0001 Fax: 307-733-0149

LARSON, HARRY THOMAS, electronics engineer, executive, consultant; b. Berkeley, Calif., Oct. 16, 1921; s. Harry Homer and Edna Clara (Petersen) L.; m. Merry Evelyn Otteson, Dec. 26, 1956 (div. Dec. 1975); children: Kristin Eve Beltz, Margit Merry Mills, Megan Marie Hoyt. BSEE summa cum laude, U. Calif., Berkeley, 1947; MSEE, UCLA, 1954. Computer engr. Inst. for Numerical Analysis Nat. Bur. Standards, L.A., 1949-51; mem. tech. staff Advanced Electronics Lab. Hughes Aircraft Co., Culver City, Calif., 1951-54; dept. mgr. bus. applications of computers Ramo-Wooldridge Co., Inglewood, 1954-56; asst. divsn. dir. command and control systems Aero. divsn. Philco-Ford Co., Newport Beach, 1956-68; asst. div. dir. software and computing ctr. TRW Systems, Redondo Beach, 1968-69; dir. planning Calif. Computer Products, Anaheim, 1969-74; sr. scientist Hughes Aircraft, Fullerton, Calif., 1978-87; pres. Larbridge Enterprises Cons., Laguna Hills, 1970—. Mem. Army Sci. Bd., Washington, 1988-92; contbd. to NASA's Mission Control Ctr. in Houston for Gemini, Apollo, Skylab and shuttle missions, Field Army tactical command and control system, first random access computer memory, early airborne digital computer, first keyboard and cathode ray tube data entry device (terminal), first-of-a-kind applications of computers in banks, factories, pension trust funds, payroll, acctg., truck scheduling, R.R. car routing, car body design and manufacture, automobile assembly plant inventory control, electrical power distbn. network, steel hot roll mill, computer programming methodologies (modularization, report generator, table-driven software), founds. for display tech. and large screen displays; lectr., organizer, chair confs., workshops, conf. sessions, 1954-74. Editor Proc. Inst. Radio Engrs., 1961; editor, pub. The Labridge Letter, 1973-76; co-editor Handbook of Automation, Computation and Control, 1959; contbr. articles to profl. jours., computer publs.; patentee in field. 1st lt. USAF, 1942-45. Fellow IEEE (life; Centennial medal); mem. IEEE Computer Soc. (co-fouder, nat. chmn. 1954-55, chmn. Social Implications of Computers, 1956-70), Soc. for Info. Display, Am. Fedn. Info. Processing Soc. (bd. govs. 1956-60), Sigma Xi, Tau Beta Pi, Eta Kappa Nu. Avocations: writing, photography. Home and Office: Larbridge Enterprises 236 Calle Aragon Unit A Laguna Woods CA 92653-3492

LARSON, JOHN WILLIAM, lawyer; b. Detroit, June 24, 1935; s. William and Sara Eleanor (Yeatman) L.; m. Pamela Jane Wren, Sept. 16, 1959; 1 dau., Jennifer Wren. BA with distinction, honors in Economics, Stanford, 1957; LLB, Stanford U., 1962. Bar: Calif. 1962. Assoc. Brobeck, Phleger & Harrison, San Francisco, 1962-68, ptnr., 1968-71, 73—, CEO, mng. ptnr., 1988-92, chmn. of firm, CEO, 1993-96; asst. sec. Dept. Interior, Washington, 1971-73; exec. dir. Natural Resources Com., Washington, 1973; counsellor to chmn. Cost of Living Coun., Washington, 1973. Faculty Practising Law Inst.; bd. dirs. Sangamo Bio Scis., Inc. Mem. 1st U.S.-USSR Joint Com. on Environment; mem. bd. visitors Stanford U. Law Sch., 1974-77, 85-87, 95-96; pres. bd. trustees The Katherine Branson Sch., 1980-83. With AUS, 1957-59. Mem. ABA, Calif. Bar Assn., San Francisco C. of C. (bd. dirs., chmn. 1996), Bay Area Coun., Calif. Acad. Sci., San Francisco Partnership, Bay Area Life Scis. Alliance, Order of Coif, Pacific Union Club, Burlingame Country Club, Bohemian Club. Home: PO Box 349 Ross CA 94957-0349 Office: Brobeck Phleger & Harrison Spear St Tower 1 Market Plz San Francisco CA 94105-1420

LARSON, MARK ALLAN, financial executive; b. Milw., June 24, 1948; s. Owen Earl and Alice May (Ulmen) L.; m. Linda Rosalie Wohlschlaeger, Jan. 3, 1970; children: Craig Allan, Emily Lin. BA, Ripon Coll., 1970; postgrad., Washington U., St. Louis, 1971-74; postgrad. in bus., St. Louis U., 1974-76. Personnel supr. Barnes Hosp., St. Louis, 1970-71; various fin. and mgmt. positions Bank Bldg. Corp., St. Louis, 1971-76, G.D. Searle & Co., Skokie, Ill., Geneva, Switzerland, 1976-85; sr. v.p., chief fin. and admistrv. officer Leaf Inc., Bannockburn, Ill., 1985-89; v.p. internat. devel. and adminstrn. Carlson Cos., Inc., Mpls., 1990-91; exec. v.p. fin. and adminstrn., travel and mktg. groups, 1992-93; exec. v.p. ops. and internat., mktg. groups, 1993-95; sr. v.p. fin. Internat. Distillers & Vintners N.Am., Hartford, Conn., 1995-96; pres. IDV Wines, San Mateo, Calif., 1997-98, United Distillers & Vintners, West, San Francisco, 1998-99; pres., COO, Golden State Vinters, Napa, Calif., 2000—. E-mail: mlarson@gsvinc.com

LARSON, MAUREEN INEZ, rehabilitation consultant; b. Madison, Minn., Mar. 10, 1955; d. Alvin John and Leona B. (Bornhorst) Larson; m. Michael Earl Klemetsrud, July 07, 1979 (div. Sept. 1988). BA in Psychology cum laude, U. Minn., 1977; MA in Counseling, U. N.D., 1978. Cert. rehab. counselor, ins. specialist; disability analyst. Employment counselor II, coordinator spl. programs Employment Security div. State of Wyo., Rawlins, 1978-80; employment interviewer Employment Security divsn. State of Wash., Tacoma, 1980; lead counselor Comprehensive Rehab. Counseling, Tacoma, 1980-81; dir. counseling Cascade Rehab. Counseling, Tacoma, 1981-87, dist. mgr., 1987-90; regional mgr. Rainier Case Mgmt., Tacoma, 1991-92; owner Maureen Larson and Assocs., Gig Harbor, Wash., 1992—. State capt. legis. div. Provisions Project Am. Personnel and Guidance Assn., 1980. Advocate Grand Forks (N.D.) Rape Crisis Ctr., 1977-78; mem. Pierce County YMCA; bd. dirs. Boys and Girls Clubs of Tacoma, 1991-98, chairperson sustaining drive, 1991-98, sec.-treas., 1992-93, pres., 1994, auction com. and spl. events com.; founding bd. dirs., bd. devel. chair, ballroom dance chair, vice chair Literacy Plus!, 1999—. State of Minn. scholar, 1973-77; recipient Alice Tweed Tuohy award U. Minn., 1977, Nat. Disting. Svcs. Registry award Libr. of Congress, 1987; named bd. mem. vol. of Yr. Boys and Girls Clubs of Tacoma, 1992. Mem. Nat. Fedn. Bus. and Profl. Women (rec. sec. 1978-80, runner-up Young Careerists' Program 1980), Nat. Rehab. Assn. (bd. dirs. Olympic chpt. 1988-97, pres. 1990-91, chairperson state conf. planning com. 1990, 93, 96), Nat. Rehab. Counseling Assn. (bd. dirs. 1993, State of Wash. Counselor of Yr. 1991, Pacific Region Counselor of Yr. 1992), Nat. Rehab. Adminstrs. Assn. (bd. dirs. 1993), Women in Workers Compensation Orgn., Washington Self-Insured Assn., Gig Harbor Yacht Club, Pi Gamma Mu. Avocations: sailing, aerobics, ballet, arts. Office: M Larson & Assocs 13504 82nd Ave NW Gig Harbor WA 98329-8642 E-mail: [illegible]

LARSON, PAUL MARTIN, lawyer; b. Tacoma, June 8, 1949; s. Charles Philip and Margeret (Kobervig) L.; m. Kristina Simonson, June 19, 1971; children: Kristin Ilene, Paul Philip, Erika Louise. AB, Stanford U., 1971; JD, Gonzaga U., 1974. Bar: Wash. 1975, U.S. Dist. Ct. (we. dist.) Wash. 1975, U.S. Dist. Ct. (ea. dist.) Wash. 1978, U.S. Ct. Appeals (9th cir.) 1981. Assoc. Hoff & Cross, Tacoma, 1975-76; ptnr., prin. Brooks & Larson, P.S., Yakima, Wash., 1976-87; ptnr. Bogle & Gates, Yakima, 1987-93, Larson & Perkins, 1994—. Author: (with others) Commercial Law Deskbook, 1981. Pres. Cardio & Pulmonary Inst., Yakima, 1981; bd. dirs. Yakima YMCA, 1981-98, pres.-elect bd. dirs. 2000, pres., 2001—; bd. dirs. Yakima Youth Commn., 1989-93, Yakima Valley chpt. ARC, 1990-93; bd. dirs. Sisters of Providence Med. Ctr.-Yakima Found., 1986-96, pres., 1992-93, Area Svc. bd. mem., 2000—; bd. dirs. Yakima Schs. Found., 1993-2000, pres., 2000. Fellow ABA (standing com. lawyer's responsibility for client protection 1984-89); mem. Wash. State Bar Assn. (spl. dist. counsel, 1985-96, pres. corp. bus. and banking sect. 1987-88, chmn. unauthorized practice of law task force 1995-96), Yakima Estate Planning Coun. (pres. 1981), Rotary. Avocations: tennis, fishing. Office: Larson & Perkins PO Box 550 Yakima WA 98907-0550 E-mail: paul@lplaw.com

LARSON, WILLIAM, electrical company executive; Pres., chmn. Network Assocs., Santa Clara, Calif. Office: Network Assocs 3965 Freedom Cir Santa Clara CA 95054-1203

LARWOOD, LAURIE, psychologist; b. N.Y., 1941; PhD, Tulane U., 1974. Pres. Davis Instruments Corp., San Leandro, Calif., 1966-71; cons., 1969—; asst. prof. orgnl. behavior SUNY, Binghamton, 1974-76; assoc. prof. psychology, chairperson dept. Claremont (Calif.) McKenna Coll., 1976-83, assoc. prof. bus. adminstrn., 1976-83, Claremont Grad. Sch., 1976-85; prof., head dept. mgmt. U. Ill., Chgo., 1983-87; dean sch. bus. SUNY, Albany, 1987-90; dean Coll. Bus. Adminstrn. U. Nev., Reno, 1990-92; dir. Inst. Strategic Bus. Issues, 1992—. Mem. western regional advisory coun. SBA, 1976-81; dir. The Mgmt. Team; pres. Mystic Games, Inc. Author: (with M.M. Wood) Women in Management, 1977, Organizational Behavior and Management, 1984, Women's Career Development, 1987, Strategies-Successes-Senior Executives Speak Out, 1988, Women's Careers, 1988, Managing Technological Development, 1988, Impact Analysis, 1999; mem. editl. bd. Sex Roles, 1979—, Consultation, 1986-91, Jour. Orgnl. Behavior, 1987—, Jour. Vocational Behavior, 1999—, Group and Orgn. Mgmt., 1982-84, editor, 1986—; founding editor Women and Work, 1983, Jour. Mgmt. Case Studies, 1983-87; contbr. numerous articles, papers to profl. jours. Mem. acad. Mgmt. (editl. rev. bd. Rev. 1977-82, past chmn. women in mgmt. div., managerial consultation divsn., tech. and innovation mgmt. divsn.), Am. Psychol. Assn., Assn. Women in Psychology. Home: 2855 Sagittarius Dr Reno NV 89509-3885 Office: U Nev Coll Bus Adminstrn Reno NV 89557-0001

LASAROW, WILLIAM JULIUS, retired federal judge; b. Jacksonville, Fla., June 30, 1922; s. David Herman and Mary (Hollins) L.; m. Marilyn Doris Powell, Feb. 4, 1951; children: Richard M., Elisabeth H. BA, U. Fla., 1943; JD, Stanford U., 1950. Bar: Calif. 1951. Counsel judiciary com. Calif. Assembly, Sacramento, 1951-52; dep. dist. atty. Stanislaus County, Modesto, Calif., 1952-53; pvt. practice law L.A., 1953-73; bankruptcy judge U.S. Cts., L.A., 1973-94; chief judge U.S. Bankruptcy Ct., Central dist., Calif., 1978-90; judge Bankruptcy Appellate Panel 9th Fed. Cir., 1980-82; fed. judge U.S. Bankruptcy Ct., L.A., 1973. Faculty Fed. Jud. Ctr. Bankruptcy Seminars, Washington, 1977-82 Contbg. author, editor legal publs.; staff: Stanford U. Law Review, 1949. Mem. ABA, Am. Coll. Bankruptcy, Am. Bankruptcy Inst., Nat. Conf. Bankruptcy Judges, Los Angeles County Bar Assn., Wilshire Bar Assn., Blue Key, Phi Beta Kappa, Phi Kappa Phi. Home: 11623 Canton Pl Studio City CA 91604-4164

LASHOF, JOYCE COHEN, public health educator; b. Phila. d. Harry and Rose (Brodsky) Cohen; m. Richard K. Lashof, June 11, 1950; children: Judith, Carol, Dan. AB, Duke U., 1946; MD, Women's Med. Coll., 1950; DSc (hon.), Med. Coll. Pa., 1983. Dir. Ill. State Dept. Pub. Health, 1973-77; dep. asst. sec. for health programs and population affairs Dept. Health, Edn., and Welfare, Washington, 1977-78; sr. scholar in residence IOM, Washington, 1978; asst. dir. office of tech. assessment U.S. Congress, Washington, 1978-81; dean sch. pub. health U. Calif., Berkeley, 1981-91, prof. pub. health Sch. Pub. Health, 1981-94, prof. emerita, 1994—. Co-chair Commn. on Am. after Roe vs. Wade, 1991-92; mem. Sec.'s Coun. Health Promotion and Disease Prevention, 1988-91; pres. APHA, 1992; chair Pres.'s Adv. Com. on Gulf War Vets. Illnesses, 1995-97. Vice chairperson editl. bd. Wellness Letter, 1983—; mem. editl. com. Ann. Rev. of Pub. Health, 1987-90. Recipient Alumni Achievement award Med. Coll. Pa., 1975, Sedgewick Meml. medal APHA, 1995. Avocation: hiking. Home: 601 Euclid Ave Berkeley CA 94708-1331 Office: U Calif Sch Pub Health 140 Earl Warren Hl Berkeley CA 94720-0001

LASKY, MOSES, lawyer; b. Denver, Nov. 2, 1907; s. Juda Eisen and Ida (Grossman) L.; m. Ruth Helen Abraham, July 6, 1933; children: Morelle, Marshall. A.B. magna cum laude, U. Colo., 1926, J.D., 1928; LHD (hon.), 1996; LL.M., Harvard U., 1929. Bar: Calif. 1930, U.S. Supreme Ct 1947. Asst. dept. econs. U. Colo., 1925-26; salesman, local sales mgr. R.C. Barnum Co., Cleve., 1927-28; assoc. Brobeck, Phleger & Harrison, San Francisco, 1929-41, partner, 1941-79, Lasky, Haas, Cohler & Munter, San Francisco, 1979-94; Lasky, Haas & Cohler, San Francisco, 1994—. Instr. Golden Gate Law Sch., 1934-35; sr. adv. bd. U.S. Ct. Appeals (9th cir.), 1984-90, chmn., 1989-90; vis. prof. law as disting. practitioner in residence Sch. Law, U. Colo., 1995. Contbr. articles in legal field and on Jewish life to jours. and mags. Pres. bd. dirs. San Francisco Mus. Modern Art, 1963, 64, now life trustee; pres. Regional Arts Coun. San Francisco, 1963-64; v.p. bd. dirs. San Francisco Art Inst., 1964; trustee War Meml. San Francisco, 1969-75; co-chmn. San Francisco Crime Com., 1968-71; bd. dirs. The Exploratorium, San Francisco, 1979-96, dir. emeritus, 1996—; bd. overseers L.A. br. Hebrew Union Coll.; nat. exec. com. Am. Jewish Com., 1947-55. Recipient Disting. Alumnus award U. Colo. Law Sch., 1977, U. Colo. medal, 1983, 50 Yr. award Am. Bar Found., 1989. Fellow Am. Coll. Trial Lawyers; mem. ABA, Phi Beta Kappa, Delta Sigma Rho. Home: 10 Mountain Spring Ave San Francisco CA 94114-2118 Office: 505 Sansome St Fl 12 San Francisco CA 94111-3106

LASORDA, THOMAS CHARLES (TOMMY LASORDA), professional baseball team manager; b. Norristown, Pa., Sept. 22, 1927; s. Sam and Carmella (Covatto) L.; m. Joan Miller, Apr. 14, 1950; children: Laura, Tom Charles. Student pub. schs., Norristown. Pitcher Bklyn. Dodgers, 1954-55, Kansas City A's, 1956; with L.A. Dodgers, 1956—, mgr. minor league clubs, 1965-73, coach, 1973-76, mgr., 1976-96, v.p. fin., 1996-98, gen. mgr., 1998—. Author: (with David Fisher) autobiography The Artful Dodger, 1985. Served with U.S. Army, 1945-47. Named Pitcher of Yr. Internat. League, 1958; L.A. Dodgers winner Nat. League pennant, 1977, 78, 81, 88, winner World Championship, 1981, 88; 2d Nat. League mgr. to win pennant first two yrs. as mgr.; named Nat. League Mgr. Yr. UPI, 1977, AP, 1977, 81, Baseball Writers' Assn. Am., 1988, Sporting News, 1988, Baseball Writers Assn. Am., 1983, 88; recipient Milton Richman Meml. award Assn. Profl. Baseball Players Am.; coach Nat. League All-Star team, 1977, 83-84, 86, 93; elected to the Baseball Hall of Fame, 1997. Mem. Profl. Baseball Players Am. Roman Catholic. Club: Variety of Calif. (v.p.). Office: c/o Los Angeles Dodgers 1000 Elysian Park Ave Los Angeles CA 90012-1112

LASSETER, JOHN P. film director, computer animator; b. Hollywood, Calif., 1957; BA in Fine Arts in Film, Calif. Inst. Arts. Exec. v.p. creative Pixar Animation Studios, Richmond, Calif. Director, writer: Luxo Jr., 1986 (Silver Berlin Bear award Berlin Internat. Film Festival, 1986 nominated Oscar for Best Short Films, Animated Films, 1986), Red's Dream, 1987, Tin Toy, 1988 (Best Short Films, Animated Films Acad. award 1988), Knickknack, 1989 (Best Short Film award Seattle Internat. Film Festival 1989), Toy Story, 1995 (nominated Oscar for Best Writing, Screenplay written Directly for Screen 1995), A Bug's Life, 1998; director: Adventures of Andre and Wally B., 1984, Toy Story 2, 1999; exec. prodr.: Luxo Jr.; exec. prodr. Geri's Game, 1997, Toy Story 2; actor: Computer Illusions, 1998. Recipient Spl Achievement award 1996 Acad. Awards; also Humanitarian award ShoWest Conv., 1997, Spl. award outstanding achievement, 1996. Office: c/p Pixar Animation Studios 1001 W Cutting Blvd Richmond CA 94804-2028

LATHAM, JOSEPH AL, JR. lawyer; b. Kinston, N.C., Sept. 16, 1951; s. Joseph Al and Margaret Lee (Tyson) L.; m. Elaine Frances Kramer, Dec. 19, 1981; children: Aaron Joshua, Adam Daniel. BA, Yale U., 1973; JD, Vanderbilt U., 1976. Bar: Calif. 1976, U.S. Dist. Ct. (cen. dist.) Calif. 1977, U.S. Ct. Appeals (9th cir.) 1977, U.S. Dist. Ct. (no. and so. dists.) Calif. 1978, Ga. 1980, U.S. Dist. Ct. (no. dist.) Ga. 1981, U.S. Ct. Appeals (5th and 11th cirs.) 1981, U.S. Dist. Ct. (mid. dist.) Ga. 1982, D.C. 1984. Assoc. Paul, Hastings, Janofsky & Walker, Orange County and L.A., 1976-80, Atlanta, 1980-83, ptnr. Orange County and L.A., 1987—; chief counsel to bd. mem. NLRB, Washington, 1983-85; staff dir. U.S. Commn. on Civil Rights, Washington, 1985-86. Instr. advanced profl. program U. So. Calif. Law Ctr., 1988, lectr. law, 1989—. Articles editor Vanderbilt Law Rev., 1975-76; editorial asst. Employment Discrimination Law, 2d edit., 1983; contbr. articles to Barron's, ABA Jour., Litigation, Employee Rels. Law Jour. Mem. Calif. Bar Assn., Ga. Bar Assn., D.C. Bar Assn., Order of Coif. Republican. Episcopalian. Office: Paul Hastings Janofsky & Walker 555 S Flower St Fl 23 Los Angeles CA 90071-2300

LATHROP, IRVIN TUNIS, retired academic dean, educator; b. Platteville, Wis., Sept. 23, 1927; s. Irvin J. and Marian (Johnson) L.; m. Eleanor M. Kolar, Aug. 18, 1951; 1 son, James I. B.S., Stout State Coll., 1950; M.S., Iowa State U., 1954, Ph.D., 1958. Tchr. Ottumwa (Iowa) High Sch., 1950-55; mem. faculty Iowa State U., 1957-58, Western Mich. U., 1958-59, Calif. State Coll., 1959-88, prof. indsl. arts, 1966-88, chmn. dept. indsl. edn., 1969-88, assoc. dean extended edn., 1978-88, prof. emeritus, 1988—. Cons. Naval Ordnance Lab., Corona, Calif., 1961-63 Author: (with Marshall La Cour) Photo Technology, 1966, rev. edit., 1977, Photography, 1979, rev. edit., 1992, The Basic Book of Photography, 1979, Laboratory Manual for Photo Technology, 1973, (with John Lindbeck) General Industry, 1969, rev. edit., 1977, 86, (with Robert Kunst) Photo-Offset, 1979; editl. cons. Am. Tech. Soc; contbr. articles to profl. jours. Mem. adv. com. El Camino and Orange Coast Coll.; mem. Orange County Grand Jury, 1989-90, Orange County Juvenile Justice Commn., 1991—. Mem. Nat. Soc. for Study Edn., Am. Council Indsl. Arts Tchr. Edn., Am. Vocat. Assn., Nat. Assn. Indsl. and Tech. Tchrs., Internat. Tech. Assn., Am. Ednl. Research Assn., Epsilon Pi Tau, Psi Chi, Phi Delta Kappa, Phi Kappa Phi. Home: PO Box 3430 Laguna Hills CA 92654-3430 Office: 1250 N Bellflower Blvd Long Beach CA 90840-0006 E-mail: ilathrop@ix.netcom.com

LATHROP, MITCHELL LEE, lawyer; b. L.A., Dec. 15, 1937; s. Alfred Lee and Barbara (Mitchell) L.; m. Lynn Mara Dalton; children: Christin Lorraine Newlon, Alexander Mitchell, Timothy Trewin Mitchell. BSc, U.S. Naval Acad., 1959; JD, U. So. Calif., 1966. Bar: D.C. 1966, Calif. 1966, U.S. Supreme Ct. 1969, N.Y. 1981; cert. arbitrator Nat. Arbitration Forum, ARIAS-US; cert. civil trial specialist Nat. Bd. Trial Advocacy. Dep. counsel L.A. County, Calif., 1966-68; with Brill, Hunt, DeBuys and Burby, L.A., 1968-71; ptnr. Macdonald, Halsted & Laybourne, L.A. and San Diego, 1971-80; sr. ptnr. Rogers & Wells, N.Y.C., San Diego, 1980-86; sr. ptnr., exec. com. Adams, Duque & Hazeltine, L.A., San Francisco, N.Y.C., San Diego, 1986-94, firm chmn., 1992-94; sr. ptnr. Luce, Forward, Hamilton & Scripps, San Diego, N.Y.C., San Francisco, L.A., 1994—. Presiding referee Calif. Bar Ct., 1984-86, mem. exec. com., 1981-88; lectr. law Calif. Judges Assn., Practicing Law Inst. N.Y., Continuing Edn. of Bar, State Bar Calif., ABA, others. Author: State Hazardous Waste Regulation, 1991, Environmental Insurance Coverage, 1991, Insurance Coverage for Environmental Claims, 1992; mem. editl. bd. Def. Counsel Jour., 1997—; editl. bd., Jous. Ins. Coverage. Western Regional chmn. Met. Opera Nat. Coun., 1971-81, v.p., mem. exec. com., 1971—, now chmn.; trustee Honnold Libr. at Claremont Colls., 1972-80; bd. dirs. Music Ctr. Opera Assn., L.A., sec., 1974-80; bd. dirs. San Diego Opera Assn., 1980—, v.p., 1985-89, pres.-elect, 1993, pres., 1994-96; bd. dirs. Met. Opera Assn., N.Y.C.; mem. nat. steering coun. Nat. Actors Theatre, N.Y. Mem. ABA, N.Y. Bar Assn., Fed. Bar Assn., Fed. Bar Council, Calif. Bar Assn., D.C. Bar Assn., San Diego County Bar Assn. (chmn. ethics com. 1980-82, bd. dirs. 1982-85, v.p. 1985), Assn. Bus. Trial Lawyers, Am. Intellectual Property Law Assn., Assn. So. Calif. Def. Counsel, Los Angeles Opera Assos. (pres. 1970-72), Soc. Colonial Wars in Calif. (gov. 1970-72), Order St. Lazarus of Jerusalem, Friends of Claremont Coll. (dir. 1975-81, pres. 1978-79), Am. Bd. Trial Advocates, Judge Advocates Assn. (dir. Los Angeles chpt. 1974-80, pres. So. Calif. chpt. 1977-78), Internat. Assn. Def. Counsel, Brit. United Services Club (dir. Los Angeles 1973-75), Mensa Internat., Calif. Soc., S.R. (pres. 1977-79), Calif. Club (Los Angeles), Valley Hunt Club (Pasadena, Calif.), Met. Club (N.Y.C.), The Naval Club (London), Phi Delta Phi. Republican. Home: 3355 Valemont St San Diego CA 92106-2430 Office: Luce Forward Hamilton and Scripps 600 W Broadway Fl 26 San Diego CA 92101-3311 also: Citicorp Ctr 153 E 53rd St 26th Fl New York NY 10022-4611 E-mail: mlathrop@luce.com

LATHROPE, DANIEL JOHN, law educator, department chairman; BSBA, U. Denver, 1973; JD, Northwestern U., 1977; LLM, NYU, 1979. Bar: Ariz. 1977, Calif. 1978. Assoc. Evans, Kitchel & Jenckes, Phoenix, 1977-78; instr. law NYU, 1979-80; assoc. prof. U. Calif. Hastings Coll. Law, San Francisco, 1980-86, prof., 1986—. Assoc. acad. dean U. Calif. Hastings Coll. Law, San Francisco, 1986-87, acting dean, 1987-88, acad. dean, 1988-90; prof., assoc. dean, dir. grad. tax program U. Fla. Coll. Law, Gainesville, 1995-96. Co-author: (with Lind, Schwarz and Rosenberg) Fundamentals of Corporate Taxation, 4th edit., 1997, (with Lind, Scharz and Rosenberg) Fundamentals of Business Enterprise Taxation, 1997, (with Lind, Schwarz and Rosenberg) Fundamentals of Partnership Taxation, 5th edit., 1998, (with Schwarz) Black Letter on Federal Taxation of Corporations and Partnerships, 2d edit., 1994, (with Freeland, Lind and Stephens) Fundamentals of Federal Income Taxation, 11th edit., 2000; author: The Alternative Minimum Tax-Compliance and Planning with Analysis, 1994. Mem. Order of Coif, Beta Gamma Sigma.

LATOUR, THOMAS W. hotel executive; m. Barbara LaTour. Degree in hotel/restaurant mgmt., Mich. State U., 1966; grad. mgmt. devel., Harvard U., 1980. Gen. mgr. Sky Chef; regional mgr. Amfac, 1983, sr. v.p. adminstrn.; pres. Kimpton Hotel and Restaurant Group, Inc., San Francisco, 1983—. Office: Kimpton Hotel Restaurant Group Inc 222 Kearny St Ste 200 San Francisco CA 94108-4510

LATTA, GEORGE HAWORTH, III, neonatologist; b. Chattanooga, Sept. 4, 1960; s. George Haworth Jr. and Charlotte (Major) L. BS in Physics, Ga. Inst. Tech., 1982; MD, East Tenn. State U., 1986. Cert. in pediats., neonatology. Intern, resident in pediat. Dartmouth (N.H.) U., 1986-88; resident in pediat. Stanford (Calif.) U., 1988-89; fellow in neonatology Vanderbilt U., Nashville, 1989-90, U. Tenn., Memphis, 1990-92; attending neonatologist Rose Med. Ctr., Denver, 1992-94, Forrest Gen. Hosp., Hattiesburg, Miss., 1994-95, Meth. Hosps., Memphis, 1995-99; neontalogist Intermountain Healthcare, Provo, Utah, 2000—. NIH pulmonary trainee grantee Vanderbilt U., 1989; March of Dimes scholar East Tenn. State U., 1981; Johnny J. Jones scholar, 1981. Fellow Am. Acad.

Pediat.; mem. Phi Eta Sigma. Roman Catholic. Avocations: snow skiing, camping, jazz music, aquariums, scuba diving. Home: 1032 S Slate Canyon Dr Provo UT 84606-6455 Office: Utah Valley Regional Med Ctr Intermountain Healthcare 1034 N 500 W Provo UT 84604-3380 E-mail: ghlatta3@earthlink.net, uvglatta@ihc.com

LATTMAN, LAURENCE HAROLD, retired academic administrator; b. N.Y.C., Nov. 30, 1923; s. Jacob and Yetta (Schwartz) L.; m. Hanna Renate Cohn, Apr. 12, 1946; children— Martin Jacob, Barbara Diane. BSChemE, Coll. City N.Y., 1948; MS in Geology, U. Cin., 1951, PhD, 1953. Instr. U. Mich., 1952-53; asst. head photogeology sect. Gulf Oil Corp., Pitts., 1953-57; asst. prof. to prof. geomorphology Pa. State U., 1957-70; prof., head dept. geology U. Cin., 1970-75; dean Coll. of Mines U. Utah, 1975-83, dean Coll. Engring., 1978-83; pres. N.Mex. Tech., Socorro, 1983-93, pres. emeritus, 1993—. Bd. dirs. Pub. Svc. Co. of N.Mex.; cons. U.S. Army Engrs., Vicksburg, Miss., 1965-69, also major oil cos. Author: (with R.G. Ray) Aerial Photographs in Field Geology, 1965, (with D. Zillman) Energy Law; Contbr. articles to profl. jours. Mem. N.Mex. Environ. Improvement Bd., 1995—. With AUS, 1943-46. Fenneman fellow U. Cin., 1953. Fellow Geol. Soc. Am.; mem. Am. Assn. Petroleum Geologists, Am. Soc. Photogrammetry (Ford Bartlett award 1968), Soc. Econ. Paleontologists and Mineralogists, AIME (Disting. mem. 1981, Mineral Industries Edn., award 1986—), Assn. Western Univs. (chmn. bd. dirs. 1986-87), Sigma Xi. Home: 11509 Penfield Ln NE Albuquerque NM 87111-6526

LATZER, RICHARD NEAL, investment company executive; b. N.Y.C., Jan. 6, 1937; s. Paul John and Alyce A. Latzer; m. Ellen Weston, Sept. 5, 1965; children: Steven, David. BA, U. Pa., 1959, MA, 1961. Chartered fin. analyst. Security analyst Mut. Benefit Life Ins. Co., Newark, 1963-66; portfolio mgr. EquitableLife Ins., Washington, 1966-68; securities analyst Investors Diversified Svcs., Mpls., 1968-69, dir. cert. and ins. investments, 1969-77, v.p. cert. and ins. investments, 1977-84, IDS Fin. Svcs., Inc., 1984-86, IDS Fin. Corp., 1987-88; v.p. investments IDS Reins. Co., 1986-88; asst. treas. Investors Syndicate Life Ins. & Annuity Co., Mpls., 1969-72; v.p. IDS Life Ins. Co., Mpls., 1973-80, v.p. investments, 1980-88; v.p. Investors Syndicate of Am., 1973-77, v.p. investments, 1977-84; v.p. Investors Syndicate Title & Guaranty Co., 1977-83; investment officer IDS Life Ins. Co. of N.Y., 1977-88; v.p. investments IDS Life Capital Resource Fund I, Inc., 1981-88, IDS Spl. Income Fund, Inc., 1981-88, Am. Enterprise Life Ins. Co., 1986-88, Reinsurance Co., 1986-88, IDS Life Series Fund, 1986-88, IDS Life Managed Fund, Inc., 1986-88, IDS Property Casualty, 1987-88; v.p. IDS Realty Corp., 1987-88; pres., chmn. bd., bd. dirs. Real Estate Svcs. Co., 1986-88, IDS Life Moneyshare Fund, Inc., 1981-88, IDS Cert. Co., 1984-88; chmn. bd., dir. IDS Real Estate Svcs. Co., 1983-86; v.p. Fireman's Fund Am. Life Ins. Co., 1985-86; dir. Investors Syndicate Devel. Corp., Mpls., 1970-88, Nuveen Realty Corp., Mpls., 1976-80; sr. v.p., chief investment officer Transamerica Corp., San Francisco, 1988—; pres., CEO Transamerica Investments Svcs., Inc., San Francisco, 1988—; dir., chief investment officer, chmn. investment com. Transamerica Occidental Life Ins. Co., L.A., 1989—; dir., chief investment officer, chmn. investment com., CEO Transamerica Life Ins. and Annuity Co., L.A., 1989—. Dir., chief investment officer, mem. investment com.Transamerica Ins. Group, Woodland Hills, 1988-93; bd. dirs., mem. exec. com. Transamerica Realty Svcs., Inc., San Francisco, 1988—, pres., CEO, 1996—; dir. Transamerica Realty Investment Corp., San Francisco, 1988—; chmn. pension investment com. Transamerica Life Ins. Co. Can., Toronto, 1991—; chief investment officer, mem. operating com. ARC Reins. Corp., Honolulu, 1993—. Lt. USN, 1960-63. Mem. Security Analysts San Francisco, Chartered Fin. Analysts. Office: Transamerica Invest Mgmt LLC 1150 S Olive St Los Angeles CA 90015-2211

LAU, CHARLES KWOK-CHIU, architect, architectural firm executive; b. Hong Kong, Oct. 19, 1954; came to U.S., 1973; s. Oi-Ting and Wai-Han L. BFA in Environ. Design, U. Hawaii Manoa, Honolulu, 1977. Registered architect, Hawaii. Designer CJS Group Architects, Honolulu, 1977-78, Fox Hawaii, Honolulu, 1978-80, Wimberly Allison Tong & Goo, Honolulu, 1980-82, Architects Hawaii, Honolulu, 1982-84; assoc., designer Stringer & Assocs., Honolulu, 1984-85; pres. AM Ptrns., Inc., Honolulu, 1985—. Instr. U. Hawaii, Honolulu, 1987. Principal works include Crystal Fantasy, Hyatt Regency Hotel, Honolulu, 1988 (Merit award Hawaii chpt. AIA 1988), Dole Cannery Sq., Honolulu, 1989 (Merit award Hawaii Renaissance 1989), Danelle Christie's, Ala Moana Hotel, Honolulu, 1989 (Hawaii Region award Illuminating Engring. Soc. N.Am. 1989, Grand and Nat. Grand awards Hawaii Renaissance 1989, Tiger Restaurant, Lahaina, Hawaii, 1990 (Gold Key Excellence in Interior Design award Am. Hotel and Motel Assn. 1990, Nat. and Merit awards Hawaii Renaissance 1990), La Pierre du Roi, ANA Kalakaua Ctr., Honolulu, 1990 (Grand and Nat. Grand awards 1990), Crazy Shirts, Honolulu, 1991 (Grand and Overall awards Hawaii Renaissance 1991), Grand Hyatt Wailea, Maui, Hawaii, 1992 (Merit award Hawaii chpt. AIA 1992), Carrera y Carrera, Ala Moana Ctr., Honolulu, 1992 (Merit award Hawaii chpt. AIA 1992), Danelle Christie's, Outrigger Waikiki Hotel, Honolulu, 1992 (Merit award Hawaii Renaissance 1992), Exec. Ctr. Hotel, Honolulu, 1992 (Merit award Hawaii Renaissance 1992), Centre Ct. Restaurant, Honolulu, 1993 (Merit award Hawaii Renaissance 1993), Lani Huli, Kailua, 1993 (Spl. Recognition award Parade of Homes 1993), 218 Plantation Club Dr., Kapalua, Maui, 1993 (Interior Design award Am. Soc. Interior Design 1993), Royal Garden Restaurant, Alamoana Hotel, Honolulu, 1994 (Brand and Overall award Hawaii Renaissance, 1994, Lani Huli, Kailua, Hawaii (Project of Yr., City and County of Honolulu 1994). Recipient 1994 Best in Am. Living award Profl. Builders, Kapalua Residence in Maui. Mem. AIA (mem. design award jury selection com. Honolulu chpt. 1990), C. of C. Hawaii, Chinese C. of C. Hawaii, Pacific Club. Office: AM Partners Inc 1164 Bishop St Ste 1000 Honolulu HI 96813-2876

LAU, FRED H. protective services official; Chief of police, San Francisco, 1996—. Office: San Francisco Police Dept 850 Bryant St Ste 525 San Francisco CA 94103-4603

LAU, H. LORRIN, obstetrician/gynecologist, inventor; b. Honolulu, Apr. 21, 1932; s. Henry S. and Helen (Lee) L.; m. Maureen Lau; children: David, Marianne, Mike, Mark, Linda. AB cum laude, Harvard U., 1950-54; MD, Johns Hopkins U., 1954-58, MPH, 1970-71. Asst. prof. Sch. Med. Johns Hopkins U. (Balt.), 1964-82; assoc. prof. U. Hawaii, 1982-84; chief ob-gyn. St. Francis West Hosp., Honolulu, 1990-92, Kuakini Hosp., Honolulu, 1994-95. Fellow AMA; mem. ACOG, Internat. Soc. Biology and Medicine. Inventor pregnancy tests, helped introduce alpha-fetoprotein tests into obstetrics in USA, 1971. Home: 925 14th Ave Honolulu HI 96816-3627 Office: 1010 S King St Honolulu HI 96814-1701

LAU, JOHN HON SHING, electronics scientist; b. China, June 17, 1946; came to U.S., 1973; s. Shui Hong and Mary Au L.; m. Teresa Yu, Sept. 2, 1972; 1 child, Judy M. BS in Civil Engring., Nat. Taiwan U., 1970; MASc in Structural Engring., U. B.C., 1973; MS in Engring. Mechanics, U. Wis., 1974; PhD in Theoretical and Applied Mechanics, U. Ill., 1977; MS in Mgmt., Fairleigh Dickinson U., 1981. Registered profl. engr., N.Y., Calif. Rsch. engr. Exxon Prodn. and Rsch. Co., Houston, 1977; structural specialist Control Data Corp., Sunnyvale, Calif., 1977-78; rsch. assoc. Internat. Paper Co., Tuxedo Park, N.Y., 1978-79; sr. engr. Ebasco Svcs. Inc., N.Y.C., 1979-81, Bechtel Power Corp., San Francisco, 1981-83; MTS Sandia Nat. Lab., N.Mex., 1983-84, Hewlett-Packard Labs., Palo Alto, Calif., 1984-95; pres. Express Packaging Sys., Inc., Palo Alto, 1995-2000; sr. scientist Agilent Techs., Inc., San Jose, 2000—. Contbr. articles to profl. jours. and 13 tech. books; assoc. editor for ASME Transaction Jour. Elec. Packaging. Fellow ASME, IEEE; mem. ASM Internat., AAAS, N.Y. Acad. Scis., Sigma Xi. Roman Catholic. E-mail: john. Home: 961 Newell Rd Palo Alto CA 94303-2929 Office: Agilent Techs Inc 350 W Trimble Rd MS 90LJ San Jose CA 95131 E-mail: lau@agilent.com

LAU, LAWRENCE JUEN-YEE, economics educator, consultant; b. Guizhou, China, Dec. 12, 1944; came to U.S., 1961, naturalized, 1974; s. Shai-Tat and Chi-Hing (Yu) Liu; m. Tamara K. Jablonski, June 23, 1984. BS with great distinction, Stanford U., 1964; MA, U. Calif., Berkeley, 1966, PhD, 1969; D.Social Sci. honoris causa, Hong Kong U. Sci. and Tech. From acting asst. prof. econs. to assoc. prof. Stanford U., Palo Alto, Calif., 1966-76, prof., 1976—, Kwoh-Ting Li prof. econ. devel., 1992—. Co-dir. Asia/Pacific Rsch. Ctr., Stanford U., 1992-96, dir. Stanford Inst. Econ. Policy Rsch., 1997-99; cons. The World Bank, Washington, 1976—; vice chmn. Bank of Canton of Calif. Bldg. Corp., San Francisco, 1981-85; dir. Bank of Canton of Calif., San Francisco, 1979-85, Property Resources Equity Trust, Los Gatos, 1987-88; vice chmn. Complete Computer Co. Far Eat Ltd., Hong Kong, 1981-89; bd. dirs. Taiwan Fund, Inc., Morningside Techs., Inc., Hong Kong, BOC Internat. Holdings Ltd., Hong Kong; vice chmn. Bank of Canton of Calif., San Francisco, 1999—. Co-author: (with D.T. Jamison) Farmer Education and Farm Efficiency, 1982, Models of Devlopment: A Comparative Study of Economic Growth in South Korea and Taiwan, 1986, rev. edit., 1990, Econometrics and the Cost of Capital: Essays in Honor of Dale W. Jorgenson, 2000, (with C.H. Yoon) North Korea in Transition: Prospects for Economic and Social Reform, 2001; contbr. articles to profl. jours. Adv. bd. Self-Help for Elderly, San Francisco, 1982—; bd. dirs. Chiang Ching-Kuo Found. for Internat. Scholarly Exch., 1989—; govs. coun. econ. policy advisors State of Calif., 1993-99; mem. Asian Art Commn., San Francisco, 1998-2001; mem. adv. coun. Innovation and Tech., Hong Kong, 2000—. John Simon Guggenheim Meml. fellow, 1973; fellow Ctr. for Advanced Study in Behavioral Scis., 1982; Overseas fellow Churchill Coll., Cambridge U., Eng., 1984 Fellow Econometric Soc.; mem. Academia Sinica (academician), Conf. Research in Income and Wealth, Chinese Acad. Social Scis. (hon.), Internat. Eurasian Acad. Scis. (academician). Republican. Episcopalian. Office: Stanford U Dept Econs Stanford CA 94305-6072 E-mail: ljlau@stanford.edu

LAUB, ALAN JOHN, engineering educator; b. Edmonton, Alta., Can., Aug. 6, 1948; came to U.S., 1970; naturalized, 1984; BSc with honors, U. B.C., 1969; MS, U. Minn., 1972, PhD, 1974. Asst. prof. Case Western Res. U., Cleve., 1974-75; vis. asst. prof. U. Toronto, Can., 1975-77; rsch. scientist MIT, Cambridge, Mass., 1977-79; assoc. prof. U. So. Calif., L.A., 1979-83; prof. U. Calif., Santa Barbara, 1983-96, chmn. dept. elec. and computer engring., 1989-92; dean Coll. of Engring. U. Calif. Davis, 1996—. Contbr. articles to profl. jours. Fellow IEEE; mem. IEEE Control Systems Soc. (pres. 1991, Disting. Mem. award 1991, Control Systems Tech. award 1993), Soc. Indsl. Applied Math., Assn. Computing Machinery. Avocations: bridge, tennis. Office: U Calif Office Dean Coll Engring One Shields Ave Davis CA 95616-5294

LAUB, WILLIAM MURRAY, retired utility executive; b. Ft. Mills, Corregidor, Philippines, July 20, 1924; s. Harold Goodspeed and Marjorie M. (Murray) L.; m. Mary McDonald, July 26, 1947; children: William, Andrew, Mary, David, John. BSBA, U. Calif., Berkeley, 1947, LLB, 1950. Bar: Calif. 1951. Practice law, Los Angeles, 1951-55; with Southwest Gas Corp., Las Vegas, Nev., 1948-88, v.p., gen. counsel, 1958 60, exec. v.p., 1960-64, pres., chief exec. officer, 1964-82, chmn., chief exec. officer, 1982-88. Pres. Boulder Dam Area council Boy Scouts Am., 1967-69, So. Nev. Indsl. Found., 1967-68, So. Nev. Meth. Found., 1967-74; chmn. Nev. Equal Rights Commn., 1966-68; Chmn. Clark County Republican Central Com., 1964-66; nat. committeeman Nev. Rep. Com., 1968-80; trustee Sch. Theology at Claremont, Calif., 1977—; trustee Inst. Gas Tech., 1983-89; nat. bd. advisors, coll. bus. and pub. adminstrn. The U. Ariz., 1985-89; bd. dirs. Alliance for Acid Rain Control, 1985-89. Served to lt. (j.g.) USNR, 1941-45. Mem. ABA, Am. Gas Assn. (bd. dirs., chmn. 1986-87), Pacific Coast Gas Assn. (chmn. 1983), Calif. Bar Assn., Nat. Coal Coun., Jonathan Club, Pauma Valley Country Club, Spanish Trail Golf and Country Club, Las Vegas Country Club. Office: 2810 W Charleston Blvd Ste 53 Las Vegas NV 89102-1906

LAUBE, ROGER GUSTAV, retired trust officer, financial consultant; b. Chgo., Aug. 11, 1921; s. William C. and Elsie (Drews) L.; m. Irene Mary Chadbourne, Mar. 30, 1946; children: David Roger, Philip Russell, Steven Richard. BA, Roosevelt U., 1942; postgrad., John Marshall Law Sch., 1942, 48-50; LLB, Northwestern U., 1960; postgrad., U. Wash., 1962-64. Cert. fin. cons. With Chgo. Title & Trust Co., Chgo., 1938-42, 48-50, Nat. Bank Alaska, Anchorage, 1950-72, mgr. mortgage dept., 1950-56, v.p., trust officer, mgr. trust dept., 1956-72; v.p., trust officer, mktg. dir., mgr. estate and fin. planning div. Bishop Trust Co., Ltd., Honolulu, 1972-82; instr. estate planning U. Hawaii, Honolulu, 1978-82; exec. v.p. Design Capital Planning Group, Inc., Tucson, 1982-83; pres., sr. trust officer, registered investment adviser Advanced Capital Advisory, Inc. of Ariz., Tucson, 1983-89; registered rep., pres. Advanced Capital Investments, Inc. of Ariz., Prescott, 1983-89; pres., chief exec. officer Advanced Capital Devel., Inc. of Ariz., Prescott, 1983-89; mng. exec. Integrated Resources Equity Corp., Prescott, 1983-89. Pres. Anchorage Estate Planning Coun., 1960-62, Charter mem., 1960-72, Hawaii Estate Planning Coun., 1972-82, v.p., 1979, pres., 1980, bd. dirs., 1981-82; charter mem. Prescott Estate Planning Coun., 1986-90, pres. 1988. Charter mem. Anchorage Community Chorus, 1946, pres., 1950-53, bd. dirs., 1953-72, Alaska Festival of Music, 1960-72; mem. Anchorage camp Gideons Internat., 1947-72, Honolulu camp, 1972-82, mem. Cen. camp, Tucson, 1982-85, Prescott, 1985-90, Port Angeles-Sequim Camp, 1990—; mem. adv. bd. Faith Hosp., Glenallen, Alaska, 1960—, Cen. Alaska Mission of Far Ea. Gospel Crusade, 1960—; sec., treas. Alaska Bapt. Found., 1955-72; bd. dirs. Anchorage Symphony, 1965-72; bd. dirs. Bapt. Found. of Ariz., 1985-90; bd. dirs., mem. investment com. N.W. Bapt. Found., 1991-97; mem. mainland adv. coun. Hawaii Bapt. Acad., Honolulu, 1982—; pres. Sabinovista Townhouse Assn., 1983-85; bd. advisers Salvation Army, Alaska, 1961-72, chmn., Anchorage, 1969-72, bd. advisers, Honolulu, 1972-82, chmn. bd. advisers, 1976-78; asst. staff judge adv. Alaskan Command, 1946-48; exec. com. Alaska Conv., 1959-61, dir. music Chgo., 1938-42, 48-50, Alaska, 1950-72, Hawaii, 1972-82, Tucson, 1982-85, 1st So. Bapt. Ch., Prescott Valley, Ariz., 1985-90; 1st Bapt. of Sequim, Wash., 1990-98; chmn. bd. trustees Hawaii, 1972-81, Prescott Valley, 1986-89, Sequim, Wash., 1991—; worship leader Waikiki Ch., 1979-82. 1st lt., JAGD, U.S. Army, 1942-48. Recipient Others award Salvation Army, 1972 Mem. Am. Inst. Banking (instr. trust div. 1961-72), Am. Bankers Assn. (legis. com., trust div. 1960-72), Nat. Assn. Life Underwriters (nat. com. for Ariz.), Yavapai County-Prescott Life Underwriters Assn. (charter), Anchorage C. of C. (awards com. 1969-71), Internat. Assn. Fin. Planners (treas. Anchorage chpt. 1969-72, exec. com. Honolulu chpt. 1972-82, Ariz. chpt. 1982-90, del. to World Congress Australia and New Zealand 1987), Am. Assn. Handbell Ringers. Baptist. Home: Sunland Country Club 212 Sunset Pl Sequim WA 98382-8515

LAUBER, MIGNON DIANE, food processing company executive; b. Detroit, Dec. 21; d. Charles Edmond and Maud Lillian (Foster) Donaker. Student Kelsey Jenny U., 1958, Brigham Young U., 1959; m. Richard Brian Lauber, Sept. 13, 1963; 1 child, Leslie Viane (dec.). Owner, operator Alaska World Travel, Ketchikan, 1964-67; founder, owner, pres. Oosick Soup Co., Juneau, Alaska, 1969—. Treas., Pioneer Alaska Lobbyists Soc., Juneau, 1977—. Mem. Bus. and Profl. Women, Alaska C. of C. Libertarian, Washington Athletic Club. Author: Down at the Water Works with Jesus, 1982; Failure Through Prayer, 1983, We All Want to Go to Heaven But Nobody Wants to Die, 1988. Home: 321 Highland Dr Juneau AK 99801-1442

LAUCHENGCO, JOSE YUJUICO, JR. lawyer; b. Manila, Philippines, Dec. 6, 1936; came to U.S., 1962; s. José Celis Sr. Lauchengco and Angeles (Yujuico) Sapota; m. Elisabeth Schindler, Feb. 22, 1968; children: Birthe, Martina, Duane, Lance. AB, U. Philippines, Quezon City, 1959; MBA, U. So. Calif., 1964; JD, Loyola U., L.A., 1971. Bar: Calif. 1972, U.S. Dist. Ct. (cen. dist.) Calif. 1972, U.S. Ct. Appeals (9th cir.) 1972, U.S. Supreme Ct. 1975. Banker First Western Bank/United Calif. Bank, L.A., 1964-71; assoc. Demler, Perona, Langer & Bergkvist, Long Beach, Calif., 1972-73; ptnr. Demler, Perona, Langer, Bergkvist, Lauchengco & Manzella, Long Beach, 1973-77; sole practice Long Beach and L.A., 1977-83; ptnr. Lauchengco & Mendoza, L.A., 1983-92; pvt. practice L.A., 1993—. Mem. commn. on jud. procedures County of L.A., 1979; tchr. Confraternity of Christian Doctrine, 1972-79; counsel Philippine Presdl. Commn. on Good Govt., L.A., 1986. Chmn. Filipino-Am. Bi-Partisan Polit. Action Group, L.A., 1978. Recipient Degree of Distinction, Nat. Forensic League, 1955. Mem. Criminal Cts. Bar Assn., Calif. Attys. Criminal Justice, Calif. Pub. Defenders Assn., Philippine-Am. Bar Assn., U. Philippines Vanguard Assn. (life), Beta Sigma. Roman Catholic. Lodge: K.C. Avocations: classical music, opera, romantic paintings and sculpture, camping, shooting. Office: 3545 Wilshire Blvd Ste 247 Los Angeles CA 90010-2388

LAUDA, DONALD PAUL, university dean; b. Leigh, Nebr., Aug. 7, 1937; s. Joe and Libbie L.; m. Sheila H. Henderson, Dec. 28, 1966; children: Daren M., Tanya R. B.S., Wayne State Coll., 1963, M.S., 1964; Ph.D., Iowa State U., 1966. Assoc. dir. Communications Center U. Hawaii, 1966-67; assoc. prof. indsl. arts St. Cloud (Minn.) State Coll., 1967-69; asst. dean Ind. State U., 1970-73; chmn. tech. edn. W.Va. U., 1973-75; dean Sch. Tech., Eastern Ill. U., Charleston, 1975-83; dean Coll. Health and Human Svcs. Calif. State U., Long Beach, 1983—. Cons. in field. Author: Advancing Technology: Its Impact on Society, 1971, Technology, Change and Society, 1978, 2d edit., 1985; contbr. articles to profl. jours. Pres. Council on Tech. Tchr. Edn.; dir. Charleston 2000 Futures Project, 1978-81. Served with USAR, 1957-59. EPDA research fellow, 1969-70; Eastern Ill. U. faculty research grantee, 1971 Mem. Future Soc. Internat. Tech. Edn. Assn., Coun. Tech. Tchr. Educators (pres., Tchr. of Yr. award 1978), World Future Soc., Internat. Tech. Edn. Assn. (pres. 1990), World Coun. Assn. Tech. Edn., Am. Vocat. Assn., Phi Kappa Phi (pres. 1993), Epsilon Pi Tau (Laureate citation 1982), Long Beach C. of C. (bd. dirs. 1995—), Japan Am. Soc. (adv. bd.). Office: Calif State U Coll Health & Human Svcs Long Beach CA 90840-0001

LAUER, GEORGE, environmental consultant; b. Vienna, Austria, Feb. 18, 1936; came to U.S., 1943; s. Otto and Alice (Denton) L.; m. Sandra Joy Comp, Oct. 1, 1983; children from previous marriage: Julie Anne, Robert L. BS, UCLA, 1961; PhD, Calif. Inst. Technology, 1967. Mem. tech. staff N.Am. Aviation, Canoga Park, Calif., 1966-69; mgr. Rockwell Internat., Thousand Oaks, 1969-75; div. mgr. ERT, Inc., Westlake Village, 1975-78; dir. Rockwell Internat., Newbury Park, 1978-85, Tetra-Tech Inc., Pasadena, 1985-86; pres. Environ. Monitoring & Svcs., Inc., 1986-88; sr. cons. Atlantic Richfield, Inc., L.A., 1988—. Rsch. prof. Desert Rsch. Inst., U. Nev., Las Vegas, 1998—; mem. adv. bd. Environment Rsch. and Tech.; mem. adv. coun. Scaqmo, 1996—. Served with U.S. Army, 1957-59. Fellow Assn. Computing Machinery; mem. Am. Chem. Soc., Am. Statis. Soc., Air Pollution Control Assn. Republican. Jewish. Home: 4449 Park Arroyo Calabasas CA 91302-2808 Office: Nat Cement 15821 Ventura # 475 Encino CA 91436 E-mail: glauer@pacbell.net

LAUER, JAMES LOTHAR, physicist, educator; b. Vienna, Austria, Aug. 2, 1920; came to U.S., 1938, naturalized, 1943; s. Max and Friederike (Rappaport) L.; m. Stefanie Dorothea Blank, Sept. 5, 1955; children: Michael, Ruth. AB, Temple U., 1942, MA, 1944; PhD, U. Pa., 1948; postgrad., U. Calif., San Diego, 1964-65. Scientist Sun Oil Co., Marcus Hook, Pa., 1944-52, spectroscopist, 1952-64, sr. scientist, 1965-77; asst. prof. U. Pa., 1952-55; lectr. U. Del., 1952-58; rsch. fellow mech. engring. U. Calif., San Diego, 1964-65; rsch. prof. mech. engring. Rensselaer Poly. Inst., Troy, N.Y., 1978-85, prof. mech. engring., 1985-93, prof. mech. engring. emeritus, 1993—; rsch. sci. Ctr. Magnetic Recording Rsch. U. Calif., San Diego, 1993-95, vis. scholar applied mechanics and engring. sci., 1995—. Sr. faculty summer rsch. fellow NASA-Lewis Rsch. Ctr., 1986-87; vis. prof. Ctr. for Magnetic Rec. Rsch., U. Calif., San Diego, 1991; cons. Digital Equipment Corp., 1992-94, NASA-Lewis Rsch. Ctr., 1993-95. Author: Infrared Fourier Spectroscopy--Chemical Applications, 1978; co-author: Handbook of Raman Spectroscopy, 2001; contbr. articles to profl. jours.; patentee in field. Active Penn Wynne Civic Assn., 1959-77, Country Knolls Civic Assn., 1978-93. Sun Oil Co. fellow, 1964-65, Air Force Office Sci. Rsch. grantee, 1974-86, NASA Lewis Rsch. Ctr. grantee, 1974-86, Office Naval Rsch. grantee, 1979-82, Army Rsch. Office grantee, 1985-89, NSF grantee, 1987-95, Innovative Rsch. award Soc. Mech. Engrs., 1991, Discovery awards NASA, 1993, 96. Fellow: Inst. Physics (U.K.); mem.: AAAS (life), Sigma Chi, Materials Rsch. Soc., Am. Chem. Soc. (emeritus), Optical Soc. Am. (emeritus), Am. Phys. Soc., Soc. Applied Spectroscopy. Jewish. Home: 7622 Palmilla Dr Apt 78 San Diego CA 92122-4710 Office: U Calif San Diego La Jolla CA 92037

LAUER, JEANETTE CAROL, college dean, history educator, writer; b. St. Louis, July 14, 1935; d. Clinton Jones and Blanche Aldine (Gideon) Pentecost; m. Robert Harold Lauer, July 2, 1954; children: Jon, Julie, Jeffrey. BS, U. Mo., St. Louis, 1970; MA, Washington U., St. Louis, 1973, PhD, 1975. Assoc. prof. history St. Louis C.C., 1974-82, U.S. Internat. U., San Diego, 1982-90, prof., 1990-94, dean Coll. Arts and Scis., 1990-94, rsch. prof., 1997—. Author: Fashion Power, 1981, The Spirit and the Flesh, 1983, Til Death Do Us Part, 1986, Watersheds, 1988, The Quest for Intimacy, 1996, 3d edit., 1993, No Secrets, 1993, The Joy Ride, 1993, For Better of Better, 1995, True Intimacy, 1996, Intimacy on the Run, 1996, How to Build a Happy Marriage, 1996, Sociology: Contours of Society, 1997, Windows on Society, 1999; Becoming Family: How to Build a Stepfamily that Works, 1999, How to Survive and Thrive in an Empty Nest, 1999, Troubled Times: Readings in Social Problems, 1999. Woodrow Wilson fellow, 1970, Washington U. fellow, 1971-75. Mem. Am. Hist. Assn., Orgn. Am. Historians. Democrat. Presbyterian. Home: 18147 Sun Maiden Ct San Diego CA 92127-3102

LAUGHLIN, ROBERT B. physics educator; b. Visalia, Calif., Nov. 1, 1950; m. Anita Rhona Perry, Apr. 22, 1979; children: Nathaniel David, Todd William. AB in Math, U. Calif., Berkeley, 1972; PhD in Physics, MIT, 1979. Postdoctoral fellow Bell Telephone Labs., 1979-81, Lawrence Livermore Nat. Lab., 1981-82; assoc. prof. physics Stanford (Calif.) U., 1985-89, prof. physics, 1989—, Anne T. and Robert M. Bass prof. Sch. Humanities and Scis., 1992—, prof. applied physics, 1993—. Lectr. in field. Contbr. articles to profl. jours. With U.S. Army, 1972-74. IBM fellow, 1976-78; recipient E.O. Lawrence award for physics, 1985, Franklin Inst. medal, 1998; named Eastman Kodak lectr., 1989, Van Vleck lectr., 1994.Nobel Prize Physics 1998 Fellow Am. Phys. Soc. (Oliver E. Buckley prize 1986); mem. AAAS, NAS, Am. Acad. Arts and Scis., Aspen Ctr. Physics. Office: Stanford U Dept Physics Stanford CA 94305

LAURANCE, DALE R. oil company executive; b. Ontario, Oreg., July 6, 1945; s. Rolland D. and Frances S. (Hopkins) L.; m. Lynda E. Dolmyer, Sept. 11, 1966; children— Catherine Megan, Brandy Nichole, Holly Elizabeth. BSChemE, Oreg. State U., 1967; MSChemE, U. Kans., 1971, PhDChemE, 1973. Mem. mgmt., research staff E.I. DuPont de NeMours, Lawrence, Kans., 1967-77; mgr. process technology Olin Corp., Lake Charles, La., 1977-80, bus. mgr. urethanes Stamford, Conn., 1980-82, gen. mgr. urethane and organics, 1982-83; sr. v.p. Occidental Chem. Corp., Darien, 1983-84; exec. v.p. Occidental Petroleum Corp., L.A., 1984-91, exec. v.p., sr. oper. officer, 1991, also bd. dirs., pres., 1997—; chmn., CEO Occidental Oil & Gas, L.A., 1999. Chmn. adv. bd., mem. dept. chem. and petroleum engring., U. Kans., Lawrence, 1985—. Contbr. articles to profl. jours. Patentee in field. Recipient Disting. Engring. Svc. award Sch. Engring., U. Kans., 1991. Mem. Am. Petroleum Inst., Chem. Mfrs. Assn., Soc. Chem. Industry, L.A. Area C. of C. (bd. dirs.). Republican. Club: Riveria Country (Los Angeles). Office: Occidental Petroleum Corp 10889 Wilshire Blvd Los Angeles CA 90024-4201

LAURIE, RONALD SHELDON, lawyer; b. San Francisco, June 30, 1942; s. Charles M. and Mimosa (Ezaoui) L.; m. Mina Heshmati, June 1, 1986. BS in Indsl. Engring., U. Calif., Berkeley, 1964; JD, U. San Francisco, 1968. Bar: Calif. 1969, U.S. Ct. Appeals (9th cir.) 1969, U.S. Patent Office 1969, U.S. Supreme Ct. 1971, U.S. Ct. Appeals (fed. cir.) 1972. Programmer, sys. engr. Lockheed Missiles & Space Co., Sunnyvale, Calif., 1960-64; patent atty. Kaiser Aluminum & Chem. Co., Oakland, 1968-70; ptnr. Townsend and Townsend, San Francisco, 1970-88, Irell & Manella, Menlo Park, Calif., 1988-91, Weil, Gotshal & Manges, Menlo Park, 1991-94, McCutchen, Doyle, Brown & Emersen, San Francisco, 1994-98; chmn. McCutchen Computers and Software Industry Group, 1995-98; ptnr. Skadden, Arps, Meagher & Flom, Palo Alto, Calif., 1998—; co-chair Skadden Arps' Computer and Info. Tech. Group, 1998—. Lectr. computer law Stanford U. Law Sch., 1993-94; advisor NAS, U.S. Copyright Office and U.S. Patent and Trademark Office, Washington, Office Tech. Assessment, U.S. Congress, World Intellectual Property Orgn., Geneva; lectr. patent law U. Calif., Berkeley, 1999—; permanent faculty World Law Inst., 1996—. Co-editor: International Intellectual Property, 1992; contbr. articles to profl. jours. Mem. Internat. Intellectual Property Assn. (exec. com.), State Bar Calif. (past mem. exec. com. intellectual property sect.), Computer Law Assn. (bd. dirs.). Avocation: vintage auto racing. Home: 107 Acacia Ave Belvedere CA 94920-2309 Office: Skadden Arps Meagher & Flom 525 University Ave Palo Alto CA 94301-1903 E-mail: rlaurie@skadden.com, roulaurie@sprintmail.com

LAURITZEN, PETER OWEN, electrical engineering educator; b. Valparaiso, Ind., Feb. 14, 1935; s. Carl W. and Edna B. (Seebach) L.; m. Helen M. Janzen, Apr. 6, 1963; children: Beth K., Margo S. B.S., Calif. Inst. Tech., 1956; M.S., Stanford U., 1958, Ph.D., 1961. Assoc. evaluation engr. Honeywell Aero. Div., Mpls., 1956-57; mem. tech. staff Fairchild Semiconductor Div., Palo Alto, Calif., 1961-65; asst. prof. elec. engring. U. Wash., Seattle, 1965-68, assoc. prof., 1968-73, prof., 1973-98, prof. emeritus, 1999—, adj. prof. social mgmt. of tech., 1977-83; engring. mgr. Avtech Corp., Seattle, 1979-80. Cons. x-ray div. Chgo. Bridge & Iron Works, 1967-71, 78, Eldec Corp., 1982-91, Energy Internat., 1986-88; conf. chair IEEE Power Electronics Specialist Conf., 1993; co-dir. NSF industry/univ. rsch. ctr., 1995-97; Fulbright lectr. IIT, Madras, India, 1997; Danfoss vis. prof. Aalborg (Denmark) U., 1999. Pres. Coalition for Safe Energy, Wash. Citizens Group, 1975-76. Danforth assoc., 1966-78; NASA-Am. Soc. Engring. Edn. summer faculty fellow, 1974 Mem. IEEE, AAAS. Home: 325 33d St Port Townsend WA 98368-5023 Office: U Wash Elec Engring Dept PO Box 352500 Seattle WA 98195-2500 E-mail: plauritz@ee.washington.edu

LAVE, CHARLES ARTHUR, economics educator; b. Phila., May 18, 1938; s. Israel and Esther Lave; 1 child, Rebecca. BA, Reed Coll., 1960; PhD, Stanford U., 1968. Mem. faculty U. Calif., Irvine, 1966—, prof. econs., chmn. dept. econs., 1978-85, 89-92. Vis. prof., vis. scholar Hampshire Coll., 1972, Stanford U., 1974, MIT, 1982, Harvard U., 1982, U. Calif., Berkeley, 1988, 94. Author: (with James March) An Introduction to Models in the Social Sciences, 1975, Energy and Auto Type Choice, 1981, Urban Transit, 1985, others. Trustee Reed Coll., Portland, Oreg., 1978-82; bd. dirs. Nat. Bur. Econ. Rsch., Cambridge, 1991-97; chmn. bd. Irvine Campus Housing Authority, Inc., 1982-96, asst. to chancellor, 1996-97. With USAF, 1957. Recipient Pyke Johnson award Transp. Rsch. Bd., 1987, Extraordinarius award U. Calif., 1993. Fellow Soc. Applied Anthropology; mem. Am. Econ. Assn., AAAS, Transp. Research Bd. Office: U Calif Dept Econs Irvine CA 92697-5100 E-mail: calave@uci.edu

LAVIDGE, ROBERT JAMES, marketing research executive; b. Chgo., Dec. 27, 1921; s. Arthur Wills and Mary Beatrice (James) L.; m. Margaret Mary Zwigard, June 8, 1946; children: Margaret, Kathleen, William, Lynn Elizabeth. AB, DePauw U., 1943; MBA, U. Chgo., 1947. Analyst Pepsodent div. Lever Bros., Chgo., 1947-48, new products mktg. rsch. mgr. Pepsodent div., 1948-49; asst. dir. mktg. Am. Meat Inst., Chgo., 1950-51; ptnr. Elrick, Lavidge and Co., Chgo., 1951-56; pres. Elrick and Lavidge, Inc., Chgo., 1956-86; pres. emeritus Elrick and Lavidge, Scottsdale, Ariz., 1987—. Lectr. mktg. research, sales adminstrn. Northwestern U., 1950-80; mem. Nat. Mktg. Adv. Com., 1967-71, also exec. com.; bd. govs. Brand Names Edn. Found., 2000—. Trustee Village Western Springs, Ill., 1957-61, pres., 1973-77; trustee McCormick Theol. Sem., 1981-90, 92-96; mem. adv. council U. Chgo. Grad. Sch. Bus. Mem. Am. Mktg. Assn. (v.p. 1963-64, pres. 1966-67, trustee found. 1992—, chmn. 1992-99), Internat. Rels. Soc. (chmn. 1961-65), Internat. Trademark Assn., Econ. Club Phoenix, De Pauw U. Alumni Assn. (pres. 1967-68), Klinger Lake Club (Mich.), Paradise Valley Country Club, Phi Beta Kappa, Beta Gamma Sigma, Sigma Delta Chi. Presbyterian.

LAVIGNE, LOUIS JAMES, JR. biotechnology company executive; b. Cheboygan, Mich., Apr. 24, 1948; s. Louis James and Shirley (Lahaie) L.; m. Rachel Joy Winikur, June 21, 1969; children: Stephanie Lynn, Gordon Scott. BSBA, Babson Coll., 1969; MBA, Temple U., 1976. Mgr. sales acctg. Pennwalt Corp., Phila., 1971-73, mgr. acctg. systems, 1973-74, mgr. acctg. info., 1974-79, asst. contr., 1979-82, Genentech Inc., South San Francisco, 1982-83, contr., 1983-84, contr., officer, 1984-86, v.p., contr., 1986-87, v.p., chief fin. officer, 1988—. Mem. Fin. Exec. Inst., Nat. Assn. Accts. Office: Genentech Inc One DNA Way South San Francisco CA 94080-4990

LAVIN, MATTHEW T. horticultural educator; Assoc. prof. biology dept. Mont. State U., Bozeman. Recipient N.Y. Botanical Garden award Botanical Soc. Am., 1993. Office: Montana State U Dept Biology 310 Lewis Hl Bozeman MT 59717-0001

LAVIN, STEPHEN MICHAEL, university basketball coach; b. San Francisco, Sept. 4, 1964; BS, Chapman U., 1987. Grad. asst. basketball coach, staff mem. Purdue U., 1988-91; staff mem. UCLA, 1991-95, asst. coach, 1995-97, recruiting coord., 1996-97, head coach, 1997—. Dir., founder Lavin Basketball Camps, 1984—; summer camp and coaches clinic spkr., 1989—; cons./advisor Korean Nat. Profl. Team, Samsung Profl. Team, 1992-96. Named Nat. Rookie Coach of Yr. Basketball Times mag., 1997; recipient Internat. Inspiration award Hugh O'Brien Youth Found., 1997. Office: UCLA 325 Westwood Plz Los Angeles CA 90095-0001

LAVINE, STEVEN DAVID, academic administrator; b. Sparta, Wis., June 7, 1947; s. Israel Harry and Harriet Hauda (Rosen) L.; m. Janet M. Sternburg, May 29, 1988. BA, Stanford U., 1969; MA, Harvard U., 1970, PhD, 1976. Asst. prof. U. Mich., Ann Arbor, 1974-81; asst. dir. arts and humanities Rockefeller Found., N.Y.C., 1983-86, assoc. dir. arts and humanities, 1986-88; pres. Calif. Inst. Arts, Valencia, 1988—. Adj. assoc. prof. NYU Grad. Sch. Bus., 1984-85; cons. Wexner Found., Columbus, Ohio, 1986-87; selection panelist Input TV Screening Conf., Montreal, Can., and Granda, Spain, 1985-86; cons., panelist NEH, Washington, 1981-85; faculty chair Salzburg Seminar on Mus., 1989; co-dir. Arts and Govt. Program, The Am. Assembly, 1991; mem. arch. selection jury L.A. Cathedral, 1996, Arch. L.A., 1998-2001. Editor: The Hopwood Anthology, 1981, Exhibiting Cultures, 1991, Museums and Communities, 1992; editor spl. issue Prooftexts jour., 1984. Bd. dirs. Sta. KCRW-FM (NPR), KCET-Pub. TV, L.A. Philharm. Assn., Endowments, Inc. Recipient Class of 1923 award, 1979, Faculty Recognition award, 1980 U. Mich.; Charles Dexter traveling fellow Harvard U., 1972, Ford fellow, 1969-74, vis. rsch. fellow Rockefeller Found., N.Y.C., 1981-83. Jewish. Office: Calif Inst Arts Office Pres 24700 McBean Pkwy Santa Clarita CA 91355-2397

LAVKULICH, LESLIE MICHAEL, soil science educator; b. Coaldale, Alta., Can., Apr. 28, 1939; s. Michael Lavkulich and Mary Alexa; m. Mary Ann Elizabeth Olah, Sept. 15, 1962; children: Gregory Michael, Miles Andrew. BS with distinction, U. Alta., Edmonton, 1961, MS, 1963; PhD, Cornell U., 1967. From asst. prof. to assoc. prof. U. B.C., Vancouver, 1967-75, prof., 1975—, dept. head, 1980-90, chair rsch. mgmt., 1979—, dir. Inst. for Resources and Environment. Contbr. 8 chpts. to books, more than 70 tech. reports, more than 150 refereed sci. publs. Mem. Internat. Soc. Soil Sci. (sec. 1976-78), Am. Soc. Soil, Can. Soc. Soil Sci. (pres. 1980-81), Pacific Regional Soc. Soil Sci. (founder 1979). Office: U BC 2206 East Mall Vancouver BC Canada V6T 1Z4 E-mail: lml@interchange.ubc.ca, ire@interchange.ubc.ca

LAW, CLARENE ALTA, innkeeper, state legislator; b. Thornton, Idaho, July 22, 1933; d. Clarence Riley and Alta (Simmons) Webb; m. Franklin Kelso Meadows, Dec. 2, 1953 (div. July 1973); children: Teresa Meadows Jillson, Charisse Meadows Haws, Steven Riley; m. Creed Law, Aug. 18, 1973. Student, Idaho State Coll., 1953. Sec., sub. tchr. Grand County Schs., Cedar City, Utah, 1954-57; UPI rep. newspaper agy. Moab, Utah Regional Papers, Salt Lake City and Denver; auditor Wort Hotel, Jackson, Wyo., 1960-62; innkeeper, CEO Elk Country Motels, Inc., Jackson, 1962—; rep. Wyo. Ho. of Reps., Cheyenne, 1991—, chmn. house travel com., 1993—, past mem. bank bd. State of Wyo., 1991-98. Bd. dirs. Jackson State Bank, Snow King Resort. Chmn. sch. bd. dirs. Teton County Schs., Jackson, 1983-86; bd. dirs. Wyo. Taxpayers Assn., Bus. Coun., 1998—. Named Citizen of Yr. Jackson C. of C., 1976, 99, Bus. Person of Yr. Jackson Hole Realtors, 1987, Wyo. Small Bus. Person SBA, 1977. Mem. Wyo. Lodging and Restaurant Assn. (pres., chmn. bd. dirs. 1988-89, Big Wyo. award 1987), Soroptimists (charter), Bus. Profl. Womens Orgn. (Woman of Yr. 1975, mem. Heritage steering com. 1996—), Gov.'s 15-Mem. Bus. Coun. Republican. Mem. LDS Ch. Avocations: grandchildren, travel, study, old cars. Address: PO Box 575 Jackson WY 83001-0575 Office: Elk Country Motels Inc 43 W Pearl Jackson WY 83001

LAW, JOHN HAROLD, biochemistry educator; b. Cleve., Feb. 27, 1931; s. John and Katherine (Frampton) L.; m. Jeannette Ward Belcher, Nov. 9, 2000. BS, Case Inst. Tech., Cleve., 1953; PhD, U. Ill., 1957; D (hon.), U. Sofia, 1995. Fellow Harvard U., Cambridge, Mass., 1958-59, from instr. to asst. prof. biochemistry, 1960-65; instr. Northwestern U., Evanston, Ill., 1959-60; prof. U. Chgo., 1965-81, U. Ariz., Tucson, 1981-91, Regents prof., 1991—, chmn. dept. biochemistry, 1981-86, dir. biotech. program, 1986-92; dir. Ctr. Insect Sci., 1993-98; assoc. dean coll. agr. U. Ariz., Tucson, 1988-90. Gov. bd. Internat. Ctr. Insects, Nairobi, Kenya, 1980-87; mem. bd. trust Gordon Rsch. Conf., 1992-98, chmn., 1996; mem. coun. Am. Soc. Biochem. Molecular Biology, 1993-96. Recipient Gregor Mendel medal Czech Acad. Sci., 1992, J.E. Purkinje medal Czech Acad. Sci., 1994. Fellow AAAS, ESA (Recognition award 1999); mem. NAS, Am. Soc. Biochem. Molecula r Biology, Am. Chem. Soc., Entomol. Soc. Am. Home: 2540 E 7th St Tucson AZ 85716-4702 Office: U Ariz Dept Biochemistry Bio Scis W 342A Tucson AZ 85721-0001 E-mail: jhlaw@u.arizona.edu

LAWRANCE, CHARLES HOLWAY, retired civil and sanitary engineer; b. Augusta, Maine, Dec. 25, 1920; s. Charles William and Lois Lyford (Holway) L.; m. Mary Jane Hungerford, Nov. 22, 1947; children: Kenneth A., Lois R., Robert J. BS in Pub. Health Engring., MIT, 1942; MPH, Yale U., 1952. Registered profl. engr., Calif. Sr. san. engr. Conn. State Dept. Health, Hartford, 1946-53; assoc. san. engr. Calif. Dept. Pub. Health, L.A., 1953-55; chief san. engr. Koebig & Koebig, Inc., Cons. Engrs., L.A., 1955-75; engr., mgr. Santa Barbara County Water Agy., Santa Barbara, Calif., 1975-79; prin. engr. James M. Montgomery Cons. Engrs., Pasadena, 1979-83; v.p. Lawrance, Fisk & McFarland, Inc., Santa Barbara, 1983-96; cons. engr., retired Santa Barbara, 1996-99. Author: The Death of the Dam, 1972; co-author: Ocean Outfall Design, 1958; contbr. articles to profl. jours. Bd. dirs. Pacific Unitarian Ch., Palos Verdes Peninsula, Calif., 1956-60, chmn. bd. 1st lt. USMCR, 1942-46, PTO. Fellow ASCE (life, Norman medal 1966); mem. Am. Water Works Assn. (life), Am. Acad. Environ. Engrs. (life diplomate), Water Environment Fedn. (life). Republican. Unitarian. Home and Office: 1340 Kenwood Rd Santa Barbara CA 93109-1224 E-mail: charleslawrance@msn.com

LAWRENCE, DAVID M. health facility administrator; b. 1940; BA, Amherst (N.Y.) Coll., 1962, DSc (hon.), 1994; MD, U. Ky., 1966; MPH, U. Wash., 1973; LittD (hon.), Colgate U., 1995. Cert. gen. preventive medicine. Intern in internal medicine, pediat.; health officer, dir. Multnomah County, Oreg.; v.p., area med. dir. N.W. Permanente Kaiser Found. Health Plan and Hosps., Portland, Maine, 1981-85, v.p., reg. mgr. Colo., 1985-88, sr. v.p., reg. mgr. N.C., 1988-89, CEO Calif., 1992—, also vice chmn. bd. dirs., 1990-91, also chmn bd. dirs. Mem. various professorships, directorships and fellowships with U. Wash., Johns Hopkins U., U. Ky.; bd. dirs. Pacific Gas and Electric Co., Hewlett Packard, Healthcare Forum, Bay Area Coun., Calif. Coll. Arts and Crafts, Colby Coll. Named Outstanding Alumnus of the Sch. Pub. Health and Cmty. Medicine U. Washington, 1980, Outstanding Alumnus of the Coll. Medicine U. Ky., 1995. Mem. APHA, Am. Hosp. Assn., Am. Coll. Preventive Medicine, Calif. Assn. Hosps. and Healty Sys., Group Health Assn. Am., Western Consortium for Pub. Health, Calif. Bus. Roundtable, The Conf. Bd. (bd. dirs.), Inst. Medicine/NAS (bd. dirs.), Alpha Omega. Office: Kaiser Found Health Plan & Hosp 1 Kaiser Plz Oakland CA 94612-3610

LAWRENCE, FREDERICK D. communications executive; BSEE, Western Mich. U. Sr. mgmt. positions AT&T, 1970-82; exec. positions Spring Corp., 1982-94; pres. transmission group ADC Telecomm., 1994-96; CEO, chmn., pres. Adaptive Broadband (formerly Calif. Microwave), Sunnyvale, 1997—. Office: Adaptive Broadband Corp 1143 Borregas Ave Sunnyvale CA 94089-1306

LAWRENCE, JEROME, playwright, director, educator; b. Cleve., July 14, 1915; s. Samuel and Sarah (Rogen) L. BA, Ohio State U., 1937, LHD (hon.), 1963; DLitt, Fairleigh Dickinson U., 1968; DFA (hon.), Villanova U., 1969; LittD, Coll. Wooster, 1983. Dir. various summer theaters, Pa. and Mass., 1934-37; reporter, telegraph editor Wilmington (Ohio) News Jour., 1937; editor Lexington Daily News, Ohio, 1937; continuity editor radio Sta. KMPC, Beverly Hills, Calif., 1938-39; sr. staff writer CBS, Hollywood, Calif. and N.Y.C., 1939-42; pres., writer, dir. Lawrence & Lee, Hollywood, N.Y.C. and London, 1945—. Vis. prof. Ohio State Univ., 1969, Salzburg Seminar in Am. Studies, 1972, Baylor Univ., 1978; prof. playwriting Univ. So. Calif. Grad. Sch., 1984—; co-founder, judge Margo Jones award, N.Y.C., 1958—; co-founder, pres. Am. Playwrights Theatre, Columbus, Ohio, 1970-85; bd. dirs. Am. Conservatory Theatre, San Francisco, 1970-80, Stella Adler Theatre, L.A., 1987—, Plumstead Playhouse, 1986—; keynote speaker Bicentennial of Bill of Rights, Congress Hall, Phila., 1991; hon. mem. Nat. Theatre Conf., 1993; adv. bd. Am. Theatre in Lit. Contemporary Arts Ednl. Project, 1993—; playwright, 1944—. Scenario writer Paramount Studios, 1941; master playwright NYU Inst. Performing Arts, 1967-69; author-dir. for: radio and television UN Broadcasts; Army-Navy programs D-Day, VE-Day, VJ-Day; author: Railroad Hour, Hallmark Playhouse, Columbia Workshop; author: Off Mike, 1944, (biography, later made into PBS-TV spl.) Actor: Life and Times of Paul Muni, 1978 (libretto and lyrics by Lawrence and Lee, music by Billy Goldenberg); co-author, dir.: (album) One God; playwright: Live Spelled Backwards, 1969, Off Mike, (mus. with Robert E. Lee) Look, Ma, I'm Dancin', 1948 (music by Hugh Martin), Shangri-La, 1956 (music by Harry Warren, lyrics by James Hilton, Lawrence and Lee), Mame, 1966 (score by Jerry Herman), Dear World, 1969 (score by Jerry Herman), (non-mus.) Inherit the Wind (translated and performed in 34 langs., named best fgn. play of year London Critics Poll 1960), Auntie Mame, 1956, The Gang's All Here, 1959, Only in America, 1959, A Call on Kuprin, 1961, Diamond Orchid (revised as Sparks Fly Upward, 1966), 1965, The Incomparable Max, 1969, The Crocodile Smile, 1970, The Night Thoreau Spent in Jail, 1970, (play and screenplay) First Monday in October, 1978, (written for opening of Thurber Theatre, Columbus) Jabberwock: Improbablilities Lived and Imagined by James Thurber in the Fictional City of Columbus, Ohio, 1974, (with Robert E. Lee) Whisper in the Mind, 1994, The Angels Weep, 1992, (novel) A Golden Circle: A Tale of the Stage and the Screen and Music of Yesterday and Now and Tomorrow and Maybe the Day After Tomorrow, 1993; Decca Dramatic Albums, Musi-Plays., Selected Plays of Lawrence and Lee, 1996; contbg. editor Dramatics mag., mem. adv. bd., contbr. Writer's Digest; Lawrence and Lee collections at Libr. and Mus. of the Performing Arts, Lincoln Ctr., N.Y., Harvard's Widener Libr., Cambridge, Mass., Jerome Lawrence & Robert E. Lee Theatre Rsch. Inst. at Ohio State U., Columbus, est. 1986. A founder, overseas corr. Armed Forces Radio Service; mem. Am. Theatre Planning Bd.; bd. dirs. Nat. Repertory Theatre, Plumstead Playhouse; mem. adv. bd. USDAN Center for Creative and Performing Arts, East-West Players, Performing Arts Theatre of Handicapped., Inst. Outdoor Drama; mem. State Dept. Cultural Exchange Drama Panel, 1961-69; del. Chinese-Am. Writers Conf., 1982, 86, Soviet-Am. Writers Conf., 1984, 85; Am. Writers rep. to Hiroshima 40th Anniversary Commemorative, Japan, 1985; mem. U.S. Cultural Exchange visit to theatre communities of Beijing and Shanghai, 1985; adv. coun. Calif. Ednl. Theatre Assn., Calif. State U., Calif. Repertory Co., Long Beach, 1984—. Recipient N.Y. Press Club award, 1942, CCNY award, 1948, Radio-TV Life award, 1948, Mirror awards, 1952, 53, Peabody award, 1949, 52, Variety Showmanship award 1954, Variety Critics poll 1955, Outer-Circle Critics award 1955, Donaldson award, 1955, Ohioana award, 1955, Ohio Press Club award, 1959, Brit. Drama Critics award, 1960, Moss Hart Meml. award, 1967, State Dept. medal, 1968, Pegasus award, 1970, Lifetime Achievement award Am. Theatre Assn., 1979, Nat. Thespian Soc. award, 1980, Pioneer Broadcasters award, 1981, 95, Diamond Circle award Pacific Pioneer Broadcasters, 1995, Ohioana Library career medal, Master of Arts award Rocky Mountain Writers Guild, 1982, Centennial Award medal Ohio State U., 1970, William Inge award and lectureship Independence Community Coll., 1983, 86—, Disting. Contbr. award Psychologists for Social Responsibility, 1985, ann. awards San Francisco State U., Pepperdine U., Career award Southeastern Theatre Conf., 1990; named Playwright of Yr. Baldwin-Wallace Coll., 1960; named to Honorable Order of Ky. Colonels, 1965, Tenn. Colonels, 1988; named to Theater Hall of Fame, 1990. Fellow Coll. Am. Theatre, Kennedy Ctr.; mem. Nat. Theatre Conf. (hon.), Acad. Motion Picture Arts and Scis. (nominating com. best fgn. films 1997), Acad. TV Arts and Scis. (2 Emmy award 1988), Authors League (coun.), ANTA (dir., v.p.), Ohio State U. Assn. (dir.), Radio Writers' Guild (founder, pres.), Writers Guild Am. (dir., founding mem. Valentine Davies award), Dramatists Guild (coun.), ASCAP, Calif. Ednl. Theatre Assn. (Profl. Artist award 1992), Century Club N.Y., Phi Beta Kappa, Sigma Delta Chi. Avocations: traveling, photography, swimming.

LAWRENCE, SALLY CLARK, academic administrator; b. San Francisco, Dec. 29, 1930; d. George Dickson and Martha Marie Alice (Smith) Clark; m. Henry Clay Judd, July 1, 1950 (div. Dec. 1972); children: Rebecca, David, Nancy; m. John I. Lawrence, Aug. 12, 1976; stepchildren: Maia, Dylan. Docent Portland Art Mus., Oreg., 1958-68; gallery owner, dir. Sally Judd Gallery, Portland, 1968-75; art ins. appraiser, cons. Portland, 1975-81; interim dir. Mus. Art Sch. Pacific Northwest Coll. Art, Portland, 1981, asst. dir., 1982-84, dir., 1984-94, pres., 1994—. Bd. dirs. Art Coll. Exch. Nat. Consortium, 1982-91, pres., 1983-84. Bd. dirs. Portland Arts Alliance, 1987—; bd. dirs. Assn. Ind. Colls. of Art and Design, 1991—, pres., 1995-96, sec., 1996—. Fellow Nat. Assn. Schs. Art and Design (life mem., bd. dirs. 1984-91, 94—, treas. bd. dirs. 1994-96, pres. 1996-99), Oreg. Ind. Coll. Assn. (bd. dirs. 1981—, exec. com. 1989-94, pres. 1992-93), Pearl Arts Found. (chmn. bd. dirs. 2000-). Office: Pacific NW Coll Art 1241 NW Johnson St Portland OR 97209-3023 E-mail: sally@pnca.edu

LAWTON, MICHAEL JAMES, entomologist, pest management specialist; b. Balt., Aug. 6, 1953; s. James William and Mary Eileen (O'Connor) L.; m. Barbara Ann Byron, Dec. 19, 1983. BS, U. Md., 1975. Cert. entomologist. Technician, tech. dir. Atlas Exterminating Co., Towson, Md., 1975-78; asst. tech. dir. Western Exterminator Co., Irvine, Calif., 1978-83, tng. and tech. dir., 1984-95, dir. sales and mktg., 1996, v.p. sales and mktg., 1997—, shareholder, 1999—. Democrat. Office: Western Exterminator Co 1732 Kaiser Ave Irvine CA 92614-5739

LAX, KATHLEEN THOMPSON, judge; b. 1945; BA, U. Kans., 1967; JD, U. Calif., L.A., 1980. Law clk. U.S. Bankruptcy Ct., L.A., 1980-82; assoc. Gibson, Dunn & Crutcher, L.A., 1982-88; judge ctrl. dist. U.S. Bankruptcy Ct., L.A., 1988—. Bd. dirs. L.A. Bankruptcy Forum, 1988—; bd. govs. Fin. Lawyers Conf., L.A., 1991-92, 94—. Bd. editors: Calif. Bankruptcy Jour., 1988—. Office: US Bankruptcy Court 21041 Burbank Blvd Woodland Hills CA 91367-6606

LAY, THORNE, geosciences educator; b. Casper, Wyo., Apr. 20, 1956; s. Johnny Gordon and Virginia Florence (Lee) L. BS, U. Rochester, 1978; MS, Calif. Inst. Tech., 1980, PhD, 1983. Rsch. assoc. Calif. Inst. Tech., Pasadena, 1983; asst. prof. geosciences U. Mich., Ann Arbor, 1984-88, assoc. prof., 1988-89; prof. U. Calif., Santa Cruz, 1989—. Cons. Woodward Clyde cons., Pasadena, 1982-84; dir. Inst. Tectonics, 1990-94, chmn. earth sci. dept., 1994-2000; dir. Inst. Geophysics and Planetary Physics, 2000—. Author: Structure and Fate of Subducting Slabs, 1997; co-author: (with T.C. Wallace) Modern Global Seismology, 1995; contbr. numerous articles to profl. jours. NSF fellow, 1978-81, Guttenberg fellow Calif. Inst. Tech., 1978, Lilly fellow Eli Lilly Found., 1984, Sloan fellow, 1985-87, Presidential Young Investigator, 1985-90. Fellow Royal Astron. Soc., Am. Geophys. Union (Macelwane medal 1991), Soc. Exploration Geophysicist, Seismol. Soc. Am., AAAS. Home: 2114 Harborview Ct Santa Cruz CA 95062-1678 Office: U Calif Santa Cruz Earth Sci Bd Santa Cruz CA 95064 E-mail: tlay@es.ucsc.edu

LAYDEN, FRANCIS PATRICK (FRANK LAYDEN), professional basketball team executive, former coach; b. Bklyn., Jan. 5, 1932; m. Barbara Layden; children: Scott, Michael, Katie. Student, Niagara U. High sch. basketball coach, L.I., N.Y.; head coach, athletic dir. Adelphi-Suffolk Coll. (now Dowling Coll.); head basketball coach, athletic dir. Niagara U.,

Niagara Falls, N.Y., 1968-76; asst. coach Atlanta Hawks, 1976-79; gen. mgr. Utah Jazz, Salt Lake City, 1979-88, head coach, 1981-88, v.p. basketball ops., until 1988, pres., 1989—. Bd. dirs. Utah Soc. Prevention Blindness; bd. dirs. Utah chpt. Multiple Sclerosis Soc., Utah Spl. Olympics. Served to 1st lt. Signal Corps, AUS. Office: Utah Jazz Delta Ctr 301 W South Temple Salt Lake City UT 84101-1216

LAYMAN, CHARLES DONALD, plastic surgeon; b. Portland, Mar. 20, 1949; MD, U Oreg. Health Scis. U., 1975. Plastic surgeon St. Vincent Med. Ctr., Portland. Clin. assoc. prof. plastic surgery U. Oreg. Health Sci. Ctr. Office: 9155 SW Barnes Rd Ste 220 Portland OR 97225-6629

LAZANO, MONICA, publishing executive; Assoc. pub. La Opinion, 1989-91, editor, 1991—; pres., CIO Lozano Comms. (parent co.). Mem. N.Y. Stock Exch. Individual Investors Adv. Com. Pub. spl. tabloid on AIDS (Advocacy award Hispanic Coalition on AIDS 1988, Best Pub. Svc. Publ., Inter-Am. Press Assn.). Trustee U. So. Calif., chair pub. affairs com.; vice-chmn. L.A. Annenberg Met. Project; mem. Calif. Citizens Commn. on Higher Edn.; bd. dirs. Venice Family Clinic, U.S., YMCA of Met. L.A., Nat. Coun. of La Raza; mem. adv. bd. Pub. Policy Inst. of Calif.; mem. Inter-Am. Dialogue and the Pacific Coun. on Internat. Policy. Recipient Distinction in Media Excellence award March of Dimes, 1991, Pub. Svc. Recognition award State Bar of Calif., 1992; named to 100 Most Influential Hispanic Women, Hispanic Bus. mag., 1987, 92, 96. Mem. Nat. Assn. of Women Bus. Owners, Nat. Assn. Hispanic Journalists, Calif. Chicano News Media Assn., Am. Soc. Newspaper Editors. Office: La Opinion 411 W 5th St Ste 1200 Los Angeles CA 90013-1028

LAZARUS, MELL, cartoonist; b. N.Y.C, May 3, 1927; s. Sidney and Frances (Mushkin) L.; m. Eileen Hortense Israel, June 19, 1949; children: Marjorie, Susan, Catherine; m. Sally Elizabeth Mitchell, May 13, 1995. Cartoonist-writer Miss Peach, 1957— , Momma, 1970— ; author anthologies Miss Peach, Miss Peach, Are These Your Children?, Momma, We're Grownups Now!; novels The Boss is Crazy, Too, 1964, The Neighborhood Watch, 1986; plays Everybody into the Lake, Elliman's Fly, Lifetime Eggcreams, 1969-70; juvenile Francine, Your Face Would Stop a Clock, 1975; co-author Miss Peach TV spl. programs Turkey Day Pageant and Annual Heart Throb Ball. Trustee Internat. Mus. Cartoon Art. With USNR, 1945, USAFR, 1951-54. Mem. Nat. Cartoonists Soc. (pres. 1989-93, chmn. membership com. 1965, nat. rep., Humor Strip Cartoonist of Yr. 1973, 79, Reuben award 1981, Silver T-Square award 2000), Writers Guild Am. West, Nat. Press Club, The Century Assn., Newspaper Features Coun. (bd. dirs.), Sigma Delta Chi. Office: Creators Syndicate Inc 5777 W Century Blvd Los Angeles CA 90045-5600

LAZARUS, RICHARD STANLEY, psychology educator; b. N.Y.C., Mar. 3, 1922; s. Abe and Matilda (Marks) L.; m. Bernice H. Newman, Sept. 2, 1945; children: David Alan, Nancy Eve. AB, CCNY, 1942; MS, U. Pitts., 1947, PhD, 1948; Dr. honoris causa, Johannes Gutenberg U., Mainz, Germany, 1988, U. Haifa, Israel, 1995. Diplomate in clin. psychology Am. Bd. Examiners in Profl. Psychology. Asst. prof. Johns Hopkins, 1948-53; psychol. cons. VA, 1952—; assoc. prof. psychology, dir. clin. tng. program Clark U., Worcester, Mass., 1953-57; assoc. prof. psychology U. Calif., Berkeley, 1957-59, prof., 1959-91, prof. emeritus, 1991—. Prin. investigator Air Force contracts dealing with psychol. stress, 1951-53, USPHS grant on personality psychol. stress, 1953-70; NIA, NIDA, and NCI grantee on stress, coping and health, 1977-81, MacArthur Found. research grantee, 1981-84; USPHS spl. fellow Waseda U., Japan, 1963-64 Author 23 books, including (autobiography) The Life and Work of an Eminent Psychologist, 1998; also numerous publs. in sci. jours. 1st lt. AUS, 1943-46. Recipient Disting. Sci. Achievement award Calif. State Psychol. Assn., 1984, Div. 38 Health Psychology, 1989; Guggenheim fellow, 1969-70; Army Rsch. Inst. rsch. grantee, 1973-75 Fellow AAAS, APA (Disting. Sci. Contbn. award 1989); mem. Western Psychol. Assn., Argentina Med. Assn. (hon.). Home: 1824 Stanley Dollar Dr Apt 3B Walnut Creek CA 94595-2833 Office: Univ Calif Dept Psychology Berkeley CA 94720-0001

LAZARUS, STEVEN S. management consultant, marketing consultant; b. Rochester, N.Y., June 16, 1943; s. Alfred and Ceal H. Lazarus; m. Elissa C. Lazarus, June 19, 1966; children: Michael, Stuart, Jean. BS, Cornell U., 1966; MS, Poly. U. N.Y., 1967; PhD, U. Rochester, 1974. Pres. Mgmt. Systems Analysis Corp., Denver, 1977—; dir. Sci. Application Intern Corp., Englewood, Colo., 1979-84; assoc. prof. Metro State Coll., Denver, 1983-84; sr. v.p. Pal Assocs. Inc., Denver, 1984-85; with strategic planning and mktg. McDonnell Douglas, Denver, 1985-86; mktg. cons. Clin. Reference Systems, Denver, 1986; pres. Mgmt. Sys. Analysis Corp., 1986-89, 95—; assoc. exec. dir. Ctr. Rsch. Ambulatory Health Care Adminstrn., Englewood, 1990-94. Spl. cons. State of Colo., Denver, 1976-81; mktg. cons. IMX, Louisville, 1986-87; speaker Am. Hosp. Assn., Chgo., 1983—; asst. sec. Work Group for Elec. Data Interchange, 1995-96, bd. dirs., 1997—, chmn. bd. elect, 2000, chmn. bd. dirs., 2001—; mng. prin., pres. Boundary Info. Group, 1995—. Contbr. chpts. to books; patentee med. quality assurance. NDEA fellow U. Rochester, 1968-71. Fellow Healthcare Info. and Mgmt. Systems Soc.; mem. Med. Group-Mgmt. Assn., Optimists (program chmn. Denver club 1976-78). Home: 7023 E Eastman Ave Denver CO 80224-2845 Office: MSA Corp 4401 S Quebec St Ste 100 Denver CO 80237-2644

LAZEAR, EDWARD PAUL, economics and labor relations educator, researcher; b. N.Y.C., Aug. 17, 1948; s. Abe and Rose (Karp) L.; m. Victoria Ann Allen, July 2, 1977; 1 child, Julia Ann A.B., A.M., UCLA, 1971; Ph.D., Harvard U., 1974; LLD (hon.), Albertson Coll., 1997. Asst. prof. econs. U. Chgo., 1974-78, assoc. prof. indsl. relations, 1978-81, prof. indsl. relations, 1981-85, Isidore and Gladys Brown prof. urban and labor econs., 1985-92; sr. fellow Hoover Instn. Stanford (Calif.) U., 1985—, coord. domestic studies Hoover Instn., 1987-90, prof. econs. and human resource mgmt. Grad. Sch. Bus., 1992-95, Jack Steele Parker prof. econs. and human resource mgmt., 1995—, mem. steering com. Stanford Inst. for Econ. Policy Rsch., 1996—. Econ. advisor to Romania, Czechoslovakia, Russia, Ukraine, Georgia; rsch. assoc. Nat. Bur. Econ. Rsch., Econs. Rsch. Ctr. of Nat. Opinion Rsch. Ctr.; chmn. rsch. adv. bd. World at Work; fellow Inst. Advanced Study, Hebrew U., Jerusalem, 1977-8; lectr. Inst. Advanced Study, Vienna, 1983-84, Nat. Productivity Bd., Singapore, 1982, 85; vis. prof. Inst. des Etudes Politiques, Paris, 1987; Wicksell lectr., Stockholm, 1993; chmn. Am. Comp. Assoc. Adv. Bd., 1999—. Author: (with R. Michael) Allocation of Income Within the Household, 1988; (with J.P. Gould) Microeconomic Theory, 1989, Personnel Economics, 1995, Personnel Economics for Managers, 1998; editor: Economic Transition in Eastern Europe and Russia, 1995; founding editor Jour. Labor Econs., 1982—; assoc. editor Jour. Econ. Perspectives, 1986-89, German Econ. Rev., 2000—; co-editor: Jour. Labor Abstracts, 1996—; contbr. numerous articles to scholarly jours. Recipient Leo Melamed prize for outstanding scholarship, 1998; NSF grad. fellow, 1971-74 Fellow Am. Acad. Arts and Scis., Econometric Soc., Soc. Labor Economists (1st v.p. 1995-96, pres. 1997-98); mem. Am. Econs. Assn. Home: 277 Old Spanish Trl Portola Valley CA 94028-8129 Office: Stanford U Grad Sch Bus Stanford CA 94305-5015 Also: Stanford Univ Hoover Inst Stanford CA 94305-6010

LEACH, ANTHONY RAYMOND, financial executive; b. Gerrards Cross, Eng., Nov. 11, 1939; came to U.S., 1969; s. John Raymond Geoffrey and Edith Eileen (Blackburn) L.; m. Shirley Ann Kidd, Apr. 17, 1965; children: Mark Irwin, Amanda Jane, Christopher John. Supr. Ernst & Whinney, London, 1957-63, San Francisco, 1967—, mgr. Paris, 1963-69; mgr. fin. acctg. Occidental Petroleum Corp., Los Angeles, 1965-74, asst. controller, 1974-81, v.p. acctg., 1981-91, v.p., contr., exec. v.p., CFO, 1991—, v.p. fin. Fellow Inst. Chartered Accts.; mem. Fin. Execs. Inst. Club: Palos Verdes Breakfast. Office: Occidental Petroleum Corp 10889 Wilshire Blvd Los Angeles CA 90024-4201

LEACH, JOHN F. editor, journalism educator; b. Montrose, Colo., Aug. 6, 1952; s. Darrell Willis and Marian Ruth (Hester) L.; m. Deborah C. Ross, Jan. 2, 1982; children: Allison, Jason. BS in Journalism, U. Colo., 1974, MA in Journalism, 1979; MA in Am. Studies, U. Sussex, Brighton, Eng., 1983. News reporter Boulder (Colo.) Daily Camera, 1974-79, The Ariz. Republic, Phoenix, 1979-85, asst. city editor, 1985-93; news editor The Phoenix Gazette, 1993-94; asst. mng. editor Phoenix Gazette, 1994-95, The Ariz. Republic and The Phoenix Gazette, 1995-97; sr. editor The Ariz. Republic, Phoenix, 1997-99, sr. editor for online news, 1999—. Faculty assoc. Ariz. State U., Tempe, 1990—; pres., dir. Best of the West, Phoenix. Bd. Regents scholar U. Colo., 1970, Rotary Found. scholar, 1982. Mem. Ariz. Press Club (treas. 1984-86, pres. 1986-87), Soc. Profl. Journalists, Soc. News Design, Newspaper Assn. Am. New Media Fedn. Office: The Ariz Republic 200 E Van Buren St Phoenix AZ 85004-2238 E-mail: john.leach@arizonarepublic.com

LEAHY, T. LIAM, business development, technology investor; b. Camp Legeunne, N.C., Apr. 15, 1952; s. Thomas James and Margaret May (Munnelly) L.; m. Shannon Kelly Brooks, Apr. 21, 1990. BS, St. Louis U., 1974, MA, 1975. V.p. sales Cablecom Inc., Chgo., 1976-80, Kaye Advt., N.Y.C., 1980-82; group pubr. Jour. Graphics Pub., N.Y.C., 1983-85; pres., gen. mgr. Generation Dynamics, N.Y.C., 1985-86; pres. Leahy & Assocs., N.Y.C., 1982-86, Tarzana, Calif., 1982—; assoc. Am Coun. of Execs. Assoc., Glendale, 1991-95. Bd. dirs. Cons. Assn., Tele-Interpreters, Inc.; dir. RBAC, 1998-2000. Contbr. articles to profl. jours. Fellow Success Mgmt. Ctrs. (sr.); mem. Turnaround Mgmt. Assn., L.A. C. of C. Avocations: music, film. Office: Leahy & Assocs 4209 Santa Monica Blvd Ste 201 Los Angeles CA 90029-3027

LEAL, GEORGE D. engineering company executive; b. 1934; B in Civil Engrng., MA, Santa Clara U., 1959. With Dames & Moore, Inc., L.A., 1959—, CEO, 1981—, now CEO, pres. Bd. dirs. BW/IP Internat. Inc. Office: Dames & Moore Inc 911 Wilshire Blvd Ste 700 Los Angeles CA 90017-3436

LEAL, STEVE, city council; married. BA in Polit. Sci., U. Calif. Property mgmt. and devel., 1985—; adminstrv. specialist Pima County, 1993—; city coun., 1989—. Cmty. svc. Salvation Army Hospitality House, Tucson-Pima County Hist. Commn., Citizens Adv. Commn. Democrat. Office: 4300 S Park Ave Tucson AZ 85714-1652

LEALE, OLIVIA MASON, import marketing company executive; b. Boston, May 5, 1944; d. William Mason and Jane Chapin (Prouty) Smith; m. Euan Harvie-Watt, Mar. 11, 1967 (div. Aug. 1979); children: Katrina, Jennifer; m. Douglas Marshall Leale, Aug. 29, 1980. BA, Vassar Coll., 1966. Cert. paralegal, beginning yoga instr. Sec. to dir. Met. Opera Guild, N.Y.C., 1966; sec. to pres. Friesons Printers, London, England, 1974-75; guide, trainer Autoguide, London, England, 1977-79; ptnr. Inmark Internat. Mktg. Inc., Seattle, 1980—; owner-mgr. Argus Ranch Facility For Dogs, 2001—. Social case worker Inner London Ednl. Authority, 1975-76. Democrat. Presbyterian. Avocations: reading, making doll house furniture, painting, knitting, dog agility. Home and Office: 1233 Shenandoah Dr E Seattle WA 98112-3727

LEAPHART, W. WILLIAM, state supreme court justice; b. Butte, Mont., Dec. 3, 1946; s. Charles William and Cornelia (Murphy) L.; m. Barbara Berg, Dec. 30, 1977; children: Rebecca, Retta, Ada. Student, Whitman Coll., 1965-66; BA, U. Mont., 1969, JD, 1972. Bar: Mont. 1972, U.S. Dist. Ct., U.S. Ct. Appeals (9th cir.) 1975, U.S. Supreme Ct. 1975. Law clk. to Hon. W.D. Murray U.S. Dist. Ct., Butte, 1972-74; ptnr. Leaphart Law Firm, Helena, Mont., 1974-94; justice Mont. Supreme Ct., Helena, 1995—. Office: Mont Supreme Ct Justice Bldg 215 N Sanders St Rm 315 Helena MT 59601-4522

LEAR, NORMAN MILTON, producer, writer, director; b. New Haven, July 27, 1922; s. Herman and Jeanette (Seicol) L.; children: Ellen, Kate B. Lear LaPook, Maggie B.; m. Lyn Davis; children: Benjamin Davis, Brianna, Madeline. Student, Emerson Coll., 1940-42, HHD, 1968. Engaged in pub. relations, 1945-49; founder Act III Comms., 1987—. Comedy writer for TV, 1950-54; writer, dir. for TV and films, 1954-59; prodr.:(films) Never Too Late, 1965, Start the Revolution Without Me, 1970, (TV) Sanford and Son, 1972, Maude, 1972, Good Times, 1974, Hot L Baltimore, 1975, All That Glitters, 1977, A Year at the Top, 1977, The Baxters, 1979, Sunday Dinner, 1991; exec. prodr.: (films) Fried Green Tomatoes, 1991, Way Past Cool, 2000, (TV), The Andy Williams Show, 1962, One Day at a Time, 1975, The Nancy Walker Show, 1976, Heartsounds, 1984, a.k.a. Pablo, 1984, 704 Hauser, 1994, Channel Umptee-3, 1997; prodr., dir., creator: (TV) All in the Family, 1971 (4 Emmy awards 1970-73, Peabody award 1977), The Powers That Be, 1992; prodr., screenwriter: (films) Come Blow Your Horn, 1963, Divorce American Style, 1967, The Night They Raided Minsky's, 1968; prodr., dir., screenwriter: Cold Turkey, 1971; screenwriter: Scared Stiff, 1953; creator: The Jeffersons, 1975, Fernwood 2-Night, 1977. Pres. Am. Civil Liberties Found. So. Calif., 1973—; trustee Mus. Broadcasting; bd. dirs. People for the American Way; founder Bus. Enterprise Trust. Served with USAAF, 1942-45. Decorated Air medal with 4 oak leaf clusters; named One of Top Ten Motion Picture Producers, Motion Picture Exhibitors, 1963, 67, 68, Showman of Yr., Publicists Guild, 1971-77, Assn. Bus. Mgrs., 1972, Broadcaster of Yr., Internat. Radio and TV Soc., 1973; Man of Yr. Hollywood chpt. Nat. Acad. Television Arts and Scis., 1973; recipient Humanitarian award NCCJ, 1976, Mark Twain award Internat. Platform Assn., 1977, William O. Douglas award Pub. Counsel, 1981, 1st Amendment Lectr. Ford Hall Forum, 1981, Gold medal Internat. Radio and TV Soc., 1981. Disting. Am. award, 1984, Mass Media award Am. Jewish Com. Inst. of Human Relations, 1986, Internat. award of Yr., Nat. Assn. TV Program Execs., 1987, Nat. Arts Medal, 1992; inducted into TV Acad. Hall of Fame, 1984. Mem. Writers Guild Am. (Valentine Davies award 1977), Dirs. Guild Am., AFTRA, Caucus Producers, Writers, and Dirs. Office: Act III Comm 1999 Avenue Of The Stars Los Angeles CA 90067-6022

LEAR, WILLIAM H. lawyer; b. 1939; BA magna cum laude, Yale U., 1961; JD, Duke U., 1965. Bar: Calif. 1966. Sr. v.p., gen. counsel, sec. Fleetwood Enterprises, Inc., Riverside, Calif. Office: Fleetwood Enterprises Inc 3125 Myers St PO Box 7638 Riverside CA 92513-7638

LEARNED, VINCENT ROY, electrical engineer, educator; b. San Jose, Calif., Jan. 21, 1917; m. Bernice Evelyn Brown, June 5, 1938; children: Daryl Vincent, Dean Charles, Craig Edwin, Kent Brudeen, Bruce Roy. BSEE, U. Calif., 1938; PhD, Stanford U., 1943. Dir. rsch. and devel. microwave tubes Sperry Rand Corp., 1943-65; prof. elec. and computer engr. San Diego State U., 1968-87, prof. emeritus, 1987—. Fellow Inst. Radio Engrs. Office: 2801 Cohasset Rd Apt 130 Chico CA 95973-0981

LEARY, DENIS, comedian; b. Boston, Aug. 18, 1957; m. Ann Lembeck; children: Jack, Devin. BFA, Emerson Coll., 1979. Films: The Sandlot, 1993, Who's the Man?, 1993, Judgment Night, 1993, Demolition Man, 1993, The Ref, 1994, Neon Bible, 1996, Wag the Dog, 1997, The Real Blonde, 1998, Suicide Kings, 1998, Monument Avenue, 1998, Love Walked In, 1998, A Bug's Life (voice), 1998, True Crime, 1999, The Thomas Crown Affair, 1999, Jesus' Son, 1999, Do Not Disturb, 1999; off Broadway appearances No Cure for Cancer, 1991-92, Lock 'n Load, 1997; TV spls. No Cure for Cancer, 1993, MTV Unplugged, 1993, A-hole, 1993, Lock 'n Load, 1997; dir., actor: Lust (Winner 1997 Cable Ace award best dir); albums include No Cure for Cancer, 1993, Lock 'n Load, 1997. Office: c/o UTA 9960 Wilshire Blvd Beverly Hills CA 90210-3116 also: Apostle Ed Sullivan Theatre 1697 Broadway New York NY 10019-5904

LEARY, G. EDWARD, state commisioner; m. Betty Chamberlain; 5 children. BS in Polit. Sci., U. Utah, 1971, MBA, 1981. Cert. Internat. Rels. With collections and lending dept. Draper Bank and Trust, 1974-77; examiner Utah Dept. Fin. Instns., Salt Lake City, 1977-82, industry supr., 1982-87, chief examiner, 1987-92, commr., 1992—. Chmn. Bd. Fin. Instns.; mem. Utah Housing Fin. Agy. Bd., Utah Appraiser Registration and Cert. Bd. With USN, 1971-73. Capt. USNR, ret. 1995. Mem. Conf. State Bank Supr. (chmn.-elect). Office: Utah Dept Fin Instns PO Box 89 Salt Lake City UT 84110-0089

LEASE, RONALD CHARLES, financial economics educator; b. Davenport, Iowa, Feb. 3, 1940; s. Mace Duane and Mary Virginia (Marsh) L.; m. Judy Ellen Gifford, Aug. 24, 1962; 1 child, Tracy Rene. BS in Engring., Colo. Sch. Mines, 1963; MS, Purdue U., 1966, PhD, 1973. Metall. engr. Aluminum Co. Am., 1963-69; prof. U. Utah, Salt Lake City, 1973-86; prof., chmn. Tulane U., New Orleans, 1986-90, endowed prof., assoc. dean, 1988-90; endowed prof. U. Utah, Salt Lake City, 1990—. Vis. assoc. prof. U. Chgo., 1978-79; vis. prof. U. Mich., Ann Arbor, 1985-86. Mem. editorial bd. Jour. Fin. Rsch., Phoenix, 1987-93, Fin. Mgmt., Tampa, 1986-98, Jour. Corp. Fin., Pitts., 1993—; contbr. articles to profl. jours. Mem. Am. Fin. Assn., Western Fin. Assn., Fin. Mgmt. Assn. (editor Survey and Synthesis in Fin. 1984-90, pres. 1992-93, chmn. bd. dirs. 1996-99), Phi Kappa Phi, Beta Gamma Sigma. Home: PO Box 486 Driggs ID 83422-0486 Office: U Utah Eccles Sch Bus Salt Lake City UT 84112

LEAVELL, CARROLL H. state legislator; b. Clovis, N.Mex., Oct. 23, 1936; BA, Eastern N.Mex. U. Ins. agt., N.Mex.; real estate broker; mem. N.Mex. Senate, Dist. 41, Santa Fe, 1996—; mem. conservation com. N.Mex. Senate, mem. pub. affairs com. Republican. Office: Drawer D Rm 423 Jal NM 88252

LEAVITT, MICHAEL OKERLUND, governor, insurance executive; b. Cedar City, Utah, Feb. 11, 1951; s. Dixie and Anne (Okerlund) L.; m. Jacalyn Smith; children: Michael Smith, Taylor Smith, Anne Marie Smith, Chase Smith, Weston Smith. BA, So. Utah U., 1978. CPCU. Sales rep. Leavitt Group, Cedar City, 1972-74, account exec., 1974-76, mgr. underwriting Salt Lake City, 1976-82, chief operating officer, 1982-84, pres., chief exec. officer, 1984-92; gov. State of Utah, 1993—. Bd. dirs. Pacificorp, Portland, Oreg., Utah Power and Light Co., Salt Lake City, Great Western Thrift and Loan, Salt Lake City. Utah Bd. Regents, chmn. instl. coun. So. Utah State U., Cedar City, 1985-89; campaign chmn. U.S. Sen. Orrin Hatch, 1982, 88, U.S. Sen. Jake Garn, 1980, 86; cons. campaign Gov. Norman Angerter, 1984; mem. staff Reagan-Bush '84. 2d lt. USNG, 1969-77. Named Disting. Alumni So. Utah State Coll. Sch. Bus., 1986. Mem. CPCU. Republican. Mormon. Avocation: golf. Office: Office Gov 210 State Capitol Building Salt Lake City UT 84114-1202*

LEAVITT, MYRON E. state supreme court justice; Justice Nev. Supreme Court, Carson City. Office: Supreme Ct Capitol Complex 201 S Carson S Carson City NV 89710-0001

LEAVY, EDWARD, judge; m. Eileen Leavy; children: Thomas, Patrick, Mary Kay, Paul. AB, U. Portland, 1950, LLB, U. Notre Dame, 1953. Dist. judge Lane County, Eugene, Oreg., 1957-61, cir. judge, 1961-76; magistrate U.S. Dist. Ct. Oreg., Portland, 1976-84, judge, 1984-87, cir. judge U.S. Ct. Appeals (9th cir.), 1987-97, sr. judge, 1997—. Office: US Ct Appeals Pioneer Courthouse 555 SW Yamhill St Ste 232 Portland OR 97204-1323*

LEBEAU, CHARLES PAUL, lawyer; b. Detroit, Dec. 11, 1944; s. Charles Henry Jr. and Mary Barbara (Moran) L.; m. Victoria Joy (Huchin), May 15, 1970; children: Jeffrey Kevin, Timothy Paul. AA, Macomb County Community Coll., Warren, Mich., 1967; BA, Wayne State U., 1969; JD, U. Detroit, 1972; grad. tax program, NYU Sch. Law, 1972-73. Bar: Mich. 1973, U.S. Tax Ct. 1973, Calif. 1987, U.S. Ct. Internat. Trade. 1988, U.S. Supreme Ct. 1988, U.S. Dist. Ct. (so. dist.) Calif. 1988. Tax atty. Ford Motor Co., Dearborn, Mich., 1973-75; assoc. Hoops & Huff, Detroit, 1975-76, Miller, Canfield, Paddock & Stone, Detroit, 1976-78; tax mgr. Oceaneering Internat., Santa Barbara, Calif., 1978-79; tax counsel Signal Cos. Inc., Beverly Hills and La Jolla, 1979-83; assoc. Gray, Cary, Ames & Frye, San Diego, 1983-84; of counsel James Watts Esq., La Jolla, 1985, Murfey, Griggs & Frederick, La Jolla, 1986; pvt. practice La Jolla and San Diego, 1987—. Lectr. grad. tax program Golden Gate U., San Diego, 1979-87; adj. prof. law U. San Diego, 1982-85, 88-89; mem. Law Rev., U. Detroit, 1971-72; lectr. in taxation. Contbr. articles on internat. tax to profl. jours.; monthly tax case commentator Taxes Internat., London, 1981-85. Campaign coord. United Way, Santa Barbara, 1979. Recipient Congrl. Medal of Merit, 1999, Presdl. Medal of Honor, 2000, Rep. of Yr., Calif., 2000. Mem. ABA, Mich. Bar Assn., Calif. Bar Assn., San Diego County Bar Assn., Pi Sigma Alpha. Republican. Roman Catholic. Avocations: sailing, tennis, walking. Home: 1999 Via Segovia La Jolla CA 92037-6441 Office: Law Offices Charles LeBeau Hist Hayward Patterson Bldg 2148 Broadway San Diego CA 92102-1829

LEBER, MIKE, advertising executive; Chief fin. officer Alcone Mktg. Group, Irvine, Calif. Office: Alcone Mktg Co 4 Studebaker Irvine CA 92618-2012

LE BERTHON, ADAM, lawyer; b. L.A., June 12, 1962; s. Edward Lynch and Veronica Rose (Franks) Le B; m. Kelly Elizabeth McKee, Mar. 23, 1996; children: John Thomas, Ryan Michael. BA cum laude with dept. honors, U. San Diego, 1985; JD, U. So. Calif., L.A., 1989. Bar: Calif. 1989, U.S. Dist. Ct. (ctrl. dist.) Calif. 1989, U.S. Ct. Appeals (9th cir.) 1989, U.S. Dist. Ct. (so. dist.) Calif. 1990, (no. dist.) Calif. 1990, (ea. dist.) Calif. 1990. Assoc. White & Case, L.A., 1989-91, Straw & Gilmartin, Santa Monica, Calif., 1991-97; ptnr. Gilmartin & Le Berthon LLP, Santa Monica, 1997-99; assoc. Arnold & Porter, L.A., 1999—. Editor So. Calif. Law Rev., 1988-89; contbr. articles to profl. jours. Recipient Am. Jurisprudence award U. So. Calif., 1987. Mem. Calif. State Bar Assn., L.A. County Bar Assn., Order of the Coif, Phi Alpha Delta, Omicron Delta Epsilon, Kappa Gamma Pi. Home: 27621 Harwick Pl Valencia CA 91354-1925 Office: Arnold & Porter 44th Fl 777 S Figueroa St Los Angeles CA 90017-5800 E-mail: adam_le_berthon@aporter.com

LE BLANC, SUZANNE, museum director; Exec. dir. Lied Discovery Children's Mus., Las Vegas, Nev. Office: Lied Discovery Childrens Mus 833 Las Vegas Blvd N Las Vegas NV 89101-2059

LEBLANC, TINA, dancer; b. Erie, Pa. m. Marco Jerkunica, May 1988; 1 child, Marinko James. Trained, Carlisle, Pa. Dancer Joffrey II Dancers, N.Y.C., 1982-83, The Joffrey Ballet, N.Y.C., 1984-92; prin. dancer San Francisco Ballet, 1992—. Guest tchr. Ctrl. Pa. Youth Ballet, 1992, 94—. Work includes roles in (with San Francisco Ballet) Con Brio, Bizet Pas de Deux, Swan Lake, Nanna's Lied, Handel -- A Celebration, La fille mal gardée, Rubies, Tchaikovsky Pas de Deux, Seeing Stars, The Nutcracker, La Pavane Rouge, Company B, Romeo and Juliet, Sleeping Beauty, The Dance House, Terra Firma, Lambarena, Fly by Night, In the Night, Ballo della Regina, The Lesson, The Tuning Game, Quartette, Etudes, Western Symphony, Maelstrom, Pacific, Criss-Cross, Giselle, Theme and Variations, Gala Performance, The Vertiginous Thrill of Exactitude, Taiko, Sandpaper Ballet, La Bayadere, Night, Serenade, Celts, Stars & Stripes, Tarantella; (with other companies) The Green Table, Les Presages, Le sacre du printemps, Les Noces, Light Rain, Romeo and Juliet, Runaway Train, Empyrean Dances, La Vivandière, L'air D'esprit, Corsaire Pas de deux, Don Quixote pas de deux, Lacrymosa, Confetti, Kettentanz Le Beau Danube, Offenbach in the Underworld, Suite Saint Saens, Forgotten Land, Dream Dances, Postcards, Remembrances, Reflections. Recipient Princess Grace Found. award, 1988, Princess Grace Statuette award, 1995. Office: San Francisco Ballet Assn 455 Franklin St San Francisco CA 94102-4471

LECHELT, EUGENE CARL, psychology educator; b. Edmonton, Alta., Can., Dec. 26, 1942; s. Adolph Carl and Natalie (Klapstein) L.; m. Sandra Dona Morris, Dec. 18, 1965; 1 child, David Patrick. BSc, U. Alta., 1964, MSc, 1966, PhD, 1969. Rsch. assoc., lectr. Princeton U., N.J., 1969-72; asst. prof. dept. psychology U. Alta., Edmonton, 1972-76, assoc. prof., 1976-82, prof., 1982—, chmn., 1986-97, dir. Vision Loss Applied Rsch. Inst. dept. psychology, 1998—. Recipient Rutherford Tchg. award, 1985, Vol. award Fed. Govt. Can., 1994; U. Alta. dissertation fellow, 1968-69; Social Scis. Rsch. Coun. Can. fellow, 1978-79. Mem. AAAS, Psychonomic Soc., Can. Psychol. Assn., N.Y. Acad. Scis., Sigma Xi. Home: # 1207 10883 Saskatchewan Dr Edmonton AB Canada T6E 4S6 Office: U Alta Dept Psychology Edmonton AB Canada T6G 2E9

LECLERC, ROBERT L. mining company executive; b. 1944; Chmn., CEO Milner Fenerty, Calgary and Edmonton, Can.; legal counsel Echo Bay Mines, Englewood, Colo., dir., chmn., 1996—, CEO, chmn. bd., 1997—. Office: Ste 1000 6400 S Fiddlers Green Cir Englewood CO 80111-4957

LEDER, MIMI, television director; b. N.Y.C., Jan. 26, 1952; d. Paul and Etyl Leder; m. Gary Werntz, Feb. 6, 1986; 1 child, Hannah. Student, Los Angeles City College, Am. Film Inst. Dir. TV movies A Little Piece of Heaven (also known as Honor Bright), 1991, Woman with a Past, 1992, Rio Shannon, 1992, Marked for Murder, 1992, There Was a Little Boy, 1993, House of Secrets, 1993, The Sandman, 1993, The Innocent, 1994; dir. TV series L.A. Law, 1986, Midnight Caller, 1988, A Year in the Life, 1988, Buck James, 1988, Just in Time, 1988, Crime Story, 1988; dir. movies, The Peacemaker, 1997, Deep Impact, 1998; supervising prodr. China Beach, 1988-91 (Emmy nominations for outstanding drama series 1989, 90, and outstanding directing in drama series 1990, 91), Nightingales, 1989, ER, 1994— (Emmy award 1995). Mem. Dirs. Guild Am. Office: c/o CAA 9830 Wilshire Blvd Beverly Hills CA 90212-1804

LEDERER, MARION IRVINE, cultural administrator; b. Brampton, Ont., Can., Feb. 10, 1920; d. Oliver Bateman and Eva Jane (MacMurdo) L.; m. Francis Lederer, July 10, 1941. Student, U. Toronto, 1938, UCLA, 1942-45. Owner Canoga Mission Gallery, Canoga Park, Calif., 1967—, cultural heritage monument, 1974—. Vice pres. Screen Smart Set women's aux. Motion Picture and TV Fund, 1973—; founder sister city program Canoga Park-Taxco, Mexico, 1963; Mem. mayor's cultural task force San Fernando Valley, 1973—; mem. Los Angeles Cultural Affairs Commn., 1980-85. Mem. Los Angeles Cultural Affairs Commn., 1980-85. Recipient numerous pub. service awards from mayor, city council, C. of C. Mem. Canoga Park C. of C. (cultural chmn. 1973-75, dir. 1973-75) Presbyn. Home: PO Box 32 Canoga Park CA 91305-0032 Office: Canoga Mission Gallery 23130 Sherman Way Canoga Park CA 91307-1402

LEDERER, RICHARD HENRY, writer, educator, columnist; b. Phila., May 26, 1938; s. Howard Jules and Leah (Perry) L.; m. Rhoda Anne Spangenberg, Aug. 25, 1962 (div. 1986); m. Simone Johanna van Egeren, Nov. 29, 1991; children: Howard Henry, Anne Labarr, Katherine Lee. BA, Haverford Coll., 1959; student, Harvard U., 1959-60, M of Arts and Teaching, 1962; PhD, U. N.H., 1980. Tchr., coach St. Paul's Sch., Concord, N.H., 1962-89. Lectr. in field. Author: Anguished English, 1987, Get Thee to a Punnery, 1988, Crazy English, 1989, The Play of Words, 1990, The Miracle of Language, 1991, More Anguished English, 1993, Building Bridge, 1994, Adventures of a Verbivore, 1994, Literary Trivia, 1994, Nothing Risqué, Nothing Gained, 1995, The Write Way, 1995, Pun and Games, 1996, Fractured English, 1996, The Word Circus, 1998. Sleeping Dogs Don't Lay, 1999 (book of the month club selection), The Bride of Anguished English, 2000, The Circus of Words, 2001, Word Play Crosswords, 2001; usage editor Random House Dictionary of the English Language Unabridged, 3d edit., 2000; weekly columnist Looking at Lang.; contbr. over 2000 articles to mags. and jours.; broadcaster various radio stas.; numerous TV appearances; host A Way With Words KPBS, San Diego. Recipient Lifetime Achievement award Columbia Scholastic Press Assn., N.Y.C., 1989, Leadership in Comms. award San Diego Toastmasters; named Internat. Punster of Yr. Internat. Save the Pun Found., Toronto, Can., 1990; Paul Harris Rotary fellow. Mem. Am. Mensa, Phi Beta Kappa, Phi Delta Kappa. Avocations: tennis, cards, film. Office: 9974 Scripps Ranch Blvd San Diego CA 92131-1825

LEDERIS, KAROLIS PAUL (KARL LEDERIS), pharmacologist, educator, researcher; b. Noreikoniai, Lithuania, Aug. 1, 1920; arrived in Can., 1969; s. Paul Augustus and Franciska (Danisevicius) L.; m. Hildegard Gallistl, Feb. 28, 1952 (dec. Nov. 2000); children: Aldona Franciska, Edmund Paul. Diploma, Tchrs. Coll., Siauliai, Lithuania, 1939; BSc, U. Bristol, U.K., 1958, PhD, 1961, DSc, 1968. From jr. lectr. to reader U. Bristol, 1961-69; prof. pharmacology and therapeutics U. Calgary, Alta., Can., 1969-89, prof. emeritus Can., 1989—. Vis. prof. univs. in Fed. Republic Germany, Austria, Chile, Argentina, Sri Lanka, Switzerland, Lithuania, France, , USA, USSR, 1963-79, U. Bristol, 1979, U. Kyoto, Japan, 1980; career investigator, mem., chair grants com. Med. Rsch. Coun., Ottawa, Ont., Can., 1970-89, coun. mem., exec., 1983-90; mem. internat. com. Centres Excellence Networks, Ottawa, 1988-89. Author, editor: 5 books on hypothalamic hormones; editor in chief Jour. Exptl. and Clin. Pharmacology, 1977-89; contbr. approximately 350 book chpts. and articles to profl. jours.; patentee hormonal peptides. Recipient Upjohn award in pharmacology, 1990, various fellowships and scholarships in U.K., Fed. Republic of Germany, U.S. Fellow NAS, Royal Soc. Can.; mem. Western Pharmacological Soc. (pres. 1982-83), Lithuanian Club (London), Men's Can. Club, Cabot Yacht and Cruise Club (Bristol). Avocations: music, sailing, golf. Home: 147 Carthew St Comox BC Canada V9M 1T4 Office: U Calgary Health Scis Centre Calgary AB Canada T2N 4N1 E-mail: klederis@home.com

LEDYARD, JOHN ODELL, economics educator, consultant; b. Detroit, Apr. 4, 1940; s. William Hendrie and Florence (Odell) L.; m. Bonnie Higginbottom, May 23, 1970; children: Stephen, J. Henry, Meg. BA, Wabash Coll., 1963; PhD, Purdue U., 1967; PhD (hon.), Purdue U./Ind. U., 1993. Asst. prof. Carnegie-Mellon U., Pitts., 1967-70; prof. Northwestern U., Evanston, Ill., 1970-85, Calif. Inst. Tech., Pasadena, 1985—, exec. officer for social sci., 1989-92, chmn. div. humanities and social scis., 1992—. Contbr. articles to profl. jours. Fellow Am. Acad. Arts and Scis., Econometric Soc.; mem. Pub. Choice Soc. (pres. 1980-82), Econ. Sci. Assn. (exec. com. 1986-88). Office: Calif Inst Tech Dept Econs Pasadena CA 91125-0001

LEE, BARBARA, congresswoman; BA, Mills Coll., 1973; M in Social Welfare, U. Calif. Berkeley, 1976. Rep. Calif. State Assembly, 1990-96; mem. Calif. State Sen., 1996-98, U.S. Congress from 9th Calif. dist., Washington, 1998—; mem. fin. svcs. com., internat. rels. com. Democrat. Office: US Ho Reps 426 Cannon Ho Office Bldg Washington DC 20515-0001*

LEE, DAVID, fiber optics company executive; Grad., McGill U.; D of Physics & Econs., Calif. Inst. Tech. CPA. With Arthur Andersen & Co.; various exec. positions Comsat; group v.p. fin. & acquisitions TRW Info. Systems Group, until 1989; with Pacific Capital Group, 1989-97; CEO Global Crossings Ltd., Beverly Hills, Calif., 1997—. Office: Global Crossings Ltd 360 N Crescent Dr Beverly Hills CA 90210-4802

LEE, DAVID MALLIN, physicist; b. Bklyn., Jan. 18, 1944; s. George Francis Lee and Winifred Rita (Jones) Wyatt; m. Judith Carol Silliman, Aug. 20, 1966; children: David, Timothy, Karen, Jeffrey, Rebecca. BS, Mannhattan Coll., 1966; PhD, U. Va., 1971. Vis. mem. staff Los Alamos (N.Mex) Nat. Lab., 1971-74, mem. staff, 1974-80, 81—; U.S. tech. expert IAEA, Vienna, Austria, 1980-81. Patentee in field. Mem. Am. Phys. Soc., AAAS, Sigma Xi. Democrat. Roman Catholic. Home: 48 Wildflower Way Santa Fe NM 87501-8616 E-mail: dLee@lanl.gov

LEE, GLENN RICHARD, medical administrator, educator; b. Ogden, Utah, May 18, 1932; s. Glenn Edwin and Thelma (Jensen) L.; m. Pamela Marjorie Ridd, July 18, 1969; children— Jennifer, Cynthia. B.S., U. Utah, 1953, M.D., 1956. Intern Boston City Hosp.-Harvard U., 1956-57, resident, 1957-58; clin. asso. Nat. Cancer Inst., NIH, 1958-60; postdoctoral fellow U. Utah, 1960-63; instr. U. Utah Coll. Medicine, 1963-64, asst. prof. internal medicine, 1964-68, assoc. prof., 1968-73, prof., 1973-96, assoc. dean for acad. affairs, 1973-76, dean, 1978-83, prof. emeritus, 1996—; chief of staff Salt Lake VA Med. Ctr., 1985-95. Author: (with others) Clinical Hematology, 10th edit, 1998; Contbr. (with others) numerous articles to profl. jours.; editorial bd.: (with others) Am. Jour. Hematology, 1976-79. Served with USPHS, 1958-60. Markle Found. scholar, 1965-70; Nat. Inst. Arthritis, Metabolic and Digestive Disease grantee, 1977-82. Mem. A.C.P., Am. Soc. Hematology, Am. Soc. Clin. Investigation, Western Assn. Physicians, Am. Inst. Nutrition. Mem. LDS Ch. Home and Office: 3781 Ruth Dr Salt Lake City UT 84124-2331 E-mail: grichardl@aol.com

LEE, HI YOUNG, physician, acupuncturist; b. Seoul, Korea, Oct. 18, 1941; came to U.S., 1965, naturalized, 1976; s. Jung S. and Hwa J. (Kim) L.; m. Sun M. Lee, June 4, 1965; children: Sandra, Grace, David. MD, Yon Sei U., Seoul, 1965. Diplomate Am. Bd. Family Practice. Intern Grasslands Hosp., Valhalla, N.Y., 1965-66; resident VA Hosp., Dayton, Ohio, 1966-70; mem. staff Eastern State Hosp., Medical Lake, Wash., 1970-74; practice family medicine, acupuncturist Empire Med. Office, Spokane, 1974—. Active staff St. Lukes Meml. Hosp., Spokane, 1974—, bd. trustees St. Georges Prep Sch., Wash., 1986—; courtesy staff Deaconess Med. Center, Spokane, 1974—, Sacred Heart Med. Ctr., Spokane, 1974—. Author: Von Recklinghousen's Disease, 1970 (McDermit award); columnist Rainier Forum Korea Post Weekly News, 1996—. Elder First Presbyn. Ch., Spokane, 1975. Fellow Am. Acad. Family Practice; mem. Ctr. for Chinese Medicine, Spokane County Med. Soc., Nat. Acupuncture Rsch. Soc., Christian Med. Soc. Home: 2006 W Liberty Ave Spokane WA 99205-2570 Office: Empire Med Office 17 E Empire Ave Spokane WA 99207-1707 E-mail: acupuncture@u.s.west.net

LEE, JERRY CARLTON, university administrator; b. Roanoke, Va., Nov. 21, 1941; m. Joan Marie Leo; 1 child, Zan. BA, W.Va. Wesleyan Coll., 1963; postgrad., W.Va. U. Grad. Sch. Indsl. Relations, 1963-64, U. Balt. Sch. Law, 1967-69; MA, Va. Poly. Inst., 1975, EdD, 1977; LLD (hon.), Gallaudet U., 1986. Mgmt. trainee Gen. Motors Corp., 1964-65; v.p. adminstrn. Comml. Credit Indsl. Corp., Washington, 1965-71; dir. gen. services Gallaudet Coll., Washington, 1971-77, asst. v.p. bus. affairs, 1978-82, v.p. adminstrn. and bus., 1982-84; pres. Gallaudet U. (formerly Gallaudet Coll.), Washington, 1984-88, Nat. U., San Diego, 1989—. Hon. bd. dirs. D.C. Spl. Olympics; commn. in adminstrn. org. Rehab. Internat.; bd. dirs. People to People, Deafness Research Found., Am. Assn. Univ. Adminstrs., Am. Coun. on Edn. Commn. on Women in Higher Edn.; hon. advocacy bd. Nat. Capital Assn. Coop. Edn.; mem. Personnel Policies Forum Bur. Nat. Affairs. Served with USAR, 1966-72. Recipient Nat. Service award, Hon. Pres. award Council for Better Hearing and Speech, 1986, One-of-a-Kind award People-to-People, 1987, Advancement Human Rights & Fundamental Freedoms award UN, U.S.A., Disting. Alumni award Va. Poly. Inst., 1985, Pres.' award Gallaudet Coll. Alumni Assn., Gallaudet Community Relations award, U.S. Steel Found. Cost Reduction Incentive award Nat. Assn. Coll. and Univ. Bus. Officers, award Am. Athletic Assn. Deaf, 1987 Mem. Am. Assn. Univ. Adminstrs. (Eileen Tosney award 1987), Consortium of Univs. Washington Met. Area (exec. com.), Nat. Collegiate Athletic Assn. (pres.' commn.), Nat. Assn. Coll. Aux. Services (jour. adv. bd., journalism award), Alpha Sigma Pi (Man of Yr. award 1983-84). Lodge: Sertoma (life, found. nat. adv. com.). Avocations: tennis, long distance running, weightlifting. Office: Nat Univ 11255 N Torrey Pines Rd La Jolla CA 92037-1011

LEE, JIMMY S.M. electronic executive; Chmn., pres., CEO Integrated Silicon Solutions, Inc., Santa Clara, Calif. Office: Integrated Silicon Solutions Inc 2231 Lawson Ln Santa Clara CA 95054-3311

LEE, JOHN MARSHALL, mathematics educator; b. Phila., Sept. 2, 1950; s. Warren W. and Virginia (Hull) L.; m. Pm Weizenbaum, May 26, 1984; children: Nathan Lee Weizenbaum, Jeremy Lee Weizenbaum. AB, Princeton U., 1972; student, Tufts U., 1977-78; PhD, MIT, 1982. Systems programmer Tex. Instruments, Princeton, N.J., 1972-74; Geophys. Fluid Dynamics Lab., GFDL/NOAA, Princeton, 1974-75; tchr. math. and physics Wooster Sch., Danbury, Conn., 1975-77; programmer and cons. info. processing svcs. MIT, Cambridge, Mass., 1978-82; asst. prof. math. Harvard U., Cambridge, 1982-87, U. Wash., Seattle, 1987-89, assoc. prof. math., 1989-96, prof. math., 1996—. Sr. tutor Harvard U., Cambridge, 1984-87. Author: Riemannian Manifolds: An Introduction to Curvature, 1997, Introduction to Topological Manifolds, 2000; contbr. articles to profl. jours. Rsch. fellow NSF, 1982. Mem. Am. Math. Soc. (Centennial fellow 1989). Avocations: hiking, wine tasting, music. Home: 5637 12th Ave NE Seattle WA 98105-2603 Office: Univ Wash Math Dept PO Box 354350 Seattle WA 98195-4350 E-mail: lee@math.washington.edu

LEE, KENNETH, secondary education educator; Tchr. Highlands Intermediate Sch., Pearl City, Hawaii, 1986—. Recipient Tchr. Excellence award Internat. Tech. Edn. Assn., Hawaii, 1992. Office: Highlands Intermediate Sch 1460 Hoolaulea St Pearl City HI 96782-2198

LEE, LORRIN L. marketing executive, architect, designer, writer, speaker; b. Honolulu, July 22, 1941; s. Bernard Chong and Betty (Lum) L.; m. Nina Christine Fedoroscko, June 10, 1981. BArch, U. Mich., 1970; MBA, PhD in Psychology, Columbia Pacific U., 1981. Registered arch., Hawaii. Arch. Clifford Young AIA, Honolulu, 1971-72, Aotani & Oka AIA, Honolulu, 1972-74, Geoffrey Fairfax FAIA, Honolulu, 1974-76; seminar leader Lorrin Lee Program, Honolulu, 1976-81; star grand master coord. Enhance Corp., 1981-83; 5-diamond supr. Herbalife Internat., L.A., 1983—, mem. global expansion team, 1993—; presdl. dir. Uni-Vite Internat., San Diego, 1989-92; rep. Internat. Pen Friends, 1995—; mgr. Cyber Media Sales, 1996-2000; dealer Cajun Country Candies, 2000—. Author: Here is Genius, 1980. Editor Honolulu Chinese Jaycees, Honolulu, 1972, v.p., 1983; active Makiki Cmty. Ctr., Honolulu, 1974. 1st lt. U.S. Army, 1967-70, Okinawa. Recipient Braun-Knect-Heimann award, 1959, 1st prize in design Kidjel Cali-Pro Internat., 1975, Kitchen Design award Sub-zero Contest, 1994; named Honolulu Chinese Jaycee of Yr., Honolulu Chinese Jaycees, 1973. Mem. Nature Conservancy, Sierra Club. Avocations: international travel, hiking, desktop publishing, photography, reading. Office: 758 Kapahulu Ave # 101 Honolulu HI 96816-1196 Fax: 808-947-8817. E-mail: lorrin@lorrinlee.com

LEE, MARGARET ANNE, psychotherapist, social worker; b. Scribner, Nebr., Nov. 23, 1930; d. William Christian and Caroline Bertha (Benner) Joens; m. Robert Kelly Lee, May 21, 1950 (div. 1972); children: Lawrence Robert, James Kelly, Daniel Richard. AA, Napa Coll., 1949; student, U. Calif., Berkeley, 1949-50; BA, Calif. State Coll., Sonoma, 1975; MSW, Calif. State U., Sacramento, 1977. Diplomate clin. social worker; lic. clin. social worker, Calif.; lic. marriage and family counselor, Calif.; tchr. Columnist, stringer Napa (Calif.) Register, 1946-50; eligibility worker, supr. Napa County Dept. Social Services, 1968-75; instr. Napa Valley Community Coll., 1978-83; practice psychotherapy Napa, 1977—; oral commr. Calif. Dept. Consumer Affairs, Bd. Behavioral Sci., 1984-90. Bd. dirs. Project Access, 1978-79. Trustee Napa Valley C.C., 1983—, v.p. bd., 1984-85, pres. bd., 1986, 90, 95, clk., 1988-89; bd. dirs. Napa County Coun. Econ. Opportunity, 1984-85, Napa chpt. March of Dimes, 1957-71, Mental Health Assn. Napa County, 1983-87; vice chmn. edn. com. Calif. C.C. Trustees, 1987-88, chmn. edn. com., 1988-89, legis. com., 1985-87, bd. dirs., 1989-99, 2d v.p., 1991, 1st v.p., 1992, pres., 1993; mem. student equity rev. group Calif. C.C. Chancellors, 1992; bd. dirs. C.C. League Calif., 1992-95, 1st v.p., 1992; appointed mem. Nape County Paratransit Coord. Coun., 1999—. Recipient Fresh Start award Self mag., award Congl. Caucus on Women's Issues, 1984; named Woman of distinction, Soroptimist Internat. and Sunrise Clubs of Napa, 1997. Mem. NASW, Calif. Elected Women's Assn. Edn. and Rsch. Democrat. Lutheran. Office: 1100 Trancas St Napa CA 94558-2908

LEE, MARTHA, artist, writer; b. Chehalis, Wash., Aug. 23, 1946; d. William Robert and Phyllis Ann (Herzog) L.; m. Peter Reynolds Lockwood, Jan. 25, 1974 (div. 1982). BA in English Lit., U. Wash., 1968; student, Factory of Visual Art, 1980-82. Reporter Seattle Post-Intelligencer, 1970; personnel counselor Theresa Snow Employment, 1971-72; receptionist Northwest Kidney Ctr., 1972-73; proprietress The Reliquary, 1974-77; travel agt. Cathay Express, 1977-79; artist, 1980—; represented by Mahler Fine Arts, Seattle, Pacific Rim Gallery, Astoria, Oreg., Cannon Beach. Painter various oil paintings; exhibited in numerous one-woman and group shows throughout Pacific N.W. and Washington; author: To The Beach and Other Poems, 1998. Avocations: horseback riding, beachcombing, reading, music. Home: PO Box 1157 Ocean Park WA 98640-1157

LEE, PHILIP RANDOLPH, medical educator; b. San Francisco, Apr. 17, 1924; divorced; 5 children; 1 stepdaughter. AB, Stanford U., 1945, MD, 1948; MS, U. Minn., 1956; DSc (hon.), MacMurray Coll., 1967; PhD (hon.), Ben Gurion U., Israel, 1995, St. George U., , 1998. Diplomate Am. Bd. Internal Medicine. Asst. prof. clin. phys. medicine and rehab. NYU, 1955-56; clin. instr. medicine Stanford (Calif.) U., 1956-59, asst. clin. prof., 1959-67; asst. sec. health and sci. affairs Dept. HEW, Washington, 1965-69; chancellor U. Calif., San Francisco, 1969-72, prof. social medicine, 1969-93, dir. inst. health policy studies, 1972-93; asst. sec. U.S. Dept. HHS, Washington, 1993-97; prof. emeritus, sr. advisor Inst. Health Policy, San Francisco, 1997—; cons. prof. human biology program Stanford U., 1997—. Mem. dept. internal medicine Palo Alto Med. Clinic, Calif., 1956-65; cons. bur. pub. health svc. USPHS, 1958-63, adv. com., 1978, nat. commn. smoking & pub. policy, 1977-78; dir. health svc. office tech. cooperation & rsch. AID, 1963-65; dep. asst. sec. health & sci. affairs HEW, 1965, mem. nat. coun. health planning & devel., 1978-80; co-dir. inst. health & aging, sch. nursing U. Calif., San Francisco, 1980-93; pres. bd. dirs. World Inst. Disability, 1984-93; mem. population com. Nat. Rsch. Coun.- Nat. Acad. Sci., 1983-86; mem. adv. bd. Scripps Clinic & Rsch. Found., 1980-86. Author of co-author 15 books; contbr. some 100 articles to profl. jours. Chmn. bd. trustees Jenifer Altman Found., 1992-93; trustee Kaiser Family Found., 1991-93, Mayo Found., 1971-75, Carnegie Fedn., 1971-79. Recipient Hugo Schaefer medal Am. Pharm. Assn., 1976. Mem. AAAS, AMA, ACP, Am. Pub. Health Assn., Am. Fedn. Clin. Rsch., Am. Geriatric Soc., Assn. Am. Med. Colls., Inst. Medicine-Nat. Acad. Sci., Alpha Omega Alpha. Achievements include research in arthritis and rheumatism, especially Rubella arthritis, cardiovascular rehabilitation, academic medical administration, health policy. Office: U Calif Inst Health Policy Studies 3333 California St Ste 265 San Francisco CA 94143-0001

LEE, RICHARD DIEBOLD, law educator, legal publisher, consultant; b. Fargo, N.D., July 31, 1935; s. Sidney Jay and Charlotte Hannah (Thompson) L.; m. Patricia Ann Taylor, June 17, 1957; children: Elizabeth Carol, Deborah Susan, David Stuart. BA with distinction, Stanford U., 1957; JD, Yale U., 1960. Bar: Calif. 1961, U.S. Dist. Ct. (no. dist.) Calif. 1961, U.S. Ct. Appeals (9th cir.) 1961. Dep. atty. gen. Office of Atty. Gen., Sacramento, 1960-62; assoc. McDonough, Holland, Schwartz, Allen & Wahrhaftig, Sacramento, 1962-66, ptnr., 1966-69; asst. dean U. Calif. Sch. Law, Davis, 1969-73, assoc. dean, 1973-76; assoc. prof. law Temple U. Sch. Law, Phila., 1976-77, vis. prof., 1975-76, prof., 1977-89; dir. profl. devel. Baker & McKenzie, Chgo., N.Y.C., 1981-83; dir. Am. Inst. for Law Tng., Phila., 1985-89; dir. profl. devel. Morrison & Foerster, San Francisco, 1989-93; dir. Continuing Edn. of the Bar, Berkeley, 1993-97. Mem. Grad. and Profl. Fin. Aid Coun., Princeton, N.J., 1974-80; trustee Law Sch. Admission Council, Washington, 1976-78; mem. internat. adv. com. Internat. Juridical Org., Rome, 1977-88; mem. bd. advisors Lawyer Hiring and Tng. Report, Chgo., 1983-95; vis. prof. law sch. law Golden Gate U., San Francisco, 1988-89. Author: (coursebook) Materials on Internat. Efforts to Control the Environment, 1977, 78, 79, 80, 84, 85, 87. Co-editor: Orientation in the U.S. Legal System annual coursebook, 1982-92. Contbr. articles to profl. jours. Bd. dirs. Lung Assn. of Sacramento-Emigrant Trails, 1962-69, pres., 1966-68; bd. dirs. Sacramento County Legal Aid Soc., 1968-74, pres., 1971-72; chmn. bd. overseers Phila. Theol. Inst., 1984-88, bd. overseers, 1979-80, 84-88; mem. bd. of council Episcopal Community Services, Phila., 1984-88; trustee Grace Cathedral, San Francisco, 1989—, chair bd. trustees, 1992-95; mem. bd. visitors John Marshall Law Sch., Chgo., 1989-93; trustee Grad. Theol. Union, Berkeley, 1991-2000, vice chair, 1994-99; trustee Coll. of Preachers, Washington Nat. Cathedral, 1999—. Mem. ABA (chmn. various coms., spl. cons. on continuing legal edn. MacCrate Task Force on Law Schs. and the Profession: Narrowing the Gap, 1991-93, standing com. on specialization 1998—), State Bar Calif. (chair standing com. on minimum continuing legal edn. 1990-92, com. mem. 1990-93), Bar Assn. San Francisco (legal ethics com., conf. of delegates 1987—), Profl. Devel. Consortium (chair 1991-93), Am. Law Inst., Yale Club (N.Y.C., San Francisco. Democrat. Episcopalian. Home and Office: 2001 Sacramento St Ste 4 San Francisco CA 94109-3342

LEE, RICHARD FRANCIS JAMES, evangelical clergyman, media consultant; b. Yakima, Wash., Sept. 13, 1967; s. Richard Francis and Dorothy Aldean (Blackwell). Diploma, Berean Coll., Springfield, Mo., 1989; BA, U. Wash., Seattle, 1990; JD, Gonzaga Sch. Law, 1997; MDiv, Fuller Theol. Seminary, 2001. Lic. clergyman; ordained Assemblies of God, So. Calif. dist., 1999. Lic. clergyman N.W. dist. Assemblies of God, Seattle, 1989. Author: Tell Me the Story, 1982, The Crimson Detective Motion Picture, 1996. Named Most Likely to be President, Franklin High Sch., Seattle, 1986. Pentecostal. Avocations: collector, writer, itinerant speaker, filmmaker. Office: 2604 E Boone Ave Spokane WA 99202-3718

LEE, RICHARD KENNETH, software company executive; b. Birmingham, Eng., Dec. 10, 1942; came to U.S., 1964; s. Kenneth Jesse Lee and Eleanor Margaret (Bellsham) Dean; m. Melinda Elena Noback, Aug. 20, 1966; children: Sonja Eleanor, Alyssa Claire. BSc with upper 2d class honours, No. Poly. U. London, 1964; MS in Inorganic Chemistry, Northwestern U., 1965; PhD in Inorganic Chemistry, U. London, 1968. Various corp. rsch. positions UOP Inc., Des Plaines, Ill., 1965-74, mgr. catalyst R & D automotive products divsn., 1974-77; v.p., gen. mgr. portable battery div. Gould Inc., St. Paul, 1977-82; v.p., gen. mgr. Elgar Corp., an Onan/McGraw Edison Co., San Diego, 1982-85; v.p. R & D, Pharmaseal div. Baxter Healthcare Corp., Valencia, Calif., 1985-88; v.p. strategic bus. ops. Manville Sales Corp., Denver, 1988-92; pres., chief exec. officer Rocklite Inc., Denver, 1992-99; prin. LeeVarage Internat., Castle Rock, 1993-00; chmn., pres., CEO Value Innovations, Inc., Denver, 1999—. Adj. prof. masters tech. program U. Coll., U. Denver, 1993-95; bd. dirs. Q.E.D., Denver; adv. bd. Kodiak, Denver, 1998-99. Author: (videotape) U.S. Competitiveness—A Crisis?, 1992; patentee for vehicle emission control system. Chmn. Summit 91, Denver, 1991, mem. organizing com. Summit 92, Pacoima, Calif., 1992; bd. dirs. Indsl. Rsch. Inst., Inc., Washington, 1991-92, co-chmn. emeriti, 1998-2000. Recipient IR-100 award Indsl. R & D, 1978; Fulbright travel scholar, 1964-65. Mem. Rocky Mountain World Trade Ctr. (vice chmn. 1992-94, exec. com. 1992-94, bd. dirs. 1990-95). E-mail: dick_lee@valueinnovations.net

LEE, ROBERT R. state legislator; b. Ashton, Idaho, Feb. 28, 1932; m. Gwen Lee; children: Robert J., Kevin, Jennifer, Vanessa, Bryan, Richard, Jared. BS in Civil Engring., U. Idaho; PhD in Civil Engring., Stanford U. Irrigation engr.; mem. Idaho Senate, Dist. 27, Boise, 1994—. Vice chair agrl. affairs com., mem. commerce and human resources, fin., resources and environment, and transp. coms. 1st lt., U.S. Army Corps of Engrs. White Ho. fellow. Mem. Rotary. Republican. Office: State Capitol PO Box 83720 Boise ID 83720-3720

LEE, RONALD DEMOS, demographer, economist, educator; b. Sept. 5, 1941; s. Otis Hamilton and Dorothy (Demetracopoulou) L.; m. Melissa Lee Nelken, July 6, 1968; children: Sophia, Isabel, Rebecca. BA, Reed Coll., 1963; MA, U. Calif., Berkeley, 1967; PhD, Harvard U., 1971. Postdoctoral fellow Nat. Demographic Inst., Paris, 1970-71; asst. prof. to prof. U. Mich., Ann Arbor, 1971-79; prof. demography and econs. U. Calif., Berkeley, 1979—. Dir. Berkeley Ctr. on Econs. and Demography of Aging; chair com. on population, NAS, 1993-97; cons. in field. Author, editor: Econometric Studies of Topics in Demographic History, 1978, Population Patterns in the Past, 1977, Population, Food, and Rural Development, 1988, Economics of Changing Age Distributions in Developed Countries, 1988, others; editor: Population Change in Asia: Transition, Development, and Aging, 2000, Demographic Change and Fiscal Policy, 2000, United States Fertility: New Patterns, New Theories, 1996; contbr. over 130 articles to profl. jours. Peace Corps. vol., Ethiopia, 1963-65. Recipient Mindel C. Sheps award Population Assn. of Am. and U. N.C. Sch. Pub. Health, 1984, MERIT award Nat. Inst. Aging, 1994-03, Taeuber award Population Assn. of Am. and Princeton U., 1999; NIH fellow, 1965-67; NSF fellow, 1968-69, fellow Social Sci. Rsch. Council, 1970-71; NIH grantee, 1973—; Guggenheim fellow, 1984-85. Fellow Brit. Acad. (corr.); mem. NAS, Population Assn. Am. (pres. 1987), Am. Econ. Assn., Internat. Union Sci. Study of Population. Democrat. Home: 2933 Russell St Berkeley CA 94705-2333 Office: U Calif Dept Demography 2232 Piedmont Ave Berkeley CA 94720-2120 E-mail: rlee@demog.berkeley.edu

LEE, THOMAS L. real estate executive; Degree in econ., Denison U.; MBA, Stanford U. Various positions The Newhall Land & Farming Co., Valencia, Calif., 1970-85, pres., COO, 1985-87, CEO, 1987—, chmn., 1989—. Bd. dirs. Blue Shield Calif., L.A. Area C. of C., chmn. bd. dirs. 1994; bd. dirs. Nat. Realty Com., bd. trustees Boys and Girls Clubs Am., Calif. Inst. Arts. With USNR, 1965-68. Mem. Calif. Bus. Roundtable, Urban Land Inst. Office: Newhall Land & Farming Co 23823 Valencia Blvd Valencia CA 91355-2103

LEE, YEU-TSU MARGARET, surgeon, educator; b. Xian, Shensi, China, Mar. 18, 1936; m. Thomas V. Lee, Dec. 29, 1962 (div. 1987); 1 child, Maxwell M. AB in Microbiology, U. S.D., 1957; MD, Harvard U., 1961. Diplomate Am. Bd. Surgery. Assoc. prof. surgery Med. Sch., U. So. Calif., L.A., 1973-83; commd. lt. col. U.S. Army Med. Corps, 1983, advanced through grades to col., 1989; chief surg. oncology Tripler Army Med. Ctr., Honolulu, 1983-98; ret. U.S. Army, 1999; assoc. clin. prof. surgery Med. Sch., U. Hawaii, Honolulu, 1984-92, clin. prof. surgery, 1992—. Author: Malignant Lymphoma, 1974; author chpts to books; contbr. articles to profl. jours. Pres. Orgn. Chinese-Am. Women, L.A., 1981, Hawaii chpt., 1988; active U.S.-China Friendship Assn., 1991—. Decorated Nat. Def. Svc. medal, Army Commendation medal, Army Meritorious Svc. medal, Army Humanitarian Svc. medal; recipient Chinese-Am. Engrs. and Scis. Assn., 1987; named Sci. Woman Warrior, Asian-Pacific Womens Network, 1983. Mem. ACS, Soc. Surg. Oncology, Assn. Women Surgeons. Avocations: classical music, movies, hiking, ballroom dancing. Address: PO Box 6486 Honolulu HI 96818-0486 E-mail: ytm_lee@hotmail.com

LEE, YUAN TSEH, chemistry educator; b. Hsinchu, Taiwan, China, Nov. 29, 1936; came to U.S., 1962, naturalized, 1974; s. Tsefan and Pei (Tasi) L.; m. Bernice Wu, June 28, 1963; children: Ted, Sidney, Charlotte. BS, Nat. Taiwan U., 1959; MS, Nat. Tsinghua U., Taiwan, 1961; PhD, U. Calif., Berkeley, 1965. From asst. prof. to prof. chemistry U. Chgo., 1968-74; prof. emeritus U. Calif., Berkeley, 1974—, also former prin. investigator Lawrence Berkeley Lab., 1974-97; pres. Academia Sinica, Taiwan, 1994—. Contbr. numerous articles on chem. physics to profl. jours. Recipient Nobel Prize in Chemistry, 1986, Ernest O. Lawrence award Dept. Energy, 1981, Nat. Medal of Sci., 1986, 90, Peter Debye award for Phys. Chemistry, 1986; fellow Alfred P. Sloan, 1969-71, John Simon Guggenheim, 1976-77; Camille and Henry Dreyfus Found. Tchr. scholar, 1971-74, Harrison Howe award, 1983. Fellow Am. Phys. Soc.; mem. NAS, AAAS, Am. Acad. Arts and Scis., Am. Chem. Soc. Office: Acad Sinica Pres Office 128 Academia Rd Sec 2 Nankang Taipei 11529 Taiwan*

LEEB, CHARLES SAMUEL, clinical psychologist; b. San Francisco, July 18, 1945; s. Sidney Herbert and Dorothy Barbara (Fishstrom) L.; m. Storme Lynn Gilkey, Apr. 28, 1984; children: Morgan Evan, Spencer Douglas. BA in Psychology, U. Calif.-Davis, 1967; MS in Counseling and Guidance, San Diego State U., 1970; PhD in Edn. and Psychology, Claremont Grad. Sch., 1973. Assoc. So. Regional Dir. Mental Retardation Ctr., Las Vegas, Nev., 1976-79; pvt. practice, Las Vegas, 1978-79; dir. biofeedback and athletics Menninger Found., Topeka, 1979-82, dir. children's div. biofeedback and psychophysiology ctr. The Menninger Found., 1979-82; pvt. practice, Claremont, Calif., 1982—; dir. of psychol. svcs. Horizon Hosp., 1986-88; dir. adolescent chem. dependency and children's program Charter Oak Hosp., Covina, Calif., 1989-91; founder, chief exec. officer Rsch. and Treatment Inst., Claremont, 1991—; lectr. in field. Contbr. articles to profl. jours. Mem. Am. Psychol. Assn., Calif. State Psychol. Assn. Office: 937 W Foothill Blvd Ste D Claremont CA 91711-3358

LEEDY, ROBERT ALLAN, SR. retired lawyer; b. Portland, Oreg., Aug. 5, 1909; s. Harry E. and Loretta (Viles) L.; m. Annapauline Rea, Sept. 14, 1935; children: Douglas Harry, Robert Allan, Jr. J.D., U. Oreg., 1933. Bar: Oreg. 1933. Practiced in, Portland, 1934-86; mem. firm Bullivant, Houser, Bailey, Pendergrass, and Hoffman, ret. Mem. Oreg. Bar Examiners, 1947-48, chmn., 1949 Chancellor Episcopal Diocese Oreg., 1970-83. U.S. Comdr. 1943-56. Mem. ABA, Oreg. Bar Assn. (pres. 1953), Multnomah County Bar Assn., Western Bar Conf. (pres. 1952), Alpha Tau Omega, Phi Delta Phi. Home: 1300 NE 16th Ave Apt 1219 Portland OR 97232-4404 Office: Pioneer Towers Portland OR 97204 E-mail: rleedy7097@aol.com

LEEFE, JAMES MORRISON, architect; b. N.Y.C., Aug. 28, 1921; s. Charles Clement and Suzanne (Bernhardt) L.; m. Miriam Danziger, Oct. 31, 1949; 1 dau., Molly Elizabeth. Cert., U.S. Mcht. Marine Acad., 1943; B.Arch., Columbia U., 1950. Practice architecture, San Francisco, 1955-60; chief architect power and indsl. div. Bechtel Inc., San Francisco, 1960-64, prin. urban designer, 1974-80; chief architect San Francisco Power div. Bechtel Power Corp., 1980-89; v.p., asst. sec. Bechtel Assos. (P.C.), N.Y., 1978-89, v.p. D.C. and Va., 1978-89; pvt. cons. architect Sausalito, Calif., 1989—; ptnr. Leefe & Ehrankrantz Architects, San Francisco, 1964-68; v.p. Bldg. Systems Devel. Inc., San Francisco and Washington, 1965-70; also dir.; dir. architecture Giffels Assos. Inc., Detroit, 1971-74. Lectr. in architecture Columbia U., 1951-52, U. Calif., Berkeley, 1954-60; mem. faculty U. for Pres's., Young Pres's. Orgn., 1967; adj. prof. U. Detroit, 1971-72; mem. adv. bd. Nat. Clearing House for Criminal Justice Planning and Architecture, 1974-76 Works include Mus. West of Am. Craftsmen's Council, San Francisco, 1964 (Archtl. Record award for interior design 1971), Wells Hydrocombine Dam and Power Generating Facility, Columbia River, Wash., 1965, Boundary Dam, Pend Orielle River, Wash., 1965 (Am. Public Power Assn. honor award 1975), Detroit Automobile Inter-Ins. Exchange Corp. Hdqrs, Dearborn, Mich., 1972 (Detroit chpt. AIA honor award 1975), PPG Industries Research Center, Allison Park, Pa., 1973 (Detroit chpt. AIA honor award 1975, Am. Inst. Steel Constrn. Archtl. award of excellence 1975, Mich. Soc. Architects honor award 1976), Gen. Electric Research Center, Twinsburg, Ohio, 1973 (Detroit chpt. AIA honor award 1977), Appliance Buyers Credit Corp. Hdqrs. Office, Benton Harbor, Mich., 1974 (Engring. Soc. Detroit Design award 1976), Standard Tng. Bldg. Commonwealth Edison, 1989-90, Strybing Arboretum, San Francisco, 1990; contbr. articles to profl. jours.; originator various techniques for analysis of human factors in the working environment. Chmn. bd. Mus. West of Am. Crafts Coun., San Francisco, 1966-68; vice chmn. Franklin (Mich.) Hist. Dist. Commn., 1973-74; trustee So. Marin Land Trust. With U.S. Mcht. Marine, 1942-46. Recipient Hirsh Meml. prize Columbia U., 1950, 1st prize (with Miriam Leefe) Dow Chem. Co. Competition for Interior Design, 1960 Fellow AIA; hon. mem. Internat. Union Architects Working Group Habitat, trustee, So. Marin Land Trust. Home and Office: James Leefe FAIA Architect 131 Spencer Ave Sausalito CA 94965-2022

LEELAND, STEVEN BRIAN, electronics engineer; b. Tampa, Fla., Dec. 27, 1951; s. N. Stanford and Shirley Mae (Bahner) L.; m. Karen Frances Hayes, Dec. 20, 1980; children: Crystal Mary, April Marie. BSEE, MSEE magna cum laude, U. South Fla., 1976. Registered profl. engr., Ariz. Engr. Bendix Avionics, Ft. Lauderdale, Fla., 1976-77; prin. engr., instr. Sperry Avionics, Phoenix, 1977-84; prin. staff engr. Motorola Govt. Electronics Group, Scottsdale, Ariz., 1984-88; engring. fellow, mgr. dept. software engring. Fairchild Data Corp., Scottsdale, 1988-98; prin. staff engr. Teledesic Sys. Arch., Motorola Space Sys. Tech. Group, 1998-99; contractor Dantel, Fresno, Calif., 1999—. Cons. Motorola Govt. Electronics Group, 1991. Patentee systolic array, 1990; contbr. articles to profl. jours. Mem. IEEE (Phoenix chpt. Computer Soc. treas. 1978-79, sec. 1979-80, chmn. 1980-81, 81-82), Tau Beta Pi, Pi Mu Epsilon, Phi Kappa Phi, Omicron Delta Kappa, Themis. Adventist. Avocations: chess, computers, bible study, exercise, health. Home: 10351 E Sharon Dr Scottsdale AZ 85260-9000 Office: Dantel PO Box 55013 2991 N Argyle Ave Fresno CA 93747-5013 E-mail: steven.leeland@worldnet.att.net

LEEMANS, WIM PIETER, physicist; b. Gent, Belgium, June 7, 1963; BS in Elec. Engring., Free U. Brussels, 1985; MS in Elec. Engring., UCLA, 1987, Ph.D. in Elec. Engring., 1991. Teaching asst. UCLA, 1986-87, rsch. asst., 1987-91; staff scientist Lawrence Berkeley Lab., Berkeley, Calif., 1991—. Group leader exptl. beam physics group, 1994—; chair ICFA panel on advanced and novel accelerators; presenter numerous seminars. Contbr. articles to profl. jours. Recipient Simon Ramo awd., Am. Physical Soc., 1992; grad. scholar IEEE Nuclear and Plasma Soc., 1987. Fellow Belgian Am. Ednl. Found., Francqui Found.; mem. IEEE (Nuclear and Plasma scis. soc. grad. scholar 1987), Soc. Photo-Optical Instrument Engrs., Am. Phys. Soc., Royal Flemish Engrs. Soc. Achievements include research in high intensity laser-plasma interaction, interaction of relativistic electrons with lasers and plasmas, novel radiation sources, advanced accelerator concepts, non-linear dynamics of free electron lasers. Office: Lawrence Berkeley Lab Divsn Accelerator Fusion Rsch 1 Cyclotron Rd Ms 71 259 Berkeley CA 94720-0001

LEESON, SUSAN M. state supreme court judge; Law clerk U.S. 9th Cir. Ct. of Appeals; Tom. C. Clark judicial fellow U.S. Supreme Ct.; prof. polit. sci., assoc. prof. law Willamette U., Salem, Oreg.; judge Oreg. Ct. Appeals, 1993-98, Oreg. Supreme Ct., 1998—. Former mem. Oreg. Criminal Justice Coun., Marion-Polk Local Govt. Boundary Commn. Office: Supreme Ct Bldg 1163 State St Salem OR 97310-1331

LEFRANC, MARGARET (MARGARET SCHOONOVER), artist, illustrator, editor, writer; b. N.Y.C., Mar. 15, 1907; d. Abraham and Sophie (Teplitz) Frankel; m. Raymond Schoonover, 1942 (div. 1945). Student, Art Students League, N.Y.C., Kunstschule des Westerns, Berlin, NYU Grad. Sch., Andre L'Hote, Paris, Acad. Grande Chaumiere, Paris. Tchr. art Adult Edn., Los Alamos, 1946, Miami (Fla.) Mus. Modern Art, 1975-76. Mem. Art in the Embassies Program, Paris, 1998—. Exhibitions include one-person show Mus. N.Mex., Santa Fe, 1948, 1951, 1953, Philbrook Art Ctr., Tulsa, Okla., 1949, 1951, Okla. Art Ctr., 1950, Recorder Workshop, Miami, Fla., 1958, St. John's Coll., Santa Fe, N.Mex., 1993, 1997, A Lifetime of Imaging (works on paper), 1921—95, Figurative Works, 1920—30, Cline Fine Art Gallery, 1997, exhibitions include group shows Salon de Tuileries, Paris, 1928, 1929, 1930, Art Inst. Chgo., 1936, El Paso Mus. Art, 1964, Mus. Modern Art, 1974, North Miami Mus. Contemporary Art, 1984, Miami Collects, 1989, Women's Caucus Invitational, 1990, Gov.'s Gallery, Santa Fe, 1992, Gene Autry Western Heritage Mus., 1995, Gilcrease Mus., Tulsa, 1996, Mus. N.Mex., Santa Fe, 1996, Brigham Young U., Provo, Utah, 1996, Art in the Embassies Program, Paris, 1998—2001, Purdue U. Women Artists of the Am. West: Past and Present, 1998, Art Trends: Miami's Trek 1: The Decades of Art in Miami, 1940s-1960s, 1999—2000, Gerald Peters Gallery Modernistic Peaks, Santa Fe, N. Mex, 1999, Ind. State Univ. and Swope Art Mus. Women Artists, Terre Haute, Ind., 1999, Belles Artes, Mex. City, Mus. Fine Arts, Santa Fe, N.Mex. Bd. dirs., pres. Artist Equity of Fla., 1964-68; v.p. Miami Art Assn., 1958-60; founder, bd. dirs. Guild Art Gallery, N.Y.C., 1935-37. Recipient Illustration award Fifty Best Books of Yr., Libr. of Congress, 1948, Hon. Mention award Rodeo Santa Fe, Mus. N.Mex., 1949, others, Gov.'s award for Excellence and Achievement in the Arts, 1996. E-mail: McKenzieHi@aol.com

LEGGE, CHARLES ALEXANDER, federal judge; b. San Francisco, Aug. 24, 1930; s. Roy Alexander and Wilda (Rampton) L.; m. Janice Meredith Sleeper, June 27, 1952; children: Jeffrey, Nancy, Laura. AB with distinction, Stanford U., 1952, JD, 1954. Bar: Calif. 1955. Assoc. Bronson, Bronson & McKinnin, San Francisco, 1956-64, ptnr., 1964-84, chmn., 1978-84; U.S. Dist. Ct. judge U.S. Dist. Ct. (no. dist.) Calif., San Francisco, 1984—. Served with U.S. Army, 1954-56. Fellow Am. Coll. Trial Lawyers; mem. Calif. Bar Assn. (past chmn. adminstrn. justice com.). Republican. Clubs: Bohemian, World Trade (San Francisco); Orinda (Calif.) Country. Office: US Dist Ct PO Box 36060 450 Golden Gate Ave Ste 36052 San Francisco CA 94102-3482

LEGINGTON, GLORIA R. middle school educator; BS, Tex. So. U, Houston, 1967; MS, U. So. Calif., L.A., 1973. Cert. adminstr. (life). Tchr., mentor L.A. Unified Sch. Dist., 1991-93. Tchr. insvc. classes for area colloquim, parents, tchrs., faculty shared decision making coun., 1993-94, mem. faculty senate, 1992-93, mem. sch. improvement, 1993-94; del. U.S. Spain Joint Conf. on Edn., Barcelona, 1995. Sponsor 8th grade, 1994-97. Named semi-finalist Nat. Libr. Poetry, 1997, recipient Editor's Choice award, 1997. Mem. NEA, Internat. Reading Assn., United Tchrs. L.A., Calif. League of Mid. Schs., Internat. Libr. Poetry. Avocations: painting, writing, collecting black memorabilia, reading, traveling.

LEGRAND, SHAWN PIERRE, computer systems programmer; b. San Diego, Nov. 27, 1960; s. Roger and Violet Louise (Howe) L. Grad. high sch., El Cajon, Calif.; student, U. Calif., San Diego, 1992-95. Cert. computer programmer; cert. in neural networks. Computer operator Grossmont CCD, El Cajon, 1978-79; computer systems programmer ICW, San Diego, 1979—. Recipient Math. Achievement award Bank of Am., 1978. Mem. IEEE Computer Soc., Assn. Computing Machinery, Soc. Indsl. and Applied Mathematicians. Republican. Office: ICW 11455 El Camino Real San Diego CA 92130-2088 E-mail: slegrand@attglobal.net

LEHMAN, I. ROBERT, biochemist, educator; b. Tauroggen, Lithuania, Oct. 5, 1924; came to U.S., 1927; s. Herman Bernard Lehman and Anne Kalin; m. Sandra Lee Lehman, July 5, 1959; children: Ellen, Deborah, Samuel. BA, Johns Hopkins U., 1950, PhD, 1954; MD, U. Gothenberg, Sweden, 1987; DSc, U. Paris, 1992. Asst. prof. Stanford (Calif.) U., 1959-62, assoc. prof., 1962-67, prof. biochemistry, 1967—. Mem. sci. adv. bd. U.S. Biochem., Cleve., 1984-98, RPI Pharms., Boulder, Colo., 1991-96, Genetrol, Oakland, Calif., 1998—; cons. Abbott Labs, Chgo., 1990-94. Author: Principles of Biochemistry, 7th edit., 1984. Sgt. U.S. Army, 1943-46, ETO. Recipient Merck award Am. Soc. Biochemistry and Molecular Biology, 1994. Democrat. Jewish. Office: Sch of Medicine Stanford U Stanford CA 94305

LEHMAN, LARRY L. state supreme court justice; Judge Wyo. County Ct., 1985-88, Wyo. Dist. Ct. (2nd dist.), 1988-94; justice Wyo. Supreme Ct., Cheyenne, 1994-98, chief justice, 1998—. Office: Supreme Court Bldg Cheyenne WY 82002-0001

LEHMAN, MARK EDWARDS, lawyer; b. St. Louis, Aug. 18, 1955; s. Donald Walter and Barbara Louise (Pohle) L.; m. Mary Eileen Robertson, Feb. 1, 1992; children: Micah Edwards, Gabriel Phillip, Madeline Eileen. BS, U. Utah, 1977; JD, Washington U., 1981. Bar: Utah 1981, U.S. Dist. Ct. Utah 1982. Jud. clk. Mo. Ct. Appeals, St. Louis, 1981-82; assoc. Kruse, Landa & Maycock, Salt Lake City, 1982-87; ptnr. Lewis & Lehman, Salt Lake City, 1987-91, Lehman, Mitchell & Waldo, Salt Lake City, 1991-93, Lehman, Jensen & Donahue, Salt Lake City, 1993—. Founding dir. Make-A-Wish Found. Utah, Salt Lake City, 1986-93, pres., 1992. Mem. Utah State Bar Assn. (mem. securities adv. com. 1989-94, officer estate planning sect. 1994—). Office: Lehman Jensen & Donahue 8 E Broadway Ste 620 Salt Lake City UT 84111-2243 also: Bear Stearns Co Inc 245 Park Ave New York NY 10167

LEHMAN, MICHAEL EVANS, computer company executive, BBA, U. Wis., 1974. Sr. mgr. Price Waterhouse, San Francisco; asst. corp. contr., external reporting mgr. Asian subsidiary Sun Microsystems, Hong Kong, dir. fin. and adminstrn. Asian subsidiary, v.p., corp. contr., CFO, v.p. corp. resources, CFO, corp. exec. officer, 1998-2000, exec. v.p. corp. resources, DFO, corp. exec. officer, 2000—. Mem. deans adv. bd. Grad. Sch. Bus., U. Wis., Madison. Mem. Am. Electronics Assn. (exec. com.). Office: Sun Microsystems Inc 901 San Antonio Rd Palo Alto CA 94303-4900

LEHMAN, STEPHEN C. direct response programming executive; Chmn. bd. dirs., CEO Nat. Media Corp., Phila., E4L Inc., Encino, Calif., 1998—. Office: E4L Inc 15821 Ventura Blvd Encino CA 91436

LEHMANN, ERICH LEO, statistics educator; b. Strasbourg, France, Nov. 20, 1917; came to U.S., 1940, naturalized, 1945; s. Julius and Alma Rosa (Schuster) L.; m. Juliet Popper Shaffer; children: Stephen, Barbara, Fia. MA, U. Calif., Berkeley, 1943, PhD, 1946; DSc (hon.), U. Leiden, 1985, U. Chgo., 1991. From asst. dept. math. to prof. U. Calif., Berkeley, 1942-55, prof. dept. stats., 1955-88, emeritus, 1988—, chmn. dept. stats., 1973-76. Vis. assoc. prof. Columbia, 1950-51, Stanford, 1951-52; vis. lectr. Princeton, 1951 Author: Testing Statistical Hypotheses, 1959, 2d edit., 1986; (with J.L. Hodges, Jr.) Basic Concepts of Probability and Statistics, 1964, 2d edit, 1970, Nonparametrics: Statistical Methods Based on Ranks, 1975, Theory of Point Estimation, 1983, (with Casella) 2nd edit., 1998, Elements of Lange Sample Theory, 1998. Recipient Fisher award Coms. of Pres. Stats. Socs. in N.Am., 1988; Guggenheim fellow, 1955, 66, 79; Miller research prof., 1962-63, 72-73; recipient Samuel S. Wilks Meml. medal Am. Statis. Assn., 1996, Gottfried Noether award Am. Statis. Assn., 2000. Fellow Inst. Math. Stats., Am. Statis. Assn., Royal Statis. Soc. (hon.); mem. Internat. Statis. Inst., Am. Acad. Arts and Scis., Nat. Acad. Scis. Office: U Calif Dept Statistics Berkeley CA 94720-0001

LEHR, JEFFREY MARVIN, immunologist, allergist; b. N.Y.C., Apr. 29, 1942; s. Arthur and Stella (Smellow) L.; m. Suzanne Kozak, June 10, 1946; children: Elisa, Alexandra, Vanessa, Ryan. BS, City Coll., Bklyn., 1963; MD, NYU, 1967. Intern, resident Beth Israel Hosp., N.Y.C., 1967-69; resident in allergy/immunology, internal medicine Roosevelt Hosp., N.Y.C., 1969-72; chief of allergy/immunology USAF, Wright Patterson AFB, Ohio, 1972-74; allergist, immunologist Monterey, Calif., 1974—. Chmn. Monterey Bay Ari Pollution Hearing Bd., 1982-95; v.p. Lyceum of Monterey, 1977-83. Fellow Am. Acad. Allergy/Immunology, Am. Coll. Allergy/Immunology, Am. Assn. Cert. Allergists; mem. Am. Lung Assn. (v.p. 1989-91), Monterey County Med. Soc. (pres. 1988-89). Avocations: tennis, jogging, golf, hiking, backpacking. Office: 798 Cass St Monterey CA 93940-2918 also: 262 San Jose St Salinas CA 93901-3901

LEIBERT, RICHARD WILLIAM, special events producer; b. N.Y.C., Nov. 11, 1948; s. Richard William and Rosemarie Martha (Bruns) L. BS, Boston U., 1966-70; student, Northwestern U., 1971. Producer Sta. WBZ AM/FM, Boston, 1968-70; prodn. dir. Sta. WMMR-FM, Phila., 1970; exec. producer Sta. WIND-AM, Chgo., 1970-72; program dir. Sta. KGB AM-FM, San Diego, 1972-80; pres. Events Mktg., Inc., L.A., 1980—. Dir. Nat. Fireworks Ensemble, Los Angeles, Calif., 1985—. Creator (mascot, publicity stunts) Sta. KGB Chicken, 1974; creator, producer (radio fireworks show) Sta. KGB Sky Show, 1976; writer, producer (network radio show) New Music News, 1983; creator, dir. (touring co.) Nat. Fireworks Ensemble, 1985. Recipient Emmy award, 1978; named Program Dir. of Yr. Billboard Mag., 1976, Radio Program of Yr. Billboard Mag., 1976. Avocations: sailing, baseball. Office: Events Mktg Inc PO Box 65694 Los Angeles CA 90065-0694

LEIBOW, RONALD LOUIS, lawyer; b. Santa Monica, Calif., Oct. 4, 1939; s. Norman and Jessica (Kellner) L.; m. Linda Bengelsdorf, June 11, 1961 (div. Dec. 1974); children: Jocelyn Elise, Jeffrey David, Joshua Aaron; m. Jacqueline Blatt, Apr. 6, 1986. AB, Calif. State U., Northridge, 1962; JD, UCLA, 1965. Bar: Calif. 1966, U.S. Dist. Ct. (cen. dist.) Calif. 1966, U.S. Dist. Ct. (no., so. and ea. dists.) Calif. 1971. Spl. asst. city atty. City of Burbank, Calif., 1966-67; from assoc. to ptnr. Meyers, Stevens & Walters, L.A., 1967-71; ptnr. Karpf, Leibow & Warner, Beverly Hills, Calif., 1971-74, Volk, Newman Gralla & Karp, L.A., L.A., 1979-81, Spector & Leibow, L.A., 1982-84, Stroock & Stroock & Lavan, L.A., 1984-94, Kaye Scholer LLP, L.A., 1994—, mng. ptnr., 1996-97. Lectr. law

UCLA, 1968-69; asst. prof. Calif. State U., Northridge, 1969-71. Contbr. articles to profl. jours. Pres. Jewish Cmty. Ctr., Greater L.A., 1983-86; vice chair Jewish Cmty. Ctr. Assn. N.Am., N.Y.C., 1988—; vice chair Jewish Fedn. Greater L.A., 1988—, chair planning and allocations com., 1998-2001; internat. bd., exec. com. Starlight Childrens Found., 1997—. Mem. ABA (bus. bankruptcy com.), Phi Alpha Delta. Avocations: writing, tennis, skiing, travel. Office: Kaye Scholer LLP 1999 Avenue Of The Stars Fl 16 Los Angeles CA 90067-6022 E-mail: rleibow@kaye.scholar.com

LEIGH, HOYLE, psychiatrist, educator, writer; b. Seoul, Korea, Mar. 25, 1942; came to U.S., 1965; m. Vincenta Masciandaro, Sept. 16, 1967; 1 child, Alexander Hoyle. MA, Yale U., 1982; MD, Yonsei U., Seoul, 1965. Diplomate Am. Bd. Psychiatry and Neurology. Asst. prof. Yale U., New Haven, 1971-75, assoc. prof., 1975-80, prof., 1980-89, lectr. in psychiatry, 1989—. Dir. Behavioral Medicine Clinic, Yale U., 1980-89; dir. psychiat. cons. svc. Yale-New Haven Hosp., 1971-89; chief psychiatry VA Med Ctr., Fresno, Calif., 1989—; prof., vice chmn. dept. psychiatry U. Calif., San Francisco, 1989—, head dept. psychiatry, 1989—; cons. Am. Jour. Psychiatry, Archives Internal Medicine, Psychosomatic Medicine. Author: The Patient, 1980, 2d edit., 1985, 3d edit., 1992; editor: Psychiatry in the Practice of Medicine, 1983, Consultation-Liaison Psychiatry: 1990's & Beyond, 1994, Biopsychosocial Approaches in Primary Care: State of the Art and Challenges for the 21st Century, 1997. Fellow ACP, Internat. Coll. Psychosomatic Medicine (v.p.), Am. Acad. Psychosomatic Medicine; mem. AMA, AAUP, World Psychiat. Assn. Avocations: reading, music, skiing. Office: U Calif Dept Psychiat 2615 E Clinton Ave Fresno CA 93703-2223

LEIGHNINGER, DAVID SCOTT, cardiovascular surgeon; b. Ohio, Jan. 16, 1920; s. Jesse Harrison and Marjorie (Lightner) L.; m. Margaret Jane Malony, May 24, 1942; children: David Allan, Jenny. BA, Oberlin Coll., 1942; MD, Western Res. U., 1945. Intern Univ. Hosps. of Cleve., 1945-46, resident, 1949-51, asst. surgeon, 1951-68; rsch. fellow in cardiovascular surgery rsch. lab. Case Western Res. U. Sch. Medicine, Cleve., 1948-49, 51-55, 57-67, instr. surgery, 1951-55, sr. instr., 1957-64, asst. prof., 1964-68, asst. clin. prof., 1968-70; resident Cin. Gen. Hosp., 1955-57; practice medicine specializing in cardiovascular surgery Cleve., 1957-70; pvt. practice medicine specializing in cardiovascular and gen. surgery Edgewater Hosp., Chgo., 1970-82, staff surgeon, also dir. emergency surg. svcs., 1970-82, Mazel Med. Ctr., Chgo., 1970-82; emergency physician Raton, N.Mex. and Trinidad, Colo., 1982-85. Assoc., courtesy, or cons. staff Marymount Hosp., Cleve., Mt. Sinai Hosp., Cleve., Geauga Cmty. Hosp., Chardon, Ohio, Bedford Cmty. Hosp. (Ohio), 1957-70. Contbr. numerous articles to med. jours., chpts. to med. texts; spl. pioneer rsch. (with Claude S. Beck) in physiopathology of coronary artery disease and CPR; developed surg. treatment of coronary artery disease; developed vein graft bypass in late 1940s; (with Claude S. Beck) achieved 1st successful defibrillation of human heart; 1st successful reversal of fatal heart attack; provided 1st intensive care of coronary patients. Tchr. tng. courses in CPR for med. personnel, police, fire and vol. rescue workers, numerous cities, 1950-70. Served to capt., M.C., AUS, 1946-48. Recipient Chris award Columbus Internat. Film Festival, 1964, numerous other awards for sci. exhibits from various nat. and state med. socs., 1953-70; USPHS grantee, 1949-68. Fellow Am. Coll. Cardiology (emeritus), Am. Coll. Chest Physicians; mem. Mont Reid Surg. Soc. (Cinn.).

LEIGHTON, ROBERT, film editor; Editor: (films) Delusion, 1981, (with Peter Thornton) Kill and Kill Again, 1981, Blood Tide, 1982, The House Where Death Lives, 1982, The Being, 1983, (with Mark Goldblatt) Wavelength, 1983, This Is Spinal Tap, 1984, The Sure Thing, 1985, Stand By Me, 1986, The Princess Bride, 1987, (with Adam Weiss) Bull Durham, 1988, When Harry Met Sally..., 1989, Blaze, 1989, Misery, 1990, (with Richard Chew) Late for Dinner, 1991, A Few Good Men, 1992, Life With Mikey, 1993, North, 1994, The American President, 1995, Courage Under Fire, 1996, Ghosts of Mississippi, 1996, Hush, 1997, The Story of Us, 1999. Address: 2258 Kenilworth Ave Los Angeles CA 90039-3010

LEIJONHUFVUD, AXEL STIG BENGT, economics educator; b. Stockholm, Sweden, Sept. 6, 1933; came to U.S., 1960; s. Erik Gabriel and Helene Adelheid (Neovius) L.; m. Marta Elisabeth Ising, June 10, 1955 (div. 1977); m. Earlene Joyce Craver, June 18, 1977; children— Carl Axel, Gabriella Helene, Christina Elisabeth Fil. kand., U. Lund, Sweden, 1960; M.A., U. Pitts., Pa., 1961; Ph.D., Northwestern U., 1967; Fil. Dr. (hon.), U. Lund, Sweden, 1983; Dr. (hon.), U. Nice, Sophia-Antipolis, France, 1995. Acting asst. prof. econs. UCLA, 1964-67, assoc. prof. econs., 1967-71, prof. econs., 1971—, chair dept. econs., 1980-83, 90-92; dir. Ctr. for Computable Econs., 1992-97; prof. monetary theory and policy U. Trento, Italy, 1995—. Co-dir. summer workshops Siena Internat. Sch. Econ. Rsch., 1987-91; participant numerous profl. confs.; cons., lectr., vis. prof. econs. various colls. and univs.; cons. Republic of Tatarstan, 1994. Author: On Keynesian Economics and the Economics of Keynes: A Study in Monetary Theory, 1968, Keynes and the Classics: Two Lectures, 1969, Information and Coordination: Essays in Macroeconomic Theory, 1981, (with D. Heymann) High Inflation, 1995, Macroeconomic Instability and Coordination: Selected Essays, 2000. Mem. econ. expert com. of pres. Kazakhstan, 1991-92. Brookings Instn. fellow, 1963-64; Marshall lectr. Cambridge U., Eng., 1974; Overseas fellow Churchill Coll., Cambridge, 1974; Inst. Advanced Study fellow, 1983-84 Mem. Am. Econ. Assn., Western Econ. Assn., History of Econs. Soc. Office: UCLA Dept Econs Los Angeles CA 90024 E-mail: axel@ucla.edu

LEINO, DEANNA ROSE, business educator; b. Leadville, Colo., Dec. 15, 1937; d. Arvo Ensio Leino and Edith Mary (Bonan) Leino Malenck; 1 adopted child, Michael Charles Bolan. BSBA, U. Denver, 1959, MS in Bus. Adminstrn., 1967; postgrad., C.C. Denver, U. No. Colo., Colo. State U., U. Colo., Met. State Coll. Cert. tchr., vocat. tchr., Colo. Tchr. Jefferson County Adult Edn., Lakewood, Colo., 1963-67; tchr. bus., coord. coop. office edn. Jefferson H.S., Edgewater, 1959-93, ret., 1993; sales assoc. Joslins Dept. Store, Denver, 1978—; mem. ea. team. clk. office automation Denver Svc. Ctr., Nat. Park Svc., 1993-94; wage hour technician U.S. Dept. Labor, 1994—. Instr. C.C. Denver, Red Rocks, 1967-81, U. Colo., Denver, 1976-79, Parks. Coll. Bus., (now Parks Jr. Coll.), 1983-98, Front Range C.C., 1998-2000; dist. advisor Future Bus. Leaders Am. Author short story. Active City of Edgewater Sister City Project Student Exch. Com.; pres. Career Women's Symphony Guild; treas. Phantoms of Opera, 1982—; active Opera Colo. Assocs. and Guild, I Pagliacci; ex-officio trustee Denver Symphony Assn., 1980-82. Recipient Disting. Svc. award Jefferson County Sch. Bd., 1980, Tchr. Who Makes a Difference award Sta. KCNC/Rocky Mountain News, 1990, Youth Leader award Lakewood Optimist Club, 1993; inducted into Jefferson H.S. Wall of Fame, 1981; named to Jefferson County Hist. Commn. Hall of Fame, 2000, countess of the Wheat Ridge Carnation Festival, 2001. Mem. NEA (life), Colo. Edn. Assn., Jefferson County Edn. Assn., Colo. Vocat. Assn., Am. Vocat. Assn., Colo. Educators for and about Bus., Profl. Secs. Internat., Career Women's Symphony Guild, Profl. Panhellenic Assn., Colo. Congress Fgn. Lang. Tchrs., Wheat Ridge C. of C. (edn. and scholarship com.), Federally Employed Women, Tyrolean Soc. Denver, Delta Pi Epsilon, Phi Chi Theta, Beta Gamma Sigma, Alpha Lambda Delta. Republican. Roman Catholic. Avocations: decorating wedding cakes, crocheting, bowling, music, world travel. Home: 3712 Allison St Wheat Ridge CO 80033-6124 E-mail: dleino@dal.dol-esa.gov

LEIPPER, DALE FREDERICK, physical oceanographer, meteorologist, educator; b. Salem, Ohio, Sept. 8, 1914; s. Robert and Myrtle (Cost) L.; m. Virginia Alma Harrison, May 14, 1942; children: Diane Louise, Janet Elizabeth, Bryan Robert, Anita Dale. BS in Edn., Wittenberg Coll., 1937; DSc (hon.), 1968; MA, Ohio State U., 1939; postgrad., UCLA, 1939-40; Ph.D., Scripps Instn. Oceanography, 1950. Tchr. city schs., San Diego, 1940-41; research oceanographer, tchr. Scripps Instn. Oceanography, U. Calif., 1945-49; mem. faculty dept. oceanography and meteorology Tex. A&M U., 1949-68, head dept., 1949-64, prof., 1964-68; prof., chmn. dept. oceanography Naval Postgrad. Sch., 1968-79; rsch. prof. U. Nev., 1996-97. Supr. rsch. program NSF, FAA, Internat. Geophys. Year, Office Naval Rsch.; mem. tech. panel oceanography, exec. vice chmn. meteorology panel U.S. Nat. Com. Internat. Geophys. Year; chmn. com. marine scis. So. Regional Edn. Bd., 1952-56; assoc. dir. Tex. A&M Rsch. Found., 1953-54. Contbr. articles on West Coast fog, oceanography, hurricane-ocean interaction, ocean currents to jours. in field. Served as maj. USAAF, 1941-45; weather officer, oceanographer. Mem. Am. Meteorol. Soc., Am. Geophys. Union, Am. Soc. Limnology and Oceanography (pres. 1957-58), Tex. Acad. Sci. (pres. 1955), Nat. Acad. Sci. (panel chmn. 1959-64), Marine Tech. Soc., Am. Soc. Oceanography (pres. 1967-68), U. Corp. for Atmospheric Rsch. (founding mem., bd. dirs.), The Oceanography Soc., Sigma Xi, Phi Kappa Phi. Club: Rotary (pres. Bryan, Tex. 1965-66). Home and Office: 716 Terra Ct Reno NV 89506-9606 E-mail: dalelr@attglobal.net

LEITH, CECIL ELDON, JR. retired physicist; b. Boston, Jan. 31, 1923; s. Cecil Eldon and Elizabeth (Benedict) L.; m. Mary Louise Henry, July 18, 1942; children: Ann, John, Paul. A.B., U. Calif. at, Berkeley, 1943, Ph.D., 1957. Exptl. physicist Lawrence Radiation Lab., Berkeley, 1946-52, theoretical physicist Livermore, Calif., 1952-68; sr. scientist Nat. Center for Atmospheric Research, Boulder, Colo., 1968-83, div. dir., 1977-81; physicist Lawrence Livermore Nat. Lab. (Calif.), 1983-90. Symons Meml. lectr. Royal Meteorol. Soc., London, 1978; chmn. com. on atmospheric scis. NRC, 1978-80, sci. program evaluation com. Univ. Corp. for Atmospheric Rsch., 1991-96; mem. joint sci. com. world climate research program World Meteorol. Organ. and Internat. Council Sci. Unions, 1976-83; mem. program adv. com. Office Advanced Sci. Computing, NSF, 1984-85. Served with AUS, 1944-46. Fellow Am. Phys. Soc., Am. Meteorol. Soc. (Meisinger award 1967, Rossby research medal 1982) Home: 627 Carla St Livermore CA 94550-2316 Office: Lawrence Livermore Nat Lab PO Box 808 Livermore CA 94551-0808

LEITMANN, GEORGE, mechanical engineering educator; b. Vienna, Austria, May 24, 1925; s. Josef and Stella (Fischer) L.; m. Nancy Lloyd, Jan. 28, 1955; children: Josef Lloyd, Elaine Michèle. BS, Columbia U., 1949, MA, 1950; PhD, U. Calif., Berkeley, 1956; D Engring. honoris causa, Tech. U. Vienna, 1988; D honoris causa, U. Paris, 1989, Tech. U. Darmstadt, 1990. Physicist, head aeroballistics sect. U.S. Naval Ordnance Sta., China Lake, 1950-57; mem. faculty U. Calif., Berkeley, 1957—, prof. engring. sci., 1963—, prof. grad. sch., 1995—, assoc. dean acad. affairs, 1981-90, assoc. dean rsch., 1990-94, acting dean, 1988, chair of the faculty, 1994-98. Cons. to aerospace industry and govt. Author: An Introduction to Optimal Control, 1966, Quantitative and Qualitative Games, 1969, The Calculus of Variations and Optimal Control, 1981, others; contbr. articles to profl. jours. Served with AUS, 1944-46, ETO. Decorated Croix de Guerre (France), Fourragere (Belgium), comdr.'s cross Order of Merit (Germany), commendatore Order of Merit (Italy); recipient Pendray Aerospace Lit. award AIAA, 1979, Von Humboldt U.S. Sr. Scientist award Von Humboldt Found., 1980, Levy medal Franklin Inst., 1981, Mechanics and Control of Flight award AIAA, 1984, Berkeley citation U. Calif.-Berkeley, 1991, von Humboldt medal Von Humboldt Found., 1991, Rufus Oldenburger medal ASME, 1995, Bellman Continuum Soc. award, 1995; named Miller Rsch. prof., 1966. Mem. NAE, Acad. Sci. Bologna, Internat. Acad. Astronautics, Argentine Nat. Acad. Engring., Russian Acad. Natural Sci., Georgian Acad. Engring., Bavarian Acad. Sci., A.V. Humboldt Assn. Am. (pres. 1994-97), Georgian Acad. Sci. Office: U Calif Coll Engring Berkeley CA 94720-0001 E-mail: gleit@uclink4.berkeley.edu

LEITZELL, TERRY LEE, lawyer; b. Williamsport, Pa., Apr. 15, 1942; s. Ernest Richard and Inez Mae (Taylor) L.; m. Lucy Acker Emmerich, June 18, 1966; children: Thomas Addison, Charles Taylor, Robert Davies. A.B., Cornell U., 1964; J.D., U. Pa., 1967. Bar: D.C. bar 1967. Consular officer Dept. State, Bombay, India, 1968-70, atty.-adv. for oceans affairs Washington, 1970-77, chief U.S. negotiator UN law of sea negotiations Geneva, also N.Y.C., 1974-77; asst. adminstr. for fisheries and dir. Nat. Marine Fisheries Service, NOAA, Dept. Commerce, Washington, 1978-81; practice law Washington, 1981-92, Seattle, 1992—; gen. counsel Icicle Seafoods, Seattle. Mem ABA, Mem. D.C. Bar Assn., Am. Soc. Internat. Law. Democrat. Home: 3150 W Laurelhurst Dr NE Seattle WA 98105-5346 Office: Icicle Seafoods 4019 21st Ave W Ste 300 Seattle WA 98199-1299 E-mail: terryl@icicleseafoods.com

LEIWEKE, TIMOTHY, sports executive, marketing professional; b. St. Louis, Apr. 21, 1957; s. John Robert and Helen (Caicuey) L.; m. Bernadette Leiweke; 1 child, Francesa Leiweke. Grad. high sch., St. Louis. Salesperson New Eng. Mut. Life Ins. Co., St. Louis, 1976-79; asst. gen. mgr. St. Louis Steamers/MISL, 1979-80; gen. mgr. Balt. Blast/MISL, 1980-81; v.p., gen. mgr. Kansas City (Mo.) Comets/MISL, 1981-84; v.p. Leiweke and Co., Kansas City, 1984-85; pres. Kansas City Comets/MISL, 1986-88; v.p. sales and mktg. div. Minn. Timberwolves, Mpls., 1988-91; sr. v.p. of bus. ops. Denver Nuggets, Denver, 1991-92, pres., 1992-96, LA Kings, Los Angeles, 1996—. Bd. dirs. Kidney Found., Minn., 1989—, Spl. Olympics, Minn., 1989—, Timberwolves Community Found., Minn., 1989—; pres. Staples Ctr. Arena. Named Rookie of the Yr., Mo. Life Underwriters, 1976, Kansas Citian of the Yr., Kansas City Press Club, 1983; recipient William Brownfield award U.S. Jaycees, 1978, William Brownfield award Mo. Jaycees, 1978, Excalibur award Am. Cancer Soc., 1987. Mem. Kansas City Mktg. and Sales Execs., Mpls. Club. Avocations: running, golf, cross-country skiing, soccer, basketball. Office: LA Arena Co 1111 S Figueroa St Ste 3100 Los Angeles CA 90017-5491

LEMAN, LOREN DWIGHT, civil engineer, state legislator; b. Pomona, Calif., Dec. 2, 1950; s. Nick and Marian (Broady) L.; m. Carolyn Rae Bratvold, June 17, 1978; children: Joseph, Rachel, Nicole. BSCE, Oreg. State U., 1972; MS in Civil, Environ. Engring., Stanford U., 1973. Registered profl. engr., Alaska. Project mgr. CH2M Hill, San Francisco, 1973, Reston, Va., 1973-74, Ketchikan, Alaska, 1974-75, Anchorage, 1975-87; mem. Alaska Ho. of Reps., 1989-93, Alaska Senate, Dist. G, Juneau, 1993—; owner Loren Leman, P.E., Anchorage, 1987—. Mem. Anchorage Hazardous Materials Commn., Local Emergency Planning Com., 1989-93. Contbr. articles to profl. jours. Mem. Breakthrough Com., Anchorage, 1978; del. to conv. Rep. Party of Alaska, 1976-90; basketball coach Grace Christian Sch., Anchorage, 1985-88; commr. Pacific States Marine Fisheries Commn.; past chmn. Pacific Fisheries Legis. Task Force. Mem. ASCE, Alaska Water Mgmt. Assn., Am. Legis. Exch. Coun., Water Environment Fedn., Toastmasters (pres.). Republican. Avocations: reading, fishing, biking, music, basketball. Home: 2699 Nathaniel Ct Anchorage AK 99517-1016 Office: Alaska State Legis 716 W 4th Ave # 520 Anchorage AK 99501-2107

LEMIEUX, LINDA DAILEY, museum director; b. Cleve., Sept. 6, 1953; d. Leslie Lee LeMieux Jr. and Mildred Edna (Dailey) Tutt. BA, Beloit Coll., 1975; MA, U. Mich., 1979; assoc. cert., Mus. Mgmt. Program, Boulder, Colo., 1987. Asst. curator Old Salem, Inc., Winston-Salem, N.C., 1979-82; curator Clarke House, Chgo., 1982-84, Western Mus. Mining and Industry, Colorado Springs, Colo., 1985-86, dir., 1987—. Author: Prairie Avenue Guidebook, 1985; editor: The Golden Years--Mines in the Cripple Creek District, 1987; contbr. articles to mags. and newspapers. Fellow Hist. Deerfield, Mass., 1974 [illegible] 1978. Mem. Am. Assn. Mus., Am. Assn. State and Local History, Colo.-Wyo. Mus. Assn., Colo. Mining Assn., Nev. Mining Assn., Mountain Plains Assn. Mus., Women in Mining. Congregationalist. Home: 1337 Hermosa Way Colorado Springs CO 80906-3050 Office: Western Mus Mining & Industry 1025 N Gate Rd Colorado Springs CO 80921-3018 E-mail: westernmuseum@aol.com, ldlemieux@gateway.net

LEMIRE, DAVID STEPHEN, school psychologist, educator; b. Roswell, N.Mex., May 23, 1949; s. Joseph Armon and Jeanne (Longwill) L.; BA, Linfield Coll., 1972, MEd, 1974; EdS, Idaho State U., 1978; postgrad. U. Wyo.; EdS in Ednl. Adminstrn. and Instructional Leadership, U. Wyo., 1988; postgrad. U. Wyo., PhD in Curriculum and Instruction Kansas State U. Cert. sch. counselor, sch. psychologist, psychotherapist. Student pers. worker, psychology instr., Calif. Sch. counselor, psychol. technician and tchr. Goshen County Sch. Dist. 1, Torrington, Wyo., counselor Aspen High Sch., Aspen, Colo.; sch. counselor Unita County Sch. Dist., Evanston, Wyo., coord. R&D Lifelong Learning Ctr. 1986-87; dir. spl. svcs. and sch. psychologist Bighorn County Sch. Dist. #4, Basin, Wyo., 1989-90; sch. psychologist Sweetwater County Sch. Dist. #2, Green River, Wyo., 1990-91; dir. housing, residence supr. Pratt (Kans.) C. C., 1991-92; tchr. Highland C.C. and Cloud County C.C., Kans., pres. David Lemire Software Enterprises, Evanston; dir. Inst. for Advanced Study of Thinkology. Mem. ASCD, Nat. Assn. Sch. Psychologists (cert.), Am. Psychol. Assn. Author: (with Richard Mueller) Instructional Psychology, Fifty or More Ethical Dilemas: Reading/Writing Activities for the Secondary and College Classroom, Twenty Simple and Inexpensive Learning Style/Personal Style/Self Concept Instruments for Professionals and Educators with Research and Supporting Documentation; former editor WACD Jour.; former mng. editor Jour. Humanistic Edn.; contbr. articles to profl. jours. Office: Creative Therapeutics Adminstrv Offices 2390 Riviera St Reno NV 89509-1144

LEMKE, HERMAN ERNEST FREDERICK, JR. retired elementary education educator, consultant; b. Argo, Ill., July 13, 1919; s. Herman and Augusta Victoria (Statt) L.; m. Geneva Octavene Davidson, Sept, 5, 1942; children: Patricia, Herman E.F. III, Gloria, John, Elizabeth. BA, George Peabody Coll., 1949, MA, 1952. Cert. social sci. tchr., Tenn., elem. tchr., Calif. Tchr. Cadd Parish Sch., Shreveport, La., 1950-55, Pacific Sch. Dist., Sacramento, 1956-58, Sacramento Sch. Dist., 1958-89; part-time tchr. Sacramento County Sch., 1974-84. Substitute tchr., 1989—. Co-author: Natural History Guide, 1963, (field guide) Outdoor World of Sacramento Region, 1975; contbr. articles to profl. jours. Asst. dist. Commn. Boys Scouts Am., Shreveport, 1954, cubmaster, 1954; leader 4-H Club, Shreveport, 1950-54; elder Faith Luth. Ch., Fair Oaks, Calif., 1981-88. Recipient Scouter award, Boy Scouts Am., Shreveport, 1954, Honorary Svc. award Am. Winn Sch. PTA, 1982, Calif. Life Diploma Elem. Schs., 1961. Mem. Calif. Congress Parents Tchrs. Inc. (life). Democrat. Avocations: backpacking, coin collecting, stamp collecting, antiques, fishing. Home: 7720 Magnolia Ave Fair Oaks CA 95628-7316

LEMLY, THOMAS ADGER, lawyer; b. Dayton, Ohio, Jan. 31, 1943; s. Thomas Moore and Elizabeth (Adger) L.; m. Kathleen Brame, Nov. 24, 1984; children: Elizabeth Hayden, Joanna Marsden, Isabelle Stafford, Kate Brame. BA, Duke U., 1970; JD with honors, U. N.C., 1973. Bar: Wash. 1973, U.S. Dist. Ct. (we. dist.) Wash. 1973, U.S. Ct. Appeals (9th cir.) 1975, U.S. Supreme Ct. 1980. Assoc. Davis Wright Tremaine, Seattle, 1973-79, ptnr., 1979—. Contbg. editor Employment Discrimination Law, 1984-87, 94—; editor Wash., Oreg., Alaska and Calif. Employment Law Deskbooks, 1987—. Chmn. Pacific Coast Labor Conf., Seattle, 1983; trustee Plymouth Congregational Ch., 1980-84, Seattle Opera Assn., 1991—. Mem. ABA (labor employment law sect. 1975—, subcom. chmn. 1984-90, govt. liaison com. 1982—), Seattle-King County Bar Assn. (chmn. labor sect.), Assn. Wash. Bus. (trustee 1992—, chmn. human resources coun. 1993—, chmn. employment law task force 1987-93), U. N.C. Bar Found. (bd. dirs. 1973-76), Seattle Duke Alumni Assn. (pres. 1979-84), Order of Coif, Wash. Athletic Club (Seattle), Rotary. Republican. Presbyterian. Home: 1614 7th Ave W Seattle WA 98119-2919 Office: Davis Wright Tremaine 2600 Century Sq 1501 4th Ave Seattle WA 98101-1688 E-mail: tomlemly@dwt.com

LEMON, LESLIE GENE, retired diversified services company executive; b. Davenport, Iowa, June 14, 1940; BS, U. Ill., 1962, LLB, 1964. Bar: Ill. 1964, Ariz. 1972. Asst. gen. counsel Am. Farm Bur. Fedn., Chgo., 1964-69; sr. atty. Armour and Co., Chgo., 1969-71; with Viad Corp (formerly The Dial Corp and Greyhound Corp.), Phoenix, 1971-99; gen. counsel The Dial Corp (formerly Greyhound Corp.), Phoenix, 1977-96, v.p., 1979-99; ret., 1999; chmn. State of Ariz. Citizens Clean Elections Commn. Vestryman All Saints Episcopal Ch., Phoenix, 1975-81; trustee Phoenix Art Mus., 1985-98; bd. dirs. Phoenix Children's Hosp., 1985-98; bd. visitors U. Calif. Med. Sch., Davis, 1983—. Mem. ABA, Nat. Conf. Uniform Law Commrs., Assn. Gen. Counsel, Maricopa County Bar Assn., State Bar Ariz., Phoenix C. of C. (bd. dirs. 1989-95), Am. Arbitration Assn. (bd. dirs. 1996—). Home: 1136 W Butler Dr Phoenix AZ 85021-4428 E-mail: l.lemon@azbar.org

LEMONE, MARGARET ANNE, atmospheric scientist; b. Columbia, Mo., Feb. 21, 1946; d. David Vandenberg and Margaret Ann (Meyer) LeMone; m. Peter Augustus Gilman; children: Patrick Cyrus, Sarah Margaret. BA in Math., U. Mo., 1967; PhD in Atmospheric Scis., U. Wash., 1972. Postdoctoral fellow Nat. Ctr. for Atmospheric Rsch., Boulder, Colo., 1972-73, scientist, 1973-92, sr. scientist, 1992—. Mem. bd. on atmospheric sci. and climate NRC, 1993-97, 2001—; mem. sci. adv. com. U.S. Weather Rsch. Program, 1997-99. Contbr. articles to profl. jours.; contbg. author: D.C. Heath Earth Science, 1983-93; editor Jour. Atmospheric Scis., 1991-95. Woodrow Wilson fellow, NSF fellow, NDEA fellow, 1967. Fellow AAAS, Am. Meteorol. Soc. (councillor, mem. exec. com. 1992-96, Editor's award); mem. Am. Geophys. Union, Nat. Acad. Engring. Achievements include research in dynamics of linear convection (roll vortices) in daytime atmospheric boundary layer and its relationship to clouds; demonstrating that bands of deep convection (like squall lines) can increase the vertical shear of horizontal wind (contrary to conventional wisdom at that time); developing technique to estimate small fluctuations in air pressure from aircraft flying over land, used to estimate pressure field around clouds and storms. Avocations: paleontology (invertebrate), reading, hiking, drawing. Home: 2048 Balsam Dr Boulder CO 80304-3618 Office: Nat Ctr Atmospheric Rsch PO Box 3000 Boulder CO 80307-3000 E-mail: lemone@ucar.edu

LENARD, MICHAEL BARRY, merchant banker, lawyer; b. Chgo., May 20, 1955; s. Henry Madart and Jacqueline Jo Anne (Silver) L.; m. Amy Jeanne Rifenbergh, Oct. 10, 1987; children: Madeline Michael, Nicholas Xavier. BBA, U. Wis., 1977; postgrad., NYU, 1981-82; JD, U. So. Calif., 1982. Assoc. Whitman & Ransom, N.Y.C., 1982-83; from assoc. to ptnr. Latham & Watkins, L.A., 1984-93; mng. dir., counselor William E. Simon & Sons, L.A., 1993—; mng. dir. Indsl. Sport, L.A., 2001—. Bd. dirs. William E. Simon & Sons (Asia), Hong Kong. With So. Calif. Law Rev. mag., 1980-81. V.p. U.S. Olympic Com., 1989-96, mem. exec. com., bd. dirs., 1985-96, mem. athletes' adv. coun., 1981-89, vice chmn. athletes' adv. coun., 1985-89; named to Internat. Coun. for Arbitration of Sport, 1994—; bd. dirs. L.A. Sports Coun., 1988—, Atlanta Com. for Olympic Games, 1990—. Named semi-finalist Outstanding Undergrad. Achievement award, 1977, USA Team Handball Athlete of Yr., 1985, USOC [illegible] Team Handball Sportsman of Yr., 1985, Nat. Champion in Team Handball, 1975, 77, 79-80, 82, 87, 95; recipient Harry A. Bullis scholarship, 1977, Disting. Svc. award U.S. Sports Acad., 1996; mem. 1984 Olympic Team, U.S. Nat. Team, 1977-85 (capt. 1985). Mem. Order of the Coif, Phi Kappa Phi, Beta Gamma Sigma, Beta Alpha Psi, Phi Eta Sigma. Office: William E Simon & Sons 10990 Wilshire Blvd Ste 500 Los Angeles CA 90024-3917 E-mail: mlenard@wesandsons.com

LENDARIS, GEORGE GREGORY, systems science educator; b. Helper, Utah, Apr. 2, 1935; s. Gregory George and Argie (Xenakis) L.; m. Irene Kokinos, June 26, 1958 (dec. July 1988); children: Miriam, Dorothy. BSEE cum laude., U. Calif., Berkeley, 1957, MSEE, 1958; PhD in Electrical Engring., 1961. Registered profl. engr., Calif., Oreg. Sr. rsch. engr., program mgr. Gen. Motors Corp., Defense Rsch. Labs., Santa Barbara, Calif., 1961-69; assoc. prof. systems sci., chmn. faculty Oreg. Grad. Ctr. for Rsch., Beaverton, 1969-71; prof. systems sci., electrical engring. Portland State U. Systems Sci. PhD Program, Oregon, 1971—; with Accurate Automation Corp., Chattanooga, 1993—, also bd. dirs. Cons. various bus.; editorial bd. Internat. Jour. of Gen. Systems (Gordon & Breach), 1974—, Systems Rsch. Jour. 1985—, IEEE Transactions on Neural Networks, 1991—; chmn. gen. Internat. Joint Conf. on Neural Networks, Oreg., 1991-93; presiding officer Faculty Senate Portland State U., 1995-96. Author jour. article Diffraction Pattern Sampling, 1970, selected reprints book IEEE, 1978, chpt. in book Conceptual Graphs & Neural Networks, 1992, numerous conf. articles. Choir dir. local chs. Greek Orthodox Ch., Santa Barbara, Portland, 1962-73, pres., chmn. various coms., 1962—, mem. justice and human rights com. local ch., Portland, 1974—; mem. Gov.'s Tech. Adv. Com., Oreg., 1970-72, oreg. State Senate Task Force on Econ. Devel., 1972-73; mem. adv. panel Portland Energy Commn., 1980. NAS fellow, 1974. Fellow IEEE; mem. AAAS, Systems, Man and Cybernetics Soc., Internat. Neural Network Soc. (bd. govs. 1996—), Internat. Soc. Knowledge Engrs., Am. Helenic Edn. Progressive Assn., Sigma Xi, Tau Beta Pi, Eta Kappa Nu. Avocations: woodworking, Greek folk dancing instructor, church choir singing. Office: Portland State U Sys Sci PhD Program PO Box 751 Portland OR 97207-0751

LENGERICH, ANTHONY WILLIAM, career officer; BA in Polit. Sci., U. Colo., 1971; MSEE, Naval Postgrad. Sch., 1982; postgrad. in mgmt., Cornell Univ., 1994. Commd. USN; various to staff comms. officer USS Oklahoma City (CLG-5), 1973-74; comms. opers. officer CINCUS-NAVEUR, E. Atlantic/Mediterranean, 1974-76; opers. officer USS Badger (FF 1071), Pearl Harbor, Hawaii, 1976-78; opers./combat systems officer Commander Destroyer Squad. Thirteen, San Diego, 1978-80; various to asst. surface opers. officer, scheduler various aircraft carriers including Nimitz, Saratoga, others, 1983-84; engring. duty officer, platform integration officer NAVELEX, JTIDS, 1984-86; project officer Command and Control Processor, 1986-88; dir. Force Systems Engring. SPAWAR, 1988-90; divsn. dir. Afloat Mission Planning Systems Program Exec. Officer Cruise Missile Project's Command, 1990-92; comdr. Naval Electronic Systems Engring. Ctr., Charleston, S.C., 1992-94; commd. Engring. East Coast Divsn. Naval Command, Control and Ocean Surveillance Ctr. In-Svc., 1994-95; comdr. NCCOSC, San Diego, 1995-97; exec. asst. to comdr. Naval Sea Systems Command, Washington, 1997-98; dir. installations and logistics/rear adm. SPAWAR, 1998—. Decorated Legion of Merit, Meritorious Svc. medal, Navy Commendation medal, Combat Action ribbon, others. Office: 4301 Pacific Hwy San Diego CA 92110-3127

LENGYEL, CORNEL ADAM (CORNEL ADAM), writer; b. Fairfield, Conn., Jan. 1, 1915; s. Elmer Alexander and Mary Elizabeth (Bismarck) L.; m. Teresa Delaney Murphy, July 10, 1933; children: Jerome Benedict, Paul Joel, Michael Sebastian, Cornelia (Mrs. Charles Burke). LittD (hon.), World Acad. of Arts and Culture, Taiwan, 1991. Editor, supr. Fed. Research Project, San Francisco, 1938-41; music critic The Coast, San Francisco, 1937-41; shipwright, personnel officer Kaiser Shipyard, Richmond, Calif., 1942-44; mgr. Forty-Nine Theatre, Georgetown, 1946-50; editor W.H. Freeman Co., San Francisco, 1952-54, founder, exec. editor Dragon's Teeth Press, Georgetown, 1969—. Vis. prof., lectr. English lit. Calif. State U., 1962-63; writer-in-residence Hamline U., St. Paul, 1968-69; guest lectr. MIT, 1969; transl. from Hungarian; editorial cons. HEW; edni. dir. ILGWU. Author: (history) American Testament: The Story of the Promised Land, 1956, Four Days in July, 1958, I, Benedict Arnold: The Anatomy of Treason, 1960, Presidents of the U.S.A., 1961, Ethan Allen and the Green Mountain Boys, 1961, Jesus the Galilean, 1966, The Declaration of Independence, 1969; (poetry) Thirty Pieces, 1933, First Psalms, 1950, Fifty Poems, 1965, Four Dozen Songs, 1970, The Lookout's Letter, 1971, Late News from Adam's Acres, 1983, El Dorado Forest. Selected Poems, 1986, Advice to a Future Poet: Poems Early and Late, 1996, Stop, I Told the Sun, 1999; (plays) The World's My Village, 1935, Jonah Fugitive, 1936, The Giant's Trap, 1938, The Atom Clock, 1951, Eden, Inc., 1954, rev. edit. The Master Plan, 1963, Will of Stratford, 1964, Three Plays, 1964, The Case of Benedict Arnold, 1975, Doctor Franklin, 1976, The Shadow Trap, 1977, The Second Coming, 1985, Mengele's Passover, 1987, A Clockmaker's Boy: Part One, 1987; (novel) Malunkyaputta: His Quest for Edification, 1996; (essay) The Creative Self, 1971, contbr. to anthologies, The Golden Year, 1960, Interpretation for Our Time, 1966, The Britannica Library of Great American Writing, 1961, The Menorah Treasury, 1964, The Courage to Grow Old, 1988, From These Hills, 1990, Blood to Remember, 1991, Anthology of Contemporary Poets, 1992, World Poetry, 1993, We Speak for Peace, 1993, also Poet Lore, The Coast, The Argonaut, Saturday Rev., Menorah Jour., Kayak, Old Crow, Mandrake Rev., Midstream, California's Characters, 2000. Served with U.S. Merchant Marine, 1944-45. Recipient Albert M. Bender award in lit., 1945; recipient 1st prize Maritime Poetry Awards, 1945, 1st prize Poetry Soc. Va., 1951, Maxwell Anderson award drama, 1950, Di Castagnola award Poetry Soc. Am., 1971, Internat. Who's Who in Poetry award, 1972; Huntington Hartford Found. resident fellow, 1951, 64; MacDowell Colony resident fellow, 1967; Ossabaw Island Found. fellow, 1968; Nat. Endowment for Arts fellow, 1976-77 Mem. MLA, AAUP, PEN, Poetry Soc. Am., Poetry Soc. Eng., Authors Guild Address: Adam's Acres Georgetown CA 95634

LENHOFF, HOWARD MAER, biological sciences educator, academic administrator, activist; b. North Adams, Mass., Jan. 27, 1929; s. Charles and G. Sarah Lenhoff; m. Sylvia Grossman, June 20, 1954; children: Gloria, Bernard. B.A., Coe Coll., 1950, D.Sc. (hon.), 1976; Ph.D., Johns Hopkins U., 1955. USPHS fellow Loomis Lab., Greenwich, Conn., 1954-56; vis. lectr. Howard U., Washington, 1957-58; rsch. assoc. George Washington U., Washington, 1957-58; postdoctoral fellow Carnegie Instn., Washington, 1958; investigator Howard Hughes Med. Inst., Miami, 1958-63; prof. biology, dir. Lab. for Quantitative Biology U. Miami, Coral Gables, 1963-69; prof. biol. scis. U. Calif., Irvine, 1969-92, prof. polit. sci., 1986-92, assoc. dean biol. scis., 1969-71, dean grad. div., 1971-73, faculty asst. to vice chancellor of student affairs, 1986-88, 90-96, chair faculty senate, 1988-90, prof. emeritus, rsch. prof., 1993—; adj. prof. psychology U. Mass., Amherst, 2001—. Adj. prof. psychology U. Mass., Amherst, 2001—; vis. scientist, Louis Lipsky fellow Weizmann Inst. Sci., Rehovot, Israel, 1968-69; vis. prof. chem. engring., Rothschild fellow Israel Inst. Tech., 1973-74; vis. prof. Hebrew U., Jerusalem, spring 1970, fall 1971, 77-78; Hubert Humphrey Inst. fellow Ben Gurion U., Beersheva, Israel, 1981; sr. rsch. fellow Jesus Coll., U. Oxford, 1988; dir. Nelson Rsch. & Devel. Co., Irvine, 1971-73; bd. dirs. BioProbe Internat., Inc., Tustin, Calif., 1983-89, chmn. bd., 1983-86. Editor/author: Biology of Hydra, 1961, Hydra, 1969, Experimental Coelenterate Biology, 1972, Coelenterate Biology— Review and Perspectives, 1974, Hydra: Research Methods, 1983, Enzyme Immunoassay, 1985, From Trembley's Polyps to New Directions in Research on Hydra, 1985, Hydra and the Birth of Experimental Biology, 1986, Biology of Nematocysts, Conception to Birth, 1988; mem. editorial bd. Jour. Solid Phase Biochemistry, 1976-80. Vice chmn. So. Calif. div. Am. Assn. Profs. for Peace in Middle East, 1972-80; bd. dirs. Am. Assn. for Ethiopian Jews, 1974-93, pres., 1978-82; bd. govs. Israel Bonds Orange County, Calif., 1974-80, Dade County Heart Assn., Miami, 1958-61, So. Calif. Technion Soc., 1976; pres. Hillel Coun. of Orange County, 1976-78; nat. chmn. faculty div. State of Israel Bonds, 1976; mem. sci. adv. bd. Am. Friends of Weizman Inst. Sci., 1980-84; bd. dirs. Hi Hopes Identity Discovery Found., Anaheim, Calif., 1982-87, pres. bd. govs., 1983-85, William Syndrome Found., trustee, 1992, 99—, pres., bd. dirs., 1993-95, exec. v.p., 1995-99; v.p. edn. Williams Syndrome Assn., 1994, bd. dirs., 1993-94; adv. bd. Berkshire Hills Music Acad., 2000—. 1st lt. USAF, 1956-58. Recipient Career Development award USPHS, 1965-69; Disting. fellow Iowa Acad. Sci., 1986. Fellow AAAS; mem. Soc. Physics and Natural History of Swiss Acad. Scis. Geneva (hon.), Am. Chem. Soc., Am. Biophys. Soc., Am. Soc. Zoologists, History of Sci. Soc., Am. Soc. Cell Biologists, Am. Soc. Biol. Chemists, Biophysics Soc., Soc. Gen. Physiologists, Soc. Growth and Devel. Home: PO Box 1511 Crescent City CA 95531 Office: U Calif Sch Biol Scis Irvine CA 92697-2300 E-mail: hmlenhof@uci.edu

LENO, JAY (JAMES DOUGLAS MUIR LENO), television personality, comedian, writer; b. New Rochelle, N.Y., Apr. 28, 1950; s. Angelo and Cathryn Leno; m. Mavis Nicholson, 1980. Grad., Emerson Coll., 1973. Worked as Rolls-Royce auto mechanic and deliveryman. Stand-up comedian playing Carneigie Hall, Caesar's Palace, others; numerous appearances on Late Night with David Letterman; exclusive guest host The Tonight Show, NBC-TV, 1987-92, host, 1992— (Emmy award, 1995); host, prodr. Showtime Spl. Jay Leno and the American Dream, 1986, Saturday Night Live, 1986, Jay Leno's Family Comedy Hour (Writers Guild Am. nomination), 1987, Our Planet Tonight; film appearances include: The Silver Bears, Fun with Dick and Jane, 1977, American Hot Wax, 1978, Americathon, 1979, Collision Course, 1988, Dave, 1993, Wayne's World 2, Major League 2, The Flintstones, 1994, The Birdcage, 1996; author: Leading with my Chin, 1996; (voice) What's up Hideous Sun Demon?, We're Back, 1995. Avocations: antique motorcycles and automobiles. Office: c/o NBC Enterprises 3500 Olive Dr 15th Fl Burbank CA 91510-7885

LENZ, PHILIP JOSEPH, municipal administrator; b. Monterey Park, Calif., Sept. 15, 1940; s. Philip George and Irene Mary (Bowers) L.; m. Mary Lou Antista, July 16, 1966; children: Brian Joseph, Jonathan Thomas. BA, Calif. State U., L.A., 1966; MS, Pepperdine U., 1974; cert. instr. total quality mgmt., Calif. State U., San Bernardino, 1993; cert. participating mgmt., Calif. State U., 1998. Dir. West Valley div. San Bernardino County (Calif.) Probation Dept., 1977-79, dir. juvenile div., 1979-82, dir. adminstrv. services, 1982-88, dir. dist. services, 1988-90; dep. chief probation officer, 1990—. Instr. dept. bus. Calif. State U., San Bernardino; instr. dept. social rels. Loma Linda U., 1988. Sec. bd. trustees Upland (Calif.) Sch. Dist., 1986—, pres. sch. bd., 1989-90, 94-96; mgr., coach Upland Am. Little League, 1981-90, bd. dirs., 1982-90; pres. Fontana (Calif.) Family Svc. Agy., 1972-74; mem. adv. com. corrections Chaffey Coll., Alta Loma, Calif., 1977-97; mem. Upland Parks and Recreation Com., 1986-97, chmn., 1989-91; bd. dirs. Highlander Ednl. Found., v.p., 1991-96; mem. Calif. Youth Authority CADRE of Cons.; mem. San Bernardino County Com. on Sch. Dist. Orgn., 1998—. Recipient Tim Fitzharris award Chief Probation Officers of Calif., 1987. Mem. Calif. Probation, Parole and Correctional Assn. (liaison, regional v.p. 1981-83, 2d v.p. 1985-86, 1st v.p. 1986—, pres. 1987—), Probation Bus. Mgr.'s Assn. (regional chmn. 1984-86, v.p. 1987), Western Correctional Assn., Assn. for Criminal Justice Rsch. (bd. dirs.), Probation Adminstrs. Assn. (regional chair 1992-93). Democrat. Roman Catholic. Avocations: baseball, bicycle riding, hiking. Home: 1375 Stanford Ave Upland CA 91786-3147 Office: San Bernardino County Dept Probation 175 W 5th St San Bernardino CA 92415-1012

LEON, BRUNO, architect, educator; b. Van Houten, N.Mex., Feb. 18, 1924; s. Giovanni and Rose (Cunico) L.; m. Louise Dal-Bo, Sept. 4, 1948 (dec. 1974); m. Bonnie Bertram, Sept. 12, 1976; children: Mark Jon, John Anthony, Lisa Rose. Student, Wayne State U., 1942, U. Detroit, 1945-48, LHD (hon.), 1984; BArch, N.C. State U., 1953. Registered architect, Mich., N.C., Mass., N.Y., N.Mex., Fla. Head design staff Fuller Research Found., Raleigh, N.C., 1954-55; archtl. designer I.M. Pei & Assos., N.Y.C., 1955-56; instr. Mass. Inst. Tech., 1956-59; designer Catalano & Belluschi (architects), Cambridge, Mass., 1958-59; asst. prof. U. Ill., Urbana, 1959-61; dean Sch. Architecture, U. Detroit, 1961-93, dean emeritus, 1993; pvt. practice architecture, 1956—. With USAAF, 1942-45. Fellow AIA (dir. Detroit 1963-64); mem. Alpha Sigma Nu (hon.), Phi Kappa Phi. Home: 9 Redonda Ct Santa Fe NM 87508-8308 E-mail: volterra@newmexico.com

LEONARD, GLEN MILTON, museum administrator; b. Salt Lake City, Nov. 12, 1938; s. Burnham J. and Allene (Green) L.; m. Karen Wright, Mar. 15, 1968; children: Cory, Kyle, Keith. BA, U. Utah, 1964, MA, 1966, PhD, 1970. Mng. editor Utah State Hist. Soc., Salt Lake City, 1970-73; sr. rsch. assoc. history divsn. Ch. of Jesus Christ of LDS, Salt Lake City, 1973-78; dir. Mus. Ch. History and Art, Salt Lake City, 1979—. Mem. adv. bd. editors Utah Hist. Quarterly, Salt Lake City, 1973-88; assoc. editor Jour. Mormon History, Provo, Utah, 1974-80; bd. dirs. Western Studies Ctr., Brigham Young U., Provo. Co-author: The Story of the Latter-day Saints, 1976; Author: A History of Davis County, 1999. Mem. Hist. Preservation Commn., Farmington, Utah, 1986-92; mem. adv. coun. Mormon Pioneer Nat. Hist. Trail, Nat. Pk. Svc., 1980-86; mem. Utah Pioneer Sesquicentennial Celebration Coordinating Coun., 1995-97. Recipient Dale Morgan Article award Utah State Hist. Soc., 1973, Mormon History Assn. Article awards, 1990, 96. Mem. Orgn. Am. Historians, Western History Assn., Am. Assn. Mus. (mus. assessment program cons.), Western Mus. Assn., Utah Mus. Assn. (bd. dirs. 1980-83), Am. Assn. State and Local History. Avocations: photography, music, gardening. Office: Mus Ch Hist & Art 45 N West Temple Salt Lake City UT 84150-3810

LEONARD, THOMAS, dean, educator, librarian; BA (hon.), Univ. Mich., 1966; PhD, Univ. Calif., 1973. Librarian Univ. Calif., Berkeley. Speaker and cons. in field. Author: Above the Battle: War-Making in America from Appomattox to Versailles, 1978, The Power of the Press: The Birth of American Political Reporting, 1986, News for All: America's Coming of Age with the Press, 1995; contbr. numerous articles to profl. jours. Office: Univ Calif Sch Library 245 Doe Library MC 6000 Berkeley CA 94720-6000

LEONDAKIS, NIKI ANNA, food service executive; b. West Springfield, Mass., Nov. 28, 1960; B in Hotel and Restaurant Mgmt., U. Mass. Restaurant and beverage mgr. Marriott, Nashville; dir. catering Ritz Carlton Hotels, Atlanta, dir. food and beverage Marina Del Rey, Calif., San Francisco; joined Klimpton Hotel and Restaurant Group, Inc., San Francisco, 1993, regional mgr. N.W., 1993-95, v.p. restaurant ops., 1995—. Named Rising Star, Restaurant Hospitality Mag. Avocations: snow skiing, running, painting, family activities. Office: Kimpton Hotel & Restaurant Group Inc 222 Kearny St Ste 200 San Francisco CA 94108

LEONE, STEPHEN ROBERT, chemical physicist, educator; b. N.Y.C., May 19, 1948; s. Dominic and Annie Frances (Sappa) L. BA, Northwestern U., 1970; PhD, U. Calif., Berkeley, 1974. Asst. prof. U. So. Calif., L.A., 1974-76; physicist/fellow Nat. Inst. Standards and Tech., Boulder, Colo., 1976-94, acting chief Quantum Physics divsn., 1994-95; adj. prof. U. Colo., Boulder, 1994-96. Contbr. over 200 articles to profl. publs.; mem. editorial bd. Optics Letters, Jour. Chem. Physics, Chem. Revs., Jour. Phys. Chemistry, Molecular Physics, Chem. Physics Letters, Progress in Reaction Kinetics; patentee in field. Recipient silver and gold medals Dept. Commerce, 1980, 85, Coblentz award Coblentz Soc., 1984, Arthur S. Flemming award U.S. Govt., 1986, Samuel Wesley Stratton award Nat. Inst. Standards and Tech., 1992; Alfred P. Sloan fellow Sloan Found., 1977-81, Guggenheim fellow, 1988. Fellow AAAS, Optical Soc. Am., Am. Phys. Soc. (chair div. chem. physics 1987-88, Herbert P. Broida prize 1989); mem. NAS, Am. Chem. Soc. (pure chemistry award 1982, nobel laureate signature award 1983). Office: JILA PO Box 440 Boulder CO 80309-0440

LEONG, MARGARET, construction executive; CFO Shapell Industries, Beverly Hills, Calif., 1993—. Office: Shapell Industries 8383 Wilshire Blvd Ste 700 Beverly Hills CA 90211-2472

LEONHARDT, THOMAS WILBURN, librarian, library director; b. Wilmington, N.C., Feb. 7, 1943; s. Thomas Beauregard and Rachel Virginia (Callicutt) L.; m. Margaret Ann Pullen, Sept. 19, 1966; children: Hilary, Thomas, Rebecca, Benjamin. AA, Pasadena (Calif.) City Coll., 1968; AB, U. Calif., Berkeley, 1970, MLS, 1973. Head gift and exch. div. Stanford (Calif.) U. Librs., 1973-76; head acquisition dept. Boise (Idaho) State U. Libr., 1976-79, Duke U. Librs., Durham, N.C., 1980-82; asst. univ. libr. U. Oreg., Eugene, 1982-87; dean librs. U. of the Pacific, Stockton, Calif., 1987-92; dir. tech. svcs. U. Okla. Librs., Norman, 1992-97; libr. dir. Oreg. Inst. Tech., Klamath Falls, 1997—. Editor RTSD Newsletter, Chgo., 1986-89, Info. Tech. & Librs., Chgo., 1990-95. Editor Advances in Collection Development and Resource Management, JAI Press, 1994—; publisher, editor Callicutt Family Chronicle; contbr. articles to profl. jours. Bd. dirs. No. Regional Libr. Facility, Richmond, Calif., 1988-92, Feather River Inst. for Libr. Acquisitions, Blairsden, Calif.; del. Online Computer Libr. Ctr. AMIGOS Bibliog. Coun., Inc., 1996—; chair Orbis Coun., 1999—; mem. Klamath Symphony, 1997—. Mem. ALA, Assn. Coll. Rsch. Librs., Libr. and Info. Tech. Assn. (pres. 1997-98), Assn. for Libr. Collections and Tech. Svcs., Ctrl. Assn. Librs. (bd. dirs. Stockton chpt. 1987-92). Democrat. Avocations: trumpet, guitar. Home: 4070 Adelaide Ave Ste C Klamath Falls OR 97603-3782 Office: Oreg Inst Tech 3201 Campus Dr Klamath Falls OR 97601-8801 E-mail: leonhart@oit.edu

LEOPOLD, GEORGE ROBERT, radiologist; b. Lewistown, Pa., 1937; MD, U. Pitts., 1962. Intern York Hosp., 1962-63; resident U. Pitts., 1965-68; chmn., prof. dept. radiology U. Calif., San Diego, 1984—. Mem. Am. Coll. Radiology (Gold medal 1996), AIUM, ARRS, AUR, RSNA. Office: U Calif San Diego Med Ctr Ultrasound Divsn 8756 200 W Arbor Dr San Diego CA 92103-8756

LEOPOLD, LUNA BERGERE, geology educator; b. Albuquerque, Oct. 8, 1915; s. Aldo and Estella (Bergere) L.; m. Barbara Beck Nelson, 1973; children: Bruce Carl, Madelyn Dennette. BS, U. Wis., 1936, DSc (hon.), 1985; M.S., UCLA, 1944; Ph.D., Harvard, 1950; D Geography (hon.), U. Ottawa, 1969; DSc (hon.), Iowa Wesleyan Coll., 1971, St. Andrews U., 1981, U. Murcia, Spain, 1988. With Soil Conservation Service, 1938-41, U.S. Engrs. Office, 1941-42, U.S. Bur. Reclamation, 1946; head meteorologist Pineapple Research Inst. of Hawaii, 1946-49; hydraulic engr. U.S. Geol. Survey, 1950-71, chief hydrologist, 1957-66, sr. research hydrologist, 1966-71; prof. geology U. Calif. at Berkeley, 1973—. Author: (with Thomas Maddock, Jr.) The Flood Control Controversy, 1954, Fluvial Processes in Geomorphology, 1964, Water, 1974, (with Thomas Dunne) Water in Environmental Planning, 1978, A View of the River, 1994, Water, Rivers and Creeks, 1997; also tech. papers. Served as capt. air weather service USAAF, 1942-46. Recipient Disting. Svc. award Dept. of Interior, 1958, Veth medal Royal Netherlands Geog. Soc., 1963, Cullum Geog. medal Am. Geog. Soc., 1968, Rockefeller Pub. Service award, 1971, Busk medal Royal Geog. Soc., 1983, Berkeley citation U. Calif., David Linton award British Geomorphol. Rsch. Group, 1986, Linsley award Am. Inst. Hydrology, 1989, Caulfield medal Am. Water Resources Assn., 1991, Nat. Medal Sci. NSF, 1991, Palladium medal Nat. Audubon Soc., 1994, Joan Hodges Queneau Palladium medal Am. Assn. Engring. Socs., 1994. Mem. NAS (Warren prize), ASCE (Julian Hinds award), Geol. Soc. Am. (Kirk Bryan award 1958, pres. 1972, Disting. Career award geomorphological group 1991, Penrose medal 1994), Am. Geophys. Union (Robert E. Horton medal 1993), Am Geological Inst. (Ian Campbell medal), Am. Acad. Arts and Scis., Am. Philos. Soc., Cosmos Club (Washington), Sigma Xi, Tau Beta Pi, Phi Kappa Phi, Chi Epsilon. Home: PO Box 1040 Pinedale WY 82941-1040 Office: U Calif Dept Geology Berkeley CA 94720-0001

LEOPOLD, RAY, electronics executive; PhD, U. N.Mex., 1973; D Telecomm. Mgmt., S.D. Sch. Mines & Tech., 1997. V.p., chief tech. officer Global Telecom Solutions Sector, Chandler, Ariz. Patentee in field. Recipient Space award Aviation Week and Space Tech., 1996; Dan Noble fellow, 1995. Fellow IEEE (3d Millenium medal 2000); mem. AIAA (Biennial Comms. award 1998). Office: Global Telecom Solutions Sector 2501 S Price Rd Chandler AZ 85248-2895

LEPPER, MARK ROGER, psychology educator; b. Washington, Dec. 5, 1944; s. Mark H. and Joyce M. (Sullivan) L.; m. Jeanne E. Wallace, Dec. 22, 1966; 1 child, Geoffrey William. BA, Stanford U., 1966; PhD, Yale U., 1970. Asst. prof. psychology Stanford (Calif.) U., 1971-76, assoc. prof., 1976-82, prof., 1982—, chmn., 1990-94, 2000—. Fellow Ctr. Advanced Study in Behavioral Scis., 1979-80; chmn. mental health behavioral scis. research rev. com. NIMH, 1982-84, mem. basic sociocultural research rev. com., 1980-82. Co-editor: The Hidden Costs of Reward, 1978; cons. editor Jour. Personality and Social Psychology, 1977-85, Child Devel., 1977-86, Social Cognition, 1981-84, Jour. Ednl. Computing Research, 1983—, Media Psychology, 1999—; contbr. articles to profl. jours. Recipient Hoagland prize Stanford U., 1990, Cattell Found. award, 1999; Woodrow Wilson fellow, 1966-67, NSF fellow, 1966-69, Sterling fellow, 1969-70, Mellon fellow, 1975, fellow Stanford U., 1988-90; grantee NSF, 1978-82, 86-88, NIMH, 1978-86, 88—, Nat. Inst. Child Health and Human Devel., 1975-88, 90—, U.S. Office Edn., 1972-73. Fellow APA, AAAS, Am. Psychol. Soc., Soc. Personality and Social Psychology, Soc. Psychol. Study Social Issues; mem. Am. Ednl. Rsch. Assn., Soc. Exptl. Social Psychology, Soc. Rsch. in Child Devel. Home: 1544 Dana Ave Palo Alto CA 94303-2813 Office: Stanford U Dept Psychology Jordan Hall Bldg 420 Stanford CA 94305-2130

LEPRINO, JAMES G. food products executive; b. 1937; With Leprino Foods Co., Denver, 1955—, now chmn. bd. Office: Leprino Foods Co 1830 W 38th Ave Denver CO 80211-2200

LERAAEN, ALLEN KEITH, financial executive; b. Mason City, Iowa, Dec. 4, 1951; s. Myron O. and Clarice A. (Handeland) L.; m. Mary Elena Partheymuller, Apr. 14, 1978. BBA in Data Processing and Acctg., No. Ariz. U., 1975. CFA. Data processing supr. Stephenson & Co., Denver, 1978-81, contr., 1981-85, arbitrageur, trader, 1985-88, v.p., 1985-90, exec. v.p., portfolio mgr., 1990—. V.p., sec. bd. dirs. Circle Corp., Denver, 1985—; v.p StarTek, Inc., Denver, 1997—. Mem. Assn. Investment Mgmt. and Rsch., Denver Soc. Security Analysts. Avocation: flying. Home: 5692 S Robb St Littleton CO 80127-1942 Office: 100 Garfield St Fl 4 Denver CO 80206-5597 E-mail: al@great.net

LERDAL, MARK D. energy company executive; b. 1959; AB, Stanford U.; JD, Northwestern. Pres., CEO, chmn. bd. dirs. Kenetech Corp., San Francisco. Office: 500 Sansome St San Francisco CA 94111-3224 Fax: (415) 391-7740

LERMAN, EILEEN R. lawyer; b. N.Y.C., May 6, 1947; d. Alex and Beatrice (Kline) L. BA, Syracuse U., 1969; JD, Rutgers U., 1972; MBA, U. Denver, 1983. Bar: N.Y. 1973, Colo. 1976. Atty. FTC, N.Y.C., 1972-74; corp. atty. Samsonite Corp. and consumer products divsn. Beatrice Foods, Denver, 1976-78, assoc. gen. counsel, 1978-85, asst. sec., 1979-85; ptnr. Davis, Lerman, & Weinstein, Denver, 1985-92, Eileen R. Lerman & Assocs., Denver, 1993—. Bd. dirs. Legal Aid Soc. of Met. Denver, 1979-80. Bd. dirs., vice chmn. Colo. Postsecondary Ednl. Facilities Authority, 1981-89; bd. dirs., pres. Am. Jewish Com., 1989-92; mem. Leadership Denver, 1983. Mem. ABA, Colo. Women's Bar Assn. (bd. dirs. 1980-81), Colo. Bar Assn. (mem. bd. govs.), Denver Bar Assn. (trustee), N.Y. State Bar Assn., Rhone Brackett Inn (pres. 1997-98), Denver Law Club, Rutgers U. Alumni Assn., Univ. Club. Home: 1018 Fillmore St Denver CO 80206-3332 Office: Lerman & Assocs PC 50 S Steele St Ste 820 Denver CO 80209-2813

LERNER, RICHARD ALAN, chemistry educator, scientist; b. Chgo., Aug. 26, 1938; s. Peter Alex and Lily (Orlinsky) L.; m. Diana Lynn Pritchett, June 1966 (div. 1977); children: Danica, Arik, Edward; m. Nicola Green, Sept. 1, 1979. Student, Northwestern U., 1956-59; BS, MD, Stanford U., 1964; MD (hon.), Karolinska Inst., 1990. Intern Palo Alto (Calif.) Stanford Hosp., 1964-65, rsch. fellow, 1965-68; assoc. mem. Wistar Inst., Phila., 1968-70; assoc. mem. dept. exptl. pathology Scripps Clinic and Rsch. Found., La Jolla, Calif., 1970-72, mem., 1972-74, mem. dept. immunopathology, 1974-82; chmn. and mem. dept. molecular biology Rsch. Inst. Scripps Clinic, La Jolla, 1982-87, prof. dept. chemistry, 1988—, dir., 1987—; pres. The Scripps Rsch. Inst., La Jolla. Cons. Johnson & Johnson, 1983—, PPG Industries, Inc., Pitts., 1987—; sci. advisor Igen Inc., Rockville, Md., 1986—; spl. advisor Genex Corp., Gaithersburg, Md., 1988—; bd. dirs. Cytel Corp.; chmn. Internat. Symposium on Molecular Basis Cell-Cell Interaction, 1977, 78, 79, 80; mem. organizing com. for Modern Approaches to Vaccines, Cold Spring Harbor, 1983-89. Contbr. over 250 sci. papers; mem. editorial bd. Jour. Virology, Molecular Biology and Medicine, Protein Engring., Vaccine, In Vivo, Peptide Rsch. Mem. sci. policy adv. com. Uppsala U. (Sweden), sci. adv. bd. Econ. Devel. Bd., Singapore. Decorated Oficial de La Orden de San Carlos (Colombia); recipient NIH AID Career Devel. award, 1970, Parke Davis award, 1978, John A. Muntz Meml. award, 1990, San Marino prize, 1990, Burroughs Wellcome Fund and FASEB Wellcome Vis. Prof. award, 1990-91, College de France award, 1991, 1oth Ann. Jeanette Piperno Meml. award, 1991, Arthur C. Cope scholar award in chemistry, 1991, Wolf Prize in Chemistry, 1994. Fellow ACS (screening com. Calif. div.); mem. NAS Inst. Med. (ad hoc com. new rsch. opportunities in immunology), Am. Soc. Virology (charter), Am. Soc. Nephrology, Am. Assn. Immunologists, Am. Soc. Exptl. Pathology, Am. Soc. Microbiology, N.Y. Acad. Scis., Biophys. Soc., Royal Swedish Acad. Sci, Nat. Cancer Inst. (cancer preclin. program project rev. com. 1985-88), Royal Swedish Acad. Scis. (fgn., Lita Annenberg Hazen prof. immunochemistry 1986), 1st Thursday Club, Phi Eta Sigma, Alpha Omega Alpha. Avocations: tennis, walking, skiing, polo. Office: Scripps Rsch Inst 10550 N Torrey Pines Rd La Jolla CA 92037-1000

LERNER, SANDY, cosmetics executive; b. Phoenix, 1955; BA, Calif. State U.; student, Claremont Coll., Stanford U. Co-founder Cisco Sys., 1984-90, Ampersand Capital, 1990—; CEO Urban Decay, Mountain View, Calif., 1996—. Office: Urban Decay 729 Farad St Costa Mesa CA 92627-4304

LERNER, VLADIMIR SEMION, computer scientist, educator; b. Odessa, Ukraine, Sept. 12, 1931; came to U.S., 1990; s. Semion N. and Manya G. (Grosman) L.; m. Sanna K. Gleyzer, Sept. 28, 1954; children: Alex, Tatyana, Olga. BSEE, Odessa Poly. Inst., 1954; MEE, Inst. Problem's Controls, Moscow, 1959; PhD in Elec. Engring., Moscow Power Inst., 1961; D Sci. in Systems Analysis, Leningrad State U., 1974. Prof. elec. engring. Kishinev (Moldova) State U., 1962-64; prof. elec. engring. and control systems Kishinev Poly. Inst., 1964-79; sr. scientist in applied math. Acad. Sci., Kishinev, 1964-79; dir. math. modeling and computer sci. lab. Rsch. Inst., Odessa, 1979-89; sr. lectr. UCLA, 1991-93, rschr., 1993—; chmn. computer sci. dept. West Coast U., L.A., 1993-97, Nat. U., L.A., 1997-99. Mem. adv. bds. Acad. Sci., Kishinev, 1964-79, Poly. Inst., Kishinev, 1964-79; vis. prof. Leningrad State U., 1971-73; cons., mem. adv. bd. Poly. Inst., Odessa, 1979-89; mem. hon. editl. adv. bd. Encyclopedia of Life Support Syss., Informational Macrodynamics. Author: Physical Approach to Control Systems, 1969, Superimposing Processes in Control Problems, 1973, Dynamic Models in Decision Making, 1974, Special Course in Optimal and Self Control Systems, 1977, Lectures in Mathematical Modelling and Optimization, 1995, Mathematical Foundations of Informational Macrodynamics, 1996, Lectures in Informational Macrodynamics, 1996, Information Systems Analysis and Modelling: An Informational Macrodynamics Approach, 1999; contbr. numerous articles to sci. jours.; holder 23 patents; founder new sci. discipline Informational Macrodynamics. Recipient Silver medal for rsch. achievements, Moscow, 1961, outstanding achievements in edn., Kishinev, 1975. Avocations: bicycling, travel. E-mail: vslerner@yahoo.com

LEROY, DAVID HENRY, lawyer, state and federal official; b. Seattle, Aug. 16, 1947; s. Harold David and Lela Fay (Palmer) L.; 2 children. B.S., U. Idaho, 1969, J.D., 1971; LL.M., NYU, 1972; JD (hon.), Lincoln Coll., 1993. Bar: Idaho 1971, N.Y. State 1973, U.S. Supreme Ct. 1976. Law clk. Idaho 4th Dist. Ct., Boise, 1969; legal asst. Boise Cascade Corp., 1970; asso. firm Rothblatt, Rothblatt, Seijas & Peskin, N.Y.C., 1971-73; dep. prosecutor Ada County Prosecutor's Office, Boise, 1973-74, pros. atty., 1974-78; atty. gen. State of Idaho, Boise, 1978-82, lt. gov., 1983-87; ptnr. Runft, Leroy Coffin & Matthews, 1983-88, Leroy Law Offices, 1988—. Candidate for Gov. of Idaho, 1986, U.S. Congress, 1994; U.S. nuclear waste negotiator, 1990-93; U.S. Presdl. elector, 1992; lectr., cons. in field. Mem. State Task Force on Child Abuse, 1975; mem. Ada County Coun. on Alcoholism, 1976; del. Rep. Nat. Conv., 1976, 80, 84; chmn. Nat. Rep. Lt. Gov.'s Caucus, 1983-86; bd. dirs. United Fund, 1975-81; del. Am. Coun. Young Polit. Leaders, USSR, 1979, Am. Coun. for Free Asia, Taiwan, 1980, U.S./Taiwan Investment Forum, 1983; del. leader Friendship Force Tour USSR, 1984; legal counsel Young Reps., 1974-81; candidate for Gov. Idaho, 1986; presdl. elector, 1992; candidate U.S. Ho. Reps. 1st Dist, Idaho, 1994. Mem. Nat. Dist. Attys. Assn., Idaho Prosecutors Assn., Am. Trial Lawyers Assn., Idaho Trial Lawyers Assn., Nat. Assn. Attys. Gen. (chmn. energy subcom., exec. com., del to China 1981), Western Attys. Gen. Assn. (vice chmn. 1980-83, chmn. 1981), Nat. Lt. Govs. Assn. (exec. bd. 1983), Idaho Bar Assn., Ada County Lincoln Day Assn. (pres. 2000), Sigma Alpha Epsilon. Presbyterian. Office: The Leroy Offices PO Box 193 Boise ID 83701-0193 E-mail: dave@dleroy.com

LE SAGE, BERNARD E. lawyer; b. Pasadena, Calif., Mar. 29, 1949; BA, U. Notre Dame, 1971; JD, Loyola U., L.A., 1974. Bar: Calif. 1974. Extern clk. to Hon. William P. Clark Calif. Supreme Ct., 1974; with Buchalter, Nemer, Fields & Younger, L.A., 1979—. Mem. ABA, State Bar Calif., Los Angeles County Bar Assn. (trustee 1982-84), Los Angeles County Bar Barristers (pres. 1983-84), Chancery Club. Office: Buchalter Nemer Fields & Younger 601 S Figueroa St Ste 2400 Los Angeles CA 90017-5709

LESCH, BARRY M. lawyer; b. N.Y.C., Apr. 26, 1945; BA, U. Pa., 1965; MA, Ind. U., 1971; JD, U. Calif., Berkeley, 1975. Bar: Calif. 1975, U.S. Supreme Ct. 1980. With Laughlin, Falbo, Levy & Moresi, Sacramento. Mem. State Bar Calif. (cert. specialist workers compensation law). Office: Laughlin Falbo Levy & Moresi 106 K St Fl 2 Sacramento CA 95814-3218

LESHER, ROBERT OVERTON, lawyer; b. Phoenix, Apr. 6, 1921; s. Charles Zaner and Alice Marguerite (Heckman) L.; children: Stephen Harrison, Janet Kay. BA, U. Ariz., 1942, LLB, 1949. Bar: Ariz. 1949, Ill. 1949. Atty. Atcheson, Topeka & Santa Fe Ry., 1949-54; pvt. practice, Tucson, 1954—. Adj. prof. Law Sch., U. Ariz., 1954-84; mem. Supreme Ct. Ariz., 1960. With AUS, 1942-46, 50-52. Fellow Am. Coll. Trial Lawyers; mem. Am. Law Inst., Am. Bd. Trial Advs. (diplomate), Internat. Assn. Ins. Counsel, Tucson Country Club. Home: 659 N Richey Blvd Tucson AZ 85716-5040

LESH-LAURIE, GEORGIA ELIZABETH, university administrator, biology educator, researcher; b. Cleve., July 28, 1938; d. Howard Frees and Josephine Elizabeth (Taylor) Lesh; m. William Francis Laurie, Aug. 16, 1969. BS, Marietta Coll., 1960; MS, U. Wis., 1961; PhD, Case Western Reserve U., 1966. Asst. prof. SUNY, Albany, 1966-69; asst., then assoc. prof. Case Western Reserve U., 1969-77, asst. dean, 1973-76; interim dir. Cleve. State U., Ohio, 1980, prof., chairperson, 1977-81, dean grad. studies, 1981-86, dean arts and scis., 1986-91, interim provost, v.p. academic and student affairs, 1989-90; vice chancellor acad. and student affairs U. Colo., Denver, 1991-95, interim chancellor, 1995-97, chancellor, 1997—. Cons. in field; reviewer numerous granting agencies, profl. jours., 1968—; advanced placement exam. Edn. Testing Service, Princeton, N.J., 1982-83. Contbr. sci. articles to profl. pubs. Trustee Marietta Coll., Ohio, 1980-84, 85-95; mem. city/univ. interchange com., Cleve., 1983-91. Fellow NSF, NIH; grantee NIH, Am. Cancer Soc., Am. Heart Assn., Research Corp., 1968—; recipient Wright fellowship Bermuda Biol. Station; named among AAUW Women of Distinction; named to Girl Scouts Women's Leadership Cir. Fellow AAAS; mem. Am. Soc. Zoologists, Soc. Devel. Biology, Am. Soc. Cell Biology, Phi Beta Kappa. Home: 1761 E Phillips Ave Littleton CO 80122-3260 E-mail: georgia.lesh-laurie@cudenver.edu

LESHY, JOHN D. lawyer, legal educator, government official; b. Winchester, Ohio, Oct. 7, 1944; s. John and Dolores (King) L.; m. Helen M. Sandalls, Dec. 15, 1973; 1 child, David Alexander. AB cum laude, Harvard U., 1966, JD magna cum laude, 1969. Trial atty. Civil Rights Divsn. Dept. Justice, Washington, 1969-72; atty. Natural Resources Def. Coun., Palo Alto, Calif., 1972-77; assoc. solicitor energy and resources Dept. Interior, Washington, 1977-80; prof. law Ariz. State U., Tempe, 1980—; spl. counsel to chair Natural Resources Com. U.S. Ho. Reps., Washington, 1992-93; solicitor (gen. counsel) Dept. Interior, 1993-2001. Cons. Calif. State Land Commn., N.Mex. Atty. Gen., Western Govs. Assn., Congl. Rsch. Svc., Ford Found.; mem. com. Onshore Oil & Gas Leasing, NAS Nat. Rsch. Coun., 1989-90; vis. prof. Sch. Law U. San Diego, 1990; disting. vis. prof. law U. Calif. Hastings Coll. Law, 2001-02. Author: The Mining Law: A Study in Perpetual Motion, 1987, The Arizona State Constitution, 1993; co-author Federal Public Land and Resources Law, 4th edit., 2000, Legal Control of Water Resources, 3rd edit., 2000; contbr. articles, book chpts. to profl. jours., environ. jours. Bd. dirs. Ariz. Ctr. Law in Pub. Interest, 1981-86, Ariz. Raft Adventures, 1982-92; mem. Gov.'s Task Force Recreation on Fed. Lands, 1985-86, Gov.'s Task Force Environ. Impact Assessment, 1990, City of Phoenix Environ. Quality Commn., 1987-90. Robinson Cox vis. fellow U. Western Australia Law Sch., Perth, 1985, rsch. fellow U. Southampton, Eng., 1986; Ford Found. grantee, Resources for the Future grantee. Democrat. Avocations: piano, hiking, whitewater rafting, photography. Office: Calif Hastings Coll Law 200 McAllister St San Francisco CA 94102-4978 E-mail: Leshy@frontiernet.net

LESLIE, LISA DESHAUN, professional basketball player; b. Gardena, Calif., July 7, 1972; Grad., U. So. Calif., 1994. Basketball player USA Women's Nat. Team, 1996, L.A. Sparks WNBA, 1997—. Mem. gold medal winning 1994 Goodwill Games Team. Named 1993 USA Basketball Female Athlete of Yr.; recipient gold medal Atlanta Olympics, 1996; named MVP 1st WNBA All-Star Game, 1999. Office: Los Angeles Sparks Great Western Forum POB 10 3900 W Manchester Blvd Inglewood CA 90306-0010

LESLIE, MARK, software company executive; BA in Physics & Math., NYU, 1966; M of Bus. Devel., Harvard U., 1980. Pres., CEO Rugged Digital Systems, Inc., 1984-89; prin., owner Leslie cons., 1989-90; pres., CEO, co-chmn. Veritas Software, Mountain View, Calif., 1997—. Office: 1600 Plymouth St Mountain View CA 94043-1232

LESLIE, ROBERT LORNE, lawyer; b. Adak, Ala., Feb. 24, 1947; s. J. Lornie and L. Jean (Conelly) L.; children: Lorna Jean, Elizabeth Allen. BS, U.S. Mil. Acad., 1969; JD, U. Calif., San Francisco, 1974. Bar: Calif. 1974, D.C. 1979, U.S. Dist. Ct. (no. dist.) Calif. 1974, U.S. Ct. Claims 1975, U.S. Tax Ct. 1975, U.S. Ct. Appeals (9th and D.C. cirs.) 1974, U.S. Ct. Mil. Appeals 1980, U.S. Supreme Ct. 1980. Commd. 2d lt. U.S. Army, 1969, advanced through grades to maj., 1980; govt. trial atty. West Coast Field Office, Contract Appeals, Litigation and Regulatory Law divsns., Office JAG, Dept. Army, San Francisco, 1974-77; sr. trial atty., team chief Office of Chief Trial Atty., Dept. of Amry, Washington, 1977-80; ptnr. McInerney & Dillon, Oakland, Calif., 1980—, Oakland, 1980—. Lectr. on govt. contracts CSC, Continuing Legal Edn. Program; lectr. in govt. procurement U.S. Army Material Command. Served to col. USAR, ret. Decorated Purple Heart, Silver Star. Mem. ABA, Fed. Bar Assn., Associated Gen. Contractors, The Beavers. Office: McInerney & Dillon Ordway Bldg Fl 18 Oakland CA 94612-3610

LESLIE, TIM (ROBERT LESLIE), state legislator; b. Ashland, Oreg., Feb. 4, 1942; s. Robert Tabor Leslie and Virginia (Hall) P.; m. Clydene Ann Fisher, June 15, 1962; children: Debbie, Scott. BA in Political Sci., Calif. State U., Long Beach, 1963; MPA, U. Southern Calif., L.A., 1969. Prin. analyst Sacramento County Exec. Office, Calif., 1965-69; cons. Assm. W. & M. Commn., Sacramento, 1965-72; prin. legis. rep. County Sups. Assn., Sacramento, 1972-80; founder bd. dirs. Comm. Act. Against Drg., Sacramento, 1975-83; v.p. Moss & Thompson, Inc., Sacramento, 1980-84; exec. v.p. Kuhl. Corp., Sacramento, 1984-86; assemblyman Calif. State Ho. Reps., Sacramento, 1986-91; senator Calif. State Senate, Sacramento, 1991—. Chmn. fin. Investment and Internat. Trade Com.; vice chmn. Appropriations Com.; mem. Ins. Com., Natural Resources Com. Rep. candidate for lt. gov., 1998. Recipient Hang Tough award Nat. Tax Limitation Com., Calif., 1987; named Legislator of Yr., Sacramento County Taxpayers League and Osteo. Surgeons of Calif., 1990, Women in Timber, 1994. Republican. Presbyterian.

LESONSKY, RIEVA, editor; b. N.Y.C., June 20, 1952; d. Gerald and Muriel (Cash) L. BJ, U. Mo., 1974. Rschr. Doubleday & Co., N.Y.C., 1975-78, Entrepreneur Mag., L.A., 1978-80, rsch. dir., 1983-84, mng. editor, 1985-86, exec. editor, 1986-87, editor Irvine, Calif., 1987-90; sr. v.p., editor dir. Entrepreneur Media, Inc., Irvine, 1990—; rsch. dir. LFP Inc., L.A., 1980-82; editor in chief Entrepreneur mag., Irvine, CA. Spkr., lect. in field. Author: Start Your Own Business, 1998, 2d edit., 2001, Young Millionaires, 1998, Get Smart!, 1999, 303 Marketing Tips, 1999; editor: Complete Guide to Owning a Home-based Business, 1990, 168 More Businesses Anyone Can Start, 1991, 111 Businesses You Can Start for Under $10,000, 1991; contbr. articles to mags. Mem. nat. adv. coun. SBA, 1994-96, 96-2000; bd. dirs. Students in Free Enterprise. Named Dist. Media Advocate of Yr., Small Bus. Adminstrn., 1993, Dist. Women in Bus. Advocate, Small Bus. Adminstrn., 1995. Mem. Women's Network for Entrepreneurial Tng. (bd. dirs., advisor, nat. steering com.), Nat. Assn. Women's Bus. Advocates (bd. dirs.). Avocations: books, magazines, baseball. Office: Entrepreneur Media Inc 2445 Mccabe Way Irvine CA 92614-6244 E-mail: rieva@entrepreneur.com

LESSER, HENRY, lawyer; b. London, Feb. 28, 1947; came to U.S., 1976; s. Bernard Martin and Valerie Joan (Leslie) L.; m. Jane Michaels, June 29, 1969. BA with honors, Cambridge (Eng.) U., 1968, MA with honors, 1972; LLM, Harvard U., 1973. Bar: Eng. 1969, N.Y. 1977, U.S. Dist. Ct. (so. and ea. dists.) N.Y. 1977, Calif. 1984, U.S. Dist. Ct. (cen. dist.) Calif. 1984. Pvt. practice, London, 1969-71; assoc. Spear & Hill, N.Y.C. and London, 1974-75, Webster & Sheffield, N.Y.C. and London, 1976-77, Wachtell, Lipton, Rosen & Katz, N.Y.C., 1977-80, ptnr., 1980-83, Gibson, Dunn & Cutcher, L.A., 1983-87, Fried, Frank, Harris, Shriver & Jacobson, L.A., 1987-91, Irell & Manella, LLC, L.A., 1991-97, Heller, Ehrman, White & McAuliffe, Palo Alto, Calif., 1997-2000, Gray, Cary, Ware & Freidenrich, Palo Alto, 2000—. Lectr. law Oxford (Eng.) U., 1968-69, Cambridge U., 1970-71, UCLA, 1989. Editor-in-chief (bi-monthly) Corporate Governance Adviser; contbr. articles to profl. publs. Harkness fellow Commonwealth Fund, N.Y., 1971. Mem. ABA, Internat. Bar Assn., Calif. Bar Assn. (chmn. corps. com. 1990-91, vice chmn. bus. law sect. exec. com. 1993-94), Am. Law Inst., Assn. Bar City N.Y. Avocations: running, golf. Office: Gray Cary Ware & Freidenrich 400 Hamilton Ave Palo Alto CA 94301-1833 E-mail: hlesser@graycary.com

LESSER, JOAN L. lawyer; b. L.A. BA, Brandeis U., 1969; JD, U. So. Calif., 1973. Bar: Calif. 1973, U.S. Dist. Ct. (cen. dist.) Calif. 1974. Assoc. Irell and Manella LLP, L.A., 1973-80, ptnr., 1980—. Mem. planning com. Ann. Real Property Inst., Continuing Edn. of Bar, Berkeley, 1990-96; speaker at profl. confs. Trustee Windward Sch.; grad. Leadership L.A., 1992; bd. dirs. L.A. chpt. Legion Lex. Mem. Orgn. Women Execs. (past pres., bd. dirs.), Order of Coif. Office: Irell & Manella LLP 1800 Avenue Of The Stars Los Angeles CA 90067-4276 E-mail: jlesser@irell.com

LESSER, WENDY, literary magazine editor, writer, consultant; b. Santa Monica, Calif., Mar. 20, 1952; d. Murray Leon Lesser and Millicent (Gerson) Dillon; m. Richard Rizzo, Jan. 18, 1985; 1 stepchild, Dov Antonio; 1 child, Nicholas. BA, Harvard U., 1973; MA, Cambridge (Eng.) U., 1975; PhD, U. Calif., Berkeley, 1982. Founding ptnr. Lesser & Ogden Assocs., Berkeley, 1977-81; founding editor The Threepenny Rev., Berkeley, 1980—. Bellagio resident Rockefeller Found, Italy, 1984. Author: The Life Below the Ground, 1987, His Other Half, 1991, Pictures at an Execution, 1994, A Director Calls, 1997, The Amateur, 1999; editor: Hiding in Plain Sight, 1993. Fellow NEH, 1983, 92, Guggenheim fellow, 1988, ACLS, 1996, Open Soc. Inst. fellow, 1998, Columbia U. Nat. Arts Journalism Program sr. fellow, 2000-01. Democrat. Office: The Threepenny Rev PO Box 9131 Berkeley CA 94709-0131

LESTER, W. HOWARD, retail executive; Chmn., CEO Williams-Sonoma Inc., San Francisco, 1986—. Office: Williams-Sonoma Inc 3250 Van Ness Ave San Francisco CA 94109

LESTER, WILLIAM ALEXANDER, JR. chemist, educator; b. Chgo., Apr. 24, 1937; s. William Alexander and Elizabeth Frances (Clark) L.; m. Rochelle Diane Reed, Dec. 27, 1959; children: William Alexander III, Allison Kimberleigh. BS, U. Chgo., 1958, MS, 1959; postgrad., Washington U., St. Louis, 1959-60; PhD, Cath. U. Am., 1964. Phys. chemist Nat. Bur. Stds., Washington, 1961-64; asst. dir. Theoretical Chemistry Inst./U. Wis., Madison, 1965-68; rsch. staff IBM Rsch. Lab., San Jose, Calif., 1968-75, mgr., 1976-78; tech. planning staff IBM T.J. Watson Rsch. Ctr., Yorktown Heights, N.Y., 1975-76; dir. Nat. Resource for Computation in Chemistry, Lawrence Berkeley (Calif.) Lab., 1978-81, also assoc. dir., staff sr. scientist, 1978-81, faculty sr. scientist, 1981—; prof. chemistry U. Calif., Berkeley, 1981—, assoc. dean Coll. Chemistry, 1991-95. Lectr. chemistry U. Wis., 1966-68; cons. NSF, 1976-77, mem. chem. divsn. adv. panel, 1981-83, adv. com. Office Advanced Sci. Computing program, 1985-87, chmn., 1987, sr. fellow for sci. and engring., asst. to dir. for human resource devel., 1995-96; mem. U.S. nat. com. Internat. Union Pure and Applied Chemistry, 1976-79; mem. com. on recommendations for U.S. Army Basic Sci. Rsch. NRC, 1984-87, mem. steering com., 1987-88; chemistry rsch. evaluation panel AF Office Sci. Rsch., 1974-78; chmn. Gordon Conf. Atomic and Molecular Interactions, 1978; mem. NRC panel on chem. physics Nat. Bur. Stds., 1980-83; mem. com. to survey chem. scis. NRC, 1982-84, Fed. Networking Coun. Adv. Com., 1991-95; mem. blue ribbon panel on high performance computing NSF, 1993; mem. com. on high performance computing and comm.: status of a major initiative NRC, 1994-95, mem. com. on math. challenges from theoretical computational chemistry, NRC, 1994-95; mem. tech. assessment bd. Army Rsch. Lab., NRC, 1996-99; coun. mem. Gordon Rsch. Conf., 1997-2000, selection and scheduling com., 2000-; mem. adv. bd. Model Instns. Excellence Spelman Coll., 1997—; mem. external vis. com. Nat. Partnership Advanced Computational Infrastructure, 1999—; mem. pres. com. Nat. Medal Sci., 2000-; mem. dept. energy adv. com. on advanced sci. computing, 2000-. Editor: Procs. of Conf. on Potential Energy Surfaces in Chemistry, 1971, Recent Advances in Quantum Monte Carlo Methods, 1997, (with J. Govaerts and M.N. Houkonnou) Contemporary Problems in Mathematical Physics, 2000; author: (with Brian L. Hammond and Peter J. Reynolds) Monte Carlo Methods in Ab Initio Quantum Chemistry, 1994; mem. editl. bd. Jour. Phys. Chemistry, 1979-81, Jour. Computational Chemistry, 1980-87, Computer Physics Comm., 1981-86; mem. adv. bd. Sci. Yr., 1989-93, Comms. on Analysis, Geometry and Physics, 1997—. Recipient Alumni award in sci. Cath. U. Am., 1983 Fellow AAAS (com. on nominations 1988-91, nat. bd. dirs. 1993-97), Calif. Acad. Scis., Am. Phys. Soc. (chmn. div. chem. physics 1986); mem. Am. Chem. Soc. (sec.-treas. Wis. sect. 1967-68, chmn. div. phys. chemistry 1979, treas. div. computers in chemistry 1974-77), Nat. Orgn. Black Chemists and Chem. Engrs. (Percy L. Julian award 1979, Outstanding Tchr. award 1986, exec. bd. 1984-87). Home: 4433 Briar Cliff Rd Oakland CA 94605-4624 Office: U Calif Dept Chemistry Berkeley CA 94720-1460 E-mail: walester@lbl.gov

LETA, DAVID EDWARD, lawyer; b. Rochester, N.Y., June 9, 1951; married; 2 children. BA, SUNY, Binghamton, 1973; JD, U. Utah, 1976. Bar: Utah, 1976, U.S. Ct. Appeals (9th and 10th cir.), U.S. Tax Ct., U.S. Supreme Ct. Assoc. Roe & Fowler, 1976-80, ptnr., 1980-82, Hansen, Jones, & Leta and predecessor firms Hansen, Jones, Maycock & Leta, Hansen & Anderson, 1982-92, Snell & Wilmer, Salt Lake City, 1992. Adj. prof. U. Utah. 1978-80; presenter, lectr. numerous seminars and legal edn. seminars. Contbr. articles to profl. jours. Trustee Ballet West. Mem. ABA (bankruptcy cts., rules and legislation subcoms. bus. bankruptcy section), Utah State Bar (first chmn. bankruptcy sec.), Utah Bankruptcy Lawyers Forum (initial trustee). Office: Snell & Wilmer 15 W South Temple Ste 1200 Salt Lake City UT 84101-1547

LETTERIE, KATHLEEN, broadcast executive; Sr. v.p. talent and casting WB Network, Burbank, Calif. Office: WB TV Network 4000 Warner Blvd Bldg 34R Burbank CA 91522-0001

LETTICH, SHELDON BERNARD, director, screenwriter; b. N.Y.C., Jan. 14, 1951; s. Max and Sonja (Shapelska) L.; m. Toni Dorthera Williams, Mar. 5, 1954; children: Micheline, Jessica, Angelique. Student, Brooks Inst., Santa Barbara, Calif., 1974; AA, Santa Monica Coll., 1974-76; student, Am. Film Inst., Beverly Hills, 1977-78. Author: (with others) play Tracers, 1980 (Los Angeles Drama Critics award, 1981), film Russkies, 1987, Rambo III, 1988; author: film Bloodsport, 1988; dir., writer films Lionheart, 1990, Only the Strong, 1993; dir., writer, co-prodr. film Double Impact, 1991; dir. films Perfect Target, 1996, The Last Patrol, 2000, The Order, 2001; writer, exec. prodr. film Legionnaire, 1999. Served to cpl. U.S.M.C., 1969-72, Vietnam. Mem. Dirs. Guild Am., Writers Guild Am. Office: Hard Corps Prodns Inc Ste 1060 10100 Santa Monica Blvd Los Angeles CA 90067-4100

LETTS, J. SPENCER, federal judge; b. 1934; BA, Yale U., 1956; LLB, Harvard U., 1960. Commd. U.S. Army, 1956, advanced through grades to capt., resigned, 1965; pvt. practice law Fulbright & Jaworski, Houston, 1960-66, Troy, Malin, Loveland & Letts, L.A., 1973-74, Hedlund, Hunter & Lynch, L.A., 1978-82, Latham & Watkins, L.A., 1982-85; gen. counsel Teledyne, Inc., 1966-73, 75-78, legal cons., 1978-82; judge U.S. Dist. Ct. (cen. dist.) Calif., L.A., 1986—. Contbr. articles to profl. jours. Mem. ABA, Calif. State Bar, Tex. State Bar, L.A. Bar Assn., Houston Bar Assn. Office: US Dist Ct 312 N Spring St Ste 243J Los Angeles CA 90012-4704

LETWIN, LEON, law educator; b. Milw., Dec. 29, 1929; s. Lazar and Bessie (Rosenthal) L.; m. Alita Zurav, July 11, 1952; children— Michael, Daniel, David Ph.B., U. Chgo., 1950; LL.B., U. Wis., 1952; LL.M., Harvard U., 1964. Bar: Wis. 1952, Calif. 1969. Teaching fellow Harvard Law Sch., Boston, 1963-64; faculty Law Sch. UCLA, 1964—, prof., 1968-92, prof. emeritus, 1993—. Coord. Native-Am. Grave Protection and Repatriation Act, UCLA, 1998—. Contbr. articles to profl. jours. Active ACLU. Mem. Lawyers Guild, State Bar Calif. Home: 2226 Manning Ave Los Angeles CA 90064-2002 Office: UCLA Law Sch 405 Hilgard Ave Los Angeles CA 90095-9000

LEUNG, FRANKIE FOOK-LUN, lawyer; b. Guangzhou, China, 1949; married; 1 child. BA in Psychology with honors, Hong Kong U., 1972; MS in Psychology, Birmingham U., Eng., 1974; BA, MA in Jurisprudence, Oxford U., Eng., 1976; JD, Coll. of Law, London, 1977. Bar: Calif. 1987. Barrister, Eng. and Hong Kong, 1977—. Lectr. Chinese law for businessmen Hong Kong U., 1984-85, 85-86; vis. scholar Harvard U. Law Sch., 1983; barrister, solicitor Supreme Ct. of Victoria, Australia, 1983—, Calif. Bar, 1987—; cons. prof. Chinese Law Diploma Program, U. East Asia, 1986-87; adj. prof. Loyola Law Sch., L.A., 1988-2000, Pepperdine U. Law Sch., 1989-90; lectr. Stanford U. Law Sch., 1995-96, U. So. Calif. Law Sch., 1998—. Author books on Chinese and Hong Kong law, Asian politics, Asian trade and bus. mgmt.; contbr. numerous articles to profl. jours., and 6 books. Bd. advisors Hong Kong Archives Hoover Instn.- Stanford U., 1988—; adv., Central Policy Unit, Hong Kong govt., 1997-99, dir. YMCA, Pasadena, Calif., 1997-99. Mem. Am. Arbitration Assn. (bd. dirs.), Calif. State Bar (mem. exec. coun. internat. sect. 1989-92, Wiley W. Manuel award 1993), Hong Kong Bar Assn., European Assn. for Chinese Law (mem. exec. coun. 1986—, country corr. 1985—), Am. C. of C. (chmn. subcom. on Chinese intellectual property law 1985-86), Am. Soc. Internat. Law (judge moot ct. 1984-96). Office: 444 S Flower St Fl 31 Los Angeles CA 90071-2901 Fax: (213) 228-8923. E-mail: frankieleunglaw@aol.com

LEUNG, KASON KAI CHING, computer specialist; b. Hong Kong, July 2, 1962; came to U.S., 1963; s. Patrick Kin Man and Esther Mo Chee (Shum) L. BA in Computer Sci., U. Calif., 1984. Microcomputer specialist Coopers & Lybrand, San Francisco, 1985-87; freelance computer specialist San Francisco, 1988-90; computer applications specialist T.Y. Lin Internat., San Francisco, 1990-92; tech. specialist Ziff-Davis Labs., Foster City, Calif., 1993-94; tech. analyst PC Mag., Foster City, 1995; sr. tech. analyst Ziff-Davis Benchmark Operation, Foster City, 1996; sr. tech. specialist Ziff-Davis Labs., Foster City, 1997-98; sys. adminstr. TurboLinux, Inc., Brisbane, 1999; sys. programmer II Office of the Pres., U. Calif., Oakland, 2000—. Mem. Assn. for Computing Machinery. Avocations: computers, sports, music, reading. Home: 90 Stanford Heights Ave San Francisco CA 94127-2318 E-mail: kason.leung@ucop.edu, kasonleung@earthlink.net

LEUTY, GERALD JOHNSTON, osteopathic physician and surgeon; b. Knoxville, Iowa, July 23, 1919; s. John William and Mable Reichard (Johnston) L.; m. Martha L. Weymouth, Jan. 24, 1940 (div. 1957); children: Maxine Joanne, Robert James, Gerald Johnston Jr., Karl Joseph; m. Norma Jean Hindman, Dec. 30, 1969; children: Barbara Jayne, Patrick Jack. AB, Kemper Mil. Sch., Boonville, Mo., 1939; postgrad., Drake U., Des Moines, 1944-45; DO, Des Moines Coll. Osteopathy, 1949; embalmer, Coll. Mortuary Sci., St. Louis, 1941. Mortician/embalmer Cauldwell-McJihon Funeral Home, Des Moines, 1939-40; aero. engr. Boeing Aircraft Co., Wichita, Kans., 1941-42; osteopathic physician and surgeon Knoxville (Iowa) Ostepathic Clinic, 1949-56; dir. Leuty Osteopathic Clinic, Earlham, Iowa, 1957-77; osteopathic physician and surgeon in pvt. practice Santa Rosa, Calif., 1977—; prof. clin. med. Western U. Health Svcs., Pomona, 1985—. Mem. Iowa's Gov. Blue Med. Adv. Bd., 1972-77. With U.S. Army, 1942-46. Named Physician of the Yr., 6th Dist. Iowa Ostepathic Soc., 1975, Disting. Leadership award, Am. Biog. Inst., 1988, others. Fellow Internat. Co.. Angiologists; mem. Am. Ostepathic Assn. (ho. of dels., life mem. 1989), Iowa Osteopathic Soc. (pres. 6th dist. 1974), Soc. Osteopathic Physicians, No. Calif. Osteopathic Med. Soc. (pres. 1981), Osteopathic Physicians and Surgeons of Calif. (pres. 1982), Am. Acad. Osteopathy (chmn. component socs. com. 1988, pres. Calif. divsn. 1987, pres. No. Calif. divsn. 1989, 91-93, 95), North Coast Osteopathic Med. Assn. (pres. 1992), Am. Med. Soc. Vienna (life mem.), Am. Legion (6th dist. comdr. 1974-75), Lions (pres. 1946). Republican. Presbyterian. Avocations: photography, travel. Home: 5835 La Cuesta Dr Santa Rosa CA 95409-3914

LEVADA, WILLIAM JOSEPH, archbishop; b. Long Beach, Calif., June 15, 1936; s. Joseph and Lorraine (Nunez) L. B.A., St. John's Coll., Camarillo, Calif., 1958; S.T.L., Gregorian U., Rome, 1962, S.T.D., 1971. Ordained priest Roman Cath. Ch., 1961, consecrated bishop, 1983. Assoc. pastor Archdiocese of L.A., 1962-67; prof. theology St. John's Sem., Camarillo, Calif., 1970-76; ofcl. Doctrinal Congregation, Vatican City, Italy, 1976-82; exec. dir. Calif. Cath. Conf., Sacramento, 1982-84; aux. bishop Archdiocese of L.A., 1983-86; archbishop Archdiocese of Portland, Oreg., 1986-95; coadjuctor archbishop of San Francisco, 1995. Trustee Cath. U. Am.; chmn. bd. dirs. Pope John XXIII Med.-Moral Rsch. and Edn. Ctr. Mem. Nat. Conf. Cath. Bishops (com. on doctrine), U.S. Cath. Conf., Cath. Theol. Soc. Am., Canon Law Soc. Am. Office: Archbishop San Francisco Pastoral Ctr 1 Peter Yorke Way San Francisco CA 94109

LEVE, ALAN DONALD, electronic materials manufacturing company owner, executive; b. Los Angeles, Dec. 15, 1927; s. Milton Lewis and Etta L.; m. Annette Einhorn, Sept. 3, 1962; children— Laura Michelle, Elise Deanne. BS, UCLA, 1951. CPA, Calif. Staff acct., mgr. Joseph S. Herbert & Co. (C.P.A.s), Los Angeles, 1951-57, ptnr., 1957-63; fin. and adminstrv. v.p., sec./treas. Mica Corp., Culver City, Calif., 1963-82, also bd. dirs., 1963-82, chmn. bd., chief exec. officer, 1982-83; v.p., bd. dirs. Micaply Internat. Inc., 1968-1982; v.p. Micaply AG, Switzerland, 1972-83, also bd. dirs. Switzerland, chief exec. officer, also bd. dirs. Switzerland, 1982-83; v.p., bd. dirs. Micaply Internat., Ltd., U.K., 1971-82; chmn. bd., mng. dir., chief exec. officer Micaply Internat. Ltd., U.K., 1982-83; v.p., bd. dirs. Titan Chem. Corp., Edgecraft Corp., Culver Hydro-Press, Inc., L.A., 1963-75; chmn. bd., pres., chief exec. officer Ohmega Techs., Inc., Culver City, Calif., 1983—, Ohmega Electronics, Inc., Culver City, 1986—. Chmn. In-Sight Editions LLC, 1998. Served with USAAF, 1946-47. Home: 16430 Dorado Dr Encino CA 91436-4118 Office: 4031 Elenda St Culver City CA 90232-3723

LEVEL, LEON JULES, information services executive; b. Detroit, Dec. 30, 1940; s. Leon and Madeline G. (Mayea) L.; m. Constance Kramer, June 25, 1966; children— Andrea, Aileen B.B.A., U. Mich., 1962, M.B.A., 1963. CPA, Mich. Asst. accountant Deloitte Haskins & Sells, Detroit, 1963-66, sr. accountant, 1966-69, prin., 1969-71; asst. corp. controller Bendix Corp., Southfield, Mich., 1971-81; v.p. fin. planning Burroughs Corp., Detroit, 1981-82, v.p., treas., 1982-86, Unisys Corp., Blue Bell, Pa., 1986-89; v.p., chief fin. officer Computer Scis. Corp., El Segundo, Calif., 1989—. Mem. U. Mich. adv. bd., Ann Arbor, 1984-90, Providence Hosp. Adv. Bd., Southfield, Mich., 1984-86, Allendale Ins. Adv. Bd., Cleve., 1985-89, 96—. Trustee Walnut St. Theatre, Phila., 1988-89 Mem. Fin. Execs. Inst. (sec. Detroit chpt. 1983-85, v.p. 1985-86, pres. 1986-87), Am. Inst. C.P.A.s, Mich. Assn. C.P.A.s, Inst. Mgmt. Accts. Office: Computer Scis Corp 2100 E Grand Ave El Segundo CA 90245-5024

LEVENSON, ALAN IRA, psychiatrist, physician, educator; b. Boston, July 25, 1935; s. Jacob Maurice and Frances Ethel (Biller) L.; m. Myra Beatrice Katzen, June 12, 1960 (div. 1993); children: Jonathan, Nancy; m. Linda Ann Nadell, Jan. 30, 1994. AB, Harvard U., 1957, MD, 1961, MPH, 1965. Diplomate: Am. Bd. Psychiatry and Neurology. Intern U. Hosp., Ann Arbor, Mich., 1961-62; resident psychiatry Mass. Mental Health Center, Boston, 1962-65; staff psychiatrist NIMH, Chevy Chase, Md., 1965-66, dir. div. mental health service programs, 1967-69; prof. psychiatry U. Ariz. Coll. Medicine, Tucson, 1969-2000, prof. emeritus, 2000—, head dept. psychiatry, 1969-89; chief exec. officer Palo Verde Mental Health Svcs., Tucson, 1971-91, chief med. officer, med. dir., 1991-93; chmn. bd. dirs., CEO Psychiatrists' Purchasing Group, 1991—; chmn. bd. dirs. Psychiatrists' Risk Retention Group, 1991-2000. Mem. staff Tucson Med. Ctr., U. Med. Ctr., Tucson. Author: The Community Mental Health Center: Strategies and Programs, 1972; Contbr. papers and articles to psychiat. jours. Bd. dirs. Tucson Urban League, 1971-78, Pima Council on Aging, 1976-83. Served with USPHS, 1965-69. Fellow Am. Psychiat. Assn. (treas. 1986-90), Am. Coll. Psychiatrists (regent 1980-83, v.p. 1983-85, pres.-elect 1985-86, pres. 1986-87), Am. Coll. Mental Health Adminstrn. (v.p. 1980-82, pres. 1982-83); mem. Group for Advancement Psychiatry, Harvard Alumni Assn. (bd. dirs. 1988-91). Office: 75 N Calle Resplendor Tucson AZ 85716-4937

LEVENSON, MARC DAVID, optics and lasers specialist, scientist, editor; b. Phila., May 28, 1945; s. Donald William and Ethyl Jean Levenson; m. Naomi Francis Matsuda, Oct. 24, 1971. SB, MIT, 1967; MS, Stanford U., 1968, PhD, 1971. Rsch. fellow Harvard U., Cambridge, Mass., 1971-74; asst. prof. physics U. So. Calif., L.A., 1974-77, assoc. prof., 1977-79; mem. rsch. staff IBM Rsch. div., San Jose, Calif., 1979-93, head mgr. OSC, 1987, mgr. quantum metrology, 1990; v.p. Focused Rsch., Inc., Sunnyvale, 1993-95; propr., cons. Marc D. Levenson Optics, Saratoga, 1993—. Vis. fellow Joint Inst. for Lab. Astrophysics, U. Colo., Boulder, 1995-96; vis. prof. Rice U., Houston, 1996. Author: Introduction to Nonlinear Laser Spectroscopy, 1988; editor: Lasers, Spectroscopy, New Ideas, 1987, Resonances, 1991; West Coast editor Solid State Tech. mag., 1993—; editor-in-chief Microlithography World Mag., 1995—; contbr. articles to profl. jours. Alfred Sloan rsch. fellow, 1975. Fellow IEEE, Optical Soc. Am. (Adolph Lomb medal 1976), Am. Phys. Soc., Bay Area Chrome Users Soc./Soc. Photog. and Instrumentation Engrs. (award 1991). Avocations: gardening, reading. E-mail: marcl@pennwell.com

LEVENSON, MILTON, chemical engineer, consultant; b. St. Paul, Jan. 4, 1923; s. Harry and Fanny M. Levenson; m. Mary Beth Novick, Aug. 27, 1950 (dec.); children: James L., Barbara G., Richard A., Scott D., Janet L. BChemE, U. Minn., 1943. Jr. engr. Houdaille-Hershey Corp., Decatur, Ill., 1944; research engr. Oak Ridge Nat. Lab., 1944-48; with Argonne (Ill.) Nat. Lab., 1948-73, assoc. lab. dir., 1973; dir. nuclear power div. Electric Power Research Inst., Palo Alto, Calif., 1973-80; exec. cons. Bechtel Power Corp., San Francisco, 1981-88; v.p. Bechtel Internat., 1984-89; pvt. exec. cons., 1990—. Lectr. in field. Contbr. over 150 articles to profl. jours., chpts. to 8 books; patentee in field. Served with C.E. U.S. Army, 1944-46. Bechtel fellow, 1981-89. Fellow AIChE (Robert E. Wilson award 1975), NAE, Am. Nuclear Soc. (pres. 1983-84). Office: 21 Politzer Dr Menlo Park CA 94025-5541

LEVEY, GERALD SAUL, internist, educator; b. Jersey City, Jan. 9, 1937; s. Jacob and Gertrude (Kantoff) L.; m. Barbara Ann Cohen, June 4, 1961; children: John, Robin. AB, Cornell U., 1957; MD, N.J. Coll. Medicine, 1961. Diplomate: Am. Bd. Internal Medicine. Med. intern Jersey City Med. Ctr., 1961-62, asst. med. resident, 1962-63; postdoctoral fellow dept. biol. chemistry Harvard U. Med. Sch., 1963-65; med. resident Mass. Gen. Hosp., Boston, 1965-66; clin. assoc. clin. endocrinology br. Nat. Inst. Arthritis and Metabolic Diseases NIH, Bethesda, Md., 1966-68, clin. assoc. Nat. Heart and Lung Inst., 1968-69, sr. investigator Nat. heart and Lung Inst., 1969-70; assoc. prof. medicine U. Miami Sch. Medicine, Fla., 1970-73, prof. medicine, 1973-79; prof., chmn. dept. medicine U. Pitts. Sch. Medicine, 1979-91; physician-in-chief Presbyn.-Univ. Hosp., Pitts., 1979-91; sr. v.p. for med. and sci. affairs Merck and Co., Inc., Whitehouse Sta., N.J., 1991-94; provost med. scis., dean Sch. of Medicine UCLA, 1994—. Harold Jeghers lectr. N.J. Coll. Medicine, 1977; Marian Blankenhorn lectr. Cin. Soc. Internal Medicine, 1982; co-prin. investigator Nat. Study of Internal Medicine Manpower, 1984—. Mem. editorial bd.: Endocrinology, 1972-76, Am. Jour. Physiology, 1972-76, Jour. Applied Physiology, 1972-76, Annals of Internal Medicine, 1981-84; cons. editor: Hosp. Medicine, 1981-91; contbr. articles to profl. jours. Bd. dirs. Am. Jewish Com., Miami, 1975-79; mem. United Jewish Fedn. Pitts. Leadership Devel., 1981-82; bd. dirs. Jewish Family and Children's Services, 1982-83. NIH grantee, 1971-91; Fla. Heart Assn. grantee, 1971-74. Fellow ACP; mem. AMA, Am. Thyroid Assn. (mem. membership com. 1977-80), Am. Fedn. Clin. Rsch. (councillor so. sect. 1973-76, pres. so. sect. 1977-78), Am. Soc. Clin. Investigation, Endocrine Soc., Assn. Profs. Medicine (chmn. ad hoc com. for use of animals in rsch. 1982-85, chmn. task force on internalmedicine manpower 1983-90, nat. pres. 1990-91), So. Soc. Clin. Investigation, Soc. Gen. Internal Medicine, Assn. Am. Physicians, Alpha Omega Alpha. Home: 1132 Laurel Way Beverly Hills CA 90210-2221 Office: UCLA Deans Office Sch Medicine 10833 Le Conte Ave Los Angeles CA 90095-3075

LEVI, DAVID F. federal judge; b. 1951; BA, Harvard U., MA, 1973; JD, Stanford U. Bar: Calif. 1983. U.S. atty. ea. dist. State of Calif., Sacramento, 1986-90; judge U.S. Dist. Ct. (ea. dist.) Calif., 1990—. Chmn. task force on race, religious and ethnic fairness U.S. Ct. Appeals (9th cir.), 1994-97, mem. jury com., 1993-95. Adv. com. on Civil Rules, 1994—, chair, 2000—; vis. com. U. Chgo. Law Sch., 1995-98. Mem. Am. Law Inst., Milton L. Schwartz Inn of Ct. (pres. 1992-95). Office: 501 I St Rm 14-230 Sacramento CA 95814-7300

LEVIN, ANDREW, state legislator; b. N.Y.C., May 4, 1946; m. Nicolette Levin. BA, U. Pa.; JD, Harvard U. Chief counsel Big Island, Legal Aid Soc., 1969-74, Aloha Airlines, 1971-74; asst. prof. U. Hawaii, Hilo, 1977-79; pvt. practice Hilo, 1974—; mem. Hawaii Senate, Honolulu, 1998—, co-chair ways and means com., mem. health/human svcs. com., mem. govt. ops. and housing com. Pres. Easter Seals; chair Carole Kai Bed Race; mem. Gov.'s Solid Waste Task Force; pres. Big Isle Mental Health Assn.; pres. East Hawaii Cultural Coun.; bd. dirs. BICA; mem. Vol. Action League, Humane Soc., ECOH, Puna Traffice and Crime Commn., Hist. Hawaii Found., Big Isle Rd. Runners; mem. Hawaii County Coun., 1975-76. Office: State Capitol 415 S Beretania St Honolulu HI 96813-2407

LEVIN, BARRY RAYMOND, rare book dealer; b. Phila., June 11, 1946; s. Sidney and Bertha (Zwerman) L.; m. Sally Ann Fudge, Aug. 19, 1983. Student, Santa Monica City Coll., 1964-65. Various aerospace positions McDonnell Douglas, AstroPeen, 1967-72; owner Barry R. Levin Sci. Fiction & Fantasy Lit., 1973—. Cons. sci. fiction, fantasy and horror films, 1976—. Author: (rare book catalogs) Titles from the Back Room, 1981, Great Works and Rarities of Science Fiction and Fantasy, 1982, One Small Step, 1983, Newsletters, 1980—, others; contbr. articles to profl. jours. With U.S. Army, 1965-67. Mem. Antiquarian Booksellers Assn. Am., Am. Booksellers Assn., Bibliog. Soc. Am., Bibliog. Soc. Great Britain, New Eng. Sci. Fiction Assn., So. Calif. Booksellers Assn., Internat. League Antiquarian Booksellers, Internat. Assn. of the Fantastic in the Arts, Internat. Platform Assn., Sci. Fiction Writers Am., Horror Writers Am., Manuscript Soc., Sci. Fiction Rsch. Assn., Assn. Sci. Fiction and Fantasy Artists, Lewis Carroll Soc., others. Jewish. Office: Barry R Levin Sci Fiction & Fantasy Lit 720 Santa Monica Blvd Santa Monica CA 90401-2602 E-mail: brl@raresf.com

LEVIN, ROBERT BARRY, motion picture company executive; b. Chgo., May 31, 1943; s. Albert Harold and Sally Ethel (Bloom) L.; children: Jordan, Leigh; m. Pamela Knussmann, Dec. 2, 1990; 1 stepchild, Taylor Thompson; 1 child, Spencer. BS in Journalism and Comm, U. Ill., 1965. Copywriter Sears Roebuck and Co., Chgo., 1965-66; pub. relations Natural Gas Pipeline Co. Am., Chgo., 1966-69; accounts exect. Hurvis Binzer and Churchill, Chgo., 1969-70; with McCann-Erickson, Chgo., 1975-82, acct. supr., 1975-79; mgmt. supr. Needham Harper Worldwide, Chgo., 1982-85; pres. mktg. Walt Disney Co., Burbank, Calif., 1985-94, chief corp. mktg. and comm., 1994-95; pres. worldwide mktg. Savoy Pictures, Santa Monica, 1995-96, Sony Pictures Entertainment, Culver City, 1996—2001, MGM Studios, 2001—.

LEVINE, ARNOLD MILTON, retired electrical engineer, documentary filmmaker; b. Preston, Conn., Aug. 15, 1916; s. Samuel and Florence May (Clark) L.; m. Bernice Eleanor Levich, Aug. 31, 1941; children: Mark Jeffrey, Michael Norman, Kevin Lawrence. BS in Radio Engring., Tri-State U., Angola, Ind., 1939, DSc, 1960; MS, U. Iowa, 1940. Head sound lab. CBS, N.Y.C., 1940-42; asst. engr., div. head ITT, N.Y.C. and Nutley, N.J., 1942-65, lab. head, lab. dir. San Fernando, Calif., 1965-71, v.p. aerospace, gen. mgr., sr. scientist Van Nuys, 1971-86; ret., 1986. Patentee fiber optics, radar, motion picture digital sound, communications and TV fields. Past mem. bd. dirs., v.p., pres. Am. Jewish Congress, L.A. Recipient San Fernando Valley Engr. of Yr. award, 1968; Profl. designation Motion Picture Art & Scis., UCLA, 1983. Fellow IEEE (life), Soc. Motion Picture and TV Engrs., USCG Aux. (vice comdr. 1990-91, flotilla cmdr. 1992-94). Avocations: sailing, amateur radio, filmmaking, swimming. Home: 10828 Fullbright Ave Chatsworth CA 91311-1737

LEVINE, C. BRUCE, lawyer; b. Liberty, N.Y., Aug. 20, 1945; Student, Stanford U.; BA magna cum laude, UCLA, 1967; JD cum laude, Harvard U., 1971. Bar: Calif. 1971. Mem. Greenberg, Glusker, Fields, Claman & Machtinger, L.A., 1971—. Editor Harvard Law Rev., 1970-71. Mem. State Bar Calif., L.A. County Bar Assn. (chmn. income tax com. tax sect. 1979-80), Beverly Hills Bar Assn. (chmn. taxation com. 1977-78), Phi Beta Kappa, Pi Gamma Mu. Office: Greenberg Glusker Fields Claman & Machtinger Ste 2100 1900 Avenue Of The Stars Los Angeles CA 90067-4502

LEVINE, JESSE E. publishing executive; b. N.Y.C., Apr. 28, 1951; one child. BA in English Lit., State U. N.Y. Sales rep. New Line Cinema, 1976-77; exec. v.p. N.Y. Syndicate Sales Corp., 1977-82; dir. L.A. Times Syndicate, 1982-88, pres., COO, 1988-93, pres., CEO, 1993—. Office: LA Times Syndicate 218 S Spring St Los Angeles CA 90012-3723

LEVINE, MARK DAVID, research laboratory administrator; b. Cleve., May 26, 1944; s. Hyman and Rebecca (Spector) L.; m. Irma Herrera, June, 1990. AB summa cum laude, Princeton U., 1966; PhD, U. Calif., Berkeley, 1975. Staff scientist Ford Found. Energy Policy Project, Washington, 1972-73; sr. energy policy analyst SRI Internat., Menlo Park, Calif., 1974-78; staff scientist Lawrence Berkeley Lab., Berkeley, 1978-84, dept. program leader, 1984-86, leader energy analysis program, 1986-96, dir. environ. energy techs. divsn., 1996—. Cons. Ford Found., TEM, Inc., Pacific Gas & Electric Co., QED Research, Inc., Energy Found., 1978—. Contbr. articles to profl. jours. Bd. dirs. Am. Coun. Energy Efficient Economy, Ctr. Clean Air Policy, Ctr. Resource Solutions, Beijing Energy Efficient Ctr. Woodrow Wilson fellow, 1966; Fulbright scholar, 1966. Fellow Calif. Coun. on Sci. and Tech. Jewish. Home: 5701 Barrett Ave El Cerrito CA 94530-1408 Office: Lawrence Berkeley Lab Bldg 90 Room 3125 Berkeley CA 94720 E-mail: mdlevine@lbl.gov

LEVINE, MICHAEL, public relations executive, writer; b. N.Y.C., Apr. 17, 1954; s. Arthur and Virginia (Gaylor) L. Student, Rutgers U., 1978. Owner, operator TV News Mag., Los Angeles, 1977-83; owner Levine/Schnieder Pub. Rels., now Levine Comms. Office, Los Angeles, 1982—. Mem. Gov.'s adv. bd. State Calif., Sacramento, 1980-82; pres. owner Aurora Pub., L.A., 1986—; moderator Thought Forum; lectr. in field; founder, moderator L.A. Media Roundtable; media expert KFWB Radio; host Access L.A. Radio Show. Author: The Address Book: How to Reach Anyone Who's Anyone, 1984, The New Address Book, 1986, The Corporate Address Book, 1987, The Music Address Book, 1989, Environmental Address Book, 1991, Kid's Address Book, 1991, Guerrilla P.R., Lessons at Halfway Point, 1995, Take It From Me, Selling Goodness, 1998, The Princess & The Package, 1998, Raise Your Social I.Q., 1998; pub., writer For Consideration newsletter; host Spiritual Seeker KRLA 1110 AM; host Spiritual Seeker Radio Show KRLA, nat. syndicated via Falk Am. Radio Network. Mem. Ronald Reagan Pres.'s Libr.; founder The Actor's Conf., Aurora Charity, 1987; bd. dirs. Felice Found., Micah Ctr.; adv. bd. Dare America; founder, moderator L.A. Media Roundtable; moderator U. Judaism Thought Forum. Mem. TV Acad. Arts and Scis., Entertainment Industries Coun., Musician's Assistance Program, West Hollywood C. of C. (bd. dirs. 1980-82). Jewish. Office: 10333 Ahston Ave Los Angeles CA 90024 E-mail: levinepr@earthlink.net, rebecca@levinepr.com

LEVINE, MICHAEL STEVEN, science educator; b. L.A., Mar. 5, 1955; married; two children. BA, U. Calif., Berkeley, 1976; PhD, Yale U., 1981. Postdoctoral staff U. Basel, 1982-83, U. Calif., Berkeley, 1983-84; asst. prof. dept. biol. scis. Columbia U., 1984-86, assoc. prof. dept. biol. scis., 1986-88, prof. dept. biol. scis., 1988-90; prof. dept. biology U. Calif., San Diego, 1991-96, prof. divsn. genetics Berkeley, 1996—. Mem. developmental biology study sect. NSF, 1988-90; mem. genetics study sect. NIH, 1990-94; co-dir. MBL Embryology, Woods Hole, Mass., 1991-96; vis. prof. Zool. Inst., U. Zürich, 1999-2000. Editor Mech. Devel., 1990-95, Devel., 1995—; mem. editl. bd. Cell, Genes & Devel., Current Opinion Cell Biology, Procs. Nat. Acad. Sci.; contbr. more than 120 articles to profl. jours. Recipient award in molecular biology NAS, 1996; Jane Coffin Childs postdoctoral fellow, 1982-84, Searle Scholars fellow, 1985-88, Alfred P. Sloan Rsch. fellow, 1985-87. Fellow Am. Acad. Arts and Scis.; mem. Nat. Acad. Sci., Phi Beta Kappa. Office: Univ Calif Dept MCB Divsn Genetics 401 Barker Hall Dept Mcb Berkeley CA 94720-3208

LEVINE, NORMAN GENE, insurance company executive; b. N.Y.C., Sept. 14, 1926; s. Harris J. and Dorothy S. (Podolsky) L.; m. Sandra Leibow, Dec. 11, 1969; children— Linda, Daniel, Donald. Student, U. Wis.-Madison, 1943-48. Agt. Aetna Life Ins. Co., N.Y.C., 1948-56, supr., 1956-59, gen. agt., 1959-75; mng. gen. agt. Mut. Benefit Life Ins. Co. in No. Calif., San Francisco, 1975-91; br. mgr. Sun Life of Can., 1991-97; pres. Levine Enterprises, Palm Springs, Calif., 1994—. Internat. speaker in field; past div. v.p. Million Dollar Round Table; nat. chmn. Life Underwriters Tng. Council, 1983-84; nat. pres. Gen. Agts. and Mgrs. Conf., 1986-87. Author: How to Build a $100,000,000 Agency in Five Years or Less, Yes You can, Life Insurance to Diversification, Selling with Silk Gloves Not Brass Knuckles, The Norman Levine Reader, High Trust Leadership, A Passion for Compassion; editor: bi-weekly news report Probe; contbr. numerous articles to profl. jours.; author tapes on ins., mgmt., photography, Americanism. Past mem. bd. dirs. Calif. Law Enforcement Needs Com.; chmn. Gama Found.; chmn. Million Dollar Round Table Mentoring Coun. Served with AUS, 1944-46, ETO. Recipient Julian Myrick award, 1969, John Newton Russell Meml. award, 1986; named to

Hall of Fame Gen. Agts. and Mgrs. Conf., 1982 Mem. N.Y.C. Assn. Life Underwriters (pres. 1967-68), N.Y. State Assn. Life Underwriters (pres. 1968-69), Nat. Assn. Life Underwriters (pres. 1974-75, dir. polit. action com. 1967-69), N.Y.C. Life Mgrs. Assn. (pres. 1974-75), Assn. Advanced Life Underwriters, Am. Soc. C.L.U.s, San Francisco Gen. Agts. and Mgrs. Assn. (pres. 1983), Golden Key Soc., Linnaean Soc., San Francisco C. of C., Audubon Soc., Am. Israel Friendship League (trustee) Mem. Order B'nai Zion (pres. 1964-67). Home: 2162 Silverado Cir Palm Springs CA 92264-9209 Office: Levine Enterprises 555 S Sunrise Way Ste 219 Palm Springs CA 92264-7869 E-mail: norman@levineenterpise.com, levineente@aol.com

LEVINE, PHILIP, poet, retired educator; b. Detroit, Jan. 10, 1928; s. A. Harry and Esther Gertrude (Priscol) L.; m. Frances Artley, July 12, 1954; children: Mark, John, Teddy. B.A., Wayne State U., 1950, A.M., 1955; M.F.A., U. Iowa, 1957, studied with John Berryman, 1954. Instr. U. Iowa, 1955-57; instr. Calif. State U., Fresno, prof. English, 1969-92, Tufts U.; tchr. Princeton U., Columbia U., U. Calif., Berkeley.; ret.; Elliston lectr. poetry U. Cin.; poet-in-residence Vassar Coll., Nat. U. Australia. Chmn. lit. panel Nat. Endowment Arts, 1985; adj. prof. NYU, Spring, 1984, Univ. prof. Brown U., spring 1985; tchr. NYU, U. Iowa, Vanderbilt U., U. Houston; part-time vis. prof. various univs. Author: On the Edge, 1961, Silent in America: Vivas for Those Who Have Failed, 1965, Not This Pig, 1968, 5 Detroits, 1970, Thistles, 1970, Pili's Wall, 1971, Red Dust, 1971, They Feed They Lion, 1972, 1933, 1974, On The Edge & Over, 1976, The Names of the Lost, 1976 (Lenore Marshall award Best Am. Book Poems 1976), 7 Years from Somewhere, 1979 (Nat. Book Critics Circle prize 1979, Notable Book award Am. Libr. Assn. 1979), Ashes, 1979 (Nat. Book Critics Circle prize 1979, Nat. Book award 1979), Don't Ask, 1979, One for the Rose, 1981, Selected Poems, 1984, Sweet Will, 1985, A Walk with Tom Jefferson, 1988 (Bay Area Book Reviewers award), What Work Is, 1991 (L.A. Times Book Prize 1991, Nat. Book award for poetry, 1991), New Selected Poems, 1991, Earth, Stars, and Writers, 1992, The Bread of Time: Toward an Autobiography, 1994, Simple Truth, 1994 (Pulitzer Prize for poetry 1995), The Mercy, 1999; editor: (with Henri Coulette) Character and Crisis, 1966, (with E. Trejo) The Selected Poems of Jaime Sabines, (with Ada Long) Off the Map, The Selected Poems of Gloria Fuertes, 1984, (with D. Wojahn and B. Henderson) The Pushcart Prize XI, 1986, The Essential Keats, 1987, Poetry, 1998. Active anti-Vietnam war movement. Recipient Joseph Henry Jackson award San Francisco Found., 1961, The Chaplebrook Found. award, 1968, Frank O'Hara Meml. prize, 1973; Amer. Academy of Arts and Letters Award of Merit, 1974; Levinson Prize, 1974; Harriet Monroe Meml. prize for poetry, 1976; Golden Rose award New Eng. Poetry Soc., 1985, Ruth Lilly Poetry Prize, Modern Poetry Assn. and Am. Council Arts, 1987, Elmer Bobst award NYU, 1990, Lit. Lion New York Public Library 1993; named outstanding lectr. Calif. State U., Fresno, 1971, outstanding prof. Calif. State U. System, 1972; Stanford U. poetry fellow, 1957, Nat. Inst. Arts and Letters grantee, 1973, Guggenheim fellow, 1973-74, 80; Nat. Endowment for Arts grantee, 1969, 70 (refused), 76, 81, 87. Mem. AAAL, Acad. Am. Poets (chancellor 2000). Address: 4549 N Van Ness Blvd Fresno CA 93704-3727 also: 106 Willow St Brooklyn NY 11201-2202

LEVINE, PHILIP, classics educator; b. Lawrence, Mass., Sept. 8, 1922; s. Samuel and Jennie (Derdak) L.; m. Dinnie Moseson, June 19, 1955; children— Jared Elliott, Harlan Alcon. A.B., Harvard, 1946, A.M., 1948, Ph.D., 1952; DHL (hon.), U. Judaism, 1986. Instr., asst. prof. classics Harvard, 1952-59; assoc. prof. classical langs. U. Tex. at Austin, 1959-61; assoc prof., prof. classics UCLA, 1961-91, prof. emeritus, 1991—; dean div. humanities U. Calif. at Los Angeles, 1965-83; Biggs resident lectr. Washington U., 1993. Info. officer Coun. U. Calif. Emeriti Assn. Author: Lo Scriptorium Vercellese da S. Eusueblo ad Attone, 1958, St. Augustine, City of God, Books 12-15, 1966; editor: Latin lt. sect. Twayne World Author Series, 1964—; adv. editor, U. Calif. Publs. in Classical Studies, 1963-72; assoc. editor, contbr. to U. Calif. Studies in Classical Antiquity, 1967-75, sr. co-editor, 1975-78; mem. editorial bd. Classical Antiquity, 1986-93. Mem. rev. com., sr. fellowship program Nat. Endowment for Humanities, 1966-70; bd. govs. U. Judaism, 1968-90, coun. visitors, 1990-94, acad. adv. coun., 1994—. With AUS, 1943-46. Sheldon fellow Italy; Guggenheim fellow; Fulbright Research grantee; recipient Bromberg Humanities award; decorated Cavaliere dell' Ordine al Merito della Repubblica Italiana. Mem. Am. Philol. Assn. (dir. 1968-70), Mediaeval Acad. Am. (exec. council 1969-72), Renaissance Soc., Am. Philol. Assn., Pacific Coast (chmn. gen. lit. 1964-65), Phi Beta Kappa. Home: 224 S Almont Dr Beverly Hills CA 90211-2507 Office: U Calif Dept Classics Los Angeles CA 90095-0001 E-mail: levine@ucla.edu

LEVINE, RAPHAEL DAVID, chemistry educator; b. Alexandria, Egypt, Mar. 29, 1938; brought to U.S., 1939; s. Chaim S. and Sofia (Greenberg) L.; m. Gillah T. Ephraty, June 13, 1962; 1 child, Ornah T. MSc, Hebrew U., Jerusalem, 1959; PhD, Nottingham (Eng.) U., 1964; DPhil, Oxford (Eng.) U., 1966; PhD honoris causa, U. Liege, Belgium, 1991, Tech. U., Munich, Germany, 1996. Vis. asst. prof. U. Wis., 1966-68; prof. theoretical chemistry Hebrew U., Jerusalem, 1969—, chmn. research ctr. molecular dynamics, 1981—, Max Born prof. natural philosophy, 1985—; faculty Dept. Chemistry and Biochemistry UCLA, L.A. Battelle prof. chemistry and math. Ohio State U., Columbus, 1970-74; Brittingham vis. prof. U. Wis., 1973; adj. prof. U. Tex., Austin, 1974-80, MIT, 1980-88, UCLA, 1989—; Arthur D. Little lectr. MIT, 1978; Miller rsch. prof. U. Calif., Berkeley, 1989, A.D. White prof. at large Cornell U., 1989-95. Author: Quantum Mechanics of Molecular Rate Processes, 1969, Molecular Reaction Dynamics, 1974, Lasers and Chemical Change, 1981, Molecular Reaction Dynamics and Chemical Reactivity, 1986, Algebraic Theory of Molecules, 1995; mem. editorial bds. several well known scientific jours.; contbr. articles to profl. jours. Served with AUS, 1960-62. Recipient Ann. award Internat. Acad. Quantum Molecular Sci., 1968, Landau prize, 1972, Israel prize in Exact Scis., 1974, Weizman prize, 1979, Rothschild prize, 1992, Max Planck prize for Internat. Cooperation, 1996; co-recipient Chemistry prize Wolf Found., 1988; Ramsay Meml. fellow, 1964-66, Alfred P. Sloan fellow, 1970-72. Fellow Am. Phys. Soc.; mem. Israel Chem. Soc., Israel Acad. Scis., Max Planck Soc. (fgn. mem.), Academia Europaea (fgn.), Am. Acad. Arts and Scis. (fgn. hon. mem.), Am. Philos. Soc. (fgn.), Royal Danish Acad. Scis. and Letters (fgn.), Natl. Acad. of Sci., US, (fgn.). Office: UCLA Dept Chemistry & Biochemistry 607 Charles E Young E Dr Los Angeles CA 90095-0001 also: Hebrew U Jerusalem Fritz Haber Rsch Ctr Molecular Dynamics Jerusalem 91904 Israel E-mail: rafi@fh.huji.ac.il

LEVINE, ROBERT ARTHUR, economist, policy writer; b. Bklyn., July 7, 1930; s. Isaac Bert and Jessie Sue (Palevsky) L.; m. Esther Carol Knudsen, Mar. 2, 1953; children: David Knudsen, Peter Kemmerer, Joseph Karl. BA, Harvard U., 1950, MA, 1951; PhD, Yale U., 1957. Economist Rand Corp., 1957-61, sr. economist, 1962-65, 69-73, 87—, sr. economist emeritus, cons., 1994-98, 98—; research assoc. Harvard U. Center Internat. Affairs, 1961-62; asst. dir. for research, plans, programs and evaluation OEO, Washington, 1966-69; pres. N.Y.C.-Rand Inst., 1973-75; dep. dir. Congl. Budget Office, Washington, 1975-79; v.p. System Devel. Corp., Santa Monica, Calif., 1979-85; pres. Canyon Analysts, 1985—. Sr. fellow Nat. Security Studies Program, UCLA, 1964-65; vis. prof. public policy Stanford U. Grad. Sch. Bus., 1972; adj. prof. econs. Pepperdine U. Sch. Bus. and Mgmt., 1984 Author: The Arms Debate, 1963, The Poor Ye Need Not Have With You, 1971, Public Planning: Failure and Redirection, 1972, Evaluation Research and Practice, 1981, Still the Arms Debate, 1990, Turmoil and Transition in the Atlantic Alliance, 1991. With USN, 1951-54. Ford Found. grantee, 1969, 85; German Marshall Fund grantee, 1979; Carnegie Corp. grantee, 1986. Mem. Inst. Strategic Studies. Club: Beverly Glen Democratic. Home and Office: 10321 Chrysanthemum Ln Los Angeles CA 90077-2812 E-mail: ral@rand.org

LEVINSON, ARTHUR DAVID, molecular biologist; b. Seattle, Mar. 31, 1950; s. Sol and Malvina (Lindsay) L.; m. Rita May Liff, Dec. 17, 1978; children: Jesse, Anya. BS, U. Wash., 1972; PhD, Princeton U., 1977. Postdoctoral fellow U. Calif., San Francisco, 1977-80; sr. scientist Genentech, South San Francisco, 1980-83, staff scientist, 1983—, dir. cell genetics dept., 1987-89, v.p. rsch., 1989-90, sr. v.p., 1992-95; pres., CEO Genentech, Inc., South San Francisco, 1995—, chmn., 1999—. Bd. dirs. Apple Computer Inc., 2001- Mem. editl. bd. Virology, 1984-87, Molecular Biology and Medicine, 1986-89, Molecular and Cellular Biology, 1987-96, Jour. of Virology, 1988-91. Mem. Am. Soc. Microbiology, Am. Soc. Biochemistry and Molecular Biology, Biotech. Industry Orgn. (bd. dirs. 1995-2000), Pharm. Rsch. and Mfrs. of Am. (bd. dirs. 1997—), Tech. Network (bd. dirs. 1997—). Office: Genentech Inc 1 DNA Way South San Francisco CA 94080-4990

LEVINSON, KATHY, multimedia executive; BA in Econs., Stanford U. With Charles Schwab, 1981-94, sr. v.p. credit svc., 1989-94; cons. E*TRADE Securities, Inc., E*TRADE Group, Palo Alto, Calif., 1995, pres., COO, 1996—, corp. sr. v.p., 1996—, dir., 1996—, corp. exec. v.p. ops., 1996; pres., COO E*Trade Group, Palo Alto, 1996—. Office: E Trade Group 4 Embarcadero Rd Palo Alto CA 94301-2321

LEVINSON, SHAUNA T. financial services executive; b. Denver, Aug. 1, 1954; d. Charles and Geraldine D. Titus; m. Kenneth L. Levinson, Dec. 21, 1986. BA cum laude, U. Puget Sound, 1976; M Bank Mktg. with honors, U. Colo., 1986. Cert. fin. planner. Fin. planning analyst Swift and Co., Chgo., 1977-79; from credit analyst to asst. v.p. Ctrl. Bank of Denver, 1979-84; v.p. fin. svcs. First Nat. Bank S.E. Denver, 1984-94; dir. mktg. First Nat. Banks, 1991-94; pres., CEO Fin. Directions, Inc., Denver, 1994—; CEO Levinson Resources, Inc., Denver, 1994—. Mem. bankers edn. com. Colo. Bankers Assn., Denver, 1992-94. Contbr. articles to profl. jours. Chmn. human resources com., mem. adminstrv. coun. Jr. League of Denver, 1983—; mem. cmty. assistance fund, placement adv. com.; fundraiser Women's Libr. Assn. U. Denver, 1990-94, 96—, Good Shepherd Cath. Sch., 1986-95, Jewish Cmty. Ctr., Denver, 1990-95, St. Mary's Acad., 1995-99 Theodor Herzl Day Sch., 1996-99; mem. Denver Campus for Jewish Edn., 2000—, Allied Jewish Fedn., 2000—. Recipient Gold Peak award Am. Bankers Assn.-Bank Mktg. Assn., 1987; named Businessperson of Week Denver Bus. Jour., 1995. Mem. Jr. League Denver, U. Denver Pioneer Hockey, St. Andrews Soc. (life), Crestmoor Gardeners (treas. 1994-2000), Betty Baur Lambert Soc. (life), Kappa Alpha Theta (Chgo. NW alumnae 1977-79, Denver alumnae 1980—, rush adv. com. 2000—), Phi Kappa Phi, Phi Chi Theta. Office: 1624 Market St Ste 475 Denver CO 80202-1518

LEVINSON, STEVEN HENRY, state supreme court justice; b. Cincinnati, OH, June 8, 1946; BA with distinction, Stanford U., 1968; JD, U. Mich., 1971. Bar: Hawaii 1972, U.S. Dist. Ct. Hawaii 1972, U.S. Ct. Appeals (9th cir.) 1972. Law clk. to Hon. Bernard H. Levinson Hawaii Supreme Ct., 1971-72; pvt. practice Honolulu, 1972-89; judge Hawaii Cir. Ct. (1st cir.), 1989-92; assoc. justice Hawaii Supreme Ct., Honolulu, 1992—. Staff mem. U. Mich. Jour. Law Reform, 1970-71. Active Temple Emanu-El. Mem. ABA (jud. adminstrn. divsn. 1989—), Hawaii State Bar Assn. (dir. young lawyers divsn. 1975-76, dir. 1982-84), Nat. Jud. Coll. (state jud. leader 1991—), Am. Judges Assn., Am. Judicature Soc. Jewish. Office: Supreme Ct Hawaii Aliiolani Hale 417 S King St Honolulu HI 96813-2912

LEVINTHAL, ELLIOTT CHARLES, physicist, educator; b. Bklyn., Apr. 13, 1922; s. Fred and Rose (Raiben) L.; m. Rhoda Arons, June 4, 1944; children— David, Judith, Michael, Daniel. B.A., Columbia Coll., 1942; M.S., Mass. Inst. Tech., 1943; Ph.D., Stanford U., 1949. Project engr. Sperry Gyroscope Co., N.Y.C., 1943-46; research assoc. nuclear physics Stanford (Calif.) U., 1946-48, sr. scientist dept. genetics Sch. Medicine, 1961-74, dir. Instrumentation Research Lab., 1961-80, assoc. dean for research affairs, 1970-73, adj. prof. genetics Sch. Medicine, 1974-80, research prof. mech. engring., dir. Inst. Mfg. and Automation Sch. Engring., 1983-90, assoc. dean for research Sch. Engring., 1986-90, assoc. dean spl. programs, 1990-91, prof. emeritus, 1991—; research physicist Varian Assocs., Palo Alto, Calif., 1949-50, dir. research, 1950-52; chief engr. Century Electronics, Palo Alto, 1952-53; pres. Levinthal Electronics, Palo Alto, 1953-61; dir. def. scis. office Def. Advanced Projects Agy., Dept. Def., Arlington, Va., 1980-83. Mem. NASA Adv. Coun., 1980-84, space studies bd., NRC, 1989-91, mem. human exploration, 1991-92, army sci. bd., 1989-91; cons. HEW; chmn. bd. dirs. CSFluids Inc. Recipient NASA Public Service medal, 1977 Mem. AAAS, IEEE, Am. Phys. Soc., Optical Soc. Am., Biomed. Engring. Soc., Sigma Xi. Democrat. Jewish. Home: 59 Sutherland Dr Atherton CA 94027-6471 Office: Stanford U Sch Engring 530 Duena St Rm 104 Stanford CA 94305-2209 E-mail: levinthal@stanford.edu

LEVIT, VICTOR BERT, lawyer, foreign representative, civic worker; b. Singapore, Apr. 21, 1930; s. Bert W. and Thelma (Clumeck) L.; divorced; children: Carson, Victoria; m. Margery K. Blum, Oct. 26, 1996. A.B. in Polit. Sci. with great distinction, Stanford, 1950; LL.B., Stanford U., 1952. Bar: Calif. 1953. Assoc. Long & Levit, San Francisco and Los Angeles, 1953-55, ptnr., 1955-83, mng. ptnr. San Francisco and L.A., 1971-83; ptnr. Barger & Wolen, San Francisco, L.A. and Newport Beach, 1983—; assoc. and gen. legal counsel U.S. Jaycees, 1959-61; legal counsel for consul gen. Ethiopia for San Francisco, 1964-71, hon. consul for Ethiopia, 1971-76. Guest lectr. Stanford U. Law Sch., 1958— , Haile Selassie I Univ. Law Sch., 1972-76; mem. com. group ins. programs State Bar Calif., 1980— ; Mem. Los Angeles Consular Corps, 1971-77; mem. San Francisco Consular Corps, 1971-77, vice dean, 1975-76; Grader Calif. Bar Exam., 1956-61; del. San Francisco Mcpl. Conf., 1955-63, vice chmn., 1960, chmn., 1961-63 Author: Legal Malpractice in California, 1974, Legal Malpractice, 1977, 2d edit., 1983; Note editor: Stanford Law Rev, 1952-53; legal editor: Underwriters' Report, 1963— ; Contbr. articles to legal jours. Campaign chmn. San Francisco Aid Retarded Children, 1960; mem. nat. com. Stanford Law Sch. Fund, 1959—; mem. Mayor's Osaka-San Francisco Affiliation Com., 1959-65, Mayor's Com. for Mcpl. Mgmt., 1961-64; mem. San Francisco Rep. Country Cen. Com., 1956-63; assoc. mem. Calif. Rep. Cen. Com., 1956-63, 70-72; campaign chmn. San Francisco Assemblyman John Busterud, 1960; bd. dirs. San Francisco Comml. Club, 1967-70, San Francisco Planning and Urban Renewal Assn., 1959-60, San Francisco Planning and Urban Renewal Assn. Nat. Found. Infantile Paralysis, 1958, Red Shield Youth Assn., Salvation Army, San Francisco, 1960-70, bd. dirs. NCCJ, San Francisco, 1959—, chmn., No. Calif., 1962 64, 68 70; mem. nat. bd. dirs., 1964-75; bd. dirs. San Francisco Tb and Health Assn., 1962-70, treas., 1964, pres., 1965-67; bd. dirs. San Francisco Assn. Mental Health, 1964-73, pres., 1968-71; mem. com. Nat. Assn. Mental Health, 1969-71; trustee United Bay Area Crusade, 1966-74, Ins. Forum San Francisco; bd. visitors Stanford Law Sch., 1969-75; mem. adv. bd. Jr. League San Francisco, 1971-75. Named Outstanding Young Man San Francisco mng. editors San Francisco newspapers, 1960, One of Five Outstanding Young Men Calif., 1961 Fellow ABA (chmn. profl. liability com. for gen. practice sect. 1979-81, council gen. practice sect. 1982-86, sec.-treas. gen. practice sect. 1986-87); mem. San Francisco Bar Assn. (chmn. ins. com. 1962, 73, chmn. charter flight com. 1962-66), State Bar Calif. (com. on group ins. programs 1980—, chmn. gen. practice sect. 1988—), Consular Law Soc., Am. Arbitration Assn. (arbitrator), World Assn. Lawyers (chmn. parliamentary law com. 1976—), Am. Law Inst. (adviser restatement of law governing lawyers 1985—), Internat. Bar Assn., San Francisco Jr. C. of C. (dir. 1959, pres. 1958), U.S. Jaycees (exec. com. 1959-61), Jaycees Internat. (life, senator), Calif. Scholarship Fedn., U.S. C. of C. (labor com. 1974-76), San Francisco C. of C. (dir.), Phi Beta Kappa, Order of Coif, Pi Sigma Alpha. Clubs: Commercial (San Francisco) (dir.); Commonwealth (quar. chmn.), California Tennis; World Trade; Bankers. Home: 2063 Broadway St San Francisco CA 94115-1537 Office: Barger & Wolen 650 California St Fl 9 San Francisco CA 94108-2702

LEVITCH, JOSEPH See LEWIS, JERRY

LEVITON, ALAN EDWARD, curator; b. N.Y.C., Jan. 11, 1930; s. David and Charlotte (Weber) L.; m. Gladys Ann Robertson, June 30, 1952; children: David A., Charlotte A. Student, NYU, 1948; AB, Stanford U., 1949, MA, 1953, PhD, 1960; postgrad., U. Nebr., 1954, Columbia U., 1948; student, U. Nebr., 1954. Asst. curator herpetology Calif. Acad. Scis., San Francisco, 1957-60, assoc. curator, 1960-61, chmn., curator, 1962-82, 89-92, curator, 1983-88, 93—, chmn. computer svcs., 1983-92, editor sci. publs., 1994—; assoc. curator zool. collections Stanford U., 1962-63, lectr. biol. sci., 1963-70; professorial lectr. Golden Gate U., 1953-63; adj. prof. biol. sci. San Francisco State U., 1967-2000, rsch. prof., 2000—. Author: North American Amphibians, 1970, Reptiles of the Middle East, 1992, T.H. Hittel's California Academy of Sciences, 1997; contbr. articles to profl. jours. Grantee Am. Philos. Soc., 1960, NSF, 1960-61, 77-79, 80, 83-89, 91-93, Belvedere Sci. Fund, 1958-59, 62; recipient Fellows' medal Calif. Acad. Scis., 1999. Fellow AAAS (coun. 1976-97, com. coun. affairs 1983-85, sec.-treas. Pacific divsn. 1975-79, exec. dir. 1980-98, 2000—, pres.-elect 1998, pres. 1999-2000), Calif. Acad. Scis., Geol. Soc. Am. (vice-chmn. history geology divsn. 1989-90, chmn. 1990-91); mem. Am. Soc. Ichthyologists and Herpetologists (mem. bd. govs. 1960-84), Soc. Systematic Zoology (sec.-treas. Pacific sect. 1970-72), Forum Historians of Sci. Am. (coord. com. 1986-88, sec.-treas. 1988-90), Herpetologists League (pres. 1961-62), History of Sci. Soc. Home: 571 Kingsley Ave Palo Alto CA 94301-3225 Office: Calif Acad Scis Golden Gate Park San Francisco CA 94118

LEVY, ALAN DAVID, real estate executive; b. St. Louis, July 19, 1938; s. I. Jack and Natalie (Yawitz) L.; m. Abby Jane Markowitz, May 12, 1968; children: Jennifer Lynn, Jacqueline Claire. Grad., Sch. Real Estate Washington U., 1960. Property mgr. Solon Gershman Inc. Realtors, Clayton, Mo., 1958-61; gen. mgr. Kodner Constrn. Co., St. Louis, 1961-63; regional mgr. Tishman Realty & Constrn. Co., Inc., N.Y.C., 1963-69; v.p. L.A., 1969-77; exec. v.p., dir. Tishman West Mgmt. Corp., 1977-78; pres. Tishman West Cos., 1988-92; chmn. Tishman Internat. Cos., 1993—. Guest lectr. on real estate mgmt. to various forums. Contbr. articles on property mgmt. to trade jours. Mem. L.A. County Mus. Art; former chmn. Am. Art Coun.; trustee Archives Am. Art, Harvard-Westlake Sch.; bd. govs. W.L.A. coun. Boy Scouts Am., Cedars-Sinai Med. Ctr.; bd. councillors USC Sch. of Social Work. Bryant fellow Met. Mus. of Art. Mem. Bldg. Owners and Mgrs. Assn., L.A. (bd. dirs.), N.J. (co-founder, hon. dir.), Inst. Real Estate Mgmt. (cert. property mgr.), Urban Land Inst., Internat. Coun. Shopping Ctrs. Office: 10900 Wilshire Blvd Ste 510 Los Angeles CA 90024-6533

LEVY, BERNARD C. electrical engineer, educator; b. Princeton, N.J., July 31, 1951; Ingenieur civil des mines, Paris, 1974; PhD in Elec. Engring., Stanford U., 1979. Prof. dept. elec. and computer engr. U. Calif., Davis, 1980—, chair dept. elec. and computer engring., 1996—. Fellow IEEE (image and multidimensional signal processing tech. com. 1992—). Office: U Calif Dept Elec & Computer Engr 1 Shields Ave Davis CA 95616-5270

LEVY, DAVID, retired lawyer, insurance company executive; b. Bridgeport, Conn., Aug. 3, 1932; s. Aaron and Rachel (Goldman) L. BS in Econs., U. Pa., 1954; JD, Yale U., 1957. Bar: Conn. 1958, U.S. Supreme Ct. 1963, D.C. 1964, Mass. 1965, N.Y. 1971, Pa. 1972; CPA, Conn. Acct. Arthur Andersen & Co., N.Y.C., 1957-59; sole practice Bridgeport, 1959-60; specialist tax law IRS, Washington, 1960-64; counsel State Mut. Life Ins. Co., Worcester, Mass., 1964-70; assoc. gen. counsel taxation Penn Mut. Life Ins. Co., Phila., 1971-81; sole practice Washington, 1982-87; v.p., tax counsel Pacific Life Ins. Co., Newport Beach, Calif., 1987-2001; ret., 2001. Author: (with others) Life Insurance Company Tax Series, Bureau National Affairs Tax Management Income Tax, 1970-71. Mem. adv. bd. Tax Mgmt., Washington, 1975-90, Hartford Inst. on Ins. Taxation, 1990-97; bd. dirs. Citizens Plan E Orgn., Worcester, 1966-70. With AUS, 1957. Mem. ABA (vice-chmn. employee benefits com. 1980-86, ins. cos. com. 1984-86, torts and ins. practice sect., subcom. chair ins. cos. com. tax sect. 1994—), Assn. Life Ins. Counsel, AICPA, Beta Alpha Psi. Jewish.

LEVY, JOSEPH WILLIAM, department stores executive; b. Fresno, Calif., 1932; m. Sharon Sorokin; children: Felicia, Jody, Bret. BS, U. So. Calif., 1954. Asst. merchandising mgr., then mgr. Gottschalks, Inc., Fresno, 1956-72, exec. v.p., 1972-82, chmn., chief exec. officer, 1982—. Chmn. exec. com. Frederick Atkins Inc., N.Y.C., 1992—, also bd. dirs. Chmn. Fresno Econ. Devel. Corp., 1982-83; mem. Calif. Transp. Commn., 1983-91, chmn., 1986-87; sec. City of Fresno Equipment Corp.; mem. bus. adv. coun. Sch. Bus. and Adminstrv. Scis., Calif. State U., Fresno; trustee Community Hosps. Cen. Calif. With USNR, 1950-58. Mem. Calif. of C. (bd. dirs.), Fresno County and City C. of C. (transp. com.), U. So. Calif. Sch. Bus. Alumni Assn., San Joaquin Country Club, U. Sequoia-Sunnyside Country Club, Downtown Club (Fresno). Home: 6475 N Sequoia Dr Fresno CA 93711-1232 Office: Gottschalks Inc PO Box 28920 Fresno CA 93729-8920

LEVY, JULIA, immunology educator, researcher; b. Singapore, May 15, 1935; came to Can. 1940; d. Guillaume Albert and Dorothy Frances (Brown) Coppens; m. Howard Bernard Gerwing, Oct. 8, 1955 (div. 1962); children— Nicholas, Benjamin; m. Edwin Levy, June 13, 1969; 1 child, Jennifer BA with honors, U. B.C., 1955; PhD, U. London, 1958. Asst. prof. U. B.C., Vancouver, 1959-65, assoc. prof., 1965-72, prof. immunology, 1972—; pres., CEO QLT Inc., Vancouver. Dir., v.p. R&D, Quadra Logic Techs., Vancouver, 1980— ; cons. Monsanto Chems., Mo., 1978-80; mem. Prime Minister's Nat. Adv. Bd. on Sci. and Tech., 1987—. Fellow Royal Soc. Can.; mem. Am. Soc. Immunology, Can. Soc. Immunology (pres. 1983-85), Can. Fedn. Biol. Sci. (pres. 1983-84) Office: QLT PhotoTherapeutics Inc QLT Inc 887 Great Northern Way Vancouver BC Canada V5T 4T5

LEVY, KENNETH, executive; CEO KLA Tencor, San Jose, Calif., chmn., 1999—. Office: KLA-TENCOR CORP One Technology Dr Milpitas CA 95035

LEVY, MARK RAY, lawyer; b. Denver, Mar. 2, 1946; s. Richard C. and Hilde (Lindauer) L.; m. Patricia Loeb, June 13, 1971; children: Betsy, Robert. BA, U. Colo., 1968, JD, 1972. Bar: Colo. 1972, U.S. Dist. Ct. Colo. 1972. Assoc. Holland & Hart LLP, Denver, 1972-78, ptnr., 1978—. Adj. prof. the lawyering process U. Denver Law Sch., 1990-93; mem. spl. adv. com. Colo. Securities Bd., 1996-97. Author: (with others) Colorado Corporations Manual, 1987, Colorado Corporation Law and Practice, 1990. Trustee Congregation Emanuel, Denver, 1984-90, mem. legal com., 1989—; chmn. Denver Alumni Phonathon U. Colo. Law Sch., 1989-90, mem. alumni bd., 1992-96, chmn. alumni bd., 1994-95; trustee Nat. Repertory Orch., 1995-96. Mem. ABA, Colo. Bar Assn. (Blue Sky Law task force 1980-81, co-chmn. Colo. securities law rev. com. 1988-91, Article 8 of UCC com. 1995-96, chmn. ann. conv. com. 1999-2000, mem. annual conv. com. 1998—, mem. planning com. annual bus. law inst. 2000), Denver Bar Assn., Rockies Venture Club. Office: Holland & Hart LLP 555 17th St Ste 3200 Denver CO 80202-3950 E-mail: mlevy@hollandhart.com

LEVY, NORMAN, motion picture company executive; b. Bronx, N.Y., Jan. 3, 1935; s. Irving and Helen (Saunders) L.; m. Hirsch, Nov. 11, 1962; children— Jordan, Brian, Matthew. BA, CCNY. Salesman Universal Pictures, 1957-67, Nat. Gen. Pictures, 1967-74; gen. sales mgr. Columbia Pictures, Burbank, Calif., 1974-75, exec. v.p. in charge domestic sales, 1975-77, exec. v.p. mktg., 1977-78, pres. domestic distbn., 1978-80, pres. Twentieth Century Fox Entertainment Group, 1980-81, vice chmn., 1981-85; mktg., distbn. cons., 1985—; chmn. New Century/Vista Film Co. L.A., 1985-91; chmn., chief exec. officer Domino Entertainment, L.A., 1991-92; pres., CEO Creative Film Enterprises, L.A., 1992—. Served with U.S. Army, 1955-57. Office: Creative Film Enterprises 4965 Queen Florence Ln Woodland Hills CA 91364-4745

LEVY, RALPH, engineering executive, consultant; b. London, Apr. 12, 1932; came to U.S., 1967, naturalized, 1978; s. Alfred and Esther L.; m. Barbara Dent, Dec. 12, 1959; children: Sharon E., Mark S. B.A., Cambridge U., 1953, M.A., 1957; Ph.D., Queen Mary Coll. U. London, 1966. Mem. sci. staff GEC, Stanmore, Middlesex, Eng., 1953-59; mem. sci. staff Mullard Research Labs., Redhill, Eng., 1959-64; lectr. dept. elec. and electronic engring. U. Leeds, 1964-67; v.p. research Microwave Devel. Labs., Inc., Natick, Mass., 1967-84; v.p. engring. KW Engring., San Diego, 1984-88; v.p. research Remec Inc., San Diego, 1988-89; R. Levy Assocs., 1989—. Author: (with J.O. Scanlan) Circuit Theory, 1970, 2d vol., 1973; contbr. articles in field; patentee in field. Fellow IEEE (editor Transactions on Microwave Theory and Techniques 1986-88, Career award IEEE Microwave Theory and Techniques Soc. 1997); mem. Instn. Elec. Engrs. (London). Office: 1897 Caminito Velasco La Jolla CA 92037-5725 E-mail: r.levy@ieee.org

LEVY, RICARDO BENJAMIN, chemical company executive; b. Quito, Ecuador, Jan. 11, 1945; came to U.S., 1962; s. Leopoldo and Kate (Bamberg) L.; m. Noella Luke, June 15, 1967; children: Tamara, Brian. BS, Stanford U., 1966, PhDChemE, 1972; MS, Princeton U., 1967. Gen. mgr. Sudamericana, Quito, 1967-70; research engr. Exxon Research & Engring. Corp. subs. Exxon Corp., Florham Park, N.J., 1972-74; v.p., co-founder Catalytica Inc., Mountain View, Calif., 1974—, exec. v.p., chief operating officer, 1982—, pres., CEO, 1991—. Bd. dirs. Catalytica, Inc., Catalytica Combustion Sys., Inc., Catalytica Fine Chems., Inc., GENXON Power Sys. Co-Author: Catalysis in Coal Conversion; patentee in field. Mem. Am. Inst. Chem. Engrs., Comml. Devel. Assn., Phi Beta Kappa. Avocation: sailing. Office: Catalytica Inc 430 Ferguson Dr Ste 3 Mountain View CA 94043-5272

LEVY, S. WILLIAM, dermatologist, educator; b. San Francisco, Sept. 28, 1920; s. Joseph and Dora (Taylor) L.; m. Elisabeth Rellstab, Mar. 17, 1974; children: David Lewis, Ann Louise. BS, U. Calif., San Francisco, 1943, MD, 1949. Practice medicine specializing in dermatology, San Francisco; research dermatologist Biomechanics Lab., U. Calif., San Francisco; mem. staff Children's Hosp. of the Calif.-Pacific Med. Ctr., Mt. Zion Hosp. and Med. Center. Cons. to Letterman Army Hosp.; central med. adv. Calif. Blue Shield, San Francisco; clin. prof. dermatology U. Calif.; cons. in field. Author: Skin Problems of the Amputee, 1983; co-author: The Skin in Diabetes, 1986, Dermatology, 3rd edit., 1992, Dermatology in General Medicine, 5th edit., 1998, Atlas of Limb Prosthetics, 2d edit., 1992, Cutis, 1995, Biomechanics, 1999, In Motion—Amputee Coalition of America, 2000. Served with USN, 1943-46. Recipient Lehn and Fink Gold Medal award. Fellow Am. Acad. Dermatology (Gold medal); mem. San Francisco Dermatol. Soc. (pres.), Pacific Dermatologic Assn. (v.p.), AMA, Calif. Med. Assn. (sci. council 1977-84), San Francisco Med. Soc. Office: Ste 305 599 Sir Francis Drake Blvd Greenbrae CA 94904-1732

LEW, RONALD S. W. federal judge; b. L.A., 1941; m. Mamie Wong; 4 children. BA in Polit. Sci., Loyola U., L.A., 1964; JD, Southwestern U., 1971. Bar: Calif. 1972. Dep. city atty. L.A. City Atty's. Office, 1972-74; ptnr. Avans & Lew, L.A., 1974-82; commr. fire and police pension City of L.A., 1976-82; mcpl. ct. judge County of L.A., 1982-84, superior ct. judge, 1984-87; judge U.S. Dist. Ct. (cen. dist.) Calif., L.A., 1987—. Bar: Calif. 1971. Mem. World Affairs Council of L.A., 1976—, Christian Businessmen's Com. of L.A., 1982—; active Com. of 100, Chinese Am. Heart Coun., Friends of the Mus. Chinese Am. History. 1st lt. U.S. Army, 1967-69. Recipient Vol. award United Way of L.A., 1979, cert. of merit L.A. Human Relations Commn., 1977, 82. Mem. Am. Judicature Soc., Calif. Assn. of Judges, So. Calif. Chinese Lawyer's Assn. (charter mem. 1976, pres. 1979), Chinese Am. Citizens Alliance, San Fernando Valley Chinese Cultural Assn., Delta Theta Phi. Office: US Dist Ct 312 N Spring St Los Angeles CA 90012-4701

LEWIN, KLAUS J. pathologist, educator; b. Jerusalem, Israel, Aug. 10, 1936; came to U.S., 1968; s. Bruno and Charlotte (Nawratzki L.; m. Patricia Coutts Milne, Sept. 25, 1964; children: David, Nicola, Bruno. Attended, King's Coll. U. London, 1954-55; MB, BS, Westminster Med. Sch. London, Eng., 1959; MD, U. London, 1966. Diplomate Am. Bd. Pathology, Royal Coll. Pathologists (London), lic. Calif. Casualty officer Westminster Med. Hosp., 1960; resident Westminster Hosp. Med. Sch., London, 1960-68; pediatric house physician Westminster Hosp. Med. Sch., Westminster Children's Hosp., 1961; house physician St. James Hosp., Balham, London, 1961; asst. prof. pathology Stanford (Calif.) U., 1979-86; assoc. prof. pathology UCLA, L.A., 1977-80, vice chmn. dept. pathology, 1970-86; attending physician Dept. Medicine Gastroenterology divsn. UCLA-Wadsworth VA Hosp., 1978—; prof. pathology UCLA Med. Sch., 1980—, prof. dept. medicine divsn. gastroenterology, 1986—; dir. divsn. surg. pathology UCLA Ctr. Health Scis., 1986-95, mem. diagnostic surg. pathology svc., dir. divsn. liver, pancreas and gastrointestinal pathology, 1996—. Resident pathologist clinical chemistry, bacteriology, hematology, blood transfusion, serology, Westminster Hosp. Med. Sch., 1961-62, registrar dept. morbid anatomy, 1962-64, rotating sr. registrar morbid anatomy, Royal Devon, Exeter Hosp., 1964-68; vis. asst. prof. pathology, Stanford U. Med. Sch., 1968-70; vice chmn. pathology UCLA, L.A., 1979-86; pres. L.A. Soc. Pathologists Inc., 1985-86; mem. curriculum com. U. Calif. Riverside, 1977-84; cons. Wadsworth VA Hosp., L.A., carcinoma of esophagus intervention study, Polyp Prevention study, Nat. Cancer Inst., Cancer Preservation Studies br., Bethesda, Md.; chief gastrointestinal liver/pancreas sect. surg. pathology; rschr. structure, function, pathologic disorders of gastrointestinal tract and liver; vis. prof. U. Leeds, Eng., Porto Alegre, Brazil, Nat. Cancer Inst., Washington, 1999. Author: (with Riddel R., Weinstein W.) Gastrointestinal Pathology and Its Clinical Implications, 1992, (with Henry Appelman) Atlas of Tumor Pathology: Tumors of the Esophagus and Stomach, 1997; editl. bd. Human Pathology, 1986—, Am. Jour. Surg. Pathology, 1990—; reviewer Gastroenterology and Archives of Pathology; contbr. 170 papers, 80 abstracts, 26 chpts. in books and more than 250 revs. and articles to profl. jours.; lectr., presenter in field. Recipient Chesterfield medal Inst. Dermatology, London, 1966; named Arris and Gale lectr. Royal Coll. Surgeons, London, 1968; Welcome Trust Rsch. grantee, 1968; fellow Found. Promotion Cancer Rsch., Tokyo, 1992. Fellow Royal Coll. Pathologists (Eng.); mem. Pathological Soc. Great Britain, Am. Gastroenterology Soc., Gastrointestinal Pathology Soc. (founder, pres. 1985-86, exec. com., edn. com. 1990-99), U.S. Acad. Pathology, Can. Acad. Pathology, Assn. Clin. Pathologists, Pathological and Bacteriological Soc. Great Britain, Internat. Acad. Pathology, L.A. Pathology Soc. (bd. dirs.), Calif. Soc. Pathology (edn. com. 1983—), So. Calif. Soc. Gastrointestinal Endoscopy, Arthur Purdy Stout Soc., Gastrointestinal Pathology Soc. (pres., by-laws com., chmn. edn. com., exec. com.). Avocations: internat. travel, geographic pathology, hiking, swimming. Home: 333 Las Casas Ave Pacific Palisades CA 90272-3307 Office: UCLA Sch Medicine Dept Pathology 10833 Le Conte Ave Los Angeles CA 90095-3075

LEWIN, LEONARD, electrical engineering educator; b. Southend-On-Sea, Eng., July 22, 1919; came to U.S., 1968; s. Abraham and Leza (Roth) L.; m. Daphne Smith, June 26, 1943; children: David Ian, Wendy Patricia. Student, pub. schs., Southend; D.Sc., U. Colo., 1967. Chartered elec. engr., U.K. Sci. officer Brit. Admiralty, Witley, Surrey, Eng., 1941-45; sr. engr. Standard Telecommunication Labs., Harlow, Essex, Eng., 1946-50, head microwave dept. Eng., 1950-60, asst. mgr. transmission research Eng., 1960-66, sr. prin. research engr. Eng., 1967-68; prof. elec. engring. U. Colo., Boulder, 1968-86, prof. emeritus, 1987—. Cons. Standard Telecommunication Labs., 1968-90, Medion Ltd., London, 1970-90, Nat. Bur. Standards, Boulder, 1978-90, Nuclear Protection Adv. Group, London, 1980-90, MIT Lincoln Labs., 1984-90, NOAA, 1984-93; Nat. Prestige lectr. Inst. Elec. Engring, New Zealand, 1987 Author: Theory of Waveguides, 1975, Polylogarithms and Associated Functions, 1981; editor: Telecommunications in the U.S.: Trends, 1981, Telecommunications: Interdisciplinary, 1985, Structural Properties of Polylogarithms, 1991. Mem. Accountability Com. Boulder Valley Schs., 1979-81; active Colo. Assn. for Gifted and Talented, Boulder, 1976-90. Grantee U.K. Sci. Research Council, 1973, 75; grantee Fulbright Commn., 1981 Fellow IEEE (Microwave award, W.G. Baker 1963, Microwave Career award 1993), Brit. Interplanetary Soc.; mem. Instn. Elec. Engrs. U.K. (Premium award 1952, 60), Internat. Sci. Radio Union (U.S nat. com.). Home: 500 Mohawk Dr Apt 108 Boulder CO 80303-3745 Office: U Colo PO Box 425 Boulder CO 80309-0425

LEWIN, RALPH ARNOLD, biologist; b. London, Apr. 30, 1921; came to U.S., 1947; s. Maurice and Ethel Lewin; m. Joyce Mary Chismore, June, 1950 (div. 1965); m. Cheng Lanna, June 3, 1969. BA, Cambridge U., Eng., 1942, MA, 1946; PhD, Yale U., 1950; ScD, Cambridge U., Eng., 1973. Instr. Yale U., New Haven, 1951-52; sci. officer Nat. Rsch. Coun., Halifax, N.S., Can., 1952-55; ind. investigator NIH, Woods Hole, Mass., 1956-59; from assoc. prof. to prof. U. Calif., La Jolla, 1960—. Editor: Physiology and Biochemistry of Algae, 1962, Genetics of Algae, 1976, Biology of Algae, 1979, Biology of Women, 1981, Origins of Plastids, 1993, Internacia Vortaro de Mikroba Genetiko, 1994; co-editor: Prochloron, a microbial enigma, 1989; transl. Winnie-La-Pu (Esperanto), 1972, La Dektri Horlogoj, 1993, Merde, 1999, Abacus & Swallows, 2000. Served with British Army, 1943-46. Mem. Phycological Soc. Am. (pres. 1970-71, Darbaker prize 1963). Avocations: Esperanto, recorders, badminton. Home: 8481 Paseo Del Ocaso La Jolla CA 92037-3024 Office: U Calif San Diego Scripps Inst Oceanogra # 0202 La Jolla CA 92093 E-mail: rlewin@ucsd.edu

LEWIS, ALAN JAMES, pharmaceutical executive, pharmacologist; b. Newport Gwent, UK; BSc, Southampton U., Hampshire, 1967; PhD in Pharmacology, U. Wales, Cardiff, 1970. Postdoctoral fellow biomedical sci. U. Guelph, Ont., Can., 1970-72; rsch. assoc. lung rsch. ctr. Yale U., 1972-73; sr. pharmacologist Organon Labs., Ltd., Lanarkshire, Scotland. 1973-79; rsch. mgr. immunoinflammation Am. home products Wyeth-Ayerst Rsch., Princeton, N.J., 1979-82, assoc. dir. exptl. therapeutics, 1982-85, dir., 1985-87, asst. v.p., 1987-89, v.p. rsch., 1989-93; pres. Signal Pharms. Inc., San Diego, 1994-96, pres., CEO, 1996-2000; pres. signal rsch. divsn. Celgene Corp., 2000—. Editor allergy sect. Agents & Actions & Internat. Archives Pharmacodynamics Therapy; reviewer Jour. Pharmacology Exptl. Therapy, Biochemical Pharmacology, Can. Jour. Physiol. Pharmacology, European Jour. Pharmacology, Jour. Pharm. Sci. Mem. Am. Soc. Pharmacological and Exptl. Therapeutics, Am. Rheumatism Assn., Mid-Atlantic Pharmacology Soc. (v.p. 1991-93, pres. 1993-94), Pulmonary Rsch. Assn., Inflammation Rsch. Assn. (pres. 1986-88), Pharm. Mfrs. Assn., Internat. Assn. Inflammation Socs. (pres. 1990-95), Bio Bd. Achievements include research in mechanisms and treatment of inflammatory diseases including arthritis and asthma cardiovascular diseases, metabolic disorders, central nervous system diseases, osteoporosis and viral diseases. Office: Signal Pharms Inc 5555 Oberlin Dr Ste 100 San Diego CA 92121-3746 E-mail: alewis@signalpharm.com

LEWIS, CARSON MCLAUGHL, retired plastic surgeon; b. Dallas, Sept. 27, 1931; MD, U. Tex., Galveston, 1956. Plastic surgeon Scripps Meml. Hosp., Calif.; dir. Total Body Wellness Inc., La Jolla. Mem. tchg. staff U. Hosp., San Diego. Mem. Internat. Soc. Aesthetic Plastic Surgeons (dir. ednl. found.). Office: 9043 Clover Cirle San Diego CA 92126-2423

LEWIS, CHARLES D. rancher, consultant; b. Denver, June 22, 1936; s. Harry Thompson and Margretta (Borrmann) L.; m. Penelope Hall, June 18, 1956; children: C. Randel, Christina, Vanda H. Student, Dartmouth Coll., 1954-55; BSBA, U. Denver, 1959, MBA, 1961. Tax mgr. Arthur Andersen & Co., Denver, 1959-64; exec. v.p., treas. Vail (Colo.) Assocs., Inc., 1964-67, Writer Constrn. Corp., Denver, 1967-69; pres., chief exec. officer, founder Copper Mountain (Colo.), Inc., 1969-82; gen. ptnr. W.F.R. Ltd., Kremmling, Colo., 1979—; gen. ptnr., dir. Boettcher & Co., Denver, 1982-85; pres. L.W.P. Svcs., Inc., Golden, Colo., 1985-95. Pres., dir. Arlberg Holding Co., 1990-97; pres. Arlberg Ins. Co., 1990-97; mng. mem. Eldora Enterprises L.L.C., 1990-97, C.D. Lewis LLC, 1997—; bd. dirs. Erie County Investment Co., Sugar Bowl Corp. Chmn. Copper Mountain Water & Sanitation Dist., 1972-82, Copper Mountain Met. Dist., 1972-82; mem. Colo. Passenger Tramway Bd., 1974-82, chmn., 1976-82. Recipient Industry and Environ. award Rocky Mountain Ctr. on Environment, 1974, Lifetime Achievement award Nat. Ski Areas Assn., 1998; named Outstanding Design, Ski Mag., 1975, Colo. Ski Hall of Fame, 1989, Alumnus of Yr. Sch. Accountancy U. Denver, 1998. Mem. Am. Arbitration Assn., Colo. Soc. CPAs, Nat. Ski Areas Assn. (chmn. 1981-83), Colo. Ski Country USA (chmn. 1978-79), Am. Ski Fedn. (vice chmn. 1980-82), Colo. Wildlife Commn. (chmn. 1998—). Republican. Episcopalian. Avocations: climbing, fishing. Home: 19752 Us Highway 40 Kremmling CO 80459-9603 Office: CD Lewis LLC 23522 Us Highway 40 Kremmling CO 80459-9600

LEWIS, CHARLES EDWIN, epidemiologist, educator; b. Kansas City, Dec. 28, 1928; s. Claude Herbert and Maudie Friels (Holaday) L.; m. Mary Ann Gurera, Dec. 27, 1963; children— Kevin Neil, David Bradford, Matthew Clinton, Karen Carleen. Student, U. Kans., 1948-49; M.D., Harvard, 1953; M.S., U. Cin., 1957, Sc.D., 1959. Diplomate Am. Bd. Preventive Medicine (Occupl. Medicine). Intern, resident U. Kans. Hosp., 1953-54; trainee USPHS, 1956-58; fellow occupational health Eastman Kodak Co., 1958-59; asst. clin. prof. epidemiology Baylor U. Sch. Medicine, 1960-61; asso. prof. medicine U. Kans. Med. Sch., 1961-62, prof., chmn. dept. preventive medicine, 1962-69; coordinator Kan. Regional Med. Program, 1967-69; prof. social medicine Harvard Med. Sch., 1969-70; prof. pub. health, head div. health adminstrn. UCLA Med. Sch., 1970-72, prof. medicine, div. head, 1972-90; prof., 1972-89; prof. nursing Sch. Nursing UCLA Med. Sch., 1973—, head div. preventive and occupational medicine, 1991-93; dir. Health Svcs. Rsch. Ctr., 1991-93, UCLA Ctr. Health Promotion and Disease Prevention, 1991—; chair acad. senate UCLA, 1995-96. Chmn. acad. senate UCLA, 1995-96; cons. Getty Trust, Walt Disney Prodns.; mem. Nat. Bd. Med. Examiners, 1964-68, 8-83, Jt. Commn. on Accreditaiton Health Care Orgns., 1989-95; mem. health svcs. rsch. study sect. USPHS, 1968-76; vis. scholar Annenberg Sch. Comm., U. So. Calif., 1980-81; mem. adv. bd. Hosp. Rsch. and Edn. Trust, 1972-75. Contbr. articles to profl. Jours. Served to capt. USAF, 1954-56. Recipient Ginsberg prize medicine U. Kans., 1954, Glasier award Soc. Gen. Internal Medicine, 1988. Master ACP (regent 1988-94, Rosenthal award 1980, Laureate award So. Calif. III 1994); fellow APHA, Acad. Occupl. Medicine; mem. Internat. Epidemiology Soc., Assn. Tchrs. Preventive Medicine (pres. coun. 1977-80), Am. Assn. Physicians. Home: 221 S Burlingame Ave Los Angeles CA 90049-3702 E-mail: lewis@ph.adm.ucla.edu

LEWIS, CHARLES JEREMY (JERRY LEWIS), congressman; b. Spokane, Wash., Oct. 21, 1934; BA, UCLA, 1956. Former life ins. underwriter; field rep. for former U.S. Rep. Jerry Pettis; mem. Calif. State Assembly, 1968-78; vice chmn. rules com., chmn. subcom. on air quality; mem. U.S. Congress from 40th (formerly 35th) Calif. dist., 1979—; mem. appropriations com. Chmn. VA-HUD subcom., mem. defense subcom., select com. on intelligence, chmn. subcom. on human intelligence; co-chair Calif. Congl. Delegation. Republican. Presbyterian. Office: US Ho Reps 2112 Rayburn Ho Office Bldg Washington DC 20515*

LEWIS, CHARLES S., III, lawyer; b. Baker, Oreg., Aug. 19, 1953; Student, U. So. Calif.; BS magna cum laude, Lewis and Clark Coll., 1975; JD magna cum laude, Willamette U., 1978. Bar: Oreg. 1978, U.S. Tax Ct. 1978. Mem. Stoel Rives, LLP, Portland, Oreg., 1978—. Co-author: The Tax Reform Act of 1986: Analysis and Commentary, 1987. Mem. ABA (taxation and bus. law sects.), Delta Mu Delta. Office: Stoel Rives LLP 900 SW 5th Ave Ste 2600 Portland OR 97204-1268

LEWIS, DONALD CLYDE, lawyer; b. Evansville, Ind., Apr. 28, 1942; s. Raymond and Helen (Newman) L.; m. Brenda Cobb, Sept. 1, 1962; children: Kelly Marie, Matthew Ryan, Elaine Janel, Nicole Renee. BS, cert. in Urban Studies, Ind. U., 1964, JD, 1967. Bar: Ind., 1967, Colo., 1989. Staff atty. N. Am. Van Lines, Ft. Wayne, Ind., 1967-72, PepsiCo Inc, Ft. Wayne, 1972-74; various legal positions Ball Corp., Muncie, Broomfield, Ind. Colo., 1974-96, asst. corp. sec., asst. gen. counsel Broomfield, Colo., 1995—.

LEWIS, EDWARD B. biology educator; b. Wilkes-Barre, Pa., May 20, 1918; s. Edward B. and Laura (Histed) L.; m. Pamela Harrah, Sept. 26, 1946; children: Hugh, Glenn (dec.), Keith. B.A., U. Minn., 1939; Ph.D., Calif. Inst. Tech., 1942; Phil.D., U. Umea, Sweden, 1982; DSc, U. Minn., 1993. Instr. biology Calif. Inst. Tech., Pasadena, 1946-48, asst. prof., 1949-56, prof., 1956-66, Thomas Hunt Morgan prof., 1966-88, prof. emeritus, 1988—. Rockefeller Found. fellow Sch. Botany, Cambridge U., Eng., 1948-49; mem. Nat. Adv. Com. Radiation, 1958-61; vis. prof. U. Copenhagen, 1975-76, 82; researcher in developmental genetics, somatic effects of radiation. Editor: Genetics and Evolution, 1961 Served to capt. USAAF, 1942-46 Recipient Gairdner Found. Internat. award, 1987, Wolf Found. prize in medicine, 1989, Rosenstiel award, 1990, Nat. Medal of Sci. NSF, 1990, Albert Lasker Basic Med. Rsch. award, 1991, Louisa Gross Horowitz prize Columbia U., 1992, Nobel Prize in Medicine, 1995. Fellow AAAS; mem. NAS, Genetics Soc. Am. (sec. 1962-64, pres. 1967-69, Thomas Hunt Morgan medal), Am. Acad. Arts and Scis., Royal Soc. (London) (fgn. mem.), Am. Philos. Soc., Genetical Soc. Great Britain (hon.). Home: 805 Winthrop Rd San Marino CA 91108-1709 Office: Calif Inst Tech Divsn Biology 1201 E California Blvd Pasadena CA 91125-0001

LEWIS, FREDERICK THOMAS, insurance company executive; b. Tacoma, Apr. 1, 1941; s. Arthur Thomas and June Louise (Levenhagen) L.; m. Sarah Carolyn Boyette, Apr. 18, 1971; adopted children: Johanna, Elizabeth, Sarah, Jonathan, Matthew. Student, Concordia Coll., Portland, Oreg., 1959-61, Dominican Coll., San Rafael, Calif., 1967-71. Registered health underwriter. Enroute coord. Trans World Airlines, N.Y.C., 1961-62, 64-66, customer svc. rep. Oakland, Calif., 1966-75; dist. rep. Aid Assn. for Luths., Twin Falls, Idaho, 1975-96, dist. mgr., 1984-88; pres. Luth. Care Ctr., Inc., Jerome, 2000—. Vocalist Oakland Symphony Chorus, 1972-75; soloist Magic Valley Chorale, Twin Falls, 1979-83. Cantor Immanuel Luth. Ch., Twin Falls, 1984-98; organizer Theos of Magic Valley, Filer, Idaho, 1984; dir. planned giving/major gifts Concordia U. Found., Portland, 1998—; chpt. leader So. Idaho Us Too!, 1998—. Mem.: Magic Valley Rose Soc. (bd. dir. 2000—01), Lions (local v.p. 1979—81, pres. 1982—83, organizer women's aux. 1983, sec. 1986—87, sec. 1992—93, treas. 1993—94, sec.-treas. multiple dist. 39 1994—95, vice-dist. gov. 39W 1995—96, dist. gov. 39W 1996—97), Nat. Assn.Life Underwriters (tng. coun. fellow 1984, Nat. Quality award Nat. Sales Achievement award Health Ins. Quality award 1978—96), So. Idaho Life Underwriters (pres. 1980—81, edn. chmn. 1984—86, nat. local com. mem. 1986—89), So. Idaho Health Underwriters (bd. dirs. 1986—88), Idaho State Assn. Life Underwriters (area v.p. 1988—89, sec. 1989—90, pres.-elect 1990—91, pres. 1991—92, state conv. exhibitor chmn. 1992—94, Bill Rankin Life Underwriter of Yr. award 1993), Idaho Fraternal Congress (ins. counselor 1976, bd. dir. 1976—85, pres. 1981—82). Republican. Avocations: ceramics, numismatics, gardening, music. Home and Office: 1612 Targhee Dr Twin Falls ID 83301-3546 E-mail: flewis@cu-portland.edu

LEWIS, GOLDY SARAH, real estate developer, corporation executive; b. West Selkirk, Man., Can., June 15, 1921; d. David and Rose (Dwor) Kimmel; m. Ralph Milton Lewis, June 12, 1941; children: Richard Alan, Robert Edward, Roger Gordon, Randall Wayne. B.S., UCLA, 1943; postgrad., U. So. Calif., 1944-45. Pvt. practice acctg., L.A., 1945-57; law office mgr. L.A., 1953-55; dir., exec. v.p. Lewis Homes, Upland, Calif., 1955—, Lewis Construction Co. Inc., Upland, 1959—, Lewis Bldg. Co., Inc., Las Vegas, 1960—, Republic Sales Co., Inc., 1956—, Kimmel Enterprises, Inc., 1959—; mng. partner Lewis Homes of Calif., 1973—; mng. ptnr. Lewis Homes of Nev., 1972—, Western Properties, 1972—, Foothill Investment Co., 1971—, Republic Mgmt. Co., 1978—. Contbr. articles to mags., jours. Mem. Dean's Coun. UCLA Grad. Sch. Architecture and Urban Planning; mem. UCLA Found., Chancellor's Assocs.; endowed Ralph and Goldy Lewis Ctr. for Regional Policy at UCLA, 1989, Ralph and Goldy Lewis Hall of Planning and Devel. at U. S.C., 1989, others. Recipient 1st award of distinction Am. Builder mag., 1963, Homer Briggs Svc. to Youth award West End YMCA, 1990, Spirit of Life award City of Hope, 1993; co-recipient Builder of Yr. award Profl. Builder Mag., 1988, Housing Person of Yr. award Nat. Housing Conf., 1990, Entrepreneur of Yr. award Inland Empire, 1990; Ralph and Goldy Lewis Sports Ctr. named in their honor City of Rancho Cucamonga, 1988, also several other parks and sports fields including Lewis Park in Claremont.; named one of Women of Yr. Calif. 25th Senate Dist., 1989, (with husband Ralph M. Lewis) Disting. Chief Exec. Officer, Calif. State U., San Bernadino, 1991, Mgmt. Leaders of the Yr. Univ. Calif., Riverside, 1993. Mem. Nat. Assn. Home Builders, Bldg. Industry Assn. So. Calif. (Builder of Yr. award Baldy View chpt. 1988), Internat. Coun. Shopping Ctrs., Urban Land Inst. Office: Lewis Homes PO Box 670 Upland CA 91785-0670

LEWIS, HUEY (HUGH ANTHONY CREGG III), singer, composer, bandleader; b. N.Y.C., July 5, 1951; s. Hugh Anthony II and Magda Cregg; m. Sidney Conroy, 1983; children: Kelly, Austin. Student, Cornell U. Mem. Clover, 1972-77; singer, composer leader Huey Lewis and the News, 1978—. Rec. artist: (with Clover) Clover, 1977, Unavailable, 1977, Love on the Wire, 1977, (with Huey Lewis and the News) Huey Lewis and the News, 1980, Picture This, 1982, Sports, 1983, Fore, 1986, Small World, 1988, Hard at Play, 1991, Best of Huey Lewis and the News, 1992, Four Chords and Several Years Ago, 1994, Time Flies...The Best of Huey Lewis, 1996, Original Gold, 2000; hit singles include Do You Believe in Love?, Workin' for a Living, I Want a New Drug, The Heart of Rock 'n' Roll (Grammy award for Best Music Video 1985), Heart and Soul, Walking on a Thin Line, Hip To Be Square, I Know What I Like, (single from Back to the Future soundtrack) The Power of Love; contbr. (single and video) We Are the World, 1984; appeared in films: Back to the Future, 1985, Short Cuts, 1993, Sphere, 1998, Shadow of Doubt, 1998, Duets, 2000, TV film: Dead Husbands, 1998, video: Twister: A Ritual Reality, 1994. Office: c/o Capitol EMI Records 1750 Vine St Hollywood CA 90028-5209

LEWIS, JASON ALVERT, JR. communications executive; b. Clarksville, Tex., Aug. 17, 1941; s. Jason Allen and Mary (Dinwiddie) L. Student, Stockton Coll., 1959-60, San Jose Jr. Coll., 1962-63. Field engr. telephone tech. Pacific Bell, San Francisco, 1983-84; systems technician AT&T, San Francisco, 1984—. Patentee in field. With U.S. Army, 1964-66. Mem. Internat. Platform Assn., Cousteau Soc., Astron. Soc. Pacific, San Francisco Zool. Soc., Planetary Soc., U.S. Naval Inst. Democrat. Avocations: photography, astronomy. Home: 139 Pecks Ln South San Francisco CA 94080-1744

LEWIS, JEROME A. petroleum company executive, investment banker; b. 1927; married. BA in Engring., U. Okla. Geologist Shell Oil Co., 1950-51; pres. Lewmont Drilling Inc., 1951-65, Border Exploration Co., 1965-68; pres., chmn. bd., CEO Petro-Lewis Corp., 1968-87; pres. Princeps Ptnrs., Inc., 1987-97; dir. DenverAmerican Petrol., 1991-97. Bd. dirs. Denver Leadership Found., Trinity Forum, Downing St. Found. Mem. Ind. Petroleum Assn. Am., Oil Investment Inst. (founding gov.), World Pres.' Orgn., Am. Assn. Petroleum Geologists, Am. Petroleum Inst., Chief Execs. Orgn. Office: Downing Ptnrs Inc 50 S Steele St Ste 328 Denver CO 80209-2808

LEWIS, JERRY (JOSEPH LEVITCH), comedian; b. Newark, Mar. 16, 1926; s. Danny and Rae Levitch; m. Patti Palmer, 1944 (div.); children: Gary, Ron, Scott, Chris, Anthony, Joseph; m. Sandra Pitnick, 1983; 1 child, Danielle Sara. Edn., Irvington (N.J.) High Sch.; DHL (hon.), Mercy Coll., 1987. Prof. cinema U. So. Calif.; pres. JAS Prodns., Inc., P.J. Prodns., Inc. Began as entertainer with record routine at Catskill (N.Y.) hotel; formed comedy team with Dean Martin, 1946-56; performed as a single, 1956—; formed Jerry Lewis Prodns. Inc., prod., dir., writer, star, 1956; films include: My Friend Irma, 1949, My Friend Irma Goes West, 1950, At War with the Army, 1950, That's My Boy, 1950, Sailor Beware, 1951, The Stooge, 1952, Jumping Jacks, 1952, Scared Stiff, 1953, The Caddy, 1953, Money From Home, 1953, Three Ring Circus, 1954, Living it Up, 1954, You're Never Too Young, 1955, Artists and Models, 1955, Partners, 1956, Hollywood or Bust, 1956, The Delicate Delinquent, 1957, The Sad Sack, 1957, The Geisha Boy, 1958, Rockabye Baby, 1958, Don't Give Up the Ship, 1959, Li'l Abner, 1959, Visit to a Small Planet, 1960, The Bellboy, 1960, Cinderfella, 1960, The Ladies Man, 1961, It's Only Money, 1962, The Errand Boy, 1962, It's a Mad, Mad, Mad, Mad World, 1963, The Nutty Professor, 1963, Who's Minding The Store, 1963, The Patsy, 1964, The Disorderly Orderly, 1964, The Family Jewels, 1965, Boeing-Boeing, 1965, Three On A Couch, 1965, Way ... Way ... Out, 1966, The Big Mouth, 1967, Don't Raise the Bridge, Lower the Water, 1968, Hook, Line and Sinker, 1969, One More Time, 1969, Which Way To the Front?, 1970, Hardly Working, 1981, King of Comedy, 1983, Smorgasbord, 1983, Slapstick, 1984, To Catch A Cop, 1984, How Did You Get In?, 1985, Cookie, 1989, Arrowtooth Waltz, 1991, Mr. Saturday Night, 1992, Arizona Dream, 1993, Funny Bones, 1995; appeared on Broadway in Damn Yankees, 1995, on tour, 1995—; author: The Total Film-Maker, 1971, Jerry Lewis in Person, 1982; principal TV appearances include master of ceremonies ann. Labor Day Muscular Dystrophy Telethon, 1966—. Comdr. Order of Arts & Letters, France, 1984; nat. chmn. Muscular Dystrophy Assn. Recipient most promising male star in TV award Motion Picture Daily's 2nd Ann. TV poll, 1950, (as team), one of TV's 10 money making stars award Motion Picture Herald - Fame poll, 1951, 53-54, 57, best comedy team award Motion Picture Daily's 16th annual radio poll, 1951-53, Nobel Peace Prize nomination, 1978. Mem. Screen Producers Guild, Screen Dirs. Guild, Screen Writers Guild. Office: Jerry Lewis Films Inc 3160 W Sahara Ave # 16C Las Vegas NV 89102-6003 also: William Morris Agy Inc 151 S El Camino Dr Beverly Hills CA 90212-2704

LEWIS, JOHN CHRISTOPHER, allergist; b. Boston, Oct. 15, 1950; MD, Loyola U., Maywood, 1982. Asst. prof. medicine Mayo Med. Sch., Scottsdale, Ariz. Office: Mayo Clinic Scottsdale 13400 E Shea Blvd Scottsdale AZ 85259-5499

LEWIS, JOHN CLARK, JR. retired manufacturing company executive; b. Livingston, Mont., Oct. 15, 1935; s. John Clark and Louise A. (Anderson) L.; m. Carolyn Jean Keesling, Sept. 4, 1960; children: Robert, Anne, James. BS, Fresno (Calif.) State U., 1957. With Service Bur. Corp., El Segundo, Calif., 1960-70, Computer Scis. Corp., 1970; with Xerox Corp., El Segundo, 1970-77, pres. bus. systems div., 1977; pres. Amdahl Corp., Sunnyvale, Calif., 1983-87, CEO, 1983, chmn., 1987-2000; ret., 2000. Served with USNR, 1957-60. Roman Catholic. Office: Amdahl Corp 1250 E Arques Ave Sunnyvale CA 94085-4730

LEWIS, JOHN R. state legislator; b. L.A., Nov. 2, 1954; m. Suzanne Henry. BA in Polit. Sci., U. So. Calif. Mem. Calif. State Assembly, 1981-92, Calif. State Senate, 1992—, chmn. Rep. caucus elections com. Mem. Reagan for Pres. Calif. Exec. Com., 1976; del. Nat. Conv. 1976. Republican. Office: Calif State Senate State Capitol Rm 3063 Sacramento CA 95814 also: 1940 W Orangewood Ave Ste 106 Orange CA 92868-2064 Fax: 714-939-0730

LEWIS, JOHN WILSON, political science educator; b. King County, Wash., Nov. 16, 1930; s. Albert Lloyd and Clara (Lewis) Seeman; m. Jacquelyn Clark, June 19, 1954; children: Cynthia, Stephen, Amy. Student, Deep Springs Coll., 1947-49; AB with highest honors, UCLA, 1953, MA, 1958, PhD, 1962; hon. degree, Morningside Coll., 1969, Lawrence U., 1986, Russian Acad. Sci., 1996. Asst. prof. govt. Cornell U., 1961-64, assoc. prof., 1964-68, Asst. prof. govt., 1961-64; prof. polit. sci. Stanford U., 1968-97, William Haas prof. Chinese politics, 1972-97, William Haas prof. emeritus, 1997—, co-dir. arms control and disarmament program, 1971-83, co-dir. NE Asia U.S. Forum on Internat. Policy, 1980-90, co-dir. Ctr. for Internat. Security and Arms Control, 1983-91, sr. fellow, 1991—; dir. Project on Peace and Cooperation in the Asian-Pacific Region, 1990—; chmn. Internat. Strategic Inst., 1983-89; chmn. joint com. on contemporary China Social Sci. Rsch. Coun.-Am. Coun. Learned Socs., 1976-79; mng. dir. Generation Ventures, 1994-99. Former vice chmn., bd. dirs. Nat. Com. on U.S.-China Rels.; cons. Senate Select Com. on Intelligence, 1977-81, Los Alamos Nat. Lab., 1987-92, Lawrence Livermore Nat. Lab., Dept. of Def., 1994-96; mem. Def. Policy Bd., 1994-96; chmn. com. advanced study in China Com. Scholarly Comm. with People's Republic of China, 1979-82; mem. com. on internat. security and arms control Nat. acad. Scis., 1980-83; organizer first univ. discussion arms control and internat. security matters Chinese People's Inst. Fgn. Affairs, 1978, first academic exch. agreement Dem. People's Repb. of Korea, 1988; negotiator first univ. tng. and exch. agreement People's Rep. of China, 1978. Author: Leadership in Communist China, 1963, Major Doctrines of Communist China, 1964, Policy Networks and the Chinese Policy Process, 1986; co-author: The United States in Vietnam, 1967, Modernization by Design, 1969, China Builds the Bomb, 1988, Uncertain Partners: Stalin, Mao, and the Korean War, 1993, China's Strategic Seapower: The Politics of Force Modernization in the Nuclear Era, 1994; editor: The City in Communist China, 1971, Party Leadership and Revolutionary Power in China, 1970, Peasant Rebellion and Communist Revolution in Asia, 1974; contbr.: Congress and Arms Control, 1978, China's Quest for Independence, 1979, others; mem. editl. bd. Chinese Law and Govt., The Pacific Rev.; mem. adv. bd. China Quarterly. Served with USN, 1954-57. Recipient Helios award, Russian Acad. Sci., 2001. Home: 541 San Juan St Stanford CA 94305-8432 Office: Stanford U Encina Hall Stanford CA 94305-6105

LEWIS, JONATHAN, health care association administrator; BS Applied Behavioral Scis., U. Calif., Davis. Founder, mng. ptnr., pres. JLA Advocates, Inc.; exec. dir. Calif. Commn. on Tchg. Profession; chief cons. State of Calif. State Senate Commn. on Property Tax Equity, 1990-91; exec. dir. Calif. Assn. Health Maintenance Orgns., Sacramento, 1990-93; founder, pres. Acad. for Internat. Health Studies, Inc., Davis, Calif., 1993—. Vis. faculty U. Calif., Berkeley; budget cons. State of Calif. Senate Pres. Office: Acad Internat Health Study 621 Georgetown Pl Davis CA 95616-1821

LEWIS, LOUISE MILLER, gallery director, art history educator; b. St. Louis, Dec. 4, 1940; d. Hugh Milton and Jeanne (Vical) Miller; m. Guy R. Lewis, Nov. 26, 1966; 1 child, Kevin. BA with distinction, 1963; cert. practique de la langue Francaise, U. Paris, 1963; MA in French, U. N.Mex., 1966, MA in Art History, 1972. Curator Art Mus. U. N.Mex., Albuquerque, 1966-70, asst. dir., 1970-72, acctg. dir., 1970, 71-72; assoc. dir. Art Gallery Calif. State U., Northridge, 1972-80, dir., 1980—; asst. prof. art history/recent art of internat. origins Calif. State U., 1972-79, assoc. prof., 1979-83, prof., 1983—, v.p. faculty, 1990-92, pres. faculty, 1992-94. Mem. Phi Beta Kappa. Office: Calif State U 18111 Nordhoff St Northridge CA 91330-0001 E-mail: louise.lewis@csan.edu

LEWIS, NATHAN SAUL, chemistry educator; b. L.A., Oct. 20, 1955; BS in Chemistry with highest honors, MS in Chemistry, Calif. Inst. Tech., 1977; PhD in Chemistry, MIT, 1981. Asst. prof. chemistry Stanford (Calif.) U., 1981-86, assoc. prof., 1986-88, Calif. Inst. Tech., 1988-90, prof., 1990—. Cons. Lawrence Livermore (Calif.) Nat. Lab., 1977-81, 84-88, Solar Energy Rsch. Assocs., Santa Clara, Calif., 1981-85, Am. Hosp. Supply, Irvine, Calif., 1983-85, Molecular Devices, Palo Alto, Calif., 1983-88; mem. U.S. Japan Joint Conf. Photochemistry and Photoconversion, 1983, Chem. Revs. Adv. Bd., 1989-92, long range planning com. Electrochem. Soc., 1991-94, Adv. Bd. Progress Inorganic Chemistry, 1992-94, vis. com. dept. applied sci. Brookhaven Nat. Lab., 1993—. Divisional editor Jour. Electrochemical Soc., 1984-90; mem. editorial adv. bd. Accounts Chem. Rsch., 1993—. Recipient Presdl. Young Investigator award, 1984-88, Fresenius award Phi Lambda Upsilon, 1990, Pure Chemistry award Am. Chem. Soc., 1991; Achievement Rewards Coll. Scientists Found. scholar Calif. Inst. Tech., 1975-77, Calif. State scholar, 1976-77, Carnation Co. Acad. Merit scholar, 1976-77, Camille and Henry Dreyfus Tchr. scholar, 1985-90; Fannie and John Hertz Found. fellow MIT, 1977-81, Alfred P. Sloan Rsch. fellow, 1985-87. Office: Calif Inst Tech Dept Chem 127 72 Pasadena CA 91125-0001 E-mail: nslewis@caltech.edu

LEWIS, NORMAN G. academic administrator, researcher, consultant; b. Irvine, Ayrshire, Scotland, Sept. 16, 1949; came to U.S., 1985; s. William F. and Agnes H. O. L.; m. Christine I. (div. Oct. 1994); children: Fiona, Kathryn; m. Laurence Beatrice Davin, July 1997; 1 child, Sebastian. BSc in Chemistry with honors, U. Strathclyde, Scotland, 1973; PhD in Chemistry 1st class, U. B.C., 1977. NRC postdoctoral fellow U. Cambridge, Eng., 1978-80; rsch. assoc. chemistry dept. Nat. Rsch. Coun., Can., 1980; asst. scientist fundamental rsch. divsn. Pulp and Paper Rsch. Inst. Can., Montreal, 1980-82, group leader chemistry and biochemistry of woody plants, grad. rsch. chemistry divsn., 1982-85; assoc. prof. wood sci. and biochemistry Va. Poly. Inst. and State U., Blacksburg, 1985-90; dir. Inst. Biol. Chemistry, Wash. State U., Pullman, 1990—; Eisig-Tode disting. prof. Cons. NASA, DOE, USDA, NIH, NSF, Am. Inst. Biol. Scis., other industries, 1985—. Mem. editl. bd. Holzforschung, 1986, TAPPI, 1986, 89, Jour. Wood Chemistry and Tech., 1987—, Polyphenols Actualities, 1992—; mem. editl. bd. The Ams., Asia regional editor Phytochemistry, 1992—; author or co-author more than 140 publs., books, articles to profl. jours. Hon. mem. Russian Assn. Space and Mankind Recipient ICI Merit awards Imperial Chem. Industries, 1968-69, 69-70, 70-71, 71-72, ICI scholar, 1971-73, Chemistry awards Kilmarnock Coll., 1969-70, 70-71; NATO/SRC scholar U. B.C., 1974-77; named Arthur M. and Kate E. Tode Disting. Prof. Mem. Am. Chem. Soc. (at-large cellulose divsn., organizer symposia, programme subcom. cellulose, paper and textile divsn. 1987-90, editorial bd.), Am. Soc. Plant Physiologists, Am. Soc. Gravitational and Space Biology (pres. 1998-99), Phytochemical Soc. N.A. (phytochemical bank com. 1989—), Chem. Inst. Can. (treas. Montreal divsn. 1982-84, Am. Inst. Chemists and Chem. Inst. Can. Montreal conf. 1982-84), Can. Pulp and Paper Assn., Tech. Assn. of Pulp and Paper Industry, Societe de Groupe Polyphenole, Gordon Rsch. Conf. (vice-chmn. raenewable resources com. 1993—). Presbyterian. Achievements include 2 patents in field. Home: 1710 NE Upper Dr Pullman WA 99163-4624 Office: Washington State U Inst Biol Chemistry Clark Hall Pullman WA 99164 Fax: 509-335-8206. E-mail: lewisn@wsu.edu

LEWIS, OLI PAREPA, curator; b. Cleve., Dec. 14, 1958; d. Raymond Joseph and Yarmila Manlet; m. Fred Lewis. BA, U. Las Vegas. Gen. mgr., curator Guinness World Records Mus., Las Vegas, Nev., 1990—. Pres. Mus. and Attractions in Nev. Recipient Voluntourism award Nev. Commn. Tourism, 1994. Office: Guinness World Records Mus 2780 Las Vegas Blvd S Las Vegas NV 89109-1102

LEWIS, ORME, JR. real estate investment company executive, land use advisor; b. Phoenix, Apr. 26, 1935; s. Orme and Barbara (Smith) L.; m. Elizabeth Bruening, Oct. 17, 1964; children: Joseph Orme, Elizabeth Blaise. BS, U. Ariz., 1958. Assoc. Coldwell Banker, Phoenix, 1959-64; v.p. Braggiotti Constrn., Phoenix, 1964-65; pvt. practice investment brokerage Phoenix, 1966-69; dep. asst. sec. Dept. Interior, Washington, 1969-73; dir. devel. Ariz. Biltmore Estates, 1973-76; exec. World Resources Co., Phoenix and McLean, Va., 1978-91; mng. mem. Applewhite Laflin & Lewis, Phoenix, 1979-96; gen. ptnr. Equity Interests, Phoenix, 1982—; mng. dir. Select Investments, Phoenix, 1996—. Co-chmn. U.S. Adv. Com. on Mining and Mineral Rsch., Washington, 1982-94; mem. U.S. Emergency Minerals Adminstrn., 1987—, Gov.'s Regulatory Rev. Coun., 1992-95, State Plant Site Transmission Line Com., Phoenix, 1974-85; co-chmn. Disease Control Rsch. Commn., 1995—. Mem. Ariz. Senate, 1966-70; chmn. Phoenix Children's Hosp., 1981—; mem. Boyce Thompson Arboretum, 1999—; mem. governing bd. Polycystic Kidney Rsch. Found., Kansas City, Mo., 1983—, Ariz. Cmty. Found., 1986-91, Ariz. Parks and Conservation Coun., 1985-96, Ariz. State U. Found., Tempe, 1981—, Ariz. Hist. Found., 1984—; mem. governing bd. Desert Bot. Garden, 1987-89, Men's Art Coun., 1983-85. Recipient Dept. Interior Conservation Svc. award, 1996; inductee Wisdom Hall of Fame, 1997. Mem. Ariz. C. of C. (dir. 1990-96), Met. Club (Washington), Ariz. Valley Field Riding and Polo Club, Paradise Valley Country Club, Rotary. Republican. Home: 4325 E Palo Verde Dr Phoenix AZ 85018-1127 Office: Select Investments LLC 4350 E Camelback Rd Ste 260E Phoenix AZ 85018-8343 E-mail: adviser_az@msn.com

LEWIS, RANDALL, home building company executive; Exec. v.p., dir. mktg. Lewis Homes Mgmt. Corp.; exec. v.p., bd. mem. Kaufman & Broad Home Corp., 1999—. Office: Kaufman & Broad Home Corp 10990 Wilshire Blvd Fl 7 Los Angeles CA 90024-3913

LEWIS, RANDOLPH VANCE, molecular biologist, researcher; b. Powell, Wyo., Apr. 8, 1950; s. William (Jack) Fredrick and Evelyn Jean (Vonburg) L.; m. Lorrie Dale Emery, May 27, 1972; children: Brian, Daryl (dec.), Karren. BS in Chemistry, Calif. Inst. Tech., 1972; MS in Chemistry, U. Calif., San Diego, 1974; PhD in Chemistry, U. Calif., 1978. Postdoctoral fellow Roche Inst. Molecular Biology, Nutley, N.J., 1978-80; asst. prof. molecular biology U. Wyo., Laramie, 1980-84, assoc. prof., 1984-89, head dept., 1986-91, prof., 1989—; dir. NSF EPSCOR Program, 1990—. Cons. NIH, Bethesda, Md., 1985-91, Hoffmann-LaRoche, Nutley, N.J., 1990-93, DuPont, Wilmington,Del., 1990-94, Protein Polymer Techs., San Diego, 1988-94, Nexia, 1999—; pres. Wyobigen, Laramie, Wyo., 1994—. Author chpts. to books; contbr. articles to profl. jours. Mem. Jr. Livestock Sale Com., Laramie, 1991-98; pres. Albany County 4-H Coun., Laramie, 1994-98. Sloan Found. fellow, 1985; recipient Research Career Devel. award NIH, 1985, Jr. Faculty award Am. Cancer Soc., 1985, Burlington-North Faculty award U. Wyo., 1986. Mem. Am. Chem. Soc., Am. Soc. Biochemists and Molecular Biologists, N.Y. Acad. Scis., Protein Soc. Republican. Baptist. Achievements include discovery of opioid peptide precursor; sequencing of first spider silk protein genes; five product licenses; 4 patents. Avocations: fly fishing, bird hunting. Home: 1948 Howe Rd Laramie WY 82070-6889 Office: U Wyo PO Box 3944 Laramie WY 82071-3944

LEWIS, ROBERT TURNER, former psychologist; b. Taft, Calif., June 17, 1923; s. D. Arthur and Amy Belle (Turner) L.; m. Jane Badham, Mar. 23, 1946; children: Jane, William, Richard. BA, U. So. Calif., 1947, MA, 1950; PhD, U. Denver, 1952. Chief psychologist Hollywood Presbyn. Hosp., L.A., 1953-58; dir. psychol. svcs. Salvation Army, Pasadena, Calif., 1958-68; dir. Pasadena Psychol. Ctr., 1964-74; successively asst. prof., assoc. prof. and prof. Calif. State U., L.A., 1952-83, prof. emeritus, 1984—. Assoc. dir. Cortical Function Lab., L.A., 1972-84; clin. dir. Diagnostic Clinic, West Covina, Calif., 1983-85; dir. Job Stress Clinic, Santa Ana, Calif., 1985-95. Author: Taking Chances, 1979, A New Look at Growing Older, 1995, Money Hangups, 1995; co-author: Money Madness, 1978, Human Behavior, 1974, The Psychology of Abnormal Behavior, 1961. Lt (j.g.) USNR, 1943-46, PTO. Mem. APA, Calif. State Pscyhol. Assn. Republican.

LEWIS, RODERIC W. technology company executive, lawyer; b. Nyssa, Oreg., May 17, 1955; BA, Brigham Young U., 1980; JD, Columbia U., 1983. Bar: Utah 1983. Assoc. LeBoeuf, Lamb, Leiby & MacRae, N.Y.C., 1983-89, Rogers, MacKay, Price & Anderson, 1989-91; asst. gen. counsel Micron Tech., 1991-95; v.p., legal and corp. sec. Micron Electronics, 1995-96; v.p. legal affairs, gen. counsel, corp. sec. Micron Techs., Inc., Boise. Vice-chmn. Utah Bus. Corp. Act Revision Com. Mem. ABA, Idaho State Bar, Utah State Bar (chmn. bus. law sect. 1988-89). Office: Mail Stop 507 PO Box 6 8000 S Federal Way Boise ID 83707 E-mail: rodlewis@micron.com

LEWIS, SHELDON NOAH, technology consultant; b. Chgo., July 1, 1934; s. Jacob Joseph and Evelyn (Mendelsohn) Iglowitz; m. Suzanne Joyce Goldberg, June 17, 1957; children: Sara Lynn, Matthew David, Rachel Ann. BA with honors, MS (Univ. fellow), Northwestern U., 1956; PhD (Eastman Kodak fellow), UCLA, 1959; postgrad. (NSF fellow), U. Basel, Switzerland, 1959-60; postgrad. cert. in research mgmt, Indsl. Research Inst., Harvard U., 1973. With Rohm & Haas Co., 1960-78, head lab., 1963-68, research supr., 1968-73, dir. splty. chem. research, 1973-74; gen. mgr. DCL Lab. AG subs., Zurich, Switzerland, 1974-75; dir. European Labs. Valbonne, France, 1975-76; corp. dir. research and devel. worldwide for polymers, resins and monomers Spring House, Pa., 1976-78; with The Clorox Co., Oakland, Calif., 1978-91, v.p. R&D, 1978, group v.p., 1978-84, exec. v.p., 1984-91, also bd. dirs.; pres. SNL Inc., Lafayette, 1991—. Mem. indsl. panel on sci. and tech. NSF. Referee: Jour. Organic Chemistry; patentee in field; contbr. articles to profl. publs. Mem. Calif. Inst. Adv. Bd., World Affairs Council, UCLA Chemistry Adv. Council, Bay Area Sci. Fair Adv. Bd., Mills Coll. Adv. Council for Sci. and Math. Recipient cert. in patent law Phila. Patent Law Assn., 1962, Roon award for coatings research Fedn. Socs. Coatings Tech., 1966, cert. of service Wayne State U. Polymer Conf. Series, 1967, cert. in mgmt. by objectives Am. Mgmt. Research, Inc., 1972 Mem. Soap and Detergent Assn. (bd. dirs.), Chem. Ind. Inst. of Toxicology (bd. dirs.), Indsl. Rsch. Inst., Am. Chem. Soc. (chmn. Phila. polymer sect. 1970-71), Soc. Chem. Industry London, Sigma Xi. Jewish. Office: SNL Inc 3711 Rose Ct Lafayette CA 94549-3030

LEWIS, SHIRLEY JEANE, psychology educator; b. Phoenix, 23 Aug. d. Herman and Leavy (Hutchinson) Smith; m. Edgar Anthony Lewis (div.); children: Edgar Anthony, Roshaun, Lucy Ann Jonathan. AA, Phoenix C.C., 1957; BA, Ariz. State U., 1960; MS, San Diego State U., 1975, MA, 1986, Azusa Pacific U., 1982; PhD, U. So. Calif., 1983. Cert. tchr. Calif. Recreation leader Phoenix Parks and Recreation Dept., 1957-62; columnist Ariz. Tribune, Phoenix, 1958-59; tchr. phys. edn. San Diego Unified Schs., 1962—; adult educator San Diego C.C., 1973—; head counselor Gomper Secondary Sch./San Diego Unified Schs., 1998-2001. Instr. psychology, health, Black studies, 1977—, counselor, 1981—; cmty. counselor S.E. Counseling and Cons. Svcs. and Narcotics Prevention and Edn. Systems, Inc., San Diego, 1973-77; counselor educator, counselor edn. dept. San Diego State U., 1974-77; marriage, family, child counselor Counseling and Cons. Ctr., San Diego, 1977—; inservice educator San Diego Unified and San Diego County Sch. Dists., 1973-77; Fulbright Exch. counselor, London, 1994-96, asst. prin. Oceanside Unifed Sch. Dist., 1997-98; lectr. in field. Contbr. articles to profl. jours. Girl Scout phys. fitness cons., Phoenix, 1960-62; vol. cmty. tutor for high sch. students, San Diego, 1963; sponsor Tennis Club for Youth, San Diego, 1964-65; troop leader Girl Scouts U.S., Lemon Grove, Calif., 1972-74; vol. counselor USN Alcohol Rehab. Ctr., San Diego, 1978; mem. sch. coun.'s adv. bd. San Diego State U. Named Woman of Yr., Phoenix, 1957, One of Outstanding Women of San Diego, 1980; recipient Phys. Fitness Sch. award and Demonstration Sch. award Pres.'s Coun. on Phys. Fitness, Taft Jr. H.S., 1975, Excel award Corp. Excellence Edn., 1989; Delta Sigma Theta scholar, 1957-60; Alan Korrick scholar, 1956. Mem. NEA, Calif. Tchrs. Assn., San Diego Tchrs. Assn., Assn. Marriage and Family Counselors, Am. Personnel and Guidance Assn., Calif. Assn. Health, Phys. Edn. and Recreation (v.p. health), Am. Alliance of Health, Phys. Edn. and Recreation, Assn. Black Psychologists (corr. sec. 1993), Assn. African-Am. Educators, Delta Sigma Theta (Delta of Yr. 1987). Democrat. Baptist. Home: 1226 Armacost Rd San Diego CA 92114-3307 Office: Gompers Secondary Sch 1005 47th St San Diego CA 92102-3699

LEWIS, THOMASINE ELIZABETH, magazine editor-in-chief; b. Manila, Phillipines, 20 Sept. d. Thomas Donald and Elizabeth Jane (Munson) L. Student, Broward C.C., 1976, Universidad de las Americas, Mexico City, 1979, U. Fla., L.A. Valley Coll., 1981, UCLA, 1984. Copy editor, reporter Mexico City News, 1979-81; mng. editor, editor-in-chief Playgirl Mag., Santa Monica, Calif., 1984-86; exec. editor mag. devel. Petersen Pub., Hollywood, 1986-87; exec. editor Japan Jour. Mag., Marina del Rey, 1987-88; assoc. pub., dir. Radio Guide Mag., L.A., 1988-90; editor-in-chief Disney Adventures Mag., Burbank, Calif., 1991-95, Sassy Mag., L.A., 1995; exec. dir. Live! Mag., L.A., 1995-98; editor, chief Teen Mag., 1998—. Bd. dirs. Santa Monica Red Cross; mem. League of Women Voters, NOW, People for the Am. Way. Avocations: traveling, writing, running.

LEWIS, TOMMI, magazine editor; Editor-in-chief Disney Adventures Walt Disney Pub. Co.; editl. dir. Radio Guide Magazine; exec. editor Japan. Journal Magazine; exec. editor mag. devel. Petersen Pub.; editor-in-chief Sassy Magazine; exec. editor LIVE! Magazine; editor-at-large Teen Magazine, 1998-2000, editor-in-chief, 2000—. Office: EMAP USA 6420 Wilshire Blvd Los Angeles CA 90048-5502

LEWITZKY, BELLA, choreographer; b. Los Angeles, Jan. 13, 1916; d. Joseph and Nina (Ossman) L.; m. Newell Taylor Reynolds, June 22, 1940; 1 child, Nora Elizabeth. Student, San Bernardino Valley (Calif.) Jr. Coll., 1933-34; hon. doctorate, Calif. Inst. Arts, 1981; PhD (hon.), Occidental Coll., 1984, Otis Parsons Coll., 1989, Juilliard Sch., 1993; DFA, Santa Clara U., 1995; DFA (hon.), Calif. State U., Long Beach, 1997. Chmn. dance dept., chmn. adv. panel U. So. Calif., Idyllwild, 1956-74; founder Sch. Dance, Calif. Inst. Arts, 1969, dean, 1969-74; vice chmn. dance adv. panel Nat. Endowment Arts, 1974-77, mem. artists-in-schs. adv. panel, 1974-75; mem. Nat. Adv. Bd. Young Audiences, 1974—, Joint Commn. Dance and Theater Accreditation, 1979. Com. mem. Am. chpt. Internat. Dance Coun. of UNESCO, 1974—; trustee Calif. Assn. Dance Cos., 1976—, Idyllwild Sch. Music and Arts, 1986-95, Dance/USA, 1988-95, Calif. State Summer Sch. of Arts, 1988—; cons. the dance project WNET, 1987—. Co-founder, co-dir. Dance Dance Assocs., L.A., 1951-55; founder, 1966; artistic dir. Lewitzky Dance Co., L.A.; choreographer, 1948-97; founder, former artistic dir. The Dance Gallery, L.A.; contbr. articles in field; choreographed works include Trio for Saki, 1967, Orrenda, 1969, Kinaesonata, 1971, Pietas, 1971, Ceremony for Three, 1972, Game Plan, 1973, Five, 1974, Spaces Between, 1975, Jigsaw, 1975, Inscape, 1976, Pas de Bach, 1977, Suite Satie, 1980, Changes and Choices, 1981, Confines, 1982, Continuum, 1982, The Song of the Woman, 1983, Nos Duraturi, 1984, 8 Dancers/8 Lights, 1985, Facets, 1986, Impressions #1, 1987, Impressions #3, 1988, Agitime, 1989, Impressions #3, 1989, Episode #1, 1990, Glass Canyons, 1991, Episode #2, 1992, Episode #3, 1992, Episode #4, 1993, Meta 4, 1994, Four Women in Time, 1996. Mem. adv. com. Actors' Fund of Am., 1986—, Women's Bldg. Adv. Council, 1985-91, Calif. Arts Council, 1983-86, City of Los Angeles Task Force on the Arts, 1986—; mem. artistic adv. bd. Interlochen Ctr. for Arts, 1988—. Recipient Mayoral Proclamation, City of L.A., 1976, 1982, ann. award Dance mag., 1978, Dir.'s award Calif. Dance Educators Assn., 1978, Plaudit Award, Nat. Dance Assn., 1979, Labor's Award of Honor for Community Svc., L.A. County AFL-CIO, 1979, L.A. Area Dance Alliance and L.A. Junior C. of C. Honoree, 1980, City of L.A. Resolution, 1980, Distguished Artist Award, City of L.A. and Music Ctr., 1982, Silver Achievement award YWCA, 1982, California State Senate Resolution, 1982, 1984, Award of Recognition, Olympic Black Dance Festival, 1984, Distinguished Women's Award, Northwood Inst., 1984, California State U. Distinguished Artist, 1984, Vesta Award, Woman's Bldg, L.A., 1985, L.A. City Council Honors for Outstanding Contributions, 1985, Woman of the Year, Palm Springs Desert Museum, Women's Committee, 1986, Disting. Svc. award Western Alliance Arts Adminstrs., 1987, Woman of Achievement award, 1988, Am. Dance Guild Ann. award, 1989, So. Calif. Libr. for Social Studies & Rsch. award, 1990, Am. Soc. Journalists & Authors Open Book award, 1990, Internat. Soc. Performing Arts Adminstrs. Tiffany award, 1990, Burning Bush award U. of Judaism, 1991, 1st recipient Calif. Gov.'s award in arts for individual lifetime achievement, 1989; honoree L.A. Arts Coun., 1989, Heritage honoree, Nat. Dance Assn., 1991, Vaslav Nijinsky award, 1991, Hugh M. Hefner First Amendment award, 1991, Artistic Excellence award Ctr. Performing Arts U. Calif., 1992, Lester Horton Lifetime Achievement award Dance Resource Ctr. of L.A., 1992, Occidental Coll. Founders' award, 1992, Dance/USA honor, 1992, Visual Arts Freedom of Expression award Andy Warhol Found., 1993, Artist of Yr. award L.A. County High Sch. Arts, 1993, Freedom of Expression honor Andy Warhol Found. Visual Arts, 1993, Calif. Alliance Edn. award, 1994, Lester Horton Sustained Achievement award, 1995 Dance Resource Ctr. of L.A., Lester Horton award for Restaging and Revival, Dance Resource Ctr. of L.A., 1996, 97, Disting. Artists of 1996, High Sch. of Performing Arts, Houston Tex., Bill of Rights award, Am. Civil Liberties Union of So. Calif., Nat. Medal of Arts, 1996, Gypsy award Profl. Dancers Soc., 1997, We. Arts Alliance Emeritus Mem. award, 1999, Capezio ann. Dance award for Significant Conbns. to Dance in U.S., 1999; grantee Mellon Found., 1975, 81, 86, Guggenheim Found., 1977-78, NEA, 1969-94; honoree Women's Internat. League Peace and Freedom, 1995; presented with Key to the City, Cin., 1997. Mem. Am. Arts Alliance (bd. dirs. 1977), Internat. Dance Alliance (adv. council 1984—), Dance/USA (bd. dirs. 1988), Phi Beta (hon.). Fax: 505-897-9259

LEYDEN, NORMAN, conductor; m. Alice Leyden; children: Robert, Constance. Grad., Yale U., 1938; MA, Columbia U., EdD, 1968. Bass clarinetist New Haven Symphony; arranger Glenn Miller Air Force Band, Eng., France; chief arranger Glenn Miller Orch., 1946-49; freelance arranger N.Y.C.; mus. dir. RCA Victor Records, Arthur Godfrey, 1956-59; with Oreg. Symphony, 1970—, assoc. conductor, 1974—, condr.; music dir. Seattle Symphony Pops, 1975-93. Tchr. Columbia U.; guest condr. over 40 Am. symphony orchs. including Boston Pops, Minn. Orch., Pitts. Symphony, St. Louis Symphony, San Diego Symphony, San Francisco Symphony, Nat. Symphony, Utah Symphony; condr. Army Air Force. Office: Oreg Symphony Orch 921 SW Washington St Ste 200 Portland OR 97205-2800

LEYLAND, JAMES RICHARD, professional baseball team manager; b. Toledo, Dec. 15, 1944; m. Katie Leyland. Player various minor league teams Detroit Tigers, 1964-69, coach minor league system, 1970-71, mgr. minor league system, 1971-81; coach Chgo. White Sox, 1981-85; mgr. Pitts. Pirates, 1985-96, Fla. Marlins, Miami, 1997-98, Colo. Rockies, Denver, 1998—. Christmas chmn. Salvation Army, 1990-91. Named Nat. League Mgr. of Yr. Baseball Writers' Assn. Am., 1988, 90, Sporting News, 1990, Man of Yr. Arthritis Found., 1989, Epilepsy Found., 1991. Office: Colorado Rockies 2001 Blake St Denver CO 80205-2000

LEYRITZ, JAMES JOSEPH, professional baseball player; b. Lakewood, Ohio, Dec. 27, 1963; m. Karri Leyritz; children: Austin, Dakota. Student, Middle Ga. Jr. Coll., U. Ky. Catcher N.Y. Yankees farm sys., 1985-90; catcher, other positions N.Y. Yankees, N.Y.C., 1991-97, 99-, Anaheim (Calif.) Angels, 1997, Tex. Rangers, 1997, Boston Red Sox, 1997-98, San Diego Padres, 1998-99, L.A. Dodgers, 2000—. Office: LA Dodgers Dodger Stadium 1000 Elysian Park Ave Los Angeles CA 90012

LIANG, CHRISTINE, import company executive; Pres., founder ASI Corp., Fremont, Calif., 1987—. Office: ASI Corp 48289 Fremont Blvd Fremont CA 94538-6510

LIANG, MARCEL, corporate executive; CEO ASI, Fremont, Calif. Office: ASI 48289 Fremont Blvd Fremont CA 94538-6510

LIBBIN, ANNE EDNA, lawyer; b. Phila., Aug. 25, 1950; d. Edwin M. and Marianne (Herz) L.; m. Christopher J. Cannon, July 20, 1985; children: Abigail Libbin Cannon, Rebecca Libbin Cannon. AB, Radcliffe Coll., 1971; JD, Harvard U., 1975. Bar: Calif. 1975, U.S. Dist. Ct. (cen. dist.) Calif. 1977, U.S. Dist. Ct. (no. dist.) Calif. 1979, U.S. Dist. Ct. (ea. dist.) Calif. 1985, U.S. Ct. Appeals. (2d cir.) 1977, U.S. Ct. Appeals (5th cir.) 1982, U.S. Ct. Appeals (7th cir.) 1976, U.S. Ct. Appeals (9th cir.) 1976, U.S. Ct. Appeals (D.C. cir.) 1978. Appellate atty. NLRB, Washington, 1975-78; assoc. Pillsbury Madison & Sutro LLP, San Francisco, 1978-83, ptnr., 1984-99; sr. counsel Pacific Telesis Group, San Francisco, 1999—. Three Guineas fellow Harvard Law Sch., 1997; dir. Alumnae Resources, San Francisco, 1991-97. Mem. ABA (labor and employment sect.), State Bar Calif. (labor law sect.), Bar Assn. San Francisco (labor law sect.), Radcliffe Club (San Francisco). Office: Pacific Telesis Group 140 New Montgomery St San Francisco CA 94105-3705

LIBERMAN, ROBERT PAUL, psychiatry educator, researcher, writer; b. Newark, Aug. 16, 1937; s. Harry and Gertrude (Galowitz) L.; m. Janet Marilyn Brown, Feb. 16, 1973; children: Peter, Sarah, Danica, Nathaniel, Annalisa. AB summa cum laude, Dartmouth Coll., 1959, diploma in medicine with honors, 1960; MS in Pharmacology, U. Calif., San Francisco, 1961; MD, Johns Hopkins U., 1963. Diplomate Nat. Bd. Med. Examiners, Am. Bd. Psychiatry and Neurology. Intern Bronx (N.Y.) Mcpl. Hosp.-Einstein Coll. Medicine, 1963-64; resident psychiatry Mass. Mental Health Ctr., Boston, 1964-68; postdoctoral fellow in social psychiatry Harvard U., 1966-68, tchg. fellow in psychiatry, 1964-68; mem. faculty group psychotherapy tng. program Washington Sch. Psychiatry, 1968-70; asst. clin. prof. psychiatry UCLA, 1970-72, assoc. clin. prof., 1972-73, assoc. rsch. psychiatrist, 1973-76, rsch. prof. psychiatry, 1976-77, prof. psychiatry, 1977—. With nat. Ctr. Mental Health Svc., Tng. and Rsch., St. Elizabeths Hosp., also mem. NIMH Clin. and Rsch. Assocs. Tng. Program, Washington, 1968-70; dir. Camarillo-UCLA Clin. Rsch. Unit, 1970-97, dir. Clin. Rsch. Ctr. Schizophrenia and Psychiat. Rehab., 1977-2001; chief Rehab. Medicine Svc., West L.A. VA Med. Ctr., Brentwood divsn., 1980-92; cons. divsn. mental health and behavioral scis. edn. Sepulveda (Calif.) VA Hosp., 1975-80; practice medicine specializing in psychiatry, Reston, Va., 1968-70, Thousand Oaks, Calif., 1977—; staff psychiatrist Ventura County Mental Health Dept., 1970-75, Ventura County Gen. Hosp.; mem. med. staff UCLA Neuropsychiat. Inst. and Hosp., 1971—, Ventura Gen. Hosp., Camarillo State Hosp., 1970-97, West L.A. VA Med. Ctr.; dir. Rehab. Rsch. and Tng. Ctr. Mental Illness, 1980-85. Author: (with King, DeRisi and McCann) Personal Effectiveness: Guiding People to Assert Their Feelings and Improve Their Social Skills, 1975, A Guide to Behavioral Analysis and Therapy, 1972, (with Wheeler, DeVisser, Kuehnel and Kuehnel) Handbook of Marital Therapy: An Educational Approach to Treating Troubled Relationships, 1980, Psychiatric Rehabilitation of Chronic Mental Patients, 1987, (with DeRisi and Mueser) Social Skills Training for Psychiatric Patients, 1989, (with Kuehnel, Rose and Storzbach) Resource Book for Psychiatric Rehabilitation, 1990, Handbook of Psychiatric Rehabilitation, 1992, (with Yager) Stress in Psychiatric Disorders, 1993, (with Corrigan) Behavior Therapy in Psychiatric Hospitals, 1994, International Perspectives on Skills Training with the Mentally Disabled, 1998; mem. editl. bd. Jour. Applied Behavior Analysis, 1972-78, Jour. Marriage and Family Counseling, 1974-78, Jour. Behavior Therapy and Exptl. Psychiatry, 1975-2000, Behavior Therapy, 1979-84, Assessment and Intervention in Devel. Disabilities, 1980-85; assoc. editor Jour. Applied Behavior Analysis, 1976-78, Schizophrenia Bull., 1981-87, Internat. Rev. Psychiatry, 1988—, Psychiatry, 1993—; contbr. over 300 articles to profl. jours. and chpts. to books. Bd. dirs. Lake Sherwood Cmty. Assn., 1978—, pres., 1979-81, 90-92, v.p., 1992-95, sec., 1995-97; mem. Conejo Valley Citizens Adv. Bd., 1979-81. Served as surgeon USPHS, 1964-68. Recipient Noyes award for Rsch. in Schizophrenia, 1992, Kolb award in Schizophrenia, 1994, Human Rights award Psychosocial Rehab., Lilly Reintegration prize, Human Rights award WHO, 2000, Reintegration award Eli Lilly, 2000, Disting. Investigator award NARSAD, 2000-01; rsch. grantee NIMH, SSA, NIDA, VA, 1972—. Mem. Assn. Advancement Behavior Therapy (exec. com. 1970-72, dir. 1972-79), Am. Psychiat. Assn. (Hibbs and Van Ameringen awards, Inst. Psychiat. Svcs. Significant Achievement award), Assn. Clin. Psychosocial Rsch. (mem. coun. 1985-98, pres. 1995-97), Phi Beta Kappa. Home: 528 Lake Sherwood Dr Thousand Oaks CA 91361-5120 Office: 300 UCLA Med Plz Los Angeles CA 90095

LIBIN, ALVIN G. business executive; LLD (hon.), U. Calgary. Co-owner Calgary Flames - NHL; chmn. Crownx Properties, Inc.; dir. Extendicare, Inc. (N.Am.), Crown Life Ins. Co. Chmn. Alberta Heritage Found. for Sci. and Engring. Rsch. Office: 255-5 Ave SW # 3200 Calgary AB Canada T2P 3G6

LICENS, LILA LOUISE, administrative assistant; b. Puyallup, Wash., Feb. 18, 1949; d. C.L. and Joan L. (Rubert) Vormestrand. Cert., Knapp Bus. Coll., 1968. Cert. profl. sec. Adminstrv. asst. Weyerhaeuser Co., Federal Way, Wash., 1968-93, adminstrv. asst. bleached paperboard Tacoma, 1993-2000, adminstrv. asst. bus. conduct office, 2000—. Mem. adv. bd. Bates Tech. Coll., 1994—. Mem. Internat. Assn. Adminstrv. Profls. (pres. Mt. Rainier chpt. 1994-2000, pres. Wash.-Alaska divsn. 1990-91, pres.-elect 1989-90, sec. 1987-89, pres. Sea-Tac chpt. 1985-87), Fed. Way Women's Network (treas. 1988, sec. 1989, pres. 1995, 96). Avocations: travel, photography, reading. Home: 771 108th St S Tacoma WA 98444-5666

LICHTENBERG, MARGARET KLEE, publishing company executive; b. N.Y.C., Nov. 19, 1941; d. Lawrence and Shirley Jane (Wickman) Klee; m. James Lester Lichtenberg, Mar. 31, 1963 (div. 1982); m. William Shaw Jones, July 2, 2000; children: Gregory Lawrence, Amanda Zoe. BA, U. Mich., 1963; postgrad., Harvard U., 1963. Book rev. editor New Woman mag., 1972-73; assoc. editor children's books Parents Mag. Press, 1974; editor, rights dir. Books for Young People, Frederick Warne & Co., N.Y.C., 1975-78; sr. editor Simon & Schuster, N.Y.C., 1979-80; dir. sales promotion Grosset & Dunlap, N.Y.C., 1980-81; ednl. sales mgr. Bantam Books, N.Y.C., 1982-84; dir. mktg. and sales Grove Press, N.Y.C., 1984-86, dir. of sales, 1986-87; dir. sales Weidenfeld & Nicolson, N.Y.C., 1986-87; mktg. dir. Beacon Press, Boston, 1988-95; bus. and pub. coach, 1995—. Writer, freelance critic, 1961—. Contbr. articles, essays, stories, poetry, revs. to mags., newspapers and anthologies. Bd. dirs. Children's Book Council, 1978. Recipient 2 Avery Hopwood awards in drama and fiction, 1962, 2 in drama and poetry, 1963; coll. fiction contest award Mademoiselle mag., 1963; Woodrow Wilson fellow, 1963. Mem. Women's Nat. Book Assn. (past pres. N.Y. chpt.), Internat. Coach Fedn., The Coaching Collective, Pubs. Mktg. Assn., Small Pubs. Assn. N.Am., N.Mex. Book Assn., SW Writers Workshop, PEN N.Mex., Pubs. Assn. of the West. Home and Office: 4 Cosmos Ct Santa Fe NM 87508-2285 E-mail: maggie@maggielichtenberg.com

LICK, WILBERT JAMES, mechanical engineering educator; b. Cleve., June 12, 1933; s. Fred and Hulda (Sunntag) L.; children— James, Sarah. B.A.E., Rensselaer Poly. Inst., 1955, M.A.E., 1957, Ph.D., 1958. Asst. prof. Harvard, 1959-66; sr. research fellow Calif. Inst. Tech., 1966-67; mem. faculty Case Western Res. U., 1967-79, prof. earth scis., 1970-79, chmn. dept., 1973-76; prof. mech. engring. U. Calif.-Santa Barbara, 1979—, chmn. dept., 1982-84. Home: 1236 Camino Meleno Santa Barbara CA 93111-1007 Office: U Calif Dept Mech & Environ Engring Santa Barbara CA 93106 E-mail: willy@erode.ucsb.edu

LIDDLE, ALAN CURTIS, retired architect; b. Tacoma, Mar. 10, 1922; s. Abram Dix and Myrtle (Maytum) L. B.Arch., U. Wash., 1948; postgrad., Eidgenoische Technische Hochschule, Zurich, Switzerland, 1950-51. Asst. prof. architecture U. Wash., 1954-55; prin. Liddle & Jones, Tacoma, 1957-67, Alan Liddle (architects), Tacoma, 1967-90, Liddle & Jacklin, Tacoma, 1990-98; ret., 1999. Architect oceanography bldgs, U. Wash., 1967, Tacoma Art Mus., 1971, Charles Wright Acad., Tacoma, 1962, Pacific Nat. Bank Wash., Auburn, 1965. Pres. bd. Allied Arts Tacoma, 1963-64, Civic Arts Commn. Tacoma-Pierce County, 1969; commr. Wash. Arts Commn., 1971; Bd. dirs. Tacoma Art Mus., Tacoma Zool. Soc., Tacoma Philharmonic, Inc. Served with AUS, 1943-46. Fellow A.I.A. (pres. S.W. Wash. chpt. 1967-68); mem. Wash. Hist. Soc., U. Wash. Alumni Assn. (all life) Home: 12735 Gravelly Lake Dr SW Lakewood WA 98499-1459 Office: 703 Pacific Ave Tacoma WA 98402-5207

LIDICKER, WILLIAM ZANDER, JR. zoologist, educator; b. Evanston, Ill., Aug. 19, 1932; s. William Zander and Frida (Schroeter) L.; m. Naomi Ishino, Aug. 18, 1956 (div. Oct., 1982); children: Jeffrey Roger, Kenneth Paul; m. Louise N. DeLonzor, June 5, 1989. BS, Cornell U., 1953; MS, U. Ill., 1954, PhD, 1957. Instr. zoology, asst. curator mammals U. Calif., Berkeley, 1957-59, asst. prof., asst. curator, 1959-65, assoc. prof., assoc. curator, 1965-69; assoc. dir. Mus. Vertebrate Zoology, 1968-81, acting dir., 1974-75, prof. zoology, curator mammals, 1969-89, prof. integrative biology, curator of mammals, 1989-94, prof., curator emeritus, 1994—. Dancer Westwind Internat. Folk Ensemble, 1994-2000, Jubilee Am. Dance Theater, 1999—; contbr. articles to profl. jours. Bd. dirs. No. Calif. Com. for Environ. Info., 1971-77; bd. trustees BIOSIS, 1987-92, chmn., 1992; N.Am. rep. steering com., sect. Mammalogy IUBS, UNESCO, 1978-89; chmn. rodent specialist group Species Survival Commn., IUCN, 1980-89; mem. sci. adv. bd. Marine World Found. at Marine World Africa USA, 1987-98; pres. Dehnel-Petrusewicz Meml. Fund, 1985-97, sec.-treas., 1999. Fellow AAAS, Calif. Acad. Scis., Polish Acad. Scis. (fgn. mem.), Explorers Club; mem. Am. Soc. Mammalogists (dir. 1969—, 2d v.p. 1974-76, pres. 1976-78, C.H. Merriam award 1986, elected hon. mem. 1995), Am. Soc. Naturalists, Berkeley Folk Dancers Club (pres. 1969, tchr. 1984—, hon. mem. 2000). Office: U Calif Mus Vertebrate Zoology Berkeley CA 94720-0001 E-mail: lidicker@socrates.berkeley.edu

LIDMAN, ROGER WAYNE, museum director; b. June 8, 1956; s. Arthur Arvid and Elna G. (Bernson) L.; m. Cynthia Louise Platt, May 26, 1988. BA in Anthropology, Ariz. State U., 1987, postgrad. studies, 1987-91. Mus. aide Pueblo Grande Mus., Phoenix, 1976-84, exhibit preparator, 1984-86, ops. coord., 1986-89, acting dir., 1989-90, dir., 1990-2001. Chair Ariz. Archaeol. Adv. Commn., 1998, 99—. Bd. mem. Ariz. Tourism Alliance, 1997—; mem. adv. coun. Ariz. State Libr., 2001—. Recipient Outstanding Personal Svc. award Mus. Assn. Ariz., 1998. Mem. Am. Assn. Mus. (officer small mus. adminstr. com. 1993-94, treas. 1994-96), Mus. Assn. Ariz. (v.p. 1994-95, pres. 1995-96), Ctrl. Ariz. Mus. Assn. (v.p. 1992, pres. 1993-94, 95-96), Papago Salado Assn. (treas. 1996-99), Western Mus. Assn. (at-large mem. 1998-2001, 1st v.p. 2001). Avocations: scuba diving, golf, natural history, guitar. Office: Pueblo Grande Mus 4619 E Washington St Phoenix AZ 85034-1909

LIDOW, ERIC, electrical parts manufacturing company executive; b. Vilnius, Lithuania, Dec. 22, 1912; came to U.S., 1937, naturalized, 1941; s. Leon and Rachel (Schwartz) L.; m. Judith Margolis, July 2, 1939 (div. 1952); 1 son, Alan; m. Elizabeth Hay, Oct. 1952; children: Derek Balfour, Alexander. M. Elec. Engring., Technische Hochschule, Berlin, Germany, 1937. Elec. engr. Super Electric Co., Berlin, Germany, 1937; elec. devel. engr. Emby Products Cal., 1939-41; co-founder, v.p. Selenium Corp. Am., 1941-46; with Internat. Rectifier Corp., El Segundo, Calif., 1946—, now pres., chmn. bd., also dir. corp. and domestic and fgn. subsidiaries. Mem. Assos. Calif. Inst. Tech. Bd. dirs. Lidow Found.; trustee City of Hope, Los Angeles County Mus. Art. Sr. mem. IEEE; mem. Am. Technion Soc. (v.p.) Achievements include patents in semiconductors. Home: 454 Cuesta Way Los Angeles CA 90077-3434 Office: Internat Rectifier Corp 233 Kansas St El Segundo CA 90245-4316

LIEBECK, ROBERT H. aerospace engineer; PhD in Aero. and Astron. Engring., U. Ill., 1968. With Boeing/McDonnell Douglas; rschr., instr. U. So. Calif.; sr. fellow The Boeing Co.; prof. dept. mech. and aerospace engring. U. Calif., Irvine, 2000—. Mem. NAE. Achievements include design for high-lift airfoils, referred to as "Liebeck airfoils"; contributor to propeller design, windmill analysis, wing design for supersonic transports, and design of high-altitude unmanned aircraft; co-developer Blended-Wing Body, a revolutionary design for subsonic transports. Office: Dept Mech and Aerospace Engring 4200 Engineering Gateway U Calif Irvine Irvine CA 92697-3975 Fax: 949-824-8585

LIEBELER, SUSAN WITTENBERG, lawyer; b. July 3, 1942; d. Sherman K. and Eleanor (Klivans) Levine; m. Wesley J. Liebeler, Oct. 21, 1971; 1 child, Jennifer. BA, U. Mich., 1963, postgrad., 1963-64; LLB, UCLA, 1966. Bar: Calif. 1967, Vt. 1972, D.C. 1988. Law clk. Calif. Ct. of Appeals, 1966-67; assoc. Gang, Tyre & Brown, 1967-68, Greenberg, Bernhard, Weiss & Karma, L.A., 1968-70; assoc. gen. counsel Rep. Corp., 1970-72; gen. counsel Verit Industries, 1972-73; spl. counsel, chmn. John S. R. Shad, SEC, Washington, 1981-82; commr. U.S. Internat. Trade Commn., Washington, 1984-88, vice-chmn., 1984-86, chmn., 1986-88, ptnr. Irell & Manella, L.A., 1988-94; pres. Lexpert Rsch. Svcs., L.A., 1995—. Vis. prof. U. Tex., summer 1982; cons. Office of Policy Coordination, office of Pres.-elect, 1981-82; cons. U.S. Ry. Assn., 1975, U.S. EPA, 1974, U.S. Price Commn., 1972; mem. Adminstrv. Conf. U.S., 1986-88. Mem. editl. adv. bd. Regulation mag. CATO Inst.; sr. editor UCLA Law Rev., 1965-66; contbr. articles to profl. jours. Bd. govs. Century City Hosp., 1992—, vice-chair, 1997-99, chair, 1999—; mem. adv. bd. U. Calif. Orientation in USA Law. Stein scholar UCLA, 1966. Mem. State Bar Calif. (treas., vice chair, chair exec. com. internat. law sect.), Practicing Law Inst. (Calif. adv. com.), Washington Legal Found. (acad. adv. bd.), Order of Coif. Jewish. E-mail: lexpert@lexpertresearch.com

LIEBER, DAVID LEO, university president; b. Stryj, Poland, Feb. 20, 1925; came to U.S., 1927, naturalized, 1936; s. Max and Gussie (Jarmush) L.; m. Esther Kobre, June 10, 1945; children— Michael, Daniel, Deborah, Susan. BA, CCNY, 1944; B.Hebrew Lit., Jewish Theol. Sem. Am., 1944, M.Hebrew Lit., 1948, D.Hebrew Lit., 1951; MA, Columbia, 1947; postgrad., U. Wash., 1954-55, UCLA, 1961-63; LDH (hon.), Hebrew Union Coll., 1982—. Ordained rabbi, 1948. Rabbi, 1948, Sinai Temple, Los Angeles, 1950-54; dir. (B'nai B'rith Hillel), Seattle, Cambridge, 1954-56; dean students U. Judaism, Los Angeles, 1956-63, Samuel A. Fryer prof. Bible, pres., 1963-92, Skovron Disting. Svc. prof. Bibl. lit., 1990—, pres. emeritus, 1992—, L.A., 1992—; lectr. Hebrew UCLA, 1957-90; vice chancellor Jewish Theol. Sem., 1972-92. Mem. exec. coun. Rabbinical Assembly, 1966-69, v.p., 1994-96, pres., 1996-98; vice chmn. Am. Jewish Com., L.A., 1972-75; bd. dirs. Jewish Fedn. Coun., L.A., 1980-86, bd. govs., 1986—. Mem. editorial bd.: Conservative Judaism, 1968-70. Served as chaplain USAF, 1951-53. Recipient Torch of Learning award Hebrew U., 1984. Mem. Assn. Profs. Jewish Studies (dir. 1970-71), Phi Beta Kappa. Office: U Judaism 15600 Mulholland Dr Los Angeles CA 90077-1519 E-mail: dllieber@aol.com

LIEBER, MICHAEL RANDALL, biochemist, educator; b. St. Louis, June 21, 1955; s. John Warren Sr. and Matilda V. (Shelby) L.; m. Chih-Lin Hsieh, Jan. 1, 1990. BA, BS, U. Mo., 1977; PhD, U. Chgo., 1981, MD, 1983. Diplomate Am. Bd. Pathology. Resident in pathology NIH, Bethesda, Md., 1983-86, postdoctoral fellow, 1986-89; asst. prof., then assoc. prof. Stanford (Calif.) U., 1989-94; assoc. prof. pathology Washington U., St. Louis, 1994-97; prof. U. So. Calif., 1997—. Editl. bd. Molecular and Cellular Biology; contbr. over 86 articles to profl. publs., including Nature, EMBO Jour., Genes & Devel. Recipient Faculty Scholar award Leukemia Soc. Am., 1994—, Award Warner-Lambert/Parke-Davis, 1998. Mem. AAAS, Am. Soc. Investigative Pathology. Achievements include patents in field. Home: 439 W Winding Way Arcadia CA 91007-7958 Office: Norris Comp Cancer Ctr Rm 5428 USC Sch Medicine MS73 1441 Eastlake Ave Los Angeles CA 90033-1048

LIEBERFARB, WARREN N. broadcast executive; Pres. Warner Home Video, Burbank, Calif., 1984—. Office: Warner Home Video 3903 W Olive Ave Burbank CA 91505-4692

LIEBERMAN, FREDRIC, ethnomusicologist, educator; b. N.Y.C., Mar. 1, 1940; s. Stanley and Bryna (Mason L.). MusB, U. Rochester, 1962; MA in Ethnomusicology, U. Hawaii, 1965; PhD in Music, UCLA, 1977; diploma in Electronics, Cleve. Inst. Electronics, 1973; cert. Inst. for Ednl. Mgmt., Harvard U., 1984. Asst. prof. music Brown U., Providence, 1968-75; assoc. prof. U. Wash., Seattle, 1975-83, chmn. dir. ethnomusicology, 1977-80, dir. sch. music, 1981-83; prof. U. Calif., Santa Cruz, 1983—, dir. divsn. arts, 1983-85, provost Porter Coll., 1983-85, chmn. dept. music, 1988-92; expert witness and forensic musicology cons. Virgin Records and others, 1991—. Fieldworker, Taiwan and Japan, 1963-64, Sikkim, winter 1970, Madras, India, winters 1977, 78, 82, 83; mem. folk arts panel Nat. Endowment for Arts, 1977-80, internat. panel, 1979-80; panelist basic rsch. divsn. NEH, 1982-84, Calif. Arts Coun., 1993, Mass. Cultural Coun., 1995; fieldworker, presenter Smithsonian Instn. Festival Am. Folklife, 1978-82; reviewer Ctr. for Scholarly Comm. with China, 1979-91; exch. lectr. U. Warsaw, Poland, spring 1980; co-dir. summer seminar for coll. tchrs. NEH, 1977; dir. Am. Mus. Heritage Found., 1991-96. Author: Chinese Music: An Annotated Bibliography, 1970, 2d edit, 1979, A Chinese Zither Tutor: The Mei-An Ch-in-P'u, 1983, (with Mickey Hart) Drumming at the Edge of Magic, 1990, Planet Drum: A Celebration of Percussion and Rhythm, 1991, (with L. Miller) Lou Harrison: Composing a World, 1998, (with Mickey Hart) Spirit into Sound: The Magic of Music, 1999; editor: (with Fritz A. Kuttner) Perspectives on Asian Music: Essays in Honor of Lawrence Picken, 1975; gen. editor Garland Bibliographies in Ethnomusicology, 1980-86; mem. editl. bd. Musica Asiatica, 1984—; contbr. numerous articles and revs. to profl. publs.; composer: Suite for Piano, 1964, Sonatina for Piano, 1964, Two Short String Quartets, 1966, Leaves of Brass (for brass quartet), 1967, Psalm 136: By the Rivers of Babylon (for chorus), 1971; records include China I: String Instruments, 1969, China II: Amoy Music, 1971, Music of Sikkim, 1975; ethnomusicology cons. 360 Degrees Prodns., 1988—; filmer, editor (with Michael Moore) Traditional Music and Dance of Sikkim, Parts I and II, 1976; prodr., dir., editor videotape Documenting Traditional Performance, 1978, South Indian Classical Music House Concert, 1994, At Home with Master Musician T.N. Krishnan, 2000. Mem. exec. bd. Pub. Radio Sta. KRAB-FM, Seattle, 1977-78; mem. King County Arts Commn., Seattle, 1977-80; bd. dirs. Young People's Symphony Orch., 1997—. Grantee Nat. Endowment for the Arts, 1978, NEH, 1978, 80, 95-97, N.Y. State Regents fellow, 1958-62, East-West Ctr. fellow and travel grantee, 1962-65, UCLA Chancellor's tchg. fellow, 1965-69, John D. Rockefeller 3d Fund rsch. fellow, 1970-71. Mem. NARAS, Music Critics Assn. N.Am., Soc. for Ethnomusicology (editor Ethnomusicology 1977-81, nat. coun. 1970-72, 74-76, 78-81, 83-86), Soc. for Asian Music (editorial bd. Asian Music 1968-77, editor publs. series 1968-83), Assn. Rsch. Chinese Music (mem. adv. bd. 1987—), Coll. Music Soc. (nat. coun. 1973-75, exec. bd. 1974-75, 76-77), Conf. on Chinese Oral and Performing Lit. (exec. bd. 1971-74, 78-80), ASCAP, Internat. Coun. Traditional Music (treas. 1991-96), Phi Mu Alpha Sinfonia. Avocations: amateur radio N7AX, photography. Office: U Calif Porter Coll Santa Cruz CA 95064 Address: 50 Charles Dr Santa Cruz CA 95060 E-mail: gagaku@cats.ucsc.edu

LIEBERMAN, MICHAEL A. electrical engineer, educator; b. N.Y.C., Oct. 3, 1940; married; 2 children. BS, MS, MIT, Cambridge, 1962; PhD, MIT, 1966. Prof. electronic rsch. labs. U. Calif., Berkeley, 1977-80; asst. prof. biochem. dept. nutrition Harvard Sch. Pub. Health, Boston, 1981-83; assoc. prof. molecular genetics, biochemistry & microbiology Coll. Medicine U. Cin., 1983-84; prof., vice-chmn. undergrad. program EECS U. Calif., Berkeley, 1984—. Study sect. cellular biology & physiology NIH, 1986-89. Fellow IEEE (award for contbns. to rsch. in plasma-assisted materials processing, nonlinear dynamics and controlled fusion). Office: U Calif Electronics Rsch Lab 189M Cory Hall Berkeley CA 94720-1714

LIEBHABER, MYRON I. allergist; b. Dec. 28, 1943; MD, U. Ariz., 1972. Allergist Coll. Hosp., Santa Barbara, Calif. Assoc. vis. clin. prof. UCLA. Office: Santa Barbara Med Found Clinic 215 Pesetas Ln Santa Barbara CA 93110-1416 E-mail: mil1258@pol.net

LIEGLER, ROSEMARY MENKE, dean, nursing educator; b. Fairfield, Iowa, Aug. 21, 1939; d. Vincent Thomas and Catherine Lucille Menke; m. Donald G. Liegler, June 8, 1963; children: Katherine, Jerry. BSN, St. Ambrose Coll., 1961; MS in Nursing, Marquette U., 1962; PhD, Claremont Grad. Sch., 1994. Asst. prof. Miami (Fla.)-Dade Jr. Coll., Georgetown U., Washington, U. Miami; prof., dean Sch. Nursing Azusa (Calif.) Pacific U. Bd. dirs. Huntington East Valley Hosp. Mem. ANA, Calif. Assn. Colls. Nursing, East San Gabriel Valley Vis. Nurses' Assn. (cmty. bd. 1995), Sigma Theta Tau. Home: 3226 E Whitebirch Dr West Covina CA 91791-3037 Office: Azusa Pacific U Sch Nursing 901 E Alosta Ave Azusa CA 91702-2769

LIGHT, JANE ELLEN, librarian; b. Crosby, N.D., May 4, 1948; d. Ralph W. and Ethel S. (Cady) Johnson; m. Donald Howard Light, June 19, 1979; children: Jessica, David. BA, Calif. State U., Sacramento, 1973; MLS, U. Calif., Berkeley, 1974. Project mgr. Peninsula Libr. Sys., San Mateo, Calif., 1974-78, sys. dir., 1979-83; program mgr. Coop. Libr. Authority, San Jose, Calif., 1978-79; asst. libr. dir. Redwood City (Calif.) Pub. Libr., 1983-84, libr. dir., 1984-97; city libr. San Jose Pub. Libr., 1997—. Libr. bldg. and mgmt. cons., Menlo Park, Calif., 1989—; del. On-line Computer Libr. Ctr. User's Coun., 1993-2000. Bd. dirs. Child Care Coordinating Coun., San Mateo, 1988-97, pres. 1992-93; bd. dirs. YMCA of Santa Clara Valley, 2001—. Mem. ALA, Calif. Libr. Assn., Pub. Libr. Assn. Office: San Jose Pub Libr Sys 180 W San Carlos St San Jose CA 95113-2005 E-mail: jane.light@ci.sj.ca.us

LIGHTFOOT, WILLIAM CARL, performing arts association executive, symphony musician; b. Indpls., May 5, 1938; s. Francis H. and Margaret (Vitz) L.; m. May C. Chu, Sept. 22, 1988; children: Melissa, Tom. BME, Butler U., Indpls., 1960; cert., Vienna Acad. Music, Austria, 1965. 2d and Eb clarinetist Honolulu Symphony Orch., 1966-84, orch. mgr., 1984-88; exec. dir. Boulder (Colo.) Philharm. Orch. (now Peak Assn. of the Arts), 1988—. Pers. mgr. Honolulu Symphony Orch., 1982-84, orch. mgr., 1984-88; exec. dir. Ensemble Players Guild, Honolulu, 1969-74; gen. mgr. Honolulu Chamber Music Series, 1978, Chamber Music Hawaii, Honolulu, 1979-84. Avocations: sailing, skiing. Office: Peak Arts 2590 Walnut St Ste 6 Boulder CO 80302-5700

LIGHTSTONE, RONALD, lawyer; b. N.Y.C., Oct. 4, 1938; s. Charles and Pearl (Weisberg) L.; m. Nancy Lehrer, May 17, 1973; 1 child, Dana. AB, Columbia U., 1959; JD, NYU, 1962. Atty. CBS, N.Y.C., 1967-69; assoc. dir. bus. affairs CBS News, N.Y.C., 1969-70; atty. NBC, N.Y.C., 1970; assoc. gen. counsel Viacom Internat. Inc., N.Y.C., 1970-75, v.p., gen. counsel, sec., 1976-80; v.p. bus. affairs Viacom Entertainment Group, Viacom Internat., Inc., 1980-82, v.p. corp. affairs, 1982-84, sr. v.p., 1984-87; exec. v.p. Spelling Entertainment Inc., L.A., 1988-91, CEO, 1991-93; chmn. Multimedia Labs. Inc., 1994-97; CEO, pres. New Star Media Inc., 1997-99, vice chmn., 1999-2000. Lt. USN, 1962-66. Mem. ABA (chmn. TV, cable and radio com.), Assn. of Bar of City of N.Y., Fed. Comm. Bar Assn.

LIKINS, PETER WILLIAM, university administrator; b. Tracy, Calif., July 4, 1936; s. Ennis Blaine and Dorothy Louise (Medlin) L.; m. Patricia Ruth Kitsmiller, Dec. 18, 1955; children: Teresa, Lora, Paul, Linda, Krista, John. BCE, Stanford U., 1957, PhD in Engring. Mechanics, 1965; MCE, MIT, 1958; PhD (hon.), Lafayette Coll., 1983, Moravian Coll., 1984, Med. Coll. Pa., 1990, Lehigh U., 1991, Allentown St. Francis de Sales, 1993, Czech Tech U., 1993. Devel. engr. Jet Propulsion Lab., Pasadena, Calif., 1958-60; asst. prof. engring. UCLA, 1964-69, assoc. prof., 1969-72, prof., 1972-76, asst. dean, 1974-75, asso. dean, 1975-76; dean engring. and applied sci. Columbia U., N.Y.C., 1976-80, provost, 1980-82; pres. Lehigh U., Bethlehem, Pa., 1982-97, U. Ariz., Tucson, 1997—. Cons. in field. Author: Elements of Engineering Mechanics, 1973, Spacecraft Dynamics, 1982; Contbr. articles to profl. jours. Mem. U.S. Pres.'s Coun. Advisors Sci. and Tech., 1990-93. Ford Found. fellow, 1970-72; named to Nat. Wrestling Hall of Fame Fellow AIAA; mem. Nat. Acad. Engring., Phi Beta Kappa, Sigma Xi, Tau Beta Pi. Office: U Ariz PO Box 210066 Tucson AZ 85721-0066 E-mail: plikins@arizona.edu

LILLA, JAMES A. plastic surgeon; b. Comfrey, Minn., June 12, 1943; MD, Stanford U., 1969. Plastic hand surgeon Sutter Cmty. Hosp., Calif. Office: Hand Surg Assocs 1201 Alhambra Blvd Ste 410 Sacramento CA 95816-5243

LILLEGRAVEN, JASON ARTHUR, paleontologist, educator; b. Mankato, Minn., Oct. 11, 1938; s. Arthur Oscar and Agnes Mae (Eaton) L.; m. Bernice Ann Hines, Sept. 5, 1964 (div. Feb. 1983); children: Brita Anna, Ture Andrew; m. Linda Elizabeth Thompson, June 5, 1983. BA, Long Beach State Coll., 1962; MS, S.D. Sch. Mines and Tech., 1964; PhD, U. Kans., 1968. Professional geologist, Wyo. Postdoctoral fellow Dept. Paleontology U. Calif., Berkeley, 1968-69; from asst. prof. to prof. zoology San Diego State U., 1969-75; from assoc. prof. to prof. geology and zoology U. Wyo., Laramie, 1975—. Program dir. NSF Systematic Biology, Washington, 1977-78; assoc. dean U. Wyo. Coll. Arts and Scis., 1984-85, temporary joint appointment Dept. Geography, 1986-87; U.S. sr. scientist Inst. for Paleontology Free U., Berlin, 1988-89; mem. adv. panel geology and paleontology program NSF, 1997-2000. Author, editor: Mesozoic Mammals the First Two Thirds of Mammalian History, 1979, Vertebrates, Phylogeny and Philosophy, 1986; mem. editl. bds. of Research and Exploration (Nat. Geographic Soc.), Jour. of Mammalian Evolution, Jour. of Vertebrate Paleontology, Cretaceous Rsch.; co-editor, contbr. Geology, Rocky Mountain Geology; contbr. articles to profl. jours. Recipient numerous rsch. grants NSF, 1970-2001, George Duke Humphrey Disting. Faculty award, Humboldt prize. Mem. Am. Soc. Mammalogists, Am. Assn. Petroleum Geologists, Paleontol. Soc., Soc. Vertebrate Paleontology (pres. 1985-86), Linnean Soc. London, Soc. Mammalian Evolution, Sigma Xi. Avocations: computer graphics, outdoor activities. E-mail: bagpipe@uwyo.edu

LILLY, LUELLA JEAN, academic administrator; b. Newberg, Oreg., Aug. 23, 1937; d. David Hardy and Edith (Coleman) L. BS, Lewis and Clark Coll., 1959; postgrad., Portland State U., 1959-61; MS, U. Oreg., 1961; PhD, Tex. Woman's U., 1971; postgrad., various univs., 1959-72. Tchr. phys. edn. and health, dean girls Cen. Linn Jr.-Sr. High Sch., Halsey, Oreg., 1959-60; tchr. phys. edn. and health, swimming, tennis, golf coach Lake Oswego (Oreg.) High Sch., 1960-63; instr., intramural dir., coach Oreg. State U., Corvallis, 1963-64; instr., intercollegiate coach Am. River Coll., Sacramento, 1964-69; dir. women's phys. edn., athletics U. Nev., Reno, 1969-73, assoc. prof. phys. edn., 1971-76, dir. women's athletics, 1973-75, assoc. dir. athletics, 1975-76; dir. women's intercollegiate athletics U. Calif., Berkeley, 1976-97. Organizer, coach Lue's Aquatic Club, 1962-64; v.p. PAC-10 Conf., 1990-91. Author: An Overview of Body Mechanics, 1966, 3d rev. edit., 1969. Vol. instr. ARC, 1951; vol. Heart Fund and Easter Seal, 1974-76, Am. Heart Assn., 1991-95, ofcl. Spl. Olympics, 1975; mem. L.A. Citizens Olympic Com., 1984; bd. dirs. Las Trampas, 1993-98, sec. 1996-98. Recipient Mayor Anne Rudin award Nat. Girls' and Women's Sports, 1993, Lifetime Sports award Bay Area Women's Sports Found., 1994, Golden Bear award Vol. of Yr., 1995; inducted Lewis and Clark Coll. Athletic Hall of Fame, 1988; named to U. Calif. First 125 Yrs. Women of Honor, 1995 Mem. AAHPER (life), AAUW, Nat. Soc. Profs., Women's Sports Found. (awards com. 1994-2000), Nat. Assn. Coll. Women Athletic Adminstrs. (divsn. I-A women's steering com. 1991-92, Lifetime Achievement award 1999), Women's Athletic Caucus, Coun. Collegiate Women Athletics Adminstrs. (membership com. 1989-92), Western Soc. Phys. Edn. Coll. Women (membership com. 1971-74, program adv. com. 1972, exec. bd. 1972-75), Western Assn. Intercollegiate Athletics for Women (exec. bd. dirs. 1973-75, 79-82), Oreg. Girls' Swimming Coaches Assn. (pres. 1960, 63), Ctrl. Calif. Bd. Women Ofcls. (basketball chmn. 1968-69), Calif. Assn. Health, Phys. Edn. and Recreation (chmn.-elect jr. coll. sect. 1970), Nev. Bd. Women Ofcls. (chmn. bd., chmn. volleyball sect., chmn. basketball sect. 1969), No. Calif. Women's Intercollegiate Conf. (sec. 1970-71, basketball coord. 1970-71), No. Calif. Intercollegiate Athletic Conf. (volleyball coord. 1971-72), Nev. Assn. Health Phys. Edn. and Recreation (state chmn. 1974), No. Calif. Athletic Conf. (pres. 1979-82, sec. 1984-85), Soroptimists Club (bd. dirs. 1988-98, v.p. 1989, 92-93, sec. 1993-95, 2001—, 1st v.p. 1996-97, corr. sec. 1997-98, pres. 1998-2000, Women Helping Women award 1991), Phi Kappa Phi, Theta Kappa. Avocation: Held Am. records in swimming, 1950's. Home and Office: 60 Margrave Ct Walnut Creek CA 94596-2511

LILLY, MARTIN STEPHEN, university dean; b. New Albany, Ind., Aug. 31, 1944; s. Raymond John and Amy Elizabeth (Peake) L.; m. Marilyn Ann MacDougall, Jan. 8, 1966; children— Matthew William, Mark Christopher, Rachel Marie, Martin Stephen, Jason Wood B.A., Bellarmine Coll., Louisville, 1966; M.A., Peabody Coll., Nashville, 1967, Ed.D., 1969. Instr. dept. spl. edn. Peabody Coll., 1967-69; asst. prof. edn. U. Oreg., 1969-71; research coordinator N.W. Regional Spl. Edn. Instructional Materials Center, 1969-71; research coordinator div. research Bur. Edn. for Handicapped U.S. Office Edn., 1971-72; assoc. prof. dept. spl. edn. U. Minn., Duluth, 1972-75; assoc. prof., chmn. dept. spl. edn. U. Ill., Urbana-Champaign, 1975-79, prof., chmn., 1979-81, assoc. dean grad. studies Coll. Edn., 1981-84; dean Coll. Edn. Wash. State U., Pullman, 1984-90, Calif. State U., San Marcos, 1990—. Cons. in field; U.S. Office Edn. fellow, 1966-69; pres. Tchr. Edn. Coun. State Colls. and Univs.; bd. dirs. San Diego County Childrens Initiative. Author: Children with Exceptional Needs: A Survey of Special Education, 1979, (with C.S. Blankenship) Mainstreaming Students With Learning and Behavior Problems, 1981; assoc. editor: Exceptional Children, 1969-79; cons. editor: Edn. Unltd, 1979-81; reviewer: Jour. Tchr. Edn, 1980— ; mem. editorial bd. Tchr. Edn. and Spl. Edn, 1980-83, co-editor, 1983-84; contbr. chpts. to books, articles to profl. jours. Mem. Coun. for Exceptional Children, Assn. Tchr. Educators, Am. Assn. Colls. Tchr. Edn., Phi Delta Kappa. Democrat. Roman Catholic. Office: Calif State U San Marcos CA 92096-0001

LILLY, MICHAEL ALEXANDER, lawyer, writer; b. Honolulu, May 21, 1946; s. Percy Anthony Jr. and Virginia (Craig) L.; children: Michael Jr., Cary J., Laura B., Claire F., Winston W. AA, Menlo Coll., Menlo Park, Calif., 1966; BA, U. Calif., Santa Cruz, 1968; JD with honors, U. of Pacific, 1974. Bar: Calif. 1974, U.S. Dist. Ct. (no., so. and ea. dists.) Calif. 1974, U.S. Ct. Appeals (9th cir.) 1974, Hawaii 1975, U.S. Dist. Ct. Hawaii 1975, U.S. Ct. Appeals (D.C. cir.) 1975, U.S. Supreme Ct. 1978, U.S. Ct. Appeals (7th cir.) 1979. Atty. Pacific Legal Found., Sacramento, 1974-75; dep. atty. gen. State of Hawaii, Honolulu, 1975-79, 1st dep. atty. gen., 1981-84, atty. gen., 1984-85; ptnr. Feeley & Lilly, San Jose, Calif., 1979-81, Ning, Lilly & Jones, Honolulu, 1985—. Author: If You Die Tomorrow-A Layman's Guide to Estate Planning. Dir. Diamond Head Theatre, U.S.S. Mo. Meml. Assn.; Lt. USN, 1968-71, Vietnam; capt. USNR. Named hon. Ky. col.; decorated Legion of Merit medal, 1997. Mem. Nat. Assn. Attys. Gen., Hawaii Law Enforcement Ofcls. Assn., Navy Res. Assn. (pres. 14th dist. 1986-89), Navy League (nat. dir., nat. dept. judge adv. to bd. Honolulu coun.), Outrigger Canoe Club. Home: 2769 Laniloa Rd Honolulu HI 96813-1041 Office: Ning Lilly & Jones 707 Richards St Ste 700 Honolulu HI 96813-4623 E-mail: malkc@hawaii.rr.com

LILLYMAN, WILLIAM JOHN, German language educator, academic administrator; b. Sydney, Australia, Apr. 17, 1937; came to U.S., 1963, naturalized, 1974; s. John and Christina Mary (Munro) L.; m. Ingeborg Wolz, Sept. 14, 1962; children: Gregory, Christina. AB, U. Sydney, 1959; PhD, Stanford U., 1964. Asst. prof. Stanford (Calif.) U., 1964-67; assoc. prof. U. Calif., Santa Cruz, 1967-72, prof. German Irvine, 1972—, dean humanities, 1973-81, vice chancellor acad. affairs, 1981-82, exec. vice chancellor, 1982-88, 98-00. Author: Otto Ludwig's Zwischen Himmel und Erde, 1967, Otto Ludwig: Romane und Romanstudien, 1977, Reality's Dark Dream The Narrative Fiction of Ludwig Tieck, 1979, Goethe's Narrative Fiction, 1983; co-editor; Probleme der Moderne, 1983, Horizonte Festschrift für H. Lehnert, 1990, Critical Architecture and Contemporary Culture, 1994. Mem. MLA, Am. Assn. Tchrs. German. Office: U Calif Exec Vice Chancellors Office 509 Administrn Bldg Irvine CA 92697-1000

LIM, ALAN YOUNG, plastic surgeon; b. St. Louis, Apr. 11, 1953; MD, U. Calif., San Diego, 1979. Plastic surgeon Kaiser-Permanente, Sacramento. Asst. clin. prof. U. Calif. Davis. Office: Plastic Surg 6600 Bruceville Rd Sacramento CA 95823

LIM, DAVID JONG-JAI, otolaryngology educator, researcher; b. Seoul, Republic of Korea, Nov. 27, 1935; came to U.S., 1964; s. Yang Sup Lim and Cha Nang Yoo; m. Young Sook Hahn, May 14, 1966; children: Michael, Robert. AB, Yonsei U., Seoul, 1955, MD, 1960. Research fellow in otolaryngology Mass. Eye & Ear Infirmary, Boston, 1965-66; research assoc. dept. otolaryngology Ohio State U. Coll. Medicine, Columbus, 1966-67, asst. prof., 1967-71, assoc. prof., 1971-76, prof. dept. otolaryngology, 1976-91, dir. otological research labs., 1967-91, prof. cell biology, neurobiology and anatomy, 1977-91, prof. emeritus otolaryngology, 1992—; rsch. prof. cell and neurobiology U. So. Calif., 1996—; dir. intramural rsch. program Nat. Inst. on Deaf and Other Communication Disorders, NIH, Bethesda, Md., 1992-94, chief lab cellular biology, 1993-95; exec. v.p., rsch. House Ear Inst., L.A., 1995—. Mem. nat. adv. neurol. and communicative disorders and stroke coun. NIH, Bethesda, Md., 1979-83; mem. adv. bd. Nat. Inst. Deafness and Other Communication Disorders, 1989-91; cons., bd. dirs. Rsch. Fund Am. Otol. Soc., 1982-87; mem. adv. bd. Cen. Inst. for Deaf, 1989-91. Contbr. articles to profl. jours., chpts. to textbooks. Pres. Korean Assn. in Columbus, 1970; chmn. bd. dirs. Cen. Ohio Korean Lang. Sch., Columbus, 1986; bd. dirs. Deafness Rsch. Found., N.Y.C., 1980—. Fogarty Internat. fellow Karolinska Inst., Stockholm, 1982; recipient Disting. Scholar award Ohio State U., 1985, Javits award NIH, 1985, Claude Pepper award, 1989, Guyot prize U. Groningen, 1994, Freedom award L.A. Sertoma Club, 1996, Grand prize for med. scis. Yonsei U., 1997, Magarotto award 1998; grantee various orgns., 1969-91. Fellow Am. Acad. Otolaryngology (Gold award 1972, Paparella award 1999); mem. Internat. Symposium Recent Advances in Otitis Media (co-founder 1975, 79, 83, 87, 91, 95, 99, co-dir.), Assn. for Research in Otolaryngology (co-founder, sec./treas. 1973-75, pres. 1976-77, editor-historian 1980-93, historian, 1993—, Merit award 1993), Am. Laryngol. Rhinol. and Otol. Soc., Collegium Oto-rhino-laryngologicum Amicitiae Sacrum (Shambaugh prize 1993, v.p. 2000—), Am. Otol. Soc., Soc. Neurosci., Am. Soc. Cell Biology, Histochem. Soc., Soc. for Mucosal Immunology, Flint Canyon Tennis Club (La Canada). Methodist. Avocations: tennis, skiing. Home: 775 Panorama Pl Pasadena CA 91105-1020 Office: House Ear Inst 2100 W 3rd St Los Angeles CA 90057-1922 E-mail: dlim@hei.org

LIM, JOHN K. state senator, business executive; b. Yeoju, South Korea, Dec. 23, 1935; came to U.S., 1966, naturalized, 1976; s. Eun Kyu and Seu Nyu (Chung) L.; m. Grace Young-Hee Park, Dec. 9, 1963; children: Peter, Billy, Gloria. BA in Religion, Seoul Theol. Coll., 1964; MDiv, Western Evang. Sem., Portland, Oreg., 1970, DHL, 1996. Chaplain U.S. Mil. Base, 1961-66; pres. Realty Resources, 1981-91; founder, chmn. Am. Royal Jelly Co., 1972—; mem. Oreg. State Senate, 1993—. Founder, chmn. Am. Royal Jelly Co., 1972—; pres. Realty Resources, 1981-91; chair Senate Trade and Econ. Devel. Com., 1995; vice chair Senate Bus. and Consumer Affairs Com., 1995; mem. Govs. Adv. Com. on DUII, 1993—; mem. sheriffs forum Multnomah County, Oreg., 1994; asst. majority leader Oreg. State Senate, 1995; exec. bd. mem. Pacific N.W. Econ. Region. Pub.: World Korean Conference Journal, 1989; editor, pub.: (directory) World Korean C. of C., 1990, The World Korean Soc. Directory, 1989. Asst. supr. Yo Kwang Orphanage, Yoju, South Korea, 1956-57; chaplain U.S. Missile Base, Yoju, 1961-66; mem. Oreg.-Korea Econ. Coop., 1986-88; pres. Korean-Am. Soc. Oreg., 1986; nat. pres. Korean-Am. C. of C. and Industry Fedn. of the USA, 1989-90; Oreg. Gubernatorial Candidate, 1990; nat. chair Asian Am. Voters Coalition, 1990-91; bd. dirs. Rep. Nat. Com. Asian Adv., 1992; mem. exec. com. Billy Graham Crusade, Portland, Oreg., 1992; mem. Cmty. Bd. Mt. Hood Med. Ctr., 1993—; com. mem. Commn. on DUII, 1993-97; bd. regents Western Evang. Sem., 1994-97; bd. mem. Western Evang. Sem., 1995—; bd. mem. George Fox U., 1996—. Mem. Oreg. Royal Rosarian Soc., Portland Rose Soc., AARP, Portland Chamber of Commerce, Oreg. PTA. Republican. Avocations: golf, fishing, skiing. Office: 3630 SE Division St Portland OR 97202-1546 Address: Oreg Senate S-205 State Capitol Salem OR 97310-0001

LIM, LARRY KAY, university official; b. Santa Maria, Calif., July 4, 1948; s. Koonwah and Nancy (Yao) L.; m. Louise A. Simon, Aug. 15, 1988. BA, UCLA, 1970, teaching cert., 197l. Asst. engr. Force Ltd., L.A., 1969; tchg. asst. UCLA, 1970-71; tchr. L.A. Sch. Dist., 197l-82; dir. pre-coll. programs Sch. Engring., U. So. Calif., L.A., 1979—. Presenter minority math.-based intervention symposium U. D.C., Washington, 1988; presenter NEMEPA/WEPAN nat. conf., 1997. Newsletter editor, 198l-92. Bd. dirs. Developing Ednl. Studies for Hispanics, L.A., 1983-88. Named Dir. of Yr., Math., Engring., Sci. Achievement Ctr. Adv. Bd., 1986, 91, 92. Fellow Inst. Advancement Engring. (educator award); mem. Nat. Assn. Pre-Coll. Dirs., Nat. Assn. Minority Engring. Program Adminstr., Lotus/West Club (pres. l98l-92). Avocation: automobile racing. Office: U So Calif Sch Engring Ohe 104 Los Angeles CA 90089-0001

LIMATO, EDWARD FRANK, talent agent; b. Mt. Vernon, N.Y., July 10, 1936; s. Frank and Angelina (Lacerra) L. Grad. high sch., Mt. Vernon. With Ashley Famous, 1966, I.F.A., N.Y.C., William Morris Agy., L.A.; talent agt. Internat. Creative Mgmt., N.Y.C., L.A., co-pres. Mem. Acad. Motion Picture Arts & Scis. (assoc.). Republican. Roman Catholic. Office: Internat Creative Mgmt 8942 Wilshire Blvd Beverly Hills CA 90211-1934

LIMBAUGH, RONALD HADLEY, retired history educator, history center director; b. Emmett, Idaho, Jan. 22, 1938; s. John Hadley and Evelyn E. (Mortimore) L.; m. Marilyn Kay Rice, June 16, 1963; 1 child, Sally Ann. BA, Coll. Idaho, 1960; MA, U. Idaho, 1962, PhD, 1967. Hist. libr. Idaho State Hist. Soc., Boise, 1963-66; instr. Boise Coll., 1964-66; asst. prof. history U. of the Pacific, Stockton, Calif., 1966-71, archivist, curator, 1968-87, prof. history, 1977-2000, Rockwell Hunt chair of Calif. history, 1989-2000; dir. Holt-Atherton Ctr., U. of the Pacific, Stockton, 1984-87. Exec. dir. Conf. of Calif. Hist. Socs., Stockton, 1973-76, 77-78, 82-86, 90-97; dir. John Muir Ctr. for Regional Studies, U. of Pacific, Stockton, 1989-2000; cons., evaluator NEH, 1983-86. Author: Rocky Mountain Carpetbaggers, 1987, John Muir's Stickeen and the Lessons of Nature

1996; co-editor: (microform) John Muir Papers, 1986, (book) Guide to Muir Papers, 1986; contbr. articles to profl. jours. With U.S. Army, 1955-56. NDEA fellow, 1960; grantee Calif. Coun. Humanities, 1976, Nat. Hist. Publs. and Records Commn., 1980-82, NEH, 1983, Inst. European Studies, 1989, Hoover Libr. Assn., 1997. Mem. Western History Assn., Mining History Assn. Christian Humanist. Avocations: hiking, golf. Office: U Pacific 3601 Pacific Ave Stockton CA 95211-0197 E-mail: limbaugh@mcn.org

LIMERICK, PATRICIA NELSON, history educator; b. Banning, Calif., May 17, 1951; BA, U. Calif., Santa Cruz, 1972; PhD, Yale, 1980. Prof. history dept. U. Colo., Boulder. Chmn. bd. dirs. Ctr. Am. West. Author: (books) Desert Passages: Encounters With the American Deserts, 1985, The Legacy of Conquest: The Unbroken Past of the American West, 1987, Something in the Soil: Legacies and Reckonings in the New West, 2000. MacArthur fellow, 1995. Office: U Colo Ctr Am West MAcky 229 282 UCB Boulder CO 80309 E-mail: patricia.limerick@colorado.edu

LIN, FRANK C. computer company executive; Chmn. bd. dirs., pres., CEO Trident Microsys. Inc., Mountain View, Calif. Office: Trident Microsystems 2450 Walsh Ave Santa Clara CA 95051-1303

LIN, LAWRENCE SHUH LIANG, accountant; b. China, July 5, 1938; s. Wan Chow and Inn Chi Lin; came to U.S., 1967, naturalized, 1979; LLB, Soochow U., 1963; MBA, Pepperdine U., 1970; JD, U. West L.A., 1998; m. Grace Yu, July 31, 1966; children: Ray, Lester. Spl. project acctg. supr. Motown Records, Hollywood, Calif., 1975; chief acct. Elektra/Asylum/Nonesuch Records, Beverly Hills, Calif., 1976-77, United Artists Music Pub. Group, Hollywood, 1977-80; contr.-adminstr. Pasadena (Calif.) Guidance Clinics (name now Pacific Clinics, 1980-86; v.p. Stew Kettle Corp., L.A., 1986-87; v.p. LKL Corp., L.A., 1987-89; internat. fin. cons. Pacific Capital Mgmt., Alhambra, Calif., 1990. Mem. Inst. Mgmt. Accts., Nat. Assn. Security Dealers. Baptist. Office: Pacific Capital Mgmt 670 Monterey Pass Rd Monterey Park CA 91754-2419

LIN, ROBERT PEICHUNG, physicist, educator, researcher; b. Kwangsi, People's Republic of China, Jan. 24, 1942; s. Tung Hua and Susan Lin; m. Lily Wong, Aug. 14, 1983; 1 stepson, Linus Sun. BS, Calif. Inst. Tech., 1962; PhD, U. Calif., Berkeley, 1967. Asst. rsch. physicist Space Sci. Lab., U. Calif., Berkeley, 1967-74, assoc. rsch. physicist, 1974-79, rsch. physicist, 1979-88, sr. fellow, 1980-88; adj. prof. astronomy dept. U. Calif., Berkeley, 1988-91, prof. physics dept., 1991—, assoc. dir. space scis. lab., 1992—. Vis. prof. geophysics program U. Wash., Seattle, 1987; mem. solar physics panel Astronomy and Astrophysics Survey, Nat. Acad. Sci., 1989-91; mem. working groups for astrophysics, solar physics, space plasma, cosmic and heliospheric physics, balloons, space and applications adv. com. NASA, 1977—, mem. various rev. panels, 1977—. Contbr. articles to Jour. Geophys. Rsch., Solar Physics, Phys. Rev. Letters, Rev. Sci. Instruments, Astrophys. Jour., Geophys. Rsch. Letters. Grantee NASA, 1980—, NSF, 1981—. Mem. Am. Geophys. Union, Am. Astron. Soc. Achievements include research on solar and interplanetary physics, high energy astrophysics, lunar and planetary science, and physics of the earth's magnetosphere. Office: U Calif Space Scis Lab Berkeley CA 94720-0001

LIN, TUNG HUA, civil engineering educator; b. Chungkin, China, May 26, 1911; s. Yao-Ching and Yue (Kuo) L.; m. Susan Z. Chiang, Mar. 15, 1939; childern: Rita P., Lin Wood, Robert P., James P. B.S., Tangshan Coll., Chiaotung U., 1933; S.M., MIT, 1936; D.Sc., U. Mich., 1953. Prof. Tsing Hua U., China, 1937-39; chief engr. Chinese 2d Aircraft Co., Nancheun, Szechuan, 1939-44; prodn. mgr. Mfg. Factory, China, 1940-44; mem. tech. mission in charge of jet aircraft design, 1945-49; prof. aero. engring. U. Detroit, 1949-55; prof. engring. and applied scis. UCLA, 1955-78, prof. emeritus, 1978—. Cons.N.Am. Aviation, N.Am. Rockwell, L.A., 1964-74, Atomic Internat., Canoga Park, Calif., 1965-68, ARA Inc., Industry City, Calif., 1964-94. Author: Theory of Inelastic Structure, 1968; contbr. articles to profl. jours.; mem. editorial bd.: Jour. Composite Materials, 1966-75; patentee in field. Chinese Nat. fellow Tsing-Hua U., 1933; recipient medal for Design of 1st Chinese twin-engine airplane, 1944, Disting. Svc. award Applied Mechanics Rev. ASME, 1966, NSF grantee, 1954-78; named prin. investigator Office Naval Rsch., 1985-93, Air Force Office of Sci. Rsch., 1988—. Fellow ASME, Am. Acad. Mechanics; mem. ASCE (life, gen. chmn. engring. mechanics conf. 1965, Theodore von Karman award 1988); mem. NAE, Academia Sinica. Home: 906 Las Pulgas Rd Pacific Palisades CA 90272-2441 Office: UCLA Dept Civil Engring 405 Hilgard Ave Los Angeles CA 90095-9000 E-mail: thlin@seas.mcra.edu

LIN, TUNG YEN, civil engineer, educator; b. Foochow, China, Nov. 14, 1911; came to U.S., 1946, naturalized, 1951; s. Ting Chang and Feng Yi (Kuo) L.; m. Margaret Kao, July 20, 1941; children: Paul, Verna. BS in Civil Engring., Chiaotung U., Tangshan, Republic of China, 1931; MS, U. Calif., Berkeley, 1933; LLD, Chinese U. Hong Kong, 1972, Golden Gate U., San Francisco, 1982, Tongji U., Shanghai, 1987, Chiaotung U., Taiwan, 1987. Chief bridge engr., chief design engr. Chinese Govt. Rys., 1933-46; asst., then assoc. prof. U. Calif., 1946-55, prof., 1955-76, chmn. div. structural engring., 1960-63, dir. structural lab., 1960-63; chmn. bd. T.Y. Lin Internat., 1953-87, hon. chmn. bd., 1987-92; pres. Inter-Continental Peace Bridge, Inc., 1968—. Cons. to State of Calif., Def. Dept., also to industry; chmn. World Conf. Prestressed Concrete, 1957, Western Conf. Prestressed Concrete Bldgs., 1960; chmn. bd. Lin Tung Yen, China, 1993—. Author: Design of Prestressed Concrete Structures, 1955, rev. edit., 1963, 3d edit. (with N.H. Burns), 1981, (with B. Bresler, Jack Scalzi) Design of Steel Structures, rev. edit., 1968, (with S.D. Statesbury) Structural Concepts and Systems, 1981, 2d edit., 1988; contbr. articles to profl. jours. Recipient Berkeley citation award, 1976, NRC Quarter Century award, 1977, AIA Honor award, 1984, Pres.'s Nat. Med. of Sci., 1986, Merit award Am. Cons. Engrs., Coun., 1987, John A. Roebling medal Bridge Engring., 1990, Am. Segmental Bridge Inst. Leadership award, 1992, Outstanding Paper of Yr. award Internat. Assn. Bridge and Structural Engring., 1993, Lifetime Achievement award Asian Am. Archs. and Engring. Assn., 1993, Outstanding Achievement award AAAE Assn. of So. Calif., Prix Albert Caquot award Assn. Française pour Construction, 1995; fellow U. Calif. at Berkeley; named Alumnus of Yr. U. Calif. Alumni Assn., 1994. Mem. ASCE (hon., life, Wellington award, Howard medal, OPAL award), Nat. Acad. Engring., Chinese Acad. Sci., Academia Sinica, Internat. Fedn. Prestressing (Freyssinet medal), Am. Concrete Inst. (hon.), Prestressed Concrete Inst. (medal of honor), Chinese Acad. Sci., Chi Epsilon (nat. hon.). Home: 8701 Don Carol Dr El Cerrito CA 94530-2734 Office: 315 Bay St San Francisco CA 94133-1923

LINAWEAVER, WALTER ELLSWORTH, JR. physician; b. San Pedro, Calif., Oct. 16, 1928; s. Walter Ellsworth and Catherine Breathed (Bridges) L.; m. Lydia Anne Whitlock, Oct. 5, 1957; children: Catherine Ann, Nancy Alyn, Walter E. III. BA cum laude, Pomona Coll., 1952; MD, U. Rochester, 1956. Diplomate Am. Bd. Allergy and Immunology, Am. Bd. Pediatrics, Am. Bd. Pediatric Allergy. Intern pediatrics Med. Ctr. U. Rochester, N.Y., 1956-57, resident pediatrics Med. Ctr., 1958-59; asst. resident pediatrics Med. Ctr. UCLA, 1957-58; fellow allergy and immunology Med. Ctr. U. Colo., Denver, 1959-61, instr. pediatrics Sch. Medicine, 1961; pvt. practice Riverside (Calif.) Med. Clinic, 1962—. Asst. clin. prof. pediatrics Loma Lida U. Med. Sch., 1965—. Elder Presbyn. Ch. Staff sgt. U.S. Army, 1946-48. Inducted into Athletic Hall of Fame Pomona Coll., Claremont, Calif., 1979. Fellow Am. Acad. Allergy, Asthma & Immunology, Am. Acad. Pediat., Southwestern Pediat. Soc. (emeritus, v.p. 1978), L.A. Acad. Medicine; mem. Riverside County Med. Soc. (councilor 1964-66), Riverside County Heart Assn. Republican. Avocations: gardening, American and British military history. Home: 1296 Tiger Tail Dr Riverside CA 92506-5475 Office: Riverside Med Clinic 3660 Arlington Ave Riverside CA 92506-3912

LINCOLN, ALEXANDER, III, financier, lawyer, private investor; b. Boston, Dec. 1, 1943; s. Alexander Jr. and Elizabeth (Kitchel) L.; m. Isabel Fawcett Ross, Dec. 27, 1969. BA, Denver U., 1967; JD, Boston U., 1971. Bar: Colo. 1972, U.S. Ct. Appeals (10th cir.) 1972, U.S. Supreme Ct. 1979. Atty. Dist. Ct. Denver, 1973-78, Colo. Ct. Appeals, Denver, 1978-80; mng. ptnr. Alexander Lincoln & Co., Denver, 1980—. Mem. Colo. Bar Assn. (fin. com. 1975-76), Colo. Soc. Mayflower Descendants (life, bd. dirs. 1975—), Order of Founders and Patriots (life). Republican. Avocations: skiing, mountain climbing, horticulture. Home and Office: 121 S Dexter St Denver CO 80246-1052

LINCOLN, GEORGIANNA, state legislator; b. Fairbanks, Alaska, Feb. 22, 1943; children: Gidget, Sean. Student, U. Alaska. Mem. Alaska Ho. of Reps., 1990-92, Alaska Senate, Dist. R, Juneau, 1992—; mem. resources, transp. and adminstrv. regulation rev. coms. Bd. dirs. Doyon Ltd., Doyon Drilling, Inc. Commr. Alaska Commn. on Jud. Conduct, 1984-90; U.S. del. East Asia and Pacific Parliamentarian's Conf. on Environment and Devel., 1993; mem. Local-State Tribal Rels. Task Force, 1994; vice-chair NCSL. Democrat. Avocation: working with children and people. Office: State Capitol 120 4th St Rm 11 Juneau AK 99801-1142 Fax: 907-465-2652. E-mail: georgiannalincoln@legis.state.ak.us

LINCOLN, HOWARD, manufacturing company and sports team executive; married; one child. Grad., U. Calif., Berkeley; JD, U. Calif. Sch. Law. Sr. v.p., gen. counsel to chmn. Nintendo Am., 1983-94, 94—; chmn., CEO Seattle Mariners. Bd. dirs. Nintendo of Am., Nintendo Co. Ltd. of Kyoto, Japan; chmn. Interactive Digital Software Assn. Instrumental in creating Nintendo's charitable contbns. program, including Starlight Found.; major initiator in Club Mario/after-sch. program with Bellevue, Wash. Boys & Girls Club; trustee Seattle Childrn's Hosp. Found., Washington Roundtable; hi-tech chmn. United Way of King County, Wash., 1999; bd. dirs. Boalt Hall Alumni Assn., U. Calif., Berkeley, The Baseball Club of Seattle, LP, Seattle Mariners, Pacific Sci. Ctr., Corp. Coun. for the Arts, others. Office: c/o Seattle Mariners Safeco Field PO Box 4100 Seattle WA 98104

LIND, MARSHALL L. academic administrator; Dean Sch. Extended and Grad. Studies U. Alaska, Juneau, until 1987, chancellor, 1987-99, Fairbanks, 1999—. Office: U Alaska Office Chancellor PO Box 757500 Fairbanks AK 99775-7500

LINDE, HANS ARTHUR, state supreme court justice; b. Berlin, Germany, Apr. 15, 1924; came to U.S., 1939, naturalized, 1943; s. Bruno C. and Luise (Rosenhain) L.; m. Helen Tucker, Aug. 13, 1945; children: Lisa, David Tucker. BA, Reed Coll., 1947; JD, U. Calif., Berkeley, 1950. Bar: Oreg. 1951. Law clk. U.S. Supreme Ct. Justice William O. Douglas, 1950-51; atty. Office of Legal Adviser, Dept. State, 1951-53; pvt. practice Portland, Oreg., 1953-54; legis. asst. U.S. Sen. Richard L. Neuberger, 1955-58; from assoc. prof. to prof. U. Oreg. Law Sch., 1959-76; justice Oreg. Supreme Ct., Salem, 1977-90, sr. judge, 1990—. Fulbright lectr. Freiburg U., 1967-68, Hamburg U., 1975-76; cons. U.S. ACDA, Dept. Def., 1962-76; mem. Adminstrv. Conf. U.S., 1978-82, Oreg. Law Commn., 1997—; disting. scholar in residence Willamette U. Coll. Law, Salem, Oreg., 1994—. Author: (with George Bunn) Legislative and Administrative Processes, 1976. Mem. Oreg. Constl. Revision Commn., 1961-62, Oreg. Law Commn., 1997—, Oreg. Commn. on Pub. Broadcasting, 1990-93; bd. dirs. Oreg. Pub. Broadcasting, 1993-99. With U.S. Army, 1943-46. Fellow Am. Acad. Arts and Scis.; mem. Am. Law Inst. (council), Order of Coif, Phi Beta Kappa. Office: Willamette U Coll Law Salem OR 97301 E-mail: hlinde@willamette.edu

LINDE, LEONARD M. pediatric cardiologist; b. N.Y.C., June 1, 1928; s. Ben and Marsha (Weinberg) L.; m. Shirley Dann, Apr. 22, 1951; children: Bruce D., Lauren G., Brian K., Peter B. BS, U. Calif., Davis, 1947; MD, U. Calif., San Francisco, 1951. Intern Morrisania City (N.Y.) Hosp., 1952; from resident to sr. resident in pediat. L.A. Childrens Hosp., 1952-56; prof. pediat. cardiology UCLA Sch. Medicine, 1956-72; chief pediat. cardiology St. Vincent Hosp., L.A., 1973-87; prof. pediat. cardiology U. So. Calif. Sch. Medicine, L.A., 1988—. Med. dir. Marion Davies Clinic, 1957-61; pediat. cons. Crippled Children Svcs. State of Calif., 1957—; chief pediat. cardiology L.A. Heart Inst., St. Vincents Med. Ctr., L.A., 1973-87; internat. adv. bd. Acta Pediat. Japonica, 1992—; book reviewer in field; nat. cons. to Surgeon Gen. USAF, 1965-78. Mem. editl. bd. USC Jour. Medicine, 1990—; contbr. articles to profl. jours. With med. corps., U.S. Army, 1953-55. UCLA Med. Ctr. fellow, 1956-57. Fellow Am. Acad. Pediat. (coun. on cardiology 1962-68, exec. coun. 1968-75); mem. Am. Pediat. Soc., Soc. Pediat. Rsch. (Ross Pediat. Rsch. award 1962), Western Soc. for Pediat. Rsch. (exec. coun. 1966-69), Calif. Soc. for Pediat. Cardiology, Alpha Omega Alpha, Alpha Zeta. Home: 2733 Manning Ave Los Angeles CA 90064-4354 Office: Childrens Hosp LA 4650 W Sunset Blvd Los Angeles CA 90027-6062 Fax: 310-836-4632. E-mail: llinde@hsc.usc.edu

LINDGREN, TIMOTHY JOSEPH, supply company executive; b. N.Y.C., Dec. 7, 1937; s. Carl Herbert and Ruth Elizabeth (Pickering) L.; m. Barbara Fiorini, Feb. 7, 1957; children: Sharon, Mark, Susan. AA, Pierce Coll., Woodland Hills, Calif., 1959; BS in Prodn. Mgmt., Calif. State U., Northridge, 1961; MBA in Indsl. Relations, UCLA, 1962. Registered profl. engr., Calif. cert. tchr., Calif. Systems analyst, methods acct. Pacific Tel. & Tel., Van Nuys, Calif., 1964-65; dir. mfg. Olga Co., Van Nuys, 1965-69; dir. prodn. Calif. Almond Orchards, Bakersfield, 1970-72, gen. mgr., 1972-73; pres. United Wholesale Lumber Co., Montebello, Calif., 1973-77; pres., chief exec. officer Fruit Growers Supply Co., Sherman Oaks, 1978—. Mem. Calif. C. of C. (chair com. on agrl. & natural resources). Office: Fruit Growers Supply Co 14130 Riverside Dr Sherman Oaks CA 91423-2313

LINDHEIM, RICHARD DAVID, television company executive, university official; b. N.Y.C., May 28, 1939; s. Gilbert R. and Pearl (Gruskin) L.; m. Elaine Lavis, Dec. 22, 1963; children: Susan Patricia, David Howard. B.S., U. Redlands, 1961; postgrad, U. So. Calif., 1963. Adminstrv. asst. story dept. CBS, L.A., 1962-64; project dir. entertainment testing ASI Market Rsch., L.A., 1964-69; v.p. program research NBC, L.A., 1969-78, v.p. dramatic programs, 1978-79; producer Universal TV, L.A., 1979-81, v.p. current programs, 1981-85, sr. v.p. series programming, 1986-87, exec. v.p. creative affairs, 1987-91; exec. v.p. program strategy MCA TV Group, 1991-92; exec. v.p. Paramount TV Group, 1992-99; exec. dir. Inst. for Creative Techs., U. So. Calif., L.A., 1999—; with ICT, Marina Del Rey, Calif. Asst. prof. Calif. State U.; sr. lectr. U. So. Calif.; lectr. UCLA; reviewer NEH; bd. dirs. Am. Fgn. Svc. Intercultural Program-USA. Author: (with Richard Blum) Primetime: Network Television Programming, 1987, Inside Television Producing, 1991; contbr. articles to profl. jours. Mem. Acad. TV Arts and Scis., Producers Guild Am., Writers Guild Am. Democrat. Jewish. Avocations: model railroading, photography, music, traveling. Office: ICT 4676 Admiralty Way Ste 1001 Marina Del Rey CA 90292

LINDHOLM, DWIGHT HENRY, lawyer; b. Blackduck, Minn., May 27, 1930; s. Henry Nathanial and Viola Eudora (Gummert) L.; m. Loretta Catherine Brown, Aug. 29, 1958; children: Douglas Dwight, Dionne Louise, Jeanne Marie, Philip Clayton, Kathleen Anne. Student, Macalester Coll., 1948-49; BBA, U. Minn., 1951, LLB, 1954; postgrad., Mexico City Coll. (now U. of Ams.), 1956-57. Bar: Minn. 1954, Calif. 1958. Sole practice, Los Angeles, 1958-65, 72-81, 84—; ptnr. Lindholm & Johnson, Los Angeles, 1965-69, Cotter, Lindholm & Johnson, Los Angeles, 1969-72; sole practice Los Angeles, 1972-81; of counsel Bolton, Dunn & Moore, Los Angeles, 1981-84. Mem. Calif. Republican Central Com., 1962-63, Los Angeles Republican County Central Com., 1962-66; bd. dirs. Family Service Los Angeles, 1964-70, v.p., 1968-70; bd. dirs. Wilshire YMCA, 1976-77; trustee Westlake Girls Sch., 1978-81; hon. presenter Nat. Charity League Coronet Debutante Ball, 1984; bd. dirs. Calif. State U.-Northridge Trust Fund, 1989-93; bd. dirs. Queen of Angeles/Hollywood Presbyn. Med. Ctr., 1990-98; chmn., CEO Queen of Angels, Hollywood Presbyn. Found., 1997-2000; bd. dirs., corp. sec. QueensCare, 1998—. Served as capt. JAG Corps USAF, 1954-56. Recipient Presdl. award Los Angeles Jr. C. of C., 1959 Mem. Calif. Bar Assn., L.A. County Bar Assn., Wilshire Bar Assn. (bd. govs. 1989-91), Internat. Genealogy Fellowship of Rotarians (founding pres. 1979-86), Calif. Club, Ocean Cruising Club Eng. (Newport Harbor port officer), Rotary (dir. 1975-78), Delta Sigma Pi, Delta Sigma Rho, Delta Theta Phi (state chancellor 1972-73). Presbyterian. Avocations: sailing, offshore cruising. Office: 3580 Wilshire Blvd Fl 17 Los Angeles CA 90010-2501 E-mail: dlindholm@earthlink.net

LINDHOLM, RICHARD THEODORE, economics and finance educator; b. Eugene, Oreg., Oct. 5, 1960; s. Richard Wadsworth and Mary Marjorie (Trunko) L. m. Valaya Nivasananda, May 8, 1987. BA, U. Chgo., 1982, MA, 1983, PhD, 1993. Ptnr. Lindholm and Osanka, Eugene, 1986-89, Lindholm Rsch., Eugene, 1995—2001, owner, 1995—, The Lindholm Co., 1995—; ptnr. DBA Lindholm Rsch., Eugene, 2001—. Guest lectr. Nat. Inst. Devel. Adminstrn., Bangkok, Thailand, 1989; pres. Rubicon Inst., Eugene, 1988—; adj. asst. prof. U. Oreg., Eugene, 1988—. Campaign co-chmn. Lane C.C. Advocates, Eugene, 1988; coord., planner numerous state Rep. Campaigns, Oreg., 1988—; campaign mgr. Jack Roberts for Oreg. State Labor Commn., 1994; mem. staff Oreg. Senate Rep. Office, 1989-90; precinct committeeperson Oreg. Rep. Party, 1987-92, 94—; bd. dirs. Rubicon Soc., Eugene, 1987—, pres., 1993-98. Republican. Lutheran. Home: 3335 Bardell Ave Eugene OR 97401-8021

LINDL, JOHN D. physicist; Scientific dir. Inertial Confinement Fusion Program. Recipient E.O. Lawrence Meml. award U.S. Dept. Energy, 1994. Office: Lawrence Livermore Nat Lab Livermore CA 94550

LINDLEY, F(RANCIS) HAYNES, JR. foundation executive, lawyer; b. L.A., Oct. 15, 1945; s. Francis Haynes and Grace Nelson (McCanne) L.; m. Hollinger McCloud Lindley, Apr. 1, 1977; 1 child, Anne Hollinger Lindley. BA, Claremont (Calif.) Men's Coll., 1967; MFA, Claremont (Calif.) Grad. Sch., 1972; JD, Southwestern U., L.A., 1976. Bar: Calif. 1976, U.S. Supreme Ct. 1980. Deputy pub. defender Office of Pub. Defender, L.A., 1977-79; staff atty., Dept. Trial Counsel The State Bar of Calif., L.A., 1979-81; pvt. practice, 1981-90; pres. John Randolph Haynes and Dora Haynes Found., L.A., 1987-97, pres. emeritus, 1997—. Trustee John Randolph Haynes and Dora Haynes Found., L.A., 1978—. Mem. bd. dirs. TreePeople, L.A., 1985-87, So. Calif. Assn. Philanthropy, L.A., 1985-89; mem. bd. fellows Claremont (Calif.) U. Ctr. and Grad. Sch., 1987—; mem. bd. dirs. Marin Agrl. Land Trust, 1995—. Recipient Disting. Svc. award The Claremont (Calif.) Grad. Sch., 1994. Avocation: sailing, art history, banjo. Home: PO Box 1404 Ross CA 94957-1404 Office: John Randolph Haynes & Dora Haynes Found 888 W 6th St Ste 1150 Los Angeles CA 90017-2737

LINDLEY, JEARL RAY, lawyer; b. Abilene, Tex., Mar. 12, 1934; s. Hardie Lindley and Hope Clement Mourant; m. Annabelle Sim Yee Lindley, May 22, 1954; children: Katheryn Ann, Michael Andrew, Carolyn Elizabeth. BS in Chemistry, N.Mex. State U., 1960; MD, U. Colo., 1964; MS, U. Ill., 1967; JD, South Tex. Coll. of Law, 1997. Asst. clin. prof. of surgery Rush Med. Coll. of Rush U., Chgo., 1969-71, U. Ill. Sch. of Medicine, Chgo., 1969-71; assoc. clin. prof. of surgery Tex. Tech. U. Sch. of Medicine, El Paso, 1976-80; atty., counselor Las Cruces, N.Mex., 1997—. Adj. prof. N.Mex. State U., Las Cruces, 1984-86. Author publs. in field (McNeil Meml. Rsch. award 1967). Bd. dirs. Meml. Gen. Hosp., Las Cruces, 1983, So. N.Mex. Regional Dialysis Ctr., Las Cruces, 1984-89; instr. ACLS, AHA, Las Cruces, 1980-86, ATLS, Am. Coll. Surgeons, Las Cruces, 1980-86; mem. emergency med. svcs. com. Dona Ana Emergency, Las Cruces, 1979, City County Hosp. Bd. Govs., Las Cruces, 1981-83; mem. internat. bd. dirs. N.Mex. State U. Alumni Assn., 1979-81; mem. bd. counselors Citizens Bank, Las Cruces, 1991-93. Named to Outstanding Young Men of Am., 1969, Marine of Yr., Marine Corps League, 1990; commd. Ky. Col., State of Ky., 1989; proclamation of Jearl R. Lindley Day/Mayor of Truth or Consequences, N.Mex., 1990; recipient Disting. Citizen medal Dept. of N.Mex. Marine Corps League, others. Fellow Am. Coll. Surgeons, Internat. Coll. of Surgeons, Southwestern Surg. Congress; mem. Internat. Endovascular Soc., Soc. Clin. Vascular Surgery, Dona Ana County Med. Soc., AHA, Am. Legion, Marine Corps Assn., Marine Corps Heritage Found., Naval Inst., Marine Meml. Club, Air Force Assn., Marine Corps League (Commandant Dept. of N.Mex. 1990-91, Dept. Commandant's medal 1991, medal with bronze star 1988-90). Republican. Mem. Ch. of Christ. Avocations: shooting, photography, travel in an RV, reading, motorcycling. Home: 4566 Mockingbird St Las Cruces NM 88011-9616

LINDSAY, GEORGE EDMUND, museum director; b. Pomona, Calif., Aug. 17, 1916; s. Charles Wesley and Alice (Foster) L.; m. Geraldine Kendrick Morris, 1972. Student, San Diego State Coll., 1936-39; B.A., Stanford U., 1951, Ph.D., 1956. Dir. Desert Bot. Gardes, Phoenix, 1939-40, San Diego Natural History Mus., 1956-63, Calif. Acad. Scis., San Francisco, 1963-82, dir. emeritus, 1982—. Served to capt. USAAF, 1943-46. Decorated Air medal with 3 clusters, Bronze Star. Fellow San Diego Soc. Natural History, Zool. Soc. San Diego, Calif. Acad. Scis., A.A.A.S., Cactus and Succulent Soc. Achievements include spl. rsch. taxonomy desert plants, Cactaceae of Baja Calif., Mex. Home: 87 Barbaree Way Tiburon CA 94920-2223 Office: Calif Acad Scis San Francisco CA 94118

LINDSEY, CASIMIR CHARLES, zoologist, educator; b. Toronto, Ont., Can., Mar. 22, 1923; s. Charles Bethune and Wanda Casimira (Gzowski) L.; m. Shelagh Pauline Lindsey, May 29, 1948. B.A., U. Toronto, 1948; M.A., U. B.C., Vancouver, 1950; Ph.D., Cambridge (Eng.) U., 1952. Div. biologist B.C. Game Dept., 1952-57; with Inst. Fisheries, also dept. zoology U. B.C., 1953-66; prof. zoology U. Man., Winnipeg, 1966-79; dir. Inst. Animal Resource Ecology, U. B.C., 1980-85; mem. Fisheries and Oceans Adv. Council, 1981-86; prof. emeritus U. B.C., 1988—. Bd. govs. Vancouver Public Aquarium, 1956-66, 80-95; external assessor univs. S ingapore and Nanyang, 1979-81; cons. in field. Author papers in field. Served with Can. Army, 1943-45. Recipient Publ. award Wildlife Soc., 1972; Saunderson award for excellence in teaching U. Man., 1977; Rh Inst. award, 1979; Nuffield Found. grantee, 1973; Killam sr. fellow, 1985-86 Fellow Royal Soc. Can.; mem. Can. Soc. Zoologists (pres. 1977-78), Can. Soc. Environ. Biologists (v.p. 1974-75), Am. Soc. Ichthyologists and Herpetologists (gov.), Fedn. Can. Artists. Office: U BC Dept of Zoology 6270 University Blvd Vancouver BC Canada V6T 1Z4

LINDSEY, GINA MARIE, airport executive; Gen. mgr. Seattle-Tacoma Internat. Airport, aviation dimension dir., 1997—, mng. dir. aviation divsn. Office: Seattle Tacoma Internat Airport PO Box 68727 Seattle WA 98168-0727

LINDSEY, JOANNE M. flight attendant, poet; b. Peoria, Ill., Aug. 27, 1936; d. George Edward and Elsie Rosetta (Mann) L.; m. Aug. 1959 (div. 1961). AA, El Camino Coll., Torrance, Calif., 1958. Exec. adminstrv. sec. Space Tech. Labs. (formerly Ramo-Woolridge), Hawthorne, Calif., 1958-64; flight attendant Am. Airlines, L.A., 1964—. Mem. acad. coun. London. Diplomatic Acad. Contbr. poems to anthologies. Attended People to People Amb. Program's So. African Tour of Women Writers, 1998. Recipient 6 Poetry Editor's Choice awards in anthologies Internat. Libr. Poetry, 1996, 97, 98, 2001. Mem. Acad. Am. Poets, Audie Murphy Rsch. Found., Internat. Soc. Poets, L.A. World Affairs Coun., Friends of Poets and Writers. Avocations: gardening, writing, skiing, mountain biking, home refurbishing. Home: 846 American Oaks Ave Newbury Park CA 91320-5572

LINDSTROM, GREGORY P. lawyer; b. Hollywood, Calif., Aug. 4, 1953; AB summa cum laude, UCLA, 1975; JD, U. Chgo., 1978. Bar: Calif. 1978. Mng. ptnr. Latham & Watkins, San Francisco. Mem. Am. Coll. Trial Lawyers, Phi Beta Kappa. Office: Latham & Watkins 505 Montgomery St Ste 1900 San Francisco CA 94111-2552

LINDSTROM, KRIS PETER, environmental consultant; b. Dumont, N.J., Oct. 18, 1948; s. Sven Rune and Moyra Hilda (Coughlan) L.; m. Annette Gail Chaplin, June 25, 1978; 1 child, Karl Pierce. MPH, U. Calif., Berkeley, 1973; MS in Ecology, U. Calif., Davis, 1983. Registered environ. health specialist, Calif. Sr. lab. analyst County Sanitation Dists. Orange County, Fountain Valley, Calif., 1970-72, environ. specialist, 1973-74, J.B. Gilbert and Assocs., Sacramento, 1974-78; prin. K.P. Lindstrom & Assocs., Sacramento, 1978-84; pres. K.P. Lindstrom, Inc., Pacific Grove, Calif., 1985—. Mem. rsch. adv. bd. Nat. Water Rsch. Inst., Fountain Valley, 1991—. Author: Design of Municipal Wastewater Treatment Plants, 1992; editor publs., 1989, 90. Chmn. City of Pacific Grove (Calif.) Mus. Bd., 1992-96, City of Seal Beach (Calif.) Environ. Bd., 1970; dir. Monterey Peninsula Water Mgmt. Dist., 1999—. Mem. Water Environ. Fedn. (chmn. marine water quality com. 1987-90), Calif. Water Pollution Control Assn., Pacific Grove Residents Assn. (bd. dirs., pres., v.p. 1992-98). Office: KP Lindstrom Inc PO Box 51008 Pacific Grove CA 93950-6008

LINEBERGER, WILLIAM CARL, chemistry educator; b. Hamlet, N.C., Dec. 5, 1939; s. Caleb Henry and Evelyn (Cooper) L.; m. Katharine Wyman Edwards, July 31, 1979. BS, Ga. Inst. Tech., 1961, MSEE, 1963, PhD, 1965. Rsch. physicist U.S. Army Ballistic Rsch. Labs., Aberdeen, Md., 1967-68; postdoctoral assoc. Joint Inst. for Lab. Astrophysics U. Colo., Boulder, 1968-70, from asst. prof. to prof. chemistry, 1970-83, E.U. Condon prof. chemistry, 1983—. Phi Beta Kappa nat. lectr., 1989. Capt. U.S. Army, 1965-67. Fellow AAAS, Joint Inst. for Lab. Physics, Am. Phys. Soc. (H.P. Broida prize 1981, Bomen Michelson prize 1987, Optical Sci. Am. Meggers prize 1988, Plyler prize 1992; mem. NAS, Am. Chem. Soc. (Irving Langmuir prize 1996), Am. Acad. Arts and Scis., Sigma Xi. Office: U Colo Joint Inst Lab Astrophysics Cb 440 Boulder CO 80309-0001

LINFORD, RULON KESLER, physicist, engineer; b. Cambridge, Mass., Jan. 31, 1943; s. Leon Blood and Imogene (Kesler) L.; m. Cecile Tadje, Apr. 2, 1965; children: Rulon Scott, Laura Linford Williams, Hilary Linford Henderson, Philip Leon. BSEE, U. Utah, 1966; MS in ElecE, Mass. Inst. Tech., 1969, PhD in ElecE, 1973. Staff CTR-7 Los Alamos (N.Mex) Nat. Lab., 1973-75, asst. group leader CTR-7, 1975-77, group leader CTR-11, 1977-79, program mgr., group leader compact toroid CTR-11, 1979-80, program mgr., asst. div. leader compact toroid CTR divsn., 1980-81, assoc. CTR divsn. leader, 1981-86, program dir. magnetic fusion energy, 1986-89, program dir., div. leader CTR div. office, 1989-91, program dir. nuclear sys., 1991-93; staff LER, 1993-94; U. Calif. coord. sci. and tech., 1994-97; assoc. vice provost for rsch. and lab. programs Office of the Pres., U. Calif., Oakland, 1997—. Contbr. articles to profl. jours. Recipient E. O. Lawrence award Dept. of Energy, Washington, 1991. Fellow Am. Physical Soc. (exec. com. 1982, 90-91, program com. 1982, 85, award selection com. 1983, 84, fellowship com. 1986); mem. Sigma Xi. Home: 1055 Aquarius Way Oakland CA 94611-1939 Office: U Calif Office Pres 1111 Franklin 11th Fl Oakland CA 94607-5200 E-mail: rulon.linford@ucop.edu

LINGAFELTER, EDWARD CLAY, JR. chemistry educator; b. Toledo, Mar. 28, 1914; s. Edward Clay and Winifred (Jordan) L.; m. Roberta Crowe Kneedler, Apr. 30, 1938; children— Robert Edward (dec. 1996), Thomas Edward, James Edward, Richard Edward, Daniel Edward. B.S., U. Calif.-Berkeley, 1935, Ph.D., 1939. Mem. faculty U. Wash., Seattle, 1939—, prof. chemistry, 1952-84, prof. emeritus, 1984—, assoc. dean Grad. Sch., 1960-68. Contbr. articles to profl. jours. Mem. Am. Chem. Soc., Am. Crystallographic Assn. (pres. 1974), Assn. Italian Cristallografia. Achievements include rsch. on solutions, molecular structures of paraffin-chain and coordination compounds. Home: 5323 27th Ave NE Seattle WA 98105-3105 Office: U Wash Dept Chemistry PO Box 351700 Seattle WA 98195-1700

LINGENFELTER, SHERWOOD GALEN, university provost, anthropology educator; b. Hollidaysburg, Pa., Nov. 18, 1941; s. Galen Miller and Kathern Margaretta (Rogers) L.; m. Judith Elaine Beaumont, Aug. 10, 1962; children: Jennifer Elaine, Joel Sherwood. BA, Wheaton Coll., 1963; PhD, U. Pitts., 1971. Dir. acad. advising U. Pitts., 1964-66; instr. SUNY, Brockport, N.Y., 1966-67, asst. prof, 1969-74, assoc. prof., 1974-82, prof. anthropology, 1982-83; NIH predoctoral fellow U. Pitts., 1967-69; prof. Biola U., La Mirada, Calif., 1983-88, provost, sr. v.p., 1988-99; dean Sch. of World Mission Fuller Theol. Sem., Pasadena, 1999—, provost, 01—. Cons. in anthropology Summer Inst. Linguistics, Dallas, 1977-96, bd. dirs., 1999; tng. cons. Liebenzell Mission of Am., Schooleys Mountain, N.J., 1981-89; evaluating cons. Trust Terr. of the Pacific Islands, Saipan, Mariana Islands, 1969-74. Author: Yap: Political Leadership, 1975, The Deni of Western Brazil, 1980, Ministering Cross-Culturally, 1986, Transforming Culture, 1992, 2nd edit., 1998, Agents of Transformation, 1996; editor: Political Development in Micronesia, 1974, Social Organization of Sabah Societies, 1990. Bd. dirs. Christian Scholars Rev., 1989-95, Grace Brethren Internat. Missions, 1994—; mem. Sr. Accrediting Commn. Western Assn. Schs. and Colls., 2000. Recipient Disting. Teaching award Biola U., 1987-88; grantee NSF, 1967-69, 79-81, SUNY Rsch. Found., 1970. Fellow Am. Anthrop. Assn., Soc. for Applied Anthropology, Am. Ethnol. Soc.; mem. Assn. Social Anthropology Oceania, Am. Conf. Acad. Deans. Democrat. Mem. Grace Brethern Ch. Office: Fuller Theol Sem Sch World Mission 135 N Oakland Ave Pasadena CA 91182-0001

LINGLE, CRAIG STANLEY, glaciologist, educator; b. Carlsbad, N.Mex., Sept. 11, 1945; s. Stanley Orland and Margaret Pearl (Ewart) L.; m. Diana Lynn Duncan, Aug. 21, 1972; 1 son, Eric Glenn. BS, U. Wash., 1967; MS, U. Maine, 1978; PhD, U. Wis., 1983. Nat. rsch. coun. resident rsch. assoc. Coop. Inst. for Rsch. in Environ. Scis., U. Colo., Boulder, 1983-84, rsch. assoc., 1984-86; program mgr. polar glaciology divsn. polar programs NSF, Washington, 1986-87; cons. Jet Propulsion Lab., Pasadena, Calif., 1987-88; nat. rsch. coun. resident rsch. assoc. NASA Goddard Space Flight Ctr., Oceans and Ice Branch, Greenbelt, Md., 1988-90; rsch. assoc. prof. Geophys. Inst., U. Alaska, Fairbanks, 1990-2000, acting dir. Alaska synthetic aperture radar facility, 1997-98, rsch. prof. geophysics, 2000—. Contbr. articles to profl. jours. Recipient Antarctic Svc. medal of U.S., NSF, 1987, Rsch. Project of Month award Office of Health and Environ. Rsch., U.S. Dept. Energy, 1990, Group Achievement award NASA, 1992. Mem. AAAS, Internat. Glaciological Soc., Am. Geophys. Union, Sigma Xi. Avocations: downhill and cross-country skiing, canoeing, hiking. Office: U Alaska Geophys Inst PO Box 757320 Fairbanks AK 99775-7320

LINGLE, LINDA, political organization administrator, former mayor; Mayor County of Maui, Hawaii; chair. Democratic Party of Hawaii. Office: County Maui 200 S High St Wailuku HI 96793-2135

LINK, GEORGE HAMILTON, lawyer; b. Sacramento, Mar. 26, 1939; s. Hoyle and Corrie Elizabeth (Evans) L.; m. Betsy Leland; children—Thomas Hamilton, Christopher Leland. AB, U. Calif., Berkeley, 1961; LLB, Harvard U., 1964. Bar: Calif. 1965, U.S. Dist. Ct. (no., ea., ctrl. and so dists.) Calif. 1965, U.S. Ct. Appeals (9th cir.) 1965. Assoc. Brobeck, Phleger & Harrison, San Francisco, 1964-69, ptnr., 1970—, mng. ptnr. L.A., 1973-93, mng. ptnr. firmwide, 1993-96. Chmn. Pacific Rim Adv. Coun., 1992-95. Bd. regents U. Calif., 1971-74; trustee Berkeley Found., Jr. Statesmen Am.; bd. govs. United Way, 1979-81; trustee, v.p. Calif. Hist. Soc., 1987—. Fellow Am. Bar Found.; mem. ABA, Calif. Bar Assn., L.A. Bar Assn., U. Calif. Alumni Assn. (pres. 1972-75), Calif. Club, Bohemian Club, Jonathan Club. Republican. Methodist. Office: Brobeck Phleger & Harrison 550 S Hope St Los Angeles CA 90071-2627 E-mail: glink@brobeck.com

LINKHART, DOUGLAS D. (DOUG), state legislator; b. Norman, Okla., Dec. 17, 1955; m. Doroth Norbie. BA, MA, U. Ariz. Bus. economist; Presdl. mgmt. intern EPA, former analyst air quality divsn.; mem. Colo. Ho. of Reps., 1994-95, Colo. Senate, Dist. 31, Denver, 1995—; mem. fin. com., mem. joint legis. audit com.; mem. health, environ., welfare and instns. com. Founder Neighborhood Resource Ctr.; bd. mem. Urban League Met. Denver; active West Denver Teen Pregnancy Prevention Task Froce, Colo. Inst. for Hispanic Edn., Econ. Devel. Bd.; mem. Mayuor's Adv. Coun., 1987-88, Denver Air Pollution Regulations Adv. Com., 1990-91; capt., co-capt. Dem. Party Dist. 2A. Democrat. Office: State Capitol 200 E Colfax Ave Ste 274 Denver CO 80203-1716 Fax: 303-866-4543. E-mail: rubyg@dnvr.us.west.net

LINKLETTER, ARTHUR GORDON, radio and television broadcaster; b. Moose Jaw, Sask., Can., July 17, 1912; s. Fulton John and Mary (Metzler) L.; m. Lois Foerster, Nov. 25, 1935; children: Jack, Dawn, Robert (dec.), Sharon, Diane (dec.). AB, San Diego State Coll., 1934. Program dir. Sta. KGB, San Diego, 1934; program dir. Calif. Internat. Expn., San Diego, 1935; radio dir. Tex. Centennial Expn., Dallas, 1936; San Francisco World's Fair, 1937-39; pres. Linkletter Prodns.; ptnr., co-owner John Guedel Radio Prodns. Chmn. bd. Linkletter Enterprises; owner Art Linkletter Oil Enterprises. Author: theme spectacle Cavalcade of Golden West, 1940; author and co-producer: theme spectacle Cavalcade of Am, 1941; writer, producer, star in West Coast radio shows, 1940-55; former star, writer: People Are Funny, NBC-TV and radio, Art Linkletter's House Party, CBS-TV and radio; Author: People Are Funny, 1953, Kids Say The Darndest Things, 1957, The Secret World of Kids, 1959, Confessions of a Happy Man, 1961, Kids Still Say The Darndest Things, 1961, A Child's Garden of Misinformation, 1965, I Wish I'd Said That, 1968, Linkletter Down Under, 1969, Oops, 1969, Drugs at My Door Step, 1973, Women Are My Favorite People, 1974, How to be a Super Salesman, 1974, Yes, You Can!, 1979, I Didn't Do It Alone, 1979, Public Speaking for Private People, 1980, Linkletter on Dynamic Selling, 1982, Old Age is not for Sissies, 1988; co-host (with Bill Cosby) series Kids Say the Darnedest Things, 1998—; lectr. convs. and univs. Nat. bd. dirs. Goodwill Industries; commr. gen. to U.S. Exhibit at Brisbane Expo 88, Australia, 1987; commr. gen. to rank of U.S. amb. to The 200th Anniversary Celebration, Australia, 1987—; bd. regents Pepperdine U.; pres. bd. advisors Ctr. on Aging, UCLA; chmn. bd. French Found. for Alzheimers Rsch. Recipient numerous awards. Address: 8484 Wilshire Blvd Ste 205 Beverly Hills CA 90211-3213

LINN, STUART MICHAEL, biochemist, educator; b. Chgo., Dec. 16, 1940; s. Maurice S. and Pauline L.; children: Matthew S., Allison D., Meagan S. B.S. with honors in Chemistry, Calif. Inst. Tech., 1962; Ph.D. in Biochemistry, Stanford U., 1967. Asst. prof. biochemistry U. Calif., Berkeley, 1968-72, assoc. prof., 1972-75, prof., 1975-87, head div. biochemistry and molecular biology, 1987-90, Berkeley, 1995-2000. Mem. editorial bd. Nucleic Acids Rsch., 1974-98, Jour. Biol. Chemistry, 1975-80, Molecular and Cellular Biology, 1987-91; contbr. articles to profl. jours., chpts. to books. Helen Hay Whitney fellow, 1966-68; John Simon Guggenheim fellow, 1974-75; recipient USPHS Merit Grant award, 1988-97. Mem. AAAS, Am. Soc. Biol. Chemists (coun.), Am. Soc. Microbiologists. Office: U Calif Divsn Biochem & Molec Bio Barker Hall Berkeley CA 94720-3202 E-mail: slinn@socrates.berkeley.edu

LINNA, TIMO JUHANI, immunologist, researcher, educator; b. Tavastkyro, Finland, Mar. 16, 1937; came to U.S., 1968, naturalized, 1981; foster s. Gustaf Lennart and Anne-Marie (Forsstrom) Ackell; m. Rhoda Margareta Popova, May 20, 1961; children: Alexander, Fredrik, Maria. MB, U. Uppsala, Sweden, 1959, MD, 1965, PhD, 1967. Intern, resident hosps., Sweden; pvt. practice medicine hosps. and clinic Sweden; asst. prof. histology U. Uppsala, 1967-71; asst. prof. microbiology and immunology Temple U., Phila., 1970-71, dir. lab. clin. immunology hosps., 1970-72, adviser clin. immunology, 1972-80, assoc. prof. microbiology, immunology, 1971-78, prof., 1978-80, research prof., 1980-90. Group leader immunology central research and devel. dept. E.I. duPont de Nemours & Co., Wilmington, Del., 1980-84, research supr., 1984-85, mgr. med. research products dept., 1986-87, assoc. med. dir., 1987-90; sr. dir. cellular immunology Applied Immune Scis., Inc., Menlo Park, Calif., 1990-91; sr. assoc. med. dir. inst. clin. immunology and infectious diseases, devel. rsch., Syntex (USA) Inc., Palo Alto, Calif., 1992-94, dir. med. rsch., 1994-95; dir. med. rsch. Roche Global Devel., Palo Alto, Calif., 1995-96; transplant med. liaison Roche Labs., Palo Alto, 1996—; immunology cons. UNDP/World Bank/WHO Spl. Program for Research and Tng. in Tropical Diseases, WHO, Geneva, 1978-79; mem. sci. adv. coun. Internat. Inst. Immunology Tng. and Research, Amsterdam, Netherlands, 1975-81. Author books; contbr. articles to profl. publs. USPHS Internat. postdoctoral research fellow, 1968-70; spl. research fellow U. Minn., 1970; Eleanor Roosevelt Am. Cancer Soc. fellow, 1976; grantee Swedish Med. Research Council, 1969-71; grantee NIH, 1972-80 Mem. Am. Assn. Cancer Research, Am. Assn. Immunologists (chmn. edn. com. 1975-80), Am. Assn. Pathologists, Am. Soc. Microbiology, Internat. Soc. Exptl. Hematology, Internat. Soc. Lymphology, N.Y. Acad. Scis., Reticuloendothelial Soc., Royal Lymphatic Soc. Uppsala, Scandinavian Soc. Immunology, Soc. Swedish Physicians, Swedish Med. Assn. Lutheran. Home: 260 Highland Ave San Carlos CA 94070-1911 Office: PO Box 10850 3401 Hillview Ave Palo Alto CA 94304-1320 E-mail: jlinna@prodigy.net

LINSK, MICHAEL STEPHEN, real estate executive; b. L.A., Apr. 20, 1940; s. Abe P. and Helen Linsk; m. Wilma M. Stahl, Aug. 11, 1979; children by previous marriage: Cari E., Steven D. BSBA, U. So. Calif., 1965, MBA, 1969. CFO Larwin Group, Inc., Encino, Calif., 1970-75; v.p. fin., dir. Donald L. Bren Co., L.A., 1976-78; v.p., CFO, treas., dir. Wilshire Mortgage/Wilshire Diversified, Burbank, Calif., 1980-81; pres., dir. subs. Wilshire Mortgage Corp., Burbank, 1981-84; pres., dir. Wilshire Realty Investments, Burbank, 1981-84, Glenfed Investments Inc., subs. Glendale Fed. Savs., 1982-84; pres. Eastern Pacific Fin. Group, L.A., 1984-85; sr. v.p. Leisure Tech., Inc., L.A., 1985-87; CEO Investec Realty Group, Inc., Encino, 1987-88; sr. v.p. L.A. Land Co., 1988-91; mng. dir. real estate consulting Price Waterhouse Coopers, 1992—. Dir. Presdl. Savs. Bank, Jewel City Ins., Glendale, Verdugo Services, Inc., Glendale. Treas. Temple Judea, Tarzana, Calif., 1982-83, trustee, 1981-83; treas., bd. dirs. Am. Theater Arts; bd. dirs. North Hollywood Cultural Ctr., Inc., A Cmty. of Friends, Inc., 1998—. Mem. Bldg. Industry Assn. (dir. L.A. chpt. 1981-88), AICPA, Calif. Soc. CPAs, Urban Land Inst., Beta Gamma Sigma. Office: Price Waterhouse Coopers 400 S Hope St Ste 2300 Los Angeles CA 90071-2889 E-mail: michaellinsk@cswebmail.com, michael.linsk@us.pwcglobal.com

LINSTONE, HAROLD ADRIAN, management and systems science educator; b. Hamburg, Fed. Republic Germany, June 15, 1924; came to U.S., 1936; s. Frederic and Ellen (Seligmann) L.; m. Hedy Schubach, June 16, 1946; children: Fred A., Clark R. BS, CCNY, 1944; MA, Columbia U., 1947; PhD, U. So. Calif., 1954. Sr. scientist Hughes Aircraft Co., Culver City, Calif., 1949-61, The Rand Corp., Santa Monica, 1961-63; assoc. dir. planning Lockheed Corp., Burbank, 1963-71; prof. Portland (Oreg.) State U., 1970—. Pres. Systems Forecasting, Inc., Santa Monica, 1971-98; cons. 1973—. Author: Multiple Perspectives for Decision Making, 1984, Decision Making for Technology Executives, 1999; co-author: The Unbounded Mind, 1993, The Challenge of the 21st Century, 1994; co-editor The Delphi Method, 1975, Technological Substitution, 1976, Futures Research, 1977; editor-in-chief Technol. Forecasting Social Change, 1969—. NSF grantee, Washington, 1976, 79, 85. Mem. Inst. Mgmt. Scis., Ops. Rsch. Soc., Internat. Soc. Systems Scis. (pres. 1993-94). Avocation: photography. Office: Portland State U PO Box 751 Portland OR 97207-0751

LINVILL, JOHN GRIMES, engineering educator; b. Kansas City, Mo., Aug. 8, 1919; s. Thomas G. and Emma (Crayne) L.; m. Marjorie Webber, Dec. 28, 1943; children: Gregory Thomas, Candace Sue. AB, William Jewell Coll., 1941; SB, Mass. Inst. Tech., 1943, SM, 1945, ScD, 1949; D of Applied Sci., U. Louvain, Belgium, 1966; DSc, William Jewell Coll., 1992. Asst. prof. elec. engring. Mass. Inst. Tech., 1949-51; tech. staff Bell Telephone Labs., 1951-55; assoc. prof. elec. engring. Stanford U., 1955-57, prof., dir. solid-state electronics lab., 1957-64, prof., chmn. dept. elec. engring., 1964-80, prof., dir. Center for Integrated Systems, 1980-90—, Canon USA prof. engring., 1988-89, prof. emeritus, 1989—; co-founder, dir. Tele Sensory Corp., 1971-2000; dir. Read-Rite Corp., 1992-2000. Author: Transistors and Active Circuits, 1961, Models of Transistors and Diodes, 1963; inventor Optacon reading aid for the blind. Recipient citation for achievement William Jewell Coll., 1963, John Scott award for devel. of Optacon, City of Phila., 1980, Medal of Achievement Am. Electronics Assn., 1983, Louis Braille Prize Deutscher Blindenverband, 1984. Fellow IEEE (Edn. medal 1976), AAAS; mem. Nat. Acad. of Engring., Am. Acad. of Arts and Scis. Home: 30 Holden Ct Portola Valley CA 94028-7913 Office: Stanford U Dept Elec Engring Stanford CA 94305

LIONAKIS, GEORGE, architect; b. West Hiawatha, Utah, Sept. 5, 1924; s. Pete and Andriani (Protopapadakis) L.; student Carbon Jr. Coll., 1942-43, 46-47; BArch., U. Oreg., 1951; m. Iva Oree Braddock, Dec. 30, 1951; 1 dau., Deborah Jo. With Corps Engrs., Walla Walla, Wash., 1951-54; architect Liske, Lionakis, Beaumont & Engberg, Sacramento, 1954-86, Lionakis-Beaumont Design Group, 1986—. Mem. Sacramento County Bd. Appeals, 1967—, chmn., 1969, 75, 76; pres. Sacramento Builders Exchange, 1976. Served with USAAF, 1943-46. Mem. AIA (pres. Central Valley chpt., 1972—), Constrn. Specifications Inst. (pres. Sacramento chpt., 1962; nat. awards, 1962, 63, 65), Sacramento C. of C. (code com., 1970—). Club: North Ridge Country (pres. 1987). Lodge: Rotarian (pres. East Sacramento 1978-79). Prin. works include Stockton (Calif.) Telephone Bldg., 1968, Chico (Calif.) Main Telephone Bldg., 1970, Mather AFB Exchange Complex Sacramento, 1970, Base Chapel Mather AFB, Sacramento, 1970, Woodridge Elementary Sch., Sacramento, 1970, Pacific Telephone Co. Operating Center Modesto, Calif., 1968, Sacramento, 1969, Marysville, Calif., 1970, Red Bluff, Calif., 1971, Wells Fargo Banks, Sacramento, 1968, Corning, Calif., 1969, Anderson, 1970, Beale AFB Exchange Complex, Marysville, 1971, Cosumnes River Coll., Sacramento, 1971, base exchanges at Bergstrom AFB, Austin, Tex., Sheppard AFB, Wichita Falls, Tex., Chanute AFB, Rantoul, Ill., McChord AFB, Tacoma, Wash., health center Chico State U., Sacramento County Adminstrn. Center, Sacramento Bee Newspaper Plant. Home: 160 Breckenwood Way Sacramento CA 95864-6968 Office: Lionakis Beaumont Design Group 1919 19th St Sacramento CA 95814-6714

LIOU, KUO-NAN, atmospheric sciences educator, researcher; b. Taipei, Taiwan, Republic of China, Nov. 16, 1944; m. Agnes L.Y. Hung, Aug. 3, 1968; children: Julia C.C., Clifford T.C. BS, Taiwan U., 1965; MS, NYU, 1968, PhD, 1970. Rsch. assoc. Goddard Inst. for Space Studies, N.Y.C., 1970-72; asst. prof. atmospheric sci. U. Wash., Seattle, 1972-74; assoc. prof. U. Utah, Salt Lake City, 1975-80, prof., 1980-97, dir. grad. studies in meteorology, 1981-84, dir. Ctr. for Atmospheric and Remote Sounding Studies, 1987-97, chmn. dept. meteorology, 1996-97, rsch. prof. physics, 1992—; prof. UCLA, 1997—, dir. Inst. Radiation and Remote Sensing, 1997—, chair dept. atmospheric scis., 2000—. Adj. prof. geophysics U. Utah, Salt Lake City, 1992-97; vis. prof. UCLA, 1981, U. Ariz., Tucson, 1995; affiliated prof. Peking U., Beijing, Chinga, 1991—; vis. scholar Harvard U., 1985; cons. NASA Ames Rsch. Ctr., Moffett Field, Calif., 1984-94, Los Alamos (N.Mex.) Nat. Lab. 1984-88. Author: An Introduction to Atmospheric Radiation, 1980, Radiation and Cloud Processes in the Atmosphere, 1992; editor: Atmospheric Radiation Progress and Prospects, 1987; contbr. articles to profl. jours. Recipient Founders Day award NYU, 1971, Creativity award Atmospheric Scis. divsn. NSF, 1996; NRC fellow, 1970, Gardner fellow, 1978. Fellow AAAS, Optical Soc. Am., Am. Meterol. Soc. (chmn. atmospheric radiation com. 1982-84, Jule G. Charney award 1997), Am. Geophys. Union; mem. NAE. Home: 1488 Paseo De Oro Pacific Palisades CA 90272-1961 Office: UCLA Dept Atmospheric Scis 7127 Math Scis Bldg 405 Hilgard Ave Los Angeles CA 90095-9000

LIPINSKI, TARA KRISTEN, professional figure skater; b. Phila., 10 June; Prof. figure skater Stars On Ice, 1998—. Competitive history includes placing 1st in Hershey's Kisses Challenge, 1997, 1st in World Championships, 1997, 1st in Champions Series Final, 1997, 1st Nat. Sr., 1997, 1st (team) U.S. Postal Svc. Challenge, 1996, 2d in Nations Cup, 1996, 3rd Trophy Lalique, 1996, 2nd place Skate Can., 1996, numerous others; recipient Mary Lou Retton award U.S. Olympic Festival, 1994; youngest-ever Olympic Festival gold medalist at age 12, 2nd place Nat. Champ., 1998, 1st place Skate, Rattle & Roll, 1998, 1st place Olympic Games, 1998, 1st place Champion Series Final, 1997,98. Avocations: reading, cooking, tennis. Office: Thorne & Co 1801 Century Park E Fl 12 Los Angeles CA 90067-2302

LIPPARD, LUCY ROWLAND, writer, lecturer; b. N.Y.C., Apr. 14, 1937; d. Vernon William and Margaret Isham (Cross) L.; m. Robert Tracy Ryman, Aug. 19, 1961 (div. 1968); 1 child, Ethan Isham Ryman. BA, Smith Coll., 1958; MA in Art History, NYU, 1962; DFA (hon.), Moore Coll. Art, 1972, San Francisco Art Inst., 1984, Maine Coll. Art, 1994, Mass. Coll. Art, 1998. Freelance writer, lectr., curator, 1964—. Prof. Sch. Visual Arts, N.Y.C., Williams Coll., Queensland U., Brisbane, Australia, U. Colo., Boulder; mem. adv. bd. Franklin Furnace, N.Y.C., 1979—; bd. dirs. Printed Matter, N.Y.C., Ctr. for Study of Polit. Graphics, L.A., Time & Space Ltd., Hudson, N.Y.; co-founder W.E.B., Ad Hoc Women Artist's Com., Artists Meeting for Cultural Change, Heresies Collective and Jour., Artists Call Against U.S. Intervention in Ctrl. Am., Polit. Art Documentation/Distbn. Author: Overlay: Contemporary Art and the Art of Prehistory, 1983, Mixed Blessings: New Art in a Multicultural America, 1990, Pop Art, 1966, The Graphic work of Philip Evergood, 1966, Changing: Essays in Art Criticism, 1971, Tony Smith, 1972, Six Years: The Dematerialization of the Art Object, 1973, From the Center: Feminist Essays on Women's Art, 1976,

Eva Hesse, 1976, (with Charles Simonds) Cracking (Brüchig Werden), 1979, Ad Reinhardt, 1981, Get the Message? A Decade of Art for Social Change, 1984, A Different War: Vietnam in Art, 1988, The Pink Glass Swan: Selected Feminist Essays on Art, 1995, The Lure of the Local: Senses of Place in a Multicentered Society, 1997, Florence Pierce: In Touch With Light, 1998, On the Beaten Track: Tourism, Art and Place, 1999, (with Alfred Barr and James Thrall Soby) The School of Paris, 1965, (novel) I See/You Mean, 1979; author, editor: Partial Recall: Photographs of Native North Americans, 1992; editor: Surrealists on Art, 1970, Dadas on Art, 1971; contbg. editor: Art in Am.; editor El Puente de Galisteo, 1997—; contbr. monthly columns Village Voice, 1981-85, In These Times, Z Mag., also numerous articles to mags., anthologies, and mus. catalogs, 1964—. Mem. Dem. Socialists Am., Atlatl, Nat. Writers Union; mem. planning and adv. com. Santa Fe County Open Land and Trails, 1999. Recipient Frederick Douglass award North Star Fund, 1994, Frank Jewett Mather award for criticism Coll. Art Assn., 1974, Claude Fuess award for pub. svc. Phillips Andover Acad., 1975, curating award Penny McCall Found., 1989, citation N.Y.C. mayor David Dinkins, 1990, Smith Coll. medal, 1992; Guggenheim fellow, 1968, ArtTable award, 1999. Avocations: hiking, amateur archaeology, sailing, local history. Home and Office: 14 Avenida Vieja Galisteo NM 87540-9783

LIPPS, JERE HENRY, paleontology educator; b. L.A., Aug. 28, 1939; s. Henry John and Margaret (Rosaltha) L.; m. Karen Elizabeth Loeblich, June 25, 1964 (div. 1971); m. Susannah McClintock, Sept. 28, 1973; children: Jeremy Christian, Jamison William. BA, UCLA, 1962, PhD, 1966. Asst. prof. U. Calif., Davis, 1967-70, assoc. prof., 1970-75, prof., 1975-88, Berkeley, 1988—, prof. paleontology, 1988-89, prof. integrative biology, 1989—; dir. Mus. Paleontology, Berkeley, 1989-97. Dir. Inst. Ecology U. Calif., Davis, 1972-73, chmn. dept. geology, 1971-72, 79-84, chmn. dept. integrative biology, Berkeley, 1991-94. Contbr. articles to sci. publs. Fellow, dir. Cushman Found. Recipient U.S. Antarctic medal NSF, 1975; Lipps Island, Antarctica named in his honor, 1979. Fellow AAAS, CSICOP (pres. 1983-84), Calif. Acad. Scis., Geol. Soc. Am., Cushman Found.; mem. Paleontol. Soc. (pres. 1996-97), Coun. for Media Integrity. Avocation: scuba diving. Office: U Calif Mus Paleontology 1101 Valley Life Sciences Bldg Berkeley CA 94720-4780 E-mail: jlipps@uclink4.berkeley.edu

LIPSEY, RICHARD GEORGE, economist, educator; b. Victoria, B.C., Can., Aug. 28, 1928; s. Richard Andrew and Faith Thirell (Ledingham) L.; m. Diana Louise Smart, Mar. 17, 1960; children: Mark Alexander (stepson), Mathew Richard, Joanna Louise, Claudia Amanda. BA with honours, U. B.C., 1950, LLD (hon.) , 1999; MA, U. Toronto, 1953; PhD, London Sch. Econs., 1958; LLD (hon.) , McMaster U., 1984, Victoria U., 1985, Carleton U., 1986, Queens U., 1990; DSc (hon.), Toronto U., 1992; DLitt (hon.) , Guelph U., 1993; LLD (hon.) , U. Western Ont., 1994; LL.D (hon.), U. Essex, 1996. Rsch. asst. B.C. Dept. Trade and Industry, 1950-53; from asst. lectr. to prof. econs. London Sch. Econs., 1955-63; prof. econs., chmn. dept., dean Sch. Social Studies, U. Essex, Eng., 1965-69; vis. prof. U. B.C., 1969-70, U. Colo., 1973-74; Irving Fisher vis. prof. Yale U., 1979-80; Sir Edward Peacock prof. econs. Queens U., Kingston, Ont., 1970-87; prof. Simon Fraser U., Vancouver, B.C., 1989-97, prof. emeritus, 1997—. Sr. rsch. advisor C.D. Howe Inst., 1983-89; dir. rsch. into growth in U.K. Nat. Econ. Devel. Coun. U.K., 1961-63; mem. coun. and planning com. Nat. Inst. Econ. and Social Rsch. U.K., 1962-69; mem. bd. Social Sci. Rsch. Coun. U.K., 1966-69. Author: An Introduction to Positive Economics, 9th edit, 1998, The Theory of Customs Unions: A General Equilibrium Analysis, 1971; co-author: An Introduction to a Mathematical Treatment of Economics, 3d edit, 1977, Economics, 12th edit., 1999, Mathematical Economics, 1976, An Introduction to the U.K. Economy, 1983, 4th edit., 1993, Common Ground for the Canadian Common Market, 1984, Canada's Trade Options in a Turbulent World, 1985, Global Imbalances, 1987, First Principles of Economics, 1988, 3d edit., 1996, Evaluating the Free Trade Deal, 1988, The NAFTA, What's In, What's Out, What Next, Business Economics, 1997, A Structuralist Assessment of Innovation Policies, 1998; editor: Rev. Econ. Studies, 1962-64. Decorated officer Order of Can.; Can. Inst. for Advanced Rsch. fellow, 1989—. Fellow Econometric Soc., Royal Soc. Can., Can. Inst. for Advanced Rsch., IC2 Soc. (Austin, Tex.); mem. Royal Econ. Soc. (council 1967-71), Econ. Study Soc. (chmn. 1965-69), Am. Econ. Assn., Can. Econ. Assn. (pres. 1980-81), Atlantic Econ. Soc. (chmn. 1986-87). Office: Simon Fraser U Harbour Centre 515 W Hastings St Vancouver BC Canada V6B 5K3 E-mail: rlipsey@sfu.ca

LIPSIG, ETHAN, lawyer; b. N.Y.C., Dec. 11, 1948; s. Daniel Allen and Haddassah (Adler) L. BA, Pomona Coll., 1969; postgrad., Oxford U., 1969-70; JD, UCLA, 1974. Bar: U.S. Dist. Ct. (cen. dist.) Calif. 1974, U.S. Ct. Appeals (9th cir.) 1974, U.S Tax Ct. 1978. Author: Individual Retirement Arrangements, 1980, Downsizing, 1996. Mem. ABA (tax and labor rels. sect.), Calif. C. of C., Order of Coif, Ctrl. City Assn., Soc. Fellows of Huntington Libr., Calif. Club, L.A. Men's Garden Club. Avocations: travel, horticulture, wine, music, art. Home: 280 California Ter Pasadena CA 91105-1515 Office: Paul Hastings Janofsky & Walker LLP 555 S Flower St Fl 23 Los Angeles CA 90071-2300

LIPSON, MELVIN ALAN, technology and business management consultant; b. Providence, June 1, 1936; s. Nathan and Esta (Blumenthal) L.; m. Jacqueline Ann Barclay, July 2, 1961; children: Donna, Robert, Michelle, Judith. BS, U. R.I., 1957; PhD, Syracuse U., 1963. Chemist ICI Organics, Providence, 1963, Philip A. Hunt Chem. Co., Lincoln, R.I., 1964-67, rsch. mgr., 1967-69; tech. dir. Dynachem div. Morton Thiokol Inc., Tustin, Calif., 1969-72, v.p., 1979-82, sr. v.p., 1972-82, Tustin, 1982-85, exec. v.p., 1985-86, pres., 1986-89; v.p. tech. devel. Morton Internat. Inc., Chgo., 1989-92; pres. Lipson Assocs., Newport Beach, Calif., 1993—. Chmn. bd., CEO Aurelon, Inc., Huntington Beach, Calif., 1993-96, Pivotech., Inc., Newport Beach, Calif., 1996-98; CEO Meltex, Inc., Huntington Beach, Calif., 1998—. Home and Office: 1715 Plaza Del Sur Newport Beach CA 92661-1417

LISS, WALTER C., JR. television station executive; Pres., gen. mgr. WABC-TV, N.Y.C.; chmn. Buena Vista TV, Burbank, Calif., 1999—; pres. ABC owned TV stas. ABC, Inc. Office: ABC Inc 500 S Buena Vista St Burbank CA 91521-4472

LISSAUER, JACK JONATHAN, astronomy educator; b. San Francisco, Mar. 25, 1957; s. Alexander Lissauer and Ruth Spector. SB in Math., MIT, 1978; Phd in Applied Math., U. Calif., Berkeley, 1982. NAS-NRC resident rsch. assoc. NASA-Ames Rsch. Ctr., Moffett Field, Calif., 1983-85; asst. rsch. astronomer U. Calif., Berkeley, 1985, vis. rschr. dept. physics Inst. for Theoretical Physics Santa Barbara, 1985-87; asst. prof. astronomy program dept. earth and space scis. SUNY, Stony Brook, 1987-93, assoc. prof., 1993-96; space scientist NASA Ames Rsch. Ctr., 1996—. Rep. Univs. Space Rsch. Assn., SUNY, Stony Brook, 1987-96; vis. scholar dept. planetary scis. and lunar and planetary lab. U. Ariz., Tucson, 1990; guest prof. dept. physics U. Paris VII et Observatoire Paris, Meudon, France, 1990; mem. Lunar and Planetary Geoscis. Rev. Panel, 1989, 91, 99; vis. asst. rsch. physicist Inst. for Theoretical Physics, U. Calif., Santa Barbara, 1992, organizer Program on Plant Formation, 1992; rsch. assoc. Inst. d'Astrophysique, Paris, 1993; vis. scholar dept. astronomy U. Calif., Berkeley, 1994-95; adj. assoc. prof. SUNY, Stony Brook, 1996—; Yuval Ne'eman Distinguished Lectr. Geophysics, Atmosphere and Space Scis., Tel Aviv U., 2001. Planetary scis. editor New Astronomy Reviews; contbr. numerous articles on planet and star formation, extrasolar planets, spiral density wave theory, rotation of planets and comets to profl. jours. including Nature, Astron. Jour., Icarus, Sci., Astrophys. Jour. Letters, Astrophys. Jour., Jour. Geophys. Rsch., Astron. Astrophysics, Ann. Rev. Astron. Astrophysics, Revs. of Modern Physics. NASA Grad. student fellow, 1981-82, Alfred P. Sloan Found. fellow, 1987-91. Mem. Am. Astronomical Assn. (divsn. planetary scis., divsn. dynamical astronomy, Harold C. Urey prize divsn. planetary scis. 1992), Internat. Astronomical Union, Am. Geophys. Union. Achievements include research in planetary accretion, extrasolar planets, dynamics of planetary rings, cratering, binary and multiple star systems, circumstellar disks, resonances and chaos. Office: NASA Ames Rsch Ctr Space Sci Divsn 245-3 Moffett Field CA 94035

LIST, ERICSON JOHN, environmental engineering science educator, engineering consultant; b. Whakatane, New Zealand, Mar. 27, 1939; came to U.S., 1962; s. Ericson Bayliss and Freda Helen (Sunkel) L.; m. Olive Amoore, Feb. 3, 1962; children: Brooke Meredith, Antonia Michael. B.E. with honors, U. Auckland, N.Z., 1961, B.Sc., M.E., U. Auckland, 1962; Ph.D., Calif. Inst. Tech., 1965. Registered profl. engr., Calif., S.C. Sr. lectr. U. Auckland, 1966-69; asst. prof. Calif. Inst. Tech., Pasadena, 1969-72, assoc. prof., 1972-78, prof. environ. engrng. sci., 1978-97, exec. officer, 1980-85, prof. emeritus, 1997; pres. Flow Sci. Inc., Pasadena, 1997—. Bd. dirs. Environ. Def. Scis., Pasadena; bd. chmn. Flow Sci. Inc., Pasadena, 1983— ; cons. So. Calif. Edison, Rosemead, Calif., 1973— , City and County of San Francisco, 1974— Author: (with Hugo B. Fischer et al), Mixing in Inland and Coastal Waters, 1979, (with W. Rodi) Turbulent Jets and Plumes, 1982, (with Roscoe Moss Co.) Handbook of Ground Water Development, 1990. Mem. Blue Ribbon Commn. City of Pasadena, 1976-78. Recipient Spl. Creativity award NSF, 1982 Fellow ASCE (editor Jour. Hydraulic Engrng. 1984-89). Republican. Club: Athenaeum (Pasadena) (chmn. wine com. 1981-83). Office: Flow Sci Inc 723 E Green St Pasadena CA 91101-2111 E-mail: ejlist@flowscience.com

LISTON, ALBERT MORRIS, investor, administrator, educator; b. Aug. 6, 1940; s. Joseph Bostick and Hazel Marie (Smalley) L.; m. Angela Lynne Carbonatto, Jan. 1998. AB in Econs., U. Calif., Davis, 1963; MA in Govt., Calif. State U., Sacramento, 1970; postgrad., U. Calif., Santa Barbara, 1980—. Rsch. analyst polit. sci. dept. Ombudsman Activities Project, U. Calif., Santa Barbara, 1970-72; asst. prof. polit. sci. dept. CAlif. State U., Fullerton, 1973-79; investor, 1980—. Lt. Supply Corps, USNR, 1963-66. Mem. Kappa Sigma, Phi Kappa Phi. Democrat. Home: PO Box 8027 Missoula MT 59807-8027

LITEWKA, ALBERT BERNARD, communications and publishing company executive; b. N.Y.C., Feb. 5, 1942; s. Joel and Leah L. B.A. summa cum laude, UCLA, 1964; postgrad., U. Calif., Berkeley, 1964-65. Mgr. purchasing McGraw-Hill Book Co., N.Y.C., 1965-67; pres. Mktg. Innovations, Inc., N.Y.C., 1967-69; v.p. Westinghouse Leisure Time Industries, N.Y.C., 1972-75; exec. v.p. mktg. The Baker & Taylor Co. (W.R. Grace & Co.), N.Y.C., 1975-77; pres. Pix of Am. (W. R. Grace & Co.), N.Y.C., 1978; v.p. consumer services group W.R. Grace & Co., N.Y.C., 1977-79; pres. Macmillan Gen. Books div., N.Y.C., 1980-82; sr. v.p. Macmillan Pub. Co., Inc., 1980-82; pres. Warner Software, Inc., 1982-85; chmn., CEO Air Creative Group, Los Angeles and N.Y.C., 1986-98, Creative Domain, Inc., Los Angeles, Calif., 1991—. Author: Warsaw: A Novel of Resistance, 1989. Internat. Ladies Garment Workers Union Nat. scholar, 1959-64, U. Calif. Regents scholar, 1959-64; Woodrow Wilson Nat. Grad. fellow, 1964-65; recipient 1st prize Acad. Am. Poets, 1964 Mem. Am. Film Inst., Third Decade Coun., Authors Guild, Authors League Am., Acad. TV Arts & Scis. Office: Creative Domain Inc 9000 W Sunset Blvd Fl 9 Los Angeles CA 90069-5801

LITMAN, ROBERT BARRY, physician, writer, television and radio commentator; b. Phila., Nov. 17, 1947; s. Benjamin Norman and Bette Etta (Saunders) L.; m. Niki Thomas, Apr. 21, 1985; children: Riva Belle, Nadya Beth, Caila Tess, Benjamin David. BS, Yale U., 1967, MD, 1970, MS, MPhil in Anatomy, 1972. Diplomate Am. Bd. Family Practice. Postdoct. rsch. fellow Am. Cancer Soc. Yale U., New Haven, 1970-73, USPHS fellow, 1974-75; resident in gen. surgery Bryn Mawr (Pa.) Hosp., 1973-74; pvt. practice in medicine and surgery Ogdensburg, N.Y., 1977-93, San Ramon, Calif., 1993—; mem. staff A. Barton Hepburn Hosp., 1977-93, John Muir Med. Ctr., 1993—, San Ramon Regional Med. Ctr., 1993—, also chmn. med. edn., chmn. dept. family practice, 1998-99. Commentator Family Medicine Stas. WWNY-TV and WTNY-Radio, TCI Cablevision, Contra Costa T.V.; moderator Ask the Dr.; clin. preceptor dept. family medicine State U. Health Sci. Ctr., Syracuse, 1978—. Author: Wynnefield and Limer, 1983, The Treblinka Virus, 1991, Allergy Shots, 1993; contbr. articles to numerous profl. jours. Pres. No. N.Y. chpt. AHA. Fellow Life Ins. med. Rsch. Fund, U. Coll. Hosp., U. London, 1969-70; recipient We. Access Video Excellence award, 1998, Bay Area Cable Excellence award, 1999, Telly award, 1999, 2000, 01. Fellow Am. Coll. Allergy, Asthma, and Immunology, Am. Acad. Family Physicians; mem. AMA (Physicians Recognition award 1970—), Calif. State Med. Assn., Alameda-Contra Costa County Med. Assn., Joint Coun. Allergy and Immunology, Nat. Assn. Physician Broadcasters (charter), Acad. Radio and TV Health Communicators, Book and Snake Soc., Gibbs Soc. Yale U. (founder), Sigma Xi, Nu Sigma Nu, Alpha Chi Sigma. Home and Office: PO Box 1857 San Ramon CA 94583-6857 E-mail: roblitmanmd@drlitman.com

LITT, IRIS FIGARSKY, pediatrics educator; b. N.Y.C., Dec. 25, 1940; d. Jacob and Bertha (Berson) Figarsky; m. Victor C. Vaughan, June 14, 1987; children from previous marriage: William M., Robert B. AB, Cornell U., 1961; MD, SUNY, Bklyn., 1965. Diplomate Am. Bd. Pediatrics (bd. dirs. 1989-94), sub-specialty bd. cert. in adolescent medicine. Intern, then resident in pediat. N.Y. Hosp., N.Y.C., 1965-68; assoc. prof. pediat. Stanford U. Sch. Medicine, Palo Alto, Calif., 1982-87, prof., 1987—, dir. divsn. adolescent medicine, 1976—, dir. Inst. for Rsch. on Women and Gender, 1990-97. Editor Jour. Adolescent Health; contbr. articles to profl. jours including Jour. Am. Med. Assn., Pediatrics. Mem. Soc. for Adolescent Medicine (charter), Am. Acad. Pediatrics (award sect. on adolescent health), Western Soc. Pediatric Rsch., Soc. Pediatric Rsch., Am. Pediatric Soc., Inst. of Medicine/NAS. Office: 750 Welch Rd Ste 325 Palo Alto CA 94304-1510 E-mail: iris.litt@stanford.edu

LITTLE, BRIAN FREDERICK, oil company executive; b. Moncton, N.B., Can., Oct. 28, 1943; s. George E. and Marion M. (McCartney) L.; m. Dianne E. Rogers, Oct. 11, 1969; children: Michael William, Sara Elizabeth. BA, Am. Internat. Coll., 1966; LLB, Osgoode Hall Law Sch., 1974; LLM, London Sch. Econs., Eng., 1975. Indsl. devel. asst. Can. Nat., Moncton and Montreal, Can., 1967-71; articling student McMillan Binch, Toronto, Ont., Can., 1975-76, assoc. Can., 1977-82, ptnr. Can., 1982-83; v.p., gen. counsel Dome Petroleum, Calgary, Alta., Can., 1983-88; v.p. law and external affairs BP Can. Energy Co., Calgary, 1988-89; sr. v.p. law Amoco Can. Petroleum Co. Ltd., Calgary, 1989-92, sr. v.p. law, gen. counsel, 1992—, gen. counsel, corp. sec., 1997—, BP Can. Energy Co., Calgary, 1999—. Trustee Can. Athletic Found. Mem. Can. Bar Assn., Law Soc. Upper Can., Law Soc. Alta., Osgoode Hall Law Sch. Alumni Assn. (bd. dirs.). Office: Amoco Can Petroleum Co Ltd 240 Fourth Ave SW Calgary AB Canada T2P 4H4

LITTLE, CAROLE, women's apparel company executive; Co-founder CL Cinema Line Films Corp., L.A.; co-founder, co-chmn. Calif. Fashion Industries, Inc., L.A. Guest design tchr. Parson's Sch. Design, N.Y.C., L.A.; contbg. designer Divine Design; sponsor many benefit fashion shows; guest designer Acad. Awards; costume designer feature film. Co-prodr. Anaconda, 1997. Mem. bds. Calif. Am. Women's Econ. Devel., Women Inc., The Trusteeship; hon. co-chair mus. Fashion Designers and Creators; mem. Pres. Circle, L.A. County Mus. Art; found. mem. Internat. House of Blues Found. Named One of Leading Women Entrepreneurs of World, Nat. Found. Women Bus. Owners, Paris, 1997. Office: CL Fashions Corp 4505 Bandini Blvd Los Angeles CA 90040-2008

LITTLE, CHARLES GORDON, radiophysicist; b. Liuyang, Hunan, China, Nov. 4, 1924; s. Charles Deane and Caroline Joan (Crawford) L.; m. Mary Zughaib, Aug. 21, 1954; children: Deane, Joan, Katherine, Margaret, Patricia. BSc with honors in Physics, U. Manchester, Eng., 1948; PhD in Radio Astronomy, U. Manchester, 1952. Jr. engr. Cosmos Mfg. Co. Ltd., Enfield, Middlesex, Eng., 1944-46; jr. physicist Ferranti Ltd., Manchester, Lancashire, Eng., 1946-47; asst. lectr. U. Manchester, 1952-53; prof. dept. geophysics U. Alaska, 1954-58, dep. dir. Geophys. Inst., 1954-58; cons. Ionosphere Radio Propagation Lab. U.S. Dept. Commerce Nat. Bur. Standards, Boulder, Colo., 1958-60, chief Upper Atmosphere and Space Physics divsn., 1960-62, dir. Central Radio Propagation Lab., 1962-65; dir. Inst. Telecommunication Sci. and Aeronomy, Environ. Sci. Services Adminstrn., Boulder, 1965-67; dir. Wave Propagation Lab. NOAA (formerly Environ. Sci. Services Adminstr.), Boulder, 1967-86; sr. UCAR fellow Naval Environ. Prediction Research Facility, Monterey, Calif., 1987-89; George J. Haltiner rsch. prof. Naval Postgrad. Sch., Monterey, 1989-90. Author numerous sci. articles. Recipient U.S. Dept. Commerce Gold medal, 1964, mgmt. and sci. research awards NOAA, 1969, 77, Presdl. Meritorious Exec. award, 1980. Fellow IEEE, Am. Meteorol. Soc. (Cleveland Abbe award 1984); mem. NAE, AIAA (R.M. Losey Atmos. Sci. award 1992). Address: 4907 Country Club Way Boulder CO 80301-3656 E-mail: cglitt@aol.com

LITTLE, LOREN EVERTON, musician, ophthalmologist; b. Sioux Falls, S.D., Oct. 28, 1941; s. Everton A. and Maxine V. (Alcorn) L.; m. Christy Gyles; 1 child, Nicole Moses; children from previous marriage: Laurie, Richard. BA, Macalester Coll., 1963; BS, U. S.D., 1965; MD, U. Wash., 1967. Prin. trumpeter Sioux Falls Mcpl. Band, 1956-65; trumpeter St. Paul Civic Orch., 1960-62; leader, owner Swinging Scots Band, St. Paul, 1960-63; trumpeter Edgewater Inn Show Room, Seattle, 1966-67, Jazztet-Arts Council, Sioux Falls, 1970-71, Lee Maxwell Shows, Washington, 1971-74; residency in ophthalmology Walter Reed Med. Ctr., Washington, 1974; co-leader, trumpeter El Paso (Tex.) All Stars, 1975; freelance trumpeter, soloist various casinos and hotels, Las Vegas, Nev., 1977—. Trumpeter (album) Journey by R. Romero Band, 1983, Sizenter, 1997; soloist for numerous entertainers including Tony Bennett, Burt Bacharach, Jack Jones, Sammy Davis Jr., Henry Mancini, Jerry Lewis Telethon, for video Star Salute to Live Music, 1989; with Stan Mark Band Nat. Pub. Radio Broadcast, 1994, 95; soloist on video Stan Mark Live at the 4 Queens Hotel, Las Vegas; pres. S&L Music, S&L Records; prodr. Carl Saunders Debut Album Out Of the Blue, 1996, Eclecticism, 2000. Trustee Nev. Sch. of the Arts, Las Vegas, 1983—; pres. S&L Music SNL Rec. Served to lt. col. U.S. Army, 1968-76, Vietnam. Decorated Silver Star, Purple Heart, Bronze Star, Air medal; fellow Internat. Eye Found., 1974; Dewitt Wallace scholar Readers Digest, 1963-65. Fellow ACS, Am. Acad. Ophthalmology; mem. Am. Fedn. Musicians, Nat. Bd. Med. Examiners. Presbyterian. Avocations: history, music, medicine, sports, skiing.

LITTLE, RICH (RICHARD CARUTHERS LITTLE), comedian, impressionist, actor; b. Ottawa, Ont., Can., Nov. 26, 1938; s. Lawrence Peniston and Elizabeth Maud (Wilson) L. Ed., Lisgar Collegiate, Ottawa, 1953-57; student drama, Ottawa Little Theatre, 1950-60. First TV appearance in U.S. on Judy Garland Show, 1964; appearances films, TV, night clubs; host: TV series The Rich Little Show, 1975-76 (Winner Entertainer of Year award 1974), You Asked For It, 1981-83; appeared on TV series Love on a Rooftop, 1966-71, The John Davidson Show, 1969, ABC Comedy Hour, 1972, The Julie Andrews Hour, 1972-73; TV film appearance Dirty Tricks, 1981, Rich Little's Christmas Card, Rich Little's Washington Follies, Parade of Stars, The Christmas Raccoons, Rich Little and Friends in New Orleans, The Late Shift, 1996, (films) Bsetter Off Dead, 1985, One Crazy Summer, 1986, (voice) Bebe's Kids, 1992; others; rec. albums include My Fellow Canadians, The First Family Rides Again; appeared in films Dirty Tricks, 1981, Happy Hour, 1987. Recipient Maple Leaf Disting. Arts and Letters award, 1983. Office: William Morris Agy 151 S El Camino Dr Beverly Hills CA 90212-2775

LITTLE, WILLIAM ARTHUR, physicist, educator; b. South Africa, Nov. 17, 1930; came to U.S., 1958, naturalized, 1964; s. William Henry and Margaret (Macleod) L.; m. Annie W. Smith, July 15, 1955; children—Lucy Claire, Linda Susan, Jonathan William. Ph.D., Rhodes U., S. Africa, 1953, Glasgow (Scotland) U., , 1957. Faculty Stanford, 1958—, prof. physics, 1965-94; prof. emeritus, 1994—. Cons. to industry, 1960— ; co-founder, chmn. MMR Techs. Inc., 1980—, 3L&T, Inc., 1999—. Recipient Deans award for disting. teaching Stanford U., 1975-76, Walter J. Gores award for excellence in teaching, Stanford U., 1979, IR-100 award Indsl. Rsch. and Devel., 1981; NRC Can. postdoctoral fellow Vancouver, Can., 1956-58, Sloan Found. fellow, 1959-63, John Simon Guggenheim fellow, 1964-65, NSF sr. postdoctoral fellow, 1970-71 Fellow Am. Phys. Soc.; mem. Am. Chem. Soc. Achievements include spl. research low temperature physics, superconductivity, neural network theory cryogenics; holder 14 patents in area of cryogenics and med. instrumentation. Home: 15 Crescent Dr Palo Alto CA 94301-3106 Office: Stanford U Dept Physics Stanford CA 94305 E-mail: bill@mmr.com

LITTLEFIELD, EDMUND WATTIS, mining company executive; b. Ogden, Utah, Apr. 16, 1914; s. Edmond Arthur and Marguerite (Wattis) L.; m. Jeannik Mequet, June 14, 1945; children: Edmund Wattis, Jacques Mequet, Denise Renee. BA with great distinction, Stanford U., 1936, MBA, 1938. With Standard Oil Co. of Calif., 1938-41, Golden State Co., Ltd., 1946-50; v.p., treas. Utah Internat. Inc. (formerly Utah Constrn. & Mining Co.), San Francisco, 1951-56, exec. com., dir., 1951—, exec. v.p., 1956, gen. mgr., 1958—, pres., 1961—, chmn. bd., 1971—, chief exec. officer, 1971-78, chmn. exec. com., dir., 1978-86. Bd. dirs. SRI Internat., FMC Gold. Served as lt. (j.g.) USNR, 1941-43; spl. asst. to dep. adminstr. Petroleum Adminstrn. for War 1943-45. Recipient Ernest C. Arbuckle award Stanford Bus. Sch. Assn., 1970, Golden Beaver award, 1970, Bldg. Industry Achievement award, 1972, Harvard Bus. Statesman award, 1974, Internat. Achievement award World Trade Club, 1986, Lone Sailor award U.S. Naval Found., 1997; named to Nat. Mining Hall of Fame. Mem. San Francisco C. of C. (pres. 1956), Bus. Council (hon. mem., past chmn.), Conf. Bd., Phi Beta Kappa, Chi Psi. Clubs: Burlingame (Calif.) Country; Pacific Union, San Francisco Golf (San Francisco); Augusta National Golf, Eldorado Country; Bohemian, Cypress Point (Pebble Beach, Calif.); Vintage.

LITTLEJOHN, DAVID, writer; b. San Francisco, May 8, 1937; s. George Thomas and Josephine Mildred (Cullen) L.; m. Sheila Beatrice Hageman, June 10, 1963; children: Victoria Schoenke, Gregory David. BA, U. Calif., Berkeley, 1959; MA, Harvard U., 1961, PhD, 1963. Asst. prof. English, U. Calif., Berkeley, 1963-69, assoc. prof. journalism, 1969-76, prof., 1976-97, vice chmn. acad. senate, chmn. senate policy com., 1984-86, assoc. dean Grad. Sch. Journalism, 1974-78, 85-86, 87-89, prof. emeritus, 1997—. Arts critic Sta. KQED-TV, San Francisco, 1965-75, PBS nationwide, 1971-72; critic and corr. London Times, 1975-89, Architecture mag., 1984-89, Wall Street Jour., 1990—. Author: Architect: The Life and Work of Charles W. Moore, 1984, The Ultimate Art: Essays Around and About Opera, 1992,

The Fate of the English Country House, 1997, The Real Las Vegas, 1999, also 9 other books, over 300 articles and 200 TV programs. Fulbright lectr., Montpellier, France, 1966-67; Am. Coun. Learned Socs. rsch. fellow, London, 1972-73; NEH grantee 1976-77. Mem. Arts Club (Berkeley, sec.). Democrat. Roman Catholic. Home and Office: 719 Coventry Rd Kensington CA 94707-1403

LITTLE RICHARD, (RICHARD WAYNE PENNIMAN), recording artist, pianist, songwriter, minister; b. Macon, Ga., Dec. 5, 1932; s. Bud and Leva Mae Penniman; m. Ernestine Campbell, 1957 (div.). BA, Oakwood Coll. Sem., Huntsville, Ala., 1961. Ordained to ministry Seventh Day Adventist Ch., 1961. Began singing and dancing on streets of Macon, Ga., 1942; won talent shows in Atlanta, 1943 and 1951; toured with Dr. Hudson's Medicine Show and other shows, 1949-51; worked with own band doing dances and clubs, 1951-52, with Tempo Toppers in New Orleans, 1953-54; recording artist Peacock Records, Houston, 1953-54, Splty. Records, 1955-58, 64; toured in Big 10 Package shows, U.S., Australia and Gt. Brit., 1957-58; recording artist Veejay Records, 1964-65. Songs include Long Tall Sally, Tutti Frutti, Slippin' and Slidin', Rip it Up, Ready Teddy, Lucille, Send Me Some Lovin', Jenny, Jenny, Miss Ann, Keep A-Knockin', Good Golly Miss Molly, Baby Face, True Fine Mama, Kansas City, Bama Lama Bama Loo, Freedom Blues, Greenwood Mississippi; albums include Here's Little Richard, 1958, Little Richard 2, 1958, The Fabulous, 1959, Well Alright, 1959, Sings Gospel, 1964, Coming Home, 1964, Sings Freedom Songs, 1964, King of Gospel Songs, 1965, Wild & Frantic, 1965, The Explosive, 1967, The Explosive & Roy Orbison, 1970, The Rill Thing, 1971, King of Rock N Roll, 1971, Second Coming, 1971, All Time Hits, 1972, Rock Hard Rock Heavy, 1972, The Very Best Of, 1975, Georgia Peach, 1980, Get Down With It, 1982, Ooh! My Soul, 1983, Lucile, 1984, Shut Up, 1988, The Specialty Sessions, 1990, Greatest Songs, 1995, Mega-Mix, 1995; film appearances include The Girl Can't Help It, 1956, Don't Knock the Rock, 1957, She's Got It, 1957, Mr. Rock and Roll, 1957, Jimi Plays Berkeley, 1970, Let the Good Times Roll, 1973, Jimi Hendrix, 1973, Down and Out in Beverly Hills, 1985 Chuck Berry Hail! Hail! Rock 'n' Roll, 1987, Purple People Eater,, 1988, Scenes from the Class Struggle in Beverly Hills, 1989, Magic Years, Vols. 1-3, 1989, Sunset Heat, 1991, The Naked Truth, 1992, The Last Action Hero, 1993, The Pickle, 1993, The History of Rock 'n' Roll, Vol. 1, 1995, Why Do Folls Fall in Love, 1998, Mystery, Alaska, 1999; TV appearances include Tonight Show, Merv Griffin Show, Mike Douglas Show, Smothers Brothers Show, American Bandstand, Glen Campbell Good Time Hour, Tom Jones Show, Midnight Special, Donny & Marie Show, The Godess of Love, 1988, Mother Goose Rock 'n' Rhyme, 1990, Happy Birthday Bugs!: 50 Looney Years, 1990, Columbo: Columbo & the Murder of a Rock Star, Sinatra: 80 Years My Way, 1995, The Late Shift, 1996, The Fifties, 1997, Motown 40: The Music is Forever, 1998, Hollywood Squares, 1998; stage appearances include Paramount Theatre, The Felt Forum, Wembley Stadium, Hollywood Paladium. Inducted Rock & Roll Hall of Fame. Office: PO Box 29 Hollywood CA 90078-0029

LITTMAN, IRVING, forest products company executive; b. Denver, Apr. 21, 1940; s. Maurice Littman and Cecile P. Zohn.; m. Gertrude Pepper, Aug. 16, 1964; children: Margaret R., Michael J., Elizabeth B. BS in Engring. (Applied Math.), U. Colo., 1964; MBA, U. Chgo., 1966. Mgr. corp. sys. Boise Cascade Corp., Idaho, 1966-68, corp. mgr. budgeting, 1968-71, asst. to pres., 1971-73, asst. contr. realty group Calif., 1973-76, dir. investor rels. Boise, 1976-84, treas., 1984-86, v.p., treas., 1986—. Bd. dirs. Idaho Humanities Coun., Boise, 1985-88, vice chair, 1987-88; trustee Boise H.S. Band Scholarship Endowment, 1987—; trustee Boise Art Mus., 1996—, treas., 1998—; referee US Soccer Fedn., 1982—; investment com. Idaho Cmty. Found., 1989—, chmn. investment com., 1991—, treas., 1997—. With U.S. Army, 1958-59. Mem. Bogus Basin Ski Area Assn. (bd. dirs. 1988-97, treas. 1989-94, vice-chmn. 1991-94, chmn. 1994-96), Treas. Club San Francisco, Fin. Execs. Inst., Crane Creek Country Club, Arid Club (Boise). Office: Boise Cascade Corp PO Box 50 Boise ID 83728-0050

LITTMAN, RICHARD ANTON, psychologist, educator; b. N.Y.C., May 8, 1919; s. Joseph and Sarah (Feinberg) L.; m. Isabelle Cohen, Mar. 17, 1941; children— David, Barbara, Daniel, Rebecca. AB, George Washington U., 1943; postgrad., Ind. U., 1943- 44; PhD, Ohio State U., 1948. Faculty U. Oreg., 1948—, prof. psychology, 1959—, chmn. dept., 1963-68, vice provost acad. planning and resources, 1971-73. Vis. scientist Nat. Inst. Mental Health, 1958-59 Contbr. articles to profl. jours. Sr. postdoctoral fellow NSF, U. Paris, 1966-67; sr. fellow Nat. Endowment for Humanities, U. London, 1973-74; Ford Found. fellow, 1952-53; recipient U. Oreg. Charles H. Johnson Meml. award, 1980. Mem. APA, Western Psychol. Assn., Am. Psychol. Soc., Soc. Research and Child Devel., Psychonomics Soc., Animal Behavior Soc., Soc. Psychol. Study of Social Issues, Internat. Soc. Developmental Psychobiology, History of Sci. Soc., Am. Philos. Assn., AAUP, Sigma Xi. Home: 3625 Glen Oak Dr Eugene OR 97405-4736 Office: U Oreg Dept Psychology Eugene OR 97403

LITVACK, SANFORD MARTIN, lawyer; b. Bklyn., Apr. 29, 1936; s. Murray and Lee M. (Korman) L.; m. Judith E. Goldenson, Dec. 30, 1956; children: Mark, Jonathan, Sharon, Daniel. BA, U. Conn., 1956; LLB, Georgetown U., 1959. Bar: N.Y. 1964, D.C. 1979. Trial atty. antitrust div. Dept. Justice, Washington, 1959-61, asst. atty. gen., 1980-81; asso. firm Donovan, Leisure, Newton & Irvine, N.Y.C., 1961-69, ptnr., 1969-80, 81-86, Dewey, Ballantine, Bushby, Palmer & Wood, N.Y.C., 1987-91; vice chmn. bd. The Walt Disney Co., Burbank, Calif., 1991—, also bd. dirs. Bd. dirs. Bet Tzedek. Fellow Am. Coll. Trial Lawyers; mem. ABA, Fed. Bar Coun., N.Y. State Bar Assn. (sec. antitrust sect. 1974-77, chmn. antitrust sect. 1985-86), Va. Bar Assn., Calif. Inst. of Arts (bd. dirs.), Am. Arbitration Assn. (bd. dirs.). Office: The Walt Disney Co 500 S Buena Vista St Burbank CA 91521-0006

LITWACK, LEON FRANK, historian, educator; b. Santa Barbara, Calif., Dec. 2, 1929; s. Julius and Minnie (Nitkin) L.; m. Rhoda Lee Goldberg, July 5, 1952; children: John Michael, Ann Katherine. BA, U. Calif., Berkeley, 1951, MA, 1952, PhD, 1958. Asst. prof., then assoc. prof. history U. Wis., Madison, 1958-65; mem. faculty U. Calif., Berkeley, 1965—, prof. history, 1971—, Alexander F. and May T. Morrison prof. history, 1987—; dir. NDEA Inst. Am. History, summer 1965. Vis. prof. U. S.C., 1975, Colo. Coll., Sept. 1974, 79, La. State U., 1985; Fulbright prof. Am. history U. Sydney, Australia, 1991, Moscow (USSR) State U., 1980; vis. lectr. Peking U., (China), 1982; Walter Lynwood Fleming lectr. La. State U., 1983; Wentworth scholar-in-residence U. Fla., Spring 1983; mem. Nat. Afro-Am. History and Culture Commn., 1981-83; mem. screening com. Fulbright Sr. Scholar Awards, 1983-86; bd. acad. advisors The American Experience Sta. WGBH-TV, 1986—, Africans in America, WGBH-TV, 1990-98; Ford Found. prof. So. studies U. Miss., 1989; mem. exec. com. of dels. Am. Coun. of Learned Socs., 1993-96. Author: North of Slavery: The Negro in the Free States, 1790-1860, 1961, Been in the Storm So Long: The Aftermath of Slavery, 1979, Trouble in Mind: Black Southerners in the Age of Jim Crow, 1998; (film) To Look for America, 1971; co-author: The United States, 1981, rev. edit., 1991, Without Sanctuary: Lynching Photography in America, 2000; editor: American Labor Movement, 1962, co-editor: Reconstruction, 1969, Black Leaders in the Nineteenth Century, 1988, Harvard Guide to African American History, 2001. Mem. Bradley Commn. on History in Schs., 1987-90, Schomburg Commn. for the Preservation of Black Culture; trustee Nat. Coun. for History Edn., 1990-96, mem. steering com. 1994 NAEP History Consensus Project; chair U. Calif. Acad. Senate Libr. Com. 1995-97. Served with AUS, 1953-55. Recipient Excellence in Teaching award U. Calif., Berkeley, 1967, 95, Disting. Tchg. award, 1971, 96. Mem. Orgn. Am. Historians (chmn. nominations bd. 1975-76, exec. bd. 1983-85, pres. 1986-87), Am. Hist. Assn. (chmn. program com. 1980-81), So. Hist. Assn., Soc. Am. Historians, Am. Acad. Arts and Scis., Am. Antiquarian Soc., U. Calif. Alumni Assn., Assn. for the Study African Am. Life and History, PEN Am. Ctr. Office: U Calif Dept History 3229 Dwinelle Hall Berkeley CA 94720-2550

LIU, CHEN-CHING, electrical engineering educator; b. Tainan, Taiwan, Dec. 30, 1954; came to the U.S., 1980; m. Judy Y. Chuvan; 1 child, Wendy. BSEE, Nat. Taiwan U., 1976, MSEE, 1978; PhD, U. Calif., Berkeley, 1983. Asst. prof. U. Wash., Seattle, 1983-87, assoc. prof., 1987-91, prof., 1991—. Program dir. NSF, Arlington, Va., 1994-95; Tokyo Electric Power chair U. Tokyo, 1991; prof. invite Swiss Fed. Inst. Tech., Lausanne, 1989. Editor: Engring. Intelligent Systems, 1993—; mem. editl. bd. Procs. of IEEE; assoc. editor: IEEE Trans. Circuits and Systems. Fellow IEEE; mem. Internat. Conf. on Intelligent System Application to Power Systems (steering com.), IEEE Power Engring. Soc. (chair history com. 1992—, mem. governing bd. 1992—). Achievements include pioneered artificial intelligence applications to power systems; development of theories for power system voltage dynamics, computational methods for power electronic circuits, knowledge engineering methods. Office: U Wash Dept Elec Engring Seattle WA 98195-0001

LIU, YOUNG KING, biomedical engineering educator; b. Nanjing, China, May 3, 1934; came to U.S., 1952; s. Yih Ling and Man Fun (Teng) L.; m. Nina Pauline Liu, Sept. 4, 1964 (div. July 1986); children— Erik, Tania; m. Anita Beeth, Aug. 14, 1994 (div. Aug. 2000). BSME, Bradley U., 1955; MSME, U. Wis.-Madison, 1959; PhD, Wayne State U., 1963. Cert. acupuncturist, Calif. Asst. prof. Milw. Sch. of Engring., 1956-59; instr. Wayne State U., Detroit, 1960-63; lectr. then asst. prof. U. Mich., Ann Arbor, 1963-69; assoc. prof. then prof. Tulane U., New Orleans, 1969-78; prof. biomed. engring., dir. dept. U. Iowa, Iowa City, 1978-93; pres. U. No. Calif., Petaluma, 1993—; interim pres., CEO Calif. Coll. Podiatric Medicine, 2000-2001. Contbr. articles to profl. jours., chpts. to books NIH spl. research fellow, 1968-69; recipient Research Career Devel. award NIH, 1971-76 Mem. Internat. Soc. Lumbar Spine (exec. com., ctrl. U.S. rep. 1983-88), Orthopedic Research Soc., Am. Soc. Engring. Edn., Sigma Xi Democrat E-mail: admits@uncm.edu, ykingliu@yahoo.com

LIVERMORE, ANN M. computer company executive; BA in Econ., U. N.C.; MBA, Stanford U. From mem. staff to pres., corp. v.p. Hewlett-Packard Co., Palo Alto, Calif., 1982-1995, corp. v.p., 1995—, pres., CEO enterprise computing divsn., 1998—, pres. enterprise computing divsn. Bd. dirs. UPS; bd. visitors Kenan-Flagler Bus. Sch. U. N.C., Chapel Hill. Office: Hewlett Packard Enterprise Computing 100 Mayfield Ave Mountain View CA 94043-4158

LIVERMORE, JOHN S. geologist; Founder Pub. Resource Assocs., Reno. Recipient Daniel C. Jackling award Soc. for Mining, Metallurgy and Exploration, 1996, Disting. Nevadan award U. Nev., 1997; named to Nat. Mining Hall of Fame, 2000. Office: Pub Resource Assocs 1755 E Plumb Ln Ste 170 Reno NV 89502-3683

LIVESAY, THOMAS ANDREW, museum administrator, lecturer; b. Dallas, Feb. 1, 1945; s. Melvin Ewing Clay and Madge Almeda (Hall) L.; m. Jennifer Clark, June 15, 1985 (div.); 1 child, Russell; m. Amanda Haralson, Nov. 12, 1994; children: Heather Marie, Seth Stover. BFA, U. Tex., Austin, 1968, MFA, 1972; postgrad., Harvard U. Inst. Arts Adminstrn., 1978. Curator Elisabet Ney Mus., Austin, 1971-73; dir. Longview (Tex.) Mus. and Arts Center, 1973-75; curator Amarillo (Tex.) Art Center, 1975-77, dir., 1977-80; asst. dir. for adminstrn. Dallas Mus. Fine Arts, 1980-85; dir. Mus. of N.Mex., Santa Fe, 1985-2000, Whatcom Mus. History and Art, Bellingham, Wash., 2000—. Mem. touring panel Tex. Commn. Arts; mem. panel Nat. Endowment Arts, Inst. Mus. Svcs.; adj. prof. U. Okla., Coll. Liberal Studies, 1992—, U. N.Mex., 1992—; chmn. N.Mex. State Records and Archives Commn., 1986—. Author: Young Texas Artists Series, 1978, Made in Texas, 1979; editor: video tape American Images, 1979, Ruth Abrams, Paintings, 1940-85, NYU Press. Served with U.S. Army, 1969-71. Mem. Am. Assn. Mus. (coun. 1986-89, commn. on ethics 1992—, accreditation commn. 1994—, chmn. acreditation commn. 1997—), Tex. Assn. Mus. (v.p. 1981, pres. 1983), Rotary. Presbyterian. Office: Whatcom Mus History & Art 121 Prospect St Bellingham WA 98225 E-mail: tlivesay@cob.org

LIVINGSTON, JOHNSTON REDMOND, manufacturing executive; b. Foochow, China, Dec. 18, 1923; s. Henry Walter V and Alice (Moorehead) L.; m. Caroline Johnson, Aug. 17, 1946 (dec.); children: Henry, Ann, Jane, David; m. Patricia Karolchuck, Sept. 4, 1965. BS in Engring. with honors, Yale U., 1947; MBA with distinction, Harvard U., 1949. With Mpls.-Honeywell Regulator Co., 1949-55; with Whirlpool Corp., 1956-66, v.p., until 1966, Redman Industries, Dallas, 1966-67; dir. Constrn. Tech., Inc., Dallas, 1967—, pres., chmn. bd. dirs. Denver, 1974-89; chmn. bd. dirs. Enmark Corp., Denver, 1979-90. Pres. Marcor Housing Sys., Inc., Denver, 1971-74. Past mem. industry adv. com. Nat. Housing Ctr.; bd. dirs., past pres. Nat. Home Improvement Coun.; pres., chmn. bd. dirs. Denver Symphony Assn., 1977-81; bd. dirs., past chmn. bd. dirs. Rocky Mountain Regional Inst. Internat. Edn.; trustee, pres. Bonfils-Stanton Found., Denver, 1979—; hon. trustee Inst. Internat. Edn., N.Y. Baker scholar Harvard U., 1949. Mem. Rocky Mountain World Trade Assn. (bd. dirs., past chmn. bd. dirs.), Denver Country Club, Yale Club N.Y., Sigma Xi, Tau Beta Pi. Home: PO Box 39484 Denver CO 80239-0484 Office: 5070 Oakland St Denver CO 80239-2724

LIVINGSTON, LOUIS BAYER, lawyer; b. N.Y.C., Dec. 12, 1941; s. Norman and Helen (Bayer) L.; m. Mari Livingston, Apr. 6, 1968; children: Diana, Alex, Ann. BA, Yale U., 1963; LLB, Harvard U., 1966. Bar: N.Y. 1967, Oreg. 1971. Atty. NLRB, Memphis, 1967-68, Poletti, Freidin et al., N.Y.C., 1968-71; ptnr. Miller Nash LLP, Portland, Oreg., 1971—. Office: Miller Nash LLP 111 SW 5th Ave Ste 3400 Portland OR 97204-3655

LIVINGSTON, STANLEY C. architect; BArch, U. So. Calif., 1961; student, U. Calif., San Diego. Lic. architect Calif., N.Mex., Nev., Ariz., Colo., Ky.; cert. Nat. Coun. Archtl. Registration. Prin. Salerno/Livingston Architects, San Diego. Lectr. numerous instns. Archtl. projects include Residence Hall Tower & Multi Purpose Bldg. San Diego State U., Pacific Southwest Airlines Adminstrv. Offices & Hangar Facility, Fujitsu Microelectronics, Inc., Belden Village Low Income Sr. Housing Project, Atkinson Marine Corp. Hdqs. & Ship Repair Facility, Campbell Industries, Islandia Hotel Tower, Marlin Club, Sportfishing Facility and 500 Boat Marina, Branch Libr., Belmont Park Master Plan, Expert Witness Projects; other comml. projects include U.S. Fin. Office Bldg., Lake Murray Office Bldg., San Diego Fed. Branch Bank (5 locations), Nat. U. Office Bldg., Harbor Boat & Yacht Shipyard Renovation, Pacific Southwest Airlines Passenger Lounges & Gates (2 locations), and others. Symposia chmn. "Frank Lloyd Wright-Living in the Wright Century...An Evaluation" San Diego Archtl. Found./San Diego Mus. Art, 1990; mem. design competition adv. panel Balboa Park Organ Pavilion Parking Garage, 1990; mem. urban design com. San Diego Centre City, 1982-86; founder Orchids and Onions Program, 1976, com. chmn. 1984, jury chmn. 1985; chmn. design adv. com. San Diego Center City Devel. Corp., 1980. Fellow AIA (San Diego chpt., past pres. 1978-79, chmn. urban design com. 1978-86, chmn. task force Balboa Pk. master plan); mem. Am. Planning Assn. (mem. bd. dirs. San Diego 1981-82), Soc. Mktg. Profl. Svcs., Am. Arbitration Assn. (mem. panel arbitrators 1988—), Urban Land Inst. (assoc.), Urban Design & Planning Com., Bldg. Industry Assn. (mem. construction quality com.), Community Assn. Inst., San Diego Archtl. Found. (bd. dirs.), SCARAB. Office: Salerno Livingston Architects 363 5th Ave Fl 3 San Diego CA 92101-6965

LIVSEY, HERBERT C. lawyer; b. Salt Lake City, Aug. 20, 1941; BS, U. Utah, 1967, JD, 1969; LLM in Taxation, NYU, 1971. Bar: Utah 1969. Shareholder, fin. dir. Ray, Quinney & Nebeker P.C., Salt Lake City, 1969—. Assoc. editor: Utah Law Review, 1968-69; graduate editor: Tax Law Review, 1970-71. Fellow Am. Coll. Trust and Estate Counsel; mem. Utah State Bar Assn. (chmn. tax sect. 1978-79), Order of the Coif, Phi Kappa Phi, Delta Theta Phi. Office: Ray Quinney & Nebeker PC PO Box 45385 Salt Lake City UT 84145-0385

LIVSEY, ROBERT CALLISTER, lawyer; b. Salt Lake City, Aug. 7, 1936; s. Robert Frances and Rosezella Ann (Callister) L.; m. Renate Karla Guertler, Sept. 10, 1962; children: Scott, Rachel, Daniel, Benjamin. BS, U. Utah, 1962, JD, 1965; LLM, NYU, 1967. Bar: Utah 1965, Calif. 1967. Prof. Haile Selassie U., Addis Ababa, Ethiopia, 1965-66; spl. asst. to chief counsel IRS, Washington, 1977-79; assoc., then ptnr. Brobeck, Phleger & Harrison, San Francisco, 1967—. Adj. prof. U. San Francisco Law Sch., 1970-77; mem. adv. com. IRS Dist. Dirs., 1986-89; mem. western region liason com IRS (chmn. 1989). Research editor U. Utah Law Rev., 1964-65; editor Tax Law Rev., 1966-67; contbr. articles to profl. jours. Bd. dirs. Gilead Group, 1986-88, East Bay Habitat for Humanity, 1987-88, Morning Song, 1992-94. Mem. ABA (chmn. subcom. real estate syndications 1981-84), State Bar Calif. (chmn. taxation sect. 1984-85), San Francisco Bar Assn. (chmn. taxation sect. 1982), Am. Coll. Tax Counsel, Am. Law Inst., Tax Litigation Club (pres. 1986-87), Order of Coif, Beta Gamma Sigma. Democrat. Mem. Evangelical Covenant Ch. Club: Commonwealth (San Francisco). Home: 128 La Salle Ave Piedmont CA 94610-1233 Office: Brobeck Phleger & Harrison 1 Market Plz Fl 31 San Francisco CA 94105-1100 E-mail: rlivsey@brobeck.com

LLAURADO, JOSEP G. nuclear medicine physician, scientist; b. Barcelona, Spain, Feb. 6, 1927; s. José and Rosa (Llaurado) Garcia; m. Deirdre Mooney, Nov. 9, 1966; children: Raymund, Wilfred, Mireya; m Catherine D. Entwistle, June 28, 1958 (dec.); children: Thadd, Oleg, Montserrat. BS, BA, Balmes Inst., Barcelona, 1944; MD, Barcelona U., 1950, PhD in Pharmacology, 1960; MSc in Biomed. Engring., Drexel U., 1963. Diplomate Am. Bd. Nuclear Medicine. Resident Royal Postgrad. Sch. Medicine, Hammersmith Hosp., London, 1952-54; fellow M.D. Anderson Hosp. and Tumor Inst., Houston, 1957-58, U. Utah Med. Coll., Salt Lake City, 1958-59; asst. prof. U. Otago, Dunedin, New Zealand, 1954-57; sr. endocrinologist Prizer Med. Rsch. Lab., Groton, Conn., 1959-60; assoc. prof. U. Pa., Phila., 1963-67; prof. Med. Coll. Wis., Milw., 1970-82, Marquette U., Milw., 1967-82; clin. dir. nuclear medicine svc. VA Med. Ctr., Milw., 1977-82; chief nuclear medicine svc. VA Hosp., Loma Linda, Calif., 1983—; prof. dept. radiation svcs. Loma Linda U. Sch. Medicine, 1983—. U.S. rep. symposium on dynamic studies with radioisotopes in clin. medicine and rsch. IAEA, Rotterdam, The Netherlands, 1970, Knoxville, Tenn., 1974. Hon. editor Internat. Jour. Biomed. Computing; dep. editor Environ Mgmt. and Health; contbr. numerous articles to profl. jours. Merit badge counselor Boy Scouts Am., 1972—; pres. Hales Corners (Wis.) Hist. Soc., 1981-83. Recipient commendation cert. Boy Scouts Am., 1980, Joan d'AlÒs prize Cardiovasc. Ctr. St. Jordi, Barcelona, 1999, XII Batista-Roca prize Inst. Exterior Projection of Catalan Culture, 2000. Fellow Am. Coll. Nutrition; mem. IEEE (life), Royal Acad. Medicine of Catalonia/Barcelona, Soc. Nuc. Medicine (computer and acad. couns.), IEEE in Medicine and Biology Soc. (nat. adminstrv. com. 1986-89), Biomed. Engring. Soc. (charter), Am. Physiol. Soc., Am. Soc. Pharmacology and Exptl. Therapeutics, Soc. Math. Biology (founding), Endocrine Soc., Am. Soc. Nuc. Cardiology, Soc. Catalana Biologia, Casal dels Catalans Calif. (pres. 1989-91)_, Calif. Med. Assn. (sci. adv. panel on nuc. medicine 1983—). Office: VA Hosp Nuclear Med Svc Rm 115 11201 Benton St Loma Linda CA 92357-0001

LLOYD, JOSEPH WESLEY, physicist, researcher; b. N.Mex., Jan. 31, 1914; s. William Washington and Mattie May (Barber) L.; m. Lenora Lucille Hopkins, Jan. 24, 1944 (dec. June 1969); 3 children (dec.); m. Ruth Kathryn Newberry, Nov. 19, 1988; children: Kathryn Ruth Jordan, Mary Evelyn Jordan. Student, Pan Am. Coll., 1942. Plumber, Pomona, Calif., 1951-57; plumber, pipefitter Marysville, 1957-79; ret., 1979. Ind. researcher in physics and magnetism, Calif., 1944—. With CAP, 1944-45. Mem. Ch. of Christ.

LLOYD, LLYN ALLAN, association executive; b. Evergreen Park, Ill., Jan. 14, 1938; s. Russell Donald and Gladys Marie (Bladholm) L.; m. Helen Elizabeth Main, Mar. 22, 1959; children: Leanne, Douglas, Bradley. BS in Pharmacy, Ohio No. U., 1960; MA in Pub. Adminstrn., Boise State U., 1980. Lic. pharmacist, Ohio, Idaho, Ariz. With various pharmacies, Ohio and Idaho, 1960-63; pharmacist, owner Arco (Idaho) Drug, 1963-76; pharmacist City of Boise, Idaho, 1976-82; exec. dir. Idaho Bd. Pharmacy, Boise, 1982-86, Ariz. State Bd. Pharmacy, Phoenix, 1986—. Chmn. Butte County unit ARC, Arco, Idaho, 1968-74; mem. forest adv. com. Challis (Idaho) Nat. Forest, 1969-72. Recipient A.H. Robbins Bowl of Hygiene award Challis Nat. Forest, 1973. Mem. Nat. Assn. Bds. Pharmacy (exec. com. 1986—), Ariz. Pharmacy Assn., Ariz. Soc. Hosp. Pharmacists (Svc. to Pharmacy award 1988), Rotary, Lions, Masons. Avocations: woodworking, rose growing, travel, fishing, golf. Home: 6030 W Kimberly Way Glendale AZ 85308-7614 Office: Ariz State Bd Pharmacy 5060 N 19th Ave Phoenix AZ 85015-3210

LLOYD, MICHAEL JEFFREY, recording producer; b. N.Y.C., Nov. 3, 1948; s. John and Suzanne (Lloyd) Sutton; m. Patricia Ann Varble, Sept. 6, 1980; children: Michael, Christopher, Jeni, Deborah. Student, U. So. Calif. V.p. artists and repertoire MGM Records, Inc., 1969-73; ind. record producer, 1973—; pres. Heaven Prodns., 1975—, Michael Lloyd Prodns., 1979—, Taines-Lloyd Film Prodns., 1984-85; music dir. TV series Happy Days; music dir. Kidsongs, Living Proof, NBC-TV movie, Kidsongs Videos; prodr. Love Lines, NBC-TV movie Swimsuit; pres., co-founder Studio M, Beverly Hills, Calif., 2000—. Guest lectr. UCLA, Pepperdine U.; judge Am. Song Festival. Composer: (music for feature films) Tough Enough, If You Could See What I Hear, Dirty Dancing, All Dogs Go to Heaven, (music and lyrics) Rudolph the Red Nose Reindeer- The Movie, 1998, Coyote Ugly, Driven, Angel Eyes; composer music for 8 Movies of the Week, 12 TV spls., 28 TV series and 42 feature motion pictures. Recipient 51 Gold Album awards, 25 Platinum Album awards, 26 Gold Single awards, 2 Platinum Single awards, 3 Grammy awards, 43 Chart Album awards, 100 Chart Single awards, 10 Broadcast Music Inc. awards, 1 Am. Music award, 1 Dove award, 2 Nat. Assn. of Record Mrnets. Mem. ASCAP (12 awards), SAG, NARAS, AFTRA, Am. Fedn. Musicians.

LLOYD, RAY DIX, health physicist; b. Mar. 10, 1930; s. Ray Ernest and Dixie (Penrose) L.; m. Louise Mortensen, July 10, 1954; children: Thomas R., Janna L. Brady, Alan T., Christopher R., Heather L. Smith. BS, U. Utah, 1954, MS, 1956, PhD, 1974; postgrad., U. Southwestern La., 1959, La. State U., 1960. Diplomate Am. Bd. Health Physics. Rsch. asst. radiobiology divsn. U. Utah, 1961, rsch. assoc. radiobiology divsn., 1961-64, rsch. instr. dept. anatomy, radiobiology divsn., 1964-74, rsch. assoc. prof. dept. pharmacology, radiobiology divsn., 1979-84, rsch. prof. dept. pharmacology, radiobiology divsn., 1984-92, part-time rsch. prof. Sch. Medicine, 1992—. Adj. asst. prof. dept. mech. engring. U. Utah, 1975-90; adj. prof. engring. U. Utah, 1997—, rsch. prof. radiology, 1998—; cons. in field;

mem. Nat. Coun. Radiation Protection and Measurements, 1980-92, consociate mem., 1992—; mem. radiol. health adv. com. Utah State Divsn. Health. Assoc. editor: (jour.) Health Physics, 1990-92; (book) Delayed Effects of Bone Seeking Radionuclides; reviewer: Radiation Rsch., Health Physics, Radiat. Protection, Internat. Jour. Radiation Biology, others; contbr. articles to profl. jours., chpts. to books; patentee radiation detector. M sgt. U.S. Army, 1948-52, Korea, 1951-52. Fellow Health Physics Soc.; mem. Am. Acad. Health Physics, Radiation Rsch. Soc., Health Physics Soc. (Great Salt Lake chpt.), Utah br. Am. Assn. for Lab. Animal Sci., Internat. Radiation Protection Assn., Sigma Xi, Phi Kappa Phi, Gamma Theta Upsilon. Office: U Utah Radiobiology 729 Arapeen Dr 2334 CAMT Salt Lake City UT 84108-1218

LLOYD, SHARON, marketing professional; Mgr. mktg. Raley's Bel Air, West Sacramento, Calif. Office: Raleys Bel Air 500 W Capitol Ave West Sacramento CA 95605-2696

LO, BERNARD, education educator; Prof. medicine, dir. med. ethics U. Calif. Office: U Calif Dept Medicine PO Box Cc-126 San Francisco CA 94143-0001

LOAR, PEGGY ANN, foundation administrator, museum administrator; b. Cin., May 14, 1948; d. Jerome Vincent and Elizabeth (Ranz) Wahl. BA in History of Art, U. Cin., 1970, MA in History of Art, 1971. Summer intern Met. Mus. Art, N.Y.C., 1968; curator edn. Indpls. Mus. Art, 1971-76, asst. to the dir., 1974-75, asst. dir., 1975-77; asst. dir. programs and policy Inst. Mus. Svcs., 1977-80; dir. Smithsonian Inst. Traveling Exhbn. Svc., Washington, 1980-87, Wolfsonian Found., Miami, Fla., 1987-96; exec. dir. Amer. Ctr. Wine, Food and Arts, Napa, Calif., 1996—. Lectr. art history U. Cin., 1970-71; lectr. art appreciation and criticism Ind. U., Purdue U., 1975-77; guest lectr. in field. Project dir.: The Art of Cameroon Exhibition Catalog, 1984, Treasures from the Smithsonian Inst. Exhibition Catalog, 1984, Paris Style 1900: Art Noveau Bing, 1986, Hollywood: Legend & Reality Exhibition Catalog, 1988. Travel grantee Japan Found., 1984; Swedish Inst. grantee; Aspen Inst. Humanistic Studies fellow, 1986-87, recipient Smithsonian Gold Medal for Disting. Service, 1987. Mem. Am. Assn. Museums (mus. ethics com. 1980), Internat. Coun. Museums (pres. U.S. nat. com., US dir.), Com. Internat. Musees d'Art Moderne. Avocations: biking, tennis, hiking, dogs. Office: COPIA Am Ctr Wine Food & Arts 1700 Soscol Ave Napa CA 94559-1347

LOARIE, THOMAS MERRITT, healthcare executive; b. Deerfield, Ill., June 12, 1946; s. Willard John and Lucile Veronica (Finnegan) L.; m. Stephanie Lane Fitts, Aug. 11, 1968 (div. Nov. 1987); children: Thomas M., Kristin Leigh Soule. BSME, U. Notre Dame, 1968; Student, U. Minn., 1969-70, U. Chgo., 1970-71, Columbia U., 1978. Registered profl. engr., Calif. Prodn. engr. Honeywell, Inc., Evanston, Ill., 1968-70; various positions Am. Hosp. Supply Co., Evanston, 1970-83, pres. Heyer-Schulte divsn., 1979-83; pres. COO Novacor Med. Corp., Oakland, Calif., 1984-85, also bd. dirs.; pres. ABA Bio Mgmt., Danville, 1985-87; chmn., CEO Keravision, Inc., Fremont, 1987-2001; founder, chmn., med. device CEO Roundtable, 1993—. Asst. prof. surgery Creighton U. Med. Sch., Omaha, 1986-94; guest lectr. Anderson Sch. Mgmt., U. Calif., L.A., 2001—; speaker in field. Contbr. articles on med. tech. and pub. policy to Wall St. Jour., others. Bd. dirs. Marymount Sch. Bd., 1981-84; bd. dirs. United Way Santa Barbara, 1981-84, assoc. chairperson, 1982-83, treas., 1983. Named One of 50 Rising Stars: Exec. Leaders for the 80's Industry Week mag., 1983. Mem. Assn. for Rsch. in Vision and Ophthalmology, Contact Lens Assn. Ophthalmology, Health Industry Mfrs. Assn. (spl. rep. bd. dirs. 1993-96, bd. dirs. 1997—, exec. com. 1997—, treas. 1998-00, chmn.-elect 2000—), Am. Entrepreneurs for Econ. Growth, Med. Tech. Leadership Forum, Calif. Healthcare Inst. (bd. dirs. 1998—, exec. com. 2000—). Roman Catholic. Achievements include leading development of Intacs corneal ring segments for treatment of nearsightedness (named One of Top 10 Medical Advances by Health Magazine/CNN 1999). Avocations: snow skiing, backpacking, oil painting, the arts. Office: KeraVision Inc 48630 Milmont Dr Fremont CA 94538-7353

LOBELL, JEANINE, cosmetics company executive; b. 1964; m. Anthony Edwards. Founder Stila Cosmetics, L.A., 1994—. Office: Stila Cosmetics 2801 Hyperion Ave Los Angeles CA 90027-2571

LOCATELLI, PAUL LEO, academic administrator; b. Santa Cruz, Calif., Sept. 16, 1938; s. Vincent Dino and Marie Josephine (Piccone) L. BS in Acctg., Santa Clara U., 1961; MDiv, Jesuit Sch. Theology, 1974; DBA, U. So. Calif., 1971. CPA, Calif.; ordained priest Roman Cath. Ch., 1974. Acct. Lautze & Lautze, San Jose, Calif., 1960-61, 73-74; prof. acctg. Santa Clara (Calif.) U., 1974-86, assoc. dean Bus. Scvh., acad. v.p., 1978-86, pres., 1988—. Bd. dirs. chair, Assn. Jesuit Colls. and Univs., JV:SV Network, NCCJ, Am. Leadership Forum Silicon Valley; bd. trustees Inst. for the Internat. Edn. of Students, Jesuit Sch. Theology, Berkeley; exec. com. Ind. Colls. and Univs. of Calif., adv. couns. Parents Helping Parents and Community Found.; past rector Jesuit Cmty. at Loyola Marymount U. Co-author: (assessment) The New Curriculum: A Guide to Professional Accounting, 1995. Past trustee U. San Francisco, Seattle U., St. Louis U., Loyola Marymount U., Regis U.; past mem. Sr. Commn. Western Assn. Schs. and Colls., Acctg. Edn. Change Commn. Mem. AICPA, Calif. Soc. CPAs (Disting. Prof. of the Yr. award 1994), Am. Acctg. Assn. Democrat. Office: Santa Clara U 500 El Camino Real Santa Clara CA 95053-0001

LOCHMILLER, KURTIS L. real estate entrepreneur; b. Sacramento, Dec. 30, 1952; s. Rodney Glen and Mary Margaret (Frauen) L.; m. Mariye Susan Mizuki, Nov. 9, 1951; children: Margaux Sian, Chase Jordan. BA in Econs. and Fin., U. Denver, 1975. Dist. sales mgr. Hertz Truck Div., Denver, 1975-76; drilling foreman Shell Oil, Alaska, Mont., Colo., 1976-79; pres., owner Kurtex Mortgage & Devel. Co., Denver, 1979—, Kurtex Properties Inc., Denver, 1980-86; pres., chief exec. officer Kurtex Inc., Denver, 1981—, Bankers Pacific Mortgage, Denver, 1980—, Bankers Fin. Escrow Corp., Denver, 1984—, Northwest Title & Escrow, Denver, 1984—. Pres., chief exec. officer Steamboat Title, Steamboat Springs, Colo., 1985—, First Escrow, Denver, 1986—, Fidelity-Commonwealth-Continental Escrow, Denver, 1984—; pres. Colonnade Ltd., Denver, 1981-88; pres., bd. dirs. Breckridge (Colo.) Brewery. V.p., founder Colfax on the Hill, Denver, 1984; mediator, arbitrator Arbitrator/Mediation Assn., Denver, 1986; mem. Police Athletic League, Denver, 1988. Recipient Pres. Spl. Achievement/Founder award Colfax on the Hill, Denver, 1984, Spl. Mayor's award, City & County of Denver, 1985. Mem. Nat. Assn.of Real Estate Appraisers, Internat. Brotherhood of Teamsters, Colo. Mortgage Bankers Assn., Mortgage Banking Assn., Denver C. of C., Phi Beta Kappa, Omicron Delta Epsilon. Clubs: U.S. Karate Assn. (Phoenix) (3d degree Black Belt), Ferrari (Portland). Lodge: Internat. Supreme Council Order of Demolay. Avocations: collecting cars, karate, fishing, art collecting. Home: 1 Carriage Ln Littleton CO 80121-2010 Office: Bankers Fin Escrow Corp 9655 E 25th Ave Ste 101 Aurora CO 80010-1056

LOCK, GERALD SEYMOUR HUNTER, retired mechanical engineering educator; b. London, June 30, 1935; arrived in Can., 1962, naturalized, 1973; s. George and Mary (Hunter) L.; m. Edna Burness, Sept. 19, 1959; children: Graeme, Gareth, Grenville. B.Sc. with honors, U. Durham, Eng., 1959, Ph.D., 1962. Asst. prof. mech. engring. U. Alta. (Can.), Edmonton, 1962-64, assoc. prof., 1964-70, prof., 1970-93, dean interdisciplinary studies, 1976-81; cons. mech. engr., Edmonton, 1993—. Chmn. Internat. Arctic Sci. Commn. Regional Bd., 1993-96. Vice chmn. Alta. Manpower Adv. Coun., 1979-84, chmn., 1984-89; chmn. Salvation Army Red Shield Appeal, 1980-82; bd. govs. Alta. Coll., chmn., 1982-85; founding pres. Alta. Poetry Festival Soc., 1981. Recipient Queen Elizabeth II Silver Jubilee medal, 1977 Fellow Engring. Inst. Can, Can. Soc. Mech. Engring. (pres. 1977-78), ASME; mem. Sci. Coun. Can., Can. Polar Commn. Mem. Progressive Conservative Party. Anglican. Home: 11711 83rd Ave Edmonton AB Canada T6G 0V2 Office: U Alta Edmonton AB Canada T6G 2G3

LOCKE, GARY, governor; b. Jan. 21, 1950; s. James and Julie Locke.; m. Mona Lee Locke, Oct. 15, 1994; children: Emily Nicole, Dylan James BA in Polit. Sci., Yale U., 1972; JD, Boston U., 1975. Dep. prosecuting atty. State of Wash., King County; mem. Wash. State Ho. of Reps., 1983-93; gov. State of Washington, 1996—. Cmty. rels. mgr. U.S. West; chief exec. King County, 1993. Named First in effectiveness among Puget Sound area lawmakers Seattle Times, 1990. Office: Office Gov PO Box 40002 Olympia WA 98504-0002*

LOCKE, VIRGINIA OTIS, writer; b. Tiffin, Ohio, Sept. 4, 1930; d. Charles Otis and Frances Virginia (Sherer) L. BA, Barnard Coll., 1953; MA in Psychology, Duke U., 1972, postgrad. Program officer, asst. corp. sec. Agrl. Devel. Coun., N.Y.C., 1954-66; staff psychologist St. Luke's-Roosevelt Med. Ctr., N.Y.C., 1973-75; freelance writer and editor N.Y.C., 1976-85; writer-editor Cornell U. Med. Coll./N.Y. Hosp. Med. Ctr., N.Y.C., 1986-89; sr. editor humanities and social scis. coll. divsn. Prentice Hall, Upper Saddle River, N.J., 1989-96; profl. writer behavioral scis., 1996—. Co-author: (coll. textbook) Introduction to Theories of Personality, 1985, The Agricultural Development Council: A History, 1989, (coll. textbook) Child Psychology: A Contemporary Viewpoint, 1999. Founder Help Our Neighbors Eat Yearround (H.O.N.E.Y.), Inc., N.Y.C., chmn., 1983-87, vol., 1987—, newsletter editor, 1992-97; reader Recording for the Blind, N.Y.C., 1978-84; vol. Reach to Recovery program Am. Cancer Soc., Bergen County, N.J., 1990-96. Recipient Our Town Thanks You award, N.Y.C., 1984, Mayor's Vol. Svc. award, N.Y.C., 1986, Cert. of Appreciation for Community Svc. Manhattan Borough, 1986, Jefferson award Am. Ins. Pub. Svc., Washington, 1986. Home and Office: 4620 Kester Ave Apt 214 Sherman Oaks CA 91403-2568 Fax: 818-728-6736. E-mail: ginnyol@mindspring.com

LOCKER, RAYMOND DUNCAN, editor; b. Dunkirk, N.Y., Apr. 15, 1960; s. Robert Smith and Margaret Ellen (Duncan) L.; m. Debbie Elizabeth Long, July 2, 1988 (div. Oct. 9, 1997); 1 child, Margaret Katherine. BA in Political Sci., U. Cin., 1982; MS in Journalism, Ohio U., 1984. Reporter Lake Wales Highlander, Lake Wales, Fla., 1982-83, The Montgomery Advertiser, Montgomery, Ala., 1985-87; political reporter The Tampa Tribune, Tampa, Fla., 1987-89, Washington corr., 1989-91, political columnist, 1991-93, night metro editor, 1993-94, political editor, 1994-97, sr. editor, 1997-2000; asst. city editor L.A. Times, 2000—. Panelist Tampa Bay Week, WEDU-TV, 1993-2000, Bayside, WTOG-TV, 1994-2000. Roman Catholic. Office: LA Times 93 S Chestnut St Ventura CA 93001-2807

LOCKLIN, PAUL G. executive; BS in Mktg., Calif. State U., Hayward. Rschr. color & chem. divsn. Hercules, Inc.; pres., CEO PCI, CIDCO, Morgan Hill, Calif., 1986-97, 98—. Office: 220 Cochrane Cir Morgan Hill CA 95037-2803

LOCKYER, BILL, state attorney general; b. Oakland, Calif., May 8, 1941; 1 child, Lisa. BA in Polit. Sci., U. Calif., Berkeley; cert. in sec. tchg., Calif. State U., Hayward; JD, U. of the Pacific. Past tchr., San Leandro, Calif.; Mem. Calif. State Assembly, 1973; state senator State of Calif., 1982; pres. pro tem, chmn. senate rules com., chmn. senate jud. com. Calif. State Senate, 1994-98; atty. gen. State of Calif., 1999—. Active San Leandro Sch. Bd., 1968-73. Past chair Alameda County Dem. Ctrl. Com. Named Legislator of Yr. Planning and Conservation League, 1996, Calif. Jour., 1997. Office: Office Atty Gen Dept Justice PO Box 944255 Sacramento CA 94244-2550

LODGE, EDWARD JAMES, federal judge; b. 1933; BS cum laude, Coll. Idaho, 1957; JD, U. Idaho, 1969. With Smith & Miller, 1962-63; probate judge Canyon County, Idaho, 1963-65; judge Idaho State Dist. Ct., 1965-88; U.S. bankruptcy judge State of Idaho, 1988; dist. judge, chief judge U.S. Dist. Ct. Idaho, 1989-99. Mem. Ninth Cir. Jud. Coun., 1997-98; chair Chief Dist. Judges for Ninth Cir., 1998-99. Recipient Kramer award for excellence in jud. adminstrn.; named three time All-Am., disting. alumnus Coll. Idaho, Boise State U., Professionalism award Idaho State Bar, 1997; named to Hall of Fame Boise State U., Coll. Idaho. Mem. Idaho Trial Lawyer Assn., Idaho State Bar Assn. (Professionalism award 1997), U.S. Fed. Judges Assn., Boise State Athletic Assn., Elks Club. Office: US Dist Ct MSC 040 550 W Fort St Fl 6 Boise ID 83724-0101

LODGE, PATTI ANNE, state senator; b. Pitts., July 29, 1942; m. Edward J. Lodge; children: Mary Jeanne, Edward, Anne Marie. BA, Maryhurst U., 1964. Edn. media specialist Caldwell Sch. Dist., 1968-99, edn. media coord., 1980-97; pres. Windridge Vineyards, 1987—; Rep. senator dist. 11 Idaho State Senate, 2000—. Del. Nat. Rep. Platform Com., 1996; cons. St. Paul's Sch., Our Lady of the Valley, 1999—. Chair Miss Rodeo Caldwell Com., 1964-80, Canyon County Reps., 1986-88, Nat. Fedn. GOP Women Resolutions, 1997-99, Day at the Legislature, 2000; dir. Idaho H.S. Rodeo Dist. # 3, 1970-78; precinct chair Canyon County Rep. Com. # 22, 1980-2000; chair bd. dirs. West Valley Med. Ctr., 1986; pres. Idaho Fedn. Rep. Women, 1991-96; bd. dirs. Idaho Cath. Found., 1992-2000; vol. Latino Voter Registration, 2000; chair Idaho Rep. Gala Celebration, 2000. Roman Catholic. Office: PO Box 96 Huston ID 83630 also: Idaho State Senate State Capitol 700 W Jefferson Boise ID 83720-0081 Fax: 208 459-7199

LOEB, RONALD MARVIN, lawyer; b. Denver, Sept. 24, 1932; s. Ellis and Lillian (Mosko) L.; m. Shirley Ross; children: Joshua Ross, Gabriel Ross, Daniel Seth, Jennifer Miriam, Rachel Sarah.. AB with highest honors, UCLA, 1954; LLB cum laude, Harvard U., 1959. Bar: Calif. 1960. Assoc. Irell & Manella, L.L.P, L.A., 1959-64, ptnr., 1964-97, of counsel, 1997-99; acting CEO Mattel, 2000; sr. v.p., gen. counsel Williams Sonoma, Inc., 1999—. Instr. Stanford Law Sch. Director's Coll., 2001, bd. dirs. Mattel, Inc., Ehama Inst.; course presenter The Esalen Inst., 1994; instr. corp. governance and social responsibility KVK Raju Internat. Leadership Acad., Hyderabad, India; task force on social cohesion sponsored by Danish Min. Pub. Affairs. Co-editor: Duties and Responsibilities of Outside Directors, 1978. Trustee Crossroads Sch. Arts and Scis., Santa Monica, Calif., 1987-99; past chmn. Pacific Crest Outward Bound Sch.; past founding trustee, dir. World Bus. Acad. Mem. ABA, State Bar Assn. Calif., Office: Williams Sonoma Inc 3250 Van Ness Ave San Francisco CA 94109 E-mail: rloeb@wsgc.com

LOEHMAN, RONALD ERNEST, materials scientist; b. San Antonio, Feb. 22, 1943; s. Roland Albert and Charlotte (Herweck) L.; m. Edna Tusak, June 26, 1965 (div. Oct. 1981), 1 child, Rachel Andrea; m. Ellen Louise Griffith, July 10, 1982; 1 child, Matthew Charles. BA, Rice U., 1964; PhD, Purdue U., 1969. Asst. prof. U. Fla., Gainesville, 1970-75, assoc. prof., 1975-78; sr. materials scientist SRI Internat., Menlo Park, Calif., 1978-82; mem. tech. staff Sandia Nat. Labs., Albuquerque, 1982-86, div. supr., 1986-87, mgr. chemistry and ceramics dept., 1987-92; co-dir. Advanced Materials Lab., Albuquerque, 1992—; nat. labs. disting. prof. U. N.Mex., 1992—; sr. scientist Sandia Nat. Labs., 1998—. Contbr. articles to profl. jours.; patentee in field. Mem. AAAS, Am. Ceramic Soc. (assoc. editor jour. 1988—, Roland Snow award 1984, Fulrath award 1988), Nat. Inst. Ceramic Engrs., Sigma Xi. Office: Advanced Materials Lab 1001 University Blvd SE Albuquerque NM 87106-4325

LOESCHER, RICHARD ALVIN, gastroenterologist; b. Brockton, Mass., Feb. 6, 1940; s. Vernon Alvin and Anna Marie (Good) L.; m. Linda Rockwell Clifford Loescher, June 5, 1965 (div. Jan. 1982); children: Steven Clifford Loescher, Laura May Loescher. BA, De Pauw U., 1961; MD cum laude, Harvard U., 1965. Diplomate Am. Bd. Internal Medicine, 1972, Am. Bd. Gastroenterology, 1973. Chief Med. Svc. U.S. Pub. Health Svc. Hosp., Lawton, Okla., 1967-69; chief Med. Staff, 1968-69; svc. unit dir., 1969; attending physician Seattle, 1970-71, U. Hosp., Seattle, 1970-71; active staff Sacred Heart Med. Ctr., Eugene, Oreg., 1973—, Eugene (Oreg.) Hosp., 1972-88; courtesy staff McKenzie-Williamette Hosp., Springfield, Oreg., 1982—. Recipient Rector scholarship DePauw U., 1957-61, Maimonides award Harvard Med. Sch., 1965. Mem. AMA, ACP-Am. Soc. Internal Medicine, Lane County Med. Soc., Oreg. Med. Assn., Am. Soc. for Gastrointestinal Endoscopy, Am. Acad. Med. Acupuncture, Alpha Omega Alpha, Phi Beta Kappa. Democrat. Unitarian. Avocations: physical fitness, personal growth, magic, outdoor activities. Home: 2345 Patterson St Apt 34 Eugene OR 97405-2974 Office: 1162 Willamette St Eugene OR 97401-3568

LOEWENSTEIN, WALTER BERNARD, nuclear power technologist; b. Gensungen, Hesse, Germany, Dec. 23, 1926; came to U.S., 1938; s. Louis and Johanna ((Katz) L.; m. Lenore C. Pearlman, June 21, 1959; children: Mark Victor, Marcia Beth. BS, U. Puget Sound, 1949; postgrad., U. Wash., 1949-50; PhD, Ohio State U., 1954. Registered profl. engr., Calif. Rsch. asst., fellow Ohio State U., Columbus, 1951-54; rsch. asst. Los Alamos Nat. Lab., 1952-54; sr. physicist, divsn. dir. Argonne (Ill.) Nat. Lab., 1954-73; dept. dir., dep. divsn. dir. Electric Power Rsch. Inst., Palo Alto, Calif., 1973-89, profl. cons., 1989—, mem. large aerosol containment experiment project bd., 1983-87. Mem. Marviken project bd. Studsvik Rsch. Ctr., Stockholm, 1978-85; mem. LOFT project bd. Nuclear Energy Agy., Paris, 1982-89; mem. tech. adv. com. nuclear safety Ontario Hydro Corp., 1990-98; mem. nuclear engring. dept. adv. com. Brookhaven Nat. Lab., 1992-96; mem. advanced tech. divsn. adv. com. Los Alamos Nat. Lab., 1994-99; mem. nuclear engring. dept. adv. com. U. Calif., Berkeley, 1994—. With USNR, 1945-46. Recipient Alumnus Cum Laude award U. Puget Sound, 1976. Fellow Am. Phys. Soc., Am. Nuclear Soc. (v.p., pres. 1988-90); mem. Am. Assn. Engring. Socs. (sec., treas. 1990), Nat. Acad. Engring. Jewish. Avocations: history, golf. Home and Office: 515 Jefferson Dr Palo Alto CA 94303 E-mail: wblo3@aol.com

LOFGREN, CHARLES AUGUSTIN, legal and constitutional historian, history educator; b. Missoula, Mont., Sept. 8, 1939; s. Cornelius Willard and Helen Mary (Augustin) L.; m. Jennifer Jenkins Wood, Aug. 6, 1986. AB with great distinction, Stanford U., 1961; AM, 1962, PhD, 1966. Instr. history San Jose State Coll., 1965-66; asst. prof. Claremont McKenna Coll., 1966-71; assoc. prof., 1971-76; prof., 1976—; Roy P. Crocker prof. Am. history and politics, 1976—. Author: Government form Reflection and Choice, 1986, The Plessy Case, 1988, Claremont Pioneers, 1996; contbr. articles to profl. jours. Served with USAR, 1957-63. Mem. Am. Soc. Legal History, Orgn. Am. Historians, Am. Hist. Assn. Republican. Roman Catholic. Office: Claremont McKenna Coll Dept History 850 Columbia Ave Claremont CA 91711-6420

LOFGREN, ZOE, congresswoman; b. San Mateo, Cailf., Dec. 21, 1947; d. Milton R. and Mary Violet Lofgren; m. John Marshall Collins, Oct. 22, 1978; children: Sheila Zoe Lofgren Collins, John Charles Lofgren Collins. BA in Polit. Sci., Stanford U., 1970; JD cum laude, U. Santa Clara, 1975. Bar: Calif. 1975, D.C. Adminstrv. asst. to Congressman Don Edwards, San Jose, Calif., 1970-79; ptnr. Webber and Lofgren, San Jose, 1979-81; mem. Santa Clara County Bd. Suprs., 1981-94, U.S. Congress from 16th Calif. dist., 1995—. Mem. com. on stds. of ofcl. conduct, jud. com., sci. com.; part-time prof. law U. Santa Clara, 1978-80. Exec. dir. Cmty. Housing Developers, Inc., 1979-80; trustee San Jose C.C. Dist., 1979-81; bd. dirs. Cmty. Legal Svcs., 1978-81, San Jose Housing Svc. Ctr., 1978-79; mem. steering com. sr. citizens housing referendum, 1978; del. Calif. State Bar Conv., 1979-82, Dem. Nat. Conv., 1976; active Assn. Immigration and Nationality Lawyers, 1976-82, Calif. State Dem. Ctrl. Com., 1975-78, Santa Clara County Dem. Ctrl. Com., 1974-78, Notre Dame H.S. Blue Ribbon Com., 1981-84, Victim-Witness Adv. Bd., 1981-94. Recipient Bancroft-Whitney award for Excellence in Criminal Procedure, 1973. Mem. Santa Clara County Bar Assn. (trustee 1979—), Santa Clara County Women Lawyers Com. (exec. bd. 1979-80), Santa Clara Law Sch. Alumni Assn. (v.p. 1977, pres. 1978), Nat. Women's Polit. Caucus, Assn. of Bay Area Govts. (exec. bd. 1981-86). Office: US Ho Reps 227 Cannon Ho Office Bldg Washington DC 20515-0516 also: 635 N 1st St Ste B San Jose CA 95112-5110*

LÖFSTEDT, BENGT TORKEL MAGNUS, classics educator; b. Lund, Sweden, Nov. 14, 1931; came to U.S., 1967; s. Ernst Martin Hugo and Sigrid (Johanson) L.; m. Maija-Leena Kekomäki, Oct. 15, 1961; children: Ragnar, Torsten, Ritva, Ingvar. M.A., U. Uppsala, Sweden, 1954, Fil. Lic. (Ph.D.), 1957, Fil. doktor, 1961. Asst. prof. Latin U. Uppsala, 1962-67; asso. prof. Mediaeval Latin U. Calif. at Los Angeles, 1967-68, prof., 1968—. Contbr. Swedish newspapers Fria Ord, Vägen Framät. Author: Studien Über die Sprache der langobardischen Gesetze, 1961, Der hibernolateinische Grammatiker Malsachanus, 1965, Zenonis Veronensis Tractatus, 1971, Ars Laureshamensis, 1977, Sedulius Scottus: In Donati artem minorem, in Priscianum, in Eutychem, 1977, Sedulius Scottus: in Donati artem miaorem, 1977, Ars Ambrosiana, 1982, Beatus Liebanensis: Adversus Elipandum, 1984 (with G.J. Gebauer) Bonifatius Ars Grammatica, 1980, (with L. Holtz and A. Kibre) Smaragdus: Liber in Partibus Donati, 1986, (with Leena Löfstedt) Maturin Cordier: De Corrupti Sermonis Emendatione, 1989, Sedulius Scottus: Kommentar zum Evangelium nach Matthäus 1,1-11,1, 1989, Sedulius Scottus: Kommentar zum Evangelium nach Matthäus, 11,2 bis Schluss, 1991, (with B. Bischoff) Anonymus ad Cuimnanum, 1992, Vier Juvenal-Kommentare aus dem 12. Jh., 1995, (with Scott Talkovic) Diego Valadés: Catholicae Assertiones, 1998, Ausgewählte Aufsätze, 2000, Hrabanus Maurus: Expositio in Matthaeum, 2000; contbr. articles to profl. jours. Served to lt. Swedish Army, 1959-60. Alexander von Humboldt-Stiftung fellow Munich, 1961-62; Humanities Inst., U. Calif. grantee, 1968, 71; Am. Philos. Soc. grantee, 1971, 74; Am. Council Learned Socs. grantee, 1972, 75 Lutheran. Office: UCLA Dept Classics 405 Hilgard Ave Los Angeles CA 90095-1417

LOFTFIELD, ROBERT BERNER, biochemistry educator; b. Detroit, Dec. 15, 1919; s. Sigurd and Katherine (Roller) L.; m. Ella Bradford, Aug. 24, 1946 (dec. Dec. 1990); children: Lore Loftfield DeBower, Eric, Linda, Norman, BjÖrn, Curtis, Katherine, Earl, Allison Dinsdale, Ella-Kari. BS, Harvard U., 1941, MA, 1942, PhD, 1946. Research assoc. MIT, Cambridge, 1946-48; research assoc. to sr. research assoc. Mass. Gen. Hosp., Boston, 1948-64; asst. to assoc. prof. biochemistry Harvard U. Sch. Medicine, Boston, 1948-64; prof. biochemistry Sch. Medicine U. N.Mex., Albuquerque, 1964-90, chmn. dept. biochemistry, 1964-71, 78-90, prof. emeritus, 1990—. Contbr. articles on protein biosynthesis and enzymology to profl. jours. Served as corp. U.S. Army, 1945-46. Fellow Damon Runyon Fund, 1952-53, Guggenheim Found., 1961-62; Fulbright fellow, 1977, 83; sr. fellow NIH, 1971-72. Mem. AAAS, Am. Soc. Biol. Chemists, Am. Chem. Soc., Am. Assn. Cancer Research, Biophys. Soc., Marine Biol. Lab. Lutheran. Avocations: sailing, hiking, camping, skiing. Home: 707 Fairway Rd NW Albuquerque NM 87107-5718 Office: U NMex Sch Medicine Dept Biochemis & Molecular Biology Albuquerque NM 87131-0001

LOFTIS, JOHN (CLYDE), JR. English language educator; b. Atlanta, May 16, 1919; s. John Clyde and Marbeth (Brown) L.; m. Anne Nevins, June 29, 1946; children: Mary, Laura, Lucy. BA, Emory U., 1940; MA, Princeton U., 1942, PhD, 1948. Instr. English Princeton, 1946-48; instr., then asst. prof. English UCLA, 1948-52; faculty Stanford U., 1952-81, prof. English, 1958-81, Bailey prof. English, 1977-81, Bailey prof. emeritus, 1981—, chmn. dept., 1973-76. Author: Steele at Drury Lane, 1952, Comedy and Society from Congreve to Fielding, 1959, La Independencia de la Literatura Norteamericana, 1961, The Politics of Drama in Augustan England, 1963, The Spanish Plays of Neoclassical England, 1973, (with others) The Revels History of Drama in English, Vol. V, 1976, Sheridan and the Drama of Georgian England, 1977, Renaissance Drama in England and Spain: Topical Allusion and History Plays, 1987; editor: (Steele) The Theatre, 1962, Restoration Drama: Modern Essays in Criticism, 1966, (with V.A. Dearing) The Works of John Dryden, Vol. IX, 1966, (Sheridan) The School for Scandal, 1966, (Nathaniel Lee) Lucius Junius Brutus, 1967, (Addison) Essays in Criticism and Literary Theory, 1975, The Memoirs of Anne, Lady Halkett and Ann, Lady Fanshawe, 1979, (with D.S. Rodes and V.A. Dearing) The Works of John Dryden, Vol. XI, 1978, (with P.H. Hardacre) Colonel Bampfield's Apology, 1993; co-editor Augustan Reprint Society, 1949-1952, English Literature, 1660-1800: A Current Bibliography, 1951-56; gen. editor: Regents Restoration Drama Series, 35 vols, 1962-81; mem. editorial bd.: Studies in English Literature, 1966-76, Huntington Library Quar., 1968-76, Wesleyan Edit. Works Henry Fielding, 1970-83 , Augustan Reprint Soc., 1985-90. Served with USNR, 1942-46, PTO. Fellow Fund Advancement Edn., 1955-56; Fulbright lectr. Am. studies Peru, 1959-60; Guggenheim fellow, 1966-67; fellow Folger Shakespeare Library, 1967; NEH fellow, 1978-79 Mem. MLA, Phi Beta Kappa, Kappa Alpha. Home: 7 Arastradero Rd Portola Vally CA 94028-8012 Office: Stanford Univ Dept English Stanford CA 94305

LOFTUS, THOMAS DANIEL, lawyer; b. Nov. 8, 1930; s. Glendon Francis and Martha Helen (Wall) L. BA, U. Wash., 1952, JD, 1957. Bar: Wash. 1958, U.S. Ct. Appeals (9th cir.) 1958, U.S. Dist. Ct. Wash. 1958, U.S. Ct. Mil. Appeals 1964, U.S. Supreme Ct. 1964. Trial atty. Northwestern Mut. Ins. Co., Seattle, 1958-62; sr. trial atty. Unigard Security Ins. Co., Seattle, 1962-68, asst. gen. counsel, 1969-83, govt. rels. counsel, 1983-89; of counsel Groshong, LeHet & Thornton, 1990-98; mem. Wash. Commn. on Jud. Conduct (formerly Jud. Qualifications), 1982-88, vice-chmn., 1987-88; judge pro tem Seattle Mcpl. Ct., 1973-81; mem. nat. panel of mediators Arbitration Forums, Inc., 1990—. Sec., treas. Seattle Opera Assn., 1980-91; pres., bd. dirs. Vis. Nurse Svcs., 1979-88; pres., v.p. Salvation Army Adult Rehab. Ctr., 1979-86; nat. committeeman Wash. Young Rep. Fedn., 1961-63, vice-chmn, 1963-65; pres. Young Reps. King County, 1962-63; bd. dirs. Seattle Seafair, Inc., 1975; bd. dirs., gen. counsel Wash. Ins. Coun., 1984-86, sec., 1986-88, v.p., 1988-90, Am. Mediation Panel of Mediators, 1990-96; bd. dirs. Arson Alarm Found., 1987-90; bd. visitors Law Sch. U. Wash., 1993—. 1st Lt. U.S. Army, 1952-54, col. Res., 1954-85. Fellow Am. Bar Found.; mem. Am. Arbitration Assn. (nat. panel arbitrators 1965—, nat. panel mediators 2000—), Am. Arbitration Forums, Inc. (nat. panel arbitrators 1992), Nat. Assn. Security Dealers (bd. arbitrators 1997—), Am. Mediation Panel, Wash. Bar Assn. (gov. 1981-84), Seattle King County Bar Assn. (sec., trustee 1977-82), ABA (ho. of dels. 1984-90), Internat. Assn. Ins. Counsel, U.S. People to People (del. Moscow internat. law-econ. conf. 1990), Def. Rsch. Inst., Wash. Def. Trial Lawyers Assn., Wash. State Trial Lawyers Assn., Am. Judicature Soc., Res. Officers Assn., Judge Advocate Gen.'s Assn., Assn. Wash. Gens., U. Wash. Alumni Assn., Coll. Club Seattle, Wash. Athletic Club, Masons, Shriners, English Spkg. Union, Ranier Club, Pi Sigma Alpha, Delta Sigma Rho, Phi Delta Phi, Theta Delta Chi. Republican. Presbyterian. Home: 3515 Magnolia Blvd W Seattle WA 98199-1841 Office: Coll Club Bldg 505 Madison St Ste 300 Seattle WA 98104-1123

LOGAN, FRANCIS DUMMER, lawyer; b. Evanston, Ill., May 23, 1931; s. Simon Rae and Frances (Dummer) L.; m. Claude Riviere, Apr. 13, 1957; children: Carolyn Gisele, Francis Dummer. B.A., U. Chgo., 1950; B.A. Juris, Oxford U., 1954; LL.B., Harvard U., 1955. Bar: N.Y. 1956, Calif. 1989. Assoc. Milbank, Tweed, Hadley & McCloy, N.Y.C., 1955-64, ptnr. N.Y.C. and L.A., 1965-96, chmn., 1992-96. Mem. vis. com. U. of Chgo. Coll.; bd. dirs. Pasadena Symphony Orchestra. Mem. Calif. State Bar, Coun. on Fgn. Rels., Am. Law Inst., Pacific Coun. on Internat. Policy, N.Y. State Bar. Home: 1726 Linda Vista Ave Pasadena CA 91103-1132

LOGAN, LEE ROBERT, orthodontist; b. L.A., June 24, 1932; s. Melvin Duncan and Margaret (Seltzer) L.; m. Maxine Nadler, June 20, 1975; children: Chad, Casey. BS, UCLA, 1952; DDS, Northwestern U., 1956, MS, 1961. Diplomate Am. Bd. Orthodontics. Gen .practice dentistry, Reseda, Calif., 1958-59; practice orthodontics Northridge, 1961—; pres. Lee R. Logan DDS Profl. Corp. Mem. med. staff Northridge Hosp.; owner Maxine's Prodn. Co.; owner Maxine's Talent Agy.; guest lectr. UCLA, U. So. Calif. Contbr. articles to profl. jours. Achievements include patent and licensing agreement with 3M for a device to attach braces, 2001. Served to lt. USNR, 1956-58. Recipient Nat. Philanthropy award, 1987, 1st Pl. winner Autistic Jogathon, 1981-2000; named (with wife) Couple of Yr., Autistic Children Assn., 1986. Mem. ADA, San Fernando Valley Dental Assn. (pres. 1998), Am. Assn. Orthodontists, Pacific Coast Soc. Orthodontists (dir., pres. so. sect. 1974-75, chmn. membership 1981-83), Foudn. Orthodontic Rsch. (charter mem.), Calif. Soc. Orthodontists (chmn. peer rev. 1982-93), G.V. Black Soc. (charter) Angle Soc. Orthodontists (pres. 1981-82, bd. dirs. 1982-2001, nat. pres. 1985-87), U. S.C. Century Club Fraternity, Xi Psi Phi, Chi Phi. Home: 4830 Encino Ave Encino CA 91316-3813 Office: 18250 Roscoe Blvd Northridge CA 91325-4226 E-mail: orthologan@aol.com

LOGAN, MARK BYRON, optics corporation executive; b. Phoenixville, Pa., Dec. 1, 1938; s. Leo Joseph and Roselyn Francis (Baker) L.; m. Sharon Kathleen Logan, Sept. 3, 1960 (div. Nov. 19, 1973); 1 son, Bret; m. Anne Herndon Jones, May 9, 1975; children: Catherine, Virginia. B.A., Hiram Coll., 1960; M.A., NYU, 1961; postgrad., Harvard U. Grad. Sch. Bus. Adminstrn. Pres. Home Products de Mex. div., Am. Home Products, N.Y.C., 1967-74; v.p., mktg. cons. products A.H. Robins Co., Richmond, Va., 1974-75; group pres. Becton Dickinson Co., Paramus, N.J., 1975-81; sr. v.p., pres. vision care group Bausch & Lomb Inc., Rochester, N.Y., 1981—, also dir.; chmn., Pres and CEO Insmed Pharmaceuticals, Inc.; chmn. and CEO VISX, Inc., Santa Clara, CA, 1994—. Dir. Upstate Health Systems, Rochester, Eastman Dental Ctr., Rochester, Abgenix, Inc., VI-VUS, Inc. Bd. dirs. Roberts Wesleyan Coll., Rochester, 1982— . Woodrow Wilson fellow, 1960-61 Clubs: County of Rochester, Genessee Valley. Home: 109 Ambassador Dr Rochester NY 14610-3403 Office: VISX Inc 3400 Central Expy Santa Clara CA 95051-0703

LOGAN, NANCY JANE, broadcast sales and marketing executive; b. Buffalo, Oct. 29, 1957; d. Harry Lee and MaryJane (Redinger) Logan. AA, Erie Community Coll., Buffalo, 1977; BS, SUNY, Brockport, 1979. Account exec. Sta. WBUF Radio, Buffalo, 1979-80; account exec. Sta. WBEN Radio, Buffalo, 1980-82; regional mgr. Westwood One Radio Networks, L.A., 1983-84; mktg. rep. TV Guide Mag., L.A., 1984-88, broadcast mktg. supr., 1988-89, western mgr. tune-in advt., 1989—; sr. dir., media licensing BMI, L.A.; pres., foundation chair. AWRT, L.A., 1999-. Mem. NATAS, Am. Women in Radio & TV (pres. so. Calif. chpt. 1988-89), Publicity Club L.A. Democrat. Presbyterian. Avocations: painting, skiing, equestrian, biking, music. Home: 2627 5th St Santa Monica CA 90405-4259 Office: BMI 8730 W Sunset Blvd Fl 3 Los Angeles CA 90069-2210

LOGANBILL, G. BRUCE, pathologist; b. Newton, Kans., Sept. 06; s. Oscar and Warrene L. B.A., Bethel Coll., Kans., 1956; M.A., U. Kans., 1958; Ph.D., Mich. State U., 1961; postdoctoral fellow, Inst. Logopedics, 1965-66. Mem. faculty Kalamazoo Coll., 1961-63; mem. faculty Fresno (Calif.) State U., 1966-68, Calif. State U., Long Beach, 1968—, prof., 1975—; voice cons. Nat. Coll. Psychiatry, Paris. Lectr. on voice modification/pathologies and interpretive comm., Argentina, Denmark, France, Hong Kong, Estonia, Switzerland, Japan, Can., India, Scotland, Czechoslovakia, USSR, Germany, Netherlands, People's Republic of China; U.S. rep. 2d Internat. Congress de Melodie-Therapie du Language en accord Nat. Coll. Psychiatry, Paris, 1990; cons. aesthetic comms., Ferrand Exhbn. Embassy of France, Washington. Author: The Bases of Voice, Articulation and Pronunciation, 1974, 6th edit., 1997, also in Japanese, 1980; contbr. more than 30 articles to profl. jours. Mem. Speech Comm. Assn., Am. Speech and Hearing Assn., Western States Comm. Assn., Internat. Assn. Logopedics and Phoniatrics, Internat. Phonetics Assn., Internat. Assn. Art Therapy (v.p. 1996—), Assn. Calif. State U. Profs. (univ. chpt. pres. 1985), Assoc. Internat. Melodic Therapy and Language (v.p. 1997-2000), Big Ten Club of L.A., others. Republican. Episcopalian. Office: Calif State U 1250 N Bellflower Blvd Long Beach CA 90840-0006

LOHMAN, LORETTA CECELIA, social scientist, consultant; b. Joliet, Ill., Sept. 25, 1944; d. John Thomas and Marjorie Mary (Brennan) L. BA in Polit. Sci., U. Denver, 1966, PhD in Am. History, 1996; MA in Social Sci., U. No. Colo., 1975. Lectr. Ariz. State U., Tempe, 1966-67; survey researcher Merrill-Werthlin Co., Tempe, 1967-68; edn. asst. Am. Humane Assn., Denver, 1969-70; econ. cons. Lohman & Assocs., Littleton, Colo., 1971-75; rsch. assoc. Denver Rsch. Inst., 1976-86; owner, rsch. scientist Lohman & Assocs., Littleton, 1986-99; affiliate Colo. Water Resources Rsch. Inst., Ft. Collins, Colo., 1989-91; Colo. Nonpoint source info./edn. coord. coop. ext. Colo. State U., 1999—. Tech. adv. com. Denver Potable Wastewater Demo Plant, 1986-90; cons. Constrn. Engring. Rsch. Lab., 1984—; peer reviewer NSF, 1985-86, Univs. Coun. Water Resources, 1989—; WERC consortium reviewer N.Mex. Univs.-U.S. Dept. Energy, 1989—, Co-Alliacne Environ. Edn. Adv. Bd., 2000—; course cons. Regis Coll., Denver, 1992—. Contbr. articles to profl. jours. Vol. Metro Water Conservation Projects, Denver, 1986-90; vol. handicapped fitness So. Suburban Parks and Recreation. Recipient Huffsmith award Denver Rsch. Inst., 1983; Nat. Ctr. for Edn. in Politics grantee, 1964-65. Mem. ASCE (social and environ. objectives com.), Orgn. Am. Historians, Pub. Hist. Assn., Sigma Xi, Pi Gamma Mu, Phi Alpha Theta. Avocations: vegetable and xeriscape gardening, traveling, miniature boxes. Home and Office: 3375 W Aqueduct Ave Littleton CO 80123-2903 E-mail: llohman@juno.com

LOHNES, WALTER F. W. German language and literature educator; b. Frankfurt, Germany, Feb. 8, 1925; came to U.S., 1948, naturalized, 1954; s. Hans and Dina (Koch) L.; m. Claire Shane, 1950; children: Kristen, Peter, Claudia. Student, U. Frankfurt, 1945-48, Ohio Wesleyan U., 1948-49, U. Mo., 1949-50; PhD, Harvard U., 1961. Asst., Inst. German Folklore, U. Frankfurt, 1947-48; instr. German U. Mo., 1949-50; head dept. German, Phillips Acad., Andover, Mass., 1951-61; asst. prof. Stanford (Calif.) U., 1961-65, assoc. prof., 1965-68, prof., 1969-95, prof. emeritus, 1995—, dir. NDEA Inst. Advanced Study, 1961-68, chmn. dept. German studies, 1973-79, dir. Inst. Basic German, 1975-95, prin. investigator NEH grant, 1978-80. Vis. prof. Woehler-Gymnasium, Frankfurt, 1956-57, Middlebury Coll., 1959, U. N.Mex., 1980, 81, 86, U. Vienna, 1990, Coll. de France, Paris, 1992; mem., chmn. various coms. of examiners Ednl. Testing Svc. and Coll. Bd.; chmn. German Grad. Record Exam. Author: (with V. Nollendorfs) German Studies in the United States, 1976, (with F. W. Strothmann) German: A Structural Approach, 1968, 4th rev. edit., 1988; (with E.A. Hopkins) Contrastive Grammar of English and German, 1982, (with Martha Woodmansee) Erkennen und Deuten, 1983, (with J.A. Pfeffer) Grunddeutsch, Texte zur gesprochenen deutschen Gegenwartssprache, 3 vols., 1984, (with D. Benseler and V. Nollendorfs) Teaching German in America: Prolegomena to a History, 1988; contbr. numerous articles to profl. jours.; editor: Unterrichtspraxis, 1971-74 Bd. dirs. Calif. Youth Symphony, 1977-78, Oakland (Calif.) Symphony Youth Orch., 1978-80, Peninsula Dem. Coalition, 1998—. Decorated Fed. Order of Merit (Germany); Medal of Honor in Gold (Austria); German Govt. grantee, 1975, 76, 78. Mem. MLA, Am. Assn. Tchrs. German (v.p. 1961-62, 70-71, Outstanding Educator award 1994; hon. 1995), Am. Assn. Applied Linguistics, Am. Coun. on Teaching Fgn. Langs., German Studies Assn., Internat. Vereinigung Germanische Sprach und Literaturwissenschaft. Home: 733 Covington Rd Los Altos CA 94024-4903 Office: Stanford U Dept German Studies Stanford CA 94305-2030

LOHRDING, RONALD K. business executive; PhD in Math. Statistics, Kans. State U. R&D mgr., scientist Los Alamos (N.Mex.) Nat. Lab., asst. dir. for indsl. and internat. initiatives, dep. assoc. dir. for environment and biosys., program dir. for energy, environment, and tech.; co-founder Cell Robotics, Albuquerque, 1988—, chmn., pres., CEO. Office: Cell Robotics Internat Office Pres 2715 Broadbent Pkwy NE Albuquerque NM 87107-1618

LOHRER, RICHARD BAKER, investment consultant; b. Boston, Nov. 30, 1932; s. Leo and Elizabeth Louise (Kaiser) L.; m. Ruth Willa Gutekunst, Feb. 15, 1958; children: Richard Baker, William L., Elizabeth L. Hall, Andrew M. AB, Harvard U., 1954; MBA, NYU, 1961. Asst. sec. comml. lending Irving Trust Co. (now Bank of N.Y.), N.Y.C., 1957-64; asst. to v.p. fin. and treas. Nat. Dairy Products Corp. (now Kraft Foods Divsn. of Philip Morris, Inc.), N.Y.C., 1964-71; asst. treas. Martin Marietta Corp. (now Lockheed Martin Corp.), N.Y.C., 1971-74; with Northrop Corp. (now Northrop Grumman Corp.), L.A., 1974-90, treas., 1977-87, v.p. trust investments, 1987-90; prin., pres. R.B. Lohrer Assocs., Inc., Palos Verdes Estates, Calif., 1990—. Bd. dirs. Cmty. Helpline, Inc., 1988-98, pres., 1992-97; bd. dirs. Presbyn. Ch. (U.S.A.) Investment and Loan Program, Inc., 1995—, vice chmn., 1995-2000, chmn. 2001—; bd. dirs., chmn. endowment fund trustees Palos Verdes Art Ctr., 1996—. Mem. L.A. Treas. Club (pres. 1981), Boston Latin Sch. West Coast Alumni Assn. (bd. dirs., pres. 1982-84), Fin. Exec. Internat., Harvard Club of So. Calif., Palos Verdes Golf Club, Masons. Republican. Presbyterian.

LOMBARDI, EUGENE PATSY, retired orchestra conductor, violinist, educator; b. North Braddock, Pa., July 7, 1923; s. Nunzio C. and Mary (Roberto) L.; m. Jacqueline Sue Davis, Mar. 1955; children: Robert, Genanne. BA, Westminster Coll., 1948; MA, Columbia U., 1948; Edn. Specialist, George Peabody Coll., 1972; MusD, Westminster Coll., 1981. Band dir. Lincoln H.S., Midland, Pa., 1948-49; orch. dir. Male H.S., Louisville, 1949-50, Phoenix Union H.S., 1950-57; orch. dir., prof. Ariz. State U., Tempe, 1957-89; ret., 1989. Condr. Phoenix Symphonette, 1954-61, 70-73, Phoenix Symphony Youth Orch., 1956-66, Phoenix Pops Orch., 1971-83, Fine Arts String Orch., Phoenix, 1995-97 With USAAF, 1943-46. Decorated Bronze Star; recipient Alumni Achievement award Westminster Coll., 1976, gold medal Nat. Soc. Arts and Letters, 1973, Disting. Tchr. award Ariz. State U. Alumni, 1974, Phoenix appreciation award, 1983 Mem. Music Educators Nat. Conf., Am. String Tchrs. Assn. (pres. Ariz. unit 1965-67), Am. Fedn. Musicians, Ariz. Music Educators Assn. (pres. higher edn. sect. 1973-75, Excellence in Teaching Music award 1989), Ind. Order Foresters, Phi Delta Kappa, Phi Mu Alpha, Alpha Sigma Phi. Republican. Methodist. Home: 920 E Manhatton Dr Tempe AZ 85282-5520

LOMBARDINI, CAROL ANN, lawyer; b. Framingham, Mass., Dec. 29, 1954; d. Harry and Sarah (Scarano) L. m. William L. Cole, Apr. 23, 1983; children: Kevin Daniel, Kristin Elizabeth. BA, U. Chgo., 1976; JD, Stanford U., 1979. Bar: Calif. 1979. Assoc. Meserve, Mumper & Hughes, L.A., 1979-80, Proskauer Rose Goetz & Mendelsohn, L.A., 1980-82; from counsel to sr. v.p. legal and bus. affairs Alliance of Motion Picture and TV Prodrs., Encino, Calif., 1982—. Trustee Dirs. Guild Contract Adminstrn., Encino, 1982—, Prodr.-Writers Guild Pension & Health Plans, Burbank, Calif., 1983—, SAG-Prodr. Pension & Health Plans, Burbank, 1986—, Dirs. Guild-Prodr. Pension & Health Plans, L.A., 1987— Avocations: hiking, cooking. Office: Alliance Motion Picture & TV Prodrs 15503 Ventura Blvd Encino CA 91436-3103

LOMICKA, WILLIAM HENRY, investor; b. Irwin, Pa., Mar. 9, 1937; s. William and Carabel L.; m. Carol L. Williams, Feb. 14, 1979; 1 son, Edward W. B.A., Coll. Wooster, Ohio, 1959; M.B.A., U. Pa., 1962. Sr. securities analyst Guardian Life Ins. Co., N.Y.C., 1962-65; treasury svcs. mgr. L.B. Foster Co., Pitts., 1966-68, Welch Foods Co., Westfield, N.Y., 1969-70; asst. treas. Ashland Oil, Inc., Ky., 1970-75; sr. v.p. fin. Humana Inc., Louisville, 1975-85; pres., fin. cons. Old South Life Ins. Co., Louisville, 1985-87; sec. econ. devel. Commonwealth of Ky., 1987-88; acting pres. Citizens Security Life Ins. Co., Louisville, 1988-89; pres. Mayfair Capital, Inc., Louisville, 1988-99; chmn. Coulter Ridge Capital, Tucson, 1999—. Bd. dirs. Pomeroy Computer Resources, Inc. Served with USAR, 1962-63. Home and Office: 7406 N Secret Canyon Dr Tucson AZ 85718-1435 E-mail: coulterridge@earthlink.net

LOND, HARLEY WELDON, editor, publisher; b. Chgo., Feb. 5, 1946; s. Henry Sidney and Dorothy (Shaps) L.; m. Marilyn Moss, Aug. 20, 1981; 1 child Elizabeth. BA in Journalism, Calif. State U., L.A., 1972. Adminstrv. dir. Century City Ednl. Arts Project, L.A., 1972-76, hon. dir., 1982—; founder, editor Intermedia mag., L.A., 1974-80; prodn. mgr. FilmRow Publs., L.A., 1981; assoc. editor Box Office mag., Hollywood, Calif., 1981-84, editor, assoc. pub., 1984-94; dir. publs. Entertainment Data, Inc., 1994-95; pres. CyberPod Prodns., 1995—; asst. news editor The Hollywood Reporter, 1995-2000, news editor, 2000—. Syndicated columnist Continental Features, Washington, Tel-Aire Publs., Dallas, 1986—; hon dir. Monterey (Calif.) Film Festival, 1987; mem. media adv. bd. Cinetex Internat. Film Festival, 1988; cons. Take 3 Info. Svc.; web architect-master, OnVideo website, 1995—. Editor: Entertainment Media Electronic Info. Svc.; contbg. editor: (video) Family Style Mag.; contbr. articles to profl. publs. Calif. Arts Council grantee, 1975, Nat. Endowment for Arts grantee, 1976-77. Mem. MLA, Soc. Profl. Journalists, Assn. for Edn. in Journalism and Mass Communication, Speech Communication Assn., Soc. for Cinema Studies. Home and Office: PO Box 17377 Beverly Hills CA 90209-3377

LONDON, ANDREW BARRY, film editor; b. Bronx, N.Y., Jan. 1, 1949; s. Max Edward and Nellie (Steiner) L. BA in Cinema magna cum laude, U. So. Calif., 1970. Represented by Mont. Artists, Santa Monica, Calif. Prin. works include: (features) Big Eden, 2000, The Meteor Man, 1993, F/X 2, 1991, Rambo III, 1988, Planes, Trains and Automobiles, 1987, Link, 1986, Cloak & Dagger, 1984, Psycho II, 1983, The True Story of Eskimo Nell, 1975, (TV shows) The Soul Collector, 1999, A Memory in My Heart, 1999, Murder at 75 Birch, 1999, Before He Wakes, 1997, Perfect Crime, 1997, Divided By Hate, 1997, The Crying Child, 1996, Evil Has a Face, 1996, Don't Talk to Strangers, 1994, Day of Reckoning, 1993, Mortal Sins, 1992, Running Delilah, 1992, True Tales, 1992, Sweet Poison, 1991, Tales from the Crypt, 1989-90, Beauty and the Beast Pilot, 1987, The Christmas Star, 1986; sound editor: Wolfen (MPSE Golden Reel award 1982), Hammett, Roadgames, Psycho II, I'm Dancing As Fast As I Can, Perfect, Protocol, Coal Miner's Daughter, The Long Riders, others. Mem. Acad. Motion Picture Arts and Scis., Motion Picture Sound Editors (Golden Reel award 1982), Phi Beta Kappa. Office: 3085 St George St #3 Los Angeles CA 90027-2532

LONEGAN, THOMAS LEE, retired restaurant corporation executive; b. Kansas City, Mo., July 4, 1932; s. Thomas F. and Edna L. (Payton) L.; m. Donna F. Ednie, Apr. 11, 1958; children: Timothy L., John M. BSME, Gen. Motors Inst., 1955; MS in Mgmt., USN Post Grad Sch., 1963; grad., Indsl. Coll. Armed Forces, Washington, 1970; postgrad., Calif. State U., Long Beach, 1979-83; grad., Coll. for Fin. Planning, Denver, 1984. Registered profl. engr., Mass.; CFP. Commd. ensign USN, 1956, advanced through grades to comdr., 1978; dir. pub. works, officer in charge of constrn. Naval Weapons Sta., Seal Beach, Calif., 1974-78; ret., 1978; dir. cen. staff McAthco Enterprises, Inc., Camarillo, Calif., 1985, exec. v.p., CFO, 1986-90, pres., CEO, 1991-93, exec. v.p., CFO, 1994-95; ret. Bd. dirs. McAthco Enterprises; exec. v.p. engring. Orange County Engring. Coun., 1977-78. Author: Analysis and Attenuation of Air Borne Noise in Industrial Plants, 1955, Formalized Training of Maintenance Personnel, 1963. Vol. various couns. Boy Scouts Am., 1968-76. Decorated Bronze Star with combat device, Meritorious Svc. medal, Jt. Svcs. Commendation medal, Navy Achievement medal; decorated Order of Chamoro (Guam); named Sr. Engr./Arch. Yr. Naval Facilities Engr. Command, 1972; recipient Silver medal Boy Scouts Am., 1974. Fellow Soc. Am. Mil. Engrs., Ret. Officers Assn., GM Inst. Robots Honor Soc.; mem. Beta Gamma Sigma. Avocations: reading, theater, music, foreign travel. Home: 8578 Amazon River Cir Fountain Valley CA 92708 E-mail: tomlonegan@aol.com

LONERGAN, KEVIN M. retail apparel company executive; With Gap Inc., 1971, other retail cos.; rejoined Gap Inc., 1989, co-creator, exec. v.p. Old Navy divsn., 1994, now exec. v.p., COO Old Navy divsn., 1999—. Office: Gap Inc 1 Harrison St San Francisco CA 94105-1602

LONERGAN, WALLACE GUNN, economics educator, management consultant; b. Potlatch, Idaho, Mar. 18, 1928; s. Willis Gerald and Lois (Gunn) L.; m. Joan Laurie Penoyer, June 1, 1952; children: Steven Mark, Kevin James. BA, Coll. Idaho, 1950; MBA, U. Chgo., 1955, PhD, 1960. Asst. dir., asst. prof. bus. Indsl. Relations Ctr. U. Chgo., 1960-70, assoc. dir., assoc. prof., 1970-74, dir., prof., 1974-84; vis. prof. Rikkyo U., Tokyo, 1985; vis. fellow Merton Coll. Oxford (Eng.) U., 1986; chair, prof. bus., econs. divsn. Albertson Coll. Idaho, Caldwell, 1987—. V.p. Human Resources Research Cons., Chgo., 1980-87. Author: Leadership and Morale, 1960, Group Leadership, 1974, Performance Appriasal, 1978, Leadership and Management, 1979. Chmn. Episcopal Commn. on Higher Edn., Chgo., 1970-80, mgmt. con. United Way Chgo., 1982-85. 1st lt. U.S. Army, 1950-53, Korea. Named Disting. Alumni Coll. Idaho, 1962; vis. scholar Internat. Anglican Exchange, N.Y.C., 1976, Tokyo, 1986. Mem. Internat. House Japan, Internat. Indsl. Relations Research Assn., Acad. Mgmt., Rotary. Avocations: power walking, hiking. Home: 812 E Linden St Caldwell ID 83605-5335 Office: Albertson Coll Idaho Bus Econs Divsn 2112 Cleveland Blvd Caldwell ID 83605-4432

LONG, ANTHONY ARTHUR, classics educator; b. Manchester, Eng., Aug. 17, 1937; came to U.S. 1983; s. Tom Arthur and Phyllis Joan (LeGrice) L.; m. Janice Calloway, Dec. 30, 1960 (div. 1969); 1 child, Stephen Arthur; m. Mary Kay Flavell, May 25, 1970 (div. 1990); 1 child, Rebecca Jane; m. Monique Marie-Jeanne Elias, Mar. 22, 1997. B.A., U. Coll. London, 1960; Ph.D., U. London, 1964. Lectr. classics U. Otago, Dunedin, N.Z., 1961-64; lectr. classics U. Nottingham, Eng., 1964-66; lectr. Greek and Latin U. Coll. London, 1966-71; reader in Greek and Latin U. London, 1971-73; Gladstone prof. Greek U. Liverpool, Eng., 1973-83; prof. classics U. Calif., Berkeley, 1982—; pub. orator U. Liverpool, Eng., 1981-83; Irving Stone prof. lit. U. Calif., Berkeley, 1991—, chmn. dept. classics, 1986-90. Mem. Inst. Advanced Study, Princeton, N.J., 1970, 79; vis. prof. U. Munich, 1973, Ecole Normale Supérieure, Paris, 1993; Cardinal Mercier prof. philosophy U. Louvain, Belgium, 1991; mem.

Mellon Fellowships Selection Com., 1984-90; mem. selection com. Stanford U. Humanities Coun., 1985-86; Corbett lectr. U. Cambridge, 1998-99; Faculty Rsch. lectr. U. Calif., Berkeley, 1999-2000. Author: Language and Thought in Sophocles, 1968 (Cromer Greek prize 1968), Problems in Stoicism, 1971, 96, Hellenistic Philosophy, 1974, 2d edit., 1986, (with Fortenbaugh and Huby) Theophrastus of Eresus, 1985, (with Sedley) The Hellenistic Philosophers, 1987, (with Dillon) The Question of Eclecticism, 1988, 96, (with Bastianini) Hierocles, 1992, (with others) Images and Ideologies, 1993, Stoic Studies, 1996, Cambridge Companion to Early Greek Philosophy, 1999; editor: Classical Quar., 1975-81, Classical Antiquity, 1987-90; gen. editor: (with Barnes) Clarendon Later Ancient Philosophers, 1987—. Served to lt. Royal Arty., Eng., 1955-57 Named hon. citizen City of Rhodes, Greece; sr. fellow humanities coun. Princeton U., 1978, Bye fellow Robinson Coll., Cambridge, 1982, Guggenheim fellow, 1986-87, sr. fellow Ctr. for Hellenic Studies, 1988-93, fellow NEH, 1990-91, Wissenschaftskolleg fellow, Berlin, 1991-92, William Evans fellow U. Otago, New Zealand, 1995. Fellow Am. Acad. Arts and Scis., Brit. Acad. (corr.); mem. Classical Assn., Aristotelian Soc., Am. Philol. Assn., Phi Beta Kappa (hon.). Avocations: music, walking, travel, bridge. Home: 32 Sunset Dr Kensington CA 94707-1139 Office: U Calif Dept Classics Berkeley CA 94720-0001 E-mail: aalong@uclink4.berkeley.edu

LONG, DAVID MICHAEL, JR. biomedical researcher, cardiothoracic surgeon; b. Shamokin, Pa., Feb. 26, 1929; s. David Michael and Elva (Christ) L.; m. Donna Rae Long, Feb. 26, 1954; children: Kurt, Raymond, Carl, Grace, Carolyn, Ruth. BS magna cum laude, Muhlenberg Coll., Allentown, Pa., 1951; MS, Hahnemann U., Phila., 1954, MD, 1956; PhD, U. Minn., 1965. Lic. physician, Ariz., Calif., Colo., Ill., Md., Minn., Pa., Tex.; diplomate Nat. Bd. Med. Examiners, Am. Bd. Surgery, Am. Bd. Thoracic Surgery; cert. trauma provider, advanced life support; advanced cardiac life support. Intern Hahnemann U. Hosp., Phila., 1956-57; resident in surgery U. Minn., Mpls., 1957-65, fellow in surgery, 1957-61, 63-65, fellow in physiology, 1959-61; pres., chmn. bd. Long Labs., San Diego, 1984-85; chmn., dir. rsch. Fluoromed Pharm., Inc., San Diego, 1985-89; chmn., dir. sci. Alliance Pharm. Corp., La Jolla, Calif., 1989-91; pres., chmn. Abel Labs., Inc., Spring Valley, 1991—; CEO, Biofield Corp., Spring Valley, 2000—. Mem. faculty Hahnemann U., 1953-54, U. Calif., San Diego, 1973-92, U. Minn., 1959-61, 63-64, Naval Med. Sch., 1962, Chgo. Med. Sch., 1965-67, Cook County Grad. Sch. Medicine, 1965-73, U. Ill., 1967-73; cons. Chgo. State Tuberculosis Sanitarium, 1967-72; asst. dir. dept. surg. rsch. Hektoen Inst. for Med. Rsch. of Cook County Hosp., 1965-68, dir., 1968-73, assoc. attending staff, 1965-73; attending staff West Side VA Hosp., 1966-73, U. Ill. Hosp., 1967-73, Villa View Hosp., 1973-85, AMI Valley Med. Ctr., 1973-85, Grossman Dist. Hosp., 1973-85, Alvarado Cmty. Hosp., 1973-85, Sharp Meml. Hosp., 1973-84; head divsn. cardiovasc. and thoracic surgery U. Ill., 1967-73; cons. continuing med. edn. com. Grossmont Dist. Hosp., 1985—; mem. continuing med. edn. com. Sharp Healthcare Sys., 1994—; cons. Docent Corp., 1975-76; com. mem. consensus devel. com. Thrombolytic Therapy in Thrombosis, NIH/FDA, 1980; trustee N.Y. Acad. Art, N.Y.C., 1997—; bd. govs., chmn. Hahnemann U. Hosp./Tenet Healthcare, Phila., 1999—. Contbr. numerous articles and abstracts to profl. jours., chpts. to books; editl. bd. Current Surgery, 1967-89; co-editor Hematrix, 1982-85. Bd. dirs. Rsch. Assocs. of Point Loma Nazarene coll., San Diego, chmn., 1984-85; bd. trustees Muhlenberg Coll., Allentown, Pa., 1992—, chmn., 1994—; bd. dirs. Grossmont Hosp. Found., Grossmont Hosp., La Mesa, Calif., 1992—; co-chmn. Calif. divsn. of campaign of Muhlenberg Coll., 1992-93; chmn. Campaign of Grossmont Hosp. Found. for David and Donna Long Cancer Treatment Ctr. and Cardiac Diagnosis Ctr., 1992-94; co-chmn. Campaign for Health Ctr., Point Loma Nazarene Coll., San Diego, 1992-94. Rsch. fellow Heart Assn. Southeastern Pa., 1953-54, Student Senate of Hahnemann U., 1955; trainee Nat. Cancer Inst., 1957-58, Nat. Heart Inst., 1958-60, 63-64; spl. rsch. fellow Nat. Heart Inst., 1960-61; established investigator Minn. Heart Assn, 1964-65; Muhlenberg Coll. scholar, 1947-51, Hahnemann U. scholar, 1952-55, Luth. Brotherhood Leadership scholar, 1951 Fellow ACS, Am. Coll. Chest Physicians (sec. cardiovascular surgery com. 1976-78), Am. Coll. Cardiology; mem. AAAS, AMA, Am. Assn. Thoracic Surgery, Am. Assn. Anatomists, Internat. Cardiovascular Surgery Soc., Internat. Soc. for Artificial Cells and Immobilization Biotechnology, Am. Heart Assn., Am. Physiol. Soc., Am. Thoracic Soc., Assn. for Advancement of Med. Instrumentation, Cajal Soc. Neuroanatomy, Calif. Med. Assn., Internat. Soc. Surgery, Internat. Soc. Hemorheology (founding mem.), N.Y. Acad. Sci., San Diego County Med. Soc., Soc. Thoracic Surgeons, Soc. Univ. Surgeons, Warren H. Cole Soc., Western Thoracic Surg. Soc. Lutheran. Achievements include 17 U.S. patents and 11 fgn. patents. Avocations: hiking, gardening, philanthropic programs, books on Winston Churchill. Office: Abel Laboratories Inc 2737 Via Orange Way Ste 108 Spring Valley CA 91978-1750

LONG, DAVID R. food products executive; BA in Agrl. Econs. with distinction, Cornell U., 1965; MS in Agrl. Econs., Ohio State U., 1970, PhD in Agrl. Econs., 1972. Ptnr. family farm, Albion, NY, 1965-68; policy planning analyst U.S. Dept. Agr., Washington, 1972-76; bus. analyst Ill. Grain Co., Bloomington, IL, 1976-78; mgr., dir., to v.p., gen. mgr. Anheuser Busch Co., Inc., St. Louis, 1978-87; v.p. transp. Staley Continental, Inc., Decatur, IL, 1987-89; pres., CEO Rice Growers Assn. Calif., Sacramento, 1989-93; pres. Calif. Pear Growers Assn., Sacramento, 1994-96; pres., CEO Snokist Growers, Inc., Yakima, WA, 1996—. Bd. dirs. Rice Millers Assn., 1989-93; mem. Am. Agrl. Econs. Assn., 1968-93, U.S.D.A. Fed. Grain Inspection adv. com., 1986-91. Mem. Boy Scouts Am.; bd. trustees Sacramento Valley Open Space Conservancy, 1992—. Mem. Rotary, Phi Kappa Phi. Office: Snokist Growers Inc PO Box 1587 Yakima WA 98907-1587 Address: 18 W Mead Ave Yakima WA 98902-6026

LONG, GREGORY ALAN, lawyer; b. San Francisco, Aug. 28, 1948; s. William F. and Ellen L. (Webber) L.; m. Jane H. Barrett, Sept. 30, 1983; children: Matthew, Brian, Michael, Gregory. BA magna cum laude, Claremont Men's Coll., Calif., 1970; JD cum laude, Harvard U., 1973. Bar: Calif. 1973, U.S. Dist. Ct. (ctrl. dist.) Calif. 1973, U.S. Ct. Appeals (9th cir.) 1976, U.S. Supreme Ct. 1977, U.S. Ct. Appeals (fed. cir.) 1984. Assoc. Overton, Lyman & Prince, L.A., 1973-78, ptnr., 1978-87, Sheppard, Mullin, Richter & Hampton, L.A., 1987—. Arbitrator L.A. Superior Ct). Fellow Am. Bar Found.; mem. ABA (young lawyers divsn. exec. coun. 1974-88, chmn. 1984-85, ho. of dels. 1983-89, exec. coun. litigation sect. 1981-83), Calif. Bar Assn. (del. 1976-82, 87-88), L.A. County Bar Assn. (exec. com. 1979-82, trustee 1979-82, barristers sect. exc. coun. 1976-82, pres. 1981-82, exec. coun. trial lawyers sect. 1984-88, chair amicus briefs com. 1989-92). Office: Sheppard Mullin Richter & Hampton 333 S Hope St Bldg 48 Los Angeles CA 90071-1406 E-mail: glong@smph.com

LONG, JEANINE HUNDLEY, state legislator; b. Provo, Utah, Sept. 21, 1928; d. Ralph Conrad and Hazel Laurine (Snow) Hundley; m. McKay W. Christensen, Oct. 28, 1949 (div. 1967); children: Cathy Schuyler, Julie Schulleri, Kelly M. Christensen, C. Brett Christensen, Harold A. Christensen; m. Kenneth D. Long, Sept. 6, 1968. AA, Shoreline C.C., Seattle, 1975; BA in Psychology, U. Wash., 1977. Mem. Wash. Ho. of Reps., 1983-87, 93-94, mem. joint com. pension policy, mem. Inst. Pub. Policy; mem. Wash. Senate, Dist. 44, Olympia, 1995—. Ranking mem. Human Svcs. and Corr. com., Wash. Senate. Mayor protem, mem. city coun. City of Brier, Wash., 1977-80. Republican. Office: PO Box 40482 Olympia WA 98504-0482 E-mail: long_je@leg.wa.gov

LONG, MARSHA TADANO, state official; b. Phoenix, Jan. 14, 1947; d. Tadashi and Michiko (Seki) Tadano; m. Merritt D. Long, Nov. 19, 1976; 1 child, Merisa Tamiko. BA, Pitzer Coll., 1968; MA, Pacific Luth. U., 1976. Vocat. counselor various orgns., 1968-73; vocat. edn. program specialist Wash. State Commn. Vocat. Edn., Olympia, 1973-82; mgr. info. systems Wash. State Dept. Licensing, Olympia, 1982-89, asst. dir., 1989-93; dep. supr. Wash. State Dept. Natural Resources, Olympia, 1993-97; dir. Wash. State Dept. Gen. Adminstrn., Olympia, 1997—. Mem. adv. com. Wing Luke Mus., Seattle, 1997. Mem. Capital High Sch. Site Based Coun., Olympia, 1996-98. Mem. Japanese-Am. Citizen League (past pres., past v.p.). Office: Wash State Dept Gen Adminstrn PO Box 41000 Olympia WA 98504-1000

LONG, ROBERT MERRILL, retail drug company executive; b. Oakland, Calif., May 19, 1938; s. Joseph Milton and Vera Mai (Skaggs) L.; m. Eliane Quilloux, Dec. 13, 1969. Student, Brown U., 1956-58; BA, Claremont Men's Coll., 1960. With Longs Drug Stores Inc., Walnut Creek, Calif., 1960—, dist. mgr., 1970-72, exec. v.p., 1972-75, pres., 1975-77, pres., chief exec. officer, 1977-91; chmn., chief exec. officer Longs Drug Stores, Walnut Creek, 1991-2000, chmn., 2000—. Mem. Nat. Assn. Chain Drug Stores (dir.) Office: Longs Drug Stores Corp PO Box 5222 141 N Civic Dr Walnut Creek CA 94596-3858

LONG, SHARON RUGEL, molecular biologist, plant biology educator; b. Mar. 2, 1951; d. Harold Eugene and Florence Jean (Rugel) Long; m. Harold James McGee, July 7, 1979; 2 children. BS, Calif. Inst. Tech., 1973; PhD, Yale U., 1979. Rsch. fellow Harvard U., Cambridge, Mass., 1979-81; from asst. prof. molecular biology to prof. Stanford U., Palo Alto, Calif., 1982-92, prof. biol. scis., 1992—. Investigator Howard Hughes Med. Inst., 1994—; adv. bd. Jane Coffin Childs Meml. Fund; bd. dirs. Ann. Revs. Inc. Assoc. Editor Jour. Bacteriology; assoc. editor Jour. Plant Physiology, 1992—; mem. editl. bd. Devel. Biology; editl. com. Ann. Review Cell Biology. Recipient award NSF, 1979, NIH, 1980, Shell Rsch. Found. award 1985, Presdl. Young Investigator award NSF, 1984-89; grantee NIH, Dept. Energy, NSF; MacArthur fellow, 1992-97, Georges Morel fellow I.N.R.A., France, 1998; fellow Noble Found. Fellow Assn. Women in Sci.; mem. NAS, Genetics Soc. Am., Am. Soc. Plant Physiology (Charles Albert Shull award 1989), Am. Soc. Microbiology, Soc. Devel. Biology. Office: Stanford U Dept Biol Scis 371 Serra Mall Stanford CA 94305-5008

LONG, WILLIAM D. grocery store executive; b. Watertown, Wis., Nov. 30, 1937; s. William D. and Olive (Piper) L.; m. Doreen Loveall, Sept. 23, 1967; children: Angela, Scott, Irene, Jeffrey, William, Jennifer. Student, U. Wis., Madison. Store mgr. Safeway, Salt Lake City, 1961-68; pres., CEO Winco Foods, Inc, Boise, Idaho, 1968—. Cpl. U.S. Army, 1957-60. Office: Winco Foods 650 N Armstrong Pl Boise ID 83704

LONGAKER, RICHARD PANCOAST, political science educator emeritus; b. Phila., July 1, 1924; s. Edwin P. and Emily (Downs) L.; m. Mollie M. Katz, Jan. 25, 1964; children— Richard Pancoast II, Stephen Edwin, Sarah Ellen, Rachel Elise. B.A. in Polit. Sci, Swarthmore Coll., 1949; M.A. in Am. History, U. Wis., 1950; Ph.D. in Govt, Cornell U., 1953. Teaching asst. Cornell U., 1950-53, vis. asso. prof., 1960-61; asst. prof. Kenyon Coll., 1953-54, asso. prof., 1955-60; asst. prof. U. Calif., Riverside, 1954-55, faculty Los Angeles, 1961 76, chmn. dept. polit. sci., 1963-67, prof., 1965-76, dean acad. affairs grad. div., 1970-71; prof. Johns Hopkins U., Balt., 1976-87, provost and v.p. for acad. affairs, 1976-87, prof. emeritus, cons. western states office Santa Monica, Calif., 1987—. Author: The Presidency and Individual Liberties, 1961; co-author: The Supreme Court and the Commander in Chief, 1976, also articles, revs. Served with AUS, 1943-45. Mem. Am. Polit. Sci. Assn. Office: 16550 Chalet Ter Pacific Palisades CA 90272-2344 E-mail: longaker@ucla.edu

LONGBRAKE, WILLIAM ARTHUR, bank executive; b. Hershey, Pa., Mar. 15, 1943; s. William Van Fleet and Margaret Jane (Barr) L.; m. Martha Ann Curtis, Aug. 23, 1970; children: Derek Curtis, Mark William, David Robert, Dorothy Eleanor Lois. BA, Coll. of Wooster, 1965; MA, U. Wis., 1968, MBA, 1969; D. Bus. Adminstrn., U. Md., 1976. Jr. asst. planner Northeastern Ill. Planning Commn., Chgo., 1966; instr. Coll. Bus. and Mgmt. U. Md., 1969-71, lectr., 1976, 79-81; fin. economist FDIC, Washington, 1971-75, sr. planning specialist Office Corp. Planning, 1975-76, spl. asst. to chmn., acting contr., 1977-78; assoc. dir. div. banking rsch. Office Compt. of Currency, Treas. Dept., Washington, 1976, dep. dir. econ. rsch. and analysis div., 1976-77, dep. compt. for rsch. and econ. programs, 1978-81, acting sr. dep. compt. for policy, 1981-82, sr. dep. compt. for resource mgmt., 1982; exec. v.p., chief fin. officer Wash. Mut. Savs. Bank, Seattle, 1982-85, exec. v.p. finance and ops., 1985-86, sr. exec. v.p., 1986-88, sr. exec. v.p., chief fin. officer, 1988—. Dir. Abarim Bus. Computers Inc., 1993—; WM Trust Co., 1989-93, WM Life Co., 1994—; trustee Washington Mutual Savings Bank Found., 1982—; small bus. cons. Assoc. editor Fin. Mgmt., 1974-78; mem. editorial adv. bd. Issues in Bank Regulation, 1977-84, Jour. Econs. and Bus., 1980-83; contbr. articles to profl. jours. Mem. College park (Md.) Citizen's Adv. Com. on Code Enforcement, 1973-74, cons., 1975; lectr. Albers Sch. Bus. Seattle U., 1985, student mentor, 1994—; bd. dirs. Pget Sound Coun. Fin. Insts., Seattle, dir., 1986-90, v.p., 1988, pres., 1989-90; mem. Seattle Mcpl. League, 1986—; treas., 1988-90, pres., 1990-93, mem. exec. com., chmn. fin. and pers. com. 1988—, devel. Com., 1992—, bus. planning com., 1992-93, strategic planning com., 1993—, Capitol Hill Housing Improvement Program, Seattle, 1988—; mem. The King County Housing Partnership, Seattle, 1988—, exec. com., 1989—, chmn. outreach and tech. assistance com., 1990-92; bd. visitors Sch. Nursing U. Wash., Seattle, 1983-92, chmn., 1986-90; mem. of local initiative support corp. Seattle/Tacoma Adv. Bd., 1989-91; bd. dirs. Diabetes Rsch. Coun., Seattle, 1984-89, v.p., 1987-88; bd. dirs. N.W. Symphony Orch., Seattle, 1987-89, treas., 1988-89, adv. bd., 1989—; trustee Kenney presbyn. Home, West Seattle, 1987—, treas., 1988—, exec. com., chmn. fin. com.; trustee Intiman Theatre Co., Seattle, 1988-92; chmn. tax com. Wash. Savs. league, 1987—, legis. regulatory com., 1991; mem. Seattle Comprehensive Plan Implement Task Force, 1993-94; chmn. adv. bd. Wash. State Affordable Housing, 1993—; dir. Nat. Assn. Housing partnerships, 1993—; mem. King County Growth Mgmt., planning coun. affordable housing task force, 1992-93; co-chair Gov.'s Task force on Affordable Housing, Washington, 1992-93, chmn. bd. dirs. Threshold Housing, 1992—; mem. Impact Fees commn., 1992-92, Coun. Washiongton's Future, arrangement's chair, 1988-91. Recipient Kenneth E. Treffz prize Western Fin. Assn., 1971, certo of recognition William A. Jump Meml. Found., 1978. Mem. Am. Econs. Assn., Am. Fin. Assn., Fin. Mgmt. Assn. (dir. 1978-80), Fin. Execs. Inst. (Puget Sound chpt., bd. dirs. 1988—, chmn. acad. rels. com. 1988-89, chmn. tec. com. 1989-90, treas. 1990-91, v.p. 1991-93, pres. 1993-94, chmn. nominating com. 1994—), Coll. of Wooster Alumni Assn. (pres. Washington Alumni Assn. 1976, pres. Seattle Alumni Assn. 1983—, trustee 1988—, mem. fin., audit, religious dimension, student rels. com. alumni bd. 1988—), Nat. Coun. Savings Instns. (mortgage fin. com. 1989), Columbia Tower Club. Presbyn. (trustee 1973-75, chmn. 1975, elder 1979-82, clk. 1980-82, deacon 1985-88, tras. 1993—). Avocations: jogging, painting, singing, piaho playing. Home: 2000 1st Ave Apt 2601 Seattle WA 98121-2172 Office: Wash Mut Savs Bank PO Box 834 1201 3d Ave Ste 1500 Seattle WA 98101-3029 also: FDIC Bd of Dirs 550 17th St NW Washington DC 20429-0001

LONGENECKER, MARTHA W. museum director; BA in Art, UCLA; MFA, Claremont Grad. Sch.; studied with Millard Sheets, Shoji Hamada, Tatsuzo Shimaoka. Owner ceramics studio, Claremont, Calif.; prof. art, now prof. emeritus San Diego State U.; founder, dir. Mingei Internat. Mus., San Diego. Coord. editing, design and prodn. of exhbn. documentary publs. Mingei Internat. Mus. World Folk Art.; condr. tours. Contbr. chpts. to books; developer videotapes; exhibited at Dalzell Hatfield Galleries. San Diego State U. Found. grantee, 1967, Calif. State U. Rsch. grantee, 1978; recipient Disting. Alumna award Claremont Grad. Sch., 1980, Essence of Life award ElderHelp of San Diego, 1993, Living Legacy award Women's Internat. Ctr., 1994, Women of Distinction award Soroptimist Internat. of La Jolla, 1994. Office: Mingei Internat Mus Balboa Park 1439 El Prado San Diego CA 92101-1617 also: Mingei Internat Mus PO Box 553 La Jolla CA 92038-0553

LONGMIRE, WILLIAM POLK, JR. physician, surgeon; b. Sapulpa, Okla., Sept. 14, 1913; s. William Polk and Grace May (Weeks) L.; m. Jane Jarvis Cornelius, Oct. 28, 1939; children— William Polk III (dec.), Gill, Sarah Jane. A.B., U. Okla., 1934; M.D., Johns Hopkins, 1938; M.D. hon. degrees, U. Athens, Greece, 1972, Northwestern U., , 1976, U. Lund, Sweden, 1976; M.D. (h.c.), U. Heidelberg, Germany, 1974. Diplomate Am. Bd. Surgery (chmn. 1961-62). Intern surgery Johns Hopkins Hosp., Balt., 1938-39, resident surgery, 1944, surgeon in charge plastic out-patient clinic, 1946-48, surgeon, 1947-48; Harvey Cushing fellow exptl. surgery Johns Hopkins, 1939-40, Halsted fellow surg. pathology, 1940, successively instr., asst. prof. assoc. prof. surgery, 1943-48; prof. surgery UCLA, 1948-81, prof. emeritus, 1981—, chmn. dept., 1948-76. Cons. surgery Wadsworth VA Hosp., Los Angeles County Harbor Hosp., 1945-76, VA disting. physician, 1982-87; guest prof. spl. surgery Free U. Berlin, Fed. Republic Germany, 1952-54; vis. prof. surgery Mayo Grad. Sch. Medicine, 1968, Royal Coll. Physicians and Surgeons of Can., 1968; chmn. surgery study sect. NIH, USPHS, 1961-64; mem. Conf. Com. on Grad. Edn. in Surgery, 1959-66, chmn., 1964-66; mem. spl. med. adv. group to med. dir. VA, 1963-68, vice chmn., 1967-68; chmn. surgery tng. com. NIH, 1969-70; mem. pres.' cancer panel Nat. Cancer Inst., 1982-91; Wade vis. prof. Royal Coll. Surgeons Edinburgh, 1972; nat. civilian cons. surgery Air Surgeon USAF; surg. cons. Surgeon Gen. U.S. Army, 1961-88; commr. Joint Commn. on Accreditation of Hosps., 1975-80. Editor: Advances in Surgery, 1975-76; editorial bd.: Annals of Surgery, 1965— . Served as maj. USAF, 1952-54; spl. cons. Air Surgeon Gen.'s Office. Recipient hon. certificate for advancement cardiovascular surgery Free U. of Berlin, 1954, certificate for high profl. achievement USAF, 1954, Gold medal UCLA, 1980, prize Societe Internationale De Chirurgie, 1987, Disting. Med. Alumni award Johns Hopkins Univ. Sch. Medicine, 1999; inducted into Okla. Hall of Fame, 1980. Fellow ACS (chmn. forum com. fundamental surg. problems 1961-62, regent 1962-71, chmn. bd. regents 1969-71, pres. 1971-73, Sheen award N.J. chpt. 1987); hon. fellow Assn. Surgeons Great Britain and Ireland, Royal Coll. Surgeons Ireland, Royal Coll. Surgeons Edinburgh, Royal Coll. Surgeons Eng., Italian Surg. Soc., Association Française de Chirurgie, Japan Surg. Soc.; mem. AMA (mem. council on med. edn. 1964-69), Soc. Scholars of Johns Hopkins U., Soc. Clin. Surgeons, Am. Surg. Assn. (pres. 1967-68), Pacific Coast Surg. Assn., Western Surg. Assn., So. Surg. Assn., Soc. U. Surgeons, Internat. Soc. Surgery, Internat. Fedn. Surg. Colls. (pres. 1984-87), Internat. Surgical Group, (pres. 1993), Am. Assn. Thoracic Surgery, Pan-Pacific Surg. Assn., Los Angeles Surg. Soc. (pres. 1956), Bay Dist. Surg. Soc., Soc. Surgery Alimentary Tract (pres. 1975-76), Calif. Med. Assn. (sec. surg. sect. 1950 51, chmn. sci. bd. 1966 67, Golden Apple award 1990), James IV Assn. Surgeons (pres. 1981), Soc. Surg. Chairmen (pres. 1970-72), Sociédad Argentina di Cirugia Digestiva (hon.), Italian Surg. Soc. (hon.), Phi Beta Kappa, Alpha Omega Alpha; corr. mem. Deutsche Gesellschaft fur Chirugie. Home: 10102 Empyrean Way Bldg 8 Los Angeles CA 90067-3825 Office: U Calif Med Ctr Los Angeles CA 90024

LONGO, LAWRENCE DANIEL, physiologist, obstetrician-gynecologist; b. Los Angeles, Oct. 11, 1926; s. Frank Albert and Florine Azelia (Hall) L.; m. Betty Jeanne Mundall, Sept. 9, 1948; children: April Celeste, Lawrence Anthony, Elisabeth Lynn, Camilla Giselle. BA, Pacific Union Coll., 1949; MD, Coll. Med. Evangelists, Loma Linda, Calif., 1954. Diplomate Am. Bd. Ob-Gyn. Intern L.A. County Gen. Hosp., 1954-55, resident in internal medicine, 1955-58; asst. prof. ob-gyn UCLA, 1962-64; asst. prof. physiology and ob-gyn U. Pa., 1964-68; prof. physiology and ob-gyn Loma Linda U., 1968—; dir. ctr. for perinatal biology Loma Linda U. Sch. Medicine, 1974—. Perinatal biology com. Nat. Inst. Child Health, NIH, 1973-77; co-chmn. reprodn. scientist devel. program NIH; NATO prof. Consiglio Nat. delle Rsch., Italian Govt. Editor: Respiratory Gas Exchange and Blood Flow in the Placenta, 1972, Fetal and Newborn Cardiovascular Physiology, 1978, Charles White and A Treatise on the Management of Pregnant and Lying-in Women, 1987; co-editor: Landmarks in Perinatology, 1975-76, Classics in Obstetrics Gynecology, 1993; editor classic pages in ob-gyn. Am. Jour. Ob-Gyn.; contbr. articles to profl. jours. Served with AUS, 1945-47. Founder Frank A. and Florine A. Longo lectureship in faith, knowledge, and human values Pacific Union Coll., 1993. Fellow Royal Coll. Ob-Gyns., Am. Coll. Ob-Gyns.; mem. Am. Assn. History Medicine (coun.), Am. Osler Soc. (bd. govs., sec.-treas.), Am. Physiol. Soc., Assn. Profs. Ob-Gyn., Perinatal Rsch. Soc., Soc. Gynecologic Investigation (past pres.), Neurosci. Soc., Royal Soc. Medicine. Adventist. Office: Loma Linda U Sch Medicine Ctr Perinatal Biology Loma Linda CA 92350-0001

LONNQUIST, GEORGE ERIC, lawyer; b. Lincoln, Nebr., Mar. 29, 1946; s. John Hall and Elizabeth Claire (Hanson) L.; m. Wendi Ann McDonough; children: Alethea, Courtenay, Barrett. BS, U. Tenn., 1968; JD, U. Nebr., 1971; LLM, NYU, 1974. Bar: Calif. 1983, Oreg. 1972, Nebr. 1971. Law clerk Oreg. Supreme Ct., Salem, 1971-72; dep. legis. counsel Oreg. Legislature, Salem, 1972-73; ptnr. Meysing & Lonnquist, Portland, 1974-78; v.p., assoc. gen. counsel Amfac, Inc., Portland and San Francisco, 1978-84; sr. v.p., gen. counsel Homestead Fin. Corp., Millbrae, Calif., 1984-91, Homestead Savs., Millbrae, 1984-93; pvt. practice, San Francisco, 1993—. Democrat. Roman Catholic. Avocation: woodcarving. Home: 1945 Beach Park Blvd Foster City CA 94404-1326 Office: 4000 E 3rd Ave Foster City CA 94404-4805 E-mail: lonn@legacypartners.com

LOO, THOMAS S. lawyer; b. 1943; BS, JD, U. So. Calif. Bar: Calif. 1969. Ptnr. Bryan Cave LLP, Santa Monica, Calif., 1986—. Office: Bryan Cave LLP 120 Broadway Ste 300 Santa Monica CA 90401-2386

LOOMIS, CHRISTOPHER KNAPP, metallurgical engineer; b. San Francisco, May 6, 1947; s. Richard and Evaline Elsie (Crandal) L.; m. Merril Ellen Purdy, Dec. 8, 1968; 1 child, Nicole Lee; m. Sandra Lee Marsh, Feb. 14, 1993. Profl. Engring. degree, Colo. Sch. Mines, 1969. Process engr. Alcan Aluminum Corp., Riverside, Calif., 1969-73, prodn. supt., 1973-76, process engr. Oswego, N.Y., 1976-78, maintenance engr., 1978-80; metall. engr. Hazelett Strip-Casting Corp., Colchester, Vt., 1980-81; chief engr. ARCO Metals Co., Chgo., 1981-84; maintenance supt. Cerro Metal Products, Paramount, Calif., 1984-85, mgr. engring. and maintenance, 1985-86; supt. tech. svcs. Golden Aluminum Co., Ft. Lupton, Colo., 1987-88, process devel. engr. Lakewood, 1988-91, corp. environ. and process engr., 1991; engr. IV Coors Brewing Co., Golden, 1991-93, materials engr. V, 1993-96, supr. maintenance svcs., 1999—; gen. ptnr. Loomis Engring. and Design, 1996-99. Mem. Am. Soc. for Metals, Metall. Soc., Colo. Sch. Mines Alumni Assn., Am. Soc. for Quality Control, Fedn. Fly Fishers (life), Trout Unltd. (life). Avocations: fishing, camping, mechanics, home repair. Office: Coors Brewing Co PO Box 4030 Golden CO 80401-0030 E-mail: loomiseng@att.net, chris.loomis@coors.com

LOONEY, NORMAN EARL, pomologist, plant physiologist; b. Adrian, Oreg., May 31, 1938; came to Can., 1966; s. Gaynor Parks and Lois Delilah (Francis) L.; m. Arlene Mae Willis, Oct. 4, 1957 (div. 1982); children: Pamela June, Patricia Lorene, Steven Paul; m. Norah Christine Keating, July 16, 1983. BSc in Agr. Edn., Washington State U., 1960, PhD in Horticulture, 1966. Rsch. scientist Agr. Can., Summerland, B.C., 1966-71, scientist, sect. head, 1972-81, sr. scientist, 1982-87, sr. scientist, sect. head, 1987-90, prin. scientist, sect. head, 1991-95; prin. scientist emeritus, 1996—. Vis. scientist food rsch. divsn. CSIRO, Sydney, Australia, 1971-72, East Malling Rsch. Sta., Maidstone, Kent, 1981-82, Dept. Horticulture Lincoln U., Christchurch, New Zealand, 1990-91; sec. Expert Com. on Horticulture, Ottawa, Ont., Can., 1986-90; chmn. Agrl. Can. Tree Fruit Rsch. Network, 1993-97; chmn. working group on growth regulators in fruit prodn. Internat. Soc. Hort. Sci., Leuven, Belgium, 1987-94, chmn. fruit sect., 1994—; pres. XXVI Internat. Hort. Congress, 1998—. Author textbook on cherries, 1995, Temperate and Subtropical Fruit Crops, 1999; contbr. numerous articles and chpts. to sci. publs. Fellow Am. Soc. Hort. Sci.; mem. Can. Soc. for Hort. Sci. (pres. 1997—). Achievements include patent for Promotion of Flowering in Fruit Trees (U.S. and foreign). Office: Agr Can Rsch Sta Summerland BC Canada V0H 1Z0

LOPACH, JAMES JOSEPH, political science educator; b. Great Falls, Mont., June 23, 1942; s. John Ernest and Alma Marie (Schapman) L.; divorced, Dec. 10, 1991; children: Christine, Paul. AB in Philosophy, Carroll Coll., 1964; MA in Am. Studies, U. Notre Dame, 1967, MAT in English Edn., 1968, PhD in Govt., 1973. Mgr. Pacific Telephone, Palo Alto, Calif., 1968-69; adminstr. City of South Bend, Ind., 1971-73; prof. U. Mont., Missoula, 1973—, chmn. dept. polit. sci., 1977-87, assoc. dean Coll. Arts and Scis., 1987-88, acting dir. Mansfield Ctr., 1984-85, spl. asst. to the univ. pres., 1988-92, assoc. provost, 1992-95, spl. asst. to provost, 1995-96. Cons. local govts., state agys., tribal govts., law firms, 1973—; expert witness. Author, editor: We the People of Montana, 1983, Tribal Government Today, 1990, 98, Planning Small Town America, 1990; contbr. articles to profl. jours. Roman Catholic. Office: U Mont Dept Polit Sci Missoula MT 59812-0001 E-mail: lopach@selway.umt.edu

LOPER, JOYCE E. plant pathologist, educator; BS in Biol. Scis., U. Calif., Davis, 1974, MS in Plant Pathology, 1978; PhD in Plant Pathology, U. Calif., Berkeley, 1983. Prof. dept. botany and plant pathology Oreg. State U., 1987—; rsch. plant pathologist USDA-Agrl. Rsch. Svc., rsch. leader Hort. Crops Rsch. Lab., 2000—. Mem. agr. bd. NRC, ecologically-based pest mgmt.: new solutions for a new century panel NAS, Washington, 1992-95, sci. adv. panel NSF Ctr. Microbial Ecology Mich. State U., 1992-96; councilor-at-large Am. Phytopathol. Soc., 1997-2000. Sr. editor Am. Phytopathol. Soc. Press, 1990-93; assoc. editor Molecular Plant-Microbe Interactions, 1996-99; mem. editorial com. Ann. Reviews of Phytopathology, 1996—; mem. editorial bd. European Jour. Plant Path., 1995—. Recipient CIBA GEIGY award Am. Phytopathological Soc., 1995. Fellow Am. Phytopathol. Soc. Office: USDA ARS Hort Crops Lab 3420 NW Orchard Ave Corvallis OR 97330-5014

LOPES, JAMES LOUIS, lawyer; b. Watsonville, Calif., Feb. 1, 1947; s. Allen M. and Norma Maxine (McElroy) L.; m. Gail R. Lopes, Mar. 24, 1979; children: Elizabeth, Jane. BS, U.Calif., Davis, 1969; JD, U. Pacific, 1974; LLM, Harvard U., 1975. Bar: Calif. 1974, U.S. Ct. Appeals (9th cir.), U.S. Dist. Ct. (no., ea., ctrl. dists.) Calif. Assoc. Gendel, Raskoff, Shapiro & Quittner, L.A., 1975-78; ptnr. Gordon, Peitzman & Lopes, San Francisco, 1978-81, Howard, Rice & Nemerovski, San Francisco, 1982—. Adv. com. bankruptcy/creditors' rights Practicing Law Inst., 1992—. Co-author: Law and Business of Computer Software, 1989; contbr. articles to profl. jours. Mem. ABA (bankruptcy com., 1980—), Calif. Bankruptcy Forum (bd. dirs. 1990-93), Calif. State Bar Assn., Turnaround Mgmt. Assn. (bd. dirs. 1996—). Avocations: flying, contract bridge. Office: Howard Rice & Nemerovski 3 Embarcadero Ctr Ste 7 San Francisco CA 94111-4074 E-mail: jlopes@hrice.com

LOPES, ROSALY MUTEL CROCCE, astronomer, planetary geologist; b. Rio de Janeiro, Jan. 8, 1957; came to U.S., 1989; d. Walmir Crocce and Atir (Mutel) Lopes; m. Thomas Nicholas Gautier, III, Nov. 17, 1990 (div.); 1 child, Thomas N. Gautier. BSc in Astronomy, U. London, 1978, PhD in Physics, 1986. Curator Old Royal Obs., Greenwich, Eng., 1985-88; rsch. assoc. Vesuvius Obs., Naples, Italy, 1989; NRC rsch. assoc. Jet Propulsion Lab., Pasadena, Calif., 1989-91, rsch. scientist Galileo Project, 1990—. Mem. Volcanic Eruption Surveillance Team, U.K., 1981; mem. coun. Assn. Astronomy Edn., London, 1988-89. Author numerous works in sci. field. Recipient Latinas in Sci. award Commn. Feminil Mexicana Nat., L.A., 1990; named Woman of the Yr. in Sci., Gems TV, 1997. Fellow Royal Astron. Soc.; mem. Internat. Astron. Union, Am. Astron. Soc., Am. Geophys. Union, Soc. Hispanic Profl. Engrs. Office: Jet Propulsion Lab Mail Stop 183-601 4800 Oak Grove Dr Pasadena CA 91109-8001 E-mail: rlopes@lively.jpl.nasa.gov

LOPEZ, BARRY HOLSTUN, writer; b. Port Chester, N.Y., Jan. 6, 1945; s. Adrian Bernard and Mary Frances (Holstun) L.; m. Sandra Jean Landers, June 10, 1967 (div. Jan. 16, 1999). BA cum laude, U. Notre Dame, 1966, MA in Teaching, 1968; postgrad., U. Oreg., 1968-69; LHD (hon.), Whittier Coll., 1988, U. Portland, 1994, Tex. Tech. U., 2000. Free-lance writer, 1970—. Assoc. Media Studies Ctr. at Columbia Univ., N.Y.C., 1985—; mem. U.S. Cultural Delegation to China, 1988; residency fellow Lannan Found., 1999, MacDowell Colony, 2001. Author: Desert Notes, 1976, Giving Birth to Thunder, 1978, Of Wolves and Men, 1978 (John Burroughs Soc. medal 1979, Christophers of N.Y. medal 1979, Pacific Northwest Booksellers award in nonfiction 1979), River Notes, 1979, Winter Count, 1981 (Disting. Recognition award Friends Am. Writers in Chgo. 1982), Arctic Dreams, 1986 (Nat. Book award in nonfiction Nat. Book Found. 1986, Christopher medal 1987, Pacific Northwest Booksellers award 1987, Frances Fuller Victor award in nonfiction Oreg. Inst. Literary Arts 1987), Crossing Open Ground, 1988, Crow and Weasel, 1990 (Parents Choice Found. award), The Rediscovery of North America, 1991, Field Notes, 1994 (Pacific Northwest Booksellers award in fiction 1995, Critics' Choice award 1996), Lessons From the Wolverine, 1997, About This Life, 1998, Apologia, 1998, Light Action in the Caribbean, 2000; also numerous articles, essays and short stories; contbg. editor Harper's mag., 1981-82, 84—, N.Am. Rev., 1977—, Ga. Rev., 2000—; works translated into Japanese, Swedish, German, Dutch, Italian, French, Norwegian, Chinese, Finnish, Spanish, Arabic. Recipient award in Lit., Am. Acad. Arts and Letters, 1986, Antarctic Svc. medal USN/NSF, 1989, Gov.'s award for Arts, 1990, Lannan Found. award, 1990, Internat. Environ. award Prescott Coll., 1992; HEA Title V fellow, 1967, John Simon Guggenheim Found. fellow, 1987. Mem. PEN Am. Ctr., Authors Guild, Poets and Writers, Nature Conservancy (hon. life).

LOPEZ, DANIEL HERALDO, academic administrator; b. Puerto de Luna, N.Mex., Feb. 14, 1946; s. Julian and Tiofila (Ocaña) L.; m. Linda Vigil, July 12, 1975. BA in Polit. Sci., U. N.Mex., 1970, MA in Polit. Sci., 1972, PhD in Polit. Sci., 1982. Cabinet sec. N.Mex. Dept. Fin. and Adminstrn., Santa Fe, 1984-86, chief of staff for senate fin. and sr. staff analyst House Appropriations and Fin. Com., Santa Fe, 1987-89; assoc. and dep. dir. terminal effects rsch. and analysis N.Mex. Inst. Mining and Tech., Socorro, 1987-89, adj. prof., 1994—; v.p. institutional devel. N.Mex. Inst. Mining and Technology, Socorro, 1989-93, pres., 1993—. Exec. dir. N.Mex. Adv. Coun. on Vocat.-Tech. Edn., 1973-82; adj. prof. U. N.Mex., Albuquerque, 1975-82, N.Mex. Inst. Mining and Tech., Socorro, 1994—; cabinet sec. N.Mex. Employment Security Dept., Albuquerque, 1983-84. Mem. League of United Latin Am. Citizens, Albuquerque; mem., past pres. Albuquerque Hispano C. of C. Staff Sgt. USAF, 1968-69, Korea. Mem. N.Mex. Tech. Rsch. Found. (v.p. 1994), N.Mex. First Exec. Com. (v.p. 1994), N.Mex. Children's Found., N.Mex. Industry Network Corp. (exec. com. 1994), N.Mex. Amigos, Rio Grande Tech. Found. Avocations: running, world travel. Home: One Olive Ln Socorro NM 87801 Office: NMex Inst Mining & Tech Office Pres 801 LeRoy Pl Socorro NM 87801

LOPEZ, JENNIFER, actress, dancer, singer; b. Bronx, N.Y., July 24, 1970; Appeared in films Money Train, 1995, Jack, 1996, Blood and Wine, 1996, Anaconda, 1997, Selena, 1997, My Family, 1995, U-Turn, 1997, Antz (voice), 1998, Out of Sight, 1998, Thieves, 1999, Pluto Nash, 1999, The Wedding Planner, 2000, The Cell, 2000, Angel Eyes, 2000; released Latin music album: On the 6. Recipient ALMA award 1998, Lasting Image award 1998, Lone Star Film and TV award 1998; nominated for Blockbuster Entertainment award, 1998, Golden Globe, 1998, Independent Spirit award 1996, MTV Movie award 1999. Office: Internat Creative Mgmt 8942 Wilshire Blvd Beverly Hills CA 90211-1934

LOPEZ, JOE EDDIE, state legislator; b. Duran, N.Mex., Dec. 8, 1939; m. Rosie Lopez; children: Debbie, Eddie. Student, Ariz. State U. Mem. Ariz. Ho. of Reps., 1991-96, Ariz. Senate, Dist. 22, 1996—; mem. appropriations com., mem. edn. com. Ariz. State Senate, mem. family svcs. com., mem. joint legis. budget com. Affirmative action adminstr. Ariz. Dept. Transp.; pres. Housing Devel. Corp. Elected ofcl. Maricopa County Bd. Suprs., Phoenix, 1972-76; mem. governing bd. Phoenix Union H.S. Dist., 1990-96; bd. dirs. Tiempo Devel.; active Los Diablos, Inc., Ariz. Hispanic Cmty. Forum, Mexican-Am. Legislators Policy Inst.; past co-founder, chmn. Chicanos Por La Causa, Inc.; past co-founder, bd. mem. Valle Del Sol, Inc., Barrio Youth Project; past chmn. Phoenix Human Rels. Commn.; past bd. mem. Boy Scouts Am., Ariz. Recipient Cmty. Leadership award Chicanos Por La Causa, 1972, Cmty. Leadership award SER, 1976, Outstanding Svc. to the Cmty. award Ariz. Hispanic/Native Am. Indian Sch. Bd. Forum, 1989, El Aguila award Alma de la Gente, 1992. Mem. Nat. Coun. State Legislators (Ariz. rep. tourism and econ. devel. com.). Democrat. Roman Catholic. Office: State Capitol Bldg 1700 W Washington St Ofc 311 Phoenix AZ 85007-2812 E-mail: jlopez@azleg.state.az.us

LOPEZ, LINDA M. state legislator; BA, MBA, Coll. of Santa Fe. Cons., N.Mex.; mem. N. Mex. Senate, Dist. 11, Santa Fe, 1996—; vice chair edn. com.; mem. jud. com. Democrat. Office: 9132 Suncrest Ave SW Albuquerque NM 87121-8846

LOPEZ, MANUEL M. mayor; Mayor, Oxnard, Calif. Address: 305 W 3rd St Oxnard CA 93030-5790

LOPICCOLO, JOHN, conductor, music director; m. Mary Lopiccolo; children: Sabrina, John Michael. MusB in Music Edn., San Francisco State U.; MusM in Orchestral Conducting, Ea. Washington U. Music dir., conductor Idaho Falls (Idaho) Symphony Soc., Inc. Founder, music dir., conductor Idaho Falls Symphony Chorale; concert programmer ann. POPS concerts, Idaho; guest condr. Charlotte, Dubuque, Spokane, S.D., Bremerton, Great Falls, Lethbridge, Walla Walla, Fla. Festival Symphonies, Mont. All-State Orch.; cover-condr. Boise Philharm., 1995-96. Guest condr. (play) Porgy and Bess, Vancouver, B.C. Judge Idaho State Civic Symphony, Idaho Falls Symphony Young Artist Competition, Idaho Falls Music Club Scholarship Awards. Recipient Outstanding Svc. award Greater Idaho Falls C. of C. Office: Idaho Symphony Soc Inc 498 A St Idaho Falls ID 83402-3617

LOPKER, PAMELA, technology industry executive; BS in Math., U. Calif., Santa Barbara, 1976—. Cert. prodn. and inventory mgmt. Sr. sys. analyst Comptek Rsch., 1976-79; founder, chmn., pres. QAD, Carpinteria, Calif., 1979—. Profiled 4 times Forbes Mag. (cover 3 times); named to Women in Tech. Internat. Hall of Fame 1997. Mem. Am. Prodn. and Inventory Control Soc. Office: QAD Inc 6450 Via Real Carpinteria CA 93013-2924

LORD, HAROLD WILBUR, electrical engineer, electronics consultant; b. Eureka, Calif., Aug. 20, 1905; s. Charles Wilbur and Rossina Camilla (Hansen) L.; m. Doris Shirley Huff, July 25, 1928; children: Joann Shirley (Mrs. Carl Cook Disbrow), Alan Wilbur, Nancy Louise (Mrs. Leslie Crandall), Harold Wayne. BS, Calif. Inst. Tech., 1926. With GE, Schenectady, N.Y., 1926-66, electronics engr., 1960-66; pvt. cons. engr. Mill Valley, Calif., 1966-90. Contbr. articles to profl. jours.; patentee in field. Fellow IEEE (life, tech. v.p. 1962, Centennial medal 1984, IEEE Magnetics Soc. Achievement award 1984, 3d Millenium medal 2000). Home: 1565 Golf Course Dr Rohnert Park CA 94928-5638

LORD, JERE JOHNS, retired physics educator; b. Portland, Oreg., Jan. 3, 1922; s. Percy Samuel and Hazel Marie (Worstel) L.; m. Miriam E. Hart, Dec. 30, 1947; children— David, Roger, Douglas. Physicist U. Calif. Radiation Lab., Berkeley, 1942-46; research asso. U. Chgo., 1950-52; asst. prof. physics U. Wash., Seattle, 1952-57, assoc. prof., 1957-62, prof., 1962-92, prof. emeritus, 1992—. Fellow AAAS, Am. Phys. Soc.; mem. Am. Assn. Physics Tchrs. Home: 720 Seneca St Apt 1004 Seattle WA 98101-2766 Office: U Wash Dept Physics Box 351560 Seattle WA 98195-1560

LORE, LINDA, retail executive; b. Calif. With Robinson's Dept. Stores, Calif., 1972-82, fragrance buyer, 1983-86; v.p. sales planning and devel. Giorgio Beverly Hills, Santa Monica, sr. v.p. mktg.; pres., CEO Giorgio Beverly Hills (acquired by Procter & Gamble Europe), Santa Monica, 1991-97; corp. v.p., gen. mgr. Giorgio Products-Worldwide Procter & Gamble, 1994-97; pres., CEO Frederick's of Hollywood, Calif., 1999—. Bd. dirs. Inst. Design Merchandising, Coalition to Preserve the Integrity of Am. Trademarks, Fragrance Found. Bd. dirs. L.A. chpt. drop-out prevention prog. Cities in Sch., Inc.; mem. Com. 200, trustee Women's Forum. Recipient Woman Achievement award Beverly Hills Women's Network, 1992, Outstanding Businesswoman award L.A. Advt. Women, 1992, Industry Leadership award So. Calif. Cosmetic Assn., 1993, Beautiful Apple Industry Leadership award Greater N.Y. March of Dimes Birth Defects Found, 1996; named Humanitarian of Year, West Coast Beauty Assn. which funded the Linda LoRe Found. for Pediatric AIDS, 1993. Achievements include winning the exclusive rights to launch the Giorgio fragrance on the West Coast; successful mktg. of Giorgio fragrances RED, RED For Men, WINGS, WINGS For Men, HUGO by Hugo Boss, Giorgio Aire, Ocean Dream, RED 2. Office: Fredericks of Hollywood PO Box 229 Hollywood CA 90078-0229

LORENZ, MARIANNE, curator; b. Denver, Nov. 5, 1949; d. Paul Frederick and Celesta (Johnson) Holscher. BA, U. Colo., 1971, MFA, 1981, MBA in Mktg., 1982. Tchr. French/German Adams County #50, Westminster, Colo., 1972-80; coord. pub. programs Colo. State History Mus., Denver, 1984-85, dir. edn., 1985-87; curator edn. Joslyn Art Mus., Omaha, 1987-89; asst. dir. collections and programs Dayton (Ohio) Art Inst., 1989; dir., chief exec. ofcr. Yellowstone Art Museum, Billings, Mont. Author: Theme and Improvisation Kandinsky and the American Avant-Garde, 1912-1950, 1992; contbr. Dictionary of Art, 1993. Fulbright grantee, 1975-76. Mem. Am. Assn. Museums, Coll. Art Assn. Avocations: skiing, running. Office: Yellowstone Art Museum 401 N 27th St Billings MT 59101

LORENZ, NANCY, artist; BFA in Painting and Printmaking, U. Mich., 1985; MFA in Painting, Tyler Sch. Art, Phila. and Rome, 1988. Instr. R.I. Sch. Design, 1996; lectr. in field. One-person shows include Temple U., Rome, 1988, Willoughby Sharp Gallery, N.Y., 1990, Genovese Gallery, Boston, 1990, 91, 94, others; exhibited in group shows at Helander Gallery, Palm Beach, 1991, 92, 93, Helander Gallery, N.Y., 90, 92, 94, N.Y. Pub. Lib., 1994, Austin Ackles Studio, N.Y., 1995, PDX, Portland, Oreg., 1996, 97, 98, Galerie Verneil des Saints-Péres, Paris, Galerie Xippas, Paris; numerous others; represented in permanent collections Senayan Hotel, Jakarta, Yokahama Hotel, Japan, Soho Grand Hotel, N.Y., MIA Ins., Pan Am. Bldg., San Francisco, Muscat Hilton, Oman, David Barton Gym, N.Y. Pub. Lib., Champion Paper, Shinwa Med. Inc., Nagoya, Japan, Aero Studios, The Boston Co., numerous others. Guggenheim fellow, 1998. Office: c/o PDX Gallery 604 NW 12th Ave Portland OR 97209-3002 E-mail: pdxgallery@aol.com

LORENZ, STEPHEN R. career officer; b. Houston, Oct. 17, 1951; BS in Internat. Affairs, USAF Acad., 1973; M in Pub. Adminstrn., U. Northern Colo., 1977; postgrad., Pa. State U., 1995. Commd. 2d lt. USAF, 1973, advanced through grades to brig. gen., 1996; co-pilot, aircraft comdr. 4th Airborne Command and Control Squadron, Ellsworth AFB, S.D., 1975-80; aide, T-39 pilot to comdr. Air Force Logistics Command, Wright-Patterson AFB, Ohio, 1980-82; congrl. liaison officer Office of Legis. Liaison The Pentagon, Washington, 1982-83, exec. officer to the dir. of legis. liaison, 1983; dep. chief Air Force Senate Liaison Office, Capitol Hill, Washington, 1983-86; KC-135 instr. pilot, flight comdr. 924th Air Refueling Squadron, Castle AFB, Calif., 1986-87; comdr. 93rd Air Refueling Squadron, Castle AFB, 1987-89; chief N.E. Asia br., Japan desk officer The Pentagon, Washington, 1990-91, chief European and North Atlantic Treaty Orgn. Policy br., 1991-92; comdr. 398th Ops. Group, Castle AFB, 1992-93, 22nd Air Refueling Wing, 722nd Air Refueling Wing, March AFB, 1993-94, 305th Air Mobility Wing, McGuire AFB, N.J., 1994-96; commandant of cadets, comdr. 34th Tng. Wing, USAF Acad., Colorado Springs, Colo., 1996-99. Decorated Legion of Merit with oak leaf cluster. Office: USAF Acad Commandant for Cadets 2354 Fairchild Dr Ste 5a10 U S A F Academy CO 80840-6299

LORENZEN, ROBERT FREDERICK, ophthalmologist; b. Toledo, Mar. 20, 1924; s. Martin Robert and Pearl Adeline (Bush) L.; m. Lucy Logdson, Feb. 14, 1970; children: Roberta Jo, Richard Martin, Elizabeth Anne. BS, MD, Duke U., 1948; MS, Tulane U., 1953. Intern Presbyn. Hosp., Chgo., 1948-49; resident Duke U. Med. Ctr., 1949-51, Tulane Grad. Sch., 1951-53; practice medicine specializing in ophthalmology Phoenix, 1953—. Mem. staff St. Joseph's Hosp., St. Luke's Hosp., Good Samaritan Hosp., Surg. Eye Ctr. of Ariz. Pres. Ophthalmic Scis. Found., 1970-73; chmn. bd. trustees Rockefeller and Abbe Prentice Eye Inst. of St. Luke's Hosp., 1975— Editor in chief Ariz. Medicine, 1963-66, 69-70. Recipient Gold Headed Cane award, 1974; named to Honorable Order of Ky. Colls. Fellow ACS, Internat. Coll. Surgeons, Am. Acad. Ophthalmology and Otolaryngology, Pan Am. Assn. Ophthalmology; mem. Am. Assn. Ophthalmology (sec. of ho. of dels. 1972-73, trustee 1973-76), Ariz. Ophthal. Soc. (pres. 1966-67), Ariz. Med. Assn. (bd. dirs. 1963-66, 69-70), Royal Soc. Medicine, Rotary (pres. Phoenix 1984-850). Republican. Office: 3333 E Camino Sin Nombre Paradise Valley AZ 85253

LORENZINI, PAUL GILBERT, electric power industry executive; b. Portland, Oreg., Apr. 16, 1942; s. Gilbert Henry and Viola Pauline (Gates) L.; m. Janet Grace Jesperson, Aug. 19, 1967; children: Christy, Michael. BS in Marine Engring., U.S. Merchant Marine Acad., 1964; PhD in Nuclear Engring., Oreg. State U., 1969; JD, Loyola U., L.A., 1975. Registered profl. engr., Calif.; bar: Calif., Oreg. Nuclear engr. Rockwell Internat., Canoga Park, Calif., 1969-76; assoc. Tooze, Kerr, Peterson, Marshall & Shenker, Portland, 1976-79; dir. health/safety/environ. Rockwell Hanford Ops., Richland, Wash., 1979-82, asst. gen. mgr., 1982-84, v.p., gen. mgr., 1984-87; dir., spl. projects Pacific Power & Light, Portland, 1987, v.p., 1987-89, exec. v.p., 1989—. Adv. bd. dept. nuclear engring. Oreg. State U., Corvallis, 1989—. Pres. Columbia Pacific Coun., Boy Scouts Am., Portland, 1991; trustee Maryhurst Coll., Lake Oswego, Oreg., 1990—; bd. dirs. Holladay Park Med. Ctr., Portland, 1990—. Recipient Tri-Cities Engr. of Yr. award NSPE, Richland, Wash., 1983-84. Mem. Arlington Club, Am. Nuclear Soc., Riverside Country Club, Oreg. Golf Club, Mountain park Tennis Club. Avocations: golf, skiing, tennis, fishing. Home: 17550 Brookhurst Dr Lake Oswego OR 97034-5095 Office: Pacific Power 920 SW 6th Ave Portland OR 97204-1239

LO SCHIAVO, JOHN JOSEPH, university executive; b. San Francisco, Feb. 25, 1925; s. Joseph and Anne (Re) Lo S. A.B., Gonzaga U., 1948, Ph.L. and M.A., 1949; S.T.L., Alma Coll., 1962. Joined S.J., Roman Catholic Ch., 1942; tchr. St. Ignatius High Sch., San Francisco, 1949-50; instr. philosophy and theology U. San Francisco, 1950-52, 56-57, 61-62, v.p. for student affairs, dean of students, 1962-68, pres., 1977-91, chancellor, 1991—. Pres. Bellarmine Coll. Prep. Sch., San Jose, 1968-75 Bd. dirs. Sch. of Sacred Heart, 1991-2000, St. Mary's Hosp., 1990-96, United Religion Initiative, 1999—. Mem. Olympic Club, Bohemian Club, Univ. Club. Office: U San Francisco 2130 Fulton St San Francisco CA 94117-1080

LOSSE, JOHN WILLIAM, JR. mining company executive; b. St. Louis, Mar. 16, 1916; s. John William and Claire (Schmedtje) L.; m. Marjorie West Penney, Mar. 7, 1942; children: John William IV, Georgia Shane, Barbara Stevens, Mary Coulter, Penney Gregersen, Jane Momberger. BS, Washington U., St. Louis, 1937; MBA, Harvard U., 1939. Sec.-treas. J.W. Losse Tailoring Co., St. Louis, 1939-41, 45-55; treas., controller, asst. sec. Uranium Reduction Co., Salt Lake City, 1955-62; v.p. finance Atlas Minerals div. Atlas Corp., Salt Lake City, 1962-64; asst. v.p., asst. treas. Am. Zinc Co., St. Louis, 1965-66, v.p. finance, treas., 1966-70; v.p. finance Conrad, Inc., St. Louis, 1970-71; v.p. finance, sec., dir. Fed. Resources Corp., Salt Lake City, 1971-82, pres., chief exec. officer, dir., 1982-84, 85-86, chief fin. officer, dir., 1986-88, v.p., treas., 1988—, also bd. dirs., 1988-89; sec.-treas. Madawaska Mines Ltd., Bancroft, Ont., Can., 1976-82, pres., bd. dirs. Can., 1983—; pres. Camp Bird Colo., Inc., Ouray, 1983-92. Pres. Utah Natural Resources Council, 1964; tax com. and fin. adv. com. Am. Mining Congress, 1965-84; bd. dirs. Episcopal Mgmt. Corp., Salt Lake City, 1988-99. Bd. dirs. St. Mark's Hosp., Salt Lake City, 1987-88, Arthritis Found., Salt Lake City, 1988-97; vice chmn., bd. dirs. St. Mark's Charities, Salt Lake City, 1987-92; mem. investment com. Corp. of the Bishop, Salt Lake City, 1989-96; mem. investment adv. com. Perpetual Trust of St. Peter and St. Paul, 1995-96. Lt. comdr. USNR, 1941-45. Mem. Utah Mining Assn. (bd. dirs., legis. and tax coms. 1971-91), Alta Club of Salt Lake City, Phi Delta Theta. Republican. Episcopalian. Office: Fed Resources Corp PO Box 806 Salt Lake City UT 84110-0806 Fax: 801-521-6400

LOTT, IRA TOTZ, pediatric neurologist; b. Cin., Apr. 15, 1941; s. Maxwell and Jeneda (Totz) L.; m. Ruth J. Weiss, June 21, 1964; children: Lisa, David I. BA cum laude, Brandeis U., 1963; MD cum laude, Ohio State U., 1967. Intern Mass. Gen. Hosp., Boston, 1967, resident in pediatrics, 1967-69, resident in child neurology, 1971-74; clin. assoc. NIH, Bethesda, Md., 1969-71; from clin. rsch. fellow to asst. prof. Harvard Med. Sch., Boston, 1971-82; clin. dir. Eunice Kennedy Shriver Ctr. for Mental Retardation, Waltham, Mass., 1974-82; assoc. prof. U. Calif., Irvine, 1983-91, prof., 1992—, chmn. dept. pediat., 1990-2000, dir. clin. neurosci. devel., 2000—. Chmn. dept. pediatrics U. Calif., Irvine, 1990-2000 , dir. pediatric neurology, 1983—, clin. neuroscience devel., 2000—; pres. Prof. Child Neurology, Mpls., 1992—. Editor: Down Syndrome-Medical Advances, 1991; contbr. articles to profl. jours. Sec., treas. Child Neurology

Soc., Mpls., 1987-90. Lt. comdr. USPHS, 1969-71. NIH grantee, 1974—; recipient Career Devel. award Kennedy Found., 1976. Fellow Am. Acad. Neurology; mem. Am. Pediatric Soc., Am. Neurol. Assn., Nat. Down Syndrome Soc. (sci. acad. bd. 1985—), Western Soc. for Pediatric Rsch. (councillor 1989-91). Achievements include research in relationship of Down Syndrome to Alzheimer's disease, neurometabolic disease, extra-corporeal membrane oxygenation in infants. Office: U Calif Irvine Med Ctr Dept Pediatrics 101 The City Dr S # 2 Orange CA 92868-3201

LOTT, RONNIE (RONALD MANDEL LOTT), retired professional football player, television broadcaster; b. Albuquerque, May 8, 1959; BS in Pub. Adminstrn., U. So. Calif., 1981. With San Francisco 49ers, 1981-90, L.A. Raiders, 1991-93, N.Y. Jets, 1993-94, Kansas City Chiefs, 1994-95; analyst NFL Fox Broadcasting Co., Beverly Hills, Calif., 1996—. Founder, All Stars Helping Kids, 1989. Named to Sporting News Coll. All-Am. team, 1980, Pro Bowl team, 1981-84, 86-91, Sporting News All-Pro team, 1981, 87, 90. Office: Fox Broadcasting Co PO Box 900 Beverly Hills CA 90213-0900

LOUGHEED, PETER, lawyer, former Canadian official; b. Calgary, Alta., Can., July 26, 1928; s. Edgar Donald and Edna (Bauld) L.; m. Jeanne Estelle Rogers, June 21, 1952; children— Stephen, Andrea, Pamela, Joseph. B.A., U. Alta., 1950, LL.B., 1952; M.B.A., Harvard U., 1954. Bar: Alta 1955. With firm Fenerty, Fenerty, McGillivray & Robertson, Calgary, 1955-56; sec. Mannix Co., Ltd., 1956-58, gen. counsel, 1958-62, v.p., 1959-62, dir., 1960-62; individual practice law, from 1962; formerly mem. Alta. Legislature for Calgary West; formerly leader Progressive Conservative Party of Alta., 1965-85; premier of Alta., 1971-85; ptnr. Bennett Jones, Calgary, 1986-99, counsel, 1999—. Office: Bennett Jones 855 2nd St SW 4500 Bankers Hall Calgary AB Canada T2P 4K7

LOUIE, STEVEN GWON SHENG, physics educator, researcher; b. Canton, China, Mar. 26, 1949; came to U.S., 1961; s. Art and Kam Shui (Lau) L.; m. Jane Yuk Wong, Aug. 3, 1975; children: Jonathan S., Jennifer Y., Sarah W. AB in Math. and Physics, U. Calif., Berkeley, 1972, PhD in Physics, 1976. IBM postdoctoral fellow IBM Watson Rsch. Ctr., Yorktown Heights, N.Y., 1977-79; mem. vis. tech. staff AT&T Bell Labs., Murray Hill, N.J., 1979; asst. prof. U. Pa., Phila., 1979-80; NSF postdoctoral fellow physics dept. U. Calif., Berkeley, 1976-77, assoc. prof., 1980-84, prof., 1984—, Miller rsch. prof., 1986, 95. Faculty scientist Lawrence Berkeley Lab., 1980-93, sr. faculty scientist, 1993—; cons. Exxon Rsch. & Engring. Co., Annandale, N.J., 1981-87. Editor Solid State Comm., 1994—; contbr. over 300 articles to sci. jours. Recipient sustained outstanding rsch. in solid state physics award Dept. Energy, 1993; fellow A.P. Sloan Found., 1980, Guggenheim fellow, 1989. Fellow Am. Phys. Soc. (Aneesur Rahman prize 1996, Davisson-Germer prize 1999); mem. Materials Rsch. Soc. Baptist. Avocations: gardening, skiing, tennis. Office: U Calif Dept Physics 366 LeConte Hall 7300 Berkeley CA 94720-7300

LOUNSBURY, JOHN FREDERICK, geographer, educator; b. Perham, Minn., Oct. 26, 1918; s. Charles Edwin and Maude (Knight) L.; m. Dorothea Frances Eggers, Oct. 3, 1943; children— John Frederick, Craig Lawrence, James Gordon. B.S., U. Ill., 1942, M.S., 1946; Ph.D., Northwestern U., 1951. Asst. dir. rural land classification program Insular Govt., P.R., 1949-52; cons., research analyst Dayton Met. Studies, Inc, Ohio, 1957-60; chmn. dept. earth scis., prof. geography Antioch Coll., 1951-61; prof. geography, head dept. geography and geology Eastern Mich. U., 1961-69; chmn. dept. geography Ariz. State U., 1969-77; dir. Ctr. for Environ. Studies, 1977-80; prof. emeritus Ariz. State U., 1987—. Project dir. Geography in Liberal Edn. Project, Assn. Am. Geographers, NSF, 1963-65, project dir. commn. on coll. geography, 1965-74; dir. environment based edn. project US. Office Edn., 1974-75; dir. spatial analysis of land use project NSF, 1975-85 Author articles, workbooks, textbooks. Mem. Yellow Springs Planning Commn., Ohio, dir. research, 1957-60; mem. Ypsilanti Planning Commn., 1961-66; research com. Washtenaw County Planning Commn., 1961-69; mem. cons. Ypsilanti Indsl. Devel. Corp., 1961-63. Served with AUS, 1942-46, ETO. Named Man of Yr., Yellow Springs C. of C., 1956-57 Fellow Ariz.-Nev. Acad. Sci.; mem. Assn. Am. Geographers (chmn. East Lakes div. 1959-61, mem. nat. exec. council 1961-64, chmn. liberal edn. com. 1961-65), Nat. Council Geog. Edn. (chmn. earth sci. com. 1961-68, regional coord. 1961-63, mem. exec. bd. 1968-71, 77-83, v.p. 1977-78, pres. 1979-80, Disting. Svc. award 1988, Disting. Mentor award 1990), Mich. Acad. Sci. Arts and Letters (chmn. pub. relations com. 1964-69, past chmn. geography sect.), Ohio Acad. Sci. (past exec. v.p.), Mich. Acad. Sci., Ariz. Acad. Sci., Am. Geog. Soc., AAAS, Sigma Xi, Delta Kappa Epsilon, Gamma Theta Upsilon. Home: 2426-2 Quarterback Ct Ypsilanti MI 48197 Office: Ariz State U Dept Geography Tempe AZ 85281

LOURD, BRYAN, talent agent; Mng. dir. Creative Artists Agy., Beverly Hills, Calif. Office: Creative Artists Agy 9830 Wilshire Blvd Beverly Hills CA 90212-1825 Fax: 310-288-4711

LOUX, GORDON DALE, religious organization administrator; b. Souderton, Pa., June 21, 1938; s. Curtis L. and Ruth (Derstine) L.; m. Elizabeth Ann Nordland, June 18, 1960; children: Mark, Alan, Jonathan. Diploma, Moody Bible Inst., Chgo., 1960; BA, Gordon Coll., Wenham, Mass., 1962; BD, No. Bapt. Sem., Oak Brook, Ill., 1965, MDiv, 1971; MS, Nat. Coll. Edn., Evanston,Ill., 1984; LHD (hon.), Sioux Falls Coll., 1985. Ordained to ministry, Bapt. Ch., 1965. Assoc. pastor Forest Park (Ill.) Bapt. Ch., 1962-65; alumni field dir. Moody Bible Inst., Chgo., 1965-66, dir. pub. rels., 1972-76; dir. devel. Phila. Coll. Bible, 1966-69; pres. Stewardship Svcs., Wheaton, Ill., 1969-72; exec. v.p. Prison Fellowship Ministries, Washington, 1976-84, pres., CEO, 1984-88, Prison Fellowship Internat., Washington, 1979-87; pres. Internat. Students, Inc., Colorado Springs, Colo., 1988-93, Gordon D. Loux & Co., LLC, Colorado Springs, 1994—, Trinity Cmty. Found., 1996—. Author: Uncommon Courage, 1987, You Can Be a Point of Light, 1991; contbg. author: Money for Ministries, 1989, Dictionary of Christianity in America, 1989. Bd. dirs. Evang. Coun. for Fin. Accountability, Washington, 1979-92, vice chmn., 1981-84, 86-87, chmn., 1987-89; vice chmn. Billy Graham Greater Washington Crusade, 1985-85; bd. dirs. Evang. Fellowship of Mission Agys., 1991-94, Ctr. for Christian Jewish Dialogue, Colorado Springs, 1996—, Hope and Home, Colorado Springs, 1998—, C2ure, Mechanicsburg, Pa., 1999—, Global Leaders Initiative. Named Alumnus of Yr., Gordon Coll., 1986. Mem. Broadmoor Golf Club (Colo. Springs). Republican. Home: 740 Bear Paw Ln N Colorado Springs CO 80906-3215 Office: PO Box 38898 Colorado Springs CO 80937-8898

LOVE, COURTNEY, singer, actress; b. San Francisco, July 9, 1965; d. Hank Harrison and Linda Carroll; m. Kurt Cobain, Feb. 1992 (dec.); 1 child, Frances Bean. Singer, writer, musician Hole. Albums include Pretty on the Inside, 1991, Live Through This, 1994; appeared in film Sid and Nancy, 1986, Feeling Minnesota, 1996, The People vs. Larry Flynt, 1996, Basquiate, 1996, Life, 1997, Man on the Moon, 1999, 200 Cigarettes, 1999; actress, co-prodr. Not Bad For a Girl, 1996; television appearance on MTV Unplugged, 1995. Office: c/o David Geffen Co 9130 W Sunset Blvd Los Angeles CA 90069-3110

LOVE, DANIEL JOSEPH, consulting engineer; b. Fall River, Mass., Sept. 27, 1926; s. Henry Aloysius and Mary Ellen (Harrington) L.; m. Henrietta Maurisse Popper, June 10, 1950 (dec. Mar. 1986); children: Amy, Timothy (dec.), Terence, Kevin; m. Adeline Aponte Esquivel, Feb. 11, 1989; stepchildren: Eric, Brian, Jason. BSEE, Ill. Inst. Tech., 1951, MSEE, 1956; MBA, Calif. State U., Long Beach, 1973. registered profl. engr., Calif., Ariz., Ill., La.; cert. fire protection, Calif. Test engr. Internat. Harvester Co., Chgo., 1951-52; designer Pioneer Svc. & Engring. Co., Chgo., 1952-53; project engr., ops. mgr. Panellit Co., Skokie, Ill., 1953-60; mktg. mgr. Control Data Co., Mpls., 1961-62; mktg. mgr., asst. to pres. Emerson Electric Co., Pasadena, Calif., 1963-65; pres., gen. mgr. McKee Automation Co., North Hollywood, 1965-68; engring. specialist Bechtel Co., Vernon and Norwalk, 1968-80, chief elec. engr. Madrid, 1980-83, engring. specialist Norwalk, Calif., 1983-87; cons. engr. Hacienda Heights, 1987—. Contbr. articles to jours. in field. Pres. Wilson High Sch. Band Boosters, Hacienda Heights. 1971-73. With USN, 1944-46. Named Outstanding Engr., Inst. for Advancement Engring., 1986; recipient 3d place prize paper award Industry Application Soc., 1995. Fellow IEEE (disting. lectr., chmn. Met. L.A. sect. 1973-74, chmn. L.A. coun. 1977-78, chmn. protection com. 1990-91, Richard Harold Kaufmann award 1994, Ralph H. Lee prize paper award 1995); mem. NSPE, Nat. Acad. Forensic Engrs., Instrument Soc. Am. (sr.), Soc. Fire Protection Engrs. Republican. Roman Catholic. Avocations: duplicate bridge, travel, walking, writing. Home: 16300 Soriano Dr Hacienda Heights CA 91745 E-mail: danlove@ieee.org

LOVE, KEITH SINCLAIR, communications executive; b. Apr. 26, 1947; s. James and Ruth L. BA, NYU, 1980. Editor N.Y. Times, N.Y.C., 1973-79; editor, polit. writer L.A. Times, 1979-90; asst. to v.p. ops. McClatchy Newspapers, Inc., 1990-92; pub. Ellensburg (Wash.) Daily Record, 1992-98; comm. dir. Gov. State of Washington, Olympia, 1998-99; v.p. comm. Stimson-Lane Vineyards & Estates, Woodinville, Wash., 1999—. Office: Stimson Lane Vineyards State Wash PO Box 1976 Woodinville WA 98072-1976

LOVE, SANDRA RAE, information specialist; b. San Francisco, Feb. 20, 1947; d. Benjamin Raymond and Charlotte C. Martin; m. Michael D. Love, Feb. 14, 1971. BA in English, Calif. State U., Hayward, 1968; MS in L.S., U. So. Calif., 1969. Tech. info. specialist Lawrence Livermore (Calif.) Nat. Lab., 1969—. Mem. Beta Sigma Phi. Democrat. Episcopalian. Office: Lawrence Livermore Nat Lab PO Box 808 Livermore CA 94551-0808

LOVE, SUSAN MARGARET, surgeon, educator, writer; b. N.J., Feb. 9, 1948; d. James Arthur and Margaret Connick (Schwab) L.; life ptnr. Helen Sperry Cooksey, Sept. 8, 1982; 1 child, Katherine Mary Love-Cooksey. BS, Fordham U., 1970; MD, SUNY, N.Y.C., 1974; DSc (hon.), Northeastern U., 1991; D of Humane Sci. (hon.), Simmons Coll., 1992; LHD (hon.), U. R.I., 1997; DSc (hon.), SUNY, N.Y.C., 1998; MBA, UCLA, 1998. Clin. fellow in surgery Harvard Med. Sch., Boston, 1977-78, clin. instr. in surgery, 1980-87; dir. breast clinic Beth Israel Hosp., Boston, 1980-88; clin. assoc. in surg. oncology Dana Farber Cancer Inst., Boston, 1981-92; dir. Faulkner Breast Ctr. Faulkner Hosp., Boston, 1988-92; asst. clin. prof. surgery Harvard Med. Sch., Cambridge, 1987-92; assoc. prof. clin. surgery UCLA Sch. Medicine, 1992-96; dir. UCLA Breast Ctr., 1992-96; adj. prof. surgery UCLA, 1966—. Adv. coun. Breast and Cervical Cancer Coun., State of Calif. Dept. Human Svcs., 1994-98; mem. NSABP Oversight Com., Pitts., 1994; mem. adv. com. Women's Health Initiative Program, Washington, 1993-95; prin. investigator Nat. Surg. Adjuvant Breast and Bowel Project, 1985-96; mem. Pres.'s Nat. Action Plan on Breast Cancer, DHHS, 1994—; co-chair Biol. Resources Working Group, 1994-98, mem. exec. and steering coms., 1995—; mem. Nat. Cancer Adv. Bd., 1998—. Author: Dr. Susan Love's Breast Book, 1990, 3d edit., 2000, Dr. Susan Love's Hormone Book, 1997, Atlas of Techniques in Breast Surgery, 1996; (book chpts.) Breast Disease, 1987, Clinics in Oncology: Breast Cancer, 1989, The Woman's Guide to Good Health, 1991; contbr. articles to profl. jours. Founder, bd. dirs. Nat. Breast Cancer Coalition, 1991—; mem. breast cancer subcom. divsn. cancer treatment Bd. Sci. Counselors, Nat. Cancer Inst., 1992-95; conf. com. co-chair Sec.'s Conf. to Establish Nat. Action Plan on Breast Cancer, 1993; med. dir. Susan Love MD Breast Cancer Found., 1996—. Recipient Rose Kushner award Am. Med. Writers Assn., 1991, Achievement award Am. Assn. Physicians for Human Rights, 1992, Women Making History award U.S. Senator Barbara Boxer, 1993, Woman of Yr. award YWCA, 1994, Frontrunner award Sara Lee Corp., 1994, Spirit of Achievement award Albert Einstein Coll. of Yeshiva U., 1995, Abram L. Sachar medallion Brandeis U., 1996, Bicentennial honoree U. Louisville, 1997, Walker prize Boston Mus. Sci., 1998, Radcliffe medal, 2000; grantee Dept. of Def., 1994, 96. Mem. Am. Med. Women's Assn. (pres. br. 39 1987), Soc. for Study of Breast Disease, Am. Soc. Preventive Oncology, Southwestern Oncology Group (women's health and breast com. 1992-96, surg. rep. 1992-96), L.A. Med. Soc., Boston Surg. Soc., N.Am. Menopause Soc., Am. Assn. Cancer Rsch., Am. Coll. Women's Health Physicians, Assn. Women Surgeons. Office: PO Box 846 Pacific Palisades CA 90272-0846 E-mail: slove@earthlink.net

LOVE, WILLIAM EDWARD, lawyer; b. Eugene, Oreg., Mar. 13, 1926; s. William Stewart and Ola A. (Kingsbury) L.; m. Sylvia Kathryn Jaureguy, Aug. 6, 1955; children: Kathryn Love Petersen, Jeffrey, Douglas, Gregory. BS, U. Notre Dame, 1946; MA in Journalism, U. Oreg., 1950, JD, 1952. Bar: Oreg. 1952. Newspaper reporter Eugene Register Guard, 1943-44, 47-52; asst. prof. law, asst. dean Sch. Law U. Wash., Seattle, 1952-56; ptnr. Cake, Jaureguy, Hardy, Buttler & McEwen, Portland, Oreg., 1956-69; pres., chmn., CEO Equitable Savs. & Loan, Portland, 1969-82; sr. ptnr. Schwabe, Williamson & Wyatt, Portland, 1983—. Chmn. Oreg. Savs. League, 1976; dir. Portland Gen. Electric, 1976-83, Fed. Home Loan Bank of Seattle, 1976-79, 85-96, adv. council Fed. Nat. Mortgage Assn., Washington, 1978-80; exec. dir. Health, Housing, Ednl. & Cultural Facilities Authority, 1990—. Author: (with Jaureguy) Oregon Probate Law and Practice, 2 vols., 1958; contbr. articles to profl. jours. Commr., past chmn. Oreg. Racing Commn., 1963-79; pres. Nat. Assn. State Racing Commrs., 1977-78; commr. Port of Portland, 1979-86, pres. 1983; referee Pac-10 football, 1960-81, Rose Bowl, 1981; active United Way, Boy Scouts Am., Portland Rose Festival, polit. campaigns; mem. adv. coun. Jockey's Guild, Inc., 1990—. Served to lt. (j.g.) USN, 1944-47. Mem. Oreg. Bar Assn., Multnomah County Bar Assn., Arlington Club, Multnomah Athletic Club, Golf Club (Portland). Republican. Home: 10225 SW Melnore St Portland OR 97225-4356 Office: Schwabe Williamson & Wyatt 1211 SW 5th Ave Ste 1800 Portland OR 97204-3713

LOVELAND, VALORIA, state legislator; Dep. treas. Franklin County, 1963-81, treas., 1982-92; mem. Wash. Legislature, Olympia, 1993—, chair ways and means com., senate majority caucus chair, 1993, Dem. caucus chair, 1997. Mem. Wash. State Pub. Disclosure Commn., 1979, 81, Tri-Cities Diversification Bd., 1988-90, Tri-Cities Diversification Com., 1987-90; mem. Nuclear Waste Adv. Coun., 1986-87. Mem. Wash. Assn. Counties (pres. 1989-90), Wash. State County Treasurers Assn. (legis. com. chair 1988, 89, 92, county treas. rep. 1984-85, pres. 1991-92), Nat. Assn. County Ofcls., Nat. Assn. County Treasurers and Fin. Officers (dir., bd. dirs.), Wash. State Fedn. Dem. Women's Club (past regional dir., past state nominating chair), Bus. and Profl. Women (Woman of Yr. award). Democrat. Office: 316 John Cherberg Bldg Olympia WA 98504-0001

LOVELL, CAROL, museum director; Dir. Kauai Mus., Lihue, Hawaii. Office: Kauai Mus 4428 Rice St Lihue HI 96766-1338

LOVELL, CHARLES C. federal judge; b. 1929; m. Ariliah Carter. BS, U. Mont., 1952, JD, 1959. Assoc. Church, Harris, Johnson & Williams, Great Falls, Mont., 1959-85; judge U.S. Dist. Ct. Mont., Helena, 1985—. Chief counsel Mont. Atty Gen.'s Office, Helena, 1969-72. Served to capt. USAF, 1952-54. Mem. ABA, Am. Judicature Soc., Assn. Trial Lawyers Am. Office: US Dist Ct Fed Bldg 5th Flr 301 S Park Ave Fl 5 Helena MT 59626-0001

LOVENTHAL, MILTON, writer, playwright, lyricist; b. Atlantic City; s. Harry and Clara (Feldman) L.; m. Jennifer McDowell, July 2, 1973. BA, U. Calif., Berkeley, 1950, MLS, 1958; MA in Sociology, San Jose State U., 1969. Researcher Hoover Instn., Stanford, Calif., 1952-53, spl. asst. to Slavic Curator, 1955-57; librarian San Diego Pub. Library, 1957-59; librarian, bibliographer San Jose (Calif.) State U., 1959-92. Tchr. writing workshops, poetry readings, 1969-73; co-producer lit. and culture radio show Sta. KALX, Berkeley, 1971-72; editor, pub. Merlin Press, San Jose, 1973—. Author: Books on the USSR, 1951-57, 57, Black Politics, 1971 (featured at Smithsonian Inst. Special Event, 1992), A Bibliography of Material Relating to the Chicano, 1971, Autobiographies of Women, 1946-70, 72, Blacks in America, 1972, The Survivors, 1972, Contemporary Women Poets an Anthology, 1977, Ronnie Goose Rhymes for Grown-Ups, 1984; co-author: (Off-Off-Broadway plays) The Estrogen Party to End War, 1986, Mack the Knife, Your Friendly Dentist, 1986, Betsy & Phyllis, 1986, The Oatmeal Party Comes to Order, 1986, (plays) Betsy Meets the Wacky Iraqi, 1991, Bella and Phyllis, 1994; co-writer (mus. comedy) Russia's Secret Plot to Take Back Alaska, 1988; lyricist Intern Girl, 1998. Recipient Bill Casey Award in Letters, 1980; grantee San Jose State U., 1962-63, 84. Mem. Assn. Calif. State Profs., Calif. Alumni Assn., Calif. Theatre Coun., Am. Assn. for Advancement of Slavic Studies, Soc. for Sci. Study of Religion. Office: PO Box 5602 San Jose CA 95150-5602

LOVERIDGE, RONALD OLIVER, mayor; b. Antioch, Calif., 1938; m. Marsha Jean White, 1964; 2 children. BA in Polit. Sci., U. Pacific, 1960; MA Polit. Sci., Stanford U., 1961, PhD in Polit. Sci., 1965. Assoc. prof. polit. sci. U. Calif., Riverside, 1965—, assoc. dean coll. social scis., 1970-72, chair acad. ednl. policy com., 1990-92; mem. Riverside City Coun., 1979-94; mayor City of Riverside, 1994—. Chair land use com. Riverside City Coun., 1980-94; exec. com. Western Riverside Coun. of Govts., 1994—. Contbr. articles to profl. jours. Chair Earth Day City of Riverside, 1990; co-chair Citrus Heritage Tourism Task Force, 1991; mem. bd. dirs. League of Calif. Cities; mem. South Coast Air Quality Mgmt. Dist. Bd., 1995—. Mem. Greater Riverside C. of C., Northside Improvement Assn., Urban League, So. Calif. Assn. Govts. (exec. com. 1994—). Office: 3900 N Main St Riverside CA 92522-0001

LOVETT, CLARA MARIA, university administrator, historian; b. Trieste, Italy, Aug. 4, 1939; came to U.S., 1962; m. Benjamin F. Brown. BA equivalent, U. Trieste, 1962; MA, U. Tex., Austin, 1967; PhD, U. Tex., 1970. Prof. history Baruch Coll. CUNY, N.Y.C., 1971-82, asst. provost, 1980-82; chief European divsn. Libr. of Congress, Washington, 1982-84; provost, v.p. acad. affairs George Mason U., Fairfax, Va., 1988-93; on leave, dir. Forum on Faculty Roles and Rewards Am. Assn. for Higher Edn., 1993-94; pres. No. Ariz. U., Flagstaff, 1994-2001, pres. emerita, 2001—. Vis. lectr. Fgn. Svc. Inst., Washington, 1979-85. Author: Democratic Movement in Italy 1830-1876, 1982 (H.R. Marraro prize, Soc. Italian Hist. Studies); Guiseppe Ferrari and the Italian Revolution, 1979 (Phi Alpha Theta book award); Carlo Cattaneo and the Politics of Risorgimento, 1972 (Soc. for Italian Hist. Studies Dissertation award), (bibliography) Contemporary Italy, 1985; co-editor: Women, War, and Revolution, 1980, (essays) State of Western European Studies, 1984; contbr. sects. to publs., U.S., Italy. Organizer Dem. clubs Bklyn., 1972-76; mem. exec. com. Palisades Citizens Assn., Washington, 1985-87; vestry mem. St. David's Episc. Ch., Washington, 1986-89; bd. dirs. Blue Cross Blue Shield Ariz., 1995—; trustee Western Govs. U., 1996—; mem. Ariz. State Bd. Edn., 1999-2001. Fellow Guggenheim Found., 1978-79, Woodrow Wilson Internat. Ctr. for Scholars, 1979 (adv. bd. West European program), Am. Coun. Learned Socs., 1976, Bunting Inst. of Radcliffe Coll., 1975-76, others; named Educator of Yr. Va. Fedn. of Bus. and Profl. Women, 1992. Mem. Am. Assn. Higher Edn. (cons. 1979—), Soc. for Italian Hist. Studies, Assn. Am. Coll. and Univs. (bd. dirs. 1990-93). Avocations: choral singing, swimming. Office: 2715 N 3d St Phoenix AZ 85003 E-mail: clara.lovett@nau.edu

LOVETT, RICHARD, talent agency executive; Pres. Creative Artists Agy. Office: Creative Artists Agy 9830 Wilshire Blvd Beverly Hills CA 90212-1825

LOVETT, WENDELL HARPER, architect, educator; b. Seattle, Apr. 2, 1922; s. Wallace Herman and Pearl (Harper) L.; m. Eileen Whitson, Sept. 3, 1947; children: Corrie, Clare. Student, Pasadena Jr. Coll., 1943-44; BArch, U. Wash., 1947; MArch, MIT, 1948. Architect, designer Naramore, Bain, Brady & Johanson, Seattle, 1948; architect, assoc. Bassetti & Morse, Seattle, 1948-51; pvt. practice architect Seattle, 1951—; instr. architecture U. Wash., 1948-51, asst. prof., 1951-60, assoc. prof., 1960-65, prof., 1965-83, prof. emeritus, 1983—. Lectr. Technische Hochschule, Stuttgart, 1959-60 Prin. works include nuclear reactor bldg. U. Wash., 1960, Villa Simonyi, Medina, Wash., 1989; patentee in field. Pres. Citizen's Planning Coun., Seattle, 1968-71; bd. dirs. Seattle Baroque Orch., 1998—. With AUS, 1943-46. Recipient 2d prize Progressive Architecture U.S. Jr. C. of C., 1949; Internat. design award Decima Triennale di Milano, 1954; Arch. Record Homes awards, 1969, 72, 74; Interiors award, 1973; Sunset-AIA awards, 1959, 62, 69, 71; Fulbright grantee, 1959; AIA fellow, 1978 Mem. AIA (sec. Wash. chpt. 1953-54, bd. dirs. Found. Seattle chpt. 1991-92, Seattle chpt. medal 1993, pres. sr. coun. 1991-92), Plestcheeff Inst. (bd. dirs. 1992). Home and Office: 420 34th Ave Seattle WA 98122-6408

LOVETT, WILLIAM LEE, surgeon; b. Natchez, Miss., June 12, 1941; s. Frank Lee and Lucille (Mullen) L.; m. Martha Lynn Gray, Aug. 15, 1964; children: Shelby Elizabeth Lovett Cuevas, Heather Lee Lovett Dunn, Michael Gray. BA, U. Miss., Oxford, 1963; MD, U. Miss., Jackson, 1967. Diplomate Am. Bd. Surgery, Am. Bd. Hand Surgery. Intern in surgery U. Va. Med. Ctr., Charlottesville, 1967-68, jr. asst. resident in surgery, 1968-69, sr. asst. resident in surgery, 1970-72, co-chief resident in surgery, 1972-73; fellow surg. rsch. dept. surgery U. Va., Charlottesville, 1969-70; physician S.W. Hand Surgeons Ltd., Phoenix, 1983—; vice chief of staff St. Joseph's Hosp., Phoenix, 1990-93, rep. orthopedic surgery com., 1990—, vice chair dept. orthopedics, 1991-92, chief of staff, 1996-98; physician S.W. Hand Surgeons Ltd., Phoenix. Mem. sports medicine adv. team Ariz. State U., 1991-95; presenter in field. Contbr. articles to profl. jours. Mem. Sch. Bd. Xavier High Sch., 1983-87, v.p., 1985-86, pres., 1986-87; chief Webelos den Roosevelt coun. Boy Scouts Am., Phoenix, 1992-93, asst. scoutmaster, 1993—. Comdr. USN, 1974-76. Fellow ACS (pres. Ariz. chpt. 1983-84); mem. AMA, Am. Soc. for Surgery of the Hand, Ariz. Med. Assn. (del. 1985), Phoenix Surg. Soc. (pres. 1985-86), Muller Surg. Soc., Scottsdale Mounted Posse. Avocations: horseback riding, fly fishing, quail hunting, canoeing. Home: 6049 N 5th Pl Phoenix AZ 85012-1219 Office: SW Hand Surgeons Ltd 300 W Clarendon Ave Ste 250 Phoenix AZ 85013-3477 E-mail: L5hand@aol.com

LOVINS, AMORY BLOCH, physicist, energy consultant; b. Washington, Nov. 13, 1947; s. Gerald Hershel and Miriam (Bloch) L.; m. L. Hunter Sheldon, 1979 (div. 1999). Student, Harvard U., 1964-65, 66-67, Magdalen Coll., Oxford, Eng., 1967-69; MA, Oxford U., Oxford, 1971; DSc (hon.), Bates Coll., 1979, Williams Coll., 1981, Kalamazoo Coll., 1983, U. Maine, 1985; LLD (hon.), Ball State U., 1983; D of Environ. Sci. (hon.), Unity Coll., 1992. Jr. research fellow Merton Coll., Oxford, England, 1969-71; Brit. rep., policy advisor Friends of the Earth, San Francisco, 1971-84; regent's lectr. U. Calif., Berkeley and Riverside, 1978, 81; CEO, CFO and dir. Rocky Mountain Inst., Old Snowmass, Colo., 1982—. Govt. and indsl. energy cons., 1971—; vis. prof. Dartmouth Coll., 1982; disting. vis. prof. U. Colo., 1982, U. St. Gallen, Switzerland, 1999; prin. tech. cons. E Source, 1989-99; prin. The Lovins Group, 1994-99; mem. Def. Sci. Bd. panel U.S. Sec. Def., 1999-2001; chmn., dir. Hypercar Inc., Basalt, Colo., 1998—. Author: (also layout artist and co-photographer) Eryri, The

Mountains of Longing, 1971, The Stockholm Conference: Only One Earth, 1972, Openpit Mining, 1973, World Energy Strategies: Facts, Issues, and Options, 1975, Soft Energy Paths: Toward a Durable Peace, 1977; co-author: (with J. Price) Non-Nuclear Futures: The Case: The Case for an Ethical Energy Strategy, 1975, (with L.H. Lovins) Energy/War: Breaking the Nuclear Link, 1980, Brittle Power: Energy Strategy for National Security, 1982, (with L.H. Lovins, F. Krause, and W. Bach) Least-Cost Energy: Solving the CO2 Problem, 1982, 89 (with P. O'heffernan, sr. author and L.H. Lovins) The First Nuclear World War, 1983, (with L.H. Lovins, sr. author and S. Zuckerman) Energy Unbound: A Fable for America's Future, 1986, (hardware reports) The State of the Art: Lighting, 1988, The State of the Art: Drivepower, 1989, The State of the Art: Appliances, 1990, The State of the Art: Water Heating, 1991, The State of the Art: Space Cooling and Air Handling, 1992, (with Ernst von Weizsaecker, sr. author and L.H. Lovins) Faktor Vier, 1995, Factor Four, 1997, (with M.M. Brylawski, D.R. Cramer, T.C. Moore) Hypercars: Materials, Manufacturing, and Policy Implications, 1995, (with Paul Hawken and L.H. Lovins) Natural Capitalism, 1999; co-photographer (book) At Home in the Wild: New England's White Mountains, 1978; author numerous poems; contbr. articles to profl. jours., reports to tech. jours.; patentee in field. Co-founder, treas. Windstar Land Conservancy, Colo., 1996-2000. Recipient Right Livelihood award Right Livelihood Found., 1983, Sprout award Internat. Studies Assn., 1977, Pub. Edn. award Nat. Energy Resources Orgn., 1978, Pub. Svc. award Nat. Assn. Environ. Edn., 1980; Mitchell prize Mitchell Energy Found., 1982, Delphi prize Onassis Found., 1989, Nissan prize Internat. Symposium Automotive Tech. and Automation, 1993, Award of Distinction, Rocky Mountain chpt. AIA, 1994, Heinz award 1997, Lindbergh award 1999, World Tech. award 1999, Happold medal U.K. Construction Industries Coun., 2000, Heroes for the Planet award Time, 2000; MacArthur fellow John D. and Catherine T. MacArthur Found., Chgo., 1993. Fellow AAAS, World Acad. Art and Sci., Lindisfarne Assn; mem. Fedn. Am. Scientists, Am. Phys. Soc., Soc. Automotive Engring., Am. Solar Energy Soc., Internat. Assn. Energy Econs. Avocations: mountaineering, photography, music. Home and Office: 1739 Snowmass Creek Rd Snowmass CO 81654-9115 E-mail: ablovins@rmi.org

LOVINS, L. HUNTER, public policy institute executive; b. Middlebury, Vt., Feb. 26, 1950; d. Paul Millard and Farley (Hunter) Sheldon; m. Amory Bloch Lovins, Sept. 6, 1979; 1 child, Nanuq. BA in Sociology, BA in Polit. Sci., Pitzer Coll., 1972; JD, Loyola U., L.A., 1975; LHD, U. Maine, 1982. Bar: Calif. 1975. Asst. dir. Calif. Conservation Project, L.A., 1973-79; co-CEO, co-founder Rocky Mountain Inst., Snowmass, Colo., 1982—. Vis. prof. U. Colo., Boulder, 1982; Henry R. Luce vis. prof. Dartmouth Coll., Hanover, N.H., 1982; pres. Nighthawk Horse Co., 1993. Co-author: Brittle Power, 1982, Energy Unbound, 1986, Least-Cost Energy Solving the CO2 Problem, 2d edit., 1989, Natural Capitalism, 1999. Bd. dirs. Point Found., Basalt and Rural Fire Protection Dist., Nighthawk Horse Co., Rocky Mountain Inst., Windstar Land Conservancy; vol. EMT and firefighter. Recipient Mitchell prize Woodlands Inst., 1982, Right Livelihood Found. award, 1983, Best of the New Generation award Esquire Mag., 1984, Nissan prize, 1995, Lindberg award, 1999, Bd. Govs.' award Loyola Law Sch., 2000, LOHAS award for svc. to bus., 2001, Shingo Prize for Excellence in Mfg. Rsch., 2001. Mem. Calif. Bar Assn., Am. Quarter Horse Assn., Am. Polocrosse Assn. Avocations: rodeo, fire rescue, polocrosse. Office: Rocky Mountain Inst 1739 Snowmass Creek Rd Snowmass CO 81654-9199

LOW, ANDREW M. lawyer; b. N.Y.C., Jan. 1, 1952; s. Martin Laurent and Alice Elizabeth (Bernstein) L.; m. Margaret Mary Stroock, Mar. 31, 1979; children: Roger, Ann. BA, Swarthmore Coll., 1973; JD, Cornell U., 1976. Bar: Colo. 1981, U.S. Dist. Ct. Colo. 1981, U.S. Ct. Appeals (10th cir.) 1986. Assoc. Rogers & Wells, N.Y.C., 1977-81, Davis, Graham & Stubbs, Denver, 1981-83, ptnr., 1984—. Editor: Colorado Appellate Handbook, 1984, 94. Pres. Colo. Freedom of Info. Coun., Denver, 1990-92, Colo. Bar Press Com., 1989, appellate practice subcom. Colo. Bar Assn. Litigation Coun., 1994—; bd. dirs. CLE in Colo., Inc., 1993-96; trustee 9 Health Fair, Denver, 1988—; mem. Colo. Sup. Ct. Joint Commn. on Appellate Rules, 1993—. Avocations: skiing, golfing, fly-fishing. Office: Davis Graham & Stubbs LLP Ste 500 1550 17th St Denver CO 80202 E-mail: andrew.low@dgslaw.com

LOW, BOON CHYE, physicist; b. Singapore, Feb. 13, 1946; came to U.S., 1968; s. Kuei Huat and Ah Tow (Tee) Lau; m. Daphne Nai-Ling Yip, Mar. 31, 1971; 1 child, Yi-Kai. BSc, U. London, Eng., 1968; PhD, U. Chgo., 1972. Scientist High Altitude Observatory Nat. Ctr. for Atmospheric Rsch., Boulder, Colo., 1981-87, sect. head, 1987-90, 97—, acting dir., 1989-90, sr. scientist, 1987—. Mem. mission operation working group for solar physics NASA, 1992-94; vis. sr. scientist Princeton Plasma Physics Lab., 1998-99. Mem. editl. bd. Solar Physics, 1991—. Named Fellow Japan Soc. for Promotion of Sci., U. Tokyo, 1978, Sr. Rsch. Assoc., NASA Marshall Space Flight Ctr., 1980. Mem. Am. Physical Soc., Am. Astron. Soc., Am. Geophysical Union. Office: Nat Ctr for Atmosph Rsch PO Box 3000 Boulder CO 80307-3000 E-mail: low@hao.ucar.edu

LOW, HARRY WILLIAM, judge; b. Oakdale, Calif., Mar. 12, 1931; s. Tong J. and Ying G. (Gong) L.; m. May Ling, Aug. 24, 1952; children: Larry, Kathy, Allan. AA, Modesto Jr. Coll., 1950; AB Polit. Sci. with honors, U. Calif., Berkeley, 1952, JD, 1955. Bar: Calif. 1955, U.S. Ct. Appeals (9th cir.) 1955. Commr. Workmen's Compensation Commn., 1966; teaching assoc. Boalt Hall, 1955-56; dep. atty. gen. Calif. Dept. Justice, 1956-66; judge Mcpl. Ct., San Francisco, 1966-74, presiding judge, 1972-73; judge Superior Ct., San Francisco, 1974-82; presiding justice Calif. Ct. Appeals, 1st dist., 1982-92; commr. Calif. Ins. Dept., San Francisco, 2000—. Pres. San Francisco Police Commn., 1992-96; pres. San Francisco Human Rights Commn., 1999-2000; mem. Jud. Arbitration and Mediation Svcs., 1992-2000, Commn. on Future of Cts., 1991-94, Commn. on Future of Legal Profession, 1993-95; Calif. Ins. commr., 2000—. Contbr. articles to profl. jours. Chmn. bd. Edn. Ctr. for Chinese, 1969-80, Chinese-Am. Internat. Sch., 1979-99; bd. visitors U.S. Mil. Acad., 1980-83; bd. dirs. Friends of Recreation and Parks, Salesian Boys Club, World Affairs Coun., 1979-85, NCCJ, San Francisco chpt. St. Vincent's Boys Home, Coro Found., 1970-76, San Francisco Zool. Trust, 1987, Union Bank Calif., 1993-2000; pres. San Francisco City Coll. Found., 1977-87, Inst. Chinese Western History U. San Francisco, 1987-89. Mem. ABA (chmn. appellate judges conf. 1990-91, commr. on minorities), San Francisco Bar Assn., Chinese Am. Citizens Alliance (pres. San Francisco chpt. 1976-77, nat. pres. 1989-93), Calif. Judges Assn. (pres. 1978-79), Calif. Jud. Coun., State Bar Calif. (rsch. editor publs. 1958-76, pub. affairs com. 1987-90, exec. bd. 1992-94), Calif. Conf. Judges (editor jour. cts. commentary 1973-76), Calif. Judges Assn. (exec. bd. 1976-79), Asian Bus. League (dir. 1986-93), Nat. Ctr. State Cts. (bd. dirs. 1986-91), San Francisco Bench Bar Media Commn. (chmn. bd. dirs. 1987-92), Boalt Hall Alumni Assn. (Distinguished Svc. award 1992, Judge Lowell Jensen award 2000), Phi Alpha Delta. Office: Calif Dept Ins 45 Fremont St 23r Fl San Francisco CA 94105

LOW, JOHN WAYLAND, lawyer; b. Denver, Aug. 7, 1923; s. Oscar Wayland and Rachel E. (Stander) L.; m. Merry C. Mullan, July 8, 1979; children: Lucinda A., Jan W. BA, Nebr. Wesleyan U., 1947; JD cum laude, U. Denver, 1951. Bar: Colo. 1951, U.S. Dist. Ct. (Colo. dist.) 1951, U.S. Ct. Appeals (10th cir.), U.S. Supreme Ct. 1960. Ptnr. Sherman & Howard LLC, Denver, 1951-93, counsel, 1993—. Trustee U. Denver, 1987—; chmn. bd. Denver Symphony Assn., 1989-90; vice chmn. Colo. Symphony Assn., 1990-96; pres. Colo. Symphony Found., 1995—; chmn. Colo. [illegible] Recipient Learned Hand award Am. Jewish Com., 1989, Outstanding Alumni award U. Denver, 1994, Evans Disting. Svc. award U. Denver, 2001.. Mem. ABA, Colo. Bar Assn., Denver Bar Assn., University Club of Denver, Garden of Gods Club (Colorado Springs). Republican. Mem. United Ch. of Christ. Office: Sherman & Howard 633 17th St Ste 3000 Denver CO 80202-3665

LOW, MERRY COOK, civic worker; b. Uniontown, Pa., Sept. 3, 1925; d. Howard Vance and Eleanora (Lynch) Mullan; m. William R. Cook, 1947 (div. 1979); m. John Wayland Low, July 8, 1979; children: Karen, Cindy, Bob, Jan. Diploma in nursing, Allegheny Gen. Hosp., Pitts., 1946; BS summa cum laude, Colo. Women's Coll., 1976. RN, Colo. Dir. patient edn. Med. Care and Rsch. Found., Denver, 1976-78. Contbr. chpt. to Pattern for Distribution of Patient Education, 1981. Bd. dirs. women's libr. assn. U. Denver, 1982—, vice chmn., 1985-86, chair, 1986-87, co-chair spl. event, 1992; bd. dirs. Humanities Inst., 1993-, pres., 1999, co-chair Founder's Day com., 1994—, chair Culturefest, 1995, 96; mem. DuArt bd. U. Denver, 1998—; docent Denver Art Mus., 1979-99, vol. exec. bd., 1988-94, nat. docent symposium com., 1991, chair collectors' choice benefits, 1988, pres. vols., trustee 1988-90; mem. alumni assn. bd. U. Denver, 1994-2000, sec., 1996-98; bd. dirs. Lamont Sch. Music Assocs., 1990-96; search com. for dir. Penrose Libr., 1991-92; trustee ch. coun., chair invitational art show 1st Plymouth Congl. Ch., Englewood, Colo., 1981-84; co-chair art auction Colo. Alliance Bus., 1992-93, com., 1994-97. Recipient Disting. Svc. award U. Denver Coll. Law, 1988, King Soopers Vol. of Week award, 1989, Citizen of Arts award Fine Arts Found., 1993, Outstanding Vol. Colo. Alliance of Bus., 1994, U. Denver Cmty. Svc. award, 1996. Mem. Am. Assn. Mus. (vol. meeting coord. 1990-91), P.E.O. (pres. Colo. chpt. DX 1982-84), U. Denver Alumni Assn. (bd. dirs., sec. 1996-98), Welcome to Colo., Women for Profit Investment Club (sec. 1999—). Republican. Congregationalist. Home: 2552 E Alameda Ave Apt 11 Denver CO 80209-3324

LOW, RANDALL, internist, cardiologist; b. San Francisco, June 24, 1949; s. Huet Hee and Betty Tai (Quan) L.; m. Dorothy Fung, May 4, 1975; children: Audrey, Madeleine, Jennifer. AA, City Coll., San Francisco, 1969; BA, U. Calif., Berkeley, 1971; MD, U. Calif., Davis, 1975. Diplomate Am. Bd. Internal Medicine, Nat. Bd. Med. Examiners, Am. Bd. Cardiovascular Diseases. Intern Hosp. of Good Samaritan, L.A., 1975-76, resident, 1976-77, chief med. resident, 1977-78, fellow in cardiology, 1979-81; mem. staff St. Francis Meml. Hosp., San Francisco, 1981—, chmn. dept. cardiology, 1995—; pvt. practice internal medicine and cardiology San Francisco, 1981—; mem. staff Chinese Hosp., San Francisco, 1981—, chief of medicine, 1991-92; asst. clin. prof. U. Calif., San Francisco, 1994-2000. Mem. courtesy staff St. Mary's Hosp., San Francisco, 1981—, Calif. Pacific Med. Ctr., San Francisco, 1990—; cardiology cons. Laguna Honda Hosp., San Francisco, 1981—. Mem. home health quality assurance com. Self Help for Elderly, San Francisco, 1991—; bd. trustees San Francisco Health Authority, 2000—; bd. dirs. Youth Advocates, San Francisco, 1992-99. Recipient Hearst Pub. Svc. award U. Calif.-Berkeley, 1970, 6th ann. homecare recognition award Self Help for Elderly, 1993. Mem. ACP, Am. Soc. Internal Medicine, Am. Coll. Cardiology, Am. Heart Assn. (bd. govs. 1983-90), Calif. Acad. Medicine, Calif. Med. Soc., San Francisco Med. Soc., bd. dirs., SF Med. Soc., 1999, (bd. dirs. 1999—), Assn. Chinese Cmty. Physicians (sec.-treas. 1986-89), Chinese Cmty. Health Care Assn. (pres. 1991-96, 99—). Office: 909 Hyde St Ste 501 San Francisco CA 94109-4853

LOWBER, JOHN M. communications executive; b. 1950; Sr. mgr. KPMG Peat Marwick; CFO Gen. Comm., Inc., Anchorage, 1987—, sec., treas., 1988—, CFO, sr. v.p., 1989—. Office: Gen Comm Inc Ste 1000 2550 Denali St Anchorage AK 99503 Office Fax: 907-265-5076

LOWBER, STEPHEN SCOTT, financial executive; b. Gainesville, Fla., Apr. 17, 1951; s. Leslie Vernon and Grace Irene (Townsend) L.; m. Susan Irene LeClair, Aug. 28, 1976; children: Jessica Renee, Allison Susanne. BA in Acctg., Western Wash. U., 1975; MBA, Seattle U., 1978. CPA, Wash. Sr. audit mgr. Ernst & Whinney, Seattle, 1978-84; v.p., chief fin. officer Xytec, Inc., Tacoma, 1984-90, Advanced Digital Info. Corp., Redmond, Wash., 1990—. Served with U.S. Army, 1969-71, Socialist Republic Vietnam. Mem. Am. Inst. CPA's, Wash. Soc. CPA's, Nat. Assn. Accts. (bd. dirs. 1983). Republican. Mem. Assembly of God. Club: Pacific West. Avocations: tennis, hiking, church activities, family. Home: 3006 161st St SE Mill Creek WA 98012-7838 Office: Cutter & Buck Inc 2701 1st Ave Ste 500 Seattle WA 98121

LOWE, KEVIN HUGH, professional hockey coach, former professional hockey player; b. Apr. 15, 1959; m. Karen Percy. Hockey player Edmonton Oilers, 1979-92, 98-99, capt., 1991-92; hockey player N.Y. Rangers, 1992-98; head coach Edmonton Oilers, 1999—. Played in NHL All-Star game 1984-86, 88-90, 93; winner Clancy Meml. Trophy, 1989-90; named Budweiser/NHL Man of Yr., 1989-90. Office: Edmonton Oilers 11230 110th St 2d Fl Edmonton AB Canada T5G 3G8

LOWE, OARIONA, dentist; b. San Francisco, June 17, 1948; d. Van Lowe and Jenny Lowe-Silva; m. Evangelos Rossopoulos, Dec. 18, 1985; children: Thanos G., Jenny Sophia. BS, U. Nev., Las Vegas, 1971; MA, George Washington U., 1977; DDS, Howard U., 1981; pediatric dental cert., UCLA, 1984. Instr. Coll. Allied Health Scis. Howard U., Washington, 1974-76, asst. prof., 1976-77; research asst. Howard U. Dental Sch., Washington, 1977-81; resident gen. practice Eastman Dental Ctr., Rochester, N.Y., 1981-82; dir. dental services City of Hope Med. Ctr., Duarte, Calif., 1984-86; dental staff Whittier (Calif.) Presbyn. Hosp., 1987—, chief dental staff, 1992-94; asst. prof. Loma Linda (Calif.) U., 1991—. Vis. lectr. pediatric dentistry UCLA; mem. oral cancer task force Am. Cancer Soc., Pasadena, Calif., 1985—; internat. spkr. Europe, Asia. Contbr. articles to profl. jours. Del. People to People Internat. Mem. ADA, Am. Soc. Dentistry for Children (v.p.), Nat. Soc. Autistic Children, Calif. Dental Assn., Am. Acad. Pediatric Dentistry (mem. comm. coun. 1999-2001), San Gabriel Valley Dental Soc. (chmn. 1991—), Tri County Dental Soc. (bd. dirs. 1996—), Calif. Dental Assn., Sigma Xi, Alpha Omega. Republican. Presbyterian. Avocations: cooking, bicycling, walking, aerobic dancing. Office: 8135 Painter Ave Ste 202 Whittier CA 90602-3175

LOWE, RICHARD GERALD, JR. computer programming manager; b. Travis AFB, Calif., Nov. 8, 1960; s. Richard Gerald and Valerie Jean (Hoeffer) L.; m. Claudia Maria Arevalo, 1993; 1 child, Alvaro Arevalo. Student, San Bernardino Valley Coll., 1978-80. Microsoft cert. sys. engr. plus Internet; A+-svc. technician network and cert. Tech. specialist Software Techniques Inc., Los Alamitos, Calif., 1980-82, sr. tech. specialist, 1982-84, mgr. tech. services, 1984-85, mgr. cons. services Cypress, 1985-86; sr. programmer BIF Accutel, Camarillo, 1986-87, systems analyst, 1987-88; mgr. project Beck Computer Systems, Long Beach, Calif., 1986-91, v.p. devel., 1991-93, dir. tech. svcs. Trader Joe's Co., S. Pasadena, 1994—. Webmaster Internet Tips and Secrets, 1999—. Author: The Autobiography of Richard G. Lowe, Jr., 1991, The Lowe Family and Their Relatives, 1992; contbr. articles to profl. jours. Vol. min., field staff mem. L.A. Found. Ch. of Scientology, 1993—; active Concerned Citizens for Human Rights. Mem. Assn. Computing Machinery, Digital Equipment Corp. Users Group, UniData Users Group, Internat. Assn. Scientologists, Inst. Elec. and Electronics Engrs., Inc., World Order Webmasters, Coalition Against Unsolicited Comml. Email, Assn. Internet Profls., HTML Writers Guild. Avocations: reading and writing science fiction, collecting movies, battlefield simulations, painting fantasy miniatures, collecting stamps. [illegible]

LOWELL, J(AMES) DAVID, geological consultant, cattle rancher; b. Nogales, Ariz., Feb. 28, 1928; s. Arthur Currier and Lavina (Cumming) L.; m. Edith Walmisly Sykes, Mar. 30, 1948; children: Susan, William, Douglas. BS in Mining Engring., U. Ariz., 1949, E.Geol., 1959; MS in Geology, Stanford U., 1957; D. Hon. Causa, U. N at. Mayor de San Marcos, Peru, 1998; Dsc (hon.) , U. Ariz, 2000. Registered profl. engr., Ariz. Mining engr. to mine foreman Asarco, Chihuahua City, Mex., 1949-51; field geologist to dist. geologist AEC, Grand Junction, Colo., 1951-54; chief geologist to v.p. S.W. ventures Ventures Ltd. and subs., Denver, Tucson, 1955-59; dist. geologist Utah Internat., San Francisco, Tucson, 1959-61; geol. cons. Lowell Mineral Exploration, Tucson, 1961—, pres. Chile, 1985—, Acuarios Mineral, Peru, 1991-96; chmn. Areguipa Resources Ltd., Can., 1993-96; pres. Exploraciones Mineras Lowell SA de CV, Mex., 1998—, Lowell Mineral Exploration LLC, Ariz., 1998—. Mem. bd. dirs. Soc. Econ. Geologists Found., 1986-91; Thayer Lindsley disting. lectr. Soc. Econ. Geologists, 1978; cons. to 26 other oil and mining cos., U.S. and fgn. countries, 1961—, to nat. govt. orgn., U.S.; cons. retainer Bechtel Corp., San Francisco, 1976—; dir. Nat. Mining Hall of Fame, 2000-. Assoc. editor Econ. Geology, New Haven, 1970-75. Recipient Disting. Citizen award U. Ariz., 1974, Soc. Econ. Geol. Thayer Lindsley Dist. Lectr., 1977, Silver Medal Soc. Econ. Geologists, 1983, Medal of Merit Am. Mineral Hall of Fame, 1994. Mem. Ariz. Geol. Soc. (pres. 1965-66), Am. Inst. Mining Engrs. (pres. Yavapai sect. 1957, Daniel Jackling award 1970, Robert Dreyer award 2000, Earll McConnell award 2000), Can. Inst. Mining and Metall. Engrs. (disting. lectr. 1972), Internat. Assn. on Genesis of Ore Deposits, Mining and Metallurgy Soc. of Am. (gold medal award 2001, Mining Club of S.W. (dir. 1969-70), Prescott Country Club, NAE. Republican. Episcopalian. Home: 789 Avenida Beatriz Rio Rico AZ 85648-2200 Office: Lowell Mineral Exploration 789 Avenida Beatriz Rio Rico AZ 85648-2200

LOWEN, ROBERT MARSHALL, plastic surgeon; b. Detroit; MD, U. Mich. Med. Sch., 1971. Diplomate Am. Bd. Plastic Surgery, cert. surgery of the hand. Internship Pacific Presbyn., San Francisco, 1971-72; resident general surgery Stanford U. Med. Ctr., 1983-85; resident plastic surgery U. Okla. HSC, Okla. City, 1985-86; fellow hand surgery U. Colo. HSC, Denver, 1986-87, resident plastic surgery, 1987-88; pvt. practice Mountain View, Calif., 1988—; mem. staff El Camino Hosp., Mountain View, 1988—. Mem. Am. Soc. Plastic and Reconstructive Surgeons, Am. Soc. Lasers in Medicine aSurgery, Calif. Med. Soc., Lipoplasty Soc. N.Am., Santa Clara County Med. Assn., Am. Soc. for Aestheric Plastic Surgery. Home and Office: 305 South Dr Ste 1 Mountain View CA 94040-4207 E-mail: rmlowen@pacbell.net

LOWENTHAL, ABRAHAM FREDERIC, international relations educator; b. Hyannis, Mass., Apr. 6, 1941; s. Eric Isaac and Suzanne (Moos) L.; m. Janet Wyzanski, June 24, 1962 (div. 1983); children: Linda Claudina, Michael Francis; m. Jane S. Jaquette, Jan. 20, 1991. A.B., Harvard U., 1961, M.P.A., 1964, Ph.D., 1971; postgrad., Harvard Law Sch., 1961-62. Tng. assoc. Ford Found., Dominican Republic, 1962-64, asst. rep. Peru, 1969-72; asst. dir., then dir. of studies Coun. Fgn. Rels., N.Y.C., 1974-76; dir. Latin Am. program Woodrow Wilson Internat. Ctr. for Scholars, Washington, 1977-83; exec. dir. Inter-Am. Dialogue, Washington, 1982-92; prof. Sch. Internat. Rels., U. So. Calif., Los Angeles, 1984—; dir., ctr. internat. studies U. So. Calif., 1992-97; pres. Pacific Coun. Internat. Policy, L.A., 1995—; v.p. Coun. on Foreign Rels., L.A., 1995—. Vis. fellow, rsch. assoc. Ctr. Internat. Studies, Princeton U., 1972-74; vis. lectr. polit.. sci. Cath. U. Santiago, Dominican Republic, 1966; lectr. Princeton U., 1974; spl. cons. Commn. U.S.-L.Am. rels., N.Y.C., 1974-76; mem. internat. adv. bd. Ctr. U.S.-Mex. Rels., U. Calif.-San Diego, 1981-94; mem. internat. adv. bd. Helen Kellogg Inst., 1984-95; cons. Ford Found., 1974-90; bd. dirs. InterAm. Dialogue, Fulbright Assn., Pacific Coun. on Internat. Policy. Author: The Dominican Intervention, 1972, 2nd edit., 1995, Partners in Conflict: The United States and Latin America in 1990s, 1991; editor, contbg. author: The Peruvian Experiment: Continuity and Change Under Military Rule, 1975, Armies and Politics in Latin America, 1976, Exporting Democracy: The United States and Latin America, 1991; co-editor, contbg. author: The Peruvian Experiment Reconsidered, 1983, The California-Mexico Connection, 1993; editor Latin Am. and Caribbean Record, vol. IV, 1985-86, vol. V, 1986-87, Latin America in a New World, 1994, Constructing Democratic Governance: Latin America, 1996; mem. editorial bd. Jour. Inter-Am. Studies and World Affairs, 1980-97, New Perspectives Quarterly, 1984—, Hemisphere, Internat. Security, 1977-85, Wilson Quar., 1977-83; contbr. articles to profl. jours. Mem. nat. adv. coun. Amnesty Internat., 1977-83, Ctr. for Nat. Policy, 1986—. Mem. Internat. Inst. Strategic Studies, Am. Polit. Sci. Assn. (coun. 1979-81), Latin Am. Studies (exec. coun. 1979-81), Coun. Fgn. Rels., Overseas Devel. Coun. Democrat. Jewish Home: 1343 Luna Vis Pacific Palisades CA 90272-2235 Office: Pacific Coun Internat Policy Los Angeles CA 90089-0035

LOWNDES, DAVID ALAN, programmer analyst; b. Schenectady, N.Y., Oct. 28, 1947; s. John Henry and Iris Anne (Hepburn) L.; m. Peggy Welco, May 3, 1970; children: Diana Justine, Julie Suzanne. AB, U. Calif., Berkeley, 1969, postgrad., 1972-73. Acct., credit mgr. The Daily Californian, Berkeley, 1973-75, bus. mgr., 1975-76; acct. Pacific Union Assurance Co., San Francisco, 1976-77, acctg. mgr., 1977-78; sr. acct. U. Calif., San Francisco, 1978-88, sr. programmer analyst, 1988—. Avocations: genealogy, microcomputing. Home: 1829 Gaspar Dr Oakland CA 94611-2350 Office: U Calif 250 Executive Park Blvd San Francisco CA 94134-3306 E-mail: dlowndes@its.ucsf.edu

LOWRY, EDWARD FRANCIS, JR. lawyer; b. L.A., Aug. 13, 1930; s. Edward Francis and Mary Anita (Woodcock) L.; m. Patricia Ann Palmer, Feb. 16, 1963; children: Edward Palmer, Rachael Louise. Student, Ohio State U., 1948-50; AB, Stanford U., 1952, JD, 1954. Bar: Ariz. 1955, D.C. 1970, U.S. Supreme Ct. 1969. Camp dir. Quarter Circle V Bar Ranch, 1954; tchr. Orme Sch., Mayer, Ariz., 1954-56; trust rep. Valley Nat. Bank Ariz., 1958-60; pvt. practice, Phoenix, 1960—; assoc. atty. Cunningham, Carson & Messinger, 1960-64; ptnr. Carson, Messinger, Elliott, Laughlin & Ragan, 1964-69, 70-80, Gray, Plant, Mooty, Mooty & Bennett, 1981-84, Eaton, Lazarus, Dodge & Lowry Ltd., 1985-86; exec. v.p., gen. counsel Bus. Realty Ariz., 1986-93; pvt. practice, Scottsdale, Ariz., 1986-88; ptnr. Lowry & Froeb, Scottsdale, 1988-89, Lowry, Froeb & Clements, P.C., Scottsdale, 1989-90, Lowry & Clements P.C., Scottsdale, 1990, Lowry, Clements & Powell, P.C., Scottsdale, 1991—. Asst. legis. counsel Dept. Interior, Washington, 1969-70; mem. Ariz. Commn. Uniform Laws, 1972—, chmn., 1976-88; judge pro tem Ariz. Ct. Appeals, 1986, 92-94; mem. Nat. Conf. Commrs. on Uniform State Laws, 1972-97, life mem., 1997—. Chmn. Coun. of Stanford Law Socs., 1968; bd. dirs. Scottsdale Prevention Inst., 1999—; vice chmn. bd. trustees Orme Sch., 1972-74, treas., 1981-83; trustee Heard Mus., 1965-91, life trustee, 1991—, pres., 1974-75; bd. visitors Stanford Sch. Law; magistrate Town of Paradise Valley, Ariz., 1976-83, town councilman, 1998—, mayor, 1998—; juvenile ct. referee Maricopa County, 1978-83. Capt. USAF, 1956-58. Fellow Ariz. Bar Found. (founder); mem. ABA, Maricopa County Bar Assn., State Bar Ariz. (chmn. com. uniform laws 1979-85), Stanford Law Soc. Ariz. (past pres.), Scottsdale Bar Assn. (bd. dirs. 1991—, v.p. 1991, pres. 1992-95), Ariz. State U. Law Soc. (bd. dirs.), Delta Sigma Rho, Alpha Tau Omega, Phi Delta Phi. Home: 7600 N Moonlight Ln Paradise Valley AZ 85253-2938 Office: Lowry Clements & Powell PC 2901 N Central Ave Ste 1120 Phoenix AZ 85012-2731 also: 6900 E Camelback Rd Ste 1010 Scottsdale AZ 85251-2444

LOWRY, MIKE, former governor, former congressman; b. St. John, Wash., Mar. 8, 1939; s. Robert M. and Helen (White) L.; m. Mary Carlson, Apr. 6, 1968; 1 child, Diane. B.A., Wash. State U., Pullman, 1962. Chief fiscal analyst, staff dir. ways and means com. Wash. State Senate, 1969-73; govtl. affairs dir. Group Health Coop. Puget Sound, 1974-75; mem. council King County Govt., 1975-78, chmn., 1977; mem. 96th-100th congresses from 7th dist. Wash., 1979-1989; governor State of Wash., 1993-96. Chmn. King County Housing and Community Devel. Block Grant Program, 1977; pres. Wash. Assn. Counties, 1978. Democrat. Address: 3326 Park Ave N Renton WA 98056-1915

LOWY, PETER, executive; Exec. dir. Westfield Corp., Inc., L.A., 1986—.

LU, NANCY CHAO, nutrition and food science educator; b. Xian, China, May 29, 1941; came to U.S. 1963; d. Lun Yuan and Shu Mei (Tsang) Chao; m. Chyi Kang Lu, Mar. 19, 1966; 1 child, Richard H. BS, Nat. Taiwan U., 1963; MS, U. Wyo., 1965; PhD, U. Calif., Berkeley, 1973. Registered dietitian. Teaching asst. dept. nutritional sci. U. Wyo., Laramie, 1963, U. Calif., Berkeley, 1964, 70, teaching assoc. dept. nutritional sci., 1978, 79; lectr. dept. nutrition and food sci. San Jose State U., 1980-82, assoc. prof. dept. nutrition and food sci., 1982-87, prof. dept. nutrition and food sci., 1987—, acting assoc. dean, dir. divsn. health professions. Contbr. articles to profl. jours. Recipient Ellsworth Dougherty award, 1976, Calif. State U. Affirmative Action Faculty Devel. award, 1984, 85, 86, Meritorious Performance and Profl. Promise award San Jose State U., 1986, Most Outstanding Nutrition and Food Sci. Prof. award, 1989, 93; San Jose State U. Found. grantee, 1986-87, 89-90, 92-93, 93-94, 94-95, NIH grantee, 1975-76, 78-79, 73-75. Mem. Am. Dietetic Assn., Am. Inst. Nutrition, Inst. Food Technologists, Soc. Nematology, Soc. for Exptl. Biology and Medicine, Iota Sigma Pi, Sigma Xi. Office: San Jose State U Divsn Health Professions San Jose CA 95192-0001

LUBATTI, HENRY JOSEPH, physicist, educator; b. Oakland, Calif., Mar. 16, 1937; s. John and Pauline (Massimino) L.; m. Catherine Jeanne Berthe Ledoux, June 29, 1968; children: Karen E., Henry J., Stephen J.C. AA, U. Calif., Berkeley, 1957, AB, 1960; PhD, U. Calif., 1966; MS, U. Ill., 1963. Research assoc. Faculty Scis. U. Paris, Orsay, France, 1966-68; asst. prof. physics MIT, 1968-69; assoc. prof., sci. dir. visual techniques lab. U. Wash., 1969-74, prof., sci. dir. visual Techniques lab., 1974-98. Vis. lectr. Internat. Sch. Physics, Erice, Sicily, 1968, Herceg-Novi, Yugoslavia Internat. Sch., 1969, XII Cracow Sch. Theoretical Physics, Zapokane, Poland, 1972; vis. scientist CERN, Geneva, 1980-81; vis. staff Los Alamos Nat. Lab., 1983-86; guest scientist SSC Lab., 1991-93; mem. physics editorial adv. com. World Sci. Pub. Co. Ltd., 1982-93; guest scientist Fermilab., 1999-2000. Editor: Physics at Fermilab in the 1990's, 1990; contbr. numerous articles on high energy physics to profl. jours. Alfred P. Sloan research fellow, 1971-75 Fellow AAAS, Am. Phys. Soc.; mem. Sigma Xi, Tau Beta Pi. Office: Elem Particle Experiment Group U Wash PO Box 351560 Seattle WA 98195-1560 E-mail: lubatti@phys.washington.edu

LUBCHENCO, JANE, marine biologist, educator; b. Denver, Dec. 4, 1947; married; 2 children. BA, Colo. Coll., 1969; MS, U. Wash., 1971; PhD in Ecology, Harvard U., 1975. Asst. prof. ecology Harvard U., Cambridge, Mass., 1975-77; from asst. prof. to assoc. prof. Oreg. State U., Corvallis, 1978-88, prof. zoology, 1988—; rsch. assoc. Smithsonian Inst., 1978—; Disting. prof., Wayne and Gladys Valley prof. marine biology Oreg. State U., Corvallis. Prin. investigator NSF, 1976— Fellow John D. and Katherine T. MacArthur Found., 1993. Mem. AAAS (pres. 1996), Ecol. Soc. Am. (George Mercer award 1979, mem. coun. 1982-84, chair awards com. 1983-86, nominating com. 1986), Phycological Soc. Am. (nat. lectr. 1987-89), Am. Soc. Naturalists, Am. Soc. Zoologists, Am. Inst. Biol. Sci. Achievements include research in population and community ecology, plant-herbivore and predator-prey interactions, competition, marine ecology, algal ecology, agal life histories, biogeography and chemical ecology. Office: Oreg State U Dept Zoology Cordley 3029 Corvallis OR 97331

LUBECK, MARVIN JAY, ophthalmologist; b. Cleve., Mar. 20, 1929; s. Charles D. and Lillian (Jay) L. A.B., U. Mich., 1951, M.D., 1955, M.S., 1959. Diplomate Am. Bd. Opthamology; m. Arlene Sue Bitman, Dec. 28, 1955; children: David Mark, Daniel Jay, Robert Charles. Intern, U. Mich. Med. Ctr., 1955-56, resident ophthalmology, 1956-58, jr. clin. instr. ophthalmology, 1958-59; pvt. practice medicine, specializing in ophthalmology, Denver, 1961—; mem. staff Rose Hosp., Porter Hosp., Presbyn. Hosp., St. Luke's Hosp.; assoc. clin. prof. U. Colo. Med. Ctr. With U.S. Army, 1959-61. Fellow ACS; mem. Am. Acad. Ophthalmology, Denver Med. Soc., Colo. Ophthalmol. Soc. Home: 590 S Harrison Ln Denver CO 80209-3517 Office: 3600 E Alameda Ave Denver CO 80209-3189

LUCAS, DONALD LEO, private investor; b. Upland, Calif., Mar. 18, 1930; s. Leo J. and Mary G. (Schwamm) L.; m. Lygia de Soto Harrison, July 15, 1961; children: Nancy Maria Lucas Thibodeau, Alexandra Maria Lucas Ertola, Donald Alexander Lucas. BA, Stanford U., 1951, MBA, 1953. Assoc. corp. fin. dept. Smith, Barney & Co., N.Y.C., 1956-59; gen., ltd. ptnr. Draper, Gaither & Anderson, Palo Alto, Calif., 1959-66; pvt. investor Menlo Park, 1966—. Bd. dirs. Cadence Design Systems, San Jose, Calif., Oracle Corp., Redwood Shores, Calif., Macromedia, San Francisco, TriCord Systems, Inc., Plymouth, Minn. Mem. bd. regents Bellarmine Coll. Prep., 1977—; regent emeritus U. Santa Clara, 1980—. 1st lt. AUS, 1953-55. Mem. Am. Coun. Capital Formation (dir.), Stanford U. Alumni Assn., Stanford Grad. Sch. Bus. Alumni Assn., Order of Malta, Stanford Buck Club, Vintage Club (Indian Wells, Calif.), Menlo Circus Club (Atherton, Calif.), Jackson Hole Golf and Tennis Club, Sand Hills Golf Club, Teton Pines Club, Bighorn Country Club, Calif., Zeta Psi. Home: 224 Park Ln Atherton CA 94027-5411 Office: 3000 Sand Hill Rd Ste 3-210 Menlo Park CA 94025-7119

LUCAS, DONNA, communications executive; m. Greg Lucas; 1 child, Katherine. Grad. in Journalism, U. So. Calif., 1982. Press sec. Gov. George Deukmejian; dir. pub. affairs State Treas. Office; CEO, pres. Nelson Comm. Group, Sacramento, NCG Porter Novelli, Sacramento. Bd. dirs. Am. Assn. Polit. Cons.; past gubernatorial appointee Calif. Commn. on Status of Women; bd. dirs. Capitol Focus; Calif. media dir. Rep. Nat. Conv., 1992; Calif. press sec. Pres. George Bush's 1988 campaign; past campaign mgr. State Treas., Tom Hayes. Office: NCG Porter Novelli 1215 K St Ste 2100 Sacramento CA 95814-3951

LUCAS, GEORGE W., JR. film director, producer, screenwriter; b. Modesto, Calif., May 14, 1944; Student, Modesto Jr. Coll.; BA, U. So. Calif., 1966. Chmn. Lucasfilm Ltd., San Rafael, Calif. Creator short film THX-1138 (Grand prize Nat. Student Film Festival, 1967); asst. to Francis Ford Coppola on The Rain People; dir. Filmmaker (documentary on making of The Rain People); dir., co-writer THX-1138, 1970, American Graffiti, 1973; dir., author screenplay Star Wars, 1977; exec. prodr. More American Graffiti, 1979, The Empire Strikes Back, 1980, Raiders of the Lost Ark, 1981, Indiana Jones and the Temple of Doom, 1984, Labyrinth, 1986, Howard the Duck, 1986, Willow, 1988, Tucker, 1988, Radioland Murders, 1994; exec. prodr., co-author screenplay Return of the Jedi, 1983; co-exec. prodr. Mishima, 1985; co-author, co-exec. prodr. Indiana Jones and the Last Crusade, 1989; exec. prodr. (TV series) The Young Indiana Jones Chronicles, 1992-93; writer, dir., exec. prodr.: Star Wars: Episode I The Phantom Menace, 1999. Office: Lucasfilm Ltd PO Box 2009 San Rafael CA 94912-2009

LUCAS, LINDA LUCILLE, dean; b. Stockton, Calif., Apr. 22, 1940; d. Leslie Harold Lucas and Amy Elizabeth (Callow) Farnsworth. BA, San Jose State Coll., 1961, MA, 1969; EdD, U. San Francisco, 1982. Dist. libr. Livermore (Calif.) Elem. Schs., 1962-64; libr. Mission San Jose High Sch., Fremont, Calif., 1964-69; media reference libr. Chabot Coll., Hayward, 1969-75; asst. dean instrn. Chabot-Las Positas Coll., Livermore, 1975-91; assoc. dean instrn. Las Positas Coll., Livermore, 1991-94, dean acad. svcs., 1994-2000. Participant Nat. Inst. for Leadership Devel., 1991. Bd. dirs. Tri-Valley Community TV, Livermore, 1991-98, Valley Choral Soc., 1993-98, Chabot-Las Positas Colls. Found., Pleasanton, Calif., 1991-94; mem. needs assessment com Performing Arts Coun., Pleasanton. Mem. ALA, Coun. Chief Librs., Assn. Calif. Community Coll. Adminstrs., Calif. Libr. Assn. Avocations: choral music, photography. Home: 4848 Golden Rd Pleasanton CA 94566-6038

LUCCHETTI, DAVID J. manufacturing executive; CEO, pres. Pacific Coast Bldg. Products, Sacramento. Office: Pacific Coast Bldg Products PO Box 160488 Sacramento CA 95816-0488 Fax: 916-325-3697

LUCCHINO, LAWRENCE, sports team executive, lawyer; b. Pitts., Sept. 6, 1945; s. Dominic A. and Rose (Rizzo) L. A.B. cum laude, Princeton U., 1967; J.D., Yale U., 1972. Bar: Calif. and Pa. 1973, D.C. 1975. Counsel Impeachment Inquiry, House Judiciary Commn., Washington, 1974; assoc. Williams & Connolly, Washington, 1975-79, ptnr., 1979—; pres., CEO Balt. Orioles, 1988-93, San Diego Padres, 1995—. Sec., bd. dirs., gen. counsel Washington Redskins Football Club, 1978-85; bd. dirs., gen. counsel Balt. Orioles Baseball Club, from 1979, v.p., 1982-88, pres., CEO, 1988-93; CEO San Diego Padres Baseball Club, 1994—; bd. dirs. Army Times, Springfield, Va. Trustee Nat. Found. on Counseling, Princeton, N.J., 1984—; bd. dirs. Nat. Aquarium Natl., Balt. Symphony, Princeton Electronic Bd., Babe Ruth Mus. Mem. ABA Democrat. Roman Catholic. Office: San Diego Padres PO Box 2000 San Diego CA 92112-2000 also: Williams & Connolly 725 12th St NW Washington DC 20005-3901

LUCE, R(OBERT) DUNCAN, psychology educator; b. Scranton, Pa., May 16, 1925; s. Robert Rennselaer and Ruth Lillian (Downer) L.; m. Gay Gaer, June 6, 1950 (div.); m. Cynthia Newby, Oct. 5, 1968 (div.); m. Carolyn A. Scheer, Feb. 27, 1988; 1 child, Aurora Newby. BS, MIT, 1945, PhD, 1950; MA (hon.), Harvard U., 1976. Mem. staff research lab electronics MIT, 1950-53; asst. prof. Columbia U., 1953-57; lectr. social relations Harvard U., 1957-59; prof. psychology U. Pa., Phila., 1959-69; vis. prof. Inst. Advanced Study, Princeton, 1969-72; prof. Sch. Social Scis., U. Calif., Irvine, 1972-75; Alfred North Whitehead prof. psychology Harvard U., Cambridge, Mass., 1976-81, prof., 1981-83, Victor S. Thomas prof. psychology, 1983-88, Victor S. Thomas prof. emeritus, 1988, chmn., 1988-94; disting. prof. cognitive sci. U. Calif., Irvine, 1988-94, dir. Irvine Rsch. Unit in math. behavioral sci., 1988-92, disting. rsch. prof. cognitive sci. and rsch. prof. econs., 1994—; dir. Inst. for Math. Behavioral Sci., 1992-98. Chmn. assembly behavioral and social scis. NRC, 1976-79 Author: (with H. Raiffa) Games and Decisions, 1957, Individual Choice Behavior, 1959, (with others) Foundations of Measurement, I, 1971, II, 1989, III, 1990, Response Times, 1986, (with others) Stevens Handbook of Experimental Psychology, I and II, 1988, Sound & Hearing, 1993, Utility of Gains and Losses, 2000. Served with USNR, 1943-46. Ctr. Advanced Study in Behavioral Scis. fellow, 1954-55, 66-67, 87-88, NSF Sr. Postdoctoral fellow, 1966-67, Guggenheim fellow, 1980-81; recipient Disting. award for Rsch. U. Calif., Irvine, 1994, medal, 2001, gold medal award Am. Psychol. Found., 2001. Fellow: AAAS (chair elect psychology sect. 1998—99, chair 1999), APA (bd. sci. affairs 1993—95, exec. com. divsn. I 2000, disting. sci. contbn. award 1970 gold medal for lifetime achievement in scientific psychology 2001), Am. Psychol. Soc. (bd. dirs. 1989—91); mem.: Sigma Xi, Tau Beta Pi, Phi Beta Kappa, Am. Acad. Arts and Sci., Am. Philos. Soc., Nat. Acad. Scis. (chmn. sect. psychology 1980—83, class behavioral and social scis. 1983—86), Am. Math. Soc., Math. Assn. Am., Fedn. Behavioral Psychol. and Cognitive Scis. (pres. 1988—90), Psychometric Soc. (pres. 1976—77), Psychonomic Soc., Soc. Math. Psychology (pres. 1979). Home: 20 Whitman Ct Irvine CA 92612-4057 Office: U Calif Social Sci Plz Irvine CA 92697-0001 E-mail: rdluce@uci.edu

LUCERO, CARLOS, federal judge; b. Antonito, Colo., Nov. 23, 1940; m. Dorothy Stuart; 1 child, Carla. BA, Adams State Coll.; JD, George Washington U., 1964. Law clk. to Judge William E. Doyle U.S. Dist. Ct., Colo., 1964-65; pvt. practice Alamosa; sr. ptnr. Lucero, Lester & Sigmund, Alamosa; judge U.S. Ct. Appeals (10th cir.), 1995—. Mem. Pres. Carter's Presdl. Panel on Western State Water Policy. Bd. dirs. Colo. Hist. Soc., Santa Fe Opera Assn. of N.Mex. Recipient Outstanding Young Man of Colo. award Colo. Jaycees, Disting. Alumnus award George Washington U.; Paul Harris fellow Rotary Found. Fellow Am. Coll. Trial Lawyers, Am. Bar Found., Colo. Bar Found. (pres.), Internat. Acad. Trial Lawyers, Internat. Soc. Barristers; mem. ABA (mem. action com. to reduce ct. cost and delay, mem adv. bd. ABA jour., mem. com. on the availability of legal svcs.), Colo. Bar Assn. (pres. 1977-78, mem. ethics com.), San Luis Valley Bar Assn. (pres.), Nat. Hispanic Bar Assn., Colo. Hispanic Bar Assn. (profl. svc. award), Colo. Rural Legal Svcs. (bd. dirs.), Order of the Coif. Office: US Ct Appeals 1823 Stout St Denver CO 80257-1823*

LUCHTERHAND, RALPH EDWARD, financial advisor; b. Portland, Oreg., Feb. 9, 1952; s. Otto Charles II and Evelyn Alice (Isaac) L.; children: Anne Michelle, Eric Alexander, Nicholas Andrew, Mistie Rose Beaudoin; m. Victoria Marie Schiffbauer, Nov. 8, 1997. BS, Portland State U., 1974, MBA, 1986. Registered profl. engr., Oreg.; cert. fin. planner; gen. securities broker NYSE/NASD, registered investment prin. Mech. engr. Hyster Co., Portland, 1971-75, svc. engr., 1975-76; project engr. Lumber Systems Inc., Portland, 1976-79; prin. engr. Moore Internat., Portland, 1979-81, chief product engr., 1981-83; project engr. Irvington-Moore, Portland, 1983, chief engr., 1983-86; ind. cons. engr., 1986; engring. program mgr. Precision Castparts Corp., Portland, 1986-87; personal fin. advisor Am. Express Fin. Advisors, Clackamas, Oreg., 1987-94, sr. fin. advisor, 1994—. Ptnr. Bacon, Luchterhand Wilmot & Assocs. (a fin. adv. br. of Am. Express Fin. Advisors), Clackamas, Oreg., 1996—, br. mgr., 1999—; apptd. to Silver Team, 1991, Gold Team, 1994. Treas., Village Bapt. Ch., Beaverton, Oreg., 1988-91; bd. dirs. Carus Cmty. Planning Orgn., Oregon City, Oreg., 1993-99; active Rolling Hills Cmty. Ch., Tualatin, Oreg., 1995—. Mem. Fin. Planning Assn., Assn. Fin. Planning Profls. Republican. Home: 24440 S Eldorado Rd Mulino OR 97042-9629 Office: Bacon Luchterhand Wilmot & Assocs Am Express Fin Advisors 8800 SE Sunnyside Rd Ste 114 Clackamas OR 97015-5702 Mailing: PO Box 1216 Mulino OR 97042 E-mail: ralph@bctonline.com

LUCIA, MARILYN REED, physician; b. Boston; m. Salvatore P. Lucia, 1959 (dec. 1984); m. C. Robert Russell; children: Elizabeth, Walter, Salvatore, Darryl. MD, U. Calif., San Francisco, 1956. Intern Stanford U. Hosps., 1956-57; NIMH fellow, resident in psychiatry Langley Porter, U. Calif., San Francisco, 1957-60; NIMH fellow, resident in child psychiatry Mt. Zion Hosp., San Francisco, 1964-66; NIMH fellow, resident in community psychiatry U. Calif., San Francisco, 1966-68, clin. prof. psychiatry, 1982—. Founder, cons. Marilyn Reed Lucia Child Care Study Ctr., U. Calif., San Francisco; cons. Cranio-facial Ctr., U. Calif., San Francisco, No. Calif. Diagnostic Sch. for Neurologically Handicapped Children; dir. children's psychiat. svcs. Contra Costa County Hosp., Martinez. Fellow Am. Psychiat. Assn., Am. Acad. Child Psychiatry; mem. Am. Cleft Palate Assn., San Francisco Med. Soc. Office: 350 Parnassus Ave Ste 602 San Francisco CA 94117-3608

LUCKOFF, MICHAEL, broadcast executive; Pres., gen. mgr. Sta. KGO-AM, San Francisco, 1975—. Office: KGO Radio 900 Front St San Francisco CA 94111-1450

LUCKOW, LYNN D. W. publishing executive; b. Hettinger, N.D., 1949; Grad., U. N.D., 1971, Ind. U., 1974. Pres., pub. Jossey-Bass Inc. Pub., San Francisco. Home: 666 Post St San Francisco CA 94109-8293 Office: Jossey Bass Inc Pub 350 Sansome St Fl 5 San Francisco CA 94104-1304

LUCZO, STEPHEN J. computer equipment company executive; Sr. mng. dir. fin., co-head Bear Stearns Global Tech. Group, until 1993; exec. v.p. corp. devel. Seagate Software; sr. mng. dir. fin. Bear Stearns; with Seagate Tech., Inc., Scotts Valley, Calif., 1993—, exec. v.p. corp. devel., pres., 1997-2000, CEO, 2000—. Office: Seagate Tech Inc 920 Disc Dr Scotts Valley CA 95066-4542

LUDGUS, NANCY LUCKE, lawyer; b. Palo Alto, Calif., Oct. 28, 1953; d. Winston Slover and Betty Jean Lucke; m. Lawrence John Ludgus, Apr. 8, 1983. BA in Polit. Sci. with honors, U. Calif., Berkeley, 1975; JD, U. Calif., Davis, 1978. Bar: Calif. 1978, U.S. Dist. Ct. (no. dist.) Calif. 1978. Staff atty. Crown Zellerbach Corp., San Francisco, 1978-80, Clorox Co., Oakland, Calif., 1980-82, Nat. Semiconductor Corp., Santa Clara, 1982-85, corp. counsel, 1985-92, sr. corp. counsel, asst. sec., 1992-2000, assoc. gen. counsel, asst. sec., 2000—. Contbr. articles to profl. jours. Mem. ABA, Am. Corp. Counsel Assn., Calif. State Bar Assn., Santa Clara County Bar Assn., Phi Beta Kappa. Democrat. Avocations: travel, jogging, opera. Office: Nat Semiconductor Corp 1090 Kifer Rd # 16135 Sunnyvale CA 94086-5301 E-mail: nancy.lucke.ludgus@nsc.com

LUEDTKE, ROGER A. lawyer; b. Wausau, Wis., Apr. 10, 1942; BS, U. Wis., 1964, MA, 1968, JD, 1974. Bar: Wis. 1974, Oreg. 1974. Atty. Schwabe, Williamson & Wyatt, Portland, Oreg., 1974—. Mem. Oreg. State Bar, Phi Eta Sigma. Address: Schwabe Williamson & Wyatt 1211 SW 5th Ave Ste 1600 Portland OR 97204-3716

LUENBERGER, DAVID GILBERT, electrical engineer, educator; b. Los Angeles, Sept. 16, 1937; s. Frederick Otto and Marion (Crumley) L.; m. Nancy Ann Iversen, Jan. 7, 1962; children: Susan Ann, Robert Alden, Jill Alison, Jenna Emmy. B.S.E.E., Calif. Inst. Tech., 1959; M.S.E.E., Stanford U., 1961, Ph.D. in Elec. Engring., 1963. Asst. prof. elec. engring. Stanford (Calif.) U., 1963-67, assoc. prof. engring.-econ. systems, 1967-71, prof., 1971—, dept. chmn., 1980-91, prof. mgmt. sci. & engring., 2000—. Tech. asst. dir. U.S. Office Sci. and Tech., Exec. Office of Pres., Washington, 1971-72; vis. prof. MIT, Cambridge, 1976; guest prof. Tech. U. of Denmark, Lyngby, 1986. Author: Optimization by Vector Space Methods, 1969, Linear and Nonlinear Programming, 1973, 2d edit., 1984, Introduction to Dynamic Systems, 1979, Microeconomic Theory, 1995, Investment Science, 1998; contbr. articles to tech. jours. Recipient Hendrik W. Bode Lecture prize Control Systems Soc., 1990, Rufus Oldenburger medal, 1998. Fellow IEEE; mem. Econometric Soc., Soc. for Advancement Econ. Theory, Soc. for Promotion of Econ. Theory, Inst. Mgmt. Sci., Soc. Econ. Dynamics and Control (pres. 1987-88), Math Programming Soc., Palo Alto Camera Club, Sigma Xi, Tau Beta Pi. Lutheran.

LUEVANO, FRED, JR. computer systems executive; b. Alamogordo, N.Mex., June 21, 1943; s. Fred Macias and Margaret (Baca) L.; m. Lupe Olmos, July 11, 1964; children: Michael, James Paul. AA in bus., Fullerton Coll., 1975; BA in Mgmt., U. Redlands, 1979, MA in Mgmt., 1985. Cert. data processing mgr., disaster recovery planner. Mgr. computer ops. Hoffman Electronics, El Monte, Calif., 1971-76; mgr. computer ops. and tech. services City of Anaheim, 1976-79; mgr. data processing Wyle Data Services, Huntington Beach, 1979-83; mgr. corp. computer ops. Northrop Grumman Corp., Pico Rivera, 1983, mgr. corp. computing, 1985—, dir. disaster revovery program, 1983—, dir. disaster recovery and security, 1988-90, with, 1990-92, mgr. data processing, 1992—, dir. cons. svcs., 2000—. Cons. on info. sys., La Habra, Calif., 1971—; chmn. cert. bd. dirs. Disaster Recovery Inst., spkr., 1991-95. Cub master Boy Scouts Am., La Habra, 1979-84, chmn. com. 1975-79; councilman candidate City of La Habra Heights, Calif., 1982; pres. Red Coach Club, 1979-80, 86-88, pres. La Habra Parents for Swimming Inc., 1986-88; chmn. bd. dirs. Pub. and Pvt. Bus., Inc., 1998; dir. Gartner Group, 1999. Served with USN, 1961-65. Named Enterprise Sys. Mgr. of Yr., Assn. for Computer Ops. Mgrs.(AFCOM), 1998. Mem. Am. Mgmt. Assn., Telecom. Assn., Assn. Computer Ops. Mgrs. (speaker 1983-94), Northrop Mgmt. Club. Republican. Roman Catholic. Avocations: fishing, basketball. Office: Northrop Grumman Corp MS 770 XC 8900 Washington Blvd Pico Rivera CA 90660-3765 E-mail: fred.luevano@gartner.com

LUFT, HAROLD S. health economist; b. Newark, Jan. 6, 1947; s. George and Kay (Grossman) L.; m. Lorraine Ellin Levinson, May 24, 1970; children: Shira Levinson, Jana Levinson. A.B., Harvard U., 1968, AM, 1970, Ph.D., 1973. Systems analyst, rsch. asst. Harvard Transport Rsch., Cambridge, Mass., 1965-68; systems analyst Harvard Econ. Rsch. Project, Cambridge, 1968-72; instr. econs. Tufts U., Medford, 1972-73; postdoctoral fellow Harvard Ctr. Community Health, Boston, 1972-73; asst. prof. health econs. Stanford U., Calif., 1973-78; prof. health econs., acting dir. Inst. Health Policy Studies, U. Calif., San Francisco, 1978-93; dir. Inst. Health Policy Studies U. Calif., San Francisco, 1993—. Cons. Applied Mgmt. Scis., Silver Spring, Md., 1979—, Robert Wood Johnson Found., Princeton, N.J., 1982—; study sect. Nat. Ctr. Health Svcs., Rockville, Md., 1981-83; mem. coun. Agy. for Health Care Policy and Rsch., 1994-99. Author: Poverty and Health, 1978, Health Maintenance Organizations, 1981, 2d edit., 1988, (with Deborah Garnick, David mark, Stephen McPhee) Hospital Volume, Physician Volume, and Patient Outcomes, 1990, HMOs and the Elderly, 1994; sr. assoc. editor Health Svcs. Rsch., 1997; contbr. chpts. to books, articles to profl. jours. Advisor, fin. planning com. Mid-Peninsula Health Service, Palo Alto, Calif., 1984— . NSF fellow, Carnegie Found. fellow, Grad. Prize fellow Harvard U., 1968-72, fellow Ctr. for Advanced Study in Behavioral Scis., 1988-89; recipient health svcs. rsch. prize AUPHA, 1998. Mem. Am. Pub. Health Assn., Am. Econ. Assn., Inst. Medicine, Western Econ. Assn., Assn. for Health Svcs. Rsch. (bd. dirs., Investigator of Yr. 1999). Home: 1020 Ramona St Palo Alto CA 94301-2443 Office: U Calif Inst Health Policy Studies 3333 California St Ste 265 San Francisco CA 94143-0001

LUIKART, JOHN FORD, investment banker; b. Washington, Apr. 9, 1949; s. Fordyce Whitney and Margaret Lucille (Clark) L.; m. Lorry Adele Haycock, June 2, 1973; children: Erin Kristine, James Benjamin, John Thomas. BA, Ohio Weslyan U., 1971. Ptnr. Prescott Ball and Turben, Cleve., 1977, sr. v.p., mgr. fixed income, 1982-86, exec. v.p., also bd. dirs., 1986-88; pres. Sutro & Co. Inc., San Francisco, 1989—, CEO, 1995—; bd. dirs. John Hancock Freedom Securities, San Francisco, 1996; chmn., CEO Sutro & Co., San Francisco. Pres. Selected Money Mkt. Fund, Chgo., 1986, 1331 Advisors, Cleve., 1986; mgr. Ohio Bond Fund, Cleve., 1983—; chmn. NASD Dist. Bus. Conduct Com., 1994; bd. dirs. Freedom Securities, Freedom Capital Mgmt. Chmn. Ohio Mcpl. Adv. Council, Cleve., 1978-79. Mem. Cleve. Bond Club (pres. 1980). Methodist. Avocations: sports, reading. Office: Sutro & Co 201 California St Ste 200 San Francisco CA 94111-5002

LUKENBILL, GREGG, real estate developer, sports promoter; b. Sacramento, Aug. 15, 1954; s. Frank and Leona L.; children: Jake, Molly, Ben. BSBA, Calif. State U., 1995, MBA, 1997. Owner, developer, builder Lukenbill Enterprises, Sacramento Valley Region; mng. gen. ptnr. Sacramento Kings Profl. Basketball/NBA, 1983-92, ARCO Arena, 1985-93; pres. Hyatt Regency, Sacramento, 1986-92; owner Sky King Inc.; pilot, pres. Lunkenbill Engerprises. Office: UNITH 3600 Power Inn Rd Sacramento CA 95826-3826

LUKER, KRISTIN, sociology educator; b. Sam Francisco, Aug. 15, 1946; d. James Wester and Bess (Littlefield) L. BA, U. Calif., Berkeley, 1968; PhD, Yale U., 1974. Postdoctoral fellow U. Calif., Berkeley, 1974-75, asst. prof. sociology San Diego, 1975-81, assoc. prof., 1981-85, prof., 1985-86, co-dir. women's studies program, 1984-85, prof. jurisprudence and social policy and sociology Berkeley, 1986—. Doris Stevens prof. women's studies, prof. sociology Princeton (N.J.) U., 1993-95. Author: Taking Chances: Abortion and the Decision Not To Contracept, 1976 (hon. mention Jessie Bernard award), Abortion and the Politics of Motherhood, 1984 (Charles Horton Dooley award, 1985). Bd. dirs. Ctr. for Women's Studies and Svcs., San Diego, Ctr. for Population Otions, Washington. Grantee Guggenheim Found., 1985. Mem. Am. Sociol. Assn., Sociologists for Women in Society. Office: U Calif Jurisprudence and Social Policy 2240 Piedmont Ave Berkeley CA 94720-2150

LULLO, THOMAS A. electronics executive; CFO Consolidated Electronics Distbrs., Westlake Village, Calif. Office: Consolidated Electronics Distbrs 31356 Via Colinas Ste 107 Westlake Village CA 91362 Office Fax: (818) 991-6858

LUM, JEAN LOUI JIN, nursing educator; b. Honolulu, Sept. 5, 1938; d. Yee Nung and Pui Ki (Young) L. BS, U. Hawaii, Manoa, 1960; MS in Nursing, U. Calif., San Francisco, 1961; MA, U. Wash., 1969, PhD in Sociology, 1972. Registered nurse, Hawaii. From instr. to prof. Sch. Nursing U. Hawaii Manoa, Honolulu, 1961-95, acting dean, 1982, dean, 1982-89, prof. emeritus, 1995—. Project coordinator Analysis and Planning Personnel Svcs., Western Interstate Commn. Higher Edn., 1977; extramural assoc. div. Rsch. Grants NIH, 1978-79; mem. mgmt. adv. com. Honolulu County Hosp., 1982-96; mem. exec. bd. Pacific Health Rsch. Inst., 1980-88; mem. health planning com. East Honolulu, 1978-81; mem. rsch. grants adv. coun. Hawaii Med. Svcs. Assn. Found., Nat. Adv. Coun. for Nursing Rsch., 1990-93. Contbr. articles to profl. jours. Trustee Straub Pacific Health Found., Honolulu; bd. dirs. Friends of the Nat. Inst. of Nursing Rsch., 1994-97. Recipient Nurse of Yr. award Hawaii Nurses Assn., 1982; named Disting. Practitioner in Nursing, Nat. Acads. of Practice, 1986; USPHS grantee, 1967-72 Fellow Am. Acad. Nursing; mem. Am. Nurses Assn., Am. Pacific Nursing Leaders Conf. (pres. 1983-87), Council Nurse Researchers, Nat. League for Nursing (bd. rev. 1981-87), Western Council Higher Edn. for Nurses (chmn. 1984-85), Western Soc. for Research in Nursing, Am. Sociol. Assn., Pacific Sociol. Assn., Assn. for Women in Sci., Hawaii Pub. Health Assn., Hawaii Med. Services Assn. (bd. dirs. 1985-92), Western Inst. Nursing, Mortar Bd., Phi Kappa Phi, Sigma Theta Tau, Alpha Kappa Delta, Delta Kappa Gamma. Episcopalian Home: 3185 Waialae Ave Honolulu HI 96816-1511 Office: U Hawaii Manoa Sch Nursing Webster Hall 2528 The Mall Honolulu HI 96822

LUMAN, ROBERT M. protective services official; b. Long Beach, Calif., Nov. 8, 1934; m. Annette Luman; 2 children. MPA, U. So. Calif.; grad., FBI Nat. Acad., 1991. From patrol officer to dep. chief Long Beach (Calif.) Police Dept., 1968-96, chief of police, 1996—. Bd. dirs. Am. Heart Assn., Long Beach, ARC, Long Beach; active Long Beach Cmty. Partnership, Nat. Conf., St. Marys Bd. Trustees. Mem. Internat. Assn. Chiefs Police, L.A. County Police Chiefs Assn., Calif. Peace Officers Assn. (Law Enforcement Profl. Achievement award 1992), Long Beach Area C. of C. (bd. dirs.), Rotary. Avocations: fishing, boating. Office: Long Beach Police Dept 400 W Broadway Long Beach CA 90802-4401

LUMBYE, BETSY, editor; Mng. editor Fresno (Calif.) Bee. Office: Fresno Bee 1626 E St Fresno CA 93706-2098

LUMMIS, CYNTHIA MARIE, state treasurer, lawyer; b. Cheyenne, Wyo., Sept. 10, 1954; d. Doran Arp and Enid (Bennett) L.; m. Alvin L. Wiederspahn, May 28, 1983; children: Annaliese Alex. BS, U. Wyo., 1976, BS, 1978, JD, 1985. Bar: Wyo. 1985, U.S. Dist Ct. of Wyo. 1985, U.S. Ct. of Appeals (10th cir.) 1986. Rancher Lummis Livestock Co., Cheyenne, 1972—; law clk. Wyo. Supreme Ct., Cheyenne, 1985-86; assoc. Wiederspahn, Lummis & Liepas, Cheyenne, 1986—; treas. State of Wyo., 1999—. Mem. Wyo. Ho. Judiciary Com., 1979-86, Ho. Agriculture, Pub. Lands & Water Resources Com., 1985-86, Wyo. State Senate, 1993-94, Senate Judiciary Com., 1993-94, Senate Mines, Minerals, Econ. Devel. Com., 1993-94, U. Wyo. Inst. for Environment and Natural Resource Policy and Rsch.; chmn. County Ct. Planning Com., Wyo., 1986-88, Ho. Rev. Com., 1987-92, Joint Revenue Interim Com., 1988-89, 91-92; mem. adv. bd. U. Mont. Ctr. for the Rocky Mountain West, 1998—. Sec. Meals on Wheels, Cheyenne, 1985-87; mem. Agrl. Crisis Support Group, Laramie County, Wyo., 1985-87; mem. adv. com. U. Wyo. Sch. Nursing, 1988-90; mem. steering com. Wyo. Heritage Soc., 1986-89. Republican. Lutheran. Club: Rep. Women's (Cheyenne) (legis. chmn. 1982). Office: State Treasurer 200 W 24th St Cheyenne WY 82002-0001

LUNA, B. MARTIN, lawyer; b. Waimea, Kauai, Hawaii, July 25, 1938; BA, Emory U., 1960, MA, 1962; LLB, George Washington U., 1967. Bar: Hawaii 1968, U.S. Dist. Ct. Hawaii, U.S. Ct. Appeals (9th cir.), U.S .Supreme Ct. Ptnr. Carlsmith Ball Wichmans Case, Wailuku, Hawaii. Office: Carlsmith Ball Wichman Case Mukai & Ichiki PO Box 1086 2200 Main St Ste 400 Wailuku HI 96793-1691

LUND, ROBERT W. newspaper editor; Editor L.A. Daily News, 1994-98, mgr. editl. ops. and fin., 1998—. Office: Los Angeles Daily News 21221 Oxnard St Woodland Hills CA 91367-5015

LUND, STEVEN JAY, lawyer; b. Mesa, Ariz., Oct. 30, 1953; s. Jay Norman and Toy (Openshaw) L.; m. Kalleen Kirk, Aug. 8, 1980; children: Christine, Ryan, Tanner, Kelsey. BA, JD, Brigham Young U., 1983. Bar: Ariz. 1984, Utah 1984. Assoc. Watson, Seiler & Orehoski, Provo, Utah, 1983-85; gen. counsel Nu Skin Internat., Inc., Provo, 1985, v.p., 1986—. Vol. rep. LDS Ch., 1973-75. Served with U.S. Army, 1975-78. Republican. Avocation: scuba diving. Office: Nu Skin Internat Inc 75 W Center St Provo UT 84601-4432

LUND, VICTOR L. retail food company executive; b. Salt Lake City, 1947; married BA, U. Utah, 1969, MBA, 1972. Audit mgr. Ernst and Whinney, Salt Lake City, 1972-77; sr. v.p. Skaggs Cos. Inc., from 1977; v.p., contr. Am. Stores Co., 1980-83, sr. v.p., contr., from 1983, exec. v.p., co-chief exec. officer, vice-chmn., chief fin. and adminstrv. officer, pres., CEO, dir., 1992-95, chmn., CEO, dir., 1995-99; vice chmn. bd. dirs. Albertsons Inc., Boise. Office: Albertsons Inc 250 Park Ctr Blvd Boise ID 83726-0001 also: Am Stores Co 709 E South Temple Salt Lake City UT 84102-1205

LUNDE, DOLORES BENITEZ, retired secondary education educator; b. Honolulu, Apr. 12, 1929; d. Frank Molero and Matilda (Francisco) Benitez; m. Nuell Carlton Lunde, July 6, 1957; 1 child, Laurelle. BA, U. Oreg., 1951, postgrad., 1951-52, U. So. Calif., L.A., 1953-54, Colo. State U., , 1957-58, Calif. State U., Fullerton, 1967-68. Cert. gen. secondary tchr., Calif.; cert. lang. devel. specialist. Tchr. Brawley (Calif.) Union High Sch. 1952-55; tchr. Fullerton (Calif.) Union High Sch. Dist., 1955-73; tchrs. aide Placentia (Calif.) Unified Sch. Dist., 1983-85; tchr. continuing edn. Fullerton Union High Sch. Dist., 1985-91; tchr. Fullerton Sch. Dist., 1988, Fullerton Union H.S. Dist., 1989-94. Presenter regional and state convs., so. Calif., 1986-88. Innovator tests, teaching tools, audio-visual aids. Vol. Luth. Social Svcs., Fullerton, 1981-82, Messiah Luth., Yorba Linda, Calif., 1981-88, 91-2001. Recipient Tchr. of Yr. award Fullerton Union High Sch. Dist., 1989. Mem. NEA, AAUW (life, bull. editor 1979-80, corr. sec. 1981-83, program v.p. 1983-84, gift honoree Fullerton br. 1985), Calif. State Tchrs. Assn., Fullerton Secondary Tchrs. Assn., Internat. Club/Spanish Club (advisor La Habra, Calif. 1965-72), Tchrs. English to Speakers Other Langs., Calif. Assn. Tchrs. English to Speakers Other Langs. Avocations: singing, folk and interpretive dance, guitar, reading, travel. Home: 4872 Ohio St Yorba Linda CA 92886-2713

LUNDEN, JOAN, television personality; b. Fair Oaks, CA, Sept. 19, 1950; d. Erle Murray and Gladyce Lorraine (Somervill) Blunden; children: Jamie Beryl, Lindsay Leigh, Sarah Emily. Student, Universidad de Las Americas, Mexico City, U. Calif., Calif. State U., Am. River Coll., Sacramento, Calif. Began broadcasting career as co-anchor and prodr. at Sta. KCRA-TV and Radio, Sacramento, 1973-75; with Sta. WABC-TV, N.Y.C., 1975—, co-anchor, 1976-80; co-host Good Morning America, ABC-TV, 1980-97; host spl. report TV for Whittle Comm.; host Everyday with Joan Lunden, 1989, Behind Closed Doors With Joan Lunden, 1994, 95, 96; film appearances include: Macho Callahan, 1970, What About Bob?, 1991, Free Willy 2, 1995, Conspiracy Theory, 1997; spl. appearances: (TV series) Murphy Brown, 1992, 93, LateLine, 1998; co-author: (with Andy Friedburg) Good Morning, I'm Joan Lunden, 1986, (with Michael Krauss) Joan Lunden's Mother's Minutes, 1986, Your Newborn Baby, Healthy Cooking For Your Family With Joan Lunden; syndicated columnist: Parent's Notes. Recipient Outstanding Mother of Yr. award, Nat. Mother's Day Com., 1982; Albert Einstein Coll. of Yeshiva U. Spirit of Achievement award; Nat. Women's Polit. Caucus award; NJ Divsn. of Civil Rights award; Baylor U. Outstanding Woman of the Year award. Office: LMNO Prodns PO Box 4361 Los Angeles CA 90028 also: 77 W 66th St New York NY 10023-6201 also: Creative Artists Agy c/o Debra Goldfarb 9830 Wilshire Blvd Beverly Hills CA 90212-1825

LUNDERVILLE, GERALD PAUL, bilingual ESL/social studies educator; b. Springfield, Mass., Feb. 22, 1941; s. Leon Albert and Florence Marion (Jolivette) L.; m. Martha Ann Sumner, Mar. 26, 1966 (div. Aug. 1971); m. Bony Lek, June 30, 1984. BA cum laude, U. N.H., 1963; MA, Middlebury Coll., 1969, U. Rochester, 1973, Calif. State U., Long Beach, 1994. Instr. Spanish Berwick Acad., South Berwick, Maine, 1963-64; tchr. French, Spanish Barnstable High Sch., Hyannis, Mass., 1967-68; instr. Spanish Cape Cod Community Coll., West Barnstable, 1968-71; tchr. French, Spanish Stevens High Sch. Annex, Claremont, N.H., 1973-74; tchr. English Centro de Estudios Norteamericanos, Valencia, Spain, 1974-75; dept. head fgn. langs. Merrimack (N.H.) High Sch., 1975-80; tchr. Spanish El Camino Coll., Torrance, Calif., 1980-85; tchr. ESL Wilson High Sch., Long Beach, 1980—, dept. head ESL, 1987-88, tchr. bilingual social studies/Spanish, 1992—, tchr. history/ELD, 1998—. Author: 20th Century Baseball Trivia, 1992; contbr. articles to Am. Atheist Mag. Active Long Beach Area Citizens Peace, 1982—, Animal Protection Inst. Am., Sacramento., 1983—; mem. Civil War Round Table of Long Beach. Served with U.S. Army, 1964-67, Vietnam. Mem. NEA, ACLU, NOW, Modern and Classical Lang. Assn. So. Calif., Tchrs. of English as a 2d Lang., Soc. for Preservation of English Lang. and Lit., VERBATIM, Nat. Humane Edn. Soc., Merrimack Tchrs. Assn. (sec. 1977-80), Lambda Pi. Avocations: cooking, tennis, reading, travel, writing. Home: 1740 Washington St Long Beach CA 90805-5535 Fax: 562-433-2731. E-mail: glunderville@lbusd.k12.ca.us

LUNDGREN, SUSAN ELAINE, counselor, educator; b. Martinez, Calif., May 31, 1949; d. Elmer Alfred and Shirley (Bright) L.; 1 child, Alicia Hadiya. AA, Diablo Valley Coll., 1969; BA in English, San Francisco State U., 1971, MA in Counseling, 1975; EdD, U. San Francisco, 1983; cert. in gen. mgmt., John F. Kennedy U., 1988. Instr., counselor Diablo Valley Coll., Pleasant Hill, Calif., 1976—, coordinator, 1986-90, women's ctr. faculty dir., 1983-85. Adj. prof. grad. career devel. John F. Kennedy U., Concord, Calif., 1982-98. Sec., bd. dirs. Rape Crisis Ctr., Concord, Calif., 1985. Named participant in leadership devel. inst. AAUW and Nat. Assn. Community Colls., 1985. Mem. Eureka Consortium (conf. speaker 1984, 86). Avocations: travel, photography. Home: 3738 Victor Ave Oakland CA 94619-1533 Office: Diablo Valley Coll 321 Golf Club Rd Pleasant Hill CA 94523-1529

LUNDIN, JOHN E. lawyer; b. Mpls., May 9, 1940; BA, U. Ariz., 1962, JD with distinction, 1967. Bar: Ariz. 1967, U.S. Supreme Ct. 1977. Mem. Gallagher & Kennedy, Phoenix, 1987—. Judge pro tem Ariz. Ct. Appeals, 1984-85, 91. With U.S. Army, 1963-65. Fellow Ariz. Bar Found.; mem. State Bar Ariz. (v.p. 1991-92), Maricopa County Bar Assn. (bd. dirs. 1977-85, pres. 1984-85), Ariz. Commn. on Judicial Performance Rev., Phi Delta Phi. Office: Gallagher & Kennedy 2600 N Central Ave Ste 1800 Phoenix AZ 85004-3099

LUNDINE, STANLEY NELSON, state government official, former congressman, lawyer; b. Jamestown, N.Y., Feb. 4, 1939; children: John Ludwig, Mark Andrew. Mayor of, Jamestown, 1969-76; mem. 95th-97th Congresses from 39th N.Y. Dist., 98th-99th Congress from 34th N.Y. Dist., 1976-87; lt. gov. State of N.Y., Albany, 1987—; exec. dir. Found. for Enterprise Devel., La Jolla, CA. Mem. banking, fin. and urban affairs coms., sci. and tech. com., select com. on aging. Office: Found for Enterprise Devel 7911 Herschel Ave Ste 402 La Jolla CA 92037-4412

LUNDQUIST, GENE ALAN, cotton company executive; b. Bakersfield, Calif., Feb. 25, 1943; s. Felix Waldemar and Elsie Geneva (Bartlett) L.; m. Susan Randour; 1 child, Nels Eric. BS, Colo. State U., 1964. Info. specialist Calcot Ltd., Bakersfield, 1969-71, field rep., 1971-74, asst. v.p., 1974-77, asst. v.p., corp. sec., 1977-80, v.p., corp. sec., 1980—. Bd. dirs. Calif. Farm Water Coalition, Water Assn. Kern County; apptd. Calif. Gov.'s Agrl. Summit; bd. dirs., chmn. bd. Agrl. Coun. Calif., 1999—. Bd. dirs. Kern County Water Agy., Bakersfield, 1975-91, dir., 1996—; bd. dirs. Bakersfield Salvation Army, 1985-88. With U.S. Army, 1965-67. Decorated Army Commendation medal; Calif. Agr. Leadership Found. fellow, 1973. Mem. Cotton Bd. (alt. dir. 1984-2000), Nat. Cotton Council Am. (del. 1984—), Calif. Cotton Growers Assn. (adv. com. 1976—), Calif. Planting Cotton Seed Distbrs. (adv. com. 1976—). Republican. Avocations: golf, tennis, running, landscaping, reading. Office: Calcot Ltd 1601 E Brundage Ln PO Box 259 Bakersfield CA 93302-0259

LUNDSTROM, MARJIE, newspaper editor and columnist; Grad., U. Nebr. Columnist, editor, nat. corr. The Denver Post, 1981-89; with The Sacramento Bee, 1989-90, 91—; nat. corr. Gannett News Svc., Washington, 1990-91. Recipient Pulitzer Prize for nat. reporting, 1991. Office: The Sacramento Bee PO Box 15779 Sacramento CA 95852-0779

LUNGREN, DANIEL EDWARD, former state attorney general; b. Long Beach, Calif., Sept. 22, 1946; s. John Charles and Lorain Kathleen (Youngberg) L.; m. Barbara Kolls, Aug. 2, 1969; children: Jeffrey Edward, Kelly Christine, Kathleen Marie. A.B. cum laude, Notre Dame U., 1968; postgrad., U. So. Calif. Law Sch., 1968-69; J.D., Georgetown U., 1971. Bar: Calif. 1972. Staff asst. Sen. George Murphy, Sen. William Brock, 1969-71; spl. asst. to co-chmn. Rep. Nat. Com., dir. spl. programs, 1971-72; assoc., selected as ptnr. Ball, Hunt, Hart, Brown & Baerwitz, Long Beach, 1973-78; mem. 96th-97th Congresses from 34th, 98th-100th Congresses from 42d Calif. Dist., 1979-1989, Rep. State Cen. Com. Calif., 1974-89; ptnr. Diepenbrock, Wulff, Plant & Hannegan, Sacramento, 1989-90; atty. gen. State of Calif., Sacramento, 1991-98; host, Dan Lungren Show Catholic Family Radio, San Diego. Bd. dirs. Long Beach chpt. ARC, Boy's Club, 1976-88; committeeman Rep. Nat. Com., Calif., 1988-96. Recipient Good Samaritan award Los Angeles Council Mormon Chs., 1976 Republican. Roman Catholic. Address: 1109 Kris Way Roseville CA 95661-5393 Office: Catholic Family Radio 8910 University Center Lane San Diego CA 92122

LUNINE, JONATHAN IRVING, planetary scientist, educator; b. N.Y.C., June 26, 1959; BS magna cum laude, U. Rochester, 1980; MS, Calif. Inst. Tech., 1983, PhD, 1985. Rsch. assoc. U. Ariz., Tucson, 1984-86, asst. prof. planetary scis., 1986-90; vis. asst. prof. UCLA, 1986, assoc. prof., 1990-95, prof., 1995—, faculty mem. program in applied math., 1992—, chair theoretical astrophys. program, 2000. Interdisciplinary scientist on joint U.S.-European Cassini mission to Saturn; mem. com. planetary and lunar exploration space sci. bd. NAS, 1986-90; chmn. NASA Solar Sys. Exploration subcom., 1990-95; chmn. Pluto Express Sci. Definition Team, 1995; disting. vis. scientist Jet Propulsion Lab., 1997—; mem. exec. com. space studies bd. NRC, 1998—, chmn. com. on origin and evolution of life in the universe of space studies bd., 2000—; mem. sci. coun. NASA Astrobiology Inst., 2001—. Author: Earth: Evolution of, 1999; contbr. articles to profl. jours.; co-editor: Protostars and Planets III, 1993. Mem. Internat. Mars Exploration Adv. Panel NASA, 1993-94, space sci. adv. com., 1990-95; exec. com. NRC Space Studies bd., 1998—. Recipient Cospar Zeldovich prize Soviet Intercosmos and Inst. for Space Rsch., 1990. 1 of the 50 emerging leaders Time Mag., 1994, Arthur Adel award Scientific Achievement No. Ariz. U., 2000; Co-Recipient James B. Macelwane Young Investigator medal Am. Geophysical Union, 1995 Fellow Am. Geophys. Union (Macelwane medal 1995); mem. Am. Astron. Soc. (Harold C. Urey prize 1988), Internat. Acad. Astronautics (corr. mem.), Internat. Coun. Sci. Unions, European Geophys. Soc., Sigma Xi. Avocation: hiking. Office: U Ariz Dept Planetary Scis PO Box 210092 Tucson AZ 85721-0092 E-mail: jlunine@lpl.arizona.edu

LUONGO, JOHN R. executive; BA in East Asian History, CUNY. Various mgmt. positions Tymshare, Inc.; sr. cons. Merrill, Pickard, Anderson & Eyre; pres. Devlyn Corp.; creator, dir. internat. divsn. Oracle Corp.; pres., CEO Vantive Corp., Santa Clara, Calif. Mem. Phi Beta Kappa. Office: 2455 Augustine Dr Santa Clara CA 95054-3002

LUPIA, ARTHUR W. political science educator; b. Buffalo, May 20, 1964; BA in Econs., U. Rochester, 1986; MS in Social Sci., Calif. Inst. Tech., 1988, PhD in Social Sci., 1991. Asst. prof. polit. sci. U. Calif., San Diego, 1990-96, assoc. prof. polit. sci., 1996-98, prof. polit. sci., 1998—. Presenter in field; panelist San Diego Headliners, KNSD-TV, 1990; election analyst L.A. Times, 1987, 88, Sol Del Valle Cmty. Ctr., 1988, Remcho, Johannson and Purcell law firm, 1989. Author: (with Mathew D. McCubbins) The Democratic Dilemma: Can Citizens Learn What They Need to Know?, 1998; contbr. articles to profl. publs.; referee for numerous publs., including Econ. Inquiry, Games and Econ. Behavior, Jour. Instnl. and Theoretical Econs., Jour. of Law, Econs. and Orgn., Pub. Opinion Quar., NAS, others. Recipient Emerging Scholar award Am. Polit. Sci. Assn., 1996, award for initiatives in rsch. NAS, 1998; fellow Ctr. for Advanced Study in Behavioral Sci., 1999-2000, John Randolph Haynes and Dora Haynes fellow, 1989, Earle D. Anthony Grad. fellow, 1986; grantee NSF, 1994, 95, U. Calif.-San Diego, 1990, 91, 94, 96, 97, 98, Ctr. for European and German Studies, 1994, World Bank, 1997. Mem. Am. Polit. Sci. Assn. (mem. exec. com. sect. on elections, public opinion and voting behavior 1996—, sec. on polit. economy, 1995—). Office: U Calif San Diego Dept Polit Sci La Jolla CA 92923-0521

LURVEY, IRA HAROLD, lawyer; b. Chgo., Apr. 6, 1935; s. Louis and Faye (Grey) L.; m. Barbara Ann Sirvint, June 24, 1962; children: Nathana, Lawrence, Jennifer, Jonathan, David, Robert. BS, U. Ill., 1956; MS, Northwestern U., 1961; JD, U. Calif., Berkeley, 1965. Bar: Calif. 1965, Nev. 1966, U.S. Dist. Ct. (cen. dist.) Calif. 1966, U.S. Tax Ct. 1966, U.S. Ct. Appeals (9th cir.) 1966, U.S. Supreme Ct. 1975. Law clk. to hon. justices Nev. Supreme Ct., Carson City, 1965-66; from assoc. to ptnr. Pacht, Ross, Warne, Bernhard & Sears, Inc., 1966-84; predecessor firm Shea & Gould, L.A.; founding ptnr. Lurvey & Shapiro, L.A., 1984—. Lectr. legal edn. programs; mem. Chief Justice's Commns. on Ct. Reform, Weighted Caseloads; mediator family law L.A. Superior Ct. Editor Community Property Jour., 1979-80, Primary Consultant CFL 2d, 1994; columnist Calif. Family Law Monthly; contbr. articles to profl. jours. Former chmn. L.A. Jr. Arts Ctr.; past pres. Cheviot Hills Homeowners Assn.; exec. v.p., counsel Hillel Acad. Sch., Beverly Hills, Calif., 1977—. With U.S. Army, 1957-58. Fellow Am. Acad. Matrimonial Lawyers (pres. So. Calif. chpt. 1991-92, mem. nat. bd. govs. 1992-94), Internat. Acad. Matrimonial Lawyers; mem. ABA (chair family law sect. 1996-97, liaison family law to sr. lawyers' divsn. 1998—, exec. com. 1991-97, governing coun. 1986—, fin. officer 1991-92, chmn. support com., chmn. CLE, chmn. policy and issues com., vice chmn. com. arbitration and mediation, bd. of editors Family Adv. mag., chmn. issues com. sr. lawyer divsn. 2001—), Calif. Bar Assn. (editor jour. 1982-85, chmn. family law sect. 1986-87, exec. com. family law sect. 1982-88, specialization adv. bd. family law 1979-82), L.A. County Bar Assn. (chmn. family law sect. 1981-82, exec. com. family law 1989-92), Beverly Hills Bar Assn. (chmn. family law sect. 1976-77,). Home: 2729 Motor Ave Los Angeles CA 90064-3441 Office: Lurvey & Shapiro Ste 1550 1333 Beverly Green Drive Los Angeles CA 90035-1018 E-mail: lurv-shap@aol.com

LUSK, HARLAN GILBERT, national park superintendent, business executive; b. Jersey City, June 22, 1943; s. Harlan H. and Mary M. (Kuhl) L.; m. Catherine L. Rutherford, Oct. 11, 1986. BA in History, Gettysburg Coll., 1965, D of Pub. Svc. (hon.), 2001. Supervisory historian Cape Hatteras Nat. Seashore, Manteo, N.C., 1968; historian Nat. Pk. Svc., Washington, 1968-69; programs specialist So. Utah Group, Cedar City, 1968-70; pk. supt. Wolf Trap Farm Pk., Vienna, 1970-72; supervisory pk. ranger Blue Ridge Pkwy., Roanoke, 1972-74; pk. supt. Appomattox (Va.) Courthouse, Nat. Hist. Pk., 1974-76, Valley Forge (Pa.), Nat. Hist. Pk., 1976-81, Big Bend (Tex.) Nat. Pk., 1981-86, Glacier Nat. Pk., West Glacier, Mont., 1986-94; pk. supt. Albright Tng. Ctr. Grand Canyon Nat. Pk., Ariz., 1994-95; chief, Divsn. Tng. and Employee Nat. Park Svc., Washington, 1995-97; retired from park svc., 1997; chmn. Gil Lusk Assocs., 1997—; group mgr. The Cholla Group, 1997—. Organizer 1st regional conf. Rio Grande Border, States on Pks. and Wildlife, Laredo, Tex., 1985 Bd. dirs. Tech. Com. on Pks. & Recreation Cen. Va. Planning Dist., 1972-74, Fed. Exec. Assn. Roanoke Valley, 1972-74, Flathead Basin Commn., 1986-94, Flathead Conv. & Visitor Assn., 1986-94, Sonoran Inst., 1995—; prin. founder, 1st pres., Appomattox County Hist. Soc., 1974-76; trustee Sci. Mus. Assn. Roanoke Valley, 1972-74, Nature Conservancy Mont., 1994—; ex-officio Friends of Valley Forge, 1977-81; founder, ex-officio, bd. dirs. Valley Forge Pk. Interpretive Assn., 1977-81; founder Big Bend Area Travel Assn., chmn., 1984-86. Recipient Meritorious Svc. award. Dept. Interior, 1986, Disting. Svc. award, 1999. Mem. Glacier Natural History Assn. (ex officio 1986-94), Glacier Nat. Pk. Assocs. (founder, ex-officio 1989-94), George Wright Soc., Lions, Rotary. Avocations: golf, antiques, computers, collecting artwork, hiking. E-mail: hglusk@msn.com, gil@rancholaioka.com

LUSKY, JOHN ANDERSON, lawyer; b. Louisville, Oct. 30, 1951; BA, Harvard U., 1973; JD, Stanford U., 1977. Bar: Oreg. 1977. Ptnr. Miller, Nash LLP (formerly known as Miller, Nash, Wiener, Hager & Carlsen), Portland, Oreg. Mem. Oreg. State Bar. Office: Miller Nash LLP 111 SW 5th Ave Ste 3500 Portland OR 97204-3638

LUSZTIG, PETER ALFRED, university dean, educator; b. Budapest, Hungary, May 12, 1930; s. Alfred Peter and Susan (Szabo) L.; m. Penny Bicknell, Aug. 26, 1961; children: Michael, Cameron, Carrie. B in Com., U. B.C., Vancouver, Can., 1954; MBA, U. Western Ont., London, Can., 1955; PhD, Stanford U., 1964. Asst. to comptroller B.C. Electric, Vancouver, 1955-57; instr. fin. U. B.C., 1957-60, asst. prof. fin., 1962-64, assoc. prof., 1968-95, Killam sr. research fellow, 1968-69, prof., 1965-68, dean faculty commerce, 1977-91, dean emeritus, 1995—. Chair, bd. trustees BC Health Benefit Trust; bd. dirs. Canfor Corp., Royal Sun Alliance (Can.) Western Assurance, Que. Assurance, Roins Fin. Holdings; fed. commr. BC Treaty Commn., 1995—; vis. prof. IMEDE, Switzerland, 1973-74, London Grad. Sch. Bur. Studies, 1968-69, Pacific Coast Banking Sch., 1977—; sr. advisor B.C. Ministry of Econ. Devel., Small Bus. and Trade, 1991. Author: Report of the Royal Commission on Automobile Insurance, 2 vols., 1968, Financial Management in a Canadian Setting, 6th rev. edit., 2001, Report of the Commission on the B.C. Tree Fruit Industry, 1990. Ford Found. faculty dissertation fellow, Stanford U., 1964. Lutheran. Office: BC Treaty Commn 203 1155 W Pender St Vancouver BC Canada V6E 2Z2 E-mail: p.lusztig@home.com

LUTES, DONALD HENRY, architect; b. San Diego, Mar. 7, 1926; s. Charles McKinley and Helen (Bjoraker) L.; m. Donnie Wageman, Aug. 14, 1949; children: Laura Jo, Gail Eileen, Dana Charles. B.Arch., U. Oreg., 1950. Pvt. archtl. practice, Springfield, Oreg., 1956-58; ptnr. John Amundson, Springfield, 1958-70; pres. Lutes & Amundson, Springfield, 1970-72; ptnr. Lutes/Sanetel, 1973-86. Adj. assoc. prof. architecture U. Oreg., 1964-66, 89-2000; chmn. Springfield Planning Commn., 1954-65, 93-99, Urban Design and Devel. Corp., 1968-70, Eugene Non-Profit Housing, Inc., 1970 Architect: Springfield Pub. Library, 1957, Mt. Hood Community Coll, 1965-79, Shoppers Paradise Expt. in Downtown Revitalization, 1957. Chmn. Springfield United Appeal, 1959. Served to 1st lt. AUS, 1943-46, 51-52. Decorate Bronze Star; named Jr. 1st Citizen, Springfield C. of C., 1957, 1st Citizen, 1968, Disting. Citizen, 1995. Fellow AIA (bd. dirs. 1987-90, v.p. 1991, doc. com. 1993-2000); mem. Rotary, Theta Chi. Home and Office: 778 Crest Ln Springfield OR 97477-3601

LUTHY, RICHARD GODFREY, environmental engineering educator; b. June 11, 1945; s. Robert Godfrey Luthy and Marian Ruth (Ireland) Haines; m. Mary Frances Sullivan, Nov. 22, 1967; children: Matthew Robert, Mara Catherine, Jessica Bethlin. BSChemE, U. Calif., Berkeley, 1967; MS in Ocean Engring., U. Hawaii, 1969; MSCE, U. Calif., Berkeley, 1974, PhDCE, 1976. Registered profl. engr., Pa.; diplomate Am. Acad. Environ. Engrs. Rsch. asst. dept. civil engring. U. Hawaii, Honolulu, 1968-69; rsch. asst. div. san. and hydraulic engring. U. Calif., Berkeley, 1973-75; asst. prof. civil engring. Carnegie Mellon U., Pitts., 1975-80, assoc. prof., 1980-83, prof., 1983—, assoc. dean Carnegie Inst. Tech., 1986-89, head dept. civil and environ. engring., 1989-96, Lord prof. environ. engring., 1996 2000; Silas H. Palmer prof. dept. civil and environ. engring. Stanford (Calif.) U., 2000—. Shimizu Corp. vis. prof. dept. civil engring. Stanford U., 1996-97; cons. sci. adv. bd. U.S. EPA, 1983—, Bioremediation Action com., 1990-92; cons. U.S. Dept. Energy, 1978—, various pvt. industries; del. water sci. and tech. bd. NAE, Washington and Beijing, 1988; mem. tech. adv. bd. Remediation Techs., Inc., Concord, Mass., 1989-94, Fostin Capital, Pitts., 1991-94, Balt. Gas & Elec., 1992-95, Pa. Dept. Environ. Protection, 1994-96; mem. sci. adv. com. Hazardous Substance Rsch. Ctr. Stanford U., 1994-99; chair Gordon Rsch. Conf. Environ. Scis., 1994, Nat. Rsch. Coun. Commn. on Innovative Remediation Tech., Com. on Intrinsic Remediation, Com. on Bioavailabilty, Water Sci. and Tech. Bd., 1997—, chair, 2000—. Contbr. articles to tech. and sci. jours. Chmn. NSF/Assn. Environ. Engring. Prof. Conf. on Fundamental Rsch. Directions in Environ. Engring, Washington, 1988. Lt. C.E. Corps, USN, 1969-72. Recipient George Tallman Ladd award Carnegie Inst. Tech., 1977. Mem. ASCE (Pitts. sect. Prof. of Yr. award 1987), Nat. Acad. Engring., Assn. Environ. Engring. Sci. Profs. (pres. 1987-88, Nalco award 1978, 82, Engring. Sci. award 1988, Svc. award 1999), Water Environ. Fedn. (rsch. com. 1982-86, awards com. 1981-84, 89-94, std. methods com. 1977—, groundwater com. 1989-90, editor jour. 1989-92, Eddy medal 1980, McKee medal 2000), Internat. Assn. on Water Quality (Foudners award U.S. Nat. Com. 1986, 93, orgnl. com. 16th Biennial Conf. Washington 1992), Am. Chem. Soc. (divsn. environ. chemistry, mem. editl. adv. bd. Environ. Sci. Tech. 1992-95). Presbyterian.

LUTIN, DAVID LOUIS, real estate development and finance consultant; b. East Hartford, Conn., Apr. 18, 1919; s. Solomon and Esther (Newman) L.; m. Dorothy Marmor, Dec. 3, 1944; children: Gary, Marnie. AB, Ohio No. U., 1946; MBA, Syracuse U., 1949. Housing economist and field rep. HHFA, Washington, 1950-57; dir. urban renewal City of Brookline, Mass., 1957-58; cons. urban renewal and housing Com. for Econ. Devel., N.Y.C., 1958-59; propr. David L. Lutin Assocs.; real estate devel. and fin. cons. Rye, N.Y., 1959-73, Phoenix, 1975—; v.p. real estate and mortgages Am. Bank and Trust Co., N.Y.C., 1973-75; assoc. prof. housing econs. MIT, 1951-52. Contbr. articles to profl. jours. Capt. AUS, 1942-46. Decorated Purple Heart. Mem. Am. Econ. Assn., Nat. Planning Assn., Mortgage Bankers Assn., Urban Land Inst., Am. Planning Assn., Am. Statis Assn., Nat. Assn. Home Builders. Home and Office: 10330 W El Rancho Dr Sun City AZ 85351-3854 E-mail: davedotl@aol.com

LUTTROPP, PETER C. city official; b. Coeur d' Alene, Idaho, Feb. 7, 1941; BS, U. Idaho, 1964; MBA, U. Calif., Berkeley, 1969. City treas. City of Tacoma, Wash., 1971-91, dir. fin., 1991—. Office: City Tacoma Tacoma Mcpl Bldg 747 Market St Ste 132 Tacoma WA 98402-3726

LUTZ, CHRIS P. research physicist; Rsch. scientist IBM Almaden Rsch. Ctr., San Jose, Calif. Recipient Newcomb Cleveland prize AAAS, 1993-94. Office: IBM Almaden Rsch Ctr 650 Harry Rd San Jose CA 95120-6099

LUTZ, WILLIAM LAN, lawyer; b. Chgo., May 18, 1944; s. Raymond Price and Sibyl (McCright) L.; m. Jeanne M. McAlister, Dec. 27, 1969; children: William Lan, David Price. BS, U. Tex., 1965, JD, 1969. Bar: Tex. 1969, N.Mex. 1970. Assoc. Martin, Lutz, Cresswell & Hubert and predecessor firms, Las Cruces, N.Mex., 1969-82; former U.S. atty. dist. N.Mex. U.S. Dept. Justice, Albuquerque, 1982-91; ptnr. Martin, Lutz, Roggow, Hosford & Eubanks, P.C., Las Cruces, 1991—. Mem. ABA, N.Mex. Bar Assn. (mem. bd. bar commrs. 1995-97); Aggie Sports Assn. (bd.dirs.) N.Mex. State U. Methodist. Office: Martin Lutz Roggow Hosford & Eubanks PC 2100 N Main St Ste 2 Las Cruces NM 88001-1183

LUYENDYK, BRUCE PETER, geophysicist, educator, institution administrator; b. Freeport, N.Y., Feb. 23, 1943; s. Pieter Johannes and Frances Marie (Blakeney) L.; 1 child, Loren Taylor Luyendyk. BS Geophysics, San Diego State Coll., 1965; PhD Marine Geophysics, Scripps Inst. Oceanography, 1969. Geophysicist Arctic Sci. and Tech. Lab. USN Electronics Lab. Ctr., 1965; lectr. San Diego State Coll., 1967-68; postgrad rsch. geologist Scripps Inst. Oceanography, 1969; postdoctoral fellow dept. geology and geophysics Woods Hole Oceanographic Instn., 1969-70, asst. scientist dept. geology and geophysics, 1970-73; asst. prof. U. Calif., Santa Barbara, 1973-75, assoc. prof., 1975-81, prof. dept. geol. scis., 1981—, acting dir. Inst. Crustal Studies, 1987-88, dir. Inst. Crustal Studies, 1988-97, chair dept. geol. scis., 1997—. Participant, chief sci. oceanographic cruises, geol. expdns.; coord. bd. So. Calif. Integrated GPS Network, 1997-2000. Editorial bd. Geology, 1975-79, Marine Geophysical Rschs., 1976-92, Jour. Geophysical Rsch., 1982-84, Tectonophysics, 1988-92, Pageoph, 1988-95; contbr. articles to profl. jours., chpts. to books, encys. Co-recipient Newcomb Cleveland prize AAAS, 1980; recipient Antarctic Svc. medal U.S. NSF, Dept. Navy, 1990, Disting. Alumni award San Diego State U., 1983, numerous rsch. grants, 1971—. Fellow Geol. Soc. Am.; mem. Am. Geophys. Union. Office: U Calif Santa Barbara Dept Geol Scis Santa Barbara CA 93106 E-mail: luyendyk@geol.ucsb.edu

LUZURIAGA, FRANCESCA, former manufacturing executive; b. Boston, 1954; Grad., Pomona Coll., 1976, U. So. Calif., 1978. Exec. v.p. fin. and adminstrn. Mattel Inc., El Segundo, Calif. Mem. Fin. Execs. Inst. Office: Mattel Inc 333 Continental Blvd El Segundo CA 90245-5012

LYDON, DANIEL T. city official; s. James and Joan (O'Brien) L.; m. Pat Lydon, 1966; children: Bridget, Daniel, Kevin, Margaret, Michael. Grad. h.s., Berkeley, Calif.; grad. exec. fire officer program, Nat. Fire Acad., Emmitsburg, Md. Firefighter, lt., capt., battalion chief City of Fremont (Calif.) Fire Dept., fire chief, 1987—. Condr. profl. seminars and courses. With USMC. Office: City Fremont Fire Dept 39100 Liberty St PO Box 5006 Fremont CA 94537-5006

LYMAN, JOHN, psychology and engineering educator; b. Santa Barbara, Calif., May 29, 1921; s. Oren Lee and Clara Augusta (Young) L. A.B. in Psychology and Math., UCLA, 1943, M.S., 1950, Ph.D. in Psychology, 1951. Research technician Lockheed Aircraft Corp., Burbank, Calif., 1940-43, mathematician, 1943-44; with dept. psychology UCLA, 1947—, assoc. prof., 1957-63, prof., 1963—, from instr. to assoc. prof. Sch. Engring. and Applied Sci., 1950-63, prof. Sch. Engring. and Applied Sci., 1963—, chmn. engring. systems dept., 1978-84, head Biotech. Lab., 1958-80, head Human-Machine-Environment Engring. Lab., 1981-96; prof. materials sci. and engring., 1984-91; prof. emeritus Sch. Engring. and Applied Sci. UCLA, 1991—; research engr. Inst. Traffic and Transp., 1967-73. Vis. prof. bioengring. Technol. Inst., Delft, Netherlands, 1965; spl. cons. Nat. Acad. Scis., Washington, 1973; cons. VA, Los Angeles, 1962-66, 67-76, NIH, 1963-66, 68-73, med. devices div. FDA, 1976-78, Perceptronics, Inc., Woodland Hills, Calif., 1968—, other agys. and cos.; bd. dirs. Perceptronics, Inc., MegaGraphics, Inc., also chmn. bd.; cons. in field. Author chpts. in books, articles in profl. jours.; editor in field. Served to lt. (j.g.) U.S. Navy, 1944-46. Recipient Japanese Govt. Research award for Fgn. Specialists (Robotics), 1985, also numerous fellowships and grants. Fellow APA, Am. Psychol. Soc., Soc. Engring. Psychologists, AAAS, Human Factors and Ergonomics Soc. (Paul Fitts award 1971, pres. 1967-68, pres. disting. svc. award 1991); mem. Biomed. Engring. Soc. (pres. 1980-81), IEEE, Am. Soc. Engring. Edn., Am. Assn. Artificial Intelligence, Robotics Internat., Robotics Soc. Japan, Soc. Mfg. Engrs., Sigma Xi, Tau Beta Pi. Office: UCLA 6732 Boelter Hall Los Angeles CA 90024

LYMAN, RICHARD WALL, foundation and university executive, historian; b. Phila., Oct. 18, 1923; s. Charles M. and Aglae (Wall) L.; m. Elizabeth D. Schauffler, Aug. 20, 1947; children: Jennifer P., Holly Lyman Antolini, Christopher M., Timothy R. BA, Swarthmore Coll., 1947, LLD (hon.), 1974; MA, Harvard U., 1948, PhD, 1954, LLD (hon.), 1980, Washington U., St. Louis, 1971, Mills Coll., , 1972, Yale U., 1975; LHD (hon.), U. Rochester, 1975, Coll. of Idaho, 1989. Teaching fellow, tutor, Harvard U., 1949-51; instr. Swarthmore Coll., 1952-53; instr., then asst. prof. Washington U., St. Louis, 1953-58; mem. faculty Stanford U., 1958-80, 88-91, prof. history, 1962-80, 88-91, Sterling prof., 1980-91, assoc. dean Sch Humanities and Scis., 1964-66, v.p., provost, 1967 70, pres., 1970-80, pres. emeritus, 1980—, dir. Inst. Internat. Studies, 1988-91; pres. Rockefeller Found., 1980-88. Spl. corr. The Economist, London, 1953-66; bd. dirs. Coun. on Founds., 1982-88, Independent Sector, 1980-88, chair, 1983-86, Nat. Com. on U.S.-China Rels., 1986-92; dir. IBM, 1978-92, Chase Manhattan Corp., 1981-91. Author: The First Labour Government, 1957; editor: (with Lewis W. Spitz) Major Crises in Western Civilization, 1965, (with Virginia A. Hodgkinson) The Future of the Nonprofit Sector, 1989; editorial bd. Jour. Modern History, 1958-61. Mem. Nat. Coun. on Humanities, 1976-82, vice chmn., 1980-82; chmn. Commn. on Humanities, 1978-80; trustee Rockefeller Found., 1976-88, Carnegie Found. Advancement of Tchg., 1976-82, World Affairs Coun. of No. Calif., 1992-98; bd. dirs. Nat. Assn. Ind. Colls. and Univs., 1976-77, Assn. of Governing Bds. of Univs. and Colls., 1994-97, Am. Alliance for Rights and Responsiblities, 1993—; chmn. Assn. Am. Univs., 1978-79. With USAAF, 1943-46. Decorated officier Legion of Honor; recipient Clark Kerr award U. Calif., Berkeley, 1981; Fulbright fellow London Sch. Econs., 1951-52, hon. fellow, 1978— ; Guggenheim fellow, 1959-60 Fellow Royal Hist. Soc.; mem. Am. Acad. Arts and Scis., Am. Hist. Assn., Council on Fgn. Relations, Am. Philos. Soc., Conf. Brit. Studies, Phi Beta Kappa. Office: Stanford U Sch Edn Stanford CA 94305

LYNCH, BEVERLY PFEIFER, education and information studies educator; b. Moorhead, Minn. d. Joseph B. and Nellie K. (Bailey) Pfeifer; m. John A. Lynch, Aug. 24, 1968. B.S., N.D. State U., 1957, L.H.D. (hon.); M.S., U. Ill., 1959; Ph.D., U. Wis., 1972. Librarian Marquette U., 1959-60, 62-63; exchange librarian Plymouth (Eng.) Pub. Library, 1960-61; asst. head serials div. Yale U. Library, 1963-65, head, 1965-68; vis. lectr. U. Wis., Madison, 1970-71, U. Chgo., 1975; exec. sec. Assn. Coll. and Research Libraries, 1972-76; univ. librarian U. Ill.-Chgo., 1977-89; dean Grad. Sch. Libr. and Info. Sci. UCLA, 1989-94, prof. Grad. Sch. Edn. and Info. Studies, 1989—; interim pres. Ctr. for Rsch. Librs., Chgo., 2000-01. Author: (with Thomas J. Galvin) Priorities for Academic Libraries, 1982, Management Strategies for Libraries, 1985, Academic Library in Transition, 1989, Information Technology and the Remaking of the University Library, 1995. Named Acad. Libr. of Yr., 1982, one of top sixteen libr. leaders in Am., 1990; fellow Indo-U.S. Subcommn. on Edn. and Culture, 1992-93. Mem. ALA (pres. 1985-86, coun. 1998—, com. on accreditation 1999—, chair 1999—), Nat. Info. Stds. Orgn. (bd. dirs. 1996—, vice chair 1999-2001, chair 2001—), Acad. Mgmt., Am. Sociol. Assn., Assn. for the Study of Higher Edn., Bibliog. Soc. Am., Caxton Club, Grolier Club, Book Club Calif., Phi Kappa Phi. Office: UCLA Grad Sch Edn Info Mailbox 951521 Los Angeles CA 90095-0001 E-mail: bplynch@ucla.edu

LYNCH, CHARLES ALLEN, investment executive, corporate director; b. Denver, Sept. 7, 1927; s. Laurence J. and Louanna (Robertson) L.; divorced; children: Charles A., Tara O'Hara, Casey Alexander; m. Justine Bailey, Dec. 27, 1992. BS, Yale U., 1950. With E.I. duPont de Nemours & Co., Inc., Wilmington, Del., 1950-69, dir. mktg., 1965-69; corp. v.p. SCOA Industries, Columbus, Ohio, 1969-72; corp. exec. v.p., also mem. rotating bd. W.R. Grace & Co., N.Y.C., 1972-78; chmn. bd., chief exec. officer Saga Corp., Menlo Park, Calif., 1978-86, also dir.; chmn., chief exec. officer DHL Airways, Inc., Redwood City, 1986-88; also dir.; pres., chief exec. officer Levolor Corp., 1988-89, also bd. dir., chmn. exec. com. of bd., 1989-90; chmn. Market Value Ptnrs. Co., Menlo Park, Calif., 1990-95; chmn., dir. Fresh Choice, Inc., Santa Clara, 1995—, chmn., 1995—; also bd. dirs.; chmn. Market Value Ptnrs. Co., 1999—. Bd. dirs. Spectrum Organic Products, Inc., SRI Internat., Shari's Mgmt. Corp., Age Wave, LLC, Mifund.com, Inc., Cloudsource, Inc. Bd. dirs. United Way, 1990-92, past chmn. Bay Area campaign, 1987; vice chmn., dir. Bay Area Coun.; past chmn. Calif. Bus. Roundtable; mem. adv. bd. U. Calif.-Berkeley Bus. Sch., Governance Bd.; chmn. bd. trustees Palo Alto Med. Found. Mem. Yale Club (N.Y.C.), Internat. Lawn Tennis Club, Menlo Country Club (Calif.), Pacific Union Club (San Francisco), Coral Beach and Tennis Club (Bermuda), Vintage Club (Indian Wells, Calif.), Menlo Circus Club. Republican. Home: 96 Ridge View Dr Atherton CA 94027-6464 Office: 333 Ravenswood Ave Ste Ag320 Menlo Park CA 94025-3453

LYNCH, DANIEL C. multimedia executive; Degree in math. and philosophy, Loyola Marymount U.; M in Math., UCLA. Mgr. computing lab. Artificial Intelligence Ctr., SRI; dir. computing facilities SRI Internat.; dir. info. processing divsn. U. So. Calif., Info. Scis. Inst., Marina del Rey; founder, chmn. bd. dirs. CyberCash, Inc., Reston, Va.; owner Lynch Enterprises, Los Altos Hills, Calif. Founder Interop Co. divsn. Softbank Expos; trustee Santa Fe Inst., Bionomics Inst., CommerceNet; founder, bd. dirs. CyberCash Inc., Reston, Va. Author: Digital Money: The New Era of Internet Commerce. Mem. IEEE. Avocation: vineyards. Office: Lynch Enterprises 25660 La Lanne Ct Los Altos CA 94022-2017

LYNCH, JOHN DANIEL, secondary education educator, state legislator; b. Butte, Mont., Sept. 17, 1947; s. Leo and Queenie Veronica Lynch; m. Shannon Christine Crawford, May 7, 1983; children: Kaitlin, Jennifer. BS, West Mont. Coll.; MS, No. Mont. Coll. Tchr. Butte H.S., 1970-78, Butte Vo-Tech, 1978-89, Adult Basic Edn., 1989—. Mem. Mont. State Legis., Helena, 1971-79, state senator, 1982—. Mem. KC. Democrat. Roman Catholic.

LYNCH, MARTIN ANDREW, retail company executive; b. Chgo., Oct. 5, 1937; s. George Irwin and Cecilia Veronica (Corley) L.; children: Kathleen Marie, Kevin Michael, Karen Ann, Daniel Patrick, Michelle Eileen. BSc, DePaul U., 1962. CPA, Ill., Calif. Audit mgr. Price Waterhouse & Co., Chgo., 1962-69; asst. to pres. Scot Lad Foods, Chgo., 1969-70; v.p. fin. N.Am. Car Corp., Chgo., 1970-76; sr. v.p. fin. Tiger Internat. Inc., L.A., 1976-83; exec. v.p., chief fin. officer Duty Free Shoppers Group Ltd., San Francisco, 1983-89, Casino USA Inc., Santa Barbara, Calif., 1989—, Smart & Final Inc., Santa Barbara, 1989—. Mem. AICPA, Calif. CPA Soc., Fin. Execs. Inst., Nat. Assn. Whole Grogery, Inst. Food Distbn. Assn., Bel Air Country Club (L.A.). Roman Catholic. Avocations: jogging, swimming, skiing, golf. Office: Smart & Final Inc 600 Citadel Dr City Of Commerce CA 90040

LYNCH, PATRICK, lawyer; b. Pitts., Nov. 11, 1941; s. Thomas Patrick and Helen Mary (Grimes) L.; m. M. Linda Maturo, June 20, 1964; children: Megan, Kevin, Colin, Brendan, Erin, Brian, Liam, Eamonn, Kilian, Caitlin, Ryan, Declan, Cristin, Mairin, Sean. BA in Philosophy, Loyola U., L.A., 1964, LLB, 1966. Bar: Calif. 1967, U.S. Dist. Ct. (cen., so., no. and ea. dists.) Calif., U.S. Ct. Appeals (9th cir.), U.S. Supreme Ct. Ptnr. O'Melveny & Myers, Los Angeles, 1966—. Panelist PLI Annual Antitrust Law Inst., 1982-2000. Bd. editors Matthew Bender Fed. Litigation Guide Reporter. Fellow Am. Coll. Trial Lawyers; mem. L.A. County Bar Assn. Office: OMelveny & Myers 400 S Hope St Los Angeles CA 90071-2899

LYNCH, PETER JOHN, former dermatologist; b. Mpls., Oct. 22, 1936; s. Francis Watson and Viola Adeline (White) L.; m. Barbara Ann Lanzi, Jan. 18, 1964; children: Deborah, Timothy. Student, St. Thomas Coll., 1954-57; BS, U. Minn., 1958, MD, 1961. Intern U. Mich. Med. Ctr., 1961-62, resident in dermatology, 1962-65, asst. prof., then assoc. prof. dermatology, 1968-73; clin. instr. U. Minn., 1965; chief dermatology and venereal disease Martin Army Hosp., Columbus, Ga., 1966-68; asso. prof. to prof. dermatology U. Ariz., Tucson, 1973 86, chief sect. dermatology, 1973-86, asso. head dept. internal medicine, 1977-86; prof., head dermatology U. Minn. Med. Sch., Mpls., 1986-95; med. dir. ambulatory care U. Minn. Health Sys., 1993-95; prof., chmn. dept. dermatology U. Calif., Davis, 1995-2000, prof. emeritus, 2000—. Author: (with S. Epstein) Burckhardt's Atlas and Manual of Dermatology and Venereology, 1977, Dermatology for the House Officer, 1982, 3rd edit., 1994, (with W.M. Sams) Principles and Practice of Dermatology, 1992, 2nd edit., 1996, (with I.E. Edwards) Genital Dermatology, 1994. With AUS, 1966-68. Decorated Army Commendation Medal; recipient Disting. Service award for faculty U. Mich., 1970, Disting. Faculty award U. Ariz., 1981 Mem. Am. Acad. Dermatology (bd. dirs. 1974-78, v.p. 1991-92), Assn. Profs. Dermatology (bd. dirs. 1976-80, pres. 1994-96), Internat. Soc. Study of Vulvar Disease (bd. dirs. 1976-79, pres. 1983), Soc. Investigative Dermatology, Am. Bd. Dermatology (bd. dirs. 1984-89), Gougerot Soc. (Bronze medal award), Alpha Omega Alpha. Democrat. Roman Catholic. Home: 332 Sandpiper Dr Davis CA 95616-7536 Office: U Calif 4860 Y St # 3400 Sacramento CA 95817-2307

LYNCH, PETER L. supermarket/drug store executive; V.p., gen. mgr. Star Markets, Boston; pres. Acme Markets subs. Am. Stores Co., Malvern, Pa.; exec. v.p. ops. Albertson's Inc., Boise, Idaho, 1999-2000, pres., COO, 2000—. Office: Albertson's Inc 250 Parkcenter Blvd Boise ID 83726

LYNN, EVADNA SAYWELL, investment analyst; b. Oakland, Calif., June 16, 1935; d. Lawrence G. Saywell; m. Richard Keppie Lynn, Dec. 28, 1962; children: Douglas, Melisa. BA, MA in Econs., U. Calif. CFA. With Dean Witter, San Francisco, 1958-61, 70-71, Dodge & Cox, San Francisco, 1961-69; fin. analyst, v.p. Clark, Dodge & Co., San Francisco, 1971-73, Wainwright Securities, N.Y.C., 1977-78; 1st v.p. Merrill Lynch Capital markets, N.Y.C., 1978-90; sr. v.p. Dean Witter Reynolds, N.Y.C., 1990-97; forest products cons., San Francisco, 1997—. Mem. Assn. for Investment Mgmt. and Rsch., San Francisco Security Analysts (treas. 1973-74), Fin. Women's Club San Francisco (pres. 1967). Office: 2355 Pacific Ave San Francisco CA 94115-1241

LYON, DAVID WILLIAM, research executive; b. Lansing, Mich., Mar. 26, 1941; s. Herbert Reid and Mary Kathleen (Slack) L.; m. Catherine McHugh Dillon, July 8, 1967. BS, Mich. State U., 1963; M in City and Regional Planning, U. Calif., Berkeley, 1966, PhD, 1972. Regional economist Fed. Res. Bank Phila., 1969-71; rsch. dir. human and econ. resources The N.Y.C.-Rand Inst., 1972-75, v.p., 1975; sr. economist The Rand Corp., Santa Monica, Calif., 1975-77, dep. v.p., 1977-79, v.p. domestic rsch. divsn., 1979-93, v.p. external affairs, 1993-94; pres., CEO Pub. Policy Inst. Calif., 1994—. Adj. prof. U. Pa., 1975; mem. adv. bd. Inst. for Civil Justice, 1987-93, Rand-Urban Inst. Program for Rsch. on Immigration Policy, 1988-91, Drug Policy Rsch. Ctr., 1989-93, So. Calif. Health Policy Rsch. Consortium, 1989-94, Rand Ctr. for U.S.-Japan Rels., 1989-93, Rand Ctr. for Asia-Pacific Policy, 1993-95; dir. Coll. Environ. Design Coun., U. Calif., Berkeley, 1979-90. Mem. publs. com. Rand Jour. Econs., 1984-94; contbr. articles to profl. jours. Bd. dirs. Ctr. for Healthy Aging, Santa Monica, Calif., 1985-94, pres., 1989-91; mem. adv. coun. Coll. Environ. Design, U. Calif., Berkeley, 2000—. Mellon fellow in city planning, 1966-68; Econ. Devel. Adminstrn. grad. fellow, 1966 Mem. Coun. on Fgn. Rels., World Affairs Coun. No. Calif. (trustee 1999—), Japan Am. Soc. So. Calif. (bd. dirs. 1990-94), Japan Soc. No. Calif., Asia Soc. (So. Calif. adv. bd.), Pacific Coun. on Intenat. Policy, Delta Phi Epsilon, Lambda Alpha Internat. Office: Pub Policy Inst Calif 500 Washington St Ste 800 San Francisco CA 94111-2919 E-mail: lyon@ppic.org

LYON, JAMES KARL, German language educator; b. Rotterdam, Holland, Feb. 17, 1934; came to U.S., 1937; s. T. Edgar and Hermana (Forsberg) L.; m. Dorothy Ann Burton, Dec. 22, 1959; children: James, John, Elizabeth, Sarah, Christina, Rebecca, Matthew, Melissa. BA, U. Utah, 1958, MA, 1959; PhD, Harvard U., 1963. Instr. German Harvard U., Cambridge, Mass., 1962-63, asst. prof., 1966-71; assoc. prof. U. Fla., Gainesville, 1971-74; prof. U. Calif. San Diego, La Jolla, 1974-94, provost

Eleanor Roosevelt Coll., 1987-94; prof. dept. Germanic and Slavic langs. Brigham Young U., Provo, Utah, 1994—. Vis. prof. U. Augsburg, Germany, 1993. Author: Konkordanz zur Lyrik Gottfried Benns, 1971, Bertolt Brecht and Rudyard Kipling, 1975, Brecht's American Cicerone, 1978, Bertolt Brecht in America, 1980, Brecht in den USA, 1994. Capt. M.I., U.S. Army, 1963-66. NEH fellow, 1970, Guggenheim Found. fellow, 1974; Ford Found. grantee, 1988, 91. Mem. MLA, Am. Assn. Tchrs. German, Internat. Brecht. Soc., Phi Beta Kappa. Democrat. Mormon. Avocations: back-packing, fishing. Office: Brigham Young U Dept Germanic & Slavic Lang 4094 Jesse Knight Human Bld Provo UT 84602-6120 E-mail: james_lyon@byu.edu

LYON, JOSEPH LYNN, physician, medical educator; b. Salt Lake City, May 13, 1939; s. Thomas Edgar and Hermana (Forsberg) L.; m. June Fetzer, July 3, 1964; children: Natalee, Joseph, Stephen, Maryanne, Rachael, Janet. BS, U. Utah, 1964, MD, 1967; MPH, Harvard U., 1969. Diplomate Am. Bd. Preventive Medicine. Intern U. Calif., San Diego, 1967-68; resident Harvard U., 1968-70, Utah State Health Dept., 1971-72; asst. prof. U. Utah, Salt Lake City, 1974-80, assoc. prof., 1980-90, prof., 1990—. Contbr. articles to profl. jours. Mem. Soc. for Epidemiologic Rsch. (sec.-treas. Balt. chpt. 1993). Mem. LDS Ch. Office: U Utah Dept Medicine Salt Lake City UT 84132-0001

LYON, RICHARD, mayor emeritus, retired naval officer; b. Pasadena, Calif., July 14, 1923; s. Norman Morais and Ruth (Hollis) L.; m. Cynthia Gisslin, Aug. 8, 1975; children: Patricia, Michael, Sean; children by previous marriage: Mary, Edward, Sally, Kathryn, Patrick (dec.), Susan. B.E., Yale U., 1944; M.B.A., Stanford U., 1953. Commd. ensign USN, 1944; advanced through grades to rear adm. SEAL, 1974; served in Pacific and China, World War II; with Underwater Demolition Team Korea; recalled to active duty as dep. chief Naval Res. New Orleans, 1978-81. Mem. Chief Naval Ops. Res. Affairs Adv. Bd., 1978-81; exec. v.p. Nat. Assn. Employee Benefits, Newport Beach, Calif., 1981-90; mem. Bd. Control, U.S. Naval Inst., 1978-81; pres. Civil Svc. Commn., San Diego County, 1990, Oceanside Unified Sch. Bd., 1991; mayor City of Oceanside, 1992-2000. Pres. bd. trustees Children's Hosp. Orange County, 1965, 72. Decorated Legion of Merit. Mem. Nat. Assn. Securities Dealers (registered prin.), Newport Harbor Yacht Club, Oceanside Yacht Club, Rotary (Anaheim, Calif. pres. 1966). Republican. Episcopalian. Home: 600 S The Strand Oceanside CA 92054-3902 E-mail: lyonclan@aol.com

LYON, RUSS, executive; Chmn. Westcor Ptnrs., Phoenix, 1989—. Office: Westcor Ptnrs 11411 N Tatum Blvd Phoenix AZ 85028-2399

LYON, WILLIAM, builder; b. 1923; Student, U. So. Calif. With Lyon & son, Phoenix, 1945-50, William Lyon Devel. Co., Newport Beach, Calif., 1954-72, pres.; with William Lyon Co., Newport Beach, 1972—, now chmn. bd., CEO. Office: William Lyon Co 4490 Von Karman Ave Newport Beach CA 92660-2000

LYONS, LINDA, health science association administrator; BA, U. Calif.; MD, Harvard Med. Sch.; internal med. training, UCLA Med. Ctr. Sr. v.p. Scripps Clinic Med. Group, San Diego; sr. v.p., health svcs., chief med. officer PacifiCare Health Systems, 1996—. Former chmn. Unified Med. Group Assn.; founding pres., chmn. Calif., Assn. Healthcare Provider Found.; bd. mem. Med. Quality Commn. Office: PacifiCare Health Sys 3120 W Lake Center Dr Santa Ana CA 92704-6917

LYONS, LIONEL DALE, city official; b. N.C. BA in Polit. Sci., N.C. Agrl. & Tech. State U.; MPA, Ohio State U. Adminstrv. intern City of Columbus (Ohio) Water Dept.; mgmt. intern City of Phoenix, 1986-87; mgmt. asst. City of Phoenix Mgr.'s Office, 1987-90; asst. to mayor City of Phoenix, 1991-94, dir. equal opportunity dept., 1995—. Bd. dirs. Valley Leadership; past mem. capital devel. program com., South Mountain YMCA; bd. dirs. Phoenix Met. YMCA, urban svcs. br. Mem. NAACP (life), Internat. City Mgmt. Assn., Nat. Forum for Black Pub. Adminstrs., Nat. Spkrs. Assn. (cert. Toastmaster 1987—), Greater Phoenix Urban League, Omega Psi Phi (pres. Phoenix chpt. 1993-95). Office: City Phoenix Equal Opportunity Dept Calvin C Goode Bldg 251 W Washington St Phoenix AZ 85003-2245

LYONS, PATRICK HILLER, state legislator; b. Clovis, N.Mex., Nov. 7, 1953; BS, N.Mex. State U., 1976; M in Agr., Colo. State U., 1977. Rancher, farmer, N.Mex.; mem. N. Mex. Senate, Dist. 7, Santa Fe, 1993—, mem. conservation com., mem. fin. com., mem. water and natural resource com. Mem. N.Mex. Farm and Livestock Bd. Republican. Home: Ima Rt Box 26 Cuervo NM 88417

LYONS, TERRENCE ALLAN, merchant banking, investment company executive; b. Grand Prairie, Alta., Can., Aug. 1, 1949; s. Allan Lynnwood and Mildred Helen (Smith) L. B in Applied Sci., U. B.C., 1972; MBA, U. Western Ont., 1974. Registered profl. engr., B.C. Gen. mgr. Southwestern Drug Co., Vancouver, B.C., Can., 1975-76; mgr. planning Versatile Corp., Vancouver, 1976-83, asst. v.p., 1983-86, v.p., dir., 1986-88; pres., mng. ptnr. B.C. Pacific Capital Corp., 1988—. Bd. dirs. Internat. Utility Structures, Ariz. Goldfields Inc., Regional Cable TV, Inc.; pres., chief exec. officer FT Capital Ltd., 1990—; chmn. Northgate Exploration Ltd. Author articles on mfg. tech. Office: BC Pacific Capital Corp Royal Ctr PO Box 11179 1632 1055 W Georgia St Vancouver BC Canada V6E 3R5 E-mail: bcpcc@direct.ca

LYSYK, KENNETH MARTIN, judge; b. Weyburn, Sask., Can., July 1, 1934; s. Michael and Anna (Maradyn) L.; m. Patricia Kinnon, Oct. 2, 1959; children: Joanne, Karen (dec.), Stephanie. B.A., McGill U., 1954; LL.B., U. Sask., 1957; B.C.L., Oxford U., 1960. Bar: Sask., B.C., Yukon, apptd. Queen's counsel 1973. Lectr. U. B.C., 1960-62, asst. prof., 1962-65, assoc. prof., 1965-68, prof., 1968-69; adviser Constl. Rev. sect. Privy Council Office, Govt. of Can., Ottawa, 1969-70; prof. Faculty of Law U. Toronto, 1970-72; dep. atty. gen. Govt. of Sask., Regina, 1972-76; dean Law Sch., U. B.C., Vancouver, 1976-82; judge Supreme Ct. of B.C., Vancouver, 1983—. Dep. judge Supreme Ct. Yukon, 1991—, N.W. Territories, 1991—; judge Ct. Martial Appeal Ct. Can., 1995—; assoc. dir. Nat. Jud. Inst., 1996-98; chmn. Alaska Hwy. Pipeline Inquiry, 1977; sole commr. Yukon Electoral Boundaries Commn., 1991. Mem. Can. Bar Assn., Internat. Commn. Jurists (Can. sect.; v.p. for B.C. 1992—), Can. Inst. for Adminstrn. of Justice (pres. 1989-91). Office: Law Ct 800 Smithe St Vancouver BC Canada V6Z 2E1 E-mail: kenneth.lysyk@courts.gov.bc.ca

LYSYK, TIMOTHY JAMES, livestock insect population ecologist, researcher; b. Aug. 6, 1959; BS (hon.) in Zoology, U. Alberta, Edmonton, 1980; MS in Entomology, South Dakota State U., 1982; PhD in Entomology, minor in statistic, N.C. State U., 1985. Summer asst. Agricultural Canada, Lethbridge, AB, 1978-80; rsch. asst. South Dakota State U, Brookings, 1980-78, N.C. State U., Raleigh, 1982-85; rsch. scientist insect population dynamics Canadian Forestry Svc. Great Lakes Forestry Ctr., 1985-89; scientist livestock insect population ecology Agriculture and Agri-Food, Lethbridge, AB, Canada, 1989—. Adj. prof. dept. of Biological Scis., U. Lethbridge, 1994—, instr., Sault Ste Marie Bd. Edn., biology enrichment program, 1988, Lab. instr., 1981. Co-editor Environmental Entomology, 1995—. Mem. LRS study selection and assessment com., 1991, 95, mem. Western Com. Livestock Pests, 1989—, vice chmn., 1990, chmn., 1992—; mem. computer com. Lethbridge Rsch. Sta., 1989-90, 94—, mem. orgn. com., chmn., geographic info. sys., and numerous others. Recipient of the C Gordon Hewitt award for outstanding achievement in Entomology, 1996. Mem. AAFC Biological Control Working Group, 1995—, Entomological Soc. of Alberta, mem. Entomological Soc., Canada, mem. Entomological Soc., Am., and numerous others. Home: 53 Lafayette Blvd W Lethridge AB Canada T1K 3Y4 Office: Agriculture & Agri Food PO Box 3000 Lethbridge AB Canada T1J 4B1

MA, FENGCHOW CLARENCE, agricultural engineering consultant; b. Kaifeng, Honan, China, Sept. 4, 1919; came to U.S., 1972; s. Chao-Hsiang and Wen-Chieh (Yang) Ma; m. Fanny Luisa Corvera-Achá, Jan. 20, 1963; 1 child, Fernando. BS in Agr., Nat. Chekiang U., Maytan, Kweichow, China, 1942; postgrad. in agrl. engring., Iowa State U., 1945-46. Cert. profl. agronomist, Republic of China, 1944; registered profl. agrl. engr., Calif. Chief dept. ops. Agrl. Machinery Operation and Mgmt. Office, Shanghai, China, 1946-49; sr. farm machinery specialist Sino-Am. Joint Commn. on Rural Reconstrn., Taipei, Taiwan, Republic of China, 1950-62; agrl. engring. adviser in Bolivia, Peru, Chile, Ecuador, Liberia, Honduras, Grenada, Bangladesh FAO, Rome, 1962-80; consulting agrl. engr. to USAID projects in Guyana & Peru IRI Rsch. Inst., Inc., Stamford, Conn., 1981-82, 83, 85; chief adviser Com. Internat. Tech. Coop., Taipei, 1984-85; pres. FCM Assocs., Inc., 1962—. Short consulting missions to Paraguay, Saudi Arabia, Indonesia, Malawi, Swaziland, Barbados, Dominica, Ivory Coast, Vietnam, Philippines, Nicaragua and others. Author papers, studies; contbr. articles to profl. publs. Mem. Am. Soc. Agrl. Engrs. Avocations: reading, stamp and coin collecting. Home: 1004 Azalea Dr Sunnyvale CA 94086-6747 Office: PO Box 70096 Sunnyvale CA 94086-0096

MABEY, RALPH R. lawyer; b. Salt Lake City, May 20, 1944; s. Rendell Noel and Rachel (Wilson) M.; m. Sylvia States, June 5, 1968; children: Rachel, Elizabeth, Emily, Sara. BA, U. Utah, 1968; JD, Columbia U., 1972. Bar: Utah 1972, U.S. Dist. Ct. Utah 1972, U.S. Ct. Appeals (10th cir.) 1976, N.Y. 1985, U.S. Supreme Ct. 1988, U.S. Ct. Appeals (4th cir.) 1988, U.S. Ct. Appeals (3d cir.) 1993. Law clk. Atty. Gen., Salt Lake City, 1970, U.S. Dist. Ct., Salt Lake City, 1972-73; ptnr. Irvine, Smith & Mabey, Salt Lake City, 1973-79; U.S. bankruptcy judge U.S. Ct., Salt Lake City, 1979-83; ptnr. LeBoeuf, Lamb, Greene & MacRae, Salt Lake City and N.Y.C., 1983—. Sr. lectr. Brigham Young U. Sch. Law, Provo, Utah, 1983—, U. Utah Coll. Law, Salt Lake City, 1983-85. Mng. editor Norton Bankruptcy Law Adviser, 1983-85; contbg. author: Collier Bankruptcy Manual, 1986—, Collier on Bankruptcy, 15th Edition. With USAR, 1968-74. Mem. ABA (bus. bankruptcy com., joint task force bankruptcy court structure and insolvency processes), Nat. Bankruptcy Conf., Am. Bankruptcy Inst., Am. Coll. Bankruptcy (pres.). Republican. Mormon. Avocation: running. Home: 253 S 1550 E Bountiful UT 84010-1350 Office: LeBoeuf Lamb Greene & MacRae 1000 Kearns Bldg 136 S Main St Salt Lake City UT 84101-1601 also: 125 W 55th St New York NY 10019-5369 E-mail: mabey@LLGM.com

MACALISTER, ROBERT STUART, oil company executive; b. L.A., May 22, 1924; s. Robert Stuart and Iris Grace (Doman) MacA.; m. Catherine Vera Willby, Nov. 15, 1947 (dec. 1994); children: Rodney James, Sara Marjorie Pfirrmann; m. Grace V. LeClerc, Dec. 2, 1995. Student, Brighton Coll., Sussex, Eng., 1945; BSME, Calif. Inst. Tech., 1947. Registered profl. engr., Tex. Petroleum engr. Shell Oil Co., 1947-56; mgmt. trainee Royal Dutch Shell, The Hague, Netherlands, 1956-57; with exec. staff, mgr. Shell Oil Co., U.S.A., 1957-68; v.p., ops. mgr. Occidental Petroleum Corp., Tripoli, Libya, 1968-71; mng. dir.various subs. London, 1971-76; mng. dir., pres. Occidental Internat. Oil, Inc., London, 1976-78; pres., chmn. bd. Can. Occidental Petroleum Ltd., Calgary Alberta, 1978-81; mng. dir. Australian Occidental Petroleum Ltd., Sydney, 1982-83, Hamilton Bros. Oil & Gas Ltd., London, 1983-86; petroleum cons. Camarillo, Calif., 1986—. Exec. U.K. Offshore Operators, London, 1972-78, 83-86. Cubmaster Boy Scouts Am., Larchmont, N.Y., 1964-65, scoutmaster, Houston, 1965-68. Sgt. U.S. Army, 1944-45, ETO. Mem. Am. Assn. Petroleum Geologists, Soc. Petroleum Engrs., Can. Petroleum Assn. (bd. govs. 1978-81), Las Posas Country Club, Gold Coast Srs., Caltech Torchbearer. Republican. Episcopalian. Avocations: carpentry, crafts, watercolor painting, golfing, gardening. Home and Office: 78 Lopaco Ct Camarillo CA 93010-8846

MACARTHUR, CAROL JEANNE, pediatric otolaryngology educator; b. Glendale, Calif., Aug. 23, 1957; d. Seth Gerald and Barbara Jeanne (Shaw) MacA.; m. Geoffery Buncke, Dec. 14, 1990; children: Keith Davis, Michelle Jeanne. BS, Occidental Coll., 1979; MD, UCLA, 1984. Diplomate Am. Bd. Otolaryngology. Intern U. Calif., Davis, 1984-85, resident in otolaryngology, 1985-90; fellow in pediatric otolaryngology Boston Children's Hosp., 1990-91; instr. dept. otolaryngology U. Calif.-Davis, Sacramemto, 1989-90; clin. fellow in otology and laryngology Harvard U. Med. Sch., Boston, 1990-91; asst. prof. U. Calif., Irvine, 1991—, asst. prof. dept. pediatrics, 1993-98, program dir. dept. otolaryngology-head and neck surgery, 1992-95, dir., 1995—. Recipient investigator devel. award Am. Acad. Facial Plastic and Reconstructive Surgery, 1993. Fellow ACS, Am. Acad. Pediatrics; mem. Am. Soc. Pediat. Otolaryngology, Soc. for Ear, Nose and Throat Advances in Children, Am. Cleft Palate Craniofacial Assn., Am. Acad. Otorhinolaryngology-Head and Neck Surgery, Alpha Omega Alpha. Office: 302 W La Veta Ave Ste 201 Orange CA 92866-2607

MACAULAY, RONALD KERR STEVEN, linguistics educator, former college dean; b. West Kilbride, Ayrshire, Scotland, Nov. 3, 1927; came to U.S., 1965; s. Robert Wilson and Mary Robb (McDermid) M.; m. Janet Grey, July 25, 1956; children: Harvey, Anna. M.A., U. St. Andrews, 1955; Ph.D., UCLA, 1971. Lectr. Brit. Inst., Lisbon, Portugal, 1955-60, Brit Council, Buenos Aires, Argentina, 1960-64; asst. prof. linguistics Pitzer Coll., Claremont, Calif., 1965-67, assoc. prof., 1967-73, prof., 1973-99, dean faculty, 1980-86, prof. emeritus, 2000—. Author: Language, Social Class and Education, 1977, Generally Speaking: How Children Learn Language, 1980, Locating Dialect in Disourse: The Language of Honest Men and Bonnie Lasses in Ayr, 1991, The Social Art: Language and Its Uses, 1994, Standards and Variation in Urban Speech: Some Examples From Lowland Scots, 1997; editor: (with R.P. Stockwell) Linguistic Change and Generative Theory, 1972, (with D. Brenneis) The Matrix of Language: Contemporary Linguistic Anthropology, 1996. Home: 317 W 7th St Claremont CA 91711-4312 Office: Pitzer Coll 1050 N Mills Ave Claremont CA 91711-3908

MACCANNELL, DEAN, anthropology educator; b. Olympia, Wash., May 25, 1940; s. Earle Hector and Helen Frances (Meskimen) MacC.; m. Juliet Flower, July 25, 1965; children: Daniel Stephan, Jason Francis. AB in Anthropology, U. Calif., Berkeley, 1964; MS in Rural Sociology, Cornell U., 1966, PhD in Rural Sociology, 1968. Lectr. Cornell U., Ithaca, N.Y., 1967-69; asst. prof. Temple U., Phila., 1969-70, 71-75; from asst. to assoc. prof. U. Calif., Davis, 1975-77, from assoc. to prof., 1977-81, exec. dir. Semiotic Soc. Am., 1985—. Research assoc. Haverford (Pa.) Coll., 1970-72; vis. prof. Am. Coll. in Paris, 1970-71; cons. U.S. Congress, Washington, 1983-86, U.S. Sec. Agriculture, Washington, 1980; U.S. Rep. Internat. Soc. Semiotic Studies, 1984-90. Author: The Tourist, 1976 (Clemens Soc. award 1976), (with Juliet MacCannell) The Time of the Sign, 1982; editor: Am. Jour. of Semiotics, 1984—. Adv. bd. mem. Calif. Agrarian Action Project, Sacramento, 1985—, Mus. Modern Mythology, San Francisco, 1983—; project rev. NSF, Washington, Guggenheim Found., N.Y.C. Sr. Humanities fellow Soc. for Humanities, 1986; recipient Policy Prize Calif. State Legis., 1978. Mem. Semiotic Soc. Am. (officer 1984—), Am. Anthropol. Assn., Am. Rural Sociol. Assn. (Dissertation award 1968), Samuel Clemens Soc., Phi Kappa Phi. Democrat. Avocations: collecting books, letters, documents. Office: U Calif Community Studies Davis CA 95616

MACCOBY, ELEANOR EMMONS, psychology educator; b. Tacoma, May 15, 1917; d. Harry Eugene and Viva May (Johnson) Emmons; m. Nathan Maccoby, Sept. 16, 1938 (dec. Apr. 1992); children: Janice Carmichael, Sarah Maccoby Blunt, Mark. BS, U Wash., 1939; MA, U. Mich., 1949, PhD, 1950. Study dir. div. program surveys USDA, Washington, 1942-46; study dir. Survey Rsch. Ctr. U. Mich., Ann Arbor, 1946-48; lectr., rsch. assoc. dept. social rels. Harvard U., Cambridge, Mass., 1950-58; from assoc. to full prof. Stanford (Calif.) U., 1958-87, chmn. dept. psychology, 1973-76, prof. emeritus, 1987—. Author: (with R. Sears and H. Levin) Patterns of Child-Rearing, 1957, (with Carol Jacklin) Psychology of Sex Differences, 1974, Social Development, 1980, (with R.H. Mnookin) Dividing the Child: Social and Legal Dilemmas of Custody, 1992, (with Buchanan and Dombusch) Adolescents after Divorce, 1996, The Two Sexes: Growing Up Apart, Coming Together, 1998; editor: (with Newcomb and Hartley) Readings in Social Psychology, 1957, The Development of Sex Differences, 1966. Recipient Gores award for Excellence in Teaching Stanford U., 1981, Disting. Contbn. to Ednl. Research award Am. Ednl. Research Assn., 1984, Disting. Sci. Contbn. to Child Devel. award Soc. for Research in Child Devel., 1987, Disting. Sci. Contbns. award Am. Psychol. Assn., 1988; named to Barbara Kimball Browning professorship Stanford U., 1979—. Fellow APA (pres. Divsn. 7, 1971-72, G. Stanley Hall award 1982), Soc. for Rsch. in Child Devel. (pres. 1981-83, mem. governing coun. 1963-66, Am. Psychol. Soc.; mem. NAS, AAAS, Am. Acad. Arts and Scis., Inst. Medicine, Western Psychol. Assn. (pres. 1974-75), Inst. for Rsch. on Women and Gender, Social Sci. Rsch. Coun. (chmn. 1984-85), Consortium of Social Sci. Assns. (pres. 1997-98), Am. Psychol. Found. (Life Achievement award 1996). Democrat. Home: 729 Mayfield Ave Palo Alto CA 94305-1016 Office: Stanford U Dept Psychology Stanford CA 94305-2130

MAC CREADY, PAUL BEATTIE, aeronautical engineer; b. New Haven, Sept. 29, 1925; BS in Physics, Yale U., 1947; MS, Calif. Inst. Tech., 1948, PhD in Aeros. cum laude, 1952. Founder, pres. Meteorology Research Inc., 1951-70, Atmospheric Research Group, 1958-70; founder, 1971, CEO, chmn. AeroVironment Inc., Pasadena, Calif., 1994, chmn., 1994—. Leader team that developed Gossamer Albatross for human-powered flight across English Channel, 1979, Solar Challenger, ultralight aircraft powered by solar cells, 1981, GM-Sunraycer, 1987, GM-Impact, 1990; cons. in field, 1951—; mem. numerous govt. tech. adv. coms. Contbr. articles to profl. jours. Recipient Collier trophy Nat. Aero. Assn., 1979, Edward Longsreth medal Franklin Inst., 1979, Gold Air medal Fedn. Aero. Internat., 1981, Inventor of Yr. award Assn. Advancement Innovation and Invention, 1981; named Engr. of Century ASME, 1980. Mem. AIAA (Reed Aero. award 1979), Nat. Acad. Engring., Am. Acad. Arts and Scis., Am. Meteorol. Soc. (chmn. com. atmospheric measurements 1968-69, councillor 1971-74). Office: Aerovironment Inc 222 E Huntington Dr Ste 200 Monrovia CA 91016-3500

MAC DIARMID, WILLIAM DONALD, physician; b. Arcola, Sask., Can., June 22, 1926; s. John Angus and Evaline (Reed) MacD.; m. Bette Nell Brown, May 16, 1953; children— John A., Margaret A., Donald G., Andrew L. B.A., U. Sask., 1947; M.D., U. Toronto, 1949. Diplomate Am. Bd. Internal Medicine. Intern Pasqua Hosp., Regina, Sask., 1949-50; family physician, mem. med. staff Pasqua Hosp. and Regina Gen. Hosp., 1950-53; mem. staff Shaunavon (Sask.) Union Hosp., 1953-58; resident in internal medicine, fellow in endocrinology and metabolism U. Utah Affiliated Hosps., Salt Lake City, 1958-62; research asst. in human genetics Univ. Coll. Hosp. Med. Sch., London, 1962-64; mem. faculty U. Utah Med. Sch., 1964-69; prof. medicine U. Man. Med. Sch., Winnipeg, 1969-75, 79-91, chmn. dept., 1979-85; physician-in-chief St. Boniface Gen. Hosp., 1969-75, St. John's Gen. Hosp. and Health Sci. Ctr., 1975-79, Health Sci. Ctr. of Winnipeg, 1979-85; health svcs. cons., 1986-91. Prof., chmn. dept. medicine Meml. U. Nfld. Med. Sch., 1975-79; pres. Swift Current and Dist. Med. Soc., 1956-57; mem. bd. Com. for Accreditation of Can. Med. Schs., 1985-91, chmn., 1988-91. Vol. Can. Cancer Soc., 1992—; bd. dirs. Man. Med. Svcs. found., 1986-91, Winnipeg Mcpl. Hosps., 1986-89; chmn. bd. Man. Cancer Treatment and Rsch. Found., 1987-88; v.p. Man. Med. Coll. Found., 1988-91; active layman United Ch. of Can., 1954-58, 69—, Presbyn. Ch. U.S.A., 1964-69. Fellow ACP, Royal Coll. Physicians and Surgeons Can., Can. Coll. Med. Geneticists; mem. Am. Soc. Human Genetics, Can. Med. Assn. (com. on ethics 1987-91, coun. on med. edn. 1988-91), Man. Med. Assn. (dir. 1981-83, 87—, chmn. bd. 1982-83, hon. sec. 1988-89, hon. treas. 1989-90, chmn. com. on ethics 1987-91). Home and Office: 4142 Cortez Pl Victoria BC Canada V8N 4R8

MACDONALD, ALAN HUGH, librarian, university administrator; b. Ottawa, Ont., Can., Mar. 3, 1943; s. Vincent C. and Hilda C. (Durney) MacD.; children: Eric Paul Henry, Nigel Alan Christopher. BA, Dalhousie U., Halifax N.S., 1963; BLS, U. Toronto, Ont., 1964. With Dalhousie U., 1964-78, law librarian, 1965-67, 69-71, asst. univ. librarian, 1970-72, health sci. librarian, 1972-78, lectr. Sch. Libr. Svcs., 1969-78; with U. Calgary, Alta., Can., 1979—, sr. advisor Info. Resources, Sch. Libr. Svcs. Can., 1999—, asst. to v.p. (acad.), provost Can., 1999—, adj. prof. faculty comm. and culture, dir. info. svcs. Can., 1988-99; libr. N.S. Barristers Soc., Can., 1969-74; univ. orator U. Calgary, Can., 1989—, dir. librs. Can., 1979-92, univ. orator Can., 1989—; dir. U. Calgary Press, 1984-90. Chair editl. Bd. U. Calgary Press, 2001—; librarian N.S. Barristers Soc., 1969-74; mem. adv. bd. Nat. Libr. Can., 1972-76, Health Scis. Resource Ctr., Can. Inst. Sci. and Tech. Info., 1977-79; mem. Coun. of Prairie Univ. Librs., 1979-92, 97-98, chair, 1984-85, 89, 91; Bassam lectr. U. Toronto Faculty Info. Studies, 1994, Lorne MacRae lectr. Libr. Assn. Alta., 1996; mem. steering com. Alta. Knowledge Network, 1999—, steering. com. Can. Digital Libr. Rsch. Inst. Initiative, 1999-2000. Mem. editorial bd. America: History and Life (ABC-CLIO), 1985-93. Pres. TELED Cmty. Media Access Orgn., Halifax, 1972—74; mem. Minister's Com. on Univ. Affairs, Alta., 1979—83; bd. dirs. Alta. Found. for Can. Music Ctr., 1985—92, Can. Inst. for Hist. Microreprodn., 1990—98, pres., 1996—97; bd. mem. Calgary Learning Ctr., 1997—, vice-chair, 2000—. Council Library Resources fellow, 1975; exec. fellow Univ. Microfilms Internat., 1986; recipient Disting. Acad. Librarian award Can. Assn. of Coll. and Univ. Libraries, 1988, U. Toronto Faculty of Info. Studies Alumni Jubilee award, 1999. Mem.: Can. Libr. Assn. (treas. 1977—79, pres. 1980—81, Award for Outstanding Svc. to Librarianship 1997), Atlantic Provinces Libr. Assn. (pres. 1977—78), Libr. Assn. Alta. (v.p. 1988—89, Pres.' award 1992), Can. Health Libr. Assn. (life; treas. 1977—79), Australian Libr. and Info. Assn. (assoc.), Foothills Libr. Assn., Can. Assn. Info. Sci. (pres. 1979—80), Can. Assn. Rsch. Librs. (bd. dirs. 1981—86, v.p. 1985—86), Calgary Cmty. Network Assn. (bd. dirs. 1994—99, chair 1996—99), Order of U. Calgary. Office: U Calgary MLT750 2500 University Dr NW Calgary AB Canada T2N 1N4 E-mail: ahmacdon@ucalgary.ca

MACDONALD, ANDREW STEPHEN, management consulting firm executive; b. Fairbanks, Alaska, July 15, 1953; s. Bernard L. and Rosemary (Unger) MacD.; m. Josephine A. Joanne, Aug. 4, 1972; children: Peter, Stephen, Charles. BA in Acctg., Seattle U., 1974. CPA, cert. mgmt. cons. Acct. Boeing Aerospace, Seattle, 1976-79; owner, pres. Triak Corp., Seattle, 1977—; pres. Exec. Cons. Group, Inc., Seattle, 1979—. Mem. AICPA, Inst. Mgmt. Cons., Wash. Soc. CPAs, Columbia Tower Club. Home: 10030 Lake Shore Blvd NE Seattle WA 98125-8158

MACDONALD, DONALD, IV, federal judge; b. 1947; Apptd. chief bankruptcy judge U.S. Dist. Ct. Alaska, 1990. Office: 605 W 4th Ave Ste 138 Anchorage AK 99501-2351 Fax: 907-271-2692

MACDONALD, ERIN E. healthcare company executive; With Sierra Health Svcs. Inc. and predecessor firms, 1978—, ops. mgr. Southwest Med. Assocs.; dir. ops. HPN Sierra Health Svcs. Inc., Reno, v.p. HMO Ops., pres. HPN, 1984, v.p. HMO and ins. ops., 1989-92, pres. SHL, 1990, sr. v.p. ops. Office: Sierra Health Svcs 2724 N Tenaya Way Las Vegas NV 89128

MACDONALD, KEN CRAIG, geophysicist; b. San Francisco, Oct. 14, 1947; m. Rachel Haymon, 1984. BS in Engring. Physics, U. Calif. Berkeley, 1970; PhD in Marine Geophysics, MIT/Woods Hole, 1975. Cecil H. and Ida Green postdoctoral scholar Scripps Instn. of Oceanography, 1975-76, asst. rsch. geophysicist, lectr., 1976-80; assoc. prof. U. Calif., Santa Barbara, 1980-83, prof., 1983—. Chief scientist on over 30 deep sea expeditions; prin. ALVIN diver on over 40 dives to the mid-ocean ridge. Assoc. editor Jour. of Geophys. Rsch., 1979-82, Earth and Planetary Sci. Letters, 1978-88; mem. editorial bd. Marine Sci. Revs., 1986—; editor Marine Geophys. Rschs., 1986-90; contbr. over 100 articles to profl. jours. Mem. ALVIN Rev. Com., 1979-82; mem. Ocean Sci. Bd. of NAS, 1980-83, Lithosphere Panel Advanced Ocean Drilling Project, 1983-85, Ocean Scis. Panel, NSF, 1984-86, COSOD II planning com.; mem. various RIDGE coms., RIDGE steering com., 1987-90; mem. NSF Ocean Scis. Strategic Plan for Rsch. and Edn. Com., 1993-94, U.S. Geodynamics Comm., 1997—. Regents scholar U. Calif., Berkeley, 1966-70, Mineral Tech. scholar, 1967-70, Cecil H. and Ida Green scholar Inst. Geophysics and Planetary Physics/U. Calif., San Diego, 1975-76; NSF Grad. fellow, 1970-73;recipient AAAS Newcomb-Cleveland prize, 1980, Robert L. and Bettie P. Cody prize and medal Scripps Instn. Oceanography, 1994; named U. Hawaii SOEST Disting. lectr., 1990. Fellow Am. Geophys. Union, Geol. Soc. Am.; mem. Phi Beta Kappa, Sigma Psi. Avocations: windsurfing, fly fishing. Office: U Calif Santa Barbara Dept Geol Sci Santa Barbara CA 93106 E-mail: macdonald@geol.ucsb.edu

MACDONALD, KIRK STEWART, lawyer; b. Glendale, Calif., Oct. 24, 1948; s. Bruce Macc and Phyllis Jeanne MacDonald. BSCE, U. So. Calif., 1970; JD, Western State U., 1982. Bar: Calif. 1982, U.S. Dist. Ct. (cen. dist.) Calif. 1982, U.S. Ct. Appeals (9th cir.) 1982, U.S. Dist. Ct. (no. dist.) Calif. 1984, U.S. Dist. Ct. (so. dist.) Calif. 1985, U.S. Dist. Ct. (ea. dist.) Calif. 1987. Dist. engr. Pacific Clay Products, Corona, Calif., 1971-76, Nat. Clay Pipe Inst., La Mirada, 1976-82; ptnr. Gill and Baldwin, Glendale, 1982—. Mem. ABA, L.A. County Bar Assn., Water Environ. Assn., Calif. Water Environ. Assn. Avocations: travel, woodworking. Office: Gill & Baldwin Ste 405 130 N Brand Blvd Glendale CA 91203-2646 E-mail: kirk@gillandbaldwin.com

MACDONALD, NORVAL (WOODROW), safety engineer; b. Medford, Oreg., Dec. 8, 1913; s. Orion and Edith (Anderson) MacD.; m. Elizabeth Ann Clifford, Dec. 8, 1937; children: Linda (Mrs. Bob Comings), Peggy (Mrs. Don Lake), Kathleen (Mrs. Michael Nissenberg). Student, U. So. Calif., 1932-34. Registered profl. safety engr., Calif. Safety engr. Todd Shipyards, San Pedro, Calif., 1942-44, Pacific Indemnity Ins. Co., San Francisco, 1944-50; area safety engring. chief safety engr. Indsl. Ind., San Francisco, 1950-76; supervising safety engr. Beaver Ins. Co., 1976-82, v.p. loss control, 1982-88; cons. safety engr. MacDonald and Assocs., 1988-99. Tchr. adult evening classes U. San Francisco, 1960-63, Golden Gate U., 1969-76. Contbr. articles to profl. jours.; producer safety training films. Mem. ASME, Am. Soc. Safety Engrs. (pres. San Francisco chpt. 1958, 59), Las Posas Country Club, Masons, Shriners. Methodist. Home: 1710 E Shoreline St Camarillo CA 93010-6018 E-mail: nmacd@aol.com

MACDONNELL, PHILIP J. lawyer; b. Boston, Apr. 22, 1948; BA magna cum laude, Harvard U., 1971, JD cum laude, 1974. Bar: Ariz. 1974, U.S. Dist. Ct. Ariz. 1975, U.S. Ct. Appeals (9th cir.) 1976, U.S. Supreme Ct. 1978. Asst. atty. gen. Ariz. Atty. Gen.'s Office, 1975-77, chief counsel special prosecutions divsn., 1977-81; asst. U.S. atty. Dist. Ariz., 1981-85; supt. Ariz. Dept. Liquor Licenses and Control, 1985-87; atty. Jennings, Strouss and Salmon, Phoenix, 1987—. Editor Harvard Law Rev., 1972-73, sr. editor, 1973-74. Office: Jennings Strouss & Salmon 1 Renaissance Sq 2 N Central Ave Ste 1600 Phoenix AZ 85004-2393

MACE, JOHN WELDON, pediatrician; b. Buena Vista, Va., July 9, 1938; s. John Henry and Gladys Elizabeth (Edwards) M.; m. Janice Mace, Jan. 28, 1962; children: Karin E., John E., James E. B.A., Columbia Union Coll., 1960; M.D., Loma Linda U., 1964. Diplomate: Am. Bd. Pediatrics, Sub-bd. Pediatric Endocrinology. Intern U.S. Naval Hosp., San Diego, 1964-65, resident in pediatrics, 1966-68; fellow in endocrinology and metabolism U. Colo., 1970-72; asst. prof. pediatrics Loma Linda (Calif.) U. Med. Center, 1972-75, prof., chmn. dept., 1975—. Med. dir. Loma Linda U. Children's Hosp., 1990-92, physician-in-chief, 1992—. Contbr. articles to profl. jours. Treas. Found. for Med. Care San Bernardino County, 1979-80, pres., 1980-82; mem. Congl. Adv. Bd., 1984-87; pres. So. Calif. affiliate Am. Diabetes Assn., 1985-86, dir., 1987-89; chmn. adv. bd. State Calif. Children's Svcs., 1986—; bd. dirs. So. Calif. Children's Cancer Svcs., 1993-94, Loma Linda Ronald McDonald House, 1991—, Aetna Health Plans of Calif., 1993-95; bd. dirs. Loma Linda U. Health Care, 1995—. Named Alumnist of Yr., Loma Linda U. Sch. Medicine, 1994. Mem. AAAS, N.Y. Acad. Sci., Calif. Med. Soc. (adv. panel genetic diseases State Calif., 1975—, chmn. acad. practice forum 1997—), Western Soc. Pediatric Rsch., Lawson Wilkens Pediatric Endocrine Soc., Assn. Med. Pediatric Dept. Chmn., Am. Acad. Pediatrics, Sigma Xi, Alpha Omega Alpha. Office: Loma Linda U Childrens Hosp 11234 Anderson St Loma Linda CA 92354-2870

MACEY, WILLIAM BLACKMORE, oil company executive; b. Buffalo, Aug. 1, 1920; s. Richard Charles and Doris (Bourne) M.; m. Jean Olive Mullins, Oct. 6, 1945; 1 dau., Barbara Jean. B.S. in Petroleum Engring, N.Mex. Sch. Mines, 1942; D.Engring. (hon.), N.Mex. Inst. Mining and Tech., 1984. Dist. engr. N.Mex. Oil Conservation Commn., 1946-48; dist. supt. Am. Republics Corp., 1948-52; chief engr. N.Mex. Oil Conservation Commn., 1952-54, state geologist, dir., 1954-56; v.p. Internat. Oil & Gas Corp. (and predecessor co., developers mineral properties), Denver, 1956-60, then pres., 1960-67; pres. Nielson Enterprises Inc., oil and gas prodn. and pipelines, livestock ranching, 1967-74; v.p., dir. Y-Tex Corp. (mfr. livestock identification tags), 1972-73; pres. GEN Oil Inc. (oil and gas prodn.), 1972-75, Col. Cody Inn (real estate and golf course devel.), 1970-73; pres., dir. Macey & Mershon Oil, Inc., 1974-93; dir. Juniper Oil and Gas Corp., Denver, 1981-83, Ruidoso (N.Mex.) State Bank Holding Co., 1987—; pres. The Macey Corp., Denver, 1985—. Chmn. Pres.'s N.Mex. Inst. Mines and Tech., 1980-82; mem. adv. bd. U. Ariz. Heart Ctr., 1997—; mem. Pres.'s U. Ariz. Found. Served from 2d lt. to capt. USAAF, 1942-45. Mem. N.Mex. Oil and Gas Assn. (exec. com. 1949-52, 60-61), Garden of the Gods, Skyline Country Club (Tucson) (dir., treas. 1980-82, pres. 1982-83), Altolakes Golf and Country Club, Tucson Country Club, Ruidoso, N.Mex. Jockey Club (bd. dirs. 1985-88, 91-93, pres. 1993), Popejoy & Pres. Club, Garden of the Gods Club. Episcopalian. Home: 7010 N Javelina Dr Tucson AZ 85718-1850 also: 10153 Masters Dr NE Albuquerque NM 87111-5894 Office: PO Box 2210 Denver CO 80201-2210

MACFARLAND, CRAIG GEORGE, natural resource management professional; b. Great Falls, Mont., July 17, 1943; s. Paul Stanley and Jean Elizabeth (Graham) MacF.; m. Janice Lee Bennett, Dec. 23, 1963 (div. 1987); children: Bennett, Francisco; m. Marilyn Ann Swanson, Mar. 19, 1988 (div. 1999). BA magna cum laude, Austin Coll., 1965; MA, U. Wis., Madison, 1969, PhD in Zoology, 1993; DSc (hon.), Austin Coll., 1978. Dir. Charles Darwin Rsch. Sta., Galapagos Islands, Ecuador, 1974-78; head Wildlands and watershed mgmt. program C.Am. Centro Agronomico Tropical de Investigacion Enseñanza, Turrialba, Costa Rica, 1978-85; pres. Charles Darwin Found. for Galapagos Islands, Ecuador, 1985-96; cons. natural resources and sustainable use in L.Am. Moscow, 1985—. Affiliate faculty dept. Resource, Recreation and Tourism, U. Idaho, Moscow, 1988—; affiliate faculty dept. natural resource recreation and tourism Colo. State U., Ft. Collins, 1992. Contbr. to numerous profl. publs. Recipient Internat. Conservation medal Zool. Soc. San Diego, 1978, Order of Golden Ark for internat. conservation, Prince Bernhard of Netherlands, 1984. Mem. World Conservation Union, World Commn. on Protected Areas, Ecol. Soc. Am., Internat. Soc. for Ecol. Econs., Internat. Soc. Tropical Foresters, Assn. Tropical Biology, Soc. Conservation Biology, Nature Conservancy, World Wildlife Fund, Greenpeace, Cultural Survival, George Wright Soc. Avocations: cross-country skiing, hiking, camping, skiing. Home and Office: Box 207 Arlee MT 59821-0207 E-mail: riverbottom@blackfoot.net, craigmacfarland@hotmail.com

MACGINITIE, WALTER HAROLD, psychologist, educator; b. Carmel, Calif., Aug. 14, 1928; s. George Eber and Nettie Lorene (Murray) MacG.; m. Ruth Olive Kilpatrick, Sept. 2, 1950; children: Mary Catherine, Laura Anne. B.A., UCLA, 1949; A.M., Stanford U., 1950; Ph.D., Columbia U., 1960. Tchr. Long Beach (Calif.) Unified Sch. Dist., 1950, 1955-56; mem. faculty Columbia U. Tchrs. Coll., 1959-80, prof. psychology and edn., 1970-80; Lansdowne scholar, prof. edn. U. Victoria, B.C., Can., 1980-84. Research assoc. Lexington Sch. Deaf, N.Y.C., 1963-69; mem. sci. adv. bd. Ctr. for Study of Reading, 1977-80, chmn. 1979-80. Co-author: Gates-MacGinitie Reading Tests, 1965, 78, 89, 2000, Psychological Foundations of Education, 1968; Editor: Assessment Problems in Reading, 1972; co-editor: Verbal Behavior of the Deaf Child, 1969. Life mem. Calif. PTA. Served with USAF, 1950-54. Fellow APA, AAAS, Am. Psychol. Soc., Nat. Conf. on Rsch. on Language and Literacy, N.Y. Acad. Scis.; mem. Internat. Reading Assn. (pres. 1976-77, Spl. Svc. award 1981), Reading Hall of Fame (pres. 1989-90). Home and Office: PO Box 1789 Friday Harbor WA 98250-1789

MACGOWAN, EUGENIA, lawyer; b. Turlock, Calif., Aug. 4, 1928; d. William Ray and Mary Bolling (Gilbert) Kern; m. Gordon Scott Millar, Jan. 2, 1970 (dec. Jan. 1997); 1 dau., Heather Mary. A.B., U. Calif., Berkeley, 1950; J.D., U. Calif., San Francisco, 1953. Bar: Calif. 1953; cert. family law specialist Calif. State Bar Bd. Legal Specialization. Research atty. Supreme Ct. Calif., 1954, Calif. Ct. Appeals, 1955; partner firm MacGowan & MacGowan, Calif., 1956-68; pvt. practice, San Francisco, 1968-99. Bd. dirs. San Francisco Speech and Hearing Center, San Francisco Legal Aid Soc., J.A.C.K.I.E. Mem. Am., Calif., San Francisco bar assns., Queen's Bench. Clubs: San Francisco Lawyers, Forest Hill Garden. Office: 236 W Portal Ave San Francisco CA 94127-1423

MACGREGOR, GEORGE LESCHER, JR. freelance writer; b. Dallas, Sept. 15, 1936; s. George Lescher and Jean (Edge) MacG.; divorced; children: George Lescher III, Michael Fordtran. B.B.A., U. Tex., 1958. Asst. cashier First Nat. Bank in Dallas, 1960-64, asst. v.p., 1964-68; v.p. Nat. Bank of Commerce of Dallas, 1968-70, sr. v.p., 1970-73, exec. v.p., 1973-74; pres., chief exec. officer Mountain Banks Ltd., Colorado Springs, 1974-77; chief exec. officer Highfield Fin. (U.S.A.) Ltd., 1978-83; chmn. bd., chief exec. officer, dir. Dominion Nat. Bank, Denver, 1981-84; chmn. bd., chief exec. officer Royal Dominion Ltd., Denver; chmn. bd., chief exec. officer, dir. Market Bank of Denver, 1983-84; vice chmn., dir. Bank of Aurora, Denver, 1983-84; chmn., pres., chief exec. officer Alamosa Bancorp. of Colo., Denver, 1983-84; pres., chief exec. officer Am. Interstate Bancorp., 1984 88; pres. Banco, Inc., 1984-89; sr. mng. ptnr. Scotland Co., Denver, London, 1988-91; free-lance writer, 1992—. Served with M.C. AUS, 1958-60. Mem. Am. Inst. Banking (hon.), Young Pres.'s Orgn., Koon Kreek Club, Broadmoore Golf Club, Oxford Club, Phi Gamma Delta. Anglican Catholic. Home and Office: 1736 Blake St Denver CO 80202-1226 Fax: 303-292-9794

MACHADO, MICHAEL JOHN, state legislator, farmer; b. Stockton, Calif., Mar. 12, 1948; s. Bill and Grace Machado; m. Diana Machado, June 20, 1970; children: Christopher, Erahm, Melissa. BA in Econs., Stanford U., 1970; MS in Agrl. Econs., U. Calif., Davis, 1974. Owner, operator, farmer, Linden, Calif., 1972—; mem. Calif. Ho. of Reps. from 17th dist., Sacramento, 1995-2000, Calif. Senate from 5th dist., Sacramento, 2001—. Mem. Dem. Ctrl. Com., San Joaquin County, 1994—, Dem. Leadership Coun., Sacramento, 1994—; pres. People's Orgn. for Land Preservation, Linden, 1976-78. Lt. USN, 1970-72. Recipient Calif. Outstanding Young Farmer Calif. Farm Bur., 1978; named Legislator of Yr. Assn. of Calif. Water Agencies, 1999, Outstanding Young Men and Women Under 40 Esquire mag., 1984. Mem. Lions Club, Rotary, San Joaquin County Farm Bur. Roman Catholic. Avocations: reading, theatre, traveling, gardening, racquetball. Office: Calif Senate State Capitol Sacramento CA 95814

MACHEN, BERNARD J. academic administrator; m. Chris; children: Maggie, Michael, Lee. DDS, St. Louis U., 1968; MS, U. Iowa, 1972, PhD in Edn. Psychology, 1974. Prof., assoc. dean U. N.C., 1983-89; pres. Am. Assn. Dental Schs., 1987; dean U. Mich. Sch. Dentistry, 1989-95; provost, exec. v.p. acad. affairs U. Mich., 1995-97; pres. U. Utah, 1998—. Mem. Inst. Medicine Com. in Future Dental Edn. Nat. Acad. Scis., 1993-95. Office: U of Utah 201 Presidents Cir Rm 203 Salt Lake City UT 84112-9008

MACHIDA, CURTIS A. research molecular neurobiologist, educator; b. San Francisco, Apr. 1, 1954; AB, U. Calif., Berkeley, 1976; PhD, Oreg. Health Scis. U., 1982. Postdoctoral scientist Oreg. Health Scis. U., Portland, 1982-88; asst. scientist div. neurosci. Oreg. Regional Primate Research Ctr., Beaverton, 1988-95, assoc. scientist divsn. neuroscience, 1995—. Rsch. asst. prof. biochemistry and molecular biology Oreg. Health Scis. U., 1989-95, mem. faculty neurosci. and molecular and cell biology grad. programs, 1989—, adj. assoc. prof. biochemistry and molecular biology, 1995—; mem. grad. faculty biochemistry and biophysics Oreg. State U., Corvallis, 1997—; mem. Institutional Ethics oversight com., Institutional Bisafety com., Instnl. Animal Care and Use com.; mem. biotech. program adv. com. Portland C.C. Editorial cons. Oreg. Health Scis. U. News, 1984-87; editor Adrenergic Receptor Protocols, 1997-99, Virus Vectors for Gene Therapy: Methods and Protocols, 2000—; ad-hoc reviewer Endocrinology, Molecular Pharmacology, Biochimica et Biophysica Acta, Am. Jour. Physiology, Lab. Animal Sci., NSF; contbr. articles, revs., and abstracts to profl. jours. and internat. confs. Recipient Leukemia Assn. award, 1981, Tartar award Med. Rsch. Found. Oreg., 1980; NIH fellow, 1980-82, 85-87, grantee, 1989, 95, 98; rsch. grantee Med. Rsch. Found. Oreg., Wills Found., Nat. Parkinson Found., Collins Med. Trust, Murdock Charitable Trust and Rsch. Corp. Mem. AAAS, Am. Soc. Biochemistry and Molecular Biology, Am. Soc. Microbiology, Soc. Neurosci., Am. Heart Assn. (basic scis. coun., established investigator 1994-99), Am. Soc. Gene Therapy, U.S.-Israel Binational Sci. Found. (reviewer). Achievements include patent on dopamine receptor and genes; cloning of several adrenergic receptor genes and simian retroviral infectious genomes; depositor, nucleotide sequence to EMBL and GenBank databases, and clones to American Type Culture Collection. Office: Oreg Regional Primate Rsch Ctr Neurosci Oreg Health Scis U 505 NW 185th Ave W Campus Beaverton OR 97006-3448 Fax: (503) 690-5384. E-mail: machidac@ohsu.edu

MACIAS, FERNANDO, state legislator, lawyer; b. Dona Ana, N.Mex., 1953; BA, N.Mex. State U.; JD, Georgetown U. Mem. N.Mex. Legislature, Santa Fe, 1984—, mem. conservation com., mem. corps. and transp. com. Democrat. Office: PO Box 1155 Mesilla NM 88046-1155

MAC INTYRE, DONALD JOHN, college president; b. Detroit, Aug. 19, 1939; s. Donald MacLellan and Ellen (McGrath) MacI.; m. Antoinette Shen, June 2, 1979; children by previous marriage: Honey, Michele, James, John. A.B., U. Detroit, 1961; M.A., U. Iowa, 1963, Ph.D., 1966. Prof. U. Pacific, Stockton, Calif., 1966-73; acad. dean/pres. St. Francis Coll., Biddeford, Maine, 1973-75; acad. v.p. U. San Francisco, 1975-79; pres. Metro. State Coll., Denver, 1979-81, Canada Coll., Redwood City, Calif., 1981-83, Skyline Coll., San Bruno, 1983-85, John F. Kennedy U., Orinda, 1985-89, Patricia Montandon & Assocs., San Francisco, 1989-91, Tie Tone, Inc., Mill Valley, Calif., 1991-92, The Fielding Inst., Santa Barbara, 1993-99; exec. v.p. e-vitro, Boulder, Colo., 1999—. Cons. Indsl. Rels. Workshops Seminars, Inc., 1978-81, State Bd. Agr. Colo., 1979; assoc. John A. Scalone & Assocs., Orinda, Calif., 1977-85; chmn. adv. com. office adult learning svcs. Coll. Entrance and Exam. Bd., 1980-81; evaluator Women's Equity in Edn. Act Program, 1981. Contbr. articles to profl. jours. Chmn. edn. div. Mile High United Way, Denver, 1980-81; bd. dirs. Nat. Hispanic Center for Advanced Studies and Policy Analysis, 1981-86, Nat. Hispanic U., 1982-86, Chinese Culture Found., 1983-89; chmn. Children As the Peacemakers Found. Recipient award for Commendable Service U. San Francisco, 1979, Henry Clay Hall award, 1976; Disting. Teaching award U. Pacific, 1971; U. Pacific grantee, 1969-71; Don Quixote award Nat. Hispanic U., 1983; hon. mem. World Trade Ctr. Club, Nanjing, Republic of China, 1985—. Mem. Assn. Public Coll. and Univ. Pres.'s (co-chmn. Colo. 1980-81), Internat. Cultural Soc. Korea, Democrat. Roman Catholic. Club: World Trade Ctr. (hon.) (Nanjing, China). Office: e-vitro 27 Midway Ave Mill Valley CA 94941-3438

MACK, J. CURTIS, II, civic organization administrator; b. Los Angeles, Dec. 22, 1944; s. James Curtis and Ahli Christina (Youngren) M.; m. Tamara Jo Kriner, Jan. 23, 1988; children: James Curtis III, Robert Lee, Edward Albert. BA cum laude, U. So. Calif., 1967, M in Pub. Adminstrn., 1969, MA, 1976. Asst. to regional dir. VA, Los Angeles, 1973-79; exec. dir. Citizens for the Republic, Santa Monica, Calif., 1979-85; asst. sec. oceans and atmosphere U.S. Dept. Commerce, Washington, 1985-88; pres. Los Angeles World Affairs Coun., 1988—. Adj. prof. Pepperdine U. Grad. Sch. Pub. Policy, 1999—; bd. dirs. Brentwood Bank of Calif. Mem. Pres.'s Commn. on White House Fellowships, 1984-85. Col. USAFR, 1969-99. Mem. Nat. Space Club (bd. dirs. 1987-88). Republican. Episcopalian. Avocation: philatelist. Office: LA World Affairs Coun 345 S Figueroa St Ste 313 Los Angeles CA 90071-1002

MACK, JAMES A. parks director; b. Chgo., July 7, 1944; BS in Wildlife Mgmt., Calif. State U., Eureka, 1968; postgrad., N. Ariz. U., 1973. With Nat. Park Svcs.; chief naturalist Haleakla, Maui, Hawaii, 1975-78; chief visitor svcs. Rocky Mt. Nat. Park, 1988-97; supt. Fort Laramie, Wyo., 1997—. Office: Nat Hist Site HC 72 Box 389 PO Box 86 Fort Laramie WY 82212-0086

MACKAY, HAROLD HUGH, lawyer; b. Regina, Sask., Can., Aug. 1, 1940; s. John Royden and Grace Madeliene (Irwin) MacK.; m. Jean Elizabeth Hutchison, Dec. 27, 1963; children: Carol, Donald. BA, U. Sask., 1960; LLB, Dalhousie U., Halifax, N.S., 1963. Bar: Sask. 1964, Queen's Counsel 1981. Assoc. MacPherson Leslie & Tyerman, Regina, 1963-69, ptnr., 1969-75, 76—, mng. ptnr., 1989-96, chmn., 1997—. Bd. dirs. Bank of Can., Can. Life Fin. Corp., IMC Global Inc.; chmn. task force Future of the Can. Fin. Svcs. Sector; chair Saskatchewan Inst. Pub. Policy. Trustee Found. for Legal Rsch. Mem. Internat. Bar Assn., Can. Bar Assn., Law Soc. Sask. Mem. United Ch. Office: 1500 1874 Scarth St Regina SK Canada S4P 4E9 E-mail: hmackay@mlt.com

MACKENBACH, FREDERICK W. welding products manufacturing company executive; b. St. Marys, Ohio, Mar. 10, 1931; s. Frederick Jacob and Mabel (Tangeman) M.; m. Jo Ann Dietrich, Oct. 21, 1953; children: John Frederick, David Dietrich. BS in Econs., Wharton Sch. Fin. & Commerce, 1953. Various sales engr. positions The Lincoln Electric Co., Indpls., Ft. Wayne, L.A., 1956-64, asst. dist. mgr. L.A., 1973-76, dist. mgr., 1976-88; pres. Lincoln Electric Mexicana, 1988-91, Lincoln Electric Latin Am., 1991-92; pres., COO The Lincoln Electric Co., Cleve., 1992-96, ret., 1996. Mem. Com. on Fgn. Rels.; bd. dirs. Torrance Meml. Med. Ctr. Health Care Found., Goodwill Industries So. Calif. Coun. mem. City of Palos Verdes Estates (Calif.) City Coun. With U.S. Army 1953-55. Mem. Econ. Roundtable in L.A., Am. Welding Soc. Office: Lincoln Electric Co 732 Via Somonte Palos Verdes Estates CA 90274-1629 E-mail: mackenbach@aol.com

MACKENZIE, JOHN DOUGLAS, engineering educator; b. Hong Kong, Feb. 18, 1926; came to U.S., 1954, naturalized, 1963; s. John and Hannah (Wong) MacK.; m. Jennifer Russell, Oct. 2, 1954; children: Timothy John, Andrea Louise, Peter Neil. BS, U. London, 1952, PhD, 1954. Research asst., lectr. Princeton U., 1954-56; ICI fellow Cambridge (Eng.) U., 1956-57; research scientist Gen. Electric Research Ctr., N.Y.C., 1957-63; prof. materials sci. Rensselaer Poly. Inst., 1963-69; prof. engring. U. Calif., Los Angeles, 1969—. U.S. rep. Internat. Glass Commn., 1964-71 Author books in field (6); editor: Jour. Non-Crystalline Solids, 1968—; contbr. articles to profl. jours.; patentee in field. Fellow Am. Ceramic Soc., Royal Inst. Chemistry; mem. Nat. Acad. Engring., Am. Phys. Soc., Electrochem. Soc., ASTM, Am. Chem. Soc., Soc. Glass Tech. Office: U Calif 6532 Boelter Hall Los Angeles CA 90095-1595

MACKENZIE, PETER SEAN, writer; b. L.A., Aug. 25, 1954; s. William Duncan and Patricia Ann (Kronschnabel) Mack; m. Carin Willette, Dec. 28, 1983; 1 child, Liam Reynolds. BA, Western Wash. U., 1976. Bus. editor Skagit Valley Herald, Mount Vernon, Wash., 1976-79; mng. editor Stanwood (Wash.)-Camano News, 1979-84; graphic artist Pacific Media Group, Seattle, 1985-90, editor, 1990-94; instnl. designer Lucent Techs. (Mosaix, Inc.), Redmond, Wash., 1994-2000; sr. tech. writer Envision Telephony, Inc., Seattle, 2000—. Instr. U. Wash. Exptl. Coll., Seattle, 1990-91, 96-97. Author: Jumper, 1989; rec. artist LP KEZX Album Project, 1987, Victory Music Vol. # 2, 1988; speaker Viacom Cable Pub. Access TV, Seattle, 1990. V.p. Stanwood, Wash. C. of C., 1983; mem. U. Unitarian Ch., Gay, Lesbian, and Straight Edn. Network Amnesty Internat. Recipient 1st place newswriting award Wash. Newspaper Pubs. Assn., 1981, 82, 2d place award for comprehensive coverage, 1982, 3d place awards in newswriting, features and spot news, 1983, 2d place investigative reporting award Soc. Profl. Journalists, 1982. Mem. Soc. for Tech. Comm. (Puget Sound chpt.). Avocations: photography, Native American spiritual teachings, political research, philosophy. Home: 316 NW 86th St Seattle WA 98117-3125 Office: Envision Telephony Inc 615 2nd Ave Fl Dave4 Seattle WA 98104-2264 E-mail: seanm11@earthlink.net

MACKEY, THOMAS B. health facility administrator; COO Tenet Healthcare Corp., Santa Barbara, Calif., 1998—. Office: Tenet Healthcare Corp PO Box 31907 Santa Barbara CA 93130-1907

MACKIE, JERRY, state legislator, business owner; b. Ketchikan, Alaska, Jan. 10, 1962; s. Ralph P. Mackie and Marge (Thompson) Young; divorced; 1 child, John. Grad. high sch., Ketchikan. Chmn. bd. Shaan Seet Inc., Craig, Alaska, 1981-90; comml. fisherman Craig, 1985—; rep. Alaska State Legislature, Juneau, 1990-96; owner fishing lodge Craig, 1985—; mem. State Senate AK, Juneau, AK, 1996—. Bd. dirs. Alaska Fed. Natives, Anchorage. Recipient Pub. Svc. commendation USCG, 1987. Mem. Alaska Native Brotherhood, Moose. Democrat. Avocations: fishing, basketball, racquetball, skiing. Home: PO Box 240118 Douglas AK 99824-0118 Office: Alaska State Legislature State Capitol St Juneau AK 99801-1182

MACKINNON, PEGGY LOUISE, public relations executive; b. Florence, Ariz., June 18, 1945; d. Lacy Donald Gay and Goldie Louise (Trotter) Martin; m. Ian Dixon Mackinnon, Oct. 20, 1973. BA, San Jose State U., 1967, postgrad., 1968. Cert. secondary tchr., Calif. Tchr. Las Lomas H.S., Walnut Creek, Calif., 1968-69; edn. officer Ormond Sch., Sydney, Australia, 1970-72; tchr. Belconnen H.S., Canberra, Australia, 1972-73; temp. exec. sec. various orgns., London, 1973-75; mktg. mgr. Roadtown Wholesale, Tortola, British Virgin Islands, 1975-80; sr. v.p., gen. mgr. Hill & Knowlton Inc., Denver, 1981-96; pres. Peggy Mackinnon Inc., Denver, 1996—. Bd. dirs. Rocky Mountain Poison and Drug Found., Denver, 1984-87, Denver C. of C., Boy Scouts Am., Denver coun. Avocations: tennis, skiing, fishing, travel. Home and Office: Apt 21 9200 Cherry Creek South Dr Denver CO 80231-4018

MACKINNON, STEPHEN R. Asian studies administrator, educator; b. Columbus, Nebr., Dec. 2, 1940; s. Cyrus Leland and Helen (Wigglesworth) MacK.; m. Janice Carolyn Rachie, July 15, 1967 (dec. Sept. 1999); children: Rebecca, Cyrus R. BA, Yale U., 1963, MA, 1964; PhD, U. Calif., Davis, 1971. Acting instr. Chinese U., Hong Kong, 1968-69; dir. Asian Studies, prof. history Ariz. State U., Tempe, 1971—; vis. assoc. Chinese Acad. Social Sci., Beijing, 1979-81, 85. Mem. U.S. State Dept. Selection Bd., Washington, 1991, Nat. Com. on U.S.-China Rels., N.Y.C., 1991—; cons. PBS film documentary "Dragon and Eagle" on U.S.-China rels., San Francisco, 1986—. Author: (book) Power/Politics China, 1980; co-author: (books) Agnes Smedley, 1988, China Reporting, 1987; co-editor: (book) Chinese Women Revolution, 1976 (ALA notable book 1976), Scars of War, 2001; lectr. on China to local orgns. and TV, 1981—. Commr. Phoenix Sister Cities, 1986-91; bd. dirs. Com. on Fgn. Rels., Phoenix, 1988—; bd. dirs. Marshall Fund Ariz., 1995—. Rsch. fellow Am. Coun. Learned Socs., Hong Kong, 1978, Fulbright Found., India, 1977-78; rsch. sr. Com. on Scholarly Com. People's Republic China, Washington-Beijing, 1992. Mem. Assn. Asian Studies (bd. dirs. 1990-91), Am. Hist. Assn. (program com. 1990-91). Avocations: tennis, hiking, jazz. Office: Ariz State U History Dept Ctr Asian Studies Tempe AZ 85287-2501 E-mail: stephen.mackinnon@asu.edu

MACLACHLAN, DOUGLAS LEE, marketing educator; b. Hollywood, Calif., Aug. 27, 1940; s. Alexander D. and Patricia E. (Culver) MacL.; m. Natalie Bowditch Knauth, July 23, 1966; children: Heather Bowditch, Trevor Douglas. A.B. in Physics, U. Calif., Berkeley, 1962, M.B.A., 1965, M.A. in Stats., 1970, Ph.D. in Bus. Adminstrn, 1971; student, Hastings Sch. Law, 1965-66. Instr. bus. adminstrn. U. Calif., Berkeley, 1969-70; v.p. Hartec Corp., Newport Beach, Calif., 1965-70; acting asst. prof. U. Wash., Seattle, 1970-71, asst. prof., 1971-74, asso. prof., 1974-78, prof., chmn. dept. mktg. and internat. bus., 1978-86, prof., acting chair dept. mktg. and internat. bus., 1993-94, Affiliate Program Disting. prof. mktg. and internat. bus., 1986-88, Nordstrom prof. retail mktg., 1988-89, Ford Motor Co. prof. mktg., 1989-90, assoc. dean Sch. Bus., 1995-99. Vis. prof. bus. adminstrn. U. Calif., Berkeley, summer 1974; vis. prof. Institu Européen des Affaires, Fontainebleau, France, 1982-83, Cath. U. Leuven, Belgium, 1991-92; dir. Univ. Book Store, 1985—. Contbr. articles profl. jours.; editorial bd.: Jour. Mktg. Research, 1975-81. Mem. Am. Mktg. Assn. (dir. Puget Sound chpt. 1975-77, 90-91, pres. 1978-79), Informs, Am. Statis. Assn., Decision Scis. Inst., Assn. Consumer Research, Clan MacLachlan Soc. (pres. n.w. br. 1995—), Alpha Kappa Psi, Kappa Delta Rho. Home: 16305 Inglewood Rd NE Kenmore WA 98028-3908 Office: U Washington Box 353200 Seattle WA 98195-3200 E-mail: macl@u.washington.edu

MACLAUGHLIN, FRANCIS JOSEPH, lawyer; b. Davenport, Iowa, Oct. 5, 1933; s. Francis Joseph and Sylvia (Boone) MacL.; m. Joan Elizabeth Pfeiffer, Oct. 17, 1959; children: Lisa Ann, Christine Ann, Francis Joseph B.A., Yale U., 1955; J.D., U. Mich., 1958. Bar: Ill. 1958, Calif. 1963. Assoc. Graham, Califf, Harper & Benson, Moline, Ill., 1958-59, Lillick, McHose & Charles, Los Angeles, 1963-70, ptnr. L.A., 1970-90, White and Case, 1990—. Lt. USN, 1959-63 Mem. ABA, Calif. Bar Assn., Los Angeles County Bar Assn., Maritime Law Assn. U.S. Republican. Office: White & Case 633 W 5th St Ste 1900 Los Angeles CA 90071-2087

MACLEOD, ALEX, newspaper editor; b. Seattle; Student, Whitman Coll. Night reporter to city editor to asst. mng. editor-news Seattle Times, 1976-84, assoc. mng. editor, 1984-86, mng. editor, 1986—. Office: Seattle Times PO Box 70 Seattle WA 98111-0070

MACLEOD, HUGH ANGUS MCINTOSH, optical science educator, physicist, consultant; b. Glasgow, Scotland, June 20, 1933; came to U.S., 1979; s. John and Agnes (Maclure) M.; m. Ann Turner, May 25, 1957; children: Hugh, Ivor, Charles, Eleanor, Alexander. BSc with honors, U. Glasgow, 1954; D of Tech., Coun. for Nat. Acad. Awards, 1979; D honoris causa, U. Aix-Marseille, 1997. Chartered physicist. Grad. apprentice Sperry Gyroscope Co. Ltd., Brentford, Eng., 1954-56, engr., 1956-60; chief engr. Williamson Mfg. Co. Ltd., London, 1961-62; sr. physicist Mervyn Instruments Ltd., Woking, Eng., 1963; tech. mgr. Sir Howard Grubb Parsons & Co. Ltd., Newcastle upon Tyne, 1964-70; reader in thin-film physics Newcastle upon Tyne Poly., 1971-79; assoc. prof. U. Aix-Marseille III, France, 1979; prof. optical scis. U. Ariz., Tucson, 1979-95, prof. emeritus, 1995—; pres. Thin Film Ctr., Inc., Tucson, 1992—; dir. Precision Optics Corp., Inc., 1997—. Author: Thin-Film Optical Filters, 1986; editor Jour. Modern Optics, London, 1988-93; contbr. over 100 articles to profl. jours., chpts. to books. Fellow Inst. Physics (London), Optical Soc. Am. (dir.-at-large 1987-89, Esther Hoffman Beller award 1997), SPIE-Internat. Soc. Optical Engring. (Gold medal 1987), Am. Vacuum Soc., Soc. Vacuum Coaters, French Vacuum Soc. (John Matteucci award 2000, Internat. Conf. on Vacuum Web Coating). Anglican. Avocation: piano. Home: 2745 E Via Rotunda Tucson AZ 85716-5227 Office: Thin Film Ctr Inc 2745 E Via Rotonda Tucson AZ 85716-5227 E-mail: angus@thinfilmcenter.com

MACMILLAN, HOKE, state attorney general; m. Becky Klemt; children: Ryan Klemt, Christopher Klemt. BA, U. Wyo., 1967, JD, 1970. Bar: Wyo., Colo., Nebr., U.S. Ct. Appeals (10th cir.), U.S. Ct. Mil. Appeals, U.S. Supreme Ct. Capt. U.S. Army JAG, 1970—74; mem. Pence and Millett, Laramie, Wyo., 1974—2001, sr. ptnr., 1982—2001; atty. gen. State of Wyo., 2001—. Fellow: Am. Bar Found.; mem.: Wyo. State Bar (pres. 1996—97), Nebr. State Bar, Albany County Bar Assn. Office: Atty Gens Office 123 Capitol Bldg 200 W 24th St Cheyenne WY 82002*

MACMILLEN, RICHARD EDWARD, biological sciences educator, researcher; b. Upland, Calif., Apr. 19, 1932; s. Hesper Nichols and Ruth Henrietta (Golder) MacM.; m. Ann Gray, June 12, 1953 (div. 1975); children: Jennifer Kathleen, Douglas Michael; m. Barbara Jean Morgan, Oct. 23, 1980; 1 child, Ian Richard. BA, Pomona Coll., 1954; MS, U. Mich., 1956; PhD, UCLA, 1961. From instr. to assoc. prof. Pomona Coll., Claremont, Calif., 1960-68, Wig Disting. prof., 1965; assoc. prof., then prof. U. Calif., Irvine, 1968—, chair dept. population and environ. biology, 1972-74, chair dept. ecology and evolutionary biology, 1984-90; prof. emeritus, 1993—. Mem. award panel NSF, Washington, 1976-80; coord. U. Calif. Multi-Campus Supercourse in Environ. Biology, White Mountain Rsch. Sta., spring 1996, 97, tchg. participant, 1998—. Contbr. numerous articles to profl. jours. Chair sci. adv. bd. Endangered Habitats League, 1991-93. Recipient rsch. awards NSF, 1961-83; Fulbright-Hays advanced rsch. fellow Monash U., Australia, 1966-67. Fellow AAAS; mem. Am. Soc. Mammalogists (life), Ecol. Soc. Am. (cert. sr. ecologist), Am. Ornithologists Union, Cooper Ornithol. Soc. (life, bd. dirs. 1982-84). Democrat. Avocations: fly fishing, camping, hiking, nature photography. Home: 705 Foss Rd Talent OR 97540-9758 E-mail: bidmac@jeffnet.org

MACNAUGHTON, ANGUS ATHOLE, finance company executive; b. Montreal, July 15, 1931; s. Athole Austin and Emily Kidder (MacLean) MacN.; children: Gillian Heather, Angus Andrew. Student, Lakefield Coll. Sch., 1941-47, McGill U., 1949-54. Auditor Coopers & Lybrand, Montreal, 1949-55; acct. Genstar Ltd., Montreal, 1955, asst. treas., 1956-61, treas., 1961-64, v.p., 1964-70, exec. v.p., 1970-73, pres., 1973-76, vice chmn., chief exec. officer, 1976-81, chmn. or pres., chief exec. officer, 1981-86; pres. Genstar Investment Corp., 1987—. Bd. dirs. Can. Pacific Ltd., Sun Life Assurance Co. Can. (U.S.), Sun Life Ins. and Annuity Co. Can. (N.Y.), Barrick Gold Corp., Diversified Collection Svcs., Inc., Varian Semiconductor Assocs., Inc.; past pres. Montreal chpt. Tax Execs. Inst. Bd. govs. Lakefield Coll. Sch.; past chmn. San Francisco Bay Area coun. Boy Scouts Am.; bd. dirs. San Francisco Opera; trustee World Affairs Coun. of No. Calif. Mem. Pacific Union Club, World Trade Club, Villa Taverna (San Francisco), Mt. Royal Club (Montreal), Toronto Club. Address: Barrick Gold Corp 200 Bay St Ste 2700 Toronto ON Canada M5J 2J3 Office: 555 California St Fl 48 San Francisco CA 94104-1502

MAC NEIL, JOSEPH NEIL, archbishop; b. Sydney, N.S., Can., Apr. 15, 1924; s. John Martin and Kate (Mac Lean) Mac N. BA, St. Francis Xavier U., Antigonish, N.S., 1944; postgrad., Holy Heart Sem., Halifax, N.S., 1944-48, U. Perugia, , 1956, U. Chgo., 1964; JCD, U. St. Thomas, Rome, 1958. Ordained priest Roman Cath. Ch., 1948. Pastor parishes in, N.S., 1948-55; officialis Chancery Office, Antigonish, 1958-59; adminstrn. Diocese of Antigonish, 1959-60; rector Cathedral Antigonish, 1961; dir. extension dept. St. Francis Xavier U., Antigonish, 1961-69, v.p., 1962-69; bishop St. John, N.B., Can., 1969-73; chancellor U. St. Thomas, Fredericton, 1969-73; archbishop of Edmonton, Alta., 1973-99; ret., 1999. Chmn. Alta Bishops' Conf., 1973-99; chmn. bd. Newman Theol. Coll., Edmonton, 1973-99, St. Joseph's Coll. U. Alta., Edmonton, 1973-99. Vice chmn. N.S. Voluntary Econ. Planning Bd., 1965-69; bd. dirs. Program and Planning Agy., Govt. of N.S., 1969; exec. Atlantic Provinces Econ. Coun., 1968-73, Can. Coun. Rural Devel., 1965-75; bd. dirs. Futures Secretariat, 1981, Ctr. for Human Devel., Toronto, Ont., Can., 1985-95; mem. bd. mgmt. Edmonton Gen. Hosp., 1983-92, Edmonton Caritas Health Group, 1992-99; mem. Nat. Com. for Can. Participation in Habitat, 1976. Mem. Can. Assn. Adult Edn. (past pres. N.S.), Can. Assn. Dirs. Univ. Extension and Summer Schs. (past pres.), Inst. Rsch. on Pub. Policy (founding mem.), Can. Conf. Cath. Bishops (pres. 1979-81, mem. com. on ecumenism 1985-91, com. on missions 1991-96, mem. permanent coun. 1993-95). Office: Archbishop Emeritus Edmonton 8421 101st Ave Edmonton AB Canada T6A 0L1

MACNEILL, BRIAN F. retired oil and natural gas company executive; b. 1939; married; 4 children. B in Comms., Mont. State U., 1965. CPA. Acct. Haskins & Sells, San Francisco, 1967; v.p., treas. Hiram Walker Resources Ltd., 1980-82; v.p. fin., CFO, bd. dirs. Home Oil Co., Ltd., 1982-2001, retired, 2001. Pres. & CEO Enbridge, Inc., Calgary, 1990—; bd. dirs. Enbridge Inc., TD, Bank, Petro Can. (chmn.), Veritas, others. Mem. Fin. Execs. Inst., CICA, Calgary Petroleum Club, Calgary Golf & Country. Office: Enbridge Inc 2900 421 7th Ave SW Calgary AB Canada T2P 4K9

MACOVSKI, ALBERT, electrical engineering educator; b. N.Y.C., May 2, 1929; s. Philip and Rose (Winogr) M.; m. Adelaide Paris, Aug. 5, 1950; children: Michael, Nancy. BEE, City Coll. N.Y., 1950; MEE, Poly. Inst. Bklyn., 1953; PhD, Stanford U., 1968. Mem. tech. staff RCA Labs., Princeton, N.J., 1950-57; asst. prof., then assoc. prof. Poly. Inst. Bklyn., 1957-60; staff scientist Stanford Research Inst., Menlo Park, Calif., 1960-71; fellow U. Calif. Med. Center San Francisco, 1971-72; prof. elec. engring. and radiology Stanford U., 1972—, endowed chair, Canon USA prof. engring., 1991—. Dir. Magnetic Resonance Systems Research Lab.; cons. to industry. Author. Recipient Achievement award RCA Labs., 1952, 54; award for color TV circuits Inst. Radio Engrs., 1958; NIH spl. fellow, 1971 Fellow IEEE (Zworykin award 1973), Am. Inst. Med. Biol. Engring., Optical Soc. Am., Internat. Soc. Magnetic Resonance in Medicine (trustee 1991-94, gold medal 97); mem . NAE, Inst. Medicine, Am. Assn. Physicists in Medicine, Sigma Xi, Eta Kappa Nu. Jewish. Achievements include patents in field. Home: 2505 Alpine Rd Menlo Park CA 94025-6314 Office: Stanford U Dept Elec Engring Stanford CA 94305 E-mail: macovski@stanford.edu

MACPHAIL, JOY K. provincial agency administrator; b. Hamilton, Ont., Canada; one child, Jack. Degree in econs., U. Western Ont.; postgrad., London Sch. Econs. With Svc. Employees Internat. Union, Brit. Columbia Govt. Employees Union; economist, trade unionist Brit. Columbia Fedn. Labour; apptd. Min. Social Svcs., 1993—, Govt. House Leader, 1996—, Min. Health, 1996—, Min. Responsible for Srs. and B.C. Transit, 1996-98, Min. Fin. & Corp. Rels., Min. Resp. Transit, 1998-2000, Min. Labor and Dep. Premier, 2000—; dep. premier Min.'s Labour, 2000—. Chair standing com. on fin. and crown corps.; vice chair pub. accts. com.; co-chair legis. constitution com.; govt. caucus chair. Active Hastings Park, Vancouver Action Plan, Cmty. Svcs. Fund, VIEW Performing Arts Soc.; mem. Kidsafe Adv. Com. Office: Mins Office Rm 152 Parliament Bldgs Victoria BC Canada V8V 1X4

MACPHERSON, SHIRLEY, clinical therapist; b. Bayonne, N.J., June 16, 1934; d. Alexander Phillip and Milldred (Gurstelle) Gottlieb; m. Duncan MacPherson, Jan. 2, 1981; children from previous marriage: Suzanne Pugsley, Brett Barber. BS, Columbia U., NYU, 1951; MS, Juilliard Sch. Music, 1955; MEd, Calif. State U., Northridge, 1967; MA in Psychology, Pepperdine U., 1992; PhD in Psychology, Pacific Western U., 1998. Concert pianist Norman Seman Prodns., N.Y.C., 1952-61; indsl. health educator Am. Med. Internat., L.A., 1968-70; cons., lectr. Hosp. Mgmt. Corp., L.A., 1970-80; regional dir. Control Data Corp., L.A., 1980-86; outplacement specialist Ind. Cons., L.A., 1986-90; psychologist, intern Airport Marina Counseling Svcs., L.A., 1990-93; staff psychologist Forensic Psychology Assocs., Sherman Oaks, Calif., 1993-94; staff clin. psychologist Pacific Psychologist Assocs., L.A., 1992-94; clin. therapist employee profiling and crisis intervention MacPherson Relationship Counseling, L.A., 1993—. Author: Rx for Brides, 1990, Understanding Your Man, 1998. Vol. Cmty. Alliance to Support and Empower, L.A., 1994-96, South Bay Free Clinic, L.A., 1995-97; mem. Town and Gown Scholarship program, U. So. Calif., L.A. Mem. AAUW, APA, Calif. Psychol. Assn., L.A. Psychol. Assn., L.A World Affairs Coun., Am. Bd. Hypnotherapy, Am. Assn. Humanistic Psychology, Am. Assn. Suidiology, Juilliard Alumni Assn., Pepperdine Allumni Assn., Internat. Wound Ballistics Assn. Avocations: French and Italian, piano, studies. E-mail: Shirlmac@ix.netcom.com

MACTAVISH, CRAIG, professional hockey coach, former hockey player; b. London, Can., Aug. 15, 1958; Hockey player Boston Bruins Nat. Hockey League, 1980-85, hockey player Edmonton Oilers, 1985-94, hockey player N.Y. Rangers, 1994, hockey player Phila. Flyers, 1994-96, hockey player St. Louis Blues, 1996-97; asst. coach N.Y. Rangers, 1997-98, Edmonton Oilers, 1998—. Mem. Stanley Cup championship team 1987, 88, 90, 94; capt. Edmonton Oilers, 1992-93, 93-94. Office: Edmonton Oilers 11230 110 St Edmonton AB Canada T5G 3GB

MACUMBER, JOHN PAUL, insurance company executive; b. Macon, Mo., Jan. 21, 1940; s. Rolland Deardorf and Althea Villa (Cason) M.; m. Marilyn Sue Ashe, Nov. 10, 1962; children: Leanne, Cheryl. BA, Cen. Meth. Coll., Fayette, Mo., 1962; Assoc. in Risk Mgmt., Ins. Inst. Am., 1978. Casualty underwriter U.S. Fidelity & Guaranty Co., St. Louis, 1962-66; automobile underwriter Am. Indemnity Co., Galveston, Tex., 1966-69; auto casualty underwriter St. Paul Cos., New Orleans, 1969-73; sr. comml. casualty underwriter Chubb/Pacific Indemnity, Portland, Oreg., 1973-75; casualty underwriter Interstate Nat. Corp., L.A., 1975-76, underwriting supr., 1976-78, v.p., br. mgr. Mpls., 1978-82, also v.p. subs. Chgo. Ins. Co.; umbrella/spl. risk supr. Guaranty Nat. Ins. Co., Englewood, Colo., 1982-85; br. mgr. Burns & Wilcox Ltd.-West, Salt Lake City, 1985-96; v.p. M.J. Kelly Ins. Brokers of Utah, Sandy, 1997—. With USAF, 1962-68. Nat. Methodist scholar, 1958; named Co. Person of Yr. Profl. Ins. Agts. Utah, 1991, Ind. Ins. Agts. of Utah, 1996. Mem. Ins. Assn. Utah (sec.-treas. 1992-93, v.p. 1993-94, pres. 1994-95), Ind. Ins. Agts. Utah, Surplus Line Assn. Utah (bd. dirs. 1994-97, 99—, sec.-treas. 2000-2001, v.p. 2001—), Nat. Assn. Profl. Surplus Lines Offices, Utah Rock Art Rsch. Assn. (v.p. 2000-2001), Optimists (charter pres. 1968) (Friendswood, Tex.), Kiwanis (charter pres. 1979, Bloomington, Minn.), Insurance Club, Blue Goose Club (Salt Lake City). Mem. Unity Ch. of Salt Lake City (v.p., bd. dirs. 1988). Home and Office: 9683 Buttonwood Dr Sandy UT 84092-3245

MACY, RICHARD J. retired state supreme court justice; b. Saranac Lake, N.Y., June 2, 1930; m. Emily Ann Macy; children: Anne, Patty, Mark. BS in Bus., U. Wyo., 1955, JD, 1958. Pvt. practice, Sundance, Wyo., 1958-85; justice Wyo. Supreme Ct., Cheyenne, 1985—. Crook County atty., 1970-85; mem. Nat. Conf. Commrs. on Uniform State Laws, 1982—. Mem. Sigma Chi (Nat. Outstanding Sig award 1986).

MADDEN, PALMER BROWN, lawyer; b. Milw., Sept. 19, 1945; m. Susan L. Paulus, Mar. 31, 1984. BA, Stanford U., 1968; JD, U. Calif., Berkeley, 1973. Bar: Calif. 1973, U.S. Dist. Ct. (no. dist.) Calif. 1973, U.S. Supreme Ct. 1982. Ptnr. McCutchen, Doyle Brown & Enersen, Walnut Creek, 1985-98; prin. ADR Svcs., Alamo, Calif., 1999—. Pres. State Bar Bd. Govs., 2000-2001. Chair bd. govs. Continuing Edn. of the Bar, 1997; judge pro tem Contra Costa Superior Ct., 1991—; pres. Contra Costa Coun., 1995, Kennedy-King Found., 1994; bd. dirs. Episcopal Homes Found., 2001. Mem. Contra Costa County Bar Assn. (pres. 1996-97). Democrat. Episcopalian. Office: ADR Svcs 3000 Danville Blvd # 543 Alamo CA 94507

MADDEN, PAUL ROBERT, lawyer, director; b. St. Paul, Nov. 13, 1926; s. Ray Joseph and Margaret (Meyer) M.; m. Rosemary R. sorel, Aug. 7, 1974; children: Margaret Jane, William, James Patrick, Derek R. Sorel, Lisa T. Sorel. Student, St. Thomas Coll., 1944; AB, U. Minn., 1948; JD, Georgetown U., 1951. Bar: Ariz. 1957, Minn. 1951, D.C. 1951. Assoc. Hamilton & Hamilton, Washington, 1951-55; legal asst. to commr. SEC, Washington, 1955-56; assoc. Lewis and Roca, Phoenix, 1957-59, ptnr., 1959-90, Beus, Gilbert & Morrill, Phoenix, 1991-94, Chapman and Cutler, Phoenix, 1994-97; of counsel Gallagher & Kennedy, Phoenix, 1997—. Bd. dirs. Mesa Air Group, Inc., Phoenix, chmn., 1998-99. Sec. Minn. Fedn. Coll. Rep. Clubs, 1947-48; chmn. 4th dist. Minn. Young Rep. Club, 1948; nat. co-chmn. Youth for Eisenhower, 1951-52; mem. Ariz. Rep. Com., 1960-62; bd. dirs. Found. Jr. Achievement Ctrl. Ariz., Cath. Community Found., Phoenix, Heritage Hills Homeowners Assn., St. Joseph the Worker, past-pres. Attys. for Family-Held Enterprises; past bd. dirs., past chmn. Camelback Charitable Trust; past bd. dirs. The Samaritan Found., Phoenix; past bd. dirs., Ariz. Club, Phoenix, 1990-93; past bd. dirs., past chmn. Found. for Sr. Living; past bd. dirs., vice chmn. Cen. Ariz. chpt. ARC; past bd. dirs., past pres. Jr. Achievement Cen. Ariz., Inc.; mem. nat. bd. vis. U. Ariz. Law Sch. With USNR, 1946-48. Mem. ABA, Ariz. Bar Assn., Maricopa County Bar Assn., Fed. Bar Assn., Maricopa County Bar Assn., Fed. Bar Assn., Fedn. Ins. Counsel, The Barristers Club (Washington, Arizona Club, Phi Delta Phi. Home: 1190 Deer Run Rd Prescott AZ 86303 Office: Gallagher & Kennedy PA 2575 E Camelback Rd Phoenix AZ 85016-9225 E-mail: PRM@gknet.com

MADDEN, RICHARD BLAINE, forest products executive; b. Short Hills, N.J., Apr. 27, 1929; s. James L. and Irma (Twining) M.; m. Joan Fairbairn, May 24, 1958; children: John Richard, Lynne Marie, Kathryn Ann, Andrew Twining. B.S., Princeton U., 1951; J.D., U. Mich., 1956; M.B.A., NYU, 1959; PhD (hon.), St. Scholastica Coll., 1994. Bar: Mich. 1956, N.Y. 1958. Gen. asst. treas.'s dept. Socony Mobil Oil Corp., N.Y.C., 1956-57, spl. asst., 1958-59, fin. rep., 1960; asst. to pres. Mobil Chem. Co.; also dir. Mobil Chems. Ltd. of Eng., 1960-63; exec. v.p., gen. mgr. Kordite Corp.; also v.p. Mobil Plastics, 1963-66; v.p. Mobil Chem. Co., N.Y.C., 1966-68, group v.p., 1968-70; asst. treas. Mobil Oil Corp., 1970-71; chmn. Mobil Oil Estates Ltd., 1970-71; pres., chief exec. Potlatch Corp., San Francisco, 1971-77, chmn. chief exec. officer, 1977-94; ret., 1994. Bd. dirs. CNF Transp. Inc., URS Corp.; former bd. dirs. Potlatch Corp., PG&E Corp., Del Monte Corp., AMFAC Inc., Bank Calif. N.A. and BankCal Tri-State Corp.; from lectr. to adj. assoc. prof. fin. NYU, 1960-63; bd. dirs. Hospitaller; Order of Malta, Western Assn.; bd. govs., mem. adminstrv. compensation, audit & labor rels. com. San Francisco Symphony. Bd. dirs. Smith-Kettlewell Eye Rsch. Inst., trustee emeritus, former chmn. Am. Enterprise Inst.; former mem. bd. Nat. Park Found.; hon. trustee Com. for Econ. Devel. Lt. (j.g.) USNR, 1951-54. Mem. N.Y. Bar Assn., Mich. Bar Assn. Roman Catholic. Clubs: Bohemian (San Francisco); Lagunitas (Ross, Calif.); Metropolitan (Washington).

MADDOCK, JEROME TORRENCE, information services specialist; b. Darby, Pa., Feb. 7, 1940; s. Richard Cotton and Isobel Louise (Mezger) M.; m. Karen Rhueama Weygand, Oct. 2, 1965. BS in Biology, Muhlenberg Coll., 1961; MS in Info. Sci., Drexel U., 1968. Editorial assoc. Biol. Abstracts, Phila., 1962-63; mgr. rsch. info. Merck & Co., West Point, Pa., 1963-72; sr. cons. Auerbach Assocs., Inc., Phila., 1972-79; mgr. libr. and info. svcs. Solar Energy Rsch. Inst., Golden, Colo., 1979-88; mgr. info. svcs. Transp. Rsch. Bd., Washington, 1988-99; project mgr. IHS Enterprise, Boulder, Colo., 1999-01. Del. Gov.;s Conf. on Libr. and Info. Svc., Pa., 1978; mem. blue ribbon panel to select archivist of U.S., Washington, 1979; U.S. del. to ops. com. on transp. rsch. info. Orgn. for Econ. Cooperation and Devel., 1988-99. Bd. dirs. Paoli (Pa.) Pub. Libr., 1976-77. With USAFR, 1962-68. Mem. AAAS, Am. Soc. Info. Sci. (chmn. 1974-75), Elks, Beta Phi Mu, Pi Delta Epsilon. Republican. Episcopalian. Achievements include projection of information science operations 10 years into the future. Home: 545 W Laurel Ct Louisville CO 80027-1116 Office: IHS Enterprise 2585 Central Ave # 100 Boulder CO 80301-2851

MADDOX, LYN E. utilities company executive; Sr. v.p. PG&E Corp., San Francisco. Office: PG&E Corp Spear Tower Ste 2400 1 Market San Francisco CA 94105

MADHAVAN, MURUGAPPA CHETTIAR, economics educator, international consultant; b. Kandramanickam, Tamilnadu, India, Dec. 17, 1932; came to U.S., 1960; s. L. Murugappa Chettiar and Adaikkammai Achi (Meyyappan) M.; m. Nachammai Manickam, May 3, 1953; children: Nachiappa, Nataraj. BA with honors, Annamalai U., India, 1955, MA, 1958; MS, U. Wis., 1963, PhD, 1969. Lectr. in econs. Annamalai U., 1955-60; economist Europe and Mid. East World Bank, Washington, 1963-66, asst. sec. econ. com., 1966-68; dir. Ctr. for Rsch. in Econ. Devel. San Diego State U., 1969-85, prof. econs., 1974—, dir. Asian Studies, 1991-2000, chmn. dept. Asian Studies, 1999-2000. Prof. econs. Nat. Inst. Bank Mgmt., Bombay, 1971-72; vis. prof. econs. Indian Inst. Tech., Madras, 1979-80; Father Carty Meml. lectr. U. Madras, 1980; vis. Fulbright prof. U. of the Philippines, 1987-88; cons. UN Devel. Program, N.Y.C., 1987-88, Gen. Atomics, San Diego, 1993-99; advisor Gov. Sim Grinio, The Philippines, 1988; vis. Fulbright prof.; Fulbright sr. specialist Faculty of Law and Econ. Svcs., Phnom Penh, Cambodia, summer 2001. Co-author: The Transfer of Knowledge Through Expatriate Nationals, 1988. Chmn. World Affairs Coun. San Diego, 1991-93; pres. Tamil Nadu Found., Inc., Chgo., 1985-87, life mem.; advisor Mingei Internat. Mus., San Diego, 1985—; pres. San Diego Indian Am. Soc., 1984-99. Fulbright fellow, 1960; recipient Hon. Am. award Ams. by Choice, 1987, Leadership and Contbn. award Tamil Nadu Found., 1994; Fulbright sr. scholar

Fulbright Program in Ho Chi Minh City, U. Econs., 2000, U. Putra Malaysia, 2000. Mem. Am. Econ. Assn., Indian Econ. Assn. (life), Assn. Indian Econ. Studies (life). Democrat. Avocations: reading, walking, organizational activities. Home: 8727 Verlane Dr San Diego CA 92119-2033 Office: San Diego State U Coll Arts & Letters Ctr Asian Studies San Diego CA 92182 E-mail: madhavan@mail.sdsu.edu

MADISON, JAMES RAYMOND, lawyer; b. White Plains, N.Y., Apr. 27, 1931; s. Raymond S. and Katherine (Sherwin) M.; m. Mary Massey, Sept. 19, 1953; children: Michael, Matthew, Molly. BS, Stanford U., 1953, LLB, 1959. Bar: Calif. 1960, U.S. Dist. Ct. (no. dist.) Calif. 1960, U.S. Ct. Appeals (9th cir.) 1960, U.S. Dist. Ct. (ctrl. dist.) Calif. 1970, U.S. Supreme Ct. 1973, U.S. Dist. Ct. (ea. dist.) Calif. 1981, U.S. Dist. Ct. (so. dist.) Calif. 1988. Assoc. Orrick, Herrington & Sutcliffe, San Francisco, 1959-67, ptnr., 1968-95; pvt. practice Menlo Park, Calif., 1996—. Trustee Antioch U., Yellow Springs, Ohio, 1980-87; bd. dirs. Planned Parenthood Alameda/San Francisco, 1984-89; pres. Calif. Dispute Resolution Coun., 2001. Lt. (j.g.) USN, 1953-56. Mem. ABA, ASCE, State Bar Calif., Bar Assn. San Francisco, San Mateo County Bar Assn., Am. Arbitration Assn. (large complex case panel arbitrators and mediators, No. Calif. regional adv. coun.). Democrat. Episcopalian. Avocation: soccer. Office: 750 Menlo Ave Ste 250 Menlo Park CA 94025-4758 E-mail: jrmcoach@aol.com

MADIX, ROBERT JAMES, chemical engineer, educator; b. Beach Grove, Ind., June 22, 1938; s. James L. and Marjorie A. (Strohl) M.; children: Bradley Alan, David Eric, Micella Lynn, Evan Scott. BS, U. Ill., 1961; PhD, U. Calif., 1964. NSF postdoctoral fellow Max Planck Inst., Göttingen, Fed. Republic of Germany, 1964-65; asst. prof, chem. engr. Stanford (Calif.) U., 1965-72, assoc. prof., chem. engr., 1972-77; prof. chem. engring. Stanford U., 1977—, chmn., chem. engr., 1983-87, prof. chemistry, 1981—. Cons. Monsanto Chem., St. Louis, 1975-84, Shell Oil Co., Houston, 1985-86; Peter Debye lectureship Cornell U., 1985; Eyring lectr. chemistry Ariz. State U., 1990; Barnett Dodge lectr. Yale U., 1996; disting. prof. lectr. U. Tex., Austin, 1980; Walter Robb Disting. lectr. Penn State U., 1996; chmn. Gordon Rsch. Conf. on Reactions on Surfaces, 1995. Assoc. editor Catalysis Rev., 1986—, Catalysis Letters, 1992—, Rsch. on Chem. Intermediates, 1994—; contbr. articles to profl. jours. Recipient Alpha Chi Sigma award AIChemE, 1990, Paul Emmett award Catalysis Soc. N.Am., 1984, Humboldt U.S. Sr. Scientist prize, 1978; Ford Found. fellow, 1969-72. Mem. AIChE, Internat. Precious Metal Inst. (Henry J. Alber award 1997), Am. Chem. Soc. (Irving Langmuir Disting. Lectr. award 1981, Arthur Adamson award 1997, Am. Phys. Soc., Am. Vacuum Soc., Calif. Catalysis Soc. Office: Stanford Univ Dept Chemical Engring Stanford CA 94305-5025

MADONNA, (MADONNA LOUISE VERONICA CICCONE), singer, actress; b. Bay City, Mich., Aug. 16, 1958; d. Sylvio and Madonna Ciccone; m. Sean Penn, Aug. 16, 1985 (div. 1989); 1 child, Lourdes. Student, U. Mich., 1976-78. Dancer Alvin Ailey Dance Co., N.Y.C., 1979; CEO Maverick Records, L.A. Albums include Madonna, 1983, Like a Virgin, 1985, True Blue, 1986, (soundtrack)Who's That Girl, 1987, (with others) Vision Quest Soundtrack, 1983, You Can Dance, 1987, Like a Prayer, 1989, I'm Breathless: Music From and Inspired by the Film Dick Tracy, 1990, The Immaculate Collection, 1990, Erotica, 1992, Bedtime Stories, 1994, Something to Remember, 1995, Ray of Light, 1998 (Grammy award for Best Pop Album 1999), (with others) Austin Powers, The Spy Who Shagged Me soundtrack, 1999; film appearances include A Certain Sacrifice, 1980, Vision Quest, 1985, Desperately Seeking Susan, 1985, Shanghai Surprise, 1986, Who's That Girl, 1987, Bloodhounds of Broadway, 1989, Dick Tracy, 1990, Truth or Dare, 1991, Madonna, 1992, Body of Evidence, 1992, A League of Their Own, 1992, Dangerous Game, 1993, Blue in the Face, 1995, Four Rooms, 1996, Girl 6, 1996, Evita, 1996 (Golden Globe, 1997); Broadway theater debut in Speed-the-Plow, 1987, TV Happy Birthday Elizabeth: A Celebration of a Life, 1997, The Next Best Thing, 2000; author: Sex, 1992. Roman Catholic. Office: 8491 W Sunset Blvd Ste 485 West Hollywood CA 90069-1911 Address: Maverick Recording Co 9348 Civic Center Dr Ste 100 Beverly Hills CA 90210-3606

MADRID, DON, electronics executive; CFO Fry's Electronics, San Jose, Calif. Office: Fry's Electronics 600 E Brokaw Rd San Jose CA 95112-1006

MADRID, PATRICIA A. state attorney general, lawyer; b. Sept. 25, 1946; BA in English and Philosophy, U. N.Mex., 1969, JD, 1973; cert., Nat. Jud. Coll., U. Nev., 1978. Bar: N.Mex. 1973. Ptnr. Messina, Madrid & Smith, P.A., Albuquerque, 1984-88; atty. gen. State of N.Mex., 1999—. Editor N.Mex. Law Rev., 1972-73. Bd. dirs. Fechin Art Inst., Taos, N.Mex.; dem. nominee Lt. Gov. N.Mex., 1994. Hon. Commdr. award USAF, 1979, award of yr. Albuquerque Bus. and Profl. Women; named Outstanding Young Women of Am., 1980-81; recipient Gov.'s award Outstanding N.Mex. Women, 1993. Mem. Hispanic Women's Coun. of N.Mex. (bd. dirs. 1989), Mex. Am. Legal Def. and Ednl. Fund (bd. dirs. 1989). Office: Atty Gens Office PO Drawer 1508 Santa Fe NM 87504-1508

MADSEN, BARBARA A, state supreme court justice; Justice Washington Supreme Ct., Olympia.

MADSEN, REGINALD B. protective services official; b. Neopit, Wis., Sept. 15, 1940; married; 2 children. AAS, Clark Coll., Vancouver, Wash., 1967. Police officer Vancouver (Wash.) Police Dept., 1966-68; supt. Oreg. State Police Dept., Salem, 1968-93, retired, 1993; U.S. marshal U.S. Marshals Svc., Dept. Justice, Portland, 1994—. With USN, 1958-64. Office: Mark O Hatfield US Courthouse 100 SW 3d Ave Rm 401 Portland OR 97204

MADSEN, SUSAN ARRINGTON, writer; b. Logan, Utah, Aug. 25, 1954; d. Leonard J. and Grace F. Arrington; m. Dean Madsen, Aug. 20, 1974; children: Emily, Rebecca, Sarah, Rachel. BS in Journalism, Utah State U., 1975. Mem. adj. faculty Logan Latter-day Saints Inst. Religion, 1991-95. Author: Christmas: A Joyful Heritage, 1984, The Lord Needs a Prophet, 1990, I Walked to Zion: True Stories of Young Pioneers on the Mormon Trail, 1994, Growing Up in Zion: True Stories of Young Pioneers Building the Kingdom, 1996, The Second Rescue: The Story of the Spiritual Rescue of the Willie and Martin Handcart Pioneers, 1998, (with Leonard J. Arrington) Sunbonnet Sisters: True Stories of Mormon Women and Frontier Life, 1984, Mothers of the Prophets, 1987; contbr. numerous articles to Collier's Ency. Yearbooks. Chair Hyde Pk. (Utah) Bd. Adjustments, 1985-94. Honoree Utah State U. Nat. Women's History Week, 1985; recipient Cmty. Svc. award Nat. Daus. Utah Pioneers, 1990. Mem. LDS Ch. Avocations: horseback riding, snow skiing, genealogy, family activities.

MAEHL, WILLIAM HENRY, historian, university administrator, educational consultant; b. Chicago Heights, Ill., June 13, 1930; s. William Henry and Marvel Lillian (Carlson) M.; m. Audrey Mae Ellsworth, Aug. 25, 1962; 1 child, Christine Amanda. B.A., U. Minn., 1950, M.A., 1951; postgrad (Fulbright fellow), King's Coll., U. Durham, Eng., 1955-56; Ph.D., U. Chgo., 1957; LHD (hon.), Fielding Inst., 1993. Asst. prof. Montclair (N.J.) State Coll., 1957-58; asst. prof. Washington Coll., Chestertown, Md., 1958-59, U. Okla., Norman, 1959-64, asso. prof., 1964-70, prof. English history, 1970-86; dean Coll. Liberal Studies, 1976-86, vice provost for continuing edn. and public service, 1979-86; pres. The Fielding Inst., Santa Barbara, Calif., 1987-93, pres. emeritus, 1993—. Prin. investigator Project for a Nation of Lifelong Learners, Regents Coll., Albany, N.Y., 1994-97; vis. prof. U. Nebr., summer 1965; vis. fellow Wolfson Coll. Oxford (Eng.) U., spring 1975; fellow Salzburg Seminar in Am. Studies, 1976. Author: The Reform Bill of 1832, 1967, Lifelong Learning at Its Best: Innovative Practices in Adult Credit Programs, 2000; editor: R.G. Gammage, Chartist Reminiscences, 1981, Continuum: Jour. of the Nat. Continuing Edn. Assn., 1980-83, also articles. Bd. dirs. Alliance for Alternative Degree Programs, 1988-90; trustee Coun. for Adult and Exptl. Learning, 1990-94; mem. coun. Nat. Ctr. for Adult Learning, 1990—; trustee Southwestern Coll., 2000—. Leverhulme Research fellow, 1961-62; grantee Am. Philos. Soc., 1961-62, 67-68, 71, 76 Fellow Royal Hist. Soc., Assn. of Grad. Liberal Studies Programs; mem. Conf. on Brit. Studies, Soc. for Study Labour History. Office: PO Box 6580 Santa Fe NM 87502-6580 E-mail: wmaehl2@cs.com

MAES, PETRA JIMENEZ, state supreme court justice; widowed; 4 children. BA, U. N.Mex., 1970, JD, 1973. Bar: N.Mex. 1973. Pvt. pratice law, Albuquerque, 1973-75; rep., then office mgr. No. N.Mex. Legal Svcs., 1975-81; dist. judge 1st Jud. Dist. Ct., Santa Fe, Los Alamos, 1981-98; chief judge, 1984-87, 92-95; state supreme ct. justice Supreme Ct. N.Mex., 1998—. Active S.W. coun. Boy Scouts Am., mem. dist. coms.; presenter pre cana St. John's Cath. Ch.; bd. dirs. Nat. Ctr. on Women and Family Law; chairperson Tri-County Gang Task Force; mem. Gov.'s Task Force on Children and Families, 1991-92; mem. adv. com. Santa Fe County Jail, 1996. Mem. N.Mex. Bar Assn. (elderly law com. 1980-81, alternative dispute resolution com. 1987-92, code of jud. conduct com. 1992—, juvenile cmty. corrections svcs. com. chairperson), Hispanic Women's Coun. (charter). Office: Supreme Court NMex PO Box 848 Santa Fe NM 87504-0848

MAES, ROMAN M., III, state legislator, lawyer; BA, N.Mex. Highlands U.; JD, U. Denver. Mem. N.Mex. Senate, Dist. 25, Santa Fe, 1998—; mem. corps. and transp. com. N.Mex. Senate, Santa Fe, mem. ways and means com. Real estate property mgr.; investment cons. Democrat. Office: 1488 S Saint Francis Dr Ste B Santa Fe NM 87505-4096

MAESTRONE, FRANK EUSEBIO, diplomat; b. Springfield, Mass., Dec. 20, 1922; s. John Battista and Margaret Carlotta (Villanova) M.; m. Jo Colwell, Jan. 20, 1951; childen: Mark, Anne. BA, Yale U., 1943; grad., Naval War Coll., 1963. With Fgn. Svc., Dept. State, 1948-84; assigned to Vienna and Salzburg, Austria, 1948, 54, Hamburg, Germany, 1949, Khorramshahr, Iran, 1960; with NATO, Paris, 1963, Brussels, 1968-71; counselor of embassy for polit. affairs Am. Embassy, Manila, 1971-73; Dept. State adviser to pres. Naval War Coll., 1973; min.-counselor Am. Embassy, Cairo, 1974, amb. to Kuwait, 1976-79; diplomat-in-residence U. Calif., San Diego, 1979; spl. rep. to Pres., dir. U.S. Ainai Support Mission, 1980; exec. dir. World Affairs Coun., San Diego, 1984-86, now bd. dirs.; adj. prof. internat. rels., amb.-in-residence U.S. Internat. U., San Diego, 1986-90. Mem. adv. bd. Hansen Inst. for World Peace, San Diego State U. Found. With AUS, 1943-46. Decorated chevalier du Merite Agricole (France). Mem. Internat. Inst. Strategic Studies. E-mail: fmaestrone@juno.com

MAFFEI, GREG, computer company executive; AB, Dartmouth Coll.; MBA, Harvard U. Dir. bus. devel. and investments Microsoft, 1993-94, treas., 1994—, v.p. corp. devel., 1996—, CFO, 1997—; pres., CEO 360 networks, Inc., Vancouver, B.C., 2000—. Bd. dirs. Citrix Sys., Comcast, CORT Bus. Svcs., Mtel. Baker scholar. Office: 360networks Inc 1500 1066 W Hastings St Redmond WA 98052-6399 also: 360 networks Inc 1500 1066 W Hastings St Vancouver BC Canada V6E 3X1

MAFFRE, MURIEL, ballet dancer; b. Enghien, Val D'Oise, France, Mar. 19, 1966; came to U.S., 1990; d. Bernard and Monique (Berteaux) M. Diploma, Paris Opera Ballet Sch., 1981; Baccalauréat (hon.), France, 1984. Dancer Hamburg Ballet, Fed. Republic Germany, 1983-84; soloist Sarragoza Ballet, Spain; premiere danseuse Monte Carlo Ballet, Monaco, 1985-90; prin. dancer San Francisco Ballet, 1990—. Guest artist with Berlinor Staatsoper and Lines Contemporary Ballet. Recipient 1st prize Nat. Conservatory, Paris, 1983, Grand prize and Gold medal Paris Internat. Ballet Competition, 1984, Isadora Duncan award, 1990. Office: San Francisco Ballet 455 Franklin St San Francisco CA 94102-4471

MAGADAN, DAVID JOSEPH, professional baseball player; b. Tampa, Fla., Sept. 30, 1962; children: Jordan, Christian. Student, U. Ala. 1st baseman-3d baseman N.Y. Mets, N.Y.C., 1986-92, Fla. Marlins, Miami, 1993; 1st-baseman-3d-baseman-designated hitter Seattle Mariners, 1993; 1st baseman-3d baseman Fla. Marlins, 1994, Houston Astros, 1995; 1st baseman-3d baseman-designated hitter Oakland (Calif.) Athletics, 1997-99, San Diego Padres, 1999—. Drafted Boston Red Sox, 1980, declined; led U. Ala. to championship game 1983 Coll. World Series, 1983, led NCAA Divsn. 1 with .525 batting average, 1983. Chmn. No Small Affair-South. Recipient Payson award for humanitarian svc., N.Y. chpt. Baseball Writers' Assn. Am.; recipient USA Baseball Golden Spikes award, 1983, named Coll. Player of Yr., Baseball Am., 1983, named All-Southeast Conf. Office: c/o San Diego Padres PO Box 2000 San Diego CA 92112-2000

MAGELITZ, LARRY L. construction company executive; CFO Dillingham Constrn. Corp., Pleasanton, Calif. Office: Dillingham Constrn Corp 5960 Inglewood Drive Pleasanton CA 94588

MAGER, ARTUR, retired aerospace company executive, consultant; b. Nieglowice, Poland, Sept. 21, 1919; arrived in U.S., 1939, naturalized, 1944; s. Herman and Ella (Kornbluh) M.; m. Phyllis R. Weisman, Aug. 19, 1942; 1 child Ilana Gail. BS, U. Mich., 1943; MS, Case Inst. Tech., 1951; PhD in Aeros., Calif. Inst. Tech., 1953. Aero. rsch. scientist NASA Lewis Labs., Cleve., 1946-51; rsch. scientist Marquardt Corp., Van Nuys, Calif., 1954-60; dir. Nat. Engring. Sic. Co., Pasadena, 1960-61; dir. spacecraft scis. Aerospace Corp., El Segundo, 1961-64, gen. mgr. applied mechanics divsn., 1964-68, v.p., gen. mgr. engring. sci. ops., 1968-78, v.p. engring. group, 1978-82, cons., 1982—. Mem. BSD Re-entry Panel, 1961—63; mem. NASA com. missile and space vehicle aerodynamics, 1963—65; mem. adv. com. AFML, 1971—72; mem. NASA Adv. Coun., 1982—86; chmn. NASA Space Applications Adv. Com., 1982—86; mem. Aeros. and Space Engring. Bd. NRC, 1982—87; mem. Space Sta. Task Force NRC, 1983—87, mem. Shuttle Critically and Hazard Analysts Rev. Bd., 1986—88; mem. DSB NASP Task Force, 1987—88, AFSB Hypersonic Task Force, 1987—88. Contbr. articles to profl. jours. Mem. alumni fund coun. Calif. Inst. Tech., 1972—74; trustee West Coast U., 1980—92; mem. devel. disabilities bd. Area X, 1976—80, chmn., 1976—78; 1st v.p. Calif. Assn. Retarded, 1983—85; pres. Exceptional Children's Found., 1970—72; bd. councilors U. So. Calif. Sch. Engring., 1976—86. Recipient Disting. Alumni award, U. Mich., 1969, Golden Rule award, Calif. Assn. Retarded, 1977, 1989. Fellow: AIAA (chmn. L.A. sect. 1967—68, bd. dirs. 1975—77, pres. 1980—81), AAAS, Inst. Advanced Engring.; mem.: Sigma Xi, Technion Soc., Nat. Acad. Engring. Home and Office: 1353 Woodruff Ave Los Angeles CA 90024-5129 E-mail: mager@icnt.net

MAGLICH, BOGDAN CASTLE, physicist; b. Yugoslavia; came to U.S., 1956, naturalized, 1972; s. Cveta and Ivanka (Bingulac) M.; children: Marko Castle, Ivanka Taylor, Roberta Cveta, Angelica Dara, Aleksandra Mara Nadine. Diploma physics, U. Belgrade, 1951; MS, U. Liverpool, Eng., 1955; PhD, MIT, 1959. Staff mem. Lawrence Berkeley Lab., 1959-62; dep. group leader Brit. group, 1962-63; leader Swiss group CERN European Orgn. Nuclear Rsch., 1964-67; vis. prof., joint faculty mem. Princeton U.-U. Pa. accelerator U. Pa., 1967-69; prof. physics, prin. investigator high energy physics Rutgers U., 1969-74; pres., chmn. Fusion Energy Corp., Princeton, N.J., 1972-81, Aneutronix, Inc., 1982-83, Sci. Transfer Assocs., Inc., 1981-84, United Scis., Inc., 1984-87, AE Labs Aneutronic Energy Lab., Inc., 1986-88; pres. Advanced Physics Corp., 1988-94; chmn. Advanced Projects Group, Inc., 1994—, HiEnergy Microdevices, Ltd., 1995—. Chmn. The Tesla Found., 1985—; resident scientist UN-ILO Seminar Econ. Devel. East Africa, Kenya, 1967; lectr. Postdoctoral Sch. Physics, Yerevan, USSR, 1965, Internat. Sch. Majorana, Italy, 1969; mem. U.S. delegation Internat. Conf. High Energy Physics, Vienna, 1968, Kiev, 1970; spl. rep. of U.S. Pres. to Yugoslavia, 1976; sci. project dir. Univ. Research Ctr., King Abdulaziz U., Saudi Arabia, 1981-82; prin. investigator for aneutronic energy USAF Weapons Lab., 1985-87, USAF Space Tech. Ctr., 1988-89. Editor: Adventures in Exptl. Physics, 1972-80, Living Physics Video Jour. Chmn. Yugoslav-Am. Bicentennial Com., 1975-76; co-chmn. Serbian-Am. Com. for a Dem. Yugoslavia, 1989—; pres. World Serbian Union, Geneva, 1990-92. Recipient White House citation, 1961; Bourgeois d'honneur de Lens Switzerland, 1973; UNESCO fellow, 1957-58 Fellow Am. Phys. Soc.; mem. Serbian Acad. Scis. and Arts (Yugoslavia), Ripon Soc. (bd. govs.), Nassau Club, MIT Club, Sigma Xi. Mem. Serbian Orthodox Ch. Achievements include discovering omega-meson, sonic spark chamber, missing-mass spectrometer, delta-meson, g-meson, S, T and U-mesons, precetron, self collider migma, aneutronic energy process, superserver and microserver, atometry, and neutron microscope; patentee in field. E-mail: maglich2@aol.com

MAGNESS, RHONDA ANN, microbiologist; b. Stockton, Calif., Jan. 30, 1946; d. John Pershing and Dorothy Waneta (Kelley) Wetter; m. Barney LeRoy Bender, Aug. 26, 1965 (div. 1977); m. Gary D. Magness, Mar. 5, 1977; children: Jay D. (dec.), Troy D. BS, Calif. State U., 1977. Lic. clin. lab. scientist Nat. Cert. Agy., Calif., med. technologist; cert. clin. lab. scientist. Med. asst. C. Fred Wilcox, MD, Stockton, 1965-66; clk. typist Dept. of U.S. Army, Ft. Eustis, Va., 1967, Def. Supply Agy., New Orleans, 1967-68; med. asst. James G. Cross, MD, Lodi, Calif., 1969, Arthur A. Kemalyan, MD, Lodi, 1969-71, 72-77; med. sec. Lodi Meml. Hosp., 1972; lab. aide Calif. State U., Sacramento, 1977; phlebotomist St. Joseph's Hosp., Stockton, 1978-79; supr. microbiology Dameron Hosp. Assn., Stockton, 1980—. Active Concerned Women Am., Washington, 1987—. Mem. Calif. Assn. Clin. Lab. Technologists, San Joaquin County Med. Assts. Assn., Nat. Geog. Soc., Nat. Audubon Soc., San Francisco Offshore. Baptist. Lodge: Jobs Daus. (chaplain 1962-63). Avocations: boating, birding, sewing, reading. Home: 9627 Knight Ln Stockton CA 95209-1961 Office: Dameron Hosp Lab 525 W Acacia St Stockton CA 95203-2405 E-mail: gnrmagness@aol.com

MAGOWAN, PETER ALDEN, professional baseball team executive, grocery chain executive; b. N.Y.C., Apr. 5, 1942; s. Robert Anderson and Doris (Merrill) M.; m. Jill Tarlau (div. July 1982); children: Kimberley, Margot, Hilary; m. Deborah Johnston, Aug. 14, 1982 BA, Stanford U., 1964; MA, Oxford U., Eng., 1966; postgrad., Johns Hopkins U., 1967-68. Store mgr. Safeway Stores Inc., Washington, 1968-70, dist. mgr. Houston, 1970-71, retail ops. mgr. Phoenix, 1971-72, divsn. mgr. Tulsa, 1973-76, mgr. internat. divsn. Toronto, Ont., Can., 1976-78, mgr. western region San Francisco, 1978-79, CEO Oakland, Calif., 1980-93, chmn. bd. dirs., 1980-98; pres., mng. gen. ptnr. San Francisco Giants, 1993—. Bd. dirs. Daimler Chrysler Corp., Caterpillar, Safeway Inc. Office: San Francisco Giants 24 Willie Mays Plz San Francisco CA 94107-2199

MAGUIRE, JOHN DAVID, academic administrator, educator, writer; b. Montgomery, Ala., Aug. 7, 1932; s. John Henry and Clyde (Merrill) M.; m. Lillian Louise Parrish, Aug. 29, 1953; children: Catherine Merrill, Mary Elizabeth, Anne King. A.B. magna cum laude, Washington and Lee U., 1953, Litt.D. (hon.), 1979; Fulbright scholar, Edinburgh (Scotland) U., 1953-54; B.D. summa cum laude, Yale, 1956, Ph.D., 1960; postdoctoral research, Yale U. and U. Tübingen, Germany, 1964-65, U. Calif., Berkeley, 1968-69, Silliman U., Philippines, 1976-77; HLD (hon.), Transylvania U., 1990. Dir. Internat. Student Ctr., New Haven, 1956-58; mem. faculty Wesleyan U., Middletown, Conn., 1960-70, asso. provost, 1967-68; vis. lectr. Pacific Sch. Religion and Grad. Theol. Union, Berkeley, 1968-69; pres. SUNY Coll. at Old Westbury, 1970-81, Claremont (Calif.) Grad. U., 1981-98. Sr. fellow Claremont Grad. U. Sch. Politics and Econs.; dir. nat. project Renewing Democracy through Interracial/Multicultural Comty. Bldg., 1998—. Author: The Dance of the Pilgrim: A Christian Style of Life for Today, 1967; also numerous articles. Mem. Conn. adv. comt. US Comn. Civil Rights , 1961—70; participant White House Conf. on Civil Rights, 1966; advisor Martin Luther King Cent. Social Change, Atlanta, 1968—, permanent trustee, 1968—, 1st chmn. bd. dirs., 1968—; bd. dirs. Nassau County Health and Welfare Coun. , 1971—81, pres., 1974—76; trustee United Bd. Christian Higher Ed in Asia, 1975—81, Inst. Int. Ed. , 1980—86; charter trustee Tom+200s Rivera Policy Inst., Claremont, Calif., 1984—, vice chmn., 1987—94, treas., 1995—; with Asn. Ind. Calif. Cols. and Univs. , 1985—98; chmn. Asn. Ind. Calif. Cols. and Univs., 1990—92, mem. exec. comt., 1992—98; with Calif. Achievement Coun., 1985—94, chmn., 1990—94; with Transylvania Univ. Bingham Trust, 1987—, Lincoln Found. and Lincoln Inst. Land Policy, Inc., 1987—94; The JL Found., 1988—; with Bus. Enterprise Trust, 1989—; with Educ. Found. African Ams., 1991—99; bd. dirs. Asn. Am. Cols. and Univs., 1981—86, chmn., 1984—85; bd. dirs. Legal Def. and Edu. Fund NAACP, 1991—, west coast div., 1981—91, Thacher Sch. , Ojai, Calif., 1982—94, vice chmn., 1986—90; with Salzburg Seminar, 1992—96; charter mem. Pacific Coun. Int. Policy , 1995—; mem. Am. Comt. US-Soviet Rels., 1981—92, Blue Ribbon Calif. Comn. Teaching Profession , 1984—86; mem. gov. coun. Aspen Inst. Wye Faculty Seminar, 1984—94; mem. Coun. Fgn. Rels., 1983—; mem. adv. bd. RAND Cent. Research Immigration Policy, 1994—, Peter F. Drucker Found. Non-Profit Mgt , 1990—, Andrew Young Sch. Policy Ga. State Univ., 1999—, The Eureka Communities , 1998—; mem. Pres.'s Adv. Coun. Comn. on Calif. Master Plan Higher Educ. , 1986—87, Los Angeles Educ. Alliance Restructuring Now, 1992—98, Calif. Bus. Higher Educ. Forum, 1992—98. Recipient Julia A. Archibald High Scholarship award Yale Div. Sch., 1956; Day fellow Yale Grad. Sch., 1956-57; Kent fellow, 1957-60; Howard Found. postdoctoral fellow Brown U. Grad. Sch., 1964-65; Fenn lectr., 7 Asian countries, 1976-77; recipient Conn. Prince Hall Masons' award outstanding contbns. human rights in Conn., 1965; E. Harris Harbison Gt. Tchr. prize Danforth Found., 1968 Fellow Soc. Values Higher Edn. (pres. 1974-81, bd. dirs. 1972-88); mem. Phi Beta Kappa, Omicron Delta Kappa Democrat. Office: Claremont Grad U Inst for Dem Renewal 170 E 10th St Claremont CA 91711-5909

MAGUIRE, ROBERT FRANCIS, III, real estate investor; b. Portland, Oreg., Apr. 18, 1935; s. Robert Francis Jr. and Jean (Shepard) M. B.A., UCLA, 1960. Vice pres. Security Pacific Nat. Bank, L.A., 1960-64; chmn. Maguire Thomas Ptnrs., L.A., 1964—. Exec. bd. med. scis. UCLA. Bd. dirs. Los Angeles County Mus. Art; trustee UCLA Found., Bard Coll.; bd. dirs. St. John's Hosp., Music Ctr. Bd. Govs., Calif. Clubs: California (Los Angeles); Valley (Montecito, Calif.), L.A. Country. E-mail: robert.maguire@maguirepartners.com

MAHAJAN, SUBHASH, electronic materials educator; b. Gurdaspur, India; m. Sushma Sondhi, Sept. 3, 1965; children: Sanjoy, Sunit, Ashish. BS with highest honors, Panjab U., India, 1959; BE in Metallyrgy with highest honors, Indian Inst. Sci., 1961; PhD in Materials Sci. and Engring., U. Calif., 1965. Rsch. asst. U. Calif., Berkeley, 1961-65; rsch. metallurgist U. Denver, 1965-68; Harwell fellow Atomic Energy Rsch. Establishment, Harwell, Eng., 1968-71; mem. tech. staff AT&T Bell Labs., Murray Hill, N.J., 1971-83, rsch. mgr., 1981-83; prof. electronic materials dept. material sci. and engring. Carnegie Mellon U., Pitts., 1983-97; prof. electronic materials Ariz. State U., Tempe, 1997—, assoc. chair, 1999, interim chair and chair dept. chem. and materials engring., 2000—. Mem. site panel Materials Rsch. Lab., 1993; vis. prof. U. Antwerp, Belgium, 1991, Ecole

Ctrl. Lyon, Ecully, France, 1993; lectr., spkr., patentee, cons. in field. Editor: (with V.G. Keramidas) Electrochemical Society Symposium volume, 1983; (with L.C. Kimerling) The Concise Encyclopedia of Semiconducting Materials and Related Technologies, 1992, Handbook on Semiconductors vol. 3, 1994; (with D. Bloor, R.J. Brook and M.C. (Flemings) The Encyclopedia of Advanced Materials, 1994; contbr. more than 190 articles to profl. jours. Mem. materials rsch. adv. com. divsn. materials rsch. NSF, 1989-92. Fellow TMS, Am. Soc. Metals Internat. (Albert Sauveur Achievement award), Minerals, Metals and Materials Soc.; mem. Materials Rsch. Soc. (editor symposium volume 1983, organizer symposium Am. Assn. Crystal Growers), Electrochem. Soc. (mem. electronics divsn. 1973-86, divisional editor 1976-86), Minerals, Metals and Materials Soc. (mem. phys. metallurgy com. 1976-83, vice chmn. mech. metallurgy com. 1978-79, mem. 1975-80, mem. electronic materials com. 1990-94, chmn. electronic, magnetic and photonic materials com. 1984-86, tech. dir. bd., John Bardeen award), Sigma Xi. Home: 8824 S Poplar St Tempe AZ 85284-4521 Office: Ariz State U Dept Chem and Materials Engring Tempe AZ 85287-6006 E-mail: smahajan@asu.edu

MAHARIDGE, DALE DIMITRO, journalist, educator; b. Cleve., Oct. 24, 1956; s. Steve and Joan (Kopfstein) M. Student, Cleve. State U., 1974-75. Free-lance reporter various publs., Cleve., 1976; reporter The Gazette, Medina, Ohio, 1977-78; free-lance reporter Cleve. Plain Dealer, 1978-80; reporter The Sacramento Bee, 1980-91; lectr. Stanford U., Palo Alto, Calif., 1992—. Author: Journey to Nowhere: The Saga of the New Underclass, 1985, repub. with introduction by Bruce Springsteen, 1996, And Their Children After Them, 1989 (Pulitzer Prize for gen. nonfiction 1990), The Last Great American Hobo, 1993, The Coming White Minority: California's Eruptions and the Nation's Future, 1996, Vintage Books edit., 1999; contbr. articles to profl. jours. Nieman fellow Harvard U., 1988; grantee Pope Found., 1994, Freedom Forum, 1995. Democrat. Office: Stanford U Dept Comm Bldg 120 Stanford CA 94305 E-mail: maharidg@leland.stanford.edu

MAHDAVI, KAMAL B. writer, researcher; b. Esfahan, Iran, Sept. 1, 1933; came to U.S., 1958, naturalized. s. Ebrahim B. and Ghamar (Jalilian) M. BA, U. Calif., Berkeley, 1964; MA, U Toronto, 1965; postgrad., U. Cambridge, Eng., 1965-69. Cert. coll. tchr., Calif. R&D rschr. U. Stockholm, 1969-71; freelance rschr., writer self-employed, San Francisco, San Diego, 1972—. Ind. legal rschr. San Francisco, San Diego, 1980—. Author (as K.M.B. Writer): Technological Innovation: An Efficiency Investigation, 1972; contbr. articles to profl. jours. Civil rights litigant. Avocations: swimming, chess. Office: PO Box 121164 San Diego CA 92112-1164

MAHER, BILL, talk show host, comedian, producer; b. N.Y.C., Jan. 20, 1956; s. Bill and Julie (Berman) M. BA, Cornell U., 1978. Creator, host Politically Incorrect, HBO, N.Y.C., 1993-96, Politically Incorrect, ABC, 1996—. Performances include (theatre) Seymour Glick is Alive But Sick (Steve Allen); (stand-up) The Bob Monkhouse Show, Late Night with David Letterman, The Tonight Show Anniversary Show, The Tonight Show, HBO Spl., 1989, 92; (TV shows) Steve Allen's Music Room, Alice, Sara, Max Headroom, Hard Knocks, Newhart, Murder, She Wrote, The Midnight Hour, Say What?; (TV movies) Out of Time, Rags to Riches, Club Med; (films) D.C. Cab, Rat Boy, House II, Cannibal Women in the Avocado Jungle of Death, Pizza Man; author: (novel) True Story, 1994. Recipient Cableace award Nat. Acad. Cable Programming, 1990, Cableace award for best talk show series, 1995, Cableace award for best talk show host, 1995. Office: Politically Incorrect c/o CBS Television City 7800 Beverly Blvd Los Angeles CA 90036-2112

MAHER, DAVID L. drug store company executive; b. Iowa City, 1939; Grad., U. Iowa, 1964. Pres., vice chmn., COO Am. Stores Co., Salt Lake City, vice chmn., COO, 1997-99. Office: American Stores Co 155 N 400 W Salt Lake City UT 84103-1111

MAHER, PETER MICHAEL, management educator; b. North Battleford, Sask., Can., Mar. 4, 1940; s. Hugh James and Florence Andrea (Showell) M.; m. Illa Horning, Sept. 5, 1964; children: Andrea, Allison, Jennifer. BE, U. Sask., 1962; MBA, U. Western Ont., 1965; PhD, Northwestern U., 1970; D in Commerce, St. Mary's U., 1996. Registered prof. engr., Sask., Alta. Devel. engr. DuPont of Can., 1962-64, new venture analyst, 1965-67; teaching asst. Sir George Williams U., 1966-70; rsch. engr. dept. indsl. engring. and mgmt. sci. Northwestern U., 1968-76; prof., rsch. coord. Faculty of Bus. Adminstrn. and Commerce, U. Alta., 1970-76; dean, prof. adminstrn. Coll. of Commerce, U. Sask., 1976-81; dean, prof. faculty of mgmt. U. Calgary, Alta., 1981-99, prof. faculty mgmt., 1999—, mem. univ. senate Alta., 1989-92. Bd. dirs. Calgary Airport Authority, Computalog Ltd., Can. Inst. for Petroleum Industry Devel., Theatre Calgary, Freehold Royalty Trust; witness House of Commons Spl. Commn. Employment Opportunities, 1981; mem. exec. com. Nu-West Ltd., 1982-88; audit com. Contbr. articles to profl. jours. Chmn. edn. div., mem. cabinet United Way, Calgary, 1989-90; creditor Northland Bank, 1985; trustee CNIB White Cane Found., 1989-91; bd. dirs. Calgary Econ. Devel. Authority, 1983-90, Banff Mountain Acad., 1990-95, Banff Sch. Advanced Mgmt., 1990—, chmn. acad. coun., 1992—, chmn. bd. dirs., 1999—; mem. corp. St. Thomas More Coll., Saskatoon, 1981—; mem. steering com. Calgary Police Commn., 1998—; bd. dirs. CMC Czech Grad. Sch. Bus., 1999—. Mem. Nat. Rsch. Coun. Can., Can. C. of C. (bd. dirs. 1984-86), Calgary C. of C. (bd. dirs. 1982-86), Am. Assembly Collegiate Schs. Bus. (faculty supply com. 1986-90, initial/continuing accreditation com. 1989-94), Can. Fedn. Deans Mgmt. and Adminstrn. Studies (vice chmn. 1981-82, chmn. 1982-84, sec.-treas. 1990-96), Internat. Labour Orgn. (UN rep. 1985-95), Can. Consortium Mgmt. Schs. (chmn. 1990-95, past chair 1995-97), Premier's Coun. on Sci. and Tech. (interman bd. dirs. 1984-95). Home: 12 Varbrook Pl NW Calgary AB Canada T3A OA2 Office: U Calgary Faculty Mgmt 2500 University Dr NW Calgary AB Canada T2N 1N4

MAHLER, RICHARD TERENCE, finance executive; b. Galt, Ont., Can., May 15, 1943; s. Lawrence Herman and Therese (Trepanier) M.; m. Susan Jane Campbell, May 25, 1968; children: Stephen, Katherine. BSc, U. Waterloo, 1966; MBA, McMaster U., Hamilton, 1975. Asst. contr. Ford Motor Can., Oakville, Ont., 1967-81; v.p. fin., chief fin. officer Amdahl Can. Ltd., Toronto, 1981-90; exec. v.p., CFO Finning Internat. Inc., Vancouver, B.C., 1990—. Chmn. Oakville Galleries, Ont., 1971-79; pres. U. Waterloo Adv. Coun., 1984-90; bd. dirs. Nat. Ballet Sch., Toronto; dir. Vancouver Bd. Trade; past chmn. coop. coun. Simon Fraser U., 1993-95; mem. bus. coun. B.C. Econ. Policy Adv. Group, 1994. Mem. Fin. Execs. Inst., Coun. Fin. Execs. Conf. Bd. Can., Hollyburn Country Club, Seymour Golf Club, Canadian Club Vancouver. Office: Finning Internat Inc 555 Great Northern Way Vancouver BC Canada V5T 1E2

MAHLUM, DALE DUANE, state legislator, small business owner; b. Bowman, N.D., June 12, 1930; s. Lloyd S. and Ragna (Paulson) M.; m. Sandra Sue Little, Dec. 21, 1956; children: Douglas, Connie, Thomas, Dee Ann, Michele. BS, U. Mont, 1956. Mgr. Super Foods, Kalispell, Mont., 1954-58; store owner Missoula, 1959-93; former thoroughbred farm owner, breeder Coast to Coast, Missoula; mem. Mont. Senate, Dist. 35, Helena, 1996—. Chmn. Mont. Bank Bd., Missoula, 1974—; bd. dirs. Mont. Hardware Implement, Helena, St. Patricks Hosp., Missoula; chmn. adv. bd. sch. bus U. Mont., Missoula, 1985-88. Mem. Western Mont. Fair Commn., Missoula, 1974—. With USN, 1950-54. Mem. Mont. Thoroughbreds Breeders Assn. (pres.), Thoroughbred Owners/Breeders Assn. Republican. Lutheran. Home: 10955 Us Highway 93 N Missoula MT 59808-9227 Office: Mont Legislature PO Box 201706 Helena MT 59620-1706

MAHLUM, KIRTLAND L. federal judge; b. Mpls., Mar. 30, 1945; BA, U. Calif., Davis, 1966; JD, Calif. Western Sch. Law, 1969. Bar: Calif. 1970. Law practice, San Diego, 1973-75, Barstow, Calif., 1975—; apptd. part-time magistrate judge cen. dist. U.S. Dist. Ct. Calif., 1980. Bd. dirs. Hi Desert Mental Health, 1976-82; bd. trustees Barstow Unified Sch. Dist., 1977-82. Mem. San Bernardino County Bar Assn., Hi Desert Bar Assn. (past pres.). Avocation: golf. Office: 240 E Williams St Barstow CA 92311-2842

MAHMOOD, AAMER, computer system architect; b. Lahore, Pakistan, Jan. 27, 1956; came to U.S., 1979; s. Muhammad Iftikhar Quereshi and Farakh (Sultana) Iftikhar; m. Samira Aftab, June 28, 1985; children: Muhammad Bilal, Umer Ali. BSEE with honors, U. Engring. & Tech., Lahore, 1979; MSEE, Stanford U., 1980, PhD in Elec. Engring., 1986. Lectr. U. Egnring. & Tech., 1979; teaching asst. Stanford (Calif.) U., 1980-82, rsch. asst., 1983-85; mem. tech. staff Rolm Milspec Computers, San Jose, Calif., 1986-88; mgr., tech. leader CPU and memory systems Amdahl/Advanced Systems, Sunnyvale, 1988-93; dir. engring. architect network hardware Cisco Systems, San Jose, 1994—. Contbr. articles to profl. jours. Bd. of Secondary Edn. merit scholar, Lahore, 1971, Bd. of Intermediate Edn. talent scholar, Lahore, 1973. Mem. IEEE (sr.), Assn. Computing Machinery, Stanford Alumni Assn. (life). Home: 1098 Cardinal Way Palo Alto CA 94303-3540 E-mail: amahmood@cisco.com

MAHONEY, DAVID L. pharmaceutical wholesale and healthcare management company executive; b. Brighton, Mass., June 24, 1954; s. Thomas H.D. and K. Phyllis (Norton) M.; m. Winn Canning Ellis, Sept. 26, 1992. AB in English, Princeton U., 1975; MBA, Harvard U., 1981. Asst. gen. mgr. Ogden Food Svc. Corp., L.A., 1975-76, concessions mgr. East Boston, Mass., 1976-77, gen. mgr., 1977-78, ops. analyst, 1978-79; assoc. McKinsey & Co., San Francisco, 1981-86, prin., 1986-90; v.p. strategic planning McKesson Corp., San Francisco, 1990-94, pres. HDS, Inc., 1994-95, pres. pharm. svcs., 1995-97, group pres. pharm svcs. & internat. group, 1997-99; exec. v.p., CEO pharm. svcs. bus. McKesson HBOC, 1999, co-CEO, 1999-2001; CEO McKesson, 2000-01. Bd. dirs. Armor All Products Corp. Mem. City Club of San Francisco, San Francisco C. of C. Avocations: outdoor activities, photography. Office: McKesson HBOC 235 Montgomery St Ste 820 San Francisco CA 94104-5292

MAHONEY, GERALD FRANCIS, manufacturing company executive; b. Bklyn., July 31, 1943; s. Francis B. and Leona (Gray) M.; m. JoAnne A. Maselli, May 2, 1971; children: G. Scott, Ryan J. BA, Adelphi U., 1965; MBA, Northeastern U., 1966. CPA, N.Y. Mgr. Arthur Andersen & Co., N.Y.C., 1966-73; asst. contr. Bairnco Corp., N.Y.C., 1973-78, v.p. fin., 1980-81, gen. mgr. Pensauken, N.J., 1979-80, v.p., div. pres. Union, 1981-83; sr. v.p. fin. and adminstrn. Polychrome Corp., Yonkers, N.Y., 1984-87; pres. Transcrit Corp., Brewster, 1987-90, Pavey Envelope & Tag Corp., Jersey City, 1991-94; chmn., CEO Mail-Well, Inc., Englewood, Colo., 1994—. Mem. AICPA, N.Y. State Soc. CPA's, Noyac Country Club (Sag Harbor, N.Y., bd. dirs. 1980-83), Glenmoor Country Club (Englewood, Colo.), Ridgewood Country Club (N.J.). Republican. Roman Catholic. Avocations: golf, tennis. Home: 21 Cherry Hills Farm Dr Englewood CO 80110-7170 Office: Mail Well Inc 23 Inverness Way E Englewood CO 80112-5711

MAHONY, CARDINAL ROGER MICHAEL, archbishop; b. Hollywood, Calif., Feb. 27, 1936; s. Victor James and Loretta Marie (Baron) M. AA, Our Lady Queen of Angels Sem., 1956; BA, St. John's Sem. Coll., 1958, BST, 1962; MSW, Cath. U. Am., 1964. Ordained priest Roman Cath. Ch., 1962, ordained bishop, 1975, created cardinal priest, 1991. Asst. pastor St. John's Cathedral, Fresno, Calif., 1962, 68-73, rector, 1973-80; residence St. Genevieve's Parish, Fresno, 1964—, adminstr., 1964-67, pastor, 1967-68; titular bishop of Tamascani, aux. bishop of Fresno, 1975-80; chancellor Diocese of Fresno, 1970-77, vicar gen., 1975-80; bishop Diocese of Stockton (Calif.), 1980-85; archbishop Archdiocese of L.A., 1985—, cardinal priest, 1991—; diocesan dir. Cath. Charities and Social Svc. Fresno, 1964-70; exec. dir. Infant of Prague Adoption Svc., Cath. Welfare Bur., Fresno, 1964-70. Chaplain St. Vincent de Paul Soc., Fresno, 1964-70; named chaplain to Pope Paul VI, 1967; mem. faculty extension div. Fresno State U., 1965-67; sec. U.S. Cath. bishops ad hoc com. on farm labor Nat. Conf. Bishops, 1970-75; chmn. com. on pub. welfare and income maintenance Nat. Conf. Cath. Charities, 1969-70; bd. dirs. West Coast Regional Office Bishops Com. for Spanish-Speaking, 1967-70; chmn. Calif. Assn. Cath. Charities Dirs., 1965-69; trustee St. Patrick's Sem., Archdiocese of San Francisco, 1974-75; mem. adminstrv. com. Nat. conf. Cath. Bishops, 1976-79, 82-85, 87-90, 92-95, 98—, com. migration and refugees, 1976-95, chmn. com. farm labor, 1981-92, com. moral evaluation of deterrence, 1986-88; cons. com., chmn. for ProLife Activities, 1990-95; mem. com. social devel. and world peace U.S. Cath. Conf., 1985-93, chmn. internat. policy sect., 1987-93; com. justice and peace, Pontifical Couns., 1984-89, 90-98, chmn. com. domestic policy, 1998—, pastoral care of migrants and itinerant people, 1986-91, social comms., 1989—. Mem. Urban Coalition of Fresno, 1968-72, Fresno County Econ. Opportunities Commn., 1964-65, Fresno County Alcoholic Rehab. Com., 1966-67, Fresno City Charter Rev. Com., 1968-70, Mexican-Am. Council for Better Housing, 1968-72, Fresno Redevel. Agy., 1970-75, L.A. 2000 Com., 1985-88, Fed. Commn. Agrl. Workers, 1987-93, Blue Ribbon Com. Affordable Housing City of L.A., 1988; mem. commn. to Draft an Ethics Code for L.A. City Govt., 1989-90; bd. dirs. Fresno Cmty. Workshop, 1965-67, Rebuild L.A., 1992-95; trustee St. Agnes Hosp., Fresno, 1969-73, Cath. U. Am., 1984-88, 98—. Named Young Man of Yr. Fresno Jr. C. of C., 1967 Mem. Canon Law Soc. Home: 555 W Temple St Los Angeles CA 90012-2707 Office: Archdiocese LA 3424 Wilshire Blvd Los Angeles CA 90010-2241

MAIER, DAVID EUGENE, computer science educator; b. Eugene, Oreg., June 2, 1953; BA in Math. and Computer Sci., U. Oreg., 1974; PhD in Elec. Engring. and Computer Sci., Princeton U., 1978. Asst. prof. dept. computer sci. SUNY, Stony Brook, 1978-82; asst. prof. dept. computer sci. and engring. Oreg. Grad. Inst., Portland, 1982-83, assoc. prof. dept. computer sci. and engring., 1983-88, prof., 1988—, acting chair, 1988. Vis. scientist GIP Altair-Inst. Nat. de Rsch. en Informatique et an Automatique, Rocquencourt, France, 1989-90; vis. prof. computer scis. dept. U. Wis., Madison, 1997-98; organizer and mem. arrangements com. various confs. and workshops; cons. and presenter in field. Author: The Theory of Relational Databases, 1983, (with D.S. Warren) Computing with Logic: Introduction to Logic Programming, 1988, Query Processing for Advanced Database Systems, 1993, Persistent Object Systems, 1995; contbr. chpts. to books and articles to profl. jours. Recipient NSF Presdl. Young Investigator award, 1984-89, Innovations award Assn. Computing Machinery/Spl. Interest Group Mgmt. Data, 1997; grantee Dept. Energy Emergency Info. Mgmt. Sys., 1979, NSF, 1979-82, 81-83, 82-84, 82-84, 86-88, 88-90, 89-91, 91-94, 92-95, 93-95, 97-99, Tektronix Computer Rsch. Lab., 1983-86, Tektronix Info. Display Group, 1984-85, Microelectronics and Computer Tech. Corp., 1985-87, Apple Computer, 1988-89, Battelle Pacific N.W. Labs., 1991-92, 91, 92, 93-94, 93, 94, Sequent Computer Sys., 1991, DARPA, 1991-94, 96-99, Office Naval Rsch., 1996-99, U.S. West Advanced Techs., 1992, others; Univ. Awards Com. fellow SUNY, 1979. Fellow Assn. for Computing Machinery. Office: Data Intensive Sys Ctr Computer Sci & Engring Dept PO Box 91000 Portland OR 97291-1000

MAIER, GERALD JAMES, corporate executive; b. Regina, Sask., Can., Sept. 22, 1928; s. John Joseph and Mary (Passler) M. Student, Notre Dame Coll. (Wilcox), U. Man., U. Alta., U. Western Ont.; LLD (hon.), U. Alberta, 1999, U Alta. With petroleum and mining industries, Can., U.S., Australia, U.K.; responsible for petroleum ops. Africa, United Arab Emirates, U.S. Asia; past chmn., pres., CEO TransCan. PipeLines, Calgary, 1985-99; vice-chmn. NOVA Chems. Corp., Calgary, 1998-2000. Bd. dirs. Stream-Flo Industries, Ltd., XPronet Inc.; past chmn. Can. Nat. Com. for World Petroleum Congresses; past chmn. Van Horne Inst. for Internat. Transp. Chmn. bd. dirs. Notre Dame Coll. Named Hon. Col. (ret.) King's Own Calgary Rgt., Resource Man of Yr. Alta. Chamber of Resources, 1990; recipient Can. Engr.'s Gold medal Can. Coun. Profl. Engrs., 1990, Disting. Alumni award U. Alta., 1992, Mgmt. award McGill U., 1993, Centennial award Alta Assn. Engrs., Geologists and Geophysicists, Hal Godwin award for excellence in internat. bus. U. Calgary, 1999, Can. Bus. Leader award U. Alberta, 1999; inductee Can. Petroleum Hall of Fame, 1999. Fellow Can. Acad. Engring.; mem. Assn. Profl. Engrs., Geologists and Geophysicists Alta. (past pres.), Can. Inst. Mining and Metallurgy (Past Pres.'s Meml. medal 1971). Avocations: golf, downhill skiing, shooting, fishing. Office: Granmar Investments Ltd 400 3rd Ave SW Ste 3300 Calgary AB Canada T2P 4H2

MAIER, PAUL VICTOR, pharmaceutical executive; b. Seattle, Nov. 6, 1947; s. Norman Alvin and Rosalie (Godek) M.; m. Shirley Diehl, Aug. 11, 1979. BS, Pa. State U., 1969; MBA, Harvard U., 1975. Fin. analyst Greyhound Corp, Phoenix, 1975-76; asst. mgr. Wells Service Wells Fargo Bank, San Francisco, 1976-78; v.p. Fin. Cummins Service and Sales, Los Angeles, 1978-84; v.p., treas. ICN Pharms, Inc., Costa Mesa, Calif., 1984-90; v.p. fin. DFS West, 1990-92; sr. v.p., CFO Ligand Pharmaceuticals, Inc., San Diego, 1992—. Chmn. audit com. Entropin Inc., 2000—, also bd. dirs. Chmn. hosp. div. United Way Region V, L.A., 1983-84; bd. dirs. The Wellness Community, San Diego, 1993—. Served with USNR, 1969-95. Mem. Fin. Execs. Inst., The Athletic Congress, Pa. State Club of S.D., Harvard Bus. Sch. Assn. So. Calif., Ctr. for Non-Profit Mgmt., Vis. Nurse Assn. L.A. (bd. dirs. 1979-92, chmn.), Protection Mut. Inst. (West Coast adv. bd. 1985-90). Republican. Roman Catholic. Office: Ligand Pharmaceuticals 10275 Science Center Dr San Diego CA 92121-1117 E-mail: pmaier@ligand.com

MAIER, RONALD VITT, surgeon; b. Wheeling, W.Va., Oct. 23, 1947; BS, U. Notre Dame, 1969; MD, Duke U., 1973. Intern Parkland Meml. Hosp., Dallas, 1973-74; resident U. Wash. Hosps., Seattle, 1974-78; rsch. assoc. Scripps Rsch. Found., La Jolla, Calif., 1978-81; surgeon-in-chief HMC, Seattle, 1993—; prof., vice chair surgery U. Wash., Seattle, 1994—. Office: Dept Surgery 359796 Harborview Med Ctr 325 9th Ave Seattle WA 98104-2499

MAIER, STEPHEN JOHN, college president; b. Newburgh, N.Y., Apr. 23, 1946; s. Gerard G. and Esther (Brandow) M.; m. Edre Jane Maier, Sept. 5, 1970. BA, St. Lawrence U., 1968; MS, SUNY, 1970; EdD, U. Colo., 1974. Dean student svcs. Miles Community Coll., Miles City, Mont., 1974-78; dean instrn. N.Mex. J.C., Hobbs, 1978-88; pres. No. Wyo. Community Coll. Dist., Sheridan, 1988—. Mem. commn. on small/rural community colls. Mem. Econ. Devel. Com., Sheridan, 1991—. Mem. C. of C. (dir. 1990—), Rotary (Sheridan chpt.). Avocations: soaring, soccer refereeing, fishing, skiing. Office: Sheridan Coll Office Pres PO Box 1500 Sheridan WY 82801

MAIMAN, THEODORE HAROLD, physicist, researcher; b. Los Angeles, July 11, 1927; BS in Engring. Physics, U. Colo., 1949; MSEE, Stanford U., 1951, PhD in Physics, 1955; PhD (hon.), U. Cordoba, Argentina, 1993. Sect. head Hughes Research Labs., 1955-61; pres., founder Korad Corp., Santa Barbara, Calif., 1961-68, Maiman Assocs., Santa Barbara, 1968—; v.p., founder Laser Video Corp., Los Angeles, 1972-75; v.p. advanced tech. and new ventures TRW Inc. Electronics and Def. Sector, Los Angeles, 1975-83. Vis. prof. Nat. U. Asuncion, Paraguay, 1993. Contbr. articles to profl. jours. With USNR, 1945-46. Recipient award Fannie and John Hertz Found., 1966, Ballantine award Franklin Inst., 1962, award for devel. laser Aerospace Elec. Soc.-Am. Astron. Soc., 1965, Light award Braille Inst., 1982, Wolf prize in physics, 1984; named Alumni of Century U. Colo., 1976; named to U.S. Nat. Inventors Hall of Fame, 1984; named Laureate Japan Prize in electro-optics, 1987. Fellow Soc. Motion Picture and TV Engrs., Am. Phys. Soc. (Oliver E. Buckley prize 1966), Optical Soc. Am. (R.W. Wood prize 1976), Soc. Photog. and Instrumentation Engrs., Royal Coll. Surgeons (hon.), 1994; mem. Nat. Acad. Engring., Nat. Acad. Scis., IEEE, Soc. Info. Display, Sigma Xi, Sigma Pi Sigma, Sigma Tau, Pi Mu Epsilon. Achievements include devel. of 1st laser. E-mail: laserinventor-.com. Home and Office: 1701 837 W Hastings St Vancouver BC Canada V6C 3N7

MAIMON, ELAINE PLASKOW, English educator, university provost; b. Phila., July 28, 1944; d. Louis J. and Gertrude (Canter) Plaskow; m. Morton A. Maimon, Sept. 30, 1967; children: Gillian Blanche, Alan Marcus. AB, U. Pa., 1966, MA, 1967, PhD, 1970. Asst. prof. Haverford (Pa.) Coll., 1971-73; lectr. Beaver Coll., Glenside, Pa., 1973-75, asst. prof., dir. writing, 1975-77, assoc. prof., 1977-83, assoc. dean, 1980-84, assoc. v.p., prof. English, 1984-86; adj. assoc. prof. U. Pa., Phila., 1982-83; assoc. dean of coll. Brown U., Providence, 1986-88; dean, prof. English Queens Coll. CUNY, Flushing, N.Y., 1988-96; campus CEO, provost Ariz. State U. West, Phoenix, 1996—; v.p. Ariz. State U., 1996—. Nat. bd. cons. NEH, 1977-81; mem. adv. bd. Cox Comms., 1997-2001—; bd. dirs. Arrowhed Cmty. Bank. Co-author: Writing in the Arts and Sciences, 1981; co-editor: Readings in the Arts and Sciences, 1984, Thinking, Reasoning and Writing, 1989. Mem. exec. bd. Sch. to Work, Western Maricopa County, 1996-98; trustee Heard Mus., Phoenix, 1999—. Recipient Golden Heart Today's Ariz. Woman, 2000; Elaine Maimon award for Excellence in Writing named in her honor Beaver Coll., 1994. Mem. MLA (exec. com., teaching of writing divsn., 1991), Nat. Coun. Tchrs. English (nominating com. 1986-87), ACE Nat. Commn. Women, Conf. on Coll. Composition Comm. (exec. com. 1985-87), Assn. Am. Colls., Phi Beta Kappa. Home: 20726 N 55th Ave Glendale AZ 85308-9342 Office: Ariz State U W PO Box 37100 4701 E Thunderbird Rd Phoenix AZ 85069-7100 E-mail: elaine.maimon@asu.edu

MAIN, JACKSON TURNER, history educator; b. Chgo., Aug. 6, 1917; s. John Smith and Dorothy Kinsey (Turner) M.; m. Gloria Jean Lund, June 16, 1956; children: Jackson Turner, Eifiona Llewelyn, Judson Kempton. B.A., U. Wis., 1939, M.A., 1940, Ph.D., 1949; LL.D. (hon.), Washington and Jefferson Coll., 1980. Asst. prof. Washington and Jefferson Coll., Washington, 1948-50; prof. San Jose State U. (Calif.), 1953-65, U. Md., College Park, 1965-66; prof. history State U. N.Y. at Stony Brook, 1966-83. Author: The Antifederalists 1781-1788, 1961, The Social Structure of Revolutionary America, 1965, The Upper House in Revolutionary America, 1967, Political Parties Before the Constitution, 1973, The Sovereign States, 1775-1783, 1973, Connecticut Society in the Era of the American Revolution, 1977, Society and Economy in Colonial Connecticut, 1985, The Social Origins of Leaders, 2000 B.C. to 1850 A.D., 1998. Served to sgt. USAF, 1941-45. Am. Council Learned Socs. fellow, 1962-63; Nat. Endowment Humanities fellow Center Advanced Studies in Behavioral Scis., Stanford, Calif., 1980-81 Mem. Am. Hist. Soc., Orgn. Am. Historians, Wis. Hist. Soc., others. Office: U Colo Dept History Boulder CO 80305-5209

MAIN, ROBERT GAIL, communications educator, training consultant, television and film producer, former army officer; b. Bucklin, Mo., Sept. 30, 1932; s. Raymond M. and Inez L. (Olinger) M.; m. Anita Sue Thoroughman, Jan. 31, 1955; children: Robert Bruce, David Keith, Leslie Lorraine. BS magna cum laude, U. Mo., 1954; grad. with honors, Army Commd. Gen. Staff Coll., 1967; MA magna cum laude in Comm., Stanford U., 1968; PhD, U. Md., 1978. Commd. 2d lt. U.S. Army, 1954, advanced [illegible]

Coll., 1968-70; chief speechwriting and info. materials divsn. U.S. Army Info. Office, 1971, chief broadcast and film divsn., 1972-73; dir. def. audiovisual activities Office of Info. for Armed Forces, 1973-76; ret., 1976; prof. instrnl. tech. Calif. State U., Chico, 1976—, dept. chair, 1993-98. Cons. in field. Author: Rogues, Saints and Ordinary People, 1988; prodr. (TV documentary) Walking Wounded, 1983, Army Info. Films, Army Radio Series, 1972-73; contbr. articles on computer based tng. and telecoms. to scientific and profl. jours. Decorated Legion of Merit, Meritorious Svc. medal, Commendation medal with oak leaf cluster, combat Inf. Badge; Vietnamese Cross of Gallantry; recipient Freedom Found. awards, 1972, 73, 74; Bronze medal Atlanta Film Festival, 1972; Best of Show award Balt. Film Festival, 1973; Creativity award Chgo. Indsl. Film Festival, 1973; Cine gold award Internat. Film Prodrs. Assn., 1974; named an Outstanding Prof. Calif. State U., 1987-88. Mem. Phi Eta Sigma, Alpha Zeta, Phi Delta Gamma, Omicron Delta Kappa, Alpha Gamma Rho.

MAINWARING, WILLIAM LEWIS, publishing company executive, author; b. Portland, Oreg., Jan. 17, 1935; s. Bernard and Jennie (Lewis) M.; m. Mary E. Bell, Aug. 18, 1962; children: Anne Marie, Julia Kathleen, Douglas Bernard. B.S., U. Oreg., 1957; postgrad., Stanford U., 1957-58. With Salem (Oreg.) Capital Jour., 1958-76, editor, pub., 1962-76; pub. Oreg. Statesman, 1974-76; pres. Statesman-Jour. Co., Inc., Salem, 1974-76, Westridge Press, Ltd., 1977—, MediAmerica, Inc., Portland, 1981-96, CEO, 1988-96. Bd. dirs. MediAmerica, Inc. Author: Exploring the Oregon Coast, 1977, Exploring Oregon's Central and Southern Cascades, 1979, Exploring the Mount Hood Loop, 1992, Government, Oregon-Style, 1996, rev. edit., 1997, 99. Pres. Salem Beautification Coun., 1968, Marion-Polk County United Good Neighbors, 1970, Salem Social Svcs. Commn., 1978-79, Salem Hosp. Found., 1978-81. 2d lt. AUS, 1958; capt. Res. Ret. Mem. Salem Area C. of C. (pres. 1972-73), Oreg. Symphony Soc. Salem (pres. 1973-75), Salem City Club (pres. 1977-78), Sigma Chi. Republican. Presbyterian. Home and Office: 1090 Southridge Pl S Salem OR 97302-5947

MAISEL, SHERMAN JOSEPH, economist, educator; b. Buffalo, July 8, 1918; s. Louis and Sophia (Beck) M.; m. Lucy Cowdin, Sept. 26, 1942; children: Lawrence C., Margaret L. A.B., Harvard U., 1939, M.P.A., 1947, Ph.D., 1949. Mem. bd. govs. FRS, 1965-72; economist, fgn. service res. officer Dept. State, 1945-46; teaching fellow Harvard U., 1947-48; asst. prof., assoc. prof., prof. bus. adminstrn. U. Calif. at Berkeley, 1948-65, 72-86; sr. economist Nat. Bur. Econ. Research-West, 1973-78; chmn., bd. dirs. Farmers Savings & Loan, 1986-88; pres. Sherman J. Maisel & Asscs. Inc., 1986—. Fellow Fund For Advancement Edn., 1952-53, Inst. Basic Math. with Application to Bus., 1959-60, Center for Advanced Study in Behavioral Scis., 1972; mem. adv. coms. to Bur. Census, FHA, State of Calif., Ford Found., Social Sci. Research Council; mem. bldg. research adv. bd. NRC. Author: Housebuilding in Transition, 1953, Fluctuations, Growth, and Forecasting, 1957, Managing the Dollar, 1973, Real Estate Investment and Finance, 1976, Risk and Capital Adequacy in Commercial Banks, 1981, Macroeconomics: Theories and Policies, 1982, Real Estate Finance, 1987, 2d edit., 1992. Bd. dirs. Berkeley Unified Sch. Dist., 1962-65. Served to capt. AUS, 1941-45. Mem. Am. Fin. Assn. (pres. 1973), Am. Econ. Assn. Home: 2164 Hyde St San Francisco CA 94109-1788 Office: U Calif Haas Bus Sch Berkeley CA 94720-0001

MAJESKE, MARK T. retail sales professional; Former sr. v.p. field opers. Hamilton Hallmark (Electronics Divsn. Avnet Corp.); group pres., retail McKesson HBOC, Inc., San Francisco, 1996—. Office: McKesson HBOC INC One Post St San Francisco CA 94104

MAJESTY, MELVIN SIDNEY, psychologist, consultant; b. New Orleans, June 6, 1928, s. Sidney Joseph and Marcella Cecilia (Kieffer) M.; m. Bettye Newanda Gordon, Dec. 18, 1955; 1 child, Diana Sue. BA, La. State U., 1949; MS, Western Res. U., 1951; PhD (USAF Inst. Tech. fellow), Case-Western Res. U., 1967. Commd. 2d lt. USAF, 1951, advanced through grades to lt. col., 1968; program mgr., ast. dir. tng. rsch. Air Force Human Resources Lab., 1967-69; dir. faculty and profl. ednl. rsch. USAF Acad., 1969-72; dir. plot tng. candidate selection program Officer Tng. Sch., Air Tng.Command, 1972-76; ret. USAF, 1976; personnel selection cons. to Calif. State Pers. Bd., Sacramento, 1976-92. Patentee listening center; founded pers. testing for ballistic missile and space systems; directed largest study of fighter pilot selection since World War II; pioneered use of phys. testing as replacement for the maximum age requirement in law enforcement jobs; developed phys. fitness tests and established psychol. screening standards for state highway patrol officer and police officers; contbr. numerous articles to profl. publs. With U.S. Army, WWII, 1944-46, Korea, Vietnam, USAF, 1951-76. Decorated Commendation medal (2), Meritorious Svc. medal (2), Am. Campaign medal, WWII Victory medal, WWII Overseas Occupation medal, Ballistic Missile badge, numerous others. Mem. Am. Psychol. Assn., Soc. Indsl. and Orgnl. Psychology, VFW, DAV, Ret. Officers Assn., Nat. Assn. for Uniformed Svcs., Am. Legion, Amvets, Vietnam Vets. Am., Mil. Order of Fgn. Wars, Am. Bible Soc., Am. Family Assn. Avocation: family. Office: 801 Capitol Mall Sacramento CA 95814-4806

MAJOR, CLARENCE LEE, novelist, poet, educator; b. Atlanta, Dec. 31, 1936; s. Clarence and Inez (Huff) M.; m. Pamela Ritter, May 8, 1980. BS, SUNY, Albany; PhD, Union Inst. Prof. U. Colo., Boulder, 1977-89, U. Calif., Davis, 1989—. Author: All-Night Visitors, 1969, 2d version, 1998, Dictionary of Afro-American Slang, 1970, No, 1973, Reflex and Bone Structure, 1975, rev. edit., 1996, Emergency Exit, 1979, My Amputations, 1986, Such Was the Season, 1987, Painted Turtle: Woman with Guitar, 1987, Fun and Games, 1990, Calling the Wind, 1993, Juba to Jive: A Dictionary of African American Slang, 1994, Dirty Bird Blues, 1996; poetry: Swallow the Lake, 1970, Symptoms & Madness, 1971, Private Line, 1971, The Cotton Club, 1972, Inside Diameter: The France Poems, 1985, Painted Turtle, 1988, Surfaces and Masks, 1988, Some Observations of a Stranger at Zuni in the Latter Part of the Century, 1989, Parking Lots, 1992, The Garden Thrives, 1996, Configurations: New and Selected Poems, 1958-1998, 1998 (Nat. Book Award finalist 1999), Clarence Major and His Art: Portraits of an African American Postmodernist, 2001, Necessary Distance, 2001; contbr. articles to Washington Post Book World, L.A. Times Book Rev., N.Y. Times Book Rev. Recipient Nat. Council on Arts award, Washington, 1970; Western States Book award, Western States Found., Santa Fe, 1986; Fulbright grantee, 1981-83. Office: U Calif Dept English 281 Voorhies Hall Davis CA 95616

MAKEPEACE, MARY LOU, mayor; 2 children. BA in Journalism, U. N.D.; MPA, U. Colo., Colorado Springs. Tchr. Am. Sch., Tananarive, Madagascar; asst. to Def. Attaché Am. Embassy, Prague, Czechoslavakia; adult edn. officer Ramstein AFB, Germany; case worker, adminstr. El Paso County Dept. Social Svcs., 1974-82; exec. dir. Cmty. Coun. Pikes Peak Region, 1982-84; dist. 1 rep. City Colorado Springs, 1985-97, vice mayor, 1997, mayor, 1997—. Exofficio mem. Econ. Devel. Coun. Bd. Dirs.; chair Econ. Devel. Com., Task Force City Svcs. to Srs., urban affairs com. Pikes Peak Area Coun. Govts.; apptd. Colo. Space Adv. Coun.; adj. prof. U. Colo.; leader Pikes Peak Program Citizen's Goals. Mem. steering com. Imagination Celebration; sr. advisor Palmer Found., Pikes Peak Partnership; mem. Nat. League Cities Leadership Tng. Coun.; past mem. Colo. Mcpl. League Exec. Bd., 1st United Meth. Ch. Gates Found. fellow, 1992; recipient Svc. Mankind award Centennial Sertoma Club, 1985; named Super Woman Women's Health Ctr., 1988, Best City Councilmem. Springs Mag., 1991. Mem. Am. Soc. Pub. Adminstrn., Pi Alpha Alpha. Office: City Colo Springs 30 S Nevada Ave Ste 401 Colorado Springs CO 80903-1898

MAKI, KAZUMI, physicist, educator; b. Takamatsu, Japan, Jan. 27, 1936; s. Toshio and Hideko M.; m. Masako Tanaka, Sept. 21, 1969. B.S., Kyoto U., 1959, Ph.D., 1964. Research asso. Inst. for Math. Scis., Kyoto U., 1964; research asso. Fermi Inst., U. Chgo., 1964-65; asst. prof. physics U. Calif., San Diego, 1965-67; prof. Tohoku U., Sendai, Japan, 1967-74; vis. prof. Universite Paris-Sud, Orsay, France, 1969-70; prof. physics U. So. Calif., Los Angeles, 1974—. Vis. prof. Inst. Laue-Langevin, U. Paris-Sud, France, 1979-80, Max Planck Inst. fur Festkorper Forschung, Stuttgart, Germany, 1986-87, U. Paris-7, 1990, Hokkaido U., Sapporo, Japan, 1993, Centre de Recherche sur Tres Basses Temperatures, Grenoble, France, 1993-94, Instituto de Ciencia de Materiales, Madrid, Spain, 1994. Assoc. editor Jour. Low Temperature Physics, 1969-91; contbr. articles to profl. jours. Guggenheim fellow, 1979-80, Japan Soc. Promotion of Sci. fellow, 1993; Fulbright scholar, 1964-65; recipient Nishina prize, 1972, Alexander von Humboldt award, 1986-87. Fellow Japan Soc. Promotion of Sci., Am. Phys. Soc.; mem. AAAS, Phys. Soc. Japan. Office: U So Calif Dept Physics and Astronomy Los Angeles CA 90089-0484 E-mail: kmaki@usc.edu

MALA, THEODORE ANTHONY, physician, consultant; b. Santa Monica, Calif., Feb. 3, 1946; s. Ray and Galina (Liss) M.; children: Theodore S., Galina T.; 1 adopted child, Christine A. Lindholm. BA in Philosophy, DePaul U., 1972; MD, Autonomous U., Guadalajara, Mex., 1976; MPH, Harvard U., 1980. Spl. asst. for health affairs Alaska Fedn. Natives, Anchorage, 1977-78; chief health svcs. Alaska State Divsn. Corrections, Anchorage, 1978-79; assoc. prof., founder, dir. Inst. for Circumpolar Health Studies, U. Alaska, Anchorage, 1982-90; founder Siberian med. rsch. program U. Alaska, Anchorage, 1982, founder Magadan (USSR) med. rsch. program, 1988; commr. Health and Social Svcs. State of Alaska, Juneau, 1990-93; pres., CEO Ted Mala, Inc., Anchorage, 1993-97; pres., ptnr. Mexican-Siberian Trading Co., Monterrey, Mex., 1994-96; CEO, Confederated Tribes of Grand Ronde, Oreg., 1998-99; dir. tribal rels. Southcentral Found., Anchorage, 1999—, Anchorage, 2000—. Traditional healing dir. Southcentral Found., Anchorage, 2000—; Alaska rsch. and publs. com. Indian Health Svc., USPHS, 1987-90; advisor Nordic Coun. Meeting, WHO, Greenland, 1985; mem. Internat. Organizing Com., Circumpolar Health Congress, Iceland, 1992-93; chmn. bd. govs. Alaska Psychiat. Inst., Anchorage, 1990-93; cabinet mem. Gov. Walter J. Hickel, Juneau, 1990-93; advisor humanitarian aid to Russian Far East U.S. Dept. State, 1992-96; cons. USAID on U.S.-Russian Health Programs, 1994; apptd. adv. com. Sec. of Health and Human Svc. on Minority Health for the U.S., 2000—. Past columnist Tundra Times; contbr. articles to profl. jours. Trustee United Way Anchorage, 1978-79; chmn. bd. trustees Alaska Native Coll., 1993-96. Recipient Gov.'s award, 1988, Outstanding Svc. award Alaska Commr. Health, 1979, Ministry of Health citation USSR Govt., 1989, Citation award Alaska State Legislature, 1989-90, 94, Commendation award State of Alaska, 1990, Alaska State Legislature, 1994, Honor Kempton Svc. to Humanity award, 1989, citation Med. Comty. of Magadan region, USSR, 1989; Nat. Indian fellow U.S. Dept. Edn., 1979. Mem. Assn. Am. Indian Physicians (pres.), N.Y. Acad. Scis., Internat. Union for Circumpolar Health (permanent sec.-gen. 1987-90, organizing com. 8th Internat. Congress on Circumpolar Health 1987-90), Russian Acad. Polar Medicine (elected). Avocations: cross-country skiing, hiking, photography, travel. E-mail: tmala@post.harvard.edu

MALAMUTH, NEIL MOSHE, psychology and communication educator; BA in Psychology summa cum laude, MA in Psychology, UCLA, 1972, PhD in Social Psychology and Personality, 1975. Lectr. dept. psychology, UCLA and postdoctoral fellow Ctr. for Behavioral Therapy, Beverly Hills, Calif., 1975-77; asst. prof. psychology U. Man., Winnipeg, Can., 1977-80, assoc. prof. Can., 1980-82; prof. comm. and psychology, chairperson dept. comm. U. Mich., Ann Arbor, 1991-94; tchg. asst. dept. psychology UCLA, 1971-73, rsch. assoc. Ctr. for Computer-Based Behavioral Studies, 1973-75, assoc. prof., 1982-86, assoc. dir. Ctr. for Study of Women, 1986-87, prof. comm. and psychology, 1982-91, 94—, chairperson comm. studies program and speech dept., 1984-91, 94—. Vis. scholar Stanford (Calif.) U., fall 1988; mem. rev. com. on violence and stress NIMH, 1989-93; Lady Davis sr. fellow Hebrew U. Jerusalem, spring 1995; participant leadership inst. Freedom Forum, Columbia U., summer 1992; participant workshop for deans and chairpersons Annenberg Programs, Washington, winter 1993; presenter various profl. and ednl. confs., most recently Oakland (Mich.) U., 1994, Nat. Assn. for Devel. of Work with Sex Offenders, Durham (Eng.) U., 1994, Soc. for Sci. Study of Sex., Miami, Fla., 1994, Ctr. for Study of Evolution and Origins of Life, UCLA, 1994, Ctr. for Evolutionary Psychology, Santa Barbara, Calif., 1995, Tel Aviv U., 1995, Bar-Ilan U., Israel, 1995, Hebrew U. Jerusalem, 1995, NRC, Washington, 1995, Soc. Exptl. Social Psychology, Washington, 1995, Nat. Assn. for Treatment of Sexual Aggression, New Orleans, 1995, Polish Nat. Acad. Sci., Warsaw U., 1995. Co-author: An Instructor's Manual and Guide for Teaching a Course in Social Psychology, 1976, Pornography, 1993; co-editor Sites and Insights in Psychology, 1976; co-editor, contbr. chpt. to: Pornography and Sexual Aggression, 1984, Sex, Power, Conflict: Evolutionary Feminist Perspectives, 1996; contbr. chpt. to: Aggression in Children and Youth, 1984, Handbook of Research on Rape and Sexual Assault, 1984, Media Violence and Pornography: An International Perspective, 1984, The psychology of Women: Ongoing Debates, 1987, Public Communication and Behavior, Vol. 2, 1989; contbr. or co-contbr. various chpts., also numerous articles; mem. editl. bd. Motivation and Emotion, 1983-89, Comm. Rsch., 1986-92, Jour. Sex Rsch., 1982-99, Sexual Abuse: A Jour. and Treatment, 1995-99; assoc. editor Comm. Concepts Series, 1989-98, Jour. Rsch. in Personality, 1990-93; co-editor issue Jour. Social Issues, 1986. Recipient John Kendall award for Outstanding Contbns. to Psychology, Gustavus Coll., Minn., 1987; rsch. grantee Social Sci. and Humanities Rsch. Coun. Can., 1979-81, NIMH, 1986-89, 89-91, 91-92; named one of 7 scholars among top 100 rschrs. in 4 categories of eminence Personality and Social Psychology Bull., 1992. Fellow APA, Am. Psychol. Soc.; mem. Internat. Comm. Assn. (presenter 1994, Top 5 Conf. Paper award mass comm. divsn. 1987), Internat. Soc. for Rsch. on Aggression, Soc. for Psychol. Study of Social Issues, Soc. for Sci. Study of Sex, Phi Beta Kappa. Office: UCLA Comm Studies Program 334 Kinsey Hl Los Angeles CA 90095-0001

MALCOLM, DAWN GRACE, family physician; b. L.A., Nov. 3, 1936; d. Thomas N. and Grace S. (Salisian) M. BA, UCLA, 1959; MD, Med. Coll. Pa., 1973. Diplomate Am. Bd. Family Practice. Tchr. elem. music Fullerton (Calif.) Sch. Dist., 1960-61; tchr. Ahlman Acad., Kabul, Afghanistan, 1961-65; intern and resident in family practice Kaiser Found. Hosp., L.A., 1973-76; family physician So. Calif. Permanente Med. Group, L.A., 1976—. Mem. faculty family practice residency program Kaiser Found. Hosp., L.A., 1976—. Fellow Am. Acad. Family Physicians. Office: So Calif Permanente Med Grp 4747 Sunset Blvd Los Angeles CA 90027-6021

MALCOLM, GAROLD DEAN, architect; b. Belle Fouche, S.D., Apr. 25, 1940; s. Gifford Garold Malcolm and Ellen Eve Liming; m. Breta Lois Bailey, 1966 (div. 1982); children; Heather Marie, Allison Clare; m. Lucia Eagon Stenson, 1991. BArch, U. Oreg., 1966. Ptnr. McAdoo, Malcolm & Youel, Architects, 1981—. Prin. works include Creston-Nelson Elec. Substation, Seattle (Honor award Wash. Aggregates and Concrete Assn.), Arboretum Visitor's Ctr., Seattle (Honor award Builders Community Awards Program, People's Choice award Seattle chpt. AIA), Des Moines (Wash.) Libr., Queen Anne Swimming Pool, Seattle. Mem. AIA, Matsumura Kenpo Karate Assn. (black belt). Office: McAdoo Malcolm & Youel Architects 1718 E Olive Way Seattle WA 98102-5683

MALCURIA, SHERRY JOANNE, real estate company executive, interior designer; b. Wendall, Idaho, Apr. 16, 1942; d. John Donald and Vera Ella (Frost) Kingery; children: Artist Roxanne, Buddy (George II), Kami JoAnne, Launi JoElla; m. Samuel Ross Malcuria, June 12, 1999. Student, Ariz. State U., 1960. Corp. sec., treas. Karbel Metals Co., Phoenix, 1963-67; sec. to pub. Scottsdale (Ariz.) Daily Progress, 1969-72; with D-Velco Mfg. of Ariz., Phoenix, 1959-62, dir., exec. v.p., sec., treas., 1972-87; mng. ptnr., financial and real estate investment Karitage, Ltd., Scottsdale, 1987—. E-mail: footnotes1@earthlink.net

MALDONADO, GREGORY MATTHEW, music director, educator; b. Merced, Calif., June 8, 1958; s. Daniel Robert and Elaine Louise (Turrey) M. MusB, UCLA, 1990. Music dir., founder L.A. Baroque Orch., 1986—; mem. faculty U. So. Calif., 1988-97; instr. in Baroque violin UCLA, 1989-91. Founder, music dir. La Stravaganza, L.A., Eroica String Quar., L.A., L.A. Fortepiano Trio, L.A. Supporter Greenpeace Internat., San Francisco, 1989, Pesticide Watch, L.A., 1990—. Mem. So. Calif. Early Music Soc. Avocations: travel, hiking, feature films, exotic foods. Home: 2844 Avenel St Los Angeles CA 90039-2071

MALECHEK, JOHN CHARLES, ecology and range science educator; b. San Angelo, Tex., Aug. 6, 1942; BS, Tex. Tech. U., 1964; MS, Colo. State U., 1966; PhD in Range Sci., Tex. A&M U., 1970. From asst. prof. to assoc. prof. Utah State U., Logan, 1970-82, prof. range sci., 1982—, head rangeland & resources. dept., 1986—. Mem. Am. Soc. Animal Sci., Soc. Range Mgmt. Office: Utah State U Dept Rangeland & Resources 5320 Old Main Hl Logan UT 84322-0001

MALENG, NORM, prosecutor; b. Acme, Wash., 1938; m. Judy Maleng; 1 child. BS in Econs., U. Wash., 1960, JD, 1966. Bar: Wash. State 1967, U.S. Supreme Ct. 1983, USOC Wash. 1973. Staff atty. U.S. Senate Com. on Commerce; pvt. practice Seattle; chief dep. civil divsn. King County, Seattle, prosecutor, 1978—. Chair Gov.'s Task Force on Cmty. Protection, 1989; vice chair Wash. Sentencing Guidelines Commn. Named Outstanding Pub. Ofcl. in King County, Mcpl. League, 1986. Mem. Wash. Assn. Pros. Attys. (pres.), Nat. Dist. Attys. Assn. (v.p., mem. exec. bd.), Wash. Assn. County Ofcls. (pres.). Office: W554 KC Courthouse 516 3d Ave Seattle WA 98104

MALETIS, ED, distribution executive; Pres., owner Columbia Distributing of Seattle, 1993—. Office: Columbia Distributing Seattle 6840 N Cutter Cir Portland OR 97217-3943

MALHOTRA, RENU, scientist; BS, MS, Indian Inst. Tech., Delhi, 1983; PhD, Cornell U., 1988. Rsch. asst. Indian Inst. Tech., New Delhi, 1983; rsch. assoc. astronomy dept. Cornell U., Ithaca, N.Y., 1988-89; rsch. assoc. planetary sci. Calif. Tech. Inst., Pasadena, 1989-91; staff scientist Lunar & Planetary Inst., Houston, 1991-2000; assoc. prof. dept. planetary sci. U. Az., Tucson, 2000—. Vis. scientist physics dept. U. Ill., Urbana, 1991-93. Contbr. articles to profl. jours. Recipient Harold C. Urey, 1997. Mem. Am. Astron. Soc. Office: U Az Planetary Sci 129 E Univ Blvd Tucson AZ 85721-0092

MALHOTRA, VIVEK, medical educator; BS with honors, Stirling U., 1982; DPhil in Biochemistry, Oxford U., 1985. Asst. prof. biology U. Calif., San Diego, 1990-95, assoc. prof. biology, 1995-99, prof. biology, 1999—. Contbr. articles to profl. jours. Recipient Established Investigator award Am. Heart Assn., 1995; postdoctoral fellow Stanford U., 1985-90, Am. Cancer Soc., Calif., 1988-90; Pirie-Reid scholar, Oxford U., 1982-85, Basil O'Connor Starter scholar, March of Dimes, 1992-95. Office: U Calif Dept Biology 9500 Gilman Dr # 0347 La Jolla CA 92093-5004

MALICK, TERRENCE (DAVID WHITNEY II), film director; b. Waco, Tex., Nov. 30, 1943; Motion picture director, writer, prodr. Films include Dirty Harry, 1971, Pocket Money, 1972, Deadhead Miles, 1972, Badlands, 1973 (Golden Seashell award 1974), The Gravy Train, 1974, Days of Heaven, 1978 (Best Dir. award Cannes Film Festival 1979, nominee Golden Globe award 1979, N.Y. Film Critics Circle award 1978), The Thin Red Line, 1998 (nominee Best Dir. Oscar 1999, nominee Best Writing Oscar 1999, Golden Berlin Bear award 1999, Chgo. Film Critics Assn. award 1999, Golden Satellite award 1999, others). Office: c/o DGA 7920 W Sunset Blvd Los Angeles CA 90046-3300 also: c/o Harley Williams 1900 Ave of the Stars Fl 17 Los Angeles CA 90067

MALIK, OM PARKASH, electrical engineering educator, researcher; b. Sargodha, Punjab, India, Apr. 20, 1932; arrived in Can., 1966; s. Arjan Dass and Kesar Bai (Ahuja) M.; m. Margareta Fagerstrom, Dec. 22, 1968; children: Ola Parkash, Mira, Maya. Nat. Diploma in Elec. Engring., Delhi (India) Poly., 1952; M in Engring., Roorkee (India) U., 1962; PhD, London U., 1965; D.I.C., Imperial Coll., London, 1966. Registered profl. engr., Ont., Alta. Asst. engr. Punjab State Elec. Bd., 1953-61, asst. to chief engr., 1957-59; rsch. engr. English Elec. Co., Eng., 1965-66; asst. prof. U. Windsor, Ont., Can., 1966-68; assoc. prof. U. Calgary, Alta., Can., 1968-74, prof. Can., 1974-97, faculty prof. Can., 1997—, assoc. dean student affairs, faculty engring. Can., 1995-98, assoc. acad. dean faculty engring. Alta., Can., 1979-90, acting dean Can., 1981. Cons. prof. Huazhong U. Sci. and Tech., Wuhan, People's Republic China, 1986—. Assoc. editor Can. Elec. and Computer Engring. Jour., 1988-97, mng. editor, 1998—; contbr. 400 articles to profl. jours. Indsl. tng. scholar Govt. India, 1952-53, sr. indsl. tng. scholar Confedn. Brit. Industries, 1959-60; recipient Can. Pacific Rwy. engring. medal Engring. Inst. Can., 1997. Fellow IEEE (life; chmn. Western Can. coun. 1983-84, chmn. student activities Can. region 1979-82, Centenniel medal 1984, Merit award 1986, Third Millenium medal 2000, A.G.L. McNaughton award 2001), EIC, Inst. Elec. Engrs.; mem. IEEE Power Engring. Soc. (machine theory subcom. 1979—, excitation sys. subcom. 1988—, sys. dynamic performance com. 1988—, energy devel. and power generation com. 1990—), Assn. Profl. Engrs., Geologists and Geophysicists Alta. (Vol. Svc. award 1990), Assn. Profl. Engrs. Ont., Am. Soc. Engring. Edn., Can. Elec. Assn. (assoc., controls com.1977-92, chmn. digital control com. 1977-85, chmn. edn. com. 1983-85, mem. expert sys. com. 1989-94), Confederacion Panamericana de Ingenieria Mecanica, Electica y Ramas Afines (v.p. 1987-2000, bd. dirs. region I, 1991-93). Hindu. Home: 4 6841 Coach Hill Rd SW Calgary AB Canada T3H 3T9 Office: U Calgary Dept Elec & Computer Engring 2500 University Dr NW Calgary AB Canada T2N 1N4 E-mail: maliko@ieee.org

MALINS, DONALD CLIVE, biochemistry, researcher; b. Lima, Peru, May 19, 1931; came to U.S., 1947; s. Richard Henry and Mabel (Madeline) M.; m. Mary Louise Leiren, 1962; children: Christopher W., Gregory S., Timothy J. BA, U. Washington, 1953; BS in Chemistry, Seattle U., 1954; PhD in Biochemistry, U. Aberdeen, 1967, DSc, 1976. Dir. environ. conservation div. Nat. Marine Fisheries Svc., Seattle, 1974-87; sr. scientific cons. U.S. Dept. Justice, Washington, 1989-91; sci. cons. NOAA, 1990-92; prin. scientist, dir. molecular epidemiology program Pacific N.W. Rsch. Inst., Seattle, 1992—; rsch. prof. dept. chemistry Seattle U., 1972-95. Affiliate prof. dept. environ. health U. Washington, 1984—, Coll. Ocean & Fishery Scis. U. Washington, 1974-91; editor-in-chief Aquatic Toxicology, 1980-95; lectr., speaker in field. Contbr. articles to profl. jours.; inventor in field. Bd. dirs. Am. Oceans Campaign, 1989-91; adv. bd. Internat. Jt. Commn., 1990-91. Recipient U.S. Dept. Commerce Gold medal, 1982. Mem. NAS, Am. Soc. Biochemistry and Molecular Biology, Am. Assn. for Cancer Rsch. Office: Pacific Northwest Rsch Inst 720 Broadway Seattle WA 98122-4302 E-mail: dmalins@puni.org

MALL, WILLIAM JOHN, JR. aerospace executive, retired Air Force general; b. Pitts., Jan. 13, 1933; s. William John and Margaret (Henry) M.; m. Vivian Lea Fenton; children— Michele, William, Catherine B.B.A., U. Pitts., 1954; M.B.A., George Washington U., 1966; sr. mgrs. in govt. program, Harvard U., 1980. Commd. officer USAF, 1954, advanced through grades to maj. gen., 1981; insp. gen. Mil. Airlift Command., Scott AFB, Ill., 1978, comdr. 436 wing Dover AFB, Del., 1979; DCS personnel Mil. Airlift Command, Scott AFB, Ill., 1979-81; comdr. Air Rescue Service, Scott AFB, 1981-83, 23d AF/MAC, Scott AFB, 1983-85; assigned to Hdqrs USAF, Bolling AFB, D.C., 1985-86; ret.; dir. integrated logistics support div. Douglas Aircraft Co., Long Beach, Calif., 1987-89, gen. mgr. human resources, 1989-91; exec. dir. LAX Two Corp., L.A., 1991-99. Decorated Legion of Merit, Bronze Star, Air medal Mem. Airlift Assn., Daedalians, Jolly Green Pilots Assn. Avocations: tennis, sailing. Office: LAX Two Corp 200 World Way Los Angeles CA 90045-5859

MALLON, PETER, archbishop; b. Prince Rupert, Can., Dec. 5, 1929; s. Joseph P. and Sheila M. (Keenan) D. Grad., Seminary Christ the King, Burnaby and Mission, B.C. ordained to ministry Roman Cath. Ch., 1956. Asst. Holy Rosary Cath., Vancouver, B.C., 1956-64, rector, 1966-82; chancellor Archdiocese Vancouver, 1964-65, dir. religious edn., 1971-73; adminstr. Guardian Angels Parish, Vancouver, 1964-65; pastor St. Anthony's, West Vancouver, 1982-89; bishop Nelson, B.C., 1989-95; archbishop of Regina Sask., Can., 1995—. Address: 445 Broad St N Regina SK Canada S4R 2X8

MALLORY, FRANK LINUS, lawyer; b. Calgary, Alta., Can., May 5, 1920; s. Frank Louis and Anna Amy (Allstrum) M.; m. Jean Ellen Lindsey, Jan. 29, 1944; children: Susan Mallory Remund, Ann, Bruce R. AB with distinction, Stanford U., 1941, LLB, 1947. Bar: Calif. 1948. Assoc. Gibson, Dunn & Crutcher, L.A., 1947-54; ptnr. L.A. and Orange County, Calif., 1955-88. Cert. specialist taxation law Calif. Bd. Legal Specialization, 1973-89. Pres. Town Hall of Calif., L.A., 1970, Boys Republic, Chino, Calif., 1962-64; pres. Braille Inst. Am., L.A., 1988-92. Lt. (j.g.) USNR, 1942-46. Mem. ABA, Calif. Bar Assn., Los Angeles County Bar Assn., Orange County Bar Assn., Newport Harbor Yacht Club, Big Canyon Country Club, Transpacific Yacht Club (staff commodore), Order of the Coif, Phi Beta Kappa. Republican. Home: 633 Bayside Dr Newport Beach CA 92660-7213 E-mail: flmallory@CS.com

MALLORY, V(IRGIL) STANDISH, geologist, educator; b. Englewood, N.J., July 14, 1919; s. Virgil Sampson and Sarah Lauris (Baum) M.; m. Miriam Elizabeth Rowan, Feb. 3, 1946; children— Charles Standish, Stefan Douglas, Peter Sommers, Ingrid Lauris. A.B., Oberlin Coll., 1943; M.A., U. Calif. at Berkeley, 1948, Ph.D. (Standard Oil of Calif. fellow in paleontology), 1952. Preparator U. Calif. Museum Paleontology, Berkeley, 1946-48, curator foraminifera, 1948-50, cons., 1951; lectr. paleontology U. Calif. at Berkeley, 1951; asst. prof. geology U. Wash., 1952-59, asso. prof., 1959-62; prof., chmn. div. geology and paleontology, curator of paleontology Burke Meml. Wash. State Mus., 1962-84, prof. emeritus, mus. curator, 1984—. Cons. in petroleum geology and mus. curation, in wines to restaurants; lectr. geology of wine; mem. Gov. of Wash. Commn. on Petroleum Regulations, 1956-57; mem. NSF Paris Basin Field Inst., Paris, Belgium and Luxembourg, 1964; co-dir. NSF Inst. Secondary Sch. Tchrs., Western Wash. State Coll., summers 1963, 65. Author: Lower Tertiary Biostratigraphy of California Coast Ranges, 1959, Lower Tertiary Foraminifera From Media Agua Creek Drainage Area, Kern County, California, 1970, Biostratigraphy— A Major Basis of Paleontologic Correlation, 1970; contbg. author: Lincoln Library Essential Knowledge, 1965, Ency. Brit., 15th edit, 1974; Editor paleontology: Quaternary Research Jour, 1970-77; Contbr. articles to profl. jours. Served with AUS, 1944-46, PTO. Am. Assn. Petroleum Geologists Revolving Fund grantee, 1957; U. Wash. Agnes Anderson Fund grantee, 1963 Fellow AAAS (coun. 1964—), Geologic Soc. Am.; mem. Am. Assn. Petroleum Geologists (sect. coun. 1964-84, com. on stratigrahic correlations 1979-85), Paleontologic Soc. (chmn. sect. 1956-58), Geol. Soc. Am., Soc. Econ. Paleontology and Mineralogy, Paleontol. Rsch. Soc., Paleontologische Gesellschaft, Geologische Gesellschaft, Internat. Paleontological Union, N.W. Sci. Soc., Am. Assn. Mus., Mineral Mus. (adv. coun. 1974-87), N.W. Fedn. Mineralogical Socs. (hon. award 1995, 96), N.W. Paleontol. Assn. (hon. mem.), Sigma Xi, Theta Tau. Home: 5209 Pullman Ave NE Seattle WA 98105-2139 Office: U Wash Burke Meml Wash State Mus Db10 Seattle WA 98195-0001

MALMSTADT, HOWARD VINCENT, university provost; b. Marinette, Wis., Mar. 17, 1922; s. Guy August and Nellie (RUsch) M.; m. Carolyn Gay Hart, Aug. 3, 1947; children: Cynthia Sue, Alice Ann, Jonathan Howard. BS, U. Wis., 1943, MS, 1948, PhD, 1950. Postdoctoral rsch. assoc. U. Wis., Madison, 1950-51; mem. faculty U. Ill., Urbana, 1951—, prof. chemistry, 1961-78, emeritus, 1978—, dir. electronic insts., 1960-74; dean sci. and tech., provost, internat. v.p. acad. affairs U. of the Nations, 1978—. Fulbright-Hays disting. prof., Romania, 1978; cons. to govt. and industry. Author textbooks and articles in field; mem. adv. bds. profl. jours.; patentee sci. instruments. Served as officer USNR, 1943-46. Recipient award in edn. Instrument Soc. Am., 1970, Outstanding Analytical Chemist award Pitts. Conf. Analytical Chemistry and Applied Spectroscopy, 1978, ISCO award for contbns. biochem. instrumentation, 1980, award for Outstanding Contbns. in Chemistry, ANACHEM, 1987; Guggenheim fellow, 1960; grantee NSF, 1965-78, NIH, 1975-80. Mem. Am. Chem. Soc. (award instrumentation 1963, award analytical chemistry 1976, award for excellence in tchg. 1984), Soc. Applied Spectroscopy (M.F. Hasler award 1995), Am. Assn. Clin. Chemists. Office: U of the Nations 75 5851 Kuakini Hwy Kailua Kona HI 96740-2136

MALMUTH, NORMAN DAVID, research scientist, program manager; b. Brooklyn, N.Y., Jan. 22, 1931; s. Jacob and Selma Malmuth; m. Constance Nelson, 1970; children: Kenneth, Jill. AE, U. Cin., 1953; MA in Aero. Engring., Polytech. Inst. of N.Y., 1956; PhD in Aeronautics, Calif. Inst. Tech., 1962. Rsch. engr. Grumman Aircraft Engring. Corp., 1953-56; preliminary design engr. N.A. Aviation Div., L.A., 1956-68; teaching asst. Calif. Inst. Tech., L.A., 1961; mem. maths. sci. group Rockwell Internat. Sci. Ctr., 1968-75, project mgr. fluid dynamics rsch., 1975-80, mgr. fluid dynamics group, 1980-82, sr. scientist, project mgr., 1982—. Cons. Aeroject Gen., 1986-89; lectr. UCLA, 1971-72; mem. adv. group for aerospace R&D Fluid Dynamics Panel, 1995; vis. scientist Rensselaer Poly. Inst. Referee AIAA Jour.; bd. editors Jour. Aircraft; contbr. articles to Jour. of Heat Transfer, Internat. Jour. Heat Mass Transfer, and others. Named Calif. Inst. Tech. fellow; recipient Outstanding Alumnus award Univ. Cin., 1990. Fellow AIAA (Aerodynamics award 1991), Am. Phys. Soc.; mem. Am. Acad. Mechanics, Am. Inst. Physics (fluid dynamics divsn.), Soc. Indsl. and Applied Math. Achievements include patent in Methods and Apparatus for Controlling Laser Welding, hypersonic transition delay; pioneering development of high aerodynamic efficiency of hypersonic delta wing body combinations, hypersonic boundary layer stability, transonic wind tunnel interference, plasma aerodynamics, flow control web dynamics, combined asymptotic and numerical methods in fluid dynamics and aerodynamics. Home: 182 Maple Rd Newbury Park CA 91320-4718 Office: Rockwell Sci Ctr PO Box 1085 1049 Camino Dos Rios Thousand Oaks CA 91360-2362 E-mail: wortham@humnet.ucla.edu

MALONE, JOHN C. telecommunications executive; b. 1941; m. Leslie. Attended Yale U., Johns Hopkins U. Formerly pres. Jerrold Electronics Corp.; pres., CEO Tele-Comms., Inc., Denver, chmn. and CEO, 1996-99; chmn. Liberty Media, Denver, 1999—. Office: Tele Comm Inc Liberty Media 9197 S Peoria St Englewood CO 80112

MALONE, KARL, professional basketball player; b. Summerfield, La., July 24, 1963; Student, La. Tech. U., 1981-85. Basketball player Utah Jazz, 1985—. Mem. U.S. Olympic Basketball Team (received Gold medal), 1992. Mem. NBA All-Star team, 1988-94; recipient NBA All-Star Game MVP award, 1989, co-recipient, 1993; mem. All-NBA first team, 1989-94; mem. All-NBA second team, 1988; mem. NBA All-Defensive second team, 1988; mem. NBA All-Rookie Team, 1986; co-leader most seasons (8) with 2000 points, 1987-95; NBA Most Valuable Player, 1997. Office: Utah Jazz Delta Ctr 301 W South Temple Salt Lake City UT 84101-1216

MALONE, KEVIN, sports team executive; b. San Diego, Aug. 6, 1957; m. Marilyn Perry; children: Shannon, Shawn. Grad., U. Louisville, 1980. Second baseman Cleve. Indians, 1980-85; scout and coach Calif. Angels, 1985-87; East Coast supr. Minn. Twins, 1989-91; coach N.Y. Penn League, 1988; dir. scouting Montreal Expos, 1991-93, gen. mgr., 1994-95, Balt. Orioles, 1995-99; exec. v.p., gen. mgr. L.A. Dodgers, 1999—.

MALONE, NANCY, actor, director, producer; b. Queens Village, N.Y. d. James and Bridget (Sheilds) M. Freelance actress, dir., producer, writer. Performer (TV series) The First Hundred Years, Naked City, The Long, Hot Summer (Best Performance by an Actress award); Broadway debut in Time Out For Ginger, other stage performances include Major Barbara, The Makropoulis Secret, A Touch of the Poet, The Trial of the Catonsville Nine; touring performances include The Chalk Garden, The Seven Yr. Itch, A Place For Dolly; actress (films) The Violators, I Cast No Shadow, An Affair of the Skin, Intimacy, The Trial of the Cantonsville Nine, The Man Who Loved Cat Dancing, Capricorn One; producer (TV series) including Bionic Woman, 1978, Husbands, Wives and Lovers, 1978, The Great Pretender, 1984, (special) Bob Hope: The First 90 Years, 1993 (Emmy award, Outstanding Variety, Musical or Comedy Special, 1993), Womanspeak, 1983; dir. (TV series) Dynasty, 1984-87, Hotel, 1984-87, Colbys, 1985, Cagney and Lacey, 1987, Star Trek Voyager, 1997, Burning Zone, 1997, Fame, Rosie O'Niel (Emmy nomination), Sisters (Emmy nomination), Melrose Place, Beverly Hills, Picket Fences; producer, dir. (film) There Were Times Dear, 1986 (John Muir Trustees award, Cine Golden Eagle, Blue Ribbon); founder Nancy Malone Prodns., 1975, Lilac Prodns., 1979. Fellow Leaky Found.; mem. Am. Film Inst. (mem. founder), Women in Film (trustee, Chrystal award, Founders award 1996). Office: Guild Mgmt PHA 9911 W Pico Blvd Los Angeles CA 90035-2703

MALONE, ROBERT JOSEPH, retired bank executive; b. Sept. 3, 1944; With Bank of Am., 1969-81; chmn., pres., CEO First Interstate Bank Boise, Idaho, 1981-84; pres., CEO First Interstate Bank Denver, 1984-90; chmn., pres., CEO Western Capital Investment Corp. (now First Bank System, Inc.), Denver, 1990-92; chmn., CEO Bank Western/Central Banks (now First Bank System, Inc.), Denver, 1992-93; CEO Colo. Nat. Bank, Denver, 1993—; chmn. U.S. Bank (formerly Colo. Nat. Bank), Denver, 1996-2001, ret., 2001. Office: US Bank 950 17th St Denver CO 80202-2815

MALONEY, ROBERT E., JR. lawyer; b. San Francisco, Sept. 17, 1942; s. Robert E. and Mara A. (Murphy) M.; children: Michael, Sarah, Paul. BA magna cum laude, U. Portland, 1964; JD summa cum laude, Willamette U., Salem, Oreg., 1967. Bar: Oreg., Wash., U.S. Dist. Ct. Oreg., U.S. Dist. Ct. (we. dist.) Wash., U.S. Dist. Ct. (ea. dist.) Wash., U.S. Ct. Appeals (9th cir.). Ptnr. Lane Powell Spears Lubersky, LLP, Portland, 1967—. Bd. dirs., sec. Norm Thompson Outfitters, Inc., Portland; chmn. bd. visitors Willamette U. Law Sch., 1993-95, bd. dirs. emeritus, 1998—; past chair, mem. exec. com. Portland Trial Dept.; lawyers del. 9th Cir. Jud. Conf., 1995-97; pres. adv. coun. U. Portland, 2001—. Bd. dirs., Oreg. chpt. Multiple Sclerosis Soc.; judge pro tem Multnomah County Cir. Ct., 1994-99; bd. dirs. Oreg. Lawyers Against Hunger, 1997-99. Mem. ABA (co-chair products liability com., trial practice com. 1990-94), Nat. Assn. R.R. Trial Counsel, Fedn. Ins. Corp. Counsel, Oreg. Assn. Def. Counsel (bd. dirs. 1987-94, sec. 1991-92, v.p. 1993-94, pres. 1994), Fed. Bar Assn. (exec. com. Oreg. divsn. 1988-96, pres. 1994-95), Multnomah Athletic Club. Republican. Roman Catholic. Office: Lane Powell Spears Lubersky LLP 601 SW Second Ave Ste 2100 Portland OR 97204-3158 Fax: 503-778-2200

MALOOF, GAVIN, professional sports team executive; Co-owner profl. basketball team Houston Rockets, 1979-82, Sacramento Kings; co-owner WNBA's Sacramento Monarchs, Sacramento Knights, ARCO Arena; vice chmn. Maloof Cos. Office: One Sports Pky Sacramento CA 95834

MALOOF, GILES WILSON, academic administrator, educator, author; b. San Bernardino, Calif., Jan. 4, 1932; s. Joseph Peters and Georgia (Wilson) M.; m. Mary Anne Ziniker, Sept. 5, 1958 (dec. Oct. 1976); children: Mary Jane, Margery Jo. BA, U. Calif., Berkeley, 1953; MA, U. Oreg., 1958; PhD, Oreg. State U., 1962. Petroleum reservoir engr. Creole Petroleum Corp., Venezuela, 1953-54; mathematician electronics divsn. rsch. dept. U.S. Naval Ordnance Rsch. Lab., Corona, Calif., 1958-59; asst. prof. math. Oreg. State U., Corvallis, 1962-68, rsch. assoc. dept. oceanography, 1963-68, vis. prof. math., 1977-78; prof. math. Boise (Idaho) State U., 1968—, head dept., 1968-75, dean grad. sch., 1970-75. Author, reviewer of coll. textbooks; contbr. to profl. jours. Served with Ordnance Corps, AUS, 1950, 54-56. Recipient Carter award, 1963, Mosser prize, 1966, Oreg. State U., Alumni Found. scholar Teaching award Boise State U., 2000. Mem. Math. Assn. Am., Am. Math. Soc., Soc. Indsl. and Applied Math., N.W. Coll. and Univ. Assn. for Sci. (dir. 1973—, pres. 1990-92), N.W. Sci. Assn. (trustee 1977-80), Assn. Western Univs. (mem. edn. and rsch. com. 1993—), Sigma Xi, Pi Mu Epsilon, Phi Kappa Phi. Home: 1400 Longmont Ave Boise ID 83706-3730 E-mail: giles@diamond.idbsu.edu

MALOOF, JOSEPH, professional sports team executive; Co-owner profl. basketball team Houston Rockets, 1979-82, Sacramento Kings, 1999—; co-owner WNBA's Sacramento Monarchs, Sacramento Knights, ARCO Arena; ptnr., pres. Maloof Cos. Mem. NBA Bd. Govs., 1999—. Office: One Sports Pky Sacramento CA 95834

MALOOF, PHILLIP J. state legislator; BUS, U. N.Mex. Exec. v.p. Maloof Hotels; mem. N.Mex. Legislature, Santa Fe, 1993—, vice chair corps. and transp. com., vice chair Indian and cultural affairs. Democrat. Office: 119 Industrial Ave NE Albuquerque NM 87107-2228

MALOTT, ADELE RENEE, editor; b. St. Paul, July 19, 1935; d. Clarence R. and Julia Anne (Christensen) Lindgren; m. Gene E. Malott, Oct. 24, 1957 B.S., Northwestern U., 1957. Coordinator news KGB Radio, San Diego, 1958-60; asst. pub. relations dir. St. Paul C. of C., 1961-63; night editor Daily Local News, West Chester, Pa., 1963-65; editor, co-pub. Boutique and Villager, Burlingame, Calif., 1966-76; sr. editor mag. The Webb Co., St. Paul, 1978-84; editor GEM Pub. Group, Reno, 1985-2001. Faculty Reader's Digest Writers' Workshops. Co-author: Get Up and Go: A Guide for the Mature Traveler, 1989, The Mature Traveler's Book of Deals, 1997; columnist The Mature Traveler, 1989—. Recipient numerous awards Soc. Am. Travel Writers, Nat. Fedn. Press Women, Calif. Newspaper Pubs. Assn., San Francisco Press Club, Calif. Taxpayers Assn., White House Citations. Mem. Internat. Assn. Bus. Communicators (Merit award 1984), Press Women Minn. (numerous awards), Press Women Nev., Soc. Am. Travel Writers (chair Western chpt. 1996-98, v.p. 1999). Avocations: historical research, golf, travel, photography, reading. E-mail: maturetrav@aol.com

MALOY, STUART, materials scientist, engineer; BS, Case Western Res. U., 1989, MS, 1991, PhD, 1994. Staff mem. Los Alamos (N.Mex.) Nat. Lab. Contbr. articles to profl. jours. Office: Los Alamos Nat Lab APT TPO MSHP09 PO Box 1663 Los Alamos NM 87545

MALTIN, LEONARD, television commentator, writer; b. N.Y.C., Dec. 18, 1950; s. Aaron Isaac and Jacqueline (Gould) M.; m. Alice Tlusty, Mar. 15, 1975; 1 child, Jessica Bennett. BA, NYU, 1972. Mem. faculty New Sch. for Social Rsch., N.Y.C., 1973-81; curator Am. Acad. Humor, N.Y.C., 1975-76; guest curator dept. film Mus. Modern Art, N.Y.C., 1976; film critic and corr. Entertainment Tonight, Hollywood, Calif., 1982—; columnist Modern Maturity, 1996-99; film critic Playboy mag., 1998—. Adj. prof. Sch. Cinema & TV, U. So. Calif., 1998—. Author: Movie Comedy Teams, 1970, rev. edit., 1985, Behind the Camera (reprinted as The Art of the Cinematographer), 1971, The Great Movie Shorts (reprinted as Selected Short Subjects), 1971, The Disney Films, 1973, rev. edit., 2000, The Great Movie Comedians, 1978, Of Mice and Magic: A History of American Animated Cartoons, 1980, rev. edit., 1987, The Great American Broadcast, 1997; co-author: Our Gang: The Life and Times of the Little Rascals, 1977, reprinted as The Little Rascals: The Life and Times of Our Gang, 1992; editor: Leonard Maltin's Movie & Video Guide, 1969, rev. annually, Leonard Maltin's Movie Encyclopedia, 1994, Leonard Maltin's Family Film Guide, 1999; producer, writer, host (video) Cartoons for Big Kids, 1989; writer (TV spl.) Fantasia: The Making of a Disney Classic, 1990; writer, host (video) The Making of The Quiet Man, 1992, The Making of High Noon, 1992, Cartoon Madness: The Fantastic Max Fleischer Cartoons, 1993, Cliffhanger!, 1993. Mem. steering com. Hollywood Entertainment Mus., 1989—. Mem. Authors Guild, Soc. for Cinephiles (pres. 1990-91, Man of Yr. 1973), L.A. Film Critics Assn. (pres. 1995-96). Office: c/o Entertainment Tonight Paramount TV 5555 Melrose Ave Los Angeles CA 90038-3112

MALTZAN, MICHAEL THOMAS, architect; b. Roslyn Heights, N.Y., Oct. 10, 1959; s. William George and Jacqualine (Cain) M.; m. Amy Louise Murphy, Sept. 25, 1988. Student, Wentworth Inst. Tech., 1977-79; BFA, RISD, 1984, BArch, 1985; MArch with letter of distinction, Harvard U., 1988. Lic. architect, Calif. Architect The Architects, Glastonbury, Conn., 1978-80, Williamd D. Warner Assocs., Exeter, R.I., 1980-83, Steven Lerner Assocs., Providence, 1983-84, Schwartz/Silver Assocs., Boston, 1984-86, Machado-Silvetti Assocs., Boston, 1986-88, Frank O. Gehry Assocs., L.A., 1988-95; pvt. practice architecture L.A., 1995—. Instr. RISD, Providence, 1987, Harvard U., Cambridge, Mass., 1988; co-instr. UCLA, 1989, U. Waterloo, 1993, RISD, 1995, Harvard U., 1999; invited jury critic Harvard U., RISD, So. Calif. Inst. Architecture, L.A., Ariz. State U., tempe, Calif. Coll. Arts and Crafts, San Francisco, U. SO. Calif., L.A., UCLA, Iowa State U., Ames, Miami (Ohio) U. Prin. works include Unitarian-Universalist Ch., Vernon, Conn., 1979, Providence Riverfront Study, 1982, Harvard Law Sch. Alumni Bldg. Addition, Cambridge, 1984, 330 Congress St. Renovation, Boston, 1985, 280 Summer St. Renovation, Boston, 1986, City of Leonforte, Italy Master Plan, 1987 (Progressive Arch. award), North Park Apt. Complex Renovation, Chevy Chase, Md., 1988, Walt Disney Concert Hall, 1988— (Progressive Arch. award), Culver City (Calif.) Retail Complex Master Plan, 1990, Villa Olympica Retail and Entertainment Complex, Barcelona, Spain, 1992, U. Toledo Art Sch., 1992 (AIA award), Inner-City Arts Sch., L.A., 1994, Harvard Westlake Art Ctr., 1997, Getty Culture Lab., 1997. Recipient Coll. Gold medal AIA. Office: 2801 Hyperion Ave # 107 Los Angeles CA 90027-2571

MAMER, JAMES MICHAEL, secondary education educator; b. L.A., Oct. 8, 1948; s. James Robert and Annette (Babue) M.; m. Jessica Puma, Aug. 31, 1963. BA in Polit. Sci., Calif. Poly. U., Pomona, 1970; MA in Internat. Studies, Immaculate Heart Coll., 1990. Tchr. Irvine (Calif.) Unified Sch. Dist., 1978—. Mentor tchr. Irvine Sch. Dist., 1988-95. Mem. editl. bd. Global Pages, L.A., 1991-96. Recipient Global Teaching award Western Internat. Studies Consortium, L.A., 1991, Am. Coun. Internat. Edn. award, 1998; Fulbright-Hays grantee, India, 1977; Coe fellow, 1984. Mem. Nat. Coun. Social Studies (Nat. Social Studies Tchr. of Yr. 1992), Irvine Tchrs. Assn. Democrat. Avocation: reading. Home: 29102 Kommers Ln Silverado CA 92676-9726

MAMER, JOHN WILLIAM, business educator; b. July 4, 1954; BA, BS, U. Calif., 1975; MS, U. Calif., Berkeley, 1978, PhD, 1982. Analyst Manalytics Inc., 1977-78; rsch. intern Xerox Corp., 1979-80; from asst. prof. to prof. U. Calif., L.A., 1981-96, prof., 1996—. Lectr. in field. Referee Mgmt. Sci., 1982—, Ops. Rsch., 1984—, Jour. Econ. Dynamics and Control, 1984, 88; contbr. over 15 articles to profl. jours. Mem. Inst. Mgmt. Sci. (organizing chmn. 1994, arangements chmn. 1995), Ops. Rsch. Soc. Am. Office: The Anderson School UCLA PO Box 951481 Los Angeles CA 90095-1481*

MAN, LAWRENCE KONG, architect, graphic, furniture and fashion designer; b. Kowloon, Hong Kong, July 4, 1953; s. Hon-Kwong Man and Sau-Ching Luk. Student, U. Redlands, 1971-72; BArch, U. Oreg., 1977; MArch, Harvard U., 1978. Registered architect, Mass., Calif. Designer, project architect Shepley Bulfinch Richardson & Abbott, Boston, 1978-86; project designer, project architect E. Verner Johnson & Assoc., Boston, 1987-91; owner Lawrence Man Architect, Cambridge, Mass., 1992-95, L.A., 1994—. Bd. dirs. Fashion Bus. Incubator. Prin. works include Fong House, San Marino, Calif., Tighe Summer House, Sagamore Beach, Mass, Frozen Fusion Juice Bar, L.A. schs., Fed. Credit Union, L.A., Pub. Mus. Grand Rapids, Mich. (AIA Grand Valley Disting. Bldg. award 1997), LCP Studio, Somerville, Mass., New Asia Restaurants, Danvers and Arlington, Mass., Tai Pan Restaurant, Cambridge, Mass. (Honor award AIA 1993, New Eng. award Excellence in Architecture 1993, Design Excellence award Nat. Orgn. Minority Architects 1993), Ti-Sales Office, Sudbury, Mass. (Design Excellence award Nat. Orgn. Minority Architects 1993), Dental Clinic, Reading, Mass. (AIA Interior Architecture award 1992, Interior Design Project award Am. Soc. Interior Designers 1991, Boston Exports citation AIA 1990, Boston Soc. of Architects/New Eng. Healthcare Assembly honor award, 1994), Mus. Ctr. Union Terminal, Cin. (Reconstrn. award 1991), Ramesses Pavilion Boston Mus. Sci. (Double Vision award/Double Silver Soc. Environ. Graphics 1990), Smithsonian South Quadrangle Mus., Washington (Boston Exports award/citation AIA 1990, Honor award AIA 1989), U. Vt. Student Ctr., Burlington, Campus Ctr. Study and Libr. addition Franklin & Marshall Coll., Andover (Mass.) Co. Corp. Hdqs., Emerson Hosp., Concord, Mass., pvt. residences, others. Mem. AIA, Am. Assn. Mus., Fashion Bus. Incubator (bd. dirs.). Avocations: dancing, traveling, music. Home: 939 1/2 Chung King Rd Los Angeles CA 90012 E-mail: lawrencemanarchitects@hotmail.com

MANASSON, VLADIMIR ALEXANDROVICH, physicist; b. Chernovtsy, Ukraine, Mar. 4, 1952; came to U.S., 1991; s. Alexander and Chaya (Finkelsteyn) M.; m. Katrine Kokhanovskaya, Aug. 2, 1975; children: Alexander, Julia. BSEE, Moscow Inst. Electronic Mfg., 1973, MSEE, 1974; PhD in Physics, Chernovtsy U., 1984. Entr. Acad. of Scis. of the Ukraine Material Sci. Inst., 1975-78, sr. engr., 1978-80, jr. rsch. assoc., 1980-85, sr. rsch. assoc., 1985-90; rsch. scientist Phys. Optics Corp., Torrance, Calif., 1991-94, sr. scientist, 1994-95; leader antenna devel. WaveBand Corp., Torrance, 1996-98, dir. rsch., 1999-2000, v.p. R&D, 2000—. Patentee several photosensitive devices and antennae. Grantee NSF, 1993-94, 97, 98, Dept. Def., 1994, 95, 96, 97, 98, 99, Dept. Transp., 1994, 97, 98, U.S. Dept. Commerce, 1997, Nat. Rsch. Coun./Nat. Acad. of Sci., 1995, 98, L.A. Regional Tech. Alliance, 1999. Mem. IEEE, Optical Soc. Am., Assn. of Old Crows. Avocations: piano improvising, reading, children, cooking. Office: 375 Van Ness Ave Torrance CA 90501-1497 E-mail: vmanasson@earthlink.net

MANCHESTER, CRAIG, construction executive; Pres. Western Pacific Homes, El Segundo, Calif., 1998—. Office: 300 Continental Blvd Ste 390 El Segundo CA 90245

MANCINO, DOUGLAS MICHAEL, lawyer; b. May 8, 1949; s. Paul and Adele (Brazaitis) M.; m. Carol Keith, June 16, 1973. BA, Kent State U., 1971; JD, Ohio State U., 1974. Bar: Ohio 1974, U.S. Tax Ct. 1977, Calif. 1981, D.C. 1981. Assoc. Baker & Hostetler, Cleve., 1974-80; ptnr. Memel & Ellsworth, L.A., 1980-87, McDermott, Will & Emery, L.A., 1987—. Bd. dirs. Health Net of Calif. Inc. Author: Taxation of Hospitals and Health Care Organizations, 2000, (with others) Hospital Survival Guide, 1984, Navigating the Federal Physician Self-Referral Law, 1998; (with F. Hill) Taxation of Exempt Organizations, 2001; co-author quar. tax column Am. Hosp. Assn. publ. Health Law Vigil, (with L. Burns) Joint Ventures Between Hosps. and Physicians, 1987; contbr. articles to profl. jours. Chmn. bd. dirs. The Children's Burn Found. Mem. ABA (tax, bus., real property, probate and trust sects., chair exempt orgns. com. 1995-97, coun. dir. 1999—), Calif. State Bar Assn. (tax, bus. law sects.), Ohio Bar Assn., Calif. State Bar, D.C. Bar Assn., Am. Health Lawyers Assn. (bd. dirs. 1986-95, pres. 1993-94), Calif. Soc. for Healthcare Attys., Bel Air Country Club, The Regency Club, Calif. Yacht Club. Office: McDermott Will & Emery 2049 Century Park E Fl 34 Los Angeles CA 90067-3101 E-mail: dmancino@mwe.com

MANCUSO, FRANK G. entertainment and communications company executive; b. Buffalo, July 25, 1933; married Ed., SUNY. Film buyer, ops. supr. Basil Enterprises, 1959-63; joined Paramount Pictures Corp., 1963, booker Buffalo br., 1963-64, sales rep. Buffalo br., 1964-67, br. mgr., 1967-70; v.p., gen. sales mgr. Paramount Pictures Can. Ltd., 1970-72, pres., 1972-76; U.S. we. divsn. mgr. Paramount Pictures Corp., L.A., 1976-77, gen. sales mgr. N.Y.C., 1977, v.p. domestic distbn., 1977-79, exec. v.p. distbn. and mktg., 1979-83, pres. motion picture divsn., 1983-84, chmn., CEO, 1984-91; chmn, CEO Metro-Goldwyn-Mayer, 1993-99. Bd. dirs. Metro-Goldwyn Mayer. Bd. dirs. Will Rogers Meml. Fund, N.Y.-Cornell Med. Ctr., Burke Rehab. Ctr., UCLA Med. Ctr., Mus. of Broadcasting, MGM Motion Picture TV Found. Mem. Acad. Motion Picture Arts and Scis. (bd. dirs.), Motion Picture Assn. (bd. dirs.), Am. Film Inst. (bd. dirs.), Motion Picture Pioneers (bd. dirs.), Variety Clubs Internat. (bd. dirs.). Office: Metro Goldwyn Mayer Inc 2500 Broadway Ste B-201 Santa Monica CA 90404-3065

MANCUSO, VINCE, advertising executive; Chief ifn. officer, sr. v.p. Rubin Postaer & Assocs., Santa Monica, Calif. Office: Rubin Postaer & Assocs 1333 2d St Santa Monica CA 90401

MANDARICH, DAVID D. real estate corporation executive; b. 1948; With Majestic Savs. and Loan, 1966-67; formerly chief operating officer, exec. v.p. MDC Holdings Inc., pres., co-chief operating officer, from 1986, now pres., chief operating officer. Office: MDC Holdings Richmond Amer Homes 3600 S Yosemite St Ste 900 Denver CO 80237-1867

MANDEL, JOSEPH DAVID, academic administrator, lawyer; b. N.Y.C., Mar. 26, 1940; s. Max and Charlotte Lee (Goodman) M.; m. Jean Carol Westerman, Aug. 18, 1963; children: Jonathan Scott, Eric David. AB, Dartmouth Coll., 1960, MBA with distinction, 1961; JD, Yale U., 1964. Bar: Calif. 1965. Law clk. U.S. Ct. Appeals, 9th cir., L.A., 1964-65; lectr. law U. So. Calif. Law Ctr., L.A., 1965-68; assoc. atty. Tuttle & Taylor, L.A., 1965-69, mem., 1970-82, 90-91, of counsel, 1984-90; vice chancellor UCLA, 1991—, lectr. in law, 1993; v.p., gen. counsel, sec. Natomas Co., San Francisco, 1983. Mem. Calif. Legal Corps, 1993—; bd. dirs. LRN, The Legal Knowledge Co. Mem. bd. editors Yale Law Jour., 1962-64. Pres. Legal Aid Found., L.A., 1978-79; trustee Southwestern U. Sch. Law, 1982, UCLA Pub. Interest Law Found., 1981-82, L.A. County Bar Found., 1974-79, 82, Coro Found., 1989-92, UCLA Armand Hammer Mus. Art and Cultural Ctr., 1995—, Geffen Playhouse, Inc., 1995-98, Coro So. Calif. Ctr., 1985-92, bd. dirs. pub. coun., 1989-94, cmty. v.p., 1992-94; mem. L.A. Bd. Zoning Appeals, 1984-90, vice-chmn., 1985-86, 89-90, chmn., 1986-87; mem. L.A. City Charter Reform Commn., 1996-99; bd. dirs. Western Justice Ctr. Found., 1989—, v.p., 1992-95, 1st v.p., 1995-97, sr. v.p., 1997-99, pres., 1999—; bd. dirs. Harvard Water Polo Found., 1990-96; bd. advisors Pub. Svc. Challenge Nat. Assn. for Pub. Interest Law, 1990—; bd. govs. Inner City Law Ctr., 1991—; mem. Blue Ribbon Screening Com. to Select Insp. Gen., L.A. Police Commn., 1999; mem. bd. overseers Inst. for Civil Justice, RAND, 1999—. Recipient Maynard Toll award Legal Aid Found. of L.A., 1991, Shattuck-Price award L.A. County Bar Assn., 1993, West Coast Liberty award Lambda Legal Def. and Edn. Fund, 1994, Cmty. Achievement award Pub. Coun., 1996; named One of Calif.'s 100 Most Influential Attys. by Calif. Bus. Jour., 2000. Mem. State Bar Calif. (legal svcs. trust fund commn. 1985-87, chmn. 1985-86), Yale U. Law Sch. Assn. (exec. com. 1983-88, 90-96, v.p. 1986-88, chmn. planning com. 1990-92, pres. 1992-94, chmn. exec. com. 1994-96), mem. alumni Coun. Dartmouth Coll., 1992-95, Dartmouth Coll. Assn. Alumni (exec. com. 1997—), Order of Coif. Democrat. Jewish. Home: 15478 Longbow Dr Sherman Oaks CA 91403-4910 Office: UCLA Office Chancellor 2135 Murphy Hl Los Angeles CA 90095-1405 E-mail: jmandel@conet.ucla.edu

MANDEL, MARTIN LOUIS, lawyer; b. L.A., May 17, 1944; s. Maurice S. and Florence (Byer) M.; m. Duree Dunn, Oct. 16, 1982; 1 child, Max Andrew. BA, U. So. Calif., 1965, JD, 1968; LLM, George Washington U., 1971. Bar: Calif. 1969, U.S. Dist. Ct. (cen. dist.) Calif. 1972, U.S. Ct. Claims 1971, U.S. Tax Ct. 1971, U.S. Supreme Ct. 1972. With office of gen. csl. IRS, Washington, 1968-72; ptnr. Stephens, Jones, LaFever & Smith, L.A., 1972-77, Stephens, Martin & Mandel, 1977-79, Fields, Fehn, Feinstein & Mandel, 1979-83; sr. v.p., gen. counsel Investment Mortgage Internat., Inc., 1983-84; ptnr. Feinstein, Gourley & Mandel, 1984-85, Mandel & Handin, San Francisco, 1985—; gen. counsel L.A. Express Football Club, 1983-85. Instr. corps. U. West L.A., 19873-83. Mem. ABA, L.A. County Bar Assn., L.A. Athletic Club, Phi Delta Phi. Office: 1510 Fashion Island Blvd San Mateo CA 94404-1596 E-mail: TMGTalent@aol.com, tmgtalent@msn.com

MANDEL, MORTON, molecular biologist; b. Bklyn., July 6, 1924; s. Barnet and Rose (Kliner) M.; m. Florence H. Goodman, Apr. 1, 1952; children: Robert, Leslie. BCE, CUNY, 1944; MS, Columbia U., 1949, PhD in Physics, 1957. Scientist Bell Telephone Labs., Murray Hill, N.J., 1956-57; asst. prof. physics dept. Stanford (Calif.) U., 1957-61; scientist Gen. Telephone & Telegraph, Mountain View, Calif., 1961-63; rsch. assoc. dept. genetics Stanford U., 1963-64; rsch. fellow Karolinska Inst., Stockholm, Sweden, 1964-66; assoc. prof. sch. of medicine U. Hawaii, Honolulu, 1966-68, prof., 1968—; founder, dir. Hawaii Biotechnology Group, Inc., 1982-95. Cons. Fairchild Semiconductor, Hewlett Packard, Lockheed, Rheem, Palo Alto, Calif., 1957-61. Contbr. articles to profl. jours. Lt. (j.g.) USN, 1944-46. Recipient Am. Cancer Soc. Scholar award Am. Cancer Soc., 1979-80, Eleanor Roosevelt Internat. Cancer fellowship, 1979; named NIH Spl. fellow Karolinska Inst., 1964-66. Fellow Am. Phys. Soc.; mem. Sigma Xi. Achievements include citation classics; optimal conditions for mutagenesis by N-methyl-N-nitro-N-nitrosoguanidine in E. coli K12; calcium dependent bacteriophage DNA infection. Office: Dept Biochemistry 1960 E West Rd Honolulu HI 96822-2319

MANDEL, OSCAR, literature educator, writer; b. Antwerp, Belgium, Aug. 24, 1926; came to U.S., 1940; m. Adrienne Schizzano. BA, NYU, 1947; MA, Columbia U., 1948; PhD, Ohio State U., 1951. Asst. prof. English U. Nebr., 1955-60; Fulbright lectr. U. Amsterdam, 1960-61; vis. assoc. prof. English Calif. Inst. Tech., 1961-62, assoc. prof. English, 1962-68, prof. Lit., 1968—. Author: A Definition of Tragedy, 1961, The Theater of Don Juan, 1963, Chi Po and the Sorcerer, 1964, The Gobble-Up Stories, 1967, Seven Comedies by Marivaux, 1968, Five Comedies of Medieval France, 1970, The Collected Plays, 1970-72, Amphitryon, 1976, The Land of Upside Down by Tieck, 1978, The Ariadne of Thomas Corneille, 1982, Collected Lyrics and Epigrams, 1981, Three Classic Don Juan Plays, 1981, Philoctetes and the Fall of Troy, 1981, Annotations to Vanity Fair, 1981, The Book of Elaborations, 1985, The Kukkurrik Fables, 1987, Sigismund, Prince of Poland, 1989, August von Kotzebue: The Comedy, The Man, 1990, The Virgin and the Unicorn: Four Plays, 1993, The Art of Alessandro Magnasco: An Essay on the Recovery of Meaning, 1994, The Cheerfulness of Dutch Art: A Rescue Operation, 1996, Two Romantic Plays: The Spaniards in Denmark and The Rebels of Nantucket, 1996, Fundamentals of the Art of Poetry, 1998, The Couble Book of Beguiling Fables, 2001; contbr. articles to profl. jours. Office: Calif Inst Tech Humanities Divsn Pasadena CA 91125-0001

MANDELSTAM, STANLEY, physicist; b. Johannesburg, South Africa, Dec. 12, 1928; came to U.S., 1963; s. Boris and Beatrice (Liknaitzky) M. BSc, U. Witwatersrand, Johannesburg, 1952; BA, Cambridge U., Eng., 1954; PhD, Birmingham U., Eng., 1956. Boese postdoctoral fellow Columbia U., N.Y.C., 1957-58; prof. math. physics U. Birmingham, 1960-63; asst. rsch. physicist U. Calif., Berkeley, 1958-60, prof. physics, 1963-94, prof. emertitus, 1994—. Vis. prof. physics Harvard U., Cambridge, Mass., 1965-66, Univ. de Paris, Paris Sud, 1979-80, 84-85. Editorial bd. The Phys. Rev. jour., 1978-81, 85-88; contbr. articles to profl. jours. Recipient Dirac medal and prize Internat. Ctr. for Theoretical Physics, 1991. Fellow AAAS, Royal Soc. London, Am. Phys. Soc. (Dannie N. Heineman Math. Physics prize 1992). Jewish. Office: U Calif Dept Physics Berkeley CA 94720-0001

MANDICH, MITCHELL, computer company executive; Grad., U. Calif., Berkeley. Tchr. sociology West Valley Coll. and San Jose State U.; sales and mgmt. posiitons Unisys; dir. U.S. sales ops., dir. Western Region ops. Tandem; sr. v.p. Ams. sales and mktg. Pyramid Tech.; v.p. worldwide sales and svcs. NeXT Software; sr. v.p. N.Am. sales Apple Computer, Inc., Cupertino, Calif., v.p. N.Am. bus. divsn., sr. v.p. worldwide sales. Office: 1 Infinite Loop Cupertino CA 95014-2083

MANDLER, GEORGE, psychologist, educator; b. Vienna, Austria, June 11, 1924; came to U.S., 1940, naturalized, 1943; s. Richard and Hede (Goldschmied) M.; m. Jean Matter, Jan. 19, 1957; children: Peter Clark, Michael Allen. BA, NYU, 1949; MS, Yale U., 1950, PhD, 1953; postgrad., U. Basel, Switzerland, 1947-48. Asst. prof. Harvard U., 1953-57, lectr., 1957-60; prof. U. Toronto, Ont., Can., 1960-65; prof. psychology U. Calif., San Diego, 1965-94, chmn. dept. psychology, 1965-70, prof. emeritus, 1994—; dir. Ctr. Human Info. Processing, U. Calif., San Diego, 1965-90. Hon. rsch. fellow Univ. Coll. London., 1977-78, 82-90, vis. prof., 1990—. Author: Mind and Emotion, 1975, (German edit.), 1980, Mind and Body, 1984, (Japanese edit.), 1987, Cognitive Psychology, 1985, Japanese edit., 1991, Human Nature Explored, 1997; co-author: (with W. Kessen) The Language of Psychology, (Italian edit.), 1959, (with J.M. Mandler) Thinking: From Association to Gestalt, 1964; contbr. articles and revs. to profl. jours.; editor: Psychol. Rev., 1970-76. Served with U.S. Army, 1943-46. Fellow Ctr. for Advanced Study in Behavioral Scis., 1959-60; vis. fellow Oxford U., Eng., 1971-72, 78; Guggenheim fellow, 1971-72. Fellow AAAS, Am. Acad. Arts and Scis.; mem. AAUP, Am. Assn. Advancement Psychology (1974-82); Psychonomic Soc. (governing bd., chmn. 1983), Am. Psychol. Soc., Am. Psychol. Assn. (pres. div. exptl. psychology 1978-79, pres. div. gen psychology 1982-83, mem. coun. reps. 1978-82, William James prize 1986), Internat. Union Psychol. Scis. (U.S. com. 1985-90), Soc. Exptl. Psychologists, Fedn. Behavioral Psychol. and Cognitive Scis. (pres. 1981). Home: 1406 La Jolla Knoll La Jolla CA 92037-5236 Office: U Calif San Diego Dept Psychology La Jolla CA 92093-0109 also: 3 Perrins Lane London NW3 1QY England E-mail: gmandler@ucsd.edu

MANDLER, JEAN MATTER, psychologist, educator; b. Oak Park, Ill., Nov. 6, 1929; d. Joseph Allen and May Roberts (Finch) Matter; m. George Mandler, Jan. 19, 1957; children: Peter Clark, Michael Allen. Student, Carleton Coll., 1947-49; BA with highest honors, Swarthmore Coll., 1951; PhD, Harvard U., 1956. Rsch. assoc. lab. social rels. Harvard U., 1957-60; rsch. assoc. dept. psychology U. Toronto, Ont., Can., 1961-65; assoc. rsch. psychologist, lectr. U. Calif. at San Diego, La Jolla, 1965-73, assoc. prof., 1973-77, prof. psychology, 1977-88, prof. cognitive sci., 1988-2000, rsch. prof., 2000—; mem. adv. com. memory and cognitive processes NSF, 1978-81. Hon. rsch. fellow U. Coll., London, 1978-89, vis. prof., 1990—; hon. mem. Med. Rsch. Coun. Cognitive Devel. Unit, 1982-98. Author: (G. Mandler) Thinking: From Association to Gestalt, 1964, Stories, Scripts and Scenes, 1984; assoc. editor Psychol. rev., 1970-76; mem. editl. bd. Child Devel., 1976-89, Discourse Processes, 1977-94, Jour. Exptl. Psychology, 1977-85, Text, 1979-97, Jour. Verbal Learning and Verbal Behavior, 1980-88, Lang. and Cognitive Processes, 1985—, Cognitive Devel., 1990-99, Jour. Cognition and Devel., 1999—; contbr. articles to profl. jours. Pres. San Diego Assn. Gifted Children, 1968-71; v.p. Calif. Parents for Gifted, 1970-71; mem. alumni council Swarthmore Coll., 1975-78. NIMH research grantee, 1968-81; NSF research grantee, 1981-99. Fellow APA (mem. exec. com. divsn. 3 1983-85), Am. Acad. Arts and Scis.; mem. Psychonomic Soc. (mem. governing bd. 1982-87, chmn. 1985-86), Soc. Rsch. in Child Devel., Cognitive Sci. Soc., Soc. Exptl. Psychologists, Phi Beta Kappa. Office: U Calif San Diego Dept Cognitive Sci La Jolla CA 92093-0515

MANDRA, YORK T. geology educator; b. N.Y.C. s. Raymond and Irene (Farruggio) M.; m. Highoohi Kechijian, Jan. 26, 1946. BA, U. Calif., Berkeley, 1947, MA in Paleontology, 1949; PhD in Geology, Stanford U., 1958. From instr. to assoc. prof. geology San Francisco State U., 1950-63, prof., 1964—, head geology sect., chmn. dept., 1960-67. Vis. prof. U. Aix-Marseille, France, 1959, Syracuse U., summer 1963, U. Maine, summer 1969, U. Calif., Santa Barbara, summers 1972—; research assoc. U. Glasgow, 1959, Calif. Acad. Scis., 1966-88; vis. scientist New Zealand Geol. Survey, fall 1970. Contbr. numerous articles to profl. jours. Pres. David S. Sohigian Found., 1975—. Served with USAAF, 1942-46. Recipient Neil A. Miner Disting. Coll. Teaching award, 1984; Danforth Found. teaching fellow, 1958, NSF fellow, 1959; NSF rsch. grantee, 1967-77. Fellow Geol. Soc. Am. (Sr.), Calif. Acad. Scis., AAAS; mem. Nat. Assn. Geology Tchrs. (pres. Far Western sect. 1953-54, 73-74, Robert Wallace Webb award 1977), Paleontol. Soc., Soc. Econ. Mineralogists and Paleontologists, Soc. for Environ. Geochemistry and Health. Avocations: walking, reading, music. Office: San Francisco State U Dept Geoscis 1600 Holloway Ave Dept Geoscis San Francisco CA 94132-1722 E-mail: ytjmandra@sfsu.edu

MANEATIS, GEORGE A. retired utility company executive; b. 1926; BSEE, Stanford U., 1949, MSEE, 1950. With GE, 1950-53, Pacific Gas & Elec. Co., San Francisco, 1953-91, v.p., 1979-81, sr. v.p., 1981-82, exec. v.p., 1982-86, pres., 1986-91, also bd. dirs. Office: Pacific Gas & Electric Co PO Box 770000 123 Mission St H17F San Francisco CA 94177

MANELLA, NORA M. federal judge; BA in Italian with highest honors, Wellesley Coll., 1972; JD, U. So. Calif., 1975. Bar: Calif. 1976, U.S. Ct. Appeals (5th cir.) 1976, D.C. Ct. Appeals 1978, U.S. Dist. Ct. (ctrl., so., no. and ea. dists.) 1980-81, U.S. Ct. Appeals (9th cir.) 1982. Law clk. to Hon. John Minor Wisdom U.S. Ct. Appeals (5th cir.), New Orleans, 1975-76; legal counsel Subcom. on Constn., Senate Com. on Judiciary, Washington, 1976-78; assoc. O'Melveny & Myers, Washington and L.A., 1978-82; asst. to U.S. Atty. U.S. Dept. Justice, L.A., 1982-90; trial asst. major crimes, 1982-85; dep. chief, criminal complaints U.S. Dept. Justice, L.A., 1986-87, chief criminal appeals, 1988-90; judge L.A. Mcpl. Ct., 1990-92; justice pro tem Calif. Ct. Appeals (2nd dist.), 1992; judge L.A. Superior Ct., 1992-93; U.S. atty. (ctrl. dist.) Calif. U.S. Dept. Justice, L.A., 1994-98; judge U.S. Dist. Ct. (cen. dist.) Calif., L.A., 1998—. Instr. U.S. Atty. Gen. Advocacy Inst., 1984-86, Calif. Jud. Coll., 1992-93; mem. Atty. Gen.'s Adv. Com., 1994-95. Mem. editl. bd. State Bar Criminal Law Newsletter, 1991-92. Mem. adv. bd. Monroe H.S. and Govt. Magnet, 1991-94; acad. specialist USAID Delegation, 1993; judge L.A. Times Cmty. Partnership Awards, 1993; bd. councilors Law Sch. U. So. Calif., 1996—. Mem. Am. Law Inst., Calif. Judges Assn., Nat. Assn. Women Judges, Calif. Women Lawyers, Women Lawyers of L.A., Order of the Coif. Office: US Dist Ct 312 N Spring St Los Angeles CA 90012-4701

MANK, EDWARD WARREN, marketing professional; b. Boothbay Harbor, Maine, Oct. 2, 1962; s. Edward Raymond Jr. and Sandra Gail (Strahan) M. Assoc. in Liberal Arts, C.C. Vt., 1985; cert. ophthalmic technician, Nat. Edn. Ctr., San Francisco, 1992; cert. real estate broker, Am. Sch. Mortgage Banking, Walnut Creek, Calif., 1994. Lic. real estate salesman, Calif.; cert. Am. Bd. Optometry Dispensing. Tng. coord. Burger King Corp., South Burlington, Vt., 1985-87, San Francisco, 1988-89; asst. mgr. Bonanza Family Restaurant, South Burlington, 1987-88; supr. U.S. Census Bur., San Francisco, 1990; sales rep. Viacom Cablevision, San Francisco, 1991; programming researcher NBC, San Francisco, 1992; mktg. cons. Calyx & Corolla, San Francisco, 1993; mktg. rep. Alliance Bancorp, Millbrae, Calif., 1993—. Sustaining mem. Rep. Nat. Com., Washington, 1989—; sponsor Heritage Found., Washington, Cato Inst., Washington. Mem. Acad. Polit. Sci., Coun. Fgn. Rels., World Affairs Coun., Nat. Rifle Assn. (life), Reason Found. Republican. Episcopalian. Home: 3401 E 18th St Apt 3 Oakland CA 94601-3003 Office: Alliance Bancorp 800 El Camino Real Millbrae CA 94030-2010 E-mail: edmank@canada.com

MANKOFF, DAVID ABRAHAM, nuclear medicine physician; b. July 10, 1959; BS in Physics summa cum laude, Yale U., 1981; MD, PhD in Bioengring., U. Pa., 1988. Diplomate Am. Bd. Internal Medicine, Am. Bd. Nuclear Medicine. Rsch. scientist UGM Med. Systems, Phila., 1988-89, dir. engring., 1989-90; rsch. assoc. nuclear medicine sect. U. Pa., Phila., 1988-90; resident in internal medicine U. Wash., Seattle, 1990-92, resident in nuclear medicine, 1992-96, asst. prof. radiology, 1996—. Office: Divsn Nuc Medicine U Wash Med Ctr Box 356113 1959 NE Pacific St Seattle WA 98195-0001 E-mail: dam@u.washington.edu

MANLEY, JOHN FREDERICK, political scientist, educator; b. Utica, N.Y., Feb. 20, 1939; s. John A. and Gertrude Manley; children from previous marriage: John, Laura; m. Kathy Lynn Sharp, 1991; 1 child, Cole Sharp Manley. B.S., Le Moyne Coll., 1961; Ph.D., Syracuse U., 1966. Asst. prof. polit. sci. U. Wis., 1966, assoc. prof., 1969-71; prof., chmn. dept. polit. sci. Stanford U., 1977-80. Fellow Center for Advanced Study in Behavioral Scis., 1976-77; vis. prof. Stanford in Oxford, 1996. Author: The Politics of Finance, 1970, American Government and Public Policy, 1976; author, co-editor: The Case Against the Constitution, 1987. Congressional fellow, 1963-64; Brookings Instn. fellow, 1965-66; Guggenheim fellow, 1974-75; Fulbright fellow U. Bologna, 1992. Office: Stanford U Dept Polit Sci Stanford CA 94305

MANLEY, RICHARD WALTER, insurance executive; b. Malone, N.Y., Dec. 26, 1934; s. Walter E. and Ruth (St. Mary) M.; m. Linda Kimberlin, Dec. 18, 1965; children: Stephanie, Christopher. BS in Bus., U. So. Miss., 1960. Cert. real estate broker. Account exec. Colonial Life and Accident, Hattiesburg, Miss., 1960-63, dist. mgr. Oklahoma City, 1963-66, regional dir. Denver, 1966-76, zone dir., 1976-82; pres. Commonwealth Gen. Group, Denver, 1982-98, Manley Properties Inc., Denver, 1982-90, Richard W. Manley Commonwealth Gen. Grps., Inc., Denver, 1982—. Cons. Capitol Am. Life Ins. Co., Cleve., 1987-96; bd. dirs. (merco) Mercy Hosp., Denver, 1982-87. With USAF, 1956-59. Mem. Cherry Hills C. of C., Rotary, Alpha Tau Omega. Roman Catholic. Avocations: golfing, racquetball, running. Home: 6510 E Lake Pl Englewood CO 80111-4411 E-mail: manleydick@aol.com

MANN, BRUCE ALAN, lawyer, investment banker; b. Chgo., Nov. 28, 1934; s. David I. and Lillian (Segal) M.; m. Naomi Cooks, Aug. 31, 1980; children: Sally Mann Stull, Jonathan Hugh, Andrew Ross. BBA, U. Wis., 1955, SJD, 1957. Bar: Wis. 1957, N.Y. 1958, Calif. 1961. Assoc. Davis, Polk & Wardwell, N.Y.C., 1957-60, Pillsbury, Madison & Sutro, San Francisco, 1960-66, ptnr., 1967-83; adminstrv. mng. dir. L.F. Rothschild Unterberg Towbin, San Francisco, 1983-87; ptnr. Morrison & Foerster, San Francisco, 1987—; sr. mng. dir. W.R. Hambrecht & Co., San Francisco, 1999—. Cons. SEC, 1978; vis. prof. law Georgetown U., 1978; lectr. in field. Author: (with Mattson) California Corporate Practice and Forms, 1999; contbr. articles to profl. jours. Served with USAR, 1957. Mem. Am. Law Inst., Am. Bar Assn. (chmn. fed. regulation of securities com. 1981-83, mem. bus. law sect. coun. 1996-99, standing com. on ethics and profl. responsibility 1997-2000, com. on venture capital 2000—), State Bar Calif., Bar Assn. San Francisco (bd. dirs. 1974-75), Nat. Assn. Securities Dealers (gov. at large 1981-83). Club: The Family. Office: Morrison & Foerster 425 Market St Ste 3100 San Francisco CA 94105-2482 E-mail: bmann@mofo.com

MANN, CLAUD PRENTISS, JR. retired television journalist, real estate agent; b. Galveston, Tex., June 30, 1925; s. Claud Prentiss and Henrietta Anno (Cline) M.; m. Loris Lea Padgett, Sept. 18, 1948; children: Beatrice Anno, Claudea Padgett, Claud Prentiss III. BS, U. Houston, 1949. Cert. tchr., Calif.; lic. real estate agt., Wash. Fellow Fund for Adult Edn. Mass Media U. Calif., Berkeley, 1958-59; anchor, reporter, writer, prodr., commentator Sta. KTVU-TV, San Francisco, Oakland, Calif., 1962-87; news dir., anchor, prodr. Sta. KTIE-TV, Oxnard, Santa Barbara, 1987-88; freelance writer, producer, pub. info. specialist, 1988—; journalism instr. Highline and South Seattle Community Colls., 1990-92. Past v.p. bd. dirs. Vashon-Maury Sr. Ctr. Recipient No. Calif. Emmy awards for reporting and anchor work, 1975, 76, 77, 79, 81, John Swett award for Edn. Reporting; commendations U.S. State Dept., City of Oakland, City of San Francisco, Calif. State Legis. Mem. AFTRA, NATAS (Silver Circle), Vashon Allied Arts (bd. dirs. 1989-91), Soc. Profl. Journalists. Home: 25115 122nd Ave SW Vashon WA 98070-7820 E-mail: cmanX2@aol.com

MANN, J. KEITH, arbitrator, law educator, lawyer; b. May 28, 1924; s. William Young and Lillian Myrle (Bailey) M.; m. Virginia McKinnon, July 7, 1950; children: William Christopher, Marilyn Keith, John Kevin, Susan Bailey, Andrew Curry. BS, Ind. U., 1948, LLB, 1949; LLD, Monmouth Coll., 1989. Bar: Ind. 1949, D.C. 1951. Law clk. Justice Wiley Rutledge and Justice Sherman Minton, 1949-50; pvt. practice Washington, 1950; with Wage Stblzn. Bd., 1951; asst. prof. U. Wis., 1952, Stanford U. Law Sch., 1952-54, assoc. prof., 1954-58, prof., 1958-88, prof. emeritus, 1988—, assoc. dean, 1961-85, acting dean, 1976, 81-82, cons. to provost, 1986-87. Vis. prof. U. Chgo., 1953; mem. Sec. of Labor's Adv. Com., 1955-57; mem. Pres.'s Commn. Airlines Controversy, 1961; mem. COLC Aerospace Spl. Panel, 1973-74; chmn., mem. Presdl. Emergency Bds. or Bds. of Inquiry, 1962-63, 67, 71-72; spl. master U.S. vs. Alaska, U.S. Supreme Ct., 1980-97. Editor book rev. and articles Ind. U. Law Jour., 1948-49. Ensign USNR, 1944-46. Sunderland fellow U. Mich., 1959-60; scholar in residence Duke U., 1972. Mem. ABA, AAUP, Nat. Acad. Arbitrators, Indsl. Rels. Rsch. Assn., Acad. Law Alumni Fellows Ind. U., Order of Coif, Tau Kappa Epsilon, Phi Delta Phi. Democrat. Presbyterian. Home: 872 Lathrop Dr Stanford CA 94305-1053 Office: Stanford U Sch Law Stanford CA 94305-8610 E-mail: jkmann@leland.stanford.edu

MANN, MICHAEL K. producer, director, writer; b. Chgo. Ed., U. Wis., London Film Sch. Dir. (documentary) 17 Days Down the Line, 1972; dir, scriptwriter (TV movie) The Jericho Mile, 1979 (Best Dir. award Dir. Guild Am., Emmy award); dir, exec. prodr., scriptwriter (film) Thief, 1981; dir, scriptwriter (films) The Keep, 1983, Manhunter, 1986; dir., co-prodr., scriptwriter (films) Last of the Mohicans, 1992, Heat, 1995, The Insider, 1999 (Dir., Screenwriter, Prodr. Acad. award nominee), (TV movie) LA Takedown, 1989; exec. prodr. (TV show) Miami Vice, Crime Story, (TV miniseries) Drug Wars: Camarena Story (Emmy award), Drug Wars: Cocaine Cartel; scriptwriter (TV episodes) Police Story, Starsky and Hutch. Mem. Writers Guild., Dirs. Guild. Office: c/o CAA 9830 Wilshire Blvd Beverly Hills CA 90212-1804

MANN, NANCY LOUISE (NANCY LOUISE ROBBINS), entrepreneur; b. Chillicothe, Ohio, May 6, 1925; d. Everett Chaney and Pauline Elizabeth R.; m. Kenneth Douglas Mann, June 19, 1949 (div. June 1979); children: Bryan Wilkinson, Laura Elizabeth. BA in Math., UCLA, 1948, MA in Math., 1949, PhD in Biostatistics, 1965. Sr. scientist Rocketdyne Divsn. Rockwell Internat., Canoga Park, Calif., 1962-75; tech. staff Rockwell Sci. Ctr., Thousand Oaks, 1975-78; rsch. prof. UCLA Biomath., L.A., 1978-87; pres., CEO, owner Quality Enhancement Seminars, Inc., L.A., 1982—; pres., CEO Quality and Productivity, Inc., L.A., 1987—. Curriculum adv. UCLA Ext. Dept. of Bus. and Mgmt., L.A., 1991—; mem. com. on Nat. Statistics, Nat. Acad. Scis., Washington, 1978-82; mem adv. bd. to supt. U.S. Naval Posgrad. Sch., Monterey, Calif., 1979-82. Co-author: Methods for Analysis of Reliability and Life Data, 1974; author: Keys to Excellence, 1985, The Story of the Deming Philosophy, 2d edit., 1987, 3d edit., 1989; contbr. articles to profl. jours. Recipient award IEEE Reliability Soc., 1982, ASQC Reliability Divsn., 1986. Fellow Am. Statis. Assn. (v.p. 1982-84); mem. Internat. Statis. Inst. Office: Quality Productivity Inc 10724 Wilshire Blvd # 711 Los Angeles CA 90024-4463

MANN, WESLEY F. newspaper editor; Editor Investor's Business Daily, L.A., 1984—. Office: Investors Business Daily 12655 Beatrice St Los Angeles CA 90066-7303

MANN, ZANE BOYD, editor, publisher; b. St. Paul, Jan. 28, 1924; s. Michael M. and Rose Lee (Reuben) M.; m. Esther Zeesman, Mar. 25, 1945; children: Michael L., Eric F. Personal Fin. Planning, U. Calif., Riverside, 1986. Registered investment advisor Securities and Exch. Commn. Mcpl. fin. cons. Ehlers Mann & Assoc., Mpls., 1956-64; v.p. mcpl. bond underwriter Ebin Robertson, Mpls., 1964-70; v.p. mcpl. dept. Piper Jaffrey & Co., Mpls., 1970-72; ret., 1972; editor, pub. monthly investment newsletter Calif. Mcpl. Bond Advisor, Palm Springs, Calif., 1984—. Author: Fair Winds and Far Places, 1978; contbr. articles to profl. jours. Mem. Twin City Met. Planning Commn., St. Paul, 1958-70; bd. dirs. CORAL, Riverside County, Calif., 1984-91. Staff sgt. U.S. Army, 1942-45. Decorated DFC with cluster, Air medal with cluster, Soldier's medal, Purple Heart U.S. Army Air Corp. Mem. Nat. Fedn. Mcpl. Analysts, Calif. Soc. Mcpl. Analysts, Internat. Combat Camera Assn., Writers Guild Am. (ret.), Com. for the Sci. Investigation of Claims of the Paranormal (assoc.), Royal Corinthian Yacht Club (life, Cowles, Eng.), Mensa., Sports Car Club Am. Avocations: sailing, racing and cruising, scuba, SCCA competition driver, pilot. Home: 1300 E Verbena Dr Palm Springs CA 92262-5873 Office: Calif Mcpl Bond Advisor 1037 S Palm Canyon Dr Palm Springs CA 92264-8378

MANNERS, NANCY, retired mayor; b. Catania, Sicily, Italy; d. Gioacchino Jack and Maria Providenza (Virzi) Marasa; m. George Manners, Dec. 20, 1941; children: Gene David, Nancy Ellen Manners Sieh, Joan Alice. BA in Pub. Adminstrn., U. La Verne, 1979. Asst. city mgr. City of Covina, 1963-74; mcpl. mgmt. cons., 1975-85; mem. city coun. City of West Covina, Calif., 1984-97; pres. Ind. Cities Risk Mgmt. Authority, West Covina, 1988; mayor City of West Covina, 1988-89, 92-93; pres. Ind. Cities Assn., 1989-90. Pres. Covina Coord. Coun., 1970-71, Altrusa Club of Covina-West, 1971-72, Ea. San Gabriel Valley Regional Occupation Program, 1974-76, San Gabriel Valley Planning Com., 1986-87, Mid-Valley Mental Health Coun., 1988-89; regional chmn. San Gabriel Valley Lung Assn., 1971-73; trustee Covina-Valley Unified Sch. Dist., 1973-77; foreman pro tem L.A. County Grand Jury, 1980-81; chmn. L.A. County Solid Waste Mgmt. Com., 1986-89; treas., bd. dirs. San Gabriel Valley Commerce and Cities Consortium, 1991, policy and steering com. Nat. League Cities, 1991-96; chmn. employee rels. policy com. League Calif. Cities; bd. dirs. L.A. County Sanitation Dist., 1992-94, San Gabriel Valley Coun. of Govts., San Gabriel Valley Mosquito Abatement Dist., 1994-97; hon. chair, grand marshall July 4th Parade, City of West Covina, 1997. Named Covina Citizen Yr., 1977, West Covina Citizen Yr., 1983, Woman Yr., Calif. State Legislature, 1990; recipient Woman of Distinction award Today's Woman Forum, 1988, Woman of Achievement award YWCA, 1987, 88, Community Svc. award West Covina C. of C., 1989, Meritorious Pub. Svc. award Rsch. Inst. Claremont McKenna Coll., 1990, Disting. Leader award San Gabriel Valley Boy Scouts of Am., 1997, others. Mem. LWV (pres. San Gabriel Valley 1978-79), Am. Heart Assn. (mem. bd. dirs.), Mcpl. Mgmt. Assocs. of So. Calif. (v.p. 1972-73), Queen of the Valley Hosp. 2100 (pres. 1996-97), Ind. Cities Assn. (v.p. 1988, pres. 1989), West Covina Hist. Soc. (v.p. 1995-99, pres. 1999-2000), West Covina Rotary (bd. dirs.). Home: 734 N Eileen Ave West Covina CA 91791-1042

MANNING, BRENT V. lawyer; b. Preston, Idaho, Jan. 18, 1950; s. Leon W. and Gwen (Briscoe) M.; m. J. Christine Coffin, Oct. 25, 1969; children: Justin, Britten, John. BA, Idaho State U., 1972; JD, Harvard U., 1975. Bar: Colo. 1975, Utah 1981, U.S. Ct. Appeals (10th cir.) 1978. Assoc. Holme Roberts & Owen, Denver, 1975-80, ptnr., 1980-97, Salt Lake City, 1981-97; founding ptnr. Manning Curtis Bradshaw & Bednar, LLC, Salt Lake City, 1997—. Mem. panel mediators and arbitrators U.S. Dist. Ct. Utah, 1993—; mediation & settlement judge pro tempore 3rd Jud. Dist. State of Utah, 1996—; mem. jud. nominating commn., 2d Jud. Dist. Ct. Utah. Trustee Bountiful (Utah) Davis Art Found., 1985-91, Utah Tibetan Resettlement Project; chair ...and Justice for All Campaign, 2001—. Mem. ABA, Utah Bar Assn. (chmn. continuing legal edn. com. 1988, mem. disciplinary com. 1991-93, cts. and judges com. 1993—, chmn. 1996-97, chmn. And Justice for All campaign, 2001—), Am. Inns of Ct. (pres. 1997-98, master of bench 1988—), Am. Alpine Club (N.Y.C.) Democrat. Avocations: climbing, bicycling, running. Home: 2079 Maple Grove Way Bountiful UT 84010-1005 Office: Manning Curtis 3d Fl Newhouse Bldg 10 Exchange Pl Salt Lake City UT 84111-2714 E-mail: BManning@mc2b.com

MANNING, ERIC, computer science and engineering educator, university dean, researcher; b. Windsor, Ont., Can., Aug. 4, 1940; g. George Gorman and Eleanor Katherine (Koehler) M.; m. Betty Goldring, Sept. 16, 1961; children: David, Paula. BSc, U. Waterloo, Ont., 1961, MSc, 1962; PhD, U. Ill., 1965. Registered profl. engr., B.C. With MIT and Bell Telephone Labs., 1965-68; prof. computer sci. U. Waterloo, 1968-86, founding dir. computer comms. networks group, 1973-82; founding dir. Inst. for Computer Rsch., 1982-86; prof., dean engring. U. Victoria, B.C., Can., 1986-92, prof. computer sci., elec. engring. Can., 1993-2000, New Media Ctr./Nortel Networks Prof. Network Performance Can., 2000—. NewMIC Chief Scientist, Networks Cluster, 2000—; dir. Natural Sci. and Engring. Rsch. Coun. Can., mem. exec. com., chair strategic grants com., 1982-87; dir. Comms. Rsch. Centre, Govt. of Can., 1995-97, Consortium for Software Engring. Rsch., Ottawa, 1997-99; trustee B.C. Advanced Sys. Found., 1986-93; dir. Sci. Coun. B.C., 1988-91; bd. dirs. Can. Microelectric Corp.; adv. com. on artificial intelligence NRC, 1987-91; IBM chair computer sci. Keio U., Yokohama, 1992-93; hon. prof. South East U. Nanjing, People's Republic of China. Author: Fault Diagnosis of Digital Systems, 1970; also numerous articles. V.p. Greater Victoria Concert Band, 1995-96; trumpet sect., Sooke Philharmonic & 5th Field Artillery Band, Royal Canadian Artillery. Fellow IEEE, Engring. Inst. Can.; mem. Assn. Computing Machinery (mem. snowbird com. 1999—), Assn. Profl. Engrs. B.C., Soc. for Computer Simulation, Can. Inst. for Advanced Rsch. (adv. com. on artificial intelligence and robotics 1986-90), Can. Assn. for Computer Sci. (pres. 1994-2000), Can. Soc. for Fifth Generation Rsch. (trustee 1987-88), B.C. Microelectronics Soc. (bd. dirs. 1986-87). Avocations: squash, scuba diving, sailing, flying, musical performance. Home: 2909 Phyllis St Victoria BC Canada V8N 1Y8 Office: U Victoria Faculty Engring PO Box 3055 Victoria BC Canada V8W 3P6 E-mail: Eric.Manning@engr.UVic.ca

MANNING, RICHARD DALE, writer; b. Flint, Mich., Feb. 7, 1951; s. Harold J. Manning and Juanita Mayo; m. Margaret B. Saretsky, June 5, 1971 (div.); 1 child, Joshua; m. Tracy M. Stone, Sept. 8, 1990. AB in Polit. Sci., U. Mich., 1973. News dir. Sta. WATZ, Alpena, Mich., 1975-79; reporter Alpena News, 1977-79; city editor Post-Register, Idaho Falls, Idaho, 1979-81; editor, columnist Wood River Jour., Hailey, 1981-82; city editor, columnist Times-News, Twin Falls, 1982-85; reporter, columnist Missoulian, Missoula, Mont., 1985-89; John S. Knight fellow in journalism Stanford (Calif.) U., 1994-95; freelance writer Lolo, Mont., 1989—. Author: Last Stand: Timber, Journalism and the Case for Humility, 1991, A Good House, 1993, Grassland, 1995, One Round River, 1997, Food's Frontier, 2000, Inside Passage, 2000. Recipient Blethen award for investigative reporting Allied Newspapers, 1986-87.

MANNING, ROBERT M. aerospace engineer; m. Dominique Manning; 1 child, Caline. Degree, Whitman Coll., Calif. Inst. Tech. With Jet Propulsion Lab., Pasadena, Calif., 1981—, mem. devel. team Galileo mission to Jupiter, mem. devel. team Magellan mission to Venus, chief engr. Cassini mission to Saturn, flight sys. chief engr. Mars Pathfinder Calif. Office: Jet Propulsion Lab 4800 Oak Grove Dr Pasadena CA 91109-8001

MANNIX, KEVIN LEESE, lawyer; b. Queens, N.Y., Nov. 26, 1949; s. John Warren Sr. and Editta Gorrell M.; m. Susanna Bernadette Chiocca, June 1, 1974; children: Nicholas Chiocca, Gabriel Leese, Emily Kemper. BA, U. Va., 1971, JD, 1974. Bar: Oreg. 1974, U.S. Ct. Appeals (9th cir.) 1976, U.S. Supreme Ct. 1978, Guam 1979. Law clk. to judge Oreg. Ct. Appeals, Salem, 1974-75; asst. atty. gen. Oreg. Dept. Justice, Salem, 1975-77, Govt. of Guam, Agana, 1977-79; judge adminstrv. law Oreg. Workers' Compensation Bd., Salem, 1980-83; assoc. Lindsay, Hart, Neil & Weigler, Portland, Oreg., 1983-86; pres. Kevin L. Mannix Profl. Corp., Salem, 1986—. Chmn. St. Joseph Sch. Bd., Salem, 1981-86; pres. Salem Cath. Schs. Corp., 1985; v.p. Salem Cath. Schs. Found., 1985-88, pres., 1988-90, 91-94, 2000—, state rep., 1989-97, 99-2001; pres. bd. dirs. Blanchet Sch.; v. chair Oregon Rep. Party, 1998—; State Senator, 1998-99. Mem. Marion Bar Assn., Rotary (bd. dirs. East Salem 1985-89, pres. 1987-88), KC. Republican. Avocations: photography, scuba diving, travel. Home: 375 18th St NE Salem OR 97301-4307 Office: 2003 State St Salem OR 97301-4349

MANOSEVITZ, MARTIN, psychologist; b. Mpls., June 22, 1938; s. Julius and Ethel (Cohen) M.; m. Carolyn Heather Margulius, Sept. 17, 1959; children— Bradley, Jason. BA, U. Minn., Mpls., 1960, PhD, 1964. Diplomate in clin. psychology, psychoanalysis Am. Bd. Profl. Psychology. Asst. prof. psychology Rutgers U., 1964-67; asst. prof. psychology U. Tex., Austin, 1967-69, assoc. prof., 1969-75, prof., 1975-87; pvt. practice clin. psychology Austin, 1975-99, Aspen, Colo., 1999—. Adj. prof. psychology U. Tex., 1987-93; dir. psychol. svcs. CPC Capital Hosp., Austin, 1987-93, Shoal Creek Hosp., Austin, 1994-99; allied profl. staff Aspen Valley Hosp., 2000—. Trustee Austin-Travis County Mental Health-Mental Retardation Center, 1978-80. Fellow APA (bd. dirs. divsn. psychoanalysis, 1999-2000, membership chmn. 1997-2000, bd. mem. at large 1999-2000), Acad. Clin. Psychology, Acad. Psychoanalytic Psychology; mem. Colo. Psychol. Assn., Austin Soc. for Psychoanalytic Psychology (pres. 1994-95), Denver Psychoanalytic Soc. E-mai. Office: Ste 304 117 Aspen Airport Bus Ctr Aspen CO 81611 E-mail: mmanosev@earthlink.net

MANROSS, MARY, mayor; m. Larry; 4 children. BS in Polit. Sci. Mayor City of Scottsdale, Ariz., 2000—. Mem. Scottsdale (Ariz.) City Coun., 1992-2000. Chmn. Scottsdale (Ariz.) Parks and Recreation Commn., Maricopa Assn. Govts. Youth Policy Adv. Com.; bd. dirs. Ariz. Women in Mcpl. Govt.; mem. Planning Commn.; vice chmn. Scottsdale Bond Com.; mem. Sub-com. TPC-Westworld, City Ct., C. of C./Econ. Devel.; mem. Govs. Task Force on Urban Planning, Ariz. Town Hall, Nat. League of Cities Energy, Environment and Nat. Resource Policy Com.; mem. steering com. NLC Transp., Infrastructure and Svcs. Address: 3939 N Drinkwater Blvd Scottsdale AZ 85251-4433 Office: City Hall 3939 N Drinkwater Blvd Scottsdale AZ 85251-4433

MANSELL, L. ALMA, state legislator; b. Midvale, Utah, Jan. 23, 1944; m. Margurite Mansell. Student, U. Utah. Lic. real estate broker. Real estate broker; mem. Utah Senate, Dist. 10, Salt Lake City, 1994—; asst. majority whip Utah Senate, 1999—; mem. legis. mgmt. com., state and local affairs com.; co-chair econ. devel. and human resources appropriations. Mem. Salt Lake Bd. Realtors (pres. 1983, Realtor of Yr. 1986), Utah Assn. Realtors (pres. 1990, Realtor of Yr. 1988, Pres.'s award 1992), Nat. Assn. Realtors (v.p. 1992), Sandy Rotary Club (past pres.). Republican. Office: 6995 Union Park Ctr Ste 100 Midvale UT 84047-4135

MANSFIELD, ELAINE SCHULTZ, molecular geneticist, automation specialist; b. Boulder, Colo., Apr. 20, 1954; d. William Varley and Juanita M. (Zingg) M.; m. Gary G. Schultz, Nov. 24, 1983; children: Matthew, Greggory Mark. BA in Molecular Biology, San Jose State U., 1975; MS in Genetics, U. Calif., Berkeley, 1978, PhD in Genetics, 1983. Diplomate Am. Bd. Med. Genetics (fellow), Am. Bd. Clin. Molecular Genetics. Customer cons. IntelliGenetics, Mountain View, Calif., 1983-86; staff scientist Applied Biosys., Foster City, 1986-93; sr. staff scientist Molecular Dynamics, Sunnyvale, 1993-98; dir. pharmacogenomics diaDexus, LLC, Santa Clara, 1998-99; prin. scientist Aclara Bio Sci., Mountain View, 1999—. Lectr. in the field. Author (with others) Mutations in the Human Genome, 1993; contb. to profl. jours.; patentee in field. U. Calif. grantee, Chancellors Patent Fund grantee U. Calif., NIH SBIR grantee, 1995-99. Mem. AAAS, Am. Soc. Human Genetics, Am. Soc. Histocompatibility and Immunogenetics, Women in Sci., Black Masque (pres. 1975). Avocations: skiing, quilting. Office: Aclara Bio Sci 1288 Pair Ave Mountain View CA 94043

MANSFIELD, ROGER LEO, astronomy and space publisher; b. Boston, Feb. 18, 1944; s. Roy D. Sr. and Nellie E. Mansfield; m. Alice Lee Waring, Nov. 1, 1969 div. Mar. 1983); 1 child, Jason Benjamin; m. Karen June Sprout, June 27, 1987. BS in Chemistry with high honors., U. Cin., 1965; MA in Math., U. Nebr., 1972. Chemist Lockheed Missiles & Space Co., Palo Alto, Calif., 1967; orbital analyst USAF, Offutt AFB, Nebr., 1967-73; instr. Dept. of Math. USAF Acad., Colorado Springs, Colo., 1973-74; aerospace engr. Philco-Ford Corp., Palo Alto, 1974-75, Data Dynamics Inc., Mountain View, Calif., 1975-76, Ford Aerospace & Communications Corp., Colorado Springs, 1976-90; prin. engr. Loral Aerospace Corp., Colorado Springs, 1990-95; owner Astron. Data Svc., 1976—; asst. prof. adjoint U. Colo., Colorado Springs, 1996—99. Pub. Skywatcher's Almanac, Local Planet Visibility Report, Photographer's Almanac, Comparative Ephemeris, Space Birds, WeatherBirds Utilities, Skywatcher; contbr. articles to profl. jours. Mem. Am. Astron. Soc., Math. Assn. Am., Internat. Planetarium Soc., Rocky Mountain Planetarium Assn., Phi Beta Kappa, Phi Eta Sigma. Avocations: satellite tracking and orbital mechanics. Home and Office: 3922 Leisure Ln Colorado Springs CO 80917-3502

MANSOUR, NED, manufacturing company executive; BS in Fin. with honors, U. So. Calif., 1970; JD with honors, U. San Diego, 1973. bd. dirs. Mattel, Inc., Toy Mfrs. of Am., Children's Miracle Network. Former tax acct. Touche Ross & Co.; former asst. to chief counsel Getty Oil Corp.; various positions from sr. atty. to sr. v.p./gen. counsel Mattel, Inc., El Segundo, Calif., 1978-99, pres., 1999-2000; ret. Office: Mattel Inc 333 Continental Blvd El Segundo CA 90245

MANSOUR, TAG ELDIN, pharmacologist, educator; b. Belkas, Egypt, Nov. 6, 1924; came to U.S., 1951, naturalized, 1956; s. Elsayed and Rokaya (Elzayat) M.; m. Joan Adela MacKinnon, Aug. 6, 1955; children—Suzanne, Jeanne, Dean. DVM, Cairo U., 1946; PhD, U. Birmingham, Eng., 1949, DSc, 1974. Lectr. U. Cairo, 1950-51; Fulbright instr. physiology Howard U., Washington, 1951-52; sr. instr. pharmacology Case Western Res. U., 1952-54; asst. prof., assoc. prof. pharmacology La. State U. Med. Sch., New Orleans, 1954-61; assoc. prof., prof. molecular pharmacology Stanford U. Sch. Medicine, 1961—, chmn. dept. pharmacology, 1977-91, Donald E. Baxter prof., 1977-98, prof. emeritus, 1999—. Cons. USPHS, WHO, Nat. Acad. Scis.; Mem. adv. bd. Med. Sch., Kuwait U.; Heath Clarke lectr. London Sch. Hygiene and Tropical Medicine, 1981 Contrbr. sci. articles to profl. jours. Commonwealth Fund fellow, 1965; Macy Found. scholar NIMR, London, 1982. Fellow AAAS; mem. Am. Soc. Pharmacology and Exptl. Therapeutics, Am. Soc. Biol. Chemists, Am. Heart Assn., Sierra Club, Stanford Faculty Club. Office: Stanford Sch Medicine Dept Molecular Pharm CCSR 269 Campus Dr Rm 3155 Stanford CA 94305-5174

MANSOURI, LOTFOLLAH (LOTFI MANSOURI), general director of opera company; b. Tehran, June 15, 1929; arrived in Can., 1976; s. Hassan and Mehri (Jalili) M.; m. Marjorie Anne Thompson, Sept. 18, 1954; 1 child, Shireen Melinda. AB, UCLA, 1953. Asst. prof. UCLA, 1957-60; resident stage dir. Zurich Opera, 1960-65; chief stage dir. Geneva Opera, 1965-75; gen. dir. Can. Opera Co., Toronto, Ont., 1976-88, San Francisco Opera, 1988—; dramatic coach Music Acad. West, Santa Barbara, Calif., 1959; dir. dramatics Zurich Internat. Opera Studio, 1961-65, Centre Lyrique, Geneva, 1967-72; artistic adviser Tehran Opera, 1973-75; opera adviser Nat. Arts Centre, Ottawa, Ont., 1977; v.p. Opera America, 1979—. Operatic cons. dir. Yes, Giorgio, MGM, 1981; dir. opera sequence for film Moonstruck (Norman Jewison), 1987. Guest dir. opera cos. including Met. Opera, San Francisco Opera (60 prodns.), N.Y.C. Opera, Lyric Opera of Chgo., Canadian Opera Co. (30 new prodns.), Houston Grand Opera, La Scala, Covent Garden, Verona Opera, Kirov Opera, Australian Opera, Vienna Staatsoper, Vienna Volksoper, Salzburg Festival, Amsterdam Opera, Holland Festival, Nice (France) Opera, Festival D'Orange, France, Verona Arena Festival; co-author: An Operatic Life, 1982. Decorated chevalier Order Arts and Letters (France), 1992. Mem. Am. Guild Mus. Artists, Can. Actors Equity Assn. Achievements include initiating above-stage projection of subtitles as a simultaneous translation of opera, 1983. Address: Columbia Artists Mngmt Crittenden Divsn 165 W 57th St New York NY 10019-2201

MANUEL, VIVIAN, public relations executive; b. Queens County, N.Y., May 6, 1941; d. George Thomas and Vivian (Anderson) M. BA, Wells Coll., 1963; MA, U. Wyo., Laramie, 1965. Mgmt. analyst Dept. Navy, 1966-68; account supr. GE Co., N.Y.C., 1968-72, corp. rep. bus. and fin., 1972-76; dir. corp. comm. Std. Brands Co., N.Y.C., 1976-78; pvt. cons. N.Y.C., 1978-80; pres. V M Comm. Inc., N.Y.C., 1980-97; pub. info. officer Mont. Dept. Commerce, Helena, 1997—. Bd. dirs. Am. Lung Assn. of No. Rockies, 1999—; mem. com. Girls Club N.Y., 1983-84; trustee Wells Coll., 1983-90; mem. adv. bd. Glenholme Sch., 1991-92; mem. audit com.-disaster relief agys. and youth orgns. United Way Mont., 1998—. Mem. AAUW, N.Y. Women in Comms. (bd. v.p. 1983-85, chair Matrix awards 1985), Women Execs. in Pub. Rels. (bd. dirs. 1985-88), Women's Econ. Roundtable. Address: 1400 Flowerree St Helena MT 59601-6024 Office: 1424 9th Ave Helena MT 59601-4503 E-mail: vmanuel@aol.com

MAO, HUAZHONG, civil engineer; Civil engr. Aquatex Corp., Edmonton, Alberta, Can. T.C. Keefer medal Can. Soc. Civil Engring., 1997. Office: Aquatex Corp 21 10405 Jasper Ave # 702 Edmonton AB Canada T5J 2S2

MAPES, JEFFREY ROBERT, journalist; b. San Francisco, Nov. 21, 1954; s. James Robert and Phyllis June (Bloemker) M.; m. Karen Jane Minkel, Aug. 20, 1978; children: Katharine, James. BA, San Jose State U., 1976. Reporter Napa (Calif.) Register, 1976-79; Washington corr. Scripps League Newspapers, 1979-83; reporter The Oregonian, Portland, 1984-87, chief polit. reporter, 1987—. Office: The Oregonian 1320 SW Broadway Portland OR 97201-3499

MAPLE, M. BRIAN, physics educator; b. Nov. 20, 1939; BS in Physics with distinction, AB in Math with distinction, San Diego State U., 1963; MS in Physics, U. Calif., San Diego, 1965, PhD in Physics, 1969. Asst. rsch. physicist U. Calif., San Diego, 1969-75, asst. prof. physics, 1973-75, assoc. prof. physics, 1975-81, prof. physics, 1981-90, Bernd T. Matthias endowed chair in physics, 1990—, dir. Ctr. Interface and Materials Sci., 1990—, dir. Inst. for Pure and Applied Phys. Scis., 1995—, assoc. rsch. physicist Inst. for Theoretical Physics Santa Barbara, 1980; Bernd T. Matthias scholar Ctr. for Materials Sci. Los Alamos Nat. Lab., 1993. Vis. scientist U. Chile, Santiago, 1971, 1973; vis. prof. Inst. de Fisica Jose Balseiro, San Carlos de Bariloche, Argentina, 1974; lectr. in field; mem. rev. com. materials sci. and tech. divsn. Argonne Nat. Lab., 1983-90, chmn., 1987; mem. rev. com. Office of Basic Energy Scis. Rev. of the Materials Sci. Program at Lawrence Livermore Nat. Lab., 1985; mem. exec. com. High Flux Isotope Reactor User's Group, Oak Ridge Nat. Lab., 1984-91; mem. user's com. Francis Bitter Nat. Magnet Lab., 1984-87; mem. rev. com. materials scis. program rev. Ames Lab., 1990-93; mem. scientific adv. bd. CONNECT, 1990—; mem. adv. coun. Glenn T. Seaborg Inst. for Transactinium Sci. Lawrence Livermore Nat. Lab., 1991—, others. Co-editor: Applied Physics A, 1983-93, Superconductivity in d- and f-Band Metals, 1980, Valence Fluctuations in Solids, 1982, Superconductivity in Ternary Compounds, Vols. 32, 34, 1982, Proceedings of the Internat. Conf. on Strongly Correlated Electron Sys., 1994; guest editor Spl. Issue of Materials Rsch. Soc. Bulletin on High Tc Superconductors, 1989, 2d Spl. Issue of Materials Rsch. Soc. Bulletin on High Tc Superconductors, 1990, Handbook on the Physics and Chemistry of Rare Earths, Vols. 30, 31, High Temperature Superconductors, 2001; mem. editl. bd. Superconductivity Review. Recipient Lockheed Leadership scholarship, 1958-60, Rotary Club scholarship, 1958-60, Calif. State scholarship, 1961-62, John Simon Guggenheim Meml. Found. fellowship, 1984, Disting. Alumnus of Yr. award U. Calif., San Diego, 1987, Disting. Alumnus of Yr. award San Diego State U. Coll. Scis., 1988, Bernd T. Matthias prize Internat. Conf. Materials and Mechanisms of Superconductivity and High Temperature Superconductors, 2000; inducted into Chula Vista H.S. Hall of Fame, 1990; recognized as one of world's most highly cited researchers ISI, 2000. Fellow AAAS, Am. Physical Soc. (various positions selection com. for internat. prize on new materials, 1982-91, mem. exec. com. divsn. condensed matter physics 1985-89, vice-chmn. to chmn. divsn. 1986-88, mem. com. on meetings 1992-96, David Adler lectureship award 1996, centennial speaker 1998-99, Humboldt Rsch. award 1998, Frank H. Spedding award 1990, James C. McGroddy prize in New Materials 2000

Bernd T. Matthias prize Internat. Conf. Materials and Mechanisms of Superconductivity and High Temperature Superconductors 2000); mem. Am. Vacuum Soc., Materials Rsch. Soc., Calif. Catalysis Soc., Sigma Xi. Achievements include research in experimental condensed matter physics including superconductivity, magnetism, valence fluctuation and heavy fermion phenomena, strongly correlated election phenomena low temperature and high pressure physics, surface science and catalysis. Office: U Calif San Diego Dept Physics 0319 9500 Gilman Dr La Jolla CA 92093-0319 E-mail: mbmaple@ucsd.edu

MARADUDIN, ALEXEI A. physics educator; b. San Francisco, Dec. 14, 1931; BS, Stanford U., 1953, MS, 1954; PhD in Physics, Bristol U., 1957. Rsch. assoc. physics U. Md., College Park, 1956-57, rsch. asst. prof., 1957-58; asst. rsch. prof. Inst. Fluid Dynamics & Applied Math., 1958-60; physicist Westinghouse Rsch. Labs., Churchill Borough, Pa., 1960-65; cons. semicondr. br. U.S. Naval Rsch. Lab., Washington, 1958-60, Los Alamos Sci. Lab., 1965-67, 83-89; cons. semiconductor br. Gen. Atomic Divsn. Gen. Dynamics Corp., 1965-71; chmn. dept. U. Calif., Irvine, 1968-71, prof. physics, 1965—. Recipient Alexander von Humboldt U.S. sr. scientist award, 1980-81. Fellow Am. Phys. Soc., Optical Soc. Am., Am. Assn. Advancement of Sci., Inst. Physics, U.K.; mem. Phi Beta Kappa, Tau Beta Pi, Sigma Xi. Office: U Calif Irvine Dept Physics & Astronomy Frederick Reines Hl # 2180 Irvine CA 92697-0001 E-mail: aamaradu@uci.edu

MARBLE, FRANK E(ARL), engineering educator; b. Cleve., July 21, 1918; m. 1943, 2 children. BS, Case Inst. Tech., 1940, MS, 1942; PhD in Aeronautics and Math., Calif. Inst. Tech., 1948. Head heat transfer and engine cooling sect. Lewis Flight Propulsion Lab., Nat. Adv. Com. Aeronautics, Cleve., 1942-44, chief compressor and turbine rsch. br., 1944-46; instr. aeronautics Calif. Inst. Tech., Pasadena, 1948-49, from asst. prof. to prof. jet propulsion and mech. engring., 1949-81, Richard L. and Dorothy M. Hayman prof., 1981-89, Richard L. and Dorothy M. Hayman prof. emeritus, 1990—. Instr. fluid dynamics and gas turbines Case Sch. Applied Sch., 1942-46; cons., 1948—; vis. prof. Cornell U., 1956, MIT, 1980-81, Chinese Acad. Sci., 1980; mem. various coms. NRC, NAS, 1956—. Fellow AIAA (Combustion and Propulsion award 1992); mem. NAE, NAS, Combustion Inst., Sigma Xi. Office: Calif Inst Tech Guggenheim Aeronaut Lab Ms 205 45 Pasadena CA 91125-0001 Fax: 818-449-2677. E-mail: marble@cco.caltech.edu

MARCELLA, JOSEPH, information system administrator; BS in Biochemistry, Temple U., 1970. Computer operator/sys. programmer, asst. mgr. King Kullen Grocery Co./Gen. Fire & Casualty, L.I., 1971-72; asst. v.p., electronic banking Bank of Am., Las Vegas, 1972-83; sr. v.p., dir. info. svcs. Primerit Bank of Nev., Las Vegas, 1983-96; dir. info. technologies City of Las Vegas, 1997—. Bd. dirs., past pres. Bank Adminstrn. Inst.; past pres., v.p. Nev. Clearing House Assn.; bd. dirs. Western Payments Alliance; mem. Rules Com. Nat. Automated Clearning House, Task Force to Build Acad. Advanced Tech., Focus Sch. Partnership program. Mem. South Nev. Entities Tech. Alliance (bd. dirs.). Office: City Las Vegas Dept Info Techs City Hall 5th Fl 400 Stewart Ave Las Vegas NV 89101-2927

MARCELYNAS, RICHARD CHADWICK, management consultant; b. New London, Conn., Aug. 21, 1937; s. Anthony F. and Elizabeth A. (Chadwick) M.; m. Betty A. Forray, July 1, 1961; children: Michael R., Thomas R. BA in Bus. Adminstrn., U. Wash., 1961; postgrad. Seattle U., 1971-72. Mgmt. trainee, installation foreman Pacific Bell, Fullerton, Calif., 1964-65; cost acct. Scott Paper Co., Everett, Wash., 1965-68; asst. v.p. pers. and adminstrn. Nat. Pub. Svc. Ins. Co., Seattle, 1968-77; pers. ops. mgr. Olympia Brewing Co., 1977-78; mgr. indsl. rels. Heath Tecna Precision Structures Inc., Kent, Wash., 1978-85; mgmt. cons., recruiter Pilon Mgmt. Co., Seattle, 1985-90; pers. adminstr. Peninsula Group Olympia, Wash., 1990-94; pres. Chadwick & Assocs., Olympia, 1994-2000; info. tech. recruiter Red Rover Solutions, Bellevue, Wash., 2000—. Served to maj. USMCR, 1961-77. Decorated commendations for bravery and tech. expertise, 1962-64; recipient Seattle chpt. Pacific N.W. Personnel Mgrs. Assn. Bd. Dirs. award, 1975. Mem. Pacific N.W. Personnel Mgrs. Assn. (past pres. Tacoma chpt.), Oreg. Lodging Assn., Human Resources Consultants Network. Office: 623 Sherman St SW Olympia WA 98502-5454

MARCH, BERYL ELIZABETH, animal scientist, educator; b. Port Hammond, B.C., Can., Aug. 30, 1920; d. James Roy and Sarah Catherine (Wilson) Warrack; m. John Algot March, Aug. 31, 1946; 1 dau., Laurel Allison. B.A., U. B.C., Vancouver, 1942, M.S.A., 1962; D.Sc., U. B.C., 1988. Mem. indsl. research staff Can. Fishing Co. Ltd., 1942-47; mem. research staff, faculty U. B.C., 1947—, prof. animal sci., 1970-85; prof. emerita. Recipient Poultry Sci. Assn.-Am. Feed Mfrs. award, 1969, Queen's Jubilee medal, 1977, Earle Willard McHenry award Can. Soc. Nutritional Sci., 1986, 125th Can. Confederation Annv. medal, 1993. Fellow Agrl. Inst. Can., Royal Soc. Can., Poultry Sci. Assn.; mem. Profl. Agrologists, Agr. Inst. Can., Can. Soc. Nutritional Sci., Am. Inst. Nutrition, Can. Soc. Animal Sci., Aquaculture Assn. Can. Avocation: researching poultry and fish nutrition and physiology. E-mail: betb@interchange.ubc.ca

MARCH, JAMES GARDNER, social scientist, educator; b. Cleve., Jan. 15, 1928; s. James Herbert and Mildred (MacCorkle) M.; m. Jayne Mary Dohr, Sept. 23, 1947; children: Kathryn Sue, Gary Clifton, James Christopher, Roderic Gunn. BA, U. Wis., 1949; MA, Yale U., 1950, PhD, 1953; PhD (hon.), Copenhagen Sch. Econs., 1978, Swedish Sch. Econs., 1979, U. Wis., Milw., 1980, U. Bergen, , 1980, Uppsala U., 1987, Helsinki Sch. Econs., 1991, Dublin City U., 1994, Göteborg U., 1998. From asst. prof. to prof. Carnegie Inst. Tech., 1953-64; prof., dean Sch. Social Scis. U. Calif., Irvine, 1964-70; prof. mgmt., higher edn., polit. sci. and sociology Stanford (Calif.) U., 1970-95, prof. emeritus, 1995—. Cons. in field; mem. Nat. Council Ednl. Research, 1975-78, Nat. Sci. Bd., 1968-74; mem. sociol.-social psychology panel NSF, 1964-66; social sci. tng. com. NIMH, 1967-68; mem. math. social sci. com. Social Sci. Research Council, 1958-60; mem. Assembly Behavioral and Social Sci., NRC, 1973-79, chmn. com. on aging, 1977-82, chmn. com. on math., sci., tech. edn., 1984-86 Author: (with H.A. Simon) Organizations, 1958, 2nd edit., 1993, (with R.M. Cyert) A Behavioral Theory of the Firm, 1963, 2nd edit., 1992, Handbook of Organizations, 1965; (with B.R. Gelbaum) Mathematics for the Social and Behavioral Sciences, 1969; (with M.D. Cohen) Leadership and Ambiguity, 1974, 2nd edit., 1986, Academic Notes, 1974; (with C.E. Lave) An Introduction to Models in the Social Sciences, 1975; (with J.P. Olsen) Ambiguity and Choice in Organizations, 1976, Aged Wisconsin, 1977, Autonomy as a Factor in Group Organization, 1980, Pleasures of the Process, 1980, Slow Learner, 1985; (with R. Weissinger-Baylon) Ambiguity and Command, 1986, Decisions and Organizations, 1988; (with J.P. Olsen) Rediscovering Institutions, 1989, Minor Memos, 1990, A Primer on Decision Making, 1994, Fornuft og Forandring, 1995; (with J.P. Olsen) Democratic Governance, 1995; The Pursuit of Organizational Intelligence, 1999, (with M. Schulz and X. Zhou) The Dynamics of Rules, 2000, Late Harvest, 2000; contbr. articles to profl. jour. Fellow Ctr. Advanced Study in Behavioral Scis., 1955-56, 73-74; recipient Wilbur Lucius Cross medal Yale U., 1968; named knight 1st class Royal Norwegian Order of Merit, 1995, Comdr. of Order of Lion of Finland, 1999. Mem. NAS, Nat. Acad. Edn., Accademia Italiana di Economia Aziendale, Royal Swedish Acad. Scis., Norwegian Acad. of Sci. and Letters, Am. Acad. Arts and Scis., Am. Econ. Assn., Am. Polit. Sci. Assn. (v.p. 1983-84, John Gaus award 1997), Am. Psychol. Assn., Am. Sociol. Assn., Acad. Mgmt. (Disting. Scholar award 1999), Russell Sage Found. (trustee 1985-94, chmn. 1990-93), Finnish Soc. Scis. and Letters, Citigroup Behavioral Scis. Rsch. Coun. (chmn. 1994-2000), Am. Philos. Soc., Phi Beta Kappa, Sigma Xi. Home: 837 Tolman Dr Stanford CA 94305-1025 Office: Stanford U 71 Cubberley Stanford CA 94305-3096 E-mail: march@stanford.edu

MARCH, KATHLEEN PATRICIA, judge; b. May 18, 1949; married; 2 children. BA, Colo. Coll., 1971; JD, Yale U., 1974. Bar: N.Y. 1975, Calif. 1978. Law clk. to hon. judge Thomas J. Griesa U.S. Dist. Ct. (so. dist.) N.Y., 1974-75; assoc. Cahill, Gordon & Reindel, N.Y.C., 1975-77; asst. U.S. atty. criminal div. Office of U.S. Atty. Cen. Dist. Calif., L.A., 1978-82; assoc. Adams, Duque & Hazeltine, L.A., 1982-85; ptnr. Demetriou, Del Guercio & Lovejoy, L.A., 1985-88; judge U.S. Bankruptcy Ct. Cen. Dist. Calif., L.A., Calif., 1988—. Bd. editors Yale U. Law Jour. Mem. ABA, Fed. Bar Assn., L.A. County Bar Assn., Women Lawyers Assn., , Nat. Assn. Women Judges, L.A. Bankruptcy Forum, Fin. Lawyers Assn., Phi Beta Kappa. Avocations: horseback riding, scuba diving, photography. Office: Roybal Fed Ct Bldg 255 E Temple St Ste 1460 Los Angeles CA 90012-3332

MARCHAK, MAUREEN PATRICIA, anthropology and sociology educator; b. Lethbridge, Alta., Can., June 22, 1936; d. Adrian Ebenezer and Wilhelmina Rankin (Hamilton) Russell; m. William Marchak, Dec. 31, 1956; children: Geordon Eric, Lauren Craig. BA, U. B.C., Vancouver, Can., 1958, PhD, 1970. Asst. prof. U. B.C., Vancouver, 1972-75, assoc. prof., 1975-80, prof., 1980—, head dept. anthropology and sociology, 1987-90, dean faculty arts, 1990-96, disting. scholar in residence Peter Wall Inst., 2000-01. Author: Ideological Perspectives on Canada, 1975, 2d edit., 1981, 3d edit., 1988, In Whose Interests, 1979, Green Gold, 1983 (John Porter award 1985), The Integrated Circus, The New Right and The Restructuring of Global Markets, 1991, Logging the Globe, 1995, Falldown, Forest Policy in British Columbia, 1999, Racism, Sexism and the University, the Political Science Affair at UBC, 1996, God's Assassins. State Terrorism in Argentina in the 1970's, 1999 (Wallace J. Ferguson prize, Hon. Mention); author, co-editor: Uncommon Property, 1987; mem. editl. bd. Can. Rev. Sociology and Anthropology, Montreal, Que., 1971-74, Studies in Polit. Economy, Ottawa, Ont., Can., 1980-87, Current Sociology, 1980-86, Can. Jour. Sociology, 1986-90, B.C. Studies, 1988-90, 2000—. Bd. dirs., chair ethics com. Univ. Hosp., 1992-93, Cedar Lodge Trust Soc., 1989-92; mem. adv. coun. Ecotrust, 1991-93, bd. dirs., 1993-97, Eco-trust Can., 1995-99; chmn. bd. dirs. B.C. Bldgs. Corp., 1992-95; mem. B.C. Forest Appeals Commn., 1992—; bd. govs. U. B.C., 1999-2001. Fellow Royal Soc. Can. (v.p. Acad. II 1994-98, pres. Acad. II 1998-2000); mem. Can. Sociology and Anthropology Assn. (pres. 1979-80, other offices), Internat. Sociol. Assn., Can. Polit. Sci. Assn., Assn. for Can. Studies, Forest History Soc. (mem. exec. com. 1991-92). Avocations: hiking, swimming, traveling. Home: 4455 W 1st Ave Vancouver BC Canada V6R 4H9 Office: U BC Dept Anthrop & Sociology 6303 NW Marine Dr Vancouver BC Canada V6T 1Z1 E-mail: pmarchak@interchange.ubc.ca

MARCHAND, RUSSELL DAVID, II, retired protective services official; b. Lafayette, Ind., May 14, 1950; s. Russell David and Mable May (Gean) M.; m. Sandra Green, June 12, 1951 (div. Nov. 1986); 1 child, Russell David III; m. Carol Bella Flashenburg, May 31, 1987 (div. Feb., 1996); m. Dorian L. Jones, Feb. 28, 2000. AA in Fire Sci., Clark County Community Coll., Las Vegas, Nev., 1979. Cert. fire service instr., supr. instr. Firefighter North Las Vegas Fire Dept., 1973-78, engr., 1978-82, capt., 1982-95, divsn. chief, officer-in-charge bldg. and constrn., 1990-2000, ret., 2000. Pres. Local 1607 Internat. Assn. Fire Fighters, Las Vegas, 1980— (v.p. 1976-80); instr. N. Las Vegas Fire Dept., 1986. Chmn. N. Las Vegas Firefighters Polit. Action Com., 1980—, Muscular Dystrophy Assn., 1980-83, 85. Sgt. USMC, 1968-72, South Vietnam. Named Fireman of Yr., Optimist Club, 1981, Lions Club Nev., 1989, Profl. Ins. Agts. of Am.; received citation of merit Muscular Dystrophy Assn., 1982, commendation City of N. Las Vegas, 1980, 83, 85. Mem. Fed. Firefighters Nev. (received commendation 1982), Internat. Assn. Fire Fighters (local 1607 pres. emeritus 1990). Avocations: sailing, computers. Office: 2626 E Carey Ave North Las Vegas NV 89030-6215

MARCHANT, DAVID JUDSON, lawyer; b. Oakland, Calif., Jan. 12, 1939; s. Luther Brusie and Marian Hand (Fisher) M.; m. Susan Robbins (div. 1980); children: Michael Hilton, Robbins Fisher, Lauren Payton. BA, U. Calif., Berkeley, 1961; JD, U. Calif., San Francisco, 1967. Bar: Calif. 1967. Atty. Calif. Pub. Utilities Commn., San Francisco, 1967-68; ptnr. Graham & James, San Francisco, 1968-1995; sr. counsel MCI Telecom. Corp., San Francisco, 1996-98; of counsel Davis, Wright, Tremaine, San Francisco, 1999-2000; ptnr. Davis Wright Tremaine LLP, San Francisco, 2001—. Mem. ABA (pub. utility law sect.). Office: Davis Wright Tremaine One Embarcadero Ctr Ste 600 San Francisco CA 94111

MARCHI, JON, former investment brokerage executive, cattle rancher, exporter; b. Aug. 6, 1946; s. John Robert and Joan Trimble (Toole) M.; m. Mary Stewart Sale, Aug. 12, 1972; children: Aphia Jessica, Jon Jacob. Student, Claremont Men's Coll., 1964-65; BS, U. Mont., 1968, MS, 1972. Sec., treas. Marchi, Marchi & Marchi, Inc., Morris, Ill., 1968-69; account exec. D. A. Davidson & Co., Billings, Mont., 1972-75, asst. v.p., office mgr., 1976-77, v.p. mktg. and adminstrn. Great Falls, 1977—. Sec., dir., v.p. fin. svcs. and exec. devel. D. A. Davidson Realty Corp., Great Falls, 1978-85, chmn. rsch. com., 1980; bd. dirs. Ligocyte Corp., Bozeman, Mont., Big Sky Airlines, Billings, chmn. bd. dirs., 1995; bd. dirs. Implemax Equipment Co., Inc., Bozeman, Energy Overthrust Found., Mansfield Found., Mont. Beverages, Mont. Venture Capital Network, Direct Advantage, Inc., Hamilton, Mont., Mont. Naturals Internat., Inc., Eclipse Techs., Inc., Mont. Small Bus. Investment Corp.; chmn., dir. Devel. Corp. Mont., Helena, 1995; cattle rancher, Polson, Mont., 1986— Chmn. Mont. Gov.'s Subcom. for Venture Capital Devel., Mont. Cmty. Fin. Corp., Helena; chmn. investment com. State of Mont. Sci. and Tech. Alliance, 1985—; chmn. seed capital com. State of Mont., bd. dirs. job svc. com.; mem. Mont. Peoples Action; sec.-treas. Valley View Assn., 1987—; trustee sch. dist. # 35, Polson, Mont., 1990—, chmn., 1991—; bd. dirs. Mont. Entrepreneurship Ctr., Missoula, Mont., 1990—; pres., dir. sec.-treas. Mont. Pvt. Capital Network, Bozeman, Mont., 1990—, pres., 1992—; chmn., dir. Mont. Naturals Internat., Inc., 1991; dir. Mont. State Rural Devel. Coun., 1992, Mont. SBA Adv. Coun., 1992; dir. Ctr. Econ. Renewal and Tech. Transfer Mont. State U., Bozeman, 1994—; del. to White House Conf. on Small Bus., Washington, 1994-95; chmn. Glacier Venture Fund, Helena, Mont., 1996—; mem. investment adv. com. DCC Growth Fund, Washington, 1998—. With U.S. Army, 1969-71; dir. Mont. State U., Billings, Coll. of Bus. Bd., 1995-, Mont. Econ. Devel. Action Group, 2001-. Mem. Nat. Cattlemen's Assn. (fgn. trade com.), Am. Wagyu Assn. (dir. 2000—), Can. Wagyu Assn., Polson C. of C. (bd. dirs.), Valley View Assn. (bd. dirs.), Mont. Cattle Feeders Assn., Mont. Angus Assn., Western Mont. Angus Assn., Am. Angus Assn., Western Mont. Stockgrowers Assn., Securities Industry Assn., Mont. Stock Growers Assn., Mont. Ambassadors (dir. 1995, pres. 2001—), Polson C. of C. (dir.), Leadership Great Falls Club, Ski Club, Mont. Club, Helena Wilderness Riders Club, Rotary. Episcopalian. Office: Marchi Angus Ranches 7783 Valley View Rd Polson MT 59860-9302

MARCIALIS, ROBERT LOUIS, planetary astronomer; b. N.Y.C., Sept. 14, 1956; s. Louis Angelo and Joan Regina (Dippolito) M. SB in Aero. and Astronautical Engring., MIT, 1978, SB in Earth and Planetary Scis., 1980; MS in Physics and Astronomy, Vanderbilt U., 1983; PhD in Planetary Scis., U. Ariz., 1990. Teaching asst. dept. earth and planetary scis. MIT, Cambridge, 1976-80; lab. instr. dept. physics and astronomy Vanderbilt U., Nashville, 1981, 82-83, rsch. asst. Arthur J. Dyer Obs., 1981-82; rsch. asst. Lunar and Planetary Lab. U. Ariz., Tucson, 1983-86, rsch. assoc., 1986-90; JPL postdoctoral fellow Jet Propulsion Lab., Pasadena, Calif., 1990-92; adj. faculty Pima C.C., Tucson, 1992—; sr. rsch. specialist U. Ariz., 1996—. Founding mem. Pluto/Charon Mut. Eclipse Season Campaign. Contbr. articles to Nature, Bull. Am. Astron. Soc., Astron. Jour., Minor Planet Circular, Lunar and Planetary Sci., Sci., Jour. Brit. Astron. Assn., Astrophys. Jour., Icarus, also others. Instr. water safety ARC, 1981-82; ednl. counselor MIT, 1983—; fastpitch softball umpire, 1975—. Rsch. fellow NASA, 1986-89. Mem. AAAS, Am. Astron. Soc., Am. Geophys. Union, Astron. Soc. Pacific, Internat. Occultation Timing Assn., Sigma Pi Sigma. Roman Catholic. Achievements include discovery of water ice on surface of Pluto's moon Charon; construction of an albedo map for surface of Pluto; research on Pluto, Charon and Triton, icy satellites, outer solar system formation and evolution, solar system photometry, occultation astronomy, construction and calibration of Imager for Mars Pathfinder and cameras for the Mars Polar Lander missions. Office: U Ariz Lunar Planetary Lab Tucson AZ 85721-0001 E-mail: umpire@lpl.arizona.edu

MARCIANO, MAURICE, apparel executive; CEO Guess?, L.A. Office: Guess Inc 1444 S Alameda St Los Angeles CA 90021-2433

MARCOTTE, BRIAN, transportation executive; BAS in Civil Engring., U. Toronto, Ont., 1971; Diploma in Local Govt. Adminstrn., U. Alta., 1985; Cert., U. Va., 1994. With Ont. Ministry of Transp., North Bay, Toronto, 1971-74, Regional Municipality of York, Newmarket, Ont., 1974-81; exec. dir. policy and planning br. Alberta Infrastructure, Edmonton, 1981—. Office: Alberta Infrastructure Policy & Planning 4999 98 Ave 3rd Flr Edmonton AB Canada T6B 2X3 Fax: 780-427-1066. E-mail: brian.marcotte@gov.ab.ca

MARCUM, WALTER PHILLIP, manufacturing executive; b. Bemidji, Minn., Mar. 1, 1944; s. John Phillip and Johnnye Evelyn (Edmiston) M.; m. Barbara Lynn Maloof, Apr. 17, 1976. BBA, Tex. Tech. U., 1967. Rschr. Collins Securities, Denver, 1968-70, Hanifin Imfoff, Denver, 1970-71; cons. Marcum-Spillane, Denver, 1971-76; with MGF Oil Corp., Midland, Tex., 1976-87, sr. v.p., 1978, exec. v.p., 1979-83, pres., CEO, 1983-87; sr. v.p. corp. fin. Boettcher & Co., Denver, 1987-90; pres., CEO Marcum Natural Gas Svcs., Inc., Denver, 1991-99, Metretek Techs., Denver, 2000—. Dir. TestAmerica Inc., Asheville, N.C., Key Energy Group, East Brunswick, N.J. Republican. Presbyterian. Home: 342 Monroe St Denver CO 80206-4445 Office: 600 17th St Ste 800 North Denver CO 80202

MARCUS, FRANK ISADORE, cardiologist, educator; b. Haverstraw, N.Y., Mar. 23, 1928; s. Samuel and Edith (Sattler) M.; m. Janet Geller, June 30, 1957; children: Ann, Steve, Lynn. BA, Columbia U., 1948; MS, Tufts U., 1951; MD cum laude, Boston U., 1953. Diplomate Am. Bd. Internal Medicine, subspecialty cardiovascular diseases. Intern Peter Bent Brigham Hosp., Boston, 1953-54, asst. resident, 1956-57, research fellow in cardiology, 1957-58; clin. fellow in cardiology Georgetown U. Hosp., 1958-59, chief med. resident, 1959-60; chief of cardiology Georgetown U. Med. Service, D.C. Gen. Hosp., Washington, 1960-68; instr. medicine Georgetown U. Sch. Medicine, 1960-63, asst. prof., 1963-68, assoc. prof., 1968; prof. medicine, chief cardiology sect. U. Ariz. Coll. Medicine, Tucson, 1969-82, disting. prof. internal medicine (cardiology), 1982-99, emeritus prof., 1999—, dir. electrophysiology, 1982—. Cons. cardiology VA Hosp., Tucson, 1969, USAF Regional Hosp., Davis-Monthan AFB, Tucson, 1969; mem. panel drug efficacy study, panel on cardiovascular drugs Nat. Acad. Scis.-NRC, 1967-68; chmn. undergrad. cardiovascular tng. grant com. HEW-NIH, 1970; dir. Arrhythmia Svcs., 1996 . Editor: Modern Concepts of Cardiovascular Disease, 1982-84; mem. editl. bd.: Circulation, 1976-81, Current Problems in Cardiology, 1976-80, Cardiovascular Drugs and Therapy, 1986—, New Trends in Arrythmias, 1984—, Jour. Am. Coll. Cardiology, 1984-87, 96-2000, Am. Jour. Cardiology, 1984—, Jour. Cardiovasc. Drugs and Therapy, 1994—, Jour. Cardiovasc. Pharmacology and Therapeutics, 1994—, Pacing and Clin. Electrophysiology, 1995—, Annals of Noninvasive Electrocardiology, 1996—, Cardiology, 2000—, others; contbr. numerous articles to med. jours. Chmn. Washington Heart Assn. High Sch. Heart Program, 1966-68. Served to capt. USAF, 1954-56. Recipient Career Devel. award NIH, 1965, Student AMA Golden Apple award Georgetown U. Sch. Medicine, 1968; Mass. Heart Assn. fellow, 1957-58; John and Mary Markle scholar, 1960-65 Fellow Coun. on Clin. Cardiology Am. Heart Assn., ACP (Ariz. laureate award 1987), Am. Coll. Cardiology (bd. govs. Ariz. 1984-87, asst. sec. 1987-89, trustee); mem. Assn. Univ. Cardiologists, Inc. (v.p. 1989-90, pres. 1990-91), Ariz. Heart Assn. (dir. 1970, v.p. 1972-73, chmn. rsch. com. 1970-72), So. Ariz. Heart Assn. (dir. 1969), N.Am. Soc. for Pacing and Electrophysiology, Alpha Omega Alpha. Home: 4949 E Glenn St Tucson AZ 85712-1212 Office: U Ariz Univ Med Ctr 1501 N Campbell Ave Tucson AZ 85724-0001

MARCUS, JANET, former city council; married; 3 children. MEd in Counseling and Guidance, U. Ariz.; MA, Radcliffe U.; BA in English, Wellesley Coll. Nat. bd. mem. Common Cause, 1976-79; pres. Planned Parenthood of Southern Ariz., 1985-87; mem. Energy & Environ. Policy Com. Nat. League Cities, 1989—; city coun., 1987-91, Tucson, 1991-99. Office: 2100 N Kolb Rd Tucson AZ 85715-3854

MARCUS, KAREN MELISSA, foreign language educator; b. Vancouver, B.C., Can., Feb. 28, 1956; came to the U.S., 1962; d. Marvin Marcus and Arlen Ingrid (Sahlman) Bishop; m. Jorge Esteban Mezei, Jan. 7, 1984 (div. Mar. 1987). BA in French, BA in Polit. Sci., U. Calif., Santa Barbara, 1978, MA in Polit. Sci., 1981; MA in French, Stanford U., 1984, PhD in French, 1990, . Lectr. in French Stanford (Calif.) U., 1989-90; asst. prof. French No. Ariz. U., Flagstaff, 1990-96, assoc. prof. French, 1996—. Cons. Houghton Mifflin, 1993, Grand Canyon (Ariz.) Natural History Soc., 1994. Vol., letter writer Amnesty Internat. Urgent Action Network, 1991-95; vol. No. Ariz. Aids Outreach Orgn., Flagstaff, 1994-95. Recipient medal for outstanding achievement in French, Alliance Française, Santa Barbara, 1978; named Scholarship Exch. Student, U. Geneva, Switzerland, 1979-80; doctoral fellow Stanford (Calif.) U., 1981-85. Mem. MLA, Am. Assn. Tchrs. French, Am. Coun. on the Tchg. Fgn. Langs., Am. Literary Translators Assn., Women in French, Coordination Internat. des Chercheurs Sur Les Litteratures Maghrebines, Phi Beta Kappa, Pi Delta Phi, Alpha Lambda Delta. Democrat. Jewish. Avocations: walking, yoga, reading, writing short stories. Office: No Ariz Univ Modern Lang Dept PO Box 6004 Flagstaff AZ 86011-0001 E-mail: melissa.marcus@nau.edu

MARCUS, RUDOLPH ARTHUR, chemist, educator; b. Montreal, July 21, 1923; came to U.S., 1949, naturalized, 1958; s. Myer and Esther (Cohen) M.; m. Laura Hearne, Aug. 27, 1949; children: Alan Rudolph, Kenneth Hearne, Raymond Arthur. BS in Chemistry, McGill U., 1943, PhD in Chemistry, 1946, DSc (hon.), 1988, U. Chgo., 1983, Poly. U., 1986, U. Göteborg, Sweden, 1987, U. N.B., Can., 1993, Queens U., 1993, U. Oxford, Eng., 1995, Yokohama Nat. U., , 1996, U. N.C., 1996, U. Ill., 1997, Technion-Israel Inst. Tech., 1998, Polytechnic U. Valencia, 1999, Northwestern U., 2000. Rsch. staff mem. RDX Project, Montreal, 1944-46; postdoctoral rsch. assoc. NRC of Can., Ottawa, Ont., 1946-49, U. N.C., 1949-51; asst. prof. Poly. Inst. Bklyn., 1951-54, assoc. prof., 1954-58, prof., 1958-64, U. Ill., Urbana, 1964-78; Arthur Amos Noyes prof. chemistry Calif. Inst. Tech., Pasadena, 1978—; vis. prof. theoretical chemistry U. Oxford, 1975-76; Baker lectr. Cornell U., Ithaca, N.Y., 1991; Linnett vis. prof. chemistry Cambridge (Eng.) U., 1996; hon. prof. Fudan U., Shanghai, 1994—; hon prof. Inst. Chemistry Chinese Acad. Scis., Beijing, 1995—; hon. fellow Univ. Coll., Oxford, Oxford, 1995—. Professorial fellow Univ. Coll., Oxford, 1975-76; mem. Courant Inst. Math. Scis., NYU, 1960-61; trustee Gordon Rsch. Confs., 1966-69, chmn.

bd. dirs., 1968-69, mem. coun., 1965-68; mem. rev. panel Argonne Nat. Lab., 1966-72, chmn., 1967-68; mem. rev. panel Brookhaven Nat. Lab., 1971-74; mem. rev. com. Radiation Lab., U. Notre Dame, 1975-80; mem. panel on atmospheric chemistry climatic impact com. NAS-NRC, 1975-78, mem. com. kinetics of chem. reactions, 1973-77, chmn., 1975-77, mem. com. chem. scis., 1977-79, mem. com. to survey opportunities in chem. scis., 1982-86; mem. math. panel Internat. Benchmarking of U.S. Rsch. Fields, 1996-97; mem. panel on accountability of federally funded rsch. Com. on Sci., Engring. and Pub. Policy, 2000-01; adv. com. for chemistry NSF, 1977-80, external adv. bd. NSF ctr. Photoinduced Charge Transfer, 1990—, mem. presdl. chairs com., Chile, 1994-96; advisor Ctr. for Molecular Scis., Chinese Acad. Scis. and State Key Lab. for Structural Chemistry of Unstable and Stable Species, Beijing, 1995—; co-hon. pres. 29th Internat. Chemistry Olympiad, 1997; hon. visitor Nat. Sci. Coun., Republic of China, 1999. Former mem. editl. bd. Jour. Chem. Physics, Ann. Rev. Phys. Chemistry, Jour. Phys. Chemistry, Accounts Chem. Rsch., Internat. Jour. Chem. Kinetics Molecular Physics, Theoretica Chimica Acta, Chem. Physics Letters, Faraday Trans., Jour. Chem. Soc.; mem. editl. bd. Laser Chemistry, 1982—, Advances in Chem. Physics, 1984—, World Sci. Pub., 1987—, Internat. Revs. in Phys. Chemistry, 1988—, Progress in Physics, Chemistry and Mechanics (China), 1989—, Perkins Transactions 2, Jour. Chem. Soc., 1992—, Chem. Physics Rsch. (India), 1992—, Trends in Chem. Physics Rsch. (India), 1992—; hon. editor Internat. Jour. Quantum Chemistry, 1996—. Alfred P. Sloan fellow, 1960-61, sr. postdoctoral fellow NSF, 1960-61; sr. Fulbright-Hays scholar, 1972; recipient Sr. U.S. Scientist award Alexander von Humboldt-Stiftung, 1976, Electrochem. Soc. Lecture award Electrochem. Soc., 1979, 96, Robinson medal Faraday divsn. Royal Soc. Chemistry, 1982, Centenary medal Faraday divsn., 1988, Chandler medal, Columbia U., 1983, Wolf prize in Chemistry, 1985, Nat. Medal of Sci., 1989, Evans award Ohio State U., 1990, Nobel prize in Chemistry, 1992, Hirshfelder prize in Theoretical Chemistry, U. Wis., 1993, Golden Plate award Am. Acad. Achievement, 1993, Lavoisier medal French Chem. Soc., 1994; named Hon. Citizen, City of Winnipeg, 1994, Treasure of L.A., Ctrl. City Assn., 1995, Oesper award U. Cin., 1997, Key to City of Taipei, Taiwan, 1999. Fellow AAAS, Am. Acad. Arts and Scis. (hon., exec. com. western sect., co-chmn. 1981-84, rsch. and planning com. 1989-91), Internat. Soc. Electrochemistry (hon.), Internat. Soc. for Theoretical Chem. Physics (hon.), Internat. Soc. theoretical Chem. Physics (hon.), Royal Soc. Chemistry (hon.), Royal Soc. London (hon.), Chinese Acad. Scis. (hon.), Internat. Acad. Quantum Molecular Sci. (hon.), Royal Soc. Can. (hon.); mem. NAS (hon.), Am. Philos. Soc. (hon., mem. coun. 1999—), Korean Chem. Soc. (hon.), Am. Phys. Soc., Am. Chem. Soc. (past divsn. chmn., mem. exec. com., mem. adv. bd. petroleum rsch. fund, Irving Langmuir award in chem. physics 1978, Pter Debye award in phys. chemistry 1988, Willard Gibbs medal Chgo. sect. 1988, S.C. Lind Lecture, East Tenn. sect. 1988, Theodore William Richards medal Northwestern sect. 1990, Edgar Fahs Smith award Phila. sect. 1991, Ira Remsen Meml. award Md. sect. 1991, Pauling medal Portland, Oreg., and Puget Sound sect. 1991, Auburn-Kosolapoff award 1996, Theoretical Chemistry award 1997, Top 75 Chem. & Engring. News award 1998). Achievements include responsibility for the Marcus Theory of electron transfer reactions in chemical systems and RRKM theory of unimolecular reactions. Home: 331 S Hill Ave Pasadena CA 91106-3405 E-mail: ram@caltech.edu

MARCY, CHARLES FREDERICK, food company executive; b. Buffalo, Aug. 25, 1950; s. Charles and Mary Jane (Frederick) M.; m. Helen Jean Shank, May 6, 1972 (div. Dec. 1986); children: Michelle Catherine, Adam Charles; m. Cynthia Louise Shockey, June 17, 1989; 1 child, Brooke Allison. BA, Washington and Jefferson Coll., Washington, Pa., 1972; MBA, Harvard U., 1974. Various mktg. and strategic planning positions Gen. Foods Corp., White Plains, N.Y., 1974-84; v.p. mktg. Sara Lee Bakery, Deerfield, Ill., 1984-86; v.p., gen. mgr. Wolferman's Inc. divsn. of Sara Lee Corp., Lenexa, Kans., 1987-89; v.p. strategy and mktg. Kraft Gen. Foods Frozen Products, Glenview, Ill., 1989-90; pres. Kraft Gen. Foods Nat. Dairy Products Corp., Phila., 1991-92, Golden Grain Co., Pleasanton, Calif., 1993-95; pres., CEO Sealright Packaging Co., Inc., DeSoto, Kans., 1995-98; prin. Marcy & Ptnrs. Strategy Cons., Leawood, 1999; pres., COO Horizon Organic Dairy, Longmont, Colo., 1999, pres., CEO, 2000. Bd. dirs. Phila. Police Athletic League, 1991-92, Boys and Girls Club of Kansas City, Mo., 1987-90, Lake Forest (Ill.) Symphony, 1984-87. Office: Horizon Organic Dairy 6311 Horizon Ln Longmont CO 80503-7176

MARDIAN, ROBERT CHARLES, JR. restaurateur; b. Orange, Calif., Feb. 1, 1947; s. Robert Charles Sr. and Dorothy Driscilla (Denniss) M.; m. Jayne Marie Garvin, June 21, 1970 (div. 1977); 1 child, Robert Charles III; m. Kathleen Frances Dixon, Oct. 13, 1984 (div. 1991); children: Alexandra Quinn, Ashley Michele. BA, Stanford U., 1969; MBA, Pepperdine U., 1986. Gen. mgr. Loft Restaurant, San Jose, Calif., 1969-71; chief exec. officer/chmn. bd. Wind & Sea Restaurants, Inc., Dana Point, 1971—. Bd. dirs. Dana Niguel Bank, cons. U.S. Olympic Com., Colorado Springs, 1984-88. Commr. Dana Point Econ. Devel. Mem. Young Pres. Orgn. Republican. Avocations: skiing, surfing, beach volleyball, running, snowboarding. Office: Wind & Sea Restaurants Inc 34699 Golden Lantern St Dana Point CA 92629-2908

MARG, ELWIN, physiological optics, optometry educator; b. San Francisco, Mar. 23, 1918; s. Sigmund and Fannie (Sockolov) M.; m. Helen Eugenia Kelly, Apr. 1, 1942; 1 child, Tamia. AB, U. Calif., Berkeley, 1940, PhD, 1950. Asst. prof. vision sci. U. Calif., Berkeley, 1950-56, assoc. prof., 1956-62, prof., 1962—. Co-founder, v.p., exec. officer Minerva Found., Berkeley. Author: Computer Assisted Eye Examination, 1980; also articles. Served to lt. col. USAF, 1941-46, 50-52, ETO. NSF fellow, Nobel Inst. Stockholm, 1957, Guggenheim, Madrid, 1964; recipient Miller Research Professorship U. Calif.-Berkeley, 1967. Fellow AAAS, Optical Soc. Am., Am. Acad. Optometry; mem. Soc. Neuroscis., Assn. Rsch. Vision and Ophthalmology, Internat. Soc. Magnetic Resonance in Medicine. Office: U Calif Sch Optometry Minor Hl Berkeley CA 94720-0001

MARGEN, SHELDON, public health educator; b. Chgo., May 19, 1919; s. Paul and Sarah M.; m. Jeanne Carmel Sholtz, Mar. 16, 1943; children: Claude, Paul, Peter, David. BA, UCLA, 1938, MA, 1939; MD, U. Calif., San Francisco, 1943. Diplomate Am. Bd. Internal Medicine. Assoc prof. U. Calif., Berkeley, 1963-68, prof. pub. health and nutrition, 1968-89, prof. emeritus, 1989—. Cons., mem. adv. coms. NIH, WHO,; bd. dirs. Omnicare. Cin., 1980—. Editor-in-chief U. Calif. Wellness Letter; author and editor 10 books on Nutrition and/or Pub. Health. Bd. dirs. Calif. Wellness Found., Woodland Hills, 1991-96. Capt. M.C., U.S. Army, 1943-48, ETO. Grantee NIH, State of Calif., Ford Found., numerous others. Fellow Am. Inst. Nutrition and many other profl. orgns. in fields of nutrition and pub. health. Office: U Calif Sch Pub Health Berkeley CA 94720-0001

MARGERUM, J(OHN) DAVID, chemist, researcher; b. St. Louis, Oct. 20, 1929; s. Donald Cameron and Ida Lee (Nunley) M.; m. Virginia Bolen, June 5, 1954; children: John Steven, Kris Alan, Julie Ellen. A.B., S.E. Mo. State Coll., 1950; Ph.D., Northwestern U., 1956. Rsch. chemist Shell Oil Co., Wood River, Ill., 1954-55; chief spectroscopy sect. U.S. Army QMR&E Center, Natick, Mass., 1957-59; research specialist Sundstrand Corp., Pacoima, Calif., 1959-62; with Hughes Research Labs., Malibu, 1962—, sr. scientist, head chemistry sect., 1967—, head material scis. sect., 1988—, asst. dept. mgr. exploratory studies dept., 1989—, mgr. dept. materials sci., lab. chief scientist, 1991—; prin. rsch. scientist, 1993—; mgr. dept. batteries polymer sensors, prin. rsch. scientist HRL Labs., Malibu, 1997—. Contbr. articles to profl. jours.; patentee in field. Served with U.S. Army, 1955-57. Recipient Holley medal ASME, 1977 Fellow AAAS; mem. Am. Chem. Soc., Electrochem. Soc., Soc. Info. Display, Inter-Am. Photochem. Soc., Internat. Liquid Crystal Soc., Sigma Xi Democrat. Unitarian. Home: 5433 Rozie Ave Woodland Hills CA 91367-5760 Office: HRL Labs LLC 3011 Malibu Canyon Rd Malibu CA 90265-4737 E-mail: jdmargerum@HRL.com

MARGETT, BOB G. state legislator; m. Beverly. Student, U. Calif. Bus. owner, engring. contractor; mem. Calif. State Senate, 2001—. Active Arcadia Tournament of Roses Assn., L.A. County Arboretum Found., L.A. Heart Assn., Arcardia Little League, past pres. Mem. ARC, Am. Roadbuilders, Assn. Gen. Contractors, Bldg. Industry Assn., L.A. Rotary. Office: 55 E Huntington Dr Ste 120 Arcadia CA 91006 E-mail: bob.margett@assembly.ca.gov*

MARGOL, IRVING, personnel consultant; b. St. Louis, May 28, 1930; s. William and Dora (Karsh) M.; m. Myrna Levy, Dec., 1960; children— Bradley, Lisa, Cynthia. B.A., Washington U., St. Louis, 1951, M.A., 1952. Employment mgr. Am. Car & Foundry div. ACF, St. Louis, 1955-59; asst. personnel dir. Vickers Inc. div. Sperry-Rand, St. Louis, 1959-60; instr. personnel mgmt. Washington U. (St. Louis), 1960-62; personnel dir. Energy Controls div. Bendix Corp., South Bend, Ind., 1962-69; exec. v.p. community/employee affairs group, community rels. dept., employee assistance program Security Pacific Nat. Bank, L.A., 1969-92; mng. dir. Southern Calif. Jannotta, Bray & Assocs., Inc., 1992—; pres. Security Pacific Found., L.A., 1989-94; mng. dir. Jannotta Bray & Assocs., L.A., 1992-94, Right and Assocs., L.A., 1995-99; prin. Eddy Assocs., Inc., 2000—. Instr. UCLA Extension Div., Los Angeles; Grad. Sch. Banking, Rutgers U., Notre Dame U.; bd. dirs. Gateway Hosp. Bd. dirs. L.A. chpt. ARC, Am. Heart Assn., Am. Cancer Soc., Nat. Conf. Christians & Jews, Braille Inst.; bd. overseers Southwestern U. Law. Mem. Am. Bankers Assn. (exec. com. 1979—), Am. Soc. Tng. and Devel., Am. Soc. Personnel Adminstrs., Am. Inst. Banking, Washington U. Alumni Assn. Democrat. Jewish. Office: Eddy Assocs Inc 3500 W Olive Ave Ste 300 Burbank CA 91505-4647

MARGOLIS, JULIUS, economist, educator; b. N.Y.C., Sept. 26, 1920; s. Sam and Fannie (Weiner) M.; m. Doris Lubetsky, Oct. 30, 1942; children— Jane S., Carl W. B.S.S., City Coll. N.Y., 1941; Ph.M. in Econs, U. Wis., 1943; M.P.A. in Econs, Harvard, 1947, Ph.D., 1949. Instr. econs. Tufts Coll., 1947-48; asst. prof. econs. and planning U. Chgo., 1948-51; asst. prof. econs. Stanford, 1951-54; prof. bus adminstrn. U. Calif. at Berkeley, 1954-64; prof. econs. and engring. econ. systems Stanford, 1964-69; prof., dir. Fels Center of Govt., U. Pa., 1969-76; prof. econs. U. Calif. at Irvine, 1976—. Dir. Ctr. on Global Peace and Conflict Studies, 1985—; cons. to govt. and industry, 1958— Author: (with others) The Public Economy of Urban Communities, 1965, The Northern California's Water Industry, 1966, Public Economics, 1969, Public Expenditure and Policy Analysis, 1984; also articles. Served with AUS, 1943-46. Mem. Am. Econ. Assn., Royal Econ. Soc. Home: 45 Whitman Ct Irvine CA 92612-4059 Office: U Calif Dept Econ Irvine CA 92697-0001 E-mail: jmargoli@uci.edu

MARGULIES, LEE, newspaper editor; Television editor Los Angeles Times, Calif., 1976—. Office: Los Angeles Times Times Mirror Sq Los Angeles CA 90053

MARINEAU, PHILIP ALBERT, apparel executive; b. Chgo., Oct. 4, 1946; s. Philip Albert and Bernice (Collins) M.; m. Susan Anne Graf, June 28, 1969; children: Philip Albert III, Anne Elizabeth. AB in History, Georgetown U., 1968; MBA, Northwestern U., 1970. Coordinator sales research The Quaker Oats Co., Chgo., 1972-73, mktg. asst., 1973-74, asst. brand mgr., then brand mgr., 1974-78, product group mgr., 1978-80, dir., then v.p. product mgmt., 1980-85, pres. grocery specialties div., 1985-87, exec. v.p. grocery specialties and market devel., 1987-88, exec. v.p. internat. grocery products, 1988, exec. v.p., U.S. grocery products, 1989-93, pres., COO, 1993-96; pres. & CEO Dean Foods Co., 1996, Pepsi-Cola N. America, 1997-99, Levi Strauss & Co., San Francisco, 1999—. Bd. dirs. Travelers and Immigrant Aid, Chgo., 1987—; trustee Northlight Theatre, Evanston, Ill., 1985—. Mem. Am. Mktg. Assn. (Steuart Hendersen Britt award 1987), Westmoreland Country Club (Wilmette, Ill.). Office: Levi Strauss & Co 1155 Battery St San Francisco CA 94111

MARINER, WILLIAM MARTIN, chiropractor; b. Balt., Jan. 2, 1949; s. William Joseph and Ellen (Dexter) M. AA, Phoenix Coll., 1976; BS in Biology, D Chiropractic summa cum laude, L.A. Coll. of Chiropractic, 1980; DD (hon.), Universal Life Ch., Modesto, Calif., 1986. Health food restaurant mgr. Golden Temple of Conscious Cookery, Tempe, Ariz., 1974-75; health food store mgr. Guru's Grainery, Phoenix, 1975; physical therapist A.R.E. Clinic, Phoenix, 1975-76; research dir., founder G.R.D. Healing Arts Ctr., Phoenix, 1974-77; aminstrv. asst., acad. dean L.A. Coll. Chiropractic, Whittier, Calif., 1977-80; faculty Calif. Acupuncture Coll., L.A., 1978-80; ednl. cons. Avanti Inst., San Francisco, 1985-91; found, dir., head clinician Pacific Healing Arts Ctr., Del Mar, Calif., 1980-93, Mt. Shasta, 1993—. Ednl. cons. John Panama Cons., San Francisco, 1991-99. Patentee in field. Co-dir. "We Care We Share" Charitable Orgn., San Diego, 1985-86. Named Outstanding Sr., L.A. Coll. Chiropractic, 1980. Mem. Calif. Chiropractic Assn., Am. Chiropractic Assn., Internat. Coll. Applied Kinesiology, Holistic Dental Assn., Brit. Homopathic Assn. Avocations: Yoga, meditation, personal growth, natural healing methods, cooking. Office: Pacific Healing Arts Ctr PO Box 192 Mount Shasta CA 96067-0192 E-mail: wmariner@jps.net

MARINO, RICHARD J. publishing executive; With Harcourt/Brace/Jovanovich; sr. v.p. advtg. and mktg. ABC Cap Cities Pub. Corp.; assoc. pub. PC World Communications, 1990-92, pub., 1992-94, pres., 1994-96, pres., CEO, 1997-99; exec. v.p. IDG, 1999-2000; pres. CNET Inc., San Francisco, 2000—. Office: CNET Inc 150 Chestnut St San Francisco CA 94111

MARIO, ERNEST, pharmaceutical company executive; b. Clifton, N.J., June 12, 1938; s. Jerry and Edith (Meijer) M.; m. Mildred Martha Daume, Dec. 10, 1961; children: Christopher Bradley, Gregory Gerald, Jeremy Konrad. B.S. in Pharmacy, Rutgers U., 1961; M.S. in Phys. Scis., U. RI., 1963, Ph.D. in Phys. Scis., 1965. Registered pharmacist, R.I., N.Y. Vice pres. mfg. Smith Kline Corp., Phila., 1975-77; v.p. mfg. ops. U.S. Pharm. Co. (divsn. E. R. Squibb), New Brunswick, NJ, 1977-79; v.p., gen. mgr. chem. div. E. R. Squibb, Princeton, 1979-81; pres. chem. and engring. div., sr. v.p. Squibb Corp., Princeton, 1981-84, v.p., 1984-86; pres., COO Glaxo Inc., 1986-88, chmn., CEO, 1988, chmn., 1989-91; CEO Glaxo Holdings plc, 1989-93, dep. chmn., 1991-93; co-chmn., CEO, Alza Corp., Palo Alto, Calif., 1993-97, chmn., ceo, 1997—. Grad. asst., instr. U. R.I., Kingston, 1961-66; research fellow Inst. Neurol. Diseases, Bethesda, Md., 1963-65. Contbr. articles to profl. jours. Trustee Duke U., Rockefeller U., U. R.I. Found.; mem. pres.'s coun. U. R.I.; chmn. Am. Found. for Pharm. Edn.; bd. dirs. Nat. Found. Infectious Diseases, Pharm. Product Devel., Catalytica Energy Sys., Inc., Cor Therapeutics, SonoSite, Inc., Orchid Bioscis. Office: 25 Haslet Ave Princeton NJ 08540

MARIOTTA, CLAUDIO, electronics executive; Diploma in engring., Swiss Inst. Tech., Zurich, Switzerland; MS, San Jose State U.; postgrad., U. Fla. With Harris Corp., SSE Telecom; from v.p. product devel. to v.p. ops. Giga-tronics Inc., San Ramon, Calif., 1999-2001, pres., gen. mgr. instrument divsn., 2001—. Office: Giga-tronics Inc 4650 Norris Canyon Rd San Ramon CA 94583-1320 Fax: 925-328-4700

MARIUCCI, ANNE L. real estate development company executive; BA in Accounting/Finance, U. Ariz. In corp. fin. KPMG Peat Marwick, Am. Continental Corp.; v.p. corp. planning & devel. Del Webb Corp., 1982-86, pres, CEO Del Webb Investment Properties, 1986-87, sr. v.p., 1988—. Office: Del Webb Corp 6001 N 24th St Phoenix AZ 85016-2018

MARIUCCI, STEVE, professional football coach, former college coach; b. Iron Mountain, Mich., Nov. 4, 1955; m. Gayle Mariucci; 4 children. Football coach No. Mich. U., 1978-79, Calif. State U., Fullerton, 1980-82; asst. head coach U. Louisville, 1983-84; receivers coach Orlando Renegades U.S. Football League, 1985; quality control coach L.A. Rams, 1985; receivers/spl. teams coach U. So. Calif., L.A., 1986, wide receivers/spl. teams coach, 1987-89, quarterbacks coach, offensive coord., 1990-91; quarterbacks coach Green Bay (Wis.) Packers, 1992-95; head coach Golden Bears U. Calif., 1996-98; head coach San Francisco 49ers, 1996—. Office: San Francisco 49ers 4949 Centennial Blvd Santa Clara CA 95054-1229

MARK, JAMES B. D. surgeon, educator; b. Nashville, June 26, 1929; s. Julius and Margaret (Baer) M.; m. Jean Rambar, Feb. 5, 1957; children: Jonathan, Michael, Margaret, Elizabeth, Katherine. BA, Vanderbilt U., 1950, MD, 1953. Intern, resident in gen. and thoracic surgery Yale-New Haven Hosp., 1953-60; instr. to asst. prof. surgery Yale U., 1960-65; assoc. prof. surgery Stanford U., 1965-69, prof., 1969-97, prof. emeritus, 1997—, Johnson and Johnson prof. surgery, 1972-97, head div. thoracic surgery, 1972-97, assoc. dean clin. affairs, 1988-92; chief staff Stanford U. Hosp., 1988-92. Governing bd. Health Systems Agy., Santa Clara County, 1978-80; sr. Fulbright-Hays fellow, vis. prof. surgery U. Dar es Salaam, Tanzania, 1972-73 Mem. editl. bd.: Jour. Thoracic and Cardiovasc. Surgery, 1986-94, World Jour. Surgery, 1995—; contbr. numerous articles to sci. jours. Bd. dirs. Stanford U. Hosp., 1992-94. With USPHS, 1955-57. Fellow ACS (pres. No. Calif. chpt. 1980-81), Am. Coll. Chest Physicians (pres. 1994-95); mem. Am. Assn. Thoracic Surgery, Am. Surg. Assn., Western Surg. Assn., Pacific Coast Surg. Assn., Halsted Soc. (pres. 1984), Western Thoracic Surg. Assn. (pres. 1992-93), Calif. Acad. Medicine (pres. 1978), Santa Clara County Med. Soc. (pres. 1976-77), Internat. Surg. Soc. Home: 921 Casanueva Pl Stanford CA 94305-1001 Office: Stanford U Med Ctr CVRB Stanford CA 94305 E-mail: jbdm@stanford.edu

MARK, SHELLEY MUIN, economist, educator, government official; b. China, Sept. 9, 1922; came to U.S., 1923, naturalized, 1944; s. Hing D. and S. (Wong) M.; m. Janet Chong, Sept. 14, 1946 (dec. Mar. 1977); children— Philip, Diane, Paul, Peter, Steven; m. Tung Chow, July 8, 1978. B.A., U. Wash., 1943, Ph.D., 1956; M.S., Columbia, 1944; postgrad. (Ford Found. fellow), Harvard, 1959-60. Fgn. news reporter CBS, N.Y., 1945-46; instr. U. Wash., 1946-48; asst. prof. Ariz. State Coll., 1948-51; territorial economist OPS, Honolulu, 1951-53; prof. econs. U. Hawaii, 1953-62, dir. econ. rsch. ctr., 1959-62; dir. planning and econ. devel. State of Hawaii, 1962-74, state land use commr., 1962-74, state energy coord., 1973-74; dir. Office Land Use Coordination EPA, Washington, 1975-77; prof. econs. U. Hawaii, 1978—. Rsch. fellow East-West Ctr., Inst. Econ. Devel. and Policy, 1984-94; Asian advisor Internat. Ctr. Econ. Growth, 1992—; sr. advisor Dept. Bus., Econ. Devel. and Tourism, Hawaii, 1995—; vis. scholar Harvard U., 1986; vis. faculty Grad. Sch. People's Bank of China, 1988; also econ. cons. Philippines Inst. Devel. Studies, Devel. Rsch. Ctr. State Coun., China, also other orgns.; mem. Gov.'s Adv. Com. Sci. and Tech., 1963-74, Oahu Transp. Policy Com., 1964-74, Regional Export Expansion Coun., 1964-74 Author: Economics in Action, 4th edit., 1969, Macroeconomic Performance of Asia-Pacific Region, 1985, Development Economics and Developing Economies, 1990, Aspects of Chinese Economic Development, 1991; editor: Economic Interdependence and Cooperation in Asia-Pacific, 1993, Asian Transitional Economies, 1996; contbr. articles to profl. jours. Bd. dirs. U. Hawaii Rsch. Corp.; bd. dirs. Coun. State Planning Agys., pres., 1973-74, hon. mem., 1975—; governing bd. Coun. State Govts., 1972-74. Recipient Sackett Meml. award Columbia, 1944 Mem. Hawaii Govt. Employees Assn. (pres. univ. chpt., dir. 1958-59), Am. Econ. Assn., Royal Econ. Soc., Western Regional Sci. Assn. (pres. 1974-75, dir.), Phi Beta Kappa, Sigma Delta Chi. Mem. United Ch. of Christ. Home: 2036 Keeaumoku St Honolulu HI 96822-2526

MARKER, MARC LINTHACUM, lawyer, investor; b. Los Angeles, July 19, 1941; s. Clifford Harry and Voris (Linthacum) M.; m. Sandra Vocom. Aug. 29, 1965; children: Victor, Gwendolyn. BA in Econs. and Geography, U. Calif.-Riverside, 1964; JD, U. So. Calif., 1967. Asst. v.p., asst. sec. Security Pacific Nat. Bank, L.A., 1970-73; sr. v.p., chief counsel, sec. Security Pacific Leasing Corp., San Francisco, 1973-92; pres. Security Pacific Leasing Svcs. Corp., San Francisco, 1977-85, dir., 1977-92. Bd. dirs., sec. Voris, Inc., 1973-86; bd. dirs. Refiners Petroleum Corp., 1977-81, Security Pacific Leasing Singapore Ltd., 1983-85, Security Pacific Leasing Can. Ltd., 1989-92; lectr. in field. Served to comdr., USCGR. Mem. ABA, Calif. Bar Assn., D.C. Bar Assn; Club: Army and Navy. Republican. Lutheran.

MARKEY, WILLIAM ALAN, health care administrator; b. Cleve., Dec. 29, 1927; s. Oscar Bennett and Claire (Feldman) M.; m. Irene Nelson, Oct. 31, 1954; children— Janet Ellen Markey-Hisakawa, Suzanne Katherine Markey-Johnson. Student, Case Inst. Tech., 1945-48; BA, U. Mich., 1950; MS, Yale U., 1954. Resident hosp. adminstrn. Beth Israel Hosp., Boston, 1953-54; asst. dir. Montefiore Hosp., Pitts., 1954-56; asst. adminstr. City of Hope Med. Ctr., Duarte, Calif., 1956-57, adminstrv. dir., 1957-66; assoc. dir. cancer hosp. project, instr. pub. health U. So. Calif. Sch. Medicine, 1966-67, asst. clin. prof. pub. health and community medicine, 1968-70, asst. prof., 1970-75, dep. dir. regional med. programs, 1967-71; adminstr. Health Care Agy., County of San Diego, 1971-74, health services cons., 1974-75; dir. Maricopa County Dept. Health Services, Phoenix, 1975-79, cons., 1979-80; adminstr. Sonoma Valley Hosp., Calif., 1980-83. Lectr. pub. health Sch. Pub. Health, UCLA, 1969-74; lectr. comty. medicine Sch. Medicine, U. Calif.-San Diego, 1973-75; cons. L.A. County Dept. Hosps., 1966-71, cons. Hosp./Health Svcs., 1983—; CEO Chinese Hosp., San Francisco, 1985-86, 90-91; adj. instr. Golden Gate U., 1992-96. Mem. bd. edn. Duarte Unified Sch. Dist., 1967-72, pres., 1970-72; bd. dirs. Hosp. Coun. So. Calif., 1963-67, sec., 1966-67, Duarte Pub. Libr. Assn., 1965-72, Duarte-Bradbury chpt. Am. Field Svc., 1965-72, Duarte-Bradbury Comty. Chest, 1961-68, Cen. Ariz. Health Svcs. Agy., 1975-80, Vis. Nurse Assn. The Redwoods, Santa Rosa, Calif., 1985-86, Sonoma Greens Homeowners Assn., 1990-95, Sonoma City Opera, 1987, 93, United Way, Sonoma, 1996—; com. chmn. Sonoma County Bd. Realtors, 1990-92; active Sonoma County Multiple Listing Svc., 1987—. With AUS, 1950-52. Fellow Am. Coll. Health Care Execs. (life); mem. Am. Hosp. Assn. (life), Am. Pub. Health Assn., Royal Soc. Health, Calif. Hosp. Assn. (trustee 1966-69, dir. 1966-69), Internat. Fedn. Hosps., Hosp. Coun. No. Calif. (dir. 1981-83), Kiwanis, Rotary (past pres. Duarte). Home: 866 Princeton Dr Sonoma CA 95476-4186 Office: PO Box F Sonoma CA 95476-0370

MARKHAM, REED B. education educator, consultant; b. Alhambra, Calif., Feb. 14, 1957; s. John F. and Reeda (Bjarason) M. BA, MA, Brigham Young U., 1982; BS, Regents Coll., 1981, MA, 1982; MPA, U. So. Calif., 1983; MA, UCLA, 1989; PhD, Columbia Pacific U., 1991. Mem. faculty Brigham Young U., Provo, Utah, 1984, Calif. State U., Fullerton and Long Beach, 1984, Northridge, 1985, El Camino Coll., Torrance, Calif., 1986, Orange Coast Coll., Costa Mesa, 1986, Pasadena (Calif.) Coll., 1986, Fullerton (Calif.) Community Coll., 1986; instr., mem. pub. rels. com. Chaffey (Calif.) Coll., 1986-87; prof., CARES dir. Calif. State Poly. U., Pomona, 1987-98; adj. prof. Calif. State U., L.A., 1992-93, dir. Ctr. for Student Retention, 1995—; prof. East L.A. Coll., 1996-98, Salt Lake C.C., 1998—. Rsch. asst. to pres. Ctr. for the Study of Cmty. Coll.,

1985; mem. faculty Riverside (Calif.) Coll., 1989-90, Rio Hondo (Calif.) Coll., 1989-90, English Lang. Inst., 1994, Calif. Poly Summer Bridge, 1989-95, East L.A. Coll.; adj. prof. Citrus Coll., 1998—; speechwriter U.S. Supreme Ct., Washington, 1980; cons. gifted children program Johns Hopkins U./Scripps Coll., Claremont, Calif., 1987-88; mem. faculty PACE Program East L.A., 1995-96; faculty East L.A. Coll., 1996-97; adj. prof. U. So. Calif., 1998—; prof. Salt Lake C. C., 1998-99; mem. Pres.'s Coalition for Am. Reads Challenge, 1999; mem. Olympic News Svc. 2002, 2001-. Author: Power Speechwriting, 1983, Power Speaking, 1990, Public Opinion, 1990, Advances in Public Speaking, 1991, Leadership 2000: Success Skills for University Students, 1995, Excellence in Public Speaking, 1997; co-author: Student Retention: Success Models in Higher Education, 1996, Upward Bound Program Grant Proposal, 1996, Making Marriage Magnificent, 1998; editor Trojan in Govt., U. So. Calif., 1983; editl. bd. mem. Edn. Digest, Speaker and Gavel, Innovative Higher End., Pub. Rels. Rev., Nat. Forensic Jour., The Forensic Educator, Clearinghouse for the Contemporary Educator, Hispanic Am. Family Mag.; writer N.Y. times, Christian Sci. Monitor; ednl. columnist San Bernardino (Calif.) Sun., 1992-98. VOICE, 2000-01. Pres. bd. trustees Regents Coll., 1986; aapointed to Pres.'s Coalition for Am. Reads Challenge; mem. Olympic News Svc., 2001—. Mem. Doctorate Assn. N.Y. Scholars, Nat. Assn. Pvt. Nontraditional Colls. (accrediting com. 1989—), Pub. Rels. Soc. Am. (dir.-at-large inland empire 1992-93, faculty advisor). LDS. Office: Salt Lake CC Comm Dept PO Box 30808 Salt Lake City UT 84130-0808 E-mail: markham@slcc.edu

MARKHAM, RICHARD GLOVER, research executive; b. Pasadena, Calif., June 18, 1925; s. Fred Smith and Maziebelle (Glover) M.; m. Jonne Louise Pearson, Apr. 29, 1950; children: Janet B., Fred S., Charles R., Richard G., Marilyn A. Student, Stanford U., 1943; BS, Calif. Inst. Tech., Pasadena, 1945; MS, Stanford U., 1947. Pres., owner Aquarium Pump Supply, Prescott, Ariz., 1957-78; 1st v.p., dir. Bank of Prescott, 1981-87; also v.p., bd. dirs. Oxycal Labs., Prescott, 1981-97, ret., 1997. Patentee in field. Mem. Ariz. Dept. Econ. Planning and Devel., 1967-72; treas. Ariz. State Rep. Com., 1970-72; active Ariz. Acad., 1974—; trustee Orme Sch., Mayer, Ariz., 1970-83, Prescott Coll., 1979-83.

MARKKULA, A. C., JR. entrepreneur, computer company executive; Co-founder, former pres., chief exec. officer Apple Computer Inc., now chmn. bd. dirs.; founder, vice chmn. Echelon, Los Gatos, Calif.; with ACM Investments, Woodside. Office: ACM Investments PO Box 620170 Woodside CA 94062-0170

MARKLAND, FRANCIS SWABY, JR. biochemist, educator; b. Phila., Jan. 15, 1936; s. Francis Swaby Sr. and Willie Lawrence (Averritt) M.; m. Barbara Blake, Jun. 27, 1959 - April 5, 1996; children: Cathleen Blake, Francis Swaby IV. B.S., Pa. State U., 1957; Ph.D., Johns Hopkins U., 1964. Postdoctoral fellow UCLA, 1964-66, asst. prof. biochemistry, 1966-73; vis. asst. prof. U. So. Calif., Los Angeles, 1973-74, assoc. prof., 1974-83, prof., 1983—, acting chmn. dept. biochemistry, 1986-88, vice-chmn., 1988-92. Cons. Clin. Lab. Med. Group, L.A., 1977-88, Cortech, Inc., Denver, 1983-88, Maret Corp., Wayne, Pa., 1996-2000; mem. biochem., endocrinology study sect. NIH, 1986-90. Mem. editl. bd. Toxicon., Internat. Jour. of Toxinology; contbr. articles, chpts. and abstracts to profl. publs.; patentee in field. Mem. Angeles Choral, L.A. Capt. USNR, 1957-59 Recipient NIH rsch. career devel. award USPHS, NIH, 1968-73; rsch. grantee Nat. Cancer Inst., 1979-86, 91-93, Nat. Heart Lung and Blood Inst., 1984-88, 95-99, State of Calif. Breast Cancer Rsch. Program, 1995—, State Calif. Cancer Rsch. Program, 2000—. Mem. AAAS, Am. Soc. Biochem. and Molecular Biology, Am. Chem. Soc., Internat. Soc. on Toxinology, Protein Soc., Soc. Fibronolysis & Proteolysis, Internat. Soc. on Thrombosis and Haemostasis (subcom. exogenous hemostatic factors, chair 1994-96, 99-2001), Am. Assn. Cancer Rsch., Am. Soc. Hematology, Protein Soc., Sigma Xi, Alpha Zeta. Avocations: singing, skiing, aerobics, golf. Office: U So Calif Keck Sch Medicine Cancer Rsch Lab Rm 106 1303 N Mission Rd Los Angeles CA 90033-1020 E-mail: markland@usc.edu

MARKLE, DAVID A. optical engineer; With Ultratech Stepper, San Jose, Calif., chief tech. officer. Recipient David Richardson medal Optical Soc. Am., 1994. Office: 3050 Zanker Rd San Jose CA 95134-2126

MARKOFF, STEVEN C. finance company executive; CEO, pres., founder A. Mark Fin., Santa Monica, Calif., 1965—. Office: A Mark Financial 100 Wilshire Blvd Fl 3 Santa Monica CA 90401

MARKOVCHICK, VINCENT J. surgeon; b. Hazleton, Pa., 1944; MD, Temple U., 1970. Intern Presbyn. Med. Ctr., Denver, 1970-71; resident emergency medicine U. Chgo. Hosps.-Clinics, 1974-76; mem. staff Denver Gen. Hosp.; assoc. prof. U.Colo. Health Sci. Ctr.; pres. Am. Bd. Emer. Med., East Lansing. Mem. Am. Coll. Emergency Physicians, Colo. Med. Soc., STEM. Office: Denver Gen Hosp Emergency Medicine Dept 777 Bannock St Denver CO 80204-4507 also: Amer Bd Emerg Med 3000 Coolidge Rd East Lansing MI 48823-6319

MARKOWITZ, HARRY M. finance and economics educator; b. Chicago, Ill., Aug. 24, 1927; s. Morris and Mildred (Gruber) M.; m. Barbara Gay. PhB, U. Chgo., 1947, MA, 1950, PhD, 1954. With research staff Rand Corp., Santa Monica, Calif., 1952-60, 61-63; tech. dir. Consol. Analysis Ctrs., Inc., Santa Monica, 1963-68; prof. UCLA, Westwood, 1968-69; pres. Arbitrage Mgmt. Co., N.Y.C., 1969-72; pvt. practice cons. N.Y.C., 1972-74; with research staff T.J. Watson Research Ctr. IBM, Yorktown Hills, N.Y., 1974-83; Speiser prof. fin. Baruch Coll. CUNY, N.Y.C., 1982-93; dir. rsch. Daiwa Securities Trust Co, Jersey City, 1990-2000. V.p. Inst. Mgmt. Sci., 1960-62. Author: Portfolio Selection: Efficient Diversification of Investments, 1959, Mean-Variance Analysis in Portfolio Choice, 1987; co-author: SIMSCRIPT Simulation Programming Language, 1963; co-editor: Process Analysis of Economic Capabilities, 1963. Recipient John von Neumann Theory prize Ops. Rsch. Soc. Am. and Inst. Mgmt. Sci., 1989, Nobel Prize in Econs., 1990. Fellow Econometric Soc., Am. Acad. Arts and Scis.; mem. Am. Fin. Assn. (pres. 1982—). Office: Ste 245 1010 Turquoise St San Diego CA 92109

MARKS, LEONARD, JR. retired corporate executive; b. N.Y.C., May 22, 1921; s. Leonard M. and Laura (Colegrove) Rose; m. Antonia Saldaña Riley, July 19, 1986; children from previous marriage: Linda, Patricia Anne, Peter K. A.B. in Econs., Drew U., 1942; M.B.A., Harvard U., 1948, D.B.A., 1961. Asst. prof. bus. adminstrn. Harvard U., 1949-55; prof. fin. Stanford U., 1955-64; asst. sec. USAF, Washington, 1964-68; v.p. corp. devel. Times Mirror Co., Los Angeles, 1968-69; sr. v.p. Wells Fargo Bank, San Francisco, 1969-72; exec. v.p. Castle & Cooke Inc., San Francisco, 1972-85; gen. ptnr. Marks-Hoffman Assocs., Venture Capital, 1985-92; corp. dir., 1992-2000, Airlease Mgmt. Svcs., Flagstaff, Ariz., 2000—. Bd. dirs. Ubizen, Inc. Co-author: Case Problems in Commercial Bank Management, 1962; contbg.: Credit Management Handbook, 1958. Capt. AUS, 1942-46, ret. brig. gen. USAFR. E-mail: proftmarks@aol.com

MARKS, MERTON ELEAZER, lawyer; b. Chgo., Oct. 16, 1932; s. Alfred Tobias and Helene Fannie (Rosner) M.; m. Radee Maiden Feiler, May 20, 1966; children: Sheldon, Elise Marks Vazelakis, Alan, Elaine Marks Ianchiou. BS, Northwestern U., 1954, JD, 1956. Bar: Ill. 1956, U.S. Ct. Mil. Appeals 1957, Ariz. 1958, U.S. Dist. Ct. Ariz. 1960, U.S. Ct. Appeals (9th cir.) 1962, U.S. Supreme Ct. 1970. Assoc. Moser, Compere & Emerson, Chgo., 1956-57; ptnr. Morgan, Marks & Rogers, Tucson, 1960-62; asst. atty. gen. State of Ariz., Phoenix, 1962-64, counsel indsl. commn., 1964-65; from assoc. to ptnr. Shimmel, Hill, Bishop & Greunder, Phoenix, 1965-74; ptnr. Lewis & Roca, Phoenix, 1974—. Lectr. on pharm., health care, product liability and ins. subjects; Judge Pro Tempore Ariz. Ct. Appeals, 1994; legal columnist Exec. Golfer mag. Contbr. articles to profl. jours. Capt. JAGC, USAR, 1957-64. Fellow Chartered Inst. Arbitrators (London); mem. ABA (tort and ins. practice sect., chmn. spl. com. on fed. asbestos legis. 1987-89, chmn. workers compensation and employers liability law com. 1983-84, dispute resolution sect., internat. law and practice sect.), Am. Bd. Trial Advocates, Acad. Hosp. Industry Attys., Am. Coll. Legal Medicine, Internat. Bar Assn. (sect. on bus. law, product liability, advt., unfair competition and consumer affairs com., internat. litigation com., ins. com., arbitration and alt. dispute resolution com.), Drug Info. Assn., Am. Soc. Pharmacy Law, State Bar Ariz. (chmn. workers compensation sect. 1969-73), Nat. Coun. Self Insurers, Ariz. Self Insurers Assn., Fedn. Ins. and Corp. Counsel (chmn. pharm. litig. sect. 1989-91, chmn. workers compensation sect. 1977-79, v.p. 1978-79, 81, bd. dirs. 1981-89, mem. products liability sect., mem. reinsurance sect.), Internat. Assn. Def. Counsel, Ariz. Assn. Def. Counsel (pres. 1976-77), Maricopa County Bar Assn., Def. Rsch. Inst. (drug and device com., chmn. workers compensation com. 1977-78), Assn. Internat. de Droit des Assurances (cert. arbitrator), Reinsurance and Ins. Arbitration Soc. (cert. arbitrator), Union Internat. des Avocats. Office: 8655 E Via De Ventura Ste G-223 Scottsdale AZ 85258

MARKS, MICHAEL E. electronics company executive; BA, MA, Oberlin Coll.; MBA, Harvard U. Formerly pres., CEO Metcal Inc.; chmn. bd. dirs. Flextronics, 1993—, CEO, 1994—. Office: Flextronics 2090 Fortune Dr San Jose CA 95131-1823

MARKS, ROBERT ARTHUR, lawyer, attorney general; b. Dayton, Ohio, Oct. 9, 1952; s. Arthur Kenneth and Patricia Marks; m. Victoria Scurlock, Oct. 21, 1978; two sons. BA, U. Wis., 1974; JD, U. Cin., 1977. Bar: Ohio 1977, Hawaii 1978, U.S. Ct. Appeals (6th cir.) Ohio 1977, U.S. Ct. Appeals (9th cir.) Hawaii 1978, U.S. Supreme Ct. 1992. Pvt. practice, Honolulu, 1978-84; dep. atty. gen. State of Hawaii, Honolulu, 1984-87, supr. dep. atty. gen., 1987-92, 1st dep. atty. gen., 1992, atty. gen., 1992-94; counsel Alston, Hunt, Floyd & Ing, Honolulu, 1995-97, Price, Okamoto Himeno & Lum, Honolulu, 1997—. Office: Price Okamoto Himeno Lum 707 Richards St Ste 728 Honolulu HI 96813-4623

MARLAR, JAMES M. federal judge; b. 1945; AB, Stanford U., 1967; JD, U. Ariz., 1970. With Teilberg, Sanders & Parks, Phoenix; pvt. practice Phoenix; judge pro tempore Ariz. Ct. Appeals, 1986, Ariz. Superior Ct., Phoenix, 1988; apptd. bankruptcy judge U.S. Dist. Ct. Ariz., 1993; apptd. 9th Cir. Bankruptcy Appellate Panel, 1999. Office: 110 S Church Ave Ste 8112 Tucson AZ 85701-1600 Fax: 520-620-7457

MARLATT, MICHAEL JAMES, lawyer; b. L.A., Jan. 15, 1957; s. James Raymond and Norma Jean (Greenfield) M.; m. Donna Marie Healey, Apr. 13, 1985. BA, U. So. Calif., Calif. Poly., Pomona, 1981; JD, Pepperdine U., 1984. Bar: Calif. 1984, U.S. Dist. Ct. (ctrl. dist.) Calif. 1985, U.S. Supreme Ct. 1990. Project liaison U. So. Calif., Sch. Medicine, L.A., 1975-78; documentation rschr. NASA-Jet Propulsion Lab., Pasadena, Calif., 1978-81; ptnr. Thompson & Colegate, Riverside, 1984—. Bd. dirs. Assn. So. Calif. Def. Counsel, L.A., U. Calif., Riverside; lectr. Calif. Trial Lawyers Assn., 1991-94, Princeton U., 1993, U. Amsterdam Law Sch., 1994, Loma Linda (Calif.) U. Sch. Medicine, 1991-94, 99, Boston Coll. Law Sch., 1997, U. London, 1998; chair Am. Legal Sys. Internat. Law Program Civil Litigation U. of Calif., 1997; lectr., spkr. to ins. cos. on health care, 1988—; bd. dirs. Mission Inn Found., v.p., 1997-99, pres., 1999—; radio commentator Stas. KCKC, KCAL, KMEN and KPRO. Mem. ctr. com. Calif. Rep. Party, Sacramento, 1990-93; bd. dirs. U. Calif., Riverside, pres., 1996-99; bd. dirs. Mission Inn Found., v.p., 1996-98, pres., 1999—; bd. dirs. Riverside County Regional Med. Ctr.; mem. bioethics com. Riverside Cmty. Hosp., 1999-2001. Mem. Am. Bd. Trial Advocates, So. Calif. Assn. Hosp. Risk Mgrs. (bylaws com. 1996-99), Victoria Country Club, Lincoln Club Riverside County, Phi Alpha Delta. Roman Catholic. Avocations: rare book collecting, collegiate athletics, traveling. Office: Thompson & Colegate PO Box 1299 3610 14th St Riverside CA 92501-3843 E-mail: mjmdmm@gateway.net

MARLEN, JAMES S. chemical, plastics and building materials manufacturing company executive; b. Santiago, Chile, Mar. 14, 1941; came to U.S., 1961; m. Carolyn S. Shields, Jan. 23, 1965; children: James, Andrew, John. Grad., U. Ala., 1965; MBA, U. Akron, 1971. With GenCorp., Akron, Ohio, 1965-93, engring., mktg. and gen. mgmt. positions domestic and internat. ops., 1965-76; pres. GTR Coated Fabrics Co., 1977-80, group pres. fabricated plastics, 1980-87; pres. consumer and indsl. sects. GenCorp Polymer Products, Akron, Ohio, 1988—; v.p. and officer GenCorp, Akron, 1988-93; pres., CEO Ameron Internat. Corp., Pasadena, Calif., 1993—. Bd. dirs., Ameron, Inc., chmn. bd. dirs., pres. and CEO, 1995—; dir. A. Schulman, Inc., Tamco Steel, Parsons Corp.; gen. and hon. chmn. Nat. Inventors Hall of Fame Induction, 1993. Bd. dirs. YMCA Met. L.A., The Employers Group of Calif., Town Hall of L.A., gov.; mem. the Beavers; dir. L.A. Sports Coun. Mem. Chem. Mfrs. Assn. (past pres.), Assocs. Caltech, Calif. C. of C., L.A. C. of C. (dir.), Portage Country Club (Akron, Ohio), Calif. Club (L.A.), Annandale Golf Club (Pasadena), L.A. Country Club, Valley Hunt Club (Pasadena), Soc. Fellows of Huntington Libr. (L.A.). Office: Ameron Internat Corp 245 S Los Robles Ave Pasadena CA 91101-2820

MARLON, ANTHONY M. healthcare company executive, cardiologist; Intern, resident, cardiology fellow Stanford (Calif.) U., 1967-72; chief cardiology U. Med. Ctr. So. Nev., 1972-85; pvt. practice cardiology, from 1972; founder, chmn. bd., CEO Sierra Health Svcs., Inc., Las Vegas, Nev. Office: Sierra Health Svcs Inc 2724 N Tenaya Way Las Vegas NV 89128

MARLOW, EDWARD A. former army officer; b. Cleve., Nov. 22, 1946; m. Gari Ann Dill, Sept. 20, 1975. AA, Long Beach City Coll., 1971; cert., Officer Candidate Sch., Ft. Benning, 1974, Basic Infantry Officer Course, 1976; student, Am. Law Inst., N.Y., 1979-80; cert., Advance Armor Officer Course, Ft. Knox, 1982, U.S. Army Command and Gen. Staff Coll., , 1986; BS in Bus. Mgmt. and Polit. Sci., SUNY, 1987; MPA, U. So. Calif., 1990; cert., Advance Intelligence Officer Course, Ft. Huachuca, 1991. Registered investment adv. with SEC, 1978-90. Commd. 2d lt. inf. U.S. Army, 1974, advanced through grades to maj., 1988; chief real property br. Mil. Dept., Sacramento, 1968—; pres. and dir. TEAM Mgmt. Corp., 1978—; pres. Western Res. Corp., Goldfield, Nev., 2000—, also bd. dirs. Mng. sr. ptnr. Caribbean Basin Latin Am. Devel. Orgn., Sacramento, 1988-98; trustee Hosp. Relief Fund Caribbean, Inc., Washington, 1989-92; mem. Caribbean Pvt. Sector Disaster Coord. subcom. White House Internat. Disaster Adv. Com., 1991-92; sr. ptnr. Caribbean Basin Latin Am. Devel. Orgn. Endowment Group, Sacramento, 1992—; chair bd. trustees CABALADO Relief Fund, Inc., 1993-99; provided disaster assistance and med. equipment to Glendon Hosp., Plymouth, Montserrat, West Indies, 1994-95. Mem. DAV (life), Am. Assn. Retired Persons. Avocations: sailing, fishing.

MARMARELIS, VASILIS ZISSIS, engineering educator, writer, consultant; b. Mytilini, Greece, Nov. 16, 1949; came to U.S., 1972; s. Zissis P. and Elpis V. (Galinos) M.; m. Melissa Emily Orme, Mar. 12, 1989; children: Zissis Eugene and Myrl Galinos. Diploma in elec. and mech. engring., Nat. Tech. U. of Athens, Greece, 1972; MS in Info. Sci., Calif. Inst. Tech., 1973, PhD in Engring. Sci., 1976. Rsch. fellow Calif. Inst. Tech., Pasadena, 1976-78; asst. prof. U. So. Calif., L.A., 1978-83, assoc. prof., 1983-88, prof., 1988—, also dir. biomed. simulations resource, 1985—, chmn. dept. biomed. engring., 1990-96; pres. Multispec Corp., L.A., 1986-2000. Author: Analysis of Physiological Systems, 1978, translated in Russian 1981, translated in Chinese 1990; Advanced Methods of Physiological Systems Modeling, vol. I, 1987, vol. II, 1989, vol. III, 1994; contbr. numerous articles to profl. jours. Fellow IEEE, Am. Inst. for Med. and Biol. Engring.; mem. N.Y. Acad. Scis., Biomed. Engring. Soc., Neural Networks Soc. Office: U So Calif Ohe 500 Los Angeles CA 90089-0001

MARMOR, JUDD, psychiatrist, educator; b. London, May 1, 1910; came to U.S., 1911, naturalized, 1916; s. Clement K. and Sarah (Levene) M.; m. Katherine Stern, May 1, 1938; 1 son, Michael Franklin. AB, Columbia U., 1930, MD, 1933; DHL, Hebrew Union Coll., 1972. Diplomate: Am. Bd. Psychiatry and Neurology, Nat. Bd. Med. Examiners. Intern St. Elizabeth Hosp., Washington, 1933-35; resident neurologist Montefiore Hosp., N.Y.C., 1935-37; psychiatrist Bklyn. State Hosp., 1937; psychoanalytic tng. N.Y. Psychoanalytic Inst., N.Y.C., 1937-41; pvt. practice psychiatry, psychoanalysis and neurology N.Y.C., 1937-46, L.A., 1946—; adj. neurologist, neurologist-in-charge clinic Mt. Sinai Hosp., N.Y.C., 1939-46; lectr. New Sch. Social Rsch., N.Y.C., 1942-43; vis. prof. social welfare UCLA, 1949-64, clin. prof. psychiatry sch. medicine, 1953-80, adj. prof. psychiatry, 1980-85, emeritus prof., 1985—. Tng. analyst, also pres. So. Calif. Psychoanalytic Inst., 1955-57; sr. attending psychiatrist L.A. County Gen. Hosp., 1954-80; dir. divs. psychiatry Cedars-Sinai Med. Ctr., L.A., 1965-72; Franz Alexander prof. psychiatry U. So. Calif. Sch. Medicine, 1972-80, emeritus, 1980— ; sr. cons. regional office social svc. VA, L.A., 1946-50; cons. psychiatry Brentwood VA Hosp., Calif., 1955-65; mem. Coun. Mental Health of Western Interstate Commn. Higher Edn., 1966-72. Editor: Sexual Inversion-The Multiple Roots of Homosexuality, Modern Psychoanalysis: New Directions and Perspectives, Psychiatry in Transition: Selected Papers of Judd Marmor, Homosexual Behavior: A Modern Reappraisal; (with S. Woods) The Interface Between the Psychodynamic and Behavioral Therapies, Psychiatrists & Their Patients: A National Study of Private Office Practice; (with S. Elsenstein and N.A. Levy) The Dyadic Transaction: An Investigation into the Nature of the Psychotherapeutic Process; (with P. Nardi and D. Sanders) Growing Up Before Stonewall; mem. editl. bd. Am. Jour. Psychoanalysis, Contemporary Psychoanalysis, Archives Sexual Behavior; contbr. articles in field to profl. jours. Served as sr. attending surgeon USPHS USNR, 1944-45. Fellow Am. Psychiat. Assn. (life mem., pres. 1975-76), N.Y. Acad. Medicine (life mem.), Am. Acad. Psychoanalysis (pres. 1965-66), Am. Orthopsychiat. Assn. (dir. 1968-71), AAAS, Am. Coll. Psychiatrists; mem. AMA, Calif. Med. Assn., Group for Advancement Psychiatry (dir. 1968-70, pres. 1973-75), Am. Fund for Psychiatry (dir. 1955-57), So. Calif. Psychiat. Soc., So. Calif. Psychoanalytic Soc. (pres. 1960-61), Am. Psychoanalytic Assn., Los Angeles County Med. Soc., Phi Beta Kappa, Alpha Omega Alpha. Home and Office: 10660 Wilshire Blvd # 1007 Los Angeles CA 90024-4526 Fax: (310) 446-4186

MARMOR, MICHAEL FRANKLIN, ophthalmologist, educator; b. N.Y.C., Aug. 10, 1941; s. Judd and Katherine (Stern) M.; m. C. Jane Breeden, Dec. 20, 1968; children: Andrea K., David J. AB, Harvard U., 1962, MD, 1966. Diplomate Am. Bd. Ophthalmology. Med. intern UCLA Med. Ctr., 1967; fellow neurophysiology NIMH, 1967-70; resident in ophthalmology Mass. Eye and Ear Infirmary, Boston, 1970-73; asst. prof. ophthalmology U. Calif. Sch. Medicine, San Francisco, 1973-74; asst. prof. surgery (ophthalmology) Stanford (Calif.) U. Sch. Medicine, 1974-80, assoc. prof., 1980-86, prof., 1986—, head. div. ophthalmalogy, 1984-88, chmn. dept., 1988 92, dir. Basic Sci. Course Ophthalmology, 1993 . Faculty mem. program in human biology Stanford U., 1982—; chief ophthalmology sect. VA Med. Ctr., Palo Alto, Calif., 1974-84; mem. sci. adv. bd. No. Calif. Soc. to Prevent Blindness, 1984-92, Calif. Med. Assn., 1984-92, Nat. Retinitis Pigmentosa Found., 1985-95. Author: The Eye of the Artist, 1997; editor: The Retinal Pigment Epithelium, 1975, The Effects of Aging and Environment on Vision, 1991, The Retinal Pigment Epithelium: Function and Disease, 1998; editor-in-chief Doc. Ophthalmologica, 1995-99; history editor: Survey of Ophthalmology; editl. bd. Healthline, MDVista, contbr. more than 200 articles to sci. jours., 50 chpts. to books. Mem. affirmative action com. Stanford U. Sch. Medicine, 1984-92. Sr. asst. surgeon USPHS, 1967-70. Recipient Svc. award Nat. Retinitis Pigmentosa Found., Balt., 1981, Rsch. award Alcon Rsch. Found., Houston, 1989; rsch. grantee Nat. Eye. Inst., Bethesda, Md., 1974-94. Fellow Am. Acad. Ophthalmology (bd. councillors 1982-85, pub. health com. 1990-93, rep. to NAS com. on vision 1991-93, Honor award 1984, Sr. Honor award 1996), Internat. Acad. Sports Vision (rsch. com.); mem. Internat. Soc. Clin. Electrophysiology of Vision (v.p. 1990-98), Assn. Rsch. in Vision and Ophthalm ology, Internat. Soc. for Eye Rsch., Macula Soc., Retina Soc. Democrat. Avocations: tennis, race-walking, chamber music (clarinet), art, medical history. Office: Stanford U Sch Medcine Dept Ophthalmology Stanford CA 94305-5308

MARNELL, ANTHONY AUSTIN, II, architect; b. Riverside, Calif., Mar. 30, 1949; s. Anthony Austin and Ida Marie (Comforti) M.; m. Sandra Jean Graf, June 24, 1972 (div.); children: Anthony, Alisa. BArch, U. So. Calif., 1972. Architect, draftsman firms in Calif. and Nev., 1969-72; project coordinator Zuni Constrn. Co., Las Vegas, Nev., 1973-74; office mgr., architect Corrao Constrn. Co., Inc., Las Vegas, 1973-74, Las Vegas, 1974-82; chmn. bd. Marnell Corrao Assocs., Las Vegas, 1976—; pres. Marinelli Internat., Inc., Las Vegas, 1978—, A.A. Marnell II, Architect, Las Vegas, 1978—, Las Vegas, 1980—, Air Continental Jet Charter, Inc., Las Vegas, 1980-99; CEO Maxwell Corrao Assocs., Las Vegas, 1999—. Mem. ethics com. Nev. Bd. Architects, 1974; chmn. bd. Rio Hotel & Casino, Inc., 1986—, Focus 2000, Inc., 1989—. Prin. works include Mirage, Rio, Maxim Hotel, Treasure Island, Boulder Station, Sundance Hotel, Sam's Town, Excalibur; additions to Caesar's Palace, Desert Inn, Sands, Stardust, California, Frontier and Dunes Hotels (all Las Vegas), Caesar's, Atlantic City, others. Mem. Founders Bd. U. Nev., Las Vegas. Mem. Nat. Council Archtl. Registration Bds., Post Tensioning Inst. YPO (Nev. chmn. 1990). Roman Catholic. Office: Marnell Corrao Assoc Inc 4495 Polaris Ave Las Vegas NV 89103-4119 also: Rio Hotel & Casino Inc 3700 W Flamingo Rd Las Vegas NV 89103-4046

MARPLE, STANLEY LAWRENCE, JR. electrical engineer, signal processing researcher; b. Tulsa, Sept. 7, 1947; s. Stanley Lawrence and Geraldine Doris M.; m. Eileen Suzanne Stevens, Aug. 31, 1974; children: Darci Leah, Rebecca Anne, Matthew Lawrence. BA, Rice U., 1969, MEE, 1970; DEng, Stanford U., 1976. Staff engr. Argo Systems, Inc., Sunnyvale, Calif., 1972-78; sr. staff engr. Advent Systems, Inc., Mountain View, 1978-79, The Analytic Scis. Corp., Mc Lean, Va., 1980-82; sr. devel. engr. Schlumberger Well Svcs., Houston, 1983-85; mgr., devel. engr. Martin Marietta Aero & Naval Systems, Balt., 1986-88; chief scientist Orincon Corp., San Diego, 1989-93, 96—, Acuson Corp., Mountain View, Calif., 1993-96. Author: Digital Spectral Analysis, 1987, Digital Time, Frequency, and Space Analysis, 1999. Capt. Signal Corps, U.S. Army, 1972-80. Fellow IEEE; mem. IEEE Signal Processing Soc. (editor Trans. on Signal Processing 1982-86, Sr. Paper award 1984, adminstrv. com. 1985-88, chmn. spectral estimation and array processing com. 1989-91). Avocations: stamp collecting, hiking, writing. Office: Orincon 9363 Towne Centre Dr San Diego CA 92121-3017

MARQUESS, LAWRENCE WADE, lawyer; b. Bloomington, Ind., Mar. 2, 1950; s. Earl Lawrence and Mary Louise (Coberly) M.; m. Barbara Ann Bailey, June 17, 1978; children: Alexander Lawrence, Michael Wade. BSEE, Purdue U., 1973; JD, W.Va. U., 1977. Bar: W.Va. 1977, Tex. 1977, U.S. Dist. Ct. (so. dist.) W.Va. 1977, U.S. Dist. Ct. (no. dist.) Tex. 1977, Colo. 1980, U.S. Dist. Ct. Colo. 1980, U.S. Ct. Appeals (10th cir.) 1980, U.S. Supreme Ct. 1984, U.S. Dist. Ct. (no. dist.) Ohio 1988, U.S. Ct. Appeals (DC cir.) 1997, U.S. Dist. Ct. Nebr. 1999. Assoc. Johnson, Bromberg, Leeds & Riggs, Dallas, 1977-79, Bradley, Campbell & Carney, Golden, Colo., 1979-82, ptnr., 1983-84, Stettner, Miller & Cohn P.C.,

1984-87, Nelson & Harding, Denver, 1987-88, Heron, Burchette, Ruckert & Rothwell, 1989-90, Harding & Ogborn, 1990-94, Otten, Johnson, Robinson, Neff & Ragonetti, Denver, 1994-2001, Littler Mendelson, P.C., Denver, 2001—. Mem. faculty Am. Law Inst. - ABA Advanced Labor and Employment Law Course, 1986, 87. Mem. ABA (labor, antitrust and litigation sects.), ACLU, Colo. Bar Assn. (co-chmn. labor law com. 1989-92), Denver Bar Assn., 1st Jud. Dist. Bar Assn., Sierra Club, Nat. Ry. Hist. Soc. Democrat. Methodist. Home: 11883 W 27th Dr Lakewood CO 80215-7000 Office: Littler Mendelson PC 1200 17th St Ste 2850 Denver CO 80202 E-mail: lmarquess@littler.com

MARQUEZ, ALFREDO C. federal judge; b. 1922; m. Linda Nowobilsky. B.S., U. Ariz., 1948, J.D., 1950. Bar: Ariz. Practice law Mesch Marquez & Rothschild, 1957-80; asst. atty. gen. State of Ariz., 1951-52; asst. county atty. Pima County, Ariz., 1953-54; adminstrv. asst. to Congressman Stewart Udall, 1955; judge U.S. Dist. Ct. Ariz., Tucson, 1980-91, sr. judge, 1991—. Served with USN, 1942-45 Office: US Dist Ct US Courthouse Rm 327 405 W Congress Ste 6180 Tucson AZ 85701-5060

MARROW, TRACY See ICE-T

MARSDEN, JERROLD ELDON, mathematician, educator, engineer; b. Ocean Falls, British Columbia, Aug. 17, 1942; married 1965; 1 child. BSc, U. Toronto, Canada, 1965; PhD in Math., Princeton U., 1968. Instr. math. Princeton U., N.J., 1968; lectr. U. Calif., Berkeley, 1968-69, asst. prof., 1969-72, assoc. prof., 1972-77, prof. math., 1977—; asst. prof. U. Toronto, Canada, 1970-71; prof. Calif. Tech., Pasadena, 1995—. Recipient Norbert Weiner Applied Math. prize Am. Math. Soc., 1990. Mem. IEEE, Am. Phys. Soc. Achievements include research in mathematical physics, global analysis, hydrodynamics, quantum mechanics, nonlinear Hamiltonian systems. Office: Control Dynamical Sys MS 107 81 Pasadena CA 91125-0001

MARSEE, STUART (EARL), educational consultant, retired; b. Gardener, Oreg., Sept. 30, 1917; s. William and Clare (Grimes) M.; m. Audrey Belfield, June 1, 1940; children: Frederic, Jeffrey, Wayne. BS, U. Oreg., 1939, MS, 1942; EdD, U. So. Calif., 1947; LLD, Pepperdine U., 1977. Asst. supt. for bus. Pasadena City Schs., Calif., 1949-57, acting supt., 1957-58, asst. supt., 1949-58; pres. El Camino Coll., 1958-82, cons., 1982—. Lectr. UCLA, 1965, U. So. Calif., 1956-57; adj. prof. Pepperdine U., 1978-79 Author: History of the Rotary Club of Torrance, 1962-74, 1974; contbr. articles to profl. jours. Recipient Disting. Service award Los Angeles County Bd. Suprs., 1958, Disting. Service Leadership award Kiwanis Internat., 1970; named Citizen of Yr., Torrance, Calif., 1981, Redondo Beach, Calif., 1986. Mem. Am. Assn. Cmty. and Jr. Colls. (pres. 1968), Nat. Commn. Accrediting (dir. 1970-74), Coun. Postsecondary Accreditation (dir. 1974-78), Western Coll. Assn. (mem. exec. com. 1978-81). Office: 358 Camino De Las Colinas Redondo Beach CA 90277-6435

MARSH, MALCOLM F. federal judge; b. Portland, Oreg., Sept. 24, 1928; m. Shari Marsh. BS, U. Oreg., 1952, LLB, 1954, JD, 1971. Bar: Oreg. 1954, U.S. Dist. Ct. Oreg. 1955, U.S. Ct. Appeals (9th cir.) 1968. Ptnr. Clark & Marsh, Lindauer & McClinton (and predecessors), Salem, Oreg., 1954-87; judge U.S. Dist. Ct. Oreg., Portland, 1987—. With U.S. Army, 1946-47. Fellow Am. Coll. Trial Lawyers; mem. ABA, Oreg. Bar Assn. Office: US Dist Ct 1507 US Courthouse 1000 SW 3d Ave Portland OR 97204

MARSH, MARY ELIZABETH TAYLOR, recreation administrator, dietician, nutritionist; b. Medina, N.Y., Dec. 10, 1933; d. Glenn Aaron and Viola Hazel (Lansill) Grimes; m. Wilbur Alvin Fredlund, Apr. 12, 1952 (div. Jan. 1980); 1 child, Wilbur Jr.; m. Frederick Herbert Taylor, Mar. 15, 1981 (dec. Dec. 1996); children: Martha Dayton, Jean Grout, Beth Stern, Cindy Hey, Carol McLellan, Cheryl Dearborn, Robert, Marilyn Ridens, Janice Emory, Gordon Marsh, Margaret Hana; m. Earl R. Marsh, Apr. 4, 1998. BS in Food and Nutrition, SUCB, Buffalo, 1973; MEd in Health Sci. Edn. and Evaluation, SUNY, 1978. Registered dietitian, 1977. Diet cook Niagara Sanitorium, Lockport, N.Y., 1953-56; cook Mount View Hosp., Lockport, 1956-60, asst. dietician, 1960-73, dietician, food svc. dir., 1973-79, cons. dietician, 1979-81; instr. Erie Community Coll., Williamsville, 1979-81; sch. lunch coord. Nye County Sch. Dist., Tonopah, Nev., 1982-93, retired, 1993; food svc. mgmt. cons., fin. mgmt. advisor pvt. practice, 1994—; activity dir. Preferred Equitity Corp. Recreation Vehicle Resort, Pahrump, Nev., 1993-95; tchr. maturing body and nutrition Nev. Cmty. Coll., Pahrump, Fall 1997; nutritionist Equal Opportunity Bd. Clark County, Las Vegas, 1997-2000; ind. travel agt. Hello World Travel, 2001—. Cons. dietitian Nye Gen. Hosp., Tonopah, 1983-88; adj. instr. Erie C.C., Williamsville, 1978-79, So. Nev. C.C., 1997; nutrition instr. for coop. extension Clark County C.C., 1990—; cons. Group Purchasing Western N.Y. Hosp. Adminstr., Buffalo, 1975-79, vice-chmn. adv. com., 1976-78; cons. BOCES, Lockport, 1979-81. Nutrition counselor Migrant Workers Clinic, Lockports, 1974-80; mem. Western N.Y. Soc. for Hosp. Food Svc. Adminstrn., 1974-81; nutritionist Niagara County Nutrition Adv. Com., 1977-81; mem. Helping Hands, Pahrump, 1997—; nutritionist Equal Opportunity Bd. Clark Conty, 1997-2000; activity dir. Perfered Equities RV Resort, 2001-. Recipient Outstanding Woman of the Yr., YWCA-UAW Lockport, 1981, Disting. Health Care Food Adminstrn. Recognition award Am. Soc. for Hosp. Food Svc. Adminstrs., 1979, USDA award Outstanding Lunch Program in Nev. and Western Region, 1986, 91. Mem. Am. Assn. Ret. Persons, Am. Sch. Food Svc. Assn. (bd. dirs. 1987, 92-93, cert. dir. II 1987, 5-yr. planning com. 1990, mem. ann. confs. 1988-93), Am. Dietetic Assn. (nat. referral system for registered dietitians 1992-93), So. Nev. Dietetic Assn. (pres. 1985-86), Nev. Food Svc. Assn. (participant ann. meetings 1990-93), Nutrition Today Soc., Nev. Sch. Food Svcs. Assn. (dietary guidelines com. 1991-93), Pahrump Kawians. Republican. Lutheran. Avocations: travel, knitting, crocheting, sewing. Home: 481 N Murphy St Pahrump NV 89060-3851 E-mail: mrshtrvl@wizard.com

MARSHAK, HARRY, plastic surgeon; b. L.A., Oct. 1, 1961; s. Herbert and Pearl (Engelson) M. BS, U. Calif., Riverside, 1981; MD, UCLA, 1984. Diplomate Am. Bd. Surgery, Am. Bd. Plastic Surgery. Pvt. practice, Beverly Hills, Calif., 1991—. Fellow ACS (hon.), Internat. Coll. Surgeons; mem. Am. Soc. Plastic and Reconstructive Surgeons, Calif. Soc. Plastic Surgery. Republican. Avocations: sports. Office: 120 S Spalding Dr Ste 300 Beverly Hills CA 90212-1841

MARSHALL, CONRAD JOSEPH, entrepreneur; b. Detroit, Dec. 23, 1934; s. Edward Louis Fedak and Maria Magdalena Berzsenyi; m. Dorothy Genieve Karnafil, Dec. 1, 1956 (div. 1963); children: Conrad Joseph Jr., Kevin Conrad, Lisa Marie; m. Beryle Elizabeth Callahan, June 15, 1965 (div. 1972); children: Brent Jasmer, Farah Elizabeth. Diploma, Naval Air Tech. Tng. Ctr., Norman, Okla., 1952; student, Wayne State U., 1956-59; Diploma, L.A. Police Acad., 1961. Dir. mktg. Gulf Devel., Torrance, Calif., 1980-83; sales mgr. Baldwin Piano Co., Santa Monica, 1977-80; dir. mktg., v.p. Western Hose, Inc., L.A., 1971-76; city letter carrier U.S. Post Office, L.A., 1969-71; writer freelance L.A., 1966—; police officer L.A. Police Dept., 1961-66; asst. sales mgr. Wesson Oil Co., Detroit, 1958-60; agt. Life Ins. Co. of Va., Wayne, Mich., 1956-58; pres. Am. Vision Mktg., L.A., 1990—, Con-Mar Prodns., L.A., 1983—; sr. v.p. Pacific Acquisition Group, 1992—, Invest. Admin. HealthCom., Int., 1993—; pres. Midway TV Co., 1994—. Tech. advisor Lion's Gate Films, Westwood, Calif., 1970-74, Medicine Wheel Prodns., Hollywood, Calif., 1965-75; mng. gen. ptnr. Encino Wireless #1, 1994—; CEO Midway TV Inc., 1995; v.p. nat. bus. affairs MMA Internat., 1997; v.p. mktg. Kidkritter, Inc., 1998; sr. prodn. exec. Alpine Pictures Inc., 1999. Author: (series) "Dial Hot Line", 1967, (screenplay) "Heads Across the Border", 1968, "The Fool Card", 1970, "Probable Cause", 1972; co-author: The Fedak File, 1995; albums include Song Shark, 1992, Conrad Marshall Quintet, 1991. Campaign vol. Dem. Ctrl. Com., L.A., 1976, Rep. Ctrl. Com., 1994. Mem. Screen Actors Guild, Internat. Platform Assn. Avocations: poetry, song writing, club singing, philosophy, theology. Home: 11853 Kling St Valley Vlg CA 91607-4073 Office: Con Mar Prodns 2026 Holly Hill Ter Hollywood CA 90068-3812

MARSHALL, CONSUELO BLAND, federal judge; b. Knoxville, Tenn., Sept. 28, 1936; d. Clyde Theodore and Annie (Brown) Arnold; m. George Edward Marshall, Aug. 30, 1959; children: Michael Edward, Laurie Ann. AA, L.A. City Coll., 1956; BA, Howard U., 1958, LLB, 1961. Bar: Calif. 1962. Dep. atty., City of L.A., 1962-67; assoc. Cochran & Atkins, L.A., 1968-70; commr. L.A. Superior Ct., 1971-76; judge Inglewood Mcpl. Ct., 1976-77, L.A. Superior Ct., 1977-80, U.S. Dist. Ct. Central Dist. Calif., L.A., 1980—. Lectr. U.S. Information Agy. in Yugoslavia, Greece and Italy, 1984, in Nigera and Ghana, 1991, in Ghana, 1992. Contbr. articles to profl. jours.; notes editor Law Jour. Howard U. Mem. adv. bd. Richstone Child Abuse Center. Recipient Judicial Excellence award Criminal Cts. Bar Assn., 1992, Ernestine Stalhut award; named Criminal Ct. Judge of Yr., U.S. Dist. Ct., 1997; inducted into Langston Hall of Fame, 2000; rsch. fellow Howard U. Law Sch., 1959-60. Mem. State Bar Calif., Century City Bar Assn., Calif. Women Lawyers Assn., Calif. Assn. Black Lawyers, Calif. Judges Assn., Black Women Lawyers Assn., Los Angeles County Bar Assn., Nat. Assn. Women Judges, NAACP, Urban League, Beta Phi Sigma. Office: US Dist Ct 312 N Spring St Los Angeles CA 90012-4701

MARSHALL, ELLEN RUTH, lawyer; b. N.Y.C., Apr. 23, 1949; d. Louis and Faith (Gladstone) M. AB, Yale U., 1971; JD, Harvard U., 1974. Bar: Calif. 1975, D.C. 1981, N.Y. 1989. Assoc. McKenna & Fitting, Los Angeles, 1975-80; ptnr. McKenna, Conner & Cuneo, Los Angeles and Orange County, Calif., 1980-88, Morrison & Foerster, LLP, Orange County, Calif., 1988—. Mem. ABA (bus. law sect., mem. savs. inst. com., mem. asset securitization com., tax sect., mem. employee benefits com.), Orange County Bar Assn. Club: Center (Costa Mesa, Calif.). Office: Morrison & Foerster LLP 19900 Macarthur Blvd Irvine CA 92612-2445

MARSHALL, KATHRYN SUE, lawyer; b. Decatur, Ill., Sept. 12, 1942; d. Edward Elda and Frances M. (Minor) Lahniers; m. Robert S. Marshall, Sept. 5, 1964 (div. Apr. 1984); m. Robert J. Arndt, June 25, 1988; children: Stephen Edward, Christine Elizabeth. BA, Lake Forest Coll., 1964; JD, John Marshall Law Sch., Chgo., 1976. Intern U.S. Atty.'s Office, Chgo., 1974-76; mng. ptnr. Marshall and Marshall Ltd., Waukegan, Ill., 1976-84; pvt. practice Waukegan, 1984-93, Preemptive Solutions, Wash., Calif. Contbr. articles to profl. jours. Cert. jud. candidate Dem. party, Lake County, Ill.; bd. mem. Camerata Soc., Lake Forest; bd. mem., v.p. Lake Forest (Ill.) Fine Arts Ensemble; bd. dirs. Island Hosp. Health Found.; mem. steering com. Equal Justice Coalition. Fellow ABA (gov. 1993-96), Ill. Bar Assn., Coll. Law Practice Mgmt.; mem. Navy League (life). Avocations: boating, reading, travel.

MARSHALL, MERYL, telecommunications executive, lawyer; b. L.A., Oct. 16, 1949; d. Jack and Nita Corinblit; m. Raymond Daniels, Aug. 19, 2000. BA, UCLA, 1971; JD, Loyola Marymount U., L.A., 1974. Bar: Calif. 1974. Dep. pub. defender County of L.A., 1975-77; sole practice L.A., 1977-78; ptnr. Markman and Marshall, L.A., 1978-79; sr. atty. NBC, Burbank, Calif., 1979-80, dir. programs, talent contracts bus. affairs, 1980, asst. gen. atty. N.Y.C., 1980-82, v.p., compliance and practices Burbank, 1982; v.p. program affairs Group W Prodns., 1987-89, sr. v.p. future images, 1989-91, TV producer, Meryl Marshall Prodns., 1991-93; pres. Two Oceans Entertainment Group, 1991—. Chmn., Nat. Women's Polit. Caucus, Westside, Calif., 1978-80; mem. Calif. Dem. Ctrl. Com., 1978-79; mem. Hollywood Women's Polit. Com., 1988. Mem.: Acad. TV Arts and Scis. (treas. 1985, treas. 1993—97, bd. govs. 1989—2001, pres. 1997—99, chmn. bd., CEO 1999—2001), Women in Film. Democrat. Jewish. Office: Two Oceans Entertainment Group 2017 Lemoyne St Los Angeles CA 90026 E-mail: twoceans@aol.com

MARSHALL, PETER, actor, singer, game show host; b. Clarksburg, W.Va., Mar. 30, 1930; s. Ralph and Jeanne (Frampton) Lacock; m. Laurie L. Stewart, Aug. 19, 1989; children: Suzanne, Peter, David, Jaime. Grad. high sch., Huntington, W.Va. Big band singer; night club entertainer; part of comedy team Noonan and Marshall; appeared in motion pictures, musicals, comedies, Broadway and tv; host Hollywood Squares (5 Emmys: Best Game Show Host, 1973-74, 74-75, 79-80, 80-81, Best Day Time Entertainer, 1973-74). Master sgt. U.S. Army. Avocations: golf, tennis. E-mail: gloent@al.com

MARSHALL, RAYMOND CHARLES, lawyer; b. Aquadilia, Puerto Rico, July 23, 1953; m. Piper Kent-Marshall; 1 child, Kyle. BA summa cum laude, Coll. Idaho, 1975; JD, Harvard U., 1978. Bar: Calif. 1978, D.C. 1989. Ptnr. McCutchen Doyle Brown & Enersen, San Francisco. Chmn. Calif. Supreme Ct. Adv. Multi-Jurisdictional Practice. Co-author: Environmental Crimes, 1992; contbr. chpt. to manual; contbr. articles to profl. jours. Bd. dirs. Nat. Multiple Sclerosis Soc. Northern Calif. chpt., 1992—; adv. bd. United Negro Coll. Fund Northern Bay Area Chpt., 1992—; bd. trustees Alta Bates Found., 1994—; mem. San Francisco leadership bd. Am. Red Cross Bay Area; adv. coun. mem. San Francisco Sports Coun. Recipient San Francisco Neighborhood Legal Assistance Found. award, 1989, Earl Warren Legal Svcs. award NAACP Legal Def. & Ednl. Found., 1990, Unity award Minority Bar Coalition, 1992, Cmty. Svc. award Wiley Manuel Law Found., 1994, Disting. Jesuit award Anti-Defemation League, 2001. Mem. ABA (met. bar caucus exec. com. 1992-94, vice-chmn. natural resources & energy litigation com. 1989-93, environmental crimes com. 1990-92, nominating com. conf. of minority ptnrs. in maj. corp. law firms 1991, commn. on women in the profession 1994-95, co-chmn. environmental crimes subcom. of white collar crime com. 1994-95), Nat. Bar Assn., Calif. State Bar (bd. govs. 1995—, pres. 1998-99), Charles Houston Bar Assn. Avocations: travel, recreational sports. Office: McCutchen Doyle Brown & Enersen Three Embarcadero Ctr San Francisco CA 94111

MARSHALL, ROBERT HERMAN, economics educator; b. Harrisburg, Pa., Dec. 6, 1929; s. Mathias and Mary (Bubich) M.; m. Billie Marie Sullivan, May 31, 1958; children: Mellisa Frances, Howard Hylton, Robert Charles. A.B. magna cum laude, Franklin and Marshall Coll., 1951; M.A., Ohio State U., 1952, Ph.D., 1957. Teaching asst. Ohio State U., 1952-57; mem. faculty, then prof. econs. U. Ariz., Tucson, 1957-95, prof. emeritus, 1995; dir. Internat. Bus. Studies Project, 1969-71. Research observer Sci.-Industry Program, Hughes Aircraft Co., Tucson, summer 1959 Author: Commercial Banking in Arizona: Structure and Performance Since World War II, 1966, (with others) The Monetary Process, 2d edit, 1980. Bd. dirs. Com. for Econ. Opportunity, Tucson, 1968-69. Faculty fellow Pacific Coast Banking Sch., summer 1974 Mem. Am. Econ. Assn., Phi Beta Kappa, Beta Gamma Sigma, Pi Gamma Mu, Phi Kappa Phi, Delta Sigma Pi. Democrat. Roman Catholic. Home: 6700 N Abington Rd Tucson AZ 85743-9795

MARSHALL, SCOTT, advertising agency executive; V.p. Ogilvy & Mather, N.Y.C., sr. v.p., 1986-88; pres. Cole & Weber, Inc., Seattle; now pres. Hal Riney & Ptnrs., Inc., San Francisco. Office: Hal Riney & Ptnrs 2001 Embarcadero San Francisco CA 94133-1531

MARSHALL, WILLIAM J., III, career officer; Grad., Villanova U., 1972; MS in Fin. Mgmt., Naval Postgrad. Sch.; MA in Nat. Security/Strategic Studies, Naval War Coll. Commd. ensign USN, advanced through ranks to rear adm.; various assignments to dep. dir. Expeditionary Warfare Divsn; comdr. Navy Region Northwest Naval Surface Group Pacific Northwest. Decorated Def. Superior Svc. medal, Legion of Merit with gold star in lieu of second award, Def. Meritorious Svc. medal. Office: 1103 Hunley Rd Silverdale WA 98315-1102

MARSTON, MICHAEL, urban economist, asset management executive; b. Oakland, Calif., Dec. 4, 1936; s. Lester Woodbury and Josephine (Janovic) M.; m. Alexandra Lynn Geyer, Apr. 30, 1966; children: John, Elizabeth. BA, U. Calif., Berkeley, 1959; postgrad. London Sch. Econs., 1961-63. V.p. Larry Smith & Co., San Francisco, 1969-72, exec. v.p. urban econ. divsn., 1969-72; chmn. bd. Keyser Marston Assocs., Inc., San Francisco, 1973-87; gen. ptnr. The Sequoia Partnership, 1979-91; pres. Marston Vineyard and Winery, 1982—, Marston Assocs., Inc., 1982—, The Ctr. for Individual and Instnl. Renewal, 1996—. Cert. rev. appraiser Nat. Assn. Rev. Appraisers and Mortgage Underwriters, 1984—. Chmn., San Francisco Waterfront Com., 1969-86; chmn. fin. com., bd. dirs., mem. exec. com., treas. San Francisco Planning and Urban Rsch. Assn., 1976-87, Napa Valley Vintners, 1986—, mem. gov. affairs com.; trustee Cathedral Sch. for Boys, 1981-82, Marin Country Day Sch., 1984-90; v.p. St. Luke's Sch., 1986-91; pres. Presidio Heights Assn. of Neighbors, 1983-84; chmn. Presidio Com. 1991—; v.p., bd. dirs., mem. exec. com. People for Open Space, 1972-87; mem. Gov.'s Issue Analysis Com. and Speakers Bur., 1966; mem. speakers bur. Am. Embassy, London, 1961-63; v.p., bd. dirs. Dem. Forum, 1966-72; v.p., trustee Youth for Service. Served to lt. USNR. Mem. Napa Valley Vintners, Urban Land Inst., World Congress Land Policy (paper in field), Order of Golden Bear, Chevalier du Tastevin, Bohemian Club, Pacific Union Club, Lambda Alpha. Contbr. articles to profl. jours. Home: 3375 Jackson St San Francisco CA 94118-2018

MARSZOWSKI, BRUNO A. finance company executive; Sr. v.p., contr., CFO The Finova Group Inc., Scottsdale, Ariz. Office: The Finova Group Inc 4800 N Scottsdale Rd Scottsdale AZ 85251-7623

MARTEL, JOHN SHELDON, lawyer, writer; b. Stockton, Calif., Jan. 1, 1931; s. Henry T. and Alice L. M.; m. Bonnie Martel; children: John Sheldon, Melissa Ann. B.S., U. Calif.-Berkeley, 1956, J.D., 1959. Bar: Calif. 1959. Dep. dist. atty., Alameda County, 1960-61; assoc. trial atty. firm Bronson, Bronson & McKinnon, San Francisco, 1961-64; ptnr. firm Farella, Braun & Martel, San Francisco, 1964—. Lectr., mem. adv. bd. Hastings Ctr. for Trial and Appelate Adv., 1983—. Author: (novels) Partners, 1988, Conflicts of Interest, 1994, The Alternate, 1999; author, editor legal publs.; composer-writer popular songs; profl. musician. Pilot USAF, 1951-54. Winner Am. Song Festival awards, 1978-80, 82, 85, 87. Fellow Am. Coll. Trial Lawyers (state chmn. 1985-87, bd. regents 1993-98); mem. ABA (litigation, antitrust, tort and ins. sects.), Calif. Bar Assn., San Francisco Bar Assn. (former chair litigation sect.), Am. Bd. Trial Advocates (bd. dirs. 1991-93), Am. Fedn. Musicians, Phi Delta Phi, Kappa Sigma. Office: Farella Braun & Martel 235 Montgomery St Ste 3100 San Francisco CA 94104-2902

MARTENS, DON WALTER, lawyer; b. Darlington, Wis., Mar. 25, 1934; s. Walter W. and Geraldine A. (McWilliams) M.; children: Kim Martens Cooper, Diane Martens Reed. BS in Engring. with hons., U. Wis., 1957; JD with honors, George Washington U., 1963. Bar: Supreme Ct. Calif. 1964, U.S. Ct. Appeals (9th cir.) 1964, U.S. Dist. Ct. (no. and cen. dists.) Calif. 1964, U.S. Supreme Ct. 1973, U.S. Dist. Ct. (so. dist.) Calif. 1977, U.S. Ct. Appeals (fed. cir.) 1982, U.S. Dist. Ct. (ea. dist.) Calif. 1984. Examiner U.S. Patent and Trademark Office, Washington, 1960-63; patent lawyer Standard Oil of Calif., San Francisco, 1963-65; ptnr. Knobbe, Martens, Olson & Bear, Newport Beach, Calif., 1965—. Mem. adv. comm. Fed. Cir. Ct. Appeals, 1991-96, 2000—. Lt. USN, 1957-60. Mem. Orange County Bar Assn. (pres. 1975), Orange County Legal Aid Soc. (pres. 1969), Orange County Patent Law Assn. (pres. 1984), L.A. Patent Law Assn. (pres. 1989), State Bar Calif. (bd. govs. 1984-87, v.p. 1986-87), Am. Intellectual Property Law Assn. (pres. 1995-96), State Bar Intellectual Property Assn. (chmn. 1977), 9th Cir. Jud. Conf. (del. 1985-88, 1995-98), Nat. Inventors Hall of Fame Found. (pres. 1998-99), Nat. Coun. Intellectual Property Law Assn. (chmn. 1998-99), Big Canyon Country Club, Santa Ana Country Club, Rancho La Quinta Country Club. Republican. Roman Catholic. Office: 620 Newport Center Dr Fl 16 Newport Beach CA 92660-6420 E-mail: dmartens@kmob.com

MARTIN, AGNES, artist; b. Maklin, Sask., Can., 1912; came to U.S., 1932, naturalized, 1950; Student, Western Wash. State Coll., 1935-38; BS, Columbia U., 1942, MFA, 1952. One-woman shows include Betty Parsons Gallery, N.Y.C., 1958, 59, 61, Robert Elkon Gallery, N.Y.C., 1961, 63, 72, 76, Nicolas Wilder Gallery, Los Angeles, 1963-66, 67, Visual Arts Ctr., N.Y.C., 1971, Kunstraum, Munich, 1973, Inst. Contemporary Art U. Pa., Phila., 1973, Pace Gallery, N.Y.C., 1975, 76, 77, 78, 79, 80-81, 81, 83, 84, 85, 86, 89, 91, 92, 94, 95, Mayor Gallery, London, 1978, 84, Galerie Rudolf Zwirner, Cologne, Fed. Republic Germany, 1978, Harcus/Krakow Gallery, Boston, 1978, Margo Leavin Gallery, Los Angeles, 1979, 85, Mus. N.Mex., Santa Fe, 1979, Richard Gray Gallery, Chgo., 1981, Garry Anderson Gallery, Sydney, Australia, 1986, Waddington Galleries Ltd., London, 1986, Stedelijk Mus., Amsterdam, 1991, Whitney Mus. Am. Art, N.Y.C., 1992; exhibited in group shows at Carnegie Inst., Pitts., 1961, Whitney Mus. Am. Art, N.Y.C., 1962, 66, 67, 74, 77, 92, Tooth Gallery, London, 1962, Gallery Modern Art, Washington, 1963, Wadsworth Atheneum, Hartford, Conn., 1963, Solomon R. Guggenheim Mus., N.Y.C., 1965, 66, 76, Mead Corp., 1965-67, Mus. Modern Art, N.Y.C., 1967, 76, 85, Inst. Contemporary Art, Phila., 1967, Detroit Inst. Art, 1967, Corcoran Gallery Art, Washington, 1967, 81, Finch Mus., N.Y., 1968, Phila. Mus., 1968, Zurich Art Mus., Switzerland, 1969, Ill. Bell Telephone Co., Chgo., 1970, Mus. Contemporary Art, Chgo., 1971, Inst. Contemporary Art U. Pa., Phila., 1972, Randolph-Macon Coll., N.C., 1972, Kassel, Fed. Republic Germany, 1972, Stedelijk Mus., Amsterdam, 1975, U. Mass., Amherst, 1976, Venice Biennale, Italy, 1976, 80, Cleve. Mus. Art, 1978, Albright-Knox Gallery, Buffalo, 1978, Inst. Contemporary Art, Boston, 1979, Art Inst. Chgo., 1979, San Francisco Mus. Modern Art, 1980, ROSC Internat. Art Exhbn., Dublin, Ireland, 1980, Marilyn Pearl Gallery, N.Y.C., 1983, Kemper Gallery, Kansas City Art Inst., 1985, Am. Acad. and Inst. Arts and Letters, N.Y.C., 1985, Charles Cowles Gallery, N.Y.C., 1986, Moody Gallery Art U. Ala., Birmingham, 1986, Butler Inst. Am. Art, 1986, Art Gallery Western Australia, Perth, 1986, Mus. Contemporary Art, Los Angeles, 1986, Boston Fine Arts Mus., 1989; represented in permanent collections Mus. of Modern Art, N.Y.C., Albright-Knox Gallery, Aldrich Mus., Ridgefield, Conn., Art Gallery Ont., Can., Australian Nat. Gallery, Canberra, Grey Art Gallery and Study Ctr., N.Y.C., Solomon R. Guggenheim Mus., High Mus. Art, Atlanta, Hirshhorn Mus. and Sculpture Garden, Washington, Israel Mus., Jerusalem, La Jolla (Calif.) Mus. Contemporary Art, Los Angeles County Mus. Art, Mus. Art R.I. Sch. Design, Providence, Mus. Modern Art, Neuegalerie der Stadt, Aachen, Fed. Republic Germany, Norton Simon Mus. Art at Pasadena, Calif., Stedelijk Mus., Amsterdam, The Netherlands, 1992, Mus. Modern Art, paris, 1992, Tate Gallery, London, Wadsworth Atheneum, Walker Art Ctr., Mpls., Whitney Mus. Am. Art, 1993, Sofia, Madrid, 1993, Huosten, 1993, Worcester (Mass.) Art Mus., Yale U. Art Gallery, New Haven; subject of various articles. Office: 414 Placitas Rd # 27 Taos NM 87571-3517

MARTIN, CHARLES, chief information officer; BS in Acctg., Ariz. State U. Formerly with Solutions Cons., Ernst & Young, LLP and Digital Equip. Corp.; former v.p. profl. svcs. ECadvantage; former group v.p. of info. svcs. MicroAge, chief info. officer Ariz., 1999—. Office: 2400 S Microage Way Tempe AZ 85282-1896

MARTIN, CRAIG LEE, engineering company executive; b. Dodge City, Kans., Nov. 23, 1949; s. Ray N. and Nadia C. Martin; m. Diane E. Hensley, Mar. 19, 1977. BSCE, U. Kans., 1971; MBA, U. Denver, 1982. Project mgr. Martin K. Eby Constrn. Co., Wichita, Kans., 1972-83; exec. v.p., COO CRSS Constructors, Inc., Denver, 1983-89; exec. v.p. CRSS Comml. Group, Houston, 1989-90; sr. v.p. CRSS Capital, Houston, 1990-92, CRSS Inc., Houston, 1992-94; pres. CRSS Architects, Inc., Houston, 1992-94; sr. v.p. ops. Jacobs Engring. Group Inc., 1994-95; pres. Jacobs Constructors, Inc., 1994-95; sr. v.p. gen. sales and mktg. Jacobs Engring. Group, Inc., 1995-2000, exec. v.p. global sales, 2000—. Adv. bd. Constrn. Bus. Rev., 1993—. Bd. govs. Woodbury U. Sch. Bus.; bd. dirs. The Wellness Cmty.-Foothills. Mem. ASCE. Avocations: golf, clay shooting. Home: 930 S El Molino Ave Pasadena CA 91106-4414 Office: Jacobs Engring Group Inc 1111 S Arroyo Pkwy Pasadena CA 91105-3254 E-mail: craig.martin@jacobs.com

MARTIN, DARRICK DAVID, professional basketball player; b. Calif., Mar. 6, 1971; Grad., UCLA, 1992. Guard Minn., 1994-95, L.A. Clippers, 1996-99, Sacramento Kings, 1999—. Avocations: reading, video games, movies. Office: Sacramento Kings ARCO Arena 1 Sports Pkwy Sacramento CA 95834-2301

MARTIN, DAVID G. rental company executive; b. 1966; Investment banker Salmon Bros., Inc.; v.p. high yield fin. and merchant banking Nomura Securities Co., Ltd., 1991-96; mng. dir. high yield fin. NationsBanc Montgomery Securities LLC, 1996-99; exec. v.p., CFO Hollywood Entertainment Corp., 1999—. Office: Hollywood Entertainment Corp 9275 SW Peyton Ln Wilsonville OR 97070 Fax: 503-570-1680

MARTIN, DEAN, state senator; Rep. senator dist 24 Ariz. State Senate. Mem. appropriations, banking and ins. and transp. coms. Ariz. State Senate, vice chair govt. com., appropriations subcom. on criminal justice, chair transp. com. Office: Ariz State Senate State Capitol Rm 302 1700 W Washington Phoenix AZ 85007-2890 E-mail: dmartin@azleg.state.az.us

MARTIN, FRED, artist, college administrator; b. San Francisco, June 13, 1927; s. Ernest Thomas and Leona (Richey) M.; m. Genevieve Catherine Fisette, Jan. 29, 1950 (dec.); children: T. Demian, Fredericka C., Anthony J.; m. Stephanie Zuperko Dudek, 1992. BA, U. Calif., Berkeley, 1949, MA, 1954; postgrad., Calif. Sch. Fine Arts, 1949-50. Registrar Oakland (Calif.) Art Mus., 1955-58; dir. exhbns. San Francisco Art Inst., 1958-65, dir. coll., 1965-75, dean acad. affairs, 1983-92; dean acad. affairs emeritus; represented by Frederick Spratt Gallery, San Jose, Calif., Ebert Gallery, San Francisco. Exhibited one man shows, Zoe Dusanne Gallery, Seattle, 1952, M.H. deYoung Meml. Mus., San Francisco, 1954, 64, Oakland Art Mus., 1958, San Francisco Mus. Modern Art, 1958, 73, Dilexi Gallery, San Francisco, 1961, Minami Gallery, Tokyo, 1963, Royal Marks Gallery, N.Y.C., 1965-70, Hansen Fuller Gallery, San Francisco, 1974, 75, 76, Quay Gallery, San Francisco, 1979, 81, 84, Natsoulas Gallery, Davis, Calif., 1991, Belcher Studios Gallery, San Francisco, 1994, Frederick Spratt Gallery, San Jose, 1996, Ebert Gallery, San Francisco, 1997, 98, 99, 2000, Art and Consciousness Gallery/John F. Kennedy U., Berkeley, 1997, Shasta Coll., 1998, Han Art Contemporaire, Montreal, 1999; represented in permanent collections, Mus. Modern Art, N.Y.C., San Francisco Mus. Modern Art, Oakland Art Mus., Whitney Mus., Fogg Mus.; author: Beulah Land, 1966, Log of the Sun Ship, 1969, Liber Studiorum, 1973, A Travel Book, 1976, From an Antique Land, 1979; Bay area corr.: Art Internat., 1967-69, 75-76; contbg. editor Art Week, 1976-93. Recipient prizes Oakland Art Mus., 1951, 58, prizes San Francisco Mus. Art, 1957, 58, prizes Richmond (Calif.) Art Center, 1962, prizes Nat. Found. for Arts, 1970 E-mail: Fred T. Home: 232 Monte Vista Ave Oakland CA 94611-4922 Office: San Francisco Art Inst 800 Chestnut St San Francisco CA 94133-2206 E-mail: Martin@IBM.net

MARTIN, GEORGE FRANCIS, lawyer; b. Yuba City, Calif., July 7, 1944; s. John Severd and Albina Marie M.; m. Linda Louise D'Aoust, Mar. 17, 1968; children: Brandon, Bry. BA in Govt., Calif. State U., Sacramento, 1968; JD, U. Calif., Davis, 1971. Bar: Calif. Adminstr. asst. Assemblyman E. Richard Barnes, Sacramento, 1967-68; with Borton, Petrini & Conron, Bakersfield, Calif., 1971—, mng. gen. ptnr., 1977—; dean Calif. Pacific Sch. Law, Bakersfield, 1993-95. Holdings numerous ventures, partnerships; lectr. in field; founder, owner theatrical bus. Mgmt. by Martin, Inc., Shower of Stars, Frantic Records, 1962-67. Editor-in-chief Verdict Jour. of Law, 1984-85, Calif. Def. Mag.; newspaper reporter Appeal Democrat, Marysville, Calif., 1959-62. Former vice chmn. Kern County Rep. Ctrl. Com.; past pres. So. Calif. Def. Counsel; past chmn. Ctrl. Calif. Heart Inst.; bd. dirs. Calif. State U. at Bakersfield Found., chair, 1998; bd. dirs. Calif. Coun. Partnerships, Kern Econ. Devel. Corp; mem. adv. bd. Automobile Club So. Calif.; chmn. adv. bd. Witkin Legal Inst. Mem. Greater Bakersfield C. of C. (bd. dirs., past pres.). Office: Borton Petrini & Conron 1600 Truxtun Ave Bakersfield CA 93301-5111

MARTIN, GEORGE M. pathologist, gerontologist, educator; b. N.Y.C., June 30, 1927; s. Barnett J. and Estelle (Weiss) M.; m. Julaine Ruth Miller, Dec. 2, 1952; children: Peter C., Kelsey C., Thomas M., Andrew C. BS, U. Wash., 1949, MD, 1953. Diplomate Am. Bd. Pathology, Am. Bd. Med. Genetics. Intern Montreal Gen. Hosp., Quebec, Can., 1953-54; resident-instr. U. Chgo., 1954-57; instr.-prof. U. Wash., Seattle, 1957—. Vis. scientist Dept. Genetics Albert Einstein Coll., N.Y.C., 1964, Rockefeller U., 1998-99; chmn. Gordon Confs. Molecular Pathology, Biology of Aging, 1974-79; chmn., nat. res. Plan on Aging Nat. Inst. on Aging, Bethesda, Md., 1985-89; dir. Alzheimer's Disease Rsch. Ctr. U. Wash., 1985—, assoc. dir., 1999—. Editor Werner's Syndrome and Human Aging, 1985, Molecular Aspects of Aging, 1995; contbr. articles in field to profl jours. Active Fedn. Am. Scientists. With USN, 1945-46. Recipient Allied Signal award in Aging, 1991, Rsch. medal Am. Agy. Assn., 1992, Kleemeier award, 1994, Paul Glenn award for aging rsch., 1998; named Disting. Alumnus, U. Wash. Sch. Medicine, 1987; USPHS rsch. fellow dept. genetics, Glasgow U., 1961-62; Eleanor Roosvelt Inst. Cancer Rsch. fellow Inst. de Biologie, PHysiologie, Chimie, Paris, 1968-69; Josiah Macy faculty scholar Sir William Din Sch. Pathology, Oxford (Eng.) U., 1978-79, Humboldt Disting. scientist dept. genetics U. Wurzburg, Germany, 1991. Fellow AAAS, Gerontol. Soc. Am. (chmn. Biol. Sci. 1979, pres. elect 2001, Brookdale award 1981, Lifetime Achievement award for rsch. on alzheimer's disease World Alzheimer's Congress, 2000), Tissue Culture Assn. (pres. 1986-88); mem. Inst. Medicine, Am. Assn. Univ. Pathologists (emeritus), Am. Soc. Human Genetics, Am. Soc. Investigative Pathology, Am. Fedn. Aging Rsch. (pres. 2000—). Democrat. Avocations: internat. travel, jazz music, biography. Home: 2223 E Howe St Seattle WA 98112-2931 Office: U Wash Sch Medicine Dept Pathology Rm K543 Seattle WA 98195 E-mail: gmmartin@u.washington.edu

MARTIN, J. LANDIS, manufacturing company executive, lawyer; b. Grand Island, Nebr., Nov. 5, 1945; s. John Charles and Lucile (Cooley) M.; m. Sharon Penn Smith, Sept. 23, 1978; children: Mary Frances, Sarah Landis, Emily Penn. BS in Bus. Adminstrn., Northwestern U., 1968, JD cum laude, 1973. Bar: Ill. 1974, D.C. 1978, Colo. 1982. Assoc. Kirkland & Ellis, Chgo., 1973-77, ptnr. Washington, 1978-81, mng. ptnr. Denver, 1981-87, firm com. mem., Chgo., 1983-87; chmn., bd. dirs. Titanium Metals Corp., 1987—, CEO, 1995—, pres.; pres., CEO NL Industries Inc., Houston, 1987—, also bd. dirs.; chmn., CEO Baroid Corp., Houston, 1987-94; chmn. bd., pres., CEO Tremont Corp., 1990—, also bd. dirs. Dir. Halliburton Co., Dallas, Aimco. Editor-in-chief: Exchange Act Guide to SEC Rule 144, 1973; articles editor Northwestern U. Law Rev., 1972-73. Pres Ctrl. City Opera House Assn., Denver, 1986-88, chmn. 1987-96; pres. Ctrl. City Opera House Endowment Fund, 1995—; vis. com. Northwestern U. Sch. Law, 1987—; mem. exec. com. Houston Grand Opera, 1991—, sr. v.p. devel. 1992-93, pres. 1993-95, chmn. 1995-97; bd. trustees Denver Art Mus., 1994—, Graland Country Day Sch., 1992-97. With U.S. Army, 1969-71. Mem. Colo. Bar Assn., D.C. Bar Assn. Clubs: Chevy Chase (Md.), John Evans (Evanston, Ill.), Denver, Denver Country, Castle Pines Golf. Office: Titanium Metals Corp 1999 Broadway Ste 4300 Denver CO 80202-5743

MARTIN, JAY HERBERT, psychoanalysist, English educator; b. Newark, Oct. 30, 1935; s. Sylvester K. and Ada M. (Smith) M.; m. Helen Bernadette Saldini, June 9, 1956; children: Helen E., Laura A., Jay Herbert. AB with honors, Columbia U., 1956; MA, Ohio State U., 1957, PhD, 1960; PhD in Psychoanalysis, So. Calif. Psychoanalytic Inst., 1983. Instr. English Pa. State U., 1957-58; instr., then asst. to assoc. prof. English and Am. Studies Yale U., New Haven, 1960-68; prof. English and comparative culture U. Calif., Irvine, 1968-79; asst. prof. psychiatry and human behavior, clin. supr. residency program Calif. Coll. Medicine Calif. Coll. Medicine U. Calif., Irvine, 1978-96; Leo S. Bing prof. English and Am. lit. U. So. Calif., L.A., 1979-96, dir. undergrad. program in Am. studies, 1968-69, dir. program in comparative culture, 1969-71, dir. edn. abroad program, 1971-75; prof. govt., Edward S. Gould prof. humanities Claremont McKenna Coll., 1996—; dir. civilization program Claremont (Calif.) McKenna Coll., 1996—, acting dir. Gould Ctr. for Humanistic Studies, 1998-2000. Instr. psychoanalysis So. Calif. Psychoanalytic Inst., 1984-96; Bicentennial prof. Am. lit. and culture Moscow State U., USSR, 1976, Dai Ho Chun (Wisdom) chair Prof. U. Hawaii, 2000-01; vis. Parmenter lectr. Children's Hosp., San Francisco, 1989, Ann. William Faulkner Lecture, 1991, Herman Serota Found. lecture, 1992; cons. to pub. houses; lectr. USSR, Poland, Norway, France, Costa Rica, Germany, Brazil, Can., U. London, Hebrew U., Jerusalem, Seoul, Rep. Korea, China, Peru, Durham, Eng., Helsinki; dir. NEH summer sems., 1976, 77; mem. evaluation com. dept. pvt. post-secondary edn. State of Calif., 1986; cons. numerous univs., pubs., NEA, NEA, J.S. Guggenheim Found., Calif. Coun. for Humanities and Pub. Policy, U.S. Congress Com. on Edn. and Labor; faculty assoc. Coun. Internat. Exch. of Scholars; frequent speaker profl. orgns. and sems., univs., confs., hosps. Author: (criticism and biography) Conrad Aiken: A Life of His Art, 1962, Harvests of Change: American Literature 1865-1914, 1967, Nathanael West: The Art of His Life, 1970 (U. Calif. Friends Libr. award), Robert Lowell, 1970, Always Merry and Bright. The Life of Henry Miller, 1978, (U. Calif. Friends of Libr. award, Phi Kappa Phi Best Faculty Publ. prize U. So. Calif., transl. in French, Japanese and German), (fiction) Winter Dreams: An American in Moscow, 1979, Who Am I This Time, Uncovering the Fictive Personality, 1988 (trans. Portuguese, Burlington No. Found. award 1989); Swallowing Tigers Whole, 1996, A Corresponding Leap of Love: Henry Miller, 1996, Henry Miller's Dream Song, 1996, Journey to Heavenly Mountain, 2002, Biography and Humanity, 2000; author one hour radio drama, William Faulkner. Sound Portraits of Twentieth-Century Humanists, starring Tennessee Williams, Glenn Close, Colleen Dewhurst, Nat. Pub. Radio, 1980; author one-act docudrama Trial Days in Coyocoan, Antioch Rev., 2001; author sects. 24 books including most recently American Writing Today, vol. I, 1982, The Haunted Dusk: American Supernatural Fiction, 1820-1902, 1983, Frontiers of Infant Psychiatry, vol.II, 1986, Centenary Essays on Huckleberry Finn, 1985, Robert Lowell: Essays on the Poetry, 1987, William Faulkner: The Best from American Literature, 1989, The Homosexualities: Reality, Fantasy and the Arts, 1991, Life Guidance Through Literature, 1992, Biography and Source Studies, 1995, William Faulkner and Psychology, 1995, Psychotherapy East and West, 1996, Readings on Huckleberry Finn, 1999, John Fante: A Critical Gathering, 2000, Uncollected Works By...Paul Laurence Dunbar, 2000 ; contbr. numerous articles and revs. to profl. jours., bulls., L.A. Times Book Rev., Partisan Rev., N.Y. Times Book Rev., Internat. Rev. Psycho-Analysis, Am. Lit., London Times Lit. Supplement, Psychoanalytic Quarterly, Jour. Applied Psychoanalysis; editor: Winfield Townley Scott (Yale series recorded poets), 1962, Twentieth Century Interpretations of the Waste Land: A Collection of Critical Essays, 1968, Twentieth Century Views of Nathanael West, 1972, A Singer in the Dawn: Reinterpretations of Paul Laurence Dunbar (with intro.), 1975, Economic Depression and American Humor (with intro.), 1986; mem. editl. bd. Am. Lit., 1978-81, Humanities in Society, 1979-1983; editor-in-chief Psychoanalytic Edn., 1984-89; editor Humanitas/Communitas, 1998-2000; appearances on TV and radio including Connie Martinson Talks Books, Barbara Brunner Nightline, Sonya Live in L.A., Oprah Winfrey Show, 1988-89 Pres. Friends of Irvine Pub. Libr., 1974-75; mem. Com. for Freud Mus. Recipient Fritz Schmidl Meml. prize for rsch. applied psychoanalysis Seattle Assn. Psychoanalysis, 1982, Marie H. Briehl prize for child psychoanalysis, 1982, Franz Alexander prize in psychoanalysis, 1984; Morse rsch. fellow, 1963-64, Am. Philos. Soc. fellow, 1966, J.S. Guggenheim fellow, 1966-67, Rockefeller Found.humanities sr. fellow, 1975-76, Rsch. Clin. fellow So. Calif. Psychoanalytic Soc. 1977-81, Rockefeller fellow, Bellagio, Italy, 1983, NEH sr. fellow, 1983-84. Mem. So. Calif. Am. Studies Assn. (pres. 1969-71), Am. Studies Assn. (exec. bd. 1969-71, del. to MLA Assembly 1974, chmn. Ralph Gabriel prize com. 1975-77), MLA (chmn. prize com. Jay B. Hubbell Silver medal in Am. lit. 1978-84), Nat. Assn. Arts and Letters (prize com. 1987-88), Nat. Humanities Faculty (advisor to Valhalla High Sch., El Cajon, Calif. 1979-81), Nat. Am. Studies Faculty, Internat. Psychoanalytic Assn., Internat. Assn. Empirical Aesthetics, Internat. Assn. U. Profs. English, Internat. Karen Horney Soc., Phi Beta Kappa. Home: 748 Via Santo Tomas Claremont CA 91711-1569 E-mail: jay_martin@mckenna.edu

MARTIN, JOHN C. medical products executive; b. 1952; PhD in Organic Chemistry, U. Chgo. With Syntex Corp., 1978-84; dir. antiviral che3mistry Bristol-Myers Squibb, 1984-90; v.p. R&D Gilead Scis., Inc., Foster City, Calif., 1990-95, COO, 1995-96, pres., CEO, dir., 1996—. Mem. Internat. Soc. for Antiviral Rsch. (pres.). Office: Gilead Scis Inc 333 Lakeside Dr Foster City CA 94404-1146 Fax: 650-573-4800

MARTIN, J(OHN) EDWARD, architectural engineer; b. L.A., Oct. 23, 1916; s. Albert C. and Carolyn Elizabeth (Borchard) M.; m. Elizabeth Jane Hines, May 27, 1944; children: Nicolas Edward, Peter Hines, Sara Jane McKinley Reynolds, Christopher Carey, Elizabeth Margaret Ferguson. Student, U. So. Calif., 1934-36; BS in Archtl. Engring., U. Ill., 1939. Registered profl. engr., Calif., Ill. Structural engr. Albert C. Martin & Assocs., L.A., 1939-42, ptnr., 1945-75, mng. ptnr., 1975-86. Founding mem. bd. trustees Thomas Aquinas Coll., Santa Paula, Calif., 1971-98, emeritus, 1998. Lt. USNR, 1942-45. Fellow ASCE; mem. Structural Engrs. Assn. Calif., Cons. Engrs. Assn. Calif., Jonathan Club (bd. dirs. 1978-81), Calif. Club, Ranchero Visitadores, Valley Hunt Club, Flintridge Riding Club, West Hills Hunt Club (Master of Fox Hounds 1975-88), Saddle & Sirloin Club, Heritage Found., Traditional Mass Soc. (founder), Pacific Legal Found. (charter). Republican. Roman Catholic. Avocation: horsemanship. E-mail: bzmartin@pacbellnet. Office: AC Martin Ptnrs 811 W 7th St Los Angeles CA 90017-3475 Fax: 626-440-0889

MARTIN, JOHN L. airport executive; Dir. San Francisco Airport Commn. Office: San Francisco Airport Commn PO Box 8097 San Francisco CA 94128-8097

MARTIN, JULIE, women's healthcare company executive; BA in Liberal Arts and Scis., MS in Exercise Physiology, San Diego State U. Propr. 2 cos., 1983-90; gen. mgr. Dale Fitzmorris, 1990-92; dir. health promotion Ctr. for Women's Medicine, 1993-96; co-CEO, As We Change, LLC, 1995-98; v.p. catalog ops. Women First HealthCare, Inc., San Diego, 1998—. Office: Women First HealthCare Inc 12220 El Camino Real Ste 400 San Diego CA 92130-2091 Fax: 619-509-1353

MARTIN, JUNE JOHNSON CALDWELL, journalist; b. Toledo, 06 Oct. d. John Franklin and Eunice Imogene (Fish) Johnson; m. Erskine Caldwell, Dec. 21, 1942 (div. Dec. 1955); 1 child, Jay Erskine; m. Keith Martin, May 5, 1966. AA, Phoenix Jr. Coll., 1941; BA, U. Ariz., 1943, 59; postgrad., Ariz. State U., 1939, 40. Freelance writer, 1944—; columnist Ariz. Daily Star, Tucson, 1956-59, 70-94, book reviewer, 1970-94, co-founder Ann. Book and Author Event; editor Ariz. Alumnus mag., Tucson, 1959-70; ind. book reviewer, audio tape columnist Tucson, 1994—. Panelist, co-producer TV news show Tucson Press Club, 1954-55, pres., 1958. Contbg. author: Rocky Mountain Cities, 1949; contbr. articles to World Book Ency., and various mags. Mem. Tucson CD Com., 1961; vol. campaigns of Samule Goddard, U.S. Rep. Morris Udall, U.S. amb. and Ariz. gov. Raul. Castro. Recipient award Nat. Headliners Club, 1959, Ariz. Press Club award, 1957-59, 96, Am. Alumni Coun., 1966, 70. Mem. Nat. Book Critics Circle, Ariz. Press Women, Jr. League of Tucson, Tucson Urban League, PEN U.S.A. West, Planned Parenthood So. Ariz., Tucson Press, Pi Beta Phi. Democrat. Methodist. Home: Desert Foothills Sta PO Box 65388 Tucson AZ 85728-5388

MARTIN, LOREN WINSTON, allergist; b. Albertsville, Ala., Apr. 20, 1938; s. Loren d. and Byrda G. (Crotwell) M.; m. Vivian Elizabeth Sanger Martin, Dec. 29, 1960; children: Lori Ann, Karen Lynn, James Winston. BA in Chemistry, Duke U., 1959; MD, U. Tenn., 1962. Lic. physician, Ariz. Rotating internship Fitzsimons Army Hosp., Denver, 1963; med. residency Honolulu, 1964-67; med. officer U.S. Army, 1962-70; fellowship allergy U. Colo., Denver, 1970-71; pvt. practice Tucson, 1971—. Decorated Bronze Star. Fellow Am. Acad. Allergy & Immunology, Am. Coll. Allergy & Immunology; mem. Pima County Med. Soc. Republican. Office: 1661 N Swan Rd Ste 300 Tucson AZ 85712-4053

MARTIN, LUCY Z. public relations executive; b. Alton, Ill., July 8, 1941; d. Fred and Lucille J. M. BA, Northwestern U., 1963. Adminstrv. asst., copywriter Batz-Hodgson-Neuwoehner, Inc., St. Louis, 1963-64; news reporter, Midwest fashion editor Fairchild Publs., St. Louis, 1964-66; account exec. Milici Advt. Agy., Honolulu, 1967; publs. dir. Barnes Med. Ctr., St. Louis, 1968-69; comms. cons. Fleishman-Hillard, St. Louis, 1970-74; comms. cons., CEO, pres. Lucy Z. Martin & Assocs., Portland, Oreg., 1974—. Spkr. Marylhurst Coll., 1991, 92, 93, Concordia Coll., 1992, Women Entrepreneurs of Oreg., 1992, Oreg. Assn. Hosps. and Health Sys. Trustees, 1992, Healthcare Assn. Hawaii, Honolulu, 1993, USBancorp for Not-for-Profits, 1993, Multnomah County Ret. Srs. Vol. Program, 1993, Healthcare Fin. Mgmt. Assn., N.W., 1993, Healthcare Comms. Oreg., 1994, Area Health Edn. Ctrs., OHSU/statewide, 1994, Columbia River chpt. Pub. Rels. Soc. Am., 1994, 96; spkr., workshop conducter Healthcare Assn. Hawaii, 1993, USBancorp Not-for-Profit, 1993, Healthcare Communicators Oreg., 1994, Pathways to Career Transition, 1995, among others; bd. dirs. Ctrs. Airway Sci., Oregon Coll. Arts & Crafts, 1989-95, Good Samaritan Hosp. Assn., 1991-94, Am. Mktg. Assn., Oreg. chap., 1992-93, Inst. Managerial and Profl. Women, 1992-94, YMCA Public Policy com., 1993-95, Jr. League Cmty. adv. bd., 1994 , Bus. Social Responsibility Steering com., 1996—, Ctrs. for Airway Sci. Bd., 1996—; spkr. in field. Featured in Entrepreneurial Woman mag.; contbr. articles to profl. jours. Chmn. women's adv. com. Reed Coll., Portland, 1977-79; mem. Oreg. Commn. for Women, 1984-87; bd. dirs. Ronald McDonald House Oreg., 1986, Oreg. Sch. Arts and Crafts, 1989—, Northwestern U. Alumni Coun., 1992—; bd. dirs. Good Samaritan Hosp. Assocs., 1991-94, chair 1993-94; mem. pub. policy com. YMCA, 1993-95; mem. adv. bd. Jr. League, 1994—; mem. steering com. Bus. for Social Responsiblity, 1996—; bd. dirs. Ctrs. for Airway Sci., 1996—. Recipient MacEachern Citation Acad. Hosp. Pub. Relations, 1978, Rosey awards Portland Advt. Fedn., 1979, Achievement award Soc. Tech. Comms., 1982, Disting. Tech. Comm. award, 1982, Exceptional Achievement award Coun. for Advancement and Support Edn., 1983, Monsoon award Internat. Graphics, Inc., 1984, William Marsh Achievement award PRSA, 1998; named Woman of Achievement Daily Jour. Commerce, 1980. Mem. Pub. Rels. Soc. Am. (pres. Columbia River chpt. 1984, chmn. bd. 1980-84, Oreg. del. 1984-86, jud. panel N. Pacific dist 1985-86, exec. bd. health care sect. 1986-87, mem. Counselors Acad., Spotlight awards 1985, 86, 87, 88, nat. exec. com. 1987-91; William Marsh Achievement award 1998), Portland Pub. Rels. Roundtable (chmn. 1985, bd. dirs. 1983-85), Assn. Western Hosps. (editl. adv. bd. 1984-85), Best of West awards 1978, 80, 83, 87), Oreg. Hosp. Pub. Rels. Orgn. (pres. 1981, chmn. bd. 1982, bd. dirs. 1992-93), Acad. Health Service Mktg., Am. Hosp. Assn., Am. Mktg. Assn. (Oreg. chpt. bd. dirs. 1992-93), Am. Soc. Hosp. Mktg. & Pub. Rels., Healthcare Communicators Oreg. (conf. keynote speaker 1994), Internat. Assn. Bus. Communicators (18 awards 1981-87), Oreg. Assn. Hosps. (keynote speaker for trustee, 1991, speaker, 1993, bd. dirs. 1992-93), Oreg. Press Women, Nat. and Oreg. Soc. Healthcare Planning and Mktg., Women in Comms. (Matrix award 1977), Bus. for Social Responsibility (steering com. 1996—), Inst. for Managerial and Profl. Women (bd. dirs. 1992-94). Office: 1881 SW Edgewood Rd Portland OR 97201-2235 Fax: 503-227-1569. E-mail: lucyz@lzma.com

MARTIN, MELISSA CAROL, radiological physicist; b. Muskogee, Okla., Feb. 7, 1951; d. Carl Leroy and Helen Shirley (Hicks) Paden; m. Donald Ray Martin, Feb. 14, 1970; 1 child, Christina Gail. BS, Okla. State U., 1971; MS, UCLA, 1975. Cert. radiol. physicist, Am. Bd. Radiology, radiation oncology, Am. Bd. Med. Physics. Asst. radiation physicist Hosp. of the Good Samaritan, L.A., 1975-80; radiol. physicist Meml. Med. Ctr., Long Beach, Calif., 1980-83, St. Joseph Hosp., Orange, 1983-92, Therapy Physics, Inc., Bellflower, 1993—. Cons. in field. Editor: (book) Current Regulatory Issues in Medical Physics, 1992. Fund raising campaign div. mgr. YMCA, Torrance, Calif., 1988-92; dir. AWANA Youth Club-Guards Group, Manhattan Beach, Calif., 1984—. Named Dir. of Symposium, Am. Coll. Med. Physics, 1992. Fellow Am. Coll. Med. Physics (chancellor western region 1992-95), Am. Assn. Physicists in Medicine (profl. coun. 1990-95, treas. 1998—, bd. dirs. 1994—), Am. Coll. Radiology (econs. com. 1992-95, govt. rels. com. 1998—); mem. Calif. Med. Physics Soc. (treas. 1991-98), Am. Soc. for Therapeutic Radiology and Oncology, Health Physics Soc. (pres. So. Calif. chpt. 1992-93), Am. Brachytherapy Soc. Baptist. Avocations: Christian youth group dir. Home: 507 Susana Ave Redondo Beach CA 90277-3953 Office: Therapy Physics Inc 9156 Rose St Bellflower CA 90706-6420 E-mail: melissamartin@compuserve.com

MARTIN, MYRON GREGORY, foundation administrator; b. Houston, Jan. 14, 1958; s. Monty Gene and Vera Mae (Saurage) M. MusB, U. North Tex., 1980; MBA, Golden Gate U., 1989. Various sales and mktg. positions Baldwin Piano Co., N.Y.C., 1980-1990, dir. concert and artists, 1990-95; exec. dir. Liberace Found., Las Vegas, Nev., 1995-98; dir. U. Las Vegas, 1998—. Mem. adv. bd. Thelonious Monk Inst., Washington, D.C., 1994-95; bd. dirs. Cystic Fibrosis Found., Chgo., 1990, Liberace Found., 1993-95, Museums and Attractions, Las Vegas, 1996—. Recipient Special award Cystic Fibrosis Found., 1990. Mem. Nev. Mus. Assn. (bd. dirs. 1997—). Avocations: tennis, judging scholarship pageants for Miss America organization. Home: 3996 Placita Del Rico Las Vegas NV 89120-2629 Office: U Las Vegas Performing Art Ctr 4505 S Maryland Pkwy Las Vegas NV 89154-9900

MARTIN, NANICE S. software company executive; Editor, writer numerous publs., including Tiger Beat, Seventeen; dir. software devel. Mattel, dir. online content; pres. PlanetGirl.com., Los Angeles. Author 4 books; prodr. CD-ROM Barbie Fashion Designer, also entertainment CD-ROMs. Office: PlanetGirlcom 1964 Westwood Blvd Ste 425 Los Angeles CA 90025-4651 Fax: 310-446-1405. E-mail: christiana@planetgirl.com

MARTIN, PATRICK J. technology company executive; b. 1941; Doctorate in Elec. Engring., George Washington U. Exec. Xerox Corp., pres. N.Am. solutions group. Office: Storage Tech 1 Storage Tek Dr Louisville CO 80028

MARTIN, PRESTON, financial services executive; b. L.A., Dec. 5, 1923; s. Oscar and Gaynell (Horne) M.; 1 child, Pier Preston. BS in Fin., U. So. Calif., 1947, MBA, 1948; PhD in Monetary Econs., U. Ind., 1952. Prof. fin. Grad. Sch. Bus. Adminstrn. U. So. Calif., 1950-60; prin. in housebldg. firm, 1952-56; with mortgage fin. and consumer fin. instns., 1954-57; commr. savs. and loan State of Calif., 1967-69; chmn. Fed. Home Loan Bank Bd., Washington, 1969-72; founder, CEO PMI Mortgage Ins. Co., 1972-80; chmn., CEO Seraco Group subs. Sears, Roebuck & Co., 1980-81, also bd. dirs. parent co.; chmn., CEO WestFed Holdings Inc., L.A., 1986-92, SoCal Holdings, Inc., L.A., 1987-93, H.F. Holdings, Inc., San Francisco, 1986. Vice-chmn. Fed. Res. Bd., Washington, 1982-86; founder Fed. Home Loan Mortgage Corp.; prof. bus. econ. and fin. Inst. per lo Studio Organizitzatione Aziendale, Italy. Author: Principles and Practices of Real Estate, 1959. Mem. President's Commn. on Housing, 1980-81; prin. Coun. Excellence in Govt., Washington. Recipient House and Home award, 1969, award Engring. News Record, 1971, Turntable award Nat. Assn. Home Builders, 1973. Mem. Lambda Chi Alpha. Presbyterian.

MARTIN, RAFAEL M., SR. construction company executive; Pres., CEO Azteca Constrn. Inc., Rancho Cordova, Calif., 1980—. Office: Azteca Constrn Inc 3871 Security Park Dr Rancho Cordova CA 95742-6920

MARTIN, RICHARD H. national park service executive; Supt. Death Valley (Calif.) Nat. Park. Office: Death Valley Nat Park PO Box 579 Death Valley CA 92328-0579

MARTIN, RICHARD J. food wholesale executive; Exec. v.p., CFO Rykoff-Sexton, Wilkes-Barre, Pa.; sr. v.p. fin. & adminstrn., CFO Cert. Grocers Calif., 1998-2000; CFO, exec. v.p. fin. & adminstrn. Unified Western Grocers, Inc., Commerce, Calif., 2000—. Office: Unified Western Grocers Inc 5200 Sheila St Commerce CA 90040

MARTIN, RICHARD JAY, medical educator; b. Detroit, May 16, 1946; s. Peter Aaron and Tillie Jean (Munch) M.; m. Helene Iris Horowitz, Dec. 23, 1967; children: Elizabeth Hope, David Evan. BS, U. Mich., 1967, MD, 1971. Diplomate Am. Bd. Internal Medicine and Pulmonary Disease. Intern, Ariz., 1971-72; resident Tulane U., New Orleans, 1974-76; pulmonary fellow, 1976-78; asst. prof. medicine U. Okla., Okla. City, 1978-80, U. Colo., Denver, 1980-85, assoc. prof., 1985-92, prof., 1992—. Dir. Cardiorespiratory Sleep Rsch., Nat. Jewish Med. and Rsch. Ctr., Denver, 1980-89, staff physician, 1980—, head divsn. pulmonary medicine, 1993—, vice chair dept. of medicine, 1997—. Author: Cardiorespiratory Disorders During Sleep, 1984, 2d edit., 1990, (with others) Current Therapy in Internal Medicine, 1984, Clinical Pharmacology and Therapeutics in Nursing, 1985, Interdisciplinary Rehabilitation of Multiple Sclerosis and Neuromuscular Disorders, 1984, Drugs for the Respiratory System, 1985, Current Therapy in Pulmonary Medicine, 1985, Abnormalities of Respiration During Sleep, 1986, Mitchell's Synopis of Pulmonary Medicine, 1987, Pulmonary Grand Rounds, 1990, Asthma and Rhinitis, 1994, The High Risk Patient: Management of the Critically Ill, 1995, Manual of Asthma Management, 1995, 2000, Severe Asthma: Pathogenesis and Clinical Management, 1995, Curret Pulmonology, 1995, Pulmonary and Respiratory Therapy Secrets, 1996, (book chpts.) Lung Biology in Health and Disease, 1995, 97, 2000, Allergy, 1997, Asthma, 1997, Emergency Asthma, 1999, Difficult Asthma, 1999, Asthma and Rhinitis, 1999, Imaging of Diffuse Lung Disease, 2000; editor: Nocturnal Asthma: Mechanisms and Interventions, 1993, Cardiothoracic Interrelationships in Clinical Practice, 1997; author, editor: Nocturnal Asthma: Mechanisms and Treatment, 1993, Combination Therapy for Asthma and Chronic Obstructive Pulmonary Disease, 2000; mem. editl. bd.: (jour.) Chronobiology Internat., 1997—, Am. Jour. of Respiratory and Critical Care Medicine, 1994-98, Bronchial Asthma: Index and Review, 1996-97; assoc. editor: Clinical Care for Asthma, 1995-97; contbr. articles, reviews, reports on respiratory and neuromuscular diseases to profl. jours. Pres. Congregation Rodef Shalom, Denver, 1984-85; regional v.p. United Synagogues of Am., Denver, 1988-89. Pulmonary fellow Am. Lung Assn., 1977-79; James F. Hamarsten Outstanding fellow U. Okla. Health Scis. Ctr., 1978; grantee Am. Lung Assn., VA, U. Okla. Lung Assn., NIH, Parker B. Francis Found.; recipient Best Paper in Internal Medicine award Okla. Soc. Interna. Medicine, 1977, 78, U. Okla. Gastroenterology sect, 1977. Mem. Am. Thoracic Soc., Am. Fedn. for Clin. Rsch., Am. Coll. Chest Physicians (rep. to Young Pulmonary Physician Conf., St. Charles, Ill. 1979), ACP, Colo. Trudeau Soc., Western Soc. Clin. Investigation. Avocations: biking, golf, karate. Office: Nat Jewish Med Rsch Ctr 1400 Jackson St Denver CO 80206-2761 E-mail: martinr@njc.org

MARTIN, ROBERT, JR. state agency administrator; b. Kake, Alaska, Feb. 26, 1942; married; two children. Diploma in electronics tech., Haskell Inst., 1962; BS in Engring. Sci., U. Alaska, 1969. Registered profl. engr., Alaska. Electronic maintenance technician FAA, Anchorage, 1962-64; with Alaska Dept. Hwys., 1972-77; chief engr. Tlingit-Haida Regional Elec. Authority, Juneau, Alaska, 1977-78, gen. mgr., CEO, 1978-81, 1989-98; elec. engr. power line and comm. divsn. Cochran Electric Co., Juneau, 1981; dep. dir. for design and constrn. S.E. region Alaska Dept. Transp. and Pub. Facilities, Juneau, 1981-84, dir. S.E. region; gen. mgr. Chugach Electric Assn., Inc., Anchorage, 1984-86; sr. elec. engr. Neubauer & Assocs., Juneau, 1986; v.p. adminstrn. Sealaska Corp., 1987-88, v.p. corp. devel., 1988-89; pvt. practice elec. engring. and mgmt. svcs. cons., 1989. Bd. dirs., chmn. Alaska Energy Authority; chmn. Goldbelt Bd. Dirs. Capt. U.S. Army, 1969-72, Vietnam. Mem. N.W. Pub. Power Assn. (trustee, pres., immediate past pres.). Office: 6860 Glacier Hwy Juneau AK 99801-7909

MARTIN, ROBERT BURTON, management and marketing consultant; b. Takoma Park, Md., Mar. 17, 1935; s. Herbert Lester and Lenora Marie (Sponseller) M.; m. Mary Lou Rushworth, Sept. 7, 1959 (div. Dec. 1982); children: Laurajean, Kenneth, Donna Beth. BEE, Cornell U., 1958; MS, Northwestern U., 1966, PhD, 1967. Dir. mgmt. systems Denver and Rio Grande Western R.R., 1967-71; v.p. Mgmt. Design Assoc., Denver, 1971-79; owner Martin & Assoc., Denver, 1979—; founder Martin Aquatics, LLC, Denver, 1993—. Treas. Rocky Mountain chpt. Inst. of Mgmt. Sci., Denver, 1968-70; opening speaker AICPAs, Las Vegas, Nev., 1988. Author, pub.: (newsletter) Martin Reports, 1981-90, Bob Martin-Chris Frederiksen Marketing and Management Report for CPAs, 1990-94. Served to lt. USN, 1958-63. Mem. Inst. Mgmt. Cons., Alpha Pi Mu, Sigma Xi. Avocations: hiking, camping, ultralight aviation, watersports. Home and Office: PO Box 6886 Denver CO 80206-0886

MARTIN, ROGER JOHN, computer scientist; b. Ft. Atkinson, Iowa, Sept. 11, 1947; s. Raymond Charles and Linda R. (Kuennen) M.; m. Jane Degnan, Nov. 21, 1970; children: John, Kathryn, Susan, Jacquelyn. BS in Computer Sci., Iowa State U., 1969, MS in Computer Sci., 1971. Computer specialist Naval Ship R & D Ctr., Bethesda, Md., 1971-76; supervisory sys. analyst Exec. Office of Pres., Washington, 1976-82; computer scientist, mgr. software engring. group Inst. Computer Scis. and Tech., Nat. Inst. Stds. and Tech., Washington, 1982-92, chief sys. and software tech. divsn., 1993-95, mgr. software methods, 1995-96; stds. straegy mgr. Sun Microsys., Palo Alto, Calif., 1996—. Program co-chmn. Conf. on Software Maintenance, 1985, gen. mgr., 1987; gen. chmn. Computer Stds. Comf., 1988. Soccer coach Montgomery Country Recreation Dept., Rickville, Md., 1979-83; treas., del. Mill Creek Towne Elem. Sch. PTA, Rockville, 1981-84, pres., 1986-87; Magruder clustr PTA coord., 1984-856; leader Cub Scouts Am., Rockville, 1983-84, asst. troop scoutmaster, 1984-92. Recipient award for tech. excellence Interagy. Com. on Info. Resources Mgmt., 1989, Fed. Computer Week award, 1992, cert. of recognition Nat. Bur. Stds., 1983, bronze medal Dept. Commerce, 1984, silver medal, 1989, Hans Karlsson award IEEE, 1995. Mem. Assn. for Computing Machinery, IEEE Computer Soc. (chmn. working group on test methods for POSIX 1986-93, tech. com. on conformance testing 1989-94, mem. tech. com. on operating sys. project mgmt. com. 1991-93, cert. of recognition 1987, Meritorious Svc. award 1991, Stds. medal 1992). Home: 1418 Rosalia Ave San Jose CA 95130-1249 Office: Sun Microsystems 901 San Antonio Rd Palo Alto CA 94303-4900 E-mail: roger.martin@sun.com

MARTIN, STEVE, national park service officer; Supt. Denali Nat. Park, Alaska. Office: Denali Nat Park PO Box 9 Denali National Park AK 99755

MARTIN, STEVE, comedian, actor; b. Waco, Tex., 1945; s. Glenn and Mary Lee Martin; m. Victoria Tennant, Nov. 20, 1986 (div. 1994). Student, Long Beach State Coll., UCLA. Exec. prodr. TV show Domestic Life, 1984. TV writer for Smothers Bros. (co-winner Emmy award 1969), Sonny and Cher, Pat Paulsen, Ray Stevens, Dick Van Dyke, John Denver, Glen Campbell; nightclub comedian; guest and host appearances NBC's Saturday Night Live, Tonight Show; appeared on Carol Burnett Show; starred in TV spls. Steve Martin: A Wild and Crazy Guy, 1978, Comedy is Not Pretty, 1980, Steve Martin's Best Show Ever, 1981; rec. comedy albums Let's Get Small, 1977 (Grammy award 1977), A Wild and Crazy Guy, 1978 (Grammy award 1978), Comedy is Not Pretty, 1979, The Steve Martin Brothers, 1982; actor, screenwriter (films) The Absent Minded Waiter, 1977 (Academy award nomination best short film 1977), The Jerk, 1979, Pennies From Heaven, 1981, Dead Men Don't Wear Plaid, 1982, The Man With Two Brains, 1983, All of Me, 1984 (Nat. Soc. Film Critics award best actor 1984, New York Film Critics' Circle award best actor 1984), Three Amigos, 1986, Roxanne, 1987, (Nat. Soc. Film Critics award best actor 1988, Los Angeles Film Critics' award best actor 1988), L.A. Story, 1991; actor (films) Sergeant Pepper's Lonely Hearts Club Band, 1978, The Muppet Movie, 1979, The Kids Are Alright, 1979, The Lonely Guy, 1984, Little Shop of Horrors, 1986, Planes, Trains and Automobiles, 1987, Dirty Rotten Scoundrels, 1988, Parenthood, 1989, My Blue Heaven, 1990, Father of the Bride, 1991, Grand Canyon, 1991, Housesitter, 1992, Leap of Faith, 1993, Mixed Nuts, 1994, Twist of Fate, 1994, Sgt. Bilko, 1995, The Spanish Prisoner, 1998, Bowfinger, 1999; (theatre) Waiting For Godot, 1988; (television) And the Band Played On, 1993; screenwriter (films) Easy Money, 1983, Bowfinger, 1999; author: Cruel Shoes, 1977, Pure Drivel, 1998; playwright Picasso at the Lapin Agile, 1993. Recipient Georgie award Am. Guild Variety Artists 1977, 78; Grammy award 1978. Office: c/o ICM 8942 Wilshire Blvd Beverly Hills CA 90211-1934 also: Rogers & Cowan c/o Michelle Bega 1888 Century Park E Ste 500 Los Angeles CA 90067-1709

MARTINETTI, RONALD ANTHONY, lawyer; b. N.Y.C., Aug. 13, 1945; s. Alfred Nathan and Frances Ann (Battipaglia) M. Student, U. Chgo., 1981-82; JD, U. So. Calif., 1982. Bar: Calif. 1982; U.S. Dist. Ct. (cen. and no. dists.) Calif. 1982, U.S. Dist. Ct. Ariz., 1992; U.S. Ct. Appeals (9th cir.) 1982. Ptnr. Kazanjian & Martinetti, Glendale, Calif., 1986—. Co-founder Am. Legends Website, 1995, Am. Legends Pub., 1996. Author: James Dean Story, 1995; co-author: Rights of Owners of Lost, Stolen or Destroyed Instruments Under UCC Section3-804: Can They Be Holders in Due Course, 1993; contbr. to Wall St. Jour., Washington Post, Newsday, Balt. Sun, The New Leader, Columbia U. Forum, 1968-76; pub. James Dean Scrapbook, 1996. Vol. trial lawyer Bet Tzedek Legal Svcs., 1987—; vol. arbitrator L.A. Sup. Ct., 1987—; judge pro tem L.A. Superior Ct., 1994—. Mem. Calif. Bar Assn. Roman Catholic. Office: Kazanjian & Martinetti 520 E Wilson Ave Glendale CA 91206-4374 Fax: 818-241-2193. E-mail: amlegends@aol.com

MARTINEZ, ALEX J. state supreme court justice; b. Denver, Apr. 1, 1951; m. Kathy Carter; children: Julia, Maggie. Diploma, Phillips Exeter Acad., N.H., 1969; student, Reed Coll., 1969-72; BA, U. Colo., 1973, JD, 1976. Bar: Colo. 1976. Dep. state pub. defender, Pueblo and Denver, 1976-83; county ct. judge Pueblo, 1983-88; dist. ct. judge Pueblo, 1988-97; justice Colo. Supreme Ct., Denver, 1997—. Supreme Ct. liaison Colo. Criminal Rules Com., Colo. Criminal Jury Instrns.; chmn. Child Welfare Appeals Workgroup, 1997; mem. standing com. Integrated Info. Svcs. Chmn. Pueblo adv. bd. Packard Found., 1993-96; chmn. site-based governing coun. Pueblo Sch. Arts and Scis., 1994-95; mem. site-based governing coun. Roncalli Mid. Sch., 1993-94; bd. dirs. Colo. U. Law Alumni. Mem. Colo. Bar Assn. (regional v.p. 1995-96), Colo. Hispanic Bar Assn., Pueblo Bar Assn. (mem. exec. coun. 1994-96), Pueblo Hispanic Bar Assn. Office: Colo Supreme Ct 2 E 14th Ave Denver CO 80203-2115 E-mail: AJMarti@aol.com

MARTINEZ, ART L. legislative staff member; b. Spain, July 4, 1952; ABA, Coll. Ea. Utah, 1966; BS, Utah State U., 1970; MBA, Brigham Young U., 1981; PhD, Am. U., 1992. Mayor City Price City, Utah, sch. bd. adminstr., sch. bd. pres.; dist. dir. Office of Rep. Merrill A. Cook, Salt Lake City, 1999—. Office: Office Rep Merril A Cook Fed Bldg 125 S State St Salt Lake City UT 84138-1102

MARTINEZ, EDGAR, professional baseball player; b. N.Y.C., Jan. 2, 1963; Student, American Coll., Puerto Rico. Baseball player Seattle Mariners, 1982—. Named. to Am. League All-Star Team, 1992, 95, 96, Am. League Silver Slugger Team, 1992, 95. Achievements include Am. League Batting Champion, 1992, 95. Office: Seattle Mariners Kingdome 1st Ave S & Atlantic Seattle WA 98107

MARTINEZ, MATTHEW GILBERT, former congressman; b. Walsenburg, Colo., Feb. 14, 1929; children: Matthew, Diane, Susan, Michael, Carol Ann. Cert of competence, Los Angeles Trade Tech. Sch., 1959. Small businessman and bldg. contractor; mem. 97th-106th Congresses from 31st Calif. dist., 1982-2001; mem. edn. and labor com., fgn. affairs com. Mem. Monterey Park Planning Commn., 1971-74; mayor City of Monterey Park, 1974-75; mem. Monterey Park City Council, 1974-80, Calif. State Assembly, 1980-82; bd. dirs. San Gabriel Valley YMCA. Served with USMC, 1947-50. Mem. Congl. Hispanic Caucus, Hispanic Am. Democrats, Nat. Assn. Latino Elected and Apptd. Ofcls., Communications Workers Am., VFW, Am. Legion, Latin Bus. Assn., Monterey Park C. of C., Navy League (dir.) Democrat. Lodge: Rotary.*

MARTINEZ, RAY, museum director; Dir. Ghost Ranch Living Mus., Albuquerque. Office: Ghost Ranch Living Mus Carson National Forest PO Box 15 Abiquiu NM 87510-0015

MARTINEZ, RICHARD C. state senator; Magistrate judge; Dem. senator dist. 5 N.Mex. State Senate. Mem. judiciary com. N.Mex. State Senate, vice chair conservation com. Home: Box 934 Espanola NM 87532 Office: NMex State Senate State Capitol Mail Rm Dept Santa Fe NM 87503 E-mail: senate@state.nm.us

MARTINEZ, ROBERT, state legislator; b. Holly, Colo., Sept. 6, 1943; BA, U. So. Colo., 1968; MA in Sociology, U. Colo., 1971. Ind. cons.; adminstr. U. So. Colo. Health Scis. Ctr.; mem. Colo. House of Reps., 1981-84, caucus chair, 1984; mem. Colo. State Senate, 1984—, mem. state, vets. and mil. affairs com. Active Nat. Mexican Am. State Legislators Policy Inst., Am. G.I. Forum, Met. Boys Club, Denver Goodwill Industries, Adams County Planning Commn. With U.S. Army, 1961-63. Mem. U.S. Hispanic C. of C., Am. Legions. Democrat. Office: State Capitol 200 E Colfax Ave Ste 274 Denver CO 80203-1716

MARTINI, ROBERT EDWARD, wholesale pharmaceutical and medical supplies company executive; b. Hackensack, N.J., 1932; BS, Ohio State U., 1954. With Bergen Brunswig Corp., Orange, Calif., 1956-92, v.p., 1962-69, exec. v.p., 1969-81, pres., 1981-92, CEO, 1990-97, chmn., 1992—. Chmn. exec. com. Bergen Brunswig Corp. Capt. USAF, 1954.

MARTINSON, IDA MARIE, nursing educator, nurse, physiologist; b. Mentor, Minn., Nov. 8, 1936; d. Oscar and Marvel (Nelson) Sather; m. Paul Varo Martinson, Mar. 31, 1962; children— Anna Marie, Peter. Diploma, St. Luke's Hosp. Sch. Nursing, 1957; B.S., U. Minn., 1960, M.N.A., 1962; Ph.D., U. Ill., Chgo., 1972. Instr. Coll. St. Scholastica and St. Luke's Sch. Nursing, 1957-58, Thornton Jr. Coll., 1967-69; lab. asst. U. Ill. at Med. Ctr., 1970-72; lectr. dept. physiology U. Minn., St. Paul, 1972-82, asst. prof. Sch. Nursing, 1972-74, assoc. prof. rsch., 1974-77, prof., dir. rsch., 1977-82; prof. dept. family health care U. Calif., San Francisco, 1982—, chmn. dept., 1982-90. Vis. rsch. prof. Nat. Taiwan U., Def. Med. Ctr., 1981; vis. prof. nursing Sun Yat-Sen U. Med. Scis., Guang Zhou, Republic of China, Ewha Women's U., Seoul, Korea; vis. prof. nursing Frances Payne Bolton Sch. Nursing, Case Western Res. U., Cleve., 1994-96; chair, prof. dept. health scis. Hong Kong Poly. U., 1996—. Author: Mathematics for the Health Science Student, 1977; editor: Home Care for the Dying Child, 1976, Women in Stress, 1979, Women in Health and Illness, 1986, The Child and Family Facing Life Threatening Illness, 1987, Family Nursing, 1989, Home Health Care Nursing, 1989; contbr. chpts. to books, articles to profl. jours. Active Am. Cancer Soc. Recipient Book of Yr. award Am. Jour. Nursing, 1977, 80, 87, 90, Children's Hospice Internat. award, 1988, Humanitarian award for pediatric nursing, 1993; Fulbright fellow, 1991. Mem. ANA, Coun. Nurse Rschrs., Am. Acad. Nursing, Inst. Medicine, Sigma Xi, Sigma Theta Tau. Lutheran. Office: U Calif Family Health Care Nursing PO Box 606 San Francisco CA 94143-0001

MARTO, PAUL JAMES, retired mechanical engineering educator, consultant, researcher; b. Flushing, N.Y., Aug. 15, 1938; s. Peter Joseph and Natalie Janet (Verrinoldi) M.; m. Mary Virginia Indence, June 10, 1961; children: Terese V. Marto Sanders, Paul J. Jr., Wayne T., Laura C. BS, U. Notre Dame, 1960; SM, MIT, 1962, ScD, 1965. Asst. prof. Naval Postgrad. Sch., Monterey, Calif., 1965-69, assoc. prof., 1969-77, prof., 1977-85, disting. prof., 1985-96, chmn. dept. mech. engring., 1978-86, dean rsch., 1990-96, disting. prof. emeritus, 1996—. Cons. Modine Mfg. Co., Racine, Wis., 1986—. Editor: Power Condenser Heat, 1981; regional editor N.Am. Jour. of Enhanced Heat Transfer, 1993-98; editor-in-chief Internat. Jour. Transport Phenomena, 1997—; contbr. articles to profl. jours. Bd. trustees Naval Postgrad. Sch. Found., Inc., 1997—. Lt. USN, 1965-67. Recipient Rear Adm. John J. Schieffelin award Naval Postgrad. Sch., 1976, Alexander von Humboldt U.S. Sr. Scientist award Humboldt Stiftung, Fed. Republic Germany, 1989-90, Disting. Civilian Svc. award Sec. of Navy, 1996. Fellow ASME (assoc. tech. editor Jour. of Heat Transfer 1984-90); mem. Am. Soc. Naval Engrs., Am. Soc. for Engring. Edn., Sigma Xi. Avocations: walking, tennis, music. Office: Naval Postgrad Sch Dept Mechanical Engring Code ME MX Monterey CA 93943

MARTONE, FREDERICK J. state supreme court justice; b. Fall River, Mass., Nov. 8, 1943; BS, Coll. Holy Cross, 1965; JD, U. Notre Dame, 1972; LLM, Harvard U., 1975. Bar: Mass. 1972, Ariz. 1974, U.S. Dist. Ct. Mass. 1973, U.S. Dist. Ct. Ariz. 1974, U.S. Ct. Appeals (1st cir.) 1973, U.S. Ct. Appeals (9th cir.) 1974, U.S. Supreme Ct. 1977. Law clk. to Hon. Edward F. Hennessey Mass. Supreme Judicial Ct., 1972-73; pvt. practice Phoenix, 1973-85; assoc. presiding judge Superior Ct. Ariz., Maricopa County, judge, 1985-92; justice Supreme Ct. Ariz., Phoenix, 1992—. Editor notes and comments Notre Dame Law Rev., 1970-72; contbr. articles to profl. jours. Capt. USAF, 1965-69. Mem. ABA, Ariz. Judges Assn., Maricopa County Bar Assn., Am. Judicature Soc., State Bar Ariz., Horace Rumpole Inn of Ct. Office: Supreme Ct Arizona 1501 W Washington St Phoenix AZ 85007-3222 E-mail: FMartone@Supreme.sp.state.az.us

MARTORI, JOSEPH PETER, lawyer; b. N.Y.C., Aug. 19, 1941; s. Joseph and Teresa Susan (Fezza) M. BS summa cum laude, NYU, 1964, MBA, 1968; JD cum laude, U. Notre Dame, 1967. Bar: D.C. 1968, U.S. Dist. Ct. D.C. 1968, U.S. Dist. Ct. Ariz. 1968, U.S. Ct. Appeals (9th cir.) 1969, U.S. Supreme Ct. 1977. Assoc. Sullivan & Cromwell, N.Y.C., 1967-68, Snell & Wilmer, Phoenix, 1968-69; pres. Goldmar Inc., Phoenix, 1969-71; ptnr. Martori, Meyer, Hendricks & Victor, P.A., Phoenix, 1971-85, Brown & Bain, P.A., Phoenix, 1985-94, chmn. corp. banking & real estate dept., 1994—; chmn. bd. ILX Resorts, Inc., Phoenix. Bd. dirs. Firstar Bank, Phoenix; chmn. ILX Inc., Varsity Clubs Am. Inc. Author: Street Fights, 1987; also articles, 1966-70. Trustee Boys' Clubs Met. Phoenix, 1974-99; consul for Govt. of Italy, State of Ariz., 1987-97. Mem. ABA, State Bar Ariz., Maricopa County Bar Assn., Lawyers Com.for Civil Rights Under Law (trustee 1976—), Phoenix Country Club, Plaza Club (founding bd. govs. 1979-90). Republican. Roman Catholic. Office: ILX Inc 2111 E Highland Ave Ste 210 Phoenix AZ 85016-4786 E-mail: jmartori@ILXresorts.com

MARTY, LAWRENCE A. magistrate; b. Leigh, Nebr., June 17, 1926; Student, Wayne State U., 1944-46, Creighton U. Sch. Law, 1946-48; JD, U. Wyo., 1954. Bar: Wyo. 1954. Sole practice, Green River , Wyo., 1954-67; ptnr. Mart & Clark, Green River, 1967-74, Marty & Ragsdale, Green River, 1975—; judge Green River Mcpl. Ct., 1956—58, U.S. Magistrate P.T. Dist. Wyo., 1958—2000, ret., 2000. Alt. del. Rep. Nat. Conv., 1964. Mem.: ABA, Wyo. Bar Assn., Sweetwater County Bar Assn. Office: 20 E Flaming Gorge Way Green River WY 82935-4210

MARTZ, CLYDE OLLEN, lawyer, educator; b. Lincoln, Nebr., Aug. 14, 1920; s. Clyde O. and Elizabeth Mary (Anderson) M.; m. Ann Spieker, May 29, 1947; children: Robert Graham, Nancy. AB, U. Nebr., 1941; LLB, Harvard U., 1947. Bar: Colo. 1948, U.S. Ct. Appeals (D.C. cir.) 1968, U.S. Supreme Ct. 1969. Prof. U. Colo., Boulder, 1947-58, 60-62; jud. adminstr. State of Colo., Denver, 1959-60; ptnr. Davis, Graham & Stubbs, Denver, 1962-67, 69-80, 81-87, of counsel, 1988—; asst. atty. gen. U.S. Dept. Justice, Washington, 1967-69; solicitor U.S. Dept. Interior, Washington, 1980-81; exec. dir. dept. natural resources State of Colo., 1987. Adj. prof. U. Denver, 1961-79, U. Colo., Boulder, 1988-96; cons. Pres. Materials Policy Commn., 1951; mem. Colo. Adv. Bd. Bur. Land Mgmt., 1967-69; bd. dirs. Natural Resources Law Ctr. Author: Cases and Materials on Natural Resources Law, 1951, Water for Mushrooming Populations, 1954; co-author: American Law of Property, 1953, Water and Water Rights, 1963; editor, co-author: American Law of Mining, 1960. Co-chmn. Jud. Reorganization Commn., 1961-63; elder Presbyn. Ch., Boulder; pres. Rocky

Mountain Mineral Law Found., 1961-62, others. Comdr. USN, 1942-58, PTO, with Res. Decorated Silver Star, Bronze Star, Letter of Commendation. Mem. ABA (chmn. natural resources sect. 1985-86), Fed. Bar Assn., Am. Health Lawyers Assn., Colo. Bar Assn. (chmn. water sect. 1957, chmn. mineral sect. 1961, award of merit 1962), Nat. Mining Assn. (Disting. Svc. award 1997), Order of Coif, Phi Beta Kappa. Democrat. Avocations: horticulture, woodworking, mountaineering, skiing. Home: 970 Aurora Ave Apt 205F Boulder CO 80302-7299 Office: Davis Graham & Stubbs PO Box 185 Denver CO 80201-0185

MARTZ, JUDY HELEN, governor; b. Big Timber, Mont., July 28, 1943; m. Harry Martz, June 23, 1965; children: Justin, Stacey. Owner, operator Martz Disposal Svc., 1971—; skater U.S. World Speed Skating Team, Japan, 1963, U.S. Olympic Team, Innsbruck, Austria, 1964; exec. dir. U.S. High Altitude Speed Skating Ctr., Butte, Mont., 1985-89; field rep. Senator Conrad Burns, 1989-96; lt. gov. State of Mont., 1997-2001, gov., 2001—. Coach Mont. Amateur Speed Skating Assn.; bd. dirs. Youth Hockey Assn.; pres. adv. bd. U.S. Internat. Speed Skating Assn. Bd dirs. St. James Cmty. Hosp., Legion Oasis HUD Housing Project. Named Miss Rodeo Mont., 1963; inducted Butte Sports Hall of Fame, 1987.*

MASLACH, CHRISTINA, psychology educator; b. San Francisco, Jan. 21, 1946; d. George James and Doris Ann (Cuneo) M.; m. Philip George Zimbardo, Aug. 10, 1972; children: Zara, Tanya. B.A., Harvard-Radcliffe Coll., 1967; Ph.D., Stanford U., 1971. Prof. psychology U. Calif.-Berkeley, 1971—, vice provost for undergrad. edn., 2001—. Author: Burnout: The Cost of Caring, 1982; co-author: Influencing Attitudes and Changing Behavior, 1977, Maslach Burnout Inventory (rsch. scale), 1981, 2d edit., 1986, 3d edit., 1996, Experiencing Social Psychology, 1979, 4th edit., 2001, Professional Burnout, 1993, The Truth About Burnout, 1997, Preventing Burnout and Building Engagement, 2000. Recipient Disting. Teaching award, 1987, Best Paper award Jour. Orgnl. Behavior, 1994, Prof. of Yr. award Carnegie/CASE, 1997. Fellow AAAS, APA, Am. Psychol. Soc., Soc. Clin. and Exptl. Hypnosis (Henry Guze rsch. award 1980), We. Psychol. Assn. (pres. 1989); mem. Soc. Exptl. Social Psychology. Democrat. Office: U Calif Office of Chancellor 200 California Hall # 1500 Berkeley CA 94720-1500 E-mail: maslach@socrates.berkeley.edu

MASON, CHERYL WHITE, lawyer; b. Champaign, Ill., Jan. 16, 1952; d. John Russell and Lucille (Birden) White; m. Robert L. Mason, Oct. 9, 1972; children: Robert L. II and Daniel G. BA, Purdue U., 1972; JD, U. Chgo., 1976. Bar: Calif. 1977. Assoc. O'Melveny & Myers LLP, L.A., 1976-81, 84-86, ptnr., 1987—; exec. dir. Public Counsel, L.A., 1981-84. Bd. dirs. Pub. Policy Inst. Calif. Chmn. State Bar, Legal Svcs. Trust Fund, 1987; trustee L.A. County Bar, 1985-88; bd. dirs. Challengers Boys and Girls Club, L.A., 1990—, Western Ctr. Law and Poverty, L.A., 1991-94; bd. dirs. James Irvine Found. Mem. ABA (co-chair environ. litigation commn. 1992-94, lawyer rep. 9th cir. jud. conf. 1993-94), Calif. Women Lawyers, L.A. County Bar Assn., Women Lawyers L.A., Black Women Lawyers L.A., Langston Bar Assn. Democrat. Office: O Melveny & Myers LLP 400 S Hope St Los Angeles CA 90071

MASON, DEAN TOWLE, cardiologist; b. Berkeley, Calif., Sept. 20, 1932; s. Ira Jenckes and Florence Mabel (Towle) M.; m. Maureen O'Brien, June 22, 1957; children: Kathleen, Alison. BA in Chemistry, Duke U., 1954, MD, 1958. Diplomate Am. Bd. Internal Medicine, Am. Bd. Cardiovasc. Diseases, Nat. Bd. Med. Examiners. Intern, then resident in medicine Johns Hopkins Hosp., 1958-61; clin. assoc. cardiology br., sr. asst. surgeon USPHS, Nat. Heart Inst., NIH, 1961-63, asst. sect. dir. cardiovascular diagnosis, attending physician, sr. investigator cardiology br., 1963-68; prof. medicine, prof. physiology, chief cardiovascular medicine U. Calif. Med. Sch., Davis-Sacramento Med. Center, 1968-82; dir. cardiac ctr. Cedars Med. Ctr., Miami, Fla., 1982-83; physician-in chief Western Heart Inst., San Francisco, 1983 ; chmn. dept. cardiovascular medicine St. Mary's Med. Ctr., San Francisco, 1986-99, hon. med. staff, 2000—. Co-chmn. cardiovascular-renal drugs U.S. Pharmacopeia Com. Revision, 1970-75; mem. life scis. com. NASA; med. rsch. rev. bd. VA, NIH; vis. prof. numerous univs., cons. in field; mem. Am. Cardiovascular Splty. Cert. Bd., 1970-78. Editor-in-chief Am. Heart Jour., 1980-96; author 25 books on cardiovasc. medicine; contbr. numerous articles to med. jours. Recipient rsch. award Am. Therapeutic Soc., 1965; Theodore and Susan B. Cummings Humanitarian award Dept. State-Am. Coll. Cardiology, 1972, 73, 75, 78; Skylab Achievement award NASA, 1974; U. Calif. Faculty Rsch. award, 1978, Award of Honor Wisdom Soc., 1997, Medal of Honor Winston Churchill Soc., 1998, Armand Hammer Creative Genius award, 1998, Dwight D. Eisenhower Admirable Am. of Achievement award, 1998, Eternal Jesus Christ award, 1998, Blessed Lord's Prayer award, 1998, Dean Towle Mason Eminent Physician of Wisdom award, 1999; named Outstanding Prof. U. Calif. Med. Sch., Davis, 1972 Master Am. Coll. Cardiology (pres. 1977-78); fellow A.C.P., Am. Heart Assn., Am. Coll. Chest Physicians, Royal Soc. Medicine; mem. Am. Soc. Clin. Investigation, Am. Physiol. Soc., Am. Soc. Pharmacology and Exptl. Therapeutics (Exptl. Therapeutics award 1973), Am. Fedn. Clin. Research, N.Y. Acad. Scis., Am. Assn. U. Cardiologists, Am. Soc. Clin. Pharmacology and Therapeutics, We. Assn. Physicians, AAUP, We. Soc. Clin. Research (past pres.), Phi Beta Kappa, Alpha Omega Alpha. Republican. Methodist. Club: El Marcero Country. Home: 44725 Country Club Dr El Macero CA 95618-1047 Office: Western Heart Inst St Marys Med Ctr 450 Stanyan St San Francisco CA 94117-1079

MASON, GREG, publishing executive; Pub. PC Computing (now Smart Bus.), San Francisco. Office: Smart Business 50 Beale St Ste 13 San Francisco CA 94105-1813

MASON, JAMES ALBERT, retired museum director, former university dean; b. Eureka, Utah, 1929; married, 1956; 3 children. BA, Brigham Young U., 1955, MA, 1957; EdD, Ariz. State U., 1970. Cons., clinician in fine arts, 1955—; former chmn. dept. music Brigham Young U., Provo, Utah, dean Coll. Fine Arts and Comm., 1982-93, dir. Mus. of Art, 1993-96; ret., 1996. Vis. prof., lectr. Ind. U., Northwestern U., Cin. Coll.-Conservatory, U. Tex., Central Conservatory, Beijing, Internat. Soc. Music Edn., Warsaw; chmn. nat. symposium Applications of Psychology to the Teaching and Learning of Music. Editor The Instrumentalist, Orch. News, Utah Music Educator, Rsch. News column, Jour. Rsch. in Music Edn. Chmn., bd. dirs. The Barlow Endowment for Music Composition; co-founder, 1st pres. Utah Valley Symphony Orch.; past condr. Utah Valley Youth Orch.; trustee Utah Opera Co.; commr. Utah Centennial of Statehood; bd. dirs. Presser Found. Mem. Music Educators Nat. Conf. (past nat. pres., coun.), Nat. Music Coun. (past bd. dirs.), Am. Music Conf. (past bd. dirs.).

MASON, JAMES OSTERMANN, public health administrator; b. Salt Lake City, June 19, 1930; s. Ambrose Stanton and Neoma (Thorup) M.; m. Lydia Maria Smith, Dec. 29, 1952; children: James, Susan, Bruce, Ralph, Samuel, Sara, Benjamin BA, U. Utah, 1954, MD, 1958; MPH, Harvard U., 1963, DPH, 1967. Diplomate Am. Bd. Preventive Medicine. Intern Johns Hopkins Hosp., Balt., 1958-59; resident in internal medicine Peter Bent Brigham Hosp.-Harvard Med. Service, Boston, 1961-62; chief infectious diseases Latter-day Saints Hosp., Salt Lake City, 1968-69; commr. Health Services Corp., Ch. of Jesus Christ of Latter-day Saints, 1970-76; dep. dir. health Utah Div. Health, 1976-78, exec. dir., 1979-83; chief epidemic intelligence service Ctr. Disease Control, Atlanta, 1959, chief hepatitis surveillance unit epidemiology br., 1960, chief surveillance sect. epidemiology br., 1961, dep. dir. bur. labs., 1964-68, dep. dir. of Ctr., 1969-70; dir. Ctrs. for Disease Control, Atlanta; adminstr. Agy. for Toxic Substances and Disease Registry, 1983-89; acting asst. sec. health HHS, Washington, 1985, asst. sec. for health, acting surgeon gen., 1989-90, asst. sec. for health, 1990-93; asst. prof. dept. medicine and preventive medicine U. Utah, Salt Lake City, 1968-69, assoc. prof., chmn. div. community medicine, dept. family and community medicine, 1978-79; v.p. planning, devel., prof. preventive medicine and biometrics Uniformed Svcs. U. Health Scis., 1993-94; 2nd quorum of Seventy LDS Ch., 1994—. Physician, cons. to med. services Salt Lake VA Hosp., 1977-83; clin. prof. dept. family and community medicine, U. Utah. Coll. Medicine, 1979-83, clin. prof. dept. pathology, 1980-83; clin. prof. community health Emory U. Sch. Medicine, 1984-86; chmn. joint residency com. in preventive medicine and pub. health Utah Coll. Medicine, 1975-80; mem. Utah Cancer Registry Research Adv. Com., 1976-83; mem. adv. com. Utah Ctr. Health Stats., 1977-79; chmn. bd. Hosp. Coop. Utah, 1977-79; chmn. exec. com. Utah Health Planning and Resource Devel. Adv. Group, 1977-79; chmn. Utah Gov.'s Adv. Com. for Comprehensive Health Planning, 1975-77; mem. recombinant DNA adv. com. NIH, 1979-83; mem. Gov.'s Nuclear Waste Repository Task Force, 1980-83, chmn., 1980-82; bd. dirs. Utah Health Cost Mgmt. Found., 1980-83; mem. adv. com. for programs and policies Ctrs. for Disease Control, 1980; mem. com. on future of local health depts., Inst. Medicine, 1980-82; mem. exec. com., chmn. tech. adv. com. Thrasher Research Found., 1980-89; mem. Robert Wood Johnson Found. Program for Hosp. Initiatives in Long-Term Care, 1982-84; mem. sci. and tech. adv. com. UNDP-World Bank-WHO Spl. Programme for Research and Tng. in Tropical Diseases, 1984-89; mem. Utah Resource for Genetic and Epidemiologic Research, 1982-85, chmn. bd., 1982-83; U.S. rep. WHO Exec. Bd., 1990-93. Author: (with H.L. Bodily and E.L. Updyke) Diagnostic Procedures for Bacterial, Mycotic and Parasitic Infections, 5th edit., 1970; (with M.H. Maxell, K.H. Bousfield and D.A. Ostler) Funding Water Quality Control in Utah, Procs. for Lincoln Inst., 1982; contbr. articles to profl. jours. Mem. nat. scouting com. Boy Scouts Am., 1974-78. Recipient Roche award U. Utah, 1957, Wintrobe award U. Utah, 1958, Disting. Alumni award U. Utah, 1973, Adminstr. of Yr. award Brigham U., 1980, spl. award for outstanding pub. svc. Am. Soc. Pub. Adminstrn. 1984, Disting. Svc. medal USPHS, 1988, LDS Hosp. Deseret Found. Legacy of Life award, 1992, Gorgas Medal and Scroll, 1993. Mem. Inst. Medicine of NAS, AMA, Am. Pub. Health Assn. (task force for credentialing of lab. personnel 1976-78, program devel. bd. 1979-81), Utah State Med. Assn. (trustee 1979-83), Utah Acad. Preventive Medicine (pres. 1982-83), Utah Pub. Health Assn. (pres. 1980-82, Beatty award 1979), Sigma Xi, Alpha Epsilon Delta, Phi Kappa Phi, Alpha Omega Alpha, Delta Omega Mem. LDS Ch. Lodge: Rotary Office: LDS 47 E South Temple Salt Lake City UT 84150-9701

MASON, JOHN E. political association executive; b. L.A., Dec. 6, 1946; m. Bianca Mason; seven children. BA with honors, UCLA, 1978; JD with highest honors, U. Calif., Berkeley, 1971. Chmn. Nev. State Rep. Party, 1995—; mem. Nat. Rep. Com., 1995—. Founder, pres. Mason, Sloane & Gilbert, 1977-90, now Law Office of John E. Mason; dir. and audit com. mem. LIVE Entertainment Inc., 1987-90; dir., mem. audit and compensations coms. Heftel Broadcasting Inc., 1992-96; v.p. music industry chpt. City of Hope, 1982-86. Assoc. editor Ecolog. Law Quar., 1969-71; mng. editor Calif. Law Rev., 1970-71. Trustee, chmn. western regional exec. bd. Nat. Found. Ileitis and Colitis, 1982-88; trustee Barton Meml. Hosp. Found., 1995-97; chmn. Nev. State Film Commn., 1996-97. Named Entertainment Lawyer of Yr. Billboard Mag., 1978, 80. Mem. Calif. Bar Assn., Nev. Bar Assn., Tenn. Bar Assn., Nat. Found. Ileitis and Colitis (Gold medal award for Humanitarian of Yr. 1986), Order of Coif. E-mail: maso007@ibm.net

MASON, JOHN LATIMER, engineering executive; b. Los Angeles, Nov. 8, 1923; s. Zene Upham and Edna Ella (Watkins) M.; m. Frances Howe Draeger, Sept. 1, 1950 (dec. June 1951); m. Mary Josephine Schulte, Nov. 26, 1954; children: Andrew, Peter, Mary Anne, John Edward. B.S. in Meteorology, U. Chgo., 1944; B.S. in Applied Chemistry, Calif. Inst. Tech., 1947, M.S. in Chem. Engring., 1948, Ph.D., 1950. Registered profl. engr., Calif. Engr. AiResearch Mfg. Co., Los Angeles, 1950-60; dir. engring. AiResearch Mfg. Co. div. Garrett Corp., Los Angeles, 1960-72; v.p. engring. Garrett Corp., Los Angeles, 1972-87; v.p. engring. and tech. Allied-Signal Aerospace Co., Los Angeles, 1987-88, cons., 1989-96; chmn. tech. adv. com. Indsl. Turbines Internat., Inc., Los Angeles, 1972-81, bd. dirs., 1980-88; adj. prof. engring. Calif. State U., Long Beach, 1992-96. Mem. tech. adv. bd. Tex. Ctr. for Superconductivity, U. Houston, 1989—; chair Calif. Coun. Sci. and Tech. Panel on Transp. R&D Ctr., 1993-94; bd. dirs. San Juan Capistrano Rsch. Inst., 1995—, sec., 1998—; cons. Capstone Turbine Corp., 1994-98; mem. tech. adv. bd. Ceryx Inc., 1998—; mem. workshop com. Transp. Rsch. Bd., 1998. Patentee in field. Chmn. energy and environment com. FISITA Coun., 1990-94. 1st lt. USAAF, 1943-45, PTO. Fellow AIAA (assoc.). Soc. Automotive Engrs. (bd. dirs. 1984-87, 90-93, pres.-elect 1989-90, pres. 1990-91), Performance Rev. Inst. (chmn. 1990-91, bd. dirs. 1992-93); mem. AAAS, NAS (com. on alternative energy R&D strategies 1989-90), Office Sci. and Tech. Policy (Nat. Critical Techs. panel 1992-93), Inst. Medicine of NAS (com. on health effects of indoor allergens 1992-93), Nat. Acad. Engring., U.S. Advanced Ceramics Assn. (chmn. tech. com., bd. dirs. 1985-88), Am. Chem. Soc., Am. Ceramic Soc., Caltech Assocs., Sigma Xi (assoc.). E-mail: JL-Mason@home.com

MASON, MARSHALL W. theater director, educator; b. Amarillo, Tex., Feb. 24, 1940; s. Marvin Marshall and Lorine (Chrisman) M. B.S. in Speech, Northwestern U., 1961. Prof. Ariz. State U., 1994—; chief drama critic New Times, Phoenix, 1994-96. Founder, artistic dir. Circle Repertory Co., 1969-87, guest artistic dir., Ctr. Theater Group, 1988; dir. Broadway prodns. Redwood Curtain, 1993, The Seagull, 1992, Solitary Confinement, 1992, Burn This, 1987, As Is, 1985 (Drama Desk award, Tony nomination), Passion, 1983, Angels Fall, 1983 (Tony nomination), Fifth of July, 1981 (Tony nomination), Talley's Folly, 1980, (Pulitzer Prize, N.Y. Drama Critics Circle award, Tony nomination), Murder at the Howard Johnsons, 1979, Gemini, 1977, Knock Knock, 1976 (Tony nomination); Off-Broadway prodns. Sympathetic Magic, 1997, Robbers, 1997, Cakewalk, 1996, A Poster of the Cosmos/The Moonshot Tape, 1994, The Destiny of Me, 1992, Sunshine, 1989, Talley and Son, 1985, Childe Byron, 1980, Hamlet, 1979, Serenading Louie, 1976 (Obie award), Knock Knock, 1976 (Obie award), The Mound Builders, 1975 (Obie award), Battle of Angeles, 1974 (Obie award), The Sea Horse, 1974, The Hot L Baltimore, 1973 (Obie award); dir. numerous prodns. including Who's Afraid of Virginia Woolf?, Tokyo, 1985, Talley's Folly, 1982, London, Home Free! and The Madness of Lady Bright, 1968, London, Nat. Tour Sleuth, 1988, Summer and Smoke, 1988, Whisper in the Mind, 1990, King Lear, 1998, The Elephant Man, London, 1998, Long Day's Journey into Night, 1998, Riga, Los Angeles, 1999, Los Alamos, 1999, Book of Days, 1999, Ginger, 2000; transl. Pirandello's Enrico IV, 2001, Ghosts, 2001; dir. numerous TV prodns. including Picnic, 1986, Kennedy's Children, 1982, The Fifth of July, 1983. Recipient Vernon Rice award, 1975, Drama Desk award, 1977, Margo Jones award, 1977, Outer Critics Circle award, 1978, Theatre World award, 1979, Shubert's Vaughan award, 1980, Obie award for Sustained Achievement, 1983, Inge Festival award for lifetime achievement, 1990, Last Frontier award, 1994, award Ariz. Press Club, 1995, Erwin Piscator award, 1996, Millennium Mr. Abbott award, 1999, Creative Achievement award ASU, 2001. Mem. Soc. Stage Dirs. and Choreographers (pres. 1983-85), Dirs. Guild Am., Actors Equity Assn., Coll. Fellow of Am. Theater. Address: 1948 E Ellis Cir Mesa AZ 85203-5825 E-mail: mwm@asu.edu

MASON, WILLIAM A(LVIN), psychologist, educator, researcher; b. Mountain View, Calif., Mar. 28, 1926; s. Alvin Frank and Ruth Sabina (Erwin) M.; m. Virginia Joan Carmichael, June 27, 1948; children: Todd, Paula, Nicole, Hunter. BA, Stanford U., 1950, MS, 1952, PhD, 1954. Asst. prof. U. Wis.-Madison, 1954-59; research assoc. Yerkes Labs. Primate Biology, Orange Park, Fla., 1959-63; head dept. behavioral sci. Delta Primate Research Ctr., Tulane U., Covington, La., 1963-71; prof. psychology, research psychologist U. Calif., Davis, 1971-91, leader behavioral biology unit Calif. Primate Rsch. Ctr., 1972-96, prof. emeritus, 1991. Bd. dirs. Jane Goodall Inst., 1978-92, Karisoke Rsch. Ctr., 1980-86. Mem. Editorial bd. Animal Learning and Behavior, 1973-76, Internat. Jour. Devel. Psychobiology, 1980-92, Internat. Jour. Primatology, 1980-90; contbr. numerous articles to profl. jours., chpts. to books. With USMC, 1944-46. USPHS spl. fellow, 1963-64. Fellow AAAS, APA (pres. divsn. 6 1982, disting. sci. contbn. award 1995), Am. Psychol. Soc., Animal Behavior Soc.; mem. Internat. Primatological Soc. (pres. 1976-80, 81-84), Am. Soc. Primatologists (pres. 1988-90, disting. primatologist award), Internat. Soc. Devel. Psychobiology (pres. 1971-72, Best Paper of Yr. award 1976), Sigma Xi. Home: 2809 Anza Ave Davis CA 95616-0257 Office: U Calif Regl Primate Rsch Ctr 1 Shields Ave Davis CA 95616 E-mail: wamason@ucdavis.edu

MASON, WILLIAM VANHORN, dermatologist; b. Pitts., Jan. 8, 1930; AB, Harvard U., 1951; MD, Baylor Coll. Medicine, Houston, 1961. Diplomate Am. Bd. Dermatology. Pvt. practice, Albuquerque, 1979—; clin. assoc. prof. dermatology U. N.Mex. Sch. Medicine, Albuquerque, 1986—. Lt. (j.g.) USN, 1951-54. Mem. Phi Beta Kappa, Alpha Omega Alpha. Office: 200 Oak St NE Albuquerque NM 87106-4740

MASOTTI, LOUIS HENRY, management and real estate educator, consultant; b. N.Y.C., May 16, 1934; s. Henry and Angela Catherine (Turi) M.; m. Iris Patricia Leonard, Aug. 28, 1958 (div. 1981); children: Laura Lynn, Andrea Anne; m. Ann Randel Humm, Mar. 5, 1988. AB, Princeton U., 1956; MA, Northwestern U., 1961, PhD, 1964. Fellow Nat. Ctr. Edn. in Politics, 1962; asst. prof. polit. sci. Case Western Res. U., Cleve., 1963-67, assoc. prof., 1967-69, dir. Civil Violence Rsch. Ctr., 1968-69; sr. Fulbright lectr. Johns Hopkins U. Ctr. Advanced Internat. Studies, Bologna, Italy, 1969-70; assoc. prof. Northwestern U., Evanston, Ill., 1970-72, prof. polit. sci. and urban affairs, 1972-83, dir. Ctr. Urban Affairs, 1971-80, dir. Program in Pub. and Not-for-Profit Mgmt., Kellogg Sch. Mgmt., 1979-80, prof. mgmt. and urban devel. Kellogg Sch. Mgmt., 1983-94, dir. Real Estate Research Ctr. Kellogg Sch. Mgmt., 1986-88. Cons. to numerous publs., govt. agys., real estate firms, and corps.; vis. assoc. prof. U. Wash. summer 1969; exec. dir. Mayor Jane Byrne Transition Com., Chgo., 1979; vis. prof. Stanford Sch. Bus., 1989-92, UCLA Sch. Mgmt., 1989-92; prof., dir. real estate mgmt. program U. Calif. Grad. Sch. Mgmt., Irvine, 1992-98, bd. dirs. Mfd. Home Communities, Inc., Facilities Mgmt. Internat., Imperial Credit Comml. Mortgage Investment Corp., 1997-2000. Author: Education and Politics in Suburbia, 1967, Shootout in Cleveland, 1969, A Time to Burn?, 1969, Suburbia in Transition, 1973, The New Urban Politics, 1976, The City in Comparative Perspective, 1976, co-editor: Metropolis in Crisis, 1968, 2d edit., 1971, Riots and Rebellion, 1968, The Urbanization of the Suburbs, 1973, After Daley: Chicago Politics in Transition, 1981, Downtown Development, 1985, 2d edit., 1987; editor Edn. and Urban Soc., 1968-71, Urban Affairs Quar., 1973-80; sr. editor Econ. Devel. Quar., 1986-92; vice chmn. bd. Illinois Issues jour., 1986-92, BOMA Office mag., 1990-95. Rsch. dir. Carl Stokes for Mayor of Cleve., 1967; mem. Cleveland Heights Bd. Edn., 1967-69; devel. coordinator for high tech. State of Ill.-City Chgo., 1982-83; advisor to various congl., gubernatorial and mayoral campaigns, Ohio, Ill., N.J., Calif.; cons. urban devel. issues corps. developers, govt. agys. and news media. Lt. USNR, 1956-59. Fellow Homer Hoyt Inst. for Advanced Real Estate Studies; recipient Disting. Service award Cleve. Jaycees, 1967; numerous fed. and found. research grants, 1963-2000. Mem. Urban Land Inst., Habitat, Nat. Trust for Hist. Preservation, Internat. Assn. Corp. Real Estate Execs., Internat. Devel. Rsch. Coun., Nat. Assn. Indsl. Office Properties, Coun. on Urban Econ. Devel., Lambda Alpha. Office: 915 Sunset Dr Healdsburg CA 95448 E-mail: lmasotti@aol.com

MASRI, MERLE SID, biochemist, consultant; b. Jerusalem, Sept. 12, 1927; came to U.S., 1947; s. Said Rajab and Fatima (Muneimné) M.; m. Maryjean Loretta Anderson, June 28, 1952 (div. 1974); children: Kristin Corinne, Allan Eric, Wendy Joan, Heather Anderson. BA in Physiology, U. Calif., Berkeley, 1950; PhD in Mammalian Physiology and Biochemistry, U. Calif. Berkeley, 1953. Rsch. asst. Dept. Physiology, Univ. Calif., Berkeley, 1950-53; predoctoral fellow Baxter Labs., Berkeley, 1952-53; rsch. assoc. hematology Med. Rsch. Inst., Michael Reese Hosp., Chgo., 1954-56; sr. rsch. biochemist Agrl. Rsch. Svc., USDA, Berkeley, 1956-87; supervisory rsch. scientist Agrl. Rsch. Svc., USDA, N.D. State U. Sta., Fargo, N.D., 1987-89; pvt. practice as cons. Emeryville, Calif., 1989—. Lectr. numerous confs. Contbr. articles to profl. jours. and books. Recipient Spl. Svc. and Merit awards USDA, 1966, 76, 77, Superior Svc. award USDA, 1977. Mem. AAAS, Am. Chem. Soc., Am. Oil Chemists Soc., Am. Assn. Cereal Chemists, N.Y. Acad. Scis., Inst. Food Technologists, Commonwealth Club Calif., Internat. Platform Assn., World Affairs Coun. of No. Calif., Sigma Xi. Achievements include patents for detoxification of aflatoxins in agricultural crops and aflatoxin contaminated milk, improved dyeability of cotton fabrics and reduced dye and electrolyte discharge in plant effluent, new closed-circuit raw wool scouring technology to conserve water and energy and control pollution, synthesis and use of polymers and modification of biopolymers for wastewater treatment, and for encapsulation, enzyme immobilization, toxic heavy metals removal and textile finishing treatment, non-polluting new technology for scouring raw wool in a closed circuit with water recycling and re-use and waste effluent control; studied chlorination of water in food processing operations and water re-use and recycle and the generation of mutagens and means of improving disinfection efficiency and reducing mutagen formation, pharmacology, metabolism, and toxicology of natural and synthetic compounds, cereal and baking technology and wheat and durum quality, carbohydrate chemistry, fermentation and enology, confectionery, and ceramic chemistry; discovered new methods and reagents for protein and amino acid residue modification and analysis, new mammalian metabolic pathways; developed other non-polluting textile finishing treatments. Home: 9 Commodore Dr Emeryville CA 94608-1652

MASSARO, MIKE, advertising executive; COO, exec. v.p. Goldberg, Moser & O'Neill, San Francisco, 1988—. Office: 600 Battery St San Francisco CA 94111-1802

MASSARO, TONI MARIE, dean, law educator; BS, Northwestern U., 1977; JD, Coll. William and Mary, 1980. With Vedder, Price, Kaufman and Kammholz; tchr. law Washington and Lee U., U. Fla.; former prof. law U. Ariz., Tucson, dean, Milton O. Riepe chair constl. law, 1999—. Vis. prof. law Stanford U., U. N.C., Johann Goethe U., Frankfurt, West Germany. Author: Constitutional Literacy: A Core Curriculum for a Multi-Cultural Nation; contbr. numerous articles to law revs. Office: U Ariz James E Rogers Coll Law PO Box 210176 1201 E Speedway Tucson AZ 85721-0176 Fax: 520-621-9140. E-mail: massaro@law.arizona.edu

MASSENGILL, MATTHEW H. retail company executive; BE, Purdue U., 1983. Product engr. Western Digital Corp., Irvine, Calif., 1985-94, v.p. mktg. personal storage divsn., 1994-97, sr. v.p., gen. mgr. enterprise storage group, 1997-99, co-chief operating officer, 1999—. Office: Western Digital Corp 8105 Irvine Center Dr Irvine CA 92618-2902

MASSEY, HENRY P., JR. lawyer; b. Montclair, N.J., Sept. 2, 1939; AB, Cornell U., 1961, JD with distinction, 1968. Bar: Calif. 1969. Ptnr. Wilson Sonsini Goodrich & Rosati, Palo Alto, Calif., 1982—. Bd. editors Cornell Law Rev., 1967-68. Mem. ABA (sects. on corp., banking and bus. law, taxation law), State Bar Calif. (mem. corps. com. bus. law sect. 1979-82), Order of Coif, Phi Kappa Phi. Office: Wilson Sonsini Goodrich & Rosati 650 Page Mill Rd Palo Alto CA 94304-1050

MASSEY, LEON R. (R.L. MASSEY), professional association administrator; b. Grand Island, Nebr., Jan. 16, 1930; s. James Moore and Iva Pearl (Richardson) M.; m. Jean M. Nielsen, June 17, 1951; children: Dean R., Maureen L. Student, U. Colo., 1948-49; BA, U. Nebr., 1955; postgrad., N.Y. Inst. Fin., 1963. Salesman consumer products Union Carbide Corp., Memphis, 1956-57, Greenville, Miss., 1957-58, Albuquerque, 1958-61, Dallas, 1962-63; regional sales mgr. GC Electric div. Textron Corp., Dayton, Ohio, 1963-64; account exec. Merrill Turben Co., Dayton, 1964-66; with Nat. Electric Contractors Assn., Dayton, 1967-72, Denver, 1972-83, exec. sec., 1967-83, also bd. dirs. Rocky Mountain chpt.; pres. RLM's Assocs., Englewood, Colo., 1983—. Instr. adult edn. Wayne State U., Dayton, 1964-66. City councilman City of Greenwood Village, Colo., 1986-90; pres. Cherry Creek Civic Assn., 1979-80, bd. dirs. 1973-74; bd. dirs. Assn. Operating Rm. Nurses, Cherry Creek Village Water Dist., 1992-95; bd. dirs. Goldsmith Gulch Sanitation Dist., 1990—, pres., 1992—; bd. dirs. The Retreat Assn., 1996-99, Highlands Ranch Met. Dist., 1999; active Dem. Party, 1960. With USAF, 1950-54, Korea. Mem. Am. Soc. Assn. Execs. (cert., bd. dirs.), Colo. Soc. Assn. Execs. (life, pres. 1979), Civitan Club, Masons, Phi Kappa Psi. Office: RLM Assocs 4935 E Greenwich Ln Highlands Ranch CO 80130

MASSIE, MICHAEL ANTHONY, state legislator, historian; b. Akron, Ohio, Jan. 8, 1954; s. Donald and Eileen Marie Massie; m. Ruth Ellen Massie; children: Kara Marie, Jedediah Mark. BS in Edn. and History, U. Akron, 1979; M in History, U. Wyo., 1980. Historian Wyo. State Hist. Preservation Office, Cheyenne, 1980-82; historian, curator South Pass City (Wyo.) State Historic Site, 1982-89; mus. dir. City of Greeley (Colo.) Mus., 1989-90; asst. dir. Wyo. Coun. for the Humanities, Laramie, 1990-99; divsn. dir. Wyo. Inst. for Disabilities, U. Wyo., Laramie, 1999—; mem. Wyo. Senate, Dist. 9, Cheyenne, 1998—. Contbr. articles to profl. jours. Founder, bd. dirs. Sublette County Hist. Preservation Bd., Pinedale, Wyo., 1984-89; bd. dirs. Albany County Hist. Preservation Bd., Laramie, 1992-95; mem. Wyo. State Legislature Senate, 1999—, Ho. of Reps., 1995-99; bd. dirs., zone warden Atlantic City Vol. Fire Dept., 1982-89; chmn., bd. dirs. Lander chapt. Employees Assn., 1984-89. Recipient Historic Preservation Citation Wyo. State Hist. Preservation Office, 1987, Whistleblower's award Wyo Assn. of Pub. Employees, 1996, Helping Woman award Laramie SAFE Project, 1996, Friend of Young Children award Wyo. Early Childhood Assn., 1999; named Legislator of Yr. Wyo. Wildlife Fedn., 1995. Mem. Wyo. Assn. of Profl. Historians (founder, bd. dirs. 1993-98), Wyo. Hist. Preservation Assn. (founder, bd. dirs. 1981-83), Laramie Sunrise Rotary Club, Laramie Area C. of C., Friends of the George Frison Inst., Wyo. State Hist. Soc. Democrat. Roman Catholic. Avocations: baseball, basketball, camping, fishing, hunting. Home: 1209 W Hill R Laramie WY 82072

MASSY, WILLIAM FRANCIS, education educator, consultant; b. Milw., Mar. 26, 1934; s. Willard Francis and Ardys Dorothy (Digman) M.; m. Sally Vaughn Miller, July 21, 1984; children by previous marriage: Willard Francis, Elizabeth BS, Yale U., 1956; SM, MIT, 1958, PhD in Indsl. Econs., 1960. Asst. prof. indsl. mgmt. MIT, Cambridge, 1960-62; from asst. prof. to prof. edn. and bus. adminstrn. Stanford U., Calif., 1962-96, assoc. dean Grad. Sch. Bus., 1971, vice provost for rsch., 1971-77, v.p. for bus. and fin., 1977-88, v.p. fin., 1988-91, prof. emeritus, 1996—; prof. edn., dir. Stanford Inst. Higher Edn. Rsch., Calif., 1988-96; sr. v.p. P.R. Taylor Assocs., 1995-99; sr. rschr. Nat. Ctr. for Postsecondary Imrprovement, 1996—; pres. The Jackson Hole Higher Edn. Group, Inc., 1996—. Bd. dirs. Diebold, Inc., 1979-95; mem. univ. grants com. Hong Kong, 1990—; mem. coun. Yale U., 1980-95; mgmt. cons.; mem. Stanford Mgmt. Co., 1991-93. Author: Stochastic Models of Buying Behavior, 1970, Marketing Management, 1972, Market Segmentation, 1972, Planning Models for Colleges and Universities, 1981, Endowment, 1991, Resource Allocation in Higher Education, 1996; mem. editl. bd. Jour. Mktg. Rsch., 1964-70, Harcourt, Brace Jovanovich, 1965-71; contbr. articles to profl. jours. Bd. dirs. Palo Alto-Stanford chpt. United Way, 1978-80, Stanford U. Hosp., 1980-91, MAC, Inc., 1969-84, EDUCOM, 1983-86. Ford Found. faculty rsch. fellow, 1966-67 Mem. Am. Mktg. Assn. (bd. dirs. 1971-73, v.p. edn. 1976-77), Inst. Mgmt. Scis. Office: The Jackson Hole Higher Edn Group Inc PO Box 9849 Jackson WY 83002-9849

MAST, ROBERT FREDERICK, structural engineer; b. Springfield, Ill., May 20, 1934; BArch, U. Ill., 1957. Registered profl. engr., Wash., Fla., Mo., Tex., Mich., Colo., Ill. Design engr. Anderson, Birkeland, Anderson & Mast, Tacoma, 1959-62, ptnr., 1963-65; exec. v.p. to chmn. bd. ABAM Engrs. Inc., 1966-86, chmn. bd., 1986-97; prin. BERGER/ABAM Engrs. Inc., Federal Way, Wash., 1997—. Contbr. articles to profl. jours. Recipient Boase award Reinforced Concrete Council, 1997, Cons. Engrs. Coun. Washington Engr. of Yr. award, 2001. Mem. Nat. Acad. Engrs., Am. Soc. Civil Engrs. (TY Lin award 1969, 73, Opal Design award 2001), Soc. Naval Archs. & Marine Engrs., Marine Tech. Soc., Reinforced Concrete Rsch. Council (Boase award 1997); fellow Prestressed Concrete Inst. (Martin P. Korn award 1992), Am. Concrete Inst. (bldg. code com. 318 1984, tech. activity com. 1988-94, v.p. 1993-96, pres. 1997) Office: BERGER/ABAM Engineers Inc 33301 9th Ave S Ste 300 Federal Way WA 98003-2600 Fax: 253-431-2250. E-mail: mast@abam.com*

MASTERS, LEE, broadcast executive; married; 2 children. Student, Temple U. Various positions including programmer, sta. mgr., owner radio stas.; exec. v.p., gen. mgr. MTV; pres., CEO E! Entertainment TV, 1990—. Conf. co-chair CTAM '96. Mem. Nat. Cable TV Assn. (Vanguard award for programmers 1995, pub. affairs com., co-chair state and local govt. com.). Office: E! Entertainment TV Inc 12312 W Olympic Blvd Los Angeles CA 90064-1033

MASTERSON, WILLIAM A. retired judge; b. N.Y.C., June 25, 1931; s. John Patrick and Helen Audrey (O'Hara) M.; m. Julie Dohrmann Cosgrove; children: Mark, Mary, Timothy, Barbara. BA, UCLA, 1953, JD, 1958. Bar: Calif. 1959, U.S. Supreme Ct. 1965.. Assoc. Sheppard, Mullin, Richter & Hampton, L.A., 1952-62, pntr., 1962-79; ptnr. Rogers & Wells, 1979-83, Skadden, Arps, Slate, Meagher & Flom, 1983-87; judge L.A. Superior Ct., 1987-92; justice Ct. Appeal, 1993-2000; ret., 2000. Author, editor: Civil Trial Practice: Strategies and Techniques, 1986. With inf. U.S. Army, 1953-55. Fellow Am. Coll. Trial Lawyers; mem. Order of Coif. Office: PO Box 190 Mendocino CA 95460 E-mail: wmasterson@pobox.com

MASYS, DANIEL RICHARD, medical school director; b. Columbus, Ohio, Mar. 6, 1949; s. Paul John and Jane Marie (Mollenauer) M.; m. Linda Suzanne Bross, June 2, 1974; 1 child, Christopher. AB in Biochemistry, Princeton U., 1971; MD, Ohio State U., 1974. Diplomate Am. Bd. Internal Medicine. Staff hematologist, oncologist U.S. Naval Hosp., San Diego, 1980-84; chief ICRDB br. NIH, Bethesda, Md., 1984-86; dir. Lister Hill Nat. Ctr. Nat. Libr. Medicine, Bethesda, 1986-94; dir. biomed. informatics, assoc. clin. prof. Sch. Medicine U. Calif., San Diego, 1994—. Assoc. editor Acad. Medicine jour., 1988-91. Mem. high performance computing White House Office of Sci., Washington, 1991-94; rep. Fed. Networking Coun., Washington, 1991-94. Capt. USPHS, 1984-94. Fellow ACP, Am. Coll. Med. Informatics (exec. com. 1989-92); mem. Am. Med. Informatics Assn. (bd. dirs. 1992-95, assoc. editor jour. 1993—, Pres.'s award 1992), Alpha Omega Alpha. Office: U Calif San Diego Sch Medicine Basic Sci 9500 Gilman Dr Bldg 1317 La Jolla CA 92093-5003

MATARAZZO, HARRIS STARR, lawyer; b. Portland, Oreg., July 24, 1957; s. Joseph Dominic and Ruth Wood (Gadbois) M.; m. Judith Grace Hudson, Jan. 2, 1988. AB in Polit. Sci., Brown U., 1979; JD, Northwestern Sch. Law, Portland, 1983. Bar: Oreg. 1986, U.S. Dist. Ct. Oreg. 1986, U.S. Ct. Appeals (9th cir.) 1986, U.S. Supreme Ct. 1992. With Aitchison, Imperati, Paull, Barnett and Sherwood, Portland, 1986; assoc. Parks & Bauer, Salem, Oreg., 1987-88; pvt. practice Portland, 1988—. Sprk. Mental Health and the Law conf. Med. Ednl. Svcs., Inc., 1995, 96. Contbr. to Criminal Law Handbook, 1994, 98. Mem. Hist. Preservation League Oreg., Portland, 1984—, Oreg. State Pub. Interest Rsch. Group, Portland, 1985—, The Old Ch. Soc., Portland, 1986; bd. dirs. Bosco Milligan Found., 1992—, Rape Survivors Inc., 1994, Lincoln H.S. Alumni Assn., 1995—, Morrison Ctr., 1996-2001, Network Housing, Inc., 1998—, Oreg. Advocacy Ctr., 1998, 2000—, Italian Businessmen's Club, 1998—, InAct, Inc., 1998—, Rosemont Treatment Ctr. and Sch., 1998-99, Friends of Simon Benson House, 1998—, Parents Anonymous, 2001—; mem. vestry Trinity Episcopal Ch., 1992-95, 2001—; mem. Oreg. Advocacy Ctr. Mental Health Adv. Coun., 1996-2000; mem. planned giving com. Multnomah County Libr., 1997—. Mem. ABA, Fed. Bar Assn., Oreg. State Bar Assn., Oreg. Criminal Def. Lawyers Assn. (spkr. State of Mind. conf. 1990, Property Crimes conf. 1999), Multnomah County Bar Assn. Office: Bank Am Fin Ctr 121 SW Morrison St Ste 1020 Portland OR 97204-3140

MATARAZZO, JOSEPH DOMINIC, psychologist, educator; b. Caiazzo, Italy, Nov. 12, 1925; (parents Am. citizens); s. Nicholas and Adeline (Mastroianni) M.; m. Ruth Wood Gadbois, Mar. 26, 1949; children: Harris, Elizabeth, Sara. Student, Columbia U., 1944; BA, Brown U., 1946; MS, Northwestern U., 1950, PhD, 1952. Fellow in med. psychology Washington U. Sch. Medicine, 1950-51; instr. Washington U., 1951-53, asst. prof., 1953-55; rsch. assoc. Harvard Med. Sch., assoc. psychologist Mass. Gen. Hosp., 1955-57; prof., head med. psychol. dept. Oreg. Health Scis. U., Portland, 1957-96, prof. behavioral neurosci., 1996—. Mem. behavioral medicine study sect. NIH; mem. nat. mental health adv. coun. NIMH; mem. bd. regents Uniformed Svcs. U. Health Scis., 1974-80. Author: Wechsler's Measurement and Appraisal of Adult Intelligence, 5th edit., 1972, (with A.N. Wiens) The Interview: Research on its Anatomy and Structure, 1972, (with Harper and Wiens) Nonverbal Communication, 1978; editor: Behavioral Health: A Handbook of Health Enhancement and Disease Prevention, 1984; editorial bd.: Jour. Clin. Psychology, 1962-96 ; cons. editor: Contemporary Psychology, 1962-70, 80-93, Intelligence: An Interdisciplinary Jour, 1976-90, Jour. Behavioral Medicine, 1977— , Profl. Psychology, 1978-94, Jour. Cons. and Clin. Psychology, 1978-85; editor: Psychology series Aldine Pub. Co, 1964-74; psychology editor: Williams & Wilkins Co, 1974-77; contbr. articles to psychol. jours. With USNR, 1943-47; capt. Res. Recipient Hofheimer prize Am. Psychiat. Assn., 1962 Fellow AAAS, APA (pres. 1989-90, divsn. health psychology 1978-89, mem. coun. reps. 1982-91, bd. dirs. 1986-90, Ann. Disting. Profl. Contbn. award 1991, Annual Gold Medal for Life Achievement in the Application of Psychology 2001); mem. Western Psychol. Assn. (pres. 1986-97), Am. Assn. State Psychology Bds. (pres. 1963-64), Nat. Assn. Mental Health (bd. dirs.), Oreg. Mental Health Assn. (bd. dirs., pres. 1962-63), Internat. Coun. Psychologists (bd. dirs. 1972-74, pres. 1976-77), Am. Psychol. Found. (pres. 1994-2000). Home: 1934 SW Vista Ave Portland OR 97201-2455 Office: Oreg Health Scis U Sch Medicine 3181 SW Sam Jackson Park Rd Portland OR 97201-3011 Fax: 503-494-5972. E-mail: matarazz@ohsu.edu

MATASEJE, VERONICA JULIA, sales executive; b. St. Ann's, Ontario, Can., Apr. 5, 1949; came to U.S., 1985; d. John and Anna Veronica M. Grad. H.S., Smithville, Can. Clk. typist, typesetter Crown Life Ins. Co., Toronto, Can., 1966-70; typesetter Toronto Life/Calendar Mag., 1970-71; typesetter, exec. sec. Cerebrus Prodns. Ltd., Toronto, 1971-74; pres. Veron Prodns. Ltd., Toronto, 1975-81, Acclaim Records Inc., Toronto, 1981-88; pvt. health care provider Las Vegas, Nev., 1989-94; retail sales mgr. Top Cats, Las Vegas, 1994-00; pres. Abracadabra Music Corp., 2000—. Campaign vol. Dist. Atty., Las Vegas, 1994; vol. pilot Angel Planes, Las Vegas, 1989. Avocations: gardening, interior design, showing cats, travel, music. Home: 4326 Caliente St Las Vegas NV 89119-5801 Office: Top Cats PO Box 61173 Las Vegas NV 89160-1173 E-mail: vm@abracadabramusic.com

MATAYOSHI, CORALIE CHUN, lawyer, bar association executive; b. Honolulu, June 2, 1956; d. Peter J. and Daisy (Look) Chun; m. Ronald F. Matayoshi, Aug. 8, 1981; children: Scot, Kelly, Alana. BA, U. Calif., Berkeley, 1978; JD, U. Calif., San Francisco, 1981. Bar: Hawaii 1981, U.S. Dist. Ct. Hawaii 1981. Trial atty. U.S. Dept. Justice Antitrust, Washington, 1981-84; assoc. Chun, Kerr, & Dodd, Honolulu, 1984-86; exec. dir. Hawaii Inst. of CLE, Honolulu, 1987-90, Hawaii State Bar Assn., Honolulu, 1990—. Arbitrator Ct. Annexed Arbitration Program, Honolulu, 1992—; adv. bd. Channel 2 TV Action Line, Honolulu, 1993—. Contbr. chapters to books. Bd. dirs. Neighborhood Justice Ctr., 1994-97, mediator, 1997—. Office: Hawaii State Bar Assn 1132 Bishop St Ste 906 Honolulu HI 96813-2814

MATEJU, JOSEPH FRANK, hospital administrator; b. Cedar Rapids, Iowa, Oct. 18, 1927; s. Joseph Frank and Adeline (Smid) M. B.A., U. N.Mex., 1951; M.A., N.Mex. State U., 1957. Sr. juvenile probation officer, San Diego County, 1958-64; adminstr. Villa Solano State Sch., Hagerman, N.Mex., 1965-67; state coordinator on mental retardation planning N.Mex. Dept. Hosps. and Instns., Santa Fe, 1969-70; adminstr. Los Lunas (N.Mex.) Hosp. and Tng. Sch., 1968-69, 70-85. Pres., bd. dirs. Intercare. Bd. dirs. Mountain-Plains region Deaf-Blind Program. Served with USAAF, 1946-47. Fellow Am. Assn. Mental Deficiency; fellow Am. Coll. Nursing Home Adminstrs.; mem. Am. Assn. Retarded Children, Albuquerque Assn. Retarded Citizens, N.Mex. Hosp. Assn., Pi Gamma Mu. Home: 405 Fontana Pl NE Albuquerque NM 87108-1168

MATERA, FRANCES LORINE, elementary educator; b. Eustis, Nebr., June 28, 1926; d. Frank Daniel and Marie Mathilda (Hess) Daiss; m. Daniel Matera, Dec. 27, 1973; children: Richard William Post, Mary Jane Post Craig. Luth. tchrs. diploma, Concordia U., Seward, Nebr., 1947, BS in Edn., 1956; MEd, U. Oreg., 1963. Elementary tchr. Our Savior's Luth. Ch., Colorado Springs, Colo., 1954-57; tchr. 5th grade Monterey (Calif.) Pub. Schs., 1957-59; tchr. 1st grade Roseburg (Oreg.) Schs., 1959-60; tchr. several schs. Palm Springs (Calif.) Unified Sch. Dist., 1960-73; tchr. 3rd grade Vista del Monte Sch., Palm Springs, Calif., 1973-93; ret., 1993. Named Tchr. of the Yr., Palm Springs Unified Schs. Mem. Kappa Kappa Iota (chpt. and state pres.). E-mail: Franmatera7@aol.com

MATHES, STEPHEN JOHN, plastic and reconstructive surgeon, educator; b. New Orleans, Aug. 17, 1943; s. John Ernest and Norma (Deutsch) M.; m. Jennifer Tandy Woodbridge, Nov. 26, 1966; children: David, Brian, Edward. BS, La. State U., 1964; MD, La. State U., New Orleans, 1968. Diplomate Am. Bd. Surgery, Am. Bd. Plastic Surgery (dir. 1993—). Asst. prof. surgery Wash. U., St. Louis, 1977-78; assoc. prof. U. Calif., San Francisco, 1978-84, prof. surgery, 1984, prof. surgery, anatomy and cell biology, 1984-85, also bd. dirs. craniofacial anomalies; head plastic surgery sect. U. Mich., Ann Arbor, 1984-85, prof. surgery, 1984-85; prof. surgery, head plastic and reconstructive surgery div. U. Calif., San Francisco, 1985—, prof. growth and devel. Sch. Dentistry, 1985—. Author: (textbook) Clinical Applications for Muscle and Musculocutaneous Flaps, 1983 (Best Med. Book award Physician's category, Am. Med. Writer's Assn., 1983), Clinical Atlas of Muscle and Musculocutaneous Flaps, 1979, Plastic Surgery Principles and Practice, 1990, Reconstructive Surgery, 1996; contbr. articles to profl. jours. including Am. Soc. Plastic Surgery, Am. Soc. Aesthetic Plastic Surgery, 1981. Recipient 1st prize plastic surgery scholarship contest, Plastic Surgery Edn. Found., 1981, 83, 84, 86, 93, 99, Spl. Achievement award Am. Soc. Plastic Surgery, 1980, Best Sci. Paper, Am. Soc. Aesthetic Plastic Surgery, 1981; grantee NIH, 1982-85, 86-90. Fellow ACS (chmn. adv. coun. on plastic and maxillofacial surgery 1999—, gov. at large); mem. Am. Assn. Plastic Surgery (Clinician of Yr. award 2001), Plastic Surgery Research Council (pres. 1988), Am. Soc. Surgery of Hand, Soc. Univ. Surgeons, Assn. of Acad. Chairmen in Plastic Surgery (pres. 2001), Plastic Surgery Ednl. Found. (bd. dirs. 1994-2000, v.p. 2001), Accreditation Coun. Grad. Med. Edn. , Residency Rev. Com. Plastic Surgery. Republican. Episcopalian. Avocations: gardening, tennis. Home: 2100 Baker St San Francisco CA 94115-1606 Office: U Calif San Francisco Dept Surgery San Francisco CA 94143-0001 E-mail: sjmathes@pacbell.net

MATHESON, ALAN ADAMS, law educator; b. Cedar City, Utah, Feb. 2, 1932; s. Scott Milne and Adele (Adams) M.; m. Milicent Holbrook, Aug. 15, 1960; children— Alan, David Scott, John Robert. B.A., U. Utah, 1953, M.S., 1957, J.D., 1959; postgrad. asso. in law, Columbia U. Bar: Utah 1960, Ariz. 1975. Asst. to pres. Utah State U., 1961-67; mem. faculty Ariz. State U., Tempe, 1967—, prof. law, 1970—, dean, 1978-84, 89, 97-98. Bd. dirs. Ariz. Center Law in Public Interest, 1979-81; bd. dirs. DNA Navajo Legal Services, 1984-97. Pres. Tri-City Mental Health Citizens Bd., 1973-74. Served with AUS, 1953-55. Mem. Utah Bar Assn., Ariz. Bar Assn., Maricopa County Bar Assn., Phi Beta Kappa, Order of Coif. Democrat. Mormon. Home: 720 E Geneva Dr Tempe AZ 85282-3737 Office: Ariz State U Coll Law Tempe AZ 85287

MATHESON, CHARLES E. federal judge; b. 1935; BS, U. Colo., 1958, LLB, 1961. Bar: Colo. 1961. Ptnr. Fairfield and Woods, Denver, 1961-86; bankruptcy judge for Colo., U.S. Bankruptcy Ct., Denver, 1986-87, chief judge, 1987—. Office: US Bankruptcy Ct US Custom House 721 19th St Denver CO 80202-2500

MATHESON, SCOTT MILNE, JR. dean, law educator; b. Salt Lake City, July 18, 1953; s. Scott Milne and Norma (Warenski) M.; m. Robyn Kuida, Aug. 12, 1978; children: Heather Blair, Briggs James. AB, Stanford U., 1975; MA, Oxford U., Eng.; JD, Yale U., 1980. Bar: D.C., 1981, Utah 1986. Assoc. Williams & Connolly, Washington, 1981-85; assoc. prof. law U. Utah, 1985-91; dep. atty. Salt Lake County Attys. Office, 1988-89; vis. assoc. prof. JFK Sch. Govt. Harvard U., Cambridge, Mass., 1989-90; assoc. dean law U. Utah, 1990-93, prof. law, 1991—, dean, 1998—; U.S. atty. Dist. Utah, 1993-97. Adv. com. on rules of evidence Utah Supreme Ct., 1987-93, Utah Constitutional Revision Commn., 1987-93, adv. com. on the local rules of practice, U.S. Dist. Ct. Utah, 1993-97. Contbr. articles to profl. jours. Chmn. U.N. Day for State of Utah, 1991; mem. Univ. Com. on Tanner Lectures on Human Values U. Utah, 1993-2000, Honors Program Adv. Com. U. Utah, 1986-88, Adv. Bd. Hinckley Inst. Politics U. Utah, 1990-93; trustee Legal Aid Soc. of Salt Lake, 1986-93, pres., 1987; trustee TreeUtah, 1992-93; campaign mgr. Matheson for Gov., 1976, 1980; vol. state dir. Clinton/Gore '92. Recipient Up'n Comers award Zions Bank, 1991, Faculty Achievement award Burlington Resources Found., 1993, Disting. Svc. to Fed. Bar award Fed. Bar Assn., Utah chpt., 1998, spl. recognition award Utah Minority Bar Assn., 1999; named one of Outstanding Young Men of Am., 1987, 1988; Rhodes scholar. Mem. ABA, Assn. Am. Law Schs. (chair sect. on mass com. law 1993), Utah State Bar, Salt Lake County Bar Assn. (exec. com. 1986-92), Golden Key Nat. Honor Soc. (hon. 1990), Phi Beta Kappa.

MATHEWS, ANNE JONES, library educator and administrator, consultant; b. Phila. d. Edmond Fulton and Anne Ruth (Reichner) Jones; m. Frank Samuel Mathews, June 16, 1951; children: Lisa Anne Mathews-Bingham, David Morgan, Lynne Elizabeth Bietenhader-Mathews, Alison Fulton Sawyer. AB, Wheaton Coll., 1949; MA, U. Denver, 1965, PhD, 1977. Field staff Intervarsity Christian Fellowship, Chgo., 1949-51; interviewer supr. Colo. Market Rsch. Svcs., Denver, 1952-64; reference libr. Oreg. State U., Corvallis, 1965-67; program dir. Ctrl. Colo. Libr. Sys., Denver, 1969-70; inst. dir. U.S. Office of Edn., Inst. Grant, 1979; dir. pub. rels. Grad. Sch. Librarianship and Info. Mgmt. U. Denver, 1970-76, dir. continuing edn., 1977-80, from assoc. prof. to prof., 1977-85; dir. office libr. programs, office ednl. rsch., improvement U.S. Dept. Edn., Washington, 1986-91; dir. Nat. Libr. Edn., Washington, 1992-94; cons. Acad. Ednl. Devel., Washington, 1994—. Cons., Waldern U., Mpls., 2001; vis. lectr. Simmons Coll. Sch. Libr. Sci., Boston, 1977; cons. USIA, 1984-85, mem. book and libr. adv. com., 1981-91; faculty assoc. Danforth Found., 1974-84; speaker in field; mem. secondary sch. curriculum com. Jefferson County Pub. Schs., Colo., 1976-78; mem. adv. com. Golden H.S., 1973-77; mem. adv. coun. White House Conf. on Librs. and Info. Svcs., 1991; del. Internat. Fedn. Libr. Assn., 1984-93. Author, editor 6 books; contbr. articles to profl. jours., numerous chpts. to books. Mem. rural librs. and humanities program Colo. planning and resource bd. NEH, 1982-83; bd. mgrs. Friends Found. of Denver Pub. Libr., 1976-82; pres. Faculty Women's Club, Colo. Sch. Mines, 1963-64; bd. dirs. Jefferson County Libr. Found., v.p., 1997-2000; mem. Engl. Speaking Union (Denver chpt. 1995—). Mem. ALA (visionary leaders com. 1987-89, coun. mem. 1979-83, com on accreditation 1984-85, orientation com. 1974-77, 83-84, pub. rels. com.), Am. Soc. Info. Sci. (pub. rels. chmn. 1971), Mountain Plains Libr. Assn. (profl. devel. com. 1979-80, pub. rels. and publs. com. 1973-75, continuing edn. com. 1973-76), Colo. Libr. Assn. (pres. 1974, bd. dirs. 1973-75, continuing edn. com. 1976-80), Assn. Libr. and Info. Sci. Edn. (comm. com. 1978-80, program com. 1977-78), Pelican Bay Women's League, Fla., Naples Philharmonic Leabue (Fla.), Cosmos Club (Washington), Mt. Vernon (Colo.) Country Club, Mountain Rep. Women's Club (v.p. 1997-2000). Avocations: travel, reading, antique collecting, mus. & gallery activities, volunteer work. Home: 492 Mount Evans Rd Golden CO 80401-9626 E-mail: afmathews2@earthlink.net

MATHEWS, BERNICE MARTIN, state legislator, small business owner; b. Jackson, Miss., Nov. 12, 1933; children: Arnold II, Anthony, Aileen, Barbara, Ruben, Clive, Allen (dec.). BSN, MEd, U. Nev. Small bus. owner; mem. Nev. Senate, Dist. 1 Washoe, Carson City, 1994—; mem. fin. com., human resources and facilities com. Nev. Senate, mem. legis. affairs and ops. com. City councilwoman, Reno; mem. Regional EMS Coun., 1974-85; past chair Reno Civil Svc. Commn., 1979-89; active Ch. Youth Dept., 1981-87, United Way Distbn. Com., 1992—, Nev. Women's Fund Adv. Bd., 1992—; bd. dirs. Trukee Meadows Boys and Girls Club, 1987—. Mem. Nev. Nurses Assn., Commn. for Women. Democrat. Office: PO Box 2032 Sparks NV 89432-2032 also: Nev State Legis Bldg 401 S Carson St Rm 208 Carson City NV 89701-4747 Fax: 706-687-8206; 702-673-2086. E-mail: bmathews@sen.state.nv.us

MATHEWS, LAURIE A. state agency administrator; m. Andrew Holecek. BS in Environ. Biology, U. Colo., Boulder, 1974; M in Environ. Engring., Stanford U., 1976. Staff mem. U.S. Senate; water cons. DeLew Cather & Co.; asst. dir. Dept. Natural Resources; acting dir. Gov. Roy Romer's Policy Office; dir. State Colo., divsn. State Parks and Outdoor Recreation, Denver, 1991—. Bd. dirs. Nat. Assn. State Park Dirs. Bd. vols. Outdoor Colo. Office: State Colo Divsn State Parks & Outdoor Rec 1313 Sherman St Ste 618 Denver CO 80203-2240 Fax: 303-866-3206

MATHEWS, MAX V. acoustical engineer, educator; Dir. Acoustical and Behavior Rsch. Ctr. Bell Labs., 1962-85; sci. advisor Inst. de Recherche et Coordination Acoustique/Musique, Paris; prof. music Stanford (Calif.) U. Recipient Silver medal in musical acoustics Acoustical Soc. Am., Chevalier dans l'order des Arts et Lettres, Republique Francaise. Mem. NAE. Achievements include research in sound and music synthesis with digital computers and with the application of computers to areas in which man-machine interactions are critical, computer methods for speech processing, studies of human speech production, studies of auditory masking, and the invention of techniques for computer drawing of typography, the effect of resonances on sound quality; development of a program (Music V) for the direct digital synthesis of sounds and a program (Groove) for the computer control of a sound synthesizer. Office: Stanford U Knoll Rm 218 Mail Code 8180 Stanford CA 94305-8180 Fax: 650-723-8468. E-mail: mvm@ccrma.stanford.edu

MATHEWS, MICH, computer company executive; Cons. to Microsoft; head corp. pub. rels. group Microsoft, Redmond, Wash., 1993, v.p. corp. comms., 1993—. Office: Microsoft Corp Comms one Microsoft Way Redmond WA 98052-6399

MATHEWS, WILLIAM EDWARD, neurological surgeon, educator; b. Indpls., July 12, 1934; s. Ples Leo and Roxie Elizabeth (Allen) M.; m. Eleanor Jayne Comer, Aug. 24, 1956 (div. 1976); children: Valerie, Clarissa, Marie, Blair; m. Carol Ann. Koza, Sept. 12, 1987; 1 child, William Kyle. BS, Ball State U., 1958; DO, Kirksville Coll. Osteo. Med., 1961; MD, U. Calif., Irvine, 1962; fellow, Armed Forces Trauma Sch., Ft. Sam Houston, Tex., 1967-68. Diplomate Am. Bd. Neurol. and Orthopedic Surgery, Am. Bd. Pain Mgmt., Am. Bd. Indsl. Medicine, Am. Bd. Spinal Surgeons (v.p. 1990-92), Am. Bd. Forensic Medicine, Am. Bd. Traumatic Stress, Am. Bd. Clin. Neurosurgery, Am. Bd. Spinal Surgery. Intern Kirksville (Mo.) Osteo. Hosp., 1961-62; resident neurosurgery Los Angeles County Gen. Hosp., 1962-67; resident in neurosurgery Rancho Los Amigos Spinal Rehab. Ctr., 1964-65; with Brooke Army Hosp., Ft. Sam Houston, 1967-68; with 8th field hosp. U.S. Army Neurosurgeon C.O. & 933 Med. Corp, Vietnam, 1968-69; chief neurosurgery Kaiser Med. Group, Walnut Creek, Calif., 1969-77; staff neurosurgeon Mt. Diablo Med. Ctr., Concord, 1977—. NIH student rsch. fellow/early rsch. on the clin. use of electromyography, 1959-61; co-chief resident neurosurgery Los Angeles County Gen. Hosp., 1962-67; asst. prof. biochemistry Kirksville Coll. Osteo. Medicine, 1958-62; asst. lecturing prof. neuroanatomy U. Calif. Coll. Medicine, 1962-65; sec. Am. Fedn. Med. Edn., 1997—; chmn. Am. Bd. Spinal Surgery, 1998, chmn. Am. Bd. Med. Accreditation, 1999—. Author: Intracerebral Missile Injuries, 1972, Intrasellar Chordoma, 1976, Intraoperative Myelography, 1982, Thin Slice Computed Tomography of the Cervical Spine, 1985, Early Return to Work Following Cervical Disc Surgery, 1991, Iatrogenic Tethering of the Spinal Cord, 1998; contbr. articles to profl. jours. Mem. adv. com. Rep. Presdl. Selection Com. Maj. U.S. Army, 1967-69, Vietnam. Recipient Disting. Svc. award Internat. Biography, 1987; scholar Psi Sigma Alpha, 1957. Fellow Congress Neurol. Surgeons (joint sect. on neurotrauma), Royal Coll. Medicine, Am. Acad. Neurologic and Orthopedic Surgeons (pres. 1981-82, bd. dirs. 1990—), Bay Area Spinal Surgery Soc., Internat. Coll. Surgeons; mem. AMA, Calif. Med. Assn., San Francisco Neurologic, Contra Costa County Med. Soc. Roman Catholic. Avocations: pen and ink art, golf, gardening. E-mail: bayareaneuro@aol.com

MATHIAS, BETTY JANE, communications and community affairs consultant, writer, editor, lecturer; b. Oct. 22, 1923; d. Royal F. and Dollie B. (Bowman) M.; 1 child, Dena. Student, Merritt Bus. Sch., 1941, 42, San Francisco State U., 1941-42. Asst. publicity dir. Oakland (Calif.) Area War Chest and Comty. Chest, 1943-46; pub. rels. Am. Legion, Oakland, 1946-47; asst. to pub. rels. dir. Cen. Bank of Oakland, 1947-49; pub. rels. dir. East Bay chpt. Nat. Safety Coun., 1949-51; propr., mgr. Mathias Pub. Rels. Agy., Oakland, 1951-60; gen. assignment reporter, teen news editor Daily Rev., Hayward, Calif., 1960-62; freelance pub. rels. and writing Oakland, 1962-66, 67-69; dir. corp. comms. Systech Fin. Corp., Walnut Creek, Calif., 1969-71; v.p. corp. comms. Consol. Capital cos., Oakland, 1972-79, v.p. comty. affairs Emeryville, Calif., 1981-84, v.p. spl. projects, 1984-85; v.p., dir. Consol. Capital Realty Svcs., Inc., Oakland, 1973-77, Centennial Adv. Corp., Oakland, 1976-77; comms. cons., 1979—. Cons. Mountainair Realty, Cameron Park, Calif., 1986-87; pub. rels. coord. Tuolumne County Visitors Bur., 1989-90; lectr. in field Editor: East Bay Mag., 1966-67, TIA Traveler, 1969, Concepts, 1979-83; editor, writer souvenir program: Little House on the Prairie Reunion, 1998. Bd. dirs. Oakland YWCA, 1944-45, ARC, Oakland, So. Alameda County chpt., 1967-69, Family Ctr., Children's Hosp. Med. Ctr. No. Calif., 1982-85, March of Dimes, 1983-85, Equestrian Ctr. of Walnut Creek, Calif., 1983-84, also sec.; mem. Women's Ambulance and Transport Corps of Calif., Oakland, 1942-46; active USO and Shrine Hospitality Ctrs., Oakland, USO-Travelers Aid Soc., Oakland, 1942-46; adult and publs. adv. Internat. Order of the Rainbow for Girls, 1953-78; comms. arts adv. com. Ohlone (Calif.) Coll., 1979-85, chmn., 1982-84; mem. adv. bd. dept. mass comms. Calif. State U.-Hayward, 1985; pres. San Francisco Bay Area chpt. Nat. Reyes Syndrome Found., 1981-86; vol. staff Columbia Actors' Repertory, Columbia, Calif., 1986-87, 89; mem. exec. bd., editor newsletter Tuolumne County Dem. Club, 1987; publicity chmn. 4th of July celebration Tuolumne County C. of C., 1988; vol. children's dept. Tuolumne County Pub. Libr., 1993-97; vol. Ann. Comty. Christmas Eve Dinner, Sonora, Calif., 1988-96; mem. adv. com. Ride Away Ctr. for Therapeutic Riding for the Handicapped, 1995-96, vol. Hold Your Horses Therapeutic Riding Acad., 1997; vol. Tuolumne County Visitors Bur. and Film Commn., 1996-99. Recipient Grand Cross of Color award Internat. Order of Rainbow for Girls, 1955. Mem. Order Ea. Star (life, worthy matron 1952, publicity chmn. Calif. state 1955). Home: 20575 Gopher Dr Sonora CA 95370-9034

MATHIAS, LESLIE MICHAEL, electronic manufacturing company executive; b. Bombay, Dec. 17, 1935; came to U.S., 1957; s. Paschal Lawrence and Dulcine (D'Souza) M.; m. Vivian Mae Doolittle, Dec. 16, 1962. BSc, U. Bombay, 1957; BS, San Jose (Calif.) State U., 1961. Elec. engr. Indian Standard Metal, Bombay, 1957; sales engr. Bleisch Engring. and Tool, Mt. View, Calif., 1958-60; gen. mgr. Meadows Terminal Bds., Cupertino, 1961-63; prodn. mgr. Sharidon Corp., Menlo Park, 1963-67, Videx Corp., Sunnyvale, 1967-68, Data Tech. Corp., Mt. View, 1968-69; pres. L.G.M. Mfg., Inc., Mt. View, 1969-83; pvt. practice plating cons. Los Altos, Calif., 1983-87; materials mgr. Excel Cirs., Santa Clara, 1987-91, 93-98, acct. mgr., 1991-93, materials mgr., 1993-98, internat. materials mgr., 2000—; buyer Planned Parenthood, San Jose, 1998-2000. Social chmn. Internat. Students, San Jose, 1958-59. Mem. Nat. Fedn. Ind. Bus., Calif. Cirs. Assn., Better Bus. Bur., Purchasing Assn., U.S. C. of C. Roman Catholic. Avocations: electronics, reading, med. jours. Home: 20664 Mapletree Pl Cupertino CA 95014-0449 E-mail: lesliemathias01@msn.com

MATHIES, ALLEN WRAY, JR. former pediatrician, hospital administrator; b. Colorado Springs, Colo., Sept. 23, 1930; s. Allen W. and Esther S. (Norton) M.; m. Lewise Austin, Aug. 23, 1956; children: William A., John N. BA, Colo. Coll., 1952; MS, Columbia U., 1956, PhD., 1958; MD, U. Vt., 1961. Rsch. assoc. U. Vt., Burlington, 1957-61; intern L.A. County Hosp., 1961-62; resident in pediatrics L.A. Gen. Hosp., 1962-64; asst. prof. pediatrics U. So. Calif., L.A., 1964-68, assoc. prof., 1968-71, prof., 1971—, assoc. dean, 1969-74, interim dean, 1974-75, dean, 1975-85, head physician Communicable Disease Svc., 1964-75; pres., CEO Huntington Meml. Hosp., Pasadena, Calif., 1985-94, So. Calif. Healthcare Sys., Pasadena, 1992-95, pres. emeritus, 1995—. Bd. dirs. Pacific Mut. Contbr. articles to med. jours. Bd. dirs. Occidental Coll. With U.S. Army, 1953-55. Mem. Am. Acad. Pediatrics, Infectious Disease Soc. Am., Am. Pediatric Soc., Soc. Pediatric Rsch. Republican. Episcopalian. Home: 314 Arroyo Dr South Pasadena CA 91030-1623 Office: Huntington Meml Hosp PO Box 7013 Pasadena CA 91109-7013

MATHIS, DANIEL R. banking officer; Formerly with United Calif. Bank, Calif. First Bank; former regional v.p. Imperial Bank, San Diego, former exec. v.p. so. Calif. and Ariz. regions, pres., COO, bd. dirs. Calif. Mem. Econ. Devel. Corp. of L.A. County, L.A. Regional Technology Alliance. Bd. dirs. Jr. Achievement of So. Calif. Vet. USN, Vietnam. Office: Imperial Bank 9920 S La Cienega Blvd # 14th Inglewood CA 90301-4423

MATHIS, HARRY, city official; City councilman City of San Diego, dep. mayor, 1999—. Capt. USN, 1953-81, ret.

MATHIS, VIRGINIA, federal judge; Apptd. magistrate judge U.S. Dist. Ct. Ariz., 1996. Office: 5025 US Courthouse 230 N 1st Ave Phoenix AZ 85025-0230

MATIJEVIC, JACOB R. aerospace scientist; BS, Ill. Inst. Tech., 1969; MS, PhD in math., U. Chgo., 1973, PhD in Math. Sys. engr. NASA Jet Propulsion Lab., Pasadena, Calif., dir., mgr. Mars Pathfinder Microrover Flight Experiment, 1994—. Recipient Aerospace Laureate award Aviation Week, Sci. Tech., 1998. Office: NASA Jet Propulsion Lab 4800 Oak Grove Dr MS264 380 Pasadena CA 91109-8001

MATSCH, RICHARD P. judge; b. Burlington, Iowa, June 8, 1930; A.B., U. Mich., 1951, J.D., 1953. Bar: Colo. Asst. U.S. atty., Colo., 1959-61; dep. city atty. City and County of Denver, 1961-63; judge U.S. Bankruptcy Ct., Colo., 1965-74, U.S. Dist. Ct. for Colo., 1974-94, 1994—. Mem. Judicial Conf. of the U.S., 1991-94, mem. com. on criminal law, 1988-94; mem. bd. dirs. Fed. Judicial Ctr., 1995-99. Served with U.S. Army, 1953-55 Mem. ABA, Am. Judicature Soc. Office: US Court House 1929 Stout St Denver CO 80294-1929

MATSEN, FREDERICK ALBERT, III, orthopedic educator; b. Austin, Tex., Feb. 5, 1944; s. Frederick Albert II and Cecilia (Kirkegaard) M.; m. Anne Lovell, Dec. 24, 1966; children: Susanna Lovell, Frederick A. IV, Laura Jane Megan. BA, U. Tex., Austin, 1964; MD, Baylor U., 1968. Intern Johns Hopkins U., Balt., 1971; resident in orthopaedics U. Wash., Seattle, 1971-74, acting instr. orthopaedics, 1974, asst. prof. orthopaedics, 1975-79, assoc. prof. orthopaedics, 1979-82, prof., 1982-85, 86—, adjunct prof. Ctr. Bioengring., 1985—, dir. residency program orthopaedics, 1978-81, vice chmn. dept. orthopaedics, 1982-85, acting chmn. dept. orthopaedics, 1983-84, prof., chmn. dept. orthopaedics, 1981—. Mem. Orthopaedic Residency Rev. Com., Chgo., 1981-86. Author: Compartmental Syndromes, 1980; editor: The Shoulder, 1990; contbr. articles to profl. jours., chpts. to textbooks; assoc. editor Clin. Orthopaedics, Jour. Orthopaedic Rsch., 1981—. Lt. comdr. USPHS, 1969-71. Recipient Traveling fellowship Am. Orthopaedic Assn., 1983, Nicholas Andry award Assn. Bone and Joint Surgery, 1979, Henry Meyerding Essay award Am. Fracture Assn., 1974. Mem. Am. Shoulder and Elbow Surgeons (founding, pres. 1991—), Am. Acad. Orthopaedic Surgeons (bd. dirs. 1984-85), Orthopaedic Rsch. Soc., Western Orthopaedic Assn., Phi Beta Kappa. Office: U Wash Dept Orthopaedics RK 10 1959 NE Pacific St Seattle WA 98195-0001

MATSEN, JOHN MARTIN, academic administrator, pathologist; b. Salt Lake City, Feb. 7, 1933; s. John M. and Bessie (Jackson) M.; m. Joneen Johnson, June 6, 1959; children: Marilee, Sharon, Coleen, Sally, John H., Martin K., Maureen, Catherine, Carl, Jeri. BA, Brigham Young U., 1958; MD, UCLA, 1963. Diplomate Am. Bd. Pediatrics, Am. Bd. Pathology, Spl. Competence in Med. Microbiology. Intern UCLA, 1963-65; resident Los Angeles County Harbor/UCLA Med. Ctr., Torrance, Calif., 1965-66; USPHS fellow U. Minn., Mpls., 1966-68, asst. prof., 1968-70, assoc. prof., 1971-74, prof., 1974, U. Utah, Salt Lake City, 1974—, assoc. dean, 1979-81, chmn. dept. pathology, 1981-93, univ. sr. v.p. health scis., dean Sch. Medicine, 1993-98. Pres. Associated Regional and Univ. Pathologists, Inc., Salt Lake City, 1983-93, chmn. bd. dirs., 1993-99. Author over 200 publs. in field. Recipient Sonnenwirth Meml. award Am. Soc. Microbiology, 1993. Mem. Acad. Clin. Lab. Physicians and Scientists (pres. 1978-79), Assn. Pathology Chmn. (pres. 1990-92). Mormon. Home: 410 South 10 West Farmington UT 84025-2203 Office: U Utah Health Scis Ctr 50 N Medical Dr Salt Lake City UT 84132-0001

MATSIK, GEORGE A. packaging executive; Various mfg., operating postions Ball Corp., metal beverage divn., 1973-93, head of intenat. packaging ops., 1993—; COO Ball Corp., packaging bus., 1996—. Office: Ball Corp 9300 W 108th Cir Broomfield CO 80021-3682

MATSON, PAMELA ANNE, environmental science educator; b. Eau Claire, Wis., Aug. 3, 1953; BS, U. Wis., 1975; MS, Ind. U., 1980; PhD, Oreg. State U., 1983. Prof. U. Calif., Berkeley, 1993-97, Stanford (Calif.) U., 1997—. MacArthur fellow, 1995. Fellow Am. Acad. Arts & Scis.; mem. Nat. Acad. Sci. Achievements include rsch. in interactions between the biosphere and the atmosphere; pioneereed research into the role of land-use changes on atmospheric change, analyzing the effects of greenhouse gas emissions resulting from tropical deforestization; investigating the effects of intensive agriculture on the atmosphere, especially the effects of tropical agriculture and cattle ranching, and is finding ways in which agricultural productivity can be expanded without increasing the level of greenhouse gasses. Office: Stanford U Dept Geology Environ Scis Stanford CA 94305-2115

MATSUI, ROBERT TAKEO, congressman; b. Sacramento, Sept. 17, 1941; s. Yasuji and Alice (Nagata) M.; m. Doris Kazue Okada, Sept. 17, 1966; 1 child, Brian Robert. AB in Polit. Sci, U. Calif., Berkeley, 1963; JD, U. Calif., San Francisco, 1966. Bar: Calif. 1967. Practiced law, Sacramento, 1967-78; mem. Sacramento City Coun., 1971-78, vice mayor, 1977; mem. 96th-107th Congresses from 5th Calif. dist., 1979—; mem. ranking minority, ways and means, s.s. subcom.; dep. chair Dem. Nat. Com., 1995—. Chmn. profl. bus. forum Dem. Congl. Campaign Com.; mem. fin. coun. Dem. Nat. Com.; mem. adv. coun. on fiscal policy Am. Enterprise Inst. Chmn. Profl. Bus. Forum of the Dem. Congl. Co. and Com.; congl. liaison Nat. Fin. Council, Dem. Nat. Com.; mem. Am. Enterprise Inst. Adv. Council on Fiscal Policy. Named Young Man of Yr. Jr. C. of C., 1973; recipient Disting. Service award, 1973 Mem. Sacramento Japanese Am. Citizens League (pres. 1969), Sacramento Met. C. of C. (dir. 1976) Democrat. Clubs: 20-30 (Sacramento) (pres. 1972), Rotary (Sacramento). Office: US Ho Reps 2308 Rayburn Hob Washington DC 20515-0505

MATSUMORI, DOUGLAS, lawyer; b. Salt Lake City, Oct. 22, 1947; BS, U. Utah, 1973; JD, Harvard U., 1976. Ptnr. Ray, Quinney & Nebeker PC, Salt Lake City. Mem. Utah State Bar, Phi Beta Kappa. Office: Ray Quinney & Nebeker PO Box 45385 Salt Lake City UT 84145-0385

MATSUNAGA, MATTHEW MASAO, state legislator, lawyer, accountant; b. Honolulu, Nov. 22, 1958; s. Spark Masayuki and Helene (Tokunaga) M.; m. Loretta Ann Sheehan, Apr. 20, 1986, children, Hannah, Sarah. BS, Bucknell U., 1980; JD, Georgetown U., 1985. Bar: Hawaii 1985, U.S. Ct. Appeals (9th cir.); CPA, Hawaii. Assoc. Carlsmith, Ball, Wichman, Murray & Case, Honolulu, 1985—; CPA Price Waterhouse, 1980-82; mem. Hawaii Senate, Dist. 9, Honolulu, 1992—. Bd. dirs. Moiliili Community Ctr., Honolulu, 1987—. Mem. ABA, Hawaii Bar Assn., Am. Judicature Soc., Hawaii Soc. CPAs. Office: Carlsmith Ball Wichman Murray & Case PO Box 656 Honolulu HI 96809-0656 Address: Hawaii State Capitol 415 S Beretania St Rm 226 Honolulu HI 96813-2407

MATSUNAKA, STANLEY T. state legislator; b. Akron, Colo., Nov. 12, 1953; m. Kathleen Matsunaka; three children. BS, Colo. State U., 1975; JD, U. San Diego. Atty.; mem. Colo. Senate, Dist. 15, Denver, 1994—. Cubmaster, den leader Boy Scouts Pack 190; active Namaqua Sch. Accountability Com. Mem. ABA, Colo. Bar Assn. (former sect. young lawyers sect.), Larimer County Bar Assn. (former sec.), Loveland Sertoma Club (pres.). Democrat. Presbyterian. Home: 2109 S County Road 21 Loveland CO 80537-9052 Office: State Capitol 200 E Colfax Ave Ste 274 Denver CO 80203-1716 also: 2881 N Monroe Ave Loveland CO 80538-3295 E-mail: stanseante@aol.com

MATSUURA, DAVID M. state legislator; b. Feb. 21, 1963; m. Elizabeth Matsuura; children: Joy, Grace, Matthew, Faith. BS in Mgrl. Econs. and Agrl. Econs., U. Calif., Davis. Pres., owner Orchid Isle Nursery, 1985—; sec. A&O Internat. Corp., 1990—; gen. mgr., corp. sec. Umikoa Ranch, 1990—; mem. Hawaii Senate, Honolulu, 1998—. Chair health and human svcs. com., vice-chair jud. com., mem. agr. com., mem. labor com., mem. tourism and intergovtl. affairs USDA/FSA; mem. pres.'s coun. Good News Prison Ministries; mem. Hilo Union Elem. Sch. PTA, Hilo Union and Waiakea Elem. Sch. Safety Bd.; active Haili Christian Ch.; mem. adv. bd. Salvation Army. Mem. Big Island Assn. Nurserymen (dir.), Big Island Dendrobium Growers Assn. (v.p., pres.), Gideons Internat., Hawaii Farm Bur., Hawaii Forest Industry assn. (v.p.), Hawaii Florist Shipper Assn., Nat. Fedn. Ind. Bus., Japanese C. of C. (dir.). Democrat. Office: State Capitol 415 S Beretania St Rm 203 Honolulu HI 96813-2407

MATTATHIL, GEORGE PAUL, communications specialist, consultant; b. Kottayam, India, May 12, 1957; came to U.S., 1985; s. Paul and Annamma M. Bs, U. Kerala (India), 1973-78; MS, Indian Inst. Tech., 1978-82. Project engr. Tekelec, Calabasas, Calif., 1986-89; sr. systems analyst Security Pacific Automation, L.A., 1989-90; sr. design. engr. Telenova, Camarillo, Calif., 1990-91. Cons. Raynet, Menlo Park, Calif., 1991, Larse, Santa Clara, Calif., 1991—, NEC, 1992—, Level One Comm., Sacramento, 1994—, DigitalLink, 1994—, Verilink, San Jose, 1994—, Telebit, Sunnyvale, 1995—, Hitachi, San Jose, 1995—, C-Cor Electronics, Fremont, 1996, Xylan, Calabasas, Calif., 1996—, GoDigital Telecomm., Fremont, 1996—, Diva Systems, Menlo Park, Calif., 1998—. Nat. Sci. Talent scholar, India, 1975-80. Mem. IEEE, Assn. Computing Machinery, Soc. Telecom. Cons., Am. Mktg. Assn. Avocations: photography, biking. Office: Silicom Inc PO Box 2264 Cupertino CA 95015-2264 E-mail: gmattathil@silicom.com

MATTES, MARTIN ANTHONY, lawyer; b. San Francisco, June 18, 1946; s. Hans Adam and Marion Jane (Burge) M.; m. Catherine Elvira Garzio, May 26, 1984; children: Nicholas Anthony, Daniel Joseph, Thomas George. BA, Stanford U., 1968; postgrad., U. Chgo., 1968-69, U. Bonn, Fed. Republic Germany, 1971; JD, U. Calif., Berkeley, 1974. Bar: Calif. 1974, U.S. Ct. Appeals (D.C., 5th and 9th cirs.) 1978, U.S. Dist. Ct. (no. dist.) Calif. 1979, U.S. Dist. Ct. (ea. dist.) Calif. 1991. Asst. legal officer Internat. Union Conservation of Nature and Natural Resources, Bonn, 1974-76; staff counsel Calif. Pub. Utilities Commn., San Francisco, 1976-79, legal advisor to pres., 1979-82, adminstrv. law judge, 1983, asst. chief adminstrv. law judge, 1983-86; ptnr. Graham & James, San Francisco, 1986-98, Nossaman Guthner Knox Elliott, LLP, San Francisco, 1998—. Adv. group. Calif. Senate Subcom. on Pub. Utilities Commn. Procedural Reform, 1994. Mng. editor Ecology Law Quar., 1973-74; contbr. articles to profl. jours. Mem. Conf. Calif. Pub. Utility Counsel (treas. 1988-90, v.p. 1990-91, pres. 1991-92), Internat. Coun. Environ. Law, San Francisco Bar Assn., Fed. Comms. Bar Assn., Power Assn. No. Calif. Office: Nossaman Guthner Knox Elliott LLP 50 California St Fl 34 San Francisco CA 94111-4624

MATTESSICH, RICHARD VICTOR (ALVARUS), business administration educator; b. Trieste, Venezia-Julia, Italy, Aug. 9, 1922; s. Victor and Gertrude (Pfaundler) M.; m. Hermine Auguste Mattessich, Apr. 12, 1952. Mech. engr., Engring. Coll., Vienna, Austria, 1940; Diplomkaufmann, Hochschule für Welthandel, Vienna, 1944; Dr.rer.pol., Hochschule für Welthandel, 1945; Accademico Ordinario, Accademia Italiana di Economia Aziendale, Bologna, 1980—; corr. mem., Austrian Acad. Scis., Vienna, 1984—; D h.c., U. Complutense, Madrid, 1998. Research fellow Austrian Inst. Econ. Research, Vienna, 1945-47; instr. Rosenberg Coll., St. Gallen, 1947-52; dep. head Mt. Allison U., Sackville, Can., 1953-59; assoc. prof. U. Calif.-Berkeley, 1958-67; prof. econs. Ruhr U., Bochum, W. Ger., 1966-67; prof. indsl. adminstrn. U. Tech., Vienna, 1976-78; prof. bus. adminstrn. U. B.C., Vancouver, 1967-87, Arthur Andersen & Co. Disting. chair, 1980-87, prof. emeritus, 1988—. Vis. prof. Free U., Berlin, 1965, U. Social Scis., St. Gallen, Switzerland, 1965-66, U. Canterbury, 1970, Austrian Acad. Mgmt., 1971, 73, City Univ. Hong Kong, 1992, Chuo U., Tokyo, 1992; mem. bd. nominations Acctg. Hall of Fame, Columbus, Ohio, 1978-87; bd. govs. Sch. Chartered Accountancy, Vancouver, 1981-82; bd. dirs. Can. Cert. Gen. Accts. Research Found., 1984-90; internat. adv. bd. CGA Rsch. Found., 1993—. Author: Accounting and Analytical Methods, 1964, Simulation of the Firm Through a Budget Computer Program, 1964, Instrumental Reasoning and Systems Methodology, 1978, Critiqie of Accounting, 1995, Foundational Research in Accounting: Professional Memoirs and Beyond, 1995, The Beginnings of Accounting and Accounting Thought, 2000; editor: Modern Accounting Research History, Survey and Guide, 1984, 89, 92, Accounting Research in the 1980s and Its Future Influence, 1991, French transl., 1993, others; mem. editl. bd. Theory and Decision Libr., Jour. Bus. Adminstrn., Economia Azlendale, Praxiology, Acctg., Bus. and Fin. History. Sec.-treas. Internat. House, U. B.C., 1969-70; bd. dirs. Can. Cert. Gen. Accts. Research Found., 1984-90. Served to lt. Orgn. Todt., 1944-45. Recipient Lit. award AICPA, 1972, Haim Falk award Can. Acad. Acctg. Assn., 1991;Ford Found. fellow, 1961-62; Disting. Erskine fellow U. Canterbury, 1970; Killam sr. fellow U. B.C., 1971-72. Fellow Accademia Italiana di Economia Aziendale (accademico ordinario 1980—); mem. Am. Acctg. Assn. (lit. award 1972), Schmalenbach Gesellschaft, Verb. d. Hochschullehrer für Betriebswirtschaft (exec. adv. council 1976-78), Inst. Chartered Accts. of B.C. (bd. of govs. 1981-82), Austrian Acad. Scis. (corr.), Acad. Acctg. Historians (life) (hon. prof. Centro Univ. Francesco de Vitoria, U. Madrid). Achievements include pioneering analytical methods in acctg. and the computerized spreadsheet. Office: U BC Dept Bus Adminstrn Vancouver BC Canada V6T 1Z2 E-mail: Richard.Mattessich@commerce.ubc.ca

MATTEUCCI, DOMINICK VINCENT, real estate developer; b. Trenton, N.J., Oct. 19, 1924; s. Vincent Joseph and Anna Marie (Zoda) M.; BS, Coll. of William and Mary, 1948; BS, Mass. Inst. Tech., 1950. Registered profl. engr., Calif.; lic. gen. bldg. contractor, real estate broker; m. Emma Irene DeGuia, Mar. 2, 1968; children: Felisa Anna, Vincent Eriberto. Owner, Matteucci Devel. Co., Newport Beach, Calif.; pres. Nat. Investment Brokerage Co., Newport Beach. Home: 2104 Felipe Newport Beach CA 92660-4040 Office: PO Box 10474 Newport Beach CA 92658-0474

MATTEUCCI, SHERRY SCHEEL, prosecutor; b. Columbus, Mont., Aug. 17, 1947; d. Gerald F. and Shirley Scheel; m. William L. Matteucci, Dec. 26, 1969 (div. June 1976); children: Cory, Cody. Student, Kinman Bus. U., 1965-66, Mont. State U., 1967-69, Gonzaga U., 1971-72; BS, Eastern Wash. State U., 1973; JD, U. Mont., 1979. Bar: Mont., U.S. Dist. Ct. Mont., U.S. Ct. Appeals (9th cir.), U.S. Supreme Ct. Mont. Spl. asst.

Commr. Higher Edn., 1974-76; assoc. Crowley, Haughey, Hanson, Toole & Dietrich, Billings, Mont., 1979-83, ptnr., 1984-93; U.S. atty. Dist. of Mont., Billings, 1993—. Bd. visitors U. Mont. Law Sch., 1988—. Mem. editorial bd. U. Mont. Law Rev., 1977-78, contbg. editor, 1978-79. Bd. dirs. Big Bros. & Sisters, Billings, 1982-85, City/County Library Bd., Billings, 1983-93, Billings Community Cable Corp., 1986, chmn., 1987; vice chmn., bd. dirs. Parmley Billings Library Found. Named one of Outstanding Young Women in Am., 1983. Mem. ABA, State Bar Mont. (chmn. jud. polling com. 1985-87, chmn. women's law sect. 1985-86, trustee, sec., treas. 1988—), Yellowstone County Bar Assn. (dir. 1984-87, pres.-elect 1986-87, pres. 1987-88), Billings C. of C. (leadership com. 1986, legis. affairs com. 1984). Democrat. Mem. Unitarian Ch. Home: 1804 Virginia Ln Billings MT 59102-3626 Office: US Attorney Western Federal Savings & Loan Bldg 2929 3rd Ave N Billings MT 59101-1944

MATTHEW, LYN, sales and marketing executive consultant; b. Long Beach, Calif., Dec. 15, 1936; d. Harold G. and Beatrice (Hunt) Matthew; m. Wayne Thomas Castleberry, Aug. 12, 1961 (div. Jan. 1976); children: Melanie, Cheryl, Nicole, Matthew. BS, U. Calif., Davis, 1958; MA, Ariz. State U., 1979. Cert. hotel sales exec., meeting profl. Pres. Davlyn Cons. Found., Scottsdale, Ariz., 1979-82; cons., vis. prof. The Art Bus., Scottsdale, 1982—; pres., dir. sales and mktg. Embassy Suites, Scottsdale, 1987-98; pres., Matthew Enterprises, Inc., Scottsdale, 1998—. Trustee Hotel Sales and Mktg. Assn. Internat. Found., 1988-90, chmn., 1991-93, mem. exec. com., 1993-95; mktg. exec. HSMAI, 1998—; vis. prof. Maricopa C.C., Phoenix, 1979—, Ariz. State U., Tempe, 1980-83; cons. Women's Caucus for Art, Phoenix, 1983-88; state dir. AOBTA, 1999—. Author: The Business Aspects of Art, Book I, 1979, Book II, 1989, Marketing Strategies for the Creative Artist, 1985, Moxibustion Manual, 1999. Bd. dirs. Rossom House and Heritage Square Found., Phoenix, 1987-88. Mem. Women Image Now (Achievement and Contbn. in Visual Arts award 1983), Women in Higher Edn., Nat. Women's Caucus for Art (v.p. 1981-83), Ariz. Women's Caucus for Art (pres. 1980-82, hon. advisor 1986-87), Ariz. Vocat. Edn. Assn. (sec. 1978-80), Ariz. Visionary Artists (treas. 1987-89), Hotel Sales and Mktg. Assn. Internat. (pres. Great Phoenix chpt. 1988-89, regional dir. 1989-90, bd. dirs. 1985-90), CHME (profl. designation tng. chair 1995, cert. commr. 1998-2000), Meeting Planners Internat. (v.p. Ariz. Sunbelt chpt. 1989-91, pres. 1991-92, Supplier of Yr. award 1988, CMP cert. trainer 1995—), Soc. Govt. Meeting Planners (charter bd. dirs. 1987, Sam Gilmer award 1992, nat. conf. co-chair 1993-94), Ariz. Visionary Artists (treas. 1987-88), Ariz. Acad. Performing Arts (v.p. bd. dirs. 1987-88, pres. 1988-89).

MATTHEW, NEIL EDWARD, artist, educator; b. Anderson, Ind., Jan. 19, 1925; s. Mark Neil and Mary Bertha (Clifford) M.; m. Jeannette Morrow, Dec. 22, 1963. BA in Edn., Ariz. State U., 1949; MFA, Ind. U., 1955; postgrad., U. Iowa, 1957-58, State Acad. of Fine Arts, Stuttgart, Germany, 1959-60. Tchr., art Covington (Ind.) Jr. H.S., 1949-50, Clay H.S., South Bend, Ind., 1955-57; instr. art Ind. U., Kokomo, 1960-64, instr. to asst. prof. art. Indpls., 1964-71; asst. to assoc. prof. art Herron Sch. Art/Ind. U. Purdue U., Indpls., 1971-87, assoc. prof. emeritus, 1987—. Art exhbit judge Kokomo Art Assn., Ind., 1970; rschr. for salary studies AAUP, Ind. U. Purdue U., 1970s, others. Painter oils, acrylics, and watercolors, 1945—; printmaker etching and woodcuts, 1953—; photographer; one-man shows include: Lyman-Snodgrass Gallery, Indpls., 1984, Lieber's Gallery, Indpls., 1962, 68, Purdue U. Gallery, 1962, Ind. U. Med. Ctr., Indpls., 1966, Ind. U. at Kokomo, 1967, Ind. U. Purdue U. Archives and Libr., 1996, 98, others; group shows include: Ind. Arts Competition, 1988, Purdue U., 1966, 69, Libr. of Congress, 1956, 58, 59, numerous others; work represented at Lieber's Gallery, Indpls., 1959-73, Assoc. Am. Artists, N.Y.C., 1965-72, Lyman-Snodgrass Gallery, Indpls., 1984-85, Ruschman Gallery, Indpls., 1989—; permanent collections include: U. Ariz. Mus. of Art, Tucson, Ctr. for Creative Photograhy, Tucson, Archives, Ind. U. -Purdue U. at Indpls., Indpls. Mus. Art, others; copper plate included in ednl. show U. Ariz. Mus. Art, 2000. Pvt. first class U.S. Army, 1950-52. Named Outstanding Art Grad., Ariz. State U., Tempe, 1949; recipient tuition scholarship U. Iowa, Iowa City, 1957-58; Fulbright grantee, Stuttgart, 1959-60. Mem. Soc. Ind. Pioneers, Coll. Art Assn., Ctr. for Creative Photography, Assocs. of Art History (bd. dirs. 1991-97), Fulbright Assn. Republican. Presbyterian. Avocations: travel, reading, art history, fiction. Home: 5233 North Via Sempreverde Tucson AZ 85750-5967

MATTHEWS, BRIAN W. molecular biology educator; b. Mount Barker, Australia, May 25, 1938; came to U.S., 1967; s. Lionel A. and Ethlinda L. (Harris) M.; m. Helen F. Denley, Sept. 7, 1963; children: Susan, Kristine. BS, U. Adelaide, Australia, 1959, BS with honors, 1960, PhD, 1964, DSc, 1986. Mem. staff Med. Rsch. Coun., Cambridge, Eng., 1963-66; vis. assoc. NIH, Bethesda, Md., 1967-69; prof. molecular biology U. Oreg., Eugene, 1969—, chmn. dept. physics, 1985-86, dir. Inst. Molecular Biology, 1980-83, 90-92; Drummond lectr. U. Calgary (Can.), 1995. Advisor NSF, Washington, 1975-77; investigator Howard Hughes Med. Inst., 1989—; mem. U.S. Nat. Commn. for Crystallography, Washington, 1980-86, 88-90. Rsch. fellow Alfred P. Sloan Found., 1971, Guggenheim fellow, 1977; recipient Career Devel. award NIH, 1973, Faculty Excellence award Oreg. Bd. Edn., 1984, Discovery award Med. Rsch. Found. Oreg., 1987, Reed Coll. Vollum award, 1994, Stein and Moore award Protein Soc., 2000. Mem. NAS, AAAS, Crystallographic Assn., Am. Chem. Soc., Protein Soc. (pres. 1995-97), Biophysical Soc. (nat. lectr. 2001). Office: U Oreg HHMI Inst Molecular Biology Eugene OR 97403 E-mail: brian@uoxray.uoregon.edu

MATTHEWS, DAVID FORT, career officer; b. Lancaster, N.H., Sept. 25, 1944; s. Clinton Fort and Mabel Sawin (Oaks) M.; m. Eva Mae Horton, Nov. 10, 1990. BA, Vanderbilt U., 1966; MA, Mid. Tenn. U., 1973. Cert. acquisition mgr. Rsch. and devel. officer U.S. Army Rsch. Inst., Washington, 1974-77; exec. officer 194th Maintenence Battalion-Camp Humphreys, Korea, 1978-79; career program mgr. U.S. Army Mil. Pers. Ctr., Washington, 1979-82; logistics staff officer Dep. Chief of Staff Logistics, Washington, 1982-83; team chief Chief of Staff Army Study Group, Washington, 1983-85; logistics div. chief Multiple Launch Rocket System Project Office, Huntsville, Ala., 1985-88; comdr. Ordanance Program Div., Riyadh, Saudi Arabia, 1988-90; project mgr. Army Tactical Missile System, Huntsville, 1990-94; sr. lectr. weapon systems acquisition Naval Postgrad. Sch., Monterey, Calif., 1994—. Decorated Legion of Merit, Bronze Star; recipient award as project mgr. of yr. Sec. of Army, 1991. Mem. Am. Ordinance Assn., Nat. Def. Indsl. Assn., Assn. U.S. Army. Avocations: spectator sports, water skiing, reading, scuba diving. Home: 83 High Meadow Ln Carmel CA 93923 Office: Naval Postgrad Sch Monterey CA 93943 E-mail: DMatthews@nps.navy.mil

MATTHEWS, DONALD ROWE, political scientist, educator; b. Cin., Sept. 14, 1925; s. William Procter and Janet Burch (Williams) M.; m. Margie C. Richmond, June 28, 1947 (div.); children: Mary, Jonathan; m. Carmen J. Onstad, July 7, 1970 (div.); children: Christopher, Amy. Student, Kenyon Coll., 1943, Purdue U., 1944-45; A.B. with high honors, Princeton, 1948, M.A., 1951, Ph.D., 1953; Dr. hon. causa, U. Bergen, 1985. Instr. Smith Coll., Northampton, Mass., 1951-53, asst. prof. govt., 1953-57; lectr. polit. sci. U. N.C., Chapel Hill, 1957-58, assoc. prof., 1958-63, prof., 1963-70; research prof. Inst. for Research in Social Sci., 1963-70; sr. fellow in govtl. studies Brookings Instn., Washington, 1970-73; prof. polit. sci. and research assoc. Inst. for Research in Social Sci., U. Mich., Ann Arbor, 1973-76; chmn. dept. polit. sci. U. Wash., Seattle, 1976-83, prof. polit. sci., 1976-94, prof. emeritus, 1995—. Guest prof. U. Bergen, Norway, 1980; fellow Ctr. for Advanced Study in the Behavioral Scis., 1964-65; cons. to U.S. Commn. on Civil Rights, 1958-60, NBC News, 1966-68, Ford Found., 1967-68, U.S. Ho. of Reps., 1970-72, others; faculty lectr. U. Wash., 1989. Author: The Social Background of Political Decision-Makers, 1954, U.S. Senators and Their World, 1960, (with James Prothro) Negroes and the New Southern Politics, 1966, Perspectives on Presidential Selection, 1973, (with William Keech) The Party's Choice, 1976, (with James Stimson) Yeas and Nays: A Theory of Decision-Making in the U.S. House of Representatives, 1975, (with Henry Valen) Parliamentary Representation: The Case of the Norwegian Storting, 1999; Contbr. articles to profl. jours. Served with USNR, 1943-46. Recipient Sr. Award for Research in Govtl. Affairs Social Sci. Research Council, 1962; Ford Found. fellow, 1969-70; Guggenheim fellow, 1980-81 Fellow Am. Acad. Arts and Scis.; mem. Am. Polit. Sci. Assn. (treas. 1970-72, v.p. 1985-86), Pacific N.W. Polit. Sci. Assn. (pres. 1977-78), Western Polit. Sci. Assn. (pres. 1979-80), So. Polit. Sci. Assn., Midwestern Polit. Sci. Assn., Inter-Univ. Consortium for Polit. Research (exec. com. 1970-72) Democrat. Home: 2125 1st Ave Apt 1301 Seattle WA 98121-2118 E-mail: drm@u.washington.edu

MATTHEWS, EUGENE EDWARD, artist; b. Davenport, Iowa, Mar. 22, 1931; s. Nickolas Arthur and Velma (Schroeder) M.; m. Wanda Lee Miller, Sept. 14, 1952; children: Anthony Lee, Daniel Nickolas. Student, Bradley U., 1948-51; BFA, U. Iowa, 1953, MFA, 1957. Prof. fine arts grad. faculty U. Colo., Boulder, 1961-96, prof. fine arts emeritus, 1996—, dir. vis. artists program, 1985-96. Vis. artist Am. Acad. Rome, 1989. One-man shows include U. Wis., Milw., 1960, Brena Gallery, Denver, 1963, 65, 67, 70, 74, 76, 78, 80, 83, 88, Colorado Springs Fine Arts Ctr., 1967, Sheldon Art Gallery, U. Nebr., 1968, Denver Art Mus., 1972, James Yu Gallery, N.Y.C., 1973, 77, Dubins Gallery, L.A., 1981, Galeria Rysunku, Poznan, 1983, CU. Art Galleries, U. Colo., Boulder, 1996, Rule Art Gallery, Denver, 1998; exhibited in numerous group shows U.S., Europe, Africa, Asia; internat. watercolor exhbn. New Orleans, 1983, Louvre, Paris, Met. Mus. of Art, N.Y.C., Internat. Art Ctr., Kyoto, Japan, Mus. of Modern Art, Rijeka, Yugoslavia, Taipei Fine Arts Mus., Taiwan, Republic of China, Internat. Watercolor Biennial-East/West, Champaign, Ill., 1997; represented in permanent collections Nat. Mus. Am. Art, Washington, Denver Art Mus., Butler Inst. Am. Art, Chrysler Art Mus., others. Recipient Penello d'Argento award Acitrezza Internazionale, 1958, S.P.Q.R. Cup of Rome, Roma Olimpionica Internazionale, 1959, Gold medal of honor Nat. Arts Club, N.Y.C., 1969, Bicentennial award Rocky Mountain Nat. Watercolor Exhbn., 1976, Am. Drawings IV Purchase award, 1982, others; fellow in painting Am. Acad. Rome, 1957-60, U. Colo. Creative Rsch. fellow, 1966-67. Mem. Watercolor U.S.A. Honor Soc. (charter). Home: 720 Hawthorn Ave Boulder CO 80304-2140

MATTHEWS, GILBERT ELLIOTT, investment banker; b. Brookline, Mass., Apr. 24, 1930; s. Martin W. and Charlotte (Cohen) M.; m. Anne Lisbeth Barnett, Apr. 20, 1958 (div. 1975); children: Lisa Joan, Diana Kory (dec. 1995); m. Elaine Rita Siegal Pulitzer, Jan. 2, 1978 (div. 1999); 1 child, Jennifer Rachel. AB, Harvard U., 1951; MBA, Columbia U., 1953. Chartered fin. analyst. Dept. mgr. Bloomingdale's, N.Y.C., 1953, 56-60; security analyst Merrill Lynch, N.Y.C., 1960; investment banker Bear, Stearns & Co., N.Y.C., 1960-95, gen. ptnr., 1979-85; mng. dir. Bear, Stearns & Co. Inc., 1985-86, sr. mng. dir., 1986-95, Sutter Securities Inc., San Francisco, 1995—, chmn. bd. dirs., 1997—. Bd. dirs. Oak Industries, Inc., Waltham, Mass. Served as lt. (j.g.) USN, 1953-56. Mem. N.Y. Soc. Security Analysts. Democrat. Jewish. Office: Sutter Securities Inc One Sansome St Ste 3950 San Francisco CA 94104

MATTHEWS, LEONARD SARVER, advertising and marketing executive; b. Glendean, Ky., Jan. 6, 1922; s. Clell and Zetta Price (Sarver) M.; m. Dorothy Lucille Fessler; children: Nancy, James, Douglas. B.S. summa cum laude, Northwestern U., 1948. With Leo Burnett Co., Inc., Chgo., 1948-75, v.p., dir., 1958-59, exec. v.p. charge mktg. services, 1959-61, exec. v.p. client svc., 1961-69, pres., 1970-75; asst. sec. commerce for domestic and internat. bus., 1976; pres., exec. com., dir. Young and Rubicam, 1977-78; pres. Am. Assn. Advt. Agys., 1979-89; co-founder Matthews & Johnston, Stamford, Conn., 1989-92; chmn. Next Century Media, 1992—. Mem. adv. bd. Adcom, Carlsbad, Calif., Ambient Capital, Beverly Hills, Calif., Scripps Capital, San Diego, D2 Media, Intuitive Design. Ensign USCGR, 1942-46. Named to Advt. Hall of Fame, 1999. Mem. Advt. Coun. (life bd. dirs.), Sky Club (N.Y.C.), Pine Valley Golf Club (N.J.), Rancho Santa Fe Golf (Calif.), Georgetown Club (Washington), Delta Sigma Pi, Beta Gamma Sigma. Republican. Lutheran. Office: PO Box 2629 Rancho Santa Fe CA 92067-2629

MATTHEWS, THOMAS M. utilities company executive; m. Sherry Matthews; children: Stephanie, Leslie. BSCE, Tex. A&M U., 1965; postgrad., U. Okla., Stanford U., Columbia U. Various engring., mgmt. and exec. positions Exxon; exec. v.p. Tenneco Gas; pres. Tenn. Gas Pipeline Co., Texaco Refining and Mktg., Inc., Dynegy, Houston; sr. exec. v.p. Avista Corp., Spokane, 1998—, chmn. bd. dirs. Bd. dirs. Wash. CEO Roundtable; mem. adv. coun., mem. vision 2020 com. Tex. A&M U. Office: Avista Corp 1411 E Mission Ave Spokane WA 99202-2600

MATTHEWS, THOMAS MICHAEL, energy company executive; b. Luling, Tex., May 20, 1943; s. Chester Raymond and Mary Lucille (Stutts) M.; m. Sherry Dianne Klein, May 25, 1968; children: Stephanie Dianne, Leslie Michelle. BSCE, Tex. A & M U., 1965; postgrad., U. Okla., 1967, UCLA, 1975, Stanford U., 1988, Columbia U., 1993. Staff engr. Exxon Co. USA, Houston, New Orleans, 1965-69, project engr. L.A., 1974-76, div. engr. Houston, 1969-74, engring. mgr. Anchorage, 1976-78; v.p. Exxon Gas, Houston, 1978-81, Tenn. Gas/Tenneco, Houston, 1981-86, pres., 1986-89; v.p., gen. mgr. Texaco USA, Houston, 1989—; pres. Texaco Gas, 1990-93; pres., CEO Texaco Refining & Mktg., Inc.; v.p. Texaco, Inc.; pres. NGC Corp., 1996-98; chmn., CEO & pres. Avista Corp., Wash. Power Co., Spokane, 1998—. Dir. Offshore Tech. Ctr., Tex. A & M U., 1987-89, adv. coun.; bd. dirs. Inroads, Inc. Contbr. articles to profl. jours.; inventor in field. Pres., chmn. Ponderosa Forest Community Council, Houston, 1980-85; mem. PTO, Scenic Pk. Sch., Anchorage, 1976-78. Mem. NSPE (bd. dirs.), Soc. Petroleum Engrs., Soc. Ga. Assn., Am. Petroleum Inst., Natural Gas Supply Assn., Gas Rsch. Inst., Petroleum Club, Northgate Forest Country Club. Republican. Lutheran. Avocations: snow skiing, golf, reading, running, singing. Office: Avista Corp 1411 E Mission Ave Spokane WA 99202-2600

MATTHEWS, WARREN WAYNE, state supreme court justice; b. Santa Cruz, Calif., Apr. 5, 1939; s. Warren Wayne and Ruth Ann (Maginnis) M.; m. Donna Stearns, Aug. 17, 1963; children: Holly Maginnis, Meredith Sample. A.B., Stanford U., 1961; LL.B., Harvard U., 1964. Bar: Alaska 1965. Assoc. firm Burr, Boney & Pease, Anchorage, 1964-69, Matthews & Dunn, Matthews, Dunn and Baily, Anchorage, 1969-77; assoc. justice Alaska Supreme Ct., Anchorage, 1977—, justice, chief justice. Bd. dirs. Alaska Legal Services Corp., 1969-70. Mem. Alaska Bar Assn. (bd. govs. 1974-77), ABA, Anchorage Bar Assn.

MATTHEWS, ZAKEE, psychiatrist, educator; Prof. psychiatry sch. medicine Stanford U., Palo Alto, Calif. Recipient Presdl. Scholar award Am. Acad. Child and Adolescent Psychiatry, 1993. Office: Stanford U Sch Med PBS Bldg C108c 401 Quarry Rd Palo Alto CA 94304-1419

MATTHEWS-BURWELL, VICKI, elementary education educator; Elem. tchr. New Plymouth Elem. Sch. Named State Tchr. of Yr. Elem., Idaho, 1993. Office: New Plymouth Elem Sch 704 S Plymouth Ave New Plymouth ID 83655-3062

MATTINGLY, GARY, city manager; b. Louisville, Oct. 26, 1943; BS in Fin., Calif. State U., L.A., 1967. Gen. mgr. L.A. Fire and Police Pensions Sys., 1982—. Recipient Disting. Alumnus award Calif. State U., 1997. Mem. Calif. Assn. Pub. Ret. Sys. (past bd. dirs.), Govt. Fin. Officers Assn., Internat. Found. Employee Benefit Plans, Nat. Conf. Pub. Employee Ret. Sys. Office: Fire Police Pensions City Los Angeles 360 E 2nd St Ste 600 Los Angeles CA 90012-4207

MATTIS, LOUIS PRICE, pharmaceutical and consumer products company executive; b. Balt., Dec. 12, 1941; s. Louis Wadsworth and Sara Helene (Myers) M.; children: Louis Wadsworth, Deborah Cook Collier. AB in Internat. Affairs, Lafayette Coll., Easton, Pa., 1962; MBA, Tulane U., 1964. V.p., gen. mgr. Warner Lambert Co., Manila, 1971-74, regional dir. Hong Kong, 1974-76, region pres. Sydney, Australia, 1976-79; exec. v.p. Americas-Far East Richardson-Vicks, Inc., 1979-81, pres. Americas-Far East, 1981-84, exec. v.p., 1985-87; group v.p. Sterling Winthrop Inc., N.Y.C., 1987-88, chmn., pres., CEO, 1988-94; dir. Salomon Bros. Fund, 1992—. Mem. Shek-o Golf Club, Turnberry Golf Club, Roaring Fork Club, Snowmass Club. Avocations: skiing, golf, woodworking. Home: 446 Oak Ridge Rd Snowmass Village CO 81615 Office: PO Box 6535 Snowmass Village CO 81615-6535

MATTOX, DONALD, metallurgist, materials scientist, physicist; MS in Solid State Physics, U. Ky., 1960. Weather officer USAF, 1950s; rsch. sci. materials and processes directorate Sandia Corp., 1961-65; supr. metall. dept. Sandia Nat. Labs., 1965-89; tech. dir. Soc. Vacuum Coaters, 1989-92, Assn. Vacuum Equipment Mfrs., 1992—. Co-owner Mgmt Plus, Inc., Albuquerque; cons. Phys. Vapor Deposition, 1989—. Inventor ion-plating process and its continued devel.; contbr. articles to profl. jours. Recipient Disting. award 9th Internat. Congress on Vacuum Metallurgy, 1988. Albert Nerken awd Am. Vaccum Soc., 1995. Mem. Am. Vacuum Soc. (pres. 1985, Albert Nerken award 1995). Office: Mgmt Plus Inc 440 Live OaK Loop NE Albuquerque NM 87122-1407

MATUSZAK, ALICE JEAN BOYER, pharmacy educator; b. Newark, June 22, 1935; d. James Emery and Elizabeth Hawthorne (Irvine) Boyer; m. Charles Alan Matuszak, Aug. 27, 1955; children: Matthew, James. BS summa cum laude, Ohio State U., 1958, MS, 1959; postgrad., U. Wis., 1959-60; PhD, U. Kans., 1963. Registered pharmacist, Ohio, Calif. Apprentice pharmacist Arensberg Pharmacy, Newark, 1953-58; rsch. asst. Ohio State U., Columbus, 1958, lab. asst., 1958-59; rsch. asst. U. Wis., Madison, 1959-60, U. Kans., Lawrence, 1960-63; asst. prof. U. of the Pacific, Stockton, Calif., 1963-67, assoc. prof., 1971-78, prof., 1978—. Vis. fgn. prof. Kobe-Gakuin U., Japan, 1992. Contbr. articles to profl. jours. Recipient Disting. Alumna award Ohio State U. Coll. Pharmacy, 1994; NIH grantee, 1965-66. Fellow Am. Pharm. Assn. (chmn. basic scis. 1990); mem. Am. Assn. Colls. of Pharmacy (chmn. chemistry sect. 1979-80, bd. dirs. 1993-95), Am. Inst. History of Pharmacy (exec. coun. 1984-88, 90-92, 92-95, chmn. contributed papers 1990-92, pres.-elect 1995-97, pres. 1997—, cert. of commendation 1990), Am. Chem. Soc., Internat. Fedn. Pharmacy, Acad. Pharm. Rsch. Sci. (pres. 1993-94), Coun. Sci. Soc. Pres., U.S. Adopted Names Coun., U.S. Pharmacopeial Conv., Clan Irwin Assn., Sigma Xi, Rho Chi, Phi Lambda Sigma, Phi Kappa Phi, Kappa Epsilon (Unicorn award, award of merit 1995), Lambda Kappa Sigma, Delta Zeta. Democrat. Episcopalian. Avocation: collecting historical pharmacy artifacts. Home: 1130 W Mariposa Ave Stockton CA 95204-3021 Office: U Pacific Sch Pharmacy Stockton CA 95211-0001

MATZDORFF, JAMES ARTHUR, investment banker, financier; b. Kansas City, Mo., Jan. 3, 1956; BS, U. So. Calif., 1978; MBA, Loyola U., Los Angeles, 1980. Comml. loan officer Bank of Am., Los Angeles, 1976-78; mng. dir. James A. Matzdorff & Co., Beverly Hills, Calif., 1978—. Mem. Rep. Nat. Com., 1980—. Mem. Am. Fin. Assn., Mercedes Benz Car Club, BMW Motorcycle Internat., Phi Delta Theta. Avocations: tennis, sailing, karate, skiing, sport target shooting. Office: 9903 Santa Monica Blvd Beverly Hills CA 90212-1671

MATZKE, RICHARD H. oil industry executive; Mem. Chevron Corp., San Francisco, 1961, corp. v.p., 1990, dir., 1997, vice chmn. worldwide oil and gas exploration and prodn., 2000; dir. Dynegy, Inc. Office: Chevron Corp 575 Market St San Francisco CA 94105

MAUGHAN, REX, natural healthcare products company executive; Founder Forever Living Products, Phoenix, 1978, pres., CEO.

MAULDING, BARRY CLIFFORD, lawyer, director; b. McMinville, Oreg., Sept. 3, 1945; s. Clifford L. and Mildred (Fisher) Maulding; m. Reva J. Zachow, Dec. 27, 1965; children: Phillip B., John C. BA in Psychology, U. Oreg., 1967, JD, 1970. Bar: Oreg. 1970. Sec., gen. counsel Alaska Continental Devel. Corp., Portland, Oreg., 1970—75, Seattle, 1970—75; gen. counsel Alaska Airlines, Seattle, 1975—84; dir. legal svcs., corp. sec. Univar Corp., Seattle, 1984—91; v.p., gen. counsel, corp. sec. Prime Source Corp., Seattle, 1991—. Mem. editl. bd.: law rev. Oreg. Law Rev. Trustee Good Neighbor Found., Seattle. Republican.

MAUPIN, A. WILLIAM, state supreme court justice; children: Allison, Michael. BA, U. Nev., 1968; JD, U. Ariz., 1971. Atty., ptnr. Thorndal, Backus, Maupin and Armstrong, Las Vegas, 1976-93; judge 8th Jud. Dist. Clark County, 1993-97; assoc. justice Supreme Ct. Nev., 1997—. Bd. govs. Nev. State Bar, 1991-95. Recipient highest rating for Retention as Dist. Ct. Judge, 1994, 96, Highest Qualitative Ratings, 1996, Las Vegas Review Jour., Clark County Bar Assn.; highest rating as Supreme Ct. Justice Clark County Bar Assn. and Las Vegas Rev. Jour. judicial poll, 1998, 2000. Mem. Nev. Supreme Ct. (study com. to review jud. elections, chmn. 1995, alternate dispute resolution implementation com. chmn. 1992-96). Office: Nev Supreme Ct 201 S Carson St Carson City NV 89701-4702

MAU-SHIMIZU, PATRICIA ANN, lawyer; b. Jan. 17, 1953; d. Herbert G. K. and Leilani (Yuen) Mau; 1 child, Melissa Rose. BS, U. San Francisco, 1975; JD, Golden Gate U., 1979. Bar: Hawaii 1979. Law clk. State Supreme Ct., Honolulu, 1979-80; atty. Bendet, Fidell & Sakai, Honolulu, 1980-81; legis. atty. Honolulu City Coun., 1981-83, House Majority Staff Office, Honolulu, 1983-84, dir., 1984-93; chief clk. Hawaii Ho. of Reps., 1993—. Mem. Hawaii Bar Assn., Hawaii Women Lawyers, Jr. League Hawaii. Democrat. Roman Catholic. Home: 7187 Hawaii Kai Dr Honolulu HI 96825-3115 Office: State House Reps 415 S Beretania St Rm 027 Honolulu HI 96813-2407

MAUZY, MICHAEL PHILIP, environmental consultant, chemical engineer; b. Keyser, W.Va., Nov. 14, 1928; s. Frank and Margery Ola (Nelson) M.; m. Nancy Shepherd Watson, Mar. 27, 1949; children: Michael P. Jr., Jeffrey A., Rebecca A. BSChemE, Va. Poly. Inst., 1950; MSChemE, U. Tenn., 1951. Registered profl. engr., Va., Ill. With Monsanto Co., St. Louis, 1951-71, dir. engring. and mfg., 1968-71; mgr. comml. devel. Kummer Corp., Creve Coeur, Mo., 1971-72; mgr. labs. Ill. EPA, Springfield, 1972-73, mgr. water pollution control, 1973-74, mgr. environ. programs, 1974-77, dir., 1977-81; v.p. Roy F. Weston, Inc., West Chester, Pa., 1981-88, Vernon Hills, Ill., 1988-93, Albuquerque, 1993-96, also bd. dirs. West Chester, Pa.; mgr. The Pangaea Group, LLC, Albuquerque, 1996—. Bd. dirs. DeTox Internat. Corp., St. Charles, Ill.; provider Congl. testimony, 1974-81; presenter various workshops, symposia and seminars, 1974—. Contbr. articles on environ. mgmt. to profl. publs., 1974—. Mem. Ohio River Valley Water Sanitary Commn., Cin., 1976-81. 1st lt. U.S. Army, 1951-53. Recipient Environ. Quality award Region V, U.S. EPA, Chgo.,

1976, Disting. Svc. award Cons. Engrs. Coun. of Ill., 1978, Ill. award Ill. Assn. Sanitary Dists., 1979, Clarence W. Klassen award Ill. Assn. Water Pollution Control Ops., 1984. Mem. Am. Pub. Works Assn., Am. Inst. Chem. Engring., Water Pollution Control Assn., Am. Mgmt. Assn. Avocations: reading, travel, home improvements.

MAX, CLAIRE ELLEN, physicist; b. Boston, Sept. 29, 1946; d. Louis William and Pearl (Bernstein) M.; m. Jonathan Arons, Dec. 22, 1974; 1 child, Samuel. AB, Harvard U., 1968; PhD, Princeton U., 1972. Postdoctoral rschr. U. Calif., Berkeley, 1972-74; physicist Lawrence Livermore (Calif.) Nat. Lab., 1974—; dir. Livermore br. Inst. Geophysics and Planetary Physics, 1984-93, dir. univ. rels., 1993-2000; assoc. dir. Ctr. for Adaptive Optics, U. Calif., Santa Cruz, 2000—. Mem. Math.-Sci. Network Mills Coll., Oakland, Calif.; mem. com. on fusion hybrid reactors NRC, 1986, mem. com. on internat. security and arms control NAS, 1986-89, mem. com. on phys. sci., math. and applications NRC, 1991-94, mem. policy and computational astrophys. panels, astron. and astgrophys. survey NRC, 1989-91; mem. sci. steering com. W.M. Keck Obs., 1992-96, mem. adaptive optics sci. team, 1994—; mem. vis. com. Space Telescope Sci. Inst., 1996-2000, Hubble Space Telescope Second Decade Com., 1998-2000. Editor: Particle Acceleration Mechanisms in Astrophysics, 1979; contbr. numerous articles to sci. jours. Fellow AAAS (coun. rep. physics sect. 2001—), Am. Phys. Soc. (exec. com. divsn. plasma physics 1977, 81-82); mem. Am. Astron. Soc. (exec. com. divsn. high energy astrophysics 1975-76), Am. Geophys. Union, Internat. Astron. Union, Phi Beta Kappa, Sigma Xi. Achievements include rsch. on adaptive optics and laser guide stars for astronomy; astrophys. plasmas. Avocations: violin, skiing. Office: Lawrence Livermore Nat Lab PO Box 808 7000 East Ave # L413 Livermore CA 94550-9516 E-mail: max1@llnl.gov

MAXFIELD, PETER C. state legislator, law educator, lawyer; b. 1941; AB, Regis Coll., 1963; JD, U. Denver, 1966; LLM, Harvard U., 1968. Bar: Colo. 1966, Wyo. 1969. Trial atty. Dept. Justice, 1966-67; assoc. Hindry, Erickson & Meyer, Denver, 1968-69; asst. prof. U. Wyo. Coll. Law, 1969-72, assoc. prof., 1972-76, prof., 1976-96, dean, 1979-87, prof. emeritus, 1996—. Vis. assoc. prof. U. N.Mex., 1972-73; Raymond F. Rice Disting. prof. U. Kans., 1984; Chapman Vis. Disting. prof., U. Tulsa, 1987; vis. prof. U. Utah, 1992. Author: (with Garr Houghton) Cases and Materials on the Taxation of Oil and Gas and Natural Resources Transactions, 1990, (with Allen Houghton) Taxation of Mining Operation, 1981, 97; (with Trelease and Dietrich) Natural Resources Law on American Indian Lands, 1977. Coord. Wyo. State Planning 1988-89; spl. asst. Gov. Wyo. 1989-90; Dem. nominee U.S. Ho. Reps., 1990; mem. Wyo. Environ. Quality Coun., 1991-93; mem. Wyo. Senate, Laramie, 1993-97. Mem. Omicron Delta Kappa, Pi Delta Phi. Home: 1159 Escalera St Laramie WY 82072-5020 Office: U Wyo Coll Law PO Box 3035 Laramie WY 82071-3035 E-mail: petemaxfield@earthlink.net, petemax@uwyo.edu

MAXSON, ROBERT C. university president; Former sr. v.p. acad. affairs U. Houston Systems, Houston; pres. U. Nev., Las Vegas, 1984-94, Calif. State U., Long Beach, 1994—. Office: Calif St Univ Long Beach BH 300 1250 N Bellflower Blvd Long Beach CA 90840-0006

MAXWELL, DONALD MALCOLM, college president, minister; b. Watford, Eng., Apr. 6, 1934; s. Arthur S. and Rachel Elizabeth (Joyce) M.; m. Eileen J. Bolander, Aug. 25, 1955; children: Wendy E. Maxwell Henderson, D. Kevin. BA in Theology and Biblical Langs., Pacific Union Coll., 1956; MA in Systematic Theology, Andrews U., 1958; PhD in Biblical Studies New Testament, Drew U., 1968. Ordained to ministry Seventh-Day Adventist Ch., 1960. Pastor No. Calif. Conf. Seventh-Day Adventists, Oakland, Calif., 1956-64; instr. in religion Union Coll., Lincoln, Nebr., 1964-65; prof. in religion Walla Walla Coll., College Place, Wash., 1965-78, v.p. acad. affairs, 1978-83; pres. Pacific Union Coll., Angwin, Calif., 1983—. Bd. trustees St. Helena Hosp., Deer Park, Calif., 1983—, Rio Lindo Acad., Healdsburg, Calif., 1983—; bd. dirs., membership com. Adventist Health/West, Roseville, Calif., 1983—. Rockefeller fellow, 1967-68; Drew U. scholar, 1967-68; named Tchr. of Yr., Wash. State Auto Assn., 1971. Mem. Soc. Biblical Lit., Rotary. Avocations: golf, boating, gardening. Office: Pacific Union Coll 1 Angwin Ave Angwin CA 94508-9713 E-mail: mmaxwell@puc.edu

MAXWELL, JENNIFER, food products executive; m. Brian Maxwell, 1988. PhD, U. Calif., Berkeley, 1988. Co-owner PowerBar Inc., Berkeley, Calif., 1986—. Office: PowerBar Inc 2150 Shattuck Ave Berkeley CA 94704-1307 Fax: 510-843-1446

MAXWELL, NEAL A. religious organization administrator; b. Salt Lake City, July 6, 1926; s. Clarence H. and Emma (Ash), m. Colleen Hinckley; four children. B in Polit. Sci., M in Polit. Sci., LLD (hon.), U. Utah, Brigham Young U.; LittD (hon.), Westminster Coll., HHD (hon.), Utah State U., Ricks Coll.; BA, U of Utah; HHD (hon.), Salt Lake C.C., 1998; MA, U of Utah; Four Hon. PhD's. Legis. asst. U.S. sen. Wallace F. Bennett, Utah; exec. v.p., Neal A. Maxwell pres. endowed chair pol. theory U. Utah, Salt Lake City; various ch. positions including bishop Salt Lake City's Univ. Sixth Ward, mem. gen. bd. youth orgn., adult correlation com. and one of first Regional Reps. of the Twelve; elder Ch. Jesus Christ Latter Day Sts., Asst. to the Council of Twelve, 1974-76, mem. of Presidency of First Quorum of the Seventy, 1976-81, mem. Coun. of Twelve Apostles, 1981—. Mem. Quorum of the Twelve Ch. of Jesus Christ of Latter-Day Saints, Salt Lake City. Recipient Liberty Bell award Utah State Bar, 1967; named Pub. Adminstr. of Yr. Inst. Govt. Service Brigham Young U., 1973. Office: LDS Church Quorum Twelve 47 E South Temple Salt Lake City UT 84150-0001

MAXWELL-BROGDON, FLORENCE MORENCY, school administrator, educational adviser; b. Spring Park, Minn., Nov. 11, 1929; d. William Frederick and Florence Ruth (LaBrie) Maxwell; m. John Carl Brogdon, Mar. 13, 1957; children: Carole Alexandra, Cecily Ann, Daphne Diana. BA, Calif. State U., L.A., 1955; MS, U. So. Calif., 1957; postgrad., Columbia Pacific U., San Rafael, Calif., 1982-86. Cert. tchr., Calif. Dir. Rodeo Sch., L.A., 1961-64; lectr. Media Features, Culver City, Calif., 1964—; dir. La Playa Sch., Culver City, 1968-75; founding dir. Venture Sch., Culver City, 1974—, also chmn. bd. dirs. Bd. dirs., v.p. Parent Coop. Preschools, Baie d'Urfe Que., Can., 1964—; del. to Ednl. Symposium, Moscow-St. Petersburg, 1992, U.S./China Joint Conf. on Edn., Beijing, 1992, Internat. Confedn. of Prins., Geneva, 1993, Internat. Conf., Berlin, 1994. Author: Let Me Tell You, 1973, Wet'n Squishy, 1973, Balancing Act, 1977, (as Morency Maxwell) Framed in Silver, 1985; (column) What Parents Want to Know, 1961—; editor: Calif. Preschooler, 1961-74; contbr. articles to profl. jours. Treas. Dem. Congl. Primary, Culver City, 1972. Mem. NASSP, Calif. Coun. Parent Schs. (bd. dirs. 1961-74), Parent Coop. Preschs. Internat. (advisor 1975—), Pen Ctr. USA West, Mystery Writers of Am. (affiliate), Internat. Platform Assn. Libertarian. Home: 10814 Molony Rd Culver City CA 90230-5451 Office: Venture Sch 11477 Jefferson Blvd Culver City CA 90230-6115 E-mail: morencee@aol.com

MAXWORTHY, TONY, mechanical and aerospace engineering educator; b. London, May 21, 1933; came to U.S., 1954, naturalized, 1961; s. Ernest Charles and Gladys May (Butson) M.; m. Emily Jean Parkinson, June 20, 1956 (div. 1974); children: Kirsten, Kara; m. Anna Barbara Parks, May 21, 1979 BS in Engring. with honors, U. London, 1954; MSE, Princeton U., 1955; PhD, Harvard U., 1959. Rsch. asst. Harvard U., Cambridge, Mass., 1955-59; sr. scientist, group supr. Jet Propulsion Lab., Pasadena, Calif., 1960-67, cons., 1968—; assoc. prof. U. So. Calif., L.A., 1967-70, prof., 1970—, Smith Internat. prof. mech. and aero. engring., 1988—, chmn. dept. mech. engring., 1979-89; cons. BBC Rsch. Ctr., Baden, Switzerland, 1972-82, J.P.L., Pasadena, Calif., 1968-80; lectr. Woods Hole Oceanographic Inst., Mass., summers 1965, 70, 72, 83. Forman vis. prof. aeronautics Technion Haifa, 1986; vis. prof. U. Poly., Madrid, 1988, Inst. Soperiore Tech., Lisbon, 1988, Swiss Fed. Inst. Tech., Lausanne, 1989; assoc. prof. IMG, U. Joseph Fourier, Grenoble, 1980—, Ecole Superieure Physics and Indsl. Chemistry, Paris, 1995—; Shimizu vis. prof. Stanford U., 1996—. Mem. editorial bd. Geophys. Fluid Dynamics, 1973-79, 88-96, Dynamic Atmospheric Oceans, 1976-83, Phys. Fluids, 1978-81, Zeitschrift fuer Angewandte Mathematik und Physik, 1987-96; contbr. articles to profl. jours. Recipient Humboldt Sr. Scientist award, 1981-93; fellow Cambridge U., 1974, 93—, Australian Nat. U., 1978, Nat. Ctr. Atmospheric Rsch., 1976, Glennon fellow U. Western Australia, 1990, F.W. Mosey fellow, 1993, Sr. Queen's fellow in marine scis. Commonwealth of Australia, 1984. Fellow Am. Phys. Soc. (chmn. exec. com. fluid dynamics divsn. 1974-79, Otto Laporte award 1990); Mem. NAE, Am. Geophys. Union, European Geophys. Soc. Office: U So Calif Dept Aerospace & Mech Engr Exposition Park Los Angeles CA 90089-1191 E-mail: maxworth@usc.edu

MAY, ADOLF DARLINGTON, civil engineering educator; b. Little Rock, Mar. 25, 1927; s. Adolf Darlington and Inez (Shelton) M.; m. Margaret Folsom, Dec. 23, 1948; children— Dolf, Barbara, David, Larry. B.Sc. in Civil Engring, So. Meth. U., 1949; M.Sc., Iowa State U., 1950; Ph.D., Purdue U., 1955. Asst. prof., then assoc. prof. Clarkson Coll. Tech., 1952-56; assoc. prof. Mich. State U., 1956-59; research engr. Thompson-Ramo Wooldridge, 1959-62; project dir. Ill. Div. Hwys., 1962-65; mem. faculty U. Calif., Berkeley, 1965—, prof. civil engring., 1965-91, prof. emeritus, 1991—. Guest prof. numerous univs., 1965— , cons. to industry, 1965— Contbr. to profl. jours., books. Served with USNR, 1944-47. Recipient Disting. Engring. Alumnus award Purdue U., 1978, Transp. Sci. and Ethics Internat. award, 1995; Fulbright scholar to Netherlands, 1977; German Humboldt scholar, 1980. Mem. ASCE (Turner award 1994), Transp. Rsch. Bd. (Disting. Lectr. award 1994), Nat. Acad. Engring. (Matson Transp. Rsch. award 1992), Am. Soc. Engring. Edn. (hon.), Inst. Traffic Engrs. (award 1995), Sigma Xi, Tau Beta Pi. Home: 1645 Julian Dr El Cerrito CA 94530-2011 Office: U Calif Dept Civil Engring 106 Mclaughlin Hall Berkeley CA 94720-1720 E-mail: amay@uclink4.berkeley.edu

MAY, BRUCE BARNETT, lawyer; b. Portland, Oreg., Apr. 16, 1948; s. Ralph Barnett May and Barbara (Newton) Evans; m. Deborah Sue Wright, Jan. 22, 1972; children: Alexander, Christopher, Elizabeth, Andrew. BA, Princeton U., 1971; JD, U. Oreg., 1978. Bar: Ariz. 1978. Ptnr. Streich Lang, Phoenix, 1978—. Lectr. various bar and trade assns. Contbr. articles to profl. jours. Dir. Phoenix Mountain Preservation Coun., 1985-89; mem. Paradise Valley Urban Village Planning Com., Phoenix, 1985-87, mem. Men's Art Coun., 1987-91; mem. adv. bd. Corp. Supportive Housing. Lt. (j.g.) USN, 1972-75. Mem. ABA (chmn. land sales regulation com., vice chair divsn. CLE, task force future of CLE, co-chmn. brokers and brokerage com.), Am. Coll. Real Estate Lawyers, Order of Coif. Republican. Episcopalian. Avocations: book collecting, running, boxing. Office: Streich Lang Renaissance 1 2 N Central Ave Fl 2 Phoenix AZ 85004-2345

MAY, PHILIP ALAN, sociology educator; b. Bethesda, Md., Nov. 6, 1947; s. Everette Lee and Marie (Lee) M.; m. Doreen Ann Garcia, Sept. 5, 1972; children: Katrina Ruth, Marie Ann. BA in Sociology, Catawba Coll., 1969; MA in Sociology, Wake Forest U., 1971; PhD in Sociology, U. Mont., 1976. NIMH predoctoral fellow U. Mont., Missoula, 1973-76; dir. health stats. and rsch. Navajo Health Authority, Window Rock, Ariz., 1976-78; asst. prof. U. N.Mex., Albuquerque, 1978-82, assoc. prof., 1982-89, prof., 1989—, dir. Ctr. on Alcoholism, Substance Abuse and Addictions, 1990-99; co-dir., 2000—; sr. rsch. scientist Ctr. on Alcoholism, Substance Abuse and Addictions, 2000—. Mem. fetal alcohol syndrome study com., Inst. of Medicine/NAS, 1994-96; cons. various govt. agys., 1976—; dir. Nat. Indian Fetal Alcohol Syndrome Prevention Program, Albuquerque, 1979-85; mem. adv. bd. Nat. Orgn. on Fetal Alcohol Syndrome, Washington, 1990—; rsch. assoc. Nat. Ctr. for Am. Indian and Alaska Native Mental Health Rsch., 1986—; mem. U.S. Surgeon Gens. Task Force on Drunk Driving, 1988-89; prin. investigator fetal alcohol syndrome epidemiology rsch. in South Africa, 1997—; mem. com. on pathophysiology and prevention of adolescent and adult suicide Inst. Medicine/NRC/NAS, 2000-2002. Contbr. chpts. to books and articles to profl. jours. V.p. Bd. Edn. Laguna Pueblo, N.Mex., 1998—. Lt. USPHS, 1970-73. Recipient Spl. Recognition award U.S. Indian Health Svc., 1992, award Navajo Tribe and U.S. Indian Health Svc., 1992, Human Rights Promotion award UN Assn., 1994, Program award for Contbns. to Mental Health of Am. Indians, U.S. Indian Health Svc., 1996, O.B. Michael Outstanding Alumnus award Catawba Coll., 2000. Mem. APHA, Am. Sociol. Assn., Population Ref. Bur., Coll. on Problems of Drug Dependence, Rsch. Soc. Alcoholism. Methodist. Home: 4610 Idlewilde Ln SE Albuquerque NM 87108-3422 Office: U NMex CASAA 2650 Yale Blvd Albuquerque NM 87106-3202 E-mail: pmay@unm.edu

MAY, RON, state senator; b. Sherman, Tex., Sept. 16, 1934; m. Onilla May. BGS, U. Nebr. Commd. 2d lt. USAF, 1953, advanced through grades, 1974; pres., owner The May Corp., Colorado Springs; Rep. rep. dist. 15 Colo. Ho. of Reps., 1980-2000; Rep. senator dist. 10 Colo. State Senate, 2000—. Mem. bus. affairs and labor and transp. and energy coms. Colo. Ho. of Reps.; mem. govt., vets. and mil. rels. and transp. coms. Colo. State Senate. Mem. Colorado Springs City Coun., 1981-85; charter pres. Acad. Blvd. Sertoma Club; mem. adv. bd. Colorado Springs Internat. Airport; mem. Village Seven Presbyn. Ch. Office: 4980 Daybreak Circle N Colorado Springs CO 80917 also: Colo State Senate State Capitol 200 E Colfax Rm 274 Denver CO 80203 E-mail: ronmay@sni.net

MAYBAY, DUANE CHARLES, recycling systems executive; b. Ft. Dodge, Iowa, Oct. 5, 1922; s. John H. and Florabel (Hibbard) Lungren; m. Mary Trible Parrish, Dec. 18, 1947 (div. Oct. 1972); children: Tina Biggs, Karen Woodward. BA in Mktg., U. Wis., 1948. Product engr. Gates Rubber Co., Denver, 1948-50; asst. dir. sales & mktg. Hi-C divsn. Hi-C and Snow Crop Divsn. Minute Maid Corp., N.Y.C., 1951-63; mktg. dir. Knudsen Foods, L.A., 1963-70; owner Mountain Foods, Altadena, Calif., 1970-76, Maybay Recycling Sys., Irvine, 1976-84; ptnr. Resource Recovery Sys., Irvine, 1984—. Served to lt. col. U.S. Army Air Corps, 1943-45, Italy. Avocation: antiques. Home: 104 Pergola Irvine CA 92612-1704 Office: Peterson Maybay Inc PO Box 17426 Irvine CA 92623-7426 E-mail: dcmaybay@aol.com

MAYDAN, DAN, chemical company executive; BSEE, MSEE, Technion; PhD in Physics, Edinburgh U. Mgr. new technology devel. Bell Labs., 1967-80; dir. technology Applied Materials, Inc., Santa Clara, Calif., 1980-87, group v.p., pres., gen. mgr. Applied Deposition Technology, 1987-94, pres., 1994—. Bd. dirs. Drexler Corp., Electronics for Imaging, Inc.; adv. bd. Komatsu Electronics. Bd. dirs. San Jose Symphony. Recipient Internat. Partnership award Calif.-Israel C. of C., 1998, Israel trade award Israel Min. Industry & Trade, 1998, jubilee award State of Israel, 1998, lifetime achievement award Semicondr. Equipment & Materials Internat., 1994. Mem. Nat. Acad. Engring. Office: Applied Materials Inc 3050 Bowers Ave Santa Clara CA 95054-3201*

MAYER, GEORGE ROY, educator; b. National City, Calif., Aug. 28, 1940; s. George Eberly and Helen Janet (Knight) M.; m. Barbara Ann Fife, Sept. 9, 1964 (div. June 1986); children: Kevin Roy, Debbie Rae Ann; m. Jocelyn Volk Finn, Aug. 3, 1986. BA, San Diego State U., 1962; MA, Ind. U., 1965, EdD, 1966. Cert. sch. psychologist; bd. cert. behavior analyst. Sch. counselor, psychologist Ind. U., Bloomington, 1964-66; asst. prof. guidance and ednl. psychology So. Ill. U., Carbondale, 1966-69; profl. edn. Calif. State U., L.A., 1966—. Cons. in field; mem. adv. bd. Dept. Spl. Edn., L.A., 1986—, Alamansor Edn. Ctr., Alhambra, Calif., 1986-90, Jay Nolan Ctr. for Autism, Newhall, Calif., 1975-86; lectr. in field; mem. study group on youth violence prevention Nat. Ctr. for Injury Prevention and Control, Divsn. Violence Prevention of the Ctrs. for Disease Control and Prevention, 1998. Author: Classroom Management: A California Resource Guide, 2000; co-author: Behavior Analysis for Lasting Change, 1991; contbr. articles to profl. jours. Recipient Outstanding Prof. award Calif. State U.-L.A., 1988; U.S. Dept. Edn. grantee, 1996—. Mem. Assn. for Behavior Analysis, Nat. Assn. Sch. Psychologists, Calif. Assn. Behavior Analysis (pres., Outstanding Contbr. to Behavior Analysis award 1997, hon. life), Cambridge Ctr. for Behavioral Studies (adv. bd.), Calif. Assn. Sch. Psychologists (chmn. practitioners conf. 1994—). Avocations: horseback riding, fishing, swimming. Home: 10600 Pinyon Ave Tujunga CA 91042-1517 E-mail: grmayer@aol.com

MAYER, JAMES HOCK, mediator, lawyer; b. Neptune City, N.J., Nov. 1, 1935; s. J. Kenneth and Marie Ruth (Hock) M.; m. Carol I. Keating, Sept. 20, 1958 (div. Feb. 1981); children: Craig, Jeffrey; m. Patrisha Renk, Mar. 28, 1981 (div. July 2001). AB with distinction, Dartmouth Coll., 1957; JD, Harvard U., 1964. Bar: Calif. 1965, U.S. Dist. Ct (no. dist., so. dist.) Calif. 1965, U.S. Ct. Appeals (9th cir.) 1965, U.S. Supreme Ct. 1974. Assoc. Pillsbury, Madison & Sutro, San Francisco, 1964-72, ptnr., 1973—; ind. mediator, 1992—. Rear adm. USNR, 1957-93. Rufus Choate scholar Dartmouth Coll., 1956-57. Mem. Newcomen Soc., Navy League, Naval Order of U.S., Harvard Club. Office: 12707 High Bluff Dr pmb 200 San Diego CA 92130-2037 E-mail: just-results@msn.com

MAYER, RICHARD EDWIN, psychology educator; b. Chgo., Feb. 8, 1947; s. James S. and Bernis (Lowy) M.; m. Beverly Linn Pastor, Dec. 19, 1971; children: Kenneth Michael, David Mark, Sarah Ann. BA with honors, Miami U., Oxford, Ohio, 1969; MS in Psychology, U. Mich., 1971, PhD in Psychology, 1973. Vis. asst. prof. Ind. U., Bloomington, 1973-75; asst. prof. psychology U. Calif., Santa Barbara, 1975-80, assoc. prof., 1980-85, prof., 1985—, pres., chmn. dept., 1987-90. Vis. scholar Learning Rsch. and Devel. Ctr., U. Pitts., 1979, Ctr. for Study of Reading, U. Ill., 1984. Author: Foundations of Learning and Memory, 1979, The Promise of Cognitive Psychology, 1981, Thinking, Problem Solving, Cognition, 1983, 2d edit., 1992, BASIC: A Short Course, 1985, Educational Psychology, 1987, The Critical Thinker, 1990, 2d edit., 1995, The Promise of Educational Psychology, 1999; editor: Human Reasoning, 1980, Teaching and Learning Computer Programming, 1988; editor jours. Instructional Sci., 1983-87, Educational Psychologist, 1983-89. Sch. bd. officer Goleta (Calif.) Union Sch. Dist., 1981—. NSF grantee, 1975-88. Fellow APA (divsn. 15 officer 1987—, G. Stanley Hall lectr. 1988), Am. Psychol. Soc.; mem. Am. Ednl. Rsch. Assn. (divsn. C officer 1986-88), Psychonomic Soc. Democrat. Jewish. Avocations: computers, hiking, bicycling, reading, dogs. Office: U Calif Dept Of Psychology Santa Barbara CA 93016

MAYERI, BEVERLY, artist, ceramic sculptor, educator; b. N.Y.C., Nov. 2, 1944; d. Bernard and Cora (Wisoff) Howard; m. Earl Melchior Mayeri, Sept. 1, 1968; 1 child, Rachel Theresa. BA, U. Calif., Berkeley, 1967; MA in Art and Sculpture, San Francisco State U., 1976. Tchr., seminar conductor, lectr. Dominican Coll., San Rafael, Calif., 1978, Sonoma State U., Rohnert Park, Calif., 1978, NYU, 1987, Calif. State U., 1989, Creative Growth, Oakland, Calif., 1990, Acad Art Coll., 1990, Foothill Coll., Los Altos Hills, 1990, Natsoulas Gallery, 1992, U. Minn., Mpls., 1993, Sonoma Stae U., Rohnert Park, Calif., 1994, Mendocino (Calif.) Art Ctr., 1995, Fresno State U., 1996, CCAC, Oakland, Calif., 1996, Edinboro (Pa.) U., 1997. Artist: solo exhibitions include Palo Alto (Calif.) Cultural Ctr., 1979, Ivory/Kimpton Gallery, San Francisco, 1981, 83, Garth Clark Gallery, N.Y., 1985, 87, Esther Saks Gallery, Chgo., 1988, 90, Dorothy Weiss Gallery, San Francisco, 1990, 92, 94, 96, San Jose Inst. Contemporary Art, 1990, Robert Kidd Gallery, Birmingham, Mich., 1993; group exhibitions include San Francisco Mus. of Art, Northern Calif. Clay Routes: Sculpture Now, 1979, Smithsonian Instn., Renwick Gallery, 1981, Ivory Kimpton Gallery, San Francisco, 1982, Prieto Meml. Gallery, Mills Coll., Oakland, Calif. 1982, Crocker Art Mus., San Francisco, 1983, Euphrate Gallery, De Anza Coll., Cupertino, Calif., 1984, 88, Fisher Gallery, U. So. Calif., L.A., traveled to Pratt Inst., N.Y.C., 1984, Arts Commn. Gallery, San Francisco, 1984, Signet Arts Gallery, St. Louis (two person show), 1984, Garth Clark Gallery, N.Y., 1985, Robert L. Kidd Gallery, Birmingham, Mich., Animals Contemporary Vision, Major Concepts: Clay, 1986, Fresno (Calif.) Arts Ctr. and Mus., 1987, Canton (Ohio) Art Inst., 1991, Soc. for Contemporary Crafts, Pitts., 1992, Triton Mus. of Art, Santa Clara, Calif., 1992, Nat. Mus. of History Taipei, Taiwan, 1993, Lew Allen Gallery, Santa Fe, New Mex., 1993, Perimeter Gallery, 1995, Duane Reed Gallery, St. Louis, 1997; works in pub. and private collections include: Nat. Mus. History, Taipei, Canton Art Inst., Long Beach (Calif.) Parks and Recreation, L.A. Arts Commn., Mr. and Mrs. Eric Lidow, L.A., Alfred Shands, Louisville, Mrs. Audrey Landy, Atlanta, Karen Johnson Boyd, Racine, Wis., Alan and Esther Saks, Chgo., Gloria and Sonny Kamm. Founder Marin Women Artists, Marin County, Calif., 1974-84. Recipient fellowship visual artist NEA, Washington, 1982, 88; grantee: Marin Arts Coun., 1987, Virgina A. Groot Found., 1991. Avocations: painting, hiking, skiing, gardening, environmentalist. Office: Dorothy Weiss Gallery 256 Sutter St San Francisco CA 94108-4409

MAYHEW, ERIC GEORGE, medical researcher, educator; b. London, June 22, 1938; came to U.S., 1964; s. George James and Doris Ivy (Tipping) M.; m. Barbara Doe, Sept. 28, 1966 (div. 1976); 1 child, Miles; m. Karen Caruana, Apr. 1, 1978 (div. 1994); children: Ian, Andrea: m. Ludmila Khatchatrian, June 29, 1995. BS, U. London, 1960, MS, 1963; PhD, 1967; DSc, U. London, 1993. Rsch. asst. Chester Beatty Rsch. Inst., London, 1960-64; cancer rsch. scientist Roswell Pk. Meml. Inst., Buffalo, 1964-68, sr. cancer rsch. scientist, 1968-72, assoc. cancer rsch. scientist, 1979-93, dep. dir. exptl. pathology, 1988-93; prin. scientist The Liposome Co., Princeton, N.J., 1993-99, May Pharm Consulting, 2000—. Assoc. rsch. prof. SUNY, Buffalo, 1979-93; ad-hoc mem. NIH study sects., 1982-94; cons. to industry, 2000—. Editor jour. Selective Cancer Therapeutics, 1989-91; contbr. articles to Jour. Nat. Cancer Inst., Cancer Rsch. and many other profl. jours. Grantee NIH, Am. Heart Assn., and pvt. industry, 1972-93. Mem. Am. Assn. Cancer Rsch., N.Y. Acad. Sci. Achievements include development of liposomes for drug delivery and patents for new chemical entities and liposome delivery. Office: May Pharm Consulting 3905 W Bertona St Seattle WA 98199-1932 E-mail: eailkmay@aol.com

MAYHEW, WILLIAM A. judge; b. Pueblo, Colo., July 21, 1940; s. Wilbren D. and Dorothy L. (Holloway) M.; m. Marianne J., May 8, 1971; children: Lance, Kevin, Christie. AA, Modesto Jr. Coll., 1959; BS, UCLA, 1961, JD, 1964. Bar: Calif. 1965, U.S. Ct. Appeals (9th cir.) 1965, U.S. Dist. Ct. (no., ea. dists.) Calif. 1965. Dep. atty. gen. State Calif., 1964-67; ptnr., pvt. practice Thompson, Mayhew & Michel, 1968-82; prof. law Miss. Coll. Sch. Law, 1982-86; atty. Sarhad & Mayhew, Turlock, Calif., 1986-88; mng. ptnr. Borton, Petrini & Conron, Modesto, 1988-94; judge Stanislaus County Mcpl. Ct., Modesto, 1994-95, Stanislaus County Superior Ct., Modesto, 1995—, presiding judge, 2000—. Assoc. prof. Coll. Law U. Toledo, 1975-76; lecturer in field. Bd. editors UCLA Law Review; contbr. articles to profl. jours. Mem. Turlock H.S. Bd. Trustees, 1989-94, pres., 1992; mem. standing com. Episcopal Diocese San Joaquin Diocesan Conv., 1991-95; vice chancelor Episcopal Bishop of San Joaquin, 1990-94. Maj. JAGC, Calif. Army N.G., 1966-77. Mem. Am. Bd. Trial Advocates (nat. bd. dirs., advocate, chair western regional conf. 1987, Miss. chpt., sec.-treas. 1985), Turlock Rotary Club, Order of Coif. Republican. Office: Stanislaus County Superior Ct PO Box 1011 Modesto CA 95353-1011

MAYNARD, CATHERINE, medical researcher; BS, U. Manchester. Mgr. core transgenic svcs. Imperial Cancer Rsch. Fund, 1988-92; various positions most recently assoc. dir. Animal Rsch. Svcs. and Microembryology, 1992-96; assoc. dir. animal rsch. svcs. & microembryology Abgenix, Inc., Fremont, Calif., 1996-98, dir. ops., 1998—. Office: Abgenix Inc 7601 Dumbarton Cir Fremont CA 94555-3616

MAYNARD, KENNETH DOUGLAS, architect; b. Hackensack, N.J., Aug. 16, 1931; s. Douglas Harry and Eva (Whiting) M.; m. Myrna Myrtle James, Feb. 4, 1956; children: Colin, Vivien Noll. Cert. in Architecture, U. Natal, Durban, Republic of South Africa, 1958. Registered architect Alaska. Draftsman Morross & Graff, Johannesburg, Republic of South Africa, 1950-51, Anglo-Am. Corp., Johannesburg, Republic of South Africa, 1951-54, Moir & Llewellyn, Empangeni, Zululand, Republic of South Africa, 1955-57; architect Pearse Aneck-Hahn & Bristol, Johannesburg, 1957-60, Manley & Mayer, Anchorage, 1960-61, FAA, Anchorage, 1961-62, Crittenden Cassetta Wirum & Jacobs, Anchorage, 1962-65; prin. Schultz & Maynard, Anchorage, 1965-68, Kenneth Maynard Assocs., Anchorage, 1968-78; pres. Maynard & Partch, Anchorage, 1978-96; prin. USKH, Inc., Anchorage, 1996—. Active Western Alaska Coun. Boy Scouts. Am., Anchorage, 1965-84; bd. dirs. Salvation Army Adv. Bd., Anchorage, 1981-87, Anchorage Mus. Assn., 1969-86, Anchorage Opera Co., 1983-90; chmn. Mayor's Comprehensive Homeless Program Strategy Group, 1992-94. Fellow AIA (pres. Alaska chpt. 1969, N.W. regional rep. for nat. com. on design 1976-89, nat. bd. mem. 1999—); mem. Constrn. Specification Inst. (pres. Cook Inlet chpt. 1993-94), Soc. Am. Mil. Engrs. Republican. Avocation: tennis. Home: 2237 Forest Park Dr Anchorage AK 99517-1324 Office: USKH 2515 A St Anchorage AK 99503-2776

MAYNARD, STEVEN HARRY, writer; b. San Diego, July 4, 1954; s. Harry Clark and Ruby Kristina (Odna). BA in Communications, U. Wash., 1976; MA in Theology, Fuller Theol. Seminary, 1979. Religion writer, gen. news reporter Walla Walla (Wash.) Union-Bulletin, 1979-84; religion writer Houston Chronicle, 1984-87; religion/ethics/values reporter The News Tribune, Tacoma, 1987—. Recipient Mng. Editors award Tex. Associated Press, 1984, Wilbur award Religious Pub. Relations Council, 1981. Mem. Religion Newswriters Assn. Office: 1950 S State St Tacoma WA 98405-2817

MAYNE, EDDIE P. state legislator, former union official; b. Sept. 16, 1945; m. Karen Hibler. Student, Snow Coll., U. Utah; LHD (hon.), Salt Lake C.C. Formerly pres. AFL-CIO; mem. Utah Senate, Dist. 11, Salt Lake City, 1994—; mem. bus., labor and econ. devel. com., mem. rules com.; mem. transp. and pub. safety com.; mem. commerce and revenue appropriations com. Mem. NAACP, VFW, United Steelworkers Am., Lions Club. Democrat. Home: 5044 Bannock Cir Salt Lake City UT 84120-4701 Fax: 801-972-9344. E-mail: emayne@le.state.ut.us

MAYORKAS, ALEJANDRO, prosecutor; b. Cuba; With Patterson, Belknap, Webb & Tyler, L.A., 1986-89; asst. U.S. atty., 1989-99; chief office's gen. crimes sect., 1996-98; U.S. atty. cen. dist. Calif. U.S. Dept. Justice, 1999—. Tchr. trial advocacy Loyala Law Sch., 1997-98. Office: US Courthouse 312 N Spring St Los Angeles CA 90012-4701

MAYTHAM, THOMAS NORTHRUP, art and museum consultant; b. Buffalo, July 30, 1931; s. Thomas Edward and Margaret (Northrup) M.; m. Daphne Chace, Dec. 30, 1960 (div.); 1 child, T.F. Gifford; m. Gloria Maytham, June 11, 1994. BA in Art History, Williams Coll., Williamstown, Mass., 1954; MA in Art History, Yale U., 1956; cert. in German, Colby Coll., 1954. Intern Wadsworth Atheneum, 1955; rsch. asst. Yale U., 1956; head dept. paintings Boston Mus. Fine Arts, 1957-67; assoc. dir., acting dir. Seattle Art Mus., 1967-74; dir. Denver Art Mus., 1974-83; art cons., pub. Artadvisors LLC, Denver, 1983—. Mus. accreditation program evaluator Am. Assn. Museums; past trustee, mem. exhbns. adv. com. Am. Fedn. Arts, N.Y.; past mem. mus. program panel, grants reviewer Nat. Endowment for Arts, Washington; reviewer Nat. Endowment for Humanities, Washington; mem. adv. panel, grants reviewer Nat. Mus. Act, Smithsonian Instn.; past mem. policy panel and adv. com., econ. impact of arts study Colo. Coun. Arts and Humanities; co-founder Consortium of Rocky Mountain Regional Conservation Ctr., U. Denver; founder dirs. assn. Denver cultural agys.; del. Inter-Am. Museums Conf., Oaxaca, Mexico; co-founder United Arts Fund, Seattle; mem. art adv. com. Airport Art Program, Port of Seattle; vis. faculty Leadership Denver program, Pres.'s Leadership class U. Colo.; cons. Aspen Ctr. Visual Arts, Sangre de Cristo Arts Ctr., Pueblo, Western States Arts Found., Santa Fe, BBHC, Cody, Wyo.; lectr. museums, colls., corporate groups and art assns. Exhbns. organized include Ernst Ludwig Kirchner Retrospective, Seattle, Pasadena and Boston museums, 1968-69, Am. Painting from the Boston and Met. Museums, Nat. Gallery, St. Louis and Seattle museums, 1970-71; contbr. articles to profl. jours.; presenter TV programs on collections and exhbns. Boston Pub. TV, WGBH-TV. Trustee Internat. Exhbns. Found., Washington. Recipient Gov.'s Arts award Seattle Airport Art Program, 1972, Denver Art mus., award Downtown Denver Inc., 1978. Mem. Assn Art Mus. Dirs. (officer, trustee, ops. com. sec., future directions. com. chmn.) Office: Maytham Artadvisors 3882 S Newport Way Denver CO 80237-1246

MAZO, ROBERT MARC, chemistry educator, retired; b. Bklyn., Oct. 3, 1930; s. Nathan and Rose Marion (Mazo) M.; m. Joan Ruth Spector, Sept. 5, 1954; children: Ruth, Jeffrey, Daniel. B.A., Harvard U., 1952; M.S., Yale U., 1953, Ph.D., 1955. Research assoc. U. Chgo., 1956-58; asst. prof. Calif. Inst. Tech., 1958-62; assoc. prof. U. Oreg., Eugene, 1962-65, prof. chemistry, 1965-95; prof. emeritus, 1996; head chemistry dept. U. Oreg., 1978-81, dir. Inst. Theoretical Sci., 1964-67, 84-87, assoc. dean Grad. Sch., 1967-71; program dir NSF, 1977-78. Alfred P. Sloan fellow, NSF Sr. Postdoctoral fellow, vis. prof. U. Libre de Bruxelles, Belgium, 1968-69; vis. prof. Technische Hochschule Aachen, Weizmann Inst., Rehovoth, Israel, 1981-82, U. New South Wales, Australia, 1989. Author: Statistical Mechanical Theories of Transport Processes, 1967; also research articles. NSF Postdoctoral fellow U. Amsterdam, Netherlands, 1955-56 Mem. Am. Phys. Soc. Home: 2460 Charnelton St Eugene OR 97405-3214 Office: U Oreg Inst Theoretical Sci Eugene OR 97403 E-mail: mazo@oregon.uoregon.edu

MAZUREK, JOSEPH P. state attorney general, former state legislator; b. San Diego, July 27, 1948; B.A., U. Mont., 1970, J.D., 1975; m. Patty Mazurek; 3 children. Bar: Mont. 1975; atty. Gough, Shanahan, Johnson, and Waterman, Helena, Mont.; mem. Mont. Senate from 23d Dist., 1981-92; Senate pres., 1991-92; atty. gen., State of Mont., 1993—; mem. Revenue Oversight Com., 1983-92; chmn. Senate Judiciary Com.; assoc. editor Mont. Law Rev., 1974-75. Served with U.S. Army, 1970-72. Mem. ABA, Beta Gamma Sigma, Phi Delta Phi, Phi Delta Theta. Office: PO Box 201401 Helena MT 59620-1401

MAZURSKY, PAUL, screenwriter, theatrical director and producer; b. Bklyn., Apr. 25, 1930; s. David and Jean (Gerson) M.; m. Betsy Purdy, Mar. 12, 1953; children— Meg, Jill. BA, Bklyn. Coll., 1951. Actor, star, TV and Films, 1951—, including film Deathwatch, Miami Rhapsody, 1995; night club comedian, 1954-60; writer Danny Kaye Show, 1963-67; co-writer film I Love You, Alice B. Toklas, 1968; writer, dir. films Bob & Carol & Ted & Alice, 1969, Alex in Wonderland, 1970, Blume in Love, 1972, Harry & Tonto, 1973, Next Stop, Greenwich Village, 1976, An Unmarried Woman, 1977-78, Willie & Phil, 1979-80, Tempest, 1982, Moscow on the Hudson, 1984; writer, prodr., dir. films Down and Out in Beverly Hills, 1986, Moon Over Parador, 1988; co-scriptwriter, prodr., dir. film Enemies, A Love Story, 1989, Scenes From a Mall, 1990, The Pickle, 1992, Faithful, 1995, Winchell, 1998. Office: ICM c/o Ken Kamins 8942 Wilshire Blvd Beverly Hills CA 90211-1934

MCALEER, WILLIAM HARRISON, technology venture capitalist; b. Pitts., Feb. 14, 1951; s. William Kearns and Helen (Harrison) McA.; m. Colleen McGinn, Aug. 9, 1975; children: William F., Lindsay J. BS, Cornell U., 1973, MBA, 1975. CPA, Wash. Sr. acct. KPMG-Peat Marwick, Seattle, 1975-78; v.p. Westin Hotels, Seattle, 1978-87; v.p. finance, CFO Ecova Corp., Seattle, 1987-88; v.p. fin., CFO, sec. Aldus Corp., Seattle, 1988-94; pres. e.liance Ptnrs.; co-founder, mng. dir. Voyager Capital, Seattle, 1996—. Bd. dirs. Avocent Corp., ClearCommerce, See Commerce. Pres., dir. Seattle Jr. C. of C., 1977-82; bd. dirs. Big Bros. King County, Seattle, 1994—. Mem. Fin. Execs. Ins., Software Pub. Assn., Wash. Software Assn., Evergreen Venture Capital Assn., Wash. Software and Digital Media Alliance, Wash. Soc. CPAs, Cornell Alumni Club, Columbia Tower Club, Sand Point Country Club. Avocations: hiking, travel, golfing, boating, gardening. Home: 3530 W Laurelhurst Dr NE Seattle WA 98105-5358 Office: Voyager Capital 800 5th Ave Ste 4100 Seattle WA 98104-3100 E-mail: mcaleer@voyagercap.com

MCALISTER, MAURICE L. savings and loan association executive; b. 1925; married. Pres., dir. Downey Savs. and Loan, Newport Beach, Calif., 1957—, chmn. bd. Office: Downey Savs & Loan Assn PO Box 6000 3501 Jamboree Rd Ste 5000 Newport Beach CA 92660-2980

MCALISTER, MICHAEL H. architect; b. Calif. s. Doyle R. and Mary E. McAlister. AA, Bakersfield Coll.; BArch, Calif. Polytech. U. Planning technition Bakersfield City Hall, 1963; carpenter Del Webb Corp., Kern City, Calif., 1964; architectural draftsman Goss & Choy Architects, Bakersfield, 1965-67; architect, v.p. D.G.C. & Assocs., Bakersfield, 1971-80; dir. architecture, v.p. N.B.A. & Assocs., Architects, Bakersfield, 1980-83; architect, pres. Michael H. McAlister, A.I.A., Bakersfield, 1983—. Nepthrology design cons. for various treatment groups and hosps., 1987—. Commr., architectural advisor Historic Preservation Commn., Bakersfield, 1986-87; bd. dirs. Camp Fire Coun., Kern County, Calif., 1980-84. Recipient Architectural Pub. Bldg. Hist. award Beautiful Bakersfield Com., City of Bakersfield's City Coun. and Hist. Preservation Commn., 1985, 87, Exterior Environ. Design Excellence Bakersfield C. of C., 1988, Comml. Design Excellence award, 1984, Design Excellence and Beautification award City of Taft, Calif., 1989, Design Excellence award State of Nev., 1992. Mem. AIA (Calif. Coun., Golden Empire chpt.). Avocations: horseback riding, art and sculpture. Office: 5030 Office Park Dr Ste B Bakersfield CA 93309-0612

MCANELLY, ROBERT D. physiatrist; b. Austin, Tex., Jan. 31, 1958; s. Robert C. and Betty J. McAnelly; m. Suzanne Marie Blickhan, Aug. 18, 1990. BS in Engring., Calif. Inst. Tech., 1979, BS in Physics, 1980; MD, U. Tex., 1987. Diplomate Am. Bd. Phys. Medicine and Rehab. Aerospace engr. Vought Corp., Dallas, 1980-82; resident U. Kans., Kansas City, 1987-91, chief resident, 1990-91; asst. prof. U. Tex. Health Scis. Ctr., San Antonio, 1991-98; dir. movement analysis lab. U. Tex., San Antonio, 1994-98; physiatrist Desert Rehab., Las Vegas, Nev., 1998-2000, Mountain Rehab., Las Vegas, 2000—. Contbr. chpt. Physical Medicine and Rehabilitation, 1996, 00, Cancer Rehabilitation, 1994. Mem. Assn. Acad. Physiatrists (mem. com. 1993—), Paralyzed Vets. Am. (assoc.). Avocations: gardening, music. Office: Mountain Rehab 653 Town Ctr Dr 514 Las Vegas NV 89144

MCANIFF, EDWARD JOHN, lawyer; b. N.Y.C., June 29, 1934; s. John Edward and Josephine (Toomey); m. Jane Reiss, June 11, 1960; children: John E., Maura T., Anne T. Annick, Jane A., Peter J., Kathleen A. AB magna cum laude, Holy Cross Coll., 1956; LLB cum laude, NYU, 1961. Bar: N.Y. 1962, Calif. 1963, D.C. 1976. Law clk. to Justice A.T. Goodwin Supreme Ct. Oreg., Salem, 1961-62; ptnr., of counsel O'Melveny & Myers, L.A., 1962—. Adj. prof. Sch. Law Stanford U., 1974-75, 94-98, Boalt Hall Law Sch., 1992-95, UCLA Law Sch., 1996—; vis. prof. U. Oreg. Law Sch., 1999—; fgn. law counsel Freehill, Hollingdale & Page, Sydney, 1981-82; bd. dirs. Mellon Fin. Corp. Bd. dirs. L.A. Master Chorale, 1979-81, 87—, chmn., 1996—; dir., exec. com. Perf. Art Ctr. Los Angeles County, 1992—; bd. dirs. Music Ctr. Found., 1992—. Capt. USNR, 1956-87. Republican. Office: O Melveny & Myers 400 S Hope St Ste 1717 Los Angeles CA 90071-2899 E-mail: tmcaniff@omm.com

MCANINCH, JACK WELDON, urological surgeon, educator; b. Merkel, Tex., Mar. 17, 1936; s. Weldon Thomas and Margaret (Canon) McA.; m. Barbara B. Buchanan, Dec. 29, 1960 (div. Aug. 1972); m. Burnet B. Sumner, Dec. 29, 1987; children: David A., Todd G., Brendan J. BS, Tex. Tech U., 1958; MS, U. Idaho, 1960; MD, U. Tex., 1964. Diplomate Am. Bd. Urology (trustee 1991-97, pres. 1996-97). Commd. capt. U.S. Army, 1964-66, advanced through grades to col., 1977, ret., 1977; col. USAR; intern then resident Letterman Army Med. Ctr., San Francisco, 1964-69; chief urol. surgery San Francisco Gen. Hosp., 1977—; prof. urol. surgery U. Calif., San Francisco, 1977—. Editor: Urogenital Trauma, 1985, Urologic Clinics of North America, 1989, Smith's General Urology, 1995; section editor: Early Care of the Injured Patient, 1990, Traumatic and Reconstructive Urology, 1996. Col. US Army, 1964-72. Recipient Disting. Alumnus award Tex. Tech U., 1994; named Disting. Alumnus U. Idaho, 1997. Fellow ACS (gov. 1992-97, regent 1998—); mem. Am. Urol. Assn. (pres. we. sect. 1992-93, bd. dirs. 1990—, pres. 1996-97), Genitourinary Reconstructive Surgeons (pres.), Am. Assn. Surgery Trauma (v.p.), Soc. Univ. Urologists, Am. Bd. Urology (pres. 1996-97). Office: San Francisco Gen Hosp Dept Urology 1001 Potrero Ave San Francisco CA 94110-3594

MCARTHUR, ELDON DURANT, geneticist, researcher; b. Hurricane, Utah, Mar. 12, 1941; s. Eldon and Denise (Dalton) McA.; m. Virginia Johnson, Dec. 20, 1963; children: Curtis D., Monica McArthur Bennion, Denise McArthur Johnson, Ted O. AS with high honors, Dixie Coll., 1963; BS cum laude, U. Utah, 1965, MS, 1967, PhD, 1970. Postdoctoral rsch. fellow, dept. demonstrator Agrl. Rsch. Coun. Gt. Britain, Leeds, Eng., 1970-71; rsch. geneticist Intermountain Rsch. Sta. USDA Forest Svc., Ephraim, Utah, 1972-75, rsch. geneticist Shrub Scis. Lab., Intermountain Rsch. Sta. Provo, 1975-83, project leader, chief rsch. geneticist, 1983-97, Rocky Mountain Rsch. Sta., USDA Forest Svc., Provo, 1997—. Adj. prof. dept. botany and range sci. Brigham Young U., Provo, 1976—. Author more than 320 rsch. papers; contbr. chpts. to books; editor symposium procs. Named USDA Forest Svc. Superior Scientist, 1990, Disting. Scientist, 1996; Sigma Xi grantee, 1970, NSF grantee, 1981, 85, 96, Coop. State Rsch., Svc. grantee, 1986, 91; recipient Eminent Sci. Publ. award Rocky Mtn. Rsch. Station, 2001. Mem. Soc. Range Mgmt. (pres. Utah sect. 1987, Outstanding Achievement award 1992), Botan. Soc. Am., Soc. Study Evolution, Am. Genetic Assn., Shrub Rsch. Consortium (chmn. 1983—), Intermountain Consortium for Aridlands Rsch. (pres. 1991—). Mormon. Avocations: hiking, cycling, basketball. Home: 555 N 1200 E Orem UT 84097-4350 Office: USDA Forest Svc Shrub Scis Lab 735 N 500 E Provo UT 84606-1856 E-mail: emcarthur@fs.fed.us, edmdixie@aol.com

MCATEE, PATRICIA ANNE ROONEY, medical educator; b. Denver, Apr. 20, 1931; d. Jerry F. and Edna E. (Hansen) Rooney; m. Darrell McAtee, Sept. 4, 1954; 1 son, Kevin Paul. BS, Loretto Heights Coll., 1953; MS, U. Colo., 1961; PhD, Union of Univs., 1976. Supr. St. Anthony Hosp., Denver, 1952-55; pub. health nurse, edn. dir. Tri-County Health Dept., Colo., 1956-58; adminstr. sch. health program Littleton (Colo.) Pub. Schs., 1958-60; asst. prof. community health, acad. adminstr. continuing edn. U. Colo., 1968-70; project dir. Western Interstate Commn. for Higher Edn., 1972-74; asst. prof. pediatrics, project co-dir. Sch. Medicine U. Colo., 1975—; mem. profl. svcs. staff Mead Johnson & Co., 1981—. Cons. Colo. Safety Coun.; treas. Vista Nueva Assocs. Editor: Pediatric Nursing, 1975-77. Chmn. bd. dirs. Found. for Urban and Neighborhood Devel.; mem. Arapahoe Health Planning Coun. Mem. NAS, APHA, Inst. Medicine, Nat. Bd. Pediatric Nurse Practitioners and Assocs. (pres.), Nat. Assn. Pediatric Nurse Practitioners (v.p.), Am. Acad. Polit. and Social Scientist, Nat. League Nursing, Western Soc. Rsch., Am. Sch. Health Assn., Sigma Theta Tau. Home: 877 E Panama Dr Littleton CO 80121-2531 Office: 4200 E 9th Ave Denver CO 80220-3706

MCAULIFFE, ROSEMARY, state legislator; b. Seattle, Aug. 1, 1940; m. James McAuliffe; 6 children. BSN, Seattle U. Owner, mgr. Hollywood Sch. House; mem. Wash. Senate, Dist. 1, Olympia, 1993—; chair edn. com. Wash. Senate, mem. environ. quality and water resources com., mem. higher edn. com., co-chairperson joint select com. on edn. restructuring, mem. student conduct task force, mem. spl. edn. adv. coun., mem. food safety adv. coun. Bd. dirs. Northshore Sch., 1977-91, bd. pres., 1981-82; mem. Northshore Econ. Devel. Com., Together for a Drug-Free Youth Com., 1989; chairwoman Bothell Downtown Mgmt. Assn., 1987-90; del. Main St. Revitalization, Pacific N.W.; mem. conf. com. and diversion com. Northshore Juvenile Ct., 1978-80; mem. Lake Health Com., 1997-98. Mem. Wash. Sch. Dir.'s Assn. (legis. network rep. 1990-91), Assn. Children with Learning Disabilities, Northshore and Woodinville C. of C. Democrat. Office: 402A John Cherberg Bldg Olympia WA 98504-0001

MCBRIDE, JOHN P. state commissioner; b. Buffalo, Mar. 23, 1951; Grad., U. Wyo., 1973, law school grad., 1976. Lawyer Jones, Vines and Hunkins, Wheatland, Wyo., 1981-89; staff atty. to dep. commr. State of Wyo. Ins. Dept., Cheyenne, 1989-92, ins. commr., 1992—. U.S. Army Judge Advocate Gen. Corps, 1977-81. Office: State Wyo Insurance Dept Herschler Bl 122 W 25th St Cheyenne WY 82002-5011

MCBRIDE, JUDITH, elementary education educator; Art tchr. Slade Elem. Sch., Laramie, Wyo., 1996, Spring Creek Elem. Sch., Laramie, 1996—. Named Wyo. State Art Tchr. of Yr., 1993. Office: Spring Creek Elem Sch 1203 Russell St Laramie WY 82070-4682

MCBRIDE, TERESA, information systems specialist; b. Grants, N. Mex., Sept. 8, 1962; 1 child. Mem. staff Family Restaurant, Grants, N. Mex.; founder, pres., CEO McBride & Assocs., Albuquerque, 1986—. Office: McBride & Assocs 5555 Mcleod Rd NE Albuquerque NM 87109-2408

MCCABE, EDWARD R. B. academic administrator, educator, physician; b. Balt., Mar. 26, 1946; BA in Biology, Johns Hopkins U., 1967; PhD in Pharmacology, U. So. Calif., 1972, MD, 1974. Diplomate Am. Bd. Pediatrics. Resident in pediatrics U. Minn. Hosps., Mpls., 1974-76; pediatric metabolism fellow Sch. Medicine U. Colo., Denver, 1976-78, instr., asst. prof., assoc. prof. pediatrics Sch. Medicine, 1978-86; from assoc. prof. to prof. genetics, pediatrics Baylor Coll. Medicine, Houston, 1986-94; prof., chmn. dept. pediatrics Sch. Medicine UCLA, 1994—. Physician-in-chief Mattel Children's Hosp. at UCLA, 1995—; mem. med. genetics residency rev. com. Accreditation Coun. Grad. Med. Edn., 1993-97; chmn. conf. gaucher disease NIH, Bethesda, Md., 1994-96, mem. NICHD coun., Bethesda, 1995-99. Editor Biochem. and Molecular Medicine, 1990-97, Molecular genetics and Metabolism, 1998—. Chair sci. adv. bd. Hereditary Disease Found., L.A., 1998-99; chmn. Basil O'Connor Award March Dimes, White Plains, N.Y., 1997-99. Mem. Am. Acad. Pediatrics (chmn. com. genetics Elk Grove Village, Ill. 1987-91, co-founder, chmn. sect. genetics Elk Grove, 1990, 93-95), Am. Bd. Med. Genetics (diplomate, bd. dirs. 1992-97, pres. Bethesda 1995-96), Am. Soc. Human Genetics, Am. Fedn. Clin. Rsch., Am. Pediatric Soc., Am. Soc. Biochemistry and Molecular Biology, Am. Coll. of Med. Genetics (pres.-elect 1999-00; co-chair newborn screening task force, maternal and child health bur. 1999-2000; chair sec.'s adv. com. ge netic testing 1998—), Soc. Pediatric Rsch. (E. Mead Johnson award, 1993), Phi Kappa Phi (L.A.), Sigma Xi (L.A.), Alpha Omega Alpha (L.A.). Achievements include first to describe the Continguous Gene Syndrome, Complex Glycerol Kinase Deficiency; first to extract DNA from blood in newborn screening blotters; first to set up molecular genetic diagnosis for sickle cell disease as part of newborn screening; developement of concept of molecular genetic triage of bacterial infection. Office: UCLA Sch Medicine Dept Pediatrics 22 412 MDCC 10833 Le Conte Ave Los Angeles CA 90095-3075

MCCABE, JOHN L. lawyer; b. Chgo., Oct. 17, 1941; BA, U. Notre Dame, 1963; LLB, Harvard U., 1966. Bar: Ill. 1967, Colo. 1967. Ptnr. Davis, Graham & Stubbs, Denver. Office: Davis Graham & Stubbs 1550 Seventeenth St Ste 500 Denver CO 80202 E-mail: john.mccabe@dgslaw.com

MCCAGHREN, MICHAEL, retail executive; b. 1960; Sr. v.p., chief info. officer Eli Witt Co., 1991-96; nat. dir. GSI Outsourcing, Inc.; sr. v.p. sys., merchandise planning, allocation, etc. Jumbo Sports, Denver, 1997-99; sr. v.p., chief info. officer Gart Sports Co., 1999—. Office: Gart Sports Co 1001 Lincoln Ave Denver CO 80203 Office Fax: 303-829-1511

MCCAIG, JEFFREY JAMES, transportation company executive; b. Moose Jaw, Sask., July 5, 1951; s. John Robert and Anne Shorrocks (Glass) McC.; m. Marilyn Graves, July 7, 1983; children: Robbert Angus, Scott Thomas, Christa Mae. Student, Can. Jr. Coll. Lausanne, Switzerland, 1970; AB, Harvard Coll., 1973; LLB, Osgoode Hall Law Sch., Can., 1976; MSc in Mgmt., Leland Stanford Jr. U., 1984. Assoc. MacKimmie Matthews, 1976-81; owner, sr. officer Jeffrey J. McCaig Profl. Corp., 1981-83; v.p. planning and corp. devel. Trimac, Calgary, Alta., Can., 1983-87, exec. v.p. Can., 1987-90, pres. Can., 1990-94, pres., CEO Can., 1994—; chmn. Bovar, Inc., Calgary, 1994—. Bd. dirs. Bovar, Inc., chmn. bd. dirs. Trimac Corp., Richland Petroleum Corp., Potash Corp. of Sask; adv. bd. Weldwood of Can. Ltd. Mem. Law Soc. Alta., Young Pres.'s Orgn., Calgary Golf and Country Club, Calgary Petroleum Club, Glencoe Club, 400 Club. Home: 708 Riverdale Ave SW Calgary AB Canada T2S OY3 Office: Trimac Corp 800 5 Ave SW Ste 2100 Calgary AB Canada T2P 5A3

MCCAMBRIDGE, DENNIS, protective services official; Chief dep. U.S. marshal U.S. Dist. Ct., Boise. Office: 550 W Fort St Msc 10 Boise ID 83724-0001

MCCAMMON, JAMES ANDREW, chemistry educator; b. Lafayette, Ind., Feb. 8, 1947; s. Lewis Brown and Jean Ann (McClintock) McC.; m. Anne Elizabeth Woltmann, June 6, 1969. BA magna cum laude, Pomona Coll., 1969; MA, Harvard U., 1970, PhD, 1976. Research fellow Harvard U., Cambridge, Mass., 1976-78; asst. prof. U. Houston, 1978-81, M.D. Anderson prof. chemistry, 1981-94, dir. Inst. for Molecular Design, 1987-94, prof. biochemistry, 1989-94, adj. prof. chemistry, 1995—. Adj. prof. molecular physiology and biophysics Baylor Coll. Medicine, Houston, 1986-94, adj. prof. biochemistry, 1992-94; Joseph E. Mayer chair theoretical chemistry U. Calif., San Diego, 1995—, prof. pharmacology, 1995—; investigator Howard Hughes Med. Inst., 2000—. Author: Dynamics of Proteins and Nucleic Acids, 1987. Recipient Tchr.-scholar award Camille and Henry Dreyfus Found., George H. Hitchings award Burroughs-Wellcome Fund, 1987, Computerworld Smithsonian Info. Tech. Leadership award for Breakthrough Computational Sci., 1995; named Alfred P. Sloan Rsch. fellow, 1980. Fellow AAAS, Am. Phys. Soc., Biophys. Soc.; mem. Am. Chem. Soc., Protein Soc., Phi Beta Kappa.

Achievements include development of the molecular dynamics simulation method for proteins and nucleic acids, of the thermodynamic cycle perturbation method for studying molecular recognition, and of the Brownian dynamics method for simulating diffusion-controlled reactions. Office: U Calif San Diego Dept Chemistry La Jolla CA 92093-0365

MCCANDLESS, BRUCE, II, aerospace engineer, former astronaut; b. Boston, June 8, 1937; s. Bruce and Sue McCandless; m. Alfreda Bernice Doyle, Aug. 6, 1960; children: Bruce III, Tracy. BS, U.S. Naval Acad., 1958; MSEE, Stanford U., 1965; MBA, U. Houston, Clear Lake, 1987. Commd. ensign USN, 1958, advanced through grades to capt., 1979, naval aviator, 1960, with Fighter Squadron 102, 1960-64; astronaut Johnson Space Ctr., NASA, Houston, 1966-90; mem. Skylab 1 backup crew Johnson Space Center, NASA, Houston, mem. STS-11 shuttle crew, mem. STS-31 Hubble Space Telescope deployment crew; ret. USN, 1990; prin. staff engr. Lockheed Martin Astronautics, Denver, 1990-97, chief scientist Reusable Space Transportation Systems, 1997—. Decorated Legion of Merit; recipient Def. Superior Service medal, NASA Exceptional Service medal, NASA Spaceflight medal, NASA Exceptional Engring. Achievement medal, Collier Trophy, 1985, Haley Space Flight award AIAA, 1991. Fellow Am. Astron. Soc.; mem. IEEE, U.S. Naval Inst., Nat. Audubon Soc., Houston Audubon Soc. (past pres.) Episcopalian. Achievements include executing 1st untethered free flight in space using Manned Maneuvering Unit. Office: Lockheed Martin Astronautics MS DC3005 PO Box 179 Denver CO 80201-0179

MC CANN, CECILE NELKEN, writer, artist; b. New Orleans; d. Abraham and Leona (Reiman) Nelken; children: Dorothy Collins, Cecile Isaacs, Annette Arnold, Denise Bachman, Albert Hews III. Student, Vassar Coll., Tulane U.; BA, San Jose State Coll., 1963, MA, 1964; postgrad., U. Calif.-Berkeley, 1966-67; hon. doctorate, San Francisco Art Inst., 1989. Tool designer Convair Corp., New Orleans, 1942-45; archtl. draftsman, various companies New Orleans and Clinton, Iowa, 1945-47, 51-53; owner, operator ceramics studio Clinton, 1953-58; instr. San Jose State Coll., 1964-65, Calif. State U., Hayward, 1964-65, Chabot Coll., Hayward, 1966-69, Laney Coll., 1967-70, San Francisco State U., 1977-78; founder, editor, pub. Artweek mag., Oakland, Calif., 1970-89; freelance writer, art advisor Kensington, 1989—. Cons. Nat. Endowment Arts, 1974-78, fellow in art criticism, 1976; panelist numerous confs. and workshops Contbr. to profl. publs.; one-woman shows at, Davenport Mus. Art, Robert North Galleries, Chgo., Crocker Art Mus., Sacramento, Calif., Calif. Coll. Arts and Crafts, Oakland, others; exhibited in group shows at, DeYoung Mus., San Francisco, Everson Mus. Art, Syracuse, N.Y., Oakland Mus., Pasadena Mus., Los Angeles County Mus. Art, others; represented in permanent collections, San Jose State Coll., Mills Coll., Coll. Holy Names, City of San Francisco, State of Calif., others. Trustee Rene and Veronica di Rosa Found; mem. Pub. Art Adv. Com., Oakland. Recipient Vesta award Woman's Bldg. mag., L.A., 1988, Honor award Art Table, 1988, Media award Bay Area Visual Arts Coalition, 1989, Achievement award Art Table, 1992. Mem. Art Table, Internat. Assn. Art Critics. Office: 244 Colgate Ave Kensington CA 94708-1122 E-mail: clem@citycom.com

MCCANN, JACK ARLAND, former construction and mining equipment company executive; b. Chestnut, Ill., Apr. 16, 1926; s. Keith Ogden and Miriam Imogene McCann; m. Marian Adele Gordon, Mar. 31, 1956; 1 child Christopher John. AB, Bradley U., 1950. Mgr. Washington Office, R.G. LeTourneau Inc., 1950-58; mgr. def. and spl. products Westinghouse Air Brake Co., 1958-64, mgr. nat. accounts, 1964-67, mng. dir. Belgian plant and European mktg., 1967-70; gen. sales mgr. WABCO divsn. Am. Std. Inc., Peoria, Ill., 1970-73, v.p. mktg., 1973-80, v.p. staff, 1980-82; ret., 1982. Communicant St. Francis-in-Valley Episcopal Ch., Green Valley, Ariz.

MCCANN, RICHARD EUGENE, lawyer; b. Billings, Mont., Aug. 14, 1939; s. Oakey O. and Edith May (Miller) McC.; m. Mona N. Miyagishima, Apr. 27, 1964; children: Tami, Todd (dec.), Jennifer. BA magna cum laude, Rocky Mountain Coll., 1965; JD with highest honors, U. Mont., 1972. Bar: Mont. 1972, Washington 1977, Alaska 1982. Law clk. to Judge W. Jameson U.S. Dist. Ct., Billings, 1972-73; assoc. Crowley, Haughey, Hansen, Toole & Dietrich, Billings, 1973-77, Perkins Coie, Seattle, 1977-80, ptnr., 1981—. Contbr. articles to profl. jours. Trustee Rocky Mountain Coll., Billings., 1973-77. Served with USMC, 1957-61. Mem. ABA, Mont. Bar Assn., Wash. Bar Assn., Alaska Bar Assn. Office: Perkins Coie 1201 3rd Ave Fl 40 Seattle WA 98101-3029 E-mail: mccar@perkinscoie.com

MCCANN, STEVEN, retail executive; Auditor Touche Ross & Co.; v.p., corp. contr. May Co.; v.p. of fin., chief acctg. officer Svc. Mgmt. Co.; sr. v.p., CFO Longs Drug Stores, Walnut Creek, Calif., 2000—. Office: Long Drug Stores Corp 141 N Civic Dr Walnut Creek CA 94596

MCCARTHY, BEA, state legislator; b. Great Falls, Mont., Apr. 17, 1935; d. Robert Joseph and Rose Mary (Krier) McKenna; m. Edward Joseph McCarthy, June 27, 1959; children: Colleen, Mary, Edward Jr., Patrick, John. BS in Elem Edn., Mont. State U., 1957. Tchr. 1st grade, Anaconda, Mont., 1968—; mem. Mont. Ho. of Reps., Dist. 66, 1991-94, Mont. Senate, Dist. 29, Helena, 1997—. Mem. Mont. Bd. Regents, 1983-90, Mont. Bd. Edn., 1983-90. Mem. AAUW, Am. Legion Aux., Ladies Ancient Order Hibernians (past pres.), Phi Beta Phi, Delta Kappa Gamma. Democrat. Roman Catholic. Avocations: needlework, painting, reading. Home: 1906 Ogden St Anaconda MT 59711-1706 Address: Capitol Station Helena MT 59620

MC CARTHY, FRANK MARTIN, oral surgeon, surgical sciences educator; b. Olean, N.Y., Aug. 27, 1924; s. Frank Michael and Joan (Quinn) McC.; m. Julia Richmond, Nov. 24, 1949; children: Robert Lee, Joan Lee. B.S., U. Pitts., 1943, D.D.S., 1945, M.D., 1949; M.S. in Oral Surgery, Georgetown U., 1954; Sc.D. (hon.), St. Bonaventure U., 1956. Med. intern Mercy Hosp., Pitts., 1949-50; practice oral surgery L.A., 1954-75; teaching fellow Georgetown U., 1952-53; rsch. fellow NIH, 1953-54; prof. oral surgery U. So. Calif. Sch. Dentistry, 1966-75, prof., chmn. sect. anesthesia and medicine, 1975-90, prof. emeritus, 1990—, chmn. dept. surg. scis., 1979-84, assoc. dean adminstrv. affairs, 1977-79, asst. dean hosp. affairs, 1979-84. Dir. anesthesiology U.So. Calif. oral surgery sect. L.A. County Hosp., 1958-89; clin. supr., lectr. dental hygiene program Pasadena City Coll., 1992—; v.p. Am. Dental Bd. Anesthesiology, 1984-89; lectr. in field; mem. adv. panel on dentistry sect. anesthesizing agts. Nat. Fire Protection Assn., 1971-79; mem. Am. Nat. Standards Com., 1974-86, 95—; cons. in field. Author: Emergencies in Dental Practice, 1967, rev., 1972, 79, Medical Emergencies in Dentistry, 1982, Safe Treatment of the Medically Compromised Patient, 1987, Essentials of Safe Dentistry for the Medically Compromised Patient, 1989; mem. editorial bd.: Calif. Dental Assn. Jour; contbr. articles to profl. publs. Bd. councilors Sch. Dentistry, U. So. Calif., 1972-75. Served as lt., M.C. USNR, 1950-52. Fellow Internat. Assn. Oral Surgeons (founder), Am. Coll. Dentists, Internat. Coll. Dentists; mem. ADA (editorial bd. jour.), Am. Dental Soc. Anesthesiology (Heidbrink award 1977), Am. Assn. Oral-Max Surgeons (chmn. anesthesia com. 1971), So. Calif. Soc. Oral Surgeons (pres. 1974), Calif., Los Angeles County dental assns., Delta Tau Delta, Psi Omega, Phi Rho Sigma, Omicron Kappa Upsilon. Home and Office: 480 S Orange Grove Blvd Apt 11 Pasadena CA 91105-1720

MCCARTHY, J. THOMAS, lawyer, educator; b. Detroit, July 2, 1937; s. John E. and Virginia M. (Hanlon) McC.; m. Nancy Irene Orrell, July 10, 1976 BS, U. Detroit, 1960; JD, U. Mich., 1963. Bar: Calif. 1964. Assoc. Julian Caplan, San Francisco, 1963-66; prof. law U. San Francisco, 1966—; vis. prof. law U. Calif., Berkeley, 1976-77, Davis, 1979-80. Cons. in field; mem. Trademark Rev. Commn., 1986-88. Author: McCarthy on Trademarks and Unfair Competition, 6 vols., 4th edit., 1996, McCarthy on Rights of Publicity and Privacy, 1987, 2d edit., 2000, McCarthy's Desk Encyclopedia of Intellectual Property, 2d edit., 1995; mem. editl. bd. Trademark Reporter. Recipient Jefferson medal N.J. Intellectual Property Assn., 1994, Ladas award Brand Names Ednl. Found., 1997, Pattishall medal Brand Names Found., 2000. Mem. Am. Intellectual Property Law Assn. (Watson award 1965, Centennial award in Trademark law 1997), Internat. Assn. for Advancement of Teaching and Rsch. in Intellectual Property, Am. Law Inst. (adv. com. on restatement of law of unfair competition), IEEE.

MCCARTHY, JOHN, computer scientist, educator; b. Boston, Sept. 4, 1927; s. Patrick Joseph and Ida McC.; children: Susan Joanne, Sarah Kathleen, Timothy Talcott. B.S., Calif. Inst. Tech., 1948; Ph.D., Princeton U., 1951. Instr. Princeton U., 1951-53; acting asst. prof. math. Stanford U., 1953-55; asst. prof. Dartmouth Coll., 1955-58; asst. and asso. prof. communications scis. M.I.T., Cambridge, 1958-62; prof. computer sci. Stanford U., 1962—, Charles M. Pigott prof. Sch. Engring., 1987-94. Served with AUS, 1945-46. Recipient Kyoto prize, 1988, Nat. Medal of Sci. NSF, 1990. Mem. NAS, NAE, Am. Acad. Arts and Scis., Assn. for Computing Machinery (A.M. Turing award 1971), Am. Math. Soc., Am. Assn. Artificial Intelligence (pres. 1983-84). Home: 885 Allardice Way Stanford CA 94305-1050 Office: Stanford U Dept Computer Sci Stanford CA 94305 E-mail: mccarthy@stanford.edu

MCCARTHY, KEVIN, broadcast executive; V.p., gen. mgr. Sta. KSDO, San Diego, 1998—. Office: KSDO Bldg 5050 Murphy Canyon Rd San Diego CA 92123-4441

MCCARTHY, LAURENCE JAMES, physician, pathologist; b. Boston, Aug. 11, 1934; s. Theodore Clifford and Mary Barrett (Moran) McC.; m. Cynthia Marion DeRoch, Aug. 28, 1978; children: Laurence J. Jr., Jeffrey A., Karen E., Patrick K., Ryan N. BA, Yale U., 1956; student, Georgetown U. Sch. Med., 1956-58; MD, Harvard U., 1960; MS, U. Minn., 1965. Cert. Am. Bd. Pathology, 1965. Intern Boston City Hosp., 1960-61; resident in pathology Mayo Clinic, Rochester, Minn., 1961-65; pathologist Honolulu Heart Program, 1965-67; chief pathology Kelsey-Seybold Clinic, Houston, 1967-68; clin. asst. pathologist M.D. Anderson Hosp., Houston, 1967-68; chief pathology Straub Clinic, Honolulu, 1968-72; assoc. pathologist Wilcox Hosp., Lihue, Hawaii, 1972-74; chief pathology A.R. Gould Hosp., Presque Isle, Maine, 1975-78; assoc. pathologist Kuakini Med. Ctr., Honolulu, 1978—. Med. dir. USPHS, 1965-67. Fellow Coll. Am. Pathologists, Am. Soc. Clin. Pathologists; mem. AMA, Hawaii Soc. Pathologists (pres. 1970), Am. Acad. Forensic Sci., Hawaii Med. Assn., Honolulu County Med. Soc. (del. 1982-83). Roman Catholic. Home: 249 Kaelepulu Dr Kailua HI 96734-3311 Office: Kuakini Med Ctr 347 N Kuakini St Honolulu HI 96817-2306

MCCARTHY, ROGER LEE, mechanical engineer; AB in Philosophy with high distinction, BSME summa cum laude, U. Mich., 1972; MS in Mech. Engring., MIT, 1973, MechE, 1975, PhD in Mech. Engring., 1977. Registered profl. engr., Calif., Ariz. Project engr. machine design and devel. engring. div. Proctor & Gamble, Inc., Cin., 1973-74; program mgr. Spl. Machinery Group Foster-Miller Assocs., Inc., Waltham, Mass., 1976-78; prin. design engr. Failure Analysis Assocs., Inc. (became Exponent Failure Analysis Assocs., Inc. in 1998), Menlo Park, Calif., 1978—; chmn. bd. dirs., 1988—; CEO The Failure Group, Inc., Menlo Park, 1988-96, chief tech. officer, 1996-98, chmn. Exponent Failure Analysis Assocs., Inc., Menlo Park, Calif., 1998—. Co-contbr. numerous articles to profl. jours. Mem. Pres.' Commn. on Nat. Medal od Sci., 1992-94. Recipient Outstanding Civilian Svc. Gold medal U.S. Army, 1998; NSF fellow, 1972-75. Mem. Am. Soc. Metals, ASME, Soc. Automotive Engrs., Am. Welding Soc., Am. Soc. for Testing and Materials, Human Factors Soc., ASHRAE, Nat. Fire Protection Assn., Phi Beta Kappa, Sigma Xi (James B. Angell scholar). Office: Exponent Failure Analysis Assn Inc 149 Commonwealth Dr Menlo Park CA 94025

MCCARTY, FREDERICK BRIGGS, electrical engineer, consultant; b. Dilley, Tex., Aug. 11, 1926; s. John Frederick Briggs and Olive Ruth (Snell) Briggs McCarty; m. Doris Mary Cox, May 03, 1950 (div. 1970); children: Mark Frederick, David Lambuth, Jackson Clare; m. Nina Lucile Butman, Aug. 17, 1973. BSEE, U. Tex., 1949. Registered profl. engr., Calif. Design engr. GE, Schenectady, N.Y., 1949-51; sr. design engr. Convair, Ft. Worth, 1951-55; sr. engr. Aerojet Gen., Azusa, Calif., 1955-61; sr. engring. specialist Garrett Corp., Torrance, alif., 1961-91; v.p., founder Patio Pacific, Inc., Torrance, 1973-84; owner, operator Textiger Co., Torrance, 1980-91; cons., 1991—. Author computer software, Textiger word processor, Tiger Tools, Big Mag and Roundrot generator synthesizers; designer (superconducting acyclic motor for) U.S. Navy and various high speed elec. machines for aerospace and transp. Served with USNR, 1944—46, PTO. Mem.: IEEE (sr.), Tau Beta Pi, Eta Kappa Nu. Democrat. Achievements include patents for patentee in field. Home and Office: 1366 Stonewood Ct San Pedro CA 90732-1550

MCCARTY, JUDY, councilman; b. June 4, 1940; m. Curt McCarty; 2 children. BS, Ind. U. Aide to Assemblyman Larry Stirling; del. UN Program for Local Environ. Initiatives, White House Conf. on Libr. and Info. Svcs.; city councilwoman 7th Dist., San Diego, 1985—. Chair select com. on govt. effeciency, fiscal reform, Mission Traisl Regional Pk. Task Force, natural resources, culture com., city rep. Pk. and Recreation Bd., San Diego Processing Corp., alt. rep. Met. Transit Devel. Bd., San Diego City Coun. Pres. Navajo Cmty. Recipient Local Legislator of Yr. award, Kate Sessions award Industry Environ. Assn. Methodist. Office: City San Diego 202 C St Fl 10 San Diego CA 92101-3860

MCCARTY, PERRY LEE, civil and environmental engineering educator; b. Grosse Pointe, Mich., Oct. 29, 1931; s. James C. and Alice C. (Marsom) McC.; m. Martha Davis Collins, Sept. 5, 1953; children: Perry Lee, Cara L., Susan A., Kathleen R. BSCE, Wayne State U., 1953; MS in Sanitary Engring., MIT, 1957, ScD, 1959; DEng (hon.), Colo. Sch. Mines, 1992. Field engr. Edwin Orr Co., Dearborn, Mich., 1951-52; engr. Pate & Hirn, Detroit, 1952-53; field engr. Hubbell, Roth & Clark, Detroit, 1953; instr. civil engring. Wayne State U., 1953-54; field engr. George Jerome & Co., Detroit, 1954; engr. Civil Engrs., Inc., Detroit, 1956; assoc. Rolf Eliassen Assocs., Winchester, Mass., 1958-61; asst. prof. sanitary engring. MIT, 1958-62; mem. faculty Stanford U., 1962—, prof. civil engring., 1967-75, Silas H. Palmer prof., 1975-99, Silas H. Palmer prof. emeritus, 1999—, chmn. dept. civil engring., 1980-85; dir. Western Region Hazardous Substance Rsch. Ctr., 1989—. Chmn. Gordon Rsch. Conf. Environ. Scis., 1972; vice chmn. environ. studies bd. NRC-NAS, 1976-80, mem. com. on phys. scis., math. and resources, 1985-88, bd. on radioactive waste mgmt., 1989-96, mem. com. geoscis., environment, resources, 1994-97. Co-author: Chemistry for Environmental Engineering, 4th edit., 1994, Environmental Biotechnology Principles and Applications, 2001. Served with AUS, 1954-56. Recipient Tyler Prize for Environ. Achievement, 1992, Clarke Prize Outstanding Achievement Water Sci. and Tech., 1997; NSF faculty fellow, 1968-69. Fellow AAAS, Am. Acad. Microbiology, Am. Acad. Arts and Scis.; mem. ASCE (Walter L. Huber Rsch. prize 1964, Simon W. Freese Environ. Engring. award 1979, James R. Croes medal 1995), NAE, Am. Water Works Assn. (hon. 1981, life 1987, chmn. water quality divsn. 1972-73, trustee rsch. divsn. 1980-85, Best Paper award 1985, A.P. Black Rsch. award 1989), Am. Soc. for Microbiology, Water Environment Fedn. (hon. 1989, Harrison P. Eddy award 1962, 77, Thomas Camp award 1975), Assn. Environ. Engring. Profs. (Disting. Faculty award 1966, Oustanding Publ. award 1985, 88, 98, Founders award 1992), Am. Soc. Engring. Edn.(vice chmn. environ. engring. divsn. 1968-69), Internat. Assn. on Water Quality, Am. Chem. Soc., Sigma Xi, Tau Beta Pi (fellow 1957-58). Home: 823 Sonoma Ter Stanford CA 94305-1024 Office: Stanford U Civil Environ Engring Dept Stanford CA 94305-4020 E-mail: mccarty@ce.stanford.edu

MCCASLIN, ROBERT L. state legislator; m. Linda Callahan. BA in Sociology and Econs., Wash. State U. Ret. real estate broker; former prodn. mgr. Kaiser Aluminum and Chem. Corp.; mem. Wash. Senate, Dist. 4, Olympia, 1980—; mem. jud. com. Wash. Senate, Olympia, mem. state and local govt. com., mem. statute law com., mem. state law and justice adv. coun., mem. select com. on vets. and mil. affairs, mem. growth mgmt. impact fee com., mem. growth mgmt. adv. com., mem. joint adminstrv. rules rev. com. With USN, 1944-46. Republican. Office: 112 Irving Newhouse Ofc Olympia WA 98504-0001

MCCAW, CRAIG O. communications executive; b. Centralia, Wash., 1949; Grad., Stanford U., 1971. Pilot; chmn., CEO McCaw Cellular Comm., Inc., 1968-88, chmn. bd. dirs., CEO Wash., 1982-94; chmn., CEO Lin Broadcasting Co., 1990—; founder, chief, co-exec. officer Teledesic Corp., Kirkland, 1990—; chmn., CEO NEXTLINK Comm. Inc., Eagle River Inc.

MCCAW, JOHN E., JR. professional sports team executive; Co-founder, bd. dirs. McCaw Comm., McCaw Cellular Comm., Inc.; owner, bd. dirs. Seattle Mariners, 1992; co-chmn. Orca Bay Sports and Entertainment, Vancouver, B.C.; chmn., gov. Vancouver Canucks. Office: Vancouver Canucks 800 Griffiths Way Vancouver BC Canada V6B 6G1

MCCLATCHY, JAMES B. newspaper publisher, editor; b. Sacramento; s. Carlos K. and Phebe (Briggs) McC.; m. Susan Brewster; children: Carlos F., William B. BA, Stanford U.; MS, Columbia U. Pub. The McClatchy Co., Sacramento. Past pres., dir. InterAm. Press Assn.; dir. Capital Region Inst., Sacramento; pres. Ctrl. Valley Found. Trustee Nat. Ctr. Internat. Schs. Office: McClatchy Co 21st & Q Sts Sacramento CA 95816

MCCLAVE, DONALD SILSBEE, professional society administrator; b. Cleve., May 7, 1941; s. Charles Green and Anne Elizabeth (Oakley) McC.; m. Christine Phyllis Mary Tomkins, Feb. 19, 1966; children: Andrew Green, Susan Elizabeth (dec.). BA, Denison U., 1963. Mktg. rsch. officer Bank of Calif., San Francisco, 1968-70; v.p. Cen. Nat. Bank, Chgo., 1970-75, First Interstate Bank, Portland, Oreg., 1975-77, sr. v.p., 1977-79, exec. v.p., 1979-86; pres., CEO Portland Met. C. of C., 1987—. Instr. Grad. Sch. Mktg. and Strategic Planning, Athens, 1982-84, Pacific Coast Sch. Banking, Seattle, 1976-78. Pres. Oreg. Episc. Sch. Bd., Portland, 1983-84; pres. Assn. Oreg. Industries Found., Salem, 1984-85; pres., co-chmn. Japan-Am. Conf. Mayors and C. of C., Portland, 1985, trustee, 1991—, exec. com., 1992-97; trustee YMCA of Columbia-Willamette, 1990-92, Portland Student Svcs. Corp., 1991-93; mem. METRO Urban Growth Mgmt. Adv. Com., 1989-92; mem. adv. com. Downtown Housing Preservation Partnership Adv. Com., 1989-94; mem. City of Portland Mayoral Transition Team, 1992, Mayor's Bus. Roundtable, 1993—; bd. dirs. Oreg. Trail chpt. ARC, 1994-95, Tri-Met, 1994—, chair fin. com., 1995—; dir. United Way Columbia Willamette, 1978-83, 2000-01; dir. Urban League Portland, 2000-01. Capt. USAF, 1963-68. Mem. Oreg. Chamber Execs. Assn. (pres. 1998). Avocations: reading, travel, golf, model building. Office: Portland Met C of C 221 NW 2nd Ave Portland OR 97209-3958

MCCLAY, BOB, broadcast executive; Bureau chief, Phoenix Metro Networks, Scottsdale, AZ, 1998—. Office: Metro Networks 14605 N Airport Dr Ste 360 Scottsdale AZ 85260-2491

MCCLEARY, LLOYD E(VERALD), education educator; b. Bradley, Ill., May 10, 1924; s. Hal and Pearl McC.; m. Iva Dene Carter, June 13, 1971; children: Joan Kay, Victoria Lea, Karen Ann. Student, Kans. U., 1941-42; B.S., U. Ill., 1948, M.S., 1950, D.Ed., 1956; postgrad., Sorbonne, Paris, 1946. Tchr., asst. prin. Portland (Oreg.) Public Schs., 1949-51; asst. prin. Univ. High Sch., Urbana, Ill., 1951-52, prin., 1953-56; asst. supt. Evanston Twp. (Ill.) High Sch., 1956-60; assoc. Roosevelt U., 1957-69; mem. faculty U. Mich., summers, 1958-59; prof. ednl. adminstrn. U. Utah, 1969—, chmn. dept., 1969-74. Assoc. CFK Ltd. Found., 1971-76; dir. projects in Latin Am. for AID, World Bank, Ford Found., Bolivian Govt.; dir. Nat. Sch. Prin. Study, 1976-79, 86-89, res. project Families in Edn., 1992-94; edn. rep. to Utah People to People Program; Keynoter Asian Conf. Edn., 1985; edn. adviser Office of the Queen, Jordan, 1985-86; advisor Nat. Commn. on Standards in the Principalship; U.S. del. Conf. on Status Children, Senegal, 1992, Yr. of the Family, Malta, 1993; J. Lloyd Trump lectr., New Orleans, 1994. Author: Organizational Analysis X-Change, 1975, Politics and Power in Education, 1976, The Senior High School Principalship, 1980, Educational Administration, Today, 1984, High School Leaders and Their Schools, vols. 1 and 2, 1990, Leadership, 1996; editor Western Hemisphere Edn. Sch. Orgn., 1989—. Served with inf. AUS, 1941-46. Decorated Bronze Star with oak leaf cluster, Army Commendation medal; S.D. Shankland fellow, 1956; Grantee Ford Found., 1968, 72, AID, 1966, 67, 70, 72, 74, 76, CFK Ltd., 1970-74, Rockefeller Family Found., 1979-80, U.S. Dept. State, 1981, 86-87, U.S. Dept. Def., 1986—; recipient Hatch Prize, 1988-89. Mem. Nat. Assn. Secondary Sch. Prins. (cert. of merit 1978, scholar-in-residence fall 1989, grantee 1969, 77, 86—), Assn. Supervision and Curriculum Devel., Nat. Assn. Elem. Sch. Prins., Phi Delta Kappa, Kappa Delta Pi. Methodist. Home: 1470 Wilton Way Salt Lake City UT 84108-2549 Office: U Utah 339 MBH Salt Lake City UT 84112

MCCLELLAN, CRAIG RENE, lawyer; b. Portland, Oreg., June 28, 1947; s. Charles Russell and Annette Irene (Benedict) McC.; m. Susan Armistead Nash, June 7, 1975; children: Ryan Alexander, Shannon Lea. BS in Econs., U. Oreg., 1969; JD magna cum laude, Calif. We. U., 1976. Bar: Calif. 1976, U.S. Dist. Ct. (so. dist.) Calif. 1976, U.S. Dist. Ct. (ea., ctrl., no. dists.) Calif. 1991, U.S. Supreme Ct. 1991. Compliance specialist Cost of Living Coun. and Price Commn., Washington, 1972-73, dir. Oil Policy subcom., 1973; ptnr. Luce, Forward, Hamilton & Scripps, San Diego, 1976-87; owner McClellan & Assocs., San Diego, 1987—. Chmn. annual fundraising auction KPBS, 1984. Capt. USMC, 1969-72. Fellow Am. Coll. Trial Lawyers; mem. Assn. Trial Lawyers Am., Am. Bd. Trial Advocates, Am. Inns of Ct. (master), Calif. State Bar Assn., San Diego County Bar Assn., Calif. Trial Lawyers Assn. (bd. govs. 1985-87), San Diego Trial Lawyers Assn. (bd. dirs. 1983-90), Nat. Forensics League, Phi Gamma Delta, Phi Alpha Delta. Presbyterian. Avocations: reading, running, tennis, chess, civic activities. Office: McClellan & Assocs 1144 State St San Diego CA 92101-3529 E-mail: mcclellanfirm@aol.com

MCCLELLAND, NORMAN P. food products executive; CEO, chmn. Shamrock Foods Co., Phoenix, 1949—. Office: Shamrock Foods Co 2228 N Black Canyon Hwy Phoenix AZ 85009-2707

MCCLENNEN, CRANE, judge; b. July 31, 1946; s. Louis McClennen and Dorothy (Petrovich) Johnson; m. Deborah Ann Hass, Feb. 19, 1995. BS, Ariz. State U., 1968, JD cum laude, 1972. Bar: Ariz. 1972, U.S. Dist. Ct. (Ariz.) 1972, U.S. Ct. Appeals (9th cir.) 1977, U.S. Supreme Ct. 1977. Atty. Snell & Wilmer, Phoenix, 1972-75; asst. atty. gen. Ariz. Atty. Gen.'s

Office, 1975-97; judge Ariz. Superior Ct., Maricopa County, 1997—. Lectr. State Bar of Ariz., 1987—, continuing legal edn. commn., 1987—, chair, 1996-97, appellate handbook com., 1985—, criminal jury inst. com., 1996—, bd. legal specialization, 1991-96, chair, 1993-95, peer review com., 1992-95, criminal rules com., 1990-94, alternative dispute resolution com., 1984-86, criminal justice sec., 1980-87, chair, 1984-86; editl. bd. Ariz. Atty., 1987-98; spkr. in field. Author: Arizona Courtroom Evidence Manual, 3rd edit., 1998, Arizona Legal Forms, Criminal Procedure, 1990. Named Disting. Public Lawyer, State Bar Ariz., 1991, Mem. of Yr. State Bar of Arizona, 1995. Fellow Ariz. Bar Found.; mem. Phi Delta Theta. Office: 201 W Jefferson St SPC 47 Phoenix AZ 85003-2244

MC CLENNEN, LOUIS, lawyer, educator; b. Cambridge, Mass., May 29, 1912; s. Edward F. and Mary (Crane) Mc C.; m. Miriam Jacobs, Apr. 25, 1969; children by previous marriage: Adams, James, Helen, Persis, Crane, Emery. AB cum laude, Harvard U., 1934, JD, 1937. Bar: Mass. 1937, Ind. 1940, Ariz. 1947. Pvt. practice, Boston, 1937-39, Indpls., 1940-42, Phoenix, 1946-95; pres. McClennen & Fels, P.C., 1974—; adj. prof. law fed. taxation Ariz. State U., 1974-80, pres. Law Soc., 1981-83. Author: (with others) Arizona Estate Tax, 1953, (with J.T. Melczer Jr.) Arizona Income Tax Regulations, 1954; contbr. articles to profl. jours. Pres. Ariz. Bd. Edn., 1965-69; trustee No. Ariz. Mus.; past pres., bd. dirs. Maricopa County Legal Aid Soc., Phoenix Symphony Assn.; v.p., bd. dirs. Phoenix United Fund; founder, sec., bd. dirs. Phoenix Country Day Sch.; bd. dirs. Ariz. Acad.; regional dir. Harvard Alumni Assn. Maj. USAAF, 1942-46. Mem. ABA, Am. Law Inst., Ariz. Bar Assn., Maricopa County Bar Assn. (dir., past v.p.), Harvard Law Sch. Assn. (v.p.) Lawyers Club Phoenix (pres.), Phoenix Country Club, Eastward Ho Country Club (Chatham, Mass.). Unitarian. Home and Office: 5311 N La Plaza Cir Phoenix AZ 85012-1415

MCCLINTOCK, JESSICA, fashion designer; b. Frenchville, Maine, June 19, 1930; d. Rene Gagnon and Verna Hedrich; m. Frank Staples (dec. 1964); 1 child Scott. BA, San Jose State U., 1963. Elem. sch. tchr., Marblehead, Mass., 1966-68, Long Island, N.Y., 1968, Sunnyvale, Calif., 1964-65, 68-69; fashion designer Jessica McClintock, Inc., San Francisco, 1969—. Active donor, AIDS and Homeless programs; scholarship sponsor Fashion Inst. Design and Merchandising. Recipient Merit award Design, 1989, Dallas Fashion award, 1988, Tommy award, 1986, Pres. Appreciation award, 1986, Best Interior Store Design, 1986, Calif. Designer award, 1985, Earnie award, 1981, numerous others. Mem. Coun. Fashion Designers of Am., Fashion Inst. Design & Merchandising (adv. bd. 1979—), San Francisco Fashion Industry (pres. 1976-78, bd. dirs. 1989). Office: Jessica McClintock Inc 1400 16th St San Francisco CA 94103-5181

MCCLINTOCK, RICHARD POLSON, dermatologist; b. Lancaster, N.H., Dec. 16, 1933; s. Richard P. and Dorothy Grace McClintock; m. Barbara Wyatt, June 1959 (div. Mar. 1970); children: Peter, Pamela; m. Mary Joy Fitzgerald, Mar. 21, 1970; children: Wayne, Patrick. BA, Dartmouth Coll., 1956; MD, Harvard U., 1960. Diplomate Am. Bd. Dermatology, Am. Bd. Dermatopathology. Intern in medicine U. N.C., Chapel Hill, 1960-61; resident in dermatology Stanford U., Palo Alto, Calif., 1964-67; pvt. practice Ukiah, 1967—; clin. instr. dermatology Stanford U., Palo Alto, 1967-78, clin. asst. prof., 1978-86, assoc. clin. prof., 1986-92, lectr., 1992-98, assoc. clin. prof., 1998—. Mem. hosp. staff Ukiah Valley Med. Ctr., chief of staff, 1974; bd. dirs. IPA and Found. Med. Care Mendocino and Lake Counties. Contbr. articles to profl. jours. Trustee Found. for Med. Care for Mendocino and Lake Counties, 1990-94, pres., 1992-94. Lt. Med. Corps, USN, 1961-64. Mem. San Francisco Dermatol. Soc., Pacific Dermatol. Assn., Am. Acad. Dermatology, Calif. Med. Soc., Mendocino Lake County Med. Soc., Internat. Soc. Dermatopathology. Office: 723 S Dora St Ukiah CA 95482-5335 E-mail: fitzmac@pacific.net

MCCLINTOCK, TOM, state senator; Rep. rep. dist. 38 Calif. Ho. of Reps., 1996-2000; Rep. senator dist. 19 Calif. State Senate, 2000—. Mem. housing and cmty. devel. Calif. Ho. of Reps. Resolutions chmn. Calif. Rep. Party; Rep. county chmn., Ventura County. Office: 10727 White Oak Ave Ste 124 Granada Hills CA 91344 also: Calif State Senate PO Box 942849 State Capitol Rm 4153 Sacramento CA 95814 Fax: 818 885-3307; 916 319-2138. E-mail: tom.mcclintock@asm.ca.gov

MCCLOSKEY, THOMAS HENRY, mechanical engineer, consultant; b. Phila., Dec. 11, 1946; s. Thomas H. McCloskey; m. Rosemary Loscalzo, July 11, 1970. BSME, Drexel U., 1969. Rsch. engr. Westinghouse Elec. Corp., Phila., 1969-80; mgr. turbo-machinery Elec. Power Rsch. Inst., Palo Alto, Calif., 1980-92, cons. turbo-machinery, 1992—. Mem. adv. bd. Internat. Pump Symposium, Houston, 1987—. Author: ASME Specification Guidelines for Large Steam Turbines, 1987; contbr. articles to profl. jours. Recipient George Westinghouse Gold medal Am. Soc. of Mechanical Engineers, 1995. Fellow ASME (dir. turbine design course 1988—, mem. rsch. bd. 1989—, Edison Elec. Prime Mover award 1984, 97, George Westinghouse Gold medal 1995). Achievements include 6 patents in turbomachinery design; development and field application of finite element/fracture mechanic techniques and erosion/corrosion resistant materials for life assessment/optimization of large turbine generators and pumps.

MCCLUGGAGE, KERRY, television executive; Chmn. Paramount TV Group, Viacom TV Group. Office: Paramount Pictures 5555 Melrose Ave Los Angeles CA 90038-3197

MCCOLLAM, CRAIG A. business executive; b. 1960; Dir. fin., corp. controller Dionex Corp, Sunnyvale, Calif., 1993-99, v.p. fin. & adminstrn., CFO, 1999—. Office: Dionex Corp PO Box 3603 1228 Titan Way Sunnyvale CA 91088-8603*

MCCOMAS, DAVID JOHN, science administrator, space physicist; b. Milw., May 22, 1958; s. Harrold James and Hazelyn (Melconian) McC.; m. Richelle Wolff, May 30, 1981; children: Random A., Koan I., Orion G. BS in Physics, MIT, 1980; MS in Geophysics and Space Physics, UCLA, 1985, PhD in Geophysics and Space Physics, 1986. Mem. staff Los Alamos (N.Mex.) Nat. Lab., 1980-91, sect. leader space plasma and planetary physics, 1991-92, NASA program mgr., group leader space and atmospheric scis., 1992-98, group leader for space and atmospheric scis., 1992-98, founding dir. Ctr. for Space Sci. and Exploration, NASA prog, 1998-2000; exec. dir. space sci. and engring. divsn. S.W. Rsch. Inst., San Antonio, 2000—. Mem. strategic planning com. earth and space scis. divsn. Los Alamos Nat. Lab, 1986; mem. advanced composition explorer phase A study team NASA, 1988-89, mem. space physics data system steering com., 1990-91, mem. inner magnetosphere imaging study team, 1991-94, prin. investigator Ulysses Solar Wind Observations Over the Poles of the Sun Experiment, Two Wide-Angle Imaging Neutral-Atom Spectrometers, Explorer Mission-of-Opportunity, Solar Wind Electron Proton Alpha Monitor (instrument on the Advanced Composition Explorer, co-investigator Medium Energy Neutral Atom instrument on IMAGE Midsized Discovery Mission, plasma instrument for Cassini mission to Saturn, GENESIS Discovery mission, ISTP Polar Spacecraft's Thermal Ion Dynamics Experiment, Cluster plasma electron instrument, team mem. New Millennium Plasma Experiment for Planetary Exploration, mem. Space Sci. Adv. Com., chmn. Sun-Earth Connections Adv. Subcom.; mem. com. solar-terrestrial rsch. Nat. Rsch. Coun., 1991-94, mem. com. space sci. tech. planning Aeronautics and Space Engring. Bd./space studies bd., 1992, mem. task group rsch. prioritization future space sci. space studies bd., 1994—; former prin. investigator series of 10 magnetospheric plasma analyzer instruments at geosynchronous orbit Dept. Energy; mem. coms. and panels Nat. Acad. Sci.'s Nat. Rsch. Coun., U. Calif., State of N.Mex., others. Assoc. editor Jour. Geophys. Rsch.-Space Physics, 1993-94; contbr. over 300 sci. papers to profl. jours.; patentee in field. Grad. fellow Inst. Geophysics and Planetary Physics, 1983-84. Fellow Am. Geophys. Union (James B. Macelwane award 1993). Office: SW Rsch Inst PO Drawer 28510 San Antonio TX 78228-0510

MC COMIC, ROBERT BARRY, real estate development company executive, lawyer; b. Selmer, Tenn., Nov. 6, 1939; s. Richard Donald and Ila Marie (Prather) McC.; children: Thomas Christopher, Robert Geoffrey. BS, Union U., 1961; LLB, Tulane U., 1964; postgrad. in law, U. Freiburg, W. Ger., 1964-65, Hague (Netherlands) Internat. Acad. Law, , 1965. Bar: Tenn. 1964, N.Y. 1966, Calif. 1971. Assoc. Donovan Leisure Newton & Irvine, N.Y.C., 1965-68; assoc. gen. counsel Avco Corp., Greenwich, Conn., 1968-70; exec. v.p., pres., CEO Avco Cmty Developers, Inc., 1973-82; chmn., CEO R.B. McComic, Inc., 1982-92, McComic Consolidated, Inc., 1992—; CEO Trans West Housing, Inc., 1994—, Globelink, LLC, 1995—; chmn. Price Smart Travel, San Diego, 2000—. Chmn. bd. dirs. Price Smart Travel. Pres. emeritus U. Calif. San Diego Found.; bd. dirs. World Affairs Coun. Honoree Human Relations Inst. Am. Jewish Com., 1981, Kellog's Celebrity Tribute, 1988. Mem. ABA, Calif. Bar Assn., San Diego County Bar Assn., Assn. of Bar of City of N.Y., San Diego Bldg. Industry Assn., San Diego Yacht Club, Order of Coif, Sigma Alpha Epsilon, Omicron Delta Kappa, Lambda Alpha. Home: 2032 Via Casa Alta La Jolla CA 92037-5732 Office: McComic Consolidated Inc 9968 Hibert St Ste 102 San Diego CA 92131 E-mail: bMcComic@Yahoo.com

MCCONNEL, RICHARD APPLETON, aerospace company official; b. Rochester, Pa., May 29, 1933; s. Richard Appleton Sr. and Dorothy (Merriman) McC.; m. Mary Francis McInnis, 1964 (div. 1984); children: Amy Ellen, Sarah Catherine; m. Penny Kendzie, 1993. BS in Naval Engring., U.S. Naval Acad., 1957; MS in Aerospace Engring., USN Postgrad. Sch., 1966. Commd. ensign USN, 1957; naval aviator Operation ASW, 1959-63, 68-71, 75-79; asst. prof. math. U.S. Naval Acad., 1966-68; program mgr. P3C update Naval Air Devel. Ctr., 1971-75; range program mgr. Pacific Missile Test Ctr., 1979-82; ret. USN, 1982; program mgr. Electromagnetic Systems div. Raytheon Co., Goleta, Calif., 1982-87; sr. engr. SRS Techs., Inc., Camarillo, 1987-92, High Tech. Solutions, Inc., Camarillo, 1992—. Mem. Internat. Test and Evaluation Assn., Assn. Old Crows. Republican. Office: High Tech Solutions 1317 Del Norte # 200 Camarillo CA 93010

MCCONNELL, HARDEN MARSDEN, biophysical chemistry researcher, chemistry educator; b. Richmond, Va., July 18, 1927; s. Harry Raymond and Frances (Coffee) McC.; m. Sophia Milo Glogovac, Oct. 6, 1956; children: Hunter, Trevor, Jane. BS, George Washington U., 1947; PhD, Calif. Inst. Tech., 1951; DSc (hon.), U. Chgo., 1991, George Washington U., 1993. NRC fellow dept. physics U. Chgo., 1950-52; research chemist Shell Devel. Co., Emeryville, Calif., 1952-56; asst. prof. chemistry Calif. Inst. Tech., 1956-58, prof. chemistry and physics, 1963-64; prof. chemistry Stanford U., Calif., 1964-79, Robert Eckles prof. chemistry, 1979—, chmn. dept., 1989—; founder Molecular Devices Corp., 1983—. Cons. in field Contbr. numerous articles to profl. publs.; patentee (in field). Pres. Found. for Basic Rsch. in Chemistry, 1990-96; hon. assoc. Neurosci. Rsch. Program. Recipient Calif. sect. award Am. Chem. Soc., 1961, award in pure chemistry Am. Chem. Soc., 1962, Harrison Howe award, 1968, Irving Langmuir award in chem. physics, 1971, Pauling medal Puget Sound and Oreg. sects., 1987, Peter Debye award in phys. chemistry, 1990; Am. Achievement award George Washington U., 1971; Disting. Alumni award Calif. Inst. Tech., 1982, Sherman Fairchild Disting. scholar, 1988; Dickson prize for sci. Carnegie-Mellon U., 1982, Wolf prize in chemistry, 1984, ISCO award, 1984; Wheland medal U. Chgo., 1988; Nat. Medal Sci., 1989, Brucker prize, 1995; Gold medal Internat. ESR Soc., Zaroisky award, 2000. Fellow AAAS, Am. Phys. Soc., Biophys. Soc.; mem. Nat. Acad. Scis. (award in chem. scis. 1988), Am. Acad. Arts and Scis., Am. Soc. Biol. Chemists, Internat. Acad. Quantum Molecular Scis., Am. Chem. Soc. (award in Surface Chemistry 1997), Serbian Acad. Scis. and Arts (Zaroisky award). Office: Stanford U Dept Chemistry Stanford CA 94305

MCCONNELL, J. DANIEL, sports marketing professional; b. Noblesville, Ind., Oct. 5, 1944; s. John Worley and Nadine Lillian (McFarlin) McC.; m. Jane Brantlinger, June 29, 1968. AB in English/Journalism, Ind. U., 1966, MS in Bus., 1968. Asst. to pres. Ind. U. Found., Bloomington, 1966-67; legis. liaison Dept. HEW, Washington, 1968; dir. pub. rels. Cummins Engine Co., Columbus, Ind., 1970-72, dir. investor comm., 1972-75, dir. exec. recruiting, 1975-77; prin., CEO The McConnell Co. Pub. Rels., Seattle, 1977-93; sr. v.p., group dir. Elgin DDB, Seattle, 1993-96, sr. v.p., mng. dir., 1997—. Founder The Mountain Summit Internat. Symposium, 1987—; co-founder Coll. Baseball Classic Found., 1990-95; bd. dirs. Great Adventures Ltd., Jersey, U.K. Bd. dirs. Child Haven, Seattle, 1985-91, Internat. Snow Leopard Trust, Seattle, 1991-95, Pacific Crest Outward Bound Sch., Portland, Oreg., 1992-2001; trustee Seattle Ctrl. C.C., 1992—, bd. pres., 1997—; mem. adv. bd. pub. rels. cert. program U. Wash., 1990—, instr., 1991—. Capt. U.S. Army, 1968-70. Mem. Pub. Rels. Soc. (Hoosier chpt. bd. dirs. 1975-77, Puget Sound bd. dirs. 1995-98). Avocations: snow skiing, mountaineering, racquetball, sailing. Office: DDB Worldwide 1008 Western Ave Ste 601 Seattle WA 98104-1032 E-mail: dan.mcconnell@sea.ddb.com

MCCONNELL, ROBERT EASTWOOD, architect, educator; b. Spokane, Wash., July 15, 1930; s. Robert Ervie and Alma (Eastwood) Mc C.; m. Beverly Ann Vincent, Sept. 12, 1953; children: Kathleen Ann, Karen Eileen, Terri Lynn. B in Archtl. Engring., Wash. State U., 1952; MArch, Mass. Inst. Tech., 1954. Project architect John W. Maloney (Architect), Seattle, 1956-62; asst. prof. architecture Ariz. State U., Tempe, 1962-66, asso. prof., 1966-67; prof. U. Kans., Lawrence, 1967-69; prof., head dept. art and architecture U. Idaho, Moscow, 1969-71; prof. U. Ariz., Tucson, 1971-92, dean Coll. Architecture, 1971-77, prof. emeritus, dean emeritus, 1992—, acting assoc. dean, 1994; partner McConnell & Peterson, Architects, Tempe, 1963-66; pvt. practice architecture, 1962-96. Author, project dir.: Land Use Planning for Ariz., Ariz. Acad, 1974; Contbr. articles to profl. jours. Chmn. Idaho Gov.'s Awards Program in Arts and Humanities, 1970; project dir. Rio Salado Conceptual Study, Phoenix, 1966; bd. dirs. Tucson Regional Plan, 1972-79. Served with USAF, 1954-56. Fellow AIA (awards 1969, 76, pres. So. Ariz. chpt. 1975-76, bd. dirs. 1971-77); mem. AIA Ariz. (mem. coun. of dels. 1971-77, chmn. honor awards jury 1975), Phi Kappa Phi, Scarab, Tau Beta Pi, Sigma Tau. Home: 930 East Camino Corrida Tucson AZ 85737

MCCORD, JOE MILTON, biochemist, educator; b. Memphis, Mar. 3, 1945; s. James Charles and Clara Elizabeth (Brown) McC. BS in Chemistry, Rhodes Coll., 1966; PhD in Biochemistry, Duke U., 1970. Research assoc. Duke U. Med. Ctr., Durham, N.C., 1971, assoc. in exptl. medicine, 1972-76, asst. med. research prof., 1976; assoc. prof. U. South Ala., Mobile, 1976-80, prof., dept. co-chmn., 1980-81, chmn. dept. biochemistry, 1981-90; prof. medicine and biochemistry Webb-Waring Inst. Biomed. Rsch. U. Colo., Denver, 1990—. Sci. cons. BioTech. Gen., N.Y., 1985—, CIBA-GEIGY Corp., Summit, N.J., 1984-85. Co-recipient Elliott Cresson medal Franklin Inst., 1997. Mem. Am. Soc. Biol. Chemists, Ala. Acad. Sci., Reticuloendothelial Soc., Am. Heart Assn. (council on basic sci.). Home: 390 S Hudson St Apt 6 Denver CO 80246-1448 Office: U Colo Webb Waring Lung Inst PO Box C-321 Denver CO 80262-0001

MC CORMACK, FRANCIS XAVIER, lawyer, former oil company executive; b. Bklyn., July 9, 1929; s. Joseph and Blanche V. (Dengel) Mc C.; m. Margaret V. Hynes, Apr. 24, 1954; children: Marguerite, Francis Xavier, Sean Michael, Keith John, Cecelia Blanche, Christopher Thomas. AB cum laude, St. Francis Coll., Bklyn., 1951; LLB, Columbia U., 1954. Bar: N.Y. 1955, Mich. 1963, Calif. 1974, Pa. 1975. Assoc. Cravath, Swaine & Moore, N.Y.C., 1956-62; sr. atty. Ford Motor Co., 1962-64, asst. gen. counsel, 1970-72; v.p., gen. counsel, sec. Philco-Ford Corp., 1964-72; v.p., gen. counsel Atlantic Richfield Co., 1972-73, sr. v.p., gen. counsel, 1973-94. Editor Columbia U. Law Rev., 1954. Decorated commendatore Ordine al Merito (Italy); Stone scholar Columbia U., 1954. Mem. Calif. Club, Chancery Club, Annandale Golf Club. Home and Office: 975 Singingwood Dr Arcadia CA 91006-1924

MCCORMICK, HOMER L., JR. lawyer; b. Frederick, Md., Nov. 11, 1928; s. Homer Lee McCormick and Rosebelle Irene Biser; m. Jacquelyn R.; children: Deidre Ann and Thomas Lee. Student, George Washington U., 1946-48; AB, San Jose State U., 1951; JD, U. Calif., San Francisco, 1961. Bar: Calif. 1961, U.S. Dist. Ct. Ctrl. Dist. Calif. 1972, U.S. Dist. No. Calif. 1961, U.S. Dist. Ct., So. Dist. Calif. 1976, U.S. Dist. Ct. of Appeals (9th cir. 1961), U.S. Tax Ct. 1977, U.S. Ct. Claims 1977, U.S. Supreme Ct. 1977. Atty. Holiway Jones State of Calif., 1961-63; atty. assoc. Rutan & Tucker, Santa Ana, Calif., 1963-66, atty. ptnr., 1966-70, atty., sr. ptnr. Costa Mesa, 1970-88, dept. head pub. law, 1974-88, mng. ptnr., 1984-88; founding ptnr., sr. ptnr. McCormick, Kidman & Behrens, Costa Mesa, 1988—. Arbitrator Am. Arbitration Assn., 1966-88; judge pro tem Orange County Superior Ct., 1975, 81, 84; spkr., lectr. Cal. Continuing Edn. of the Bar, 1976-88; profl. designation Internat. Right of Way Assn.; elected mem. Cal. Condemnation Lawyers, 1994—. Contbg. author: Real Property Remedies, 1982; contbr. articles to profl. jours. Mem. bd. govs. Bus. Com. Arts, Orange County Philharm. Soc. Lt. USMCR, 1951-56; pilot, Korea. Named Alumnus of Year Hastings Law Sch., 1992. Mem. ABA (com. chair 1991), Am. Bd. Trial Adv. (pres. O.C. chpt. 1973), Orange City Atty. Assn. (pres. 1972), Fed. Bar Assoc., Consumer Attys. Calif., Am. Judicature Soc., Orange County Bar Assn. (com. chair 1991-92), Orange County Bus. Trial Lawyers, Order Coif, Thurston Soc., Hastings Alumni Assn. (pres. 1973), Springs Country Club, Delta Theta Pi. Republican. Episcopalian. Avocations: boating, fishing, flying, golf, foreign travel.

MCCORMICK, RICHARD LEVIS, academic administrator; b. New Brunswick, N.J., Dec. 26, 1947; s. Richard Patrick and Katheryne Crook (Levis) McC.; m. Suzanne Dee Lebsock, Aug. 30, 1984; children: Elizabeth, Michael. BA in Am. Studies, Amherst Coll., 1969; PhD in History, Yale U., 1976. From asst. prof. to prof. Rutgers U., New Brunswick, N.J., 1976-92, dean Faculty Arts and Scis., 1989-92; exec. vice chancellor, provost, vice chancellor acad. affair U. N.C., Chapel Hill, 1992-95; pres. U. Wash., Seattle, 1995—. Author: From Realignment to Reform: Political Change in New York State, 1893-1910, 1981, The Party Period and Public Policy: American Politics from the Age of Jackson to the Progressive Era, 1986. Rsch. fellow Am. Coun. Learned Socs., 1978-79, fellow John Simon Guggenheim Meml. Found., 1985. Mem. Phi Beta Kappa. Home: 806 36th Ave E Seattle WA 98112-4320 Office: U Wash Seattle WA 98195-0001

MCCOVEY, WILLIE LEE, former professional baseball player; b. Mobile, Ala., Jan. 10, 1938; s. Frank and Ester (Jones) McC. Minor league baseball player, 1955-59; first baseman San Francisco Giants, 1959-73, 77-80, active in pub. rels., 1981-86, spl. asst. to pres., 1986-94; mem. San Diego Padres, 1974-76, Oakland Athletics, 1976-81. Named Nat. League Rookie of Year, 1959, Most Valuable Player, 1969; Home Run Champion, 1963, 68, 69; Runs Batted In Leader, 1968, 69; Comeback Player of Year, 1977; 10th on All-Time Major League List of Career Home Runs (521); All-Time Nat. League leader in grand slam home runs (18); mem. Nat. League All-Star Team, 1963, 66, 68-71; inducted into Baseball Hall of Fame, 1986 Office: c/o San Francisco Giants 3 Compark at Candlestick Pk San Francisco CA 94124 also: Baseball Hall Fame PO Box 590 Cooperstown NY 13326-0590

MCCOY, HARRY E., II, lawyer; b. Parkersburg, W.Va., June 27, 1938; BA, U. Utah, 1967, JD, 1970. Bar: Utah 1970, Tex. 1974. Ptnr. Ballard Spahr Andrews & Ingersoll, LLP, Salt Lake City. Founding dir. ARDA Internat. Found., 1983—; bd. dirs., chair legis. coun., Am. Resort Devel. Assn. Mem. Utah State Bar. Office: Ballard Spahr Andrews & Ingersoll LLP 201 S Main St Ste 600 Salt Lake City UT 84111-2221 E-mail: mccoy2@ballardspahr.com

MCCRACKEN, STEVEN CARL, lawyer; b. Artesia, Calif., Oct. 29, 1950; s. Glenn A. and Helen V. (Fears) McCracken; m. Susan Lee Waggener, July 29, 1979; children: Casey James, Scott Kevin. BA magna cum laude, U. Calif., Irvine, 1972; JD, U. Va., 1975. Bar: Calif. 1975, U.S. Dist. Ct. (cen. dist.) Calif. 1975, U.S. Ct. Appeals (9th cir.) 1976, U.S. Dist. Ct. (no. dist.) Calif. 1977, D.C. 1979, U.S. Supreme Ct. 1985, U.S. Dist. Ct. (so. dist.) Calif. 1990. Assoc. Gibson, Dunn & Crutcher, L.A., 1975-82, ptnr. Irvine, Calif., 1983-94; v.p., sec. and gen. counsel Callaway Golf Co., Carlsbad, 1994-96, exec. v.p., gen. counsel and sec., 1996-97, exec. v.p. licensing, chief legal officer, sec., 1997-2000, sr. exec. v.p., chief legal officer, sec., 2000—. Lawyer rep. Ninth Cir. Jud. Conf., 1989-91. Editor Va. Law Rev., 1973-75, mng. bd. 1974-75, bd. editors The Computer Lawyer, 1984-96. Mem. ABA (antitrust sect.), Orange County Bar Assn. (bd. dirs. 1988-90, chmn. fed. ct. com. 1988-89, chmn. bus. litigation sect. 1990, sec. 1991, treas. 1992, pres.-elect 1993, pres. 1994). Democrat. Office: Callaway Golf Co 2180 Rutherford Rd Carlsbad CA 92008-8815

MCCRANK, MICHAEL NEIL, government official; b. Bourlamaque, Que., Can., May 9, 1943; s. Ernest Martin and Anna Mary (Amyotte) McC.; married, Aug. 26, 1967; children: Jason, Kelly, Darren, Matthew. BSc, Queen's U., Kingston, Ont., Can., 1966, LLB, 1969. Assoc. Lang, Michener, Toronto, Ont., 1969-73; asst. crown atty. Regional Municipality of Durham, Whitby, 1973-79; spl. prosecutor Alta. Atty. Gen., Edmonton, Can., 1979-82, dir. spl. prosecutions Can., 1982-84, asst. dep. min. criminal justice Can., 1984-90, acting dep. Can., 1989, dep. atty. gen. Can., 1990, dep. min. justice Can., 1993-98; chmn. AB Energy Utilities Bd., Calgory, Can., 1998—. Chmn. liaison officers com. Can. Ctr. for Justice. Bd. dirs. Cath. Social Svcs., Edmonton, 1988-92, chmn. bd. dirs., 1992-93; chmn. bd. dirs. Edmonton Cath. Charities, 1994-99. Recipient Commemorative medal for 125th Anniversary of Confedn. Can., 1992. Office: AB Energy Utilities Bd 640 5th Ave SW Calgary AB Canada T2P 3G4

MCCRAVEN, EVA STEWART MAPES, health service administrator; b. L.A., Sept. 26, 1936; d. Paul Melvin and Wilms Zech (Ziegler) Stewart; m. Carl Clarke McCraven, Mar. 18, 1978; children: David Anthony, Lawrence James, Maria Lynn Mapes. ABS magna cum laude, Calif. State U., Northridge, 1974; MS, Cambridge Grad. Sch. Psycholoy, 1987, PhD, 1991. Dir. spl. projects Pacoima Meml. Hosp., 1969-71, dir. health edn., 1971-74; ast. exec. dir., v.p. Hillview Cmty. Mental Health Ctr., Lakeview Terrace, Calif., 1974-99, exec. dir., 1999—, former dir. clin. svcs. Past dir. dept. consultation and edn. Hillview Ctr., developer, mgr. long-term residential program, 1986-90; former program mgr. crisis residential program, transitional residential program and day treatment program for mentally ill offenders, past dir. mentally ill offenders svcs.; former program dir. Valley Homeless Shelter Mental Health Counseling Program; dir. Integrated Svcs. Agy., Hillview Mental Health Ctr., Inc., 1993-98, dir. clin. programs, 1996-99, exec. dir. 1999—. Former pres. San Fernando Valley Coordinating Coun. Area Assn., Sunland-Jujunga Coordinating Coun.; bd. advisors Pacoima Sr. Citizens Multi-Purpose Ctr.; bd. dirs. N.E. Valley Health Corp., 1970-73, Golden Gate Cmty. Mental Health Ctr., 1970-73. Recipient resolution of commendation State of Calif., 1988, commendation award, 1988, spl. mayor's plaque, 1988, commendation awards for cmty. svcs. City of L.A., 1989, County of Los Angeles, 1989, Calif. Assembly, 1989, Calif. Senate, 1989, award Sunland-Tujunga Police Support Coun., 1989, Women of Achievement award Sunland-Tujunga Bus and Profl. Women, 1990. Mem. Health Svcs. Adminstrn. Alumni Assn. (past v.p.), Sunland-Jujunga Bus. and Profl. Women, LWV, Valley Philharm. Soc. Office: Hillview Cmty Mental Health Ctr 11500 Eldridge Ave Lake View Terrace CA 91342-6523

MCCRAW, LESLIE G. retired engineering and construction company executive; b. Sandy Springs, S.C., Nov. 3, 1934; s. Leslie Gladstone and Cornelia (Milam) McC.; m. Mary Earle Brown; children: Leslie Gladstone III, James B., John. BSCE, Clemson U., 1956. Registered profl. engr., Del. Design engr. Gulf Oil Corp., Phila., 1956-57; various engring. and constrn. positions E.I. DuPont Co., Wilmington, Del., 1960-75; v.p., mgr. div. Daniel Constrn. Co., Greenville, S.C., 1975-82, pres., 1982-84; pres., chief exec. officer Daniel Internat., Greenville, 1984-86, Fluor Daniel, Greenville and Irvine, Calif., 1986-88; pres. Fluor Corp., Irvine, 1988-90, vice chmn., chief exec. officer, 1990-91, chief exec. officer, chmn. bd. dirs., 1991-97; ret., 1997. Bd. dirs. Allergan, N.Y. Life Ins. Co., U.S.-China Bus. Coun.; trustee Hampden-Sydney Coll., Va.; adv. bd. rsch. found., pres.'s adv. coun. Clemson U.; bd. visitors U. Calif. Grad. Sch. Mgmt.; internat. adv. bd. Br.-Am. Bus. Coun. Mem. NAM (bd. dirs.), Bus. Roundtable, Constrn. Industy's Presidents' Forum, Calif. Bus. Roundtable, Palmetto Bus. Forum, Pres.'s Export Coun. Republican. Presbyterian.

MCCRAY, RICHARD ALAN, astrophysicist, educator; b. L.A., Nov. 24, 1937; s. Alan Archer and Ruth Elizabeth (Woodworth) McC.; m. Sandra Broomfield; children: Julia, Carla BS, Stanford U., 1959; PhD, UCLA, 1967. Rsch. fellow Calif. Inst. Tech, Pasadena, 1967-68; asst. prof. astronomy Harvard U., Cambridge, Mass., 1968-71; assoc. prof. astrophysics U. Colo., Boulder, 1971-75, prof., 1975—, chmn. Joint Inst. Lab. Astrophysics, 1981-82, chmn. Ctr. for Astrophysics and Space Astronomy, 1985-86, George Gamow prof. astrophysics, 1998—; corr. prof. astronomy Nanjing (China) U., 1996—. Contbr. articles to profl. jours. Guggenheim fellow, 1975-76 Mem. NAS, Am. Astron. Soc. (councilor 1980-83, chmn. high energy astrophysics div. 1986-87, Heineman Prize for Astrophysics, 1990), Internat. Astron. Union Office: U Colo Joint Inst Lab Astrophysics Boulder CO 80309-0001 E-mail: dick@jila.colorado.edu

MCCREADY, KENNETH FRANK, past electric utility executive; b. Edmonton, Alta., Can., Oct. 9, 1939; s. Ralph and Lilian McCready; children: John, Janet, Brian. BSc, U. Alta., 1963. Supr. data processing and systems Calgary (Alta.) Power Ltd., 1965-67, supr. rates and contracts, 1967-68, adminstrv. asst. to exec. v.p., 1968-72, asst. mgr. mgmt. cons. div., 1972-75; mgr. mgmt. systems dept., gen. mgr. Montreal Engring. Co., Calgary, 1975-76; v.p. adminstrn. Calgary (Alta.) Power Ltd., 1976-80; sr. v.p. ops. TransAlta Utilities, Calgary, 1980-85, pres., COO, 1985-89, also bd. dirs., 1988-96; pres., CEO TransAlta Corp., 1989-96; CEO TransAlta Energy Corp., 1989-96; pres. K. F. McCready & Assocs. Ltd., Calgary, 1996—. Bd. dirs. PanCan. Petroleum Ltd., ABB Asea Brown Boveri Environment adv. bd., Zurich,, Colonia Corp., Calgary, Airborne Techs. I. Adv. Bd., Calgary, Computer Modelling Group, Calgary, Can. Environ. Tech. Advancement Corp., Calgary, Internat. Inst. Sustainable Devel., Winnipeg; past chmn. Conf. Bd. Can.; past chmn. bd. Advanced Computing Techs., Inc.; mem. Dow Chem. Corp. Adv. Coun., Midland, Tata Energy Rsch. Inst. adv. bd., Washington; past mem. World Bus. Coun. for Sustainable Devel.; past chair Conf. Bd. Can.; past moderator Premier's Forum, Govt. of Alta. Past dep. chmn. bd. govs. So. Alta. Inst. Tech.; past chair Alta. Round Table on Environment and Econ.; past mem. com. on trade and environment Govt. Can. Internat. Trade Adv.; past pres. Western Electric Power and Light Assn.; past chair environ. task force Bus. Coun. Nat. Issues. Mem. Assn. Profl. Engrs., Geologists and Geophysicists of Alta., Ranchmen's Club. Avocations: computers, cycling, photography. E-mail: ken.mccready@cadvision.com

MCCREARY, DEBORAH DENNIS, oncology nurse; b. Washington, Oct. 6, 1952; d. Eldon Hugh Dennis and Janice Sylvia (North) Saunders; m. James Leo McCreary, May 21, 1988. BSN, Ohio State Sch. Nursing, 1976. Nurse Ohio State U. Hosp., Columbus, 1976-77; asst. head nurse Riverside Meth. Hosp., Columbus, 1977-80; nurse Good Samaritan Hosp., San Jose, Calif., 1980-82; asst. head nurse Valley West Hosp., San Jose, 1982; outpatient oncology nurse Southbay Med. Oncology, San Jose, 1982-88; oncology nurse specialist, office mgr. Menlo Med. Clinic, Menlo Park, Calif., 1988-98. Cons. Schering Corp., Dallas, 1991, Berlix, Menlo Park, 1992, spkr., 1994, Ortho Biotech, San Francisco, 1995. Mem. Oncology Nursing Soc. (Santa Clara chpt. sec. 1982-84, membership chair 1984-85, cert. oncology nurse). Republican. Avocations: classical music, piano, gourmet cooking, hiking, travel. Home: 23750 Ravensbury Ave Los Altos CA 94024-6341 E-mail: debbiemccreary@hotmail.com

MCCRONE, ALISTAIR WILLIAM, university president; b. Regina, Can., Oct. 7, 1931; BA, U. Sask., 1953; MSc, U. Nebr., 1955; PhD, U. Kans., 1961. Instr. geology NYU, 1959-61, asst. prof., 1961-64, assoc. prof., 1964-69, prof., 1969-70, supr. Rsch. Ship Sea Owl on L.I. Sound, 1959-64, asst. dir. univ. program, 1965-66, resident master Rubin Internat. Residence Hall, 1966-69, chmn. dept. geology, 1966-69, assoc. dean Grad. Sch. Arts and Scis., 1969-70; prof. geology, acad. v.p. U. Pacific, 1970-74, acting pres., 1971; prof. geology, pres. Calif. State U. Sys. Humboldt State U., Arcata, 1974—. Mem. sys. exec. coun. Calif. State U. Sys., 1974—, acad. senate Humboldt State U., 1974—, mem. chancellor's com. on innovative programs, 1974-76, trustees' task force on off-campus instrn., 1975-76, exec. com. Chancellor's Coun. of Pres., 1976-79, Calif. state del. Am. Assn. State Colls. and Univs., 1977-80; mem. Commn. on Edni. Telecomm., 1983-86; chair Calif. State U. Statewide Task Force on Earthquake and Emergency preparedness, 1985-88, 95; chmn., mem. accreditation teams Western Assn. Schs. and Colls.; chair com. on energy and environ. Am. Assn. State Colls. and Univs., 1980-84; chair program com. Western Coll.Assn., 1983-84, panelist, 1983; mem. bd. dirs. Assn. Am. Colls., 1989-93, chair, 1992-93. Contbr. articles to profl. jours.; lectr. on geology Sunrise Semester program CBS Nat. Network, 1969-70; various appearances on local TV stas. Bd. trustees Presbyn. Hosp.-Pacific Med. Ctr., San Francisco, 1971-74; mem. Calif. Coun. for Humanities, 1977-82; mem. local campaign bd. United Way, 1977-83; mem. Am. Friends Wilton Park, 1980—; bd. dirs. Humboldt Convention and Visitors Bur., 1980-87, Redwood Empire Assn., 1983-87; bd. dirs. Calif. State Automobile Assn., 1988—, Am. Automobile Assn., 1990-93; bd. trustees Calif. State Parks Found., 1994-2000. Shell fellow in geology U. Nebr., 1954-55; Danforth assoc. NYU, 1964. Fellow Calif. Acad. Scis.; mem. AAAS, Geol. Soc. Am., Am. Assn. U. Adminstrs. (nat. bd. 1986-89, 96-99, 2001—), St. Andrews Soc. N.Y. (life), Rotary, Sigma Xi (pres. NYU chpt. 1967-69), Phi Kappa Phi. Avocation: golf. Office: Humboldt State U Univ Campus Arcata CA 95521

MCCROSKEY, WILLIAM JAMES, aeronautical engineer; b. San Angelo, Tex., Mar. 9, 1937; s. J. M. and W. Elizabeth McC.; m. Elizabeth W. Wear, Jan. 31, 1960; children: Nancy E., Susan C. BS, U. Tex., 1960; MS, Princeton U., 1962, PhD, 1966. Rsch. assoc. Princeton U., 1966; rsch. engr. U.S. Army Aeromechanics Lab., Moffett Field, Calif., 1966-80; sr. rsch. scientist U.S. Army and NASA Aeronautics Directorate, 1980—. Exch. scientist Office Nat. Etudes et Recherches Aérospatiale, Châtillon, France, 1972-73; mem. fluid dynamics panel NATO Adv. Group for Aerospace R & D, 1976-94, chmn., 1989-91. With U.S. Army, 1966-68. Recipient French Medaille l'Aeronautique, 1994, AGARD von Kármán medal, 1995, Nat. Acad. Engring., 1996. Fellow AIAA (Outstanding Engr. San Francisco sect. 1975, fluid dynamics tech com. 1984-88, internat. activities com. 1990—); mem. ASME (Freeman scholar award 1976), Am. Helicopter Soc. (Howard Hughes award 1991). Office: Ames Rsch Ctr N258-1 Moffett Field CA 94035

MC CULLOCH, SAMUEL CLYDE, history educator; b. Ararat, Australia, Sept. 3, 1916; came to U.S., 1936, naturalized, 1944; s. Samuel and Agnes Almond (Clyde) McC.; m. Sara Ellen Rand, Feb. 19, 1944; children: Ellen (Mrs. William Henry Meyer III), David Rand, Malcolm Clyde. A.B. with highest honors in History, UCLA, 1940, M.A. (grad. fellow history), 1942; Ph.D., U. Calif. at Los Angeles, 1944. Asst. U. Calif. at Los Angeles, 1943-44; instr. Oberlin Coll., 1944-45; asst. prof. Amherst Coll., 1945-46; vis. asst. prof. U. Mich., 1946-47; mem. faculty Rutgers U., 1947-60, prof. history, assoc. dean arts and scis., 1958-60; dean coll., prof. history San Francisco State Coll., 1960-63; dean humanities, prof. history U. Calif. at Irvine, 1963-70, prof., 1970-87, prof. emeritus, 1987—, coordinator Edn. Abroad Program, 1975-85, dir. Australian Study Ctr., 1986, 87. Vis. summer prof. Oberlin Coll., 1945, 46, U. Calif. at Los Angeles, 1947, U. Del., 1949; Fulbright Research prof. Monash U., Melbourne (Australia) U., 1970; Am. Philos. Soc. grantee, 1970 Author: British Humanitarianism, 1950, George Gipps, 1966, River King: The Mc Culloch Carrying Company and Echura, 1865-1898, 1986, Instant University: A History of U.C.I., 1957-1993, 1995, William McCulloch, 1932-1909, 1997, A Collection of Book Reviews, 1948-93, 2000; contbr. numerous articles, revs. to profl. jours.; assoc. editor Jour. Brit. Studies, 1960-68, bd. advisors, 1968-70; bd. corrs. Hist. Studies: Australia and New Zealand, 1949-83. Mem. Calif. Curriculum Commn., 1961-67, Highland Park (N.J.) Bd. Edn., 1959-60. Grantee Am. Philos. Soc., Social Sci. Research Council and Rutgers U. Research Council to Australia, 1951; Fulbright research fellow U. Sydney, Australia, 1954-55; grantee Social Sci. Research Council to Eng., summer 1955 Fellow Royal Hist. Soc.; mem. Am. Hist. Assn., Church, Royal Australian hist. socs., A.A.U.P., Conf. Brit. Studies (exec. sec. 1968-73, pres. 1975-77), English Speaking Union (pres. New Brunswick 1957-59), Phi Beta Kappa, Pi Gamma Mu. Episcopalian (vestry). Home: 2121 Windward Ln Newport Beach CA 92660-3820 Office: U Calif Dept History Irvine CA 92717

MCCUNE, ELLIS E. retired university system chief administrator, higher education consultant; b. Houston, July 17, 1921; s. Ellis E. and Ruth (Mason) McC.; m. Hilda May Whiteman, Feb. 8, 1946; 1 son, James Donald. Student, Sam Houston State U., 1940-42; B.A., UCLA, 1948, Ph.D., 1957; LHD, Golden Gate U., 1994. Teaching asst. UCLA, 1949-51; from instr. to assoc. prof. polit. sci. Occidental Coll., Los Angeles, 1951-59, chmn. applied politics and econs. curriculum, 1951-56; asst. prof. Calif. State U., Northridge, 1959-61, assoc. prof., chmn. dept. polit. sci., 1961-63, prof., 1963, dean letters and sci., 1963; dean acad. planning Calif. State Univs. and Colls., 1963-67; pres. Calif. State U., Hayward, 1967-90, pres. emeritus, 1991—; acting chancellor The Calif. State U. System, 1990-91, ret., 1991. Cons. govtl. units and agys.; lectr., panelist; mem. Calif. State Scholarship and Loan Commn., 1964-68, chmn., 1967-68; pres. Govtl. Adminstrn. Group Los Angeles, 1959; chair planning com., mem. exec. com., bd. dirs. Eden Med. Ctr. Found., 1994—, pres.-elect, 1995-97, pres., 1997-99. Chmn. univs. and colls. div. United Bay Area Crusade, 1969-70, 73-74; bd. dirs. Oakland (Calif.) Museum Assn., 1974-77, 86-88, Hayward Area Hist. Soc., 1998—; vice chmn. higher edn. div., East Bay United Way, 1989-90; mem. arts adv. council, 1986-87, devel. com., 1988-89, Bay Area Urban League, bd. trust Calif. Coun. Econ. Edn. No. sect., Emergency Shelter Program Adv. Coun., Hayward Area Hist. Assn., NAACP Hayward chpt.; trustee Calif. Council Econ. Edn.; sec. bd. dirs. Eden Community Found., 1978-79; rsch. fellow Haynes Found, 1957. With USAAF, 1942-46. Mem. Am. Coun. Edn. (adv. com. 1970-72, inst. coll. & univ. adminstrs. 1973 74, bd. dirs. 1985-86), Western Assn. Schs. and Colls. (accrediting commn. sr. colls. and univs. 1974-78, chmn., 1978-82, pres. 1979-81), N.W. Assn. Schs. and Colls. (commn. colls. 1974-80), Assn. Am. Colls. (bd. dirs. 1972-75, vice chmn. 1975-76), Assn. Western Univs. (bd. dirs.), Coun. Postsecondary Accreditation (bd. dirs. 1977-88, exec. com. 1979-88, chmn. 1985-87, immediate past chmn., 1988-89, chmn. com. recognition 1982-84), Am. Assn. State Colls. and Univs. (chmn. accreditation com. 1983-86, com. acad. pers. and acad. freedom 1987-88, com. on acad. affairs 1988-91), Calif. Coun. Edn. (trustee), Western Polit. Sci. Assn. (exec. coun. 1958-61), Hayward C. of C. (dir. 1968-71, 73-76, 77-80, 82-85, 86-90), Regional Assn. East Bay Colls. and Univs. (exec. com. 1974-90, sec. 1975-76, 87-88, vice chmn. 1976-77, 84-85, chmn. 1977-79, 85-86), Rotary, Phi Beta Kappa, Pi Gamma Mu, Pi Sigma Alpha. Club: Bohemian (San Francisco). Home: 22012 Sevilla Rd # 85 Hayward CA 94541 2735 Office: Calif State U Pres Emeritus LI 3167 Hayward CA 94542-3053 Fax: 510-537-3581. E-mail: EMcCune@worldnet.att.net

MCCUNE, SARA MILLER, foundation executive, publisher; b. N.Y.C., Feb. 4, 1941; d. Nathan M. and Rose (Glass) M.; m. George D. McCune, Oct. 16, 1966 (dec. May 1990). BA, Queens Coll., 1961. Asst. to v.p. sales Macmillan Pub. Co., N.Y.C., 1961-63; sales mgr. Pergamon Press Ltd., Oxford, England, 1963-64; pres., pub., founder Sage Publs. Inc., N.Y.C., 1965-66, pres., pub. Beverly Hills, Calif., 1966-83, pub., chmn. Newbury Park, 1984—; bd. dirs. Sage Publs. Ltd., London, chmn., 1990-95; bd. dirs. Sage Publs. India, New Delhi; pres. McCune Found., Newbury Park, Calif., 1990—. Mem. bd. dirs. UCSB Comm. Dept. Adv. Bd., Santa Barbara, Calif., 1994—, USCB Bd. Trustees, 1994—, The Fielding Inst., 1994—, Am. Acad. Pol. Scis., Phila., 1994—. Bd. dirs. USCB Found. Bd. Trustees, 1994—, sec., 1996-97, treas., 1997-98, vice-chair, 1998—. Mem. Am. Evaluation Assn. (spl. award for disting. contbns. 1988). Office: Sage Publications Inc 2455 Teller Rd Newbury Park CA 91320-2234

MCDANIEL, RODERICK ROGERS, petroleum engineer, consultant; b. High River, Alta., Can., 1926; s. Dorsey Patton and Daisy (Rogers) McD.; m. Trudy Ethier, Apr. 15, 2000; children: Nancy, Leslie. BS, U. Okla., 1947. Petroleum reservoir engr. Creole Petroleum Corp., 1947, Imperial Oil Ltd., 1948-52, chief reservoir engr., 1952-55; founder McDaniel Cons., Calgary, 1955—; chmn. Can. Airlines Ltd., Calgary, 1974-91, Can. Regional Airlines, Calgary, 1991-92. Bd. dirs. Prudential Steel Ltd. Hon. dir. Calgary Exhbn. and Stampede, 1979-88, hon. bd. dirs., 1988—; dir. Calgary Stampeder Football Team, 1988, Corp. Commissionaires S.A.B. Mem. Assn. Profl. Engrs. Alta (hon. life), Can. C. of C. (bd. dirs. 1973), Calgary C. of C. (past pres.), Calgary Petroleum Club (past pres.), Calgary Highlanders (hon. col. ret.), Ranchmen's Club, Calgary Golf and Country Club, Outrigger Club (Honolulu), Mission Hills Country Club. Mem. Progressive Conservative Party. Home: # 2200 255 5 Ave SW Calgary AB Canada T2P 3G6 Office: McDaniel & Assoc 2200 255 5th Ave SW Calgary AB Canada T2P 3G6

MCDAVID, DOUGLAS WARREN, systems consultant; b. San Francisco, Feb. 25, 1947; s. James Etheridge and Elizabeth Rae (Warren) McD.; m. Nancy Kathleen Somers, June 1968 (div. 1982); 1 child, Amy Kemp; m. Carleen Ann Richmond, Feb. 14, 1987; 1 child, Amanda Claire. BA in Sociology, U. Calif., Santa Cruz, 1969; MA in Libr. Sci., San Jose State U., 1972. Libr. Palo Alto (Calif.) City Libr., 1969-81; systems analyst Tymnet (Tymshare), Cupertino, Calif., 1981-84; mgr. systems architecture Tymnet McDonnell Douglas, San Jose, 1984-86; data modeling cons. Fireman's Fund Ins., Terra Linda, 1986-87, Bank of Calif., San Francisco, 1988; systems cons. Pacific Bell, San Ramon, Calif., 1989-93; prin. Integrated Info., 1993—; exec. cons. IBM Global Svcs., 1995—. Mem. IBM Acad. Tech., 2000—; spkr. Entity/Relationship Conf. Internat., Burlingame, Calif., 1991, DAMA Internat. Conf., 1994—; sr. cons. in bus. semantic modeling for object oriented applications IBM Corp., 1994—; 1996 spkr. Bus. Rules Conf. OOPSLA, IBM Object Technology Conf., Ind. Labor & Mgmt. Coun.; cons. IBM, 1994-98, mgr. knowledge devel., 1999—; spkr. in field. Assoc. editor: Handbook of Object Technology. Mem. IEEE, Assn. for Computing Machinery, Data Adminstrn. Mgmt. Assn. (San Francisco bd. dirs. 1987-91, Sacramento bd. dirs. 1992, speaker 1991, 92), Data Processing Mgmt. Assn. (speaker 1992), Am. Assn. Artificial Intelligence (speaker 1993). Avocations: golf, gardening, creative writing, investing, swimming. Home and Office: 8611 Kingslynn Ct Elk Grove CA 95624-3135 E-mail: mcdavid@us.ibm.com

MCDERMOTT, JAMES A. congressman, psychiatrist; b. Chicago, Ill., Dec. 28, 1936; children: Katherine, James. BS, Wheaton Coll., 1958; MD, U. Ill., 1963. Intern Buffalo Gen. Hosp., 1963-64; resident in adult psychiatry U. Ill. Hosps., Chgo., 1964-66; resident in child psychiatry U. Wash. Hosps., Seattle, 1966-68; asst. clin. prof. dept. psychiatry U. Wash., Seattle, 1970-83; mem. Wash. Ho. of Reps., 1971-72, Wash. Senate, 1975-87; regional med. officer U.S. Fgn. Svc., 1987-88; mem. U.S. Congress from 7th Wash. dist., 1989—; former chmn. standards of ofcl. conduct com.; mem. ways and means com., budget com. Mem. exec. and edn. com. Nat. Conf. State Legislatures, chair ethics com.; chmn. congressional task force internat. HIV/AIDS. Mem. Wash. State Arts Commn., Wash. Coun. for Prevention Child Abuse and Neglect; Dem. nominee for gov., 1980. Lt. comdr. M.C., USN, 1968-70. Mem. Am. Psychiat. Assn., Wash. State Med. Assn., King County Med. Soc. Democrat. Episcopalian. Office: US Ho Reps 1035 Longworth Ho Office Bldg Washington DC 20515*

MCDERMOTT, JOHN E. lawyer; b. Ravenna, Ohio, Oct. 25, 1946; BA, Ohio Wesleyan U., 1968; JD, Harvard U., 1971. Bar: Calif. 1972. Mem. ABA, State Bar Calif., Los Angeles County, Phi Beta Kappa. Office: Howrey & Simon 555 S Hope St Los Angeles CA 90071-2603

MCDERMOTT, THOMAS JOHN, JR. lawyer; b. Santa Monica, Calif., Mar. 23, 1931; s. Thomas J. Sr. and Etha Irene (Cook) McD.; m. Yolanda Amante Jatap; children: Jodi Friedman, Kimberly E., Kish S. BA, UCLA, 1953, JD, 1958. Bar: Calif. 1959. Ptnr. Gray, Binkley and Pfaelzer, L.A., 1964-67, Kadison, Pfaelzer, Woodward, Quinn and Rossi, L.A., 1967-87, Rogers & Wells, L.A., 1987-93, Bryan Cave, L.A., 1993-95, Manatt, Phelps & Phillips, LLP, L.A., 1995-99, Shanks and Herbert, San Diego. Served with U.S. Army, 1953-56, Korea. Fellow Am. Coll. Trial Lawyers; mem. ABA, Assn. Bus. Trial Lawyers (pres. 1980-81, mem. exec. com. 9th cir. jud. conf. 1993—, chair 1997), State Bar Calif. (chair litigation sect. 1993-94), UCLA Law Alumni Assn. (pres. 1961-62), Order of Coif. Office: Shanks & Herbert Ste 330 4350 La Jolla Village Dr San Diego CA 92122

MCDEVITT, CHARLES FRANCIS, retired state supreme court justice, lawyer; b. Pocatello, Idaho, Jan. 5, 1932; s. Bernard A. and Margaret (Hermann) McD.; m. Virginia L. Heller, Aug. 14, 1954; children: Eileen A., Kathryn A., Brian A., Sheila A., Terrence A., Neil A., Kendal A. LLB, U. Idaho, 1956. Bar: Idaho 1956. Ptnr. Richards, Haga & Eberle, Boise, 1956-62; gen. counsel, asst. sec. Boise Cascade Corp., 1962-65; mem. Idaho State Legislature, 1963-66; sec., gen. counsel Boise Cascade Corp., 1965-67, v.p. sec., 1967-68; pres. Beck Industries, 1968-70, group v.p. Singer Co., N.Y.C., 1970-72, exec. v.p., 1973-76; pub. defender Ada County, Boise, 1976-78; co-founder Givens, McDevitt, Pursley & Webb, Boise, 1978-89; justice Idaho Supreme Ct., Boise, 1989-97, chief justice, 1993-97; ptnr., founder McDevitt & Miller, LLP, Boise, 1997—. Served on Gov.'s Select Com. on Taxation, Boise, 1988-89; mem. State Select Com. on Campaign Ethics and Campaign Finances, State Select Com. on Legis. Compensation. Chair Idaho Jud. Coun., 1993-97, Cts. Advisors Coun., 1994-98; mem. Multi-State Tax Com. Home: 4940 Boise River Ln Boise ID 83716-8816 Office: McDevitt & Miller LLP 537 W Bannock St Ste 215 Boise ID 83702-5759 E-mail: chas@McDevitt.org

MCDEVITT, HUGH O'NEILL, immunologist, educator; b. Cin., Aug. 26, 1930; M.D., Harvard U., 1955. Diplomate: Am. Bd. Internal Medicine. Intern Peter Bent Brigham Hosp., Boston, 1955-56, sr. asst. resident in medicine, 1961-62; asst. resident Bell Hosp., 1956-57; research fellow dept. bacteriology and immunology Harvard U., 1959-61; USPHS spl. fellow Nat. Inst. Med. Research, Mill Hill, London, 1962-64; physician Stanford U. Hosp., Calif., 1966—; assoc. prof. Stanford U. Sch. Medicine, 1969-72, prof. med. immunology, 1972—, prof. med. microbiology, 1980—, Burt and Marian Avery Prof. Immunology, 1990—. Cons. physician VA Hosp., Palo Alto, Calif., 1968— Served as capt. M.C., AUS, 1957-59. Mem. NAS, AAAS, Am. Fedn. Clin. Rsch., Am. Soc. Clin. Investigation, Am. Assn. Immunologists, Transplantation Soc., Inst. Medicine, Royal Soc. (fgn.). Office: Sherman Fairchild Bldg Stanford U Sch of Medicine 299 Campus Dr MC5124 Stanford CA 94305-5124 E-mail: hughmcd@stanford.edu

MCDONALD, ALAN ANGUS, federal judge; b. Harrah, Wash., Dec. 13, 1927; s. Angus and Nell (Britt) McD.; m. Ruby K., Aug. 22, 1949; children: Janelle Jo, Saralee Sue, Stacy. BS, U. Wash., 1950, LLB, 1952. Dep. pros. atty. Yakima County, Wash., 1952-54; assoc. Halverson & Applegate, Yakima, 1954-56; ptnr. Halverson, Applegate & McDonald, Yakima, 1956-85; judge U.S. Dist. Ct. (ea. dist.) Wash., Yakima, 1985-95, sr. judge, 1995—. Fellow Am. Coll. Trial Lawyers; Yakima C. of C. (bd. dirs.). Clubs: Yakima Country, Royal Duck (Yakima). Office: US Dist Ct PO Box 2706 Yakima WA 98907-2706

MCDONALD, CRAYDON DEAN, psychologist; b. Denver, Dec. 22, 1946; s. Donald D. and Irene (Dunlavy) McD.; children: Ian, Brendan, Tavis, Morgynne. BFA, Parsons Sch. Design, N.Y.C., 1970; MDiv cum laude, St. Paul Sch. Theology, Kansas City, Mo., 1979; D of Ministry, Wesley Theol. Sem., Washington, 1982; PhD, Boston U., 1987. Diplomate Am. Bd. Profl. Psychology; lic. psychologist, Mass., Wis., Ill., Ariz.; approved supr. Am. Assn. Marriage & Family Therapy; ordained to ministry United Meth. Ch., 1982. Psychologist Worcester (Mass.) Pastoral Counseling Ctr., 1982-87; assoc. prof., asst. program dir. Loyola U., Chgo., 1987-88; clin. psychologist Lake Geneva, Wis., 1987-93. Psychology faculty No. Ariz. U., 1993—; chief psychologist Drs. McDonald & Assocs., Inc., 1982—; examiner Am. Bd. Profl. Psychology. Author: Personality and Cognitive Theology, 1982, Type A Coronary Prone Behavior and Narcissism, 1987. Fellow The Acad. Family Psychology (bd. dirs.); mem. APA (program com. divsn. 43), Human Factors Soc., Am. Assn. Pastoral Counselors. Democrat. Home: 612 N William Flagstaff AZ 86001 Office: 1100 N San Francisco St Ste C Flagstaff AZ 86001-3260

MCDONALD, DANIEL ROBERT, state legislator; b. Seattle, Feb. 4, 1944; s. Robert William and Josephine Dorothy (Quigley) McD.; m. Norah Jane Cornwall, Dec. 28, 1966; children: Tod Robert, Evan Daniel. BSME, U. Wash., 1965, MA in Econs., 1975. Registered profl. engr., Calif., Wash. Mem. Wash. Ho. of Reps., Olympia, 1979-83, floor leader, 1983; mem. Wash. Senate, Dist. 48, Olympia, 1983—; floor leader Wash. Senate, Olympia, 1985-86, chmn. Ways and Means Com., 1988-92. Mem. revenue forecast coun. Olympia, 1984—, chmn. 1984-85; mem. legis. evaluation and accountability program, Olympia, 1983-90; commr. exec. bd. Western Interstate Com. on Higher Edn., 1983-87; mem. State Investment Bd. Mem. Seattle/King County Drug Commn., 1978-79, Mcpl. League, Seattle, 1979—. Served to lt. (j.g.) USN, 1966-69, Vietnam. Mem. Am. Pub. Works Assn., Am. Waterworks Assn., Bellevue (Wash.) C. of C., Rotary, Spec. Olympics Bd., Municipal League. Republican. Presbyterian. Lodge: Rotary. Home: 4650 92nd Ave NE Bellevue WA 98004-1335 Office: Wash State Senate 204 Irving Newhouse Ofc Bldg Olympia WA 98504-0001

MCDONALD, HENRY (HARRY MCDONALD), research center administrator; b. Glasgow, Scotland, Jan. 24, 1937; came to U.S., 1965, naturalized U.S. citizen. m. June McDonald; 3 children. BS in Aero. Engring., U. Glasgow, 1960, DEng, 1985, hon. degree, 1997. Supr. wind tunnel testing Brit. Aircraft Corp., Wharton, Eng., 1960-65; rsch. engr. United Techs. Rsch. Ctr., East Hartford, Conn., 1965-76; founder pres., CEO, Sci. Rsch. Assocs. Inc., Glastonbury, 1976-92; prof. mech. engring. Pa. State U., State College, 1991-96, asst. dir. computational scis. Applied Rsch. Lab., 1991-96; dir. NASA Ames Rsch. Ctr., Moffett Field, Calif., 1996—. Former mem. adv. panels in aero. field. Contbr. numerous articles on aero. R & D to sci. jours. Former mem. RAF Res. Co-recipient Small Businessman of Yr. award for high tech. State of Conn. Mem. aero. assns, NAE. Achievements include co-patentee of novel ultra-high frequency ventilator providing life support to critically ill patients suffering from adult respiratory distress syndrome; research on heat transfer and gas dynamics relative to aircraft engine performance and design. Avocation: sailing. Office: NASA Ames Rsch Ctr Office Dir Mail Stop 200 Moffett Field CA 94035-1000

MCDONALD, JOHN GREGORY, financial investment educator; b. Stockton, Calif., 1937; m. Melody McDonald. BS, Stanford U., 1960, MBA, 1962, PhD, 1967. Mem. faculty Grad. Sch. Bus. Stanford U., Calif., 1968—, now The IBJ prof. fin. Grad. Sch. Bus. Vis. prof. U. Paris, 1972, Columbia Bus. Sch., 1975, Harvard Bus. Sch. 1986; gov., vice chmn., bd. govs. NASD/NASDAQ Stock Market, 1987-90; mem. adv. bd. InterWest Venture Capital; dir. Investment Co. of Am., New Perspective Fund, Inc., Scholastic Corp., Varian Inc., EuroPacific Growth Fund. Contbr. articles to profl. jours. Bd. overseers vis. com. Harvard U. Bus. Sch., Cambridge, Mass., 1994-2000. Fulbright scholar, Paris, 1967-68. Office: Stanford U Grad Sch Business Stanford CA 94305

MC DONALD, JOHN RICHARD, lawyer; b. Connersville, Ind., Aug. 8, 1933; s. Vernon Louis and Thelma (Venham) McD.; m. Mary Alice Boyd, Aug. 17, 1957; children: Anne Elizabeth, John Richard, Colleen Lynn. B.A., U. Ariz., 1957, LL.B., 1960. Bar: Ariz. 1960. Since practiced in, Tucson; assoc. Richard N. Roylston, 1961-62; pvt. practice, 1963-65; ptnr. McDonald & Rykken, 1965-68, DeConcini & McDonald (now DeConcini, McDonald, Yetwin, Lacy, P.C.), 1968—. Mem. adv. bd. Dependable Nurses, Inc., 1994—. Mem. Ariz. Law Rev. Pres., bd. dirs. emeritus Comstock Children's Hosp. Found.; v.p. Ariz. Sch. Bds. Assn., 1979, pres., 1981; v.p. All Ariz. Sch. Bd., 1981; v.p., bd. dirs. Tucson Assn. for Blind, 1966-86; trustee Catalina Foothills Sch. Dist., 1976-82; bd. dirs. Tucson Unified Sch. Dist. Ednl. Enrichment Found., 1994—, Ariz. Acad., 1981-89, Tucson Symphony Soc., 1997—, Catalina Foothills Sch. Dist. Found.; mem. Am. Park Svcs. Mem. Ariz. Bar Assn., Ariz. Law Rev. Assn. (pres. 1994), Pima County Bar Assn. (dir. 1978-86, pres. 1984-85), Nat. Coun. Sch. Attys. (dir. 1992-96), Delta Chi. Republican. Presbyterian. Home: 6151 N Camino Almonte Tucson AZ 85718-3729 Office: 2525 E Broadway Blvd Tucson AZ 85716-5398 E-mail: jmcdonald@dmyl.com, mjr44@qwest.net

MCDONALD, JOSEPH LEE, insurance broker; b. Bremerton, Wash., Aug. 15, 1931; s. Joseph Okane and Ida Elizabeth (Finholm) McD.; m. Glorietta Maness, Jan. 22, 1954 (dec. 1984); children: Holly Ann Chaffin, Andrew Lee McDonald; m. Beverly Mae Falkner, June 22, 1986. BS, U. Wash., 1954. Various mgmt. positions AT&T, 1956-62; broker, ptnr. McDonald & McGarry Co., Seattle, 1962-84; ptnr., exec. McDonald Ins. Group, Kirkland, Wash., 1984—. V.p., bd. dirs. Chimayo Inc., Seattle, 1990-94, Santa Fe Food Corp., Seattle, 1991-96. City councilman City of Bellevue, 1971-75; commr. Water Dist. #97, Bellevue, 1967-71, Lake Hills Sewer Dist., Bellevue, 1965-71; pres. Wash. State Assn. of Sewer Dists., Seattle, 1969. With U.S. Army, 1954-56. Mem. Coll. Club of Seattle, Overlake Golf and Country Club, Western Assn. of Ins. Brokers, Ind. Ins. Agts. Assn., Seattle Master Builders Assn., Nat. Wildlife Fedn., Nature Conservancy, Apt. Assn. of Seattle and King County, Roche Harbor Yacht Club, Chi Phi. Avocations: skiing, sailing, tennis. Home: 7235 91st Pl SE Mercer Island WA 98040-5803 Office: McDonald Ins Group 416 6th St S Kirkland WA 98033-6718 E-mail: jlm@mcdonaldins.com

MCDONALD, MARIANNE, classicist; b. Chgo., Jan. 2, 1937; d. Eugene Francis and Inez (Riddle) McD.; children: Eugene, Conrad, Bryan, Bridget, Kirstie (dec.), Hiroshi. BA magna cum laude, Bryn Mawr Coll., 1958; MA, U. Chgo., 1960; PhD, U. Calif., Irvine, 1975; doctorate (hon.), Am. Coll. Greece, 1988; diploma (hon.), Am. Archaeol. Assn.; DLitt (hon.), U. Athens, 1994, U. Dublin, 1994, Aristotle U., 1997, U. Thessalonika, 1997, Nat. U. Ireland, 2001. Instr. Greek, Latin, English, mythology, cinema U. Calif., Irvine, 1975-79; founder, rsch. fellow Thesaurus Linguae Graecae Project, 1975-97. Tchg. asst. U. Calif., Irvine, 1974; bd. dirs. Centrum. Author: (novels) Terms for Happiness in Euripides, 1978, Semilemmatized Concordances to Europides' Alcestis, 1977, Cyclops, Andromache, Medea, 1978, Heraclidae, Hippolytus, 1979, Hecuba, 1984, Hercules Furens, 1984, Elecra, 1984, Ion, 1985, Trojan Women, 1988, Iphigenia in Taurus, 1988, Euripides in Cinema: The Heart Made Visible, 1983; translator The Cost of Kindness and Other Fabulous Tales (Shinichi Hoshi), 1986, (chpt.) Views of Clytemnestra, Ancient and Modern, 1990, Classics and Cinema, 1990, Modern Critical Theory and Classical Literature, 1994, A Challenge to Democracy, 1994, Ancient Sun/Modern Light: Greek Drama on the Modern Stage, 1990, Star Myths: Tales of the Constellations, 1996, Sole Antico Luce Moderna, 1999, Mythology of the Zodiac: Tales of the Constellations, 2000, Antigone by Sophocles, 2000, Mythology of the Zodiac, 2000, Sing Sorrow: Classics, History, and Heroines in Opera, 2001. Bd. dirs. Am. Coll. of Greece, 1981-90, Scripps Hosp., 1981, Am. Sch. Classical Studies, 1986—; mem. bd. overseers U. Calif., San Diego, 1985—; nat. bd. advisors Am. Biog. Inst., 1982—; pres. Soc. for the Preservation of the Greek Heritage, 1990—; founder Hajime Mori Chair for Japanese Studies, U. Calif., San Diego, 1985, McDonald Ctr. for Alcohol and Substance Abuse, 1984, Thesaurus Linguarum Hiberniae, 1991—; vis. prof. U. Dublin, 1990—, U. C. Dublin, 1999, U. Ulster, Ireland, 1997; adj. prof. theatre U. Calif., San Diego, 1990, prof. theatre and classics, 1994—. Recipient Ellen Browning Scripps Humanitarian award, 1975, Disting. Svc. award U. Calif.-Irvine, 1982, 2001, Irvine medal, 1987; named one of the Cmty. Leaders Am., 1979-80, Philanthropist of Yr., 1985, Headliner San Diego Press Club, 1985, Philanthropist of Yr. Honorary Nat. Conf. Christians and Jews, 1986, Woman of Yr. AHEPA, 1988, San Diego Woman of Distinction, 1990, Woman of Yr. AXIOS, 1991; recipient Bravissimo gold medal San Diego Opera, 1990, Gold Medal Soc. Internationalization of Greek Lang., 1990, Athens medal, 1991, Piraeus medal, 1991, award Desmoi, 1992, award Hellenic Assn. of Univ. Women, 1992, Acad. of Achievement award AHEPA, 1992, Woman of Delphi award European Cultural Crr. Delphi, 1992, Civis Universitatis award U. Calif., San Diego, 1993, Hypatia award Hellenic U. Women, 1993, Am.-Ireland Fund Heritage award, 1994, Contribution to Greek Letters award Aristotle U. Thessaloniki, 1994, Mirabella Mag. Readers Choice One of 1000 Women for the Nineties, 1994, citations from U.S. Congress and Calif. Senate, Alexander the Gt. award Hellenic Cultural Soc., 1995, made hon. citizen of Delphi and gold medal of the Amphiktuonon, Del. Bus. award for Fine Arts San Diego Bus. Jour., 1995, Vol. of Decade Women's Internat. Ctr., 1994, 96, Gold Star award San Diego Arts League, 1997, Golden Aeschylus award Inst. Nat. Drama Antkg. Siracusa, 1998, Women Who Mean Bus., Fine Arts award San Diego Bus. Jour., 1998, Fulbright award, 1999, Ellis Island award, 1999, Spirit of Scripps award 1999; Theatre Excellence award KPBS Patte, 2001. Mem. MLA, AAUP, Am. Philol. Assn. (disting. svc. award 1999), Soc. for the Preservation of the Greek Heritage (pres.), Libr. of Am., Am. Classical League, Philol. Assn. Pacific Coast, Am. Comparative Lit. Assn., Modern and Classical Lang. Assn. So. Calif., Hellenic Soc. (coun. award 2000), Calif. Fgn. Lagn. Tchrs. Assn., Internat. Platform Assn., Royal Irish Acad., Greece's Order of the Phoenix (commdr. 1994), KPBS Producers Club, Hellenic Univ. Club (bd. dir.). Avocations: karate, harp (medieval), skiing, diving. Home: PO Box 929 Rancho Santa Fe CA 92067-0929 Office: U Calif at San Diego Dept Theatre La Jolla CA 92093

MC DONALD, MEG, public relations executive; b. Santa Monica, Calif., Oct. 11, 1948; Dir. radio & TV svcs. Fran Hynds Pub. Rels., 1969-75; owner, CEO Mc Donald Media Svcs., 1975—. Recipient Buccaneer award PIRATES, 1980, 82, Prisms award Pub. Rels. Soc. Am., 1981, Pro awards Publicity Clubs. of L.A. Mem. Pub. Rels. Soc. Am. (sec. 1985), Radio ane TV News Assn. of So. Calif. (mem. bd. dirs. 1973-88), Publicity Club of L.A. (pres. 1979-80), L.A. Advt. Women (v.p. 1984-85), Print Interactive Radio and TV Ednl. Soc. (pres. 1998-00), Radio and TV News Assn. Office: Mc Donald Media Svcs 11076 Fruitland Dr Studio City CA 91604-3541

MCDONALD, MICHAEL BRIAN, economist, consultant; b. Tulsa, Jan. 1, 1948; s. William Gerald and Agnes Gertrude (Sellman) McD.; m. Jane Anne Fahey, Aug. 25, 1969; children: Kelly, Anne. BA in Econs. cum laude, Georgetown U., 1969; PhD in Econs., U. Pa., 1978. Teaching fellow U. Pa., Phila., 1976-77; rsch. fellow Logistics Mgmt. Inst., Washington, 1977-78; assoc. dir. Bur. Bus. and Econ. Rsch. U. N.Mex., Albuquerque, 1978-82, dir. Bur. Bus. and Econ. Rsch., 1982—. Dir. Kirtland Fed. Credit Union, Albuquerque, 1982—. Contbr. articles to profl. jours. Lt-Col. USAFR, 1978—. Capt. USAF, 1972-76. NDEA Title IV fellow U. Pa., 1969-72. Mem. Phi Beta Kappa. Avocations: tennis, golf, fishing.

MCDONALD, MICHAEL LEE, clinic administrator, retired naval officer; b. Salt Lake City, Oct. 23, 1949; s. Jack Alex and Dorothy Elsie (Mantle) McD.; m. Celia McKean Smoot, June 23, 1975; children: Sarah Lynn, Michelle Elise, AnnMarie, Jeffrey Michael, Matthew David, Emily Jane. BA, U. Utah, 1973; MA, U. Iowa, 1977. Commd. ensign USN, 1975; advanced through grades to comdr., 1991; patient adminstr. Naval Hosp., Great Lakes, Ill., 1977-80, Oakland, Calif., 1980-82; med. recruiter Navy Recruiting Dist., San Francisco, 1982-84; adminstr. Navy Environ. and Preventative Medicine Unit # 7, Naples, Italy, 1984-87; staff officer Navy Med. Commd. Europe, London, 1987-89; healthcare advisor U.S. Naval Forces Europe, London, 1989-91; exec. officer Naval Med. Clinic, Seattle, 1991-93, commdg. officer, 1993-94; officer in charge Branch Med. Clinic, Everett, Wash., 1994-96; ret., 1996; clinic adminstr. Medalia Healthcare, 1996—, Providence Med. Group, 1999—. Coach Northshore Little League, Bothell, Wash., 1992-93; scoutmaster Boy Scouts Am., Dublin, Calif., 1981-85, instl. sponsor, Naples, Italy, 1985-87; bd. dirs. North Bothell Little League, 1998—. Fellow Am. Coll. Healthcare Execs. Mem. LDS Ch. (bishop). Avocations: golf, basketball, English literature, cycling. Home and Office: 19225 4th Dr SE Bothell WA 98012-7013 E-mail: michael.mcdonald@swedish.org

MCDONNELL, BARBARA, health facility administrator; B, Univ. Ill.; M, Univ. Iowa; JD magna cum laude, Univ. Pa. Law Sch. With Sherman & Howard, 1982-87; staff atty. Colo. Ct. Appeals, 1988-89; law clerk Phila.; legal adv. Gov. Romer, dep. dir. policy and rsch., 1989-90; exec. dir. Colo. Dept. Human Svcs., 1991-99; chief dep. atty. gen. Office of Atty. Gen., Denver, 1999—. Rep. Nursing Adv. bd., team leader Policy Acad. Team on Families & Children At Risk. Office: Office Atty Gen 1525 Sherman St Denver CO 80203-1702

MCDONOUGH, PATRICK DENNIS, academic administrator; b. Virginia, Minn., Jan. 30, 1942; s. James Morris and Vivian S. McDonough; children: Jeffrey, Anne; m. Karen Howe, June 27, 1981. BA cum laude, Moorhead State U., 1964; MA, U. Kans., 1969; PhD, U. Minn., 1972. Asst. prof. theatre Emporia (Kans.) State U., 1966-70; dir. sales, mktg. Guthrie Theater, Mpls., 1971, 72; asst. prof. speech, dir. of forensics Moorhead (Minn.) State U., 1972-73; assoc. prof., mng. dir., chair Marshall Performing Arts Ctr. U. Minn., Duluth, 1973-76; dean fine arts, prof. U. Evansville (Ind.), 1976-81; vice chancellor, prof. U. Wis., Stevens Point, 1981-84; program dir. (edn. and leadership) W.K. Kellogg Found., Battle Creek, Mich., 1984-89; 15th pres., prof. theatre and mgmt. Marietta (Ohio) Coll., 1989-95, exec. dir. McDonough Ctr. for Leadership and Bus.; assoc. vice chancellor planning and analysis Calif. State U. Sys., Long Beach, 1995-97, prof. theatre, 1997—; exec. v.p. higher edn. practice The Charitable Resources Group, Pitts. Pres. Emporia chpt. AAUP, 1969; cons. Lexington (Ky.) Children's Theatre, 1979; festival evaluator Am. Coll. Theatre Festival, 4 states, 1975-76; mem. theatre panel Ind. Arts Commn., Indpls., 1977-79; arts orgn. panel Mich. Arts Bd., Detroit, 1985-89; presenter in field. Producer, dir. 100 plays and musicals, 1964-84; contbr. articles to profl. jours. Bd. visitors U. Wis., Stevens Point, 1988-90; dist. organizer Eugene McCarthy Presdl. Campaign, Emporia, 1968; mem. leadership commn. Am. Coun. Edn., 1989-94; mem. exec. com. Campus Compact, 1990-95; bd. dirs. numerous civic and arts orgns., 1973-90; chmn. govs. adv. com. on vol. svc., Ohio, 1990-93; mem. leadership studies project U. Md., 1994—. Recipient Disting. Alumnus award Moorhead State U., 1989; grantee Minn. Arts Bd., 1974-76, Ind. Arts Commn., 1976-79. Mem. Am. Assn. Higher Edn., Univ. and Coll. Theatre Assn. (v.p. 1982-83), Marietta Country Club, Stevens Point Country Club, Athletic Club of Columbus. Democrat. Episcopalian. Avocations: travel, international relations, arts. Office: Dept Theatre 1250 N Bellflower Blvd Long Beach CA 90840-0006 E-mail: mcdonou@gte.net

MCDONOUGH, RUSSELL CHARLES, retired state supreme court justice; b. Glendive, Mont., Dec. 7, 1924; s. Roy James and Elsie Marie (Johnson) McD.; m. Dora Jean Bidwell, Mar. 17, 1946; children: Ann Remmich, Michael, Kay Jensen, Kevin, Daniel, Mary Garfield. JD, George Washington U., 1949. Bar: Mont. 1950. Pvt. practice, Glendive, Mont., 1950-83; judge Gen. Jurisdiction State of Montana, Glendive, 1983-87; justice Mont. Supreme Ct., Helena, 1987-93, ret., 1993. City atty. City of Glendive, 1953-57; county atty. Dawson County, Mon., 1957-63; del. Mont. Constl. Conv., Helena, 1972. 1st lt. AC, U.S. Army, 1943-45, ETO. Decorated DFC. Mem. Mont. Bar Assn. Roman Catholic. Home: PO Box 60 Circle MT 59215-0060

MCDOUGALL, DUANE C. manufacturing executive; Grad., Ohio State U. With Willamette Industries, exec. v.p. bdlg. materials group, pres., COO. Past pres. Portland Rotary Charitable Trust Found. Office: Willamette Industries Inc 1300 SW 5th Ave Ste 3800 Portland OR 97201-5671

MCDOUGALL, IAIN ROSS, nuclear medicine educator; b. Glasgow, Scotland, Dec. 18, 1943; came to U.S., 1976; s. Archibald McDougall and Jean Cairns; m. Elizabeth Wilson, Sept. 6, 1968; children: Shona, Stewart. MB, ChB, U. Glasgow, 1967, PhD, 1973. Diplomate Am. Bd. Nuclear Medicine (chmn. 1985-87), Am. Bd. Internal Medicine (gov. 1984-86). Lectr. in medicine U. Glasgow, 1969-76; fellow Harkness-Stanford Med. Ctr., 1972-74; assoc. prof. radiology and medicine Stanford (Calif.) U., 1976-84, prof. radiology and medicine, 1985—. Contbr. numerous articles to sci. jours. Fellow Royal Coll. Physicians (Glasgow), Am. Coll. Physicians; mem. Am. Thyroid Assn., Soc. Nuclear Medicine, Western Assn. for Clin. Research. Office: Stanford U Med Ctr Divsn Nuclear Medicine Stanford CA 94305

MCDOUGALL, JOHN ROLAND, civil engineer; b. Edmonton, Alta., Can., Apr. 4, 1945; s. John Frederick and Phyllis Eirene (Sladden) McD.; m. Susan Carley, July 2, 1971 (div. 1995); children: John Christopher, Jordan Page, Michael Tait; m. Irene Makar, May 15, 1996. BSCE, U. Alta., Edmonton, 1967. Registered profl. engr., Alta. Engr. Imperial Oil Ltd., Calgary, Alta., 1967-69, sr. engr. Edmonton, 1969-75; treas. McDougall & Secord, Edmonton, 1969-85; v.p. McDougall & Secord, Ltd., 1975-90, pres., 1990—; pres., chief exec. officer Dalcor Cos., Edmonton, 1975-91; chmn. Trade Innoventures, Inc., 1992—; chair engring. mgmt. U. Alta., Edmonton, 1991-98. Chmn. D.B. Robinson & Assocs., Edmonton; CEO Alberta Rsch. Coun., 1997—; chmn. World Trade Centre, Edmonton, 1994-98; mem. adv. bd. Royal Trust Corp., 1984-94, Royal Glenora Club, Faculty Club; dir. PFB Corp. Chmn. Edmonton Civic Govt. Assn., 1975-77; mem. Premiers Coun. on Sci. and Tech., 1990. Fellow Can. Acad. Engrs. (bd. dirs. 1992—); mem. Can. Coun. Profl. Engrs. (pres. 1990-91), Assn. Profl. Engrs. Alta. (hon. life, pres. 1980-81), Can. Engring. Manpower Bd. (chmn. 1985-88), Edmonton C. of C. (pres. 1989), Loyal Edmonton Regiment (hon.), Edmonton Club (pres. 1983-84), 8 Field Engring. Regiment (hon. col.). Anglican. Avocations: skiing, travel, cycling, philately, railroad modeling. Office: Alberta Rsch Coun 250 Karl Clark Rd Edmonton AB Canada T6N 1E4

MCDOUGALL, RODERICK GREGORY, lawyer; BBA in Econs., JD, U. Ariz. Bar: Ariz. 1965, U.S. Ct. Claims 1965, U.S. Supreme Ct. 1970, U.S. Dist. Ct. Airz. 1972, U.S. Ct. Appeals (9th cir.) 1972. Law clk. Ariz. Supreme Ct., 1964, Ariz. Ct. Appeals, 1965; dep. county atty. Maricopa County, 1965-67; staff atty. Ariz. State Senate, 1967; asst. atty. gen., 1967-74; chief asst. Atty. Gen., Ariz., 1974-84; city atty. City of Phoenix, 1984-2000. Advisor Ariz. Supreme Ct. Mem. ABA, Internat. Mcpl. Lawyers Assn. (bd. dirs. 1994-2000), Ariz. Bar Assn., Maricopa County Bar Assn. Office: Office City Atty 200 W Washington St Ste 1300 Phoenix AZ 85003-1611

MCDOWELL, JENNIFER, sociologist, composer, playwright, publisher; b. Albuquerque; d. Willard A. and Margaret Frances (Garrison) McD.; m. Milton Loventhal, July 2, 1973. BA, U. Calif., 1957; MA, San Diego State U., 1958; postgrad., Sorbonne, Paris, 1959; MLS, U. Calif., 1963; PhD, U. Oreg., 1973. Tchr. English Abraham Lincoln H.S., San Jose, Calif., 1960-61; free-lance editor Soviet field, Berkeley, 1961-63; rsch. asst. sociology U. Oreg., Eugene, 1964-66; editor, pub. Merlin Papers, San Jose, 1969-80, Merlin Press, San Jose, 1973—; rsch. cons. sociology San Jose, 1973—; music pub. Lipstick and Toy Balloons Pub. Co., San Jose, 1978—; composer Paramount Pictures, 1982-88. Tchr. writing workshops; poetry readings, 1969-73; co-producer radio show lit. and culture Sta. KALX, Berkeley, 1971-72. Author: (with Milton Loventhal) Black Politics: A Study and Annotated Bibliography of the Mississippi Freedom Democratic Party, 1971 (featured at Smithsonian Inst. Spl. Event 1992), Contemporary Women Poets, 1977; co-author: (plays off-off Broadway) Betsy and Phyllis, 1986, Mack the Knife Your Friendly Dentist, 1986, The Estrogen Party To End War, 1986, The Oatmeal Party Comes to Order, 1986, (plays) Betsy Meets the Wacky Iraqui, 1991, Bella and Phyllis, 1994; contbr. poems, plays, essays, articles, short stories, and book revs. to lit. mags., news mags. and anthologies; rschr. women's autobiog. writings, contemporary writing in poetry, Soviet studies, civil rights movement, and George Orwell, 1962—; writer: (songs) Money Makes a Woman Free, 1976, 3 songs featured in Parade of Am. Music, 1976-77; co-creator mus. comedy Russia's Secret Plot To Take Back Alaska, 1988, Our Women Are Strong, 2001. Recipient 8 awards Am. Song Festival, 1976-79, Bill Casey Award in Letters, 1980; doctoral fellow AAUW, 1971-73; grantee Calif. Arts Coun., 1976-77. Mem. AAUW, Am. Assn. for Advancement of Slavic Studies, Soc. Sci. Study of Religion, No. Calif. Songwriters Assn., Am. Sociol. Assn., Dramatists Guild, Phi Beta Kappa, Sigma Alpha Iota, Beta Phi Mu, Kappa Kappa Gamma. Democrat. Office: c/o Merlin Press PO Box 5602 San Jose CA 95150-5602

MC DUFFIE, MALCOLM, oil company executive; b. San Francisco, Nov. 14, 1915; s. William Chester and Mary (Skaife) McD.; m. Mary Sutherland de Surville, Dec. 8, 1951; children: Cynthia de Surville, Duncan de Surville. A.B. in Econs, Stanford U., 1940. With O.C. Field Gasoline Corp., 1940-41, Wilmington Gasoline Corp., 1941-42; with Mohawk Petroleum Corp., 1945-80, pres., dir., 1969-80; dir. Res. Oil & Gas Co., 1973-80, sr. v.p., 1977-80; sp. asst. to pres. Getty Oil Co., Los Angeles, 1980-82. Bd. overseers Huntington Library, Art Gallery and Bot. Gardens, 1972-98; bd. dirs. Calif. Inst. Tech. Assos., 1976-82. Mem. Nat. Petroleum Refiners Assn. (Dir. 1970-80), Ind. Refiners Assn. Calif. (pres. 1967-69, 77-78, dir. 1950-80), Rancheros Visitadores. Republican. Episcopalian. Clubs: California (Los Angeles); Bohemian (San Francisco); Valley Hunt (Pasadena, Calif.), Annandale Golf (Pasadena, Calif.); Birnam Wood (Santa Barbara, Calif.), Valley (Montecito, Calif.). Fax: 805-969-2818

MCDYESS, ANTONIO, professional basketball player; b. Quitman, Miss. Forward Denver Nuggets. Named to NBA All-Rookie First Team, 1995-96, All-NBA Third Team, 1998-99. Avocations: bowling, rythem and blues. Office: Denver Nuggets 1000 Chopper Cir Denver CO 80204-5809

MCEACHERN, ALEXANDER, electronics company executive; b. Boston, Feb. 18, 1955; s. Alexander William and Elisabeth Helena McEachern; m. Barbara Ruth Pereira, Dec. 18, 1975; children: Alexander Wallis, Ian Wallis. V.p. Mac Systems, 1975-79; dir. R&D Lomac Corp., Santa Clara, Calif., 1979-80; chmn., founder Basic Measuring Instruments, Santa Clara, 1981-99; pres. Electrotek Concepts, Inc., 1996-97, Power Stds. Lab., 2000—. Dir. WPT, 1997—, Dranetz/BMI/Electrotek, 1997—; founder Infrastructure Instruments Inc., 1996—; bd. dirs. Basic Measuring Instruments. Author: Handbook of Power Signatures; contbr. articles to profl. jours. Mem. IEEE (sr.). Office: PSL 2000 Powell St Ste 1200 Emeryville CA 94608-1856

MCEACHERN, ALLAN, Canadian justice; b. Vancouver, B.C., Can., May 20, 1926; s. John A. and Blanche L. (Roadhouse) McE.; m. Gloria, July 17, 1953 (dec. Sept. 1997); children: Jean Williams, Joanne Evans. BA, U. B.C., Vancouver, 1949; LLB, U. B.C., 1950, LLM (hon.), 1990. Assoc., sr. ptnr., barrister, solicitor Messrs. Russell & DuMoulin, Vancouver, B.C., 1950-78; chief justice Supreme Ct. B.C., Vancouver, 1979-88, Ct. Appeals B.C., Vancouver, 1988—. Pres. Kats Rugby Club, Vancouver, 1953-64, B.C. Lions Football Club, Vancouver, 1967, 68. 69, We. Football Conf., 1964, Can. Football League, 1967-68, commr. 1967-68. Mem. Can. Bar Assn. (bd. dirs.), Vancouver Bar Assn. (bd. dirs.), Legal Aid Soc. (pres. 1977-78), Law Soc. B.C. (bencher 1971-79). Avocations: sailing, gardening, walking, summer cottage. Office: Law Cts 800 Smithe St Vancouver BC Canada V6Z 2E1

MCELHANY, ANDY, state senator; b. San Francisco, Apr. 28, 1940; Student, Colo. Sch. Mines, 1958-59, U. Mo. Lic. real estate broker. Rep. rep. dist. 17 Colo. Ho. of Reps., 1994-2000; Rep. senator dist. 12 Colo. State Senate, 2000—. Mem. transp. and energy coms. Colo. Ho. of Reps., chair vets. and mil. affairs com.; mem. bus. affairs and labor, capitol devel. and pub. policy and planning coms. Colo. State Senate. Chmn. adv. bd. Colo. Springs Pk. and Recreation, 1992-94. Recipient Disting. Svc. award, 1989-90, Realtor of Yr. award, 1992. Mem. Pikes Peak Assn. Realtors. Office: 95 W Boulder Colorado Springs CO 80903 also: Colo State Senate State Capitol 200 E Colfax Rm 274 Denver CO 80203

MCELHINNEY, JAMES LANCEL, artist, educator; b. Abington, Pa., Feb. 3, 1952; s. James and Joan Howland (Carpenter) McE.; m. Victoria Maria Dávila, Sept. 12, 1981 (div.). Scholarship student, Skowhegan (Maine) Sch. of Art, 1973; BFA, Temple U., 1974; MFA, Yale U., 1976. Asst. prof. Moore Coll. Art, Phila., 1977-78, Skidmore Coll., Saratoga Springs, N.Y., 1979-87; adj. instr. UCLA, 1983, Moore Coll. Art, 1983, Tyler Sch. Art, Phila., 1983-86, U. of Arts, Phila., 1985-89; instr. Milw. Inst. Art and Design, 1991-93; vis. artist East Carolina U., Greenville, N.C.,

1994-98; head painting and drawing program visual arts dept. U. Colo., Denver, 1998—; dir. study abroad program Feltre, Italy, 2000—. Artist in residence Harper's Ferry Nat. Hist. Park, 1999; lectr. USAF Acad., 2001. Exhibited paintings in solo shows at Peninsula Ctr. for the Fine Arts, Newport News, Va., 1993, Danville (Va.) Mus., 1993, Second Street Gallery, Charlottesville, Va., 1995, F.A.N. Gallery, Phila., 1995, 98, Greenville (N.C.) Mus. Art, 1996, Lee Hansley Gallery, Raleigh, N.C., 1996, Asheville (N.C.) Art Mus., 1996, 1998, Lee Hansley Gallery, 1998; one-man show, Lee Hansley Gallery, 1999; group shows at Chrysler Mus., Norfolk, Va., Allen Sheppard Gallery, N.Y.C., 1999, Ucross Found., 2000, Nicolayseu Mus., 2000. Vol. Richmond (Va.) Nat. Battlefield Park, 1991—. Grantee: (painting) NEA, Washington, 1987-88, Ptnrs. in the Arts, Richmond Arts Coun., 1995. Mem. Coll. Art Assn. Home: 1050 Sherman St Denver CO 80203-2815 Office: U Colo Coll Arts Media Box 177 PO Box 173364 Denver CO 80217-3364

MCELHINNY, HAROLD JOHN, lawyer; b. San Francisco, Jan. 5, 1947; s. Harold James and Margaret I. (Mahoney) McE.; m. Mary Ellen McElhinny, June 22, 1968; children: Hannah, Jennifer, William. BA in Polit. Sci., U. Santa Clara, 1970; JD, U. Calif., Berkeley, 1975. Bar: Calif. 1976, U.S. Supreme Ct. 1983. Vol. Peace Corps., Tripoli, Libya, 1968-69; juvenile counselor Santa Clara County (Calif.) Juvenile Hall, 1969-72; law clk. U.S. Dist. Ct., Hartford, Conn., 1975-76; ptnr. Morrison & Foerster, San Francisco, 1976—. Mem. ABA, Calif. Bar Assn., State Bar Calif. (rev. dept. 1986-89, chmn. 1988), San Francisco Bar Assn., Am. Intellectual Property Law Assn., Assn. Bus. Trial Lawyers (bd. govs. 1992-97, pres. 1997). Democrat. Roman Catholic. Office: Morrison & Foerster 425 Market St Fl 30 San Francisco CA 94105-2482 E-mail: hmcelhinny@mofo.com

MCELHINNY, WILSON DUNBAR, banker; b. Detroit, July 27, 1929; s. William Dunbar and Elizabeth (Wilson) McE.; m. Barbara Cheney Watkins, June 6, 1952 (dec.); children: David Ashton, Ward Cheney, Edward Wilson, William Dunbar; m. Lisa Lesher, Mar. 27, 1993. BA, Yale U., 1953. With Union and New Haven Trust Co., 1952-63, Reading Trust Co., Pa., 1963-68, pres., 1968-70, Nat. Central Bank (formerly Reading Trust Co.), 1970-79, chief exec. officer, 1975-79; chmn. bd. dirs., pres., chief exec. officer Hamilton Bank (formerly Nat. Central Bank), Lancaster, 1979-81, chmn. bd. dirs., chief exec. officer, 1981-83, chmn. bd. dirs., 1981-90; pres. CoreStates Fin. Corp., Phila., 1983-86, vice chmn., 1986-90; pres., chmn. Hamilton Bank, Lancaster, Pa., 1988-90. Bd. dirs. Reading Eagle Co., 1st Bank Idaho, SIGCO, Portland, Maine. Bd. dirs. UAI Group LP, Sinking Spring, Pa., Nature Conservancy of Idaho; mem. cmty. coun. St. Luke's Wood River Med. Ctr. Mem. Pa. C. of C. (chmn. 1990-92), Yale Club N.Y., The Valley Club. Home and Office: PO Box 3070 Ketchum ID 83340-3070

MCELROY, LEO FRANCIS, communications consultant, journalist; b. Los Angeles, Oct. 12, 1932; s. Leo Francis and Helen Evelyn (Silliman) McE.; m. Dorothy Frances Montgomery, Nov. 3, 1956 (div. 1981); children: James, Maureen, Michael, Kathleen; m. Judith Marie Lewis, May 30, 1992. BS in English, Loyola U., L.A., 1953. News dir. KFI, KRLA, KABC Radio, L.A., 1964-72; pub. affairs host TV Sta. KCET, L.A., 1967-74; v.p. Sta. KROQ AM/FM, L.A., 1972-74; polit. editor Sta. KABC-TV, L.A., 1974-81; pres. McElroy Comm., Sacramento, 1981—. Pres. sec. Lt. Gov.'s Office, Sacramento, 1982-84; chmn. Calif. AP Broadcasters, 1972-74; cons. State Office Migrant Edn., Sacramento, 1974, Californians for Water, L.A., 1982, Calif. Water Protection Coun., Sacramento, 1982, Planning and Conservation League, Sacramento, 1984—, Common Cause, Sacramento, 1988—. Author: Uneasy Partners, 1984; author plays: Mermaid Tavern, 1956, To Bury Caesar, 1952 (Christopher award), Rocket to Olympus, 1960, The Code of Whiskey King, 1995. State del. Western Am. Assembly on Prison Reform, Berkeley, Calif., 1973; chmn. State Disaster Info. Task Force, Calif., 1973-74; campaign media cons. statewide issues, various candidates, Sacramento, L.A., 1981—; bd. dirs. Vols. in Victim Assistance, Sacramento, 1984, Rescue Alliance, Sacramento, 1987-92, Mental Health Assn., Sacramento, 1985-89, Leukemia Soc., 1992-97. Recipient Gabriel award Cath. Archdiocese, L.A., 1972, Golden Mike award Radio-TV News Assn., L.A., 1973; Hon. Resolution, Calif. State Assembly, Sacramento, 1981. Mem. ASCAP, AFTRA, Screen Actors Guild, Am. Assn. Polit. Cons. Roman Catholic. Home: 2262 Swarthmore Dr Sacramento CA 95825-6608 Office: McElroy Comm 2410 K St Ste C Sacramento CA 95816-5002 E-mail: mcelcom@ns.net

MC ELWAIN, JOSEPH ARTHUR, retired power company executive; b. Deer Lodge, Mont., Nov. 13, 1919; s. Lee Chaffee and Johanna (Petersen) McE.; m. Mary Cleaver Witt, Mar. 8, 1945 (dec. June 1992); m. Mary E. McLaughlin, Oct. 9, 1996 (dec. Sept. 1998); children— Lee William and Lori Louise (twins). B.A., U. Mont., 1943, LL.B., 1947. Bar: Mont. 1947. Individual practice law, Deer Lodge, 1947-63; Washington legis. counsel Mont. Power Co., Butte, 1954-63, counsel, 1963-65, asst. to pres., 1965-67, v.p., 1967-70, exec. v.p., dir., 1970, then chmn., chief exec. officer, now ret. Dir. Mont. Power Co., First Bank System 1975-84, Devel. Credit Corp. Mont.; MHD Devel. Corp. 1986—; mem. U.S. nat. com. World Energy Conf.; Mont. dir. for U.S. Savs. Bonds, 1980-81; cons. in field Mem. Mont. Pub. Land Law Rev. Adv. Com. City atty. Deer Lodge, 1950-57, 60-63; mem. Mont. Ho. of Reps., 1949-55, majority floor leader, 1951; mem. Mont. State Senate, 1962-64; state chmn. Republican Central Com., Mont., 1952-54; mem. adv. com. Edison Electric Inst., U. Mont. Found., Missoula, Rocky Mountain Coll., Billings; bd. dirs. Mont. Internat. Trade Commn. Served with AUS, World War II and Korea. Recipient Judstin Miller award, 1947 Mem. Mont., Am. bar assns. Episcopalian. Clubs: Masons, Shriners, Kiwanis. Home: 307 Aspen Way Butte MT 59701-3992 Office: 40 W Broadway St Butte MT 59701-9222

MCELYEA, ULYSSES, JR. veterinarian; b. Ft. Collins, Colo., Oct. 29, 1941; s. Ulysses and Hazel (Hall) McE.; m. Rexanna Bell, Dec. 29, 1975 (div. 1980); m. Natalia B. Zarzosa, Apr. 29, 2000. BS in Pharmacy, U. N.Mex., 1963; DVM, Colorado State U., 1967, MS, 1968. Diplomate Am. Bd. Vet. Practicioners; cert. in companion animals. Owner Alta Vista Animal Clinic, Las Cruces, N.Mex., 1970—; attending vet. N.Mex. State U., 1995—. Bd. dirs. N.Mex. Acad. Vet. Practice, Albuquerque, bd. dirs. state of N.Mex. Bd. Vet. Examiners, v.p., 1988-98, vice chair, 1992, chair, 1992-96, Bank of the Rio Grande; adj. prof. N.Mex. State U., 1998—. Pres. Las Cruces Community Theater, 1974; founder, bd. dirs. Dona Ann Arts Coun., Las Cruces, 1976-80. Capt. U.S. Army, 1968-70. Mem. AVMA, Am. Pharm. Assn., Am. Assn. Feline Practitioners, Am. Soc. Vet. Ophthalmologists, N.Mex. Vet. Med. Assn. (bd. dirs. 1976-82), So. N.Mex. Vet. Assn. (pres. 1974, 84), N.Mex. State U. Athletic Assn. 9bd. dirs. 1976—, pres.-elect 1992-93, pres. 1993-94), N.Mex. State U. Pres.'s Assn. 9bd. dirs. 1988-91), U. N.Mex. Alumni Assn. (bd. dirs. 1976-80). Republican. Home: 2635 Fairway Dr Las Cruces NM 88011-5044 Office: Alta Vista Animal Clinic 725 S Solano Dr Las Cruces NM 88001-3244 E-mail: umcelyea@zianet.com

MCENERY, TOM, professional sports team executive; married; three children. BA, MA degress, Santa Clara U. Mayor City of San Jose, Calif., 1983-90; vice-chmn. San Jose Sharks. Lectr. Stanford U., 1991-92. Contbr. editl. to L.A. Times, 1995; author: The New City-State: Change and Renewal in America's Cities, California Cavalier; editor: A New Ireland. Presdl. scholar Santa Clara U., 1992-93. Office: San Jose Sharks 525 W Santa Clara St San Jose CA 95113-1500

MCEVOY, NAN TUCKER, publishing company executive, olive rancher; b. San Mateo, Calif., July 15, 1919; d. Nion R. and Phyllis (de Young) Tucker; m. Dennis McEvoy, 1948 (div.); 1 child, Nion Tucker McEvoy. Student, Georgetown U., 1975. Newspaper reporter San Francisco Chronicle, 1944-46, N.Y. Herald Tribune, N.Y.C., 1946-47, Washington Post, 1947-48; rep. in pub. rels. John Homes, Inc., Washington, 1959-60; spl. asst. to dir. U.S. Peace Corps, Washington, 1961-64; mem. U.S. delegation UNESCO, Washington, 1964-65; dir. Population Coun., Washington, 1965-70; co-founder, dep. dir. Preterm, Inc., Washington, 1970-74; former chmn. bd. Chronicle Pub. Co., San Francisco, 1975-95, dir. emeritus, 1995—. Mem. nat. bd. dirs. Smithsonian Instn., Washington, 1994—; bd. dirs. Am. Farmland Trust; mem. coun. Brookings Instn., Washington, 1994—; mem. U. Calif. San Francisco Found., 1993—; dir. emeritus Nat. Mus. Am. Art; mem. Nat. Coun. Fine Arts Museums; formerly arbitrator Am. Arbitration Assn., Washington. Named Woman of Yr., Washingtonian Mag., 1973. Mem. Am. Art Forum, Burlingame Country Club, The River Club, Commonwealth Club of Calif., World Affairs Coun., Villa Taverna. Avocation: overseeing Marin County, California olive grove ranch producing fine extra virgin olive oil. Office: 655 Montgomery St Ste 1430 San Francisco CA 94111-2635

MCEVOY, NION TUCKER, editor; b. San Mateo, Calif., May 23, 1952; s. Dennis Griffin and Nan (Tucker) McE.; m. Karen Ira Polcyn, July 19, 1986. BA, U. Calif., Santa Cruz, 1974; JD, Hastings Coll. Law, San Francisco, 1979. Bar: Calif. 1980, Oreg. 1984. Bus. affairs exec. William Morris Agy., Beverly Hill, Calif., 1980-83; atty. Legal Svcs. Orgn., Portland, Oreg., 1983-84; dir. of bus. affairs Wescom Prodns., L.A., 1984-86; editor Chronicle Books, San Francisco, 1986-87, editor-in-chief, 1990—. Office: Chronicle Books 85 2nd St Fl 6 San Francisco CA 94105-3464

MCEWEN, ALFRED SHERMAN, planetary geologist; b. Lawrence, Kans., July 22, 1954; s. William Edwin and Miriam (Sherman) McE.; m. Eileen Haney; 1 child, Ian. B.S., SUNY-Syracuse, 1975; B.S. No. Ariz. U., 1981, M.S., 1983; PhD Ariz. State U., 1988. Vol. Peace Corps, Guatemala, Central Am., 1975-77; soil conservationist Soil Conservation Service, USDA, 1978-80; geologist U.S. Geol. Survey, Flagstaff, Ariz., 1981-96, U. Ariz., 1996—, dir. Planetary Image Rsch. Lab. Mem. Galileo, Cassini, Mars Global Surveyor, and Clementine Spacecraft Sci. Teams. Contbr. articles to profl. jours. Mem. Am. Geophys. Union, Am. Astron. Soc. Home: 4135 E Cooper St Tucson AZ 85711-3464 Office: U Ariz Dept Planetary Sci Lunar Planetary Lab 1629 E University Blvd Tucson AZ 85721-0001

MCFADDEN, DANIEL LITTLE, economics educator; b. Raleigh, N.C., July 29, 1937; s. Robert S. and Alice (Little) McF.; m. Beverlee Tito Simboli, Dec. 15, 1962; children: Nina, Robert, Raymond. BS, U. Minn., 1957, PhD, 1962; LLD, U. Chgo., 1992. Mellon fellow U. Pitts., Pa., 1962-63; asst. prof. U. Calif., Berkeley, 1963-65, assoc. prof., 1965-67, prof., 1967-77; research prof. Yale U., New Haven, 1977-78; prof. MIT, Cambridge, Mass.; E. Morris Cox prof. of economics Coll. of Letters & Sci., U. Calif., Berkeley; dir. Econometrics Lab., U.Calif., Berkeley. Mem. econs. adv. panel NSF, 1969-71, Universities Nat. Bur., 1974-77, rev. com. Calif. Energy Com. Forecasts, 1979, Sloan Found. Book Com., 1977-79, NAS Com. on Basic Research in Social Scis., 1982—, NAS Com. on Energy Demand Modeling, 1983-84; chmn. AEA Awards Com., 1981-84, NSF-NBER Conf. on the Econs. of Uncertainty, 1970—; bd. dirs. Nat. Bur. Econ. Research, 1976-77, 1980-83; dir. Econometrics Lab. U. Calif. Berkeley, 1991—; mem. NAS Commn. Behavioral and Social Scis. and Edn., 1989—. Editor: Jour. Statis. Physics, 1968-70, Econometric Soc. monographs, 1980-83; bd. editors: Am. Econ. Rev., 1971-74, Jour. Math. Econs., 1973-77, Transp. Research, 1978-80; assoc. editor: Jour. Econometrics, 1977-78. Mem. adv. com. Transp. Models Project, Met. Transp. Commn., 1975, City of Berkeley Coordinated Transit Project, 1975-76; exec. com. Transp. Research Bd., 1975-78. Recipient John Bates Clark medal, 1975, Outstanding Teacher award MIT Econ. Dept., 1981, Frisch medal, 1986, Nobel Prize in Economics, 2000. Mem. Am. Acad. Arts and Scis., Nat. Acad. Sci., Am. Econ. Assn. (exec. com. 1985-87, v.p. 1994), Econometric Soc. (exec. com. 1983-86, v.p. 1984, pres. 1985), Am. Statis. Assn., Math. Assn. Am., Transp. Rsch. Bd. Democrat. Avocations: biking, tennis, squash, sailing, skiing. Home: 1370 Trancas St # 152 Napa CA 94558-2912 Office: U Calif-Berkeley Dept Economics 549 Evans Hall # 3880 Berkeley CA 94720-1775

MCFANN, MAURICE L., JR. career officer; b. June 10, 1950; BA, Calif. State U., Chico, 1972; MS, Vanderbilt U., 1981. Commd. 2d lt. USAF, 1972, advanced through grades to brig. gen., 1997; flight examiner 100th Air Refueling Wing, Beale AFB, Calif., 1973-77; pilot tng. 82nd Flying Tng. Wing, Williams AFB, Ariz., 1977-78; flight examiner 1st Tactical Reconnaissance Squadron, Royal Air Force, Alconbury, Eng., 1979-82; flight comdr. 12th Tactical Reconnaissance Squadron, Bergstrom AFB, Tex., 1982-83; air-to-surface br. chief, inspector's gen.'s office Hdqrs. Tactical Command, Langley AFB, Va., 1983-85; asst. chief tactical forces divsn., dep. chief of staff Hdqrs. USAF, The Pentagon, Washington, 1986-88, dep. dir. modeling and simulation, dep. chief of staff, 1994-95, exec. officer, dep. chief of staff to dep. dir. of ops., 1995-96; comdr. 363rd Tactical Fighter Wing, Shaw AFB, S.C., 1988-90, 12th Ops. Group, 12th Flying Tng. Wing, Randolph AFB, Tex., 1991-92; chief Joint Simulation and Interoperability Divsn. The Joint Staff, The Pentagon, Washington, 1992-94; comdr. E-3A component NATO Airborne Early Warning Force, Geilenkirchen AB, Germany, 1996-98; comdr. 552nd Air Control Wing, Tinker AFB, Okla., 1998—. Dir. plans, NORAD, Colorado Springs. Deocrated Legion of Merit. Office: Hdqs NORAD 250 S Peterson Blvd Ste 116 Colorado Springs CO 80914-3180

MC FARLAND, NORMAN FRANCIS, bishop; b. Martinez, Calif., Feb. 21, 1922; student St. Patrick's Sem., Menlo Park, Calif.; J.C.D., Cath. U. Am. Ordained priest Roman Catholic Ch., 1946, consecrated bishop, 1970; titular bishop of Bida and aux. bishop of San Francisco, 1970-74; apostolic adminstr. Diocese of Reno, 1974-76; bishop Diocese of Reno-Las Vegas, 1976-87, Diocese of Orange, Calif., 1987-98. Office: 200 W La Veta Ave Orange CA 92866-1936

MCFARLANE, WILLIS MCKEE, buffalo company executive; b. Cleve., May 27, 1933; BA in Econs. cum laude, Amherst Coll., 1955. Exec. Nowthwestern Mut. Life Ins., 1955-60; ptnr. life ins. co. Files, Cristal, and McFarlane, 1956—; founder AIRCOA, Cleve., 1968-79, Denver, 1979-90; co-owner Denver Buffalo Mktg. Co., 1990—, Buffalo Bar, Idaho Springs, 1995—. Chmn. bd. dirs. Colo. Symphony Orch.; bd. dirs. Colo. Wildlife Heritage Found. Mem. Cherry Hills Country Club. Office: Denver Buffalo Co 1120 Lincoln St Ste 905 Denver CO 80203-2138

MCFEE, RICHARD, electrical engineer, physicist; b. Pitts., Jan. 24, 1925; s. William and Beatrice (Allender) McF.; m. Anne Stauffer, June 26, 1947 (div. 1960); m. 2d., Joanellen Lewis, Dec. 31, 1974. BEE, Yale U., 1947; MS in Physics, Syracuse U., 1949; PhDEE, U. Mich., 1955. Rsch. asst. Syracuse U. Med. Sch., 1947-48; instr. Syracuse U. elec. enging. dept., 1948-49; rsch. assoc. U. Mich. Med. Sch., 1949-51; engr. Electro-Mech. Rsch. Inc., Ridgefield, Conn., 1951-52; mem. tech. staff Bell Telephone Labs., Whippany, N.J., 1952-57; prof. elec. engring. Syracuse U., 1957-82; ind. researcher Union Springs, N.Y., 1982-86, Hawi, Hawaii, 1986—. Cons. Arthur D. Little Inc., Cambridge, Mass., 1960-61, cardiovascular study sect. NIH, GE Inc., Crouse Hinds Inc., Syracuse, N.Y., 1970, Stanford U. physics dept., 1974-75. Contbr. articles on electronics, electrocardiography, magnetocardiography, superconductivity, circuit theory, thermodynamics, elec. measurements; patentee in field. Sgt. U.S. Army, 1943-46. Sci. Faculty fellowship NSF, Stanford U., 1970. Fellow IEEE; mem. AAAS, Sigma Xi. Home and Office: PO Box 989 Kapaau HI 96755-0989 E-mail: jermcfee@aol.com

MC FERON, DEAN EARL, mechanical engineer, educator; b. Portland, Oreg., Dec. 24, 1923; s. Wallace Suitor and Ruth Carolyn (Fessler) McF.; m. Phyllis Grace Ehlers, Nov. 10, 1945; children: David Alan, Phyllis Ann, Douglas Dean, Donald Brooks. Student, Oreg. State Coll., 1942-43; BSME with spl. honors, U. Colo., 1945, MSME, 1948; PhD, U. Ill., 1956. Instr. U. Colo., Boulder, 1946-48; assoc. prof. U. Ill., 1948-58; rsch. assoc. Argonne (Ill.) Nat. Lab., 1957-58; prof. mech. engring., assoc. dean U. Wash., Seattle, 1958-82, prof. emeritus, 1983—. Cons. to industry, 1959-80 Served with USNR, 1942-46, to comdr. Res., 1946-72. Co-recipient Outstanding Tech. Applications Paper award ASHRAE, 1974; Ednl. Achievement award Soc. Mfg. Engrs., 1970; NSF faculty fellow, 1967-68 Mem. ASME, Am. Soc. Engring. Edn., U.S. Naval Inst. (life), Sigma Xi (nat. dir. 1972-80, nat. pres. 1978), Tau Beta Pi, Sigma Tau, Pi Tau Sigma. Home: 4008 NE 40th St Seattle WA 98105-5422 Office: U Wash Dept Mech Engring Seattle WA 98195-0001

MCGAGH, WILLIAM GILBERT, financial consultant; b. Boston, May 29, 1929; s. Thomas A. and Mary M. (McDonough) McG.; m. Sarah Ann McQuigg, Sept. 23, 1961; children: Margaret Ellen, Sarah Elizabeth. BSBA, Boston Coll., 1950; MBA, Harvard U., 1952; MS, MIT, 1965. Fin. analyst Ford Motor Co., Dearborn, Mich., 1953-55; mem. staff treas. office DaimlerChrysler, Detroit, 1955-64, compt., treas. Canadian divsn. Windsor, 1965-67, staff exec.-fin. Latin Am. ops. Detroit, 1967-68, asst. treas., 1968-75, treas., 1975-76, v.p., treas., 1976-80; sr. v.p. fin., dir. Northrop Grumman Corp., L.A., 1980-88; owner McGagh Assocs., Beverly Hills, Calif., 1988—. Chmn. bd. dirs. Pacific Am. Income Shares, Inc., Western Asset Funds, Inc. Vice-chmn., bd. regents Mt. St. Mary's Coll.; bd. dirs. L.A. Orthop. Hosp., John Tracy Clinic, chmn. bd. dirs., 1998—. Sloan fellow MIT, 1965. Mem. Fin. Execs. Inst. (pres. Detroit chpt. 1979-80), Harvard Club (N.Y.C. and Boston), Beach Club (Santa Monica, Calif.), L.A. Country Club, Calif. Club (L.A.), Eastward Ho Country Club (Chatham, Mass.). Home: 2189 Century Hl Los Angeles CA 90067-3516 Office: McGagh Assocs 9601 Wilshire Blvd Ste 600 Beverly Hills CA 90210-5208

MCGAGIN, NANCY, public affairs executive; Mgr. pub. affairs Raley's Bel Air, West Sacramento, Calif., mgr. corp. consumer affairs. Office: Raleys Bel Air 500 W Capitol Ave West Sacramento CA 95605-2696

MCGANN, JOHN MILTON, real estate executive; b. Omaha, Mar. 18, 1948; s. John Byron and Donna M. (Rehnquist) McG.; m. Barbara June Scott, June 2, 1978. BSBA, cert. real estate, U. Nebr., Omaha, 1971. Property mgr. Boetel & Co., Omaha, 1971-73; asst. office bldg. mgr. The Irvine Co., Newport Beach, Calif., 1973-74; property mgr. Harbor Investment Co., Corona Del Mar, 1974-76, Robert A. McNeil Corp., Santa Ana, 1976-78; gen. mgr. Daon Mgmt., Newport Beach, 1978-80; v.p. August Mgmt. Inc., Long Beach, Calif., 1980-82, Calif. Fed. Asst. Mgmt., L.A., 1982-83; pres. Wespac Mgmt. Realty Corp., Newport Beach, 1983-87; v.p., dir. asset mgmt., pres. CalFed Asset Mgmt. Co., L.A., 1987-90; v.p. com. ops. Pinnacle Realty (formerly Sovereign/Ring), Santa Monica, 1990-95; pres., ptnr. Churchill McGann, LLC, 1995-97; pres. McGann Enterprises Inc. dba Churchill McGann & Round Table Pizza, Lakewood, Long Beach, Calif., 1997—. Mem. Inst. Real Estate Mgmt. (L.A. chpt., cert. property mgr.), Internat. Coun. Shopping Ctrs. (cert. shopping ctr. mgr.), Lambda Chi Alpha, Delta Sigma Pi, Rho Epsilon (pres.). Republican. Mem. Christian Sci. Ch. Home: 3834 Pine Ave Long Beach CA 90807-3234 Office: McGann Enterprises Inc dba Churchill McGann 4201 Long Beach Blvd Ste 306 Long Beach CA 90807-2021 also: Round Table Pizza 5250 Faculty Ave Lakewood CA 90712-2508 E-mail: jbmcgann@earthlink.net

MC GAUGH, JAMES LAFAYETTE, psychobiologist; b. Long Beach, Calif., Dec. 17, 1931; s. William Rufus and Daphne (Hermes) McG.; m. Carol J. Becker, Mar. 15, 1952; children: Douglas, Janice, Linda. BA, San Jose State U., 1953; PhD (Abraham Rosenberg fellow), U. Calif. - Berkeley, 1959; sr. postdoctoral fellow, NAS-NRC, Istituto Superiore di Sanitá, Rome, 1961-62; DSc (hon.), So. Ill. U., 1991. Asst. prof., assoc. prof. psychology San Jose State U., 1957-61; assoc. prof. psychology U. Oreg., 1961-64; assoc. prof. U. Calif., Irvine, 1964-66, founding chmn. dept. psychobiology, 1964-67, 71-74, 86-89, prof., 1966-94; rsch. prof., 1994—; dean Sch. Biol. Sci. U. Calif., Irvine, 1967-70, vice chancellor acad. affairs, 1975-77, exec. vice chancellor, 1978-82, founding dir. Ctr. Neurobiology of Learning and Memory, 1983—. Mem. adv. coms. NIMH, 1965-78, Mental Health Coun. NIMH, 1992-95. Author: (with J.B. Cooper) Integrating Principles of Social Psychology, 1963, (with H.F. Harlow, R.F. Thompson) Psychology, 1971, (with M.J. Herz) Memory Consolidation, 1972, Learning and Memory: An Introduction, 1973, (with R.F. Thompson and T. Nelson) Psychology I, 1977, (with C. Cotman) Behavioral Neuroscience, 1980; editor: (with N.M. Weinberger, R.E. Whalen) Psychobiology, 1966, Psychobiology-Behavior from a Biological Perspective, 1971, The Chemistry of Mood, Motivation and Memory, 1972, (with M. Fink, S.S. Kety, T.A. Williams) Psychobiology of Convulsive Therapy, 1974, (with L.F. Petrinovich) Knowing, Thinking, and Believing, 1976, (with R.R. Drucker-Colín) Neurobiology of Sleep and Memory, 1977, (with S.B. Kiesler) Aging, Biology and Behavior, 1981, (with G. Lynch and N.M. Weinberger) Neurobiology of Learning and Memory, 1984, (with N.M. Weinberger and G. Lynch) Memory Systems of the Brain, 1985, Contemporary Psychology, 1985, (with C.D. Woody and D.L. Alkon) Cellular Mechanisms of Conditioning and Behavioral Plasticity, 1988, (with N.M. Weinberger and G. Lynch) Brain Organization and Memory: Cells, Systems and Circuits, 1990, (with R.C.A. Frederickson and D.L. Felten) Peripheral Signaling of the Brain, 1991, (with L. Squire, G. Lynch and N.M. Weinberger) Memory: Organization and Locus of Change, 1991; (with N.M. Weinberger and G. Lynch) Brain and Memory: Modulation and Mediation of Neuroplasticity, 1995; author over 400 sci. papers; founding editor Behavioral Biology, 1972-78, Behavioral and Neural Biology, 1979-94, Neurobiology of Learning and Memory, 1995-98, Plasticity in the Central Nervous System; Learning and Memory, 1995, Brain Processes and Memory, 1996. Recipient medal U. Calif., Irvine, 1992; recipient John P. McGovern award, 1996. Fellow AAAS, Am. Acad. Arts and Scis., Soc. Exptl. Psychologists, Am. Psychol. Soc. (William James fellow 1989, pres. 1989-91), Western Psychol. Assn. (pres. 1992-93); mem. NAS (chmn. psychol. secat. 1992-95), APA (chief sci. advisor 1986-88, Sci. Contbn. award 1981), Internat. Brain Rsch. Orgn., Soc. Neurosci., Am. Coll. Neuropsychopharmacology, Brazilian Acad. Sci. (fgn. mem.), Collegium Internat. Neuropsychopharmacologicum, Psychonomic Soc., European Behavioral Pharmacology Soc., Phi Beta Kappa, Sigma Xi. Office: U Calif Dept Neurobiology Behavior Ctr Neurobiology Learning Irvine CA 92697-0001

MCGEE, JAMES SEARS, historian, educator; b. Houston, July 12, 1942; s. William Sears and Mary Elizabeth (Peterson) McG.; m. Mary Arnall Broach, Aug. 20, 1966; children: Elizabeth, Claude. BA, Rice U., 1964; MA, Yale U., 1966, M in Philosophy, 1968, PhD, 1971. Asst. prof. Ga. So. Coll., Statesboro, 1969-71; asst. prof. history U. Calif., Santa Barbara, 1971-78, assoc. prof., 1978-84, prof., 1984—, chmn. dept., 1990-95. Pres. Pacific Coast Conf. on Brit. Studies, 1998-2000. Author: The Godly Man in Stuart England, 1976; co-author: The West Transformed, 2000; editor: The Miscellaneous Works of John Bunyan, Vol. 3, 1987. Named Disting.

Tchr. in Soc. Scis., U. Calif., Santa Barbara, 1989; fellow Abraham Found., 1962-63; Woodrow Wilson fellow, 1964-65; recipient summer stipend NEH, 1975. Fellow Royal Hist. Soc.; mem. Am. Soc. Ch. History, Am. Hist. Assn., N.Am. Conf. on Brit. Studies. Democrat. Episcopalian. Avocation: gardening. Office: U Calif Dept History Santa Barbara CA 93106

MCGEE, MICHAEL JAY, protective services official, educator; b. Ft. Worth, June 9, 1952; s. Cecil Carl McGee and Helen Ruth (Peeples) McGee-Furrh; m. Carol Lee Garbarino, Sept. 18, 1982; children: Megan Rose, John Michael, Molly Caitlin. Student, U. Tex., 1970-73, Western Oreg. State U., 1983; AAS in Fire Protection Tech., Colo. Mountain Coll., 1990. Lic. fire suppression systems insp., Colo., vocat. educator, Colo.; cert. hazardous materials technician, Colo., 1992, EMT, Colo.; cert. fire safety hazardous materials instr., evaluator. Driver Massengale Co., Austin, Tex., 1970-73; gen. mgr. Sundae Palace, Austin, 1973-74; staff mem. Young Life, Colorado Springs, Colo., 1970-75; mgr. Broadmoor Mgmt. Co., Vail, 1974-76; technician Vail Cable Communications, 1976-77; fire marshal, dep. chief fire marshal Vail Fire Dept., 1977—, fire sci. coord., 1995—, emergency med. program coord., 1996—; v.p. HAZPRO (Hazardous Materials and Fire Safety Consulting Firm), 1996—; pres. Fire Protection Tng. & Consulting, Inc., 1999. Dist. rep. Joint Coun. Fire Dist. Colo., 1983-85; co-chmn. Eagle County Hazardous Materials, 1984-85, mem. planning com., 1987-90; mem. accountability com. Eagle County Sch. Dist., 1991-96, mem. budget rev. com., 1991-93, vice chair accountability com. 1992-93, chmn. accountability com., 1993-96; mem. policy rev. com., 1993-96, bldg. coord., team coach Odyssey of the Mind at Eaglevalle Elem. Sch., 1995; invited dir. workshops Colo. Dept. Edn. Dist. Accountability Convention, Colo. Springs, 1995; pres. Fire Protection Tng. and Cons., Inc.; instr., trainer EMP Am. Inc. Chmn. Eagle County chpt. ARC, 1980-83, disaster chmn., 1977-80; tng. officer Eagle Vol. Fire Dept., 1988-90; mem. parish coun. St. Mary's Parish, Eagle County, 1989-90; mem. citizen's adv. com. Colo. Mountain Coll., 1990-91, bd. dirs. 1990; bldg. coord., team coach Odessey of the Mind, Eagle Valley Elem. Sch., 1994-95, 97-98, 98-99, coach Destination Imagination, 1999-2000; mem. facilities master planning com. Engle County Sch. Dist., 1996-97; mem. planning com. 1999 World Alpine Ski Championships; program coord. Eagle County Driver's Edn. Mem. Internat. Assn. Arson Investigators (Colo. chpt.), Internat. Platform Assn., Nat. Fire Protection Assn., Colo. State Fire Marshals Assn., Colo. State Fire Chiefs Assn. Office: Vail Fire Dept 42 W Meadow Dr Vail CO 81657-5000 E-mail: mmcgee@ci.vail.co.us

MCGEE, TERRY, geography educator; BA, MA in Geography, PhD in Geography, U. Wellington. Lectr. U. Malaya, 1958—65, Victoria U. Wellington, 1966—68; prof. U. Hong Kong, 1968—73; sr. fellow dept. human geography Rsch. Sch. Pacific Studies Australian Nat. U. , Australia, 1978—; prof. dept. geography faculty of arts Inst. Asian Rsch., U. B.C., Vancouver, Can. Cons. UN Devel. Program, Internat. Devel. Rsch. Ctr., Can. Internat. Devel. Agy., UN Ctr. for Human Settlements; presenter in field. Author, editor: (with I. Robinson) The Mega-Urban Regions of Southeast Asia: Policy Challenges and Response, 1995, (with R.F. Watters) New Geographies of the Asia Pacific Regiona, 1997, (with E. Laquian and A. Laquian) The Silent Debate: Asian Immigration and Racism in Canada, 1997; contbr. chpts. to books. Erskine fellow U. Canterbury, New Zealand, 2000. Mem. Can. Assn. Geographers (Scholarly Distinction award 2000). Achievements include research on urbanization in developing countries, The Pacific Rim particularly S.E. Asia, geography of development. Office: U BC Inst Asian Rsch 254-1855 West Mall Vancouver BC Canada V6T 1Z2 Fax: 604-822-5207. E-mail: tmcgee@interchange.ubc.ca

MCGEER, EDITH GRAEF, neurological science educator; b. N.Y.C., Nov. 18, 1923; d. Charles and Charlotte Annie (Ruhl) Graef; m. Patrick L. McGeer, Apr. 15, 1954; children: Patrick Charles, Brian Theodore, Victoria Lynn. BA, Swarthmore Coll., 1944; PhD, U. Va., 1946; DSc (hon.), U. Victoria, 1987, U. B.C., 2000. Research chemist E.I. DuPont de Nemours & Co., Wilmington, Va., 1946-54; research assoc. div. neurological sci. U. B.C., Vancouver, Can., 1954-74, assoc. prof., 1974-76, prof., acting head, 1976-83, prof., head., 1983-89, prof. emerita, 1989—. Author: (with others) Molecular Neurobiology of the Mammalian Brain, 1978, 2d. edit., 1987; editor: (with others) Kainic Acid as a Tool in Neurobiology, 1978, Glutamine, Glutamate, and GABA, 1983; contbr. articles to profl. jours. Decorated officer Order of Can.; recipient Citation Am. Chem. Soc., 1958, Rsch. Prize in Psychiatry Clarke Inst., 1992, Lifetime Achievement spl. award Sci. Coun. B.C., 1995, Hon. Alumnus award, 1996. Fellow Can. Coll. Neuropsychopharmacology; mem. Can. Biochemical Soc., Internat. Brain Research Orgn., Internat. Soc. Neurochemistry, Soc. Neuroscience, Am. Neurochemical Soc. (councilor 1979-83), North Pacific Soc. Neurology and Psychiatry (hon. fellow), Lychnos Soc., Sigma Xi, Phi Beta Kappa Office: U BC Divsn Neurol Scis 2255 Wesbrook Mall Vancouver BC Canada V6T 1Z3 E-mail: mcgeer@interchange.ubc.ca

MCGETTIGAN, CHARLES CARROLL, JR. investment banker; b. San Francisco, Mar. 28, 1945; s. Charles Carroll McGettigan and Molly (Fay) McGettigan Pedley; m. Katharine Havard King, Nov. 1, 1975 (div. 1981); m. Meriwether Lewis Stovall, Aug. 6, 1983; 1 child, Meriwether. AB in Govt., Georgetown U., 1966; MBA in Fin., U. Pa., 1969. Assoc., asst. v.p., v.p. Blyth Eastman Dillon, N.Y.C., 1970-75, 1st v.p., 1975-78, sr. v.p. San Francisco, 1978-80, Dillon, Read & Co., San Francisco, 1980-83; gen. ptnr. Woodman Kirkpatrick & Gilbreath, San Francisco, 1983-84; prin. corp. fin. Hambrecht & Quist, Inc., San Francisco, 1984-88; mng. dir., founder McGettigan, Wick & Co., Inc., San Francisco, 1988—; gen. ptnr., founder Proactive Ptnrs., L.P., San Francisco, 1990—, Proactive Investment Mgrs., L.P., San Francisco, 1991—. Gen. ptnr. Fremont Proactive Ptnrs., 1991-2001; bd. dirs. Cuisine Solutions, Inc., Alexandria, Va., Tanknology-NDE Corp., Austin, Tex., PMR Corp., San Diego, Sonex Rsch., Inc., Annapolis, Md., Modtech, Inc., Perris, Calif.; chmn. Onsite Energy Corp., Carlsbad, Calif.; adv. dir. Chesapeake Ventures, Balt., 1984-94. Trustee St. Francis Meml. Hosp., San Francisco, 1980-86; mem. United San Francisco Rep. fin. com., 1983—, steering com., 1986—; adv. bd. dirs. Leavey Sch. Bus. Adminstrn., Santa Clara U., Calif., 1984-90. With USN, 1966. Named Confrerie des Chevaliers du Tastevin, 1991. Mem. Soc. Calif. Pioneers, The Brook, Racquet and Tennis Club (N.Y.), The Pacific Union Club, Bohemian Club (San Francisco), San Francisco Golf Club, Burlingame Country Club (Hillsborough, Calif.), Boston (New Orleans), White's (London). Republican. Roman Catholic. Home: 3375 Clay St San Francisco CA 94118-2006 Office: McGettigan Wick & Co Inc 50 Osgood Pl San Francisco CA 94133-4622 E-mail: Chas@McGettigan-Wick.com

MC GILL, ARCHIE JOSEPH, venture capitalist; b. Winona, Minn., May 29, 1931; s. Archibald Joseph and Anne (Lettner) McG.; m. Jeanne Sullivan, Mar. 17, 1974; children: Archibald Joseph, III, Mark E., Gregory P., Debora, Susan, Brian. BA in Econs., St. Mary's Coll., Winona, 1956. With IBM Corp., 1956-69, v.p. market ops. N.Y., 1956-69; founder, pres. McGill Assocs., White Plains, 1970-73; dir. market mgmt. AT&T Co., 1973-78, v.p. bus. mktg., 1978-83; pres. Advanced Info. Systems Am. Bell, Inc., 1983; pres., chief exec. officer Rothschild Ventures, Inc., 1983; now pres. Chardonnay, Inc. Dir. various cos. Bd. dirs. Steadman/Hawkins Found. With USAF, 1951-54. Named Mktg. Statesman of Year Sales Execs Club 1978

MCGILL, THOMAS CONLEY, physics educator; b. Port Arthur, Tex., Mar. 20, 1942; s. Thomas Conley and Susie Elizabeth (Collins) McG.; m. Toby Elizabeth Cone, Dec. 27, 1966; children: Angela Elizabeth, Sara Elizabeth. BS in Math., Lamar State Coll., 1963, BEE, 1964; MEE, Calif. Inst. Tech., 1965, PHD, 1969. NATO postdoctoral fellow U. Bristol, Eng., 1969-70; NRC postdoctoral fellow Princeton (N.J.) U., 1970-71; from asst. to assoc. prof. applied physics Calif. Inst. Tech., Pasadena, 1971-77, prof., 1977—. Cons. United Techs. Corp., 1988-95, Advance Projects Agy./Def. Sci. Rsch. Coun., Arlington, Va., 1979—; chief Naval Ops. Exec. Panel, 1995-2000; mem. Semiconductor Tech. Coun., 1995-98; mem. adv. bd. Sematech U., 1992-95. Alfred P. Sloan Found. fellow, 1974. Fellow Am. Physical Soc.; mem. AAAS, IEEE, Am. Vacuum Soc., Sigma Xi. Office: Calif Inst Tech Mail Code 128 # 95 Pasadena CA 91125-0001

MCGILLICUDDY, JOAN MARIE, psychotherapist, consultant; b. Chgo., June 23, 1952; d. James Neal and Muriel (Joy) McG. BA, U. Ariz., 1974, MS, 1976; PhD, Walden U., 1996. Cert. nat. counselor. Counselor ACTION, Tucson, 1976; counselor, clin. supr. Behavioral Health Agy. Cen. Ariz., Casa Grande, 1976-81; instr. psychology Cen. Ariz. Coll., Casa Grande, 1978-83; therapist, co-dir. Helping Assocs., Inc., Casa Grande, 1982—, v.p., sec., 1982—; cert. instr. Silva Method Mind Devel., Tucson, 1986—. Mem. Mayor's Com. for Handicapped, Casa Grande, 1989-90, Human Svcs. Planning, Casa Grande, 1985-95. Named Outstanding Am. Lectr. Silva Mind Internat., 1988-99. Mem. ACA. Avocations: jogging, singing. Office: Helping Assocs Inc 1901 N Trekell Rd Casa Grande AZ 85222-1706

MCGINNESS, MIKE W. state legislator; b. Fallon, Nev., Apr. 12, 1947; m. Dee Pearce; children: Ryan, Brett, Shannon. BA, U. Nev. Radio sta. mgr.; mem. Nev. Assembly, 1989-91, Nev. Senate, Central Nev., 1992—; mem. judiciary com., mem. natural resources com. Nev. Senate, chair taxation com. Past chair Churchill County Rep. Ctrl. Com., Churchill County Sch. Bd., Churchill County Pks. and Recreation Commn., 1986-87; past pres. Citizens for Pvt. Enterprise-Fallon Chpt., 1987-88, Nev. State Fair Bd. Dirs., 1985 . With Nev. Air Nat. Guard, 1969-75. Mem. Nat. Conf. State Legislatures, Churchill County Ducks Unltd. (steering com.), Churchill County C. of C. (past pres. 1975-76), Kiwanis Club Fallon (past pres., sec., treas.). Republican. Home: 770 Wildes Rd Fallon NV 89406-7843 Office: Nev State Legis Bldg 401 S Carson St Rm 242 Carson City NV 89701-4747 Fax: 702-687-8206. E-mail: mmcginness@sen.state.nv.us

MCGINNIS, ROBERT E. lawyer; b. Caldwell, Ohio, May 1, 1931; s. Earl Peregoy and Mary Ethel (Richner) McG.; m. Jane Ann Lindenmeyer, Sept. 12, 1953; children: Sharon Ann, David E. BA, Ohio Weslayan U., 1952; JD summa cum laude, Ohio State U., 1954. Bar: Ohio 1954, Calif. 1956. Asst. judge advocate USAF, 1954-56; sr. ptnr. Luce, Forward, Hamilton, & Scripps, San Diego, 1956—. Counsel to pub. utilities, pub. agys., savs. and loan instns., ins. cos. and contractors. Trustee Wesley Meth. Ch., San Diego, Fine Arts Soc., First Meth. Ch., La Mesa, Calif.; counsel Kensington Community Ch.; dir. San Diego Opera Assn., corp. sec., v.p. Mem. Order of Coif. Republican. Mem. United Ch. Christ. Office: Luce Forward Hamilton & Scripps 600 W Broadway Ste 2600 San Diego CA 92101-3372 E-mail: rmcginnis@luce.com

MC GOVERN, MAUREEN THERESE, entertainer; b. Youngstown, Ohio, July 27, 1949; d. James Terrence and Mary Rita (Welsh) McG. Student pub. schs., Youngstown. Exec. sec. Youngstown Cartage Co., 1968-69; sec. Assocs. in Anesthesiology, Youngstown, 1970-71. Entertainer, 1972— ; stage appearances include: The Sound of Music, 1981, The Pirates of Penzance, 1981, South Pacific, 1982, Nine, 1984, Brownstone, 1984, Guys and Dolls, 1984, Three Penny Opera, 1989; cameo appearance in movie The Towering Inferno, 1975; appeared in film Ky. Fried Theater's Airplane, 1979; albums recorded include: The Morning After, 1973 (Gold Record award), Nice To Be Around, 1974, Academy Award Performance, 1975, Maureen McGovern, 1979, Another Woman In Love, 1987, Naughty Baby, 1989, Baby I'm Yours, 1992, Music Never Ends, 1997, The Pleasure of His Company, 1998; composer: Midnight Storm, 1973, If I Wrote You a Song, 1973, All I Want, 1974, Memory, 1974, Little Boys and Men, 1974, Love Knots, 1974, You Love Me Too Late, 1979, Thief in the Night, 1979, Don't Stop Now, 1979, Hello Again, 1979, Halfway Home, 1980, others. Recipient Gold Record for single The Morning After, Record Industry Assn. Am., 1973; Can. RPM Gold Leaf award, 1973; Australian gold award, 1975; resolution for bringing fame and recognition to Ohio, Ohio Senate, 1974; Grand prize Tokyo Music Festival, 1975 Mem. ASCAP, Am. Fedn. Musicians, AFTRA, Screen Actors Guild. Office: c/o Warner Bros Records 3300 Warner Blvd Burbank CA 91505-4632

MC GOVERN, WALTER T. federal judge; b. Seattle, May 24, 1922; s. C. Arthur and Anne Marie (Thies) McG.; m. Rita Marie Olsen, June 29, 1946; children: Katrina M., Shawn E., A. Renee. B.A., U. Wash., 1949, LL.B., 1950. Bar: Wash. 1950. Practiced law in, Seattle, 1950-59; mem. firm Kerr, McCord, Greenleaf & Moen; judge Municipal Ct., Seattle, 1959-65, Superior Ct., Wash., 1965-68, Wash. Supreme Ct., 1968-71, U.S. Dist. Ct. (we. dist.) Wash., 1971-87, chief judge, 1975-87, sr. judge, 1987—. Mem. subcom. on supporting personnel Jud. Conf. U.S., 1981-87, chmn. subcom., 1983, mem. adminstrn. com., 1983-87, chmn. jud. resources com., 1987-91. Mem. Am. Judicature Soc., Wash. State Superior Ct. Judges Assn., Seattle King County Bar Assn. (treas.), Phi Delta Phi. Club: Seattle Tennis (pres. 1968). Office: US Dist Ct US Courthouse 5th Fl 1010 5th Ave Ste 215 Seattle WA 98104-1189

MCGOWN, JOHN, JR. lawyer; b. Bowling Green, Ky., June 15, 1949; s. John Stanley and Margaret (Deatherage) McG.; m. Mary Grunewald, Apr. 20, 1978; children: Erin Margaret, Brenna Kathryn. BS, U. Ky., 1971; JD, U. Colo., 1974; LLM in Taxation, U. Denver, 1981. Bar: Colo. 1975, U.S. Tax Ct. 1981, Idaho 1982. Dep. dist. atty. Weld County, Colo., 1974-78; assoc. Montgomery, Little, Young, Campbell, & McGrew, Denver, 1979-80; rschr. appellate divsn. IRS, Denver, 1980-81; mem. staff tax dept. Price Waterhouse, Denver, 1981-82; ptnr. Hawley, Troxell, Ennis & Hawley, LLP, Boise, Idaho, 1982-99, of counsel, 2000—. Adj. prof. Boise State U., 1983, assoc. prof., 2000—; guest lecturer U. Idaho Coll. Law, Moscow, 1990; guest speaker various tax seminars, 1983—. Contbr. over 80 articles to profl. jours. Bd. dirs. Assn. for Retarded Citizens Ada County, Inc., 1987-93, pres. 1991-92, Assoc. Taxpayers Idaho, Inc., 1993—, exec. com., 1995—; audit review panel United Way Ada County, 1986-91; IRS vol. tax asst. program 1982, 87. Fellow Am. Coll. of Trust and Estate Counsel; mem. ABA (taxation sect.), Idaho State Bar Assn. (founding mem., taxation probate and trust law sect.), Idaho Soc. CPAs (fed. and state taxation com. 1984-89, bus. legis. com. 1989-91), Boise Bar Assn., Toastmasters (pres. 1991), Beta Gamma Sigma, Sigma Chi. Home: 262 S Mobley Ln Boise ID 83712-8329 Office: Hawley Troxell Ennis & Hawley LLP 877 Main St Ste 100 Boise ID 83702-5883 also: Boise State U Dept Acctg Coll Bus B 214 1910 University Dr Boise ID 83725-1610 E-mail: jmcgown@boise.stae.edu

MCGRATH, DON JOHN, banker; b. Springfield, Ill., June 15, 1948; s. Donald John and Wilma P. (Beck) McG.; m. Patriaia Ratti, May 7, 1983. BS in Mktg., U. Ill., 1970; MBA, Boston U., 1973. Investment officer Banque Nationale de Paris, San Francisco, 1975-76, treas. San Francisco and L.A., 1976-78, v.p., treas., 1978-80, Bank of the West, San Francisco, 1980, v.p., CFO, 1980-81, sr. v.p., CFO, 1981-84, sr. exec. v.p., CFO, 1984-87, sr. exec. v.p., COO, 1987-91, pres., COO, 1991-95, pres., CEO, 1996—; pres., COO, dir. BancWest Corp., 1998—. Bd. dirs. Commonwealth Club Calif., Nature Conservancy Calif., Dominican Coll. San Rafael, Calif. Mem. Calif. Bankers Assn., Univ. Club, St. Francis Yacht Club (San Francisco), Diablo (Calif.) Country Club. Office: BancWest Corp 1450 Treat Blvd Walnut Creek CA 94596-7579

MCGRATH, MIKE, lawyer; b. Rapid City, S.D., Aug. 22, 1947; s. John E. and Jean F. (Funk) McG.; m. Joy L. Rasmusson, May 22, 1971; children— Patrick John, Christopher Paul. B.S., U. Mont., 1970; J.D., Gonzaga U., 1975. Bar: Wash. 1975, Mont. 1977, U.S. Ct. Appeals (9th cir.) 1980, U.S. Supreme Ct. 1980. Legal intern Spokane Legal Services, Spokane, 1973-75; atty. Washoe County Legal Services, Reno, Nev., 1975-76, Bradbury & Bliss, Anchorage, 1976; asst. atty. gen. State of Mont., Helena, 1977-82; county atty. Lewis and Clark County, Helena, 1983—2001; atty. gen. State of Mont., 2001- . Chmn. rules com. Mont. Dem. Party, 1983—; pres. Mont. Legal Services Assn., 1984-85, 95-96, bd.dirs. 1980—; bd. dirs. Mountain chpt. Nat. Com. for Prevention of Child Abuse, 1985-90, Big Bros. and Sisters, Helena, 1977-83; bd. dirs. Friendship Ctr. Helena, 1989—, pres., 1995-97. Served with USAF, 1970-72. Mem. Mont. Bar Assn., Nat. Dist. Attys. Assn., Mont. County Attys. Assn. (pres. 1996-97). Democrat. Home: 514 Hayes Ave Helena MT 59601-6106 Office: 215 N Sanders 3d Fl PO Box 201401 Helena MT 59620*

MCGRATH, PATRICK JOSEPH, bishop; b. Dublin, July 11, 1945; came to U.S., 1970; Grad., St. John's Coll. Sem., Waterford, Ireland; student, Lateran U., Rome. Ordained priest Roman Cath. Ch., 1970, titular bishop of Allegheny. Aux. bishop Archdiocese San Francisco, 1989-98; co-adjutor bishop Diocese of San Jose, 1998-99, bishop, 1999—. Office: Diocese San Jose 900 Lafayette St Ste 301 Santa Clara CA 95050-4934

MCGRAW, DONALD JESSE, biologist, science historian, writer; b. Altadena, Calif., Oct. 27, 1943; s. Jesse E. and Mary L. (Hajostek) McG.; m. Laura Lee Hansen, July 13, 1968; children: Adrienne, Holly, Rachel. BS in Biol. Scis., Calif. State Poly. Coll., 1965; MS, Utah State U., 1967; PhD, Oreg. State U., 1976. Registered microbiologist Am. Acad. Microbiology. Research asst. microbiology Utah State U., 1965-66, teaching asst. food and aquatic microbiology, 1966-67; grad. teaching asst. gen. biology Oreg. State U., 1970-72, instr., 1972-73; tchr. phys. and biol. scis. U.S. Bur. Indian Affairs Boarding Sch., Shonto, Ariz., 1974-75; asst. prof. biology Franklin Coll., Ind., 1975-78; adj. asst. prof. biology Ind. Central U., Indpls., 1977-78; adj. asst prof. Ind. U.-Purdue U., Columbus, 1978; mem. faculty Yavapai Community Coll., Prescott, Ariz., 1978-79; assoc. dir. Ute Research Lab., Ft. Duchesne, Utah, 1980-81, dir., 1981-82; vis. prof. biology Bard Coll., N.Y., Spring 1984, Coll. St. Thomas, Minn., 1985-87; asst. prof. biology, assoc. provost U. San Diego, 1988—, adjunct prof., 2001—; ranger-naturalist U.S. Nat. Park Svc., summers, 1970-79, 83-86. Writer, 1968—; adj. faculty Southwestern Coll., 1989-92. Contbr. numerous articles on history of microbiology and history of antibiotics to sci. publs. Commr. San Diego County Columbian Quincentenary Commn., 1990-93, chmn. edn. com., 1990-93; mem. pres.'s adv. com. San Diego Zool. Soc., 1995-97; trustee Quail Bot. Gardens Found., 1995-98. Recipient Disting. Alumnus award, Calif. State Poly. U., 1991, Monrovia High Sch., 1991; Eli Lilly doctoral grantee Oreg. State U., 1973-74; NSF grantee, 1998. Mem. AAAS, History of Sci. Soc., Cabrillo Hist. Assn. (bd. dirs. 1989-94, vice chair 1992, chair 1993, 94), Alpha Scholastic Honor Soc. of Franklin Coll. (pres. 1976-78), Sigma Xi (sec. San Diego chpt. 1996-97, v.p. 1997-98, pres. 1999-2000assoc. dir. S.W. region 2000—), Beta Beta Beta. Office: U San Diego Office Provost 5998 Alcala Park San Diego CA 92110-2429

MCGRAW, JACK WILSON, federal agency administrator; b. Balt., May 19, 1943; s. P.W. and Nina (Gwinn) McG.; m. Nancy F. Foster, Aug. 31, 1974; children— David, Mark B.A., Morris Harvey Coll., 1964; B.Div., Tex. Christian U., 1967. Ordained minister Christian Ch. (Disciples of Christ). Dir. temporary housing HUD, Washington, 1979-82; asst. assoc. dir. Fed. Emergency Mgmt. Agy., Washington, 1982, dep. asst. dir., 1982-83; dep. asst. adminstr. EPA Office Solid Waste and Emergency Response, Washington, 1983-88, acting asst. adminstr.; dep. regional adminstr. EPA Regional Office, Denver, 1988—. Nominee William H. Jump award HUD, 1972; recipient Presdl. Meritorious award, Presdl. Disting. Exec. award. Presbyterian Avocation: skiing. Home: 8074 S Oneida Ct Englewood CO 80112-3128 Office: EPA Regional Office 999 18th St Denver CO 80202-2499

MCGRAW, JOHN, political organization administrator; State chmn. Calif. Rep. Party, 1999—. Mem. Rep. Nat. Com. Western State Chmn. Assn., 1999—. Office: 1903 W Magnolia Blvd Burbank CA 91506-1727

MCGREGOR, RUTH VAN ROEKEL, state supreme court justice; b. Le Mars, Iowa, Apr. 4, 1943; d. Bernard and Marie Frances (Janssen) Van Roekel; m. Robert James McGregor, Aug. 15, 1965. BA summa cum laude, U. Iowa, 1964, MA, 1965; JD summa cum laude, Ariz. State U., 1974. Bar: Ariz. 1974, U.S. Dist. Ct. Ariz. 1974, U.S. Ct. Appeals (9th cir.), U.S. Supreme Ct. 1982. Assoc. Fennemore, Craig, von Ammon, Udall & Powers, Phoenix, 1974-79, ptnr., 1980-81, 82-89; law clk. to justice Sandra Day O'Connor U.S. Supreme Ct., Washington, 1981-82; judge Ariz. Ct. Appeals, 1989-98, vice chief judge, 1993-95, chief judge, 1995-98; justice Ariz. Supreme Ct., 1998—. Mem. disciplinary commn. Ariz. Supreme Ct., 1984-89, City of Mesa jud. adv. bd., 1997—. Mem., newsletter editor Charter 100, Phoenix, 1981—; bd. dirs., mem. Ctr. for Law in Pub. Interest, Phoenix, 1977-80. Mem. ABA (chmn. state memberships 1985—), Ariz. Bar Assn. (disciplinary com. 1984—), Ariz. Judges Assn. (exec. com. 1990—, sec. 1991-92, v.p. 1992-93, pres. 1993-94), Nat. Assn. Women Judges (chair first time attendees com. 1990-91, 1994 conv. com.; exec. com. 1995—). Democrat. Lutheran. Lodge: Soroptomists. Office: Arizona Supreme Court 1501 W Washington St Phoenix AZ 85007-3222

MCGUCKIN, JOHN HUGH, JR. lawyer; b. Bryn Mawr, Pa., Nov. 8, 1946; AB magna cum laude, Harvard Coll., 1968, JD, 1971. Bar: Mass. 1971, Calif. 1973. Assoc. Orrick, Herrington, Rowley & Sutcliffe, 1972-79; sr. counsel legal divsn. Bank Am., 1979-81; exec. v.p., gen. counsel UnionBanCal Corp./Union Bank Calif., N.A., San Francisco, 1981—, UnionBanCal Corp., 1998—. Adj. instr. Hastings Coll. Law U. Calif., 1980-82; judge pro tem San Francisco Superior Ct. Contbr. articles to profl. jours. Mem. ABA, State Bar Calif. (v.p., treas., bd. govs., chmn. subcom. duties and liabilities trustees probate and trust law sect. 1985-86, legal svcs. trust fund commn. 1989-90, minimum CLE com.), Calif. Bankers Assn. (legal affairs com. 1988-90), Bar Assn. San Francisco (chmn. probate and trust law sect. 1985, exec. com., vice chmn. corp. law dept. sect. 1985-87), Phi Beta Kappa. Office: Union Bank Calif NA 400 California St Ste 1200 San Francisco CA 94104-1320

MCGUIRE, MICHAEL FRANCIS, plastic and reconstructive surgeon; b. St. Louis, Oct. 4, 1946; s. Arthur Patrick and Virginia Claribel (Gannon) McG. BA, Columbia U., 1968, MD, 1972. Diplomate Am. Bd. Surgery, Am. Bd. Plastic Surgery. Intern UCLA, 1972-73, resident in gen. surgery, 1973-77, resident in plastic surgery, 1978-80; fellow in plastic surgery rsch. Stanford (Calif.) U., 1977-78; traveling fellow in plastic surgery Gt. Britain, 1980; chief plastic surgery L.A. County-Olive View Med. Ctr., Sylmar, Calif., 1980-85; pvt. practice Santa Monica, 1980—; chief plastic surgery St. John's Health Ctr., 1990—; asst. clin. prof. surgery UCLA, 1980-97, assoc. clin. prof., 1998—. Bd. dirs. Calif. Med. Rev., Inc., sec.-treas., 1997, v.p., 1997-99, chmn. bd. dirs. 1999—; chmn. surg. rev. St. Johns Health Ctr., 1996-98; pres. Pacific Coast Plastic Surgery Ctr.,

1988—. Charter patron L.A. Music Ctr. Opera, 1983—; sponsoring patron Los Angeles County Art Mus., 1986—; patron Colleague Helpers in Philanthropic Svc., Bel Air, Calif., 1987, 93, 95; pres. Found. for Surg. Reconstrn., 1996—. Fellow ACS, Royal Soc. Medicine; mem. Am. Soc. Plastic Surgeons (membership chmn. 1997-2000), Am. Soc. Aesthetic Plastic Surgery (ethics chmn. 1998-99), Am. Health Quality Assn. (bd. dirs. 1999—), L.A. County Med. Assn. (v.p. 1995-97, sec.-treas. 1997-99), Calif. Med. Assn. (del., exec. com., splty. delegation 1994-99), Calif. Soc. Plastic Surgery (exec. com., auditor 1988-89, program chmn. 1990, exec. coun. 1991-94, treas. 1994-97, v.p. 1997-98, acting pres. 1997, pres.-elect 1998-99, pres. 1999-2000; nominating com. chmn. 2000-01; strategic planning com. chmn. 2001—), Am. Assn. Accreditation of Ambulatory Surgery (facilities ops. com. 1995-96, bd. dirs. 1996, treas. 1996-98, sec. 1998-2000, v.p. 2000—), Alpha Omega Alpha. Avocations: golf, travel, collecting antique Irish glass, opera, modern art. Office: 1301 20th St Ste 460 Santa Monica CA 90404-2054

MCGUIRE, SUSAN GRAYSON, legislative staff member; BA in Polit. Sci., U. Mich., 1962. Legis. asst. select com. on equal ednl. opportunity U.S. Senate, Washington, 1970-73; staff dir. subcom. on employment opportunities U.S. Ho. of Reps., Washington, 1973-84, staff dir. com. on edn. and labor, 1984-91; pub. policy cons. McGuire & Assocs., Cedar Crest, N.Mex., 1991-93; exec. dir. Indian Arts and Crafts Assn., Albuquerque, 1995-98; state dir. U.S. Senator Jeff Bingaman, Albuquerque, 1998—. Pres. N.Mex. Arts and Crafts Fair, Albuquerque; sec. bd. dirs. Albuquerque Literacy Program; active N.Mex. Clinton for Pres. Com., 1992. Office: 625 Silver Ave SW Ste 130 Albuquerque NM 87102-3185 Fax: 505-346-6780. E-mail: Susan_McGuire@Bingaman.senate.gov

MCGUIRE, THOMAS ROGER, distribution company executive; b. Marshfield, Wis., Aug. 29, 1943; s. James Gilbert and Gene Elizabeth (Connor) McG.; m. Patricia Mae Ainsworth, Aug. 25, 1962; children: Elizabeth Anne, Amy Lynn. Chief exec. officer, chmn. bd. dirs. Coast Fabrication, Inc., San Jose, Calif., 1964-83, Coast R.V., Inc., San Jose, 1977—. Republican. Methodist. Avocation: basketball. Home: 1480 Calaveras Ave San Jose CA 95126-2502 Office: Coast Distbn System PO Box 1449 Morgan Hill CA 95038-1449

MCGULPIN, ELIZABETH JANE, nurse; b. Toledo, Oct. 18, 1932; d. James Orville and Leah Fayne (Helton) Welden; m. David Nelson Buster, Apr. 9, 1956 (div. Nov. 1960); children: David Hugh, James Ray, Mark Stephen; m. Fredrick Gordon McGulpin, Oct. 7, 1973. AA in Nursing, Pasadena City Coll., 1968. RN, Wash. Lic. nurse Las Encinas Hosp., Pasadena, Calif.; nurse Hopi Indian Reservation HEW, Keams Canyon, Ariz., 1969-70; nurse, enterostomal therapist Pasadena Vis. Nurse Assn., 1972-74; nurse Seattle King County Pub. Health, 1977-81; home care nurse Victorville, Calif., 1983-85; nurse Adult Family Home, Woodinville, Wash., 1986—. Vol. nurse, counselor Child Protective Svcs., Victorville, 1984; realtor Century 21, Lynden, Wash., 1993—. Vol. nurse Am. Cancer Soc., Pasadena, 1973-75, United Ostomy Assn., Los Angeles, Victorville, 1973-84; RN, ARC, 1996—. Am. Cancer Soc. grantee. Mem. Nat. Assn. Realtors, Wash. Assn. Realtors, Whatcom County Assn. Realtors, Vis. Nurse Assn. (Enterostomal Therpay grantee 1973). Avocations: reading, gardening, travel. Home: 106 Kale St Everson WA 98247-9660

MCHENRY, HENRY MALCOLM, anthropologist, educator; b. Los Angeles, May 19, 1944; s. Dean Eugene and Emma Jane (Snyder) McH.; m. Linda Jean Conway, June 25, 1966; children: Lindsay Jean, Annalisa Jane. BA, U. Calif., Davis, 1966, MA, 1967; PhD, Harvard U., 1972. Asst. prof. anthropology U. Calif., Davis, 1971-76, assoc. prof. anthropology, 1976-81, prof. anthropology, 1981—, chmn. dept. anthropology, 1984-88. Fellow Am. Anthrop. Assn., Calif. Acad. Sci.; mem. Am. Assn. Phys. Anthropologists (exec. com. 1981-85), Soc. Study Evolution, Soc. Vertebrate Paleontology, Phi Beta Kappa, Phi Kappa Phi. Democrat. Buddhist. Avocation: winemaker. Home: 330 11th St Davis CA 95616-2010 Office: U of Calif Davis Dept Of Anthropology Davis CA 95616

MCHENRY, JULIE, communications executive; BJ, U. Mo.; MBA in Mktg., U. Portland. Adv. prog. supr. Tektronix, Inc., Beaverton, Oreg.; acct. exec. Regis McKenna Inc., Portland; co-founder, v.p. The Waggener Group; co-founder Global Tech. Comm., Wilson McHenry Co. Spkr. in field. Office: Wilson McHenry Co 393 Vintage Park Dr Ste 140 Foster City CA 94404-1172

MCHUGH, HEATHER, poet; b. Calif., Aug. 20, 1948, BA, Radcliffe Coll., 1970; MA, U. Denver, 1972. Assoc. prof. English SUNY, Binghamton, 1976-82; prof. English, Milliman writer-in-residence U. Wash., Seattle, 1983—. Vis. prof. Columbia U., 1987; Holloway lectr. U. Calif., Berkeley, 1987; judge Nat. Poetry Series book award, 1986, 95. Author: (poetry) Dangers, 1977, A World of Difference, 1981, To the Quick, 1987, Shades, 1988, Hinge & Sign: Poems, 1968-93, 1994 (Nat. Book award nomination 1994), The FAther of the Predicaments, 1999, (essays) Broken English: Poetry and Partiality, 1993; translator: D'Apres Tout: Poems by Jean Follain, 1981; (with Nikolai Popov) Because the Sea Is Black: Poems by Blaga Dimitrova, 1989, (with Nikolai Popov) Glottal Stop: 101 Poems by Paul Celan, 2000, (with David Konstan) Cyclops of Euripides, 2000. Recipient Harvard U./Pollock prize, 1995, Lila Wallce/Reader's Digest Writer's award, 1996, PEN Voelcker prize, 2000. Mem. Acad. Am. Poets (chancellor 1999), Am. Acad. Arts and Scis. Office: U Washington Dept English Box 354330 Seattle WA 98195-4330

MCHUGH, PETER, mayor; b. Boston; m. Gail Marie Parnagian; children: Sean Michael, Tatia Marie. Student, Boston U. Sch. Bus. Adminstrn., 1963; BS in Bus. Adminstrn., UCLA, 1969. With IBM, 1964; mem. city coun. Milpitas, Calif., 1976-78, 82-90; mayor Milpitas, 1978-82, 90-96; bd. suprs. dist. 3 County of Santa Clara, 1996—. Recipient numerous honors and acknowledgments for cmty. svc. including Calif. State Assembly, Calif. State Senate, U.S. Congress. Office: 70 W Hedding St Fl 10 San Jose CA 95110-1705

MCILWAIN, CARL EDWIN, physicist; b. Houston, Mar. 26, 1931; s. Glenn William and Alma Ora (Miller) McI.; m. Mary Louise Hocker, Dec. 30, 1952; children— Janet Louise, Craig Ian. B.A., N. Tex. State Coll., Denton, 1953; M.S., State U. Iowa, 1956, Ph.D., 1960. Asst. prof. State U. Iowa, 1960-62; assoc. prof. physics U. Calif.-, San Diego, 1962-66; prof. U. Calif., 1966—. Mem. space scis. steering com., fields and particles subcom. NASA, 1962-66; mem. anti-submarine warfare panel President's Sci. Adv. Com., 1964-67; mem. com. potential contamination and interference from space expts. Space Sci. Bd., Nat. Acad. Scis.-NRC, 1964-71; mem. advisory com. for radiation hazards in supersonic transports FAA, 1967-71; mem. Fachbeirat Inst. Extraterrestrial Physics, Max Planck Inst., Garching, Fed. Republic Germany, 1977-83, Space Sci. Bd., NRC, 1983-86. Author; patentee in field. Guggenheim fellow, 1968, 72; recipient Space Sci. award Am. Inst. Aeros. and Astronautics, 1970, Computer Art award U.S. Users Automatic Info. Display Equipment, 1971, Sr. U.S. Scientist award Alexander von Humboldt Found., Ger., 1976, Hannes Alfven medal European Geogphys. Soc., 2000. Fellow Am. Geophys. Union (John A. Fleming award 1975); mem. Am. Phys. Soc., Am. Astron. Soc. Home: 6662 Avenida Manana La Jolla CA 92037-6228 Office: U Calif San Diego Cass 0424 La Jolla CA 92093-0424 E-mail: cmcilwain@ucsd.edu

MCINNIS, SCOTT STEVE, congressman, lawyer; b. Glenwood Springs, Colo., May 9, 1953; s. Kohler McInnis and Carol Kreir; m. Lori McInnis; children: Daxon, Tessa, Andrea. BA, Ft. Lewis Coll., 1975; JD, St. Mary's Law Sch., 1980. Atty. Delaney & Balcomb P.C., Glenwood Springs, Colo., 1981—; mem. Colo. State Ho. of Reps., 1984-93, chmn. agrl. livestock and natural resources com., 1986-90, majority leader, 1990-92; mem. U.S. Ho. Reps. 103d-106th Congresses from 3d Colo. Dist., 1993—; mem. rules com. U.S. Ho. Reps., 1998, mem. house ways and means com., 2001—, chmn.resources subcom. on forests and forest health. Recipient Florence Sabin award, 1984, Guardian of Small Bus. award Nat. Fed. Ind. Bus., 1990, Lee Atwater Leadership award, 1991, and various awards from United Vets. Commn.; named Legislator of Decade and Legislator of Yr by Colo. Ski Country and Colo. Wildlife Found. Mem. Elks, Rotary, Phi Delta Phi. Republican. Roman Catholic. Office: US Ho Reps 320 Cannon Hob Washington DC 20515

MC INTOSH, J(OHN) RICHARD, biologist, educator; b. N.Y.C., Sept. 25, 1939; s. Rustin and Millicent Margaret (Carey) McI.; m. Marjorie Rogers Keniston, Aug. 30, 1961; children— Robert K., Elspeth R., Craig T. B.A. in Physics, Harvard U., 1961, Ph.D. in Biophysics, 1968. Instr. in math. and physics Cambridge Sch., Weston, Mass., 1961-63; asst. prof. biology Harvard U., 1968-70; asst. prof. U. Colo., Boulder, 1970-72, assoc. prof., 1972-76, prof., 1977—, chmn. dept. molecular, cellular and devel. biology, 1977-78, dir. Lab for High Voltage Electron Microscopy, 1986—, disting. prof., 1999—. Mem. editl. bd. Jour. Cell Biology, 1978-82, 86-90, Cell Motility, 1986-87, Jour. Structural Biology, 1990-97, Molecular Biology Cell, 1995—; contbr. articles to profl. jours. Recipient Teaching Recognition award U. Colo., 1974, Scholar award Am. Cancer Soc., 1976, 90; Am. Cancer Soc. grantee, 1971-90, NSF grantee, 1970-82, NIH grantee, 1973-78, 80—; Eleanor Roosevelt Internat. Cancer fellow, 1984; Guggenheim fellow, 1990-91. Mem. Am. Soc. Cell Biology (coun. 1977-80, 86-89, pres. 1994), Am. Cancer Soc. (cell biology panel 1983-87, rsch. prof. 1994—, adv. coun. 1997—), NIH (molecular cytology study sect. 1988-92), Nat. Acad. Sci., Am. Acad. Arts and Sci. Home: 870 Willowbrook Rd Boulder CO 80302-7439 Office: U Colo Dept Molec Devel & Devel Bio Boulder CO 80309-0001

MCINTOSH, L(ORNE) WILLIAM, marketing executive; b. Kingston, Ont., Can., May 1, 1945; s. Jack Lorne and Lillian (Oaks) McI.; m. Siobhan McAfee, May 18, 1998. BSBA, Lehigh U., 1967, MBA, 1968. Asst. prof. Union Coll., Cranford, N.J., 1968-72; sr. market rsch. analyst Merck, Sharp & Dohme, West Point, Pa., 1972-75, advt. copywriter, 1975-77, product mgr., 1977-80, assoc. dir. advt., 1980-82, dir. licensing and acquisitions, 1982, sr. dir. mktg., 1983-86; exec. v.p. mktg. Medco Containment Svcs., Inc., Fair Lawn, N.J., 1987-88; v.p. mktg. and bus. devel. Boehringer Mannheim Pharms., Rockville, Md., 1988-92; chmn. bd., chief exec. officer Target Mktg. Systems, Inc., Blue Bell, Pa., 1992-93; sr. v.p. bus. devel. and com. ops. Zynaxis, Inc., Malvern, 1993-95; sr. cons. SmithKline Beecham, Phila., 1995-97; sr. v.p. of bus. devel. & Finance and CFO Nexell Theraputics, Irvine, CA, 1997-98, pres. and COO, 1998—. Mem. Am. Econ. Assn., Am. Mktg. Assn., Lic. Execs. Soc., Antique Automobile Club Am., Model A Ford Club Am., Vintage Chevrolet Club Am., Pontiac Oakland Owners Club, Beta Gamma Sigma. Avocations: antique automobiles, woodworking, antique furniture restoration, music. Home: 31201 Paseo Miraloma San Juan Capistrano CA 92675-5505 E-mail: Mcamci@msn.com

MCINTOSH, TERRIE TUCKETT, lawyer; b. Ft. Lewis, Wash., July 20, 1944; d. Robert LeRoy and Elda (Perry) Tuckett; m. Clifton Dennis McIntosh, Oct. 13, 1969; children: Alison, John. BA, U. Utah, 1967; MA, U. Ill., 1970; JD, Harvard U., 1978. Bar: N.Y. 1979, Utah 1980. Assoc. Hughes, Hubbard & Reed, N.Y.C., 1978-79, Fabian & Clendenin, Salt Lake City, 1979-84, shareholder, 1984-86; staff atty. Questar Corp., Salt Lake City, 1986-88, sr. atty., 1988-92, sr. corp. counsel, 1992—. Instr. philosophy Douglass Coll. Rutgers U., New Brunswick, N.J., 1971-72; mem. adv. com. civil procedure Utah Supreme Ct., Salt Lake City, 1987—; mem. jud. nominating com. 5th Cir. Ct., Salt Lake City, 1986-88. Mem. Utah State Bar (ethics and discipline screening panel 1989-96, vice chair ethics and discipline com. 1996-99, co-chair law related edn. com. 1985-86), Women Lawyers of Utah (chair exec. com. 1986-87), Salt Lake Legal Aid Soc. (trustee 1999—), Harvard Alumni Assn. Utah (bd. dirs. 1987—), Phi Beta Kappa, Phi Kappa Phi. Office: Questar Corp PO Box 45433 180 E 1st S Salt Lake City UT 84111-1502

MCINTYRE, BRUCE MARTIN, oil company executive; b. Denver, Aug. 1, 1927; s. Paul Joseph and Alice Herschel (Martin) McI.; m. Mary Ellen Neale, Nov. 20, 1954; children: Betsy, John. AB, Harvard Coll., 1950; MBA, Harvard Grad. Sch. of Bus., 1952. Dist. landman Sinclair Oil & Gas Co., Denver, 1952-63; mgr., investments Jenney Oil Co., Chestnut Hill, Mass., 1963-69; v.p., treas. C&K Petroleum Inc., Houston, 1969-81; pres. Bruce M. McIntyre & Co., Houston, 1981—; CEO Benton Oil & Gas Co., Carpinteria, Calif. Bd. dirs. Res. Industries Corp., Albuquerque, Benton Oil and Gas, Ventura, Calif. With USNR, 1945-46, PTO. Mem. Boston Soc. Security Analysts, Fin. Execs. Inst., Coronado, Willow Creek Golf. Republican. Episcopalian. Avocations: golf, curling, backgammon. Home: 6154 San Felipe St Houston TX 77057-2802 Office: Benton Oil & Gas Co 6267 Carpinteria Ave Ste 200 Carpinteria CA 93013

MC INTYRE, JAMES A. diversified financial services executive; b. 1932; BS, U. So. Calif., 1954. With Ernst & Ernst, L.A., 1958-63; pres. Fremont Indemnity Co., 1963-80; pres., CEO, chmn. Fremont Gen. Corp., Santa Monica, Calif., 1980—. Office: Fremont Gen Corp 2020 Santa Monica Blvd Ste 600 Santa Monica CA 90404-2060

MCINTYRE, JERILYN SUE, academic administrator; m. W. David Smith. Student, Stanford U., Italy, 1962; AB in History with distinction, Stanford U., 1964, MA in Journalism, cert. Summer Radio-TV Inst., Stanford U., 1965, tchrs. cert., 1968; PhD in Comms., U. Washington, 1973; postgrad. Inst. Ednl. Mgmt., Harvard U., 1993. Corr. World News Bureau McGraw-Hill Pub. Co., L.A., 1965-67; asst. prof. dept. mass comm. Chico (Calif.) State Coll., 1968-70; asst. prof. Sch. Journalism U. Iowa, Iowa City, 1973-77; assoc. prof., prof. dept. comm. U. Utah, Salt Lake City, 1977-2000, assoc. dean Coll. Humanities, 1984-88, assoc. v.p. acad. affairs, 1988-90, interim pres., 1997, v.p. acad. affairs, 1990-98; pres. Ctrl. Wash. U., Ellensburg, 2000—. Dir. Wall St. Jour. Publs. workshop Chico State Coll., 1968; mem. ednl. adv. bd. NFL, 1996-98; mem. exec. com. coun. acad. affairs Nat. Assn. State Univs. and Land Grant Colls., 1995-98, chair, 1997-98; mem. steering com. Utah Edn. Network, 1995-98. Editl. asst. Chemical Week Mag., 1965-66, World News Bureau, 1966-67; mem. editl. bd. Journalism History; co-author: Symbols & Society; contbr. articles to profl. jours., chpts. to books. Mem. Utah Women's Forum; cmty. adv. bd. YWCA. David P. Gardner fellow, 1984; recipient Yesterday's Girl Scout Today's Successful Woman award Utah Girl Scout Coun., 1996. Mem. AAUW (Dist. Woman Utah Salt Lake City chpt. 1994), Assn. Edn. in Journalism and Mass Comm. Office: 400 E 8th Ave Ellensburg WA 98926-7501

MCINTYRE, NORMAN F. petroleum industry executive; b. Pangman, Sask., Can., Oct. 21, 1945; s. Donald and Jean (Cruickshank) McI.; m. Lana Jean, June 10, 1967; children: Jason Lee, Spencer James. BSc in Petroleum Engring., U. Wyo., 1971; MS in Mgmt., MIT, 1991. Various positions with Mobil Oil, U.S., Can., to 1982; group mgr. engring. offshore divsn. Petro-Can., 1982-83, gen. mgr. frontier devel. offshore divsn., 1983, v.p. frontier devel., 1983-86, v.p. prodn. devel., 1986-89; sr. v.p. western region Petro-Can. Products, 1989-90; pres. Petro-Can. Resources, Calgary, Alta., Can., 1990-95, exec. v.p. Can., 1995—. Past chmn., dir. Panarctic Oils Ltd. Campaign chair United Way of Calgary and Area. Mem. Can. Assn. of Petroleum Producers (chmn. 1998), Can. Assn. World Petroleum Congresses (chmn.), Assn. of Profl. Engineers, Geologists and Geophysists of Alberta, Assn. Profl. Engrs., Glencoe Golf and Country Club, Calgary Petroleum Club (bd. mem.). Office: Petro Canada 150 6th Ave SW PO Box 2844 Calgary AB Canada T2P 3E3

MC INTYRE, VONDA NEEL, writer; b. Aug. 28, 1948; d. H. Neel and Vonda Barth (Keith) McI. B.S., U. Wash., Seattle, 1970. Author: The Exile Waiting, 1976, 85, Dreamsnake, 1978 (Hugo award, Nebula award), Fireflood and Other Stories, 1979, The Entropy Effect, 1981, The Wrath of Khan, 1982, Superluminal, 1983, The Search for Spock, 1984, Barbary, 1986, Enterprise: The First Adventure, 1986, The Voyage Home, 1986, Starfarers, 1989, Transition, 1991, Metaphase, 1992, Nautilus, 1993, Star Wars: The Crystal Star, 1994, The Moon and the Sun, 1997 (Nebula award); editor: (with Susan Janice Anderson) Aurora: Beyond Equality, 1976. Mem. ACLU. Recipient Nebula award, 1973, 78 Mem. Sci. Fiction Writers Am., Planetary Soc., Cousteau Soc., NOW, Space Studies Inst., Authors Guild, Greenpeace, Nature Conservancy. Office: PO Box 31041 Seattle WA 98103-1041

MCKAY, LAURA L. banker, consultant; b. Watonga, Okla., Mar. 3, 1947; d. Frank Bradford and Elizabeth Jane (Smith) Drew; m. Cecil O. McKay, Sept. 20, 1969; 1 child, Leslie. BSBA, Oreg. State U., 1969. Cert. cash mgr., Treasury Mgmt. Assn. New br. research U.S. Bank, Portland, Oreg., 1969-80, cash mgmt. officer, 1980-82, asst. v.p., 1982-87, v.p., 1987-94; founder, cons. LLM Cons., Milw., 1994-97; co-founder, mng. ptnr. DMC & Assocs. LLC, Portland, 1997—; v.p. treasury mgmt., sales mgr. West Coast Bank, 2000—. Cert. trainer Achieve Global and Edge Learning. Chmn. Budget Com., North Clackamas Sch. Dist., 1982-84. Mem. ASTD, Assn. for Fin. Profls., Nat. Assn. Bank Women (chmn. Oreg. group 1979-80), Portland Cash Mgrs. Assn., Portland C. of C. Republican. Office: DMC & Assocs 5686 SE Viewcrest Dr Portland OR 97267-4146 E-mail: lauramckay@aol.com

MCKAY, MICHAEL DENNIS, lawyer; b. Omaha, May 12, 1951; s. John Larkin and Kathleen (Tierney) McK.; m. Christy Ann Cordwin, Apr. 22, 1978; children: Kevin Tierney, Kathleen Lindsay, John Larkin. BA in Polit. Sci. with distinction, U. Wash., 1973; JD, Creighton U., 1976. Bar: Wash. 1976, U.S. Dist. Ct. (we. dist.) Wash. 1978, U.S. Dist. Ct. (ea. dist.) Wash. 1982, U.S. Ct. Appeals (9th cir.) 1982, U.S. Supreme Ct. 1993. Sr. dep. pros. atty. King County, Seattle, 1976-81; ptnr. McKay & Gaitan, Seattle, 1981-89; U.S. atty. we. dist. Wash. Seattle, 1989-93; ptnr. Lane Powell Spears Lubersky, Seattle, 1993-95, McKay Chadwell PLLC, Seattle, 1995—. Bd. dirs. Mental Health North, Seattle, 1982-85, St. Joseph Sch. Bd., 1984-87, Our Lady of Fatima Sch. Commn., 1994-97, Creighton U., 1988-90; mem. stadium adv. bd. Seattle Kingdome, 1987-89; mem. U.S. Atty. Gen. Adv. Com., 1991-93, vice chmn., 1992; mem. Washington Citizens' Commn. on Salaries for Elected Officials, 1997—; vice chmn., 1999—; vice chmn. Seattle Expert Rev. Panel, 1999; co-chair Washington State George W. Bush Campaign, 2000. Mem. Creighton U. Alumni Assn. (pres. 1988-90, nat. alumni bd. 1988-92), Wash. Athletic Club, Columbia Tower Club. Republican. Roman Catholic. Avocations: swimming, golf. Office: McKay Chadwell PLLC 701 5th Ave Seattle WA 98104-7097 E-mail: mckay@mckay-chadwell.com

MCKAY, MONROE GUNN, federal judge; b. Huntsville, Utah, May 30, 1928; s. James Gunn and Elizabeth (Peterson) McK.; m. Lucile A. Kinnison, Aug. 6, 1954; children: Michele, Valanne, Margaret, James, Melanie, Nathan, Bruce, Lisa, Monroe. B.S., Brigham Young U., 1957; J.D., U. Chgo., 1960. Bar: Ariz. 1961. Law clk. Ariz. Supreme Ct., 1960-61; assoc. firm Lewis & Roca, Phoenix, 1961-66, ptnr., 1968-74; assoc. prof. Brigham Young U., 1974-76, prof., 1976-77; judge U.S. Ct. Appeals for 10th Cir., Denver, 1977-91, chief judge, 1991-94, sr. judge, 1994—. Mem. Phoenix Community Council Juvenile Problems, 1968-74; pres. Ariz. Assn. for Health and Welfare, 1970-72; dir. Peace Corps, Malawi, Africa, 1966-68; bd. dirs., pres. Maricopa county Legal Aid Soc., 1972-74. Served with USMCR, 1946-48. Mem. Ariz. Bar Assn. Mem. LDS Ch. Office: US Ct Appeals 10th Cir Fed Bldg 125 S State St Ste 6012 Salt Lake City UT 84138-1181*

MCKEAN, KEVIN S. publishing executive; Staff writer Discover mag., 1981-87, sr. editor, 1981-87, Money mag., 1987-97, founding new media editor; asst. mng. editor bus. and fin. Time Inc. New Media; exec. editor Forbes.com, 1999-2000; v.p., editl. dir. PC World, PCWorld.com, San Francisco, 2000—. Office: PC World IDG Comm 501 2d St Ste 600 San Francisco CA 94107-1496

MCKEE, CHRISTOPHER FULTON, astrophysics and astronomy educator; b. Washington, Sept. 6, 1942; m. Suzanne P. McKee; 3 children. AB in Physics summa cum laude, Harvard U., 1963; PhD in Physics, U. Calif., Berkeley, 1970. Physicist Lawrence Livermore (Calif.) Labs., 1969-70, cons., 1970—; rsch. fellow in astrophysics Calif. Inst. Tech., Pasadena, 1970-71; asst. prof. astronomy Harvard U., Cambridge, 1971-74; asst. prof. physics and astronomy U. Calif., Berkeley, 1974-77, assoc. prof., 1977-78, prof., 1978—, Miller Rsch. prof., 1984-85, 99; chair dept. physics, 2000—; assoc. dir. Space Scis. Lab., Berkeley, 1978-83, acting dir., 1983-84, dir., 1985-98, Theoretical Astrophysics Ctr., Berkeley, 1985. Co-chair Astronomy and Astrophysics Survey com., NRC, 1998—. Fannie and John Hertz Found. fellow, 1963-69, Guggenheim fellow, 1998; Sherman Fairchild Disting. scholar, 1981, Nat. Acad. Scis., 1992. Fellow AAAS, Am. Phys. Soc. (exec. com. astrophysics div. 1986-88); mem. Am. Astron. Soc. (councillor 1981-84), Internat. Astron. Union, Phi Beta Kappa. Office: U Calif Dept Physics Berkeley CA 94720-0001

MC KEE, JOHN ANGUS, oil company executive; b. Toronto, Ont., Can., Aug. 31, 1935; s. John William and Margaret Enid (Phippen) McK.; m. Susan Elizabeth Harley, May 30, 1970; children: John Andrew, Mary Susan. Student, U. Toronto, 1954-58, Upper Can. Coll., Port Hope, Ont., Trinity Coll. Sch. With Dominion Securities Corp. Ltd., Toronto, 1958-60; mng. dir. Patino Mining Group, Toronto and London, Eng., 1960-71; with Consolidated Tin Smelters, Brit. Tin Investment Corp., Amalagamated Metal Corp., 1964-71; pres. J. Angus McKee & Assoc., 1971-83; pres., chief exec. officer Can. Occidental Petroleum Ltd., 1983-93; bd. dirs. chmn. Gulfstream Resources Can., Ltd., Calgary, Alta., 1993—. Bd. dirs. Conor Pacific Environ. Techs. Inc., Big Rock Brewery Ltd., Hankin Atlas Industries Ltd. Bd. govs. Trinity Coll. Sch.. Mem. Toronto Club, York Club, Badminton and Racquet Club, Ranchmen's Club, Calgary Petroleum Club, Knickerbocker Club (N.Y.C.), Craigleith Ski Club, Internat. Order of St. Hubert, Goodwood Club, Alpha Delta Phi (bd. govs. and dir.). Office: Gulfstream Resources Ltd 855 2d St SW 34th Fl Calgary AB Canada T2P 4J8

MCKEE, KATHRYN DIAN GRANT, human resources consultant; b. L.A., Sept. 12, 1937; d. Clifford William and Amelia Rosalie (Shacher) G.; m. Paul Eugene McKee, June 17, 1961; children: Scott Alexander, Grant Christopher. BA, U. Calif., Santa Barbara, 1959; grad. Anderson Sch. Mgmt. Exec. Program, UCLA, 1979. Cert. compensation and benefits. Mgr. Mattel, Inc., Hawthorne, Calif., 1963-74; dir. Twentieth Century Fox Film Corp., L.A., 1975-80; sr. v.p. 1st Interstate Bank, Ltd., L.A., 1980-93; sr. v.p. and human resources dir. Am.'s Std. Chartered Bank, 1993-95; pres. Human Resources Consortia, Santa Barbara, Calif., 1995—. V.p. cons. Right Mgmt. Cons., 1997-98; dir. Accordia benefits of Southern Calif., 1991-96, mem. exec. com. H.R. div. of Am. Bankers Assn., 1991-93; bd. dirs. Bank Certification Inst. Am. Bankers Assn., 1992-94; treas. Pers.

Accreditation Inst., 1983-86, pres., 1986. Contbr. articles to profl. jours. Pres. GEM Theatre Guild, Garden Grove, Calif., 1984-86; bd. dirs. Vis. Nurses Assn., L.A., 1984-88, SHRM, 1986-92, treas., 1989, vice-chmn., 1990, chmn., 1991, pres. SHRM Found., 1994, 95; bd. dirs. Laguna Playhouse, 1996-2000, pres., 1998-99; dir. Ctr. for Info. Tech. and Society; mem. U. Calif. Santa Barbara Found., 2001—. Recipient Sr. Honor Key award U. Calif., Santa Barbara, 1959, William Winter award Am. Compensation Assn., 1986, Excellence award L.A. Pers. Indsl. Rels. Assn., 1990, Profl. Excellence award SHRM, 1994; named Outstanding Sr. Woman, 1959. Mem. Internat. Assn. Pers. Women (various offices, past nat. pres., Mem. of Yr. 1986), U. Calif. Santa Barbara Alumni Assn. (bd. dirs. 1995—, pres.-elect 1999, pres. 1999-2000). Office: Human Resources Consortia 3730 Cedar Vis Santa Barbara CA 93110-1578 E-mail: kmckee3730@home.com

MCKEE, ROGER CURTIS, retired federal judge; b. Waterloo, Iowa, Feb. 11, 1931; s. James A. and Leonace (Burrell) McK.; m. Roberta Jeanne Orvis, Sept. 3, 1954; children: Andrea Jane, Brian Curtis, Paul Robert. BA, State Coll. of Iowa, 1955; MA, U. Ill., 1960; JD, U. San Diego, 1968. Bar: Calif. 1970, U.S. Dist. Ct. (so. dist.) Calif. 1969, U.S. Ct. Appeals (9th cir.) 1971. Telegrapher, agt. Ill. Cen. R.R., 1950-55; tng. asst. No. Ill. Gas Co., Aurora, 1959-60; with indsl. rels. dept. Convair div. Gen. Dynamics Corp., San Diego, 1960-68; contract adminstr. and supr. Datagraphix div. Gen. Dynamics Corp., San Diego, 1968-69, asst. counsel, 1969-70; ptnr. Powell & McKee, San Diego, 1970-75, Millsberg, Dickstein & McKee, San Diego, 1975-83; magistrate judge U.S. Dist. Ct. for So. Dist. Calif., San Diego, 1983-97; presiding magistrate judge, 1993-97. Bd. trustees So. Calif. Presbyn. Homes, L.A., 1979-81; moderator Presbytery of San Diego, 1980. Capt. USNR, 1949-85. Mem. Calif. Bar Assn., Fed. Magistrate Judges Assn., Navy League U.S., Naval Res. Officers Assn., Res. Officers Assn., Dixieland Jazz Soc. (bd. dirs. San Diego chpt. 1984—). Republican. Fax: (858) 277-0444. E-mail: rcmckee10@cs.com

MCKEEVER, JEFFREY D. computer company executive; b. Marion, Ind., 1942; Grad., U. Ariz., Tucson, 1965; MBA, U. Ariz., 1973. V.p. First Interstate Bank of Arizona; chmn., CEO, co-founder MicroAge Inc., Tempe, Ariz., 1976—. Office: MicroAge Inc 1330 W Southern Ave Tempe AZ 85282-4545

MCKELL, CYRUS M. retired college dean, plant physiologist; b. Payson, Utah, Mar. 19, 1926; s. Robert D. and Mary C. (Ellsworth) McK.; m. Betty Johnson; children: Meredith Sue, Brian Marcus, John Cyrus. BS, U. Utah, 1949, MS, 1950; PhD, Oreg. State U., 1956; postgrad., U. Calif., Davis, 1957. Instr. botany Oreg. State U., Corvallis, 1955-56; range rsch. plant physiologist U. Calif. USDA-Agrl. Research Service, Davis, 1956-60; prof., dept. chmn. U. Calif., Riverside, 1960-69; prof. dept. head., dir. Utah State U., Logan, 1969-80; v.p. research NPI, Salt Lake City, 1980-88; dean Coll. of Sci. Weber State U., Ogden, Utah, 1988-94; pres., prin. Applied Ecol. Svcs. Inc., Logan, 1995—. Cons. Ford Found. 1968-72, Rockefeller Found., 1964-70, 89, UN, 1978, 90, NAS, 1980, 89, 91, 92, 93, USAID, 1972, UN Devel. Program, 1989. Editor: Grass Biology and Utilization, 1971, Useful Wildland Shrubs, 1972, Rehabilitation of Western Wildlife Habitat, 1978, Paradoxes of Western Energy Development, 1984, Resource Inventory and Baseline Study Methods for Developing Countries, 1983, Shrub Biology and Utilization, 1989, Wilderness Issues, Arid Lands of the Western United States, 1992; contbr. over 230 articles to profl. jours. Chmn. Cache County Planning Commn., Logan, 1974-79; mem. Utah Energy Conservation and Devel. Coun., 1976-79, Gov.'s Sci. Adv. Coun., 1988-97, chmn., 1990-91, 96-97; mem. Commn. of the Californians, Riverside, 1965-68. Recipient Utah Gov.'s Sci. and Tech. medal, 1990, Gardner Prize in Sci., awarded by Utah Acad. Scis., Arts and Letters, 1999; Fulbright scholar Spain, 1967-68; World Travel grantee Rockefeller Found., 1964. Fellow AAAS (com. chmn. 1979-89, sci. exchange to China grantee 1984-85, 89, sci. panel U.S.-Chile 1987); mem. Am. Soc. Agronomy, Soc. Range Mgmt. (pres. Calif. sect. 1965, pres. Utah sect. 1982). Mem. LDS Ch. Avocations: travel, photography. Home: 2248 E 4000 S Salt Lake City UT 84124-1864 Office: 550 N Main St Ste 302 Logan UT 84321-3957 E-mail: cmmckell@xmission.com

MCKELVEY, JUDITH GRANT, lawyer, educator, university dean; b. Milw., July 19, 1935; d. Lionel Alexander and Bernadine R. (Verdun) Grant. B.S. in Philosophy, U. Wis., 1957, J.D., 1959. Bar: Wis. 1959, Calif. 1968. Atty. FCC, Washington, 1959-62; adj. prof. U. Md., Europe, 1965; prof. law Golden Gate U. Sch. Law, San Francisco, 1968-99, dean, 1974-81. Mem. State Jud. Nominees Evaluation Commn., 1981-82. Contbr. to: Damages Book, 1975, 76. Bd. dirs. San Francisco Neighborhood Legal Assistance Found. Fellow Am. Bar Found.; mem. ABA, Wis. Bar Assn., Calif. Bar Assn., San Francisco Bar Assn. (dir. 1975-77, chmn. legis. com., sec.-treas., pres.-elect 1980-83, pres. 1984), Calif. Women Lawyers (1st pres.), Law in a Free Soc. (exec. com.), Continuing Edn. of Bar (chmn. real estate subcom., mem. joint adv. com.), Legal Svcs. to Children Inc. (pres. 1987-89), San Francisco Neighborhood Legal Assistance Found. (dir. and exec. com. 1985-87), Lawyers Com. for Urban Affairs (dir. and exec. com. 1985-87, co-chairperson 1988-90). Office: Golden Gate U Sch Law 536 Mission St San Francisco CA 94105-2921

MCKENNON, KEITH ROBERT, chemical company executive; b. Condon, Oreg., Dec. 25, 1933; s. Russel M. and Lois E. (Edgerton) McK.; m. Patricia Dragon, Sept. 30, 1961; children: Brian, Marc, Kevin. B.S., Oreg. State U., 1955. Rsch. chemist Dow Chem. Co., Pittsburg, Calif., 1955-67, sales mgr. Houston, 1967, research mgr. Midland, Mich., 1968-69, bus. mgr., 1969-80, v.p., 1980-83, group v.p., 1983-87, exec. v.p., 1987-92, also bd. dirs.; pres. Dow USA, 1987-90; chmn., chief exec. officer Dow Corning Corp., 1992-94, also bd. dirs.; chmn. PacifiCorp, Portland, Oreg., 1994-99, CEO, 1998-99. Bd. dirs. Scottish Power. Patentee. Recipient Chemical Industry medal Soc. of Chemical Industry, 1994 Republican. Presbyterian. Home: 6079 N Paradise View Dr Paradise Vly AZ 85253-3828 Office: Pacific Corp 825 NE Multnomah St Ste 2000 Portland OR 97232-2135

MCKEON, ELAINE, museum administrator; Chmn. San Francisco Mus. of Modern Art, Calif. Office: San Francisco Mus Modern Art 151 3rd St San Francisco CA 94103-3107

MCKEON, HOWARD P. (BUCK MCKEON), congressman, former mayor; b. L.A. m. Patricia; 6 children. BS, Brigham Young U. Mem. Coun. City of Santa Clarita, Calif., 1987-92, mayor, 1987-88; mem. edn. and workforce, armed svcs. and vet. affairs 103rd-106th Congresses from 25th Calif. dist., 1993—. Founding dir., chmn. Valencia Nat. Bank; co-owner Howard & Phil's Western Wear, Inc. Hon. chmn. Leukemia Soc. Celebrity program, 1990, Red Cross Community Support Campaign, 1992; active Dist. Com. Boy Scouts Am.; chmn., trustee William S. Hart Sch. dist., 1979-87; chmn., dir. Henry Mayo Newhall Meml. Hosp., 1983-88; mem. Calif. Rep. State Ctrl. Com., 1988-92; bd. dirs. Santa Clarita Valley Sml. Bus. Devel. Ctr., 1990-92, Canyon Country C. of C., 1988-92. Office: US Ho Reps 2242 Rayburn Ho Ofc Bldg Washington DC 20515 E-mail: tellbuck@mail.house.gov

MCKEOWN, MARY MARGARET, federal judge; b. Casper, Wyo., May 11, 1951; d. Robert Mark and Evelyn Margaret (Lipsack) McK.; m. Peter Francis Cowhey, June 29, 1985; 1 child, Megan Margaret. BA in Internat. Affairs and Spanish, U. Wyo., 1972; JD, Georgetown U., 1975. Bar: Wash. 1975, D.C. 1982. Assoc. Perkins Coie, Seattle, 1975-79, Washington, 1979-80; White House fellow U.S. Dept. Interior and White House, Washington, 1980-81; [illegible] Perkins Coie, Seattle, 1981-98, mng. dir. strategic planning and client rels., 1990-95; judge U.S. Ct. Appeals for 9th Circuit, Seattle, from 1998, San Diego. Trustee The Pub. Defender, Seattle, 1982-85; rep. 9th Cir. Judicial Conf., San Francisco, 1985-89, mem. gender bias task force, 1992-93. Author: Girl Scout's Guide to New York, 1990; contbr. chpt. to book and articles to profl. jours. Nat. bd. dirs. Girl Scouts U.S., N.Y.C., 1976-87; bd. dirs. Family Svcs., Seattle, 1982-84; mem. exec. com. Corp. Coun. for the Arts, Seattle, 1988-98; bd. gen. counsel Downtown Seattle Assn., 1986-89; mem. exec. com. Wash. Coun. Internat. Trade, 1994—; bd. mem. YMCA Greater Seattle, 1998—. Recipient Rising Stars of the 80's award Legal Times Washington, 1983, 100 Young Women of Promise, Good Housekeeping, 1985; named Washington's Winningest Trial Lawyers Washington Journal, 1992; Japan leadership fellow, 1992-93, Top 50 Women Lawyers, Nat. Law Jour., 1998; featured in article Newsweek, July 10, 2000. Fellow ABA (ho. of dels. 1990—); Fed. Bar Assn. (trustee western dist. Wash. 1980-90), Wash. Bar Assn. (chmn. jud. recommendations 1989-90), Seattle-King County Bar Assn. (trustee, sec. 1984-85, Outstanding Lawyer award 1992), Legal Found. Wash. (trustee, pres. 1989-90), Washington Women Lawyers (bd. dirs., pres. 1978-79), Nat. Assn. Iolta Programs (bd. dirs. 1989-91), White House Fellows Found. (bd. dirs. 1998—, pres. 2000-01). Avocations: travel, classical piano, hiking, gourmet cooking, tennis. Office: US Ct Appeals 401 West A St Ste 2000 San Diego CA 92101-7908

MCKIBBEN, BILLY, state legislator; BA, BS, N.Mex. State U. Mem. N.Mex. Legislature, Santa Fe, 1980—, mem. corps. and transp. com., mem. fin. com. Investor; developer. Republican. Office: 505 E Alto Dr Hobbs NM 88240-4003

MCKIBBEN, HOWARD D. federal judge; b. Apr. 1, 1940; s. James D. and Bernice McKibben; m. Mary Ann McKibben, July 2, 1966; children: Mark, Susan. BS, Bradley U., 1962; MPA, U. Pitts., 1964; JD, U. Mich., 1967. Assoc. George W. Abbott Law Office, 1967-71; dep. dist. atty. Douglas County, Nev., 1969-71, dist. atty., 1971-77; dist. ct. judge State of Nev., 1977-84; judge U.S. Dist. Ct. Nev., Reno, 1984—. Mem. Nev. Bar Assn., Am. Inns of Ct. (pres. Nev. chpt. 1986-88). Methodist. Avocations: tennis, golf, racquetball. Home: PO Box 588 Verdi NV 89439-0588 Office: US Dist Ct 400 S Virginia St Ste 804 Reno NV 89501-2197

MCKIBBEN, RYAN TIMOTHY, newspaper executive; b. Watertown, S.D., June 25, 1958; s. Bernard Dean and Patricia Martha (Loehr) McK.; m. Mary Elizabeth O'Donnell, Oct. 3, 1981; children: Sean Robert, Michael Patrick. Grad. high sch., Janesville, Wis. Classified advt. exec. Green Bay (Wis.) Press Gazette, 1977-79; display advt. exec. Racine (Wis.) Jour. Times, 1979-80; advt. dir. Oshkosh (Wis.) Northwestern, 1980-82, dir. sales/mktg., 1982-84; advt. dir. Reno Gazette-Jour., 1984-85, Madison (Wis.) Newspapers Inc., 1985-88; v.p., advt. dir., sr. v.p. advt. and mktg. Denver Post, 1988-90, exec. v.p., gen. mgr., 1990-93, pub., 1993-98; pres. Western Color Print, Denver, 1998—. Bd. dirs. Newspapers First, N.Y.C. Mem. mktg. com. Metro Area Boys Clubs, Denver, 1988—; bd. dirs. Nat. Jewish Ctr. for Immunology and Respiratory Medicine, Denver, Denver Metro Conv. Bur., Denver Ctr. for Performing Arts, Colo. Symphony, Colo. Forum, Colo. Concer, Castle Pines Golf Club. Mem. Am. Press Inst., Newspaper Advt. Coop. Network (bd. dirs. 1989—), Internat. Newspaper Advt./Mktg. Execs., (com. mem. 1989—), Denver Advt. Fedn., Boys and Girls Club, Columbine Country Club. Republican. Roman Catholic. Home: 5350 S Race Ct Littleton CO 80121-1430 Office: Western Color Print 1600 Stout St Ste 1520 Denver CO 80202-3133

MCKINLEY, LOREN DHUE, museum director; b. Tillamook, Oreg., Feb. 1, 1920; s. Henry Raymond and Flora (Phillips) McK.; m. Mary Eileen Sessions, May 22, 1942; children: Candace Eileen, Scott Dhu, Kevin Loren, Laurie Lee, Maris Colleen. Student, Oreg. State U., U. Oreg.; D.Sc., U. Portland, 1973. Advt. mgr. Headlight Herald, Tillamook, 1946; partner Kenwood Press, Tillamook, 1949; dir. Oreg. Mus. Sci. and Industry, Portland, 1960-78, chief exec. officer, 1978—. Bd. dirs. Fred Hutchinson Cancer Rsch. Ctr. Found., Oreg. Mus. Sci. and Industry; sr. devel. officer Office of Devel. Oreg. State U. Mayor of Tillamook, 1954-60; pres. Leukemia Assn. Oreg. Inc., 1983—; bd. dirs. St. Mary's Acad., 1993—; bd. trustees Oreg. Mus. Sci. and Industry; mem. Oreg. State U Found. Served with AUS, World War II, ETO, MTO. Decorated Bronze Star with oak leaf cluster; named 1st Citizen of Oreg., 1951; recipient award Oreg. Mus. Sci. and Industry, 1965, Elsie M.B. Naumberg award as outstanding sci. mus. dir., 1968, citation for outstanding svc. Oreg. Acad. Sci., 1971, Aubrey Watzek award Lewis and Clark Coll., 1973, Barbara Stallcup Miller Profl. Achievement award Willamette Valley Devel. Officers, 1999; named alumni of yr. Oreg. State U., 1999, recipient heart of gold award, 1999. Mem. Assn. Sci. and Tech. Ctrs. Am. (pres. 1973—), League Oreg. Cities (past pres.), Kappa Sigma. Republican. Home and Office: 11925 SW Belvidere Pl Portland OR 97225-5805

MCKINLEY, PATRICK, prosecutor; Chief of police, Fullerton, Calif.; now asst. dist. atty. County of Santa Barbara. Office: Office Dist Atty Courthouse 1105 Santa Barbara St Santa Barbara CA 93101-2007

MCKINNEY, JUDSON THAD, broadcast executive; b. Sacramento, Aug. 21, 1941; s. Judson Bartlett and Mildred Eoline (Taylor) McK. Student, Sacramento State U., 1959-61, Western Bapt. Bible Coll., 1961-62, Am. River Coll., 1962-63. Prodn. dir. Sta. KEBR, Sacramento, 1962-65; prodn. dir. Sta. KEAR, Merced, Calif., 1965-68; sta. mgr. Sta. KAMB, 1968-75, Sta. KEAR, San Francisco, 1975-78, 79-88, WFME, Newark, 1978; western regional mgr. Family Stas. Inc., 1988—. Pres. Abounding Love Ministries, 2000—. Chmn. bd. 1st Bapt. Ch. of San Francisco, 1985-91. Mem. Nat. Religious Broadcasters., Nat. Assn. Evangs., Gideons. Republican. Baptist. Note, exact names of churches are not listed unless an office is held therein, per style. Office: Family Stations Inc 290 Hegenberger Rd Oakland CA 94621-1436

MCKINNEY, SALLY VITKUS, state official; b. Muncie, Ind., Aug. 6, 1944; d. Robert Brookins and Mary (Mann) Gooden; m. Alan George Vitkus (div. Jan. 1979); m. James Larry McKinney, Feb. 1, 1986. AA, William Woods U., 1964; BS, U. Ariz., 1966; postgrad., U. Nev., Las Vegas, 1966-68. Tchr. Las Vegas Day Sch., 1972-76; salesperson Globe Realty, Las Vegas, 1976-79; owner, pres. Realty West, Las Vegas, 1979-96; chief investigator State of Nev. Real Estate Divsn., 1996-2000. Rec. sec. Clark County Rep. Cen. Com., Las Vegas, 1982, 1st vice chmn., 1985; vice chmn. Nev. Rep. com., 1986, chmn., 1987-88; mem. Assistance League Las Vegas; state chmn. Nev. Rep. Party. Recipient award Nat. Assn. Home Builders, 1981, 82, 83. Mem. Nat. Assn. Realtors, Las Vegas Bd. Realtors, Greater Las Vegas C. of C., Gen. Fedn. Womens Clubs (nominee Outstanding Young Woman Am. 1979, exec. bd. 1980-82), Jr. League Las Vegas, Mesquite Club (chmn. pub. affairs com. 1986-87, past pres., secret witness exec. bd. 1994-96, vice chmn.). Presbyterian. Avocations: bridge, fly fishing. Home: 460 Golden State St Henderson NV 89012-2509

MCKINNON, F(RANCIS) A(RTHUR) RICHARD, utility executive; b. Delburne, Alta., Can., Mar. 5, 1933; s. John Donald and Ruth Rebecca (Sundberg) McK.; m. Elma Lorraine Lebsack, June 1, 1957; children: Kenneth Richard, Stephen David, Karen Diane. B. Commerce, U. Alta., 1954; postgrad., Stanford Exec. Program, Stanford U., 1982. With Alta. Gas Trunk Line Co. Ltd., Calgary, 1960-75, treas., 1971-75; dir. fin. TransAlta Utilities Corp. (formerly Calgary Power Ltd.), 1975—, treas., 1976-81, v.p. fin., 1981—, Trans Alta Energy Corp., Trans Alta Corp.; pres. ELM FARMS CONS., INC., Calgary, 1996—. Bd. dirs. AEC Power Ltd. Past bd. dirs. Foothills Gen. Hosp., Calgary. Fellow Inst. Chartered Accts. of Alta.; mem. Can. Inst. Chartered Accts., Fin. Execs. Inst. Can. (past chmn., past pres., bd. dirs. Calgary chpt., v.p.), Fin. Execs. Inst. (bd. dirs.). Clubs: Calgary Petroleum, Canyon Meadows Golf and Country. Office: ELM FARM CONS INC 1412 Windsor St NW Calgary AB Canada T2N 3X3

MCKIRAHAN, RICHARD DUNCAN, classics and philosophy educator; b. Berkeley, Calif., July 27, 1945; s. Richard Duncan and Helen Marion (Hixson) McK.; m. Voula Tsouna, June 3, 1961; 1 child, Helen Hamilton. AB, U. Calif., Berkeley, 1966; BA, U. Oxford, Eng., 1969; MA, Oxford U., Eng., 1979; PhD, Harvard U., 1973. Teaching fellow, tutor Harvard U., Cambridge, Mass., 1971-73; asst. prof. classics and philosophy Pomona Coll., Claremont, Calif., 1973-79, assoc. prof., 1979-87, E.C. Norton prof. classics and philosophy, 1987—, chair dept. classics, 1992—. Marshall Aid Commemoration Commn. scholar, U. Oxford, 1966-69, Fulbright Sr. scholar, 1999, Overseas Vis. scholar St. John's Coll., Cambridge, 1999; Woodrow Wilson Found. fellow, 1966-67; NEH grantee, 1975, 85, 90, 98. Mem. Am. Philol. Assn., Soc. Ancient Greek Philosophy, Phi Beta Kappa. Office: Pomona Coll Dept Classics 140 W 6th St Claremont CA 91711-4301 E-mail: rmckirahan@pomona.edu

MCKNIGHT, FREDERICK L. lawyer; b. Kansas City, Mo., Nov. 28, 1947; s. Harry A. and Donna Ruth (Breining) McK.; m. Linda Jean McKnight, June 20, 1970; children: Justin Teague, Cristin Ruth. AB honors, Princeton U., 1969; JD, U. Calif., Berkeley, 1972. Bar: Calif. 1973, N.Y. 1973. Regional mng. ptnr. Jones Day Reavis & Pogue, L.A., 1997—. Adv. com. Jones, Day, Reavis & Pogue, Cleve., 1991—, Calif. regional mng. ptnr., 1997—. Bd. dirs. Econ. Devel. Corp., L.A., 1992—, St. Vincent Med. Ctr. Found., L.A., 1994—. Fellow Am. Coll. of Trial Lawyers; mem. Assn. Bus. Trial Lawyers. Office: Jones Day Reavis & Pogue 555 W 5th St Ste 4600 Los Angeles CA 90013-1025 E-mail: fmcknight@jonesday.com

MC KNIGHT, WILLIAM WARREN, JR. publisher; b. Normal, Ill., June 9, 1913; s. William Warren and Isabel Alida (Travis) McK.; m. Alice McGuire, Oct. 30, 1937; children: William Warren, III, Michael Joe, John James. B.S. in Bus. Adminstrn., Northwestern U., 1938. With McKnight Pub. Co., Bloomington, Ill., 1938-83, sec.-treas., 1949-56, pres., 1956-67, chmn. bd., 1968-79. Bd. dirs. Gen. Telephone Co. Ill., Champion Fed. Savs. & Loan Assn., chmn. bd. Pres. Bloomington Rotary Club, 1952, Bloomington C. of C., 1954; mem. Ill. Commn. Higher Edn., 1956-60; chmn. Bloomington-Normal Airport Authority, 1965-70, CETA Pvt. Industry Council Ill. Balance of State, 1979-81. Served with USNR, 1942-46. Recipient Disting. Service award Bloomington Kiwanis Club, 1963, Disting. Service award Normal C. of C., 1973; Good Govt. award Bloomington Jaycees, 1970; Edn. Constrn. award Edn. Council Graphic Arts Industry, 1974; Disting. Alumni award Ill. State U., 1978; Disting. Service award Spirit of McLean County, 1982; Disting. Service citation Epsilon Pi Tau, 1983; award of Merit Am. Vocat. Assn., 1990; disting. assoc. award Coun. on Tech. Tchr. Edn., 1995. Mem. Graphic Arts Edn. Assn., Internat. Tech. Edn. Assn., Nat. Assn. Indsl. and Tech. Tchrs. Educators, Ill. C. of C. (dir. 1964-69), Ill. Mfrs. Assn. (dir. 1954-62) Republican. Presbyterian. Clubs: Coll. Alumni, Bloomington Country. Home: 7788 E Stallion Rd Scottsdale AZ 85258-3485

MC KOY, BASIL VINCENT CHARLES, theoretical chemist, educator; b. Trinidad, W.I., Mar. 25, 1938; came to U.S., 1960, naturalized, 1973; s. Allan Cecil and Doris Augusta McK.; m. Anne Ellen Shannon, Mar. 18, 1967; 1 son, Christopher Allan. B.Chem. Eng., N.S. Tech. U., 1960; Ph.D. in Chemistry (Univ. fellow), Yale U., 1964. Instr. chemistry Calif. Inst. Tech., 1964-66, asst. prof. chemistry, 1966-69, asso. prof., 1969-75, prof. theoretical chemistry, 1975—, chmn. of faculty, 1985-87. Cons. Lawrence Livermore Lab., U. Calif., Livermore, 1974— , Inst. Def. Analysis, 1984—; vis. prof. Max Planck Inst., Munich, Ger., 1976— , U. Paris, 1968— , U. Campinas, Brazil, 1976— ; lectr. Nobel Symposium, Goteborg, Sweden, 1979. Contbr. articles to Jour. Physics, London, chem. Physics Lettters, Phys. Rev., Jour. Chem. Physics; bd. editors; Chem. Physics Jour., 1977-79, mem. adv. editoral bd., 1992—; co-editor: Electron-Molecule and Photon-Molecule Collisions, 1979, 83, Swarm Studies and Inelastic Electron-Molecule Collisions, 1986; co-author: Electron-Molecule Collisions and Photoionization Processes, 1982. Recipient medal Gov.-Gen. Can., 1960; Alfred P. Sloan Found. fellow, 1969-73; Guggenheim fellow, 1973-74 Fellow Am. Phys. Soc. Home: 3855 Keswick Rd La Canada Flintridge CA 91011-3945 Office: Calif Inst Tech Divsn Chemistry Pasadena CA 91125-0001

MCKUSICK, MARSHALL KIRK, computer scientist; b. Wilmington, Del., Jan. 19, 1954; s. Blaine Chase and Marjorie Jane (Kirk) McK.; domestic ptnr. Eric P. Allman. BSEE with distinction, Cornell U., 1976; MS in Bus. Adminstrn., U. Calif., Berkeley, 1979, MS in Computer Sci., 1980, PhD in Computer Sci., 1984. System designer Hughes Aircraft Co., 1977-79; software cons., 1982—; rsch. computer scientist U. Calif., Berkeley, 1984-93. Author: The Design and Implementation of the 4.4BSD Operating System, 1996 (trans. into German, 1997, Japanese, 1997, French, 1997); contbr. articles to profl. publs. Mem. IEEE, Usenix Assn. (Lifetime Achievement award 1992, pres. 1990-92, bd. dirs. 1986-92), Assn. Computing Machinery. Democrat. Avocations: swimming, scuba diving, wine collecting. Office: 1614 Oxford St Berkeley CA 94709-1608 E-mail: mkm@mckusick.com

MCLAIN, CHRISTOPHER M. lawyer; b. San Luis Obispo, Calif., July 21, 1943; s. James Latane and Marjorie Patricia (McNalley) McL.; m. Barbara McFarland, Nov. 23, 1968; children: Beth, Brian, Amy. BS in Bus. Adminstrn., U. Calif.-Berkeley, 1965, JD, 1968. Assoc. Knox, Goforth & Ricksen, Oakland, Calif., 1968-69, Donahue, Gallagher, Thomas & Woods, Oakland, 1969-73, ptnr., 1973-83; sec., counsel Lucky Stores, Inc., Dublin, 1984-89, v.p., 1985-89; ptnr. Sonnenschein, Nath & Rosenthal, San Francisco, 1989-90; sr. v.p., gen. counsel, sec. Transam. Corp., San Francisco, 1990-94; of counsel Sonnenschein Nath & Rosenthal, San Francisco, 1994-95; sr. v.p., gen. counsel, sec. Crown Vantage Inc., Oakland, Calif., 1995-99; ptnr., sr. v.p., gen. counsel Sequoia Assocs., LLC, Menlo Park, 1999—. Mem. ABA, State Bar Calif., Alameda County Bar Assn., San Francisco Bar Assn., Am. Soc. Corps. Secs. Avocation: skiing. Office: Sequoia Assocs LLC Bldg 2 Ste 140 3000 Sand Hill Rd Menlo Park CA 94025

MCLANE, FREDERICK BERG, lawyer; b. Long Beach, Calif., July 24, 1941; s. Adrian B. and Arlie K. (Burrell) McL.; m. Lois C. Roberts, Jan. 28, 1967; children: Willard, Anita. BA, Stanford U., 1963; LLB, Yale U., 1966. Bar: Calif. 1967, U.S. Dist. Ct. (cen. dist.) Calif. 1967. Assoc. prof. law U. Miss., Oxford, 1966-68; assoc. O'Melveny & Myers, L.A., 1968-74, ptnr., 1975—. Com. of counsel HUD, Los Angeles, 1979-84; lectr. in field. Pres., bd. dirs. Legal Aid Found., L.A., 1974-83; deacon Congl. Ch., Sherman Oaks, Calif., 1979-83; vice-chair L.A. Music Ctr., Unified Fund, 1992-94; bd. dirs. Calif. Sci. Ctr. Found., 1991-2000. Mem. ABA (banking com., fed. regulation of securities com.), Calif. Bar Assn. (fin. insts. com., uniform comml. codes), L.A. Bar Assn., Order of Coif, Calif. Club (L.A.), L.A. Country Club (bd. dirs.), Lakeside Golf Club (L.A.). Democrat. Avocations: golf, walking, reading. Office: O'Melveny & Myers 400 S Hope St Los Angeles CA 90071-2899 E-mail: fmclane@omm.com

MCLAUGHLIN, CALVIN STURGIS, biochemistry educator; b. St. Joseph, Mo., May 29, 1936; s. Calvin Sturgis and Agnes Jane McLaughlin; m. Chin Helen Moy, Sept. 7, 1960; children: Heather Chin Chu, Christine Leng Oy, Andrew Calvin Moy BS, King Coll., 1958; postgrad., Yale U., 1958-59; PhD, MIT, 1964. Postdoctoral fellow Institut de Biologie Physico-Chimique, Paris, 1964-66; prof. biochemistry U. Calif., Irvine, 1966—, dir. Cancer Rsch. Inst., 1981-83; vis. prof. Sch. Botany Oxford U., Eng., 1976, 80. Mem. peer rev. panels Am. Cancer Soc., NSF, NIH, VA Contbr. numerous articles to profl. jours.; mem. editl. bds. Jour. Bacteriology, 1975-80, Exptl. Mycology, 1980-86; reviewer profl. jours. Bd. dirs. Am. Cancer Soc., Orange County, 1980-89; mem. Traffic Affairs Com., Newport Beach, Calif., 1972-78. Named Outstanding Tchr. U. Calif.-Irvine, 1978, Gabriel Lester Meml. Lectr. Reed Coll., 1979; fellow Rockefeller Found., 1958-59, Upjohn Found., 1959-60, Nutrition Found., 1960-61, NIH, 1961-64, Am. Cancer Soc., 1964-66 Mem. Genetics Soc. Am., Am. Soc. Biochemistry and Molecular Biology, Am. Soc. Microbiology, Am. Soc. Mycology, Am. Soc. for Cell Biology, Yeast Genetics and Molecular Biology Soc. Am. (co-chair 1986-88), Electrophoresis Soc. Presbyterian Office: U Calif Irvine Dept Biol Chemistry Irvine CA 92697-0001 E-mail: cal@uci.edu

MCLAUGHLIN, GLEN, financial services company executive; b. Shawnee, Okla., Dec. 21, 1934; s. Champe and Mattie Bet (Jenkins) McL.; m. Ellen Marr Schnake, Aug. 29, 1964; children: Helen Elizabeth, Glen Wallace. B.B.A., U. Okla., 1956; M.B.A., Harvard U., 1964. Asst. treas. Foremost-McKesson, Inc., San Francisco, 1964-69; exec. v.p., dir. MacFarlane's Candies, Oakland, Calif., 1969-70; dir. fin. and adminstrn. Memorex Corp., London, 1970-71; sr. v.p. fin. Four-Phase Systems, Inc., Cupertino, Calif., 1971-82; pres., chmn. Four-Phase Fin., Inc., Cupertino, 1977-82; chmn. bd. Four-Phase Systems, Ltd., Toronto, Ont., Can., 1977-82, Four-Phase Systems Internat., Inc., 1977-82, DeAnza Ins. Co. Ltd., Cayman Islands, 1979-82; gen. ptnr. Matrix Ptnrs., L.P., San Jose and Boston, 1982-86; chmn. bd. Venture Leasing Assocs., 1986—; chmn. bd. dirs. Cupertino Nat. Bank, Calif., 1990-96; dir. Greater Bay Bancorp, Palo Alto, 1996—. Author: The Mapping of California as an Island, 1995. Served USAF 1956-62, USAFR 1964-65 (capt. and pilot), pres. Jr. Achievement Santa Clara County, 1978-79, chmn. bd., 1980-81; chmn. bd. Jr. Achievement Found. Santa Clara County, 1980-87; mem. bus. sch. adv. bd. U. Santa Clara, 1981-84; pres. Boy Scouts Am., Santa Clara County, 1986-87, mem. exec. coun., 1982—, pres. No. Calif. Area, 1988-91; pres. BSA Meml. Found., 1991-95; mem. pvt. sector investment adv. panel City of San Jose, 1984-92; bd. visitors Sch. Acctg., Coll. Bus. Adminstrn., U. Okla., 1991-94, endowed chair in bus. ethics, 1997, bd. advs., 1998—; trustee Gould Acad., Bethel, Maine, 1993—, O'Connor Hosp. Found., San Jose, 1994-97; bd. dirs. Am. Cancer Soc., Santa Clara County, 1994-98, Libr. Congress Map Divn., Phillips Soc., 1995—, co-chair, 1998—; founding angel Band of Angels, Silicon Valley, Calif., 1995—. Recipient Silver Leadership award Jr. Achievement, 1981, Silver Beaver award Boy Scouts Am., 1985, Silver Antelope award Boy Scouts Am., 1990, Disting. Eagle Scout award Boy Scouts Am., 1994, pub. svc. citations Calif. State Senate, Calif. State Assembly, Santa Clara County Suprs.; Baden-Powell World fellow, 1986; decorated Order of St. John, 1989. Fellow Royal Geog. Soc.; mem. Fin. Execs. Inst., English Speaking Union, Commonwealth Club, Harvard U. Bus. Sch. Club, Roxburghe Club, Book Club Calif., Beta Gamma Sigma, Sigma Alpha Epsilon. Home: 14016 Camino Barco Saratoga CA 95070-5661

MC LAUGHLIN, JEROME MICHAEL, lawyer, shipping company executive; b. St. Louis, Jan. 11, 1929; s. John Thomas and Mary Adelaide (White) McL.; m. Delphine M. McClellan, June 15, 1957; children— Margaret D., Mary Martha, Elizabeth O., Jerome Michael, John T. A.B., St. Louis U., 1950, J.D., 1954. Bar: Mo. 1954, U.S. Supreme Ct. 1972. V.p. Internat. Indemnity, St. Louis, 1955-56; asst. circuit atty. City of St. Louis, 1957-58; partner firm Willson, Cunningham & McClellan, St. Louis, 1958-78; v.p., gen. counsel Alexander & Baldwin, Inc., Honolulu, 1978-79; sr. v.p. Philippines, Micronesia & Orient Navigation Co., San Francisco, 1979-87, exec. v.p., 1987—, chmn. bd. dirs., 1996—. Instr. philosophy St. Louis U., 1955-60 Served to capt. USMC, 1951-53, Korea. Mem. Mo. Bar Assn., Maritime Law Assn. U.S., Soc. Maritime Arbitrators San Francisco (past pres.). Republican. Roman Catholic. Home: 820 Smoketree Ct San Marcos CA 92078-4980 Office: 353 Sacramento St San Francisco CA 94111-3620

MCLAUGHLIN, JOSEPH MAILEY, lawyer; b. L.A., July 10, 1928; s. James Aloysius and Cecilia Ann (Mailey) McL.; m. Beverly Jane Walker, July 24, 1949; children: Stephen Joseph, Lawrence James, Suzanne Carol, Eileen Louise. JD, Loyola U., L.A., 1955. Bar: Calif. 1955, U.S. Supreme Ct. 1959. Mem. firm McLaughlin and Irvin, L.A., 1955—. Lectr. labor relations Loyola U., L.A., 1958-60, mem. bd. visitors law sch., 1987—; pres. Food Employers Coun., Inc., 1984-89; pres. L.A. Stock Exch., 1972. Contbg. author: Labor Law for General Practitioners, 1960. Served to 1st lt. USAF, 1951-53. Mem. San Francisco, Long Beach, Los Angeles County, Fed., Am., Internat., Inter-Am. Bar Assns., State Bar Calif., Am. Judicature Soc., Assn. Bus. Trial Lawyers, Am. Soc. Internat. Law, Calif. Club. Office: 11957 Wood Ranch Rd Granada Hills CA 91344

MCLAUGHLIN, LEIGHTON BATES, II, journalism educator, former newspaperman; b. Evanston, Ill., Apr. 10, 1930; s. Leighton Bates and Gwendolyn I. (Markle) McL.; m. Beverly Jean Jeske, May 5, 1962; children: Leighton Bates III, Jeffrey, Steven, Patrick. Student English lit., Kenyon Coll., Gambier, Ohio, 1948-50, Northwestern U., , 1951; BA in English lit., UCLA, 1983; MA in communications, Calif. State U., Fullerton, 1990. Copyboy, reporter, rewriteman City News Bur., Chgo., 1957-58; reporter, rewriteman Chgo. Sun-Times, 1958-62; rewriteman, asst. city editor Ariz. Jour., Phoenix, 1962; reporter Miami (Fla.) Herald, 1962-64; successively rewriteman, night city editor, 1st asst. city editor, telegraph editor Chgo. Sun-Times, 1964-74; dir. Chgo. Daily News/Sun-Times News Service, 1974-79; editorial coord. electronics newspaper div. Field Enterprises, 1975-79; adminstr. reference libr. and communications ctr. Field Newspapers, 1976-79; editor News Am. Syndicate, Irvine, Calif., 1979-85; mng. editor San Gabriel Valley Daily Tribune, 1986; assoc. prof. journalism Riverside (Calif.) C.C., 1987-96, chmn. performing arts and media dept., 1993-96, coll. publs. editor, ret., 1996-99; lectr. in journalism Calif. State U.-Fullerton, 1984-96; fill-in editor The Press-Enterprise, Riverside, Calif., 1988-95. Lectr., condr. seminars in field. Author articles in field. Served to 1st lt. USMC, 1951-54. Recipient Stick-o-Type award for best feature story Chgo. Newspaper Guild, 1961, Best News story award Ill. AP and UPI, 1967 Mem. Soc. Profl. Journalists, Verban Soc., Psi Upsilon. Office: Riverside CC 4800 Magnolia Ave Riverside CA 92506-1242

MCLAUGHLIN, MARGUERITE P. state legislator, logging company executive; b. Matchwood, Mich., Oct. 15, 1928; d. Harvey Martin and Luella Margaret (Livingston) Miller; m. George Bruce McLaughlin, 1947; children: Pamela, Bruce Jr., Cynthia. Owner, operator contract logging firm, Orofino, Idaho; mem. Idaho Ho. of Reps., 1978-80, Idaho Senate, 1980—, asst. Dem. Leader, 1990-93, Dem. leader, 1997-98. Chair Democrat Caucus, 1995-96; mem. Senate Fin. Com., 1987—, Gov.'s Adv. Coun. Workers Compensation, 1990-96, State of Idaho Endowment Fund Investment Bd., 1991-95, legis. coun., 1989-94, 95—. Mem. State of Idaho Job Trg. Coun., 1989-98, State Ins. Fund Commn., 1998—; trustee Joint Sch. Dist. 171, 1976-80; pres. Oro Celebration, Inc. Office: Idaho State Senate State Capital Boise ID 83720-0001

MCLEAN, HUGH ANGUS, management consultant; b. Salt Lake City, Feb. 19, 1925; s. George Mark and Rose (Powell) McL.; m. Martha Lane Green, Nov. 23, 1949; children: Michael Hugh, Merrie Smithson. Student, U. Kans., 1943-44; BSME, Iowa State U., 1946; postgrad., U. Utah, 1946, 61-66. Registered profl. engr., Utah. With Utah Oil Refining Co., Boise, Idaho, Twin Falls, Idaho and Salt Lake City, 1953-61, Am. Oil Co., Salt Lake City and 11 western states, 1961-66; cons. Standard Oil (Ind.), Chgo., 1966-69; v.p. Mahler Assocs., Midland Park, N.J., 1969-76; pres. McLean Mgmt. Systems, Wyckoff, 1976-84, Heber City, Utah, 1984—. Author: There Is a Better Way to Manage, 1982, Developmental Dialogues, 1972, Career Planning Program, 1975; creator, host (TV) live shows and commls., 1956-57; creator stewardship mgmt. system, 1987. Rep. election judge, Salt Lake City, 1964, Operation Eagle Eye, Chgo., 1968; pub. communications dir. Ch. Jesus Christ Latter-Day Saints, N.Y. metro area, 1981-84; introduced SAFE HOMES in county and state, 1987; chmn. bd. dirs. Town Hall Playhouse, 1990-96; elected Daniel Twp. Planning Commn., 1996-2000; emergency preparedness coord. Daniels Canyon area of Wasatch County, Utah, 2000—. Served to lt. (j.g.) USNR, 1943-46. Recipient Silver award Am. Petroleum Inst., 1957. Mem. Am. Soc. Tng. Devel. (chmn. N.Y. metro chpt. field trips 1972-74). Office: McLean Mgmt Sys PO Box 251 Heber City UT 84032-0251

MCLUCAS, KATE, magazine editor; Exec. editor, testing dir. Infoworld, San Mateo, Calif. Office: Infoworld 155 Bovet Rd Ste 800 San Mateo CA 94402-3150

MC LURE, CHARLES E., JR. economist, consultant; b. Sierra Blanca, Tex., Apr. 14, 1940; s. Charles E. and Dessie (Evans) McL.; m. Patsy Nell Carroll, Sept. 17, 1962. BA, U. Kans., 1962; MA, Princeton U., 1964, PhD, 1966. Asst. prof. econs. Rice U., Houston, 1965-69, assoc. prof., 1969-72, prof., 1972-79, Allyn R. and Gladys M. Cline prof. econs., 1973-79; exec. dir. for research Nat. Bur. Econ. Research, Cambridge, Mass., 1977-78, v.p., 1978-81; sr. fellow Hoover Instn., Stanford U., 1981—; dep. asst. sec. Dept. Treasury, 1983-85. Sec. Dept. Treasury, 1983-85; sr. staff economist Coun. Econ. Advisers, Washington, 1969-70; vis. lectr. U. Wyo., 1972; vis. prof. Stanford U., 1973; cons. U.S. Treasury Dept., Labor Dept., World Bank, UN, OAS, Interam. Devel. Bank, Tax Found., Com. Econ. Devel., IMF, Internat. Tax and Investment Ctr., govts. Can., Colombia, Malaysia, Panama, Jamaica, Bolivia, Indonesia, New Zealand, Brazil, Trinidad and Tobago, Venezuela, Guatemala, Peoples Republic China, Egypt, Malawi, Mex., Bulgaria, Brazil, Russia, Ukraine, Romania, Kazakhstan, South Africa, Vietnam, Chile, Argentina. Author: Fiscal Failure: Lessons of the Sixties, 1972, (with N. Ture) Value Added Tax: Two Views, 1972, (with M. Gillis) La Reforma Tributaria Colombiana de 1974, 1977, Must Corporate Income Be Taxed Twice?, 1979, Economic Perperspectives on State Taxation of Multijurisdictional Corporations, 1986, The Value Added Tax: Key to Deficit Reduction, 1987; co-author: Taxation of Income from Business and Capital in Colombia, 1989; also numerous articles on econs. and public finance. Ford Found. faculty research fellow, 1967-68 Mem. Am. Econ. Assn., Nat. Tax Assn., Beta Theta Pi. Home: 250 Yerba Santa Ave Los Altos CA 94022-1609 Office: Stanford U Hoover Instn Stanford CA 94305-6010 E-mail: mclure@hoover.stanford.edu

MCMAHON, BRIAN, publishing executive; Pub. Car and Driver Hachette Filipacchi Mags., Inc., Ann Arbor, Mich. Office: Hachette Filipacchi Mags Inc 1499 Monrovia Ave Newport Beach CA 92663-2752 also: Car & Driver 2002 Hogback Rd Ann Arbor MI 48105-9736

MCMAHON, JAMES W. federal magistrate judge; b. 1941; BA, Santa Clara U., 1962; LLB, Harvard U., 1968. Pvt. practice, L.A., 1986-94; apptd. magistrate judge cen. dist. U.S. Dist. Ct. Calif., 1994. Dep. pub. defender L.A. County, 1969-79. With Peace Corps, 1963-65. Office: Courtroom 580 255 E Temple Los Angeles CA 90012-4712 Fax: 213-984-4402

MCMANIS, JAMES, lawyer; b. Haverhill, Mass., May 28, 1943; s. Charles and Yvonne (Zinn) McM.; m. Sara Wigh, Mar. 30, 1968. BA, Stanford U., Palo Alto, Calif., 1964; JD, U. Calif., Berkeley, 1967. Bar: Calif. 1967, U.S. Dist. Ct. (no. dist.) Calif. 1967, U.S. Ct. Appeals (9th cir.) 1967, U.S. Supreme Ct. 1971. Dep. dist. atty. Santa Clara County Dist. Atty., 1968-71; mem. McManis, Faulkner & Morgan, San Jose, Calif., 1971—. Spl. master tech. equities litigation, 1987—; spl. examiner State Bar Calif., 1995-98; prof. law Lincoln U. Law Sch., San Jose, 1972-82; lectr. Calif. Continuing Edn. of Bar, 1989-90; instr. U. Calif. Law Sch., 1992-96, Stanford U. Sch. Law, 1994-99. Pres. Santa Clara County Bar Assn. Law Found., 1996, dir., 1987—. Fellow Am. Coll. Trial Lawyers; mem. ABA, State Bar Calif., Calif. Trial Lawyers Assn., Santa Clara County Bar Assn., Boalt Hall Alumni Assn. Avocations: history, books, travel, running. Office: McManis Faulkner & Morgan Inc 160 W Santa Clara St Fl 10 San Jose CA 95113-1701 Fax: 408-279-3244. E-mail: jmcmanis@mfmlaw.com

MCMANUS, DANA C. construction company executive; b. Exeter, Calif., Dec. 25, 1949; BA, Fresno State U.; MBA, Golden Gate U., 1973, MS, 1975. CFO S.J. Amoroso Constrn. Co., Foster City, Calif., 1981-95, CEO, 1995—. Mem. Constrn. Employer Assn. (pres. 1997-98). Office: SJ Amoroso Constrn Co 348 Hatch Dr Foster City CA 94404-1106

MCMANUS, MICHAEL S. federal judge; b. 1953; BA, U. Calif., Berkeley, 1975; JD, UCLA, 1978. With Morris & Polich, 1978-79, Diepenbrock, Wulff, Plant & Hannegan, 1979-94; apptd. bankruptcy judge ea. dist. U.S. Courthouse, 1994. Office: 501 I St Ste 3-200 Sacramento CA 95814 Fax: 916-930-4552. E-mail: michael_mcmanus@ce9.uscourts.gov

MCMANUS, PATRICK FRANCIS, educator, writer; b. Sandpoint, Idaho, Aug. 25, 1933; s. Francis Edward McManus and Mabel Delana (Klaus) DeMers; m. Darlene Madge Keough, Feb. 3, 1954; children: Kelly C., Shannon M., Peggy F., Erin B. BA in English, Wash. State U., 1956, MA in English, 1962, postgrad., 1965-67. News reporter Daily Olympian, Olympia, Wash., 1956; editor Wash. State U., Pullman, 1956-59; with Ea. Wash. U., Cheney, 1959—; ret., 1983; news reporter Sta. KREM-TV, 1960-62; assoc. prof. Ea. Wash. U., Cheney, 1971-74, prof., 1974-83, prof. emeritus, 1983—. Author: A Fine and Pleasant Misery, 1978, Kid Camping form Aaaaiii! to Zip, 1979, They Shoot Canoes, Don't They?, 1981, Never Sniff a Gift Fish, 1983, The Grasshopper Trap, 1985, Rubber Legs & White Tail-Hairs, 1987, The Night The Bear Ate Goombaw, 1989, Whatchagot Stew, 1989, Real Ponies Don't Go Oink!, 1991, The Good Samaritan Strikes Again, 1992, How I Got This Way, 1994, Never Cry "Arp!" and Other Great Adventures, 1996, Into the Twilight, Endlessly Grousing, 1997, The Deer on a Bicycle, Excursions Into the Writing of Humor, 2000, (stage play) A Fine and Pleasant Misery: The Humor of Patrick F. McManus, 1994, Misery II: McManus In Love, 1995, Pat McManus, Endlessly Grousing, 1997, Pott's Luck, 1999; assoc. editor Field & Stream mag., 1977-81; editor-at-large Outdoor Life, 1981—. Recipient Booksellers award P.N.W. Booksellers, 1983, Trustees medal EWU, 1984, Gov.'s award Wash. State Libr., 1985, Excellence in Craft award OWAA, 1986, Disting. Achievement award WSU, 1994, Founder's Day award EWU, 1994; named to Idaho's Hall of Fame, 1995. Mem. Authors Guild, Outdoor Writers Am. (bd. dirs. 1981-84, Excellence award 1986). Roman Catholic. Avocations: outdoor sports, woodworking, traveling. Office: PO Box 28216 Spokane WA 99228-8216

MCMANUS, RICHARD PHILIP, lawyer, agricultural products company executive; b. Keokuk, Iowa, Oct. 20, 1929; s. Edward William and Kathleen (O'Connor) M.; m. Marjorie Theresa Mullaney, Nov. 5, 1955; children: Michael L., Mark J., Matthew A. BA, St. Ambrose U., Davenport, Iowa, 1949; JD, U. Mich., 1952; MBA, Roosevelt U., Chgo., 1965. Bar: Calif. 1982, Ill. 1958, Iowa 1952. Ptnr. McManus & McManus, Keokuk, 1953-63; div. counsel USN Facility Engring. Command, Great Lakes, Ill., 1963-66; v.p., dir. law Household Fin. Corp., Chgo., 1966-81; exec. v.p., sec. Security Pacific Fin. Svcs., Inc., San Diego, 1981-91; exec. v.p./sec. Bank Am. Fin. Svcs., San Diego, 1991-92; pres., bd. dirs. Mosamac Co., Inc., 1992—. Mem. gen. com. Conf. Consumer Fin. Law, Chgo., 1975-92. Contbr. articles to profl. jours. Bd. dirs., treas., atty. Tijuana/San Diego Habitat for Humanity, Inc., 1992-95; trustee Village of Lake Bluff, Ill., 1974-78. Recipient of the San Diego Vol. Lawyer Disting. Svc. award, 1995-2000, Pres. Calif. Bar Pro Bono Svs., award, 1998. Mem. Calif. Bar Assn., San Diego Bar Assn., Calif. Fin. Svcs. Assn. (chmn. law com. 1981-92), Am. Fin. Svcs. Assn. (chmn. law forum 1980-81, Disting. Svc. award 1990), Lions, Elks, KC, Beta Gamma Sigma. Democrat. Roman Catholic. Avocations: golf, flying, sailing, woodworking. E-mail: mcman1000@cs.com

MCMASTER, JULIET SYLVIA, English language educator; b. Kisumu, Kenya, Aug. 2, 1937; emigrated to Can., 1961, naturalized, 1976; d. Sydney Herbert and Sylvia (Hook) Fazan; m. Rowland McMaster, May 10, 1968; children: Rawdon, Lindsey. B.A. with honors, Oxford U., 1959; M.A., U. Alta., 1963, Ph.D., 1965. Asst. prof. English U. Alta., Edmonton, Can., 1965-70, assoc. prof., 1970-76, prof. English, 1976-86, Univ. prof., 1986—. Author: Thackeray: The Major Novels, 1971, Jane Austen on Love, 1978, Trollope's Palliser Novels, 1978, (with R.D. McMaster) The Novel from Sterne to James, 1981, Dickens the Designer, 1987, Jane Austen the Novelist, 1995; co-editor: Jane Austen's Business, 1996, Cambridge Companion to Jane Austen, 1997; gen. editor Juvenilia Press, 1993—; illustrator/editor children's picture book: (by Jane Austen) The Beautifull Cassandra, 1993; contbr. articles to profl. jours. Fellow Can. Coun., 1969-70, Guggenheim Found., 1976-77, Killam Found., 1987-89; recipient Molson prize in Humanities for Outstanding Contbn. to Canadian Culture, 1994. Fellow Royal Soc. Can.; mem. Victorian Studies Assn. Western Can. (founding pres. 1972), Assn. Can. Univ. Tchrs. English (pres. 1976-78), MLA, Jane Austen Soc. N.Am. (dir. 1980-91). Office: U Alta Dept English Edmonton AB Canada T6G 2E5 E-mail: juliet.mcmaster@ualberta.ca

MCMICHAEL, J(ACK) RICHARD, real estate developer; b. Berkeley, Calif., Mar. 9, 1943; s. Jack R. and Dorothy (Dwyer) McM.; m. Karen Lois Moore, Nov. 15, 1964; children: J. Richard IV, Erik C. BA, U. Calif., Berkeley, 1964, JD, 1969. Bar: Calif.; lic. real estate broker, Calif. Assoc. Pettit and Martin, San Francisco, 1969-71; pres. Sutter Hill Ltd., Palo Alto, Calif., 1971-78; exec. v.p. Genstar Pacific Corp., San Francisco, 1978-79; gen. mgr. investment property div. Citation Builders, San Leandro, Calif., 1979-84; prin. JRM Properties, Palo Alto, 1984-88; pres. The Fairway Land Co., Laguna Niguel, Calif., 1988-90; v.p., gen. mgr. Quadrant Corp., San Ramon, 1990-92; v.p. Weyerhauser Real Estate Co., Federal Way, Wash., 1992-95. Bd. dirs., Western Real Estate Fund, Inc., Menlo Park, Calif. Chmn., Scholar Opera, Palo Alto, 1982-85; bd. mgrs., Palo Alto YMCA, 1987-91; chmn. troop com., Palo Alto area Boy Scouts Am., 1987-88. Comdr. USN, 1964-66, Vietnam. Mem. Internat. Coun. Shopping Ctrs. Republican. Presbyterian. Avocations: running, golf. Office: Weyerhaeuser Real Estate Co EC3-3B9 PO Box 9777 Federal Way WA 98063 E-mail: rick.mcmichael@wreco1.com

MCMILLAN, M. SEAN, lawyer; Diploma, U. Munich, 1963; cert., Internat. Sch., Copenhagen, Denmark, 1962; SB, U. So. Calif., 1967; JD, Qarvard U., 1970. Bar: Calif. 1971. Spl. projects dir. Mass. Gen. Hosp., Boston, 1967-70; ptnr. Keatinge, Libbott, Bates & Loo, Los Angeles, 1970-74, Loo, Merideth & McMillan, Los Angeles, 1974-85, Bryan Cave LLP, Los Angeles/Santa Monica, 1986—. Editor: Harvard Internat. Law Jour., 1968-70.. Mem. Assn. Computing Machinery, ABA, Am. Soc. Internat. Law, Phi Beta Kappa, Phi Kappa Phi. Office: Bryan Cave LLP 120 Broadway Ste 300 Santa Monica CA 90401-2386

MCMILLAN, PAUL FRANCIS, chemistry educator; b. Edinburgh, Scotland, June 3, 1955; BSc with honors, U. Edinburgh, 1977; PhD, Ariz. State U., 1981. Asst. prof. Ariz. State U., Tempe, 1983-88, assoc. prof., 1988-92, prof. chemistry, 1992—, presdl. prof. scis., dir., 1998—. Dir. Materials Rsch. Ctr. Ariz. State U., 1996—, dir. Ctr. for Solid State Sci., 1997—. Editor: Structure and Dynamics of Silicate Melts, 1995, Spl. Issue European Jour. Solid State Inorganic Chemistry, 1997; contbr. articles to profl. jours. Materials Rsch. Ctr. grant NSF, 1996. Fellow Mineralogical Soc. Am.; mem. Fgn. Assn., Materials Rsch. Soc., Am. Chem. Soc. Achievements include 2 patents on nitride glasses; research on density driven phase transition in liquids, synthesis of icosahedral borides. Office: Ariz State U Dept Chemistry Ctr Solid State Sci Tempe AZ 85287-1604

MCMILLAN, TERRY L. writer, educator; b. Port Huron, Mich., Oct. 18, 1951; d. Edward McMillan and Madeline Washington Tillman; 1 child, Solomon Welch. BA in Journalism, U. Calif., Berkeley, 1979; postgrad., Columbia Univ., N.Y.C., 1979. Instr. U. Wyoming, Laramie, 1987-88; prof. U. Ariz., Tucson, 1988-91. Author: Mama, 1987, Disappearing Acts, 1989, Waiting to Exhale, 1992, How Stella Got Her Groove Back, 1996, A Day Late & A Dollar Short, 2001; editor: Breaking Ice: An Anthropology of Contemporary African-American Fiction, 1990; screenwriter (with Ron Bass) (movies) Waiting to Exhale, 1995, How Stella Got Her Groove Back, 1998. Recipient National Endowment for the Arts fellowship, 1988.

MCMORRIS, JERRY, transportation company executive, sports team executive; Past CEO NW Transport Svc, Denver; chair, pres., CEO Colorado Rockies, Denver, 1995-. Office: NW Transport Svc 717 17th St Ste 500 Denver CO 80202-3330

MCMURDO, C(HARLES) GREGORY, state official, lawyer; b. Klamath Falls, Oreg., Apr. 30, 1946; s. Charles Andrew and Juanita Berniece (Bell) McM.. BA Oreg. State U., 1968, JD Lewis and Clark Coll., 1972. Bar: Oreg. 1972, U.S. Dist. Ct. Oreg. 1975, U.S. Ct. Appeals (9th cir.) 1980, U.S. Supreme Ct. 1984. Legal counsel Oreg. Ho. of Reps., Salem, 1972—76; asst. sec. state State of Oreg. , Salem, 1976—81, dep. sec. state, 1981—85; mem. Workers Compensation Bd., 1985—88; dir. of govt. rels. Metro, Portland, 1988—90; dep. supt. of pub. instrn. State of Oreg., 1990—2000, exec. legal officer, 2000—. Mem.: Oreg. State Bar. Republican. Episcopalian. Office: Oreg Dept Edn Pub Svc Bldg 255 Capitol St NE Salem OR 97310-1341

MCMURRAY, RON, political candidate, former political association executive; Chmn. Idaho State Rep. Party, 1995-99; candidate for election U.S. Ho. Reps., 1999—.

MCNALL, SCOTT GRANT, sociology educator; b. New Ulm, Minn., Jan. 16, 1941; s. Everett Herman and Dorothy Grant (Brown) McN.; m. Sally Anne Allen, Oct. 31, 1960; children— Miles Allen, Amy Ellen BA, Portland State U., 1962; PhD, U. Oreg., 1965. Instr. sociology U. Oreg., Eugene, 1964-65; asst. prof. U. Minn., Mpls., 1965-70; from assoc. prof. to prof. Ariz. State U., Tempe, 1970-76; prof., chmn. dept. sociology U. Kans., Lawrence, 1976-89, prof, chmn. dept. Am. studies, 1989-90; dean coll. arts and scis. U. Toledo, 1990-94; provost, v.p. acad. affairs Calif. State U., Chico, 1994—. Author: The Sociological Experience, 1969, 3d edit., 1974, The Greek Peasant, 1974, Social Problems Today, 1975, Career of a Radical Rightist, 1975, (with Sally A. McNall) Plains Families: Exploring Sociology Through Social History, 1983, The Road to Rebellion, 1988; editor: The Sociological Perspective, 1968, 4th edit., 1977, Theoretical Perspectives in Sociology, 1979, Current Perspectives in Social Theory, 1980, 6th edit., 1985, Political Economy: A Critique of American Society, 1981, (jour.) Current Perspectives in Social Theory, 1980-87, (with others) Studies in Historical Social Change, 1986—, The Road to Rebellion: Class Formation and Kansas Populism, 1865-1900, 1988, (with Rhonda Levine) Bringing Class Back In, 1991, (with Sally A. McNall) Sociology, 1992; assoc. editor: The Am. Sociologist, 1975-78, Jour. Polit. and Mil. Sociology, 1982—; adv. editor: Sociol. Quar., 1969-72; contbr. articles to profl. jours. Fulbright lectr., Greece, 1968-69; East-West Center vis. fellow, 1978; Mid-Am. State U. Assn. vis. lectr., 1982-83; Fulbright grantee, 1983 Mem. Midwest Sociol. Soc. (pres. 1982-83), Am. Sociol. Assn. (chair Marxist sect. 1989-90), Pacific Sociol. Soc. Democrat. Congregationalist Home: 520 Crestwood Dr Paradise CA 95969-3825 Office: Calif State U VPAA Office Chico CA 95929

MCNALLY, THOMAS CHARLES, III, lawyer; b. San Francisco, Dec. 5, 1938; s. Thomas Charles and Claire Marie (Egan) McN.; m. Paula Ann Berger, Sept. 3, 1960; children: Megan, Martin, J. Tevis. BS, U. San Francisco, 1960; JD, U. Calif., San Francisco, 1963. Bar: Calif. 1964. Dep. atty. gen., State Calif., 1964; assoc. firm Bohnert, Flowers & McCarthy, San Francisco, 1965-68; asst. sec., counsel DiGiorgio Corp., San Francisco, 1968-73, sec., counsel, 1974-75; sec., gen. counsel Consol. Fibres, Inc., San Francisco, 1975-88, v.p., 1981-88, also bd. dirs.; of counsel McInerney & Dillon, P.C., Oakland, Calif., 1989-91; pvt. practice San Francisco, 1991—. Lectr. McGeorge Bar Rev., 1964-65, Continuing Edn. of Bar, U. Calif., 1975-76; judge moot ct. U. San Francisco, 1974-84; arbitrator Am. Arbitration Assn., NASD, 1988—. Co-chmn. Mill Valley Citizens Adv. Com., 1974-76; mem. pub. affairs com. San Francisco Assn. Mental Health, 1965-69; commr. Mill Valley Park and Recreation Commn., 1988-93, chmn., 1990; lector Roman Cath. ch. Mem. ABA, State Bar Calif., San Francisco Bar Assn., Olympic Club (bd. dirs. 1999—, v.p. 2001), Scott Valley Tennis Club (founder, bd. dirs. 1971-76, 80-82, pres. 1980-82), World Trade Club. Republican. Home: 108 Hawthorne Ave Larkspur CA 94939 Office: 455 Market St Ste 1900 San Francisco CA 94105-2448 E-mail: tmcnally@lmi.net

MC NAMARA, JOSEPH DONALD, researcher, retired police chief, novelist; b. N.Y.C., Dec. 16, 1934; s. Michael and Eleanor (Shepherd) McN.; divorced; children: Donald, Laura, Karen. BS, John Jay Coll., 1968; fellow, Harvard Law Sch., 1970; DPA (Littauer fellow), Harvard U., 1973. Served to dep. insp. Police Dept., N.Y.C., 1956-73; police chief Kansas City, Mo., 1973-76, San Jose, Calif., 1976-91; rsch. fellow Hoover Instn., Stanford U., 1991—. Adj. instr. Northeastern U., 1972, John Jay Coll., 1973, Rockhurst Coll., 1975-76, San Jose State U., 1980; cons. U.S. Civil Rights Commn., 1978; lectr., appearances on nat. TV; apptd. nat. adv. bd. U.S. Bur. Justice Stats., 1980, U.S. Drug Control Policy Office, 1993; commentator Pub. Broadcasting Radio. Author: (non-fiction) Safe and Sane, 1984, (novel) The First Directive Crown, 1985, Fatal Command, 1987, The Blue Mirage, 1990, Code 211 Blue, 1996; contbr. articles to profl. publs. Bd. dirs. Drug Policy Found., Washington; active NCCJ. Served with U.S. Army, 1958-60. Named one of 200 Young Am. Leaders Time mag., 1975; recipient disting. alumni award John Jay Coll., 1979, Pres.'s award Western Soc. Criminology1979, Morrison Gitchoff award Western Soc. Criminology, 1992, H.B. Spear award Drug Policy Found., 1992; Kansas City police named Best in Country by Nat. Newspaper Enterprises, 1974, San Jose Police Dept. named Nat. Model U.S. Civil Rights Commn., 1980; named Law Enforcement Officer of Yr., Calif. Trial Lawyers Assn., 1991. Mem. Internat. Assn. Chiefs of Police, Calif. Police Chiefs Assn., Calif. Peace Officers Assn., Major Cities Police Chiefs Assn., Police Exec. Research Forum (dir.) Office: Hoover Instn Stanford CA 94305

MCNAMARA, MARGARET M. pediatrician; MD, U. Conn., 1990. Diplomate Am. Bd. Pediatrics. Resident in pediatrics U. Calif., San Francisco; chief of pediatrics U. Calif. San Francisco/Mount Zion Pediatric Practice, San Francisco. Office: UCSF Mount Zion Pediat Practice 2330 Post St Ste 320 San Francisco CA 94115-3466

MCNAMEE, STEPHEN M. federal judge; b. 1942; B.A., U. Cinn., 1964; M.A., J.D., U. Ariz., 1969. U.S. atty. Dist. of Ariz., Phoenix, 1985-90; chief judge U.S. Dist. Ct. Ariz., Phoenix, 1990—. Office: US Dist Judge Sandra Day O'Connor US Ct 401 W Washington St SPC 60 Phoenix AZ 85003-2158

MCNEAL, DALE WILLIAM, JR. biological sciences educator; b. Kansas City, Kans., Nov. 23, 1939; s. Dale William and Geraldine Estelle (Reed) McN.; m. Arlene Joyce Purvis, Feb. 26, 1966. B.A., Colo. Coll., 1962; M.S., SUNY Coll. Environ. Sci. and Forestry, Syracuse, 1964; Ph.D., Wash. State U., 1969. Asst. prof. dept. biol. scis. U. Pacific, Stockton, Calif., 1969-74, assoc. prof., 1974-79, prof., 1979—, chmn. dept., 1978-84. Contbr. articles to profl. jours. Served with U.S. Army, 1964-66. Mem. Am. Bot. Soc., Calif. Bot. Soc. (pres. 1987-88), Am. Soc. Plant Taxonomists, Internat. Soc. Plant Taxonomy, Calif. Acad. Scis., Sigma Xi. Republican. Episcopalian. Office: U Pacific Dept Biol Scis Stockton CA 95211-0001

MCNEALY, SCOTT G. computer company executive; b. 1954; BA, Harvard U., 1976; MBA, Stanford U., 1980. With Rockwell Internat. Corp., Troy, Mich., 1976-78, sales engr.; staff engr. FMC Corp., Chgo., 1980-81; dir. ops. Onyx Systems, San Jose, Calif., 1981-82; chmn. bd., pres., CEO, Sun Microsystems Inc., Palo Alto, 1982—, also bd. dirs., 1985. Office: Sun Microsystems Inc 901 San Antonio Rd Palo Alto CA 94303-4900

MCNEILL, DANIEL RICHARD, writer; b. San Francisco, June 1, 1947; s. Daniel Harry and Maureen Evangeline (Sherriff) McN.; m. Rosalind Deborah Gold, Dec. 20, 1984. AB, U. Calif., Berkeley, 1975; JD, Harvard U., 1982. Author: Fuzzy Logic, 1993 (L.A. Times Book prize in sci. and tech. 1993), The Face, 1998. Mem. Authors Guild. Avocations: photography, bodybuilding. Home and Office: 8110 Redlands St #306 Playa Del Rey CA 90293

MCNEILL, JOHN HUGH, pharmaceutical sciences educator; b. Chgo., July 5, 1938; s. John and Agnes Margaret (McLean) McN.; m. Sharon Keneffly, July 27, 1963; children: Sandra, Laurie. BS, U. Alta., Can., 1960, MS, 1962; PhD, U. Mich., 1967. Lectr. pharmacy Dalhousie U., 1962-63, U. Alta., 1963; research assoc. U. Mich., Ann Arbor, 1963-65, teaching fellow, 1965-66; asst. instr. Mich. State U., East Lansing, 1966-67, asst. prof., 1967-71; assoc. prof. U. B.C., 1971-72, assoc. prof., chmn. div. pharmacology and toxicology, 1972-75, dir. research and grad. studies Faculty Pharm. Scis., 1977-78; prof. Faculty Pharm. Scis., 1975—; asst. dean U. B.C., 1978-81, research prof. Med. Research Council, 1981-82, prof., assoc. dean research and grad. studies, 1982-84, dean Faculty Pharm. Scis., 1985-96. Contbr. over 400 tech. articles to profl. jours. Fellow Royal Soc. Can.; mem. Pharm. Soc. Can. (various coms. 1974-88, coun. 1977-83, v.p. 1979, pres. 1980-81), Am. Soc. for Pharm. and Therapeutics (J.J. Abel award com. 1981, Upjohn award com., 1978-80, chmn. mem. com. 1983-86), Western Pharm. Soc. (coun. 1977-81, pres. 1979-80, past pres. 1980-81), N.Y. Acad. Scis., Internat. Soc. for Heart Rsch. (coun. 1986-95), AAAS, B.C. Coll. Pharms. (coun. 1985-96), Internat. Union Pharmacologists (Can. rep. 1982-88), Am. Pharm. Assn. Office: Univ BC Fac Pharm Scis 2146 East Mall Vancouver BC Canada V6T IZ3 E-mail: jmcneill@interchange.ubc.ca

MCNEIL STAUDENMAIER, HEIDI LORETTA, lawyer; b. Preston, Iowa, Apr. 7, 1959; d. Archie Hugo and Heidi (Waltert) McN.; m. L. William Staudenmaier III; children: Kathleen Louise McNeil Staudenmaier, Jacob William Staudenmaier. BA in Journalism and Broadcasting with distinction, U. Iowa, 1981, JD with distinction, 1985. Bar: Ariz. 1985, U.S. Dist. Ct. Ariz. 1985, U.S. Ct. Appeals (9th cir.) 1985, U.S. Ct. Appeals (10th cir.) 1990. Sports journalist The Daily Iowan, Iowa City, 1977-81, Quad City Times, Davenport, Iowa, 1981-82; ptnr. Snell & Wilmer, Phoenix, 1985—. Judge pro tem, Maricopa County, Phoenix, 1992—, Ariz. Ct. Appeals, 1998—. Mem. ABA (mem. domestic violence commn. 1995-98, Ho. of Dels. 1995-98, 2001—, chair young lawyers career issues com. 1992-93, mem. affiliate assistance program com. 1992-93, dir. 1993-94, spl. projects coord. 1994-95, bus. law sect., mem. editl. bd. bus. Law Today), Internat. Assn. Gaming Attys., Ariz. Bar Assn. (Indian law sect. exec. coun. and chair, 1995-99, young lawyers exec. coun. 1991-94), Maricopa County Bar Assn. (bd. dirs. 1991—, young lawyers divsn. 1987-93, pres. 1991-92, 99-2000), Ariz. Women Lawyers, Phoenix Assn. Def. Counsel, Native Am. Bar Assocs., Phi Beta Kappa, Phi Eta Sigma. Lutheran. Avocations: running, golf, skiing, hiking, bicycling.

MCNIFF, PETER J. federal judge; b. 1940; Bankruptcy judge U.S. Bankruptcy Ct. Wyo., Cheyenne, 1994—. Office: 2120 Capitol Ave Rm 8024 Cheyenne WY 82001-3633

MCNULTY, JAMES F. export company executive; BS in Engring., U.S. Mil. Acad., 1964; MS in Nuc. Physics, Ohio State U., 1970; MS in Mgmt., MIT, 1985. Rsch. assoc. Lawrence Livermore Nat. Lab., 1972-74; asst. dir. Office Mil. Applications U.S. Dept. Energy, 1978-80; officer nuc. weapon requirements Ops. and Plans Office Dept. U.S. Army, 1980-82, sys. mgr. Pershing II Missle Sys., 1982-84, program mgr. ground based laser sys., 1985-88; dir. bus. devel. Parsons Corp., 1988-89, v.p., 1991-92, sr. v.p., mgr. sys. divsn., 1992-95, pres. infrastructure and tech. group, 1996, pres., CEO Calif., from 1996, now chmn., CEO. Office: Parsons Corp 100 W Walnut St Pasadena CA 91124-0001

MCNULTY, JOHN KENT, lawyer, educator; b. Buffalo, Oct. 13, 1934; s. Robert William and Margaret Ellen (Duthie) McN.; m. Linda Conner, Aug. 20, 1955 (div. Feb. 1977); children: Martha Jane, Jennifer, John K. Jr.; m. Babette B. Barton, Mar. 23, 1978 (div. May 1988). A.B. with high honors, Swarthmore Coll., 1956; LL.B., Yale U., 1959. Bar: Ohio 1961, U.S. Supreme Ct. 1964. Law clk. Justice Hugo L. Black, U.S. Supreme Ct., Washington, 1959-60; vis. prof. Sch. Law U. Tex., summer 1960; assoc. Jones, Day, Cockley & Reavis, Cleve., 1960-64; prof. law U. Calif., Berkeley, 1964-91, Roger J. Traynor prof. law, 1991—. Of counsel Baker and McKenzie, San Francisco, 1974-75; acad. visitor London Sch. Econs., 1985, Cambridge U., 1994, U. Edinburgh, 1994; vis. fellow Wolfson Coll., Cambridge, 1994, U. Innsbruck, 1996, Trinity Coll., Dublin, 1997; vis. prof. Yale U., U. Tex., U. Leiden, U. Tilburg, U. Tokyo, U. San Diego, others; lectr. univs. Cologne, Hamburg, Hitotsubashi, Kansei, Kyoto, London, Munich, Seoul, Tokyo, Tilburg, Amsterdam, Rotterdam, Vienna Econ., Tohoku, Tübingen, others; mem. adv. bd. Tax Mgmt. Author: Federal Income Taxation of Individuals, 6th edit., 1999, Federal Estate and Gift Taxation, 5th edit., 1994, Federal Income Taxation of S Corporations, 1992; (with Westin & Beck) Federal Income Taxation of Business Enterprises, 1995, 2d edit., 1999; mem. bd. overseers Berkeley Jour. Internat. Law. Guggenheim fellow, 1977 Mem. ABA, Am. Law Inst. (life), Internat. Fiscal Assn. (coun. U.S. br.), Order of Coif, Phi Beta Kappa. Home: 1176 Grizzly Peak Blvd Berkeley CA 94708-1741 Office: U Calif Sch Law 335 Boalt Hl Berkeley CA 94720-7200 E-mail: mcnultyj@law.berkeley.edu

MCNUTT, WALTER L. state legislator; b. Worland, Wyo., Nov. 8, 1940; m. Karen McNutt. BS, Coll. of Great Falls, 1969. Agrl. equipment dealer; small bus. owner; mem. Mont. Senate, Dist. 50, Helena, 1996—; chair conf. com., chair select com. on constnl. amendments; vice chair agr., livestock and irrigation com.; mem. com. on coms., jud. com., labor/employment rels. com. Bd. dirs. First United Bank, Sidney, Mont. Mem. Airport Authority, Richland County, Mont.; mem. Solid Waste Dist., Richland County; mem. Econ. Devel. Richland County. Republican. Home: 110 12th Ave SW Sidney MT 59270-3614 E-mail: walt@lyrea.com

MCPHERSON, BRUCE, state legislator; b. Santa Cruz; m. Mary McPherson; children: Tori, Hunter. Mem. Calif. State Assembly, 1993-96, Calif. State Senate, 1996—, vice-chair edn. com., mem. appropriations com., environ. quality com., pub. safety com., revenue and taxation com. Mem. joint coms. on arts, headwaters forest and fisheries/aquaculture. Active Santa Cruz City Sch. Dist.; active literacy program Santa Cruz County. Recipeint Friend of Higher Edn. award Calif. State U. Alumni Coun., 1995, Simon Wiesenthal Mus. of Tolerance award, 1998; named Legislator of Yr., U. Calif. Alumni Assn., 1997, Pub. Ofcl. of Yr., Monterey Bay Nat. Marine Sanctuary Coun., 1997, 1998 Friend of C.C., Assn. Calif. C.C. Adminstrs., 1998. Mem. Calif. Coastal Conservancy, Santa Cruz Rotary Club (pres.). Republican. Office: State Capitol Rm 3076 Sacramento CA 95814 also: 701 Ocean St Rm 318A Santa Cruz CA 95060-4027 also: 7 John St Ste A Salinas CA 93901-3303

MCPHERSON, GARY LEE, lawyer, state representative; b. Auburn, Wash., Dec. 4, 1962; s. Percy Ivan and Vicki Mae (Voyles) McP.; children: Christina, Elizabeth, Ashley. BS in Bus. Adminstrn., Union Coll., 1985; JD, U. Nebr., 1988. Bar: Colo. 1989, Nebr. 1989, U.S. Dist. Ct. Colo. 1989, U.S. Ct. Appeals (10th cir.) 1989. Legal/legis. aide Knudsen, Berkheimer & Richardson, Lincoln, Nebr., 1981-85; law clk. Crosby, Guenzel & Davis, Lincoln, 1986; law clk. ethics com. Nebr. State Bar Assn., Lincoln, 1987; assoc. Hall & Evans, Denver, 1987-89, Elrod, Katz, Preeo & Look, P.C., Denver, 1989-90, Fortune & Lawritson, P.C., Denver, 1990-93; ptnr. McPherson & Hull, P.C., Aurora, Colo., 1993-98, Kissinger & Fellman, P.C., Denver, 1998—; state rep. State of Colo., Denver, 1994—. Author: Handbook on Professional Malpractice, 1987, rev. edit., 1988; contbr. articles to profl. jours. Bd. dirs. Arapahoe Park and Recreation Bd., Aurora 1991-95; dist. capt. Arapahoe County Rep. Dist. 8, Aurora, 1992-95; vice chmn. Ho. Dist. 40, Aurora, 1993-95, state rep.; chmn. Senate Dist. 28, Aurora, 1993-95. Recipient Internat. Acad. Trial Lawyers award, 1987, 88, Aurora Pub. Schs. Supts. award, 1992. Mem. ABA (bd. dirs., litigations com. 1992-93, chmn. young lawyers divsn. prelaw counseling com. 1992-94), Colo. Bar Assn. (sec., treas. young lawyers divsn. 1991-93, chair-elect 1993-94, chmn. 1994-95), Arapahoe County Bar Assn., Aurora Rep. Forum, Arapahoe County Rep. Mens Club. Avocations: aviation, scuba, politics, backpacking, snow skiing. Office: 3773 Cherry Creek North Dr Denver CO 80209-3804

MC PHERSON, ROLF KENNEDY, clergyman, religious organization administrator; b. Providence, Mar. 23, 1913; s. Harold S. and Aimee (Semple) McP.; m. Lorna De Smith, July 21, 1931 (dec.); children—Marlene (dec.), Kay; m. Evangeline Carmichael, Jan. 31, 1997. Grad., So. Cal. Radio Inst., 1933; D.D. (hon.), L.I.F.E. Bible Coll., 1944; LLD (hon.), L.I.F.E. Bible Coll., Los Angeles, 1988. Ordained to ministry Internat. Ch. Foursquare Gospel, 1940. Pres. Internat. Ch. Foursquare Gospel, L.A., 1944-88, dir., 1944-92; pres. emeritus, 1988—; pres., dir. L.I.F.E. Bible Coll., Inc., L.A., 1944-88. Mem. Echo Park Evangelistic Assn. (pres. 1944—). Office: Internat Ch Foursquare Gospel 1910 W Sunset Blvd Ste 200 Los Angeles CA 90026-3295 E-mail: drrolfe@pacbell.net

MCQUAID, ROBERT A., JR. federal judge; Apptd. magistrate judge U.S. Dist. Ct. Nev., 1996. Office: US Courthouse 400 S Virginia St Rm 405 Reno NV 89501 2193 Fax: 775 686 5865

MCQUEEN, JUSTICE ELLIS (L. Q. JONES), actor, director; b. Beaumont, Tex., Aug. 19, 1927; s. Justice Ellis and Pat (Stephens) McQ.; m. Sue Helen Lewis, Oct. 10, 1950 (dec.); children: Marlin Randolph, Marilyn Helen, Steven Lewis. Student, Lamar Jr. Coll., 1944, Lon Morris Coll., 1949, U. Tex., 1950-51. Actor, writer, dir.: motion picture films including A Boy and His Dog, 1975 (recipient Hugo award, Sci. Fiction achievement award for dramatic presentation); actor White Line Fever, 1975, Mother, Jugs & Speed, 1976, Winterhawk, 1976, Fast Charlie, The Moonbeam Rider, 1979, Timerider: The Adventures of Lyle Swann, 1982, The Beast Within, 1982, Sacred Ground, 1983, Lone Wolf McQuade, 1983, Bulletproof, 1988, River of Death, 1989, The Legend of Grizzly Adams, 1990, Lightning Jack, 1994, The Friends of Harry, 1995, Casino, 1995, Ben Johnson: Third Cowboy on the Right, 1996, The Edge, 1997, The Patriot, 1998, The Mask of Zorro, 1998, numerous others; tv movies include The Sacketts, 1979, Tornado!, 1996, In Cold Blood, 1996, The Jack Bull, 1999, numerous others; appeared in tv series including Gunsmoke, 1955, Alias Smith and Jones, 1971, Cannon, 1971, Cade's County, 1971, Kung Fu, 1972, Matt Helm, 1975, Charlie's Angels, 1976, Columbo: The Conspirators, 1978, The Dukes of Hazzard, 1979, The Fall Guy, 1981, The Yellow Rose, 1983, The A-Team, 1983, Walker, Texas Ranger, 1993, numerous others; producer The Big Thickett, Come In, Children, The Witchmaker; author, prodr.: The Brotherhood of Satan, 1971; dir., prodr. The Devil's Bedroom, 1964, (tv series) The Incredible Hulk, 1978. Served with USNR, 1945-46. Nominee 4 Emmy awards. Mem. Screen Actors Guild. Republican. Methodist. Home and Office: 2144 1/2 N Cahuenga Blvd Los Angeles CA 90068-2708

MCQUERN, MARCIA ALICE, newspaper publishing executive; b. Riverside, Calif., Sept. 3, 1942; d. Arthur Carlyle and Dorothy Louise (Krupke) Knopf; m. Lynn Morris McQuern, June 7, 1969. BA in Polit. Sci., U. Calif., Santa Barbara, 1964; MS in Journalism, Northwestern U., 1966. Reporter The Press-Enterprise, Riverside, 1966-72, city editor, 1972-74, capitol corrs., 1975-78, dep. mng. editor news, 1984-85, mng. editor news, 1985-87, exec. editor, 1988-94, pres., 1992—; editor, publisher, 1994—; asst. metro editor The Sacramento Bee, 1974-75; editor state and polit. news The San Diego Union, 1978-79, city editor, 1979-84. Juror Pulitzer Prize in Journalism, 1982, 83, 92, 93. Bd. advisors U. Calif.-Berkeley Grad. Sch. Journalism, 1991-96, U. Calif.-Riverside Grad. Sch. Mgmt., 1994-2000; mem. Riverside Cmty. Coll. Found., 1993—, pres., 1996-98; trustee U. Calif. Riverside Found., 1996—. Recipient Athena award YWCA, 1994; named Newspaper Exec. of Yr., Calif. Press Assn., 2000. Mem. Am. Soc. Newspaper Editors (bd. dirs. 1992-98), Calif. Soc. Newspaper Editors (bd. 1988-95), Calif. Newspaper Pubs. Assn. (bd. dirs. 1992—), Calif. Press Assn. (bd. dirs. 1996-99), Soc. Profl. Journalists, U. Calif.-Santa Barbara Alumni Assn. (bd. dirs. 1983-89). Home: 5717 Bedford Dr Riverside CA 92506-3404 Office: Press-Enterprise Co 3512 14th St Riverside CA 92501-3878

MCRAE, HAMILTON EUGENE, III, lawyer; b. Midland, Tex., Oct. 29, 1937; s. Hamilton Eugene and Adrian (Hagaman) McR.; m. Betty Hawkins, Aug. 27, 1960; children: Elizabeth Ann, Stephanie Adrian, Scott Hawkins BSEE, U. Ariz., 1961; student, USAF Electronics Sch., 1961-62; postgrad., U. Redlands, Calif., 1962-63; JD with honors and distinction, U. Ariz., 1967; LHD (hon.), Sterling Coll., 1992; vis. fellow, Darwin Coll. and Martin Ctr., Cambridge (Eng.) U., 1996-97. Bar: Ariz. 1967, U.S. Supreme Ct. 1979; cert. real estate specialist, Ariz. Elec. engr. Salt River Project, Phoenix, 1961; assoc. Jennings, Strouss & Salmon, Phoenix, 1967-71, ptnr., 1971-85, chmn. real estate dept., 1980-85, mem. policy com., 1982-85, mem. fin. com., 1981-85, chmn. bus. devel. com., 1982-85; ptnr. and co-founder Stuckey & McRae, Phoenix, 1985—; co-founder, chmn. bd. Republic Cos., Phoenix, 1985—. Magistrate Paradise Valley, Ariz., 1983-85; juvenile referee Superior Ct., 1983-85; pres., dir. Phoenix Realty & Trust Co., 1970—; officer Indsl. Devel. Corp. Maricopa County, 1972-86; instr. and lectr. in real estate; officer, bd. dirs. other corps.; adj. prof. Frank Lloyd Wright Sch. Architecture, Scottsdale, Ariz., 1989—; instr. Ariz. State U. Coll. Architecture and Environ. Design; lead instr. ten-state-bar seminar on Advanced Real Estate Transactions, 1992; evaluation com. for cert. real estate specialist Ariz. Bar, 1994-96; mem. real estate adv. commn. Ariz. Bar, 1996—. Exec. prodr. film documentary on relief and devel. in Africa, 1990; contbr. articles to profl. jours. Elder Valley Presbyn. Ch., Scottsdale, Ariz., 1973-75, 82-85, 96-98, chair evangelism com. 1973-74, corp. pres., 1974-75, 84-85, trustee, 1973-75, 82-85, chmn. exec. com., 1984, mem. mission com. 1993—, chmn. 1998; trustee Upward Found., Phoenix, 1977-80, trustee, Valley Presbyn. Found., 1982-83, Ariz. Acad., 1971—; trustee, mem. exec. com. Phi Gamma Delta Ednl. Found., Washington, 1974-84; trustee Phi Gamma Delta Internat., 1984-86; bd. dirs. Archon, 1986-87; founder, Hall of Fame (Ariz.), 99, trustee, pres. McRae Found., 1980—; founder Hall of Fame, Ariz., 1999; bd. dirs. Food for Hungry Inc. (Internat. Relief), 1985-95, exec. com., 1986-95, chmn. bd. dirs., 1987-92; chmn. bd. dirs. Food for Hungry Internat., 1993-95, pres. adv. coun., 1995—, mem. building com., 1999—; trustee, mem. exec. com. Ariz. Mus. Sci. and Tech., 1984—, 1st v.p., 1985-86, pres., 1986-88, chmn. bd. dirs., 1988-90, exec. com. 1984-90, exhibits com. 1990—, strategic planning com., 1999—, svc. recognition 1999; Lambda Alpha Internat. Hon. Land Econs. Soc, 1988-98; sec.-treas. Ariz. State U. Coun. for Design Excellence, 1989-90, bd. dirs. 1988-99, pres. 1990-91, trustee 1999—; mem. Crisis Nursery Office of the Chair, 1988-89, Maricopa Community Colls. Found., 1988—, sec. 1990-91, 2d v.p. 1993-94, 1st v.p. and pres. elect 1994-95, pres. 1995-96, mem. Elsner scholarship com., 1999—, web site com., 1999, capital campaign cabinet, 1995-96, 98-99, mem. of chair, 1998-99, mem. nominating com., 1997—, deferred gifts com., 1999—, strategic planning com., 2000—, Phoenix Cmty. Alliance, 1988-90, Interchurch Ctr. Corp., 1987-90, Western Art Assocs., bd. dirs., 1989-91, Phoenix Com. on Fgn. Rels., 1988-99, U. Ariz. Pres.'s Club, 1984—, chmn., 1991-92; bd. dirs. Econ. Club of Phoenix, 1987— , sec.-treas., 1991-92, v.p., 1992-93, pres. 1993-94; bd. dirs. Ctrl. Ariz. Shelter Svcs., 1995—, bd. dir., Ariz. Community Found., 1996—, invest. com., 1996—, chair, 2000, exec. com. 1997—, treas. 1997—, chair nominating com. 1997-98, vice chair bd. dirs., 1999—, chair devel. com., 1999—, advancement com., 1999—, chair, 1999—, fin. and adminstrn. com. 1999—; founding mem. Alliance linking poverty and homelessness, 1996-98, bd. dirs., 1996-98, mem. exec. com., 1996-98, co-chair long range planning com., 1997-98; mem. adv. bd. Help Wanted USA, 1990-92; vol. fund raiser YMCA, Salvation Army, others; bd. dirs. Frank Lloyd Wright Found., 1992—, chair fin. com. 1997-98, chmn. bd. dirs., 1998—; mem. Taliesin Coun., 1985—; bd. dirs. Taliesin Arch., 1992-98, Taliesin Conservation Com. (Wis.), 1992—; founding mem. Frank Lloyd Wright Soc., 1993—; mem. fin. com. Kyl for Congress, 1985-92, bd. dir. campaign bd. Kyl for U.S. Senate, 1993-94, 99—; Senator Kyl Council, 1995—; campaign com. Symington for Gov. '90, 1989-90, mem. gubernatorial adv. bd., 1990-91; mem. Gov.'s Selection Com. for State Revenue Dir., 1993; mem. bond com. City of Phoenix, 1987-88; mem. Ariz. State U. Coun. of 100, 1985-89, investment com., 1985-89; bd. govs. Twelve Who Care Hon Kachina, 1991; mem. adv. coun. Maricopa County Sports Authority, 1989-93; mem. Ariz. Coalition for Tomorrow, 1990-92; founding mem., bd. dirs. Waste Not Inc., 1990-94, pres., 1990-92, chmn., 1992-94, adv. bd. 1996—; bd. dirs. Garden Homes at Teton Pines Home Owners Assn., 1996—; selected as bearer for the Olympic Torch Relay Team, 1996; adv. bd. KAET TV PBS (Channel 8). 1st lt. USAF, 1961-64. Recipient various mil. awards; 1st place award Ariz. Bar exam, 1967; named to Ariz. Hall of Fame, 1999. Mem. ABA, AIEE, AIME, Ariz. Bar Assn., Maricopa County Bar Assn., U. Ariz. Alumni Assn., Nat. Soc. Fund Raising Execs.

(Philanthropy award Ariz. chpt. 1991, 97), Clan McRae Soc. N.Am. Phoenix Exec. Club, Internat. Platform Assn., Am. Friends of the U. Cambridge (Eng.), Jackson Hole Racquet Club, Teton Pines Country Club, Tau Beta Pi. Republican. Address: Republic Cos 11811 N Tatum Blvd Ste 1005 Phoenix AZ 85028-1617 E-mail: repcos@aol.com

MCREYNOLDS, NEIL LAWRENCE, management consultant; b. Seattle, July 27, 1934; s. Dorr E. and Margaret (Gillies) McR.; m. Nancy Joyce Drew, June 21, 1957; children: Christopher, Bonnie. BA in Journalism, U. Wash., 1956, postgrad. bus. and fin., 1973-76. Assoc. editor Bellevue (Wash.) Am., 1956-60, editor, 1960-67; press sec. to Gov. Dan Evans State of Wash., Olympia, 1967-73; N.W. regional mgr. for pub. rels. and pub. affairs ITT Corp., Seattle, 1973-80; v.p. corp. rels. Puget Sound Power & Light, Bellevue, 1980-87, sr. v.p., 1987-95; prin. McReynolds & Assocs., Seattle, 1995-97; v.p. external affairs Kaiser/Group Health, Seattle, 1997-99; pres. Donworth-McReynolds Co., Seattle, 1999—. Bd. dirs. HomeStreet Bank, Seattle, Wash. Dental Svcs., Seattle, Adinfonitum, Inc., Seattle, Eastern Wash. U., Cheney; chmn. exec. adv. com. Edison Electric Inst., 1984-85; mem. rsch. adv. coun. Electric Power Rsch. Inst., 1989-90. Bd. dirs. Seattle Symphony, 1980-89, Ind. Colls. of Wash., 1984-95, Mus. of History and Industry, 1995—, Corp. Coun. for Arts, 1985-94, Wash. Nat. Parks Fund, 1995-2000, Seattle Repertory Theatre, 1996—; chmn. bd. dirs. Fred Hutchinson Cancer Rsch. Ctr., 1993-95, Leadership Tomorrow, Seattle, 1987, Seattle-King County Econ. Devel. Coun., 1994; pres. Seattle Ctr. Found., 1979-80; chair U. Wash. Bus. and Econ. Devel. Program, 1996-98; nat. pres. Electric Info. Coun., 1988; chmn. bd. trustees Bellevue C.C., 1976-77; state chmn. Nature Conservancy, 1988-90; mem. Wash. State Commn. on Trial Cts., 1990; chmn. King County 2000, 1988-90; mem. campaign cabinet United Way of King County, 1998-2001. Named Citizen of Yr., Bellevue, One of Wash. State's Three Outstanding Young Men; recipient Pres. medal Pacific Luth. U. Mem. Pub. Rels. Soc. Am. (accredited), N.W. Elec. Light and Power Assn. (pres. 1982-83), Greater Seattle C. of C. (officer 1979-81), Soc. Profl. Journalists, Rainier Club (trustee 1995-01, v.p. 1997-98, pres. 1999-2000), Overlake Golf and Country Club (trustee 1993-96), Rotary (pres. Downtown Seattle Club 1991-92). Republican. Episcopalian. Avocations: golf, hiking, skiing, photography, mountain climbing. Home: 14315 SE 45th St Bellevue WA 98006 Office: McReynolds Assocs Inc 2033 Sixth Ave Ste 1001 Seattle WA 98121 E-mail: nmcreyolds@qwest.net

MC SHEFFREY, GERALD RAINEY, architect, educator, city planner; b. Belfast, Ireland, Aug. 13, 1931; s. Hugh and Jane (Piggot) McS.; m. Norma Isabella Lowry, June 4, 1956; children: Laurence, Niall, Aidan. Student, Belfast Coll. Tech., 1950-56; Diploma in Architecture, Univ. Coll., U. London, 1959; Diploma in Civic Design, U. Edinburgh, Scotland, 1963. Archtl. asst. various archtl. firms, Belfast, 1950-57; design architect Munce and Kennedy, Belfast, 1957-62; architect/planner Liverpool (Eng.) City Planning Dept. and Livingston New Town, 1963-65; asso. partner James Munce Partnership, Belfast, 1965-68; prin. planning officer (design) Belfast City Planning Dept., 1968-71; prof. architecture U. Kans., 1971-73, dir. archtl. studies, 1976-79; Belfast regional architect, dir. devel. No. Ireland Housing Exec., 1973-76; prof. architecture, dean Coll. Architecture, Planning and Design, Ill. Inst. Tech., 1979-82; dean Coll. Architecture and Environ. Design Ariz. State U., Tempe, 1982-86, prof. architecture, 1988-98; v.p. Ariz. State U., West Campus, Phoenix, 1985-88; prof. and dean emeritus, 1998—. Vis. fellow Princeton (N.J.) U., 1989; external examiner in urban design and landscape studies U. Edinburgh, 1973-76 Author: (with James Munce Partnership) Londonderry Area Plan, 1968, Planning Derry: Planning and Politics in Northern Ireland, 2000. Fulbright award, 1965 Fellow Royal Inst. Brit. Architects; mem. AIA. Episcopalian. Office: Ariz State U Coll Architecture & Environ Design Tempe AZ 85287-1605

MCSORLEY, CISCO, state legislator, lawyer; b. Albuquerque, July 8, 1950; s. Frank N. and Virginia E. (Norton) McS., m. Joanne Kuestner McSorley. BA, U. N.Mex., 1974, JD, 1979; postdoctoral sch. govt., Harvard U., 1986. Bar: N.Mex. 1980, U.S. Dist. Ct. N.Mex. 1980. Tchr. Academia Cotopaxi, Quito, Ecuador, S. Am., 1973-76; sole practice Albuquerque, 1980—; mem. N.Mex. Ho. of Reps., 1984-96, N.Mex. Senate, Dist. 16, Sante Fe, 1996—. Mem. ABA, N. Mex. Bar. Assn., N. Mex. Trial Lawyers Assn., Assn. Trial Lawyers Am. Democrat. Mem. Soc. of Friends.

MCSWEENEY, FRANCES KAYE, psychology educator; b. Rochester, N.Y., Feb. 6, 1948; d. Edward William and Elsie Winifred (Kingston) McS. BA, Smith Coll., 1969; MA, Harvard U., 1972, PhD, 1974. Lectr. McMaster U., Hamilton, Ont., Can., 1973-74; asst. prof. Wash. State U., Pullman, 1974-79, assoc. prof., 1979-83, prof. psychology, 1983—, chmn. dept. psychology, 1986-94. Cons. in field. Contbr. articles to profl. jours. Woodrow Wilson fellow, Sloan Fellow, 1968-69; NSF fellow, 1970-72; NIMH fellow, 1973. Fellow APA, Am. Psychol. Soc.; mem. Psychonomic Soc., Assn. Behavior Analysis, Phi Beta Kappa, Sigma Xi, Phi Kappa Phi. Home: 860 SW Alcora Dr Pullman WA 99163-2053 Office: Wash State U Dept Psychology Pullman WA 99164-4820

MCVANEY, C. EDWARD, computer softwarm executive; b. 1940; Ptnr. Alexander, Grant & Co.; co-founder, chmn. bd. dirs., CEO J.D. Edwards & Co., 1977—. Office: JD Edwards & Co One Technology Way Denver CO 80257

MCVEIGH-PETTIGREW, SHARON CHRISTINE, communications consultant; b. San Francisco, Feb. 6, 1949; d. Martin Allen and Frances (Roddy) McVeigh; m. John Wallace Pettigrew, Mar. 27, 1971; children: Benjamin Thomas, Margaret Mary. B.A. with honors, U. Calif.-Berkeley, 1971; diploma of edn. Monash U., Australia, 1975; M.B.A., Golden Gate U., 1985. Tchr., adminstr. Victorian Edn. Dept., Victoria, Australia, 1972-79; supr. Network Control Ctr., GTE Sprint Communications, Burlingame, Calif., 1979-81, mgr. customer assistance, 1981-84, mgr. state legis. ops., 1984-85, dir. revenue programs, 1986-87; communications cons. Flores, Pettigrew & Co., San Mateo, Calif., 1987-89; mgr. telemarketing Apple Computer, Inc., Cupertino, Calif., 1989-94; prin. The Call Ctr. Group, San Mateo, Calif., 1995—; telecomm. cons. PPG Svcs., 1994—; telecomm. spkr. Dept. Consumer Affairs, Sacramento, 1984. Panelist Wash. Gov.'s Citizens Council, 1984; founding mem. Maroondah Women's Shelter, Victoria, 1978; organizer nat. conf. Bus. Women and the Polit. Process, New Orleans, 1986; mem. sch. bd. Boronia Tech. Sch., Victoria, 1979. Recipient Tchr. Spl. Responsibilities award Victoria Edn. Dept., 1979. Mem. Women in Telecommunications (panel moderator San Francisco 1984), Am. Mgmt. Assn., Peninsula Profl. Women's Network, Am. Telemktg. Assn. (bd. dirs. 1992), Women's Econ. Action League. Democrat. Roman Catholic.

MCVEY, LARRY, household cleaner manufacturing executive; V.p. fin. Orange Glo Internat., Englewood, Calif. Office: Orange Glo Internat 8765 E Orchard Rd #703 Englewood CO 80111-5009

MCWILLIAMS, ROBERT HUGH, federal judge; b. Salina, Kans., Apr. 27, 1916; s. Robert Hugh and Laura (Nicholson) McW.; m. Catherine Ann Cooper, Nov. 4, 1942 (dec.); 1 son, Edward Cooper; m. Joan Harcourt, Mar. 8, 1986. A.B., U. Denver, 1938, LL.B., 1941. Bar: Colo. bar 1941. Colo. dist. judge, Denver, 1952-60; justice Colo. Supreme Ct., 1961-68, chief justice, 1969-70; judge U.S. Ct. Appeals (10th cir.), Denver, 1970—, now sr. judge. Served with AUS, World War II. Mem. Phi Beta Kappa, Omicron Delta Kappa, Phi Delta Phi, Kappa Sigma. Republican. Episcopalian. Home: 137 Jersey St Denver CO 80220-5918 Office: Byron White US Courthouse 1823 Stout St Rm 216 Denver CO 80257-1823

MCWRIGHT, MICHAEL J. historic site administrator; b. Mandan, N.D., July 5, 1950; Mem. pk. svc. staff Colo. region, 1974-75; facility mgr. Grant-Kohrs Ranch Nat. Hist. Site, Deerlodge, Mont., 1975—. Office: Grant Kohrs Ranch Nat Hist Site PO Box 790 Deer Lodge MT 59722-0790

MEAD, CARVER ANDRESS, computer science educator; b. Bakersfield, Calif., May 1, 1934; B.S., Calif. Inst. Tech., 1956, M.S., 1957, Ph.D., 1960; hon. doctorate, U. of Lund, 1987, U. So. Calif., 1991. Prof. Calif. Inst. Tech., Pasadena, 1957—, Gordon and Betty Moore prof. engring. and applied sci., 1980-99, Gordon and Betty Moore prof. engring./applied sci. emeritus, 1999—. Author: Introduction to VLSI Systems, 1979 (Electronic Achievements award 1981, Harold Pender award 1984, John Price Wetherill award 1985), Analog VLSI and Neural Systems, 1989, Collective Electrodynamics, 2000. Recipient T.D. Callinan award Electrochem. Soc., 1971, Centennial medal IEEE, 1984, Harry Goode Meml. award Am. Fedn. Info. Processing Socs., Inc., 1985, award for Outstanding Rsch., INNS, 1992, Robert Dexter Conrad award USN, 1994, Phil Kaufman awrd EDAC, 1995, Allen Newell award ACM, 1997, Lemelson-MIT award, 1999. Fellow IEEE (John von Neumann medal 1996), Am. Phys. Soc., Franklin Inst. (life), Am. Acad. Arts and Scis.; mem. NAE, NAS, Royal Swedish Acad. Engring. Sci. (fgn.), Sigma Xi. Office: Calif Inst Tech Dept Engring 1200 E California Blvd Pasadena CA 91125-0001

MEAD, TRAY C. museum director; b. Mesa, Ariz., Apr. 1, 1950; s. Norman Wesley and Peggy Lee (Barrows) M.; Barbara Celaya, Feb. 9, 1981; children: Michael Adam, Kristiana Nicole. BA in Edn., Ariz. State U., 1973. Cert. tchr., Ariz. Publisher Ariz. Northland Mag., Flagstaff, 1973-77; mus. dir. Mesa Southwest Mus., 1977—. Founding dir. Ariz. Fed. Credit Union, Phoenix, 1980-85. Author: Mesa, Beneath the Superstitions, 1988, Sirrine House Story, 1992; editor: Mesa Grande, 1979, Capturing the Canyon, 1987; field editor Ariz. White Mountain Mag., 1965—; contbg. editor Tonto Trails Mag., 1970—. Founding dir. Mesa Conv. and Tourism Bureau, 1989—; founding chmn. S.W. Svc. Corp., Phoenix, 1981-85; bd. dirs., founding pres. Arts in Mesa, 1980—. Recipient Excellence award Centennial Com., 1978, Golden Quill award Caligraphic Soc. Ariz., 1987, Native Am. Heritage award U.S.M.C. Netherlands, 1991; named Hon. Medicine Man, Ft. Apache Tribe, 1973, Hon. Chmn. Mesa Parade, Mayor City of Mesa, 1980. Mem. Nat. Trust Hist. Preservation, Am. Assn. State and Local Histories, Am. Assn. Mus., Mus. Assn. Ariz. (founding mem., v.p. 1982—), Ctrl. Ariz. Mus. Assn. (founding pres. 1978—), Mesa C. of C. (com. chmn. 1979-89). Avocations: sculpting, painting, hiking, reading. Home: 370 E Pinon Way Gilbert AZ 85234-4573 Office: Mesa Southwest Mus 53 North MacDonald Dr Mesa AZ 85201-7325

MEADOWS, JUDITH ADAMS, law librarian, educator; b. Spartanburg, S.C., June 5, 1945; d. Thomas Taylor and Virginia (Dayton) Adams; m. Bruce R. Meadows; children: Beth Ann Blackwood, Ted Adams Meadows. BA, Am. U., 1967; MLS, U. Md., 1979. Law libr. Aspen Sys. Corp., Gaithersburg, Md., 1979-81; dir. Fairfax (Va.) Law Libr., 1981-84, State Law Libr., Helena, Mont., 1984—. Vis. prof. U. Wash., Seattle, 1994; adj. prof. U. Great Falls, Mont., 1989-96; presiding ofcl. Gov.'s Conf. on Libr. Info. Svc., Helena, Mont., 1991. Author: (book chpts.) From Yellow Pads to Computers, 1991, Law Librarianship, 1994; contbr. articles to profl. jours. Bd. dirs. Helena Presents, 1986-92, Holter Mus. Art, 1995—. Recipient Disting. Svc. award State Bar of Mont., 1991. Mem. Am. Assn. Law Librs. (treas. 1992-95, v.p., v.p. 1996—, pres. 1997-98, past pres. 1998—), N.W. Consortium of Law Librs. (pres.), Mont. Libr. Assn. (sec. 1986-88). Avocations: gourmet cooking, cross-country skiing, reading, gardening. Office: State Law Libr PO Box 203004 Helena MT 59620-3004 E-mail: jmeadows@state.mt.us

MEALS, PAMELA F. publishing executive; b. Ill. 1 child, Laura. Student, We. Oreg. State Coll. With advtsg. The Oreg. Statesman and Capital Jour., Salem; advtsg. mgr. The Idaho Statesman, Boise, 1979, pres., publ., 1994-99; publ. Coffeyville (Kans.) Jour., 1979-82, The Palladium-Item, Richmond, Ind., 1982-85, The Olympian, Olympia, Wash., 1985-94, Bellingham Herald, Bellingham, 1999—. Bd. dirs. Boise Pub. Schs. Edn. Found., Idaho Shakespeare Festival, Albertson Coll. Annual Fund, FUNDSY, William Allen White Found. Mem. Boise Area C. of C. (bd. dirs.), Rotary Club, Idaho Bus. Coun., Pacific N.W. Newspaper Assn. (bd. dirs.), Newspaper Assn. Am. Office: The Bellingham Herald 1155 N State St Ste 1 Bellingham WA 98225-5086

MEANS, JAMES ANDREW, engineer; b. Heavener, Okla., Oct. 11, 1937; s. Edward Andrew and Lorena (Nobles) M.; Therese Louise Zimmermann, Feb. 21, 1959; children: James A. Jr., William R., Charles E., Vicky M. Locken. BSEE, U. Ariz., 1962, MSEE, 1966; PhD, U. Calif., Santa Barbara, 1972; MS in Computer Sci., Chapman U., Orange, Calif., 1988. Engr. Pacific Missile Test Ctr., Pt Mugu, Calif., 1962-72, engr. mgr., 1972-79; tech. dir. Space and Missile Test Orgn., Vandenberg AFB, Calif., 1979-89; sr. tech. advisor SRI Internat., Menlo Park, 1990—. Cons. Agri-Craft, Camarillo, Calif., 1968-70, Astro-Geo-Marine, Ventura, Calif., 1972-74. Patentee in field. Mem. Internat. Found. for Telemetering (pres. 1989-95), Internat. Test and Evaluation Assn. (Allen R. Mattews Award, 1991). Democrat. Baptist. Avocations: water skiing, fishing, hunting, old cars. Home and Office: 284 St Andrews Way Lompoc CA 93436-1355 E-mail: jim.means@sri.com

MEAUX, ALAN DOUGLAS, facilities technician, sculptor; b. Joliet, Ill., Sept. 10, 1951; s. Berry Lee and Luella Ann (Ferguson) M.; m. Letta Sue Nygaard, Sept. 15, 1984; children: Ashley Nicole, Lacey Marie. Student, Joliet Jr. Coll., 1969-71, Bradley U., 1971-72, U.S. Dept. Agr. Grad. Sch., 1972, Skagit Valley Coll., 1983-85. Photographer J.J.C. Blazer, Joliet Herald News, Joliet, 1969-71; auto mechanic Pohanka Olds and Fiat, Hillcrest Heights, Md., 1972-74, Hoffman Olds and Rolls Royce, Hartford, Conn., 1974-75; carpenter Klappenbach Constrn. Co., Moscow, 1975-79; property mgr. Olympic Builders, Oak Harbor, Wash., 1979-86; maintenance technician Troubleshooters Inc., Oak Harbor, 1986-87; facilities technician Island County Govt., Coupeville, Wash., 1987—. Chmn. safety com. Island County Govt., 1997, 98, 99, 2000; bronze sculptor Ronin Art Prodns., Oak Harbor, 1979—; appraiser class A Mid-Am. Appraisers Assn., Springfield, Mo., 1986—; bd. dirs. North West Token Kai, U. Wash., Seattle, 1989—, lectr., 1985; contbr. Nanka Token Kai, L.A., 1985—. Author: Japanese Samurai Weapons, 1989; prin. works exhibited at Mini Guild Children's Orthopedic Show, Ballard, Wash., 1986, Worldfest/Ethnic Heritage Coun., Seattle, 1988, 89, 90, Stanwood (Wash.) Invitational Art Show, 1988. Asst. coach Whidbey Islanders Soccer League, 1997-99; safety com. chmn. Island County Govt., 1998-2000. Mem. NRA (life), Law Enforcement Alliance Am. (life), Japanese Sword Soc. U.S. (life), N.W. Token Kai (charter, bd. dirs. 1989-91), Western Mus. Conf., Wash. Mus. Assn., Ethnic Heritage Coun., Nanka Token Kai, Japan Soc., Wash. Arms Collectors Assn., North Whidbey Sportmen's Assn. (chmn. range com., trustee), Leisure Acres Water Assn. (pres. 1998-2000), Internat. Defensive Pistol Assn., Ctrl. Whidbey Sportmen's Club, Whidbey Islanders Futbol Club (asst. coach for girls under 12, 1997-99). Avocations: hunting, fishing, woodworking, reading, collecting Japanese antiques. Office: Ronin Art Prodns 1287 E Hideaway Ln Oak Harbor WA 98277

MECHANIC, WILLIAM M. television and motion picture industry executive; b. Detroit; BA in English, Mich. State U.; PhD in Film, U. So. Calif. Dir. programming SelecTV, 1978-80, v.p. programming, 1980-82; v.p. pay TV Paramount Pictures Corp., 1982-84; v.p. pay TV sales Walt Disney Pictures and TV, 1984-85, sr. v.p. video, 1985-87, pres. internat. theatrical distbn. and worldwide video, 1987-93; pres., COO 20th Century Fox Film Entertainment, 1993—; now pres. Fox Inc., Beverly Hills, Calif.; now chmn., CEO 20th Century Fox Film Entertainment. Office: Fox Inc PO Box 900 Beverly Hills CA 90213-0900

MECKEL, PETER TIMOTHY, arts administrator, educator; b. Yankton, S.D., Nov. 28, 1941; s. Myron Eugene and Cynthia Ann (Tunblom) M.; m. Louise Gloria Mudge, Sept. 8, 1962; children: Christina Louise, Christopher Mark; m. Adrienne Dawn Maravich, Dec. 30, 1972; children: Moya Anne, Jon-Peter. Ed., Rockford Coll., Occidental Coll. Founder, gen. dir. Hidden Valley Music Seminars, Carmel Valley, Calif., 1963—; dir. Hidden Valley Opera Ensemble, Masters Festival of Chamber Music, Master Class Series. Cons. in field. Mem. Music Educators Nat. Conf. Congregationalist. Office: Hidden Valley Opera Ensemble PO Box 116 Carmel Valley CA 93924-0116 E-mail: hvms@aol.com

MEDOFF, MARK HOWARD, playwright, screenwriter, novelist; b. Mt. Carmel, Ill., Mar. 18, 1940; s. Lawrence Ray and Thelma Irene (Butt) M.; m. Stephanie Thorne, June 24, 1972; children: Debra, Rachel, Jessica. B.A., U. Miami, Fla., 1962; M.A., Stanford U., 1966; D.H.L., Gallaudet Coll., 1981. Instr. English and drama N.Mex. State U., 1966-79, dramatist in residence, 1974—, head dept. drama, 1978-87, prof. drama, 1979-93, artistic dir., 1982-87, Am. S.W. Theatre Co., 1984-87. Author: (plays) When You Comin' Back, Red Ryder?, 1974, The Wager, 1975, The Kramer, 1975, The Halloween Bandit, 1978, The Conversion of Aaron Weiss, 1978, Firekeeper, 1978, The Last Chance Saloon, 1979, Children of a Lesser God, 1980 (Soc. West Theatres best play award 1982), The Majestic Kid, 1981, The Hands of Its Enemy, 1984, Kringle's Window, 1985, The Heart Outright, 1986, Road to a Revolution, 2001, (novel) Dreams of Long Lasting: (films) When You Comin' Back, Red Ryder?, 1979, Off Beat, 1986, Apology, 1986, Children of a Lesser God, 1986, Good Guys Wear Black, 1978, Clara's Heart, 1988, The Majestic Kid, 1988, City of Joy, 1992, Homage, 1995, Santa Fe, 1997, Who Fly On Angel's Wings, 2000; works appear in Best Plays, 1973-74, 75-75, 79-80, Best Short Plays, 1975, The Homage that Follows, 1987; plays Stumps, 1989, Stefanie Hero, 1990, Showdown On Rio Road, 1995, Gila, 1995, A Christmas Carousel, 1996, Crunch Time, 1996, Gunfighters, A Gulf War Chronicle, 1997, A Christmas Carousel, 1998, Tommy J and Sally, 2000. Guggenheim fellow, 1974-75; recipient Obie award, Drama Desk award, Outer Critics Circle award, Media award Pres.'s Com. Employment Handicapped, Tony award; Oscar award nominee for Best Screenplay for Children of A Lesser God, 1987. Mem. SAG, Coll. Fellows Am. Theater, Dramatists Guild, Writers Guild Am., Actors Equity Assn., Pen, Coll. Fellows of the Am. Theatre. Office: PO Box 3072 Las Cruces NM 88003-3072

MEDVED, ROBERT ALLEN, lawyer; b. Cleve., July 22, 1945; s. Joseph Jack and Mary (Blasko) M. BBA, Kent State U., 1968, JD cum laude, U. Puget Sound, 1975. Bar: Wash. 1976, U.S. Ct. Appeals (9th cir.) 1976, U.S. Dist. Ct. (we. dist.) Wash. 1976, U.S. Dist. Ct. (ea. dist.) Wash. 1979, U.S. Supreme Ct. 1981, U.S. Ct. Appeals (D.C. cir.) 1989. Fin. analyst Ford Motor Co., Sandusky, Ohio, 1972; rsch. asst. U. Puget Sound, 1973; arbitration asst. to labor arbitrator, Tacoma, 1975; law clk. to judge U.S. Ct. Appeals (9th cir.), Seattle, 1974, to judge U.S. Dist. Ct. Cen. Dist. Calif., L.A., 1976; assoc. Graham & Dunn, Seattle, 1976-82, ptnr., 1982-83; ptnr. Drake and Whiteley, Bellevue, Wash., 1983-86, Foster Pepper & Shefelman, Seattle, 1986-97; Bellevue, Wash., 1997—; spl. dist. counsel 8th Congl. Dist. Wash., 1983-96. Editor-in-chief U. Puget Sound Law Rev. Bd. dirs. Bellevue C.C. Found., 1986—. Lt. USN, 1968-71. U. Puget Sound scholar, 1974. Mem. ABA, Wash. State Bar Assn., Seattle C. of C., Bellevue C. of C. Roman Catholic. Office: 212 108th Ave SE Bellevue WA 98004-6209

MEE, C(HARLES) DENIS, physicist; b. Loughborough, Eng., Dec. 28, 1927; BS, Univ. London, 1948; PhD, Univ. Nottingham, 1951, DSc, 1967. Magnetics engr. Steel Co., Wales, 1951-54; magnetic engr. MSS Recording Co., 1954-57; tech. dir. magnetics group CBS Labs., 1957-62; tech. mgr. IBM, 1962-93; cons., 1993—. Lectr. Chinese Magnetic Tech. Soc., Taiwan, 1996, Info. Storage Material Rsch. Consortium, Toyota Tech. Inst., 1996. Contbr. over 30 articles to profl. jours.; patentee in field. Recipient Audio Soc. Achievement award, 1964, Reynold B. Johnson award, 1994, Achievement award IEEE Magnetic Soc., 2000. Fellow IEEE; mem. Nat. Acad. Engr. Home: 105 Stonybrook Rd Los Gatos CA 95032-5643 Office: IBM Almaden Rsch Ctr 650 Harry Rd San Jose CA 95120-6099

MEECHAM, WILLIAM CORYELL, engineering educator; b. Detroit; s. William Edward and Mabel Catherine (Wilcox) M.; m. Barbara Jane Brown, Sept. 4, 1948 (dec.); children: Janice Lynn, William James; m. Della Fern Carson BS, MS, U. Mich., 1948; PhD in Physics, U. Mich. and Brown U., 1954. Head acoustics lab. Willow Run Labs., Ann Arbor, Mich., 1959-60; asst. prof. U. Mich., Ann Arbor, 1958-60; prof. U. Minn., Mpls., 1960-67; prof. fluid mechanics and acoustics UCLA, 1967—, chmn. dept. mechanics and structures, 1972-73. Cons. Aerospace Corp., El Segundo, Calif., 1975-80, Rand Corp., Santa Monica, Calif., 1964-74, Bolt, Beranek and Newman, Cambridge, Mass., 1968-73, Arete Assocs., Encino, Calif., 1976—, CRT Corp., Chatsworth, Calif., 1985—; expert witness numerous cmty. noise ct. cases, L.A., Las Vegas, 1986—. Author: (with R. Lutomirski) Lasar Systems, 1973; author 140 papers on fluid mechanics and acoustics. Treas. Unitarian Ch., Ann Arbor, Mich., 1958-60; advisor U.S. Congress Com. on Pub. Works, Congl. Record Report N.J., 1972; mem. Calif. Space and Def. Council, U.S. Congress, 1982— . Served with U.S. Army, 1944-46. Mich. Alumni scholar 1942-44, Donovan scholar U. Mich., 1944-45; UCLA senate rsch. grantee, 1968—, NASA rsch. grantee, 1971—, Office Naval Rsch. grantee, 1977-85; recipient Disting. Svc. award U.S. Army. Fellow Acoustical Soc. Am. (gen. chmn. meeting 1973), AIAA (assoc. fellow); mem. Internat. Inst. Acoustics and Vibration, Am. Phys. Soc. (fluid dynamics div.), Inst. Noise Control Engring., Sigma Xi, Tau Beta Pi Home: 927 Glenhaven Dr Pacific Palisades CA 90272-2202 Office: UCLA Sch Engring & Applied Sci Los Angeles CA 90024

MEEHAN, MICHAEL JOSEPH, lawyer; b. St. Louis, Aug. 28, 1942; s. Joseph Michael and Frances (Taylor) M.; m. Sharon Kay McHenry (div. 1988); m. Patricia Ann Shive, July 8, 1989 (dec. 1999). BS in Engring., U.S. Coast Guard Acad., 1964; JD with high distinction, U. Ariz., 1971. Bar: Ariz. 1971, U.S. Ct. Appeals (6th, 8th, 9th and 10th cirs.), U.S. Supreme Ct. 1975. Law clk. Assoc. Justice William H. Rehnquist, U.S. Supreme Ct., 1972; assoc. Molloy, Jones & Donahue, P.C., Tucson, 1971-75, shareholder, 1975-93; chmn. exec. com., head trial dept., 1986-93; founder Meehan & Assocs., Tucson, 1993-2001; ptnr. Quarters & Brady/Striech Long, Tucson, 2001—. Mem. fed. appellate rules adv. com. Jud. Conf. U.S., 1994-99. Author chpt. on appellate advocacy: State Bar of Arizona Appellate Practice Handbook. Fellow Am. Acad. Appellate Lawyers (treas.); mem. ABA (sect. on litig., sect. on intellectual property), Ariz. Bar Assn. (exec. coun., past chair appellate practice sect. 1995-99). Republican. Lutheran. Avocation: golf. Office: Quartes & Brady 1 S Church Ave Ste 1700 Tucson AZ 85701-1621 E-mail: mmeehan@quartes.com

MEEKER, ROBERT ELDON, retired manufacturing company executive; b. Moline, Ill., Sept. 6, 1930; s. Paul Edwin and Esther (Carlson) M.; m. Dorothy Elaine Nelson, Dec. 23, 1951; children: Julie Lynn Meeker Gratton, Laurie Allison Meeker Gamel, Bradford Nelson (dec.). BS in Chemistry, Ill. Wesleyan U., 1952; PhD in Phys. Chemistry, Northwestern U., 1955. Chemist, supr. Shell Devel. Co., Emeryville, Calif., 1955-64; mgr.-dir. synthetic rubber tech. ctr. Shell Chem. Co., Torrance, 1964-66, mgr. new projects N.Y.C., 1966-69; dir. exploratory sci., exploration and prodn. rsch. ctr. Shell Devel. Co., Houston, 1969-71; gen. mgr., head new enterprises divsn. Royal Dutch-Shell Co., London, 1971-72; v.p. comml., gen. mgr. Billiton Aluminum B.V. Billiton Internat. Metals subs. Shell Co., The Hague, The Netherlands, 1972-74; pres. Roxana Shale Oil Co. subs. Shell Co., Houston, 1974-76; v.p., gen. mgr. energy systems mgmt. div. TRW, Inc., Redondo Beach, Calif., 1976-80, v.p., gen. mgr. maj. programs, 1980-86; pvt. practice cons., real estate developer Tucson, 1986-94. Patentee in field Trustee Ill. Wesleyan U., Bloomington, 1982-94, trustee emeritus, 1994—; v.p., bd. dirs. Cobblestone Homeowners Assn., 1991-92, pres., bd. dirs., 1992-94, security chmn., 1994-97. Recipient Disting. Alumnus award Ill. Wesleyan U., 1981 Mem. Am. Parkinson Disease Assn. Inc. (pres. Ariz. chpt. 1996-2000, nat. bd. dirs. 1996—), Mercedes Benz Club Am. (pres. Chaparral sect. 1992-94). Republican. Lutheran Avocations: photography; swimming; travel. Home and Office: 7240 N Star Fury Pl Tucson AZ 85718-1345 E-mail: remeeker@theriver.com

MEHDIZADEH, PARVIZ, insurance company executive; b. Tehran, Iran, Sept. 15, 1934; came to U.S., 1981; s. Alexander and Sedigheh (Siavooshy) M.; m. Manijeh Sadri, Sept. 12, 1961; children: Sheida, Peyman, Pejman. BS, Forestry Sch., Tehran, 1958; MS, N.C. State U., 1963, PhD, 1966. Pres. Rsch. Inst. Natural Resources, Tehran, 1968-73; assoc. prof. U. Tehran, 1973-74; prof. environ. sci. U. Tabriz, Iran, 1974-76; chmn. resolution com. FAO, Rome, 1976-77; chmn. natural resources Ctrl. Treaty Orgn., Ankars, Turkey, 1977-78; spl. adviser to sec. Ministry of Agr., Tehran, 1978-79; dist. mgr. Am. Family Life Assurance Co., Beverly Hills, Calif., 1981—; v.p. Point Internat. Corp. Inc., Los Angeles, 1986—; pres. ZMS Fin. Network Corp. Inc., Beverly Hills, Calif., 1995-98, Active Universal Corp., 1998—. Cons. Ministry of Sci., Tehran, 1972-75, UN U., Tokyo, 1975-76; gen. agt. AFLAC, 1995. Author: Flowering Plants of Semi-Arid Regions, 1976, Economizing of Water Use in Agriculture, 1977; editor Khandamhayeh Hafteh, 1979. Mem. U.S. Senatorial Club, Washington, 1984; charter mem. Rep. Presdl. Task Force, Washington, 1984. Mem. Life Underwriters Assn. (L.A. chpt., Health Ins. Quality award 1985, 88, 89), Rotary (chmn. dist. 5280 1992, Paul Harris Fellow award 1989). Avocations: tennis, golf.

MEHLIS, DAVID LEE, publishing executive; m. Marjie Bauman; children: Michelle, Stephen. BA in History, Wheaton Coll., 1965; postgrad., Trinity Evang. Sem., 1965-67. Various positions in mktg., then v.p. and gen. mgr. David C. Cook Pub. Co., Elgin, Ill., 1967—; now pres., CEO Cook Comm. Ministries., Colorado Springs, Colo. Trustee Judson Coll., Elgin, 1991. Bd. mem. Scripture Press Ministries, Colorado Springs Symphony, Kids Around the World, Kingsway Publ. Ltd. Mem. Christian Booksellers Assn., Evang. Christian Pub. Assn. (bd. dirs.). Office: Cook Comm Ministries 4050 Lee Vance Vw Colorado Springs CO 80918-7102

MEHRING, CLINTON WARREN, engineering executive; b. New Haven, Feb. 14, 1924; s. Fred Emmett and Florence Edith (Hutson) M.; m. Carol Jane Adams, Mar. 9, 1946; children: James Warren, Charles David, John Steven (dec.), Martha Jane. B.S., Case Inst. Tech., 1950; M.S., U. Colo., 1956. Registered profl. engr., Wyo., Colo., Nev. Design engr. U. S. Bur Reclamation, Denver, 1950-56; design engr. Tipton & Kalmbach, Denver, 1956-58, asst. resident engr. Quito, Equador, 1959-61, asst. chief design engr. Lahore, Pakistan, 1962-65, v.p. Denver, 1966-73, exec. v.p., 1973-79, pres., bd. dirs., 1979-2001; sr. assoc. Stantec Cons. Inc., Denver, 2001—. Served with AUS, 1943-45. Recipient Theta Tau award as outstanding grad. Case Inst. Tech., 1950. Fellow ASCE (life); mem. Am. Cons. Engrs. Coun., U.S. Com. on Large Dams, Am. Concrete Inst., U.S. Com. Irrigation and Drainage (life), Sigma Xi, Tau Beta Pi, Theta Tau, Sigma Chi, Blue Key. Methodist. Club: Denver Athletic. Home: 1821 Mt Zion Dr Golden CO 80401-1733 Office: 2135 S Cherry St Denver CO 80222 E-mail: tandkay@home.com

MEHRINGER, CHARLES MARK, medical educator, educator; b. Dickinson, N.D., Nov. 21, 1945; m. Ruth Herrman; 1 child, Sydney. BS in Biology, Lamar U., 1966; MD, U. Tex., 1970. Diplomate Am. Bd. Radiology, Am. Bd. Neuroradiology. Intern UCLA Hosp., 1970-71; resident in diagnostic radiology Harbor-UCLA Med. Ctr., Torrance, Calif., 1971-74, fellow in neuroradiology, 1976-77; asst. prof. dept. radiology UCLA Sch. Medicine, 1977-80, dir. spl. procedures, 1980-94, assoc. prof. dept. radiology, 1986-96, prof. dept. radiology, 1996—, acting chmn. radiology, 1996—. Vice-chmn. dept. radiological scis. UCLA Sch. Medicine, Torrance, 1992—, acting chmn. dept. radiology, 1992—, chief diagnostic radiology, 1983-92; chief radiological svcs., cons. U.S. Air Force for Japan and Korea, 1974-76; cons. U. Calif./Irvine (Calif.) Med. Ctr., 1988—, St. Marys Med. Ctr., Long Beach, Calif., 1986—, Long Beach VA Hosp., 1979—, L.A. County Dept. Chief Med. Examiner-Coroner, 1977—; bd. dirs. Rsch. and Ednl. Inst.; presenter in field. Co-author: (with others) Neurological Surgery of the Ear and Skull Base, 1982, Vascular Surgery, 1984, 2d edit., 1994, Youman's Neurological Surgery, 1990, Common Problems in Infertility and Impotence, 1990, Intraluminal Imaging of Vascular and Tubular Organs: Diagnostic and Therapeutic Applications, 1993, Neuroradiology, A Study Guide, 1995; contbr. articles to profl. jours. Bd. dirs., exec. com. Med. Found. Harbor-UCLA Med. Ctr., 1992—. Recipient numerous grants for rsch., 1977—. Mem. Am. Coll. Radiology, Am. Soc. Neuroradiology (sr. mem.), Western Neuroradiologic Soc., L.A. Radiologic Soc. Office: Harbor UCLA Med Ctr Box 27 1000 W Carson St Torrance CA 90502-2004

MEHTA, SHAILESH J. banker; b. Bombay, India, Apr. 22, 1949; came to U.S., 1971; s. Jayantilal B. and Manjula J. Mehta; m. Kalpa S. Doshi, Dec. 19, 1973; children: Sameet, Sheetal B.S. in Mech. Engring., Indian Inst. Tech., 1971; M.S. in Ops. Research, Case Western Res. U., 1973, Ph.D. in Ops. Research and Computer Sci., 1975. Sr. ops. analyst Cleve. Trust Co., 1973-75, ops. officer, 1975-76, asst. v.p. card ops., 1976-77, v.p. corp. ops. adminstrn., 1979; v.p. advanced systems planning, 1977-78, v.p. info. systems, 1979-82; exec. v.p. banking services AmeriTrust, Cleve., 1974-86; exec. v.p., COO First Deposit Corp., San Francisco, 1986-88, pres., CEO, 1988—; chmn. bd. First Deposit Nat. Bank, Tilton, N.H., 1986—; pres., chief exec. officer, chmn. bd. First Deposit Savs. Bank, Redding, Calif., 1986-90; CEO, chmn. bd. First Deposit Nat. Credit Card Bank, Concord, N.H., 1990-93; exec. v.p. Providian Corp., San Francisco, 1993-94, pres., COO, 1994-97, chmn., CEO, 1998—. Pres., dir. A.T. Venture Capital Group, Cleve., 1982-86. Mem. community adv. coun. U. Calif., Berkeley, 1991—. Mem. Am. Bankers Assn. (telecommunications group 1984—), Ohio Venture Assn., Calif. Commn. for Econ. Devel.'s Adv. Coun. on Asia. Office: Providian Corp 201 Mission St San Francisco CA 94105-1831

MEHTA, SIDDARTH N. credit services company executive; b. 1958; BS, London Sch. Econs.; MS, U. Chgo. V.p. Info. Bus. Divsn. Citicorp; sr. v.p. Boston Cons. Group, L.A.; joined Household Internat. Inc., 1996—, group exec. domestic MC/Visa bus., 1998—. Office: Household Internat Inc 1441 Schilling Pl Salinas CA 93901-4543

MEHTA, ZUBIN, conductor, musician; b. Bombay, India, Apr. 29, 1936; came to U.S., 1961; s. Mehli Nowrowji and Tehmina (Daruvala) M.; m. Nancy Diane Kovack; children: Zarina, Merwan. Student, St. Xavier's Coll., Bombay, 1951-53, State Acad. Music, Vienna, Austria, 1954-60; LL.D., Sir George Williams U., Montreal, 1965; D.Mus. (hon.), Occidental Coll.; hon. doctorate, Colgate U., Brooklyn Coll., Westminster Choir Coll., Juilliard Sch., Weizmann Inst. Sci. (Israel). Music dir. Montreal Symphony Orch., 1961-67, L.A. Philharm. Orch., 1962-78; mus. dir. Israel Philharmonic, from 1969, appointed dir. for life, 1981; music dir. N.Y. Philharm., 1978-91, Munich Opera, 1998—; guest condr. Met. Opera, Salzburg (Austria) Festival, Vienna Philharmonic, Berlin Philharmonic, La Scala, Milan, Italy, music dir., Maggio Musicale Florence, Italy, rec. artist for, Decca, CBS, RCA, New World Records, (recipient 1st prize Liverpool (Eng.) Condrs. Competition 1958); gen. music dir. Barian State Opera, Munich, 1998—. Decorated Padma Bhushan India, 1967, commendatore of Italy

MEI, TOM Y. K. lawyer; b. Kuantan, Malaysia, July 24, 1940; came to U.S., 1958. s. Hung Po and Hannah (Chung) M.; m. Margene Suzuki Mei, Sept. 1964; children: Rodney, Todd. BA in econ., Calif. State U. at L.A., 1963; JD, Western State U. Coll. Law, 1975. Bar: Calif. 1976. Claim rep. CNA Ins., L.A., 1964-66, claim supr. San Diego, 1966-76; assoc. attorney Murchison & Cumming, Santa Ana, 1976-88, ptnr., 1988—. Pres. San Diego Claims Mgr. Council, 1973. Mem. Am. Bd. Trial Advocates (bd. dirs.), Defense Rsch. Inst., Orange County Bar Assoc. Avocation: snow sking and traveling. Office: Murchison & Cumming 200 W Santa Ana Blvd Ste 801 Santa Ana CA 92701-4134

MEIER, CURT, state legislator, farmer, rancher; b. Greeley, Colo., Jan. 1, 1953; m. Charlene Meier. Mem. Wyo. Senate, Cheyenne, 1994—, mem. agr., pub. lands, and water resources com., mem. labor, health, and social svcs. com. Chair adv. coun. Rep. Nat. Com.; mem. Wyo. State Bd. Edn., Wyo. Agrl. Leadership Coun. Mem. Wyo. Stockgrowers, Farm Bur., LaGrange C. of C. Republican. Office: Bear Creek Rt Rt 77 Wycross Ranch Lagrange WY 82221 also: Wyo Senate State Capitol Cheyenne WY 82002-0001 Fax: 307-834-2300

MEIER, GERALD MARVIN, economics educator; b. Tacoma, Feb. 9, 1923; s. Max and Bessie (Nagel) M.; m. Gilda Slote, Oct. 23, 1954; children: David, Daniel, Jeremy, Andrew. BA in Econs., Reed Coll., 1947; BLitt in Econs., Oxford (Eng.) U., 1952; PhD, Harvard U., 1953; MA (hon.), Wesleyan U., Middletown, Conn., 1959. Instr. Williams Coll., Williamstown, Mass., 1952-54; asst. prof. Wesleyan U., 1954-59, prof. econs., 1959-63, Stanford (Calif.) U., 1963—. Research assoc. Oxford U., 1957-58; vis. lectr. Yale U., New Haven, 1955-56, vis. assoc. prof., 1956-59, vis. prof., 1959-61; vis. prof. Stanford U., 1962; cons. Asia Soc., Bank Am., East-West Ctr., Food and Agrl. Orgn., Goodyear Internat., NSF, others; internat. lectr. in field. Author: International Trade and Development, 1963, Leading Issues in Development Economics, 1964, The International Economics of Development, 1968, 2d edit., 1978, Leading Issues in Economic Development: Studies in International Poverty, 7th edit., 2000; (with R.E. Baldwin) Economic Development, 1957; gen. editor: Econ. Devel. Series, Econ. Theory and the Underdevel. Countries, Human Resources as the Wealth of Nations, 1973, Fin. Deepening in Econ. Devel., 1975, Agrl. and Structural Transformation, 1975, Gen. X-Efficiency Theory of Econ. Devel., 1978; editor: International Economic Reform: Collected Papers of Emile Despres, 1973, Problems of Trade Policy, 1973, Problems of a World Monetary Order, 1982, Problems of Cooperation for Development, 1977, Toward a New International Development, 1982, La Nueva Era de Desarollo, 1978, Internat. Econs. of Development, International Economics: Theory of Policy, 1982, New International Development Policy, 1982, Pricing Policy for Development Management, 1983, Pioneers in Development, 1985, Emerging from Poverty: The Economics that Really Matters, 1984, Financing Asian Development, 1986, Pioneers in Development, 1987, Asian Development: Economic Success and Policy Lessons, The International Environment of Business, 1998, (with Joseph Stiglitz) Frontiers of Development Economics, 2000; author numerous chpts. to books and articles to profl. jours. Rhodes scholar, 1948-52, Rockefeller Found. Study Ctr. resident scholar, 1981; Guggenheim fellow, 1957-58, Brookings Nat. Research fellow, 1961-62, Russel Sage Found. resident fellow, 1976-77; Social Sci. Research Council Faculty research grantee, 1968, Internat. Legal Ctr. research grantee, 1970, Rockefeller Found. research grantee, 1974-75 Mem. Am. Assn. Rhodes Scholars, Am. Econ. Assn., Royal Econ. Soc., Am. Soc. Internat. Law, Phi Beta Kappa. Home: 774 Santa Ynez St Stanford CA 94305-8441 Office: Stanford U Grad Sch Bus Stanford CA 94305-5015 E-mail: meier_gerald@gsb.stanford.edu

MEIER, MARK FREDERICK, research scientist, glaciologist, educator; b. Iowa City, Dec. 19, 1925; s. Norman C. and Clea (Grimes) M.; m. Barbara McKinley, Sept. 16, 1955; children: Lauren G., Mark S., Gretchen A. BSEE, U. Iowa, 1949, MS in Geology, 1951; PhD in Geology and Applied Mechanics, Calif. Inst. Tech., 1957. Instr. Occidental Coll., L.A., 1952-55; chief glaciology project office U.S. Geol. Survey, Tacoma, 1956-85; dir. Inst. Arctic and Alpine Rsch. U. Colo., Boulder, 1985-94. Vis. prof. Dartmouth Coll., Hanover, N.H., 1964; rsch. prof. U. Wash., Seattle, 1964-86; prof. geol. scis. U. Colo., 1985-96, prof. emeritus, 1997—; pres. Internat. Comn. on Snow and Ice, 1967-71; pres. Internat. Assn. Hydrol. Scis., 1979-83; Mendenhall lectr. U.S. Geol. Survey, 1982, Walter Orr Roberts Disting. lectr. Aspen Global Change Inst., 1992. Contbr. articles to profl. jours. With USN, 1945-46. Recipient 3 medals Acad. Scis., Moscow, 1970-85, Disting. Svc. award (Gold medal) U.S. Dept. Interior, 1968, Internat. Hydrology prize Internat. Assn. Hydrol. Scis./World Meteor. Orgn./UNESCO, 1999; Meier Valley, Antarctica named in his honor U.S. and U.K. Bd. Geog. Names. Fellow AAAS (John Wesley Powell Meml. lectr. 1994), Am. Geophys. Union (com. chmn., Robert E. Horton medal 1996), Geol. Soc. Am., (com. mem.), Internat. Glaciological Soc. (v.p., coun., Seligman Crystal 1985), Arctic Inst. N.Am. (gov. 1987-93). Office: U Colo Inst Arctic Alpine Rsch 1560 30th St Boulder CO 80309-0450 E-mail: mark.meier@colorado.edu

MEIER, MATTHIAS S(EBASTIAN), historian; b. Covington, Ky., June 4, 1917; s. Matthias J. and Mary (Berberich) M.; married; 5 children. BA, U. Miami, 1948; MA, Mexico City Coll., 1949; PhD in Latin Am. History, U. Calif.-Berkeley, 1954. Lectr. U.S. history San Francisco State Coll., summers 1953-55; lectr. U.S. And Latin Am. history Bakersfield Coll., 1955-63; asst. prof. Fresno State Coll., summer 1956, fall 1962; asst. prof. Latin Am. history Santa Clara U., 1963-66, assoc. prof., 1966-72, prof., 1972-89, Patrick A. Donohoe prof. history, 1983-89, emeritus. Fulbright lectr. Nat. U. Tucuman and Inst. Nacional de Profesorado Secundario, Buenos Aires, Argentina, 1958-59; lect. U. Ibero-Am., summer 1965; vis. prof. San Jose State Coll., spring 1968 Author: (with Feliciano Rivera) The Chicanos: A History of Mexican Americans, 1972, A Bibliography for Chicano History, 1972; editor: (with Feliciano Rivera) Readings on La Raza: Twentieth Century, 1973, Dictionary of Mexican American History, 1981, Bibliography of Mexican American History, 1984, Mexican American Biographies, 1988, update of Carey McWilliams's North From Mexico (publ. 1949), 1990, revision, update The Chicanos (new title Mexican Americans/American Mexicans), 1993, Notable Latino Americans, 1997, Encyclopedia of the Mexican American Civil Rights Movement, 2000. Served with Signal Corps U.S. Army, 1942-46. Mem. Pacific Coast Council Latin Am. Studies (pres. 1964-65, 76-77), Latin Am. Studies Assn., Conf. Latin Am. Historians, Assn. Borderlands Scholars, Nat. Assn. for Chicano Studies. Office: Santa Clara U Dept History Santa Clara CA 95053-0001 E-mail: mmeier@scu.edu

MEIERAN, EUGENE STUART, material scientist; b. Dec. 23, 1937; s. Elias and Rae (Linetsky) M.; m. Rosalind Berson, Mar. 25, 1962; children: Sharon Elizabeth, Andrew Marc. BS in Metallurgy, MIT, 1961, ScD in Material Sci., 1963. Mem. tech. staff Fairchild R&D, Palo Alto, Calif., 1963-73; engring. mgr. Intel Corp., Santa Clara, 1973-77, sr. mgr. quality assurance, 1977-84, Intel fellow, 1984—, mgr. applications lab., 1989—. Dir. rsch. LFM program MIT, 1993—; vis. lectr. Technion, Haifa, Israel, 1970-71, H.H. Wills Physics Lab., Bristol, Eng., 1970-71; mem. adv. bd. Lawrence Berkeley Lab., 1984—. Contbr. articles to profl. jours. AEC fellow, 1960; recipient Internat. Reliability awards, 1970, 79, 85; appt. Disting. Engring. Alumnus Purdue U., 1988. Mem. AIME (chmn. electronic material symposium 1973—), NAE, Electron Microscope Soc. U.S.A., Tau Beta Pi, Phi Lambda Upsilon. Democrat. Jewish. Home: 5421 E Camello Rd Phoenix AZ 85018-1910 Office: Intel Corp 5000 W Chandler Blvd Chandler AZ 85226-3699

MEIGHAN, STUART SPENCE, hospital consultant, internist, writer; b. Glasgow, Scotland, Jan. 30, 1923; came to U.S., 1962; s. Stuart Spence and Annie Louise (Brown) M; m. Anne Stewart Henderson, Nov. 4, 1952 (div. 1968); children: Jane Spence, Stuart Spence; m. Louise Rhys McGregor, July 7, 1985. MB, U. Glasgow, 1945. Registrar, sr. registrar Nat. Health Svc., U.K., 1948-57; sr. staff mem. Allan Blair Meml. Clinic, Regina, Sask., Can., 1957-62; internist Cleland Clinic, Oregon City, Oreg., 1962-64; dir. med. affairs Good Samaritan Hosp., Portland, 1964-78; pres. Spence Meighan and Assocs., Portland, 1978—. Cons. several hosps. and orgns. Contbr. over 100 articles to profl. jours. Lt. Royal Navy, 1946-48. Recipient Disting. Svc. award Am. Soc. Internal Medicine. Fellow Am. Coll. Physicians, Royal Coll. Physicians. Avocations: sailing, tennis, theater, rugby football, music. Home and Office: 408 NW Rainier Ter Portland OR 97210-3347

MEIKLEJOHN, ALVIN J., JR. state legislator, lawyer, accountant; b. Omaha, June 18, 1923; m. Lorraine J. Meiklejohn; children; Pamela Ann, Shelley Lou, Bruce Ian, Scott Alvin. BS, U. Denver, JD, 1951; LLD (hon.), U. No. Colo., 2000. Mem. Colo. state Senate from 19th Dist., 1976-96, chmn. com. edn.; mem. Edn. Commn. of States, 1981-96; chmn. Colo. Commn. on Ach. in Edn., 1995, mem., 1993-96, Jefferson Sch. Dist. No. R-1 Bd. Edn., 1971-77, pres., 1973-77; commr. Commn. on Uniform State Laws, 1988-96. Dir. Red Rocks C.C. Found., Wings Over the Rockies Aviation and Aerospace Mus. Capt. U.S. Army, 1940-46; maj. USAF, 1947-51. Mem. Colo. Soc. CPA's, Arvada C. of C., Masons, Shriners, Transp. Lawyers Assn. (pres. 1972-73). Republican. E-mial. Home: 7540 Kline Dr Arvada CO 80005-3732 Office: Jones & Keller PC 1625 Broadway Ste 1600 Denver CO 80202-4727 E-mail: ajmeiklejohn@joneskeller.com

MEINDL, ROBERT JAMES, English language educator; b. Wausau, Wis., Sept. 17, 1936; s. George Martin and Adeline Emilie (Goetsch) M.; m. Victoria Lynn Chavez; children: Karin Rose, George Andrew, Damian Kurt, Erika Wittmer, Christopher Smith, Gabrielle Remelia. BS, U. Wis., 1958; MA, U. Conn., 1960; PhD, Tulane U., 1965; postdoctoral studies, U. Calif., Berkeley, 1967-68, Goethe Inst., Liblar, Germany, 1879, U. Cologne, Germany, 1970. Teaching asst. U. Conn., Storrs, 1958-60; teaching fellow Tulane U., 1960-62; lectr. U. Wis., Green Bay, 1963-65; from asst. to full prof. English Calif. State U., Sacramento, 1965—. Translator: Studies in John Gower, 1981; book rev. editor Studia Mystica Jour., 1984-89; contbr. numerous articles to profl. jours. With USNR, 1953-61, 79-96. Nat. Endowment for the Humanities fellow Stanford U., 1982. Mem. MLA, Medieval Acad. Am., Medieval Assn. of Pacific, Early English Text Soc., John Gower Soc., New Chaucer Soc. Home: 2301 Pennland Dr Sacramento CA 95825-0329 Office: Calif State U 6000 J St Sacramento CA 95819-2605

MEISINGER, LOUIS M. lawyer; b. N.Y.C., Dec. 12, 1942; BA, UCLA, 1964, JD, 1967. Bar: Calif. 1968. Atty. Hill Wynne Troop & Meisinger, L.A.; exec. v.p., gen. coun. Walt Disney Co., Burbank, Calif., 1997—. Editor: UCLA Law Rev., 1965-67. Mem. State Bar Calif., L.A. County Bar Assn., Century City Bar Assn., Order of Coif, Phi Beta Kappa, Sigma Delta Pi, Phi Delta Phi. Office: Walt Disney Co 500 S Buena Vista St Burbank CA 91521-0006

MEISSNER, KATHERINE GONG, city official; b. 1955; BA, U. Phoenix, Stockton, Calif., 1999. Mem. comty. planning dept. staff City of Stockton, Calif., 1982-85, exec. asst. city clk., 1985-96, city clk., 1996—. Office: City Stockton Office City Clk 425 N El Dorado St Stockton CA 95202-1997

MELCHER, TRINI URTUZUASTEGUI, accounting educator; b. Somerton, Ariz., Dec. 1, 1931; d. Francisco Juan and Dolores (Barraza) Urtuzuastegui; m. Arlyn Melcher, Aug. 3, 1957 (div. Feb. 1972); children: Teresa Dolores, Michael Francis, Jocelyn Marie. BS, Ariz. State U., 1954; MBA, Kent State U., 1964; PhD, Ariz. State U., 1977. Acct. CPA firm, L.A., 1954-56; instr. L.A. Sch. Dist., 1956-58, Dolton (Ill.) Sch. Dist., 1958-61; asst. prof. Kent (Ohio) State U., 1962-72; prof. Calif. State U., Fullerton, 1976-89, founding faculty mem. San Marcos, 1990—. Author: Intermediate Accounting Study Guide, 1984. Treas. Community Devel. Coun., Santa Ana, 1985-88, chmn. bd., 1989; mem. com. U.S. Dept. Labor, 1989—. Named Outstanding Educator, League of United Latin Am. Citizens, Stanton, Calif., 1987, Mex. Am. Women's Nat. Assn., Irvine, Calif., 1987; recipient Outstanding Faculty award Calif. State U. Sch. Bus., 1983, Pub. Svc. award Am. Soc. Women CPAs, San Antonio, 1989; Affirmative Action grantee, 1990. Mem. AICPA (editorial bd. The Woman CPA), Am. Acctg. Assn., Calif. Soc. CPAs (Merit award 1991), Hispanic CPAs. Avocations: music, travel. Home: 2024 Sequoia St San Marcos CA 92069-5454 Office: Calif State U San Marcos CA 92096-0001

MELDRUM, PETER DURKEE, venture capital/biotechnology company executive; b. Salt Lake City, June 26, 1947; s. Benjamin Nibley and Grace Natalie (Durkee) M.; m. Catherine Roper, June 16, 1970; children: Christopher Shawn. BSChemE, U. Utah, 1970, MBA, 1974. Asst. to pres. Terra Tek, Inc., Salt Lake City, 1974-78; pres., CEO Resource Enterprises, Inc., Salt Lake City, 1978-81, AgriDyne Techs., Salt Lake City, 1981-91, Founder's Fund Inc., 1991-95, Myriad Genetics Inc., Salt Lake City, 1992—. Bd. dirs. Dairy Equipment Co. Utah, Salt Lake City, Paradigm Bioscis. Inc., Alaxis, Inc., Manticore Pharms. Vice-chmn. fundraising Salt Lake Boy's Club, 1978-79; bd. dirs., vice chmn. ARC Golden Spike, Salt Lake City, 1980-90; mem. State of Utah Council Sci. and Tech., 1984-89; adv. bd. High Tech Mktg. Rev., Austin, Tex., 1986-88; mem. Gov.'s Task Force on Entrepreneurship; mem. rev. panel Utah Tech. Fin. Corp., Gov.'s Com. on Biomed. Industry, 1988-91; mem. bioengring. adv. bd. U. Utah, bus. adv. bd. Coll. Bus. Weber State U.; bd. arbitrators NASD, 1991-98. 1st lt. USAR, 1970-72. Mem. Utah Life Scis. Assn. (bd. dirs. 1995—), Tau Beta Pi, Phi Kappa Phi, Beta Gamma Sigma. Republican. Presbyterian. Avocations: skiing, backpacking, basketball, racquetball. Home: 1808 Mohawk Way Salt Lake City UT 84108-3363 Office: Myriad Genetics 320 Wakara Way Salt Lake City UT 84108-1214

MELENDEZ, ROSA MARIA, protective services official; b. Salt Lake City, Oct. 24, 1952; Diploma, Wash. State Criminal Justice, 1978. U.S. marshall We. dist. U.S. Marshall Svc., Wash., 1994—. Office: 300 US Courthouse 1010 5th Ave Seattle WA 98104-1195

MELICHER, RONALD WILLIAM, finance educator; b. St. Louis, July 4, 1941; s. William and Lorraine Norma (Mohart) M.; m. Sharon Ann Schlarmann, Aug. 19, 1967; children: Michelle Joy, Thor William, Sean Richard. BSBA, Washington U., St. Louis, 1963, MBA, 1965, DBA, 1968. Asst. prof. fin. U. Colo., Boulder, 1969-71, assoc. prof., 1971-76, prof. fin., 1976—, chmn. fin. div., 1978-86, 90; chmn. fin. and econ. div., 1993-2000; MBA/MS programs dir. U. Colo., Boulder, 1990-93. Assoc. dir. space law bus. and policy ctr. U. Colo., 1986-87; rsch. cons. FPC, Washington, 1975-76, GAO, Washington, 1981, RCG/Hagler, Bailly, Inc., 1985—, Ariz. Corp. Commn., 1986-87, Conn. Dept. Pub. Utility Control, 1989, U.S. SEC, 1992-95; cons. tech. edn. IBM Corp., 1985-91; dir. ann. Exch. Program for Gas Industry, 1975-94; instr. ann. program Nat. Assn. Regulatory Utility Commrs., Mich. State U., 1981-94. Co-author: Real Estate Finance, 1978, 2d edit. 1984, 3d edit, 1989, 5th edit., 1982; Finance: Introduction to Markets, Institutions and Management, 1980, 84, 88, 92, Finance: Introduction to Institutions, Investments, and Management, 9th edit., 1997, 10th edit., 2000; assoc. editor Fin. Mgmt. Jour., 1975-80, The Fin. Rev., 1988-91. Recipient News Ctr. 4 TV Teaching award, 1987, MBA/MS Assn. Teaching award, 1988, Boulder Faculty Assembly Teaching award, 1988, Grad. Bus. Students Teaching award, 1995, 98; grantee NSF, 1974, NASA, 1986, 87; scholar W.H. Baughn Disting., 1989-2000, U. Colo. Pres.'s Teaching, 1989—. Mem. Fin. Mgmt. Assn. (mem. com. 1974-76, regional dir. 1975-77, v.p. ann. mtg. 1985, v.p. program 1987, pres. 1991-92, exec. com. 1991-93, bd. trustees 1992-99, chmn. 25th Anniversary com. 1994-95, mem. search. com. for editor of Financial Mgmt. Jour., 1995-96, chmn. search com. editor of Fin. Practice and Edn. Jour. 1996, mem. search com. for sec./treas. 1999, 2001), Am. Fin. Assn. Western Fin. Assn. (bd. dirs. 1974-76), Fin. Execs. Inst. (acad. mem. 1975—), Ea. Fin. Assn., Southwestern Fin. Assn., Midwest Fin. Assn. (bd. dirs. 1978-80), Alpha Kappa Psi, Beta Gamma Sigma. Presbyterian. Home: 6348 Swallow Ln Boulder CO 80303-1456 Office: U Colo Coll Bus PO Box 419 Boulder CO 80303 E-mail: Ronald.Melicher@colorado.edu

MELLINKOFF, SHERMAN MUSSOFF, medical educator; b. McKeesport, Pa., Mar. 23, 1920; s. Albert and Helen (Mussoff) M.; m. June Bernice O'Connell, Nov. 18, 1944; children: Sherrill, Albert. BA, Stanford U., 1941, MD, 1944; LHD (hon.), Wake Forest U., 1984, Hebrew Union Coll., L.A., 1988. Diplomate Am. Bd. Internal Medicine, Am. Bd. Gastroenterology, Am. Bd. Nutrition. Intern asst. resident Stanford U. Hosp., San Francisco, 1944-45; asst. resident Johns Hopkins Hosp., Balt., 1947-49, chief resident, 1950-51, instr. in medicine, 1951-53; fellow in gastroenterology Hosp. of U. Pa., Phila., 1949-50; from asst. prof. to prof. medicine UCLA Sch. of Medicine, L.A., 1962-86; dean UCLA Sch. Medicine, L.A., 1962-86, emeritus prof. of medicine, 1990—; disting. physician of VA Wadsworth VA Medical Ctr., L.A., 1990-93. Mem. sci. adv. panel Rsch. to Prevent Blindness, Inc., N.Y.C., 1975-93; mem. program devel. com. Nat. Med. Fellowships, Inc., N.Y.C., 1984—. Editorial bd. The Pharos, 1986; contbr. articles to profl. jours. Apptd. by Gov. of Calif. to McCone Com., 1965. Capt. U.S. Army, 1945-47. Recipient Abraham Flexner award Assn. Am. Med. Colls., 1981, J.E. Wallace Sterling Disting. Alumnus award Stanford U. Sch. of Medicine, 1987. Master ACP; fellow Royal Coll. of Physicians; mem. Am. Gastroenterol. Assn. Assn., of Am. Physicians, Inst. of Medicine of NAS, Am. Acad. of Arts and Scis., The Johns Hopkins Soc. of Scholars. Avocations: reading, hiking. Office: UCLA Dept Medicine 44 138 Chs Los Angeles CA 90095-0001

MELLOR, RONALD JOHN, history educator; b. Bklyn., Sept. 30, 1940; s. Ronald Green and Eleanor Teresa (Walsh) M.; m. Anne Tidaback Kostelanetz, June 7, 1969; 1 child, Ronald Blake. AB, Fordham Coll., 1962; cert., U. Louvain, Belgium, 1961; AM, Princeton U., 1964, PhD in Classics, 1968. Asst. prof. Classics Stanford (Calif.) U., 1965-75; assoc. prof. history UCLA, 1976-82, prof. history, 1982—. Vice-chmn. history UCLA, 1991-92, chmn. history, 1992-97; visitor Princeton Inst. Advanced Studies, 1997-98. Author: Thea Rhome, 1975, Tacitus, 1993, Tacitus and the Classical Tradition, 1995, The Roman Historians, 1999; editor: From Augustus to Nero: The First Dynasty of Imperial Rome, 1990, The Historians of Ancient Rome, 1997, Text and Tradition: Studies in Greek History and Historiography in Honor of Mortimer Chambers, 1999, The Roman Historians, 1999. Fellow NEH, 1969, Am. Coun. Learned Socs., 1972, Humanities Rsch. Ctr. Australian Nat. U., Canberra, Australia, 1990; hon. fellow U. Coll. London, Eng., 1969, 72, 83-85. Mem. Am. Hist. Assn., Am. Philol. Assn., Am. Inst. Archaeology, Assn. Ancient Historians, Soc. for the Promotion of Roman Studies. Democrat. Avocations: opera, travel, theater, tennis. Home: 2620 Mandeville Canyon Rd Los Angeles CA 90049-1004 Office: UCLA Dept History 405 Hilgard Ave Los Angeles CA 90095-9000 E-mail: mellor@history.ucla.edu

MELMON, KENNETH LLOYD, internist, biologist, pharmacologist, consultant; b. San Francisco, July 20, 1934; s. Abe Irving and Jean (Kahn) M.; m. Elyce Edelman, June 9, 1957; children: Bradley S., Debra W. AB in Biology with honors, Stanford U., 1956; MD, U. Calif. at San Francisco, 1959. Intern, then resident in internal medicine U. Calif. Med. Ctr., San Francisco, 1959-61; clin. assoc., surgeon USPHS, Nat. Heart, Lung and Kidney Inst., NIH, 1961-64; chief resident in medicine U. Wash. Med. Ctr., Seattle, 1964-65; chief div. clin. pharmacology U. Calif. Med. Ctr., 1965-78; chief dept. medicine Stanford U. Med. Ctr., 1978-84, Arthur Bloomfield prof. medicine, prof. pharmacology, 1978-86, prof. medicine and molecular pharmacology, 1978-2000; assoc. dean postgrad. med. edn., 1994-2000; dir. tech. transfer program Stanford U. Hosp., 1986-93, Arthur L. Bloomfield prof. emeritus, 2000—. Mem. sr. staff Cardiovasc. Rsch. Inst.; chmn. joint commn. prescription drug use Senate Subcom. on Health, Inst. Medicine and HEW-Pharm. Mfrs. Assn.; mem. Nat. Bd. Med. Examiners, 1987-97; pres. Bio 2000, Woodside, Calif., 1983-85; co-founder Immulogic, Waltham, Mass., 1988, Shine Inc., Stanford, Calif., 1999; sci. advisor Epoch, Vysis, SurroMed, Cellergy, Artecel, Stanford E-Skolar, others; founder Skolar MD/Stanford, Chief Med. Officer; cons. FDA, 1965-82, Office Tech. Assessment, 1974-75, Senate Subcom. on Health, 1975-98; bd. dirs. Vysis, Chgo., Immologic, Boston, Epoch, Seattle, Skolar, MD Inc., Stanford, DNA Scis., Articel, PFerin; cons. to govt.; founder Inst. Biol. and Clin. Investigation, Ctr. for Molecular and Genetic Medicine, Stanford Cmty. of Internists Stanford Med. Group, Intergrate Ctr. Clin. Immunology, Stanford Health Info. Network Edn.; chmn. acad. senate Sch. Medicine, Stanford U., 1996-99, chmn. steering com. univ. acad. senate, 1996-98; founder Iceberg Med. Knowledge, 1998, Shine LLC, Stanford, 1999. Author articles, chpts. in books, sects. encys.; Editor: Clinical Pharmacology: Basic Principles in Therapeutics, 4th edit., 2000, Cardiovascular Therapeutics, 1974; assoc. editor: The Pharmacological Basis of Therapeutics (Goodman and Gilman), 1984; mem. editl. bd. numerous profl. jours. Surgeon USPHS, 1961-64. Burroughs Wellcome clin. pharmacology scholar, 1966-71; John Simon Guggenheim fellow Weizman Inst., Israel, 1971, NIH spl. fellow, Bethesda, 1971. Fellow AAAS (nat. coun. 1985-89); mem. Am. Fedn. Clin. Rsch. (pres. 1973-74), Am. Soc. Clin. Investigation (pres. 1978-79), Assn. Am. Physicians, Western Assn. Physicians (pres. 1983-84), Am. Soc. Pharmacology and Exptl. Therapeutics, Am. Soc. Clin. Pharmacology and Therapeutics (Oscar Hunter award in therapeutics 1994), Inst. Medicine of NAS, Am. Physiol. Soc., Calif. Acad. Medicine, Med. Friends of Wine, Phi Beta Kappa. Democrat. Jewish. Achievements include initiation of founding of Ctr. of Molecular and Genetic Medicine, The Integrated Ctr. for Clin. Immunology, Stanford, Stanford Health Info. Network for Edn., others. Home: 51 Cragmont Way Woodside CA 94062-2307 Office: E Skolar MD 3155 Porter Dr Palo Alto CA 94304 E-mail: KMelmon@Skolar.com

MELNICK, ALICE JEAN (AJ MELNICK), counselor; b. St. Louis, Dec. 25, 1931; d. Nathan and Henrietta (Hausfater) Fisher; m. Harold Melnick, May 24, 1953; children: Susan, Vikki, Patrice. BJ, U. Tex., Austin, 1952; MEd, U. North Tex., 1974. Lic. profl. counselor. Reporter San Antonio Light, 1952-53; instr. journalism project Upward Bound So. Meth. U., Dallas, 1967-71. Instr. writing El Centro Dallas County C.C., Dallas, part time 1972-74; instr. human devel. Richland C.C., Dallas, part-time 1974-79; tchr. English, journalism and psychology Dallas Ind. Sch. Dist., 1969-81; counselor Ursuline Acad., 1981-94; part-time instr. human devel. Sante Fe C.C.; freelance documentary photographer. Mem. Dallas Sports Car Club, N.Mex. Jewish Hist. Soc., Temple Beth Shalom. Jewish. Home: 101 Monte Alto Rd Santa Fe NM 87505-8865 E-mail: aj@melnick.net

MELNICK, ROB, research administrator; b. Mt. Vernon, N.Y., May 6, 1950; BA in Govt., Dartmouth Coll., 1972; postgrad., NYU, 1972; MA in Media, Ariz. State U., 1973, PhD in Ednl. Tech., 1980. Dir. media ctr., tchr. social studies Glendale (Ariz.) Union H.S., 1973-75; instr. dept. ednl. tech., assoc. dir. univ. media sys. Ariz. State U., Tempe, 1975-80; v.p. Desert Mountain Assocs. Inc., Phoenix, 1980-82; sr. rsch. fellow, v.p. Hudson Inst., Indpls., 1982-87; dir. Morrison Inst. for Pub. Policy Ariz. State U., Tempe, 1987—. Cons. in areas of policy analysis, prodn. of pub. info. and program evaluation for numerous govt., corp., and ednl. orgns.; mass media presentations. Contbr. numerous articles to profl. jours. Bd. dirs. Noble Ctrs., Inc., Indpls., 1986, Phoenix Ctr. for Law-Related Studies, 1987—, Inst. for Ednl. Leadership of Ariz., 1990—, Succes by Six, 1990—, Work Force Solutions for Am.'s Future Inc., 1992—; mem. Phoenix Commn. on Edn., 1987-92; bd. dirs., sec. Ariz. Sch.-to-Work Partnership, Inc., 1990—; mem., moderator Gov.'s Task Force on Edn., 1991; mem., facilitator State Supt.'s Task Force on Sch. Violence, 1993, Gov.'s Task Force on Employment and Tng., 1993; other activities. Project dir., author or co-author numerous funded policy studies. Office: Morrison Inst Pub Policy PO Box 874405 Tempe AZ 85287-4405

MELODY, MICHAEL EDWARD, publishing company executive; b. Streator, Ill., Dec. 22, 1943; s. Giles Lambert and Rose Mary (Moreschi) M.; m. Carol Ann Weir, June 8, 1968 (div.); 1 dau., Alison Anne; m. Bonnie Kaye Binkert, Mar. 26, 1983. BA, Ala. Coll., 1966. Exec. editor, asst. v.p. Prentice-Hall, Inc., Englewood Cliff, N.J., 1974-79; v.p., editor-in-chief coll. div. Macmillan Pub. Co., N.Y.C., 1979-80, sr. v.p., pres. coll. div., 1980-87, pres. sch. div., 1987-88; v.p. higher edn. group Simon & Schuster, N.Y.C., 1988-90; sr. v.p. Houghton Mifflin Co., Boston, 1990-91, exec. v.p., 1991-95; prin. Michael E. Melody Cons., Boston, 1995-96; v.p., gen. mgr. info. prod. Inso Corp., Boston, 1996-99; pres, CEO Sage Pubs., Inc., Thousand Oaks, Calif., 1999—, also bd. dirs. Chmn. bd. dirs. Appleton & Lange, N.Y.C., 1989-90; bd. dirs. Sage Publs., Ltd., London. Bd. overseers Huntington Theatre Co., Boston, 1993-96; bd. advisors Boston U. Sch. for the Arts, 1997-2000; bd. dirs. Judge Baker Ctr. for Children, Harvard U. Med Sch., 1997-99, mem. exec. com.; pres. avd. coun. Calif. Luth. U., 2001—. Mem. Assn. Am. Pubs. (vice chmn. coll. divsn. 1981-83, chmn. coll. divsn. 1983-86, exec. com. sch. divsn. 1987-88, exec. com. higher edn. divsn. 1990—), Nat. Assn. Coll. Stores (trustee 1986-87, 94-95).

MELTON, ARTHUR RICHARD, healthcare executive; b. Ysleta, Tex., Apr. 28, 1943; s. Francis Charles and Jean (Graham) M.; m. Frances Bay, Aug. 19, 1965; children: David Bay, Amy Elizabeth. BS, U. Utah, 1969; MPH, U. N.C., 1974, D in Pub. Health, 1976. Dir. labs. S.D. Dept. Health, Pierre, 1976-87; microbiologist Utah Dept. Health, Salt Lake City, 1970-73, dir. divsn. lab. svcs., 1987-92, dep. dir., 1992-96, 98—. Mem.: Am. Pub. Health Assn. (governing coun. 1980—83), S.D. Pub. Health Assn. (pres. 1980—81), Assn. State and Territorial Health Ofcls. (pres. elect 1999—2000, pres. 2000—01). Mormon. Home: 6835 Heather Way West Jordan UT 84084-2304 Office: PO Box 142802 Salt Lake City UT 84114-2802 Personal E-mail: armelton@qwest.net; Business E-Mail: dmelton@dho.state.ut.us

MELTZER, DAVID, author, musician, educator; b. Rochester, N.Y., Feb. 17, 1937; s. Louis and Roseamunde (Lovelace) M.; m. Christina Meyer, Apr. 1, 1958; children— Jennifer, Margaret, Amanda, Adam Benjamin ben David. Student, Los Angeles City Coll., 1955-56, U. Calif. at Los Angeles, 1956-57. Mem. cons. bd. Coordinating Coun. of Lit. Mags.; instr. M.A. program in poetics New Coll., San Francisco, 1980—, coord. writing and lit. program in undergrad. humanites program, 1987—. Author: numerous books of poetry, including Tens, Selected Poems, 1973, Six, 1976, Two-Way Mirror: Notebook on Poetry, 1977, The Art, The Veil, 1981, The Name: Selected oetry, 1973-83, 1983; editor: The San Francisco Poets, 1971, Birth, 1973, The Secret Garden: Anthology of the Classic Kabbalah, 1977, revised edit., 1998, Birth: An Anthology of Ancient Texts, Songs, Prayers, and Stories, 1981, Death: An Anthology of Ancient Texts, Songs, Prayers and Stories, 1983, The Book Within the Book: Approaching the Kabbalah, 1990, Arrows: Selected Poetry: 1952-92, 1994, Reading Jazz, 1993, Writing Jazz, 1999, No Eyes: Lester Young, 2000, San Francisco Beat: Innterviews with the Poets, 2001, Tree; editor, pub. The Agency, 1968, The Agency Trilogy, 1994, Under, 1995, also Tree Books; songwriter, musician, vocalist: Serpent Power, 1968, Poet Song, 1970, Green Morning, 1999; soundtrack for Chance, 1978. Bd. dirs. Before Columbus Found., 1977— . Coordinating Coun. of Lit. Mags. grantee, 1973-74, 81, Nat. Endowment of Arts grantee for creative writing, 1974, for pub., 1975, Calif. Arts Coun. grantee, 1979; recipient Tombstone award for poetry John Ryan Morris Meml. Found., 1992. Office: PO Box 9005 Berkeley CA 94709-0005 E-mail: dmelt@ccnet.com

MELVILL-JONES, GEOFFREY, internist, educator; b. Cambridge, Eng., Jan. 14, 1923; emigrated to Can., 1961, naturalized, 1974; s. Benett and Dorothy Laxton (Jotham) Melvill J.; m. Jenny Marigold Burnaby, June 21, 1953; children— Katharine F., Francis H., Andrew J., Dorothy H. BA, Cambridge U., 1944, MA, 1947, MB, BChir, 1949. House surgeon Middlesex (Eng.) Hosp., 1950; sr. house surgeon in otolaryngology Addenbrooke's Hosp., Cambridge, 1950-51; sci. officer Med. Rsch. Coun. Gt. Britain, 1955-61; assoc. prof. physiology McGill U., Montreal, Que., Can., 1961-68, prof., 1968-92, prof. emeritus, 1992—, Hosmer rsch. prof., 1978-92, dir. aerospace med. rsch. unit, 1961-89. Adj. prof. dept. clin. neurosci., faculty medicine U. Calgary, 1992—; vis. prof. Stanford U., 1971-72, College de France, 1979, 95; Ashton Graybiel lectr. U.S. Naval Aerospace Lab., Fla. Author: Mammalian Vestibular Physiology, 1979, Adaptive Mechanisms in Gaze Control, 1985; contbr. numerous articles to profl. publs. Flying pers. med. officer RAF, 1951-55. Recipient SkyLab Achievement award NASA, 1974, Dohlman medal Toronto U., 1986, Wilbur Franks award Can. Soc. Aerospace Medicine, 1988. Fellow Can. Aero. and Space Inst., Aerospace Med. Assn. (Harry G. Armstrong Lectureship award 1968, Arnold D. Tuttle award 1971), Royal Soc. (London), Royal Soc. Can. (McLaughlin medal 1991), Royal Aero. Soc. (London) (Stewart Meml. award 1989, Buchanan Barbour award 1990); mem. U.K. Physiol. Soc., Can. Physiol. Soc., Can. Soc. Aviation Medicine, Internat. Collegium Otolaryngology, Soc. Neurosci., Bárány Soc. (Gold medal 1988). Office: U Calgary Dept Clin Neurosci 3330 Hospital Dr NW U2813 Calgary AB Canada T2N 4N1

MENDE, HOWARD SHIGEHARU, mechanical engineer; b. Hilo, Hawaii, Nov. 19, 1947; s. Tsutomu and Harue (Kubomitsu) M. BSME, U. Hawaii, 1969; MSME, U. So. Calif., 1975. Registered profl. engr., Calif. Mem. tech. staff I Rockwell Internat., Anaheim, Calif., 1970-71, L.A., 1971-73, mem. tech. staff II, 1973-77, mem. tech. staff IV, 1984-86; devel. engr. AiRsch. Mfg. Co., Torrance, Calif., 1977-83; mech. engr. Def. Contracts Mgmt. Dist. West, Santa Ana, 1987-94, electronics engr., 1994—. Lectr. Pacific States U., L.A., 1974-75. Mem. ASME. Democrat. Buddhist. Home: 1946 W 180th Pl Torrance CA 90504-4417 Office: Def Contracts Mgmt 2525 W 190th St Torrance CA 90504-6002 E-mail: hmende@dcmdw.dcma.mil

MENDEL, JERRY MARC, electrical engineering educator; b. N.Y.C., May 14, 1938; s. Alfred and Eleanor (Deutch) M.; m. Letty Susan Grossman, June 26, 1960; children: Jonathan, Aileen. BMechE cum laude, Poly. U., 1959, MEE, 1960, PhD in Elec. Engring., 1963. Registered profl. engr., Calif. Instr. elec. engring. Poly. Inst. Bklyn., 1960-63; engring. scientist and sect. chief McDonnell-Douglas Astronautics Co., Huntington Beach, Calif., 1963-74; prof. dept. elec. engring. systems U. So. Calif., L.A., 1974—, chmn. dept., 1984-91, dir. Signal and Image Processing Inst., 1991-94, assoc. dir. edn. Integrated Media Sys. Ctr., 1996—. Pres., founder MENTECH, Culver City, Calif., 1983—; pres. United Signals and Systems, Inc., 1989—. Author: Discrete Techniques of Parameter Estimation: The Equation Error Formulation, 1973, Optimal Seismic Deconvolution: An Estimation Based Approach, 1983 (Phi Kappa Phi award 1984), Lessons in Digital Estimation Theory, 1987, Maximum-Likelihood Deconvolution, 1990, Lessons in Estimation Theory for Signal Processing, Communications and Control, 1995; editor: Prelude to Neural Networks: Adaptive and Learning Systems, 1994, Uncertain Rule-Based Fuzzy Logic Systems: Introduction and New Directions, 2001; co-editor: Adaptive Learning and Pattern Recognition Systems, 1970. Fellow IEEE (Centennial medal 1984Third Millennium medal 2000); mem. IEEE Control Systems Soc. (Disting. mem.; pres. 1986). Office: U So Calif Dept Elec Engring Sys Eeb 400 Los Angeles CA 90089-0001 E-mail: mendel@sipi.usc.edu

MENDELSOHN, HAROLD, sociologist, educator; b. Jersey City, Oct. 30, 1923; s. Louis and Bessie (Yulinsky) M.; m. Irene Sylvia Gordon, Apr. 10, 1949; 1 dau., Susan Lynn. B.S., CCNY, 1945; M.A., Columbia U., 1946; Ph.D., New Sch. Social Research, 1956. Sr. survey analyst U.S. Dept. State, Washington, 1951-52; research assoc. Bur. Social Sci. Research, Am. U., Washington, 1952-56; assoc. mgr. mktg. communications McCann-Erickson Advt., N.Y.C., 1956-58; assoc. dir. Psychol. Corp., N.Y.C., 1958-62; prof. dept. mass communications U. Denver, 1962-89, prof. emeritus, 1989—, chmn., 1970-78, dean faculty social scis., 1984-86, spl. asst. to chancellor, 1986-88. Morton vis. disting. prof. Ohio U., spring 1981; cons. FTC, Denver Rsch. Inst., U.S. Consumer Product Safety Commn., The Gallup Orgn., Ford Found., Fedn. Rocky Mountain States, CBS, ABC, Children's TV Workshop. (Emmy award Nat. Acad. TV Arts Scis. 1968, Gold Camera award U.S. Indsl. Film Festival 1972); Author: Mass Entertainment, 1966, (with David H. Bayley) Minorities and the Police: Confrontation in America, 1969, (with Irving Crespi) Polls, Television and the New Politics, 1970, (with others) Television and Growing Up: The Impact of Televised Violence, 1972, (with Garrett O'Keefe) The People Choose a President, 1976; editor: Mass Communications series, 1967-69; contbr. articles to profl. jours. Mem. Denver Coun. Pub. TV, 1970-78; mem. U.S. Surgeon Gen.'s Sci. Adv. Com. on TV and Social Behavior, 1969-71; bd. dirs. Nat. Safety Coun., 1963-69; mem. pub. affairs adv. bd. Air Force Acad. Found., 1972-76; mem. cancer control and rehab. adv. com. Nat. Cancer Inst., 1976-81; mem. adv. coun., prevention div. Nat. Inst. Alcoholism and Alcohol Abuse, 1977-82; trustee Colo. Med. Svc., Inc., 1973-78. Recipient award TV Bur. Advt., 1962, Met. Life award Nat. Safety Council, 1967; Gold Eagle award, 1973; Silver award Internat. Festival Film and TV, 1974 Fellow Am. Psychol. Assn., Am. Sociol. Assn.; mem. Am. Assn. Pub. Opinion Research (pres. 1973-74), AAAS, N.Y. Acad. Scis., Sigma Delta Chi, Omicron Delta Kappa. Club: Chicago Press. Home: 1451 E Cornell Pl Englewood CO 80110-3013 Office: U Denver Dept Mass Comm Denver CO 80208-0001

MENDELSON, ALAN CHARLES, lawyer; b. San Francisco, Mar. 27, 1948; s. Samuel Mendelson and Rita Rosalie (Spindel) Brown; children: Jonathan Daniel, David Gary; m. Agnés Marie Barbariol. BA with great distinction, U. Calif., Berkeley, 1969; JD cum laude, Harvard U., 1973. Bar: Calif. 1973. Assoc. Cooley Godward LLP, San Francisco, 1973-80, ptnr. Palo Alto, 1980-2000, mng. ptnr. Palo Alto office, 1990-95, 96-97; sec. gen. counsel Amgen Inc., Thousand Oaks, Calif., 1990-91; acting gen. counsel Cadence Design Sys., Inc., San Jose, 1995-96; sr. ptnr. Latham & Watkins, Menlo Park, 2000—. Bd. dirs. Valentis Inc., Axys Pharms., Inc., Aviron, USSearch.com, iScribe, Inc., Connectix Corp.; mem. mgmt. com. Cooley Godward, LLP, chmn. Cos. Practice Group, 1990—, Life Sci. Group, 1998-2000. Chmn. Piedmont (Calif.) Civil Svc. Commn., 1978-80; den leader Boy Scouts Am., Menlo Park, Calif.; fundraiser Crystal Springs Upland Sch., Hillsborough, Calif., Harvard Law Sch. Fund, Berkeley, Lucille Packard Children's Hosp.; coach Menlo Park Little League, 1982-86; pres., mem. exec. com., bd. dirs. No. Calif. chpt. Nat. Kidney Found., 1986-98. With USAR, 1969-75. Recipient Disting. Svc. award Nat. Kidney Found., 1992; named U. Calif. Berkeley Alumni scholar, 1966, Scaife Found. scholar, 1966, One of 100 Most Influential Attys. in U.S. Nat. Law Jour., 1994, 97, 2000 (Best Lawyers in Am., 1993-2000). Mem. Bohemian Club, Phi Beta Kappa. Jewish. Home: 76 De Bell Dr Atherton CA 94027-2253 Office: Latham & Watkins 135 Commonwealth Dr Menlo Park CA 94025 E-mail: alan.mendelson@lw.com

MENDELSON, LEE M. film company executive, writer, producer, director; b. San Francisco, Mar. 24, 1933; s. Palmer C. and Jeanette D. (Wise) M.; children: Glenn, Linda, Jason, Sean. BA, Stanford U., 1954. With Sta. KPIX-TV, 1961-63; chmn. bd., pres. Lee Mendelson Film Prodns. Inc., Los Angeles and Burlingame, Calif., 1963—. Guest instr. in communications Stanford U. Exec. producer, co-writer (miniseries) This Is America, Charlie Brown; producer: Charlie Brown, Cathy, Betty Boop, (TV spls.) John Steinbeck's Travels with Charley, American and Americans, The Fantastic Funnies, You Asked for It, Here Comes Garfield, (animated films) A Boy Named Charlie Brown, Snoopy Come Home, Race for Your Life Charlie Brown, Peanuts, Bon Voyage Charlie Brown (And Don't Come Back), Garfield and Friends, Mother Goose and Grim. Served to 1st lt. USAF, 1954-57. Recipient 7 Emmy awards, 3 Peabody awards. Mem. Writers Guild Am., Dirs. Guild Am. Office: Lee Mendelson Film Prodn Inc 330 Primrose Rd Ste 310 Burlingame CA 94010-4028

MENDENHALL, HARRY BARTON, lawyer; b. Oct. 31, 1946; BA, Colo. Coll., 1968; JD, U. Colo., 1971. Bar: Colo. 1971. Ptnr. Mendenhall & Malouff, R.L.L.P., Rocky Ford, Colo., 1971—. Mem. nominating com. Colo. Supreme Ct., Denver, 1986-91; pres. Colo. Lawyer Trust Account Found., Denver, 1995-97. Mem. Colo. Bar Assn. (pres. 1999-2000). Office: Mendenhall & Malouff 805 Chestnut Ave Rocky Ford CO 81067-1224 E-mail: bmendenhall@rmi.net

MENDIUS, PATRICIA DODD WINTER, editor, educator, writer; b. Davenport, Iowa, July 9, 1924; d. Otho Edward and Helen Rose (Dodd) Winter; m. John Richard Mendius, June 19, 1947; children: Richard, Catherine M. Graber, Louise, Karen M. Chooljian. BA cum laude, UCLA, 1946; MA cum laude, U. N.Mex., 1966. Cert. secondary edn. tchr., Calif., N.Mex. English teaching asst. UCLA, 1946-47; English tchr. Marlborough Sch. for Girls, L.A., 1947-50, Aztec (N.Mex.) High Sch., 1953-55, Farmington (N.Mex.) High Sch., 1955-63; chair English dept. Los Alamos (N.Mex.) High Sch., 1963-86; sr. technical writer, editor Los Alamos Nat. Lab., 1987—. Adj. prof. English, U. N.Mex., Los Alamos, 1970-72, Albuquerque, 1982-85; English cons. S.W. Regional Coll. Bd., Austin, Tex., 1975—; writer, editor, cons. advanced placement English test devel. com. Nat. Coll. Bd., 1982-86, reader, 1982-86, project equality cons., 1985-88; book selection cons. Scholastic mag., 1980-82. Author: Preparing for the Advanced Placement English Exams, 1975; editor Los Alamos Arts

Coun. bull., 1986-91. Chair Los Alamos Art in Pub. Places Bd., 1987-92; chair adv. bd. trustees U. N.Mex., Los Alamos, 1987-93; pres. Los Alamos Concert Assn., 1972-73, 95-98; chair Los Alamos Mesa Pub. Libr. Bd., 1990-94, chair endowment com., 1995-99. Mem. Soc. Tech. Communicators, AAUW (pres. 1961-63, state bd. dirs. 1959-63, Los Alamos coordinating coun. 1992-93, pres. 1993-94), DAR, Order Ea. Star, Mortar Bd., Phi Beta Kappa (pres. Los Alamos chpt. 1969-72, 99, v.p. 1996-99, pres. 2000-01), Phi Kappa Phi, Delta Kappa Gamma, Gamma Phi Beta. Avocations: swimming, reading, hiking, astronomy, singing. Home: 124 Rover Blvd Los Alamos NM 87544-3634 Office: Los Alamos Nat Lab Diamond Dr Los Alamos NM 87544 E-mail: mendius@qwest.net, pmendius@lanl.gov

MENDOZA, STANLEY ATRAN, pediatric nephrologist, educator; b. Pitts., May 7, 1940; s. Joseph William and Marian Ruth (Atran) M.; m. Carole Ann Klein, June 23, 1963; children: Daniel, Joseph. Student, Harvard U., 1957-59; B.A., Johns Hopkins U., 1961, M.D., 1964. Diplomate: Am. Bd. Pediatrics. Intern Johns Hopkins Hosp., Balt., 1964-65; jr. asst. resident dept. medicine Children's Hosp. Med. Ctr., Boston, 1965-66; asst. attending physician, dir. renal rsch. labs Children's Meml. Hosp., Chgo., 1969-71; asst. prof. pediatrics Sch. Medicine U. Calif., San Diego, 1971-73, assoc. prof., 1973-79, prof. pediatrics, dept. pediatrics, div. pediatric nephrology, 1979—, vice chmn. dept. pediatrics, 1986-87, chmn. dept. pediatrics, 1992-2000. Contbr. article in field to profl. publ. Served With USPHS, 1966-69. Fogarty Sr. Internat. fellow, 1978-79; Alan J. Wurtzburger research scholar, 1964; recipient Johns Hopkins Med. Soc. award, 1964, hon. mention Borden Undergrad. research award in medicine, 1964; Eleanor Roosevelt internat. fellow Internat. Union Against Cancer, 1984-85 Mem. Am. Fedn. Clin. Research, Am. Pediatric Soc., Am. Physiol. Soc., Am. Soc. Nephrology, Am. Soc. Pediatric Nephrology, Internat. Soc. Nephrology. Office: U Calif San Diego Dept Pediat 9500 Gilman Dr # 0696 La Jolla CA 92093-5004 E-mail: samendoza@ucsd.edu

MENHALL, DALTON WINN, lawyer, insurance executive, professional association administrator; b. Edgerton, Wis., Aug. 1, 1939; s. Joseph Laurence and Mary Winn (Dalton) M.; m. Lilian Marilyn Christie, Oct. 19, 1968; children: Dalton Winn II, Rebecca Lynn, Katherine Elizabeth BA, Ill. Coll., 1962; JD, Vanderbilt U., 1965. Bar: Wis. 1965; cert. assn. exec. Staff asst. State Bar of Wis., Madison, 1965-72, dir., 1972-76, legis. counsel, dir. continuing legal edn., 1972-76; exec. dir. N.J. State Bar Assn., Trenton, 1976-86; nat. programs dir. Herbert L. Jamison & Co., 1987-91; v.p. Edward Poll & Assocs., 1995; exec. dir. San Diego County Bar Assn., 1995—. Trustee St. Patricks' Day Sch., 1994-96. Exec. v.p. Phi Alpha Delta Pub. Svc. Ctr., Washington, 1991-94; exec. dir. Phi Alpha Delta Law Frat. Internat., Granada Hills, Calif., 1992-94; bd. dirs. San Diego unit Am. Cancer Soc., 1996-98, sec.-treas., 1998, pres.-elect, 1998-99, pres., 1999-2000, bd. dirs. Calif. divsn., 1999—; mem. vestry St. John's Episcopal Ch., 1997, sr. warden, 1998-99. Fellow Am. Bar Found.; mem. ABA (cons., youth edn. and citizenship com 1993-97), Nat. Assn. Bar Execs. (pres. 1985-86), N.J. State Bar Assn., State Bar Wis., Am. Soc. Assn. Execs., Am. Judicature Soc., Nat. Assn. Bar Execs. (hon.), So. Calif. Soc. Assn. Execs., San Diego Soc. Assn. Execs. (bd. dirs. 1997-98, sec. 1998-99).

MENKES, JOHN HANS, pediatric neurologist; b. Vienna, Austria, Dec. 20, 1928; came to U.S., 1940; s. Karl and Valerie (Tupler) M.; m. Miriam Trief, Apr. 14, 1957 (div. Feb. 1978); m. Joan Simon Feld, Sept. 28, 1980 (dec. Nov. 2000); children: Simon, Tamara, Rafael C. AB, U. So. Calif., 1947, MS, 1951; MD, Johns Hopkins U., 1952. Diplomate Am. Bd. Pediatrics, Am. Bd. Psychiatry and Neurology. Intern, jr. asst. resident Children's Med. Ctr., Boston, 1952-54; asst. resident pediatrics Bellevue Hosp., N.Y.C., 1956-57; resident neurology, trainee pediatric neurology Columbia-Presbyn. Med. Ctr., Neurological Inst. N.Y., N.Y.C., 1957-60; asst. prof. pediatrics Johns Hopkins U., Balt., 1960-63, assoc. prof., 1963-66, asst. prof. neurology, 1964-66, chief pediatric neurology div., 1964-66; prof. pediatrics and neurology UCLA, 1966-74, chief pediatric neurology div., 1966-70, prof. psychiatry, 1970-74; chief Neurology-Neurochem. Lab. Brentwood (Calif.) VA Hosp., 1970-74; clin. prof. psychiatry, neurology and pediatrics UCLA, 1974-77, clin. prof. pediatrics and neurology, 1977-84, prof. pediatrics and neurology, 1985-89, prof. emeritus pediatrics and neurology, 1989—. Dir. pediatric neurology Cedars-Sinai Med. Ctr., 1997-99, dir. emeritus pediat. neurology, 1999—; mem. metabolism study sect. NIH, 1968-70, project com., 1969-70; mem. adv. com. Nat. Inst. Child Health and Human Devel., 1985-87; mem. Dept. Health Svcs., Calif., 1980-87; mem. vaccine safety commn. Nat. Inst. Medicine, 1995—; mem. Coun. Child Neurology Soc., Dysautonomia Found., med. adv. bd. Nat. Orgn. Rare Diseases, Nat. Wilson's Disease Found.; trustee Dystonia Med. Rsch. Found., Vancouver, Can., 1985—. Author: Textbook of Child Neurology, 6th edit., 2000; (play) The Last Inquisitor, 1985 (Drama-Logue Critics award 1985), The Salvation of Miguel Toruna, 1987; (screen play) Miguel, Open Ward, 1989, The Countess of Sligo, 1992, The White Darkness, 1996, Lady Macbeth Gets a Divorce, 2001; (novel) The Secret Diary of Alice in Wonderland, 1998, The Angry Puppet Syndrome, 1999, After the Tempest, 1999, The Waiting Game, 2000, A View of Fuji, 2000; contbr. numerous articles to profl. jours. Served with USAF, 1954-56. Mem. Am. Acad. Neurology, Am. Acad. Pediatrics, Am. Chem. Soc., Soc. for Pediatric Rsch., Sociedad Peruana de Neuro-Psiquiatria (hon.), Am. Neurochem. Soc., Am. Neurol. Assn., Am. Pediatric Soc., Child Neurology Soc. (Hower award 1980), Dramatist Guild, PEN. Jewish. Home: 1201 Park Way Beverly Hills CA 90210-3334 Office: 9320 Wilshire Blvd Beverly Hills CA 90212-3216 E-mail: jmenkes@ucla.edu

MENNELLA, VINCENT ALFRED, automotive manufacturing and airplane company executive; b. Teaneck, N.J., Oct. 7, 1922; s. Francis Anthony and Henrietta Vernard (Dickson) M.; m. Madeleine Olson, Aug. 18, 1945; children: Bruce, Cynthia, Mark, Scott, Chris. BA in Acctg., U. Wash., 1948. Various sales and bus. mgmt. positions Ford divsn. Ford Motor Co., 1949-55; founder, pres. Southgate Ford, Seattle, 1955-80; pres. Flightcraft, Inc., Seattle, 1973-86; chmn. bd. Stanley Garage Door Co., Seattle, 1981-86, Zman Magnetics, Seattle, 1990—. Past chmn. March of Dimes. Capt. USNR, 1942-45. Mem. Rainier Golf Club, Seattle Tennis Club, Rotary (past pres. Seattle). Republican. Roman Catholic. Home: 1400 SW 171st Pl Seattle WA 98166-3453 E-mail: vinmad@juno.com

MENNIS, EDMUND ADDI, investment management consultant; b. Allentown, Pa., Aug. 12, 1919; s. William Henry and Grace (Addi) M.; m. Selma Adinoff, Sept. 25, 1945; children: Ardith Grace, Daniel Liam. BA, CCNY, 1941; MA, Columbia U., 1946; PhD, NYU, 1961. Security analyst Eastman, Dillon & Co., N.Y.C., 1945-46; sr. rsch. asst. Am. Inst. Econ. Rsch., Great Barrington, Mass., 1946-50; security analyst Wellington Mgmt. Co., Phila., 1950-61, dir. rsch., 1958-61, v.p., mem. investment com., 1958-66, economist, 1953-66; sr. v.p., chmn. trust investment com. Republic Nat. Bank, Dallas, 1966-72; sr. v.p., chmn. investment policy com. Security Pacific Nat. Bank, L.A., 1973-81; pres., dir. Bunker Hill Income Securities, Inc., 1973-81; chmn. bd. Security Pacific Investment Mgrs., Inc., 1977-81; ind. cons. to investment mgmt. orgns., 1982—. Tech. cons. Bus. Coun., Washington, 1962-66, 72-77, 79-81; econ. adviser sec. commerce, 1967-68; mem. investment adv. panel Pension Benefit Guaranty Corp., 1981-83 Author: How the Economy Works, 1991, 2d edit., 1999; assoc. editor Fin. Analysts Jour., 1960-88; editor: C.F.A. Digest, 1971-86, Bus. Econs., 1985-99, editor emeritus, 2000—; editor: Banker's Econ. & Investment Alert, 1993—; author or editor books, chpts., numerous articles in field of econs. and investments. Trustee Fin. Analysts Rsch. Found., 1981-86. 1st lt. USAAF, 1942-45; capt. USAF, 1951-53. Fellow Nat. Assn. Bus. Economists (coun. 1967-69, David L. Williams Lifetime Achievement award 1996); mem. Fin. Analysts Fedn. (dir. 1970-72, Graham and Dodd award 1972, Molodovsky award 1972), Am. Econ. Assn., Am. Fin. Assn., L.A. Soc. Fin. Analysts, Conf. Bus. Economists (vice chmn. 1977, chmn. 1978), Inst. CFAs (pres. 1970-72, trustee 1968-74, C. Stewart Sheppard award 1978) Home: 721 Paseo Del Mar Pls Vrds Est CA 90274-1222 Office: PO Box 1146 Palos Verdes Estates CA 90274-7946 E-mail: eamennis@home.com

MENOR, RON, state legislator; b. Hilo, Hawaii, Sept. 29, 1955; m. Patricia Ann Menor. BA in Polit. Sci., UCLA, 1977; JD, Georgetown U., 1980. Pvt. atty.; Dem. rep. dist. 18 Hawaii Ho. of Reps., 1982-85; Dem. senator dist. 18 Hawaii State Senate, 1986-90; Dem. rep. dist. 18 Hawaii Ho. of Reps., 1992—. Mem. Mililani Lions Club; bd. dirs. Mililani YMCA. Mem. commerce, consumer protection, edn., transp., mil. affairs and govtl. affairs coms. Hawaii Ho. of Reps., chair housing com. E-mail: Sen.Menor. Office: Hawaii Ho of Reps Hawaii State Capitol Rm 219 415 S Beretania St Honolulu HI 96813 Fax: 808 586-6829

MENSE, ALLAN TATE, research and development engineering executive; b. Kansas City, Mo., Nov. 29, 1945; s. Martin Conrad Mense and Nancy (Tate) Johnson; children from previous marriage: Melanie Georgia, Eileen Madelaine. BS, U. Ariz., 1968, MS, 1970; PhD, U. Wis., 1976; MS in Indsl. Engring., Ariz. State U., 1999. Scientist Oak Ridge (Tenn.) Nat. Lab, 1976-79; sr. staff sci. and tech. comm. U.S. Ho. Reps., Washington, 1979-81; sr. scientist McDonnell Douglas Astro. Co., St. Louis, 1981-85; from dep. chief scientist to chief scientist Dept. Def. Strategic Def. Initiative Orgn., Washington, 1985-88; v.p. rsch. Fla. Inst. Tech., Melbourne, 1988-92; pres. Advanced Tech. Mgmt., Inc., Tempe, Ariz., 1992-97; program mgr. Motorla Space Sys. Tech. Group, Chandler, 1998—. Vis. scholar Sloan Sch., MIT, 1995-96. Contbr. over 60 articles to profl. jours. Ariz. State U. scholar, 1996-97. Mem. AIAA (sr. mem.), IEEE (chmn. energy com. 1985—, sr. mem.), Am. Def. Preparedness Assn., Am. Phys. Soc., Am. Nuclear Soc., Inst. Indsl. Engrs., Fla. Com. Nat. Space Club (charter), Sigma Xi, Theta Tau, Pi Mu Alpha. Episcopalian. Home: 2292 W Myrtle Dr Chandler AZ 85248-4126 Office: 8075 S River Pkwy Tempe AZ 85284

MERCER, JOHN A. state legislator; b. Missoula, Mont., Jan. 21, 1957; m. Tine Mercer; children: Thomas, Michael. BA in Bus., U. Mont., 1979; JD, Northwestern U., 1982. Pvt. practice, Polson, Mont., 1982; mem. Mont. Ho. of Reps., 1984—, minority whip, 1989-90, minority leader, 1991-92, house spkr., 1993—, mem. rules com., mem. legis. administrv. com. Office: PO Box 460 Polson MT 59860-0460 also: PO Box 200400 Helena MT 59620-0400 E-mail: house@state.mt.us

MERCHANT, ROLAND SAMUEL, SR. hospital administrator, educator; b. N.Y.C., Apr. 18, 1929; s. Samuel and Eleta (McLymont) M.; m. Audrey Bartley, June 6, 1970; children: Orelia Eleta, Roland Samuel, Huey Bartley. BA, NYU, 1957, MA, 1960; MS, Columbia U., 1963, MSHA, 1974. Asst. statistician N.Y.C. Dept. Health, 1957-60, statistician, 1960-63, N.Y. Tb and Health Assn., N.Y.C., 1963-65; biostatistician, adminstrv. coord. Inst. Surg. Studies, Montefiore Hosp., Bronx, N.Y., 1965-72; resident in adminstrn. Roosevelt Hosp., N.Y.C., 1973-74; dir. health and hosp. mgmt. Dept. Health, City of N.Y., 1974-76; from asst. adminstr. to adminstr. West Adams Cmty. Hosp., L.A., 1976; spl. asst. to assoc. v.p. for med. affairs Stanford U. Hosp., Calif., 1977-82, dir. office mgmt. and strategic planning, 1982-85, dir. mgmt. planning, 1986-90; v.p. strategic planning Cedars-Sinai Med. Ctr., L.A., 1990-94; cons. Roland Merchant & Assocs., L.A., 1994—. Clin. assoc. prof. dept. family, community and preventive medicine Stanford U., 1986-88, dept. health rsch. and policy Stanford U. Med. Sch., 1988-90. With U.S. Army, 1951-53. USPHS fellow. Fellow Am. Coll. Healthcare Execs., APHA; mem. Am. Hosp. Assn., Nat. Assn. Health Svcs. Execs., N.Y. Acad. Scis. Home: 27335 Park Vista Rd Agoura Hills CA 91301-3639

MERENDINO, K. ALVIN, surgical educator; b. Clarksburg, W.Va., Dec. 3, 1914; s. Biagio and Cira (Bivona) M.; m. Shirley Emojane Hill, July 6, 1943; children: Cira Anne Watts, Nancy Jane Napuunoa, Susan Hill Mitchell, Nina Merendino-Sarich, Maria King Merendino-Stillwell. BA, Ohio U., 1936, LLD (hon.), 1967; MD, Yale U., 1940; PhD, U. Minn., 1946. Diplomate Am. Bd. Surgery, Am. Bd. Thoracic Surgery. Intern Cin. Gen. Hosp., 1940-41; resident U. Minn. Hosp., Mpls., 1941-45; rsch. asst. Dr. Owen H. Wangensteen, 1942-43; trainee Nat. Cancer Inst., 1943-45; dir. program in postgrad. med. edn. in surgery Ancker Hosp., St. Paul, 1946-48; instr. dept. surgery U. Minn., Mpls., 1944-45, asst. prof. dept. surgery, 1945-48; assoc. prof. dept. surgery U. Wash., Seattle, 1949-55, dir. exptl. surgery labs., dept. surgery, 1950-72, prof. dept. surgery, 1955-81, prof. emeritus, 1981—, prof. and adminstrv. officer dept. surgery, 1957-64, prof., chmn., 1964-72; chmn. dept. surgery King Faisal Specialist and Rsch. Ctgr., Riyadh, Saudi Arabia, 1976, dir. med. affairs Saudi Arabia, 1976-79, dir. Cancer Therapy Inst., spl. cons. to Coun., supr. for exec. mgmt., assoc. dir. med. affairs Saudi Arabia, 1981-82; dir. ops. King Faisal Med. City, Riyadh, 1981-85. Mem. adv. com. for med. rsch., Boeing Airplane Co., 1959-67, chmn., 19621 cons. Children's Orthopedic Hosp., Seattle, 1972-82; mem. adv. com. on heart disease and surgery for crippled children's svc., Wash. State Dept. Health and Div. Vocational Rehab., 1961; mem. surgery study sect. NIH, 1958-62, subcom. on prosthetic valves for cardiac surgery, chm. 1st Nat. Conf., 1960, mem. adv. com. 2d Nat. Conf. on Prosthetic Heart Valves, 1969, Surgery A study sect. chmn., 1970-72, Nat. Heart and Lung Inst. Tng. Com., 1965-69; cons. VA, Seattle, 1949-59, 65-81; mem. adv. com. on hosps. and clinics, USPHS, 1963-66; mem. surgery test com. Nat. Bd. Med. Examiners, 1963-67; mem. surgery resident rev. com., Conf. Com. on Grad. Edn. in Surgery, 1963-73, vice-chmn., 1972-73; chmn. 2d Saudi Arabian Med. Conf., Riyadh, 1978; mem. com. on postgrad. med. edn., Kingdom of Saudi Arabia Ministry of Health, 1978-79. Editor in chief: Prosthetic Valves for Cardiac Surgery, 1961; assoc. editor: Prosthetic Heart Valves, 1969; mem. editorial bd. Am. Jour. Surgery,. 1958-83, Jour. Surg. Rsch., 1961-69, Pacific Medicine and Surgery, 1964-68, King Faisal Hosp. Medicine Jour. (renamed Annals of Saudi Medicine), 1981-85; contbr. articles to profl. jours., chpts. to books; producer movies on surgery. Recipient cert. of merit Ohio U. Alumni Assn., 1957, Outstanding W.Va. Italian-Am. award W.Va. Italian Heritage Festival Inc., Clarksburg, W.Va., 1984, Spirit of Freedom award A. James Mancin, Sec. State W.Va., 1984, Disting. W. Virginian award State of W.Va., 1984, John Baird Thomas Meml. award Ohio U.; named Surgery Alumnus of Yr., U. Minn., 1981, Disting. Citizen Wash. State, Lt. Gov. John Cherberg, 1981; NIH grantee, 1951-76; Verdi scholar Yale U. Fellow ACS (numerous coms., bds.), Soc. of Univ. Surgeons (councilman at large 3 yrs.), Internat. Soc. Surgery; mem. Am. Surg. Assn. (adv. mem. com. 1959-64, v.p. 1972-73), Am. Assn. for Thoracic Surgery, Halsted Soc., Henry N. Harkins Surg. Soc., N. Pacific Coast Surg. Assn., Seattle Surg. Soc. (honored special tribute annual meeting 1997), So. Surg. Soc. (Arthur H. Shipley award 1972), Am. Bd. Surgery 1958-64 (vice chmn. 1962-63, chmn. 1963-64, emeritus 1964—); University Club, Seattle Golf Club, Phi Beta Kappa, Sigma Xi, Beta Theta Pi (sec., pres.), Phi Beta Pi (hon.). Republican. Episcopalian. Avocations: golf, fly fishing, bird hunting, gardening. Home: The Highlands Seattle WA 98177 Office: U Wash Sch Med Dept Surgery Seattle WA 98195-0001

MERIGAN, THOMAS CHARLES, JR. internist, medical researcher, educator; b. San Francisco, Jan. 18, 1934; s. Thomas C. and Helen M. (Greeley) M.; m. Joan Mary Freeborn, Oct. 3, 1959; 1 son, Thomas Charles III. BA with honors, U. Calif., Berkeley, 1955; MD, U. Calif., San Francisco, 1958. Diplomate: Am. Bd. Internal Medicine. Intern 2d and 4th Harvard med. services Boston City Hosp., 1958-59, asst. resident medicine, 1959-60; clin. assoc. Nat. Heart Inst., NIH, Bethesda, Md., 1960-62; assoc. Lab. Molecular Biology, Nat. Inst. Arthritis and Metabolic Diseases, NIH, 1962-63; practice medicine specializing in internal medicine and infectious diseases Stanford, Calif., 1963—; asst. prof. medicine Stanford U. Sch. Medicine, 1963-67, assoc. prof. medicine, 1967-72, head div. infectious diseases, 1966-92, prof. medicine, 1972—, George E. and Lucy Becker prof. medicine, 1980—. Dir. Diagnostic Microbiology Lab., Univ. Hosp., 1966-72, Diagnostic Virology Lab., 1969-99, Ctr. AIDS Rsch. Stanford U., 1988—; hosp. epidemiologist, 1966-88; mem. microbiology rsch. tng. grants com. NIH, 1969-73, virology study sect., 1974-78; cons. antiviral substances program Nat. Inst. Allergy and Infectious Diseases, 1970-94, mem. AIDS clin. drug devel. commn., 1986-94; mem. Virology Task Force, 1976-78, bd. sci. counselors, 1980-85; mem. U.S. Hepatitis panel U.S. and Japan Coop. Med. Sci. Program, 1979-90, AIDS subcom. Nat. Adv. Allergy and Infectious Diseases Coun., 1988-89; co-chmn. interferon evaluation Group Am. Cancer Soc., 1978-81; vaccines and related biol. products adv. com. Ctr. for Drugs and Biols., FDA, 1984-88; internat. adv. com. on biol. sci. Sci. Council, Singapore, 1985-88; adv. com. J.A. Hartford Found., 1979-84; mem. Albert Lasker awards jury, 1981-84; peer review panel U.S. Army Med. Rsch. and Devel. Com., 1986-88; nat. com. to rev. current procedures for approval New Drugs for Cancer and AIDS, 1989-90; mem. Com. to Study Use of Coms. within FDA, 1991-92. Contbr. articles on infectious diseases, virology and immunology to profl. jours.; editor: Antivirals with Clinical Potential, 1976, Antivirals and Virus Diseases of Man, 1979, 4th edit., 1997, Regulatory Functions of Interferon, 1980, Interferons, 1982, Interferons as Cell Growth Inhibitors, 1986; assoc. editor: Virology, 1975-78, Cancer Research, 1987-91; co-editor: monograph series Current Topics in Infectious Diseases, 1975-92, Cytomegalovirus Infect and Ganciclovir, 1988, Focus on Didanosine (ddI), 1990, Practical Diagnosis of Viral Infection, Textbook of AIDS Medicine, 1994, 2d edit., 1999, Surrogate Markers for HIV Infection, 1995, Antimicrobial Therapy in Vaccines, 1999; mem. editl. bd. Archives Internal Medicine, 1971-81, Jour. Gen. Virology, 1972-77, Infection and Immunity, 1973-81, Intervirology, 1973-85, Proc. Soc. Expt. Biology and Medicine, 1978-87, Reviews of Infectious Diseases, 1979-89, Jour. Interferon Rsch., 1980-89, Antiviral Rsch., 1980-86, Jour. Antimicrobial Chemotherapy, 1981-91, Molecular and Cellular Biochemistry, 1982-89, AIDS Rsch. and Human Retroviruses, 1983—, Jour. Virology, 1984-89, Biotechnology Therapeutics, 1988-98, Jour. Infectious Diseases, 1989-94, Clinical Drug Investigation, 1989—, HIV: Advances in Rsch. and Therapy, 1990-00, Internat. Jour. Antimicrobial Agts. 1990-99, The AIDS Reader, 1991—, AIDS, 1993, Clinical Immunotherapeutics, 1994—, Antiviral Therapy, 1996-99. Recipient Borden award for Outstanding Rsch., Am. Assn. Med. Colls., 1973, Merit award, Nat. Inst. Allergy and Infectious Diseases, 1988, Maxwell Finland Lectureship award Infectious Diseases Soc. Am., 1988; Guggenheim Meml. fellow, 1972. Fellow AAAS; mem. AMA, Assn. Am. Physicians, Western Assn. Physicians, Am. Soc. Microbiology, Am. Soc. Clin. Investigation (coun. 1977-80), Am. Assn. Immunologists, Am. Fedn. Clin. Rsch., Western Soc. Clin. Rsch., Soc. Exptl. Biology and Medicine (publ. com. 1985-89), Infectious Diseases Soc. Am., Am. Soc. Virology, inst. Medicine, Pan Am. Group for Rapid Viral Diagnosis, Internat. Soc. Interferon Rsch. (coun. 1983-89), Calif. Med. Assn., Santa Clara County Med. Soc., Calif. Acad. Medicine, Royal Soc. Medicine, Alpha Omega Alpha. Home: 148 Goya Rd Portola Valley CA 94028-7307 Office: Stanford U Sch Medicine Divsn Infectious Diseases Stanford CA 94305

MERINOFF, HERMAN I. vintager, wine and spirits executive; Chmn., pres., CEO Sonoma Vineyards, Healdsburg, Calif.; CEO Charmer Industries Inc., Queens, N.Y. Vintager, wine and spirits executive. Chmn., pres., chief exec. officer Sonoma Vineyards, Healdsburg, Calif; chief exec. officer, Charmer Industries Inc., Queens, New York. Office: Sonoma Vineyards 11455 Old Redwood Hwy Healdsburg CA 95448-9523

MERKER, STEVEN JOSEPH, lawyer; b. Cleve., Feb. 21, 1947; s. Steven Joseph and Laverne (Zamenik) M.; m. Janet L. Whyatt; children: Steven, Rena, Ashley, Matthew. BS, Case Inst. Tech., 1968; MS, U. Fla., 1973. Bar: Ohio 1976, U.S. Dist. Ct. (no. dist.) Ohio, 1976, U.S. Dist. Ct. Colo. 1979, U.S. Ct. Appeals (10th cir.) 1979, U.S. Supreme Ct. 1989. Assoc. Jones, Day, Reavis & Pogue, Cleve., 1976-78, Davis, Graham & Stubbs, Denver, 1978-82, ptnr., 1983-96, chmn. labor and employment group, 1989-96; chmn. litigation and labor and employment groups Merrick, Calvin & Merker, LLP, 1996-97; ptnr. Dorsey & Whitney LLP, Denver, 1997—, mng. ptnr. Denver office, 2000—. Mem. Tenth Cir. Adv. Com., 1997-2000. Legal counsel Coloradans for Lamm-Dick campaign, Denver, 1982, Nancy Dick for U.S. Senate Com., Denver, 1984, Cantrell for Dist. Atty., Jefferson County, Colo., 1984; bd. dirs. Very Spl. Arts, Colo., 1994—. Capt. USAF, 1969-72. Mem. ABA, Colo. Bar Assn., Denver Bar Assn. Office: Dorsey & Whitney LLP 370 17th St Ste 4400 Denver CO 80202-5644 E-mail: werker.steve@dorseylaw.com

MERKIN, ALBERT CHARLES, pediatrician, allergist; b. Chgo., Sept. 4, 1924; s. Harry A. and Goldie (Lamasky) M.; m. Eunice Aprill, Aug. 22, 1948; children: Audrey, Ellen, Joseph. Student, U. Ill., 1942-44; MD, U. Ill., Chgo., 1949. Diplomate Am. Bd. Allergy and Immunology, Am. Bd. Pediatrics. Intern, resident Cook County Hosp., Chgo.; resident Children's Meml. Hosp., Chgo.; with Valley Pediatric and Allergy Clinic, Las Vegas, Nev. Capt. USAF, 1950-53. Fellow Am. Acad. Pediatrics (state chmn. Nev. 1961-64, sect. allergy and immunology), Am. Coll. Allergy; mem. Am. Acad. Allergy, Allergy Subsplty. Group of Acad. Pediatrics (cert. pediatric allergist). Avocations: reading, travel. Office: Valley Pediat & Allergy Clinic 222 S Rainbow Blvd Ste 119 Las Vegas NV 89145-5343

MERRIFIELD, DONALD PAUL, university chancellor; b. Los Angeles, Nov. 14, 1928; s. Arthur S. and Elizabeth (Baker) M. B.S. in Physics, Calif. Inst. Tech., 1950; M.S., U. Notre Dame, 1951; A.M., Ph.L. in Philosophy, St. Louis U., 1957; Ph.D., MIT, 1962; S.T.M., U. Santa Clara, Calif., 1966; S.T.D. (hon.), U. So. Calif., 1969; D.H.L. (hon.), U. Judaism, 1984, Hebrew Union Coll.-Jewish Inst. Religion, 1986. Joined Soc. of Jesus, 1951; ordained priest Roman Cath. Ch., 1965; instr. physics Loyola U., Los Angeles, 1961-62; lectr. Engring. Sch., Santa Clara, 1965; cons. theoretical chemistry Jet Propulsion Lab., Calif. Inst. Tech., 1962-69; asst. prof. physics U. San Francisco, 1967-69; pres. Loyola Marymount U., Los Angeles, 1969-84, chancellor, 1984—. Mem. Sigma Xi. Home: Jesuit Cmty at Loyola Marymount U Box 45041 Los Angeles CA 90045 E-mail: dmerrifi@lmu.edu

MERRILL, HARVIE MARTIN, manufacturing executive, director; b. Detroit, Apr. 26, 1921; s. Harvie and Helen (Nelson) M.; m. Mardelle Merrill; children— Susan, Linda. B.S. in Chem. Engring, Purdue U., 1942. Devel. engr. Sinclair Refining Co., 1946-47; research and gen. mgr. 3M Co., St. Paul, 1947-65; v.p. fabricated products Plastics div. Stauffer Chem. Co., N.Y.C., 1965-69; with Hexcel Corp., San Francisco, 1969-86, pres., chief exec. officer, 1969-86, chmn. bd., 1976-88. With USAF, 1942-46. Mem. Pacific-Union Club, Bohemian Club San Francisco, Villa Taverna (San Francisco), Burlingame Country Club. Home: 1170 Sacramento St San Francisco CA 94108-1943

MERRILL, RICHARD JAMES, educational director; b. Milw., Apr. 15, 1931; s. Henry Baldwin and Doris (Lucas) M.; m. Kathleen Emden Keely, June 14, 1953 (dec. Jan. 1974); children— Wendy Ann, Vicki Louise, Robin Kay, Christina Suzanne; m. Terry Bradley Alt, Aug. 10, 1974 (div. 1976); m. Shannon Ann Lynch, June 19, 1977. B.S., U. Mich., 1953; M.A., Columbia U., 1957, Ed.D., 1960. Tchr. sci. Ramona High Sch., Riverside, Calif., 1958-62; secondary sci. coordinator Riverside city schs., 1960-62; exec. dir. chem. edn. material study Harvey Mudd Coll. and U. Calif. at Berkeley, 1962-65; curriculum specialist Mt. Diablo Unified Sch. Dist., Concord, Calif., 1965-91, dir. curriculum, 1980-81; assoc. dir. Inst. for Chem. Edn. and Project Phys. Sci., U. Calif., Berkeley, 1990-94. Bd. dirs.

San Francisco Bay Area Sci. Fair; mem. sci. adv. com. Calif. Assessment Program, 1983-89, also mem. assessment adv. com. to state supt., pub. instrn., 1984-86; dir. N. Calif. W. Nev. Jr. Sci. and Humanities Symposium, 1993—; lectr. Calif. State U., Hayward, 1996—. Author: (with David W. Ridgway) The CHEM Study Story, 1969; co-author: National Science Teachers Association Guidelines for Self-Assessment of Secondary Science Programs, 1975, Science Framework for California Public Schools, 1978, 84; co-author, editor: The Physical Science of Living in California, 1993. Bd. dirs. Ctr. for New Ams., Concord, Calif., 1984-91. Served from ensign to lt. (j.g.) USN, 1953-56. Mem. Nat. Sci. Tchrs. Assn. (past pres., past mem. exec. com.), Nat. Sci. Suprs. Assn., Elem. Sch. Sci. Assn. (coun. 1975-82, pres. 1983), Calif. Sci. Tchrs. Assn. (Disting. Svc. award 1990), Assn. Calif. Sch. Adminstrs., Acacia, Phi Delta Kappa. Home: 1862 2nd Ave Walnut Creek CA 94596-2553 Office: U Calif Lawrence Hall Of Sci Berkeley CA 94720-0001

MERRIN, SEYMOUR, computer marketing company executive; b. Bklyn., Aug. 13, 1931; s. Joseph and Esther Bella (Manelis) M.; m. Elaine Cohen, Sept. 4, 1960 (dec. May 1962); m. Elizabeth Jenifer Slack, Oct. 12, 1963 (dec. Mar. 1995); children: Charles Seymour, Marianne Jenifer Weights. BS, Tufts Coll., 1952; MS, U. Ariz., 1954; PhD, Pa. State U., 1962. Geologist Magma Copper Co., Superior, Ariz., 1954; geologist U.S. Geol. Survey, 1956-58; chemist IBM, Poughkeepsie, N.Y., 1962-64; mgr. package devel., mgr. reliability and failure analysis Sperry Semicondr. div. Sperry Rand, Norwalk, Conn., 1965-68; cons. materials tech. Fairfield, 1967-69; v.p., dir. Innotech Corp., Norwalk, 1969-74; div. mgr. Emdex div. Exxon Enterprises, Milford, Conn., 1974-78; chmn., dir. Computerworks, Westport, 1978-85; v.p., dir. personal computing service Gartner Group, Inc., Stamford, 1984-87; pres. Merrin Resources, Southport, 1987-89, Merrin Info. Svcs., Inc., Palo Alto, Calif., 1987—. Bd. dirs. Micrografx Corp., Allen, Tex.; mem. adv. panel Apple Computer Co., Cupertino, Calif., 1982-83; mem. adv. bd. Compaq Computer Corp., Houston, 1984-85, Computer and Software News, N.Y.C., 1984-89; mem. program adv. bd. Comdex, Boston, 1985—; lectr. in field. Contbr. numerous articles to profl. publs.; patentee in field Served with U.S. Army, 1954-56 Fellow Geol. Soc. Am., Am. Inst. Chemists; Computing Tech. Industry Assn. (founder, pres. 1981-83, bd. dirs. 1981-84). Home and Office: 560 Los Nidos Dr Santa Fe NM 87501-8356 E-mail: smerrin@aol.com

MERRITT, LAVERE BARRUS, engineering educator, civil engineer; b. Afton, Wyo., Mar. 11, 1936; s. Joseph M. and Lera (Barrus) M.; m. Jackie Call, Jan. 5, 1956 (dec. Sept. 1999); m. Diane Mainord, July 14, 2001; children: Teri F., Lynn T., Rachel R., Shaun S. BSCE, U. Utah, 1963, MSCE, 1966; PhD, U. Wash., 1970. Registered profl. engr., Utah, Ariz. Prof. civil and environ. engring. Brigham Young U., Provo, Utah, 1970—, chmn. dept. civil engring., 1986-92; co-chmn. faculty senate, 1996-97. Spl. cons. Utah Div. Health, Salt Lake City, 1973-74; cons. engring. firms, 1970— Chmn. Provo Met. Water Bd., Utah, 1978-87. Named Utah Engring. Educator of the Yr. Utah Joint Enring. Coun., 1987. Mem. ASCE (nat. dir. 1982-85), Am. Acad. Environ. Engrs., Water Environment Fedn. (nat. dir. 1981-84, Bedell award), Am. Water Works Assn., Am. Soc. Engring. Edn., Sigma Xi. Republican. Mormon. Home: 562 E 3050 N Provo UT 84604-4264 Office: Brigham Young U 370 CB Provo UT 84602-4067 E-mail: merrittl@byu.edu

MERRITT, NANCY-JO, lawyer; b. Phoenix, Sept. 24, 1942; d. Robert Nelson Meeker and Violet Adele Gibson; children: Sidney Kathryn, Kurt, Douglas. BA, Ariz. State U., 1964, MA, 1974, JD, 1978. Bar: Ariz. 1978, U.S. Dist. Ct. Ariz. 1978, U.S. Ct. Appeals (9th cir.) 1984. Assoc. Erlichman, Fagerberg & Margrave, Phoenix, 1978-79, Pearlstein & Margrave, Phoenix, 1979-81, Corwin & Merritt, P.C., Phoenix, 1982-87; with Nancy-Jo Merritt & Assocs., P.C., Phoenix, 1987-88; ptnr. Bryan Cave, Phoenix, 1988-97, Bacon and Merritt, Phoenix, 1997-98; of counsel, mng. atty. Fragomen, Del Rey, Bernsen & Loewy, Phoenix, 1998—. Author: Understanding Immigration Law, 1993; sr. editor: Immigration and National Law Handbook, 1993—; contbr. articles to profl. jours. Chair bd. dirs. TERROS, 1995-97. Fellow Ariz. Bar Found.; mem. ABA, Am. Immigration Lawyers Assn. (chairperson Ariz. chpt. 1985-87, several coms., Pro Bono award), Am. Immigration Law Found. (trustee), Ariz. Bar Assn. (immigration sect.), Nucleus Club. Democrat. Avocations: modern literature, South American literature, hiking, gardening. Office: Fragomen Del Rey Bernsen & Loewy 3101 N Central Ave Ste 1470 Phoenix AZ 85012-2643 E-mail: njmerritt@fdbl.com

MERTA DE VELEHRAD, JAN, diving engineer and marine safety specialist, scientist, psychologist, inventor, educator, civil servant; b. Stare Mesto, Czechoslovakia, Apr. 24, 1944; arrived in Can., 1968; s. Jan and Marie (Sebkova) M.; m. Margaret; 1 child, Iveta. Diploma, Ucnovská Skola Technická, Slusovice, 1962, Coll. Social Law, Prague, 1968; BS, McGill U., Montreal, 1971; PhD in Psychology, U. Aberdeen, Scotland, 1978. Pres., pub. Jan's Pub. Co., Montreal, 1972-74; deep sea diver, diving supr. North Sea, Middle East, Africa, 1974-78; dir. R&D Wharton-Williams Ltd., Aberdeen, 1978-79, Oceaneering, Inc., Houston, 1979-81; chief insp. diving Govt. of Can., 1981-2000; specialist, insp. officer, health and safety officer. Co-author: Exploring The Human Aura, 1976, Canadian Oil and Gas Diving Regulations, 1989, 99. Chmn. com. for survival suits Can. Gen. Standards Bd., 1983-96; br. chmn. Czech Assn. of Can., 1986-91; hon. appt. bd. Seneca Coll. Ont., 1983; chmn. com. for diving competency Can. Stds. Assn., 1994-2000; chmn. Z-275 com. Can. Stds. Assn., 2000—. Decorated Order of Can., Alta. Order of Excellence; recipient Spl. Industry award Can. Assn. Diving Contrators, 1985, award for svc. to sub-sea industry, 1988, Ietarnat. Cultural Diploma of Honour, 1989, Commemorative Medal of Honour, 1988, Silver Shield of Valor, 1992; named Pursuivant, Spanish Coll. Arms, 1990, to Internat. Leadership Hall of Fame, 1988, Internat. Hall of Leaders, 1988; named Man of Yr., U.K., 1990, World Intellectual, 1993, One in a Million, U.K., 1992, hon. citizen Town of Modra, Czech Republic, 2001. Fellow Inst. Diagnostic Engrs., Inst. Petroleum; mem. Soc. Fire Protection Engrs., Brit. Psychol. Soc., Internat. Soc. Hyperbaric Medicine (v.p. 1990-96), Undersea Med. Soc., Soc. Petroleum Engrs., Submarine Pilot Assn., Soc. Naval Archs. and Marine Engrs. Soc. rank: H.S.H. Prince of Armavir, Duke of Melk, Baron de Velehrad, Chevalier Ordre Royal de La Couronne de Boheme, Capt., Sea Eagle Legion. Achievements include 2 British patents; patents pending. Avocations: photography, exploration, literary investigation. Office: Nat Energy Bd 311 6th Ave S W Calgary AB Canada T2P 3H2 Address: PO Box 22244 Bankers Hall Calgary AB Canada T2P 4J6

MERTENS, LYNNE G. retail executive; CEO, pres. Waller, The Graphics Resource, San Francisco. Office: Waller 339 Harbor Way South San Francisco CA 94080-6919 Fax: 650-589-0578

MERTZ, EDWIN THEODORE, retired biochemist, emeritus educator; b. Missoula, Mont., Dec. 6, 1909; s. Gustav Henry and Louise (Sain) M.; m. Mary Ellen Ruskamp, Oct. 5, 1936; children: Martha Ellen, Edwin T.; m. Virginia T. Henry, Aug. 1, 1987. B.A., U. Mont., 1931, D.Sc. (hon.), 1979; M.S. in Biochemistry, U. Ill., 1933, Ph.D. in Biochemistry, 1935; D.Agr. (hon.), Purdue U., 1977. Rsch. biochemist Armour & Co., Chgo., 1935-37; instr. biochemistry U. Ill., 1937-38; rsch. assoc. in pathology U. Iowa, 1938-40; instr. agrl. chemistry U. Mo., 1940-43; rsch. chemist Hercules Powder Co., 1943-46; prof. biochemistry Purdue U., West Lafayette, Ind., 1946-76, emeritus prof., 1976—. Vis. prof. U. Notre Dame, South Bend, Ind., 1976-77; cons. in agronomy Purdue U., 1977-94; affiliate prof. crops and soils Mont. State U., Bozeman, 1995—. Author: Elementary Biochemistry, 1969; author, editor: Quality Protein Maize, 1964-94. Recipient McCoy award Purdue U., 1967; John Scott award City of Phila., 1967; Hoblitzelle Nat. award Tex. Research Found., 1968; Congressional medal Fed. Land Banks, 1968; Disting. Service award U. Mont., 1973; Browning award Am. Soc. Agronomy, 1974; Pioneer Chemist award Am. Inst. Chemists, 1976 Mem. AAAS, AAUP, Nat. Acad. Scis., Am. Soc. Biol. Chemists, Am. Inst. Nutrition (Osborne-Mendel award 1972), Am. Chem. Soc. (Spencer award 1970), Am. Assn. Cereal Chemists. Lutheran. Achievements include co-discovering high lysine corn, 1963. Office: Montana State Univ Dept Plant And Soils Bozeman MT 59717-0001

MESAROS, KENNETH LEE, state legislator, rancher; b. Great Falls, Mont., June 17, 1950; s. Albert and Hilda (Heiman) M.; m. Rebecca Lynn Mesaros; children: Mathew, Michael, Scot, Kimberly. BS in Agr. Edn., Mont. State U., 1973. Owner, operator Mesaros Ranch, Cascade, Mont., 1969—; senator State of Mont., Helena, 1992—. Dir. Am. Inst. Cooperatives, Mpls., 1978; chmn., dir. Foothill Livestock Assn., Cascade County, Mont., 1982-88, Equity Co-op Assn., Ulm, Mont., 1977-84. Sch. bd. chmn. Sch. Dist. # 95, Deep Creek, Mont., 1986-90. Staff sgt. Mont. Air N.G., 1969-75. Mem. Mont. Stockgrowers Assn. (dir. 1990-94), Cascade Lions Club, Great Falls Elks Club, NRA, Mont. Farm Bureau, Mont. Cattleman's Assoc., Mont. Graingrowers Assoc. Republican. Roman Catholic. Avocations: hunting, fishing, skiing, golf. Home: 2191 Milligan Rd Cascade MT 59421-8001

MESCHKOW, JORDAN M. lawyer; b. Bklyn., Mar. 25, 1957; s. Gerald Meschkow and Florence Y. (Katz) Silverman; m. Susan G. Scher, Aug. 10, 1980; children: Sasha Hayley, Alisha Sadie. BS in Biology, SUNY, Stony Brook, 1979; JD, Chgo. Kent Coll. Law, 1982. Bar: Ariz. 1982, Fla. 1983; registered U.S. Patent and Trademark Office 1983. Assoc. James F. Duffy, Patent Atty., Phoenix, 1982; ptnr. Duffy & Meschkow, Phoenix, 1983-84; sole practice Phoenix, 1984-92; sr. ptnr. Meschkow & Gresham, P.L.C., Phoenix, 1992—. Frequent talk radio guest and spkr. at seminars on patent, trademark and copyright law. Contbr. article series to profl. jours.; patentee in field. Exec. bd. City of Phoenix Fire Pub. Awareness League, 1996—. Mem. Am. Intellectual Property Law Assn., State Bar Ariz. (intellectual property sect. 1982—), State Bar Fla. Avocations: gardening, motorcycling, bicycling, skating, swimming. Office: 5727 N 7th St Ste 409 Phoenix AZ 85014-5818 E-mail: JM@patentmg.com

MESSENGER, GEORGE CLEMENT, engineering executive, consultant; b. Bellows Falls, Vt., July 20, 1930; s. Clement George and Ethel Mildred (Farrar) M.; m. Priscilla Betty Norris, June 19, 1954; children: Michael Todd, Steven Barry, Bonnie Lynn. BS in Physics, Worcester Poly U., 1951; MSEE, U. Pa., 1957; PhD in Engring., Calif. Coast U., 1986. Rsch. scientist Philco Corp., Phila., 1951-59; engring. mgr. Hughes Semicondr., Newport Beach, Calif., 1959-61; divsn. mgr. Transitron Corp., Wakefield, Mass., 1961-63; staff scientist Northrop Corp., Hawthorne, Calif., 1963-68; cons. engr. Las Vegas, Nev., 1968—. Lectr. UCLA, 1969-75; v.p., dir. Am. Inst. Fin., Grafton, Mass., 1970-78; gen. ptnr. Dargon Fund, Anaheim, Calif., 1983—; v.p., tech. dir. Messenger and Assoc., 1987—, registered investment adviser, 1989—. Co-author: The Effects of Radiation on Electronic Systems, 1986, Single Event Phenomena, 1997; contbg. author: Fundamentals of Nuclear Hardening, 1972, Nonvolatile Semiconductor Memory Technology, 1998; contbr. articles to profl. jours.; patentee microwave diode, hardened semicondrs. Recipient Naval Rsch. Lab. Alan Berman award, 1982, Best Paper award HEART Conf., 1983, Spl. Merit award, 1983, Pete Haas award, 1992, Goddard award for outstanding profl. achievement Worcester Poly. Inst., 1996. Fellow IEEE (Merit award 1986); mem. Rsch. Soc. Am., Am. Phys. Soc. Congregationalist. Home and Office: 3111 Bel Air Dr Apt 7F Las Vegas NV 89109-1510 E-mail: gpmessenger@prodigy.net

MESSER, DONALD EDWARD, theological school president, theology educator; b. Kimball, S.D., Mar. 5, 1941; s. George Marcus and Grace E. (Foltz) M.; m. Bonnie Jeanne Nagel, Aug. 30, 1964; children: Christine Marie, Kent Donald. BA cum laude, Dakota Wesleyan U., 1963; M. Divinity magna cum laude, Boston U., 1966, PhD, 1969; LHD (hon.), Dakota Wesleyan U., 1977. Asst. to commr. Mass. Commn. Against Discrimination, Boston, 1968-69; asst. prof. Augustana Coll., Sioux Falls, S.D., 1969-71; assoc. pastor 1st United Meth. Ch., Sioux Falls, 1969-71; pres. Dakota Wesleyan U., Mitchell, S.D., 1971-81, Iliff Sch. Theology, Denver, 1981-2000, pres. emeritus and prof. practical theology, 2000—. Author: Christian Ethics and Political Action, 1984, Contemporary Images of Christian Ministry, 1989, Send Me? The Intineracy in Crisis, 1991, The Conspiracy of Goodness, 1992, Caught in the Crossfire: Helping Christians Debate Homosexuality, 1994, Calling Church and Seminary Into the 21st Century, 1995, Unity, Liberty, and Charity: Building Bridges Under Icy Waters, 1996, How Shall We Die? Helping Christians Debate Assisted Suicide, 1997, The Befuddled Stork: Helping Persons of Faith Debate Beginning of life Issues, 2000; contbr. articles to Face to Face, The Christian Century, The Christian Ministry. Active Edn. Commn. of U.S., 1973-79; co-chmn. Citizens Commn. Corrections, 1975-76; vice chmn. S.D. Commn. on Humanities, 1979-81. Dempster fellow, 1967-68; Rockefeller fellow, 1968-69. Mem. Soc. Christian Ethics, Am. Acad. Religion, Assn. United Meth. Theol. Schs. (v.p. 1986-91, pres. 1991-92). Democrat. Office: Iliff Sch Theology 2201 S University Blvd Denver CO 80210-4798

MESSERLE, KENNETH C. state senator; b. Coos Bay, Oreg., May 8, 1940; m. Lola Messerle; children: Anthony, Blaine, Molly. BS, Oreg. State U., 1962. Owner, mgr. Messerle and Sons, Cattle and Timber, 1962-96; dir. Security Bank Holding Co., 1992—, Lincoln Security Bank, 1997—; Rep. rep. dist. 48 Oreg. Ho. of Reps., 1996-2000; Rep. senator dist. 24 Oreg. State Senate, 2000—. Mem. full ways and means com. Oreg. Ho. of Reps., mem. Pacific fisheries legis. task force, 1997—, natural resources ways and means subcom., 1999, interim task force on children and families, gen. govt. ways and means subcom., 1999, environ. and land use transp. task force, 1999—, co-chair salmon recovery and stream restoration. Chmn. Port of Bandon Relending Corp.; commr. Port of Bandon; dir. Coquille Sch. Bd.; mem. Coos County Water Resources Com.; dir. Coos Soil and Water Dist. Mem. Oreg. Coastal Zone Mgmt. Assn. Roman Catholic. Office: 94271 Coos Sumner Ln Coos Bay OR 97420 also: Oreg State Senate H-381 State Capitol Salem OR 97310 Fax: 541 269-2510; 503 986-1336. E-mail: repMessLola@harborside.com, messerle.rep@state.or.us

MESSERLI, DOUGLAS, writer, publisher; b. Waterloo, Iowa, May 30, 1947; s. John H. and Lorna (Caspers) M.; companion Howard N. Fox. BA in English, U. Md., 1972, MA in English, 1974, PhD in English, 1979. Admissions coord. U. Wis., Madison, 1967-69; asst. head protocol Columbia U., N.Y.C., 1969-70; grad. asst., tchr., coord. interns U. Md., 1973-77; pub. Sun & Moon Press, L.A., 1976—; prof. dept. English Temple U., Phila., 1979-84; dir. The Contemporary Arts Ednl. Project, Inc., 1983—; pub. Green Integer, 1998—. Part-time faculty mem. Calif. Inst. Tech., Pasadena, 1987-89, Otis-Parsons Sch. Arts, L.A., 1989; pub. Green Integer, 1998—. Author: (poetry) Dinner on the Lawn, 1979, Some Distance, 1982, River to Rivet: A Manifesto, 1985, River to Rivet: A Poetic Trilogy, 1985, Maxims from My Mother's Milk/Hymns to Him: A Dialogue, 1988, An Apple, A Day, 1993, After, 1998, primerias palavras, 1999, (drama) Silence All Round Marked: An Historical Play in Hysteria Writ, 1992, (as Kier Peters) The Confirmation, 1993, (fiction/film/poetry) Along Without: A Fiction in Film for Poetry, 1993, The Walls Come True: An Opera for Spoken Voices, 1996, (fiction as Joshua Haigh) Letters from Hanusse, 2000, (poetry) Primeiras palavras, 1999; editor: From the Other Side of the Century: A New American Poetry 1960-1990, 1994, The Sun & Moon Guide to Eating Through Literature and Art, 1994, 50: A Celebration of Sun & Moon Classics, 1995, From the Other Side of the Century II: A New American Drama 1960-95, 1998, The PIP Anthology of World Poetry of the 20th Century. Recipient Carey-Thomas award Pubs. Weekly, 1987, Harry Ford Editor's award, 1994, Am. Book award, 1998. Mem. MLA, Am. Booksellers Assn. Office: Sun & Moon Press 6026 Wilshire Blvd Los Angeles CA 90036-3607

MESSIER, MARK DOUGLAS, professional hockey player; b. Edmonton, Alta., Can., Jan. 18, 1961; With Indpls. Racers, 1978, Cin. Stingers, 1979, Edmonton Oilers, 1979-91, team capt., 1988-91; with N.Y. Rangers, 1991-1997; center Vancouver Canucks, Vancouver, B.C., Can, 1997—. Player NHL All-Star Game, 1982-84, 86, 88-92, 94, Stanley Cup Championship Game, 1984, 85, 87, 88, 90, 94. Recipient Conn Smythe trophy, 1984, Lester B. Pearson award, 1989-90, 91-92, Hart trophy, 1990, 92; named NHL Player of Yr., 1989-90, 91-92; named to Sporting News All-Star Team, 1981-82, 82-83, 89-90, 91-92. Office: Vancouver Canucks 800 Griffiths Way Vancouver BC Canada V6B 6G1

MESSINGER, SHELDON L(EOPOLD), law educator; b. Chgo., Aug. 26, 1925; s. Leopold J. and Cornelia (Eichel) M.; m. Mildred Handler, June 30, 1947; children— Adam J., Eli B. Ph.D. in Sociology, UCLA, 1969. Assoc. rsch. sociologist Ctr. Study Law and Soc. U. Calif., Berkeley, 1961-69, rsch. sociologist, 1969-70, prof. criminology, 1970-77, prof. law jurisprudence and social policy program, 1977-88, Elizabeth J. Boalt prof. law, 1988-91, prof. law emeritus, 1991—, prof. grad. sch., 1995-97, vice chmn., 1961-69, acting dean criminology, 1970-71, dean criminology, 1971-75, chmn. program, 1983-87. Author, co-author numerous books, articles. Mem. Coun. U. Calif. Emeriti Assns. (chair-elect 1999-2000, chair 2000-01). Home: 860 Indian Rock Ave Berkeley CA 94707-2051 Office: U Calif Sch Law Boalt Hall Berkeley CA 94720 E-mail: slm@uclink.berkeley.edu

MESSMER, HAROLD MAXIMILIAN, JR. financial services executive; b. Jackson, Miss., Feb. 20, 1946; s. Harold Maximilian and Margaret (Dee) M.; m. Marcia Elizabeth Nesmith, Apr. 5, 1973; children: Michael Christopher, Matthew Gordon. A.B. summa cum laude, Loyola U., 1967; J.D. cum laude, NYU, 1970. Ptnr. corp. law and securities O'Melveny & Myers, Los Angeles, 1970-81; sr. v.p., gen. counsel Pacific Holding Corp., Los Angeles, 1981-82, pres., chief operating officer, 1982-85; pres., dir., chief operating officer Cannon Mills Co. (subs.), Kannapolis, N.C., 1982-85; chmn., dir. Castle & Cook Inc., San Francisco, 1985; chmn., pres., chief exec. officer Robert Half Internat. Inc., San Francisco, 1985—; dir. Nat. Bank N.C., Charlotte. Adj. prof. Claremont Grad. Sch. Bus.(exec. mgmt. program), 1979-82; bd. dirs. Health Care Property Investors, Los Angeles, BF Enterprises Inc., N.C. Nat. Bank, Charlotte. Trustee Davidson (N.C.) Coll., 1984—; appointee Pres. Reagan's Adv. Com. on Trade Negotiations, 1985-87. Served with USAR, 1971-75. Mem. ABA, Los Angeles County Bar Assn., Calif. Bar Assn. Served with USAR, 1971-75. Office: Robert Half Internat Inc 2884 Sand Hill Rd Ste 200 Menlo Park CA 94025-7059

MESTRES, RICARDO A., III, motion picture company executive; b. N.Y.C., Jan. 23, 1958; s. Ricardo Angelo Jr. and Ann (Farnsworth) M.; m. Tracy Stewart; children: Alexander Carson, Carrie Ann. AB, Harvard U., 1980. Creative exec. Paramount Pictures, L.A., 1981-82, exec. dir. prodn., 1982-84, v.p. prodn., 1984-85, Walt Disney Pictures, Burbank, Calif., 1985-86, sr. v.p. prodn., 1986-88; pres. prodn. Touchstone Pictures, Burbank, 1988-89; pres. Hollywood Pictures, Burbank, 1989-94; co-founder Great Oaks Entertainment, Burbank, 1995-97; prin. Ricardo Mestres Prodns., Disney Studios, Burbank, 1997—. Prodr: Jack, 101 Dalmations, Flubber, Home Alone 3, The Visitors, The Hunted. Mem. Acad. Motion Picture Arts and Scis. Office: Ricardo Mestres Prodns 500 S Buena Vista St Burbank CA 91521-0001

METCALF, JACK, former congressman, retired state senator; b. Marysville, Wash., Nov. 30, 1927; s. John Read and Eunice (Grannis) M.; m. Norma Jean Grant, Oct. 3, 1948; children: Marta Jean, Gayle Marie, Lea Lynn, Beverlee Ann. Student, U. Wash., 1944-45; BA, BEd, Pacific Luth. U., 1951. Tchr. Elma (Wash.) pub. schs., 1951-52, Everett (Wash.) pub. schs., 1952-81; mem. Wash. Ho. of Reps., 1960-64, Wash. Senate, 1966-75, 80-92, U.S. Ho. of Reps. from 2d Wash. dist., 1995-2001. Chmn. environment and natural resources com., 1988-92; mem. domestic & internat. monetary policy, fin. instns. & consumer credit, aviation, surface transp. coms. Mem. Coun. State Govts., Wash. Edn. Assn. (bd. dirs.), Wash. Assn. Profl. Educators (state v.p. 1979-81, state pres. 1977-79), Nat. Conf. State Legislatures, Western States Recycling Coalition, South Whidbey Kiwanis, Deer Lagoon Grange. Republican. Home: 4693 E Saratoga Rd Langley WA 98260-9694*

METCALF, WAYNE C., III, insurance commissioner; m. Shirley Imada Metcalf. BA in Polit. Sci., U. Hawaii, 1975; JD, 1978; student, Tufts U., 1992-93. Atty. pvt. practice, 1979—; spl. cons. UN, 1994; ins. commr. Dept. Commerce and Consumer Affairs State Hawaii, 1994-97, 99—. Staff Senate Jud. Com., 1973-75; staff dir. Senate Pres.'s Office, 1975-78; vice-chmn. House Com. on Jud., 1984-86; chmn. House Com. on Jud., 1986-92;; mem. house coms. Comsuner Protection and Commerce, 1984-92, Land Use and Hawaiian Affairs Plannong, 1984-86, Labor and Pub. Employment Transp., 1985-88, Housing, Health Humand Svcs, 1988-90, Housing, Health, 1990-92. Recipient Disting. Alumni award U. hawaii, 1988, Disting. Legislator award, Nat. Dem. State LEgis. Leaders Assn., 1988; named one of Hawaii's five best legislators by polit. columnist Dan Boylan, 1990, 92. Office: Ins Divsn Dept Commerce Consumer Affairs PO Box 3614 Honolulu HI 96811-3614

METSGER, RICK T. state legislator; b. Sandy, Oreg., Aug. 16, 1951; m. Kay Metsger. BA, Lewis & Clark Coll., 1972, MAT, 1975. Tchr. Sam Barlow H.S., 1973-76; news reporter, anchor Sta. WOIN-TV, 1977-92; pub. affairs bus. owner, 1992—; mem. Oreg. Legislature, Salem, 1998—, mem. bus. and consumer affairs, mem. ways and means com., mem. subcom. on natural resources. Bd. dirs., vice chair Portland Tchrs. Credit Union. Mem. Oreg. Film and Video Found. (bd. dirs.), North Clakamas C. of C. Democrat. Protestant. Office: PO Box 287 Welches OR 97067-0287

METTE, JOE, museum director; Dir. California State Capitol Mus., Sacramento; dist. supt. pks. and recreation dist. office San Luis Obispo (Calif.) Coast Dist., 1998—. Office: Pks Recreation Dist Office 3220 S Higuera St Ste 311 San Luis Obispo CA 93401-6984

METZ, MARY SEAWELL, foundation administrator, retired academic administrator; b. Rockhill, S.C., May 7, 1937; d. Columbus Jackson and Mary (Dunlap) Seawell; m. F. Eugene Metz, Dec. 21, 1957; 1 dau., Mary Eugena. BA summa cum laude in French and English, Furman U., 1958; postgrad., Institut Phonetique, Paris, 1962-63, Sorbonne, 1962-63; PhD magna cum laude in French, La. State U., 1966; HHD (hon.), Furman U., 1984; LLD (hon.), Chapman Coll., 1985; DLT (hon.), Converse Coll., 1988. Instr. French La. State U., 1965-66, asst. prof., 1966-67, 1968-72, assoc. prof., 1972-76, dir. elem. and intermediate French programs, 1966-74, spl. asst. to chancellor, 1974-75, asst. to chancellor, 1975-76; prof. French Hood Coll., Frederick, Md., 1976-81, provost, dean acad. affairs, 1976-81; pres. Mills Coll., Oakland, Calif., 1981-90; dean of extension U. Calif., Berkeley, 1991-98; pres. S.H. Cowell Found., San Fransisco, 1999—. Vis. asst. prof. U. Calif.-Berkeley, 1967-68; mem. commn. on leadership devel. Am. Coun. on Edn., 1981-90, adv. coun. Stanford Rsch. Inst., 1985-90, adv. coun. Grad. Sch. Bus., Stanford U.; assoc. Gannett Ctr. for Media Studies, 1985—; bd. dirs. PG&E, Pacific

Telesis, PacTel & PacBell, Union Bank, Longs Drug Stores, S.H. Cowell Found. Author: Reflets du monde francais, 1971, 78, Cahier d'exercices: Reflets du monde francais, 1972, 78, (with Helstrom) Le Francais a decouvrir, 1972, 78, Le Francais a vivre, 1972, 78, Cahier d'exercices: Le Francais a vivre, 1972, 78; standardized tests; mem. editorial bd. Liberal Edn., 1982— . Trustee Am. Conservatory Theater. NDEA fellow, 1960-62,, 1963-64; Fulbright fellow, 1962-63; Am. Council Edn. fellow, 1974-75 Mem. Western Coll. Assn. (v.p. 1982-84, pres. 1984-86), Assn. Ind. Calif. Colls. and Univs. (exec. com. 1982-90), Nat. Assn. Ind. Colls. and Univs. (govt. rels. adv. coun. 1982-85), So. Conf. Lang. Teaching (chmn. 1976-77), World Affairs Coun. No. Calif. (bd. dirs. 1984-93), Bus.-Higher Edn. Forum, Women's Forum West, Women's Coll. Coalition (exec. com. 1984-88), Phi Kappa Phi, Phi Beta Kappa. Address: PO Box 686 Stinson Beach CA 94970-0686 also: 9 Regulus Ct Alameda CA 94501-1015 Office: SH Cowell Found 120 Montgomery St San Francisco CA 94104-4303

METZENBERG, ROBERT L. education educator; Prof. rsch. and biol. scis. Stanford U. Office: Stanford U Gilbert Hall Dept Biol Sci Stanford CA 94305-5020

METZGER, ROBERT STREICHER, lawyer; b. St. Louis, Sept. 27, 1950; s. Robert Stanley and Jean Harriet (Streicher) M.; m. Stephanie Joy Morgan, Nov. 16, 1980; children: Michael, Kristen, Marisa. BA, Middlebury Coll., 1974; JD, Georgetown U., 1977. Bar: Calif. 1978, D.C. 1978. Legis. aide U.S. Rep. Robert F. Drinan, Washington, 1972-73; legis. asst. U.S. Rep. Michael J. Harrington, Washington, 1973-75; rsch. fellow Ctr. for Sci. and Internat. Affairs Harvard U., Cambridge, Mass., 1977-78; assoc. Latham & Watkins, L.A., 1978-84, ptnr., 1984-90, Kirkland & Ellis, L.A., 1990-93, Troop, Meisinger, Steuber & Pasich and predecessor, L.A., 1993-97, Gibson, Dunn & Crutcher LLP, L.A., 1997—. Chmn. Aerospace & Govt. Practice Group, 1997—; cons. Congl. Rsch. Svc., Washington, 1977-78. Contbr. articles to profl. jours. Mem. ABA (litigation pub. contracts sect.), Internat. Inst. for Strategic Studies, Jonathan Club. Office: Gibson Dunn & Crutcher LLP 333 S Grand Ave Los Angeles CA 90071-3197

METZLER, ROGER JAMES, JR. lawyer; b. East Orange, N.J., Feb. 4, 1945; s. Roger James and Dorothy Marie (Clark) M.; m. Marilyn Carol Schick, Apr. 19, 1969; children: Andrea C., Maria N. BS, Brown U., 1967; JD, Santa Clara U., 1975. Bar: Calif. 1975. Ptnr. Farrand, Cooper, Metzler & Bruiniers, San Francisco, 1975-88, McQuaid, Bedford, Clausen & Metzler, San Francisco, 1988-89, Keck, Mahin & Cate, Chgo. and San Francisco, 1990-96, McQuaid, Metzler, Bedford & Van Zandt, San Francisco, 1996—. Avocation: soccer referee. Office: McQuaid Metzler Bedford Van Zandt 221 Main St Fl 16 San Francisco CA 94105-1936

METZNER, RICHARD JOEL, psychiatrist, psychopharmacologist, educator; b. L.A., Feb. 15, 1942; s. Robert Gerson and Esther Rebecca (Groper) M.; children: Jeffrey Anthony, David Jonathan; m. Leila Kirkley, June 26, 1993. BA, Stanford U., 1963; MD, Johns Hopkins U., 1967. Diplomate Am. Bd. Psychiatry and Neurology. Intern Roosevelt Hosp., N.Y.C., 1967-68; resident in psychiatry Stanford U. Med. Ctr., 1968-71; staff psychiatrist divsn. manpower and tng. NIMH-St. Elizabeths Hosp., Washington, 1971-73; chief audiovisual edn. sys. VA Med. Ctr. Brentwood, L.A., 1973-79; from asst. prof. psychiatry to assoc. clin. prof. UCLA Neuropsychiat. Inst., 1980-96, clin. prof., 1996—. Lectr. Sch. Social Welfare, 1975-84; pvt. practice medicine specializing in psychiatry, Bethesda, Md., 1972-73, L.A., 1973—, Sedona, Ariz., 1997—; dir. Western Inst. Psychiatry, L.A., 1977—; pres. Psychiat. Resource Network, Inc., 1984-90. Contbr. articles to profl. jours.; prodr., writer numerous films and videotapes. With USPHS, 1968-71. Recipient 6 awards for film and videotape prodns., 1976-80. Fellow Am. Psychiat. Assn.; mem. So. Calif. Psychiat. Soc., Mental Health Careerists Assn. (chmn. 1972-73), UCLA Psychiatric Clin. Faculty Assn. (pres. 2001—), Phi Beta Kappa. Democrat. Jewish. E-mail: rmetzner@ucla.edu, rmetzner@earthlink.net

MEYER, ANN JANE, human development educator; b. N.Y.C., Mar. 11, 1942; d. Louis John and Theresa Meyer. BA, U. Mich., 1964; MA, U. Calif., Berkeley, 1967, PhD, 1971. Asst. prof. dept. human devel. Calif. State U., Hayward, 1972-77, assoc. prof., 1977-84, prof., 1984—. Mem. APA. Office: Calif State U Dept Human Devel Hayward CA 94542 E-mail: ameyer@csuhayward.edu

MEYER, C. RICHARD, architect; BArch, U. Calif., Berkeley, 1968. Registered architect, Wash. With The Callison Partnership, Seattle, 1977—, dir. quality assurance. Mem. adv. bd. cert. program project mgmt. U. Wash.; contracts rev. panelist Soc. Archtl. Adminstrs.; mem. faculty Pacific real estate symposium N.W. Real Estate Inst.; guest lectr. Archtl. Registration Exam. Seminar; guest lectr. coll. architecture and urban planning U. Wash.; guest panelist Internat. Conf. of Bldg. Ofcls. Nat. Conf., 1991. Mem. AIA (treas. Seattle chpt., mem. steering com. Pacific NW regional conf., vice-chair nat. risk mgmt. com., mem. steering com. nat. practice com., liaison to Am. Arbitration Assn.), Nat. Inst. Bldg. Scis. Office: The Callison Partnership Ltd 1420 5th Ave Ste 2400 Seattle WA 98101-2343

MEYER, CHARLES G. museum director; Exec. dir. Bakersfield (Calif.) Mus. Art, 1995—. Office: Bakersfield Mus Art PO Box 1911 Bakersfield CA 93303-1911

MEYER, CHRISTOPHER HAWKINS, lawyer; b. Springfield, Mo., Sept. 29, 1952; s. Richard DeWitt and Nancy (Hawkins) M.; m. Karen Anne Adams, Aug. 8, 1987; 1 child, C. Andrew Meyer. BA in Econs. magna cum laude, U. Mich., 1977, JD cum laude, 1981. Bar: D.C. 1981, U.S. Ct. Appeals (D.C. cir.) 1982, U.S. Ct. Appeals (9th cir.) 1983, Colo. 1985, U.S. Ct. Appeals (10th cir.) 1985, Idaho, U.S. Ct. Appeals (8th cir.). Counsel water resources program Nat. Wildlife Fedn., Washington, 1981-84, assoc. prof. adjoint, counsel Rocky Mountain Natural Resources Clinic Boulder, Colo., 1984-91; ptnr. Givens Pursley, Boise, 1991—. Contbr. articles to profl. publs. Mem. steering com. Idaho Environ. Forum; bd. dirs. Land Trust of the Treasure Valley. Recipient Lawyer of Yr. award Environ. Policy Inst., 1984, Water Conservationist of Yr. Nebr. Wildlife Fedn., 1989. Mem. Phi Beta Kappa. Democrat. Roman Catholic. Home: 2460 E Bergeson St Boise ID 83706-6012 Office: Givens Pursley LLP 277 N 6th St Ste 200 Boise ID 83702-7720

MEYER, DANIEL KRAMER, real estate executive; b. Denver, July 15, 1957; s. Milton Edward and Mary (Kramer) M. Student, Met. State Coll., Denver, 1977-78, U. Colo., , 1978-80. Ptnr., developer RM & M II (Ltd. Partnership), Englewood, Colo., 1981-87; pres. Centennial Mortgage and Investment, Ltd., Englewood, 1984-87; prin. Capriole Properties, Greenwood Village, 1983—. Alumni mem. bd. trustees Kent Denver Country Day Sch., 1981-83; sec. dist. 37 ctrl. and vacancy com. Colo. Ho. of Reps., 1991-92. Recipient Pamela Davis Beardsley devel. award Kent Denver Sch., 1995. Mem. Greenwood Athletic Club. Republican. Avocations: climbing, rollerblading, political economy, 20th century English lit., metaphysics.

MEYER, DAVID J. energy executive, lawyer; m. Anni Ryan; 4 children. BA in Polit. Sci., BA in Econs., Valparaiso U.; JD, Cornell U., 1978. Ptnr. Paine Hamblen et. al., 1978-98; sr. v.p., gen. counsel Avista Corp., Spokane, Wash., 1998—. Pres. bd. dirs. Lilac Blind Found. Mem. Fed. Energy Bar Assn., Wash. State Bar Assn., Spokane County Bar Assn. Office: Avista Corp 1411 E Mission Ave Spokane WA 99202-2600

MEYER, EDMOND GERALD, energy and natural resources educator, resources scientist, entrepreneur, former chemistry educator, university administrator; b. Albuquerque, Nov. 2, 1919; s. Leopold and Beatrice (Ilfeld) M.; m. Betty F. Knobloch, July 4, 1941; children: Lee Gordon, Terry Gene, David Gary. BS in Chemistry, Carnegie Mellon U., 1940, MS, 1942; PhD, U. N.Mex., 1950. Chemist Harbison Walker Refractories Co., 1940-41; instr. Carnegie Mellon U., 1941-42; asst. phys. chemist Bur. Mines, 1942-44; chemist research div. N.Mex. Inst. Mining and Tech., 1946-48; head dept. sci. U. Albuquerque, 1950-52; head dept. chemistry N.Mex. Highlands U., 1952-59; dir. Inst. Sci. Rsch., 1957-63; dean Grad. Sch., 1961-63, Coll. Arts and Sci., U. Wyo., 1963-75, v.p., 1974-80, prof. energy and natural resources, 1981-89, prof. and dean emeritus, 1989—. Exec. cons. Diamond Shamrock Corp., 1980; bd. dirs. Carbon Fuels Corp., First Nat. Bank, Laramie; sci. adviser Gov. of Wyo., 1964-90; pres. Coal Tech. Corp., 1981—; cons. Los Alamos Nat. Lab., NFS, HHS, GAO, Wyo. Bancorp; contractor investigator Rsch. Corp., Dept. Interior, AEC, NIH, NSF, Dept. Energy, Dept. Edn.; Fulbright exch. prof. U. Concepcion, Chile, 1959; chmn. Advanced Coal Tech., 2001. Co-author: Chemistry-Survey of Principles, 1963, Legal Rights of Chemists and Engineers, 1977, Industrial Research & Development Management, 1982; contbr. articles to profl. jours.; patentee in field. Chair, Laramie Regional Airport Bd., 1989-93, treas., 1994-97, chair; active Laramie City Coun., 1997-2001, vice mayor, 1998-2001. Lt. comdr. USNR, 1944-46, ret. Recipient Disting. Svc. award Jaycees; rsch. fellow U. N.Mex., 1948-50. Fellow AAAS, Am. Inst. Chemists (hon. fellow; pres. 1992-93, chmn. 1994-95); mem. Assoc. Western Univs. (chmn. 1972-74), Am. Chem. Soc. (councilor 1962-90, chmn. Wyo. sect. 1997), Biophys. Soc., Coun. Coll. Arts and Scis. (pres. 1971, sec.-treas. 1972-75), dir. Washington office 1973), Laramie C. of C. (pres. 1984), Sigma Xi. Home: 1058 Colina Dr Laramie WY 82072-5015 Office: U Wyo Coll Arts Scis Laramie WY 82071-3825 E-mail: egmeyer@uwyo.edu

MEYER, FREDERICK G. lawyer; b. Temple, Tex., 1945; BA, Dartmouth Coll., 1967; JD, Columbia U., 1970; LLM, NYU, 1979. Bar: Conn. 1970, N.Y. 1971, Colo. 1979. Atty. Holland & Hart, Denver, Reinhart, Boerner, Van Deuren, Norris & Rieselbach, P.C., Denver, 1998—. Vis. lectr. grad. tax program law sch. U. Denver, 1982-83. Co-author: Colorado Probate: Beyond the Basics, 1984, Colorado Probate & Estate Planning, 1986, An Attorney's Look at Tax Planing for the Small Business Owner, Rancher and Farmer: Asset Protection Planning, 1996; co-editor: Colorado Estate Planning Handbook, rev. edit., 1989; editor trust and estate forum Colo. Lawyer, 1981-82; contbr. articles to profl. jours. Fellow Am. Coll. Trust and Estate Counsel, Colo. Bar Found.; mem. ABA (vice chair agrl. tax com. 1996-97), Greater Denver Tax Counsels Assn., Rocky Mountain Estate Planning Council (pres. 1987). Office: Reinhart Boerner Van Deuren Norris and Rieselbach PC 1775 Sherman St Ste 2100 Denver CO 80203-4320

MEYER, JAROLD ALAN, oil company research executive; b. Phoenix, July 28, 1938; s. Lester M. and Anita (Walker) M.; m. Diane Louise Wheeler; children: Ronald Alan, Sharon Lynne. BSChemE, Calif. Inst. Tech., 1960, MS, 1961. Mgr. process devel. Chevron Rsch., Richmond, Calif., 1978-82; tech. mgr. Chevron U.S.A., El Segundo, 1982-84; v.p. process rsch. Chevron Rsch., Richmond, 1984-86, pres., 1986—; sr. v.p. Chevron Rsch. and Tech., Richmond, 1990-93; ret., 1993; prin. J.A. Meyer Assocs., Martinez, Calif., 1993—. Bd. dirs. Solvent Refined Coal Internat., Inc., San Francisco; mem. adv. bd. Surface Sci. and Catalysis Program Ctr. for Advanced Materials, Lawrence Berkeley Lab., 1988-91; mem. adv. coun. Lawrence Hall Sci., 1989-94; indsl. advisor Accreditation bd. for Engring. and Tech. Inventor petroleum catalysts; contbr. articles to profl. jours. Bd. visitors U. Calif., Davis, 1986-93, trustee found., 1989—. Mem. Nat. Acad. Engring., Am. Chem. Soc., Nat. Petroleum Refining Assn., Indsl. Rsch. Inst., Conf. Bd. Internat. Rsch. Mgmt. Coun., Accreditation Bd. for Engring. and Tech. Indsl. Advisor, Sigma Xi, Tau Beta Pi. Avocations: electronics design and constrn., photography. Home and Office: 849 Corte Briones Martinez CA 94553-5950

MEYER, JEROME J. diversified technology company executive; b. Caledonia, Minn., Feb. 18, 1938; s. Herbert J. and Edna (Staggemeyer) M.; m. Sandra Ann Beaudoin, June 18, 1960; children— Randall Lee, Lisa Ann, Michelle Lynn Student, Hamline U., 1956-58; B.A., U. Minn., 1960. Devel. engr. Firestone Tire & Rubber Co., Akron, Ohio, 1960-61; v.p., gen. mgr. Sperry Univac, St. Paul, 1961-79; group v.p. Honeywell, Inc., Mpls., 1979-84; pres., chief operating officer Varian Assocs., Palo Alto, Calif., 1984-86, also bd. dirs.; pres., chief exec. officer Honeywell Inc., 1986-90; from pres. to chmn., CEO Tektronix Inc., Beaverton, Oreg., 1990-99, chmn., 1999—. Bd. dirs. Oreg. Pub. Broadcasting, Esterline Tech., Oregon Bus. Coun., AMP, Std. Ins. Co. Trustee Oreg. Grad. Inst., Willamette U., Oreg. Children's Found. Mem. Oregon Golf Club. Avocation: golf. Office: Tektronix Inc PO Box 500 14200 SW Karl Braun Dr Beaverton OR 97077-0001

MEYER, JOSEPH B. state official, former academic administrator; b. Casper, Wyo., 1941; m. Mary Orr; children: Vincent, Warren. Student, Colo. Sch. Mines; BA, U. Wyo., 1964, JD, 1967; postgrad., Northwestern U., 1968. Dep. county atty. Fremont County, Wyo., 1967-69; assoc. Smith and Meyer, 1968-71; asst. dir. legis. svc. office State of Wyo., Cheyenne, 1971-87, atty. gen., 1987-95; spl. asst. to pres. Univ. Wyo., Laramie, 1995-98; sec. of state State of Wyoming, 1999—. Conductor numerous govt. studies on state codes including Wyo. probate, criminal, state adminstrn., banking, domestic rels., game and fish, state instn., employment security, worker's compensation, motor vehicle, others; conductor legis. rev. of adminstrv. rules; negotiator with Office of Surface Mining for Wyo. state preemption; instr. Wyo. Coll. Law, fall 1986; lectr. Rocky Mountain Mineral Law Found., 1977; chmn. Conf. Western Atty. Gen., 1992-93; mem. exec. com. Nat. Assn. Attys. Gen. Bd. dirs. Cheyenne Jr. League, 1982-85, Jessup PTO, 1980-81; instr. Boy Scouts Am. Mem. Rotary. Congregationalist. Avocations: golf, tennis, gardening, wood carving, rock hunting. Office: State Capital Bldg Cheyenne WY 82002-0001 E-mail: jmeyer3@state.wy.us

MEYER, LYNN NIX, lawyer; b. Vinita, Okla., Aug. 10, 1948; d. William Armour and Joan Ross Nix; children: Veronica, Victoria, David. BA, Baldwin Wallace Coll., 1978; JD, Case Western Res. U., 1981. Bar: Ky. 1982, Colo. 1984. Paralegal Texaco Devel., Austin, Tex., 1976-77; legal asst. Alcan Aluminum, Cleve., 1977-79; assoc. Wyatt, Tarrant & Combs, Lexington, Ky., 1982-83; ptnr. Meyer, Meyer & Assocs., P.C., Denver, 1984-85; gen. counsel Carbon Fuels Corp., 1985-95; in pvt. practice Denver, 1996-97; asst. gen. counsel products Gambro, Inc., Lakewood, Colo., 1997—. Mem. ABA, Colo. Bar Assn., Ky. Bar Assn., Arapahoe County Bar Assn. Home: 10487 E Ida Ave Englewood CO 80111-3746 Office: 10810 W Collins Ave Lakewood CO 80215-4439 E-mail: lynn.meyer@gambrobct.com

MEYER, MARGARET ELEANOR, microbiologist, educator; b. Westwood, Calif., Feb. 8, 1923; d. Herman Henry and Eleanor (Dobson) M. B.S., U. Calif., Berkeley, 1945; Ph.D., U. Calif., Davis, 1961. Pub. health analyst USPHS, Bethesda, Md., 1945-46; swine Brucellosis control agt. Dept. Agr., Davis, 1946-47; bacteriologist U. Calif., Davis, 1947-61; research microbiologist U. Calif. (Sch. Vet. Medicine), 1961-77, prof. vet. pub. health and microbiologist exptl. sta., 1977—; research microbiologist U. Calif. Med. Sch., Los Angeles, 1961-77; supr. Brucella identifications lab. WHO, U. Calif.-Davis, 1964—, prof. vet. pub. health, 1973—; also dir. M.A. program in preventive vet. medicine. Cons. subcom. on Brucella Internat. Com. Bacterial Taxonomy, 1962—, mem., 1966—; mem. 5th Pan Am. Congress Veterinary Medicine, Venezuela, 1966; mem. Internat. Congress Microbiology, Moscow, 1966, Mexico City, 1970, Munich, Ger., 1978, mem., officer, Eng., 1986; mem. Internat. Conf. Culture Collections, Tokyo, 1968; mem. adv. com. to Bergey's Manual Determative Bacteriology, 1967; cons. in resident Pan Am. Health Orgn., Zoonoses Lab., Buenos Aires, 1968; mem. brucellosis tech. adv. com. U.S. Animal Health Assn., 1977; FAO cons. on brucellosis control in dairy animals, Tripoli, Libya, 1981, mem. 3d internat. brucellosis symposium, Algiers, 1983; cons. Alaska Dept. Fish and Game, 1976, FAO, Libya, 1981, Bering Straits Reindeer Herders Assn., Nome, Alaska, 1981; invited speaker Internat. Symposium on Advances in Brucellosis Rsch., Tex. A&M U., 1989, Internat. Bison Conf.; resident cons. on brucellosis control in sheep and goats Am. Near East Refugee Aid, East Jerusalem, 1989; cons. on brucellosis in Yellowstone Nat. Pk., Nat. Pk. Svc., 1991—; invited mem. nat. symposium on brucellosis in the Greater Yellowstone Area, Jackson Hole, Wyo., 1994; cons. on brucellosis control in livestock for Armenia, 1994—. Contbr. articles to profl. jours. Bd. dirs. Carmichael Park and Recreation Dist., Calif., 1975; mem. Sacramento County Grand Jury, 1999-2000. Recipient Research Career Devel. award USPHS-NIH, 1963 Fellow Am. Pub. Health Assn., Am. Acad. Microbiology; mem. Soc. Am. Microbiologists, N.Am. Conf. Animal Disease Research Workers, Am. Coll. Vet. Microbiologists (hon. affiliate), U.S. Animal Health Assn. (chmn. brucellosis tech. advisory com. 1978-79), Internat. Assn. Microbiol. Socs. (mem. 1st intersect. congress 1974), AAUW, No. Calif. Women's Golf Assn., U. Calif. Alumni Assn., Sigma Xi. Clubs: U. Calif. Faculty (Davis); El Dorado Royal Country (Shingle Springs, Calif.); Reno Women's Golf. Home: 5611 Fair Oaks Blvd Carmichael CA 95608-5503 Office: U Calif Sch Vet Medicine Dept Epidemiology & Preventive Medicine Davis CA 95616

MEYER, MICHAEL EDWIN, lawyer; b. Chgo., Oct. 23, 1942; s. Leon S. and Janet (Gorden) M.; m. Catherine Dieffenbach, Nov. 21, 1982; children: Linda, Mollie, Patrick, Kellie. BS, U. Wis., 1964; JD, U. Chgo., 1967. Bar: Calif. 1968, U.S. Supreme Ct. 1973. Assoc. Lillick & McHose, L.A., 1967-73, ptnr., 1974-90, mng. ptnr., 1986-87; ptnr. Pillsbury Madison Sutro, 1990—, mem. mgmt. com., 1990-92, chmn., 1999—. Judge pro tem Beverly Hills Mcpl. Ct., Calif., 1976-79, Los Angeles Mcpl. Ct., 1980-86; lectr. in field. Bd. dirs. Bldg. Owners and Mgrs. Assn. Greater L.A., L.A. coun. Boy Scouts Am., L.A. Sports and Entertainment Commn.; pub. counsel United Way Greater L.A., Los Angeles County Bar Found., trustee, 1997—, Reviving Baseball in Inner Cities; mem. L.A. County Sheriff Youth Found. Recipient Good Scout award L.A. coun. Boy Scouts Am., 1992, Man of Yr. award United Way, 1996. Mem. ABA, Am. Arbitration Assn. (arbitrator), Calif. Bar Assn., Los Angeles County Bar Assn. (trustee 1997—), L.A. Bar Assn., U. Chgo. Alumni Assn. So. Calif. (pres. 1980-82), Calif. Club, U. L.A. Club (dir. 1979-85, pres. 1984-85), L.A. Country Club. Jewish. Home: 759 31st St Manhattan Beach CA 90266-3456 Office: Pillsbury Winthrop 725 S Figueroa St Los Angeles CA 90017-5524 E-mail: mmeyer@pillsburywinthrop.com

MEYER, PAUL I. lawyer; b. St. Louis, Jan. 5, 1944; AB magna cum laude, Harvard U., 1966, JD cum laude, 1969. Bar: Calif. 1970. Atty. Latham & Watkins, San Diego. Capt. USMCR, 1970-73. Mem. ABA (Profl. Merit award 1970), San Diego County Bar Assn., Phi Beta Kappa. Office: Latham & Watkins 701 B St Ste 2100 San Diego CA 92101-8197 E-mail: Paul.Meyer@LW.com

MEYER, ROBERT LEE, secondary education educator; b. St. Joseph, Mo., July 9, 1952; s. Robert James and Jerry Lee (Patterson) M.; m. Barbara Anita Stickles, Aug. 2, 1986. BS in Edn., Mo. Western State Coll., 1974; MA in Edn., U.S. Internat. U., 1988. Cert. tchr., Calif., Mo.; cert. specialist learning handicapped, resource specialist cert., adminstr., Calif. Spl. edn. tchr., learning handicapped Mann Jr. High Sch., San Diego, 1978-80, Serra High Sch., San Diego, 1980-84, Morse High Sch., San Diego, 1984-85; magnet seminar tchr. Bell Jr. High Sch., San Diego, 1985-91; project resource tchr., dir. student activities Serra High Sch., San Diego, 1991-94, resource specialist, 1994-95; magnet coord. Ctr. for Sci., Math. and Computer Tech. Samuel Gompers Secondary Sch., San Diego, 1995-97; dean of students, attendance coord. Scripps Ranch H.S., nonathletic event coord., 1997-98; asst. prin. Mountain Empire Jr./Sr. H.S., 1998—. Chmn. resource com. Western Assn. Schs. & Colls. accreditation Serra High Sch., San Diego, 1995, chmn. process com. Western Assn. Schs. and Colls. accreditation Gompers Secondary Sch., San Diego, 1996-97, sch. site coun., 1992-97, gov. team mem., 1992-95, chair spl. edn. dept., 1983, mem. sch. leadership team, 1992-95, sr. class advisor, 1994-95, liaison Partnerships in Edn., 1996-97; monitor City Schs. Race Human Rels. Monitoring Team, 1991-92, African Am. students pupil advocate program adv. coun., 1995-97; restructuring coord. Senate Bill 1274 Grant, 1993-95, resource specialist, 1994-95; chmn. process com. Western Assn. Schs. and Colls. accreditation Gompers Sec. Sch., adv. com. mem. African Am. students program; co-chmn. race/human rels. com. Scripps Ranch H.S., 1997-98. Contbr.: (book) History of Andrew Meyer Family, 1989. Alternate del. Dem. Party 6th Dist. and State Conventions, Holt County, Mo., 1976; mem. Nat. Conf. Minitown Race/Human Rels. Camp Coord., Scripps Ranch H.S. Recipient star adminstr. award Calif. FFA, 2000. Mem. Assn. Calif. Sch. Adminstrs., Optimist Club, Delta Chi. Democrat. Roman Catholic. Avocations: collecting political buttons, antiques, travel. E-mail: meyer@adcoe.k12.ca.us

MEYER, RON, agent; b. 1944; m. Kelly Chapman; children, Jennifer, Sarah, Carson, Eli. With Paul Kohner Agency, 1964-1970; agent William Morris Agency, Beverly Hills, CA, 1970-1975; co-founder, pres. Creative Artists Agency, Inc., Beverly Hills, 1975-95; pres., COO Universal Studios Inc., Universal City, 1995—. Served with USMC. Office: Universal Studios Inc 100 Universal City Plz Universal City CA 91608 E-mail: susan.fleishman@unistudios.com

MEYER, THOMAS JAMES, editorial cartoonist; b. Fort Benning, Ga., May 8, 1955; s. Edward Charles and Carol (McCunniff) M. B.A., U. Mich., 1977. Congl. aide U.S. Ho. of Reps., Washington, 1977-79; free lance cartoonist, illustrator Washington Post, Fed. Times, Bus. Rev. of, Washington, 1979-81; editorial cartoonist San Francisco Chronicle, 1981—. Roman Catholic Office: San Francisco Chronicle 901 Mission St San Francisco CA 94103-2905

MEYEROWITZ, ELLIOT MARTIN, biologist, educator; b. Washington, May 22, 1951; s. Irving and Freda (Goldberg) M.; m. Joan Agnes Kobori, June 17, 1984; 2 children. AB, Columbia U., 1973; MPhil, Yale U., 1975, PhD, 1977. Rsch. fellow Stanford U., Calif., 1977-79; asst. prof. biology Calif. Inst. Tech., Pasadena, 1980-85, assoc. prof., 1985-89, prof., 1989—, chair, 2000—. Mem. editl. bd. Trends in Genetics, Current Biology, Cell, Devel., Genome Biology; contbr. articles to profl. jours. Recipient LVMH Sci. pour l'Art Sci. prize, 1996, Internat. prize for biology, Japan, 1997, Mendel medal, U.K., 1997, Wilbur Cross medal Yale U., 2001; Jane Coffin Childs Meml. fund fellow, 1977-79, Sloan Found. fellow, 1980-82. Fellow AAAS; mem. NAS (Lounsbery award 1999), Am. Philos. Soc., Am. Acad. Arts and Scis., Am. Soc. Plant Physiologists (Gibbs medal 1995), Bot. Soc. Am. (Pelton award 1994), Genetics Soc. Am. (medal 1996, v.p. 1998, pres. 1999), Internat. Soc. for Plant Molecular Biology (pres. 1995-97). Office: Calif Inst Tech Divsn Biology Pasadena CA 91125-0001 E-mail: meyerow@caltech.edu

MEYERROSE, DALE WILLIAM, career officer; BS in Econs., USAF Acad., 1975; MBA, U. Utah, 1978. Commd. 2d lt. USAF, 1975, advanced through grades to brig. gen., 1998; maintenance officer 4th Combat Comms. Group, Altus AFB, Okla., 1976-77; aide-de-camp, asst. exec. officer to the comdr. European Comms. Divsn., Kapuan Air Sta., West

Germany, 1977-79; aide-de-camp to the comdr. Air Force Comms. Command, Scott AFB, Ill., 1979-80; chief of maintenance 1974th Comms. Group, Scott AFB, 1980-82; mem., air staff tng. program officer Sec. of the Air Pers. Coun., The Pentagon, Washington, 1982-83; various assignments Hdqrs. USAF, The Pentagon, Washington, 1983-85, chief future concepts, dep. chief of staff, 1990-91; comdr. 2048th Comms. Squadron, Carswell AFB, 1985-87; comms. support officer Nat. Mil. Command Ctr. the Joint Staff, the Pentagon, Washington, 1987-90; comdr. 3rd Combat Comms. Group, Tinker AFB, Okla., 1992-94; dir. comms. Operation Southern Watch, Riyadh, Saudi Arabia, 1993; dir. comms. and info. Hdqrs. USAF in Europe, Ramstein AB, Germany, 1994-96, Hdqrs. Air Combat Command, Langley AFB, Va., 1996—. Brig. gen., U.S. Base Command, Peterson AFB, Colorado Springs. Decorated Legion of Merit. Office: US Base Command J6 250 S Peterson Blvd # J6 Colorado Springs CO 80914-3285

MEYERS, ALBERT IRVING, chemistry educator; b. N.Y.C., Nov. 22, 1932; s. Hyman and Sylvia (Greenberg) M.; m. Joan Shepard, Aug. 10, 1957; children: Harold, Jill, Lisa BS, NYU, 1954, PhD, 1957. Rsch. chemist Cities Svc. Oil Co., Cranbury, N.J., 1957-58; asst., assoc. prof., prof. La. State U., New Orleans, 1958-70, Boyd prof., 1969; prof. Wayne State U., Detroit, 1970-72, Colo. State U., Fort Collins, 1972—, disting. prof., 1986—, John K. Stille prof. chemistry, 1993—. Spl. postdoctoral fellow Harvard U., Cambridge, 1965-66; cons. G.D. Searle Co., Skokie, Ill., 1972-84, Mid-West Rsch. Inst., Kansas City, Mo., 1974-77, NIH, Bethesda, Md., 1977-79, 85-89, Bristol-Myers Squibb Co., 1983-95, Roche Bioscience, 1989—, Smith Kline Beecham Co., 1994—; scientific adv. bd. Trega Bioscis., La Jolla, Calif., Avanir Bioscis., La Jolla. Editor Jour. Am. Chem. Soc., 1979-85; mem. editl. adv. bd. Jour. Organic Chemistry, 1990-95, Tetrahedron, 1990—, Jour. Chem. Soc. Perkin, 1993, Jour. Chem. Soc. Chem. Commn., 1996, Heterocycles, 1974—; contbr. over 450 articles to profl. jours. Recipient Alexander von Humboldt award Fed. Republic of Germany, 1984, Disting. Alumni award NYU, 1990, award in synthetic chemistry Am. Chem. Soc., 1985, A.C. Cope Scholar award, 1987, Yamada prize, Japan, 1996, award Internat. Soc. Heterocyclic Chemistry, 1997; named Man of Yr., New Orleans Jaycees, 1968, Boyd Prof. La. State U., 1969; recipient pioneer award Am. Insts. Chemists, 1998. Fellow AAAS, Nat. Acad. Sci.; mem. Royal Soc. Chemistry (silver medalist 1982), Phila. Organic Chemistry Soc. (Allan Day award 1987). Home: 1500 Hepplewhite Ct Fort Collins CO 80526-3822 Office: Colo State Univ Dept Chemistry Fort Collins CO 80523-0001 E-mail: aimeyers@lamar.colostate.edu

MEYERS, ANN ELIZABETH, sports broadcaster; b. San Diego, Mar. 26, 1955; d. Robert Eugene and Patricia Ann (Burke); m. Donald Scott Drysdale, Nov. 1, 1986; children: Donald Scott Jr., Darren John, Drew Ann. Grad., UCLA, 1978. Profl. basketball player N.J. Gems, 1979-80; profl. basketball player Ind. Pacers NBA, 1979; sports broadcaster Ind. Pacers, 1979-80; sportscaster men's basketball U. Hawaii, Honolulu, 1981-82; sportscaster men's and women's basketball UCLA, 1982-84, 89—; sportscaster volleyball, basketball, softball, tennis ESPN, 1981—; sportscaster Olympic Games ABC, L.A., 1984; sportscaster volleyball, softball, tennis, basketball, soccer Sportsvision, 1985-87; sportscaster volleyball, basketball, softball Prime Ticket, 1985-97; sportscaster CBS-TV, 1991—, ESPN Women's Basketball, Fox Women's Basketball, WNBA-NBC World Championships; sportscaster Olympic Games NBC, Sydney, Australia, 2000. Sportscaster Goodwill Games, WTBS, 1986, 90; sportscaster basketball NBC and ESPN, 1996-97, WNBA, NBA, ESPN, 1996—. Winner Silver medal Montreal Olympics, 1976, Gold medal Pan Am. Games, 1975, Silver medal, 1979, All Am. UCLA, 1975, 76, 77, 78; 1st woman named to Hall of Fame UCLA, 1987; named to Women's Sports Hall of Fame, 1987, Orange County Sports Hall of Fame, 1985, Calif. H.S. Hall of Fame, 1990, Basketball Hall of Fame, 1993, Nat. H.S. Hall of Fame, 1995, NBC Hoop It Up, 1995, 96, 97, Cath. Youth Orgn. Hall of Fame, 1996, Women's Basketball Hall of Fame, 1999. Office: c/o Lampros and Roberts 16615 Lark Ave Ste 101 Los Gatos CA 95032-7645

MEYERS, DAVID L. food products executive; CFO Del Monte Foods, San Francisco. Office: Del Monte Foods PO Box 193575 San Francisco CA 94119-3575

MEYERS, GERALD A. metal products executive; With Logan Aluminum Inc., Bowling Green, Ky., Alcan & Logan, U.S. and Canada; pres., coo Ravenswood Aluminum Corp., W.Va., pres. & CEO, Century Aluminum Corp., Monteray, Calif., 1992—. Office: Century Aluminum Corp 2511 Garden Rd Monterey CA 93940

MEYERS, MARLENE O. retired hospital administrator; m. Eugene Meyers; children: Lori, Lisa, Dean. BSN, U. Sask., 1962; postgrad., U. Oslo, Norway, 1973; MSc, U. Calgary, Alta., Can., 1976; postgrad., Harvard U., 1980, Banff Sch. Mgmt., 1985, U. Western Ont., Can., 1993; EMT-B, Scottsdale C.C., 2000. RN, Ariz. Various nursing positions, Alta. and B.C., Can., 1962-69; instr., chair Mount Royal Coll. Allied Health, Calgary, 1969-82; asst. exec. dir. Rockyview Hosp., Calgary, 1982-85; v.p. patient svcs. Calgary Gen. Hosp., 1985-91, pres., CEO, 1991-95, Meyers and Assocs. Health Care Mgmt. Cons., Calgary, 1995—; now ret. Surveyor Can. Coun. on Health Facilities Accreditation, 1986-97. Rotary Intl. Named Calgary Woman of Yr. in field of Health, 1982; recipient Heritage of Svc. award, 1992. Mem. Alta. Assn. RNs (hon. mem., 1996), Can. Coll. Health Svcs. Orgn., Can. Exec. Svcs. Orgn., Can. Soc. for Internat. Health (bd. dirs. 1997—), Rotary Internat. Home and Office: 244 Osprey Cir Hope ID 83836-9664 also: 10464 E Cannon Dr Scottsdale AZ 85258-4929 E-mail: marlyo@coldreams.com

MEYERSON, BRUCE ELLIOT, lawyer; b. N.Y.C., Apr. 10, 1947; BS, Ariz. State U., 1968; JD, Georgetown U., 1972. Bar: Ariz. 1972. Exec. dir. Ariz. Ctr. for Law in Pub. Interest, 1974-82; judge Ariz. Ct. Appeals, 1982-86; gen. counsel Ariz. State U., 1986-90; ptnr. Steptoe & Johnson, Phoenix. Adj. prof. law Ariz. State U., 1985-88. Mem. nat. governing bd. Common Cause, 1978-81; bd. dirs. Community Legal Svcs., 1979-81; chair ad hoc com. on human rels. City of Phoenix, 1984. Office: Steptoe & Johnson Two Renaissance Sq Phoenix AZ 85004-4424

MEYERSON, IVAN D. lawyer, holding company executive; AB, U. Calif., Berkeley, 1966; JD, Stanford U., 1969. Bar: Calif. 1970. Assoc. Herzstein & Maier, San Francisco, 1970-75, ptnr., 1976-78; atty. SEC, 1975-76; assoc. gen. counsel McKesson Corp, San Francisco, 1984-87; v.p., gen. counsel McKesson Corp., San Francisco, 1987-98; sr. v.p., gen. counsel McKesson - HBOC Inc., San Francisco, 1998—. Office: McKesson Corp 1 Post St Ste 3275 San Francisco CA 94104-5292

MEYERSON, RONALD L. city official; b. Mar. 23, 1947; BA, U. Ariz. Adminstrv. asst. II City of Tucson, 1974-76, adminstrv. asst. III, 1976-80, asst. dir. ops., 1980-89, dir. ops., 1989—. Office: City Tucson PO Box 27210 Tucson AZ 85726-7210

MEZEY, ROBERT, poet, educator; b. Phila., Feb. 28, 1935; s. Ralph and Clara (Mandel) M.; m. Olivia Simpson (div.); children: Naomi, Judah, Eve. Student, Kenyon Coll., 1951-53; BA, U. Iowa, 1959; postgrad., Stanford U., 1960-61. Lectr. Western Res. U., Cleve., 1963-64, Franklin & Marshall Coll., Lancaster, Pa., 1965-66; asst. prof. Fresno (Calif.) State U., 1967-68, U. Utah, Salt Lake City, 1973-76; prof., poet-in-residence Pomona Coll., Claremont, Calif., 1976-99; ret., 1999. Author: (poems) The Lovemaker, 1960 (Lamont award), White Blossoms, 1965, The Door Standing Open, 1970, Selected Translations, 1981, Evening Wind, 1988 (Bassine citation, PEN prize 1989), Collected Poems 1952-1999, 2000; editor Naked Poetry, 1968, Poems from the Hebrew, 1973, Collected Poems of Henri Coulette, 1990, Selected Poems of Thomas Hardy, 1998, The Poetry of E.A. Robinson, 1999; translator: Tungsten (César Vallejo), 1987. With U.S. Army, 1953-55. Fellow Ingram Merrill, 1973, 89, Guggenheim Found., 1977, Stanford U., 1960, NEA, 1987; recipient Poetry prize Am. Acad. Arts and Letters, 1982. Avocations: tennis, chess. Home: 1663 Chattanooga Ct Claremont CA 91711-2917 Office: Pomona Coll Dept English 140 W 6th St Claremont CA 91711-4301

MEZGER, JEFFREY T. real estate company executive; Sr. v.p., regional mgr. S.W. divsn. Kaufman and Broad Homes Corp., L.A., exec. v.p., COO, 1999—. Office: Kaufman and Broad Home Corp 10990 Wilshire Blvd 7th Fl Los Angeles CA 90024

MICHAEL, ERNEST ARTHUR, mathematics educator; b. Zurich, Switzerland, Aug. 26, 1925; came to U.S., 1939; s. Jakob and Erna (Sondheimer) M.; m. Colette Verger Davis, 1956 (div. 1966); children: Alan, David, Gerard; m. Erika Goodman Joseph, Dec. 4, 1966; children: Hillary, Joshua. B.A., Cornell U., 1947; M.A., Harvard U., 1948; Ph.D., U. Chgo., 1951. Mem. faculty dept. math. U. Wash., Seattle, 1953—, asst. prof., 1953-56, assoc. prof., 1956-60, prof., 1960-93, prof. emeritus, 1993—. Mem. Inst. for Advanced Study, Princeton, 1951-52, 56-57, 60-61, 68, Math. Research Inst., E.T.H., Zürich, 1973-74; vis. prof. U. Stuttgart, Ger., 1978-79, U. Munich, Fed. Republic Germany, 1987, 88, 92-93. Editor: Procs. Am. Math. Soc., 1968-71, Topology and Its Applications, 1972-94, Set-Valued Analysis, 1993—; contbr. articles to profl. jours. Served with USNR, 1944-46. Grantee AEC; Grantee Office Nav. Research; Grantee NSF; Grantee Guggenheim Found.; Grantee Humboldt Found. Mem. Am. Math. Soc., Math. Assn. Am., ACLU, Amnesty Internat. Jewish. Home: 22200 Chinook Rd Woodway WA 98020-7200 Office: U Washington Dept Math Box 354350 Seattle WA 98195-4350

MICHAEL, GARY G. retail supermarket and drug chain executive; b. 1940; married. BS in Bus., U. Idaho, 1962. Staff acct. Ernst & Ernst, CPA's, 1964-66; with Albertson's, Inc., Boise, Idaho, 1966—, acct., 1966-68, asst. controller, 1968-71, controller, 1971-72, v.p., controller, 1972-74, sr. v.p. fin., treas., 1974-76, exec. v.p., 1976-84, vice chmn., CFO, corp. devel. officer, 1984-91, chmn., CEO, 1991—, also dir. Served to 1st lt. U.S. Army, 1962-64. Office: Albertsons Inc PO Box 20 250 E Parkcenter Blvd Boise ID 83726

MICHAEL, MARK DIXWELL, lawyer; b. Palo Alto, Calif., Feb. 27, 1951; s. J.L. and Elizabeth (Ketcham) M.; m. Eileen Susan Landauer; children: Sarah Kristen Michael, Emily Christine Landauer. BA, Stanford U., 1972; JD, UCLA, 1977. Bar: Hawaii 1977, Calif. 1979. Assoc. Carlsmith, Carlsmith, Wichman & Case, Honolulu, 1977-78, Char, Hamilton, Taylor & Thom, Honolulu, 1979-81, Law Offices of Jerry E. Berg, San Francisco, 1981-84; sr. v.p., gen. counsel, sec. 3Com Corp., Santa Clara, Calif., 1984—. Mem. ABA, Am. Soc. Corp. Secs., Silicon Valley Assn. Gen. Counsel, Calif. State Bar Assn., Hawaii State Bar Assn. Office: 3 Com Corp 5400 Bayfront Plz Santa Clara CA 95054-3601 E-mail: Mark_Michael@3com.com

MICHAEL, WILLIAM BURTON, psychologist, educator; b. Pasadena, Calif., Mar. 6, 1922; s. William Whipple and Helen Augusta (Schultz) M.; m. Martha Walker Hennessey, Aug. 30, 1947 (dec. 1959); m. Joan Yvonne Johnson, Aug. 26, 1966 A.B., UCLA, 1943; M.S. in Edn., U. So. Calif., Los Angeles, 1945, M.A. in Psychology, 1946, Ph.D., 1947. Lectr. engring. math. Calif. Inst. Tech., Pasadena, 1942-45; lectr. math., psychology and edn. U. So. Calif., L.A., 1944-47; asst. prof. psychology Princeton U., N.J., 1947-50; rsch. assoc. Rand Corp., Santa Monica, Calif., 1951-52; dir. testing bur. U. So. Calif., L.A., 1952-62, prof. edn. and psychology, 1957 62, 1967 , U. Calif., Santa Barbara, 1962 67. Cons. in field. Author: Teaching for Creative Endeavor, 1967; co-author: Psychological Foundations of Learning and Teaching, 2d edit., 1974, Handbook in Research and Evaluation, 3d edit., 1995 (standardized tests) Study Attitudes and Methods Survey, Dimensions of Self-Concept; editor Ednl. and Psychol. Measurement, 1985-95; cons. editor Jour. Pers. Evaluation in Edn., Ednl. Rsch. Quar., Spanish Jour. Psychology; contbr. chpts. to books and articles to profl. jours. Mem., bd. dirs. Neuro-Psychiat. Clinic, L.A. and Pasadena, 1958— ; mem. L.A. Philharm. Assn., 1965— ; advisor Sch. of Comm., Arcadia, Calif., 1981—. Fellow APA; mem. Am. Ednl. Rsch. Assn. (exec. com., editor Rev. Edn. Rsch. 1962 65), Western Psychol. Assn., Northeastern Ednl. Rsch. Assn., Nat. Coun. on Measurement in Edn., Calif. Ednl. Rsch. Assn. (pres. 1965), Phi Beta Kappa, Sigma Xi, Phi Kappa Phi, Psi Chi, Phi Delta Kappa. Congregationalist. Avocations: Music; travel; reading; ice cream gourmet. Home: 325 Callita Pl San Marino CA 91108-2311 Office: U So Calif Sch Edn Los Angeles CA 90089-0031

MICHAILIDES, THEMIS J. plant pathology educator; Prof. plant pathology U. Calif., Parlier. Recipient Lee M. Hutchins award Am. Phytopathological Soc., 1995. Office: U Calif Kearny Agrl Ctr 9240 S Riverbend Ave Parlier CA 93648-9757

MICHALKO, JAMES PAUL, library association administrator; b. Cleve., May 13, 1950; s. Paul James and Lillian (Fanta) M.; 1 child, Alexandra. BA, Georgetown U., 1971; MLS, MBA, U. Chgo., 1974. Asst. to v.p., adminstrn. Technicare Inc. (formerly BCC Industries), Cleve., 1971-72; asst dir., adminstrn. U. Pa. Librs., Phila., 1974-80; dir. bus. and fin. Rsch. Librs. Group, Stanford, Calif., 1980-85, v.p. fin. and adminstrn., 1985-87, acting pres., 1988-89, pres. Mountain View, 1989—. Contbr. to Libr. Quar., Coll. & Rsch. Librs.; reviewer for Libr. Quar., Coll. & Rsch. Librs., Acad. of Mgmt. Rev., Jour. Acad. Librarianship, Jour. Libr. Adminstrn. Office: Rsch Librs Group Inc 1200 Villa St Mountain View CA 94041-1106

MICHEL, BERNARD, civil engineering educator, consultant; b. Chicoutimi, Que., Canada, May 31, 1930; s. Joseph Williams and Jeanne (Tremblay) M.; m. Mariette Boivin, Sept. 7, 1954; children: Marianne, Francois, Luc, Jacques, Charles, Christine. B.Applied Sci., Laval U., 1954; Dr. Engring., Grenoble U., 1962. Registered profl. engr., Que. Research engr. Lasalle Hydraulic Lab., Quebec, 1956-60; head dept. civil engring. Laval U., Quebec, 1960-63, prof., 1963—; chmn., CEO Cameco Corp., Saskatoon, Can. V.p. Arctec Can. Ltd., Ottawa, Ont., 1973-78; cons. Recherches Bermic, Inc., Quebec, 1978— Author: Ice Mechanics, 1978; patentee in field. Recipient Gzowski medal Engring. Inst. Can., 1963 Fellow Engring. Inst. Can., Can. Soc. Civil Engring. (Keefer medal 1977, 81, Prix Camille A. Dagenais 1983); mem. Royal Soc. Can., mem. Internat. Assn. Hydraulic Research (chmn. com. ice problems 1970-76) Office: Cameco Corp 2121 11th St W Saskatoon SK Canada S7M 1J3

MICHEL, MARY ANN KEDZUF, nursing educator; b. Evergreen Park, Ill., June 1, 1939; d. John Roman and Mary (Bassar) Kedzuf; m. Jean Paul Michel, 1974. Diploma in nursing, Little Company of Mary Hosp., Evergreen Park, 1960; BSN, Loyola U., Chgo., 1964; MS, No. Ill. U., 1968, EdD, 1971. Staff nurse Little Co. of Mary Hosp., 1960-64; instr. Little Co. of Mary Hosp. Sch. Nursing, 1964-67, No. Ill. U., DeKalb, 1968-69, asst. prof., 1969-71; chmn. dept. nursing U. Nev., Las Vegas, 1971-73, prof. nursing, 1975—, dean Coll. Health Scis., 1973-90; pres. PERC, Inc.; mgmt. cons., 1993—. Mgmt. cons. Nev. Donor Network, 1993; mem. So. Nev. Health Manpower Task Force, 1975; mem. manpower com. Plan Devel. Commn., Clark County Health Sys. Agy., 1977-79, mem. governing body, 1981-86; mem. Nev. Health Coordinating Coun., Western Inst. Nursing, 1971-85; mem. coordinating com. assembly instnl. adminstrs. dept. allied health edn. and accreditation AMA, 1985-88; mem. bd. advisors So. Nev. Vocat. Tech. Ctr., 1976-80; sec.-treas. Nev. Donor Network, 1988-89, chmn. bd., 1988-90. Contbr. articles to profl. jours. Trustee Desert Spring Hosp., Las Vegas, 1976-85; bd. dirs. Nathan Adelson Hospice, 1982-88, Bridge Counseling Assocs., 1982, Everywoman's Ctr., 1984-86; chair Nev. Commn. on Nursing Edn., 1972-73, Nursing Articulation Com., 1972-73, Yr. of Nurse Com., 1978; moderator Invitational Conf. Continuing Edn., Am. Soc. Allied Health Professions, 1978; mgmt. cons. Nev. Donor Network, 1994-95, Donor Organ Recovery Svc., Transplant Recipient Internat. Orgn., S.W. Eye Bank, S.W. Tissue Bank. Named Outstanding Alumnus, Loyola U., 1983; NIMH fellow, 1967-68. Fellow Am. Soc. Allied Health Professions, 1991, (chair nat. resolutions com. 1981-84, treas. 1988-90, sec's. award com. 1982-83, 92-93, nat. by-laws com. 1985, conv. chair 1987); mem. AAUP, Am. Nurses Assn., Nev. Nurses Assn. (dir. 1975-77, treas. 1977-79, conv. chair 1978), So. Nev. Area Health Edn. Coun., Western Health Deans (co-organizer 1985, chair, 1988-90), Nat. League Nursing, Nev. Heart Assn., So. Nev. Mem. Hosps. (nursing recruitment com. 1981-83, mem. nursing practice com. 1983-85), Las Vegas C. of C. (named Woman of Yr. Edn.) 1988, Slovak Catholic Sokols, Phi Kappa Phi (chpt. sec. 1981-83, pres.-elect 1983, pres. 1984, v.p. Western region 1989-95, editl. bd. jour. Nat. Forum 1989-93), Alpha Beta Gamma (hon.), Sigma Theta Tau, Zeta Kappa. Office: U Nev Las Vegas 4505 S Maryland Pky Las Vegas NV 89154-9900

MICHELS, DOUG, computer company executive; Grad., U. Calif., Santa Cruz. Pres., CEO SCO, Santa Cruz, Calif., 1979—; pres. UniForums, 1989-90. Office: 425 Encinal St PO Box 1900 Santa Cruz CA 95060

MICHELSON, LILLIAN, motion picture researcher; b. Manhattan, N.Y., June 21, 1928; d. Louis and Dora (Keller) Farber; m. Harold Michelson, Dec. 14, 1947; children: Alan Bruce, Eric Neil, Dennis Paul. Vol. Goldwyn Libr., Hollywood, Calif., 1961-69; owner Former Goldwyn Rsch. Libr., Hollywood, 1969—; ind. location scout, 1973—. Bd. dirs Beverlywood After Care Ctr., L.A., 1988—; mem. Friends of L.A. Pub. Libr. Mem. Acad. Motion Picture Arts and Scis. Office: c/o Dreamworks SKG Rsch Libr 1000 Flower St Glendale CA 91201-3007 Fax: 818-695-6450. E-mail: hmichelson@dreamworks.com

MICHIE, SARA H. pathologist, educator; b. Tulsa, Okla., Jan. 3, 1955; BS in Biology, Stephen F. Austin U., 1977; MD, U. Tex., Houston, 1981. Diplomate Am. Bd. Pathology. Resident anatomic pathology Stanford (Calif.) U. Med. Ctr., 1981-83, postdoctoral fellow immunology dept. pathology, 1983-84, 86-87, postdoctoral fellow diagnostic immunopathology, 1984-85; resident dept. pathology U. Iowa, Iowa City, 1985-86, postdoctoral fellow, 1986; assoc. investigator lab. svc. VA Hosp., Palo Alto, Calif., 1988-89, staff physician, 1989—, assoc. investigator, 1990-91; clin. instr. pathology dept. Stanford U., 1989-92, asst. prof. pathology, 1992—. Contbr. articles to profl. jours. Recipient Rsch. award Am. Diabetes Assn., 1996. Mem. Am. Soc. Investigative Pathology, Soc. Investigative Pathology, Bay Area Flow Cytometry Group, Sigma Xi, Alpha Omega Alpha. Office: VA Hosp Palo Alto 3801 Miranda Ave Stop 154F Palo Alto CA 94304-1207

MICKUS, DONALD V. real estate development corporation executive; BS in Acctg., Wayne State U. CPA. Mgr. Ernst & Young, Greyhound Corp., Del Webb Corp., Phoenix, 1983-85, v.p., treas., sec., 1985—. Office: Del Webb Corp 6001 N 24th St Phoenix AZ 85016-2018

MIDDLEBROOK, DIANE WOOD, English language educator; b. Pocatello, Idaho, Apr. 16, 1939; d. Thomas Isaac and Helen Loretta (Downey) Wood; m. Jonathan Middlebrook, June 15, 1963 (div. 1972); 1 child, Leah Wood Middlebrook; m. Carl Djerassi, June 21, 1985. BA, U. Wash., 1961; MA, Yale U., 1962, PhD, 1968; LittD (hon.), Kenyon Coll., 1999. Asst. prof. Stanford (Calif.) U., 1966-73, assoc. prof., 1973-83, prof., 1983-2001, D, dir. Ctr. for Rsch. on Women, 1977-79. Author: Walt Whitman and Wallace Stevens, 1974, Worlds into Words: Understanding Modern Poems, 1980, Anne Sexton, A Biography, 1991, Suits Me: The Double Life of Billy Tipton, 1998, (poems) Gin Considered as a Demon, 1983; editor: Coming to Light: American Women Poets in the Twentieth Century, 1985. Founding trustee Djerassi Resident Artists Program, Woodside, Calif., 1980-83, chair, 1994; trustee San Francisco Art Inst., 1993. Ind. study fellow NEH, 1982 83, Bunting Inst. fellow Radcliffe Coll., 1982 83, Guggenheim Found. fellow, 1988-89, Rockefeller Study Ctr. fellow, 1990; recipient Yale Prize for Poetry; finalist Nat. Book award, 1991. Mem. MLA. Avocations: collecting art, theater. Home: 1101 Green St Apt 1501 San Francisco CA 94109-2012 Office: Stanford U Dept English Stanford CA 94305-2087 E-mail: dwm@stanford.edu

MIDDLEBROOK, ROBERT DAVID, electronics educator; b. England, May 16, 1929; BA, Cambridge U., England, 1952, MA, 1956; MS, Stanford U., 1953, PhD in Elec. Engring., 1955. Sr. tech. instr., mem. trade testing bd. Radio Sch. No. 3, Royal Air Force, Eng., 1947-49; asst. prof. electrical engring. Calif. Inst. Tech., Pasadena, 1955-58, assoc. prof., 1958-65, prof. electronics, 1965-98, prof. emeritus, 1998—. Mem. hon. editorial adv. bd. Solid State Electronics, 1960-74; mem. WESCON tech. program com., 1964; lectr. 23 univs. and cos. in Eng., The Netherlands, Germany, 1965-66; mem. rsch. and tech. adv. coun. com. on space propulsion and power, NASA, 1976-77; gen. chmn. Calif. Inst. Tech. Indsl. Assocs. Conf. Power Electronics, 1982; cons. in field. Author: An Introduction to Transistor Theory, 1957, Differential Amplifiers, 1963, (with S. Cuk) Advances in Switched-Mode Power Conversion, Vols. I and II, 1981, 2d edit., 1983, Vol. III, 1983; mem. editorial bd. Internat. Jour. Electronics, 1976-82; presented 77 profl. papers; patentee in field. Recipient Nat. Profl. Group Indsl. Engrs. award, 1958, Indsl Rsch. 100 award Indsl. Rsch. Mag., 1980, award for the Best Use of Graphics Powercon 7, 1980, Powercon 8, 1981, William E. Newell Power Electronics award Inst. Elec. & Electronics Engrs., 1982, PCIM award for Leadership in Power Electronics Edn., 1990, Edward Longstreth Medal Franklin Inst., 1991, Richard P. Feynman prize for excellence in tchg. Calif. Inst. Tech., 1997. Fellow IEEE (exec. com. San Gabriel Valley sect. 1964-65, treas. 1977-78, gen. chmn. power electronics specialists conf. 1973, AES-S elec. power/energy systems panel 1977-87, program chmn. applied electronics conf. 1986, 87), Instn. Elec. Engrs. (Eng.); mem. Sigma Xi. Achievements include research in new solid state devices, their development, representation and application; electronics education (design-oriented analysis techniques); power conversion and control. Office: Calif Inst Tech 136 93 Engring Applied Sci Pasadena CA 91125-0001

MIDDLEKAUFF, ROBERT LAWRENCE, history educator, administrator; b. Yakima, Wash., July 5, 1929; s. Harold and Katherine Ruth (Horne) M.; m. Beverly Jo Martin, July 11, 1952; children: Samuel John, Holly Ruth. B.A., U. Wash., 1952; Ph.D., Yale U., 1961. Instr. history Yale U., New Haven, 1959-62; asst. prof. history U. Calif.-Berkeley, 1962-66, assoc. prof., 1966-70, prof., 1970-80, Margaret Byrne prof. history, 1980-83; dir. Huntington Library, Art Gallery and Bot. Gardens, San Marino, Calif., 1983-88; prof. history U. Calif., Berkeley, 1988-92, Preston Hotchkiss prof., 1992—; Harmsworth prof. history Oxford (Eng.) U., 1996-97. Mem. council Inst. Early Am. History and Culture, Williamsburg, Va., 1974-76, 85-88. Author: Ancients and Axioms, 1963, The Mathers, 1971, The Glorious Cause: The American Revolution, 1763-1789, 1982, Benjamin Franklin and His Enemies, 1996. Served to 1st lt. USMC, 1952-54, Korea. Recipient Bancroft prize, 1972; recipient Commonwealth Club Gold medal, 1983; fellow Am. Council Learned Socs., 1965, NEH, 1973, Huntington Library, 1977 Fellow Am. Acad. Arts and Scis.; mem.

Am. Hist. Assn., Orgn. Am. Historians, Am. Philos. Soc., Soc. Am. Historians, Am. Antiquarian Soc., Assocs. Early Am. History and Culture (mem. exec. com.), Colonial Soc. Mass. (corr.) Home: 5868 Ocean View Dr Oakland CA 94618-1535 Office: Univ Calif Dept History Berkeley CA 94720-0001 E-mail: rlmiddlek@juno.com

MIDDLETON, JAMES ARTHUR, oil and gas company executive; b. Tulsa, Mar. 15, 1936; s. James Arthur and Inez (Matthews) M.; m. Victoria Middleton; children: Robert Arthur, James Daniel, Angela Lynn; stepson: Andrew Davis Fitzhugh. B.A., Rice U., 1958, B.S. in Mech. Engring., 1959. With Atlantic Richfield Co., 1959-96; design engr. Dallas, 1962-67; tech. planner, 1967-69; mgr. shale devel. Grand Junction, Colo., 1969-72; mgr. engring. dept. Los Angeles, 1972-74; mgr. Prudhoe Bay project Pasadena, Calif., 1974-80; v.p., mgr. corp. planning Los Angeles, 1980-81; pres. ARCO Coal Co., Denver, 1981-82; sr. v.p. ARCO Oil and Gas Co., Dallas, 1982-85, pres., 1985-90, sr. v.p. parent co., 1981-87, exec. v.p. parent co., 1987-94, also bd. dirs.; chmn., CEO Crown Energy Corp., Salt Lake City, 1996-2000. Bd. dirs. Tex. Utilities Co., Dallas., ARCO Chem. Co., Berry Petroleum Co. Corp. rep. Circle Ten coun. Boy Scouts Am.; bd. dirs. L.A. coun. Boy Scouts Am., United Way Met. Dallas, Dallas Coun. on World Affairs, Jr. Achievement So. Calif. 2d lt. C.E., AUS, 1959-60 Reicpient ASME Petroleum div. Oil Drop award. Mem. Soc. Petroleum Engrs. of AIME, Tex. Mid-Continent Oil and Gas Assn., Am. Petroleum Inst., Rocky Mountain Oil and Gas Assn., We. States Petroleum Assn. (chmn. bd. dirs.), Nat. Gas Suppliers Assn. (chmn.), L.A. C. of C. (bd. dirs.), L.A. Music Ctr. Founders, Ctr. for Strategic and Internat. Studies (CSIS)-Dallas Round Table, Am. Enterprise Forum Chief Execs. Round Table, Dallas Petroelum Club, Tower, Northwood, Calif. Club, Bel-Air Country Club, L.A. Country Club. Office: 574 Chapala Dr Pacific Palisades CA 90272-4429

MIDDLEWOOD, MARTIN EUGENE, technical communications specialist, writer, consultant; b. Galesburg, Ill., Mar. 21, 1947; s. Martin and Bernetta Maxine (Henderson) M.; m. Mona Marie Jarmer, Sept. 10, 1971; children: Erin, Martha, Emily, Margaret. BA, Ea. Wash. U., 1973, MA, 1980. Writer tech. manuals Tektronix, Inc., Beaverton, Oreg., 1976-77, tech. writer, 1977-79, sr. tech. writer, 1979-82, supr. pub. rels., 1982-84, mgr. pub. rels., 1984-85, mgr. mktg. communications Vancouver, Wash., 1985-86; dir. info. strategy and svcs. Waggener Edstrom, Portland, Oreg., 1986-98; pub. Cognizer Report, Portland, 1990-94. Chmn. adv. bd. sci. and tech. writing, Clark Coll., Vancouver, 1984—; owner communications cons. firm, Vancouver, 1978-98; pres., owner Frontline Strategies, Inc., 1998—. Author: (ednl. brochure series) Oscilloscope Measurements, 1979 (award of excellence Willamette Valley chpt., Network Svcing., won Awd. of Distinction, 1980, Soc. Tech. Communication, 1980); contbr. articles to profl. jours. Served with USMC, 1967-70. Recipient cert. recognition Clark Coll., Vancouver, 1984, 86, 89, 92-99, award of excellence Pacific N.W. chpt. Internat. Assn. Bus. Communicators, 1985. Mem. Soc. Tech. Communication (sr., pres. Willamette Valley chpt. 1983-85, award of recognition 1986, chpt. pub. achievement award 1985, awards of distinction, 1980, 81). Avocations: photography, martial arts. Home and Office: 1107 SE 98th Ave Vancouver WA 98664-4119 E-mail: martinm@pacific.com

MIDGETT, LEON A. manufacturing executive; b. Flat Rock, Ill., Oct. 31, 1942; BA, U. Ill., 1965. Plant contr., metal beverage container plant Ball Corp., Findlay, Ohio, 1972-74, adminstr. mgr., Findlay and Fairfield plants, 1974-78, mgr. mfg. svcs., 1978, dir. mfg. svcs. Colo., 1979-90, v.p., mfg., 1990-, pres., 1995-00, COO, 2000—. Office: Ball Corp 9300 W 108th Cir Broomfield CO 80021-3682

MIDKIFF, ROBERT RICHARDS, financial and trust company executive, consultant; b. Honolulu, Sept. 24, 1920; s. Frank Elbert and Ruth (Richards) M.; m. Evanita Sumner, July 24, 1948; children: Mary Lloyd, Robin Starr, Shelley Sumner, Robert Richards Jr., David Wilson. BA, Yale U., 1942; grad. Advanced Mgmt. Program, Harvard U., 1962. Asst. sec. Hawaiian Trust Co., 1951-56, asst. v.p., 1956-57, v.p., 1957-65; dir. Am. Factors, Ltd., 1954-65; v.p. Amfac, Inc., 1965-68; exec. v.p., dir. Am. Security Bank, Honolulu, 1968-69, pres., dir., 1969-71; pres., CEO, dir. Am. Trust Co. Hawaii, Honolulu, 1971-93; chmn. bd. dirs. Bishop Trust Co. Ltd., Honolulu, 1984-93; pres., CEO Am. Fin. Svcs. of Hawaii, 1984-93. Bd. dirs. Persis Corp., Honolulu. Co-chmn. Gov.'s Archtl. Adv. Com. on State Capitol, 1960-65; co-chmn. Gov.'s Adv. Com. on Fine Arts for State Capitol, 1965-69; past chmn., bd. dirs. Hawaii Visitors Bur.; past pres., bd. dirs. Downtown Improvement Assn., Lahaina Restoration Found., Hawaii Cmty. Found.; bd. dirs., pres. Atherton Family Found.; past chmn. Profit Sharing Rsch. Found.; bd. dirs. Coun. on Founds.; chmn. bd. dirs. Hawaii Theatre Ctr.; chmn. bd. dirs. Good Beginnings Alliance. Mem. Coun. on Founds., Profit Sharing Coun. Am. (past bd. dirs.), Small Bus. Coun. Am. (past bd. dirs.), Pacific Club, Waialae Golf Club, Phi Beta Kappa. Democrat. Episcopalian. Office: 4477 Kahala Ave Honolulu HI 96816-4924 Fax: 808-737-9007. E-mail: rrmhi@aol.com

MIDLER, BETTE, singer, entertainer, actress; b. Honolulu, Dec. 1, 1945; m. Martin von Haselberg, 1984; 1 child, Sophie. Student, U. Hawaii. Debut as actress film Hawaii, 1965; mem. cast Fiddler on the Roof, N.Y.C., 1966-69, Salvation, N.Y.C., 1970, Tommy, Seattle Opera Co., 1971; nightclub concert performer on tour, U.S., from 1972; appearance Palace Theatre, N.Y.C., 1973, Radio City Music Hall, 1993; TV appearances include The Tonight Show, Bette Midler: Old Red Hair is Back, 1978, Gypsy, 1993 (Golden Globe award best actress in a mini-series or movie made for television 1994, Emmy nomination, Lead Actress - Special, 1994), Seinfeld, 1996, Diva Las Vegas, 1997, Murphy Brown, 1998; appeared Clams on The Half-Shell Revue, N.Y.C., 1975; recs. include The Divine Miss M, 1972, Bette Midler, 1973, Broken Blossom, 1977, Live at Last, 1977, The Rose, 1979, Thighs and Whispers, 1979, Songs for the New Depression, 1979, Divine Madness, 1980, No Frills, 1984, Mud Will Be Flung Tonight, 1985, Beaches (soundtrack), 1989, Some People's Lives, 1990; motion picture appearances include Hawaii, 1966, The Rose, 1979 (Academy award nomination best actress 1979), Divine Madness, 1980, Jinxed, 1982, Down and Out in Beverly Hills, 1986, Ruthless People, 1986, Outrageous Fortune, 1987, Oliver and Company (voice), 1988, Big Business, 1988, Beaches, 1988, Stella, 1990, Scenes From a Mall, 1991, For the Boys, 1991 (Academy award nomination best actress 1991), Hocus Pocus, 1993, Get Shorty, 1995, The First Wives Club, 1996, That Old Feeling, 1997, Get Bruce, 1999, Isn't She Great, 1999; appeared in cable TV (HBO) prodn. Bette Midler's Mondo Beyondo, 1988; author: A View From A Broad, 1980, The Saga of Baby Divine, 1983. Recipient After Dark Ruby award, 1973; Grammy awards, 1973, 1990; spl. Tony award, 1973; Emmy award for NBC Spl., Ol' Red Hair is Back, 1978; 2 Golden Globe awards for The Rose, 1979, Golden Globe award for The Boys, 1991; Emmy award The Tonight Show appearance, 1992. Office: c/o All Girl Prodns 100 Universal City Plz Universal City CA 91608 also: c/o Warner Bros Records 3300 Warner Blvd Burbank CA 91505 Fax: 818-866-5871

MIEL, VICKY ANN, city official; b. South Bend, Ind., June 20, 1951; d. Lawrence Paul Miel and Virginia Ann (Yeagley) Hernandez. BS, Ariz. State U., 1985. Word processing coordinator City of Phoenix, 1977-78, word processing adminstr., 1978-83, chief dep. city clk., 1983-88, city clk. dir., 1988—. Assoc. prof. Phoenix Community Coll., 1982-83, Mesa (Ariz.) Community Coll., 1983; speaker in field, Boston, Santa Fe, Los Angeles, N.Y.C. and St. Paul, 1980—. Author: Phoenix Document Request Form, 1985, Developing Successful Systems Users, 1986. Judge Future Bus. Leaders Am. at Ariz. State U., Tempe, 1984; bd. dirs. Fire and Life Safety League, Phoenix, 1984. Recipient Gold Plaque, Word Processing Systems Mag., Mpls., 1980, Green Light Productivity award City of Phoenix, 1981, Honor Soc. Achievement award Internat. Word Processing Assn., 1981, 1st Ann. Grand Prize Records Mgmt. Internat. Inst. Mcpl. Clks., 1990, Olsten Award for Excellence in Records Mgmt., 1991, Tech. Award of Excellence, 1995. Mem. ASPA, Assn. Info. Systems Profls. (internat. dir. 1982-84), Internat. Inst. Mcpl. Clks. (cert., 2d v.p. 1996-97, 1st v.p. 1997-98, pres. 1998-99, tech. award of excellence 1995, immediate past pres. 1999-2000), Am. Records Mgrs. Assn., Assn. Image Mgmt., Am. Mgmt. Assn. Office: City Phoenix 200 W Washington St Ste 1500 Phoenix AZ 85003-1611

MIELKE, CLARENCE HAROLD, JR. hematologist; b. Spokane, Wash., June 18, 1936; s. Clarence Harold and Marie Katherine (Gillespie) M.; m. Marcia Rae, July 5, 1964; children: Elisa, John, Kristina. BS, Wash. State U., 1959; MD, U. Louisville, 1963. Intern San Francisco Gen. Hosp., 1963-64; resident in medicine Portland VA Hosp., 1964-65, San Francisco Gen. Hosp., 1965-67; fellow in hematology U. So. Calif., 1967-68; tchg. fellow, asst. physician, instr. Tufts-New Eng. Med. Ctr. Hosps., Boston, 1968-71; sr. scientist Med. Rsch. Inst., San Francisco, 1971-90; chief hematology Presbyn. Hosp., San Francisco, 1971-82; asst. prof. clin. medicine U. Calif. Sch. Medicine, San Francisco, 1971-80, assoc. clin. prof., 1979-90, bd. dirs. Inst. Cancer Rsch., 1992—. Trustee, bd. dirs. Med. Rsch. Inst. San Francisco, Sacred Heart Hosp. Found., 1997-2000, Rockwood Clinic Found., 1994—; dir. emeritus Inst. Cancer Rsch.; trustee emeritus, bd. dirs. Med. Rsch. Inst., 1988—; dir. Health Rsch. and Edn. Ctr., Wash. State U., 1989—, prof. pharmacology, 1989—, prof. vet. medicine, 1989—, assoc. dean rsch., 1992—. Editor emeritus Jour. Clin. Aphesis, 1981; contbr. chpts. to books, articles to med. jours. Named Nat. Disting. Eagle Scout, 1998; NIH grantee, 1973-88. Fellow ACP; mem. AAAS, AMA, Internat. Acad. Clin. and Applied Thrombosis and Hemostasis, Internat. Soc. Hematology, Am. Coll. Angiology; mem. Am. Soc. Internal. Medicine, Internat. Soc. Thrombosis and Hemostasis, Am. Heart Assn., N.Y. Acad. Scis., Spokane Med. Soc., Internat. Soc. Angiology. Office: Wash State U Health Rsch & Edn Ctr 601 W 1st Ave Spokane WA 99201-3825

MIELKE, PAUL WILLIAM, JR. statistician, consultant; b. St. Paul, Feb. 18, 1931; s. Paul William and Elsa (Yungbauer) M.; m. Roberta Roehl Robison, June 25, 1960; children: William, Emily Spear, Lynn. BA, U. Minn., 1953, PhD, 1963; MA, U. Ariz., 1958. Teaching asst. U. Ariz., Tucson, 1957-58, U. Minn., Mpls., 1958-60, statis. cons., 1960-62, lectr., 1962-63; from asst. to assoc. prof. dept. statistics Colo. State U., Fort Collins, 1963-72, prof. dept. statistics, 1972—. Co-author: (boo) Permutation Methods: A Distance Function Approach; contbr. articles to Am. Jour. Pub. Health, Jour. of Statis. Planning and Inference, Ednl. and Psychol. Measurement, Biometrika, Earth-Sci. Revs., Weather and Forecasting, Jour. Behavioral and Ednl. Stats. Capt. USAF, 1953-57. Recipient Banner I. Miller award Am. Meteorological Assn., 1994 Fellow Am. Statis. Assn.; mem. Am. Meteorol. Soc. (Banner I. Miller award 1994), Biometric Soc. Achievements include proposal that common statistical methods (t test and analysis of variance) were based on counter intuitive geometric foundations and provided alternative statistical methods which are based on appropriate foundations. Home: 736 Cherokee Dr Fort Collins CO 80525-1517 Office: Colo State U Dept Stats Fort Collins CO 80523-1877

MIGHT, THOMAS OWEN, newspaper company executive; b. Fort Walton Beach, Fla., Apr. 22, 1951; s. Gerald William and Rosina (Bugner) M.; m. Sept. 22, 1973; children— Matthew, Daniel B.S. in Indsl. Engring., Ga. Tech. U., 1972; M.B.A., Harvard Bus. Sch., 1978. Asst. to pub. Washington Post, 1978-80, mgr. plant, 1980-81, v.p. prodn., v.p. marketing; now pres., CEO, divsn. Cable One The Washington Post Co., Phoenix, 1981—. Served to capt. U.S. Army, 1972-76 Roman Catholic

MIGIELICZ, GERALYN, photojournalist; b. St. Louis, Feb. 15, 1958; d. Edward J. and Mary Ann (McCarthy) M. BJ, U. Mo., 1979. Photographer Emporia (Kans.) Gazette, 1979-80; chief photographer St. Joseph (Mo.) News-Press & Gazette, 1980-83; photo editor, photographer Seattle Times, 1984; picture editor Rocky Mountain News, Denver, 1985-86; graphics editor San Jose (Calif.) Mercury News, 1986-92, dir. photography, 1992—. Mem. faculty Poynter Inst., U. Mo. Workshop, Latin Am. Photojournalism Conf. Recipient Individual Editing awards Soc. Newspaper Designers, 1988-98, Editing awards, 91-98; named for Overall Excellence in Editing, Picture of Yr. Contest, U. Mo., 1993. Office: San Jose Mercury News 750 Ridder Park Dr San Jose CA 95131-2432

MIHALAS, DIMITRI MANUEL, astrophysicist, educator; b. Los Angeles, Mar. 20, 1939; s. Emmanuel Demetrious and Jean (Christo) M.; children: Michael Demetrious, Genevieve Alexandra. B.A. with highest honors, UCLA, 1959; M.S., Calif. Inst. Tech., 1960, Ph.D., 1964. Asst. prof. astrophys. scis. Princeton U., 1964-67; asst. prof. physics U. Colo., 1967-68; asso. prof. astronomy and astrophysics U. Chgo., 1968-70, prof., 1970-71; adj. prof. astrogeophysics, also physics and astrophysics U. Colo., 1972-80; sr. scientist High Altitude Obs., Nat. Center Atmospheric Research, Boulder, Colo., 1971-79, 82-85; G.C. McVittie prof. astronomy U. Ill., 1985-98; astronomer Sacramento Peak Obs., Sunspot, N.Mex., 1979-82; staff mem. Los Alamos Nat. Lab., 1998—. Cons. Los Alamos Nat. Lab, 1981-98; vis. prof. dept. astrophysics Oxford (Eng.) U., 1977-78; sr. vis. fellow dept. physics and astronomy Univ. Coll., London, 1978; mem. astronomy adv. panel NSF, 1972-75 Author: Galactic Astronomy, 1969, 2d edit, 1981, Stellar Atmospheres, 1970, 2d edit., 1978, Theorie des Atmospheres Stellaires, 1971, Foundations of Radiation Hydrodynamics, 1984; assoc. editor Astrophys. Jour, 1970-79, Jour. Computational Physics, 1981-87, Jour. Quantitative Spectroscopy, 1984-94; mem. editorial bd. Solar Physics, 1981-89. NSF fellow, 1959-62; Van Maanen fellow, 1962-63; Eugene Higgins vis. fellow, 1963-64; Alfred P. Sloan Found. Research fellow, 1969-71; Alexander von Humboldt Stiftung sr. U.S. scientist awardee, 1984. Mem. U.S. Nat. Acad. Sci., Internat. Astron. Union (pres. commn. 36 1976-79), Am. Astron. Soc. (pub. bd. 1995-99, mem. coun. 2000—, Helen B. Warner prize 1974), Astron. Soc. Pacific (dir. 1975-77) Home: PO Box 806 Los Alamos NM 87544-0806 Office: Los Alamos Nat Lab X-3 MS-D413 Los Alamos NM 87545-0001 E-mail: dmihalas@lanl.gov

MIKEL, THOMAS KELLY, JR. laboratory administrator; b. East Chicago, Ind., Aug. 27, 1946; s. Thomas Kelly and Anne Katherine (Vrazo) M.; BA, San Jose State U., 1973; MA, U. Calif.-Santa Barbara, 1975. Asst. dir. Santa Barbara Underseas Found., 1975-76; marine biologist PJB Labs., Ventura, Calif., 1976-81; lab. dir. CRL Environ., Ventura, 1981-88; lab. dir. ABC Labs, Ventura, 1988—; instr. oceanography Ventura Coll., 1980-81. Chair joint task group, section author 20th edit. Std. Methods Examination Water & Wastewater APHA, 1996. With U.S. Army, 1968-70. Mem. Assn. Environ. Profls., Soc. Population Ecologists, ASTME (rsch. contbr. 10th ann. symposium 1986), Soc. Environ. Toxicology and Chemistry. Biol. coord. Anacapa Underwater Natural trail U.S. Nat. Park Svc., 1976; designer ecol. restoration program of upper Newport Bay, Orange County, Calif., 1978; rsch. contbr. 3d Internat. Artificial Reef Conf., Newport Beach, Calif., 1983, Ann. Conf. Am. Petroleum Inst., Houston. Democrat.

MIKULA, JULIE, aerospace engineer; married; 2 children. Grad., Mich. State U. Mech. engr. NASA Ames Rsch. Ctr., Calif., mgr. flight simulation labs. facility. Office: NASA Ames Rsch Ctr Moffett Field CA 94035

MIKULAS, MARTIN M., JR. aerospace engineer, educator; BS, MS, PhD, Va. Polytechnic Inst. Vis. prof. aerospace structures U. Colo., Boulder. Mem. NAE. Office: Aerospace Structures U Colo Campus Box 429 Boulder CO 80309 E-mail: Martin.Mikulas@Colorado.edu

MILANOVICH, NORMA JOANNE, training and development company executive; b. Littlefork, Minn., June 4, 1945; d. Lyle Albert and Loretta (Leona) Drake; m. Rudolph William Milanovich, Mar. 18, 1943 (dec.); 1 child, Rudolph William Jr. BS in Home Econs., U. Wis., Stout, 1968; MA in Curriculum and Instrn., U. Houston, 1973, EdD in Curriculum and Program Devel., 1982. Instr. human svcs. dept. U. Houston, 1971-75; dir. videos project U. N.Mex., Albuquerque, 1976-78, dir. vocat. edn. equity ctr., 1978-88, asst. prof. occupational edn., 1982-88, coord. occupational vocat. edn. programs, 1983-88, dir. consortium rsch. and devel. in occupational edn., 1984-88; pres. Alpha Connection Tng. Corp., Albuquerque, 1988—; exec. dir. Trinity Found., 1991—; pres. Athena Leadership Ctr., 1999—. Adj. instr. Cen. Tng. Acad., Dept. Energy, Wackenhut; mem. faculty U. Phoenix; adj. faculty So. Ill. U., Lesley Coll., Boston. Author: Model Equitable Behavior in the Classroom, 1983, Handbook for Vocational-Technical Certification in New Mexico, 1985, A Vision for Kansas: Systems of Measures and Standards of Performance, 1992, Workplace Skills: The Employability Factor, 1993; editor: Choosing What's Best for You, 1982, A Handbook for Handling Conflict in the Classroom, 1983, Starting Out...A Job Finding Handbook for Teen Parents, Going to Work...Job Rights for Teens; author: JTPA Strategic Marketing Plan, 1990, We, The Arcturians, 1990, Sacred Journey to Atlantis, 1991, The Light Shall Set You Free, 1996; editor: Majestic Raise newsletter, 1996—, Celestial Voices newsletter, 1991—. Bd. dirs. Albuquerque Single Parent Occupational Scholarship Program, 1984-86; del. Youth for Understanding Internat. Program, 1985-90; mem. adv. bd. Southwestern Indian Poly. Inst., 1984-88; com. mem. Region VI Consumer Exch. Com., 1982-84; ednl. lectures, tng., tour dir. internat. study tours to Japan, Austria, Korea, India, Nepal, Mex., Eng., Greece, Egypt, Australia, New Zealand, Fed. Republic Germany, Israel, Guatemala, Peru, Bolivia, Chile, Easter Island, Tibet, China, Hong Kong, Turkey, Italy, Russia, Ukraine, Sweden, Norway, France, Kenya, Tanzania, Zimbabwe, North Pole Arctic Region, Antarctica, Argentina, Ireland, Scotland, New Zealand, Fiji, Australia, Bali, Palau, The Amazon, Galapagos Islands, Ethiopia, Mongolia, Gobi Desert, Portugal, Spain, Poland, Austria, Sicily, U.S.; facilitator, dir. Ann. Worldwide Confs., 1999, 00; keynote spkr., workshop tng. presenter worldwide; coord. Worldwide Conf. for Peace on Earth in Portugal, India, 1999, 2000, Rome, 2001, Jordan, 2002, Washington, 2002. Grantee N.Mex. Dept. Edn., 1976-78, 78-86, 83-86, HEW, 1979, 80, 81, 83, 84, 85, 86, 87. Mem. ASTD, Am. Vocat. Assn., Vocat. Edn. Equity Coun., Nat. Coalition for Sex Equity Edn., Am. Home Econs. Assn., Inst. Noetic Scis., N.Mex. Home Econs. Assn., N.Mex. Vocat. Edn. Assn., N.Mex. Adv. Coun. on Vocat. Edn., Greater Albuquerque C. of C., NAFE, Phi Delta Kappa, Phi Upsilon Omicron, Phi Theta Kappa. Democrat. Roman Catholic. Office: Athena Leadership Ctr Scottsdale AZ 85259 E-mail: info@athenalctr.com

MILAVSKY, HAROLD PHILLIP, real estate executive; b. Limerick, Sask., Can., Jan. 25, 1931; s. Jack and Clara M. B in Commerce, U. Sask., Saskatoon, Can., 1953; LLD (hon.), U. Sask., 1995, U. Calgary, 1995. Chief acct., treas., controller Loram Internat. Ltd. div. Mannix Co. Ltd., Calgary, Alta., Can., 1956-65; v.p., chief fin. officer Power Corp. Devels. Ltd., Calgary, Can., 1965-69; exec. v.p., bd. dirs. Great West Internat. Equities Ltd. (name now Trizec Corp. Ltd.), Calgary, Can., 1976-94; pres. Trizec Corp. Ltd., Calgary, Can., 1976-86, bd. dirs. Can., 1976-94, chmn. Can., 1986-93, Quantico Capital Corp., Calgary, 1994—. Bd. dirs. Consol. Properties Ltd., Citadel Diversified Mgmt., Ltd., Calgary, ENMAX Corp., Prime West Energy Inc., Calgary, Aspen Properties, Ltd., Calgary, Torode Realty, Ltd., Calgary. Past dir. Terry Fox Humanitarian Award Program; past dir. Conf. Bd. Can.; past. gov. Acctg. Edn. Found. Alta.; hon. col. 14th Svc. Battalion, Calgary; bd. dirs. Tennis Can. Recipeint B'nai Brith award of merit, 1952, Commemorative medal 125th Birthday of Can., 1992. Fellow Inst. Chartered Accts. Alta.; mem. Inst. Chartered Accts. Sask., Can. Inst. Pub. Real Estate Cos. (past pres., bd. dirs.), Can. C. of C. (past chmn.), Internat. Profl. Hockey Alumni (founding dir.), Petroleum Club, Ranchmen's Club. Avocations: skiing, tennis, horseback riding. Office: Quantico Capital Corp 1920-855 Second St SW Calgary AB Canada T2P 4J7

MILEDI, RICARDO, neurobiologist; b. Mexico City, Sept. 15, 1927; m. Ana Mela Garces, Dec. 17, 1955; 1 child, Rico. BSc, Instituto Cientifico y Literario, Chihuahua, Mex., 1945; M.D., U. Nacional Autonoma de Mex., 1955; Doctor Honoris Causa, Universidad del Pais Vasco, 1992, U. Trieste, Italy, 2000, U. Chihuahua, Mex., 2000. Researcher Instituto Nacional de Cardiologia, Mex., 1954-56; fellow John Curtin Sch. Med. Res., Canberra, Australia, 1956-58; mem. faculty U. Coll., London, 1959-85, Foulerton research prof. of Royal Soc., 1975-85, head dept. biophysics, 1978-85; Disting. prof. dept. neurobiology and behavior U. Calif., Irvine, 1984—. Editor Archives of Med. Rsch. Trustee The Grass Found., PEW L.Am. Fellows Program. Recipient Principe de Asturias prize, Spain, 1999. Fellow Royal Soc. London (Royal medal 1999), Am. Acad. Arts and Scis.; mem. AAAS, NAS, 3d World Acad. Scis., (titular) European Acad. Arts, Scis., Humanities, N.Y. Acad. Scis., Hungarian Acad. Scis. (hon.), Mex. Acad. Scis., Mex. Acad. Medicine. Home: 9 Gibbs Ct Irvine CA 92612-4032 Office: U Calif Dept Neurobiology Behavior 2205 Bio Sci Ii Irvine CA 92697-4550 E-mail: rmiledi@uci.edu

MILES, DON CLIFFORD, architect; b. Ft. Knox, Ky., Sept. 17, 1942; s. Don and Kathrine Eva (Gray) M.; m. Pamela Wait, Aug. 6, 1972; children: Katherine Wait, Lesley Gray, Nicole Conel. BArch with honors, U. Wash., 1966; MArch, M of City Planning in Urban Design, Harvard U., 1971. Registered architect, Wash. Assoc. ptnr. Zimmer, Gunsul, Frasca Partnership, Seattle. Cons., lectr. numerous orgns., cities, corps. Prin. projects include Pedestrian Corridor, Major Pub. Open Spaces, CBD Transit Ctr., Bellevue, Wash., Banfield Light Rail Project, Portland, Boise (Idaho) Downtown Major Pub. Open Space, Street Improvements and Transit Malls, Honolulu Rapid Transit Project, Revitalization of State St., Chgo., Midway Corridor Project, Mpls., High Capacity Transit Project, Seattle, Ctrl. Orange County Aerial Fixed Guideway, Mission Valley West Extension Light Rail Project, San Diego, Master Plan for Capitol of State of Wash., Seattle Union Sta. Redevel. Plan, Weyerhauser Corp. Campus, Quadrant Corp. site, Lake Union, Seattle, Whitman Coll. Bd. dirs., founder Project for Pub. Spaces, 1975—; bd. dirs. Seattle Children's Mus., 1978-82; trustee Queen Ann Community Coun., 1978-80. Fellow AIA, Inst. Urban Design. Avocations: skiing, jogging. Home: 611 W Comstock St Seattle WA 98119-3422 Office: Zimmer Gunsul Frasca 1191 2nd Ave Ste 800 Seattle WA 98101-2949

MILES, DONALD F. lawyer; b. Marysville, Calif., Apr. 11, 1949; AB with honors, Stanford U., 1971; JD, U. Calif., San Francisco, 1974. Bar: Calif. 1974, U.S. Dist. Ct. (no. dist.) Calif. 1974, U.S. Dist. Ct. (ea. dist.) Calif. 1977, U.S. Dist. Ct. (so. dist.) Calif. 1986, U.S. Supreme Ct. 1987, U.S. Dist. Ct. (ctrl. dist.) Calif. 1991. Law clk. to Hon. William P. Clark Jr. Supreme Ct. Calif., 1974-75; mem. Howard, Rice, Nemerovski, Canady, Falk & Rabkin, P.C., San Francisco. Spl. master U.S. Dist. Ct. (no. dist.) Calif.; instr., adj. faculty mem. Hastings Coll. Law U. Calif.; faculty mem., bd. dirs. Hastings Nat. Coll. Advocacy; mem. adv. com. Calif. Legis. Joint Com. Tort Liability. Author: (with others) Civil Procedure During Trial, vol. II, 1984, 95, California Liability Insurance Practice, 1991, Continuing Education of the Bar Action Guide, 1991; author, narrator: (videotape) Laying a Foundation to Introduce Evidence, 1989; contbr. articles to profl. jours. Bd. chmn. The Glenwood Sch. Found. Mem. ABA (sect. torts and ins. practice), State Bar Calif., Assn. Def. Counsel No. Calif., Bar Assn. of San Francisco, Internat. Assn. Def. Counsel, Def. Rsch. Inst., Thurston Soc., Order of Coif. Office: Howard Rice Nemerovski Canady Falk & Rabkin PC 3 Embarcadero Ctr Ste 700 San Francisco CA 94111-4074

MILES, JACK (JOHN RUSSIANO), journalist, educator; b. Chgo., July 30, 1942; s. John Alvin and Mary Jean (Murphy) M.; m. Jacqueline Russiano, Aug. 23, 1980; 1 child, Kathleen. LittB, Xavier U., Cin., 1964; PhB, Pontifical Gregorian U., Rome, 1966; student, Hebrew U., Jerusalem, 1966-67; PhD, Harvard U., 1971. Asst. prof. Loyola U., Chgo., 1970-74; asst. dir. Scholars Press, Missoula, Mont., 1974-75; postdoctoral fellow U. Chgo., 1975-76; editor Doubleday & Co., N.Y.C., 1976-78; exec. editor U. Calif. Press, Berkeley, 1978-85; book editor L.A. Times, 1985-91, mem. editl. bd., 1991-95; dir. Humanities Ctr. Claremont (Calif.) Grad. Sch., 1995-97; Mellon vis. prof. Calif. Inst. Tech., 1997-98; sr. advisor to pres. J. Paul Getty Trust, L.A., 1999—. Contb. editor Atlantic Monthly, 1995—. Author: Retroversion and Text Criticism, 1984, God: A Biography, 1995, Christ: A Crisis in the Life of God, 2001; contbr. learned and popular articles to various periodicals; book reviewer. Recipient Pulitzer prize for biography, 1996; Guggenheim fellow, 1990-91. Mem. PEN, Nat. Book Critics Circle (pres. 1990-92), Am. Acad. Religion, Amnesty Internat. Episcopalian. Office: J Paul Getty Trust 1200 Getty Center Dr Ste 1100 Los Angeles CA 90049-1188

MILES, JOANNA, actress, playwright, director; b. Nice, France, Mar. 6, 1940; came to U.S., 1941, naturalized, 1941; d. Johannes Schiefer and Jeanne Miles; m. William Burns, May 23, 1970 (div. 1977); m. Michael Brandman, Apr. 29, 1978; 1 child, Miles. Grad., Putney (Vt.) Sch., 1958. Mem. Actors Studio, Playwrites and Dirs. Workshop, N.Y.C., 1966; co-founder, mem. L.A. Classic Theatre, 1986. Founder, mem. Playwrights Group/LAWW, 1991-98, L.A. Writer's Workshop, 1996-98. Appeared in: (motion pictures) The Way We Live Now, 1969, Bug, 1975, The Ultimate Warrior, 1975, Golden Girl, 1978, Cross Creek, 1983, As Is, 1986, Blackout, 1988, Rosencrants and Guildenstern are Dead, 1991, The Rhinghart Theory, 1994, Judge Dredd, 1994, Alone, 1996; numerous television films including In What America, 1965, My Mothers House, 1963, Glass Managerie, 1974, Born Innocent, 1974, Aloha Means Goodbye, 1974, The Trial of Chaplain Jensen, 1975, Harvest Home, 1977, Fire in the Sky, 1978, Sophisticated Gents, 1979, Promise of Love, 1982, Sound of Murder, 1983, All My Sons, 1987, The Right to Die, 1987, The Habitation of Dragons, 1991, Heart of Justice, 1991, Water Engine, 1991, Cooperstown, 1992, Legionnaires, 1992, Life Lessons, 1992, Willing to Kill, 1992, The American Clock, 1993, Dark Reflections, 1993, Outcry, 1994, Everything to Gain, 1995, Small Vices, 1998, Crossfire Trail, 1999, Thin Aire, 1999; episodes in numerous TV series including: Barney Miller, Dallas, St. Elsewhere, The Hulk, Trapper John, Kaz, Cagney and Lacey, Studio 5B, 1989, Star Trek: The Next Generation, 1990, 91, Life Stories, 1991, HBO Life Stories, 1993, Total Security, 1997, Nothing Sacred, 1998, Chicago Hope, 1998-99, ER, 2000, Family Law, 2000; stage plays include Once in a Life Time, 1963, Cave Dwellers, 1964, Drums in the Night, 1968, Dracula, 1968, Home Free, 1964, One Night Stands of a Noisy Passenger, 1972, Dylan, 1973, Dancing for the Kaiser, 1976, Debutante Ball, 1985, Kramer, 1977, One Flew Over the Cuckoo's Nest, 1989, Growing Gracefully, 1990, Cut Flowers, 1994; performed in radio shows Sta. KCRW Once in a Lifetime, 1987, Babbit, 1987, Sta. KPFK, Grapes of Wrath, 1989, The White Plague, Sta. KCRW, 1991, Chekhov Short Stories, Sta. KCRW, 1992; playwright, v.p. Brandman Productions; author; (plays) Ethanasia, A Woman in Reconstruction, Hostages, Feathers, On the Shelf. Pres. Children Giving to Children. Recipient 2 Emmy awards, 1974, Women in Radio and TV award, 1974, Actors Studio Achievement award, 1980, Dramalogue award, 1996; nominated Golden Globe, 1994. Mem. Acad. Motion Picture Arts and Scis., Acad. TV Arts and Scis., Dramatists Guild Office: Brandman Prodns 2062 Vine St Apt 5 Hollywood CA 90068-3928 also: The Artists Agy 10000 Santa Monica Blvd Los Angeles CA 90067-7007 E-mail: jmilesb@aol.com

MILES, RAYMOND EDWARD, former university dean, organizational behavior and industrial relations educator; b. Cleburne, Tex., Nov. 2, 1932; s. Willard Francis and Wilma Nell (Owen) M.; m. Lucile Dustin, Dec. 27, 1952; children: Laura, Grant, Kenneth. B.A. with highest honors, U. North Tex., 1954, M.B.A., 1958; Ph.D., Stanford U., 1963. Clk. Santa Fe R.R., Gainesville, Tex., 1950-55; instr. mgmt. Sch. Bus. U. North Tex., Denton, 1958-60; asst. prof. organizational behavior and indsl. relations Sch. Bus. Adminstrn. U. Calif.-Berkeley, 1963-68, assoc. prof., 1968-71, prof., 1971—, assoc. dean Haas Sch. of Bus., 1978-81, dean, 1983-90; dir. Inst. Indsl. Relations, 1982-83; cons. various pvt., pub. orgns. Author: Theories of Management, 1975, (with Charles C. Snow) Organization Strategy, Structure and Process, 1978, (with Charles C. Snow) Fit, Failure, and the Hall of Fame, 1994; co-author: Organizational Behavior: Research and Issues, 1976; co-editor, contbg. author: Organization by Design: Theory and Practice, 1981. Served to 1st. lt. USAF, 1955-58. Mem. Indsl. Relations Research Assn., Acad. Mgmt. Democrat. Unitarian. Home: 8640 Don Carol Dr El Cerrito CA 94530-2733 Office: U Calif Walter A Haas Sch Bus Berkeley CA 94720-0001 E-mail: miles@haas.berkeley.edu

MILES, RICHARD ROBERT, art historian, writer; b. Tokyo, Apr. 1, 1939; s. Robert Henri and Eleanor Alfrida (Child) Perreau-Saussine. BA, UCLA, 1972. Novelist, screenwriter various, 1965-72; dir. Meilinki Enterprises Ltd., 1980—. Bd. dirs. Balcom Trading Co., Tokyo, 1979-82. Author: That Cold Day in the Park, 1965 (Dell Book award 1965), Angel Loves Nobody, 1967 (Samuel Goldwyn award UCLA, 1969); (art history) Prints of Paul Jacoulet, 1982, Elizabeth Keith-The Prints, 1989, The Watercolors of Paul Jacoulet, 1992, Printmaker in Paradise: Charles W. Bartlett, 2001, others. Mem. Internat. Soc. of Fine Art Appraisers, New Eng. Appraisers Assn., Writers Guild of Am. West, Acad. of Am. Poets. Office: Meilinki Enterprises Ltd 214 N Bowling Green Way Los Angeles CA 90049-2816

MILGRIM, DARROW A. insurance broker, recreation consultant; b. Chgo., Apr. 30, 1945; s. David and Miriam (Glickman) M.; m. Laurie Stevens, Apr. 15, 1984; children: Derick, Jared, Kayla. BA, Calif. State U., San Bernardino, 1968; postgrad., U. So. Calif., 1972. Accredited ins. adv.; cert. ins. counselor; cert. sch. adminstr. Tchr. Rialto (Calif.) Unified Sch. Dist., 1969-70, Las Virgenes Unified Sch. Dist., Westlake Village, Calif., 1970-78; instr. Calif. State U., Northridge, 1980-84; pres. Darrow Milgrim Ins, Svcs., Inc.; ins. broker, dir. Speare Ins. Brokers, Blade Ins. Svcs., Brentwood, Calif., 1984—. Dir. Calamigos Star C Ranch Summer Camp, Malibu, Calif., Calamigos Environ. Edn. Ctr., Malibu. Editor: Legislation and Regulations for Organized Camps, 1987. Pres. Calif. Camping Adv. Coun., Long Beach, 1985-87, 99-2000; bd. dirs. Calif. Collaboration for Youth, Sacramento, 1985—, Camp Ronald McDonald for Good Times, 1989-95; commr. dept. parks and recreation City of Agoura Hills, Calif., 1987-93; cons. Ronald McDonald House Charities, S.C., L.A., 1986-95, ACA Legis Task Force and Nat. Pub. Policy Com. Mem. Am. Camping Assn. (bd. dirs. So. Calif. sect., mem. nat. pub. policy com. Martinsville, Ind., 1980-98, nat. bd. dirs. 1990-95, legis. liaison, regional honor 1986), Ins. Brokers and Agts. of L.A. Coun., Agts. and Brokers State Legis. Coun. Office: Speare Co Ins Brokers PO Box 250024 Los Angeles CA 90025-0660 E-mail: dmilgrim@speare.com

MILLAR, ROBERT, artist; b. L.A., Mar. 6, 1958; s. Thomas A. and Josephine E. (Alford) M. BA, Calif. State U., Northridge, 1980. Exhibited work at L.A. Metro Rail Sta., 1990 (progressive Arch. citation 1992), Newport Harbor Art Mus., 1991, Rose Theatre Site, London, 1992, S.D. Alvarado Filtration Plant, 1993. Arts commr. City of Manhattan Beach, Calif., 1985-94; mem. pub. art adv. com. Calif. Arts Coun., 1992. Grantee Pollock-Krasner Found., 1989. Studio: 1420 Old Topanga Canyon Rd Topanga CA 90290-3923

MILLARD, NEAL STEVEN, lawyer; b. Dallas, June 6, 1947; s. Bernard and Adele (Marks) M.; m. Janet Keast, Mar. 12, 1994; 1 child, Kendall Layne. BA cum laude, UCLA, 1969; JD, U. Chgo., 1972. Bar: Calif. 1972, U.S. Dist. Ct. (cen. dist.) Calif. 1973, U.S. Tax Ct. 1973, U.S. Ct. Appeals (9th cir.) 1987, N.Y. 1990. Assoc. Willis, Butler & Schiefly, Los Angeles, 1972-75; ptnr. Morrison & Foerster, Los Angeles, 1975-84, Jones, Day, Reavis & Pogue, Los Angeles, 1984-93, White & Case, L.A., 1993—. Instr. Calif. State Coll., San Bernardino, 1975-76; lectr. Practising Law Inst., N.Y.C., 1983-90, Calif. Edn. of Bar, 1987-90; adj. prof. USC Law Ctr., 1994—. Citizens adv. com. L.A. Olympics, 1982-84; trustee Altadena (Calif.) Libr. Dist., 1985-86; bd. dirs. Woodcraft Rangers, L.A., 1982-90, pres., 1986-88; bd. dirs. L.A. County Bar Found., 1990-2000, pres., 1997-98; mem. Energy Commn. of County and Cities of L.A., 1995-99; bd. dirs. Inner City Law Ctr., 1996-99; mem. jud. procedures commn. L.A. County, 1999—, chair, 2000—. Mem. ABA, Calif. Bar Assn., N.Y. State Bar Assn., L.A. County Bar Assn. (trustee 1985-87), Pub. Counsel (bd. dirs. 1984-87, 90-93), U. Chgo. Law Alumni Assn. (pres. 1998—), USC Inst. for Corporate Counsel (advisory bd. 1998—), Calif. Club, Phi Beta Kappa, Pi Gamma Mu, Phi Delta Phi. Office: White & Case 633 W 5th St Ste 1900 Los Angeles CA 90071-2087 E-mail: nmillard@whitecase.com

MILLARD, RICHARD STEVEN, lawyer; b. Pasadena, Calif., Feb. 6, 1952; s. Kenneth A. and Kathryn Mary (Paden) M.; m. Jessica Ann Edwards, May 15, 1977; children: Victoria, Elizabeth, Andrew. AB, Stanford U., 1974; JD magna cum laude, U. Mich., 1977. Bar: Calif. 1977, Ill. 1985. Assoc. Heller, Ehrman, White & McAuliff, San Francisco, 1977-81, Mayer, Brown & Platt, Chgo., 1982-83, ptnr., 1984-99, Weil, Gotshal & Manges, Menlo Park, Calif., 1999—. Mem. ABA, Order of Coif. Office: Weil Gotshal & Manges 2882 Sand Hill Rd Menlo Park CA 94025-7064 E-mail: richard.millard@weil.com

MILLENDER-MCDONALD, JUANITA, congresswoman, former school system administrator; b. Birmingham, Ala., Sept. 7, 1938; d. Shelly and Everlina (Dortch) M.; m. James McDonald III, July 26, 1955; children: Valeria, Angela, Sherryll, Michael, Roderick. BS, U. Redlands, Calif., 1980; MS in Edn., Calif. State U., L.A., 1986; postgrad., U. So. Calif. Manuscript editor Calif. State Dept. Edn., Sacramento; dir. gender equity programs L.A. Unified Sch. Dist.; mem. U.S. Congress from 37th Calif dist., Washington, 1996—; mem. small bus. com., transp. and infrastructure com. City councilwoman, Carson; bd. dirs. S.C.L.C. Pvt. Industry Coun. Policy Bd., West Basin Mcpl. Water Dist., Cities Legis. League (vice chmn.; mem. Nat. Women's Polit. Caucus; mem. adv. bd. Comparative Ethnic Tng. U. So. Calif.; founder, exec. dir. Young Advocates So. Calif. Mem. NEA, Nat. Assn. Minority Polit. Women, NAFE, Nat. Fedn. Bus. and Profl. Women, Assn. Calif. Sch. Adminstrs., Am. Mgmt. Assn., Nat. Coun. Jewish Women, Carson C. of C., Phi Delta Kappa. Democrat. Office: US House Reps 125 Cannon Bldg Washington DC 20515-0537*

MILLER, ANN (LUCILLE ANN COLLIER), actress, dancer, singer; b. Houston; d. John Alfred and Clara Emma (Birdwell) Collier. Student, Lawlors Profl. Sch., Los Angeles, 1937. Appeared in numerous motion pictures, including: You Can't Take It With You, 1939, Room Service, 1939, Easter Parade, 1949, Kiss Me Kate, 1956, On the Town, 1950, Hit the Deck, 1955, Opposite Sex, 1956, Great American Pastime, 1956, That's Entertainment, Part 1, 1976, Part 2, 1977, Won Ton Ton, 1976, That's Entertainment!III, 1994; star: stage show Mame on Broadway, 1969-70, also in, Los Angeles, Fla., Ohio, Ga., 1970-71; Broadway show Sugar Babies, 1979-82 (Tony nomination 1980), (on tour), 1982-84; appeared: TV shows including Perry Como, 1961, Magic of Christmas, 1968, Bob Hope Show, 1961, Jonathan Winters Show, 1969, Ed Sullivan Show, 1958, 59, 4 Palace Shows, 1966-68, also, Heinz Soup Comml, 1971; appeared in: TV shows including Hello Dolly in, Ohio and Indpls., 1971; tour with Cactus Flower, 1978-79; TV spl. Dames at Sea, 1971, Can Can, 1972; appearances on all talk shows; semi-regular on: Merv Griffin Show; Author: Miller's High Life, 1972, Tops in Taps, 1981. Created dame Knights of Malta; recipient Israeli Cultural award, 1980; Woman of Yr. award Anti-Defamation League, 1980 Office: The Artists Group 10100 Santa Monica Blvd Los Angeles CA 90067-4003

MILLER, ARNOLD, electronics executive; b. N.Y.C., May 8, 1928; s. Sam and Mina (Krutalow) M.; m. Beverly Shayne, Feb. 5, 1950; children: Debra Lynn, Marla Jo, Linda Sue BS in Chemistry, UCLA, 1948, PhD in Phys. Chemistry, 1951. Registered profl. engr., Calif. Rsch. phys. chemist Wrigley Rsch. Co., Chgo., 1951; supr. phys. chemistry Armour Rsch. Found., Chgo., 1951-54, mgr. chemistry and metals, 1954-56; chief materials sci. dept. Borg-Warner Rsch. Ctr., Des Plaines, Ill., 1956-59; dir. rsch. Rockwell Corp., Anaheim, Calif., 1959-66, dir. microelec. ops., 1967-68; group exec. materials ops. Whittaker Corp., L.A., 1968-70; pres. Theta Sensors, Orange, Calif., 1970-72; mgr. xeroradiography Xerox Corp., Pasadena, 1972-75, corp. dir. rsch. and adv. devel. Stamford, Conn., 1975-78, El Segundo, Calif., 1978-81, v.p. electronics div., 1981-84, pres. electronics div., 1984-87, corp. officer Stamford, 1984-87; pres. Tech. Strategy Group, Fullerton, Calif., 1987—. Bd. dirs. Spectro Diode Labs, San Jose, Calif., Semicondr. Rsch. Corp., Colorep Inc., Carlsbad, Calif.; bd. dirs., chair audit com. Merisel Computer Products, El Segundo, Calif., lead dir., 1989—; mem. vis. com. on materials sci. U. So. Calif., L.A., 1966-68; mem. State of Calif. Micro Bd., 1984-2000. Editorial adv. bd. Advances in Solid State Chemistry; co-editor Electronics Industry Development; contbr. numerous articles to profl. jours. and monographs; patentee in field. Mem. civilian adv. group Dept. Commerce, 1959-60; mem. 5th decade com., also adv. com. on engring. and mgmt. program UCLA, 1984—; mem. com. on scholarly commn. with People's Republic of China, Tech. Transfer Task Force, Nat. Acad. Sci., Washington, 1985; bd. dirs. Orange County Pacific Symphony, Fullerton, Calif., 1982—; mem. univ.'s adv. bd. Calif. State U.-Fullerton, 1986—, chair, 1991—; v.p., bd. dirs. Heritage Pointe Home for the Aging, 1987-97; chmn. Indsl. Assocs. sch. engring. and computer sci. Calif. State U., 1987-97, trustee continuing learning ctr., 1993—; mem. Overseas Devel. Coun., 1988—; mem. Nat. Com. U.S.-China Rels., 1990—; trustee So. Calif. Coll. of Optometry, 1996—, sec.-treas. 1997—; bd. mem. Cmty. Found., 1995—, v.p., 1997—. Recipient Sci. Merit award Navy Bur. Ordnance/Armour Rsch. Found., 1952, IR-100 award, 1964, 69; named hon. alumnus Calif. State U., Fullerton, 1996. Fellow AAAS; mem. IEEE, AIME, Am. Chem. Soc., So. Calif. Coalition Edn. Mfg. Engring. (bd. dirs. 1994-98), Elec. Industry Assn. (past chmn. microelectronics), Phi Beta Kappa, Sigma Xi, Phi Lamda Upsilon Home: 505 Westchester Pl Fullerton CA 92835-2706 Office: Tech Strategy Group PO Box 5769 Fullerton CA 92838-0769 E-mail: amiller@fullerton.edu

MILLER, BARBARA STALLCUP, development consultant; b. Montague, Calif., Sept. 4, 1919; d. Joseph Nathaniel and Maybelle (Needham) Stallcup; m. Leland F. Miller, May 16, 1946; children: Paula Kay, Susan Lee, Daniel Joseph, Alison Jean. BA, U. Oreg., 1942. Women's editor Eugene (Oreg.) Daily News, 1941-43; law clk. to J. Everett Barr, Yreka, Calif., 1943-45; mgr. Yreka C. of C., 1945-46; Northwest supr. Louis Harris and Assocs., Portland, Oreg., 1959-62; dir. pub. rels. and fund raising Columbia River coun. Girl Scouts U.S.A., 1962-67; pvt. practice pub. rels. cons. Portland, 1967-72; adviser of student publs., asst. prof. comms. U. Portland, 1967-72, dir. pub. rels. and info., asst. prof. comms., 1972-78, dir. devel., 1978-79; exec. dir. devel., 1979-83; assoc. dir. St. Vincent Med. Found., 1983-88; dir. planned giving Good Samaritan Found., 1988-95; planned giving cons., 1995—. Contbr. articles to profl. jours. Pres. bd. dirs. Vols. of Am. of Oreg., Inc., 1980-84, pres. regional adv. bd., 1982-84; chmn. bd. dirs. S.E. mental Health Network, 1984-88; nat. bd. dirs. Vols. of Am., Inc., 1984-96; pres., bd. dirs. Vol. Bur. Greater Portland, 1991-93; mem. U. Oreg. Journalism Advancement Coun., 1991—. Named Oasis Sr. Role Model, 1992, pres. Oasis adv. coun., 2000—, pres. Ont. Presdl. Citation, Oreg. Communicators Assn., 1973, Matrix award, 1976, 80, Miltner award U. Portland, 1977, Communicator of Achievement award Oreg. Press Women, 1992, Willamette Valley Devel. Officers award, 1992 (Barbara Stallcup Miller Profl. Achievement award 1992). Mem. Nat. Coast Trail Assn. (pres. bd. dirs. 1997—), Nat. Soc. Fundraising Execs., Nat. Planned Giving Coun., Women in Comm. (NW regional v.p. 1973-75, Offbeat award 1988), Nat. Fedn. Press Women, Oreg. Press Women (dist. dir.), PRSA (dir. local chpt., Marsh award 1989), Oreg. Fedn. Womens Clubs (comms. chmn. 1978-80), Alpha Xi Delta (found. trustee, editor 1988-95), Portland Zenith (pres. 1975-76, 81-82). Unitarian. Home and Office: 1706 Boca Ratan Dr Lake Oswego OR 97034-1624 E-mail: bmiller@teleport.com

MILLER, BARRY, research administrator, psychologist; b. N.Y.C., Dec. 25, 1942; s. Jack and Ida (Kaplan) M.; m. Susan Hallermeier; children: Eric, Arianne, Kristina, Barrie. BS in Psychology, Bklyn. Coll., 1965; MS in Psychology, Villanova U., 1967; PhD in Psychiatry, Med. Coll. Pa., 1971. Instr. psychology Villanova (Pa.) U., 1971-73; asst. dir. dept. behavioral sci., med. rsch. scientist Ea. Pa. Psychiatric Inst., Phila., 1971-73, sr. med. rsch. scientist, 1973-80; dir. Pa. Bur. Rsch. and Tng., Harrisburg, 1973-81; asst. prof. psychology U. Pa. Med. Sch., Phila., 1975-78, asst. clin. prof. psychology, 1978—; assoc. prof. psychiatry Med. Coll. Pa., Phila., 1981-90, rsch. assoc. prof. medicine, 1983-90, assoc. dean for rsch., 1981-90; dir. for rsch. devel. Albert Einstein Healthcare Network, Phila., 1990-95; dir. The Permanente Med. Group Rsch. Inst., Oakland, Calif., 1995-99; adj. assoc. prof. psychiatry Med. Coll. Pa., Phila., 1990—; rsch. assoc. prof. psychiatry Temple U. Sch. Med., Phila., 1990—; asst. dir. rsch. planning and devel. Divsn. Rsch., Oakland, Calif., 1999—. Mem. sci. and tech. task force Pa. Econ. Devel. Partnership, Harrisburg, 1987-88, adv. com. Clin. Rsch. Ctr. Psychopathology of Elderly, Phila., 1985-88; mem. cancer control prgram Pa. Dept. Health, 1994; vis. rsch. assoc. prof. Med. Coll. Pa., Phila., 1991—. Contbr. articles to profl. jours.; mem. editorial bd. Jour. Mental Health Adminstrn., 1988—, assoc. editor, 1989—. Bd. dirs. Community Mental Health Ctr. 6A, Phila., 1969-73, Northwest Jewish Youth Ctrs., Phila., 1974-75; mem. Lafayette Hill Civic Assn., 1973-86, Citizens Coun. Whitemarsh (Pa.) Twp., 1975-86; pres., bd. dirs. Golden Eagle Luxury Homeowners Assn., Pleasanton, Calif., 1995-97. Grantee HHS, NIH. Mem. AAAS, Am. Psychol. Assn., Assn. Mental Health Adminstrs., Assn. Univ. Tech. Mgrs., Soc. Rsch. Adminstrs., Calif. Psychol. Assn. Avocation: tennis. Office: The Permanente Med Group 1800 Harrison St Oakland CA 94612-3429

MILLER, BRUCE, advertising executive; Pres, new bus. contact Suissa Miller Advt, L.A. Office: Suissa Miller Advt 11601 Wilshire Blvd Fl 16 Los Angeles CA 90025-1770

MILLER, CAROLE ANN LYONS, editor, publisher, video and marketing specialist; b. Newton, Mass. d. Markham Harold and Ursula Patricia (Foley) Lyons; m. David Thomas Miller, July 4, 1978. BA, Boston U., 1964; bus. cert., Hickox Sch., Boston, 1964; cert. advt. and mktg. profl., UCLA, 1973; cert. retail mgmt. profl., Ind. U., 1976. Editor Triangle Topics, Pacific Telephone, L.A.; programmer L.A. Ctrl. Area Spkrs. Bur., 1964-66; mng. editor, mktg. dir. Teen mag., L.A. and N.Y.C., 1966-76; advt. dir. L.S. Ayres & Co., Indpls., 1976-78; v.p. mktg. The Denver, 1978-79; founder, editor, pub. Clockwise mag., Ventura, Calif., 1979-85; mktg. mgr., mgr. pub. rels. and spl. events Robinson's Dept. Store, L.A., 1985-87; exec. v.p., dir. mktg. Harrison Svcs., L.A., San Francisco, 1987-93; pres. divsn. Miller & Miller MillerMania, Video Image and Mktg., Camino, Calif., 1993—. Instr. retail advt. Ind. U., 1977-78. Recipient Pres.'s award Advt. Women of N.Y., 1974; Seklemian award, 1977; Pub. Svc. Addy award, 1978. Mem. Advt. Women N.Y., Retail Advt. and Mktg. Assn., Fashion Group Internat., Bay Area Integrated Mktg., San Francisco Fashion Group, UCLA Alumni Assn. (life, Sacramento chpt.), Media Coms. (Sacramento chpt.), Assn. Image Cons. Internat. E-mail: 2m@compuserve.com

MILLER, CARROLL S. state legislator, dentist; b. Aurora, Ill., Jan. 6, 1926; s. F. Herbert and Anna Karine (Stordock) M.; m. Carol Jean Buckendahl, Nov. 25, 1950; children: Robin, Mark, Susan. Student, U. Richmond, 1943-45; BA, U. Ill., Chgo., 1947, DDS, 1949. Pres. Aurora Dental Soc., 1953-54; asst. prof. U. Ill. Coll. Dentistry, Chgo., 1977-81; dentist Greybull (Wyo.) Dental Clinic; mem. Wyo. Legislature, Cheyenne, 1986-92, Wyo. Senate, Dist. 19, Cheyenne, 1992—. Served with USN, 1943-45. Mem. ADA, Kiwanis (pres. 1970-71), Rotary (pres. 1987-88, Paul Harris fellow 1989), Elks, Am. Legion, Farm Bur. Republican. Avocations: hunting, fishing, horses, hiking, gardening. Home: 2185 Beaver Creek Rd Shell WY 82441-9713 Office: Greybull Dental Clinic 337 Greybull Ave Greybull WY 82426-2049

MILLER, CHARLES DALE, self-adhesive materials company executive; b. Hartford, Conn., 1928; married. Grad., Johns Hopkins U. Sales and mktg. mgr. Yale & Towne Mfg. Co., 1949-59; assoc. Booz, Allen & Hamilton, 1959-64; with Avery Internat. Corp., Pasadena, Calif., 1964—; v.p., mng. dir. Materials Europe, 1965-68; v.p. Fasson Internat. Ops., 1968; group v.p. materials group Avery Internat. Corp., Pasadena, 1969-75, pres., bd. dirs., COO, 1975-77, pres., CEO, 1977-83; chmn., CEO Avery Dennison Corp. (formerly Avery Internat. Corp.), Pasadena, 1983-98, chmn., 1998-00. Office: Nationwide Health Properties Inc 610 Newport Center Dr Ste 1150 Newport Beach CA 92660

MILLER, CHERYL DEANN, professional basketball coach, broadcaster; b. Riverside, Calif., Jan. 3, 1964; BA in Broadcast Journalism, U. So. Calif., 1985. Basketball player Jr. Nat. Team, 1981, U.S. Nat. Team, 1982, U.S. Olympics, 1984; commentator ABC Sports; head coach women's basketball U. So. Calif., 1993-94; commentator TNT Sports, Atlanta, 1996; gen. mgr., head coach Phoenix Mercury, 1997—. Player JC Penney All-Am. Team Five, U. So. Calif. Women's Basketball Team, World Championship Team, 1983. Recipient Sports Illustrated Player of Yr., 1986, Naismith Player of Yr. award, Kodak All-Am. award, more than 1,140 trophies and 125 plaques including Nat. Sports Festival, 1981, Pan Am. Games, 1983, FIBA World Championship, Goodwill Games, gold medal 1984 Olympic Games; elected to Naismith Basketball Hall of Fame, 1995. Office: Phoenix Mercury America West Arena 201 E Jefferson St Phoenix AZ 85004-2412

MILLER, CLIFFORD ALBERT, merchant banker, business consultant; b. Salt Lake City, Aug. 6, 1928; s. Clifford Elmer and LaVeryl (Jensen) M.; m. Judith Auten, Sept. 20, 1976; 1 child, Courtney; children by previous marriage, Clifford, Christin, Stephanie. Student, U. Utah, 1945-50, UCLA, 1956. Pres. Braun & Co., L.A., 1955-82, chmn., 1982-87; exec. v.p. Gt. Western Fin. Corp., Beverly Hills, Calif., 1987-91; chmn. Clifford Group, Inc., bus. cons., 1992—; mng. dir. Shamrock Holdings, Inc., 1992—, Shamrock Capital Advisors, L.P., 1992—. Bd. dirs. Frontier Bank, Park City, Utah, Triad Broadcasting Co., Inc. Monterey, Calif.; cons to White House, 1969-74. Trustee Harvey Mudd Coll., Claremont, Calif., 1974—, chmn. bd. trustees, 1991-98; chmn. bd. dirs. L.A. Master Chorale, 1989-93, chmn. emeritus, 1993; mem. chmn.'s coun. Music Ctr. Unified Fund Campaign; bd. trustees Keck Grad. Inst. Applied Life Scis., Claremont, 1997—. Mem. Calif. Club, Wilshire Country Club, Park Meadows Country Club, Pi Kappa Alpha. Office: Shamrock Holdings Inc PO Box 7774 4444 W Lakeside Dr Burbank CA 91510-7774

MILLER, CLIFFORD JOEL, lawyer; b. L.A., Oct. 31, 1947; s. Eugene and Marian (Millman) M. BA, U. Calif., Irvine, 1969; JD, Pepperdine U., 1973. Bar: Calif. 1974, Hawaii 1974, U.S. Dist. Ct. Hawaii 1974. Ptnr. Rice, Lee & Wong, Honolulu, 1974-80, Goodsill Anderson Quinn & Stifel, Honolulu, 1980-89, McCorriston Miller Mukai MacKinnon, Honolulu, 1989—. Mem. ABA, Calif. Bar Assn., Hawaii Bar Assn., Am. Coll. Real Estate Lawyers. Avocations: sailing, volleyball, swimming, history. Office: McCorriston Miller Mukai MacKinnon 5 Waterfront Plz 500 Ala Moana Blvd Ste 400 Honolulu HI 96813-4920 E-mail: cmiller@m4law.com

MILLER, DAVID C. airport manager; b. Salina, Kans., Mar. 6, 1943; m. Cora (Brown) M.; 4 children. BBA, U. Denver (Colo.), 1965; MPA, U. No. Colo., Greeley, 1975. Cert. Commercial Pilot. Comm. 2d. lt. USAF, 1966, various positions, 1966-88; ast. dir. Bishop Internat. Airport Authority, Flint, Mich., 1988-89; airport dir. Bismarck Mcpl. Airport, Bismarck, N.D., 1989-95; airport mgr. Juneau Internat. Airport, Juneau, AK, 1995-99, Ketchikin Airport, 1999—. Mem. CAP, Am. Radio Relay League Decorated Air medal with six leaf clusters. Mem. Am. Assn. of Airport Execs., USAF ASSN., Order of Daedalions. Office: Juneau Internat Airport Ste 10 1000 Airport Terminal Way Ketchikan AK 99901

MILLER, DIANE WILMARTH, human resources director; b. Clarinda, Iowa, Mar. 12, 1940; d. Donald and Floy Pauline (Madden) W.; m. Robert Nolen Miller, Aug. 21, 1965; children: Robert Wilmarth, Anne Elizabeth. AA, Colo. Women's Coll., 1960; BBA, U. Iowa, 1962; MA, U. No. Colo., 1994. Cert. tchr., Colo.; vocat. credential, Colo.; cert. sr. profl. in human resources. Sec.-counselor U. S.C., Myrtle Beach AFB, 1968-69, instr. Conway, 1967-69; tchr. bus. Poudre Sch. Dist. R-1, Ft. Collins, Colo., 1970-71; travel cons. United Bank Travel Svc., Greeley, 1972-74; dir. human resources Aims Community Coll., Greeley, 1984—2001. Instr. part-time Aims Community Coll., Greeley, 1972—. Active 1st Congl. Ch., Greeley. Mem. Coll. Univ. Assn. (chpt. Profl. for Human Resources), Colo. Coll. Univ. Profl. Assn. for Human Resources, No. Colo. Human Resource Assn., Soc. Human Resource Mgmt., Philanthropic Ednl. Orgn. (pres. 1988-89), Women's Panhellenic Assn. (pres. 1983-84), Scroll and Fan Club (pres. 1985-86), WTK Club, Questers. Home: 3530 Wagon Trail Pl Greeley CO 80634-3405 Office: Aims CC PO Box 69 Greeley CO 80632-0069

MILLER, DWIGHT RICHARD, personal care industry executive, cosmetologist, consultant; b. Johnstown, Pa., Jan. 24, 1943; Grad., Comer & Doran Sch., San Diego; DSci. (hon.), London Inst. for Applied Rsch., 1973. Cert. aromatherapist; lic. cosmetologist., instr.; Brit. Mastercraftsman. Styles dir. Marinello-Comer, Hollywood, Calif., 1965-67; expert Pivot Point Internat., Chgo., 1967-68; styles dir. Lapins, L.A., 1969; dir. Redken, L.A., 1970, Vidal Sassoon, London, 1971-74; world amb. Pivot Point, New Zealand and Australia, 1974-75, internat. artistic dir., 1975-78; internat. dir., co-founder Hair Artists Inst. & Registry, 1978-81; internat. artistic dir. Zotos Internat., Darien, Conn., 1981-87, Matrix Essentials, Inc., Solon, Ohio, 1987-92; bd. dirs., founder, v.p. creative Anasazi Exclusive Salon Products, Inc., Dubuque, Iowa, 1992-96; pres. Anasazi Salon Sys., Santa Fe, 1996-98; cons., 1998—. Judge hairdressing competitions including Norwegian Masters, Australian Nat. Championships; pres. Intercrimpers, London, 1974-75; cons. Amos, Clairol, John Frieda, John Sahag, J.C. Penney, NCA, Matrix, Zotos/ISO, 1998—, Hairworld Author: (book) Sculptic Cutting Pivot Point 75, Prismatics, 1983, Milady's Standard System of Salon Skills, 1998, Amos Master Cutting System, 2000; prodr.(and dir.): (documentaries, 15), (numerous tech. and industry videos-);contbr. articles and photographs to popular mags. Cons. American Crew; with USMC, 1960-64. Named Artistic Dir. Yr. Am. Salon mag., Intercoiffure Educator of the Century; presented with Order of White Elephant, 1976; recipient London Gold Cup for Best Presentation London Beauty Festival, 1982, Dr. Everett G. McDonough award for Excellence in Permanent Waving, World Master award Art and Fashion Group, 1992, N.Am. Hairstylist of the Yr. award, 2000. Mem. Cercle des Arts et Techniques de la Coiffure, Intercoiffure, Haute Coiffure Franchaise, Soc. Cosmetic Chemists, Hair Artists Great Britain, Internat. Assn. Trichogists, Nat. Cosmetologists Assn. (HairAmerica, cert. instr.), Am. Soc. Phytotherapy and Aromatherapy, HairChicago (hon.), Art and Fashion Group (pres. 1993), 'Dressers MC (pres. 1990—), London's Alternative Hair Club (patron), The Salon Assn., Am. Beauty Assn., Beauty and Barber Suppy Inst. Achievements include development of several profl. product lines including Vidal Sassoon-London, Design Freedom, Bain de Terre, Ultra Bond, Vavoom!, Systeme Biolage. Home and Office: 707 Don Gaspar Ave Santa Fe NM 87505-2629 E-mail: dwight@DwightMiller.com

MILLER, ELDON EARL, corporate business publications consultant, retired manufacturing company executive; b. Hutchinson, Kans., Jan. 1, 1919; s. Robert Dewalt and Martha Velva (Stauffer) M.; m. Margaret Borgsdorf, Mar. 26, 1950. B.A., UCLA, 1941. Formerly newspaper editor, mag. editor, pub. relations cons., polit. writer; with Purex Industries, Inc., Lakewood, Calif., 1950-85, asst. sec., 1971-72, v.p. corp. relations, 1972-85, cons. bus. publs., corp. relations, 1985—. Republican. Presbyterian. Home and Office: 26685 Westhaven Dr Laguna Hills CA 92653-5767

MILLER, ELIZABETH RODRIGUEZ, city official; b. Tucson, Feb. 22, 1954; d. Tony S. Martinez and Maria (Corral) Rodriguez; m. Marc Alan Miller, Nov. 5, 1972; children: Andrea Eve, Matthew Luke, Meredith C. BA in Spanish, U. Ariz., 1976, MLS, 1978. Unit mgr. S. Tucson Libr., 1978-80; activities coord. community cable com. City of Tucson, 1980; info./reference mgr. Tucson Pub. Libr., 1981-84, agy. mgr., 1984-85, regional mgr., 1985-87, asst. dir. pub. svcs., 1987-89; dep. exec. dir. divsn. ALA Libr. Adminstrn. & Mgmt. Assn., Chgo., 1990; dep. dir. Tucson Pima Libr., 1990-91, libr. dir., 1991-96; asst. city mgr. City of Tucson, 1996—. Co-editor: Great Library Promotion Ideas V, 1990; contbr. articles to profl. jours. Mem. adv. bd. libr. power grant Tucson Unified Sch. Dist., 1992-95; bd. dirs. Tucson area Literacy Coalition, 1992-95, YWCA, 1998—; active Hispanic Profl. Action Com., 1992—. Mem. ALA (mem. pres. program com. 1987, mem. nominating com. 1991-93), REFORMA (chair elections com. 1983-84, 85, chair conf. program 1987, pres. 1987-88), Libr. Adminstrn. and Mgmt. Assn. (mem. cultural diversity com. 1991-92, chair 1992-93, mem. nominating com. 1992-93), Pub. Libr. Assn. (mem. Pub. Libr. Assn.-Libr. Adminstrn. and Mgmt. Assn. cert. com. 1991-92, chair 1992-93, chair Allie Beth Martin Award com. 1987-88, mem. 1989), Ariz. Libr. Assn. (Libr. of Yr. 1995), Ariz. State Libr. Assn. (chair svcs. to Spanish-speaking Roundtable 1980-82, pres. pub. libr. divsn. 1984-85, chair ann. conf. 1986), Internat. City/County Mgmt. Assn. (assoc., participant Comparative Performance Measurement Consortium 1994-96—, U. Ariz. Hispanic Alumni Assn., Women at the Top, Office: City Mgrs Office City Hall 10th Fl West PO Box 27210 Tucson AZ 85726-7210

MILLER, EUGENE H. lawyer; b. Chgo., Dec. 21, 1947; s. Clifford and Birdie M.; m. Judith Miriam Bolef, June 15, 1969; children: Adam, Rachel. BS, U. Ill., 1969, JD, 1973. Bar: Ill. 1973, Calif. 1973, U.S. Dist. Ct. (no. dist.) Calif. 1973, U.S. Supreme Ct. 1977, U.S. Tax Ct. 1983. Acct. Lester Witte, Chgo., 1969-70, Price Waterhouse, Oakland, Calif., 1973-74; atty. Heizel, Leighton, Brunn & Deal, Oakland, 1974-77, Brunn, Leighton & Miller, Oakland, 1977-79, Miller, Starr & Regalia, Oakland, 1980—, mng. ptnr. Author: (with others) Closely Held Corporations, 1988. Office: Miller Starr & Regalia 1331 N California Blvd Fl 5 Walnut Creek CA 94596-4537

MILLER, GALE TIMOTHY, lawyer; b. Kalamazoo, Sept. 15, 1946; s. Arthur H. and Eleanor (Johnson) M.; m. Janice Lindvall, June 1, 1968; children: Jeremy L., Amanda E., Timothy W. AB, Augustana Coll., 1968; JD, U. Mich., 1971. Bar: Mich. 1971, Colo. 1973, U.S. Dist. Ct. Colo. 1973, U.S. Ct. Appeals (10th cir.) 1979, U.S. Supreme Ct. 1997. Trial atty. FTC, Washington, 1971-73; assoc. Davis Graham & Stubbs LLP Denver 1973-77, ptnr., 1978—, chmn. exec. com., 1998—. Bd. dirs. Sr. Housing Options, Inc., 1980-93, Colo. Jud. Inst., 1999—; chair Colo. Lawyers Com., 1989-91, bd. dirs., 1987—, Individual Lawyer of Yr., 1994. Recipient Cmty. Svc. award Colo. Hispanic Bar Assn., 1996. Mem. ABA (antitrust sect. task force on model civil antitrust jury instrns.), Colo. Bar Assn. (chair antitrust sect. 1996-98), Denver Bar Assn. Democrat. Lutheran. Office: Davis Graham & Stubbs LLP 1550 17th St Ste 500 Denver CO 80202

MILLER, GARY G. congressman; b. Huntsville, Ark., 1948; m. Cathy, 1972; 4 children. Student, Mt. San Antonio C.C. Founder G. Miller Devel. Co.; mem. U.S. Congress from 4th Calif. dist., Washington, 1999—; mem. budget com., fin. svcs. com., sci. com. Bd. dirs. Sonrise Christian Sch., 1982; appointed to Diamond Bar (Calif.) Mcpl. Adv. Coun., 1988; elected to 1st Diamond Bar City Coun., 1989; mayor, 1992; elected to Calif. State Assembly, 1995 (chmn. budget com. and banking and fin. com., vice chmn. transp. com.). With U.S. Army. Republican. Achievements include proposing 24 bills signed into law, successfully negotiated funding of 1st class size reduction program, and produced balanced budget that reduced the bus. tax. to 1973 levels while maintaing a $310 million reserve. Office: US Ho Reps 1037 Longworth Ho Office Bldg Washington DC 20515-0001*

MILLER, GEORGE, congressman; b. Richmond, Calif., May 17, 1945; s. George and Dorothy (Rumsey) M.; m. Cynthia Caccavo, 1964; children: George, Stephen. B.A., San Francisco State Coll., 1968; J.D., U. Calif., Davis, 1972. Legis. counsel Calif. senate majority leader, 1969-73; mem. U.S. Congress from 7th Calif. dist., 1975—; mem. edn. and workforce resources com. Chmn. subcom. on oversight and investigations, 1985—, chmn. subcom. on labor stds., 1981-84, chmn. select com. on children, youth and families, 1983-91, chmn. com. on natural resources, 1991-94; mem. com. on edn. and lab., dep. majority whip, 1989-94; vice chair Dem. Policy Com., 1995—. Mem. Calif. Bar Assn. Office: House of Reps 2205 Rayburn Ho Office Bldg Washington DC 20515-0001*

MILLER, GEORGE, former mayor; b. Detroit, 1922; m. Roslyn Girard; 4 children. BA, U. Ariz., 1947, MEd, 1952. Tchr. high schs.; owner, prin. painting contracting co., until 1989; mayor City of Tucson, 1991-99. Active mem. Dem. Party So. Ariz., 1960—, treas. Pima County div., state chmn. Presdl. Del. Selection Reform Commn.; bd. dirs. Tucson Jewish Community Ctr., Anti-Defamation League of B'nai B'rith; councilman Tucson City Coun., 1977-91, also vice mayor. With USMC, WWII. Decorated Purple Heart; recipient Recognition award United Way, Cmty. Svcs. Support award Chicano Por La Causa (2), Met. Edn. Commn. Crystal Apple award, cert. appreciation San Ignacio Yaqui Coun., Old Pasqua, Dr. Martin Luther King Jr. Keep the Dream Alive award, 1995; named Father of Yr. 1995, Man of Yr. So. Ariz. Home Builders Assn., Outstanding Pub. Ofcl. Ariz. Parks and Recreation Assn., 1995.

MILLER, GORDON HOLMAN, chemical, nuclear and environmental engineering consultant; b. Kansas City, Mo., Jan. 12, 1916; s. Mervin Thurmond and Alice Henshaw (Snively) M.; m. Marjorie Jane Trimble, Feb. 14, 1942. AS, Kansas City Jr. Coll., Mo., 1934; BSChemE, U. Kans., Lawrence, 1936; MSChemE, Pa. State U., 1939; PhD in Nuclear Engring., U. Mich., 1962. Chemist, Kansas City Testing Labs., Mo., 1936; chief chemist Certain-Teed Products Corp., Kansas City, 1937; from chemist to supr. Texaco Inc., Port Arthur, Tex., 1939-56, sr. engr. radiation research, Beacon, N.Y., 1956-62, environ. coordinator, Denver, 1974-82; research assoc. Texaco Experiment Inc., Richmond, Va., 1962-74; cons. chem., nuclear and environ. engring. Texaco Inc., Littleton, Colo., 1982-84; pvt. cons. chem., nuclear and environ. engring., Littleton, 1982—. Patentee in field. Recipient Thiokol award Am. Rocket Soc., 1959. Mem. Am. Chem. Soc. (sect. chmn. 1955-56), N.Y. Acad. Scis. (Boris Pregel award 1962), AAAS, Am. Forestry Assn., Research Soc. Am. (sec. chmn. 1962), Sigma Xi, Tau Beta Pi, Sigma Tau, Pi Mu Epsilon. Home and Office: 1321 E Costilla Ave Littleton CO 80122-1300

MILLER, HAROLD WILLIAM, nuclear geochemist; b. Walton, N.Y., Apr. 21, 1920; s. Harold Frank and Vera Leona (Simons) M. BS in Chemistry, U. Mich., 1943; MS in Chemistry, U. Colo., 1948, postgrad. Control chemist Linde Air Products Co., Buffalo, 1943-46; analytical research chemist Gen. Electric Co., Richland, Wash., 1948-51; research chemist Phillips Petroleum Co., Idaho Falls, Idaho, 1953-56; with Anaconda (Mont.) Copper Co., 1956; tech. dir., v.p. U.S. Yttrium Co., Laramie, Wyo., 1956-57; tech. dir. Colo. div. The Wah Chang Co., Boulder, Colo., 1957-58; analytical chemist The Climax (Colo.) Molybdenum Co., 1959; with research and devel. The Colo. Sch. of Mines Research Found., Golden, 1960-62; cons. Boulder, 1960—; sr. research physicist Dow Chem. Co., Golden, 1963-73. Bd. dirs. Sweeney Mining and Milling Corp., Boulder; cons. Hendricks Mining and Milling Co., Boulder; instr. nuclear physics and nuclear chemistry Rocky Flats Plant, U. Colo. Contbr. numerous articles to profl. jours. Recipient Lifetime Achievement award Boulder County Metal Mining Assn., 1990. Mem. Sigma Xi. Avocations: mineralogy, western U.S. mining history. Home and Office: PO Box 1092 Boulder CO 80306-1092

MILLER, HARRIET SANDERS, former art center director; b. Apr. 18, 1926; d. Herman and Dorothy (Silbert) S.; m. Milton H. Miller, June 27, 1948; children: Bruce, Jeffrey, Marcie. BA, Ind. U., 1947; MA, Columbia U., 1949; MS, U. Wis., 1962, MFA, 1967. Dir. art sch. Madison (Wis.) Art Ctr., 1963-72; acting dir. Ctr. for Contg. Edn., Vancouver, B.C., 1975-76; mem. fine arts faculty Douglas Coll., Vancouver, B.C., 1972-78; exec. dir. Palos Verdes (Calif.) Arts Ctr., 1978-84; dir. Jr. Arts Ctr., L.A., 1984-98. One woman exhibits at Gallery 7, Vancouver, 1978, Gallery 1, Toronto, Ont., 1977, Linda Farris Gallery, Seattle, 1975, Galerie Allen, Vancouver, 1973.

MILLER, JACK DAVID R. radiologist, physician, educator; b. Johannesburg, South Africa, Apr. 15, 1930; s. Harold Lewis and Inez (Behrman) M.; m. Miriam Sheckter, Dec., 1988. B.Sc., M.B., Ch.B., U. Witwatersrand, Johannesburg, 1956. Diplomate: Am. Bd. Radiology. Intern Coronation Hosp., Johannesburg, 1957-58; resident in radiology Passavant Meml. Hosp., Chgo., 1959-62, Wesley Meml. Hosp., Chgo., 1959-62; fellow in radiology Northwestern U. Med. Sch., 1962-63; chmn. dept. radiology U. Hosp., Edmonton, Alta., Can., 1971-83; prof. emeritus radiology U. Alta., 1997—. Clin. prof. radiology U. Alta., 1971— Fellow Royal Coll. Physicians Can., Am. Coll. Radiology. Office: U Alberta Dept Radiology Edmonton AB Canada

MILLER, JAMES MCCALMONT, pediatrician; b. Springfield, Mass., Sept. 25, 1938; s. John Haynes and Josephine (Darrah) M.; m. Jane Rose, July 7, 1975; children: John, Charlotte, Willard. AB, Hamilton Coll., 1960; MD, Cornell U., 1964. Resident U. Colo. Med. Ctr., Denver, 1964-67; staff pediatrician Kaiser Permanente Med. Ctr., Walnut Creek, Calif., 1969-87, chief pediatrician, 1971-82, Pleasanton, 1982-87; staff pediatrician Appalachian Regional Health, Hazard, Ky., 1987-92, N.W. Pediat. Ctr., Centralia, Wash., 1992—. Clin. assoc. U. N.Mex., Albuquerque, 1967-69; instr. U. Calif., San Francisco, 1969-87, U. Ky., Lexington, 1988-92. With U.S. Army, 1967-69. Fellow Am. Acad. Pediat.; mem. Wash. State Med. Assn. Office: Northwest Pediatric Ctr 908 S Scheuber Rd Centralia WA 98531-9027 E-mail: jmiller@localaccess.com

MILLER, JAN DEAN, metallurgy educator; b. Dubois, Pa., Apr. 7, 1942; s. Harry Moyer and Mary Virginia (McQuown) M.; m. Patricia Ann Rossman, Sept. 14, 1963; children: Pamela Ann, Jeanette Marie, Virginia Christine. BS, Pa. State U., 1964; MS, Colo. Sch. of Mines, 1966, PhD, 1969. Rsch. engr. Anaconda Co., Mont., 1966; asst. prof. metallurgy U. Utah, Salt Lake City, 1968-72; rsch. engr. Lawrence Livermore Lab., Calif., 1972; assoc. prof. U. Utah, 1972-78, prof., 1978-2000, Ivor D. Thomas prof., 2000—. Cons. on processing of mineral resources to various cos. and govt. agys. Editor: Hydrometallurgy, Research, Development, and Plant Practice, 1983, others; contbr. over 300 articles to profl. jours.; 24 patents in field. Recipient Marcus A. Grossman award Am. Soc. Metals, 1974, Van Diest gold medal Colo. Sch. Mines, 1977, Extractive and Processing Lectr. award The Minerals, Metals and Materials Soc., 1992, Disting. Achievement medal Colo. Sch. of Mines, 1994; Centennial fellow Coll. of Earth and Mineral Scis., Pa. State U., 1996, Best Paper award for fundamental rsch. 2000 TAPPI Recycling Symposium, 2000. Mem. NAE, AIME (Henry Krumb lectr. 1987, Richards award 1991, Mineral Industry Edn. award 1997), Soc. Mining, Metallurgy and Exploration (chmn. mineral processing divsn. 1980-81, Disting. Mem. 1992, Antoine M. Gaudin award 1992), Fine Particle Soc., Am. Chem. Soc., Soc. Mining Engrs. (bd. dirs. 1980-83, program chmn. 1982-83, Taggart award 1986, Stefanko award 1988), Metall. Soc. (Extractive Metallurgy Tech. award 1988); clubs: Salt Lake Swim and Tennis; U. Utah Faculty. Baptist. Office: U Utah Metall Engring 135 S 1460 E Rm 412 Salt Lake City UT 84112-0114 E-mail: jdmiller@mines.utah.edu

MILLER, JEAN RUTH, retired librarian; b. St. Helena, Calif., Aug. 4, 1927; d. William Leonard and Jean (Stanton) M. BA, Occidental Coll., 1950; MLS, U. So. Calif., Los Angeles, 1952. Base librarian USAF, Wethersfield, Eng., 1952-55; post librarian USMC Air Sta., El Toro, Calif., 1955-63; data systems librarian Autonetics (Rockwell), Anaheim, 1963-65; mgr. library services Beckman Instruments, Inc., Fullerton, 1966-92. Mem. adv. com. Library Technician Program, Fullerton Coll., 1969—. Author: (bibliography) Field Air Traffic Control, 1965, Electrical Shock Hazards, 1974. Chair Fullerton Are U. So. Calif. Scholarship Alumni Interview Program, Fullerton, 1974—; vol. Beckman Heritage Ctr. Mem. Prange County Libr. Assn., Spl. Libraries Assn. (pres. So. Calif. chpt. 1975-76, chair Sci./Tech. Div. 1985-86). Republican. Avocations: travel, reading, swimming. Home: 4701 E Fairfield St Anaheim CA 92807-3651

MILLER, JON HAMILTON, forest products company executive; b. Des Moines, Jan. 22, 1938; s. Victor George and Virginia Adelaide (Hamilton) M.; m. Sydney Gail Fernald, June 4, 1966; children: Emily, Sara. AB in Econs., Stanford U., 1959, MBA in Mktg. and Fin., 1961. Asst. to pres. Boise (Idaho) Cascade Corp., 1961-62, prodn. service mgr., 1962-65, sr. v.p. bus. products and services and packaging Oreg., 1971-74; exec. v.p. paper and paper products Boise Cascade Corp., Boise, Idaho, 1974-76, exec. v.p. timber/wood products/bldg. materials, 1976-78, pres. and chief operating officer, 1978—, also dir. Bd. dirs. Northwestern Mut. Life Ins. Co., St. Luke's Regional Med. Ctr., Idaho Power Co. Mem. bd. trustees Inst. Paper Science and Technology. With U.S. Army, 1959-60. Recipient Top Mgmt. award Sales & Mktg. Execs. of Boise, 1984; named Idaho Bus Leader of Yr. Alpha Kappa Psi, Idaho State U., 1986. Mem. Greater Boise C. of C. (pres. 1977) Bronco Athletic Assn. (bd. dirs. 1987—). Republican. Methodist. Clubs: Arid (Boise) (bd. dirs. 1987); Multnomah Athletic (Portland). Home: 3330 Mountain View Dr Boise ID 83704-4637 Office: Idacorp Inc 1221 W Idaho St PO Box 70 Boise ID 83707-0070

MILLER, JON PHILIP, marketing professional, pharmaceutical executive; b. Moline, Ill., Mar. 30, 1944; s. Clyde Sheldon and Alice Lenora (Taes) M.; m. Shirley Ann Hymes, Aug. 21, 1965; children: Melissa, Elizabeth. AB, Augustana Coll., 1966; PhD, St. Louis U., 1970; MBA, Pepperdine U., 1983. Rsch. assoc. to sr. biochemist ICN Pharm., Inc., Irvine, Calif., 1970-72, leader molecular pharmacology group, 1972-73, head molecular pharmacology/drug metabolism dept., 1973-76, dir. biology div., 1975-76; dir. SRI-NCI liaison group SRI Internat. (formally Stanford Rsch. Inst.), Menlo Park, 1976-78, sr. bioorganic chemist, 1978-80, head medicinal biochemistry program, 1980-84, dir. biotech. rsch. dept., 1982-85, dir. biotech. and biomed. rsch. lab., 1985-92, assoc. dir. life scis. div., 1989-92; dir. bus. devel., strategic mktg. MDS Panlabs, Inc., Bothell, Wash., 1992-98; dir. pharm. mktg. Applied Biosystems, Foster City, Calif., 1998—. Office: Applied Biosystems 850 Lincoln Centre Dr Foster City CA 94404-1128

MILLER, JOSEPH ARTHUR, retired manufacturing engineer, educator, consultant; b. Brattleboro, Vt., Aug. 28, 1933; s. Joseph Maynard and Marjorie Antoinette (Hammerberg) M.; m. Ardene Hedwig Barker, Aug. 19, 1956; children: Stephanie L., Jocelyn A., Shana L., Gregory J. BS in Agrl., Andrews U., Berrien Springs, Mich., 1955; MS in Agrl. Mechs., Mich. State U., 1959; EdD in Vocat. Edn., UCLA, 1973. Constrn. engr. Thornton Bldg. & Supply, Inc., Williamston, Mich., 1959-63, C & B Silo Co., Charlotte, 1963-64; instr. and dir. retraining Lansing (Mich.) C.C., 1964-68; asst. prof./prog. coord./coop coord. San Jose State U., 1968-79; mfg. specialist Lockheed Martin Missiles and Space (and predecessor cos.), Sunnyvale, Calif., 1979-81, rsch. specialist, 1981-88, NASA project mgr., 1982-83, staff engr., 1988-96, rsch. staff engr., 1996-98, coord. flexible mfg. system simulation project, 1994-96, team mem. federally funded AIMS Agile Mfg. project, 1995-97, team mem. corp funded machining outsource initative project, 1995-97, coord. productivity improvement program, 1996-98; engring. and constrn. cons., Berry Creek, 1998—. Agrl. engring. cons. USDA Poultry Expt. Sta., 1960-62; computer numerical control cons. Dynamechtronics, Inc., Sunnyvale, 1987-90; machining cons. Lockheed, Space Sys. Div., 1986-96; instr. computer numerical control DeAnza Coll., Cupertino, Calif., 1985-88, Labor Employment Tng. Corp., San Jose, Calif., 1988-93; instr. computer-aided mfg. and non traditional machining San Jose (Calif.) State U., 1994-97; team leader Pursuit of Excellence machine tool project Lockheed Martin Missiles and Space, Sunnyvale, Calif., 1990-95, coord. safety award program, 1997-98, mem. quality awareness program screening com., 1998. Author: Student Manual for CNC Lathe, 1990; contbr. articles to profl. jours. Career counselor Pacific Union Coll., Angwin, Calif., 1985-92. UCLA fellow, 1969-73. Mem. Soc. Mfg. Engrs. (sr. mem. 1980-92, chmn. edn. com. local chpt. 1984-85, career guidance counselor 1986-88), Nat. Assn. Indsl. Tech. (pres. industry divsn. 1987-88, bd. cert. 1991-92, mem., chmn. accreditation visitation teams 1984—), Calif. Assn. Indsl. Tech. (pres. 1974-75, 84-85), Am. Soc. Indsl. Tech. (pres. 1980-81). Seventh-day Adventist. Avocations: violin, camping, designing and building homes, traveling. Home: PO Box 190 Berry Creek CA 95916-0190

MILLER, JOSEPH S. astronomy researcher; b. L.A., Sept. 7, 1941; s. William George and Bertha Florence (Standard) M.; m. Nina Armstrong Parker, Dec. 22, 1971; children: Miriam Q., Samuel A. BA, UCLA, 1963; MA, U. Wis., 1966, PhD, 1967. Dir. U. Calif. Lick Observatory, Santa Cruz, Calif., 1967-68; prof. astronomy Lick Obs., Santa Cruz, 1968—, dir., 1991—. Fellow Am. Acad. Arts and Scis. Office: Lick Obs Univ Calif Santa Cruz CA 95064

MILLER, JUDSON FREDERICK, lawyer, former military officer; b. Tulsa, Dec. 5, 1924; s. Herbert Frederick and Martha (Davidson) M.; m. June Hirakis, Aug. 4, 1967; children by previous marriage: Kathleen, Shelley, Douglas, Judson Frederick. BS, U. Md., 1961; postgrad., Army War Coll., 1961-62; MA, George Washington U., 1962; JD, U. Puget Sound, 1980. Bar: Wash. 1981. Commd. 2d lt. U.S. Army, 1943, advanced through grades to maj. gen., 1975; platoon leader, co. comdr. 4th Cav. Group, Europe, 1944-46, 82d Airborne Div., 1947-50; with 187th Airborne RCT and Hdqrs. 8th Army, 1950-52; instr. Armored Sch., 1953-56; bn comdr. 14th Armored Cav., 1958-60; with Hdqrs. U.S. Strike Command, 1963-65; brigade comdr., chief of staff 4th Inf. Div., Vietnam, 1966-67; mem. gen. staff Dept. Army, 1967-68; dep. comdg. gen. Ft. Ord, Cal., 1968-69; asst. chief of staff Hdqrs. Allied Forces Central Europe, 1969-71; asst. comdr. 3d Inf. Div., Germany, 1971-73; chief of staff I Corps Group, Korea, 1973-75; dep. comdg. gen. VII Corps, Germany, 1975-77; ret., 1977; assoc. F.G. Enslow and Assocs., Tacoma, 1981—. Decorated Silver Star, Legion of Merit, Bronze Star with V device and oak leaf cluster, Joint Service Commendation medal, Air medal with 8 oak leaf clusters, Purple Heart, Vietnamese Gallantry Cross with palm; named to Okla. Mil. Acad. Hall of Fame, 1988. Mem. ABA, Assn. U.S. Army. Club: Tacoma Country, Lakewood Racquet. Home: 8009 75th St SW Tacoma WA 98498-4817 Office: Tacoma Mall Office Bldg 4301 S Pine St Ste 205 Tacoma WA 98409-7205

MILLER, KEN, state legislator; b. Fort Collins, Colo., Feb. 1, 1957; m. Peggy Miller. Student, Ft. Collins VoTech. Farmer; roofing and wood mfg. contractor; mem. Mont. Senate, Dist. 11, Helena, 1994—; chair bills and jour. com., vice chair local govt. com. Mont. Senate; mem. joint appropriations subcom. on edn./cultural resources Mont. State Senate, mem. natural resources com., mem. fin. and claims com. Republican. Home: PO Box 186 Laurel MT 59044-0186 E-mail: Ken@cw2.com

MILLER, KIRK EDWARD, lawyer, health foundation executive; b. San Jose, Calif., June 9, 1951; BA in Polit. Sci., U. Calif., Riverside, 1973; JD, Syracuse U., 1976. Bar: Colo. 1976, Calif. 1980, Tex. 1993. Assoc. Hughes & Dorsey, Denver, 1977-78; v.p., assoc. gen. counsel Am. Med. Internat., Inc., Dallas, 1979-88, v.p., sec., gen. counsel, 1988-91; with McGlinchey Stafford Lang, Dallas, 1991-94; sr. v.p., sec., gen. counsel Kaiser Found. Health Plan, Inc., Kaiser Found. Hosps., Inc., Oakland, Calif., 1994—. Instr. Syracuse U., 1975-76. Mem. ABA (co-vice chair com. health care fraud and abuse 1995-96). Office: Kaiser Found Health Plan 1 Kaiser Plz Oakland CA 94612-3610

MILLER, LARRY H. professional sports team executive, automobile dealer; b. Salt Lake City; m. Gail Miller; 5 children. Formerly with auto parts bus., Denver and Salt Lake City; now owner auto dealerships, Salt Lake City, Albuquerque, Denver and Phoenix; part-owner Utah Jazz, NBA, Salt Lake City, 1985-86, owner, 1986—. Office: c/o Utah Jazz 301 W South Temple Salt Lake City UT 84101-1216 also: Larry H Miller Group 5650 S State St Murray UT 84107-6131

MILLER, LORRAINE, business owner; BA in History, U. Utah. Lab. technician U. Utah Med. Ctr., 1972-75; pres. Cactus & Tropicals, Inc., Salt Lake City, 1975—. Mem. adv. bd. Utah Securities Commn., 1994; panelist Am. Arbitration Assn., 1991; pres., bd. dirs. Phoenix Inst., 1986-87. Vol. VISTA, 1966-69; mem. Gov.'s Task Force Entrepreneurism, 1988, Gov.'s Task Force Work Force Devel., 1994; mentor Women's Network Entrepreneurial Tng., Small Bus. Adminstrn., 1990; mem. adv. bd. Utah Dem. Health Care Task Force, 1991, Women's Bus. Devel. Office State of Utah, 1990-92; employer Supportive Employment for the Handicapped, 1990-92. Recipient Pathfinder award Salt Lake C. of C., 1986, Women of Achievement award YWCA, 1992; named Nat. Small Bus. Person of Yr. by U.S. Small Bus. Adminstrn., 1994. Mem. Nat. Assn. Women's Bus. Owners (pres. Salt Lake chpt. 1992), Utah Assn. Women's Bus. Owners (pres. 1992, 1st v.p. 1991, bd. dirs. 1985, 89-90, named Woman Bus. Owner of Yr. 1987), Wasatch Cactus & Succulent Soc. (co-founder). Office: Cactus & Tropicals 2735 S 2000 E Salt Lake City UT 84109-1749

MILLER, LOUIS RICE, lawyer; b. Frankfort, Ind., Feb. 28, 1914; s. Louis A. and Josephine (Rice) M.; m. Jean Preston Russell, Feb. 1, 1941; 1 child, Mary Melissa Emery. A.B., U. Chgo., 1935, J.D., 1937. Bar: Ill. 1938. Assoc. Gardner, Carton & Douglas, Chgo., 1937-40; atty. Armour & Co., Chgo., 1940-71, Phoenix, 1971-79; v.p., chief legal officer Armour & Co., (acquired by Greyhound Corp. 1970), 1967-79; v.p., gen. counsel Greyhound Corp. (now The Viad Corp.), Phoenix, 1972-79. Served with AUS, 1941; Served with USNR, 1942-45. Mem. ABA, Assn. Gen. Counsel. Club: Paradise Valley Country (Phoenix). Home: 12000 N 90th St Unit 1072 Scottsdale AZ 85260-8630 Office: Viad Corp Phoenix AZ 85077-0001

MILLER, MAYNARD MALCOLM, geologist, educator, research institute director, explorer, legislator; b. Seattle, Jan. 23, 1921; s. Joseph Anthony and Juanita Queena (Davison) M.; m. Joan Walsh, Sept. 15, 1951; children: Ross McCord, Lance Davison. BS magna cum laude, Harvard U., 1943; MA, Columbia U., 1948; MPhil, PhD (Fulbright scholar), St. John's Coll., Cambridge U., Eng., 1957; student, Naval War Coll., Air War Coll., Oak Ridge Inst. Nuclear Sci.; D of Sci. (hon.), U. Alaska, 1990. Registered profl. geologist, Idaho. Asst. prof. naval sci. Princeton (N.J.) U., 1946; geologist Gulf Oil Co., Cuba, 1947; rsch. assoc., coord., dir. Office Naval Rsch. Juneau Icefield Rsch. Project, Am Geog. Soc., N.Y.C., 1948-53; staff scientist Swiss Fed. Inst. for Snow and Avalanche Rsch., Davos, 1952-53; instr. dept. geography Cambridge U., 1953-54, 56; assoc. producer, field unit dir. film Seven Wonders of the World Cinerama Corp., Europe, Asia, Africa, Middle East, 1954-55; rsch. assoc. Lamont Geol. Obs., N.Y.C., 1955-59; sr. scientist dept. geology Columbia U., N.Y.C., 1957-59; asst. prof. geology Mich. State U., East Lansing, 1959-61, assoc. prof., 1961-63, prof., 1963-75; dean Coll. Mines and Earth Resources U. Idaho, Moscow, 1975-88, prof. geology, dir. Glaciological and Arctic Scis. Inst., 1975—; dir., state geologist Idaho Geol. Survey, 1975-88; mem. Legislature of State of Idaho, Boise, 1992-2000. Prin. investigator, geol. cons. sci. contracts and projects for govt. agys., univs., pvt. corps., geographic socs., 1946—; geophys. cons. Nat. Park Svc., NASA, USAF, Nat. Acad. Sci.; organizer leader USAF-Harvard Mt. St. Elias Expdn., 1946; chief geologist Am. Mt. Everest Expdn., Nepal, 1963; dir. Nat. Geographic Soc. Alaskan Glacier Commemorative Project, 1964—; organizer field leader Nat. Geographic Soc. Joint U.S.-Can. Mt. Kennedy Yukon Meml. Mapping Expdn., 1965, Muséo Argentino de Ciencias Naturales, Patagonian expdn. and glacier study for Inst.. Geologico del Peru & Am. Geog. Soc., 1949-50, participant adv. missions People's Republic of China, 1981, 86, 88, 98, geol. expdns. Himalaya, Nepal, 1963, 84, 87, USAF mission to Ellesmere Land, North Pole and Polar Sea, 1951; organizer, ops. officer USN-LTA blimp geophysics flight to Ice Island T-3 and North Pole area for Office Naval Rsch., 58; prin. investigator U.S. Naval Oceanographic Office sea and pack ice Rsch. Ice Island T-3 Polar Sea, 1967-68, 70-73; dir. lunar field sta. simulation program USAF-Boeing Co., 1959-60; co-prin., prin. investigator Nat. Geographic Soc. 30 Yr. Remap of Lemon, Taku and Cathedral Massif Glaciers, Juneau Icefield, 1989-2000; exec. dir. Found. for Glacier and Environ. Rsch., Pacific Sci. Ctr., Seattle, 1955-95, 1997—, chmn., 1992—, pres., 1955-85, trustee, 1960—, organizer, dir. Juneau (Alaska) Icefield Rsch. Program (JIRP), 1946—; cons. Dept. Hwys. State of Alaska, 1965; chmn., exec. dir. World Ctr. for Exploration Found., N.Y.C., 1968-71; dir., mem. adv. bd. Idaho Geol. Survey, 1975-88; chmn. nat. coun. JSHS program U.S. Army Rsch. Office and Acad. Applied Sci., 1982-90; sci. dir. U.S. Army Rsch. Office and DOD Nat. Sci. and Humanities Symposia program, 1991—; disting. guest prof. China U. Geoscis., Wuhan, 1981—, Changchun U. Earth Scis., People's Republic of China, 1988—; adj. prof. U. Alaska, 1986—. Author: Field Manual of Glaciological and Arctic Sciences; co-author books on Alaskan glaciers and Nepal geology; contbr. over 200 reports, sci. papers to profl. jours., ency. articles, chpts. to books, monographs; prodr., nat. lectr. films and videos. Past mem. nat. exploring com., nat. sea exploring com. Boy Scouts Am.; past mem. nat. adv. bd. Embry Riddle Aero. U.; bd. dirs. Idaho Rsch. Found.; pres. state divsn. Mich. UN Assn., 1970-73; mem. Centennial and Health Environ. Commns., Moscow, Idaho, 1987—. With USN, 1943-46, PTO. Decorated 11 campaign and battle stars; named Leader of Tomorrow Seattle C. of C. and Time mag., 1953, one of Ten Outstanding Young Men U.S. Jaycees, 1954; recipient commendation for lunar environ. study USAF, 1960, Hubbard medal (co-recipient with Mt. Everest expdn. team) Nat. Geog. Soc., 1963, Elisha Kent Kane Gold medal Geog. Soc. Phila., 1964, Karo award Soc. Mil. Engrs., 1966, Franklin L. Burr award Nat. Geog. Soc., 1967, Commendation Boy Scouts Am., 1970, Disting. Svc. commendation plaque UN Assn. U.S., Disting. Svc. commendation State of Mich. Legis., 1975, Outstanding Civilian Svc. medal U.S. Army Rsch. Office, 1977, Outstanding Leadership in Minerals Edn. commendations Idaho Mining Assn., 1985, 87, Nat. Disting. Tchg. award Assn. Am. Geographers, 1996; recipient numerous grants NSF, Nat. Geog. Soc., NASA, ARO, M.J. Murdock Trust, others, 1948—. Fellow Geol. Soc. Am., Arctic Inst. N.Am., Explorers Club; mem. councilor AAAS (Pacific divsn. 1978-88), AIME, Am. Geophys. Union, Internat. Glaciological Soc. (past councilor), ASME (hon. nat. lectr.), Assn. of Am. State Geologists (hon.), Am. Legis. Exchange Coun., Am. Assn. Amateur Oarsmen (life), Am. Alpine Club (past councilor, life mem.), Fulbright Assn., Alpine Club (London), Appalachian Club (hon. corr.), Brit. Mountaineering Assn. (hon., past v.p.), The Mountaineers (hon.), Cambridge U. Mountaineering Club (hon.), Himalyan Club (Calcutta), English Speaking Union (nat. lectr.), Naval Res. Assn. (life), Dutch Treat Club, Circumnavigators Club (life), Adventurers Club N.Y. (medalist), Am. Legion, VFW, Harvard Club (N.Y.C. and Seattle), Sigma Xi, Phi Beta Kappa (pres. Epsilon chpt. Mich. State U. 1969-70), Phi Kappa Phi. Republican. Methodist. Avocations: skiing, mountaineering, photography. Home: 514 E 1st St Moscow ID 83843-2814 Office: U Idaho Coll Mines & Earth Resources Moscow ID 83844-3022 also: Found Glacier & Environ Rsch 4470 N Douglas Hwy Juneau AK 99801-9403 E-mail: jirp@uidaho.edu

MILLER, MIKE, state legislator, small business owner; b. Fairbanks, Alaska, Aug. 7, 1951; m. Susan Miller; children: Teffonie, Carissa. Student, U. Alaska. Owner, mgr. Santa Claus House; mem. Alaska State Senate, senate pres., 1997-98, chair health edn. and social svcs. com., chair legis. coun., mem. com. on coms., rules com., transp. com. Bd. mem. Project 714 (STARS); active Drug Intervention and Prevention Program for Secondary Schs. With Alaska Air Nat. Guard. Mem. NRA, Nat. Fedn. Ind. Bus., Alaska Pvt. Home Educators Assn., North Pole C. of C. Republican. Avocations: coin and stamp collecting, sports, family activities, church activities, Alaska and U.S. history. Office: State Capitol 120 4th St Rm 119 Juneau AK 99801-1142 Fax: 907-465-3883. E-mail: senatormikemiller@legis.state.ak.us

MILLER, MILTON ALLEN, lawyer; b. L.A., Jan. 15, 1954; s. Samuel C. and Sylvia Mary Jane (Silver) Miller; m. Mary Ann Toman, Sept. 10, 1988; 1 child Mary Ann. AB With distinction and honors in Econs., Stanford U., 1976; JD with honors, Harvard U., 1979. Bar: Calif. 1979, U.S. Dist. Ct. (cen., no. and so. dists.) Calif., U.S. Ct. Appeals 99th cir.) 1979, U.S. Supreme Ct. 1989. Law clk. U.S. Ct. Appeals (9th cir.), Sacramento, 1979—80; assoc. Latham & Watkins, L.A., 1979—87, ptnr., 1987—. Author: (non-fiction) Attorney Ethics; editor (articles): (law rev.) Harvard Law Rev., 1978—79. Mem.: ABA, ATLA, Am. Cancer Soc. (L.A. chpt.), Phi Beta Kappa, Calif. State Bar Assn. (mem. com. on profl. responsibility), L.A. County Bar Assn. (chmn. profl. responsibility and ethics com.). Office: Latham & Watkins 633 W 5th St Ste 4000 Los Angeles CA 90071-2005

MILLER, MILTON HOWARD, psychiatrist; b. Indpls., Sept. 1, 1927; s. William and Helen L. (Lefkovits) M.; m. Harriet Sanders, June 27, 1948; children— Bruce, Jeffrey, Marcie. B.S., Ind. U., 1946, M.D., 1950; diploma in psychiatry, Menninger Sch., Topeka, 1953. Intern Indpls. Gen. Hosp., 1950-51; resident Menninger Sch. Psychiatry, Topeka, 1951-53; with dept. psychiatry Univ. Hosps., U. Wis., Madison, 1955-71, prof., 1961-71, chmn., 1962-71; dir. Wis. Psychiat. Inst., 1962-71; vis. prof. Nat. Taiwan U., Taipei, 1969-70; prof. psychiatry U. B.C., Vancouver, 1972-78, head dept. psychiatry, 1972-78; dir. WHO-U. B.C. Mental Health Tng. Centre, Vancouver, 1974-78; dep. dir coastal region Dept. of Mental Health, L.A. County, 1978-86; chmn. dept. psychiatry Harbor-UCLA Med. Ctr., Torrance, Calif., 1978—; prof., vice chmn. dept. psychiatry UCLA, 1978—; dep. med. dir. Dept. of Mental Health, L.A., 1986-96; hon. prof. Hunan (China) Med. U., 1996—. Cons. in field. Author: Psychiatry: A Personal View, 1981; Contbr. articles to profl. jours. Fellow Am. Psychiat. Assn., Royal Coll. Psychiatry; mem. Can. Psychiat. Assn., Royal Coll. Physicians and Surgeons (examiner 1973—), Can. Med. Assn., World Fedn. for Mental Health (mem. exec. bd. 1973—) Home: 1321 W Paseo Del Mar San Pedro CA 90731-6054 Office: Harbor UCLA Med Ctr Dept Psychiatry Torrance CA 90509-2910

MILLER, PERCY, record company executive; b. New Orleans; Student, U. Houston. CEO No Limit Records, Richmond, Calif. & L.A., 1989—. Rapper, releasing debut album: The Ghetto Is Trying to Kill Me, 1991, The Last Don, 1998; prodr.: (video) I'm 'Bout It, 'Bout It, 1998; writer, prodr. movie: I Got the Hook Up, 1998. Office: Priority Records 6430 W Sunset Blvd Ste 900 Los Angeles CA 90028-7913

MILLER, RANDY, state legislator, educator, lawyer; b. Portland, Oreg., Dec. 10, 1946; m. Gini Miller; 4 children. BS, U. Oreg., 1968, MEd, 1970; JD, Lewis & Clark U., 1974. Mem. Oreg. Legislature, Salem, 1992—, mem. bus. and consumer affairs com., chair rev. com., vice chair rules and elections com., mem. subcom. on edn. Mem. Nat. Policy Forum on the Environment; chair State Rep. Orgn. Mem. Oreg. State Bar Assn. Republican. Presbyterian. Office: PO Box 1795 Lake Oswego OR 97035-0524 E-mail: rm13@teleport.com

MILLER, RANNE B. lawyer; b. Claremore, Okla., Aug. 22, 1940; BBA, U. Wash., 1963; JD, U. N.Mex., 1967. Bar: N.Mex. 1967. Sr. ptnr. Miller, Stratvert & Torgerson, Albuquerque. Bd. editors Nat. Resources Jour., 1966-67. Fellow N.Mex. State Bar Found.; mem. Am. Bd. Trial Advocates (pres. N.Mex. chpt. 1976-77), Am. Coll. Trial Lawyers, Fed. Bar Com., State Bar N.Mex., Albuquerque Bar Assn., Phi Kappa Phi. Office: Miller Stratvert & Torgerson PO Box 25687 Albuquerque NM 87125-0687

MILLER, RICHARD ALAN, agricultural consultant, hypnotherapist; b. Everett, Wash., Mar. 16, 1944; s. John Harrison and Katheryn Ada (Nelson) M.; m. Patricia Merz, June 30, 1964 (div. 1972); 1 child, Paula Anne. BS in Physics, Washington State U., 1966; Degree in Fluidics (hon.), MIT, 1967; MS in Physics, U. Del., 1968; engr. in tng./profl. engr., U. Wash., 1969. Cert. giophysicist, 1972, hypnotherapist, 1987. Physicist instruments products div. Dupont, Wilmington, Del., 1966-68; physicist The Boeing Co./MASD, Seattle, 1968-71; biophysicist dept. anesthesiology U. Wash., Seattle, 1971-73; owner, mgr. The Beltane Corp., Inc., Seattle, 1973-80; ltd. ptnr. Western Herb Farms/Country Spice, Seattle, 1980-82; owner, mgr., writer Orgn. Advancement of Knowledge, Grants Pass, Oreg., 1983—; owner, mgr., broker Northwest Bots., Inc., Grants Pass, 1987—; ptnr., mgr., telemktg. program Florals, N.W., Grants Pass & Vancouver, B.C., Can., 1994; ptnr.,mgr. broker Nat. Collection Co., Grants Pass & Denman, Can., 1992; ptnr., mgr. telemktg. program N.W. Naturals, Inc., Grants Pass, 1991. Ptnr., sales mgr. Coltsfoot, Inc., Grants Pass, 1986—; advisor Ariz. Herb Growers Assn., Phoenix, 1988—; mem. New Crops Devel. Oreg. Dept. Agriculture; cons. in field; lectr. in field. Author: The Magical Mushroom Handbook, 1977, The Magical and Ritual Use of Herbs, 1978, The Magical and Ritual Use of Herbs, 1983, German edit., Spanish edit., 1995, The Potential of Herbs as a Cash Crop, 1985, The Magical and Ritual Use of Aphrodisiacs, 1985, German hardback and softback edit., 1992, The Magical and Ritual Use of Perfumes, 1990, German hardback edit., 1991, Spanish softback edit., 1990, Native Plants of Commercial Importance, 1991, The Modern Alchemist, 1991, Pantheon: Archetypal Gods in Daily Living, 1992, The Diamond Body: A Modern Alchemical View of the Philosopher's Stone, 1992, The Modern Alchemist, 1994, spl. hardback edit., 1995, Farming Echinacea angustifolia Root, A New Pharmaceutical, 2000, Farming Comfrey Leaf, A New Cattle Food Alternative, 2000, Farming Chamomile Flowerheads, Including a Flowerhead Harvester Design, 2000, Wildcrafting Prince's Pine Herb, A Primary Ingredient for the Micro Brewery, 2000, Gleaning Hydrangea Flowerheads, A New Floral Product, 2000, A Centralized Processing Facility for Botanical Alternatives, 2000, Economic Outlooks for Herbs and Spice for the Year 2000, 2000, Marketing Tips and Protocols, including Cottage Industry Examples, 2000; contbr. articles to profl. jours., chpts. to books. Amb. All Am. City, Grants Pass, 1987—. Small Bus. Innovative Rsch. grantee USDA, 1986, Neighborhood Devel. grantee SBA, 1977, USDA grantee, 1985, 95. Mem. Am. Coun. Hypnotist Examiners, Masons. Home and Office: Northwest Botanicals Inc 493 Coutant Ln Grants Pass OR 97527-6104 E-mail: drram@magick.net

MILLER, RICHARD SHERWIN, law educator; b. Boston, Dec. 11, 1930; s. Max and Mollie Miller; m. Doris Sheila Lunchick, May 24, 1956; children: Andrea Jayne Armitage, Matthew Harlan. BSBA, Boston U., 1951, JD magna cum laude, 1956; LLM, Yale U., 1959. Bar: Mass. 1956, Mich. 1961, Hawaii 1977. Pvt. practice law, Boston, 1956-58; assoc. prof. law Wayne State U., Detroit, 1959-62, prof., 1962-65, Ohio State U., Columbus, 1965-73, dir. clin. and interdisciplinary program, 1971-73; prof. U. Hawaii, Honolulu, 1973-95, prof. emeritus, 1995—, dean, 1981-84. Vis. prof. law USIA/U. Hawaii, Hiroshima U. Affiliation Program, Japan, fall 1986, Victoria U., Wellington, N.Z., Spring 1987; del. Hawaii State Jud. Conf., 1989-92; cons. Hawaii Coalition for Health, 1997—. Author: Courts and the Law: An Introduction to our Legal System, 1980; editor: (with Roland Stanger) Essays on Expropriations, 1967; editor-in-chief: Boston U. Law Rev., 1955-56; contbr. articles to profl. jours. Mem. Hawaii Substance Abuse Task Force, 1994-95; arbitrator Hawaii Ct. Annexed Arbitration Program, 1995-99; bd. dirs. Drug Policy Forum Hawaii, 1996—; mem. Save our Star-Bulletin Com., 1999—. 1st lt. USAF, 1951-53. Sterling-Ford fellow Yale U., 1958-59; named Lawyer of Yr. Japan-Hawaii Lawyers Assn., 1990; recipient Cmty. Svc. award Hawaii Med. Assn. Alliance, 1999. Mem. ABA, Hawaii State Bar Assn., Hawaii ACLU, Am. Inn of Ct. IV (emeritus founding mem., master of the bench), Am. Law Inst., Honolulu Cmty-Media Coun. (pres. 1994-98, v.p. 1998-2000, treas. 2000—). Office: U Hawaii Richardson Sch Law 2515 Dole St Honolulu HI 96822-2328

MILLER, ROBERT CARMI, JR. microbiology educator, university administrator; b. Elgin, Ill., Aug. 10, 1942; s. Robert C. and Melba I. (Steinke) M.; m. Patricia A. Black, Aug. 29, 1964; children: Geoffrey T., Christopher J. BS in Physics, Trinity Coll., Hartford, Conn., 1964; MS in Biophysics, Pa. State U., 1965; PhD in Molecular Biology, U. Pa., 1969. USPHS trainee U. Pa., Phila., 1966-69; postdoctoral fellow U. Wis., Madison, 1969-70; rsch. assoc., Am. Cancer Soc. postdoctoral fellow MIT, Cambridge, 1970-71; asst. assoc. prof. U. B.C., Vancouver, 1971-79, prof. microbiology, 1980-96, head dept. microbiology, 1982-85, dean sci., 1985-88, v.p. rsch., 1988-95, univ. senate, 1985-88; assoc. vice provost for rsch., dir. technology transfer U. Wash., Seattle, 1995-2000, vice provost, 2000—. Vis. prof. Inst. Molecular Biology, U. Geneva, Switzerland, 1976; mem. grants com. on genetics Med. Rsch. Coun., 1980-82; mem. Grants Panel A Nat. Cancer Inst., 1981-85; biotech. com. B.C. Sci. Coun., 1981-87, univ./industry program grant com., 1987-92; biotech. com. Med. Rsch. Coun., 1983; assoc. com. for biotech. NRC, 1983-86; strategic grant com. biotech. NSERC, 1985-87; bd. dirs. Paprican, Discovery Found., Sci. Coun. B.C., TRIUMF. Assoc. editor Virology, 1974-85, Jour. Virology, 1975-84; contbr. 100 articles to profl. jours.; author research papers. Recipient gold medal Nat. Sci. Coun. B.C., 1993; grantee Natural Sci. and Engring. Rsch. Coun., 1971-96, Med. Rsch. Coun., 1981, 86-89, Nat. Cancer Inst., 1982-86. Fellow Royal Soc. Can., 1993. Office: Univ Wash Office Tech Transfer 1107 NE 45th St Ste 200 Seattle WA 98105-4631 E-mail: rcmjr@u.washington.edu

MILLER, ROBERT HAROLD, otolaryngologist, educator; b. Columbia, Mo., July 2, 1947; s. Harold Oswald and Ruth Nadine (Ballew) M.; m. Martha Guillory, Apr. 18, 1981; children: Morgan Guillory, Reed Thurston. BS in Biology, Tulane U., 1969, MD, 1973; cert. in otolaryngology-head/neck surg., UCLA Med. Ctr., 1978; MBA, Tulane U., 1996. Diplomate Am. Bd. Otolaryngology. From asst. prof. to assoc. prof. otolaryngology-HNS Baylor Coll. Medicine, Houston, 1978-87; prof., chmn. otolaryngology-HNS Tulane Sch. Medicine, New Orleans, 1987-98, vice-chancellor for clin. affairs, 1997-99; dean U. Nev. Sch. Medicine, 1999—. Bd. dirs. Am. Bd. Otolaryngology; chief of staff Tulane Hosp., 1995-96. Mem. editl. bd. Archives of Otolaryngology, 1986—, Head & Neck Surgery, 1987—, Larynoscope '96. Named Outstanding Young Man, Houston C. of C., 1980; Robert Wood Johnson Health Policy fellow, 1996-97. Fellow ACS, Am. Soc. Head & Neck Surgery, Am. Acad. Oto-Head & Neck Surgery (Disting. Svc. award 1994, Honor award 1991), Triological Soc. (exec. sec. 1992-97). Avocations: tennis, computers. Office: Univ Nevada Sch Medicine 2040 W Charleston Blvd Ste 400 Las Vegas NV 89102-2249

MILLER, ROBERT JOSEPH, lawyer, former governor; b. Evanston, Ill., Mar. 30, 1945; s. Ross Wendell and Coletta Jane (Doyle) M.; m. Sandra Ann Searles, Oct. 17, 1949; children: Ross, Corrine, Megan. BA in Polit. Sci., U. Santa Clara, 1967; JD, Loyola U., Los Angeles, 1971. First legal advisor Las Vegas (Nev.) Met. Police Dept., 1973-75; justice of the peace Las Vegas Twp., 1975-78; dep. dist. atty. Clark County, Las Vegas, 1971-73, dist. atty., 1979-86; lt. gov. State of Nev., 1987-89, gov., 1989-98, 1991-98; sr. ptnr. Jones Vargas, Las Vegas, 1999—. Chmn. Nev. Commn. on Econ. Devel., Carson City, 1987-91, Nev. Commn. on Tourism, Carson City, 1987-91; mem. Pres. Reagan's Task Force on Victims of Crime, 1982; chmn. Nev. divsn. Am. Cancer Soc., 1988-90. Mem. Nat. Dist. Attys. Assn. (pres. 1984-85), Western Govs. Assn. (chmn. 1993-94), Nat. Govs. Assn. (vice chmn. exec. com. 1995-96, chmn. 1996-97, past chmn. com. on justice and pub. safety, chmn. legal affairs com. 1992-94, lead gov. on transp. 1992—), Nev. Dist. Attys. Assn. (pres. 1979, 83). Democrat. Roman Catholic. Office: Jones Vargas 3rd Fl S 3773 Howard Hughes Pkwy Las Vegas NV 89109-0949

MILLER, ROBERT NOLEN, lawyer; b. Monmouth, Ill., May 30, 1940; s. Robert Clinton and Doris Margaret (Nolen) M.; m. Diane Wilmarth, Aug. 21, 1965; children: Robert Wilmarth, Anne Elizabeth. BA, Cornell Coll., Mt. Vernon, Iowa, 1962; JD, U. Colo., 1965. Bar: Colo. 1965. Assoc. firm M. Quiat, Denver, 1965-66, Fischer & Beaty, Ft. Collins, Colo., 1969-70; dist. atty. Weld County Dist. Atty's. Office, Greeley, 1971-81; U.S. atty. U.S. Dept. Justice, Denver, 1981-88; chief counsel litigation and security US West Inc., Englewood, Colo., 1988-93; of counsel Patton, Boggs & Blow, Denver, 1993-94; ptnr., head litigation LeBoeuf, Lamb, Greene & Mac Crae, Denver, 1994—. Instr. bus. law Am. U., U. S.C., Myrtle Beach, 1966-69; mem. Gov.'s Commn. for Columbine and Civil Justice Reform, 1999—; mem. Supreme Ct. Nominating Commn., 1999—. Co-author: Deathroads, 1978 Bd. dirs. Boys Club, Greeley, 1974-78, 1st Congl. Ch., Greeley, 1975-78; Rep. candidate for atty. gen. Colo., 1977-78. Capt. USAF, 1966-69. Recipient Citizen of Yr. award Elks Club, Greeley. Mem. Fed. Bar Assn. (pres. Colo. chpt. 1983-84), Colo. Dist. Atty's Coun. (pres. 1976-77), Colo. Bar Assn., Weld County Bar Assn., Rotary (pres. local chpt. 1980-81). Republican. Avocations: fishing, hunting, golf, tennis, reading. Office: LeBoeuf Lamb Greene MacRae 633 17th St Ste 2000 Denver CO 80202-3620

MILLER, RONALD ALFRED, family physician; b. Orange, Calif., Sept. 27, 1943; s. Alfred Casper and Inez Geraldine (Gunderson) M.; m. Jean Ilene Andrews, June 18, 1966; children: Jon, Lauri, Bryan. BA, Pacific Luth. U., 1965; MD, U. Wash., 1969. Diplomate Am. Bd. Family Practice (bd. dirs. 1985-90, pres. bd. 1989-90). Intern in medicine Parkland Meml. Hosp., Dallas, 1969-70; gen. practice residency USPHS Gallup Indian Med. Ctr., Gallup, N.Mex., 1970-72; prin. Medical Doctor Glacier Med Assocs., Whitefish, Mont., 1972—. Clin. prof. U. Wash., Seattle, 1975—; coord. community clin. unit in family medicine, U. Wash., Whitefish, 1975—; bd. dirs. Utah Med. Ins. Assn., Salt Lake City, 1987—. Bd. dirs. Whitefish Housing Authority, 1977-82; mem. alumni bd. Pacific Luth. U., Tacoma, 1976-81, pres., 1979-80; mem. Glacier Community Chorale, Whitefish, 1984—, bd. dirs., 1990-92. Lt. comdr. USPHS, 1970-72. Mem. Am. Acad. Family Physicians (com. on continuing med. edn. 1977-81, com. on edn. 1984-89, Mead Johnson award Grad. Edn. in Family Practice 1972), Mont. Acad. Family Physicians (bd. dirs., sec./treas, v.p., pres. 1982-83, del. nat. congress 1978-84), Rotary, Alpha Omega Alpha. Republican. Lutheran. Avocations: hunting, fishing, skiing, backpacking, choral singing. Home: 1046 7th St W Whitefish MT 59937-3227 Office: Glacier Med Assocs 401 Baker Ave Whitefish MT 59937-2499

MILLER, RONALD GRANT, writer, critic; b. Santa Cruz, Calif., Feb. 28, 1939; s. Fred Robert and Evelyn Lenora Miller; m. Darla-Jean Irene Rode, Nov. 2, 1963. AA, Monterey Peninsula Coll., 1958; BA, San Jose State U., 1961. Reporter Santa Cruz (Calif.) Sentinel, 1959-62; reporter, chief news bur. San Jose (Calif.) Mercury News, 1962-77, editor T.V., 1977-99; syndicated TV columnist Knight Ridder Syndicate, 1978-99; journalist, author, 1998—. Commentator, critic Sta. KLOK, San Jose, 1981-83; panelist, guest speaker various orgns., 1978—; nat. judge Cableace awards, 1987. Author: (foreword) Les Brown's Encyclopedia of Television, 1992; co-author: Masterpiece Theatre, 1995, Author: Mystery! A Celebration, 1996 (Agatha, Anthony, and Macavity award nominee 1996-97); contbr. articles and short fiction to various mags.; columnist TheColumnists.com website, 1999—; mystery columnist Alibris.com. website, 2000—; writer, co-exec. prodr. TV spl. The History of Mystery. Recipient Nat. Spot News Photo award Sigma Delta Chi, 1961, Outstanding Alumnus award San Jose State U. Dept. Journalism and Mass Comm., 1985, Nat. Headline award Press Club Atlantic City, 1994. Mem. TV Critics Assn. (nat. pres. 1981). Democrat. Home and Office: 1554 Arbor Ave Los Altos CA 94024-5913

MILLER, SARAH PEARL, librarian; b. Wilkensburg, Pa., Aug. 31, 1938; d. Samuel Henry and Anna Deborah (Shirley) Lyons; m. Paul Victor Miller, Apr. 15, 1989; children: Cheryl, Michael, Daniel, Lorel. BS, Indiana U. of Pa., 1960; MREM, Denver Conservative Bapt. Sem., 1965; MA, U. Denver, 1966. Libr. Denver Conservative Bapt. Sem., 1966—. Mem. Am. Theol. Libr. Assn. (bd. dirs. 1978-81, 90-91, index bd. 1983-90). Home: 15707 E Grand Ave Aurora CO 80015-1708

MILLER, STANLEY LLOYD, chemistry and biochemistry educator; b. Oakland, Calif., Mar. 7, 1930; s. Nathan Harry and Edith (Levy) M. BS, U. Calif., Berkeley, 1951; PhD, U. Chgo., 1954. F.B. Jewett fellow Cal-Tech., Pasadena, Calif., 1954; asst. prof. Coll. Physicians and Surgeons, N.Y.C., 1955-60; from asst. to full prof. U. Calif., San Diego, 1960—. Mem. Am. Chem. Soc., Am. Soc. Biol. Chemists, Nat. Acad. Sci., Internat. Soc. Study of the Origin of Life (pres. 1986-89). Office: Univ Calif San Diego Dept Chemistry & Biochem 9500 Gilman Dr Dept & La Jolla CA 92093-0506 E-mail: smiller@ucsd.edu

MILLER, THOMAS G. career officer; b. Ft. Bragg, N.C., July 12, 1952; Brig. gen., dep. dir. for ops. J-3 U.S. Pacific Command, 1998—. Office: US Pacific Command Camp H M Smith HI 96867

MILLER, THOMAS ROBBINS, lawyer, publisher; b. Chgo., Mar. 8, 1938; s. William Whipple and Helen (Robbins) M.; m. Tran Tuong Nhu, July 3, 1974; children: Toby, Teddy, Nathalie, Gabriella. BA, Yale U., 1960; LLB, Stanford U., 1965; cert., Parker Sch. Fgn. and Comparative Law, Columbia U., 1966. Bar: N.Y. 1966, Calif. 1974. Assoc. Webster & Sheffield, N.Y.C., 1965-68; sole practice N.Y.C., 1968-74, Berkeley, 1974-89; pub. Lancaster Miller Pubs., Berkeley, 1974-89; sr. ptnr. Miller & Ngo, PLC, Oakland, Calif., 1989—. Founder, pres. Internat. Children's Fund, Berkeley, 1974—; cons. Peace Corps, Washington, 1961, Ctr. for Constl. Rights, UNICEF, N.Y.C., 1973-76; dep. dir. Calif. Rural Legal Assistance, San Francisco, 1977-79. Named 1 of 10 Outstanding Young Men in U.S., U.S. Jaycees, 1974 Democrat Office: 725 Washington St Oakland CA 94607-3924

MILLER, TIMOTHY ALDEN, plastic and reconstructive surgeon; b. Inglewood, Calif., Dec. 11, 1938; s. Henry Bernard and Florence Algena (Maddock) M.; 1 child, Matthew Christopher. Student, U. Calif., Berkeley; MD, UCLA, 1963. Diplomate Am. Bd. Surgery, Am. Bd. Plastic Surgery (dir. 1991-97). Intern Vanderbilt U. Hosp., Nashville, 1963-64; resident in surgery, dept. surg. pathology UCLA, 1966-67, resident, then chief resident gen. and thoracics sugery, 1967-69, acting asst. prof., 1969-70, prof. surgery, 1981—; asst. surg. resident John Hopkins Hosp., 1967; fellow plastic and reconstructive surgery U. Pitts., 1970-72; chief plastic surgery West L.A. VA Med. Ctr., 1973—. Author: (novel) Practice to Deceive, 1991; assoc. editor Jour. Plastic & Reconstructive Surgery, 1987-93, co-editor, 1994—. Trustee Children's Inst. Internat., 1995—. Capt. U.S. Army, 1964-66, Vietnam. Decorated Bronze Star; recipient Thomas Symington award Pitts. Acad. Medicine, 1971. Mem. Am. Soc. for Plastic Surgery (co-editor Jour. Plastic and Reconstructive Surgery), Am. Soc. for Aesthetic Plastic Surgery (bd. dirs. 1990-95), Plastic Surgery Ednl. Found. (bd. dirs. 1991-95). Office: UCLA Med Ctr 200 Ucla Medical Plz Ste 465 Los Angeles CA 90095-8344

MILLER, WALKER DAVID, judge; m. Susanne Hauk; 3 children. LLB, U. Colo., 1963; M in Comparative Law, U. Chgo., 1965. Bar: Colo., 1963. Asst. prof. Sch. Law, U. Kans., Lawrence, 1966-69; ptnr. Miller & Ruyle, Greeley, Colo., 1969, Miller, Ruyle, Steinmark & Shade, Greeley, 1970-74; solo practice, Greeley, Colo., 1974-92; ptnr. Karowsky, Witwer, Miller and Oldenburg, Greeley, 1992-96; judge U.S. Dist. Ct. Colo., Denver, 1996—. Office: US Dist Ct Colo 1929 Stout St Rm C-530 Denver CO 80294-1929

MILLER, WALTER LUTHER, pediatrician, educator; b. Alexandria, Va., Feb. 21, 1944; s. Luther Samuel and Beryl (Rinderle) M. SB, MIT, 1965; MD, Duke U., 1970. Diplomate Am. Bd. Pediatrics. Intern, then resident Mass. Gen. Hosp., Boston, 1970-72; staff assoc. NIH, Bethesda, Md., 1972-74; sr. resident U. Calif., San Francisco, 1974-75, rsch. fellow, 1975-78, asst. prof. pediatrics, 1978-83, assoc. prof., 1983-87, prof., 1987—, dir. Child Health Rsch. Ctr., 1992—, faculty biomed. scis. grad. program, 1982—, faculty genetics grad. program, 1998—, assoc. prof. metabolic rsch. unit, 1983-87, prof., 1987—, chief divsn. endocrinology, 2000—. Editor DNA Jour., 1983—; mem. editl. bds. numerous sci. jours.; contbr. articles to profl. jours. Del. Dem. Nat. Conv., N.Y.C., 1976. Served with USPHS, 1972-74. Recipient Nat. Rsch. Svc. award NIH, 1975, Clin. Investigator award, 1978, Albion O Bernstein award N.Y. Med. Soc., 1993, Clin. Endocrinology Trust medal Brit. Endocrine Soc., 1993, Henning Andersen prize European Soc. Pediatric Endocrinology, 1993, Samuel Rosenthal Found. prize for excellence in acad. pediatrics, 1999. Fellow AAAS, Molecular Medicine Soc.; mem. Am. Soc. for Microbiology, Assn. Am. Physicians, Am. Acad. Pediatrics, Am. Pediatric Soc., Soc. Pediatric Rsch., We. Soc. Pediatric Rsch. (Ross rsch. award 1982), Endocrine Soc. (fin. com. 1999—, Edwin B. Astwood lecture award 1988), Am. Soc. Human Genetics, Am. Soc. Clin. Investigation, Japanese Soc. for Pediatric Endocrinology (hon.), European Soc. for Paediatric Endocrinology (hon.), Lawson Wilkins Pediatric Endocrine Soc. (edn. com. 1992-96, coun. 1995-98), Theta Delta Chi. Office: U Calif Med Ctr Dept Pediat 1466 4th Ave San Francisco CA 94122-2656

MILLER, WILLIAM, broadcast executive; b. Chgo., June 17, 1943; Gen. mgr. KTVK-TV, Phoenix, 1994—. Office: KTVK TV 5555 N 7th Ave Phoenix AZ 85013-1701

MILLER, WILLIAM CHARLES, college dean, architect; b. San Francisco, May 11, 1945; s. Francis Leland and Ethel Lorene (Britt) M.; m. Beverly Jean McConnell, Dec. 22, 1968; children: Britt A., David A. BArch, U. Oreg., 1968; MArch, U. Ill., 1970. Registered architect, Ariz., Kans., Utah. Architect various firms, San Francisco, Sacramento, Calif., Tucson and Oak Harbor, Wash.; asst. prof. Coll. Architecture U. Ariz., Tucson, 1970-73, 74-77; assoc. prof. dept. architecture Kans. State U., Manhattan, 1977-86, prof., 1986-92, head dept., 1990-92; dean, prof. Grad. Sch. Architecture U. Utah, Salt Lake City, 1992—. Guest lectr. over 40 schs. architecture; presenter numerous profl. socs. and orgns.; dir. west ctrl. region Assn. Collegiate Schs. Architecture, 1988-91, chair theme paper sessions ann. meeting, San Francisco, 1990, chair regional paper sessions ann. meeting, Washington, 1991, co-chair adminstrv. conf., Milw., 1995; bd. dirs. Nat. Archtl. Accrediting Bd., 1996-99; mem. Utah Architects Lic. Bd., 2000—. Author: Alvar Aalto: An Annotated Bibliography, 1984; co-editor: The Architecture of the In-Between, 1990, Architecture: Back to Life, 1991; contbr. articles to profl. jours., chpts. to books. Bd. dirs. Assist, Inc., Artspace, Inc., Contemporary Arts Group. Recipient Svc. awards Assn. Collegiate Schs. Architecture, Nat. Coun. Archtl. Registration Bds., Nat. Archtl. Accrediting Bd. Fellow AIA (pres-elect Flint Hills, treas. Utah, exec. com., treas., exec. com. Western Mountain region, elected coll. of fellows 1997); mem. Am.-Scandinavian Found., Soc. for Advancement Scandinavian Studies, Tau Sigma Delta. Office: U Utah Grad Sch Architecture Salt Lake City UT 84112 E-mail: miller@arch.utah.edu

MILLER, WILLIAM FREDERICK, research company executive, educator, business consultant; b. Vincennes, Ind., Nov. 19, 1925; s. William and Elsie M. (Everts) M.; m. Patty J. Smith, June 19, 1949; 1 son, Rodney Wayne. Student, Vincennes U., 1946-47; BS, Purdue U., 1949, MS, 1951, PhD, 1956; DSc (hon.), 1972. Mem. staff Argonne Nat. Lab., 1955-64, assoc. physicist, 1956-59, dir. applied math. div., 1959-64; prof. computer sci. Stanford U., Palo Alto, Calif., 1965-97, Herbert Hoover prof. pub. and pvt. mgmt. emeritus, 1997—, assoc. provost for computing, 1968-70, v.p. for rsch., 1970-71, v.p., provost, 1971-78; mem. Stanford Assocs., 1972—; pres., CEO SRI Internat., Menlo Park, Calif., 1979-90; chmn. bd., CEO SRI Devel. Co., Menlo Park, David Sarnoff Rsch. Ctr., Inc., Princeton, N.J. Chmn. bd. dirs. Borland Software; bd. dirs. XPEED, Inc., Data Digest; chmn. bd. dirs. Sentris Corp.; professorial lectr. applied math. U. Chgo., 1962-64; vis. prof. math. Purdue U., 1962-63; vis. scholar Ctr. for Advanced Study in Behavioral Scis., 1976; fellow McKenna Group; mem. adv. coun. BHP Internat., 1990-97; computer sci. and engring bd. NAS, 1968-71; mem. Nat. Sci. Bd., 1982-88; corp. com. computers in edn. Brown UU., 1971-79; mem. policy bd. EDUCOM Planning Coun. on Computing in Edn., 1974-79, chmn., 1974-76; mem. ednl. adv. bd. Guggenheim Meml. Found., 1976-80; com. postdoctoral and doctoral rsch. staff NRC, 1977-80, computer sci. and telecom.; dir. Fund Am., 1977-91, Fireman's Fund Ins., 1977-91, Wells Fargo Bank and Co., 1996-97, Varian Assocs. Inc., 1973-96, Veo Systems Inc., 1996-99. Mem. editl. bd. Pattern Recognition Jour, 1968-72, Jour. Computational Physics, 1970-74. Served to 2d lt. F.A. AUS, 1943-46. Recipient Frederic B. Whitman award United Way Bay Area, 1982, Sarnoff Founders medal, 1997, David Packard Civic Entrepreneurship Team award, 1998, Robert K. Jaedicke Silver Apple award Stanford U. Bus. Sch. Alumni, 1998, The Dongbaeg medal Order of Civil Merit, The Rep. of Korea, 2000, The Okawa prize, The Okawa Found. for Info. and Telecoms., 2000; named to Silicon Valley Engring. Hall of Fame, 2001. Fellow IEEE, Am. Acad. Arts and Scis., AAAS; mem. Am. Math. Soc., Am. Phys. Soc., Soc. Indsl. and Applied Math., Assn. Computing Machinery, Nat. Acad. Engring., Sigma Xi, Tau Beta Pi (Eminent Engr. 1989). Office: Stanford U Grad Sch Bus Stanford CA 94305

MILLER, WILLIAM HUGHES, theoretical chemist, educator; b. Kosciusko, Miss., Mar. 16, 1941; s. Weldon Howard and Jewel Irene (Hughes) M.; m. Margaret Ann Westbrook, June 4, 1966; children: Alison Leslie, Emily Sinclaire. BS, Ga. Inst. Tech., 1963; AM, Harvard U., 1964, PhD, 1967. Jr. fellow Harvard U., 1967-69; NATO postdoctoral fellow Freiburg (Germany) U., 1967-68; asst. prof. chemistry U. Calif., Berkeley, 1969-72, assoc. prof., 1972-74, prof., 1974—, dept. chmn., 1989-93, chancellor's prof., 1998—, Kenneth S. Pitzer disting. prof., 1999—. Fellow Churchill Coll., Cambridge (Eng.) U., 1975-76; hon. prof. Shandong U., People's Republic of China, 1994. Alfred P. Sloan fellow, 1970-72; Camille and Henry Dreyfus fellow, 1973-78; Guggenheim fellow, 1975-76, Christensen fellow St. Catherine's Coll., Oxford, 1993; recipient Alexander von Humboldt-Stiftung U.S. Sr. Scientist award, 1981-82, Ernest Orlando Lawrence Meml. award, 1985, Hirschfelder prize in theoretical chemistry, U. Wis., 1996, Alumni Achievement award Ga. Inst. Tech., 1997, Spiers medal Faraday divsn. Royal Soc. Chemistry, London, 1998. Fellow AAAS, Am. Acad. Arts and Scis., Am. Phys. Soc. (Irving Langmuir award 1990); mem. NAS, Am. Chem. Soc. (Theoretical Chemistry award 1994, Ira Remsen award 1997), Internat. Acad. Quantum Molecular Sci. (Ann. prize 1974). Office: U Calif Dept Chemistry Berkeley CA 94720-0001

MILLER, WILLIAM NAPIER CRIPPS, lawyer; b. Long Branch, N.J., June 7, 1930; adopted s. Julia (Erwin) M.; m. Carolyn Anderson, Jan. 19, 1951 (div. 1963); children: Bruce Douglass, Jennifer Erwin; m. Hannelore Steinbeck, Dec. 4, 1970 A.A., Coll. Marin, 1949; student, U. Calif.-Berkeley, 1949-51, J.D., 1955. Bar: N.Y., Calif. 1956, U.S. Supreme Ct. 1983. Assoc. Mudge, Stern, Baldwin & Todd, N.Y.C., 1955-58, Pillsbury, Madison & Sutro, San Francisco, 1959-65, ptnr., 1966—; staff NYU Law Sch., 1957-58; ct. adv. com. Calif. State Assembly Judiciary Com., 1979-80. Bd. dirs. Laguna Honda Hosp., San Francisco, 1966— ; bd. visitors U. Calif.-Hastings Law Sch. Served with USAF, 1951-52. Recipient Bur. Nat. Affairs award U. Calif.-Hastings, 1955; recipient Thurston Soc. award, 1953 Fellow Am. Coll. Trial Lawyers; mem. ABA, San Francisco Bar Assn., Order of Coif, St. Francis Yacht Club, Silverado Country Club. Home: 16 George Ln Sausalito CA 94965-1890 Office: Pillsbury Winthrop LLP PO Box 7880 San Francisco CA 94120-7880

MILLER, WILLIAM RICHEY, JR. lawyer; b. Oklahoma City, Apr. 4, 1947; s. William Richey and Edna Rosalind (Nielsen) M.; m. Susan Hammond, Aug. 2, 1970; children: Brooke, Karen. BA, Pomona Coll., Claremont, Calif., 1969; MA, Claremont Grad. Sch., 1972; JD, Lewis and Clark Coll., 1975. Bar: Oreg. 1975, U.S. Dist. Ct. Oreg. 1976, U.S. Ct. Appeals (9th cir.) 1976. Staff atty. Oreg. Ct. Appeals, Salem, 1975-76; with firm Griffith, Bittner, Abbott & Roberts, Portland, Oreg., 1976-83; ptnr. Davis Wright Termaine, Portland, 1983—. Adj. prof. Lewis and Clark Law Sch., 1975-78. Bd. dirs. Portland Civic Theatre, 1988-91, Am. Lung Assn. Oreg., Portland, 1985-88, Oreg. Bus. Com. for the Arts, Portland, 1991-93. Mem. Oreg. State Bar (sect. chair 1990-91), Comml. Fin. Assn., Oreg. Bankers Assn., Lewis and Clark Alumni Assn. (bd. dirs. 1989-92). Presbyterian. Home: 843 Lakeshore Rd Lake Oswego OR 97034-3704 Office: Davis Wright Tremaine 1300 SW 5th Ave Ste 2300 Portland OR 97201-5682

MILLER, ZOYA DICKINS (MRS. HILLIARD EVE MILLER JR.), civic worker; b. Washington, July 15, 1923; d. Randolph and Zoya Pavlovna (Klementinovska) Dickins; m. Hilliard Eve Miller, Jr., Dec. 6, 1943; children: Jeffrey Arnot, Hilliard Eve III. Grad., Stuart Sch. Costume Design, Washington, 1942; student, Sophie Newcomb Coll., 1944, New Eng. Conservatory Music, 1946, Colo. Coll., 1965; grad., Internat. Sch. Reading, 1969. Lic. pvt. pilot. Instr. Stuart Summer Sch. Costume Design, Washington, 1942; fashion coord. Julius Garfinckel, Washington, 1942-43; fashion coord., cons. Mademoiselle mag., 1942-44; star TV show Cowbelle Kitchen, 1957-58, Flair for Living, 1958-59; model mags. and comml. films, also nat. comml. recs., 1956-80; dir. rsch. devel. Webb-Waring Inst. for Biomed. Rsch., Denver, 1973—. Contbr. articles, lectrs. on health care sys. and fund raising. Mem. exec. com., bd. dirs. El Paso County chpt. Am. Lung Assn. Colo., 1965-84, bd. dirs., 1965-87, chmn. radio and TV coun., 1963-70, mem. med. affairs com., 1965-70, pres., 1965-66, procurer found. funds, 1965-70; developer nat. radio ednl. prodns. for internat. use Am. Lung Assn., 1963-70, coord. statewide pulmonary screening programs Colo., other states, 1965-72; chmn. benefit fund raising El Paso County Cancer Soc., 1963; co-founder, coord. Colorado Springs Debutante Ball, 1967—; coord. Nat. Gov.'s Comprehensive Health Planning Coun., 1967-74, chmn., 1971-72; chmn. Colo. Chronic Care Com., 1969-73, chmn. fund raising, 1970-72, chmn. spl. com. conl. studies on nat. health bills, 1971-73; mem. Colo.-Wyo. Regional Med. Program Adv. Coun., 1969-73; mem. Colo. Med. Found. Consumers Adv. Coun., 1972-78; mem. decorative arts com. Colorado Springs Fine Arts Ctr., 1972-75; founder, state coord. Nov. Noel Pediat. Benefit Am. Lung Assn., 1973-87; founder, chmn. bd. dirs. Newborn Hope, Inc., 1987—; mem. adv. bd. Wagon Wheel Girl Scouts, 1991-94, Cmty. in Schs., 1995—; mem. cmty. adv. coun. Beth-El Nursing Sch., 1998—; bd. dirs. Episcopal Columbarium Assn., 2001. Zoya Dickins Miller Vol. of Yr. award established Am. Lung Assn. of Colo., 1979; recipient James J. Waring award Colo. Conf. on Respiratory Disease Workers, 1963, Nat. Pub. Rels. award Am. Lung Assn., 1979, Gold Double Bar Cross award, 1980, 83, Jefferson award Am. Inst. Pub. Svc., 1991, Thousand Points of Light award The White House, 1992, Recognition award So. Colo. Women's C. of C., 1994, Silver Spur Cmty. award Pikes Peak Range Riders, 1994, Silver Bell award Assistance League Colorado Springs, 1996, Svc. to Mankind award Centennial Sertoma Club, 1997, Help Can't Wait award Pikes Peak chpt. ARC, 1997, Cmty. Weaver award The Independent News, 1997, Apgar award Colo. March of Dimes, 1998; named Humanitarian of Yr., Am. Lung Assn. of Colo., 1987, One of 50 Most Influential Women in Colorado Springs by Gazette Telegraph Newspaper, 1990, One of 5 Leading Ladies Colo. Homes & Lifestyles Mag., 1991. Mem. Colo. Assn. Fund Raisers, Denver Round Table for Planned Giving, Nat. Soc. Fund Raising Execs., Nat. Cowbell Assn. (El Paso county pres. 1954, TV chmn., chmn. nat. Father of Yr. contest Colo. 1956-57), Broadmoor Garden Club. Home: 74 W Cheyenne Mountain Blvd Colorado Springs CO 80906-4336

MILLIGAN, SISTER MARY, theology educator, religious consultant; b. Los Angeles, Jan. 23, 1935; d. Bernard Joseph and Carolyn (Krebs) M. BA, Marymount Coll., 1956; Dr. de l'Univ., U. Paris, 1959; MA in Theology, St. Mary's Coll., Notre Dame, Ind., 1966; STD, Gregorian U., 1975; D. honoris causa, Marymount U., 1988. Tchr. Cours Marymount, Neuilly, France, 1956-59; asst. prof. Marymount Coll., Los Angeles, 1959-67; gen. councillor Religious of Sacred Heart of Mary, Rome, 1969-75, gen. superior, 1980-85; asst. prof. Loyola Marymount U., Los Angeles, 1977-78, provost, 1986-90, prof., 1990—, dean liberal arts, 1992-97, provincial superior, 1997—. Pres. bd. dirs. St. John's Sem., Camarillo, Calif., 1986-89; mem. exec. com. Internat. Union Superiors Gen., Rome, 1983-85; mem. planning bd. spiritual renewal program Loyola Marymount U., Los Angeles, 1976-78. Author: That They May Have Life, 1975; compiler analytical index Ways of Peace, 1986; contbr. articles to profl. jours. Vis. scholar Grad. Theol. Union, Berkeley, 1986. Mem. Calif. Women in Higher Edn., Coll. Theology Soc., Cath. Biblical Assn. Democrat. Roman Catholic. Home: 3216 Eagle St Los Angeles CA 90063-3121 E-mail: mmilliga@earthlink.net

MILLIKAN, CLARK HAROLD, physician; b. Freeport, Ill., Mar. 2, 1915; s. William Clarance and Louise (Chamberlain) M.; m. Gayle Margaret Gross, May 2, 1942 (div. Apr. 1966); children: Terri, Clark William, Jeffry Brent; m. Janet T. Holmes, July 21, 1966 (div. Dec. 1987); m. Nancy Futrell, Dec. 28, 1987. Student, Parsons (Kans.) Jr. Coll., 1935; MD, U. Kans., 1939. Diplomate Am. Bd. Psychiatry and Neurology. Intern St. Luke's Hosp., Clev., 1939-40, asst. resident medicine, 1940-41; from resident neurology to asst. prof. neurology State U. Iowa, Iowa City, 1941-49; staff Mayo Clinic, Rochester, Minn., 1949—, cons. neurology, 1958—; dir. Mayo Center for Clin. Rsch. in Cerebrovascular Disease; prof. neurology Mayo Sch. Medicine; physician-in-chief pro tem Cleve. Clinic, 1970; prof. neurology U. Utah Sch. Medicine, Salt Lake City, 1976-87, U. Miami (Fla.) Sch. Medicine, 1987-88; scholar in residence, dept. neurology Henry Ford Hosp., Detroit, 1988-92; prof. neurology Sch. of Medicine Creighton U., Omaha, 1992-94; clin. prof. neurology Med. Coll. Ohio, Toledo, 1994-97; dir. acad. affairs Intermountain Stroke Rsch. Found., Salt Lake City, 1997—. Asst. chmn., editor trans. 2d Princeton Conf. Cerebrovascular Disease, 1957, chmn. confs., 1961, 64; chmn. com. classification and nomenclature cerebrovascular disease USPHS, 1955-69; mem. council Nat. Inst. Neurologic Diseases and Blindness, NIH, USPHS, 1961-65, div. regional med. program, 1965-68; A.O.A. lectr. Baylor U., Waco, Tex., 1952; James Mawer Pearson Meml. lectr., Vancouver, B.C., Can., 1958; Conner Meml. lectr. Am. Heart Assn., 1961; Peter T. Bohan lectr. U. Kans., 1965, 73 Editor: Jour. Stroke, 1970-76, assoc. editor, 1976—. Recipient Outstanding Alumnus award U. Kans., 1973 Fellow ACP, Am. Acad. Neurology (founding chmn. sect. on stroke and vascular neurology 1994), Royal Soc. Medicine; mem. AMA, AAUP, AAAS, Assn. Rsch. Nervous and Mental Disease (pres. 1961), Am. Neurol. Assn. (1st v.p. 1969-70, pres. 1973-74), Minn. Med. Assn., Four County Med. Soc. South Minn., Cen. Neuropsychiat. Assn., N.Y. Acad. Sci., Am. Heart Assn. (chmn. coun. cerebrovascular disease 1967-68, Gold Heart award 1976, Spl. Merit award 1981), Nat. Stroke Assn. (pres. 1986, editor Jour. Stroke and Cerebrovascular Disease 1990—), Sigma Xi. E-mail: clarkmillikan@yahoo.com

MILLIN, LAURA JEANNE, museum director; b. Elgin, Ill., June 11, 1954; d. Douglas Joseph and PAtricia Ruth (Feragen) M. BA in Interdisciplinary Studies, The Evergreen State Coll., 1978. Dir. On The Boards, Seattle, 1979; art dir. City Fair Merocenter YMCA, Seattle, 1980; dir. Ctr. on Contemporary Art, Seattle, 1981; co-owner Art in Form Bookstore, Seattle, 1981-89; co-dir. 3d internat festical of films by women dirs. Seattle Art Mus.. & 911 Contemporary Arts, 1988; auction coord. Allied Arts of Seattle, 1989; dir. Missoula (Mont.) Mus. of the Arts, 1990—. Dir. Visual AIDS Missoula Missoula Mus. of the Arts, 1989; curator Radio COCA, Ctr. on Contemproary Art, Seattle, 1986, co-curator, 1981, 83; lectr. in field. Co-editor: AnOther (ind. feminist newspaper), Seattle, 1989, editor: (exhibition catalog) James Turrell: Four Light Installations, 1981. Bd. dirs. Internat. Festival of Films by Women Dirs., Seattle, 1987, 89, Nine One One Comtemporary Arts Ctr., Seattle, 1981-87, bd. chmn. 1981-85; bd. advisors REFLEX (art mag.), Seattle, 1988-89, Ctr. on Contemporary Art, Seattle, 1983-86; state vis. Mont. Arts. Coun., Missoula, 1991, NEA, Mpls., 1988, Chgo., 1987; ; panelist Mont. Arts Coun., Helena, 1990; cons. Seattle Arts Commn., 1989, juror, 1985. Home: 1721 S 9th St W Missoula MT 59801-3432 Office: Art Mus Missoula 335 N Pattee St Missoula MT 59802-4520

MILLIS, ROBERT LOWELL, astronomer; b. Martinsville, Ill., Sept. 12, 1941; married, 1965; 2 children. BA, Ea. Ill. U., 1963; PhD in Astronomy, U. Wis., 1968. Astronomer Lowell Obs., Flagstaff, Ariz., 1967-86, assoc. dir., 1986-90, dir., 1990—. Mem. Am. Astron. Soc., Internat. Astronomy Union, Divsn. Planetary Sci. (sec.-treas. 1985-88, chmn. 1994-95). Achievements include research in planetary satellites and ring systems; occultation studies of solar system objects; research on comet and Kuiper belt objects. Office: Lowell Observatory 1400 W Mars Hill Rd Flagstaff AZ 86001-4499

MILLON, JEAN-PIERRE, health care executive; b. Paris, June 30, 1950; s. Andre and Marie-France (Parachaud) M.; m. Monique Triffoz, Dec. 15, 1979; children: Sebastien, Véronique. B in Econ, U. Lyons, France, 1974; degree in ME, Ecole Centrale, Lyons, 1974; M in Mgmt., Northwestern U., 1976. Head fin. planning dept. Eli Lilly France, Strasbourg, 1976-78, fin. planning mgr. Paris, 1978-80; fin. advisor Eli Lilly Europe, London, 1980-81; fin. dir. Eli Lilly Benelux, Brussels, 1981-82, Eli Lilly Germany, Badhomburg, 1982-85; gen. mgr. Carribbean and Ctrl. Am. Eli Lilly Co., San Juan, P.R., 1985-88, dir. mkt. rsch. and planning Indpls., 1988-91, dir. strategic planning, 1991-92; pres. Eli Lilly Japan, Kobe, 1992-95; pres., CEO PCS Health Systems, Scottsdale, Ariz., 1995—. V.P. Am. C. of C., Tokyo, 1993-95; mem. Scottsdale Leadership Coun., 1996—; bd. dirs. Phoenix Symphony, exec. com., 1996—; advisor Thunderbird Internat. Sch. Bd., 1995—, Ariz. State U., 1995—; mem. Kellogg Grad. Sch. Advisor Bd., 1996—; bd. trustee Barrows Neurol. Found., 1997— Avocations: skiing, traveling. Office: PCS Health Sys 9501 E Shea Blvd Scottsdale AZ 85260-6704

MILLS, REBECCA, national park administrator; BA, Swarthmore Coll., 1961; MSW, U. Calif., Berkeley, 1968. Cmty. and individual social work, 1963-69; adminstrv. analyst Statewide Pres.'s Office U. Calif., 1969-72; exec. dir. Advocates for Women Econ. Devel. Ctr., 1972-76; cons. in fundraising and tng. Stanford U., Girl Scouts USA, others, 1976-78; equal opportunity mgr., chief youth programs Western Regional Nat. Park Svc., 1978-95; supr. Gt. Basin Nat. Park, 1995—. Office: Great Basin Nat Pk Hwy 488 Baker NV 89311

MILNER, CLYDE A., II, historian; b. Durham, N.C., Oct. 19, 1948; s. Charles Fremont and Eloyse (Sargent) M.; m. Carol Ann O'Connor, Aug. 14, 1977; children: Catherine Carol, Charles Clyde. AB, U. N.C., 1971; MA, Yale U., 1973, MPhil, 1974, PhD, 1979. Admissions counselor Guilford Coll., Greensboro, N.C., 1968-70; acting instr. Yale U., New Haven, 1974-75; research fellow McNickle Ctr., Chgo., 1975-76; instr. Utah State U., Logan, 1976-79, asst. prof., 1979-82, assoc. prof., 1982-88, prof., 1988—; dir. Mountain West Ctr. for Regional Studies, 1997-2000. Reader of manuscripts History Book Club, Inc., 1986—; exec. dir. Am. Studies program, Utah State U., 1997-2000. Author: With Good Intentions, 1982; editor: Major Problems in the History of the American West, 1989, co-editor 2d edit., 1997; editor: A New Significance: Re-envisioning the History of the American West, 1996; assoc. editor The Western Hist. Quar., 1984-87, co-editor, 1987-89, editor, 1990-97, exec. editor, 1998—; co-editor: Churchmen and the Western Indians, 1985, Trails: Toward a New Western History, 1991, Oxford History of the American West, 1994 (Western Heritage award for non-fiction Nat. Cowboy Hall of Fame 1994, Caughey Western History Assn. award for best book on history of Am. West 1995). Recipient Paladen Writing award The Montana Mag. Western History, 1987, Faculty Svc. award Associated Students Utah State U., 1987, Outstanding Social Science Researcher award Utah State U., 1983, (with Carol A. O'Connor) Charles Redd prize Utah Acad. Scis., Arts and Letters, 1996. Mem. Western History Assn., Orgn. Am. Historians, Phi Alpha Theta, Phi Beta Kappa. Society of Friends. Home: 1675 E 1400 N Logan UT 84341-2975 Office: Utah State U Dept Of History Logan UT 84322-0001 E-mail: cmilner@hass.usu.edu

MILNER, DANIEL PAUL, publishing executive, composer, producer; b. San Diego, June 17, 1952; s. Gerald Herbert and Dolores Rose (Englund) M. Student, U. Minn., 1970-72. Freelance rec. engr. various studios, Los Angeles, Mpls., 1966-68, 72-78; rec. artist 20th Century Records, Los Angeles, 1970-74, record producer, 1972-74; staff songwriter Warner Bros. Records, Los Angeles, 1973-76; chief rec. engr. Studio West Rec., San Diego, Los Angeles, 1978-83; owner, exec. prodr. Milner and Sullivan Music, San Diego, Los Angeles, 1982-89; owner, pres. Wintermoon Music, San Diego, Los Angeles, 1983—; owner, exec. prodr. Broadcast Design Group, 1996—. Music dir. The Arthur Co., L.A., 1978-92; audio cons. Studio C, San Diego, 1984-92, Wanna Be Doll Corp., 1986—; judge Clio Awards com., 1987-88. Composer, producer, arranger, engr.: (TV scores) Ace Diamond Private Eye, 1985, Safe at Home, 1984-87, Rocky Road, 1984-87, Down to Earth, 1983-86, The O'Briens, 1987, Here to Stay, 1987, Airwolf, 1986-88, The Munsters, 1987-90, The American Gladiators, 1993-97, (pilots) On the Line, 1985, Safe at Home, 1984, Operation Watchdog, 1987, (jingles) Budweiser, NBC Theme Song, Michelob, Firestone, thousands more; engr., producer: (feature film scores) A Minor Miracle, Happy Hour, Iced. Bd. dirs. Wildlife Rehabilitation, San Diego, 1978-84; mem. San Diego Zool. Soc., 1985-90; music producer United Way, San Diego, 1986-87, San Diego Pops Orch., 1986; conductorial mem. San Diego Pops Summer Orch. (Golden Baton 1985). Recipient 20 Clio nominations, 1 Emmy nomination, 21 Internat. Broadcast awards, 12 Addys, 1 Chgo. Film Festval, 6 Tellys, 2 N.Y. Film Festival, 3 Best in West, 1 Golden Peel, 28 Las Vegas Addys, 2 N.Y. Andys, 71 Utah Fedn., 3 Beldings, hundreds more. Mem. BMI, Am. Fedn. Musicians, San Diego Advt. Club (11 Homburg awards 1980—), San Diego Communicating Arts Group (8 awards 1984—). Roman Catholic. Avocations: falconry, jet-skiing, painting, pigeon racing. Office: Wintermoon Music 12432 Kestrel St San Diego CA 92129-3535

MILNER, HAROLD WILLIAM, hotel executive; b. Salt Lake City, Nov. 11, 1934; s. Kenneth W. and Olive (Schoettlin) M.; m. Susan Emmett, June 19, 1959 (div. 1976); children— John Kenneth, Mary Sue; m. Lois Friemuth, Aug. 14, 1977; 1 dau., Jennifer Rebecca. B.S., U. Utah, 1960; M.B.A., Harvard, 1962. Instr. Brigham Young U., Provo, Utah, 1962-64; v.p. Gen. Paper Corp., Mpls., 1964-65; dir. finance Amalgamated Sugar Co., Ogden, Utah, 1965-67; corp. treas. Marriott Corp., Washington, 1967-70; pres., chief exec. officer, trustee Hotel Investors, Kensington, Md., 1970-75; pres., chief exec. officer Americana Hotels Corp., Chgo., 1975-85, Kahler Corp., Rochester, Minn., 1985-97; pres., CEO The Kensington Co., Salt Lake City, 1997—. Trustee Baron Asset Funds, 1987—. Author: A Special Report on Contract Maintenance, 1963. Served as lt. AUS, 1960. Mem. Minn. Bus. Partnership (dir. 1991—). Mem. LDS Ch. Office: The Kensington Co 2293 Morning Star Dr Park City UT 84060-6725 E-mail: hmilner@aol.com

MILONE, ANTHONY M. bishop; b. Omaha, Sept. 24, 1932; Grad., North American Coll. (Rome). Ordained priest Roman Catholic Ch., 1957. Ordained titular bishop of Plestia and aux. bishop Diocese of Omaha, 1982; bishop Diocese of Great Falls-Billings, Great Falls, Mont., 1987—. Office: Diocese Gt Falls Billings PO Box 1399 121 23rd St S Great Falls MT 59403

MILONE, EUGENE FRANK, astronomer, educator; b. N.Y.C., June 26, 1939; arrived in Can., 1971; s. Frank Louis and Vera Christine (Joeckle) M.; m. Helen Catherine Louise (Ligor), Mar. 1, 1959; children: Bartholomew Vincenzo Llambro, Marie Christina Milone Jack. AB, Columbia U., 1961; MSc, Yale U., 1963, PhD, 1967. Astronomer space sci. div. rocket spectroscopy br. Naval Rsch. Lab., Washington, 1967-84; asst. prof. Gettysburg (Pa.) Coll., 1968-71; asst. prof. dept. physics and astronomy U. Calgary, Alta., Can., 1971-75, assoc. prof. Can., 1976-81, prof. Can., 1981—; co-dir. Rothney Astrophys. Obs., 1975—. Organizer Internat. Symposium on the Origins, Evolution and Destinies of Binary Stars in Clusters, U. Calgary, June 1995; chair rsch. grants com. U. Calgary, 1995-96. Editor: Infrared Extinction and Standardization, 1989; co-author: Challenges of Astronomy, 1991, Eclipsing Binary Stars: Modeling and Analysis, 1999, Exploring Ancient Skies, 2001; editor: Light Curve Modeling of Eclipsing Binary Stars, 1993, The Origins, Evolution, and Destinies of Binary Stars in Clusters, 1996; contbr. more than 150 articles to profl. jours. Elected mem. com. for coll. and univ. svcs. Evang. Luth. Ch. in Can., Synod of Alberta and the Territories, Edmonton, Alta., 1989-93. Operating and Equipment grantee Natural Scis. and Engring. Rsch. Coun. Can., 1972—; Killam Resident fellow Killam Found. U. Calgary, 1982, 88; Province of Alta. Innovation andSci. program grantee, 2001—. Mem. Internat. Astron. Union (mem. organizing com., commn. 25 1985-91, 94—, chair infrared astronomy working group 1988—), Am. Astron. Soc. (chmn. local organizing com. Calgary meeting 1981), Can. Astron. Soc., Sigma Xi (pres. U. Calgary chpt. 1979-80). Liberal Democrat. Lutheran. Achievements include development of Rothney Astrophysical Observatory, the Rapid Alternate Detection System, of light curve modeling techniques; research on the O'Connell Effect, on a new passband system for infrared photometry. Home: 1031 Edgemont Rd NW Calgary AB T2N 1N4 Canada T3A 2J5 Office: U Calgary Dept Physics Astronomy 2500 University Dr NW Calgary AB Canada T2N 1N4 E-mail: milone@ncalgary.ca

MILOSZ, CZESLAW, poet, writer, educator; b. Lithuania, June 30, 1911; came to U.S., 1960, naturalized, 1970; s. Aleksander and Weronika (Kunat) M. M Juris, U. Wilno, Lithuania, 1934; LittD (hon.), U. Mich., 1977; honoris causa, Cath. U. Lublin, 1981, Brandeis U., 1985, Harvard U., 1989, Jagiellonian U., Poland, 1989, U. Rome, , 1992. Programmer Polish Nat. Radio, 1935-39; diplomatic service Polish Fgn. Affairs Ministry, Warsaw, 1945-50; vis. lectr. U. Calif., Berkeley, 1960-61, prof. Slavic langs. and lits., 1961-78, prof. emeritus, 1978—. Author: The Captive Mind, 1953, Native Realm, 1968, Post-War Polish Poetry, 1965, The History of Polish Literature, 1969, Selected Poems, 1972, Bells in Winter, 1978, The Issa Valley, 1981, Separate Notebooks, 1984, The Land of Ulro, 1984, The Unattainable Earth, 1985, Collected Poems, 1988, Provinces, 1991, Beginning With My Streets, 1992, A Year of the Hunter, 1994, Facing the River, 1995, A Book of Luminous Things, 1996, Striving Towards Being, 1996, Roadside Dog, 1998. Recipient Prix Littéraire Européen Les Guildes du Livre, Geneva, 1953, Neustadt Internat. prize for lit. U. Okla., 1978, citation U. Calif., Berkeley, 1978, Nobel prize for lit., 1980, Nat. Medal of Arts, 1990; Nat. Culture Fund fellow, 1934-35; Guggenheim fellow, 1976 Mem. AAAS, Am. Acad. Arts and Scis., Am. Acad Arts and Letters, Polish Inst. Letters and Scis. in Am., PEN Club in Exile. Office: U Calif Dept Slavic Langs Lits Berkeley CA 94720-0001

MILSOME, DOUGLAS, cinematographer; Cinematographer: (TV movies) Dirty Dozen, Family of Spies, 1986, Hollywood Detective, Spies, Diana: Her True Story, Seasons of the Heart, Following Her Heart, 1995, Glory and Honor, (TV mini-series) Great Expectations, 1988, Lonesome Dove (Emmy nomination), Lonesome Dove II-The Return (Emmy nomination, ASC award), Old Curiosity Shop, Elizabeth Taylor, (films) Race for the Yankee Zephyr, Wild Horses, Full Metal Jacket (British Critics Cir. award 1987, Oscar nomination 1987), 1985, Hawks, The Beast, 1987, Desperate Hours, If Looks Could Kill-Teenagent, 1989, Robin Hood-Prince of Thieves, Last of the Mohicans (1st 7 weeks of the 1st Unit principal photography), 1990, Sunset Grill, Body of Evidence, Rumpelstulskin, Sunchaser, Breakdown, 1996, Legionnaire, Dungeons and Dragons; 2d unit dir./2d unit dir. of photography: (TV miniseries) Buffalo Girls, (movies) The Bounty, The Shining. Office: Mirisch Agy 1801 Century Park E Ste 1801 Los Angeles CA 90067-2320

MILSTEIN, LAURENCE BENNETT, electrical engineering educator, researcher; b. Bklyn., Oct. 28, 1942; s. Harry and Sadie (Kaplan) M.; m. Suzanne Barbara Hirschman, Oct. 3, 1969; children— Coreen Roxanne, Renair Marissa B.E.E., CUNY, 1964; M.S.E.E., Poly. Inst. Bklyn., 1966, Ph.D. in Elec. Engring., 1968. Mem. tech. staff Hughes Aircraft Co., El Segundo, Calif., 1968-69, staff engr., 1969-72, sr. staff engr., 1972-74; asst. prof. Rensselaer Poly. Inst., Troy, N.Y., 1974-76, U. Calif.-San Diego, La Jolla, 1976-79, assoc. prof., 1979-82, prof. elec. engring., 1982—, chmn. dept., 1984-88. Cons. Hughes Aircraft Co., Culver City, Calif., 1976-78, Lockhead Missiles & Space Co., Sunnyvale, Calif., 1978-93, Motorola Satellite Comm., 1992-96, InterDigital Comm. Corp, 1992-96, Golden Bridge Tech., 1995—, various govt. agys., pvt. cos., 1975—. Co-editor: Tutorials in Modern Communications, 1983; Spread Spectrum Communications, 1983; contbr. articles to profl. jours. Recipient Outstanding Tchr. award Warren Coll., U. Calif.-San Diego, La Jolla, 1982, Disting. Tchg. award, 1999; grantee Army Rsch. Office, 1977-80, 81-84, 86-89, 91-94, 95—, Office of Naval Rsch., Arlington, Va., 1982—, TRW, San Diego, 1983-89, 92-97, NSF, 1993-96, 97—. Fellow IEEE (Millennium medal 2000, Edwin Armstrong Achievement award 2000, MILCOM long term tech. achievement award 1998), IEEE Coms. Soc. (bd. govs. 1983, 85-87, 93-95, v.p. for tech. activities 1990-91), IEEE Info. Theory Soc. (bd. govs. 1989-94). Jewish Office: U Calif San Diego Dept Elec Computer Engring La Jolla CA 92093 E-mail: milstein@ece.ucsd.edu

MINAHAN, JOHN ENGLISH, writer; b. Albany, N.Y., Apr. 30, 1933; s. John English and Constance Madeline (Langdon) M.; m. Verity Ann Hill, Apr. 27, 1966. Student, Cornell U., 1955-57, Harvard U., 1958-59, Columbia U., 1959-60. Staff writer Time mag., 1960-61; chief TV writer J. Walter Thompson Co., N.Y.C., 1961-65; free-lance writer N.Y.C., 1965-73, L.A., 1976-79, Miami, 1981-95; editor, pub. American Way mag., N.Y.C., 1973-76; contbg. editor L.A. mag., 1978-79; dir. corp. comms. The Wackehut Corp., Coral Gables, Fla., 1990-95; free-lance writer Palm Springs, Calif., 1995—. Cons. Universal-MCA Inc., 1976-79; instr. novel writing workshop Harvard U. Ctr. Lifelong Learning, 1987-89. Author: (novels) A Sudden Silence, 1963, The Passing Strange, 1965, Jeremy, 1973, Sorcerer, 1977, Nine/Thirty/Fifty-Five, 1977, Almost Summer, 1978, Nunzio, 1978, The Complete American Graffiti, 1979, Eyewitness, 1981, The Great Hotel Robbery, 1982, The Great Diamond Robbery, 1984, Mask, 1985, The Face Behind the Mask, 1986, The Great Pyramid Robbery, 1987, The Great Harvard Robbery, 1988, The Great Grave Robbery, 1989, Forests of the Night, 2000; (biographies) The Dream Collector, 1972, The Quiet American: A Biography of George R. Wackenhut, 1994, The Torment of Buddy Rich, 2000; translation from French: The Fabulous Onassis, 1972; screenplays: A Sudden Silence, 1965, The Passing Strange, 1979; TV play: First Flight, 1968; contbg. editor book and theater revs., Miami Herald, 1983-95; also articles in N.Y. Times, Saturday Rev., Time-Life Spl. Reports. Recipient Doubleday award, 1960 Mem. Nat. Soc. Lit. and Arts, Faculty of Harvard U. Clubs, Alpha Delta Phi. Home and Office: 5289 E Cherry Hills Dr Palm Springs CA 92264-5903 E-mail: jvminahan@msn.com

MINAMI, ROBERT YOSHIO, artist, graphic designer; b. Seattle, May 1, 1919; s. Kichitaro and Suma (Fujita) M.; m. Shizu Tashiro, May 30, 1953; 1 child, Ken. Artist; student, Art Inst., Chgo., 1957, Am. Acad. Art, 1980-81. Graphic artist Filmack Studios, Chgo., 1945-48, S. Taylor & Leavitt Assocs., Chgo., 1949-50; head graphic designer NBC-TV, Chgo., 1950-82; fine artist Robert Minami's Studio, Oceanside, Calif., 1983—. Artist Goodman Theatre Design, Chgo., 1955-56; mem. Oceanside Mus. Art Exhbn. Com.; art instr. Mus. Sch. Art, Oceanside, 1997-98, 99. Exhibits include Oceanside Mus. Art, 1996. Active Supporters for City Couns., Oceanside, 1984—. Recipient Merit award Artist Guild Chgo., 1956, People's Choice award Carlsbad Oceanside Art League, 1986, Dick Blick award, 1992, 1st place award Mixed Media Collage, 1993, Nat. Watercolor award Watercolor West, 1994, Best of Watercolor Painting, Texture award, 1997. Mem. San Diego Watercolor Soc., United Scenic Artists (life), Am. Fine Art Connection, San Diego Art Inst., Nat. Watercolor Soc. (assoc.), Watercolor West Juried Assn., Internat. Soc. Exptl. Art, San Diego Artists Guild, San Diego Mus. Fine Arts. Avocations: painting, travel, movies, concerts, opera.

MINC, HENRYK, mathematics educator; b. Lodz, Poland, Nov. 12, 1919; s. Izrael and Haja (Zyngler) M.; m. Catherine Taylor Duncan, Apr. 16, 1943; children: Robert Henry, Ralph Edward, Raymond. MA with honors, Edinburgh (Scotland) U., 1955; PhD, 1959. Tchr. Morgan Acad., Dundee, Scotland, 1956-58; lectr. Dundee Tech. Coll., 1957-58, U. B.C., Vancouver, Can., 1958-59, asst. prof. Can., 1959-60; assoc. prof. U. Fla., Gainesville, 1960-63; prof. U. Calif., Santa Barbara, 1963-90; emeritus, 1990—. Vis. prof. Technion Isreael Inst. Tech., Haifa, 1969-80. Author: A Survey of Matrix Theory and Matrix Inequalities, 1964, Russian translation, 1972, Chinese translation, 1990, Introduction to Linear Algebra, 1968, Spanish translation, 1968, Modern University Algebra, 1966, Elementary Linear Algebra, Spanish translation, 1971, New College Algebra, 1968, Elementary Functions and Coordinate Geometry, 1969, Algebra and Trigonometry, 1970, College Algebra, 1970, College Trigonometry, 1971, Integrated Analytic Geometry and Algebra with Circular Functions, 1973, Permanents, 1978, Russian translation, 1980, Chinese translation, 1991, Nonnegative Matrices, 1988, Chinese translation, 1991; contbr. over 80 rsch. articles to math. jours., 9 rsch. papers to archaeol. and ancient numismatic jours., articles to Burns Chronicle; referee and reviewer math. jours. 2nd lt. Polish Army, 1940-48, France, U.K. Recipient Lester Ford award Math. Assn. Am., 1966, rsch. contract Office Naval Rsch., 1985-88, Air Force Office Sci. Rsch. grantee, 1960-83, Lady Davis fellow, 1975-78. Fellow Soc. Antiquaries of Scotland; mem. Am. Math. Soc., Robert Burns World Fedn. (hon. pres.), Inst. Antiquity and Christianity, Scottish Soc. Santa Barbara (past chieftain), Scots Lang. Soc. Saltire Soc., L.A. Burns Club, James Hogg Soc., Clan Fraser Soc. N. Am. Democrat. Home: 4076 Naranjo Dr Santa Barbara CA 93110-1213 Office: U Calif Dept Math Santa Barbara CA 93106 E-mail: hmincburns@aol.com

MINDEL, LAURENCE BRISKER, restaurateur; b. Toledo, Oct. 27, 1937; s. Seymour Stewart and Eleanor (Brisker) M.; m. Deborah Dudley, Oct. 20, 1978; children: Katherine Dudley, Nicolas Laurence; children by previous marriage, Michael Laurence, Laura Beth, Anthony Jay. BA, U. Mich., 1959. Gen. mgr. Western Coffee Instants, Inc., Burlingame, Cal., 1962-64, dir., ptnr., 1964, chmn., dir. Caswell Coffee Co., San Francisco, 1964-70; pres. Coffee Instants, Inc., Long Island City, N.Y., 1966-70; v.p. Superior Tea and Coffee Co., 1970-72; chmn., chief exec. officer Spectrum Foods, Inc., 1970-85; pres. Restaurant Group Saga Corp., Menlo Park, Calif., 1985-86; chmn., chief exec. officer Il Fornaio (Am.) Corp., 1987—. Mem. adv. bd. Stanislaus Ptnrs.; adv. bd., hospitality mgmt. bd. McLaren Coll. Bus. U. San Francisco; trustee The Branson Sch. Mem. World Pres'. Orgn., Inst. Am. Entrepreneurs. Home: 86 San Carlos Ave Sausalito CA 94965-2048 Office: Il Fornaio Am Corp 770 Tamalpais Dr Ste 400 Corte Madera CA 94925

MINER, JOHN BURNHAM, industrial relations educator, writer; b. N.Y.C., July 20, 1926; s. John Lynn and Bess (Burnham) M.; children by previous marriage: Barbara, John, Cynthia, Frances; m. Barbara Allen Williams, June 1, 1979; children: Jennifer, Heather. AB, Princeton U., 1950, PhD, 1955; MA, Clark U., 1952. Lic. psychologist, N.Y. Rsch. assoc. Columbia U., 1956-57; mgr. psychol. svcs. Atlantic Refining Co., Phila., 1957-60; mem. faculty U. Oreg., Eugene, 1960-68; prof., chmn. dept. orgnl. sci. U. Md., College Park, 1968-73; rsch. prof. Ga. State U., Atlanta, 1973-87, Disting. prof., 1974; pres. Orgnl. Measurement Systems Press, Eugene, Oreg., 1976—; prof. human resources SUNY, Buffalo, 1987-94, chmn. dept. orgn. and human resources, 1989-92; profl. practice Eugene, Oreg., 1995—. Cons. McKinsey & Co., N.Y.C., 1966-69; vis. lectr. U. Pa., Phila., 1959-60; vis. prof. U. Calif., Berkeley, 1966-67, U. South Fla., Tampa, 1972; researcher on orgnl. motivation, theories of orgn., human resource utilization, bus. policy and strategy, entrepreneurship. Author many books and monographs including Personnel Psychology, 1969, Personnel and Industrial Relations, 1969, 73, 77, 85, The Challenge of Managing, 1975, (with Mary Green Miner) Policy Issues Personnel and Industrial Relations, 1977, (with George A. Steiner) Management Policy and Strategy, 1977, James A. Hamilton-Hosp. Adminstrs. Book award 1982, 86), (with M.G. Miner) Employee Selection Within the Law, 1978, Theories of Organizational Behavior, 1980, Theories of Organizational Structure and Process, 1982, People Problems: The Executive Answer Book, 1985, The Practice of Management, 1985, Organizational Behavior: Performance and Productivity, 1988, Industrial-Organizational Psychology, 1992, Role Motivation Theories, 1993, (with Donald P. Crane) Human Resource Management: The Strategic Perspective, 1995, The 4 Routes to Entrepreneurial Success, 1996, (with Michael H. Capps) How Honesty Testing Works, 1997, A Psychological Typology of Successful Entrepreneurs, 1997, Organizational Behavior: Foundations, Theories and Analyses, 2002; contbr. numerous articles, papers to profl. jours. Served with AUS, 1944-46, ETO. Decorated Bronze Star, Combat Infantryman's badge. Fellow APA, Acad. of Mgmt. (editor Jour. 1973-75, pres. 1977-78), Soc. for Personality Assessment, Am. Psychol. Soc.; mem. Soc. for Human Resource Mgmt., Indsl. Rels. Rsch. Assn., Internat. Coun. for Small Bus., Strategic Mgmt. Soc., Internat. Pers. Mgmt. Assn., Human Resource Planning Soc. Republican. Home and Office: 34199 Country View Dr Eugene OR 97408-9440

MINER, JOHN RONALD, bioengineer; b. Scottsburg, Ind., July 4, 1938; s. Gerald Lamont and Alice Mae (Murphy) M.; m. Betty Katheron Emery, Aug. 4, 1963; children: Saralena Marie, Katherine Alice, Frederick Gerald. B.S. in Chem. Engring, U. Kans., 1959; M.S.E. in San. Engring, U. Mich., 1960; Ph.D. in Chem. Engring. and Microbiology, Kans. State U., 1967. Lic. profl. engr., Kans., Oreg. San. engr. Kans. Dept. Health, Topeka, 1959-64; grad. research asst. Kans. State U., Manhattan, 1964-67; asst. prof. agrl. engring. Iowa State U., 1967-71, assoc. prof., 1971-72; assoc. prof. agrl. engring. Oreg. State U., 1972-76, prof., 1976—, head dept., 1976-86, acting assoc. dean Coll. Agrl. Sci., 1983-84, assoc. dir. Office Internat. Research and Devel., 1986-90, extension water quality specialist, 1991—; environ. engr. FAO of UN, Singapore, 1980-81. Fulbright scholar U. Malawi, 1997-98; internat. cons.; cons. to livestock feeding ops., agrl. devel. firms. Co-author 2 books on livestock waste mgmt.; author 3 books of children's sermons; contbr. numerous articles on livestock prodn., pollution control, control of odors associated with livestock prodn. to profl. publs. Fellow Am. Soc. Agrl. Engrs. (bd. dirs. 1985-87); mem. Water Pollution Control Fedn., Sigma Xi, Gamma Sigma Delta, Alpha Epsilon, Tau Beta Pi. Presbyterian. Office: Oreg State U Dept Bioengring Corvallis OR 97331 E-mail: minerj@engr.orst.edu

MING, JENNY, retail apparel company executive; Mdse. mgr. brand activewear Gap Inc., 1986, v.p., divsn. mdse mgr., co-creator Old Navy subs., 1994; pres. Old Navy subs. Gap Inc. Office: Gap Inc 1 Harrison St San Francisco CA 94105-1602

MINK, PATSY TAKEMOTO, congresswoman; b. Paia, Maui, Hawaii, Dec. 6, 1927; d. Suematsu and Mitama (Tateyama) Takemoto; m. John Francis Mink, Jan. 27, 1951; 1 child, Gwendolyn. Student, Wilson Coll., 1946, U. Nebr., 1947; BA, U. Hawaii, 1948; LLD, U. Chgo., 1951; DHL (hon.), Chaminade Coll., 1975, Syracuse U., 1976, Whitman Coll., 1981. Bar: Hawaii. Pvt. practice, Honolulu, 1953-65; lectr. U. Hawaii, 1952-56, 59-62, 79-80; atty. Territorial Ho. of Reps., 1955; mem. Hawaii Ho. of Reps., 1956-58, Ter. Hawaii Senate, 1958-59, Hawaii State Senate, 1962-64, Congresses from 2nd Hawaii dist., 1965-77, 90—; mem. edn. and workforce com., mem. budget com.; mem. com. on govt. reform 106th Congresses from 2d dist. Hawaii. Mem. govt. reform com., mem. U.S. del. to UN Law of Sea, 1975-76, Internat. Woman's Yr., 1975, UN Environ. Program, 1977, Internat. Whaling Commn., 1977; asst. sec. of state U.S. Dept. State, 1977-78. Charter pres. Young Dem. Club Oahu, 1954-56, Ter. Hawaii Young Dems., 1956-58; del. Dem. Nat. Conv., 1960, 72, 80; nat. v.p. Young Dem. Clubs Am., 1957-59; v.p. Ams. for Dem. Action, 1974-76, nat. pres., 1978-81; mem. nat. adv. com. White House Conf. on Families, 1979-80; mem. nat. adv. coun. Federally Employed Women. Recipient Leadership for Freedom award Roosevelt Coll., Chgo., 1968, Alii award 4-H Clubs Hawaii, 1969, Nisei of Biennium award, Freedom award Honolulu chpt. NAACP, 1971, Disting. Humanitarian award YWCA, St. Louis, 1972, Creative Leadership in Women's Rights award NEA, 1977, Human Rights award Am. Fedn. Tchrs., 1975, Feminist of Yr. award Feminist Majority Found., 1991, Margaret Brent award ABA, 1992, Outstanding Woman of Yr. award Nat. Assn. Profl. Am. Women, 1992, Environ. Leadership award Nat. League Conservation Voters, 1993, Jessie Bernard Wise Women award Ctr. for Women Policy Studies, 1993, Hawaii's Health Mother award, 1994, Hispanic Health Leadership award, 1995, Women Work! Nat. Network for Women's Employment, 1995, Women at Work Pub. Policy award, 1995, Justice in Action award Asian Am. Legal Def. and Edn. Fund, 1996, Daniel K. Inouye award Hawaii Psychol. Assn., 1996, Indsl. Union Dept. Lewis-Murray-Reuther Social Justice award AFL-CIO, 1996, Top Rating for Global Internat. Trade Watch, Pub. Citizens/Nat. Farmers Union/Friends of the Earth, 1996, award Inferfaith IMPACT for Justice and Peace, 1996, Hawaii Coun. on Lang. Planning and Policy cert. for opposition to English-only legislation, 1996, Hawai'i Women Lawyers Lifetime Achievement award 1997, Legis. Leadership award Nat. Assn. of WIC Dirs., 1997. Office: US Ho Reps 2210 Rayburn HOB Washington DC 20515-0001*

MINNAUGH, MIKE, political organization administrator; Chmn. fin. Rep. Party, Ariz., 1998; fin. com. Ariz. Rep. Party, 1998, state chmn., 1999—. Mem. Rep. Nat. Com. Western State Chmn. Assn., 1999—. Office: 3501 N 24th St Phoenix AZ 85016-6607

MINNICH, DIANE KAY, legal association administrator; b. Iowa City, Feb. 17, 1956; d. Ralph Maynard Minnich and Kathryn Jane (Obye) Tompkins. BA in Behavioral Sci., San Jose State U., 1978. Tutorial program coord./instr. Operation SHARE/La Valley Coll., Van Nuys, Calif., 1979-81; field exec. Silver Sage Girl Scout Coun., Boise, Idaho, 1981-85; continuing legal edn. dir. Idaho State Bar/Idaho Law Found. Inc., Boise, 1985-88, dep. dir., 1988-90, exec. dir., 1990—. Mem. adv. bd. legal asst. program Boise State U. Mem. Assn. CLE Adminstrs., Chgo., 1985-90; bd. dirs. Silver Sage coun. Girl Scouts, Boise, 1990-93, 99—, mem. nominating com., 1990-94, 97—, chair nominating com., 1991-92; mem. legal asst. program adv. bd. Boise State U. Named one of Outstanding Young Women in Am., 1991. Mem. Nat. Orgn. Bar Execs. (membership com. 1992-97, chair 1996-97), Zonta Club Boise (pres. 1991-92, bd. dirs. 1989-93), Rotary Club Boise (chair mem. com. 1994-97, bd. dirs. 1996-97, 99—). Avocations: softball, jogging, golf. Office: Idaho State Bar Idaho Law Found PO Box 895 525 W Jefferson St Boise ID 83702-5931

MINNICK, MALCOLM DAVID, lawyer; b. Indpls., July 5, 1946; s. Malcolm Dick and Frances Louise (Porter) M.; m. Heidi Rosemarie Klein, May 24, 1972. BA, U. Mich., 1968, JD, 1972. Bar: Calif. 1972, U.S. Dist. Ct. (cen. dist.) Calif. 1972, U.S. Ct. Appeals (9th cir.) 1984, U.S. Dist. Ct. (no. dist.) Calif. 1986, U.S. Supreme Ct. 1986. Assoc. Lillick McHose & Charles, Los Angeles, 1972-78; ptnr. Lillick & McHose, Los Angeles, 1978-91, Pillsbury Winthrop LLC, San Francisco, 1991—. Group mgr. Creditors Rights and Bankruptcy Group, 1993-98; panelist Calif. Continuing Edn. of Bar, L.A., 1982-86, 88, Practicing Law Inst., 1992, 93, 94, Banking Law Inst., 1999, 2000; bd. govs. Fin. Lawyers Conf., L.A., 1981-84; mem. exec. com. Lillick & McHose, 1982-85. Co-author: Checklist for Secured Commercial Loans, 1983. Pres. Ross Sch. Found., 1997-98. Mem. ABA (corp., banking and bus. law sect.), Calif. Bar Assn. (Uniform Comml. Code com. 1983-86), L.A. County Bar Assn. (exec. com. comml. law and bankruptcy sect. 1987-90), Bar Assn. San Francisco (comml. law and bankruptcy sect.), L.A. Country Club, Univ. Club (bd. dirs. 1983-86, pres. 1985-86). Avocation: golf. Office: Pillsbury Winthrop LLC 50 Fremont St San Francisco CA 94105-2230 E-mail: dminnick@pillsburywinthrop.com

MINNIS, JOHN MARTIN, state legislator, protective services official; b. Garden City, Kans., Dec. 14, 1953; s. Elbert William and Helen R. Logerwell) M.; m. Karen Marie Bartrug, Oct. 14, 1972; children: Steven, Michael, Jennifer. Student, Portland State U. Machinist-apprentice Bingham-Willamette Co., Portland, Oreg., 1973-74; rsch. dep. sheriff Multnomah County, 1976; police officer Portland Police Dept., 1976-92, detective, 1992—; mem. Oreg. Ho. of Reps., Salem, 1985-98, minority whip, 1989, asst. majority leader, 1991, also co-chmn. joint ways and means com.; mem. Oreg. Senate from 11th dist., Salem, 2001—. Sgt. USAF and Oreg. Air Guard, 1972-78. Mem. Am. Legis. Exch. Coun., Nat. Conf. State Legislatures (vice chmn. com. on fed. budget and taxation), Am. Profl. Soc. on Abuse of Children. Home: 23765 NE Holladay St Troutdale OR 97060-2903

MINOGUE, ROBERT BROPHY, retired nuclear engineer; b. Covington, Ky., Jan. 31, 1928; s. Joseph and Catherine Ann (Brophy) M.; m. Marie Joan Clarke, June 12, 1954; children: Patrick, Margaret, Marie, Francis. B.S., Thomas More Coll., 1949; M.S., U. Cin., 1951; grad., Oak Ridge Sch. Reactor Tech., 1952. Nuclear engr., then head nuclear tech. sect. naval reactors br. AEC, Washington, 1952-56; head research reactor design and enngring., then head nuclear power plant engring. sect. Gen. Atomic div. Gen. Dynamics Corp., 1957-67; chief spl. projects br. div. reactor standards AEC, Washington, 1967-72, asst. dir., then dep. dir. regulatory standards, 1972-74; dir. office standards devel. Nuclear Regulatory Commn., Washington, 1975-80, dir. office research, 1980-86; pvt. practice Temecula, Calif., 1986—. U.S. mem. sr. adv. group Safety Standards IAEA, 1974-86; mem. Com. on Interagy. Radiation Research and Policy Coordination, 1982-86. Author: Reactor Shielding Design Manual, 1956; patentee: Triga Research Reactor. Served with AUS, 1946-48. Recipient Bernard F. Langer award, ASME, 1982. Mem. ASTM (dir. 1975-76, 77-80). Roman Catholic. Home and Office: 29743 Marhill Cir Temecula CA 92591-1809

MINOR, HALSEY, multimedia company executive; Grad., U. Va. Investment banker Merrill Lynch Capital Markets, San Francisco, 1991; founder Global Publ. Corp., San Francisco; chmn., CEO CNET: The Computer Network, San Francisco, 1992-2000; chmn. CNET Networks Inc., 2000—. Office: C NET Networks Inc 150 Chestnut St San Francisco CA 94111-1004

MINSON, DIXIE L. legislative staff member; Student, Weber State U. Dir. dept. bus. regulation Utah's Divsn. Consumer Protection; dep. chief of staff Office of Gov. Norman H. Bangerter, Utah; commr. safety, health and indsl. accidents divsn. Indsl. Commn. Utah; state dir. Office of Senator Robert F. Bennett, Salt Lake City, 1993—. Active Utah Hearing Panel for Safety Auto and Inspection Stas., League Utah Consumers; Utah liaison U.S. Product Safety Commn.; v.p. Wester Assn. Worker's Compensation Bd. and Commn.; rep. Funeral Svc. Consumer Action Panel for Western States and Hawaii. Mem. Nat. Assn. Govtl. Labor Ofcls., Nat. Assn. Consumer Agy. Adminstrs., Nat. Assn. Unemployment Ins. Appellate Bds. Office: 111 S State St Fed Bldg Rm 4225 Salt Lake City UT 84138-1102

MINTON, TORRI, journalist; b. San Rafael, Calif., Oct. 7, 1956; d. John and Mary. BA in Ethnic Studies, U. Calif., Berkeley, 1983; M of Journalism, Columbia U., 1984. Reporter Associated Press, San Francisco, 1984, San Francisco Chronicle, 1986—, assigning editor, 2000—. Vice chmn. San Francisco Chronicle No. Calif. Newspaper Guild, 1992, 97, 2000; rep. assembly del., 1992, 93, 94, 95, 96; instr. newswriting U. Calif., Berkeley, 1995—; instr. journalism, lead advisor Golden Gater Newspaper, San Francisco State U., 2000; instr. journalism U. San Francisco, 2000—. Community devel. vol. Oper. Crossroads Africa, Tiriki, Kenya, 1979. Mem. Phi Beta Kappa. Office: San Francisco Chronicle 901 Mission St San Francisco CA 94103-2905 E-mail: tminton@sfchronicle.com

MINTS, GRIGORI EFROIM, mathematics specialist; b. Leningrad, USSR, June 7, 1939; s. Efroim B. and Lea M. (Novick) M.; m. Maryanna Rozenfeld, July 21, 1987; 1 child, Anna. Diploma, Leinigrad U., 1961, PhD, 1965, ScD, 1989. Rsch. assoc. Steklov Inst. Math., Leningrad, 1961-79; with Nauka Pubs., Leningrad, 1979-85; sr. rsch. assoc. Inst. Cybernetics, Tallinn, Estonia, 1985-91; prof. dept. philosophy Stanford (Calif.) U., 1991—. Mem. ed. bd. Jour. Symbolic Logic, 1987-90; mem. program orgn. com. Logic in Computer Sci., 1991-94, ASL mtg., CSLI Workshop on Logic, Language and Computation. Author: (book) A Short Introduction to Modal Logic, 1992, Selected Papers in Proof Theory, 1992, A Short Introduction to Intuitionistic Logic, 2000; editor: Mathematical Investigation of Logical Deduction, 1967, COLOG-88, 1989, Logic Colloquium, 1996; mem. editl. bd.: jour. Jour. Philos. Logic, mem. editl. bd.: jour. Jour. of Logic and Computation, mem. editl. bd.: jour. IGPL, mem. editl. bd.: jour. Math. Structures in Computer Sci.;contbr. articles to profl. jours. Mem. Assn. Symbolic Logic (mem. coun. 1990-93), Internat. Union History and Philosophy and Sci. (assessor 1991-95).

MINTZ, MARSHALL GARY, lawyer; b. Detroit, May 28, 1947; BA, UCLA, 1968, JD, 1971. Bar: Calif. 1972. Law clk. appellate dept L.A. County Superior Ct., 1971-72; ptnr. Kelly Lytton Mintz & Vann, LLP, L.A., Calif., 1995-2001; of counsel Sidley & Bell LLP, L.A., 2001—. Moderator, panelist Calif. Continuing Edn. of Bar, 1980—; mem. arbitration adminstrv. com. L.A. County Superior Ct., 1979, mem. 1984 Olympics spl. settlement panel; mem. arbitration panel L.A. Superior Ct., 1999—. Mem. ABA, State Bar Calif., L.A. County Bar Assn. (arbitrator arbitration and client rels. com. 1978-99), Assn. Bus. Trial Lawyers (bd. govs. 1976-77, program chmn. 1976). Office: Sidley & Bell LLP 2940 Westwood Blvd 2d Fl Los Angeles CA 90064 E-mail: mgmintz@earthlink.net

MINUDRI, REGINA URSULA, librarian, consultant; b. San Francisco, May 9, 1937; d. John C. and Molly (Halter) M. BA, San Francisco Coll. for Women, 1958; MLS, U. Calif., Berkeley, 1959. Reference libr. Menlo Park (Calif.) Pub. Libr., 1959-62; regional libr. Santa Clara County (Calif.) Libr., 1962-68; project coord. Fed. Young Adult Libr. Svcs. Project, Mountain View, Calif., 1968-71; dir. profl. svcs. Alameda County (Calif.) Libr., 1971, asst. county libr., 1972-77; libr. dir. Berkeley Pub. Libr., 1977-94; city libr. San Francisco Pub. Libr., 1997-2000. Lectr. U. San Francisco, 1970-72, U. Calif., Berkeley, 1977-81, 91-93, San Jose State U., 1994-97; cons., 1975-90; mem. adv. bd. Miles Cutter Ednl., 1992-98. Author: Getting It Together, A Young Adult Bibliography, 1970; contbr. articles to publs. including Sch. Libr. Jour., Wilson Libr. Bull. Bd. dirs. No. Calif. ACLU, 1994-96, Cmty. Memory, 1989-91, Berkeley Pub. Libr. Found., 1996—; bd. dirs. Berkeley Cmty. Fund, 1995—, chair youth com., 1994-96; mem. bd. mgrs. ctrl. br. Berkeley YMCA, 1988-93. Recipient proclamation Mayor of Berkeley, 1985, 86, 94, Citation of Merit, Calif. State Assembly, 1994; named Woman of Yr., Alameda County North chpt. Nat. Women's Polit. Caucus, 1985, Outstanding Alumna, U. Calif. Sch. Libr. and Info. Scis., Berkeley, 1987. Mem. ALA (pres. 1986-87, exec. bd. 1980-89, coun. 1979-88, 90-94, Grolier award 1974), Calif. Libr. Assn. (pres. 1981, coun. 1965-69, 79-82), LWV (dir. Berkeley chpt. 1980-81, v.p. comm. svcs. 1995-97). Office: Reality Mgmt 836 The Alameda Berkeley CA 94707-1916

MINZNER, DEAN FREDERICK, aviation company executive; b. July 20, 1945; s. Frederick Louis and Winifred (Hughes) M. BA, Franklin and Marshall Coll., 1967; MBA, Columbia U., 1972. Dist. exec. Greater N.Y. couns. Boy Scouts Am., N.Y.C., 1972-76; sales exec. Coast Avia, Long Beach, Calif., 1976-78, Performance Aircraft, Inc., Hayward, 1978; owner, pres. Western Aviation Consultants, Inc., Hayward, 1978-82, Cal-Pacific Assocs., Inc., Hayward, 1979—, Cal-Pacific Enterprises, Hayward, 1982—. Mem. Assn. MBA Execs., Columbia U. Grad. Sch. Bus. Alumni Assn., Aircraft Owners and Pilots Assn. Office: PO Box 6206 Hayward CA 94540-6206 E-mail: dminz@hotmail.com

MINZNER, PAMELA BURGY, state supreme court justice; b. Meridian, Miss., Nov. 19, 1943; BA cum laude, Miami U., 1965; LLB, Harvard U., 1968. Bar: Mass. 1968, N.Mex. 1972. Pvt. practice, Mass., 1968-71, Albuquerque, 1971-73; adj. prof. law U. N.Mex., Albuquerque, 1972-73, asst. prof., 1973-77, assoc. prof., 1977-80, prof. law, 1980-84; judge N.Mex. Ct. Appeals, Albuquerque, 1984-94, chief judge, 1993-94; justice N.Mex. Supreme Ct., Santa Fe, 1994—, chief justice, 1999-01. Mem. faculty Inst. Preparativo Legal U., N.Mex. Sch. Law, 1975, 79; participant NEH Summer Seminar for Law Tchrs. Stanford Law Sch., 1982, U. Chgo. Law Sch., 1978. Author: (with Robert T. Laurence) A Student's Guide to Estates in Land and Future Interests: Text, Examples, Problems & Answers, 1981, 2d edit. 1993. Mem. ABA, State Bar N.Mex. (co-editor newsletter 1979-83, bd. dirs. 1978-79, 83-84, sect. on women's legal rights and obligations), Gamma Phi Beta. Democrat. Avocations: reading, bridge, movies. Office: NMex Supreme Ct Supreme Ct Bldg 237 Don Gaspar Santa Fe NM 87504-0848

MIRACLE, ROBERT WARREN, retired banker; b. Casper, Wyo. m. Maggie Zanoni; children: Mark, John BS in Law, U. Wyo., 1951; grad. with honors, Pacific Coast Banking Sch., 1960. With Wyo. Nat. Bank (now Norwest Bank Casper N.A.), 1954-91; exec. v.p. Wyo. Nat. Bank of Casper, 1967; pres., chief exec. officer Wyo. Nat. Bank of Casper (now Norwest Bank Casper N.A.)_, 1968-87; chmn. Wyo. Nat. Bank of Casper (formerly Norwest Bank Casper N.A.), 1983-91, also bd. dirs.; pres., chief exec. officer, dir. Wyo. Nat. Bancorp. (formerly Affiliated Bank Corp Wyo.), Casper, 1970-91; mgr. Kemmerer LaBarge Royalties LLC, 1999—. Instr. bank mgmt. U. Colo., 1971-75. Bd. dirs. United Fund of Natrona County, Wyo., 1963-85, campaign co-chmn., 1973-78; trustee The Myra Fox Skelton Found., 1963—, Goodstein Found., 1992—; bd. dirs., pres. Investment in Casper, 1967-70; Wyo. treas. Radio Free Europe, 1967-72; trustee Casper Coll. Foun., 1967-91, pres., 1973-75, 85-91; trustee U. Wyo. Found., 1972-87; chmn. Casper Downtown Improvement Assn., 1974-75; bd. dirs. Cen. Wyo. Fair Bd., 1974-79, pres., 1977-78; dir. Mountain States Employers Coun., 1979-91; bd. dirs. Wyo. Natural Gas Pipeline Authority, 1991-97; trustee Meml. Hosp. Natrona County, 1993-96, pres. 1995-96; bd. dirs. Wyo. Med. Ctr., 1996-99. Capt. USMC, 1951-53. Recipient James C. Scarboro Meml. award Colo. Sch. Banking., 1977; Disting. Service in Bus. award U. Wyo. Coll. Commerce and Industry, 1980 Mem. Wyo. Bankers Assn. (chmn. legis. com. 1969-80, pres. 1974-75), Am. Bankers Assn. (mem. governing coun. 1974-75, 81-83), Am. Mgmt. Assn., Rocky Mountain Oil and Gas Assn., Newcomer Soc. in N.Am., Casper C. of C. (pres. 1965-66, Disting. Svc. award 1981), VFW, Casper Petroleum Club, Casper Country Club (pres. 1993-94), Casper Rotary Club (hon. Rotarian award 1996-97), Masons, Lions.

MIRISCH, LAWRENCE ALAN, motion picture agent; b. L.A., Oct. 10, 1957; s. Walter and Patricia (Kahan) M. BA Radio & TV, Film, Calif. State U., Northridge, 1980. Apprentice film editor, 1975-77; 2nd asst. dir., 1979-81; agent The Gersh Agency, Los Angeles, CA, 1982-84, Adams, Ray & Rosenberg, Los Angeles, 1984, Triad Artists, Los Angeles, 1984-92; pres. The Mirisch Agency, Los Angeles, 1992—. Mem. Mot. Picture Editors Guild, 1975; Directors Guild of Amer., 1978; Academy of Motion Pictures Arts & Sciences, 1987; Amer. Cinema Editors, 1988; adv. bd., Amer. Film Inst., 1990; special products comm., Dir. Guild of Amer., 1991. Bd. of governors, Cedars Sinai Hosp., 1991. Office: The Mirisch Agency 1801 Century Park E Ste 1801 Los Angeles CA 90067-2320

MIRSKY, PHYLLIS SIMON, librarian; b. Petach Tikva, Israel, Dec. 18, 1940; d. Allan and Lea (Prizant) Simon; m. Edward Mirsky, Oct. 21, 1967; 1 child, Seth (dec.). BS in Social Welfare, Ohio State U., 1962; postgrad., Columbia U., 1962-63; AMLS, U. Mich., 1965. Caseworker field placement Children's Aid Soc., N.Y.C., 1962-63; hosp. libr. hosp. and instns. divsn. Cleve. Pub. Libr., 1963-64; reference libr. UCLA Biomed. Libr., 1965-68, reference/acquisitions libr., 1968-69, head cons./continuing edn. Pacific S.W. Regl. Med. Libr. Sv., 1969-71, asst. dir. Pacific S.W. Regl. Med. Libr. Sv., 1971-73, faculty coord. Biomed. Libr. program Cen. San Joaquin Valley Area Health Edn. Ctr., 1973-77, assoc. dir. Pacific S.W. Regl. Med. Libr. Sv., 1973-79; head reference sect., coord. libr. assoc. program Nat. Libr. of Medicine, Bethesda, Md., 1979-81; asst. univ. libr., scis. U. Calif.-San Diego, La Jolla, 1981-86, acting univ. libr., 1985, 92-93, 98-99, asst. univ. libr. adminstrv. and pub. svcs., 1986-87, assoc. univ. libr. adminstrv. and pub. svcs., 1987-92, assoc. univ. libr., 1993-95; dep. univ. libr., 1995—. Guest lectr. Libr. Schs. UCLA and U. So. Calif., 1967-78, Grad. Sch. Libr. Sci. Cath. U., Washington, 1980, Grad. Sch. Libr. and Info. Sci. UCLA, 1984; mem. task force on role of spl. libr. nationwide network and coop. programs Nat. Commn. on Libr. and Info. Svcs./Spl. Libr. Assn., 1981-83; facilitator AASLD/MLA Guidelines Scenario Writing Session, L.A., 1984; mem. users coun. OCLC Online Computer Libr. Ctr., Inc., 1991-94; U. Calif.-San Diego rep. Coalition for Networked Info., 1992—; instr. Assn. Rsch. Librs., Office Mgmt. Studies, Mgmt. Inst., 1987; peer reviewer Coll. Libr. Tech. and Cooperation Grant Program U.S. Dept. Edn., 1988-94; cons. Nat. Libr. Medicine, Bethesda, Md., 1988, San Diego Mus. Contemporary Art Libr., La Jolla, Calif., 1993, Salk Inst., 1995; mem. Libr. of Congress Network Adv. Com., 1994-96, chair steering com., 1995-96. Contbr. articles to profl. jours. and bulls. Mem. fin. com. City of Del Mar, 1995-98, chair, 1997-98. NIH fellow Columbia U., 1962-63; sr. fellow UCLA/Coun. on Libr. Resources, 1987. Fellow Med. Libr. Assn. (bd. dirs. 1977-80); mem. ALA (site visitors panel com. on accreditation 1990-92, libr. adminstrn. and mgmt. assn. 1990-92), Med. Libr. Group Soc. Calif. and Ariz. (sec. 1970-71, v.p. 1971-72, pres. 1972-73), Documentation Abstracts, Inc. (bd. dirs. 1985-90, vice chair bd. dirs. 1988-90), Med. Libr. Assn. (pres. 1984-85), U. Mich. Sch. Libr. Sci. Alumni Assn. Office: U Calif San Diego U Libr 0175G 9500 Gilman Dr La Jolla CA 92093-5003

MISA, KENNETH FRANKLIN, management consultant; b. Jamaica, N.Y., Sept. 24, 1939; s. Frank J. and Mary M. (Soszka) M. BS in Psychology cum laude, Purdue U., 1963; PhD in Psychology, St. John's U., 1966. Cert. mgmt. cons.; lic. psychologist, Calif. Staff psychologist Rohrer, Hibler & Replogle, L.A., 1966-67; assoc. A.T. Kearney, Inc., L.A., 1968-71, sr. assoc., 1972-74, prin., 1975-78, v.p., ptnr., 1979-86; pres. HR Cons. Group, 1987—. Mem. APA, Am. Psychol. Soc., Calif. State Psychol. Assn., Soc. for Human Resources Mgmt., Human Resources Planning Soc., Indsl. Rels. Rsch. Assn., Soc. for Indsl. and Orgnl. Psychology, World Affairs Coun. L.A., Town Hall So. Calif., Glendale C. of C., Jonathan Club. Republican. Roman Catholic. Home: 804 S Orange Grove Blvd Pasadena CA 91105-1715 Office: HR Cons Group 100 N Brand Blvd Ste 200 Glendale CA 91203-2642 Fax: 626-441-9584. E-mail: kfmhrcg@aol.com

MISCHER, DONALD LEO, television director and producer; b. San Antonio, Mar. 5, 1940; s. Elmer Frederick and Lillian Alma. B.A., U. Tex., 1961, M.A., 1963. Mem. faculty U. Tex., 1962-63; producer/dir. USIA, Washington, 1965-68; with Charles Guggenheim Prodns., 1969-71. Pres. Don Mischer Prodns., pres. Mischer Enterprises, Inc., Beverly Hills, Calif., prodr., dir., and program packager for network television programs, 1971—. Television programs include: The Opening and Closing Ceremonies of the 1996 Centennial Olympic Games, Atlanta, The Kennedy Center Honors: A Celebration of the Performing Arts (Emmy Awards 1981, 87); The Tony Awards (Emmy Awards 1987-88); Michael Jackson's Super Bowl XXVII Halftime Show; Baryshnikov by Tharp (Emmy Award 1985); Gregory Hines, Tap Dance America; Carnegie Hall: Live at 100; It's Garry Shandling's Show; Mowtown 25: Yesterday, Today, Tomorrow (Emmy Award 1983); The Muppets Celebrate Jim Henson; Motown Returns to the Apollo (Emmy Award 1985); Baryshnikov in Hollywood, Goldie and Liza Together, Shirley MacLaine— Illusions, Making Television Dance with Twyla Tharp, An Evening with Robin Williams, Am. Film Inst. Salute to Gene Kelly; producer additional programs with Bob Hope (Bob Hope: The First 90 Years - Emmy award Outstanding Variety, Music or Comedy Special, 1993), Barbara Walters, Goldie Hawn, others. Recipient: Primetime Emmy awards (10), Director's Guild awards for Outstanding Directorial Achiement (8), NAACP Image awards (3), Peabody award, Golden Rose of Montreux award, Gabriel award, Ohio State award. Mem. Dirs. Guild Am., Nat. Acad. TV Arts and Scis. Gov., Am. Film Inst. Office: Brillstein Grey Entertainment 9150 Wilshire Blvd Ste 350 Beverly Hills CA 90212-3453

MISCHLER, HARLAND LOUIS, investment company executive; b. Troy, Ohio; m. Jean O'Connor; children: Marilyn West, Thomas O'Connor. BS, MBA, Ohio State U. CPA, Ohio. Mgr. DeLoitte & Touche, Cin., 1959-66; mgr. internat. fin., v.p., controller, treas. Hobart Corp., Troy, Ohio, 1966-81; v.p. fin. Bausch & Lomb Inc., Rochester, N.Y., 1981-84; vice chmn., exec. v.p. fin. Applied Research Labs., Rochester, 1984-87; CEO, COO HLM Capital Resources Inc., Boca Raton, Fla., 1987—. Bd. dirs., exec. v.p., fin. officer, Gradco Systems Inc., Las Vegas, Nev., 1990—. Past pres., bd. dirs. Troy C. of C., Stouder Meml. Hosp., Miami County Hosp. Assn.; mem. Ohio State adv. coun. Served to maj. USAF. Mem. Fin. Execs. Inst. (pres. Dayton chpt. 1981), Am. Inst. CPA's, Alpha Kappa Psi, Sigma Alpha Epsilon. Republican. Episcopalian. Lodge: Rotary. Home: 17037 Brookwood Dr Boca Raton FL 33496-5930 Office: Gradco Systems Inc 3753 Howard Hughes Pkwy Ste 200 Las Vegas NV 89109

MISENER, TERRY RICHARD, dean, nursing educator; b. Apr. 11, 1943; BSN, U. Colo., 1966; M in Health Sci., U. Calif., Davis, 1973; PhD, U. Ill., 1981. Ret. lt. col. U.S. Army Nurse Corps, 1964-87; prof., dept. chair nursing sys. U. Portland, Oreg., 1987-98, nursing prof., 1998—. Fellow Am. Acad. Nursing. Office: U Portland Sch Nursing Portland OR 97203

MISHELEVICH, DAVID JACOB, medical company executive, consultant; b. Pitts., Jan. 26, 1942; s. Benjamin and Sarah (Bachrach) M.; m. Bonnie Gray McKim, Dec. 6, 1981; 1 child, Cory Jane. BS in Physics, U. Pitts., 1962; MD, Johns Hopkins U., 1966, PhD in Biomed. Engring., 1970. Lic., Md., Tex. Intern in medicine Balt. City Hosps., 1966-67; staff assoc. Nat. Inst. Neurol. Diseases and Stroke, NIH, Bethesda, Md., 1967-69; exec. v.p. Nat. Ednl. Consultants, Balt., 1971-72; prof., dept. chairperson, dir. med. computing resources ctr. U. Tex. Health Sci. Ctr., Dallas, 1972-82; attending physician/sr. attending physician internal med. Dallas County Hosp., Dist. Parkland Meml. Hosp., 1973-82; v.p. computer and software tech. EAN-TECH, Mountain View, Calif., 1983-84; CEO Garden Gate Software, Cupertino, 1984-86; dir., then v.p. and gen. mgr. applications and rsch. divsn. IntelliCorp, Inc., Mountain View, 1986-89; v.p. mktg. and sales Viewpoint Engring., Mountain View, 1989-90; v.p. engring. AirWays Med. Techs., Inc., Palo Alto, Calif., 1991-93; dir., then v.p. R&D, chief tech. officer Circadian, Inc., San Jose, 1993-95, v.p., gen. mgr. AirWays Asthma Ctrs. divsn., 1995-96; CEO Sterling Healthcare Outcomes, Inc., Cupertino, 1996—; founder, exec. v.p., chief tech. officer OFNM.com, 1999-2001;

chief tech. officer HealthShore, Inc., 2001—. Pres. Mishelevich Assocs., Dallas, 1982-83, Cupertino, 1990-91; mem. biomed. libr. rev. com. NIH-Nat. Libr. Medicine, 1978-82; cons. in field. Former tech. reviewer IBM Sys. Jour., Jour. of AMA; contbr. numerous articles to profl. jours.; patentee in field. V.p. Dallas chpt. Am. Jewish Congress, 1980-84, Am. Jewish Fund, 1980-81. Fellow Am. Coll. Med. Informatics; mem. AAAS, IEEE and IEEE Computer Soc. (exec. bd. tech. com. on computational medicine 1981-83), Am. Assn. for Artificial Intelligence, Assn. for Computing Machinery (chair Dallas chpt. 1974-75), Am. Med. Informatics Assn., Internat. Med. Outcomes Trust, Internat. Tandem Users Group (past pres.), Phi Beta Kappa, Omicron Kappa. Democrat. Jewish. Home: 20902 Garden Gate Dr Cupertino CA 95014-1808 Office: QENMcom 1400 Fashion Island Blvd San Mateo CA 94404

MISHELL, DANIEL R., JR. obstetrician/gynecologist, educator; b. Newark, May 7, 1931; s. Daniel R. and Helen Mishell; m. Carol Goodrich; children: Sandra, Daniel III, Tanya. BA, Stanford U., 1952, MD, 1955. Diplomate Am. Bd. Ob-Gyn. (examiner 1975-95, bd. dirs., dir. subspecialty divsn. reproductive endocrinology 1985-89, pres. 1986-90, chmn. 1990-94). Intern L.A. County Harbor Gen. Hosp., Torrance, 1955-56; resident in internal medicine Bellevue Hosp., N.Y.C., 1956-57; resident in ob-gyn. UCLA-Harbor Gen. Hosp., Torrance, 1959-63; rsch. fellow Univ. Hosp., Uppsala, Sweden, 1961-62; from asst. prof. to assoc. prof. dept. ob-gyn. UCLA Sch. Medicine, 1963-69; prof. U. So. Calif., L.A., 1969—, assoc. chmn. dept., 1972-78, chmn. dept. ob/gyn., 1978—. Editor-in-chief Contraception, 1969—; editor Jour. Reproductive Medicine, 1982—, Year Book of Obstetrics and Gynecology, 1987—, Year Book of Infertility, 1989-96; adv. com. Core Jours. in Ob-gyn., 1982—; mem. editl. bd. New Trends in Gynecology and Obstetrics, 1998—. Capt. USAF, 1957-59. Recipient Lester T. Hibbard award U. So. Calif., L.A., 1983, Joseph Bolivar DeLee Humanitarian award Chgo. Lying-In Hosp., 1985, Arthur and Edith Wippman Sci. Rsch. award Planned Parenthood Fedn. Am., 1992, Disting. Scientist award Soc. Gynecologic Investigation, 1994. Mem. Am. Gyn-Ob Soc., Am. Soc. Reproductive Medicine, Am. Coll. Obstetricians and Gynecologists, Am. Fedn. Clin. Rsch., Endocrine Soc., Soc. for Gynecologic Investigation (pres. 1985-86), L.A. Ob-Gyn. Soc. (v.p. 1984-85, pres. 1985-86), Assn. Profs. Gynecology and Obstetrics (exec. coun. 1982-85), Pacific Coast Fertility Soc. (pres. 1973-74), Salerni Collegium, L.A. Athletic Club, Phi Beta Kappa, Alpha Omega Alpha. Avocations: tennis, fishing. Office: U So Calif 1240 N Mission Rd Los Angeles CA 90033-1019 E-mail: mishell@hsc.usc.edu

MISHKIN, PAUL J. lawyer, educator; b. Trenton, N.J., Jan. 1, 1927; s. Mark Mordecai and Bella (Dworetsky) M.; m. Mildred Brofman Westover; 1 child, Jonathan Mills Westover. AB, Columbia U., 1947, JD, 1950; MA (hon.), U. Pa., 1971. Bar: N.Y. State bar 1950, U.S. Supreme Ct. bar 1958. Mem. faculty Law Sch. U. Pa., Phila., 1950-72; prof. law U. Calif., Berkeley, 1972-75, Emanuel S. Heller prof., 1975—. Cons. City of Phila., 1953; reporter study div. jurisdiction between state and fed. cts. Am. Law Inst., 1960-65; mem. faculty Salzburg Seminar in Am. Studies, 1974; Charles Inglis Thompson guest prof. U. Colo., 1975; John Randolph Tucker lectr., 1978, Owen J. Roberts Meml. lectr., 1982; vis. fellow Wolfson Coll., Cambridge U., 1984; vis. prof. Duke U. Law Sch., 1989. Author: (with Morris) On Law in Courts, 1965, (with others) Federal Courts and the Federal System, 2d edit, 1973, 3d edit, 1988; contbr. articles to profl. jours. Trustee Jewish Publ. Soc. Am., 1966-75; mem. permanent com. Oliver Wendell Holmes Devise, 1979-87. With USNR 1945-46. Rockefeller Found. rsch. grantee, 1956; Center for Advanced Study in Behavioral Scis. fellow, 1964-65; recipient Russell Prize for Excellence in Teaching, 1996. Fellow Am. Acad. Arts Scis., Am. Bar Found.; mem. Am. Law Inst., Order of Coif, Phi Beta Kappa. Home: 91 Stonewall Rd Berkeley CA 94705-1414 Office: U Calif Sch Law Boalt Hall Berkeley CA 94720

MISHLER, WILLIAM, II, political science educator; b. Miami, Fla., Oct. 14, 1947; s. William Thomas Earle and Marie Katheryn (Schmitz) M. BA, Stetson U., 1969; MA, Duke U., 1972, PhD, 1973. Asst. prof. Duke U., Durham, N.C., 1972-78; assoc. prof. SUNY, Buffalo, 1978-82, prof., chmn., 1984-86; dir. polit. sci. program NSF, Washington, 1982-84; prof., chmn. U. S.C., Columbia, 1986-89, prof., 1989-97, James F. and Maude B. Byrnes prof. govt., 1995-97; prof., head dept. polit. sci. U. Ariz., Tucson, 1997—. Vis. prof. U. Strathclyde, Glasgow, Scotland, 1976-77; vis. scientist, dir. polit. sci. program NSF, Washington, 1990-91. Author: Influence in Parliament, Political Participation in Canada, Representative Democracy in the Canadian Provinces, Resurgence of Conservatism, Controversies in Political Economy, Democracy and its Alternatives; mem. editl. bds. Jour. Politics, 1982 88, Legis. Studies Quar., 1988 91, 99 , Electoral Studies, 1998—. Capt. U.S. Army, 1972. Mem. Am. Polit. Sci. Assn., So. Polit. Sci. Assn., Midwest Polit. Sci. Assn., Can. Polit. Sci. Assn., Internat. Studies Assn., Assn. Can. Studies (U.S. chpt.). Office: U Ariz Dept Polit Sci Tucson AZ 85721-0001 E-mail: mishler@u.arizona.edu

MISRACH, RICHARD LAURENCE, photographer; b. L.A., July 11, 1949; s. Robert Laskin and Lucille (Gardner) M.; m. Debra Bloomfield, Jan. 18, 1981 (div. 1987); 1 son, Jacob Luke; m. Myriam Weisang, Apr. 17, 1989. AB in Psychology, U. Calif., Berkeley, 1971. Instr. Assoc. Students Studio, U. Calif., Berkeley, 1971-77; vis. lectr. U. Calif.-Berkeley, 1982; lectr. U. Calif.-Santa Barbara, 1984. Juror Nat. Endowment Arts, 1986; lectr. Calif. Inst. for Arts, 1990. Author: The Sky Book, arena edits., 2000; exhbns. include Whitney Biennial, 1981, 91, Musèe d'Art Moderne, Paris, 1979, Mus. Modern Art, N.Y.C., 1978, Grapestake Gallery, San Francisco, 1979, 81, Young-Hoffman Gallery, Chgo., 1980, Oakland Mus., 1982, 87, San Franciso Mus. Modern Art, 1983, Centre Georges Pompidou, Paris, 1983, L.A. County Mus. Art, 1984, Fraenkel Gallery, San Francsico, 1985, 89, 91, 95, 97, 99, Min Gallery, Tokyo, 1975-87, Univ. Art Mus., Berkeley, Curt Marcus Gallery, 1995, 96, 97, 2000, James Danziger Gallery, 1995, Robert Mann Gallery, N.Y., 1999, Melbourne Internat. Festival, Australia, 1995, G. Gibson Gallery, 2000, High Mus. Art, Atlanta, 2000, others; one person exhbns. at Art Inst. Chgo., 1988, Milw. Art Mus., 1988, Carpenter Ctr., Harvard U., 1988, Fotomann, Inc., N.Y., 1989, 91, Photographers Gallery, 1990, Parco Gallery, Tokyo, 1990, Arles Festival, France, 1990, Jan Kesner Gallery, 1990, 91, 94, 2000, Houston Mus. Fine Arts, 1996, Ctr. Creative Photography, Tucson, 1996, Mus. Contemporary Art, Chgo., 1997, Contemporary Mus. of Art Art, Hawaii, 1997, San Jose Mus. of Art, 1998, Diputacion de Granada, Spain, 1999; art commn. cover Time mag., July 4, 1988; books include Telegraph 3 A.M., 1974, Grapestake Gallery, 1979, (A Photographic Book), 1979, Hawaii portfolio, 1980, Graecism dye-transfer portfolio, 1982, Desert Cantos, 1987, (Internat. Ctr. of Photography award 1988), Bravo 20: The Bombing of the American West, 1990 (Pen Ctr. U.S. A. West award for nonfiction 1991), Richard Misrach, Minn. Gallery, 1988, Violent Legacies, Aperture, 1992, Crimes and Splendors, 1996, Cantos del Desierto, Di putacion de Granada, 1999, The Ski Book Carena Editions, 2000. Guggenheim fellow, 1978; Ferguson grantee, 1976; NEA grantee, 1973, 77, 84, 92; AT&T commn., 1979; Eureka fellow, 1991; recipient Koret Israel prize, 1992.

MISSETT, JUDI SHEPPARD, dancer, jazzercise company executive; b. Iowa; BA in Theater, Radio/TV, Northwestern U., Chgo., 1966. Profl. dancer, Chgo., 1966-77; jazzercise instr., choreographer, tchr. Calif., 1977—; pres. worldwide dance-fitness franchise orgn. Jazzercise, Inc., Carlsbad; prin. JM TV Prodns.; prin. mail-order catalog bus. Jazzertogs. Instr. convs., children's fitness progs. Author: (comprehensive nutrition prog.) The Jazzercise Know More Diet; author weekly fitness column for Los Angeles Times Syndicate; performer, prodr. home exercise videos. Mem. Calif. Gov.'s Coun. on Phys. Fitness & Sports; bd. dirs. San Diego Inner-City Games; contbr. millions of dollars for charities by leading spl., large-scale workout classes. Recognized for contbns. to growth and advancement of fitness industry by Pres. Reagan in his White House Conf. on Women in Bus., 1986, Aerobics and Fitness Assn. Am., Am. Coun. on Exercise, Pres.' Coun. on Phys. Fitness & Sports; named Entrepreneur of Year, Working Woman Mag., 1988; recipient Lifetime Achievement award Internat. Assn. Fitness Profls., 1991, Women Who Mean Bus. award San Diego Bus. Jour., 1995, A Woman of Accomplishment award Soroptimist Internat. of San Diego, 1996; inducted into Internat. Assn. Fitness Profls. Hall of Fame, 1992. Mem. Nat. Fitness Leaders Assn. (exec. dir., Charles Bucher Meml. award 1996). Office: Jazzercise Inc 2460 Impala Dr Carlsbad CA 92008-7226

MITCHELL, BRIANE NELSON, lawyer; b. Seattle, July 4, 1953; s. Robert Max and Frances Marie (Nelson) M.; m. Suzanne Harmatz; children: Brianne Nelson, Brittany Suzanne. AB, Columbia U., 1975; JD, U. Idaho, 1978. Law clk. U.S. Ct. Appeals (9th cir.), 1978-80; assoc. Debevoise & Plimpton, N.Y.C., 1980-84, Paul, Hastings, Janofsky & Walker, L.A., 1984-86, ptnr., 1986-93; with McCambridge, Deixler & Marmaro, L.A., 1994-95; ptnr. Shapiro, Mitchell & Dupont LLP, Santa Monica, 1996-2000, Manatt, Phelps & Phillips LLP, L.A., 2000—. Mem. ABA, Idaho Bar Assn., N.Y. State Bar Assn., Calif. Bar Assn. Office: Manatt Phelps & Phillips LLP 11355 W Olympic Blvd Los Angeles CA 90064-1614 E-mail: bnmitchell@manatt.com

MITCHELL, BRUCE TYSON, lawyer; b. San Francisco, Nov. 6, 1928; s. John Robert and Lorraine C. (Tyson) M.; m. Adrienne Means Hiscox, Oct. 14, 1951; 1 son, Mark Means. AB with great distinction, Stanford U., 1949, JD, 1951. Bar: Calif. 1952, U.S. Dist. Ct. (no. dist.) Calif 1952, U.S. Ct. Appeals (9th cir.) 1952, U.S. Supreme Ct. 1971. Estate adminstr. Crocker Nat. Bank, San Francisco, 1955-57; atty. Utah Internat. Inc., San Francisco, 1957-87, sec., 1974-87, sr. counsel, 1961-87. Mem. non-securities panel arbitrators N.Y. Stock Exch., Pacific Stock Exchange, NASD Bd. Arbitrators. Chmn. San Mateo County Rep. Cen. Com., 1964-70; mem. Calif. Rep. Central Com., 1964-74, 77-83; alt. del. Rep. Nat. Conv., 1968; co-chmn. San Mateo (Calif.) County Pres. Ford Com., 1976; mem. bd. visitors sch. law Stanford U., 1980-83; exec. v.p., bd. dirs. San Francisco Jr. C. of C., 1961; bd. dirs. No. Calif. chpt. Arthritis Found., 1972-85, 1987-92, St. Francis Hosp. Found., San Francisco, 1992-98, 99—, hon. dir., 1998-99—. Lt. (j.g.) USNR, 1952-55, Japan. Mem. ABA, Calif. Bar Assn., San Francisco Bar Assn., Am. Judicature Soc., Am. Soc. Corp. Secs. (v.p. 1976-77, dir. 1976-79), Assn. Former Intelligence Officers, Commonwealth Club of Calif. (pres. San Francisco 1973), Stanford Assocs., Pacific Union Club, Olympic Club, Capitol Hill Club, Travelers Century Club, Masons. Congregationalist. Home: 165 Redwood Dr Hillsborough CA 94010-6971 Office: 225 Bush St Fl 16 San Francisco CA 94104-4213

MITCHELL, DAVID WALKER, lawyer; b. Oakland, Calif., Nov. 11, 1935; s. Theodore Boyd and Helen Louise (Walker) M.; m. Carolyn Hilliard Graves, July 29, 1961; children: Sarah, Betsy. AB in History, Stanford U., 1957; JD, Harvard U., 1960. Bar: Calif. 1961. Assoc. Kindel & Anderson, L.A., 1961-65, Weir, Hopkins, Donovan, San Jose, Calif., 1965-68; ptnr. Hopkins, Mitchell & Carley, San Jose, 1968-87, McCutchen, Doyle, Brown & Enersen, San Jose, 1987-93, Hoge, Fenton, Jones & Appel, San Jose, 1993-2000, of counsel, 2001—. Bd. dirs. Peninsula Open Space Trust, Menlo Park, Calif., 1982—, pres., 1984-92; bd. dirs. Cmty. Found. Silicon Valley., San Jose, 1977-94, 99—; chair bd. trustees United Way Santa Clara County, 1983-85. Fellow Am. Bar Found., Am. Leadership Forum (sr.); mem. Santa Clara County Bar Assn. (trustee 1972-75), San Jose C. of C. (bd. dirs. 1975-80). Mem. United Ch. of Christ. Avocations: music, hiking. Office: Hoge Fenton Jones Appel 60 S Market St Ste 1400 San Jose CA 95113-2396 E-mail: dwm@hogefenton.com

MITCHELL, HARRY E. state legislator, former mayor, educator; b. Tempe, July 18, 1940; s. Harry Casey and Irene Gladys (Childres) M.; m. Marianne Prevratil, May 5, 1962; children: Amy, Mark. BA, Ariz. State U., 1962, MPA, 1981. Tchr. Tempe (Ariz.) H.S., 1964—. Councilman City of Tempe, 1970-76, vice mayor, 1976-78, mayor, 1978—; mem. Ariz. State Senate. Bd. dirs. Tempe Sister City; trustee Tempe St. Lukes Hosp., Rio Salado Devel. Dist.; state rep. Sister Cities Internat., Washington; mem. Ariz. State U. Liberal Arts Alumni Adv. Bd., Adv. Council Ctr. Pub. Affairs, Ariz. Commn. Post Secondary Edn.; mem. Nat. League Cities Resolutions Com.; exec. com. League Ariz. Cities; bd. dirs. Ariz. Mcpl. Water Users. Recipient Disting. Svc. award Tempe Jaycees, Pub. Programs Disting. Achievement award, Ariz. State U. Mem. Ariz. State U. Alumni Bd. (chmn.), Ariz. State U. Advanced Pub. Exec. Program. Democrat. Roman Catholic. Office: Ariz Senate 1700 W Washington St Phoenix AZ 85007-2812

MITCHELL, JOHN HENDERSON, management consultant, retired career officer; b. Atlanta, Sept. 9, 1933; s. William Lloyd and Jessie (Henderson) M.; m. Joan Ann Cameron, Apr. 8, 1961; children: John Cameron, Christopher Lloyd, Colin MacKenzie. BABA, St. Bonaventure U., 1956, PhD in Sci., 1991; MA in Pub. Adminstrn., Shippensburg State U., 1973. Commd. 2nd lt. U.S. Army, 1956, advanced through grades to maj. gen., 1982, comdr. 8th Bn., 6th Arty., 1st Inf. divsn. Vietnam, 1968; chief officer assignments Field Arty. br. Officer Pers. Directorate, U.S. Army, Washington; chief of staff 8th divsn. U.S. Army, 1973-75, asst. dept. chief of staff for personnel, Hdqrs. U.S. Army Europe and 7th Army Germany, 1975-77, comdr. Arty. divsn., chief of staff 1st Inf. divsn. Ft. Riley, Kans., 1977-79, comdr., Field Command, Def. Nuclear Agy. Kirtland AFB, N.Mex., 1979-81, dir. Human Resources Devel. Office, dept. chief staff for pers. Washington; U.S. comdr. Berlin, 1984-88; ret., 1989; pres. Intersys., Inc., Englewood, Colo., 1989-94, Pease, Orr, Mitchell Enterprises, Colorado Springs, 1994-97; chmn. Berlin Sculpture Fund, Denver, 1997—. Bd. dirs. Nat. Safety Coun., 1982-84. Decorated D.S.M. with oak leaf cluster, Legion of Merit with oak leaf cluster, D.F.C. with oak leaf cluster, Bronze Star with oak leaf cluster and V., Air medals. Mem. Assn. U.S. Army, VFW, Army Navy Club, Army War Coll. Alumni, Soc. of First Inf. Div. Republican. Roman Catholic. Avocations: tennis, history, reading. Home: 375 Hidden Creek Dr Colorado Springs CO 80906-4386

MITCHELL, REGINALD EUGENE, mechanical engineering educator; b. Houston, May 16, 1947; s. Clifford Eugene and Juanita Beatrice (Thomas) M.; 1 child, Erika Gene; m. Shirley Ann Myers, Nov. 9, 1990. BS in Chem. Engring., U. Denver, 1968; MS in Chem. Engring., N.J. Inst. Tech., Newark, 1970; ScD in Chem. Engring., MIT, 1975. Mem. tech. staff Sandia Nat. Labs., Livermore, Calif., 1975-89, disting. mem. tech. staff, 1989-91; assoc. prof. mech. engring. dept. Stanford (Calif.) U., 1991—. Recipient Outstanding Tchr. award Tau Beta Pi, 1994. Mem. Nat. Orgn. Black Chemists and Chem. Engrs. (exec. bd., chair western region, Percy Julian award 1987), Combustion Inst., Sigma Xi. Avocations: board games, card games, tennis. Home: 6143 Viewcrest Dr Oakland CA 94619-3728 Office: Stanford U Mech Engring Dept Bldg 520 Rm 520C Stanford CA 94305-3032 E-mail: reggie@navier.stanford.edu

MITCHELL, TERENCE EDWARD, materials scientist; b. Haywards Heath, Sussex, Eng., May 18, 1937; came to U.S., 1963, naturalized, 1978; s. Thomas Frank and Dorothy Elizabeth (Perrin) M.; m. Marion Wyatt, Dec. 5, 1959; children: Robin Norman, Jeremy Neil. BA, St. Catharine's Coll., Cambridge (Eng.) U., 1958, MA, PhD in Physics, St. Catharine's Coll., Cambridge (Eng.) U., 1962; ScD, U. Cambridge, 1994. Research fellow Cavendish Lab., Cambridge, 1962-63; asst. prof. metallurgy Case Inst. Tech., 1963-66; assoc. prof. Case Western Res. U., 1966-75, prof., 1975-87, adj. prof., 1987—, chmn. dept., 1983-86, dir. high voltage electron microscopy facility, 1970-82, co-dir. materials research lab., 1982-83; vis. scientist NASA at Ames Lab., Stanford U. and Electric Power Research Inst., Palo Alto, Calif., 1975-76; scientist Ctr. Materials Sci. Los Alamos (N.Mex.) Nat. Lab., 1987—, lab fellow, 1991—; lab fellows chair Los Alamos (N.Mex.) Nat. Lab., 1993-95. Chmn. steering com. Electron Microscopy Ctr. Argonne (Ill.) Nat. Lab., 1979-83; cons. in field; mem. vis. com. metals and ceramics div. Oak Ridge Lab., 1987-91; vis. com. solid state scis. div. Ames Lab., 1987-89; sci. adv. com. Sci. and Tech. Ctr. for Superconductivity, 1989-93. Materials sci. editor Microscopy Rsch. and Technique, 1986—; sr. editor North Am., 1994—; contbr. 400 articles to profl. jours. Pres. Cleve. Ethical Soc., 1970-72; bd. dirs Am. Ethical Union, 1972-74; steward Los Alamos Unitarian Ch., 1992-94; mem. policy com. Univ. Materials Coun., 1986-89; mem. policy com. Argonne Electron Microscopy Steering Com., chmn. 1978-82. Electric Power Research Inst. fellow, 1975-76; NSF grantee, 1966-88; Dept. Energy grantee, 1970-86, 87—; NIH grantee, 1969-72; NASA grantee, 1974-77, 81-87; USAF Office Sci. Research grantee, 1974-85; U.S. Army Research Office grantee, 1970-75, 79-83, EPRI grantee, 1986-89; spl. issue in his honor Philos. Mag. A, Sept. 1998. Fellow Am. Soc. Metals, Am. Phys. Soc., Am. Ceramics Soc. (assoc. editor jour. 1989—, v.p. 1999-2000), Minerals, Metals & Materials Soc., Los Alamos Nat. Lab.; mem. Japan Soc. Promotion of Sci., Electron Microscopy Soc. Am. (program chmn. 1981-82, dir. 1984-86, pres.-elect 1994, pres. 1995, past pres. 1996), Materials Rsch. Soc., Soc. Francaise de Microscopie Electronique (sci. com. 1982-90). Office: Los Alamos Nat Lab Ctr Materials Sci Ms # K-765 Los Alamos NM 87545-0001 E-mail: temitchell@lanl.gov

MITCHELL, THEODORE REED, academic administrator; b. San Rafael, Calif., Jan. 29, 1956; s. Theodore Robert and Genevieve Dolores (Doose) M.; m. Christine M. Beckman, July 8, 1995; 1 child, Caroline Mitchell Beckman. BA, Stanford U., 1978, MA, 1980, PhD, 1983. Asst. prof. Dartmouth Coll., Hanover, N.H., 1981-86, assoc. prof., 1986-87, chair dept. edn., 1987-91; dep. to pres. and provost Stanford U., 1991-92; dean Sch. Edn. and Info. Studies UCLA, 1992-96, vice chancellor, 1996-98; v.p. for edn. and strategic initiatives The J. Paul Getty Trust, L.A., 1998-99; pres. Occidental Coll., L.A., 1999—. Trustee Stanford U., 1985-90, Thetford (Vt.) Acad., 1989-91; bd. dirs. L.A. Edn. Partnership, L.E.A.R.N., L.A. Author: Political Education, 1985, Sociology of Education, 1998. Bd. dirs. Children Now, Oakland, Calif., 1994—, Gateway Learning Corp., 1996—. Office: Occidental Coll Office President Los Angeles CA 90041

MITCHELL, THOMAS, editor; m. Jo Mitchell; children: Jeffery, Jay. Grad., Colo. State U. City editor Mid-Cities Daily News, Hurst, Tex.; editor Lewisville (Tex.) Daily Leader; city editor Shreveport (La.) Jour.; asst. city editor The Miami News; mng. editor Las Vegas Rev. Jour., 1989-92, editor, 1992—. Recipient First place prize for editl. writing Best of the West journalism competition, 1990, First place prize Nev. Press Assn., 1995. Mem. Am. Soc. Newspaper Editors, Investigative Reporters and Editors. Office: 1111 W Bonanza Rd Las Vegas NV 89106-3545

MITRA, SANJIT KUMAR, electrical and computer engineering educator; b. Calcutta, West Bengal, India, Nov. 26, 1935; came to U.S., 1958; MS in Tech., U. Calcutta, 1956; MS, U. Calif., Berkeley, 1960, PhD, 1962; D of Tech. (hon.), Tampere (Finland) U., 1987; Academician, Acad. Finland, 2000. Asst. engr. Indian Statis. Inst., Calcutta, 1956-58; from teaching asst. to assoc. Univ. Calif., Berkeley, 1958-62; asst. prof. Cornell U., Ithaca, N.Y., 1962-65; mem. tech. staff Bell Telephone Labs., Holmdel, N.J., 1965-67; prof. U. Calif., Davis, 1967-77, prof. elec. and computer engring. Santa Barbara, 1977—, chmn. dept. elec. and computer engring., 1979-82; dir. Ctr. for Info. Processing Rsch., 1993-96. Cons. Lawrence Livermore (Calif.) Nat. Lab., 1974-95; cons. editor Van Nostrand Reinhold Co., N.Y.C., 1977-88; mem. adv. bd. Coll. Engring. Rice U., Houston, 1986-89; mem. adv. coun. Rsch. Inst. for Math. and Computing Sci., U. Groningen, The Netherlands, 1995—; mem. adv. bd. Internat. Signal Processing Ctr., Tampere U. of Tech., Finland, 1997—; external assessor Faculty of Engring., U. Putra Malaysia, Serdang, 1997—. Author: Analysis and Synthesis of Linear Active Networks, 1969, Digital and Analog Integrated Circuits, 1980; co-editor: Modern Filter Theory and Design, 1973, Two-Dimensional Digital Signal Processing, 1978, Miniaturized and Integrated Filters, 1989, Multidimensional Processing of Video Signals, 1992, Handbook for Digital Signal Processing, 1993, Digital Signal Processing: A Computer-Based Approach, 1997, 2d edit., 2000, Nonuniform Discrete Fourier Transform and Its Signal Processing Applications, 1998, Digital Signal Processing Laboratory Using MATLAB, 1999, Nonlinear Image Processing, 2000. Named Disting. Fulbright Prof., Coun. for Internat. Exch. of Scholars, 1984, 86, 88, Disting. Sr. Scientist, Humboldt Found., 1989, Mac Van Valkenburg award, IEEE Circuits & Sys. Soc., 1999, Bleinlein-Browne-Willans premium IEE, 2000. Fellow AAAS, IEEE (Edn. award Crcts. and Systems Soc. 1988, disting. lectr. Crcts. and Systems Soc. 1991-96, Tech. achievement award Signal Processing Soc. 1996, Golden Jubilee medal 1999, Millennium medal 2000), Internat. Soc. Optical Engring.; mem. Am. Soc. for Engring. Edn. (F.E. Terman award 1973, AT&T Found. award 1985), European Assn. for Signal Processing, Acad. of Finland. Achievements include patents for two-port newtorks for realizing transfer functions; non-reciprocal wave translating device; discrete cosine transform-based image coding and decoding method; method and apparatus for multipath channel shaping; method and apparatus for multipath channel shaping. Office: Univ Calif Dept Elec Computer Eng Santa Barbara CA 93106

MITTERMILLER, JAMES JOSEPH, lawyer; b. Washington, Apr. 13, 1953; s. Jack and Alice Marie (Froeba) M.; m. Elizabeth Gaillard Simons, June 23, 1979; children: Samuel Stoney, Paul Andrew, Laurie Alice, Claire Mary. Student, U. Heidelberg, 1973-74; BA, Claremont McKenna Coll., 1975; JD, U. Calif. Berkeley, 1978. Bar: Calif., U.S. Dist. Ct. (so., ctrl. and ea. dists.) Calif., U.S. Ct. Appeals (9th cir.), U.S. Supreme Ct. Assoc. Sheppard, Mullin, Richter & Hampton, L.A., 1978-86, ptnr., 1986—. Panelist Calif. Continuing Edn. of Bar, L.A. and San Diego, 1984—. Dir. Legal Aid Soc. of San Diego, 1990—, pres., 1998-2000. Recipient Wiley Manuel Pro Bono award Calif. State Bar, 1992, 2001. Mem. Assn. Bus. Trial Lawyers (bd. dirs. 1998-2001), Am. Inns of Ct., Claremont McKenna Coll. Alumni Assn. San Diego (bd. dirs.). Avocations: swimming, surfing. Office: Sheppard Mullin Richter & Hampton 501 W Broadway Fl 19 San Diego CA 92101-3536

MITZNER, KENNETH MARTIN, electrical engineering consultant; b. Bklyn., May 7, 1938; s. Louis Bernard and Dora (Sandler) M.; m. Ruth Maria Osorio, Dec. 26, 1968; children: Camille Lorena Mitzner Zeiter, Esther Jeannette Mitzner Lin, Sharon Michelle Mitzner Mentkowski. BS, MIT, 1958; MS, Calif. Inst. Tech., 1959, PhD, 1964. Mem. tech. staff Hughes Aircraft, Malibu, Calif., 1959-64; prin. engr. B-2 divsn. Northrop Corp., Pico Rivera, 1964-94; owner Mitzner Sci. and Tech., Oceanside, 1995—. Instr. U. Calif., Santa Barbara, 1964-65; lectr. in field. Author: (handbook) Demonstrations Against Abortion & Death Selection, 1970; contbr. articles to profl. jours. Pres. Mobilization for the Unnamed, Oceanside, Calif., 1970—; bd. dirs. Ams. United for Life, 1971-94, Nat. Right to Life Com., 1980-81, Jewish Life Issues Com., Solana Beach, 1983—; sec. Calif. Pro Life Coun., Sacramento, 1972; mem. L.A. County Select Citizens Com. on Life Support Policies, L.A., 1983-85 Named Patron of Life Calif. Pro Life Coun., 1976, Pres's award, 1979; Howard Hughes fellow, 1959-64; grantee Fullbright Found., Govt. Italy, 1961-62. Fellow IEEE; mem. U.S. Nat. Commn. Internat. Union Radio Sci. (del. to 20th gen. assembly), Electromagnetics Acad. Avocations: historic research, stamp collecting.

MIURA, ROBERT MITSURU, mathematician, researcher, educator; b. Selma, Calif., Sept. 12, 1938; emigrated to Can., 1975; s. Richard Katsuki and Frances Yoneko Miura; m. Kathryn Bannai; children: Derek Katsuki, Brian Robert, Jared Bannai Nagae, Sean Takeo. BS, U. Calif.-Berkeley, 1960, MS, 1962; MA, Princeton U., 1964, PhD, 1966. Rsch. assoc. Princeton U. Plasma Physics Lab., 1965-67; assoc. rsch. scientist Courant Inst. Math. Sci., N.Y.C., 1967-68; asst. prof. math. NYU, 1968-71; assoc. prof. math. Vanderbilt U., 1971-75, U. B.C., Vancouver, B.C., Can., 1975-78, prof. Can., 1978—. Chmn. joint com. on math. in life scis. Am. Math. Soc.-Soc. Indsl. and Applied Math., 1981-84; bd. dirs. Soc. for Math. Biology, 1995-98. Editor: Backlund Transformations, 1976, Nonlinear Phenomena in Physics and Biology, 1981, Some Mathematical Questions in Biology-Neurobiology, 1982, Muscle Physiology, 1986, DNA Sequence Analysis, 1986, Plant Biology, 1986; assoc. editor Can. Applied Math. Quar.; adv. bd. Jour. Math. Biology, 1982-99; co-editor-in-chief Methods and Applications of Analysis, 1992-99, Analysis and Applications; mem. editl. bd. Integrative Neurosci.; contbr. articles to profl. jours. Mem. steering com. Ctr. Math. Rsch., U. Montreal, 1990-94. John Simon Guggenheim fellow, 1980-81; U. B.C. hon. Killam fellow, 1980-81 Fellow Royal Soc. Can.; mem. AAAS (nominating com., math. sect.), Am. Math. Soc., Soc. Indsl. and Applied Math., Can. Applied Indsl. Math. Soc., Can. Math. Soc. (internat. affairs com.), Soc. Math. Biology, Pacific Inst. Math. Sci. (interim exec. bd. 1996), Sigma Xi. Office: U BC Dept Math 1984 Mathematics Rd Vancouver BC V6T 1Z2 Canada V6T 1Z2

MIYAHIRA, NEAL, state budget and finance administrator; Dir. Hawaii Budget & Fin. Dept., Honolulu. Office: Hawaii Budget & Fin Dept PO Box 150 Honolulu HI 96810-0150

MIYASAKI, GEORGE JOJI, artist; b. Kalopa, Hawaii, Mar. 24, 1935; BFA, Calif. Coll. Arts and Crafts, 1957, MFA, 1958. Asst. prof. art Calif. Coll. Arts and Crafts, Oakland, 1958-64; mem. faculty dept. art U. Calif., Berkeley, 1964-94, prof. emeritus. John Hay Whitney fellow, 1957-58; Tamarind printing fellow, 1961; Guggenheim fellow, 1963-64; Nat. Endowment for Arts fellow, 1980-81, 85-86. Mem. NAD. Home: 2844 Forest Ave Berkeley CA 94705-1309

MIYATA, KEIJIRO, culinary arts educator; b. Tokyo, Mar. 8, 1951; came to U.S., 1967; s. Yataro Miyata and Hekkiken (Liu) Choy; m. Connie Joyce Nelson, Mar. 8, 1976; children: Michelle, Kelly, Adam. Assoc. in Occupational Study, Culinary Inst. Am., Hyde Park, N.Y., 1972, cert. of nutrition, 1991; cert., Seattle Wine Sch., 1991. Cert. exec. chef; cert. culinary educator. Garde mgr. Mid-Pacific Country Club, Kailua, Hawaii, 1972; working chef Waikiki Yacht Club, Honolulu, 1972-74, Sagano Japanese Restaurant, New Rochelle, N.Y., 1974-76; asst. pastry chef Rye Town (N.Y.) Hilton Hotel, 1976-77; working chef The Explorer, Everett, Wash., 1977-79; exec. chef Holiday Inn, Everett, 1979-81, Mill Creek (Wash.) Country Club, 1981; culinary art instr. Everett Community Coll., 1981-85, North Seattle (Wash.) Community Coll., 1985-90, Seattle Cen. Community Coll., 1990—. Cons. Chalon Corp., Redmond, Wash., Chiang-Mai Restaurant, Mukilteo, Wash., 1988, Holiday Inn Crown Plaza, Seattle, Satsuma Japanese Restaurant, 1996. Participant Nagano Winter Olympic Ice Sculpture Festival, Karuizawa, Japan, 1998. Recipient Gold awards Am. Culinary Fedn., Oreg. State Chef's Assn., Portland, 1983, Gold and Bronze medals World Culinary Olympic, Frankfurt, Germany, 1984, 88, Grand Champion award U.S. Nat. Ice Carving Contest, N.Y.C., 1986, 2d place award All Japan Ice Carving Assn., Asahikawa, 1988, Ednl. Excellence award Oreg. and Wash. Community Coll. Couns. Wash. Fedn. of Tchrs. & Am. Fedn. of Tchrs., AFL-CIO, 1988, 89; ACF Seafood Challenge State finalist, Charlotte, N.C., 1989, New Orleans, 1990; 1st place Pacific Rim Invitational World Ice Sculpting Classic, 1989; 1st place Seymour Ice Sculpting Competition, 1991; 1st place 3d Ann. Internat. Ice Sculpting Competition, Lake Louise, Alta., Can., 1993, Award of Excellence Wash. Fedn. Tchrs./Am. Fedn. Tchrs./AFL-CIO, 1993, 1st place Wash. State Seafood Festival Recipe Contest, Shelton, Wash., 1993, Grand Cahmpion, 1994, 1st place ICE ART'94 Ice Sculpting Competition, Fairbanks, Alaska, 1994, Most Artistic award AsahiKawa Internat. Ice Sculpting Competition, 1996, 1st place IceCarver's Choice, People's Choice Awards--8th Internat. Ice Carving Championship, Anchorage, Alaska, 1997; selected as Snow Sculpting Team Mem. of Sister City of Portland, Internat. Snow Sculpting Competition, Sapporo, Japan, 1997; participant Nagano Winter Olympic Ice Sculpture Festival, Karuizawa, Japan, 1998, 1st place People's Choice awards 6th annual Internat. Ice Sculpting competition, Lake Louise, Alberta, Canada, 1999, NICA (Natl. Ice Carving Assn.), Gold Medal Ice Carver's Choice Awd., People's awd., Crystal Gall. of Ice, Internatl. Carving Comp., Alaska, 1999, 1st Place People's Choice Awards--7th Annual Internat. Ice Sculpting Competition, Lake Louise, Alberta, Canada, 2000, 2d Place Hokkaido Newspaper award Asahikawa Internat. Ice Sculpting competition, 2000. Mem. Wash. State Chefs Assn. (bd. dirs. 1982, 83, 86, 87, 88, cert. chmn. 1986-92, Chef of Yr. 1986), Am. Acad. Chefs, Nat. Ice Carving Assn. Office: Seattle Ctr Cmty Coll 1701 Broadway Seattle WA 98122-2413 E-mail: KMIYAT@sccd.ctc.edu

MIZEL, LARRY A. housing construction company executive; b. 1942; married BA, U. Okla., 1964; JD, U. Denver, 1967. Chmn. bd., chmn. exec. com., dir. MDC Holdings Inc., Denver, 1972—, chmn. bd., pres., CEO, 1988—, chmn. bd., CEO. Office: MDC Holdings Inc 3600 S Yosemite St Ste 900 Denver CO 80237-1867

MIZGALA, HENRY F. physician, consultant, retired medical educator; b. Montreal, Nov. 28, 1932; s. Louis and Mary (Ropeleski) M.; m. Pauline Barbara Delaney, Oct. 26, 1957; children: Paul Stephen, Cynthia Louise, Liane Mary Mizgala Sizemore, Melanie Frances Mizgala Dressler, Nancy Elizabeth Mizgala Lewis. B.A. magna cum laude, Loyola Coll., Montreal, 1953; M.D., C.M., McGill U., 1957. Rotating intern, then resident in medicine St. Mary's Hosp., Montreal, 1957-59, asst. physician, 1963-66; resident in medicine Royal Victoria Hosp., Montreal, 1959-60; Dazian fellow cardiology Mt. Sinai Hosp., N.Y.C., 1960-61, USPHS fellow cardiology, 1961-62; resident in cardiology Montreal Gen. Hosp., 1962-63, assoc. physician, 1966-74; asst. physician, cons. cardiology Lachine (Que.) Gen. Hosp., 1964-80; cardiologist Montreal Heart Inst., also dir. CCU, 1974-80; cons. Centre Hosp. Baie des Chaleurs, Gaspe, Que., 1975-80; hon. cons. Montreal Heart Inst., 1980—; prof. medicine U. B.C., 1980-97; hon. attending med. staff, cardiologist The Vancouver (B.C.) Hosp. and Health Scis. Ctr.; cons. B.C. Cancer Agy., Vancouver, 1981—; cons. staff Univ. Hosp., U. B.C. site, 1981-94; mem. faculty McGill U. Med. Sch., Montreal, 1968-74, asso. prof. medicine, 1973-74; assoc. prof., then prof. Montreal U. Med. Sch., 1974-81; prof. medicine, head div. cardiology U. B.C., 1980-87, prof. medicine emeritus, 1998—. Mem. editl. bd. Can. Jour. Cardiol. 1988-99, Jour. Am. Coll. Cardiology, 1992-95; contbr. numerous articles to med. jours. Fellow Royal Coll. Phys. and Surg. Can., Am. Coll. Cardiology, Am. Heart Assn. (council clin. cardiology); mem. Can. Med. Assn., Can. Cardiovascular Soc. (treas. 1974-90), Que. Med. Assn., B.C. Med. Assn., B.C. and Yukon Heart and Stroke Found. (bd. dirs., sr. bd. dirs.), Alpha Omega Alpha. Office: U BC Div Cardiology Dept Med 865 W 10th Ave Vancouver BC Canada V5Z IL7 E-mail: [illegible]

MIZUGUCHI, NORMAN, state official; b. Hilo, Hawaii, May 26, 1939; m. Harriet Mizuguchi; 1 child, Reid. BS, Springfield Coll.; MS, Mich. State U.; PhD, U. Utah. Mem. state house State of Hawaii, 1974-78, state senator, 1978—, pres. state senate, 1994—; pres. Hawaiian Emporium Inc., Sundance Circle Inc.; tchr., edn. officer Dept. of Edn. Sec. Pearl city Makule Softball League; mem. Barbers Point coun., Navy League, Hawaiian Edn. Coun., Hui Kokua Kinipopo Booster Club, Japanese Am. Citizens League Honolulu, Aiea Hongwanji. Democrat. Office: Hawaiian Senate Hawaii State Capitol Rm 003 415 S Beretania St Honolulu HI 96813-2407

MLADENICH, RONALD E. publishing executive; BA in Bus. Adminstrn., U. Puget Sound, 1965. Buyer Boeing Co., Renton, Wash., 1965-68; sales/contracts Stellar Hydraulics, Sun Valley, Calif., 1968-74; circulation mgr. News Tribune, Tacoma, 1974—, transp. mgr., 1999—. Carl Burkheimer Meml. scholar N.W. Internat. Circulation Execs., 1993. Mem. Internat. Circulation Mgr. Assn. (promotions award chairperson 1986), N.W. Internat. Circulation Execs. (pres. 1984-92), Western Conf. Circulation Execs. (pres. 1985, 86). Office: News Tribune 1950 S State St Tacoma WA 98405-2817

MOAK, DAVID, geologist; BS in Geology, U. Mich., 1975; MS in Geolgoy, U. Wash., 1978, PhD in Geology, 1984. Prof. geology dept. earth scis. Montana State U., Bozeman. Contbr. articles to publications. Mem. Am. Geophys. Union (Excellence in Geophys. Edn. award 2000). Achievements include research in the evolution of the Archean continental crust of southwestern Montana and related petrogenetic processes in the middle crust. Office: Montana State U Dept Earth Scis Bozeman MT 59715

MOBERLY, LINDEN EMERY, educational administrator; b. Laramie, Wyo., Jan. 4, 1923; s. Linden E. and Ruth (Gathercole) M. BS, Coll. Emporia, 1952; MS, Kans. State Tchrs. Coll., 1954; m. Viola F. Mosher, Apr. 29, 1949. Tchr. sci., Florence, Kans., 1952-54, Concordia, Kans., 1954-56, Grand Junction, Colo., 1957-60; asst. prin. Orchard Mesa Jr. High Sch., Grand Junction, 1960-66, prin., 1967-84; field cons. Nat. Assn. Secondary Sch. Prins., 1985—. Sgt. USMC, 1941-46. Recipient Outstanding Secondary Prin. award Colo. Assn. Sch. Execs., 1978. Mem. NEA, VFW, Nat. Assn. Secondary Prins. (bd. dir. 1979-83), Colo. Edn. Assn. (bd.dir. 1968-71), Colo. North Central Assn. Colls. and Secondary Schs., Colo. Assn. Secondary Sch. Prins. (bd. dir. 1974-77), Lions, Sons of the Revolution, Marine Corps League (life), VFW (life), Masons (award of Excellence 1990). Home: 2256 Kingston Rd Grand Junction CO 81503-1221

MOCK, HENRY BYRON, lawyer, writer, consultant; b. Greenville, Tex., Feb. 1, 1911; s. Henry Byron and Ellena (Edmonds) M.; m. Mary Morris, Nov. 11, 1949. A.B., U. Ariz., 1933; J.D., Georgetown U., 1939, George Washington U., 1940. Asst. sec. to Congresswoman Isabella Greenway of Ariz., 1934-35; office mgr., legal research asst., recreation div. WPA, Washington, 1935-38, asst. atty., 1938; legal adv. President's Adv. Com. on Edn., 1938-39; asst. solicitor Dept. Interior, 1939-41; chief counsel U.S. Grazing Service, Salt Lake City, 1941-42; adminstr. region IV U.S. Bur. Land Mgmt., Colo., Utah, 1947-54, area adminstr. Idaho, Ariz., Utah, Nev., 1954-55; exec. resource cos., 1955—. Adj. prof. law U. Utah, 1979—. Contbr. profl. publs. Chmn. Dept. Interior storm relief com. Western U.S., 1949; mem. U.S. Pub. Land Law Rev. Commn., 1964-70, vice chmn., 1965-70; mem. Interior Oil Shale Com., 1964. Served pvt. to capt. with AUS, 1942-46, MTO. Mem. D.C., Va., Utah bar assns. Bar Supreme Ct. of U.S., Am., Fed. bar assn., U.S. C. of C., Bar of Ct. Mil. Appeals, Am. Inst. Mining and Metall. Engrs., Am. Soc. Range Mgmt., Am. Soc. Pub. Adminstrn. (past Utah pres.), Western Polit. Sci. Assn., Am. Forestry Assn., Pi Kappa Alpha. Clubs: Rotary (Salt Lake City), Alta (Salt Lake City). Home and Office: 900 Donner Way Apt 101 Salt Lake City UT 84108-4113

MOCK, THEODORE JAYE, accounting educator; b. Traverse City, Mich., May 28, 1941; s. Raymond Doris and Georgeann (Lardie) M.; m. Mary Jo Icenhower, Mar. 25, 1962; children— Christopher, Cameron B.S. in Math., Ohio State U., 1963, M.B.A. in Fin., 1964; Ph.D. in Bus. Adminstrn., U. Calif.-Berkeley, 1969. Dir. AIS Research Ctr. UCLA, 1969-73; dir. Ctr. Acctg. Research, Arthur Andersen Alumni prof. acctg. U. So. Calif., 1982—. Vis. prof. Norwegian Sch. Econs. and Bus., Bergen, 1988, Bond U., Gold Coast, Australia, 1990, 92, So. Cross U., Lismore, Australia, 1994; adj. prof. U. Limburg, The Netherlands, 1991—; hon. prof. Hong Kong City U., 1995-98; bd. dirs. Maastricht (The Netherlands) Acctg. Rsch. Ctr., U. Limburg, 1991—; Shaw prof. Nanyang Tech. U., Singapore, 1997, Tang Peny Yets vis. prof. Nat. U. Singapore, 2000. Author: (monographs) Risk Assessment, 1985, Internal Accounting Control (Am. Acctg. Assn. Wildman medal), 1983, Measurement and Accounting Information Criteria, 1976, Impact of Future Technology on Auditing, 1988, Auditing and Analytic Review, 1989; mem. editorial bd. Auditing: A Jour. of Practice and Theory, 1983-86, 88-93, 99—, editor, 1993-96; mem. editorial bd. The Acctg. Rev., 1972-78, Internat. Jour. Auditing, 1998—. Recipient CPA Faculty Excellence award Calif. CPA Found. for Edn. and Rsch., 1983, Collaboration award AICPA/AAA, 1998; Fulbright scholar U. Otago, Dunedin, New Zealand, 1988, U. Limburg, Maastricht, The Netherlands, 1993. Mem. Acctg., Orgns. and Soc. (editorial bd. 1978-93), Am. Acctg. Assn. (dir. rsch. 1982-84, acad. vice chmn. auditing sect. 1990-91, chair auditing sect. 1991-92). Office: U So Calif Sch Acctg Los Angeles CA 90089-0001

MOCKARY, PETER ERNEST, clinical laboratory scientist, researcher, medical writer; b. Zghorta, Lebanon, Jan. 6, 1931; came to U.S., 1953; s. Ernest Peter and Evelyn (Kaddo) M.; m. Yvette Fadlallah, Aug. 27, 1955; children: Ernest, Evelyn, Paula, Vincent, Marguerite. BA in Philosophy, Coll. des Freres, Tripoli, Lebanon, 1948; MB, Am. U. Beirut, 1950, postgrad., 1950-52. Cert. clin. lab. scientist, Calif.; cert. clin. lab. scientist Nat. Certification Agy. Chief hematology unit VA Wadsworth Med. Ctr., West Los Angeles, Calif., 1956-81; CEO Phoenicia Trading Co., 1981-88; dir. Coagulation Lab. Orthopaedic Hosp., L.A., 1988-97. Lab. supr. Westside Hosp., L.A., 1964-79; lectr. hematology UCLA, West Los Angeles, 1970-78. Pres. World Lebanese Cultural Union, L.A., 1978-79. With U.S. Army, 1954-56. Recipient outstanding performance award lab. svc. VA Wadsworth Med. Ctr., 1972-76. Republican. Roman Catholic. Avocations: billiards, reading, classical music. Home: 3103 Gilmerton Ave Los Angeles CA 90064-4319 E-mail: pemocrary@aol.com

MOCKLER, ESTHER JAYNE, state legislator; b. Jackson, Wyo., Sept. 21, 1957; d. Franklin and Nancy (Fisher) Mockler. BA in Polit. Sci., Wellesley Coll., 1980. Legal asst., 1981-84; legal adminstr., 1984-87; rschr., cons., 1987—; exec. dir. Wyo. Democratic Party, 1993-95; mem. from Dist. 44 Wyo. Senate, Cheyenne, 1992-96, mem. from Dist. 8, 1996—. Mem. Medicaid adv. coun. Dept. Health; mem. Gov.'s Coun. on Devel. Disabilities; mem. United Med. Ctr. Aux. Mem., Medicaid Advisory Council/Dept. of Health, Unified Med. Ctr. Aux., Gov. Council on Developmental Disabilities. Office: PO Box 1857 Cheyenne WY 82003-1857 E-mail: jmockler@wyoming.com

MOE, STANLEY ALLEN, architect, consultant; b. Fargo, N.D., May 28, 1914; s. Ole Arnold and Freda Emily (Pape) M.; m. Doris Lucille Anderson, July 25, 1937 (dec. 2000); children: Willa Moe Crouse, Myra Moe Galther. BArch, U. Minn., 1936; D of Engring. (hon.), U. N.D., 1993. lic. architect several states; cert. Nat. Coun. Archtl. Registration Bds. Project architect several firms in Midwest, 1936-42; project architect U.S. Army Corps Engrs., Africa, 1942-43; ptnr. H.S. Starin, Architects & Engrs., L.A., 1947-54; ptnr., gen. mgr., exec. v.p. Daniel, Mann, Johnson & Mendenall, L.A., 1954-71, corp. v.p., 1972-79; prin. Stanley A. Moe, AIA, L.A., 1979—. Dir. design of major mil. projects in Eritrea, Sudan, Egypt, Yemen for Allied Forces, 1942-43; chmn. control com. DMJM & Assocs., dir. design prototype, tng. & operational facilities Titan I Intercontinental Ballistic Missiles Program USAF, 1958-63; project dir. Space Shuttle facilities Kennedy Space Ctr., 1973; project dir. for design of aircraft maintenance complex Iranian Aircraft Industries, 1978; project mgr. for design of major med. facility program Min. of Def. and Aviation, Saudi Arabia, 1975-76; project mgr. design of Boufarik Internat. Airport, Algeria, 1983. Pres. San. Fernando Valley Young Reps., 1952, Van Nuys (Calif.) Jaycees, 1950. Recipient Disting. Svc. award for cmty. svc. Van Nuys Jaycees, 1949, Sioux award U. N.D. Alumni Assn., 1985, Trustees Soc. award U. Minn., 1992; inducted into N.D. Entrepreneur Hall of Fame, 2000. Mem. AIA (Calif. coun.), Rotary, Delta Tau Delta. Republican. Presbyterian. Avocations: world travel, hunting, fishing, historic restoration, woodworking. Home and Office: 447 S Plymouth Blvd Los Angeles CA 90020-4706

MOEHLE, JACK P. civil engineer, engineering executive; BSCE, MSCE, U. Ill., 1977, PhD, 1980. Registered civil engr., Calif. From asst. to assoc. prof. U. Calif., Berkeley, 1980-90, prof., 1990—, Roy W. Carlson Disting. prof. civil engring., vice-chair tech. svcs. civil engring., 1990-91, dir. earthquake engring. rsch. ctr., 1991—. Tech. advisor Double Deck Peer Rev. Panel, Caltrans, 1990—; mem. sci. adv. com. Nat. Ctr. Earthquake Engring. Rsch.; proposal reviewer NSF; cons. in field; bd. dirs. Calif. Univs. Rsch. Earthquake Engring., Cooperating Orgns. No. Calif. Earthquake Rsch. and Tech. Contbr. articles to profl. jours.; reviewer tech. papers. Recipient Chi Epsilon Excellence Teaching award, 1986; Regents Jr. Faculty fellow, 1981. Fellow Am. Concrete Inst. (chmn. detail and proportion earthquake resisting structural elements and systems com. 1988—, mem. various coms.); mem. ASCE (publs. sec. com. seismic effects, Huber Rsch. prize 1990), Structural Engrs. Assn. Calif. (mem. seismology com., reinforced concrete com., bd. dirs.), Earthquake Engring. Rsch. Inst. Office: U Calif Berkeley Earthquake Engring Rsch Ctr 1301 S 46th St Richmond CA 94804-4600

MOERBEEK, STANLEY LEONARD, lawyer; b. Toronto, Ont., Can., Nov. 12, 1951; came to U.S., 1953; s. John Jacob and Mary Emily Moerbeek; m. Carol Annette Mordaunt, Apr. 17, 1982; children: Sarah, Noah. BA magna cum laude, Calif. State U., Fullerton, 1974; student, U. San Diego-Sorbonne, Paris, 1977; JD, Loyola U., 1979. Bar: Calif. 1980; cert. in internat. bus. transactions, bankruptcy and bus. rehab., and civil trial practice. From law clk. to assoc. McAlpin Doonan & Seese, Covina, Calif., 1977-81; assoc. Robert L. Baker, Pasadena, 1981-82, Miller Bush & Minnott, Fullerton, 1982-83; prin. Law Office of Stanley L. Moerbeek, Fullerton, 1984—. Judge pro tem Orange County Superior Ct., Calif., 1984—; notary pub., lt. gov. 9th cir. law student divsn. ABA, 1979. Mem. Heritage Found., Washington, 1989—. Calif. Gov.'s Office scholar, 1970; recipient Plaque of Appreciation, Fullerton Kiwanis, 1983. Mem. Calif. Assn. Realtors (referral panel atty. 1985—), Orange County Bar Assn. (Coll. of Trial Advocacy 1985), Calif. C. of C., Phi Kappa Phi. Roman Catholic. Avocations: history, politics, sports. Office: 1370 N Brea Blvd Ste 210 Fullerton CA 92835-4128 E-mail: slmlaw@netzero.net

MOFFITT, DONALD EUGENE, transportation company executive; b. Terre Haute, Ind., May 22, 1932; s. James Robert and Margaret Mary (Long) M.; m. Billie Duffy, Feb. 21, 1989; 1 child, Jaime. BA, Ind. State U., 1954; postgrad., Ind. U., 1956; grad., Advanced Mgmt. Program, Harvard U., 1972. Acct. Foster Freight Lines, Indpls., 1955-56; with Consol. Freightways Inc., San Francisco, 1956-88, v.p. planning, 1961-69; v.p. fin., motor carrier subs. Consol. Freightways Corp. Del., 1969-75; v.p. fin., treas. parent co. Consol. Freightways Inc., San Francisco, 1975-81, exec. v.p. Palo Alto, Calif., 1981-86; vice chmn. parent co. bd. Consol. Freightways, Inc., Palo Alto, 1986-88; chmn., CEO Circle Express, Indpls., 1988-90; pres., CEO Consol. Freightways, Inc., Palo Alto, Calif., 1990-96; chmn., CEO Consol. Freightways, Inc. (name now CNF Transp. Inc.), Palo Alto, 1995—, also bd. dirs. Chmn. bd. dirs. all subsidiaries CNF Transport, 1990—; chmn., pres., CEO CNF Transp. Inc., 1996—. Bd. dirs. Bay Area Coun., Calif. Bus. Roundtable, Conf. Bd., Boy Scouts Am., ARC, Hoover Instn.; bd. dirs., exec. com. Hwy. Users Fedn.; bd. trustees Automotive Safety Found.; bus. adv. coun. Northwestern U. Transp. Ctr. Mem. Nat. C. of C. (vice-chmn., bd. dirs.). Office: CNF Transp Inc 3240 Hillview Ave Palo Alto CA 94304-1201

MOGEL, LEONARD HENRY, writer; b. Bklyn., Oct. 23, 1922; s. Isaac and Shirley (Goldman) M.; m. Ann Vera Levy, Oct. 23, 1949; children: Wendy Lynn, Jane Ellen. B.B.A., Coll. City N.Y., 1947. Salesman N.Y. Printing Co., N.Y.C., 1946-48; sales mgr. Pollak Printing Co., N.Y.C., 1948-52; advt. dir. Diners Club, Inc., N.Y.C., 1952-56; pub. Diners Club for Signature and Bravo mags., 1956-67; pres. Leonard Mogel Assos., Inc. (nat. advt. reps.), N.Y.C., 1952-67; prin. owner San Francisco Warriors Profl. Basketball Team, 1963-64; pres. Twenty First Century Communications Inc., N.Y.C., 1967-72; pub. Cheetah and Weight Watchers mags., 1967-75; dir. Regents Pub. Co. div. Simon & Schuster, 1960-67; advt. cons. Harvard Lampoon, 1968; pub. Nat. Lampoon, 1970-86, Liberty mag., 1971-73, Ingenue mag., 1973-75, Heavy Metal mag., 1977-86. Adj. prof. NYU Sch. Continuing Edn., 1973-78; panelist Folio Mag. Pub. Conf., 1975-76. Exec. prodr.: (feature films) Heavy Metal, 1981; author: Everything You Need to Know to Make It in the Magazine Business, 1979, Making It in the Media Professions, 1988, Making It in Advertising, 1993, Making It in Public Relations, 1993, Making It in Broadcasting, 1994, Making It in Book Publishing, 1996, Creating Your Career in Communications, the Media and Entertainment, 1998, The Newspaper: Everything You Need to Know to Make It in the Newspaper Business, 2000. Sponsor Albert Einstein Med. Coll., Birch Wathen Sch., N.Y.C. Served with AUS, 1942-46, CBI.

MOGENSEN, DENNIS, agricultural products company executive; CFO J.R. Simplot Co., Boise, Idaho. Office: JR Simplot Co PO Box 27 Boise ID 83707-0027

MOGUL, LESLIE ANNE, business development and marketing consultant; b. Balt., Mar. 9, 1948; d. Harry and Elaine Mogul; m. William Kasper. AS, Miami Dade Jr. Coll., 1969; BA, Temple U., 1976; MBA, U. Phoenix, 1996. Accredited pub. rels. Account exec. Gray & Rogers, Inc., Phila., 1976-80; pres. Leslie Mogul, Inc., Phila., 1980-84; v.p. McKinney, Inc., Phila., 1984-87; assoc. dir. comm. Scripps Meml. Hosps., San Diego, 1987-93; dir. pub. rels. Scripps Health, San Diego, 1993, dir. customer rels. and mktg., 1994-95; dir. bus. devel. Harborview Med. Ctr. Hosp., San Diego, 1995-96; cons. Projectworks, San Diego, 1996—, pres., 1996. Recipient over 25 awards local and nat. pub. rels. and comm. orgns. Mem. Pub. Rels. Soc. Am. (dir.-at-large 1993-94), Alumni Leadership Calif. Office: Project Works PO Box 301395 Escondido CA 92030-1395 E-mail: lmogul3586@aol.com

MOHAJER, DINEH, cosmetics company executive; b. Bloomfield Hills, Mich., Sept. 2, 1972; d. Reza and Shahnaz Mohajer. Student, U. So. Calif. Founder, CEO Hard Candy, Inc., Beverly Hills, Calif., 1996—. Office: [illegible]

MOHAMED, JOSEPH, SR. real estate broker, farmer; b. Omar, W.Va., Mar. 19, 1928; s. Mose and Minnie Elizabeth (Martin) M.; m. Shirley Ida Medeiros; children: Joseph Jr., John W., James R., Leslie Louise. AA in Bus. Adminstrn., Sacramento City Coll., 1950; BBA Personnel, Sacramento State U., 1952; postgrad., U. Pacific, U. Calif., Davis, Am. River Coll. Farmer, 1949—; founder comml. trucking operation Calif., 1949-52, Baja, Mex., 1953; founder Mexican Co. of Agr. and Livestock Ltd., Ensenada, Baja, Mex., 1953-57; owner Quintair, Inc., 1954—; contractor, real estate developer, 1949—; owner Joseph's Landscape Svc., Sacramento, 1952-72, Joseph Mohamed Enterprises, 1982—. Pest control adviser, Calif., 1970—. Mem. Rep. Nat. Com., Rep. Presdl. Task Force, Sacramento Regional Arts Coun., 1965—, Govs.' Emergency Drought Task Force, 1977, Civil Affairs Assn., Calif. Rental Assn., 1975—, Sacramento Apartment Assn., Calif. Apartment Assn., Nat. Apartment Assn.; dir. McClellan Aviation Museum Found., Sacramento County Sheriff's Mounted Posse, 1961—. Served with U.S. Army, 1946-48, USAR, 1949-78. Decorated Legion of Merit; recipient Master Aviator Badge. Mem. Sacramento U. Alumni Assn., Sacramento State Horseman's Assn., Calif. State Horseman's Assn., Sacramento Metro. C. of C., Navy League of U.S., Reserve Officer's Assn., Assn. of U.S. Army, Elk Grove C. of C., Sacramento Bd. of Realtors, Calif. Assn. Realtors, Nat. Assn. Realtors. Clubs: Comstock (Sacramento), Commonwealth (San Francisco). Lodges: Masons, Shriners.

MOHAN, CHANDRA, research biochemistry educator; b. Lucknow, India, Aug. 3, 1950; came to U.S., 1977; s. Prithivi Nath and Tara Rani (Sharma) Shastri; m. Nirmala Devi Sharma, July 23, 1978; children: Deepak, Naveen. BS, Bangalore (India) U., 1970, MS, 1972, PhD, 1976. Research assoc. U. So. Calif. Med. Sch., Los Angeles, 1977-83, asst. prof., 1983-93; dir. tech. svc., sr. tech. writer CalBioChem Corp., San Diego, 1993—. Assoc. editor Biochem. Medicine, Los Angeles, 1986-93; contbr. articles to profl. jours. Recipient BRSG award U. So. Calif., 1983. Mem. AAAS, Am. Diabetes Assn., N.Y. Acad. Scis., Soc. Exptl. Biology and Medicine, Am. Inst. Nutrition. Hindu. Avocations: photography, coin collecting. Home: 13638 Dicky St Whittier CA 90605-2949 Office: CalBioChem Corp 10394 Pacific Center Ct San Diego CA 92121-4340

MOHEBBI, AFSHIN, telecommunications industry executive; Telecom. engrng. cert., UCLA; BSEE, U. Calif., Irvine; MBA, U. Calif. Pres., mng. dir. Brit. Telecom.; pres., COO Qwest Comm., 1999—. Office: Qwest Comm Internat Inc 1801 California St Denver CO 80202

MOHL, ARNIE, state legislator; b. Beulah, N.D., Aug. 27, 1936; m. Maggie Mohl. AA, Allan Hancock Coll., Santa Barbara, Calif. Owner paving and concrete constrn. co.; mem. Mont. Senate, Dist. 39, Helena, 1995—; chair hwy. and transp. com.; vice chair jt. appropriation subcom. corrections/pub. safety. Served with U.S. Army. Republican. Home: 32303 Hwy 2 E Kalispell MT 59901-6653 Office: Capitol Sta Helena MT 59620

MOHR, GARY ALAN, physician; b. Erie, Pa., Aug. 17, 1952; s. Arthur John and Sue (Richardson) M.; children: Benjamin, Nathan, Elizabeth, Katelyn, Eric. BS, Pa. State U., 1975; MD, Jefferson Med. Coll., 1979. Cert. Am. Bd. Family Practice. Intern, resident in family medicine St. Vincent Health Ctr., Erie, Pa., 1979-82; pvt. practice Canon City, Colo., 1982—. Asst. clin. prof. family medicine U. Colo. Health Scis. Ctr. Founder, treas. Jefferson Soc., Fremont County, Colo., 1991. Fellow Am. Acad. Family Physicians; mem. Fremont County Med. Soc. (past pres.), Mensa. Lutheran. Achievements include climbing Mt. Kilimajaro, Oct. 2000. Avocations: hiking, scuba, philately, numismatics, computing. Office: 730 Macon Ave Canon City CO 81212-3314 E-mail: garyamohr@compuserve.com

MOHRAZ, JUDY JOLLEY, foundation administrator; b. Houston, Oct. 1, 1943; d. John Chesler and Mae (Jackson) Jolley; m. Bijan Mohraz; children: Andrew, Jonathan. BA, Baylor U., 1966, MA, 1968; PhD, U. Ill., 1974. Lectr. history Ill. Wesleyan U., 1972-74; asst. prof. history So. Meth. U., Dallas, 1974-80, coord. women's studies, 1977-81, assoc. prof. history, 1980-94, asst. provost, 1983-88, assoc. provost for student academics, 1988-94; pres. Goucher Coll., Towson, Md., 1994-2000, Virginia G. Piper Charitable Trust, Scottsdale, Ariz., 2000—. Cons. Ednl. Testing Svc., Princeton, N.J., 1984-93, Nat. Park Svcs., Seneca Falls, N.Y., 1992-93; bd. dirs. Balt. Equitable Soc., The Assocs. First Capital; bd. visitors U.S. Naval Acad., 1996—. Trustee The Lamplighter Sch., 1991-94, St. Mark's Sch. Tex., 1993-94; adv. bd. U. Tex. Southwestern Med. Sch., 1992-94; active Leadership Dallas, 1994; bd. dirs. Nat. Assn. Ind., The Balt. Cmty. Found. Recipient Disting. Alumni award Baylor U., 1993; named Woman of Merit, Omicron Delta Kappa, 1993. Office: Virgina G Piper Charitable Trust 6720 N Scottsdale Rd Scottsdale AZ 85253

MOHRMAN, KATHRYNJ, academic administrator; Pres. The Colo. Coll., Colo. Springs. Office: Colo Coll Office Pres 14 E Cache La Poudre St Colorado Springs CO 80903

MOIN, PARVIZ, mechanical engineering educator; b. Tehran, Iran, Oct. 23, 1952; came to U.S., 1970; s. Mahmood and Manijeh (Shojai) M.; m. Linda Gray, Apr. 10, 1978; children: Darius, Ryan. BME, U. Minn., 1974; MME, Stanford U., 1975, MS in Math., PhD in Mech. Engring., Stanford U., 1978. Engr. asst. U. Minn., Mpls., 1972-74; rsch. asst. Stanford (Calif.) U., 1975-78, acting asst. prof. mech. engring., 1980-82, assoc. prof., 1986-89, prof., 1989—; fellow Nat. Rsch. Coun. NASA Ames Rsch. Ctr., Moffett Field, Calif., 1978-80, rsch. scientist, 1982-86; dir. Ctr. Turbulence Rsch., Stanford, 1987—. Author book revs., chpts. to books, symposium proceedings, abstracts, jour. articles. Recipient Lawrence Sperry award AIAA, 1986, Franklin P. and Caroline M. Johnson Endowed Chair, 1990, Alexander von Humboldt prize Fed. Republic of Germany, 1995, Fluid Dynamics prize Am. Physical Soc., 1996. Fellow Am. Phys. Soc. (elected 1992, Fluid Dynamics prize 1996), NAE. Office: Stanford U Dept Mech Engring Bldg 500 Stanford CA 94305-3030

MOLASKY-ARMAN, ALICE ANNE, state commissioner; Commr. ins. State of Nev., 1995—. Office: Divsn Ins 788 Fairview Dr Ste 300 Carson City NV 89701-5491

MOLDAW, STUART G. venture capitalist, retail clothing stores executive; b. 1927; Student, Syracuse U. With Allied Stores, N.Y.C., 1949-51, G. Fox Co., Hartford, Conn., 1951-55; founder Foxmoor Casuals, 1959; co-founder U.S. Venture Ptnrs., 1981; chief exec. officer Ross Store Inc., Newark, from 1987, chmn. bd., 1988—. Office: Gymboree Corp 700 Airport Blvd Ste 200 Burlingame CA 94010

MOLINDER, JOHN IRVING, engineering educator, consultant; b. Erie, Pa., June 14, 1941; s. Karl Oskar and Carin (Ecklund) M.; m. Janet Marie Ahlquist, June 16, 1962; children: Tim, Karen. BSEE, U. Nebr., 1963; MSEE, Air Force Inst. Tech., 1964; PhD EE, Calif. Inst. Tech., 1969. Registered profl. engr., Calif. Project officer Ballistic Systems Div., Norton AFB, Calif., 1964-67; sr. engr. Jet Propulsion Lab., Pasadena, 1969-70; prof. engring. Harvey Mudd Coll., Claremont, 1970—; prin. engr. Qualcomm Inc., 1996-97, part-time, 1997—; contractor Boeing Satellite Systems, 2000—. Part-time lectr. Calif. State U., L.A.,, 1970-74; mem. tech. adv. panel Kinemetrics, Pasadena, 1985-86; part-time mem. tech. staff Jet Propulsion Lab., Pasadena, 1974-97, rep. NASA Hdqrs., Washington, 1979-80; vis. prof. elec. engring. Calif. Inst. Tech., 1982-83. Contbr. articles to profl. jours. Served to capt. USAF, 1963-67. Mem. IEEE. Avocations: bicycling, reading, computers. Office: Harvey Mudd Coll Dept Engring 301 E 12th St Dept Of Claremont CA 91711-5901

MOLINSKY, BERT, tax consultant; b. Bronx, N.Y., Feb. 25, 1938; s. Joseph and Ida G. (Rosenberg) M.; m. Donna L. Thurman, June 26, 1964; children: Avery, Lucy, Lois, Sarah. Student, U. Ariz., 1956-61, Diablo Valley Coll., 1986-88, Calif. State U., Hayward, 1988-92. CFP; CLU; ChFC; Enrolled Agt. Field supt. INA Life, Phoenix, 1968-72; regional life mgr. Sentry Life Ins. Co., Oklahoma City, 1972-73, Mpls., 1973-75, San Francisco, 1975-78; mgr. Acacia Mutual Life, Oakland, Calif., 1978-80; gen. agt. Am. United Life, Concord, 1980-82; owner East Bay Triple Check Tax Svcs., Walnut Creek, 1982—, Tax Tactics, LLC, Peoria, Ariz., 1993—. Instr. Golden Gate U. CPD, San Francisco, 1983-93, Mt. Diablo Sch. Dist., Concord, 1986-93; faculty Coll. for Fin. Planning, Denver, 1983-99; bd. dirs. Triple Check Licensee Coun. Contbr. articles to profl. jours. Nat. dir. U.S. Jaycees, Phoenix, 1967; pres. Bnai Brith Coun. of Lodges, San Francisco, 1986. With USNR, 1955-72. Named Jaycee of Yr. Ariz. Jaycees, 1967. Fellow Nat. Tax Practice Inst.; mem. Enrolled Agts., East Bay Assn Life Underwriters (pres. 1985-86), Peoria Sunset Lions (past pres.), Ariz. State Enrolled Agts. Assn. (past pres.), Nat. Assn. Enrolled Agents (mem. affiliates task force, 1997-99, bd. dirs. 1999—). Avocation: sports. Office: Plaza Del Rio Ctr 9401 W Thunderbird Rd Ste 140 Peoria AZ 85381-4817 also: PO Box 5129 Peoria AZ 85385-5129 E-mail: bertmol@aol.com

MOLLARD, JOHN DOUGLAS, engineering and geology executive; b. Regina, Sask., Can., Jan. 3, 1924; s. Robert Ashton and Nellie Louisa (McIntosh) M.; m. Mary Jean Lynn, Sept. 18, 1952; children: Catherine Lynn, Jacqueline Lee, Robert Clyde Patrick. BCE, U. Sask., 1945; MSCE, Purdue U., 1947; PhD, Cornell U., 1952; LLD (hon.), U. Regina, 1995. Registered profl. engr., profl. geologist Sask., Alta. and B.C., Can. Resident constrn. engr. Sask. Dept. Hwys and Transp., 1945; grad. asst. Purdue U., West Lafayette, Ind., 1946-47; rsch. engr. sch. civil engring. Cornell U., Ithaca, N.Y., 1950-52; air surveys engr., soil and water conservation and devel. Prairie Farm Rehab. Adminstrn., Govt. of Can., 1947-50, chief, airphoto analysis and engring. geology divsn., 1953-56; pres. J.D. Mollard and Assocs. Ltd., Regina, 1956—. Aerial resource mapping surveys tech. adv. Colombo plan, Govts. Ceylon and Pakistan, 1954-56; advisor Shaw Royal Commn. on Nfld. Agr.; Disting. lectr. series Ea. Can. Geotech. Soc., 1969; Cross Can. disting. lectr. Can. Geotech Soc., 1993; C.J. Mackenzie Disting. Grad. Meml. lectr. Coll. Engring. U. Sask., 1994; guest lectr., vis. lectr., instr. over 50 short courses on remote sensing interpretation aerial photos and satellite imagery numerous univs., cities and provinces in Can., also Cornell U., Ithaca, N.Y., Harvard U., Cambridge, Mass., U. Calif., Berkeley, U. Wis., Madison, U. Hawaii, 1952—. Author: Landforms and Surface Materials of Canada, 8 edits.; co-author: Airphoto Interpretation and the Canadian Landscape, 1986; contbr. over 100 articles to profl. pubs. Organizer, canvasser United Appeal campaigns; former bd. dirs. Regina Symphony Orch. Recipient Engring. Achievement award Assn. Profl. Engrs. Sask., 1984, Massey medal Royal Can. Geog. Soc., 1989, Allied Arts medal Royal Archtl. Inst. Can., 1998. Julian C. Smith medal, Engring. Inst. Can., 1999. Fellow ASCE, Geol. Soc. Can., Geol. Soc. Am., Am. Soc. Photogrammetry and Remote Sensing (award for contbns. airphoto interpretation and remote sensing 1979), Can. Acad. Engring., Internat. Explorers Club; mem. Engring. Inst. Can. (Keefer medal 1948, Julian C. Smith medal 1999), Assn. Cons. Engrs. Can., Can. Geotech. Soc. (1st R.M. Hardy Meml. Keynote lectr. 1987, Thomas Roy award with engring. geology divsn. 1989, R.F. Legget award 1992), Regina Geotech. Soc., Geol. Soc. Sask., Can. Soc. Petroleum Engrs., Regina YMCA (former dir.), Rotary (former dir. Regina club). Mem. United Ch. of Can. Avocations: jogging, reading, golf, tennis, nature study. Home: 2900 McCallum Ave Regina SK Canada S4S 0R2 Office: 810 Avord Tower 2002 Victoria Ave Regina SK Canada S4P 0R7 Fax: 306-352-8855. E-mail: mollard@sk.sympatico.ca

MOLLEUR, RICHARD RAYMOND, lawyer; b. Adams, Mass., May 14, 1932; s. Raymond Emory and Germaine (Ouellette) M.; m. Rita M. Desaulniers, Sept. 5, 1955; children: Denis Richard, Michelle Annette, Suzanne Nicole, Celeste Marie. A.B., Assumption Coll., Worcester, Mass., 1954; J.D., Georgetown U., 1957. Bar: D.C. 1958. Counsel Office of Architect of the Capital, Washington, 1957-60; trial atty. U.S. Dept. Justice, Washington, 1960-65; dir. D.C. bail project Georgetown Law Center, Washington, 1965-66, D.C. bail agy., 1966, asst. dean, asso. prof. law, 1967-69; v.p., gen. counsel Fairchild Industries, Inc., Germantown, Md., 1979-85; ptnr. Herron & Burchett, 1986-90, Winston & Strawn, 1990; corp. v.p., gen. counsel Northrop Corp., L.A., 1991—. Author: Bail Reform in Nation's Capital, 1966. Recipient Alumni Achievement award Georgetown Law Center, 1966 Office: Northrop Corp 1840 Century Park E Los Angeles CA 90067-2199

MOLLMAN, JOHN PETER, book publisher, consultant electronic publishing; b. Belleville, Ill., Feb. 8, 1931; s. Kenneth John and Maurine (Farrow) M.; m. Carol J. Piper, Apr. 4, 1998; children— Sarah Chase, Eric Cleburne BA, Washington U., St. Louis, 1952. Advt. specialist Gen. Electric Co., Schenectady and Boston, 1952-54; mgr. Enterprise Printing Co., Millstadt, Ill., 1956-66; gen. mgr. Monarch Pub. Co., N.Y.C., 1966-67; dir. prodn. Harper & Row Pubs., N.Y.C., 1967-74; pub. Harper's Mag. Press, N.Y.C., 1971-74; v.p. prodn. Random House Inc., N.Y.C., 1974-81; sr. v.p. World Book-Childcraft Inc., Chgo., 1981-88; pres. World Book Pub., 1988-91; pub. cons., 1991-92; dir. intellectual property devel. Multimedia Publishing Microsoft, 1992-96; cons. in electronic pub. Carmel, Calif., 1996—. Bd. dirs. Helicon Pub. Co., Oxford, Eng. Mem. vis. com. Washington U.; mem. pub. com. Art Inst. Chgo.; bd. dirs. Yevba Buena Ctr. for the Arts, San Francisco, Internat. ebook Award Found., N.Y. Mem. Golf Club at Quail Lodge, Phi Delta Theta, Sigma Delta Chi, Omicron Delta Kappa. Unitarian. Home: 25340 Vista Del Pinos Carmel CA 93923-8804 E-mail: pmollman@msn.com

MOLLOY, DONALD WILLIAM, lawyer; BA, U. Mont., 1968, JD with honors, 1976. Bar: Mont. 1976, U.S. Dist. Ct. Mont. 1976, U.S. Ct. Appeals (9th cir.) 1977, U.S. Supreme Ct. 1984. Aviation lt. USNR, 1968-72; law clk. to James F. Bettin U.S. Dist. Ct., Billings, Mont., 1976-78; ptnr. Beyer, Anderson, Sinclair & Murphy, Billings, 1978-81, Anderson, Edwards & Molloy, Billings, 1981-90, Anderson & Molloy, Billings, 1990-91; ptnr., sr., owner The Molloy Law Offices, Billings, 1991-96; judge U.S. Dist. Ct. Mont., Missoula divsn., 1996—. Contbr. articles to profl. jours. State chair Supreme Ct. Hist. Soc., Washington, 1991-93; lawyer rep. 9th Cir. Jud. Conf., San Francisco, 1989-92. Mem. ABA, Yellowstone County Bar Assn. (pres. 1984-95), Mont. Trial Lawyers Assn. (Trial Lawyer of Yr. 1993), Am. Trial Lawyers, Am. Bd. Trial Advocates, Am. Judicature Soc., Mont. Bar Assn., Pa. Trial Lawyer's Assn., Tex. Trial Lawyers Assn. Roman Catholic. Avocations: aviation, pilot. Office: US Dist Ct Dist Mont PO Box 7309 Missoula MT 59807-7309

MOLONEY, STEPHEN MICHAEL, lawyer; b. L.A., July 1, 1949; s. Donald Joseph and Madeline Marie (Sartoris) M.; m. Nancy Paula Barile, Jan. 15, 1972; children: Michael, John, Kathleen. Student, St. John's Sem., Camarillo, Calif., 1967-69; BS, U. Santa Clara, 1971, JD, 1975. Bar: Calif. 1975, U.S. Dist. Ct. (cen. dist.) Calif. 1976, U.S. Supreme Ct. 1990. Assoc. Gilbert, Kelly, Crowley & Jennett, L.A., 1975-80, from ptnr. to sr. ptnr., 1980—. Arbitrator, settlement officer Los Angeles Superior Ct., 1985—. Contbr. articles to profl. jours. Dir. Calif. Def. Polit. Action Com., Sacramento, 1991—. With USAR. Recipient Svc. award to Pres. of So. Calif. Def. Counsel, Def. Rsch. Inst., Chgo., 1992. Mem. Assn. So. Calif. Def. Counsel (pres. 1992-93), Calif. Def. Counsel (dir. 1991—), L.A. County Bar Assn. (vols. in parole, 1976-77, exec. com. alternative dispute resolution com. 1992-96), Oakmont Country Club, La Quinta Resort and Club. Democrat. Roman Catholic. Avocations: politics, golf, reading, travel. Office: Gilbert Kelly Crowley & Jennett 1200 Wilshire Blvd Ste 6 Los Angeles CA 90017-1908 E-mail: smm@gilbertkelly.com

MONAGHAN, KATHLEEN M. art museum director; b. Waterville, Maine, Sept. 6, 1936; d. Russell Vernon and Gloria Beatrice (LeClair) M. B.A. in Art History, U. Calif.-Santa Barbara, 1979, M.A. in Art History, 1981. Curatorial fellow Whitney Mus., N.Y.C., 1979, dir. Equitable Br., 1985-93; asst. curator Santa Barbara Mus., Calif., 1980-81, curator of art, 1983-84; curator, dir. Akron Art Mus., Ohio, 1984-85; dir. The Hyde Collection, Glens Falls, N.Y., 1994; exec. dir. Fresno Metropolitan Museum, Fresno, Calif. Mem. Internat. Com. on Mus., Coll. Art Assn. Address: Fresno Met Museum 1515 Van Ness Ave Fresno CA 93721

MONARCHI, DAVID EDWARD, management scientist, information scientist, educator; b. Miami Beach, Fla., July 31, 1944; s. Joseph Louis and Elizabeth Rose (Muller) M.; 1 child by previous marriage, David Edward. BS in Engring. Physics, Colo. Sch. Mines, 1966; PhD (NDEA fellow), U. Ariz., 1972. Asst. dir. bus. rsch. divsn. U. Colo., Boulder, 1972-75, asst. prof. mgmt. sci./info. sys., 1972-75, assoc. prof. mgmt. sci. and info. sys., 1975-97, prof. info. sys., 1997—, assoc. dir. divsn. info. sci. rsch., 1982-84, chair info. sys. divsn., 1999—. Chair, Information System Divn., 1999—, prin. investigator of socio-econ. environ. systems for govtl. agys., and local govt. orgns., State of Colo., also info. systems for pvt. firms, 1972-77, use of virtual reality in distance learning Colo. Commn. Higher Edn., 1996—. Contbr. numerous articles on socio-econ. modeling, object-oriented sys., info. sys. and artificial intelligence to profl. jours. Mem. Gov.'s Energy Task Force Com., 1974. Mem. IEEE, Inst. for Mgmt. Sci., Assn. Computing Machinery, Am. Assn. Artificial Intelligence. Home: 32 Benthaven Pl Boulder CO 80305-6210 Office: U Colo Grad Sch Bus Boulder CO 80309-0001

MONGER, DOUG J. state agency administrator; Park ranger State Mont. Fish, Wildlife and Parks Dept., Mont., park mgr., regional mgr., adminstr., 1998—. Office: State Mont Fish Wildlife & Park Dept PO Box 200701 Helena MT 59620-0701 Fax: 406-444-4952

MONISMITH, CARL LEROY, civil engineering educator; b. Harrisburg, Pa., Oct. 23, 1926; s. Carl Samuel and Camilla Frances (Geidt) M. BSCE, U. Calif., Berkeley, 1950, MSCE, 1954. Registered civil engr., Calif. From instr. to prof. civil engring. U. Calif., Berkeley, 1951—, chmn. dept. civil engring., 1974-79, Robert Horonjeff prof. civil engring., 1986—, prof. emeritus, 1996. Cons. Chevron Rsch. Co., Richmond, Calif., 1957-93, U.S. Army CE Waterways Expt. Sta., Vicksburg, Miss., 1968—, B.A. Vallerga, Inc., Oakland, Calif., 1980-98, ARE, Austin, Tex. and Scotts Valley, Calif., 1978-92; cons. Bechtel Corp., San Francisco, 1982-86. Contbr. numerous articles to profl. jours..Served to 2d lt. C.E., U.S. Army, 1945-47. Recipient Rupert Myers medal U. NSW, 1976; named Henry M. Shaw Lectr. in Civil Engring., N.C. State U., 1993; sr. scholar Fulbright Found., U. NSW, 1971; named Disting. Engring. Alumnus, Coll. Engring., U. Calif., Berkeley, 1996. Fellow AAAS; mem. NAE, ASCE (hon. mem., pres. San Francisco sect. 1979-80, ednl. activities com. 1989-91, State of Art award 1977, James Laurie prize 1988), ASTM, Assn. Asphalt Paving Technologists (hon. mem., pres. 1968, W.J. Emmons award 1961, 65, 85), Transp. Rsch. Bd. (assoc., chmn. pavement design sect. 1973-79, K.B. Woods award 1972, 1st disting. lectureship 1992, Roy W. Crum award 1995), Am. Soc. Engring. Edn., Internat. Soc. for Asphalt Pavements (chmn. bd. dirs. 1988-90), Asphalt Inst. (roll of honor 1990), U. Calif. (Berkeley citation 1996). Avocations: swimming, stamp collecting. Office: U Calif Dept Civil Engring 115 Mclaughlin Hall Berkeley CA 94720-1721 E-mail: clm@newton.berkeley.edu

MONK, ALLAN JAMES, baritone; b. Mission City, B.C., Can., Aug. 19, 1942; m. Marlene Folk; 3 children. Student, Elgar Higgin and Boris Goldovsky. Operatic debut in Old Maid and the Thief, San Francisco, 1967; joined touring co., later main co. San Francisco Opera; appeared with Tulsa Opera, Pitts. Opera, Edmonton Opera, Vancouver Opera, So. Alta. Opera, Chgo. Opera, Balt. Opera, Miami Opera, Colo. Opera, Mont real Opera, Hawaii Opera Theatre, Portland Opera.;, 1976. Met. Opera debut as Schaunard in La Boheme, 1976, sang title role in Wozzeck, Wolfram in Tannheuser, Dr. Malatesta in Don Pasquale, Rodrigo in Don Carlo, Sharpless in Madame Butterfly, Herald in Lohengrin; sang with Can. Opera Co. as Abelard in Heloise and Abelard, Macbeth, Rigoletto, Belcore in L'Elisir D'Amoure, Jago in Otello, as Ford in Falstaff, four villains in Les Contes d'Hoffman; with Nat. Arts Ctr. Opera Festival, Ottawa, Ont., Can., title role in Don Giovanni, Almaviva in Le Nozze Di Figaro, gulielmo in Cossi Fan Tutti, Tomsky in Pique Dame, Marcello in La Boheme; Carnegie Hall debut as Vladislav in Dalibor, 1977; European debut as Wozzeck, 1980; solo recitalist; toured with Nat. Arts Ctr. Orch. in USSR, Poland, Italy, 1973; movie debut as Baron Douphol in La Traviata, 1983. Named Artist of Yr. Can. Music Council, 1983, laureat Order of Can., 1985. Office: 14415 Parkland Blvd SE Calgary AB Canada T2J 4L5

MONK, DIANA CHARLA, artist, stable owner; b. Visalia, Calif., Feb. 25, 1927; d. Charles Edward and Viola Genevieve (Shea) Williams; m. James Alfred Monk, Aug. 11, 1951; children: Kiloran, Sydney, Geoffrey, Anne, Eric. Student, U. Pacific, 1946-47, Sacramento Coll., 1947-48, Calif. Coll. Fine Arts, San Francisco, 1948-51, Calif. Coll. Arts & Crafts, Oakland, 1972. Art tchr. Mt. Diablo Sch. Dist., Concord, Calif., 1958-63; pvt. art tchr. Lafayette, 1963-70; gallery dir. Jason Aver Gallery, San Francisco, 1970-72; owner, mgr. Monk & Lee Assocs., Lafayette, 1973-80; stable owner, mgr. Longacre Tng. Stables, Santa Rosa, Calif., 1989—. One-person shows include John F. Kennedy U., Orinda, Calif., Civic Arts Gallery, Walnut Creek, Calif., Vallery Art Gallery, Walnut Creek, Sea Ranch Gallery, Gualala, Calif., Jason Aver Gallery, San Francisco; exhibited in group shows at Oakland (Calif.) Art Mus., Crocker Nat. Art Gallery, Sacramento, Le Salon des Nations, Paris. Chair bd. dirs. Walnut Creek (Calif.) Civic Arts, 1972-74, advisor to dir., 1968-72; exhibit chmn. Valley Art Gallery, Walnut Creek, 1977-78; juror Women's Art Show, Walnut Creek, 1970, Oakland Calif. Art. Home and Office: Longacre Tng Stables 1702 Willowside Rd Santa Rosa CA 95401-3922 E-mail: longacrestables@msn.com

MONSEES, JAMES EUGENE, engineering executive, consultant; b. Sedalia, Mo., Mar. 27, 1937; s. Olen Owen and Ruth Caroline (Weiffenbach) M.; m. Leda L. Hoehns, Oct. 8, 1961; children: Brenda G., Mark E. BSCE, U. Mo., 1960, MSCE, 1961; PhDCE, U. Ill., 1970. Registered profl. engr., Ill., Md., Washington, Ohio, Calif., Wash., Colo. Grad. asst. U. Mo., Columbia, 1958-61; project mgr. USAF Spl. Weapons Ctr., Albuquerque, 1961-64; engr. Exxon, Baton Rouge, 1964-66; rsch. assoc. U. Ill., Champaign, 1967-69; sr. v.p. A.A. Mathews, CRS Engrs., Arcadia, Calif. and Rockville, Md., 1969-80; dept. mgr. Battelle Meml. Inst., Columbus, Ohio, 1980-82; v.p.-engr. Lachel L. Hanson & Assocs., Golden, Colo., 1982-83; chief tunnel engr. Metro Rail Transit Couns., L.A., 1983-1990; project mgr. Collider/SSC The PB/MK Team, Dallas, 1990-94; sr. v.p., tech. dir., prin. profl. assoc. Parsons Brinckerhoff, N.Y.C. Mem. Seismic Lifeline Com., San Francisco, 1987—; mem. exec. com. Rapid Excavation/Tunnel Conf., Denver, 1989—. Author: (with others) Guidelines for Tunnel Lining Design, 1984, Mining Handbook, 1992, Tunnel Engineering, 1994, Tunnel Engineering Handbook, 1996. Mem. U.S. Nat. Com. for Rock Mechanics, Wash., D.C., 1983-86, 88-94, Internat. Soc. for Rock Mechanics, 1983—. 1st Lt. USAF, 1961-64. Recipient Mo. Honor award U. Mo., 1992. Fellow ASCE; mem. NAE, Am. Underground Space Assn. (bd. dirs. 1995—), The Moles, Underground Tech. Rsch. Coun. Republican. Avocations: shooting, biking, tennis, reading, dog training. Home: 10141 Hummingbird Cir Orange CA 92861-4155 Office: Parsons Brinckerhoff 505 S Main St Ste 900 Orange CA 92868-4529

MONSEN, ELAINE RANKER, nutritionist, educator, editor; b. Oakland, Calif., June 6, 1935; d. Emery R. and Irene Stewart (Thorley) Ranker; m. Raymond Joseph Monsen, Jr., Jan. 21, 1959; 1 dau., Maren Ranker. B.A., U. Utah, 1956; M.S. (Mead Johnson grad. scholar), U. Calif., Berkeley, 1959, Ph.D. (NSF fellow), 1961; postgrad. NSF sci. faculty fellow, Harvard U., 1968-69. Dietetic intern Mass. Gen. Hosp., Boston, 1956-57; asst. prof. nutrition, lectr. biochemistry Brigham Young U., Provo, Utah, 1960-63; mem. faculty U. Wash., 1963—, prof. nutrition and medicine, 1984—, prof. nutrition, adj. prof. medicine, 1976-84, chmn. div. human nutrition, dietetics and foods, 1977-82, dir. grad. nutritional scis. program, 1994-99, mem. Council of Coll. Arts and Scis., 1974-78, mem. U. Wash. Press com., 1981—; chmn. Nutrition Studies Commn., 1969-83. Vis. scholar Stanford U., 1971-72; mem. sci. adv. com. food fortification Pan-Am. Health Orgn., São Paulo, Brazil, 1972; tng. grant coordinator NIH, 1976-97. Editor-in-chief Jour. Am. Dietetic Assn., 1983—; mem. editorial bd. Coun. Biology Editors, 1992-96; author research papers on lipid metabolism, iron absorption. Bd. dirs. A Contemporary Theatre, Seattle, 1969-72; trustee, bd. dirs. Seattle Found., 1978-95, vice chmn., 1987-91, chmn., 1991-93; pres. Seattle bd. Santa Fe Chamber Music Festival, 1984-85; mem. Puget Sound Blood Ctr. Bd., 1996-99. Grantee Nutrition Found., 1965-68, Agrl. Rsch. Svc., 1969-84; recipient Disting. Alumnus award U. Utah, F. Fischer Meml. Nutrition Lectr. award, 1988, L.F. Cooper Meml. Lectr. award, 1991, L. Hatch Meml. Lectr. award, 1992, Goble Lectr. award Purdue U., 1997. Mem. Am. Inst. Nutrition, Am. Soc. Clin. Nutrition (sec. 1987-90), Am. Dietetic Assn., Soc. Nutrition Edn., Am. Soc. Parenteral and Enteral Nutrition, Wash. Heart Assn. (nutrition council 1973-76), Phi Beta Kappa, Phi Kappa Phi. Office: U Wash PO Box 353410 Seattle WA 98195-3410

MONSON, JAMES EDWARD, electrical engineer, educator; b. Oakland, Calif., June 20, 1932; s. George Edward and Frances Eleanor (Fouche) M.; m. Julie Elizabeth Conzelman, June 25, 1954; children— John, Jamie, Jennifer. BSEE, Stanford U., 1954, MSEE, 1955, PhD in Elec. Engring., 1961. Mem. tech. staff Bell Telephone Labs., Murray Hill, N.J., 1955-56; devel. engr. Hewlett-Packard Co., Palo Alto, Calif., 1956-61; Robert C. Sabini prof. engring. emeritus Harvey Mudd Coll., 1961—. Mem. governing bd. Claremont Unified Sch. Dist., 1966-71, pres., 1969-70; pres. Claremont Civic Assn., 1974-75; bd. dirs. Claremont YMCA, 1978-82. Fellow NSF, 1954-55, Japan Soc. Promotion Sci., 1984; Fulbright Rsch. grantee, 1975-76; Fulbright sr. lectr., 1980. Fellow IEEE; mem. Phi Beta Kappa, Sigma Xi. E-mail: james. Home: PO Box 1029 Point Reyes Station CA 94956-1029 Office: Harvey Mudd Coll 301 E 12th St Claremont CA 91711-5901 E-mail: monson@hmc.edu

MONSON, THOMAS SPENCER, religious organization administrator, former publishing company executive; b. Salt Lake City, Aug. 21, 1927; s. George Spencer and Gladys (Condie) M.; m. Frances Beverly Johnson, Oct. 7, 1948; children— Thomas L., Ann Frances, Clark Spencer. BS with honors in mktg, U. Utah, 1948; MBA, Brigham Young U., 1974, LLD (hon.), 1981. With Deseret News Press, Salt Lake City, 1948-64, mgr., 1962-64; mem. Council Twelve Apostles, Ch. of Jesus Christ of Latter Day Saints, 1963-85, bishop, 1950-55; pres. Canadian Mission, 1959-62; mem. first presidency Ch. of Jesus Christ of Latter-day Sts., 1985—; chmn. bd. Deseret News Pub. Co., 1977-96. Vice chmn. Deseret Mgmt. Corp.; pres. Printing Industry Utah, 1958; bd. dirs. Printing Industry Am., 1958-64; mem. Utah exec. bd. U.S. West Communications. Mem. Utah Bd. Regents; mem. nat. exec. bd. Boy Scouts Am.; trustee Brigham Young U.. With USNR, 1945-46. Recipient Recognition award, 1964, Disting. Alumnus award U. Utah, 1966; Silver Beaver award Boy Scouts Am., 1971; Silver Buffalo award, 1978; Bronze Wolf award World Orgn. of the Scout Movement, 1993. Mem. Utah Assn. Sales Execs., U. Utah Alumni Assn. (dir.), Salt Lake Advt. Club, Alpha Kappa Psi. Club: Exchange (Salt Lake City). Office: LDS Ch 47 E South Temple Salt Lake City UT 84150-9701

MONTAGUE, L. DAVID, aerospace engineer; b. Washington, Apr. 17, 1933; Bachelor's, Cornell U., 1956. Assoc. engr. Lockheed Missiles & Space Co., 1956-65; chief Poseidon Missile Devel.; project engr., mgr. Poseidon Sys. Engring.; mgr. Advance Def. Sys.; v.p. Tactical & Def. Sys.; program mgr., asst. chief engr. Missile Sys. Div.; v.p. Missile Sys Div., pres., 1988-96, L. David Montague Assocs., Menlo Park, Calif. Advisor Dept. Def.; mem. Def. Sci. Bd. Task Force. Contbr. articles to profl. jours.; patentee in field. Fellow AIAA (Missile Sys. award 1991); mem. NAE. Office: L David Montague Assocs 1205 Hillview Dr Menlo Park CA 94025

MONTANA, JOSEPH C., JR. former professional football player; b. New Eagle, Pa., June 11, 1956; s. Joseph C. Montana, Sr., and Theresa M.; m. 1st, Kim Monses, 1975 (div.); m. 2nd, Cass Castillo (div. 1983); m. 3rd, Jennifer Wallace, 1984; 2 children, Alexandra, Elizabeth. B.B.A. in Mktg., U. Notre Dame, 1978. Quarterback San Francisco 49ers, 1979-93; mem. Super Bowl Championship Team, 1982, 85, 90; named to Pro Bowl, 1981, 83, 84, 85, 87, 89, 90, 93; quarterback Kansas City Chiefs, 1993-95; formerly with new bus. devel. dept. Viking Components Inc., Rancho Santa Margarita, Calif., 1999-2000. Author (with Alan Steinberg): Cool Under Fire, 1989. Named MVP at Super Bowl, 1982, 85, MVP at NFL, 1989, Player of Yr., The Sporting News, 1989, Man of Yr., The Sporting News, 1989; named to Pro Bowl 1981, 83-85, 87, 89, 90, 93, nominated Pro Football Hall of Fame, 2000. Achievements include holding NFL career records for highest completion percentage (63.67), highest passer rating (93.5), NFL single-season record for highest passer rating (112.4), 1989, NFL record for most consecutive games with 300 or more yards passing (5), 1982, most consecutive passes completed (22), 1987. Office: Super Joe Official J Montana Fan Club PO Box 2409 Menlo Park CA 94026-2409

MONTEITH, DICK, state legislator; b. Los Banos, Feb. 7, 1932; B in Sociology, Stanford U. Ptnr. Monteith Tractor/Truck Co.; with mktg. dept. Gallo Wines; sales rep. Weyerhaeuser Co.; gen. mgr. sales and distbn. Middleton Pkg.; mem. Calif. State Senate, mem. edn. com., agr. com., water resources com., vice chmn. housing and cmty. devel. com., vice chmn. natural resources and wildlife com. Recipient Gold award Merced-Mariposa Calif. Tchrs. Assn. Uni-Serv; named Freshman Legislator of Yr., Calif. Sch. Bd. Asn., 1998. Republican. Office: State Capitol Rm 2048 Sacramento CA 95814 also: 1620 N Carpenter Rd Ste A4 Modesto CA 95351-1154 also: 777 W 22nd St Ste B Merced CA 95340-3606

MONTGOMERY, DAVID BRUCE, marketing educator; b. Fargo, N.D., Apr. 30, 1938; s. David William and Iva Bernice (Trask) M.; m. Toby Marie Franks, June 11, 1960; children: David Richard, Scott Bradford, Pamela Marie. BSEE, Stanford U., 1960, MBA, 1962, MS in Stats., 1964, PhD in Mgmt. Sci., 1966; D honoris causa, Limburgs U. Centrum, Belgium, 1998. Asst. prof. mgmt. MIT, 1966-69, assoc. prof., 1969-70; assoc. prof. mktg. and mgmt. sci. Stanford U., 1970-73, prof., 1973-78, Robert A. Magowan prof. mktg., 1978-92, Sebastian S. Kregge prof. mktg. strategy, 1992-99, prof. emeritus, 1999—. Prin. The MAC Group Inc., 1969-91; mem. adv. bd. LEK Partnership, London; mem. sci. adv. bd. Univ. Connection, Bonn, Germany; acad. trustee Mktg. Sci. Inst., 1994-2000, exec. dir., 1995-97. Author: (with Glen L. Urban) Management Science in Marketing, 1969, (with Massy and Morrison) Stochastic Models of Buying Behavior, 1970, (with Day et al) Planning: Cases in Computer and Model Assisted Marketing, 1973, (with others) Consumer Behavior: Theoretical Sources, 1973, (with G. J. Eskin) Data Analysis, 1975; editor 5 books; assoc. editor Jour. Internat. Mktg., 2000—; mem. editl. bd. Mgmt. Sci., Jour. Mktg., Jour. Mktg. Rsch., Mktg. Sci., Jour. Internat. Mktg.; contbr. more than 90 articles and tech. reports to sci. and profl. jours. Trustee Family Service Assn. of Mid Peninsula, 1972-73. Recipient citation for [illegible] 1977, [illegible] award for outstanding contbn. to strategic mgmt. Strategic Mgmt. Soc., 1996. Fellow Royal Statis. Soc.; mem. Inst. Mgmt. Scis., Am. Mktg. Assn., Econometric Soc., Am. Inst. Decision Scis., Tau Beta Pi. Republican. Congregational Home: 960 Wing Pl Stanford CA 94305-1028 Office: Stanford U Grad Sch Bus Stanford CA 94305 E-mail: montogomery-david@gab.stamford.edu

MONTGOMERY, JAMES FISCHER, savings and loan association executive; b. Topeka, Nov. 30, 1934; s. James Maurice and Frieda Ellen (Fischer) M.; m. Diane Dealey; children: Michael James, Jeffrey Allen, Andrew Steven, John Gregory. BA in Acctg., UCLA, 1957. With Price, Waterhouse & Co., C.P.A.'s, Los Angeles, 1957-60; controller Conejo Valley Devel. Co., Thousand Oaks, Calif., 1960; asst. to pres. Gt. Western Fin. Corp., Beverly Hills, 1960-64; pres. United Financial Corp of Calif., Los Angeles, 1964-75; chmn., CEO Great Western Financial Corp., Chatsworth, Calif., 1975-96, now chmn. bd. dirs. 1996-97; chmn., CEO Frontier Bank, Park City, Utah, 1997—. Fin. v.p., treas. United Fin. Corp., Los Angeles, 1964-69, exec. v.p., 1969-74, pres., 1975; pres. Citizens Savs. & Loan Assn., Los Angeles, 1970-75. Served with AUS, 1958-60. Office: Frontier Bank 5217 Allott Ave Sherman Oaks CA 91401-5902

MONTGOMERY, MICHAEL DAVIS, physics/astrophysics company executive, consultant; b. San Luis Obispo, Calif., June 4, 1936; s. Herold Ray and Elva Dee (Davis) M.; m. Rita Martin, Dec. 28, 1957 (div. Sept. 1975); children: Jeanne, Gwen, Michele. MSEE, Stanford U., 1959; PhD, U. N.Mex., 1967. Group leader Max Planck Inst. for Astrophysics, Munich, 1974-76; group leader advanced concepts Los Alamos (N.Mex.) Nat. Labs., 1976-83; program mgr. for simulation Maxwell Labs. Inc., San Diego, 1983-84, dep. for DNA programs, 1984-85, v.p. rsch. and devel., 1986-91, sr. v.p. applied tech., 1991-92; sr. cons., 1993-96; owner Casa Del Mar Inn, Santa Barbara, Calif., 1991-97; real estate investor Jamach Ctr. LLC, 1997—; cons., owner All Santa Fe Reservations. Assoc. editor Jour. Geophys. Research; contbr. articles to sci. jours. Served to lt. comdr. USN, 1959-62. Recipient (charter) Sr. Scientist award Alexander Von Humboldt Found., 1972. Mem. AAAS, Am. Phys. Soc., Phi Beta Kappa, Sigma Xi, Tau Beta Pi. Avocation: amateur radio, W5MGT. Home and Office: 8 San Juan Ranch Rd Santa Fe NM 87501-7539 E-mail: mikedmont@aol.com, mike@all-santafe.com

MONTGOMERY, MIKE, university basketball coach; b. Long Beach, Calif., Feb. 27, 1947; m. Sarah Montgomery; children: John, Anne. BA in Phys. Edn., Calif. State U., Long Beach, 1968; MS in Phys. Edn., Colo. State U., 1976. Coach U. Fla., The Citadel, Colo. State U., USCG Acad.; asst. coach Boise State U.; head basketball coach U. Mont., Missoula, 1978-86, Stanford (Calif.) U., 1986—. Named Head Coach of Yr. USA Men's 22 and Under Select Team, U.S. Basketball Men's Collegiate Com., 1996, U.S. Basketball Devel. Coach of Yr., 1996, U.S. Olympic Com. Basketball Devel. Coach of Yr., 1996. Office: Stanford U Athletic Dept Basketball Dept Stanford Stadium Stanford CA 94305

MONTGOMERY, ROBERT F. state legislator, retired surgeon, cattle rancher; b. Ogden, Utah, May 13, 1933; s. William Floyd and Adrianna (Van Zweden) M.; m. Jelean Skeen, June 24, 1953; children: Lance, Dana, Kristen, Keri, Tanya. AS, Weber State U., 1953; BS, Brigham Young U., 1957; MD, U. Utah, 1961. Pvt. practice, Anaheim, Calif., 1966-88; senator Utah State Senate, 1992—. Chief surgery Anaheim Gen. Hosp., 1970, Anaheim Meml. Hosp., 1972-74. Rep. chmn. Weber County, Utah, 1991-93; pres. Am. Cancer Soc., Salt Lake City, 1992-93. Sgt. U.S. Army, 1953-55, Korea. Mem. Rotary, Utah Elephant Club, Travelor's Century Club. Mormon. Avocations: traveling, reading, hunting, fishing, golfing. Home: 1825 Mountain Rd Ogden UT 84414-2903

MONTOYA, MICHAEL A. state official, accountant; b. Albuquerque, May 4, 1952; s. Orlando (Reno) and Nancy (Maestas) M. BS, U. Colo., 1982. CPA, N.Mex. Tax mgr. Ernst and Young, Albuquerque, 1985-90; dep. state auditor State of N.Mex., Santa Fe, 1993-94, treas., 1995—. V.p., bd. dirs. Albuquerque Hispano C. of C., 1986-90; bd. dirs. Belen (N.Mex.) C. of C., 1986-90; bd. dirs. Healthnet of N.Mex., Albuquerque, 1987-90, Recreational Health Occupl. Ctr., Inc., Albuquerque, 1986-90. Mem. AICPAs, Assn. Hispanic CPAs. Democrat. Avocations: racquetball, hunting, fishing. Home: PO Box 414 Los Lunas NM 87031-0414 Office: NMex State Treasurer PO Box 608 Santa Fe NM 87504-0608

MOODY, DAVID L. career officer; BS, U.S. Air Force Acad., 1974; Diploma, Squadron Officer Sch., 1980; MS in Mgmt. and Supervision, Cen. Mich. U., 1983; Diploma, Armed Forces Staff Coll., 1985, Nat. War Coll., 1991; postgrad., Syracuse U., 1997. Commd. 2d lt. USAF, 1974, advanced through ranks to brig. gen., 1999; various assignments todep. dir. opers. and tng. Dep. Chief of Staff Air/Space Opers./Hdqtrs USAF/Pentagon, Washington, 1998-99; comdr. 57th Wing Air Combat Comman, Nellis AFB, Nev., 1999—. Decorated Def. Superior Svc. medal, Legion of Merit, Disting. Flying Cross, Meritorious Svc. medal with two oak leaf clusters, Air medal with oak leaf cluster, Air Force Commendation medal, Air Force Achievement medal, Combat Readiness medal with oak leaf clusters, Nat. Def. Svc. medal with svc. star, NATO medal, Kuwait Liberation medals, others. Office: 57 WG CC 4430 Grissom Ave Ste 206 Nellis AFB NV 89191-6536

MOODY, FREDERICK JEROME, mechanical engineer, consultant; b. Apr. 2, 1935; s. Frederick J. and Ruth K. (King) M.; m. Phyllis Arlene Ivemeyer, Aug. 27, 1955; children: David, John, Paul, Daniel. BSME, U. Colo., 1958; MSME, Stanford U., 1965, PhD in Mech. Engring., 1971. Engr. GE, San Jose, Calif., 1958-78, prin. engr., 1978-81, cons. engr., 1981—. Adj. prof. San Jose State U., 1971—; consulting engr. thermal-hydraulics GE, 1958-99. Author: Introduction to Unsteady Thermofluid Mechanics, 1990; co-author: The Thermal-Hydraulics of a Boiling Water Nuclear Reactor, 1977, 2d edit., 1993, The Day I Almost Quit-and Other Stretching Events, 1997. Chmn. bd. dirs. Med. Inst. Chaplains, San Jose, 1984. Named to Silicon Valley Engring. Hall of Fame, 2000. Fellow ASME (George Westinghouse Gold medal 1980, Pressure Vessels and Piping medal 1999); mem. Nat. Acad. Engring. Republican. Home and Office: 827 Larkspur Ln Murphys CA 95247-9694 E-mail: fmoody@goldrush.com

MOON, RONALD T. Y. state supreme court chief justice; b. Sept. 4, 1940; m. Stella H. Moon. B in Psychology and Sociology, Coe Coll., 1962, LLD, 2001; LLB, U. Iowa, 1965. Bailiff, law clk. to Chief Judge Martin Pence U.S. Dist. Ct., 1965-66; dep. prosecutor City and County of Honolulu, 1966-68; assoc. Libkuman, Ventura, Ayabe, Chong & Nishimoto (predecessor firm Libkuman, Ventura, Moon & Ayabe), Honolulu, 1968-72, ptnr., 1972-82; judge 9th div. 1st cir., Cir. Ct., State of Hawaii, Honolulu, 1982-90; assoc. justice Supreme Ct., State of Hawaii, Honolulu, 1990-93, chief justice, 1993—. Adj. prof. law U. Hawaii, 1986, 87, 88; lectr., guest spkr. numerous events. Mem. ABA, Hawaii Bar Assn., Assn. Trial Lawyers Am., Am. Bd. Trial Advocates (pres. 1986-93, nat. sec. 1989-91), Am. Inns of Cts. IV (bencher 1983—), Am. Judicature Soc., Hawaii Trial Judges' Assn., Conf. Chief Justices (bd. dirs.). Office: Supreme Ct Hawaii 417 S King St Honolulu HI 96813-2902 E-mail: cjrmoon@yahoo.com

MOONEY, HAROLD ALFRED, plant ecologist; b. Santa Rosa, Calif., June 1, 1932; s. Harold Walter and Sylvia Anita Stefany; m. Sherry Lynn Gulmon, Aug. 15, 1974; children— Adria, Alyssa, Arica. AB, U. Calif., Santa Barbara, 1957; MA, Duke U., 1958, PhD, 1960. From instr. to assoc. prof. UCLA, 1960-68; assoc. prof. Stanford U., 1968-73, prof. biology, 1975—, Paul S. Achilles prof. environ. biology, 1976—. Author: Mediterranean type Ecosystems, 1973, Convergent Evolution in Chile and California, 1977, Components of Productivity of Mediterranean Climate Regions, 1981, Disturbance in Ecosystems, 1983, Physiological of Plants in the Wet Tropics, 1984, Physiological Ecology of North American Plant Communities, 1985, Ecology of Biological Invasions of North America and Hawaii, 1986, Biological Invasions, A Global Perspective, 1989, Biodiversity and Ecosystem Function, 1993, Seasonally Dry Tropical Forests, 1995, CO2 and Terrestrial Ecosystems, 1995, Functional Roles of Biodiversity, 1996. Served with AUS, 1953-55. Recipient Humboldt award, 1989, Max Planck Forscgungs Preis award Alexander von Humboldt Soc., 1992; Inst. Ecology prize, 1990; Guggenheim fellow, 1974; Nat. Acad. Scis. fellow, 1982. Fellow AAAS, Am. Acad. Arts and Scis., Am. Philos. Soc.; mem. Ecol. Soc. Am. (pres. 1988-89, Mercer award 1961, Eminent Ecologist 1996), Brit. Ecol. Soc. (hon. mem.), Am. Inst. Biol. Scis. (pres. 1994), Internat. Coun. Sci. Unions (sec. gen. 1996—). Home: 2625 Ramona St Palo Alto CA 94306-2315 Office: Stanford U Dept Biol Sci 477 Herrin Lab Stanford CA 94305

MOONEY, JEROME HENRI, lawyer; b. Salt Lake City, Aug. 7, 1944; s. Jerome Henri and Bonnie (Shepherd) M.; m. Carolyn Lasrich, Aug. 10, 1965 (div. Dec. 1978); 1 child, Dierdre Nicole; m. Kaitlyn Cardon, Sept. 23, 1995. BS, U. Utah, 1966, JD, 1972. Bar: Utah 1972, Calif. 1998, U.S. Ct. Appeals (10th cir.) 1974, U.S. Supreme 1984, U.S. Ct. Appeals (7th cir.) 1999. Sole practice, Salt Lake City, 1972-75, 79-83; sr. ptnr. Mooney, Jorgenson & Nakamura, Salt Lake City, 1975-78, Mooney & Smith, Salt Lake City, 1983-87, Mooney & Assoc., Salt Lake City, 1987-94, Mooney Law Firm, Salt Lake City, 1995-98, Larsen & Mooney Law, Salt Lake City, 1999—. Bd. dirs. Mooney Real Estate, Salt Lake City. Mem. Gov.'s Coun. on Vet. Affiars, Salt Lake City, 1982-89; trustee Project Realty, Salt Lake City, 1976—, P.E.A.C.E.; SAMHSA sponsor Project Reality, 1994—; vice chair State Mil. Acad. Assoc. USANG, 1992-93. Mem. ABA (criminal justice sect. U.S. Sentencing Commn. com.), Utah Bar Assn. (chmn. criminal bar sect. 1987-88), Nat. Assn. Recording Industry Profls., Utah NG Assn. (trustee 1976), 1st Amendment Lawyers Assn. (v.p. 1986-88, pres. 1988-89), Nat. Assn. Criminal Def. Lawyers, Families Against Mandatory Minimums (adv. coun.), VFW. Democrat. Jewish. Avocations: sailng, computers. Home: 128 I St Salt Lake City UT 84103-3418 Office: 50 W Broadway Ste 100 Salt Lake City UT 84101-2066 E-mail: JerryM@MooneyLaw.com

MOONEY, MICHAEL JOSEPH, college president; b. Evansville, Ind., Dec. 15, 1942; s. Joseph Thomas and Marie Louise (DeJean) M.; children: Susanne, Julia. AB summa cum laude, St. Meinard Coll., 1964; STL magna cum laude, Univ. Innsbruck, Austria, 1968; M in Philosophy, Columbia U., 1973, PhD, 1982. Lectr. dept. religious studies, St. Mary's U., Halifax, N.S., Can., 1968-70, Union Theol. Sem., N.Y.C., 1972-74; project coord. Columbia U., N.Y.C., 1973-74, preceptor dept. religion, 1975-76, spl. asst. to exec. v.p. for acad. affairs, 1976-77, asst. provost, 1977-79, assoc. provost, 1979-82, dep. provost, 1982-89; pres. Lewis and Clark Coll., Portland, Oreg., 1989—. Visitor Inst. for Advanced Study, Princeton, N.J., 1984; trustee Jour. Philosophy, 1982—; bd. dirs. Nat. Assn. Ind. Colls. and Univs., 1995—; mem. exec. com. NAICU, 1997, sec., 1998—; mem. Com. Women in Higher Edn., Am. Coun. Edn., 1997; mem. Commn. on Internat. Edn., Am. Coun. on Edn., 1993-95;; bd. dirs. Reid Hall, Inc., N.Y.C. and Paris, 1977-89, v.p., 1983-89. Author: Vico in the Tradition of Rhetoric, 1985 (Gottschalk prize Am. Soc. 18th Century Studies 1985); editor: Renaissance Thought and Its Sources, 1979; co-editor: Toward a Theology of Christian Faith: Readings in Theology, 1968, Vico and Contemporary Thought, 1976, Small Comforts for Hard Times: Humanists on Public Policy, 1977. Bd. dirs. Roothbert Fund, 1980-92, Portland Opera Assn., 1992-93; trustee Scuola d'Italia, N.Y.C., 1986-90, World Affairs Coun., 1992—, pres., 1999-2000; mem. adv. bd. I Have A Dream Found.-Oreg., 1997—; trustee Oreg. Ballet Theater, 1992—. Recipient Rome prize Am. Acad. in Rome, 1989; Roothbert Fund fellow, 1972, Kent fellow Danforth Found., 1972, Woodrow Wilson fellow, 1972, Presdl. fellow Columbia U., 1972, F.J.E. Woodbridge Disting. fellow Columbia U., 1973; NEH grantee, 1984; Cavaliere Ufficiale, Order Merit, Republic of Italy, 1991. Fellow Italian Acad. for Advanced Studies in Am. (sr.); mem. Soc. for Values in Higher Edn., Am. Soc. for Eighteenth-Century Studies, Internat. Soc. for History of Rhetoric, Renaissance Soc. Am., Am. Acad. Religion, Am. Philos. Assn., Phi Beta Kappa (hon.). Office: Lewis & Clark Coll Office Pres 0615 SW Palatine Hill Rd Portland OR 97219-7879 E-mail: pres@lclark.edu

MOONVES, LESLIE, television company executive; b. N.Y.C., Oct. 6, 1949; s. Herman and Josephine (Schleifer) M.; m. Nancy Wiesenfeld, Dec. 17, 1978; children: Adam, Sara, Michael. BA, Bucknell U., 1971. Devel. exec. Catalina Prodns., Burbank, Calif., 1980-81; v.p. devel. Saul Ilson Prodns. Columbia Pictures TV, Burbank, 1981-82; v.p. movies and mini-series 20th Century Fox, L.A., 1982-85, Lorimar, Inc., Culver City, Calif., 1985-87; exec. v.p. creative affairs Lorimar-Telepictures, Culver City, 1987-90; pres. Lorimar TV, Burbank, 1990-93, Warner Bros. TV, Burbank, 1993-95; pres., CEO CBS TV, Los Angeles, 1995—. Developer, producer TV series including Dallas, Dark Justice, Guns of Paradise, Knots Landing, Midnight Caller, Sisters, Family Matters, Full House, Perfect Strangers, Family Man, I'll Fly Away, Reasonable Doubts, Step by Step, Hangin' with Mr. Cooper, the Jackie Thomas Show, Crossroads, Homefront, Going to Extremes, Shaky Ground, It Had to Be You, Time Trax, Against the Grain, Lois & Clark: The Adventures of Superman, Cafe Americain, How'd They Do That, Living Single, Family Album, Getting By. Bd. dirs. L.A. Free Clinic. Mem. Acad. TV Arts and Scis. (exec. com.), Hollywood Radio & TV Soc. (bd. dirs. 1988-91, pres. 1991). Democrat. Jewish. Office: CBS TV 51 W 52nd St New York NY 10019

MOORE, ANNETTE B. legislative staff member; b. Salt Lake City, Nov. 8, 1946; Sec., chief adminstrv. officer Utah State Senate, Salt Lake City, 1994—. Office: Utah State Senate State Capitol Rm 319 Salt Lake City UT 84114

MOORE, BROOKE NOEL, philosophy educator; b. Palo Alto, Calif., Dec. 2, 1943; s. Ralph Joseph and Dorothy Louise (Noll) M.; children: Sherry, Bill. BA, Antioch Coll., 1966; PhD, U. Cin., 1973. Asst. prof. Calif. State U., Chico, 1970-74, assoc. prof., 1974-79, prof., 1980—. Author: Philosophical Possibilities Beyond Death, 1981; co-author: Critical Thinking, 1987, 5th edit., 1997, 6th edit., 2000, The Power of Ideas, 1990, 4th edit., 1998, The Cosmos, God and Philosophy, 1992, Moral Philosophy, 1993, The Power of Ideas: A Brief Edition, 1995, Making Your Case, 1995; mem. editl. bd. Tchg. Philosophy, 1972. Mem. Am. Philos. Assn. Office: Calif State U Chico Dept Of Philosophy Chico CA 95929-0001

MOORE, BRUCE, executive; Grad., Stanford U., 1976. With IBM; pres., CEO Diasonics Ultrasound, Inc., Auspex, Santa Clara, 1995—. Office: 2300 Central Expy Santa Clara CA 95050-2516

MOORE, CARLETON BRYANT, geochemistry educator; b. N.Y.C., Sept. 1, 1932; s. Eldridge Carleton and Mabel Florence (Drake) M.; m. Jane Elizabeth Strouse, July 25, 1959; children: Barbara Jeanne, Robert Carleton; m. Diane Beets, Apr. 23, 2000. BS, Alfred U., 1954, DSc (hon.), 1977; PhD, Cal. Inst. Tech., 1960. Asst. prof. geology Wesleyan U., Middletown, Conn., 1959-61; mem. faculty Ariz. State U., Tempe, 1961—; nat. rsch. coun. rsch. assoc. NASA Ames Rsch. Ctr., 1974; prof., dir. Ctr. for Meteorite Studies Ariz. State U., Regents' prof., 1988—. Vis. prof. Stanford U., 1974; Prin. investigator Apollo 11-17; preliminary exam. team Lunar Receiving Lab., Apollo, 12-17. Author: Cosmic Debris, 1969, Meteorites, 1971, Principles of Geochemistry, 1982, Grundzügeder Geochemie, 1985; editor: Researches on Meteorites, 1961, Jour. Meteoritical Soc.; contbr. articles to profl. jours. Asteroid 5046 named Carletonmoore in his honor, 2000. Fellow Am. Geophys. Union, Ariz.-Nev. Acad.

Sci. (pres. 1979-80), Meteoritical Soc. (life hon., pres. 1966-68), Geol. Soc. Am., Mineral. Soc. Am., AAAS (council 1967-70); mem. Geochem. Soc., Am. Chem. Soc., Am. Ceramic Soc., Sigma Xi. Home: 507 E Del Rio Dr Tempe AZ 85282-3764 Office: Ariz State U Ctr Meteorite Studies Tempe AZ 85287-2504 E-mail: cmoore@asu.edu

MOORE, CHARLES AUGUST, JR. psychologist; b. Medford, Oreg., Feb. 22, 1944; s. Charles August and Bernadine (Newlun) M. BS, Lewis and Clark Coll., 1965; MA, U. Colo., 1967, PhD, 1972. Lic. psychologist, Calif., Oreg. Teaching asst. U. Colo., Boulder, 1965-66, 70-71, rsch. asst., counselor, practicum supr., 1966-67, 71-72; asst. psychologist State Home and Tng. Sch., Grand Junction, Colo., 1967; intern in psychology Camarillo (Calif.) State Hosp., 1968-69; psychology assoc., program psychologist Camarillo Drug Abuse Program (The Family), 1969-70; intern in psychology Oxnard (Calif.) Mental Health Ctr., 1969; clin. psychologist, dir. intern tng. Rural Clinics, Reno, 1972; clin. psychologist Kern County Mental Health Svcs., Bakersfield, Calif., 1972-74; clin., cons. psychologist San Diego County Mental Health Svcs., 1974-88; pvt. practice La Jolla (Calif.) Clinic, 1976-78; August Ctr., Chula Vista, Calif., 1978-85; staff psychologist Dept. Vet.'s Affairs Domiciliary, White City, Oreg., 1988—. Guest lectr. Calif. State Coll., Bakersfield, 1973-74; mem. Health Systems Agy. Mental Health Task Force, 1979; mem. doctoral dissertation com. U.S. Internat. U., 1975-76; mem. mental health task force San Diego County Bd. Suprs., 1979. Contbr. articles to profl. jours. Mem. Univ. City Community Coun., San Diego, 1976-78; bd. dirs. Pub. Employees Assn., 1976-77. Recipient Experiment in Internat. Living European Study award Lewis and Clark Coll., 1962; USPHS fellow, 1967-68; U. Colo. Grad. Sch. Rsch. grantee, 1971; recipient Hands and Heart award Dept. Vets. Affairs, 1989-90, Domiciliary Spl. Contbn. and Outstanding Performance awards, 1990, 91. Mem. APA, Am. Psychology and Law Soc., Calif. Psychol. Assn., Western Psychol. Assn., San Diego County Psychol. Assn., Assn. County Clin. Psychologists San Diego, San Diego Psychology and Law Soc., San Diego Soc. Clin. Psychologists. Office: Dept VA Domiciliary Psychology Svc 8495 Crater Lake Hwy White City OR 97503-3011

MOORE, DAN STERLING, insurance executive, sales trainer; b. Lincoln, Nebr., June 27, 1956; s. Jack Leroy and Carolyn Marie (Bachman) M.; m. Marla Janine Collister, June 2, 1979; children: Tyler David, Anna Rose. Student, Red Rocks Coll., 1977. Lic. ins. exec. Asst. mgr. European Health Spa, Englewood, Colo., 1975-78; sales mgr. Colo. Nat. Homes, Westminster, 1979-80; sales assoc. Dale Carnegie, Denver, 1981; sales mgr. Paramount Fabrics, Denver, 1981-84; sales assoc. Mighty Distbg., Arvada, Colo., 1984-87; divsn. mgr. Nat. Assn. for Self Employed/United Group Assn., Englewood, 1987—. Divsn. mgr. Communicating for Agr. Assn., 1993-98, Am. Bus. Coalition, 1997-2000, Am. for Financial Security, 1999—. Leader, trainer Alpine Rescue Team, Evergreen, Colo., 1971-74; minister Jehovah's Witnesses, 1972—. Avocations: golf, skiing, backpacking, scuba diving, tennis. Home: 892 Nob Hill Trl Franktown CO 80116-7917 Office: Nat Assn Self Employed/United Group 10579 W Bradford Rd Ste 100 Littleton CO 80127-4247 E-mail: sterlingmoore@netscape.net

MOORE, DANIEL ALTON, JR. retired state supreme court justice; b. 1933; BBA, U. Notre Dame, 1955; JD, U. Denver, 1961. Dist. ct. magistrate judge, Alaska, 1961-62; pvt. practice law, 1962-80; judge 3d Jud. Dist. Superior Ct., 1980-83; justice Alaska Supreme Ct., Anchorage, 1983-92, chief justice, 1992-95; ret., 1995. Mediator for J.A.M.S./Endispute, 1996—.

MOORE, DANIEL CHARLES, internist; b. Cin., Sept. 9, 1918; s. Daniel Clark and May (Strebel) M.; m. Betty Maxine Tobias, Aug. 5, 1945 (div. 1988); children: Barbara, Nancy, Daniel, Susan. Grad., Amherst (Mass.) Coll., 1940; M.D., Northwestern U., 1944. Diplomate: Am. Bd. Anesthesiologists. Intern Wesley Meml. Hosp., Chgo., 1944, resident, 1945; dir. anesthesia Va. Mason Hosp., Seattle, 1947-72; anesthesiologist (Mason Clinic), 1947-72, sr. cons. in anesthesia, 1972-83. Clin. prof. U. Wash. Sch. Medicine, 1963— Author: Regional Block, 1953, Stellate Ganglion Block, 1954, Complications of Regional Anesthesia, 1955, Anesthetic Techniques for Obstetrical Anesthesia and Analgesia, 1964, also papers. Served as capt. M.C. AUS, 1945-47. Recipient Ralph M. Waters award Ill. Soc. Anesthesiologists, Carl Koller Gold medal European Soc. Regional Anaesthesia, 1995. Mem. Am. Soc. Anesthesiologists (1st v.p. 1953-54, 2d v.p. 1954-55, pres. 1958-59, distinguished service award 1976), AMA (sec. anesthesiology sect. 1956-58), Am. Acad. Anesthesiology, Am. Soc. Regional Anesthesia (adv. bd., Gaston Labat award 1977), Wash. Soc. Anesthesiologists (pres. 1949-50), Wash. Med. Soc., King County Med. Soc., Faculty Anaesthetists Royal Coll. Surgeons (hon.), Northwest Forum, Beta Theta Pi, Nu Sigma Nu. Home: Madison Park Pl # 103 2000 43rd Ave E Seattle WA 98112-2704 Office: PO Box 900 Seattle WA 98111-0900

MOORE, DAVID GENE, academic administrator; b. Tonasket, Wash., Oct. 2, 1938; s. Leonard W. and Peggy (Furst) M.; m. Diane Russell, June 15, 1965 (div. 1984); children: John, Kathy, Alan. BA in Polit. Sci., Seattle U., 1960; MBA, U. Puget Sound, 1973; MS in Computer Sci., Kans. State U., 1978; postgrad., U. Mich., 1978—. Commd. 2d lt. U.S. Army, awd, 1960, advanced through grades to col., ret., 1980; dean mgmt. info. systems Mott Community Coll., Flint, Mich., 1980-82, dean mgmt., 1982-84, pres., 1985-92; pres DeVry Inst. Tech., Los Angeles, CA, 1992-94; pres. Nat. Edn. Centers, Inc., 1994-95; pres and CEO Corinthian Colleges, Inc., Santa Ana, CA, 1995—. Bd. dirs. Greater Flint Edn. Consortium. Contbr. numerous articles to profl. jours. Bd. dirs. United Way, Flint, 1987—, Human Services Network, Flint, 1988—; chmn. Bus. Resource Ctr., Flint, 1988—; sec. I-75 Corridor, 1987—; active Pvt. Industry Coun., Flint, 1985—. Decorated Silver Stars (2), Legion of Merit (2); recipient numerous civic and profl. awards. Mem. Soc. Automotive Engrs. (chmn. robotics sect. 1986—), Data Processing Mgmt. Assn., COMBASE (bd. dirs.), Coun. North Cen. Community Colls. (bd. dirs.), Mich. Community Coll. Assn. (bd. dirs.), Rotary, Univ. Club. Avocations: skiing, woodworking. Office: Corinthian Colleges Inc 6 Hutton Centre Dr Ste 400 Santa Ana CA 92707-5764

MOORE, DONALD WALTER, academic administrator, school librarian; b. Culver City, Calif., June 9, 1942; s. Raymond Owen and Jewel Elizabeth (Young) M.; m. Dagmar Ulbrich, Mar. 28, 1968; 1 child, Michael. AA, L.A. Valley Coll., 1967; BA in History, Calif. State U., Northridge, 1970; MA in Learning Disability, Calif. State U., 1973; MLS, U. So. Calif., 1974. Part time librarian L.A. Pierce Coll., Woodland Hills, Calif., 1974—; instr. reading L.A. Trade Tech. Coll., 1978-80, pres.'s staff asst., 1983-87; instr. learning skills L.A. City Coll., 1987-88, dir. amnesty edn., 1988-92, dir. Citizenship Ctr., 1992—. Adj. instr. computer sci. L.A. Trade-Tech. Coll., 1983—. Author: A Guidebook to U.S. Army Dress Helmets, 2000; contbr. fiction, articles, revs. to various publs. Mem. Ednl. Writers Am., Co. Mil. Historians, Edpress, Little Big Horn Assn., Planetary Soc. Republican. Roman Catholic. Avocations: writing, collecting U.S. frontier military memorabilia, computing. Office: LA City Coll Citizenship Program 855 N Vermont Ave Los Angeles CA 90029-3516

MOORE, EDWARD, JR. career officer; b. Little Rock; s. Edward M., Sr.; m. Deborah Marcia Cooper; children: Kimberly, Erica, Stacey. Grad., So. Ill. U., 1968; MBA, Naval Postgrad. Sch., 1974. Commd. ensign USN, 1968; advanced through grades to rear admiral; gunnery and comms. officer, navigator USS Severn; from comms. officer to ops. officer PRECOMUNITLANG USS Lang; weapons officer USS Sterett; exec. officer USS Buchanan; commdg. officer USS Lewis B. Puller; 1st commdg. officer USS Cowpens, 1993; comdr. Carl Vinson task group, cruiser-destroyer group three, 1996; jr. officer assignment officer, coord. shore assignments Bur. Naval Personnel; opd. analyst mem. staff of Comdr. in Chief U.S. Pacific Cmd.; asst. chief of staff manpower, personnel mem. staff Comdr. in Chief U.S. Pacific Fleet; commandant naval dist. Washington; dir. strategy and policy divsn. (N51); asst. dep. chief naval ops. (plans, policy ops., N3/N5B) Washington, 1997-98; vice admiral Com. Naval Surface Force, U.S. Pacific Fleet, San Diego, 1998—. With USNR, 1963-68. Decorated Legion of Merit with three gold stars, Navy Achievement medal. Mem. Nat. Naval Officers Assn., Kappa Alpha Psi. Office: Vice Admiral Moore 2841 Rendova Rd San Diego CA 92155-5490

MOORE, EMMETT BURRIS, JR. physical chemist, educator; b. Bozeman, Mont., June 14, 1929; s. Emmett Burris and Iris Marie (Brown) M.; m. Diane Elizabeth Girling, Oct. 1, 1960; children: Karen Elizabeth, Robin Diane. BS in Chemistry with honors, Wash. State U., 1951; PhD in Phys. Chemistry (Shell fellow), U. Minn., 1956. Teaching asst. U. Minn., Mpls., 1951-55, asst. prof. physics Duluth, 1957-59; mem. staff Boeing Sci. Research Labs., Seattle, 1959-73. Lectr. chemistry Seattle U., 1973; dir. power plant siting Minn. Environ. Quality Bd., St. Paul, 1973-76; gen. mgr. Richland (Wash.) Divsn. Olympic Engrng. Corp., 1976-78; staff scientist Pacific N.W. Nat. Lab., 1978-96; mem. environ. engrng. rev. panel EPA, 1989-95; alt. mem. Hanford Adv. Bd., 1995-2000; adj. prof. environ. sci. Wash. State U., 1990—. Author: (book) The Environmental Impact Statement Process and Environmental Law, 1997, 2d edit., 2000, An Introduction to the Management and Regulation of Hazardous Waste, 2000; contbr. articles to profl. jours. Trustee Mid-Columbia Symphony Soc., 1978-85, v.p., 1980-81, pres., 1981-83; trustee Richland Light Opera Co., 1984-88, bus. mgr., 1984-88. Recipient Land Grant Faculty Excellence award Wash. State U., 1999. Fellow AAAS; mem. Am. Phys. Soc., Am. Chem. Soc. (chmn. Pauling award com. 1971, sec. Puget Sound sect. 1971-73, mem. energy panel of com. on chemistry and pub. affairs 1983-86), Am. Assn. Physics Tchrs. (v.p. Wash. sect. 1965-66, pres. 1966-67), N.W. Sci. Assn., Phi Beta Kappa, Phi Kappa Phi, Phi Eta Sigma, Alpha Chi Sigma, Phi Lambda Upsilon, Sigma Alpha Epsilon (v.p. province 1972-73) Episcopalian (vestryman 1967-69, 76-79, 91, sr. warden 1969, del. diocesan conv. 1969-72). Home: 2323 Greenbrook Blvd Richland WA 99352-8427 Office: Wash State U 2710 University Dr Richland WA 99352-1671 E-mail: emoore@tricity.wsu.edu

MOORE, ERNEST EUGENE, JR. surgeon, educator; b. Pitts., June 18, 1946; s. Ernest Eugene Sr. and Mary Ann (Burroughs) M.; m. Sarah Van Duzer, Sept. 2, 1978; children: Hunter Burroughs, Peter Kitrick. BS in Chemistry, Allegheny Coll., 1968; MD, U. Pitts., 1972. Surg. resident U. Vt., Burlington, 1972-76; chief of trauma Denver Health Med. Ctr., 1976—, chief dept. surgery, 1984—. Chief div. of trauma and EMS U. Colo., Denver, 1984—, prof. surgery, vice chmn. dept., 1985-99; dir. facilities Colo. Trauma Inst., Denver, 1984-98. Editor: Critical Decisions in Trauma, 1987, Trauma, 1988, rev. edits., 1991, 96, 00, Early Care of the Injured, 1989; assoc. editor Jour. Trauma, Am. Jour. Surgery, Surgery-Problem Solving Approach, 2d edit., 1994, others; patentee retrohepatic vena cava shunt. Fellow ACS (com. on trauma, vice chair 1990), Soc. Univ. Surgeons (pres. 1989), Am. Assn. Surgery of Trauma (pres. 1993), Internat. Assn. Surgery of Trauma and Surg. Intensive Care (pres. 1998-99), Pan Am. Trauma Assn. (pres. 1991), Southwestern Surg. Congress (pres. 1998), Western Trauma Assn. (pres. 1989). Republican. Avocations: skiing, hockey, hunting, ultramarathons, fishing, camping. Home: 2909 E 7th Avenue Pky Denver CO 80206-3839 Office: Denver Health Med Ctr Dept Surgery Denver CO 80204 E-mail: Ernest.Moore@DHHA.org

MOORE, EVERETT LEROY, library administrator; b. Eugene, Oreg., May 24, 1918; s. Clinton L. Moore and Elsie LaVerne (Crowder) Morgan; m. Fern Irene Owen, July 13, 1942; children: David LeRoy, Richard Eugene, Patricia Elaine. BA, Wheaton Coll., 1949; MA, Pasadena Coll., 1954; MA in Libr. Sci., Vanderbilt U., 1960; PhD, U. So. Calif., 1973. Cert. C.C. chief adminstrv. officer, Calif. Libr. Evangel Coll., Springfield, Mo., 1955-57; head tech. svcs. North Coastal Regional Libr., Tillamook, Oreg., 1957-60; head social sci. and bus. libr. Calif. State U., Chico, 1960-62; dir. libr. svcs. Coll. of the Desert, Palm Desert, Calif., 1962-75; dir. univ. libr. Am. U. Cairo, 1970-72; dir. libr. svcs. Woodbury U., L.A., 1976-87, dir. libr. svcs., prof. emeritus, 1987—. Pres. so. region Jr. Coll. Round Table, Calif. Libr. Assn., Sacramento, 1965-66; chair tech. svcs. com. Calif. C.C. Libr. Coop., 1968-70, chmn. Desert area, 1974-75. Contbr. to profl. jours. Avocations: reading, computers, politics. Home: 1395 W 12th Ave Chico CA 95926 Office: 1395 W 12th Ave Chico CA 95926

MOORE, GEORGE EUGENE, surgeon; b. Minn., Feb. 22, 1920; s. Jesse and Elizabeth (MacRae) M.; m. Lorraine Hammell, Feb. 22, 1945; children— Allan, Laurie, Linda, Cathy, Donald. B.A., U. Minn., 1942, M.A., 1943, B.S., 1944, B.M., 1946, M.D., 1947, Ph.D. in Surgery, 1950. Intern surgery U. Minn. Hosps., 1946-47; med. fellow gen. surgery, 1947; dir. tumor clinic, 1951-53; sr. research fellow USHPS, 1947-48; faculty U. Minn. Med. Sch., 1948-53, cancer coordinator, 1951-53; chief surgery Roswell Park Meml. Inst., Buffalo, 1953-72, dir., 1953-67; dir. pub. health research N.Y. State Health Dept., Albany, 1967-73; clin. prof. surgery State U. N.Y. at Buffalo, 1962-73, also prof. research biology, 1955-69; dir. surg. oncology Denver Gen. Hosp., 1973-97; prof. surgery U. Colo., 1973-97, prof. emeritus, 1997—. Author: Diagnosis and Localization of Brain Tumors, 1950, Cancerous Diseases, 1970; contbr. 660 articles to profl. jours. Recipient Outstanding Citizen award Buffalo Evening News, 1958, Outstanding Sci. Achievement award, 1959, Disting. Achievement award Modern Medicine mag., 1962, Chancellor's medal U. Buffalo, 1963, Charles Evans Hughes award pub. administrn. Albany, 1963, Bronfman prize Am. Pub. Health Assn., 1964, Tchr. of Yr. award Dept. Surgery, U. Colo., 1977, Disting. Svc. award U. Colo., 1990, Meritorious Svc. Regents award U. Colo., 1990. Mem. Soc. U. Surgs., Halsted Soc., Am. Surg. Assn., Colo. Oncology Found. (pres.). Home: 12048 Black Hawk Dr Conifer CO 80433-7137 Office: Denver Gen Hosp 645 Bannock St PO Box 1806 Denver CO 80201-1806 E-mail: moore@WCOX

MOORE, GORDON E. electronics company executive; b. San Francisco, Jan. 3, 1929; s. Walter Harold and Florence Almira (Williamson) M.; m. Betty I. Whittaker, Sept. 9, 1950; children: Kenneth, Steven. BS in Chemistry, U. Calif., 1950; PhD in Chemistry and Physics, Calif. Inst. Tech., 1954. Mem. tech. staff Shockley Semicondr. Lab., 1956-57; mgr. engrng. Fairchild Camera & Instrument Corp., 1957-59, dir. research and devel., 1959-68; exec. v.p. Intel Corp., Santa Clara, Calif., 1968-75, pres., chief exec. officer, 1975-79, chmn., chief exec. officer, 1979-87, chmn., 1987-95, chmn. emeritus, 1995—. Bd. dirs. Varian Assocs. Inc., Transamerica Corp. Fellow IEEE (Founders medal 1997); mem. Nat. Acad. Engrng., Am. Phys. Soc. Office: Intel Corp 2200 Mission College Blvd Santa Clara CA 95054-1549

MOORE, HAL G. mathematician, educator; b. Vernal, Utah, Aug. 14, 1929; s. Lewis Henry and Nora (Gillman) M.; m. D'On Empey, July 20, 1956; children: David, Nora (Mrs. Bret C. Hess), Alison (Mrs. Samuel M. Smith). BS, U. Utah, 1952, MS, 1957; PhD, U. Calif., Santa Barbara, 1967. Tchr. Salt Lake City Public Schs., 1952-53; instr. math. Carbon Jr. Coll., also Carbon High Sch., Price, Utah, 1953-55, Purdue U., Lafayette, Ind., 1957-61, adminstrv. asst. dept. math, 1960-61; from asst. prof. math. to assoc. prof. math. Brigham Young U., Provo, 1961-71, prof., 1971-95; prof. emeritus, 1995—; assoc. chmn. dept. Math. Brigham Young U., 1986-89. Author: Precalculus Mathematics, 2d edit, 1977, (with Adil Yaqub) Elementary Linear Algebra With Applications, 1980, College Algebra and Trigonometry, 1983, A First Course in Linear Algebra, 1992, 3d edit., 1998; contbr. articles to profl. jours. Mem. High Coun., Ch. of Jesus Christ of Latter Day Saints, 1985-91, MTC br. pres., 1991-94, Bishop, 1958-61, 78-82. NSF faculty fellow U. Calif., Santa Barbara, 1964-66. Mem. Am. Math Soc., Math Assn. Am. (bd. govs. 1989-92), Utah State Math. Coalition (planning dir. 1990, bd. dirs. 1991-92), Sigma Xi (dir. 1974-80, 82-85, com. chmn. 1982-90), Phi Kappa Phi. Home and Office: 631 W 650 S Orem UT 84058-6027 E-mail: mooreh@math.byu.edu

MOORE, JAMES C. museum director; Assoc. dir. Albuquerque Mus., now dir. Office: Albuquerque Mus 2000 Mountain Rd NW Albuquerque NM 87104-1459

MOORE, JAMES R. lawyer; b. Longview, Wash., Sept. 14, 1944; s. James Carlton and Virginia (Rice) M.; m. Patricia Riley, Aug. 25, 1967 (div. 1978); 1 child, Katherine M.; m. Christine M. Monkman, July 14, 1979 (div. 1996); stepchildren: Amy McKenna, John McKenna; 1 foster child, Zia Sunseri; m. Kathryn Lindquist, Aug. 26, 1996; stepchildren: Matthew Elggren, Adam Elggren, Erin Elggren, David Heilner. BA, Whitman Coll., 1966; JD, Duke U., 1969. Bar: Wash. 1970, U.S. Ct. Appeals (4th cir.) 1972, U.S. Supreme Ct. 1973, U.S. Ct. Appeals (9th cir.) 1974, D.C., 1995. Law clk. to Hon. J. Barnes U.S. Ct. Appeals (9th cir.), L.A., 1969-70; trial atty. pollution control, land/natural resources div. U.S. Dept. Justice, Washington, 1970-74; asst. U.S. atty. U.S. Atty.'s Office, Seattle, 1974-82; regional counsel U.S. EPA Region 10, Seattle, 1982-87; counsel Perkins Coie, Seattle, 1987-88, ptnr., 1989-98; sr. environ. counsel, v.p. Huntsman Corp., Salt Lake City, 1999—. Trainer, speaker on environ. litigation, negotiation and law. Contbr. articles to profl. jours. Bd. dirs. Environ. Law Inst., 1995-2000; chair audit com. Whitman Coll., 1994—; ethics com. Bd. Environ. Auditors Cert., 1998—. Mem. ABA (sect. natural resources 1987—), Wash. State Bar Assn. (environ. and land use sect. 1974—, spl. dist. coun. 1988-95). Democrat. Office: Huntsmen Corp 500 Huntsman Way Salt Lake City UT 84108-1235 E-mail: jim_moore@huntsman.com

MOORE, JAY WINSTON, director cytogenetics laboratory; b. Madison, Wis., Apr. 20, 1942; s. Millard Harold and Leona J. (Miller) M.; m. Nancy E. Shimits; children: Meredith, Steven. BS, Cedarville Coll., 1964; MS, U. Nebr., 1966; PhD, U. Mass., 1970. Diplomate Am. Bd. Med. Genetics. From asst. prof. to prof. Eastern Coll., St. David's, Pa., 1970-84; fellow pediatric genetics Johns Hopkins Sch. of Medicine, Balt., 1984-86; asst. dirs. cytogenetics U. Iowa, Iowa City, 1986-90; dir. cytogenetics lab. Children's Hosp., Columbus, Ohio, 1990-98; asst. clin. prof. Ohio State U., Columbus, 1991-98; dir. cytogenetics lab. Genzyme Genetics, Santa Fe, 1998—. Fellow Am. Coll. Med. Genetics; mem. Am. Soc. Human Genetics. Office: Genzyme Genetics 2000 Vivigen Way Santa Fe NM 87505-5600 E-mail: jay.moore@genzyme.com

MOORE, JOHN ALEXANDER, biologist; b. Charles Town, W.Va., June 27, 1915; s. George Douglas and Louise Hammond (Blume) M.; m. Anna Betty Clark, 1938; 1 child. Student, Columbia Coll., Columbia U. Asst. zoology dept. Columbia U., N.Y.C., 1936-39, chair zoology dept., 1949-52, prof., 1954-68; tutor in biology Bklyn. Coll., 1939-41; instr. Queens Coll., 1941-43; asst. prof. zoology Barnard Coll., 1943-47, assoc. prof., 1947-50, prof., 1950-68, chair zoology dept., 1948-54, 60-66; rsch. assoc. Am. Mus. Natural History, 1942—; prof. biology U. Calif., Riverside, 1969-82, prof. emeritus, 1982—. Mem. com. on human resources NRC, 1979-82, mem. coord. coun. for edn. 1991-95, mem. com. on undergrad. sci. edn., 1992—, Nat. Sci. Resources Ctr., 1994—, com. on K-12 sci. edn., 1996—; Walker Ames prof. U. Wash., 1966; mem. Biol. Scis. Curriculum Study, 1959-76; mem. Commn. on Sci. Edn., 1967-73, chair, 1971-73. Author: Principles of Zoology, 1957, Heredity and Development, 1963, 2d edit., 1972, A Guide Book to Washington, 1963, Biological Science: An Inquiry into Life, 1963, 3d edit., 1973, (with others) Interaction of Man and the Biosphere, 1970, 3d edit., 1979, Science for Society: A Bibliography, 1970, 2d edit., 1971, Readings in Heredity and Development, 1972, Science as a Way of Knowing - Evolutionary Biology, 1984, Science as a Way of Knowing - Human Ecology, 1985, Science as a Way of Knowing - Genetics, 1986, Science as a Way of Knowing - Developmental Biology, 1987, Science as a Way of Knowing - Form and Function, 1988, Science: A Way of Knowing - A Conceptual Framework for Biology, Part I, 1989, Part II, 1990, Part III, 1991, Science as a Way of Knowing: The Foundations of Modern Biology, 1993, Nature in the New World, 1989, Nature Portrayed-the Natural World of the Americas, 1989; editor: Physiology of the Amphibia, 1964, Ideas in Modern Biology, 1965, Ideas in Evolution and Behavior, 1970, Dobzhansky's Genetics of Natural Populations, 1981; supr.: Biological Science: An Inquiry into Life, 1963, 3d edit., 1973, Genes, Cells and Organisms-Great Books in Experimental Biology, 17 vols., 1988. Fulbright rsch. scholar, Australia, 1952-53; Guggenheim fellow, 1959. Mem NAS, AAAS (mem. project 2061 1985-89), Genetics Soc. Am., Am. Soc. Zoologists (pres. 1974), Am. Soc. Naturalists (pres. 1972), Soc. for Study Evolution (pres. 1963), Am. Acad. Arts and Scis. Avocations: photography, history of American science, history of illumination. Home: 11522 Tulane Ave Riverside CA 92507-6649 Office: U Calif Dept Biology Riverside CA 92521-0001

MOORE, MARY FRENCH (MUFFY MOORE), potter, community activist; b. N.Y.C., Feb. 25, 1938; d. John and Rhoda (Teagle) Walker French; m. Alan Baird Minier, Oct. 9, 1982; children: Jonathan Corbet, Jennifer Corbet, Michael Corbet. BA cum laude, Colo. U., 1964. Ceramics mfg., Wilson, Wyo., 1969-82, Cheyenne, 1982—. Commr. County Teton (Wyo.), 1976-83, chmn. bd. commrs., 1981, 83, mem. dept. pub. assistance and social svc., 1976-82, mem. recreation bd., 1978-81, water quality adv. bd., 1976-82. Bd. dirs. Teton Sci. Sch., 1968-83, vice chmn., 1979-81, chmn., 1982; bd. dirs. Grand Teton Music Festival, 1963-68, Teton Energy Coun., 1978-83, Whitney Gallery of Western Art, Cody, Wyo., 1995—, Opera Colo., 1998—; mem. water quality adv. bd. Wyo. Dept. Environ. Quality, 1979-83; Dem. precinct committeewoman, 1978-81; mem. Wyo. Dem. Ctrl. Com., 1981-83; vice chmn. Laramie County Dem. Ctrl. Com., 1983-84, Wyo. Dem. nat. committeewoman, 1984-87; chmn. Wyo. Dem. Party, 1987-89; del. Dem. Nat. Conv., 1984, 88, mem. fairness commn. Dem. Nat. Com., 1985, vice-chairwoman western caucus, 1986-89; chmn. platform com. Wyo. Dem. Conv., 1982; mem. Wyo. Dept. Environ. Quality Land Quality Adv. Bd., 1983-86; mem. Gov.'s Steering Com. on Troubled Youth, 1982, dem. nat. com. Compliance Assistance Commn., 1986-87; exec. com. Assn. of State Dem. Chairs, 1989; mem. Wyo. Coun. on the Arts, 1989-95, chmn., 1994-95, Dem. Nat. Com. Jud. Coun., 1989—; legis. aide for Gov. Wyo., 1985, 86; project coord. Gov.'s Com. on Childrens' Svcs., 1985-86; bd. dirs. Wyo. Outdoor Coun., 1984-85; polit. dir., dep. mgr. Schuster for Congress, 1994-95; pres.' adv. com. on the performing arts John F. Kennedy Ctr. for the Performing Arts, 1999-2001. Recipient Woman of Yr. award Jackson Hole Bus. and Profl. Women, 1981, Dem. of Yr. Nellie Tayloe Ross award Wyo. Dems., 1990. Mem. Alden Kindred of Am., Jackson Hole Art Assn. (bd. dirs., vice chmn. 1981, chmn. 1982), Assn. State Dem. Chairs, Soc. Mayflower Descendents, Pi Sigma Alpha. Home: 8907 Cowpoke Rd Cheyenne WY 82009-1234 E-mail: marym6@aol.com

MOORE, OMAR KHAYYAM, experimental sociologist; b. Helper, Utah, Feb. 11, 1920; s. John Gustav and Mary Jo (Crowley) M.; m. Ruth Garnand, Nov. 19, 1942; 1 child, Venn. BA, Doane Coll., 1942; MA, Washington U., St. Louis, 1946, PhD, 1949. Instr. Washington U., St. Louis, 1949-52; teaching assoc. Northwestern U., Evanston, Ill., 1950-51; rsch. asst., prof. sociology Tufts Coll., Medford, Mass., 1952-53; researcher Naval Rsch. Lab., Washington, 1953-54; asst. prof. sociology Yale U., New Haven, 1954-57, assoc. prof. sociology, 1957-63; prof. psychology Rutgers U., New Brunswick, N.J., 1963-65; prof. social psychology, sociology U. Pitts., 1965-71, prof. sociology, 1971-89, prof. emeritus, 1989—; scholar-in-residence Nat. Learning Ctr.'s Capital Children's Mus.,

Washington, 1989-90. Pres. Responsive Environ. Found., Inc., Estes Park, Colo., 1962—; assessor of rsch. projects The Social Scis. and Humanities Rsch. Coun. Can., 1982—; adj. prof. U. Colo., Boulder, 1992—. Contbg. editor Educational Technology; contbr. numerous articles to profl. jours.; patentee in field; motion picture producer and director. Recipient Award The Nat. Soc. for Programmed Instruction, 1965, Award Doane Coll Builder Award, 1967, Ednl. Award Urban Youth Action, Inc., 1969, Award House of Culture, 1975, Cert. of Appreciation, 1986, Cert. of Appreciation D.C. Pub. Schs., 1987, da Vinci Award Inst. for the Achievement of Human Potential, 1988, Cert. of Appreciation Capital Children's Museum, 1988, award Jack & Jill of America Found., 1988, Cert. of Appreciation U.S. Dept. of Edn., 1988, Cert. of Appreciation D.C. Pub. Schs., 1990, Person of Yr. in Ednl. Tech. award Ednl. Tech. mag., 1990. Mem. AAAS, Am. Math. Soc., Am. Psychol. Assn., Internat. Sociol. Assn., Am. Sociol. Assn., Assn. for Symbolic Logic, Assn. for Anthrop. Study of Play, Philosophy Sci. Assn., Psychonomics Soc., Soc. for Applied Sociology, Soc. for Exact Philosophy, Math. Assn. Am. Republican. Avocation: mountaineering. Home and Office: 2341 Upper High Dr PO Box 1673 Estes Park CO 80517-1673 E-mail: okmoore@aol.com

MOORE, RICHARD, academic administrator; m. Susan Moore; children: Betsy, Parker. BS in Econs., Claremont Men's Coll., 1955, PhD, 1965; MBA, U. Calif., 1956. Asst. prof. mktg. San Jose (Calif.) State U., 1959-61; instr., divsn. dir. San Bernardino Valley (Calif.) Coll., 1961-66; dean instrn. Moorpark Coll., Calif., 1966-74; pres., supt. Santa Monica (Calif.) Coll., 1974-94; pres. C.C. So. Nev., Las Vegas, 1994-99, Nev. State Coll., Henderson, 2000—. Active C.C. H.S. program Clark County Sch. Dist., Boys & Girls Clubs, Learning and Earning Program, Weekend Coll., Silver Sage Coll., Peace Officers Acad., Video Distance Edn., other acad. programs. Lt. U.S. Army, 1957-59. Office: Nev State Coll Henderson City Hall 240 S Water St Ste 201 Henderson NV 89015-7227

MOORE, RICHARD ALAN, landscape architect; b. St. Louis, Jan. 17, 1930; s. Ira Mack and Helen Adoline (Fakes) M.; m. Patricia Ruth Burke, Mar. 15, 1952 (div. 1967); children: Sheryl Louise, Richard Dennis, Sara Lynn, Sandra Lee. BS, U. Mo., 1951; MLA, U. Oreg., 1957. Registered landscape architect, Calif., Hawaii. Asst. prof. landscape architecture Calif. State Poly. Coll., Pomona, 1957-61; assoc. prof., head dept. landscape architecture N.C. State U., Raleigh, 1962-67; pvt. practice landscape architecture Pomona, Calif., 1957-61; dir. land devel. and planning Oceanic Properties Inc., Honolulu, 1967-69; pvt. practice Honolulu, 1969-70, 79—; dir. ops. Eckbo, Dean, Austin & Williams, Honolulu, 1970-71, v.p. ops., 1971-73; pres. EDAW, Inc., San Francisco, 1973-76, chmn. bd., 1976-78; prof. landscape architecture Tex. A&M U., Bryan, 1977-79. Prin. works include Whispering Pines Motor Lodge, N.C., 1964 (award of merit N.C. chpt. AIA 1964), North Shore Devel. Plan, Kauai, Hawaii, 1973, Comprehensive Zoning Ordinance, County of Kauai, 1973 (Am. Soc. Landscape Architects honor award 1973, HUD honor award 1974), Lihue Devel. Plan, Kauai, 1975, Koloa, Poipu, Kalaheo Devel. Plan, Kauai, 1978, Gen. Plan Update, Kauai, 1982, Mililani Town Devel. Plan, 1967-69 (Am. Soc. Landscape Architects merit award 1970), Lanai Land Mgmt. and Devel. Study, 1969 (Am. Soc. Landscape Architects merit award 1970), Wailea Master Devel. Plan, 1971, Kukuiula Devel. Plan, 1983, Lanai Project Dist. Master Plan, 1983-89, Maliu Ridge Devel. Plan, North Kohala, 1985, Mililani Mauka Devel. Plan, 1988, Devel. Plan, Lanai City Comml. Dist., 1990, Dandan Golf Course, Guam, 1991. Lst lt. U.S. Army, 1951-53, Korea. Fellow Am. Soc. Landscape Architects; mem. Masons. Avocations: sports, drawing, painting.

MOORE, ROB, professional football player; b. N.Y.C., Oct. 27, 1968; BS in Psychology, Syracuse U., 1990. With N.Y. Jets, 1990-94; wide receiver Ariz. Cardinals, Phoenix, 1994—. Named to Sporting News Coll. All-Am. Team, 1989, NFL Pro Bowl Team, 1994. Office: Ariz Cardinals PO Box 888 Tempe AZ 85280-0888

MOORE, THOMAS CARROL, botanist, retired educator; b. Sanger, Tex., Sept. 22, 1936; s. Thomas M. and Willie Mae M.; m. Arvida Inmon DePriest, Sept. 1, 1956; children— Cynthia, Linda, Alan. B.A. in Biology, U. N. Tex., Denton, 1956; M.A. in Botany, U. Colo., 1958, Ph.D. (Outstanding Grad. Student in Biology award 1960, USPHS predoctoral fellow 1960-61), 1961. Instr. biology, then part-time instr. U. Colo., 1958-60; asst. prof. Ariz. State Coll., Flagstaff, 1961-63; mem. faculty Oreg. State U., Corvallis, 1963-93, prof. botany, 1971-93, prof. emeritus, 1993—, chmn. dept. botany and plant pathology, 1973-86, asst. to v.p. for rsch. and grad. studies, 1972-73. Vis. prof. Colo. State Coll., 1963. Mem. editorial bd. Plant Physiology, 1981-86; editor in chief Jour. Plant Growth Regulation, 1982-99; contbr. articles to profl. jours. Recipient Mosser award outstanding undergrad. teaching Oreg. State U., 1966 Mem. Am. Soc. Plant Physiologists, Bot. Soc. Am., Am. Phytopathol. Soc., Internat. Plant Growth Substances Assn., Plant Growth Regulator Soc. Am., Sigma Xi. Democrat. Lodge: Elks. Home: 560 NW Merrie Dr Corvallis OR 97330-6524

MOORE, THOMAS DAVID, academic administrator; b. Rochester, N.Y., July 26, 1937; s. Robert Franklin and Hilda (Kennedy) M.; m. Virginia Muller, June 13, 1959; children: Kathleen Mary, Michael David, Thomas David. BSS, St. John Fisher Coll., 1959; MS, SUNY, Brockport, 1962; EdD, Rutgers U., 1966. Tchr. Rochester City Schs., 1959-62; grad. asst. Rutgers U., New Brunswick, N.J., 1963-65; from asst. to full prof. Kent (Ohio) State U., 1965-93, asst. v.p. acad. affairs, 1976-83, v.p. faculty affairs and personnel, 1984-86, provost, v.p. acad. and student affairs, 1987-91, prof. emeritus ednl. philosophy, 1991—; provost, v.p. acad. affairs Ctrl. Washington U., 1993-97, prof. edn. and philosophy, 1997—. Roman Catholic. Avocations: sports, film, public affairs, music.

MOORE, WALTER DENGEL, rapid transit system professional; b. Chgo., Sept. 16, 1936; s. Walter D. and Velma Louise (Rhode) M.; m. Sandra M. Stetzel, Jan. 23, 1965 (div. 1980); children: Thomas, Timothy; m. Janice Masilun, Nov. 30, 1996. BA in Liberal Arts and Scis., U. Ill., 1958; BSEE, Ill. Inst. Tech., 1972. Cert. keel boat sailor. Supt. maintenance of way Chgo. Transit Authority, 1963-89; supr. track and rail tech. support Met. Transp. Assn. Los Angeles County, L.A., 1989-99, ret., 1999; cons. in rapid transit maintenance and tech. support, 1999—. With U.S. Army, 1958-60. Mem. Am. Pub. Transp. Assn. (vice chmn. power com. 1974-75), Am. Ry. Engring. Assn. (vice chmn. subcom. on power signals and comm. 1990—), Underwater Soc. Am. (N.Am. record in spear-fishing 1988), Calif. Pub. Utilities Commn. (gen. order 1995), Nat. Rsch. Coun., NAS (transp. rsch. bd.), Nat. Acad. Engrs. (project C3 and D6 light rail track manual), Morro Bay Art Assn. (exhibitor), Morro Bay Yacht Club, Baywood Navy Retirees. Avocations: free diving, theater, sailing. Home: 1180 9th St Los Osos CA 93402-1325

MOORES, JOHN, professional sports team executive; b. July 9, 1944; m. Becky Moores, 1963; children: Jennifer, John Jr. With IBM, Shell Oil; founder, CEO BMC Software, 1980-89, chmn., 1980-92; chmn., co-owner San Diego Padres, 1994—; owner Peregrine Sys., Inc., Del Mar, Calif. Founder Padres Found., 1995—, Padres Scholars Program, 1995—; chmn. JMI Svcs. Inc.; mem. adv. bd. San Diego Hall of Champions. Trustee Carter Ctr. of Emory U.; founder, chmn. River Blindness Found. Office: San Diego Padres PO Box 2000 San Diego CA 92112-2000

MOORHEAD, CARLOS J. former congressman; b. Long Beach, Calif., May 6, 1922; s. Carlos Arthur and Florence (Gravers) M.; m. Valery Joan Tyler, July 19, 1969; children: Theresa, Catharine, Steven, Teri, Paul. BA, UCLA, 1943; JD, U. So. Calif., 1949. Bar: Calif. 1949, U.S. Supreme Ct. 1973. Pvt. practice law, Glendale, Calif., 1949-72; dir. Lawyers Reference Service, Glendale, 1950-66; mem. 93d-104th Congresses from 22d (now 27th) Dist. Calif., 1973-96; mem. judiciary com.; chmn. subcom. on cts. and intellectual property; vice chmn. commerce com.; mem. subcom. on energy & power, subcom. on telecomm. & fin.; dean Calif. Congl. Rep. Delegation. Apptd. to Fed. Cts. Study Com.; sr. fellow Sch. Pub. Policy, UCLA. Pres. Glendale Hi-Twelve Club; mem. Verdugo Hills council Boy Scouts Am.; mem. Calif. Assembly, 1967-72; mem. Calif. Law Revision Commn., 1971-72; pres. 43d Dist. Republican Assembly, Glendale Young Republicans; mem. Los Angeles County Rep. Central Com., Calif. Rep. Central Com.; bd. dirs. Glendale La Crescenta Camp Fire Girls, Inc.; mem. Found. Bd., Glendale Hosp., Glendale C.C.; mem. adv. bd. Salvation Army of Glendale. Served to lt. col. AUS, 1942-46. Recipient Man of Yr. award USO, 1979 Mem. Calif. Bar Assn. L.A. County Bar Assn., Glendale Bar Assn. (past pres.), Glendale C. of C., Masons, Shriners, Lions, Moose, VFW. Presbyterian. Office: 1354 J Lee Cir Glendale CA 91208-1730

MOOS, RUDOLF H. psychologist, researcher; b. Berlin, Sept. 10, 1934; s. Henry R. and Herta M. (Ehrlich) M.; m. Bernice Schradski, June 9, 1963; children: Karen, Kevin. B.A. in Psychology, U. Calif. at Berkeley, 1956; Ph.D., U. Calif.-Berkeley, 1960. Mem. faculty psychiatry Stanford (Calif.) U., 1962—, dir. psychiatry research tng. program, 1967-92, prof. psychiatry, 1972—, dir. social ecology lab., 1967-92; chief research, research career scientist VA Med. Center, Palo Alto, Calif., 1975—, dir. Ctr. for Health Care Evaluation, 1984—, dir. Program Evaluation and Resource Ctr., 1990-99. Vis. prof. Inst. Psychiatry, also Maudsley and Royal Bethlem Hosp., London, 1969-70 Author: Issues in Social Ecology, 1974, Evaluating Treatment Environments, 1974, Health and the Social Environment, 1974, Evaluating Correctional and Community Settings, 1975, Human Adaptation Coping with Life Crises, 1976, The Human Context, 1976, Environment and Utopia, 1977, Coping with Physical Illness, 1977, Evaluating Educational Environments, 1979, Coping with Physical Illness: New Perspectives, 1984, Coping with Life Crises: An Integrated Approach, 1986, Alcoholism Treatment: Content, Process and Outcome, 1990, Group Residential Facilities for Older Adults, 1994, Evaluating Residential Facilities, 1996, The Quality of Psychiatric and Substance Abuse Programs, 1997; mem. editl. bd. Jour. Behavioral Medicine, Internat. Jour. Therapeutic Comtys., Prevention in Human Svcs., Psychosomatic Medicine, Jour. Personality and Social Psychology, 1985-91, Health Psychology: An Internat. Jour., Violence, Agression, and Terrorism, Jour. Substance Abuse, Jour. Applied Gerontology, Jour. Cmty. and Applied Social Psychology, Psychology and Aging, 1986-91, Evaluation and Program Planning, Environment and Behavior, 1987-91, Indian Jour. Clin. Psychology, 1996—, Jour. Studies on Alcohol, 1997. Fellow APA, Acad. Behavioral Medicine, Soc. Behavioral Medicine, Am. Orthopsychiat. Assn., Nat. Inst. on Alcohol Abuse and Alcoholism (mem. coun.); mem. Am. Sociol. Assn., Am. Psychosomatic Assn. (mem. coun.). Home: 25661 W Fremont Rd Los Altos CA 94022-1600 Office: Stanford U Dept Psychiatry MC 5550 Palo Alto CA 94305

MOOSSA, A. R. surgery educator; b. Port Louis, Mauritius, Oct. 10, 1939; s. Yacoob and Maude (Rochecoute) M.; m. Denise Willoughby, Dec. 28, 1973; children: Pierre, Noel, Claude, Valentine. BS, U. Liverpool, Eng., 1962, MD (hon.), 1965; postgrad., Johns Hopkins U., 1972-73, U. Chgo., 1973-74. Intern Liverpool Royal Infirmary, 1965-66; resident United Liverpool Hosps. and Alder Hey Children's Hosp., 1966-72; from asst. prof. surgery to assoc. prof. U. Chgo., 1975-77, prof., dir. surg. rsch., chief gen. surgery svc., vice chmn. dept., 1977-83; chmn. dept. surgery U. Calif.-San Diego Med. Ctr., 1983—. Litchfield lectr. U., Oxford, Eng., 1978; praelector in surgery U. Dundee, Scotland, 1979; Hampson Trust vis. prof. U. Liverpool, Eng., 1992, G.B. Ong. vis. prof. U. Hong Kong, 1993, Philip Sandblon vis. prof. U. Lund, Sweden. Editor: Tumors of the Pancreas, 1982, Essential Surgical Practice, 1983, 4th edit., 2000, Comprehensive Textbook of Oncology, 1985, 2d edit., 1991, Gastrointestinal Emergencies, 1985, Problems in General Surgery, 1989, Operative Colorectal Surgery, 1993. Fellow Royal Coll. Surgeons (Hunterian prof. 1977); mem. ACS, Am. Surg. Assn., Soc. Univ. Surgeons, Am. Soc. Clin. Oncology. Office: U Calif San Diego Med Ctr 200 W Arbor Dr San Diego CA 92103-9000

MORAN, RACHEL, lawyer, educator; b. Kansas City, Mo., June 27, 1956; d. Thomas Albert and Josephine (Portillo) M. AB, Stanford U., 1978; JD, Yale U., 1981. Bar: Calif. 1984. Assoc Heller, Ehrman, White & McAuliffe, San Francisco, 1982-83; prof. law U. Calif., Berkeley, 1984—, Robert D. and Leslie-Kay Raven prof. law, 1998—. Vis. prof. UCLA Sch. Law, 1988, Stanford (Calif.) U Law Sch., 1989, N.Y.U. Sch. of Law, 1996, U. Miami Sch. Law, 1997, U. Tex. Law Sch., 2000; chair Chicano/Latino Policy Project, 1993-96. Contbr. numerous articles to profl. jours. Recipient Disting. Tchg. award U. Calif. Mem. ABA, Assn. of Am. Law Schs. (mem. exec. com.), Am. Law Inst., Calif. Bar Assn., Phi Beta Kappa. Democrat. Unitarian. Avocations: jogging, aerobics, reading, listening to music. Office: U Calif Sch Law Boalt Hall Berkeley CA 94720

MORAND, BLAISE E. bishop; b. Tecumseh, Ont., Can., Sept. 12, 1932; Ordained priest Roman Cath. Ch., 1958. Ordained coadjutor bishop Diocese of Prince Albert, Sask., Can., 1981, bishop Can., 1983—. Office: Diocese Prince Albert 1415 4th Ave W Prince Albert SK Canada S6V 5H1

MORAVCSIK, JULIUS MATTHEW, philosophy educator; b. Budapest, Hungary, Apr. 26, 1931; came to U.S., 1949; s. Julius and Edith (Fleissig) M.; m. Marguerite Germain Truninger, Sept. 14, 1954; children: Adrian Clay, Peter Matthew. BA, Harvard U., 1953, PhD, 1959. Asst. prof. U. Mich., Ann Arbor, 1960-66, assoc. prof., 1966-68; prof. Stanford (Calif.) U., 1968—. Author: Understanding Language, 1975, Thought and Language, 1990, Plato and Platonism, 1992, Meaning, creativity, and the Partial Inscrutability of the Human Mind, 1998. Recipient Sr. Humanist prize Humboldt Found., 1983; fellow Ctr. Advanced Studies Behavioral Scis., 1986-87, Inst. Advanced Studies, 1988. Fellow Inst. Advanced Studies Budapest; mem. Am. Philos. Assn. (pres. Pacific divsn. 1987-88), Am. Soc. Aesthetics (trustee 1988-92), Soc. Ancient Greek Philosophy (pres. 1989-91, bd. dirs. Jour. History Philosophy, James Wilbur Award Value Theory 2000), Hungarian Acad. Arts and Scis. (external mem.). Avocations: golf, tennis. Office: Stanford U Dept Of Philosophy Stanford CA 94305 E-mail: julius@csli.stanford.edu

MORENO, ERNEST H. college president; BA in Polit. Sci., Calif. State U., L.A.; MPA in Ednl. Adminstrn., Calif. State U., Long Beach. Employee rels. specialist, pers. analyst L.A. Cmty. Coll. Dist., 1969-78, asst. dir. of labor rels., 1978-85; v.p. acad. affairs East L.A. Coll., 1991-93, pres., 1993—. Instr. L.A. Trade Tech. Coll., 1976-84, West L.A. Coll., 1984-94. Bd. dirs. Santa Marta Hosp.; pres., bd. trustees Santa Clarita C.C. Dist.; bd. trustees L.A. County Med. Ctr. Sch. of Nursing; chmn. ARC; mem. pers. com. United Way, East L.A. Occpl. Ctr., Bienvenidos Family Ctr., LAPD Hispanic Cmty. Forum. With U.S. Army, 1970-72. Mem. Assn. of Negotiations and Contract Adminstrs., Assn. of Calif. Coll. Adminstrs., Am. Coun. on Edn. (commr.), Hispanic Assn. of Colls. and Univs., East L.A. Rotary, East L.A. C. of C., Am. Diabetes Assn. Office: East Los Angeles Coll 1301 Avenida Cesar Chavez Monterey Park CA 91754-6001

MORENO, MANUEL D. bishop; Educator U. of Calif., L.A., St. John's Sem., Camarillo, Calif. Ordained priest Roman Cath. church, 1961. Ordained aux. bishop of Los Angeles, titular bishop of Tanagra, 1977; installed as bishop of Tucson, 1982—. Office: Diocese Tucson PO Box 31 Tucson AZ 85702-0031

MORETTI, AUGUST JOSEPH, lawyer; b. Elmira, N.Y., Aug. 18, 1950; s. John Anthony and Dorothy M. (De Blasio) M.; m. Audrey B. Kavka, Nov. 8, 1981; children: David Anthony, Matthew Alexander. BA magna cum laude, Princeton U., 1972; JD cum laude, Harvard U., 1975. Assoc. Heller, Ehrman, White and McAuliffe, San Francisco, 1976-82, ptnr., 1982-2000; CFO and gen. counsel Surro Med, Inc., 2001—. Lectr. bus. adminstrn. U. Calif. Berkeley, 1977-79; bd. dirs. AviGenics. Bd. dirs. Ann Martin Children's Ctr.; mem. adv. panel U. Calif. Berkeley Entrepreneur Program. Mem. ABA.

MOREY, CHARLES LEONARD, III, theatrical director; b. Oakland, Calif., June 23, 1947; s. Charles Leonard Jr. and Mozelle Kathleen (Milliken) M.; m. Mary Carolyn Donnet, June 10, 1973 (div. 1975); m. Joyce Miriam Schilke, May 29, 1982; 1 child, William. AB, Dartmouth Coll., 1969; MFA, Columbia U., 1971. Artistic dir. Peterborough (N.H.) Players, 1977-88, Pioneer Theatre Co., Salt Lake City, 1984—. Actor: N.Y. Shakespeare Festival, Playwrights Horizons, New Dramatists, ARK Theatre Co., Ensemble Studio Theatre, Cubiculo, Folger Theatre, Syracuse Repertory Theatre, Theatre by Sea, others; over 150 plays acted in or directed; guest dir. Ensemble Studio Theatre, ArK Theatre, Am. Stage Festivel, McCarter Theatre, Pioneer Theatre Co., PCPA Theatrefest, The Repertory Theater of St. Louis, Meadow Brook Theatre, Utah Shakespearean Festival; author Laughing Stock and new adaptations Alexander Dumas' The Three Musketeers, Bram Stoker's Dracula, Charles Dickens' A Tale of Two Cities, Victor Hugo's The Hunchback of Notre Dame, Alexandre Dumas' The Count of Monte Cristo. Trustee Utah Arts Endowment, Inc., Nat. Theatre Conf.; panelist Nat. Endowment for Arts. Mem. Soc. Stage Dirs. and Choreographers, AEA, SAG, AFTRA, Salt Lake City C. of C. (Honors in the Arts award 1991), Utah Assn. Gifted Children (Community Svc. award 1991), Peterborough Players (Edith Bond Stearns award 1990). Democrat. Episcopalian. Office: Pioneer Theatre Co 300 S 1400 E Salt Lake City UT 84112-0660 E-mail: chuck@ptc.utah.edu

MORGAN, ALFRED VANCE, management consulting company executive; b. Liberal, Kans., Apr. 13, 1936; s. Forrest Francis and Gertrude Irene (Henning) M.; m. Peggy Ann Riley, June 29, 1960; children: Trudie Marie, Vance Riley, Allen Forrest, Bradley Augustus, Kelly James. BBA, U. Kans., 1958; MBA, U. So. Calif., 1966; postgrad., Am. Inst. Banking, 1965. Asst. mgr. Fruehauf Trailer Co., L.A., Calif., 1960-61; asst. mktg. dir. Security Pacific Nat. Bank, 1961-65; mktg. exec. Doyle, Dane, Bernbach Advt., 1965-66; cons. Harbridge House, Inc., Boston, 1966-71; pres. Morgan Bus. Assocs., Inc., Santa Barbara and Boston, 1971—; instr. bus. L.A. City Coll., 1971-72; instr. mgmt. Santa Barbara City Coll., 1973. Contbr. articles to profl. publs. With AUS, 1958-60. Mem. ASTD, Am. Mktg. Assn. L.A., Am. Soc. Profl. Cons., U. So. Calif. Grad. Sch. Bus. Alumni Assn. Office: Morgan Bus Assocs Inc 990A Cindy Ln Carpinteria CA 93013-2900

MORGAN, BEVERLY CARVER, pediatrician, educator; b. N.Y.C., May 29, 1927; d. Jay and Florence (Newkamp) Carver; children— Nancy, Thomas E. III, John E. M.D. cum laude (Mosby Scholar), Duke U., 1955. Diplomate Am. Bd. Pediatrics (oral examiner 1984-90, mem. written examination com. 1990—), Nat. Bd. Med. Examiners. Intern, asst. resident Stanford U. Hosp., San Francisco, 1955-56; clin. fellow pediatrics, trainee pediatric cardiology Babies Hosp.-Columbia Presbyn. Med. Center, N.Y.C., 1956-59; research fellow cardiovascular diagnostic lab. Columbia-Presbyn. Med. Center, N.Y.C., 1959-60; instr. pediatrics Coll. Physicians and Surgeons, Columbia U., 1960; dir. heart sta. Robert B. Green Meml. Hosp., San Antonio, 1960-62; lectr. pediatrics U. Tex., 1960-62; spl. research fellow in pediatric cardiology Sch. Medicine, U. Wash., Seattle, 1962-64, from instr. to prof. pediatrics, 1962-73, chmn. dept. pediatrics, 1973-80; mem. staff U. Wash. Hosp., chief of staff, 1975-77; mem. staff Harborview Med. Ctr., Children's Orthopedic Hosp. and Med. Ctr., dir. dept. medicine, 1974-80; prof., chmn. dept. pediatrics U. Calif., Irvine, 1980-88, prof. pediat. and pediat. cardiology, 1980—; pediatrician in chief Children's Hosp. Orange County, 1988. Mem. pulmonary acad. awards panel Nat. Heart and Lung Inst., 1972-75; mem. grad. med. edn. nat. advisory com. to sec. HEW, 1977-80; mem. Coun. on Pediatric Practice; chmn. Task Force on Opportunities for Women in Pediatrics, 1982; mem. nursing rev. com. NIH, 1987-88. Contbr. articles to profl. jours.; mem. editorial bd. Clin. Pediatrics, Am. Jour. Diseases of Children, Jour. of Orange County Pediatric Soc., Jour. Am. Acad. Pediatrics, Los Angeles Pediatric Soc. Recipient Women of Achievement award Matrix Table, Seattle, 1974; Distinguished Alumnus award Duke U. Med. Sch., 1974; Ann. award Nat. Bd. Med. Coll. Pa., 1977; USPHS career devel. awardee, 1966-71 Mem. Am. Acad. Pediat. (chmn. com. on pediat. manpower 1984-86), Am. Coll. Cardiology, Soc. for Pediat. Rsch., Am. Fedn. Clin. Rsch., Am. Pediat. Soc., Assn. Med. Sch. Pediat. Dept. Chmn. (sec.-treas. 1981-87), Western Soc. for Pediat. Rsch., Alpha Omega Alpha. Office: U Calif Irvine Med Ctr Dept Pediatrics 101 The City Dr S Orange CA 92868-3201 E-mail: bcmorgan@vci.edu

MORGAN, CHRISTINA, venture capital firm executive; Student, Am. U., Beirut; BS in Fin., MBA in Fin., Ariz. State U. With Memorex, Qume Corp., 1977-82; securities analyst Hambrecht & Quist LLC Investment Bankers, San Francisco, 1982-84, investment banking prin., 1984-90, mng. dir., 1990-94, mng. dir., co-head investment banking, 1994—, Chase H&Q, San Francisco. Bd. dirs. Visigenic Software. Office: Chase H&Q 1 Bush St San Francisco CA 94104-4425

MORGAN, GWYN, oil and gas executive; b. Didsbury, Alta., Can., Nov. 4, 1945; s. Ian and Margaret (Hergenhein) M. BSc in Mech. Engring., U. Alta., 1967; postgrad., U. Calgary, Cornell U. Petroleum engr. Alta. Energy Resources Conservation Bd.; mgr. ops. and engring. Consolidated Natural Gas Ltd., Consolidated Pipelines Ltd., Norlands Petroleums Ltd.; with Alta. Energy Co., Ltd., Calgary, 1975—, pres., CEO. Bd. dirs. HSBC-Bank Can. Dir. Bus. Coun. on Nat. Issues; trustee Fraser Inst. Mem. Can. Assn. Petroleum Prodrs. Avocations: sailing, hiking, skiing, physical fitness, cycling. Office: Alberta Energy Co Ltd 3900 421 7th Ave SW Calgary AB Canada T2P 4K9

MORGAN, JAMES C. electronics executive; b. 1938; BSME, MBA, Cornell U.; DEng (hon.), De Anza Coll., 1994. Mem. corp. staff Textron Inc., 1963-72; sr. ptnr. West Ven Mgmt., San Francisco, 1972-76; chmn. bd., pres., CEO Applied Materials, Inc., Santa Clara, Calif., 1976-87, chmn. bd., CEO, 1987—. Co-author Cracking the Japanese Market: Strategies for Success in the New Global Economy. Apptd. by Pres. Clinton to Commn. U.S.-Pacific Trade and Investment Policy, 1996; past mem. Nat. Adv. Com. Semiconductors. Recipient Cmty. Svc. award NCCJ, 1995, Nat. Medal of Tech., Pres. Clinton, 1996; named to Jr. Achievement Hall of Fame, 1991; named Internat. Citizen of Yr., World Forum of Silicon Valley, 1995. Mem. Am. Electronics Assn. (past bd. dirs.), SEMI/SEMATECH (past bd. dirs.), World Presidents Orgn., Congrl. Econ. Leadership Inst. (bd. dirs.), Nat. Ctr. Asia-Pacific Econ. Cooperation (bd. dirs.), Coun. Competitiveness, Pacific Basin Econ. Coun. (chmn.'s circle), Semiconductor Equipment and Materials Internat. (dir. emeritus, past pres.). Office: Applied Materials Inc 3050 Bowers Ave Santa Clara CA 95054-3208

MORGAN, JAMES EARL, librarian, administrator; b. Wheeling, W.Va., June 30, 1941; s. James H. L. and Ethel Irene (Goodwin) M.; m. Carman H. Head, Dec. 23, 1966; 1 child, Scott Andrew BS in Edn., Ariz. State Coll., 1965; MSLS, Fla. State U., 1966. Reference asst. social scis. Fla. State U., Tallahassee, 1965-66; head pub. services Ga. Coll., Milledgeville, 1967-69; dir. pub. services U. Tex. Med. Br., Galveston, 1969-73; dir. libraries U. Conn. Health Ctr., Farmington, 1973-76, Oreg. Health Sci. U., Portland, 1976—. Contbr. articles to profl. jours. Grantee Nat. Library Medicine, 1974-76, 78-81 Mem. ALA (life), Med. Libr. Assn. (chmn. Pacific N.W. chpt. 1981), Oreg. Health Scis. Librs. Assn., Pacific N.W. Libr. Assn., Spl. Libr. Assn., Oreg. Libr. Assn., Portland Area Spl. Librarians Assn., Assn. Coll. and Rsch. Librs., Am. Med. Informatics Assn., Nat. Rural Health Assn. Democrat Office: Oreg Health Scis U Libr Biomedical Info Comm Ctr 3181 SW Sam Jackson Park Rd Portland OR 97201-3098 E-mail: morgan@ohsu.edu

MORGAN, JAMES JOHN, environmental engineering educator; b. N.Y.C., June 23, 1932; s. James and Anna (Treanor) M.; m. Jean Laurie McIntosh, June 15, 1957; children— Jenny, Johanna, Eve, Michael, Martha, Sarah BCE, Manhattan Coll., 1954; MSCE, U. Mich., 1956; postgrad., U. Ill., 1956-60; PhD, Harvard U., 1964; ScD (hon.), Manhattan Coll., 1989. Instr. civil engring. U. Ill., Urbana, 1956-60; assoc. prof. U. Fla., Gainesville, 1963-65, Calif. Inst. Tech., Pasadena, 1965-69, prof. environ. engring., 1969-87, Marvin L. Goldberger prof. environ. engring. sci., 1987—, dean of students, 1972-75, dean grad. studies, 1981-84, v.p. student affairs, 1980-89; exec. officer environ. engring. sci., 1993-96. Mem. environ. studies bd., NRC, 1974-80; chmn. Acid Deposition Sci. Adv. Com., Calif., 1983-98; chmn. Gordon Rsch. Conf. on Environ. Sci.; Water, 1970. Author: (with Werner Stumm) Aquatic Chemistry, 1970, 2d edit., 1981, 3rd edit. 1996; editor Environ. Sci. and Tech., 1966-74; contbr. articles to profl. jours. Recipient Stockholm Water prize, 1999, Clarke Water prize, 1999. Mem. ASCE (award 1997), Am. Chem. Soc. (award 1980), AAAS, Am. Soc. Limnology and Oceanography (editorial bd. 1977-80), Nat. Acad. Engring., Assn. Environ. Engring. Profs. (award 1981, 83, 94), Am. Water Works Assn. (award 1963), Sigma Xi, Chi Epsilon. Democrat. Roman Catholic. Club: Athenaeum Avocations: tennis; folk music. E-mail: morgan. E-mail: j@caltech.edu

MORGAN, JEFF SCOTT, research engineer; b. Salt Lake City, Sept. 3, 1954; s. David Nyle and Dene Huber (Olsen) M.; m. Linda Mae Marquez, May 28, 1982 (div.); m. Stephanie Sugamura, Oct. 25, 1998. BS, U. Calif., San Diego, 1976; MS, U. Hawaii, 1978, PhD, 1982. Rsch. assoc. U. Hawaii, Honolulu, 1982-85; sr. rsch. assoc. Stanford U., Palo Alto, Calif., 1985-91; rsch. engr. U. Wash., Seattle, 1991—. Mem. Am. Astron. Soc. Office: U Wash Dept Astronomy PO Box 351580 Seattle WA 98195-1580

MORGAN, LANNY, musician; b. Des Moines, Mar. 30, 1934; s. Harold Ira and Ruth (Maddick) M.; m. Marty Shelton Morgan; children: Breck, Wynter. Student, L.A. (Calif.) City Coll., 1952. Instr. Stanford U. Summer Jazz Workshops, L.A. Jazz Workshop, Grove Sch. Music, Many others; guest artist, instr. at coll., high schs. throughout U.S.; played on recordings, films, TV; guest solo U.K. clubs, festivals. Played lead alto saxophone with Maynard Ferguson, Rey De Michele Orch., Oliver Nelson, Bill Holman Band, Bob Florence Band, Supersax; appeared, recorded Steely Dan, Natalie Cole, Diane Schurr, Shirley Horn, Andy Williams, Mel Torme, Frank Sinatra, Julie Andrews, and many others; lead quartet/quintet in L.A.; recordings include Lanny Morgan Quartet, 1993, Pacific Standard, 1997. With U.S. Army, 1957-59. Home: 6470 Gaviota Ave Van Nuys CA 91406-6401

MORGAN, MARILYN, federal judge; b. 1947; m. James R. Grube; 1 child, Terrence M. Adamson. BA, Emory U., 1969, JD, 1976. Bar: Ga. 1976, Calif. 1977. Ptnr. Morgan & Towery, San Jose, Calif., 1979-88; bankruptcy judge U.S. Bankruptcy Ct. (no. dist.) Calif., 1988—. Mem. bankruptcy adv. com. U.S. Dist. Ct., 1984-88; law rep. 9th Cir. Jud. Conf., 1987-88. Mem. adv. bd. Downtown YMCA, 1984-88; dir. The Women's Fund, 1987-88; bd. dirs. Consumer Credit Counselors of San Francisco, 1999—, Cathedral Found., 2001—. Mem. Santa Clara County Bar Assn. (chmn. debtor and creditor and insolvency com. 1979, 81, treas. 1982, pres. 1985-86), Santa Clara County Bar Assn. Law Found. (trustee 1982, 86-88, pres. 1985, law related edn. trustee 1986-88), Nat. Assn. Bankruptcy Trustees (founding mem., v.p., sec. 1981-88), Rotary Club San Jose (bd. dirs. 1992-95), Nat. Assn. Bankruptcy Trustees (founder). Office: US Bankruptcy Ct 280 S 1st St Rm 3035 San Jose CA 95113-3010

MORGAN, MARK QUENTEN, astrophysics educator; b. Topeka, Dec. 27, 1950; s. Walter Quenten and Barbara Gene (Haynes) M. BA in Astronomy, San Diego State U., 1972; PhD in Astronomy, U. Addison, Ont., Can., 1976. Jet engine and power plant engr. N.Am. Aviation, Palmdale, Calif., 1966-68; astron. observer San Diego State U., 1970-74; engr., solar observer U. Md.-Clark Lake Radio Obs., Borrego Springs, Calif., 1978-82; engr., lectr. Sci. Atlanta, San Diego, 1979-97; adv. rsch. engr. Intel Corp., 1998—. Inventor continuous wave laser, 1965, high intensity sound acoustic screening system, 1979. Mem. Inst. Environ. Scis., Acoustic Soc. Am., Astrophys. Soc. Am., Union Concerned Scientists, Planetary Soc. Office: Sci Atlanta PO Box 4254 San Diego CA 92164-4254

MORGAN, MICHAEL BREWSTER, publishing company executive; b. L.A., Dec. 30, 1953; s. Brewster Bowen and Eleanor (Boysen) M.; m. Debra Hunter, July 20, 1986. BA, Conn. Coll., 1975. Coll. sales rep. Addison Wesley Pub. Co., Chapel Hill, N.C., 1977-81, sponsoring editor Reading, Mass., 1981-84; chief exec. officer Morgan Kaufmann Pubs., San Francisco, 1984—. Mem. Am. Assn. for Artificial Intelligence, Assn. for Computing Machinery. Office: Morgan Kaufmann Pubs 340 Pine St San Francisco CA 94104-3205

MORGAN, NEIL, writer, newspaper editor, lecturer, columnist; b. Smithfield, N.C., Feb. 27, 1924; s. Samuel Lewis and Isabelle (Robeson) M.; m. Caryl Lawrence, 1945 (div. 1954); m. Katharine Starkey, 1955 (div. 1962); m. Judith Blakely, 1964; 1 child, Jill. AB, Wake Forest Coll., 1943. Columnist San Diego Daily Jour., 1946-50; columnist San Diego Evening Tribune, 1950-92, assoc. editor, 1977-81, editor, 1981-92; assoc. editor, sr. columnist San Diego Union-Tribune, 1992—. Syndicated columnist Morgan Jour., Copley News Service, 1958— ; lectr.; cons. on Calif. affairs Bank of Am., Sunset mag. Author: My San Diego, 1951, It Began With a Roar, 1953, Know Your Doctor, 1954, Crosstown, 1955, My San Diego 1960, 1959, Westward Tilt, 1963, Neil Morgan's San Diego, 1964, The Pacific States, 1967, The California Syndrome, 1969, (with Robert Witty) Marines of Margarita, 1970, The Unconventional City, 1972, (with Tom Blair) Yesterday's San Diego, 1976, This Great Land, 1983, Above San Diego, 1990, (with Judith Morgan) Dr. Seuss & Mr. Geisel, 1995, (with Judith Morgan) Roger: The Biography of Roger Revelle, 1997; conbr. non-fiction articles to Nat. Geog., Esquire, Redbook, Reader's Digest, Holiday, Harper's, Travel and Leisure, Ency. Brit. Lt. USNR, 1943-46. Recipient Ernie Pyle Meml. award, 1957, Bill Corum Meml. award, 1961, Disting. Svc. citation Wake Forest U., 1966, Grand award for travel writing Pacific Area Travel Assn., 1972, 78, Fourth Estate award San Diego State U., 1988, The Morgan award Leadership Edn. Awareness Devel. San Diego, 1993; co-recipient Ellen and Roger Revelle award, 1986; named Outstanding Young Man of Yr. San Diego, 1959, 1st place news commentary, Calif. News Pub. Assn., 1993, Harold Keen award, 1996, Chancellors medal, U. Calif., San Diego, 2000; named Mr. San Diego, Rotary, 1999. Mem. Authors Guild, Soc. Profl. Journalists (award for best column 1999), Soc. of Am. Travel Writers, Bohemian Club, Phi Beta Kappa. Home: 7930 Prospect Pl La Jolla CA 92037-3721 Office: PO Box 191 San Diego CA 92112-4106 E-mail: neil.morgan@uniontrib.com

MORGAN, RICHARD J. dean, educator; JD, UCLA, 1971. Bar: Calif. Assoc., ptnr. Krueger & Marsh, L.A., 1972-80; dean, prof. U. Wyo. Coll. Law, 1987-89; assoc. dean Ariz. State U. Coll. Law, Tempe, 1983-87, dean, prof., 1990-97; dean, prof. William S. Boyd Sch. Law U. Nev., Las Vegas, 1997—. Office: U Nev William S Boyd Sch Law 4505 S Maryland Pkwy Las Vegas NV 89154-9900

MORGAN, STANLEY CHARLES, plastic and reconstructive surgeon; b. Phoenix, July 23, 1935; s. Fred Charles and Hazel (King) M.; m. Doris Anne Duke, Sept. 8, 1956; children: Pamela Anne, Cheryl Lynn, Mark Thomas. BS, U. Ariz.; MD, St. Louis Sch. Medicine. Diplomate Am. Bd. Plastic Surgery. Intern UCLA Ctr. Health Svcs., 1961-62, resident plastic surgery, 1966-68; resident gen. surgery Wadsworth Vets. Hosp., L.A., 1962-66; practice medicine specializing in plastic surgery Pasadena, Calif., 1970—. Asst. clin. prof. U. So. Calif. Sch. Medicine, Los Angeles, 1981—, UCLA Ctr. Health Scis., 1970-81. Lt. col. U.S. Army, 1968-70. Fellow ACS, Am. Soc. Plastic and Reconstructive Surgeons, Am. Soc. Aesthetic Plastic Surgery, Calif. Soc. Plastic Surgeons.

MORGAN, STEPHEN CHARLES, academic administrator; b. Upland, Calif., June 2, 1946; s. Thomas Andrew and Ruth Elizabeth (Miller) M.; m. Ann Marie McMurray, Sept. 6, 1969; 1 child, Kesley Suzanne. BA, U. La Verne, 1968; MS, U. So. Calif., 1971; EdD, U. No. Colo., 1979. Devel. officer U. La Verne, Calif., 1968-71, asst. to pres., 1971-73, dir. devel., 1973-75, v.p. devel., 1975-76, pres., 1985—; dir. devel. U. So. Calif., L.A., 1976-79; exec. dir. Ind. Colls. No. Calif., San Francisco, 1979-85. Dir. Ind. Colls. So. Calif., L.A., 1985—. Bd. dirs. Mt. Baldy United Way, Ontario, Calif., 1988-98, McKinley Children's Ctr., San Dimas, Calif., 1989-99; chair nat. com. on higher edn. Ch. of Brethren, Elgin, Ill., 1988-90; dir. Pomona Valley Hosp. Med. Ctr., 1992-98, 99—, Inter Valley Health Plan, 1992-97. Mem. Assn. Ind. Calif. Colls. and Univs. (exec. com. 1989—, vice-chmn. 1996-2000, chmn. 2000—), L.A. County Fair Assn. (bd. dirs.), Western Coll. Assn. (exec. com. 1992-98, pres. 1996-98), Western Assn. Schs. and Colls. (sr. accrediting commn. 1996-2001), Pi Gamma Mu. Avocations: orchid culture, fly fishing, golf. Home: 2518 N Mountain Ave Claremont CA 91711-1579 Office: U LaVerne Office Pres 1950 3rd St La Verne CA 91750-4401 E-mail: morgans@ulv.edu

MORGAN, THOMAS OLIVER, bishop; b. Jan. 20, 1941; s. Charles Edwin and Amy Amelia (Hoyes) M.; m. Lillian Marie Textor, 1963; three children. BA, U. Sask., Can., 1962; BD, King's Coll., London, 1965; DD (hon.), Coll. of Emmanuel and St. Chad, Sask., 1986. Curate Ch. of the Saviour, Blackburn, Lancashire, Eng., 1966-69; rector Ch. of the Good Shepherd, Porcupine Plain, Sask., Can., 1969-73, Ch. of the Saviour, Kinistino, 1973-77, Shellbrook, 1977-83; Archdeacon Sask., 1983-85; bishop Diocese of Saskatoon, Prince Albert, 1985-93, 1993-2001; archbishop Diocese of Saskatoon and Met. of Rupert's Land, 2001—. Office: Diocese of Saskatoon PO Box 1965 Saskatoon SK Canada S7K 3S5

MORGENROTH, EARL EUGENE, entrepreneur; b. Sidney, Mont., May 7, 1936; s. Frank and Leona (Ellison) M.; m. Noella Nichols, Aug. 2, 1958; children: Dolores Roxanna, David Jonathan, Denise Christine. BS, U. Mont., 1961. From salesman to gen. mgr. Sta. KGVO-AM Radio, Missoula, Mont., 1958-65; sales mgr. Stas. KGVO-TV, KTVM-TV and KCFW-TV, Missoula, Butte, Kalispell, 1965-66, gen. mgr., 1966-68, Sta. KCOY-TV, Santa Maria, Calif., 1968-69; v.p., gen. mgr. Western Broadcasting Co., Missoula, 1966-69, gen. mgr., pres., 1969-81, numerous cos., Mont., Calif. Idaho, P.R., Ga., 1966-84; pres., chmn. Western Broadcasting Co., Missoula, 1981-84, Western Communications, Inc., Reno, 1984-90; prin. Western Investments, Reno, 1984—. Chmn. Western Fin., Inc., Morgenroth Music Ctrs., Inc., Mont., Mont. Band Instruments, Inc.; chmn. E & B Music Inc., Times Square, Inc., Rio de Plumas Ranches, LLC; presdl. adv. coun. Univ. Mont., 1996—, biology sch. adv. coun., 2001— . Mem. Mont. Bank Bd., Helena; commencement spkr. U. Mont., 1988; bd. dirs. U. Mont. Found., 1985-95. With. U.S. Army, 1954-57. Named Boss of Yr. Santa Maria Valley J.C.s, 1968, Alumnus of the Yr., U. Mont. Bus. Sch., 1998. Mem. U. Mont. Century Club (pres.), Missoula C. of C. (pres.), Rocky Mountain Broadcasters Assn. (pres.), Craighead Wildlife-Wildlands Inst. (bd. dirs. 1991-97), Boone and Crockett Club (pres. 2001—), Grizzly Riders Internat. (bd. dirs., v.p.), Bldg. A Scholastic Heritage (bd. dirs. 1987-97). Republican. Methodist.

MORGENSEN, JERRY LYNN, construction company executive; b. Lubbock, Tex., July 9, 1942; s. J.J. and Zelline (Butler) M.; m. Linda Dee Austin, Apr. 17, 1965; children: Angela, Nicole BCE, Tex. Tech U., 1965. Area engr. E.I. Dupont Co., Orange, Tex., 1965-67, div. engr. La Place, La., 1967 73; project mgr. Hensel Phelps Constrn. Co., Greeley, Colo., 1973-78, area mgr., 1978-80, v.p., 1980-85, pres., CEO, 1985—. Office: Hensel Phelps Constrn Co 420 SIXTH AVE Greeley CO 80632

MORGENSTERN, NORBERT RUBIN, civil engineering educator; b. Toronto, Ont., Can., May 25, 1935; s. Joel and Bella (Skornik) M.; m. Patricia Elizabeth Gooderham, Dec. 28, 1960; children: Sarah Alexandra, Katherine Victoria, David Michael Gooderham. BASc, U. Toronto, 1956, DEng h.c., 1983; DIC, Imperial Coll. Sci., 1964; PhD, U. London, 1964; DSc h.c., Queen's U., 1989. Rsch. asst., lectr. civil engring. Imperial Coll. Sci. and Tech., London, 1958-68; prof. civil engring. U. Alta., Edmonton, Can., 1968-83, Univ. prof. Can., 1983—, chmn. dept. civil engring. Can., 1994-97. Cons. engr., 1961— Contbr. articles to profl. jours. Bd. dirs. Young Naturalists Found., 1977-82, Edmonton Symphony Soc., 1978-85. Athlone fellow, 1956; recipient prize Brit. Geotech. Soc., 1961, 66, Huber prize ASCE, 1971, Legget award Can. Geotech. Soc., 1979, Alta. order of Excellence, 1991. Fellow Royal Soc. Can., Can. Acad. Engring., Indian Nat. Acad. Engring. (fgn.); mem. U.S. Nat. Acad. Engring. (fgn. assoc.), Royal Acad. Engring. (fgn. mem.), Cancian Geosci. Coun. (pres. 1983), Can. Geotechnical Soc. (pres. 1989-91), Internat. Soc. for Soil Mechanics and Found. Engring. (pres. 1989-94), Royal Glenora Club, Athenaeum (London), various other profl. assns. Home: 106 Laurier Dr Edmonton AB Canada T5R 5P6 Office: U Alta Dept Civil Engring Edmonton AB Canada T6G 2G7

MORGESE, JAMES N. broadcast executive; b. Bronx, N.Y., Jan. 5, 1951; s. George N. and Tina C. (Papa) M.; m. Zoe A. Larsen, July 11, 1976; children: Mila, Lane. BA in Mass Comm., U. Denver, 1973, MA in Pub. Comm., 1979. Prodn. asst. NBC, N.Y.C., 1971-74; mem. creative staff Prodns. Unltd., Denver, 1974-75; prodn. asst. Sta. KOA-TV, Denver, 1975-79; prodn. mgr. WKYU-TV, Bowling Green, Ky., 1980-82; mgr. prodn. ops. Sta. KUID-TV, Moscow, 1982-85; local program mgr. Sta. WUFT-TV, Gainsville, Fla., 1985-86, sta. mgr., 1986-90, KRMA-TV, Denver, 1990-93, pres., gen. mgr., 1993-97, Rocky Mountain Pub. Broadcasting Network, Denver, 1997—. Exec. prodr. Borah Symposium, Moscow, 1980; adv. bd. Alachua County Cable T.V. , Fla., 1989-90; exec. in charge prodn. And Learning For All, Denver, 1992-93, A Place to Call Home, Denver, 1992-93; bd. dirs. 5 Points Media Ctr.; mem. state bd. Am.'s Pub. Telephone. Mem. adv. commn. U. Denver Alumni, 1991-92. Mem. NATAS, Colo. Hispanic Media Assn., Denver Advertising Fedn., Urban League Met. Denver, Rotary. Office: 1089 Bannock St Denver CO 80204-4067

MORGNER, AURELIUS, economist, educator; b. N.Y.C., May 23, 1917; s. Oscar A. and Anna G. (Hoffmeister) M. B.S. in Bus. Adminstrn., U. Mo., 1938, M.A. in Econs., 1940; Ph.D., U. Minn., 1955. Investigator Dept. Labor, 1941; project dir. Employment Stblzn. Research Inst., 1941-42; instr. bus. adminstrn. U. Minn., 1942-46; lectr. Northwestern U., 1946-47; assoc. prof. Tex. A&M U., 1947-56, prof., 1956-58; vis. prof. U. São Paulo, Brazil, 1958-60, dir. grad. social studies, 1959-60; prof. econs. U. So. Calif., L.A., 1960—, chmn. dept., 1962-69; prof. internat. econs. Sch. Internat. Relations, 1960—. Pub. panel mem. Chgo. Regional War Labor Bd., 1943-45; pub. rep. minimum wage com. Dept. Labor, 1942,43; cons. Govt. Eucador, 1965-68, Govt. Guyana, 1968, state Nev., 1970, Philippines, 1971-72, Yemen Arab Republic, 1974-75; U.S. State Dept. vis. lectr., Brazil, summer 1966 Co-author: Local Labor Markets, 1948, Problems in Economic Analysis, 1948, Problems in the Theory of Price, 1954 (trans. Spanish 1965, Portuguese 1967). Ford faculty fellow Columbia U., 1954-55 Mem. So. Calif. Econ. Assn. (pres. 1965-66), Am. Econs. Assn., Western Econ. Assn., Am. Arbitration Assn., Internat. Studies Assn. Office: U So Calif Dept Econs Los Angeles CA 90089-0001

MORGRIDGE, JOHN P. computer business executive; m. Tashia Morgridge; three children. BBA, DSc (hon.), U. Wis.; MBA, Stanford U. Mktg. profl. Honeywell Info. Systems, 1960-80; v.p. mkgt., sales and svc. Stratus Co., Inc., 1980-86; pres., chief ops. officer GRiD Systems (now part of Tandy Corp.), 1986-88; pres., CEO Cisco Systems, 1988-95, pres., CEO, chmn., 1995-98, chmn., 1998—. Recipient Leadership in Tech. award Tech. Corps, 1988. Office: Cisco Systems 170 W Tasman Dr San Jose CA 95134-1700

MORI, ALLEN ANTHONY, university dean, consultant, researcher; b. Hazleton, Pa., Nov. 1, 1947; s. Primo Philip and Carmella (DeNoia) M.; m. Barbara Epoca, June 26, 1971; 1 child, Kirsten Lynn. BA, Franklin and Marshall Coll., Lancaster, Pa., 1969; MEd, Bloomsburg U. Pa., 1971; PhD, U. Pitts., 1975. Spl. edn. tchr. White Haven (Pa.) State Sch. and Hosp., 1969-70, Hazleton Area Sch. Dist., 1970-71, Pitts. Pub. Schs., 1971-74; supr. student tchrs. U. Pitts., 1974-75; prof. spl. edn. U. Nev., Las Vegas, 1975-84; dean coll edn. Marshall U., Huntington, W.Va., 1984-87; dean sch. edn. Calif. State U., L.A., 1987—. Hearing officer pub. law 94-142 Nev. Dept. Edn., Carson City, 1978—; mem. Nev. Gov.'s Com. on Mental Health and Mental Retardation, 1983-84; cons. Ministry Edn., Manitoba, Can., 1980-82; pres. Tchr. Edn. Coun. State Colls. and Univs., 1993-94. Author: Families of Children with Special Needs, 1983; co-author: Teaching the Severely Retarded, 1980, Handbook of Preschool, Special Education, 1980, Adapted Physical Education, 1983, A Vocational Training Continuum for the Mentally and Physically Disabled, 1985, Teaching Secondary Students with Mild Learning and Behavior Problems, 1986, 93, 99; author numerous articles, book revs. and monographs. Bd. dirs. Assn. Retarded Citizens San Gabriel Valley, ElMonte, 1989-94. Recipient grants U.S. Dept. Edn., 1976-91, Nev. Dept. Edn., W.Va. Dept. Edn., Calif. State U. Chancellor's Office. Mem. Assn. Tchr. Educators, Coun. for Exceptional Children (div. on Career Devel. exec. com. 1981-83), Nat. Soc. for Study of Edn., Phi Beta Delta, Phi Delta Kappa, Pi Lambda Theta. Avocations: jogging, travel. Office: Calif State U 5151 State University Dr Los Angeles CA 90032-4226

MORIE, G. GLEN, lawyer, manufacturing company executive; BA, Bowdoin Coll., 1964; LLB, U. Pa., 1967. Bar: Wash. 1968. Pvt. practice law, Wash., 1970-73; asst. counsel PACCAR, Inc., Bellevue, 1973-79, asst. gen. counsel, 1979-83, gen. counsel, 1983-85, v.p., gen. counsel, 1985—. Office: PACCAR Inc PO Box 1518 Bellevue WA 98009-1518

MORIGUCHI, TOMIO, gift and grocery store executive; b. Tacoma, Apr. 16, 1936; s. Fujimatsu and Sadako (Tsutakawa) M.; m. Lovett Keiko Tanaka, Nov. 15, 1969; children: Tyler Minoru, Denise Ritsuko. BSME, U. Wash., 1961. With missile div. Boeing Co., Seattle, 1961-62; with Uwajimaya Inc., Seattle, 1962—, pres., 1965—. Bd. dirs. Seafirst Corp., Seattle 1st Nat. Bank, Wash. Energy Co. Bd. dirs. Wash. Inst. Applied Tech., Seattle, Seattle Found., Leadership Tomorrow, Pacific Celebration; mem. Wash. Econ. Devel. Bd., Wash. Adv. Council on Internat. Trade and Devel.; v.p., bd. dirs., past chmn. Nikkei Concerns, Inc., treas. Nat. Japanese Am. Citizens League, 1974-76; trustee Seattle Community Coll. Dist., 1985—, also past chmn.; past chmn. Chinatown-Internat. Dist. Preservation and Devel. Authority; bd. dirs., past pres. Internat. Dist. Improement Assn., many others. Recipient Outstanding Vol. Civic Leadership award Four Seasons Hotel, Seattle, 1987; named Alumni Legend, U. Wash., 1987. Mem. Seattle C. of C. (past v.p.), Internat. Dist. Econ. Assn. (v.p., past pres.), Japan Am. Soc. State Wash. (pres. 1985), Rotary. Office: Uwajimaya Inc 519 6th Ave S Seattle WA 98104-2812

MORIS, LAMBERTO GIULIANO, architect; b. Siena, Tuscany, Italy, Mar. 29, 1944; came to U.S., 1972; s. Gualtiero Luigi and Giovanna (Avanzati) M.; m. Tracy P. Schilling, 1970 (div. 1985); children: Giacomo, Stefano; m. Beverly Chiang, Mar. 28, 1986; 1 child, Christopher. MA in Arch., U. Florence, Italy, 1970. Assoc. Marquis Assocs., San Francisco, 1972-78, prin., 1978-85, Simon Martin-Vegue Winkelstein Moris, San Francisco, 1985—. Tchr. San Francisco City Coll.; juror DuPont Antron Design Awards, 1989; mem. adv. com. Acad. of Art-Coll., San Francisco, 1991—. Mem. San Francisco Opera Guild. Fellow AIA (mem. Coll. Fellows, mem. interior arch. sect., juror Honor Award for interiors 1996); mem. Italingua Inst. (bd. dirs.), Oakland Met. C. of C., The Engrs. Club, Il Cenacolo Club. Roman Catholic. Avocations: coin collecting, skiing, travel. Office: SMWM 989 Market St 3d Fl San Francisco CA 94103 Fax: (415) 88207098. E-mail: lmoris@smwm.com

MORISHITA, AKIHIKO, trading company executive; b. Osaka, Japan, Oct. 14, 1941; came to U.S., 1981; s. Sueyoshi and Toshiko Morishita; m. Fumiko Okamura; children: Shizuko, Kumiko, Okamura. BA in Econs., Wakayama U., Wakayama, Japan, 1965. Mgr. Hanwa & Co. Ltd., Osaka, 1965-80; cons. oil dept. Pacific Southwest Trading Co., San Diego, 1981-82; exec. Pacific Marine Bunkering, Inc., L.A., 1982—. Mem. Woodland Hills Country Club. Home: 4610 Don Pio Dr Woodland Hills CA 91364-4205

MORITA, RICHARD YUKIO, microbiology and oceanography educator; b. Pasadena, Calif., Mar. 27, 1923; s. Jiro and Reiko (Yamamoto) M.; m. Toshiko Nishihara, May 29, 1926; children— Sally Jean, Ellen Jane, Peter Wayne B.S., U. Nebr., 1947; M.S., U. So. Calif., 1949; Ph.D., U. Calif., 1954. Microbiologist Mid-Pacific Expdn., 1950, Danish Galathea Deep-Sea Expdn., 1952, Trans-Pacific Expdn.; Postdoctoral fellow U. Calif., Scripps Inst. Oceanography, 1954-55; asst. prof. U. Houston, 1955-58; asst. prof., assoc. prof. U. Neb., 1958-62; prof. microbiology and oceanography Oreg. State U., Corvallis, 1962-89, prof. emeritus microbiology and oceanography, 1989—. Prog. dir. biochemistry NSF, 1968-69; Disting. vis. prof. Kyoto Univ.; cons. NIH, 1968-70; researcher in field. Contbr. articles to sci. lit. Patentee in field. Served with U.S. Army, 1944-46 Grantee NSF, 1962—, NIH, 1960-68, NASA, 1967-72, Office Naval Research, 1966-70, Dept. Interior, 1968-72, NOAA, 1975-82, Bur. Land Mgmt., 1982, EPA, 1986—; recipient awards including King Fredericus IX Medal and Ribbon, 1954, Sr. Queen Elizabeth II Fellowship, 1973-74, Hotpack lectr. and award Can. Soc. Fellow Japan Soc. for Promotion Sci.; mem. Am. Soc. Microbiology (Fisher award). Office: Oreg State U Dept Microbiology Corvallis OR 97331

MORITZ, TIMOTHY BOVIE, psychiatrist; b. Portsmouth, Ohio, July 26, 1936; s. Charles Raymond and Elisabeth Bovie (Morgan) M.; m. Joyce Elizabeth Rasmussen, Oct. 13, 1962 (div. Sept. 1969); children: Elizabeth Wynne, Laura Morgan; m. Antoinette Tanasichuk, Oct. 31, 1981; children: David Michael, Stephanie Lysbeth. BA, Ohio State U., 1959; MD, Cornell U., 1963. Diplomate Am. Bd. Psychiatry and Neurology. Intern in medicine N.Y. Hosp., N.Y.C., 1963-64, resident in psychiatry, 1964-67; spl. asst. to dir. NIMH, Bethesda, Md., 1967-69; dir. Community Mental Health Ctr., Rockland County, N.Y., 1970-74, Ohio Dept. Mental Health, Columbus,

Ohio, 1975-81; med. dir. psychiatry Miami Valley Hosp., Dayton, 1981-82; med. dir. N.E. Ga. Community Mental Health Ctr., Athens, Ga., 1982-83, Charter Vista Hosp., Fayetteville, Ark., 1983-87; clin. dir. adult psychiatry Charter Hosp., Las Vegas, Nev., 1987-94; pvt. practice psychiatry Las Vegas, 1987—; med. dir. Problem Gambling Cons., Las Vegas, 2000—. Prof. Wright State U., Dayton, Ohio, 1981-82; asst. prof. Cornell U., N.Y.C., 1970-73; mem. human subjects biomed. scis. rev. com. U. Nev., Las Vegas, 2000—; cons. NIMH, Rockville, Md., 1973-83. Author: (chpt.) Rehabilitation Medicine and Psychiatry, 1976; mem. editorial bd. Directions in Psychiatry, 1981— Dir. dept. mental health and mental retardation Gov.'s Cabinet, State of Ohio, Columbus, 1975-81. Recipient Svc. award Ohio Senate, 1981, Svc. Achievement award Ohio Gov., 1981. Fellow Am. Psychiat. Assn. (Disting. Svc. award 1981); mem. AMA, Nev. Assn. Psychiat. Physicians, Nev. State Med. Assn., Am. Assn. Chronic Fatigue Syndrome, Clark County Med. Soc., Cornell U. Med. Coll. Alumni Assn. Office: 1640 Alta Dr Ste 11 Las Vegas NV 89106-4165 E-mail: TMB72636@aol.com

MORK, STUART R. chief financial officer land and farming company; BS in Fin., Acctg., MBA in Fin., Acctg., U. So. Ca. Treas. The Newhall Land & Farming Co., 1987-92, v.p., fin., 1992-95, CFO, 1995-98, sr. v.p., CFO, 1998—. Mem. Urban Land Inst., exec. com. mem. Lusk Ctr. Real Estate Devel. USC, bd. dirs. Henry May Newhall Meml. Hosp., bd. dirs. Boy Scouts Am. L.A. Coun., trustee San Marino Schs. Found. Office: The Newhall Land & Farming Co 23823 Valencia Blvd Valencia CA 91355-2103

MOROLES, JESUS BAUTISTA, sculptor; b. Corpus Christi, Tex., Sept. 22, 1950; AA, El Centro Coll., Dallas, 1975; BFA, No. Tex. State U., 1978. Bd. dirs. Internat. Sculpture Ctr., Washington; instr. Nat. Mus. Am. Art Symposium, 1992. One-person shows include Davis-McClain Gallery, Houston, 1982, 84, 86, 88, 90, 92, Janus Gallery, Santa Fe, 1984, 85, 86, 89, 90, 92, Marilyn Butler Gallery, Scottsdale, Ariz., 1986, 89, Richard Green Gallery, L.A., 1989, 91, N.Y., 1989, Santa Monica, Calif., 1990, Chgo. Internat. Art Exposition, Klein Art Works, Chgo., 1991, Mus. S.E. Tex., Beaumont, 1992, Wirtz Gallery, San Francisco, 1990, Escultura, 1991, Expositum, Polanco, Mex., 1991, Adams-Middleton Gallery, Dallas, 1992, Carl Schlosberg Fine Art, Sherman Oaks, Calif., 1992; commd. Tex. Commerce Bank, Dallas, 1983, Riata Devel., Houston, 1984, Siena Sq., Boulder, Colo., 1985, Nat. Health Ins. Co., Dallas, 1986, IBM, Raleigh, N.C., 1986; represented in permanent collections Albuquerque Mus., Mus. Fine Arts, Santa Fe, Old Jail Art Ctr., Albany, Tex., U. Houston, Mint Mus., Charlotte, N.C., Dallas Mus. Art, Nat. Mus. Am. Art, Smithsonian, Washington. Visual Art fellow Southeastern Ctr. Contemporary Art, Winston-Salem, N.C., 1982; Pres. Citation award U. No. Tex., 1992; Matching grnatee Nat. Endowment Arts, Birmingham Botanical Gardens, 1984. Office: Attn Jesus B Moroles c/o Imago Gallery 45 450 Hwy 74 Palm Desert CA 92260-4336

MORRILL, RICHARD LELAND, geographer, educator; b. L.A., Feb. 15, 1934; s. Robert W. and Lillian M. (Riffo) M.; m. Joanne L. Cooper, 1965; children: Lee, Andrew, Jean. B.A., Dartmouth Coll., 1955; M.A., U. Wash., 1957, Ph.D., 1959. Asst. prof. geography Northwestern U., 1959-60; NSF research fellow U. Lund, Sweden, 1960-61; asst. prof. U. Wash., Seattle, 1961-65, asso. prof., 1965-69, prof., 1969—, chmn. dept. geography, 1974-83, asso. dir. environ. studies, 1974-98; chmn. urban planning PhD program, 1992-98. Vis. asso. prof. U. Chgo., dir. Chgo. Regional Hosp. Study, 1966-67; cons. population, regional and urban planning. Author: Geography of Poverty, 1970, Spatial Organization of Society, 1973, Political Redistricting and Geographic Theory, 1981, Spatial Diffusion, 1987. Mem. King County Boundary Rev. Bd. Guggenheim fellow, 1983-84 Mem. Assn. Am. Geographers (Meritorious Contbn. award 1970, mem. coun. 1970-73, sec. 1979-81, pres. 1981-82), Regional Sci. Assn., Wash. Regional Sch. Assn. (pres. 1993-94), Population Assn. Am., Lambda Alpha. Office: U Wash Dept Geography Seattle WA 98195-0001

MORRILL, THOMAS CLYDE, insurance company executive; b. Chgo., July 1, 1909; s. Walter and Lena Elpha (Haney) M.; m. Hazel Janet Thompson, Oct. 18, 1930; children: Dorothy Mae (Mrs. Gerald L. Kelly), Charles T. Student, Cen. Coll. Arts and Scis., Chgo., 1928-29, Northwestern U., , 1929-30. With Alfred M. Best Co., Inc., 1929-45, assoc. editor, 1940-45; with N.Y. State Ins. Dept., 1945-50, dep. supt. ins., 1947-50; with State Farm Mut. Automobile Ins. Co., Bloomington, Ill., 1950-77, v.p., 1952-77; chmn. bd. State Farm Fire and Casualty Co., Bloomington, 1970-86, State Farm Gen. Ins. Co., Bloomington, 1970-91; cons. State Farm Ins. Cos., Bloomington, 1991—. Founder, chmn., dir. Ins. Inst. for Highway Safety. Chmn. exec. subcom. Nat. Hwy. Safety Adv. Com., 1971-73; chmn. tech. com. on transp. White House Conf. on Aging, 1971; mem. Pres.'s Task Force on Hwy. Safety. Clubs: Union League (Chgo.); Union Hills Country, Lakes (Sun City, Ariz.).

MORRIS, ARLENE MYERS, marketing professional; b. Washington, Dec. 29, 1951; d. Frank Hayes Myers and Lula Irene (Slusser) Kolcun; m. John L. Sullivan, Feb. 17, 1971 (div. July 1982); m. David Wellons Morris, July 27, 1984. BA, Carlow Coll., 1974; postgrad., Western New England Coll., 1981-82. Sales rep. Syntex Labs., Inc., Palo Alto, Calif., 1974-77; profl. sales rep. McNeil Pharm., Spring House, Pa., 1977-78, mental health rep., 1978-80, asst. product dir., 1981-82, dist. mgr., 1982-85, new product dir., 1985-87, exec. dir. new bus. devel., 1987-89, v.p. bus. devel., 1989-93, Scios Inc., Mountain View, Calif., 1993-96, Coulter Pharma., 1996—. Mem. Found. of Ind. Colls., Phila., 1989. Mem. Pharm. Advt. Coun., Am. Diabetes Assn., Am. Acad. Sci., Healthcare Bus. Womens Assn., Lic. Execs. Soc. Home: 11701 Winding Way Los Altos CA 94024-6331 Office: Coulter Pharm 600 Gateway Blvd South San Francisco CA 94080-7014

MORRIS, BRIAN, advertising executive; Pres. Dailey & Assoc., L.A., Calif. Office: Dailey & Assoc 8687 Melrose Ave Ste G300 West Hollywood CA 90069-5725

MORRIS, DAVID JOHN, mining engineer, consultant, mining executive; b. Seattle, May 6, 1945; s. Jack Abraham and Alice Jean (Hanson) M.; m. Melania F. Kearney, July 28, 1978; children: Whitney Elizabeth, Benton James, Sienna Elise. BA in Math. and Physics, Whitman Coll., 1968; BS in Mining Engring., Columbia U., 1968. Registered profl. engr., Colo., Utah, Wash. Mining engr. Union Oil of Calif., Los Angeles, 1968-69, John T. Boyd Co., Denver, 1974-76, sr. mining engr., 1976-78, v.p., mgr., 1978-87; sr. cons., 1998—; mng. ptnr. Palmer Coaking Coal Co., Black Diamond, Wash., 1976-82, 90—; pres. Pacific Coast Coal Co., Black Diamond, 1982—, Pacific Hydropower Devel., Inc., Seattle, 1995—. Mem. Bd. Overseers Whitman Coll., Walla Walla, Wash., 1986—, vice chair, 1993-95, chmn. Rep. campaign for Whitman, Denver, 1985; coach youth athletics. Served as lt. USN, 1969-74. Vietnam. Henry Krumb scholar Columbia U., N.Y.C., 1967-68. Mem. NSPE, Soc. Mining Engrs. (admissions com. 1985-88, Howard Eavenson award com. 1984-87, Woomer award com. 1990-93, chair 1993—, Ramsay award com. 1992-95, 99—, chair 1995—), Nat. Coal Assn. (bd. dirs. 1990-98, exec. com. 1993-94, 96-98), Nat. Coal Coun. (appointed by Sec. of Energy 1992, 94, 96, 98, 2000), Nat. Mining Assn. (bd. dirs. 1995-98), Seattle C. of C. (chmn. energy com. 1991-94), Western Rugby Football Union (sec. 1980), Broadmoor Golf Club, Rotary. Republican. Avocations: golf, hunting, fishing, gardening, handball. Home: 3711 E Madison St Seattle WA 98112-3838 Office: Pacific Coast Coal Co Inc PO Box 450 Black Diamond WA 98010-0450 E-mail: dimorris@aol.com

MORRIS, DONALD CHARLES, commercial real estate mergers and acquisitions; b. Iowa City, Nov. 15, 1951; s. Lucien Ellis and Jean (Pinder) M.; m. Barbara Louise Small, Apr. 28, 1973 (div. Apr. 1980); m. Jana Susan Moyer, Aug. 28, 1982; children: Alexander Charles, Elisa Jean. Student, Cantab Coll., Toronto, Can., 1970-71; BSC, U. Guelph, Can., 1974; MSC, U. Guelph, 1975; PhD, U. B.C., Vancouver, 1978. Instr. U. B.C., Vancouver, 1975-77; pres. Morley Internat., Inc., Seattle, 1976-81; self-employed Comml. Investment Real Estate, Seattle, 1981-83; v.p., regional mgr. DKB Corp., Seattle, 1983-86; pres. Morris Devel. Svcs., Inc., Seattle, 1986—, Washington Group, Inc., Seattle, 1986—; sec.-treas. Interactive Imagination Corp., Seattle, 2000—. Bd.dirs., sec., treas. Interactive Imagination Corp., Seattle, 2000—. Bd. dirs. Perservation Action, Washington, 1985-90; mem. Nat. Trust for Historic Preservation. Mem. Nat. Assn. Realtors, Wash. Assn. Realtors. Avocations: skiing, sailing, boating. Office: Wash Group Morris Devel PO Box 4584 Rollingbay WA 98061-0584

MORRIS, GRANT HAROLD, law educator; b. Syracuse, N.Y., Dec. 10, 1940; s. Benjamin and Caroline Grace (Judelson) M.; m. Phyllis Silberstein, July 4, 1967; children: Joshua, Sara. AB, Syracuse U., 1962, JD, 1964; LLM, Harvard U., 1971. Bar: N.Y. 1964. Atty. N.Y. Mental Hygiene Law Recodification Project, Inst. Public Adminstrn., N.Y.C., 1964-66; faculty Wayne State U. Law Sch., 1967-70, prof., 1970-73, dean acad. affairs, 1971-73; prof. U. San Diego Law Sch., 1973—, Univ. prof., 1996-97, acting dean, 1977-78, 88-89, assoc. dean grad. legal edn., 1978-81, interim dean, 1997-98; prof. law in psychiatry Wayne State U. Med. Sch., 1970-73; adj. prof. U. Calif. Med. Sch., San Diego, 1974-84, clin. prof. dept. psychiatry, 1984—. Legal counsel Mich. Legis. Com. to Revise Mental Health Statutes, 1970-73; organizer law and psychiatry sect. Assn. Am. Law Schs., 1973, chmn., 1973-74; patients advocate, San Diego County, 1977-78; cons. Criminal Code Commn., Ariz. Legis., 1974; reporter task force on guidelines governing roles of mental health profls. in criminal process Am. Bar Assn. standing com. on assn. standards for criminal justice, 1981-84; cert. rev. hearing officer San Diego Superior Ct., 1984-90, ct. commr./judge pro tem, 1990-92, mental health hearing officer, 1992-97; hearing officer San Diego Housing Commn., 1988-92; mem. exec. com. sect. law and mental disability Assn. Am. Law Schs., 1990-97. Author: The Insanity Defense: A Blueprint for Legislative Reform, 1975; co-author: Mental Disorder in the Criminal Process: Stan Stress and the Vietnam/Sports Conspiracy, 1993; editor, contbr.: The Mentally Ill and the Right to Treatment, 1970. Mem. Atascadero State Hosp. adv. bd., 2000—. Mem. Phi Alpha Delta (faculty adv. 1970-73, 75-92). Home: 8515 Nottingham Pl La Jolla CA 92037-2125 Office: U San Diego Law Sch 5998 Alcala Park San Diego CA 92110-2429 E-mail: gmorris@acusd.edu

MORRIS, JAMES, national monument administrator; Supt. Craters of the Moon Nat. Monument, Arco, Idaho. Office: Craters Moon Nat Monument PO Box 29 Arco ID 83213-0029

MORRIS, JOHN DAVID, research institute administrator, geology educator; b. Mpls., Dec. 7, 1946; s. Henry Madison and Mary Louise (Beach) M.; m. Dalta Jan Eads, Sept. 3, 1977; children: Chara Mischelle, Timothy Adam, Beth Anna. BSCE, Va. Tech., 1969; MS in Geol. Engring., U. Okla., 1977, PhD in Geol. Engring., 1980. Civil engr. City of L.A. Pub. Works, 1969-73; adj. rsch. scientist Inst. for Creation Rsch., Santee, Calif., 1972-84, prof. geology, 1984-95, pres., 1995—; asst. prof. geol. engr. U. Okla., 1980-84. Author: Adventure on Ararat, 1973, The Ark on Ararat, 1976, Tracking Those Incredible Dinosaurs, 1980, Noah's Ark and the Lost World, 1988, Science, Scripture and the Young Earth, 1989, Grand Canyon: Monument to Catastrophe, 1994, The Young Earth, 1994, Noah's Ark and Ararat Adventure, 1994 (Gold Medal 1994), Abraham's Family, 1998, The Creation, 1998, A Trip to the Ocean, 2000, The Geology Book, 2000, others; co-author: Science, Scripture and the Young Earth, 1989, Modern Creation Trilogy, 1996, others; contbr. articles to profl. jours. Republican. Mem. Bible Ch. Office: Inst for Creation Rsch 10946 Woodside Ave N Santee CA 92071-2833

MORRIS, JOHN THEODORE, planning official; b. Denver, Jan. 18, 1929; s. Theodore Ora and Daisy Allison (McDonald) M.; BFA, Denver U., 1955; m. Dolores Irene Seaman, June 21, 1951; children: Holly Lee, Heather Ann, Heidi Jo, Douglas Fraser. Apprentice landscape architect S.R. DeBoer & Co., Denver, summer 1949, planning technician (part-time), 1954-55; sr. planner and assoc. Trafton Bean & Assocs., Boulder, Colo., 1955-62; prin. Land Planning Assocs., planning cons., Boulder, 1962-65; planning dir. and park coord. Boulder County, 1965-67; sch. planner Boulder Valley Sch. Dist., 1967-84, also dir. planning and engring., 1967-84, supr. facility improvement program, 1969-84; pvt. sch. planning cons., 1984—; cons. U. Colo. Bur. Ednl. Field Svcs., 1974. Bd. dirs. Historic Boulder, 1974-76; mem. parks and recreation adv. com. Denver Regional Coun. Govts., 1975-84. Served with USCG, 1950-53. Mem. Am. Inst. Cert. Planners, Am. Planning Assn., Longmont Artist Guild. Home and Office: 7647 32nd St Boulder CO 80302-9327

MORRIS, MICHAEL H. computer company executive; b. 1948; BA, Northwestern U., 1970; JD, U. Mich., 1974. Ptnr. DeFrancesco & Morris, St. Joseph, Mich., 1977-79; gen. coun., sec. ROLM Corp., 1979-86, US Teleceters Corp., 1986-87, Sun Microsystems, Inc., Mountain View, Calif., 1987-2000, sr. v.p., gen. coun., sec., 2000—. Office: Sun Microsystems Inc MS PAL 1 521 901 San Antonio Rd Palo Alto CA 94303

MORRIS, SANDRA JOAN, lawyer; b. Chgo., Oct. 13, 1944; d. Bernard and Helene (Davies) Aronson; m. Richard William Morris, May 30, 1965 (div. Jan. 1974); children: Tracy Michelle, Bretton Todd; m. William Mark Bandt, July 12, 1981; 1 child, Victoria Elizabeth. BA, U. Ariz., 1965; JD, Calif. Western U., 1969. Bar: Calif. 1970, U.S. Dist. Ct. (so. dist.) Calif. 1970; diplomate Am. Coll. Family Trial Lawyers. Ptnr. Morris & Morris, APC, San Diego, 1970-74; sole practice San Diego, 1974—. Mem. Adv. Commn. on Family Law, Calif. Senate, 1978-79. Contbr. articles to profl. jours. Pres. San Diego Community Child Abuse Coordinating Coun., 1977; mem. human rsch. rev. bd. Children's Hosp., San Diego, 1977-92. Fellow Am. Acad. Matrimonial Lawyers (chpt. pres. 1987-88, nat. bd. govs. 1987-89, 93-94, parliamentarian 1989-91, treas. 1994-97, v.p. 1997-2000, 1st v.p. 2000—), Internat. Acad. Matrimonial Lawyers; mem. ABA (family law sect exec. com. marital property 1982-83, 87-94, faculty mem. Trial Advocacy Inst., 2001—), State Bar Calif. (cert. family law specialist 1980—), Lawyers Club San Diego (bd. dirs. 1973), San Diego Cert. Family Law Specialists (chair 1995-96). Republican. Jewish. Avocations: skiing, travel. Office: 3200 4th Ave Ste 101 San Diego CA 92103-5716

MORRIS, SANDRA K. computer company executive; b. Paxtang, Pa., 1954; BS with honors and distinction, U. Del., 1976, MS, 1981; postgrad., U. Pa. Faculty mem. U. Del.; with RCA Corp. David Sarnoff Rsch. Ctr.; product mgr. Intel Corp., 1985, v.p. e-bus. group, 1999—. Co-author: Multimedia Application Development Using Indeo video and DVI Technology, 1982. Office: Intel Corp PO Box 58119 2200 Mission College Blvd Santa Clara CA 95052-8119

MORRIS, SHARON HUTSON, city manager; BA in Home Econs., Calif. State U., 1976; MA in Urban Planning, UCLA, 1979. Legislative analyst So. Calif. Gas Co., L.A., 1983-86, dist. mgr., 1986-90, cmty. outreach coord., 1990; dir. intergovt. affairs South Coast Air Quality Mgmt. Dist., Diamond Bar, Calif., 1990-94; commr. Bd. Pub. Works City of L.A., 1994-96, dep. mayor Office of Mayor Richard J. Riordan, 1996-97, gen. mgr. Dept. Animal Regulation, 1997-98, exec. dir. Dept. on Disability, 1998—; alt. pub. mem. South Coast Air Quality Hearing Bd., 1998—. Mem. KCET cmty. adv. bd. Hollywood Cmty. Housing Corp. Recipient Outstanding Alumna award Calif. State U., L.A., 1997. Mem. Am. Assn. Blacks in Energy, Nat. Forum for Black Pub. Adminstrn., The Ethnic Coalition (bd. dirs.), Women of Color, Inc. (past co-presiding officer), Calif. League Conservative Voters (bd. dirs.), Alpha Kappa Alpha, Phi Kappa Phi. Office: City Los Angeles Dept Disability 700 E Temple St Rm 380 Los Angeles CA 90012-4046

MORRISON, CHARLES E. think-tank executive; b. Billings, Mont., 1944; m. Chieko; children: Karen, Erica, Kenneth, Douglas. BA in Internat. Studies, MA, PhD, Johns Hopkins U. Legis. asst. U.S. Senate, 1972-80; part-time sr. rsch. assoc. Japan Ctr. for Internat. Exch., 1980-92; asst. to pres. East-West Ctr., 1986-92, dir. program on internat. econs. and politics, 1992-95, pres., 1998—; dir. Asia Pacific Econ. Coun. Study Ctr., 1996-98; chair U.S. Consortium of APEC Study Ctrs., 1996-98. Editor: Asia-Pacific Security Outlook books, 1996—; author: wide range of books, papers and analyses; widely quoted by major news media on issues of regional cooperation, internat. rels., U.S. Asia policy and trade policies, U.S.-Japan rels. and the Asian economic crisis. Office: East West Ctr 1601 E West Rd Honolulu HI 96848-1601

MORRISON, DAVID, science administrator, researcher; b. Danville, Ill., June 26, 1940; s. Donald Harlan Morrison and Alice Lee (Douglass) Guin; m. Nancy Dunlap, June 19, 1966 (div. 1977); m. Janet L. Irick, Aug. 23, 1981. BA, U. Ill., 1962; PhD, Harvard U., 1969. Prof. astronomy U. Hawaii, Honolulu, 1969-88, vice chancellor rsch., 1983-85, dir. IRTF telescope, 1985-88; dep. assoc. adminstr. NASA Office Space Sci., Washington, 1981; chief space sci. div. NASA Ames Rsch. Ctr., Moffett Field, Calif., 1988-96, dir. astrobiology and space rsch., 1996—. Pres. Astron. Soc. of the Pacific, San Francisco, 1982-84; chmn. Divsn. for Planetary Scis., Washington, 1980-81; councillor Am. Astron. Soc., Washington, 1982-85; pres. Internat. Astron. Union Commn. on Planets, 1991-94. Author: Exploration of the Universe, 1987, 91, 95, The Planetary System, 1988, 96, Cosmic Catastrophes, 1989, Exploring Planetary Worlds, 1993, Voyages Through the Universe, 1996; editor: Satellites of Jupiter, 1982; contbr. articles to profl. jour. Fellow AAAS, 1982, Com. for Sci. Investigation of Claims of Paranormal, 1983, Calif. Acad. Sci. Mem. Cosmos Club. Achievements include advanced research for Voyager and Galileo planetary exploration missions. Home: 14660 Fieldstone Saratoga CA 95070 Office: NASA Ames Rsch Ctr MS 200 7 Moffett Field CA 94035

MORRISON, DAVID FRED, software company executive; b. Columbus, Ohio, Aug. 15, 1953; s. Fred Liew and Sophie Ann (Snider) M.; 1 child, Ian. BA, Stanford U., 1975; MBA, U. So. Calif., 1978. Sr. corp. planning analyst Tiger Internat., L.A., 1978-80, mgr. new bus. devel., 1980-81; dir. planning and controls Hall's Motor Transit Co., Mechanicsburg, Pa., 1981-82; mng. dir., gen. mgr. Consol. Freightways Export-Import Svc., San Francisco, 1984-86; asst. treas. McKesson Corp., San Francisco, 1987-90, treas., 1990-91; dir. strategic planning Consol. Freightways, Inc., Palo Alto, Calif., 1982-84, 86-87, v.p., treas., 1991-96; exec. v.p., CFO Consol. Freightways Corp., 1996-99; CEO The Ladder Group, 1999—. Bd. dirs. Am. Sports Inst., Mill Valley, Calif., 1992-99; trustee Ctrl. States Pension Fund, 1997-99. Fellow State of Calif., 1977, Commerce Assocs., 1977. Mem. Fin. Execs. Inst. (silver medal 1978), Turnaround Mgmt. Assn, San Francisco Treas. Club (pres.). Avocations: cycling, scuba, skiing.

MORRISON, DAVID LEE, librarian, educator; b. New London, Conn., Aug. 28, 1948; s. Samuel and Beatrice (Kinslinger) M. BA in Classics with highest honors, U. Calif., Santa Barbara, 1979; MLS, U. Ariz., 1986. Documents libr. Marriott Libr., U. Utah, Salt Lake City, 1987—, instr. libr. literacy course, 1990—. Patent fellowship libr. U.S. Patent and Trademark Office, 1996-97; workshop presenter in field; guest lectr. U. Ariz. Grad. Libr. Sch., fall 1988-94; participant confs. in field. Fay and Lawrence Clark Powell scholar U. Ariz., 1983. Mem. ALA (govt. docs. round table info. tech. com. 1987-89), Utah Libr. Assn. (GODORT bylaws com. 1987-88, 91-92, chmn. nominating com. 1987-88, continuing edn. com. 1987-89, vice chmn., chmn.-elect 1992-93, chmn. GODORT 1993-94), Patent and Trademark Depository Libr. Assn. (fin. com. 1988-97, sec.-treas. 1989-90, 92—), Patent Documentation Soc. Home: 859 S Blair St Salt Lake City UT 84111 Office: U Utah Documents Div Marriott Libr Salt Lake City UT 84112

MORRISON, DONALD GRAHAM, business educator, consultant; b. Detroit, Feb. 26, 1939; s. Roderick and Ethelyne (Murray) M.; m. Sherie Leaver, Sept. 12, 1964; children: Heather Margaret Cloonan, Tracey Michelle Oliva. B.S.M.E., MIT, 1961; Ph.D. in Ops. Research, Stanford U., 1965. Instr. Stanford U., Calif., 1965-66, vis. prof., 1982-97; mem. faculty Columbia U., N.Y.C., 1966-87, prof., 1973-87, Armand G. Erpf prof. bus., 1985-87; William E. Leonard prof. Anderson Grad. Sch. Mgmt., UCLA, 1987—. Vis. prof. U. Calif., Berkeley, 1970-71; cons. in field, UCLA faculty athletic rep. to NCAA. Editor in chief Mgmt. Sci., 1983-90; founding editor Mktg. Sci., 1980-82. Elder Hitchcock Presbyn. Ch., Scarsdale, N.Y., 1978-84, Westwood Presbyn. Ch., L.A., 1991-94, 95-98; treas. Scarsdale Jr. H.S. PTA, 1977-78; acad. trustee Mktg. Sci. Inst., 1986-92; mem. Decision, Risk and Mgmt. Sci. rev. bd. NSF, 1989-91. Mem. Inst. Mgmt. Sci. (pres. 1990-92), Ops. Rsch. Soc. Am., Am. Statis. Assn. Presbyterian. Avocations: golf; jogging; bridge. Office: UCLA Anderston Grad Sch Mgmt 110 Westwood Plz Los Angeles CA 90095-0001

MORRISON, GLENN LESLIE, minister; b. Cortez, Colo., Feb. 26, 1929; s. Ward Carl Morrison and Alma Irene (Butler) Anderson; m. Beverely Joanne Buck, Aug. 26, 1949; children: David Mark, Betty Jo Morrison Mullen, Gary Alan, Judith Lynn Morrison Oltmann, Stephen Scott. Student, San Diego State U., 1948-49, Chabot Coll., 1968-69. Ordained to ministry Evang. Ch. Alliance, 1961. Dir. counseling and follow-up Oakland (Calif.) Youth for Christ, 1954-56; pres. Follow Up Ministries, Inc., Castro Valley, Calif., 1956—. Assoc. pastor 1st Covenant Ch., Oakland, 1956-58; exec. dir. East Bay Youth for Christ, Oakland, 1960-66; supervising chaplain Alameda County (Calif.) Probation Dept., 1971-90; vol. chaplain Alameda County Sheriff's Dept., 1971—; seminar leader Calif. Dept. Corrections, Sacramento, 1978—, mem. chaplains coordinating com., 1988—; founder, dir. God Squad Vol. Program for Prison Workers, 1972—. Author: Scripture Investigation Course, 1956. Mem. Am. Correctional Assn., Am. Protestant Correctional Chaplains Assn. (regional pres., sec. 1980-86, nat. sec. 1986-88, nat. 2nd v.p. 1996-98). Office: Follow Up Ministries Inc PO Box 2514 Castro Valley CA 94546-0514 E-mail: fumi2000@email.msn.com

MORRISON, GUS (ANGUS HUGH MORRISON), mayor, engineer; b. Buffalo, Sept. 13, 1935; s. John Weir and Mary (Norton) Morrison; m. Joy Rita Hallenbarter, Feb. 7, 1959; children: Frank, Gloria, Heather. Technician Bell Aircraft Corp., Niagara Falls, N.Y., 1956-58, Lockheed Missiles and Space Corp., Sunnyvale, Calif., 1958-63, test. engr., 1963-78, group engr., 1978-86, dept. mgr., 1986-94; ret., 1994. Mayor Fremont, Calif., 1985-99, 94—, council mem., 1978-85, 91-94, planning commr., 1977-78; bd. dirs. Tri City Ecology Ctr., 1976—. Served with USN, 1953-56. Democrat. Roman Catholic. Avocations: computers, photography, seriography. Office: Office Mayor PO Box 5006 Fremont CA 94537-5006

MORRISON, JOHN HADDOW, JR. engineering company executive; b. Bozeman, Mont., Aug. 24, 1933; s. John Haddow Sr. and Rosalie (Lehrkind) M.; m. Shirley Easbey, Sept. 11, 1954; children: Robert, Richard; m. Minh Le, Apr. 25, 2001. BS, Mont. State U., 1955. Registered profl. engr., Mont., Nev., Utah, Ariz., Calif.; registered land surveyor,

Mont. Project engr. Morrison-Maierle, Inc., Helena, Mont., 1957-64, chief airport design, 1964-73, chief exec. officer, 1973-88, chmn., 1988-2000, dir. emeritus, 2000—. Bd. dirs. Mont. State U. Found., Inc., 1983—, chmn. 1992-94; sec.-treas. Helena YMCA, 1977-80. With U.S. Army 1955-57. Mem. ASCE, NSPE (pres. Helena chpt. 1968-69, Outstanding Young Engr., Helena chpt. 1965), Cons. Engrs. Council Mont. (past sec., past v.p., pres. 1986-87). Methodist. Lodges: Kiwanis, Masons. Avocations: golf, photography. Home: 4221 E Ray Rd # 2034 Phoenix MT 85044-0603 Office: Morrison Maierle Inc 120 N 44th St Ste 410 Phoenix AZ 85034-1822 E-mail: jmorrison@m-m.net

MORROW, BARRY NELSON, screenwriter, producer; b. Austin, Minn., June 12, 1948; s. Robert Clayton and Rose Nell (Nelson) M.; m. Beverly Lee McKenzie, Mar. 3, 1969; children: Clayton McKenzie, ZoeAnna Rachel. BA, St. Olaf Coll., 1970; DHL (hon.), U. La Verne, Calif., 1990. Media specialist U. Iowa, Iowa City, 1974-81; freelance screenwriter Los Angeles, 1981-90; pres. Morrow-Heus Prodns., 1990-00. Storywriter (TV film) Bill, 1981 (Emmy award 1982); screenwriter: (TV films) Bill: On His Own, 1983, Conspiracy of Love, 1987, Silent Victory, 1988, The Karen Carpenter Story, 1989, (feature film) Rain Man, 1988 (co-recipient Acad. award Best Original Screenplay 1989); screenwriter, exec. prodr.: Christmas on Division Street, 1991; exec. prodr.: Switched at Birth, 1991 (Emmy nomination), Gospa, 1995, The Fifties, 1997, Behind the Mask, 1999; screenwriter, prodr. Race the Sun, 1996; monologist: Bill for Short, 1992. Recipient Pres.'s award Am. Acad. for Devel. Medicine, 1978, Outstanding Contbn. award Mid-Am. Congress on Aging, 1983, SI award NASW, 1991, Pope John XXIII award Viterbo Coll., 1992. Mem. Writers Guild Am. West, Acad. TV Arts and Scis., Acad. Motion Picture Arts and Scis., Motion Picture Screen Cartoonists Guild.

MORROW, BILL, state legislator; b. Monterey Park, Calif., Apr. 19, 1954; divorced; 1 child. BA, U. Calif., L.A., 1976; JD, Pepperdine U., 1979. Commd. officer, mil. judge adv. USMC, 1979-87; civil litigation atty., 1987—; mem. Calif. State Assembly, 1993-98, Calif. State Senate, 1998—, vice chmn. judiciary com., mem. coms. on transp., indsl. rels., health and human svcs. Active Spl. Olympics, Boys and Girls Club, Salvation Army. Named Legislator of Yr., Orange County League of Cities., Legislator of Yr. Pro-Life PAC Orange County, 1995, Civil Justice Reform Legislator of Yr., Orange County Citizens Against Lawsuit Abuse, 1996, Legislator of Yr., Calif. Rep. Assembly, 1996, Legislator of Yr. Golden State Mobilehome Owners League Calif., 1997. Mem. NRA, Am. Legion, Marine Corps League, Gun Owners Calif., Ducks Unlimited, Calif. Waterfowl Assn., Oceanside C. of C., San Juan C. of C., North County Armed Forces, Amvets, Kiwanis, YMCA. Republican. Protestant. Office: State Capitol Rm 4062 Sacramento CA 95814 also: 27126A Paseo Espada # 1621 San Juan Capistrano CA 92675-2725 also: 2755 Jefferson St Ste 101 Carlsbad CA 92008-1714 E-mail: bill.morrow@assembly.ca.gov

MORROW, CHARLES TABOR, aerospace consulting engineer; b. Gloucester, Mass., May 3, 1917; s. Charles Harvey and Melissa Luella (Tabor) M.; m. Julia Buxton Brown, June 4, 1949; children: Hope Elizabeth, Anne Barbara. AB, Harvard U., 1937, SM, 1938, SD, 1946. Sr. project engr. Sperry Gyroscope Co., Great Neck, N.Y., 1946-51; research physicist Hughes Aircraft Co., L.A., 1951-55; mgr. sci. and engring. relations Ramo Wooldridge Co., L.A., 1955-60; mgr. tech. relations Aerospace Corp., L.A., 1960-67; staff scientist LTV Research Ctr., Anaheim, Calif. and Dallas, 1967-76. Cons. in field., Dallas and Encinitas (Calif.), 1977—. Author: Shock and Vibration Engineering, 1963; also numerous articles to profl. jours. Pres. Covey Aux. San Diego Mus. Natural History, 1983-85. Fellow Acoustical Soc. Am., Inst. Environ. Scis. (Vigness award 1971), AIAA (assoc.); mem. IEEE (life), Inst. Noise Control Engring. (founding), Am. Soc. Engring. Edn., Sigma Xi. Avocations: music, photography, natural history, travelling. Home and Office: 1345 Cherrytree Ct Encinitas CA 92024-4011

MORROW, JAMES FRANKLIN, lawyer; b. Shenandoah, Iowa, Oct. 23, 1944; s. Warren Ralph and Margaret Glee (Palm) M. BS, Kans. State U., 1967; JD, U. Ariz., 1973. Bar: Ariz. 1973, U.S. Dist. Ct. Ariz. 1973. Ptnr. Bilby, Shoenhair, Warnock & Dolph, Tucson, 1973-83, Quarles & Brady Streich Lang LLP, Tucson, 1984—. Mng. editor U. Ariz. Law Rev., 1972-73. Past chmn. bd. trustees Palo Verde Mental Health Svcs.; past pres. U. Ariz. Alumni Assn.; past chmn. bd. Palo Verde Hosp., Ariz. Tech. Devel. Corp.; past pres. bd. Cath. Cmty. Svcs.; past chmn. bd. dirs. U. Ariz. Found. Capt. U.S. Army, 1967-70. Mem. Am. Coll. Real Estate Lawyers, Am. Coll. Mortgage Attys., State Bar Ariz. (cert. real estate specialist, adv. com. real estate specialists, past chmn. real estate property sect.), Pima County Bar Assn., Calif. Bar Assn. Democrat. Roman Catholic. Avocation: golf. Office: Quarles & Brady Streich Lang LLP Ste 1700 One South Church Ave Tucson AZ 85701

MORROW, WINSTON VAUGHAN, financial executive; b. Grand Rapids, Mich., Mar. 22, 1924; s. Winston V. and Selma (von Egloffstein) M.; m. Margaret Ellen Staples, June 25, 1948 (div.); children: Thomas Christopher, Mark Staples; m. Edith Burrows Ulrich, Mar. 2, 1990. AB cum laude, Williams Coll., 1947; JD, Harvard U., 1950. Bar: R.I. 1950, U.S. Dist. Ct., U.S. Supreme Ct. Assoc. atty. Edwards & Angell, Providence, 1950-57; exec. v.p., asst. treas., gen. counsel, bd. dirs. Avis, Inc. and subs., 1957-61; v.p., gen. mgr. Rent A Car div. Avis, Inc., 1962-64, pres., bd. dirs., 1964-75; chmn., chief exec. officer, bd. dirs. Avis, Inc. and Avis Rent A Car System, Inc., 1965-77; chmn., pres., bd. dirs. Teleflorists Inc. and subs., 1978-80; pres. Westwood Equities Corp., L.A., 1981-95, CEO, 1984-95, also bd. dirs.; chmn., pres., chief exec. officer Ticor Title Ins. Co., 1982-91, also bd. dirs.; chmn. TRTS Data Svcs. Inc., 1985-91; bd. dirs. AECOM Tech. Corp., L.A., 1990-99. Mem. Pres.'s Industry and Govt. Spl. Travel Task Force, 1968, travel adv. bd. U.S. Travel Svcs., 1968-76, L.A. City-wide Airport Adv. Com., 1983-85; co-chmn. L.A. Transp. Coalition, 1985-91. Mem. juvenile delinquency task force Nat. Coun. Crime and Delinquency, 1985-86, L.A. Mayor's Bus. Coun., 1983-86, Housing Roundtable, Washington, 1983-85; chmn., pres. Spring St. Found., 1991—; bd. dirs. Police Found., Washington, 1983-91; trustee Com. for Econ. Devel., Washington, 1987-91; trustee Adelphi U., 1970-75. Decorated Stella Della Solidarieta Italy, Gold Tourism medal Austria). Mem. R.I. Bar Assn., Car and Truck Rental Leasing Assn. (nat. pres. 1961-63), Am. Land Title Assn. (bd. govs. 1989-90), L.A. Area C. of C. (bd. dirs. 1983-90), Williams Club, L.A. Tennis Club, Phi Beta Kappa, Kappa Alpha. Home: 4056 Farmouth Dr Los Angeles CA 90027-1314 also: Meadowview Farm 286 Cushing Corner Rd Freedom NH 03836-0221

MORRY, G. RICHARD, retired lawyer; b. Seattle, Mar. 2, 1943; BA cum laude, U. Wash., 1965, JD with honors, 1970. Bar: Wash. 1971, Hawaii 1973, U.S. Ct. Appeals (9th cir.) 1973, U.S. Supreme Ct. 1974. Ptnr. Rush Moore Craven Sutton Morry & Beh, Honolulu, of counsel, 1998—. Pres. Hawaii Inst. for CLE, 1996. Exec. editor Wash. Law Rev., 1969-70; bd. editors Hawaii Bar Jour., 1975-97. Mem. ABA, Wash. State Bar Assn., Hawaii State Bar Assn., Am. Judicature Soc., Maritime Law Assn. of U.S. Address: Rush Moore Craven Sutton Morry & Beh 20th Fl Hawaii Tower 745 Fort Street Mall Honolulu HI 96813-3800

MORSE, DANIEL E. biochemistry educator, science administrator; b. N.Y.C., May 20, 1941; BA, Harvard U., 1963; PhD in Molecular Biology, Albert Einstein Coll. Medicine, 1967. Fellow in molecular genetics Stanford U., 1967-69; from Silas Arnold Houston asst. prof. to Silas Arnold Houston assoc. prof. med. sch. Harvard U., 1969-73; prof. molecular genetics and biochemistry U. Calif., Santa Barbara, 1973—, chmn. sect. molecular biology and biochemistry dept. biol. sci., 1981-85, chmn. Marine Biotechnology Ctr., 1986—. Mem. NRC, U.S. Nat. Com. Internat. Union Biol. Sci., 1986—; chmn. task force biotechnology in ocean sci. NSF, 1987—. Fellow AAAS; mem. Am. Soc. Molecular Biology and Biochemistry, Am. Soc. Limnology and Oceanography, Am. Soc. Microbiology, Am. Soc. Zoology, N.Y. Acad. Sci., Internat. Soc. Chem. Ecology. Achievements include research on molecular mechanisms controlling reproduction, larval metamorphosis, development and gene expression; signal molecules, receptors, and transducers; molecular marine biology; molecular neurobiology; molecular chemosensory mechanisms. Office: U Calif Marine Biotech Ctr Dept Biology Santa Barbara CA 93106

MORSE, JACK HATTON, management consultant; b. San Diego, June 4, 1923; s. John Henderson and Alberta (Peterson) M.; m. Kathleen Clark (div.); children: David Eugene, Steven Allen; m. Jean Larson. BA, San Diego State U., 1956, M in Bus. Sci., 1971. Exec. San Diego Gas & Electric, 1947-89; pres. S.D. Pub. Safety Com., 1981-82; chmn. mil. affairs San Diego C. of C., 1982-84; pres. Project Handclasp, 1991—. Cons. Pub., contbr. Sea Power mag., 1987-89. Pres. Cystic Fibrosis Found., San Diego, 1980-83; pres. Oceans Found., 1992-94, chmn., 1996-99. Comdr. USNR, 1943-46, 52-54. Recipient Dr. Frederick Patterson award United Negro Coll. Fund, San Diego, 1989. Mem. IEEE, Pacific Coast Elec. Assn., Pacific Coast Gas Assn. (Silver medal 1981), Navy League U.S. (nat. pres., chmn. adv. com. 1987-89, Disting. Svc. award 1979, 88, 89, Hoover Hi Hall of Fame 1998), La Jolla Beach and Tennis Club, Masons (Knight Comdr. Ct. of Honor), Rotary. Republican. Mem. LDS Ch. Avocations: traveling, public speaking. Home and Office: 6125 Terryhill Dr La Jolla CA 92037-6837

MORSE, JOHN MOORE, architect, planner; b. Brookline, Mass., Aug. 23, 1911; s. Arthur Moore and Helen (Stearns) M.; m. Emily Hall (dec. 1988); children: David Hall, Catherine Morse Wikkerink; m. Helen Taverniti, Aug. 5, 1989. AB, Harvard U., 1934, MArch, 1940. Registered architect, Wash. Tchr. Loomis Sch., Windsor, Conn., 1934-36; ptnr. Bassetti & Morse, Seattle, 1947-62; prin. John Morse & Assocs., Seattle, 1962-78; ptnr. Morse Stafford Ptnrship., Seattle, 1978-85; prin. John Morse Architect & Planner, Seattle, 1985—. Mem. King County (Wash.) Planning Commn., 1965-70, Design Rev. Bd., Mill Creek, Wash., 1987-89; chmn. Seattle Urban Design Bd., 1966; bd. dirs. Cornish Coll. Arts, Seattle, 1974-80. Fellow AIA (pres. Seattle chpt. 1969, Seattle chpt. medal 1996, various local and nat. awards). Democrat. Office: 7027 32nd Ave NE Seattle WA 98115-5906

MORSE, JOSEPH GRANT, chemistry educator; b. Colorado Springs, Colo., Oct. 16, 1939; s. Grant Addison and Faris Ellen (Winninger) M.; m. Karen Dale Williams, Apr. 6, 1963; children: Robert Grant, Geoffrey Easton. BS, S.D. State Coll., 1961; MS in Chemistry, U. Mich., 1963, PhD, 1966. Instr. U. Mich., Ann Arbor, 1965-66; asst. prof. Utah State U., Logan, 1968-74, assoc. prof., 1974-93; prof. Western Wash. U., Bellingham, 1993-2000, dir. sci. edn., 1996-2000. Councilman Cache County, Utah. Capt. U.S. Army, 1966-68. Fellow AAAS; mem. Am. Chem. Soc. Office: Western Wash U Chemistry Dept Bellingham WA 98225 E-mail: mjkaren@qwest.net

MORSE, KAREN WILLIAMS, academic administrator; b. Monroe, Mich., May 8, 1940; m. Joseph G. Morse; children: Robert G., Geoffrey E. BS, Denison U., 1962; MS, U. Mich., 1964, PhD, 1967; DSc (hon.), Denison U., 1990. Rsch. chemist Ballistic Rsch. Lab., Aberdeen Proving Ground, Md., 1966-68; lectr. chemistry dept. Utah State U., Logan, 1968-69, from asst. to assoc. prof. chemistry, 1969-83, prof. chemistry dept., 1983-93, dept. head Coll. Sci., 1981-88, dean Coll. Sci., 1988-89, univ. provost, 1989-93; pres. Western Wash. U., Bellingham, 1993—. Mem., chair Grad. Record Exam in chemistry com., Princeton, N.J., 1980-89, Gov.'s Sci. Coun., Salt Lake City, 1986-93, Gov.'s Coun. on Fusion, 1989-91, ACS Com. on Profl. Tng., 1984-92; cons. 1993; nat. ChemLinks adv. com. NSF, 1995; bd. advisor's orgn. com. 2008 summer Olympic Games, Seattle, 1995; faculty Am. Assn. State Colls. and Univs. Pres.'s Acad., 1995, 96; chair Wash. Coun. of Pres., 1995-96; bd. dirs. Whatcom State Bank; NCAA Divsn. II Pres.'s Coun., 1999—, CHEA bd., 2000—; Nat. Rsch. Coun. Chem. Svcs. Roundtable, 1999—. Contbr. articles to profl. jours. Mem. Cache County Sch. Dist. Found., Cache Valley, Logan, 1988-93; swim coach, soccer coach; trustee First United Presbyn. Ch., Logan, 1979-81, 82-85; adv. bd. Sci. Discovery Ctr., Logan, 1993, KCTS-TV, Bellingham, 1996—, Seattle Opera Bd., 1999—; mem. bd. dirs. United Way, Whatcom County, 1993—; exec. com. Bellingham-Whatcom Econ. Devel. Com., 1993—. Recipient Disting. Alumni in Residence award U. Mich., 1989, Francis P. Garvan and John M. Olin medal, 1997. Fellow AAAS; mem. Am. Chem. Soc. (Utah award Salt Lake City and Cen. dists. 1988, Garvan-Olin medal 1997), Am. Assn. State Colls. and Univs. (mem. policy and purposes com. 1995, chair 1996), Bus. and Profl. Women Club (pres. 1984-85), Philanthropic Edn. Orgn., Phi Beta Kappa, Sigma Xi, Phi Beta Kappa Assocs., Phi Kappa Phi, Beta Gamma Sigma. Avocations: skiing, biking, photography. Office: Western Washington U Office Pres 516 High St Bellingham WA 98225-5946

MORSE, RICHARD JAY, human resources and organizational development consultant, manufacturers' representative company executive; b. Detroit, Aug. 2, 1933; s. Maurice and Belle Rosalyn (Jacobson) M. BA, U. Va., 1955; MA in Clin. Psychology, Calif. State U., L.A., 1967. Area pers. adminstr. Gen. Tel. Co. of Calif., Santa Monica, 1957-67; sr. v.p. human resources The Bekins Co., Glendale, Calif., 1967-83; pvt. cons. human resources and orgn. devel. Cambria, 1983—. Contbr. articles to profl. jours. Fund raiser various orgns., So. Calif., 1970—. Mem. Internat. Soc. Performance Improvement (founding mem. 1958—). Republican. Jewish. Avocations: travel, tennis, walking, swimming. Home and Office: 6410 Cambria Pines Rd Cambria CA 93428-2009 E-mail: dickmorse@earthlink.net

MORTENSEN, WILLIAM S. banking executive; b. 1932; Chmn. bd., pres., CEO 1st Fed. Bank Calif., Santa Monica, 1955—, CEO, until 1997, chmn., bd., 1999—; CEO, pres. Babette Heinbuch, 1997—. Office: 1st Fed Financial Corp 401 Wilshire Blvd Santa Monica CA 90401-1490

MORTIMER, KENNETH P. academic administrator; Pres. Western Wash. U., Bellingham, 1988-93, U. Hawaii Sys., Honolulu, 1993—. Office: U Hawaii Sys Bachmann Hall 202 2444 Dole St Honolulu HI 96822-2302

MORTIMER, WENDELL REED, JR. judge; b. Alhambra, Calif., Apr. 7, 1937; s. Wendell Reed and Blanche (Wilson) M.; m. Cecilia Vick, Aug. 11, 1962; children: Michelle Dawn, Kimberly Grace. AB, Occidental Coll., 1958; JD, U. So. Calif., L.A., 1965. Bar: Calif. 1966. Trial atty. Legal div. State of Calif., L.A., 1965-73; assoc. Thelen, Marrin, Johnson & Bridges, L.A., 1973-76, ptnr., 1976-93; pvt. practice San Marino, Calif., 1994-95; judge L.A. Superior Ct., 1995—, mem. complex litigation panel, 2000—. With U.S. Army, 1960-62. Mem. ABA, Internat. Acad. Trial Judges, Los Angeles County Bar Assn., Calif. Judges Assn., Am. Judicature Soc., Am. Judges Assn., Legion Lex., ABOTA, San Marino City Club, Pasadena Bar Assn., Balboa Yacht Club. Home: 1420 San Marino Ave San Marino CA 91108-2042

MORTON, BOB, state legislator; m. Linda Morton; children: Bettina, Laura, Shawn, Scott, Roxanne. BA in History and Polit. Sci., BD, Alfred U. Mem. Wash. Senate, Dist. 7, Olympia, 1994—. Mem. Citizens for a Great N.W., Kettle River Grange; past bd. dirs. Pacific N.W. Endurance Riders, v.p., pres.; mem. Orient Cmty. Ch. Recipient 100 Percent Voting Record Wash. State Farm Bur. Mem. Wash. State Pilots Assn., Kettle Falls C. of C., Stevens County Cattlemen's Assn., Wash. Cattlemen's Assn. Republican. Office: 115D Irving Newhouse Ofc Olympia WA 98504-0001

MORTON, DONALD CHARLES, astronomer; b. Kapuskasing, Ont., Can., June 12, 1933; s. Charles Orr and Irene Mary (Wightman) M.; m. Winifred May Austin, Dec. 12, 1970; children: Keith James, Christine Elizabeth. BA, U. Toronto, 1956; PhD, Princeton U., 1959. Astronomer U.S. Naval Rsch. Lab., Washington, 1959-61; from rsch. assoc. to sr. rsch. astronomer with rank of prof. Princeton (N.J.) U., 1961-76; dir. Anglo-Australian Obs., Epping and Coonabarabran, Australia, 1976-86; dir. gen. Herzberg Inst. Astrophysics, NRC of Can., Ottawa and Victoria, Ont., 1986-2000; rschr. emritus NRC of Can., 2000—. Contbr. numerous articles to profl. jours. Fellow Australian Acad. Sci.; mem. Internat. Astron. Union, Royal Astron. Soc. (assoc. 1980), Astron. Soc. Australia (pres. 1981-83, hon. mem. 1986), Royal Astron. Soc. Can., Am. Astron. Soc. (councilor 1970-73), Can. Astron. Soc. Australian Inst. Physics (Pawsey Meml. lectr. 1985), Can. Assn. Physicists, U.K. Alpine Club, Am. Alpine Club, Alpine Club Can. Avocations: mountaineering, rock climbing, ice climbing, marathon running. Office: Herzberg Inst Astrophysics NRC Can 5071 W Saanich Rd Victoria BC Canada V9E 2E7

MORTON, JOHN DOUGLAS, retail executive; b. 1951; With Wolfe's Sporting Goods, 1972-80; dist. mgr. sporting goods divsn. Malone and Hyde, 1980-86; divsn. mgr. Utah region Gart Sports Co., Denver, 1986-88, divsn. v.p. Utah region, 1988-90, v.p. ops., 1990-94, exec. v.p., 1994-95, pres., CEO, chmn. bd., 1995—. Office: Gart Sports Co 1001 Lincoln Ave Denver CO 80203 Fax: 303-829-1511

MORTVEDT, JOHN JACOB, soil scientist, researcher; b. Dell Rapids, S.D., Jan. 25, 1932; s. Ernest R. and Clara (Halvorson) M.; m. Marlene L. Fodness, Jan. 23, 1955; children: Sheryl Mortvedt Jarratt, Lori Mortvedt Klopf, Julie Mortvedt Stride. BS, S.D. State U., 1953, MS, 1959; PhD, U. Wis., 1962. Soil chemist TVA, Muscle Shoals, Ala., 1962-87, sr. scientist, 1987-92, regional mgr. field programs dept., 1992-93; ext. soils specialist Colo. State U., Ft. Collins, 1994-95, ext. environ. and pesticide edn. specialist, 1996. Agr. cons. U.S. Borax, 1997—. Co-author: Fertilizer Technology and Application, 1999; editor: Micronutrients in Agriculture, 1972, 2d edit., 1991; contbr. articles to profl. jours. 1st lt. U.S. Army, 1953-57. Fellow AAAS, Soil Sci. Soc. Am. (pres. 1988-89, editor-in-chief 1982-87, Profl. Svc. award 1991, Disting. Svc. award 1996), Am. Soc. Agronomy (exec. com. 1987-90); mem. Internat. Soil Sci. Soc., Colombian Soil Sci. Soc. (hon.), Exch. Club (pres. Florence, Ala. chpt. 1987-88), Toastmasters (pres. Florence chpt. 1964-65), Phi Kappa Phi. Avocations: photography, golf. Office: Colo State U Dept Soil And Crop Scis Fort Collins CO 80523-0001

MOSBY, DOROTHEA SUSAN, municipal official; b. Sacramento, May 13, 1948; d. William Laurence and Esther Ida (Lux) M. AA in Sociology, Bakersfield (Calif.) Coll., 1966-69; BS in Recreation, San Jose State U., 1969-72; MPA, Calif. State U. Dominguez Hills, Carson, 1980-82. Asst. dept. pers. officer San Jose Pks. and Recreation Dept., 1972-73, neighborhood ctr. dir., 1973-74; sr. recreation leader Santa Monica Recreation and Pks. Dept., 1974-76, recreation supr., 1976-83; head bus. divsn. Santa Monica Recreation and Parks Dept., 1983-88; bus. adminstr. Santa Monica Cultural & Recreation Svcs., 1988-91; dir. pks. and recreation City of South Gate, Calif., 1991—. Bd. dirs., officer Santa Monica City Employees Fed. Credit Union, 1980-89, pres. 1986-87; mem. citizens adv. com. L.A. Olympic Organizing Com., 1982-84. Mem. choir, flute soloist Pilgrim Luth. Ch., Santa Monica, 1974-98, treas. Luth. ch. coun., 1984-86; mem. choir, flute soloist Christ Luth. Ch., Downey, Calif., 1999—; vol. driver XXIII Olympiad, L.A., 1984; contbr. local housing assistance U.S. Olympic Com., L.A., 1984; mem. adv. com. Windsor Sq. Hancock Park Hist. Soc., L.A., 1983, dir. Christmas carolling, 1980—, chmn. Olympic com., 1984, trustee, 1984-90, chmn. pub. programs, 1985, co-chmn. pub. programs, 1986, co-vice chair, 1987, chmn., 1988, 89; Downey Symphony Guild; bd. dirs. Downey Symphony; mem. Samuel C. May Grad. Student Rsch. Paper Judging Com., Western Govt. Rsch. Assn., 1994; trustee Calif. Found. for Parks and Recreation. Recipient Outstanding Profl. of Yr. award Los Angeles Basin Pk. and Recreation Commrs. and Bd. Mems., 1993. Mem. Calif. Pk. and Recreation Soc. (bd. dirs. 1979-82, 86, mem. Calif bd. pk. and recreation cert. 1990—, Scholarship Found. Bd. 1992—, chair 1996, 97, 98—, dist. 10 v.p. 1994, 95, 96, Dist. 10 Spl. Recognition award 1998, Citation award 1999), Nat. Recreation and Pk. Assn., Calif. Found. Pks. Recreation (trustee), Mgmt. Team Assocs. (sec., treas. 1979-83), Western Govtl. Rsch. Assn., Nat. Assn. Univ. Women, South Gate C. of C., Kiwanis Club (past pres.), Chi Kappa Rho (pres. 1986), Pi Alpha Alpha. Avocations: flute, piano, reading, bicycling, tennis. Home: 9329 Elm Vista Dr Apt 103 Downey CA 90242-2992 Office: City of South Gate Dept Pks & Recreation 4900 Southern Ave South Gate CA 90280-3462

MOSELEY, COLIN, lumber company executive; MBA, Northwestern U. CEO Simpson Investment Co., Seattle, chmn. Office: Simpson Investment Co 1301 5th Ave Ste 2800 Seattle WA 98101-2675

MOSELEY, JOHN TRAVIS, university administrator, research physicist; b. New Orleans, Feb. 26, 1942; s. Fred Baker and Lily Gay (Lord) M.; m. Belva McCall Hudson, Aug. 11 1964 (div. June 1979); m. Susan Diane Callow, Aug. 6, 1979; children: Melanie Lord, John Mark, Stephanie Marie, Shannon Eleanor. BS in Physics, Ga. Inst. Tech., 1964, MS in Physics, 1966, PhD in Physics, 1969. Asst. prof. physics U. West Fla., Pensacola, 1968-69; sr. physicist SRI Internat., Menlo Park, Calif., 1969-75, program mgr., 1976-79; vis. prof. U. Paris, 1975-76; assoc. prof. U. Oreg., Eugene, 1979-81, dir. chem. physics inst., 1980-84, prof. physics, 1984—, head physics dept., 1984-85, v.p. rsch., 1985-94, v.p. acad. affairs, provost, 1994-2001, sr. v.p., 2d provost, 2001—. Mem. exec. com., coun. on acad. affairs NASULGC, 1994-2000, chair, 1996-97; bd. dirs. Oreg. Resource and Tech., Portland; mem. com. on Atomic and Molecular Sci., 1983-85. Contbr. numerous articles to profl. jours. Mem. So. Willamette Rsch. Corridor, Eugene, 1985—, Lane Econ. Devel. Com., Eugene, 1988-94; bd. dirs. Eugene/Springfield Metro Partnership, 1985—, Oreg. Bach Festival, Eugene, 1987-94, Eugene Arts Found., 1995-97. Recipient Doctoral Thesis award Sigma Xi, 1969; Fulbright fellow, 1975; numerous rsch. grants, 1969—. Fellow AAAS, Am. Physical Soc.; mem. AAUP, Am. Chem. Soc. Avocations: skiing, backpacking. Home: 2140 Essex Ln Eugene OR 97403-1851 Office: U Oreg Office VP Acad Affairs & Provost Eugene OR 97403-1258 E-mail: jtm@oregon.uoregon.edu

MOSER, ROBERT HARLAN, physician, educator, writer; b. Trenton, N.J., June 16, 1923; s. Simon and Helena (Silvers) M.; m. Linda Mae Salsinger, Mar. 18, 1989; children from previous marriage: Steven Michael, Jonathan Evan. BS, Loyola U., Balt., 1944; MD, Georgetown U., 1948. Diplomate Am. Bd. Internal Medicine. Commd. 1st lt. U.S. Army, 1948, advanced through grades to col., 1966, intern D.C. Gen. Hosp., 1948-49, fellow pulmonary disease D.C. Gen. Hosp., 1949-50, bn. surgeon Korea, 1950-51; asst. resident Georgetown U. Hosp., 1951-52; chief resident Georgetown U. Hosp. U.S. Army, 1952-53, chief med. service U.S. Army Hosp. Austria, 1953-55, Wurzburg, Fed. Republic Germany, 1955-56, resident in cardiology Brooke Gen. Hosp., 1956-57, asst. chief dept. medicine Brooke Gen. Hosp., 1957-59, chief Brooke Gen. Hosp., 1967-68, fellow hematology U. Utah Coll. Medicine, 1959-60, asst. chief

U.S. Army Tripler Gen. Hosp., 1960-64, chief William Beaumont Gen. Hosp., 1965-67, chief Walter Reed Gen. Hosp., 1968-69, ret., 1969; chief of staff Maui (Hawaii) Meml. Hosp., 1969-73, chief dept. medicine, 1975-77; exec. v.p. Am. Coll. Physicians, Phila., 1976-86; v.p. med. affairs The NutraSweet Co., Deerfield, Ill., 1986-91. Assoc. prof. medicine Baylor U., 1958-59; clin. prof. medicine Hawaii U., 1969-77, Washington U., 1970-77, Abraham Lincoln Sch. Medicine, 1974-75; adj. prof. medicine U. Pa., 1977-86, Northwestern U., 1987-91; adj. prof. Uniformed Svcs. U. Health Scis., 1979-97; clin. prof. medicine U. N.Mex. Coll. Medicine, 1992-96, emeritus, 1996—; flight contr. Project Mercury, 1959-62; cons. mem. med. evaluation team Project Gemini, 1962-66; cons. Project Apollo, 1967-73, Tripler Gen. Hosp., 1970-77, Walter Reed Army Med. Ctr., 1974-86; sr. med. cons. Canyon Cons. Corp., 1991—; mem. cardiovasc. and renal adv. com. FDA, 1978-82; chmn. life scis. adv. com. NASA, 1984-87, mem. NASA adv. coun., 1983-88, chmn. gen. med. panel Hosp. Satellite Network, 1984-86; mem. adv. com. NASA Space Sta., 1988-93; mem. Dept. Def. Com. on Grad. Med. Edn., 1986-87; mem. Life Scis. Strategic Planning Study Group, 1986-88; mem. space studies bd. NRC, 1988-93, space exploration initiation study, 1990, NASA Space Sta. Commn., 1992-93, mem. com. adv. tech. human supp. space, 1996-97. Author: Diseases of Medical Progress, 1955, rev. edit., 1969, House Officer Training, 1970; co-author: Adventures in Medical Writing, 1970, Decade of Decision, 1992; editor, chief div. sci. publs. Jour. AMA, Chgo., 1973-75; contbg. editor Med. Opinion and Rev., 1966-75; chmn. editorial bd. Diagnosis mag., 1986-89; mem. editorial bd. Hawaii Med. Jour., Family Physicians, Archives of Internal Medicine, 1967-73, Western Jour. Medicine, 1975-87, Chest, 1975-80, Med. Times, 1977-84, Quality Rev. Bull., 1979-91, The Pharos, 1991—, Emergency Med., 1993—, Travel Medicine, 1994-96; contbr. over 200 articles to med. sci. jours and med. books. Master ACP (exec. v.p. 1977-86); fellow Am. Coll. Cardiology, Royal Coll. Physicians and Surgeons Can. (hon.), Am. Clin. and Climatol. Assn.; mem. AMA (adv. panel registry of adverse drug reactions 1960-67, coun. on drugs 1967-73),), Am. Med. Writers Assn., Am. Therapeutic Soc., Am. Osler Soc., Inst. Med., Nat. Assn. Phys. Broadcasters, Chgo. Soc. Internal Medicine, Coll. Physicians Phila., Soc. Med. Cons. to Armed Forces, Alpha Sigma Nu, Alpha Omega Alpha. Democrat. Jewish. Avocations: hiking, international travel, white water rafting. Home and Office: PO Box 616 Canones Rd Chama NM 87520

MOSER, ROYCE, JR. physician, medical educator; b. Versailles, Mo., Aug. 21, 1935; s. Royce and Russie Frances (Stringer) M.; m. Lois Anne Hunter, June 14, 1958; children: Beth Anne Moser McLean, Donald Royce. BA, Harvard U., 1957, MD, 1961; MPH, Harvard Sch. Pub. Health, Boston, 1965. Diplomate Am. Bd. Preventive Medicine (trustee 1989-98), Am. Bd. Family Practice. Commd. officer USAF, 1962, advanced through grades to col., 1974; resident in aerospace medicine USAF Sch. Aerospace Medicine, Brooks AFB, Tex., 1965-67; chief aerospace medicine Aerospace Def. Command, Colorado Springs, Colo., 1967-70; comdr. 35th USAF Dispensary Phan Rang, Vietnam, 1970-71; chief aerospace medicine br. USAF Sch. Aerospace Medicine, Brooks AFB, 1971-77; comdr. USAF Hosp., Tyndall AFB, Fla., 1977-79; chief clin. scis. div. USAF Sch. Aerospace Medicine, Brooks AFB, 1979-81, chief edn. div., 1981-83, sch. comdr., 1983-85, ret., 1985; prof. dept. family and preventive medicine U. Utah Sch. Medicine, Salt Lake City, 1985—, vice chmn. dept., 1985-95; dir. Rocky Mountain Ctr. for Occupl. and Environ. Health, Salt Lake City, 1987—. Cons. in occupational, environ. and aerospace medicine, Salt Lake City, 1985—; presenter nat. and internat. med. meetings. Author: Effective Management of Occupational and Environmental Health and Safety Programs, 1992, 2d edit. 1999; contbr. book chpts. and articles to profl. jours. Mem., past pres. 1st Bapt. Ch. Found., Salt Lake City, 1987-89; mem., chmn. numerous univ. coms., Salt Lake City, 1985—; bd. dirs. Hanford Environ. Health Found., 1990-92; mem. preventive medicine residency rev. com. Accreditation Coun. Grad. Med. Edn., 1991-97; mem. ednl. adv. bd. USAF Human Sys. Ctr., 1991-96; chmn. long-range planning com. Am. Bd. Preventive Medicine, 1992-95. Decorated Legion of Merit (2); recipient Harriet Hardy award New England Coll. Occupl. and Environ. Medicine, 1998. Fellow Aerospace Med. Assn. (pres. 1989-90, chair fellows group 1994-97, Harry G. Mosely award 1981, Theodore C. Lyster award 1988, Eric Liljencrantz award 2001), Am. Coll. Preventive Medicine (regent 1981-82), Am. Coll. Occupl. and Environ. Medicine (v.p. med. affairs 1995-97, Robert A. Kehoe award 1996), Am. Acad. Family Physicians; mem. Internat. Acad. Aviation and Space Medicine (selector 1989-94, chancellor 1994-98), Soc. of USAF Flight Surgeons (pres. 1978-79, George E. Schafer award 1982), Phi Beta Kappa. Avocations: photography, fishing. Home: 664 Aloha Rd Salt Lake City UT 84103-3329 Office: Rocky Mountain Ctr Occupl & Environ Health 75 S 2000 E Salt Lake City UT 84112-8930 E-mail: rmoser@rmcoeh.utah.edu

MOSES, LINCOLN E. statistician, educator; b. Kansas City, Mo., Dec. 21, 1921; s. Edward Walter and Virginia (Holmes) M.; m. Jean Runnels, Dec. 26, 1942; children— Katherine, James O'D., William C., Margaret, Elizabeth; m. Mary Louise Coale, 1968. A.B., Stanford, 1941, Ph.D., 1950. Asst. prof. edn. Columbia Tchrs. Coll., 1950-52; faculty Stanford U., 1952—, prof. stats., 1959—, exec. head dept., 1964-68; assoc. dean Stanford U. (Sch. Humanities and Scis.), 1965-68, 85-86, dean grad. studies, 1969-75; faculty Stanford U. (Med. Sch.), 1952—; adminstr. Energy Info. Adminstrn., Dept. of Energy, 1978-80. L.L. Thurstone disting. fellow U. N.C., 1968-69; com. mem. Am. Friends Svc. Com., intermittently 1954—, chmn. No. Calif. chpt., 1972-76, 84-88. Bd. dirs. Am. Found. for AIDS Rsch., 1992-97. Guggenheim fellow, 1960-61; fellow Ctr. for Advanced Study in Behavioral Scis., 1975 Fellow Am. Acad. Arts and Scis., Inst. Math. Stats. (coun. 1969-72); mem. Inst. Medicine of NAS, Am. Statis. Assn. (coun. 1966-67), Biometric Soc. (pres. Western N.Am. region 1969), Internat. Statis. Inst. Office: Stanford U Med Ctr Divsn Biostats Stanford CA 94305

MOSES, RAPHAEL JACOB, lawyer; b. Girard, Ala., Nov. 6, 1913; s. William Moultrie and Anna (Green) M.; m. Marian Eva Beck, Aug. 22, 1938 (dec. Feb. 1976); 1 child, Marcia (Mrs. William S. Johnson); m. Fletcher Lee Westgaard, Jan. 20, 1979. A.B., U. Colo., 1935, J.D., 1937. Bar: Colo. 1938. Practiced in, Alamosa, 1938-62, Boulder, 1962—; pres. Moses, Wittemyer, Harrison & Woodruff (P.C.), from 1970, now of counsel. Spl. asst. atty. gen. Rio Grande Compact, 1957-58; mem. Colo. Water Conservation Bd., 1952-58, chmn., counsel, 1958-76, cons., 1976-77; research asso., faculty law U. Colo., 1962-66, vis. lectr., 1966-76, resident counsel, 1964-66, regent, 1973-74; grad. faculty Colo. State U., 1963-67; mem. Western States Water Council, 1965-77, chmn., 1966-70. Trustee Rocky Mountain Mineral Law Inst., 1964-66; bd. dirs. U. Colo. Found., 1977-97, chmn., 1977-79, mem. chancellor's adv. coun., 1981-97; bd. dirs. Colo. Open Lands, 1983-91, U. Colo. Improvement Corp., 1980-90, Colo. Endowment for Humanities, 1986-89; mem. adv. bd. Natural Resources Ctr., U. Colo. Sch. Law, 1983-92, chmn., 1986-88. Served to lt. (s.g.) USNR, 1942-45. Recipient William E. Knous award U. Colo. Sch. Law, 1971, Norlin award U. Colo., 1972; Raphael J. Moses Disting. Natural Resources professorship established U. Colo., 1994. Fellow Am. Bar Found. (life), Colo. Bar Found. (trustee 1977-90), Am. Coll. Trial Lawyers; mem. ABA (chmn. water rights com. sect. natural resources 1959-60), Colo. Bar Assn. (pres. 1959-60, Award of Merit 1972), San Luis Valley Bar Assn. (pres. 1942), Am. Counsel Assn., Order of Coif (hon.) Presbyterian (elder). Clubs: Univ. (Denver); Boulder Country; Garden of the Gods (Colorado Springs). Home: 4913 Clubhouse Cir Boulder CO 80301-3713 E-mail: [illegible]

MOSICH, ANELIS NICK, accountant, writer, educator, consultant; b. Croatia, Aug. 30, 1928; came to U.S., 1939, naturalized, 1951; s. Dinko and Josephine (Ursich) M.; m. Dorothy V. Rasich, June 15, 1958; children: Lori, Lisa, Jeffrey. BS, UCLA, 1951, MBA, 1953, PhD (fellow), 1963. CPA, Calif. Mem. faculty UCLA, 1955-63, Calif. State U., Northridge, 1963-64; examiner for Calif. State Bd. Accountancy, 1964-70; prof. acctg. U. So. Calif., Los Angeles, 1964-74, William C. Hallett prof. acctg., 1974-81, Ernst & Young prof., 1981-90, chmn. acctg. dept., 1970-74, 77-78, prof. emeritus, 1993. Cons. various bus. orgns., 1953—; expert witness; bd. dirs. Casden Properties, Inc.; guest speaker various profl. and bus. groups in Calif., Oreg., N.Y., Tex., Fla., and Hawaii, 1963-93. Author: Intermediate Accounting, rev. 6th edit., 1989, Financial Accounting, 1970, 75, Accounting: A Basis for Business Decision, 1972, Modern Advanced Accounting, 4th edit., 1988, The CPA Examination: Text, Problems and Solutions, 1978; editor: Education column Calif. CPA Quar., 1965-66; contbg. editor: Education and Professional Training column Jour. Accountancy, 1971-77; contbr. numerous articles to jours. and acctg. Mem. productivity commn. City of L.A., 1993-94. With U.S. Army, 1953-55. Recipient Dean's award Sch. Bus. Adminstrn., U. So. Calif., 1973, 78, Fred B. Olds Support Group award U. So. Calif., 1994, Disting. Svc. award for Leventhal Sch. Acctg., 1999. Office: U So Calif Leventhal Sch Acctg University Park Los Angeles CA 90089-0001

MOSIER, ARVIN RAY, chemist, researcher; b. Olney Springs, Colo., June 11, 1945; s. Isaac James Ellen Rena (Ross) M.; m. Susan Minnick, Dec. 30, 1965; children: Andrew, Katherine. BS, Colo. State U., 1967, MS, 1967-68, PhD, 1974. Chemist agr. research services USDA, Ft. Collins, 1967—. Contbr. papers and book chpt. to profl. publ. Mem. AAAS, Am. Soc. Agronomy, Soil Sci. Soc. Am., Internat. Soil Sci. Sco., Council Agrl. Sci. Tech., Phi Kappa Phi, Sigma XI, Gamma Sigma Delta. Republican. Methodist. Avocations: tennis, soccer. Home: Unit 40 950 Southridge Greens Blvd Fort Collins CO 80525-6728 Office: USDA Agrl Rsch Svc PO Box E Fort Collins CO 80522-0470 E-mail: amosier@lamar.colostate.edu

MOSIER, HARRY DAVID, JR. physician, educator; b. Topeka, May 22, 1925; s. Harry David and Josephine Morrow (Johnson) M.; m. Nadine Oclea Merilatt, Aug. 24, 1949; children: Carolyn Josephine Mosier Pohlmeyer, William David, Daniel Thomas, Christine Elizabeth Mosier Mahoney; m. Marjorie Knight Armstrong, Sept. 26, 1963. B.S. magna cum laude, U. Notre Dame, 1948; M.D., Johns Hopkins U., 1952. Diplomate Am. Bd. Pediatrics, Am. Bd. Pediatric Endocrinology. Intern Johns Hopkins Hosp., Balt., 1952-53; resident in pediat. Los Angeles Children's Hosp., 1953-54, resident pediatric pathology, 1954-55; fellow pediatric endocrinology Johns Hopkins U., 1955-57; asst. prof. pediat. UCLA, 1957-61, assoc. prof., 1961-63; dir. rsch. Ill. State Pediatric Inst., Chgo., 1963-67; assoc. prof. U. Ill., 1963-67; prof. pediat. U. Calif.-Irvine, 1967—; head divsn. pediat. endocrinology, 1967-2000; staff Children's Hosp. Med. Ctr., Long Beach, Calif., 1970—, U. Calif. Irvine Med. Ctr., Orange, 1979—; dist. cons. Med. Bd. Calif., 1995—. Contbr. articles to med. jours. With AUS, 1943-46, col. U.S. Army Med. Corps, 1990-91, Persian Gulf War. USAR Med. Corps. 1952-62, 83-93 (ret.). Office: U Calif Dept Pediat 101 City Dr S Orange CA 92868-3201

MOSK, RICHARD MITCHELL, lawyer; b. L.A., May 18, 1939; s. Stanley and Edna M.; m. Sandra Lee Budnitz, Mar. 21, 1964; children: Julie, Matthew. AB with great distinction, Stanford U., 1960; JD cum laude, Harvard U., 1963. Bar: Calif. 1964, U.S. Supreme Ct. 1970, U.S. Ct. Mil. Appeals 1970, U.S. Dist. Ct. (no., so., ea., and cen. dists.) Calif 1964, U.S. Ct. Appeals (9th dist.) 1964. Staff Pres.'s Commn. on Assassination Pres. Kennedy, 1964; rsch. clk. Calif. Supreme Ct., 1964-65; ptnr. Mitchell, Silberberg & Knupp, L.A., 1965-87; prin. Sanders, Barnet, Goldman, Simons & Mosk, PC, L.A., 1987-2000. Spl. dep. Fed. Pub. Defender, L.A., 1975-76; instr. U. So. Calif. Law Sch., 1978; judge Iran-U.S. Claims Tribunal, 1981-84, 97—, substitute arbitrator, 1984-97; mem. L.A. County Jud. Procedures Commn., 1973-82, chmn., 1978; co-chmn. Motion Picture Assn. Classification and Rating Adminstrn., 1994-2000; mem. panel Ct. Arbitration for Sport-Geneva. Contbr. articles to profl. jours. Mem. L.A. City-County Inquiry on Brush Fires, 1970; bd. dirs. Calif. Mus. Sci. and Industry, 1979-82, Vista Del Mar Child Ctr., 1979-82; trustee L.A. County Law Libr., 1985-86; bd. govs. Town Hall Calif., 1986-91; mem. Christopher Commn. on L.A. Police Dept., 1991; mem. Stanford U. Athletic Bd., 1991-95. With USNR, 1964-75. Hon. Woodrow Wilson fellow, 1960; recipient Roscoe Pound prize, 1961. Fellow Am. Bar Found.; mem. ABA (coun. internat. law sect. 1986-90), FBA (pres. L.A. chpt. 1972), L.A. County Bar Assn., Beverly Hills Bar Assn., Internat. Bar Assn., Am. Arbitration Assn. (comml. panel, large complex case panel, entertainment panel, internat. panel), Hong Kong Internat. Arbitration Ctr. (mem. panel 1986—), Am. Film Mktg. Assn. (arbitration panel), B.C. Internat. Arbitration Ctr. (mem. panel), World Intellectual Property Orgn. (mem. arbitration panel), Ct. Pub. Resources (arbitration panel), Ct. Arbitration Sport-Geneva (arbitration panel, NASD arbitration panel), Calif. Tribal Labor Panel, Phi Beta Kappa. Office: Ste 700 1901 Avenue Of The Stars Los Angeles CA 90067-6078

MOSKOWITZ, BARRY T. judge; BA, Rutgers Coll., 1972, JD, 1975. Judge U.S. Dist. Ct. (so. dist.) Calif., 1996—. Office: US Courthouse 940 Front St San Diego CA 92101-8994

MOSKOWITZ, JOEL STEVEN, lawyer; b. N.Y.C., Jan. 14, 1947; s. Jack I. and Myra (Shor) M.; m. Anna Boucher; children: David, Michael, Ellen. BA, UCLA, l967, JD, l970. Bar: Calif. l97l, U.S. Ct. Appeals (9th cir.) l97l, U.S. Ct. Appeals (D.C. cir.) l975, U.S. Supreme Ct. l975, U.S. Ct. Appeals (2d cir.) l979. Dep. atty. gen. Calif. Dept. Justice, Sacramento, l970-83; dep. dir. Calif. Dept. Health Svcs., Sacramento, l983-85; of counsel Gibson, Dunn & Crutcher, L.A., 1985-88, ptnr., 1988-96, Moskowitz, Brestoff, Winston & Blinderman LLP, 1996—. Author: Environmental Liaibility in Real Property Transactions, 1995; contbr. articles to legal publs. Mem. Phi Beta Kappa. Office: 1880 Century Park E Ste 350 Los Angeles CA 90067-1603 E-mail: jsm6@ix.netcom.com

MOSS, ARTHUR J. physician, educator; b. St. Paul, May 12, 1914; s. David and Anna M.; m. Alice Sylvia Litman, Oct. 19, 1941; children— Stephanie, Patricia, Tom. B.S., U. Minn., 1935, M.B., 1937, M.D., 1938, M.S., 1942. Diplomate: Am. Bd. Pediatrics. Health service physician U. Minn., Mpls., 1946; practice medicine, specializing in pediatrics Inglewood, Calif., 1946-60; chmn. dept. pediatrics Los Angeles Harbor Gen. Hosp., Torrance, 1948-51; head dept. pediatrics Methodist Hosp., Los Angeles, 1951; mem. faculty UCLA, 1952—, prof. pediatrics, 1964-81, prof. emeritus, 1981—; dir. fibrocystic center UCLA Med. Center, 1963-79, chmn. dept. pediatrics, 1967-77; chief of staff UCLA Hosps. and clinics, 1976-78. Author: (with Forrest H. Adams) Problems of Blood Pressure in Childhood, 1962, Heart Disease in Infants and Children, 1967, also articles.; Editorial bd.: (with Forrest H. Adams) Pediatrics Digest, 1962-79, Am. Jour. Cardiology, 1973-78, Jour. Tropical Pediatrics and Environ. Child Health, 1973— . Fellow Am. Coll. Cardiology; mem. Am. Acad. Pediatrics, Am., Calif., Los Angeles heart assns., Am., Calif., Los Angeles County med. assns., Soc. Exptl. Biology and Medicine, Sigma Xi. Office: U Calif Sch Medicine Dept Pediatrics Los Angeles CA 90024 Address: Pediatric Dignostic Ctr 3400 Loma Vista Rd Ste 100 Ventura CA 93003-3033

MOSS, ERIC OWEN, architect; b. L.A., July 25, 1943; BA, UCLA, 1965; MArch with honors, U. Calif., Berkeley, 1968, Harvard U., , 1972. Prof. design So. Calif. Inst. Architecture, 1974—; prin. Eric Owen Moss Archs., Culver City, Calif., 1975—; Eliot Noyes chair Harvard U., Cambridge, Mass., [illegible] Lectr. Hirshhorn Mus. Symposium, Washington, 1990, Nat. AIA Conv., 1990, Mus. Contemporary Art, L.A., 1991, N.Y. Archtl. League, 1991, Archtl. Assn. Ireland, Dublin, Archtl. Assn., London, 1991, Royal Coll. Art, London, 1991, Smithsonian Inst., Washington, 1992, U. Calif., Berkeley, 1992, Osterreichiaches Mus. fur Angewandte Kunst, Vienna, Austria, 1992, UCLA, 1992, Royal Danish Acad. Fine Arts, Copenhagen, 1993, U. Lund, Sweden, 1993, Mus. Finnish Architecture, Helsinki, 1993, Royal Acad. Arts, London, 1993, U. Pa., Phila., 1994, others; tchr. U. Tex., Austin, 1983, Wash. U., St. Louis, 1984, U. Ill., Chgo., 1985, Tulane U., New Orleans, 1985, U. Minn., Mpls., 1985, Columbia U., N.Y.C., 1986, Rice U., Houston, 1988; participant various confs. Exhbns. of work include World Biennial of Architecture, Sofia, Bulgaria, 1989, Salle des Tirages du Credit Foncier de France, Paris, 1990, Bartlett Sch. Architecture and Urban Design, London, 1991, Gallery of Functional Art, Santa Monica, Calif., 1992, GA Gallery, Tokyo, 1992, Mus. fur Gestaltung Zurich, Switzerland, 1993, Santa Monica (Calif.) Mus. Art, 1993, Fonds Regional D'Art Contemporain du Centre, 1993, Aspen (Colo.) Art Mus., 1993, Centro de Arte y Comunicacion, Buenos Aires, 1993, Contemporary Arts Ctr., Cin., 1993, Philippe Uzzan Galerie, Paris, 1993, Contemporary Arts Ctr., Tours, France, 1993, Internat. Exhbn. Contemporary Architecture, Havana, Cuba, 1994, others. Recipient Progressive Architecture Design award, 1978, 92, Winning Interior Archtl. Record award, 1984, Interiors Design award, 1991. Fellow AIA (L.A. awards 1977, 79, 83, 88, 90, Calif. Coun. awards 1981, 86, 88, L.A. Honor awards 1991, Nat. Honor awards 88, 89, Calif. Coun. Urban Design/Adaptive Re-Use awards 1991, Nat. Interior Design awards 1992, 94, L.A. Design awards 1992, 93). Achievements include being subject of monographs and numerous articles in mags. and jours. Office: 8557 Higuera St Culver City CA 90232-2535

MOSS, JOEL M. physicist; BS, Fort Hayes State U., 1964; PhD in Nuclear Chem., U. Calif., Berkeley, 1969. Postdoc. fellow Ctr. Nuclear Studies, Saclay, France, 1969-71, Physics Dept U. Minn., Mpls., 1971-73; faculty Physics Dept. Texas A&M U., 1973-79; Los Alamos (N. Mex.) Nat. Lab., 1979—. Mem. Nuclear Scis. Adv. Com. Recipient Tom W. Bonner prize 1998. Fellow Am. Physical Soc. Office: Los Alamos Nat Lab PO Box 1663 Los Alamos NM 87545-0001

MOSS, LYNDA BOURQUE, museum director; Dir. Western Heritage Ctr., Billings, Mont. Office: Western Heritage Ctr 2822 Montana Ave Billings MT 59101-2305

MOSS, MYRA ELLEN (MYRA MOSS ROLLE), philosophy educator; b. L.A., Mar. 22, 1937; m. Andrew Rolle, Nov. 5, 1983. BA, Pomona Coll., 1958; PhD, The Johns Hopkins U., 1965. Asst. prof. Santa Clara (Calif.) U., 1968-74; prof. Claremont McKenna Coll., 1975—, chmn. Dept. of Philosophy, 1992-95. Assoc. dir. Gould Ctr. for Humanities, Claremont, Calif., 1993-94; adv. coun. Milton S. Eisenhower Libr./Johns Hopkins U., 1994-96. Author: Benedetto Croce Reconsidered, 1987; translator: Benedetto Croce's Essays on Literature & Literary Criticism, 1990; co-author: Values and Education, 1998; assoc. editor Special Issues; Journal of Value Inquiry, 1990-95 (Honorable Mention, Phoenix award); cons. editor Jour. Social Philosophy, 1988—; assoc. editor: Value Enquiry Book Series, 1990-95; editor: The Philosophy of José Gaos, by Pio Colonnello, Value Equiry Book Series, 1997. Dir. Flintridge (Calif.) Riding Club, 1991. Bogliasco fellow, Liguria, Italy, 2000. Mem. Am. Philos. Assn., Am. and Internat. Soc. for Value Inquiry, Soc. for Aesthetics, Collingwood Soc. (life), Phi Beta Kappa (hon.). Avocations: gardening, horseback riding. Office: Claremont McKenna Coll 850 Columbia Ave Claremont CA 91711-3901

MOSSMAN, THOMAS MELLISH, JR. broadcasting consultant; b. Honolulu, Nov. 20, 1938; s. Thomas Mellish and Marian (Ledwith) M.; children: Thomas Mellish III, James Michael; m. Jan Carla MacAlister, Dec. 31, 1989. Student, U. Hawaii, 1954-57; BA, U. Denver, 1958, MA, 1965. Producer-dir. KRMA-TV, Denver, 1960-64, KCET-TV, L.A., 1964-72; pres. Mosaic Films, L.A., 1972-73; prodn. and operations dir. KLCS-TV, L.A., 1973-78, sta. mgr., 1978—87, L.A., 1996-2000; dept. dir. Archdiocese of L.A., 1987-96. Instr. Calif. State U., Northridge, 1981-94; chairperson, founder L.A. Community TV, 1987-95. Chmn. exec. bd. Regional Ednl. TV Adv. Coun., 1989-93; chmn., founding mem., chmn. Alliance for Distance Edn. in Calif., 1991-95; pres. Cath. TV Network, 1993-96; bd. dirs. L.A. Cable TV Access Corp. Mem.: ATAS, Dirs. Guild Am., Alliance for Cmty. Media. Episcopalian. Office: 10701 Commerce Ave Tujunga CA 91042 E-mail: tmossmanl@juno.com

MOSSOP, GRANT DILWORTH, geologist, researcher; b. Calgary, Alta., Can., Apr. 15, 1948; s. Cyril S. and Freida E. (Dilworth) M.; m. Ruth Shaver, May 24, 1969; children: Jenny, Jonathan, David. BSc in Geology, U. Calgary, 1970, MSc in Geology, 1971; PhD, DIC in Geology, Imperial Coll., U. London, 1973. Postdoctoral fellow U. Calgary, Alta., Can., 1974; asst. rsch. officer Alta. Rsch. Coun., Edmonton, 1975-77, assoc. rsch. officer, 1977-80, head geol. survey dept., 1980-84, sr. rsch. officer, 1985-91; dir. Geol. Survey of Can., Calgary, 1991-2001, rsch. scientist, 2001—. Acad. visitor dept. earth sci. Oxford (Eng.) U., 1984-85. Project mgr., editor Geol. Atlas of Western Canada Sedimentary Basin. Fellow Geol. Assn. Can. (pres. 1986-87); mem. Can. Soc. Petroleum Geologists. Home: 68 Colleen Cres SW Calgary AB Canada T2V 2R3 Office: Geol Survey Can 3303 33d St NW Calgary AB Canada T2L 2A7 E-mail: gmossop@nrcocn.gc.ca

MOTTEK, FRANK, broadcaster, journalist; b. Irvington, N.J., Feb. 17, 1962; s. Peter Mottek and Brigitte (Seidler) Fuller. AA, Broward C.C., Ft. Lauderdale, Fla., 1985; B.Liberal Studies, Barry U., Miami, Fla., 1988. News dir./anchor WMJX-FM Radio, Miami, 1978-81; news anchor/reporter WINZ Radio, Miami, 1981-92; news anchor space shuttles CBS Radio Network, Kennedy Space Ctr., Fla., 1985-91; news anchor, reporter WTVJ-TV 4, Miami, 1986-92; bus. news anchor, reporter PBS-WPBT TV Nightly Bus. Report, Miami, 1989-91; news anchor, reporter KNX Radio/KCBS-TV, L.A., 1992—; lectr. Annenberg Sch. for Comm. U. So. Calif., 1999—. Reporter, bus. news anchor Sta. KTLA-TV, 1999—. Recipient 1st place excellence in med. journalism Fla. Med. Assn., 1985, 1st place for news series AP, Fla., 1988, 1st place nat. award for documentary UPI, Washington, 1989, 1st place for spot news, Golden Mike award, 1996, 99, L.A. press Club 1st place spot news, 1996. Mem. AFTRA, Radio/TV News Dirs. Assn. (1st place regional documentary award 1992), Fla. Assoc. Press Broadcasters (pres. 1988-89, bd. dirs. 1986-92), Radio/TV News Assn. of So. Calif. Office: KNX CBS Radio 6121 W Sunset Blvd Los Angeles CA 90028-6493

MOTTO, JEROME ARTHUR, psychiatry educator; b. Kansas City, Mo., Oct. 16, 1921; MD, U. Calif., San Francisco, 1951. Diplomate Am. Bd. Neurology and Psychiatry. Intern San Francisco Gen. Hosp., 1951-52; resident Johns Hopkins Hosp., Balt., 1952-55; sr. resident U. Calif., San Francisco, 1955-56, from asst. prof. to prof. emeritus., 1956—. Contbr. articles to profl. jours. With AUS, 1942-46; ETO. Fellow Am. Psychiatric Assn. (life).

MOTULSKY, ARNO GUNTHER, geneticist, physician, educator; b. Fischhausen, Germany, July 5, 1923; came to U.S., 1941; s. Herman and Rena (Sass) Molton; m. Gretel C. Stern, Mar. 22, 1945; children: Judy, Harvey, Arlene. Student, Cen. YMCA Coll., Chgo., 1941-43, Yale U., , 1943-44; BS, U. Ill., 1945, MD, 1947, DSc (hon.), 1982, MD (hon.), 1991. Diplomate Am. Bd. Internal Medicine, Am. Bd. Med. Genetics. Intern, fellow, resident Michael Reese Hosp., Chgo., 1947-51; staff mem. charge [illegible] Army Med. Service Grad. Sch., Walter

Reed Army Med. Ctr., Washington, 1952-53; research assoc. internal medicine George Washington U. Sch. Medicine, 1952-53; from instr. to assoc. prof. dept. medicine U. Wash. Sch. Medicine, Seattle, 1953-61, prof. medicine, prof. genetics, 1961—; head div. med. genetics, dir. genetics clinic Univ. Hosp., Seattle, 1959-89; dir. Ctr. for Inherited Diseases, Seattle, 1972-90. Attending physician Univ. Hosp., Seattle; cons. Pres.'s Commn. for Study of Ethical Problems in Medicine and Biomed. and Behavioral Research, 1979-83; cons. various coms. NRC, NIH, WHO, others. Editor Am. Jour. Human Genetics, 1969-75, Human Genetics, 1969-97. Commonwealth Fund fellow in human genetics Univ. Coll., London, 1957-58; John and Mary Markle scholar in med. sci., 1957-62; fellow Ctr. Advanced Study in Behavioral Scis., Stanford U., 1976-77, Inst. Advanced Study, Berlin, 1984. Fellow ACP, AAAS; mem. NAS, Internat. Soc. Hematology, Am. Fedn. Clin. Research, Genetics Soc. Am., Western Soc. Clin. Research, Am. Soc. Human Genetics, Am. Soc. Clin. Investigation, Am. Assn. Physicians, Inst. of Medicine, Am. Acad. Arts and Scis. Home: 4347 53rd Ave NE Seattle WA 98105-4938 Office: U Wash Divsn Med Genetics PO Box 356423 Seattle WA 98195-6423 E-mail: agmot@u.washington.edu

MOU, THOMAS WILLIAM, physician, medical educator and consultant; b. Phila., May 17, 1920; s. Thomas Simonsen and Ellen Marie (Mathiesen) M.; m. Marie Elizabeth Hartmann, Dec. 29, 1945 (div. Oct., 1976); children: Susan, Roberta; m. M. Delma Jane Schreiber, Nov. 11, 1976. BSc in Bacteriology, Phila. Coll. Pharm & Sci., 1941; MD, U. Rochester, 1950. Diplomate Nat. Bd. Med. Examiners. Instr. medicine and bacteriology U. Rochester (N.Y.) Sch. of Medicine, 1954-56; asst. prof. preventive medicine to prof. cmty. medicine SUNY at Syracuse, 1956-70; exec. dean to assoc chancellor health sci. SUNY Ctrl. Adminstrn., Albany, 1970-77; dean clin. campus W. Va. U., Charleston, 1977-85; pres. Ednl. Commn. for Fgn. Med. Grads., Phila., 1986-88; dean emeritus W. Va. U. Med. Ctr., Morgantown, 1986—; geriatric practice Adult Medicine Specialists, Pueblo, Colo., 1990-2000. Cons. Carnegie Commn. for Advancement of Tchg., Princeton, N.J., 1987-88, Charles A. Dana Found., N.Y.C., 1988, Geriatric Pharmacy Inst. of Phila. Coll. of Pharmacy and Sci., 1988. Contbr. 36 article or presentations to profl. jours or sci. confs. Trustee Phila. Coll. Pharmacy and Sci., 1972-81. Capt. Sanitary Corps, 1941-45 Recipient Disting. Alumnus award Phila. Coll. Pharmacy and Sci., 1975, award of distinction and honor Ben Franklin Soc. SUNY, N.Y.C., 1975, Koch medal Am. Optometric Soc., N.Y.C., 1976; T.W. Mou Endowed Lectureship W. Va. U., Charleston, 1985. Fellow Am. Coll. Physicians, Am. Coll. Preventive Medicine, Phila. Coll. Physicians, Infectious Diseases Soc. Am. (founding fellow). Avocations: violin, travel. Home: 3050 Valleybrook Ln Colorado Springs CO 80904-1154 Office: Adult Medicine Specialists 314 W 16th St Pueblo CO 81003-2728

MOULDS, JOHN F. federal judge; m. Elizabeth Fry, Aug. 29, 1964; children: Donald B., Gerald B. Student, Stanford U., 1955-58; BA with honors, Calif. State U., Sacramento, 1960; JD, U. Calif, Berkeley, 1963. Bar: U.S. Supreme Ct., U.S. Dist. Ct. (no. dist.) Calif., U.S. Dist. Ct. (ea. dist.) Calif. 1968, U.S. Ct. Claims 1982, U.S. Ct. Appeals (9th cir.) 1967, Calif. Rsch. analyst Calif. State Senate Fact-Finding Com. on Edn., 1960-61; adminstrv. asst. Senator Albert S. Rodda, Calif., 1961-63; staff atty. Calif. Rural Legal Assistance, Marysville, 1966-68, dir. atty. Marysville field office and Sacramento legis. adv. office, 1968-69; staff atty. Sacramento Legal Aid, 1968-69; ptnr. Blackmon, Isenberg & Moulds, 1969-85, Isenberg, Moulds & Hemmer, 1985; magistrate judge U.S. Dist. Ct. (ea. dist.) Calif., 1985—, chief magistrate jdge, 1988-97. Moot ct. and trial practice judge U. Calif. Davis Law Sch., 1975—, U. of Pacific McGeorge Coll. Law, 1985—; part-time U.S. magistrate judge U.S. Dist. Ct. (ea. dist.) Calif., 1983-85; mem. 9th Cir. Capital Case Com., 1992—, U.S. Jud. Conf. Com. on the Magistrate Judge Sys., 1992—, Adv. Com. to the Magistrate Judges' Divsn. Adminstv. Office of U.S. Jud. Conf., 1989—. Author: (with others) Review of California Code Legislation, 1965, Welfare Recipients' Handbook, 1967; editor: Ninth Circuit Capital Punishment Handbook, 1991. Atty. Sacramento Singlemen's Self-Help Ctr., 1969-74; active Sacramento Human Relations Commn., 1969-75, chair, 1974-75; active community support orgn. U. Calif. at Davis Law Sch., 1971—; mem., atty. Sacramento Community Coalition for Media Change, 1972-75; bd. dirs. Sacramento Country Day Sch., 1982-90, Sacramento Pub. Libr. Found., 1985-87; active various polit. orgns. and campaigns, 1960-82. Mem. ABA, Fed. Bar Assn., Nat. Coun. Magistrates (cir. dir. 1986-88, treas. 1988-89, 2d v.p. 1989-90, 1st v.p. 1990-91), Fed. Magistrate Judges Assn. (pres.-elect 1991, pres. 1992-93), Calif. State-Fed. Jud. Coun. Conf. (panelist capital habeas corpus litigation 1992), Fed. Jud. Ctr. Training Conf. for U.S. Magistrate Judges (panel leader 1993), Milton L. Schwartz Inns of Ct. Office: 8240 US Courthouse 501 I St Ste 8-240 Sacramento CA 95814-7300

MOULIN, JANE ANN FREEMAN, ethnomusicology educator, researcher; b. Oak Park, Ill., Mar. 4, 1946; d. James Frederic and Georgia Charlotte (Rahn) Freeman; m. Jacques Edouard Moulin, Apr. 26, 1975; children: Jean-Philippe Keala, Marie-Chantal Mahala. BA in Music cum laude, U. Hawaii, 1969; MA in Music, UCLA, 1971; PhD in Music, U. Calif., Santa Barbara, 1991. Libr. Music Libr UCLA, 1970-71; tchr. English Companions, Osaka, Japan, 1972; dancer Te Maeva and Tahiti Nui, Papeete, Tahiti, 1973-76; rsch. fellow U. Auckland, New Zealand, 1989; fellow East-West Ctr., Honolulu, 1984-85, 91; assoc. prof. Hawaii Loa Coll., Kaneohe, 1980-92; prof. U. Hawaii, Honolulu, 1992—. Dir. Europa Early Music Consort, Honolulu, 1981-2000; primary rschr. field work in French Polynesia, 1973-77, 85, 89, 95, 98, 2000, Territorial Survey Oceanic Music, Marquesas Islands, 1989; cons. Video series Dancing, WNET Channel 13, N.Y.C., 1989-92. Author: The Dance of Tahiti, 1979, Music of the Southern Marquesas Islands, 1994, (audio catalog) Music of the Southern Marquesas Islands, 1991, ency. and jour. articles on Tahitian and Marquesan performing arts, field recordings of Tahitian and Marquesan music; edtl. bd. Jour. Perfect Beat, 1993—, Pacific Islands Monograph Series, 1997—; bd. dirs. Hawaii Assn. Music Socs., Honolulu, 1983-88. Bd. dirs. Tahiti-USA Assn., Honolulu, 1997-2000; mem. adv. bd. folk arts State Found. Culture and Arts, Honolulu, 1985-87. Recipient Regents' fellowship U. Calif., 1970-71, 88-89, rsch. grant UNESCO/Archives of Maori and Pacific Music, Auckland, 1989, regents' award for excellence in tchg. U. Hawaii, Honolulu, 1997, First Prize Thèse-Pac Assn. Competition, New Caledonia, 1994. Mem. Soc. Ethomusicology (mem. coun. 1995-97), Internat. Coun. Traditional Music, Polynesia Soc., Pacific Arts Assn., Viola da Gamba Soc. Am. Avocations: Tahitian dance, hula, consort playing. Office: U Hawaii Music Dept 2411 Dole St Honolulu HI 96822-2329

MOULTON, JENNIFER T. city official, architect; BA cum laude, Colo. Coll., 1971; MArch with honors, U. Colo., Denver, 1978. Registered arch., Colo. Corp. legal asst. Davis, Graham & Stubbs, Denver, 1972-75; mem. staff Ctr. for Cmty. Devel. and Design, Denver, 1976-77; assoc. Barker Rinker Seacat & Ptnrs., Archs., Denver, 1978-84; v.p., owner Anthony Pellecchia Archs., P.C., Denver, 1984-89; pres. Hist. Denver, Inc., 1989-91; dir. Denver Planning and Devel. Office, 1992—. Mem. master plan com. Colo. Coll., Colorado Springs, 1994-95, juror Ctrl. States Regional Awards of Excellence, 1995; team mem. Mayor's Inst. for City Design, Harvard U., 1996, Design Workshop for Oklahoma City, Nat. Endowment for Arts, 1995; mem. dean's search com. Sch. Architecture and Planning, U. Colo., Denver, 1986, mem. dean's adv. com., 1986-89, vis. lectr., 1979-81; instr. corp. paralegal courses U. Denver Coll. Law, Arapahoe C.C., C.C. Denver, 1973-75; lectr. Jr. League Denver, 1987-88, Colo. Coll. Alumni Assn., 1985. Prin. works include Grant Humphries Mansion restoration, Denver, also offices for Colo. Coun. on Arts and Humanities in carriage house therein, Washington Park Pavilion restoration, Denver, Goss Residence, Boulder, Colo., Georgetown (Colo.) Downtown Redevel. Project, Georgetown Loop R.R. Master Plan, Malo Mansion project, Denver. Founder, pres. Women for Downtown Housing, 1980-81; co-chmn. urban design and land use task force comprehensive plan adv. com. City of Denver, 1986-87, mem. parks and recreation adv. com., 1983-89; atrustee, chmn. preservation com. Hist. Denver, Inc., 1986-89; mem. Citizens for Denver's Future, 1989; vice chmn. Colo. Passenger Tramway Safety Bd., 1981-89; mem. design competition jury Denver Pub. Libr., 1990-91; chmn. design rev. com. Ctrl. Denver Pub. Libr., 1992-94; trustee Colo. Hist. Found., 1990—; mem. South Platte River Commn., 1995— Recipient Disting. Svc. award U. Colo. Sch. Architecture and Planning, 1987, Louis T. Benezet award for outstanding profl. achievements Colo. Coll., 1991. Mem. AIA (chmn. design awards program Denver chpt. 1983, bd. dirs. 1977-87, treas. 1982, sec. 1983, 2d v.p. 1984, pres.-elect 1985, pres. 1986), Colo. Soc. Archs. (chmn. design awards program 1980-82). Office: Denver Planning & Devel Office 200 W 14th Ave Ofc Ste 203 Denver CO 80204-2732

MOUNTAIN, CLIFTON FLETCHER, surgeon, educator; b. Toledo, Apr. 15, 1924; s. Ira Fletcher and Mary (Stone) M.; children: Karen Lockerby, Clifton Fletcher, Jeffrey Richardson. AB, Harvard U., 1946; MD, Boston U., 1954. Diplomate Am. Bd. Surgery. Dir. dept. statis. rsch. Boston U., 1947-50; cons. rsch. analyst Mass. Dept. Pub. Health, 1951-53; intern U. Chgo. Clinics, 1954, resident, 1955-58, instr. surgery, 1958-59; sr. fellow thoracic surgery Houston, 1959. Mem. staff U. Tex. Anderson Cancer Ctr.; asst. prof. thoracic surgery U. Tex., 1960-73, assoc. prof surgery, 1973-76, prof., 1976-94, prof. emeritus, 1995—, prof. surgery Sch. Medicine, 1987—, chief sect. thoracic surgery, 1970-79, chmn. thoracic oncology, 1979-84, chmn. dept. thoracic surgery, 1980-85, cons. dept. thoracic and cardiovascular surgery, 1996—, chmn. program in biomath. and computer sci., 1962-64, Mike Hogg vis. lectr. in S. Am., 1967; prof. surgery U. Calif., San Diego, 1996—; mem. sci. mission on cancer USSR, 1970-78, and Japan, 1976-84; mem. com. health, rsch. and edn. facilities Houston Cmty. Coun., 1964-78; cons. Am. Joint Com. on Cancer Staging and End Result Reporting, 1964-74, Tex. Heart Inst., 1994-96; mem. Am. Joint Com. on Cancer, 1974-86, chmn. lung and esophagus task force; mem. working party on lung cancer and chmn. com. on surgery Nat. Clin. Trials Lung Cancer Study Group, NIH, 1971-76; mem. plans and scope com. cancer therapy Nat. Cancer Inst., 1972-75, mem. lung cancer study group, 1977-89, chmn. steering com., 1973-75, mem. bd. sci. counselors divsn. cancer treatment, 1972-75; hon. cons. Shanghai Chest Hosp. and Lung Cancer Ctr., Nat. Cancer Inst. of Brazil; sr. cons. Houston Thorax Inst., 1994-96. Editor The New Physician, 1955-59; mem. editl. bd. Yearbook of Cancer, 1960-88, Internat. Trends in Gen. Thoracic Surgery, 1984-91; contbr. articles to profl. jours., chpts. to textbooks. Chmn. profl. adv. com. Harris County Mental Health Assn.; bd. dirs. Harris County Chpt. Am. Cancer Soc. Lt. USNR, 1942-46. Recipient award Soviet Acad. Sci., 1977, Garcia Meml. medal Philippine Coll. Surgeons, 1982, Disting. Alumni award Boston U., 1988, Disting. Achievement U. Tex. M.D. Anderson Cancer Ctr., 1990, Disting. Svc. award Internat. Assn. for the Study of Lung Cancer, 1991, Disting. Alumnus award Boston U. Sch. of Medicine, 1992, ALCASE Internat. award for excellence, 1997, Rudolf Nissen medal German Soc. Cardiovascular and Thoracic Surgery, 1998, named hon. pres. First Internat. Congress on Thoracic Surgery, 1997; Fellow ACS Am. Coll. Chest Physicians (chmn. com. cancer 1967-75), Am. Assn. Thoracic Surgery, Inst. Environ. Scis., N.Y. Acad. Sci., Assn. Thoracic and Cardiovascular Surgeons of Asia (hon.), Hellenic Cancer Soc. (hon.), Chilean Soc. Respiratory Diseases (hon., hon. pres. 1982). Mem. AAAS, Am. Assn. Cancer Rsch., AMA, So. Med. Assn., Am. Thoracic Soc., Soc. Thoracic Surgeons, Soc. Biomed. Computing, Am. Fedn. Clin. Rsch., Internat. Assn. Study Lung Cancer (pres. 1976-78), Am. Radium Soc., European Soc. Thoracic Surgeons, Pan-Am Med. Assn., Houston Surg. Soc., Soc. Surg. Oncology, James Ewing Soc., Sigma Xi. Achievements include conception and development of program for application of mathematics and computers to the life sciences, of resource for experimental designs, applied statistics and computational support; concept and implementation of multidisciplinary, site specific cancer mgmt. clinics; first clinical use of physiological adhesives in thoracic surgery; demonstration of clinical behavior of undifferentiated small cell lung cancer; first laser resection of lung tissue at thoracotomy; development of international system for staging of lung cancer. E-mail: cmountain@ucsd.edu

MOUNTJOY, RICHARD, state legislator; b. L.A. m. Earline Winnett; children: Michael, Dennis, Judy. Mayor, city councilman City of Monrovia, Calif., 1968-76; mem. Calif. Assembly, 1978-95, mem. assembly rules com., Rep. caucus chmn., 1982-84; mem. Calif. State Senate, Sacramento, 1995—, mem. appropriations com., vice chair energy, utilities and comm. com., vice chair indsl. rels. com., health and human svcs. com. With USN, Korea. Named Legislator of Yr., Calif. Wildlife Fedn., Calif. Rep. Assembly, San Gabriel Valley Units, Calif. Bus. Properties Assn., Calif. Rifle and Pistol Assn., Roofing Contractors Assn., Rep. Statesman of Yr., United Reps. Calif., Outstanding State Assemblyman, Young Ams. for Freedom. Mem. Commn. of the Californias, Associated Builders and Contractors Calif., Aircraft Owners and Pilots Assn. (Presdl. citation), Elks (hon. life, past exalted ruler), Monrovia Kiwanis Club, VFW (life). Republican. Avocations: fishing, hunting, flying. Office: State Capitol Rm 4052 Sacramento CA 95814 also: 500 N 1st Ave Ste 3 Arcadia CA 91006-7100

MOW, WILLIAM, apparel executive; b. Apr. 19, 1936; BEE, Rensselear; PhD, Purdue U., 1967. With Honeywell Inc., Boston, 1963-65; program mgr. Litton Industries, L.A., 1967-69; founder, pres., chmn. bd. MacroData Corp., L.A., 1969-76; sci. advisor Cutler Hammer, L.A., 1976-77; with Bugle Boy Industries, Inc., Simi Valley, Calif., 1977—, now chmn., CEO. Office: Bugle Boy 2900 N Madera Rd Simi Valley CA 93065-6230

MOWE, GREGORY ROBERT, lawyer; b. Aberdeen, Wash., Feb. 23, 1946; s. Robert Eden and Jeannette Effie (Deyoung) M.; m. Rebecca Louise Nobles, June 14, 1969; children: Emily, Tom. BA, U. Oreg., 1968, MA, 1969; JD magna cum laude, Harvard Law Sch., 1974. Bar: Oreg. 1974, U.S. Dist. Ct. Oreg. 1974, U.S. Ct. Appeals (9th cir.) 1974. Assoc. atty. Stoel Rives Boley Jones & Grey, Portland, Oreg., 1974-79; ptnr. Stoel Rivis Boley Jones & Grey, Portland, 1979—. Pres. bd. dirs. Planned Parenthood of Columbia/Willamette, Portland, 1989-90. 1st lt. U.S. Army, 1969-71, Vietnam. Mem. ABA, Phi Beta Kappa. Office: Stoel Rives Boley Jones & Grey 900 SW 5th Ave Ste 2300 Portland OR 97204-1229

MOXLEY, JOHN HOWARD, III, internist; b. Elizabeth, N.J., Jan. 10, 1935; s. John Howard, Jr. and Cleopatra (Mundy) M.; m. Doris Banchik; children: John Howard IV, Brook, Mark. BA, Williams Coll., 1957; MD, U. Colo., 1961; DSc (hon.), Sch. Medicine Hannemann U. Bar: Diplomate Am. Bd. Internal Medicine. Intern Peter Bent Brigham Hosp., Boston, 1961-62, resident in internal medicine, 1962-66; with Nat. Cancer Inst., USPHS, 1963-65; asst. to dean, instr. medicine Harvard Med. Sch., Boston, 1966-69; dean Sch. Medicine, U. Md., 1969-73; vice chancellor health scis., dean Med. Sch., U. Calif.-San Diego, 1973-79; asst. sec. for health affairs Dept. Def., Washington, 1979-81; sr. v.p. Am. Med. Internat., Beverly Hills, Calif., 1981-87; pres. MetaMed. Inc., Playa Del Rey, 1987-89; mgr. dir. Korn/Ferry Internat., L.A., 1989—. Cons. FDA, NIH; dir. Nat. Fund for Med. Edn., 1986—, chmn., 1993—; dir. Henry M. Jackson Found. for Adv. Mil. Medicine. Contbr. articles to profl. jours. Dir. Polyclinic Health Svcs. Games of XXIII Olympiad. Recipient gold and silver award U. Colo. Med. Sch., 1974, commr.'s citation for outstanding svc. to over-the-counter drug study FDA, 1977, spl. achievement citation Am. Hosp. Assn., 1983, Sec. of Def. medal for disting. pub. svc., 1981. Fellow ACP, Am. Coll. Physicians Execs. (Disting.); mem. Inst. Medicine NAS, AMA (chmn. coun. sci. affairs 1985), Calif. Med. Assn. (chmn. sci. bd. 1978-83, councilor), San Diego C. of C., Soc. Med. Adminstrs., Am. Hosp. Assn. (trustee 1979-81), Alpha Omega Alpha. Rotary. Office: Korn Ferry Internat 1800 Century Park E Ste 900 Los Angeles CA 90067-1512 E-mail: moxleyj@kornferry.com

MOYA, PATRICK ROBERT, lawyer; b. Belen, N.Mex., Nov. 7, 1944; s. Adelicio E. and Eva (Sanchez) M.; m. Sara Dreier, May 30, 1966; children: Jeremy Brill, Joshua Dreier. AB, Princeton U., 1966; JD, Stanford U., 1969. Bar: Calif. 1970, Ariz. 1970, D.C. 1970, U.S. Dist. Ct. (no. dist.) Calif. 1970, U.S. Ct. Claims 1970, U.S. Tax Ct. 1970, U.S. Ct. Appeals (D.C. cir.) 1970, U.S. Supreme Ct. 1973. Assoc. Lewis and Roca, Phoenix, 1969-73, ptnr., 1973-83; sr. ptnr. Moya, Bailey, Bowers & Jones, P.C., Phoenix, 1983-84; ptnr., mem. nat. exec. com. Gaston & Snow, Phoenix, 1985-91; ptnr. Quarles & Brady, LLP, Phoenix, 1991—, mem. nat. mgmt. com., 2000—. Instr. sch. of law Ariz. State U., 1972; bd. dirs. Bige Realestate, Inc. Mem. Paradise Valley Bd. Adjustment, 1976-80, chmn., 1978-80; mem. Paradise Valley Town Coun., 1980-82; bd. dirs. Phoenix Men's Arts Coun., 1973-81, pres., 1979-80; bd. dirs. The Silent Witness, Inc., 1979-84, pres., 1981-83; bd. dirs. Enterprise Network, Inc., 1989-94, pres., 1991-92; bd. dirs. Phoenix Little Theatre, 1973-75, Interfaith Counseling Svc., 1973-75; precinct committeeman Phoenix Rep. Com., 1975-77; dep. voter registrar Maricopa County, 1975-76; mem. exec. bd. dirs. Gov.'s Strategic Partnership for Econ. Devel.; pres. GSPED, Inc.; mem. of Steering Com. for Sonora-Ariz. Joint Econ. Plan; mem. Gov.'s Adv. Com., Ariz. and Mex., Ariz. Corp. Commn. Stock Exch. Adv. Coun., Ariz. Town Hall. Mem. ABA, Nat. Hispanic Bar Assn., Los Abogados Hispanic Lawyers Assn., Nat. Assn. Bond Lawyers, Ariz. Bar Assn., Maricopa County Bar Assn., Nat. Mgmt. Com., Paradise Valley Country Club, Univ. Club. Office: Quarles & Brady LLP One Renaissance Sq Two North Central Ave Phoenix AZ 85004-2391

MOYER, ALAN DEAN, retired newspaper editor; b. Galva, Iowa, Sept. 4, 1928; s. Clifford Lee and Harriet (Jacques) M.; m. Patricia Helen Krecker, July 15, 1950; children: Virginia, Stanley, Glenn. BS in Journalism, U. Iowa, 1950. Reporter, copy editor Wis. State Jour., Madison, 1950-53; reporter, photographer Bartlesville (Okla.) Examiner-Enterprise, 1953; telegraph editor Abilene (Tex.) Reporter-News, 1954-55; makeup editor Cleve. Plain Dealer, 1955-63; mng. editor Wichita (Kans.) Eagle, 1963-70; exec. editor Wichita Eagle and Beacon, 1970-73; mng. editor Phoenix Gazette, 1973-82, Ariz. Republic, 1982-89; ret., 1989. Pres., dir. Wichita Profl. Baseball, Inc., 1969-75; mem. jury Pulitzer Prizes, 1973-74, 85, 86, 88. Mem. AP Mng. Editors Assn. (dir. 1973-78), Am. Soc. Newspaper Editors, Wichita Area C. of C. (dir. 1970-72), Sigma Delta Chi. Office: Phoenix Newspaper Inc 200 E Van Buren St Phoenix AZ 85004-2238 E-mail: patmoyusa@netscape.net

MOYER, J. KEITH, newspaper editor; Exec. editor The Fresno (Calif.) Bee, pub., 1997—. Office: The Fresno Bee 1626 E St Fresno CA 93786-0002

MOYES, JERRY C. transportation executive; Chmn., pres., CEO Swift Transp. Co., Inc., Phoenix, 1974—. Office: Swift Transp Co 2200 S 75th Ave Phoenix AZ 85043-7410 also: PO Box 29243 Phoenix AZ 85038-9243 Fax: 623-907-7380

MOYLAN, STEVE, publishing executive; Pub., CEO Infoworld, San Mateo, Calif., CEO. Office: Infoworld Pub 155 Bovet Rd Ste 800 San Mateo CA 94402-3150

MOYLE, PETER BRIGGS, fisheries and biology educator; b. May 29, 1942; s. John Briggs and Evelyn (Wood) M.; m. Marilyn Arneson, June 11, 1966; children: Petrea Ruth, John Noah. BA, U. Minn., 1964, PhD, 1969; MS, Cornell U., 1966. Asst. prof. Calif. State U., Fresno, 1969-72; from asst. prof. to prof. U. Calif., Davis, 1972—, chmn. dept. wildlife and fisheries, 1982-87. Head, Delta Native Fishes Recovery Team, 1993-95. Author: Inland Fishes of California, 1976, 2d edit., 2001, Fishes: An Introduction to Ichthyology, 4th edit., 2000, Distribution and Ecology of Stream Fishes of Sacramento San Joaquin Drainage, 1982, Fish: An Enthusiast's Guide, 1993. Fellow Calif. Acad. Sci.; mem. Am. Fisheries Soc. (life, award of excellence West divsn. 1991, Outstanding Educator award 1995), Ecol. Soc. Am., Am. Soc. Ichthyologists and Herpetologists, Soc. Conservation Biology, Natural Heritage Inst. (v.p. 1994—). Home: 612 Eisenhower St Davis CA 95616-3031 Office: Dept Wildlife Fish & Conservation Biology U Calif Davis CA 95616 E-mail: pbmoyle@ucdavis.edu

MOZENA, JOHN DANIEL, podiatrist; b. Salem, Oreg., June 9, 1956; s. Joseph Iner and Mary Teresa (Delaney) M.; m. Elizabeth Ann Hintz, June 2, 1979; children: Christine Hintz, Michelle Delaney. Student, U. Oreg., 1974-79; B in Basic Med. Scis., Calif. Coll. Podiatric Medicine, D in Podiatric Medicine, 1983. Diplomate Am. Bd. Podiatric Surgery. Resident in surg. podiatry Hillside Hosp., San Diego, 1983-84; pvt. practice podiatry Portland, Oreg., 1984—; dir. residency Med. Ctr. Hosp., Portland, 1985-91. Lectr. Nat. Podiatric Assn. Seminar, 1990, Am. Coll. Gen. Practitioners, 1991, Am. Coll. Family Physician, 1995; adj. faculty health profl. sect. Portland C.C., 1999. Cons. editor Podiatry Today Mag., 1999—, Podiatry Today, 1999—; contbr. articles to profl. jours.; patentee sports shoe cleat design, 1985. Podiatric adv. coun. Oreg. Bd. Med. Examiners, 1994-97. Named Clinician of the Yr., Eastmoreland Hosp., 2000-01. Fellow Am Coll. Ambulatory Foot Surgeons, Am. Coll. Foot Surgeons. Republican. Roman Catholic. Avocations: softball, basketball, piano, jogging, electric bass guitar, coaching children's sports programs. Office: Town Ctr Foot Clinic 8305 SE Monterey Ave Ste 101 Portland OR 97266-7728

MOZILO, ANGELO R. diversified financial services company executive; Ptnr., co-founder Countrywide Credit Industries, Inc., Calabasas, Calif., 1969—, CEO, 2000—, also vice chmn.; chmn., CEO Countrywide Home Loans, Inc. subs., Calabasas, chmn., CEO, pres. Vice chmn. Office: Countrywide Credit Industries Inc 4500 Park Granada Calabasas CA 91302-1613

MRACKY, RONALD SYDNEY, marketing and promotion executive, travel consultant; b. Sydney, Australia, Oct. 22, 1932; came to U.S., 1947, naturalized, 1957; s. Joseph and Anna (Janousek) M.; m. Sylvia Frommer, Jan. 1, 1960; children: Enid Hillevi, Jason Adam. Student, English Inst., Prague, Czechoslovakia, 1943-47; grad., Parsons Sch. Design, N.Y.C., 1950-53; postgrad., NYU, 1953-54. Designer D. Deskey Assocs., N.Y.C., 1952-53; art dir., designer ABC-TV, Hollywood, Calif., 1956-57; creative dir. Neal Advt. Assocs., L.A., 1957-59; pres. Richter & Mracky Design Assocs., L.A., 1959-68; pres., CEO Richter & Mracky-Bates divsn. Ted Bates & Co., L.A., 1968-73, Regency Fin., Internat. Fin. Svcs., Beverly Hills, Calif., 1974-76; sr. ptnr. Sylron Internat., L.A., 1973—, mgmt. dir. for N.Am. Standard Advt.-Tokyo, 1978-91. CEO Standard/Worldwide Cons. Group, L.A., Tokyo, 1981-87; officer, bd. dirs. Theme Resorts, Inc., Denver, 1979—; prin., officer Prodn. Travel & Tours, Universal City, 1981—, Eques Ltd., L.A., 1988—; mng. ptnr. GO! Pubs., 1993—; cons. in field; exec. dir. Inst. for Internat. Studies and Devel. L.A., 1976-77; mng. ptnr. Africa Consult Group, 1998—. Contbr. articles to profl. jours.; mem.

editl. bd., mktg. dir. The African Times and Africa Quar., 1990—. With U.S. Army, 1954-56. Recipient nat. and internat. awards design and mktg. Mem. Am. Mktg. Assn., African Travel Assn. (amb.-at-large, internat. secretariat), L.A. Publicity Club, Pacific Asia Travel Assn., S.Am. Travel Assn., Am. Soc. Travel Agents. Office: 10554 Riverside Dr Toluca Lake CA 91602-2441

MUCHMORE, DON MONCRIEF, museum, foundation, educational, financial fund raising and public opinion consulting firm administrator, banker; b. Wichita, Kans., Dec. 26, 1922; s. Floyd Stephen and Ivy Fay (Campbell) M.; m. Virginia Gunn, June 18, 1949 (div. Dec. 1978); children— Melinda, Marcia BA, Occidental Coll., Los Angeles, 1945; postgrad., U. So. Calif. Law Sch., 1945, UCLA. Intern Nat. Inst. Pub. Affairs, Washington, 1944; exec. asst. to congressman Washington, 1946-48; teaching asst. UCLA, 1949-50; mem. faculty San Diego State U., 1950-51; asst. prof., adminstr. Calif. State U., Long Beach, 1951-56; pres., chief exec. officer The Campbell Found., L.A., 1956—; spl. asst. to supt. pub. instrn. Calif. Dept. Edn., Sacramento, 1956-57; exec. mus. dir. Calif. Mus. Sci. and Industry, L.A., 1957-62, 82-89; exec. v.p., chief exec. officer Calif. Mus. Found., L.A., 1957-62, 82-89; dep. dir. (on loan from mus.) Calif. Dept. Fin., Sacramento, 1960; exec. vice chancellor Calif. State Colls. and Univs. System, Long Beach, 1962-64; first exec. asst. to chmn. and chief exec. officer Calif. Fed. Savs. and Loan Assn., L.A., 1964-66; sr. v.p. Calif. Fed. Savs. and Loan Assn, L.A., 1966-82; pres., CEO PE Conservation Svcs., Inc., 1990-94. Chmn. bd. dirs., CEO Opinion Rsch. of Calif., Opinion Surveyors, The State Poll and Mkt. Surveys, Inc., Long Beach, 1948-71, syndicated by L.A. Times, 1961-70, also M-R Assocs. campaigns; cons. in pub. opinion mus. mgmt. and fund raising, 1948-71; chmn., CEO, cons. DMM & Assocs., Long Beach, 1961—; sec., treas. EVENUP for the Homeless, 1994-97; mem. Inst. Mus. Svcs., 1983-88. Contbr. chpts. to books. Participant in pub. opinion work Dem. and Rep. campaigns, 1954-72; mem., chmn. 4 presdl. commns., 1970-82, Just Say No Internat., 1989-91, Reading is Fundamental, 1989—, The Buckley Sch., 1989-90; cons. overseas traveling sci. exhibit, planning mus., 1984-96, sr. adminstr., advisor, cons. to PCS (South Ctrl. L.A.) Sr. Citizens, 1995-96; cons. Long Beach Com. Improvement League, 1995-96; lead cons. New Solution to Homeless, 1993-98; prin. officer Peruvians Cultural Exhibit, 1988-96; prin. cons. cultural exhibit Wonders of World, 1992-95, Queensway Bay, Long Beach, 1992-98; bd. dirs. Bus. Tele Network, 1995-97; active Even Up for the Homeless, 1996-98; cons. to Christian Outreach Agy., 1998-99; pres. bd. trustees East Village Cmty. Ch., 1998—, pres., 1999—; pres. Harborplace Tower Home Owners Assn., 1999— Recipient Highest Mus. Edn. award Sigma Alpha Epsilon, 1992, Chpt. Advisor of Yr., Sigma Alpha Epsilon, 1999, Citizen of Yr. award and numerous other awards from nat., state and local groups; named Pollster of Yr., Newsweek, 1968; Elks Nat. scholar. Mem. AAAS, Am. Assn. Mus., Calif. Mus. Assn. (pres. 1960, bd. dirs. 1982-88), Assn. Sci. and Tech. Ctrs. (bd. dirs. 1982-88), Am. Assn. Pub. Opinion Rsch., Am. Polit. Sci. Assn. Office: The Campbell Found DMM & Associates 525 E Seaside Way Unit 209 Long Beach CA 90802-8001 Fax: 562-983-1143

MUDD, JOHN O. lawyer; b. 1943; BA, Cath. U., 1965, MA, 1966; JD, U. Mont., 1973; LLM, Columbia U., 1986; JSD of Law, 1994. Bar: Mont. 1973. Pntr. Mulroney, Delaney, Dalby & Mudd, Missoula, Mont., 1973-79; lectr. U. Mont., Missoula, 1973-74, 75-76, prof. law, dean, 1979-88; ptnr. Garlington, Lohn & Robinson, Missoula, 1988-1999; sr. v.p. Providence Svcs., 2000—. Pres. Mid-Continent Assn. Law Schs., 1982-83. Editor: Mont. Law Rev., 1972-73. Bd. dirs. St. Patrick Hosp., 1985-90, Providence Svcs. Corp., 1992-97, Ascension Health, 1999—; elected Dem. candidate U.S. Senate, 1994; chmn. Mont. Commn. Future of Higher Edn., 1980-81. With U.S. Army, 1967-73. Mem. ABA, Am. Judicature Soc. (bd. dirs. 1985-89), State Bar Mont.

MUDGE, LEWIS SEYMOUR, theologian, educator, university dean; b. Phila., Oct. 22, 1929; s. Lewis Seymour and Anne Evelyn (Bolton) M.; m. Jean Bruce McClure, June 15, 1957; children: Robert Seymour, William McClure, Anne Evelyn. BA, Princeton U., 1951, M Div, 1955, PhD (Kent fellow), 1961; BA with honors in Theology, Oxford (Eng.) U., 1954, MA (Rhodes scholar), 1958. Ordained to ministry Presbyn. Ch., 1955. Presbyn. univ. pastor Princeton, 1955-56; sec. dept. theology World Alliance Ref. Chs., Geneva, 1957-62; minister to coll. Amherst Coll., 1962-68, asst. prof. philosophy and religion, 1962-64, assoc. prof., 1964-70, prof. philosophy and religion, 1970-76, chmn. dept. philosophy and religion, 1968-69, 75-76; dean faculty, prof. theology McCormick Theol. Sem., Chgo., 1976-87, San Francisco Theol. Sem., 1987—; prof. Grad. Theol. Union, Berkeley, Calif., 1987-95; dir. Ctr. for Hermeneutical Studies, Grad. Theol. Union/U. Calif., Berkeley, 1990-97; Stuart prof. theology Grad. Theol. Union, Berkeley, Calif., 1995—. Mem. commn. on faith and order Nat. Council Chs., 1965-70; sec. spl. com. on confession faith United Presbyn Ch., 1965-67, chmn. spl. com. on theology of the call, 1968-71; chmn. theol. commn. U.S. Consultation on Ch. Union, 1977-89; co-chmn. Internat. Ref.-Roman Cath. Dialogue Commn., 1983-90; observer Extraordinary Synod Bishops, 1985. Author: One Church: Catholic and Reformed, 1963, Is God Alive?, 1963, Why is the Church in the World?, 1967, The Crumbling Walls, 1970, The Sense of a People: Toward a Church for the Human Future, 1992, The Church as Moral Community, 1998, Rethinking the Beloved Community, 2001; also numerous articles and revs.; editor: Essays on Biblical Interpretation (Paul Ricoeur), 1980, (with James Poling) Formation and Reflection: the Promise of Practical Theology, 1987, (with Thomas Wieser) Democratic Contracts for Sustainable and Caring Societies, 2000. Pres. Westminster Found. in New Eng., 1963-67; chmn. bd. Nat. Vocation Agy., 1972-75; mem. com. selection Rhodes Scholars, Vt., 1966, Wis., 1983-85, Iowa, 1986. Mem. Phi Beta Kappa. Democrat. Home: 2444 Hillside Ave Berkeley CA 94704-2529 Office: Grad Theol Union 2905 Dwight Way Berkeley CA 94704-2514 E-mail: lmudge@sfts.edu, lewismudge@aol.com

MUEGGE, LYN, advertising executive; CFO, exec. v.p. Publicis & Hal Riney (formerly Hal Riney & Ptnrs. Inc.), San Francisco. Office: Publicis & Hal Riney 2001 The Embarcadero San Francisco CA 94133-5200

MUEHLEISEN, GENE SYLVESTER, retired protective services administrator, state official; b. San Diego, Dec. 28, 1915; s. Adolph and Vesta C. (Gates) M.; m. Elsie Jane Conover, Sept. 14, 1940 (dec. Mar. 17, 1999); 1 son, John Robert. Student, San Diego State Coll., 1935-39, San Diego Jr. Coll., 1957. U.S. park ranger Yosemite Nat. Park, summers 1936-39, 79-84; with San Diego Police Dept., 1940-60, dir. tng., 1957-59, comdg. officer patrol div., capt., 1958-60; exec. dir. Commn. on Peace Officer Standards and Tng., Calif. Dept. Justice, Sacramento, 1960-65, 67-76; assoc. dir. Pres.'s Commn. on Law Enforcement and Adminstrn. of Justice, Nat. Crime Commn., 1965-67; chmn. police sci. adv. com. San Diego Jr. Coll., 1957-60, police sci. faculty, 1957-60; staff instr. San Diego Police Acad., 1954-60; guest instr. police adminstrn. Sacramento State Coll., 1964; grad. FBI Nat. Acad. 51st Session, 1953, pres. of class, guest faculty, 1963-66; cons. Ford Found. Internat. Assn. Chiefs of Police Project, 1964-67. Cons. U.S. Nat. Park Svc., 1965-84, spl. asst. to regional dir. Western region, 1977-79; adviser Royal Can. Mounted Police, 1961—; guest lectr., 1960—. Mem. tng. com. Internat. Assn. Chiefs of Police, 1963— ; mem. adv. com. on police tng. Ford Found., 1964— ; U.S. rep. Interpol Symposium on Police Edn. and Tng., Paris, 1965; chmn. Atty. Gen.'s Com. on Law Enforcement Standards, 1957-59; vice chmn. Calif. Commn. Peace Officer Standards and Tng., 1959-60; chmn. police services task force Calif. Council Criminal Justice, 1968-78 ; mem. Atty. Gen.'s Commn. Police-Community Relations, 1971— ; mem. adv. com. FBI, 1972— ; mem. Gov.'s Pub. Safety Planning Council, 1974— ; Pres. San Diego Police Officers Assn., San Diego Police and Fire Retirement System; bd. dirs. San Diego Hist. Soc. Served to capt. USNR, World War II. The Gene Muehleisen Nature Area, Valley Oak Park, Sacramento dedicated, 1992. Mem. Nat. Conf. Police Assns. (com. chmn.), Calif. Peace Officers Assn. (com. chmn.), Peace Officers Research Assn. Calif. (pres. 1959-60, com. chmn.), Am. Soc. Pub. Adminstrn. (dir. San Diego County chpt.), Nat. Assn. State Dirs. Law Enforcement Tng. (pres. 1972-73), Am. Corrections Assn., Calif. Assn. Adminstrn. of Justice Educators, Park Rangers Assn. of Calif., Internat. Police Assn. (life, v.p. region 29 USA), Internat. Assn. Chiefs of Police (life), Calif. Parks and Recreation Soc. (Citizen of Yr. 1992), Sacramento Tree Found. (tech. adv. com. 1983—). Clubs: Kiwanis, San Diego Ski (pres.). Home and Office: 4221 Corona Way Sacramento CA 95864-5301

MUELLER, CARL RICHARD, theater arts educator, author; b. St. Louis, Oct. 7, 1931; s. Anton John and Bonita Blanche (Lacy) M. BS, Northwestern U., 1954; MA, UCLA, 1960, PhD, 1967; cert., Freie U., Berlin, 1961. Prof. theater dept. Sch. Theater, Film and Television UCLA, 1967—; dramaturg New Theatre, Inc., L.A., 1975-2000. Cons. U. Calif. Press., 1972—. Translator plays published include Buechner: Complete Plays and Prose, 1963, Brecht: The Visions of Simone Machard, 1965, Brecht: The Measures Taken, 1977, Hauptmann: The Weavers, 1965, Hebbel: Maria Magdalena, 1962, Strindberg: A Dream Play and The Ghost Sonata, 1966, Strindberg: Five Major Plays, 2000, Schnitzler: La Ronde and Game of Love, 1964, Hofmannsthal: Electra, 1964, Wedekind: The Marquis of Keith, 1964, Wedekind: The Lulu Plays, 1967, Wedekind: Four Major Plays, 2000, Zuckmayer: The Captain of Koepenick, 1972, Horváth: Tales from the Vienna Woods, 1998, Schnitzler: Four Major Plays, 1999, Sophocles: The Complete Plays, 2000, Pirandello: Three Major Plays, 2000, Kleist: Three Major Plays, 2000; translator plays produced include Anon: The Puppet Play of Dr. Johannes Faustus, Hauptmann: The Beaver Coat, Schnitzler: Dr. Bernhardi, Schnitzler: Anatol, Sternheim: The Underpants, Brecht: Mother Courage, Brecht: Caucasian Chalk Circle, Brecht: The Trial of Joan of Arc, Brecht: In the Jungle of Cities, Brecht: Man is Man, Brecht: He Who Says Yes, Brecht: He Who Says No, Brecht: The Exception and the Rule, Brecht: Round Heads, Peaked Heads, Brecht: Schweyk in the Second World War, Kleist: The Broken Jug, 1992, Lessing: Nathan the Wise, 1993, Toller, The Blind Goddess, 1993, Sophokles, Elektra, 1994, Zweig, Volpone, 1995, Sternheim, The Snob, 1996; gen. editor Visual Resources, Inc., 1976-2000; theater editor Mankind mag., 1975-82; editor New Theater/Teatro Nuevo, 1985-87; author catalogue and slides A Visual History of European Theater Arts, 1978, A Visual History of European Experimental Theater, 1983, Greek and Roman Classical Theatre Structures and Performance Iconography, 1991, Medieval Theater and Performance Iconography, 1991, The Theater of Meyerhold, 1992, Stanislavsky and the Moscow Art Theater, 1992, The Commedia dell'Arte, 1992, Russian Scene and Costume Design, vols. 1 and 2, 1993, The Baroque Stage, 1993, 18th and 19th Cen. European Theater Structures, Performance Iconography and Costume Designs, 1994, Renaissance Theater Structures, Performance Iconography and Costume Designs, 1994, The Genius of the Russian Theatre 1900-1990, 1995, 20th Century World Theater, From Appia to Dali, 1900-50, vol. 1, 1996, 20th Century World Theater, From Mother Courage to Hair, 1951-68, vol. 2, 1996, 20th Century World Theater, From Svoboda to Hockney, 1968-91, vol. 3, 1996, The Genius of the Russian Theater, From Meyerhold to the Present, 1996, Contemporary European Experimental Theater, vol. 1, Italy and Germany, 1996, The Classical Experience: The Greek Theater and Its World, 1996, The Classical Experience: The Roman Theater and Its World, 1996; dir.: (plays) Spring's Awakening, Endangered Species, Hedda Gabler, My Body, Frankly Yours, Hamlet, Macbeth, Dionysos. Served with U.S. Army, 1954-56. Recipient Samuel Goldwyn Creative Writing award Goldwyn Found., 1959; Fulbright exchange grantee Berlin, 1960-61 Mem. Internat. Arthur Schnitzler Research Assn., UCLA Center for Medieval and Renaissance Studies (mem. adv. com. 1980-83) Democrat. Office: UCLA Dept Theater Sch Theater Film TV 102 E Melnitz Box 951622 Los Angeles CA 90095-1622 E-mail: cmueller@tft.ucla.edu

MUELLER, NANCY, food products executive; BS in chemistry, Russel Sage Coll., 1965. Founder, pres. Nancys Specialty Foods, Newark, 1977—. Bd. trustees Rensselaer Polytechnic Inst., Palo Alto Med. Found.; bd. dirs. Sr. Coord. Coun. Palo Alto; mem. Com. 200; bus. adv. coun. Stanford Grad. Sch. Office: Nancys Specialty Foods 6500 Overlake Pl Newark CA 94560-1084

MUELLER, ROBERT SWAN, III, lawyer, former federal official; b. N.Y.C., Aug. 7, 1944; s. Robert Swan Jr. and Alice (Truesdale) M.; m. Ann Standish, Sept. 3, 1966; children: Cynthia, Melissa. BA, Princeton U., 1966; MA, NYU, 1967; JD, U. Va., 1973. Bar: Mass., U.S. Dist. Ct. Mass., U.S. Ct. Appeals (1st cir.), Calif., U.S. Dist. Ct. (no. dist.) Calif., U.S. Ct Appeals (9th cir.). Assoc. Pillsbury, Madison & Sutro, San Francisco, 1973-76; asst. U.S. atty. U.S. Atty.'s Office, No. Dist. Calif., San Francisco, 1976-80; chief unit spl. prosecutions, Calif. no. dist. U.S. Atty.'s Office, San Francisco, 1980-81, chief criminal div., 1981-82, chief criminal div. Mass. dist. Boston, 1982-85, 1st asst. U.S. atty. in Boston, 1985, U.S. atty. for Mass. dist., 1986-87, dep. U.S. atty. for Mass. dist., 1987-88; ptnr. Hill and Barlow, Boston, 1988-89; asst. to atty. gen. for criminal matters U.S. Dept. Justice, Washington, 1989-90, asst. atty. gen. for criminal div., 1990-93; lawyer Hale & Dorr, Washington, 1993—; interim U.S. arry. no. dist. Calif. U.S. Dept. Justice, 1998—. Capt. USMC, 1967-70; Vietnam. Decorated Bronze Star, Purple Heart, Vietnamese Cross of Gallantry. Office: US Atty Box 36055 450 Golden Gate Ave Fl 4 San Francisco CA 94102-3404

MUELLER, WILLIAM MARTIN, former academic administrator, metallurgical engineering educator; b. Denver, Jan. 14, 1917; s. Charles Franklin M. and Nydia (Hough) Mueller; m. Kathryn C. Connor, Nov. 3, 1942; children: Kathryn Irene Ingram, Joann Elaine Goss. Met.E., Colo. Sch. Mines, 1940, M.S., 1949, D.Sc., 1952. Registered profl. engr., Colo. Metallurgist ALCOA, New Kensington, Pa., 1940-45; engr. Gates Rubber Co., 1945-47; instr. Colo. Sch. Mines, Golden, 1947-52, prof. metall. engring., dept. head, 1974-79, v.p., 1979-83; staff metallurgist Dow Chem. Co., Rocky Flats, Colo., 1952-57; div. head Denver Research Inst., 1957-65; dir. edn. Am. Soc. Metals, Metals Park, Ohio, 1965-74; cons. Western Forge Corp., Colorado Springs, Colo., 1975-83. Invited lectr. Beijing U., 1980; del. leader for People to People to China, 1984, to S.E. Asia, 1986, to USSR, 1990, to Russia, 1993. Author: (with Blackledge and Libowitz) Metal Hydrides, 1968, (with McCall) Microstructural Analysis, 1973; editor: Energetics in Metallurgical Phenomena, 4 vols., 1965-68, (with McCall) Metallographic Specimen Preparation, 1974; sr. editor: Advances in X-Ray Analysis, 1960-66. Recipient Waltman award Colo. Sch. Mines, 1940, Disting. Achievement award, 1972, Halliburton award, 1983. Fellow Am. Soc. Metals (life, trustee 1964-65); mem. ASTM (dir. 1980-83), AIME (life, com. chmn. 1980-83), Am. Soc. Engring. Edn., Mining and Metall. Soc. Am. Home: 3832 Lee Cir Wheat Ridge CO 80033-4149 Office: Colo Sch Mines Hill Hall Golden CO 80401 E-mail: wwilkaym@aol.com

MUETH, JOSEPH EDWARD, lawyer; b. St. Louis, Aug. 8, 1935; s. Joseph and Marie Clare (Reher) M.; m. Ellen Agnes O'Heron, Dec. 24, 1973; children: Erin R., Patricia A. B.Chem. Engring., U. Dayton, 1957; LL.B., Georgetown U., 1960, LL.M., 1961. Bar: Calif. 1964. Practice law, L.A.; ptnr. Wills, Green & Mueth, L.A., 1974-83; pvt. practice law Calif., 1983-94; of counsel Sheldon & Mak, Pasadena, 1994—. Adj. prof. law U. Calif. Hastings Coll. Law, San Francisco, 1972-75; lectr. Claremont Grad. Sch., 1982—. Author: Copyrights Patents and Trademarks, 1974. Chmn. bd. Rio Hondo council Camp Fire Girls Inc., 1967-72. Mem. AAAS, Am., Los Angeles County bar assns., State Bar Calif., N.Y. Acad. Scis., L.A. Athletic Club. Home: PO Box 3369 1217 Seal Way Seal Beach CA 90740-6419 Office: 225 S Lake Ave Ste 800 Pasadena CA 91101-4858

MUGGERIDGE, DEREK BRIAN, dean, engineering consultant; b. Godalming, Surrey, U.K., Oct. 10, 1943; arrived in Can., 1956; s. Donald William and Vera Elvina (Jackson) M.; m. Hanny Meta Buurman, Dec. 4, 1965; children: Karen Julie, Michael Brent. BS in Aero. Engring., Calif. State Polytech. U., 1965; MASc in Aerospace Engring., U. Toronto, 1966, PhD in Aerospace Engring., 1970. Spl. lectr. U. Toronto, Ont., Can., 1971; indsl. post-doctoral fellow Fleet Mfg. Co., Fort Erie, 1970-72; from asst. prof. to prof. Meml. U. of Nfld., St. John's, 1972-93, univ. rsch. prof., 1990-93; dir. Ocean Engring. Rsch. Ctr., 1982-93; dean Okanagan U. Coll., Kelowna, B.C., Can., 1993—, assoc. v.p. rsch. Can., 1998—. Pres. Offshore Design Assocs. Ltd., Portugal Cove, Nfld., 1980—; sec., ptnr. Nfld. Ocean Cons., St. John's, 1981-93; ptnr. LNF Joint Venture Ltd., St. John's, 1984-90; vis. prof. U. Victoria, B.C., 1988-89. Co-author: Ice Interaction with Offshore Structures, 1988; contbr. articles to profl. jours.; contbr. conf. articles, reports. U. Toronto Grad. fellow, 1965, Nat. Rsch. Coun. Can. Grad. fellow U. Toronto, 1966-70. Mem. Assn. Profl. Engrs. & Geoscis. of Province of B.C. Marine and Naval. Avocations: windsurfing, sailing, rock collecting. Home: 16438 Carr's Landing Rd Lake Country BC Canada V4V 1C3 Office: Okanagan Univ Coll 3333 College Way Kelowna BC Canada V1V 1V7

MUGLER, LARRY GEORGE, regional planner; b. Chgo., June 22, 1946; s. Warren Franklin and Elaine Mae (Mittag) M.; m. Judy Ann Allison, Aug. 3, 1968; children: Jonathan, Allison. BSCE, Northwestern U., 1968; postgrad., Evang. Theol. Sem., 1968-70; MS in Urban and Regional Planning, U. Wis., 1972. Planning analyst State of Wis., Madison, 1970-72; dir. community devel. Cen. Okla. Econ. Devel. Dist., Shawnee, 1972-74; planner Denver Regional Council of Govts., 1974-80, dir. environ. services, 1980-83, dir. devel. services, 1983—. Adj. faculty mem. U. Colo., Denver. Contbr. chpts. into books. Pres. bd. dirs. Leawood Met. Recreation and Park Dist., Littleton, Colo., 1978-98; chair planning and rsch. com., bd. stewards Rocky Mountain Conf. The United Meth. Ch. Named one of Outstanding Young Men in Am., Jaycees, 1974; Lasker Found. fellow, 1971; recipient Disting. Svc. award Spl. Dist. Assn. of Colo., 1989. Mem. Am. Planning Assn. (sec. Colo. chpt. 1970-96), ASCE (subcom. chmn. 1985-86, 88-91, div. exec. com. 1991-99, vice chair 1994-96, chair 1996), Am. Inst. Cert. Planners, Urban Land Inst. Republican. Methodist. Avocations: soccer referee, choir. Office: Denver Regional Coun Govts 2480 W 26th Ave Ste 200B Denver CO 80211-5326

MUHLBACH, ROBERT ARTHUR, lawyer; b. Los Angeles, Apr. 13, 1946; s. Richard and Jeanette (Marcus) M.; m. Kerry Eldene Mahoney, July 26, 1986. BSME, U. Calif., Berkeley, 1967; JD, U. Calif., San Francisco, 1976; MME, Calif. State U., 1969; M in Pub. Adminstrn., U. So. Calif., 1976. Bar: Calif. 1976. Pub. defender County of Los Angeles, 1977-79; assoc. Kirtland & Packard, Los Angeles, 1979-85, ptnr., 1986—. Chmn. Santa Monica Airport Commn., Calif., 1984-87, chmn., bd. dirs. Hawthorne Airport Cmty. Assn. Inc. Served to capt. USAF, 1969-73. Mem. ABA, AIAA, Internat. Assn. Def. Counsel, Am. Bd. Trial Advs. Office: Kirtland & Packard Ste 2600 1900 Avenue Of The Stars Los Angeles CA 90067-4507 E-mail: ram@kirtland-packard.com

MUHLESTEIN, ROBERT M. state senator; b. Price, Utah, Oct. 10, 1965; m. Amy L. Muhlestein; 3 children. BA in Am. Studies with honors, Brigham Young U., 1990, MA in Internat. and Area Studies, 1991. With State of Utah Dept. Human Svcs., 1991-96; mem. Utah State Senate, 1996—, chair human svcs. com., mem. health and environment com., co-chair health and human svcs. appropriations. Republican. Home: 7092 S 2610 W Benjamin UT 84660-4614

MUIR, WILLIAM KER, JR. political science educator; b. Detroit, Oct. 30, 1931; s. William Ker and Florence Taylor (Bodman) M.; m. Paulette Irene Wauters, Jan. 16, 1960; children: Kerry Macaire, Harriet Bodman. B.A., Yale U., 1954, Ph.D., 1965; J.D., U. Mich., 1958. Bar: N.Y. 1960, Conn. 1965. Instr. U. Mich. Law Sch., 1958-59; assoc. firm Davis Polk & Wardwell, N.Y.C., 1959-60; lectr. in polit. sci. Yale U., 1960-64, 65-67; from assoc. to ptnr. Tyler Cooper Grant Bowerman & Keefe, New Haven, 1964-68; prof. polit. sci. U. Calif.-Berkeley, 1968-98, dept. chmn., 1980-83; speechwriter v.p. U.S., 1983-85; columnist Oakland (Calif.) Tribune, 1992-93; writer Gov. of Calif., Sacramento, 1994. Sr. cons. Calif. State Assembly, Sacramento, 1975-76; cons. Oakland (Calif.) Police Dept., 1969-74; vis. prof. polit. sci. Harvard U., summers 1976, 79; vis. disting. scholar Hawaii Pacific U., 2000; vis. lectr. U. Ariz., 2001. Author: Prayer in the Public Schools, 1967, later republished as Law and Attitude Change, 1974, Police: Streetcorner Politicians, 1977, Legislature: California's School for Politics, 1982, The Bully Pulpit: The Presidential Leadership of Ronald Reagan, 1993. Mem. Berkeley (Calif.) Police Rev. Commn., 1981-83; chmn. New Haven Civil Liberties Coun., 1965-68; Rep. candidate Calif. State Assembly, 1996. Recipient Hadley B. Cantril Meml. award, 1979, Disting. teaching award U. Calif., Berkeley, 1974, Phi Beta Kappa No. Calif. Assoc. Excellence In Teaching award, 1994. Mem. Am. Polit. Sci. Assn. (Edward S. Corwin award 1966) Republican. Presbyterian. Home: 59 Parkside Dr Berkeley CA 94705-2409 Office: Dept Polit Sci U Calif Berkeley CA 94720-1950 E-mail: sandymuir@aol.com

MUIRHEAD, BRIAN K. aerospace engineer; BSME, U. N.Mex.; MSAE, Calif. Inst. Tech. Scientist Jet Propulsion Lab., Pasadena, Calif., 1978—, builder flight hardware Galileo spacecraft, mgr. Advanced Spacecraft Devel. Group, leader SIr-C Antenna Mech. sys., leader MSTI I mech. subsys., leader Mars Pathfinder flight sys., 1992-97, project mgr. Mars Pathfinder, mgr. Deep Space 4/Champollion project. Office: Jet Propulsion Lab 4800 Oak Grove Dr Pasadena CA 91109-8001

MUKHERJEE, AMIYA K, metallurgy and materials science educator; PhD, Oxford (Eng.) U., 1962. Prof. U. Calif., Davis. Recipient Alexander von Humboldt award Fed. Republic Germany, 1988, Albert Easton White Disting. Tchr. award Am. Soc. Materials, 1992, Pfeil medal and prize Inst. Materials, 1993, U. Calif. prize and citation, 1993, Anatoly Bochvar medal U. Moscow, 1996, Inst. medal Max Planck Inst. for Metallforschung, 1997. Office: U Calif Davis Dept Chem Engring & Material Sci Davis CA 95616 E-mail: akmukherjee@ucdavis.edu

MULFORD, RAND PERRY, business executive; b. Denver, Sept. 30, 1943; s. Roger Wayne and Ann Louise (Perry) M.; 1 child, Conrad Perry; m. Paula Marie Skelley, 1987. BS in Basic Engring., Princeton U., 1965; MBA, Harvard U., 1972. Mgmt. cons. McKinsey & Co. Inc., Chgo., 1972-80, v.p. planning and control splty. chem. group Occidental Chem. Co., Houston, 1980-82; pres. Technivest Inc., Houston, 1982-85; exec. dir. corp. planning Merck & Co., Inc., Rahway, N.J., 1985-88; v.p. fin. Advanced Tissue Scis., Inc., La Jolla, Calif., 1989-90; CEO Chiron Mimotopes Peptide Systems, San Diego, 1991-94; COO Xytronyx, Inc., San Diego, 1994-95; chmn. of bd. Medication Delivery Devices, San Diego, 1991-95; CEO World Blood, Inc., 1997-99; mng. dir. bus strategy Spencer Trask, Inc. Bd. dirs. ZymeTx, Inc., Oklahoma City, Diamonex Inc., Allentown, Pa. Lt. USN, 1965-70. Home: 2178 Caminito Del Barco Del Mar CA 92014-3619 Office: The Immune Response Corp 6935 Darwin Ct Carlsbad CA 92008

MULLARKEY, MARY J. state supreme court chief justice; b. New London, Wis., Sept. 28, 1943; d. John Clifford and Isabelle A. (Steffes) M.; m. Thomas E. Korson, July 24, 1971; 1 child, Andrew Steffes Korson. BA, St. Norbert Coll., 1965; LLB, Harvard U., 1968; LLD (hon.), St. Norbert Coll., 1989. Bar: Wis. 1968, Colo. 1974. Atty.-advisor U.S. Dept. Interior, Washington, 1968-73; asst. regional atty. EEOC, Denver, 1973-75; 1st atty. gen. Colo. Dept. Law, Denver, 1975-79, solicitor gen., 1979-82; legal advisor to Gov. Lamm State of Colo., Denver, 1982-85; ptnr. Mullarkey & Seymour, Denver, 1985-87; justice Colo. Supreme Ct., Denver, 1987—, chief justice, 1998—. Recipient Alumni award St. Norbert Coll., De Pere, Wis., 1980, Alma Mater award, 1993. Fellow ABA Found., Colo. Bar Found.; mem. ABA, Colo. Bar Assn., Colo. Women's Bar Assn. (recognition award 1986), Denver Bar Assn., Thompson G. Marsh Inn of Ct. (pres. 1993-94). Office: Supreme Ct Colo Judicial Bldg 2 E 14th Ave Denver CO 80203-2115

MULLEN, JAMES HARRY, city manager; m. Patricia Staudt; children: Kevin, Jay. Diploma, U.S. Air Force Acad., 1966; MPA, U. Colo., Denver, 1976. Adminstrv. asst. to mayor City of Charleston, S.C.; asst. city mgr. Casper, Wyo.; city adminstr. Greenwood Village, Colo.; dep. city mgr. Aurora; county exec. Prince William County, Va.; city mgr. Colorado Springs, Colo., 1996—. Office: Office of City Mgr City Adminstrn Bldg 30 S Nevada Ave Ste 401 Colorado Springs CO 80903-1802

MULLEN, JOHN H. corporate executive; b. Middletown, N.Y., Apr. 16, 1942; BA cum laude, St. Johns U.; LLB, Columbia U.; LLM in Tax., N.Y. U. Bar: N.Y., 1968, Calif., 1997. Lawyer; with Northrop Grumman, 1975—, dep. gen. counsel, 1994-95, sr. corp. counsel, 1995-98, acting sect., 1998-99, corp. v.p., sect., 1999—. Office: Northrop Grumman Corp 1840 Century Park E Los Angeles CA 90067-2101

MULLEN, WILLIAM JOSEPH, III, military analyst, retired career officer; b. Plattsburg, N.Y., Dec. 26, 1937; s. William Joseph Jr. and Georgia (Cook) M.; m. Norma Sturgeon, Aug. 6, 1962; 1 child, William Joseph IV. BS, U.S. Mil. Acad., West Point, N.Y., 1959; MS in Internat. Affairs, George Washington U., 1971. Commd. 2d lt. U.S. Army, 1959, advanced through grades to brig. gen., 1987; various assignments in U.S., Vietnam, Korea, Panama, Germany, Saudi Arabia, 1959-92; mem. staff, faculty U.S. Mil. Acad., West Point, 1967-70; comdr. 1st Brigade, 1st Inf. Div., Ft. Riley, Kans., 1983-86; asst. div. comdr. 5th Inf. Div., Ft. Polk, La., 1986-87; comdg. gen. U.S. Army Combined Arms Tng. Activity, Ft. Leavenworth, Kans., 1987-89, 1st Inf. Div. (Forward), Germany, 1989-91; dep. dir. ops. J3 Forces Command, Ft. McPherson, Ga., 1991-92; sr. mgr. mil. tng. and analysis sys. BDM Fed., Inc., Monterey, Calif., 1992-98; sr. mgr. mil. tng. sys. TRW (formerly BDM Fed., Inc.), Monterey, 1998—. Co-author: Changing an Army, An Oral History of Gen. W.E. DePuy, 1979; contbr. articles, book revs. to Mil. Rev. Chmn. Officers of the 1st Divsn. Dinner, 1999—. Decorated D.S.C., D.S.M. Mem. Assn. U.S. Army, Soc. of 1st Div. (chpt. officer 1968, assoc. 1989-93, trustee found. 1989-93, bd. dirs.), Legion of Valor. Avocations: sports, reading.

MULLER, ANTHONY RICHARD, electronics company executive; b. Santa Elena, Ecuador, Feb. 17, 1943; s. Rudolph E. and Elizabeth (Steiner) M.; m. Lary Lynn Hovermale, Oct. 26, 1975; 1 child, Lesley Caroline. BA, U. Pa., 1965; MBA, Stanford U., 1971. Cons. Boston Cons. Group, 1971-73; mgr. corp. devels. Spectra-Physics, Inc., Mountain View, Calif., 1973-78; v.p. fin. Econics Corp., Sunnyvale, 1978-83, Menlo Corp., Santa Clara, 1983-85, Silicon Valley Group, Inc., San Jose, 1985-90; sr. v.p. ops., CFO Centigran Comms. Corp., 1990-96; sr. v.p., CFO Micro Focus Group PlC, 1996-98; exec v.p., CFO JDS Uniphase Corp., 1998—. Bd dirs. Uniphase Corp., Sunnyvale, Rofu Design Group, Menlo Park, Calif. Served to lt. USN, 1965-69. Mem. Stanford Golf Club. Club: University (Palo Alto, Calif.). Office: JDS UNIPHASE CORPORATION 163 BAYPOINTE PKWY San Jose CA 95134

MULLER, EDWARD ROBERT, lawyer; b. Phila., Mar. 26, 1952; s. Rudolph E. and Elizabeth (Steiner) M.; m. Patricia Eileen Bauer, Sept. 27, 1980; children: Margaret Anne, John Frederick. AB summa cum laude, Dartmouth Coll., 1973; JD, Yale U., 1976. Assoc. Leva, Hawes, Symington, Martin & Oppenheimer, Washington, 1977-83; dir. legal affairs Life Scis. group Whittaker Corp., Arlington, Va., 1983-84; v.p. Whittaker Health Svcs., Arlington, 1984-85; v.p., gen. counsel, sec. Whittaker Corp., L.A., 1985-93, chief adminstrv. officer, 1988-92, CFO, 1992-93, bd. dirs., 1993-99; v.p., gen. counsel, sec. BioWhittaker, Inc., Walkersville, Md., 1991-93; pres., CEO, bd. dirs. Edison Mission Energy, Irvine, Calif., 1993-2000; Bd of Dirs Global Marine Inc., Houston, 1997-. Mem. Brookings Task Force on Civil Justice Reform, 1988-89; chmn. U.S.-Philippines Bus. Com., 1998-2000; mem. adv. bd. Tennenbaum & Co., 1997—; mem. Coun. on Fgn. Rels., 1998—; mem. Pacific Coun. on Internat. Policy, 1988—, corp. bd. advisors, 2001—; dep. chmn. Contact Energy Ltd., 1999-2000; bd. dirs. Interval, Inc., Santa Monica, Calif., Strategic Data Corp. Trustee Exceptional Children's Found., L.A., 1988-94, treas., 1988-93; bd. dirs. Oasis Resdl., Inc., 1995-98; co-chair Internat. Energy Devel. Coun., Washington, 1993-2000; bd. govs. Jr. Achievement of Orange County and the Inland Empire, 1995-96. Home and Office: 502 20th St Santa Monica CA 90402-3028

MULLER, H(ENRY) NICHOLAS, III, foundation executive; b. Pitts., Nov. 18, 1938; s. Henry N. Jr. and Harriet (Kerschner) M.; m. Nancy Clagett, June 20, 1959 (div. 1985); children: Charles T., Brook W.; m. Carol A. Cook, Jan. 4, 1986. BA, Dartmouth Coll., 1960; PhD, U. Rochester, 1968. Instr. Dartmouth Coll., Hanover, N.H., 1964; lectr. Mt. Allison U., Sackville, N.B., Can., 1964-66; asst. prof. history U. Vt., Burlington, 1966-69; assoc. prof. history, 1970-73; prof. history U. Vt., Burlington, 1974-78, asst. dean Coll. Arts and Scis., 1969-70, assoc. dean Coll. Arts and Scis., 1970-73, dir. Living/Learning Ctr., 1973-78; pres. Colby-Sawayer Coll., New London, N.H., 1978-85; dir. State His. Soc. Wis., Madison, 1985-96; pres., CEO Frank Lloyd Wright Found., Spring Green, Scottsdale, Wis. Ariz., 1996—. Chmn. State Hist. Records Adv. Bd., 1985-96, Wis. Burial Sites Bd., 1988-96, Wis. Submerged Cultural Resources, 1993-96, Standex Internat. Corp., Salem, N.H., 1984—, Nat. Trust for Hist. Preservation, 1989-98; mem. Gov. Coun. on Tourism, 1987-96. Co-author: An Anxious Democracy, 1982; co-editor: Science, Technology and Culture, 1974, In a State of Nature, 1982; sr. editor Vt. Life mag., 1975-87; editor Vt. History, 1977-85. Chmn. Bicentennial Com., Burlington, 1976, Vt. Coun. Hist. Preservation, 1975-78; fin. chmn. Vt. Bicentennial Commn., 1970-77; mem. Wis. Sesquicentennial Commn., 1995-99; mem. N.H. Postsecondary Edn. Commn., 1983-85; trustee Vt. Hist. Soc., 1972-85, v.p., 1975-82; bd. dirs. USS Wisconsin, 1989-93, Wis. Preservation Fund Inc., 1989—; trustee, pres. Taliesin Preservation Commn., 1990—; bd. dirs. Taliesin Archs., 1999—, interim chmn., 2000—; trustee Frank Lloyd Wright Found., 1996—, interim chair 2000; v.p. Ind. Coll. Univ. Coun. Ariz., 1998-2000, mem. bd., 1998—. Fellow Ctr. for Rsch. on Vt.; mem. Nat. Coun. on Pub. History (bd. dirs. 1988-90), Am. Assn. State and Local History (councillor 1988-91), Vt. Archeol. Soc. (pres. 1971-74), Madison Club. Office: Frank Lloyd Wright Found Taliesin West Scottsdale AZ 85261-4430

MULLER, JEROME KENNETH, photographer, art director, editor; b. Amityville, N.Y., July 18, 1934; s. Alphons and Helen (Haberl) M.; m. Nora Marie Nestor, Dec. 21, 1974. BS, Marquette U., 1961; postgrad., Calif. State U., Fullerton, 1985-86; MA, Nat. U., San Diego, 1988; postgrad., Newport Psychoanalytic Inst., 1988-90. Comml. and editorial photographer, N.Y.C., 1952-55; mng. editor Country Beautiful mag., Milw., 1961-62, Reprodns. Rev. mag., N.Y.C., 1967-68; editor, art dir. Orange County (Calif.) Illustrated, Newport Beach, 1962-67, art editor, 1970-79, exec. editor, art dir., 1968-69; owner, CEO Creative Svcs. Advt. Agy., Newport Beach, 1969-79. Founder, CEO Mus. Graphics, Costa Mesa, Calif., 1978—; tchr. photography Lindenhurst (N.Y.) High Sch., 1952-54, comic art U. Calif., Irvine, 1979, publ. design Orange Coast Coll., Costa Mesa, Calif., 1997—; guest curator 50th Anniversary Exhbn. Mickey Mouse, 1928-78, The Bowers Mus., Santa Ana, Calif., 1978; organized Moving Image Exhbn. Mus. Sci. and Industry, Chgo., Cooper-Hewitt Mus., N.Y.C., William Rockhill Nelson Gallery, Kansas City, 1981; collector original works outstanding Am. cartoonists at major mus. One-man shows include Souk Gallery, Newport Beach, 1970, Gallery 2, Santa Ana, Calif., 1972, Cannery Gallery, Newport Beach, 1974, Mus. Graphics Gallery, 1993, White Gallery Portland State U., 1996, U. Calif., Irvine, 1997, Nat. Telephone and Comm., Irvine, Calif., 1998, Robert Mondavi Wine and Food Center, Costa Mesa, 2000; author: Rex Brandt, 1972, Publication Design and Production, 2000; contbr. photographs and articles to mags. Mem. Cultural Arts Com., City of Costa Mesa. With USAF, 1956-57. Recipient two silver medals 20th Ann. Exhbn. Advt. and Editorial Art in West, 1965. Mem. APA, Mus. Modern Art (N.Y.C.), Met. Mus. Art, Art Mus. Assn. Am., L.A. Press Club, Orange County Mus. Art, Alpha Sigma Nu. Home: 2438 Bowdoin Pl Costa Mesa CA 92626-6304 Office: PO Box 11155 Costa Mesa CA 92627-1155

MULLER, RICHARD STEPHEN, electrical engineer, educator; b. Weehawken, N.J., May 5, 1933; s. Irving Ernest and Marie Victoria Muller; m. Joyce E. Regal, June 29, 1957; children: Paul Stephen, Thomas Richard. ME, Stevens Inst. Tech., Hoboken, N.J., 1955; MSEE, Calif. Inst. Tech., 1957, PhD in Elect. Engring. and Physics, 1962. Engr.-in-tng., 1955. Test engr. Wright Aero/Curtiss Wright, Woodridge, N.J., 1953-54; mem. tech. staff Hughes Aircraft Co., Culver City, Calif., 1955-61; instr. U. So. Calif., L.A., 1960-61; asst. prof., then assoc. prof. U. Calif., Berkeley, 1962-72, prof., 1973—. Guest prof. Swiss Fed. Inst. Tech., 1993; founder, dir. Berkeley Sensor and Actuator Ctr., 1985—. Co-author: Device Electronics for Integrated Circuits, 1977, 2d rev. edit., 1986, Microsensors, 1990; editor-in-chief IEEE/ASME Jour. Microelectromech. Sys., 1998—; contbr. more than 200 articles to profl. jours. Pres. Kensington (Calif.) Mcpl. Adv. Coun., 1992-98; trustee Stevens Inst. of Technology, 1996—. Fellow Hughes Aircraft Co., 1955-57, NSF, 1959-62, NATO postdoctoral fellow, 1968-69, Fulbright fellow, 1982-83, Alexander von Humboldt prize, 1993, Tech. U. Berlin, 1994; Berkeley citation, 1994, Stevens Renaissance award, 1995, Career Achievement award Internat. Conf. on Sensors and Actuators, 1997, Cledo Brunetti award IEEE, 1998. Fellow IEEE (life, Millennium prize 2000); mem. IEEE Press Bd., NAE, Nat. Materials (adv. bd. 1994—), Electron Devices Soc. (adv. com. 1984—), Internat. Sensor and Actuator Meeting (chmn. steering com.). Achievements include 18 U.S. and foreign patents; construction of first operating micromotor. Office: U Calif Dept EECS 401 Cory Hl Berkeley CA 94720-0001 E-mail: r.muller@ieee.org

MULLER, WILLARD C(HESTER), writer; b. Havre, Mont., May 7, 1916; s. Chester Rudolph and Clara (Hansen) M.; m. Carolyn Elfrid Bue, Jan. 27, 1945; children: Marolyn Jean, Barbara Anne, Nancy Eleanor. BA, Stanford U., 1941; MPA, Maxwell Grad. Sch. Govt. Adminstrn., 1943; student, Nat. War Coll., 1961-62. Newspaper reporter, short story writer Bremerton (Wash.) Daily Searchlight, 1934-36; White House corr. Bremerton Daily Searchlight and Port Angeles Evening News, Washington, 1941; mgmt. analyst USDA, 1942, 46-47; mem. staff for food, agr. and forestry U.S. Dept. Army and U.S. High Commr. for Germany, Munich and Frankfurt, Fed. Republic Germany, 1948-50; dist. adminstr., Am. consul U.S. Trust Territory of Pacific Islands, Truk, Caroline Islands, 1951-55; dep. dir. ICA, U.S. Ops. Mission to Nepal, Kathmandu, 1956-58; dir. U.S. Ops. to Somali Republic, 1958-61, Office East and Southern African Affairs, AID, Dept. State, Washington, 1962-65, AID, Kampala, Uganda, 1965-70, assoc. dir. for land reform Saigon, Republic of Vietnam, 1970-73, ret., 1973, cons., 1974-81; free lance writer, 1973—. Author various short stories; contbr. articles to profl. jours. Chmn. steering com. 4-state program dialogue on peace Pacific NW dist. Am. Luth. Ch., Seattle, 1983-85; mem. Clallam br. Wash. State Centennial Commn., 1986-89; mem. Food Bank Bd., Port Angeles, Wash., 1986-90. Lt. USNR, 1943-45, PTO. Mem. Am. Soc. Pub. Adminstrn., Am. Forestry Assn., Am. Fgn. Service Assn., Pacific N.W. Morgan Horse Assn. Lodge: Kiwanis. Avocations: horseback riding, world travel. Home and Office: 3624 S Mount Angeles Rd Port Angeles WA 98362-8910 E-mail: muller@tenfornard.com

MULLINEAUX, DONAL RAY, geologist; b. Weed, Calif., Feb. 16, 1925; s. Lester Ray and Mary Lorene (Drew) M.; m. Diana Suzanne Charais, Nov. 21, 1951; children: Peter, Lauren, Keith. Student, U. Wash., 1942, BS in Math, 1947, BS in Geology, 1949, MS in Geology, 1950, PhD in Geology, 1961. Drilling insp. U.S. Army C.E., 1948; geologist U.S. Geol. Survey, 1950-86; contracting geologist, 1987-90; scientist emeritus U.S. Geol. Survey, 1990—. Author articles on volcanic activity and hazards, Mt. St. Helens, other Cascade Range volcanoes, stratigraphy and engring. geology of Puget Sound Lowland, Wash. With USNR, 1943-54, active duty, 1943-46, 51-53. Rsch. fellow Engring. Expt. Sta. U. Wash., 1949-50. Fellow Geol. Soc. Am. (E.B. Burwell Jr. award 1983); mem. Colo. Sci. Soc. Unitarian. Home: 14155 W 54th Ave Arvada CO 80002-1513 Office: PO Box 25046 Denver CO 80225-0046 E-mail: ddmullin@home.com

MULLINS, RUTH GLADYS, nurse; b. Westville, N.S., Can., Aug. 25, 1943; came to U.S., 1949, naturalized, 1955; d. William G. and Gladys H.; Leonard E. Mullins, Aug. 27, 1963; children: Deborah R., Catherine M., Leonard III. BS in Nursing, Calif. State U., Long Beach, 1966; MSN, UCLA, 1973; PhD, Columbia Pacific U. Cert. pediatric nurse practitioner. Pub. health nurse Los Angeles County Health Dept., 1967-68; nure Meml. Hosp. Med. Ctr., Long Beach, 1968-72; dir. pediatric nurse practitioner program Calif. State U., Long Beach, 1973-97, asst. prof., 1975-80, assoc. prof., 1980-85, prof., 1985—. Health svc. credential coord. Sch. Nursing Calif. State U., Long Beach, chmn., 1979-81, coord. grad. programs, 1985-92; mem. Calif. Maternal, Child and Adolescent Health Bd., 1977-84; vice chair Long Beach/Orange County Health Consortium, 1984-85, chair 1985-86. Author: (with B. Nelms) Growth and Development: A Primary Health Care Approach; contbg. author: Quick Reference to Pediatric Nursing, 1984; asst. editor Jour. Pediatric Health Care. Tng. grantee HHS, Divsn. Nursing Calif. Dept. Health. Fellow Nat. Assn. Pediatric Nurse Assocs. and Practitioners (exec. bd., pres. 1990-91), Nat. Fedn. Nursing Splty. Orgns. (sec. 1991-93); mem. APHA, Nat. Alliance Nurse Practitioners (governing body 1990-92), Assn. Faculties Pediatric Nurse Practitioenr Programs. L.A. and Orange County Assn. Pediatric Nurse Practitioners and Assocs. (treas. 1998—), Am. Assn. Univ. Faculty, Ambulatory Pediatric Assn. Democrat. Methodist. Home: 6382 Heil Ave Huntington Beach CA 92647-4232 Office: Calif State U Dept Nursing 1250 N Bellflower Blvd Long Beach CA 90840-0001 E-mail: rgmullins@sprintmail.com, rmullins@csulb.edu

MULLIS, KARY BANKS, biochemist; b. Lenoir, N.C., Dec. 28, 1944; s. Cecil Banks Mullis and Bernice Alberta (Barker) Fredericks; children: Christopher, Jeremy, Louise. BS in Chemistry, Ga. Inst. Tech, 1966; PhD in Biochemistry, U. Calif., Berkeley, 1973; DSc (hon.), U. S.C., 1994. Lectr. biochemistry U. Calif., Berkeley, 1972, postdoctoral fellow San Francisco, 1977-79, U. Kans. Med. Sch., Kansas City, 1973-76; scientist Cetus Corp., Emeryville, Calif., 1979-86; dir. molecular biology Xytronyx, Inc., San Diego, 1986-88; cons. Specialty Labs, Inc., Amersham, Inc., Chiron Inc. and various others, Calif., 1988-96; chmn. StarGene, Inc., San Rafael; v.p. Histotec, Inc., Cedar Rapids, Iowa; v.p. molecular biology chemistry Vyrex Inc., La Jolla, Calif. Disting. vis. prof. U.S.C. Coll. of Sci. and Math. Contbr. articles to profl. jours.; patentee in field. Recipient Preis Biochemische Analytik award German Soc. Clin. Chem., 1990, Allan award Am. Soc. of Human Genetics, 1990, award Gairdner Found. Internat., 1991, Nat. Biotech. award, 1991, Robert Koch award, 1992, Chiron Corp. Biotechnology Rsch. award Am. Soc. Microbiology, 1992, Japan prize Sci. and Tech. Found. Japan, 1993, Nobel Prize in Chemistry, Nobel Foundation, 1993; named Calif. Scientist of Yr., 1992, Scientist of Yr., R&D Mag., 1991. Mem. Am. Chem. Soc., Am. Acad. Achievement, Inst. Further Study (dir. 1983—). Achievements include invention of Polymerase Chain Reaction (PCR). Office: PO Box 333 A Encinitas CA 92024

MULRYAN, HENRY TRIST, mineral company executive, consultant; b. Palo Alto, Calif., Jan. 6, 1927; s. Henry and Marian Abigail (Trist) M.; m. Lenore Hoag, Aug. 25, 1948; children: James W., Carol. Student, Yale U., 1945-46; AB in Econs., Stanford U., 1948; postgrad., Am. Grad. Sch. Internat. Bus., 1949, Columbia U., 1983. V.p. mktg. Sierra Talc Co., South Pasadena, Calif., 1955-65, United Sierra, Trenton, N.J., 1965-67, v.p., gen. mgr., 1967-70, pres., 1970-77; v.p. Cyprus Mines Corp., Los Angeles, 1978-80; sr. v.p. ops. Cyprus indsl. minerals div. Amoco Minerals Co., Englewood, Colo., 1980-85; pres. Cyprus Indls. Minerals Co., Englewood, 1985-87; v.p. Cyprus Minerals Co., Englewood, 1985-87, sr. v.p. mktg., corp. adminstr., 1987-89; pres. Mineral Econs. Internat., 1989—; chmn. Persistent Vision, LLC, 1998—; pres., CEO Carpathian Marble, Inc., 1999—. Vol. exec. Internat. Exec. Svc. Corps., Zimbabwe, 1998, Romania, 1998, Jordan, 2000, 01. Served with U.S. Army, 1944-46. Clubs: Jonathan (Los Angeles). Lodge: Rotary (pres. South Pasadena club 1964-65) (bd. dirs. Princeton, N.J. club 1969-75). Office: 539 Muskingum Ave Pacific Palisades CA 90272-4252 E-mail: htmulryan@gte.net

MUMFORD, CHRISTOPHER GREENE, corporate financial executive; b. Washington, Oct. 21, 1945; s. Milton C. and Dorothea L. (Greene) M. BA, Stanford U., 1968, MBA, 1975. Cons. Internat. Tech. Resources Inc., 1974; asst. v.p. Wells Fargo Bank, San Francisco, 1975-78; treas. Arcata Corp., San Francisco, 1978-82, v.p. fin., 1982-87, exec. v.p. fin., 1987-94. Gen. ptnr. Scarff, Sears & Assocs., San Francisco, 1986-95, mng. dir. Questor Ptnrs. Fund, L.P., San Francisco, 1995-98; v.p. bd. dirs. Triangle Pacific Corp., Dallas, 1986-88, Norton Enterprises Inc., Salt Lake City, 1988-90; bd. dirs. Community Home Med. Enterprises, Inc., Crown Pacific Ltd., Portland, Oreg., IMPCO Technologies Inc., Cerritos, Calif., 1998-2000. Office: PO Box 1340 Mill Valley CA 94942-1340 E-mail: cgmumford@aol.com

MUND, GERALDINE, judge; b. L.A., July 7, 1943; d. Charles J. and Pearl M. BA, Brandeis U., 1965; MS, Smith Coll., 1967; JD, Loyola U., 1977. Bar: Calif. 1977. Bankruptcy judge U.S. Ctrl. Dist. Calif., 1984—, bankruptcy chief judge, 1997—. Past pres. Temple Israel, Hollywood, Calif.; past mem. Bd. Jewish Fedn. Coun. of Greater L.A. Mem. ABA, L.A. County Bar Assn. Office: 21041 Burbank Blvd Woodland Hills CA 91367-6606

MUNECHIKA, KEN KENJI, research center administrator; b. Waimea, Kauai, Hawaii, June 18, 1935; s. Masako (Yasutake) Kitamura; m. Grace Shizue Wakayama, June 10, 1958; children: Curtis K., Stacy M., Kenny K. BS, U. Hawaii, 1958; MS, U. So. Calif., 1976, PhD, 1979. Commd. 2d lt. USAF, 1958, advanced through grades to col., 1980, ret., 1989; exec. dir. State of Hawaii, Honolulu, 1992-93; dir. Ames Rsch. Ctr. NASA, Mountain View, Calif., 1994-96, dir. Moffett Fed. Airfield, 1996—. Mem. AIAA, Air Force Assn. Baptist. Avocations: golf, jogging, fishing. Office: 98 809 Kahaea Pl Aiea HI 96701-2771

MUNGER, EDWIN STANTON, political geography educator; b. LaGrange, Ill., Nov. 19, 1921; s. Royal Freeman and Mia (Stanton) M.; m. Ann Boyer, May 2, 1970; 1 child, Elizabeth Stanton Gibson. B.Sc., U. Chgo., 1948, M.Sc., 1949, Ph.D., 1951. Fulbright fellow Makerere U., 1949-50; research fellow U. Chgo.; field assoc. Am. Univs. Field Staff, 1950-60; faculty Calif. Inst. Tech., Pasadena, 1961—, prof. polit. geography, 1960—. Research fellow Stellenbosch U., 1955-56; vis. prof. U. Warsaw, 1973 Author books including Afrikaner and African Nationalsim, 1968, The Afrikaners, 1979, Touched by Africa: An Autobiography, 1983, Cultures, Chess and Art: A Collector's Odyssey Across Seven Continents, Vol. 1 Sub Saharan Africa, 1996, Vol. 2, Americas, 1997, Pacific Islands and the Asian Rim, Vol. 3, 1999; editor books including Munger Africana Library Notes, 1969-82; contbr. chpts. to books and numerous articles to profl. jours. Evaluator Peace Corps, Uganda, 1966, Botswana, 1967; chmn. State Dept. Evalustion Team South Africa, 1971; trustee African-Am. Inst., 1956-62; acting pres. Pasadena Playhouse, 1966; chmn. bd. trustees Crane Rogers Found., 1979-82, fellow, 1950-54; mem. exec. com. NAACP, Pasadena, 1979—, nat. del., 1984, 85; trustee Leakey Found., 1968—, pres., 1971-84; pres. Cape of Good Hope Found., 1985—; pres. Internat. Vis. Coun., L.A., 1991-93, bd. dirs., 1979-93. Recipient Alumni Citation award for pub. svc. U. Chgo., 1993. Fellow South African Royal Soc., Royal Soc. Arts, African Studies Assn. (founding bd. dirs. 1963-66); mem. PEN USA West (v.p.), Coun. Fgn. Rels., Cosmos Club, Athenaeum Club, Twilight Club, Chess Collectors Internat. (bd. dirs. 1998—). Office: Calif Inst Tech Divsn Humanities & Social Scis 1201 E California Blvd Pasadena CA 91125-0001 E-mail: munger@hss.caltech.edu

MUNITZ, BARRY, foundation administrator; b. Bklyn., July 26, 1941; s. Raymond J. and Vivian L. (LeVoff) M.; m. Anne Tomfohrde, Dec. 15, 1987. BA, Bklyn. Coll., 1963; MA, Princeton U., 1965, PhD, 1968; cert., U. Leiden, Netherlands, 1962. Asst. prof. lit. and drama U. Calif., Berkeley, 1966-68; staff assoc. Carnegie Commn. Higher Edn., 1968-70; mem. presdl. staff, then assoc. provost U. Ill. System, 1970-72, acad. v.p., 1972-76; v.p., dean faculties Central campus U. Houston, 1976-77, chancellor, 1977-82, chmn. coordinating bd. faculty workload, 1976-80; chmn. Tex. Long Range Planning, 1980-82; pres., COO Federated Devel. Co., 1982-91; vice chmn. Maxxam Inc., L.A., 1982-91; chancellor Calif. State U. System, Long Beach, Calif., 1991-98; prof. English lit. Calif. State U., L.A., 1991—; pres., CEO J.Paul Getty Trust, L.A., 1998—. Bd. dirs. Sta. KCET-TV, Nat. Bus. Higher Edn. Forum, Kaufman and Broad, SLM Holdings, KB Home, USA Edn.; cons. in presdl. evaluation and univ. governance; bd. trustees Princeton Univ., Harvard U. Author: The Assessment of Institutional Leadership, 1977, also articles, monographs. Mem. task force NSF, Art Mus. Vis. com. Recipient Disting. Alumnus award Bklyn. Coll., 1979, U. Houston Alumni Pres.'s medal, 1981; Woodrow Wilson fellow, 1963. Mem. Young Pres. Orgn., Heritage Club, Phi Beta Kappa. Office: J Paul Getty Trust 1200 Getty Center Dr Ste 400 Los Angeles CA 90049-1681 E-mail: bmunitz@getty.edu

MUNK, WALTER HEINRICH, geophysics educator; b. Vienna, Austria, Oct. 19, 1917; came to U.S., 1933; m. Edith Kendall Horton, June 20, 1953; children: Edith, Kendall. BS, Calif. Inst. Tech., 1939, MS, 1940; PhD in Oceanography, U. Calif., 1947; PhD (hon.), U. Bergen, Norway, 1975, Cambridge (Eng.) U., , 1986, U. Crete, 1996. Asst. prof. geophysics Scripps Inst. Oceanography, U. Calif., San Diego, 1947-54, prof., 1954—; dir. Inst. Geophysics and Planetary Physics, U. Calif., La Jolla, 1960-82; prof. geophysics, dir. heard island expt. Scripps Inst., U. Calif. Author: (with Mac Donald) The Rotation of the Earth: A Geophysical Discussion, 1960; (with Worcester & Wunsch) Ocean Acoustic Tomography, 1995; contbr. over 200 articles to profl. jours. Recipient Albatross award Am. Misc. Soc., 1959, gold medal Royal Astron. Soc., 1968, Nat. Medal Sci., 1985, award Marine Tech. Soc., 1969, Capt. Robert Dexter Conrad award Dept. Navy, 1978, G. Unger VVetlesen prize Columbia U., 1993, Presdl. award N.Y. Acad. Scis., 1993, Rolex Lifetime Achievement award, 1997, Kyoto Prize, 1999; named Calif. Scientist of Yr., Calif. Mus. Sci. and Industry, 1969; fellow Guggenheim Found., 1948, 55, 62, Overseas Found., 1962, 81-82, Fulbright Found., 1981-82, sr. Queen's fellow, 1978. Fellow Am. Geophys. Union (Maurice Ewing medal 1976, William Bowie medal 1989), AAAS, Am. Meteorol. Soc. (Sverdrup Gold medal 1966), Acoustical Soc. Am., Marine Tech. Soc. (Compass award 1991); mem. Nat. Acad. Scis. (Agassiz medal 1976, chmn. ocean studies bd. 1985-88), Am. Philos. Soc., Royal Soc. London (fgn. mem.), Russian Acad. of Sci., Deutsche Akademie der Naturforscher Leopoldina, Am. Acad. Arts and Scis. (Arthur L. Day medal 1965), Am. Geol. Soc., NY Acad. of Scis. (Presidl. Awd., 1994) Office: U Calif San Diego Scripps Inst Oceanography 0225 La Jolla CA 92093 E-mail: wmunk@ucsd.edu

MUNLU, KAMIL CEMAL, business educator, executive; b. Istanbul, Turkey, July 14, 1954; came to U.S., 1981; s. Adnan and Jale Sidika (Konari) M. BA in Econs., Calif. State U., Long Beach, 1983; MBA in Bus. Adminstrn., Nat. U., San Diego, 1986, MS in Logistics, 1988; M in Internat. Bus. Adminstrn., U.S. Internat. U., San Diego, 1990; DPA, U. La Verne, Calif., 1995. Adj. prof. Woodbury U., Burbank, Calif., 1998—. Adj. prof. Nat. U., San Diego, 1999, U. La Verne, Calif., 2000. Mem. Turkish Army, 1984-85. Avocations: art, boating, golfing, reading, travel.

MUNNS, CHARLES L. career officer; BS in Physics, U.S. Naval Acad., 1973; MS in Computer Sci., U. Colo., 1980; postgrad., MIT, 1993-94. Commd. ensign USN, 1973, advanced through ranks to rear adm.; various assignments to chief of staff Comdr. Submarine Force U.S. Pacific Fleet, 1996-98; dep. chief of staff C41 Resources, Requirements, Assessments Comdr.-in-Chief/U.S. Pacific Fleet, 1998—. Decorated Disting. Svc. medal (2 times), Legion of Merit (3 times), Meritorious Svc. medal (2 times), Navy Commendation medal (3 times), Navy Achievement medal. Office: 250 Makalapa Dr Pearl Harbor HI 96860-3131

MUNOZ, JOHN JOSEPH, retired transportation company executive; b. Salinas, Calif., Jan. 18, 1932; s. John Fernando and Naomal (Smith) M.; m. Phyllis Taylor, Feb. 6, 1961 (div. 1978); children: Sam, Kathy, Toni; m. Rachel Canales, Nov. 24, 1979; children: Michelle, Monique. AA, Allan Hancock Coll., 1956; student, San Jose State U., 1981, Western Sierra Law Sch. Ops. mgr. So. Pacific Milling Co., Santa Maria, Calif., 1971-77; cons. Govt., Venezuela, 1977-78; fleet supt. Granite Rock Co., San Jose, Calif., 1978-80; plant mgr. Granite Constrn. Co., Greenfield, 1980-85; mgr. transpn. Ball, Ball. & Brosmer Inc., Danville, 1985-86; ops. mgr., bd. dirs. Sorrento Ready Mix Co., Del Mar, 1986-89; trans. cons. Greenfield, 1991-96; ret., 1996. Cons. Dept. Agrl. Devel., Maricaibo, Venezuela, 1976—. Commr. Planning Commn., Greenfield, Calif., 1982-85; mem. fund raising com. Broccoli Festival, Greenfield, 1983-85; dir. Soledad Prison Vocat. Tng., 1982-85. Lt. 11th Ranger Airborne, U.S. Army, 1950-52, Korea. Mem. Am. Concrete Inst., Calif. Trucking Assn., Los Californianos, Rotary, Lions, Elks. Republican. Avocations: hunting, fishing, auto racing, photography. Home and Office: PO Box 3654 Greenfield CA 93927-3654 E-mail: 11ranger@onemain.com

MUNRO, RALPH DAVIES, state official; b. Bainbridge Island, Wash., June 25, 1943; s. George Alexander and Elizabeth (Troll) M.; m. Karen Hansen, Feb. 17, 1973; 1 son, George Alexander. BA in History and Edn. (scholar), Western Wash. U. Indsl. engr. Boeing Co., 1966-68; sales mgr. Continental Host, Inc.; asst. dep. dir. ACTION Agy., 1971; spl. asst. to gov. State of Wash., 1970-76; gen. mgr. Tillicum Enterprises & Food Services Co.; dir. Found. for Handicapped, 1976-80; pres. Northwest Highlands Tree Farm; sec. of state State of Wash., 1980—. Chmn. community service com. Seattle Rotary Club 4; founder 1st pres. Rotary Youth Job Employment Center, Seattle. Named Man of Yr. Assn. Retarded Citizens, Seattle, 1970 Mem. Nat. Assn. Secs. State (pres.), Nat. Assn. Retarded Children, Wash. Historic Mus. (dir.), Wash. Trust Historic Preservation (founder), Nature Conservancy. Republican. Lutheran. Office: Sec State Legislative Bldg PO Box 40220 Olympia WA 98504-0220

MUNSON, JOHN BACKUS, computer systems consultant, retired computer engineering company executive; b. Chgo., May 1, 1933; s. Mark Frame and Catherine Louise (Cherry) M.; m. Anne Lorraine Cooper, July 6, 1957; children: David B., Sharon A. BA, Knox Coll., 1955. With Unisys Corp., McLean, Va., 1957-93, v.p. corp. software engring., 1977-81, v.p. tech. ops., 1981-84, v.p. gen. mgr. space transp. systems, 1984-89, 89-93, v.p., gen. mgr. Space Systems divsn., 1989-94, ret., 1994. Mem. sci. adv. bd. USAF, 1981-86, mem. USN panel on F14D issues, 1987-88. Mem. bd. advisors U. Houston, Clear Lake, 1988-93, chmn. 1990-92; bd. dirs. Bay Area YMCA, 1988-93, chmn. 1992, Clear Lake Am. Heart Assn., 1989-93; co-chmn. Bay Area United Way, 1988—, chmn., 1992; Disting. visitor IEEE Computing Soc., 1981-94. Capt. U.S. Army, 1955-57. Recipient Exceptional Civilian Svc. award USAF, 1986, Superior Pub. Svc. award USN, 1988, cert. of appreciation NATO, 1984; named to Mgmt. Assn. Hall of Fame, 1994. Fellow IEEE (editor Trans. of Software Engring. 1982-84, bd. dirs. tech. com. software engring. 1982—); mem. AIA, Am. Astronautical Soc. (bd. dirs. S.W. sect. 1989-94), Aerospace Industries Assn. (space com. 1989-94), U.S. Army Assn., Nat. Security Indsl. Assn., Armed Forces Comm. Electronics Assn. (pres. Houston chpt. 1987-90), S.W. Regional Coun. Corp. CEOs. Home and Office: 1018 Westcreek Ln Westlake Village CA 91362-5462

MUNTZ, ERIC PHILLIP, aerospace and mechanical engineering and radiology educator, consultant; b. Hamilton, Ont., Can., May 18, 1934; came to U.S., 1961, naturalized, 1985; s. Eric Percival and Marjorie Louise (Weller) M.; m. Janice Margaret Furey, Oct. 21, 1964; children: Sabrina Weller, Eric Phillip. B.A.Sc., U. Toronto, 1956, M.A.Sc., 1957, Ph.D., 1961. Halfback Toronto Argonauts, 1957-60; group leader Gen. Electric, Valley Forge, Pa., 1961-69; assoc. prof. aerospace engring. and radiology U. So. Calif., Los Angeles, 1969-71, prof., 1971-87, chmn. aerospace engring., 1987-97, A.B. Freeman prof. engring., 1992—, chmn. aerospace and mech. engring., 2000—. Cons. to aerospace and med. device cos., 1967—; mem. rev. of physics (plasma and fluids) panel NRC, Washington, 1983-85 Contbr. numerous articles in gas dynamics, micromech. sys., and med. diagnostics to profl. publs., 1961—; patentee med. imaging, isotope separation, nondestructive testing, net shape mfg., transient energy release micromachines, microscale vacuum sys., micropropulsion sys. Mem. Citizens Environ. Avc. Coun., Pasadena, Calif., 1972-76. Pilot RCAF, 1955-60. U.S. Air Force grantee, 1961-74, 82—; NSF grantee, 1970-76, 87—; FDA grantee, 1980-86. Fellow AIAA (aerospace Contbn. to Soc. award 1987), Am. Phys. Soc.; mem. NAE. Epsicopalian. Home: 1560 E California Blvd Pasadena CA 91106-4104 Office: U So Calif Univ Pk Los Angeles CA 90089-1191 E-mail: muntz@spock.usc.edu

MURAI, KEVIN, electronics company executive; BSEE, U. Waterloo, Ontario. Former mgr. Verifact, Inc., Ontario, Can.; various positions to CEO, acting pres. Ingram Micro, Inc., Santa Ana, Calif., 1989-00, 2000—; pres. Ingram Micro U.S., 2000, exec. v.p., pres., 2000—. Office: Ingram Micro Inc 1600 E St Andrew Pl Santa Ana CA 92705

MURANE, WILLIAM EDWARD, lawyer; b. Denver, Mar. 4, 1933; s. Edward E. and Theodora (Wilson) M.; m. Rosemarie Palmerone, Mar. 26, 1960; children: Edward Wheelock, Peter Davenport, Alexander Phelps. AB, Dartmouth Coll., 1954; LLB, Stanford U., 1957. Bar: Wyo. 1957, Colo. 1958, D.C. 1978, U.S. Supreme Ct. 1977. Assoc. then ptnr. Holland & Hart, Denver, 1961-69; dep. gen. counsel U.S. Dept. Commerce, Washington, 1969-71; gen. counsel FDIC, Washington, 1971-72; ptnr. Holland & Hart, Denver, 1972—. Pub. mem. Adminstrv. Conf. of the U.S., Washington 1978-81. Bd. dirs. Ctr. for Law and Rsch., Denver, 1973-76, Acad. in the Wilderness, Denver, 1986—; trustee Colo. Symphony Orch., 1994-2000; mem. bd. visitors Stanford U. Law Sch. Capt. USAF, 1958-61. Fellow Am. Coll. Trial Lawyers; mem. ABA (ho of dels. 1991-96), U. Club, Cactus Club. Republican. Avocations: fishing, classical music. Office: Holland & Hart 555 17th St Ste 2700 Denver CO 80202-3950

MURDOCH, COLIN, cultural organization administrator; Pres. San Francisco Conservatory Music, Calif., 1992—. Office: San Francisco Conservatory Music Office Pres 1201 Ortega St San Francisco CA 94122-4411

MURDOCK, DAVID H. diversified company executive; b. Kansas City, Mo., Apr. 10, 1923; m. Maria Ferrer, Apr., 1992. LLD (hon.), Pepperdine U., 1978; LHD (hon.), U. Nebr., 1984, Hawaii Loa Coll., 1989. Sole proprietor, chmn., chief exec. officer Pacific Holding Co., L.A.; chmn. Dole Food Co. (formerly Castle & Cooke, Inc.), L.A., 1985—, also bd. dirs. Trustee Asia Soc., N.Y.C., L.A.; founder, bd. dirs. Found. for Advanced Brain Studies, L.A.; bd. visitors UCLA Grad. Sch. Mgmt.;bd. govs. Performing Arts Coun. of Music Ctr., L.A.; bd. govs. East-West Ctr., L.A.; patron Met. Opera, N.Y.C. With USAAC, 1943-45. Mem. Regency Club (founder, pres.) Bel-Air Bay Country Club, Sherwood Country Club (founder, pres.), Met. Club (N.Y.C.). Office: Dole Food Co Inc 31365 Oak Crest Dr Westlake Vlg CA 91361-4633 also: Pacific Holding Co 10900 Wilshire Blvd Ste 1600 Los Angeles CA 90024-6530

MURDY, WAYNE WILLIAM, mining company executive, financial officer; b. Los Angeles, July 4, 1944; s. Lee Robert and Louise Marie (Kleinemas) M.; m. Diana Yvonne DeCruse, Nov. 23, 1968; children: Dawn Marie, Christopher John, Joseph William, Elizabeth Anne. A.A., El Camino Coll., 1966; B.S., Calif. State U., Long Beach, 1968. C.P.A., Calif. With Atlantic Richfield Co., Los Angeles, 1969-78; gen. auditor Getty Oil Co., Los Angeles, 1978-81; group v.p. Texaco Trading & Transp. Inc., Denver, 1981-87; sr. v.p., chief fin. officer Apache Corp., Denver, 1987-92, Newmont Mining Corp. and Newmont Gold Co., Denver, 1993—. Mem. Am. Inst. C.P.A.s Roman Catholic. Clubs: University (Denver); Village (Cherry Hills Village, Colo.) Office: Newmont Mining Corp 1 Norwest Ctr 1700 Lincoln St Denver CO 80203-4500

MUREN, DENNIS E. visual effects director; b. Glendale, Calif., Nov. 1, 1946; s. Elmer Ernest and Charline Louise (Clayton) M.; m. Zara Pinfold, Aug. 29, 1981; children: Gregory, Gwendolen. AA, Pasadena (Calif.) City Coll., 1966; student, Calif. State U., L.A. Freelance spl. effects expert, 1968-75; camera operator Cascade of Calif., Hollywood, 1975-76; visual effects dir. photography Indsl. Light & Magic, San Rafael, Calif., 1976-80, visual effects dir., 1980—. Guest speaker Berlin Film Festival, UCLA, Film Dept., U. Calif. Berkeley Film Series, Liverpool (Eng.) U. Film Program, Mill Valley Film Festival Program, Siggraph '86, Siggraph '87, Am. Film Inst., Portland Creative Conf. '89. Cameraman, photographer various films including Star Wars, 1977, Close Encounters of the Third Kind, 1977, Battlestar Galactica, 1978, The Empire Strikes Back, 1980 (Oscar award); visual effects supr. films include Dragonslayer, 1981 (Oscar nomination), ET: The Extraterrestrial, 1982 (Oscar award), Return of the Jedi, 1983 (Oscar award, Brit. Acad. of Film and TV award), Indiana Jones and the Temple of Doom, 1984 (Oscar award, Brit. Acad. of Film and TV award), Young Sherlock Holmes, 1985 (Oscar nomination), Captain Eo, 1986, Star Tours, 1986, Innerspace, 1987 (Oscar award), Empire of the Sun, 1987, Willow, 1988 (Oscar nomination), Ghostbusters II, 1989, The Abyss, 1989 (Oscar award), Terminator 2, 1991 (Oscar award, Brit. Film and TV award), Jurassic Park, 1993 (Oscar award, Brit. Film and TV award), Casper, 1995; effects supr. Jurassic Park-The Lost World, 1997; creative advisor Twister, 1996, Mission Impossible, 1996; visual effects supr. (TV program) Caravan of Courage (Emmy award); creative advisor Twister, 1995, Mission Impossible, 1995, Jurassic Park: The Lost World, 1997 (Academy award nomination), Star Wars: The Phantom Menace, 1999, A.I., 2001. Recipient Academy Scientific/Technical Award for the development of a Motion Picture Figure Mover for animation photography, 1981, star on Hollywood Walk of Fame, 1999. Mem. Am. Soc. Cinematographers, Acad. Motion Picture Arts and Scis.

MURKOWSKI, FRANK HUGHES, senator; b. Seattle, Mar. 28, 1933; s. Frank Michael and Helen (Hughes) M.; m. Nancy R. Gore, Aug. 28, 1954; children: Carol Victoria Murkowski Sturgulewski, Lisa Ann Murkowski Martell, Frank Michael, Eileen Marie Murkowski Van Wyhe, Mary Catherine Murkowski Judson, Brian Patrick. Student, Santa Clara U., 1952-53; BA in Econs, Seattle U., 1955. With Pacific Nat. Bank of Seattle, 1957-58, Nat. Bank of Alaska, Anchorage, 1959-67; asst. v.p., mgr. Nat. Bank of Alaska (Wrangell br.), 1963-66; v.p. charge bus. devel. Nat. Bank of Alaska, Anchorage, 1966-67; commr. dept. econ. devel. State of Alaska, Juneau, 1967-70; pres. Alaska Nat. Bank, Fairbanks, 1971-80; senator from Alaska U.S. Senate, Washington, 1981—, ranking mem. Com. on Energy and Natural Resources, mem. Com. on Fin., Vets Affairs Com., Indian Affairs Com., Japan-US Friendship Com. Rep. nominee for U.S. Congress from Alaska, 1970; chmn. Can.-U.S. Interparliamentary Group. Former v.p. B.C. and Alaska Bd. Trade; mem. U.S. Holocaust Mus. Coun. Served with U.S. Coast Guard, 1955-57. Mem. AAA, AMVETS, NRA, Am. Legion, Polish Legion Am. Vets., Ducks Unltd., Res. Officer's Assn., Alaska Geog. Soc., Alaska World Affairs Coun., Fairbanks Hist. Preservation Found., Coalition Am. Vets., Alaska Native Brotherhood, Naval Athletic Assn., Am. Bankers Assn., Alaska Bankers Assn. (pres. 1973), Young Pres.'s Orgn., Alaska C. of C. (pres. 1977), Anchorage C. of C. (bd. dirs. 1966), B.C. C. of C., Fairbanks C. of C. (bd. dirs. 1973-78), Pioneers of Alaska, Internat. Alaska Nippon Kai, Capital Hill Club, Shilla Club, Army Athletic Club, Congl. Staff Club, Diamond Athletic Club, Washington Athletic Club, Elks, Lions. Office: US Senate 322 Hart Senate Bldg Washington DC 20510-0001

MURKOWSKI, LISA, state legislator; b. Ketchikan, Alaska, May 22, 1957; m. Verne Martell; children: Nicholas, Matthew. BA, Georgetown U., 1980; JD, Willamette Coll. Dist. atty., Anchorage, 1987-89; comml. atty. Hoge and Lekisch, 1989-96; atty. pvt. practice, 1997—; rep. Alaska Ho. Reps., Anchorage, 1998—. Dir. First Bank; mem. Mayor's Tasl Force Homeless, 1990-91; state ctrl. com. Dist. 14 Rep. chair, 1993-98; commr. Anchorage Equal Rights Commn., 1997—; citizens adv. bd. Joint Com. Mil. Bases in Alaska, 1998—. Trustee Cath. Svcs.; pres. Govt. Hill Elem. PTA; dir. Alaskan Drug Free Youth; mem. YWCA, Artic Power. Mem. Alaska Bar Assn., Anchorage Bar Assn., Alaska Fedn. Rep. Women (bd. dirs.), Anchorage Rep. Womens Club, Midnight Sun Rep. Women. Republican. Roman Catholic. Office: Ho of Reps Alaska State Capitol Rm 406 Juneau AK 99801-1182 also: 716 W 4th Ave Ste Tba Anchorage AK 99501-2107

MURPHY, EDWARD FRANCIS, executive; b. Chgo., July 30, 1947; s. Edward F. and Marjorie (Mooney) M.; m. Kay A. Worcester, Apr. 17, 1970; 1 child, Dean D. BA in Mktg., No. Ill. U., 1976. Dist. mgr. Midas Internat. Corp., Chgo., 1977-85; sales mgr. Raybestos, McHenry, Ill., 1985-89, Wagner Brakes, St. Louis, 1989-99; owner Displays of Distinction, Mesa, Ariz., 1998—. V.p. Associated Roof Structures, Mesa, 1999—. Author: Vietnam Medal of Honor Heroes, 1987, Heroes of World War II, 1990, Korea's Heroes, 1990, Dak To, 1993, Semper Fi-Vietnam, 1996, Khe Sahn-The Hill Fights, 2000; hist. cons. (book) Above and Beyond, 1985. Sgt. U.S. Army, 1965-68. Recipient Dist. Svc. award Congl. Medal of Honor Soc., 1989. Mem. Medal of Honor Hist. Soc. (founder, pres. 1975—). Republican. Avocations: writing, flying. Home: 2659 E Kael St Mesa AZ 85213-2363

MURPHY, FRANCIS SEWARD, retired journalist; b. Portland, Oreg., Sept. 9, 1914; s. Francis H. and Blanche (Livesay) M.; m. Clare Eastham Cooke, Sept. 20, 1974 (dec. Apr. 1990). BA, Reed Coll., 1936. With The Oregonian, Portland, 1936-79, TV editor, Behind the Mike columnist, 1952-79. Archeol. explorer Mayan ruins, Yucatan, Mex., 1950-87, mem. Am. Quintana Roo Expdn., 1965, 66, 68. Author: Dragon Mask Temples in Central Yucatan, 1988. With U.S. Army, 1942-46. Mem. Am. Philat. Soc. (life), Royal Asiatic Soc., City Club, Am. Club of Hong Kong, Explorer's Club, Oreg. Hist. Soc., Soc. Am. Archaeology, Hong Kong Philat Soc., World Wide Fund Nature, Hong Kong Jockey Club. Democrat. Congregationalist. Home: 4213 NE 32nd Ave Portland OR 97211-7149

MURPHY, FREDERICK AUGUSTUS, virologist, researcher; b. N.Y.C., June 14, 1934; s. Frederick A. and Louise A. (Knizak) M.; m. Irene M. Warwas, July 2, 1960; children: Frederick A., W. Timothy, John G., Terence D. BS, Cornell U., 1957, DVM, 1959; PhD, U. Calif., Davis, 1964; MD honoris causa, U. Turku, Finland, 1986. Chief viral pathology br. Ctrs. for Disease Control, Atlanta, 1964-78; assoc. dean Coll. Vet. Medicine Colo. State U., Ft. Collins, 1978-83; dir. divsn. viral diseases Ctrs. for Disease Control, Atlanta, 1983-87, dir. Nat. Ctr. for Infectious Diseases, 1987-91; dean Sch. Vet. Medicine U. Calif., Davis, 1991-96, prof., 1996—, dean emeritus. Program chair virology divsn. Internat. Union Microbiol. Socs., 1978-81, chair virology divsn., 1981-84; pres. Internat. Com. on Taxonomy of Viruses, 1990-96; chair adv. bd. biology/biotech. divsn. Lawrence Livermore Nat. Lab., 1996-99. Editor: (book) Virus Taxonomy, 1995, (book series) Advances in Virus Research, 1983—; editor-in-chief: (jour.) Archives of Virology, 1984—; co-author: (book) Veterinary Virology, 1992. Capt. U.S. Army, 1959-62; comdr. USPHS, 1964-68. Recipient Presdl. Rank award U.S. Govt., 1992, K.F. Meyer Gold Headed Cane, Am. Vet. Epidemiology Soc., 1986. Fellow Infectious Diseases Soc. Am.; mem. Am. Soc. Virology (founding coun. mem.), Am. Soc. Tropical Medicine, German Acad. Natural Scis. (elected mem.). Democrat. Roman Catholic. Office: U Calif Sch Vet Medicine Davis CA 95616

MURPHY, GEORGE, special effects expert; Computer graphics artist, visual effects supr. Indsl. Light & Magic, San Rafael, Calif. Films include: Hook, 1991, Death Becomes Her, 1992, Jurassic Park, 1993, Forrest Gump, 1994 (Acad. award best visual effects, Brit. Acad. Film and TV award for best visual effects 1994), Mission Impossible, 1995, Congo, 1995, Star Trek: First Contact, 1996, Starship Troopers, 1997, Mercury Rising, 1998, Mission to Mars, 1999, Impostor, 1999, Planet of the Apes, 2001; commls. include 1st Union Launch (gold Clio for visual effects 1999), 1st Union Noise (silver Clio for visual effects 1999), Hefty Gingerbread Man (bronze Clio for visual effects 1999); music videos include Will Smith Willenium. Mem. Acad. Motion Picture Arts and Scis. (visual effects br.). Office: PO Box 751300 Petaluma CA 94975 E-mail: george@georgemurphy.com

MURPHY, IRENE HELEN, publishing executive; b. Boston; d. Charles Leo and Irene Muriel (Finney) M. BA, Regis Coll., 1958; MA, Boston Coll., 1963, Northeastern U., Boston, 1968, Manhattanville Coll., , 1969. Tchr. elem. sch., Boston; high sch. dir. guidance Boston; ednl. adminstr. Boston; prof. master tchr. program Boston, 1969—; prof. N.Y.C.; dir. sch. svcs. Glencoe/McGraw Hill Pub. Co., Woodland Hills, Calif., 1969—; v.p. Glencoe Pub. Co., Mission Hills. Vis. lectr. univs., including Boston Coll., Sacred Heart U., St. John, Nfld., Regis Coll., Teachers Coll., Sidney, Australia, Teachers Coll., Melbourne, Australia, McGill U., Mont., Providence (R.I.) Coll. Author series ednl. games for children. Recipient Gold Seal Recognition award Today's Cath. Tchr., 1987, Leadership award in religious edn., 1992. Mem. AAUW, Nat. Cath. Edn. Assn., Nat. Assn. Female Execs., Jordan Hosp. Club, St. Peter Cath. Women's Club, Adminstrs. Club, Passport Club, Admirals Club. Roman Catholic. Avocations: sports, music, art work, poetry, literature. Home: 59 Summer St Plymouth MA 02360-3462 also: 2677 SW Thunderbird Trl Stuart FL 34997-8944 Office: Benziger Pub Co 21600 Oxnard St Ste 500 Woodland Hills CA 91367-4947

MURPHY, JEREMIAH T. professional sports team executive/constuction services; BA, Bernard Baruch Coll. CPA, Calif. Sr. ptnr. Bowman and Co., 1971-82; CFO A.G. Spanos Companies, Stockton, Calif., 1982—. Mem. Am. Soc. CPAs (Calif. chpt.). Office: The Spanos Companies 1341 W Robinhood Dr Ste 1A Stockton CA 95207

MURPHY, KATHLEEN ANNE FOLEY, advertising agency executive; b. Fresh Meadows, N.Y., Oct. 15, 1952; d. Thomas J. and Audrey L. Finn; m. Timothy Sean Murphy, Sept. 26, 1992; 1 child, G. David. BA, Marymount Coll., 1974; postgrad., Smith Coll., 1985. V.p. acct. supr., sr. v.p. mgmt. supr., sr. v.p. group dir. Ogilvy & Mather Inc., N.Y.C., 1974-90; sr. v.p., worldwide account dir. Young & Rubicam, San Francisco, 1990-92, sr. v.p., dir. account svcs., 1992-95, exec. v.p., dir. acct. svcs., 1995-97, exec. v.p., gen. mgr., 1997—. Mem. Advt. Edn. Found. Roman Catholic. Home: One Brookside Ave Berkeley CA 94705 Office: Young & Rubicam 100 1st St San Francisco CA 94105-2600 E-mail: tsmurphy@pacbell.net

MURPHY, MARY ANN, human services administrator; b. Salt Lake City, Feb. 13, 1943; d. Wallace L. and Irene (Hummer) Matlock; m. Robert A. Glatzer, Dec. 31, 1977; children: Gabriela, Jessica, Nicholas. BA, U. Wash., 1964; MS, Ea. Wash. U., 1975. House counselor Ryther Child Ctr., Seattle, 1966-67; tchr. presch. Head Start, L.A. and Seattle, 1967-70, Children's Orthopedic Hosp., Seattle, 1970-72; faculty Ea. Wash. U., Cheney, 1973-82; exec. dir. Youth Help Assn., Spokane, Wash., 1983-88; mgr. regional ctr. for child abuse and neglect Deaconess Med. Ctr., Spokane, 1988-97; dir. Casey Family Ptnrs., Spokane, 1997—. Pres. Wash. State Alliance for Children, Youth and Families, Seattle, 1985-87; chairperson Gov.'s Juvenile Justice Adv. Commn., Olympia, Wash., 1987—. Mem. Nat. Coun. on Juvenile Justice, 1994-98. Recipient Alumni Achievement award Ea. Wash. U., 1994; named Outstanding Women Leader in Health Care YWCA, 1992, Outstanding Children's Advocate, Wash. State Children's Alliance, 1996. Avocations: reading, swimming, backpacking. Home: 1950 W Clarke Ave Spokane WA 99201-1306 Office: Casey Family Ptnrs 613 S Washington St Spokane WA 99204-2535

MURPHY, MICHAEL JOSEPH, state official; b. Seattle, May 24, 1947; s. John Anthony and Helen Elizabeth (Domick) M.; m. Theresa Ann Smith. BA in History, Seattle U., 1969; MBA, Pacific Luth. U., 1978. Chief adjudicator vet.'s program Office of the State Treas., Olympia, Wash., 1972-75, adminstr. pub. deposit protection commn., 1975-81, internal auditor to state treas., 1981-87; treas. Thurston County, Olympia, 1987-96, State of Wash., Olympia, 1997—. Mem. adv. bd. asset/liability com. Twin County Credit Union, Olympia, 1987-96; instr. profl. orgns., govt. Treas. Thurston County Dems., 1973-77. Mem. Wash. Assn. County Treasurers (bd. dirs., officer 1987-96, legis. coord. 1989-96, Pres. award 1994), Wash. Assn. County Ofcls. (bd. dirs. 1989-90), Wash. Mcpl. Treasurers Assn. (bd. dirs. 1990—, Cert. Excellence for investment policy 1992), Wash. Fin. Officers Assn. (profl. fin. officer 1988—, bd. dirs. 1997—), Nat. Assn. State Treasurers, Olympia Yacht Club, Olympia Country and Golf Club, Valley Athletic Club. Roman Catholic. Avocations: sailing, golf, travel. Home: PO Box 1342 Olympia WA 98507-1342 Office: Legis Bldg 2d Fl Wash State Treas Olympia WA 98504-0200

MURPHY, MICHAEL R. federal judge; b. Denver, Aug. 6, 1947; s. Roland and Mary Cecilia (Maloney) M.; m. Maureen Elizabeth Donnelly, Aug. 22, 1970; children: Amy Christina, Michael Donnelly. BA in History, Creighton U., 1969; JD, U. Wyo., 1972. Bar: Wyo. 1972, U.S. Ct. Appeals (10th cir.) 1972, Utah 1973, U.S. Dist. Ct. Utah 1974, U.S. Dist. Ct. Wyo.

1976, U.S. Ct. Appeals (5th cir.) 1976, U.S. Tax Ct. 1980, U.S. Ct. Appeals (9th cir.) 1981, U.S. Ct. Appeals (fed. cir.) 1984. Law clk. to chief judge U.S. Ct. Appeals (10th cir.), Salt Lake City, 1972-73; with Jones, Waldo, Holbrook & McDonough, Salt Lake City, 1973-86; judge 3d Dist. Ct., Salt Lake City, 1986-95, pres. judge, 1990-95; judge U.S. Ct. Appeals (10th cir.), Salt Lake City, 1995—. Mem. adv. com. on rules of civil procedure Utah Supreme Ct., 1985-95, mem. bd. dist. ct. judges, 1989-90; mem. Utah State Sentencing commn., 1993-95, Utah Adv. Com. on child Support Guidelines, 1989-95, chair 1993-95; mem. Utah Child Sexual Abuse Task Force, 1989-93. Recipient Freedom of Info. award, Soc. Profl. Journalists, 1989, Utah Minority Bar Assn. award, 1995, alumni Achievement citation, Creighton U., 1997; named Judge of Yr., Utah State Bar, 1992. Fellow Am. Bar Found.; mem. ABA (editl. bd. Judges' Jour. 1997-99), Utah Bar Assn. (chmn. alternative dispute resolution com. 1985-88), Sutherland Inn of Ct. II (past pres.). Roman Catholic. Office: 5438 Federal Bldg 125 S State St Salt Lake City UT 84138-1102

MURPHY, PETER E. corporate financial officer; BA, Dartmouth Coll.; MBA, Wharton Sch. Bus. With The Walt Disney Co., Burbank, Calif., 1988—; sr. v.p., CFO ABC, Inc., Burbank, 1997-98; exec. v.p., chief strategic officer The Walt Disney Co., Burbank, 1998-99, sr. exec. v.p., chief strategic officer, 1999—. Office: The Walt Disney Co 500 S Buena Vista St Burbank CA 91521

MURPHY, PHILIP EDWARD, broadcast executive; b. Chgo., May 11, 1945; s. Edward Curtis and Mary Francis (D'Incecco) M.; m. Carol Jean Sefton, Mar. 11, 1967 (div. 1985); children: Mandy Jean, Patrick Jeffrey; life ptnr. Robert G. McCracken, 1985—. BS, Ind. U., 1967. Prodn. mgr. Sta. WFIU-FM, Bloomington, Ind., 1968; news reporter, photographer, editor Sta. WTHR-TV, Indpls., 1969, sr. account exec., 1970-80; acct. exec. Blair TV, L.A., 1980-81; pres. Am. Spot Cable Corp., Hollywood, Calif., 1981-82; sr. v.p. TV group ops., overseer asset protection program Paramount Pictures, Hollywood, 1982—. Responsible for tech. preparation and distbn. material provided to worldwide electronic ancillary markets United Paramount Network Ops.; spkr. film preservation, in field; advisor Libr. of Congress, Washington, Nat. Archives, Washington. Lighting designer Civic Theatre, Indpls., 1979; tech. dir. Footlite Mus., Indpls., 1970-78; bd. dirs. Cathedral Arts, Indpls., 1978-80. Mem. Assn. Moving Image Archivists, Human Rights Campaign (Washington), Gay and Lesbian Alliance Against Defamation L.A., Hollywood Supports Assn., Soc. Motion Picture and TV Engrs. Avocations: photography, videography, audio, theatre. Office: Paramount Pictures TV Stage 3 212 5555 Melrose Ave Los Angeles CA 90038-3197

MURPHY, ROBERT F. lawyer; Pvt. practice law; with FHP Internat., Fountain Valley, Calif., 1986-95; gen. counsel and sec. Sun Healthcare Group, Albuquerque, 1996—. Office: Sun Healthcare Group 101 Sun Ave NE Albuquerque NM 87109

MURPHY, TERENCE MARTIN, biology educator; b. Seattle, July 1, 1942; s. Norman Walter and Dorothy Louise (Smith) M.; m Judith Baron, July 12, 1969; 1 child, Shannon Elaine. BS, Calif. Inst. Tech., 1964; PhD, U. Calif. San Diego, La Jolla, 1968. Sr. fellow dept. biochemistry U. Wash., Seattle, 1969-70; asst. prof. botany U. Calif., Davis, 1971-76, assoc. prof., 1976-82, prof. plant biology, 1982—, chmn. dept. botany, 1986-90. Author: Plant Molecular Development, 1988; co-author: Plant Biology, 1998; N.Am. exec. editor, N.Am. office, Physiologia Plantarum, 1988-98; contbr. articles to profl. jours. Mem. AAAS, Am. Soc. Plant Physiologists, Am. Soc. Photobiology, Scandinavian Soc. Plant Physiology. Home: 725 N Campus Way Davis CA 95616-3518 Office: U Calif Sect Plant Biology Davis CA 95616 E-mail: tmmurphy@ucdavis.edu

MURRAY, ANDY, professional hockey coach; Coach Phila. Flyers, 1988-90, Minn. North Stars, 1990-92, Winnipeg Jets, 1993-95; head coach Can. Nat. Team, 1996-98, L.A. Kings, 1999—. Office: c/o L A Kings Staples Ctr 111 S Figueroa St Los Angeles CA 90015

MURRAY, JEAN RUPP, communications executive, writer, speaker; b. Portland, Oreg., Aug. 29, 1943; d. Edward Howard and Dorothy Eugenia (Ross) Brown. BA in English, Portland State U., 1965. Cert. tchr., Oreg. Tchr., dept. head Beaverton (Oreg.) Sch. Dist., 1967-88; pres., founder Write Communications, Portland, 1988—. Adj. faculty Portland C.C., Concordia U., Portland State U.; nat. trainer, cons.State of Oreg., City of Portland, Nike, Inc., Oreg. Health Scis. U., Oreg. Mil. Acad., Oreg. Fin. Instns. Assn., Freightliner, Automated Data Processing, Calif. State U. Systems, others, 1988—; spkr. Tektronix, Fred Meyer, Pacific Power, Am. Inst. of Banking, Utah Power, Pacific Telecom, Inc., other; writing dir. U.S. Army C.E., USDA Forest Svcs., PacifiCare, LawTalk MCLE, Wash. State Bar Assn., others, 1989-90. Author: Flawless Grammar at Your Fingertips: An Instant Guide to Perfect Grammar for Everybody in Business, 1994; TV appearances include Stas. KATU-TV and KGW-TV. Vol. Dove Lewis Emergency Vet. Clinic, Portland, 1989—, Doerbecher Children's Hosp., Oreg. Humane Soc. Mem. Oreg. Speakers Assn. (pres. bd. dirs. 1997—), Nat. Speakers Assn., Ctr. for Marine Conservation. Republican. Avocations: target-shooting, travel, speaking, exercise, animals. Office: Write Comm PMB # 200 14657 SW Teal Blvd Beaverton OR 97007-6194 E-mail: jean@paws4thoughts.com

MURRAY, KEVIN, state legislator; b. 1960; BS in Bus. Adminstrn. and Acctg., Calif. State U., Northridge, 1981; MBA, Loyola Marymount U., 1983; JD, Loyola U., 1987. Bar: Calif.; lic. real estate brooker. Talent agt. William Morris Agy.; mem. Calif. State Assembly, 1994-98, mem. rules com., asst. Dem. floor leader, majority whip; mem. Calif. State Senate, Sacramento, 1998—, chair senate elections and reapportionment com., vice-chair fin., investment and internat. trade com., mem. bus. and professions com., transp. com., others. Senate rep. Calif. Film Commn.; chmn. Calif. Legis. Black Caucus; mem. Dem. Nat. Com. Democrat. Office: State Capitol Rm 4082 Sacramento CA 95814 also: 600 Corporate Pointe Ste 1020 Culver City CA 90230-7663

MURRAY, PATRICIA, computer company executive; JD, U. Mich., 1986. Employment litigator Morrison & Foerster, Palo Alto, Calif., until 1990; atty. human resource's legal staff Intel Corp., 1990-91, mgr. human resoure's legal staff, 1992-95, dir., v.p. human resources, 1996—. Office: Intel Corp PO Box 58119 2200 Mission College Blvd Santa Clara CA 95052-8119 E-mail: patricia.murray@intel.com

MURRAY, PATTY, senator; b. Bothell, Wash., Oct. 10, 1950; d. David L. and Beverly A. (McLaughlin) Johns; m. Robert R. Murray, June 2, 1972; children: Randy P., Sara A. BA, Wash. State U., 1972. Sec. various cos., Seattle, 1972-76; citizen lobbyist various ednl. groups, Seattle, 1983-88; legis. lobbyist Orgn. for Parent Edn., Seattle, 1977-84; instr. Shoreline Community Coll., Seattle, 1984-88; mem. Wash. State Senate, Seattle, 1989-92; senator from Wash. U.S. Senate, 1993—. Mem. Appropriations Com. ranking minority mem. subcom. mil. constrn.; vice chmn. Dem. Senatorial Campaign Com.; mem. Com. on Labor and Human Resources, Budget Com., Health, Edn., Labor and Pensions Com., Com. on Vets. Affairs. Mem. bd. Shoreline Sch., Seattle, 1985-89; mem. steering com. Demonstration for Edn., Seattle, 1987; founder, chmn. Orgn. for Parent Edn., Wash., 1981-85; lst Congl. rep. Wash. Women United, 1983-85. Recipient Recognition of Svc. to Children award Shoreline PTA Coun., 1986, Golden Acorn Svc. award, 1989; Outstanding Svc. award Wash. Women United, 1986, Outstanding Svc. to Pub. Edn. award Citizens Ednl. Ctr. NW, Seattle, 1987. Democrat. Office: US Senate 173 Russell Senate Office Bldg Washington DC 20510-0001*

MURRAY, TY (KING OF THE COWBOYS), professional rodeo cowboy; b. Phoenix, Oct. 11, 1969; s. Harold "Butch" and Joy M. Student, Odessa (Tex.) Coll. Seven-time world champion all-around world cowboy Profl. Rodeo Cowboys Assn., 1989-94, 98, two-time world champion bullrider, 1993, 98. Named Nat. H.S. Rodeo All-Around Champion, 1987, PRCA Rookie of the Year Profl. Rodeo Cowboy Assn., 1988, Nat. Intercollegiate Rodeo All-Around Champion, 1988, World Champion All Around Cowboy, World Champion Bull Rider, 1998. Achievements include holding the record for single season earnings, 1991. Office: Profl Rodeo Cowboy Assn 101 Pro Rodeo Dr Colorado Springs CO 80919-4300 also: R&R Advt Tony Garritano 8076 W Sahara Ave Las Vegas NV 89117-1957

MUSFELT, DUANE CLARK, lawyer; b. Stockton, Calif., Sept. 14, 1951; s. Robert H. and Doris E. (Roth) M.; m. Linh T. To, Sept. 6, 1980. Student, U. Calif., Davis, 1969-71; BA in Econs., U. Calif., Berkeley, 1973; JD, UCLA, 1976. Bar: Calif. 1976, U.S. Dist. Ct. (cen. dist.) Calif. 1977, U.S. Ct. Appeals (9th cir.) 1980, U.S. Dist. Ct. (no. dist.) Calif. 1982, U.S. Dist. Ct. (ea. and so. dists.) Calif. 1983, U.S. Supreme Ct. 1987. Assoc. Haight, Dickson, Brown & Bonesteel, L.A., 1976-77, Mori & Ota, L.A., 1977-79, Lewis, D'Amato, Brisbois & Bisgaard, L.A., 1979-82, ptnr. San Francisco, 1982—. Mem. State Bar Calif., No. Calif. Assn. Defense Counsel, Bar Assn. San Francisco. Democrat. Presbyterian. Avocations: tennis, skiing, bridge. Office: Lewis DAmato Brisbois & Bisgaard 1 Sansome St Ste 1400 San Francisco CA 94104-4431 E-mail: Musfelt@ldbb.com

MUSGRAVE, MARILYN N. state legislator; b. Greeley, Colo., Jan. 27, 1949; m. Steven Musgrave. BA, Colo. State U. Co-owner Musgrave Bale Stacking; mem. Colo. Ho. of Reps., 1994-98, Colo. Senate, Dist. 1, Denver, 1998—; chmn. transp. com.; mem. health, environment, welfare and instns. com.; mem. state, vets. and mil. affairs com. Past pres. Morgan County Rep. Women; former bd. mem. RE-3 Sch. Dist. Republican. Office: State Capitol 200 E Colfax Ave Ste 346 Denver CO 80203-1716 also: 15484 Rd 18 1/2 Ft Morgan CO 80701 Fax: 303-867-4640

MUSGROVE, GEORGE, city official; EdD, U. Mass., 1974. Dep. city mgr. for human svcs. programs and policy City of Richmond (Va.); asst. city mgr. Oakland, Calif., 1998—. Mem. Behavioral Health Authority. Office: City Manager City Hall 1 Frank Ogawa Plz 3 Fl Oakland CA 94612

MUSMANN, KLAUS, librarian; b. Magdeburg, Germany, June 27, 1935; came to U.S., 1957; s. Ernst Hans and Eva (Grunow) M.; m. Gladys H. Arakawa, June 15, 1963 (div. 1973); children: Carlton, Michelle; m. Lois Geneva Steele, Dec. 27, 1986. BA, Wayne State U., 1962; MALS, U. Mich., 1963; MA, Mich. State U., 1967; PhD, U. So. Calif., 1981. Libr. Detroit Pub. Libr., 1962-65; asst. serials libr. Mich. State U., East Lansing, 1965-67; head of acquisitions Los Angeles County Law Libr., L.A., 1968-84; coll. devel. libr. U. Redlands, Calif., 1984 , acting dir., 1994-96, dir., 1996—. Author: Helen and Vernon Farquhar Collection: A Bibliography, 1987, Diffusion of Innovations, 1989, Technological Innovations in Libraries, 1850-1950, 1993; contbr. articles to profl. jours. Grantee Coun. on Libr. Resources, 1990. Mem. ALA, Assn. Coll. and Rsch. Librs., Soc. for History of Tech., Fortnightly Club. Avocations: photography, travel. Home: 220 W Highland Ave Redlands CA 92373-6768 Office: U Redlands Redlands CA 92374 E-mail: klaus_musmann@redlands.edu

MUSOLF, LLOYD DARYL, political science educator, institute administrator; b. Yale, S.D., Oct. 14, 1919; s. William Ferdinand and Emma Marie (Pautz) M.; m. Berdyne Peet, June 30, 1944; children— Stephanie, Michael, Laura. B.A., Huron Coll., 1941; M.A., U. S.D., 1946; Ph.D., Johns Hopkins U., 1950. Mem. faculty Vassar Coll., Poughkeepsie, N.Y., 1949-59, assoc. prof. polit. sci., 1955-59; chief of party adv. group Mich. State U., Republic South Vietnam, 1959-61, prof. polit. sci., 1961-63, U. Calif.-Davis, 1963-87, dir. Inst. Govtl. Affairs, 1963-84, prof. emeritus, 1988—. Vis. prof. Johns Hopkins U., Balt., 1953, U. Del., 1954, U. Mich., 1955-56; U.S. Nat. rapporteur for Internat. Congress Adminstrv. Scis., Berlin, 1983; cons. and lectr. in field Author: Federal Examiners and the Conflict of Law and Administration, 1953, Public Ownership and Accountability: The Canadian Experience, 1959, Promoting the General Welfare, Government and the Economy, 1965, (with others) American National Government-Policies and Politics, 1971, Mixed Enterprise-A Developmental Perspective, 1972, (with Springer) Malaysia's Parliamentary System-Representative Politics and Policymaking in a Divided Society, 1979, Uncle Sam's Private Profitseeking Corporations-Comsat, Fannie Mae, Amtrak and Conrail, 1983; editor: (with Krislov) The Politics of Regulation, 1964, Communications Satellites in Political Orbit, 1968, (with Kornberg) Legislatures in Developmental Perspective, 1970, (with Joel Smith) Legislatures in Development-Dynamics of Change in New and Old States, 1979; contbr. monographs, chpts. to books, articles to profl. jours. Served to lt. USNR, 1942-45 Johnston scholar Johns Hopkins U., 1946-48; Faculty fellow Vassar Coll., 1954-55; sr. assoc. East-West Ctr., Honolulu, 1968-69; vis. scholar Brookings Instn., Washington, 1980. Mem. Am. Soc. Pub. Adminstrn. (exec. council 1967-70), Nat. Assn. Schs. Pub. Affairs and Adminstrn. (exec. council 1972-75), Western Govtl. Research Assn. (exec. bd. 1966-68), Am. Polit. Sci. Assn., Nat. Assn. State Univs. and Land Grant Colls. (rsch. com. fiftr. urban affairs 1980-81). Home: 844 Lake Blvd Davis CA 95616-2611 Office: U Calif Dept Polit Sci Davis CA 95616

MUSSEHL, ROBERT CLARENCE, lawyer; b. Washington, May 1, 1936; s. Chester Carl and Clara Cecelia (Greenwalt) Mussehl; children: Debra Lee, David Lee; m. Misook Chung, Mar. 22, 1987; 1 child, Omar. BA, Am. U., 1964, JD, 1966. Bar: Wash. 1967, U.S. Dist. Ct. (we. dist.) Wash. 1967, U.S. Ct. Appeals (9th cir.) 1968, U.S Supreme Ct. 1971. Sr. ptnr. Thom, Mussehl, Navoni, Hoff, Pierson & Ryder, Seattle, 1967-78, Neubauer & Mussehl, Seattle, 1978-80, Mussehl & Rosenberg, Seattle, 1980—. Speaker law convs. and other profl. orgns.; moot ct. judge Nat. Appelate Advocacy Competition, San Francisco, 1987; panel mem. ABA Symposium on Compulsory Jurisdiction of World Ct., San Francisco, 1987; chmn. bd., chief exec. officer The Seattle Smashers profl. volleyball club, 1976-80. Contbr. numerous articles to legal publs. Mem. Wash. Vol. Lawyers for Arts, 1976-80; statewide chair Lawyers for Durning for Gov., 1976; mem. task force on the single adult and ch. Ch. Coun. Greater Seattle, 1976-78; bd. dirs. Wash. State Pub. Interest Law Ctr., 1976-81; founder, immediate past chair Lawyers Helping Hungry Children campaign, Wash. State Lawyers Campaign for Hunger Relief, 1991—. Recipient Jefferson award for pub. svc. State of Wash., 1997. Fellow Am. Bar Found., Am. Acad. Matrimonial Lawyers; mem. ABA (ho. of dels. 1979-91, spl. adv. com. on internat. activities 1989-91, chair marriage and family counseling and conciliation com. family law sect. 1981-83, mem. world order under law standing com. 1983-89, chair, 1986-89, chair ad hoc com. on the assembly 1986-89, mem. assembly resolutions com. 1979-91, mem. blue ribbon com. for world ct. 1987-88, mem. standing com. on dispute resolution, 1992-93; exec. coun. sect. dispute resolution 1993-95, asst. budget officer, 1995-97, budget officer 1997-99, vice-chair 1999—, chair elect 2000—, Achievement award), Wash. State Bar Assn. (exec. com. family law sect. 1973-75, chmn. internat. law com. 1974-76, sec.-treas., exec. com. world peace through law sect. 1980—, chair 1981-82, mem. edit. bd. Family Law Deskbook 1987-89), Wash. State Trial Lawyers Assn., Seattle-King County Bar Assn. (family law sect. 1971-90, other coms. 1970—, chmn. young lawyers sect. 1971-72, sec. 1972-73, trustee), Am. Arbitration Assn. (panel arbitrators), World Assn. Lawyers of World Peace Through Law Ctr. (founding mem.), Heritage Club YMCA Greater Seattle (charter 1977—), UN Assn. U.S.A. (bd. dirs. Seattle chpt. 1989-91). Avocations: biking, tennis, weight training, painting, religious studies. Home: One Pacific Tower 2000 1st Ave Apt 902 Seattle WA 98121-2167 Office: 1111 3rd Ave Ste 2626 Seattle WA 98101-3210 E-mail: rcmpi@juno.com

MUSSER, SANDRA G. retired lawyer; b. Hollywood, Calif., July 23, 1944; d. Donald Godfrey Gumpertz and Gloria G. (Rosenblatt) King; m. Michael R.V. Whitman, Feb. 19, 1980. BA, UCLA, 1965; JD, Hastings Coll. of Law, 1970. Bar: Calif. 1971, U.S. Dist. Ct. (no. dist.) Calif. 1971, U.S. Ct. Appeals (9th cir.) 1971. Clk. 9th Cir. Ct. of Appeals, 1971-72; lawyer pvt. practice of family law, 1972-86; ptnr. Musser & Ryan, San Francisco, 1986-97; pvt. practice San Francisco, 1997-98; ret., 1998. Judge pro tem San Francisco County Superior Ct., 1988-98; dealer antique Chinese rugs and textiles, 1996—. Contbr. articles to profl. jours. Mem. adv. coun. Textile Mus., Washington, 1996—. Fellow Acad. Matrimonial Lawyers; mem. ABA (chair litig. sect. domestic rels. and family law com. 1993-94), State Bar Calif. (state bar family law sect. 1977—, chair 1982-83, advisor 1983-84), Bar Assn. San Francisco. Office: 361 Oak St San Francisco CA 94102-5615

MUSSEY, JOSEPH ARTHUR, health and medical product executive; b. Cleve., July 17, 1948; s. Arthur Glenn and Mary Jane (Silvaroli) M.; m. Mary Elizabeth Stone, July 11, 1975; 1 child, Joanna Lee. BS in Indsl. Engring. with distinction, Cornell U., 1970; MBA, Harvard U., 1976. Engring. mgmt. officer U.S. Navy Pub. Works Ctr., Pearl Harbor, Hawaii, 1971-75; mktg. exec. B.F. Goodrich, Akron, Ohio, 1976-80, fin. exec., 1980-84; v.p. fin. Combustion Engring., Stamford, Conn., 1984-85, v.p. ops., 1985-86; exec. v.p. Process Automation Bus. Combustion Engring., Columbus, Ohio, 1987-90; pres., CEO Danninger Med. Tech., Inc., Columbus, 1990—; treas., dir. Danninger Med. Tech. Inc. Served as lt. U.S. Navy, 1971-75. Decorated Disting. Naval Grad. (USN), 1971, Disting. Grad. U.S. Navy Civil Engring. Corps., 1971. Mem. Alpha Pi Mu, Tau Beta Pi, Phi Eta Sigma. Republican. Roman Catholic. Club: Skull & Daggar. Home: 27662 Pinestrap Cir Laguna Hills CA 92653-7810 Office: Interpore Cross International 181 Technology Dr Irvine CA 92618

MUZYKA-MCGUIRE, AMY, marketing professional, nutrition consultant; b. Chgo., Sept. 24, 1953; d. Basil Bohdan and Amelia (Rand) Muzyka; m. Patrick J. McGuire, June 3, 1977; children: Jonathan, Elizabeth. BS, Iowa State U., 1975, postgrad., 1978—; registered dietitian, St. Louis U., 1980. Cert. dietitian. Home economist Nat. Livestock and Meat Bd., Chgo., 1975-77; dietary cons. various hosps. and nursing homes, Iowa, 1978-79; supr. foodsvc. Am. Egg Bd., Park Ridge, Ill., 1980-83; assoc. dir., mgr. foodsvc. Cole & Weber Advt., Seattle, 1984-85; prin., owner Food and Nutrition Comms., Federal Way, Wash., 1986—. Co-author: Turkey Foodservice Manual, 1987; editor: (newsletter) Home Economists in Business, 1975-77, Dietitians in Business and Industry, 1982-85; Food Net on Internet, 1995—; contbr. articles to profl. jours. Active Federal Way Women's Network, 1986-87. Named Outstanding Dietitian of Yr. North Suburban Dietetic Assn., 1983. Mem. Am. Dietetic Assn., Internat. Foodsvc. Editorial Coun., Consulting Nutritionists, Vegetarian Nutrition, Home Economists in Bus. Avocations: gardening, travel, music, food and beverage tastings. Home: 5340 SW 315th St Federal Way WA 98023-2034

MYCIELSKI, JAN, mathematician, educator; b. Wisniowa, Poland, Feb. 7, 1932; s. Jan and Helena (Bal) M.; m. Emilia Przezdziecka, Apr. 25, 1959. MS, U. Wroclaw, Poland, 1955, PhD, 1957. With Inst. Math., Polish Acad. Scis., Wroclaw, 1956-68; prof. math. U. Colo., Boulder, 1969—. Vis. prof. Case Western Res. U., Cleve., 1967, U. Colo., 1967, Inst. des Hautes Etudes Scientifiques, Bures-sur-Yvette, 1978-79, dept. math. U. Hawaii, 1987; attache de recherche Centre National de la Recherche Scientifique, Paris, 1957-58; asst. prof. U. Calif., Berkeley, 1961-62, 70; long-term vis. staff mem. Los Alamos Nat. Lab., 1989-90. Author over 150 rsch. papers. Recipient Stefan Banach prize, 1965, Alfred Jurzykowski award, 1977, Waclaw Sierpinski medal, 1990. Mem. Am. Math. Soc., Polish Math. Soc., Assn. for Symbolic Logic. Office: U Colo Dept Math Boulder CO 80309-0001

MYERNICK, GLENN, professional soccer coach; b. Dec. 29, 1954; Student, Hartwick Coll. Professional soccer player Dallas Tornado, 1977-79, Portland, 1980-82, Tampa Bay, Fla., 1983-84; asst. coach U. Tampa, 1985-86, Hartwick Coll., 1986-89; nat. coaching coord. U.S. Soccer Team, 1989-96; asst. coach U.S. Olympic Team, 1996; head coach Colo. Rapids, Denver, 1996—. Capt. U.S. Pan Am. Team, 1975, U.S. Olympic Team, 1976. Recipient Hermann Trophy as College Player of the Yr., 1976; named U.S. Soccer Fedn. Coach of the Yr. by U.S. Olympic Com., 1998. Office: c/o Colorado Rapids 555 17th St Ste 3350 Denver CO 80202-3903

MYERS, ALBERT F. transportation executive; b. New Orleans, Jan. 11, 1946; BS in Mech. Engring., U. Idaho, 1969, MS in Mech. Engring., 1971; MS in Indl. Mgmt., MIT, 1992. Active duty U.S. Army, 1972-75; various positions Dryden Flight Rsch. Ctr., 1975-81; mgr. flight controls engring. Northrop Grumman, 1981, corp. v.p., Bus. Stategy, 1992-94, corp. v.p., treas., 1994—. Office: Northrop Grumman Corp 1840 Century Park E Los Angeles CA 90067-2101

MYERS, BARTON, architect; b. Norfolk, Va., Nov. 6, 1934; s. Barton and Meeta Hamilton (Burrage) M.; m. Victoria George, Mar. 7, 1959; 1 child, Suzanne Lewis. BS, U.S. Naval Acad., 1956; MArch with honors, U. Pa., 1964. Commd. 2d lt. USAF, 1956, resigned, 1961; architect Louis I. Kahn, Phila., 1964-65, Bower, Fradley, Phila., 1967-68; architect, prin. A.J. Diamond & Barton Myers, Toronto, Ont., Can., 1968-75, Barton Myers Assocs., Toronto, 1975-96, architect, pres. Los Angeles, 1981—. Disting. vis. prof. Ariz. State U., Tempe, 1986; sr. prof. UCLA, 1981—; Thomas Jefferson Prof. U. Va., Charlottesville, 1982; vis. prof., lectr., Harvard U., U. Pa., other univs. U.S. and Can., 1968—. Prin. works include Myers Residence, Toronto (Ont. Assn. Architects Toronto Chpt. Annual Design award, 1971, Can. Housing Design Coun. award, 1971), Wolf Residence, Toronto (Archtl. Record: Record Houses of 1977, Twenty-five Yrs. of Record Houses, 1981), Housing Union Bldg., Edmonton (Can. Housing Design Coun. award, 1974, Design in Steel award, 1975), Citadel Theatre, Edmonton (City of Edmonton Design award, 1978, Stelco Design award, 1978), Seagram Mus., Waterloo, Ont. (Gov. Gen.'s Medal for Architecture, 1986), Howard Hughes Ctr. Master Plan and Wang Tower, L.A., 1986, Phoenix Mcpl. Govt. Ctr. (Winning Competition Entry, 1985), Portland Ctr. for the Performing Arts, Portland (Progressive Architecture Design award, 1984, USITT Merit award, 1994), Art Gallery Ont. expansion (Winning Competition Entry, 1987), Film and Drama Facility York U., Toronto, 1987, Cerritos (Calif.) Ctr. Performing Arts, 1987 (USITT Honor Award, 1994), N.J. Performing Arts Ctr., Newark, 1991, Ivan Reitman Prodn. Studio, 1994, Scripps Ocean Atmosphere Rsch. Facility, 1995; others. Recipient Gov. Gen.'s award for Architecture Woodsworth Coll., 1992, RAIC Gold Medal, 1994, Royal Archtl. Inst. Canada Fellow AIA, Royal Archtl. Inst. Can.; mem. Soc. Archtl. Historians, Royal Can. Acad. Art, Tau Sigma Delta. Avocations: travel, reading. Office: U Calif Dept Architecture Los Angeles CA 90095-0001

MYERS, DOUGLAS GEORGE, zoological society administrator; b. L.A., Aug. 30, 1949; s. George Walter and Daydeen (Schroeder) M.; m. Barbara Firestone Myers, Nov. 30, 1980; children: Amy, Andrew. BA, Christopher Newport Coll., 1981. Tour and show supr. Annheuser-Busch (Bird Sanctuary), Van Nuys, Calif., 1970-74, mgr. zool. ops., 1974-75, asst. mgr. ops., 1975-77, mgr. ops., 1977-78; gen. services mgr. Annheuser-

Busch (Old Country), Williamsburg, Va., 1978-80, park ops. dir., 1980-81; gen. mgr. wild animal park Zool. Soc. San Diego, 1981-83, dep. dir. ops., 1983-85, exec. dir., 1985—; chief exec. ofcr. San Diego Wild Animal Park, Escondido, Calif. Cons. in field. Mem. adv. com. of pres.' assn. Am. Mgmt. Assn. Fellow Am. Assn. Zool. Parks and Aquariums (profl., bd. dirs.), Internat. Union Dirs. Zool. Gardens; mem. Internat. Assn. Amusement Parks and Attractions, Am. Mgmt. Assn. (adv. com. pres. assn.), Calif. Assn. Zoos and Aquariums, Mus. Trustee Assn., Rotary. Office: San Diego Zoo PO Box 551 San Diego CA 92112-0551

MYERS, ELMER, social worker, psychiatrist; b. Blackwell, Ark., Nov. 12, 1926; s. Chester Elmer Myers and Irene (Davenport) Lewis; widowed; children: Elmer Jr., Keith, Kevin. BA, U. Kans., 1951, MA, 1962; student, U. Calif., Santa Barbara, 1977-78. Lic. clin. social worker; C.C. counselor credentials. Psychiat. social worker Hastings (Nebr.) State Hosp., 1960-62, State of Calif. Bur. Social Tng. Com., Sacramento, 1962-75; supr. psychiat. social worker State of Calif., Sacramento, 1975-80, Alta Calif. Regional Ctr., Sacramento, 1980-85. Exec. dir. Tri-County Family Services, Yuba City, Calif., 1966-69; cons. to 3 convalescent Hosps., Marysville, Calif., 1969-71; lectr. Yuba Coll., Marysville, 1971-76; assoc. prof. Calif. State U., Chico, 1972-73; cons. in field, Marysville, 1985—; group therapist Depot Homeless Shelter, 1996—, counselor 1995—; cons., therapist New Millennium Group Home, 2000. Juror Yuba County Grand Jury, Marysville, 1965, 87-88; sec. Y's Men's Club, Yuba City, 1964-65; chmn. Tri-County Home Health Agy., Yuba City, 1974-76; vice-chmn. Gateway Projects, Inc., Yuba City, 1974-75; bd. dirs. Christian Assistance Network, 1993, Habitat for Humanity, 1993, Yuba County Truancy Bd., Marysville, 1964-67, Golden Empire Health Sys. Agy., Sacramento, 1972-76, Youth Svcs. Bur., Yuba City, 1967, Bi-County Mental Retardation Planning Bd., Yuba City, 1972, Yuba County Juvenile Justice Commn., Marysville, 1982-90, Am. Cancer Soc., Marysville, 1985-92, Yuba County Rep. Ctrl. Com., 1983-90, Salvation Army, 1990—, faciltitor care project, 1992; asst. dir. Marysville Adult Activity Ctr., 1990—; active Yuba-Sutter United Way, 1971-73, 91-92, Tri-County Ethnic Forum, sec., 1991-1993;steering com. Yuba County Sr. Ctr. Assn., 1992, 95—; chmn. Yuba County Cmty. Svcs. Commn., 1997-99, Yuba-Sutter Gleaners, 1997—, Yuba-Sutter Commn. on Aging, 1996, bd. dirs., 1998, 2001; chmn. H.E.L.P. Working Group, HIV prevention, 2000. Recipient Cert. Spl. Recognition, Calif. Rehab. Planning Project, 1969, Cert. Spl. Recognition, State of Calif., 1967, Cert. Spl. Recognition, Alta Calif. Regional Ctrs., 1985; named Vol. of Week, Appeal Dem. newspaper, 1999. Mem. Nat. Assn. Social Workers (cert.), Kern County Mental Health Assn. (chmn. 1978-79). Lodge: Rotary (bd. dirs. Marysville club 1975-76). Avocations: fgn. lang. study, gardening, reading, computers. Home and Office: 3920 State Hwy 20 Marysville CA 95901-9003 E-mail: elm@syix.com

MYERS, GREGORY EDWIN, aerospace engineer; b. Harrisburg, Pa., Jan. 1, 1960; s. Bernard Eugene and Joyce (Calhoun) M.; m. Susan Ann Hayslett, Dec. 30, 1983 (div. 1999); children: Kimberly, Benjamin. BS in Aerospace Engring., U. Mich., 1981; MS in Aerospace Engring., Air Force Inst. Tech., 1982. Aerospace engr. Sperry Comml. Flight Systems group Honeywell, Inc., Phoenix, 1987-90, sr. project engr. satellite systems ops. Glendale, Ariz., 1990-92, sr. project engr. air transport systems Phoenix, 1992-93, prin. engr., 1993-97; prin. software engr. Orbital Scis. Corp., Chandler, Ariz., 1997—, sr. prin. software engr., 1999—. Presenter in field. Contbr. articles to profl. jours. Active Aviation Week Rsch. Adv. Panel, 1990-91. Recipient Certs. of Recognition and Appreciation Lompoc Valley Festival Assn., Inc., 1983, Arnold Air Soc. (comdr. 1979), Cert. of Appreciation Instrument Soc. Am., 1991. Mem. AIAA (sr.). Lutheran. Avocations: softball, tennis, reading, computer programming. Office: Orbital Scis Corp 3380 S Price Rd Chandler AZ 85248-3534

MYERS, HARDY, state attorney general, lawyer; b. Electric Mills, Miss., Oct. 25, 1939; m. Mary Ann Thalhofer, 1962; children: Hardy III, Christopher, Jonathan. AB with distinction, U. Miss., 1961; LLB, U. Oreg., 1964. Bar: Oreg., U.S. Ct. of Appeals (9th cir.), U.S. Dist. Ct. Law clerk U.S. Dist. Judge William G. East, 1964-65; pvt. practice Stoel Rives LLP, 1965-96; atty. gen. State of Oregon, 1997—. Mem. Oreg. Ho. of Reps., 1975-85, speaker of the ho., 1979-83. Pres. Portland City Planning Commn., 1973-74; chair Oreg. Jail Project, 1984-86, Citizens' Task Force on Mass Transit Policy, 1985-86, Oreg. Criminal Justice Coun., 1987-91, Portland Future Focus, 1990-91, Metro Charter com., 1991-92, task force on state employee benefits, 1994; co-chair gov. task force on state employee compensation, 1995. Office: Oreg Atty Gen Justice Dept 1162 Court St NE Salem OR 97310-1320

MYERS, HOWARD MILTON, pharmacologist, educator; b. Bklyn., Dec. 12, 1923; s. Charles and Rose (Nassberg) M.; m. Louise Perry, Mar. 14, 1972; children by previous marriage: Clifford Raymond, Nancy Rose, Stephen Andrew. D.D.S., Western Res. U., 1949; MSc, U. Calif., San Francisco, 1953; Ph.D., U. Rochester, 1958; M.A. (hon.), U. Pa., 1974; M.A., San Francisco State U., 1964. Prof. oral biology U. Calif., San Francisco, 1965-71; prof. biochemistry U. Pacific Sch. Dentistry, San Francisco, 1971-74; dir. Center for Oral Health Research, U. Pa., Phila., 1974-78; prof. pharmacology Sch. of Dental Medicine, 1974-86; dir. research/tchr. tng. grant U. Calif., San Francisco, 1960-71; prof. emeritus pharmacology U. Pa. Adj. prof. pharmacology U. Calif.-San Francisco Sch. Medicine, Calif. Coll. Podiatric Medicine; adj. prof. oral biology U. Calif.-San Francisco Sch. Dentistry, 1987-95; pharmacology cons. Nat. Bd. Podiatric Examiners, 1992-95; reviewer U.S.-Israel Binat. Sci. Found., 1982-95. Contbr. articles to profl. jours.; editor: Monographs in Oral Science, 1972-97. Served with U.S. Army, 1942-45. NIH fellow Karolinska Inst., Stockholm, 1964-65; Fogarty Sr. Internat. Research fellow U. Geneva, 1980-81 Mem. AAAS (chmn. sect. dentistry 1974), Am. Assn. Dental Research (pres. 1973-75), Council Biology Editors., Am. Chem. Soc. Home and Office: 3649 Market St Apt 601 San Francisco CA 94131-1307

MYERS, JOHN WESCOTT, aviation executive; b. L.A., June 13, 1911; s. Louis Wescott and Blanche (Brown) M.; m. Lucia Raymond, Mar. 21, 1941 (dec. Mar. 1999); children: Louis W. (dec.), Lucia E. A.B., Stanford U., 1933; J.D., Harvard U., 1936. Bar: Calif. 1936. Ptnr. law firm O'Melveny & Myers, L.A., 1936-42; from test pilot to sr. v.p., dir. Northrop Corp., 1942-54, 1954-79; chmn. bd. Pacific Airmotive Corp., 1954-79, Airflite, Long Beach, Calif., 1970-89, Flying M Assocs., Long Beach, 1989—. Owner Flying M Ranches, Merced, Calif., 1959—. Dir. Smithsonian Nat. Air and Space Dulles Ctr. Project. Fellow Soc. Exptl. Test Pilots; mem. Calif. Bar Assn., Los Angeles Bar Assn., Inst. Aerospace Scis., Order of Daedalians (hon.). Republican. Clubs: Bohemian, California, Los Angeles Country, Los Angeles Yacht, Sunset, Aviation Country, Conquistadores del Cielo. Home: 718 N Rodeo Dr Beverly Hills CA 90210-3210 Office: 3200 Airflite Way Long Beach CA 90807-5312

MYERS, MARILYN GLADYS, pediatric hematologist and oncologist; b. Lyons, Nebr., July 17, 1930; d. Leonard Clarence and Marian N. (Manning) M.; m. Paul Frederick Motzkus, July 24, 1957 (dec. Aug. 1982). BA cum laude, U. Omaha, 1954; MD, U. Nebr., 1959. Diplomate Am. Bd. Pediatrics. Intern Orange County Gen. Hosp., Orange, Calif., 1959-60, resident, 1960-62; fellow in hematology/oncology Orange County Gen. Hosp./Children's Hosp. L.A., 1962-64; assoc. in rsch., chief dept. hematology/oncology Children's Hosp., Orange, 1964-80, dir. outpatient dept., 1964-7[illegible], assoc. dir. leukapheresis unit, 1971-80; chmn. practice hematology, oncology, rheumatology Orange, 1964-80; instr. Coll. Medicine U. Calif., Irvine, 1968-71, asst. clin. prof. pediatrics, 1971—; pvt. practice hematology, oncology, rheumatology Santa Ana, Calif., 1980—. Clin. rsch. exptl. drugs. Contbr. articles to med. jours. Mem. med. adv. com. Orange County Blood Bank Hemophiliac Found. Grantee Am. Leukemia Soc., 1963, Am. Heart Assn., 1964. Fellow Am. Acad. Pediatrics; mem. AMA, Calif. Med. Assn., L.A. County Med. Assn., Orange County Med. Assn., Orange County Pediatric Soc., Southwestern Pediatric Soc., L.A. Pediatric Soc., Internat. Coll. Pediatrics, Orange County Oncologic Soc., Am. Heart Assn. (Cardiopulmonary Coun.). Republican. Methodist. Avocation: reading. Office: 2220 E Fruit St Ste 217 Santa Ana CA 92701-4459

MYERS, MIKE, actor, writer; b. Toronto, Ont., Can., May 25, 1963; s. Eric and Bunny (Hind) M.; m. Robin Ruzan, 1993. Stage appearences: The Second City, Toronto, 1986-88, Chgo., 1988-89; actor, writer: Mullarkey & Myers, Can., 1984-86, (TV show) Saturday Night Live, 1989-94 (Emmy award for outstanding writing in a comedy or variety series 1989), (film) Wayne's World, 1992, So I Married an Axe Murderer, 1993, Wayne's World II (also screenwriter, prodr.), 1993, Austin Powers: International Man Of Mystery (also screenwriter, prodr.), 1997, Meteor, 1998, McClintock's Peach, 1998, Just Lke Me, 1998, It's a Dog's Life, 1998, 54, 1998, Austin Powers: The Spy Who Shagged Me (also screenwriter, prodr.), 1999, Austin Powers: The Animated Series, 1999, Pete's Meteor, 1999; actor: (TV movie) John and Yoko, 1985, Elvis Stories, 1989, Saturday Night Live: The Best of Phil Hartman, 1998, Saturday Night Live: the Best of Mike Myers, 1998, Saturday Night Live: 25th Anniversary, 1999, Madonna: The Video Collection 93.99, 1999; screenwriter: (tv movie) Murderers Among Us: The Simon Wiesenthal Story, 1989, Saturday Night Live: The Best of Mike Myers, 1998; TV appearances The Littlest Hobo, 1979, Russell Gilbert Show, 1998; dir. (film) The Bacchae, 1999. Recipient Can. comedy award, 2000.

MYERS, MILES ALVIN, educator, educational association administrator; b. Newton, Kans., Feb. 4, 1931; s. Alvin F. and Katheryn P. (Miles) M.; m. Celeste Myers; children: Royce, Brant, Roslyn. BA in Rhetoric, U. Calif., Berkeley, 1953, MAT in English, 1979, MA in English, PhD in Lang. and Literacy, U. Calif., 1982. Cert. secondary tchr. English. Tchr. English Washington Union High Sch., Fremont, Calif., 1957-59, Oakland (Calif.) High Sch., 1959-67, 69-74, Concord High Sch., Mt. Diablo, Calif., 1967-69; chmn. bd. dirs. Alpha Plus Corp. Preschs., Piedmont, 1968—; dir. All City High, 1973-74; tchr. English Castlemont High Sch., Oakland, 1974-75; mem. faculty U. Calif., Berkeley, 1975-85; adminstrv. dir. Bay Area writing project Sch. Edn. U. Calif.., Berkeley, 1976-85; adminstrv. dir. nat. writing project Sch. Edn. U. Calif., Berkeley, 1979-85; pres., CEO Calif. Fedn. Tchrs., 1985-90; exec. dir. Nat. Coun. Tchrs. of English, Urbana, Ill., 1990-97, EdSchool.com of Edvantage/Riverdeep, 1999—. Co-dir. Nat. Standards Project for English Language Arts, 1992-96; adj. prof. English U. Ill., Champaign-Urbana, 1991-94; exec. dir. Calif. Subject Matter Projects, U. Calif., 1997-98, Edn. Sch. com., 1999—; vis. lectr. at numerous colleges and Univs.; rschr. in field. Author: The Meaning of Literature, 1973; co-author: Writing: Unit Lessons in Composition, Book III, 1965, The English Book-Composition Skills, 1980; author: A Procedure for Holistic Scoring, 1980, Changing our Minds, 1996; co-author: Exemplars of Standards for English Language Arts, 3 vols., 1997; editor Calif. Tchr., 1966-81; contbr. articles to profl. jours.; pub. monographs. Sgt. U.S. Army, 1953-56. Recipient cert. of Merit, Ctrl. Calif. Coun. Tchrs. of English, 1969, Commendation award Oakland Fedn. Tchrs., 1970, First Place award Internat. Labor Assn., 1971, Disting. Svc. award Calif. Coun. Classified Employees, 1991, Svc. award Nat. Writing Project, 1996. Fellow Nat. Conf. Rsch. in English; mem. Nat. Coun. Tchrs. of English, Nat. Conf. on Rsch. in English, Am. Fedn. of Tchrs. (legis. dir. Calif. Fedn. of Tchrs. 1971-72, Union Tchr. Press awards 1969-75, 86-89, 91, Ben Rust award Calif. Fedn. of Tchrs. 1994), Am. Edn. Rsch. Assn., Calif. Assn. Tchrs. of English (Disting. Svc. award 86), Internat. Reading Assn., U. Calif./Berkeley Alumni Assn., Phi Delta Kappa. Home: 5823 Scarborough Dr Oakland CA 94611-2721 Office: Dir Inst Rsch on Learning & Tchg Berkeley CA 94704 Fax: 510-531-1734. E-mail: miles.myers@worldnet.att.net

MYERS, R. DAVID, library director, dean; b. Hutchinson, Kans., Mar. 27, 1949; s. William Raymond and Elizabeth (Haas) M.; m. Barbara Jean Burridge, Sept. 15, 1973; 1 child, John David. BA, U. No. Colo., 1972, MA, 1974; ABD, U. Mich., 1976; MA, U. Denver, 1979. Manuscript curator Western History Collection, Denver, 1976-79; rsch. assoc. Colo. Legis. Coun., Denver, 1979-81; reference specialist Libr. of Congress, Washington, 1981-84, reference supr., 1984-88; libr. dir. State Hist. Soc. of Wis., Madison, 1988-94; assoc. dean univ. libr. N.Mex. State U., Las Cruces, 1994-2001; dir. Fogelson libr., prof. history Coll. Santa Fe, 2001—. Editor Am. history Macmillan Pub., N.Y.C., 1991-94; cons. history of medicine dept. U. Wis., Madison, 1993-94. Author bibliographies for Libr. of Congress, 1987, 88. Mem. ALA, Am. Hist. Assn., Orgn. Am. Historians, Wis. Libr. Assn. Avocations: research, writing, baseball, mysteries. Office: Fogelson Libr Coll Santa Fe 1600 St Michaels Dr Santa Fe NM 87505

MYERS, R(ALPH) CHANDLER, lawyer; b. L.A., Jan. 9, 1933; s. Ralph Cather and Winifred (Chandler) M.; m. Rebecca Blythe Borkgren, Jan. 11, 1963. BA, Stanford U., 1954, JD, 1958; LLD (hon.), Whittier Coll., 1988. Bar: Calif. 1959, U.S. Dist. Ct. (cen. dist.) Calif. 1959, U.S. Supreme Ct. 1971. Law clk., then assoc. Parker, Stanbury, Reese & McGee, L.A., 1958-63; assoc. Nicholas, Kolliner & Van Tassel, L.A., 1963-65; ptnr. Myers & D'Angelo and predecessors, L.A. and Pasadena, Calif., 1965—. Nat. panelist Am. Arbitration Assn., L.A., 1964— ; bd. visitors Stanfor d U. Law Sch., Calif., 1970-73; mem. judge pro tem panel L.A. Mcpl. Ct., 1971-81; mem. Los Angeles County Dist. Atty.'s Adv. Coun.., 1976-83 Bd. dirs. Opera Guild So. Calif., L.A., 1971-83, pres., 1980-82; bd. dirs. Guild Opera Co. L.A., 1974-83, pres., 1975-77; bd. dirs. Western Justice Ctr. Found., 1993—, treas. 1996-99, 2d v.p., 1999—; pres. L.A. Child Guidance Clinic, 1977-79, bd. dirs., 1972-83; nat. vice chmn. Keystone Gifts, Stanford Centennial Campaign, 1987-92; trustee Whittier Coll., Calif., 1973— , chmn. bd. trustees, 1981-87; bd. dirs. Opera Assocs. of the Music Ctr., L.A., 1976-78; trustee Flintridge Prep. Sch., La Canada Flintridge, Calif., 1981-88, chmn. bd. trustees, 1985-88; co-founder Whittier Law Sch., Calif., 1975, trustee, 1975—, chmn. bd. trustees, 1981-87. Recipient Stanford Assocs. award, 1984, Centennial Medallion award, 1991, Gold Spike award Stanford U., 1989, Disting. Svc. award Whittier Law Sch., 1993, Outstanding Achievement award Stanford Assocs., 1998. Mem. Wilshire Bar Assn. (bd. govs. 1972-81, pres. 1979-80), L.A. County Bar Assn. (trustee 1979-81), Stanford Law Soc. So. Calif. (bd. dirs. 1967-72, pres. 1970-71), Stanford Assocs. (bd. govs. 1992-97, treas. 1995-97), Jonathan Club, University Club (Pasadena), Stanford Club of L.A. (bd. dirs. 1963-70, pres. 1968-69). Home: La Canada 5623 Burning Tree Dr La Canada Flintridge CA 91011-2861 Office: Myers & D'Angelo 301 N Lake Ave Ste 800 Pasadena CA 91101-4108

MYERS, RICHARD B. career officer; BSME, Kans. State U., 1965; MBA, Auburn U., 1977; Diploma, Air Command/Staff Coll., Maxwell AFB, Ala., 1977, U.S. Army War Coll., , 1981; postgrad., Harvard U., 1991. Commd. 2d lt. USAF, 1965, advanced through ranks to gen., 1997; various assignments to comdr. U.S. Forces Japan and 5th Air Force, Yokota Air Base, Japan, 1993-96; asst. to chmn. of Joint Chiefs of Staff The Pentagon, Washington, 1996-97; comdr. Pacific Air Forces, Hickam AFB, Hawaii, 1997-98; comdr.-in-chief N.Am. Aerospace Def. Comm./U.S. Space Command, Peterson AFB, Colo., 1998—. Decorated Def. Disting. Svc. medal with oak leaf cluster, Disting. Svc. medal, Legion of Merit, Disting. Flying Cross with oak leaf cluster, Meritorious Svc. medal with three oak leaf clusters, Air medal with 18 oak leaf clusters, Air Force Commendation medal, others. Office: USCINCSPACE CINCNORAD 250 S Peterson Blvd Ste 116 Colorado Springs CO 80914-3206

MYERS, ROBERT DAVID, judge; b. Springfield, Mass., Nov. 20, 1937; s. William and Pearl (Weiss) M.; m. Judith G. Dickenman, July 1, 1962; children— Mandy Susan, Jay Brandt, Seth William. A.B., U. Mass., 1959; J.D., Boston U., 1962. Bar: Ariz. 1963. Practice in, Phoenix, 1963-89; presiding judge civil dept. Superior Ct. of Arizona in Maricopa County, 1991-92; presiding judge probate and mental health dept. Superior Ct. of Ariz., Maricopa County, Ariz., 1992-95, presiding judge, 1995-2000; pro tem judge Ariz. Ct. Appeals; judge Ariz. Superior Ct., 1989—. Adj. prof. Ariz. State U. Sch. Law, 1997—; chmn. com. on exams and admissions Ariz. Supreme Ct., 1974-75, chmn. com. on character and fitness, 1975-76, mem. multi-state bar exam. com., 1976-85; bd. dirs. Nat. Conf. Met. Judges, 1997—, pres., 1998-99. Pres. Valley of Sun chpt. City of Hope, 1965-66, Cmty. Orgn. for Drug Abuse Control, 1972-73, Valley Big Bros., 1975; chmn. Mayors Ad Hoc Com. on Drug Abuse, 1974-75; bd. dirs. Maricopa County Legal Aid Soc., 1978, Phoenix Jewish Cmty. Ctr. Recipient award for outstanding svc. and dedication to improving the legal profession and professionalism of the bar and bench Maricopa County Bar Assn., 1999, Superior Svc. award Ariz. chpt. ASPA, 2000. Mem. ATLA (nat. chmn. gov.), Ariz. Bar Assn. (gov., com. chmn., sect. pres.), Maricopa County Bar Assn. (dir., pres. 1979-80), Ariz. Trial Lawyers Assn. (pres., dir., co-editor newsletter), Phoenix Trial Lawyers Assn. (pres., dir.), Western Trial Lawyers Assn. (pres. 1977), Am. Judicature Soc. (spl. merit citation outstanding svc. improvement of adminstrn. justice 1986), Am. Bd. Trial Advocates, Sandra Day O'Connor Inn of Ct. (pres. 1991-92). Office: Justice Ctr 201 W Jefferson St Phoenix AZ 85003-2205

MYERS, WALTER E. protective services official; Chief of police, Salem, Oreg. Office: 555 Liberty St SE Rm 130 Salem OR 97301-3513

MYERS, WILLIAM GERRY, III, lawyer; b. Roanoke, Va., July 13, 1955; s. William Gerry and Ruby Grey (Pollard) M.; m. Susan Louise Benzer, Aug. 27, 1988; children: Katherine Coulter, Molly Benzer. AB, Coll. of William and Mary, 1977; JD, U. Denver, 1981. Bar: Colo. 1981, Wyo. 1982, D.C. 1987, U.S. Supreme Ct. 1990, Idaho 1997. Assoc. Davis & Cannon, Sheridan, Wyo., 1981-85; legis. counsel U.S. Sen. Alan K. Simpson, 1985-89; asst. to atty. gen. U.S. dept. Justice, Washington, 1989-92; dep. gen. counsel for programs U.S. Dept. Energy, Washington, 1992-93; dir. fed. lands Nat. Cattlemen's Assn., 1993-97; exec. dir. Pub. Lands Coun., Washington, 1993-97; atty. Holland and Hart, Boise, 1997—. Guest lectr. Yale U., Georgetown U. Sch. Law, Am. U., U. Colo. Sch. Law, U. Idaho, Nat. Park Svc. Tng. Ctr., Nat. Acad. Scis., Grazing Lands Forum, Wyo. State Bar. Editl. staff Denver Law Jour., Denver Jour. Internat. Law and Policy; contbr. articles to profl. jours. Office: Holland and Hart 101 S Capitol Blvd Ste 1400 Boise ID 83702-7714 E-mail: wmyers@hollandhart.com

MYERSON, ALAN, film and television director; b. Cleve., Aug. 8, 1936; s. Seymour A. and Vivien I. (Caplin) M.; m. Irene Ryan, June 2, 1962; 1 son, Lincoln; m. Leigh French, May 15, 1977; children: Sierra Jasmine French-Myerson, Darcy Anna French-Myerson. Student, Pepperdine Coll., 1956-57, UCLA, 1957. Mem. drama faculty U. Calif., Berkeley, 1966, San Francisco State U., 1967 Dir. Broadway and Off Broadway Prodns., 1958-64, including This Music Crept By Me Upon the Waters, The Committee; dir.: Second City, N.Y.C. and Chgo., 1961, 62; founder, producer, dir. The Committee, San Francisco, L.A. and N.Y., 1963-74; dir.: (films) Steelyard Blues, 1972, Private Lessons, 1981, Police Academy 5, 1988, It's Showtime, 1976; numerous TV shows, 1975—, including Ally McBeal, Larry Sanders Show, Friends, Frazier, Picket Fences, Miami Vice, Dynasty, Bob Newhart Show, Laverne and Shirley; TV films The Love Boat, 1976, Hi, Honey, I'm Dead, 1991, Bad Attitudes, 1991, Holiday Affair, 1996. Active in civil rights, anti-war, anti-nuclear power movements, 1957— . Recipient Emmy nomination 1997, Cable ACE award nominations, 1995, 96, 97, TV Comedy award nomination Dirs. Guild, 1997. Mem. ASCAP, Acad. Motion Picture Arts and Scis., Acad. TV Arts and Scis., Dirs. Guild Am.

MYHRE, BYRON ARNOLD, pathologist, educator; b. Fargo, N.D., Oct. 22, 1928; s. Ben Arnold and Amy Lillian (Gilbertson) M.; m. Eileen Marguerite Scherling, June 16, 1953; children: Patricia Ann, Bruce Allen. B.S., U. Ill., 1950; M.S., Northwestern U., 1952, M.D., 1953; Ph.D., U. Wis., 1962. Intern Evanston (Ill.) Hosp., 1953-54; resident Children's Meml. Hosp., Chgo., 1956-57, U. Wis. Hosp., Madison, 1957-60; assoc. med. dir. Milw. Blood Ctr., 1962-66; sci. dir. L.A. Red Cross Blood Ctr., 1966-72; dir. Blood Bank Harbor-UCLA Med. Ctr., Torrance, Calif., 1972-85, chief clin. pathology, 1985-2000; prof. pathology UCLA, 1972-2000, prof. emeritus, 2000—. Author: Quality Control on Blood Banking, 1974, (with others) Textbook of Clinical Pathology, 1972, Paternity Testing, 1975; editor seminar procs.; contbr. articles to med. jours., chpts. to books. Served with USAF, 1954-56. Mem. AMA, Am. Soc. Clin. Pathology (dep. commr. commn. on continuing edn.), Am. Assn. Blood Banks (pres. 1978-79), Coll. Am. Pathologists (chmn. blood bank survey com.), Assn. Clin. Scientists (pres. 1993), Calif. Med. Assn., Calif. Blood Bank Systems (past pres.), Wis. Blood Bank Assn. (past pres.), L.A. Acad. Medicine (past pres.), Harbor-UCLA Faculty Soc. (past pres.), Palos Verdes Breadfast Club (past pres.). Home: 4004 Via Larga Vis Palos Verdes Peninsula CA 90274-1122 Office: Harbor UCLA Med Center 1000 W Carson St Torrance CA 90502-2004

MYHRVOLD, NATHAN, technology executive; B in Math., M in Geophysics and Space Physics, U. Calif., 1979; M in Math. Econs., Princeton U., 1981; D in Theoretical and Math. Physics, 1983. Fellow dept. applied math. and theoretical physics Cambridge U., 1981-83; founder, pres., CEO Dynamical Sys., 1984-86; dir. spl. projects Microsoft Corp., Redmond, Wash., 1986, v.p. applications and content; chief tech. officer Advanced Tech. and Rsch., Redmond, Microsoft Corp., Redmond; founder, mgr. Microsoft Rsch., chief tech. officer; pres. Intellectual Ventures, Bellevue, Wash. Bd. trustees Inst. Advanced Study, Princeton, N.J.; mem. Nat. Info. Infrastructure Adv. Coun.; adv. bd. Princeton U. dept. physics. Office: Intellectual Ventures 1422 130th Ave NE Bellevue WA 98005-2220

MYLROIE, WILLA WILCOX, transportation engineer, regional planner; b. Seattle, May 30, 1917; d. Elgin Roscoe and Ruth B. (Begg) Wilcox; m. John Ellis Mylroie (dec. 1947); children: Steven Wilcox Mylroie, Jo Mylroie Sohneronne; m. Donald Gile Fassett, Dec. 30, 1966. BS in Civil Engring., U. Wash., 1940, MS in Regional Planning, 1953. Lic. profl. civil engr. Civil engr. U.S. Engring. Dept. C.E., Seattle, 1941-46; affiliate prof. civil engring. U. Wash., Seattle, 1948-51, research asst. prof. civil engring., 1951-56; assoc. prof. civil engring. Purdue U., Lafayette, Ind., 1956-58; research engr. and planner Wash. State Dept. Hwys., Olympia, 1958-69; head research and spl. assignment div. Wash. State Dept. Transp., Olympia, 1969-81; adv. cons. civil engring. and regional planning Thurston County, Wash., 1981-97. Cons. King County Design Commn., Seattle, 1981-89; advisor Coll. Engring. U. Wash., 1978-86, affiliate prof. civil engring., 1981-84; advisor Wash. State U. Coll. Engring., Pullman, 1977-85. Active Girls Scouts county coun., Boy Scouts Am., Olympia, Renton, 1950-56; pres. high sch. PTA, Olympia; commr. Thurston County Planning Commn., Olympia; U.S. Coast Guard Auxilliary, 1982-89, U.S. Power Squadron, 1967—; citizen amb. People to People Trip, Moscow, St. Petersburg, Russia and Muensk, Bolarus. Recipient Profl. Recognition award Women's Transp., Spokane, Spl. Svc. award Transp. Rsch. Bd. Coun., Washington, U. Wash. Coll. Engring. Alumni Achievement award, 1993. Fellow ASCE (ad hoc vis. com. engring. coun. for profl. devel., Edmund Friedman Profl. Recognition award 1978), Inst. Transp. Engrs. (hon. mem., internat. bd. dirs., Tech. Coun. award 1982); mem. Planning Assn. Wash. (bd. dirs.), Sigma Xi. Avocations: sailing, gardening, travel, music, vol. community activities. Home and Office: 7501 Boston Harbor Rd NE Olympia WA 98506-9720

MYRLAND, DOUG, broadcast executive; BS in Bus. Adminstrn., St. Mary's Coll. Program dir., ops. mgr. KJZZ-FM, Phoenix; dir. broadcast and affiliate svcs., dir. mktg. Am. Pub. Radio, Mpls.; mktg. and comm. mgr. KPBS, San Diego, 1991-93, gen. mgr., sta. mgr., 1993—. Chmn. Chandler (Ariz.) Salvation Army Adv. Bd. Mem. Pub. Radio Program Dirs. Assn., Queen Creek, Ariz. Kiwanis, San Diego Rotary. Office: KPBS San Diego State U 5200 Campanile Dr San Diego CA 92182-1901

MYSTROM, RICK, mayor; m. Mary; children: Nick, Richard, Jenni. Mayor City of Anchorage, 1994-97; owner Am. Multiplex Properties; owner, pres. Mystrom Advertising. Mem. Advt. Fed. Ala. (pres.). Mem. PTA (pres.); pres./founder Big Brothers/Big Sisters of Anchorage; chmn. United Way Fund Dr.; co-chmn. Alaska H.S. Basketball Classic; mem. rotary, Anchorage Mcpl. Assembly (chmn, 1983-84). Recipient Boys and Girls Club Golden Man award, Nat. Multiple Sclerosis Soc. Hope award, Alaskan of the Year Denali award; named Alaskan Advt. Person of Year, Alaska Small bus. Person of Year, one of Am. top Three Small businessmen. Office: PO Box 196650 Anchorage AK 99519-6650

NABORS, JAMES THURSTON, actor, singer; b. Sylacauga, Ala., June 12, 1930; s. Fred Nabors. Grad. in bus. adminstrn., U. Ala. Formerly film editor, then jr. cutter for TV; singer at cabaret-theatre, The Horn, Santa Monica, Calif.; first TV appearance on Steve Allen Show; appeared in: own series Gomer Pyle-USMC, 1964-72, Andy Griffith Show, 1963-64, Jim Nabors Hour, 1969-71, Lost Saucer, 1975-76, Sylvan in Paradise, 1986, The Jim Nabors Show, 1987; TV guest appearances on Redd Foxx Show; dramatic appearances in The Rookies; night club headliner in Las Vegas and Lake Tahoe, Nev.; recs. include albums Very Special, The Special Warmth of Jim Nabors, 1986; also 16 single recs.; star: Jim Nabors Polynesian Extravaganza, Honolulu, 1979-81; movie appearances include The Best Little Whorehouse in Tex., 1982, Stroker Ace, 1983, Cannon Ball II, 1984; other TV work includes (movie) Return to Mayberry. Recipient 5 gold albums, 1 platinum album Office: c/o William Morris Agy 151 S El Camino Dr Beverly Hills CA 90212-2704

NACCHIO, JOSEPH P. communications executive; m. Anne Nacchio; children: David, Michael. BSEE, MBA, NYU; MS in Mgmt., MIT. Former head consumer and bus. market divsns. AT&T; chmn., CEO Qwest Comm. Internat. Inc., Denver, 1997—. Bd. dirs. Qwest Comm. Corp. Avocation: running. Office: Qwest Comm 1801 Calif St Denver CO 80202-5555

NACHT, SERGIO, biochemist; b. Buenos Aires, Apr. 13, 1934; came to U.S., 1965; s. Oscar and Carmen (Scheiner) N.; m. Beatriz Kahan, Dec. 21, 1958; children: Marcelo H., Gabriel A., Mariana S., Sandra M. BA in Chemistry, U. Buenos Aires, 1958, MS in Biochemistry, 1960, PhD in Biochemistry, 1964. Asst. prof. biochemistry U. Buenos Aires, 1960-64; asst. prof. medicine U. Utah, Salt Lake City, 1965-70; rsch. scientist Alza Corp., Palo Alto, Calif., 1970-73; sr. investigator Richardson-Vicks Inc., Mt. Vernon, N.Y., 1973-76, asst. dir., dir. rsch., 1976-83, dir. biomed. rsch. Shelton, Conn., 1983-87; sr. v.p. rsch. and devel. Advanced Polymer Sys., Redwood City, Calif., 1987-93, sr. v.p. sci. and tech., 1993-98, sr. v.p. dermatology and skin care, 1998-2000, Enhanced Derm Techs., Redwood City, 2000—. Lectr. dermatology dept. SUNY Downstate Med. Ctr., Blkyn., 1977-87. Contbr. articles to profl. jours.; patentee in field. Mem. Soc. Investigative Dermatology, Soc. Cosmetic Chemists (award 1981), Dermatology Found., Am. Physiol. Soc., Am. Acad. Dermatology. Democrat. Jewish. Home: 409 Wembley Ct Redwood City CA 94061-4308

NACKEL, JOHN GEORGE, technology executive; b. Medford, Mass., Nov. 4, 1951; s. Michael and Josephine (Maria) N.; m. Gail Helen Becker, Oct. 30, 1976; children: Melissa Anne, Allison Elizabeth. BS, Tufts U., 1973; MS in Pub. Health and Indsl. Engring., U. Mo., 1975, PhD, 1977. Sr. mgr. Ernst & Young, Chgo., 1977-83; nat. dir. health care cons. Cleve., 1983-87; regional dir. health industry svcs. Cleve., 1987-91; mng. dir. health care Ernst & Young, Cleve., 1991-93; mng. dir. Health Consulting, L.A., 1994-99, New Ventures, 1999-2000; exec. v.p. Cap Gemini Ernst & Young, L.A., 2000-01; CEO Sogeti USA, LLC, 2001—. Editorial bd. Jour. Med. Systems, 1983—. Author: Cost Management for Hospitals, 1987 (Am. Hosp. Assn. book award 1988); contbr. articles to profl. jours. Grantee Dept. Health Edn. Welfare, Washington, 1973-76. Fellow Am. Coll. Healthcare Execs., Healthcare Info. and Mgmt. Systems Soc. (articles award); mem. Inst. Indsl. Engrs. (sr.), U. Mo. health Svcs. Mgmt. Alumni Assn. (pres.), Canterbury Golf Club (Cleve.), L.A. Country Club, Annandale Golf Club, Jonathan Club. Republican. Avocations: golf, tennis, squash, paddle, photography. Home: 666 Linda Vista Ave Pasadena CA 91105-1145

NADLER, GEORGE L. orthodontist; b. Bklyn., Jan. 13, 1939; s. Rudolph M. and Hannah (Helfman) N.; m. Essie Rubinstein, June 4, 1961; children: Rudolph M., Eric Marc. Student, Bkly. Coll., 1956-59; DDS, NYU Coll. of Dentistry, 1963, postgrad., 1966-70. Diplomate Am. Bd. Orthodontia, 1979. Intern L.I. Coll. Hosp., Bklyn., 1963-64; pvt. practice Bklyn., 1966-70, Tucson, 1970—. Cons. El Rio Health Ctr., Tucson, 1973—. Contbr. articles to profl. jours. Cons. Ariz. Crippled Children Svc., Tucson, 1973—; exec. bd. Congregation Anshei Israel, 1988—. With USPHS, 1964-66. Fellow NIH, 1961, 62. Mem. ADA, Ariz. Dental Assn., So. Ariz. Dental Assn., Am. Assn. Orthodontists, Pacific Coast Orthodontic Assn., Ariz. Orthodontic Study Club, Tucson Orthodontic Study Club, Tucson Orthodontic Soc. (pres. 1980-81), Ariz. State Orthodontic Soc. (pres. 1988-90), Angle Orthodontic Soc., Golden Key, Skyline Country Club, Omicron Kappa Upsilon. Avocations: tennis, golf, gardening. Home: 6822 N Longfellow Dr Tucson AZ 85718-2422 Office: 5610 E Grant Rd Tucson AZ 85712-2239

NADLER, GERALD, management consultant, educator; b. Cin., Mar. 12, 1924; s. Samuel and Minnie (Krumbein) N.; m. Elaine Muriel Dubin, June 22, 1947; children: Burton Alan, Janice Susan, Robert Daniel. Student, U. Cin., 1942-43; BSME, Purdue U., 1945, MS in Indsl. Engring, 1946, PhD, 1949. Instr. Purdue U., 1948-49; asst. prof. indsl. engring. Washington U., St. Louis, 1949-52, assoc. prof., 1952-55, prof., head dept. indsl. engring., 1955-64; prof. U. Wis., Madison, 1964-83, chmn. dept. indsl. engring., 1964-67, 71-75; prof., chmn. dept. indsl. and sys. engring. U. So. Calif., L.A., 1983-93, IBM chair engring. mgmt., 1986-93, IBM chair emeritus, prof. emeritus, 1993—; v.p. Artcraft Mfg. Co., St. Louis, 1956-57; dir. Intertherm Inc., St. Louis, 1969-85. Pres. Ctr. for Breakthrough Thinking Inc., L.A., 1989—; vis. prof. U. Birmingham, Eng., 1959, Waseda U., Tokyo, 1963, Ind. U., 1964, U. Louvain, Belgium, 1975, Technion-Israel Inst. Tech., Haifa, 1976; speaker in field. Author: The Planning and Design Approach, 1981; (with S. Hibino) Breakthrough Thinking, 1990, 2d edit., 1994, Creative Solution Finding, 1995; (with G. Hoffherr, J. Moran) Breakthrough Thinking in Total Quality Management, 1994; contbr. articles to profl. jours.; reviewer books, papers, proposals. Mem. Ladue Bd. Edn., St. Louis County, 1960-63, L.A. County Quality and Productivity Commn., 1997—; chmn. planning com. Wis. Regional Med. Program, 1966-69; bd. dirs. USC Credit Union, 1994—. Served with USN, 1943-45. 24510894t Gilbreth medal Soc. Advancement Mgmt., 1961, Editorial award Hosp. Mgmt. Mag., 1966, Disting. Engring. Alumnus award Purdue U., 1975, Outstanding Indsl. Engr. award, 1997; Book of Yr. award Inst. Indsl. Engrs., 1983, Frank and Lillian Gilbreth award, 1992; Phi Kappa Phi Faculty Recognition award U. So. Calif., 1990, Engring. Disting. Svc. award U. Wis. Madison, 2000. Fellow AAAS, Inst. Indsl. Engrs. (pres. 1989-90), Inst. for Advancement Engrs., Am. Soc. Engring. Edn.; mem. NAE, Inst. Operations Rsch. and Mgmt. Scis., Japan Work Design Soc. (hon. adv. 1968—), World Futurs Soc., Acad. Mgmt. Soc., Engring. Mgmt. Soc., Sigma Xi, Alpha Pi Mu (nat. officer), Pi Tau Sigma, Omega Rho, Tau Beta Pi. Office: Univ Park GER 240 Dept Of I&se Los Angeles CA 90089-0193 E-mail: nadler@usc.edu

NADLER, HENRY LOUIS, pediatrician, geneticist, medical educator; b. N.Y.C., Apr. 15, 1936; s. Herbert and Mary (Kartiganer) N.; m. Benita Weinhard, June 16, 1957; children: Karen, Gary, Debra, Amy. A.B., Colgate U., 1957; M.D., Northwestern U., 1961; M.S., U. Wis., 1965. Diplomate: Am. Bd. Pediatrics, Am. Bd. Med. Genetics. Intern NYU Med. Ctr., 1961-62, sr. resident pediatrics, 1962-63, chief resident, 1963-64; teaching asst. NYU Sch. Medicine, 1962-63, clin. instr., 1963-64, U. Wis. Sch. Medicine, 1964-65; practice medicine specializing in pediatrics Chgo., 1965—; fellow Children's Meml. Hosp. dept. pediatrics Northwestern U., 1964-65; assoc. in pediatrics Northwestern U. Med. Sch., 1965-66, asst. prof., 1967-68, assoc. prof., 1968-70, prof., 1970-81, chmn. dept. pediatrics, 1970-81; prof. Northwestern U. Med. Sch. (Grad. Sch.), 1971-80; mem. staff Children's Meml. Hosp., 1965-81, head div. genetics, 1969-81, chief of staff, 1970-81; dean, prof. pediatrics, ob-gyn Wayne State U. Med. Sch., Detroit, 1981-88; prof. U. Chgo., 1988-89, U. Ill., 1989—; pres. Michael Reese Hosp. and Med. Ctr., Chgo., 1988-91; market med. dir. Aetna Health Plans, Phoenix, 1993-94, mktg. v.p., CEO, 1994-95; v.p. managed care/physician integration, med. dir. Am. Healthcare Sys., San Diego, 1995. Mem. vis. staff, div. medicine Northwestern Meml. Hosp., 1972-81; staff Children's Hosp. of Mich., 1981-88. Mem. editorial bd. Comprehensive Therapy, 1973-84, Am. Jour. Human Genetics, 1979-83, Pediatrics in Rev., 1980-83, Am. Jour. Diseases of Children, 1983-91; contbr. articles to profl. jours. Recipient E. Mead Johnson award for pediatric rsch., 1973, Meyer O. Cantor award for Disting. Svc. Internat. Coll. Surgeons, 1987; Irene Heinz Given and John La Porte Given rsch. prof. pediatrics, 1970-81. Fellow Am. Acad. Pediatrics; mem. Am. Soc. for Clin. Investigation, Am. Soc. Human Genetics, Am. Pediatric Soc., Soc. for Pediatric Rsch., Midwest Soc. for Pediatric Rsch., Pan Am. Med. Assn., Alpha Omega Alpha. Home and Office: 25150 N Windy Walk Dr Unit 23 Scottsdale AZ 85255-8105 E-mail: hlnadler@aol.com

NADY, JOHN, electronics company executive; b. Agfalva, Hungary, Feb. 13, 1945; came to U.S., 1951; s. John and Hermine Nady. BSEE, Calif. Inst. Tech., 1965; MSEE, U. Calif., Berkeley, 1968. Elec. engr. Lawrence Radiation Lab., Livermore, 1966-71, Westinghouse Corp., Oakland, Calif., 1971-72; owner, chief exec. officer Nady Systems, Inc., Oakland, 1976—, Calif. Concerts, Inc., Oakland, 1985-93. Patentee in field. Recipient Emmy award Pioneering Devel. Wireless Microphones, 1996. Mem. Nat. Assn. Broadcasters, Audio Engring. Soc., Nat. Assn. Music Merchants. Avocations: electric guitar, skiing, tennis, golfing. Office: Nady Systems Inc 6701 Shellmound St Emeryville CA 94608-1023

NAEGELE, CARL JOSEPH, university academic administrator, educator; b. Newark, Jan. 1, 1939; s. Carl Joseph Sr. and Mabel (Flood) N.; n. Elizabeth C. McVey, June 19, 1971; children: Jennifer, Erin. BS, Kean Coll., 1965; MS, Syracuse U., 1969; PhD, Cornell U., 1974. Tchr. physics Summit (N.J.) High Sch., 1965-68; instr. physics Kean Coll., Union, N.J., 1968-70; physics instr. Cornell U., Ithaca, N.Y., 1973-75; prof. Mich. State U., East Lansing, 1975-79; program dir. NSF, Washington, 1979-81, 91-92; dean coll. arts and scis. U. San Francisco, 1981-91; dir. Sci. Inst., 1984—; prof. physics and computer sci. U. San Francisco, 1981—. Computer cons. San Rafael, Calif., 1981—. Author: Physics for the Life and Health Sciences, 1974, Laboratory Experiment in General Physics, 1976, Electronic Mail and Communications Networks, 1984, Computer Systems and Applications, 1998, Experiments in Physical Science, 1998; contbr. articles to profl. jours. Served with U.S. Army, 1959-61, Korea. Recipient Outstanding Tchg. award Mich. State U., 1978, Leadership award U. San Francisco, 1985; grantee NSF, 1968, 78, 94-99, Coun. for Basic Edn., 1984-89. Mem. Am. Phys. Soc., Am. Assn. Physics Tchrs., Am. Assn. Univ. Adminstrs., Assn. for Computing Machinery. Avocations: flying, boating, skiing, tennis, running. Office: U San Francisco Coll Arts & Scis Ignatian Heights San Francisco CA 94117-1080

NAEGLE, SHIRL R. museum director; Dir. Nev. State Mus. and Hist. Soc., Las Vegas, 1991—. Office: Nev State Mus & Hist Soc State Mail Complex Las Vegas NV 89158-0001

NAFILYAN, GUY, vice president home building corporation; Grad., U. Paris. Lawyer, real estate law firm Paris; dir., France divn. Kaufman & Broad Home, 1977, sr. v.p., bd. dirs., 1987—, pres., CEO, France divn., exec. v.p. Bd. dirs. Fedn. Nat. des Promoteurs Constructeurs. Office: Kaufman & Broad Home 10990 Wilshire Blvd Fl 7 Los Angeles CA 90024-3913

NAGANO, KENT GEORGE, conductor; b. Morro Bay, Calif. BA in Sociology & Music (high honors), U of Calif., Santa Cruz; MA in Composition, San Francisco State U.; studied with, Laszlo Varga. Former asst. Opera Co. Boston; former prin. guest condr. Ensemble InterContemporain & the Dutch Radio Orch.; mus. dir. & condr. Berkeley Symphony, 1978—; mus. dir. Opéra de Lyon, 1989—; assoc. prin. & guest condr. LSO, London, England, 1990; mus. dir., prin. condr. designate Hallé Orch., England, 1991-94, mus. dir., prin. condr. England, 1994-2000, Deutsche Symphonie, Berlin, 2000—. Has performed with numerous orchestras around the world; recordings include: Songs of the Auvergne, Peter and the Wolf, Turandot and Arlecchino (Grammy nom.), La Boheme, Dialogues of the Carelites, The Death of Klinghoffer (Grammy nom.), Love for Three Oranges (Grammy nom.), Susannah (Grammy award), La damnation de Faust, The Rite of Spring, Rodrgue et chimene. Recipient Seaver/NEA Conducting award, 1985; Record of Yr. award Gramophone; named "officer" of France's Order of Arts and Letters, 1993. Office: Vincent Farrell & Assocs 157 W 57th St New York NY 10019-2210 also: Berkeley Symphony Berkeley CA 94704

NAGATA, ROLSTON H. state agency administrator; Dir. State of Hawaii, Dept. Land and Natural Resources, Honolulu, 1998—. Office: State Hawaii Divsn State Parks Dept Land & Nat Resources 1151 Punchbowl St Rm 310 Honolulu HI 96813

NAGATANI, PATRICK ALLAN RYOICHI, artist, art educator; b. Chgo., Aug. 19, 1945; s. John Lee and Diane Yoshiye (Yoshimura) N.; m. Rae Jeanean Bodwell, June 17, 1979; children: Methuen, Hart Gen, Louis-Thomas. BA, Calif. State U., L.A., 1967; MFA, UCLA, 1980. Cert. tchr. K-12, Calif. Instr. Alexander Hamilton High Sch., L.A., 1968-80, West. L.A. C.C., 1980-83; artist in residency Calif. Arts Coun., Juvenile Ct. and Cmty. Schs., L.A., 1986-87; instr. Otis Art Inst. Parson Sch. of Design, L.A., 1987; asst. prof. dept. art/art history Loyola Marymount U., L.A., 1980-87; prof. dept. art & art history U. N.Mex., Albuquerque, 1987—. Instr. Fairfax Cmty. Adult Sch., L.A., 1976-79; vis. artist/instr. The Sch. of the Art Inst., Chgo., 1983; conductor numerous seminars and workshops; lectr. in field. One man shows include Pal Gallery, Evergreen State U., Olympia, Wash., 1976, BC Space, Laguna Beach, Calif., 1978, Cityscape Gallery, Pasadena, Calif., 1978, Exploratorium Gallery, Calif. State U., L.A., 1979, Orange Coast Coll., Costa Mesa, Calif., 1980, Susan Spiritus Gallery, Newport Beach, Calif., 1981, 83, 85, Canon Photo Gallery, Amsterdam, The Netherlands, 1982, John Michael Kohler Arts Ctr., Sheboygan, Wis., 1983, 86, Arco Ctr. Visual Arts, L.A., 1983, Clarence Kennedy Gallery, Boston, 1984, Colo. Mountain Coll., Breckenridge, 1984, Jayne H. Baum Gallery, N.Y.C., 1985, 87, 89, 91, 94, Torch Gallery, Amsterdam, 1985, 87, Fotografie Forum Frankfurt, Fed. Rep. Germany, 1986, Frederick S. Wight Art Gallery, U. Calif., L.A., 1987, San Francisco Cameraworks, 1988, Koplin Gallery, L.A., 1988, 90, 92, 95, Shadai Gallery, Tokyo Inst. Polytech., 1989, Lubbock (Tex.) Fine Arts Ctr., 1990, Haggerty Mus. Art, Marquette U., Milw., 1991, Richard Levy Gallery, Albuquerque, 1992, Stanford (Calif.) Mus. Art, 1993, numerous others; exhibited in group shows at Friends of Photography, Carmel, Calif., 1976, 81, 85, Ctrl. Wash. State Coll., Ellensburg, 1977, Humboldt State U., Arcata, Calif., 1977, Soho/Cameraworks Gallery, L.A., 1978, Libra Gallery, Claremont (Calif.) Grad. Sch., 1978, Cirrus Gallery, L.A., 1979, Skidmore Coll. Art Gallery, Saratoga, N.Y., 1980, Tortue Gallery, Santa Monica, Calif., 1981, Palos Verdes (Calif.) Cmty. Art Ctr., 1982, Fine Arts Gallery, Cypress (Calif.) Coll., 1982, Fay Gold Gallery, Atlanta, 1982, Mus. Photographic Arts, San Diego, 1983, 84, Jayne H. Baum Gallery, N.Y.C., 1983, 87, Arco Ctr. Visual Art, L.A., 1984, Alt. Mus., N.Y.C., 1984, 88, Black Gallery, L.A., 1985, Mus. N.Mex., Santa Fe, 1986, Whitney Mus. Am. Art, Stamford, Conn., 1986, Balt. Mus. Art, 1987, Ctr. Photography, Woodstock, N.Y., 1988, Oakland Mus., Calif., 1989, Alinder Gallery, Gualala, Calif., 1990, 92, Coll. Santa Fe, 1990, Art Ctr., Waco, Tex., 1991, Lintas Worldwide, N.Y.C., 1991, Dirs. Guild of Am., L.A., 1992, Burden Gallery, N.Y.C., 1992, Nat. Arts Club, N.Y.C., 1992, Knoxville (Tenn.) Art Mus., 1993, G. Ray Hawkins Gallery, L.A., 1994, Houston FotoFest, 1994, Riverside (Calif.) Art Mus., 1994, Mass. Coll. Art, Boston, 1994, numerous others; represented in permanent collections Albuquerque Mus., Balt. Art Mus., Continental Ins., N.Y.C., Chrysler Mus. Art, Norfolk, Va., Denver Art Mus., Ga. Power Co., Atlanta, Honolulu Advertiser, L.A. County Mus. Art, Loyola Marymount U., L.A., Mass. Coll. Art, Boston, Met. Mus. Art, N.Y.C., Mus. Fine Arts, Houston, Mus. N.Mex., Santa Fe, Nev. Mus. Art, Reno, Oakland (Calif.) Mus., Prudential Ins. Co. Am., Newark, Roswell (N.Mex.) Mus., St. Louis Art Mus., Shearson/Am. Express, N.Y.C., Tampa (Fla.) Mus. Art, Tokyo Inst. Polytech., numerous others. Travel grantee Ford Found., 1979; Faculty Rsch. grantee Loyola Marymount U., L.A., 1981, 83, U. N.Mex., 1988, 90; Artist-In-Residence grantee Calif. Arts Coun., 1982-83; Visual Artist fellow Nat. Endowment for the Arts, 1984-85, 92-93; Brody Arts Fund fellow, 1986; Polaroid fellow, 1983-90; named Art Waves competition and exhbn. finalist Cmty. Redevel. Agy. L.A., 1987; recipient Calif. Disting. Artist award Nat. Art Edn. Assn. Conv., Mus. Contemporary Art, L.A., 1988, Kraszna-Krausz award and Photographic Book Innovation award Kraszna-Krausz Found., 1992. Avocations: gardening, gambling.

NAGEL, DARYL DAVID, retail executive; b. Arlington, Minn., Apr. 13, 1939; s. Paul Charles and Frieda L. (Oldenburg) N.; m. Joan Clare Dacey, Dec. 23, 1961; children: Kelly, Andrew, Maureen. BME, U. Minn., 1962; diploma in Advanced Mgmt. Program, Harvard U., 1978. Asst. mdse. mgr. Res. Supply Co., Mpls., 1962-65, mdse. mgr., 1965-66, v.p., gen. mgr., 1966-69; v.p. area gen. mgr. United Bldg. Ctrs., Winona, Minn., 1969-78, exec. v.p., chief ops. officer, 1978-84, pres., CEO, 1984-87, Lanoga Corp., Seattle, 1987-2001, ret., 2001. Bd. dirs. Lanoga Corp., Seattle, 1987—, Badger Foundry, Winona, 1984-87. Bd. dirs. United Way, Winona, 1978-84; chmn. Home Ctr. Inst., 1997-99. Mem. Home Ctr. Leadership Coun., C. of C. (bd. dirs. 1964-69, 73, 78), Sahalee Country Club. Republican. Lutheran. Avocations: golf, gardening, skiing.

NAGLER, MICHAEL NICHOLAS, classics and comparative literature educator; b. N.Y.C., Jan. 20, 1937; s. Harold and Dorothy Judith (Nocks) N.; m. Roberta Ann Robbins (div. May 1983); children: Jessica, Joshua. BA, NYU, 1960; MA, U. Calif., Berkeley, 1962, PhD, 1966. Instr. San Francisco State U., 1963-65; prof. classics, peace studies and comparative lit. U. Calif., Berkeley, 1966-91, prof. emeritus, 1991—. Author: Spontaneity and Tradition, 1974, America Without Violence, 1982, Is There No Other Way: The Search for a Nonviolent Future, 2001; co-author: The Upanishads, 1987; contbr. articles to profl. publs. Pres. bd. dirs. METTA Ctrs. for Nonviolence Edn. Fellow Am. Coun. Learned Socs., NIH; MacArthur Found. grantee, 1988. Mem. Am. Philolog. Soc. (editor Oral Tradition). Office: U Calif Peace and Conflict Studies Berkeley CA 94720-0001 E-mail: mnagler@igc.org

NAGRIN, DANIEL, dancer, educator, choreographer, lecturer, writer; b. N.Y.C., May 22, 1917; s. Harry Samuel and Clara (Wexler) N.; m. Helen Tamiris, 1946 (dec. 1966); m. Phyllis A. Steele, Jan. 24, 1992. BS in Edn., CCNY, 1940; DFA, SUNY, Brockport, 1991; DHL, Ariz. State U., 1992; studied dance with Martha Graham, Anna Sokolow, Helen Tamiris, Mme. Anderson-Ivantzova, Nenette Charisse and Edward Caton, studied acting with Miriam Goldina, Sanford Meisner and Stella Adler, , 1936-56. Tchr. Silvermine Guild Art, New Canaan, Conn., 1957-66, SUNY, Brockport, 1967-71, U. Md., College Park, 1970, Davis Ctr. Performing Arts, CCNY, 1973-75, Nat. Theatre Inst., Eugene O'Neill Found., Waterford, Conn., 1974, Hartmann Theatre Conservatory, Stamford, 1975-77; long-term resident tchr., Nat. Endowment for Arts sponsorship U. Hawaii, 1978-80, tchr., 1981, Bill Evans Dance Workshop, Seattle, 1981; prof. dance dept. Ariz. State U., Tempe, 1982-92; tchr. grad. liberal studies program Wesleyan U., Middletown, Conn., 1984, Dance Workshop for Movement Rsch., N.Y.C., 1984, Improvisation Workshop, Seattle, 1985, Improvisation, Choreography and Acting Technique for Dancers, Seattle, 1985, Dance Workshop, Glenwood Springs, Colo., 1990; prof. emeritus dance Ariz. State U., 1992. Tchr. summer sessions Conn. Coll., New London, 1959, 74; Am. Dance Festival at Conn. Coll., 1960, 77, Duke U., Durham, N.C., 1978, 80, 82, 87, 88, 92, Balasaraswati/Joy Ann Dewey Beinecke Chair Dising. Tchg., 1992; summer dance program Conn. Coll., 1979, E. La Tour Dance Workshop, Sedgewick, 1982, 83; dance workshop U. Minn. at Mpls., 1984, Stanford U., 1990; co-dir. Tamiris-Nagrin Summer Dance Workshop, Sedgewick, 1960-61, (with Tamiris) summer dance session C. W. Post Coll., Greenville, N.Y., 1962-63; dir. summer dance workshop Johnson (Vt.) State Coll., 1972, 73, 75, 76. Featured dance soloist on Broadway: Annie Get Your Gun, Lend an Ear, Touch and Go, Plain and Fancy (Billboard Donaldson award 1954-55), 1940-56; appearance in film, Just for You; adapted and performed one-man theatre piece The Fall, from novel by Albert Camus, 1977-79, choreographer (solo works) Spanish Dance, 1948, Man of Action, 1948, Strange Hero, 1948, Indeterminate Figure, 1957, With My Eye and With My Hand, 1968, Jazz: Three Ways, 1958, 66, Path-Silence, 1965, Not Me, But Him, 1965, The Peloponesian War, 1967-68, Untitled, 1974, Ruminations, 1976, Getting Well, 1978, Poems Off the Wall, 1981, Apartment 18C, 1993, Crosscurrents, 1997, Lost and Never Found, 1998, Someone for Theater X, Tokyo, Japan, What Did You Say?, 2001, others; (for groups) Faces from Walt Whitman, 1950, An American Journey, 1962; asst. choreographer original Broadway prodns.: Up in Central Park, Stovepipe Hat, Show Boat, Annie Get Your Gun, By the Beautiful Sea, others; dir. off-Broadway: Volpone, 1957, The Firebugs, 1960, The Umbrella, 1961, Emperor Jones, (Boston), 1963, others; film choreography: His Majesty O'Keefe: acted in video The Art of Memory, 1985, play, Three Stories High, others; extensive touring U.S., Europe, The Pacific, and Japan, 1957-84; conceived and directed videos: Steps, 1972, The Edge is Also a Circle, 1973, Nagrin Videotape Library of Dances, 1985; author: How to Dance Forever: Surviving Against the Odds, 1988, Dance and the Specific Image: Improvisation, 1993, The Six Questions: Acting Technique for Dance Performance, 1997. With spl. svcs. Army Airforce, 1942-43. Grantee Rebekah Harkness Found., 1962, Logan Found., 1965, N.Y. State Coun. on Arts and Nat. Found. for Arts and Humanities, 1967-68, N.Y. State Coun. on Arts, 1971-72, 73-74, 75-76, 76-77, 78-79, 80-81, Anne S. Richardson Fund, 1971, 73, 74, 75, 76, 78, Nat. Endowment for Arts, 1975, 79, 81, 83, Ariz. State U., 1983, 84, 85, 86,

88; CAPS fellow N.Y. State Coun. on Arts, 1977-78; fellow NEA, 1977-78, 80, 82, 83, 90, 91, Minn. McKnight Nat. fellow, 1996-97; commd. ballet Rebekah Harkness Ballet Found., 1986. Mem. Actors' Equity, Phi Kappa Phi (hon.). Avocation: reading. Home and Office: 208 E 14th St Tempe AZ 85281-6707 Fax: (480) 829-3933. E-mail: nagrin@imap2.asu.edu

NAGY, BOB, editor periodical; Exec. editor Motor Trend, L.A., 1983—. Office: Motor Trend 6420 Wilshire Blvd Fl 7 Los Angeles CA 90048-5502

NAGY, STEPHEN MEARS, JR. physician, allergist; b. Yonkers, N.Y., Apr. 1, 1939; s. Stephen Mears and Olga (Zahoruiko) N.; m. Branda Yu Nagy, 1966; children: Catherine, Stephen III. BA, Princeton U., 1960; MD, Tufts U., 1964. Diplomate Am. Bd. Internal Medicine, Am. Bd. Allergy and Immunology. Pvt. practice, Sacramento, 1971-2000; prof. Sch. Medicine U. Calif., Davis, 1974—. Author, editor Evaluation & Management of Allergic and Asthmatic Diseases, 1981; mem. editl. bd. Clinical Reviews in Allergy; creator Famous Teachings in Modern Medicine-Allergy Series slide collection. Capt. U.S. Army, 1966-68, Vietnam. Fellow Am. Acad. Allergy, Am. Coll. Allergy; mem. CMA, Sacramento-El Dorado Med. Soc. (bd. dirs. 1971-95, 1989-95). Avocations: cycling, book collecting, opera, fencing. Office: 4801 J St Ste A Sacramento CA 95819-3746

NAHAT, DENNIS F. artistic director, choreographer; b. Detroit, Feb. 20, 1946; s. Fred H. and Linda M. (Haddad) N. Hon. degree, Juilliard Sch. Music, 1965. Prin. dancer Joffrey Ballet, N.Y.C., 1965-66; prin. dancer Am. Ballet Theatre, N.Y.C., 1968-79; co-founder Cleve. Ballet, 1976, Sch. of Cleve. Ballet, 1972; founder, artistic dir. San Jose Cleve. Ballet, 1985, Sch. Cleve. San Jose Ballet, 1996; founder New Sch. of Cleve. San Jose Ballet, 1996—. Co-chair Artists Round Table Dance USA, 1991; trustee Cecchetti Coun. Am., 1991; mem. adv. bd. Ohio Dance Regional Dance Am. Prin. performer Broadway show Sweet Charity, 1966-67; choreographer Two Gentlemen of Verona (Tony award 1972), 1969-70; (ballet) Celebrations and Ode (resolution award 1985), 1985, Green Table, Three Virgins and a Devil (Isadora Duncan award 1985); conceived, directed, choreographed Blue Suede Shoes, PBS, 1997-98. Grantee Nat. Endowment Arts, 1978, Andrew Mellow Found., 1985; recipient Outstanding Achievement award Am. Dance Guild, 1995, 96, 2000—. Avocation: master chef. Office: Cleve San Jose Ballet 3615 Euclid Ave Ste 1A Cleveland OH 44115-2527 also: Cleve San Jose Ballet PO Box 1666 San Jose CA 95109-1666 also: San Jose Cleve Ballet 40 N 1st St San Jose CA 95113-1200

NAHMAN, NORRIS STANLEY, electrical engineer; b. San Francisco, Nov. 9, 1925; s. Hyman Cohen and Rae (Levin) N.; m. Shirley D. Maxwell, July 20, 1968; children: Norris Stanley, Vicki L., Vance W., Scott T. B.S. in Electronics Enging, Calif. Poly. State U., 1951; M.S.E.E., Stanford U., 1952; Ph.D. in Elec. Enging, U. Kans., 1961. Registered profl. engr., Colo. Electronic scientist Nat. Security Agy., Washington, 1952-55; prof. elec. enging., dir. electronics rsch. lab. U. Kans., Lawrence, 1955-66; sci. cons., chief pulse and time domain sect. Nat. Bur. Standards, Boulder, Colo., 1966-73, chief time domain metrology, sr. scientist, 1975-83, group leader field characterization group, 1984-85; v.p. Picosecond Pulse Labs, Inc., Boulder, 1986-90, scientific advisor, co-chair tech. adv. bd., 1990—; cons. elec. engr., 1990—; prof., chmn. dept. elec. engring. U. Toledo, 1973-75;; prof. elec. enging. U. Colo., Boulder, 1966—; affiliate staff Los Alamos (N.Mex.) Nat. Lab., 1990—. Disting. lectr., prin. prof. Ctr. Nat. d' Etude des Telecomm. Summer Sch., Lannion France, 1978; disting. lectr. Harbin Inst. Tech., Peoples Republic China, summer 1982; mem. faculty NATO Advanced Study Inst., Castelvecchio, Italy, 1983, Internat. Radio Sci. Union/NRC; chmn. Internat. Intercomm. Group Waveform Measurements, 1981-90, chmn. Commn. A, 1985-86. Contbr. rsch. articles profl. jours.; patentee in field. Asst. scoutmaster Longs Peak coun. Boy Scouts Am., 1970-73, 75-89. With U.S. Mcht. Marine, 1943-46, U.S. Army, 1952-55. Ford Found. faculty fellow MIT, 1962; Nat. Bur. Standards sr. staff fellow, 1978-79; recipient Disting. Alumnus award Calif. Poly. State U., 1972, Order of Arrow Boy Scouts Am., 1976. Fellow IEEE (life), Internat. Sci. Radio Union; mem. Instrumentation and Measurement Soc. of IEEE (admstrv. com. 1982-84, editorial bd. Trans., 1982-86, Andrew H. chi Best Tech. Paper award 1984, Tech. Leadership and Achievement award 1987), Am. Assn. Engring. Edn., U.S. Mcht. Marine Veterans World War II, Am. Legion, Calif. Poly. State U. Alumni Assn. (life), Stanford U. (life), U. Kans. (life), Am. Radio Relay League Club (life), Sigma Pi Sigma, Tau Beta Pi, Eta Kappa Nu, Sigma Tau, Sigma Xi. E-mail: nsnahman@ieee.org

NAIDORF, LOUIS MURRAY, architect; b. Los Angeles, Aug. 15, 1928; s. Jack and Meriam (Abbott) N.; m. Dorise D. Roberts, June 1948 (div.); children: Victoria Beth Naidorf-Slifer; m. Patricia Ann Shea, June 1, 1968 (div.); m. Patricia Ruth Allen, Dec. 6, 1992. BA, U. Calif., Berkeley, 1949, MA, 1950; Doctorate (hon.), Woodbury U., 2000. Registered architect, Calif. Designer Welton Becket Assocs., L.A., 1950-51, Pereira and Luckman, L.A., 1951-52; project designer Welton Becket Assocs., L.A., 1952-55, sr. project designer, 1955-59, v.p. asst., dir. design, 1959-70, sr. v.p., dir. rsch., 1970-73; sr. v.p., design prin. Ellerbe Becket Assocs., L.A., 1973-95; dean Sch. Architecture and Design Woodbury U., L.A., 1990-2000. Mem. peer rev. panel Nat. Endowment Arts, 1995—; vis. lectr. Calif. Poly. Sch. Architecture, San Luis Obispo, 1975-82; instr. UCLA Sch. Architecture, 1985, UCLA Landscape Archtl. Program, 1980-85, Otis-Parsons, L.A., 1986-92. Prin. works include Capitol Records Bldg., Century City, Los Angeles, Hyatt Regency, Dallas, Restoration Calif. State Capitol Bldg. Bd. dirs. Inst. for Garden Studies, L.A., 1986—, ARC, 2000; trustee Woodbury U., 2000. Recipient Honor award Nat. Trust for Hist. Preservation, 1985. Fellow AIA (bd. dirs. Los Angeles chpt. 1977-79, Silver Medal 1950, Nat. Honor award 1985, Educator of Yr. 1997). Office: Woodbury Univ 7500 N Glenoaks Blvd Burbank CA 91504-1099

NAIMARK, NORMAN M. academic administrator; b. N.Y.C. BA, Stanford U., 1966, PhD, 1972. Prof. History Boston U.; fellow Russian Rsch. Ctr. Harvard U., 1994-97; former vis. Catherine Wasserman Davis chair of Slavic Studies Wellesley Coll.; Robert and Florence McDonnell chair in East European Studies Stanford U. Chmn. dept. History, sr. fellow Hoover Instn.; dir. Stanford's Ctr. Russian and East European Studies; joint com. Am. Coun. Learned Soc.; program com. Internat. Rsch. and Exchange Corp.; exec. com. Am. Assn. Advancement Slavic Studies. Author: The Russians in Germany, 1995, Terrorists and Social Democrats, 1983; lectr., author, co-editor in field. Grantee IREX, ACLS, Alexander von Humbolt Fund, Fulbright-Hays, Nat. Coun. Soviet and East European Studies, Hist. Commn. in Berlin; recipient Officer's Cross of Order of merit, Fed. Republic of Germany, 1996, Richard W. Lyman award, 1995. Office: Stanford U Dept History Stanford CA 94305

NAKAMURA, ROBERT MOTOHARU, pathologist; b. Montebello, Calif., June 10, 1927; s. Mosaburo and Haru (Suematsu) N.; m. Shigeyo Jane Hayashi, July 29, 1957; children: Mary, Nancy. AB, Whittier Coll., 1949; MD, Temple U., 1954. Cert. of spl. qualification in pathologic anatomy, clin pathology, immunopathology, Am. Bd. Pathology. Prof. pathology U. Calif., Irvine, 1971-74, adj. prof. pathology, 1974-75; chmn. dept. pathology Scripps Clinic and Rsch. Found., La Jolla, Calif., 1974-92; sr. cons., 1992—; pres. Scripps Clinic Med. Group, La Jolla, 1981-91; prof. dept. immunology and exptl. and molecular medicine Scripps Rsch. Inst., 1997-99; chmn. pathology Scripps Clinic, 1998-99, chmn. emeritus pathology 1999— Adj prof pathology U Calif San Diego 1975-93 Author editor profl. publs.; co-editor Jr. Clin. Lab. Analysis, 1989—. Fellow: Coll. Am. Pathologists, Am. Soc. Clin. Pathologists, Assn. Clin. Scientists, Am. Coll. Nutrition; mem. Internat. Acad. Pathology. Avocation: reading. [illegible]

NAKANISHI, DON TOSHIAKI, Asian American studies educator, writer; b. L.A., Aug. 14, 1949; m. Marsha Hirano; 1 child, Thomas. BA in Polit Sci. cum laude, Yale U., 1971; PhD in Polit. Sci., Harvard U., 1978. Instr. dept. urban studies Yale U., 1971; lectr. Coun. on Ednl. Devel. UCLA, 1973, instr. Asian Am. Studies Ctr., 1974, acting asst. prof. dept. polit. sci., 1975-78; vis. scholar Sophia U., Inst. Internat. Relations, Tokyo, 1978-89; adj. asst. prof. dept. polit. sci. UCLA, 1979-82, asst. rschr. Asian Am. Studies Ctr., 1979-82, from asst. prof. to full prof. Grad. Sch. Edn., 1982—, assoc. dir. Asian Am. Studies Ctr., 1985-87, chair interdepartmental program Asian Am. studies, 1989-90, dir. Asian Am. Studies Ctr., 1990—. Co-founder and publr. Amerasia Jour., 1970-75, edtl. bd., 1975—; researcher Social Sci. Rsch. Coun. of N.Y. and the Japan Soc. for the Promotion of Sci. of Tokyo Joint-Project on Am.-Japanese Mut. Images, 1971-73; mem. Asian Am. task force for social studies guideline evaluation, Calif. State Dept. Edn., 1973; guest spkr. Ctr. for the Study of Ednl. Policy, Grad. Sch. Edn., Harvard U., 1974, Metropathways, Ethni-City Sch. Desegregation Program, Boston, 1974; researcher, co-project chair Hispanic Urban Ctr., Project Sch. Desegregation, L.A., 1974; numerous coms. UCLA; numerous conf. chmns.; cons., rschr., speaker, presenter in field. Co-editor: (with Marsha J. Hirano-Nakanishi) The Education of Asian and Pacific Americans: Historical Perspectives and Prescriptions for the Future, 1983, (with Halford H. Fairchild, Luis Ortiz-Franco, Lenore A. Stiffarm) Discrimination and Prejudice: An Annotated Bibliography, 1991, (with Tina Yamano Nishida) The Asian Pacific American Educational Experience: A Sourcebook for Teachers and Students, 1995, (with James Lai) National Asian Pacific American Political Almanac, 1996, 98, 2000; contbr. numerous articles to profl. jours., monographs, book reviews and reports. Chair Yale U. Alumni Schs. Com. of So. Calif., 1978—; bd. dirs. Altamed and La Clinica Familiar Del Barrio of East L.A., 1982—; commr. Bd. Transp. Commrs., City of L.A., 1984-90; v.p. Friends of the Little Tokyo Pub. Libr., 1986-88; co-chair nat. scholars adv. com. Japanese Am. Nat. Mus., 1987—; mem., bd. govs. Assn. of Yale Alumni, 1988-91; mem. exec. coun. Mayor's LA's Best Aftersch. Program, City of Los Angeles, 1988-90. Rsch. fellow Japan Soc. for the Promotion of Sci., 1978; recipient Nat. Scholars awrd for Outstanding Rsch. Article on Asian Pacific Am. Edn., Nat. Assn. for Asian and Pacific Am. Edn., 1985, Civil Rights Impace award Asian Am. Legal Ctr. of So. Calif., 1989; grantee Chancellors' Challenge in the Arts and Humanities, 1991, Calif. Policy Seminar, 1992, U. Calif. Pacific Rim Studies, 1992; recipient numerous other research and conference grants. Mem. Nat. Assn. for Interdisciplinary Ethnic Studies (bd. dirs. 1976-79), Assn. Asian Am. Studies (nat. pres. 1983-85), Nat. Assn. for Asian and Pacific Am. Edn. (exec. bd. dirs., v.p. 1983—). Home: 4501 N Berkshire Ave Los Angeles CA 90032 Office: UCLA Asian Am Studies Ctr 3230 Campbell Ave Los Angeles CA 90024-1546 E-mail: dtn@ucla.edu

NAKATA, ROBERT, state legislator; b. Apr. 2, 1941; m. JoAnna Nakata; children: Michelle, Sarah Angelina. BS in Physics, U. Hawaii at Manoa, 1963, Ms in Physics, 1965; MDiv, Union Theol. Sem., 1972. Meth. min.; cmty. planner Kokua Kalihi Valley; mem. Hawaii Ho. of Reps., Honolulu, 1982-86, Hawaii Senate, Dist. 23, Honolulu, 1986—; chair labor and environ. com., mem. ways and means com. Hawaii Senate, Honolulu, mem. water, land, and Hawaiian affairs com. Mem. Minami County Found. Bd.; mem. adv. bd. Hawaii Cmty. Found.; mem. nat. adv. bd. Meth. Cmty. Devel. Program. Democrat. Office: State Capitol 415 S Beretania St Honolulu HI 96813-2407

NAKAYAMA, PAULA AIKO, state supreme court justice; b. Honolulu, Oct. 19, 1953; m. Charles W. Totto; children: Elizabeth Murakami, Alexander Totto. BS, U. Calif., Davis, 1975; JD, U. Calif., 1979. Bar: Hawaii 1979. Dep. pros. atty. City and County of Honolulu, 1979-82; ptnr. Shim, Tam & Kirimitsu, Honolulu, 1982-92; judge 1st Cir. Ct. State of Hawaii, Oahu, 1992-93; justice State of Hawaii Supreme Ct., Honolulu, 1993—. Mem. Am. Judicature Soc., Hawaii Bar Assn., Sons and Daughters of 442. Office: Ali'iolani Hale Hawaii Supreme Ct 417 S King St Honolulu HI 96813-2902

NALCIOGLU, ORHAN, physics educator, radiological sciences educator; b. Istanbul, Turkey, Feb. 2, 1944; came to U.S., 1966, naturalized, 1974; s. Mustafa and Melina Nalcioglu. BS, Robert Coll., Istanbul, 1966; MS, Case Western Res. U., 1968; PhD, U. Oreg., 1970. Postdoctoral fellow dept. physics U. Calif., Davis, 1970-71; rsch. assoc. dept. physics U. Rochester, N.Y., 1971-74, U. Wis., Madison, 1974-76; sr. physicist EMI Med. Inc., Northbrook, Ill., 1976-77; prof. depts. radiol. scis., elec. engring., medicine and phs U. Calif., Irvine, 1977—, head divsn. physics and engring., 1985—, dir. biomed. magnetic resonance rsch., 1987—, dir. Rsch. Imaging Ctr., 1992—. Cons. UN, 1980-86; gen. chmn. IEEE Nuclear Sci. Symposium and Med. Imaging Conf., 1996, 99. Editor several books; guest editor IEEE Nuclear Sci. Symposium and Med. Imaging Conf., 1997; contbr. articles to profl. jours. Mobil scholar, 1961-66; recipient Athalie Clarke award for rsch. excellence, 2001. Fellow IEEE (pres. Nuclear and Plasma Scis. Soc. 1993-94, Millennium medal 2000, NPSS Richard Shea award 2000), Am. Assn. Physicists in Medicine, Internat. Soc. Magnetic Resonance in Medicine; mem. Nuclear and Plasma Scis. Soc., Internat. Soc. Maj. Rsch. in Medicine. Office: U Calif Health Scis Rsch Imaging Ctr Irvine CA 92697-0001

NALDER, ERIC CHRISTOPHER, investigative reporter; b. Coulee Dam, Wash., Mar. 2, 1946; s. Philip Richard and Mibs Dorothy (Aurdal) N.; m. Jan Christiansen, Dec. 20, 1968; 1 child, Britt Hillary. BA in Communications, U. Wash., 1968. News editor Whidbey News-Times, Oak Harbor, Wash., 1971; reporter Lynnwood (Wash.) Enterprise, 1972, Everett Herald, Lynnwood, 1972-75; gen. assignment reporter Seattle Post-Intelligencer, 1975-78, edn. writer, 1977-78, investigative reporter, 1978-83; chief investigative reporter Seattle Times, 1983-2001; investigative reporter San Jose Mercury News, 2001—. Author: Tankers Full of Trouble, 1994. Recipient Edn. Writers Assn. award Charles Stewart Mott Found., 1978, Hearst Comty. Svc. award, 1978, C.B. Blethen awards (13), Outstanding Govt. Reporting award Seattle Mcpl. League, Pub. Svc. in Journalism award Sigma Delta Chi, 1987, Edward J. Meeman award Scripps Howard Found., 1987, Thomas Stokes award, Washington Journalism Ctr., 1990, Pulitzer prize for nat. reporting, 1990, Nat. Headline award, 1991, AP Sports Editors' Investigative Reporting award, 1992, Pub. Svc. award AP Mags. Editors Assn., 1992, Goldsmith prize for investigative reporting, 1992, Worth Bingham prize for investigative reporting, 1992, Headliner award, 1992, Investigative Reporters and Editors award, 1992, 95, Silver Gavel award ABA, 1995, Pulitzer prize for investigative reporting, 1997, John B. Oakes award for disting. environ. journalism, 1998, Edward J. Meeman award, Scripps Howard Found., 1999, Robert L. Kozik award Nat. Press Club, 1999, Susan Hutchinson Bosch award Soc. for Profl. Journalism, 2000, Headliner award and Best of the West in Investigative Reporting, 2000, Clarion award for investigative series, Headliner award, 2000. Mem. Investigative Reporters and Editors, Pacific N.W. Newspaper Guild. Avocation: downhill skiing. Office: Seattle Times 1120 John St Seattle WA 98109-5321 Address: PO Box 70 Seattle WA 98111-0070

NANAO, KENJILO, artist, educator; b. Aomori, Japan, July 26, 1929; came to U.S., 1960; s. Yosaburo Hirano and Tama Nanao; m. Gail Carol Chadell, Aug. 24, 1965; 1 child, Max Harunobu. Student, Nihon U., Tokyo, 1950-53, Calif. Sch. Fine Arts, San Francisco, 1960-63; MFA, San Francisco Art Inst., 1970. Lectr. art San Jose (Calif.) State U., 1970; prof. art Calif. State U., Hayward, 1970-91, prof. emeritus, 1991—. Vis. prof. U. N.H., 1973, Stanford U., 1992. One-man shows include Tsubaki Kindai Gallery, Tokyo, 1965, Smith Andersen Gallery, Palo Alto, Calif., 1971, 74, 78, 80, 88, Santa Barbara Mus., 1977, [illegible] 1973, Dubins Gallery, L.A., 1985, 86, 89, 92, others; exhibited in group shows at Gump's Gallery, San Francisco, 1971-76, Anchorage Fine Arts and Hist. Mus., 1976, Bklyn. Mus., 1976, 78, Crocker Art Mus., Sacramento, Calif., 1980, Palo Alto Cultural Ctr., 1992, Galerie Sho, Tokyo, 1994, J.J. Brookings Gallery, San Francisco, 1997, others; represented in permanent collections Biblioteque Nationale, Paris, Mus. Modern Art, N.Y.C., Libr. of Congress, Washington, Nat. Gallery of Art, Washington, others. Recipient 4 Purchase prizes Honolulu Acad. Arts, 1973-78, Purchase prize City of Phila., 1973, Bklyn. Mus. Art, 1972; Ford Found. grantee, 1968; Nat. Endowment for the Arts fellow, 1980. Home: 640 Santa Rosa Ave Berkeley CA 94707-1547

NANDA, VED PRAKASH, law educator, university official; b. Gujranwala, India, Nov. 20, 1934; came to U.S., 1960; s. Jagan Nath and Attar (Kaur) N.; m. Katharine Kunz, Dec. 18, 1982; 1 child, Anjali. MA, Punjab U., 1952; LLB, U. Delhi, 1955, LLM, 1958, Northwestern U., 1962; postgrad., Yale U., 1962-65; LLD, Soka U., Tokyo, 1997, Bundelkhand U., Jhansi, India, 2000. Asst. prof. law U. Denver, 1965-68, assoc. prof., 1968-70, prof. law, dir. Internat. Legal Studies Program, 1970—, Thompson G. Marsh prof. law, 1987—, Evans Univ. prof., 1992—, asst. provost, 1993-94, vice provost, 1994—; sst. prof. law . Denver, 965-68, ssoc. prof., 968-70, rof. law, dir. Internat. Legal Studies Program, 970—, hompson G. Marsh prof. law, 987—, vans Univ. prof., 992—, sst. provost, 993-94, ice provost, 994—. Is. prof. Coll. Law, U. Iowa, Iowa City, 1974-75, Fla. State U., 1973, U. San Diego, 1979, U. Colo., 1992; disting. vis. prof. internat. law Chgo. Kent Coll. Law, 1981, Calif. We. Sch. Law, San Diego, 1983-84; disting. vis. scholar Sch. Law, U. Hawaii, Honolulu, 1986-87; cons. Solar Energy Rsch. Inst., 1978-81, Dept. Energy, 1980-81. Uthor: (with David Pansius) Litigation of International Disputes in U.S. Courts, 1987; editor: (with M. Cherif Bassiouni) A Treatise on International Criminal Law, 2 vols., 1973, Water Needs for the Future, 1977; (with George Shepherd) Human Rights and Third World Development, 1985; (with others) Global Human Rights, 1981, The Law of Transnational Business Transactions, 1981, World Climate Change, 1983, Breach and Adaption of International Contracts, 1992, World Debt and Human Conditions, 1993, Europe Community Law After 1992, 1993, International Environmental Law and Policy, 1995; (with William M. Evan) Nuclear Proliferation and the Legality of Nuclear Weapons, 1995, (with others) European Union Law After Maastricht, 1996, (with S.P. Sinha) Hindu Law and Legal Theory, 1996, (with D. Krieger) Nuclear Weapons and the World Court, 1998; editor, contbr.: Refugee Law and Policy, 1989; editl. bd. Jour. Am. Comparative Law, Indian Jour. Internat. Law, Transnational Pubs. O-chmn. Colo. Pub. Broadcasting Fedn., 1977-78; mem. Gov.'s Commn. on Pub. Telecommunications, 1980-82. Em. World Jurist Assn. (v.p. 1991—, pres. 1997—), World Assn. Law Profs. (pres. 1987-93), UN Assn. (v.p. Colo. divsn. 1973-76, pres. 1986-88, 93-96, nat. coun. UNA-USA 1990—, mem. governing bd. UNA-USA 1995—), World Fedn. UN Assns. (vice-chmn. 1995—), Am. Assn. Comparative Study Law (bd. dirs. 1980—), Am. Soc. Internat. Law (v.p. 1987-88, exec. coun. 1969-72, 81-84, bd. rev. and devel. 1988-91, hon. v.p. 1995—), Assn. Am. Law Schs., U.S. Inst. Human Rights, Internat. Law Assn. (mem. exec. com. 1986—), Colo. Coun. Internat. Orgns. (pres. 1988-90), Assn. U.S. Mems. Internat. Inst. Space Law (bd. dirs., mem. exec. com. 1980-88), Internat. Acad. Comparative Law (assoc.), Order St. Ives (pres.), Rotary, Cactus Club. Office: U Denver Coll Law 1900 Olive St Denver CO 80220-1857 E-mail: vnanda@mail.law.du.edu

NAPIER, GRAHAM R.F. transportation executive; BSc in Engring. Product Design, MSc in Engring. Prodn., MBA. Various positions Lucas Industries; dir. acct. mgmt. Ryder Integrated Logistics, N.Am. and Europe, gen. mgr. internat. N.Am. and Europe; v.p., gen. mgr. strategic bus. devel. and supply chain svcs. Allied Signal Aerospace; exec. v.p. engring. Fritz Cos., Inc., San Francisco, 1999-2000, COO, 2000—. Office: Fritz Cos Inc 706 Mission St Fl 9 San Francisco CA 94103

NAPLES, CAESAR JOSEPH, law and public policy educator, lawyer, consultant; b. Buffalo, Sept. 4, 1938; s. Caesar M. and Fannie A. (Occhipinti) N.; children: Jennifer, Caesar; m. Sandra L. Harrison, July 16, 1983. AB, Yale U., 1960; JD, SUNY, 1963. Bar: N.Y. 1963, Fla. 1977, Calif. 1988, U.S. Supreme Ct. 1965. Assoc. Moot & Sprague, Buffalo, 1965-69; asst. dir., employee rels. N.Y. Gov. Office, Albany, 1969-71; asst. v. chancellor SUNY, Albany, 1971-75; vice chancellor and gen. counsel Fla. State U. System, 1975-82; v. chancellor Calif. State U. System, 1983-92; vice chancellor emeritus Calif. State U., 1992—; prof. law and fin. Calif. State U. System, Long Beach, 1983—; bd. dirs., gen. counsel, corp. sec. Open U., Denver and Wilmington, Del., 1999—. Cons. Govt. of Australia, U. Nev. Sys., Assn. Can. Colls. and Univs., Que., also other univs. and colls. Contbr. articles to profl. jours.; co-author: Romanov Succession, 1989 with J.Victor Baldridge. Bd. dirs., gen. counsel Walden U., 1997—; mem. Metlife Resources Adv. Bd., 1986—, chmn., 1992—; mem. Meml. Heart Inst. Long Beach Meml. Hosp., 1993—, bd. dirs., chmn. 1998—, found. bd., 1996—; bd. dirs. Calif. Acad. Math. and Scis., 1995—. Capt. U.S. Army, 1963-65. Mem. Acad Pers. Adminstrn. (founder), Nat. Ctr. for Study Collective Bargaining Higher Edn. (bd. dirs.). Avocations: opera. Office: 816 N Juanita Ave Ste B Redondo Beach CA 90277-2200 Fax: 310-798-0065. E-mail: cjnaples@csulb.edu

NAPOLES, VERONICA KLEEMAN, graphic designer, consultant; b. N.Y.C., July 9, 1951; d. Florencio Andres and Elena (Colomar) N.; m. Michael Jeffrey Kleeman, May 5, 1985; 1 child, Samuel Andres. BA, U. Miami, 1972; BArch, U. Calif., Berkeley, 1979. Account supr. Marsh & McLennan, Miami, Fla., 1974-76; designer Mus. of Anthropology, San Francisco, 1977-79; project dir. Landor & Assocs., San Francisco, 1979-81; prin. Communications Planning, Kentfield, Calif., 1981—. Bd. dirs. Mind Fitness, Mill Valley, Calif., Main Arts Coun., Mykytyn Cons. Group; instr. U. Calif.-Berkeley, San Francisco, 1983—, Sonoma State U., Santa Rosa, Calif., 1983-84; tchr. Dynamic Graphics Ednl. Found., San Francisco. Author: Corporate Identity Design, 1987; exhibited at San Francisco Airport, 1992. Bd. dirs. Marin Arts Coun. Recipient Bay Area Hispanic Bus. Achiever award, 1988, Design award PRINT, 1988, Excellence award Am. Corp. Identity, 1989, 90, 91, 92, 93, 94, 95, 96, Excellence award N.Y. Art Dirs. Show, 1989; finalist Sundance Inst., 1991. Mem. Am. Inst. Graphic Arts, Women in Communications. Avocations: painting, writing. Office: Napoles Design 189 Madrone Ave Larkspur CA 94939-2113

NAPOLITANO, GRACE F. congresswoman; b. Brownsville, Tex., Dec. 4, 1936; d. Miguel and Maria Alicia Ledezma Flores; m. Frank Napolitano, 1982; 1 child, Yolando M., Fred Musquiz Jr., Edward M., Michael M., Cynthia M. Student, Cerritos Coll., L.A. Trade Tech, Tec Southwest Coll. Mem. Calif. Assembly, 1993-98, U.S. Congress from 34th Calif. dist., Washington, 1999—; mem. resources com., sml. bus. com. U.S. Ho. Reps. Councilwoman City of Norwalk, Calif., 1986-92, mayor, 1989-90; active Cmty. Family Guidance. Mem. Cerritos Coll. Found., Lions Club. Democrat. Roman Catholic. Office: US Ho Reps 1609 Longworth Ho Office Bldg Washington DC 20515-0001 also: Assembly mem Grace F Napolitanto PO Box 408 Sacramento CA 90651-0408*

NAPOLITANO, JANET ANN, state attorney general; b. N.Y.C., Nov. 29, 1957; d. Leonard Michael and Jane Marie (Winer) N. BS summa cum laude, U. Santa Clara, Calif., 1979; JD, U. Va., 1983. Bar: Ariz. 1984, U.S. Dist. Ct. Ariz. 1984, Ct. Appeals (9th cir.) 1984, U.S. Ct. Appeals (10th cir.) 1988, U.S. Ct. Appeals (5th cir.), U.S. Ct. Appeals, U.S. Ct. Appeals (7th cir.), U.S. Ct. Appeals (8th Cir.). Law clk. to Hon. Mary Schroeder U.S Ct. Appeals (9th Cir.), 1983-84; assoc. Lewis & Roca, Phoenix, 1984-89, ptnr., 1989-93; U.S. atty. Dist. Ariz., Phoenix, 1993-97; atty. Lewis and Roca, [illegible]

Gen.'s Adv. Com., 1993—, chair, 1995-96; mem., chmn. victims rights subcom. Ariz. Criminal Justice Commn.; chmn. Ariz. High Intensity Drug Traficking Area; mem. Ariz. Peace Officer Stds. and Tng. Bd., Ariz. Pros. Attys.' Adv. Coun.; former mem. com. to study civil litigation abuse, cost and delay Ariz. Supreme Ct.; past pres. Ariz. Cmty. Legal Svcs. Corp.; former judge pro tem Ariz. Ct. Appeals. Contbr. articles to legal jours. 1st vice chmn. Ariz. Dem. Com., 1990-92; mem. Dem. Nat. Com., 1990-92; chmn. Ariz. del. Dem. Nat. Conv., 1992, co-chmn., 2000; chmn. Nucleus, 1989-91; mem. Ariz. Bd. Tech. Registration, 1989-92; Phoenix Design Standards Rev. Com., 1989-91; bd. dirs. Ariz. Cmty. Legal Svcs. Corp., 1987-92, Ariz. Fire Fighters and Emergency Paramedics Meml., Phoenix Children's Hosp., Actors' Lab Ariz., Inc., Ariz. Peace Officers Meml.; mem. Ariz. Women's Forum, Charter 100; bd. regents Santa Clara U., 1992—; hon. chmn. Camp Fire Boys and Girls, 1999. Recipient Leader of Distinction award Anti-Defamation League, Human Betterment award Roots and Wings, Golden Apple award West Valley NOW, award Nat. Network To End Domestic Violence, Woman of Distinction award Crohns and Colitis Disease Found., Women Making History award Nat. Mus. Women's History, Tribute to Women award YWCA; named Ariz. Dem. of Yr., 1989; scholar Truman Scholarship Found., 1977; Dillard fellow. Fellow Ariz. Bar Found.; mem. ABA, Am. Law Inst., Nat. Assn. Attys. Gen. (exec. com., tobacco bankruptcy working group, health care fraud group, co-chmn. civil rights com., stop underage smoking com., mem. exec. working group on prosecutorial rels.), Ariz. Bar Assn. (former mem. com. on minorities in law, past chmn. civil practice and procedure com.), Maricopa County Bar Assn. (past mem. long range planning com.), Am. Judicature Soc., Ariz. State Bar (chmn. civil practice and procedure com. 1991-92), Ariz. Women Lawyers Assn., Sandra Day O'Connor Inn of Ct. (barrister), Raven Soc., Phi Beta Kappa, Alpha Sigma Nu. Avocations: hiking, trekking, travel, reading, film. Office: 1275 W Washington St Phoenix AZ 85007-2926

NAPOLITANO, LEONARD MICHAEL, anatomist, university administrator; b. Oakland, Calif., Jan. 8, 1930; s. Filippo Michael and Angela (De Fiore) N.; m. Jane M. Winer, July 9, 1955; children— Leonard M., Janet Ann, Nancy Angela. B.S., Santa Clara U., 1951; M.S., St. Louis U., 1954, Ph.D., 1956. Instr. anatomy Cornell Med. Coll., N.Y.C., 1956-58; instr. U. Pitts. Sch. Med., 1958-59, asst. prof., 1959-64; asso. prof. U. N.Mex., 1964-68; prof. dept. anatomy U. N.Mex. (Sch. Medicine), 1968—, acting chmn. dept., 1971-72, dean pro tem, 1972-73, dean, 1973—, interim v.p. for health scis., 1976—; dir. U. N.Mex. (Med. Center); dean U. N.Mex. (Sch. Medicine), 1977-86, dean emeritus, 1996—. Mem. NIH Rsch. Resource Coun., 1988-91, ret. cons., 1994. Contbr. articles on lipid research and ultra structure of cholesterol to profl. jours.; Asso. editor: Anatomical Record, 1968-74. Mem. Am. Assn. Anatomists, Am. Soc. Cell Biology, Electron Microscope Soc. Am., Albuquerque, Bernalillo county Med. Assn. (hon.), Assn. Am. Med. Colls. Council of Deans. Home: 2308 Calle De Panza NW Albuquerque NM 87104-3070 Office: U N Mex Dean Sch Medicine Health Sci Center Albuquerque NM 87131

NARASIMHAN, PADMA MANDYAM, physician; b. Bangalore, India; came to U.S., 1976; d. Alasingracher Mandyam and Alamela Mandyam Narasimhan; 1 child, Ravi. MD, Maulana Azad Med. Coll., New Delhi, 1970. Diplomate Am. Bd. Internal Medicine. Intern in internal medicine Flushing Hosp., N.Y.C., 1976-77; resident in internal medicine Luth. Med. Ctr., N.Y.C., 1977-79; fellow hematology, oncology Beth-Israel Med. Ctr., N.Y.C., 1979-81; asst. prof. King Drew Med. Ctr., L.A., 1983-87, Harbor UCLA, Torrance, 1987—. Mem. editorial bd. Jour. Internal Medicine, 1986—. Mem. ACP, AAPI, Am. Soc. Clin. Oncology, So. Calif. Acad. Clin. Oncology. Hindu. Avocations: travel, reading, meeting people, music, walking. Home: 6604 Madeline Cove Dr Palos Verdes Peninsula CA 90275-4608 Office: Harbor UCLA 100 W Carson St Torrance CA 90509

NASH, CHARLES PRESLEY, chemistry educator; b. Sacramento, Mar. 15, 1932; s. Clarence and Mildred Vida (Johnson) N.; m. Lois Olive Brown, May 29, 1955 (dec. May 1999); children: Nancy Caroline, Sandra Lee, James Roy. BS, U. Calif., Berkeley, 1952; PhD, UCLA, 1958. Instr. chemistry UCLA, 1956-57; from instr. to assoc. prof. U. Calif., Davis, 1957-70, prof., 1970-93, prof. emeritus, 1993—, chmn. acad. senate, 1987-90, chmn. faculty assn., 1993-97; v.p. external rels. Coun. U. Calif. Faculty Assns., 1997—. Vis. sr. lectr. Imperial Coll., London, 1968-69; disting. vis. prof. USAF Acad., Colorado Springs, 1979-80. Contbr. articles to profl. jours. Bd. pres. Explorit Sci. Ctr., 1995-97. Recipient Disting. Teaching award U. Calif. Davis, 1978; named Disting. Alumnus of Yr. Sacramento City Coll., 2000. Mem. Am. Chem. Soc., Sigma Xi, Phi Lambda Upsilon. Office: U Calif at Davis Dept Chemistry Davis CA 95616

NASH, CYNTHIA JEANNE, journalist; b. Detroit, Dec. 24, 1947; d. Frederick Copp and Carolyn (Coffin) N.; 1 child, Lydia Anne Maza; m. Richard Zahler, July 22, 1994. BA, U. Mich., 1969. Reporter Detroit News, 1970-75, sports columnist, 1975-77, Life Style columnist 1977-79, Life Style editor, 1979-82; news features editor Seattle Times, 1983; asst. mng. editor Sunday Seattle Times, 1983-86, assoc. mng. editor, 1986-97, dir. content devel., 1986-2000, dir., brand and content devel., 2000—. Mem. Harbor Sq. Club. Office: Seattle Times PO Box 70 Fairview Ave N & John St Seattle WA 98111-0070 E-mail: cnash@seattletimes.com

NASH, FRANK ERWIN, lawyer; b. Pendleton, Oreg., Feb. 27, 1916; s. Frank Lee and Gertrude (Walbridge) N.; m. Elizabeth Ann Kibbe, Apr. 20, 1943; children: Thomas K., Robert L., Carl F., Frances L. B.S., U. Oreg., 1937, J.D., 1939. Bar: Oreg. 1939. Since practiced in, Portland; with firm Miller, Nash (and predecessors), 1939-91, ptnr., 1948-91, ret., 1991. Bd. dirs. Tri-County United Good Neighbors, 1961-66, pres., 1963-64; pres. U. Oreg. Found., 1979-81; bd. dirs. Med. Research Found., pres., 1980-81; bd. dirs. Library Assn. Portland, pres., 1978-81; bd. visitors U. Oreg. Law Sch. Served to lt. col., inf. AUS, 1941-46, PTO. Recipient Pioneer award U. Oreg., 1980, Meritorious Svc. award., 1992. Fellow Am. Bar Found.; mem. ABA, Multnomah Bar Assn. (pres. 1964-65), Oreg. State Bar, Order of Coif, Phi Delta Phi, Phi Delta Theta. Republican. Methodist. Clubs: Arlington (Portland) (dir. 1963-65), Multnomah Amateur Athletic (Portland) (dir. 1963-65, pres. 1965-66), Waverley (Portland) (pres. 1979-80). Home: Apt D111 32200 SW French Prairie Dr Wilsonville OR 97070-7471 Office: 111 SW 5th Ave Fl 35 Portland OR 97204-3604

NASH, STEVEN ALAN, curator, art historian; b. Wadsworth, Ohio, Apr. 8, 1944; s. Frank W. N. and LaDema (Siffert) N.; m. Carol Ostrowski, June 14, 1969; children: Colin H., Jessica K. BA, Dartmouth Coll., 1966; PhD, Stanford U., 1973. Curator Albright-Knox Art Gallery, Buffalo, 1973-80; dep. dir., chief curator Dallas Mus. Art, 1980-88; assoc. dir., chief curator, European Arts Fine Arts Mus. of San Francisco, 1988—. Panelist Nat. Endowment for the Arts, Washington, 1986—, Inst. Mus. Svcs., Washington, 1979—; bd. dirs. Oberlin (Ohio) Intermus. Conservation Labs., 1976-80. Author: Catalogue: Albright-Knox Art Gallery, 1976, Ben Nicholson, 1977, Naum Gabo: Constructivism, 1986, Century of Modern Sculpture, 1987. Bd. dirs. Lakehill Prep. Sch., Dallas, 1987-88, Buffalo Archtl. Guidebook, 1979-80. Mus. Profl. fellow Nat. Endowment for Arts, 1980; fellow Mabelle McLeod Lewis Found., 1970-71. Mem. Coll. Art Assn., Am. Assn. Mus., Dartmouth Alumni Club. Office: Fine Arts Mus San Francisco Legion Honor Lincoln Pk San Francisco CA 94121-1693

NASH, SYLVIA DOTSETH, religious organization executive, consultant; b. Montevedio, Minn., Apr. 25, 1945; d. Owen Donald and Selma A. (Tollefson) Dotseth; divorced; 1 child, Elizabeth Louise. Grad., Calif. Luth. Bible Sch., 1965; doctorate (hon.), Pilgrims Theol. Seminary, 1994. Office mgr. First Congl. Ch., Pasadena, Calif., 1968-75; adminstrv. asst. Pasadena Presbyn. Ch., 1975-78; dir. adminstrv. svcs. Fuller Theol. Sem., Pasadena, 1978-81; CEO Christian Mgmt. Assn., Diamond Bar, Calif., 1981-94; pres. Christian Healthcare Network, La Mirada, 1994-95; sr. cons. Lillestrand and Assocs., Chino, 1996—. Cons. various orgns., 1985—. Author: Inspirational Management, 1992 (Your Church Mag. award 1992); editor: The Clarion, 1975-78, The Christian Mgmt. Report, 1981-94; mem. editl./adv. bd. Your Church Mag.; mem. editl. bd. Jour. Ministry Mktg. and Mtmg.; contbr. articles to profl. jours. Bd. dirs. Evang. Coun. for Fin. Accountability, Campus Crusade for Christ Internat. Sch. Theology, Nat. Network of Youth Ministries, The Mustard Seed, Inc., Nat. Assn. of Ch. Bus. Adminstrn., Found. for His Ministry, Lamb's Players, Gospel Lit. Internat., Rosemead, Calif. Mem. NAFE, Nat. Assn. Ch. Adminstrs. (sec. 1979-81), Am. Soc. Assn. Execs., So. Calif. Soc. Assn. Execs. Office: Lillestrand & Assocs PO Box 546 Chino Hills CA 91709

NASON, ROCHELLE, conservation organization administrator; b. Oakland, Calif., May 21, 1959; d. Milton and Ann Frances (Reed) N. BA, U. Calif., Berkeley, 1984; JD, U. Calif., San Francisco, 1987. Bar: Calif. 1987. Law clk. to Chief Justice Malcolm Lucas Supreme Ct. of Calif., San Francisco, 1987-88; litigation assoc. Morrison & Foerster, San Francisco, 1988-92; staff lawyer League to Save Lake Tahoe, South Lake Tahoe, Calif., 1992-93, exec. dir., 1993—. Adj. instr. Sierra Nev. Coll., Incline Village, 1992-94, Lake Tahoe C.C., 1992-96. Editor: The Traynor Reader, 1987; sr. rev. editor Hastings Law Jour., 1986-87; editor jour. Keep Tahoe Blue, 1992—; columnist (newspaper) Tahoe Daily Tribune; contbr. articles to profl. jours. V.p., bd. dirs. Jewish Cmty. South Lake Tahoe/Temple Bat Yam, 1992-99; mem. leadership coun. Tahoe-Truckee Regional Econ. Coalition, Stateline, Nev., 1992-94; bd. dirs. Tahoe Ctr. for Sustainable Future, Glenbrook, Nev., 1995-98. Mem. Thurston Soc., Order of Coif. Jewish. Avocations: back-packing, skiing. Office: League to Save Lake Tahoe 955 Emerald Bay Rd South Lake Tahoe CA 96150-6410

NASSIF, THOMAS ANTHONY, business executive, former ambassador; b. Cedar Rapids, Iowa, July 22, 1941; s. George Joseph and Clara Christine (Nofal) N.; m. Zinetta Marie Meherg, Sept. 14, 1968; children— Jaisa Diane, Matthew Christian BS, Calif. State U.-Los Angeles, 1965; JD, Calif. Western Sch. Law, 1969, LLD (hon.), 1988. Ptnr. Gray, Cary, Ames & Frye, El Centro, Calif., 1980-81; dep. and acting chief of protocol Dept. State, Washington, 1981-83; dep. asst. sec. Bur. Near Eastern and South Asian Affairs, Dept State, Washington, 1983-85; U.S. ambassador to Morocco, 1985-88; chmn. bd. Gulf Interstate Internat. Corp., San Diego, 1988-95; chmn. of bd. Gulf Intern. Inc., Houston, 1988-95, Gulf Internat. Consulting Inc., San Diego, 1992—. Chmn. Am. Task Force for Lebanon, Washington, 1991—; pres. Los Alamos Internat., Inc., San Diego, 1988—; mng. ptnr. Aequintas Internat. Cons., 2001—. Active campaign Reagan for Pres., 1980; mem. Calif. State Rep. Cen. Com. Served with U.S. Army and USNG, 1960-67. Recipient disting. alumnus award Calif. State U., L.A., Ellis Island Medal of Honor, 1993. Office: Gulf Internat Consulting Inc Ste 1025 4660 La Jolla Village Dr San Diego CA 92122-4608

NATCHER, STEPHEN DARLINGTON, lawyer, business executive; b. San Francisco, Nov. 19, 1940; s. Stanlus Zoch and Robena Lenore Collie (Goldring) N.; m. Carolyn Anne Bowman, Aug. 23, 1969; children: Tanya Michelle, Stephanie Elizabeth. A.B. in Polit. Sci., Stanford U., 1962; J.D., U. Calif., San Francisco, 1965. Bar: Calif. 1966. Assoc. firm Pillsbury, Madison & Sutro, San Francisco, 1966-68; counsel Douglas Aircraft div. McDonnell Douglas Corp., Long Beach, Calif., 1968-70; v.p., sec. Security Pacific Nat. Bank, 1971-79; asst. gen. counsel Security Pacific Corp., 1979-80; v.p., sec., gen. counsel Lear Siegler, Inc., Santa Monica, Calif., 1980-87; v.p., gen. counsel Computer Sci. Corp., El Segundo, 1987-88; exec. v.p., gen. counsel, sec. CalFed Inc., 1989-90; sr. v.p. adminstrn., gen. counsel, sec. Wyle Electronics, Irvine, Calif., 1991-98; gen. counsel VEBA Electronics LLC, Santa Clara, 1998-2001. With USCG, 1965-71. Mem. St. Francis Yacht Club (San Francisco), The Pacific Club (Newport Beach). Republican. E-mail: snatcher@veba-electronics.com

NATHWANI, BHARAT NAROTTAM, pathologist, consultant; b. Bombay, Jan. 20, 1945; came to U.S., 1972; s. Narottam Pragji and Bharati N. (Lakhani) N. MBBS, Grant Med. Coll., Bombay, 1969, MD in Pathology, 1972. Intern Grant Med. Coll., Bombay U., 1968-69; asst. prof. pathology Grant Med. Coll., 1972; fellow in hematology Cook County Hosp., Chgo., 1972-73; resident in pathology Rush U., Chgo., 1973-74; fellow in hematopathology City of Hope Med. Ctr., Duarte, Calif., 1975-76, pathologist, 1977-84; prof. pathology, chief hematopathology U. So. Calif., L.A., 1984—. Contbr. numerous articles to profl. jours. Recipient Grant awards Nat. Libr. Medicine, Bethesda, Md., Nat. Cancer Inst., 1991. Mem. AAAS, Internat. Acad. Pathology, Am. Soc. Clin. Pathology, Am. Soc. Hematology, Am. Soc. Oncology. Office: U So Calif Sch Medicine HMR 209 2011 Zonal Ave Los Angeles CA 90033-1034

NATSUYAMA, HARRIET HATSUNE, mathematician, educator; b. Honolulu, Sept. 2, 1937; d. Kenjiro and Yakue Natsuyama; children: Julia, Conan. BA, U. Hawaii, 1959, MS, 1960; PhD, Kyoto U., 1965. Math. Rand Corp., Santa Monica, Calif., 1961-68, cons., 1968-77; adj. assoc. prof. U. So. Calif., L.A., 1974-79; sr. scientist Hughes Aircraft Co., El Segundo, 1979-87; chief engr. Infotec Devel. Inc., Camarillo, 1987-89; prof. systems engring. Calif. State U., Fullerton, 1990-96; v.p. Advanced Indsl. Materials, 1996-97. Fgn. spl. vis. prof. Oita U., 1995, Kyoto Sch. of Computer Sci., 1997—; vis. prof. Sci. U. Tokyo, 1998. Author: Invariant Imbedding and Time-Dependent Transport Processes, 1963, System Identification: Methods and Applications, 1974, Integral Equations via Imbedding Methods, 1974, Multiple Scattering Processes: Inverse and Direct, 1975, Numerical Derivatives and Nonlinear Analysis, 1986, Terrestrial Radiative Transfer: Modeling, Computation, Data Analysis, 1998. Mem. Grad. Women in Sci. (pres. 1990-91), Phi Beta Kappa, Phi Kappa Phi. E-mail: hnatsu@mediaone.net

NAUGHTEN, ROBERT NORMAN, pediatrician; b. Stockton, Calif., Oct. 13, 1928; s. Norman Stafford and Junetta (Doherty) N.; m. Ann Louise Charkins, June 26, 1954; children: Robert James, Annette Marie Naughten-Dessel, Patricia Louise Schoof. AA, San Jose City Coll., San Jose, Calif., 1948; BA, U. Calif., Berkeley, 1950; MA, Stanford U., 1955; MD, Hahnemann U., 1959. Lic. physician and surgeon, Calif. Intern Highland-Alameda County Hosp., Oakland, Calif., 1959-60; rsch. fellow Nat. Cancer Inst., Stanford, 1960-61; resident pediat. Stanford Med. Ctr., 1961-63; pvt. practice specializing in pediat. Los Gatos, Calif., 1963—. Instr. Santa Clara Valley Med. Ctr., San Jose, 1963—, Dept. of Pediat., Stanford, 1963-73; cons. drug abuse San Jose Police Dept., 1963-68; cons. child abuse Dist. Atty., San Jose, 1984—; cons. dept. social svcs. State of Calif., 1989—. Contbr. articles to profl. jours. Bd. dirs., v.p. Outreach and Escort, Inc., San Jose, 1985-88. Named Alumnus of Yr. San Jose City Coll., 1967, Chef of the West Sunset Mag., 1989; fellow Coll. of Physicians, Phila., 1986. Mem. AMA, Calif. Assn., Santa Clara Med. Assn. (v.p. 1986-88), Am. Acad. Pediatrics, Am. Acad. Allergy and Clin. Immunology, Calif. Alumni Assn. (Berkeley), Stanford Alumni Assn., Commonwealth Club (San Francisco), Soc. of the Sigma Xi. Democrat. Roman Catholic. Avocations: gourmet cooking, stamp collecting, sailing, art. Home: 13601 Riverdale Dr Saratoga CA 95070-5229 Office: 777 Knowles Dr Ste 3 Los Gatos CA 95032-1417

NAUGHTON, JAMES LEE, internist; b. 1946; AB, Dartmouth Coll., 1968; MD, Harvard U., 1972. Intern U. Calif. Moffitt Hosp., San Francisco, 1972-73; resident in medicine U. Calif. Affiliated Hosps., San Francisco, 1973-75, San Francisco Gen. Hosp., 1975-76; fellow in nephrology U. Calif., San Francisco, 1976-77, assoc. clin. prof. medicine, 1982—; pvt. practice internal medicine, ptnr. Alliance Med. Group, Pinole, Calif., 1982—. Mem. Am. Bd. Internal Medicine (bd. dirs. 1995—, exec. com. 1997—). Office: Alliance Med Group 2160 Appian Way Ste 200 Pinole CA 94564-2524

NAUGLE, DAVID N. federal judge; b. 1943; BA, Stanford U., 1965, JD, 1967. With U.S. Army, 1968-73. Mem. ABA, San Bernardino County Bar Assn., Riverside County Bar Assn. Office: 3420 12th St Riverside CA 92501-3801

NAULTY, SUSAN LOUISE, archivist; b. Abington, Pa., May 28, 1944; d. Charles J. and Ruth E. (Schick) N. BA, Whittier Coll., 1967; MA, Loyola U., L.A., 1972. Tchr. history and English, Whittier (Calif.) H.S., 1968-70; from libr. asst. to asst. curator Huntington Libr., San Marino, Calif., 1972-91; archivist Richard Nixon Libr. and Birthplace, Yorba Linda, 1991—. Office: Richard Nixon Libr and Birthplace 18001 Yorba Linda Blvd Yorba Linda CA 92886-3903

NAVA, CYNTHIA L. state legislator; b. Dona Ana, N. Mex., 1953; BS, Western Ill. U.; MA, Ea. Ill. U. Dep. supt. Gadsden Schools; mem. N.Mex. Senate, Dist. 31, Santa Fe, 1992—; mem. rules com., fin. com. N.Mex. Senate, chair legis. edn. study com., excellence in higher edn. com., health & human svcs. com., 1997—. Home: 3002 Broadmoor Dr Las Cruces NM 88001-7501 Office: N Mex Senate State Capitol Rm 301 Santa Fe NM 87503-0001

NAVARRO, EDWARD, historic site administrator; Dist. supt. Old Town San Diego State Park. Office: c/o San Diego Coast Dist 9609 Naples Ste 2000 San Diego CA 92121

NAVARRO, MANUEL, protective services official; b. Oakland, Calif. AA in Fire Sci., BA in Pub. Adminstrn. Cert. master fire instr., Colo. Fire fighter, 1966-67, Lawrence Radiation Lab. Fire Dept., 1967-72; various positions to asst. chief Oakland (Calif.) Fire Dept., 1972-93; fire chief Colorado Springs (Colo.) Fire Dept., 1993—. Mem. FEMA Urban Search and Rescue Mgmt. and Control Com. Mem. Mex.-Am. Polit. Assn. (chairperson). Office: Colorado Springs Fire Dept 31 S Weber St Colorado Springs CO 80903-1913

NAYLOR, BRUCE GORDON, museum director; b. Midale, Sask., Can., Aug. 19, 1950; s. John Raymond Naylor and Mary Lynn (Frisby) Redeberg; m. Marlene Johnstone, Dec. 19, 1981 (dec. July 1992); m. Judith Jeune, June 11, 1994; children: John Raymond, Connor Harold. BS with high honors, U. Sask., 1972; PhD, U. Alta., 1978. Postdoctoral fellow U. Toronto, Ont., 1978-80; lectr. U. Calif., Berkeley, 1979; asst. prof. U. Alta., Edmonton, 1980-82; curator Tyrrell Mus., Drumheller, Alta., 1982-86; asst. dir. Royal Tyrrell Mus., Drumheller, 1986-92, dir., 1992—. Adj. prof. U. Alta., 1983-99; sen. U. Calgary, Alta., 1989-90; bd. dirs. Yoho-Burgess Shale Rsch. Found. Contbr. articles to sci. publs. Operating grantee Nat. Sci. & Engring. Rsch. Coun., Ottawa, 1981-82. Fellow Geol. Assn. Can.; mem. Soc. Vertebrate Paleontology. Avocations: horseback riding, gardening. Office: Royal Tyrrell Mus Box 7500 Drumheller AB Canada T0J 0Y0 E-mail: bruce.naylor@gov.ab.ca

NEAL, JOSEPH M., JR. state legislator; b. Mounds, La., July 28, 1935; m. Estelle Ann DeConge; children: Charisse, Tania, Withania, Dina Amelia, Joseph. BA, So. U.; postgrad., Inst. Applied Sci. Mem. Nev. Senate, Dist. 4, 1972—; asst. majority fl. leader Nev. Senate, 1985, 87; minority fl. leader Nev. State Senate, 1989, pres. pro tempore, 1991, mem. fin. com., mem. govt. affairs com., mem. taxation com. Active State Dem. Ctrl. Com., Clark County Dem. Ctrl. Com., Nev. Cath. Welfare; past chair Clark County Econ. Opportunity Bd., Greater Las Vegas Plan; candidate Nev. Gov., 1998. Mem. Elks Lodge, Phi Beta Sigma. Democrat. Home: 304 Lance Ave North Las Vegas NV 89030-3844 Office: Nev State Legis Bldg 401 S Carson St Rm 204 Carson City NV 89701-4747 Fax: 702-687-8206. E-mail: jneal@sen.state.nv.us

NEAL, PHILIP MARK, diversified manufacturing executive; b. San Diego, Aug. 28, 1940; s. Philip Mark and Florence Elizabeth (Anderson) N.; children: Brian, Kevin. B.A., Pomona Coll., 1962; M.B.A., Stanford U., 1964. Mgr. financial planning and analysis CBS, Hollywood, 1964-66; cons. McKinsey & Co., L.A., 1966-73; v.p., contr. Avery Internat. Corp., L.A., 1974-78, sr. v.p. fin. Pasadena, Calif., 1979-88, group v.p. materials group, 1988-90, exec. pres., 1990, pres., COO, 1990-98, pres., CEO, 1998-2000, chmn., CEO, 2000—. Bd. dirs. Ind. Colls. of So. Calif. Trustee Pomona Coll; gov. Town Hall of Calif. Bd. Govs. Mem. Fin. Execs. Inst. Republican. Episcopalian. Office: Avery Dennison Corp 150 N Orange Grove Blvd Pasadena CA 91103-3534

NEALE, E(RNEST) R(ICHARD) WARD, retired university official, consultant; b. Montreal, Que., Can., July 3, 1923; s. Ernest John and Mabel Elizabeth (McNamee) N.; m. Roxie Eveline Anderson, June 3, 1950; children— Richard Ward, Owen Curtis B.Sc., McGill U., Montreal, 1949; M.S., Yale U., 1950, Ph.D., 1952; LL.D. (hon.), Calgary U., Alta., Can., 1977; DSc (hon.), Meml. U., Nfld., Can., 1989. Asst. prof. geology U. Rochester, N.Y., 1952-54; sect. chief Geol. Survey Can., Ottawa, Ont., 1954-63, div. chief, 1965-68, Calgary, 1976-81; commonwealth geol. liaison officer London, 1963-65; prof., head geology Meml. U., St. John's, Nfld., Can., 1968-76, v.p. acad., 1982-87; cons., Calgary, Alta., Can., 1987—. Chmn. nat. adv. bd. on sci. publs. NRC-Natural Scis. and Engring. Rsch. Coun., Ottawa, 1982-88. Author: Geology and Geophysics in Canadian Universities, 1980. Editor: Some Guides to Mineral Exploration, 1967, Geology in the Atlantic Region, 1968, The Geosciences in Canada, 1968; Editor: Can. Jour. of Earth Science, 1974-79, Science and the Public, 1988. Bd. dirs. Unitarian Ch. Calgary, 1993—, pres., 1995-96. Petty officer Royal Can. Navy, 1943-45. Decorated officer Order of Can., 1990; recipient Queen's Jubilee medal Govt. of Can., 1977, Can. 125 medal, 1992 Fellow Royal Soc. Can. (coun. 1972-75, chmn. com. pub. awareness of sci. 1987-91, Bancroft medal 1975), Geol. Assn. Can. (pres. 1973-74, Ambrose medal 1986, 1st E.R. Ward Neale medal 1995), Can. Geosci. Coun. (pres. 1975-76, R.T. Bell medal Can. Mining Jour. 1977), Geol. Soc. Am.; mem. Assn. Earth Sci. Editors, Nat. Def. (chmn. biol. and chem. def. rev. com. 1990-93), Univ. Club Calgary, Chancellor's Club, Crows Nest Club, Calgary Sci. Network (pres. 1989), Sigma Xi (nat. lectr. New Haven 1976, chmn. Avalon chpt. 1986). Avocations: golf, cross-country skiing, hiking, canoeing. Home and Office: 5108 Carney Rd NW Calgary AB Canada T2L 1G2

NEAR, TIMOTHY, theater director; Grad., San Francisco State U., Acad. Music and Dramatic Art, London. Artistic dir. San Jose Repertory Theatre, 1987—. Past actress, dir. with numerous prestigious theaters including The Guthrie Theatre, Berkeley (Calif.) Repertory Theater, La Jolla (Calif.) Playhouse, The Alliance Theatre, Atlanta, The Mark Taper Forum, L.A., Ford's Theatre, Washington, Repertory Theatre of St. Louis, N.Y. Shakespeare Festival, Stage West, Mass., A.C.T., Seattle. Dir. Ghosts on Fire, La Jolla Playhouse (DramaLogue award), Singer in the Storm, Mark Taper Forum (DramaLogue award), Thunder Knocking on the Door (DramaLogue award). Recipient 1997 Woman of Achievement in the Arts, San Jose Mercury News and The Woman's Fund. Office: San Jose Repertory Theatre 101 Paseo De San Antonio San Jose CA 95113-2603

NEARY, PATRICIA ELINOR, ballet director; b. Miami; d. James Elliott and Elinor (Mitsitz) N. Corps de ballet Nat. Ballet of Can., Toronto, Ont., 1957-60; prin. dancer N.Y.C. Ballet, 1960-68; ballerina Geneva Ballet, Switzerland, 1968-70, ballet dir. Switzerland, 1973-78; guest artist Stuttgart Ballet, Germany, 1968-70; asst. ballet dir., ballerina West Berlin Ballet, 1970-73; ballet dir. Zurich Ballet, Switzerland, 1978-86, La Scala di Milano ballet co., Italy, 1986-88; tchr. Balanchine ballets, Balanchine Trust, 1987—. E-mail: laneary@aol.com

NEARY, THOMAS H. career officer; b. Idaho; B in Geography, U. Idaho, 1968, M in Statis. Geography, 1969; disting. grad., Squadron Officer Sch., 1974, Air Command and Staff Coll., 1978; student, Nat. War Coll., 1986; student program sr. execs. nat. and internat. security, John F. Kennedy Sch., 1995. Commd. 2d lt. USAF, 1969, advanced through grades to maj. gen., 1997; cartographic officer 15th Reconnaissance Tech. Squadron, March AFB, Calif., 1969-72; missile combat crew comdr. 341st Strategic Missile Wing, Malmstron AFB, Mont., 1972-77, wing sr. standardization crew comdr. and wing plans officer, 1972-77; vice comdr. 341st Missile Wing, Malmstron AFB, 1992-93; missile ops. staff officer, chief missile tactics div. Hdqs. Strategic Air Command/Joint Strategic Target Planning, Offutt AFB, Nebr., 1978-81; planning/programming officer, asst. chief strategic forces Hdqs. USAF, Washington, 1981-85; dep. comdr. ops. 485th Tactical Missile Wing, Florennes Air Base, Belgium, 1986-87; spl. asst. to chief of staff Supreme Hdqs. Allied Powers Europe, Mons, Belgium, 1987-89; sr. Air Force fellow Coun. Fgn. Rels., N.Y.C., 1989-90; asst. dep. comdr. maintenance 351st Strategic Missile Wing, Whiteman AFB, Mo., 1990-91; comdr. 90th Missile Wing, Francis E. Warren AFB, Wyo., 1993-94; stationed at U.S. Strategic Command, Offutt AFB, 1994-97; dir. nuc. and counterproliferation, dep. chief of staff air and space ops. Pentagon, Washington, 1997-98. Decorated Legion of Merit. Office: 20 AF CC 6610 Headquarters Dr Ste 1 Fe Warren AFB WY 82005-3943

NEBELKOPF, ETHAN, psychologist; b. N.Y.C., June 13, 1946; s. Jacob and Fannie (Carver) N.; m. Karen Horrocks, July 27, 1976; children: Demian David, Sarah Dawn. BA, CCNY, 1966; MA, U. Mich., 1969; PhD, Summit U., 1989. Social worker Project Headstart, N.Y.C., 1965; coord. Project Outreach, Ann Arbor, 1968-69; program dir. White Bird Clinic, Eugene, Oreg., 1971-75; counseling supr. Teledyne Econ. Devel. Corp., San Diego, 1976-79; dir. planning and edn. Walden House, San Francisco, 1979-89, dir. tng., 1990-93; program evaluator United Indian Nations, Oakland, Calif., 1994-96; clin. dir., Family and Child Guidance Clinic Indian Health Ctr., Oakland, 1997—; clin. dir. Family and Child Guidance Clinic Native Am. Health Ctr., Oakland, 1997—. Adj. prof. dept. social work San Francisco State U., 1982-87; cons. Berkeley (Calif.) Holistic Health Ctr., 1979-84, Medicine Wheel Healing Co-op, San Diego, 1976-79; alternate del. Nat. Free Clinic Coun., Eugene, 1972-74; clin. dir. Urban Indian Health Bd., Oakland, Calif., 1997. Author: White Bird Flies to Phoenix, 1973, The New Herbalism, 1980, The Herbal Connection, 1981, Hope Not Dope, 1990. Mem. Mayor's Task Force on Drugs, San Francisco, 1988; mem. treatment com. Gov.'s Policy Coun. on Drugs, Sacramento, 1989; task force Human Svcs. Tng., Salem, Oreg., 1972; organizer West Eugene Bozo Assn., 1973; founder Green Psychology, 1993. Named Outstanding Young Man of Am., U.S. Jaycees, 1980; recipient Silver Key, House Plan Assn., 1966. Fellow Am. Orthopsychiat. Assn.; mem. Calif. Assn. Family Therapists, World Fedn. of Therapeutic Communities, Nat. Writer's Club, N.Y. Acad. Scis., Internat. Assn. for Human Rels. Lab. Tng., Calif. Assn. of Drug Programs and Profls. (pres. 1988-90), Phi Beta Kappa. Avocations: herbs, rocks, cactus, yoga, baseball cards. Office: 6641 Simson St Oakland CA 94605-2220

NEBLETT, CAROL, soprano; b. Modesto, Calif., Feb. 1, 1946; m. Philip R. Akre; 3 children. Studies with, William Vennard, Roger Wagner, Esther Andreas, Ernest St. John Metz, Lotte Lehmann, Pierre Bernac, Rosa Ponselle, George London, Jascha Heifetz, Norman Treigle, Sol Hurak, Dorothy Kirsten, Maestros Julius Rudel, Claudio Abbado, Daniel Barenboin, Erich Leinsdorf, James Levine, others. Soloist with Roger Wagner Chorale; performed in U.S. and abroad with various symphonies; debut with Carnegie Hall, 1966, N.Y.C. Opera, 1969, Met. Opera, 1979; sung with maj. opera cos. including Met. Opera, N.Y.C., Lyric Opera Chgo., Balt. Opera, Pitts. Opera, Houston Grand Opera, San Francisco Opera, Boston Opera Co., Milw. Florentine Opera, Washington Opera Soc., Covent Garden, Cologne Opera, Vienna (Austria) Staatsoper, Paris Opera, Teatro Regio, Turin, Italy, Teatro San Carlo, Naples, Italy, Teatro Massimo, Palermo, Italy, Gran Teatro del Liceo, Barcelona, Spain, Kirov Opera Theatre, Leningrad, USSR, Dubrovnik (Yugoslavia) Summer Festival, Salzberg Festival, others; rec. artist RCA, DGG, EMI; appearances with symphony orchs., also solo recitals, (film) La Clemenza di Tito; filmed and recorded live performance with Placido Domingo, La Fancuilla del West; numerous TV appearances. Office: DA CAPO PO Box 180369 Coronado CA 92178-0369

NEDNEY, JOSEPH THOMAS, professional football player; b. San Jose, Mar. 22, 1973; m. Gina. B of Recreation Adminstrn., San Jose State U., 1998. Kicker Oakland (Calif.) Raiders, 1995, Miami (Fla.) Dolphins, 1996, N.Y. Jets, 1997, Ariz. Cardinals, Phoenix, 1997-99, Oakland Raiders, 1999—. Office: Oakland Raiders 1220 Harbor Bay Pkwy Alameda CA 94502-6570

NEE, D. Y. BOB, think tank executive, engineering consultant; b. Shanghai, Dec. 13, 1935; came to U.S., 1953; m. Flora Hsu, Sept. 19, 1959; children: Winifred, Vivian, William BS, Purdue U., 1957; PhD, 1963; MS, U. Mo., Rolla, 1959. Sr. engr. Westinghouse Electric, Pitts., 1967-83; project mgr. U.S. Govt., San Francisco Bay, 1984-91; founder, pres. Inst. for Sys. Monitor, Tiburon, Calif., 1992—; pres. World Humanity Inst., Honolulu, 1995—. Pres. Acad. for Critical Edn.; sci. and tech. cons. ASTM, 1994. Author: Radicalizing the World Through Social Engineering, 1993, Destiny of Humanity, 1998, The New Millennium World Report, 2001. Mem. adv. bd. Reagan for Pres., Washington, 1980. Mem. ASME. Office: Inst for Sys Monitor PO Box 26723 San Francisco CA 94126-6723 E-mail: whi187114@aol.com

NEEDLEMAN, JACOB, philosophy educator, writer; b. Phila., Oct. 6, 1934; s. Benjamin and Ida (Seltzer) N.; m. Carla Satzman, Aug. 30, 1959 (div. 1989); children: Raphael, Eve; m. Gail Anderson, Dec. 1990. BA, Harvard U., 1956; grad., U. Freiburg, 1957-58; PhD, Yale U., 1961. Clin. psychology trainee West Haven (Conn.) Veterans Hosp. Adminstrn., 1960-61; rsch. assoc. Rockefeller Inst., N.Y., 1961-62; from asst. prof. to assoc. prof. philosophy San Francisco State U., 1962-66, prof philosophy, 1967—, chair dept. philosophy, 1968-69. Vis. scholar Union Theol. Seminary, 1967-68; dir. Ctr. Study New Religions, 1977-83; lectr. psychiatry, cons. med. ethics U. Calif., 1981-84. Author: Being-in-the-World, 1963, The New Religions, 1970, Religion for a New Generation, 1973, A Sense of the Cosmos, 1975, On the Way to Self-Knowledge: Sacred Tradition and Psychotherapy, 1976, Lost Christianity, 1980, Consciousness and Tradition, 1982, The Heart of Philosophy, 1982, Sorcerers, 1986, Sin and Scientism, 1986, Lost Christianity: A Journey of Rediscovery to the Centre of Christian Experience, 1990, Money and the Meaning of Life, 1991, Modern Esoteric Spirituality, 1992, The Way of the Physician, 1993, The Indestructible Question, 1994, A Little Book on Love, 1996, Time and the Soul, 1998; (trans.) The Primary World of Senses, 1963, Essays on Ego Psychology, 1964; editor Care of Patients with Fatal Illness, 1969, The Sword of Gnosis, 1973, Sacred Tradition and Present Need, 1974, Understanding the New Religions, 1978, Speaking of My Life: The Art of Living in the Cultural Revolution, 1979, Real Philosophy: An Anthology of the Universal Search for Meaning, 1991; contbr. Death and Bereavement, 1969, To Live Within, 1971, My Life with a Brahmin Family, 1972, The New Man, 1972, The Universal Meaning of the Kabbalah, 1973, The Phenomenon of Death. Grantee Religion in Higher Edn., 1967-68, Marsden Found., Ella Lyman Cabot Trust, 1969, Marsda Found, Far West Inst., 1975; Fulbright scholar Germany, 1957-58; Fels Found. fellow Munich, 1959; fellow Rockefeller Found. Humanities, 1977-78. Office: San Francisco State U Dept Philosophy 1600 Holloway Ave San Francisco CA 94132-1722

NEELD, MICHAEL EARL, public affairs executive, communications specialist; b. Portland, Oreg., May 13, 1955; s. Carl Eugene and Frances Karlene (Riggers) N.; m. Ann Pelissier. BA in Journalism and Polit. Scis., U. Oreg., 1977. Advt. rep. Post Publs., Camas, Wash., 1977; chpt. cons. Kappa Sigma Internat. Fraternity, Charlottesville, Va., 1977-79; fundraising dir. Am. Cancer Soc., Richmond, 1979-80; news editor, polit. rep. Sta. KYXI, Portland, 1980-84; comms. dir. Moshofsky for Congress, Portland, 1984; pub. info. officer Wash. State Ho. of Reps., Olympia, 1984-85; comms. dir. Paulus for Gov., Portland, 1985-86; sr. info. officer Wash. State Ho. of Reps., Olympia, 1986-91, rep. staff coord., 1991-96, pub. rels. coord., 1996-99; pub. affairs dir. Washington Health Care Assn., 1999—. Founder, ptnr. Pacific N.W. Advocates Pub. Affairs Cons., Olympia, 1989-96; instr. polit. strategy, tactics, fundraising and media Wash. State Rep. Party, Tukwila, 1991-92; campaign dir. House Rep. Orgnl. Com., Olympia, 1991-92. Recipient Best Coverage of Breaking News award Oreg. AP/Broadcast, 1982. Mem. U. Oreg. Alumni Assn., Trumpeters, City Club of Portland, Fremont Grove Soc. (founder), Indian Summer Golf and Country Club (v.p. 1998-2000), Wash. State Golf Assn. (club rep. 1999—), Pacific N.W. Golf Assn. (club rep. 1999—), Kappa Sigma (alumni, housing corp. bd. dirs. 1980-84). Presbyterian. Avocations: politics, reading, golf. Home: 7224 Deerfield Park Dr NE Olympia WA 98516-2132 Office: Wash Health Care Assn 2120 State Ave NE # 102 Olympia WA 98506-6514 E-mail: m.neeld@worldnet.att.net

NEELY, SALLY SCHULTZ, lawyer; b. L.A., Mar. 2, 1948; BA, Stanford U., 1970, JD, 1971. Bar: Ariz. 1972, Calif. 1977. Law clk. to judge U.S. Ct. appeals (9th cir.), Phoenix, 1971-72; assoc. Lewis and Roca, Phoenix, 1972-75; asst. prof. Law Sch. Harvard U., Cambridge, Mass., 1975-77; assoc. Shutan & Trost, P.C., L.A., 1977-79; ptnr. Sidley & Austin, L.A., 1980—. Mem. faculty Am. Law Inst.-ABA Chpt. 11 Bus. Reorgns., 1989-95, 97—, Banking and Comml. Lending Law, 1997-99, Nat. Conf. Bankruptcy Judges, 1988, 90, 95, 96, 97, 99, Fed. Jud. Ctr., 1989, 90, 94-95, Workshop Bankruptcy and Bus. Reorganization NYU, 1992—; rep. 9th cir. jud. conf., 1989-91; mem. Nat. Bankruptcy Conf., 1993—. Chair Stanford U. Law Sch. Reunion Giving, 1996; bd. vis. Stanford U. Law Sch., 1990-92; atty. mem. editl. bd. Am. Bankruptcy Law Jour. Mem. ABA, Am. Coll. Bankruptcy, Calif. Bar Assn. Office: Sidley & Austin 555 W 5th St Ste 4000 Los Angeles CA 90013-3000

NEIDHART, JAMES ALLEN, oncologist, educator; b. Steubenville, Ohio, Aug. 30, 1940; s. James Leonard and Mary Jane (Daniels) N.; m. Patricia Irene Harpkamp, Aug. 16, 1966 (div. Apr. 1985); children—James, Jeffrey, Jennifer; m. Mary Gagen, Feb. 1986; children: Andrew, Rae Ann. B.S., Union Coll., Alliance, Ohio, 1962; M.D., Ohio State U., 1966. Diplomate Am. Bd. Internal Medicine, Am. Bd. Hematology and Oncology. Intern Bronson Hosp., Kalamazoo, 1966-67; resident Ohio State U., Columbus, Ohio, 1969-71; postdoctoral fellow Coll. Medicine, Ohio State U., Columbus, 1972-74, asst. prof. medicine, 1974-78, assoc. prof., 1978-84, dir. interdisciplinary oncology unit Comprehensive Cancer Ctr., 1975-80, dep. dir. Comprehensive Cancer Ctr., 1980-84; prof. medicine U. Tex.-Houston-M.D. Anderson Hosp. and Tumor Inst., 1984-86, Hubert L. and Olive Stringer prof. oncology, 1984-86, dep. head div. medicine, 1984-86, chmn. dept. med. oncology, 1984-86; dir. Cancer Rsch. and Treatment Ctr., U. N.Mex., Albuquerque, 1986-96, chief hematology and oncology, 1986-91; dir. Cancer Rsch. and Treatment Ctr. San Juan Regional Cancer Ctr., 1996—. Contbr. chpts. to Recent Advances in Clinical Therapeutics, Clinical Immunotherapy Former mem. bd. dirs. Am. Cancer Soc., Columbus; former v.p. Ohio Cancer Research Assocs. Served to lt. USN, 1967-69, Vietnam Mem. Am. Soc. Hematology, Am. Soc. Clin. Oncology, Am. Assn. Cancer Research, ACP, S.W. Oncology Group, Wilderness Soc., Sierra Club Home: 66 Road 2577 Aztec NM 87410-1020 Office: San Juan Regional Cancer Ctr Farmington NM 87401

NEIL, GARY LAWRENCE, pharmaceutical company research executive, biochemical pharmacologist; b. Regina, Sask., Can., June 13, 1940; came to U.S., 1962; s. Bert Lawrence and Barbara Jessie (Robinson) N.; m. Beverly May Hendry, Apr. 16, 1939; children: Deborah Nadine, Michael Lawrence. BS with honors, Queen's U., Kingston, Ont., Can., 1962; PhD, Calif. Inst. Tech., 1966. Rsch. scientist The Upjohn Co., Kalamazoo, 1966-73, rsch. head, 1973-79, rsch. mgr., 1979-82, group mgr., 1982-83, exec. dir., 1983-85, v.p., 1985-89; sr. v.p. Wyeth-Ayerst, Radnor, Pa., 1989-90, exec. v.p., 1990-93; pres., CEO Therapeutic Discovery Corp., Palo Alto, Calif., 1993-97, Crescendo Pharm. Corp., Palo Alto, 1997—. Editor Investigational New Drugs, 1983-88; contbr. over 50 articles to profl. jours. Mem. Am. Chem. Soc., Am. Assn. Cancer Rsch., Am. Soc. Clin. Pharmacology and Exptl. Therapeutics. Presbyterian. Avocation: sailing. Office: Crescendo Pharm Corp 2000 Charleston Rd Ste 300 Mountain View CA 94043-1632

NEILL, VE, make-up artist; b. Riverside, Calif., May 13, 1951; d. Charles and Eileen Anne (Bernasco) Flores. Grad., Louisville H.S., Woodland Hills, Calif. Credits include (TV movies) Cry for Help, 1978, The London Affair, 1978, Sultan and the Rock Star, 1979, Muppets Go to the Movies, 1981, First Lady of the World, 1982, Money on the Side, 1982, Jane Doe, 1986; (TV Spls.) Sold Out-Lily Tomlin, 1981, Lily for President, 1982, Comedy Store 15th Yr. Reunion, 1988; (TV pilots) One Night Band, 1981, T.J. Hooker, 1981, Madeline (Madeline Kahn), 1982, Girls Life, 1982, A-Team, 1982, Rock & Roll Mom, 1987, Kowalski Loves, 1987, Stephen King's The Shining, 1996 (Emmy award Best Make Up), From the Earth to the Moon, 1997 (Emmy award nomination); (TV show) Pee Wee's Playhouse (Emmy award 1988, Emmy award nominee 1989); (feature films) Star Trek: The Motion Picture (Saturn award 1981), The Incredible Shrinking Woman, 9 to 5, Monty Python at the Hollywood Bowl, Sword and the Sorcerer, The Last Star Fighter, All of Me, The Lost Boys, 1986 (Saturn award 1987), Beetlejuice, 1987 (Acad. award 1987, Saturn award 1988, Brit. Acad. award nominee 1988), Cocoon II, 1988, Big Top Pee Wee, 1988, Dick Tracy, 1989, Flatliners, 1989, Edward Scissorhands, 1990 (Acad. award nominee 1989, Brit. Acad. award nominee 1990), Curly Sue, 1990, Hook, 1991, Batman Returns, 1991 (Saturn award 1992, Acad. award nominee 1992, Brit. Acad. award nominee 1992), Hoffa, 1992 (Acad. award nominee 1992), Rising Sun, 1992, Mrs. Doubtfire, 1993 (Acad. award 1993), Ed Wood, 1993 (Acad. award 1994), Cobb, 1994, Junior, 1994, Batman Forever, 1995, Matilda, 1995, Evening Star, 1996, Mars Attack, 1996, Gattaca, 1996, Batman and Robin, 1996, Amistad, 1997, Stigmata, 1998, Man on the Moon, 1998, Galaxy Quest, 1999, How the Grinch Stole Christmas, 1999, Blow, 2000, A.I., 2000, Death to Smochy, 2001, (commercial) Sony Mini Disc, 1997, (mag.) Vanity Fair Hollywood Issue, 1998. Mem. Acad. Motion Picture Arts and Scis. (mem. exec. bd.), Brit. Acad. Film and TV Avocations: collecting antiques, beading with antique Am. trade beads, hiking, traveling the U.S. Office: IATSE Local 706 828 N Hollywood Way Burbank CA 91505

NEILSEN, CRAIG H. business executive; b. 1942; Prse. Cactus Pete, Inc., Jackpot, Nev., 1984—, Ameristar Casino Vicksburg, Miss., 1993—. Office: Ameristar Casinos Inc 3773 Howard Hughes Pkwy Las Vegas NV 89109

NEINAS, CHARLES MERRILL, athletic association executive; b. Marshfield, Wis., Jan. 18, 1932; s. Arthur Oscar and Blanche Amelia (Reeder) N.; children: Andrew, Toby. B.S., U. Wis., 1957. Asst. exec. dir. Nat. Collegiate Athletic Assn., Kansas City, Mo., 1961-71; commr. Big Eight Conf., Kansas City, 1971-81; exec. dir. Coll. Football Assn., 1981—; Dr. Patricia L. Pacey prof. econs. U. Colo., Boulder, 1981—, econ. cons., 1981—. Adviser Am. Football Coaches Assn., 1997—; cons. NCAA Football, 1997—. Served with USNR, 1952-54. Home: 7398 Windsor Dr Boulder CO 80301-3651 Office: Neinas Sports Svcs 6688 Gunpark Dr Boulder CO 80301-3372

NEISER, BRENT ALLEN, public affairs and personal finance consultant, speaker; b. Cin., Sept. 16, 1954; s. Rodger and Hazel Neiser; m. Marion, Apr. 1, 1978; children: Christy Jean, Steven José, April Reneé. BA in Pub. Affairs, George Washington U., 1976; MA in Urban Studies, Occidental Coll., 1978; MBA, U. Louisville, 1979; postgrad. in internat. affairs, U. Denver, 1987-90. Cert. fin. planner, 1985; cert. assn. exec., 1994; chartered mut. fund counselor, 1996; accredited asset mgmt. specialist, 1998. Project mgr., analyst Legis. Research Com., Frankfort, Ky., 1978-84; pres. Moneyminder, Denver and Frankfort, 1983-91; dir. edn., govt. affairs and ethics Inst. Cert. Fin. Planners, Denver, 1985-91, exec. dir., 1991-94; pub. affairs, govt. rels. bus. strategies cons. The Brent Neiser Co., Englewood, Colo., 1994—; dir. Nat. Endowment for Fin. Edn., 1995—. Mng. dir. Fin. Products Stds. Bd., Denver, 1985-91; co-creator Personal Econ. Summit '93, Washington. Author: EPCOT/World Showcase External Directions, Walt Disney Imagineering, 1977, Personal Management, 1996; co-inventor: Trivia Express (game) Denver, 1986. Vol., v.p. Big Bros./Big Sisters, Frankfort, 1982; del. Colo. Model Constnl. Conv., 1987; mem. citizens budget rev. com. Greenwood Village; parent trainer The Adoption Exch., Denver, 1988, mem. long range planning com., 1992-93, bd. dirs., 1993-99; polit. action dir. Frankfort NAACP, 1983, legis. chmn. state conf., 1984; troop com. mem., asst. scoutmaster Boy Scouts Am., Englewood, 1993-99; bd. dirs. Young Ams. Bank Edn. Found., 1993-99, chair edn. coun.; bd. dirs. Leadership Denver, 1993; vol. host com. Denver Summit of the Eight, 1997; nat. spokesperson Protect our Children Campaign, 1996; active Annie E. Casey Found.: Nat. Foster Care Awareness Project, 1999-2000; citizen's panelist News Hour with Jim Lehrer (PBS), 1998—; founding ptnr. Social Venture Ptnrs., Denver, Colo. Coun. of Advisors on Consumer Credit, 2000—; mem. CFP bd. Consumer Adv. Coun. on Fin. Planning, 2001— . Lt. (j.g.) USNR, 1985-92. Recipient Assn. Advance Am. award Excellence, 1996, 98; named Man of Yr., Frankfort NAACP, 1983; Pub. Affairs fellow Coro Found., 1976-77. Mem. Investors Edn. Assn. Colo. (bd. dirs.), Nat. Assns. in Colo., Denver C. of C. (pub. affairs coun.), Adoptive Families of Am., Assn. for Fin. Counseling and Planning Edn., Am. Soc. Assn. Execs., Inst. Mgmt. Cons., N.Am. Securities Adminstrs. Assn. (investment adviser and fin. planner adv. com.), Nat. Soc. Compliance Profls. (bd. dirs. 1987-89), Am. Film Inst. (writers workshop), Am. Polit. Items Collectors, Fin. Planning Assn. Ind. Sector. Office: 5860 Big Canyon Dr Englewood CO 80111-3516 E-mail: ban@nefe.org

NEITER, GERALD IRVING, lawyer; b. L.A., Nov. 11, 1933; s. Harry and Ida Florence (Alperin) N.; m. Margaret P. Rowe, Mar. 5, 1961; children: David, Karen, Michael. BSL, JD, U. So. Calif., 1957. Bar: Calif. 1958. Judge pro tem Mcpl. Cts., L.A. and Beverly Hills, 1970-94; judge pro tem and mediator Calif. Superior Ct., L.A. County, 1974-94, family law mediator, 1976—; prin. Gerald I. Neiter, P.C., L.A., 1981—. Lectr. State Bar of Calif., 1968, 76, 79, 81; former referee State Bar Ct.; arbitrator Am. Arbitration Assn. Mem. Am., Los Angeles County (arbitrator), Beverly Hills, Century City bar assns., State Bar Calif. Office: 1925 Century Park E Ste 200 Los Angeles CA 90067-2701 E-mail: Neitlaw@aol.com

NELIPOVICH, SANDRA GRASSI, artist; b. Oak Park, Ill., Nov. 22, 1939; d. Alessandro and Lena Mary (Ascareggi) Grassi; m. John Nelipovich Jr., Aug. 19, 1973. BFA in Art Edn., U. Ill., 1961; postgrad., Northwestern U., 1963, Gonzaga U., Florence, Italy, 1966, Art Inst. Chgo., , 1968; diploma, Accademia Universale Alessandro Magno, Prato, Italy, 1983. Tchr. art Edgewood Jr. High Sch., Highland Park, Ill., 1961-62, Emerson Sch. Jr. High Sch., Oak Park, 1962-77; batik artist Calif., 1977—; illustrator Jolly Robin Publ. Co., Anaheim, 1988—, Assistance League of Anaheim, 2000—. Supr. student tchrs., Oak Park, 1970-75; adult edn. tchr. ESL, ceramics, Medinah, Ill., 1974; mem. curriculum action group on human dignity, EEO workshop demonstration, Oak Park, 1975-76; guest lectr. Muckenthaler Ctr., Fullerton, Calif., 1980, 92, Niguel Art Group, Dana Point, Calif., 1989, Carlsbad A.A., 1990, ARt League, Oceanside Art Group, 1992; 2d v.p. Anaheim Hills Women's Club, 1990-91, rec. sec. 1991-92; fabric designer for fashion designer Barbara Jax, 1987; illustrator Assistance League Anaheim (Calif.), 2000—. One-Woman shows include Lawry's Calif. Ctr., L.A., 1981-83, Whittier (Calif.) Mus., 1985-86, Anaheim Cultural Ctr., 1986-88, Ill. Inst. Tech., Chgo., 1989, Muckenthaler Cultural Ctr., Fullerton, 1990; also gallery exhibits in Oak Brook, 1982, La Habra, Calif., 1983, Millard Sheets Gallery, Pomona, Calif., 1996; represented in permanent collections McDonald's Corp., Oak Brook, Glenkirk Sch., Deerfield, Ill., Emerson Sch., Oak Park, Calif.; poster designer Saratoga Fine Arts. Active Assistance League, Anaheim, Calif., 1992—, 2d v.p. ways and means com., 1995-96, 97-98. Recipient numerous awards, purchase prizes, 1979—; featured in Calif. Art Rev., Artists of So. Calif., Vol. II, Nat. Artists' Network, 1992, Batik for Artists and Quilters, 2001. Mem. AAUW (hospitality chmn. 1984-85), Soc. Children's Book Writers and Illustrators, Assistance League Anaheim, Orange Art Assn. (jury chmn. 1980). Roman Catholic. Avocations: cooking, gardening, travel. Home and Office: 5922 E Calle Cedro Anaheim CA 92807-3207

NELLERMOE, LESLIE CAROL, lawyer; b. Oakland, Calif., Jan. 26, 1954; d. Carrol Wandell and Nora Ann (Conway) N.; m. Darrell Ray McKissic, Aug. 9, 1986; 1 child, Devin Anne. BS cum laude, Wash. State U., 1975; JD cum laude, Willamette U., 1978. Bar: Wash. 1978, U.S. Dist. Ct. (ea. dist.) Wash. 1979, U.S. Dist. Ct. (we. dist.) Wash. 1983. Staff atty. Wash. Ct. Appeals, Spokane, 1978-79; asst. atty. gen. Wash. Atty. Gen. Office, Spokane, 1979-83, Olympia, 1983-85; assoc. Syrdal, Danelo, Klein, Myre & Woods, Seattle, 1985-88; ptnr. Heller Ehrman White & McAuliffe, Seattle, 1990—. Bd. dirs. N.W. Environ. Bus. Coun., 1996—, Campfire Boys & Girls, Seattle, 1991-97. Mem. ABA, Wash. State Bar Assn., King County Bar Assn., Wash. Environ. Industry Assn. (bd. dirs.). Office: Heller Ehrman White & McAuliffe 701 5th Ave 6100 Columbia Ctr Seattle WA 98104-7043

NELSON, BERNARD WILLIAM, foundation executive, educator, physician; b. San Diego, Sept. 15, 1935; s. Arnold B. and Helene Christina (Falck) N.; m. Frances Davison, Aug. 9, 1958; children— Harry, Kate, Anne, Daniel AB, Stanford U., 1957, MD, 1961. Asst. prof., asst. dean medicine Stanford U., Palo Alto, Calif., 1965-67, assoc. dean medicine, 1968-71, cons. assoc. prof., 1980-86; assoc. dean U. Wis., Madison, 1974-77, acting vice chancellor, 1978-79; exec. v.p. Kaiser Family Found., Menlo Park, Calif., 1979-81, Menlo Park, 1981-86; prof., chancellor U. Colo. Health Sci. Ctr., Denver, 1986-95, prof. dept. preventive med. and biometrics, 1995—. Mem., v.p., pres. Nat. Med. Fellowships, 1969-77 Trustee Morehouse Med. Sch., 1981-83 Fellow Inst. Medicine; mem. Calif. Acad. Sci., Alpha Omega Alpha (bd. dirs. 1978—) Avocations: fishing, photography, gardening, carpentry. Office: U Colo Health Sci Ctr Box C245 4200 E 9th Ave Denver CO 80262-3706

NELSON, CRAIG ALAN, management consultant; b. San Rafael, Calif., July 11, 1961; s. Kenneth Alfred and Anne Catherine (Laurie) N. BS in Fin., San Diego State U., 1984. Loan assoc. Union Bank, San Diego, 1984-85, comml. loan officer, 1985-86, corp. banking officer, 1986-87, asst. v.p., 1987-89, v.p. corp. banking, 1989-93; v.p. Alexander & Alexander,

San Diego, 1993-95; sr. assoc. Goreham-Moore & Assocs., San Diego, 1995-98; v.p. Sedgwick Tech. Group Sedgwick of Calif., Inc., San Diego, 1998; v.p., dir. tech. Marsh Inc., La Jolla, Calif., 1998—; regional v.p. Comerica Tech. Banking Group, San Diego. V.p. Sedgwick Tech. Group, 1997. Corp. recruiter United Way, San Diego, 1988; community group chair San Diego chpt. Am. Cancer Soc., 1989; mem. com. Juvenile Diabetes Assn.; bd. dirs. San Diego State Found., 1989—. Mem. San Diego State U. Young Alumni Assn. (pres. 1988-89, bd. dirs. emeritus 1989). Home: 1233 San Dieguito Dr Encinitas CA 92024-5116 Office: Comerica Tech Group 600 B St Ste 100 San Diego CA 92101

NELSON, CYNTHIA J. city official; Re-devel. project mgr. City of Long Beach, Calif., until 1983, City of Santa Ana, 1983—, exec. dir. Santa Ana Cmty. Devel. Agy. Mem. Calif. Assn. Local Econ. Devel. (past chairperson Orange County chpt.), Calif. Redevel. Assn. (bd. dirs.)

NELSON, DAVID, state legislator, farmer, lawyer; b. Pendleton, Oreg., Aug. 6, 1941; m. Alice Nelson. BA in Polit. Sci., Oreg. U.; JD, Mont. U. Mem. Oreg. Legislature, Salem, 1996—, chair bus. and consumer affairs com., mem. info. mgmt. and tech. com., mem. jud. com., mem. stream restoration and species recovery com., mem. subcom. on edn.; dist. atty. Pondera County, Mont. Republican. Office: 1407 NW Horn Ave Pendleton OR 97801-1257 E-mail: sennelson@oregontrail.net

NELSON, DENNIS R. energy executive; Sr. v.p. gen. coun., corp. sec. UniSource Energy Corp., Tucson, 1997—. Office: UniSource Energy Corp 220 W 6th St Tucson AZ 85701-1014

NELSON, DOROTHY WRIGHT (MRS. JAMES F. NELSON), federal judge; b. San Pedro, Calif., Sept. 30, 1928; d. Harry Earl and Lorna Amy Wright; m. James Frank Nelson, Dec. 27, 1950; children: Franklin Wright, Lorna Jean. B.A., UCLA, 1950, J.D., 1953; LL.M., U. So. Calif., 1956; LLD honoris causa, U. San Diego, 1997, U. So. Calif., 1983, Georgetown U., 1988, Whittier U., 1989, U. Santa Clara, 1990; LLD (honoris causa), Whittier U., 1989. Bar: Calif. 1954. Research assoc. fellow U. So. Calif., 1953-56; instr., 1957; asst. prof., 1958-61; assoc. prof., 1961-67; prof., 1967; assoc. dean., 1965-67; dean., 1967-80; judge U.S. Ct. Appeals (9th cir.), 1979-95, sr. judge, 1995—. Cons. Project STAR, Law Enforcement Assistance Adminstrn.; mem. select com. on internal procedures of Calif. Supreme Ct., 1987—; co-chair Sino-Am. Seminar on Mediation and Arbitration, Beijing, 1992; dir. Dialogue on Transition to a Global Soc., Weinacht, Switzerland, 1992. Author: Judicial Adminstration and The Administration of Justice, 1973, (with Christopher Goelz and Meredith Watts) Federal Ninth Circuit Civil Appellate Practice, 1995; Contbr. articles to profl. jours. Co-chmn. Confronting Myths in Edn. for Pres. Nixon's White House Conf. on Children, Pres. Carter's Commn. for Pension Policy, 1974-80, Pres. Reagon's Madison Trust; bd. visitors U.S. Air Force Acad., 1978; bd. dirs. Council on Legal Edn. for Profl. Responsibility, 1971-80, Constnl. Right Found., Am. Nat. Inst. for Social Advancement, Pacific Oaks Coll., Childrens Sch. & Rsch. Ctr., 1996-98; adv. bd. Nat. Center for State Cts., 1971-73; adv. bd. World Law Inst., 1997—; chmn. bd. Western Justice Ctr., 1986—; mem. adv. com. Nat. Jud. Edn. Program to promote equality for woman and men in cts.; bd. advisors Tahirih Justice Inst., Washington, 1998—; chair 9th Cir. Standing Com. on Alternative Dispute Resolution, 1998—. Named Law Alumnus of Yr. UCLA, 1967, Times Woman of Yr., 1968, Disting. Jurist, Ind. U. Law, 1994; recipient Profl. Achievement award, 1969, AWARE Internat. award, 1970, U. Judaism Humanitarian award, 1973, Ernestine Stalhut Outstanding Woman Lawyer award, 1972, Pub. Svc. award Coro Found., 1978, Pax Orbis ex Jure medallion World Peace thru Law Ctr., 1975, Hollzer Human Rights award Jewish Fedn. Coun., L.A., 1988, Medal of Honor UCLA, 1993, Emil Gumpert Jud. ADR Recognition award L.A. County Bar Assn., 1996, Julia Morgan award YWCA Pasadena, 1997, Samuel E. Gates Litigation award Am. Coll. Trial Lawyers, 1999, D'Alemberte/Raven award ABA Dispute Resolution Sect., 2000, Bernard E. Witkin award State Bar Assn. Calif., 2000; Lustman fellow Yale U. 1977. Fellow Am. Bar Found., Davenport Coll., Yale U.; mem. Bar Calif. (bd. dirs. continuing edn. bar commn. 1967-74), Am. Judicature Soc. (dir., Justice award 1985), Assn. Am. Law Schs. (chmn. com. edn. in jud. adminstrn.), ABA (sect. on jud. adminstrn., chmn. com. on edn. in jud. adminstrn. 1973-89), Phi Beta Kappa, Order of Coif (nat. v.p. 1974-76), Jud. Conf. U.S. (com. to consider standards for admission to practice in fed. cts. 1976-79) Office: US Ct Appeals Cir 125 S Grand Ave Ste 303 Pasadena CA 91105-1621

NELSON, GARY, councilman, electrical engineer; b. Spokane, Wash., Apr. 11, 1936; s. Nels Alfred and Laura Marie (Winberg) Nelson; m. JoAnne Laura Knudson, Nov. 27, 1959; children: Grant, Geoffrey, Gregory. BSEE, Wash. State U., 1958; MSEE, U. Wis., 1963. Engr. RCA, Camden, N.J., 1958-59; officer USAF, Madison, Wis., 1959-62; mgr. U.S. West, Seattle, 1963-90; pvt. practice Edmonds, Wash., 1990-94. Bd. dirs. Stevens Hosp. Found., Edmonds, Snohomish County Health Dist., 1994—, United Way of Snohomish County, Everett, 1986-92, Cmty. Transit; Wash. State Legislator, 1972-94. Mem. planning commn. City of Edmonds, 1964-67, city coun., 1968-74; bd. dirs. Stevens Hosp. Found., Edmonds, 1982-90, United Way of Snohomish County, Everett, 1986-92, Snohomish County Health Dist., 1994—, Cmty. Transit, 1995—, Conv. and Performing Arts Dist., 1995—; Wash. State legislator, 1972-94. Capt. USAF, 1959-62. Mem. Sons of Norway, Rotary. Republican. Lutheran. Home: 9710 Wharf St Edmonds WA 98020-2363 Office: Snohomish County Coun 3000 Rockefeller Ave # 609 Everett WA 98201-4046 E-mail: garynelson@prodigy.net

NELSON, GRANT STEEL, lawyer, educator; b. Mitchell, S.D., Apr. 18, 1939; s. Howard Steel and Clara Marie (Winandy) N.; m. Judith Ann Haugen, Sept. 22, 1962; children: Mary Elizabeth, Rebekah Anne, John Adam. BA magna cum laude, U. Minn., 1960; JD cum laude, 1963. Bar: Minn. 1963, Mo. 1971. Assoc. Faegre & Benson, Mpls., 1963-67; mem. law faculty U. Mo., Columbia, 1967-91, assoc. prof., 1970-72, prof., 1972-91, Enoch H. Crowder prof. law, 1974-91; prof. UCLA, 1991—. Mem. bd. legal advisors Gt. Plains Legal Found., 1978-85; vis. asst. prof. U. Mich., Ann Arbor, 1969-70, Brigham Young U., Provo, Utah, summer 1976; vis. prof. U. Minn., Mpls., 1981-82, UCLA, 1989-90; disting. vis. prof. Pepperdine U., 1987-88; vis. endowed Campbell prof. U. Mo., Columbia, 1996-98; commr. Nat. Conf. Commrs. Uniform State Laws, 1983-91; mem. West Pub. Law Sch. Adv. Bd. Author: (with Van Hecke and Leavell) Cases and Materials on Equitable Remedies and Restitution, 1973, (with Whitman) Cases and Materials on Real Estate Finance and Development, 1976, Cases and Materials on Real Estate Transfer, Finance and Development, 1981, (with Osborne and Whitman) Real Estate Finance Law, 1979, (with Leavell and Love) Cases and Materials on Equitable Remedies and Restitution, 1980, (with Whitman) Land Transactions and Finance, 1983, rev. edit., 2001, (with Whitman) Real Estate Finance Law, 1985, rev. edit., 1994, (with Leavell and Love) Cases and Materials on Equitable Remedies, Restitution and Damages, 1986, rev. edit., 1994, rev. edit., 2000, (with Whitman) Cases and Materials on Real Estate Transfer, Finance and Development, 1987, (with Browder, Cunningham, Stoebuck and Whitman) Basic Property Law, 1989, (with Stoebuck and Whitman) Contemporary Property, 1996, (with Whitman) Cases and Materials on Real Estate Transfer, Finance and Development, 1992, rev. edit., 1998; co-reporter ALI Restatement of Property-Mortgages; contbr. articles to profl. jours. 1st lt. AUS, 1964-65. Recipient award for meritorious service and achievement U. Mo. Law Sch. Found., 1974; recipient Disting. Faculty Service award U. Mo.-Columbia Alumni Assn., 1978, Disting. Faculty award, 1986, Disting. Non-Alumnus award, 1991, Rutter award for excellence in tchg. UCLA Law Sch., 2000. Mem. Am. Law Inst., Assn. Am. Law Schs. (sect. chmn. 1976-77), Am. Coll. Real Estate Lawyers, Mo. Bar Assn. (vice chmn. property law com. 1974-75, chmn. 1975-77), Order of Coif, Phi Beta Kappa, Phi Delta Phi. Office: UCLA Sch Law Hilgard Ave PO Box 951476 Los Angeles CA 90095-1476

NELSON, HAROLD BERNHARD, museum director; b. Providence, May 14, 1947; s. Harold B. and Eleanor (Lavina) N. BA, Bowdoin Coll., 1969; MA, U. Del., 1972. Rsch. fellow NMAA Smithsonian Inst., Washington, 1976-77; curator Am. art Mus. Art & Archeol., U. Mo., Columbia, 1977-79; registrar Solomon R. Guggenheim Mus., N.Y.C., 1979-83; exhibition program dir. Am. Fedn. Arts, N.Y.C., 1983-89; dir. Long Beach (Calif.) Mus. of Art, 1989—. Juror Annual Art Exhibition Mus. Art, Sci. & Industry, Bridgeport, Conn., 1988, Annual Art Exhibition, Clark County Dist. Libr., Las Vegas, Nev., 1984; speaker Am. Assn. Mus. Annual Conf., Detroit, 1985, annual meeting Western Mus. Conf., Portland, Oreg., 1987, Grantmakers in Art Symposium, N.Y.C., 1986, annual meeting Western Mus. Conf., Salt Lake City, 1985; mem. adv. com. APA, Assn. Sci. and Tech. Ctrs.; panelist Aid to Spl. Exhibitions, NEA, Washington, 1986; participant Am. Legal Assn., ABA Conf., San Francisco, 1986; observer, respondent Mus. Symposium, NEA, Dallas, 1985. Author: Sounding the Depths: 150 Years of American Seascape, 1989, New Visions: Selina Trieff, 1997, Bountiful Harvest: American Decorative Arts from the Gail-Oxford Collection, 1997, For a New Nation: American Decorative Arts from the Gail-Oxford Collection, 1998, In Ye Grandest Manner and After Ye Newest Fashion, 2000, Conjunction: The Melba and Al Langman Collection, 2000, Tulips, Pomegranates and Kings: Delftware from the Collection of Benjamin F. Edwards III, 2000, Imps on a Bridge: Wedgwood Fairyland and Other Lustres, 2001. Office: Long Beach Mus Art 2300 E Ocean Blvd Long Beach CA 90803-2442

NELSON, HARRY, journalist, medical writer; b. Interlachen, Fla., Apr. 18, 1923; s. Knut Alfred and Edith Farr (Wilkes) N.; m. Diane Gabriella Meerschaert, Aug. 29, 1948 (div. 1977); children— Tanya Ann, Lawrence Stephen, Ronald Gerard, James Anthony, John Christopher; m. Gita Doris Wheelis, Jan. 29, 1984 B.A., U. So. Calif., 1949. Reporter, photographer Bakersfield Press, Calif., 1949; reporter, photographer Bakersfield Community Chest, 1949; promotion writer Los Angeles Times, 1949-57, reporter, 1957-58, med. writer, 1958-88, sr. writer, 1977-80; freelance med. writer, 1988—; staff writer Milbank Meml. Fund, 1993—. Charter mem. bd. dirs. Los Angeles County Comprehensive Health Planning Assn., Los Angeles, 1968-69. Served with USAAF, 1941-45 Recipient spl. commendation AMA, 1974, John Hancock award John Hancock Ins. Co., 1978, Journalism award Am. Acad. Pediatrics, 1979, Disting. Svc. by nonphysician award Calif. Med. Assn., 1988, Lifetime Achievement in med. writing award AMA, 1988, Peter Lisagor award for exemplary journalism Chgo. Headliners Club, 1988. Mem. Nat. Assn. Sci. Writers (pres. 1966). Avocations: sailing; hiking; ceramics. Address: Med Writers Internat PO Box N 14016 Yellowstone Dr Frazier Park CA 93222

NELSON, HELEN MARTHA, retired library director; b. Anaconda, Mont., Dec. 20, 1929; d. Ole Bertin and Caroline Helen (Massey) N. BA with honors, U. Mont., 1951; MLS, U. Wash., 1960. Asst. documents and serials libr. U. Mont., Missoula, 1951-52; tchr. English and history, libr. Laurel H.S., 1952-54; tchr. English, libr. Beaverhead County H.S., 1954-56; tchr. English, journalism Anaconda Sr. H.S., 1956-59; libr., adminstr. U.S. Army, 1960-68; libr. dir. Oceanside (Calif.) Libr., 1968-94. Chmn. Serra Coop. Libr., 1973-74, 84-85, 90-91; mem. coun. Serra Coop. Sys., 1969-94. Chmn. Christian Sponsors, Oceanside, 1975; congl. pres. King of Kings Luth. Ch., Oceanside, 1974, 77, 84, mem. coun. 1971-77, 82-84, 92-94; bd. dirs. Oceanside/Carlsbad ARC, 1970-71; del. Calif. Gov.'s Conf. Librs. and Info. Sci. Mem. ALA, AAUW, LWV (Action award 1998), Mont. Libr. Assn., Calif. Libr. Assn. (coun. 1978-80, v.p. Palomar chpt. 1978), Pub. Libr. Execs. of So. Calif., Oceanside C. of C., Calif. Inst. Libr. (bd. dirs. 1978-80). Avocations: photography, travel, crewel embroidery. E-mail: hnelson23@home.com

NELSON, HOWARD JOSEPH, geographer, educator; b. Gowrie, Iowa, Jan. 12, 1919; s. Joseph A. and Hannah (Swanson) N.; m. Betty Marie Garlick, June 18, 1944; children: Linda Ann, James Allan. B.A. with high honors, Iowa State Tchrs. Coll., 1942; M.A., U. Chgo., 1947, Ph.D., 1949. Mem. faculty UCLA, 1949—, prof. geography, 1963-86, prof. emeritus, 1986—, chmn. dept., 1966-71. Author: (with W.A.V. Clark) Los Angeles, The Metropolitan Experience, 1976, The Los Angeles Metropolis, 1983. Served with AUS, 1943-46. Mem. Assn. Am. Geographers (regional councillor 1968-71), Sigma Xi. Home: 6136 Kentland Ave Woodland Hills CA 91367-1719 Office: Univ Calif Dept Geography Los Angeles CA 90024

NELSON, JAMES ALONZO, radiologist, educator; b. Cherokee, Iowa, Oct. 20, 1938; s. Joe George and Ruth Geraldine (Jones) N.; m. Katherine Metcalf, July 16, 1966; children: John Metcalf, Julie Heaps. AB, Harvard U., 1961, MD, 1965. Asst. prof. radiology U. Calif., San Francisco, 1972-74; assoc. prof. U. Utah, Salt Lake City, 1974-79, prof., 1979-86, U. Wash., Seattle, 1986-2000, prof. emeritus, 2000—. Co-founder Circulation, Inc.; dir. radiol. rsch. U. Calif./Ft. Miley VA Hosp., 1973-74, U. Utah, 1974-85, U. Wash., 1986-98; mem. bd. sci. advisors NeoVision, 1995-96, Oreg. Life Scis., 1995—; co-founder Circulation, Inc., 1996; mem. adv. panel on non-radioactive diagnostic agts. USP, 1984-96. Contbr. chpts. to books, articles to Am. Jour. Roentgenology, Radiology, Investigative Radiology, others. Capt. USAF, 1967-69. John Harvard scholar, 1957-61, James Picker Found. scholar, 1973-77; recipient Mallinkrodt prize Soc. Body Computerized Tomography, 1990, Roscoe Miller award Soc. Gastrointestinal Radiology, 1991. Fellow Am. Coll. Radiology (diplomate); mem. Radiol. Soc. N.Am., Assn. Univ. Radiology. Achievements include patents (with others) for Non-Surgical Peritoneal Lavage, Recursive Band-Pass Filter for Digital Angiography, for Unsharp Masking for Chest Films, Oral Hepatobiliary MRI Contrast Agent, non-surgical myocardial revascularization. Office: U Wash Dept Radiology Diagnostic Imaging Sci Ctr PO Box 357115 Seattle WA 98195-7115 E-mail: jimnel@mindspring.com

NELSON, JAMES AUGUSTUS, II, real estate executive, architect, banker; b. Damrascotta, Maine, July 26, 1947; s. Robert Maynard and Margret Rebbeca (Harmision) N.; m. Linda Ray, Aug. 15, 1975 (div. 1985); m. Tina Nides, Oct. 22, 1986 (div. 1991); 1 child, Jennifer Alexandria. BArch, Columbia U., 1973, MBA, 1974. Resident v.p. Citibank, N.Y.C., 1974-77; group v.p. Bank of Am., San Francisco, 1977-82; assoc. John Portman and Assocs., Atlanta, 1983-85; pres. J.A. Nelson and Assocs., L.A., 1986-88; dir. real estate planning and devel. Universal Studios, L.A., 1988-94; founder Mother Co., Hollywood, Calif., 1995. Master planner, Internat. Gateway of the Ams., San Yisedro, Calif. Author: Banker's Guide to Construction, 1978, Doing Business in Saudi Arabia, 1979. Chmn. Eco. Dev. Com., L.A. Conservancy-Broadway Iniative, Laurel Canyon Coalition, L.A.; bd. dirs. Laurel Canyon Assn., Hollywood Heritage, Hillside Fedn., L.A., Lookout Mountain Assocs., L.A.; developer Universal CityWalk Project. Recipient Innovative Design award for Universal CityWalk, Internat. Coun. Shopping Ctrs., 1994, best new home of yr. award Metro. Home, 1989, commendation and pres.'s award Hillside Fedn., 1989, 1992. Avocations: gardening, architecture. Office: Mother Co 8306 Grand View Dr Los Angeles CA 90046-1918 E-mail: motherco@aol.com

NELSON, JAMES C, state supreme court justice; b. Idaho; m. Chari Werner; 2 children. BBA, U. Idaho, 1966; JD cum laude, George Washington U., 1974. Fin. analyst SEC, Washington; pvt. practice Cut Bank; county atty. Glacier County; assoc. judge Mont. Supreme Ct., 1993—. Former mem. State Bd. Oil and Gas Conservation, also chmn.; former mem. State Gaming Adv. Counsel, Gov. Adv. Coun. on Corrections and Criminal Justice Policy; liaison to Commn. of Cts. of Ltd. Jurisdiction, mem. adv. com. Ct. Assessment Program. Served U.S. Army. Office: Justice Bldg Supreme Ct Mont PO Box 203001 215 N Sanders St Rm 315 Helena MT 59624-3001

NELSON, JERRY EARL, astrophysics educator; b. Glendale, Calif., Jan. 15, 1944; BS, Calif. Inst. Tech., 1965; PhD in Physics, U. Calif., Berkeley, 1972. Fellow in particle physics Lawrence Berkeley Lab. U. Calif., Berkeley, 1972-75, prof. astrophysics, 1975-96, prof. Santa Cruz, 1996—. Recipient Joseph Fraunhofer/Robert M. Burley prize Optical Soc. Am., 1997. Mem. Am. Phys. Soc., Am. Astron. Soc. (Dannie Heineman prize for Astrophysics 1995). Office: U Calif Santa Cruz Santa Cruz CA 94710-1625

NELSON, JOHN C. obstetrician/gynecologist; b. 1944; m. Linda Nelson; 8 children. MPH, U. Utah, 1993, MD. Diplomate Am. Bd. Ob-Gyn. Intern Providence Hosp., Portland, Oreg.; resident U. Utah Sch. of Medicine. Charter mem. Prospective Payment Assessment Commn.; dep. dir. Utah's Dept. of Health; leader govs. task force on child abuse and neglect, teenage pregnancy prevention. Com. mem. Utah Domestic Violence adv. com.; bd. dirs. Salt Lake City Boys and Girls Club. With U.S. Army. Recipient Light of Learning award Utah State Office of Edn. Fellow Am. Coll. of Ob-Gyn.; mem. AMA (bd. trustees 1994, del. to AMA policy making house 1981), Utah Med. Assn. (former pres.), Salt Lake City County Med. Soc. Office: 370 9th Ave Ste 101 Salt Lake City UT 84103-3186 also: AMA 515 N State St Chicago IL 60610-4325

NELSON, JONATHAN, computer communications company executive; Prodr. music industry; co-founder Wired mag.; CEO Organic Online, San Francisco, 1993—. Office: Organic Online 510 3rd St Ste 540 San Francisco CA 94107-3803

NELSON, LINDA J. state legislator; b. Plentywood, Mont., June 12, 1942; m. Roger Nelson. Grad., Medicine Lake H.S. Farmer, rancher; mem. Mont. Ho. of Reps., 1989-94, Mont. Senate, Dist. 49, Helena, 1994—; mem. ethics com., mem. rules com., mem. fin. and claims com.; mem. agr., livestock and irrigation com.; mem. jt. appropriations subcom. natural resources/commerce; minority whip Mont. Senate, 1999-2000. Mem. Medicine Lake (Mont.) Sch. Bd., 1981-88, chair, 1984-88; active Mont. Dem. Party. Mem. Women Involved in Farm Econs., Nat. Order Legis. Women, N.E. Mont. Land and Mineral Owners Assn., Mont. Grain Growers, Sheridan County Dem. Women. Democrat. Lutheran. Home: 469 Griffin Medicine Lake MT 59247-9708

NELSON, MARK BRUCE, interior designer; b. Los Angeles, Dec. 8, 1921; s. Mark Bruce and Rubie (Henrionnet) N. B.A. in Art, U. Calif., Los Angeles, 1943, postgrad., 1949-50, Art Center Sch., 1946-49. Tchr. Pasadena (Calif.) City Coll., 1950-54; propr. Mark Nelson Interiors, Los Angeles, 1954—; designer DuPont Corp. exhibit N.Y. World's Fair, 1964; co-chmn. Los Angeles show com. Am. Inst. Interior Designers, 1960-67, Living with Famous Paintings, 1964-65. Mem. Los Angeles adv. council Am. Arbitration Assn., 1971-72; chmn. Los Angeles N.C.I.D.Q., 1973-80, Design House West, 1978 Mem. Los Angeles Beautiful Com., 1966. Served as officer USNR, 1942-46, 52-53, ETO, Korea. Fellow Am. Soc. Interior Designers (life mem., exam. chmn. 1972— , chmn. nat. by-laws com. 1973, pres. Los Angeles 1969-71, Calif. regional v.p. 1970-73, pres. Los Angeles found. 1980, Presdl. citation 1973); mem. Phi Kappa Sigma. Home and Office: 554 Lillian Way Los Angeles CA 90004-1106

NELSON, MAURICE S., JR. metal products company executive; CEO Earle M Jorgensen Co., Brea, Calif. Office: Earle M Jorgensen Co PO Box 2315 3050 E Birch St Brea CA 92822-2315

NELSON, PAUL WILLIAM, real estate broker; b. Mpls., Mar. 7, 1952; s. William H. and Jean (Darrington) N.; m. Jill Brownson, Oct. 18, 1986 (dec. Nov. 1990); children: Emily J., Joshua C.; m. Robin K. Carpenter, Aug. 14, 1993. BS, U. Colo., 1974. Lic. real estate broker, Colo. Advt. dir. Denver Beechcraft, 1976-77; real estate broker Coldwell Banker, Grand Junction, Colo., 1977—. Bd. dirs. Colo. Assn. Realtors, Denver, 1981-83. Mem. Grand Junction City Coun., 1985-93, also mayor pro tem; mem. Downtown Devel. Authority, Grand Junction, 1985-91; bd. dirs. Mesa County Planning Commn., Grand Junction, 1980-85, Colo. Nat. Monument Assn., 1989-91, Grand Junction Visitors and Conv. Bur., 1993-96; Lobbying Group; mem. Mesa County Uranium Mill Tailings Removal Citizens Com.; mem. co-chmn. Mesa County Riverfront Commn., 1993-99; mem. dist. resource adv. coun. Bur. Land Mgmt., 1990-92, Grand Junction Visitors and Conv. Bur. bd. dirs., 1992-96; mem. Colo. Juvenile Parole Bd., 2000—; trustee Colo. Riverfront Found., 1999—. Recipient Citizen Svc. award Mesa County, 1985, winner Parade Mag. MIlennium Photo Contest. Mem. Mesa County Assn. Realtors (bd. dirs. 1981-83, treas. 1999—), Rotary, Club 20 (bd. dirs. 1994-96). Republican. Avocations: pvt. pilot, skiing. Office: Coldwell Banker PO Box 3117 Grand Junction CO 81502-3117 E-mail: pablonelsoni@yahoo.com

NELSON, ROGER HUGH, management educator, business executive; b. Spring City, Utah, Mar. 7, 1931; s. Hugh Devere and Maudella Sarah (Larsen) N.; m. DeEtte Munk, Aug. 26, 1955 (dec. Sept. 1998); children— Steven R., Deanne, Mark L. B.S., U. Utah, 53, M.S., 1953; Ed.D., Columbia U., 1958. Mem. faculty U. Utah Coll. Bus., 1953-97, prof. mgmt., 1970-97, prof. emeritus, 1997—, dir. programs in emerging bus., 1989-97, chmn. mgmt. dept., 1976-82, asst. dean, 1969-74; dir. MBA integrative field studies, 1993-96; pres. David Eccles Sch. of Bus. Faculty, 1995-96; mem. faculty Utah Mgmt. Inst., 1968-75; v.p. Computer Logic Corp., 1970-73; pres. Am. Leisure & Sports Investment Corp., 1973-75, Oil Resources, Inc., 1980-88, Puma Energy Corp., 1981-88, The Ultimate Choice Catalog Co., 1986—. Fin. and mgmt. cons., 1965— ; founder Utah Small Bus. Devel. Center, U. Utah, 1979; trustee Utah Tech. Fin. Corp., 1998—; chmn. Am. Recreation and Sports, Inc., 1996—. Author: Personal Money Management, 1973, The Utah Entrepreneur's Guide, 1995, also articles, reports, manuals. Active local Am. Heart Assn., Am. Cancer Soc. campaigns; mem. exec. bd. Utah Opera Co., 1981-85, gen. bd., 1985-89. Danforth Teaching fellow, 1957 Mem. Acad. Mgmt., Adminstrv. Mgmt. Soc., NEA, AAUP, Phi Kappa Phi, Beta Gamma Sigma, Phi Delta Kappa, Delta Phi Epsilon. Inventor comml. color separation camera and related dye-transfer processes. Home: 2662 Skyline Dr Salt Lake City UT 84108-2855 Office: U Utah David Eccles Sch Bus Salt Lake City UT 84112

NELSON, RONALD L. film company executive; Exec. v.p., CFO Paramount Comm. Inc. (formerly Gulf & Western Inc), 1987-94, bd. dirs., 1992; CFO, founding mem. DreamWorks SKG, Univeral City, Calif., 1994—. Bd. dirs. Advanced Tissue Scis., Inc., 1997—. Office: DreamWorks SKG 100 Universal Plaza Universal City CA 91608

NELSON, RUSSELL MARION, surgeon, educator; b. Salt Lake City, Sept. 9, 1924; s. Marion C. and Edna (Anderson) N.; m. Dantzel White, Aug. 31, 1945; children: Marsha Nelson McKellar, Wendy Nelson Maxfield, Gloria Nelson Irion, Brenda Nelson Miles, Sylvia Nelson Webster, Emily Nelson Wittwer (dec.), Laurie Nelson Marsh, Rosalie Nelson Ringwood, Marjorie Nelson Helsten, Russell Marion Jr. BA, U. Utah, 1945, MD, 1947; PhD in Surgery, U. Minn., 1954; ScD (hon.), Brigham Young U., 1970; DMS (hon.), Utah State U., 1989; LHD (hon.), Snow Coll., 1994. Diplomate: Am. Bd. Surgery, Am. Bd. Thoracic Surgery (dir. 1972-78). Intern U. Minn. Hosps., Mpls., 1947, asst. resident surgery, 1948-51; first asst. resident surgery Mass. Gen. Hosp., Boston, 1953-54; sr.

resident surgery U. Minn. Hosps., Mpls., 1954-55; practice medicine (specializing in cardiovascular and thoracic surgery), Salt Lake City, 1959-84; staff surgeon Latter-day Saints Hosp., Salt Lake City, 1959-84, dir. surg. research lab., 1959-72, chief cardiovascular-thoracic surg. div., 1967-72, also bd. govs., 1970-90, vice chmn., 1979-89; staff surgeon Primary Children's Hosp., Salt Lake City, 1960; attending in surgery VA Hosp., Salt Lake City, 1955-84, Univ. Hosp., Salt Lake City, 1955-84; asst. prof. surgery Med. Sch. U. Utah, Salt Lake City, 1955-59, asst. clin. prof. surgery, 1959-66, asso. clin. prof. surgery, clin. prof., 1966-69, research prof. surgery, 1970-84, clin. prof. emeritus, 1984—; staff services Utah Biomed. Test Lab., 1970-84. Dir. tng. program cardiovascular and thoracic surgery at Univ. Utah affiliated hosps., 1967-84; mem. policyholders adv. com. New Eng. Mut. Life Ins. Co., Boston, 1976-80 Contbr. articles to profl. jours. Mem. White House Conf. on Youth and Children, 1960; bd. dirs. Internat. Cardiol. Found.; bd. govs. LDS Hosp., 1970-90, Deseret Gymnasium, 1971-75, Promised Valley Playhouse, 1970-79; mem. adv. com. U.S. Sec. of State on Religious Freedom Abroad, 1996-99. 1st lt. to capt. M.C., AUS, 1951-53. Markle scholar in med. scis., 1957-59; Fellowship of Medici Publici U. Utah Coll., 1967; Gold Medal of Merit, Argentina, 1974; named Hon. Prof. Shandong Med. U., Jinan, People's Republic of China, 1985; Old People's U., Jinan, 1986; Xi-an (People's Republic of China) Med. Coll., 1986, Legacy of Life award, 1993. Fellow A.C.S. (chmn. adv. council on thoracic surgery 1973-75), Am. Coll. Cardiology, Am. Coll. Chest Physicians; mem. Am. Assn. Thoracic Surgery, Am. Soc. Artificial Internal Organs, AMA, Dirs. Thoracic Residencies (pres. 1971-72), Utah Med. Assn. (pres. 1970-71), Salt Lake County Med. Soc., Am. Heart Assn. (exec. com. cardiovascular surgery 1972, dir. 1976-78, chmn. council cardiovascular surgery 1976-78), Utah Heart Assn. (pres. 1964-65), Soc. Thoracic Surgeons, Soc. Vascular Surgery (sec. 1968-72, pres. 1974), Utah Thoracic Soc., Salt Lake Surg. Soc., Samson Thoracic Surg. Soc., Western Soc. for Clin. Research, Soc. U. Surgeons, Am., Western, Pan-Pacific surg. assns., Inter. Am. Soc. Cardiology (bd. mgrs.), Phi Beta Kappa, Sigma Xi, Alpha Omega Alpha, Phi Kappa Phi, Sigma Chi. Mem. Ch. of Jesus Christ of Latter-day Saints (pres. Bonneville Stake 1964-71, gen. pres. Sunday sch. 1971-79, regional rep. 1979-84, Quorum of the Twelve Apostles 1984—). Home: 1347 Normandie Cir Salt Lake City UT 84105-1919 Office: 47 E South Temple Salt Lake City UT 84150-1200

NELSON, SARAH MILLEDGE, archaeology educator; b. Miami, Fla., Nov. 29, 1931; d. Stanley and Sarah Woodman (Franklin) M.; m. Harold Stanley Nelson, July 25, 1953; children: Erik Harold, Mark Milledge, Stanley Franklin. BA, Wellesley Coll., 1953; MA, U. Mich., 1969, PhD, 1973. Instr. archaeology U. Md. extension, Seoul, Republic Korea, 1970-71; asst. prof. U. Denver, 1974-79, assoc. prof., 1979-85, prof. archaeology, 1985—, chair dept. anthropology, 1985-95, dir. women's studies program, 1985-87, John Evans prof., dir. Asian studies, 1996, vice provost for rsch., 1998—. Vis. asst. prof. U. Colo., Boulder, 1974; resident Rockefeller Ctr. in Bellagio, Italy, 1996. Co-editor: Powers of Observation, 1990, Equity Issues for Women in Archaeology, 1994; author: Archaeology of Korea, 1993, Gender in Archaeology: Analyzing Power and Prestige, 1997, (novel) Spirit Bird Journey, 1999; co-author: Denver: An Archaeological History, 2001; editor: The Archaeology of Northeast China, 1995, Ancestors for the Pigs: Pigs in Prehistory, 1998; co-editor: In Pursuit of Gender: Worldwide Archaeological Perspectives, 2001. Active Earthwatch, 1989. Recipient Outstanding Scholar award U. Denver, 1989; grantee S.W. Inst. Rsch. on Women, 1981, Acad. Korean Studies, Seoul, 1983, Internat. Cultural Soc. Korea, 1986, Colo. Hist. Fund, 1995-97, Rockefeller Found. Residency, Bellagio, Italy. Fellow Am. Anthrop. Assn.; mem. Soc. Am. Archaeology, Assn. Asian Studies, Royal Asiatic Soc., Sigma Xi (sec.-treas. 1978-79), Phi Beta Kappa. Democrat. Avocations: skiing, gardening. Home: 5878 S Dry Creek Ct Littleton CO 80121-1709 Office: U Denver Dept Anthropology Denver CO 80208-0001 E-mail: snelson@du.edu

NELSON, STEWART, computer company executive; With IBM; sr. v.p. Novell, 1994, COO, 2000—. Office: Novell Inc 122 E 1700 S Provo UT 84606-6194

NELSON, THOMAS G. federal judge; b. 1936; Student, Univ. Idaho, 1955-59, LLB, 1962. Ptnr. Parry, Robertson, and Daly, Twin Falls, Idaho, 1965-79, Nelson, Rosholt, Robertson, Tolman and Tucker, Twin Falls, from 1979; judge U.S. Ct. of Appeals (9th cir.), Boise, Idaho, 1990—. With Idaho Air N.G., 1962-65, USAR, 1965-68. Mem. ABA (ho. of dels. 1974, 87-89), Am. Bar Found., Am. Coll. Trial Lawyers, Idaho State Bar (pres., bd. commrs.), Idaho Assn. Def. Counsel, Am. Bd. Trial Advocates (pres. Idaho chpt.), Phi Alpha Delta, Idaho Law Found. Office: US Ct Appeals 9th Circuit 304 N Eighth St PO Box 1339 Boise ID 83701-1339*

NELSON, WALTER WILLIAM, computer programmer, consultant; b. Seattle, May 7, 1954; s. Arne A. and Helen R. (Truitt) N.; m. Paula E. Truax, Dec. 21, 1985. BA in Zoology, U. Wash., 1976, BS in Psychology, 1977; PhC in Psychology, U. Minn., 1982. Systems analyst Dept. of Social and Health Svcs., State of Wash., Seattle, 1986-89; computer info. cons. Dept. of Health, State of Wash., Seattle, 1989-90; pres. Data Dimensions, Inc. (name now Nelson Consulting, Inc.), Seattle, 1990—. Pres. Tech. Alliance, Renton, Wash., 1990-91, Nelson Family Homes, Inc., 1996—, Women's Fin. Resources, Inc., 1998—. Contbr. articles to profl. jours. Mem. Tech Alliance, Berkeley Macintosh Users Group, Seattle Downtown Macintosh Bus. Users Group, 4th Dimension Spl. Interest Group (founder, pres. 1990—), Am. Singles Golf Assn. (founder Seattle chpt. 1999). Avocations: tennis, golf, thoroughbred horse racing. Office: Nelson Consulting Inc 6729 20th Ave NW Seattle WA 98117-5707

NELSON, WILLIAM RANKIN, surgeon, educator; b. Charlottesville, Va., Dec. 12, 1921; s. Hugh Thomas and Edith (Rankin) N.; m. Nancy Laidley, Mar. 17, 1956 (div. 1979); children: Robin Page Nelson Russel, Susan Kimberly Nelson Wright, Anne Rankin Nelson Cron; m. Pamela Morgan Phelps, July 5, 1984. BA, U. Va., 1943, MD, 1945. Diplomate Am. Bd. Surgery. Intern Vanderbilt U. Hosp., Nashille, 1945-46; resident in surgery U. Va. Hosp., Charlottesville, 1949-51; fellow surg. oncology Meml. Sloan Kettering Cancer Ctr., N.Y.C., 1951-55; instr. U. Colo. Sch. Medicine, Denver, 1955-57, asst. clin. prof., 1962-87, clin. prof. surgery, 1987—. Asst. prof. Med. Coll. Va., Richmond, 1957-62; mem. exec. com. U. Colo. Cancer Ctr.; mem. nat. bd., nat. exec. com. Am. Cancer Soc. Contbr. articles to profl. jours. and chpts. to textbooks. Capt. USAAF, 1946-48. Recipient Nat. Div. award Am. Cancer Soc., 1979. Fellow Am. Coll. Surgeons (bd. govs. 1984-89); mem. AMA, Internat. Soc. Surgery, Brit. Assn. Surg. Oncology, Royal Soc. Medicine (U.K.), Soc. Surg. Oncology (pres. 1975-76), Soc. Head and Neck Surgeons (pres. 1986-87), Am. Cancer Soc. (pres. Colo. div. 1975-77, exec. com., nat. bd. dirs., del. dir. from Colo. div. 1985-94), Am. Soc. Clin. Oncology, Western Surg. Assn. Colo. Med. Soc., Denver Med. Soc., Denver Acad. Surgery, Rocky Mt. Oncology Soc., Univ. Club, Rotary. Republican. Episcopalian. Avocations: skiing, backpacking, travel, bicycling, fly fishing. E-mail: wrn12@gwest.net

NEMIR, DONALD PHILIP, lawyer; b. Oakland, Calif., Oct. 31, 1931; s. Philip F. and Mary (Shavor) N. AB, U. Calif., Berkeley, 1957, JD, 1960. Bar: Calif. 1961, U.S. Dist. Ct. (no. dist.) Calif. 1961, U.S. Ct. Appeals (9th cir.) 1961, U.S. Dist. Ct. (ctrl. dist.) Calif. 1975, U.S. Supreme Ct. 1980. Pvt. practice, San Francisco, 1961—. Pres. Law Offices of Donald Nemir, A Profl. Corp. Mem. Calif. State Bar Assn. Home: PO Box 1089 Mill Valley CA 94942-1089

NEMIRO, BEVERLY MIRIUM ANDERSON, author, educator; b. St. Paul, May 29, 1925; d. Martin and Anna Mae Anderson; m. Jerome Morton Nemiro, Feb. 10, 1951 (div. May 1975); children: Guy Samuel, Lee Anna, Dee Martin. Student, Reed Coll., 1943-44; BA, U. Colo., 1947; postgrad., U. Denver. Tchr. Seattle Pub. Schs., 1945-46; fashion coord., dir. Denver Dry Goods Co., 1948-51; fashion dir. Denver Market Week Assn., 1952-53; free-lance writer Denver, 1958—. Moderator TV program Your Presch. Child, Denver, 1955-56; instr. writing and comm. U. Colo. Denver Ctr., 1970—, U. Calif., San Diego, 1976-78, Met. State Coll., 1985; dir. pub. rels. Fairmont Hotel, Denver, 1979-80; freelance fashion and TV model. Author, co-author: The Complete Book of High Altitude Baking, 1961, Colorado a la Carte, 1963, Colorado a la Carte, Series II, 1966, (with Donna Hamilton) The High Altitude Cookbook, 1969, The Busy People's Cookbook, 1971 (Better Homes and Gardens Book Club selection 1971), Where to Eat in Colorado, 1967, Lunch Box Cookbook, 1965, Complete Book of High Altitude Baking, 1961, (under name Beverly Anderson) Single After 50, 1978, The New High Altitude Cookbook, 1980. Co-founder, pres. Jr. Symphony Guild, Denver, 1959-60; active Friends of Denver Libr., Opera Colo.; mem. Friends of Painting and Sculpture, Denver Art Mus. Recipient Top Hand award Colo. Authors' League, 1969, 72, 79-82, 100 Best Books of Yr. award N.Y. Times, 1969, 71; named one of Colo.'s Women of Yr., Denver Post, 1964. Mem. Am. Soc. Journalists and Authors, Colo. Authors League (dir. 1969-79), Authors Guild, Authors League Am., Friends Denver Libr., Opera Colo. Guild, Denver Women's Press Club, Rotary, Kappa Alpha Theta. Address: Park Towers 1299 Gilpin St Apt 15W Denver CO 80218-2556

NEN, ROBERT ALLEN (ROBB NEN), professional baseball player; b. San Pedro, Calif., Nov. 28, 1969; s. Dick Nen. Grad. high sch., Los Alamitos, Calif. With Tex. Rangers, 1993; pitcher Fla. Marlins, 1993-97, San Francisco Giants, 1997—. Office: San Francisco Giants 3 Com Park 24 Willie Mays Plz San Francisco CA 94107-2199

NEPTUNE, JOHN ADDISON, chemistry educator, consultant; b. Barnesville, Ohio, Nov. 27, 1919; s. George Addison and Lola Mae (Skinner) N.; m. Ruth Elizabeth Dorsey, Aug. 24, 1947; 1 child, Benjamin BS summa cum laude, Muskingum Coll., 1942; MS, U. Wis., 1949, PhD, 1952. Instr. chemistry Muskingum Coll., New Concord, Ohio, 1943-44, 45-48; foreman Tenn. Eastman Corp., Manhattan Project, 1944-45; asst. prof. chemistry Bowling Green State U., Ohio, 1949-50; instr. pharm. chemistry U. Wis.-Madison, 1952-55; asst. prof. chemistry San Jose State U., Calif., 1955-58, assoc. prof., 1958-61, prof., 1961-90, chmn. dept., 1973-86. Mem. Am. Chem. Soc., AAUP Methodist Home: 50 Cherokee Ln San Jose CA 95127-2513 Office: San Jose State U Dept Chemistry San Jose CA 95192-0001

NESMITH, MICHAEL, film producer, video specialist; b. Houston, Dec. 30, 1942; s. Warren and Bette Nesmith; m. Phyliss Nesmith; children: Christian, Jonathan, Jessica; m. 2d, Kathryn Nesmith. Chmn., chief exec. officer Pacific Arts Corp. (div. Nesmith Enterprises), L.A., 1987—. Author, producer, performer various records, 1968-77; mem. (rock group) The Monkees; co-author, exec. producer: (films) including Timerider; actor: (films) Head, 1968, Burglar, 1987, (TV series) The Monkees, Hey Hey It's the Monkees, 1997; exec. producer: (films) Repo Man, 1984, Square Dance, 1986, Tapeheads, 1988; exec. producer, actor: (video) Dr. Duck's Super Secret All-Purpose Sauce, Michael Nesmith Live, 1992; producer: (series) Television Parts, 1985; co-author, producer: (pilot) for TV Pop Clips, original concept for MTV.; creator PBS Home Video. Trustee Gihon Found., 1970—, McMurray Found., 1970—. Recipient 1st Video Grammy for Elephant Paris Christian Scientist. Office: William Morris Agy 151 S El Camino Dr Beverly Hills CA 90212-2775

NESTER, EUGENE WILLIAM, microbiology educator; b. Johnson City, N.Y., Sept. 15, 1930; married, 1959; 2 children. BS, Cornell U., 1952; PhD, Western Reserve U., 1959. Am. Cancer Soc. rsch. fellow genetics Stanford U., 1959-62, instr. microbiology, 1962-63, from asst. to assoc. prof. microbiology and genetics, 1963-72; prof. microbiology U. Wash., Seattle, 1972—, chmn. microbiology, 1982-96. Recipient Chiron Corp. Biotechnology Rsch. award, Australia prize, 1990. Fellow NAS, AAAS, Am. Acad. Microbiology; mem. Am. Soc. Microbiology. Achievements include bacterial-plant relationships. Office: U Wash Microbiology Dept Box 357242 Seattle WA 98195-7242

NETHERCUTT, GEORGE RECTOR, JR. congressman, lawyer; b. Spokane, Wash., Oct. 7, 1944; s. George Rector and Nancy N.; m. Mary Beth Socha Nethercutt, Apr. 2., 1977; children: Meredith, Elliott. BA in English, Wash. State U., 1967; JD, Gonzaga U., 1971. Bar: D.C. 1972. Law clk. to Hon. Raymond Plummer U.S. Dist. Ct. Alaska, Anchorage, 1971; staff counsel to U.S. Senator Ted Stevens Washington, 1972; chief of staff to U.S. Senator Ted Stevens Washington, 1972-76; pvt. practice Spokane, Wash., 1977-94; mem. 106th Congress from 5th Wash. dist., Washington, 1994—. Mem. house appropriations and sci. coms. Chmn. Spokane County Rep. Party, 1990-94, co-founder Vanessa Behan Crisis Nursery, pres. Spokane Juvenile Diabetes Found., 1993-94. Mem. Masons (lodge #34), Lions Club (Spokane Ctrl.), Sigma Nu. Republican. Presbyterian. Avocations: running, handball, squash. Office: US House Reps 223 Cannon HOB Washington DC 20515-0001

NETZEL, PAUL ARTHUR, fund raising management executive, consultant; b. Tacoma, Sept. 11, 1941; s. Marden Arthur and Audrey Rose (Jones) N.; BS in Group Work Edn., George Williams Coll., 1963; m. Diane Viscount, Mar. 21, 1963; children: Paul M., Shari Ann. Program dir. S. Pasadena-San Marino (Calif.) YMCA, 1963-66; exec. dir. camp and youth programs Wenatchee (Wash.) YMCA, 1966-67; exec. dir. Culver-Palms Family YMCA, Culver City, Calif., 1967-73; v.p. met. fin. devel. YMCA Met. Los Angeles, 1973-78, exec. v.p. devel., 1979-85; pres. bd. dirs. YMCA Employees Credit Union, 1977-80; chmn. N.Am. Fellowship of YMCA Devel. Officers, 1980-83; adj. faculty U. So. Calif. Coll. Continuing Edn., 1983-86, Loyola Marymount U., L.A., 1986-90, Calif. State U., L.A., 1991-92, UCLA Extension, 1991—; chmn., CEO Netzel Assocs., Inc., 1985—; pvt. practice cons., fund raiser. Chmn. Culver-Palms YMCA, Culver City, 1991-93, chmn. 1989-91, bd. mgrs. 1985—; pres. bd. Culver City Guidance Clinic, 1971-74; mem. Culver City Bd. Edn., 1975-79, pres., 1977-78; mem. Culver City Edn. Found., 1982-91; bd. dirs. Los Angeles Psychiat. Svc., 1971-74, Goodwill Industries of So. Calif., 1993-97; mem. Culver City Council, 1980-88, vice-mayor, 1980-82, 84-85, mayor, 1982-83, 86-87; mem. Culver City Redevel. Agy., 1980-88, chmn., 1983-84, 87-88, vice chmn, 1985-86; bd. dirs. Los Angeles County Sanitation Dists., 1982-83, 85-87, Western Region United Way, 1986-93, vice chmn, 1991-92; chmn. bd. dirs. Calif. Youth Model Legislature, 1987-92; mem. World Affairs Coun., 1989—; mem. adv. bd. Automobile Club of So. Calif., 1996—. Recipient Man of Yr. award Culver City C. of C., 1972. Mem. Nat. Soc. Fund Raising Execs. (nat. bd. dirs. 1989-91, vice chmn. 1994, v.p. bd. dirs. Greater L.A. chpt. 1986-88, pres. bd. dirs. 1989-90, Profl. of Yr. 1983), Calif. Club, Rotary (L.A. # 5, pres. 1992-93, treas. L.A. found. 1995-96), Rotary Internat. (gov. dist. 5280 1997-98), Mountain Gate Country. Address: Netzel Assocs Inc 9696 Culver Blvd Ste 204 Culver City CA 90232-2753

NEU, CARL HERBERT, JR. management consultant; b. Miami Beach, Fla., Sept. 4, 1937; s. Carl Herbert and Catherine Mary (Miller) N.; BS, MIT, 1959; MBA, Harvard U., 1961; m. Carmen Mercedes Smith, Feb. 8, 1964; children— Carl Bartley, David Conrad. Cert. profl. mgmt. cons. Indsl. liaison officer MIT, Cambridge, 1967-69; coord. forward planning Gates Rubber Co., Denver, 1969-71; pres., co-founder Dyna-Com Resources, Lakewood, Colo., 1971-77; pres., founder Neu & Co., Lakewood, 1977— ; mng. dir. Pro-Med Mgmt. Systems, Lakewood, 1981— ; lectr. Grad. Sch. Pub. Affairs, U. Colo. Denver, 1982-84. Mem. exec. coun. Episcopal Diocese Colo., 1974; mem. Lakewood City Coun., 1975-80, pres., 1976; chmn. Lakewood City Charter Commn., 1982, Lakewood Civic Found., Inc., 1986-91; pres. Lakewood on Parade, 1978, bd. dirs., 1978-80; pres. Classic Chorale, Denver, 1979, bd. dirs., 1978-83; pres. Lakewood Pub. Bldg. Authority, 1983—; bd. dirs. Metro State Coll. of Denver Found., 1990—, treas., 1994-97; bd. dirs. Kaiser Permanente Health Adv. Com., 1990—, chair, 1997. With U.S. Army, 1961-67. Decorated Bronze Star medal, Army Commendation medal; recipient Arthur Page award AT&T, 1979; Kettering Found. grantee, 1979-80. Mem. Internat. City Mgrs. Assn., Lakewood-So. Jefferson County C. of C. (bd. dirs. 1983-89, chmn. 1988, chmn. 1987-88), Jefferson County C. of C. (chmn. 1988). Republican. Episcopalian. Contbr. articles to profl. jours. Home: 8169 W Baker Ave Denver CO 80227-3129

NEUBURGER, KAREN, apparel executive; Retail buyer Maurice's, Emporium, San Francisco; v.p. merchandising Eber Internat., 1980-91; founder, pres., design dir. Karen Neuburger Sleepwear, San Rafael, Calif., 1991—. Guest appearence Oprah Winfrey TV show. Office: Karen Neuburger Sleepwear 3100 Ferner Blvd Ste J San Rafael CA 94901

NEUFELD, ELIZABETH FONDAL, biochemist, educator; b. Paris, Sept. 27, 1928; U.S. citizen; m. 1951 PhD, U. Calif., Berkeley, 1956; DHC (hon.), U. Rene Descartes, Paris, 1978; DSc (hon.), Russell Sage Coll., Troy, N.Y., 1981, Hahnemann U. Sch. Medicine, , 1984, Queens Coll., 1996. Asst. research biochemist U. Calif., Berkeley, 1957-63; with Nat. Inst. Arthritis, Metabolism and Digestive Diseases, Bethesda, Md., 1963-84, research biochemist, 1963-73, chief sect. human biochem. genetics, 1973-79, chief genetics and biochem. br., 1979-84; prof., chmn. dept. biol. chemistry UCLA Sch. Medicine, 1984—. Passano Found. sr. laureate, 1982; named Calif. Scientist of Yr., 1990; recipient Dickson prize U. Pitts., 1974, Hillenbrand award, 1975, Gairdner Found. award, 1981, Albert Lasker Clin. Med. Rsch. award, 1982, William Allan award, 1982, Elliott Cresson medal, 1984, Wolf Found. prize, 1988, Christopher Columbus Discovery award for biomed. rsch., 1992, Nat. Medal of Sci., 1994. Fellow AAAS; mem. NAS, Inst. Medicine of NAS, Am. Acad. Arts and Scis., Am. Philos. Soc., Am. Soc. Human Genetics, Am. Chem. Soc., Am. Soc. Biochemistry and Molecular Biology (pres. 1992-93), Am. Soc. Cell Biology, Am. Soc. Clin. Investigation, Am. Soc. Gene Therapy. Office: UCLA Sch Medicine Dept Biol Chemistry Los Angeles CA 90095-1737 E-mail: eneufeld@mednet.ucla.edu

NEUFELD, MACE, film company executive; b. N.Y.C., July 13, 1928; s. Philip M. and Margaret Ruth (Braun) N.; Feb. 28, 1954; children: Bradley David, Glenn Jeremy, Nancy Ann. BA, Yale U., 1948; postgrad., NYU, 1958-60. Photographer various N.Y. pubs., 1943-45; prodn. asst. Raymond E. Nelson, 1949-50; founder, owner Ray Bloch Assos., Inc., N.Y.C., 1951-59; ptnr. BNB Prodns., N.Y.C., 1959-70, Neufeld-Davis Prodns., Inc., Beverly Hills, Calif., 1981—. Trustee Am. Film Inst., 1978— ; chmn. life achievement award nominating com. and scholarship fund. Producer in assn. with Harvey Bernhard The Omen, 1976, Damien - Omen II, 1977, Omen III - The Final Conflict, 1980; producer: The Frisco Kid, 1979, Angel on My Shoulder, 1980, The American Dream, 1980; ABC-TV mini-series East of Eden, 1981; CBS-TV series Cagney and Lacey, 1984; MGM film The Aviator, 1984, ABC-TV A Death in California, 1985; producer films Transylvania 6-5000, 1985, No Way Out, 1987, The Hunt for Red October, 1989, Flight of the Intruder, 1990, Necessary Roughness, 1991, Patriot Games, 1992, Clear and Present Danger, 1994, Gettysburg, 1994, Beverly Hills Cop 3, 1994, The Saint, 1996, The General's Daughter, 1998. Photograph entitled Sammy's Home voted Picture of Yr. N.Y. World Telegram-Sun, 1955; recipient Grand prize Eastman Kodak's First Nat. Salon of Photography, 1945; named N.A.T.O./Showest Producer of the Yr., 1993. Mem. Acad. TV Arts and Scis., Acad. Motion Picture Arts and Scis., ASCAP, Am. Film Inst. Democrat. Clubs: Friars, Yale of N.Y. Office: Sony Pictures Ste 220 10202 W Washington Blvd Culver City CA 90232

NEUGEBAUER, GERRY, retired astrophysicist, educator; b. Göttingen, Germany, Sept. 3, 1932; came to U.S., 1939; s. Otto E. and Grete (Brück) N.; m. Marcia MacDonald, Aug. 26, 1956; children: Carol, Lee. B.S., Cornell U., 1954; Ph.D., Calif. Inst. Tech., 1960. Mem. faculty Calif. Inst. Tech., Pasadena, 1962—, prof. physics, 1970—, Howard Hughes Prof. Physics, 1985—, chmn. divsn. physics, math and astronomy, 1988-93; mem. staff Hale Obs., 1970-80; acting dir. Palomar Obs., 1980-81, dir., 1981; prof. physics Calif. Inst. Tech., Pasadena, now ret. Served with AUS, 1961-63. Recipient Except. Sci. Achievement medal NASA, 1972, 1984, Richtmyer Lectr. award, 1985, Space Sci. award Am. Inst. Aeronaut and Astronaut, 1985, Rumford Premium Am. Acad. Arts & Sci., 1986, Henry Norris Russell Lectureship Am. Astron. Soc., 1996. Fellow Am. Acad. Arts and Scis.; mem. NAS, Am. Philos. Soc., Am. Astron. Soc., Royal Astron. Soc., Internat. AStron. Union. Office: Calif Inst Tech Down Lab Physics 320 47 Pasadena CA 91125-0001

NEUGEBAUER, MARCIA, physicist, administrator; b. N.Y.C., Sept. 27, 1932; d. Howard Graeme MacDonald and Frances (Townsend) Marshall; m. Gerry Neugebauer, Aug. 25, 1956; children: Carol, Lee. B.S., Cornell U., 1954; M.S., U. Ill., 1956; D of Physics (hon.), U. New Hampshire, 1998. Grad. asst. U. Ill., Urbana, 1954-56; vis. fellow Clare Hall Coll., Cambridge, Eng., 1975; sr. research scientist Jet Propulsion Lab. Calif. Inst. Tech., Pasadena, 1956-96, disting. vis. scientist Jet Propulsion Lab., 1996—; vis. prof. planetary sci. Calif. Inst. Tech., Pasadena, 1986-87. Mem. com. NASA, Washington, 1960-96, NAS, Washington, 1981-94; Regents lectr. UCLA, 1990-91. Contbr. numerous articles on physics to profl. jours. Named Calif. Woman Scientist of Yr. Calif., Mus. Sci. and Industry, 1967, to Women in Tech. Internat. Hall of Fame, 1997; recipient Exceptional Sci. Achievement medal NASA, 1970, Outstanding Leadership medal NASA, 1993, Disting. Svc. medal NASA, 1997, COSPAR award for space sci., 1998. Fellow Am. Geophys. Union (sec., pres. solar planetary relationships sect. 1979-84, editor-in-chief Rev. Geophysics 1988-92, pres.-elect 1992-94, pres. 1994-96) mem. governing bd. Amer. Inst. Physics, 1995-97. Democrat. Home: 1720 Braeburn Rd Altadena CA 91001-2708 Office: Calif Inst Tech Jet Propulsion Lab/MS 169-506 4800 Oak Grove Dr Pasadena CA 91109-8001

NEUKOM, WILLIAM H. lawyer; b. Chgo., Nov. 7, 1941; s. John Goudey and Ruth (Horlick) N.; m. Diane McMakin, Dec. 28, 1963 (div. Jun. 1977); children: Josselyn, Samantha, Gillian, John. BA, Dartmouth Coll., 1964; LLB, Stanford U., 1967. Bar: Calif., Wash., U.S. Dist. Ct. (we. dist.) Wash., U.S. Dist. Ct. (no. dist.) Calif., U.S. Ct. Appeals (9th cir.) 1968, U.S. Supreme Court 1974. Atty. MacDonald, Hoague & Bayless, Seattle, 1968-77; ptnr. Shidler, McBroom, Gates & Lucas, Seattle, 1978-85; v.p., law, corp. affairs Microsoft Corp., Redmond, Wash., 1985-93, sr. v.p. law & corp. affairs, sec., 1994—. Trustee Seattle Art Mus., 1993-99; mem. Assn. Gen. Counsel, 1994—; bd. dirs. Greater Seattle C. of C., 1987—, exec. com. 1988—, YMCA Greater Seattle, 1988—, Corporate Coun. Arts, 1988—, exec. com. 1993—, Nature Conservance (Wash. chpt.), 1991-99, Oreg. Shakespeare Festival, 1993-99. Fellow ABA (bd. editors ABA Jour. 1987-93, alternate dispute resolution com. 1987-91, exec. coun. sect. individual rights and responsibilities 1972-75, 87-92, sec. 1983-87, asst. sec. 1979-83, chmn. young lawyers divsn. 1977-78); mem. Seattle-King County Bar Assn. (long range planning com. 1972-75, 88-91, mgmt., orgn. and planning com. 1986-87, indigent defense svcs. task force 1981-83, trustee legal aid bur. 1974-77, chmn. young lawyers sect. 1972-73), Wash. State Bar Assn., (sec. 1983, pres., chmn., 1977-78, task force professionalism 1986-89, judicial recommendation com. 1985-88, planning com., faculty mem. Pacific Rim Computer Law Inst. 1984-91, orgn. and govt. of bar com. 1973-75, trustee young lawyers sect. 1973-76), Wash. State Trial Lawyers Assn. Avocations: fly-fishing, skiing, running, golf, jazz. Office: Microsoft Corp 1 Microsoft Way Redmond WA 98052-8300

NEUMAN, SHLOMO P. hydrology educator; b. Zilina, Czechoslovakia, Oct. 26, 1938; came to U.S., 1963, naturalized, 1970; s. Alexander Neumann and Klara (Pikler) Lesny; m. Yael B. Neuman, Jan. 30, 1965; children: Gil, Michal, Ariel. BSc in Geology, Hebrew U., Jerusalem, 1963; MS in Engring. Sci., U. Calif., Berkeley, 1966, PhD in Engring. Sci., 1968. Cert. profl. hydrogeologist. Acting asst. prof., asst. rsch. engr. dept. civil engring. U. Calif., Berkeley, 1968-70, vis. assoc. prof. dept. civil engring., 1974-75; sr. scientist, assoc. rsch. prof. Inst. Soil and Water Agrl. Rsch. Orgn., Bet-Dagan, Israel, 1970-74; prof. hydrology dept. hydrology and water resources U. Ariz., Tucson, 1975-88, Regents' prof. dept. hydrology and water resources, 1988—. Cons. to U.S., Can. and Swedish govts. on hydrologic issues concerning nuc. waste disposal; vis. scientist dept. isotope Weizmann Inst. Sci., Rehovot, Israel, 1976; maitre de rsch. Ctr. d'Informatique Geologique, Ecole Mines Paris, Fountainebleau, France, 1978, dir. rsch., 1981; vis. prof. dept. fluid mechanics and heat transfer Tel-Aviv U., 1981; hon. appointment concurrent prof. Nanjing U., China; disting. lectr. in field; hon. prof. Nanjing Hydraulic Rsch. Inst., China, 1998—. Mem. editl. bd. Jour. Hydrology, 1977-84, Water Sci. and Tech. Libr. (The Netherlands), 1983-86, Stochastic Hydrology and Hydraulics, 1992—; mem. editl. bd. Water Resources Rsch. Jour., 1987-93, Hydrogeology Jour., 1999—; guest editor spl. issue in memory of Eugene S. Simpson Hydrogeology Jour., 1997-98; contbr. over 230 articles to profl. jours. Hebrew U. scholar, 1962-63, Edwin Letts Oliver scholar, 1965-66; Jane Lewis fellow, 1966-68; recipient Cert. of Appreciation award USDA, 1975, C.V. Theis award Am. Inst. Hydrology, 1990. Fellow Geol. Soc. Am. (O.E. Meinzer award 1976, Birdsal Disting. Lectr. 1987), Am. Geophys. Union (4th Walter B. Langbein lectr. hydrology 1996, Robert E. Horton award 1969, original mem. ISI highly cited rschrs. database 2000); mem. Soc. Petroleum Engrs. of AIME, NAE, Assn. Groundwater Scientists and Engrs. of Nat. Well Water Assn. (Sci. award 1989), Ariz. Hydrol. Soc., Internat. Assn. Hydrogeologists. Jewish. Office: U Ariz Dept Hydrology & Water Resou Tucson AZ 85721-0001 E-mail: neuman@hwr.arizona.edu

NEUMAN, TOM S. emergency medical physician, educator; b. N.Y.C., July 23, 1946; s. Otto and Susan Ann (Baltaxe) N.; m. Doris Rubin, Aug. 24, 1969; children: Allison Rachel, Russell Solomon. AB, Cornell U., 1967; MD, NYU, 1971. Diplomate Nat. Bd. Med. Examiners, Am. Bd. Internal Medicine, Am. Bd. Pulmonary Diseases, Am. Bd. Preventive Medicine in Occupl. Medicine and Underseas and Hyperbaric Medicine), Am. Bd. Emergency Medicine. Intern Bellevue Hosp., N.Y.C., 1971-72, resident, 1972-73; commd. med. officer USN, 1973; advanced through grades to capt. USNR, 1990; instr. Naval Undersea Med. Inst., New London, Conn., 1973-74; staff med. officer Submarine Devel. Group One, San Diego, 1974-76, 78-80; emergency room physician Chula Vista (Calif.) Community Hosp., 1975-80; attending physician VA Med. Ctr., La Jolla, Calif., 1976-78; fellow in pulmonary medicine and physiology U. Calif. Sch. Medicine at San Diego, 1976-78, clin. instr., 1978-80, asst. clin. prof., 1980-84, flight physician Life Flight Aeromed. Program, 1980-86, asst. dir. dept. emergency medicine, 1980-94, assoc. dir. dept. emergency medicine, 1994—, attending physician pulmonary divsn., 1980-99, assoc. clin. prof. medicine and surgery, 1984-87, base hosp. physician, 1984—, dir. Hyperbaric Med. Ctr., 1984—; med. officer UDT/SEAL Res. Unit 119, San Diego, 1980-84, Mobile Diving and Salvage Unit One, USNR, San Diego, 1984-86, PRIMUS Unit 1942-A, U. Calif. at San Diego, 1988-90; sr. med. officer Seal Teams 1/3/5, USNR, Coronado, Calif., 1986-87; asst. officer in charge Med. Unit 1942-A U. Calif. Sch. Medicine, San Diego, 1990-95, prof. clin. medicine, 1996—. Mem. med. adv. bd. western regional underwater lab. program U. So. Calif. Marine Sci. Ctr., Catalina, 1982-85; assoc. adj. prof. medicine and surgery U. Calif. Sch. Medicine at San Diego, 1987-90, adj. prof. medicine and surgery, 1990-96, prof. clin. medicine and adj. prof. surgery, 1996—; mem. San Diego Coroner's com. for investigation of diving fatalities, 1974—; mem. diving cons. Vocat. Diver Tng. Facility, Calif. Inst. Med., Chino, Calif., 1967; mem. task force City Mgr. on Carbon Monoxide Poisoning, San Diego, 1991; mem. com. for minimal course content for recreational scuba instr. cert. Am. Nat. Stds. Inst., 1992-94; chmn. emergency med. physician quality improvement com., 1992-94; mem. undersea and hyperbaric medicine exam subcom. Am. Bd. Preventative Medicine, 1999; mem. com. on creating vision for space medicine beyond earth orbit NAS; cons. NASA. Author book chpts.; contbr. articles to profl. jours. Fellow ACP, Am. Coll. Preventive Medicine; mem. Am. Thoracic Soc., Am. Lung Assn., Undersea and Hyperbaric Med. Soc. (program com. 1981-82, nominations com. 1982-83, chmn. 1988-89, mem. edn. com. 1982-87, chmn. awards com. 1983-84, v.p. exec. com. 1983-84, co-chmn. credentials com. 1984-85, editor-in-chief Undersea and Hyperbaric Medicine 1995—), Profl. Assn. Diving Instrs. (emeritus). Avocations: scuba diving, fishing, photography. Office: U Calif Med Ctr Dept Emergency Medicine 200 W Arbor Dr Dept 8676 San Diego CA 92103-8676 E-mail: tneuman@ucsd.edu

NEUMANN, EDWARD SCHREIBER, transportation engineering educator; b. Harvey, Ill., Mar. 6, 1942; s. Arthur Edward Schreiber and Adeline Ruth (Spenks) N.; m. Carole Ann Dunkelberger, Apr. 19, 1969; children: Edward Schreiber, Jonathan David. MS, Mich. Technol. U., 1964, Northwestern U., 1967, PhD, 1969, Cert. in Prosthetics, 2000. Registered profl. engr., W.Va., Nev. Mem. faculty W.Va. U., Morgantown, 1970-90, prof. transp. engring., 1980-90, interim dir. Harley O. Staggers Nat. Transp. Ctr., 1982-95, dir., 1985-90; prof. U. Nev., Las Vegas, 1991—, chmn. dept., 1991-99, dir. Transp. Rsch. Ctr., 1991-98. Editor numerous conf. procs.; contbr. articles and rsch. reports to profl. lit. Bd. dirs. Mason Dixon Hist. Park Assn., 1978-90; chmn. new transp. systems and tech. com. TRB, 1998—. Capt., C.E., AUS, 1969-70. Resources for Future fellow, 1969. Fellow Inst. Transp. Engrs.; mem. ASCE (chmn. com. on automated people movers, chmn. exec. com. urban planning and devel. divsn., chmn. exec. com. urban transp. divsn., James Laurie prize 1996), Nat. Soc. Profl. Engrs., Am. Soc. Engring. Edn., OITAF-NACS, Advanced Transit Assn. (bd. dirs., pres. 1988-90), Sigma Xi, Tau Beta Pi, Phi Kappa Phi, Phi Eta Sigma, Chi Epsilon. Methodist. Home: 935 E Eldorado Ln Las Vegas NV 89123-0515 Office: UNLV Dept Civil Environ Engring Las Vegas NV 89154-4015

NEUMANN, HERSCHEL, physics educator; b. San Bernardino, Calif., Feb. 3, 1930; s. Arthur and Dorothy (Greenhood) N.; m. Julia Black, June 15, 1951; 1 child, Keith. BA, U. Calif., Berkeley, 1951; MS, U. Oreg., 1959; PhD, U. Nebr., 1965. Theoretical physicist Gen. Electric Co., Richland, Wash., 1951-57; instr. physics U. Nebr., Lincoln, 1964-65; asst. prof. physics U. Denver, 1965-71, assoc. prof. physics, 1971-85, prof. physics, 1985—, chmn. physics and astronomy, 1985-97. Contbr. over 20 articles to profl. jours. Dir. numerous pub. outreach programs in physics. Mem. Am. Assn. Physics Tchrs. Home: 2425 S St Paul St Denver CO 80210-5516 Office: U Denver Dept Physics Astronomy Denver CO 80208-2238 E-mail: hneumann@du.edu

NEUMANN, PETER GABRIEL, computer scientist; b. N.Y.C., Sept. 21, 1932; s. J.B. and Elsa (Schmid) N.; m. Elizabeth Susan Neumann; 1 child, Helen K. AB, Harvard U., 1954, SM, 1955; Dr rerum naturarum, Technische Hochschule, Darmstadt, Fed. Republic Germany, 1960; PhD, Harvard U., 1961. Mem. tech. staff Bell Labs, Murray Hill, N.J., 1960-70; Mackay lectr. Stanford U., 1964, U. Calif., Berkeley, 1970-71; prin. scientist SRI Internat., Menlo Park, Calif., 1971—. Adj. prof. U. Md., 1999. Author: Computer-Related Risks, 1995. Fulbright grantee, 1958-60. Fellow AAAS, IEEE, Assn. for Computing Machinery (editor jour. 1976-93, chmn. com. on computers and pub. policy 1985—). Avocations: music, tai chi, holistic health. Office: SRI Internat EL-243 333 Ravenswood Ave Menlo Park CA 94025-3493 E-mail: pneumann@acm.org

NEUMEYER, ZACHARY T. hotel executive; Pres., CEO Sage Hospitality Resources LP, Denver. Office: Sage Hospitality Resources LLC 1512 Larimer St Ste 800 Denver CO 80202-1623

NEURATH, HANS, biochemist, educator; b. Vienna, Oct. 29, 1909; came to U.S., 1935; s. Rudolf and Hedda (Samek) N.; m. Hilde Bial, June, 1935 (div. 1960); 1 child, Peter Francis; m. Susi Ruth Spitzer, Oct. 11, 1960 PhD, U. Vienna, Austria, 1933; DSc (hon.), U. Geneva, Switzerland, 1970, U. Tokushima, Japan, 1977, Med. Coll. Ohio, , 1989, U. Montpellier, France, 1989, Kyoto U., Japan, 1990. George Fisher Baker fellow Cornell U., Ithaca, N.Y., 1936-38; prof. biochemistry Duke U., Durham, N.C., 1938-50, U. Wash., Seattle, 1950—, chmn. dept. biochemistry, 1950-75, prof. emeritus biochemistry, 1980—; sci. dir. Fred Hutchinson Cancer Rsch. Inst., Seattle, 1976-80; dir. German Cancer Research Ctr., Heidelberg, Fed. Republic Germany, 1980-81. Hon. prof. U. Heidelberg, 1980—; fgn. sci. mem. Max Planck Inst. for Exptl. Medicine, Goettingen, Fed. Republic Germany, 1982—; cons. Battelle Meml. Inst., Columbus, 1970-75. Editor: (compendium) The Proteins (3 edits.), 1953-79; editor Biochemistry Jour., 1962-91, Protein Sci., 1991-98; contbr. numerous articles to sci. publs. Advisor NIH, Bethesda, Md., 1954-70; mem. med. adv. bd. Howard Hughes Med. Inst., Miami, Fla., 1969-79, Virginia Mason Rsch. Ctr., Seattle, 1982-98. Guggenheim fellow, 1955; named hon. mem. Japanese Biochem. Soc., 1977; recipient Disting. Alumnus award Duke U. Med. Sch., 1970, Stein and Moore award Protein Soc., 1989. Fellow AAAS; mem. NAS (nat. bd. grad. edn. 1971-75), Inst. of Medicine (sr.). Avocations: music, skiing. Home: 5752 60th Ave NE Seattle WA 98105-2036 Office: U Wash Dept Biochemistry PO Box 357350 Seattle WA 98195-7350

NEUREUTHER, ANDREW R. engineering educator; b. Decatur, Ill., July 30, 1941; BSEE, U. Ill., 1963, MSEE, 1964, PhD in Elec. Engring., 1966. With U. Calif., Berkeley, 1966—, prof. Cons. lithography modeling IBM Almaden Rsch. Ctr., 1977-90, optical lithography inspection Siemens, Perlach, 1984. Contbr. articles to IEEE Trans., SPIE, Jour. Vac. Sci. Tech. Fellow IEEE; mem. NAE. Achievements include research in microelectronics process technology and simulation, lithographic materials and tool characterization, simulation of lithography and inspection, wafer topography simulation. Office: U Calif Electronics Rsch Lab 5th Fl Berkeley CA 94720-1774

NEUWIRTH, BEBE, dancer, actress; b. Newark, 31 Dec. d. Lee Paul and Sydney Anne Neuwirth. Student, Juilliard Sch., 1976-77. Appeared on Broadway and internationally as Sheila in A Chorus Line, 1978-81; other stage appearances include West Side Story, 1981, (on Broadway) Little Me, 1982, Upstairs at O'Neal's, 1982-83, The Road to Hollywood, 1984, Just So, 1985, (on Broadway) Sweet Charity, 1985-87 (Tony award for Best Supporting Actress in a Musical 1985-86), Waiting in the Wings: The Night the Understudies Take the Stage, 1986, Showing Off, 1989, Chicago, 1992 (L.A. Drama Critics Circle award), Kiss of the Spider Woman (London), 1993, (on Broadway) Damn Yankees, 1994, Pal Joey, 1995, Chicago, 1996 (Tony award for Best Leading Actress in a Musical, 1997); prin. dancer on Broadway Dancin', 1982; leading dance role Kicks, 1984; TV series Cheers, 1984-93 (Emmy award for Best Supporting Actress in a Comedy Series 1990, 91); TV guest appearances Frasier, 1994, Aladdin, 1994; TV movies Without Her Consent, 1990, Unspeakable Acts, 1990, Wild Palms, 1993; films Say Anything, 1989, Green Card, 1990, Bugsy, 1991, Painted Heart, 1992, Malice, 1993, Jumanji, 1994, Pinocchio, 1995, Celebrity, 1998, The Faculty, 1998, Summer of Same, 1999, Dash and Lilly, 1999, Liberty Heights, 1999, Getting to Know You, 1999. Vol. performances for March of Dimes Telethon, 1986, Cystic Fibrosis Benefit Children's Ball, 1986, Ensemble Studio Theater Benefit, 1986, Circle Repertory Co. Benefit, 1986, all in N.Y.C. Recipient Tony award Leading Actress in a Musical, 1997. Democrat. Office: Internat Creative Mgmt 8942 Wilshire Blvd Beverly Hills CA 90211-1934 also: 40 W 57th St New York NY 10019-4001

NEVILLE, ROY GERALD, scientist, chemical management and environmental consultant; b. Bournemouth, Dorsetshire, Eng., Oct. 15, 1926; came to U.S., 1951, naturalized, 1957; s. Percy Herbert and Georgina Lallie (Jenkins) N.; m. Jeanne Frances Russ, July 26, 1952; children: Laura Jean, Janet Marilyn. BSc with honors, U. London, 1951; MSc, U. Oreg., 1952, PhD, 1954; FRIC, Royal Inst. Chemistry, London, 1963, DSc (hon.), 1973. Research chemist Monsanto Chem. co., Seattle, 1955-57; sr. chem. engr. Boeing Co., Seattle, 1957-58; sr. research scientist Lockheed Missiles & Space Co., Palo Alto, Calif., 1958-61; sr. staff scientist Aerospace Corp., El Segundo, 1961-63; prin. scientist Rockwell Internat. Corp., Los Angeles, 1963-67; head dept. materials Scis. Lab., Boeing Sci. Research Labs. Boeing Co., Seattle, 1967-69; sr. environ. engring. specialist Bechtel Corp., San Francisco, 1969-73; pres. Engring. & Tech. Cons., Inc., Redwood City, Calif., 1973—. Contbr. numerous sci. articles on inorganic and organic synthesis, thermally stable polymers, pollution control processes to profl. jours. and books; many U.S. and fgn. patents in field; associateship Southampton U., England, 1951. Fulbright scholar to U.S., 1951; USPHS fellowship, 1951-52, Research Corp. fellow, 1952-54; chartered chemist, London. Fellow Royal Soc. Chemistry (London), Am. Inst. Chemists, AAAS; mem. Am. Chem. Soc., Am. Inst. Chem. Engrs., History Sci. Soc., Soc. Study Early Chemistry, Royal Instn. Great Britain, Research Soc. Am., Soc. Mining Engrs. of AIME, Calif. Mining Assn., Sigma Xi. Office: ETC Inc 1068 Eden Bower Ln Redwood City CA 94061-1806

NEVIN, DAVID WRIGHT, real estate broker, mortgage broker; b. Culver City, Calif., July 27, 1947; s. Wilbur D. and Anita J. (Hulderman) N.; m. Shirley Grimes, Nov. 12, 1977; children: Jenny, David Wright Jr. BA, Calif. State Poly. U., 1974. Rural manpower asst. employment devel. State Calif., Riverside, 1970-74; pers. mgr. Lindsay Olive Growers, 1974-79; employee rels. mgr. Morton Salt Co., Newark, 1979-80; real estate salesman Valley Realty, Fremont, 1980-85; owner Nevin & Nevin Inc., Fremont, 1984-88, CitiDesign, Fremont, 1989—. Co-owner Brokers Exch., Inc., 1985-86; dir., officer CitiBrokers Real Estate, Inc., 1986-94; owner Nevin Fin/Mortgage Exchange 1992—; br. mgr. Brandt Property Mgmt. Group, 1994-95; mgr. Internat. Trade Corp., Saigon, Vietnam, 1997. Sustaining mem. Rep. Nat. Com., Washington, 1984; mem. Presdl. Task Force, Washington, 1984, Cornerstone Fellowship. With U.S. Army, 1967-69. Mem. Realtors Nat. Internat. Real Estate Fedn., So. Alameda County Bd. Realtors (local govt. rels. com. 1983-86). Address: 2209 Carol Ann Dr Tracy CA 95377-6614 E-mail: davidwnevin@yahoo.com

NEWALL, JAMES EDWARD MALCOLM, manufacturing company executive; b. Holden, Alta., Can., Aug. 20, 1935; 3 children. B.Comm., U. Sask., 1958. With Du Pont Can., Inc., 1957—, v.p. mktg. Que., 1975, exec. v.p., 1975-78, dir., 1976-78, pres., 1978-89, chief exec. officer, 1978-91, chmn. bd., 1979-91; pres., chief exec. officer Nova Corp., Calgary, Alta., 1991-98; chmn. Newall & Assocs., Calgary, 1998—, Nova Chems., Pitts., 1998—. Bd. dirs. Alcan Aluminum Ltd., BCE Inc., Nova Corp., Molson Cos. Ltd., Pratt & Whitney Can. Inc., Royal Bank Can. Mem. exec. compensation in the pub. svc. Adv. Group to the Prime Min.; chmn. Bus. Coun. on Nat. Issues. Office: Newall & Assocs 855 2nd St SW Calgary AB Canada T2P 4J7

NEWBERG, DOROTHY BECK (MRS. WILLIAM C. NEWBERG), portrait artist; b. Detroit, May 30, 1919; d. Charles William and Mary (Labedz) Beck; student Detroit Conservatory Music, 1938; m. William C. Newberg, Nov. 3, 1939; children: Judith Bookwalter Bracken, Robert Charles, James William, William Charles. Trustee Detroit Adventure, 1967-71, originator A Drop in Bucket Program for artistically talented inner-city children. Cmty. outreach coord. Reno Police Dept.; bd. dirs. Bloomfield Art Assn., 1960-62, trustee 1965-67; bd. dirs. Your Heritage House, 1972-75, Franklin Wright Settlement, 1972-75, Meadowbrook Art Gallery, Oakland U., 1973-75, Sierra Nevada Mus. Art, 1978-80, NCCJ; mem. adv. bd. Gang Alternatives Partnership Adv. Bd. Recipient Heart of Gold award, 1969; Mich. vol. leadership award, 1969, Outstanding Vol. award City of Reno, 1989-90. Mem. Nevada Mus. Art, No. Nev. Black Cultural Awareness Soc. (bd. dirs.), Hispanic 500 C. of C. No. Nev. Roman Catholic. Home: 2000 Dant Blvd Reno NV 89509-5193

NEWBERG, WILLIAM CHARLES, stock broker, real estate broker, automotive engineer; b. Seattle, Dec. 17, 1910; s. Charles John and Anna Elizabeth (Anderson) N.; BSME, U. Wash., 1933; MME, Chrysler Inst. Engring., 1935; LLB (hon.), Parsons Coll., 1958; m. Dorothy Beck, Nov. 3, 1939; children: Judith N. Newberg Bookwalter, Robert Charles, James William, William Charles. Salesman, Am. Auto Co., Seattle, 1932-33; student engr. Chrysler Corp., Detroit, 1933-35, exptl. engr., 1935-42, chief engr. Chgo. plant, 1942-45, mem. subs. ops. staff, Detroit, 1945-47, pres. airtemp. divsn., Dayton, Ohio, 1947-50, v.p., dir. Dodge divsn., Detroit, 1950-51, pres. Dodge divsn., 1951-56, group v.p., Detroit, 1956-58, exec. v.p., 1958-60, pres., 1960; corp. dir. Detroit Bank & Trust, Detroit, 1955-60; corp. cons., Detroit, 1960-76; realtor Myers Realty, Inc., Reno, 1976-79; owner Bill Newberg Realty, 1979— ; account exec. Allied Capital Corp., Reno, 1980— ; chmn. Newberg Corp., 1982; treas. Perfect "10" Industries. Elder, St. John's Presbyn. Ch., Reno, 1976— ; mem. exec. bd. Detroit Area coun. Boy Scouts Am., 1955-74, Nev. Area coun. Boy Scouts Am., 1976— ; Mich. state chmn. March of Dimes, 1967-68. Mem. Soc. Automotive Engrs., Am. Def. Preparedness Assn. (life), Automotive Orgn. Team (life), U. Wash. Alumni Assn. (life), Newcomen Soc., Franklin Inst., Alpha Tau Omega. Clubs: Prospectors, Harley Owners Group. Home: 2000 Dant Blvd Reno NV 89509-5193

NEWBOLD, GREGORY S. career officer; b. Denver, 1948; m. Kathleen Lewis; children: Kerry, Cameron. Student, USMC Command and Staff Coll., Nat. War Coll. Commd. 2nd lt. USMC, 1970, advanced through grades to brig. gen.; comdr. 15th Marine Expeditionary Unit, Operation Restore Hope, Somalia; officer assignment officer USMC Hdqrs., Washington; warfare policy planner USMC Joint Staff; mil. asst. to sec. USN; head enlisted assignment br. USMC Hdqrs., Washington, dir. manpower plans and policy divsn.; now dep. comdr., brig. gen. USMC, Camp Pendleton, Calif. Decorated Legion of Merit. Office: USMC Deputy CG 1st Marine Exped Force Cmp Pendleton CA 92055-0001

NEWBRUN, ERNEST, oral biology and periodontology educator; b. Vienna, Austria, Dec. 1, 1932; came to U.S., 1955; s. Victor and Elizabeth (Reichl) N; m. Eva Miriam, June 17, 1956; children: Deborah Anne, Daniel Eric, Karen Ruth. BDS, U. Sydney (New South Wales), 1954; MS, U. Rochester, 1957; DMD, U. Ala., 1959; PhD, U. Calif., San Francisco, 1965; Odont. Dr. (hon.), U. Lund, Sweden, 1988; DDSc (hon.), U. Sydney, 1997. Cert. periodontology, 1983. Rsch. assoc. Eastman Dental Ctr., Rochester, N.Y., 1955-57, U. Ala. Med. Ctr., Birmingham, 1957-59; rsch. fellow Inst. Dental Rsch., Sydney, Australia, 1960-61; rsch. tchr. trainee U. Calif., San Francisco, 1961-63, postdoctoral fellow, 1963-65, assoc. prof., 1965-70, prof. oral biology, 1970-83, prof. oral biology and periodontology, 1983-94, prof. emeritus, 1994—. Cons. FDA, 1983—. Author: Cariology, 1989, Pharmacology and Therapeutic Dentistry, 1989, (with others) Pediatrics, 1991; editor: Fluorides and Dental Caries, 1986; mem. editorial bd. Jour. Periodontal Rsch., 1985-90, Jour. Periodontology, 1990—. Bd. dirs. Raoul Wallenberg Dem. Club, San Francisco, 1987-92. Fellow AAAS (chmn. dental section, 1988-89), Internat. Assn. Dental Rsch. (pres. 1989-90); mem. Dental Health Foun. (chmn. bd. dirs., 1985-92). Jewish. Avocations: gardening, hiking, skiing, opera, theatre.

NEWCOM, JENNINGS JAY, lawyer; b. St. Joseph, Mo., Oct. 18, 1941; s. Arden Henderson and Loyal Beatrice (Winans) N.; m. Cherry Ann Phelps, Apr. 4, 1964; children: Shandra Karine, J. Derek Arden. BA, Graceland U., Lamoni, Iowa, 1961; JD, Harvard U., 1968; LLD (hon.), Graceland U., 1999. Bar: Ill. 1968, Calif. 1973, Mo. 1979, Kans. 1981, Colo. 1999. Atty. McDermott, Will & Emery, Chgo., 1968-73; ptnr. Rifkind, Sterling & Lockwood, Beverly Hills, Calif., 1973-79, Shook, Hardy & Bacon L.L.P., Kansas City, Mo., 1979-99, Davis, Graham & Stubbs, LLP, Denver, 1999—; gen. counsel Putnam, Lovell Capital Ptnrs., Inc., L.A., 1999—; dir. Stein Roe Investment Counsel, Chicago. Chmn. bd. Graceland Coll. Trustee Hubbard Found., Linde Found. Mem. Denver Bar Assn., State Bar Assn. Calif. Office: Davis Graham & Stubbs LLP 1550 17th St Ste 500 Denver CO 80202-1500

NEWCOMB, BRUCE, state legislator, farmer, rancher; b. Burley, Idaho, Mar. 2, 1940; m. Celia Gould; 5 children. Student, N.W. Christian Coll., Stanford; BS, U. Oreg. Mem. Idaho Ho. of Reps., Boise, 1987, past majority leader, caucus chmn., house spkr. Methodist. Avocations: fly fishing, hunting, family. Office: State Capitol Boise ID 83720-0001 Fax: 208-334-2491. E-mail: infocenter@lso.state.id.us

NEWCOMBE, GEORGE MICHAEL, lawyer; b. Newark, Nov. 11, 1947; s. George Anthony and Mary Hellen Newcombe; m. Joan Sharon Hanlon, May 30, 1969; children: Sean Michael, Scott Ryan, Jennifer Leigh. BSChemE, N.J. Inst. Tech., 1969; JD, Columbia U., 1975. Bar: N.J. 1975, N.Y. 1976, U.S. Dist. Ct. N.J. 1975, U.S. Ct. Appeals (2d cir.) 1975, U.S. Dist. Ct. (so. dist.) N.Y. 1976, U.S. Dist. Ct. (we. dist.) Tex. 1985, U.S. Ct. Appeals (5th cir.) 1986, U.s. Supreme Ct. 1987, U.S. Ct. Appeals (3d cir.) 1992, U.S. Ct. Appeals (fed. cir.) 1995, Calif. 1999, U.S. Dist. Ct. (no., ea., and so. dists.) Calif. 1999, U.S. Ct. Appeals (9th cir.) 1999. Ptnr. Simpson, Thacher & Bartlett, N.Y.C., 1975—. Dir. Columbia Law Sch. Assn., Inc., Columbia Jour. Environ. Law; dir., legal sec. Am. Ditchley Found., 1994; bd. visitors Columbia Law Sch., 1997—; bd. overseers N.J. Inst. Tech., 1998—. Mem. coun. com. law offices vol. divsn. Legal Aid Soc., N.Y.C., 1980-86. Lt. USPHS, 1970-72. James Kent scholar Columbia Law Sch., 1974, Harlan Fiske Stone scholar Columbia Law Sch., 1975. Mem. Am. Law Inst., ABA, AICE, Assn. of Bar of City of N.Y., Tau Beta Epsilon, Omicron Delta Kappa. Office: Simpson Thacher & Bartlett 3373 Hillview Ave Palo Alto CA 94304-1204

NEWCOMBE, RICHARD SUMNER, newspaper syndicate executive; b. Chgo., Aug. 8, 1950; s. Leo Raymond and Ann (Lombard) N.; m. Caroline Eleanor Bermeo; children: Sara Caroline Ann, John Richard D'Arcy. BA, Georgetown U., 1972; postgrad. in bus., U. Chgo., 1973-74. Reporter/editor UPI, Balt., 1974-78; v.p., gen. mgr. Los Angeles Times Syndicate, 1978-84; pres., chief exec. officer News Am. Syndicate, Irvine, Calif., 1984-87, Creators Syndicate, Los Angeles, 1987—. Bd. dirs., 1st v.p. Newspaper Features Coun., Greenwich, Conn.; chmn. The Jester's Com. Author: Businessman's Guide to Shaping Up, 1983. Mem. Phi Beta Kappa. Avocations: weightlifting, jogging. Office: Creators Syndicate 5777 W Century Blvd Ste 700 Los Angeles CA 90045-5675

NEWHART, BOB, entertainer; b. Oak Park, Ill., Sept. 29, 1929; m. Virginia Quinn, Jan. 12, 1963; 4 children. BS, Loyola U., Chgo., 1952. Acct. U.S. Gypsum Co.; copywriter Fred Niles Film Co.; appeared on Jack Paar Show, 1960; TV performer numerous guest appearances, 1961—; star TV series Newhart, 1982-90. Rec. artist (album) Button Down Mind on TV; royal command performance, London, 1964, appeared in films Hot Millions, 1968, Catch 22, 1970, Cold Turkey, 1971, First Family, 1980, Little Miss Marker, 1982; TV films include Thursday's Game, 1978, Marathon, 1980. Grand marshall Tournament Roses Parade, 1991. With U.S. Army, 1952-54. Recipient Emmy award, 1961, Peabody award, 1961, Sword of Loyola award, 1976, Legend to Legend award, 1993; named to Acad. Hall of Fame, 1993. Office: c/o Capell Duitch Franklin 11601 Wilshire Blvd Ste 2350 Los Angeles CA 90025-1759

NEWIRTH, RICHARD SCOTT, cultural organization administrator; b. N.Y.C. BA in Maths. magna cum laude, Brown U., 1980; MBA, U. Calif., Berkeley, 1990. Dividend analyst, actuarial asst. Met. Life Ins. Co., San Francisco, 1980-83, sr. underwriter, 1983-85, mgr. renewal svcs., 1985-87, dir. fin. analysis, 1988; benefits and ins. adminstr. San Francisco Symphony, 1990-92; asst. dir. San Francisco Art Commn., 1993-95, dir. cultural affairs, 1995—. Cons. Berkeley (Calif.) Repertory Theatre, 1990; spkr. Nat. Conf. State Legislators, 1997, Far W. Region Cultural Tourism Leadership Forum, 1997; dist. chair Calif. Assembly of Local Arts Agys.; v.p. Urban Arts Fedn., 1998-99, pres., 2000. Mem. mktg. com., vol. Under One Roof. Office: City San Francisco San Francisco Art Comm 25 Van Ness Ave Ste 240 San Francisco CA 94102-6053 Fax: 415-252-2595

NEWITT, JAY, construction management educator; Tchr. Brigham Young U., Provo, Utah. Recipient John Trimmer Merit Shop Tchg. award Excellence Edn. Construction Found., 1992. Office: Brigham Young U Construc Mang Dept 230 Snell Bldg Provo UT 84602-1127

NEWLAND, CHESTER ALBERT, public administration educator; b. Kansas City, Kans., June 18, 1930; s. Guy Wesley and Mary Virginia (Yoakum) N. BA, U. N. Tex., Denton, 1954; MA, U. Kans., 1955, PhD, 1958. Social Sci. Rsch. Coun. fellow U. Wis. and U.S. Supreme Ct., 1958-59; instr. polit. sci. Idaho State U., Pocatello, 1959-60; mem. faculty U. North Tex., Denton, 1960-66, prof. govt., 1963-66, dir. dept. govt., 1963-66; prof. polit. sci. U. Houston, 1967-68; dir. Lyndon Baines Johnson Libr., Austin, Tex., 1968-70; prof. pub. adminstrn. U. So. Calif., 1966-67, 68-71, 76-82, 84-92, Duggan disting. prof. pub. adminstrn., 1992—; prof. George Mason U., Fairfax, Va., 1982-84. Mem. faculty Fed. Exec. Inst., 1971-76, dir. 1973-76, 80-81; mgr. task force on fed. labor-mgmt. rels. U.S. Pers. Mgmt. Project, Pres.'s Reorgn., Washington, 1977-78. Editor in chief Pub. Adminstrn. Rev., 1984-90; contbr. articles to profl. jours. Chmn. Mcpl. Rsch. Coun., Denton, 1963-64; city councilman, Denton, 1964-66; mem. Pub. Sector Commn. on Productivity and Work Quality, 1974-78; trustee Sacramento (Calif.) Mus. History, Sci. and Tech., 1993-95; mem. UN Devel. Program Kazakhstan, 1997-2000, Moldova, 1994, Kuwait, 1991, 95-96; cons. Poland, 1990-91, Hungary, 1991, Czech and Slovak Republics, 1992,, Bank of Greece, 1999-2001. Mem. Nat. Acad. Pub. Adminstrn., Southwestern Social Sci. Assn. (chmn. govt. sect. 1964-65), Am. Soc. Pub. Adminstrn. (pres. Dallas-Ft. Worth chpt. 1964-65, nat. coun. 1976, 78-81, editorial bd. jour. 1972-76, chmn. publ. com. 1975-79, program chmn. 1977, nat. pres. 1981-82, Dimock award 1984), Am. Polit. Sci. Assn., Internat. Pers. Mgmt. Assn. (program chmn. 1978, Stockberger award 1979), Am. Acad. Polit. and Social Sci., Internat. City Mgmt. Assn. (hon.), Nat. Assn. Schs Pub. Affairs and Adminstrn. (Staats Pub. Svc. award 1989). Office: Univ Southern California 1800 I St Sacramento CA 95814-3004

NEWLAND, RUTH LAURA, small business owner; b. Ellensburg, Wash., June 4, 1949; d. George J. and Ruth Marjorie (Porter) N. BA, Cen. Wash. State Coll., 1970, MEd, 1972; EdS, Vanderbilt U., 1973; PhD, Columbia Pacific U., 1981. Tchr. Union Gap (Wash.) Sch., 1970-71; owner Newland Ranch Gravel Co., Yakima, Wash., 1998; ptnr. Arnold Artificial Limb, Yakima, 1981-86, owner, pres. Yakima and Richland, Wash., 1986—. Owner Newland Ranch, Yakima, 1969—. Contbg. mem. Nat. Dem. Com., Irish Nat. Caucus Found.; mem. Pub. Citizen, We The People, Nat. Humane Edn. Soc.; charter mem. Nat. Mus. Am. Indian. George Washington scholar Masons, Yakima, 1967. Mem. NAFE, NOW, Am. Orthotic and Prosthetic Assn., Internat. Platform Assn., Nat. Antivisection Soc. (life), Vanderbilt U. Alumni Assn., Peabody Coll. Alumni Assn., Columbia Pacific U. Alumni Assn., World Wildlife Fund, Nat. Audubon Soc., Greenpeace, Mus. Fine Arts, Humane Soc. U.S., Wilderness Soc., Nature Conservancy, People for Ethical Treatment of Animals, Amnesty Internat., The Windstar Found., Rodale Inst., Sierra Club (life), Emily's List. Democrat. Avocations: reading, gardening, sewing, handcrafts, people. Home: 2004 Riverside Rd Yakima WA 98901-8540 Office: Arnold Artificial Limb 9 S 12th Ave Yakima WA 98902-3106

NEWLIN, DOUGLAS RANDAL, lead information engineer; b. Denver, Mar. 26, 1940; s. Loren Randall and Nola Berniece (Paris) N.; m. Sandra Temple, June 22, 1968; children: Jason Britt, Jeremy Owen. BS in Journalism, U. Colo., 1968. Advt. prodn. mgr. Am. Sheep Producers Council, Denver, 1968-70; promotion dir. Sta. KLZ-AM-FM, Denver, 1970-71; account mgr. Curran-Morton Advt., Denver, 1971-72; advt. and sales promotion specialist Gates Rubber Co., Denver, 1972-78; mktg. communications mgr. Hewlett Packard Co., Ft. Collins, Colo., 1978-90; lead learning products engr., 1990—. Vis. lectr. U. Colo., Boulder, 1972-73, statis. quality control course George Washington U., Washington, 1984; web page designer. Author hardware and software catalogs, 1984-90, UNIX Tech. Documentation, 1990-99, Hewlett-Packard Visualize Worksta. User Documentation, 1999—; U.S. newsletter editor Ted Heath Music Appreciation Soc. of U.K. (Eng.); contbr. articles to profl. jours. Pres. Lake Sherwood Homeowners Assn., Ft. Collins, 1982; treas. Lake Sherwood Lake Com., Ft. Collins, 1983-85. Served with U.S. Army, 1959-61. Recipient Gold Key award Bus. and Profl. Advt. Assn., 1976. Mem. Big Bands Internat. Republican. Avocation: bicycling, teaching swing dancing. Home: 4112 Mt Vernon Ct Fort Collins CO 80525-3335 Office: Hewlett Packard Co 3404 E Harmony Rd Fort Collins CO 80528-9599

NEWLIN, L. MAX, parks and recreation director; b. June 4, 1942; BS, Wilmington Coll., 1968. Mgr. Massacre Rocks State Pk., American Falls, Idaho, 1996—. Exec. dir. Friends Massacre Rocks Inc.; v.p. S.E. Idaho Travel Coun. Idaho Parks and Recreation Assn. fellow, 1990. Mem. Power County/Am. Falls Hist. Soc. (chmn.). Office: Massacre Rocks State Pk 3592 Park Ln American Falls ID 83211-5556

NEWMAN, ANITA NADINE, surgeon; b. Honolulu, June 13, 1949; d. William Reece Elton and Margie Ruth (Pollard) Newman; m. Frank E.X. Ward, Sept. 9, 1995; children: Justin Ellis, Chelsea Newman, Andrew Frank, Tyler William. BA, Stanford U., 1971; MD, Dartmouth Coll., 1975. Diplomate Am. Bd. Otolaryngology. From intern to resident in gen. surgery Northwestern Meml. Hosp., Chgo., 1975-77, resident in otolaryngology, 1977-78; resident UCLA Hosp. and Clinics, 1979-82; assoc. prof. UCLA, 1982-96; rsch. fellow in neurotology, 1984-88; surgeon USC Head and Neck Group, 1997-2000; staff surgeon Wadsworth VA Hosp., L.A., 1982-84; pvt. practice L.A., 2000—. Contbr. articles to profl. jours. Mem. alumni admissions support com. Dartmouth Med. Sch. Alumni Coun., 1983-87. Fellow ACS; mem. Am. Acad. Otolaryngology, Am. Med. Women's Assn., L.A. County Med. Women's Assn., Assn. Rsch. Otolaryngology, Stanford Women's Honor Soc. Democrat. Office: 8631 W 3d St Ste [illegible] Los Angeles CA 90048 [illegible]

NEWMAN, CAROL L. lawyer; b. Yonkers, N.Y., Aug. 7, 1949; d. Richard J. and Pauline Frances (Stoll) N. AB/MA summa cum laude, Brown U., 1971; postgrad., Harvard U. Law Sch., 1972-73; JD cum laude, George Washington U., 1977. Bar: D.C. 1977, Calif. 1979. With antitrust divsn. U.S. Dept. Justice, Washington and L.A., 1977-80; assoc. Alschuler, Grossman & Pines, L.A., 1980-82, Costello & Walcher, L.A., 1982-85, Rosen, Wachtell & Gilbert, L.A., 1985-88, ptnr., 1988-90, Keck, Mahin & Cate, L.A., 1990-94; pvt. practice L.A., 1994-2001. Adj. prof. Sch. Bus., Golden Gate U., spring 1982. Commr. L.A. Bd. Transp. Commrs., 1993—98, v.p., 1995—96; pres. Bd. Taxicab Commrs., 1999—2001; Cand. for State Atty. Gen., 1986; bd. dirs. Women's Progress Alliance, 1996—98. Mem. ABA, State Bar Calif., L.A. County Bar Assn., L.A. Lawyers for Human Rights (co. pres. 1991-92), Log Cabin (bd. dirs. 1992-97, pres. 1996-97), Calif. Women Lawyers (bd. dirs., bd. govs. 1991-94), Order of Coif, Phi Beta Kappa. E-mail: cnewman540@aol.com

NEWMAN, DAVID WHEELER, lawyer; b. Salt Lake City, Apr. 5, 1952; s. Donnell and Vera Mae (Siratt) N.; m. Mahnaz Navai, Mar. 14, 1981; 1 child, Anthony Dara. BA cum laude, Claremont Men's Coll., 1973; JD, UCLA, 1977; LLM in Taxation, NYU, 1979. Bar: Calif. 1978, U.S. Dist. Ct. Calif. 1978, U.S. Tax Ct. 1979. Tax ptnr. Mitchell, Silberberg & Knupp, L.A., 1982—. Mem. exec. com. tax sect. L.A. County Bar, 1991-2000. Bd. trustees New Visions Found., 1995—, Calif. Youth Theatre, 1998—; bd. trustees, pres. New Rds. Sch., 2000—, Hollywood Youth Arts Ctr., 2000—. Mem. Calif. Club, Men's Garden Club L.A. (dir. 2000—). Avocations: tennis, skiing, gardening. Office: Mitchell Silberberg & Knupp 11377 W Olympic Blvd Los Angeles CA 90064-1625

NEWMAN, DEAN GORDON, business consultant; b. North Branch, Iowa, Mar. 17, 1929; s. Floyd William and Hazel Jane (Covault) N.; m. Maggie Newman; children: Gary Dean, Craig William. BA, Simpson Coll., 1950; MBA, Stanford U., 1952. Trainee GE, Schenectady, N.Y., 1952, Syracuse, 1955-56, Chgo., 1956-58, mem. employee and cmty. rels. staff, 1958-62, mgr. employee and cmty. rels. Milw., 1962-67, DeKalb, Ill., 1967-69; v.p. employees and pub. rels. United Nuclear Corp., Elmsford, N.Y., 1969-71; v.p. employee and indsl. rels. Apache Corp., Mpls., 1971-83, v.p. human resources and comm., 1983-87; v.p. mktg. Nelson Cons. Group, Mpls., 1989-92; chmn. Linear Fitness Systems, Inc., Allenspark, Colo., 1998—. Pres. Apache Found., 1973—87; v.p., bd. dirs. Boys Clubs, Mpls., 1978—85; chmn. Boys and Girls Club Mpls., 1985—88, exec. com., 1988—89; v.p. fin., bd. Boys and Girls Club Larimer County, 1993—96; vice chmn. Bus. Econs. Edn. Found., 1986—88, chmn. fin. com., 1988—89; com. mem., treas. Allenspark Sr. Adv. Com., 1999—; bd. dirs., treas. Allenspark Fire Protection Dist., Allenspark Area Club. With USNR, 1952—55, Korea. Fellow Hicks fellow, Stanford U., 1952. Mem.: Alpha Tau Omega, Epsilon Sigma, Sigma Tau Delta, Pi Gamma Mu, Nat. Assn. Mfrs. (dir. 1981—87). Republican. Methodist. Home and Office: 125 County Road 84 W Allenspark CO 80510-9713 E-mail: newman85@earthlink.net

NEWMAN, FRANCIS A. medical device company executive; b. 1947; Sr. v.p. merchandising F.W. Woolworth, 1980-84, exec. v.p. household merchandising, 1984-85; pres., CEO, dir. F&M Distributors, Inc., 1986-93; pres., COO Eckerd Fleet, Inc., Largo, Fla., 1993-98, pres., COO, chmn., 1998-2000; pres., CEO More.com, San Francisco, 2000—. Address: PO Box 4689 Clearwater FL 33758-4689 Office: More com 520 3rd St Fl 2 San Francisco CA 94107

NEWMAN, JOHN SCOTT, chemical engineer, educator; b. Richmond, Va., Nov. 17, 1938; s. Clarence William and Marjorie Lenore (Saucerman) N.; m. Nguyen Thanh Lan, June 30, 1973; children— Natalie Diane, Michael Alexander. B.S., Northwestern U., 1960; M.S., U. Calif., Berkeley, 1962, Ph.D., 1963. Asst. prof. chem. engring. U. Calif., Berkeley, 1963-67, assoc. prof., 1967-70, prof., 1970—; prin. investigator environ. energy tech. divsn. Lawrence Berkeley Nat. Lab., 1963—; Omsanger prof. Norwegian U. Sci. and Tech., 2002. Vis. prof. U. Wis., Madison, 1973; summer participant Oak Ridge Nat. Lab., 1965, 66 Author: Electrochemical Systems, 1973, rev. edit. 1991; assoc. editor Jour. Electrochem. Soc., 1990-2000; contbr. articles to profl. jours. Fellow Electrochem. Soc. (Young Author's prize 1966, 69, David C. Grahame award 1985, Henry B. Linford award 1990, Olin Palladium medal 1991); mem. AIChE (Excellence in Indsl. Rsch. award no. Calif. sect. 2000), NAE. Home: 114 York Ave Kensington CA 94708-1045 Office: U Calif Dept Chem Engring Berkeley CA 94720-1462 E-mail: newman@newman.cchem.berkeley.edu

NEWMAN, MARJORIE YOSPIN, psychiatrist; b. N.Y.C., July 8, 1945; d. Toby and Audrey (Kreinik) Yospin; children: Eric, David. Student, Smith Coll., 1963-64; AB, Barnard Coll./Columbia U., 1967; MD, Med. Coll. Pa., 1971. Diplomate Am. Bd. Psychiatry and Neurology. Psychiatry intern, resident Albert Einstein Coll. Medicine, N.Y.C., 1971-75; asst. prof. psychiatry U. Tex. Health Sci. Ctr., San Antonio, 1975-77, UCLA Sch. Medicine, 1977-80; dir. residency tng. in psychiatry Harbor-UCLA Med. Ctr., 1977-79; asst. clin. prof. psychiatry UCLA Sch. Medicine, 1980—; pvt. practice Pasadena, Calif., 1983—. Mem. admissions com. UCLA Med. Sch., 1995—. NSF grantee, London, Eng., 1969; Am. Field Svc. Internat. scholar, Argentina, 63. Fellow L.A. Acad. Medicine (bd. govs. 2000—); mem. Am. Psychiat. Assn., So. Calif. Psychiat. Soc. (regional councillor 2001—), Smith Coll. Alumna Assn., Barnard Coll. Alumna Assn., Columbia U. Alumni Assn., Ivy League Assn. So. Calif. Avocations: travel, music, art, swimming, cycling. Office: Cotton Med Ctr South 50 Alessandro Pl Ste 340 Pasadena CA 91105-3184

NEWMAN, MORRIS, mathematician, educator; b. N.Y.C., Feb. 25, 1924; s. Isaac and Sarah (Cohen) N.; m. Mary Aileen Lenk, Sept. 18, 1948; children: Sally Ann, Carl Lenk. A.B., N.Y.U., 1945; M.A., Columbia U., 1946; Ph.D., U. Pa., 1952. Mathematician applied math div. Nat. Bur. Standards, Washington, 1951-63, chief numerical analysis sect., 1963-70, sr. rsch. mathematician, 1970-76; prof. math. U. Calif., Santa Barbara, 1976-94, prof. emeritus, 1994—; dir. Inst. Interdisciplinary Applications of Algebra and Combinatorics, 1976-80. Lectr. U. B.C., 1960, U. Calif.-Santa Barbara, 1965, Am. U., Cath. U., U. Md. Author: Matrix Representations of Groups, 1968, Integral Matrices, 1972; editor: Jour. Research Nat. Bur. Standards, 1966-76, Math. of Computation, 1975-86; assoc. editor: Jour. Linear and Multilinear Algebra, 1973—, Letters in Linear Algebra, 1979—; contbr. articles to profl. jours. Recipient Gold medal U.S. Dept. Commerce, 1966 Mem. Am. Math. Soc. (council 1980-86), London Math. Soc., Math. Assn. Am., Washington Acad. Scis., AAAS, sigma Xi Home: 1050 Las Alturas Rd Santa Barbara CA 93103-1608 Office: U Calif Dept Math Santa Barbara CA 93106 E-mail: newman@math.ucsb.edu

NEWMAN, MURRAY ARTHUR, aquarium administrator; b. Chgo., Mar. 6, 1924; emigrated to Can., 1953, naturalized, 1970; s. Paul Jones and Virginia (Murray) N.; m. Katherine Greene Rose, Aug. 8, 1952; 1 child, Susan. B.Sc., U. Chgo., 1949; postgrad., U. Hawaii, 1950; M.A., U. Calif., Berkeley, 1951; Ph.D., U. B.C. (Can.), Vancouver, 1960. Curator fisheries UCLA, 1951-53, Ichthyology Museum, U. B.C., 1953-56; curator Vancouver Public Aquarium, 1956-66, dir., 1966-93; pres. Mana Aquarium Cons. Fgn. adv. Nat. Mus./Aquarium Project, Taiwan; past chmn. adv. com. Western Can. Univs. Marine Biol. Soc.; co-chmn. Enoshima (Japan) Internat. Aquarium Symposium, 1997; spl. advisor Enoshima Aquarium, 1998, Port of Nagoya Pub. Aquarium, 1999, 2000; hon. com. Fifth Internat. Congress, Monaco, 2000. Author: Life in a Fishbowl: Confessions of an Aquarium Director, 1994. Served with USN, 1943-46. Decorated Order of Can.; recipient Man of Yr. award City of Vancouver, 1964; Centennial award Govt. Can., 1967, cert. of merit, 1988; Harold J. Merilees award Vancouver Visitors Bur., 1976, 76 Achievement award, 1987, Silver [illegible] medal Royal Soc. Canada, 1992, Canada 125 medal, 1992. Mem. Am. Assn. Zool. Parks and Aquariums, Internat. Union Dirs. Zool. Gardens, Can. Assn. Zool. Parks and Aquariums (pres. 1978-79), Vancouver Club, Round Table Club. Office: Vancouver Pub Aquarium PO Box 3232 Vancouver BC Canada V6B 3X8

NEWMAN, RICHARD, engineering executive; BCE, Bucknell U; MCE, Columbia U. With Cahn Gengr Inc., L.A., 1960-77; pres. of subsidiary Daniel Mann Johnnson & Mendenhall, L.A., 1977-88; pres. Aecom Tech Corp., L.A., 1989—, now chmn. bd. dirs., pres., CEO. Office: Aecom Tech Corp 3250 Wilshire Blvd # 5 Los Angeles CA 90010-1577

NEWMAN, STEVEN HARVEY, insurance company executive, director; b. Bklyn., Apr. 26, 1943; s. Charlotte (Segal) Newman Bart; m. Lenore Blaustein, June 14, 1964; children: Richard, Michael, Stephanie. BS, Bklyn. Coll., 1963. Actuarial asst. Royal Globe Ins. Co., N.Y.C., 1963-65; asst. sec. Ins. Rating Bd., N.Y.C., 1965-69; v.p., sr. casualty actuary Am. Internat. Group, N.Y.C., 1969-82; exec. v.p. Home Ins. Co., N.Y.C., 1982-85, pres., 1985-86, also bd. dirs.; chmn., CEO Underwriters Reinsurance Co., Woodland Hills, Calif., 1987—; now chmn. Underwriters Re Group, Woodland Hills. Chmn. GCR Holdings, 1993-97, Reins. Assn. Am., 1995-96. Fellow Casualty Actuarial Soc. (pres. 1981-82); mem. Am. Acad. Actuaries, Internat. Actuarial Assn. Address: PO Box 4030 Woodland Hills CA 91365-4030

NEWMAN-GORDON, PAULINE, French language and literature educator; b. N.Y.C., Aug. 5, 1925; d. Bernard and Eva Newman; m. Sydney A. Gordon, Sept. 13, 1959 (dec.); m. Richard Yellin, Feb. 9, 1997. BA, Hunter Coll., 1947; MA, Columbia U., 1948; PhD, Sorbonne U., Paris, 1951. Instr. French Wellesley (Mass.) Coll., 1952-53; mem. faculty Stanford (Calif.) U., 1953—, prof. French lit., 1969-93, prof. emerita, 1994—. Author: Marcel Proust, 1953, Eugene Le Roy, 1957, Corbiere, Laforgue and Apollinaire, 1964, Helen of Troy Myth, 1968, (poetry) Mooring to France, (prose poem) Sydney: editor: Dictionary of Ideas in Marcel Proust, 1968, also articles in field; contbr. articles to profl. jours. Scholar Internat. Inst. Edn., 1948-51, MLA, 1956-57, AAUW, 1962-63, Am. Philos. Soc., 1970-71, NEH, 1989; elected to Hall of Fame, Alumni Assn. Hunter Coll. of CUNY, 1990 Mem. MLA, Am. Assn. Tchrs. French, Soc. Friends Marcel Proust. Office: Stanford U Dept French Italian Stanford CA 94305

NEWMARK, LEONARD DANIEL, linguistics educator; b. Attica, Ind., Apr. 8, 1929; s. Max Jacob and Sophie (Glusker) N.; m. Ruth Broessler, Sept. 16, 1951; children: Katya, Mark. AB, U. Chgo., 1947; MA, Ind. U., 1951, PhD, 1955. Instr. English U. Ill., Urbana, 1951; vis. asst. prof. linguistics U. Mich., Ann Arbor, 1961; assoc. prof. English Ohio State U., 1954-62; assoc. prof. linguistics Ind. U., Bloomington, 1962-63; prof. linguistics U. Calif., San Diego, 1963-91, prof. emeritus, 1992—, chmn. dept., 1963-71, 79-85, head program in Am. lang. and culture, 1979-84, rsch. linguist Ctr. for Rsch. in Lang., 1992—. Author: Linguistic History of English, 1963, Spoken Albanian, 1997, Standard Albanian, 1982, Albanian-English Dictionary, 1998, Albanian Handbook, 1999; inventor memory aid device. Mem. Linguistics Soc. Am., Dictionary Soc. N.Am., Phi Beta Kappa. Home: 2643 St Tropez Pl La Jolla CA 92037-3541 Office: U Calif San Diego Dept Linguistics La Jolla CA 92093 E-mail: ldnewmark@ucsd.edu

NEWMEYER, FREDERICK JARET, linguist, educator; b. Phila., Jan. 30, 1944; s. Alvin S. and Fritzie B. (Nisenson) N.; m. Carolyn V. Platt, Apr. 28, 1968 (div. 1974); m. Marilyn M. Goebel, Dec. 25, 1993. BA, U. Rochester, 1965, MA, 1967; PhD, U. Ill., 1969. Asst. prof. linguistics U. Wash., Seattle, 1969-75, assoc. prof., 1975-81, prof., 1981—, chair, 1990-2000. Vis. prof. U. London, 1979, Cornell U., 1981, U. Md., 1982, UCLA, 1982-83, La Trobe U., Australia, 1987. Author: English Aspectual Verbs, 1975, Linguistic Theory in America, 1980, Grammatical Theory, 1983, Politics of Linguistics, 1986, Generative Linguistics, 1995, Language Form and Language Function, 1998; editor: Linguistics: The Cambridge Survey, 1988, Natural Language and Linguistic Theory, 1987—; assoc. editor: Language, 1980-85. NEH fellow, 1973-74. Mem. Linguistic Soc. Am. (sec.-treas. 1989-94, v.p. 2001—). Avocations: gardening. Home: 4621 NE 107th St Seattle WA 98125-6947 Office: U Wash Dept Linguistics Seattle WA 98195-4340

NEWSOME, RANDALL JACKSON, judge; b. Dayton, Ohio, July 13, 1950; s. Harold I. and Sultana S. (Stony) N. BA summa cum laude, Boston U., 1972; JD, U. Cin., 1975. Bar: Ohio 1975, U.S. Dist. Ct. (so. dist.) Ohio 1977, U.S. Ct. Appeals (6th cir.) 1979, U.S. Supreme Ct. 1981. Law clk. to chief judge U.S. Dist. Ct. (so. dist.) Ohio, 1975-77; assoc. Dinsmore & Shohl, Cin., 1978-82; judge U.S. Bankruptcy Ct. (so. dist.) Ohio, 1982-88, U.S. Bankruptcy Ct. (no. dist.) Calif., Oakland, 1988—. Faculty mem. Fed. Jud. Ctr., ALI-ABA, 1987—; mem. Nat. Conf. of Bankruptcy Judges, 1983—, mem. bd. govs., 1987-88, pres., 1998-99. Contbg. author: Chapter 11 Theory and Practice, 1994—, Collier on Bankruptcy, 1997—. Fellow Am. Coll. Bankruptcy; mem. Am. Law Inst., Phi Beta Kappa. Democrat. Office: US Bankruptcy Ct PO Box 2070 Oakland CA 94604-2070

NEWTON, JAMES QUIGG, JR. lawyer; b. Denver, 1911; s. James Quigg and Nelle (Singleton) N.; m. Virginia Shafroth, June 6, 1942; children: Nancy Grusin, Nelle Grainger, Abby Hornung, Virginia Rice. AB, Yale U., 1933, LLB, 1936, MA (hon.), 1951; DPS (hon.), U. Denver, 1952; LLD, Adams State Coll., 1960, Colo. Coll., 1962, U. Colo., 1975. Bar: Colo. 1938. Legal sec. to W.O. Douglas SEC, 1936-37; practiced in Denver, 1938-42, 46-47; lectr. U. Denver, 1938-41; with Ford Found., N.Y.C., 1955-56, v.p., 1956; pres. U. Colo., 1956-63, Commonwealth Fund, N.Y.C., 1963-75, vice chmn., 1975-76, dir., 1951-55, 57-78; sr. cons. Henry J. Kaiser Family Found., Menlo Park, Calif., 1978-80; of counsel firm Davis, Graham & Stubbs, 1981—. Dir. N.Y. Life Fund, 1972-95, Kaiser Found. Hosps./Health Plan, 1972-80; trustee Dry Dock Savs. Bank; mem. Yale Corp., 1951-55, Western Interstate Com. Higher Edn., 1957-63; mem. nat. adv. mental health coun. NIH, 1964-68; mem. Inst. Medicine, Nat. Acad. Scis., 1972—, VA Spl. Med. Adv. Group, 1968-74; fellow Ctr. for Advanced Study in Behavioral Scis., 1977-78. Mayor, City and County of Denver, 1947-55; Sec. bd. trustees U. Denver, 1938-42, pres., 1946-47; pub. trustee Nutrition Found.; chmn. bd. YMCA Greater N.Y., 1976-77. Served with USNR, 1942-46. Fellow Acad. Arts and Scis.; mem. Am. Municipal Assn. (pres. 1950), Am. Council Edn. (dir. 1959-62), Am. Arbitration Assn. (dir., exec. com.), Fgn. Bondholders Protective Council (dir. 1975—), Phi Delta Phi, Alpha Delta Phi. Home: 2552 E Alameda Ave Denver CO 80209-3320

NG, BETTY, electronics executive; Pres. Reliance Tech Svcs., Sunnyvale, Calif., 1981—. Office: Reliance Tech Svcs 895 Kifer Rd Sunnyvale CA 94086-5205 Fax: 408-720-0838. E-mail: info@RTSII.com

NG, LAWRENCE MING-LOY, pediatrician; b. Hong Kong, Mar. 21, 1940; came to U.S., 1967, naturalized, 1977; s. John Iu-cheung and Mary Wing (Wong) N.; m. Bella May Ha Kan, June 25, 1971; children: Jennifer Wing-mui, Jessica Wing-yee. B in Medicine, U. Hong Kong, 1965; B in Surgery, 1965. Diplomate Am. Bd. Pediatrics. House physician Queen Elizabeth Hosp., Hong Kong, 1965-66, med. officer Hong Kong, 1966-67; resident physician Children's Hosp. of Los Angeles, 1967-68, Children's Hosp. Med. Ctr., Oakland, Calif., 1968-70; fellow in pediatric cardiology, 1970-72; now mem. teaching staff; practice medicine specializing in pediatrics and pediatric cardiology, San Leandro, Calif., 1972—, Oakland, 1982—; mng. ptnr. Pediatric Med. Assocs. of East Bay, 1990—. Chief of pediatrics Oakland Hosp., 1974-77; chief of pediatrics Vesper Meml.

Hosp., 1977-79, sec. staff, 1984, v.p. staff, 1985; chief pediatrics Meml. Hosp., San Leandro, 1986-88; founder Pediatric Assocs. of East Bay, 1990. Active Republican Party. Fellow Am. Acad. Pediatrics; mem. AMA, Calif. Med. Assn., Am. Heart Assn., Alameda County Assn. Primary Care Practitioners (membership chmn. 1993-97, sec. treas. 1994-97), Los Angeles Pediatric Soc., East Bay Pediatric Soc., Smithsonian Assocs., Nat. Geog. Soc., Orgn. Chinese Ams. (chpt. pres. 1984), Chinese-Am. Physicians Soc. (sec. 1980, pres. 1983, exec. dir. 1997—), Fedn. Chinese Med. Socs. (dir. 1998—), Chinese-Am. Polit. Assn. (life), Ethnic Health Inst. (bd. dirs. 1998—), Oakland Mus. Assns., Oakland Chinatown C. of C. (bd. dirs. 1986-91, adv. bd. 1992—), Oakland Asian Cultural Ctr. (dir. 1996-99, treas. 1996-99), Friends of Hong Kong U. (bd. dirs. 2001-), Hong Kong U. Alumni Assn. (sec. No. Calif. chpt. 1992-96, pres. 1997-2000, bd. chair 2001—), Children's First Healthcare Network (bd. dirs. 1997—), Stanford U. Alumni Assn. (life), Chancellor's Assocs. U. Calif. at Berkeley, Chancellor's Assocs. U. Calif. at San Francisco, Commonwealth Club, Consumer's Union (life), Oakland Chinatown C. of C. (cmty. svc. award 2000), Chinese Am. Golf Club. Buddhist. Office: 345 9th St Ste 204 Oakland CA 94607-4206 also: 101 Callan Ave Ste 401 San Leandro CA 94577-4523 E-mail: larryn@pedmed.com

NGUYEN, ANN CAC KHUE, pharmaceutical and medicinal chemist; b. Kieu Moc, Sontay, Vietnam, Nov. 12, 1949; d. Nguyen Van Soan and Luu Thi Hieu. BS, U. Saigon, 1973; MS, San Francisco State U., 1978; PhD, U. Calif., San Francisco, 1983. Teaching and research asst. U. Calif., San Francisco, 1978-83, postdoctoral fellow, 1983-86, research scientist, 1987—. Contbr. articles to profl. jours. Recipient Nat. Research Service award, NIH, 1981-83; Regents fellow U. Calif., San Francisco, 1978-81. Mem. AAAS, Am. Chem. Soc., N.Y. Acad. Scis., Bay Area Enzyme Mechanism Group, Am. Assn. Pharm. Scientists. Roman Catholic. Home: 1488 Portola Dr San Francisco CA 94127-1409 Office: U Calif PO Box 446 San Francisco CA 94143-0001 E-mail: cackhue@itsa.ucsf.edu

NGUYEN, HUONG TRAN, English language professional, federal agency official; b. Haiphong, Vietnam, Nov. 16, 1953; came to the U.S., 1971; d. Joe (Quang) Trong Tran and Therese (Nguyet-Anh) (Do) Dotran; m. Tony (Phu) The Nguyen; children: Long Tran Nguyen, Ty Tran Nguyen. B in Liberal Studies, San Diego State U., 1976, tchg. credential grades K-12, 1977; M in Curriculum Devel., Point Loma Coll., 1984; lang. devel. specialist cert., Calif. Commn. Credentialing, 1991. ESL tchr. San Diego (Calif.) Job Corps, 1978-80; resource tchr. grades K-12 San Diego (Calif.) Unified Sch. Dist., 1980-82; resource tchr. SEAL project grades K-12 Long Beach (Calif.) Unified Sch. Dist., 1982-83, ESL specialist, 1983-85, 85-92, English lang. devel. tchr., chair, 1992-95; adminstr., 1996-98; sr. fellow officer U.S. Dept. Edn., Office Bilingual & Minority Lang. Affairs, Washington, 1995-96; disting. tchr.-in-residence Calif. State U., Long Beach, 1998—. Named Outstanding Tchr. of 1994, Disney Co. Am. Tchr. Awards, Washington, 1994, Outstanding Tchr. in Fgn. Lang./ESL, Disney Co. Am. Tchr. Awards, Washington, 1994. Mem. NEA, TESOL, Calif. Lang. Tchrs. Assn., Calif. Tchr. Assn., Calif. Assn. for Bilingual Edn., Tchr. Assn. Long Beach, Assn. Curriculum and Supervision. Avocations: reading, traveling, gardening, visiting museums. Home: 6262 Cherokee Dr Westminster CA 92683-2004 Office: Calif State U Coll Edn Dept Tchr Edn 1250 N Bellflower Blvd Long Beach CA 90840-0001

NGUYEN, LAM DUC, business executive, consultant; b. Ninh Binh, Vietnam, July 20, 1945; came to the U.S., 1975; s. Phuong-Duc and Thien-Thi Nguyen; m. Trang Thu Nghiem, June 17, 1978; children: Katherine, Andrew, Alexander. BA, U. Saigon, 1968; diploma in TEFL, U. Sydney, Australia, 1973; postgrad., Furman U., 1977, San Jose State U., 1980; AS in Computer Sci., Condie Coll., 1981; MS in Telecomm. Sys. Mgmt., Nat. U., Calif., 1996, postgrad., 1997—. Cert. Emergency Specialist Tchg. credential ESL grades K-12; Calif. C.C. tchg. credential for ltd. svcs. in basic edn.; Calif. C.C. instr. credential in computer scis. Materials/mfg. sys. analyst, project leader Shugart Corp., Sunnyvale, Calif., 1979-84; mgr. programming and sys. devel. Televideo Sys., Inc., San Jose, 1984-86; sales and mktg. sys. analyst, project leader Spectra-Physics, San Jose, 1986; project mgr. U.S. Wind Power, Livermore, Calif., 1986-87; asst. mgr. ops. Burger King Corp., San Jose, 1987-88; dir. programs, dep. exec. dir. IRCC Inc., San Jose, 1988-93; pres., founder WIN-Visions, San Jose, 1993—. Asst. chief tng. team Combined Document Exploitation Ctr., 1965-68; lang. instr. Military Asst. Command Civil Ops. for Rural Devel. Strategies/USAID, Bien Hoa, Vietnam, 1968-69; tchr. ESL/EFL Vietnamese-Am. Assn., Saigon, 1970-75; lectr. med. English U. Saigon-Med. Coll., 1974-75; spl. asst. to dir. refugee liaison officer, chief interpreter staff Refugee Camp, Eglin AFB, Fla., 1975; refugee camp mgmt. counselor Indochinese Inter-Agy. Task Force, U.S. State Dept., Indiantown Gap Refugee Camp, Pa., 1975; statis. quality control Michelin Tire Corp., S.C., 1976-78, others; part-time ESL instr. Foothill-De Anza Coll., San Jose, Calif., 1979-80; bilingual elem. and ESL tchr. San Jose Unified Sch. Dist., 1979-80; spkr., panelist in field. Co-author: Affirmative Action and Viet Community, 1996; author: Annotated Bibliography of Selected Materials for Family/Community Involvement, 1997; editor VIET mag., Thi Truong Tu Do mag.; co-editor, reporter Tin Bien News; contbr. articles to profl. jours.; host, prodr. ednl. radio shows. Active Nat. Asian Pacific Islanders Am. Adv. Coun., Democratic Nat. Com., 1991—, San Jose City Mayor's Gang Prevention Policy Team, 1992—, Coalition of Asian Pacific-Ams., No. Calif., 1992—, Nat. Immigration Forum, 1994; nat. co-chair Nat. Vietnamese-Am. Voter's League, 1992—, Nat. League Indochinese Am. Voters, 1992—; pres. Vietnamese-Ams. Civic Action Com., 1992—; mem., contbr. World Affairs Coun., 1993—; mem. adv. com. on voter registration and Get Out To Vote, Santa Clara County, co-chair, 1993, 94; mem. Dem. Congl. Campaign Com., 1992—; charter mem. Senate Task Force, 1992—; mem. Dem. Nat. Com.; mem. nat. steering com. Clinton/Gore, 1996; mem. Calif. State Adv. Coun. Refugee Assistance, 1992—, mem. various coms.; chair Vietnamese-Ams. Com. for Clinton/Gore, No. Calif., 1992, 96; chair fund raising com. Tet Festival, 1988-91, spl. event com., 1992-97; leader Vietnamese Ams. Dukakis' Presdl. Campaign, 1988; mem. Nat. Asian Pacific Am. Governing Coun., Clinton/Gore, 1996. Recipient Appreciation cert. Nat. ARC, 1975, Appreciation cert. and letter of commendation Refugee Liaison Office, USAF, 1975, Achievement cert. Dept. Army, 1975, Outstand Svc. to Refugee citation World YMCA, 1975, Peter Casey Asian Am. Leadership award, 1987, Letter of Commendation, Senator Art Torres, 1989, Letter Commendation, Santa Clara County Greater Ave. for Independence/Refugee Employment and Social Svcs. Adminstrn., 1990, Appreciation cert. State Calif. Dept. Social Svcs., 1990, Appreciation Cert. Calif. Dept. Health Svcs., Tobacco Control, 1991, Appreciation cert. U. Berkeley, Extended Foods and Nutrition Edn. Program, 1991, Merit award Coalition of Nationalist Vietnamese Orgns. of No. Calif., 1991, Leadership award No. Calif. Asian Pacific Americans, 1992, Cmty. Svc. award City of San Jose, 1993, Spirit of Democracy award State of Calif., 1994, Spl. Recognition award Alum Rock Union Elem. Sch. Dist., 1999, others. Democrat. Buddhist. Avocations: bilingual ballot, civil and human rights, writing, reading, traveling. Home and Office: WIN Visions 4864 Miramar Ave San Jose CA 95129-1004

NGUYEN, TAI ANH, minister; Supt. Vietnamese Ministry Dist. of the Christian and Missionary Alliance, 1989. Office: 2275 W Lincoln Ave Anaheim CA 92801-6551

NGUYEN, THINH VAN, internist; b. Vietnam, Apr. 16, 1948; came to U.S., 1971; s. Thao Van and Phuong Thi (Tran) N.; m. Phi Thi Ho, Jan. 2, 1973; children: Anh-Quan, Andrew. BS, U. Saigon, 1970; MS, U. Mo., 1973; MD, U. Tex., 1982. Diplomate Am. Bd. Internal Medicine, Am. Acad. Pain Mgmt., Fed. Lic. Examination. Rsch. asst. U. Tex. Med. Sch., Dallas, 1974-78; intern U. Tex. Med. Br., Galveston, 1982-83, resident, 1983-85; internist Family Health Plan, Inc., Long Beach, Calif., 1985-88, internist, area chief, 1988-89; pvt. practice San Jose, 1990—; chmn. quality assurance/UM com. Premier Care of No. Calif. Med. Group, Inc., 1996-99, also bd. dirs.; chief medical officer Healthglobe, Inc., 2000—. Chmn. interdisciplinary com. Charter Cmty. Hosp., Hawaiian Gardens, Calif., 1988-89, San Jose Med. Ctr., 1993—. Fellow ACP-Am. Soc. Internal Medicine, Am. Acad. Otolaryngic Allergy (affiliate), Am. Soc. Laser Med. Surgery, 1998—; mem. AMA, Am. Acad. Pain Mgmt., Calif. Assn. Med. Dirs. (bd. dirs. 1988-92), Calif. Med. Assn., Santa Clara County Med. Assn. Office: 2470 Alvin Ave Ste 5 San Jose CA 95121-1664

NICE, CARTER, conductor, music director; b. Jacksonville, Fla., Apr. 5, 1940; s. Clarence Carter and Elizabeth Jane (Hintermister) N.; m. Jennifer Charlotte Smith, Apr. 4, 1983; children: Danielle, Christian, Olivia. MusB, Eastman Sch. Music, 1962; MusM, Manhattan Sch. Music, 1964. Asst. condr., concert master New Orleans Philharm., 1967-79; condr., music dir. Sacramento Symphony, 1979-92; music dir., condr. Bear Valley Music Fest., 1985—. Office: 7729 Rio Barco Way Sacramento CA 95831-4458 E-mail: ccniii@aol.com

NICHOL, ALICE J. state legislator; b. Denver, Feb. 6, 1939; m. Ron Nichol; 4 children. Grad. H.S. Ret. sch. sec.; beauty cons. Mary Kay; mem. Colo. Ho. of Reps., 1992-98, Colo. Senate, Dist. 24, Denver, 1998—. Active Tri-City Bd. Health, Grassroots Adams City Dem. Party. Democrat. Roman Catholic. Office: State Capitol 200 E Colfax Ave Ste 274 Denver CO 80203-1716 also: 891 E 71st Ave Denver CO 80229-6806 Fax: 303-287-7742

NICHOLAS, HENRY THOMPSON, III, communications engineering executive; BSEE, MSEE, PhD in EE, UCLA. With TRW; dir. microelectronics PairGain Techs.; pres., CEO Broadcom Corp., Irvine, Calif., 1991—. Recipient Entrepreneur of the Yr. award Ernst & Young, 1996; named Top 20 Entrepreneurs 1997 Red Herring, 1997, World's Top 50 Cyber Elite 1997 Time Digital Mag., 1997. Office: Broadcom Corp PO Box 57013 Irvine CA 92619-7013 Fax: 949-450-8710

NICHOLAS, THOMAS PETER, municipal official; b. Laramie, Wyo., Dec. 6, 1948; s. Thomas Lloyd Nicholas and Frances (Collins) Chambers; m. Tanya Michelle Villont; 1 child, Ja'el Michelle. AA in Fine Arts, Cabrillo Coll., 1970; BA in English, U. Colo., 1972; MS in Librarianship and Info. Sci., U. Denver, 1982. Real estate salesperson Sun Country, Lakewood, Colo., 1972-74; v.p. Nicholas Properties, Denver, 1971-77; libr. City of Aurora, Colo., 1975-80, system support mgr., 1981-83, dir. libr. and TV svcs., 1984-95, dir. libr., recreation & TV svcs., 1995-2000, dir. libr. & recreation svcs., 2000—. Pres. bd. Irving Libr. Network Inc., Denver, 1985—; adv. CL System Inc., Boston, 1985—; acting pers. dir. City of Aurora; Denver Regional Coun. of Govt. award for Cmty. Svc. and Govt. Coop., 1995. Exec. producer TV programs: Election Night 85 (Franny award 1986), Miss Plumjoy's Place, 1988 (Starwards 1988), Aurora's Can't Afford Not To, 1988 (Starwards 1988). Mem. exec. bd., chmn. Arapahoe Pub. Access to Librs., 1984-85; site coordinator Am. Cancer Soc., Aurora, 1988; adv. Youth at Risk, Aurora, 1989; bd. dirs. Cen. Colo. Libr. System, Lakewood, 1985-87; mem. exec. bd. Colo. Libr. Legis. Com., Denver, 1988—; pres. Greater Metro Cable Consortium, 1992—; acting dep. city mgr. City of Aurora, 1993—. Mem. ALA, Colo. Libr. Assn. (advisor 1982-83, dir. libr., recreation and TV 1995—, Programming award 1982, 1st Colo. Childrens Program award 1983, 88), Nat. Assn. Telecommunications Officers and Advisors (regional pres. 1983-84, T.V. Program award 1986), Rotary (program chmn. 1987-88, v.p. 1997-98), Eastgate Lions Club (pres. 1989-90), pres. elect Gatway Rotary, 1998. Democrat. Greek Orthodox. Avocations: fine art, poetry, automobile restoration, martial arts (Black Belt). Office: Aurora Pub Libr 14949 E Alameda Dr Aurora CO 80012-1500

NICHOLAS, WILLIAM RICHARD, lawyer; b. Pontiac, Mich., June 19, 1934; s. Reginald and Edna Irene (Bartlett) N.; m. Diana Lee Johnson, Aug. 20, 1960; children: Susan Lee, William Richard Jr. BS in Bus., U. Idaho, 1956; JD, U. Mich., 1962. Bar: 1963. Of counsel Latham & Watkins, Los Angeles, 1962-96. Contbr. numerous articles on taxation. Lt. (j.g.) USN, 1956-59. Mem. Calif. Bar Assn., Los Angeles County Bar Assn., Am. Coll. Tax Counsel. Home: 1808 Old Ranch Rd Los Angeles CA 90049-2207 Office: Latham & Watkins 633 W 5th St Ste 4000 Los Angeles CA 90071-2005

NICHOLS, ANDREW WILKINSON, state legislator, public health physician, educator; b. Bardstown, Ky., Jan. 29, 1937; s. Andrew Wilkinson and Catherine May (Garrison) N.; m. Ann Marie Weaver, June 1965; children: Catherine Ann, Michael Garrison, Miles Andrew. AB, Swarthmore Coll., 1959; MD, Stanford U., 1964; MPH, Harvard U., 1970. Diplomate Am. Bd. Preventive Medicine, Am. Bd. Family Practice. Asst. resident in medicine, then resident in medicine St. Luke's Hosp., N.Y.C., 1964-66, 68-69; med. officer U.S. Peace Corps, Lima, Peru, 1966-68; prof. family & community medicine U. Ariz., Tucson, 1970—, dir. Rural Health Office, 1980—; mem. Ariz. Ho. Reps., Dist. 13, 1992-00, Ariz. Senate, Dist. 13, Phoenix, 2000—. Pres. Ariz.-Mex. Border Health Found., Tucson, 1985—, U.S.-Mex. Border Health Assn., El Paso, Tex., 1989-90, Nat. Orgn. AHEC Program Dirs., Washington, 1991-93, Ariz. Pub. Health Assn., 1982-83; chmn. bd. dirs. Jour. Rural Health, Kansas City, Mo., 1988, 89, 90; dir. Ariz. Area Health Edn. Ctr., 1984—, S.W. Border Rural Health Rsch. Ctr., 1988—, WHO Collaborating Ctr. Rural and Border Health, 1992—. Co-author: Public Health and Community Medicine, 1980; contbr. articles to health publs. Bd. dirs. Habitat for Humanity, Tucson, 1979-93, div. higher edn. Christian Ch., St. Louis, 1988-92. Robert Wood Johnson Found. Health Policy fellow, 1977-78; sr. fellow Fogaty Internat. Ctr.-NIH, 1985-87; named Outstanding Health Worker of Yr. U.S.-Mex. Border Health Assn., 1986. Fellow Am. Coll. Preventive Medicine, Am. Acad. Family Physicians. Mem. Disciples of Christ Ch. Avocation: photography.

NICHOLS, IRIS JEAN, illustrator; b. Yakima, Wash., Aug. 2, 1938; d. Charles Frederick and Velma Irene (Hacker) Beisner; (div. June 1963); children: Reid William, Amy Jo; m. David Gary Nichols, Sept. 21, 1966. BFA in Art, U. Wash., 1978. Freelance illustrator, graphic designer, Seattle, 1966—; med. illustrator, head dept. illustration Swedish Hosp. Med. Ctr., Seattle, 1981-86; owner, med. and scientific illustrator Art for Medicine, Seattle, 1986—. Part-time med. illustrator U. Wash., Seattle, 1966-67; part-time med. illustrator, graphic coord. dept. art The Mason Clinic, 1968-78; instr. advanced illustration Cornish Coll. Arts, Seattle, 1988-90. Illustrator various books including Bryophytes of Pacific Northwest, 1966, Microbiology, 1973, 78, 82, 94, 98, Introduction to Human Physiology, 1980, Understanding Human Anatomy and Physiology, 1983, Human Anatomy, 1984 Regional Anesthesia, 1990, many other med. and sci. books, and children's books on various subjects; exhibited in group shows at Seattle Pacific Sci. Ctr., summer 1979, 82, Am. Coll. Surgeons (1st prize 1974), N.W. Urology Conf. (1st prize 1974, 76, 2d prize 1975); pub. illustrations Constellation Pk. and Marine Res., City Seattle Pk., 1999. Pres. ArtsWest (formerly West Seattle Arts Coun.), 1983; active Seattle Art Mus. Named to West Seattle H.S. Alumni Hall of Fame, 1986, Matrix Table, 1986-96. Mem. Assn. Med. Illustrators (Murial McLatchie Fine Arts award 1981), Nat. Mus. Women in the Arts (Wash. state com., bd. dirs. 1987-95, pres. 1993-94), Women Painters of Wash. (pres. 1987-89), U. Wash. Alumni Assn., Lambda Rho (pres. 1995-98). Avocations: artwork, printmaking, small books, entering juried art exhibitions. E-mail: artformed@aol.com

NICHOLS, MARK EDWARD, aerospace engineer; b. Schenectady, N.Y., Sept. 3, 1950; s. John Burton and Betty Jane (Paulsen) N.; m. Cornelia Rocas. BS in Engring. Physics, U. Calif., Berkeley, 1972; MS in Sci. and Engring. Mgmt., West Coast U., 1984; postgrad., Ind. Coll. Armed Forces, 1977. Cert. in Nat. Security Mgmt. Inst. and mech. technician Wetzel-Moreau Engring. Co., Inglewood, Calif., 1970-71; sales engr., supr. United Tech. Industries/Turbocooler Divsn., Manhattan Beach, 1972-73; wind tunnel test engr. Space Divsn. Rockwell Internat., Downey, 1973-76, flight and sys. engr. Space Sys. Divsn. Palmdale, 1976-78, aero. test engr. Space Sys. Divsn. Downey, 1980-85, project engr. payloads-cargo integration Aerospace Divsn., 1985-96; flight test integration engr. Gen. Dynamics/Convair, San Diego, 1978-80; project engr. mission/manifest integration requirements Boeing Space Sys. Divsn., 1996-99; lead flight interface engr. Boeing Reusable Space Systems, 1999-2001; sr. lead flight integration engr., reconfiguration engring. Boeing Human Space Flight and Exploration. Instr. Aerodynamics and Aeronautics, Adv. Career Tng., Downey, 1986—; instrnl. aide, lectr. Discover-E, Downey, 1992—. Columnist, Long Beach Press-Telegram, 1987-90. With USN, 1968-69. Judge L.A. County and Calif. State Sci. and Engring. Fairs, 1987—. Recipient Achievement award Bank of Am., 1968, Silver Snoopy Achievement award NASA, 1978; Gov.'s scholar, 1968. Mem. ASME, AIAA, Nat. Mgmt. Assn., Am. Legion #270, Planetary Soc., Moose #1739, Los Amigos Men's Club. Republican. Avocations: golf, skiing, sailing, travel, motorcycling. Home: 11682 Lakewood Blvd Downey CA 90241-5272 Office: Boeing Human Space Flight & Exploration Divsn 5301 Bolsa Ave Huntington Beach CA 92647

NICHOLS, MIKE, stage and film director; b. Berlin, Nov. 6, 1931; s. Nicholaievitch and Brigitte (Landauer) Peschowsky; m. Patricia Scott, 1957 (div.); m. Margot Callas, 1974 (div.); m. Annabel Davis-Goff (div.); m. Diane Sawyer, Apr. 29, 1988. Student, U. Chgo., 1950-53; student acting, Lee Strasberg. Ptnr. with Elaine May in comedy act; first appeared at Playwrights Theatre Club, Compass Theatre, Chgo.; N.Y. debut An Evening with Mike Nichols and Elaine May, 1960; acted in A Matter of Position, Phila., 1962; dir.: (plays) Barefoot in the Park, 1963 (Tony award best dir.), The Knack, 1964, Luv, 1964 (Tony award best dir.), The Odd Couple, 1965 (Tony award best dir.), The Apple Tree, 1966, The Little Foxes, 1967, Plaza Suite, 1968 (Tony award best dir.), The Prisoner of 2d Avenue, 1971 (Tony award best dir.), Uncle Vanya (co-adapted), 1973, Streamers, 1976, Comedians, 1976, The Gin Game, 1977, (L.A. Drama Critics award), Drink Before Dinner, 1978, Lunch Hour, 1980, Fools, 1981, The Real Thing, 1984 (Tony award 1984,), Hurlyburly, 1984, Social Security, 1984, Elliot Loves, 1990, Death and the Maiden, 1992; (films) Who's Afraid of Virginia Woolf?, 1966, (Academy award nomination best director 1966), The Graduate, 1967 (Academy award best director 1967), Catch-22, 1970, Carnal Knowledge, 1971, The Day of the Dolphin, 1973, The Fortune, 1975, Silkwood, 1983 (Academy award nomination best director 1983), Heartburn, 1986, Biloxi Blues, 1987, Working Girl, 1988 (Academy award nomination best director 1988), Postcards From the Edge, 1990, Regarding Henry, 1991, Wolf, 1994, The Bird Cage, 1995, Primary Colors, 1998; dir., prodr.: What Planet Are You From?, 2000; prodr. All the Pretty Horses, 2000; prodr.: (musical) Annie, 1977; performed at N.Y. musical Pres. Johnson's Inaugural Gala, 1965; TV appearances include Today Show.

NICHOLS, STEVEN, shoe and clothing manufacturing executive; b. 1942; With Nichols Foot Form Corp., 1962-79; pres. Stride Rite Retail Corp., 1979-82, Stride Rite Footwear, 1982-86, dir., v.p. merchandise, 1980-86; pres., chmn. bd. K-Swiss, Inc., Westlake Village, Calif., 1987—. Office: K-Swiss Inc 31248 Oak Crest Dr Westlake Village CA 91361-4643 Fax: (818) 706-5390

NICHOLS, WILLIAM FORD, JR. foundation executive, business executive; b. Palo Alto, Calif., July 4, 1934; s. William Ford and Elizabeth (Woodyatt) N.; m. Rosemary Peterson, 1988; children: Deborah, John, Andrew. AB, Stanford U., 1956, MBA, 1958. CPA, Calif. With Price Waterhouse, San Francisco, 1958-69, Price Waterhouse & Co., Sydney, Australia, 1966; asst. contr. Saga Corp., Menlo Park, Calif., 1969-72, contr., 1972—, asst. treas., 1981-83; assoc. prof. San Jose State U., 1983-88; treas. William and Flora Hewlett Found., Menlo Park, 1985-2000. Trustee Investment Fund for Founds., 1991-2001. Bd. dirs. Lucile Packard Found. for Children's Health, Palo Alto, Calif., 1999—. Mem. AICPA, Calif. Soc. CPA's, Inst. Mgmt. Accts. (nat. v.p. 1974-75, bd. dirs.), Fin. Execs. Inst. (pres. Santa Clara Valley chpt. 1979-80). Home: 330 August Cir Menlo Park CA 94025-5829

NICHOLSON, JOSEPH BRUCE, real estate developer; b. San Jose, Calif., Jan. 21, 1940; s. Wilmot Joseph and Ruth (Russell) N.; m. Susan Knight, Nov. 1963 (div. 1972); children: Kelsey Erin, Craig Wilmot; m. Linda Mirassou, Aug. 1992. BArch, U. Oreg., 1963. Exec. v.p. Nicholson-Brown Inc., Santa Clara, Calif., 1967-80; prin. Nicholson Assocs., Aptos, 1977—; v.p., gen. mgr. Nicholson-Wilson Co., Santa Clara, 1980-83; prin. The Nicholson Co., Campbell, Calif., 1984—; v.p. Pacific Property Ventures Inc., Campbell, 1988—; pres. Nicholson Constrn. Inc., Campbell, 1989—; v.p. Nicholson Property Mgmt. Inc., Campbell, 1989—; pres. The Nicholson Family Found., 1996—. Bd. dirs. Transmetrics Inc., San Jose. Bd. dirs. Triton Mus., Santa Clara, 1979, Hope Rehab. Svc., San Jose, 1979, United Way Cen. Area, San Jose, 1991. Devel. Engring. Rsch. Inst., Carmel, Calif., 1999—; pres. adv. bd. de Saisset Mus., Santa Clara U., 1991; trustee Mus. of Art and History, Santa Cruz, 1993. Lt. USN, 1963-67. Mem. Rotary, Commonwealth Club (San Francisco), World Trade Club (San Francisco), Santa Cruz Yacht Club, Tennis Club Rio Del Mar. Republican. Avocations: travel, reading, art collecting, cooking, tennis. Home: 218 Shoreview Dr Aptos CA 95003-4621 Office: The Nicholson Co 75 Cristich Ln Campbell CA 95008-5403 E-mail: brucenicholson@thenicholsonco.com

NICHOLSON, MARILYN LEE, arts administrator; b. San Jose, Calif., Feb. 7, 1949; d. John Hart Nicholson and Betty Ann (Price) Shepardson; m. Neal Luit Evenhuis. BA in English and History, U. Ariz., 1972; BFA in Studio, MA in English, U. Hawaii-Manoa, 1977, AS, 1984. Edn. coord., dir. Bishop Mus. Arts and Crafts Sch., Honolulu, 1977-79; owner Fiber Arts Store, Kailua, Hawaii, 1978-82; field coord. Hawaii State Found. on Culture and Arts, Honolulu, 1981-85; exec. dir. Sedona (Ariz.) Arts Ctr., 1986-92, Volcano (Hawaii) Art Ctr., 1992—. Mem. bd. artist selection com. Ariz. Indian Living Treasures, 1988-92; bd. dirs., treas. Sedona Cultural Arts Ctr., 1987-92; conf. speaker Nat. Assembly Arts Agys., 1988. Founding Chmn. Sedona Gallery Assn., 1990-92; mem. com. Sedona Acad., 1986-92; mem. steering com. community plan City of Sedona, 1989-91; commr. Arts & Cultural Ctr., Sedona, 1989-91; mem. exec. com. planning Volcano Community Assn., 1993-96. Recipient Mayor's award for Disting. Svc., Sedona City Coun., 1992. Mem. Hawaii Mus. Assn. (bd. dirs. 1995—), Cooper Ctr. Coun. (bd. dirs. 1992—), Aloha Festivals-Hawaii Island (bd. dirs. 1992—). Office: Volcano Art Ctr PO Box 104 Hawaii National Park HI 96718-0104

NICHOLSON, STEPHEN P. diversified electrical products company executive; b. 1953; Grad., Mich. State U., 1976. CPA, Mich. With Total Petroleum (N.A.) Ltd.; treas., CFO, v.p. fin. Katy Industries, Inc., Englewood, Colo., 1996—. Office: Katy Industries Inc 6300 S Syracuse Way #300 Englewood CO 80111-6723 Fax: (303) 290-9344

NICHOLSON, WILL FAUST, JR. bank holding company executive; b. Colorado Springs, Colo., Feb. 8, 1929; s. Will Faust and Gladys Olivia (Burns) N.; m. Shirley Ann Baker, Nov. 26, 1955; children: Ann Louise Nicholson Naughton, Will Faust III. S.B., M.I.T., 1950; M.B.A., U.

Denver, 1956. V.p. Van Schaack & Co., Denver, 1954-66; pntr. N. G. Petry Constrn. Co., Denver, 1966-70; sr. v.p. Colo. Nat. Bankshares, Inc., Denver, 1970-75, pres., 1975-95, chmn. bd., chief exec. officer, 1985-95; chmn. Rocky Mountain Bankcard Sys., Denver, 1995—. Bd. dirs. Boys and Girls Clubs of Metro Denver; active Downtown Denver, Inc., Colo. Assn. of Commerce and Industry, chmn. 1990-91, Denver Urban Renewal Authority, 1958-59, Denver Bd. Water Commrs., 1959-65, pres. 1964, 65; Nat. Western Stock Show; bd. Health One. With USAF, 1950-53. Mem. Assn. Bank Holding Cos. (bd. dirs. 1979-87, 89-91, exec. com. 1980-85, vice chmn. 1981-82, chmn. 1983-84), U.S. C. of C. (bd. dirs. 1990—, chmn. 1999-2000), U.S. Golf Assn. (exec. com. 1974-82, v.p. 1978, 79, pres. 1980, 81), Denver Country Club, Univ. Club Colo., Univ. Club N.Y., Castle Pine Golf Club, Royal and Ancient Golf Club (St. Andrews, Scotland), Augusta (Ga.) Nat. Golf Club. Republican. Episcopalian. Home: 37 Polo Club Cir Denver CO 80209-3307 Office: Rocky Mountain BankCard Sys Inc PO Box 5168 Denver CO 80217-5168

NICITA, RICK, agent; Agent Creative Artists Agy., co-chmn. Calif., 1995—. Office: Creative Artists Agy 9830 Wilshire Blvd Beverly Hills CA 90212-1825

NICKERSON, GUY ROBERT, lumber company executive; b. Salt Lake City, May 20, 1956; s. Charles Augustus and Florence May (Fogel) N.; m. Maggie Rose McDonnell, May 30, 1992; children: Melissa Marie, Rebecca Rose. B Acctg., U. Utah, 1977, M Profl. Accountancy, 1978. CPA, Utah. Sr. mgr. Deloitte Haskins & Sells, Salt Lake City and N.Y.C., 1978-87; v.p. fin. Anderson Lumber Co., Ogden, Utah, 1987-96, v.p. ops., 1996—. Office: Anderson Lumber Co 4700 Harrison Blvd Ogden UT 84403-4305

NICOL, ROBERT DUNCAN, architect; b. La Jolla, Calif., Sept. 16, 1936; s. Duncan and Catherine (Muffly) N.; m. Susann Kay Larson; 1 child, Jennifer E. AA, Principia Coll., 1956; BArch, U. Calif., Berkeley, 1961. Registered arch., Ariz., Calif., Mont., Wash. Designer Kawneer Mfg. Co., Richmond, Calif., 1961-62, Claude Oakland, San Francisco, 1962-64; project arch. David T. Johnson, Oakland, Calif., 1964-68; pvt. practice Oakland, 1968—. Mem. bd. appeals City of Alameda, 1971-73, vice chair planning commn., 1973-77, founder, chair, vice chair design rev. bd., 1974-80, founder, chair, vice chair hist. adv. bd., 1976—, co-founder, chair, vice chair mayor's com. for handicapped, 1980-86; mem. Calif. State Access Bd., 1995—. Recipient Design award Am. Registered Archs., 1969, Harper Plz. Design award Calif. Bldg. Ofcls. Assn., 1985. Fellow AIA; mem. Soc. Am. Registered Archs., Nat. Coun. Archtl. Registration Bds. (sr.), Alexander Graham Bell Assn. for Deaf (lectr.), Oral Hearing Impaired Sec., San Leandro Hist. Railway Soc. (founder, charter mem., chair, vice-chair), Alameda Jr. C. of C. (project dir. 1969), Alameda Victorian Preservation Soc. Republican. Office: 455 17th St Ste 300 Oakland CA 94612-2101

NICOLAI, THOMAS R. lawyer; b. Frazer, Mich., Dec. 1, 1943; BA cum laude, Kalamazoo Coll., 1965; JD, U. Mich., 1970. Bar: Ill. 1972, Oreg. 1973. Fellow in Econs. U. Bonn., Germany, 1965-67; fellow Alexander von Humbolt Found. at Max Planck Inst. for Fgn. and Internat. Patent, Copyright and Unfair Competition Law, Munich, West Germany, 1970-72; ptr. Stoel Rives LLP, Portland, Oreg., 1973—. Mem. ABA (mem. real property, probate and trust law, bus. law and internat. law and practice sects.), Phi Beta Kappa, Phi Alpha Delta. Office: Stoel Rives LLP 900 SW 5th Ave Ste 2600 Portland OR 97204-1229

NICOLAOU, K. C. chemistry educator; b. Karavas, Kyrenia, Cyprus, June 5, 1946; came to U.S., 1972; s. Costa and Helen (Yettimi) N.; m. Georgette Karayianni, July 15, 1973; children; Colette, Alexis, Christopher, Paul. BSc, Bedford Coll., London, 1969; PhD, U. Coll., London, 1972; DSc, U. London, 1994; PhD (hon.), U. Athens, 1995. Rsch. assoc. Columbia U., N.Y.C., 1972-73, Harvard U., Cambridge, Mass., 1973-76; from asst. prof. to Rhodes-Thompson prof. chemistry U. Pa., Phila., 1976-89; Darlene Shiley prof. chemistry, chmn. dept. The Scripps Rsch. Inst., La Jolla, Calif., 1989—; prof. chemistry U. Calif. at San Diego, La Jolla, 1989—. Vis. prof. U. Paris, 1986; mem. exec. com. Diann. Cyprus Conf. on Drug Design; mem. med. study sect. D, NIH, 1988-90; mem. internat. adv. bd. Angewandte Chemie, 1994—. Author: (with N. A. Petasis) Selenium in Natural Products Synthesis, 1984, (with E. J. Sorensen) Classics in Total Synthesis, 1996; co-editor: Synthesis, Germany, 1984-90, Chemistry and Biology, 1994; editl. bd. Prostaglandins, Leukotrienes and Medicine, 1978-88, Synthesis, 1990—, Accounts of Chem. Rsch., 1992—, Carbohydrate Letters, 1993—, Chemistry-A European Jour., 1994—, Perspectives in Drug, Discovery and Design, 1994—, Indian Jour. of Chemistry, Sect. B, 1995—; mem. bd. consulting editors Tetrahedron Publs., 1992—; mem. adv. bd. Contemporary Organic Synthesis, 1993—; mem. regional adv. bd. J. C. S. Chem. Comm., 189—, J. C. S. Perkin I, 1991—; contbr. articles to profl. jours.; patentee in field. Recipient Japan Soc. for Promotion Sci. award 1987-88, U.S. Sr. Scientist award Alexander von Humboldt Found., 1987-88, Alan R. Day award Phila. Organic Chemists Club, 1993, Pfizer Rsch. award, 1993-94, Paul Janssen Prize, 1994, Alexander the Great Award Hellenic Cultural Soc. of San Diego, 1994, Rhone-Poulenc medal Royal Soc. of Chemistry, 1995, Chem. Pioneer Am. Inst. of Chemists, 1996, Inhoffen Medal of Gesellscaft fur Biotechnologische Forschung mbH (GBF) Tech. U. of Braunschweig, 1996, Linus Pauling award, 1996; fellow A.P. Sloan Found., 1979-83, J. S. Guggenhiem Found., 1984; Camille and Henry Dreyfus scholar, 1980-84, Arthur C. Cope scholar, 1987. Fellow N.Y. Acad. Scis., AAAS; mem. Am. Chem. Soc. (Creative Work in Synthetic Organic Chemistry award 1993, William H. Nichols medal N.Y. sect. 1996, Ernest Guenther award in chemistry of natural products 1996), Chem. Soc. London, German Chem. Soc., Japanese Chem. Soc. Office: Scripps Rsch Inst Dept Chemistry 10550 N Torrey Pines Rd La Jolla CA 92037-1000

NIEDERAUER, GEORGE H. bishop; b. Los Angeles, CA, June 14, 1936; s. George and Elaine N. B.A. Philosophy, St. John's Seminary, Camarillo, CA, 1959; B.A. Sacred Theology, Catholic U., Washington, DC, 1962; M.A. English Lit., Loyola U., Los Angeles, CA, 1962; Ph.D. English Lit., USC, 1966. ordained priest April 30, 1962; named prelate of honor (monsignor) 1984; named bishop of Diocese of Salt Lake City, Nov. 3, 1994. Asst. pastor Our Lady of the Assumption Parish, Claremont, CA, 1962-63; priest in residence Holy Name of Jesus Parish, Los Angeles, 1963-65; instr. English Lit. St. John's Seminary Coll., Camarillo, 1965-79; instr. of English Lit. Mt. St. Mary's Coll., Los Angeles, 1967-74; English Dept. chmn. St. John's Seminary Coll., Camarillo, 1968-77, spiritual dir., 1972-79; part-time instr. of Spiritual Theology St. John's Seminary Theologate, 1976-79, full-time instr. of Spiritual Theology, 1979-87; part-time instr. of English Lit. St. John's Seminary Coll., 1979-92; rector St. John's Seminary, 1987-92, spiritual dir., 1979-95; co-dir. Cardinal Manning House of Prayer for Priests, Los Angeles, CA, 1992-95; bishop Salt Lake City, 1995—. Mem. Nat. Fedn. of Spiritual Dirs. (pres. 1975-77); mem. Alpha Sigma Nu (Jesuit Honor Soc. - LMU Chapter); pres. Western Assn. of Spiritual Dirs., 1973-75; mem. bd. of the Comm. of Priests' Retreat, Archdiocese of Los Angeles; mem. select comm. for the revision of the U.S. Catholic Conf. "Program for Priestly Formation" 3rd edition; mem. Vatican Visitation Team for Theologates; speaker World Vision Internat, Fuller Theological Seminary, Calif. Lutheran Coll.; mem. Camarillo Ministerial Assn. Avocations include: classical music, stamp collecting, reading. [illegible] Office: Chancery Office 27 C St Salt Lake City UT 84103-2302

NIEHAUS, ED, executive; Degree in engring., Duke U. Pres., CEO Neuhaus Ryan Wong, Inc., South San Francisco. Bd. dirs. Foresight Inst., Inst. Molecular Mfg., Software Forum. Office: 601 Gateway Blvd Ste 900 South San Francisco CA 94080-7006

NIELDS, MORGAN WESSON, medical supply company executive; b. Springfield, Mass., Jan. 25, 1946; s. Robert Littleton and Florence (Wesson) N.; m. Belinda Gammon, Aug. 14, 1968; children: William, Michael, Stefan, Morgan, Lindsey, Hunter. Cert. d'Etudes Francaises, Université de Lausanne, Switzerland, 1966; BA, Williams Coll., 1968; MBA, Dartmouth Coll., 1970. Mgr. mgmt. svcs. Graco Inc., Paris, 1970-73; chmn., chief exec. officer Fischer Imaging Corp., Denver, 1973—, also bd. dirs.; pres., chief operating officer Diasonics Inc., Milpitas, Calif., 1983-84. Bd. dirs. Scinticor, Inc., Milw., Columbia Hosp. Corp., Ft. Worth. Trustee Humana, Mountain View Hosp., Thornton, Colo., 1988-89. Mem. Nat. Elec. Mfrs. Assn. (bd. govs. 1986-87, 91—, bd. dirs. diagnostic imaging and therapy systems div. 1976-89), U.S. Ski Assn. (masters div., pres. Rocky Mountain region 1987-88). Avocations: ski racing, tennis, golf. Office: Fischer Imaging Corp 12300 N Grant St Denver CO 80241-3128

NIELSEN, GREG ROSS, lawyer; b. Provo, Utah, Sept. 24, 1947; s. Ross T. and Carma (Peterson) N.; m. Jo Rita Beer, Sept. 3, 1971; children: Jennifer, Jerilyn, Eric Michael, Brittany Anne. BA in Polit. Sci. magna cum laude, Brigham Young U., 1971; JD cum laude, Harvard U., 1975. Bar: Ariz. 1975, U.S. Dist. Ct. Ariz. 1975, U.S. Ct. Appeals (9th cir.) 1977, Utah 1990. Assoc. Snell & Wilmer, Phoenix, 1975-80, ptnr., 1981-91, mng. ptnr. Salt Lake City, 1991—, adminstrv. coord. real estate practice group Phoenix, 1988-90. Mem. dist. com. Theodore Roosevelt coun. Boy Scouts Am., 1988-90, Valley Partnership, Phoenix, 1989-90; trustee Utah Heritage Found., 1998-2000. Hinckley scholar Brigham Young U., 1970; fellow Ford Found., 1970. Mem. ABA, State Bar Ariz., Utah Bar Assn. Republican. Mem. LDS Ch. Office: Snell & Wilmer 15 West South Temple Ste 1200 Salt Lake City UT 84101 E-mail: gnielsen@swlaw.com

NIELSEN, JAKOB, computer interface engineer; b. Copenhagen, Oct. 5, 1957; came to U.S., 1990; s. Gerhard and Helle (Hopfner) N.; m. Hannah Kain, Feb. 18, 1984. MS in Computer Sci., Aarhus (Denmark) U., 1983; PhD in Computer Sci., T.U. of Denmark, 1988. Rsch. fellow Aarhus U., 1983-84; vis. scientist IBM User Interface Inst., Yorktown Heights, N.Y., 1985; adj. asst. prof. T.U. Denmark, Lyngby, 1986-90; mem. rsch. staff Bell Comm. Rsch., Morristown, N.J., 1990-94; disting. engr. Sun Microsystems, Mountain View, Calif., 1994-98; principal Nielsen Norman Group, Mountain View, CA, 1998—. Author: Hypertext and Hypermedia, 1990, Usability Engineering, 1993, Multimedia and Hypertext: The Internet and Beyond, 1995, Designing Web Usability: The Practice of Simplicity, 2000, Homepage Usability: 50 Websites Deconstructed, 2001; editor: Coordinating User Interfaces for Consistency, 1989, Designing User Interfaces for International Use, 1990, Usability Inspection Methods, 1994, International User Interfaces, 1996; editl. bd. Behavior and Info. Tech., 1989—, Hypermedia Jour., 1989-95, Interacting with Computers, 1989—, Internat. Jour. Human-Computer Interaction, 1989—, Internat. Jour. Man-Machine Studies, 1991-94, ACM Networker, 1997-2000, Personal Technologies, 1997—; contbr. 53 articles to profl. jours.; holder 58 patents in field. Mem. Assn. for Computing Machinery (spl. interest group on computer human interaction, papers co-chair internat. conf. 1993, editl. bd. Networker 1997—). Achievements include founding of discount usability engineering approach; invention (with R. Molich) of heuristic evaluation method for cost-effective improvement of user interfaces; demonstration (with T.K. Landauer) that user testing and heuristic evaluation both follow same mathematical model; definition of the parallel design method for rapidly exploring user interface alternatives.

NIELSEN, KENNETH RAY, academic administrator; b. Oct. 15, 1941; s. Frank and Elinor (Hansen) N.; children: Elizabeth, Mary. BEd, U. Wis., Whitewater, 1965; MS, U. Wis., Stout, 1966; EdD, U. Wyo., 1968. Dir. student activities Cornell U., Ithaca, N.Y., 1968-72; adminstr., prof. Tchr. Tng. Coll., San Juan, P.R., 1974-77; v.p. student affairs Northland Coll., Ashland, Wis., 1972-77; v.p. student life Seattle U., 1977-84; pres. Coll. St. Mary, Omaha, 1984-96, Woodbury U., Burbank, Calif., 1996—. Bd. dirs. Boy Scouts Am., Girl Scouts U.S.A., Nat. Coun. Christians and Jews, Providence Hosp. Found.; chmn. edn. sect. United Way Bd.; mem. Gov.'s Community Svcs. and Continuing Edn. Mem. Am. Coun. Edn., Am. Assn. Higher Edn., Am. Assn. Univ. Adminstrs., Coun. Ind. Colls. Roman Catholic. Avocations: reading, exercising. Office: Woodbury U 7500 N Glenoaks Blvd Burbank CA 91504-1099

NIELSEN, WILLIAM FREMMING, federal judge; b. 1934; BA, U. Wash., 1956, LLB, 1963. Law clk. to Hon. Charles L. Powell U.S. Dist. Ct. (ea. dist.) Wash., 1963-64; mem. firm Paine, Hamblen, Coffin, Brooke & Miller, 1964-91; judge to chief judge U.S. Dist. Ct. (ea. dist.) Wash., Spokane, 1991—. Lt. col. USAFR. Fellow Am. Coll. Trial Lawyers; mem. ABA, Wash. State Bar Assn., Spokane County Bar Assn. (pres. 1981-82), Fed. Bar Assn. (pres. 1988), Spokane County Legal Svcs. Corp. (past pres.), Lawyer Pilot Bar Assn., Assn. Trial Lawyers Am., Wash. State Trial Lawyers Assn., Assn. Def. Trial Attys., Am. Inns of Ct., Charles L. Powell Inn (pres. 1987), The Spokane Club, Rotary, Alpha Delta Phi, Phi Delta Phi. Office: US Dist Ct PO Box 2208 920 W Riverside Ave 9th Fl Spokane WA 99210-2208

NIELSON, HOWARD CURTIS, state legislator, retired educator, former congressman; b. Richfield, Utah, Sept. 12, 1924; s. Herman Taylor and Zula May (Curtis) N.; m. Julia Adams, June 18, 1948; children: Noreen (Mrs. Stephen Astin), Elaine (Mrs. Stanley Taylor), John, Mary Lee (Mrs. Paul Jackson), James, Jean (Mrs. Clay Cundick), Howard Curtis Jr. BS in Math., U. Utah, 1947; MS in Math., U. Oreg., 1949; MBA, Stanford U., 1956, PhD in Bus. Adminstrn. and Stats., 1958. Statistician C & H Sugar Refining Corp., 1949-51; rsch. economist and statistician Stanford Rsch. Inst., 1951-57; mem. faculty Brigham Young U., Provo, Utah, 1957-82, prof. statistics, 1961-82, chmn. dept., 1960-63; sr. devel. engr. Hercules, Inc., 1960-66; dir. Ctr. for Bus. and Econ. Rsch., 1971-72; sr. statistician, acting field mgr. C.E.I.R, Inc., 1963-64, mgr., cons., 1964-65; prin. scientist GCA Corp., 1965-67; dir. econ. rsch. Eyring Rsch. Inst., 1974-75; assoc. commr. higher edn. State of Utah, 1976-79; mem. 98th-101st Congresses from 3d dist. Utah; missionary LDS Ch., Australia, 1991-92, Hungary, 1993-94; mem. Utah Senate, Salt Lake City, 1996—2001. Econ. adviser Kingdom of Jordan, Ford Found., 1970-71; prof. Am. U., Beirut, 1970; adj. prof. U. Utah, 1972-76 Author: The Efficiency of Certain Truncated Order Statistics in Estimating the Mean of Various Distributions, 1949, Population Trends in the United States Through 1975, 1955, The Hows and Whys of Statistics, 1963, Experimental Designs Used in industry, 1965, Membership Growth of the Church of Jesus Christ of Latter-Day Saints, 1957, 67, 71, 75, 78, Evaluation of the Seven Year Plan for Economic Development in Jordan, 1971, Economic Analysis of Fiji, Tonga, Western and Am. Samoa, 1972; co-author: The Newsprint Situation in the Western Region of North America, 1952, America's Demand for Wood, 1954, also reports. Mem. Utah Gov.'s Econ. Rsch. Adv. Coun., 1967-72, Utah Sci. Adv. Coun., 1973-76; dir. bur. ch. studies Ch. of Jesus Christ of Latter-day Saints, 1958-63; rsch. dir. Utah Republican Party, 1967-68; mem. Utah Ho. of Reps, 1967-75, majority leader, 1969-71, speaker, 1973-75, mem. legis. budget-audit com., 1967-73, chmn., 1971-73; chmn. legis. coun., 1973-75; mem. Utah 3d Dist., U.S. Ho. of Reps., 1983-91; chmn. Utah County Rep. Com., 1979-81; mem. Utah Senate, 1997-2001. Mem. Am. Statis. Assn. [illegible] Order of Artus, Phi Beta Kappa, Phi Kappa Phi, Sigma Xi, Pi Mu Epsilon.

NIELSON, THEO GILBERT, protective services official, university official; b. Roosevelt, Utah, June 29, 1938; s. John Gilbert and Mazie (Alexander) N.; m. Martha Perez, May 22, 1961; children: Lucille Marie, Sherry Lou, Mark Andrew, Rex Alexander, Theo Gilbert Jr., Cristal Ina, Gregory Angus, Mazie Leah, Rosanna Alma. Grad., FBI Nat. Acad., 1970; BA, Ariz. State U., 1975, MS, 1977. Officer Univ. Police, Ariz. State U., Tempe, 1963-67, sgt., 1967-70, lt., 1970-79; chief police Douglas (Ariz.) Police Dept., 1979-82; div. adminstr. Ariz. Criminal Intelligence Systems Agy., Tucson, 1982-84; dir. campus safety and security No. Ariz. U., Flagstaff, 1984-92; chief of capitol police Ariz. Dept. Adminstrn., Phoenix, 1992—. Mem. Am. Soc. for Indsl. Security (chmn. No. Ariz. chpt. 1987), Internat. Assn. Chiefs Police, Internat. Assn. Campus Law Enforcement Adminstrs., Ariz. Assn. Campus Law Enforcement (pres. 1989-90). Republican. Mormon. Avocations: genealogy, hiking, grandchildren. Home: 3335 E Hampton Ave Mesa AZ 85204-6410 Office: Ariz State Capitol Police 1700 W Washington St Ste B15 Phoenix AZ 85007-2812 E-mail: budnielson@mstar2.net, theo.nielson@ad.state.az.us

NIEMETH, CHARLES FREDERICK, lawyer; b. Lorain, Ohio, Nov. 25, 1939; s. Charles Ambrose and Christine Cameron (Mollison) N.; m. Anne Marie Meckes, Oct. 12, 1968. B.A., Harvard U., 1962; J.D., U. Mich., 1965. Bar: Calif. 1966, N.Y. 1984. Assoc. O'Melveny & Myers, Los Angeles, 1965-72, ptnr., 1973—. Mem. nat. com. Mich. Law Sch. Fund; trustee Challengers Boys and Girls Club, 1968-83; mem. bus. adv. coun. UCLA, 1979-83; mem. exec. com. Internat. Student Ctr., 1979-83; bd. dirs. Olympic Tower Condominium, 1986-92; bd. visitors Mich. Law Sch., mem. Tri-Bar Opinion Com. Mem. Riviera Tennis Club, Regency Club, N.Y. Athletic Club, Field Club (Greenwich, Conn.), Bel-Air Bay Club. Democrat. Roman Catholic. Home: 10660 Bellagio Rd Los Angeles CA 90077-3713 also: 70 Oneida Dr Greenwich CT 06830-7131 Office: O'Melveny & Myers 1999 Avenue Of The Stars Los Angeles CA 90067-6035 also: 153 E 53rd St Fl 54 New York NY 10022-4611 E-mail: cniemeth@omm.com

NIEMI, JANICE, retired lawyer, former state legislator; b. Flint, Mich., Sept. 18, 1928; d. Richard Jesse and Norma (Bell) Bailey; m. Preston Niemi, Feb. 4, 1953 (div. 1987); children: Ries, Patricia. BA, U. Wash., 1950, LLB, 1967; postgrad., U. Mich., 1950-52; cert., Hague Acad. Internat. Law, The Netherlands, 1954. Bar: Wash. 1968. Assoc. firm Powell, Livengood, Dunlap & Silverdale, Kirkland, Wash., 1968; staff atty. Legal Svc. Ctr., Seattle, 1968-70; judge Seattle Dist. Ct., 1971-72, King County Superior Ct., Seattle, 1973-78; acting gen. counsel, dep. gen. counsel SBA, Washington, 1979-81; mem. Wash. State Ho. of Reps., Olympia, 1983-87, chmn. com. on state govt., 1984; mem. Wash. State Senate, 1987-95; sole practice Seattle, 1981-94; superior ct. judge King County, 1995-2000; chief criminal judge King County, 1997-2000; ret., 2000. Mem. White House Fellows Regional Selection Panel, Seattle, 1974-77, chmn., 1976, 77; incorporator Sound Savs. & Loan, Seattle, 1975. Bd. dirs. Allied Arts, Seattle, 1971-78, Ctr. Contemporary Art, Seattle, 1981-83, Women's Network, Seattle, 1981-84, Pub. Defender Assn., Seattle, 1982-84; bd. visitors dept. psychology U. Wash., Seattle, 1983-87, bd. visitors dept. sociology, 1988-98; mem. adv. bd. Tacoma Art Mus., 1987—. Named Woman of Yr. in Law, Past Pres.'s Assn., Seattle, 1971, Woman of Yr., Matrix Table, Seattle, 1973, Capitol Hill Bus. and Profl. Women, 1975. Mem. Wash. State Bar Assn., Wash. Women Lawyers. Democrat. Home: PO Box 20516 Seattle WA 98102-1516

NIERENBERG, NORMAN, urban land economist, retired state official; b. Chgo., May 8, 1919; s. Isadore Isaac and Sadie Sarah (Dorfman) N.; m. Nanette Joyce Fortgang, Feb. 9, 1950; children: Andrew Paul, Claudia Robin. AA, U. Chgo., 1939; AB, Calif. State Coll., L.A., 1952; MA, U. So. Calif., 1956. Lic. real estate broker, Calif.; cert. supr. and coll. instr., Calif. Right-of-way agt. Calif. Dept. Transp., L.A., 1951-61, 85-90, sr. agt. San Francisco, 1988-89; instr. UCLA, 1960-61, 67-75, 81-85; coord. continuing edn. in real estate U. Calif., Berkeley, 1961-64. Coord. econ. benefits study Salton Sea, Calif. Dept. Water Resources, L.A., 1968-69; regional economist L.A. dist. CE, 1970-75, chief economist, 1981-85; regional economist Bd. Engrs. for Rivers and Harbors, Ft. Belvoir, Va., 1975-81; faculty resource person Oakland Project, Ford Found., U. Calif., Berkeley, 1962-64; project reviewer EPA, Washington, 1972-73. Editor: History of 82d Fighter Control Squadron, 1945; assoc. editor Right of Way Nat. Mag., 1952-55. Capt. USAAF, 1942-46, ETO, Lt. Col. USAFR ret. Mem. NEA, Am. Econ. Assn., Calif. Tchrs. Assn., Calif. Assn. Real Estate Tchrs. (bd. dirs. 1962), L.A. Coll. Tchrs. Assn., Ret. Officers Assn., Omicron Delta Epsilon. Democrat. Jewish. Home: Unit 4 21931 Burbank Blvd Woodland Hills CA 91367-6456

NIGAM, BISHAN PERKASH, physics educator; b. Delhi, India, July 14, 1928; came to U.S., 1952; s. Rajeshwar Nath and Durga (Vati) N.; m. Indira Bahadur, Nov. 14, 1956; children— Sanjay, Shobhna, Ajay. B.S., U. Delhi, 1946, M.S., 1948; Ph.D., U. Rochester, N.Y., 1955. Research fellow U. Delhi, 1948-50; lectr. in physics, 1950-52, 55-56; postdoctoral fellow Case Inst. Tech., Cleve., 1954-55; postdoctoral research fellow NRC, Ottawa, Can., 1956-59; research assoc. U. Rochester, 1959-60, asst. prof. physics, part-time 1960-61; prin. scientist Gen. Dynamics/Electronics, Rochester, N.Y., 1960-61; assoc. prof. physics SUNY, Buffalo, 1961-64; prof. physics Ariz. State U., Tempe, 1964—, U. Wis., Milw., 1966-67. Author: (with R.R. Roy) Nuclear Physics, 1967; also articles. Govt. of India scholar U. Rochester, 1952-54 Fellow Am. Phys. Soc. Office: Ariz State U Dept Physics Box 871504 Tempe AZ 85287-1504

NIGG, BENNO MAURUS, biomechanics educator, researcher; b. Walenstadt, St. Gallen, Switzerland, Apr. 10, 1938; s. Josef B. Nigg and Edwina Nigg-Widrig; m. Margaretha J. Bolleter, Aug. 28, 1965; children: Andreas, Reto, Claudio, Sandro. Diploma in physics, ETH, Zurich, Switzerland, 1965, Dr. sci. nat., 1975. Instr. Lyceum Alpinum Zuoz, Switzerland, 1965-71; rschr. Biomechs. Lab. Eidgenössische Technische Hochschule (ETH), Zurich, 1971-76, dir., 1976-81; prof. U. Calgary, 1981—, dir. Human Performance Lab., 1981—. Cons. Adidas, Germany, 1976—, Nike, 1981-85; mem. steering com. World Congress on Biomechs., 1988—; co-chair Olympic Acad. Sci.; chair selection com. Internat. Olympic Com. Olympic Prize, Pfizer. Recipient Michael Jaeger award Gesellschaft für Orthopaedie und Traumatologie in Sport, Munich, 1986, Wartenweiler Meml. award Internat. Soc. for Biomechs., UCLA, 1989, NOVEL award, Vienna, 1991, Alta. Sci. and Tech. award, Can., 1993, Clin. Biomech. award Jyvåskylå, 1995, Olympic Order, 1998. Mem. Am. Soc. Biomechanics, Can. Soc. Biomechanics, Internat. Soc. Biomechanics (pres. 1983-85), Internat. Acad. Biology and Engring. in Medicine. Office: U Calgary Human Performance Lab Calgary AB Canada T2N 1N4 E-mail: nigg@ucalgary.ca

NIJENHUIS, ALBERT, mathematician, educator; b. Eindhoven, Netherlands, Nov. 21, 1926; came to U.S., 1952, naturalized, 1959; s. Hendrik and Lijdia (Koornneef) N.; m. Marianne Dannhauser, Aug. 14, 1955; children: Erika, Karin, Sabien, Alaine. Candidaat, U. Amsterdam, Netherlands, 1947, Doctorandus, 1950, Doctor cum laude, 1952. Assoc. Math. Ctr., Amsterdam, Netherlands, 1951-52; asst. Inst. Advanced Study, Princeton, N.J., 1955, mem., 1953-55, 61-62; instr., rsch. assoc. U. Chgo., 1955-56; faculty U. Wash., Seattle, 1956-63, prof., 1961-63, affiliate prof., 1988—; prof. math. U. Pa., Phila., 1963-87, prof. emeritus, 1987—; Fulbright lectr. U. Amsterdam, 1963-64; vis. prof. U. Geneva, Switzerland, 1967-68, Dartmouth Coll., 1977-78. Researcher and author publs. on subjects including differential geometry, deformation theory in algebra, combinatorics, especially [illegible] Author: Combinatorial Algorithms, 1975, 78; editor: Jour. Algorithms, Jour.

Differential Geometry Conidin. Postdoctoral fellow Princeton, 1952-53; Fulbright grantee, 1952-53, 63-64; Guggenheim fellow, 1961-62 Mem. Am. Math. Soc., Math. Assn. Am., Netherlands Math. Soc., AAUP, Royal Netherlands Acad. Scis. (corr.) Office: U Wash Dept Math PO Box 354350 Seattle WA 98195-4350 E-mail: nijenhuis@math.washington.edu

NIKODINOV, ANGELA, professional figure skater, Olympic athlete; b. Spartanburg, S.C., 09 May; Mem. U.S. World Olympic Team, Sydney, 2000. Competitive history includes 2d place Pacific Coast Jr., 1994, 3rd place Southwest Pacific Jr., 1994, 5th place U.S. Championships Jr., 1994, 2d place Pacific Coast Jr., 1995, 3d place Southwest Pacific Jr., 1995, 5th place U.S. Championships Jr., 1995, 6th place World Jr. Selections Competition, 1996, 2d place Pacific Coast Sr., 1996, 5th place U.S. Olympic Festival, 1995, 1st place Southwest Pacific Sr., 1996, 3d place O. Nepela Meml., 1996, 1st place Pacific Coast Sr., 1997, 3d place World Jr. Selection Competition, 1997, 2d place Pokal Der Blauen Scwerter, 1996, 4th place U.S. Championships, 1997, 4th place Skate America, 1997, 5th place U.S. Championships, 1998, 11th place World Jr. Championships, 1998, 4th place Goodwill Games, 1998, 2d place Keri Lotion Figure Skating Classic, 1998, 3d place Four Continents Championships, 1999, 3d place Skate America, 1998, 3d place U.S. Championships, 1999, 12th place World Championships, 1999, 7th place Skate America, 1999, 4th place U.S. Championships, 2000, 5th place Keri Lotion Figure Skating Classic, 1999, 4th place Cup of Russia, 1999, 1st place Four Continents, 2000. Avocations: water skiing, snow skiing, rollerblading, jet skiing. Office: USFSA 20 1st St Colorado Springs CO 80906-3624

NILES, JOHN GILBERT, lawyer; b. Dallas, Oct. 5, 1943; s. Paul Dickerman and Nedra Mary (Arendts) N.; m. Marian Higginbotham, Nov. 21, 1970; children: Paul Breckenridge, Matthew Higginbotham. BA in History, Stanford U., 1965; LLB, U. Tex., 1968. Bar: Tex. 1968, Calif. 1969, U.S. Dist. Ct. (cen. dist.) Calif. 1973, U.S. Ct. Appeals (9th cir.) 1973, U.S. Dist. Ct. (so. dist.) Calif. 1977, U.S. Supreme Ct. 1979, U.S. Dist. Ct. (no. dist.) Calif. 1983. Assoc. O'Melveny & Myers, Los Angeles, 1973-77, ptnr., 1978-99; of counsel, 1999—. Judge pro tem mcpl. ct. L.A.; spkr., panel mem. Practicing Law Inst., Calif. C.E.B. Served to lt. comdr. USNR, 1968-72, Vietnam. Mem. ABA, Los Angeles County Bar Assn., Am. Judicature Soc. Clubs: Bel-Air Bay (Pacific Palisades, Calif.); Calif. (Los Angeles). Avocation: sailing. Home: 1257 Villa Woods Dr Pacific Palisades CA 90272-3953 Office: O'Melveny & Myers 400 S Hope St Los Angeles CA 90071-2899

NILLES, JOHN MATHIAS (JACK NILLES), futurist; b. Evanston, Ill., Aug. 25, 1932; s. Elmer Edward and Hazel Evelyn Nilles; m. Laila Padorr, July 8, 1957. BA magna cum laude, Lawrence Coll., 1954; MS in Engring., UCLA, Los Angeles, 1964. Sr. engr. Raytheon Mfg. Co., Santa Barbara, Calif., 1956-58; section head. Ramo-Woodridge Corp., L.A., 1958-59; project engr. Space Technology Lab., L.A., 1960; dir. The Aerospace Corp., L.A., 1961-67; sr. systems engr. TRW Systems, L.A., 1967-69; assoc. group dir. The Aerospace Corp., L.A., 1969-72; dir. interdisciplinary programs U. So. Calif., L.A., 1972-81, dir. info. technology program, 1981-89; pres. JALA Internat. Inc., L.A., 1980—. Coord. EC Telework Forum, Madrid, 1992—; dir. Internat. Telework Assocs., & Coun., 1991-97, pres., 1993-94; chmn. Telecommuting Rsch. Inst., Inc., L.A., 1990—. Author: The Telecommunications Transportation Tradeoff, 1976, Japanese edit., 1977, Exploring the World of the Personal Computer, 1982, French edit., 1985, Micros and Modems, 1983, French edit., 1986, Making Telecommuting Happen, 1994, Portuguese edit., 1997, Managing Telework, 1998; mem. editl. bd. Revista Portuguesa de Gestao, 2000—. Capt. USAF, 1954-56. Recipient Rod Rose award Soc. Rsch. Adminstrs., 1976, Environ. Pride award L.A. Mag., 1993, Environ. Achievement award Renew Am., 1994-96, Commendation, L.A. County Bd. Suprs., 1997; inducted into Telework Hall of Fame, 1998. Mem. IEEE, IEEE Computer Soc., AAAS, Assn. Computing Machinery, Inst. Ops. Rsch. and Mgmt. Scis., World Future Soc., Calif. Yacht Club. Avocations: sailing, photography. Office: JALA Internat Inc 971 Stonehill Ln Los Angeles CA 90049-1412 E-mail: jnilles@jala.com

NILLES, LAILA PADORR, musician, record producer; b. Chgo., July 25, 1929; d. Abraham Leonard Ginsburg and Jeanette Padorr; m. Jack Mathias Nilles, July 8, 1957. MusB, B of Music Edn., Northwestern U., 1947, M of Music, 1949; postgrad., Julliard Sch. Music, 1950, 51, Ecoles d'Art Am. Fontainebleau, France, 1953. Founder, dir. Padorr Trio, Chgo. and Los Angeles, 1951-55, 56-72; dir. Concerts at the Mt., Los Angeles, 1958-60; mgr., dir. Concerts West, Los Angeles, 1965-75; freelance musician Los Angeles, 1975-77; asst. dir. Protone Records, Los Angeles, 1977-82, assoc. dir., 1982—; v.p. Jala Internat., Inc., Los Angeles, 1982—. Dir. design for Sharing UCLA, L.A., 1984-89, Friends of Music U. So. Calif., 1984-90, Am. Youth Symphony, 1981-88. Soloist: (record) music for Flute and Piano by Four Americans, 1976; co-producer 42 records, cassettes and compact discs, 1977—. Recipient First prize Coleman Auditions, 1956, Young Artists League, 1956. Mem. Audio Engring. Soc., Nat. Acad. Recording Arts and Scis., Musicians Union Local 47. Club: Calif. Yacht (Marina Del Ray). Avocations: photography, sailing, astronomy. Home and Office: 971 Stonehill Ln Los Angeles CA 90049-1412 E-mail: lnilles@jala.com

NILSSON, A. KENNETH, investor; b. L.A., Mar. 16, 1933; s. Arthur V. and Esther (Dean) N.; m. Lesley Swanson, Sept., 1965; children: Kerstin, Keith. BA, U. So. Calif., 1955; MA, U. Calif., 1960; grad., U.S. Defense Language Inst., 1956. Founder Koken, Ltd., Tokyo, 1960-63; mng. dir. Pfizer Internat., Tokyo, 1963-66; pres. Pfizer Inc., Manila, The Philippines, 1966-68, Max Factor & Co. Japan Ltd., Tokyo, 1968-72, Cooper Labs Internat., Inc., Geneva and Brussels, 1972-80, Cooper Labs, Inc., N.Y.C. and Palo Alto, Calif., 1980-85, Cooper Lasersonics, Inc., Palo Alto, 1982-85; dir. Monterey County Bank, Monterey, Calif., 1982-86; vice chmn. The Cooper Cos., 1986-89; chmn. Eureka Group, Monterey, 1989—. Chmn. Monterey Inst. Internat. Studies, 1983-99; dir. U.S. China Indsl. Exch., 1996—, Calif. State Automobile Assn., 2000—. Contbr. articles to profl. jours. Mem. Coun. on Foreign Rels., World Affairs Coun., Pacific Coun. on Internat. Policy. 1st lt. U.S. Army, 1955-58. Fellow Am. Soc. Laser Medicine, Internat. Inst. Strategic Studies. Avocation: philology.

NISBET, TOMA A. nursing administrator; Diploma with honors, St. Mark's Hosp. Sch. Nursing, 1967; BSN with honors, No. Ill. U., 1969, MSN with honors, 1973. Internship Winnebago County Dept. Pub. Health-Health Adminstrn. & Family Planning; night staff nurse Sycamore Municipal Hosp., Ill., 1967-68; evening relief supr., charge nurse DeKalb County Nursing Home, 1969; pub. health nurse DeKalb County Health Dept., 1969-71; divsn. dir. nursing svcs. Winnebago County Dept. Pub. Health, Rockford, 1974-84; pub. dir. nursing svcs. divsn. of health & med. svcs. State of Wyo., Cheyenne, 1985-87, policy devel. & spl. projects state program mgr. divsn. of health & med. svcs., 1987-88, state bd. nursing exec., 1988—. Spokesperson for NLX D-A-Y Pub. Rels. for Burroughs Welcome, N.Y.C., 1987; project coord. for health svcs. No. Ill. U. Sch. Nursing, DeKalb, 1973-74, instr. 1979-84. Author of numerous articles. Awarded numerous rsch. grants. Mem. ANA, Nat. Coun. State Bds. of Nursing (del. 1988-95, AEC com. mem. 1990-94, mem. nomination com. 1991-92, ednl. program task force 1994-95, alternate examination com. 1994-95), Wyo. Commn. on Nursing & Nursing Edn., Wyo. Orgn. Nurse Execs., Wyo. State Bd. of Nursing Home Adminstrs. (sec. 1988-89, vice-chmn. 1990-95), Wyo. Advanced Practitioner of Nursing Orgn. Office: Wyo State Bd Nursing 2020 Carey Ave Ste 110 Cheyenne WY 82002-0001

NISHIMURA, KOICHI, electronics manufacturing company executive; B Elec. Engring., M Elec. Engring., San Jose State U.; D Materials Sci. and Engring., Stanford U. Mgr. disk film design, tech. and mfg. divsns. IBM; COO Solectron, Milpitas, Calif., 1988-90, pres., COO, 1990-92, co-CEO, pres., pres., CEO, 1992—, chmn. bd., 1996—. Chmn. bd. Santa Clara Valley Mfg. Groups; mem. bds. Merix Corp., Ctr. Quality Mgmt.; mem. adv. bd. Santa Clara U. Tearney Sch. Bus. Past bd. mem. Tech. Mus. Innovation, San Jose, Calif.; active Japanese Western U.S. Assn., Ku-Ai Kai Sr. Cmty. Ctr., San Jose. Recipient Malcolm Baldrige Nat. Quality award, 1991, 97. Mem. IEEE, Soc. Mfg. Engrs. Office: Solectron 777 Gibraltar Dr Bldg 5 Milpitas CA 95035-6332

NISHIMURA, PETE HIDEO, oral surgeon; b. Hilo, Hawaii, Aug. 7, 1922; s. Hideichi and Satsuki N.; m. Tomoe Nishimura, June, 1949; children— Dennis Dean, Grant Neil, Dawn Naomi. Student, U. Hawaii, 1940-44; D.D.S., U. Mo., 1947; M.S.D., Northwestern U., 1949. Practice dentistry specializing in oral surgery, Honolulu, 1952—; pres. Oral Surgery Group, 1978—. Mem. coun. Nat. Bd. Dental Examination; dir. Hawaii Dental Svc., 1962-85, pres., 1970-72, 76-78; pres. State Bd. Dental Examiners, Delta Sigma Delta, Fedn. Dentaire Internat. Served with U.S. Army, 1952-54. Fellow Am. Coll. Dentists, Internat. Coll. Dentists; mem. Hawaii Dental Assn. (past pres.), Delta Dental Plans Assn. (dir.), Honolulu County Dental Soc., ADA, Hawaii Soc. Oral Surgeons, Am. Assn. Oral and Maxillofacial Surgeons, Western Soc. Oral and Maxillofacial Surgeons, Am. Assn. Dental Examiners, Pierre Fauchard Acad. (citation for outstanding contbn. to arts and sci. of dentistry 1987). Democrat. Home: 494 Halemaumau St Honolulu HI 96821-2135 Office: 848 S Beretania St Honolulu HI 96813-2551 E-mail: hilopete@aol.com

NISHIOKA, TERUO (TED NISHIOKA), electrical engineer; b. Crystal City, Tex., Sept. 6, 1945; s. Kazuto Benjamin and Kofumi (Shinkawa) N.; m. Suzanne Nayeko Hayashi, June 24, 1978; 1 child, Stephanie. BSEE, Calif. State Poly. U., 1970. Engr. Salt River Project, Phoenix, 1970-72, Pacific Gas and Electric, San Francisco, 1972-74; power plant engr. Wismer and Becker, Sacramento, 1975-78; sr. elec. engr. Ariz. Pub. Svc., Phoenix, 1978—. Author: Underground Cable Thermal Backfill, 1981. Active Japanese-Am. Citizens League, Phoenix, 1978—, bd. dirs. 1991—; v.p. Ariz. Buddhist Ch., Phoenix, 1987-88, pres., 1989-91; mem. Matsuri steering com., 1992—. With U.S. Army, 1966-68. Mem. IEEE, Power Engring. Soc., Elec. Insulation Soc. Avocations: hunting, jogging, swimming, dancing, tennis. Office: Ariz Pub Svc PO Box 53999 Phoenix AZ 85072-3999

NISHITANI, MARTHA, dancer; b. Seattle, Feb. 27, 1920; d. Denjiro and Jin (Aoto) N. B.A. in Comparative Arts, U. Wash., 1958; studied with, Eleanor King, Mary Ann Wells, Perry Mansfield, Cornish Sch., Conn. Coll. Sch. Dance, Long Beach State U. Founder, dir. Martha Nishitani Modern Dance Sch. and Co., Seattle, 1950—; dance dir. Helen Bush Sch. and Central YWCA, 1951-54; choreographer U. Wash. Opera Theater, 1955-65, Intiman Theater, 1972—; dance instr. Elementary and Secondary Edn. Act Program, 1966; dance specialist spl. edn. program Shoreline Pub. Schs., 1970-72; condr. workshops and concerts King County Youth Correctional Instns., 1972-73. Dance adv. counsel Wash. Cultural Enrichment Program; dance adv. bd. Seattle Parks and Recreation; mem. multimedia Japanese-Am. legacy project to capture history and testimony of Japanese Americans, 1999. Dancer Eleanor King Co., Seattle, 1946-50, dance films, 1946-51, Channel 9, Ednl. TV, 1967-68; lectr. demonstrator numerous colls., festivals, convs., childrens theater.; author articles on dance; one of the subjects: A Celebration of 100 Years of Dance in Washington, 1989. Trustee Allied Arts Seattle, 1967. Recipient Theta Sigma Phi Matrix Table award, 1968, Asian Am. Living Treasure award Northwest Asian Am. Theater, 1984, Small Bus. award Seattle Mayor, 1998; listed Dance Archives, N.Y.C. Libr., 1991, N.Y.C. Lincoln Ctr. Dance Archives, 1991, U. Wash. Libr. Archives, 1993, exhibit of Japanese Am. Women of Achievement, Burke Mus., 1997, Ploudit award nat. Dance Assn., 1999, 50th Anniversary of Martha Nishitani Modern Dance Sch. and Creative Dance for Children in Sch., 2000; selected for DENSHO-the Japanese-Am. Legacy Project, 1998. Mem. Am. Dance Guild (exec. com. 1961-63), Com. Research in Dance, Seattle Art Mus., Internat. Dance Alliance (adv. council 1984), Smithsonian Assos., Progressive Animal Welfare Soc. Address: 4205 University Way NE PO Box 45264 Seattle WA 98145-0264

NISSINEN, MIKKO PEKKA, dancer; b. Helsinki, Finland, Mar. 4, 1962; came to U.S., 1987; s. Pekka and Pirkko (Pulkkinen) N. Grad., Finnish Nat. Ballet Sch., 1977; postgrad., Leningrad Acad. Ballet Sch., 1979-80. Mem. corps de ballet Finnish Nat. Ballet, Helsinki, 1977-79, soloist, 1980-82; grand sujete Dutch Nat. Ballet, Amsterdam, The Netherlands, 1982-84; soloist Basel (Switzerland) Ballet, 1984-87, San Francisco Ballet, 1987-88, prin. dancer, 1988-96; artistic dir. Marin Ballet, 1996-97, Alberta Ballet, Calgary, Can., 1998—. Guest artist La Bayadere, Nat. Ballet Can., 1989, Oberlin Dance Collective, 1993; bd. dirs. Le Don Des Etoiles, 1989—; guest tchr. Royal Acad. of Dancing, 1993, Kennedy Ctr. Ednl. Program, 1994, Nat. Ballet Sch., Toronto, 1994; lectr. on dance history and state of dance today Stanord U., Leathbridge U., St. Mary's Coll., Christensen Soc. Repertoire as dancer includes (with San Francisco Ballet) The Sleeping Beauty, Swan Lake, Bizet Pas de Deux, Handel-a Celebration, Haffner Symphony, Con Brio, Ballet d'Isoline, Giuliani: Variations on a Theme, Tchaikovsky Pas de Deux, Symphony in C, Theme and Variations, Ballo della Regina, The Nutcracker, Airs de Ballet, Variations de Ballet, Rodin, Rodeo, Maelstrom, Dark Elegies, Harvest Moon, Napoli, Job, The Wanderer Fantasy, In the middle, somewhat elevated, Calcium Light Night, Le Corsaire Pas de Deux, Dreams of Harmony, Pulcinella, The Dream; (with other cos.) Don Quixote, Giselle, A Midsummer Night's Dream, Les Biches, Sleeping Beauty, Pyrrich Dances, Masse, Le Tombeau de Couperin, Symphony in C, The Four Temperaments, The Prodigal Son, Rodin, Pierrot Lunaire, La Fille mal gardée, Swan Lake, Henze, Five Tangos, In and Out, Bits and Pieces, Jeu de Cartes; appeared in the Gala Des Etoiles Canadian Internat. Ballet Gala, 1989, 90, 91, 92, 93, 94, 95, Reykjavik Arts Festival, 1990, Internat. Ballet Gala, Kuodio, Finland, 1992, Internat. Ballet Gala, Vail, Colo., 1993, Night of Stars Ballet Gala, Helsinki, 1993; profiled in nat. and internat. radio and TV programs, including CNN Worldwide Report, 1992; featured on cover of Dance Mag., 1992; choreographer Full Evening Nutcracker, Marin Ballet, 1996, Alta. Ballet, 2000. Recipient 1st prize 1st Nat. Dance Competition Kuopio, Finland, 1978. Office: Nat Cristie Ctr 141 18th Ave SW Alberta AB Canada T25 0B8 E-mail: mikkoN@albertaballet.com, Mikko403@aol.com

NISWENDER, GORDON DEAN, physiologist, educator; b. Gillette, Wyo., Apr. 21, 1940; s. Rex Lel and Inez Irene (Dillinger) N.; m. Joy Dean Thayer, June 14, 1964; children: Kevin Dean, Kory Dean. B.S., U. Wyo., 1962; M.S., U. Nebr., 1964; Ph.D., U. Ill., 1967. NIH postdoctoral fellow U. Mich., 1967-68, asst. prof. physiology, 1968-72; mem. faculty Colo. State U., Ft. Collins, 1972—, prof. physiology, 1975—; assoc. dean research Coll. Veterinary Medicine and Biomed. Scis., 1982-95, dir. animal reproduction and biotech. lab., 1986—, disting. prof., 1987—. Mem. rev. panels NIH; cons. FDA. Recipient Merit award NIH, 1988-99, grantee, 1968—. Mem. Am. Assn. Animal Scientists (Outstanding Young Scientist award western sect. 1974, Animal Physiology and Endocrinology award 1983), Soc. for Study Reprodn. (treas. 1972-75, pres. 1981-82, editor-in-chief Biology of Reprodn. 1995-99), rsch. award 1988). Office: Colo State U Animal Reprod & Biotech Lab College Of Veterinary Med Fort Collins CO 80523-0001

NITTA, JEFFREY W. real estate executive; V.p. Weyerhaeuser Real Estate Co., Tacoma, 1997—. Office: Weyerhaeuser Co CHIK35C PO Box 2999 Tacoma WA 98477-2999

NIX, JAMES RAYFORD, nuclear physicist, consultant; b. Natchitoches, La., Feb. 18, 1938; s. Joe Ebbin and Edna (Guin) N.; m. Sally Ann Wood, Aug. 19, 1961; children: Patricia Lynne, David Allen. BS in Physics, Carnegie Inst. Tech., 1960; PhD in Physics, U. Calif., Berkeley, 1964. Sumemr phjysicist Lawrence Livermore Nat. Lab., Livermore, Calif., 1961; rsch. asst. Lawrence Berkeley Lab., Berkeley, 1961-64, postdoctoral physicist, 1966-68; NATO postdoctoral fellow Niels Bohr Inst., Copenhagen, Denmark, 1964-65; mem. staff Los Alamos Nat. Lab., 1968-77, 89-94, group leader, 1977-89, fellow, 1994-98, sci. cons., 1998—. Vis. prof. Centro Brasileiro de Pesquisas Fisicas, Rio de Janeiro, 1974; cons. Calif. Inst. Tech., Pasadena, 1976, Pasadena, 79; chmn. Gordon Research Conf. Nuclear Chemistry, New London, NH, 1976; chmn. physics divsn. adv. com. Oak Ridge Nat. Lab., 1976, 97; chmn. nuclear sci. divsn. vis. com. Lawrence Berkeley Lab., 1979—80. Contbr. articles to numerous publs. Recipient Alexander von Humboldt Sr. U.S. Scientist award, Univ. Munich and Max-Planck Inst. for Nuclear Physics, 1980—81; fellow, Phi Kappa Phi, Berkeley, Calif., 1960—61; scholar, Alfred P. Sloan Found., Pitts., 1956—60. Fellow: Am. Phys. Nuclear Physics (exec. com. 1973—75); mem.: AAAS, Sigma Xi, Phi Kappa Phi. Democrat. Home and Office: 12 Los Pueblos Los Alamos NM 87544-2659 E-mail: j.nix@starband.net

NIX, NANCY JEAN, librarian, designer; b. Denver; d. James Frederik and Josephine (Britt) N. AB in History, U. So. Calif., L.A., 1959, MLS, 1960; prof. 1st level, Ikenobo Ikebana, L.A. Exhibited in group shows including Ikenobo Ikebana Historical Flower Arrangement Exhibit, 1992, 97. Mem. guiding com. Art Assn. Egg and the Eye Gallery and Restaurant, 1973-76; participant Arts & Humanities Symposium, Palm Desert, Calif., 1974; patron cultural symposium L.A. Garden Club, 1975. Recipient Kakan Monpyo award Ikenobo Ikebana Soc. Floral Art, 1988. Mem. Ikebana Internat. (bd. dirs. L.A. chpt. 1972—, mem. chmn. 1980-82), Japanese Am. Citizens League (exec. bd. L.A. Downtown chpt. 1990—, chpt. historian), Japanese Am. Nat. Mus. (charter), Japanese Am. Cultural and Cmty. Ctr, L.A. Nisei (Woman of Yr. selection com. 1990—). Republican. Jewish.

NIXON, CAROL HOLLADAY, park and recreation director; b. Salt Lake City, Dec. 25, 1937; m. William L. Nixon; children: William H., Joan, Michael, Jennifer, Jacqueline, John. Student, Brigham Young U. Dep. chief of staff, then chief of staff State of Utah, Salt Lake City, 1991-93; dir. Dept. Cmty. Devel. Divsn., Salt Lake City, 1993-96; pres., CEO This Is the Place Heritage Park, Salt Lake City, 1996—. Office: This Is the Place Heritage Park 2601 East Sunnyside Ave Salt Lake City UT 84108-1453 Fax: 801-584-8325

NIXON, ROBERT OBEY, SR. business educator; b. Pitts., Feb. 14, 1922; s. Frank Obey and Margurite (Van Buren) N.; m. Marilyn Cavanagh, Oct. 25, 1944 (dec. 1990); children: Nan Nixon Friend, Robert Obey, Jr., Dwight Cavanagh. BS in bus. adminstrn., U. Pitts., 1948; MS, Ohio State U., 1964; MBA, U. Phoenix, 1984. Commd. 2d lt. USAF, 1943, advanced through grades to col., 1970, master navigator WWII, Korea, Vietnam; sales, adminstrn. U.S. Rubber Corp., Pitts., 1940-41; asst. engr. Am. Bridge Corp., Pitts., 1941-42; underwriter, sales Penn Mutual Life Ins. Corp., Pitts., 1945-50; capt., nav. instr. USAF Reserves, 1945-50; ret. USAF Col., divsn. chief Joint Chiefs of Staff, 1973; educator, cons. U. Ariz., 1973-79; bus. dept. chmn., coord., founder weekend coll. Pima C.C., Tucson, 1979-90, prof. mgmt., 1991-98, coord. weekend coll. program, 1991—. Adj. faculty Pima C.C., 1998—; founder, pres. Multiple Adv. Group ednl. cons., Tucson, 1978—. Author: Source Document: On Accelerated Courses and Programs at Accredited Two- and Four-Year Colleges and Universities, 1996; contbr. articles to profl. jours. Mem. Soc. Logistics Engrs. (sr., charter mem.), Phi Delta Theta. Presbyterian. Avocations: tennis, hiking, swimming. Home: 1824 S Regina Cleri Dr Tucson AZ 85710-8664 Fax: 520-885-2378. E-mail: eb58271@goodnet.com, bnixon@pimacc.pima.edu

NIZZE, JUDITH ANNE, retired physician assistant; b. L.A., Nov. 1, 1942; d. Robert George and Charlotte Ann (Wise) Swan; m. Norbert Adolph Otto Paul Nizze, Dec. 31, 1966 (div. Sept. 2000). BA, UCLA, 1966, postgrad., 1966-76; grad. physician asst. tng. program, Charles R. Drew Sch. Postgrad., L.A., 1979; BS, Calif. State U., Dominguez, 1980. Cert. physician asst., Calif. Staff rsch. assoc. I-II Wadsworth Vet. Hosp., L.A., 1965-71; staff rsch. assoc. III-IV John Wayne Clinic Jonsson Comprehensive Cancer Ctr., UCLA, 1971-78; clin. asst. Robert S. Ozeran, Gardena, Calif., 1978; physician asst. family practice Fred Chasan, Torrance, 1980-82; sr. physician asst. Donald L. Morton prof., chief surg. oncology Jonsson Comprehensive Cancer Ctr., UCLA, 1983-91; adminstrv. dir. immunotherapy John Wayne Cancer Inst., Santa Monica, Calif., 1991-98; ret. Cons. cilin. rsch. orgn. devel. John Wayne Cancer Inst., 1998—. Contbr. articles to profl. jours. Fellow Am. Acad. Physician Assts., Am. Assn. Surgeons Assts., Calif. Acad. Physician Assts.; mem. Assn. Physician Assts. in Oncology. Republican. Presbyterian. Avocations: sailing, tennis, skiing, securities trading, computers. Home: 13243 Fiji Way Unit J Marina Del Rey CA 90292

NOBE, KEN, chemical engineering educator; b. Berkeley, Calif., Aug. 26, 1925; s. Sidney and Kiyo (Uyeyama) N.; m. Mary Tagami, Aug. 31, 1957; children: Steven Andrew, Keven Gibbs, Brian Kelvin. B.S., U. Calif., Berkeley, 1951; Ph.D., UCLA, 1956. Jr. chem. engr. Air Reduction Co., Murray Hill, N.J., 1951-52; asst. prof. chem. engring. UCLA, 1957-62, assoc. prof., 1962-68, prof., 1968—, chmn. dept. chem., nuclear and thermal engring., 1978-83, founding chmn. chem. engring., 1983-84. Mem. tech. staff Ramo-Wooldridge Corp., El Segundo, Calif., 1958-59. Div. editor: Jour. Electrochem. Soc, 1967-91, Electrochimica Acta, 1977-85 Served with U.S. Army, 1944-46. Mem. Electrochem. Soc. (Henry B. Linford award 1992), Am. Chem. Soc., Nat. Assn. Corrosion Engrs., Internat. Soc. Electrochemistry, Sigma Xi. Office: UCLA Dept Chemical Engring Los Angeles CA 90095-1592

NOBLE, ERNEST PASCAL, pharmacologist, biochemist, educator; b. Baghdad, Iraq, Apr. 2, 1929; came to U.S., 1946; s. Noble Babik and Barkev Grace (Kasparian) Babikian; m. Inga Birgitta Kilstromer, May 19, 1956; children— Lorna, Katharine, Erik B.S. in Chemistry, U. Calif.-Berkeley, 1951; Ph.D. in Biochemistry, Oreg. State U., 1955; M.D., Case Western Res. U., 1962. Diplomate Nat. Bd. Med. Examiners. Sr. instr. biochemistry Western Res. U., Cleve., 1957-62; intern Stanford Med. Ctr., Calif., 1962-63, resident in psychiatry, 1963-66, research assoc., asst. prof., 1965-69; assoc. prof. psychiatry, psychobiology and pharmacology U. Calif.-Irvine, 1969-71, prof., chief neurochemistry, 1971-76, 79-81; dir. Nat. Inst. Alcohol Abuse and Alcoholism HEW, 1976-78, assoc. adminstr. sci., alcohol, drug abuse and mental health, 1978-79; Pike prof. alcohol studies, dir. Alcohol Research Ctr. UCLA Sch. of Medicine, 1981—. Mem. various med./sci. jour. editorial bds.; contbr. numerous articles to profl. jours., chpts. to books V.p. Nat. Coun. on Alcoholism 1981-84; pres. Internat. Commn. for the Prevention of Alcoholism and Drug Dependency, 1988. Fulbright scholar, 1955-56; Guggenheim fellow, 1974-75; Sr. Fulbright scholar, 1984-85; recipient Career Devel. award NIMH, HEW, 1966-69 Fellow Am. Coll. Neuropsychopharmacology; mem. Internat. Soc. Neurochemistry, Am. Soc. Pharmacology and Exptl. Therapeutics, Research Soc. on Alcoholism. Office: UCLA 760 Westwood Plz Los Angeles CA 90095-8353

NOBLE, PHILLIP D. lawyer; b. Oakland, Calif., Aug. 1, 1946; BA, AD in Bus., U. Wash., 1968, JD, 1971. Bar: Wash. 1971. Law clk. to Hon. Morell Sharp Wash. State Supreme Ct., 1971, U.S. Dist. Ct. (we. dist.) Wash., 1972; ptnr. Helsell, Fetterman LLP, Seattle, 1978—. Editor: Justice on Trial, 1971. Mem. ABA, Wash. State Bar Assn., Seattle-King County Bar Assn. Office: Helsell Fetterman LLP 1500 Puget Sound Plz PO Box 21846 Seattle WA 98111-3846

NOCAS, ANDREW JAMES, lawyer; b. L.A., Feb. 2, 1941; s. John Richard and Muriel Phyliss (Harvey) N.; 1 child, Scott Andrew. BS, Stanford U., 1962, JD, 1964. Bar: Calif. 1965. Assoc. Thelen, Marrin, Johnson & Bridges, L.A., 1964-71, ptnr., 1972-91; pvt. practice, L.A., 1992-2000; with Office L.A. City Atty., 2000—. Del. Calif. Bar Conv., 1972-92. Served to capt. JAGC, USAR. Fellow Am. Bar Found.; mem. Los Angeles County Bar Assn. (chmn. sect. law office mgmt. 1980-82, chair errors and ommissions com. 1987-88, chair litigation sect. 1988-89), ABA (chmn. arbitration com. 1981), Am. Bd. Trial Advocates, Los Angeles County Bar Found. (trustee 1992-99). Office: Office LA City Aty 200 No Main St 18th Fl Los Angeles CA 90012 E-mail: anocas@atty.lacity.org

NOCE, WALTER WILLIAM, JR. hospital administrator; b. Neptune, N.J., Sept. 27, 1945; s. Walter William and Louise Marie (Jenkins) N.; m. Cinda Ann Miller, Apr. 15, 1967; children: Krista Suzanne, David Michael. B.A., LaSalle Coll., Phila., 1967; M.P.H., UCLA, 1969. Regional coordinator USPHS, Rockville, Md., 1969-71; v.p. Hollywood Presbyn. Hosp., Los Angeles, 1971-75; sr. v.p. Hollywood Presbyn. Med. ctr., 1975-77; v.p. adminstrn. Huntington Meml. Hosp, Pasadena, Calif., 1977-83; pres., chief exec. officer St. Joseph Hosp., Orange, 1983-90; pres. so. Calif. region St. Joseph Health System, 1987-90, exec. v.p., 1990-94; pres., CEO Children's Hosp., L.A., 1995—. Preceptor UCLA Health Services Mgmt. Program, 1977— ; chmn. bd. Health Plan of Am., 1985-91; chmn. Hosp. Coun. So. Calif., 1989. Exec. v.p. Mental Health Assn. in Los Angeles County, 1979-82; regional v.p. Calif. Mental Health Assn., 1982-83. W. Glenn Ebersole finalist Assn. Western Hosp., 1969; recipient USPHS letter commendation, 1971, leadership in health affairs award Healthcare Assn. So. Calif., 1997. Mem. Am. Coll. Hosp. Adminstrs., Am. Hosp. Assn. (ho. of dels. 1994—), Nat. Assn. Children's Hosps. (bd. dirs. 1995—), Calif. Assn. Cath. Hosps. (chmn. 1990-91), Calif. Assn. Hosps. and Health Sys. (chmn. 1992), UCLA Hosp. Adminstrn. Alumni Assn. (pres. 1979-80), Pasadena C. of C. (v.p. 1980-82). Home: 1012 Glen Oaks Blvd Pasadena CA 91105-1108 Office: Childrens Hosp Los Angeles 4650 W Sunset Blvd Los Angeles CA 90027-6062

NOCHIMSON, DAVID, lawyer; b. Paterson, N.J., June 19, 1943; s. Samuel S. and Mildred (Singer) N.; m. Roberta Maizel, June 5, 1966 (div. 1972); m. Gail Burgess, May 26, 1978. BA, Yale U., 1965; LLB, Columbia U., 1968; LLM, Australian Nat. U., Canberra, 1969. Bar: N.Y. 1970, Calif. 1977. Assoc. Paul, Weiss, Rifkind, Wharton and Garrison, N.Y.C., 1970-72; sr. v.p. Comprop Equities Corp., N.Y.C., 1972-76; assoc. Mitchell, Silberberg and Knupp, L.A., 1977-80, ptnr., 1980-83, Ziffren, Brittenham, Branca & Fischer, L.A., 1983—. Adv. com. UCLA Entertainment Symposium, 1979-99, co-chmn., 1981-82. Contbr. articles to Encyclopedia of Investments, 1982, profl. jours. Pres. Friends of the L.A. Free Clinic, 1994-96; trustee Santa Monica (Calif.) Mus. of Art, 1995—. Fulbright scholar, Australia, 1968-69. Mem. ABA (forum com. on entertainment and sports industries 1982—, editor The Entertainment and Sports Lawyer 1982-89, chmn. 1989-92), Internat. Bar Assn. (Vice chmn. entertainment com. 1986-90), Am. Bar Found., Beverly Hills Bar Assn. Democrat. Jewish. Avocations: tennis, racquetball, playing piano, hiking. Office: Ziffren Brittenham Branca & Fischer 1801 Century Park W Los Angeles CA 90067-6406

NODAL, ADOLFO V. city manager; b. Cienfuegos, Cuba, Mar. 6, 1950; AA, Miami Dade C.C., 1970; BA in Graphics/Art History, Fla. Sttae U., 1972; MA in Contemporary Art, San Francisco State U., 1976; postgrad. cert., U. Calif., Berkeley, 1982. Exec. dir. Washington Project for the Arts, 1978-83; dir. MacArthur Park Pub. Art Program, L.A.; dir. exhbns. Exhbn. Ctr. Otis Parsons Sch. of Design, L.A., 1983-87; exec. dir. Contemporary Arts Ctr., New Orleans, 1988; gen. mgr. Cultural Affairs Dept. City of L.A., 1988—. Mem. selection panel NEA, 1979-81, D.C. Commn. for the Arts, 1981, Md. State Arts Coun., 1981, Awards for the Visual Arts, 1983, Calif. State Arts Coun., 1985-87, City of L.A. Cultural Affairs Dept., 1985, Capp Street Project, San Francisco, 1986-91, City of Palo Alto Bixbee Park Renovation, 1986, Long Beach Corp. for the Arts Press Art Project, 1987, City of Concord, 1987, Fleishaker Found. Artists Fellowship, 1987. Founding bd. dirs. L.A. Works, 1991; v.p. MacArthur Park Found., 1988-90; sec. MacArthur Park Cmty. Coun., 1984-87; mem. Diverse Works Art Ctr., Houston, 1984-87, New Music Am. '85, 1984-85, Cultural Alliance of Greater Washington, 1982; mem. adv. com. Market Sq. Park, Houston, 1985-88, L.A. Children's Mus., 1986, L.A. Edn. Alliance for Restructuring Now, 1992; mem. overview panel NEA, 1988; mem. art adv. com. Cmty. Redevel. Agy. L.A., 1986-88; mem. Mayor Tom Bradley's Arts Task Force, 1987; mem. founding com. Latino Mus., 1990; mem. cultural masterplan com. Arts Coun. New Orleans, 1988; mem. design adv. group Pershing Sq. Mgmt. Assn., 198; mem. Metro-Dade County Pub. Art program Crandon Park Zoo, Miami, Fla., 1987; mem. pub. art in Am. conf. Fairmount Park Art Assn., Phila., 1986. Recipient Washingtonian of Yr. Washingtonian Mag. and Washington Jaycees, 1981, Mayor's Art award Washington Project for the Arts, Mayor Marion Barry, 1981, numerous pub. svc. citations, Padrino award Bilingual Found. for the Arts, 1991, Humanitarian award Ctrl. Am. Refugee Ctr,. 1991, Japan Found., 1990. Mem. Am. Coun. for the Arts, So. Calif. Inst. Arch., Wilshire Blvd. C. of C., Nat. Assn. Artists Orgn., Nat. Assembly Local Arts Agys., Ams. for the Arts (adv. com. 1996—), Office: City Los Angeles Cultural Affairs Dept 433 S Spring St Fl 10 Los Angeles CA 90013-2009

NOH, LAIRD, state legislator; b. Twin Falls, Idaho, Sept. 28, 1938; m. Kathleen Noh; children: John, Susan. BS in Bus. and Agr., U. Idaho; MBA, U. Chgo. Sheep prodr.; mem. Idaho Senate, Dist. 23, Boise, 1980—. Chair resources and environment com., mem. agrl. affairs and edn. coms. Republican. Protestant. Office: State Capitol PO Box 83720 Boise ID 83720-3720

NOKES, JOHN RICHARD, retired newspaper editor, writer; b. Portland, Oreg., Feb. 23, 1915; s. James Abraham and Bernice Alfaretta (Bailey) N.; m. Evelyn Junkin, Sept. 13, 1936; children: Richard Gregory, William G., Gail (Mrs. William M. Hulden), Douglas J., Kathy E. B.S., Linfield Coll., 1936, LHD (hon.), 1988. With The Oregonian, Portland, 1936-82, city editor, 1950-65, asst. mng. editor, 1965-71, mng. editor, 1971-75, editor, 1975-82; disting. vis. prof. journalism Linfield Coll., 1982-85. Cons. editor The Hong Kong Standard, 1994. Author: American Form of Government, 1939, Columbia's River: The Voyages of Robert Gray 1787-1793, 1991, Almost a Hero: The Voyages of John Meares to China, Hawaii and the Pacific Northwest, 1998; editor Oreg. Edn. Jour., 1944. Bd. dirs. Portland U.S.O., 1968-72, U.S. Coast Guard Acad. Found., 1972-74, Portland Opera Assn., 1976-78; trustee Linfield Coll., 1977-93; v.p. Oreg. UN Assn., 1983-85, chmn. Oreg. UN Day, 1983. Lt. (j.g.) USNR, 1944-46; comdr. Res. (ret.). Mem. Navy League U.S. (pres. Portland coun. 1969-71), Linfield Coll. Alumni Assn. (pres. 1940), World Affairs Coun. Oreg. (pres. 1973-74), AP Mng. Editors Assn. (dir. 1973-80), Am. Soc. Newspaper Editors, N.W. China Coun., Sigma Delta Chi (pres. Willamette Valley chpt. 1975-76) Republican. Methodist. Club: Multnomah Athletic (Portland). Home: 11780 SW Queen Elizabeth King City OR 97224-2601

NOLAN, MARK GREGORY, advertising executive; b. San Francisco, July 3, 1958; Founder, chief exec. officer Mark Nolan & Assocs., Inc., Citrus Heights, Calif., 1981-87; v.p., ptnr. Nolan Mktg. Group Inc., Citrus Heights, 1987—; mktg. dir., ptnr. Fin. Mktg. Corp., Citrus Heights, 1989—. Keynote speaker Marin Self-Pubs. Assn., Ross, Calif., 1986; featured speaker Community Entrepreneurs Assn., Sacramento, 1986, home-based bus. conf., 1991; treas. COSMEP, San Francisco, 1986-88; lectr. UCLA, 1987. Author: The Instant Marketing Plan, 1995; co-author: Health Secrets of the Rich and Famous, 1998, editor: Info. Mktg., 1985-87. Mem. Better Bus. Bur., Eagle Scouts. Mem. S.C. Publicists Assn., Community Entrepreneurs Assn., Internat. Assn. Self-Pubs. (treas. 1986-88), Com. of Small Mag. Editors and Pubs., C. of C., Turtles, Oregon Advt. Club, Entrepreneurs Am., Active 20-30 Club. Avocations: wine appreciation, classic automobiles. Office: Nolan Mktg Group Inc PO Box 2570 Fair Oaks CA 95628-9570

NOLAN, OWEN, professional hockey player; b. Belfast, Northern Ireland, Feb. 12, 1972; Selected 1st round NHL entry draft Que. Nordiques, 190, right wing, 1990-96, San Jose Sharks, 1996—. Named to OHL All-Star 1st team, 1989-90; played in NHL All-Star Game 1992, 96. Recipient Emms Family award, 1988-89, Jim Mahon Meml. Trophy, 1989-90. Office: c/o San Jose Sharks 525 W Santa Clara St San Jose CA 95113-1520

NOLL, ROGER GORDON, economist, educator; b. Monterey Park, Calif., Mar. 13, 1940; s. Cecil Ray and Hjordis Alberta (Westover) N.; m. Robyn Schreiber, Aug. 25, 1962 (dec. Jan. 2000); 1 child, Kimberlee Elizabeth. B.S., Calif. Inst. Tech., 1962; A.M., Harvard U., 1965, Ph.D. in Econs, 1967. Mem. social sci. faculty Calif. Inst. Tech., 1965-84, prof., 1973-82, Inst. prof., 1982-84, chmn. div. humanities and social scis., 1978-82; prof. econs. Stanford U., 1984—, dir. pub. policy program, 1986—, Morris M. Doyle centennial prof. of pub. policy, 1990—; Jean Monnet prof. European U. Inst., 1991; vis. fellow Brookings Instn., 1995-96, nonresident sr. fellow, 1996—. Sr. staff economist Coun. of Econ. Advisors, Washington, 1967-69; sr. fellow Brookings Instn., Washington, 1970-73; mem. tech. adv. bd. Com. for Econ. Devel., 1978-82; mem. adv. coun. NSF, 1978-89, SERI, 1982-90, NASA, 1978-81; mem. Pres.'s Commn. for Nat. Agenda for the Eighties, 1980; chmn. L.A.Sch. Monitoring Com., 1978-79; mem. Commn. on Behavioral Social Scis. and Edn., NAS, 1984-90; mem. energy rsch. adv. bd. Dept. Energy, 1986-89; mem. Sec. of Energy Adv. Bd., 1990-94; mem. Calif. Coun. on Sci. and Tech., 1995-2000; mem. bd. on sci., tech. and econ. policy NAS, 2000—. Author: Reforming Regulation, 1971, The Economics and Politics of Deregulation, 1991, The Economics and Politics of the Slowdown in Regulatory Reform, 1999; co-author: Economic Aspects of Television Regulation, 1973, The Political Economy of Deregulation, 1983, The Technology Pork Barrel, 1991; editor: Government and the Sports Business, 1974, Regulatory Policy and the Social Sciences, 1985, Challenges to Research Universities, 1998; co-editor: Constitutional Reform in California, 1995, Sports, Jobs and Taxes, 1997, A Communications Cornucopia, 1998; supervisory editor Info. Econs. and Policy Jour., 1984-92. NSF grantee, 1973-82; Recipient 1st ann. book award Nat. Assn. Ednl. Broadcasters, 1974; Guggenheim fellow, 1983-84 Mem. Am. Econ. Assn. Democrat. Home: 4153 Hubbartt Dr Palo Alto CA 94306-3834 Office: Stanford U Dept Econs Stanford CA 94305

NOMURA, MASAYASU, biological chemistry educator; b. Hyogo-Ken, Japan, Apr. 27, 1927; s. Hiromichi and Yaeko N.; m. Junko Hamashima, Feb. 10, 1957; children— Keiko, Toshiyasu. Ph.D., U. Tokyo, 1957. Asst. prof. Inst. Protein Research, Osaka (Japan) U., 1960-63; assoc. prof. genetics U. Wis., Madison, 1963-66, prof., 1966-70, Elvehjem prof. in Life Sci. genetics and biochemistry, 1970-84, co-dir. Inst. for Enzyme Research, 1970-84; prof. biol. chemistry, Grace Bell chair U. Calif., Irvine, 1984—. Recipient U.S. Steel award in molecular biology Nat. Acad. Scis., 1971; recipient Acad. award Japanese Acad. Arts and Sci., 1972 Mem. Am. Acad. Arts and Scis., Nat. Acad. Scis., Royal Danish Acad. Scis. and Letters, Royal Netherlands Acad. Arts and Scis., Japanese Biochem. Soc. Home: 74 Whitman Ct Irvine CA 92612-4066 Office: U Calif Dept Biol Chemistry 240D Med Sci I Dept Irvine CA 92697-1700 E-mail: mnomura@uci.edu

NOOLAN, JULIE ANNE CARROLL, management consultant; b. Adelaide, South Australia, Australia, June 14, 1944; came to U.S., 1966; d. Archibald Henry and Norma Mae (Gillett) Noolan; m. Daniel Thuering Carroll, Aug. 20, 1977. M.A., U. Chgo., 1968, Ph.D., 1974, Exec. M.B.A., 1983. With State Library of South Australia, 1962-63, Repatriation Dept. South Australia, 1962-66; asst. librarian U. Chgo. Libraries, 1966-68; dir. edn. Med. Library Assn., Chgo., 1972-77; exec. dir. Assn. Coll. and Research Libraries, Chgo., 1977-84; COO Carroll Group, Inc., Chgo., 1984-95; pres. COO Carroll Group, Inc., Chgo., 1995—. Mem. faculty U. Chgo., 1968-89, Am. U., 1995—. Author: Libraries and Accreditation in Higher Education; contbr. articles to jours. U. Chgo. fellow, 1967-68, Higher Edn. Act fellow, 1969-72; Nat. Library of Medicine grantee, 1967-69; named Outstanding Young U.S. Leader 1985 Coun. on the U.S.., Mem. ALA, Am. Soc. Assn. Execs., Am. Mgmt. Assn., Spol. Librs. Assn., Am. Soc. for Info. Scis. (past pres., doctoral award, Watson Davis award), ASTD, Nat. Tng. Labs. (bd. dirs. 1990-94), Orgn. Devel. Network, Internat. Assn. Neuro-Linguistic Programming (bd.dirs. 1990-93), Internat. Plant Genetic Resources Inst. (Rome, bd. dirs. 1991-98), Internat. Ctr. Agrl. Rsch. in Dry Areas (Syris, bd. dirs. 1992-98), Planning Forum, Beta Phi Mu.

NOONAN, JOHN T., JR. federal judge, law educator; b. Boston, Oct. 24, 1926; s. John T. and Marie (Shea) N.; m. Mary Lee Bennett, Dec. 27, 1967; children: John Kenneth, Rebecca Lee, Susanna Bain. B.A., Harvard U., 1946, LL.B., 1954; student, Cambridge U., 1946-47; M.A., Cath. U. Am., 1949, Ph.D., 1951, LHD, 1980; LL.D., U. Santa Clara, 1974, U. Notre Dame, 1976, Loyola U. South, 1978; LHD, Holy Cross Coll., 1980; LL.D., St. Louis U., 1981, U. San Francisco, 1985; student, Holy Cross Coll., 1980, Cath. U. Am., 1980, Gonzaga U., 1986, U. San Francisco, 1986. Bar: Mass. 1954, U.S. Supreme Ct. 1971. Mem. spl. staff Nat. Security Council, 1954-55; pvt. practice Herrick & Smith, Boston, 1955-60; prof. law U. Notre Dame, 1961-66, U. Calif., Berkeley, 1967-86, chmn. religious studies, 1970-73, chmn. medieval studies, 1978-79; judge U.S. Ct. Appeals (9th cir.), San Francisco, 1985-96, sr. judge, 1996—. Oliver Wendell Holmes, Jr. lectr. Harvard U. Law Sch., 1972, Pope John XXIII lectr. Cath. U. Law Sch., 1973, Cardinal Bellarmine lectr. St. Louis U. Div. Sch., 1973, Ernest Messenger lectr. Cornell U., 1982, John Dewey Meml. lectr. U. Minn., 1986, Baum lectr. U. Ill., 1988, Strassberger lectr. U. Tex., 1989; chmn. bd. Games Rsch., Inc., 1961-76; overseer Harvard U., 1991—. Author: The Scholastic Analysis of Usury, 1957; Contraception: A History of Its Treatment by the Catholic Theologians and Canonists, 1965; Power to Dissolve, 1972; Persons and Masks of the Law, 1976; The Antelope, 1977; A Private Choice, 1979; Bribes, 1984, The Responsible Judge, 1993, Professional and Personal Responsibilities of the Lawyer, 1997, The Lustre of Our Country, 1998; editor: Natural Law Forum, 1961-70. Am. Jour. Jurisprudence, 1970, The Morality of Abortion, 1970 Chmn. Brookline Redevel. Authority, Mass., 1958-62; cons. Papal Commn. on Family, 1965-66, Ford Found., Indonesian Legal Program, 1968; NIH, 1973, NIH, 1974; expert Presdl. Commn. on Population and Am. Future, 1971; cons. U.S. Cath. Conf., 1979-86; sec., treas. Inst. for Research in Medieval Canon Law, 1970-88; pres. Thomas More-Jacques Maritain Inst., 1977—; trustee Population Council, 1969-76, Phi Kappa Found., 1970-76, Grad. Theol. Union, 1970-73, U. San Francisco, 1971-75; mem. com. theol. edn. Yale U., 1972-77; exec. com. Cath. Commn. Intellectual and Cultural Affairs, 1972-75; bd. dirs. Ctr. for Human Values in the Health Scis., 1969-71, S.W. Intergroup Relations Council, 1970-72; Inst. for Study

Ethical Issues, 1971-73 Recipient St. Thomas More award U. San Francisco, 1974, Christian Culture medal, 1975, Laetare medal U. Notre Dame, 1984, Campion medal Cath. Book Club, 1987; Guggenheim fellow, 1965-66, 79-80, Laetare medal U. Notre Dame, 1984, Campion medal, 1987, Alemany medal Western Dominican Province, 1988; Ctr. for advanced Studies in Behavioral Scis. fellow, 1973-74; Wilson Ctr. fellow, 1979-80. Fellow Am. Acad. Arts and Scis., Am. Soc. Legal Historians (hon.); mem. Am. Soc. Polit. and Legal Philosophy (v.p. 1964), Canon Law Soc. Am. (gov. 1970-72), Am. Law Inst., Phi Beta Kappa (senator United chpts. 1970-72, pres. Alpha of Calif. chpt. 1972-73) Office: US Ct Appeals 9th Cir PO Box 193939 San Francisco CA 94119-3939

NOORDA, RAYMOND J. computer software company executive; b. Ogden, Utah. BSEE, Utah, 1949. CEO Novell Inc., 1982-94; chmn. MTI Inc. (now MTI Tech. Corp.), Anaheim, Calif., 1994—. Office: MTI Technology Corp 4905 E La Palma Ave Anaheim CA 92807-1915

NORA, AUDREY HART, physician; b. Picayune, Miss., Dec. 5, 1936; d. Allen Joshua and Vera Lee (Ballard) H.; m. James Jackson Nora, Apr. 9, 1966; children: James Jackson Jr., Elizabeth Hart. BS, U. Miss., 1958, MD, 1961; MPH, U. Calif., 1978. Diplomate Am. Bd. Pediatrics, Am. Bd. Hematology and Oncology. Resident in pediatrics U. Wis. Hosp., Madison, 1961-64; fellow in hematology/oncology Baylor U., Tex. Childrens Hosp., Houston, 1964-66, asst. prof. pediatrics, 1966-70; assoc. clin. prof. pediatrics U. Colo. Sch. Medicine, Denver, 1970—; dir. genetics Denver Childrens Hosp., 1970-78; cons. maternal and child health USPHS, Denver, 1978-83, asst. surgeon gen. regional health adminstr., 1983-92, dir. maternal & child health bur., health resources and svc. adminstrn., 1992-99, commd. med. officer, 1978, advanced through grades to asst. surgeon gen., 1983. Adv. com. NIH, Bethesda, 1975-77; adv. bd. Metronet Health, Inc., Denver, 1986—, Colo. Assn. Commerce and Industry, Denver, 1985—. Author: (with J.J. Nora) Genetics and Counseling in Cardiovascular Diseases, 1978, (with others) Blakiston's Medical Dictionary, 1980, Birth Defects Encyclopedia, 1990, (with J.J. Nora and K. Berg) Cardiovascular Diseases: Genetics, Epidemiology and Prevention, 1991; contbr. articles to profl. jours. Recipient Virginia Apgar award Nat. Found., 1976. Fellow Am. Acad. Pediatrics; mem. Am. Pub. Health Assn. (governing coun. 1990-92, coun. mem. maternal and child health 1990—), Commd. Officers Assn., Am. Soc. Human Genetics, Teratology Soc., Western Soc. Pediatric Rsch. Presbyterian. Avocations: quilting, cooking, hiking. Office: 1973 S Kenton Ct Aurora CO 80014-4709

NORA, JAMES JACKSON, physician, writer, educator; b. Chgo., June 26, 1928; s. Joseph James and Mae Henrietta (Jackson) N.; m. Barbara June Fluhrer, Sept. 7, 1949 (div. 1963); children: Wendy Alison, Penelope Welbon, Marianne Leslie; m. Audrey Faye Hart, Apr. 9, 1966; children: James Jackson Jr., Elizabeth Hart Nora. AB, Harvard U., 1950; MD, Yale U., 1954; MPH, U. Calif., Berkeley, 1978. Diplomate Am. Bd. Pediatrics, Am. Bd. Cardiology, Am. Bd. Med. Genetics. Intern Detroit Receiving Hosp., 1954-55; resident in pediatrics U. Wis. Hosps., Madison, 1959-61, fellow in cardiology, 1962-64; fellow in genetics McGill U. Children's Hosp., Montreal, Can., 1964-65; assoc. prof. pediatrics Baylor Coll. Medicine, Houston, 1965-71; prof. genetics, preventive medicine and pediatrics U. Colo. Med. Sch., Denver, 1971—. Dir. genetics Rose Med. Ctr., Denver, 1980—; dir. pediatric cardiology and cardiovascular tng. U. Colo. Sch. Medicine, 1971-78; mem. task force Nat. Heart and Lung Program, Bethesda, Md., 1973; cons. WHO, Geneva, 1983—; mem. U.S.-U.S.S.R. Exchange Program on Heart Disease, Moscow and Leningrad, 1975. Author: The Whole Heart Book, 1980, 2d rev. edit., 1989; (with F.C. Fraser) Medical Genetics, 4th rev. edit., 1994, Genetics of Man, 2d rev. edit., 1986, Cardiovascular Diseases: Genetics, Epidemiology and Prevention, 1991; (novels) The Upstart Spring, 1989, The Psi Delegation, 1989, The Hemingway Sabbatical, 1996, Songs from Brazen Bull, 2001. Com. mem. March of Dimes, Am. Heart Assn., Boy Scouts Am. Served to lt. USAAC, 1945-47. Grantee Nat. Heart, Lung and Blood Inst., Nat. Inst. Child Health and Human Devel., Am. Heart Assn., NIH; recipient Virginia Apgar Meml. award. Fellow Am. Coll. Cardiology, Am. Acad. Pediatrics, Am. Coll. Med. Genetics; mem. Am. Pediatric Soc., Soc. Pediatric Rsch., Am. Heart Assn., Teratology Soc., Transplantation Soc., Am. Soc. Human Genetics, Authors Guild, Authors League, Acad. Am. Poets, Mystery Writers Am., Rocky Mountain Harvard Club. Democrat. Presbyterian. Avocations: writing fiction, poetry.

NORBECK, JANE S. nursing educator; b. Redfield, S.D., Feb. 20, 1942; d. Sterling M. and Helen L. (Williamson) N.; m. Paul J. Gorman, June 28, 1970. BA in Psychology, BSN, U. Minn., 1965; MS, U. Calif., San Francisco, 1971, DNSc, 1975. Psychiat. nurse Colo. Psychiat. Hosp., Denver, 1965-66, Langley Porter Hosp., San Francisco, 1966-67; pub. health nurse San Francisco Health Dept., 1968-69; prof. U. Calif. Sch. of Nursing, San Francisco, 1975—, dept. chair, 1984-89, dean, 1989-99. Chair study sect. Nat. Inst. of Nursing Rsch., 1990-93, mem. editl. bd. Archives of Psychiat. Nursing, 1985-95, Rsch. in Nursing and Health, 1987—, Western Jour. of Medicine. Co-editor: Annual Review of Nursing Research, 1996-97; contbr. articles to profl. jours. Mem. ANA, Am. Acad. Nursing, Inst. of Medicine, Sigma Theta Tau. Office: U Calif Sch Nursing 521 Parnassus Ave San Francisco CA 94143-0001

NORBERG, DEBORAH DORSEY, curator; b. New Haven, Jan. 31, 1950; d. Gray Lankford and Jeanne (DeVall) Dorsey; m. Henry F. Norberg, Sept. 11, 1971; children: Sarah E., Daniel G. BA, Stanford U., 1968; M in Mus. Practice, U. Mich., 1974; JD, Stanford U., 1980. Rsch. asst. San Jose (Calif.) Mus. Art, 1975, asst. to curator, 1975-76, exhibition coord., 1987-88, asst. curator, 1988-89, assoc. registrar, assoc. permanent collection curator, 1989-90, registrar, assoc. permanent collection curator, 1990—; assoc. Hopkins and Carley, San Jose, 1980-82. Bd. dirs. Explorer Presch., San Jose, 1987-88; sch. site coun. Oster Sch., San Jose, 1990—. Ford Found. fellow, 1972. Mem. Am. Assn. Mus. (registrars com.), Western Mus. Conf. (registrars com.), Phi Beta Kappa. Office: San Jose Mus Art 110 S Market St San Jose CA 95113-2383

NORBY, MARK ALAN, lawyer; b. Cadillac, Mich., July 5, 1955; s. Walter Carl and Nadine Kaye (Hunt) N.; m. Connie Lynn Perrine, Feb. 26, 1983. BS in Polit. Sci., Agr., Oreg. State U., 1977; JD, U. Mich., 1980. Bar: Oreg. 1980, U.S. Dist. Ct. Oreg. 1980. Assoc. Stoel, Rives, Boley, Fraser & Wyse, Portland, 1980-86; ptnr. Stoel, RivesLLP, Portland, 1986—. Office: Stoel Rives LLP 900 SW 5th Ave Ste 2600 Portland OR 97204-1268

NORCROSS, DAVID WARREN, physicist, researcher; b. Cin., July 18, 1941; s. Gerald Warren and Alice Elizabeth (Downey) N.; children: Joshua David, Sarah Elizabeth. AB, Harvard Coll., 1963; MSc, U. Ill., 1965; PhD, Univ. Coll., London, 1970. Research assoc. U. Colo., Boulder, 1970-74; physicist Nat. Bur. Standards, Boulder, 1974—; chief quantum physics divsn. Nat. Inst. Stds. and Tech., 1989-93, dir. Boulder Labs., 1994—; fellow Joint Inst. Lab. Astrophysics, Boulder, 1976—. Contbr. articles to profl. jours. Recipient Bronze medal Nat. Bur. Standards, 1982, Silver medal U.S. Dept. Commerce, 1994. Fellow Am. Phys. Soc. Office: Nat Inst Standards & Tech 325 Broadway St Boulder CO 80305-3337

NORD, LARRY B. federal judge; BA, San Jose State U., 1961; JD, U. Calif., San Francisco, 1963. Pvt. practice, Eureka, Calif.; dep. dist. atty. Humboldt County, 1968-70; apptd. part-time magistrate judge no. dist. U.S. Dist. Ct. Calif., 1971. Office: 518 W Clark St Eureka CA 95501-0103 Fax: 707 443 6505

NORDBY, GENE MILO, engineering educator, educator; b. Anoka, Minn., May 7, 1926; s. Bert J. and Nina Grace N.; m. Arlene Delores Anderson, Aug. 27, 1949 (dec. Nov. 1974); children: Susan Pamela, Brett Gene, Lisa Lea; m. Dusilla Anne Rycroft, July 8, 1975 (div. July 1988); m. Catherine Lynn Short, Dec. 23, 1992. BSCE, Oreg. State U., 1948; MSCE, U. Minn., 1949, Ph.D. in Civil Engring., 1955. Registered profl. engr., Colo. Ariz. Grad. asst. U. Minn., 1948-50; structural designer Pfeiffer and Shultz, Mpls., summer 1950; instr., then asst. prof. civil engring. U. Colo., Boulder, 1950-56; assoc. prof., rsch. engr. Joint Hwy. Rsch. Project Purdue U., East Lafayette, Ind., 1956; engr. program dir. engring. scis. NSF, Washington, 1956-58; lectr. civil engring. George Washington U., Washington, 1956-58; dir., then chmn. adv. com. Ariz. Transp. and Traffic Inst. at univ., 1959-62; prof. engring. U. Okla., Norman, 1962-77, dean Coll. Engring, 1962-70, v.p. for adminstrn. and fin. Coll. Engring, 1969-77; v.p. for bus. and fin., prof. civil engring. Ga. Inst. Tech., Atlanta, 1977-80; chancellor U. Colo., Denver, 1980-85; chancellor emeritus, 1985—; prof. civil engring. U. Colo., Denver and Boulder, 1985-86; prof. civil engring, head dept. civil engring. U. Ariz., 1958-62, prof. agrl. engring., 1986-94, prof. emeritus, 1994—, head dept. agrl. engring., 1986-91. Mem. Reinforced Concrete Rsch. Coun. Engring. Found., 1954-60; trustee Frontiers of Sci. Found., Okla., 1963-70; pres. Tetracon Assos., Inc., 1968-86; cons. structural engring., rsch. financing and programming, ednl. facilities planning and constrn., reinforced concrete, also higher edn. adminstrn., engring. program accreditation, NSF, 1984-87, panel engring. ctrs. of excellence, 1983-87; bd. dirs. Higher Edn. and the Handicapped, Am. Coun. on Edn., 1980-83; pres. Accreditation Bd. for Engring. and Tech., 1985-86, fellow, mem. Related Accreditation Commn., 1986-95, chair, 1993-94; gen. chmn. Nat. Congress on Engring. Edn., Washington, 1986; commr. at large N. Ctrl. Assn. Schs. and Colls., 1988-92; adj. prof. U. Colo., Denver, 1998—. Co-author: Introduction to Structural Mechanics, 1960; cons. editor, MacMillan Co., 1962-70. Mem. bd. vis. Air Force Inst. Tech., 1985-87. With AUS, 1943-46. Recipient Citation for Svc., State of Okla. Ho. Reps., 1977, Linton E. Grinter Disting. Svc. award Accreditation Bd. for Engring. and Tech., 1982. Fellow ASCE (com. on engring edn., 1964-68, com. on rsch. needs, 1965-70, com. on ednl. rsch., 1976-79, Edmund Friedman Profl. Devel. award 1982); mem. Am. Soc. Engring. Edn. (projects bd. 1969-70, chmn. Curtis W. McGraw award com. 1968, Dean's Inst. com. 1966-69, accreditation process com. 1979-81), Nat. Soc. Profl. Engrs., Am. Arbitration Assn., Am. Soc. Agrl. Engrs. (com. in engring. and tech. accreditation 1987-93), Engrs. Coun. for Profl. Devel. (chmn. engring. edn. and accreditation com. 1970, dir. 1976-79, 83-87), Ariz. Soc. Profl. Engrs., Okla. Soc. Profl. Engrs. (dir. 1966-69), Nat. Assn. State Univs. and Land Grant Colls. (commn. edn. engring. profession 1966, 70-73), Engring. Colls. Adminstrv. Coun. (mem. exec. bd. 1966), Ga. Soc. Profl. Engrs. (bd. dirs. Atlanta chpt. 1978-79), Nat. Assn. Coll. and Univ. Bus. Officers (chmn. personnel com. 1977-79), Sigma Tau, Omicron Delta Kappa, Tau Beta Pi, Chi Epsilon, Alpha Epsilon. Club: Mason. E-mail: gmn5@juno.com

NORDLUND, DONALD CRAIG, lawyer; b. Chgo., May 23, 1949; s. Donald E. and Jane (Houston) N.; m. Sally Baum, Sept. 7, 1975; children: Courtney Elizabeth, Michael Andrew, Laurie Katherine. AB, Stanford U., 1971; JD, Vanderbilt U., 1974. Assoc. Ware & Freidenrich, Palo Alto, Calif., 1974-77; atty. Hewlett-Packard Co., Palo Alto, 1977-87, assoc. gen. counsel, sec., 1987-99; sr. v.p., gen. counsel, sec. Agilent Technologies, Inc., 1999—. Sec. Agilent Technologies Found. and various Agilent Tech. subsidiaries, 1999—; panelist ann. disclosure documents seminar Practicing Law Inst., 1982-2001, also contbg. author to course handbook; cons. pub. guide series, CEB, 1991; bd. dirs. Hewlett Packard Employees Fed. Credit Union. Chmn., bd. dirs. Santa Clara County chpt. Jr. Achievement, 1995-97. Mem. Am. Soc. Corp. Secs. Inc. (pres. San Francisco region 1986-88, bd. dirs. 1987-90, mem. exec. com. 1988-89, chmn. securities law com. 1995-98), Am. Corp. Counsel Assn. (bd. dirs. San Francisco chpt. 1984-2000, nat. bd. dirs. 1995—, pres. 1989-90, nat. chmn. 1999-2000), Foothills Tennis and Swimming Club (Palo Alto). Avocations: tennis, skiing, sailing, golf. Office: Agilent Technologies Inc 395 Page Mill Rd Palo Alto CA 94306-2024

NORDSTROM, BLAKE W. retail executive; Pres. Nordstrom, Inc., Seattle. Office: Nordstrom Inc 1617 Sixth Ave Seattle WA 98101-1742

NORDSTROM, BRUCE A. department store executive; b. 1933; married. BA, U. Wash., 1956. With Nordstrom, Inc., Seattle, 1956—, v.p., 1964-70, pres., 1970-75, chmn., 1975-77, co-chmn., 1977—, dir. Office: Nordstrom Inc 1617 6th Ave Seattle WA 98101-1742

NORDSTROM, JOHN N. department store executive; b. 1937; married. BA, U. Wash., 1958. With Nordstrom, Inc., Seattle, 1958—, v.p., 1965-70, exec. v.p., 1970-75, pres., 1975-77, co-chmn., 1977—, dir. Bd. dirs. Fed. Res. Bank San Francisco. Office: Nordstrom Inc 1617 6th Ave Seattle WA 98101-1742

NORMAN, E. GLADYS, business computer educator, consultant; b. Oklahoma City, June 13, 1933; d. Joseph Eldon and Mildred Lou (Truitt) Biggs; m. Joseph R.R. Radeck, Mar. 1, 1953 (div. Aug. 1962); children: Jody Norman, Ray Norman, Warren Norman (dec. May 1993), Dana Norman; m. Leslie P. Norman, Aug. 26, 1963 (dec. Feb. 1994); 1 child, Elayne Pearce. Student, Fresno (Calif.) State Coll., 1951-52, UCLA, 1956-59, Linfield Coll., 1986-95. Math. aid U.S. Naval Weapons Ctr., China Lake, Calif., 1952-56, computing systems specialist, 1957-68; systems programmer Oreg. Motor Vehicles Dept., Salem, 1968-69; instr. in data processing, dir. Computer Programming Ctr., Salem, 1969-72; instr. in data processing Merritt-Davis Bus. Coll., Salem, 1972-73; sr. programmer, analyst Teledyne Wah Chang, Albany, Oreg., 1973-79; sr. systems analyst Oreg. Dept. Vets. Affairs, Albany, 1979-80; instr. in bus. computers Linn-Benton C.C., Albany, 1980-95; ret., 1995. Computer cons. for LBCC Ret. Sr. Vol. Program, 1995—; presenter computer software seminars State of Oreg., 1991-93, Oreg. Credit Assoc. Conf., 1991, Oreg. Regional Users Group Conf., 1992; computer tchr. Linn-Benton C.C., 1999-2001; computer cons. Oremet-Wah Chang, 1996—, Oreg. State Yr. 2000 Project, 1997-98; adj. prof. Chemeketa C.C., 2000-2001; computer cons. in field. Mem. Data Processing Mgmt. Assn. (bd. dirs. 1977-84, 89-95, region sect. 1995-96, assoc. v.p. 1988, Diamond Individual Performance award 1985). Assn. Info. Tech. Profls. (region treas. 1999, region sec. 2000-2001). Democrat. Avocations: drawing, painting, sewing. E-mail: gladys_norman@juno.com, gladys.norman@wahchang.com

NORMAN, JEAN REID, journalist; b. Phoenix, Feb. 13, 1957; d. James August and V. Janice (Radford) R.; m. James E. Norman, Jr., Dec. 30, 1982; children: James R., Janiece C. BS in Journalism, Northwestern U., 1979. Reporter Fallon (Nev.) Eagle-Standard, 1979-80; reporter, spl. sections editor North Las Vegas Valley Times, 1980-81; mng. editor Good Times, Santa Cruz, Calif., 1981-83; copy editor Daily Review, Hayward, 1983-85, Journal-Bulletin, Providence, 1986-89, Contra Costa Times, Walnut Creek, Calif., 1989, The Washington Post, 1990, USA Today Money Sect., Rosslyn, Va., 1990-93; mng. editor Navy Times, Springfield, 1993-98; asst. metro editor Las Vegas Sun, 1998—. Vestry mem. St. Mark's Episcopal Ch., 1996-98. Democrat. Office: Las Vegas Sun 800 S Valley View Blvd Las Vegas NV 89107-4411

NORMAN, JOHN BARSTOW, JR. designer, educator; b. Paola, Kans., Feb. 5, 1940; s. John B. and Ruby Maxine (Johnson) N.; m. Roberta Jeanne Martin, June 6, 1967; children: John Barstow III, Elizabeth Jeanne. BFA, U. Kans., 1962, MFA, 1966. Designer and illustrator Advt. Design, Kansas City, Mo., 1962-64; asst. instr. U. Kans., Lawrence, 1964-66; art dir. Hallmark Cards, Inc., Kansas City, 1966-69; instr. dept. art U. Denver, 1969-73, asst. prof., 1973-78, assoc. prof., 1978-93, disting. prof., 1980-93, prof. emeritus, 1993—; sr. designer Mo. Coun. Arts & Humanities, 1966-67; cons. designer Rocky Mt. Bank Note Corp., Denver, 1971—. Cons. designer Signage identity System, U. Denver; bd. dirs. comm. U. Denver; tech. cons. Denver Art Mus., 1974—, designed exhbns, 1974-75; adv. cons. Jefferson County (Colo.) Sch. System, 1976—; chmn. Design and Sculpture Exhbn., Colo. Celebration of the Arts, 1975-76. One-man shows include GalleryCortina, Aspen, Colo., 1983; commd. works include Jedda, Saudi Arabia, Synegistics Corp., Denver; represented in permanent collections Pasadena Ctr. for Arts, N.Y. Arts Dirs. Club, Calif. State U./Fiber Collection, Pasadena Ctr. Arts, N.Y. Art Dirs. Club, Midland Art Coun./Fiber Collection, Geologic Soc. Am.; represented in traveling exhbns. L.A. Art Dirs. Show and N.Y. Art Dirs. Show, U.S., Europe, Japan, 1985; featured in Denver Post, 1984, Post Electric City Mag., 1984, Rocky Mt. News, 1984, Douglas County Press, 1984, Mile High Cable Vision, 1985, Sta. KWGN-TV, 1985, Les Krantz's Am. Artists, 1988; illustrated Survey of Leading Contemporaries, 1988, U.S. Surface Design Jour., 1988; co-work represented in film collectin Mus. Modern Art, N.Y.C.; selected fashion show designs displayed Sister City dels., Denver, 1987. Recipient Silver medal award N.Y. Internat. Film and Video Competition, 1976, Design awards Coun. ADvancement and Support Edn., 1969, 71, 73, 76, Honor Mention award L.A. Art Dirs. Club, 1984, Honor Mention award N.Y. ARt Dirs. Club, 1984, Native Am. Wearable Art Competition, 1985, 5th pl. Nat. Wind Sail Am. Banners Competition, Midland, Mich., 1985, also awards for surface designs in Colo. Ctr. for Arts Wearable ARt Competition, 1984-85, Foothills Art Gallery Nat. Wearable Competition, 1984-85, Fashion Group Denver Competition, 1984-85. Mem. Art Dirs. Club Denver (Gold medals 1974-82, Best of Show Gold medal 1983, Honor Mentin award 1984, 3 gold medals 1989), Univ. Dirs. Assn. Home: PO Box 507 Lake George CO 80827-0507

NORMAN, JOHN EDWARD, petroleum landman; b. Denver, May 22, 1922; s. John Edward and Ella (Warren) N.; m. Hope Sabin, Sept. 5, 1946; children— J. Thomas, Gerould W., Nancy E., Susan G., Douglas E. BSBA, U. Denver, 1949, MBA, 1972. Clk., bookkeeper Capitol Life Ins. Co., Denver, 1940-42, 45-46; salesman Security Life and Accident Co., Denver, 1947; bookkeeper Central Bank and Trust Co., Denver, 1947-50; automobile salesman H.A. Hennies, Denver, 1950; petroleum landman Continental Oil Co. (name changed to Conoco Inc. 1979), Denver, 1950-85; ind. petroleum landman, 1985; ind. investor 1985—. Lectr. pub. lands Colo. Sch. Mines, 1968-85; lectr. mineral titles and landmen's role in oil industry Casper Coll., 1969-71. Mem. Casper Mcpl. Band Commn., 1965-71, mem. band, 1961-71, mgr., 1968-71; former musician, bd. dirs. Casper Civic Symphony; former bd. dirs. Jefferson Symphony, performing mem., 1972-75. Served with AUS, World War II. Mem. Am. Assn. Petroleum Landmen (dir. at large, chmn. publs. for regional dir.), Wyo. Assn. Petroleum Landmen (pres.), Denver Assn. Petroleum Landmen, Rocky Mountain Oil and Gas Assn. (pub. lands com. 1981-85), Rocky Mountain Petroleum Pioneers. Episcopalian (mem. choir, vestryman, past dir. acolytes). Club: Elks. Home and Office: 2710 S Jay St Denver CO 80227-3856

NORMAN, MARC, screenwriter, producer; Grad., U. Calif., Berkeley. Writer films Oklahoma Crude, 1973, Zandy's Bride, 1974, The Killer Elite, 1975, Breakout, 1975, The Aviator, 1985, Cutthroat Island, 1995; prodr., writer Shakespeare in Love, 1998 (Oscar award 1999, Silver Berlin Bear award 1999, British Acad. award 1999, Broadcast Film Critics Assn. award 1999, Golden Globe award 1999, Golden Satellite award 1999, others). Mem. Phi Beta Kappa. Office: c/o WGA West Inc 7000 W 3d St Los Angeles CA 90048

NORRIS, ALFRED LLOYD, bishop; b. Bogalusa, La., Feb. 6, 1938; s. Leslie Henry Peter and Adele Theresa (Washington) N.; m. Mackie Lyvonne Harper, Sept. 9, 1961; children: Alfred Lloyd II, Angela Renee. BA, Dillard U., 1960; MDiv, Gammon Theol. Sem., Atlanta, 1964, DD (hon.), 1976, Centenary Coll., , 1989; LLD, Dillard U., 1989; DD, McMurry U., 1995. Ordained ministry United Meth. Ch., 1963. Pastor Haven United Meth. Ch., New Orleans, 1963-66, Peck United Meth. Ch., New Orleans, 1966-68, First Street United Meth. Ch., New Orleans, 1972-74, Mt. Zion United Meth. Ch., New Orleans, 1980-85; dist. supt. New Orleans dist. United Meth. Ch., New Orleans, 1974-80; dir. recruitment Gammon Theol. Sem., 1968-72, pres., 1985-92; now bishop United Meth. Ch., 1992; bishop N.W. Tex./N. Mex. Episcopal Area, 1992—. Mem. Latin Am. Preaching Mission, 1967; mem. bd. publs. United Meth. Pub. House, Nashville, 1980-92; bd. dirs. Gulfside Assembly, Waveland, Miss., 1975-97; mem. La. Conf. Bd. Higher Edn. and Campus Ministry; chmn. bd. ordained ministry La. Ann. Conf., 1980-88; guest preacher Liberia, West Africa, 1988. Trustee Centenary Coll., Shreveport, La., 1979-92; mem. exec. com. NAACP, New Orleans, 1980-85; bd. dirs. New Orleans Urban League, 1981-84, Wesley Homes, Inc., Atlanta, 1986-92, So. Meth. U.; mem. exec. com. Met. Area Com., New Orleans, 1983-85; chmn. bd. dirs. Lafon Home for Elderly, New Orleans, 1983-85; chmn. dept. devel. Africa U. Crusade scholar, 1961-63. Mem. Assn. United Meth. Theol. Schs. (sec. 1986-88), Adminstrv. Deans' Coun. (v.p. 1986—), Masons, Sigma Pi Phi, Theta Phi. Democrat. Avocations: reading, spectator sports.

NORRIS, WILLIAM ALBERT, former federal judge; b. Turtle Creek, Pa., Aug. 30, 1927; s. George and Florence (Clive) N.; m. Merry Wright, Nov. 23, 1974; children: Barbara, Donald, Kim, Alison; m. Jane Jelenko. Student, U. Wis., 1945; B.A., Princeton U., 1951; J.D., Stanford U., 1954. Bar: Calif. and D.C. 1955. Assoc. firm Northcutt Ely, Washington, 1954-55; law clk. to Justice William O. Douglas U.S. Supreme Ct., Washington, 1955-56; sr. mem. firm Tuttle & Taylor, Inc., L.A., 1956-80; judge U.S. Ct. Appeals (9th cir.), L.A., 1980-94, sr. judge, 1994-97; lawyer, ptnr., mediator Ct. of Appeals Folger, Levin & Kahn, L.A., 1997—. Spl. counsel Pres.' Kennedy's Com. on Airlines Controversy, 1961; mem., v.p. Calif. State Bd. Edn., 1961-67 Trustee Calif. State Colls., 1967-72; pres. L.A. Bd. Police Commrs., 1973-74; Democratic nominee for atty. gen. State of Calif., 1974; founding pres. bd. trustees Mus. Contemporary Art, L.A., 1979— ; trustee Craft and Folk Art Mus., 1979— . With USN, 1945-47. Home: 1473 Oriole Dr West Hollywood CA 90069-1155 Office: Folger Levin & Kahn 1900 Ave Of Stars Fl 28 Los Angeles CA 90067-4301

NORTH, PATRICK, broadcasting executive; b. Kansas City, Mo., 1950; BS in Mass. Comm., Kans. State U., 1972. V.p., gen. mgr. KPHO-TV, Phoenix, 1992—. Bd. trustees Cronkite Found./Ariz. State U. Mem. Ariz. Broadcasters Assn. (bd. dirs.). Office: KPHO TV 4016 N Black Canyon Hwy Phoenix AZ 85017-4792

NORTH, ROBERT CARVER, political science educator; b. Walton, N.Y., Nov. 17, 1914; s. Arthur W. and Irene (Davenport) N.; m. Dorothy Anderson, Mar. 12, 1977; children by previous marriage: Woesha Kristina, Mary Davenport, Elizabeth Katrynka, Robert Cloud, Renya Catarina. A.B., Union Coll., 1936; M.A., Stanford U., 1948, Ph.D., 1957. Tchr. English, History Milford (Conn.) Sch., 1939-42; research asst. Hoover Instn., Stanford, Calif., 1948-50, research assoc., 1950-57; assoc. prof. polit. sci. Stanford (Calif.) U., 1957-62, prof., 1962-85, prof. emeritus, 1985—. Author: Revolt in San Marcos, 1941 (Commonwealth Gold medal), Moscow and Chinese Communists, 1952, The World That Could Be, 1976, (with Nazli Choucri) Nations in Conflict, 1975, War, Peace, Survival, 1990, (with Nazli Choucri and Susumu Yamakage) The Challenge of Japan: Before World War II and After, 1992. Served to capt. USAAF, 1942-46. Recipient Prix Mondial, U. Geneva, Hautes Etudes Internats., 1998. Mem. Am. Polit. Sci. Assn. (Conflicts Processes Sect. Lifetime Achievement award 1993), Internat. Studies Assn. (Disting. scholar award in fgn. policy analysis, pres. 1970-71), Internat. Peace-Sci. Assn., Explorers Club Democrat. Unitarian. Office: Stanford U Dept Polit Sci Stanford CA 94305

NORTH, ROBERT L. computer software executvie; b. Topeka, Sept. 19, 1935; BEE, Stanford U., 1953, MEE, 1958; postgrad., UCLA Grad. Bus. Sch., 1977; post grad., Stanford Grad. Bus. Sch., 1981. Tech. staff mem. Aerospace Corp., 1962-65; various positions TRW, 1965-81, v.p., gen. mgr., 1981-86; CEO HNC Software, Inc., San Diego, 1987-2000, chmn., 2000—. Mem. San Diego C. of C., 1983-84; bd. dir. San Diego Econ. Devel. Coun., 1983-84, United Way Pres. Coun., 1984 Office: HNC Software Inc 5935 Cornerstone Ct W San Diego CA 92121-3728

NORTH, WHEELER JAMES, marine ecologist, educator; b. San Francisco, Jan. 2, 1922; s. Wheeler Orrin and Florence Julia (Ross) N.; m. Barbara Alice Best, Apr. 25, 1964; children: Hannah Catherine, Wheeler Orrin. BS in Engring, Calif. Inst. Tech., 1944, BS in Biology, 1949; MS in Oceanography, U. Calif. at San Diego, 1953; Ph.D., 1953. NSF postdoctoral fellow Cambridge (Eng.) U.; Electronics engr. U.S. Navy Electronics Lab., Point Loma, Calif., 1947-48; asst. research biologist Scripps Inst. Oceanography, U. Calif. at San Diego, 1953, Rockefeller postdoctoral fellow, 1955-56; asst. research biologist Inst. Marine Resources Scripps Inst. Oceanography, 1956-63; assoc. prof. Calif. Inst. Tech., Pasadena, 1963-70, prof., 1970-92, prof. emeritus, 1992—. Cons. marine biology U.S. Govt., State of Calif., San Francisco, Los Angeles, San Diego, numerous industries, 1957— ; Phi Beta Kappa vis. scholar, 1973-74; mem. Calif. Adv. Commn., 1972-73, Nav. and Ocean Devel. Commn., 1973-76; dir. Marine Biol. Cons. Contbr. articles to profl. jours. Recipient NOGI award Underwater Soc. Am., 1975, John Olguin Marine Environ. award, 1999. Mem. Am. Littoral Soc. (James Duggan award), AAAS, Am. Soc. Limnology and Oceanography, Am. Soc. Zoology, Soc. Gen. Physiology, Calif. Acad. Sci., Fish Protective Assn. (dir.), N.Y. Acad. Sci., Am. Geophys. Union, Smithsonian Instn., Am. San Diego museums, Marine Tech. Soc., Western Soc. Naturalists, Calif. Soc. Profl. Engrs., Am. Zoomalac Soc., Internat. Oceanographic Found., Sigma Xi. Home: 387 W Bay St Apt 17 Costa Mesa CA 92627-2049 Office: Calif Inst Tech Divsn Engring Applied Sci Pasadena CA 91125-0001

NORTON, DELMAR LYNN, candy company executive; b. Vernal, Utah, Sept. 6, 1944; s. La Mar and Velma (Hullinger) N.; m. Connie Jean Bryan, Mar. 10, 1967; children: Bryan Lynn, Christopher Max, Wendy, Nicholas Delmar. Student, U. Utah, 1962-63, Famous Artists Sch., 1966-69. Nat. sales mgr. Maxfield Candy Co., Salt Lake City, 1965-72; sec.-treas. Ice Cream & Candy Shops, Salt Lake City, 1972-73; pres., gen. mgr. Ostlers' Candy Co., Salt Lake City, 1973—; chmn. bd. Nat. Mktg. Co., Salt Lake City, 1974—; pres., gen. mgr. Rent-A-Flick, Inc., Salt Lake City,; v.p. Redi-Therm Insulation, Inc., Salt Lake City., 1991 94; nat. sales mgr. Uphill Down U.S.A., 1994—. Mem. Ch. Jesus Christ of Latter-Day Saints (missionary). Home: 4240 S 1650 E Salt Lake City UT 84124-2556 Office: PO Box 71470 Salt Lake City UT 84171-0470

NORTON, GALE ANN, secretary of the interior; b. Wichita, Mar. 11, 1954; d. Dale Bentsen and Anna Jacqueline (Lansdowne) N.; m. John Goethe Hughes, Mar. 26, 1990. BA, U. Denver, 1975, JD, 1978. Bar: Colo. 1978, U.S. Supreme Ct. 1981. Jud. clk. Colo. Ct. of Appeals, Denver, 1978-79; sr. atty. Mountain States Legal Found., Denver, 1979-83; nat. fellow Hoover Instn. Stanford (Calif.) U., 1983-84; asst. to dep. sec. USDA, Washington, 1984-85; assoc. solicitor U.S. Dept. of Interior, Washington, 1985-87; pvt. practice law Denver, 1987-90; atty. gen. State of Colo., Denver, 1991-99; atty. Brownstein, Hyatt & Farber, P.C., sr. counsel, 1999-2000; sec. U.S. Dept. Interior, Washington, 2001—. Lectr. U. Denver Law Sch., 1989; transp. law program dir. U. Denver, 1978-79. Contbr. chpts. to books, articles to profl. jours. Past chair Nat. Assn. Attys. Gen. Environ. Com.; co-chair Nat. Policy Forum Environ. Coun.; candidate for 1996 election to U.S. Senate; chair environ. commn. Rep. Nat. Lawyers Assn. Named Young Career Woman Bus. and Profl. Wome, 1981, Young Lawyer of Yr., 1991, Mary Lathrop Trailblazer award Colo. Women's Bar Assn., 1999. Mem. Federalist Soc., Colo. Women's Forum, Order of St. Ives. Republican. Methodist. Avocation: skiing. Office: Dept of the Interior Office of the Sec 1849 C St NW Washington DC 20240

NORTON, KAREN ANN, accountant; b. Nov. 1, 1950; d. Dale Francis and Ruby Grace (Gehlhar) N. BA, U. Minn., 1972; postgrad., U. Md., 1978; MBA, Calif. State Poly. U., Pomona, 1989. CPA, Md. Securities transactions analyst Bur. of Pub. Dept., Washington, 1972-79, internal auditor, 1979-81, IRS, Washington, 1981; sr. acct. World Vision Internat., Monrovia, Calif., 1981-83, acctg. supr., 1983-87; sr. sys. liaison coord. Home Savs. Am. (name changed to Washington Mut.), 1987-97, sys. auditor, 1997-2000, sect. mgr., 2000—. Cons. (vol.) info. systems John M. Perkins Found., Pasadena, Calif., 1985-86. Author: (poetry) Ode to Joyce, 1985 (Golden Poet award 1985). 2d v.p. chpt. Nat. Treasury Employees Union, Washington, 1978, editor chpt. newsletter; mem. M-2 Prisoners Sponsorship Program, Chino, Calif., 1984-86. Recipient Spl. Achievement award Dept. Treasury, 1976, Superior Performance award Dept. Treasury, 1977-78; Charles and Ellora Alliss scholar, 1968. Mem. Angel Flight, Flying Samaritans. Avocations: flying, chess, racquetball, whitewater rafting.

NORTON, KENNETH HOWARD, JR. professional football player; b. Jacksonville, Ill., Sept. 29, 1966; s. Ken Norton. Degree in sociology, UCLA. Linebacker Dallas Cowboys, 1988-93, San Francisco 49ers, 1994—. Selected to Pro Bowl, 1991-95; played in Super Bowls XXVII-XXIX, 1992-94. Office: San Francisco 49ers 4949 Centennial Blvd Santa Clara CA 95054-1229

NORWOOD, DEBORAH ANNE, law librarian; b. Honolulu, Nov. 12, 1950; d. Alfred Freeman and Helen G. (Papsch) N.; 1 child, Nicholas. BA, U. Wash., 1972; JD, Willamette U., 1974; M in Law Librarianship, U. Wash., 1979. Bar: Wash., U.S. Dist. Ct. (we. dist.) 1975, U.S. Ct. Appeals (9th cir.) 1980. Ptnr. Evans and Norwood, Seattle, 1975-79; law librarian U.S. Courts Library, Seattle, 1980-89; state law librarian Wash. State Law Libr., Olympia, 1989—, reporter of decisions, 1994-2001. Mem. ALA, Spl. Librs. Assn., Am. Assn. Law Librs. (chmn. state, ct. and county spl. interest section 1995-96, chair legal info. svcs. to pub. spl. interest sect. 2001—). Office: Wash State Law Libr PO Box 40751 Temple of Justice Olympia WA 98504-0751 E-mail: debby.norwood@courts.wa.gov

NOSLER, PETER COLE, construction company executive; b. Portland, Oreg., May 7, 1940; s. Lyle and Elizabeth (Lewis) N.; m. Kay Hanson, Apr. 25, 1971; 1 child, Alexander. BS in Physics and Math., Walla Walla Coll., 1962; postgrad., U. Wash., 1962-63, U. Calif., Berkeley, 1965-70. Physicist GE, Richland, Wash., 1963-65; pvt. practice Portland, 1970-72; project mgr. Stolte Constrn., San Leandro, Calif., 1972-75; v.p. ops. Rudolph & Sletten, Foster City, 1975-90; pres. DPR Constrn. Inc., Redwood City, 1990—, CEO. Lectr. Stanford U., Palo Alto, Calif., 1988—. Recipient Young Constrn. Profl. of Yr. award Jour. Bldg. Design and Constrn., 1978. Mem. Soc. Model Exptl. Engring. Avocation: model engineering and construction, history. Office: DPR Constrn Inc 1450 Veterans Blvd Redwood City CA 94063-2612

NOTARI, PAUL CELESTIN, communications executive; b. Chgo., Sept. 8, 1926; s. Peter and Mae Rose (Luvisi) N.; m. Marlene Fineman, Feb. 21, 1969; children: Cathy Notari Davidson, Kenneth, Sharon Notari Christian, Mindy Nielsen, Debbie McGrath. BS in Physics, DePaul U., 1952; MS in Comml. Sci., Rollins Coll., 1968. Mgr. publs. and tng. Motorola Inc., Chgo., 1952-65; supr., publs. engr. Martin Co., Orlando, Fla., 1966-67; dir. comm. Bus. Equipment Mfrs. Assn., N.Y.C., 1967-70; dir. publs., pub. jour. Am. Water Works Assn., Denver, 1971-79; mgr. tech. info. Solar Energy Research Inst., Denver, 1979-91; pres. SciTech Comm., Inc., Denver, 1992—. Lectr. bus. communications Northwestern U. Served with USNR, 1944-46. Mem. Assn. Computer Programmers and Analysts (founding pres. 1970-73), Soc. Tech. Writers and Pubs. (chmn. chpt. 1965-66), Am. Solar Energy Soc. (nat. chmn. 1990-91). Office: SciTech Comm Inc 1000 S Monaco Pky Ste 77 Denver CO 80224-1603 E-mail: paulnotari@cs.com

NOTTINGHAM, EDWARD WILLIS, JR. federal judge; b. Denver, Jan. 9, 1948; s. Edward Willis and Willie Newton (Gullett) N.; m. Cheryl Ann Card, June 6, 1970 (div. Feb. 1981); children: Amelia Charlene, Edward Willis III; m. Janis Ellen Chapman, Aug. 18, 1984 (div. Dec. 1998); 1 child, Spencer Chapman. AB, Cornell U., 1969; JD, U. Colo., 1972. Bar: Colo. 1972, U.S. Dist. Ct. Colo. 1972, U.S. Ct. Appeals (10th cir.) 1973. Law clk. to presiding judge U.S. Dist. Ct. Colo., Denver, 1972-73; assoc. Sherman & Howard, Denver, 1973-76, 78-80, ptnr., 1980-87, Beckner & Nottingham, Grand Junction, Colo., 1987-89; asst. U.S. atty. U.S. Dept. Justice, Denver, 1976-78; U.S. dist. judge Dist. of Colo., Denver, 1989—. Mem. Jud. Conf. of the U.S. Com. on Automation and Tech., 1994-2000, chmn., 1997-2000. Bd. dirs. Beaver Creek Met. Dist., Avon, Colo., 1980-88, Justice Info. Ctr., Denver, 1985-87, 21st Jud. Dist. Victim Compensation Fund, Grand Junction, Colo., 1987-89. Mem. ABA, Colo. Bar Assn. (chmn. criminal law sect. 1983-85, chmn. ethics com. 1988-89), Order of Coif, Denver Athletic Club, Delta Sigma Rho, Tau Kappa Alpha. Episcopalian. Office: US Dist Ct 1929 Stout St Denver CO 80294-1929 E-mail: Edward_W._Nottingham@cod.uscourts.gov

NOVAK, JAMES F. physician; b. Portland, May 5, 1944; s. John Martin and Mary Ruth Novak; m. Marilynn L. Grosso, July 10, 1971; children: Vincent, Mark. BS, U. San Francisco, 1966; MD, Oreg. Health Science U., Portland, 1970. Diplomate Am. Bd. Family Practice; cert. Md. Intern Hennepin County Gen. Hosp., Mpls., 1970-71; physician emergency room Merle West Med. Ctr., Klamath Falls, Oreg., 1971-72; physician and ptnr. Klamath (Oreg.) Med. Clinic, 1972—; clin. instr. Cascade East Family Practice Residency, Klamath Falls, 1994—. Chief of staff Merle West Meml. Ctr., Klamath Falls, 1978-79; pres. Oreg. Acad. Family Practice, 1997-98; past pres., bd. dirs. Klamath Youth Devel. Ctr., Klamath Falls, 1980—. Pres. Klamath County Rotary Club, 1995-96. Fellow Am. Acad. Family Practice; mem. AMA, Oreg. Med. Assn., Klamath County Med. Soc. (pres.). Roman Catholic. Avocations: sailing, fishing, skiing, wine making. Office: Klamath Med Clinic 1905 Main St Klamath Falls OR 97601-2649

NOVAK, TERRY LEE, public administration educator; b. Chamberlain, S.D., Sept. 1, 1940; s. Warren F. and Elaine M. N.; m. Barbara Hosea, Aug. 29, 1981; 1 child, David. B.Sc., S.D. State U., 1962; postgrad. (Rotary fellow), U. Paris, 1962-63; M.P.A., Colo. U., 1965, Ph.D., 1970. Asst. city mgr. City of Anchorage, 1966-68; city mgr. City of Hopkins, Minn., 1968-74, City of Columbia, Mo., 1974-78, City of Spokane, Wash., 1978-91; v.p. bus. and fin. Ea. Wash. U., Cheney, 1991-92, prof. public adminstrn., 1992—, dir. grad. program pub. administrn., 1994-95; dir. Spokane Joint Ctr. for Higher Edn., 1995-98; bus. mgr. Riverpoint campus Wash. State U., 1998-99; prof pub. adminstrn. Eastern Wash. U., 1999—. Asst. adj. prof. U. Mo., Columbia, 1975, 77; adj. instr. Gonzaga U., Spokane, 1986-88; mem. nat. adv. coun. on environ. policy and tech. EPA. Author: Special Assessment Financing in American Cities, 1970; contbr. articles to profl. jours. Mem. ASPA, Internat. Pers. Mgmt. Assn., Internat. City Mgrs. Assn. (Acad. Profl. Devel.). Episcopalian. Office: 668 N Riverpoint Blvd Spokane WA 99202-1677 E-mail: tnovak@terynovak.net

NOVINS, DOUGLAS K. psychiatrist, educator; Prof. psychiatry divsn. child and adolescent psychiatry U. Colo., Denver. Recipient Presdl. Scholar award Am. Acad. Child and Adolescent Psychiatry, 1993. Office: U CO Divsn Child & Adolescent Psychiatry Health Scis Ctr PO Box C-259 42 Denver CO 80262-0001

NOWICK, JAMES S. chemistry educator; AB, Columbia U., 1985; PhD, MIT, 1990. Postdoc. fellow Mass. Inst. Tech., Cambridge, 1990-91; prof. U. Calif., Irvine, 1991. Contbr. articles to profl. jours. includingJ. Am. Chem. Soc., J. Organic Chem. Recipient Nat. Sci. Found. fellowship, Am. Chem. Soc. Division of Organic Chemistry grad. fellowship, Camille and Henry Dreyfus Found. Disting. New Faculty award 1991, Am. Cancer Soc. Jr. Faculty Rsch. award 1992, Nat. Sci. Found. Young Investigator award 1992, Arnold and Mabel Beckman Found. Young Investigator award 1994, Camille Dreyfus Tchr.-Scholar award 1996, Alfred P. Sloan rsch. fellowship 1997, Arthur C. Cope Scholar award 1998. Office: U Calif Irvine Dept Chemistry 535B Psi Irvine CA 92697-0001

NOWINSKI, PETER A. federal judge; b. 1943; BA, San Jose State U., 1966; JD, U. Calif., San Francisco, 1969. Ptnr. Wilke, Fleury, Hoffelt, Gould & Birney; chief assoc. dep. atty. gen.; 1st asst., U.S. atty. ea. dist. U.S. Dist. Ct. Calif.; dir. torts br. civil divsn. Dept. Justice, Washington; apptd. magistrate judge ea. dist. U.S. Dist. Ct. Calif., 1991. Office: 5074 US Courthouse 650 Capitol Mall Sacramento CA 95814-4708

NOWLAN, GODFREY S. geologist; BA in Geology with honors, Trinity Coll., Dublin, Ireland, 1971; MSc in Geology, Meml. U. Newfoundland, 1973; PhD in Biology, U. Waterloo, 1976. Postdoctoral fellow NSERC, 1976-77; rsch. micropaleontologist Geol. Survey Can., Ottawa, 1977-85, head eastern paleontology sect., 1985-88, chief paleontologist, 1988-92, sr. rsch. scientist, 1992—. Adj. prof. U. Ottawa, 1984-88, U. Calgary, 1988-91. Editor GEOLOG, 1982-85; asst. editor Geosci. Can., 1983-98; contbr. over 85 publs. to sci. jours. Recipient Bancroft award Royal Soc. Can., 1992, McNeil medal Royal Soc. Can., 1996. Mem. Geol. Assn. Can. (chmn. paleontology divsn. 1980-81, mem. exec. com., chair publs. com. 1985-88, pres. 1997-98, E.R.W. Neale medal 1995), Paleontol. Soc. (Golden Trilobite award 1993), Calgary Sci. Network (co-founder, pres. 1988—), Sigma Xi. Achievements include research in Lower Paleozoic biostratigraphy, paleontology and regional geology. Office: Geol Survey Can 3303 33rd St NW Calgary AB Canada T2L 2A7 E-mail: gnowlan@nrcan.gc.ca

NOYES, FRANCIE, state official; BA, U. Mass.; M in Creative Writing and Lit., U. Wyo. Bus. reporter Ariz. Rep., Ariz. Bus. Gazette, Phoenix Bus. Jour.; film critic City Life, Phoenix, 1985-86; features editor, columnist, movie critic Progress, 1988-92; polit. reporter Scottsdale Progress, Ariz. Daily Star, Tribune, 1992-97; press sec. Gov. Jane Dee Hull, Phoenix, 1997—. Panelist Horizon, Sta. KAET-TV. Recipient Don Schellic award Ariz. Press Club, 1991. Office: 1700 W Washington St Phoenix AZ 85007-2812 Fax: 602-542-7602

NOYES, H(ENRY) PIERRE, physicist; b. Paris, Dec. 10, 1923; s. William Albert and Katharine Haworth (Macy) N.; m. Mary Wilson, Dec. 20, 1947; children— David Brian, Alan Guinn, Katharine Hope. AB magna cum laude, Harvard U., 1943; Ph.D., U. Calif., Berkeley, 1950. Physicist MIT, 1943-44, U. Calif., Berkeley, 1949-50; Fulbright fellow U. Birmingham, Eng., 1950-51; asst. prof. U. Rochester, N.Y., 1951-55; group leader Lawrence Livermore Lab., 1955-62; Leverhulme lectr. U. Liverpool, Eng., 1957-58; adminstrv. head theory sect. Stanford Linear Accelerator Center, 1962-69; asso. prof. Stanford U., 1962-67, prof., 1967-2000, prof. emeritus, 2000—. Vis. scholar Center Advanced Study Behavioral Scis., Stanford, 1968-69; cons. in field. Author papers in field. Chmn. Com. for Direct Attack on Legality of Vietnam War, 1969-72; mem. steering com. Faculty Political Action Group, Stanford U., 1970-72; mem. policy com. U.S. People's Com. on Iran, 1977-79. Served with USNR, 1944-46. Fellow NSF, 1962; Fellow Nat. Humanities Faculty, 1970; recipient Alexander von Humboldt U.S. Sr. Scientist award, 1979. Mem. Alternative Natural Philosophy Assn. (pres. 1979-87, 1st alternative natural philosopher award 1989), Am. Phys. Soc., AAAS, Sigma Xi. E-mail: noyes@slac.stanford.edu

NOYES, RICHARD HALL, bookseller; b. Evanston, Ill., Feb. 12, 1930; s. George Frederick and Dorothy (Hall) N.; m. Judith Claire Mitchell, Oct. 10, 1953; children— Catherine, Stephanie, Matthew. B.A., Wesleyan U., 1952. Tng. program, elementary-high sch. salesman Rand McNally & Co., Colo., Utah, Idaho, Wyo., 1955-59; founder, owner, mgr. The Chinook Bookshop, Colorado Springs, Colo., 1959—. Contbr. to A Manual on Bookselling, 1974, The Business of Book Publishing, 1984; contbr. articles to newspapers and trade jours. Co-chmn. Colo. Media Coalition, 1974—; bd. dirs. Colorado Springs Fine Arts Ctr., 1977-81, Citizens Goals for Colorado Springs, 1976-88; trustee Fountain Valley Sch., 1979-81; vice chmn. Colorado Springs Charter Rev. Commn., 1991-92; mem. adv. com. U. Colo., Colorado Springs, 1997—, Downtown Partnership, 1998—. Served with AUS, 1952-54. Recipient Intellectual Freedom award Mountain Plains Librs. Assn., 1977, Disting. Svc. award U. Colo., 1980, Recognition award Pikes Peak Arts Coun., 1989, Charles S. Haslam award, 1990), Entrepreneur of Yr. award U. Colo., 1992, Gordon Saull award for outstanding bookseller Mountains and Plains Booksellers Assn., 1996. Mem. Am. Booksellers Assn. (pres., dir.) Home: 1601 Constellation Dr Colorado Springs CO 80906-1609 Office: The Chinook Bookshop Inc 210 N Tejon St Colorado Springs CO 80903-1385

NUCKOLLS, JOHN HOPKINS, physicist, researcher; b. Chgo., Nov. 17, 1930; s. Asa Hopkins and Helen (Gates) N.; m. Ruth Munsterman, Apr. 21, 1952 (div. 1983); children: Helen Marie, Robert David; m. Amelia Aphrodite Liaskas, July 29, 1983 B.S., Wheaton Coll., 1953; M.A., Columbia U., 1955; D.Sc. (hon), Fla. Inst. Tech., 1977. Physicist U. Calif., Lawrence Livermore Nat. Lab., 1955—, assoc. leader thermonuclear design div., 1965-80, assoc. leader laser fusion program, 1975-83, div. leader, 1980-83, assoc. dir. physics, 1983-88, dir., 1988-94, assoc. dir. at large, 1994-97, dir. emeritus, 1997—. Mem. U.S. Strategic Command Strategic adv. group; tech. adv. bd. Network Physics, Inc.; cons. def. sci. bd. Dept. Def. Recipient E.O. Lawrence award Pres. and AEC, 1969, Fusion Leadership award, 1983, Edward Teller medal Internat. Workshop Laser Interaction and Related Plasma Phenomena, 1991, Resolution of Appreciation, U. Calif. Regents, 1994, Sec. of Def. Outstanding Pub. Svc. medal, 1996, Disting. Assoc. award U.S. Dept. Energy, 1996, Career Achievement award Fusion Power Assocs., 1996. Fellow AAAS, Am. Phys. Soc. (J.C. Maxwell prize 1981); mem. NAE. Office: Lawrence Livermore Nat Lab PO Box 808 Livermore CA 94551-0808

NUFFER, DAVID O. federal judge; b. 1952; BA, JD, Brigham Young U. Magistrate judge U.S. Dist. Ct. Utah, St. George. Office: 192 E 200 N Fl 3 Saint George UT 84770-2866

NUGENT, CHARLES ARTER, internist, educator; b. Denver, Nov. 18, 1924; s. Charles Arter and Florence (Cohn) N.; m. Margaret Flint, Aug. 30, 1950; children— Stephen, Sara, Daniel (dec.). Student, U. Chgo., 1941-43, Ill. Inst. Tech., 1943, U. Minn., 1944, U. S.D., 1945-46; M.D., Yale U., 1951. Intern, asst. resident New Haven Hosp., 1951-53; resident Salt Lake County Gen. Hosp., Salt Lake City, 1954-56; mem. faculty U. Utah Coll. Medicine, 1956-67, assoc. prof. medicine, 1965-67; prof. dept. internal medicine U. Hawaii Med. Sch., 1967-70; prof. sect. endocrinology dept. internal medicine U. Ariz. Coll. Medicine, Tucson, 1970-98, prof. emeritus, 1998—. Contbr. articles to profl. jours. Served with U.S. Army, 1943-46, 53. James Hudson Brown Meml. fellow, 1949-50 Mem. AAUP, Endocrine Soc., Western Assn. Physicians, Physicians Forum, Am. Soc. Clinical Investigation. Home: 3242 E 5th St Tucson AZ 85716-4902 Office: PO Box 245021 1501 N Campbell Ave Tucson AZ 85724-0001 E-mail: nugent@u.arizona.edu

NUGENT, ROBERT J., JR. fast food company executive; b. 1942; BBA, U. Cin., 1964. Loan officer Citizens Savs., 1964-67; asst. v.p. Gem City Savs., 1967-69; v.p. Ponderosa System Inc., 1969-78, Ky. Fried Chicken, 1978-79, Foodmaker Inc., San Diego, from 1979, exec. v.p. ops., mktg., 1985-95, CEO, pres., 1995-99, Jack in the Box, Inc., San Diego, 1999—. Office: Jack in the Box Inc 9330 Balboa Ave San Diego CA 92123-1598

NULL, PAUL BRYAN, minister; b. Oakland, Calif., May 7, 1944; s. Carleton Elliot and Dorothy Irene (Bryan) N.; m. Renee Yvonne Howell, Aug. 23, 1969; children: Bryan Joseph, Kara Renee. BS, Western Bapt. Coll., 1973; MDiv, Western Conservative Bapt. Sem., 1979; DMin, Trinity Theol. Sem., 1994. Ordained to ministry Bapt. Ch., 1982. Asst. pastor Bethel Bapt. Ch., Aumsville, Oreg., 1972-74, sr. pastor, 1974-87, The Calvary Congregation, Stockton, Calif., 1987-94; pastor Sierra Comty. Ch., South Lake Tahoe, 1994-98; exec. pastor Dayspring Fellowship, Salem, Oreg., 1998—. Trustee Conservative Bapt. Assn. of Oreg., 1982-85, mem. Ch. extension com., 1975-85. Radio show commentator Food for Thought, 1987. Panel mem. Presdl. Anti-Drug Campaign, 1984; vice chmn. bd. Western Bapt. Coll., Salem, Oreg., 1998—. Served with U.S. Army, 1965-67. Named Outstanding Young Man Am., 1979. Mem. Conservative Bapt. Assn. of Am., No. Calif. Conservative Bapt. Assn. (pres. 1992-93), Delta Epsilon Chi. Avocations: weight training, aerobics, writing, hiking, cross-country skiing. Home: 575 Belmont St NE Salem OR 97301-1255 Office: Dayspring Fellowship 1755 Lockhaven Dr NE Keizer OR 97303-2071 E-mail: paul_null@vaitoo.com

NUNN, ROBERT WARNE, lawyer; b. Salem, Oreg., Sept. 20, 1950; s. Warne Harry and Delores Nunn; m. Kandis Brewer; 1 child, Hayley Elisabeth. Student, U. Vienna, Austria, 1971; BS, Willamette U., 1972; MS in Acctg., Northeastern U., Boston, 1973, MBA, 2000; JD, U. Oreg., 1976. Bar: Oreg 1976, U.S. Dist. Ct. Oreg. 1977, U.S. Ct. Appeals (9th cir.) 1977, U.S. Supreme Ct. 1982, Wash. 1986. Ptnr. Schwabe, Williamson &, Wyatt, Portland, Oreg., 1976-92; ptnr., chmn. corp. dept. Preston, Gates & Ellis, Portland, 1992-96; founder, mng. ptnr. Nunn Motschenbacher & Blattner LLP, Portland, 1996—. Dir. Oreg. State Bar Profl. Liability Fund, 1999—. Mem. exec. com. Am. Leadership Forum, 1988-94, sr. fellow, 1988—; bd. mgrs. Multnomah Metro Br. YMCA, Portland, 1983-86, chmn., 1984-85; pres. Oreg. divsn. Am. Cancer Soc., Portland, 1986-87, bd. dirs., 1982-88; trustee Marylhurst Coll., Oreg., 1985-91, Willamette U., 1991—; trustee World Affairs Coun. Oreg., 1991-97, pres., 1995-96; bd. dirs. United Way of Columbia-Willamette, Portland, 1984-87. Am. Leadership fellow, 1987; named Order of Red Sword Am. Cancer Soc., 1985. Mem. ABA, Oreg. Bar Assn. (past chmn. CPA joint com., past chmn. legal assts. and legal investigators com., cert. subcom., fee arbitration panel), Profl. Liability Fund (dir. 1999—), Univ. Club, Multhnomah Athletic Club (Portland). Republican. Lutheran. Avocations: computers, skiing, sailing. Office: Nunn Motschenbacher & Blattner LLP 117 SW Taylor St Ste 200 Portland OR 97204-3029

NUSBAUM, BENNETT, printing/copying company executive; CFO Kinko's Inc., Ventura, Calif. Office: Kinko's Inc 255 W Stanely Ave Ventura CA 93002

NUSSBAUM, LUTHER JAMES, computer company executive; b. Decatur, Ind., Jan. 13, 1947; s. Leo Lester and Janet Nell (Gladfelter) N.; m. Ginger Mae McCown, Aug. 24, 1968; children: Kari, Kris. BA, Rhodes Coll., 1968; MBA, Stanford U., 1972. Dir. compensation Cummins Engine Co., Columbus, Ind., 1974-75, v.p. distbn. cos., 1977-79, v.p. parts bus., 1979-82, v.p. strategic planning, 1982-83, gen. mgr. Mex. region Mexico City, 1975-77; v.p. field ops. Businessland, San Jose, Calif., 1983-84, v.p. ops., 1984-85, sr. v.p. mktg., ops., 1985-86; pres., chief operating officer Ashton-Tate, Torrance, 1986—. Bd. dirs. Interbase, Bedford. Mem. Dem. Nat. Fin. Council, 1986—, Dem. Nat. Bus. Council, 1987—. Mem. Young Pres's. Orgn., Phi Beta Kappa. Avocations: tennis, running. Home: 5818 E Bay Shore Walk Long Beach CA 90803-4463 Office: FIRST CONSULTING GROUP, INC 111 W OCEAN BLVD., Ste 1000 Long Beach CA 90802

NUTTALL, RICHARD NORRIS, management consultant, physician; b. Hamilton, Ont., Can., Feb. 7, 1940; s. James William and Margaret Gay (Walsh) N.; m. Ethel Jane Pickering, July 9, 1977; children: Andrew Richard, John Patrick. BSA, U. Toronto, 1961; MPA, Harvard U., 1964; MB, BS, U. London, Eng., 1974. Cert. Coll. Family Physicians Can., Mgmt. Cons. Zone dir. Health and Welfare Can., Prince Rupert, B.C., 1977-79, regional dir. Edmonton, Alta., 1980-82; pres. Rutland Consulting Group, Ltd., Vancouver, B.C., 1982-87, Richmond Assocs. Internat., Vancouver, 1988-90; med. health officer Govt. N.W. Ters., Yellowknife, B.C., 1990-93, Regina Health Dist., 1993-97; pres. Anjohn Med. Svcs., Inc., Victoria, 1997—. Staff physician Royal Jubilee Hosp., Victoria Gen. Hosp. Fellow Am. Coll. Preventive Medicine, Am. Coll. Healthcare Execs., Can. Coll. Health Svc. Execs.; mem. Can. Pub. Health Assn. (bd. dirs. 1991-93). Office: 1494 Fairfield Rd Victoria BC Canada V8S 1E8

NUTTING, PAUL ALBERT, medical educator, medical science administrator; b. Aug. 24, 1944; m. Kaia M. Gallagher; children: Paul James, Kaia Elise. AB in Psychology, Cornell U., 1966; MD, U. Kans., 1970; MSPH, U. Colo., 1988. Diplomate Am. Bd. Family Practice, Am. Bd. Preventive Medicine. Intern in pediat. U. Pitts., 1970-71; resident in preventive medicine U. Ariz., 1973-75; clin. dir. Santa Rosa (Ariz.) Clinic Indian Health Svc., 1971-72, maternal and child health officer Sells (Ariz.) Svc. Unit, 1972-73, med. rsch. office Office of R&D, 1973-77, assoc. dir. rsch. Office of R&D, 1977-83; sr. scholar-in-residence Inst. Medicine-NAS, Washington, 1983-84; dir. Office of Primary Care Studies Health Resources and Svc U.S. Dept. Health and Human Svcs., Rockville, Md., 1984-86; resident in family medicine Mercy Med. Ctr., Denver, 1986-88; dir. rsch. Indian Health Svc., Tucson, 1989-90; dir. divsn. primary care and dep. dir. Ctr. for Gen. Health Svcs. Rsch., DHHS, Rockville, 1990-93; dir. Ambulatory Sentinel Practice Network, Denver, 1993—; prof. family medicine dept. family medicine U. Colo. Health Scis. Ctr., 1993—; dir. rsch. Ctr. for Rsch. Strategy, Denver, 1999—. Rsch. assoc. prof. dept. family and cmty. medicine U. Ariz., 1981-87, 88-90; clin. assoc. prof. dept. cmty. and family medicine Georgetown U. Sch. Medicine, 1983-86; mem. subcom. on cardiovascular disease Sec.'s Task Force on Black and Minority Health, 1984-85; mem. interagy. com. on infant mortality USHPS, 1990-93, chair rsch. sub-com., clin. preventive svcs. steering com., 1991-93, nat. steering com. primary care-substance abuse linkage initiative, 1991-93; chairperson Workshop on Early Detection of Prostate Cancer, Nat. Cancer Inst., Bethesda, Md., 1993; cons. in field. Author: (with L.A. Green) From Research to Policy to Practice: Closing the Loop in Clinical Policy Development in Primary Care, 1994; editor: Community-Oriented Primary Care: From Principle to Practice, 1987, co-editor: Primary Care Research: Theory and Methods, 1991; mem. editl. bd. Jour. Cmty. Health, 1981-84, Jour. Family Practice, 1990—, Am. Family Physician, 1990—, Jour. Rural Health, 1994—; contbr. chpts. to books and articles to profl. jours. Capt. USPHS, 1982. Recipient Cert. appreciation Nat. Indian Health Bd., 1982, Modern Medicine award for disting. achievement, 1993. Mem. APHA (sect. in med. care, epidemiology, internat. health), Inst. Medicine-NAS, Am. Acad. Family Physicians (liaison mem. com. on rsch. 1993—), Am. Acad. Pediat. (mem. steering com. pediat. rsch. in office settings 1993—), N.Am. Primary Care Rsch. Group (bd. dirs. 1994—, chair com. on bldg. capacity for rsch. in family practice 1994—), Soc. for Epidemiologic Rsch., Soc. Tchrs. Family Medicine. Office: Ctr Rsch Strategy 225 E 16th Ave Ste 1150 Denver CO 80203-1694

NUTZLE, FUTZIE (BRUCE JOHN KLEINSMITH), artist, writer, cartoonist; b. Lakewood, Ohio, Feb. 21, 1942; s. Adrian Ralph and Naomi Irene (Rupert) Kleinsmith; children: Adrian David, Arielle Justine and Tess Alexandra (twins); m. Halina Renatta Kleinsmith. Author: Modern Loafer, Thames and Hudson, 1981, (authobiography) Futzie Nutzle, 1983, Earthquake, 1989, Run the World: 50 Cents Chronicle Books, 1991; illustrator: The Armies Encamped Beyond Unfinished Avenues (Morton Marcus), 1977, Box of Nothing, 1982, The Duke of Chemical Birds (Howard McCord), 1989, Book of Solutions, 1990, Fact and Friction, 1990, Managing for the 90s, 1992, Soundbites for Success, 1994; feature cartoonist Rolling Stone, N.Y.C., 1975-80, The Japan Times, Tokyo and L.A., 1986—, The Prague Post, Czechoslovakia, 1991-92; contbr. exhbns. include Inaugural, 1966, Cupola, 1967, Rolling Renaissance, San Francisco, 1968, 100 Acres, O.K. Harris 1971, N.Y.C., San Francisco Mus. Art, 1972, Indpls. and Cin. Mus. Art, 1975, Leica, L.A., 1978, Santa Barbara Mus. Annex, Calif., 1978, Swope, Santa Monica, West Beach Cafe, Venice, Calif., 1985, Les Oranges, Santa Monica, Correspondence Sch., 1970-78, 1st Ann. Art-A-Thon, N.Y.C., 1985, Am. Epiphany with Phillip Hefferton, 1986, Polit. Cartoon Show, Braunstein, San Francisco, Komsomolskaya Pravda, 1988, retrospective Eloise Packard Smith, 1990, exemplary contemporary, Cowell, U. Calif. Santa Cruz, 1991, Silicon Graphics Inc., Computer Graphics for NAB, Las Vegas, 1993, Prague Eco-Fair, 1991; represented in pvt. and pub. collections (complete archives) Spl. Collections, McHenry Libr., U. Calif., Santa Cruz, Mus. Modern Art, N.Y.C., San Francisco Mus. Modern Art, Oakland Mus., San Francisco Mus. Cartoon Art, Whitney Mus. Am. Art, N.Y.C. regular contbr. The Japan Times. Ltd., Tokyo. Address: PO Box 325 Aromas CA 95004-0325 also: Fools Gold 34A Polk St San Juan Bautista CA 95045

NUXOLL, CARLA, federal official; m. Jim Braukmann. Degree in polit. sci. and history, Gonzaga U. English tchr. Mead H.S., Spokane, 1972; pres. Wash. Edn. Assn., 1989-93; apptd. sec.'s regional rep. U.S. Dept. Edn. Region X, Seattle, 1994—. Avocations: avid fly fisherwoman, bridge player, reader of detective novels. Office: US Dept Edn Region X Jackson Fed Bldg 915 2nd Ave Seattle WA 98174-1009

NYCUM, SUSAN HUBBELL, lawyer; BA, Ohio Wesleyan U., 1956; JD, Duquesne U., 1960; postgrad., Stanford U. Bar: Pa. 1962, U.S. Supreme Ct. 1967, Calif. 1974. Sole practice law, Pitts., 1962-65; designer, adminstr. legal rsch. sys. U. Pitts., Aspen Sys. Corp., Pitts., 1965-68; mgr. ops. Computer Ctr., Carnegie Mellon U., Pitts., 1968-69; dir. computer facility Computer Ctr., Stanford U., Calif., 1969-72, Stanford Law and Computer fellow, 1972-73; cons. in computers and law, 1973-74; sr. assoc. MacLeod, Fuller, Muir & Godwin, Los Altos, Los Angeles and London, 1974-75; ptnr. Chickering & Gregory, San Francisco, 1975-80; ptnr.-in-charge high tech. group Gaston Snow & Ely Bartlett, Boston, NYC, Phoenix, San Francisco, Calif., 1980-86; mng. ptnr. Palo Alto office Kadison, Pfaelzer, Woodard, Quinn & Rossi, Los Angeles, Washington, Newport Beach, Palo Alto, 1986-87; sr. ptnr., chmn. U.S. intellectual property/info. tech. practice group Baker & McKenzie, Palo Alto, 1987—, mem. U.S. leadership team 1987-97, mem. Asia Pacific regional coun., 1995—. Trustee EDUCOM, 1978-81; mem. adv. com. for high tech. Ariz. State U. Law Sch., Santa Clara U. Law Sch., Stanford Law Sch., U. So. Calif. Law Ctr., law sch. Harvard U., U. Calif.; U.S. State Dept. del. OECD Conf. on Nat.

Vulnerabilities, Spain, 1981; invited speaker Telecom, Geneva, 1983; lectr. N.Y. Law Jour., 1975—, Law & Bus., 1975—, Practicing Law Inst., 1975—; chmn. Office of Tech. Assessment Task Force on Nat. Info. Sys., 1979-80. Author:(with Bigelow) Your Computer and the Law, 1975, (with Bosworth) Legal Protection for Software, 1985, (with Collins and Gilbert) Women Leading, 1987; contbr. monographs, articles to profl. publs. Mem. Town of Portola Valley Open Space Acquisition Com., Calif., 1977; mem. Jr. League of Palo Alto, chmn. evening div., 1975-76 NSF and Dept. Justice grantee for studies on computer abuse, 1972— Fellow Assn. Computer Machinery (mem. at large of coun. 1976-80, nat. lectr. 1977—, chmn. standing com. on legal issues 1975—, mem. blue ribbon com. on rationalization of internat. propr. rights protection on info. processing devel. in the '90s 1990—), Coll. Law Practice Mgmt.; mem. ABA (chmn. sect. on sci. and tech. 1979-80), Internat. Bar Assn. (U.S. mem. computer com. of corps. sect.), Computer Law Assn. (v.p. 1983-85, pres. 1986—, bd. dirs. 1975—), Calif. State Bar Assn. (founder first chmn. econs. of law sect., vice chmn. law and computers com.), Nat. Conf. Lawyers and Scientists (rep. ABA), Strategic Forum on Intellectual Property Issues in Software of NAS, Internat. Coun. for Computer Comm. (gov. 1998). Home: 35 Granada Ct Portola Vally CA 94028-7736 Office: Baker & McKenzie PO Box 60309 Palo Alto CA 94306-0309

NYE, ERIC WILLIAM, English language and literature educator; b. Omaha, July 31, 1952; s. William Frank and Mary Roberta (Lueder) N.; m. Carol Denison Frost, Dec. 21, 1980; children: Charles William, Ellen Mary. BA, St. Olaf Coll., 1974; MA, U. Chgo., 1976, PhD, 1983; postgrad., Queens' Coll., Cambridge, England, 1979-82. Tutor in coll. writing com. U. Chgo., 1976-79, tchg. intern, 1978; tutor Am. lit. Cambridge (Eng.) U., 1979-82; asst. prof. English, Religious Studies U. Wyo., Laramie, 1983-89, assoc. prof., 1989—. V.p., bd. dirs. Plainview Tel. Co., Nebr.; hon. vis. fellow U. Edinburgh (Scotland) Inst. for Advanced Studies in the Humanities, 1987; guest lectr. NEH summer Inst., Laramie, Wyo., 1985, Carlyle Soc. of Edinburgh, 1987, Wordsworth summer Conf., Grasmere, Eng., 1988, cons. NEH. Contbr. articles and reviews to profl. jours. Mem. Am. Friends of Cambridge U., Friends of Cambridge U. Libr. (life), Gen. Soc. Mayflower Descendants; elected mem. Wyo. Coun. for Humanities, 1992-96, mem. exec. com., 1993-94; mem. adv. bd. Wyo. Ctr. for the Book, 1995—; leader Boy Scouts Am. Named Nat. Merit Scholar St. Olaf Coll., 1970-74; recipient Amb. Fellowship, Rotary Found., 1979-80, grant Am. Coun. of Learned Socs., 1988, Disting. Alumnus award, Lincoln (Neb.) E. High Sch., 1986. Mem. MLA (del. assembly 1991-93), Bibliog. Soc. London, Assn. for Computers and the Humanities, Assn. for Lit. and Linguistic Computing, Assn. Literary Scholars and Critics, Coleridge Soc. (life), Friends of Dove Cottage (life), Jane Austen Soc. N.Am. (life), Charles Lamb Soc., Carlyle Soc. (life), Rsch. Soc. for Victorian Periodicals, Soc. for History of Authorship, Reading, and Pub., Wyo. State Hist. Soc. (life), The Victorians Inst., The Tennyson Soc. (life), Royal Oak Found., Penn Club (London), Queens' Coll. Club (Cambridge) Phi Beta Kappa (pres., v.p., sec. Wyo. chpt. 1988-98). Home: 1495 Apache Dr Laramie WY 82072-6966 Office: U Wyo Dept English PO Box 3353 Laramie WY 82071-3353

NYGREN, DAVID ROBERT, physicist, researcher; BA in Mathematics, Whitman Coll., 1960; PhD in Physics, U. Wash., 1967. Rsch. assoc. Nevis Labs. Columbia U., N.Y.C.; assoc. prof. Physics Columbia U., 1969; divsn. fellow Lawrence Berkeley (Calif.) Nat. Lab., 1973-75, sr. physicist, 1975—. Distinguished visiting scientist Jet Propulsion Lab., Pasadena, Calif.; exec. com. mem. Am. Physical Soc. Divsn. Particles and Fields. Recipient E.O. Lawrence award, W.H.K. Panofsky prize in Experimental Particle Physics 1998. Fellow Am. Physicl Soc. Office: Lawrence Berkeley Nat Lab U Calif Mailstop 50B 6208 One Cyclotron Rd Berkeley CA 94720

NYHAN, WILLIAM LEO, pediatrician, educator; b. Boston, Mar. 13, 1926; s. W. Leo and Mary N.; m. Christine Murphy, Nov. 20, 1948; children: Christopher, Abigail. Student, Harvard U., 1943-45; MD, Columbia U., 1949; MS, U. Ill., 1956, PhD, 1958; hon. doctorate, Tokushima U., Japan, 1981. Intern Yale U.-Grace-New Haven Hosp., 1949-50, resident, 1950-51, 53-55; asst. prof. pediatrics Johns Hopkins U., 1958-61, assoc. prof., 1961-63; prof. pediatrics, biochemistry U. Miami, 1963-69, chmn. dept. pediatrics, 1963-69; prof. U. Calif., San Diego, 1969—, chmn. dept. pediatrics, 1969-86. Mem. FDA adv. com. on Teratogenic Effects of Certain Drugs, 1964-70; mem. pediatric panel AMA Council on Drugs, 1964-70; mem. Nat. Adv. Child Health and Human Devel. Council, 1967-71; mem. research adv. com. Calif. Dept. Mental Hygiene, 1969-72; mem. med. and sci. adv. com. Leukemia Soc. Am., Inc., 1968-72; mem. basic adv. com. Nat. Found. March of Dimes, 1973-81, mem. Basil O'Connor Starter grants com., 1973-93; mem. clin. cancer program project rev. com. Nat. Cancer Inst., 1977-81; vis. prof. extraordinario U. del Salvador (Argentina), 1982 Author: (with E. Edelson) The Heredity Factor, Genes, Chromosomes and You, 1976,Genetic & Malformation Syndromes in Clinical Medicine, 1976, Abnormalities in Amino Acid Metabolism in Clinical Medicine, 1984, Diagnostic Recognition of Genetic Disease, 1987, (with P. Ozand) Atlas of Metabolic Disease, 1998; editor: Amino Acid Metabolism and Genetic Variation, 1967, Heritable Disorders of Amino Acid Metabolism, 1974; mem. editorial bd. Jour. Pediatrics, 1964-78, King Faisal Hosp. Med. Jour., 1981-85, Western Jour. Medicine, 1974-86, Annals of Saudi Medicine, 1985-87, mem. editorial com. Ann. Rev. Nutrition, 1982-86; mem. editorial staff Med. and Pediatric Oncology, 1975-83. Served with U.S. Navy, 1944-46; U.S. Army, 1951-53. Nat. Found. Infantile Paralysis fellow, 1955-58; recipient Commemorative medallion Columbia U. Coll. Physicians and Surgeons, 1967, Guthrie award Am. Assn. Mental Retardation, 1998, Pool of Bethesda award Bethesda Luth. Homes and Svcs., 1999. Fellow Am. Acad. Pediat. (Borden award 1980, Lifetime Achievement award 1999); mem. AAAS, Am. Fedn. Clin. Rsch., Am. Chem. Soc., Soc. Pediatric Rsch. (pres. 1970-71), Am. Assn. Cancer Rsch., Am. Soc. Pharmacology and Exptl. Therapeutics, Western Soc. Pediatric Rsch. (pres. 1976-77), N.Y. Acad. Sci., Am. Pediatric Soc., Am. Inst. Biol. Scis., Soc. Exptl. Biology and Medicine, Am. Soc. Clin. Investigation, Am. Soc. Human Genetics (dir. 1978-81), Am. Assn. Clin. Chemists, Am. Coll. Med. Genetics, Inst. Investigaciones Citologicas (Spain, corr.), Biochem. Soc., Société Française de Pediatrie (corr.), South African Human Genetics (hon.), Sigma Xi, Alpha Omega Alpha. Office: U Calif San Diego Dept Pediatrics # 0830 9500 Gilman Dr La Jolla CA 92093-0830

NYMAN, MICHAEL S. company executive; BA, U. So. Calif., 1986. Prin. Bragman, Nyman, Cafarelli, Inc., Beverly Hills, Calif., 1990—. Office: Bragman Nyman Cafarelli Inc 9171 Wilshire Blvd Ste 300 Beverly Hills CA 90210-5515

OAK, CLAIRE MORISSET, artist, educator; b. St. Georges, Quebec, Can., May 31, 1921; came to U.S., 1945; d. Louis and Bernadette (Coulombe) Morisset; m. Alan Ben Oak, July 2, 1947. Student, Ecole des Beaux Arts, 1938-42, Parsons Sch. Design, N.Y.C., 1945, Art Students League, 1945-46. Staff artist Henry Morgan & R. Simpson, Montreal, 1942-45; artist illustrator W.B. Golovin Advt. Agy., N.Y.C., 1947-49; freelance illustrator Arnold Constable & Advt. Agy., N.Y.C., 1948-50, Le Jardin des Modes, Paris, 1950-51, May & Co., L.A., 1956, Katten & Marengo Advt., Stockton, Calif., 1962-84; pvt. practice illustrator, designer San Joaquin Valley, 1984-92; art instr. San Joaquin Delta Coll., Stockton, 1973—. Owner Fashion Illustrator's Workshop, N.Y.C., 1953-54; instr. Bauder Coll., Sacramento, 1975-76; painting workshop leader Lodi Art Ctr., 1991—; watercolor workshop leader D'Pharr Painting Adventures, Virginia City, Nev., 1992; on-going watercolor workshop Galerie Iona, Stockton, Calif., 1993—. Named S.B. Anthony Woman of Achievement in the Arts, U. Pacific, 1982. Mem. Stockton Art League, Lodi Art Ctr., Ctrl. Calif. Art League, The League of Carmichael Artists, Delta Watercolor Soc. (bd. mem. 1988—). Avocations: outdoor painting, drawing from a model. Home: 2140 Waudman Ave Stockton CA 95209-1755

OAKLEY, CAROLYN LE, state legislator, small business owner; b. Portland, Oreg., June 28, 1942; d. George Thomas and Ruth Alveta Victoria (Engberg) Penketh; children: Christine, Michelle. BS in Edn., Oreg. State U., 1965. Educator Linn County (Oreg.) Schs., 1965-76; owner Linn County Tractor, 1965-90; mem. Oreg. Legis. Assembly, Salem, 1989—, asst. majority leader, 1993—, majority whip, 1994. Mem. exec. bd. Oreg. Retail Coun., 1987-90. Chmn. Linn County Rep. Ctrl. Com., 1982-84; chmn. bd. dirs. North Albany Svc. Dist., 1988-90; chair Salvation Army, Linn and Benton Counties, 1987—; vice chmn. bd. trustees Linn-Benton C.C. Found., 1987—; pres. Women for Agr., Linn and Benton Counties, 1984-86; mem. STRIDE Leadership Round Table, 1991—; state chair Am. Legis. Exch. Coun., 1991-96; nat. bd. dirs., 199-99, exec. com., 1995, 1st vice chair, 1998; mem. Edn. Commn. of the States, 1991—, com. policies and priorities, 1993—, steering com., 1998—, exec. com., 1998; mem. Leadership Coun. on Higher Edn., 1995—; mem. nat. policy bd. Danforth Found., 1995—; state dir., Women in Govt., 1996—; state dir., Nat. Order Women Legislators, 1993—; hon. mem. Linn-Benton Compact Bd., 1993—; active Linn County Criminal Justice Coun., 1994—. Named Woman of Yr. Albany chpt. Beta Sigma Phi, 1970. Mem. Nat Conf. State Legislators (chmn. edn. com. 1992—), Albany C. of C. (bd. dirs. 1986-93, 96—), Linn County Rep. women (legis. chmn. 1982-91). Republican. Methodist. Avocations: gardening, camping. Home: 3197 NW Crest Loop Albany OR 97321-9627 Office: Oreg Legis Assembly State Capital Salem OR 97310-0001

OAKS, DALLIN HARRIS, lawyer, church official; b. Provo, Utah, Aug. 12, 1932; s. Lloyd E. and Stella (Harris) O.; m. June Dixon, June 24, 1952 (dec. July 1998); children: Sharmon, Cheri Lyn, Lloyd D., Dallin D., TruAnn, Jenny June; m. Kristen McMain, Aug. 25, 2000. BA with high honors, Brigham Young U., 1954, LLD (hon.), 1980; JD cum laude, U. Chgo., 1957; LLD (hon.), Pepperdine U., 1982, So. Utah U., 1991. Bar: Ill. 1957, Utah 1971. Law clk. to Chief Justice Earl Warren U.S. Supreme Ct., 1957-58; with firm Kirkland, Ellis, Hodson, Chaffetz & Masters, Chgo., 1958-61; mem. faculty U. Chgo. Law Sch., 1961-71, assoc. dean and acting dean, 1962, prof., 1964-71, mem. vis. com., 1971-74; pres. Brigham Young U., Provo, Utah, 1971-80; also prof. law J. Reuben Clark Law Sch., 1974-80; justice Utah Supreme Ct., 1981-84; mem. Coun. of Twelve Apostles Ch. Jesus Christ of Latter Day Sts., 1984—. Legal counsel Bill of Rights com. Ill. Constl. Conv., 1970 Author: (with G.G. Bogert) Cases on Trusts, 1967, 78, (with W. Lehman) A Criminal Justice System and The Indigent, 1968, The Criminal Justice Act in the Federal District Courts, 1969, (with M. Hill) Carthage Conspiracy, 1975, Trust Doctrines in Church Controversies, 1984, Pure in Heart, 1988, The Lord's Way, 1991, His Holy Name, 1998; editor: The Wall Between Church and State, 1963. Mem. Wilson coun. Woodrow Wilson Internat. Ctr. for Scholars, 1973-80; trustee Intermountain Health Care Inc., 1975-80; mem. adv. com. Nat. Inst. Law Enforcement and Criminal Justice, 1974-76; bd. dirs. Notre Dame Ctr. for Constl. Studies, 1977-80, Rockford Inst., 1980-2000; bd. dirs. Pub. Broadcasting Svc., 1977-85, chmn., 1980-85; bd. dirs. Polynesian Cultural Ctr., 1987-96, chmn., 1988-96. Fellow Am. Bar Found. (exec. dir. 1970-71); mem. Am. Assn. Pres. Ind. Colls. and Univs. (pres. 1975-78, dir. 1971-78), Order of Coif. Mem. Ch. of Jesus Christ of Latter-day Saints (regional rep. 1974-80; past 1st counselor Chgo. South Stake). Office: Quorum of Twelve 47 E South Temple Salt Lake City UT 84150-9701

O'BARA, KENNETH J. physician; b. Detroit, Feb. 27, 1947; s. John Joseph and Catherine (Levens) O'Bara; m. Marianne Schwartz, July 29, 1972; children: Thomas, Mickel. BSE, U. Mich., Ann Arbor, 1969, MD, 1976. Diplomate Am. Bd. Emergency Medicine. Resident Truman Med. Ctr., Kansas City, Mo., 1976-79; mem. staff St. Joseph Mercy Hosp., Ann Arbor, 1979-80, Centralia (Wash.) Gen. Hosp., 1980-81, St. Helen's Hosp., Chehalis, Wash., 1980-81, Valley Med. Ctr., Renton, 1981—. ACLS affiliate faculty Am. Heart Assn., Seattle, 1982-86; co-dir. Assn. Emergency Physicians, Seattle, 1983-85. Fellow Am. Coll. Emergency Physicians, Wash. State Med. Soc., King County Med. Soc. Office: 8009 S 180th St Ste 103 Kent WA 98032-1042

OBERG, LARRY REYNOLD, librarian; b. Midvale, Idaho; s. Gustav Wilhelm and Esther Marie (Watkins) O.; m. Marilyn Ann Gow, Jan. 1, 1964 (div. 1985); 1 child, Marc Aurelien. AB in Anthropology, U. Calif., Berkeley, 1977, MLS, 1978. Reference librarian Stanford (Calif.) U., 1979-80, U. Calif., Berkeley, 1981-82, dir. libr. Lewis-Clark State Coll., Lewiston, Idaho, 1984-86; dir. library Albion (Mich.) Coll., 1986-92; univ. libr. Willamette U., Salem, Oreg., 1992—. Author: Human Services in Postrevolutionary Cuba, 1985 (named a Choice Outstanding Acad. Book, Choice Editors 1984-85); mem. adv. bd. Jour. Info. Ethics; contbr. numerous articles to profl. jours. Mem. Am. Library Assn. (chair coll. librs. sect. 1997-98), Oreg. Library Assn., Phi Beta Kappa. Democrat. Office: Willamette U Mark O Hatfield Libr 900 State St Salem OR 97301-3931

OBERLANDER, CORNELIA HAHN, landscape architect; b. Muelheim-Ruhr, Germany, June 20, 1924; arrived in U.S., 1939; d. Franz and Lotte Beate (Jastrow) H.; m. H. Peter Oberlander, Jan. 2, 1953; children: Judith A., Timothy A., Wendy E. BA, Smith Coll., 1944; B of Landscape Architecture, Harvard U., 1947; LLD (hon.), U. British Columbia, 1991. Guest prof. U. B.C. Dept. Landscape Architecture, 1992; lectr. for guided tour Renaissance Gardens of No. Italy, Smith Coll. Alumni Assn., 1988; mem. adv. com. on design Nat. Capital Commn., 1975-82; mem. adv. panel, co-founder Children's Play Resource Centre, Vancouver, 1978—; lectr. in field. Prin. works include C.K. Choi Bldg., Inst. Asian Rsch., U. B.C., 1992-96, New Pub. Library, 1992—, Thunderbird Housing, U. B.C., 1992—, Kwantlen Coll., 1991—, Cariboo Coll., 1991—, N.W. Territories Legis. Bldg., 1991—, UN Peacekeeping Meml., 1990—, Ritsumeikan U. B.C. Ho., 1990—, Ottawa City Hall, 1989—, Environ. Sci. Bd., Ward Environ. Garden, Trent U., 1989—, Nat. Gallery Can., 1983-88, Canadian Chancery, Washington D.C., 1983-89. Recipient medal Smith Coll., 1982, Regional Honor award and Nat. Merit award Christopher Phillips Landcape Architects, Inc., 1992, Allied Arts medal Royal Archtl. Inst. Can., 1995, Nat. Gallery of Can., Ottawa, Ontario, Can. Chancery Am. Assn. of Nurseymen, 1990, Grand award for L'Ambassade du Can., Landscape Contractors Assn., 1989, Can. Architect award of Excellence, Matsuzaki Wright Architects, Inc., 1989, Amenity award City of Vancouver for Robson Square, 1986, Citation award Can. Soc. of Architects for Chancery & Nat. Gallery, 1990. Fellow Am. Soc. Landscape Architects, Can. Soc. Landscape Architects; mem. Order of Can., Royal Can. Acad. Arts, Archtl. Inst. B.C. (hon.). Home: 1372 Acadia Rd Vancouver BC Canada V6T 1P6

O'BERRY, CARL GERALD, former career officer, electrical engineer; b. Lansing, Mich., Apr. 11, 1936; s. Gerald Ray and Edith Lenore (Watson) O'B.; m. Charlene Marice Bussche, June 21, 1958; children: Brian, Eileen, Kevin, Bradley, Kathleen. BSEE, N.Mex. State U., 1972; MS in Systems Mgmt., Air Force Inst. Tech., 1977. Commd. 2d lt. USAF, 1961, advanced through grades to lt. gen., 1993; comdr. 2019 Communications Squadron, Griffiss AFB, N.Y., 1974-76; project engr. Rome Air Devel. Ctr., Griffiss AFB, 1979-81; asst. dep. chief of staff requirements Air Force Systems Command, Andrews AFB, Md., 1982-84; comdr. Rome Air Devel. Ctr., Griffiss AFB, 1984-86; joint program mgr. WWMCCS info. system Hdqrs. USAF, Washington, 1986-88; dir. command, control and communications U.S. European Command, Stuttgart, Fed. Republic Germany, 1988-90; dir. command control systems and logistics U.S. Space Command, Peterson AFB, Colo., 1990-92; command control comm. and computers DCS, HQ USAF, Washington, 1992-95; v.p., dir. strategic planning Motorola Space and Sys. Tech. Group, Scottsdale, Ariz., 1995-98; tech. cons. Def. Sci. Bd., Washington, 1998—; v.p., gen. mgr. govt. info. and comms. sys., space group The Boeing Co., Anaheim, Calif., 2000—. V.p. Motorola, Inc. Mem. Air Force Assn., Armed Forces Communications-Electronics Assn., Soc. Logistics Engrs. Roman Catholic. carl.g.o'berry@boeing.com. Office: The Boeing Co PO Box 4921 3370 Miraloma Ave Anaheim CA 92803

OBNINSKY, VICTOR PETER, lawyer; b. San Rafael, Calif., Oct. 12, 1944; s. Peter Victor and Anne Bartholdi (Donston) O.; m Clara Alice Bechtel, June 8, 1969; children: Mari, Warren. BA, Columbia U., 1966; JD, U. Calif., Hastings, 1969. Bar: Calif. 1970. Sole practice, Novato, Calif., 1970-2001, Tiburon, 2001—. Arbitrator Marin County Superior Ct., San Rafael, 1979—; superior ct. judge pro tem, 1979—; lectr. real estate and partnership law. Author: The Russians in Early California, 1966. Bd. dirs. Calif. Young Reps., 1968-69, Richardson Bay San. Dist., 1974-75, Marin County Legal Aid Soc., 1976-78; baseball coach Little League, Babe Ruth League, 1970-84; mem. nat. panel consumer arbitrators Better Bus. Bur., 1974-88; leader Boy Scouts Am., 1970-84; permanent sec. Phillips Acad. Class of 1962, 1987—; mem. Phillips Acad. Alumni Coun., 1991-95; bd. cmty. advisors Buck Ctr. for Rsch. on Aging, 1990-2001. Mem ABA, State Bar Calif., Marin County Bar Assn. (bd. dirs. 1985-91, treas. 1987-88, pres.-elect 1989, pres. 1990), Phi Delta Phi, Phi Gamma Delta. Republican. Russian Orthodox. Office: 6 Mateo Drive Tiburon CA 94920-1046

O'BRIEN, DAVID PETER, business executive; b. Montreal, Que., Can., Sept. 9, 1941; s. John Lewis and Ethel (Cox) O'B.; m. Gail Baxter Corneil, June 1, 1968; children: Tara, Matthew, Shaun. B.A. with honors in Econs., Loyola Coll., Montreal, 1962; B.C.L., McGill U., Montreal, 1965. Assoc. and ptnr. Ogilvy, Renault, Montreal, 1967-77; v.p., gen. counsel Petro-Can., Calgary, Alta., 1977-81, sr. v.p., 1982-85, sr. v.p. fin. and planning, 1982-85, exec. v.p., 1985-89; pres., chief exec. officer Noverco Inc., Montreal, 1989; chmn. bd., pres., chief exec. officer PanCan. Petroleum Ltd., Calgary, Alta., Can., 1990-94; pres., COO Can. Pacific Ltd., Montreal, 1995-96, chmn., pres., CEO Calgary, 1996—. Bd. dirs. Air Can., Inco Ltd., Royal Bank Can., Conf. Bd. Can., C.D. Howe Inst., Can. Pacific Ltd.; chmn. bd. dirs. PanCan. Petroleum Ltd., Bus. Coun. Nat. Issues; mem. exec. com. Bus. Coun. on Nat. Issues. Bd. govs. U. Calgary. Mem. Quebec Bar Assn., Glencoe Club, Calgary Petroleum Club, Calgary Golf and Country Club. Office: 1800 Bankers Hall East 855 2nd St SW Calgary AB Canada T2P-4Z5

O'BRIEN, ELMER JOHN, librarian, educator; b. Kemmerer, Wyo., Apr. 8, 1932; s. Ernest and Emily Catherine (Reinhart) O'B.; m. Betty Alice Peterson, July 2, 1966. A.B., Birmingham So. Coll., 1954; Th.M., Iliff Sch. Theology, 1957; M.A., U. Denver, 1961. Ordained to ministry Methodist Ch., 1957; pastor Meth. Ch., Pagosa Springs, Colo., 1957-60; circulation-reference librarian Boston U. Sch. Theology, 1961-65; asst. librarian Garrett-Evang. Theol. Sem., Evanston, Ill., 1965-69; librarian, prof. United Theol. Sem., Dayton, Ohio, 1969-96, prof. emeritus, 1996—; abstractor Am. Bibliog. Center, 1969-73; dir. Ctr. for Evang. United Brethren Heritage, 1979-96; acting libr. Iliff Sch. Theology, 2000—01. Chmn. div. exec. com. Dayton-Miami Valley Libr. Consortium, 1983-84; rsch. assoc. Am. Antiquarian Soc., 1990. Author: Bibliography of Festschriften in Religion Published Since 1960, 1972, Religion Index Two: Festschriften, 1960-69; contbg. author: Communication and Change in American Religious History, 1993, Essays in Celebration of the First Fifty Years, 1996; pub. Meth. Revs. Index, 1818-1985, 1989-91; contbr. essay to profl. jour. Recipient theol. and scholarship award Assn. Theol. Schs. in U.S. and Can., 1990-91; Assn. Theol. Schs. in U.S. and Can. library staff devel. grantee, 1976-77, United Meth. Ch. Bd. Higher Edn. and Ministry research grantee, 1984-85 Mem. ALA, Acad. Libr. Assn. Ohio, Am. Theol. Libr. Assn. (head bur. personnel and placement 1969-73, dir. 1973-76, v.p. 1977-78, pres. 1978-79), Am. Antiquarian Soc. (rsch. assoc. 1990), Delta Sigma Phi, Omicron Delta Kappa, Eta Sigma Phi, Kappa Phi Kappa. Club: Torch Internat. (v.p. Dayton club 1981-82, pres. 1982-83). Home: 4840 Thunderbird Dr Apt 281 Boulder CO 80303-3829 E-mail: Ejobr@aol.com

O'BRIEN, JACK GEORGE, artistic director; b. Saginaw, Mich., June 18, 1939; s. J. George and Evelyn (MacArthur Martens) O'B. A.B., U. Mich., 1961, M.A., 1962. Asst. dir. APA Repertory Theatre, N.Y.C., 1963-67, asso. dir., 1967-69; worked with San Diego Nat. Shakespeare Festival, 1969-82, A.C.T., 1970-80, Loretto Hilton, 1975, Ahmanson, Los Angeles, 1978-80, San Francisco Opera, Houston Grand Opera, Washington Opera Soc.; artistic dir. N.Y.C. Opera, 1982. Lyricist: Broadway prodn. The Selling of the President, 1972; dir.: on Broadway Porgy and Bess (Tony award nominee 1977), Most Happy Fella, Street Scene, Two Shakespearean Actors, 1993, Damn Yankees, 1994, Hapgood, 1994, others; artistic dir.: Old Globe Theatre, San Diego, 1981. Mem. Actors' Equity, Am. Soc. Composers and Performers, Soc. Stage Dirs. and Choreographers, Dirs. Guild Am.

O'BRIEN, JOHN CONWAY, economist, educator, writer; b. Hamilton, Lanarkshire, Scotland; s. Patrick and Mary (Hunt) O'B.; m. Jane Estelle Judd, Sept. 16, 1966; children: Kellie Marie, Kerry Patrick, Tracy Anne, Kristen Noël. B.Com., U. London, 1952, cert. in German lang., 1954; tchr.'s cert., Scottish Edn. Dept., 1954; AM, U. Notre Dame, 1959, PhD, 1961. Tchr. Scottish High Schs., Lanarkshire, 1952-56; instr. U. B.C., Can., 1961-62; asst. prof. U. Sask., 1962-63, U. Dayton, Ohio, 1963-64; assoc. prof. Wilfrid Laurier U., Ont., Can., 1964-65; from asst. to full prof. Econs. and Ethics Calif. State U., Fresno, 1965—. Vis. prof. U. Pitts., 1969-70, U. Hawaii, Manoa, 1984, U. Queensland, Brisbane, Australia, 1994; keynote speaker Wageningen Agrl. U., The Netherlands, 1987; presenter papers 5th, 6th, 10th World Congress of Economists, Tokyo, 1977, Mexico City, 1980, Moscow, 1992; presenter Schmoller Symposium, Heilbronn am Neckar, Fed. Republic Germany, 1988, paper The China Confucius Found. and "2540" Conf., Beijing, 1989, 6th Internat. Conf. on Cultural Econs., Univ. Umeä, Sweden, 1990, Internat. Soc. Intercommunication New Ideas, Sorbonne, Paris, 1990, European Assn. for Evolutionary Polit. Economy, Vienna, Austria, 1991; active rsch. U. Göttingen, Fed. Republic Germany, 1987; acad. cons. Cath. Inst. Social Ethics, Oxford; presenter in field. Author: Karl Marx: The Social Theorist, 1981, The Economist in Search of Values, 1982, Beyond Marxism, 1985, The Social Economist Hankers After Values, 1992; editor: Internat. Rev. Econs. and Ethics, Internat. Jour. Social Econs., Ethical Values and Social Econs., 1981, Selected Topics in Social Econs., 1982, Festschrift in honor of George Rohrlich, 3 vols., 1984, Social Economics: A Pot=Pourri, 1985, The Social Economist on Nuclear Arms: Crime and Prisons, Health Care, 1986, Festschrift in honor of Anghel N. Rugina, Parts I and II, 1987, Gustav von Schmoller: Social Economist, 1989, The Eternal Path to Communism, 1990, (with Z. Wenxian) Essays from the People's Republic of China, 1991, Festschrift in Honor of John E. Elliott, Parts I and II, 1992, Communism Now and Then, 1993, The Evils of Soviet Communism, 1994, Ruminations on the USSR, 1994, The Future Without Marx, 1995, Essays in Honour of Clement Allan Tisdell, 1996, Essays in Honor of Clement Allan Tisdell, Part I, 1996, Part II and III, 1997, Part IV and V, 1998, Part VI, 1999, Part VII and VIII, 2000, Social Economists at Work, 1999, Our Fragile Civilization, 2001; translator econ. articles from French and German into English; contbr. numerous articles to profl. jours. With British Royal Army Service Corps, 1939-46, ETO, NATOUSA, prisoner of war, Germany. Recipient GE Corp. award Stanford U., 1966, Ludwig Mai Svc. award Assn. for Social Econs., Washington, 1994; named Disting. Fellow of Internat. Soc. for Intercomm. of New Ideas, Paris, 1990. Fellow Internat. Inst. Social Econs. (mem. coun., program dir. 3d World Cong. Social Econs. Fresno Calif. 1983, keynote spkr. 4th conf. Toronto 1986), Internat. Soc. for Intercomm. New Ideas (disting.); mem. Assn. Social Econs. (dir. west region 1977—, pres.-elect 1988-89, program dir. conf. 1989, pres. 1990, presdl. address Washington 1990, Thomas Divine award 1997), Western Econ. Assn. (organizer, presenter 1977-95), History Econs. Soc., Soc. Reduction Human Labor (exec. com.), European Assn. Evolutionary Polit. Econs., Ga. Acad. Econ. Scis. (Republic of Ga. fgn. mem.). Roman Catholic. Avocations: jogging, collecting miniature paintings, soccer, tennis, photography. Home: 2733 W Fir Ave Fresno CA 93711-0315 Office: Calif State U Econs And Ethics Dept Fresno CA 93740-0001 E-mail: john_obrien@csu.fresno.edu

O'BRIEN, KEVIN E. lawyer; b. Teaneck, N.J., Nov. 22, 1952; BA, U. Notre Dame, 1975; JD, U. Denver, 1977. Bar: Colo. 1980. Mem. Hall & Evans, L.L.C., Denver, 1984—. Instr. Nat. Inst. Trial Advocacy, 1987. With USAR, 1972-78. Office: Hall & Evans LLC 1200 17th St Ste 1700 Denver CO 80202-5817

O'BRIEN, RAYMOND FRANCIS, transportation executive; b. Atchison, Kans., May 31, 1922; s. James C. and Anna M. (Wagner) O'B.; m. Mary Ann Baugher, Sept. 3, 1947; children: James B., William T., Kathleen A., Christopher R. B.S. in Bus. Adminstrn., U. Mo., 1948; grad., Advanced Mgmt. Program, Harvard, 1966. Accountant-auditor Peat, Marwick, Mitchell & Co., Kansas City, Mo., 1948-52; contr., treas. Riss & Co., Kansas City, 1952-58; regional contr. Consol. Freightways Corp. of Del., Indpls., also, Akron, Ohio, 1958-61; contr. Consol. Freightways, Inc., San Francisco, 1961—, v.p., treas., 1962-63, bd. dirs., 1966, v.p. fin., 1967-69, exec. v.p., 1969-75, pres., 1975—, chief exec. officer, 1977-88, 90-91, chmn., 1988—; now chmn. emeritus CNF Transportation. Pres. CF Motor Freight subs. Consol. Freightways, Inc., 1973; dir. Transam. Corp., Watkins-Johnson, Inc.; past chmn. WesternHwy. Inst., Champion Road Machinery, Ltd. Former mem. bus. adv. bd. Northwestern U., U. Calif., Berkeley; bd. dirs., regent, former chmn. bd. trustees St. Mary's Coll.; bd. dirs., regent Charles Armstrong Sch., 1991—; mem. Pres.'s Adv. Herbert Hoover Boys and Girls Club; dir. Boy Scouts Am. Bay Area Coun. Served to 1st lt. USAAF, 1942-45. Recipient Disting. Svc. Citation Automotive Hall Fame, 1991; named Outstanding Chief Exec. five times Financial World Mag. Mem. Am. Trucking Assn. (bd. dirs. Found., exec. com.), Pacific Union Club, World Trade Club, Commonwealth Club (San Francisco), Menlo Country Club. Home: 26347 Esperanza Dr Los Altos CA 94022-2601 Office: CNF Transportation Bldg #2 3000 Sand Hill Rd Ste 130 Menlo Park CA 94025-7113

O'BRIEN, SUE, journalist; b. Waukon, Iowa, Mar. 6, 1939; d. John Gordon and Jean (Schadel) O'B.; m. John Seifert, Sept. 14, 1991; children from previous marriage: Peter, Sarah, Andrew. BA, Grinnell Coll., 1959; MPA, Harvard U., 1985. Reporter KTLN/KTLK Radio, Denver, 1968-70; anchor, reporter KBTR-AM, Denver, 1970-73; anchor, reporter, commentator KOA-AM/TV, Denver, 1973-75; corr. NBC Radio, N.Y.C., 1975-76; news. dir., exec. editor KOA AM/FM/TV, Denver, 1976-80; press sec. Gov. Colo., Denver, 1980-85; campaign mgr. Roy Romer, 1985-86; asst. city editor The Denver Post, 1987-88; assoc. prof. journalism, dir. masters program Sch. Journalism & Mass Comm., U. Colo., Boulder, 1988-95; editor Editl. Page, The Denver Post, 1995—. Adj. assoc. prof. U. Colo. Grad. Sch. Pub. Adminstrn., 1986-95. Chmn. Christian Social REls. divsn. Episc. Diocese Colo., 1964-68; bd. dirs. Colo. Journalism Rev., 1974-75; press sec. Coloradans for Lamm/Dick, 1982. Recipient Headliner award Women in Comm. Colo., 1972, Women of Achievement award, 1992, Big Hat award U. Colo. Soc. Profl. Journalists, 1973, Alumni award Grinnell Coll., 1974. Mem. Soc. Profl. Journalists (v.p. 1977-78), Assn. for Edn. in Journalism & Mass Comm. (head newspaper divsn. 1992—), Radio and TV News Dirs. Assn., Denver Press Club, Martar Bd., Phi Beta Kappa. Democrat. Episcopalian. Office: Denver Post 1560 Broadway Denver CO 80202-5177

O'BRIEN, THOMAS JOSEPH, bishop; b. Indpls., Nov. 29, 1935; Grad., St. Meinrad Coll. Sem. Ordained priest Roman Catholic Ch., 1961. Bishop of Phoenix, 1982—. Office: Cath Diocese Phoenix 400 E Monroe St Phoenix AZ 85004-2336

O'BYRNE, MICHAEL, management consultant; b. Butte, Mont., Dec. 26, 1938; s. Michael E. and Margaret F. (Turner) O'B.; m. Penny L. Graham, Nov. 14, 1964; children: Jennifer L. McLellan, Gregory M. O'Byrne, Andrew G. O'Byrne. BSME, U. Wash., 1961. Cert. engr., Wash. V.p. PACCAR, Inc., Bellevue, Wash., 1969-84; pres. Mobi-Dock, Inc., Mercer Island, 1985-86; ptnr. The Catalyst Group, Mercer Island, 1986-89; pres. Raima Corp., Bellevue, 1988-89, Pacific North Equiptment Co., Kent, Wash., 1990-95; cons. Master Performance, Inc., Bellevue, 1995-2000, Vehicle Monitor Corp., Redmond, Va., 1996—. Council mem. Hunts Point, Wash., 1980-97; mem. bd. dirs. Mcpl. League of King County, Seattle, 1994-95; dist. chmn. Boy Scouts Am., Seattle, 1994-98; pres. USO Puget Sound Area, 1997—. Lt. comdr. USN, 1961-69. Mem. Soc. Automotive Engrs., Assoc. Equipment Distributors (chpt. pres. 1994-95), Rotary Internat., Seattle Yacht Club. Republican. Avocations: sailing, skiing, fishing. Home and Office: 4224 Hunts Point Rd Bellevue WA 98004-1106 E-mail: obyrne184@aol.com

OCCHIATO, MICHAEL ANTHONY, city official; b. Pueblo, Colo. s. Joseph Michael and Joan Occhiato; m. Peggy Ann Stefonowicz, June 27, 1964 (div. Sept. 1983); children: Michael, James, Jennifer. BBA, U. Denver, 1961; MBA, U. Colo., 1984; postgrad., U. So. Colo. Grad. Real Estate Inst. Sales mgr. Tivoli Brewing Co., Denver, 1965-67, acting brewmaster, prodn. control mgr., 1967-68, plant mgr., 1968-69; adminstrv. mgr. King Resources Co., Denver, 1969-70; ops. mgr. Canners Inc., Pepsi-Cola Bottling Co., Pueblo, 1970-76; pres. Pepsi-Cola Bottling Co., Pueblo, 1978-82; gen. mgr. Pepsi-Cola Bottling Group div. PepsiCo., Pueblo, 1982, area v.p., 1982-83; ind. cons. Pueblo, 1983—; broker assoc. Sound Venture Realty, Pueblo, 1996-98, Jones Healy Better Homes & Gardens, 1998—. V.p. Colo. Soft Drink Assn., 1978, pres., 1979; regional dir. Pepsi Cola Mgmt. Inst. divsn. Pepsi Co., 1979-82; pres. Ethnic Foods Internat. dba Taco Rancho, Pueblo; chmn. Weifang (China) Sister City Del., 1991—; bd. dirs. HMO So. Colo. Health Plan, 1988-93, Pueblo Diversified Industries; rancher, 1976—; land devel. real estate broker assoc., 1996—; real estate designator, GRI. V.p. Colo. Soft Drink Assn., 1979-80, pres., 1980-81; mem. coun. City of Pueblo, 1978-93, pres., 1986, 87, 90, 91; mem. bd. health, 1978-80, regional planning commn., 1980-81, Pueblo Action Inc., 1978-80, Pueblo Planning and Zoning Commn., 1985; chmn. Pueblo Area Coun. Govts., 1980-82; mem. Pueblo Econ. Devel. Corp., 1983-91; chmn. fundraising Pueblo chpt. Am. Heart Assn., 1983—; bd. dirs. El Pueblo Boys Ranch, 1971-73; del. 1st World Conf. Local Elected Orcls. to 1st UN Internat. Coun. for Local Environ. Initiative; active Earth Wise Pueblo, 1991. Lt. USN, 1961-65. Mem. So. Colo. Emergency Med. Technicians Assn. (pres. 1975), Am. Saler Assn., Am. Quarter Horse Assn., Colo. Cattle Assn., Pueblo C. of C., Rotary, Pi Kappa Alpha (v.p. 1960). Home and Office: 11 Harrogate Ter Pueblo CO 81001-1723

OCHS, ELINOR, linguistics educator; Prof. dept. TESL and applied linguistics UCLA. Co-editor: Developmental Pragmatics, 1979, Language Socialization Across Cultures, 1986, Interaction with Grammar, 1996; author: Culture and Language Development: Language Acquisition and Language Socialization in a Samoan Village, 1988, (with L. Capps) Constructing Panic, The Discourse of Agoraphobia, 1995, contbr. articles to profl. publs. MacArthur fellow J.D. and C.T. MacArthur Found.; grantee NSF, 1986-89, Nat. Inst. Child Health and Devel., 1986-89, Spencer Found., 1990-93, 94-97, U.S. Dept. Edn., 1993-96 Achievements include research on discourse structures, grammar in context, language and affect, spoken and written language, cross-cultural communication. Office: UCLA Dept Applied Linguistics TESL 330 Rolfe Hall Room 3326 PO Box 951531 Los Angeles CA 90095-1531

OCKEY, RONALD J. lawyer; b. Green River, Wyo., June 12, 1934; s. Theron G. and Ruby O. (Sackett) O.; m. Arline M. Hawkins, Nov. 27, 1957; children: Carolyn S. Ockey Baggett, Deborah K. Ockey Christiansen, David, Kathleen M. Ockey Hellewell, Valerie Ockey Sachs, Robert. BA, U. Utah, 1959, postgrad., 1959-60; JD with honors, George Washington U., 1966. Bar: Colo. 1967, Utah 1968, U.S. Dist. Ct. Colo. 1967, U.S. Dist. Ct. Utah 1968, U.S. Ct. Appeals (10th cir.) 1969, U.S. Ct. Claims 1987. Missionary to France for Mormon Ch., 1954-57; law clk. to judge U.S. Dist. Ct. Colo., 1966-67; assoc. ptnr., shareholder, v.p., treas., dir. Jones, Waldo, Holbrook & McDonough, Salt Lake City, 1967-91; pres. IntelliTrans Internat. Corp., 1992-94; mem. Utah Ho. of Reps., 1988-90, Utah State Senate, 1991-94; of counsel Mackey Price & Williams, Salt Lake City, 1995-98; asst. atty. gen. Utah, 1998—. Trustee SmartUtah, Inc., 1995—, bd. dirs., mem. exec. com., 1995—; trustee Utah Tech. Fin. Corp., 1995-98; lectr. in securities, pub. fin. and bankruptcy law. Mem. editl. bd. Utah Bar Jour., 1973-75; mem. staff and bd. editors George Washington Law Rev., 1964-66; contbr. articles to profl. jours. Stae govtl. affairs chair Utah Jaycees, 1969; del. state Rep. Convs., 1972-74, 76-78, 80-82, 84-86, 94-96, del. Salt Lake County Rep. Conv., 1978-80, 88-92; sec. Wright for Gov. campaign, 1980; legis. dist. chmn. Utah Rep. Party, 1983-87; trustee Food for Poland, 1981-85, pres., trustee Unity to Assist Humanity Alliance, 1992-95; bd. dirs. Utah Opera Co., 1991-94; trustee Utah Info. Tech. Assn., 1991-2000. Lt. U.S. Army, 1960-66, to capt. JAG, USAR, 1966-81. Mem. ABA, Utah State Bar Assn. (various coms.), Nat. Assn. Bond Lawyers (chmn. con. on state legislation 1982-85), George Washington U. Law Alumni Assn. (bd. dirs. 1981-85), Order of Coif, Phi Delta Phi. Home: 4502 Crest Oak Cir Salt Lake City UT 84124-3825 E-mail: rao@netutah.net

O'CONNELL, HUGH MELLEN, JR. retired architect; b. Oak Park, Ill., Nov. 29, 1929; s. Hugh M. and Helen Mae (Evans) O'C.; m. Frances Ann Small, Apr. 13, 1957; children: Patricia Lynn, Susan Marie, Jeanette Maureen. Student mech. engring., Purdue U., 1948-50; B.S. in Archtl. Engring, U. Ill., 1953. Registered architect, Ariz., Calif., La., Nev., Nat. Council Archtl. Registration Bds. Designer John Mackel; structural engr. Los Angeles, 1955-57; architect Harnish & Morgan & Causey, Ontario, Calif., 1957-63; self-employed architect Ventura, 1963-69; architect Andrews/O'Connell, Ventura, 1970-78; dir. engring. div. Naval Constrn. Bn. Center, Port Hueneme, Calif., 1978-91, supervisory architect, 1991-93; ret., 1993. Mem. tech. adv. com. Ventura Coll., 1965-78; sec. Oxnard Citizens' Adv. Com., 1969-79, v.p., 1970-72, pres., 1972—; chmn. Oxnard Beautification Com., 1969, 74, Oxnard Cmty. Block Grant adv. com., 1975-76; mem. Oxnard Planning Commn., 1976-86, vice chmn., 1978-79, chmn., 1980-81. Mem. Oxnard Art-in-Pub. Places Commn., 1988—. Served with AUS, 1953-55. Mem. AIA (emeritus, pres. Ventura chpt. 1973), Am. Concrete Inst., Soc. Am. Registered Architects (Design award 1968, dir. 1970), Am. Legion, Soc. for Preservation and Encouragement of Barbershop Quartet Singing in Am. (chpt. pres. 1979, chpt. sec. 1980-83), Acad. Model Aeros. (#9190 1948—), Channel Islands Condors Club (treas. 1986—), Sports Flyers Assn., Alpha Rho Chi (Anthemios chpt.). Presbyterian (elder 1963, deacon 1967). Lodges: Kiwanis (pres. 1969, div. sec. 1974-75), Elks. Home and Office: 520 Ivywood Dr Oxnard CA 93030-3527 E-mail: hughoarch@aol.com

O'CONNELL, JACK, state legislator; b. Glen Cove, N.Y., Oct. 8, 1951; m. Doree O'Connell; 1 child, Jennifer Lynn. Student, Ventura Coll.; BA, Calif. State U., Fullerton; cert. secondary tchr., Calif. State U., Long Beach, 1975. Tchr. various high schs.; mem. Calif. State Assembly, 1982-94, Calif. State Senate, 1994—, chair budget sucbom. on edn., chair majority caucus and coastal caucus, mem. bus. and professions com., constnl. amendments com., mem. edn. com., environ. quality com., others. Recipient awards Small Bus. Assn., Calif. State U. Alumni Coun., Faculty Assn. Calif. C.C., Hispanic C. of C., Internat. Sr. Citizens Assn., Planning and Conservation League, Calif. Sch. Bds. Assn., Calif. Bldg. Industry Assn., Doris Day Animal League, Calif. assn. for the Physically Handicapped, Bus. and Profl. Women, MADD, Calif. Healthcare Inst. Democrat. Office: State Capital Rm 5035 Sacramento CA 95814 also: 228 W Carrillo St Ste F Santa Barbara CA 93101-6162 also: 1260 Chorro St Ste A San Luis Obispo CA 93401-3669 also: 89 S California St Ste E Ventura CA 93001-2897

O'CONNELL, KEVIN, lawyer; b. Boston, Sept. 4, 1933; s. Michael Frederick and Kathryn Agnes (Kelley) O'C.; m. Mary Adams, July 14, 1990; children: Tiffany W., Elizabeth H., Dana A., Liesel E. A.B., Harvard, 1955, J.D., 1960. Bar: Calif. 1961. Assoc. firm O'Melveny & Myers, L.A., 1960-63; asst. U.S. atty. criminal div. Cen. Dist. Calif., L.A., 1963-65; staff counsel Gov. Calif. Commn. to Investigate Watts Riot, L.A., 1965-66; ptnr. Tuttle & Taylor, L.A., 1966-70, Coleman & O'Connell, L.A., 1971-75; pvt. practice law L.A., 1975-78; of counsel firm Simon & Sheridan, L.A., 1978-89; ptnr. Manatt, Phelps & Phillips, L.A., 1989—. Bd. editors: Harvard Law Rev, 1958-60. Mem. Los Angeles County (Calif.) Democratic Central Com., 1973-74; bd. dirs. Calif. Supreme Ct. Hist. Soc. Lt. USMCR, 1955-57. Mem. Am. Law Inst. Home: 426 N Mccadden Pl Los Angeles CA 90004-1026 Office: Manatt Phelps & Phillips Trident Ctr E Tower 11355 W Olympic Blvd Los Angeles CA 90064-1614 E-mail: koconnell@manatt.com

O'CONNELL, MARY ANN, state legislator, business owner; b. Albuquerque, Aug. 3, 1934; d. James Aubrey and Dorothy Nell (Batsel) Gray; m. Robert Emmett O'Connell, Feb. 21, 1977; children: Jeffery Crampton, Gray Crampton. Student, U. N.Mex., Internat. Coun. Shopping Ctrs. Exec. dir. Blvd. Shopping Ctr., Las Vegas, Nev., 1968-76, Citizen Pvt. Enterprise, Las Vegas, 1976; media supr. Southwest Advt., Las Vegas, 1977—; owner, operator Meadows Inn, Las Vegas, 1985—99, 3 Christian bookstores, Las Vegas, 1985-99; state senator Nev. Senate, 1985—. Chmn. govtl. affairs; vice chmn. commerce and labor; mem. taxation com.; vice chmn. Legis. Commn., 1985-86, 95-96, chair, 1999-2001; mem., 1987-88, 91-93, mem. edn. com. to rewritten standards; commr. Edn. Commn. States; rep. Nat. Conf. State Legislators; past vice chair State Mental Hygiene & Mental Retardation Adv. Bd; chmn. Legis. Commn., 1999-2001. Pres. explorer div. Boulder Dam Area coun. Boy Scouts Am., Las Vegas, 1979-80, former mem. exec. bd. mem. adv. bd. Boulder Dam chpt.; pres., bd. dirs. Citizens Pvt. Enterprise, Las Vegas, 1982-84, Secret Witness, Las Vegas, 1981-82, vice chmn. Gov.'s Mental Health-Mental Retardation, Nev., 1983—; past mem. community adv. bd. Care Unit Hosp., Las Vegas; past mem. adv. bd. Kidney Found., Milligan Coll., Charter Hosp.; tchr. Young Adult Sunday Sch. Recipient Commendation award Mayor O. Grayson, Las Vegas, 1975, Outstanding Citizenship award Bd. Realtors, 1975, Silver Beaver award Boy Scouts Am., 1980, Free Enterprise award Greater Las Vegas C. of C., Federated Employers Assn., Downtown Breakfast Exch., 1988, Award of Excellence for Women in Politics, 1989, Legislator of Yr. award Bldg. and Trades, 1991, Legislator of Yr. award Nat. ASA Trade Assn., 1991, 94, Guardian of Liberty award Nev. Coalition of Conservative Citizens, 1991, Internat. Maxi Awards Promotional Excellence, Guardian of Small Bus. award Nat. Fedn. Ind. Bus., 1995-96; named Legislator of Yr., Nev. Retail Assn., 1992, New Assn. Bldg. Contractors, 1999, Nev Polit. Med. Action Com., 1999; inducted into Nev. Vets. Citizens Hall of Fame, 1999, Legislator of Yr. award Nev. Med. Polit. Com., 1999, Legislator of Yr. award Assoc. Builders and Contractors, Legislator of Yr., New Mortgage Brokers, 2000, Nev. Ind. Check Cashing Assn., 2001. Mem. Retail Mchts. Assn. (former pres., bd. dirs.), Taxpayers Assn. (bd. dirs.), Greater Las Vegas C. of C. (past pres., bd. dirs., Woman of Achievement Politics women's coun. 1988). Republican. Mem. Christian Ch. Avocations: china painting, reading. Office: Nev Legislature Senate 401 S Carson St Carson City NV 89701-4747

O'CONNOR, DAVID, talent agent; Talent agt. Creative Artists Agy., Beverly Hills, Calif., ptnr., mng. dir., 1996—. Office: Creative Artists Agy 9830 Wilshire Blvd Beverly Hills CA 90212-1825

O'CONNOR, G(EORGE) RICHARD, ophthalmologist; b. Cin., Oct. 8, 1928; s. George Leo and Sylvia Johanna (Voss) O'C. AB, Harvard U., 1950; MD, Columbia U., 1954. Resident in ophthalmology Columbia-Presbyn. Med. Center, N.Y.C., 1957-60; research fellow Inst. Biochemistry, U. Uppsala, Sweden, 1960-61, State Serum Inst., Copenhagen, 1961-62; asst. prof. ophthalmology U. Calif., San Francisco, 1962-68, prof., 1972-84; dir. Francis I. Proctor Found. for Research in Ophthalmology, 1970-84. Mem. Nat. Adv. Eye Council NIH, 1974-78 Author: (with G. Smolin) Ocular Immunology, 1981; asso. editor: Am. Jour. Ophthalmology, 1976-81. Served with USPHS, 1955-57. Recipient Janeway prize Coll. of Physicians and Surgeons, Columbia U., 1954; Doyne medal Oxford U., 1984; NIH grantee, 1962-84 Mem. Am. Bd. Ophthalmology (examiner), Assn. for Rsch. in Vision and Ophthalmology (trustee 1979-83, pres. 1982-83, Weisenfeld award 1990), Am. Ophthal. Soc., Calif. Med. Assn., Frederic C. Cordes Eye Soc., Pan Am. Ophthal. Assn. Republican. Presbyterian. Club: Faculty. Home: 22 Wray Ave Sausalito CA 94965-1831 Office: U Calif Med Ctr 315 S San Francisco CA 94143-0001 E-mail: rconnor@itsa.ucsf.edu

O'CONNOR, KARL WILLIAM (GOODYEAR JOHNSON), lawyer; b. Washington, Aug. 1, 1931; s. Hector and Lucile (Johnson) O'C.; m. Sylvia Gasbarri, Mar. 23, 1951 (dec.); m. Judith Ann Byers, July 22, 1972 (div. 1983); m. Eleanor Celler, Aug. 3, 1984 (div. 1986); m. Alma Hepner, Jan. 1, 1987 (div. 1996); children: Blair, Frances, Brian, Brendan; m. Allie O'Connor, Jul. 15, 2000. BA, U. Va., 1952, JD, 1958. Bar: Va. 1958, D.C. 1959, Am. Samoa 1976, Calif. 1977, Oreg. 1993. Law clk. U.S. Dist. Ct. Va., Abingdon, 1958-59; practice law Washington, 1959-61; trial atty. U.S. Dept. Justice, Washington, 1961-65; dep. dir. Men's Job Corps OEO, Washington, 1965-67; mem. civil rights div. Dept. of Justice, chief criminal sect., prin. dep. asst. atty. gen., 1967-75, spl. counsel for intelligence coordination, 1975; v.p., counsel Assn. of Motion Picture and Television Producers, Hollywood, Calif., 1975-76; assoc. justice Am. Samoa, 1976; chief justice Am. Samoa, 1977-78; sr. trial atty. GSA Task Force, Dept. Justice, 1978-81; insp. gen. CSA, 1981-82; spl. counsel Merit Systems Protection Bd., Washington, 1983-86; U.S. atty. for Guam and the No. Marianas, 1986-89; ret.; pvt. practice Medford, Oreg., 1989—; Am. counsel O'Reilly Vernier Ltd., Hong Kong, 1992-93; ptnr. O'Connor & Vernier, Medford, Oreg., 1993-94; pvt. practice Medford, 1994—. Served with USMC, 1952-55. Mem. Oreg. Bar Assn., D.C. Bar Assn., Va. Bar Assn., Calif. Bar Assn., Am. Samoa Bar Assn., Soc. Colonial Wars, Phi Alpha Delta, Sigma Nu. Home: Box 126 6743 Griffin Ln Jacksonville OR 97530 Office: 916 W 10th St Medford OR 97501-3018

O'CONNOR, KEVIN JOHN, psychologist, educator; b. Jersey City, July 18, 1954; s. John Lanning and Marilyn (Reynolds) O'C.; m. Ryan Michael, Matthew Benham. BA, U. Mich., 1975; PhD, U. Toledo, 1981. Clin. psychologist Blythedale Children's Hosp., Valhalla, N.Y., 1980-83; dir. psychol. svcs. Walworth Barbour Am. Internat. Sch., Kfar Shmaryahu, Israel, 1983-84; adj. asst. prof. dept. psychology Iona Coll., New Rochelle, N.Y., 1984; clin. psychologist No. Westchester Guidance Clinic, Mt. Kisco, 1985; exec. dir., newsletter editor Assn. for Play Therapy, Fresno, Calif., 1982-97; cons. psychologist Fresno (Calif.) Treatment Ctr., 1986-87, Diagnostic Sch. for Neurologically Handicapped Children, Fresno, Calif., 1986-90; adj. faculty Pacific Grad. Sch. of Psychology, Palo Alto, 1987—, Calif. Sch. Profl. Psychology, Berkeley, 1988-89; prof. Alliant Internat. U., Calif. Sch. Profl. Psychology, Fresno, 1985—. Contbr. numerous presentations in field. Named Psychologist of Yr. San Joaquin Psychol. Assn., 1994. Fellow APA; mem. Assn. for Play Therapy. Democrat. Avocations: travel, art, ceramics. Office: Calif Sch Profl Psych Alliant Internat U 5130 E Clinton Way Fresno CA 93727-2014

O'CONNOR, KEVIN THOMAS, religious organization administrator; b. Dubuque, Iowa, Oct. 9, 1950; s. Francis John and Marion Helen (Rhomberg) O'C.; m. Abbie J. O'Connor, July 17, 1993; 1 child, Sean Francis. BS, Regis Coll., Denver, 1973. Spl. agt. Northwestern Mut. Life, Denver, 1973-78; account exec. Blue Cross/Blue Shield of Colo., Denver, 1978-82; pres., owner O'Connor Ins. Cons., Denver, 1982-92; dir. devel. Archdiocese of Denver, 1992-95, mgr. Cath. appeal, 1995-96; dir. devel. Archdiocese of L.A., 1996—. Chmn. Regis Coll. Telefund, Denver, 1987-88, 90-91; treas., 1st vice chmn. Serra Trust Fund for Vocations, 1988-93, chmn., 1993-96; mem. fin. coun. St. James Parish, 1988-95, chmn. autumn bazaar, 1985, 87, mem. choir, 1993-95; sec. Mother Teresa Com., 1989; co-founder Pueblo Serra Club, 1992, Colorado Springs Serra Club, 1995, Greeley Serra Club, 1996; pres. Denver Serra Club, 1991-92; dist. 6 gov. Serra Internat., 1995-96. Recipient Share Serra Comm. award Serra Internat., 1989, Spl. Project award Dist. 6, 1986, 88, Spl. Recognition award, 1989, Outstanding Serran award, 1995, Jan Berbers award, 1996, Alumni Svc. award Regis Coll., 1990, Disting. Alumnus award Wahlert H.S., 1994. Mem. Serra Club L.A., Serra Internat. (trustee 1997—, sec. bd. 1998-2001, chmn. internat. vocation com. 2000-01, v.p. 2001—). Roman Catholic. Avocations: golf, tennis, mountain climbing, handball, running. Home: 3510 Fallenleaf Pl Glendale CA 91206-4803 Office: Archdiocese LA 3424 Wilshire Blvd Los Angeles CA 90010-2241 E-mail: ktoconnor@la-archdiocese.org, kevinabbie@earthlink.net

O'CONNOR, PAUL DANIEL, lawyer; b. Paterson, N.J., Nov. 24, 1936; s. Paul Daniel and Anne Marie Christopher O'C.; m. Melissa Monson; children: Steven Paul, Sheryl Lynn, Laura Ann. BS in Engring, U.S. Naval Acad., 1959; LLB, U. Va., 1965. Bar: N.Y. 1965, Calif. 1995. Assoc. firm Winthrop, Stimson, Putnam & Roberts, N.Y.C., 1965-72, partner, 1972-80; sr. v.p., gen. counsel Singer Co., Stamford, Conn., 1980-86; chief exec. officer Citation Builders, 1986-95; trustee Valley Trusts, Oakland, Calif., 1986—. 1st lt. USAF, 1959-62. Mem. Assn. Bar City N.Y., Bar Assn. San Francisco, Sonoma County Bar Assn., Am. Horse Shows Assn., Fairfield County Hunt Club. Home: 1150 Lombard St # 2 San Francisco CA 94109-9103 Office: Valley Trusts 1939 Harrison St Ste 555 Oakland CA 94612-3586 also: 141 North St Healdsburg CA 95448-3821

ODA, YOSHIO, physician, internist; b. Papaaloa, Hawaii, Jan. 14, 1933; s. Hakuai and Usako (Yamamoto) O.; AB, Cornell U., 1955; MD, U. Chgo., 1959. Diplomate Am. Bd. Internal Medicine. Intern U. Chgo. Clinics, 1959-60; resident in pathology U. Chgo., 1960-62, Queen's Hosp., Hawaii, 1962-63, Long Beach (Calif.) VA Hosp., 1963-65; resident in allergy, immunology U. Colo. Med. Center, 1966-67; pvt. practice, L.A., 1965-66; pvt. practice internal medicine, allergy and immunology, Honolulu, 1970—; asst. clin. prof. medicine U. Hawaii, Honolulu, 1970—. Maj., AUS, 1968-70. Mem. ACP, Am. Acad. Allergy. Office: Piikoi Med Bldg 1024 Piikoi St Honolulu HI 96814-1925

O'DAY, ANITA BELLE COLTON, entertainer, singer; b. Chgo., Dec. 18, 1919; d. James and Gladys (Gill) C. Student, Chgo. public schs. Singer and entertainer various Chgo. Music Clubs, 1939-41; singer with Gene Krupa's Orch., 1941-45, Stan Kenton Orch., 1944, Woody Herman Orch., 1945, Benny Goodman Orch., 1959; singing tours in U.S. and abroad, 1947—;

rec. artist Polygram, Capitol, Emily Records, Verve, GNP Crescendo, Columbia, London, Signature, DRG, Pablo; million-seller songs include Let Me Off Uptown, 1941, And Her Tears Flowed Like Wine, 1944, Boogie Blues, 1945; appeared in films Gene Krupa Story, 1959, Jazz on a Summer's Day, 1960, Zigzag, 1970, Outfit, 1974; TV shows 60 Minutes, 1980; Tonight Show, Dick Cavett Show, Today Show, Big Band Bash, CBS Sunday Morning, CNN Showbiz Today; inductee Jazz Hall of Fame, Tampa, 1997, Nat. Endowment Fellowship. Author: High Times, Hard Times, 1981, rev. edit., 1989; performed 50 yr. anniversary concert Carnegie Hall, 1985, Avery Fisher Hall, 1989, Tanglewood, 1990, JVC Festival Town Hall, 1993, Rainbow and Stars, 1995, JVC Festival Carnegie Hall, 1996, JVC Festival Avery Fisher Hall, 1999, Hollywood Palladium, 1999, Blue Note, N.Y.C., 2000, Atlas Supper Club, Los Angeles, 2000; currently touring worldwide; albums include Drummer Man, Kenton Era, Anita, Anita Sings The Most, Pick Yourself Up, Lady is a Tramp, An Evening with Anita O'Day, At Mr. Kelly's, Swings Cole Porter, Travelin' Light, All the Sad Young Men, Waiter Make Mine Blues, With the Three Sounds, I Told Ya I Love Ya Now Get Out, Uptown, My Ship, Live in Tokyo, Anita Sings the Winners, Incomparable, Anita 1975, Live at Mingos, Anita O'Day/The Big Band Sessions, Swings Rodgers and Hart, Time for Two, Tea for Two, In a Mellowtone (Grammy nomination 1990), At Vine St. Live, Mello'Day, Live at the City, Angel Eyes, The Night Has a Thousand Eyes, The Rules of the Road, Jazz Masters, Skylark, Swingtime in Hawaii, SS 'Wonderful (Carnegie Hall), Jazz Past Midnight, Compact Jazz, Let Me Off Uptown, The Complete Verve/Cleff Sessions, Ultimate Anita O'Day, After Midnight, Hi-Ho Trailus Bootwhip, Legends of the Swing Era. Jazz Masters fellow Nat. Endowment for the Arts, 1997. Mem. AFTRA, Screen Actors Guild, BMI. Office: Alan Eichler 6064 Selma Ave Los Angeles CA 90028-6415

ODELL, JOHN H. construction company executive; b. Toledo, Oct. 31, 1955; s. John H. and Doris Odell; m. Kathryn Lau, Oct. 1, 1988; children: Ceara, Heather, Victoria. B of Environ. Design, U. Miami, Oxford, Ohio, 1977. Staff architect Richard Halford and Assocs., Santa Fe, 1978-79; ptnr. B.O.A. Constrn., Santa Fe, 1980-84; owner John H. Odell Constrn., Santa Fe, 1985—; v.p. Los Pintores Inc., Santa Fe, 1990-92; pres. Uncle Joey's Food Svcs. Inc., 1991—, John H. Odell Assocs. Inc., Santa Fe, 1995—. Musician Santa Fe Community Orch., 1982, Huntington Community Orch., Huntington, W.Va., 1972-73; mem. citizen rev. com. Santa Fe Sch. Bd., 1999—, mem. bond and mill levy com., 2000—. Recipient Historic Preservation award City of Santa Fe, 1997. Mem. AIA (assoc., treas., bd. dirs. Santa Fe chpt. yearly 1988—, mem. liaison com. on design 1987—, Cmty. Svc. award 1993), Vine and Wine Soc. (N.Mex. No. Rio Grande chpt. pres., bd. dirs., v.p.), Nat. Assn. of Home Builders. Avocations: skiing, scuba, handball, racquetball. Home: PO Box 2967 Santa Fe NM 87504-2967 Office: John H Odell Assn 1523 Taos St Santa Fe NM 87505-3835 E-mail: johnoinc@aol.com

ODELL, WILLIAM DOUGLAS, endocrinologist, educator; b. Oakland, Calif., June 11, 1929; s. Ernest A. and Emma L. (Mayer) O.; m. Margaret F. Reilly, Aug. 19, 1950; children: Michael, Timothy, John D., Debbie, Charles. AB, U. Calif., Berkeley, 1952; MD, MS in Physiology, U. Chgo., 1956; PhD in Biochemistry and Physiology, George Washington U., 1965. Intern, resident, chief resident in medicine U. Wash., 1956-60, postdoctoral fellow in endocrinology and metabolism, 1957-58; sr. investigator Nat. Cancer Inst., Bethesda, Md., 1960-65; chief endocrine service NICHD, 1965-66; chief endocrinology Harbor-UCLA Med. Center, Torrance, Calif., 1966-72, chmn. dept. medicine, 1972-79; vis. prof. medicine Auckland Sch. Medicine, New Zealand, 1979-80; prof. medicine and physiology U. Utah Sch. Medicine, Salt Lake City, 1980-99, chmn. dept. internal medicine, 1980-96, prof. medicine and physiology, 1996-99, emeritus prof. medicine and physiology, 1999—. Pres. med. staff U. Utah Sch. Medicine, 1995-96. Mem. editorial bds. med. jours.; author, editor 8 books in field; contbr. over 330 articles to med. jours. With USPHS, 1960-66. Recipient Disting. Svc. award U. Chgo., 1973, Pharmacia award for outstanding contbns. to clin. chemistry, 1977, Gov.'s award State of Utah Sci. and Tech., 1988, also rsch. awards, Mastership award ACP, 1987. Mem. Am. Soc. Clin. Investigation, Am. Physiol. Soc., Assn. Am. Physicians, Am. Soc. Andrology (pres.), Endocrine Soc. (v.p., Robert Williams award 1991), Soc. Study of Reprodn. (bd. dirs.), Pacific Coast Fertility Soc. (pres.), Western Assn. Physicians (pres.), Western Soc. Clin. Rsch. (Mayo Soley award), Soc. Pediatric Rsch., Alpha Omega Alpha. Office: U Utah Med Ctr 50 N Medical Dr Salt Lake City UT 84132-0001 E-mail: owodell@aol.com

ODER, KENNETH WILLIAM, lawyer; b. Newport News, Va., July 9, 1947; s. Thomas William and Joy Reletta (McNeil) O.; m. Lucinda Ann Fox, July 20, 1969; children: Joshua, Devon, Chelsea. BA, U. Va., 1969, JD, 1975. Bar: Calif. 1975, U.S. Dist. Ct. (cen. dist.) Calif. 1975, U.S. Dist. Ct. (so. and no. dists.) Calif. 1977, U.S. Ct. Appeals (9th cir.) 1977, D.C. 1979. Assoc. Latham & Watkins, Los Angeles, 1975-77, 79-82, ptnr., 1982-94, assoc. Washington, 1978-79; exec. v.p. Safeway Inc., Oakland, 1994—. Exec. editor U. Va. Law Rev., 1973-74. Coach San Marino Little League, Calif., 1983—, Am. Youth Soccer Orgn., Rosemeade, Calif., 1984—. Mem. Calif. Bar Assn. (employment law sect.), Los Angeles County Bar Assn., D.C. Bar Assn. Republican. Methodist. Avocations: jogging, hiking, fishing. Office: Safeway Inc 5918 Stoneridge Mall Rd Pleasanton CA 94588-3229

ODERMAN, JEFFREY M. lawyer; b. Orange, N.J., Oct. 30, 1949; BA summa cum laude, UCLA, 1971; JD, Stanford U., 1974. Bar: Calif. 1975, U.S. Supreme Ct., U.S. Ct. Appeals (9th cir.), U.S. Dist. Ct. (ctrl. and no. dists.) Calif. Mem. Rutan & Tucker, Costa Mesa, Calif. Mem. State Bar Calif., Phi Beta Kappa, Order of Coif. Office: Rutan & Tucker PO Box 1950 611 Anton Blvd Ste 1400 Costa Mesa CA 92626-1931

ODERMATT, ROBERT ALLEN, architect; b. Oakland, Calif., Jan. 3, 1938; s. Clifford Allen and Margaret Louise (Budge) O.; m. Diana Birtwistle, June 9, 1960; children: Kristin Ann, Kyle David. BArch, U. Calif., Berkeley, 1960. Registered architect, Calif., Oreg., Nev., Colo., Hawaii; cert. Nat. Coun. Archtl. Registration Bds. Draftsman Anderson Simonds Dusel Campini, Oakland, 1960-61; architect James R. Lucas, Orinda, Calif., 1961-62, ROMA Architects, San Francisco, 1962-76, architect, pres., 1976-84; prin. ROMA Design Group, San Francisco, 1962-92; pres. The Odermatt Group, Orinda, Calif., 1992—. Prin. speaker Internat. Conf. on Rebuilding Cities, Pitts., 1988; mem. U.S. Design in Am. Program, Sofia, Bulgaria, Armenian Disaster Assn. Team, 1989; prin. State of Calif. Bay Area Facilities Plan, 1992; princ. Greece Resort Privatization Program, 1993. Prin. designer U.S. Embassy, Bahrain, Grand Canyon Nat. Park, 1977, Yosemite Nat. Park, 1987; prin. planner hotel complex Westin Hotel, Vail, Colo., 1982, Kaanapali Resort, 1987, Las Montanas Resort, San Diego; master plan U. Calif., Berkeley, 1988, Kohanaiki and Mauna Lani resorts, 1989, Calif. State Strategic Real Estate Plan, 1992, Greek Resort/Marina Privatization Program, 1993, Tektronix Strategic Plan, 1994, United Labs, Manila Master Plan, 1995, State of Calif. Reorganization Plan, 1996, Ford Island Pearl Harbor Master Plan, 1996, Pearl Harbor Visitor Ctr. Plan, 1997, Albiano Resort Study, 1998; master plans include Trefethen Vineyards, Bell Garden, Napa Valley Expo, Wheatland Manor. Mem. Santa Cruz Downtown Assessment, Oakland Mayor's Com. on High Density Housing, 1982, Oakland Gen. Plan Congress, 1994, waterfront plan adv. com. City of Oakland, 1996. Fellow AIA (dir. East Bay chpt. 1969-71, pres. 1980-81, dir. Calif. coun. 1979-81, Disting. Svc. award 1991, nat. dir. 1983-86, nat. v.p. 1986-87, chair AIA internat. steering com. 1993-94, graphic stds. adv. com. 1991-92, U. Calif. archtl. review commn. 1992-96, exec. com. Coll. Fellows 1996-98, vice chancellor Coll. Fellows 1998, chancellor 2000, East Bay medal 1997), Am. Archtl. Found. (regent).

ODETTE, G. ROBERT, mechanical and environmental engineering educator; PhD, MIT, 1970. Prof. mech. & environ. engring. U. Calif., Santa Barbara. Office: U Calif Dept Mech & Environ Engring Santa Barbara CA 93106

ODGEN, ROGER, television station executive; Pres., mng. dir. NBC Europe; pres., gen. mgr. Sta. KUSA-TV, Gannett TV, Denver, 1997—. Office: KUSA TV 500 E Speer Blvd Denver CO 80203-4187

ODGERS, RICHARD WILLIAM, lawyer; b. Detroit, Dec. 31, 1936; s. Richard Stanley and Elsie Maude (Trevarthen) O.; m. Gail C. Bassett, Aug. 29, 1959; children: Thomas R., Andrew B. AB, U. Mich., 1959, JD, 1961. Bar: Calif. 1962. Assoc. Pillsbury Winthrop, San Francisco, 1961-69, ptnr., 1969-87, 98-2000; exec. v.p., gen. counsel Pacific Telesis Group, San Francisco, 1987-98; ptnr. Pillsbury Winthrop, San Francisco, 2001—. Chmn., bd. dirs. Legal Aid Soc. San Francisco; dir. Legal Cmty. Against Violence; dir., sec./treas. Van Loben Sels Charitable Found. Served with USNR. Fellow Am. Bar Found., Am. Judicature Soc., Am. Coll. Trial Lawyers; mem. ABA, Am. Law Inst., Coll. Law Practice Mgmt. Office: Pillsbury Winthrop 50 Fremont St San Francisco CA 94105-2228 E-mail: rwodgers@pillsburywinthrop.com

O'DONNELL, PIERCE HENRY, lawyer; b. Troy, N.Y., Mar. 5, 1947; s. Harry J. and Mary (Kane) O'D.; m. Dawn Donley, Mar. 17, 1995; children: Meghan Maureen, Brendan Casey, Courtney Dawn, Pierce Dublin, Aidan Yeats. BA, Georgetown U., 1969, JD, 1972; LLM, Yale U., 1975. Bar: D.C. 1973, U.S. Supreme Ct. 1975, Calif. 1978. Law clk. to Justice Byron R. White U.S. Supreme Ct.; law clk. to Judge Shirley M. Hutstedler U.S. Dist. Ct. (9th cir.); assoc. Williams & Connolly, Washington, 1975-78; ptnr. Beardsley, Hufstedler & Kemble, L.A., 1978-81, Hufstedler, Miller, Carlson & Beardsley, L.A., 1981-82, O'Donnell & Gordon, L.A., 1982-87, Kaye, Scholer, Fierman, Hays & Handler, L.A., 1988-95, O'Donnell & Shaeffer, L.L.P., L.A., 1996—; pres. Premiore Media, Inc., 1999—. Exec. asst. U.S. Sec. Edn., 1979; spl. counsel Commn. Jud. Performance, San Francisco, 1979; chmn. Nat. Media, Inc., 1984-92. Co-author: Fatal Subtraction: The Inside Story of Buchwald v Paramount, 1992, Toward A Just and Effective Sentencing System: Agenda for Legislative Reform, 1976; author: Dawn's Early Light, 20010; contbr. articles to profl. jours. Chmn. Friends Calif. Tech. YMCA, 1983-84, Verdugo-San Rafael Urban Mountain Park Fund, 1980-84; bd. dirs. Friends of Altadena Libr., 1979-81, Pasadena-Foothill Urban League, E. Altadena Little League, 1993-97; bd. dirs. Foothill Family Svc., 1979-85, chmn., 1984-85; bd. dirs. Interfaith Ctr. To Reverse Arms Race, 1984-90, pres., 1987-88; mem. Econ. Round Table of L.A., 1979—, pres. 2000-01. Mem. PEN, NAACP, Am. Law Inst., Calif. Tech. Assocs., Siera Club, Bel Air Country Club, Gridiron Club (Georgetown U.), Calif. Club. Roman Catholic. Home: 405 Linda Vista Ave Pasadena CA 91105-1237 Office: O'Donnell & Shaeffer LLP 633 W 5th St Ste 1700 Los Angeles CA 90071-2027 E-mail: podonnell@oslaw.com

O'DONNELL, WILLIAM RUSSELL, state legislator; b. Quincy, Mass., Jan. 16, 1951; s. Alfred Joseph and Ruth Irene (McCausland) O.; m. Mary Hogan, June 13, 1976; children: Meagan, Patrick, Kevin, Colleen, Kyle. BS in Bus. and Econs., U. Nev., Las Vegas, 1979. Patrolman Las Vegas Met. Police, 1973-74; realtor Coldwell-Banker, Las Vegas, 1988—; pres. Computer System Concepts, Las Vegas, 1980—; mem. Nev. Senate, Dist. 5 Clark County, Carson City, 1987—, Nevada Assembly, 1985-86. Nev. state assemblyman, Las Vegas, 1985-86; alt. legis. commn. Nev., 1987-89; majority Whip Rep. Party Nev., 1989; mem. Nev. Child Watch Adv. Bd., Assn. for the Handicapped, Pro-Life Nev., Citizens for Responsible Govt.; pres. Sect. 10 Homeowners Assn., Las Vegas, 1986—, Spring Valley Town Bd., 1984—, bd. dirs. Home of the Good Shepherd, St. Rose de Lima Hosp., 1985—. Mem. Las Vegas Bd. Realtors, Rotary, Nev. Assoc. of the Handicapped, St. Rose de Lima Hosp., Las Vegas Chamber of Commerce, Nev. Devel. Authority. Republican. Roman Catholic. Address: Nev Senate 401 S Carson St Rm 244 Carson City NV 89701-4747 Office: 2780 S Jones Blvd Las Vegas NV 89146-5625

O'DONNELL, WILLIAM THOMAS, management consultant; b. Latrobe, Pa., Feb. 22, 1939; s. William Regis and Kathryn Ann (Coneff) O'D; m. Judith Koetke, Oct. 1, 1965; children: William Thomas, William Patrick, Allison Rose, Kevin Raymond. Student Ea., N. Mex. U., 1961-65; student in mktg., John Carrol U., 1961-65; student, Inst. Tech., 1965-66; BSBA, U. Phoenix, 1982, MBA with distinction, 1984; PhD applied orgnl. mgmt. personel psychographics, Union Inst., 1999. Various positions Hickok Elec. Instrument Co., Cleveland, 1961-65; with Fairchild Semicondr., Mpls., 1965-67, Transitron Semicondr., Mpls., 1967-69; regional sales mgr. Burroughs Corp., Plainfield, N.J., 1967-71; mktg. mgr. Owens-Ill., Co., 1972-73; v.p. mktg. Pantek Co. subs. Owens-Ill. Co., Lewiston, Pa., 1973-75; v.p. mktg., nat. sales mgr. Toledo, 1975-76; mktg. mgr. Govt. Electronics divsn. group Motorola co., Scottsdale, Ariz., 1976-80, U.S. mktg.mgr. radar positioning syss., 1981; gen. mgr. J.K. Internat., Scottsdale, 1980-81; mgmt. cons., pres. Cambridge Grp., 1987—; v.p. mktg. Pinnacle Surg. Products, 1989, Kroy, Inc., 1992-94; mgmt. cons., 1994; v.p. mktg. and bus. devel. Kroy, inc., 1992. Adj. prof. Union Grad. Sch; Guest lectr. U. Mich. Grad. Sch. Bus. Administrn.; instr. U. Phoenix, 1984-88, chair strategic mgmt. 1988, pres. faculty, 1989—, area chair mktg., 1995—, area chair grad. assessment, 1999; lectr. Scottsdale Community Coll., Paradise Valley Community Coll; talk show host Sta. KFNN, 1992-95; area chmn gen. mgmt. Union Grad. Sch. Maricopa Community Coll., U. Phoenix Chmn., Rep. precinct, Burnsville, Minn., 1968-70; bd. dirs. Pacific Gateway. Chmn. City fin., Burnsville; dir. community devel. U.S. Jaycees, Mpls., 1968-69;mem. Scottsdale 2000 Com. With USAF, 1957-61. Recipient Outstanding Performance award Maricopa Community Coll. System, 1987, Faciliation award, Maricopa Community Coll.; Citation for Faciliation Ability, U. Phoenix, 1986, 90, 93, 99; named Hon. Citizen, Donaldsville, La., 1978. Mem. Am. Mktg. Assn., Afron-Am. Small Bus. Assn), Phoenix Indian Ctr., Inc. (bd. dirs. 1994), Amateur Athletic Union (swimming ofcl. 1980-82), Phoenix Execs. Club, U. Phoenix Faculty Club (bd. dirs., pres., 1988-91 recipient Presdl. Designation award, officer), North Cape Yacht Club, Scottsdale Racquet Club, Toftness country Club. Roman Catholic. Home: 33144 N 72d Way Scottsdale AZ 85262 E-mail: wto@att.net

O'DOWD, DONALD DAVY, retired university president; b. Manchester, N.H., Jan. 23, 1927; s. Hugh Davy and Laura (Morin) O'D.; m. Janet Louise Fithian, Aug. 23, 1953; children: Daniel D., Diane K., James E., John M. BA summa cum laude, Dartmouth Coll., 1951; postgrad. (Fulbright fellow), U. Edinburgh, Scotland, 1951-52; MA, Harvard U., 1955, PhD, 1957. Instr., asst. prof. psychology, dean freshmen Wesleyan U., Middletown, Conn., 1955-60; assoc. prof., prof. of psychology, dean Univ. Oakland Univ., Rochester, Mich., 1960-65, provost, 1965-70; pres. Oakland U., Rochester, 1970-80; exec. vice chancellor SUNY, Albany, 1980-84; pres. U. of Alaska Statewide System, 1984-90. Sr. cons. Assn. Governing Bds. Univs. and Colls. Carnegie Corp. fellow, 1965-66 Mem. APA, AAAS, Phi Beta Kappa, Sigma Xi. Home and Office: 1550 La Vista Del Oceano Santa Barbara CA 93109-1739

OEHLER, RICHARD WILLIAM, lawyer; b. N.Y.C., Nov. 24, 1950; s. John Montgomery and Florence Mae (Jahn) O.; m. Linda Tyson. BA, Dartmouth Coll., 1972; JD, Harvard U., 1976. Bar: Calif. 1976, Wash. 1987, D.C. 1988, U.S. Dist. Ct. (no. dist.) Calif. 1976, U.S. Dist. Ct. Wash. 1987, U.S. Claims Ct. 1979, U.S. Ct. Appeals (fed. cir.) 1982. Assoc. Pillsbury, Madison & Sutro, San Francisco, 1976-78; trial atty. U.S. Dept. Justice, Washington, 1978-87; of counsel Perkins Coie, Seattle, 1987-90, ptnr., 1990—. Mem. ABA, Nat. Contract Mgmt. Assn. (Spl. Achievement award 1990-92), Wash. State Bar Assn. Office: Perkins Coie 1201 3rd Ave Fl 40 Seattle WA 98101-3029 E-mail: oehlr@perkinscoie.com

OEHLKE, JACK W. computer company executive; b. 1946; Dir. ops., dir. quality Microswitch divsn. Honeywell, Inc., 1968-93; v.p. mfg. ops. Key Tronic Corp., Spokane, Wash., 1993-95, sr. v.p. ops., 1995, COO, 1995-97, pres., CEO, 1997—. Office: Key Tronic Corp N 4424 Sullivan Rd Spokane WA 99216 Fax: 509-927-5248

OELSTROM, TAD JEROME, retired lieutenant general United States Air Force; b. Milw. m. Sandra Illing; children: Kristin, Stephanie, Megan. BS in Engring., U.S. Air Force Acad., 1965; grad., Squadron Officer Sch, Maxwell AFB, Ala., 1969, Air Command and Staff Coll., 1977; MBA, Auburn U., 1977; student, Indsl. Coll. Armed Forces, Fort Lesley J. McNair, Washington, 1980, Army War Coll., Carlisle Barracks, Pa., 1981. Commd. 2d Lt. USAF, 1965, advanced through grades to Lt. Gen., 1997; F-4 pilot 417th Tactical Fighter Squadron USAF, Ramstein, Germany, and Mnt. Home, ID., 1968-70; F-4E instr. pilot, standardization, evaluation officer 421st Tactical Fighter Squadron, 366th Tactical Fighter Wing, Da Nang Air Base, S. Vietnam, 1970-71; instr. pilot, chief weapons and tactics divsn., later standardization and evaluation chief 33d Fighter Wing, Eglin AFB, Fla., 1971-74; Hawker-Hunter fighter weapons instr. Tactical Weapons Unit, Royal Air Force, Chivenor, Eng., Brawdy, Wales, 1974-76; staff officer, dep. chief of staff for requirements Hdqtrs. Tactical Air Command, Langley AFB, Va., 1977-80; wing weapons chief, 4th tactical fighter wing, then comdr. 337th Tactical Fighter Squadron, Seymour Johnson AFB, N.C., 1981-84; dep. comdr. ops. 33d fighter wing Eglin AFB to dir. fighter ops. hdqtrs. tactical air command, USAF, Langley AFB, Va., 1984-87; vice comdr. to comdr. 81st tactical fighter wing RAF, Bentwaters, Eng., 1987-90; exec. officer to dep. comdr. in chief U.S. European Command, Stuttgart, Germany, 1990-91; inspector gen. hdqtrs. U.S. Air Forces in Europe, Ramstein Air Base, Germany, 1991-92; comdr. 86th fighter wing and Kaiserslautern Mil. Comty., Germany, 1992-93; comdr. 3d air force RAF, Middenhall, 1995-97; supt. U.S. Air Force Acad., Colo. Springs, Colo., 1997-2000; ret.; vice comdr. 9th air force Shaw AFB, SC, 1993—95. Decorated Disting. Svc. medal, Defense Superior Svc. medal, Legion of Merit, Disting. Flying Cross with oak leaf cluster, Meritorious Svc. medal with 4 oak leaf clusters, Air Medal with 15 oak leaf clusters. Address: 4909 Oakcrest Dr Fairfax VA 22030 Office: Kennedy Sch Govt Cambridge MA 02138 E-mail: tofalcon@aol.com

OEMLER, AUGUSTUS, JR. astronomer, educator; b. Savannah, Ga., Aug. 15, 1945; s. Augustus and Isabelle Redding (Clarke) O.; children: W. Clarke, Bryan S. AB, Princeton U., 1969; MS, Calif. Inst. Tech., 1970, PhD, 1974. Postdoctoral assoc. Kitt Peak Nat. Obs., Tucson, 1974-75; instr. astronomy Yale U., New Haven, 1975-77, asst. prof., 1977-79, assoc. prof., 1979-83, prof., 1983-96, chmn. dept., 1988-96; dir. Obs. Carnegie Instn. Washington, Pasadena, Calif., 1996—. Contbr. articles to profl. jours. Alfred P. Sloan fellow, 1978-80 Mem. Am. Astronom. Soc., Internat. Astronom. Union. Republican. Roman Catholic. Home: 741 Burleigh Dr Pasadena CA 91105-2241 Office: Carnegie Obs 813 Santa Barbara St Pasadena CA 91101-1232

OESTING, DAVID W. lawyer; b. Chgo., Aug. 6, 1944; AB, Earlham Coll., 1967; JD, Wash. U., 1970. Bar: Wash. 1970, Alaska 1981. Ptnr. in charge of Anchorage Office Davis Wright Tremaine, Anchorage, 1980—. Editor-in-chief Wash. U. Law Quarterly, 1969-70. Mem. ABA, Am. Coll. Trial Lawyers, Wash. State Bar Assn., Alaska Bar Assn., Anchorage Bar Assn., Order of Coif. Office: Davis Wright Tremaine 701 W 8th Ave Ste 800 Anchorage AK 99501-3467 E-mail: daveoesting@dwt.com

OFFENBERGER, ALLAN ANTHONY, electrical engineering educator; b. Wadena, Sask., Can., Aug. 11, 1938; s. Ivy Viola (Hagglund) O.; m. Margaret Elizabeth Patterson, Apr. 12, 1963; children: Brian, Gary. BS, U. B.C., 1962, MS, 1963; PhD, MIT, 1968. Asst. prof. U. Alta., Edmonton, Can., 1968-70, assoc. prof. Can., 1970-75, prof. Can., 1975-95, prof. emeritus Can., 1996—. Cons. Lawrence Livermore (Calif.) Nat. Lab., 1996-98; vis. prof. U.K. Atomic Energy Agy., Abingdon, Oxon, Eng., 1975-76; project dir. Laser Fusion Project, Edmonton, 1984-91; mem. strategic adv. com. Nat. Fusion Program, Atomic Energy of Can. Ltd., Chalk River, Ont., 1987-96; vis. prof. U. Oxford, U.K., 1992, U. Osaka, Japan, 2000. Mem. editorial bd. Laser and Particle Beams, 1987—; contbr. over 150 sci. articles on lasers and plasma physics. Killam Rsch. fellow Can. Coun., 1980-82. SERC rsch. fellow, Eng., 1992. Mem. Can. Assn. Physicists (exec. officer, v.p. elect 1987-88, pres. 1989-90), Am. Phys. Soc., Sigma Xi. Home: 412 Lessard Dr Edmonton AB Canada T6M 1A7 Office: U Alta Dept Elec Computer Engring Edmonton AB Canada T6G 2G7

OFFER, STUART JAY, lawyer; b. Seattle, June 2, 1943; m. Judith Spitzer, Aug. 29, 1970; children: Rebecca, Kathryn. BA, U. Wash., 1964; LLB, Columbia U., 1967. Bar: D.C. 1968, U.S. Tax Ct. 1968, Calif. 1972. Atty., advisor U.S. Tax Ct., Washington, 1967-68; assoc. Morrison & Foerster, LLP, San Francisco, 1972-76, ptnr., 1976—. Trustee Am. Tax Policy Inst. Served as capt. U.S. Army, 1968-72. Mem. ABA (chmn. taxation sect., corp. tax com. 1991-92, coun. dir. 1995-98, vice chair adminstrn. 1998-2000), Internat. Fiscal Assn., Am. Coll. Tax Counsel. Office: Morrison & Foerster LLP 425 Market St San Francisco CA 94105-2482 E-mail: soffer@mofo.com

OFTE, DONALD, retired environmental executive, consultant; b. N.Y.C., Aug. 23, 1929; s. Sverre and Ingeborg Ofte; m. Margaret Mae McHenney, July 23, 1955; children: Marc Christian, Nancy Carolyn Appleby, Kirk Donald Jr. BA in Chemistry, Dana Coll., 1952; postgrad. study metall. engring., Ohio State U., 1958-60. Jr. chemist Inst. Atomic Research, Ames, Iowa, 1952-53; sr. research chemist Monsanto Research Corp., Miamisburg, Ohio, 1958-66; ops. engr. AEC, Miamisburg, 1966-69, br. chief, div. dir. ops. office Albuquerque, 1969-73, mgr. Pinellas area office Largo, Fla., 1973-79; mgr. Rocky Flats area office Dept. Energy, Golden, Colo., 1979-82, asst. mgr. devel. and prodn. Albuquerque, 1982-83, dep. mgr. ops. office, 1983-84; prin. dep. asst. sec. Dept. Energy Defense Programs, Washington, 1984-87; mgr. ops. office Dept. Energy, Idaho Falls, Idaho, 1987-89; mgmt. cons. Idaho Falls, 1989-92; v.p. govt. ops. United Engrs. & Constructors (Raytheon Engrs. & Constrn.), Denver, 1992-93; v.p. Adv. Scis., Inc., Albuquerque, 1993-94; pres. FERMCO (also known as Fluor Daniel, Fernald), Cin., 1994-96; ret., 1996. V.p. Fluor-Daniel, Inc., 1994-96; affiliate prof. Idaho State U., 1990-92; bd. dirs. Denver Fed. Exec. Bd., 1979-82. Author: (with others) Plutonium 1960, 1965, Physicochemical Methods in Metallurgical Research; contbr. articles to profl. jours. on metallurgy and ceramics. Campaign chmn. United Way Pinellas, St. Petersburg, Fla., 1978; bd. dirs. Bonneville County United Way, Idaho Rsch. Found.; mem. adv. bd. Teton Peaks Council Boy Scouts of Am., 1987-92, Eastern Idaho Tech. Coll.; chmn. Excellence in Edn. Fund Com., 1990-92; vice chmn., bd. dirs. Rio Grande Ch. ARC, Albuquerque, 1982-84; trustee, bd. dirs. Nat. Atomic Mus., 1999—. Served to lt. (j.g.) USN, 1953-57. Recipient citation AEC for Apollo 12 SNAP 27 Radioisotope Generator, 1969, High Quality Performance award AEC, 1968, Group Achievement award NASA, 1972; Meritorious Svc. award Dept. Energy, 1985, Disting. Career Svc. award, 1989. Mem. Am. Chem. Soc., Am. Nuclear Soc., Am. Soc. Metals, Nat. Contract Mgmt. Assn., Am. Soc. Pub. Adminstrs., Suncoast Archeol. Soc., Idaho Falls C. of C. (bd. dirs., cmty. svc. award 1990), Rotary Internat. (Paul Harris fellow). Avocations: reading, bridge, gardening, golf. Home: 1129 Salamanca St NW Albuquerque NM 87107-5643 E-mail: dofte@aol.com

OGDEN, VALERIA MUNSON, management consultant, state representative; b. Okanogan, Wash., Feb. 11, 1924; d. Ivan Bodwell and Pearle (Wilson) Munson; m. Daniel Miller Ogden Jr., Dec. 28, 1946; children: Janeth Lee Ogden Martin, Patricia Jo Ogden Hunter, Daniel Munson Ogden. BA magna cum laude, Wash. State U., 1946. Exec. dir. Potomac Coun. Camp Fire, Washington, 1964-68, Ft. Collins (Colo.) United Way, 1969-73, Designing Tomorrow Today, Ft. Collins, 1973-74, Poudre Valley Community Edn. Assn., Ft. Collins, 1977-78; pres. Valeria M. Ogden, Inc., Kensington, Md., 1978-81; nat. field cons. Camp Fire, Inc., Kansas City, Mo., 1980-81; exec. dir. Nat. Capital Area YWCA, Washington, 1981-84, Clark County YWCA, Vancouver, Wash., 1985-89; pvt. practice mgmt. cons. Vancouver, 1989—; mem. Wash. Ho. of Reps., 1991—, spkr. pro tempere, 1999—. Mem. adj. faculty pub. adminstrn. program Lewis and Clark Coll., Portland (Oreg.) State U., 1979-94; mem. Pvt. Industry Coun., Vancouver, 1986-95; mem. regional Svcs. Network Bd. Mental Health, 1993—. Author: Camp Fire Membership, 1980. County vice-chair Larimer County Dems., Ft. Collins, 1974-75; mem. precinct com. Clark County Dems., Vancouver, 1986-88; mem. Wash. State Coun. Vol. Action, Olympia, 1986-90; treas. Mortar Bd. Nat. Found., Vancouver, 1987-96; bd. dirs. Clark County Coun. for Homeless, Vancouver, 1989—, chmn., 1994; bd. dirs. Wash. Wil life and Recreation Coalition, 1995—, Human Svcs. Coun., 1996—; chair arts and tourism com. Nat. Coun. State Legis., 1996-97, exec. com., 2000—; bd. Wash. State Hist. Soc., 1996—; Dem. spkr. pro tem Wash. Ho. of Reps., 1999; pres. Nat. Order of Women, 1999-2001. Named Citizen of Yr. Ft. Collins Bd. of Realtors, 1975, State Legislator of Yr., Wash. State Labor Coun., 2000; recipient Gulick award Camp Fire Inc., 1956, Alumna Achievement award Wash. State U. Alumni Assn., 1988; named YWCA Woman of Achievement, 1991. Mem. Internat. Assn. Vol. Adminstrs. (pres. Boulder 1989-90), Nat. Assn. YWCA Exec. Dirs. (nat. bd. nominating com. 1988-90), Sci. and Soc. Assn. (bd. dirs. 1993-97), Women in Action, Philanthropic and Ednl. Orgn., Phi Beta Kappa. Democrat. Avocation: hiking, travel. Home: 3118 NE Royal Oak Dr Vancouver WA 98662-7435 E-mail: ogden_va@leg.wa.gov

OGDON, WILBUR (WILL OGDON), composer, music educator; b. Redlands, Calif., Apr. 19, 1921; s. Alfred Benjamin and Ethel (Brooks) O.; m. Beverly Jean Porter, Aug. 22, 1958; children— Bethany, Benjamin, Erica. MusB, U. Wis., 1942; MA, Hamline U., 1947; postgrad., U. Calif., Berkeley, 1949-50; pvt. composition studies with René Leibowitz, Paris, 1952-53; composition studies with Ernst Krenek, composition studies with Roger Sessions; Ph.D., Ind. U., 1955. Asst. prof. U. Tex., 1947-50; prof. Coll. St. Catherine, St. Paul, 1955-56; assoc. prof. Ill. Wesleyan U., 1956-65; dir. music Pacifica Found., KPFA, Berkeley, Calif., 1962-64; coordinator music programming U. Ill., 1965-66; prof. music U. Calif., San Diego, 1966-91, chmn. dept. music, 1966-71, research fellow Project for Music Expt., 1973-74. Author: (with Krenek and Stewart) Horizons Circled, 1974; mem. editorial bd. Perspective of New Music; composer: Three Sea Choruses, 1960-62, String Quartet, 1960, By the Isar, 1969, Un Tombeau de Cocteau, I, 1964, II, 1972, III, 1975, Sappho, The Awakening (chamber opera), 1976-80, Capriccio and Five Comments for Orch, 1980, Images, A Winter's Calendar (Soprano, piano and 3 winds), 1980, Six Small Trios for trumpet, marimba and piano, 1982, Five Preludes for violin and piano, 1982, Summer Images and Reflections, 1984-85, Five Preludes for Violin and Chamber Orchestra, 1985, Two Serenades for Wind Quintet, 1987, 90-94, Two Sea Chanteys for soprano, baritone and percussion, 1987-88, Seven Piano Pieces, 1987, 7 pieces and a Capriccio for violin and piano, 1988-89, Four D.H. Lawrence Songs for Soprano and Chamber Ensemble, 1989, 13 Expressions for solo violin and chamber ensemble, 1993, Variation Suite for violin and viola, 1995-96, Introduction and Nine Trios for two violins and piano, 1998, String Quartet, 1999, Chamber Suite for wind quintet, string quartet and piano, 2000, others. Bd. dirs. San Diego Opera Inc., 1967-70, La Jolla Civic Orch. and Chorus Assn., 1967-72, 80-82; hon. dir. N.C. Gov.'s Bd. Music, 1964— . Served with AUS, 1942-46. Nat. Endowment of Arts fellow, 1975 Mem. Anton Webern Soc. (charter), Music Execs. Calif., Calif. Profl. Music Tchrs. Assn. (hon.) Home: 482 15th St Del Mar CA 92014-2521

OGILVIE, LLOYD JOHN, clergyman; b. Kenosha, Wis., Sept. 2, 1930; s. Vard Spencer and Katherine (Jacobson) O.; m. Mary Jane Jenkins, Mar. 25, 1951. B.A., Lake Forest Coll., 1952, Garrett Theol. Sem., 1956; postgrad., New Coll., U. Edinburgh, Scotland, 1955-56; D.D., Whitworth Coll., 1973; L.H.D., U. Redlands, 1974; D.Humanities, Moravian Coll., 1975; LLD, Ea. U., 1988. Ordained to ministry Presbyn. Ch., 1956; student pastor Gurnee, Ill., 1952-56; first pastor Winnetka (Ill.) Presbyn. Ch., 1956-62; pastor 1st; Presbyn. Ch., Bethlehem, Pa., 1962-72; 1st Presbyn. Ch., Hollywood, Calif., 1972—. Preacher Chgo. Sunday Evening Club, 1962— , also frequent radio and TV personality weekly syndicated TV program Let God Love You. Author: A Life Full of Surprises, 1969, Let God Love You, 1974, If I Should Wake Before I Die, 1973, Lord of the Ups and Downs, 1974, You've Got Charisma, 1975, Cup of Wonder, 1976, Life Without Limits, 1976, Drumbeat of Love, 1977, When God First Thought of You, 1978, The Autobiography of God, 1979, The Bush Is Still Burning, 1980, The Radiance of the Inner Splendor, 1980, Congratulations, God Believes in You, 1981, Life as it Was Meant to Be, 1981, The Beauty of Love, The Beauty of Friendship, 1981, The Beauty of Caring, The Beauty of Sharing, 1981, God's Best for My Life, 1981, God's Will in Your Life, 1982, Ask Him Anything, 1982, Commentary on Book of Acts, 1983, Praying with Power, 1983, Falling into Greatness, 1983, Freedom in the Spirit, 1984, Making Stress Work For You, 1984, The Lord of the Impossible, 1984, Why Not Accept Christ's Healing and Wholeness, 1984, If God Cares, Why Do I Still Have Problems?, 1985, Understanding the Hard Sayings of Jesus, 1986, 12 Steps to Living Without Fear, 1987, A Future and a Hope, 1988, Enjoying God, 1990, Silent Strength, 1990, The Lord of the Loose Ends, 1991; gen. editor: Communicator's Commentary of the Bible, 1982; host: (TV and radio program) Let God Love You. Office: 1760 N Gower St Los Angeles CA 90028-5422

OGLE, JAMES, performing company executive; m. Mary Davis; children: Matthew, Ryan. Student, Nat. ConservatoryMusic; studied with Seiji Ozawa, Leonard Bernstein, Andre Previn, Sir Collin Davis, Boston. Music dir. Boise Philharmnonic Assn., Idaho; assoc. condr. N.C. Symphony; condr.-in-residence Appalachian State U. Cannon Music Camp. Guest condr. Music from Bear Valley, Winston-Salem Symphony, South Bend Symphony, Nebr. Chamber Orchestra; guest clinician and condr. La. State U. Symphony Orchestra and Wind Ensemble; guest artist-in-residence U. N.C.; founder, condr., artistic dir. summer residence N.C. Symphony, 1982-94., Recipient James Bland Meml. Scholarship, Malko Internat. Condr. award, 1974. Mem. Downtown Rotary Club. Office: Boise Philharmonic Assn 516 S 9th St Boise ID 83702-7005

OGLESBY, ROGER, publishing executive, editor; BJ, U. Mo.; JD, U. Calif. With Knight-Ridder's San Jose (Calif.) Mercury News, Omaha World Herald; CEO, pres. California Community News; editor, v.p. Allentown (Pa.) Morning Call; pres. Los Angeles Times (Orange County edit.); pub., editor Seattle-Post Intelligencer, 2000—. Office: Seattle Post-Intelligencer Hearst Newspapers PO Box 1909 Seattle WA 98111-1909

OGREAN, DAVID WILLIAM, sports executive; b. New Haven, Feb. 7, 1953; s. Richard Berton and Dorothy (Nystrom) O.; m. Maryellen Harvey, Aug. 10 1974; children: Matthew David, Tracy Erin, Dana Marie. BA in English cum laude, U Conn., 1974; MS in Film, Boston U., 1978. Asa S. Bushnell intern [illegible] Coll. Athletic Conf., [illegible], Mass., 1977-78, pub. rels. dir. Amateur Hockey Assn. U.S., Colorado Springs, Colo., 1978-80; mng. editor Am. Hockey and Arena mag., 1979-80; comm. rep. ESPN, Inc., Bristol, Conn., 1980-83, program mgr., 1983-88; asst. exec. dir. for TV Coll. Football Assn., Boulder, Colo., 1988-90; dir. of broadcasting U.S. Olympic Com., Colorado Springs, 1990-93; exec. dir. USA Hockey, Colorado Springs, 1993-99; chmn. Colorado Springs Sports Corp., 1996-97; dep. exec. dir. mktg. U.S. Olympic Com., Colorado Springs, 1999-2000; pres., CEO Colorado Springs Sports Corp., 2000—. Chmn. legis. com. U.S. Olympic Com., 1997-99. Mem. Country Club Colo., Broadmoor Golf Club. Office: Colorado Springs Sports Corp 219 W Colorado Ave Colorado Springs CO 80903-3338

OH, ANGELA E. lawyer; b. L.A., Sept. 8, 1955; BA, UCLA, 1977, MPH, 1981; JD, U. Calif., Davis, 1986. Bar: Calif. 1986. With Beck, DeCorso, Daly, Barrera & Oh, Redondo Beach, Calif., 1987—. Lawyer del. 9th Cir. Jud. Conf., 1995-96, lawyer rep.; mem. Senator Boxer's Jud. Noms. Com. for Ctrl. Dist. Calif., 1994-95; bd. mem. Calif. Women's Law Ctr., Lawyers Mutual Ins. Co., Lawyer Representive to the 9th Cir. Judicial Conf. Contbr. articles to profl. jours. and newspapers such as L.A. Times, L.A. Sentinel; spkr. in field including Dartmouth Coll., Hastings Sch. Law, Columbia Univ., Harvard Law Sch., Princeton Theology Seminary. Spl. counsel to the Assembly Spl. Com. on the L.A. Crisis; active Lawyers' Mutual Ins. Co.; active cmty. adv. bd. First Interstate Bank Calif.; bd. dirs. Calif. Women's Law Ctr. Mem. ABA, State Bar Calif., Korean-Am. Bar Assn. So. Calif. (pres.), L.A. County Bar Assn. Office: Beck DeCorso Daly Barrera & Oh PO Box 7000 639 Redondo Beach CA 90277

O'HARA, CATHERINE, actress, comedienne; b. Toronto, Mar. 4, 1954; m. Bo Welch, 1992. Actress, writer with Second City, Toronto, 1974; co-founder of SCTV, 1976 (Emmy award); films include After Hours, 1985, Heartburn, 1986, Beetlejuice, 1988, Dick Tracy, 1990, Betsy's Wedding, 1990, Home Alone, 1990, Little Vegas, 1990, There Goes The Neighborhood, 1992, Home Alone II: Lost In New York, 1992, (voice) The Nightmare Before Christmas, 1993, The Paper, 1994, Wyatt Earp, 1994, A Simple Twist of Fate, 1994, Tall Tale, 1995, Waiting for Guffman, 1996, The Last of the high Kings, 1996, (voice) Pippi Longstocking, 1997, Home Fries, 1998, The Life Before This, 1999, (voice) Bartok the Magnificient, 1999; TV, SCTV, Comic Relief, Dream On (dir.), Hope, 1997; co-writer SCTV, Cinemax, 1984, Really Weird Tales, HBO, 1986; dir. (TV series) Dream On, 1990; writer Really Weird Tales, 1987; TV guest appearances The Simpsons Show, The Larry Sanders Show, 1992, The Outer Limits, 1995.

OHARAH, JACK, academic administrator; m. Elaine Oharah; 3 children. BS, MS, Kans. State Coll.; EdS in C.C. Adminstrn., PhD Higher Edn., C.C. Admin./Vocat. Ed., U. Iowa. Dean coll., acting pres. Muscatine C.C., Iowa, 1976-86; instr. Scott C.C., Davenport; exec. v.p. instrn. and devel. Butler County C.C., El Dorado, Kans., 1986-96; pres. Edmonds C.C., Lynnwood, Wash., 1996—. Mem. ACCT Pres.' Adv. Com., Corrections Edn. Com. Operating Budget Com.; mem. exec. com. State Computer Info. Svcs. Wash. Comty. and Tech. Colls.; mem. AACC Commn. on Publs. and Pub. Rels., Edmonds Alliance for Econ. Devel. Bd., Wash. State Higher Edn. Bd.'s Project Coord. Team. Hon. bd. dirs. Cascade Symphony Orch., Big Bros./Big Sisters; vice-chmn. Puget Sound Ctr. for Tchg., Learning and Tech. Mem. South Snohomish County C. of C. (co-chair), Snohomish County Econ. Devel. Bd. Office: Edmonds C C 20000 68th Ave W Lynnwood WA 98036-5912 Fax: 425-640-1532. E-mail: joharah@edcc.edu

O'HEARN, MICHAEL JOHN, lawyer; b. Akron, Ohio, Jan. 29, 1952; s. Leo Ambrose and Margaret Elizabeth (Clark) O'H. BA in Econs., UCLA, 1975; postgrad., U. San Diego, 1977; JD, San Fernando Valley Coll. Law, 1979; postgrad., Holy Apostles Sem., 1993-94. Bar: Calif. 1979, U.S. Dist. Ct. (ctrl. dist.) Calif. 1979. Document analyst Mellonics Info. Ctr., Litton Industries, Canoga Park, Calif., 1977-79; pvt. practice Encino, 1979-80; atty. VISTA/Grey Law Inc., L.A., 1980-81; assoc. Donald E. Chadwick & Assocs., Woodland Hills, Calif., 1981-84, Law Offices of Laurence Ring, Beverly Hills, 1984-85; atty., in-house counsel Coastal Ins. Co., Van Nuys, 1985-89; atty. Citrus Glen Apts., Ventura, 1989-92; pvt. practice Ventura County, 1992-2000; arbitrator, 1995—; propr., property mgr. Channel Islands Village Mgmt. Co., 1998-2000. Life mem. Rep. Nat. Com. Recipient Cert. of Appreciation, Agy. for Vol. Svc., 1981, San Fernando Valley Walk for Life, 1988, Cert. of Appreciation, Arbitrator for the Superior and Mcpl. Cts., Ventura County Jud. Dist., 1996. Mem. KC, Ventura County Bar Assn., Ventura County Trial Lawyers Assn., Secular Franciscan Order., Pioneer Total Abstinence Assn. of the Sacred Heart. Republican. Roman Catholic. Avocations: golf, yachting, fishing. Home: 1941 Fisher Dr Apt B Oxnard CA 93035-3022 Office: 3650 Ketch Ave Oxnard CA 93035-3029 E-mail: mohearn_brightstar@yahoo.com

OHMAN, DIANA J. state official, former school system administrator; b. Sheridan, Wyo., Oct. 3, 1950; d. Arden and Doris Marie (Carstens) Mahin. AA, Casper Coll., 1970; BA, U. Wyo., 1972, MEd, 1977, postgrad., 1979—. Tchr. kindergarten Natrona County Sch. Dist., Casper, Wyo., 1971-72; tchr. rural sch. K-8 Campbell County Sch. Dist., Gillette, 1972-80, rural prin. K-8, 1980-82, prin. K-6, 1982-84, assoc. dir. instrn., 1984-87; dir. K-12 Goshen County Migrant Program, Torrington, 1988-89; prin. K-2 Goshen County Sch. Dist., Torrington, 1987-90; state supt. pub. instrn. State of Wyo., Cheyenne, 1991-94, secretary of state, 1995-98. Chmn. Campbell County Mental Health Task Force, 1986-87; mem. Legis. Task Force on Edn. of Handicapped 3-5 Yr. Olds, 1988-89. State Committeewoman Wyo. Rep. Party, 1985-88. Recipient Wyo. Elem. Prin. of Yr. award, 1990; named Campbell County Tchr. of Yr. 1980, Campbell County Profl. Bus. Woman of Yr. 1984, Outstanding Young Woman in Am., 1983. Mem. Coun. of Chief of State Sch. Officers (Washington chpt.), Internat. Reading Assn., Wyo. Assn. of Sch. Adminstrs., N.Am. Securities Adminstrs. Assn., Kappa Delta Pi, Phi Kappa Phi, Phi Delta Kappa. Republican. Lutheran. Office: Sec State Office Attn Karla State Capitol Cheyenne WY 82002-0001

OJALVO, MORRIS, civil engineer, educator; b. N.Y.C., Mar. 4, 1924; s. Nissim and (Fanny) O.; m. Anita Bedein, Dec. 26, 1948; children— Lynne, Joseph, Howard, Isobel. B.C.E., Rensselear Poly. Inst., Troy, N.Y., 1944, M.C.E., 1952; Ph.D., Lehigh U., Bethlehem, Pa., 1960; J.D., Ohio State U., Columbus, 1978. Bar: Ohio bar 1979. Draftsman Am. Bridge Co., Elmira, N.Y., 1946-47; tutor civil engring. CCNY, 1947-49; instr. Rensselear Poly. Inst., 1949-51; asst. prof. Princeton U., 1951-58; research instr. Lehigh U., 1958-60; mem. faculty Ohio State U., 1960—, prof. civil engring., 1964-82, prof. emeritus, 1982—; vis. prof. U. Tex.-Austin, 1982-83. Author: Thin-Walled Bars With Open Profiles, 1990; contbr. papers in field; patentee warp restraining device. Served with USNR, 1944-46. Mem. ASCE, Structural Stability Research Council. Home and Office: 1024 Fairway Ln Estes Park CO 80517-7156

OKAMURA, ARTHUR SHINJI, artist, educator, writer; b. Long Beach, Calif., Feb. 24, 1932; s. Frank Akira and Yuki O.; m. Elizabeth Tuomi, Aug. 7, 1953 (div.); children: Beth, Jonathan, Jane, Ethan; m. Kitty Wong, 1991. Student, Art Inst. of Chgo., 1950-54, U. Chgo., 1951, 52, 57, art seminar Yale, 1954. Faculty Ctrl. YMCA Coll., Chgo., 1956, 57, Evanston (Ill.) Art Center, 1956-57, Art Inst. Chgo., North Shore Art League, Winnetka, Ill., Acad. Art, San Francisco, 1957, Calif. Sch. Fine Arts, 1958, Ox Bow Summer Art Sch., Saugatuck, Mich., 1963, Calif. Coll. Arts and Crafts, Oakland, 1958-59, prof. arts, 1966-97, prof. emeritus, 1997—. Instr. watercolor painting, 1987; dir. San Francisco Studio Art, 1958; tchr. watercolor workshops, Bali, Indonesia, 1989, 92; lectr. in field. Author: [illegible] Ox-Herding, 1971, (with Robert Bly) Basho, 1972, Ten Poems by Issa, 1992, (with Steve Kowit) Passionate Journey, 1984, Magic Rabbit, 1995, The Paper Propeller, 2000; one-man shows include Charles Feingarten Galleries, Chgo., 1956, 58, 59, San Francisco, 1957, Santa Barbara Mus. Art, 1958, Oakland Mus. Art, 1959, Legion Honor, San Francisco, 1961, Dallas, 1962, La Jolla (Calif.) Mus., 1963, U. Utah, 1964, San Francisco Mus. Art, 1968, Hanssen Gallery, 1968, 71, Ruth Braunstein, San Francisco, 1981, 82, 84, 86-88, 90, 94, 97, 2000; exhibited in group shows including Pa. Acad. Fine Art, U. Chgo., U. Wash., U. Ill., Art Inst. Chgo., L.A. County Mus., Am. Fedn. Art, Denver Mus., NAD, De Young Mus., San Francisco, Knoedler Gallery, N.Y.C., Feingarten Galleries, Whitney Mus. Art, others; retrospective at Bolinas Mus. and Claudia Chapline Galleries, Stinson Beach, Calif., 1995; represented in permanent collections including Art Inst. Chgo., Borg-Warner Collections, Chgo., Whitney Mus. Art, N.Y.C., Santa Barbara Mus. Art, San Francisco Mus. Art, Ill. State Normal, Corcoran Mus., Nat. Collection Fine Arts, Smithsonian Instn., 1968, many others. Served as pvt. AUS, 1955-56. Recipient 1st prize religious art U. Chgo., 1953; Ryerson travelling fellow, 1954; Martin Cahn award contemporary Am. paintings Art Inst. Chgo., 1957; purchase award U. Ill., 1959; purchase award Nat. Soc. Arts and Letters, N.Y.C., 1960; Neysa McMein purchase award Whitney Mus. Art, 1960; Schwabacher-Frey award 79th Ann. of San Francisco Mus. Art, 1960 Mem. Commonweal (bd. dirs. 1993-98). Home: 210 Kale Rd Bolinas CA 94924

OKAMURA, HIDEO, manufacturing executive; b. Kochi-City, Japan, May 30, 1943; came to U.S., 1968; s. Junki and Hiroka Okamura; divorced; 1 child, Jennifer H. Prodn. mgr. Power Axle Corp., Compton, Calif., 1984-87; dir. tech. prodn. Dynamic Axle Co., Inc., Long Beach, 1988-90; mng. dir. Aragon Engring., Inc., Rancho Dominguez, 1991-96. Mem. Am. Soc. of Metal, Acad. of Magical Arts, Inc. Avocations: scuba diving, landscaping, photography, golf, travel. Home: 16889 Helena Cir Fountain Vly CA 92708-2815 Office: Transpower Techs Inc 6301 Orangethorpe Ave Buena Park CA 90620-1340

OKE, ROBERT EUGENE, state legislator; b. West Seattle, Sept. 4, 1940; m. Judy Oke; 3 children. With USN; mem. Wash. Senate, Dist. 26, Olympia, 1990—; mem. natural resources, parks and recreation com.; Rep. whip Wash. Senate, Olympia, 1993, 94; mem. transp. com.; mem. labor and workforce devel. com.; mem. senate com. on vets. and mil. affairs; mem. Blue Ribbon panel on ferry safety; mem. organized crime adv. bd.; mem. joint legis. audit and rev. com.; mem. legis. oversight com. Pacific Fisheries Task Force; mem. panel transp. beneficiaries; mem. aquatic nuisance species planning com. Former chmn. South Kitsap Parks and Recreation Commn.; mem. Wash. State Coalition Teaming with Wildlife; mem. cmty. correction steering com. Kitsap County; mem. Kitsay County Law and Justice Coun. Recipient Wash. State Sportsmen's Coun. awatrd, 1991, Nat. Sr. Citizen Hall of Fame award, 1994, Cert. of Appreciation Wash. State Farm Bur., 1995-96, 97-98, Cornerstone award Assn. Wash. Bus., 1997. Mem. Port Orchard C. of C., Kiwanis (Port Orchard), Kitsap Poggie Club. Republican. Office: 110 Irving Newhouse Ofc Olympia WA 98504-0001

O'KEEFE, EDWARD FRANKLIN, lawyer; b. S.I., N.Y., June 9, 1937; s. Francis Franklin and Bertha (Hall) O'K.; m. Toni Lynne McGohan; children: Kira Kathleen, Douglas Franklin, Andrew Franklin, Alison Elizabeth, Theadore William, Nigel Francis. A.B., U. N.C., 1959; J.D., U. Denver, 1961. Bar: Colo. 1962. Law clk. Colo. Supreme Ct., Denver, 1962-63; assoc. gen. counsel Hamilton Mgmt. Corp., Denver, 1966-69, sec., 1968-76, v.p. legal, gen. counsel, 1969-76; now mng. ptnr. Moye, Giles O'Keefe, Vermeire & Gorrell, Denver. Assoc. gen. counsel, sec. ITT Variable Annuity Ins. Co., Denver, 1969, v.p. legal, gen. counsel, 1969-70; sec. Hamilton Funds Inc., Denver, 1968-76 Served with USNR, 1963-66. Mem. Nat. Assn. Security Dealers (dist. conduct com., chmn. 1976), Colo. Assn. Corporate Counsel (pres. 1974-75) Home: 1225 17th St Ste 2900 Denver CO 80202-5535 also: 2680 Mariners Way SE Southport NC 28461 Office: Moye Giles O'Keefe Vermeire 1225 17th St Fl 29 Denver CO 80202-5534 E-mail: efokeefe@mgovg.com

O'KEEFE, MARK DAVID, state official; b. Pittston, Pa., July 10, 1952; s. Gervase Frances and Anne Regina (Faltyn) O'K.; m. Lucy Bliss Dayton, Sept. 24, 1983; children: Margaret, Angus, Greer. BA in Environ. Studies, Calif. State U., Sacramento, 1977; MS in Environ. Studies, U. Mont., 1984. Mgr. adjudication program Mont. Dept. Nat. Resources, Helena, 1979-81, dir. water devel., 1981-83; owner, operator Glacier Wilderness Guides, West Glacier, Mont., 1983-89; mem. Mont. Ho. Reps., Helena, 1989-92; state auditor State of Mont., Helena, 1993—. Bd. dirs. Boyd Andrew Chem. Dependency Treatment Ctr., Helena, 1991—. With U.S. Army, 1971-73. Democrat. Avocations: backpacking, jogging, rafting, fly fishing. Home: 531 Power St Helena MT 59601-6115 Office: State Auditors Office PO Box 4009 Helena MT 59604-4009

OKERLUND, ARLENE NAYLOR, university official; b. Emmitsburg, Md., Oct. 13, 1938; d. George Wilbur and Ruth Opal (Sensenbaugh) Naylor; m. Michael Dennis Okerlund, June 6, 1959 (div. Apr. 1983); 1 dau., Linda Susan. B.A., U. Md., 1960; Ph.D., U. Calif.-San Diego, 1969. Instr. sci. Mercy Hosp. Nursing Sch., Balt., 1959-63; prof. English San Jose State U., Calif., 1969-80, 94—, dean humanities and arts, 1980-86, acad. v.p., 1986-93. Cons. Ednl. Testing Service, Berkeley, Calif., 1976-80 Editor: San Jose Studies, 1975-80; contbr. articles on the humanities to profl. jours. Bd. dirs. World Forum Silicon Valley, Am. Beethoven Soc.; mem. Peninsula Banjo Band. Grantee NEH, 1979; grantee San Jose State U., 1971-72 Mem. Philol. Assn. Pacific Coast (sec.-treas. 1975-78), MLA (del. to assembly, west coast rep. 1976-77), Internat. Coun. Fine Arts Deans, Calif. Coun. Fine Arts Deans (pres. 1984-86), Am. Beethoven Soc. (bd. dirs.), Peninsula Banjo Band. Democrat. Office: San Jose State U Dept English Washington Sq San Jose CA 95192-0001 E-mail: okerlund@email.sjsu.edu

OKINAGA, LAWRENCE SHOJI, lawyer; b. Honolulu, July 7, 1941; s. Shohei and Hatsu (Kakimoto) O.; m. Carolyn Hisako Uesugi, Nov. 26, 1966; children: Carrie, Caryn, Laurie. BA, U. Hawaii, 1963; JD, Georgetown U., 1972. Bar: Hawaii 1972, U.S. Dist. Ct. Hawaii 1972, U.S. Ct. Appeals (9th cir.) 1976. Adminstrv. asst. to Congressman Spark Matsunaga, Honolulu, 1964, 65-69; law clk. to chief judge U.S. Dist. Ct. Hawaii, Honolulu, 1972-73; assoc. Carlsmith Ball, Honolulu, 1973-76, ptnr., 1976—. Mem. Gov.'s Citizens Adv. Com. Coastal Zone Mgmt., 1974-79; sec. Hawaii Bicentennial Corp., 1975-77, chmn., 1985-87, vice chmn., 1983-85; mem. Jud. Selection Commn., State of Hawaii, 1979-87, vice chmn., 1986; mem. consumer adv. coun. Fed. Res. Bd., 1984-86; chmn. State of Hawaii Jud. Conduct Commn., 1991-94; apptd. mem. Fed. Savings and Loan Adv. Council, Washington, 1988-89; mem. nat. adv. coun. U.S. Small Bus. Adminstrn., 1994-2000; mem. adv. coun. Fed. Res. Bank of San Francisco, 1995—. Bd. dirs. Moiliili Cmty. Ctr., Honolulu, 1965-68, 73-86, trustee 1993—; bd. visitors Georgetown U. Law Ctr., 1993—; trustee Kuakini Med. Ctr., 1984-88, 89-96. Capt. USAFR, 1964-72, 74-76. Mem. ABA (ho. of dels. 1991-94, standing com. on jud. selection tenure and compensation 1993-96, standing com. on jud. independence 1999—), Hawaii Bar Assn. (sec., bd. dirs. 1981), Am. Judicature Soc. (bd. dirs. 1986—, treas. 1995-97, pres. 1997-99), Georgetown U. Law Alumni Assn. (bd. dirs. 1986-91), Omicron Delta Kappa. Office: Carlsmith Ball PO Box 656 Honolulu HI 96809-0656

OLAFSON, FREDERICK ARLAN, philosophy educator; b. Winnipeg, Man., Can., Sept. 1, 1924; s. Kristinn K. and Fredericka (Björnson) O.; m. Allie Lewis, June 20, 1952 (dec.); children— Peter Niel, Christopher Arlan, Thomas Andrew. A.B., Harvard U., 1947, M.A., 1948, Ph.D., 1951. [illegible] then assoc. prof. Vassar Coll., 1954-60; assoc. prof. Johns Hopkins U., 1960-64; prof. edn. and philosophy Harvard Grad. Sch. Edn., 1964-71; prof. philosophy U. Calif., San Diego, 1971-91, chmn. dept., 1973-76, assoc. dean grad. studies and research, 1980-85. Author: Principles and Persons, 1967, Ethics and Twentieth Century Thought, 1973, The Dialectic of Action, 1979, Heidegger and the Philosophy of the Mind, 1987, What Is A Human Being?, 1995, Heidegger and the Ground of Ethics, 1998. Served to lt. (j.g.) USNR, 1943-46. Mem. Nat. Acad. Edn. Home: 6081 Avenida Chamnez La Jolla CA 92037-7404

OLAH, GEORGE ANDREW, chemist, educator; b. Budapest, Hungary, May 22, 1927; came to U.S., 1964, naturalized, 1970; . Julius and Magda (Krasznai) O.; m. Judith Agnes Lengyel, July 9, 1949; children: George John, Ronald Peter. PhD, Tech. U. Budapest, 1949, D (hon.), 1989; DSc (hon.), U. Durham, 1988, U. Munich, 1990, U. Crete, Greece, 1994, U. Szeged, Hungary, 1995, U. Veszprem, 1995, Case Western Res. U., , 1995, U. So. Calif., 1995, U. Montpellier, 1996, SUNY, 1998, U. Pecs, Hungary, 2001. Mem. faculty Tech. U. Budapest, 1949-54; assoc. dir. Ctrl. Chem. Rsch. Inst., Hungarian Acad. Scis., 1954-56; rsch. scientist Dow Chem. Can. Ltd., 1957-64, Dow Chem. Co., Framingham, Mass., 1964-65; prof. chemistry Case Western Res. U., Cleve., 1965-69, C.F. Mabery prof. rsch., 1969-77; Donald P. and Katherine B. Loker disting. prof. chemistry, dir. Hydrocarbon Rsch. Inst., U. So. Calif., L.A., 1977—. Vis. prof. chemistry Ohio State U., 1963, U. Heidelberg, Germany, 1965, U. Colo., 1969, Swiss Fed. Inst. Tech., 1972, U. Munich, 1973, U. London, 1973-79, L. Pasteur U., Strasbourg, 1974, U. Paris, 1981; hon. vis. lectr. U. London, 1981-95; cons. to industry. Author: Friedel-Crafts Reactions, Vols. I-IV, 1963-64; (with P. Schleyer) Carbonium Ions, Vols. I-V, 1969-76, Friedel-Crafts Chemistry, 1973, Carbocations and Electrophilic Reactions, 1973, Halonium Ions, 1975; (with G.K.S. Prakash and J. Somer) Superacids, 1984; (with Prakash, R.E. Williams, L.D. Field and K. Wade) Hypercarbon Chemistry, 1987; (with R. Malthotra and S.C. Narang) Nitration, 1989, Cage Hydrocarbons, 1990; (with Wade and Williams) Electron Deficient Boron and Carbon Clusters, 1991; (with Chambers and Prakash) Synthetic Fluorine Chemistry, 1992; (with Molnar) Hydrocarbon Chemistry, 1995 (with Laali, Wang, Prakash) Onium Ions, 1998, A Life of Magic Chemistry, 2001; also chpts. in books, numerous papers in field; patentee in field. Recipient Alexander von Humboldt Sr. U.S. Scientist award, 1979, Calif. Scientist of Yr. award, 1989, Pioneer of Chemistry award Am. Inst. Chemists, 1993; Mendeleev medal Russian Acad. Scis., 1992, Kapitsa medal Russian Acad. Natural Scis., 1995; Nobel prize in Chemistry, 1994; Guggenheim fellow 1972, 88. Fellow AAAS, Chem. Inst. Can., Brit. Chem. Soc. (hon., Centenary lectr. 1978); mem. NAS, Italian NAS Lincei, Royal Soc. London (fgn.), Royal Soc. Can., European Acad. Arts, Scis. and Humanities, Royal Chem. Soc. (hon.), Italy Chem. Soc. (hon.), Hungarian Acad. Sci. (hon.), Am. Chem. Soc. (award petroleum chemistry 1964, Leo Hendrik Baekeland award N.J. sect. 1966, Morley medal Cleve. sect. 1970, award Synthetic organic chemistry 1979, Roger Adams award in organic chemistry 1989, Arthur C. Cope award 2001), Am. Philos. Soc. Home: 2252 Gloaming Way Beverly Hills CA 90210-1717 Office: U So Calif Labor Hydrocarbon Rsch Inst Los Angeles CA 90007 E-mail: olah@usc.edu

O'LAUGHLIN, JOANIE, broadcast executive; b. Pasadena, Calif. Student, San Diego St. Sales rep. Blair TV, 1961-63, nat. sales coord., traffic mgr., 1963-75, ops. mgr., 1975-82, sta. mgr., 1982-95; v.p., gen. mgr. Sta. XETV-TV, San Diego, 1996—. Adv. bd. Shared Vision Found.; bd. trustees San Diego Lions Club Welfare Found. Office: Sta XETV TV 8253 Ronson Rd San Diego CA 92111-2004

OLDFIELD, JAMES EDMUND, nutrition educator; b. Victoria, B.C., Can., Aug. 30, 1921; came to U.S., 1949; s. Henry Clarence and Doris O. Oldfield; m. Mildred E. Atkinson, Sept. 4, 1942; children: Nancy E. Oldfield McLaren, Kathleen E. Oldfield Sansone, David J., Jane E. Oldfield Imper, Richard A. BSA, U. B.C., 1941, MSA, 1949; PhD, Oreg. State U., 1951. Faculty Oreg. State U., Corvallis, 1951-90, head dept. animal sci., 1967-83, dir. Nutrition Research Inst., 1986-90. Mem. nat. tech. adv. com. on water supply U.S. Dept. Interior, Washington, 1967-68; bd. dirs. Coun. for Agrl. Sci. and Tech., Ames, Iowa, 1978-84; mem. nutrition study sect. NIH, Bethesda, Md., 1975-80, 85-87; cons. Selenium Tellurium Devel. Assn., Grimbergen, Belgium, 1990—. Editor: Selenium in Biomedicine, 1967, Sulphur in Nutrition, 1970, Selenium in Biology and Medicine, 1987; author: Selenium in Nutrition, 1971, Selenium World Atlas, 1999. Served to maj. Can. Army, 1942-46, ETO, Mil. Cross award. Recipient Klaus Schwarz medal Internat. Assn. Bioinorganic Scientists, 1998; Fulbright rsch. scholar U.S. Dept. State, 1974, Massey U., New Zealand. Fellow Am. Soc. Animal Sci. (pres. 1966-67, Morrison award 1972), Am. Inst. Nutrition; mem. Am. Chem. Soc., Am. Registry Profl. Animal Scientists (pres. 1990, editor: Profl. Animal Scientist 1993-96), Fedn. Am. Socs. Exptl. Biol., Pacific Fisheries Technologists (pres. 1966), Kiwanis (pres. 1964, lt. gov. 1986). Republican. Episcopalian. Home: 1325 NW 15th St Corvallis OR 97330-2604 Office: Oreg State Univ Dept Animal Sci Corvallis OR 97331 Fax: 541-737-4174. E-mail: James.E.Oldfield@orst.edu

OLDHAM, WILLIAM GEORGE, electrical engineering and computer science educator; b. Detroit, May 5, 1938; m. Nancy Dereich; children: Katherine Ann, William James. B.S., Carnegie Mellon Inst., 1960, M.S., 1961, Ph.D., 1963. Staff scientist Siemens-Schuckert, Erlangen, W.Ger., 1963-64; mem. faculty elec. engring. and computer scis. dept. U. Calif., Berkeley, 1964—, prof., 1972—, dir. Electronics Research Lab., 1985-90; project mgr. Intel Corp., Santa Clara, Calif., 1974-75. Author: An Introduction to Electronics, 1972, Electrical Engineering, An Introduction, 1984. NSF fellow, 1970; Guggenheim fellow, 1985-86. Fellow IEEE; mem. NAE. Office: U Calif Berkeley Electronic Rsch Lab 509 Cory Hl Berkeley CA 94720-0001

O'LEARY, MARION HUGH, university dean, chemist; b. Quincy, Ill., Mar. 24, 1941; s. J. Gilbert and Ruth Elizabeth (Kerr) O'L.; m. Sandra E. Eisemann, Sept. 5, 1964 (div. 1979); children— Catherine, Randall, Jessica; m. Elizabeth M. Kean, Jan. 24, 1981. B.S., U. Ill., 1963; Ph.D., MIT, 1966. Asst. prof. chemistry U. Wis., Madison, 1967-73, assoc. prof., 1973-78, prof. chemistry and biochemistry, 1978-89; prof. and head dept. biochemistry U. Nebr., Lincoln, 1989-96; dean Coll. Natural Scis. and Math., Calif. State U., Sacramento, 1996—. Cons. Institut Pertanian Bogor, Indonesia, 1983-84; vis. prof. Universitas Andalas, Padang, Indonesia, 1984-85, Australian Nat. U., 1982-83. Author: Contemporary Organic Chemistry, 1976. Editor: Isotope Effects on Enzyme-Catalyzed Reactions, 1977. Contbr. articles to sci. publs. Grantee, NSF, U.S. Dept. Agr., Dept. Energy, NIH; Guggenheim Found. fellow, 1982-83; Sloan Found. fellow, 1972-74. Fellow AAAS; mem. Am. Chem. Soc., Am. Soc. Biochemistry and Molecular Biology. Home: 6428 Orange Hill Ln Carmichael CA 95608-4580 Office: Calif State U Coll Natural Scis Math 6000 J St Sacramento CA 95819-6123 E-mail: moleary@csus.edu

O'LEARY, PRENTICE L. lawyer; b. L.A., May 6, 1942; BA, UCLA, 1965, JD, 1968. Bar: Calif. 1969. Ptnr. Sheppard, Mullin, Richter & Hampton, L.A., 1974—. Bd. dirs. Legal Aid Found. L.A., 1987-93. Mem. ABA (bus. bankruptcy com.), State Bar Calif., Los Angles County Bar Assn. (chmn. bankruptcy com., chmn. comml. law and bankrupt sect. 1985-86), Am. Coll. Bankruptcy Profls., Order of Coif. Office: Sheppard Mullin Richter & Hampton 333 S Hope St Fl 48 Los Angeles CA 90071-1406

O'LEARY, THOMAS MICHAEL, lawyer; b. N.Y.C., Aug. 16, 1948; s. James and Julia Ann (Connolly) O'L.; m. Luise Ann Williams, Jan. 13, 1978; 1 child, Richard Meridith. BA, CUNY, 1974; JD, Seattle U., 1977. Bar: Wash. 1977, U.S. Ct. Mil. Appeals 1978, U.S. Ct. Appeals (9th cir.), U.S. Supreme Ct. 1983. Dep. pros. atty. Pierce County, Tacoma, 1978; commd. 1st lt. U.S. Army, 1978, advanced through grades to capt., 1978; chief trial counsel Office of Staff Judge Adv., Ft. Polk, La., 1978-79, trial def. counsel, trial def. svc., 1979-81; chief legal advisor Office Insp. Gen., Heidelberg, Fed. Republic of Germany, 1981-82; sr. def. counsel Trial Def. Svc., Giessen, Fed. Republic of Germany, 1982-84; asst. chief adminstrv. law U.S. Army Armor Ctr., Ft. Knox, Ky., 1984-85, chief adminstrv. law, 1985, chief legal asst., 1985-86; ret. U.S. Army, 1996; sr. trial atty. Immigration and naturalization Svc., Phoenix, 1987; sector counsel, spl. asst. U.S. atty., U.S. Border Patrol, Tucson, 1987-90; enforcement counsel U.S. Immigration and Naturalization Svc., Tucson, 1990-95, asst. dist. counsel Phoenix litigation, 1995-97. Apptd. U.S. Immigration Judge, U.S. Immigration Ct., Imperial, Calif., 1997-2000, apptd. sr. U.S. Immigration Judge, Tucson, 2000—. Decorated Purple Heart, Cross of Gallantry (Vietnam). Mem. Judge Advs Assn., Wash. State Bar Assn. E-mail: Thomas.O'Leary@usdoj.gov. Home: 9080 E 25th St Tucson AZ 85710-8675 Office: US Immigration Ct 1705 E Hanna Rd Ste 366 Eloy AZ 85231-9612

O'LEARY, TIM, controller; Contr. Shea Homes, Walnut, Calif., 1993—. Office: J F Shea Co Inc PO Box 489 Walnut CA 91788-0489

OLEJKO, MITCHELL J. lawyer; b. Jersey City, June 15, 1951; s. Frank Edward and Eugenia Joan Olejko; m. Jill Wolcott, Aug. 5, 1988. AB, Boston Coll., 1973; JD, Washington U., St. Louis, 1977. Bar: Wash. 1977, Oreg. 1992, Calif. 1998, U.S. Dist. Ct. (we. dist.) Wash. 1977, (ea. dist.) Wash. 1978, U.S. Dist. Ct. Oreg. 1992, U.S. Ct. Appeals (9th cir.) 1980, U.S. Dist. Ct. (no. dist.) Calif. 1999. Assoc. Davis, Wright, Todd, Riese & Jones, Seattle, 1977-82; ptnr. Davis, Wright & Jones, Seattle, 1982-92; chief legal officer, sr. v.p. Legacy Health System, Portland, Oreg., 1992-98; ptnr. Morrison & Foerster, San Francisco, 1998—. Contbr. Ambulatory Care Management, 2d edit., 1991. Mem. Am. Acad. Hosp. Attys., Wash. State Soc. Hosp. Attys. (pres. 1991-92). Office: Morrison & Foerster 425 Market St San Francisco CA 94105-2482

OLERUD, JOHN GARRETT, professional baseball player; b. Seattle, Aug. 5, 1968; s. John E. Olerud. Student, Washington State U. Infielder Toronto Blue Jays, 1989-96, NY Mets, 1997-99, Seattle Mariners, 1999—. Mem. Am. League All-Star Team, 1993. winner A.L batting title, 1993. Office: Seattle Mariners 1st Ave S & Atlantic Seattle WA 98104

OLES, STUART GREGORY, lawyer; b. Seattle, Dec. 15, 1924; s. Floyd and Helen Louise (La Violette) O.; m. Ilse Hanewald, Feb. 12, 1954; children: Douglas, Karl, Stephen. BS magna cum laude, U. Wash., 1947, JD, 1948. Bar: Wash., 1949, U.S. Supreme Ct. 1960. Dep. pros. atty. King County, Wash., 1949, chief civil dept., 1949-50; gen. practice law Seattle, 1950-95; sr. ptnr. firm Oles, Morrison & Rinker and predecessor, 1955-90, of counsel, 1991-95. Author: A View From the Rock, 1994, On Behalf of My Clients -- A Lawyer's Life, 1998. Chmn. Seattle Cmty. Concert Assn., 1955; pres. Friends Seattle Pub. Libr., 1956; mem. Wash. pub. Disclosure Commn., 1973-075; trustee Ch. Divinity Sch. of Pacific, Berkeley, Calif., 1974-75; mem. bd. curators Wash. State Hist. Soc., 1983; former mem. Seattle Symphony Bd.; pres. King County Ct. House Rep. Club, 1950, U. Wash. Young Rep. Club, 1947; Wash. conv. floor leader Taft, 1952, Goldwater, 1964; Wash. chmn. Citizens for Goldwater, 1964; chmn. King County Rep. convs., 1966, 68, 76, 84, 88, 90, 92, 96, Wash. State Rep. Conv., 1980. Served with USMCR, 1943-45. Mem. ABA (past regional vice-chmn. pub. contract law sect.), Wash. Bar Assn., Order of Coif, Scabbard and Blade, Am. Legion, Kapoho Bay Club (pres.), Am. Highland Cattle Assn. (v.p. and dir.), Phi Beta Kappa, Phi Alpha Delta. Home: 22715 SE 43rd Ct Issaquah WA 98029-5200 also: RR 2 Pahoa HI 96778-9802

OLIN, KENT OLIVER, banker; b. Chgo., July 27, 1930; s. Oliver Arthur and Beatrice Louise Olin; m. Marilyn Louise Wood, May 27, 1956. BS in Econs., Ripon Coll., 1955. Dist. sales rep. Speed Queen Corp., Ripon, Wis., 1955-57; v.p. United Bank, Denver, 1957-71; exec. v.p., pres. Bank One Boulder (formerly Affiliated First Nat. Bank), Boulder, Colo., 1971-74; pres., CEO Bank One Colorado Springs, Colorado Springs, 1974-86, Bank One Colo. (formerly Affiliated Bankshares of Colo.), Denver, 1986-91, vice chmn. bd., 1992-94, also bd. dirs. Trustee Colo. Coll., Colorado Springs, 1983-89, Falcon Found., Colorado Springs, 1983—; trustee El Pomar Found., Colorado Springs, 1992—, chair exec. com.; trustee Colorado Springs Fine Arts Ctr., 1992-95; sec.-treas. Air Force Acad. Found., Colorado Springs, 1988; dir., chair exec. com. Garden City (Kans.) Co.; bd. dirs. Rocky Mountain Arthritis Found., Denver, 1989-94, Goodwill Industries, Colorado Springs, 1993-99. Staff sgt. USAF, 1950-54. Mem. Broadmoor Golf Club (dir. 1975-88, 93-98). Office: El Pomar Found 10 Lake Cir Colorado Springs CO 80906-4201

OLIVER, DALE HUGH, lawyer; b. Lansing, Mich., June 26, 1947; s. Alvin Earl and Jean Elizabeth (Stanton) O.; m. Mylbra Ann Chorney, Aug. 16, 1969; children: Nathan Corey, John Franklin. BA, Mich. State U., 1969; JD cum laude, Harvard U., 1972. Bar: D.C. 1973, U.S. Dist. Ct. (D.C. dist.) 1973, U.S. Ct. Appeals (D.C. cir.) 1976, U.S. Supreme Ct. 1980, U.S. Ct. Appeals (fed. cir.) 1983, U.S. Ct. Claims 1983, Calif. 1991. Assoc., ptnr. Jones, Day, Reavis & Pogue, Washington, 1975-79; ptnr. Crowell & Moring, Washington, 1979-84; ptnr. Gibson, Dunn & Crutcher, Washington, 1984-87; ptnr. Jones, Day, Reavis & Pogue, Washington, 1987-92; ptnr. Quinn Emanuel Urquhart & Oliver, L.A., 1992—. Editor jour. Pub. Contracts Law, 1980-86; contbr. articles to profl. jours. Spl. counsel 1980 Presdl. Inaugural Com., Washington, 1980; bd. dirs. L.A. coun. Boy Scouts Am., 1991—. Capt. USAF, 1973-75. Mem. ABA (com. chmn. pub. contract sect. 1979—), Nat. Contract Mgmt. Assn., Nat. Security Indsl. Assn., Harvard Law Sch. Assn., Mich. State U. Alumni Club of Washington (pres., dir. 1984-88). Home: 1414 Paseo La Cresta Palos Verdes Estates CA 90274-2073 Office: Quinn Emanuel Urquhart & Oliver & Hedges 865 S Figueroa St Fl 10 Los Angeles CA 90017-2543

OLIVER, TRAVIS, advertising agency executive; COO Alcone Mktg. Group, Irvine, Calif. Office: Alcone Mktg Group 13 Whatney Irvine CA 92618-2837

OLLER, THOMAS R. state senator; b. Fresno, Calif., July 16, 1958; m. Londa Oller; 4 children. BA, Stanislaus State U., 1980. Owner, entrepreneur Material Ventures, Inc., 1981—; Rep. rep. dist. 4 Calif. Ho. of Reps., 1996-2000; Rep. senator dist. 1 Calif. State Senate, 2000—. Mem. banking and fin., consumer protection, govtl. efficiency and econ. devel., transp. and water, pks. and wildlife coms. Calif. Ho. of Reps., vice chair ins., labor and employment and natural resources coms. Past chmn. Turner Pk. Com; past exec. bd. dirs. Progressive Club San Andreas; past mem. Calaveras County Fish and Game Commn.; sponsor Match-2 Prisoner Outreach, 1990; mem. bd. trustees Cmty. Covenant Ch., 1990-93, chmn., 1993. Mem. Calaveras County C. of C. Office: 2999 Douglas Blvd Ste 120 Roseville CA 95661 also: Calif State Senate State Capitol Rm 4208 Sacramento CA 95814 Fax: 916 774-4433; 916 319-2104. E-mail: ao4o@assembly.ca.gov

OLLMAN, ARTHUR LEE, museum director, photographer; b. Milw., Mar. 6, 1947; s. Benn and Shirley O. B.A., U. Wis., 1969; student, San Francisco Art Inst., 1974; M.F.A., Lone Mountain Coll., 1977. Mus. dir. Mus. Photog. Arts, San Diego. Founder, dir., producer Photo History Video Project; author: Samuel Bourne, Images of India, 1983, Arnold Newman, Five Decades, 1986, William Klein: An American in Paris, 1987, Revelaciones, The Art of Manuel Alvarez Bravo, 1990, Fata Morgana: The American Way of Life, 1992, Seduced by Life: The Art of Lou Stoumen, 1992, Points of Entry: A Nation of Strangers, 1995, The Model Wife, 1999; exhibited in one-man shows including Grapestake Gallery, San Francisco, 1979, Centre Georges Pompidou, Musee Nat. D'Art et De Culture, Paris, 1979, Inst. Contemporary Art, Boston, 1985, Night: Photograph Gallery, N.Y.C., 1981, Kodak Gallery, Tokyo, 1988; exhibited in group shows at Milw. Art Ctr., 1979, U. Hawaii, 1979-81, San Francisco Mus. Modern Art, 1980, Monas Heiroglyphicas, Milan, Italy, 1978, Mus. Modern Art, N.Y.C., 1978, Whitney Mus. Am. Art, N.Y.C., 1981, Detroit Inst. Arts, 1994, Mus. Contemporary Art, L.A., 1994, Tower of David Museum, Jerusalem, 1996; represented in permanent collections, including, Mus. Modern Art, N.Y.C, Centre Georges Pompidou, Bibliotheque Nationale, Paris, Tokyo Inst. Polytechnics, Met. Mus. Art, N.Y.C., Nat. Mus. Am. Art, Washington, Chase-Manhattan collection, N.Y.C., J. Paul Getty Mus., L.A. NEA fellow, 1979; Calif. Arts Council grantee, 1977-78, NEA grantee, 1978, exhbn. aid grantee, 1979-80. Mem. San Francisco CAMERAWORK (pres. bd. dirs. 1978-83), Am. Assn. Mus. Jewish. Address: 4310 Goldfinch St San Diego CA 92103-1315 also: Mus Photographic Arts MOPA Balboa Park 1649 El Prado San Diego CA 92101-1662

OLLSON, MICKEY LOUIS, zoo owner; b. Phoenix, May 12, 1941; s. William Archie and Edith Iris (Curnow) O.; m. Donna Marie Ollson, Dec. 5, 1965 (div. Feb. 1975); children: Micalin, Louis Michael. AA, Phoenix Coll., 1961; BS, Ariz. State U., 1963. Owner, dir. Ollson's Exotic Animal Farm, Glendale, Ariz., 1965-83, Wildlife World Zoo, Glendale, 1983—. Contbr. articles to profl. publs. Mem. Am. Assn. Zool. Parks and Aquariums (profl.), Am. Fedn. Aviculture (v.p. 1976-77), Am. Game Bird Fedn. (bd. dirs. 1988-, pres. 1984-89, Outstanding Mem. of Yr. award 1968), Internat. Soc. Zooculturists (charter; treas. 1987-88), Am. Pheasant and Waterfowl Soc. (bd. dirs. 1972-78), Avondale-Goodyear-Litchfield Park C. of C. (bd. dirs. 1985-88), Kappa Sigma (pres. Rho chpt. 1964). Republican. Office: Wildlife World Zoo 16501 W Northern Ave Litchfield Park AZ 85340-9466

OLMSTEAD, MARJORIE ANN, physics educator; b. Glen Ridge, N.J., Aug. 18, 1958; d. Blair E. and Elizabeth (Dempwolf) O. BA in Physics, Swarthmore Coll., 1979; MA in Physics, U. Calif., Berkeley, 1982, PhD, 1985. Rsch. staff Palo Alto (Calif.) Rsch. Ctr. Xerox Corp., 1985-86; asst. prof. physics U. Calif., Berkeley, 1986-90, U. Wash., Seattle, 1991-93, assoc. prof., 1993-97, prof., 1997—. Prin. investigator materials sci. divsn. Lawrence Berkeley Lab., 1988-93. Contbr. articles to profl. jours. Named Presdl. Young Investigator, Nat. Sci. Found., 1987; recipient Devel. awards IBM, 1986, 87, A. von Humboldt Found. Rsch. award, 2000. Fellow Am. Vacuum Soc. (Peter Mark Meml. award 1994); mem. Am. Assn. Physics Tchrs., Am. Phys. Soc. (chair com. on status of women in physics 1999, Maria Goeppart-Mayer award 1996), Materials Rsch. Soc., Assn. Women in Sci., Phi Beta Kappa, Sigma Xi. Office: U Washington Dept Physics PO Box 351560 Seattle WA 98195-1560

OLOWOKANDI, MICHAEL, professional basketball player; b. Apr. 3, 1975; Studen, U. Pacific, 1998. Guard, center L.A. Clippers, 1998—. Named to Schick All-Rookie Second Team, 1998-99. Achievements include recording 16 points and game-highs of 17 rebounds and 3 steals against the Vancouver Grizzlies; scored in double figures in six consecutive games; logged two double-doubles. Office: Los Angeles Clippers 3939 S Figueroa St Los Angeles CA 90037-1200

OLSEN, ALFRED JON, lawyer; b. Phoenix, Oct. 5, 1940; s. William Hans and Vera (Bearden) O.; m. Susan K. Smith, Apr. 15, 1979. B.A. in History, U. Ariz., 1962; MS in Acctg., Ariz. State U., 1964; J.D., Northwestern U., 1966. Bar: Ariz. 1966, Ill. 1966, U.S. Tax Ct. 1970, U.S. Supreme Ct. 1970; C.P.A., Ariz., Ill. cert. tax specialist. Acct. Arthur Young & Co., C.P.A.s, Chgo., 1966-68; dir. firm Ehmann, Olsen & Lane (P.C.), Phoenix, 1969-76; dir. Streich, Lang, Weeks & Cardon (P.C.), Phoenix, 1977-78; v.p. Olsen-Smith, Ltd., Phoenix, 1978—. Chmn. tax adv. commn. Bd. Legal Specialization, 1990-92. Bd. editors: Jour. Agrl. Law and Taxation, 1978-82, Practical Real Estate Lawyer, 1983-95. Mem. Phoenix adv. bd. Salvation Army., 1973-81. Fellow Am. Coll. Trust and Estate Counsel, Am. Coll. Tax Counsel; mem. AICPA, Ariz. Soc. CPAs, State Bar Ariz. (chmn. tax sect. 1977-78), ABA (chmn. com. on agr., sect. taxation 1976-78, chmn. CLE com. sect. taxation 1982-84), Am. Law Inst. (chmn. tax planning for agr. 1971-82), Cen. Ariz. Estate Planning Coun. (pres. 1972-73), Nat. Cattlemen's Assn. (tax com. 1979-88), Internat. Acad. Estate and Trust Law (exec. coun. 1994-99), Sigma Nu Internat. (pres. 1986-88), Phi Beta Kappa, Beta Gamma Sigma, Phi Kappa Phi. Office: 3300 Virginia Fin Pla 301 E Virginia Ave Phoenix AZ 85004-1218

OLSEN, CLIFFORD WAYNE, retired physical chemist, consultant; b. Placerville, Calif., Jan. 15, 1936; s. Christian William and Elsie May (Bishop) O.; m. Margaret Clara Gobel, June 16, 1962 (div. 1986), remarried, Mar. 4, 2000; children: Anne K. Olsen Cordes Bothe, Charlotte Marie; m. Nancy Mayhew Kruger, July 21, 1990 (div. 1993). AA, Grant Tech. Coll., Sacramento, 1955; BA, U. Calif.-Davis, 1957, PhD, 1962. Physicist, project leader, program leader, task leader Lawrence Livermore Nat. Lab., Calif., 1962-93; ret., 1993; lab. assoc., 1993-95, 96—; cons. Holmes & Narver, 1995, Keystone Internat., 1996—, Am. Techs. Inc., 1997, Profl. Analysis, Inc., 1997-99. Mem. Containment Evaluation Panel, U.S. Dept. Energy, 1984—, mem. Cadre for Joint Nuclear Verification Tests, 1988; organizer, editor procs. for 2nd through 7th Symposiums on Containment of Underground Nuclear Detonations, 1983-93. Contbr. articles to profl. jours. Mem. bd. convocators Calif. Luth. U., 1976-78. Recipient Chevalier Degree, Order of DeMolay, 1953, Eagle Scout, 1952. Mem. AAAS, Am. Radio Relay League, Seismol. Soc. Am., Livermore Amateur Radio Klub (pres. 1994-96), Sigma Xi, Alpha Gamma Sigma (life), Gamma Alpha (U. Calif.-Davis chpt. pres. 1960-61). Democrat. Lutheran. Avocations: photography, amateur radio, music, cooking.

OLSEN, DONALD BERT, biomedical engineer, experimental surgeon, research facility director; b. Bingham, Utah, Apr. 2, 1930; s. Bertram Hansen and Doris (Bodel) O.; m. Joyce Cronquist; children: Craig, Kathy, Debbie, Jeff, Gary. BS, Utah State U., 1952; DVM, Colo. State U., 1956. Gen. practice vet. medicine, Smithfield, Utah, 1956-63; extension veterinarian U. Nev., Reno, 1963-65, researcher Deseret Rsch. Inst., 1965-68; postdoctoral fellow U. Colo. Med. Sch., Denver, 1968-72; researcher U. Utah, Salt Lake City, 1972—, rsch. prof. surgery, 1973—, dir. artificial heart lab., 1976—, rsch. prof. pharmaceutics, 1981—, rsch. prof. biomed. engring., 1986—, dir. Inst. Biomed. Engring., 1986—, prof. surgery, 1986—. Mem. sci. adv. bd. Link Resources, Inc., 1987 Contbr. articles to profl. jours.; patentee in field. Recipient Clemson award Soc. Biomaterials, N.Y.C., 1987, Centennial award for outstanding alumni Utah State U., Logan, 1988, Gov.'s medal for Sci. and Tech., 1988; named Alumnus of Yr. Colo. State U., 1986. Mem. Am. Soc. Artificial Internal Organs (trustee 1985—, mem. fellowship rev. com. 1983, chmn. program com. 1988-89, sec., treas. 1989-90, pres. elect. 1990-91, pres. 1991-92), Internat. Soc. Artificial Organs (v.p. 1987—), Am. Coll. Vet. Surgeons (hon.), Utah Vet. Med. Assn. (trustee 1985-88), Alpha Zeta Mem. LDS Ch. Avocations: fishing, hunting, camping, hiking. Office: U Utah Inst Biomed Engring 803 N 300 W Salt Lake City UT 84103-1414

OLSEN, FRANCES ELISABETH, law educator, theorist; b. Chgo., Feb. 4, 1945; d. Holger and Ruth Mathilda (Pfeifer) O.; m. Harold Irving Porter, June 8, 1984. Cert., Roskilde (Denmark) Højskole, 1967; BA, Goddard Coll., 1968; JD, U. Colo., 1971; SJD, Harvard U., 1984. Bar: Colo. 1972, U.S. Dist. Ct. Colo. 1972. Law clk. hon. Arraj U.S. Dist. Ct. Colo., Denver, 1972; lawyer Am. Indian Movement, Wounded Knee, S.D., 1973; pvt. practice Denver, 1973-74; law prof. U. Puget Sound, Tacoma, 1975-79, St. John's U., Jamaica, N.Y., 1982-83, UCLA, 1984—. Vis. fellow New Coll., Oxford (Eng.) U., 1987; vis. prof. U. Mich., Ann Arbor, 1988, Harvard U., Cambridge, Mass., 1990-91, Ochanomizu U., Tokyo, 1997, U. Tokyo,

1997, Cornell U., 1997, French UN Reunion, 2000; sr. Fulbright prof. U. Frankfurt, Germany, 1991-92; overseas fellow Churchill Coll., Cambridge, Eng., 1997-99; mem. faculty law Cambridge U., 1997-99; del. UN 4th World Conf. on Women, Beijing, China, 1995, NGO Forum, Huairou, China, 1995. Co-author: Cases and Materials on Family Law: Legal Concepts and Changing Human Relationships, 1994; editor: Feminist Legal Theory I: Foundations and Outlooks, 1995, Feminist Legal Theory II: Positioning Feminist Theory Within the Law, 1995; contbr. articles to law revs. Named Outstanding Alumnus U. Colo., 1989. Mem. Assn. Am. Law Schs. (chair jurisprudence sect. 1987-88, chair women in law tchg. sect. 1995-96), Conf. on Critical Legal Studies, European Conf. Critical Legal Studies. Avocations: wind-surfing, bicycling, mountain climbing, hiking. Office: UCLA Sch Law 405 Hilgard Ave Los Angeles CA 90095-9000

OLSEN, HAROLD FREMONT, lawyer; b. Davenport, Wash., Oct. 17, 1920; s. Oscar E. and Dorothy (Sprowls) O.; m. Jeanne L. Rounds, Aug. 30, 1942; children: Eric O., Ronald R., Margaret Ruth. B.A., Wash. State U., 1942; LL.B., Harvard U., 1948. Bar: Wash. 1948, U.S. Ct. Claims 1970, U.S. Supreme Ct. 1982; C.P.A., Wash. Instr. Oxford Bus. Sch., Cambridge, Mass., 1946-47; examiner Wash. State Dept. Pub. Utilities, 1948; with firm Perkins Coie (and predecessors), Seattle, 1949—, ptnr., 1954-88, of counsel, 1989—. Bd. dirs. Exotic Metals Forming Co.; dir. Barker Ranch, Inc., pres., 1997—; trustee Exec. Svcs. Corp. Wash., 1990-96. Bd. dirs. Northwest Hosp. Found., Northwest Hosp., 1980-90; trustee Wash. State U. Found., chmn. 1986-88; mem. adv. coun. Wash. State U. Sch. Bus. and Econs., 1978-90; trustee, mem. exec. com., pres. Mus. of Flight, 1991-92, chmn., 1993; trustee Horizon House, 1994-97. Maj. USAAF, 1942-45, NATOUSA, Mid. East, ETO. Decorated Silver Star. Mem. ABA, Wash. Bar Assn., Seattle Bar Assn., Aircraft Industry Assn. (chmn. legal com. 1957), Nat. Contract Mgmt. Assn., Alumni Assn. Wash. State U. (pres. 1956), Mcpl. League Seattle and King County, Seattle C. of C., Internat. Law Soc., Am. Judicature Assn., Phi Beta Kappa, Phi Kappa Phi, Tau Kappa Epsilon, Rainier Club, Queenstown (New Zealand) Golf Club, Seattle Golf Club (pres. 1986-87), Sr. N.W. Golf Assn. Congregationalist. Home: 8875 Overlake Dr W Medina WA 98039-5347 Office: 1201 3rd Ave Ste 4500 Seattle WA 98101-3029 E-mail: olseh@perkinscole.com, olseh@seanet.com

OLSEN, HARRIS LELAND, real estate and international business executive, educator, diplomat; b. Rochester, N.H., Dec. 8, 1947; s. Harries Edwin and Eva Alma (Turmelle) O.; m. Mimi Kwi Sun Yi, Mar. 15, 1953; children: Garin Lee, Gavin Yi, Sook Ja. AS, SUNY, Albany, 1983, BS, 1988; MA in Polit. Sci., U. Hawaii, 1990; PhD in Internat. Bus. Adminstrn., Kennedy Western U., Idaho, 1993. Enlisted USN, 1967, advanced through grades to, served in various nuclear power capacities Conn., 1971-76, Hawaii, 1976-87, ret., 1987; v.p. Waiono Land Corp., Honolulu, 1981-92, dir., 1993-95; v.p. Asian Pacific Electricity, Honolulu, 1988-89, Kapano Land Assocs., Honolulu, 1988-92, 94-95, MLY Networks, Inc., Honolulu, 1989-99, THO Consultants Cor., 1991—, Clarix Internat. Corp., 1994; consulate gen. Papua New Guinea. Staff cons. Mariner-Icemakers, Honolulu, 1982-84, Transpacific Energy Corp., Honolulu, 1982-84; dir. Asian Pacific Devel. Bank, 1983; sr. cons. Western Rsch. Assocs., Honolulu, 1984-87, 94-95; quality assurance cons. Asian Pacific, Inc., Honolulu, 1987-88; instr., lectr. Asian history and culture U. Chaminade in Honolulu, 1991; nuclear reactor plant specialist Pearl Harbor Emergency Recall Team, 1991-95; instr. nuclear reactor theory Pearl Harbor, Hawaii, 1992-95; v.p. Schwartz, Inc., 1992-98, dir. Schwartz Jewelry Sch., 1996-98; cons. Waiono/Kapano Devel. Co., 1993; bd. dirs., sec. Pacific Internat. Engring. Corp., 1994-95; Keiretsu sec. Global Ocean Cons., Inc. and Assocs., 1994-95; joint venture Premier Fisheries Pty. Ltd., Papua New Guinea, 1995-98; cons. BFD Devel. Group, 1995-96; co-drafter Nat. Tuna Industry Devel. Plan for Papua New Guinea, 1995; quality analyst, Pearl Harbor, 1995; rep. for Min. for Fisheries, Papua New Guinea, Bi-lateral Fisheries Access Rights Japan and Papua New Guinea, 1996-97, drafter Bi-Lateral Fishing Treaty Japan and Papua New Guinea, 1996; U.S. del. to 4th World Tuna Conf., Manila, 1995, U.S. del. to 5th Aquatic Coninent Conf., Maui, Hawaii, 1995, 6th, 1996; apptd. rep. Abau Electorate, Papua New Guinea Timber Sales, 1995-98; apptd. hon. consul gen. and trade rep., dep. trade min. for Govt. of Papua New Guinea in Honolulu, 1996—; bd. dirs. Island Art; cons. Pew Global Devel. Corp., 1998-99, NIUGINI Enterprises LLC, 1999—, Niugini Millenium Co., Ltd., 1999—. Inventor, alternate power supply system; contbr. articles to profl. publs. Head coach USN Men's Softball, Honolulu, 1978-79; pres. Pearl Harbor (Hawaii) Welfare and Recreation Com., 1983-84; mem. Bishop Mus, Rep. Senatorial Inner Cir.; commd. hon. consul gen. Ind. State Papua New Guinea, 1996; mem. Consular Corps of Hawaii. Named Alumnus of Yr., Kennedy Western U., 1993; recipient Citation of Leadership, Rep. Nat. Com., 1996, Letter of Commendation for Svc. During Aitape Tidal Wave Disaster in Papua New Guinea, 1998; selected to represent Hawaii at Presdl. Inauguration, Rep. Leadership U.S. Senate, 2001. Mem. AAAS, Internat. Fedn. Profl. and Tech. Engrs., Am. Polit. Sci. Assn., N.Y. Acad. Scis., USCG Aux., Am. Legion, Fleet Res. Assn., Navy League, U.S. Naval Inst., Pacific and Asian Affairs Coun., Alliance Francaise Hawaii, UN Assn., Honolulu Acad. Arts, Plaza Club, Pacific & Asian Affairs Coun., Delta Epsilon Sigma. Republican. Roman Catholic and Buddhist. Avocations: chess, philosophy, Japanese haiku poetry, native American cultures. Home and Office: 94 1025 Anania Cir Apt 56 Mililani HI 96789-2045 E-mail: HarryTho@aol.com

OLSHEN, RICHARD A. statistician, educator; b. Portland, Oreg., May 17, 1942; s. A.C. and Dorothy (Olds) O.; m. Susan Abroff, 1979. AB, U. Calif., Berkeley, 1963; PhD, Yale U., 1966. Rsch. staff statistician, lectr. Yale U., New Haven, 1966-67; asst. prof. stats. Stanford (Calif.) U., 1967-72; assoc. prof. stats. and math. U. Mich., Ann Arbor, 1972-75; assoc. prof. math. U. Calif., San Diego, 1975-77, prof. math., 1977-89, dir. lab. for math. and stats., 1982-89; prof. biostats. Sch. Medicine Stanford U., 1989—, prof. by courtesy dept. stats., 1990—, prof. by courtesy dept. elec. engring., 1995—, chief divsn. biostats., 1998—, assoc. chair dept. health rsch. and policy, 1999-2001. Office: Stanford U Sch Medicine Hrp Bldg Stanford CA 94305-5405 E-mail: olshen@stat.stanford.edu

OLSON, A. CRAIG, retail executive; m. Cathy; 1 child, Sarah. BS in Acctg., U. Idaho, 1974. CPA, Idaho. From checker to sr. v.p., CFO Albertson's, Inc., Boise, Idaho, 1967-91, sr. v.p., CFO, 1991—. Adv. bd. U. Idaho Coll. Bus. & Econs., bd. dirs. Bogus Basin Recreational Assn. Mem. Am. Inst. CPAs, Idaho Soc. CPAs, Financial Exec. Inst. Avocations: family, sailing, running, snow skiing. Office: Albertsons Inc PO Box 20 Boise ID 83726-0020

OLSON, DALE C. public relations executive; b. Fargo, N.D., Feb. 20, 1934; s. Arthur Edwin and Edith (Weight) Olson Neubauer. Sr. v.p., prin., pres. motion picture divsn. Rogers and Cowan, Inc., Beverly Hills, Calif., 1967-85; prin. Dale C. Olson & Assocs., Beverly Hills, 1985—. Cons. Filmex, L.A., 1972-83; U.S. del. Manila Film Festival, 1982-83. Editor L.A. edit. Theatre ann. Best Plays, 1963-67. V.p. Diamond Cir. City of Hope, Duarte, Calif., 1980-83; mem. adv. bd. Calif. Mus. Sci. and Industry, L.A., 1975-81; mem. bd. govs. Film Industry Workshops, Inc., 1965-80; pres. Hollywood Press Club, 1963-66; assoc. Los Angeles County Art Mus., 1981-83; bd. trustees Hollywood Arts Coun., chair 1999 jury USA Film Festival, Dallas; cons. L.A. 2000. Recipient Golden Key, Pub. Rels. News, 1982, Les Mason and pub. svc. awards Publicists Guild, Golden Satellite award for lifetime achievement Internat. Press Acad., 1999, Prism award for pub. svc. Entertainment Industries Coun., 2000. Mem. NATAS, Acad. Motion Picture Arts and Scis. (chmn. pub. rels. coordinating com. 1982—), Actors Fund Am. (chmn. Western coun. 1991, trustee 1992, exec. com. 1998), Hollywood Arts Coun. (bd. dirs.), Pres.'s Club, Thalians. Lutheran. E-mail: dolson2000@earthlink.net

OLSON, DAVID JOHN, political science educator; b. Brantford, N.D., May 18, 1941; s. Lloyd and Alice Ingrid (Black) O.; m. Sandra Jean Crabb, June 11, 1966; 1 dau., Maia Kari. B.A., Concordia Coll., Moorhead, Minn., 1963; Rockefeller fellow Union Theol. Sem, N.Y.C., 1963-64; M.A. (Brookings Instn. predoctoral research fellow 1968-69), U. Wis., Madison, 1966, Ph.D. (univ. fellow 1967), 1971. Community planner Madison Redvel. Authority, 1965-66; lectr. U. Wis., 1966-67; from lectr. to asso. prof. polit. sci. Ind. U., Bloomington, 1969-76; prof. polit. sci. U. Wash., Seattle, 1976—, chmn. dept., 1983-88, Harry Bridges endowed chairlabor studies, 1992-94; bd. dirs. Harry Bridges Inst.; dir.Ctr. Labor Studies U. Wash., 1992-94; Disting. lectr. in labor studies San Francisco State U., 1994. Vis. prof. U. Bergen, 1987, Harvard U., 1988-89, U. Hawaii, 1989, U. Calif., Berkeley, 1996. Co-author: Governing the United States, 1978, Commission Politics, 1977, To Keep the Republic, 1975, Black Politics, 1971; co-editor: Theft of the City, 1974. Recipient Disting. Teaching award Ind. U., 1973, faculty fellow, 1973, Alumni Achievement award Concordia Coll., 1998. Mem. Am. Polit. Sci. Assn., Western Polit. Sci. Assn. (v.p. 1984, pres. 1985), Midwest Polit. Sci. Assn., So. Polit. Sci. Assn. Democrat. Lutheran. Home: 6512 E Green Lake Way N Seattle WA 98103-5418 Office: U Wash Dept Polit Sci Seattle WA 98195-0001

OLSON, DONALD, state senator; b. Nome, Alaska, June 18, 1953; BA in Chemistry, U. Minn.; MD, Oral Roberts U.; postgrad. in Law, U. Colo.; postgrad., Cambridge (Eng.) U. Lic. airline transport pilot, comml. pilot airplane and helicopters, airframe and power plant mechanic; cert. insp. Seattle Pacific Coll.; aviation med. examiner. Pres., CEO Olson Air Svc., Inc., Donald Olson Enterprises, Inc., Olson Ventures, LLC; Dem. senator dist. S Alaska State Senate, 2000—. Appointed to Alaska State Med. Bd., 1995. Mem. Amundson Edn. Ctr.; mem. adv. bd. Missionary Aviation Repair Ctr. Mem. Alaska State Med. Assn., Explorers Club N.Y. Avocations: polar exploration, ivory carving, reindeer herding, aviation collectibles, reading. Office: Alaska State Senate State Capitol Rm 510 Juneau AK 99801-1182 Fax: 907 465-4821. E-mail: Senator_Donny_Olson@legis.state.ak.us

OLSON, GENE L. food products executive; Sr. v.p. fin. Golden State Foods, Irvine, Calif. Office: Golden State Foods 18301 Von Karman Ave Ste 1100 Irvine CA 92612-0133

OLSON, JAMES WILLIAM PARK, architect; b. St. Louis, Oct. 6, 1940; s. James William Park; s. Louis Garfield and Gladys Helen (Schuh) O.; m. Katherine Fovargue, June 11, 1971; children: Park, Reed. BArch, U. Wash., 1963. Registered architect, Wash., Oreg., Calif., Ill., Colo., Hawaii, Ga., Fla. Ptnr. Olson Sundberg Kundig Allen Architects, Seattle, 1985—. Assoc. architect New Seattle Art Mus., 1991. Prin. works include Pike and Virginia Bldg. (AIA Honor award 1980), Seattle's Best Coffee Retail Locations (AIA Honor award 1984), Hauberg Residence (AIA Honor award 1997), Mayer Lodo residence, Denver (AIA honor award 1998, AIA N.W. and Pacific Regional Merit award 1999), St. Mark's Cathedral Renovation (AIA Commendation award), Seattle (IFFRA award 1998, AIA citation 1998), numerous residences nationwide. Bd. dirs. Ctr. Contemporary Art, Seattle, 1982-86, Artist Trust, Seattle, 1986-90, U. Wash. Henry Art Gallery, Seattle, 1986-92, Seattle Art Mus., 1996—. Recipient Best Architect award Seattle Mag., 1985. Fellow AIA; mem. NEA (juror). Avocation: art. Work published in numerous mags, jours., including The AD 100 Architects, N.Y. Times, Archtl. Digest, Archtl. Record, Global Architecture and others. Office: Olson Sundberg Kundig Allen Architects 108 1st Ave S Ste 4 Seattle WA 98104-2557

OLSON, KRISTINE, prosecutor; b. N.Y.C., Aug. 9, 1947; d. Harold John and Arline (Schneider) Olson; children: Karin, Tyler. B.A., Wellesley Coll., 1969, J.D., Yale U., 1972. Bar: Oreg. 1973, U.S. Dist. Ct. Oreg. 1974, U.S. Ct. Appeals (9th cir.) 1975. Asst. U.S. atty. Dept. Justice, Portland, Oreg., 1974-84; vice chair State Indigent Def. Bd., Salem, Oreg., 1985-87; assoc. dean, prof. law Lewis & Clark Coll., 1989-94; U.S. atty. Dept. Justice, Dist. Oreg., Portland, 1994—; adj. prof. Lewis and Clark Coll. Northwestern Sch. Law, 1975-89, U. Oreg. Law Ctr., 1984—; mem. 9th Cir. Task Force on Tribal Cts. Contbr. articles to profl. jours. Bd. dirs., chmn. bd. Oreg. Council on Crime and Delinquency, 1981-87; bd. dirs. State Bd. Police Standards and Tng., 1976-80; chmn. Community Corrections Adv. Bd. Multnomah County, Portland, 1978-80; chmn. women's rights project ACLU Oreg., 1977; mem. World Affairs Council Oreg.; commr., mem. exec. com. Met. Human Relations Commn., mayor's appointee, 1986—. Root Tilden fellow, 1969. Mem. Soc. Am. Archaeology Native Am. Rights Fund, Earthwatch, 1000 Friends of Oreg., Archaeol. Conservancy, Nature Conservancy. Democrat. Clubs: Early Keyboard Soc., City Club of Portland (bd. govs. 1984—, pres.-elect 1995), Multnomah Athletic (Portland). Home: 900 SW 83rd Ave Portland OR 97225-6308 Office: US Dept Justice Mark O Hatfield U S Courthouse 1000 SW 3rd Ave Ste 600 Portland OR 97204-2936

OLSON, LUTE, university athletic coach; b. Mayville, N.D., Sept. 22, 1934; s. Albert E. and Alinda E. (Halvorson) O.; m. Roberta R. Russell, Nov. 27, 1953; children: Vicki, Jodi, Gregory, Christi, Steven. B.A., Augsburg Coll., Mpls., 1956; M.A., Chapman Coll., Orange, Calif., 1964. Cert. counselor. Head basketball coach Mahonomen High Sch., Minn., 1956-57, Two Harbors High Sch., 1957-61; dean of boys Baseline Jr. High Sch., Boulder, Colo., 1961-62; head basketball coach Loara High Sch., Anaheim, Calif., 1962-64, Marine High Sch., Huntington Beach, 1964-69, Long Beach City Coll., 1969-73, Long Beach State U., 1973-74, U. Iowa, Iowa City, 1974-83, U. Ariz. Wildcats, 1983—, head coach NCAA Divsn. 1A basketball, ranked #10, 1992, head coach NCAA Tournament winner West Region, semifinalist (overall), 1994, head coach NCAA Tournament champions, 1997. Author: Passing Game Offense, 1980, Multiple Zone Attack, 1981, Pressure Defense, 1981, Match-up Zone, 1983. Crusade chmn. Am. Cancer Soc., Iowa, 1982. Named Coach of Yr. Orange League, 1964; named Coach of Yr. Sunset League, 1968, Coach of Yr. Met. Conf. Calif., 1970-71, Coach of Yr. PCAA, 1974, Coach of Yr. Big Ten Conf., 1979, 80 Mem. Nat. Assn. Basketball Coaches (Coach of Yr. 1980) Lutheran.

OLSON, MARIAN KATHERINE, management executive, consultant, publisher; b. Tulsa, Oct. 15, 1933; d. Sherwood Joseph and Katherine M. (Miller) Lahman; m. Ronald Keith Olson, Oct. 27, 1956 (dec. May 1991). BA in Polit. Sci., U. Colo., 1954, MA in Elem. Edn., 1962; EdD in Ednl. Adminstrn., U. Tulsa, 1969. Tchr. pub. schs., Wyo., Colo., Mont., 1956-67; tchg. fellow, adj. instr. edn. U. Tulsa, 1968-69; asst. prof. edn. Eastern Mont. State Coll., 1970; program assoc. rsch. adminstrn. Mont. State U., 1970-75; on leave with Energy Policy Office of White House then with Fed. Energy Adminstrn., 1973-74; with Dept. Energy and predecessor, 1975—, program analyst, 1975-79, chief planning and environ. compliance br., 1979-83; regional dir. Region VIII Fed. Emergency Mgmt. Agy., 1987-93; exec. dir. Search and Rescue Dogs of the U.S., 1993—. Pres. Marian Olson Assocs., Bannack Pub. Co.; mem. Colo. Nat. Hazards Mitigation Coun. Contbr. articles in field. Bd. dirs. Disaster Preparedness and Emergency Response Assn. Internat. Grantee Okla. Consortium Higher Edn., 1969, NIMH, 1974. Mem. Internat. Assn. Emergency Mgrs., Am. Soc. for Info. Sci., Am. Assn. Budget and Program Analysis, Assn. of Contingency Planners, Nat. Inst. Urban Search and Rescue (bd. dirs.), Nat. Assn. for Search and Rescue, Colo. Search and Rescue, Search and Rescue Dogs of U.S., Colo. Emergency Mgmt. Assn., Front Range Rescue Dogs, Kappa Delta Pi, Phi Alpha Theta, Kappa Alpha Theta. Republican. Home: 203 Iowa Dr Golden CO 80403-1337 Office: Marian Olson Assocs 203 Iowa Dr Ste B Golden CO 80403-1337 E-mail: mlolson@ix.netcom.com

OLSON, RICHARD EARL, lawyer, state legislator; b. Elmhurst, Ill., Apr. 24, 1953; s. Earl Leroy and Helen Ellen (Wanamaker) O.; m. Patricia Michelle McKinney, May 16, 1976; children: Shelley, Rachel, Eric. BA, U. Miss., Oxford, 1975; JD, So. Meth. U., 1978. Bar: N.Mex. 1978. Ptnr. Hinkle, Cox, Eaton, Coffield & Hensley, Roswell, N.Mex., 1978—; mem. N.Mex. Ho. of Reps., 1989-95, mem. various coms. Bd. trustees Eastern N.Mex. Med. Ctr., 1995-98. Mem. Roswell City Coun., 1986-88, chmn. sts. and alleys com., mem. various other coms.; past chmn. pastor-parish rels. com. 1st United Meth. Ch., Roswell; bd. dirs. Roswell Econ. Forum, Roswell Mus. and Art Ctr. Found., city coun. liaison; bd. dirs. Assurance Home, 1980—, former v.p.; mem. N.Mex. 1st, former bd. dirs. Mem. ABA, Am. Legis. Exec. Coun. (civil justice task force), Def. Rsch. Inst., Noon Optimist Club, Order of Coif, Phi Kappa Phi. Republican. Home: 5003 Thunderbird Ln Roswell NM 88203-9386 Office: Hinkle Cox Eaton Coffield & Hensley PO Box 10 Roswell NM 88202-0010

OLSON, STEVEN STANLEY, social service executive; b. Longview, Wash., Aug. 5, 1950; s. Robert Martin and Martha Virginia (Duffin) O.; 1 child, Derek Thomas Dailey. BA, Wash. State U., 1972; MEd, Auburn U., 1977; postgrad., Seattle U., 1981-83. Cert. rehabilitation mgmt. Agrl. extensionist Action/Peace Corps, Popayan, Colombia, 1972-73; supr. Stonebelt Ctr. for the Mentally Retarded, Bloomington, Ind., 1974; adjustment counselor Exceptional Industries, Bowling Green, Ky., 1974-75, vocat. evaluator, 1975-76; alcohol counselor E. Ala. Mental Health, Opelika, 1976; intern Auburn Univ./Ptnrs. of the Americas, Guatemala City, Guatemala, 1976; planner, rschr. Marion County Mental Health, Salem, Oreg., 1977-78; assoc. dir. Reliable Enterprises, Centralia, Wash., 1979-80, exec. dir., 1980-98, Olympia (Wash.) Child Care Ctr., 1999—. Cons. in field, 1998-99; v.p. govt. affairs Rehab. Enterprises Wash., Olympia, 1984-86, chmn. regional rep., 1986-89, pres., 1990-91; treas. Arc of Wash., Olympia, 1983-85, 99—, govt. affairs chmn., 1983-89, v.p., 1989-90, sec., 1996-97; adv. coun. Lewis/Mason/Thurston Area Agy. on Aging, 1993-99. Contbr. articles to Vocat. Evaluation and Work Adjustment Bull., 1976, Rehab. World, 1977. Treas. Communities United for Reponsible Energy, Lewis County, Wash., 1979—; vice chairperson Wash. Solar Coun., Olympia, Wash., 1980-83; co-chair Early Childhood Help Orgn., Olympia, 1988. Home: 4333 Maytown Rd SW Olympia WA 98512-9239 Office: Olympia Child Care Ctr PO Box 7305 Olympia WA 98507

OLSON, WALTER GILBERT, lawyer; b. Stanton, Nebr., Feb. 2, 1924; s. O.E. Olson and Mabel A. Asplin; m. Gloria Helen Bennett, June 26, 1949; children: Clifford Warner, Karen Rae Olson. BS, U. Calif., Berkeley, 1947, JD, 1949. Bar: Calif. 1950, U.S. Dist. Ct. (no. dist.) Calif. 1950, U.S. Tax Ct. 1950, U.S. Ct. Appeals (9th cir.) 1950. Assoc. Orrick, Herrington and Sutcliffe (formerly Orrick, Dahlquist, Herrington and Sutcliffe), San Francisco, 1949-54, ptnr., 1954-88, of counsel, 1989—. Bd. dirs. Alltel Corp., Little Rock, 1988-94; mem. Commn. to Revise Calif. Corp. Securities Law, 1967-69, Securities Regulatory Reform Panel, 1978-80; mem. corp. security adv. com. Calif. Commr. of Corps, 1975-88. Editor-in-chief Calif. Law Review, 1948-49. Bd. dirs. Internat. Ho., Berkeley, 1981-86. With U.S. Army, 1943-46, ETO. Fellow Am. Bar Found.; mem. ABA (trust divsn. nat. conf. of lawyers and reps. of Am. Bankers Assn.), Calif. Bar Assn. (chmn. corps com. 1975-76, exec. com. bus. law sect. 1977-78), San Francisco Bar Assn., U. Calif. Alumni Assn., Boalt Hall Alumni Assn. (bd. dirs. 1982-90, sec. 1985, v.p. 1987, pres. 1988), Order of Coif, Menlo Country Club (Woodside, Calif.), Pacific-Union Club. Office: Orrick Herrington & Sutcliffe 400 Sansome St San Francisco CA 94111-3143

OLSSON, RONALD ARTHUR, computer science educator; b. Huntington, N.Y., Nov. 16, 1955; s. Ronald Alfred and Dorothy Gertrude (Hofmann) O. BA and MA, SUNY, 1977; MS, Cornell U., 1979; PhD, U. Ariz., 1986. Teaching asst. Cornell U., Ithaca, N.Y., 1977-79, rsch. asst., 1979; lectr. SUNY, Brockport, 1979-81; rsch. assoc. U. Ariz., Tucson, 1981-86; prof., vice chair Computer Sci. Dept. U. Calif., Davis, 1986—. Author (book) The SR Programming Language: Concurrency in Practice, 1993; contbr. articles to profl. jours. Grantee MICRO U. Calif., 1987, 92, NSF, 1988, 96, Dept. Energy, 1988-92, Advanced Rsch. Projects Agy., 1993—. Mem. Assn. for Computing Machinery. Avocations: bicycling, hiking, cross-country skiing, movies. Home: 2741 Brandywine Pl Davis CA 95616-2904 Office: U Calif Dept Computer Sci Davis CA 95616-8562

OLSTAD, ROGER GALE, science educator; b. Mpls., Jan. 16, 1934; s. Arnold William and Myra (Stroschein) O.; m. Constance Elizabeth Jackson, Aug. 20, 1955; children: Karen Louise, Kenneth Bradley. B.S., U. Minn., 1955, M.A., 1959, Ph.D., 1963. Instr. U. Minn., Mpls., 1956-63; asst. prof. U. Ill., Urbana, 1963-64; mem. faculty U. Wash., Seattle, 1964—, asso. prof. sci. edn., 1967-71, prof., 1971-95, asso. dean grad. studies Coll. Edn., 1971-85; prof. emeritus, 1995—. Chair environ. quality commn. City of Lake Forest Park, Wash., 1997-2000, city coun., 2000—. Fellow AAAS; mem. NSTA (bd. dirs.) Wash. Sci. Tchrs. Assn. (pres. 1973-74), Nat. Assn. Rsch. Sci. Teaching (pres. 1977-78, bd. dirs.), N.W. Sci. Assn. (chmn. 1966-68), Assn. Edn. Tchrs. in Sci. (regional pres. 1966-68, pres. 1991-92), Nat. Assn. Biology Tchrs., Biol. Scis. Curriculum Study (chmn., bd. dirs. 1989-94), U. Wash. Faculty Club, Phi Delta Kappa. Home: 20143 53rd Ave NE Seattle WA 98155-1801 Office: U Wash Coll Edn Seattle WA 98195-0001

O'MALLEY, EDWARD, psychiatrist, consultant; b. Hudson, N.Y., May 30, 1926; s. Thomas Patrick and Helen Mary (Cornell) O. BS, St. John's U., Bklyn., N.Y., 1949; MS, Loyola U., Chgo., 1952, PhD, 1954; MD, SUNY, Bklyn., 1958. Diplomate Am. Bd. Forensic Examiners, Am. Bd. Psychiatry and Neurology. Psychiat. cons. dept. of corrections N.Y.C., 1962-68; psychiatrist Cath. Charities, N.Y.C., 1963-68; dir. of mental health Suffolk County Govt., Hauppauge, N.Y., 1968-70; commr. of mental health Orange County, Goshen, 1970-72; dir. drug abuse services State of N.Y., Bronx, 1972-78; lic. sch. psychiatrist N.Y.C. Bd. of Edn., 1962-82; chief psychiatry services VA, Huntington, W.Va., 1982-86; med. cons. State of Calif., San Diego, 1986—, psychiat. cons. dept. of corrections, 1987—. Asst. prof. psychiatry N.J. Med. Sch., Newark, 1975—; examiner Am. Bd. of Psychiatry and Neurology, Los Angeles, 1980; assoc. prof. psychiatry U. Calif., San Diego, 1980—; prof. psychiatry Marshall U. Sch. of Medicine, Huntington, 1982-86; dir. com. on sea cadets Navy League, San Diego, 1987—; cons. HHS, Social Security Adminstrn., Office of Hearings and Appeals, 1989—. Contbr. articles to profl. jours. Bd. dirs. Suffolk Community Council, Hauppauge, 1968-70, United Fund of Long Island, Huntington, 1968-70. Capt. ret. USNR, 1960-86. Scholar N. Y. State Coll., 1946-49, SUNY Joseph Collins Med. Sch., 1955-58; Teaching and Research fellow Loyola U., 1952-54. Fellow Am. Psychiat. Assn.; mem. San Diego Psychiat. Soc., Soc. of Med. Cons. to the Armed Forces, Soc. of Mil. Surgeons of U.S.A., N.Y. Celtic Med. Soc., Union Am. Physicians and Dentists (steward 1990—), State Employed Physicians Assn. (bd. dirs. 1993—). Roman Catholic. Home: 3711 Alcott St San Diego CA 92106-1212 E-mail: omalleyedwr@aol.com

O'MALLEY, JAMES TERENCE, lawyer; b. Omaha, Nov. 24, 1950; s. John Austin and Mayme Bernice (Zentner) O'M.; m. Colleen L. Kizer, [illegible] laude, U. Notre Dame, 1972; JD, Stanford U., 1975. Bar: Calif. 1975, Tex. 1998. Ptnr. Gray, Cary, Ames & Frye, San Diego, 1975-87, of counsel, 1987-91, ptnr., 1991—; vice chmn., exec. v.p., gen. counsel Noble

Broadcast Group, Inc., San Diego, 1987-91; chmn. CEO Gray Care Ware & Freidenrich LLP, San Diego, 1996—. Bd. dirs. The Corky McMillin Cos. Bd. dirs. San Diego Regional Econ. Devel. Corp., 1997—. Mem. San Diego Taxpayers Assn. (pres. 1986-87), Order of Coif. Avocation: jogging, music. Office: Gray Cary Ware & Freidenrich LLP 401 B St Ste 1700 San Diego CA 92101-4297 E-mail: tomalley@graycary.com

O'MALLEY, ROBERT EDMUND, JR. mathematics educator; b. Rochester, N.H., May 23, 1939; s. Robert E. and Jeanette A. (Dubois) O'M.; m. Candace G. Hinz, Aug. 31, 1968; children: Patrick, Timothy, Daniel. B.S. in Elec. Engring., U. N.H., 1960, M.S., 1961; Ph.D., Stanford U., 1966. Mathematician Bell Labs., Gen. Electric Research Co., RCA, summers 1961-63; asst. prof. U. N.C., Chapel Hill, 1965-66; vis. mem. Courant Inst., NYU, 1966-67; research mem. Math. Research Ctr., Madison, Wis., 1967-68; asst. prof., assoc. prof. NYU, N.Y.C., 1968-73; prof. math. U. Ariz., Tucson, 1973-81, chmn. applied math. program, 1976-81; prof. math. Rensselaer Poly. Inst., Troy, N.Y., 1981-90, chmn. dept. math. scis., 1981-84, Ford Found. prof., 1989-90; prof., chair applied math. U. Wash., Seattle, 1990-93, prof., 1993—. Sr. vis. fellow U. Edinburgh, (Scotland), 1971-72; guest prof. Tech. U. Vienna, 1987-88; vis. Univ. Lyon 1 and Univ. of Cambridge, 1994-95. Author: Introduction to Singular Perturbations, 1974; editor: Asymptotic Methods and Singular Perturbations, 1976, Singular Perturbation Methods for Ordinary Differential Equations, 1991, Thinking About Ordinary Differential Equations, 1997; editor ICIAM 91 procs.; co-editor Multiscale Phenomena, 1999; contbr. numerous articles to profl. jours. Mem. Soc. for Indsl. and Applied Math. (pres. 1991-92), Am. Math. Soc. Roman Catholic. Home: 3415 W Laurelhurst Dr NE Seattle WA 98105-5345 Office: U Wash Dept Applied Math Box 352420 Seattle WA 98195-2420 E-mail: omalley@amath.washington.edu

O'MEARA, SARA, nonprofit organization executive; b. Knoxville, Tenn., 09 Sept. m. Robert O'Meara (dec.); children: John Hopkins, Charles Hopkins (dec.); m. Robert Sigholtz, Nov. 1986; stepchildren: Taryn, Whitney. Attended, Briarcliff Jr. Coll.; BA, The Sorbonne, Paris; D (hon.), Endicott Coll. Co-founder, chmn. bd., CEO CHILDHELP USA (formerly Children's Village USA), Scottsdale, Ariz., 1960—. Bd. dirs. Nat. Soc. for Prevention of Child Abuse and Neglect of Gt. Britain, Children to Children, Inc.; hon. com. mem. Learning Disabilities Found., Inc.; mem. Mayor's adv. bd., Defense for Children Internat., Nat. Soc. Prevention Cruelty to Children, World Affairs Coun.; adv. bd. mem. Ednl. Film Co.; bd. dirs. Internat. Alliance on Child Abuse and Neglect; sustaining mem. Spastic Children's League, past pres.; mem., past recording sec. Assistance League So. Calif. Recipient Cross of Merit, Knightly Order of St. Brigitte, 1967, Victor M. Carter Diamond award Japan-Am. Soc., 1970, Dame Cross of Merit of Order of St. John of Denmark, 1980, Official Seal of 34th Gov. Calif., 1981, Woman of Achievement award Career Guild, 1982, Women Making History award Nat. Fedn. Bus. Profl. Women's Clubs, 1983, Disting. Am. award for svc., 1984, Humanitarian award Nat. Frat. Eagles, 1984, Nat. Recognition award outstanding leadership Am. Heritage Found., 1986, Notable Am. award svc. to Calif., 1986, Dove of Peace award Pacific Southwest and Ctrl. Pacific Regions B'nai B'rith, 1987, Paul Harris fellow award Rotary Found., 1989, Internat. Collaboration to Prevention Child Abuse award HRH Queen of Eng., 1989, Living Legacy award Women's Internat. Ctr., 1989, Love and Help the Children award, 1990, Presdl. award, 1990, Kiwanis World Svc. medal, 1991, Family Circle award Family Circle Mag., 1992, Outstanding Woman for Tenn. award Nat. Mus. Women in Arts, 1993, Nat. Caring award Nat. Caring Inst., 1993, Hubert Humphrey award Touchdown Club Washington, 1993, numerous others. Mem. SAG, AFTRA, Victory Awards (exec. com.), Am. Biographical Inst. (nat. bd. advisors), Alpha Delta Kappa (hon.). Office: Childhelp USA 15757 N 78th St Scottsdale AZ 85260-1629

OMER, GEORGE ELBERT, JR. orthopaedic surgeon, educator; b. Kansas City, Kans., Dec. 23, 1922; s. George Elbert and Edith May (Hines) O.; m. Wendie Vilven, Nov. 6, 1949; children: George Eric, Michael Lee. BA, Ft. Hays Kans. State U., 1944; MD, Kans. U., 1950; MSc in Orthopaedic Surgery, Baylor U., 1955. Diplomate Am. Bd. Orthopaedic Surgery, 1959, (bd. dirs. 1983-92, pres. 1987-88), re-cert. orthopaedics and hand surgery, 1983, cert. surgery of the hand, 1989. Commd. 1st lt. U.S. Army, 1949; advanced through grades to col., 1967; ret. U.S. Army, 1970; rotating intern Bethany Hosp., Kansas City, 1950-51; resident in orthopaedic surgery Brooke Gen. Hosp., San Antonio, 1952-55, William Beaumont Gen. Hosp., El Paso, Tex., 1955-56; chief surgery Irwin Army Hosp., Ft. Riley, Kans., 1957-59; cons. in orthopaedic surgery 8th Army Korea, 1959-60; asst. chief orthopaedic surgery, chief hand surgeon Fitzsimons Army Med. Center, Denver, 1960-63; dir. orthopaedic residency tng. Armed Forces Inst. Pathology and Walter Reed Army Med. Ctr., Washington, 1963-65; chief orthopaedic surgery and chief Army Hand Surg. Center, Brooke Army Med. Center, 1965-70; cons. in orthopaedic and hand surgery Surgeon Gen. Army, 1967-70; prof. orthopaedics, surgery, and anatomy, chmn. dept. orthopaedic surgery, chief div. hand surgery U. N.Mex., 1970-90, med. dir. phys. therapy, 1972-90, acting asst. dean grad. edn. Sch. Medicine, 1980-81. Mem. active staff U. N.Mex. Hosp., Albuquerque, 1970—, chief of med. staff, 1984-86; cons. staff other Albuquerque hosps.; cons. orthopedic surgery USPHS, 1966-85, U.S. Army, 1970-92, USAF, 1970-78, VA, 1970-2000; cons. Carrie Tingley Hosp. for Crippled Children, 1970-99, interim med. dir., 1970-72, 86-87, mem. bd. advisor 1972-76, chair, 1994-96. Mem. bd. editors Clin. Orthopaedics, 1973-90, Jour. AMA, 1973-74, Jour. Hand Surgery, 1976-81; trustee Jour. Bone and Joint Surgery, 1993-99, sec., 1993-96, chmn., 1997-99; contbr. more than 300 articles to profl. jours., numerous chpts. to books. Decorated Legion of Merit, Army Commendation medal with 2 oak leaf clusters; recipient Alumni Achievement award Ft. Hays State U., 1973, Recognition plaque Am. Soc. Surgery Hand, 1989, Recognition plaque N.Mex. Orthopaedic Assn., 1991, Recognition award for hand surgery Am. Osteo. Acad. Orthopaedics, 1982, Pioneer award Internat. Socs. for Surgery Hand, 1995, Rodey award U. N.Mex. Alumni Assn., 1997, Cornerstone award U. N.Mex. Health Scis. Ctr., 1997; recognized with Endowed Professorship U. N.Mex. Sch. Medicine, 1995; recognized with named Annual Orthop. Seminar and Alumni Day Brooke Army Med. Ctr., 1999. Fellow ACS, Am. Orthopaedic Assn. (pres. 1988-89, exec. dir. 1989-93), Am. Acad. Orthopaedic Surgeons, Assn. Orthopaedic Chmn., N.Mex. Orthopaedic Assn. (pres. 1979-81, 1999-2000), La. Orthopaedic Assn. (hon.), Korean Orthopaedic Assn. (hon.), Peru Orthopaedic Soc. (hon.), Caribbean Hand Soc., Am. Soc. Surgery Hand (pres. 1978-79), Am. Assn. Surgery of Trauma, Assn. Bone and Joint Surgeons, Assn. Mil. Surgeons U.S., Riordan Hand Soc. (pres. 1967-68), Sunderland Soc. (pres. 1981-83), Soc. Mil. Orthopaedic Surgeons, Brazilian Hand Soc. (hon.), S.Am. Hand Soc. (hon.), Groupe D'Etude de la Main, Brit. Hand Soc., Venezuela Hand Soc. (hon.), South African Hand Soc. (hon.), Western Orthopaedic Assn. (pres. 1981-82), AAAS, Russell A. Hibbs Soc. (pres. 1977-78), 38th Parallel Med. Soc. (Korea) (sec. 1959-60); mem. AMA, Phi Kappa Phi, Phi Sigma, Alpha Omega Alpha, Phi Beta Pi. Achievements include pioneer work in hand surgery. Home: 316 Big Horn Ridge Rd NE Sandia Heights Albuquerque NM 87122 Office: U N Mex Dept Orthopaedic Surgery 2211 Lomas Blvd NE Albuquerque NM 87106-2745

ONAK, THOMAS PHILIP, chemistry educator; b. Omaha, July 30, 1932; s. Louis Albert and Louise Marie (Penner) O.; m. Sharon Colleen Neal, June 18, 1954. BA, Calif. State U., San Diego, 1954; PhD, U. Calif., Berkeley, 1957. Research chemist Olin Mathieson Chem. Corp., Pasadena, Calif., 1957-59; asst. prof. Calif. State U., Los Angeles, 1959-63, assoc. prof., 1963-66, prof. chemistry, 1966-99, prof. emeritus, 1999. Author: Organoborane Chemistry, 1975; Contbr. articles to profl. jours., chpts. to books. Recipient Rsch. Career award NIH, 1973-78, Nat. award Am. Chem. Soc., 1990, Outstanding Prof. award Calif. State U., System, 1993-94; named Calif. Prof. of Yr. Carnegie Found. and Coun. for the Advancement and Support of Edn., 1995; Fulbright Rsch. fellow U. Cambridge, Eng., 1965-66. Home: 230 E Highcourte Ln Tucson AZ 85737-6859 Office: Calif State U Dept Chemistry 5151 State U Dr Los Angeles CA 90032

O'NEAL, SHAQUILLE RASHAUN, professional basketball player; b. Newark, Mar. 6, 1972; s. Philip A. Harrison and Lucille O'Neal. Student, La. State U. Center Orlando Magic, 1992-96, L.A. Lakers, 1996—. Appeared in movie Blue Chips, 1994, Kazaam, 1996. Named to Sporting News All-American first team, 1990-91; recipient Rookie of the Yr. award NBA, 1993; mem. NBA All-Star team, 1993, 94, Dream Team II, 1994; first pick overall, 1992 draft. Office: LA Lakers 3900 W Manchester Blvd Inglewood CA 90305-2200

O'NEIL, JERRY, state senator; b. Kalispell, Mont., May 10, 1943; children: David, Wendy, Sara, Laura, Maria. AA, Flathead Valley C.C.; student, Mont. State U., U. Mont. Mgr. Lumber Co.; owner Mediator and Ind. Paralegal, 1984—; Rep. senator dist. 42 Mont. State Senate, 2000—. Pres. DREAM, Disable Ski Program. Office: 202 Helena Flats Kalispell MT 59901-2429 Fax: 406 752-8904. E-mail: oneil@in-tch.com

O'NEIL, MICHAEL JOSEPH, opinion survey executive, marketing consultant; b. Springfield, Mass., June 22, 1951; s. James Francis and Mary Helen (Apolis) O'N.; m. Catherine Mary Zirkel, Sept. 10, 1983; children: Heather Rose, Sean Michael, Ryan Joseph, Matthew James. BA, Brown U., 1974, MA, 1975; PhD, Northwestern U., 1977. Faculty Northwestern U., 1976-77, U. Ill., Chgo., 1977, U. Mich., Ann Arbor, 1977-79, fellow Survey Rsch. Ctr., Inst. Social Rsch., 1977-79; dir. Pub. Opinion Rsch. Ctr. Ariz. State U., Tempe, 1979-81; pres. O'Neil Assocs., Tempe, 1981—. Reviewer grant proposals NSF, Washington, 1977—; mem. mktg. com. Phoenix Art Mus., 1992-96; bd. dirs. Phoenix Children's Hosp. Found., vice-chmn., 1999—. Manuscript reviewer Social Problems, 1977—, Pub. Opinion Quar., 1977—, Urban Affairs Quar., 1977—, Jour. Ofcl. Statistics, 1990—, Sociological Methods and Rsch., 1993; contbr. articles to profl. jours. Chmn. Tempe Union H.S. Dist. Bus. Edn. adv. com., 1986-88; mem. mktg. com. Mesa Assn. Retarded Citizens, 1985-87; bd. dirs. East Valley Camelback Hosp., Mesa, 1985-90, v.p., 1988-90; bd. dirs. Valley Leadership, Ariz., 1997-99; active Acad./Ariz. Town Halls, Maricopa County Citizens' Jud. Adv. Coun.; v.p. Ariz. Coalition for Tomorrow, 1998-99, pres., 1999—; mem. Phoenix Pride Commn., 1991-94. Mem. Am. Mktg. Assn., Am. Assn. Pub. Opinion Rsch., Alumni Assn. Brown U. (nat. bd. dirs. 1985-90, Ariz. pres. 1984—), Phoenix City Club (bd. dirs. 1987-93, pres. 1990-91), East Valley Partnership (mem. bd. dirs. 1993—), Phi Beta Kappa. Democrat. Avocation: tennis. Office: O'Neil Assocs 412 E Southern Ave Tempe AZ 85282-5212 E-mail: mike.oneil@alumni.brown.edu, oneil@oneilresearch.com

O'NEIL, THOMAS MICHAEL, physicist, educator; b. Hibbing, Minn., Sept. 2, 1940; married; 1 child. BS, Calif. State U., Long Beach, 1962; MS, U. Calif., San Diego, 1964, PhD in Physics, 1965. Rsch. physicist Gen. Atomic, 1965-67; prof. physics U. Calif., San Diego, 1967—. Mem. adv. bd. Inst. Fusion Studies, 1980-83, Inst. Theoretical Physics, 1983-86. Assoc. editor Physics Review Letters, 1979-83; correspondent Comments Plasma Physics & Controlled Fusion, 1980-84. Alfred P. Sloan fellow, 1971; recipient Disting. Alumnus award Sch. Natural Sci. CSULB, 1985, Alumni Disting. Tchg. award UCSD, 1996. Fellow Am. Phys. Soc. (award for excellence in plasma physics 1991, James Clerk Maxwell prize 1996). Achievements include research in theoretical plasma physics with emphasis on nonlinear effects in plasmas and on non-neutral plasmas. Office: Dept Physics 9500 Gilman Dr La Jolla CA 92093-5003 E-mail: toneil@ucsd.edu

O'NEIL, WILLIAM SCOTT, publishing executive; V.p., portfolio mgr. William O'Neil Inc., L.A., 1992—. Office: Investors Bus Daily 12655 Beatrice St Los Angeles CA 90066-7303

O'NEILL, BEVERLY LEWIS, mayor, former college president; b. Long Beach, Calif., Sept. 8, 1930; d. Clarence John and Flossie Rachel (Nicholson) Lewis; m. William F. O'Neill, Dec. 21, 1952 AA, Long Beach City Coll., 1950; BA, Calif. State U., Long Beach, 1952, MA, 1956; EdD, U. So. Calif., 1977. Elem. tchr. Long Beach Unified Sch. Dist., 1952-57; instr., counsellor Compton (Calif.) Coll., 1957-60; curriculum supr. Little Lake Sch. Dist., Santa Fe Springs, Calif., 1960-62; women's advisor, campus dean Long Beach City Coll., 1962-71, dir. Continuing Edn. Ctr. for Women, 1969-75, dean student affairs, 1971-77, v.p. student svcs., 1977-88, supt.-pres., 1988—, exec. dir. LBCC, 1983—; mayor City of Long Beach, Calif., 1994—. Advisor Jr. League, Long Beach, 1976—, Nat. Coun. on Alcoholism, Long Beach, 1979—, Assistance League, Long Beach, 1982—; bd. dirs. NCCJ, Long Beach, 1976—, Meml. Hosp. Found., Long Beach, 1984-92, Met. YMCA, Long Beach, 1986-92, United Way, Long Beach, 1986-92. Named Woman of Yr., Long Beach Human Rels. Commn., 1976, to Hall of Fame, Long Beach City Coll., 1977, Disting. Alumni of Yr., Calif. State U., Long Beach, 1985, Long Beach Woman of Yr. Rick Rackers, 1987, Assistance League Aux., 1987, Woman of Yr., Calif. Legislature 54th Dist., 1995; recipient Hannah Solomon award Nat. Coun. Jewish Women, 1984, Outstanding Colleague award Long Beach City Coll., 1985, NCCJ Humanitarian award, 1991, Woman of Excellence award YWCA, 1990, Community Svc. award Community Svcs. Devel. Corp., 1991, Citizen of Yr. award Exch. Club, 1992, Pacific Regional CEO award Assn. Community Coll. Trustees, 1992. Mem. Assn. Calif. Community Coll. Adminstrs. (pres. 1988-90, Harry Buttimer award 1991), Calif. Community Colls. Chief Exec. Officers Assn., Rotary, Soroptomists (Women Helping Women award 1981, Hall of Fame award 1984). Democrat. Office: Office Mayor Civic Ctr Plz 333 W Ocean Blvd Fl 14 Long Beach CA 90802-4604

O'NEILL, BRIAN, national recreation area administrator; Gen. supt. Golden Gate Nat. Recreation Area, San Francisco; supt. Muir Woods Nat. Monument, San Francisco. Office: Golden Gate Nat Rec Area Fort Mason Bldg 201 San Francisco CA 94123

O'NEILL, JOHN, hotel executive; Pres., CEO O'Neill Hotels & Resorts Mgmt. Ltd., Vancouver, B.C., Can. Office: ONeill Hotels & Resorts 210 1333 Johnston St Vancouver BC Canada V6H 3R9

O'NEILL, MICHAEL E. bank executive; b. Oct. 31, 1946; BA in European Civilization, Princeton U., 1969; MBA, U. Va., 1974. With Continental Bank Corp (now BankAm. Corp.), 1974—, with internat. banking svcs. Belgium, 1975-78, 2d v.p. multinat. banking svcs., 1978-79, v.p., 1979-80, mgr. multinat. banking svcs. Hong Kong, 1980-83, mgr. spl. industries svcs. in Europe London, 1983-84, U.K. country mgr., 1984-85, mng. dir., head mergers and acquisitions, 1989-90, chief of staff continental capital markets investments, 1990-92, CFO capital markets investments and trading sector, 1992-94, mgr. global equity investments U.S. corp. group, 1994-95, CFO, 1995-00; pvt. practice cons. to banks and corps., 1985-88; chmn., CEO Bank of Hawaii, Honolulu, 2000—, Pacific Century Financial Corp., Honolulu, 2000—. Lt. USMC, 1969-71. Address: Pacific Century Financial Corp 130 Merchant St Honolulu HI 96813

O'NEILL, ROB, hotel executive; Chmn. O'Neill Hotels & Resorts Mgmt., Ltd., Vancouver, B.C., Can. Office: ONeill Hotels & Resorts 210-1333 Johnston St Vancouver BC Canada V6H 3R9

O'NEILL, RUSSELL RICHARD, engineering educator; b. Chgo., June 6, 1916; s. Dennis Alysious and Florence Agnes (Mathurin) O'N.; m. Margaret Bock, Dec. 15, 1939; children: Richard A., John R.; m. Sallie Boyd, June 30, 1967. BSME, U. Calif., Berkeley, MSME, 1940; PhD, UCLA, 1956. Registered profl. engr., Calif. Design engr. Dowell, Inc., Midland, Mich., 1940-41; design engr. Dow Chem. Co., Midland, 1941-44, Airesearch Mfg. Co., Los Angeles, 1944-46; lectr. engring. UCLA, 1946-56, prof. engring., 1956, asst. dean engring., 1956-61, assoc. dean, 1961-73, acting dean, 1965-66, dean, 1974-83, dean emeritus, 1983—; staff engr. NAS-NRC, 1954; dir. Data Design Labs., 1977-86, dir. emeritus, 1986—. Mem. engring. task force Space Era Edn. Study Fla. Bd. Control, 1963; mem. regional Export Expansion Coun. Dept. Commerce, 1960-66, Los Angeles Mayor's Space Adv. Com., 1964-69; mem. Maritime Transp. Rsch. Bd., 1974-81; bd. advisers Naval Postgrad. Sch., 1976-84; mem. Nat. Nuclear Accreditation Bd., 1983-88; mem. accrediting bd. Dept. Energy, 1992—. Trustee West Coast U., 1981-90; bd. dirs. Western region United Way, 1982-90. Mem. NAE, Am. Soc. Engring. Edn., Sigma Xi, Tau Beta Pi. Home: 15430 Longbow Dr Sherman Oaks CA 91403-4910 Office: UCLA SEAS 405 Hilgard Ave Los Angeles CA 90095-1600 E-mail: russ@ea.ucla.edu

OPEL, WILLIAM, medical research administrator; BA, Pepperdine U., 1968; MBA, U. So. Calif., 1993; PhD, Claremont Grad. U., 1998. Mem. staff Pasadena (Calif.) Found. Med. Rsch., Pasadena, Calif., 1961-63, rsch. assoc., 1964-70, asst. to dir., 1970-72, adminstr., 1972-76, exec. dir., 1976-82; acting exec. dir. Huntington Inst. Applied Med. Rsch., 1978-82; exec. dir. Huntington Med. Rsch. Inst., Pasadena, Calif., 1982—. Lectr. in technology, mgmt., Pepperdine U.; adj. prof. tech. mgmt. Claremont Grad. U. Mem. Beta Gamma Sigma, Phi Kappa Phi. Office: Huntington Med Rsch Insts 734 Fairmount Ave Pasadena CA 91105-3104

OPITZ, JOHN MARIUS, clinical geneticist, pediatrician; b. Hamburg, Germany, Aug. 15, 1935; came to the U.S., 1950, naturalized, 1957; s. Friedrich and Erica Maria (Quadt) O.; m. Susan O. Lewin; children: Lea, Teresa, John, Chrisanthi, Felix, Emma. BA, State U. Iowa, 1956, MD, 1959; DSc (hon.), Mont. State U., 1983; MD (hon.), U. Kiel, Germany, 1986, U. Bologna, Italy, 1999. Diplomate Am. Bd. Pediat., Am. Bd. Med. Genetics. Intern State U. Iowa Hosp., 1959-60, resident in pediat., 1960-61; resident, chief resident in pediat. U. Wis. Hosp., Madison, 1961-62; fellow in pediat. and med. genetics U. Wis., 1962-64, asst. prof. med. genetics and pediat., 1964-69, assoc. prof., 1969-72, prof., 1972-79; dir. Wis. Clin. Genetics Ctr., 1974-79; clin. prof. med. genetics and pediat. U. Wash., Seattle, 1979—; prof. pediat., human genetics and ob-gyn. U Utah, SLC, 1997—. Adj. prof. medicine, biology, history and philosophy, vet. rsch. and vet. sci. Mont. State U., Bozeman, 1979-94, McKay lectr., 1992, univ. prof. med. humanities, 1994—; adj. prof. pediat., med. genetics U. Wis., Madison, 1979—, Class of 1947 Disting. prof., 1992; coord. Shodair Mont. Regional Genetic Svcs. Program, Helena, 1979-82; chmn. dept. med. genetics Shodair Children's Hosp., Helena, 1983-94; dir. Found. Devel. and Med. Genetics, Helena, Mont., 1994-96; pres. Heritage Genetics P.C., Helena, 1996; Farber lectr. Soc. Pediat. Pathology, 1987; Joseph Garfunkel lectr. So. Ill. U., Springfield, 1987, McKay lectr. Mont. State U., 1992; Warren Wheeler vis. prof. Columbus (Ohio) Children's Hosp., 1987, 2001; Bea Fowlow lectr. in med. genetics U. Calgary, 1996; 1st vis. prof. Hanseatic U. Found. of Lübeck, 1996; Lew Barness lectr. U. South Fla., 2001; Enid Gilbert Barness lectr. U. Wis., 2001—; vis. prof. U. Catholica del Sacro Cuore, Rome, 2001—. Editor, author 14 books; founder, editor in chief Am. Jour. Med. Genetics, 1977-2000; mng. editor European Jour. Pediat., 1977-85; contbr. numerous articles on clin. genetics. Chair Mont. Com. for Humanities, 1991. Recipient Pool of Bethesda award for excellence in mental retardation rsch. Bethesda Luth. Home, 1988, Med. Alumni citation U. Wis., 1989, Col. Harlan Sanders Lifetime Achievement award for work in field of genetic scis. March of Dimes, Purkinje medal Czech Soc. Medicine, Mendel medal Czech Soc. Med. Genetics, 1996, Internat. prize Phoenix-Anni Verdi for Genetic Rsch., 1996. Fellow AAAS, Am. Coll. Med. Genetics (founder); mem. German Acad. Scientists Leopoldina, Am. Soc. Human Genetics, Am. Pediat. Soc., Soc. Pediat. Rsch., Am. Bd. Med. Genetics, Birth Defects Clin. Genetic Soc., Am. Inst. Biol. Scis., Am. Soc. Zoologists, Teratology Soc., Genetic Soc. Am., European Soc. Human Genetics, Soc. Study Social Biology, Am. Acad. Pediat., German Soc. Pediat. (hon.), Western Soc. Pediat. Rsch. (emeritus), Italian Soc. Med. Genetics (hon.), Israel Soc. Med. Genetics (hon.), Russian Soc. Med. Genetics (Hon.), So. Africa Soc. Med. Genetics (hon.), Japanese Soc. Human Genetics (hon.), Sigma Xi. Democrat. Roman Catholic. Home: 2930 E Craig Dr Salt Lake City UT 84109-3636 Office: U Utah Sch Medicine Primary Childrens Med Ctr 100 N Medical Dr Salt Lake City UT 84113-1103 E-mail: john.opitz@hsc.utah.edu

OPOTOWSKY, MAURICE LEON, newspaper editor; b. New Orleans, Dec. 13, 1931; s. Sol and Fannie (Latter) O.; m. Madeleine Duhamel, Feb. 28, 1959 (dec.); children: Didier Sol Duhamel, Joelle Duhamel, Arielle Duhamel (dec.); m. Bonnie Feibleman, May 4, 1991. Student, Tulane U., 1949-51; BA cum laude, Williams Coll., 1953. Reporter Berkshire Eagle, Pittsfield, Mass., 1951-53; pub. Sea Coast Echo, Bay St. Louis, Miss., 1953-54; reporter UPI, 1956-62; feature editor Newsday, Ronkonkoma, N.Y., 1962-64, Suffolk day editor, 1964-65, Nassau night editor, 1965-67, nat. editor, 1967-70, Suffolk editor, 1970-72; dir. L.I. Mag., 1972; day editor Press-Enterprise, Riverside, Calif., 1973-84, mng. editor features/adminstrn., 1984-87, sr. mng. editor, 1987-92, mng. editor, 1992-98, ombudsman, 1998—. Chief N.Y. State Syndicate Service, 1961-74; mem. Calif. Freedom of Info. Exec. Com., sec., 1979-80, treas., 1980-81, v.p., 1981-82, pres., 1982-83; Pulitzer prize juror. Trustee Harbor Country Day Sch., 1970-72; bd. dirs. Calif. Newspaper Editor Conf. Bd., 1978-83; mem. Smithtown (N.Y.) Hunt, 1970-73, West Hills Hunt, 1976-80, Santa Fe Hunt, Whip, 1985— ; co-chmn. Calif. Bench-Bar Media Com.; mem. adv. coun. dept. comm. Calif. State U., Fullerton, 1995-66, instr. dept. comms. 1998—. Served with AUS, 1954-56. Recipient Lifetime Achievement award Calif. 1st Amendment Assembly, 1997. Mem. AP News Execs. Calif. (chmn. 1986-87), Calif. 1st Amendment Coalition (pres., treas.), Calif. Soc. Newspaper Editors (bd. dirs., vice chmn. steering com. 1983), AP Mng. Editors Assn., Am. Soc. Newspaper Editors. Office: Press Enterprise Co 3512 14th St Riverside CA 92501-3878

OPPEDAHL, JOHN FREDRICK, newspaper publisher, publishing executive; b. Duluth, Minn., Nov. 9, 1944; s. Walter H. and Lucille (Hole) O.; m. Alison Owen, 1975 (div. 1983); m. Gillian Coyro, Feb. 14, 1987; 1 child, Max. B.A., U. Calif., Berkeley, 1967; M.S., Columbia U., 1968. Reporter San Francisco Examiner, 1967; reporter, asst. city editor Detroit Free Press, 1968-75, city editor, 1975-80, exec. city editor, 1981, exec. news editor, 1981-82, asst. mng. editor, 1983; nat. editor Dallas Times Herald, 1983-85, asst. mng. editor, 1985-87; mng. editor/news L.A. Herald Examiner, 1987-89; mng. editor Ariz. Republic, Phoenix, 1989-93; exec. editor Phoenix Newspapers, 1993-95; pub., CEO Phoenix Newspapers, Inc., 1996—. Trustee Walter Cronkite Sch. Journalism and Telecomm., Ariz. State U.; bd. dirs. Found. for Am. Comms., Downtown Phoenix Partnership, Phoenix Cmty. Alliance; trustee Phoenix Art Mus.; bd. advisors Morrison Inst.; campaign chmn. Valley of the Sun United Way, 1999; mem. Greater Phoenix Leadership; past chmn. COMPAS; bd. visitors Columbia U. Journalism Sch. Mem. Am. Soc. Newspaper Editors, AP Mng. Editors, Newspaper Assn. of Am. Office: The Arizona Republic 200 E Van Buren St Phoenix AZ 85004-2238

OPPEDAHL, PHILLIP EDWARD, computer company executive; b. Renwick, Iowa, Sept. 17, 1935; s. Edward and Isadore Hannah (Gangstead) O.; m. Sharon Elaine Ree, Aug. 3, 1957 (dec. Aug. 1989); children: Gary Lynn, Tamra Sue, Sue Ann, Lisa Kay. BS in Naval Sci., Navy Postgrad. Sch., 1963, MS in Nuclear Physics, 1971; MS in Sys. Mgmt., U. S.C., 1978. Commd. ensign U.S. Navy, 1956, advanced through grades to capt., 1977; with Airborne Early Warning Squadron, 1957-59, Anti-Submarine Squadron, 1959-65; asst. navigator USS Coral Sea, 1965-67; basig jet flight instr., 1967-69; test group dir. Def. Nuclear Agy., 1972-74; weapons officer USS Oriskany, 1974-76; program mgt. for armament Naval Air Sys. Command, Washington, 1977-79; test dir. Def. Nuclear Agy., Kirtland AFB, N.Mex., 1979-82, dep. comdr., 1982-83; pres., CEO Am. Systems, Albuquerque, 1983—. Bd. dirs. BASIS Internat., 1991—. Author: Energy Loss of High Energy Electrons in Beryllium, 1971, Understanding Contractor Motivation and Incentive Contracts. Decorated DSM. Mem. Nava. Inst., Am. Nuclear Soc., Aircraft Owners and Pilots Assn., Assn. Naval Aviation, Navy League. Lutheran. Home and Office: 13504 Desert Zinnia Ct Albuquerque NM 87111-7156

ORBACH, RAYMOND LEE, physicist, educator; b. Los Angeles, July 12, 1934; s. Morris Albert and Mary Ruth (Miller) O.; m. Eva Hannah Spiegler, Aug. 26, 1956; children: David Miller, Deborah Hedwig, Thomas Randolph. BS, Calif. Inst. Tech., 1956; PhD, U. Calif., Berkeley, 1960. NSF postdoctoral fellow Oxford U., 1960-61; asst. prof. applied physics Harvard U., 1961-63; prof. physics UCLA, 1963-92, asst. vice chancellor acad. change and curriculum devel., 1970-72, chmn. acad. senate L.A. divsn., 1976-77, provost Coll. Letters and Sci., 1982-92; chancellor U. Calif., Riverside, 1992—. Mem. physics adv. panel NSF, 1970-73; mem. vis. com. Brookhaven Nat. Lab., 1970-74; mem. materials rsch. lab. adv. panel NSF, 1974-77; mem. Nat. Commn. on Rsch., 1978-80; chmn. 16th Internat. Conf. on Low Temperature Physics, 1981; Joliot Curie prof. Ecole Superieure de la Physique et Chimie Industrielle de la Ville de Paris, 1982, chmn. Gordon Rsch. Conf. on Fractals, 1986; Lorentz prof. U. Leiden, Netherlands, 1987; Raymond and Beverly Sackler lectr. Tel Aviv U., 1989; faculty rsch. lectr. UCLA, 1990; Andrew Lawson lectr. U. Calif., Riverside, 1992; mem. external rev. com. Nat. High Magnetic Fields Lab., 1994—. Author: (with A.A. Manenkov) SpinLattice Relaxation in Ionic Solids, 1966; divsn. assoc. editor Phys. Rev. Letters, 1980-83, Jour. Low Temperature Physics, 1980-90, Phys. Rev., 1983—; contbr. articles to profl. jours. Recipient Whitney M. Young Humanitarian award Urban League of Riverside and San Bernardino, 1998, El Sol Azteca award La Prensa Hispana, 2000; Alfred P. Sloan Found. fellow, 1963-67; NSF sr. postdoctoral fellow Imperial Coll., 1967-68; Guggenheim fellow Tel Aviv U., 1973-74. Fellow Am. Phys. Soc. (chmn. nominations com. 1981-82, counselor-at-large 1987-91, chmn. divsn. condensed matter 1990-91); mem. AAAS (chairperson steering group physics sect.), NSF (mem. rsch. adv. com. divsn. materials 1992-93), Phys. Soc. (London), Univ. Rsch. Assn. (chair coun. pres. 1993), Sigma Xi, Phi Beta Kappa, Tau Beta Pi. Home: 4171 Watkins Dr Riverside CA 92507-4738 Office: U Calif Riverside Chancellors Office 4148 Hinderaker Hl Riverside CA 92521-0001

ORCHARD, HENRY JOHN, electrical engineer; b. Oldbury, Eng., May 7, 1922; came to U.S., 1961, naturalized, 1973; s. Richard John and Lucy Matilda O.; m. Irene Dorothy Wise, Sept. 13, 1947; 1 child, Richard John; m. Marietta Eugenie Gayet, Aug. 2, 1971. B.Sc., U. London, 1946, M.Sc., 1951. Prin. sci. officer Brit. Post Office, London, 1947-61; sr. staff GTE Lenkurt Inc., San Carlos, Calif., 1961-70; mem. faculty UCLA, 1970—, prof. elec. engring., 1970-91, prof. emeritus, 1991—, vice chmn. dept., 1982-91. Author over 50 pub. papers; patentee in field. Fellow IEEE (Best Paper award group circuit theory 1968), Cirs. and Systems Soc. (Golden Jubilee medal 1999). Republican. Home: 828 19th St Apt E Santa Monica CA 90403-6705 Office: UCLA Elec Engring Dept Los Angeles CA 90095-1594

ORCUTT, JOHN ARTHUR, geophysicist, researcher; b. Holyoke, Colo., Aug. 29, 1943; married, 1967; 2 children. BS, U.S. Naval Acad., 1966; MSc, U. Liverpool, 1968; PhD in Earth Scis., U. Calif., San Diego, 1976. Rsch. geophysicist Scripps Inst. Oceanography, La Jolla, Calif., 1977—, assoc. prof., 1982-84, prof. geophysics, 1984—, dir. Inst. Geophysics & Planetary Physics, 1984—. Recipient Newcomb Cleveland prize AAAS, 1980, Maurice Ewing medal Am. Geophys. Union, 1994 Mem. Am. Geophys. Union, Soc. Exploration Geophysicists, Seismological Soc. Am. Office: U Calif Inst Geophys & Planetary Physics 9500 Gilman Dr La Jolla CA 92093-5004

ORDEN, TED, gasoline service stations executive; b. 1920; With Thrifty Oil Co., Inc., Downey, Calif., 1959—, now pres., also bd. dirs. Santa Fe Springs.

ORDIN, ANDREA SHERIDAN, lawyer; m. Robert Ordin; 1 child, M. Victoria; stepchildren: Allison, Richard. AB, UCLA, 1962, LLB, 1965. Bar: Calif. 1966. Dep. atty. gen. Calif., 1965-72; So. Calif. legal counsel Fair Employment Practices Commn., 1972-73; asst. dist. atty. L.A. County, 1975-77; U.S. atty. Central Dist. Calif. L.A., 1977-81; adj. prof. UCLA Law Sch., 1982; chief asst. atty. gen. Calif. L.A., 1983-90; ptnr. Morgan, Lewis & Bockius, L.A., 1993—. Mem. L.A. County Bar Assn. (past pres., past exec. dir.). Office: Morgan Lewis & Bockius 300 S Grand Ave Ste 22 Los Angeles CA 90071-3109

O'REGAN, DEBORAH, association executive, lawyer; b. New Prague, Minn., Aug. 30, 1953; d. Timothy A. and Ermalinda (Brinkman) O'R.; m. Ron Kahlenbeck, Sept. 29, 1984; children: Katherine, Ryan. BA, Coll. of St. Catherine, 1975; JD, William Mitchell Coll. of Law, 1980. Bar: Ala. 1982, Minn. 1980. Asst. city atty. City of Bloomington, Minn., 1978-81, asst. city mgr., 1981-82; CLE dir. Alaska Bar Assn., Anchorage, 1982-84, exec. dir., 1985—. Mem. task force on gender equality State Fed. Joint Commn., Anchorage, 1991—; mem. selection com. U.S. Magistrate Judge, U.S. Dist of Ala., 1992; mem. adv. bd. Anchorage Daily News, 1991-93. Mem. Nat. Assn. Bar Execs. (exec. com. 1993-97). Avocations: travel, outdoors, rollerblading. Office: Alaska Bar Assn 510 L St Ste 602 Anchorage AK 99501-1959

O'REILLY, DAVID J. oil company executive; Various positions to v.p. Chevron Products Co., San Francisco, 1968-91, 91-94, pres., 1994-98, dir., vice-chmn., 1998-2000, chmn. bd. dirs., CEO, 2000—; CEO, chmn. Chevron Corp., San Francisco, 2001—. Office: Chevron Corp 575 Market St San Francisco CA 94105

O'REILLY, RICHARD BROOKS, journalist; b. Kansas City, Mo., Feb. 19, 1941; s. Charles Alfred and Wilma Faye (Brooks) O'R.; m. Anne Pustmeuller, June 27, 1964 (div. 1978); children— Kathleen Marie, Randall Charles; m. Joan Marlene Sweeney, Jan. 1, 1981 (div. 1996). B.A., U. Denver, 1966. Reporter Washington Park Times, Denver, 1963-64; mng. editor Aurora Advocate, Colo., 1964; police reporter Rocky Mountain News, Denver, 1964-66, night rewrite reporter, 1966, city hall reporter, 1966-67, statehouse reporter, 1967-68, investigative reporter, 1971-74; minority affairs reporter Denver Post, 1968-70; freelance writer St. Georges, Grenada, 1970; investigative reporter Orange County edition Los Angeles Times, 1974-78, chief county bur., 1978, asst. met. editor, 1978-80, environ. reporter, 1980-84, computer columnist, syndicated columnist, 1985-90, coord. tech. resources, 1984-89, dir. [illegible] computer analysis, 1989—. Adj. prof. journalism U. So. Calif., 1990-92; mem. electronic filing adv. com. Calif. Sec. of State, 1995. Named Colo. Journalist of Yr., Sigma Delta Chi, 1972; recipient Pub. Svc. award U.S. Justice Dept., 1973, McWilliams award Denver Press Club, 1974, Investigative Reporting award Orange Country Press Club, 1977, 95, Los Angeles Times, 1977, 97, Nat. Journalism award Soc. Profl. Engrs., 1983, Clean Air award Am. Lung Assn., 1985, award for non-deadline reporting Sigma Delta Chi, 1996, medal for investigative reporting Investigative Reporters and Editors, 1996. Democrat Avocations: flying; sailing; camping. Office: Los Angeles Times 202 W 1st St Los Angeles CA 90012

O'REILLY, THOMAS EUGENE, human resources consultant, retired; b. Wichita, Kans., Sept. 7, 1932; s. Eugene William and Florence Irene (Gustner) O'R.; m. Lorraine Bryant, Feb. 9, 1957; children: Thomas Jr., Patricia, Susan, Gregory, Pamela. BA, Iona Coll., 1954; MBA, NYU, 1958. Mem. human resources staff Chase Manhattan Bank, N.Y.C., 1957-69, dir. employee rels., 1969-71, mgr. internat. personnel, 1971-75, dir. internal staffing, 1976-77, dir. mgmt. resources, 1978-80, dir. exec. resources, 1980-87; v.p., sr. cons. Lee Hecht Harrison, Inc., N.Y.C., 1988-93; ret. Spl. agt. counter-intelligence corps, U.S. Army, 1954-57. Mem. Nat. Fgn. Trade Coun., Exec. Issues Forum. Republican. Roman Catholic. Home: 6200 E Cielo Run N Cave Creek AZ 85331-7645

O'REILLY, TIM, company executive; Founder, pres. O'Reilly & Assoc., Sebastopol, Calif. Office: OReilly & Assocs 101 Morris St Sebastopol CA 95472-3858

ORESKES, NAOMI, science historian; b. N.Y.C., Nov. 25, 1958; d. Irwin Oreskes and Susan Eileen Nagin Oreskes; m. Kenneth Belitz, Sept. 28, 1986; children: Hannah Oreskes Belitz, Clara Oreskes Belitz. BSc with honors, Imperial Coll., London, 1981; PhD, Stanford U., 1990. Geologist Western Mining Corp., Adelaide, Australia, 1981-84; rsch. and tng. asst. Stanford (Calif.) U., 1984-89; vis. asst. prof. Dartmouth Coll., Hanover, N.H., 1990-91, asst. prof., 1991-96; assoc. prof. Gallatin Sch. NYU, 1996-98, U. Calif., San Diego, 1998—. Consulting geologist Western Mining Corp., 1984-90; consulting historian Am. Inst. Physics, N.Y.C., 1990-96. Author: The Rejection of Continental Drift, 1999: Theory and Method in American Earth Science, 1999; contbr. articles to profl. jours. Recipient Lindgren prize Soc. Econ. Geologists, 1993, Young Investigator award NSF, 1994-99; fellow NEH, 1993. Mem. Geol. Soc. Am., History Sci. Soc. Jewish. Home: 14174 Bahama Cv Del Mar CA 92014-2901 Office: U Calif San Diego 9500 Gilman Dr La Jolla CA 92093-5004 E-mail: noreskes@ucsd.edu

ORFORD, ROBERT RAYMOND, consulting physician; b. Winnipeg, Manitoba, Can., Apr. 18, 1948; came to U.S., 1988; s. Robert Raymond and Sarah Gloria L. (Gullden) O.; m. Dale Laura Stuart, June 2, 1972; children: Carolyn Tiffany, Andrew Craig, Loren Brent. BS, McGill U., 1969, MD, 1971; MS, U. Minn., 1975; MPH, U. Wash., 1976. Assoc. prof. cmty. medicine U. Alberta, Edmonton, Can., 1978-88; dir. med. svcs. Govt. of Alberta, Edmonton, Can., 1979-81, exec. dir. occupational health svcs. Can., 1981-85, deputy min. cmty. occupational health Can., 1985-88; med. dir. employee health U. Alberta Hosp., Edmonton, Can., 1988; sr. assoc. cons. Mayo Clinic, Rochester, Minn., 1988-91, cons. preventive medicine, 1991-96, Scottsdale, Ariz., 1996—. Asst. prof. Mayo Med. Sch., Rochester, 1988—; mem. Alberta Energy Resource Conservation Bd., 1988-89; chmn. divsn. preventive and occupl. medicine, dir. exec. health program, Mayo Clinic, Scottsdale, 1999—. Contbr. articles to profl. jours. Mem. Olmsted County Environ. Commn., Rochester, 1991-96, chair, 1994. Govt. of Can. Nat. Health fellow, 1975-76. Fellow Royal Coll. Physicians & Surgeons Can., Am. Coll. Occupational and Environ. Medicine, Am. Coll. Preventive Medicine, Aerospace Med. Assn.; mem. Internat. Commn. Occupational Health Medicine (nat. sec. 2001—). Presbyterian. Avocations: volleyball, skiing, travel. Home: 15516 E Acacia Way Fountain Hills AZ 85268-3158 Office: Mayo Clinic Scottsdale Divsn Preventive Medicine 13400 E Shea Blvd Scottsdale AZ 85259-5499 E-mail: rorford@mayo.edu

ORIANS, GORDON HOWELL, biology educator; b. Eau Claire, Wis., July 10, 1932; s. Howard Lester and Marion Meta (Senty) O.; m. Elizabeth Ann Newton, June 25, 1955; children: Carlyn Elizabeth, Kristin Jean, Colin Mark. BS, U. Wis., 1954; PhD, U. Calif., Berkeley, 1960. Asst. prof. zoology U. Wash., Seattle, 1960-64, assoc. prof., 1964-68, prof., 1968-95, prof. emeritus, 1995—. Active Wash. State Ecol. Commn., Olympia, 1970-75, ecology adv. com. EPA, Washington, 1974-79; assembly life scis. NAS/NRC, Washington, 1977-83, environ. studies and toxicology bd., 1991—. Author: Some Adaptations of Marsh Nesting Blackbirds, 1980, Blackbirds of the Americas, 1985, Life: The Science of Biology, 2000; editor: Biodiversity and Ecosystem Processes in Tropical Forests, 1996. 1st lt. U.S. Army, 1955-56. Mem. AAAS, NAS, Am. Inst. Biol. Scis. (Disting. Svc. award 1994), Am. Ornithologists Union (Brewster award 1976), Am. Soc. Naturalists, Animal Behavior Soc., Royal Netherlands Acad. Arts and Scis., Orgn. for Tropical Studies (pres. 1988-94), Ecol. Soc. Am. (v.p. 1975-76, pres. 1995-96, Eminent Ecologist award 1998). Avocations: hiking, opera. Office: U Wash Dept Zoology PO Box 351800 Seattle WA 98195-1800 E-mail: blackbrd@serv.net

ORLEBEKE, WILLIAM RONALD, retired lawyer, writer; b. El Paso, Tex., Jan. 5, 1934; s. William Ronald and Frances Claire (Cook) O.; m. Barbara Raye Pike, 1955 (div. 1981); children: Michelle, Julene David; m. Susan K. Nash, 2000. BA, Willamette U., 1956; MA, Kans. U., 1957; JD, Willamette U., 1966. Bar: Calif. 1966, U.S. Dist. Ct. (no. dist.) Calif. 1967, U.S. Ct. Appeals (9th cir.) 1967, U.S. Ct. Appeals (7th cir.) 1989, U.S. Dist. Ct. (no. dist.) Ill. 1989, U.S. Dist. Ct. (cen. dist.) Calif. 1989. Mem. staff Travelers Ins. Co., Sacramento, 1957-61; branch claim mgr. N.Y. Life Ins. Co., 1961-62, Transamerica Ins. Co., San Francisco, 1962-63; assoc. Eliassen & Postel, San Francisco, 1966-69; ptnr. Coll, Levy & Orlebeke, Concord, Calif., 1969-77, Orlebeke & Hutchings, 1977-89; prin. Law Offices W. Ronald Orlebeke, 1989-98; hearing officer Constra Costa County, Calif., 1981-98; arbitrator Contra Costa County Superior Ct., 1977-98, U.S. Dist. Ct. No. Calif., 1978-98, Mt. Diablo Mcpl. Ct., 1987-89; ret., 1998. Judge pro tem Mt. Diablo Mcpl. Ct., 1973-77; adj. prof. Willamette U. Coll. of Law, 2001—. Author: Orlebeke Family in Europe and America, 1570-1990, 1988. Alumni bd. dirs. Willamette U., 1978-81, trustee, 1980-81 scholar chmn. Concord Elks, 1977-79; del. Joint U.S./China Internat. Trade Law Conf., Beijing, 1987. With USMCR, 1952-59. Sr. scholar Willamette U., 1955-56; Woodrow Wilson fellow Kans. U., 1956-57, U.S. Bur. Nat. Affairs fellow, 1966, others. Mem. SAR, Sons of Confederate Vets. (award of Merit 1989), Sons of Union Vets. Civil War, First Marine Divsn. Assn., Order Ea. Star (worthy patron 1980), Masons, Shriners, Elks, Rotary (charter pres. Clayton Valley/Concord Sunrise club 1987-88, chmn. dist. 5160 Calif. membership devel. 1989-90, dist. govs. liaison dist. 5160 1990-92, dist. Rotarian of Yr. 1989-90, Paul Harris fellow 1988, 1992 dist. conf. chmn. benefactor 1990, award of Merit 1990). Republican.

ORLOFF, CHET, historian; b. Bellingham, Wash., Feb. 22, 1949; s. Monford A. and Janice (Diamond) O.; m. Wendy Lynn Lee, Sept. 20, 1970; children: Callman Labe, Hannah Katya, Michele Alison. BA, Boston U., 1971; MA, Portland State U., 1978. Tchr. Peace Corps, Afghanistan, 1972-75; asst. dir. Oreg. Hist. Soc., Portland, 1975-86, exec. dir., 1991-2000, Ninth Cir. Hist. Soc., Pasadena, Calif., 1987-91. Adj. prof. Portland State U. Editor: Western Legal History, 1987-91, Law for the Elephant, 1992; sr. editor: Oreg. Hist. Quar.; contbr. articles to profl. jours. Commr. [illegible] Commn., Portland, 1987-91, Portland Planning Commn., 1987-92; pres. Nat. Lewis and Clark Bicentennial Coun., 1996—. Mem. Phi Alpha Theta. Avocations: reading, tennis. Office: Oreg Hist Soc 3332 NW Savier St Portland OR 97210

ORLOFF, NEIL, lawyer, artist; b. Chgo., May 9, 1943; s. Benjamin R. and Annette (Gibraltar) O.; m. Jan Krigbaum, Oct. 9, 1971 (div. 1979); m. Gudrun Mirin, Oct. 2, 1992. BS, MIT, 1964; MBA, Harvard U., 1966; JD, Columbia U., 1969. Bar: D.C. 1969, N.Y. 1975, Calif. 1989, Utah 1993. Ops. officer World Bank, Washington, 1969-71; dir. regional liaison staff EPA, Washington, 1971-73; legal counsel Pres.'s Council on Environ. Quality, Washington, 1973-75; prof. dept. environ. engring. Cornell U., Ithaca, N.Y., 1975-88; sch. law UCLA, 1992; dir. Ctr. for Environ. Rsch., 1984-87, Am. Ecology Corp., 1986-88; of counsel Morgan, Lewis & Bockius, N.Y.C., 1986-87; ptnr. Irell & Manella, L.A., 1986-92, Parsons, Behle & Latimer, Salt Lake City, 1992—. Vice chmn. bd. dirs. S.W. Research and Info. Ctr., Albuquerque, 1975-84; vice chmn. air quality commn. ABA, Chgo., 1983-92, co-chmn. intensive course in environ. law ABA, 1994-96, co-chmn. roundtable sr. environ. lawyers ABA, 1996-97, membership officer sect. on natural resources, energy and environ. law, 1997-98; coun. mem. sect. on environ., energy and natural resources, 1998—; adviser Internat. Joint Com. Can., 1979-81; governing bd. N.Y. Sea Grant Inst., 1984-87; vice chmn. City of Ithaca Environ. Commn., 1976-77; adviser N.Y. Dept. Environ. Conservation, 1984-87; artist-in-residence MacDowell Colony, 2000, Yaddo, 2001; vis. prof. art Cornell U., 2001. Author: The Environmental Impact Statement Process, 1978, The National Environmental Policy Act, 1980, Air Pollution-Cases and Materials, 1980, Community Right-to-Know Handbook, 1988, Under the Fifth Street Overpass, 2000; mem. editl. bd. Natural Resources and Environ., 1984-87. E-mail: norloff@alum.mit.edu

ORMAN, JOHN LEO, software engineer, writer; b. San Antonio, Mar. 19, 1949; s. Alton Woodlee and Isabel Joan (Paproski) O. BS in Physics, N.Mex. Inst. Mining & Tech., 1971, BS Math., MS Physics, 1974. Rsch. asst. N.Mex. Inst. Mining & Tech., Socorro, 1967-74; computer programmer State of N.Mex., Santa Fe, 1974-76; computer analyst Dikewood Corp., Albuquerque, 1976-83; nuclear engr. Sandia Nat. Labs., Albuquerque, 1983-88, software engr., 1988—. Author numerous poems. NSF fellow, 1971-74; recipient 2d place award N.Mex. State Postry Soc., 1987. Mem. IEEE Computer Soc., Am. Assn. Physics Tchrs., Assn. for Computing Machinery, Nat. Writer's Club (poetry award 1987), Southwest Writers Workshop (3d place award non-fiction 1987), N.Mex. Mountain Club. Avocations: photography, travel, skiing, hiking, tennis. Home: 719 Vista Abajo Dr NE Albuquerque NM 87123-2246 Office: Sandia Nat Labs MS 0974 PO Box 5800 Albuquerque NM 87185-0100 E-mail: jlorman@sandia.gov

ORMASA, JOHN, retired utility executive, lawyer; b. Richmond, Calif., May 30, 1925; s. Juan Hormaza and Maria Inocencia Olondo; m. Dorothy Helen Trumble, Feb. 17, 1952; children: Newton Lee, John Trumble, Nancy Jean Davies. BA, U. Calif.-Berkeley, 1948; JD, Harvard U., 1951. Bar: Calif. 1952, U.S. Supreme Ct. 1959. Assoc. Clifford C. Anglim, 1951-52; assoc. Richmond, Carlson, Collins, Gordon & Bold, 1952-56, ptnr., 1956-59; with So. Calif. Gas Co., L.A., 1959-66, gen. atty., 1963-65, v.p., gen. counsel, 1965-66; v.p., sys. gen. counsel Pacific Lighting Service Co., Los Angeles, 1966-72; v.p., gen. counsel Pacific Lighting Corp., Los Angeles, 1973-75, v.p., sec., gen. counsel, 1975. Acting city atty., El Cerrito, Calif., 1952. Served with U.S. Navy, 1943-46. Mem. ABA, Calif. State Bar Assn., Richmond (Calif.) Bar Assn. (pres. 1959), Kiwanis (v.p. 1959). Republican. Roman Catholic.

ORME, ANTONY RONALD, geography educator; b. Weston-Super-Mare, Somerset, Eng., May 28, 1936; came to U.S., 1968; s. Ronald Albert and Anne (Parry) O.; m. Amalie Jo Brown, Nov. 18, 1984; children: Mark Antony, Kevin Ronald, Devon Anne. B.A. with 1st class honors, U. Birmingham, 1957, Ph.D., 1961. Lectr. Univ. Coll., Dublin, Ireland, 1960-68; mem. faculty UCLA, 1968—, prof. geography, 1973—, dean social scis., 1977-83. Cons. geomorphology various orgns., throughout U.S., 1968— Editor-in-chief Phys. Geography. Recipient Award of Merit Am. Inst. Planners, 1975; recipient Outstanding Service award USAF, 1977-80 Mem. Geol. Soc. Am., Assn. Am. Geographers, Assn. Geography Tchrs. Ireland (pres. 1964-68), Inst. Brit. Geographers, Internat. Geog. Union Home: 5128 Del Moreno Dr Woodland Hills CA 91364-2426 Office: UCLA Dept Geography Los Angeles CA 90095-0001 E-mail: orme@geog.ucla.edu

ORNDUFF, ROBERT, botany educator; b. Portland, Oreg., June 13, 1932; s. Robert and Kathryn (Davis) O. B.A., Reed Coll., 1953; M.Sc., U. Wash., 1956; Ph.D., U. Calif.-Berkeley, 1961. Asst. prof. Reed Coll., 1962, Duke U., 1963; asst. prof. botany U. Calif., Berkeley, 1963-66, assoc. prof., 1966-69, prof., 1969-93, prof. emeritus, 1993—, dir. Jepson Herbarium, 1968-83, dir. Univ. Herbarium, 1975-83, exec. dir. Miller Inst. for Basic Research in Sci., 1984-87, chmn. dept. botany, 1986-89. Dir. Stanley Smith Hort. Trust, 1992—. Fellow AAAS, Calif. Acad. Scis., Calif. Native Plant Soc. (pres. 1972-73); mem. Am. Soc. Plant Taxonomists (pres. 1975) Home: 490 Arlington Ave Berkeley CA 94707-1609 Office: U Calif Dept Integrative Biology Berkeley CA 94720-0001

ORNSTEIN, DONALD SAMUEL, mathematician, educator; b. N.Y.C., July 30, 1934; s. Harry and Rose (Wisner) O.; m. Shari Richman, Dec. 20, 1964; children— David, Kara, Ethan. Student, Swarthmore Coll., 1950-52; Ph.D., U. Chgo., 1957. Fellow Inst. for Advanced Study, Princeton, N.J., 1955-57; faculty U. Wis., Madison, 1958-60, Stanford (Calif.) U., 1959—, prof. math., 1966—. Faculty Hebrew U., Jerusalem, 1975-76 Author: Ergodic Theory Randomness and Dynamical Systems, 1974. Recipient Bocher prize Am. Math. Soc., 1974 Mem. NAS, Am. Acad. Arts and Sci. Jewish. Office: Stanford U Dept Math Stanford CA 94305

O'ROURKE, C. LARRY, lawyer; b. Colusa, Calif., Dec. 10, 1937; s. James Harold and Elizabeth Janice (Jenkins) O'R.; m. Joy Marie Phillips, May 22, 1965; children: Ryan, Paula. BSEE, Stanford U., 1959, MBA, 1961; JD, George Washington U., 1972. Bar: Va. 1971, D.C. 1974, U.S. Ct. Appeals (fed. cir.) 1973, U.S. Patent and Trademark Office 1971, U.S. Supreme Ct. Patent atty. Westinghouse Elec., Washington, 1969-70, Pitts., 1970-73; assoc. Finnegan, Henderson, Farabow, Garrett & Dunner, Washington, 1974-79, ptnr., 1979—, mng. ptnr. Palo Alto, Calif. Dir. Zest Inc., Md., 1988, chmn. bd. dirs., 1990-95. Mem. ABA, Am. Intellectual Property Law Assn. Democrat. Presbyterian. Office: Finnegan Henderson Farabow Garrett & Dunner 700 Hansen Way Palo Alto CA 94304-1016

O'ROURKE, DENNIS, advertising executive; Former CFO, sr. v.p. Goldberg, Moser & O'Neill, San Francisco; exec. v.p., CFO, Goldberg, Moser & O'Neill/Hill Holliday. Office: GMO Hill Holliday 600 Battery St San Francisco CA 94111

ORR, DOMINIC, information technology company executive; BS in Physics, CUNY; MS, PhD, Calif. Inst. Tech. Pres., CEO Alteon Web Sys., 1996—. Office: Alteon Web Sys 50 Great Oaks Blvd San Jose CA 95119-1310

ORR, FRANKLIN MATTES, JR. petroleum engineering educator; b. Baytown, Tex., Dec. 27, 1946; s. Franklin Mattes and Selwyn Sage (Huddleston) O.; m. Susan Packard, Aug. 30, 1970; children: David, Katherine. BSChemE, Stanford U., 1969; PhDChemE, U. Minn., 1976. Asst. to dir. Office Fed. Activities EPA, Washington, 1970-72; research engr. Shell Devel. Co., Houston, 1976-78; sr. engr. N.Mex. Petroleum [illegible] Stanford (Calif.) U., 1985-87, prof., 1987—, interim dean Sch. Earth Scis., 1994-95, dean Sch. Earth Scis., 1995—. Contbr. articles to profl. jours. Bd. dirs. Wolf Trap Found. for the Performing Arts, 1988-94, Monterey Bay

Aquarium Rsch. Inst., 1987—, Am. Geol. Inst. Found., 1997—, David and Lucile Packard Found., 1999—; chair sci. adv. com. David and Lucile Packard Found. Fellowships for Sci. and Engring. With USPHS, 1970-72. Recipient AIME Robert Earll McConnell award, 2001. Mem. NAE, AIChE, AAAS, AIME (Robert Earll McConnell award 2000), Soc. Petroleum Engrs. (Disting. Lectr. award 1988-89, Disting. Achievement award for petroleum engring. faculty 1993), Soc. Indsl. and Applied Math. Office: Stanford U Sch Earth Scis Mitchell Bldg Rm 101 Stanford CA 94305-2210

ORR, RONALD STEWART, lawyer; b. L.A., Nov. 19, 1946; s. Ashley S. and Nancy (McKenna) O.; divorced; children: Justin, Hailey. BSEE, Leland Sanford Jr. U., 1968; JD, U. So. Calif., 1972, MBA, 1987. Bar: Calif. 1973, U.S. Dist. Ct. (so. dist.) Calif. 1973, U.S. Ct. Appeals (2nd, 3rd, 5th and 9th cirs.) 1974, U.S. Supreme Ct. 1983. Mem. tech. staff Hughes Aircraft Co., L.A., 1968-72; ptnr. Shutan and Trost, L.A., 1972-80, Gibson, Dunn and Crutcher, L.A., 1980-97, Ron Orr & Profls., Inc., Marina Del Rey, Calif., 1997—. Commr. Calif. Law Revison Commn., 1998-99, Co-author: Secured Creditors Under the New Bankruptcy Code, 1979, Entertainment Contracts, 1986. Trustee U. So. Calif., L.A., 1986-91; exec. com. Nancy Reagan Ctr., L.A., 1988-89; chmn. Firestone for Lt. Gov. and Firestone for Congress, 1996-98. Mem. U. So. Calif. Alumni Assn. (bd. dirs. 1984-89), Order of Coif. Office: 520 Washington Blvd # 389 Marina Dl Rey CA 90292-5442 Fax: 310 301-6549. E-mail: RonOrrEsq@aol.com

ORR, SUSAN PACKARD, business owner; BA in Econs., Stanford U., 1968, MBA, 1970; MS in Computer Sci., N.Mex. Inst. Mining and Tech., 1984. Chmn. David and Lucile Packard Found., Los Altos, Calif.; CEO Tech. Resource Assistance Ctr., Palo Alto, 1986—. Bd. dirs. Hewlett-Packard Co. Trustee Stanford U., 1998—. Office: The Packard Found 300 2nd St Ste 200 Los Altos CA 94022-3643

ORRICK, WILLIAM HORSLEY, JR. federal judge; b. San Francisco, Oct. 10, 1915; s. William Horsley and Mary (Downey) O.; m. Marion Naffziger, Dec. 5, 1947 (dec. Feb. 1995); children: Mary-Louise, Marion, William Horsley III; m. Suzanne Rogers, Jan. 19, 1996. Grad., Hotchkiss Sch., 1933; B.A., Yale, 1937; LL.B., U. Calif.-Berkeley, 1941. Bar: Calif. 1941. Partner Orrick, Dahlquist, Herrington & Sutcliffe, San Francisco, 1941-61; asst. atty. gen. civil div. Dept Justice, 1961-62, antitrust div., 1963-65; dep. under sec. state for adminstrn. Dept. State, 1962-63; practice law San Francisco, 1965-74; former partner firm Orrick, Herrington, Rowley & Sutcliffe; U.S. dist. judge No. Dist. Calif., 1974-85, sr. judge, 1985—. Past pres. San Francisco Opera Assn., Trustee, World Affairs Council; former trustee San Francisco Law Library, San Francisco Found., Children's Hosp. San Francisco, Grace Cathedral Corp. Served to capt. M.I. AUS, 1942-46. Recipient Alumnus of Yr. award Boalt Hall Alumni Assn., U. Calif., 1980. Fellow Am. Bar Found.; mem. Bar Assn. San Francisco (past trustee, treas.) Office: US Dist Ct PO Box 36060 450 Golden Gate Ave San Francisco CA 94102-3482

ORSATTI, ALFRED KENDALL, organization executive; b. Los Angeles, Jan. 31, 1932; s. Alfredo and Margaret (Hayes) O.; m. Patricia Decker, Sept. 11, 1960; children: Scott, Christopher, Sean. B.S., U. So. Calif., 1956. Assoc. prodr., v.p. Sabre Prodns., L.A., 1957-58; assoc. prodr. Ror Vic Prodns., L.A., 1958-59; bus. rep. AFTRA, L.A., 1960-61; Hollywood exec., sec. SAG, L.A., 1961-81, nat. exec. dir., 1981—, trustee Pension Welfare Plan, 1971—. Del. Los Angeles County Fedn. Labor, Los Angeles, Hollywood Film Council, Los Angeles; v.p., mem. exec. Calif. Fedn. Labor; pres. Calif. Theatrical Fedn.; chmn. arts, entertainment and media com. dept. profl. employees AFL-CIO Mem. Mayor's Film Devel. Com., Los Angeles. Mem. Actors and Artists Am. Assn. (1st v.p.) Office: SAG 5757 Wilshire Blvd Los Angeles CA 90036 3635

ORTIZ, ANTONIO IGNACIO, public relations executive; b. Mexico City, Feb. 22, 1961; came to U.S., 1988; s. Antonio and Sylvia (Vega) O.; m. Socorro Chinolla, June 12, 1982. B Bus., Autonoma U. Baja Calif., Tijuana, 1984. With acctg. dept. Bank of Atlantic, Tijuana, 1979-83; mgr. Aldaco, Tijuana, 1983-84; dir. pub. rels. Oh! Laser Club, Tijuana, 1984-88, Iguanas, Tijuana, 1988-90, Euebe, S.A., Tijuana, 1990-2000, R. Noble Enterprises, La Jolla, Calif., AAP, Inc., Chula Vista, SPD Transport Inc., Chula Vista. Cons. R.P. Noble Enterprises, La Jolla, Ca.; dir. pub. rels. R. Noble Enterprises, AAP, Inc., Chula Vista, Calif., 2000-; gen. ptnr. SPD Transport, Inc., Chula Vista, Calif., 2001-. Avocations: swimming, watching TV. Home: PO Box 431859 San Diego CA 92143-1859 Office: SPD Transport Inc 744 Design Ct Ste 203 Chula Vista CA 91911-5108

ORTIZ, DEBORAH V. state legislator; b. Sacramento, Mar. 19, 1957; Student, U. Calif., Davis, 1975-81; JD, U. of the Pacific, 1987. Mem. Calif. State Assembly, 1996-98, chair select com. on taxpayer's rights; mem. Calif. State Senate, 1998—. Mem. Sacramento City Coun., 1993-96; chair ad hoc com. Neighborhood Svcs. Dept., 1993. Recipient Sacramento Housing Alliance award. Democrat. Roman Catholic. Office: State Capitol Rm 4032 Sacramento CA 95814 also: 1020 N St Ste 576 Sacramento CA 95814-5606 also: 5975 Birdcage Centre Ln # 145 Citrus Heights CA 95610-8001

ORTIZ, JOHN MICHAEL, provost; BUS, U. N.Mex., 1970, MA, 1971; PhD, U. N.C., 1981. Spl. edn. tchr., Albuquerque, 1969-72; instr. Appalachian State U., Boone, N.C., 1972, asst. prof. dept. spl. edn., 1972-75, assoc. prof. grad. faculty dept. spl. edn., 1976-81, interim dept. chair, prof. grad. faculty, 1982-83, dept. chair, prof. grad. faculty, 1983-85, dir. Office Extension Instrn., prof. lang., 1985-90; prof. spl. edn., dean continuing edn., dir. summer sch. U. Southern Colo., 1990-93, assoc. provost, prof. spl. edn., 1993-95, interim provost, prof. spl. edn., 1995-96; assoc. provost, prof. spl. edn. Calif. State U., Fresno, 1996-97, provost, v.p acad. affairs ad interim, prof. spl. edn., 1997-99, provost, v.p. acad. affairs, 1999—. Cons., evaluator North Ctrl. Assn. of Colls. and Schs., 1995-97; pres. N.C. Fedn. of the Coun. for Exceptional Children, 1984-85, state advisor 1979-80; spl. advisor Pres. Com. on Mental Retardation; presenter in field. Contbr. articles to profl. publs. Recipient numerous grants. Mem. ASCD, Am. Assn. of Higher Edn., Nat. U. Continuing Edn. Assn., Am. Assn. for Adult and Continuing Edn., Assn. of the Severely Handicapped, Coun. for Exceptional Children. Office: Calif State U 5241 N Maple Ave MSTA 54 Fresno CA 93740-0001 Fax: 559-278-7987

ORTIZ Y PINO, GERALD, municipal official; BA in Latin Am. Studies, U. N.Mex., 1965; MSW, Tulane U., 1968. Lic. N.Mex. Bd. Social Work Examiners. Social svcs. specialist Dona Ana and San Miguel Counties N.Mex. Health and Social Svc. Dept., Albuquerque, 1968-69, cmty. worker Taos Welfare Office, 1969-71; asst. prof. social work, dir. cmty. mental health tng. Coll. Santa Fe, 1971-75; chief program devel. bur. Social Svcs. divsn. N.Mex. Human Svcs. Dept., Albuquerque, 1975-78; assoc. dir. Albuquerque Tng. Svcs. Ctr., 1978-79; exec. dir. N.Mex. Youth Work Alliance, Albuquerque, 1979-82; chief maternal, child and adolescent health bur. N.Mex. State Dept. Health, Albuquerque, 1982-83; dir. Social Svcs. divsn. N.Mex. Human Svcs. Dept., Albuquerque, 1983-84, social worker V, 1984-87; social worker Vista Sandia Psychiat. Hosp., Children's Psychiat. Hosp., Albuquerque, 1987-88; dir. Human Affairs Internat., Albuquerque, 1988-91; pvt. practice Albuquerque, 1991-92; dir. planning and resource allocation United Way Ctrl. N.Mex., Albuquerque, 1992-95; exec. dir. N.Mex. Adv. for Children and Families, Albuquerque, 1995-97; dept. dir. family and cmty. svcs. City of Albuquerque, 1997—. Instr. Webster U., Albuquerque, 1984-89, Coll. St. Francis, Albuquerque, 1986-89, Chapman Coll., Albuquerque, 1986, U. N.Mex., Albuquerque, 1977; social worker La Familia, 1987—; cons. in field. Columnist Santa Fe Reporter, 1988—. Mem. NASW, Acad. Cert. Social Workers. Home: 400 12th St NW Albuquerque NM 87102-1820 Office: City Albuquerque Dept Family & Cmty Svcs 400 Marquette Ave NW Rm 504 Albuquerque NM 87102-2167

ORTOLANO, LEONARD, civil engineering educator, water resources planner; b. Bklyn., Sept. 26, 1941; s. Salvatore Thomas and Anna Ortolano. BSCE, Poly. Inst. Bklyn., 1963; MS in Engring., Harvard U., 1966, PhD, 1969. Sanitary engr. USPHS, Denver, 1963-65; rsch. scientist Ctr. for the Environment and Man, Hartford, Conn., 1969-70; prof. civil engring. Stanford (Calif.) U., 1970—, dir. program on urban studies, 1980—. Vis. prof. Inst. Ricerca sulle Acqua, Rome, 1979, South China Environ. Inst. Sci., Guanzhou, 1987, Ecole Nat. des Ponts et Chaussées, Paris, 1987-88, Inst. Universitario Architecture Venice, Italy, 1996, 98, Nat. Poly. Inst. of Toulouse, France, 2000; vis. scholar Kyoto (Japan) U., 1992; vis. lectr. Nat. Sci. Coun. China, 1991. Author: Environmental Planning and Decision Making, 1984 (Chinese edit. 1989), Environmental Regulation and Impact Assessment, 1997; co-author: Implementing Environmental Policy in China, 1995, Environmental Regulation in China, 2000. Resources for the Future Natural Resources fellow, 1968-69; Fulbright-Hays grantee, 1979, 87. Mem. Internat. Water Resources Assn., Internat. Assn. for Impact Assessment. Office: Stanford U Dept Civil Engring Stanford CA 94305

ORTON, WILLIAM H. (BILL ORTON), former congressman, retired lawyer; b. North Ogden, Utah, Sept. 22, 1948; BS, Brigham Young U., 1973, JD, 1979. Adj. prof. Portland (Oreg.) State U./Portland C.C., 1974-76, Brigham Young. U., Provo, Utah, 1984-85; tax auditor IRS, 1966-77; owner/lectr. Tax Tng. Inst., Inc., 1978-90; lectr. continuing edn. seminars Real Estate Tax Inst., N.W. Ctr. Profl. Edn., and Tax Tng. Inst., various locations in U.S., 1978-90; corp. counsel WI Forest Products, Inc., Portland, Oreg., 1980-81; of counsel Merritt & Tenney, Atlanta, 1986-90; tax atty. pvt. practice, Utah, 1980-90, Washington, 1986-90; atty., 1980-90; mem. 102d-104th Congresses from 3f Utah dist., 1990-97, fgn. affairs com., small bus. com., budget, banking and fin. svcs. coms.; ptnr. Jones, Waldo, Holbrook & McDonough, Washington, 1997-99. Democrat. Mormon. Office: Jones Waldo Holbrook & McDonough 1500 Wells Fargo Plz 170 S Main St Salt Lake City UT 841011-1605 also: Jones Waldo Holbrook & McDonough 411 Constitution Ave NE Washington DC 20002-5923

ORULLIAN, B. LARAE, bank executive; b. Salt Lake City, May 15, 1933; d. Alma and Bessie (Bacon) O. Cert., Am. Inst. Banking, 1961, 63, 67; grad. Nat. Mortgage Sch., Ohio State U., 1969-71. With Tracy Collins Trust Co., Salt Lake City, 1951-54, Union Nat. Bank, Denver, 1954-57; exec. sec. Guaranty Bank, Denver, 1957-64, asst. cashier, 1964-67, asst. v.p., 1967-70, v.p., 1970-75, exec. v.p., 1975-77, also bd. dirs.; chair, CEO, pres. The Women's Bank N.A., Denver, 1977-97, Colo. Bus. Bankshares, Inc., 1980-97; vice chmn. Guaranty Bank and Trust Co., Denver, 1998—. Bd. dirs. Guaranty Corp., Anthem Ins. Co., Indpls., Lange Golf Co., Holladay (Utah) Bank; chmn. bd. dirs. Frontier Airlines. Treas. Girl Scouts U.S., 1981-87, 1st nat. v.p., chair exec. com., 1987-90, nat. pres., 1990-96; 1st vice chair world bd. World Assn. Girl Guides Girl Scouts, London. Recipient Woman Who Made a Difference award Internat. Women's Forum, 1994; named to Colo. Women Hall of Fame, 1988; named Colo. Entrepreneur of Yr., Inc. Mag. and Arthyr Young and Co., 1989, Woman of Yr., YWCA, 1989, Citizen of Yr., EMC Lions Club, 1995, laureate Colo. Bus. Hall of Fame, 1999. Mem. Bus. and Profl. Women Colo. (3d Century award 1977), Internat. Women's Forum, Am. Bankers Assn. (adv. bd. edn. found.), Com. of 200. Republican. Mormon. Home: 35 S Ammons St Lakewood CO 80226-1330

OSBORNE, RICHARD HAZELET, anthropology and medical genetics educator; b. Kennecott, Alaska, June 18, 1920; s. Clarence Edward and Margaret Jerenne (Hazelet) O.; m. Barbara White, Oct. 14, 1944; children: Susan, Richard, David; m. Barbara Teachman, Sept. 1, 1970. Student, U. Alaska, 1939-41; BS, BA, U. Wash., 1949; postgrad., Harvard U., 1949-50; PhD (Viking Fund Pre-doctoral fellow, Spl. fellow Inst. for Study Human Variation), Columbia, 1956; hon. doctor odontology, U. Oulu, Finland, 1994; DSc (hon.), U. Alaska, Fairbanks, 2001. Research asso. Columbia U., 1953-58; asst. Sloan-Kettering Inst., N.Y.C., 1958-60, asso., 1960-62, asso. mem., head sect. human genetics, 1962-64; prof. anthropology and med. genetics U. Wis., Madison, 1964-86, prof. emeritus, 1986—; rsch. assoc. Quatenary Ctr. U. Alaska, Fairbanks, 1993—. Asso. prof. preventive medicine Cornell Med. Coll., 1962-64; clin. geneticist Meml. Hosp. for Cancer, N.Y.C., 1963-65; vis. scientist Forsyth Dental Center, Boston, 1969-71; cons. human genetics Newington (Conn.) Childrens Hosp., 1971-73; Mem. com. on epidemiology and vets. follow up studies NRC, 1969-73; mem. perinatal research com. Nat. Inst. Neurol. Diseases and Stroke, NIH, 1970-72; mem. cultural anthropology fellowship and rev. NIMH, 1969-73 Author: Genetic Basis of Morphological Variation, 1959, Biological and Social Meaning of Race, 1971; Editor: Social Biology, 1961-77, 81— ; contbr. articles to profl. jours. Served to maj. USAAF, 1942-46. Decorated D.F.C., Air medal with 3 oak leaf clusters.; Named Health Research Council Career Scientist City N.Y., 1962-64 Fellow Explorers Club; Mem. Am. Assn. Phys. Anthropology (exec. com. 1965-67, v.p. 1968-70), Am. Soc. for Human Genetics (dir. 1960-61, 67-69), Behavior Genetics Assn. (pres. pro-tem 1970-71), Soc. for Study Social Biology (editor Social Biology 1961-99, dir. 1981-83, 86-99), Pioneers of Alaska (life), Sigma Xi. Office: 1129 E 8th St Port Angeles WA 98362-6628 E-mail: rho6@columbiau.edu

OSBY, ROBERT EDWARD, protective services official; b. San Diego, Oct. 29, 1937; s. Jesse William and Susie Lillian (Campbell) O.; m. Clydette Deloris Mullen, Apr. 11, 1961; children: Daryl Lawrence, Gayle Lorraine. AA in Fire Sci., San Diego Jr. Coll., 1970; BA in Mgmt., Redlands U., 1985. Recreation leader San Diego Parks and Recreation Dept., 1955-58; postal carrier U.S. Postal Service, San Diego, 1958-59; fire fighter San Diego Fire Dept., 1959-67, fire engr., 1967-71, fire capt., 1971-76, fire bn. chief, 1976-79; fire chief Inglewood (Calif.) Fire Dept., 1979-84, San Jose (Calif.) Fire Dept., 1985—. Served to 2d lt. Calif. NG, 1960-65. Mem. Calif. Met. Fire Chiefs (chmn. 1987—), Internat. Assn. Black Firefighters (regional dir. 1974-77), Brothers United (pres. 1972-75). Democrat. Avocations: fishing, jogging, landscaping. Home: 28203 Engelmann Oak Trl Escondido CA 92026-6960 Office: San Diego Fire Dept 1010 2nd Ave Ste 400 San Diego CA 92101-4970

O'SCANNLAIN, DIARMUID FIONNTAIN, judge; b. N.Y.C., Mar. 28, 1937; s. Sean Leo and Moira (Hegarty) O'S.; m. Maura Nolan, Sept. 7, 1963; children: Sean, Jane, Brendan, Kevin, Megan, Christopher, Anne, Kate. BA, St. John's U., 1957; JD, Harvard U., 1963; LLM, U. Va., 1992. Bar: Oreg. 1965, N.Y. 1964. Tax atty. Standard Oil Co. (N.J.), N.Y.C., 1963-65; assoc. Davies, Biggs, Strayer, Stoel & Boley, Portland, Oreg., 1965-69; dep. atty. gen. Oreg., 1969-71; public utility commr. of Oreg., 1971-73; dir. Oreg. Dept. Environ. Quality, 1973-74; sr. ptnr. Ragen, Roberts, O'Scannlain, Robertson & Neill, Portland, 1978-86; judge, U.S. Ct. Appeals (9th cir.), San Francisco, 1986—, mem. exec. com., 1988-89, 1993-94, mem. Jud. Coun. 9th Cir., 1991-93; mem. U.S. Judicial Conf. Com. on Automation and Tech., 1990—; cons. Office of Pres.-Elect and mem. Dept. Energy Transition Team (Reagan transition), Washington, 1980-81; chmn. com. adminstrv. law Oreg. State Bar, 1980-81. Mem. council of legal advisers Rep. Nat. Com., 1981-83; mem. Rep. Nat. Com., 1983-86, chmn. Oreg. Rep. Party, 1983-86; del. Rep. Nat. Convs., 1976, 80, chmn. Oreg. del., 1984; Rep. nominee U.S. Ho. of Reps., First Congl. Dist., 1974; team leader Energy Task Force, Pres.'s Pvt. Sector Survey on Cost Control, 1982-83, trustee Jesuit High Sch.; mem. bd. visitors U. Oreg. Law Sch., 1988—; mem. citizens adv. bd. Providence Hosp., 1986-92. Maj. USAR, 1955-78. Mem. Fed. Bar Assn., ABA (sec. Apellate Judges Conf. 1989-90, exec. com. 1990—, chmn.-elect 1994—), Arlington Club, Multnomah Club. Roman Catholic. Office: US Ct Appeals 313 Pioneer Courthouse 555 SW Yamhill St Ste 104 Portland OR 97204-1321*

OSE, DOUGLAS, congressman; b. Sacramento, 1955; m. Lynnda ose; children: Erika, Emily. BS, U. Calif., Berkeley, 1977. Project mgr. Ose Properties, Sacramento, 1977-85; owner real estate devel. and investment co., 1986—; mem. U.S. Congress from 3d Calif. dist., 1999—; mem. agr., fin. svcs., and govt. reform coms. Former bd. dirs. Citrus Heights C. of C., Sacramento Housing and Redevel. Commn.; mem. Citrus Heights Incorporation Project. Republican. Office: 215 Cannon Ho Office Bldg Washington DC 20515-0001*

OSHEROFF, DOUGLAS DEAN, physicist, researcher; b. Aberdeen, Wash., Aug. 1, 1945; s. William and Bessie Anne (Ondov) O.; m. Phyllis S.K. Liu, Aug. 14, 1970 B.S. in Physics, Calif. Inst. Tech., 1967; M.S., Cornell U., 1969, Ph.D. in Physics, 1973. Mem. tech. staff Bell Labs., Murray Hill, N.J., 1972-82, head solid state and low temperature physics research dept., 1982-87; prof. Stanford (Calif.) U., 1987—, J.G. Jackson and C.J. Wood prof. physics, 1992—; chair physics, 1993-96. Researcher on properties of matter near absolute zero of temperature; co-discoverer of superfluidity in liquid 3He, 1971, nuclear antiferromagnetic resonance in solid 3He, 1980 Co-recipient Simon Meml. prize Brit. Inst. Physics, 1976, Oliver E. Buckley Solid State Physics prize, 1981, Nobel prize in physics, 1996; John D. and Catherine T. MacArthur prize fellow, 1981 Fellow Am. Phys. Soc., Am. Acad. Arts and Scis., Nat. Acad. Scis. Office: Stanford U Dept Physics Stanford CA 94305-4060

OSHEROW, JACQUELINE SUE, poet, English language educator; b. Phila., Aug. 15, 1956; d. Aaron and Evelyn Hilda (Victor) O.; m. Saul Korewa, June 16, 1985; children: Magda, Dora, Mollie. AB Magna cum laude, Radcliffe Coll., Harvard U., 1978; postgrad., Trinity Coll., Cambridge U., 1978-79; PhD in English and Am. Lit., Princeton U., 1990. Prof. English C. Utah, Salt Lake City, 1989—. Author: (poetry) Looking for Angels in New York, 1988, Conversations with Survivors, 1994, With a Moon in Transit, 1996, Dead Men's Praise, 1999. Recipient Witter Bynner prize Am. Acad. and Inst. Arts and Letters, 1990; Ingram Merrill Found. grantee, 1990; Guggenheim fellow, 1997-98, Nat. Endowment for the Arts fellow, 1999—. Mem. Poetry Soc. Am. (John Masefield Meml. award 1993, Lucille Medwick Meml. award 1995, Cecil Hemley Meml. award 1997). Jewish. Office: U Utah Dept English 255 S Central Campus Dr Rm 3500 Salt Lake City UT 84112-0494

OSHMAN, M. KENNETH, computer company executive; Pres., CEO Rolm Corp.; pres., CEO, chmn. Echelon Corp., Palo Alto, Calif. Mem. NAE. Office: Echelon Corp 4015 Miranda Ave Palo Alto CA 94304-1218

OSIANDER, LOTHAR, professional soccer coach; b. Munich, Germany, Nov. 8, 1939; came to U.S., 1958; children: Kurt, Erik. AA in Gen. Edn., San Francisco City Coll.; BA in Phys. Edn. and Modern Langs., U. San Francisco. Head coach U.S. Nat. Team, 1986-88, Los Angeles Galaxy, 1996-98, San Jose Earthquakes, 1999—. Coach Calif. Soccer Assn., 1972-89; head coach U.S. Nat. Team, U.S. Olympic Team. Named Coach of Yr., A-League, 1995. Office: San Jose Earthquakes 3550 Stevens Creek Blvd Ste 100 San Jose CA 95117-1031

OSSERMAN, ROBERT, mathematician, educator, writer; b. N.Y.C., Dec. 19, 1926; s. Herman Aaron and Charlotte (Adler) O.; m. Maria Anderson, June 15, 1952; 1 son, Paul; m. Janet Adelman, July 21, 1976; children—Brian, Stephen. BA, NYU, 1946; postgrad., U. Zurich, U. Paris; MA, Harvard U., 1948, PhD, 1955. Tchg. fellow Harvard U., 1949-52, vis. lectr., rsch. assoc., 1961-62; instr. U. Colo., 1952-53; mem. faculty Stanford U., 1955-94, prof. emeritus, 1994—, prof. math., 1966—, chmn. dept. math., 1973-79, Mellon Prof. Interdisciplinary Studies, 1987-90; dep. dir. Math. Scis. Rsch. Inst., Berkeley, Calif., 1990-95, dir. spl. projects, 1995—. Mem. NYU Inst. Math. Scis., 1957-58, Math. Scis. Rsch. Inst., Berkeley,., 1983-84, head math. br. Office Naval Rsch., 1960-61; researcher and author publs. on differential geometry, complex variables, differential equations, astronomy, cosmology, especially minimal surfaces, isoperimetric inequalities. Author: Two-Dimensional Calculus, 1968, A Survey of Minimal Surfaces, 1969, 2d edit., 1986, Poetry of the Universe, 1995; author videos: Fermat's Last Theorem, 1994, Mathematics in Arcadia, 1999, Galileo: A Dialog, 2000. Fulbright lectr. U. Paris, 1965-66; Guggenheim fellow, 1976-77; vis. fellow U. Warwick, Imperial Coll., U. London. Fellow AAAS; mem. Am. Math. Soc., Math. Assn. Am., Astron. Soc. Pacific. Office: Math Sci Rsch Inst 1000 Centennial Dr Berkeley CA 94720-5070

OSTER, RICHARD, financial executive; Bachelors Degree, U. N.C.; MBA, Rutgers U. CPA. Various positions Crowley Maritime Corp., 1981-93, sr. v.p., CFO, 1995—, Inchcape Shipping Svcs., 1993-95. Office: Crowley Maritime Corp 155 Grand Ave Oakland CA 94612-3758

OSTERBROCK, DONALD E(DWARD), astronomy educator; s. William Carl and Elsie (Wettlin) O.; m. Irene L. Hansen, Sept. 19. 1952; children: Carol Ann, William Carl, Laura Jane. PhB, BS, U. Chgo., 1948, SM, 1949, PhD, 1952; DSc (hon.), Ohio State U., 1986, U. Chgo., 1992, U. Wis., Madison, 1997. Postdoctoral fellow, mem. faculty Princeton, 1952-53; mem. faculty Calif. Inst. Tech., 1953-58; faculty U. Wis.-Madison, 1958-73, prof. astronomy, 1961-73, chmn. dept. astronomy, 1966-67, 69-72; prof. astronomy and astrophysics U. Calif., Santa Cruz, 1972-92, prof. emeritus, 1993—. Dir. Lick Obs., 1972-81; mem. staff Mt. Wilson Obs., Palomar Obs., 1953-58; vis. prof. U. Chgo., 1963-64, Ohio State U., 1980, 86; Hill Family vis. prof. U. Minn., 1977-78. Author: Astrophysics of Gaseous Nebulae, 1974, James E. Keeler, Pioneer American Astrophysicist and the Early Development of American Astrophysics, 1984, Astrophysics of Gaseous Nebulae and Active Galactic Nuclie, 1989, Pauper and Prince: Ritchey, Hale and Big American Telescopes, 1993, Yerkes Observatory, 1892-1950: The Birth, Near Death and Resurrection of a Scientific Research Institution, 1997, Walter Baade: A Life in Astrophysics, 2001; co-author: (with John R. Gustafson and W.J. Shiloh Unruh) Eye on the Sky: Lick Observatory's First Century, 1988; editor: (with C.R. O'Dell) Planetary Nebulae, 1968, (with Peter H. Raven) Origins and Extinctions, 1988, (with J.S. Miller) Active Galactic Nuclei, 1989; Stars and Galaxies: Citizens of the Universe, 1990; letters editor Astrophys. Jour., 1971-73. With USAAF, 1943-46. Recipient Profl. Achievement award U. Chgo. Alumni Assn., 1982, Antoinette de Vaucouleurs Meml. lecture and medal U. Tex., Austin, 1994, Hans Lippershey medal Antique Telescope Soc., 1999, Alumni medal U. Chgo. Alumni Assn., 2000; Guggenheim fellow Inst. Advanced Studies, Princeton, N.J., 1960-61, 82-83, Ambrose Monnell Found. fellow, 1989-90, NSF sr. postdoctoral rsch. fellow U. Coll., London, 1968-69. Mem. NAS (chmn. astronomy sect. 1971-74, sec. class math. and phys. sci. 1980-83, chmn. class math and phys. sci. 1983-85, councilor 1985-88), Am. Acad. Arts and Scis., Internat. Astron. Union (pres. commn. 34 1967-70), Royal Astron. Soc. (assoc., Gold medal 1997), Am. Astron. Soc. (councilor 1970-73, v.p. 1975-77, pres. 1988-90, vice chmn. hist. astronomy div. 1985-87, chmn. 1987-89, Henry Norris Russell lectr. 1991), Astron. Soc. Pacific (chmn. history com. 1982-86, Catherine Wolfe Bruce medal 1991, bd. dirs. 1992-95), Wis. Acad. Scis. Arts and Letters, Am. Philos. Soc., State Hist. Soc. Wis. Congregationalist. Home: 120 Woodside Ave Santa Cruz CA 95060-3422 E-mail: don@ucolick.org

OSTERGAARD, JONI HAMMERSLA, lawyer; b. Seattle, May 26, 1950; d. William Dudley and Carol Mae (Gillett) Hammersla; m. Gregory Lance Ostergaard, May 22, 1976 (div. 1985); 1 child, Bennett Gillett; m. William Howard Patton, Jan. 1, 1988; 1 child, Morgan Hollis; stepchildren: Colin W., Benjamin C. BS, U. Wash., 1972; MS, Purdue U., 1974; JD, U. Wash., 1980. Bar: Wash. 1980, U.S. Dist. Ct. (we. dist.) Wash. 1980, U.S. Ct. Appeals (9th cir.) 1981, U. S. Ct. Claims 1983. Clin. psychol. intern Yale Med. Sch., 1976-77; law clk. U.S. Ct. Appeals (9th cir.), Seattle, 1980-81; assoc. Roberts & Shefelman, Seattle, 1982-86, ptnr., 1987, Foster Pepper & Shefelman, Seattle, 1988-92; sole practitioner Seattle, 1996—. Contbr. articles to profl. jours.; notes and comments editor Wash. Law Rev., 1979-80. Recipient Sophia and Wilbur Albright scholarship U. Wash. Law Sch., 1979-80, law sch. alumni scholarship U. Wash. Law Sch., 1978-79; fellow NIMH. Avocations: gardening, reading. Fax: 206-725-8121. E-mail: jostergaard@worldnet.att.net

OSTERGARD, PAUL MICHAEL, not for profit executive; b. Akron, Ohio, Apr. 1, 1939; s. Paul and Janette Beryl (Laube) O.; m. Elizabeth K. McCombs, Jan. 1965 (div. Nov. 1971). AB magna cum laude, Case-Western Res. U., 1961; JD, U. Mich., 1964; MPA, Harvard U., 1969; diploma in hispanic studies, U. Madrid, Spain, 1960. Bar: Ohio 1964. Atty. U.S. Steel Corp., Pitts., 1967-69; gen. atty. TWA Inc., N.Y.C., 1969-71; v.p. adminstrn., sec., counsel Pa. Co. (now Penn Ctrl. Corp.), 1971-74, and subs. Buckeye Pipe Line Co., N.Y.C., 1972-74; pub. affairs exec. GE, Fairfield, Conn., 1974-84; pres. GE Found., Fairfield, 1984-90; chmn., CEO, bd. dirs. Citigroup Found., N.Y.C., 1990-99; pres. Com. to Encourate Corp. Philanthropy, N.Y.C., 1999-2001; pres., CEO Jr. Achievement Internat., 2001—. Bd. dirs. Found. for a Civil Soc. Capt. USAF, 1965-68, Vietnam. Decorated Bronze Star, Legion of Merit (Vietnam); Univ. scholar, 1957-61; Littauer fellow, 1968-69 Mem. Harvard Club, Wexford Plantation Club, Phi Beta Kappa, Omicron Delta Kappa. Episcopalian. Home: 10 Hayestead Rd # 23 Darbury CT 06811-2350 Office: JA Internat 2780 Javitell Rd Colorado Springs CO 80906 E-mail: Paulnmo39@aol.com

OSTERHAUS, WILLIAM ERIC, television executive; b. N.Y.C., July 31, 1935; s. Eric Hugo and Helen (McAuliff) O.; m. Nancy Jean Heinemann, June 19, 1960 (dec.); children: Eric Frank, Marc Andrew; m. Annemarie Clark, Dec. 28, 1985 Student, Fordham U., 1953-54, Harvard U. Bus. Sch., summer 1970. Staff producer news and spl. events dept. Sta. WNBC-AM-TV, N.Y.C., 1956-61; exec. producer Sta. KYW-TV, Cleve., 1961-64, Sta. KPIX, San Francisco, 1964-67, gen. mgr., 1969-73; program mgr. Sta. KYW-TV, Phila., 1967-69; pres., gen. mgr. Sta. KQED Inc., San Francisco, 1973-78; pres. SiteLine Comms., Inc., San Francisco, 1979—; chmn. bd. VariCom Inc., San Francisco, 1982-86. Chmn. TV adv. com. Calif. Pub. Broadcasting Commn., 1977-78; mem. joint com. on film and broadcasting Indo-U.S. Subcommn. on Edn. and Culture., 1975-85; chmn. TV com. San Rafael Redevel. Agy., Calif., 1977-78; mem. citizens adv. com. CATV, San Rafael, 1976-77, Dominican Coll., San Rafael, 1972-80; bd. dirs. Downtown Parking Corp. Bd. dirs. The Ctr. for the Arts, San Francisco, 1985—; bd. dirs. Zeum, 1995—. 1st lt. U.S. Army, 1958-60. Recipient Peabody award and Hillman award for One Nation Indivisible documentary, 1968. Office: 703 Market St Ste 1108 San Francisco CA 94103-2121

OSTERHELD, R(OBERT) KEITH, chemistry educator; b. Bklyn., Apr. 19, 1925; s. Albert Henry and Hilda Pearl (Heatlie) O.; m. Jean Drake Evans, June 28, 1952; children: Robert Keith, Albert Laighton, James Evans, Thomas Heatlie. BS in Chemistry, Poly. Inst. Bklyn., 1945; PhD in Inorganic Chemistry, U. Ill., 1950. Instr. Cornell U., Ithaca, N.Y., 1950-54; asst. prof. chemistry U. Mont., Missoula, 1954-58, assoc. prof., 1958-65, prof., 1965-90, prof. emeritus, 1990—, chmn. dept., 1973-90. Contbr. articles to profl. jours. Mem. Florence (Mont.) Sch. Bd., 1969-75, chmn., 1972-73, 74-75; bd. dirs. Mont. Sch. Bd. Assn., Helena, 1973-75; council mem. Florence-Carlton Community Ch., 1965-90, treas., 1965-90. Served to sgt. USAAF, 1945-47. Mem. Am. Chem. Soc., N.Am. Thermal Analysis Soc., Sigma Xi. Home: 524 Larry Creek Loop Florence MT 59833-6705 Office: U Montana Dept Chemistry Missoula MT 59812-0001

OSTERHOFF, JAMES MARVIN, retired telecommunications company executive; b. Lafayette, Ind., May 18, 1936; s. Abel Lyman and Mildred Paulene (Post) O.; m. Marilyn Ann Morrison, Aug. 24, 1958; children: Anne Michelle Bitsie, Amy Louise Olmsted, Susan Marie BSME, Purdue U., 1958; MBA, Stanford U., 1963. Staff asst. FMC Corp., San Jose, Calif., 1963-64; with Ford Motor Co., Dearborn, Mich., 1964-84; v.p. fin. Ford Motor Credit Co., Dearborn, 1973-75; controller car ops. N. Am. Automotive Ops., Ford Motor Co., Dearborn, 1975-76, asst. controller, 1976-79; controller tractor ops. Ford Motor Co., Troy, Mich., 1979-84; v.p. fin., CFO Digital Equipment Corp., Maynard, Mass., 1985-91; exec. v.p., CFO U.S.West Inc., Englewood, Colo., 1991-95. Bd. dirs. Arkwright Mutual Ins. Co., FSA Ltd., GenCorp, Inc., Pvt. Sector Coun., Colo. Neurol. Inst., Goodwill Industries of Denver. Served to lt. (j.g.) USN, 1958-61. Recipient Disting. Engring. Alumnus award Purdue U.; named Outstanding Mech. Engring. Alumnus, Purdue U.

OSTLER, CLYDE W. banker; b. 1947; BA, U. Calif. San Diego, 1968; MBA, U. Chgo., 1976. With Touche Ross & Co., San Diego, 1970-71; with Wells Fargo Bank NA, San Francisco, 1971, v.p., 1977-81, sr. v.p., 1981-83, gen. auditor, 1983-85, exec. v.p, 1985-86, CFO, from 1986; with Wells Fargo & Co., San Francisco, 1971—, exec. v.p., CFO, from 1986, vice chmn., now group exec. v.p. internet svcs. Office: Wells Fargo & Co 420 Montgomery St San Francisco CA 94104-1205

OSTROW, JAY DONALD, gastroenterology educator, researcher; b. N.Y.C., Jan. 1, 1930; s. Herman and Anne Sylvia (Epstein) O.; m. Judith Fargo, Sept. 9, 1956; children: George Herman, Bruce Donald, Margaret Anne. B.S. in Chemistry, Yale U., 1950; M.D., Harvard U., 1954; M.Sc. in Biochemistry, Univ. Coll., London, 1970. Diplomate Am. Bd. Internal Medicine, Am. Bd. Gastroenterology. Intern Johns Hopkins Hosp., Balt., 1954-55; resident Peter Bent Brigham Hosp., Boston, 1957-58; NIH trainee in gastroenterology, 1958-59; NIH trainee in liver disease Thorndike Mem. Lab. Boston City Hosp., 1959-62; instr. in medicine Harvard U., Boston, 1959-62; asst. prof. medicine Case-Western Res. U., Cleve., 1962-70; assoc. prof. U. Pa., Phila., 1970-76, prof., 1977-78; Sprague prof. medicine Northwestern U., Chgo., 1978-89, prof. medicine, 1989-95, prof. emeritus, 1995—, chief gastroenterology sect., 1978-87; vis. prof. gastrointestinal and hepatology dept. Acad. Med. Ctr., U. Amsterdam, The Netherlands, 1995-98; vis. prof. medicine GI/Hepatology divsn. U. Wash., Seattle, 1999—. Med. investigator VA Hosp., Phila., 1973-78, VA Med. Ctr. Lakeside, Chgo., 1990-95. Editor, contbg. author: Bile Pigments and Jaundice, 1986. Asst. scoutmaster Valley Forge council Boy Scouts Am., Merion, Pa., 1972-78; asst. scoutmaster Northeast Ill. council Boy Scouts Am., 1978-81; vestryman St. Matthew's Episcopal Ch., Evanston, Ill., 1979-82; treas. Classical Children's Chorale, Evanston, 1982. Served to lt. comdr. M.C. USN, 1955-57. Recipient Gastroenterology Rsch. award Beaumont Soc., El Paso, 1979, Sr. Disting. Scientist award Alexander von Humboldt Found., Germany, 1989-90; NIH fellow, 1958-62, grantee, 1962-92; VA grantee, 1970-95. Mem. Am. Assn. Study Liver Diseases (councillor 1983-85, v.p. 1985-86, pres. 1987), Am. Gastroent. Assn. (chmn. exhibit com. 1969-72, mem. undergrad. tchg. project 1972-88), Am. Soc. Clin. Investigation, Am. Physiol. Soc. (assoc. editor [illegible]), Internat. Assn. Study Liver. Office: Rsch Svc GI/Hepatol Lab (151L) DVA Puget Sound Health Care Svs 1660 S Columbian Way Seattle Divsn Seattle WA 98108-1597 E-mail: jostrow@seanet.com

OSTROW, ROBERT, publishing executive; Pub. PC World, San Francisco. Office: PC World IDG Comm 501 2d St Ste 600 San Francisco CA 94107-1496

OTELLINI, PAUL S. communications executive; b. San Francisco; BA in Econs., U. San Francisco, 1972; MBA, U. Calif., Berkeley, 1974. Various positions to exec. v.p. sales and mktg. Intel Architecture Bus. Grop, Santa Clara, Calif., 1974-96, exec. v.p., gen. mgr., 1996—. Office: Intel Corp 2200 Mission College Blvd Santa Clara CA 95052-8119

O'TOOLE, JAMES JOSEPH, business educator; b. San Francisco, Apr. 15, 1945; s. James Joseph and Irene (Nagy) O'T.; m. Marilyn Louise Burrill, June 17, 1967; children: Erin Kathleen, Kerry Louise. BA, U. So. Calif., L.A., 1966; DPhil, Oxford (Eng.) U., (Eng.), 1970. Corr. Time-Life News Service, L.A., 1967-68, Nairobi, Kenya, 1967-68; mgmt. cons. McKinsey & Co., San Francisco, 1969-70; coordinator field investigations Pres.'s Comm. on Campus Unrest, Washington, 1970; spl. asst. to sec. HEW, Washington, 1970-73; prof. mgmt. U. So. Calif., L.A., 1973-93, Univ. Assocs. Chair of Bus., 1982-93; v.p. Aspen Inst., 1994-97; mng. dir. Booz-Allen & Hamilton Leadership Ctr., San Francisco, 1997—; rsch. prof. Ctr. for Effective Orgn., U. So. Calif., 1999—. Chmn. sec.'s com. work in Am. HEW, Washington, 1971-72; exec. dir. The Leadership Inst., 1990-93; bd. dirs. Radica Games. Prin. author: Work in America, 1973, Energy and Social Change, 1976; author: Work, Learning and the American Future, 1977, Making America Work, 1982 (Phi Kappa Phi prize 1982), Vanguard Management, 1985, The Executive's Compass, 1993, Leading Change, 1995, Leadership A to Z, 1999; bd. editors: Ency. Britannica, 1981-87; editor: New Management, 1983-89, The American Oxonian, 1996-98. Active Project Paideia, Chgo., 1981-83. Rhodes scholar, 1966; recipient Mitchell prize Woodlands Conf., 1979. Mem. Phi Beta Kappa. Home: 23852 Pacific Coast Hwy Ste 364 Malibu CA 90265-4879 Office: U So Calif Ctr Effective Orgns Los Angeles CA 90089-0806 E-mail: otoole_jim@bah.com

OTOSHI, TOM YASUO, electrical engineer, consultant; b. Seattle, Sept. 4, 1931; s. Jitsuo and Shina O.; m. Haruko Shirley Yumiba, Oct. 13, 1963; children: John, Kathryn. BSEE, U. Wash., 1954, MSEE, 1957. Tech. staff Hughes Aircraft Co., Culver City, Calif., 1956-61; tech. sr. staff Jet Propulsion Lab. Calif. Inst. Tech., Pasadena, 1961—. Cons. in field. Contbr. articles to profl. jours.; patentee in field. Treas. West L.A. United Meth. Ch., 1958-60; active Foothill Master Chorale, Pasadena, L.A. Bach Festival Chorale. Recipient New Tech. NASA award, Exceptional Svc. medal, 1994. Fellow IEEE (life); mem. Sigma Xi, Tau Beta Pi. Home: 3551 Henrietta Ave La Crescenta CA 91214-1136 Office: Jet Propulsion Lab 4800 Oak Grove Dr Pasadena CA 91109-8001

OTT, DAVID MICHAEL, engineering company executive; b. Glendale, Calif., Feb. 24, 1952; s. Frank Michael and Roberta (Michie) O.; m. Cynthia Dianne Bunce. BSEE, U. Calif., Berkeley, 1974. Electronic engr. Teknekron Inc., Berkeley, 1974-79; chief engr. TCI, Berkeley, 1979-83; div. mgr. Integrated Automation Inc., Alameda, Calif., 1983-87, Litton Indsl. Automation, Alameda, 1987-92; founder, chmn. Picture Elements Inc., Berkeley, 1992—. Inventor method for verifying denomination of currency, method for processing digited images, automatic document image revision. Mem. IEEE, AAAS, Assn. Computing Machinery, Union of Concerned Scientists. Office: Picture Elements Inc 777 Panoramic Way Berkeley CA 94704-2538

OTT, GEORGE WILLIAM, JR. management consulting executive; b. Chgo., May 5, 1932; s. George William and Isabelle (Salkeld) O.; m. Joan Virginia Vasseur; June 20, 1954; children: Lisa Joan, George William III, Robert Alexander. BSBA, U. So. Calif., L.A, 1954, MBA, 1960. CPA, Tex. Engr. adminstr. Douglas Aircraft, El Segundo, Calif., 1956-59; adminstrv. engr. Lear Corp., Santa Monica, 1959-61; co. adminstr. Plasmadyne Corp., Santa Ana, 1961-63; ptnr. Peat Marwick Mitchell & Co., L.A. and Houston, 1963-71; v.p. Korn/Ferry Internat., L.A., 1971-76; founder., pres., chief exec. officer Ott and Hansen, Inc., Pasadena, Calif., 1976—. Bd. dirs. Virco Mfg. Co.; mem. adv. bd. Compensation Resource Group Inc., 1988—. Past pres., bd. dirs. Career Encores, 1989—; chmn., bd. dirs. Salvation Army, L.A. Metro, 1989—. Lt. (j.g.) USN, 1954-56. Mem. Nat. Assn. Corp. Dirs. (pres. So. Calif. chpt.), Calif. Exec. Recruiters Assn. (pres. 1992), Jonathan Club (L.A.), Rotary. Avocations: golf, model railroading. Office: Ott & Hansen 136 S Oak Knoll Ave Ste 300 Pasadena CA 91101-2635

OTT, WAYNE ROBERT, environmental engineer; b. San Mateo, Calif., Feb. 2, 1940; s. Florian Funstan and Evelyn Virginia (Smith) O.; m. Patricia Faustina Bertuzzi, June 28, 1967 (div. 1983). BA in Econs., Claremont McKenna Coll., 1962; BSEE, Stanford U., 1963, MS in Engring, 1965, MA in Comm., 1966, PhD in Environ. Engring., 1971. Commd. lt. USPHS, 1966, advanced to capt., 1986; chief lab. ops. br. U.S. EPA, Washington, 1971-73, sr. systems analyst, 1973-79, sr. rsch. engr., 1981-84, chief air toxics and radiation monitoring rsch. staff, 1984-90; vis. scientist dept. stats. Stanford (Calif.) U., 1979-81, 90—; vis. scholar Ctr. for Risk Analysis and dept. stats., civil engring., 1990-93; sr. environ. engr., EPA Atmospheric Rsch. and Exposure Assessment Lab, 1993-95; consulting prof. of civil engring. Stanford (Calif.) U., 1995—; dir. field studies Calif. Environ. Tobacco Smoke Study, 1993-95. Author: Environmental Indices: Theory and Practice, 1976, Environmental Statistics and Data Analysis, 1995; contbr. articles on indoor air pollution, total human exposure to chems., stochastic models of indoor exposure, motor vehicle exposures, personal monitoring instruments, and environ. tobacco smoke to profl. jours. Decorated Commendation medal USPHS, 1977; recipient Nat. Statistician award for outstanding contribution to environ. statistics EPA, 1995, Commendable Svc. Bronze medal for assessing human exposure from motor vehicle pollution, 1996. Mem. Internat. Soc. Exposure Analysis (v.p. 1989-90, Jerome J. Weselowski Internat. award for career achievement in exposure assessmemt 1995), Am. Statis. Assn., Am. Soc. for Quality Control, Air and Waste Mgmt. Assn., Internat. Soc. Indoor Air Quality and Climate, Phi Beta Kappa, Sigma Xi, Tau Beta Pi, Kappa Mu Epsilon. Democrat. Clubs: Theater, Jazz, Sierra. Avocations: hiking, photography, model trains, jazz recording. Developer nationally uniform air pollution index, first total human exposure activity pattern models. Home: 1008 Cardiff Ln Redwood City CA 94061-3678 Office: Stanford U Dept Stats Sequoia Hall Stanford CA 94305

OTTEN, ARTHUR EDWARD, JR. lawyer, corporate executive; b. Buffalo, Oct. 11, 1930; s. Arthur Edward Sr. and Margaret (Ambrusko) O.; m. Mary Therese Torri, Oct. 1, 1960; children: Margaret, Michael, Maureen Staley, Suzanne Hoodecheck, Jennifer. BA, Hamilton Coll., 1952; JD, Yale U., 1955. Bar: N.Y. 1955, Colo. 1959. Assoc. Hodges, Silverstein, Hodges & Harrington, Denver, 1959-64; ptnr. Hodges, Kerwin, Otten & Weeks (predecessor firms), Denver, 1964-73, Davis, Graham & Stubbs, Denver, 1973-86; gen. counsel Colo. Nat. Bankshares, Inc., 1973-93; mem. Otten, Johnson, Robinson, Neff & Ragonetti, P.C., Denver, 1986—. Rec. sec. Colo. Nat. Bankshares, Inc., Denver, 1983-93; gen. counsel Regis U., Denver, 1994-99; mediator Denver Dist. Ct., 1997-99; com. bd. Centura Health, Denver, St. Anthony Hosps., Denver. Bd. dirs. Cath. Charities Archdiocese of Denver, 1998—. Lt. USN, 1955-59. Mem. ABA, Colo. Bar Assn., Denver Bar Assn., Am. Arbitration Assn. (panel arbitrators, large complex case panel, mediator panel), Nat. Assn. Securities Dealers (bd. arbitrators), Law club, Univ. Club, Denver Mile High Rotary (pres. [illegible] biking, church activities. Home: 3774 S Niagara Way Denver CO 80237-1248 Office: Otten Johnson Robinson Neff & Ragonetti PC 950 17th St Ste 1600 Denver CO 80202-2828 E-mail: aeotten@ojrnr.com

OTTEN, ROBIN DOZIER, state agency administrator; Supt. regulation and licensing dept. State of N. Mex., Santa Fe. Office: Off Supt Reg Licensing Dept 725 Saint Michaels Dr Santa Fe NM 87505-7605

OTTER, CLEMENT LEROY (BUTCH OTTER), congressman; b. Caldwell, Idaho, May 3, 1942; s. Joseph Bernard and Regina Mary (Buser) O.; m. Gay Corinne Simplot, Dec. 28, 1964; children: John Simplot, Carolyn Lee, Kimberly Dawn, Corinne Marie. BA in Polit. Sci., Coll. Idaho, 1967; PhD, Mindanao State U., 1980. Mgr. J.R. Simplot Co., Caldwell, Idaho, 1971-76, asst. to v.p. adminstrn., 1976-78, v.p. adminstrn., 1978-82, internat. pres., from 1982, now v.p.; lt. gov. State of Idaho, Boise, 1987-2000; mem. U.S. Congress from Idaho 1st Dist., 2001—; mem. transp. and infrastructure, resources and govt. reform coms. Mem. Presdl. Task Force-AID, Washington, 1982-84; com. mem. invest tech. devel. State Adv. Council, Washington, 1983-84; mem. exec. council Bretton Woods Com., 1984—; mem. U.S. C. of C., Washington, 1983-84. Mem. Young Pres.' Orgn., Sales and Mktg. Execs., Idaho Assn. Commerce and Industry, Idaho Agrl. Leadership Council, Idaho Ctr. for Arts, Idaho Internat. Trade Council, Pacific N.W. Waterways Assn., N.W. Food Producers, Ducks Unltd. Republican. Roman Catholic. Clubs: Arid, Hillcrest Country. Lodge: Moose, Elks. Avocations: jogging, music, art collecting, horse training, fishing. Office: US Ho of Reps 1711 Longworth HOB Washington DC 20515*

OTTERHOLT, BARRY L. technology management consultant; b. Richland, Wash., Aug. 15, 1953; s. Ernest D. and Jean T. Otterholt; m. Nancy L. Musgrave, Dec. 13, 1985; children: Casey J., Kris K., Cody M.E. BA in Computer Sci. Acctg., Western Wash. U., 1980; MBA in Bus. Adminstrn., Seattle Pacific U., 1982. Mgr. Robinson's, Wenatchee, Wash., 1971-75; purchasing agt. Sound Ctrs., Inc., Bellingham, 1975-79; chief oper. officer Speakerlab/Compulab, Seattle, 1979-82; mgmt. cons. Deloitte & Touche, Seattle, 1982-88; founder, prin. Solutions Consulting Group LLC, Bellevue, Wash., 1988—. Mem. Inst. Mgmt. Cons. (cert.). Office: Solutions Consulting Group 1400 112th Ave SE Bellevue WA 98004-6901

OTTO, FRED DOUGLAS, chemical engineering educator; b. Hardisty, Alta., Can., Jan. 12, 1935; BSc, U. Alta., 1957, MSc, 1959; PhD in Chem. Engring., U. Mich., Ann Arbor, 1963. From asst. prof. to assoc. prof. U. Alta., Edmonton, 1962-70, chmn., 1975-84, prof. chem. engring., 1970-96, dean engring., 1985-94, prof. emeritus, 1996—; pres., CEO DB Robinson & Assocs. Ltd., 1998—. Mem. governing coun. NRC, 1991-94. Recipient donald L. Katz award Gas Processors Assn., 1998. Fellow Can. Acad. Engring.; mem. AIChE, Can. Soc. Chem. Engrs. (pres. 1986-87), Assn. Profl. Engrs., Geologists and Geophysicsts of Alta. (1st v.p. 1995-96, pres. 1996-97, Centennial award 1993), Can. Coun. Profl. Engrs. (bd. dirs. 1997—). Office: 9419 20th Ave Edmonton AB Canada T6N 1E5

OTUS, SIMONE, public relations executive; b. Walnut Creek, Calif., Jan. 10, 1960; d. Mahmut and Alexa (Artemenko) O. BA, U. Calif., Berkeley, 1981. Account exec. Marx-David Advt., San Francisco, 1981-82; freelance writer Mpls. and San Francisco, 1982-83; account exec. D'Arcy, MacManus & Masius, San Francisco, 1983; account supr. Ralph Silver Assocs., San Francisco, 1984-85; ptnr., co-founder Blanc & Otus Pub. Relations, San Francisco, 1985—. Address: Blanc & Otus Pub Rels 444 Castro St Fl 6 Mountain View CA 94041-2017

OUTLAW, LANNY F. gas company executive; B in Engring., S.D. Sch. Mines and Tech. Various positions Shell Oil Co., 1958-87, Western Gas Resources, Inc., Denver, 1987-96, exec. v.p. ops., bus. devel. and engring., pres., COO, 1996-99, CEO, pres., 1999—. Office: Western Gas Resources Inc 12200 N Pecos St Denver CO 80234-3439

OUZTS, EUGENE THOMAS, minister, secondary education educator; b. Thomasville, Ga., June 7, 1930; s. John Travis and Livie Mae (Strickland) O.; m. Mary Olive Vineyard, May 31, 1956. BA, Harding U., Searcy, AR, 1956, MA, 1957; postgrad., Murray State U., KY, U. Ark., U. Ariz., Ariz. State U., No. Ariz. U. Cert. secondary tchr., Ark., Mo., Ariz.; cert. c.c. tchr., Ariz.; ordained minister Church of Christ, 1956. Min. various chs., Ark., Mo., Tex., 1957-65; tchr. various pub. schs., Ark., Mo., Ariz., 1959-92; min. Ch. of Christ, Clifton and Morenci, Ariz., 1965—; 1st lt. CAP/USAF, 1980, advanced through grades to lt. col., 1989, chaplain Ariz., 1982—, asst. wing chaplain, 1985—. Adviser student activities Clifton (Ariz.) Pub. Schs., 1965-92; bd. dirs. Ariz. Ch. of Christ Bible Camp, Tucson, 1966—. Mem. airport adv. bd. Greenlee County, Clifton, Ariz., 1992—. Recipient Meritorious Svc. award, 1994, Exceptional Svc. award, 1997, Civil Air Patrol; named Ariz. Wing Chaplain of Yr, 1984, Thomas C. Casaday Unit Chaplain of Yr., 1985, Ariz. Wing Safety Officer of Yr., 1989, Ariz. Wing Sr. Mem. of Yr., 1994, Southwest Region Sr. Mem. of Yr., 1995, Civil Air Patrol. Mem. Mil. Chaplains Assn., Disabled Am. Vets., Am. Legion, Elks. Democrat. Avocations: flying, building and flying model aircraft, reading. Home and Office: HC 1 Box 557 Duncan AZ 85534-9720

OVERGAARD, WILLARD MICHELE, retired political scientist, jurisprudent; b. Montpelier, Idaho, Oct. 16, 1925; s. Elias Nielsen and Myrtle LaVerne (Humphrey) O.; m. Lucia Clare Cochrane, June 14, 1946; children: Eric Willard, Mark Fredrik, Alisa Claire. B.A., U. Oreg., 1949; Fulbright scholar, U. Oslo, 1949-50; M.A. (non-resident scholar 1954-55), U. Wis., Madison, 1955; Ph.D. in Polit. Sci. (adminstrv. fellow 1955-56, research fellow 1962-64), U. Minn., 1969. Instr., Soviet and internat. affairs Intelligence Sch., U.S. Army, Europe, 1956-62, dir. intelligence rsch. tng. program, 1958-61; asst. prof. internat. affairs George Washington U., 1964-67; sr. staff polit. scientist Ops. Research Inst., U.S. Army Inst. Advanced Studies, Carlisle, Pa., 1967-70; assoc. prof. polit. sci., chmn. dept., dir. Internat. Studies Inst., Westminster Coll., New Wilmington, 1970-72; prof. polit. sci. and pub. law Boise (Idaho) State U., 1972-94, chmn. dept., 1972-87, acad. dir. M.P.A. degree program, personnel adminstr., mem. humanities council interdisciplinary studies in humanities, 1976-87, prof. of pub. law emeritus, 1994—, dir. Taft Inst. Seminars for Pub. Sch. Tchrs., 1985-87, coord. Legal Asst. Program, 1990-95. Mem. comml. panel Am. Arbitration Assn., 1974—; mem. Consortium for Idaho's Future, 1974-75; adv. com. Idaho Statewide Tng. Program Local Govt. Ofcls., 1974-78; adv. group Gov. Idaho Task Force Local Govt., 1977; co-dir. Idaho State Exec. Inst., Office of Gov., 1979-83; grievance hearing officer City of Boise, 1981-85; arbitrator U.S. Postal Svc., 1988-90; cons. in field. Author: The Schematic System of Soviet Totalitarianism, 3 vols, 1961, Legal Norms and Normative Bases for the Progressive Development of International Law as Defined in Soviet Treaty Relations, 1945-64, 1969; co-author: The Communist Bloc in Europe, 1959; editor: Continuity and Change in International Politics, 1972; chief editor: Idaho Jour. Politics, 1974-76. Served with USAAF, 1943-45; with AUS, 1951-54; ret. maj. USAR. Named Disting. Citizen of Idaho Idaho Statesman, 1979; named Outstanding Prof. of Sch. Social Scis. and Pub. Affairs, Boise State U., 1988. Mem. ABA (assoc.), Res. Officers Assn. (life), Am. Legion. Home: 2023 S Five Mile Rd Boise ID 83709-2316 E-mail: wgaard@earthlink.net

OVERMAN, LARRY EUGENE, chemistry educator; b. Chgo., Mar. 9, 1943; s. Lemoine Emerson and Dorothy Jane Overman; m. Joanne Louise Dewey, June 5, 1966; children: Michael, Jackie. BA in Chemistry, Earlham Coll., 1965; PhD in Organic Chemistry, U. Wis., 1969. Asst. prof. chemistry U. Calif., Irvine, 1971-76, assoc. prof. chemistry, 1976-79, prof. [illegible] try, 1994—. Mem. sci. adv. bd. Pharmacopeia, Inc., 1993—; co-chair bd. chem. scis. and tech. NRC, 1997-2000. Editor-in-chief Organic Reactions, 1999—, bd. editors Organic Reactions, 1984-97, Organic Syntheses,

1986-94; hon. mem. editl. adv. bd. Ann. Reports in Hetero Chem., 1989-95, Synlett, 1989—, Jour. Am. Chem. Soc., 1996-99, Chem. Revs., 1996-2000, Accounts Chem. Rsch., 1996-99; mem. cons. editors Tetrahedron Publs., 1995—; mem. editl. bd. Procs. NAS, 1998-2000. Recipient Sr. Scientist award Alexander von Humboldt Found., 1985-87, Jacob Javits award Nat. Inst. Neurol. Sci., 1985-92, 92-99, Disting. Faculty award Earlham Coll., 1999, S.T. Li prize for achievements in sci. and tech., 1999, fellowship Japan Soc. for Promotion of Sci., 2000; predoctoral fellow NIH, 1966-69, postdoctoral fellow, 1969-71; fellow A.P. Sloan Found., 1975-77, Guggenheim fellow, 1993-94, Japan Soc. Promotion Sci. fellow, 2000; Arthur C. Cope scholar, 1989. Fellow NAS, AAAS, Am. Acad. Arts and Scis.; mem. Am. Chem. Soc. (exec. com. organic divsn., Cope Scholar award 1989, Creative Work in Synthetic Organic Chemistry award 1995), Royal Soc. Chemistry (Centenary medal 1997). Achievements include research in new methods for organic synthesis, natural products synthesis, medicinal chemistry. Office: U Calif Irvine Dept Chemistry 516 Rowland Hl Irvine CA 92697-0001 E-mail: leoverma@uci.edu

OVERMYER, DANIEL LEE, Asian studies educator; b. Columbus, Ohio, Aug. 20, 1935; s. Elmer Earl and Bernice Alma (Hesselbart) O.; m. Estella Velazquez, June 19, 1965; children: Rebecca Lynn, Mark Edward. BA, Westmar Coll., LeMars, Iowa, 1957; BD, Evang. Theol. Sem., Naperville, Ill., 1960; MA, U. Chgo., 1966, PhD, 1971. Pastor Evangel. United Brethren Ch., Chgo., 1960-64; asst. prof. dept. religion Oberlin (Ohio) Coll., 1970-73; prof. Asian studies U. B.C., Vancouver, Can., 1973—, acting head religious studies Can., 1984-85, head Asian studies Can., 1986-91. Vis. prof. Princeton U., 1983, U. Heidelberg, 1993; prof. Chinese U. Hong Kong, 1996-98; hon. prof. Shanghai Normal U., 1997—. Author: Folk Buddhist Religion, 1976, Religions of China, 1986; (with David Jordan) The Flying Phoenix, 1986, Precious Volumes: An Introduction to Chinese Sectarian Scriptures From the Sixteenth and Seventeenth Centuries, 1999; contbr. articles to encys. and profl. jours. Chmn. Sch. Consultative Com., Vancouver, 1976-77; coord. Vancouver Boys Soccer League, 1979-81; adult edn. coord. United Ch. Can., Vancouver, 1981-84; co-chmn. Endowment Lands Regional Park Com., 1987-90; co-chair China and Inner Asia Coun., Assn. Asian Studies, 1992—. With USNR, 1953-61. Recipient Killam faculty rsch. prize U. B.C., 1986, Killiam faculty tchg. prize, 2000; NEH fellow, 1978, 79, China Rsch. fellow, 1981, sr. fellow coun. humanities Princeton U., 1983, Wang Inst. Grad. Studies fellow, 1985-86. Fellow Royal Soc. Can.; mem. Am. Soc. Study Religion, Soc. Study Chinese Religions (pres. 1985-88), Assn. Asian Studies. Democrat. Methodist. Avocations: photography, swimming, hiking, gardening. Home: 3393 W 26th Ave V Vancouver BC Canada V6S 1N4 Office: U BC Dept Asian Studies Vancouver BC Canada V6T 1Z2 E-mail: dano@interchange.ubc.ca

OVERSTREET, JAMES WILKINS, obstetrics and gynecology educator, administrator; BA in Biology magna cum laude, U. South, 1967; BA in Natural Scis., U. Cambridge, Eng., 1970, PhD in Reproductive Physiology, 1973, MA in Natural Scis., 1974; MD, Columbia U., 1974. Diplomate Nat. Bd. Med. Examiners; lic. physician, Calif. NIH Med. Scientist Tng. fellow dept. anatomy coll. physicians ans surgeons Columbia U., 1970-72, NIH Med. Scientist Tng. fellow Internat. Inst. for Study Human Reproduction, 1972-74; asst. resident in ob-gyn. Presbyn. Hosp., N.Y.C., 1974; Ford Found. Postdoctoral Rsch. fellow dept. ob-gyn. Cornell U. Med. Coll., 1975-76; asst. prof. human anatomy and ob-gyn. sch. medicine U. Calif., Davis, 1976-80, assoc. prof. human anatomy, 1980-84, assoc. prof. ob-gyn. sch. medicine, 1980-85, prof. ob-gyn. sch. medicine, 1985—, chief divsn. reproductive biology and medicine dept. ob-gyn. sch. medicine, 1983-86, dir. lab. for energy-related health rsch., 1985 88, dir. Inst. Toxicology and Environ. Health, unit leader devel. and reproductive biology Primate Rsch. Ctr., 1988—. Mem. sci. rev. panel for health rsch., reviewer test rules dept. and reproductive abd devel. toxicology brs. U.S. EPA; mem. ad hoc study sect., cons. Nat. Inst. for Occupational Safety and Health; chair AIDS and related rsch. rev. group NIH; chmn. spl. study sect., mem. site visit team, mem. ad hoc reproductuve endocrinology study sect. Nat. Inst. Child Health and Human Devel.; reviewer, mem. site visit team Nat. Inst. Environ. Health Scis./NIH, Med. Rsch. Coun. Can.; mem. tech. adv. com. and site visit team contraceptive rsch. and devel. project Agy. for Internat. Devel./Ea. Va. Med. Sch.; temp. advisor spl. program rsch. devel. and rsch. tng. in human reproduction WHO; mem. reproductive and devel. toxicology program rev. panel Chem. Industry Inst. Toxicology; mem. exec. com. systemwide toxic substances rsch. and tng. program U. Calif.; reviewer NSF, Office Health and Environ. Rsch., U.S. Dept. Energy, March of Dimes Reproductive Hazards in the Workplace Rsch. Grants Program, Mt. Sinai Hosp., Alta. Heritage Cancer Grants, U.S.-Israel Binational Agrl. Rsch. and Devel. Fund; clin. cons. lab. surveys program Coll. Am. Pathologists; cons. Ctr. for Drugs and Biologics, U.S. FDA, Inst. for Internat. Studies in Natural Family Planning, Georgetown U., Internat. Devel. Rsch. Ctr. Assoc. editor Molecular Reproduction and Devel.; mem. editorial bd. Biology of Reproduction, 1983-86, Jour. In Vitro Fertilization and Embryo Transfer, 1984-89, Reproductive Toxicology, Fertilty and Sterility, 1984-92, Jour. Andrology, 1990-92; referee Jour. Reproduction and Fertilty, Jour. Exptl. Zoology, Am. Jour. Physiology, Am. Jour. Ob-Gyn., Jour. Urology, Science, Jour. Clin. Endocrinology and Metabolism, Archives Internal Medicine, Internat. Jour. Andrology, Reproduction, Nutrition, Devel., Western Jour. Medicine, Contraception, Human Reproduction, Proceedings Royal Soc. Series B.; invited lectr. in field. Georgia Fulbright scholar, 1967-68; recipient Rsch. Career Devel. award NIH, 1978-83, Disting. Career in Clin. Investigation award Columbia Presbyn. Med Ctr., 1992; grantee Syntex Rsch. Divsn., 1978-81, NIH, 1978-81, 78-83, 79-90, 81-90, 85-88, 86—, 87—, 88—, 89—, 90— (two grants), 91—, 92—, 93—, U. Calif., 1981-82, U.S. EPA, 1981-84, 82-84, Nat. Inst. for Occupational Safety and Health, 1982-84, U.S. Dept. Energy, 1985-88, Georgetown U., 1987-89, 92—, Merck Rsch. Labs., 1988-90, 92, 92—, March of Dimes, 1988-90, Semiconductor Industry Assn., 1989-92, Tobacco Related Disease Rsch. Program, 1990-93, Andrew W. Mellon Found., 1993—, Mem. Am. Fertility Soc., Am. Soc. Andrology (exec. coun. 1986-89), Soc. for Study Fertility, Soc. for Study Reproduction, Phi Beta Kappa. Achievements include research in physiology of mammalian spermatozoa, sperm transport in the female reproductive tract, in vivo and in vitro mammalian fertilization, diagnosis and therapy of human male infertility, reproductive toxicology, environmental and occupational hazards to male and female fertility, contraceptive development, reproductive endocrinology. Office: U Calif Davis Inst Toxicology & Enviro Health Rsch Office Davis CA 95616

OVERSTREET, KAREN A. federal judge; BA cum laude, Univ. of Wash., 1977; JD, Univ. of Oregon, 1982. Assoc. Duane, Morris & Heckscher, Phila., 1983-86; ptnr. Davis Wright Tremaine, Seattle, 1986-93; bankruptcy judge U.S. Bankruptcy Ct. (we. dist.) Wash., Seattle, 1994—. Assoc. editor Oregon Law Review; dir. People's Law Sch.; mem. advisory com. U.S. Bankruptcy Ct. (we. dist.) Wash. Mem. Nat. Conf. of Bankruptcy Judges, Wash. State Bar Assn. (creditor-debtor sec.), Seattle-King County Bar Assn. (bankruptcy sec.), Am. Bar Assn., Wash. Women Lawyers Assn. Office: US Bankruptcy Ct Park Place Bldg 1200 6th Ave Ste 315 Seattle WA 98101-3130

OVIATT, LARRY ANDREW, retired secondary school educator; b. Boone, Iowa, Mar. 13, 1939; s. Eli Charles and T. Mae (Lathrop) O.; children: Julia, Vanessa, Dana. BA, Drake U., Des Moines, 1962; MS, San Diego State U., 1975. Tchr. art San Diego City Schs., 1969-96, mentor tchr., 1992-96; owner Perfect Travel of La Jolla, 1989-97; prof. art edn. Calif. State U., Northridge, 1998—. Prof. art edn. Calif. State U., Northridge. San Diego dir. Anderson for Pres., 1976; dist. coord. Hedgecock for Mayor, San Diego, 1984; dir. elder Help Corp., San Diego, 1988; v.p. Afrian Am. Mus., 1989-92; pres. Sushi Gallery, 1980-82; bd. dirs. Mingei Internat. Mus., 1983-87; pres. Cmty. Svc. Assn., 1984-88; past pres. Diversionary Theatre, African Am. Mus.; dir. AIDS Walk for Life, 1988, 89; bd. dirs. AIDS Art Alive. Named 1986 Tchr. of Yr. Urban League, 1986, Sec. Art Tchr. of Yr. Calif. Art Tchrs. Assn., 1988, Art Tchr. of Yr. Calif. Art Tchrs. Assn., 1992, Vol. of Yr. San Diego City Schs., 1993. Mem. So. Calif. Art Tchrs. Assn. (pres. 1984-89), Calif. Art Edn. Assn. (dir. 1984-89, conf. adminstr., Art Edn. Tchr. of Yr. award 1992), Nat. Art Edn. Assn. (dir. 1987-93). Avocations: reading, basketball, art. Home: 1571 E Orange Grove Pasadena CA 91104-4727 E-mail: rsmith4720@aol.com

OVITT, GARY C. mayor; b. May 3, 1947; BA, U. Redlands, 1969. Tchr. Chaffey H.S., Ontario, Calif.; mayor City of Ontario, 1998—. Chmn. dept. edn. Chaffey Joint Unified Sch. Dist., 1970—. Mem. Ontario (Calif.) City Coun., 1992-99. Office: City Hall 303 E B St Ontario CA 91764-4105

OVITZ, MICHAEL S. communications executive; b. 1946; m. Judy Reich, 1969; 3 children. Grad., UCLA, 1968. With William Morris Agy., 1968-75; co-founder, chmn. Creative Artists Agy., L.A., 1975-95; pres. Walt Disney Co., Burbank, Calif., 1995-97; owner CKE Cos., Beverly Hills, 1998—. Chmn. exec. bd. dirs. UCLA Hosp. and Med. Ctr.; bd. advisors Sch. Theater, Film and TV UCLA; bd. dirs. Livent, Inc., Gulfstream Aero. Corp., J. Crew Group, Inc. Trustee St. John's Hosp. and Health Ctr., Santa Monica, Calif., Mus. Modern Art, N.Y.C.; bd. govs. Cedars-Sinai Hosp., L.A.; mem. exec. adv. bd. Pediatric AIDS Found.; bd. dirs. Calif. Inst. Arts, Sundance Inst. Mem. Coun. Fgn. Rels., Zeta Beta Tau. Avocations: contemporary art, African antiques, Chinese furniture. Office: Artists Management Group 9465 Wilshire Blvd Ste 212 Beverly Hills CA 90212-2610

OWADES, RUTH MARKOWITZ, marketing company executive; b. Los Angeles, Sept. 2, 1944; d. David and Yonina (Graf) Markowitz; m. Joseph L. Owades, Sept. 7, 1969. BA with honors, Scripps Coll., Claremont, Calif., 1966; MBA, Harvard U., 1975; postgrad. U. Strasbourg (France), 1966-67. Exec. asst. Los Angeles Econ. Devel. Bd., N.Y.C., 1968-69; copywriter D'Arcy Advt. Co., St. Louis, 1970-71; asst. program dir. KMOX-AM Radio, St. Louis, 1971-72; assoc. producer WCVB-TV, Boston, 1972-73; mktg. project mgr. United Brands Co., Boston, 1975; mktg. dir. CML Group Inc., Concord, Mass., 1975-78; founder, pres. Gardener's Eden Inc., Boston, 1978-82; pres. Gardener's Eden, div. Williams-Sonoma Inc., Emeryville, Calif., 1982-87; founder, pres. Calyx & Carolla, Inc., 1988—; bd. dirs. Hellenic Breweries S.A., Athens, Greece. Bd. of advisors An Income of Her Own; trustee Scripps Coll. Recipient Bausch & Lomb award, 1962, Disting. Alumna award Scripps Coll., 1989, Woman of Achievement award Woman's City Club Cleve., 1991, Woman Who Has Made a Difference award Internat. Women's Forum, 1991, Woman of the Yr. award Woman's Direct Response Group N.Y., 1992, Cataloger of Yr. award Target Marketing Mag., 1992, Direct Marketer of Yr. award, No. Calif. Direct Mktg. Club, 1993; Fulbright scholar, 1966; named student Goodwill Ambassador to Nagoya, Japan, 1960. Mem. Direct Mktg. Assn., Phi Beta Kappa. Club: Harvard (N.Y.C.), Women's Forum West (v.p. and treas.), Com. of 200. Home: 2164 Hyde St San Francisco CA 94109-1788 Office: 185 Berry St Ste 6200 San Francisco CA 94107-1750

OWEN, BRADLEY SCOTT, lieutenant governor; b. Tacoma, May 23, 1950; s. Laural Willis, m. Linda Knoll, Jan. 20, 1983; children: Shanie, Dana, Mark, Sherrie, Adam, Royce. Student pub. sch., Germany. State rep. Wash. Ho. Rep., Olympia, 1976-82; state senator Wash. State Senate, Olympia, 1983-96; lt. gov. State of Wash., Olympia, 1997—. Mem. Wash. State substance abuse coun., 1997—. Mem. Elks. Democrat. Office: Wash State Lt Gov PO Box 40400 Olympia WA 98504-0400

OWEN, DAVID TURNER, state legislator, owner, operator; b. N.Y.C., June 9, 1931; s. William Myrou Owen and Cynthia Foster Wolf; m. Marilyn Laura Clarks BA, Colo. Coll., 1955; postgrad, Northern Va. Coll., 1978. With U.S. Army, Wash., 1955-79; owner, operator Greeley (Colo.) Tonis Sales, 1979-; mem. Colo. Ho. of Reps., 1988-98, Colo. Senate, Dist. 16, Denver, 1998—. Mem. Am. Legis. Exchange Council, Nat. Assn. Antique Collecters, Western Legis., Nat. Fed. Bus. Republican. Home: 2722 W Buena Vista Dr Greeley CO 80634-7717 Office: State Capitol 200 E Colfax Ave Denver CO 80203-1776

OWEN, JOHN, retired newspaper editor; b. Helena, Mont., June 10, 1929; s. John Earl and Ella Jean (McMillian) O.; m. Alice Winnifred Kesler, June 9, 1951; children— David Scott, Kathy Lynn. B.A. in Journalism, U. Mont., 1951. Sports editor Bismarck (N.D.) Tribune, 1953-55; wire editor Yakima (Wash.) Herald, 1956; with Seattle Post-Intelligencer, 1956-94, sports editor, 1968-80, assoc. editor, 1980-94, columnist, 1968-94. Author: Intermediate Eater Cookbook, 1974, Gourmand Gutbusters Cookbook, 1980, Seattle Cookbook, 1983, Great Grub Hunt Cookbook, 1989, Press Pass, 1994, Gluttony Without Guilt, 1997, Seattle Walks, 2000; also short stories. Served with AUS, 1951-52. Named Top Sports Writer in Wash. Nat. Sportswriters Orgn., 1966, 68, 69, 71, 74, 85, 88. Home: 611 Bell St Apt 4 Edmonds WA 98020-3065

OWEN, MICHAEL LEE, lawyer; b. L.A., Aug. 17, 1942; s. Richard M. Owen and Betty Hamilton; m. Espy Bolivar-Owen. AB in Econ. with distinction, Stanford U., 1964; LLB, Harvard U., 1967. Bar: Calif., 1968, N.Y. 1968. Assoc. Reid & Priest, N.Y.C., 1967-69; mem. legal dept. Bank of Am. NT&SA, San Francisco, 1969-81; corp. sec. BRE Properties, San Francisco, 1970-75; v.p., assoc. gen. counsel Bank of Am. NT&SA, L.A., 1979-81; ptnr. and chair L.Am. practice group Paul, Hastings, Janofsky & Walker, LLP, L.A., 1981—. Vice chmn. Ctr. for Am. and Internat. Law (formerly Southwestern Legal Found.). Contbr. articles to profl. jours. regarding legal issues affecting financing and investment in Latin Amer. Bd. dirs. Constnl. Rights Found. Mem. Am. Arbitration Assn. (internat. panel of arbitrators), U.S.-Mex. Law Inst. (bd. dirs.), U.S.-Mex. C. of C. (bd. dirs. Pacific chpt.). Office: Paul Hastings Janofsky & Walker LLP 555 S Flower St 24th Fl Los Angeles CA 90071-2300 E-mail: michaelowen@paulhastings.com

OWEN, RAY DAVID, biology educator; b. Genesee, Wis., Oct. 30, 1915; s. Dave and Ida (Hoeft) O.; m. June J. Weissenberg, June 24, 1939; 1 son, David G. BS, Carroll Coll., Wis., 1937, ScD, 1962; PhD, U. Wis., 1941, ScD, 1979, U. of Pacific, 1965. Asst. prof. genetics, zoology U. Wis., 1944-47; Gosney fellow Calif. Inst. Tech., Pasadena, 1946-47, assoc. prof. div. biology, 1947-53, prof. biology, 1953-83, also chmn., v.p. for student affairs, dean of students, prof. emeritus, 1983—. Research participant Oak Ridge Nat. Lab., 1957-58; Cons. Oak Ridge Inst. Nuclear Studies; mem. Pres.'s Cancer Panel. Author: (with A.M. Srb) General Genetics, 1952, 2d edit. (with A.M. Srb, R. Edgar), 1965; Contbr. articles to sci. jours. Recipient Gregor Mendel medal Czech Acad. Scis., 1965, Medawar prize The Transplantation Soc., 2000. Fellow AAAS; mem. Genetics Soc. Am. (pres., Thomas Hunt Morgan medal 1993), Am. Assn. Immunologists (Excellence in Mentoring award 1999), Am. Soc. Human Genetics, Western Soc. Naturalists, Am. Soc. Zoologists, Am. Genetics Assn., Nat. Acad. Scis., Am. Acad. Arts and Scis., Am. Philos. Soc., Am. Acad. Allergy and Immunology (hon.), Internat. Soc. Animal Genetics (hon.), Sigma Xi. Home: 1583 Rose Villa St Pasadena CA 91106-3524 Office: Calif Inst Tech # 156-29 Pasadena CA 91125-0001

OWENS, BILL, governor; b. Ft. Worth, Oct. 22, 1950; m. Frances Owens; children: Monica, Mark, Brett. BA, Stephen F. Austin State U.; MPA, U. Tex. With Touche Ross & Co., Gates Corp.; state repr. Colo. Ho. Reps., 1983-89; state sen. Colo. State Sen., 1989-94; state treas. State of Colo., 1994-98, gov., 1999—. Guest host Mike Rosen, Ken Hamblin and Chuck Baker talk shows; lectr. Russia. Contbr. more than 50 articles to profl. jours. Named One of Country's Ten Up-and-Coming leaders Robert Novak. Office: Office Gov 136 State Capitol Bldg Denver CO 80203-1792*

OWENS, JACK BYRON, lawyer; b. Orange, Calif., Oct. 14, 1944; s. Jack Byron and Lenna Mildred (Gobar) O.; children: John Byron, David Harold, James Paul, Alexandra Grace. A.B., Stanford U., 1966, J.D., 1969. Bar: Calif. 1970, D.C. 1970. Law clk. U.S. Ct. Appeals 9th Circuit, 1969-70; asso. firm Wilmer, Cutler & Pickering, Washington, 1970-71, 74-75; atty. adv. Dept. Air Force, 1971-73; law clk. U.S. Supreme Ct., 1973-74; prof. law Boalt Law Sch., U. Calif., Berkeley, 1975-79; partner firm Orrick, Herrington & Sutcliffe, San Francisco, 1978-81; exec. v.p., gen. counsel E & J Gallo Winery, 1981—. Adj. prof. Georgetown U. Law Sch. Contbr. articles legal publns. Served with USAF, 1971-73. Mem. Am. Law Inst., Am. Bar Assn., Phi Beta Kappa, Order of Coif. Office: E & J Gallo Winery PO Box 1130 600 Yosemite Blvd Modesto CA 95354-2760

OWENS, MICHAEL L. radio station executive; b. Phoenix, Mar. 8, 1950; m. Kristin Owens; 2 children. Gen. mgr. KNIX Radio, 1978—; owner New Frontier Comm., Inc., Midland/Odessa, Tex., 1988—; COO, mgr. Owens Broadcasting Co., LLC, 1995—. Mgr., ptnr. KEZ-FM Radio. Mem. Nat. Assn. Broadcasters, Radio Advt. Bur., Country Music Assn., Acad. Country Music. Avocations: exercise, golf. Office: KNIX FM 600 E Gilbert Dr Tempe AZ 85281-2021

OWEN-TOWLE, CAROLYN SHEETS, clergywoman; b. Upland, Calif., July 27, 1935; d. Millard Owen and Mary (Baskerville) Sheets; m. Charles Russell Chapman, June 29, 1957 (div. 1973); children: Christopher Charles, Jennifer Anne, Russell Owen; m. Thomas Allan Owen-Towle, Nov. 16, 1973. BS in Art and Art History, Scripps Coll., 1957; postgrad. in religion, U. Iowa, 1977; DD, Meadville/Lombard Theol. Sch., Chgo., 1994. Ordained to ministry Unitarian-Universalist Ch., 1978. Minister 1st Unitarian Universalist Ch., San Diego, 1978—. Pres. Ministerial Sisterhood, Unitarian Universalist Ch., 1980-82; mem. Unitarian Universalist Svc. Com., 1979-85, pres., 1983-85. Bd. dirs. Planned Parenthood, San Diego, 1980-86; mem. clergy adv. com. to Hospice, San Diego, 1980-83; mem. U.S. Rep. Jim Bates Hunger Adv. Com., San Diego, 1983-87; chaplain Interfaith AIDS Task Force, San Diego, 1988—. Mem. Unitarian Universalist Ministers Assn. (exec. com. 1988, pres. 1989-91, African Am. minister's action com. 1995-98). Avocations: reading, walking, combating racism, promoting human rights, designing environments. Office: 1st Unitarian Universalist Ch 4190 Front St San Diego CA 92103-2030

OWINGS, DONALD HENRY, psychology educator; b. Atlanta, Dec. 7, 1943; s. Markley James and Loyce Erin (White) O.; m. Sharon Elizabeth Calhoun, Jan. 29, 1966; children: Ragon Matthew, Anna Rebekah. BA in Psychology, U. Tex., 1965; PhD, U. Wash., 1972. Asst. prof. psychology U. Calif., Davis, 1971-78, assoc. prof., 1978-83, prof., 1983—, chair dept., 1989-93. Editor: (with M.D. Beecher & N.S. Thompson) Perspectives in Ethology, Vol. 12: Communication, 1997, (with R.G. Coss & K.R. Henry) Introduction to Psychobiol., 1998, 99 (2nd edit.); author: (with E.P. Morton) Animal Vocal Communication: A New Approach, 1998; contbr. articles to profl. jours., book chpts. NSF rsch. grantee, 1978-80, 82-84. Fellow Animal Behavior Soc.; mem. Internat. Soc. for Ecol. Psychology, Internat. Soc. for Behavioral Ecology, Internat. Soc. for Comparative Psychology. Democrat. Avocations: hiking, music, bird watching, reading. Home: 815 Oeste Dr Davis CA 95616-1856 Office: U Calif Dept Psychology 1 Shields Ave Davis CA 95616-8686 E-mail: dhowings@ucdavis.edu

OXARART, FRANK, broadcast executive; Gen. mgr. Sta. KCBS-AM, San Francisco, 1989—. Office: KCBS 1 Embarcadero Ctr Ste 3200 San Francisco CA 94111-3720

OYLER, DAVID L. real estate development executive; V.p., Melody Homes, Colo. divsn. Schuler Homes Inc., Honolulu, 1998—. Office: Schuler Homes Inc 828 4th St Mall Fl 4th Honolulu HI 96813-4321

OYLER, JAMES RUSSELL, JR. manufacturing executive; b. Gettysburg, Pa., Mar. 18, 1946; s. James Russell and Gail Louise (Dinwiddie) O.; m. Clare Marie Walther, Sept. 16, 1967; children: Catherine Meredith, Amanda Christine, Margaret Anne. BSEE magna cum laude, Lehigh U., 1967; MA in Econs. with honors, Cambridge U., Eng., 1969. Cert. mgmt. acct. Assoc. Booz, Allen & Hamilton, N.Y.C., 1972-76, product dir. Harris Corp., Dallas, 1976-79, v.p. Ft. Lauderdale, Fla., 1979-82, gen. mgr. Melbourne, 1982-86, sr. v.p., 1986-90; also bd. dirs. Harris Iberica, Madrid; pres. Am. Mfg. Group Inc., Vero Beach, Fla., 1990-93, AMG Inc., Harvard, Mass., 1993-94; pres., CEO Evans & Sutherland Computer Corp., Salt Lake City, 1994—, also bd. dirs. Bd. dirs. Ikos Systems, Inc., sec. audit com., 1992—; bd. dirs. Silicon Light Machines. Bd. dirs. Utah Opera. 1st lt. U.S. Army, 1969-72. Fellow Am. Chem. Soc.; mem. IEEE, Nat. Am. Electronics Assn. (bd. dirs. Fla. chpt. 1984-87, nat. bd. dirs. 1988), Corp. for Open Systems (bd. dirs. 1986-88), Utah Info. Tech. Assn. (chmn.), Tau Beta Pi. Republican. Roman Catholic. Avocations: tennis, photography. Home: 1873 Carrigan Cir Salt Lake City UT 84109-1475 Office: PO Box 58700 600 Komas Dr Salt Lake City UT 84158

OZAKI, JOSEPH, finance company executive; Contr., treas. and sec. A-Mark Fin., Santa Monica, Calif. Office: A-Mark Financial 100 Wilshire Blvd 3d Fl Santa Monica CA 90401 Office Fax: (310) 319-0346

OZANICH, CHARLES GEORGE, real estate broker; b. Aug. 11, 1933; s. Paul Anthony and Alma Bertha (Sablotna) O.; m. Betty Sue Carman, Feb. 20, 1955; children: Viki Lynn, Terri Sue, Charles Anthony, Nicole Lee. Student, Am. River Coll.; degree, Sierra Coll. Owner, broker Terrace Realty, Basic Realty, Grass Valley, Calif., 1971—. Compliance inspector Dept. Vets. Affairs. Mem. Grass Valley Vol. Fire Dept., 1965-93. Served with USAF, 1951-55, Korea. Decorated Bronze Star with three oak leaf clusters, Korean Presdl. citation, UN citation. Mem. Nevada County Bd. Realtors (dir. 1973-74). Lodges: Am. Legion, Masons, Shriners, Moose (charter mem.). Achievements include receiving the Nat. Champion award Truck Drivers Rodeo class 5 semi-trailer 18 wheeler divsn., 1954. Home and Office: 15053 Chinook Ln Grass Valley CA 95945-8846 E-mail: cozanich@hotmail.com

OZIER, IRVING, physicist, educator; b. Montreal, Que., Can., Sept. 7, 1938; s. Harry and Peppi (Schwartzwald) O.; m. Joyce Ruth Weinstein, July 4, 1963; children: Elizabeth, David, Douglas. BA, U. Toronto, 1960; AM, Harvard U., 1961, PhD, 1965. Rsch. fellow Harvard U., Cambridge, Mass., 1965-67, MIT, Cambridge, 1966-67; tech. staff Rockwell Internat. Sci. Ctr., Thousand Oaks, Calif., 1966-70; assoc. prof. physics U. B.C., Vancouver, B.C., Can., 1970-77, prof. Can., 1977—. Vis. rsch. fellow Cath. U., Nijmegen, The Netherlands, 1976-77, U. Nijmegen, 1997; vis. rsch. officer Nat. Rsch. Coun. Can., Ottawa, 1982-83; vis. prof. Eidgenossische Technische Hochschule, Zurich, Switzerland, 1988-89, 98. Author research articles in molecular spectroscopy. Alfred P. Sloan research fellow, 1972-74; Izaak Walton Killiam Meml. Sr. fellow U. B.C., 1982-83 Mem. Am. Phys. Soc., Can. Assn. Physicists Office: U BC Dept Physics & Astron 5224 Agricultural Rd Vancouver BC Canada V6T 1Z1

PACE, THOMAS M. lawyer; b. Mesa, Ariz., Feb. 5, 1952; s. Lemuel Max and Ann (Green) P.; m. Vi Garrett Pace, Jan. 24, 1981; children: Melanie, Brittany. BA, Stanford U., 1973; JD, U. Ariz., 1976. Bar: Ariz.; cert. real estate specialist. Assoc. Martin, Feldhacker & Freidl, Phoenix, 1976-77, Trew & Woodford, Phoenix, 1977-78; ptnr. Hecker, Phillips & Hooker, Tucson, 1978-88; sr. ptnr. O'Connor Cavanagh, Tucson, 1988-95; pvt. practice Law Office of Thomas M. Pace, Tucson, 1995—. Mem. Mayor's Housing Task Force, Tucson, 1993; bd. dirs. Tucson Urban League, 1986-96; chmn. So. Ariz. Homebuilders Polit. Action Com., 1995, 96. Mem. So. Ariz. Homebuilders (tech. com), Stanford Club So. Ariz. Democrat. Office: 2525 E Broadway Blvd Ste 102 Tucson AZ 85716-5398 E-mail: tpace2@mindspring.com

PACHECO-RANSANZ, ARSENIO, Hispanic and Italian studies educator; b. Barcelona, Spain, Feb. 8, 1932; s. Arsenio Pacheco and Jacoba Ransanz-Alvarez; m. Mercedes Olivella-Sole, Sept. 1, 1956; children: Arsenio-Andrew, David-George. MA, U. Barcelona, 1954, PhD, 1958. Tutor Colegio Mayor Hispanoamericano Fray Junipero Serra, Barcelona, 1954-56; lectr. Hochschüle für Wirtschaft und Sozialwissenschaften, Nurnberg, 1956; asst. lectr. U. Glasgow, Scotland, 1957-59; lectr. U. St. Andrews, Scotland, 1960-70; vis. prof. U. Pitts., 1966; prof. Hispanic and Italian studies U. B.C., Vancouver, Can., 1970-97, prof. emeritus, 1997—. Editor: Historia de Xacob Xalabin, 1964, Testament de Bernat Serradell, 1971, Varia fortuna del soldado Pindaro, 1975, Obres de Francesc de la Via, 1997; contbr. articles to profl. jours. Bd. dirs. Can. Fedn. Humanities, 1981-84. Fellow Royal Soc. Can.; mem. Can. Assn. Hispanists (pres. 1978-81), Asociacion Internacional de Hispanists, MLA, Assn. Hispanists Gt. Britain and Ireland, N.Am. Catalan Soc. (v.p. 1984-87, pres. 1987-90), Anglo Catalan Soc., Associacio Internacional de Llengua i Literatura Catalana. Roman Catholic. Office: U BC Dept Frnch Hispanic Ital Vancouver BC Canada V6T 1Z1 E-mail: arp@interchange.ubc.ca

PACHINO, BARTON P. lawyer; BA in Pol. Sci. magna cum laude, Duke U.; JD cum laude, Northwestern U. Law Sch. Assoc. corp. counsel KB Home, 1987-89, corp. counsel, 1989-91, v.p., 1991-93, sr. v.p., gen. counsel, 1993—. Bd. dirs. Bet Tzecek Legal Svcs., former chmn. corp. law dept. section Century City Bar Assn. Mem. Am. Bar Assoc., Ca. Bar Assoc., L.A. County Bar Assoc. Office: KB Home 10990 Wilshire Blvd Fl 7 Los Angeles CA 90024-3913 E-mail: bpachino@kbhome.com

PACHOLSKI, RICHARD FRANCIS, retired securities company executive, financial advisor, consultant; b. Seattle, June 18, 1947; s. Theodore Francis and Nellie (Tarabochia) P.; m. Dorothy Irene Nelson, May 25, 1974; children: Nicolas, Tara. BA cum laude, U. Wash., 1969, MBA summa cum laude, 1970. CPA, Wash. Mgr. Arthur Andersen & Co., Seattle, 1970-76; v.p., contr. SNW Enterprises, Seattle, 1976-82; sr. v.p., treas., sec., dir. Seattle N.W. Securities, 1982-93; cons. Carl & Co., Portland, Oreg., 1984-88, Ellis & Carl Inc., Portland, 1979-83; pres. R. Pacholski, P.C., Redmond, Wash., 1979—. Adj. prof. U. Wash., Seattle, 1976-80. Mem. AICPA, Nat. Assn. Securities Dealers (past bd. dirs. local dist.), Wash. Athletic Club, PacWest Club (Redmond, Wash.). Roman Catholic. Home and Office: 5060 164th Ct NE Redmond WA 98052-5294 E-mail: pacholski@prodigy.net

PACHON, HARRY PETER, politics educator; b. Miami, Fla., June 4, 1945; s. Juan and Rebeca (Perez) P.; children: Marc, Melissa, Nicholas. BA, Calif. State U., Los Angeles, 1967, MA, 1968; PhD, Claremont (Calif.) Grad. Sch., 1973. Adminstrv. aide U.S. Ho. of Reps., Washington, 1977-81; assoc. prof. CUNY, 1981-86; Kenan prof. politics Pitzer Coll., Claremont, 1987—. Pres. Tomas Rivera Ctr., 1993—; cons. Ford & Carnegie Founds., U.S. A.I.D. Co-author: Hispanics in the U.S., 1985, Americans by Choice, 1994; contbr. articles to profl. jours. NEH fellow, 1973-74, Nat. Assn. Schs. Pub. Affairs and Adminstrn. postdoctoral fellow, 1976-77. Mem. Am. Polit. Sci. Assn. (coun. fgn. rels.), Am. Soc. Pub. Adminstrs., Nat. Assn. Latino Elected and Appointed Ofcls. (chmn. edn. found.). Democrat. Home: 404 Damien Ave La Verne CA 91750-4104 Office: Scripps Coll Steele Hall Toms River Ctr Claremont CA 91711

PACK, RUSSELL T. theoretical chemist; b. Grace, Idaho, Nov. 20, 1937; s. John Terrell and Mardean (Izatt) P.; m. Marion Myrth Hassell, Aug. 21, 1962; children: John R., Nathan H., Allen H., Miriam, Elizabeth, Quinn R., Howard H. BS, Brigham Young U., 1962; PhD, U. Wis., 1967. Postdoctoral fellow U. Minn., Mpls., 1966-67; asst. prof. Brigham Young U., Provo, 1967-71, assoc. prof., 1971-75, adj. prof., 1975-88; staff scientist Los Alamos (N.Mex.) Nat. Lab., 1975-83, fellow, 1983—, assoc. grp. leader, 1979-81. Vis. prof. Max Planck Institut, Gottingen, 1981; chmn. Gordon Rsch. Conf., 1982; lectr. in field. Contbr. articles to profl. jours. Named Sr. U.S. Scientist, Alexander Vol Humboldt Found., 1981. Fellow Am. Phys. Soc. (sec.-treas. div. Chem. Physics 1990-93); mem. Am. Chem. Soc., Sigma Xi. Mem. Ch. of Jesus Christ of Latter Day Saints. Home: 240 Kimberly Ln Los Alamos NM 87544-3526 Office: Los Alamos Nat Lab T 12 Ms # B268 Los Alamos NM 87545-0001 E-mail: pack@lanl.gov

PACKARD, JULIE, aquarium administrator; d. David and Lucile P. Exec. dir. Monterey Bay Aquarium, Monterey, Calif., 1984—. Recipient Edward H. Bean Awd., Am. Assn. Zoological Parks and Aquariums, 1993. Office: Monterey Bay Aquarium 886 Cannery Row Monterey CA 93940-1023

PACKARD, RONALD C. former congressman; b. Meridian, Idaho, Jan. 19, 1931; m. Jean Sorenson, 1952; children: Chris, Debbie, Jeff, Vicki, Scott, Lisa, Theresa. Student, Brigham Young U., 1948-50, Portland State U., 1952-53; D.M.D., U. Oreg., Portland, 1953-57. Gen. practice dentistry, Carlsbad, Calif., 1959-82; mem. 98th-106th Congresses from 48th (formerly 43d) Calif. dist., 1983-2001; chmn. appropriations legis. com.; former mem. pub. works and transp. com., sci., space, tech.; also chmn. appropriations fgn. ops. and transp. subcoms. Mem. Carlsbad Sch. Dist. Bd., 1962-74; bd. dirs. Carlsbad C. of C., 1972-76; mem. Carlsbad Planning Commn., 1974-76, Carlsbad City Coun., 1976-78; Carlsbad chmn. Boy Scouts Am., 1977-79; mayor City of Carlsbad, 1978-82; mem. North County Armed Svcs. YMCA, North County Transit Dist., San Diego Assn. Govts., Coastal Policy Com., Transp. Policy Com.; pres. San Diego div. Calif. League of Cities. Served with Dental Corps USN, 1957-59. Republican. Mem. Ch. LDS.*

PADEREWSKI, SIR CLARENCE JOSEPH, architect; b. Cleve., July 23, 1908; BArch, U. Calif., 1932. Chief draftsman Sam W. Hamill, 1939-44; with Heitschmidt-Matcham-Blanchard-Gill & Hamill, 1943; prin. C.J. Paderewski, 1944-48; pres. Paderewski, Mitchell, Dean & Assoc., Inc. (and predecessor), San Diego, 1948-78. Instr. adult edn. San Diego city schs., 1939-44, U. Calif. extension div., 1945, 56; lectr. in field. Prin. works include Charactron Labs, Gen. Dynamics Corp., Convair, S.D., 1954, South Bay Elem. Schs., S.D., 1948-74; additions to El Cortez Hotel; including first exterior passenger glass elevator in the world and New Travolator Motor Hotel, S.D., 1959, Palomar Coll., San Marcos, 1951-80, San Diego County U. Gen. Hosp., San Diego Internat. Airport Terminal Bldgs., Fallbrook Elem. Schs., 1948-74, Silver Strand Elem. Sch., Coronado, Tourmaline Terrace Apt. Bldg., San Diego Salvation Army Office Bldg. Mem. adv. bd. Bayside Social Service Center, 1953-75, San Diego Polonia Newspaper, 1994—; mem. San Diego Urban Design Com.; adv. bd. Camp Oliver, 1963—, pres., 1975-76; bd. dirs. San Diego Symphony Orch. Assn., 1954-62, San Diego chpt. ARC, 1971-74; bd. dirs., chmn. comms., pres. San Diego Downtown [illegible] Archtl. Registration Bds., 1958-66, bd. dirs. other offices, 1961-64, pres., 1965-66, chmn. internat. relations com., 1967-68, Salvation Army, vice-chmn., 1989, life mem. adv. bd., 1993—, Copernicus Found., 1994—; mem. Calif. Bd. Archtl. Examiners, 1949-61, past pres., commr., 1961—; mem. Nat. Panel Arbitrators, 1953—, Nat. Council on Schoolhouse Constrn.; hon. chmn. Ignacy Jan Paderewski Meml. Com., 1991; adv. bd. S.D. Balboa Park Cmty. Endowment Fund, 1995—. Decorated Knight Order Polonia Restituta, Polish govt. in exile, 1982; recipient Award of Merit for San Diego County Gen. Hosp., San Diego chpt., AIA, 1961, Honor award for San Diego Internat. Airport Terminal, Honor award Portland Cement Co., Golden Trowel award Plastering Inst., 1958-60, 4 awards Masonry Inst., 1961, award Prestressed Concrete Inst., 1976, Outstanding Community Leadership award San Diego Downtown Assn., 1963-65, 80, Polish Engring. award for outstanding arch. and achievement, 2000, Gold award Engring. Soc., 2000, Outstanding INdividual Polish Am. award Polish Ctr. of L.A., 2001. Fellow AIA (pres. San Diego chpt. 1948, 49, bd. dirs. 1947-53, chmn. several coms., spl. award 1977, Calif. Coun. Spl. award 1979, Calif. Coun. Disting. Svc. award 1982, Lifetime Achievement award 2000); mem. San Diego C. of C. (bd. dirs. 1959-62, 64-67), Am. Arbitration Assn. (San Diego adv. coun. 1969—), Sister City Soc. (bd. dirs.), Lions (past pres. Hillcrest Club, Lion of Yr. 1990, fellow internat. found. 1991), Father Serra Club (charter, past pres.), Outboard Boating Club San Diego, Chi Alpha Kappa, Delta Sigma Chi. Home: 2837 Kalmia Pl San Diego CA 92104-5418

PAEZ, RICHARD A. federal judge; b. 1947; BA, Brigham Young U., 1969; JD, U. Calif., Berkeley, 1972. Staff atty. Calif. Rural Legal Assistance, Delano, Calif., 1972-74, Western Ctr. on Law and Poverty, 1974-76; sr. counsel, dir. litigation, acting exec. dir. Legal Aid Found. of L.A., 1976-81; judge L.A. Mcpl. Ct., 1981-94, U.S. Dist. Ct. (ctrl. dist.) Calif., L.A., 1994-2000, U.S. Dist. Ct. (9th cir.), Pasadena, Calif., 2000—. Active Hollywood-Los Feliz Jewish Cmty. Ctr. Mem. Calif. State Bar Assn., L.A. County Bar Assn., Mex.-Am. Bar Assn. L.A. County, Calif. Jud. Coun. Office: US Ct Appeals Edward R Roybal Ctr & Fed Bldg 125 S Grand AveRm 204 Pasadena CA 91105-1652*

PAFFENBARGER, RALPH SEAL, JR. epidemiologist, educator; b. Columbus, Ohio, Oct. 21, 1922; s. Ralph Seal and Viola Elizabeth (Link) P.; m. Mary Dale Higdon, Sept. 19, 1943 (dec.); children: Ralph, James (dec.), Ann, Charles, John (dec.), Timothy; m. Jo Ann Schroeder, July 20, 1991. AB, Ohio State U., 1944; MB, Northwestern U., 1946, MD, 1947; MPH, Johns Hopkins U., 1952, DrPH, 1954; ScD honoris causa, U. Laval, 1998. Intern Evanston (Ill.) Hosp., 1946-47; research asst. pediatrics La. State U. and Charity Hosp., New Orleans, 1949-50; practice medicine, specializing in geriatrics Framingham, Mass., 1960-68; clin. asst. prof. preventive medicine U. Cin., 1955-60; lectr. biostatistics Sch. Pub. Health, Harvard U., 1961-62, clin. assoc. preventive medicine Med. Sch., 1963-65, lectr. epidemiology Sch. Pub. Health, 1965-68, vis. lectr., 1968-83, vis. prof. epidemiology, 1983-85, vis. lectr., 1986-88, adj. prof. epidemiology, 1988—; prof. epidemiology in-residence U. Calif. Sch. Pub. Health, Berkeley, 1968-69, adj. prof., 1969-80; prof. epidemiology Stanford U., 1977-93, prof. emeritus, 1993—; rsch. epidemiologist U. Calif., Berkeley, 1993—. Commd. officer USPHS, 1947, med. dir., Atlanta, Ga., 1947-53, Bethesda, Md., 1953-55, Cin., 1955-60, Framingham, 1960-68, ret., 1968; mem. epidemiology and disease control study sect. NIH, 1972-76 Assoc. editor: Am. Jour. Epidemiology, 1972-75, 80-98, editor, 1975-79; contbr. articles to profl. publs. Founding mem. Internat. Olympic Com. Olympic Acad. Sport Scis., 1999. Recipient prize for Sports Scis. Internat. Olympic Com., 1996. Mem. AAAS, AMA, APHA, Am. Epidemiol. Soc., Am. Heart Assn., Internat. Epidemiol. Assn., Soc. Epidemiol. Rsch., Rsch. Soc. Am., Internat. Soc. Cardiology, Am. Assn. Suicidology, Marcé Soc., Am. Coll. Sports Medicine, Am. Acad. Sports Physicians, Nat. Fitness Leaders Assn., Royal Soc. Medicine, Phi Eta Sigma, Pi Kappa Epsilon, Delta Omega. Home: 892 Arlington Ave Berkeley CA 94707-1938 Office: Stanford U Sch Medicine Stanford CA 94305

PAGE, ALBERT LEE, soil science educator, researcher; b. New Lenox, Ill., Mar. 19, 1927; s. Thomas E. and Hattie O. (Pease) Pugh; m. Shirley L. Jessmore, Sept. 14, 1952; children— Nancy, Thomas BA in Chemistry, U. Calif.-Riverside, 1956; PhD in Soil Sci., U. Calif.-Davis, 1960. Prof. soil sci. U. Calif.-Riverside, 1960—. Dir. Kearney Found., Univ. Calif.-Riverside, program of excellence in energy research Editor: Methods of Soil Analysis, 1983, Utilization of Municipal Wastewater and Sludge on Land, 1983, Heavy Metals in the Environment, 1977 Served as QMQ1 USN, 1945-52 Recipient Environ. Quality Research award Am. Soc. Agronomy, 1984, Disting. Teaching award U. Calif., Riverside, 1976, Disting. Svc. award USDA, 1991; Fullbright scholar, 1966-67; Guggenheim Meml. Found. fellow, 1966-67 Fellow AAAS, Am. Soc. Agronomy, Soil Sci. Soc. Am.; mem. Internat. Soil Sci. Soc., Western Soil Sci. Soc., Soc. Environ. Geochemistry and Health, Sigma Xi. Home: 5555 Canyon Crest Dr Apt 1F Riverside CA 92507-6443 Office: U Calif Dept Soil & Environ Sci Riverside CA 92521-0001 E-mail: albert.page@ucr.edu

PAGE, LESLIE ANDREW, disinfectant manufacturing company executive; b. Mpls., June 5, 1924; s. Henry R. and Amelia Kathryn (Steinmetz) P.; m. DeEtte Abernethy Griswold, July 6, 1952 (div. Sept. 1975); children: Randolph, Michael, Kathryn, Caroline; m. Mary Ellen Decker, Nov. 26, 1976. BA, U. Minn., 1949; MA, U. Calif., Berkeley, 1953, PhD, 1956. Asst. microbiologist, lectr. U. Calif., Davis, 1956-61; cons. San Diego Zoological Soc. Zoo Hosp., 1957-60; microbiologist, research leader Nat. Animal Disease Ctr., USDA, Ames, Iowa, 1961-79; ret., 1979; specialist in Chlamydial nomenclature and disease; med. text cons. Bay St. Louis, Miss., 1979-85; founder, pres., chmn. bd. Steri-Derm Corp., San Marcos, Calif., 1987—. Cons. McCormick Distilling Co., Weston, Mo., 1994-95. Editor: Jour. Wildlife Diseases, 1965-68, Wildlife Diseases, 1976; contbr. chpts. to med. texts, over 70 articles to profl. jours.; patentee Liquid Antiseptic Composition, 1989. Pres. Garden Island Comty. Assn., Bay St. Louis, Miss., 1980-81; chief commr. East Hancock fire Protection Dist., Bay St. Louis, 1982-83; treas. Woodridge Escondido Property Owners Assn., 1986-88. Fellow Am. Acad. Microbiology (emeritus); mem. Wildlife Disease Assn. (pres. 1972-73, Disting. Svc. award 1980, Emeritus award 1984), Am. Soc. for Microbiology, Zool. Soc. San Diego, Sigma Xi, Phi Zeta (hon.). Home and Office: 1784 Deavers Dr San Marcos CA 92069-3359 E-mail: steriderm@hotmail.com, steriderm@home.com

PAGE, ROY CHRISTOPHER, periodontist, scientist, educator; b. Campobello, S.C., Feb. 7, 1932; s. Milton and Anny Mae (Eubanks) P. BA, Berea Coll., 1953; DDS, U. Md., 1957; PhD, U. Wash., 1967; ScD (hon.), Loyola U., Chgo., 1983. Cert. in periodontics. Pvt. practice periodontics, Seattle, 1963-98; asst. prof. U. Wash. Schs. Medicine and Dentistry, Seattle, 1967-70, prof., 1974—, Disting. prof. dentistry, 1996-98, dir. Ctr. Research in Oral Biology, 1976-96; dir. grad. edn. U. Wash. Sch. Dentistry, 1976-80, dir. rsch., 1976-94, dir. Regional Clin. Dental Rsch. Ctr., 1990—, assoc. dean rsch., 1994-2000. Vis. scientist MRC Labs., London, 1971-72; cons., lectr. in field; fellow Pierre Fauchard Acad. Author: Periodontal Disease, 1977, 2d edit., 1990, Periodontitis in Man and Other Animals, 1982. Recipient Gold Medal award U. Md., 1957; recipient Career Devel. award NIH, 1967-72, Disting. Alumnus award U. Wash. Sch. Dentistry, 2000. Fellow Internat. Coll. Dentists, Am. Coll. Dentists, Am. Acad. Periodontology (Gies award 1982, fellowship award 1989, spl. citation 1998); mem. ADA (Norton Rose award for clin. rsch. 1998), Am. Assn. [illegible] 1990-92, [illegible] award 2001), Am. Soc. Exptl. Pathology, Internat. Assn. Dental Rsch. (pres. 1987, basic periodontal rsch. award 1977). Home: 5583 171st Ave SE Bellevue WA 98006-5503 E-mail: roypage@u.washington.edu

PAGET, JOHN ARTHUR, mechanical engineer; b. Ft. Frances, Ont., Can., Sept. 15, 1922; s. John and Ethel (Bishop) P.; B. in Applied Sci., Toronto, 1946; m. Vicenta Herrera Nunez, Dec. 16, 1963; children: Cynthia Ellen, Kevin Arthur, Keith William. Chief draftsman Gutta Percha & Rubber, Ltd., Toronto, Ont., 1946-49; chief draftsman Viceroy Mfg. Co., Toronto, 1949-52; supr., design engr. C.D. Howe Co. Ltd., Montreal, Que., Can., 1952-58, sr. design engr. Combustion Engring., Montreal, 1958-59; sr. staff engr. Gen. Atomic, Inc., La Jolla, 1959-81. Mem. ASME, Soc. for History Tech., Inst. Mech. Engrs., Brit. Nuclear Energy Soc. Patentee in field. Home: 3183 Magellan St San Diego CA 92154-1515

PAGNI, ALBERT FRANK, lawyer; b. Reno, Jan. 28, 1935; s. Bruno and Daisy Rose (Recami) P.; m. Nancy Lynne Thomas, Aug. 12, 1961; children: Elisa, Michelle, Melissa, Michael. AB, U. Nev., 1961; JD, U. Calif.-Hastings Coll. Law, 1964. Bar: Nev. 1964. Assoc. Vargas, Dillon, Bartlett & Dixon, Reno, 1965-70; ptnr. Vargas & Bartlett and Jones Vargas, Reno, 1970—. Mem. adminstrv. council U. Nev., 1974-81; treas. U. Nev. Legis. Commn., 1973-74, pres., 1975; bd. dirs. Better Bus. Bur.; mem. Nev. Dist. Appeal Bd.; mem. hospice coun. St. Mary's Hosp. With U.S. Army, 1955-57. Recipient Outstanding Alumni award U. Nev., 1978. Fellow Am. Coll. Trial Lawyers (state chair), Nev. Law Found. (trustee, vice chair), Am. Inns Ct. (Master Bruce Thompson, Am. Bd. Trial Advs. (nat. bd.); mem. ABA, Washoe County Bar Assn., Nev. Trial Lawyers Assn., ATLA, Def. Research Inst., Assn. Def. Counsel Calif. and Nev. (no. state chmn. 1983-85), Am. Softball Found. (bd. dirs.), Am. Judicature Assn., State Bar Nev. (bd. govs. 1976-87, v.p. 1984-85, pres. elect 1985-86, pres. 1986-87), Order of Coif, Wolf Club, Elks. Office: 12th Fl 100 W Liberty St Fl 12 Reno NV 89501-1962

PAGNI, PATRICK JOHN, mechanical and fire safety engineering science educator; b. Chgo., Nov. 28, 1942; s. Frank and Helen P.; m. Carol DeSantis, Dec. 26, 1970 (div. Jan. 2000); children: Christina Marie, Catherine Ann, Patrick John Jr. B in Aeronautical Engring. magna cum laude, U. Detroit, 1965; SM, MIT, 1967, ME, 1969, PhD, 1970. Registered profl. mechanical engr., Calif., fire protection engr., Calif. Research asst. MIT, Cambridge, 1965-70; asst. prof. Mech. Engring. Dept. U. Calif., Berkeley, 1970-76, assoc. prof., 1976-81, prof., 1981—, vice chmn. grad. study, 1986-89; acting assoc. dean Coll. Engring. U. Calif., 1990; assoc. faculty scientist Lawrence Berkeley Lab., 1976—. Vis. scientist Factory Mut. Research Corp., Norwood, Mass., 1980; cons. on fire safety sci. various orgns., 1972—; affiliate prof. fire protection engring. dept. Worcester Poly. Inst., 2000—; vis. rsch. scholar U. Ulster, No. Ireland, 2000—. Editor: Fire Science for Fire Safety, 1984, Fire Safety Science--Procs. of the First Internat. Symposium, 1986, Procs. of the Second Internat. Symposium, 1989; contbr. articles to profl. jours. Grantee NSF, NASA, Nat. Bur. Standards, Nat. Inst. Standards and Tech., 1971—; Applied Mechanics fellow Harvard U., 1974, 77; Pullman Found. scholar, 1960. Mem. ASME, Am. Phys. Soc. (life), Combustion Inst., Soc. Fire Protection Engrs. (Bono award for best paper 1999), Internat. Assn. Fire Safety Sci. (vice chmn., exec. com., chmn. program com.), Tau Beta Pi, Pi Tau Sigma, Alpha Sigma Nu. Democrat. Roman Catholic. Home: 1901 Ascot Dr Moraga CA 94556-1412 Office: U Calif Coll Engring Mech Engring Dept Berkeley CA 94720-1740 E-mail: pjpagni@me.berkeley.edu

PAGTER, CARL RICHARD, lawyer; b. Balt., Feb. 13, 1934; s. Charles Ralph and Mina (Amelung) P.; m. Judith Elaine Cox, May 6, 1978; 1 child by previous marriage: Corbin Christopher. AA, Diablo Valley Coll., 1953; BA, San Jose State U., 1955; LLB, U. Calif., Berkeley, 1964. Bar:Calif. 1965, D.C. 1977, U.S. Supreme Ct. 1976. Law clk. Kaiser Industries Corp., Oakland, Calif., 1963-64, counsel, 1964-70, assoc. counsel Washington, 1970-73, counsel Oakland, Calif., 1973-75, dir. govt. affairs Washington, 1975-76; v.p., sec., gen. counsel Kaiser Cement Corp., Oakland, Calif., 1976-88, cons., gen. counsel San Ramon, 1988-98, cons., 1998—. Author: (with A. Dundes) Urban Folklore from the Paperwork Empire, 1975, More Urban Folklore from the Paperwork Empire, 1987, Never Try to Teach a Pig to Sing, 1991, Sometimes the Dragon Wins, 1996, Why Don't Sheep Shrink When It Rains, 2000. With USNR, 1957-61, to comdr., 1978. Mem. ABA, Calif. Bar, Am. Folklore Soc., Calif. Folklore Soc., Calif. Bluegrass Assn. (founder), Mariners Square Athletic Club, Univ. Club. Republican. Home and Office: 17 Julianne Ct Walnut Creek CA 94595-2610

PAINE, DAVID M. public relations executive; b. N.Y.C., Sept. 25, 1956; BA in Polit. Sci., Union Coll., 1979. Press advanceman The White House, Washington, 1980; with N.Y. State Assembly Judiciary Com.; acct. exec. Burson-Marsteller, N.Y.C.; founder, pres. Paine & Assocs., Costa Mesa, Calif., 1986—. Mem. Pub. Rels. Soc. Am. Office: Paine & Assocs 535 Anton Blvd Ste 450 Costa Mesa CA 92626-7688

PAISLEY, CHRISTOPHER B. business educator; B in Econ., U. Calif., Santa Barbara; MBA, UCLA. Various acctg. and fin. positions Hewlett Packard Co.; v.p. fin. Ridge Computers, 1982-85; v.p. fin., CFO, 3Com Corp., Santa Clara, Calif., 1985-2000; prof. Santa Clara (Calif.) U. Leavey Sch. Bus., 2000—. Bd. dirs. Applied Digital Access, Inc., DisCopy, ShareData. Mem. Fin. Execs. Inst. Office: Santa Clara U Leavey Sch Bus 500 El Camino Real Santa Clara CA 95053

PAKE, GEORGE EDWARD, research executive, physicist; b. Jeffersonville, Ohio, Apr. 1, 1924; s. Edward Howe and Mary Mabel (Fry) P.; m. Marjorie Elizabeth Semon, May 31, 1947; children— Warren E., Catherine E., Stephen G., Bruce E. B.S., M.S., Carnegie Inst. Tech., 1945; Ph.D., Harvard U., 1948. Physicist Westinghouse Research Labs., 1945-46; mem. faculty Washington U., St. Louis, 1948-56, 62-70, prof. physics, provost, 1962-69, exec. vice chancellor, 1965-69, Edward Mallinckrodt prof. physics, 1969-70; v.p. Xerox Corp.; mgr. Xerox Palo Alto (Calif.) Research Center, 1970-78, v.p. corp. research, 1978-83, group v.p., 1983-86; dir. Inst. for Research on Learning, Palo Alto, Calif., 1987-91, dir. emeritus, 1991—. Prof. physics Stanford U., 1956-62 Author: (with E. Feenberg) Quantum Theory of Angular Momentum, 1953, Paramagnetic Resonance, 1962, (with T. Estle) The Physical Principles of Electron Paramagnetic Resonance, 1973. Mem. gov. bd. Am. Inst. Physics, 1957-59; bd. dirs. St. Louis Research Council, 1964-70; mem. physics adv. panel NSF, 1958-60, 63-66; chmn. physics survey com. Nat. Acad. Sci.-NRC, 1964-66; Mem. St. Louis County Bus. and Indl. Devel. Commn., 1963-66; chmn. bd. Regional Indsl. Devel. Corp., St. Louis, 1966-67, St. Louis Research Council, 1967-70; mem. President's Sci. Adv. Com., 1965-69; Bd. dirs. St. Louis Country Day Sch., 1964-70, Central Inst. for Deaf, 1965-70; trustee Washington U., 1970— , Danforth Found., 1971-99, U. Rochester, 1982— ; trustee Ctr. for Advanced Study in Behavioral Scis., Palo Alto, 1986-92, The Exploratorium, San Francisco, 1987-98; bd. overseers Superconducting Super Collider, Univs. Rsch. Assn., 1984-89. Recipient Nat. Medal Science, 1987. Fellow Am. Phys. Soc. (pres. 1977); mem. Am. Assn. Physics Tchrs., AAUP, AAAS, Am. Acad. Arts and Scis., Nat. Acad. Sci., Sigma Xi, Tau Beta Pi. Office: Xerox Palo Alto Rsch Ctr 3333 Coyote Hill Rd Palo Alto CA 94304-1314

PAKULA, ANITA SUSAN, dermatologist; b. L.A., Nov. 20, 1961; BA, Pomona Coll., 1983; BS, Calif. Luth. Coll., 1985; MD, U. Calif., Irvine, 1988. Diplomat Am. Bd. Dermatology, NAt. Bd. Med. Examiners. Intern Evanston (Ill.) Hosp., 1988-89; resident Northwestern U. Med. Sch., Chgo., 1989-93; asst. clin. prof. dermatology UCLA MEd. Ctr., 1993—, Presenter in field. Contbr. articles to profl. jours. Fellow Am. Acad. Dermatology; mem. Soc. Pediatric Dermatology. Office: 3180 Willow Ln Ste 200 Westlake Vlg CA 91361 [illegible]

PAL, PRATAPADITYA, curator; b. Bangladesh, Sept. 1, 1935; came to U.S., 1967; s. Gopesh Chandra and Bidyut Kana (Dam) P.; m. Chitralekha Bose, Apr. 20, 1968; children— Shalmali, Lopamudra. M.A., U. Calcutta, 1958, D.Phil., 1962; Ph.D. (U. K. Commonwealth Scholar), U. Cambridge, Eng., 1965. Research assoc. Am. Acad. of Benares, India, 1966-67; keeper Indian collections Mus. Fine Arts, Boston, 1967-69; sr. curator Indian and Southeast Asian art Los Angeles County Mus. Art, L.A., 1970-95, acting dir., 1979; vis. curator Indian and S.E. Asian art Art Inst. Chgo., 1995—; cons. curator Norton Simon Mus., Pasadena, Calif., 1995—. Adj. prof. fine arts U. So. Calif., 1971-89; vis. prof. U. Calif., Santa Barbara, 1980, Irvine, 1994-95; William Cohn lectr. Oxford U., 1983; Catherine Mead meml. lectr. Pierpont Morgan Libr., N.Y.C., 1986; Ananda K. Coomaraswamy meml. lectr. Prince of Wales Mus., Bombay, 1987; D.J. Sibley prehistoric art lectr. U. Tex., Austin, 1989; Anthony Gardner meml. lectr. Victoria and Albert Mus., London, 1993, keynote spkr. 1st Internat. Conf. on Tibetan Art, 1994; mem. commr.'s art adv. panel IRS, Washington, 1986-96. Author: The Arts of Nepal, vol. 1, 1974, vol. 2, 1979, The Sensuous Immortals, 1977, The Ideal Image: Gupta Sculptures and its Influence, 1978, The Classical Tradition in Rajput Painting, 1978, Elephants and Ivories, 1981, A Buddhist Paradise: Murals of Alchi, 1982, Art of Tibet, 1983, Tibetan Painting, 1984, Art of Nepal, 1985, From Merchants to Emperors, 1986, Indian Sculpture, vol. 1, 1986, Icons of Piety, Images of Whimsey, 1987, Indian Sculpture, vol. 2, 1988, Buddhist Book Illuminations, 1988, Romance of the Taj Mahal, 1989, Art of the Himalayas, 1991, Pleasure Gardens of the Mind, 1993; Indian Painting, vol. 1, 1993, The Peaceful Liberators: Jain Art from India, 1994, On the Path to Void, 1996, A Collecting Odyssey, 1997, Divine Images, Human Visions, 1997, Tibet Change and Tradition, 1997, Desire and Devotion, 2001; gen. editor: Marg mag., 1993—. Bd. dirs. Music Circle, Pasadena, Calif. John D. Rockefeller III Fund fellow, 1964, 69, fellow NEA, 1974; Getty scholar, 1995-96. Fellow Asia Soc. (Bombay, hon.); mem. Asiatic Soc. (Calcutta, B.C. Law gold medal 1993).

PALACIO, JUNE ROSE PAYNE, nutritional science educator; b. Hove, Sussex, Eng., June 14, 1940; came to U.S., 1949; d. Alfred and Doris Winifred (Payne) P.; m. Moki Moses Palacio, Nov. 30, 1968. AA, Orange Coast Coll., Costa Mesa, Calif., 1960; BS, U. Calif., Berkeley, 1963; PhD, Kans. State U., 1984. Registered dietitian. Asst. dir. food svc. and res. halls Mills Coll., Oakland, Calif., 1964-66; staff dietitian Servomation Bay Cities, Oakland, 1966-67; commissary mgr. Host Internat., Inc., Honolulu, 1967-73; dir. dietetics Straub Clinic and Hosp., Honolulu, 1973-80; instr. Kans. State U., Manhattan, 1980-84; prof. and program dir. Calif. State U., L.A., 1984-85; prof., asst. dean Pepperdine U., Malibu, Calif., 1985—. Instr. Kapiolani Community Coll., Honolulu, 1973-79, U. Hawaii, Honolulu, 1975-80, Ctr. for Dietetic Edn., Woodland Hills, Calif., 1986—; cons. Clevenger Nutritional Svcs., Calabasas, Calif., 1985—, Calif. Mus. Sci. and Industry, L.A., 1989—, Calif. State Dept. Edn., Sacramento, Calif., 1985—. Author: Foodservice in Institutions, 1988, Introduction to Foodservice, 1992, 97, 2001, The Profession of Dietetics, 1996, 2000. Mem. Am. Dietetic Assn. (del. 1977-80, 86-89, commr. Commn. for Accreditation of Dietic Edn. 1997—), Calif. Dietetic Assn. (pres. 1992-93), L.A. Dist. Dietetic Assn., Foodsvc. Systems Mgmt. Edn. Coun., Dietetic Educators of Practitioners, Gamma Sigma Delta, Omicron Nu, Phi Upsilon Omicron. Republican. Episcopalian. Avocations: tennis, running, reading, traveling. Home: 24319 Baxter Dr Malibu CA 90265-4728 Office: Pepperdine U 24255 Pacific Coast Hwy Malibu CA 90263-0002 E-mail: june.palacio@pepperdine.edu

PALADE, GEORGE EMIL, biologist, educator; b. Jassy, Romania, Nov. 19, 1912; came to U.S., 1946, naturalized, 1952; s. Emil and Constanta (Cantemir) P.; m. Irina Malaxa, June 12, 1941 (dec. 1969); children— Georgia Teodora, Philip Theodore; m. Marilyn G. Farquhar, 1970. Bachelor, Hasdeu Lyceum, Buzau, Romania; M.D., U. Bucharest, Romania. Instr., asst. prof., then assoc. prof. anatomy Sch. Medicine, U. Bucharest, 1935-45; vis. investigator, asst. assoc., prof. cell biology Rockefeller U., 1946-73; prof. cell biology Yale U., New Haven, 1973-83, sr. research scientist, 1983-89; prof.-in-residence, dean sci. affairs Med. Sch., U. Calif., San Diego, 1990—. Author sci. papers. Recipient Albert Lasker Basic Research award, 1966, Gairdner Spl. award, 1967, Horwitz prize, 1970, Nobel prize in Physiology or Medicine, 1974, Nat. Medal Sci., 1986. Fellow Am. Acad. Arts and Scis.; mem. Nat. Acad. Sci., Pontifical Acad. Sci., Royal Soc. (London), Leopoldina Acad. (Halle), Romanian Acad., Royal Belgian Acad. Medicine. Achievements include discovery by electon microscopy of new structural elements in eukaryotic cells, correlated morphological and biochemical studies by cell fractionation of subcellular components, elucidation of the secretory, exocytic pathway and studies on membrane biogenesis and regulation of proteins and membrane traffic in animal eukaryotic cells.

PALAU, LUIS, evangelist; b. Ingeniero-Maschwitz, Argentina, Nov. 27, 1934; came to the U.S., 1960; s. Luis and Matilde Palau; m. Patricia M. Scofield, Aug. 5, 1961; children: Kevin, Keith, Andrew, Stephen. BA, St. Alban's Coll.; DD, Talbot Theol. Sem., 1977, Wheaton Coll., 1985, George Fox Coll., 1993. Missionary-evangelist Overseas Crusades Internat., 1961-66, pres., 1976-78; evangelist Luis Palau Evangelistic Team, 1967-76; pres., evangelist Luis Palau Evangelistic Assn., Portland, Oreg., 1978—. Author: Say Yes!, 1991, Healthy Habits for Spiritual Growth, 1994, Calling America and the Nations to Christ, 1994. Avocations: church history, theology. Office: Luis Palau Evangelistic Assn 1500 NW 167th Pl Beaverton OR 97006-7342

PALLOTTI, MARIANNE MARGUERITE, foundation administrator; b. Hartford, Conn., Apr. 23, 1937; d. Rocco D. and Marguerite (Long) P. BA, NYU, 1968, MA, 1972. Asst. to pres. Wilson, Haight & Welch, Hartford, 1964-65; exec. asst. Ford Found., N.Y.C., 1965-77; corp. sec. Hewlett Found., Menlo Park, Calif., 1977-84, v.p., 1985—. Bd. dirs. N.Y. Theatre Ballet, N.Y.C., 1986-98, Austin Montessori Sch., 1993, Djerassi Resident Artists Program, 1998—, Mexican Mus., 1999—; mem. women's adv. com., nat. coun.World Wildlife Fund, 1997—; mem. program com. Ind. Sector, Washington, 1998—. Mem. Women in Founds., No. Calif. Grantmakers. Office: William & Flora Hewlett Found 525 Middlefield Rd Ste 200 Menlo Park CA 94025-3448

PALM, CHARLES GILMAN, university official; b. Havre, Mont., Apr. 25, 1944; s. Victor F. and Laura (McKinnie) P.; m. Miriam Willits, Sept. 15, 1968. AB, Stanford U., 1966; MA, U. Wyo., 1967; MLS, U. Oreg., 1970. Asst. archivist Hoover Instn., Stanford (Calif.) U., 1971-74, dep. archivist, 1974-84, archivist, 1984-87, head libr., 1986-87, assoc. dir., 1987-90; dep. dir. Stanford U., Palo Alto, Calif., 1990—. Co-author: Guide to Hoover Institution Archives, 1980, Herbert Hoover, Register of His Papers in the Hoover Institution Archives, 1983; mem. editl. bd. Internat. Democracy Found., Moscow. Mem. Calif. Heritage Preservation Commn., Sacramento, 1988—, vice chmn., 1993-97, chmn., 1997—; mem. Nat. Hist. Records and Publs. Commn., Washington, 1990-96; mem. history & edn. ctr. adv. bd. ARC, 1994—; trustee Golden State Mus. Corp., 1997—. Fellow Soc. Am. Archivists; mem. Soc. Calif. Archivists (pres. 1983-84), Bohemian Club. Republican. Office: Hoover Instn Stanford CA 94305

PALM, GERALD ALBERT, lawyer; b. Seattle, Nov. 4, 1942; s. Albert Nels and Gladys Elizabeth (Danberg) P.; m. Nancy Lee Himes, Dec. 6, 1969; children: Jason E., Kimberly A. BA, Dartmouth Coll., 1964; LLB, Harvard U., 1967. Bar: Wash. 1967, U.S. Dist. Ct. (we. dist.) Wash. 1967, U.S. Ct. Appeals (9th cir.) 1981, U.S. Dist. Ct. (ea. dist.) Wash. 1982. Assoc. Jones, Grey, Bayley, Kehoe, Hooper & Olsen, Seattle, 1967-68, Williams, Kastner and Gibbs, Seattle, 1968-74, ptnr., 1974-95; sole practitioner Seattle, 1995—. Youth basketball coach Jewish Community Ctr., Mercer Island, Wash., 1984-88; deacon, youth commn. Mercer Island Covenant Ch., 1988-95; bd. dirs. Nordic Heritage Mus., 1998-2000, Mercer Island Kiwanis, 1982-92, pres. 1986. Mem. FBA, Am. Bd. Trial Advocates (pres. Wash. chpt. 1989), Def. Rsch. Inst., Wash. Def. Trial Lawyers Assn. (trustee 1971), Wash. State Bar Assn., King County Bar Assn., Dartmouth Lawyers Assn., Mercer Island Country Club (trustee 1991-94, pres. 1993-94), Wash. Athletic Club, Swedish Am. C. of C. (sec. bd. dirs. 1994—). Republican. Mem. Covenant Ch. Avocations: tennis, water skiing, snow skiing, running, attending musicals and theatre. Home: 7400 E Mercer Way Mercer Island WA 98040-5819 Office: Washington Mut Tower 1201 3rd Ave Ste 2830 Seattle WA 98101-3029 E-mail: the-palms@msn.com

PALMA, JACK D. lawyer; b. N.Y.C., Sept. 15, 1946; BA, Allegheny Coll., 1968; JD with honors, U. Denver, 1974. Bar: Colo. 1975, Wyo. 1976. Ptnr. Holland & Hart, Cheyenne, Wyo., 1984—. Mem. ABA, Colo. Bar Assn., Wyo. State Bar, Order St. Ives. Office: Holland & Hart PO Box 1347 Cheyenne WY 82003-1347

PALMATIER, MALCOLM ARTHUR, editor, consultant; b. Kalamazoo, Nov. 11, 1922; s. Karl Ernest and Cecile Caroline (Chase) P.; m. Mary Elizabeth Summerfield, June 16, 1948 (dec. Oct. 1982); children: Barnabus, Timothy K., Duncan M.; m. Marie-Anne Suzanne van Werveke, Jan. 12, 1985. BS in Math., Western Mich. U., 1945; MA in English, UCLA, 1947; MA in Econs., U. So. Calif., 1971. Instr. English Pomona Coll., Claremont, Calif., 1949-51; editor Naval Ordnance Test Sta., Pasadena, 1951-54; head editl. unit Rocketdyne, L.A., 1954-55; editor The RAND Corp., Santa Monica, Calif., 1955-87, cons. editor, 1987—. Instr. English UCLA, L.A., summer 1950. Mng. editor, cons. editor Jour.: Studies in Comparative Communism, L.A., 1968-80; co-editor Perspectives in Economics, 1971; contbr. chpts. to book, book revs. and articles to profl. jours. Chmn. bd. New Start, West L.A., 1982-84. With USNR, 1943-45. Mem. Jonathan Club. Avocations: music, travel. Home: 516 Avondale Ave Los Angeles CA 90049-4804 Office: The RAND Corp 1700 Main St Santa Monica CA 90407-2138 E-mail: Malcolm_Palmatier@rand.org

PALMER, BEVERLY BLAZEY, psychologist, educator; b. Cleve., Nov. 22, 1945; d. Lawrence E. and Mildred M. Blazey; m. Richard C. Palmer, June 24, 1967; 1 child, Ryan Richard. PhD in Counseling Psychology, Ohio State U., 1972. Lic. clinical psychologist, Calif. Adminstrv. assoc. Ohio State U., Columbus, 1969-70; rsch. psychologist Health Svcs. Rsch. Ctr. UCLA, 1971-77; commr. pub. health L.A. County, 1978-81; pvt. practice clin. psychology Torrance, Calif., 1985—; prof. psychology Calif. State U., Dominguez Hills, 1973—. Reviewer manuscripts for numerous textbook pubs; contbr. numerous articles to profl. jours. Recipient Proclamation County of L.A., 1972, Proclamation County of L.A., 1981. Mem. Am. Psychol. Assn. Office: Calif State U Dominguez Hills Dept Psychology Hls Carson CA 90747-0001

PALMER, DAVID GILBERT, lawyer; b. Lakewood, N.J., Jan. 10, 1945; s. Robert Dayton and Lois (Gilbert) P.; m. Susan Edmundson Walsh, Aug. 17, 1968; children: Jonathan, Megan. AB, Johns Hopkins U., 1967; JD, U. Colo., 1970. Bar: Colo. 1970, U.S. Dist. Ct. Colo. 1970, U.S. Ct. Appeals (9th and 10th cirs.) 1970, U.S. Supreme Ct. 1970. Ptnr., chmn. litigation dept. Holland & Hart, Denver, 1970-87, Gibson, Dunn & Crutcher, Denver, 1987-97; ptnr. Zevnik, Horton, Palmer, Denver, 1997-2001, Greenberg Taurig LLP, Denver, 2001—. Chmn. N.W. region Am. Heart Assn., Dallas, 1986—, bd. dirs., 1986—, sec., 1990—, nat. chmn., 1992-93; pres., bd. dirs. Colo. Heart Assn., Denver, 1974; bd. dirs. C.H. Kempe Nat. Ctr. for Prevention of Child Abuse, Denver, 1984-90, pres., 1989-90; bd. dirs. Goodwill Industries, Denver, 1981-84. Mem. ABA, Colo. Bar Assn., Denver Law Club, Univ. Club, Mile High Club. E-mial. Home: 3120 Ramshorn Dr Castle Rock CO 80104-9073 Office: Greenberg Taurig 1200 17th St Ste 2400 Denver CO 80202 E-mail: palmerdg@gtlaw.com

PALMER, DOUGLAS S., JR. lawyer; b. Peoria, Ill., Mar. 15, 1945; AB cum laude, Yale U., 1966; JD cum laude, Harvard U., 1969. Bar: Wash. 1969. Mem. Foster Pepper & Shefelman PLLC, Seattle, 1975—. Office: Foster Pepper & Shefelman PLLC 1111 3rd Ave Ste 3400 Seattle WA 98101-3299

PALMER, EARL A. ophthalmologist, educator; b. Winchester, Ohio, July 2, 1940; m. Carolyn Mary Clark; children: Andrea, Aaron, Genevieve. BA, Ohio State U., 1962; MD, Duke U., 1966. Diplomate Am. Bd. Pediatrics, Am. Bd. Ophthalmology. Resident in pediatrics U. Colo. Med. Ctr., Denver, 1966-68; resident in ophthalmology Oreg. Health Scis. U., Portland, 1971-74; fellow Baylor Coll. Medicine, Houston, 1974-75; asst. prof. Pa. State U., Hershey, 1975-79; prof. Oreg. Health Scis. U., 1979—. Chmn. Multicenter Outcome Study of Retinopathy of Prematurity; eye alignment specialist. Contbr. articles to profl. jours. Fellow: Am. Acad. Ophthalmology Honor award; mem.: Am. Assn. Pediatric Ophthalmology and Strabismus (pres. 1996—97). Avocation: golf. Office: Casey Eye Inst 3375 SW Terwilliger Blvd Portland OR 97201-4197

PALMER, GARY ANDREW, portfolio manager; b. Stamford, Conn., Dec. 30, 1953; s. Andrew and Edna Balz (Brogan) P.; m. Suzanne Branyon, Oct. 10, 1981; children: Gregory Allen, Kimberly Lynn. BS in Bus. Adminstrn., U. Vt., 1977; MBA, U. N.C., 1979. Sr. fin. analyst Carolina Power and Light Co., Raleigh, N.C., 1979-80; dir. fin. planning and analysis Fed. Home Loan Mortgage Corp., Washington, 1980-85; sr. v.p. capital markets Imperial Corp. of Am., San Diego, 1985-90; sr. v.p., treas. Pacific 1st Fin. Corp., Seattle, 1990-92, Gentral Capital Corp., Seattle, 1993-95; CFO So. Pacific Funding Corp., Lake Oswego, Oreg., 1995-97; pvt. practice Lake Oswego, 1998-99; CFO FiNet.com, Inc., San Ramon, Calif., 1999-2000; exec. v.p. Capital Mkts., LoanCity.com, San Jose, 2001—.

PALMER, JAMES DANIEL, protective services official; b. Oklahoma City, Aug. 11, 1936; s. Athol Ford and Marjorie Lorraine (Ward) P.; m. Gail Dorothy Myers, June 1954 (div. Sept. 1956); 1 child, James Douglas; m. Gloria Jean West, Dec. 14, 1963; children: Diana Lorraine, Elana Louise, Sheri Francis. AB in Police Sci. with honors, San Jose (Calif.) State U., 1963, AB in Psychology, 1964; MPA, Golden Gate U., 1972. Cert. Calif. police officers standards and tng. Asst. foreman Hunts Foods, Inc., Hayward, Calif., 1959-64; spl. investigator Dept. A.B.C. State of Calif., Oakland, 1964-67; criminal inspector Contra Costa County Dist. Atty., Martinez, Calif., 1967-72, lt. of inspectors, 1972-92; ret., 1992. Pres. Contra Costa County Peace Officers, Richmond, 1974-75; past v.p. Contra Costa County Dist. Atty's Inv. Assn., Martinez, 1971, tng. officer, 1990-92. Contbr. articles to profl. jours. Past pres. South Hayward (Calif.) Dem. Club, 1976, 77, San Leandro (Calif.) Dems., 1975; mem. Gov's Law Enforcement Adv. Commn., Sacramento, Calif., 1972-76, Calif. Dem. Coun., 1972-73; rev. Am. Fellowship Protestant Ch., 1990—, min., 1990—. With USAF, 1955-58. Avocations: stocks, bonds, real estate, family, church. Home: 2788 Sydney Way Castro Valley CA 94546-2738

PALMER, JERRY PHILIP, medical educator, researcher, internist; b. N.Y.C., Apr. 5, 1944; BA in Biology, SUNY, 1966; MD cum laude, Upstate Med. Ctr., Syracuse, N.Y., 1970. Diplomate Am. Bd. Internal Medicine, Am. Bd. Endocrinology and Metabolism. Intern Dartmouth Affiliated Hosps., Hanover, N.H., 1970-71, resident, 1971-72; sr. rsch. fellow divsn. endocrinology dept. medicine U. Wash., Seattle, 1972-74, acting instr. dept. medicine, 1974-75, dir. adminstrn. core diabetes endocrinology ctr., 1975—, dir. clin. rsch. core diabetes endocrinology rsch. ctr., 1975-88, 91—, acting asst. prof. dept. medicine, 1975-77, asst. prof. dept. medicine, 1977-80, dep. dir. diabetes endocrinology rsch. ctr., 1977-96, assoc. prof. dept. medicine, 1980-86, prof. dept. medicine, 1986—, dir. Diabetes Endorcinology Rsch. Ctr., 1996—; assoc. med. staff Univ. Hosp., Seattle, 1975—; attending physician Seattle Pub. Health Hosp., 1975-82, Pacific Med. Ctr., Seattle, 1982-89; mem. med. staff Providence Med. Ctr., Seattle, 1988-89, VA Med. Ctr., Seattle, 1989—; chief divsn. endocrinology, metabolism and nutrition Seattle VA Med. Ctr., 1989—; dir. diabetes care ctr. U. Wash. Med. Ctr., 1991—. Pfizer vis. prof. U. Tex., Houston, 1996. Assoc. editor: Diabetes, 1984, 85, 86. Mem. Am. Diabetes Assn. (Wash. affiliate bd. dirs. 1975-83, Wash. affiliate v.p. 1976, 77, Wash. affiliate chmn. peer rev. com. 1984, 85, 86, mem. rsch. com. 1985, 86, 87, 88, ad hoc expert com. on immunotherapy of IDDM 1990, chmn. task force on profl. membership 1991-92, mem. publs. policy com. 1993-95, bd. dirs. 1994-96, mem. scientific and med. meetings oversight com. 1995—, clin. rsch. grant 1996), Am. Fedn. for Clin. Rsch., Am. Soc. for Clin. Investigation, Endocrine Soc., King County Med., Assn. Am. Physicians, We. Assn. Physicians, We. Soc. for Clin. Rsch., Immunology Diabetes Soc. (pres. 1994-95), Alpha Omega Alpha. Office: VA Puget Sound Healthcare Sys 1660 S Columbian Way Seattle WA 98108-1532

PALMER, ROBERT, state official; b. Colo. m. Linda Haywood, Jan. 1987; 1 child, Ross. BS in Internat. Bus. and Mktg., U. Colo., 1981. With an oil and gas svc. co., 1981-83; intern Nat. Ctr. for Initiative Rev., 1983-84; press and comms. asst. Colo. State Senate, 1984-90; chief of staff Rep. Wayne Allard U.S. Ho. of Reps., Washington, 1991-96; chief of staff Senator Wayne Allard U.S. Senate, Colo., 1996-98; chief of staff Gov. of Colo., 1998—. Office: State Colo 125 State Capitol Denver CO 80203

PALMER, ROBERT ARTHUR, private investigator; b. St. Augustine, Fla., May 20, 1948; m. Christine Lynn Creger, May 14, 1974. AA, Glendale C.C., 1975; BS, U. Phoenix, 1981; MA, Prescott Coll., 1993; PhD, Union Inst., 1999. Lic. pvt. investigator, Ariz.; bd. cert. forensic examiner. Dep. sheriff Maricopa County Sheriff's Office, Phoenix, 1971-79; owner Palmer Investigative Svcs., Prescott, Ariz., 1980-90; pres. The Magnum Corp., Prescott, 1990—. V.p. Mountain Club Homeowners, Prescott, 1986—. Mem. Internat. Assn. Chem. Testing, World Assn. Detectives, Nat. Assn. Legal Investigators, Nat. Assn. Profl. Process Servers, Am. Coll. Forensic Examiners, Ariz. Assn. Lic. Pvt. Investigators (pres. 1984), Ariz. Process Servers Assn. (pres. 1985-86), Prescott C. of C. (v.p. 1987-90). Avocations: photography, collecting western art. Office: Palmer Investigative Svcs PO Box 10760 Prescott AZ 86304-0760

PALMER, ROBERT BRIAN, physicist; b. London, Feb. 28, 1934; s. Reginald William and Beatrice M. (Carter) P.; m. Magdalena Wipf, Dec. 29, 1961; children: Susannah, Malcolm. BS, Imperial Coll., London, 1956, PhD, 1959. Research assoc. Imperial Coll., 1959-60; physicist Brookhaven Nat. Lab., Upton, N.Y., 1960—, assoc. dir. for high energy physics, 1983-86; physicist Stanford (Calif.) Linear Accelerator Corp., 1987—. Mem. high energy physics adv. panel Dept. Energy, Washington, 1983-86. 2 Patents in field; contbr. 71 articles on particle and accelerator physics. Mem. Am. Phys. Soc. (div. particles and fields). Democrat. Avocations: sailing, skiing, climbing. Office: Stanford Linear Accelerator Corp Sand Hill Walk Rd # 4349 Palo Alto CA 94304 also: Brookhaven Nat Lab Physics Dept Bldg 901A PO Box 5000 Upton NY 11973-5000 also: IRT Corp 6020 Cornerstone Ct W Ste 300 San Diego CA 92121-3707

PALMER, ROBERT L. lawyer; b. Bryn Mawr, Pa., Aug. 15, 1946; BA, Georgetown U., 1968; JD, Columbia U., 1971. Bar: D.C. 1972, Ariz. 1976. Law clerk to Hon. Harold Leventhal U.S. Ct. Appeals (D.C. cir.), 1971-72; with Covington & Burling, Washington, 1972-73, 75; asst. spec. prosecuter Watergate spec. prosecution force U.S. Dept. Justice, 1973-74; mem. Meyer, Hendricks, Victor, Osborn & Maledon, Phoenix, 1976-95, Hennigan, Mercer & Bennett (name now Hennigan, Bennett & Dorman), L.A., 1995—. Adj. prof. law U. Ariz., 1983.; bd. dirs. Ariz. Ctr. for Law in Pub. Interest, 1990-96, pres., 1990-92. Notes and comments editor Columbia Law Rev., 1970-71. Mem. ABA (assoc. editor litigation jour. sect. litigation 1979-82). Office: Hennigan Bennett & Dorman 601 S Figueroa St Ste 3300 Los Angeles CA 90017-5708

PALMER, SAMUEL COPELAND, III, lawyer; b. Phila., June 9, 1934; s. Samuel Copeland Jr. and Vivian Gertrude (Plumb) P.; divorced; children: Samuel C. IV, Sarah Anne, Bryan Douglas. Grad., Harvard Sch., Los Angeles, 1952; student, Yale U., 1953; A.B., Stanford U., 1955; JD, Loyola-Marymount U., Marymount, 1958. Bar: Calif. 1959, U.S. Dist. Ct. (cen., ea. and so. dists. Calif.) 1959, U.S. Ct. Appeals (9th cir.) 1970, U.S. Supreme Ct. 1971. Dep. city atty., Los Angeles, 1959-60; assoc. firm Pollock & Deutz, Los Angeles, 1960 63; ptnr. firm Pollock & Palmer, Los Angeles, 1963-70, Palmer & Bartenetti, Los Angeles, 1970-81, Samuel C. Palmer III, P.C., 1981-85; ptnr. Thomas, & Snell, 1985—. Adj. prof. Calif. State U., Fresno, 1993. Trustee Western Ctr. Law and Poverty; bd. dirs. Big Bros./Big Sisters, Fresno, Arte Ams., Lively Arts Found., Nat. Sleep Found., Vols. in Parole; pres., bd. dirs. Poverello House; founder, pres. Fresno Crime Stoppers. Mem. ABA, State Bar Calif. (disciplinary subcom., bar examiners subcom.), Fresno County Bar Assn. (pres., bd. dirs. 1988-93), Pickwick Soc., Am. Bd. Trial Advocates, Chancery Club, Downtown Club, Calif. Club, Fig Garden Tennis Club, Rotary, Delta Upsilon, Phi Delta Phi. Office: 2445 Capitol St Fresno CA 93721-2224 also: 820 Suffolk St Cambria CA 93624 E-mail: spalmer@thomasnell.com

PALMER, WENDY, professional basketball player; b. Aug. 12, 1974; BA in History, U. Va., 1996. Forward Oviedo, Spain, 1996-97, WMBA - Utah Starzz, Salt Lake City, 1997-99, Detroit Shock, 1999—. Named to All-Am., 1995, 96. Avocations: horseback riding, music, seafood. Office: 2 Championship Auburn Hills MI 48326

PALMREUTER, KENNETH RICHARD LOUIS, principal; b. Vassar, Mich., Feb. 8, 1939; s. Clarence L. and Louise M. (Koch) P.; m. Martha Marie Zoellick, June 16, 1962; children: Pauline, Karen, Joel. BS in Edn., Concordia Tchrs. Coll., 1962; MA in Elem. Sch. Adminstrn., U. Mich., 1967; postgrad., Wayne State U., 1976-78, U. Colo., 1988-89; LLD, Concordia Tchrs. Coll., Seward, Nebr., 1993. Tchr. Grace Luth. Sch., River Forest, Ill., 1960-61, Calvary Luth. Sch., Lincoln Park, Mich., 1962-63, prin., tchr. jr. high, 1963-76; asst. prin. Luth. High Sch. West, Detroit, 1976-78, prin., 1978-87; exec. dir. Luth. High Sch., Denver, 1987—. Mem. Commn. on Theology and Ch. Rels., Luth. Ch.-Mo. Synod, 1995—, mem. planning coun. for mission and ministry, 1988-90; adv. team Luth. High Schs., 1984-88, 94—, Concordia Centennial adv. com., 1992; day sch. com. Rocky Mountain Dist., 1990-94, tchrs. conf. chmn., 1990-94, dist. conv. com., 1988, 91; nominations com. Mich. Dist., 1987, bd. social ministry, 1980-84, dist. conv. com., 1972, student aid com., 1974-78; conf. program com. Mich. Assn. Non-Pub. Schs., 1984-85; adv. coun. Wayne County Cmty. Coll., 1986-87. Named Outstanding Young Educator, Lincoln Park Jaycees, 1973; nominated Nat. Disting. Luth. Prin., 1992. Mem. NASSP, ASCD, Assn. Luth. Secondary Schs., Luth. Edn. Assn. Home: 2783 S Depew St Denver CO 80227-4106 Office: Lutheran High Sch 3201 W Arizona Ave Denver CO 80219-3941

PALOLA, HARRY JOEL, international affairs executive, consultant; b. Kaukola, Viipuri, Finland, May 13, 1943; came to U.S., 1961; s. Heikki and Mary Dagmar (Ahokas) P.; m. Rita Hannele Ahokas, Sept. 15, 1968 (div. July 1992); children: Christine, Kathy, Kimberly. AA, L.A. City Coll., 1966; BS in Mech. Engring., Calif. State U., Long Beach, 1971; MA in Internat. Affairs, Calif. State U., Sacramento, 1995. Registered engr.-in-tng., Calif. Design engr. Northrop Corp., Hawthorne, Calif., 1971-77, Ford Aerospace and Comm. Corp., Newport Beach, 1977-81, B&M Assocs.,

San Diego, 1982; mech. engr. Raytheon Corp., Goleta, Calif., 1982-84; electronic packaging engr. LPL Tech. Svc., Seattle, 1984-86; design/test engr. Boeing Co., Seattle and Vandenberg, Calif., 1986-92; CEO Internat. Consultancy Corp., Santa Ynez, 1993—. Cons. in basic and applied rsch. in human comm., 1993—. Author: International Finnish Studies: Language, History and Culture, 1995, The Karjala Question-Thoughts on Religious Directions, 1997. Econ. devel. student intern City of Sacramento, 1992-93. Sgt. USNG, 1966-72. Republican. Lutheran. Avocations: ocean sailing, private flying, Finno-Urgic and Ural-Altaic languages. Office: Internat Consultancy Corp 1041 N Refugio Rd Santa Ynez CA 93460-9316 E-mail: chrissy@syv.com

PAMPLIN, ROBERT BOISSEAU, SR. retired textile manufacturing executive; b. Sutherland, Va., Nov. 25, 1911; s. John R. and Pauline (Beville) P.; m. Mary K. Reese, June 15, 1940; 1 child, Robert Boisseau Jr. BBA, Va. Poly. Inst. & State U., 1933; postgrad., Northwestern U., 1933-34; LLD (hon.), U. Portland (Oreg.), 1972; LHD (hon.), Warner Pacific Coll., 1976. With Ga.-Pacific Corp., Portland, 1934-76, sec., from 1936, adminstrv. v.p., 1952-55, exec. v.p., 1955-57, pres., 1957-67, chmn. bd., chief exec. officer, from 1967; ret., 1976; with R.B. Pamplin Corp., 1957—, chmn. bd., CEO, to 1996, Mt. Vernon Mills Inc. (subs. R.B. Pamplin Corp.), Greenville, S.C., retired, 1996. Office: R B Pamplin Corp 805 SW Broadway Ste 240 Portland OR 97205-3341

PAMPLIN, ROBERT BOISSEAU, JR. manufacturing company executive, minister, writer; b. Augusta, Ga., Aug. 3, 1941; s. Robert Boisseau and Mary Katherine (Reese) P.; m. Marilyn Joan Hooper; children: Amy Louise, Anne Boisseau. Student, Va. Poly. Inst., 1960-62, BS in Acctg., 1965, BS in Econs., 1966; BS (hon.), Va. Tech., 2001; LHD (hon.), Va. Poly. Inst., 1995, Pacific U., 2001; DHL (hon.), Va. Poly. Inst., 1995; MBA, U. Portland, 1968, LLD (hon.), 1972, MEd, 1975; MCL, Western Conservative Bapt. Sem. (name now Western Sem.), 1978, DMin, 1982, D of Sacred Letter (hon.), 1991, MA, 2000; PhD, Calif. Coast U.; DHL (hon.), Warner Pacific Coll., 1988; LLD (hon.), Western Baptist Coll., 1989; cert. in wholesale mgmt., Ohio State U., 1970; cert. labor mgmt., U. Portland, 1982; cert. in advanced mgmt., U. Hawaii, 1975; DD (hon.), Judson Baptist Coll., 1984; DBA (hon.), Marquis Giuseppe Scicluna Internat. U. Found., 1986; LittD (hon.), Va. Tech. Inst. and State U., 1987, LHD (hon.), Western Seminary, 1991; DD, Western Evang. Sem., 1994; DBA (hon.), U. S.C., 1996; D Pub. Svc. (hon.), DHL, U. Puget Sound, Pacific U., 1999, 2001; BS in Bus. Adminstrn. (hon.), Va. Inst. Tech., 2001. Pres., CEO R.B. pamplin Corp., Portland, Oreg., 1964—. Chmn. bd., CEO Columbia Empire Farms Inc., Lake Oswego, Oreg., 1976—, Pamplin Comms.; chmn. bd., CEO Mt. Vernon Mills Inc.,; pres., CEO Ross Island Sand & Gravel; lectr. bus. adminstrn. Lewis and Clark Coll., 1968-69; adj. asst. prof. bus. adminstrn., U. Portland, 1973-76; pastor Christ Cmty. Ch., Lake Oswego; lectr. in bus. adminstrn. and econs. U. Costa Rica, 1968, Va. Tech. Found., 1986; chmn. bd. dirs. Christian Supplly Ctrs. Inc.; prof. with tenure U. Portland, 1999. Author: Everything is Just great, 1985, The Gift, 1986, Another Virginian: A Study of the Life and Beliefs of Robert Boisseau Pamplin, 1986, (with others) A Portrait of Colorado, 1976, Three in One, 1974, The Storybook Primer on Managing, 1974, One Who Believed, Vol. I 1988, vol. II, 1991, Climbing the Centuries, 1993, Heritage the Making of an American Family, 1994, American Heroes, 1995, Prelude to Surrender, 1995; editor Oreg. Mus. Sci. and Industry Press, 1973, trustee, 1971, 74—; editor Portrait of Oregon, 1973, (with others) Oregon Underfoot, 1975. Trustee Lewis and Clark Coll., 1989—, chmn. bd. trustees, 1991; hon. life pres. Western Conservative Bapt. Sem.; chmn. regents Western Sem., 1994; mem. nat. adv. coun. on vocat. Edn., 1975—; mem. Western Interstate Com. on Higher Edn., 1981-84; co-chmn. Va. Tech. $50 Million Campaign for Excellence, 1984-87, Va. Tech. Found., 1986—, Va.-Oreg. State Scholarship Commn., 1974—, chmn. 1976-78; mem. Portland dist. adv. coun. SBA, 1973-77; mem. rewards rev. com., City of Portland, 1973-78, chmn., 1973-78; bd. regents U. Portland, 1971-79, chmn. bd., 1975-79, regent emeritus, 1979—; trustee Oreg. Episc. Schs., 1979, Linfield Coll., U. Puget Sound, 1989—; dr. pub. svc., U. Puget Sound, 1999. Recipient Disting. Alumnus award Lewis and Clark Coll., 1974, ROTC Disting. Svc. award USAF, 1974, Albert Einstein Acad. bronze medal, 1986, Disting. Leadership medal Freedoms Found., Disting. Bus. Alumnus award U. Portland, 1990, Nat. Caring award Caring Inst., 1991, Pride of Portland award Portland Lions Club, Hero Ath,E,lete award 1994, Herman Lay Entrepreneurship award, 1995, Thomas Jeffersonard Oreg. Hist. Soc. 1998, Aubrey R. Watzek award Lewis and Clark Coll., 1998, Leadership award Portland Living Mag., 1998, Unique Contbns. to Comms. award Portland Advt. Fedn., 2001; named Outstanding Philanthropist of Yr. award Nat. Soc. Fund Raising Execs., 1997, Textile World's Top 10, 1999, Portland First Citizen, Portland Met. Assn. Realtors, 1999; Va. Tech. Coll. Bus. Adminstrn. renamed R.B. Pamplin Coll. Bus. Adminstrn. in his honor; Govs. Arts Award, 2001, Western Conservative Bapt. Sem. Lay Inst. for Leadership, Edn. Devel. and Rsch. named for R.B. Pamplin Jr., 1988. Mem. Acad. Mgmt., Delta Epsilon Sigma, Beta Gamma Sigma, Sigma Phi Epsilon, Waverley Country Club, Arlington, Multnomah Athletic Clulb, Capitol Hill Club, Greenville Country Club, Poinsett Club, Eldorado Country Club, Thunderbird Country Club, Rotary. Republican. Episcopalian. Office: RB Pamplin Corp Inc 900 SW 5th Ave Ste 1800 Portland OR 97204-1259

PANELLI, EDWARD ALEXANDER, retired state supreme court justice; b. Santa Clara, Calif., Nov. 23, 1931; s. Pilade and Natalina (Della Maggiora) P.; m. Lorna Christine Mondora, Oct. 27, 1956; children: Thomas E., Jeffrey J., Michael P. BA cum laude, Santa Clara U., 1953, JD cum laude, 1955, LLD (hon.), 1986, Southwestern U., L.A., 1988. Bar: Calif. 1955. Ptnr. Pasquinelli and Panelli, San Jose, Calif., 1955-72; judge Santa Clara County Superior Ct., 1972-83; assoc. justice 1st Dist. Ct. of Appeals, San Francisco, 1983-84; presiding justice 6th Dist. Ct. of Appeals, San Jose, 1984-85; assoc. justice Calif. Supreme Ct., San Francisco, 1985-94. Chief judicial officer JAMS/Endispute, 1995—; instr. Continuing Legal Edn., Santa Clara, 1976-78. Trustee West Valley Community Coll., 1963-72; trustee Santa Clara U., 1963—, chmn. bd. trustees, 1984—. Recipient Citation, Am. Com. Italian Migration, 1969, Community Legal Svcs. award, 1979, 84, Edwin J. Owens Lawyers of Yr. award Santa Clara Law Sch. Alumni, 1982, Merit award Republic of Italy, 1984, Gold medal in recognition of Italians who have honored Italy, Lucca, Italy, 1990, St Thomas More award, San Francisco, 1991, Filippo Mazzei Internat. award, Florence, Italy, 1992; Justice Edward A. Panelli Moot Courtroom named in his honor Santa Clara U., 1989. Mem. ABA, Nat. Italian Bar Assn. (inspiration award 1986), Calif. Trial Lawyers Assn. (Trial Judge of Yr. award Santa Clara County chpt. 1981), Calif. Judges Assn. (bd. dirs. 1982), Jud. Coun. Calif. (vice-chair 1989-93), Alpha Sigma Nu, Phi Alpha Delta Law Found. (hon. mem. Douglas Edmonds chpt.). Republican. Roman Catholic. Avocations: golf, jogging, sailing. Office: JAMS Endispute Inc 160 W Santa Clara St San Jose CA 95113-1701

PANETTA, LEON EDWARD, federal official, former congressman; b. Monterey, Calif., June 28, 1938; s. Carmelo Frank and Carmelina Maria (Prochilo) P.; m. Sylvia Marie Varni, July 14, 1962; children: Christopher, Carmelo, James. B.A. magna cum laude, U. Santa Clara, Calif., 1960, LL.B., J.D., 1963. Bar: Calif. bar 1965, U.S. Supreme Ct. 1965, U.S. Dist. Ct. (no. dist.) Calif. 1965, U.S. Ct. Appeals 1965. Legis. asst. to U.S. Sen. Thomas Kuchel, Washington, 1966-69; dir. U.S. Office Civil Rights, HEW, Washington, 1969-70; exec. asst. to Mayor of N.Y.C., 1970-71; ptnr. Panetta, Thompson & Panetta, Monterey, 1971-76; mem. 95th-103d Congresses from 17th Calif. dist., 1977-93, chmn. budget com., mem. agr. com., adminstrn. com., also com. dep. majority whip for budget issues, mem. select com. on hunger; dir. U.S. Office Mgmt. and Budget, Washington, 1993-94; chief of staff The White House, Washington, 1994-97; founder Panetta Inst., CA State U., Monterey, Monterey Bay, CA, 1998—. Author: Bring Us Together, 1971. Counsel Monterey Regional Park Dists.; counsel NAACP, 1971-76; bd. trustees U. Santa Clara Law Sch.; founder Monterey Coll. Law; mem. Monterey County Dem. Cen. Com., 1972-74; v.p. Carmel Valley Little League, 1974-75. Served with AUS, 1964-66. Recipient Lincoln award NEA, 1970, Disting. Svc. award NAACP, 1972, Bread for World award, 1978, Nat. Hospice Orgn. award, 1984, Golden Plow award Am. Farm Bur. Fedn., Pres.'s award Am. Coun. on Tchr. of Fgn. Langs., 1991, Coastal and Ocean Mgmt. award Coastal Zone Found., 1991, Food Rsch. and Action Ctr. award, 1991; named Lawyer of Yr., Law Sch. U. Santa Clara, 1970. Mem. Calif. Bar Assn. Roman Catholic. Office: The Panetta Inst Calif State U Monterey 100 Campus Ctr Bldg 86E Seaside CA 93955-8000

PANIC, MILAN, pharmaceutical and health products company executive; b. Belgrade, Yugoslavia, Dec. 20, 1929; came to U.S., 1956, naturalized, 1963; s. Spasóje and Zorka (Krunich) P.; children: Dawn, Milan (dec.), Vivian; stepchildren: Jane, Mark, Patricia. B.S., HU Belgrade, 1955; postgrad., U. Heidelberg, Germany, 1955-56, U. So. Calif., , 1957-59. Metallurgist Kaiser Steel Corp., 1956-57; chemist Cyclo-Chem. Corp., Los Angeles, 1957-58; research asst. dept. chemistry U. So. Calif., 1958-59; research chemist Biochem. Research, Los Angeles, 1959-61; chmn. bd., chief exec. officer ICN Pharms., Inc., Costa Mesa, Calif., pres., chmn. bd., chief exec. officer, 1961—; prime min. Govt. of Yugoslavia, Belgrade, 1992-93; chmn. Ribapharm Inc. Assoc. Calif. Inst. Tech. Trustee Intra-Sci. Research Found.; sponsoring com. program health scis. and tech. Harvard-Mass. Inst. Tech.; bd. dirs. Freedom's Found., Valley Forge, Pa. Served with Yugoslavian Army in Partisan Resistance, WWII. Recipient Ellis Island Medal of Honor, 1986. Mem. Serbian Orthodox Ch. Office: ICN Pharms Inc ICN Plaza 3300 Hyland Ave Costa Mesa CA 92626-1503

PANICCIA, PATRICIA LYNN, journalist, writer, lawyer, educator; b. Glendale, Calif., Sept. 19, 1952; d. Valentino and Mary (Napoleon) P.; m. Jeffrey McDowell Mailes, Oct. 5, 1985; children: Alana Christine, Malia Noel. BA in Comm., U. Hawaii, 1977; JD, Pepperdine U., 1981. Bar: Hawaii 1981, Calif. 1982, U.S. Dist. Ct. Hawaii 1981. Extern law clk. hon. Samuel P. King U.S. Dist. Ct., Honolulu, 1980; reporter, anchor woman Sta. KEYT-TV, Santa Barbara, Calif., 1983-84; reporter Sta. KCOP-TV, L.A., 1984-88, CNN, L.A., 1989-93; corr. Cable News Network (CNN), L.A., 1989—. Adj. prof. comm. law Pepperdine Sch. Law, 1987, gender & the law, 1994—, adj. prof.; prof. surfer, 1977-81. Author: Worksmarts for Women: The Essential Sex Discrimination Survival Guide, 2000. Recipient Clarion award Women in Comm., Inc., 1988. Mem. ABA (chair of law and media com. young lawyers divsn. 1987-88, nat. conf. com. lawyers and reps. of media 1987-91), Calif. State Bar (mem. com. on fair trial and free press 1983-84, pub. affairs com. 1985-87), Hawaii Bar Assn., Phi Delta Phi (historian 1980-81). Office: PO Box 881 La Canada CA 91012-0881

PANIK, SHARON MCCLAIN, primary education educator, writer; b. Detroit, May 29, 1952; d. Robert and Phyllis L. McClain; m. Steven Panik, May 25, 1974; 1 child, Todd. BS, Ctrl. Mich. Univ., 1973; MA, U. No. Colo., 1978. Tchr. primary grades Poudre R-1, Fort Collins, 1974—. Co-author: (with Marilyn Parke) A Quetzalcoatl Tale of Corn, 1992 (Parents' Choice Gold award paperback of yr. 1992), A Quetzalcoatl Tale of the Ball Game, 1992, A Quetzalcoatl Tale of Chocolate, 1994. Mem. Internat. Reading Assn., Soc. Children's Book Writers and Illustrators, Nat. Edn. Soc., Colo. Coun. Internat. Reading Assn. (membership dir.). Office: 1209 Parkwood Dr Fort Collins CO 80525-1930

PANKOW, JAMES F. environmental science and engineering educator; BA in Chemistry with honors, SUNY, Binghamton, 1973; MS in Environ. Engring. Sci., Calif. Inst. Tech., 1976, PhD in Environ. Engring. Sci., 1979. Grad. rsch. and tchg. asst. Calif. Inst. Tech., Pasadena, 1973-78; prof., asst. head dept. environ. sci. and engring. Oreg. Grad. Inst. Sci. and Tech., Beaverton, 1978—. Mem. rev. panel Office and Sci. Tech. Policy; mem. adv. panel U.S. Geol. Survey. Author: Dense Chlorinated Solvents in Porous and Fractured Media, 1988, Aquatic Chemical Concepts, 1991, Aquatic Chemistry Problems, 1992, Dense Chlorinated Solvents. . ., 1995; co-editor: Dense Chlorinated Solvents and Other DNAPLs in Groundwater History, Behavior and Remediation; contbr. articles to profl. publs. Office: Oreg Grad Inst Sci and Tech Dept Environ Sci & Engring 20000 NW Walker Rd Beaverton OR 97006-8921

PANKRATZ, FRANK D. real estate company executive; B in Commerce, U. Sask., 1971; chartered accts. degree, McGill U., 1974. With Del Webb Corp., Phoenix, 1987—. Sr. v.p. Del Webb Corp., G.M. So. Nev. active adult ops. and regional v.p. Nev. and Calif. active adult ops., Henderson, Nev. Office: Del Webb Corp PO Box 29040 Phoenix AZ 85016

PANNER, OWEN M. federal judge; b. 1924; Student, U. Okla., 1941-43, LL.B., 1949. Atty. Panner, Johnson, Marceau, Karnopp, Kennedy & Nash, 1950-80; judge, now sr. judge U.S. Dist. Ct. Oreg., Portland, 1980—, sr. judge, 1992—. Recipient Am. Bd. Trial Advocates Trial Lawyer of Yr., 1973. Mem. Am. Coll. Trial Lawyers, Am. Bd. Trial Advs., Order of Coif. Office: US Dist Ct 1000 SW 3rd Ave Ste 1207 Portland OR 97204-2942

PANOFSKY, WOLFGANG KURT HERMANN, physicist, educator; b. Berlin, Germany, Apr. 24, 1919; came to U.S., 1934, naturalized, 1942; s. Erwin and Dorothea (Mosse) P.; m. Adele Du Mond, July 21, 1942; children: Richard, Margaret, Edward, Carol, Steven. A.B., Princeton U., 1938, DSc (hon.), 1983; Ph.D., Calif. Inst. Tech., 1942; D.Sc. (hon.), Case Inst. Tech., 1963, U. Sask., 1964, Columbia U., 1977, U. Hamburg, Germany, 1984, Yale U., , 1985; hon. degree, U. Beijing, 1987; DSc (hon.), U. Rome, 1988; hon. degree, Uppsala U., Sweden, 1991. Mem. staff mem. radiation lab. U. Calif., 1945-51, asst. prof., 1946-48, asso. prof., 1948-51; prof. physics Stanford U., 1951-62, prof. Stanford Linear Accelerator Ctr., 1962-89, prof. emeritus, 1989—; dir. Stanford (High Energy Physics Lab., Stanford Linear Accelerator Center), 1962-84, dir. emeritus, 1984—. Am. del. Conf. Cessation Nuclear Tests, Geneva, 1959; mem. President's Sci. Adv. Com., 1960-64; cons. Office Sci. and Tech., Exec. Office Pres., 1965-73, U.S. ACDA, 1968-81; mem. gen. adv. com. to White House, 1977-81; mem. panel Office Sci. and Tech. Policy, 1977; with nat. def. rsch. Calif. Inst. Tech. and Los Alamos, 1942-45; mem. JASON, 1965—; chmn. bd. overseers Superconducting Supercollider Univs. Rsch. Assn., 1984-93; mem. com. to provide interim oversight Dept. Energy nuclear weapons complex NAS, 1988-89; mem. panel on nuclear warhead dismantlement and special materials control Dept. Energy, 1991-92; mem. Commn. on Particles and Field of Internat. Union Pure and Applied Physics, 1985-93. Decorated officier Legion of Honor; recipient Lawrence prize AEC, 1961, Nat. Medal Sci., 1969, Franklin medal, 1970, Ann. Pub. Service award Fedn. Am. Scientists, 1973, Enrico Fermi award Dept. Energy, 1979, Shoong Found. award for sci., 1983, Hilliard Roderick prize Sci. AAAS, 1991, Matteucei medal, 1997; named Calif. Scientist Yr., 1966 Fellow Am. Phys. Soc. (pres. 1974); mem. NAS (mem. com. on internat. security and arms control 1985—, chmn. com. 1985-93, mem. scis. com. on scholarly comm. with China 1987-92), AAAS, Am. Philos. Soc. (pres. 1974-75), [illegible] Phi Beta Kappa, Sigma Xi. Home: 25671 Chapin Rd Los Altos CA 94022-3413 Office: Stanford Linear Accelerator Ctr PO Box 20450 Stanford CA 94309-0450

PANTALEO, JACK, writer, composer, social worker, harpist; b. Melrose Park, Ill., Nov. 30, 1954; s. Jack Sam Pantaleo and Sophia Mannozzi Pantaleo Cicero. Psychiat. Tech., C.C., San Francisco, 1981; BA in Humanities, New Coll. Calif., San Francisco, 1986; MA in Writing, U. San Francisco, 1988. Lic. psychiat. technician. Asst. to dean U. San Francisco Sch. Nursing, 1984-88; grammar sch. tchr. St. Michael's Cath. Sch., San Francisco, 1989-91; instr. English Vista C.C., Berkeley, Calif., 1990-93; social worker City and County of San Francisco, 1991—. Founder, dir. Evangelicals Concerned, San Francisco, 1978-85; co-founder, co-dir. AIDS InterFaith Network, San Francisco, 1983-88. Author: (novel) Mother Julian and the Gentle Vampire, 2000; Playwright/composer musical The Gospel According to the Angel Julius translated into German and performed in Hamburg, Germany, 1999; (one-act play): Uncle Fred's Ex-Staight Ministry in Wilma Loves Betty, 1999; contbg. author: (collection of meditations) The Road to Emmaus, 1990; author booklet and articles. Caregiver for babies with AIDS, The Bridge, San Francisco, 1989-93. Work included in Silver Quill, The David Ross Meml. Competition, Wichita, 1996. Mem. Social Workers Union, Nat. Writers Union. Democrat. Episcopalian. Avocations: harp, lecturing. E-mail: jackp100@onebox.com

PANTENBURG, MICHEL, hospital administrator, health educator, holistic health coordinator; b. Denver, Oct. 6, 1926; d. Arthur Robert and Alice (McKenna) P. Diploma, Providence Nursing Sch., Kansas City, Kans., 1951; B.S. in Nursing Edn., St. Mary Coll., Leavenworth, Kans., 1958; M. in Nursing, Cath. U. Am., 1960. Joined Sisters of Charity, Roman Catholic Ch., 1945; lic. amateur radio operator. Dir. nursing Providence Hosp., Kansas City, Kans., 1958-62; nursing coordinator Sisters of Charity, Leavenworth, 1962-67; hosp. adminstr. St. Mary Hosp., Grand Junction, Colo., 1967-73, St. Vincent Hosp., Billings, Mont., 1973-84; dir. focus on leadership program Gonzaga U., Spokane, Wash., 1985-92; chaplain pastoral care dept. St. Marys Hosp. and Med. Ctr., Grand Junction, Colo., 1994-99, integrative medicine, 1999—. Dir. Norwest Bank, Billings Co-author, editor: Management of Nursing (CHA award 1969), 1967 Bd. dirs. De Paul Hosp., Cheyenne, Wyo., 1980-85, Ronald McDonald House, Billings, 1982-85, St. Joseph Hosp., Denver, 1994-97. Named Woman of Yr., Bus. and Profl. Women, Billings, 1979 Mem. Cath. Hosp. Assn. (bd. dirs., sec.), Am. Hosp. Assn. (regional del. 1975-80), Am. Coll. Hosp. Adminstrn., Mont. Hosp. Assn. (pres.), Billings C. of C. (v.p. 1977-78). Avocations: hiking; skiing. Office: Pastoral Care Dept St Marys Hosp & Med Ctr Grand Junction CO 81502

PANY, KURT JOSEPH, accounting educator, consultant; b. St. Louis, Mar. 31, 1946; s. Joseph Francis and Ruth Elizabeth (Westerman) P.; m. Darlene Dee Zabish, June 3, 1971; children: Jeffrey, Michael. BSBA, U. Ariz., 1968; MBA in Mgmt., U. Minn., 1971; PhD in Accountancy, U. Ill., 1977. CPA, Ariz., cert. fraud examiner. Staff auditor Arthur Andersen & Co., Mpls., 1968-69, Touche Ross & Co., Phoenix, 1971-73; teaching asst. U. Minn., Mpls., 1969-71; teaching asst. auditing and acctg. U. Ill., Urbana, 1972-76; asst. prof. acctg. Ariz. State U., Tempe, 1977-81, assoc. prof., 1981-85, Arthur Andersen/Don Dupont prof. acctg., 1985-91. Mem. acctg. and auditing standards com. State of Ariz., Phoenix, 1989—; reviewer Jour. Acctg. and Pub. Policy, 1983—. Contbg. author: CPA Exam. Rev., 1983—; co-author: Principles of Auditing, 1988—, Auditing, 1993—; co-editor Auditing: A Jour. Practice and Theory, 1984-88; mem. editl. bd. Advances in Acctg., 1982—, Jour. Acctg. Edn., 1983—; reviewer Acctg. Rev., 1984—, ad hoc editor, 1989—; contbr. numerous articles to profl. jours. Active various child-related orgns. Peat, Marwick, Mitchell & Co. Found. grantee, 1985. Fellow AICPA (auditing stds. divsn. 1989-90, acctg. lit. selection com. 1989-90, acctg. lit. awards com. 1979-83, mem. auditing stds. bd. 1995—); mem. Am. Acctg. Assn. (tech. program com. 1980-81, chairperson Western region auditing sect. 1981-83, acctg. lit. nominating com. 1982-84, 88-89, acctg. lit. selection com. 1989-90, dir. auditing stds., chmn. auditing stds. com. 1989-90), Ariz. Soc. CPA's (auditing stds. com. 1978-81, ethics com. 1981-84). Avocation: baseball. Address: 7411 S Rita Ln Unit 116 Tempe AZ 85283-4792 Office: Ariz State U Sch Accountancy Tempe AZ 85287

PAPAKONSTANTINO, STACY, English language educator; b. San Francisco, Feb. 27, 1967; d. Demetrios and Eugenia (Yiallely) P. AA, City. Coll. of San Francisco, 1987; BA in English Lit., San Francisco State U., 1989, MA in English Lang. Studies, 1991. Cert. in tchg. composition and postsecondary reading. English, ESL tutor City Coll. of San Francisco, 1986-87, instr. of English, 1991—; Greek instr. Holy Trinity Sch., 1988-90. Chair student grade and file rev. com., City Coll. of San Francisco, 1996—, resource mem. student success com., 1997—, mem. student complaint com., 1997—, mem. composition/lit./reading com., 1996—. Mem. Nat. Coun. Tchrs. of English. Democrat. Orthodox. Avocations: reading, movies and plays, helping needy people, spiritual worship, fitness. Home: 48 Westpark Dr Daly City CA 94015-1055 Office: City Coll San Francisco 50 Phelan Ave San Francisco CA 94112-1821 E-mail: spapak@hotmail.com

PAPEN, MARY KAY, state senator; Car dealer; Dem. senator dist. 38 N.Mex. State Senate. Mem. pub. affairs com. N.Mex. State Senate, vice chair edn. com. Avocations. Home: 904 Conway Ave Las Cruces NM 88005 Office: NMex State Senate State Capitol Mail Rm Dept Santa Fe NM 87503 E-mail: senate@state.nm.us

PAPIANO, NEIL LEO, lawyer; b. Salt Lake City, Nov. 25, 1933; s. Leo and Ruth Ida (Cotten) P. B.A., Stanford, 1956, M.A. in Polit. Sci, 1957; J.D., Vanderbilt U., 1961. Bar: Calif. bar 1961. Partner Iverson, Yoakum, Papiano & Hatch (and predecessor firm), Los Angeles, 1961—. Bd. dirs. Nederlander Orgn. and related cos., SCOA Industries, Inc., Ocean Tech., Inc., King Nutronics, Inc. V.p. Los Angeles County Welfare Planning Coun., 1966-71; chmn. L.A. Forward, 1970-71; vice chmn. Cal. Com. for Welfare Reform, 1972; mem. Calif. Jud. Selection Com., 1972-74; co-finance chmn. Rep. State Central Com., 1975; treas. L.A. Opera Co., 1964, bd. dirs., 1965; treas. So. Calif. Choral Music Assn., 1964, bd. dirs., 1964-73; bd. dirs. Citizens Adv. Coun. on Pub. Transp., Orthopaedic Hosp., Stanford U. Athletic Bd., Nat. Athletic Health Inst., L.A. Music Ctr. Operating Co., L.A. Light Opera; bd. govs. USO, 1967-71, Performing Arts Coun. L.A. Music Ctr., 1981-87, Greater L.A. Homeless Partnership, 1985—, L.A. Olympic Com., 1986-88; bd. trustees The Am. U., 1981-95. Mem. Am., Calif. bar assns., Los Angeles Area C. of C. (pres. 1966, dir. 1964-67, 72-75), California Club, Los Angeles Country Club, Rotary, Phi Delta Theta. Office: Iverson Yoakum Papiano & Hatch One Wilshire Bldg 27th Floor 624 S Grand Ave Ste 2700 Los Angeles CA 90017-3328

PAPP, HARRY, science association administrator; Pres. Ariz. Zool. Soc., The Phoenix Zoo, from 1995, now former pres. Office: Elroy Papp & Assocs 6225 N 24th St Ste 150 Phoenix AZ 85016-2036 also: Phoenix Zoo 455 N Galvin Pkwy Phoenix AZ 85008-3431

PAPPAS, JIM D. federal bankruptcy judge; b. 1952; Chief bankruptcy judge U.S. Bankruptcy Ct., Boise, 1993—. Office: US Bankruptcy Ct 550 W Fort St Msc 042 Boise ID 83724-0001

PAQUETTE, RICHARD, airport executive; V.p. airport devel. Calgary Airport, AB, Can.; pres., CEO airport performance group Calgary Airport Authority Co.; pres., CEO Victoria Airport, Sidney, B.C., Can., 1999—. [illegible] C. Avocations: golf, skiing, bike riding, photography, hockey. Office: Victoria Internat Airport Box 201 1640 Electra Blvd Sidney BC Canada V8L 5V4

PARDEN, ROBERT JAMES, engineering educator, management consultant; b. Mason City, Iowa, Apr. 17, 1922; s. James Ambrose and Mary Ellen (Fahey) P.; m. Elizabeth Jane Taylor, June 15, 1955; children— Patricia Gale, James A., John R., Nancy Ann. B.S. in Mech. Engring, State U. Iowa, 1947, M.S., 1951, Ph.D., 1953. Reg. profl. engr. Iowa, Calif.; lic. gen. contractor Calif. Indsl. engr. LaCrosse Rubber Mills, 1947-50; asso. dir. Iowa Mgmt. Course, 1951-53; asso. prof. indsl. engring. Ill. Inst. Tech., 1953-54; prof. engring. mgmt. Santa Clara U., 1955—, dean Sch. Engring., 1955-82; prin. Saratoga Cons. Group (Calif.), 1982—. Mem. Sec. Navy's Survey Bd. Grad. Edn., 1964 Mem. Saratoga Planning Commn., 1959-61. Served to 1st lt., Q.M.C. AUS, 1943-46. Named to Silicon Valley Engring. Hall of Fame Silicon Valley Engring. Coun., 1993. Mem. ASME (chmn. Santa Clara Valley sect. 1958), Am. Soc. Engring. Edn. (chmn. Pacific N.W. sect. 1960), Am. Inst. Indsl. Engrs. (edn. chmn. 1958-63, dir. ASEE-ECPD affairs 1963-68), Nat. Soc. Profl. Engrs., Engrs. Council Profl. Devel. (dir. 1964-65, 66-69), Soc. Advancement Mgmt., ASEM, Sigma Xi, Tau Beta Pi. Roman Catholic. Home: 19832 Bonnie Ridge Way Saratoga CA 95070-5010 Office: Santa Clara U Sch Engring Santa Clara CA 95053-0001 E-mail: bobparden@home.com, rparden@scu.edu

PARDUE, A. MICHAEL, retired plastic and reconstructive surgeon; b. Nashville, June 23, 1931; s. Andrew Peyton and Ruby (Fly) P.; m. Lilavati Sharma, Dec. 1996. BS, U. of the South, 1953; MD, U. Tenn., 1957. Resident in gen. surgery Pittsfield (Mass.) Affiliated Hosps., 1966; resident in plastic surgery N.Y. Hosp./Cornell Med. Ctr., 1968; plastic surgeon A. Michael Pardue, M.D., Thousand Oaks, Calif., 1968-98. Lt. comdr. USN, 1956-62. Fellow ACS; mem. Am. Soc. Plastic and Reconstructive Surgeons, Am. Soc. Aesthetic Plastic Surgery, Calif. Soc. Plastic Surgeons. Episcopalian. Avocations: fly fishing, skiing, golf, equestrian, African safaris. Also: 3217 Augusta Dr Bozeman MT 59715-8792

PARENTI, KATHY ANN, sales professional; b. Gary, Ind., Sept. 24, 1957; d. Lee Everett Huddleston and Barbara Elizabeth (Daves) Tilley; m. Michael A. Parenti, Mar. 31, 1979 (div. Sept. 1990); m. S. Curtis McCoy, Sept. 6, 1996. Student, Ind. U., Gary, 1977; cert., U. Nev., Las Vegas, 1978; diploma, Interior Design Inst., Las Vegas, 1984. Supr. Circus Circus Hotel, Las Vegas, 1980-87; owner Interior Views, Las Vegas, 1984-87; sales rep. Win-Glo Window Coverings, 1987-88; owner Dimension Design, 1988-90; sales rep. Sidney Goldberg & Assoc., Las Vegas, 1990-99; sales rep.. Parenti & Assocs., 1990—. Mem.: Am. Soc. Interior Designers, Network of Exec. Women in Hospitality, Construction Specification Inst., Rep Network. Avocations: exercise, reading, playing piano.

PARIKH, MIHIR, executive; PhD, U. Calif., Berkeley. Varius mgmt. positions IBM, N.Y.C., San Jose, Calif., Hewlett-Packard Labs., Palo Alto; pres., CEO ASYST technologies, Inc., Fremont, 1984—, chmn., 1992—. Contbr. articles to profl. jours. Office: ASYST Technologies Inc 48761 Kato Rd Fremont CA 94538-7313

PARIS, KATHLEEN, secondary school educator; Biology tchr. Bethel High Sch., Spanaway, Wash. Named Wash. State Biology Tchr. of Yr., 1993; recipient Presdl. award in secondary sci., 1997. Office: Bethel High Sch 22215 38th Ave E Spanaway WA 98387-6824

PARISEAU, WILLIAM G. mining engineer, educator; Prof. dept. mining & engring. U. Utah, Salt Lake City. Recipient Rock Mechanics award Soc. Mining, Metallogy & Exploration, 1990. Office: U Utah Dept Mining & Engring 313 Browning Building Salt Lake City UT 84112-1118

PARISI, PAULA ELIZABETH, writer, photographer, editor; b. N.Y.C., Feb. 27, 1960; d. Alfred John and Patricia Ann (Delucas) P. BA, Rutgers U., 1982; photography classes, Phila. Coll. Art, 1978-82. Reporter TVSM Inc./The Cable Guide, Horsham, Pa., 1982-84; assoc. editor Home Viewer Publs., Phila., 1984-85, mng. editor, 1985-87; home video cable TV, technology editor The Hollywood Reporter, Los Angeles, 1987—, editorial dir. CA, 2000—. Contbr. articles to Billboard, Film & Video Prodn., Mix, Hollywood Reporter, Phila. Inquirer; photographs published in Phila. Inquirer, Washington Jour., Miami Herald, Circus, Us, Sixteen, others. Republican. Roman Catholic. Office: The Hollywood Reporter 5055 Wilshire Blvd Ste 600 Los Angeles CA 90036-4396

PARK, CHAN HO, professional baseball player; b. Kong Ju City, Korea, June 30, 1973; Student, Hang Yan U., Seoul, Korea. Pitcher Los Angeles Dodgers, 1994—. Achievements include being the first Korean to play in Major Leagues. Address: LA Dodgers 1000 Elysian Park Ave Los Angeles CA 90012-1112

PARK, EDWARD CAHILL, JR. retired physicist; b. Wollaston, Mass., Nov. 26, 1923; s. Edward Cahill and Fentress (Kerlin) P.; m. Helen Therese O'Boyle, July 28, 1951. AB, Harvard U., 1947; postgrad., Amherst Coll., 1947-49; PhD, U. Birmingham, Eng., 1956. Instr. Amherst (Mass.) Coll., 1954-55; mem. staff Lincoln Lab., Lexington, Mass., 1955-57, Arthur D. Little, Inc., Cambridge, 1957-60, group leader electronic systems Santa Monica, Calif., 1960-64; sr. staff engr., head laser system sect. Hughes Aircraft Co., Culver City, 1964-68, sr. scientist El Segundo, 1986-88; mgr. electro optical systems sect. Litton Guidance and Control Systems, Woodland Hills, 1968-70; sr. phys. scientist The Rand Corp., Santa Monica, 1970-72; sr. scientist R&D Assocs., Marina Del Rey, Calif., 1972-1986, cons., 1986-89; sr. tech. specialist Rockwell Internat., N.Am. Aircraft, Seal Beach, 1988-94. Contbr. articles to profl. jours.; patentee in field. Served to 1st lt. USAAF, 1943-46. Grantee Dept. Indsl. and Sci. Research, 1953. Fellow Explorers Club (sec. So. Calif. chpt. 1978-79); mem. IEEE, Optical Soc. Am., Soc. Archtl. Historians, N.Y. Acad. Scis., Acad. Am. Poets, Sigma Xi. Democrat. Clubs: 20-Ghost (Eng.), Harvard (So. Calif.). Avocations: music, art, architecture, body surfing, gardening. Home: 932 Ocean Frnt Santa Monica CA 90403-2410

PARK, JANIE C. provost; children: Christopher, Eric. BSN, Baylor U., 1968; MS in Cell and Molecular Biology, Fla. Inst. Tech., 1979, PhD in Cell and Molecular Biology, 1982. Nurse Holmes Regional Med. Ctr., Melbourne, Fla., 1968-69; grad. student tchg. asst. Fla. Inst. Tech., Melbourne, 1977-82, instr. biol. scis., 1982-84, asst. prof. biol. scis., 1984-89, chair preprofl./premed. program, 1986-93, assoc. prof. biol. scis., 1989-93, assoc. dean coll. sci. and liberal arts, 1990-93; dean coll. arts and scis., prof. biol. scis. Mont. State U., Billings, 1993-96, provost, acad. vice chancellor, prof. biol. scis., 1996—. Rsch. dir. Ctr. for Interdisciplinary Rsch. in Aging, 1988-90; rsch. dir. elctron microscopy svcs. Joint Ctr. Advanced Therapy and Biomed. Rsch. Fla. Inst. Tech. and Holmes Regional Med. Ctr., 1991-93; spkr. in field. Contbr. articles to profl. jours. Bd. dirs. St. Vincent's Regional Med. Ctr., Youth Dynamics, Inc.; mem. steering com. Billings Town and Gown; mem. Bldg. a Healthy Cmty. Task Force. Mem. Microscopy Soc. Am., Am. Assn. of State Colls. and Univs., Southeast Electron Microscopy (sessions chair ann. meeting 1991, 92), Soc. for Neurosci., Rocky Mountain Deans' Assn. (ann. meeting organizer 1995), Assn. for Rsch. in Otolaryngology (mem. membership com. 1991-97, chair membership com. 1993-97), Fla. Soc. for Electron Microscopy (v.p. 1983, bd. dirs. 1983-93, session chair ann. meeting 1989-92, pres.-elect 1989, pres. 1990-91, mem. local arrangements com. 1991, meeting registration chair 1990—), Coun. Colls. of Arts and Scis. (session chair ann. meeting 1995), Coun. Arts and Scis. of Urban Univs., Billings Rotary Internat., Leadership Billings Alumni Assn. Office: Mont State U Office Acad Vice Chancellor 1500 N 30th St Billings MT 59101-0245

PARK, LEE (LEE PARKLEE), artist; b. Seoul, South Korea; s. Chung-Kun Park and Mil-Hwa Kim; m. Chae Kyung Lim, June 3, 1994. MA, Fla. State U., 1986. Group shows include Shinpara Gallery, L.A., Up-Stairs Gallery, L.A., Beverly Plz. Hotel, Pacific Mus., Pasadena, Calif., Barnsdall Art Gallery, Hollywood, Calif., Brand XXII The Assn. of Brand Art Ctr., Glendale, Calif., Asia Invitation Art Exhibn., Sejong Cultural Ctr., Seoul, la Peintre Moderne Coreend '93, Paris, Korea-Japan Interchange Exhbn., Tokyo, 1994, Downtown Lives '96 Art Exhbn., L.A., City Hall of Paris, 4, Biennale Internat. de Paris, 1994, Musee d'Art Moderne de la Commanderie d'Unet, Paris, 1994, Bridgeport U., N.Y., 1995, San Bernardino County Mus., 1995, Kong-Ja Culture Art Exhbn., China, 1995, His Majesty the King's 50th Anniversary Art Exhbn., Thailand, 1996, 1st Venice Annual Internat. Open Art Exhbn., Venice, 1998, 1st Internat. Biennial Contemporary Art, Perugia, Italy, 1998, Heukyong-gangsung Internat. Art Exhbn., China, 1998, Ting Shao-Kuang Fine Art Ctr., Beverly Hills, Articulture Gallery, Hermosa Beach, Calif., 1998, '99 World Peace Art Exhbn., Sejong Cultural Ctr., Seoul, 1999; 2 person shows include Cosmos Gallery, Honolulu, The City of L.A. Cultural Affairs Dept.; solo exhibits include Modern Art Gallery, L.A., Olympic Gallery, L.A., Sun Space Gallery, L.A., Gallery Nuevo, Pusan, Korea; publ. artwork in American References, Art of California mag., Artweek mag., The Biweekly Art Jour., Seoul, Artprint mag., Washington, Art Exposure mag., Calif., Encyclopedia of Living Artists mag., Calif., Art 2000, Seoul, Art Diary Internat. 98/99, Milan, Italy. Recipient Bronze award Art of Calif., 1993, Gold award Art Addiction, Stockholm, 1997. Avocations: collecting stamps and antiques, music, reading books, jogging, playing tennis. Home: 1935 S La Salle Ave Apt 31 Los Angeles CA 90018-1627

PARK, SAM-KOO, transportation executive; BA in Econs., Yonsei U., 1967. Exec. dir. internat. trading Samyang Tire Indsl. Co., 1967-68; mng. dir. Korea Synthetic Rubber Indusl. Co., 1968-73, Kumho & Co., 1973-74, pres. L.A. br., 1974-79, v.p., 1979-80, pres., 1980-91; pres., CEO Asiana Airlines, Inc., 1991—. Office: Asiana Airlines Inc 3530 Wilshire Blvd Ste 1450 Los Angeles CA 90010-2328 also: Kang Seo Ku Osai Dong 47 157 600 Asaiana Town Seoul Korea

PARK, WILLIAM ANTHONY (TONY), lawyer; b. Blackfoot, Idaho, June 4, 1934; s. William Clair and Thelma Edelweiss (Shear) P.; m. Elizabeth Taylor, Aug. 26, 1961 (div.); children: Susan E., W. Adam, Patricia A.; m. Gail Chaloupka, Aug. 6, 1983. AA, Boise Jr. Coll., 1954; BA, U. Idaho, 1958; JD, U. Idaho, 1963. Bar: Idaho 1963. Sole practice, Boise, Idaho, 1963-70, 82-83; atty. gen. State of Idaho, 1971-75; ptnr. Park & Meuleman, Boise, 1975-81, Park & Burkett, Boise, 1983-84, Martin, Chapman, Park & Burkett, Boise, 1984-90, Park, Costello & Burkett, Boise, 1990-93, Park, Redford, Thomas & Burkett, Boise, 1994-97, Park, Thomas, Burkett & Williams, Boise, 1997-99; of counsel Huntley, Park, Thomas, Burkett, Olsen & Williams, Boise, 1999—. Chmn. Idaho Bicentennial Commn., 1971-77; bd. dirs Radio Free Europe/Radio Liberty, Inc., 1977-82, Am. Lung Assn., 1978-90; bd. dirs. ACLU of Idaho, 1995-2000, rpes., 1997-99; bd. dirs. Am. Lung Assn. of Idaho/Nev., 1976-96, 99—, pres., 1991-95; chair Idaho State Dem. Party, 1998-99. Served with U.S. Army, 1956-58. Recipient Disting. Svc. award. Home: 706 Warm Springs Ave Boise ID 83712-6420 Office: PO Box 2188 Boise ID 83701-2188 E-mail: gchaloupka@msn.com

PARKE, MARILYN NEILS, writer; b. Libby, Mont., June 5, 1928; d. Walter and Alma M. Neils; m. Robert V. Parke, Aug. 25, 1951; children: Robert, Richard, Gayle Crawford, Lynn Parke Castle. BA, U. Mont., 1950; MEd, Colo. State U., 1973. Tchr. Poudre R-1, Fort Collins, 1973—. Co-author: (with Sharon Panik) A Quetzalcoatl Tale of Corn, 1992, A Quetzalcoatl Tale of the Ball Game, 1992 (Parent's Choice Gold award paperback of yr. 1992), A Quetzalcoatl Tale of Chocolate, 1994. Mem. Internat. Reading Assn., Soc. Children's Book Writers and Illustrators, Nat. Edn. Assn., Colo. Coun. Internat. Reading Assn. Avocations: gardening, cooking, sports, reading, travel.

PARKER, DONALD FRED, college dean, human resources management educator; b. Oilton, Okla., Nov. 7, 1934; s. Robert Fred Parker and Georgia Marie (Culley) Meek; m. Jo Ellen Dunfee, Apr. 6, 1963; children: Margaret Elizabeth, Emily Lyle. BA in Sociology, U. Okla., 1957; MS in Personnel Adminstrn., George Washington U., 1966; PhD in Human Resource Mgmt., Cornell U., 1975. Commd. ensign USN, 1957, advanced through grades to capt., 1977, staff officer with chief naval ops., 1969-71, comdg. officer, exec. officer, Patrol Squadron Ten Brunswick, Maine, 1974-76, prof. Naval War Coll. Newport, R.I., 1976-78, comdg. officer Navy Personnel Research & Devel. Ctr. San Diego, 1978-80, ret., 1980; asst. prof. Grad. Sch. Bus., U. Mich., Ann Arbor, 1980-84; prof. human resources mgmt., dean Coll. Commerce and Industry U. Wyo., Laramie, 1984-91; Sara Hart Kimball dean bus., prof. human resources mgmt. Oreg. State U., Corvallis, 1991—. Advisor U.S. West Wyo. State Bd. Advisors, Cheyenne, 1986-91; ex-officio dir. Wyo. Indsl. Devel. Corp., Casper, 1987; vis. prof. Acad. Internat. Econ. Affairs, Hsinchu, Taiwan, 1986-91. Author numerous articles, book chpts., case studies. Mem. Acad. of Mgmt. (human resource mgmt. divsn. dir. 1983-85), Midwest Assn. Deans and Dept. Chairs in Bus. (pres.), Western Assn. Collegiate Schs. Bus. (bd. dirs., pres. 1999), Phi Kappa Phi, Beta Gamma Sigma (pres. 1998-2000, past pres. 2000—). Avocations: jogging, hiking. Home: 4400 NW Honeysuckle Dr Corvallis OR 97330-3355 Office: Oreg State U Coll Bus 200 Bexell Hall Corvallis OR 97331-8527 E-mail: parker@bus.orst.edu

PARKER, GERHARD H. communications professional; BSEE, Calif. Inst. Technology, 1965, MSEE, 1966, D Elec. Engring., 1969. Quality engr. to various positions Intel Corp., Santa Clara, Calif., 1969-99, exec. v.p., gen. mgr. New Bus. Group, 1999—. Office: Intel Corp 2200 Mission College Blvd Santa Clara CA 95052-8119

PARKER, HARRY S., III, museum director; b. St. Petersburg, Fla., Dec. 23, 1939; s. Harry S. Parker and Catherine (Baillie) Knapp; m. Ellen McCance, May 23, 1964; children: Elizabeth Day, Thomas Baillie, Samuel Ferguson, Catherine Allan. A.B. magna cum laude, Harvard U., 1961; M.A., NYU, 1966. Exec. asst., adminstrv. asst. to dir. Met. Mus. Art, N.Y.C., 1963-66, exec. asst. to pres., 1966-67, exec. asst. to dir., 1967, chmn. dept. edn., 1967-71, vice dir. edn., 1971-73; dir. Dallas Mus. Art, 1974-87, Fine Arts Mus. San Francisco, 1987—. Mem. Am. Assn. Mus. (v.p.) Assn. Art Mus. Dirs., Century Assn., Bohemian Club. Home: 171 San Marcos Ave San Francisco CA 94116-1462 Office: Fine Arts Mus San Francisco 233 Post St Fl 5 San Francisco CA 94108

PARKER, JAMES AUBREY, federal judge; b. Houston, Jan. 8, 1937; s. Lewis Almeron and Emily Helen (Stuessy) P.; m. Florence Fisher, Aug. 26, 1960; children: Roger Alan, Pamela Elizabeth. BA, Rice U., 1959; LLB, U. Tex., 1962. Bar: Tex. 1962, N.Mex. 1963. With Modrall, Sperling, Roehl, Harris & Sisk, Albuquerque, 1962-87; judge U.S. Dist. Ct. N.Mex., Albuquerque, 1987—. Mem. Standing Commn. on Rules of Practice and Procedures of U.S. Cts., 1993-99, N.Mex. Commn. on Professionalism, 1986—; bd. visitors U. N.Mex. Law Sch., 1996—. Articles editor Tex. Law Rev., 1961-62. Mem. Fed. Judges Assn., Am. Judicature Soc., Am. Bd. Trial Advocates, N.Mex. Bar Assn. (Outstanding Judge award 1994), Albuquerque Bar Assn. (Outstanding Judge award 1993, 2000), Order of Coif, Chancellors, Phi Delta Phi. Avocations: ranching, fly fishing, running, skiing. Office: US Dist Ct 333 Lomas Blvd NW Ste 770 Albuquerque NM 87102-2277 Fax: 505 348-2225. E-mail: jparker@mncourt.fed.us

PARKER, JOHN MARCHBANK, consulting geologist; b. Manhattan, Kans., Sept. 13, 1920; s. John Huntington and Marjorie Elizabeth (Marchbank) P.; m. Agnes Elizabeth Potts, Mar. 17, 1978; m. Jan Goble, July 18, 1941 (div. 1968); children— Susan Kelly, Elizabeth Douglass, Deirdre Parker, John Eric; m. Nancy Booth, Jan. 24, 1970 (div. 1974). Student U. Minn., 1937, U. Wyo., 1938; B.S., Kans. State U., 1941. Cert. petroleum geologist Am. Inst. Profl. Geologists. Geologist, U.S. Pub. Roads Adminstrn., Alaska Hwy., Can., 1942-43; Field geologist Imperial Oil Ltd., Northwest Ter., Can., 1943-44; dist. geologist Stanolind Oil & Gas Co., Casper, Wyo., 1944-52; v.p. exploration Kirby Petroleum Co., Houston, 1952-74; v.p. exploration Northwest Exploration Co., Denver, 1974-75; cons. geologist Denver, 1975— . Contbr. articles to profl. jours. Recipient Disting. Service in Geology award Kans. State U., 1983. Fellow AAAS, Geol. Soc. Am.; mem. Am. Assn. Petroleum Geologists (pres. 1982-83, adv. council Tulsa 1983-84, Hon. Mem. award), Rocky Mountain Assn. Geologists (explorer of yr. 1979; pres. 1980-81). Home: 25422 Sea Bluffs Dr Unit 207 Dana Point CA 92629-2192

PARKER, OMAR SIGMUND, JR. lawyer; b. Jacksonville, Fla., Apr. 10, 1945; s. Omar Sigmund and Dorothea (Heath) P.; children: Omar Sigmund, Christopher Michael, Julie Anne, Melissa Suzanne, Amy Kathleen. BA, U. Wash., 1968; JD, U. Oreg., 1971. Bar: Wash. 1971, U.S. Dist. Ct. (we. dist.) Wash. 1971, U.S. Ct. Appeals, 1972. Ptnr. Perkins Coie, Seattle, 1971—. Contbr. articles to profl. jours. Bd. dirs. YMCA Youth and Govt. Program, Seattle, 1973-75. Mem. ABA, Wash. State Bar Assn., King County Bar Assn., Am. Coll. Real Estate Lawyers, Am. Coll. Mortgage Attys., Overlake Golf and Country Club, Order of Coif. Avocations: golf, youth coaching. Home: 411 108th Ave NE Ste 1800 Bellevue WA 98004-8420 Office: Perkins Coie 1201 3rd Ave Fl 40 Seattle WA 98101-3029

PARKER, PAM, apparel manufacturing company executive; b. San Francisco, 1960; BA, U. Calif., Berkeley; MBA, Stanford U., 1989. Cons. Bain and Co.; co-founder, co-pres. Ariat Internat., Inc., San Carlos, Calif., 1990—.

PARKER, ROBERT ALLAN RIDLEY, federal agency administrator, astronaut; b. N.Y.C., Dec. 14, 1936; s. Allan Elwood and Alice (Heywood) P.; m. Joan Audrey Capers, June 14, 1958 (div. 1980); children: Kimberly Ellen, Brian David Capers; m. Judith S. Woodruff, Apr. 2, 1981. AB, Amherst Coll., 1958; PhD, Calif. Inst. Tech., 1962. NSF postdoctoral fellow U. Wis., 1962-63, asst. prof., then assoc. prof. astronomy, 1963-74; astronaut NASA, Johnson Space Ctr., 1967-91; dir. policy plan Office Space Flight, NASA Hdqs., Washington, 1991, dir. space ops. utilization program, 1992-97; dir. NASA Mgmt. Office, JPL, Pasadena, Calif., 1997—. Mem. support crew Apollo XV and XVII, mission scientist Apollo XVII, program scientist Skylab program, mission specialist for Spacelab 1, 1983, ASTRO-1, 1990. Mem. Am. Astron. Soc., Phi Beta Kappa. Office: NMO 180 801 JPL 4800 Oak Grove Dr Pasadena CA 91109-8001 E-mail: rparker@nmo.jpl.nasa.gov

PARKER, ROBERT GEORGE, radiation oncology educator, academic administrator; b. Detroit, Jan. 29, 1925; s. Clifford Robert and Velma (Ashman) P.; m. Diana Davis, June 30, 1977; children by previous marriage: Thomas Clifford, James Richardson. BS, U. Wis., 1946, MD., 1948. Diplomate Am. Bd. Radiology (trustee 1978-90, pres. 1988-90). Intern U. Nebr. Hosp., Omaha, 1948-49; resident in pathology Western Res. U., Cleve., 1949-50; resident in radiology U. Mich., Ann Arbor, 1950, 52-54, instr. in radiology, 1954-55; staff radiotherapist Swedish Hosp. Tumor Inst., Seattle, 1955-58; prof. radiology U. Wash., Seattle, 1958-77; prof. radiation oncology UCLA, 1977—. Lt. USNR, 1950-52. Fellow Am. Coll. Radiology; mem. AMA (radiology residence rev. com.), Am. Soc. Therapeutic Radiologists (pres. 1975-76), Radiol. Soc. N.Am. (bd. dirs. 1984-90, pres. 1991-92), Am. Radium Soc. (bd. dirs. 1988-92, pres. 1992). Office: UCLA 200 Ucla Medical Plz Ste B265 Los Angeles CA 90095-8344

PARKHURST, VIOLET KINNEY, artist; b. Derby Line, Vt., Apr. 26, 1926; d. Edson Frank and Rosa (Beauchiene) Kinney; student Sch. Practical Arts, Boston, 1941-42, Baylor U., Waco, Tex., 1943, Calif. State U., Los Angeles, 1950-51; m. Donald Winters Parkhurst, Apr. 10, 1948. Fgn. corr. 5 Brazilian mags., 1946-53; tech. illustrator, 1954-55; owner five galleries including Ports of Call, San Pedro, Calif.; artist, specializing in seascapes; work included in permanent collection of Stockholm Mus., many pvt. collections including Presidents Richard M. Nixon, Ford, Reagan, Bush, Gov. Wilson, Mayor of Kobe, Japan, Mayor Yorty of L.A., Rory Calhoun, Barbara Rush, Jim Arness, David Rose; one-shows shows at prominent galleries; numerous paintings published. Winner 30 blue ribbons for art. Fellow Am. Inst. Fine Arts. Mem. Ch. of Religious Sci. Author: How to Paint Books, 1966; Parkhurst on Seascapes, 1972. Paintings reproduced on covers South West Art, Arizona Living; ltd. edit. prints published, also ltd. edit. plates. Office: Parkhurst Gallery Ports of Call Village San Pedro CA 90731

PARKIN, STUART STEPHEN PAPWORTH, materials scientist; IBM fellow IBM Almaden Rsch. Ctr., San Jose, Calif., 1983—. Recipient Internat. prize for new materials Am. Phys. Soc., 1994, C.V. Boys prize Inst. Physics, London, 1991, Inaugural Outstanding Young Investigator award Materials Rsch. Soc., 1991, Europhysics prize Hewlett-Packard, 1997, Indsl. Applications of Physics prize Am. Inst. Physics, 1999-2000. Fellow Am. Phys. Soc., Royal Soc. London, Inst. Physics (London). Office: IBM Almaden Rsch Ctr K11 D2 650 Harry Rd San Jose CA 95120-6099 E-mail: parkin@almaden.ibm.com

PARKINSON, BRADFORD WELLS, astronautical engineer, educator; b. Madison, Wis., Feb. 16, 1935; s. Herbert and Metta Tisdale (Smith) P.; m. Virginia Pinkham Wier, Nov. 26, 1977; children: Leslie, Bradford II, Eric, Ian, Bruce, Jared Bradford. BS, U.S. Naval Acad., 1957; MS, MIT, 1961; PhD, Stanford U., 1966; grad. (disting.), USAF Command and Staff Coll., 1969, Naval War Coll., 1972. Commd. 2d lt. USAF, 1957, advanced through grades to col., 1972; divsn. chief AF Test Pilot Sch., 1966-68; chair dept. astronautics and computer sci. USAF Acad., 1969-71; dir. engring. ABRES, 1972; program mgr. NAVSTAR GPS, 1972-78; ret. USAF, 1978; prof. mech. engring. Colo. State U., Ft. Collins, 1978-79; v.p. advanced engring. Rockwell Internat., Downey, Calif., 1979-80; gen. mgr., v.p. Intermetrics, Inc., Cambridge, Mass., 1980-84; prof., dir. gravity probe-B Stanford (Calif.) U., 1984—; CEO, pres. Trimble Navigation Ltd., 1998-99; prof. aerospace & astronautics Stanford U. Chair adv. coun. NASA; dir. Trimble Navigation Ltd., Sunnyvale, Calif., Draper Lab., Cambridge, Integrinautics, Palo Alto, Calif., Aerospace Corp., El Segundo, Calif. Decorated Def. Superior Svc. medal, AF Commendation medal with oak leaf cluster, Meritorius Svc. medal, Presdl. Unit citation, Bronze Star, Legion of Merit, Air medal with oak leaf cluster; recipient Pub. Svc. award NASA, 1984, Thurlow award Inst. Navigation, 1986, Burka award, 1987, Kepler award, 1991, von Karman Lectureship Am. Inst. of Aeronautics and Astronautics, 1996, Magellan Premium, Am. Philos. Soc., 1997, Gold medal Space Tech. Hall of Fame of U.S. Space Found., 1998, Williams Space medal Soc. Logistics Engrs., 1996. Fellow AIAA, Royal Inst. Navigation (Gold medal 1983), Inst. Navitation; mem. IEEE (Kirchner award 1986, Pioneer award 1994, Sperry award 1999), AAS, NAE, Internat. Acad. Astronautics, Sigma Xi, Tau Beta Pi. Avocations: hiking, skiing, running, sailing. Home: 1359 Cuernavaca Circulo Mountain View CA 94040-3570 Office: Stanford U 4085 Mail Code Stanford CA 94305

PARKLEE, LEE See PARK, LEE

PARKS, DEBORA ANN, private school director; b. Homestead, Fla., July 23, 1954; d. Jack Wesley and Blanche Margaret (Shawver) Hardin; m. Lewis O'Dell Parks, Apr. 12, 1970 (div. May 1980); 1 child, Kerri Shane Parks. BS in Early Childhood Edn., U. Ala., Tuscaloosa, 1983, MA in Spl. Edn., 1984, MA in Early Childhood Edn., 1987, PhD in Elem. Edn., 1991. Kindergarten tchr. Martin Luther King Jr. Elem. Sch., Tuscaloosa, 1983-85; tchr. gifted grades 2-5 Martin Luther King Jr. Elem. Sch. and Univ. Place Elem. Sch., Tuscaloosa, 1985-86; early childhood edn. instr. Shelton State C.C., Tuscaloosa, 1985-88; instr. U. Ala., Tuscaloosa, 1987; elem. tchr. 1st grade Martin Luther King Jr. Elem. Sch., Tuscaloosa, 1988-89; tchr. gifted grades 3-6 Carthay Elem. Sch., L.A. Unified Sch. Dist., 1991; faculty-in-residence Sunset Village Residence Halls and Hitch Stes. UCLA, 1991-95; tchr. gifted grades K-8 Maimonides Acad., L.A., 1992-94; asst. rschr. So. Calif. Injury Prevention Rsch. Ctr. Sch. Pub. Health, UCLA, 1993-95; faculty liaison on campus housing com.'s darkroom UCLA, 1993-95, instr. dept. edn., 1994, 95, instr., rschr., 1989-95; tchr. gifted grades 2-8 Maimonides Acad., L.A., 1995, gen. studies prin., 1995—. Grad. tchg. asst. elem. edn. U. Ala., Tuscaloosa, 1986-87; field coord., instr. Tchr. Edn. Lab., Grad. Sch. Edn., UCLA, 1989-93; enrichment tchr. grades 3-5 The Buckley Sch., Sherman Oaks, Calif., summer, 1991, 92, 93; evaluation coach/cons. Stanford Rsch. Inst., SB 620 Statewide Healthy Start Initiative Program, L.A., 1993-95; spl. faculty advisor UCLA Photographic Soc., 1993-95; evaluator lang. arts program, curriculum and tchrs. Maimonides Acad., L.A., 1994; enrichment tchr. grades 4-5 Buckley Sch., Sherman Oaks, Calif., summer 1994, enrichment tchr., summer 1995; evaluation coach, cons. Stanford Rsch. Inst., L.A., 1993-95; mem. governing bd. Nat. Assn. Creative Children and Adults, Ohio, 1992-94; rsch. adviser Phi Delta Kappa, UCLA chpt., 1992-94; mem. Adopt-A-Sch. Coun., L.A. Unified Sch. Dist., 1990-95; chairperson Tuscaloosa City Sch.'s Kindergarten Math. Com., 1984; presenter confs. and workshops. Author: The Newspaper Workbook, 1983, Pedestrian and Bicyclist Safety Curriculum for Grades K-5, 1994, Adopt-A-School Programs: A Guide for Pre-Service Teachers, 1995, Exercises and Tests in English Grammar, 2000; manuscript asst. editor Am. Mid. Sch. Edn., 1986-87; asst. editor Adopt-A-School Newsletter, 1993; contbr. articles to profl. jours; Photog. Exhib., Paralel 45 Pub. House, Pitesti, Romania, 2001/ Vol. Rebuild L.A., 1992-93 Recipient award NEA and Kodak, N.Y. and Ala., 1985, scholarships Am. Bus. Women's Assn., Ala., 1988, Beta Chi of Delta Kappa Gamma, 1983, Epsilon chpt. Alpha Delta Kappa, 1984, Yewell R. Thompson Endowed scholarship, 1988; designee Ala. Tchr. of Yr. Program, 1984-85, 85-86. Mem. Phi Delta Kappa. Democrat. Avocations: photography, calligraphy, graphic arts, genealogy. Home: 311 Westbourne Dr West Hollywood CA 90048-1909 Office: Maimonides Acad 310 N Huntley Dr Los Angeles CA 90048-1919 E-mail: dparks555@yahoo.com

PARKS, HAROLD RAYMOND, mathematician, educator; b. Wilmington, Del., May 22, 1949; s. Lytle Raymond Jr. and Marjorie Ruth (Chambers) P.; m. Paula Sue Beaulieu, Aug. 21, 1971 (div. 1984); children: Paul Raymond, David Austin; m. Susan Irene Taylor, June 6, 1985; 1 stepchild, Kathryn McLaughlin. AB, Dartmouth Coll., 1971; PhD, Princeton U., 1974. Tamarkin instr. Brown U., Providence, 1974-77; asst. prof. Oreg. State U., Corvallis, 1977-82, assoc. prof., 1982-89, prof. math., 1989—. Vis. assoc. prof. Ind. U., Bloomington, 1982-83. Author: Explicit Determination of Area Minimizing Hypersurfaces, vol. II, 1986, (with Steven G. Krantz) A Primer of Real Analytic Functions, 1992, (with G. Musser, R. Burton, W. Siebler) Mathematics in Life, Society and the World, 1997, 2d edit., 2000, (with Steven G. Krantz) The Geometry of Domains in Space, 1999; contbr. articles to profl. publs. Cubmaster Oregon Trail Coun. Boy Scouts Am., 1990-92. NSF fellow, 1971-74. Mem. Am. Math. Soc., Math. Assn. Am., Soc. Indsl. and Applied Math., Phi Beta Kappa. Republican. Mem. Soc. of Friends. Home: 33194 Dorset Ln Philomath OR 97370-9555 Office: Oreg State U Dept Math Corvallis OR 97331-4605 E-mail: parks@math.orst.edu

PARKS, MICHAEL CHRISTOPHER, journalist; b. Detroit, Nov. 17, 1943; s. Robert James and Rosalind (Smith) P.; m. Linda Katherine Durocher, Dec. 26, 1964; children: Danielle Anne, Christopher, Matthew. AB, U. Windsor, Ont., Can., 1965. Reporter Detroit News, 1962-65; corr. Time-Life News Service, N.Y.C., 1965-66; asst. city editor Suffolk Sun, Long Island, N.Y., 1966-68; polit. reporter, foreign corr. The Balt. Sun, Saigon, Singapore, Moscow, Cairo, Hong Kong, Peking, 1968-80; fgn. corr. L.A. Times, L.A., Peking, Johannesburg, Moscow, Jerusalem, 1980-95, dpty. fgn. editor, 1995-96, mng. editor, 1996-97, editor, 1997-2000, v.p., 1996-97, sr. v.p., 1997-98, exec. v.p., 1998-2000; v.p. Times Mirror Co., 1998-2000; vis. prof. Annenberg Sch. Comm. U. So. Calif., L.A., 2000—, interim dir. Annenberg Sch. Comm., 2001—. Disting. fellow Pacific Coun. Internat. Policy; trustee Found. Am. Comms. Recipient Pulitzer Prize, 1987. Mem. Am. Soc. Newspaper Editors, Pacific Coun. on Internat. Policy, Internat. Press Inst., Royal Commonwealth Soc. London, Soc. Profl. Journalists, Fgn. Corr. Club (Hong Kong), City Club (L.A.), Coun. on Fgn. Rels. Office: Annenberg Sch U So Calif Los Angeles CA 90089-0281 E-mail: mparks@usc.edu

PARKS, MICHAEL JAMES, publisher, editor; b. Spokane, Wash., June 3, 1944; s. Floyd Lewis and C. Marie (McHugh) P.; m. Janet K. Holter, Aug. 12, 1967; children: Michael J., Gregory F., Sarah M. BA, Seattle U., 1966. Reporter The Seattle Times, 1966-74, fin. editor, 1974-77; pub., editor Marple's Bus. Newsletter, Seattle, 1977—. Bd. govs. Seattle U. Alumni Assn.; trustee Seattle Rotary Service Found. Fellow Am. Press Inst., N.Y.C., 1973. Roman Catholic. Lodge: Rotary. Avocations: public speaking, reading, camping, hiking, swimming. Office: Marples Bus Newsletter 117 W Mercer St Ste 200 Seattle WA 98119-3953

PARKS, PATRICIA JEAN, lawyer; b. Portland, Oreg., Apr. 2, 1945; d. Robert and Marion (Crosby) P.; m. David F. Jurca, Oct. 17, 1971 (div. 1976). BA in History, Stanford U., 1963-67; JD, U. Penn., Phila., 1967-70. Bar: N.Y. 1971, Wash. 1974. Assoc. Milbank, Tweed, Hadley & McCoy, N.Y.C., 1970-73, Shidler, McBroom, Gates & Lucas, Seattle, 1974-81, ptnr., 1981-90, Preston, Thorgrimson, Shidler, Gates & Ellis, Seattle, 1990-93; pvt. practice Seattle, 1993-99; spl. counsel Karr Tuttle Campbell, 1999—. Active Vashon Allied Arts, Mountaineers. Mem. ABA, Wash. State Bar Assn. (past pres. tax sect., past chair gift and estate tax com.), Washington Women in Tax, Washington Women Lawyers, Seattle-King County Bar Assn., Employee Stock Ownership Plan Assn., Western Pension Conf., Pension Roundtable, Wash. Athletic Club, Vashon Athletic Club. Avocations: kayaking, hiking, Contra dancing, bird watching, karate. Office: 1201 3rd Ave Ste 2900 Seattle WA 98101-3284

PARKS, RICHARD E. manufacturing executive; B in Indsl. Engring., Purdue U.; MBA, U. Ill. With Delco Remy, Olin Corp.; various Fleetwood Enterprises, Inc., Riverside, Calif., 1983—, v.p. motor homes, sr. v.p. recreational vehicles, 1997—. Office: Fleetwood Enterprises Inc PO Box 7638 3125 Myers St Riverside CA 92513-7638

PARKS, ROBERT MYERS, appliance manufacturing company executive; b. Nevada, Mo., July 18, 1927; s. Cecil R. and Marcella (Myers) P.; m. Audrey Lenora Jones, June 18, 1955; children— John Robert, Janet M. Parks Huston. BS, U. Mo., 1949; MBA, Harvard U., 1952. Asst. dept. mgr. Jewett & Sherman Co., Kansas City, Mo., 1949-50; staff cons. Harbridge House, Inc., Boston, 1952; v.p. Electronic Splty. Co., Inc., Los Angeles, 1952-57; founder, chmn. bd. Parks Products, Inc., Hollywood, Calif., 1957—; pres. Generalist Industries, Inc., Hollywood, 1960-73. Chmn. bd. Shaver Corp. Am., L.A., 1965—; lectr. mktg. UCLA Extension divsn., 1960-61. Contbr. articles to profl. jours.; patentee in field. Active YMCA; bd. dirs. Hollywood Presbyn. Med. Center Found., Presbyn. Homes Found.; mem. chan's adv. council U. Mo. Bus. Sch., mayor's task force on L.A. River Cahuenga Pass Coalition. With USNR, 1944-45. Named in his honor Grad. Bus. Sch., U. Mo. Mem. Sales and Marketing Execs. Assn., C. of C., Navy League, World Affairs Council, Calif. Caballeros, Rangers, Vaqueros del Desierto, Los Caballeros, Rancheros Visitadores, E Clampus Vitus, Delta Sigma Pi, Sigma Chi. Presbyn. Clubs: Mason (Shriner), L.A. Breakfast, Braemar Country, Saddle and Sirloin. Home: 7421 Woodrow Wilson Dr Los Angeles CA 90046-1322 Office: 3611 Cahuenga Blvd Hollywood CA 90068-1205

PARLETTE, LINDA EVANS, state senator; m. Bob Parlette; 5 children. BS in Pharmacy, Wash. State U. Pharmacist; orchardist; Rep. rep. dist. 12 Wash. Ho. of Reps., 1997-2000; Rep. senator dist. 12 Wash. State Senate, 2000—. Mem. agr. and internat. trade, health and long-term care, higher edn. and ways and means coms. Wash. State Senate; chair Nat. Coun. State Legislators' Children, Family and Health Com.; bd. dirs. Wash. State Ag-Forestry Edn. Found. Mem. Lake Chelan United Meth. Ch.; former chair Lake Chelan Sch. Bd.; former mem. Lake Chelan Hosp. Guild. Recipient Trail Blazer award Lewis and Clark Elem. Sch., Margaret Chase Smith award Wash. State Rep. Women, 1995, award Friend of Rural Health Care, 1997-98, Rural Legislator of Yr. award Wash. State Hosp., 2000, Outstanding Legislator award Nat. Fedn. Ind. Bus., 2000. Mem. Wash. State Pharm. Assn., Wash. State Hort. Assn., Wenatchee Rotary (founder Lunch Buddy program). Office: PO Box 40412 106A Irv Newhouse Bldg Olympia WA 98504-0412 Fax: 360-786-7819. E-mail: parlette_li@leg.wa.gov

PARMELEE, ARTHUR HAWLEY, JR. pediatric medical educator; b. Chgo., Oct. 29, 1917; s. Arthur Hawley and Ruth Frances (Brown) P.; m. Jean Kern Rheinfrank, Nov. 11, 1939; children: Arthur Hawley III, Ann (Mrs. John C. Minahan Jr.), Timothy, Ruth Ellen. BS, U. Chgo., 1940, MD, 1943. Diplomate Am. Bd. Pediatrics (examiner 1966—). Intern U.S. Naval Hosp., Bethesda, Md., 1943-44; extern Yale Inst. Child Devel., 1947, New Haven Hosp., 1947-48, L.A. Children's Hosp., 1948-49; mem. faculty UCLA Med. Sch., 1951—, prof. pediat., 1967-88, prof. emeritus, 1988, dir. divsn. child devel., 1964-88; mem. Brain Rsch. Inst., 1966-88, Mental Retardation Rsch. Ctr., 1970-88. Rsch. prof. pediat. U. Göttingen, Germany, 1967-68; mem. com. child devel. rsch. and pub. policy NRC, 1977-81; cons. Nat. Inst. Child Health and Human Devel., 1963-70, Holy Family Adoption Svc., 1949-80. Author articles, chpts. in books. Trustee Los Angeles Children's Mus., 1979. Served with USN, 1943-47. Recipient C. Anderson Aldrich award in child devel., 1975; Commonwealth fellow Centre de Recherches Biologiques Neonatales, Clinique Obstetricale Baudelocque, Paris, 1959-60; fellow Ctr. Advanced Study in Behavioral Scis., Stanford U., 1984-85; hon. lectr. Soc. for Developmental and Behavioral Pediat., 1996. Mem. AMA, Am. Pediat. Soc., Soc. Pediat. Rsch., Western Soc. Pediat. Rsch., Am. Acad. Pediat. (chmn. com. sect. child devel. 1966), Assn. Ambulatory Pediat. (mem. coun. 1966-69), Soc. Rsch. in Child Devel. (pres. 1983-85, Disting. Sci. Contbns. to Child Devel. award 1993), Assn. Psychophysiol. Study of Sleep, Los Angeles County Med. Soc., Phi Beta Kappa. Home: 764 Iliff St Pacific Palisades CA 90272-3927 Office: Univ Calif Dept Pediatrics Los Angeles CA 90024

PARMENTER, ROBERT HALEY, physics educator; b. Portland, Maine, Sept. 19, 1925; s. LeClare Fall and Esther (Haley) P.; m. Elizabeth Kinnecom, Oct. 27, 1951; children: David Alan, Douglas Ian. B.S., U. Maine, 1947; Ph.D., Mass. Inst. Tech., 1952. Mem. staff solid state and molecular theory group Mass. Inst. Tech., 1951-54; guest scientist Brookhaven Nat. Lab., 1951-52; mem. staff Lincoln Lab., 1952-54, RCA Labs., 1954-66, vis. scientist Switzerland, 1958, acting head solid state research group, 1962-65; prof. physics U. Ariz., 1966-96, chmn. dept., 1977-83, prof. emeritus, 1996—. Mem. NASA rsch. adv. com. electrophysics, 1964-68, chmn., 1966-68, mem. rsch. and tech. adv. com. basic rsch., 1966-68; vis. lectr. Princeton (N.J.) U., 1960-61. Served with USNR, 1944-46. Fellow AAAS, Am. Phys. Soc. (chmn. div. condensed matter physics 1967-68); mem. Sigma Xi, Tau Beta Pi. Achievements include predicting the existence of the acoustoelectric effect, the enhancement of the transition temperature of a superconductor by means of tunneling extraction; demonstration of the conditions under which deterministic chaos occurs in quantum mechanical systems. Home: 1440 E Ina Rd Tucson AZ 85718-1175 Office: U Ariz Physics Dept Tucson AZ 85721-0001

PARNELL, FRANCIS WILLIAM, JR. otolaryngologist; b. Woonsocket, R.I., May 22, 1940; s. Francis W. and Dorothy V. (Lalor) P.; m. Diana DeAngelis, Feb. 27, 1965; children: Cheryl Lynn, John Francis, Kathleen Diana, Alison Anne, Thomas William. Student, Coll. Holy Cross, 1957-58; AB, Clark U., 1961; MD, Georgetown U., 1965. Diplomate: Nat. Bd. Med. Examiners, Am. Bd. Otolaryngology. Intern Univ. Hosps., Madison, Wis., 1965-66, resident in gen. surgery, 1966-67, otolaryngology, 1967-70; pvt. practice medicine specializing in otolaryngology San Rafael, Calif., 1972-75, Greenbrae, 1972-75, 78—; chmn., pres., CEO Parnell Pharms., Larkspur, 1982—. Cons. corp. med. affairs, 1978-82; corp. med. dir. Becton, Dickinson & Co., Rutherford, N.J., 1976-78; clin. instr. U. Calif. at San Francisco, 1972-75, asst. clin. prof., 1975-76; Alt. del., U.S. Del. 27th World Health Assembly WHO, Geneva, 1974. Contbr. articles to profl. jours. Candidate Calif. State Assembly, 1988; bd. dirs. Marin Coalition, 1980-96, 97—, chmn., 1986-87; trustee Ross (Calif.) Sch. Dist., 1981-89; mem. governing bd. Marin Cmty. Coll. Dist., 1995—, pres., 1999-00. Maj. M.C. AUS, 1970-72, lt. col. M.C., USAR, 1985-94. Fellow ACS (gov. 1988-94), Am. Acad. Otolaryngology. Home: PO Box 998 Ross CA 94957-0998 Office: 1100 S Eliseo Dr Greenbrae CA 94904-2017

PARNELL, SEAN, state legislator, lawyer; b. Hanford, Calif., Nov. 19, 1962; m. Sandy Parnell; children: Grace, Rachel. BBA, Pacific Luth. U., 1984; JD, U. Puget Sound, 1987. Pvt. practice law; mem. Alaska State Senate, co-chair fin. com., mem. resources com., legis. budget and audit com. Vol. mentor for H.S. youth groups and orgns., 1988-91; mem. Telecom. Info. Coun., Energy Coun., Western Legis. Timber Task Force, Bayshore-Klatt Cmty. Coun., Uniform Code Revision Commn.; dissenting mem. Long Range Fin. Planning Commn. Mem. Nat. Fedn. Ind. Bus. Republican. Avocations: family, teaching and coaching high school youth, running, reading, softball. Office: State Capitol 120 4th St Rm 518 Juneau AK 99801-1142 also: 716 W 4th Ave Ste 530 Anchorage AK 99501-2107 Fax: 907-465-6592. E-mail: senatorseanparnell@legis.state.ak.us

PARNES, ANDREW H. financial executive; V.p. fin., treas., CFO Standard Pacific Corp., Costa Mesa, Calif., 1996—. Office: Standard Pacific Corp 1565 W MacArthur Blvd Costa Mesa CA 92626

PARODE, ANN, lawyer; b. L.A., Mar. 3, 1947; d. Lowell Carr and Sabine (Phelps) P. BA, Pomona Coll., 1968; JD, UCLA, 1971. Bar: Calif. 1972, U.S. Dist. Ct. (so. dist.) Calif. 1972, U.S. Ct. Appeals (9th cir.) 1975. Assoc. Luce, Forward et al, San Diego, 1971-75; gen. counsel, exec. v.p., sec. San Diego Trust & Savings, 1975-94. Judge pro tem San Diego Mcpl. Ct., 1978-84; campus counsel U. Calif., San Diego, 1997—. Bd. dirs. San Diego Cmty. Found., 1989-97, chmn., 1994-96; bd. dirs. The Burnham Inst., 1995—. Mem. Calif. Bar Assn. (corp. law com. 1980-83, client trust fund commn. [illegible] 1000-00), San Diego County Bar Found. (founder, bd. dirs. 1979-86, 98—, pres. 1980-83), San Diego Bar Asns. (bd. dirs. 1977-81, v.p. 1977-78, 80-81, treas. 1979-80), Law Libr. Justice Found. (pres. 1994). E-mail: aparode@ucsd.edu

PARROTT, DENNIS BEECHER, retired insurance executive; b. St. Louis, June 13, 1929; s. Maurice Ray and Mai Ledgerwood (Beecher) P.; m. Vivian Cleveland Miller, Mar. 24, 1952; children: Constance Beecher, Dennis Beecher, Anne Cleveland. BS in Econs., Fla. State U., Tallahassee, 1954; postgrad., Princeton U., 1964; MBA, Pepperdine U., 1982. With Prudential Ins. Co. Am., 1954-74, v.p. group mktg., 1971-74; sr. v.p. Frank B. Hall Cons. Co., L.A., 1974-83; v.p. Johnson & Higgins, L.A., 1983-95; exec. v.p. Arthur J. Gallagher & Co., L.A., 1995-98; ret., 1998. Spkr. in field. Chmn. Weekend with the Stars Telethon, 1976-80; chmn. bd. dirs. United Cerebral Palsy/Spastic Children's Found., L.A. County, 1979-82, chmn. bd. govs., 1982-83; bd. dirs. Nat. United Cerebral Palsy Assn., 1977-82, pres., 1977-79; bd. dirs. L.A. Emergency Task Force, 1992; mem. cmty. adv. coun. Birmingham High Sch., Van Nuys, Calif., 1982-85; sect. chmn. United Way, L.A., 1983-84; bd. dirs. The Betty Clooney Found. for Brain Injured, 1986-88; mem. com. to fund an endowed chair in cardiology at Cedars-Sinai Med. Ctr., 1986-88; adv. coun. Family Health Program, Inc., 1986-88; bd. deacons Bel Air Presbyn. Ch., 1990-92, chmn., 1991-92, elder, 1993-96; mem. adv. coun. Blue Cross Calif., 1996-98; chmn. Danny Arnold Meml. Golf Classic at Riviera Country Club benefitting John Wayne Cancer Inst., 1997. 1st lt. AUS, 1951-53. Mem. Am. Soc. C.L.U.s., Internat. Found. Employee Benefits, Merchants and Mfrs. Assns. 44th Ann. Mgmt. Conf. (chmn. 1986), Employee Benefits Planning Assn. So. Calif., L.A. Club, Woodland Hills Country Club, Jonathan Club (L.A.). Republican. Presbyterian. Home: 17023 Encino Hills Dr Encino CA 91436-4009 E-mail: dparr63374@aol.com

PARROTT, JOEL J. zoo director; b. Lake George, N.Y., Aug. 21, 1952; married; 2 children. BS in Biology, Colo. State U., 1975, DVM, 1980. Intern Denver Zoo, 1979; veterinarian in pvt. practice Castro Valley, Calif., 1980-84; asst. dir. Oakland (Calif.) Zoo, 1984, exec. dir., 1985—. Office: The Oakland Zoo PO Box 5238 9777 Golf Links Rd Oakland CA 94605-4925

PARRY, ATWELL J., JR. state legislator, retail executive; b. Ogden, Utah, June 14, 1925; s. John Atwell and Nina Virginia (McEntire) P.; m. Elaine Hughes, Feb. 6, 1946; children: Bonnie, Michael, Jay, Donald, David, Delbert, Kent. Student pub. sch., Nampa, Idaho. Salesman King's Packing Co., Nampa, 1947-54, credit mgr., 1954-55; plant mgr. Stone Poultry Co., Nampa, 1955-56; salesman Nestle Chocolate Co., 1956-64; owner, mgr. Melba Foods, Idaho, 1964-82; mem. Idaho Senate, 1981—. Bd. dirs. Western Idaho Tng. Ctr., 1987-90; chmn. Senate Finance Com. and co-chmn. Joint Fin. and Appropriations Com., 1987—; chmn. Idaho State Bd. for Nat. Ctr. for Constl. Studies, 1988-90. Bd. dirs. Alcohol Treatment Ctr., Nampa, 1976-81; mem. Melba City Coun., 1971-74; mem. adv. bd. Mercy Med. Ctr., Nampa, 1976-81. Recipient Silver Beaver award Boy Scouts Am., 1959, Svc. award Mercy Med. Ctr., Outstanding Rep. Legislator in Idajo State award, 1993, Friend of Small Bus. award, 1987-88, 90, 92, Friend of Agrl. award, 1989-90, 91-92, 94-95, Melba Citizen of Yr. award, 1996, Canyon County Rep. Hall of Fame Outstanding Rep., 1998, Support of Scouting award Ore-Ida Coun. Boy Scouts Am., 2000, Silver Medallion award Boise (Idaho) State U., 2000, Spl. Recognition award Idaho Profl. Technician Edn., 2000. Office: State Capitol PO Box 83720 Boise ID 83720-3720

PARRY, ROBERT WALTER, chemistry educator; b. Ogden, Utah, Oct. 1, 1917; s. Walter and Jeanette (Petterson) P.; m. Marjorie J. Nelson, July 6, 1945; children: Robert Bryce, Mark Nelson. BS, Utah State Agr. Coll., 1940; MS, Cornell U., 1942; PhD, U. Ill., 1946; DSc (hon.), Utah State U., 1985, U. Utah, 1997. Rsch. asst. NDRC Munitions Devel. Lab. U. Ill., Urbana, 1943-45, tchg. fellow, 1945-46; mem. faculty U. Mich., Ann Arbor, 1946-69, prof. chemistry, 1958-69; Disting. prof. chemistry U. Utah, Salt Lake City, 1969-97, prof. emeritus, 1997—. Indsl. cons., 1952—; chmn. bd. trustees Gordon Rsch. Conf., 1967-68. Founding editor Inorganic Chemistry, 1960-63. Recipient Mfg. Chemists award for coll. tchg., 1972, Sr. U.S. Scientist award Alexander Von Humboldt-Stiftung, West Germany, 1980, First Govs. medal of Sci., State Utah, 1987. Mem. AAAS (chmn. chemistry sect. 1983), Internat. Union Pure and Applied Chemistry (chmn. U.S. nat. com., chmn. com. tchg. chemistry 1968-74), Am. Chem. Soc. (bd. editors jour. 1969-80, dir. 1973-83, pres.-elect 1981, pres. 1982, Disting. Svc. to Inorganic Chemistry award 1965, Disting. Svc. to Chem. Edn. award 1977, Utah award Utah sect. 1978, Priestly medal 1993), Sigma Xi. Achievements include research and publications on some structural problems of inorganic chemistry and incorporation results into theoretical models, chemistry of phosphorus, boron and fluorine. Home: 5002 Fairbrook Ln Salt Lake City UT 84117-6205 Office: U Utah Dept Chemistry 315 South 1400 East Rm 2174 Salt Lake City UT 84112-0850 Fax: 801-278.8224. E-mail: parry@chemistry.chem.utah.edu, rwpmnp@quest.net

PARSA, FEREYDOUN DON, plastic surgeon; b. Tehran, Iran, May 20, 1942; came to U.S., 1970; s. Issa and Zahra (Bismark) P.; m. Touri Akhlaghi, June 17, 1972; children: Natalie, Alan, Sean. MD, Lausanne U., Switzerland, 1969. Diplomate Am. Soc. Plastic Surgery. Chief of plastic surgery, prof. surgery U. Hawaii, Honolulu, 1981—. Contbr. articles to profl. jours. Mem. Am. Cancer Soc. Avocations: painting. Office: U Hawaii Sch Med Surg 1356 Lusitana St Honolulu HI 96813-2421 also: U Hawaii 1329 Lusitana St Honolulu HI 96813-2429 E-mail: fparsa@hotmail.com

PARSKY, GERALD LAWRENCE, lawyer; b. West Hartford, Conn., Oct. 18, 1942; s. Isadore and Nettie (Sanders) P.; m. Susan Haas, June 26, 1966; children: Laura, David; m. Robin Cleary, Jan. 27, 1980. A.B., Princeton U., 1964; J.D., U. Va., 1968. Bar: N.Y. 1969, D.C. 1974, Calif. 1983. Assoc. Mudge Rose Guthrie & Alexander, N.Y.C., 1968-71; spl. asst. to under sec. U.S. Treasury Dept., Washington, 1971-73, exec. asst. to dep. sec. Fed. Energy Office, 1973-74, asst. sec. internat. affairs, 1974-77; sr. ptnr. Gibson, Dunn & Crutcher, Los Angeles, 1977-90; of counsel Gibson, Dunn & Cruther, L.A., 1990-92; chmn. Aurora Capital Ptnrs., L.A., 1990—. Bd. govs. Performing Arts Council, Los Angeles Music Ctr. Recipient Alexander Hamilton award U.S. Treasury, 1976 Mem. ABA, Coun. Fgn. Rels., N.Y. Princeton Club, Calif. Club, Racquet Club, Anandale Club, Beach Club. Office: Aurora Capital Group 10877 Wilshire Blvd Ste 2100 Los Angeles CA 90024-4376

PARSONS, A. PETER, lawyer; b. Norwood, Mass., May 29, 1945; s. Charles A.A. and Elizabeth P. (Coombs) P.; children: A. Peter, Christopher P.; m. Elizabeth A. Lee, Aug. 24, 1991; 1 child Alex W. AA, Palm Beach Jr. Coll., 1968; BS Fla. Atlantic U., 1969; JD, Duke U., 1973. Bar: Wash. 1973, U.S. Dist. Ct. (ea. and we. dists.) Wash. 1974, U.S. Ct. Appeals (9th cir.) 1974; CPA, Fla., Wash. Acct., Haskins & Sells, Ft. Lauderdale, 1969-70; tax cons. Arthur, Young & Co., Portland, Oreg., 1972; law clk. Wash. Supreme Ct., 1973-74; atty. Perkins, Coie, Seattle, 1974-77; mem., mng. dir. Weinrich, Gilmore & Adolph, Seattle, 1978-87; ptnr. Davis Wright Tremaine LLP, 1988—; adj. prof. U. Puget Sound, 1974-75; lectr. U. Wash., 1978-81. Mem. editorial bd. Duke U. Law Jour., 1971-73. Contbr. articles to legal jours. Chmn. bd. dirs. PIVOT, non-profit corp., Seattle, 1975-78; Group Theater, Seattle, 1984-86; chmn. bd. dirs. MIT Enterprise Forum, Seattle, 1984-92 ; Wash. State Biotechnology Assn. 1991-94, Washington Software Alliance, Bellevue, 1996-98, Midisoft Corp., Issaquah, 1996-98, Info. Technol. World Congress N.Am., 1998—, BC Softworld Soc., 1998—. Served with USAF, 1963-67. Mem. ABA, Wash. Bar Assn., Am. Intellectual Property Law Assn., Computer Law Soc., Am. Inst. CPAs, Wash. Soc. CPAs, Seattle-King County Bar Assn., Am. Coll. of Mediators, Rainier Club, Seattle Yacht Club. Home: 1864 Broadmoor Dr E Seattle WA 98112-2312 Office: Davis Wright Tremaine LLP 2600 Century Sq 1501 4th Ave Seattle WA 98101-1688

PARSONS, ELMER EARL, retired clergyman; b. Cloverland, Wash., Oct. 4, 1919; s. Claud Solomon and Bessie Lillian (Campbell) P.; m. Marjorie Emma Carlson, Aug. 29, 1942; children— Karl Elmer, James Myron, Helen Joy, Ann Elizabeth, Lois Marie, Louise Melba. BA, Seattle Pacific U., 1942; STB, Bibl. Sem. N.Y., 1945; STM, Asbury Theol. Sem., Wilmore, Ky., 1955; DD (hon.), Greenville (Ill.) Coll., 1958. Ordained to ministry Free Methodist Ch., 1944; acad. dean Wessington Springs (S.D.) Coll., 1945-47; missionary to China, 1947-49; missionary to Japan, 1949-54; supt. Japan Free Meth. Mission, 1950-54; pres. Central Coll., McPherson, Kans., 1955-64, Osaka (Japan) Christian Coll., 1964-74; Asia area sec.; Free Meth. Ch., 1964-74; bishop Free Meth. Ch. N.Am., 1974-85. Author: Witness to the Resurrection, 1967. Chmn. Free Meth. Study Commn. on Doctrine, 1990-95. Named Alumnus of Year Seattle Pacific U., 1976 Mem. Wesleyan Theol. Soc.

PARSONS, ERIC E. financial company executive; Degree, Lewis & Clark Coll., Northwestern U. V.p. Standard Ins. Co., pres. mortgage and real estate subs.; sr. v.p., CFO StanCorp Fin. Group/Standard Ins. Co., Portland, Oreg. Trustee Oreg. Zoo Found.; bd. dirs. Portland Opera; mem. Metro Bus. Adv. Coun.; mem. Portland Mayor's Bus. Roundtable. Fellow Life Office mgmt. Inst. Office: StanCorp Fin Group Inc 1100 SW 6th Ave Portland OR 97204

PARTHEMORE, JACQUELINE GAIL, internist, educator; b. Harrisburg, Pa., Dec. 21, 1940; d. Philip Mark and Emily (Buvit) Parthemore; m. Alan Morton Blank, Jan. 7, 1967; children: Stephen Eliot, Laura Elise. BA, Wellesley Coll., 1962; MD, Cornell U., 1966. Diplomate Am. Bd. Internal Medicine. Resident in internal medicine N.Y. Hosp., Cornell, 1966-69; fellow in endocrinology Scripps Clinic and Rsch. Found., La Jolla, Calif., 1969-72; rsch. edn. assoc. VA Hosp., San Diego, 1974-78; staff physician VA San Diego Health Care Sys., 1978-79, asst. chief, med. svc., 1979-83, acting chief, med. svc., 1980-81, chief of staff, 1984—; asst. prof. medicine U. Calif. Sch. Medicine, San Diego, 1974-80, assoc. prof. medicine, 1980-85, prof. medicine, assoc. dean, 1985—. Mem. nat. rsch. resources coun. NIH, Bethesda, Md., 1990-94. Contbr. articles to profl. jours., chpts. to books. Bd. dirs. San Diego Vets. Med. Rsch. Found.; mem. adv. bd. San Diego Opera; mem. Roundtable and Channel 10 Focus Grp., San Diego Millennium Proj., 1999. Recipient Bullock's 1st Annual Portfolio award, 1985, San Diego Pres.'s Coun. Woman of Yr. award, 1985, YWCA Tribute to Women in Industry award, 1987, San Diego Women Who Mean Bus. award, 1999. Fellow ACP; mem. Endocrine Soc., Nat. Assn. VA Chiefs Staff (pres. 1989-91), Am. Assn. Clin. Endocrinologists, Wellesley Coll. Alumnae Assn. (1st v.p. 1992-95), San Diego Wellesley Club (pres. 1997-99). Avocations: gardening, reading, sailing, cooking, travel. Office: VA San Diego Healthcare Sys 3350 La Jolla Village Dr San Diego CA 92161-0002 E-mail: jparthemore@ucsd.edu

PARTIDA, GILBERT A. executive; b. Nogales, Ariz., July 27, 1962; s. Enrique Gilberto and Mary Lou (Flores) P.; m. Soncee Ray Brown, July 30, 1992. BA with distinction, U. Ariz., 1984; JD cum laude, Pepperdine U., 1987; LLD (hon.), Calif. Western Sch Law, San Diego, 1993. V.p., bd. mem. Partida Brokerage, Inc., Nogales, 1983-91; law clk. Office of Ariz. Atty. Gen., Tucson, 1985; assoc. Gray, Cary, Ames & Frye, San Diego, 1986-89, sr. assoc., 1990-92, chmn. Mex. Practice Group, 1992; pres. Greater San Diego C. of C., 1993-98; pres., CEO Price Smart, San Diego, 1998—. Corp. counsel San Diego Incubator Corp., 1990—. Contbr. articles to profl. jours. Mem. United Way Latino Future Scan Com., 1990; mentor Puente, 1991; leadership tng. mentor Chicano Fedn., 1992; dinner com. Young at Art, 1991; mem. Children's Initiative, 1993, Superbowl Task Force, 1993, San Diego Dialogue, 1993; hon. mem. Sister City, 1993, LEAD, 1993; hon. chair Easter Seals Telethon, 1994; vice chmn. Border Trade Alliance, 1989-91; mem. nat. gala com. HDI Ednl. Svcs., 1990; Calif. state del. U.S.-Mexico Border Govs.' Conf., 1990, 92; exec. com. San Diego Conv. and Visitors Bur. Mem. San Diego County Hispanic C. of C. (chmn. 1991, pres. 1990-91, v.p. 1989-90, internat. com. chair 1989-90, sec. 1989, founding bd. mem. 1988), Consejo Nacional de Maquiladoras, Calif. Hispanic C. of C. (state conv. joint venture com. 1991, spl. projects chair 1991), San Diego/Tijuana Sister Cities Soc. (adv. coun. 1993—), San Diego County Bar Assn. (U.S./Mexico liaison com.), ABA (U.S./Mexico bar liaison com.), Hispanic Alliance for Free Trade, Rotary Club San Diego. Avocations: tennis, running, creative writing. Office: Price Smart Inc 4649 Morena Blvd San Diego CA 92117-3650

PARTLOW, BOB, broadcast executive; Bureau chief Gannett News Service, Olympia, WA. Office: Gannett News Svc 1417 S Columbia St Fl 2 Olympia WA 98504-0001

PARTRIDGE, BRUCE JAMES, lawyer, educator, writer; b. Syracuse, N.Y., June 4, 1926; came to Can., 1969; s. Bert James and Lida Marion (Rice) P.; m. Mary Janice Smith, June 13, 1948 (dec. 1986); children: Heather Leigh, Eric James, Brian Lloyd, Bonnie Joyce; m. May S. Archer, May 28, 1988; stepchildren: Sheila Archer, Laurel Archer. AB cum laude, Oberlin Coll., Ohio, 1946; LLB, Blackstone Coll., Chgo., 1950, JD, 1952; LLB, U. B.C., 1974. Bar: B.C. 1976, N.W.T. 1980. Rsch. physicist Am. Gas Assn., Cleve., 1946-48; bus. mgr., purchasing agt., asst. treas. Rochester Inst. Tech., N.Y., 1953-58; bus. adminstr. Baldwin-Wallace Coll., Berea, Ohio, 1951-53; bus. mgr. Cazenovia (N.Y.) Coll., 1948-51; v.p. bus. and mgmt. U. Del., Newark, 1958-63; v.p. adminstrn. Johns Hopkins U., Balt., 1963-69; pres. U. Victoria, B.C., Can., 1969-72; assoc. Clark, Wilson & Co., Vancouver, Can., 1975-78; successively solicitor, mng. solicitor, gen. solicitor, v.p. law and gen. counsel, sec. Cominco Ltd., Vancouver, 1978-88; exec. dir. Baker & McKenzie, Hong Kong, 1988-90; v.p. Pacific Creations, Inc., 1990-92; faculty Camosun Coll., 1992-99. Author: Management in Canada: The Competitive Challenges, 2000; co-author: College and University Business Administration, 1968; chmn. editl. com. Purchasing for Higher Education, 1962; contbr. numerous articles to profl. jours. Chmn. commn. on adminstrv. affairs Am. Coun. on Edn., Washington, 1966-69; mem. Pres.'s Com. on Employment of Handicapped, Washington, 1967-69; mem. adv. coun. Ctr. for Resource Studies, Queen's U.; bd. dirs. L'Arche in the Americas; mem. adv. coun. Westwater Rsch. Ctr., U. B.C. Mem. Law Soc. B.C., Law Soc. of N.W. Ters., Assn. Can. Gen. Counsel, Fedn. Ins. and Corp. Counsel, Def. Rsch. Inst. (product liability com.), Am. Corp. Counsel Assn., Vancouver Club, Aberdeen Marina Club, Hong Kong Football Club. Unitarian. Office: Camosun Coll 4461 Interurban Rd Victoria BC Canada V8X 3X1 E-mail: brucepart@sprint.ca

PASAHOW, LYNN H(AROLD), lawyer; b. Ft. Eutiss, Va., Mar. 13, 1947; s. Samuel and Cecelia (Newman) P.; m. Leslie Aileen Cobb, June 11, 1969; 1 child, Michael Alexander. AB, Stanford U., 1969; JD, U. Calif., Berkeley, 1972. Bar: Calif. 1972, U.S. Ct. Appeals (9th cir.) 1972, U.S. Dist. Ct. (no. dist.) Calif. 1973, U.S. Dist. Ct. (cen. dist.) Calif. 1974, U.S. Supreme Ct. 1976, U.S. Dist. Ct. (ea. dist.) Calif. 1977, U.S. Ct. Appeals (fed. cir.) 1990. Law clk. judge U.S. Dist. Ct. (no. dist.) Calif., San Francisco, 1972-73; assoc. McCutchen, Doyle, Brown & Enersen, Palo Alto, Calif., 1973-79, ptnr. San Francisco, 1979-2001, Fenwick & West LLP, 2001—. Attys. adv. panel Bay Area Biosci. Ctr., 1993—; mem. adv. bd. Berkeley Ctr. for Law and Tech., 1998—. Author: Pretrial and Settlement Conferences in Federal Court, 1983; co-author: Civil Discovery and Mandatory Disclosure: A Guide to Effective Practice, 1994; contbr. articles to profl. jours. Mem. ABA, Calif. Bar Assn. Democrat. Office: Fenwick & West LLP Two Palo Alto Sq Palo Alto CA 94306 E-mail: lpasahow@fenwick.com

PASCAL, AMY, film company executive; Pres. Columbia Pictures, Culver City, Calif., 1996-99, chmn., 1999—. Office: Columbia Pictures 10202 Washington Blvd Culver City CA 90232-3119

PASCAL, C(ECIL) BENNETT, classics educator; b. Chgo., May 4, 1926; s. Jack and Goldie (Zeff) P.; m. Ilene Joy Shulman, Feb. 1, 1959; 1 child, Keith Irwin. BA, UCLA, 1949, MA, 1950, Harvard U., 1953, PhD, 1956. Instr. U. Ill., Champaign, 1955-56, Cornell U., Ithaca, N.Y., 1957-60; asst. prof., then assoc. prof. U. Oreg., Eugene, 1960-75, prof. classics, 1975-96, prof. emeritus, 1996—, head dept., various years - 1965-85. Author: Cults of Cisalpine Gaul, 1964; contbr. articles to profl. jours. Active Eugene Bicycle Com., 1971-83. Wwith USN, 1944-46. Traveling fellow, Italy, Harvard U., 1956-57, Fulbright-Hays fellow, Rome, 1967-68. Mem. Am. Philol. Assn., Classical Assn. Pacific N.W. (pres. 1965-66), AAUP, Archeol. Inst. of Am. (past pres., sec. Eugene Soc.) Democrat. Jewish. Avocations: skiing, fishing, novel writing. Home: 330 Fulvue Dr Eugene OR 97405-2788 Office: U Oreg Dept Classics Eugene OR 97403 E-mail: cbpasc@darkwing.uoregon.edu

PASCAL, NAOMI BRENNER, editor-in-chief, publishing executive; b. Bklyn., Mar. 13, 1926; d. Mortimer and Sylvia (Freehof) Brenner; m. Paul Pascal, June 27, 1948; children: David Morris, Janet Brenner. BA, Wellesley Coll., 1946. Editor Vanguard Press, Inc., N.Y.C., 1946-48, U. N.C. Press, Chapel Hill, N.C., 1948-50, 52-53, U. Wash. Press, 1953-75, editor-in-chief, 1976—, assoc. dir., 1985—. Dir. Assn. Am. Univ. Presses, 1976-78; cons. editor Scholarly Pub. jour., Toronto, Ont., Can., 1979— ; del. Wash. State Gov.'s Conf. on Library and Info. Services, Olympia, 1978-79. Co-author: Glossary Typesetting Terms, 1994; contbr. chpts. to books, articles to profl. jours. Durant scholar, 1945; recipient constituency award Assn. Am. Univ. Presses, 1991. Mem. Women in Scholarly Pub., Assn. Asian Am. Studies, Native Am. Art Studies Assn., Phi Beta Kappa (treas. Alpha of Wash. chpt. 1975-78). Office: U Wash Press PO Box 50096 Seattle WA 98145-5096

PASCOE, PATRICIA HILL, state legislator, writer; b. Sparta, Wis., June 1, 1935; d. Fred Kirk and Edith (Kilpatrick) Hill; m. D. Monte Pascoe, Aug. 3, 1957; children: Sarah, Edward, William. BA, U. Colo., 1957; MA, U. Denver, 1968, PhD, 1982. Tchr. Sequoia Union High Sch. Dist., Redwood City, Calif. and Hayward (Calif.) Union High Sch. Dist., 1957-60; instr. Met. State Coll., Denver, 1969-75, Denver U., 1975-77, 81, research asst. bur. ednl. research, 1981-82; tchr. Kent Denver Country Day, Englewood, Colo., 1982-84; freelance writer Denver, 1985—; mem. Colo. Senate, Dist. 32, Denver, 1989-93, 95—; chair minority caucus Colo. Senate, Denver, 1996-2000, chair policy and planning com., 2000—. Commr. Edn. Commn. of the States, Denver, 1975-82. Contbr. articles to numerous publs. and jours. Bd. dirs. Samaritan House, 1990-94, Cystic Fibrosis Found., 1989-93; pres. East H.S. Parent Tchr. and Student Assn., Denver, 1984-85; mem. Moore Budget Adv. Com., Denver, 1966-72; legis. chmn. alumni bd. U. Colo., Boulder, 1987-89; del. Dem. Nat. Conv., San Francisco, 1984, N.Y.C., 1992; mem. Denver Woman's Press Club, 1986—, Colo. Arts Coalition, 1988-97; bd. dirs. Opera Colo., 1996—. Mem. Soc. Profl. Journalists, Common Cause (bd. dirs. Denver chpt. 1986-88), Colo. Endowment for Humanities, Phi Beta Kappa. Presbyterian.

PASCOTTO, ALVARO, lawyer; b. Rome, Mar. 8, 1949; came to U.S., 1984; s. Antonio and Anna Ludovica (Habig) P.; m. Linda Haldan, July 20, 1985. JD, U. Rome, 1973. Bar: Italy 1976, Calif. 1987, U.S. Dist. Ct. (cen. dist.) Calif. 1987, U.S. Ct. Appeals (9th cir.) 1987. Ptnr. Studio Legale Pascotto, Rome, 1976-86, Pascotto, Gallavotti & Gardner, L.A. and Rome, 1986-90, Pascotto & Gallavotti, L.A., 1990—; of counsel Irell & Manella LLP, L.A., 1994—. Ofcl. counsel Consulate Gen. Italy, L.A., 1987—. Mem. ABA, Calif. Bar Assn., Italian-Am. Bar Assn., Am. Mgmt. Assn., Consiglio dell'Ordine Degli Avvocati e Procuratori di Roma. Clubs: Circolo del Golf (Rome); Malibu (Calif.) Racquet Club, Regency Club (L.A.), L.A. Country Club. Home: 6116 Merritt Dr Malibu CA 90265-3847 Office: Pascotto & Gallavotti Ste 900 1800 Avenue Of The Stars Los Angeles CA 90067-4212 Fax: 310-284-3021

PASHGIAN, MARGARET HELEN, artist; b. Pasadena, Calif., Nov. 7, 1934; d. Aram John and Margaret (Howell) P. BA, Pomona Coll., 1956; MA in Fine Arts, Boston Univ., 1958; student, Columbia U., 1957. Art instr. Harvard-Newton Program Occidental Coll., 1977-78; artist in residence Calif. Inst. Tech., 1970-71. Grants panelist Calif. Arts Coun., Sacramento, 1993. Artist: solo shows include Rex Evans Gallery, L.A., 1965, 67, Occidental Coll., 1967, Kornblee Gallery, N.Y.C., 1969 72, U. Calif., Irvine, 1975, U. Calif. Santa Barbara, 1976, Stella Polaries Gallery, L.A., 1981, 82, Kaufman Galleries, Houston, 1982, Modernism Gallery, San Francisco, 1983, Works Gallery, Long Beach, Costa Mesa, Calif., 1986, 87, 88, 89, 90, 91, 92, Malka Gallery, L.A., 1997; group exhibitions include Pasadena Art Mus., 1965, Carson Pirie Scott, Chgo., 1965, Calif. Palace of Legion of Honor, San Francisco, 1967, Esther Bear Gallery, Santa Barbara, 1967, 69, Lytton Ctr. of the Visual Arts, L.A., 1968, Salt Lake Art Inst., Salt Lake City, 1968, Mus. Contemporary Crafts, Internat. Plastics Exhibition, 1969, Second Flint (Mich.) Invitational, 1969, Milw. Art Ctr., 1969, U.S.I.S. Mus., N.Y.C., Mus. Contemporary Art, Chgo., 1970, Studio Merconi, Milan, 1970, Calif. Inst. Tech., Baxter Art Galley, 1971, 1980, Calif. Innovations, Palm Springs Dessert Mus., 1981, Calif. Internat. Arts Found. Mus. of Modern Art, Paris, 1982, L.A. Artists in Seoul, Donsangbang Gallery, 1982, An Artistic Conversation, 1931-82, Poland, USA, Ulster Mus., Belfast, Ireland, 1983, Madison (Wis.) Art Ctr., 1994, Calif. State U., Fullerton, 1995, Oakland (Calif.) Mus., 1995; represented in pub. collections at River Forest (Ill.) State Bank, Atlantic Richfield Co., Dallas, Frederic Weisman Collection, L.A., Security Pacific Bank, L.A., Singapore, Andrew Dickson White Mus. of Art, Cornell U., Ithaca, N.Y., L.A. County Mus. of Art, Santa Barbara Art Mus., Laguna Beach Mus. of Art. Trustee, Pomona Coll, Claremont, Calif., 1987—; parade judge Tournament of Roses Centennial Parade, Pasadena, 1987; bd. dirs. L.A. Master Chorale, 1992—. NEA grantee, 1986. Home: 731 S Grand Ave Pasadena CA 91105-2424

PASHLER, HAROLD E. psychologist, educator; AB in Logic and Philosophy of Sci., ScB in Psychology magna cum laude, Brown U., 1980; PhD in Psychology, U. Pa., 1985. Asst. prof. dept. psycholgoy U. Calif., San Diego, 1985-90, assoc. prof., 1990-93, prof. dept. psychology, 1993—. Mem. various coms. U. Calif. San Diego; ad hoc reviewer Hong Kong Rsch. Coun., Natural Sci. and Engring. Rsch. Coun., Can., NSF, Behavioral and Neural Scis., USAF Office Sci. Rsch. Life Scis. Program. Assoc. editor Psychonomic Bull. and Rev., 1998—; mem. editl. bd. Perception & Psychophysics, 1988—, Psychol. Rsch., 1989—, Cognitive Psychology, 1992-98, Visual Cognition, 1994—, Psychonomic Bull. and Rev., 1994-97, Am. Jour. Psychology, 1998—; ad hoc reviewer Am. Jour. Psychology, Attention and Performance XII, XIV, Cognition, Cognitive Psychology, Cognitive Sci., Current Directions in Psychol. Sci., Ency. Human Biology, Exptl. Brain Rsch., Jour. Exptl. Psychology: Human Perception and Performance, Jour. Exptl. Psychology: Learning, Memory and Cognition, Memory and Cognition, Nature, Nature Neurosci., Perception, Perception & Psychophysics, Psychol. Rsch., Psychol. Rev., Quarterly Jour. Exptl. Psychology, Spatial Vision, Vision Rsch. Recipient Troland Rsch. award NAS, 1999; NSF grad. fellow, 1981-84, IBM grad. fellow, 1984-85. Fellow Am. Psychol. Soc.; mem. Phi Beta Kappa, Sigma Xi. Office: Dept Psychology 0109 U Calif San Diego La Jolla CA 92093 E-mail: hpashler@ucsd.edu

PASICH, KIRK ALAN, lawyer; b. La Jolla, Calif., May 26, 1955; s. Chris Nick and Iva Mae (Tormey) P.; m. Pamela Mary Woods, July 30, 1983; children: Christopher Thomas, Kelly Elizabeth, Connor Woods. BA in Polit. Sci., UCLA, 1977; JD, Loyola Law Sch., L.A., 1980. Bar: Calif. 1980, U.S. Dist. Ct. (no., so., ea. and cen. dists.) Calif. 1981, U.S. Ct. Appeals (9th cir.) 1982, U.S. Ct. Appeals (1st cir.) 1992. Assoc. Paul, Hastings, Janofsky & Walker, L.A., 1980-88, ptnr., 1988-89, Troop Steuber Pasich Reddick & Tobey, LLP, L.A., 1989-2000, Howrey Simon Arnold & White LLP, L.A., 2001—. Author: Casualty and Liability Insurance, 1990, 2000; co-author: Officers and Directors: Liabilities and Protections, 1996, 2000, The Year 2000 and Beyond: Liability and Insurance for Computer Code Problems, 2000; contbg. editor: West's California Litigation Forms: Civil Procedure Before Trial, 2000; entertainment law columnist, ins. law columnist L.A. and San Francisco Daily Jour., 1989—; contbr. articles to profl. jours. Active bd. dirs. Nat. Acad. Jazz, L.A., 1988-89, chmn. bd. dirs. Woody Herman Found., L.A., 1989-92, Constnl. Rights Found., 2000; active L.A. City Atty's. Task Force for Econ. Recovery, 1992-93. Named to Calif's. Legal Dream Team as 1 of state's top 25 litigators, Calif. Law Bus., 1992, as one of the nation's top 45 lawyers under age 45, The Am. Lawyer, 1995. Mem. ABA (mem. Task Force on Complex Insurance Coverage Litigation). Home: 10419 Lindbrook Dr Los Angeles CA 90024-3323 E-mail: pasichk@howrey.com

PASK, JOSEPH ADAM, ceramic engineering educator; b. Chgo., Feb. 14, 1913; s. Adam Poskoczem and Catherine (Ramanauskas) P.; m. Margaret J. Gault, June 11, 1938; children: Thomas Joseph, Kathryn Edyth. B.S., U. Ill., 1934, Ph.D., 1941; M.S., U. Wash., 1935. Ceramic engr. Willamina Clay Products Co., Oreg., 1935-36; teaching asst. ceramic engring. U. Ill., 1938, instr., 1938-41; asst. ceramic engr. electrotech. lab. U.S. Bur. Mines, 1941; assoc. ceramic engr. N.W. Exptl. Sta., 1942-43; asst. prof. ceramic engring., head dept. Coll. of Mines, U. Wash., Seattle, 1941-43; research ceramist, lamp div. Westinghouse Electric Corp., N.J., 1943-46, research engr. ceramic sect., 1946-48; assoc. prof. ceramic engring., head ceramic group div. materials sci. and engring. U. Calif. at Berkeley, 1948-53, founder program ceramic engring. and sci., 1948, prof., 1953-80, prof. emeritus, 1980—, vice chmn. div., 1956-57, chmn. dept., 1957-61; asso. dean grad. student affairs U. Calif. at Berkeley (Coll. Engring.), 1969-80; sr. faculty scientist Lawrence Berkeley Lab. John Dorn Meml. lectr. Northwestern U., 1977; mem. clay mineral com. NRC; mem. materials adv. bd., chmn. ad hoc com. ceramic processing, adv. commn. metallurgy div. U.S. Bur. Standards; chmn. NSF study objective criteria in ceramic engring. edn., U.S.-China Seminar on Basic Sci. of Ceramics, Shanghai, 1983 Recipient John F. Bergeron Meml. Svc. award Ceramic Engring. div. U. Wash., Seattle, 1969, gold medal for research and devel. French Soc. for Research and Devel., 1979, Berkeley citation U. Calif., 1980, Alumni honor award for disting. service in engring. U. Ill. Coll. Engring., 1982, Outstanding Achievement in Edn. award Com. of Confucius, 1982, Internat. Prize Japan Fine Ceramics Assn., 1988, Engring. Alumni Achievement award U. Wash. Coll. Engring., 1991. Fellow AAAS, Am. Ceramic Soc. (disting. life mem., v.p. 1953-54, pres. ednl. coun. 1954-55, trustee 1959-62, chmn. electronics div. 1959-60, John Jeppson award 1967, Ross Coffin Purdy award 1979), Mineral Soc., Acad. Dental Materials; mem. NAE, Nat. Inst. Ceramics Engrs., N.Y. Acad. Scis., Am. Soc. Matls, Brit. Ceramic Soc., Internat. Acad. Ceramics,, Am. Soc. Engring. Edn. (chmn. materials com. 1961-63, Centennial Cert. 1993), Clay Minerals Soc., Ceramics Soc. Japan (hon., Centennial medal 1991), Materials Rsch. Soc. Japan (hon.), Keramos, Sigma XI, Tau Bet Pi, Alpha Sigma Mu. Home: 994 Euclid Ave Berkeley CA 94708-1437 Office: U Calif Dept Ceramic Engring Berkeley CA 94720-0001

PASTEGA, RICHARD LOUIS, retired retail specialist; b. Klamath Falls, Oreg., Mar. 25, 1936; s. Louie and Jennie (Borgialli) P. BS, So. Oreg. State Coll., 1960; MS, Mont. State U., Bozeman, 1961. Tchr. social studies Henley High Sch., Klamath Falls, Oreg., 1962-63, Juneau (Alaska) Douglas High Sch., 1964-67, Thessaloniki (Greece) Internat. High Sch., 1967-69; editor, pub. Breakdown Newspaper, Klamath Falls, Oreg., 1971-73; mgr. Pastega's Market, Klamath Falls, 1975-98, ret., 1998. Del. Dem. Nat. Conv., N.Y.C., 1976, Oreg. Dem. Platform conv., Eugene, Beaverton and Ashland, 1978-80, 82; councilor City of Klamath Falls, 1986-88; bd. dirs. Basin Transit Svc., Klamath Falls, 1981-87; chair Klamath County Dem. Ctrl. Com., 1983-86, sec. 1992-94; Klamath County alt. del. Oreg. Dem. State Ctrl. Com., 1998—. Mem. Sons of Italy, Klamath Solar Assn. (bd. dirs. 1998—). Democrat. Home: 428 S 9th St Klamath Falls OR 97601-6126 E-mail: pastega@cdsnet.net

PASTER, JANICE DUBINSKY, lawyer, former state legislator; b. St. Louis, Aug. 4, 1942; BA, Northwestern U., 1964; MA, Tufts U., 1967; JD, U. N.Mex., 1984. Bar: N.Mex. 1984. Atty. in pvt. practice, 1984—; mem. N.Mex. State Senate from 10th dist., 1988-96. Democrat. Home and Office: 5553 Eakes Rd NW Albuquerque NM 87107-5529

PASTOR, EDWARD, congressman; b. Claypool, Ariz., June 28, 1943; m. Verma Mendez; children: Yvonne, Laura. BA, Ariz. State U., 1966, JD, 1974. Mem. Maricopa County Bd. Suprs., Phoenix, 1976-91; mem. U.S. Congress from 2d Ariz. dist., Washington, 1991—; mem. appropriations com. Democrat. Office: Ho Reps 2465 Rayburn HOB Washington DC 20515*

PASTOR, JENNIFER, sculptor; b. Hartford, 1966; BFA, Sch. Visual Arts, 1988; MFA in Sculpture, UCLA, 1992. One-person shows include Richard Telles Fine Art, 1994, Studio Guenzani, Milan, 1995, Mus. Contemporary Art, Chgo., 1996; exhibited in group shows at Regen Projects, L.A., 1993, Richard Telles Fine Art, L.A., 1994, Studio Guenzani, Milan, 1996, La. Mus. Modern Art, Humleback, Denmark, 1997, Whitney Mus. Am. Art, N.Y.C., 1997, Mus. Modern Art, San Francisco, 1997, others. Louis Comfort Tiffany grantee, 1995. Office: c/o Richard Telles Fine Art 7380 Beverly Blvd Los Angeles CA 90036-2501

PASTORE, MICHAEL ANTHONY, college administrator; b. Fresno, Calif., Aug. 31, 1932; s. Michele Constantino and Rosa Maria (Damiani) P.; m. Elizabeth Anne York, Dec. 23, 1955; children: Michael Anthony, Christi Anna, Maria Delisa. AA, Coll. of Sequoias, Visalia, Calif., 1952; BS, U. San Francisco, 1954; MA, Fresno State Coll., 1969; PhD, U. Wash., 1976. Agt., M.A. Pastore Ins. Co., Fresno, 1963-69; instr., coordinator, div. chmn. Edmonds Community Coll., Lynwood, Wash., 1969-73; founder, pres. City Univ. Seattle, 1973— . Served with U.S. Army, 1956-57. Roman Catholic. Clubs: Wash. Athletic, Rainier (Seattle); Glendale Country (Bellevue, Wash.). Home: 618 175th Pl NE Bellevue WA 98008-4242 Office: City Unversity 335 116th Ave SE Bellevue WA 98004-6407

PASTREICH, PETER, orchestra executive director; b. Bklyn., Sept. 13, 1938; s. Ben and Hortense (Davis) P.; m. Jamie Garrard Whittington; children by previous marriages: Anna, Milena, Emanuel, Michael. A.B. magna cum laude, Yale Coll., 1959; postgrad., N.Y. U. Sch. Medicine, 1959-60; studied trumpet, with Robert Nagle at Yale U., with Raymond Sabarich, Paris. Asst. mgr. Denver Symphony, Balt. Symphony; mgr. Greenwich Village Symphony, N.Y.C., 1960-63; gen. mgr. Nashville Symphony, 1963-65, Kansas City Philharmonic, 1965-66; asst. mgr., mgr. St. Louis Symphony, 1966-78, exec. dir., 1966-78, San Francisco Symphony, 1978-98. Instr. orch. mgmt. Am. Symphony Orch. League; bd. dirs. Nat. Com. for Symphony Orch. Support; founder San Francisco Youth Orch.; rep. planning and constrn. Davies Symphony Hall, San Francisco Symphony, 1980. Author: TV comml., 1969 (CLIO award); contbr. articles to various newspapers. Mem. recommendation bd. of the Avery Fisher Artist Program, Yale U. Council com. on music; past mem. adv. panel Nat. Endowment for the Arts, co-chmn. music panel, 1985; founding mem. bd.

dirs. St. Louis Conservatory, mem. policy com. Maj. Orch. Mgrs. Conf., chmn., 1980; bd. dirs. Laumeier Sculpture Park, St. Louis, Stern Grove Festival, San Francisco Conv. and Visitors Bur.; chmn. fund campaign French-Am. Internat. Sch., San Francisco. Served with U.S. Army, 1960. Recipient First Disting. Alumnus award Yale U. Band, 1977, cert. Merit Yale Sch. Music, 1984. Mem. Am. Symphony Orch. League (dir., chmn., former chmn. task force on mgmt. tng.; mem. exec. and long-range planning com., chmn. standing com. on adminstrv. policy), Assn. Calif. Symphony Orchs. (dir.), Bankers Club of San Francisco. Club: Yale (N.Y.C.).

PATÉ-CORNELL, MARIE-ELISABETH LUCIENNE, management and engineering educator; b. Dakar, Senegal, Aug. 17, 1948; came to U.S., 1971; d. Edouard Pierre Lucien and Madeleine (Tournissa) Paté; m. C. Allin Cornell, Jan. 3, 1981; children: Phillip, Ariane. Eng. Degree, Inst. Polytechnique de Grenoble, France, 1971; MS in Ops. Rsch., Stanford U., 1972, PhD in Engring.-Econ. Systems, 1978. Asst. prof. in civil engring. MIT, 1978-81; asst. prof. indsl. engring. Stanford (Calif.) U., 1981-84, assoc. prof. indsl. engring., 1984-91, prof. indsl. engring., 1991—, chmn. dept. indsl. engring., 1997-99, chmn. dept. mgmt. sci. and engring., 2000—. Cons. EPA, 1980, Electric Power Rsch. Inst., 1985, WHO, 1988, Shell Oil, 1990, Texaco, 1992, Electric Power Rsch. Inst., 1995, SRI Internat. 1993, Atty. Gen. of N.Mex., 1995, Halliburton, 2000; mem. NASA Adv. Coun., 1995-98, Marine Bd. of the NRC, 1995-97, Army Sci. Bd., 1995-97, Air Force Sci. Bd., 1998—, Calif. Coun. on Sci. and Tech., 2000—. Contbr. numerous articles to profl. jours. Numerous rsch. grants. Mem. Soc. for Risk Analysis (councilor 1985-86, pres. 1995), Ops. Rsch. Soc. Am., Inst. for Mgmt. Scis., Nat. Acad. Engring. (councilor 2001—). Avocations: tennis, swimming, chess, music. Home: 110 Coquito Way Menlo Park CA 94028-7404 Office: Stanford U Dept Mgmt Sci and Engring Stanford CA 94305 E-mail: mep@leland.stanford.edu

PATEL, CHANDRA KUMAR NARANBHAI, communications company executive, educator, researcher, entrepreneur; b. Baramati, India, July 2, 1938; came to U.S., 1958, naturalized, 1970; s. Naranbhai Chaturbhai and Maniben P.; m. Shela Dixit, Aug. 20, 1961; children: Neela, Meena. B.Engring., Poona U., 1958; M.S., Stanford U., 1959, Ph.D., 1961. Mem. tech. staff Bell Telephone Labs., Murray Hill, N.J., 1961-93, head infrared physics and electronics rsch. dept., 1967-70, dir. electronics rsch. dept., 1970-76, dir. phys. rsch. lab., 1976-81, exec. dir. rsch. physics and acad. affairs div., 1981-87, exec. dir. rsch., materials sci., engring. and acad. affairs div., 1987-93; trustee Aerospace Corp., L.A., 1979-88; vice chancellor rsch. UCLA, 1993-2000, prof. dept. physics and astronomy, dept. chemistry, 2000—, prof. dept. elec. engring., 2000—; chmn., CEO Pranalytica, Inc, Santa Monica, Calif., 2001—. Mem. governing bd. NRC, 1990-91; bd. dirs. Newport Corp.; chmn. bd. Calif. Accuwave Corp., 1994-98; founder, chmn. bd. Pranalytica, Inc., Santa Monica, Calif.; co-founder Photuris, Inc. Contbr. articles to tech. jours. Chmn. Calif. Biomed. Found., 1994-2000; mem. exec. bd. Calif. Healthcare Inst., 1995-2000; mem. L.A. Regional Tech. Alliance, 1997—. Recipient Ballantine medal Franklin Inst., 1968, Coblentz award Am. Chem. Soc., 1974, Honor award Assn. Indians in Am., 1975, Founders prize Tex. Instruments Found., 1978, award N.Y. sect. Soc. Applied Spectroscopy, 1982, Schawlow medal Laser Inst. Am., 1984, Thomas Alva Edison Sci. award N.J. Gov., 1987, William T. Ennor Manufacturing Technology award ASME, 1995, Nat. Medal of Sci., 1996. Fellow AAAS, IEEE (Lamme medal 1976, medal of honor 1989, Millennium medal 2000), Am. Acad. Arts and Scis., Am. Phys. Soc. (coun. 1987-91, exec. com. 1987-90, George E. Pake prize 1988, pres. 1995), Optical Soc. Am. (Adolph Lomb medal 1966, Townes medal 1982, Ives medal 1989), Indian Nat. Sci. Acad. (fng.); mem. NAS (coun. 1988-91, exec. com. 1989-91), NAE (Zworykin award 1976), Gynecol. Laser Surgery Soc. (hon.), Am. Soc. for Laser Medicine and Surgery (hon.), Third World Acad. Scis. (assoc.), Calif. Biomed. Found. (pres. 1994-2000), Calif. Healthcare Inst. (exec. com. 1995-2000), Sigma Xi (pres. 1994-96). Home: 1171 Roberto Ln Los Angeles CA 90077-2302 Office: Pranalytica Inc 1101 Colorado Ave Santa Monica CA 90401 also: Pranalytica Inc 1101 Colorado Ave Santa Monica CA 90401 E-mail: patel@pranalytica.com

PATEL, MARILYN HALL, judge; b. Amsterdam, N.Y., Sept. 2, 1938; d. Lloyd Manning and Nina J. (Thorpe) Hall; m. Magan C. Patel, Sept. 2, 1966; children: Brian, Gian. B.A., Wheaton Coll., 1959; J.D., Fordham U., 1963. Bar: N.Y. 1963, Calif. 1970. Mng. atty. Benson & Morris, Esq., N.Y.C., 1962-64; sole practice N.Y.C., 1964-67; atty. U.S. Immigration and Naturalization Svc., San Francisco, 1967-71; sole practive San Francisco, 1971-76; judge Alameda County Mcpl. Ct., Oakland, Calif., 1976-80, U.S. Dist. Ct. (no. dist.) Calif., San Francisco, 1980—; now chief judge U.S. Dist. Ct. for No. Dist. Calif., San Francisco, 1998—. Adj. prof. law Hastings Coll. of Law, San Francisco, 1974-76 Author: Immigration and Nationality Law, 1974; also numerous articles Mem. bd. visitors Fordham U. Sch. Law. Mem. ABA (litigation sect., jud. adminstrn. sect.), ACLU (former bd. dirs.), NOW (former bd. dirs.), Am. law Inst., Am. Judicature Soc. (bd. dirs.), Calif Conf. Judges, Nat. Assn. Women Judges (founding mem.), Internat. Inst. (bd. dirs.), Advs. for Women (co-founder), Assn. Bus. Trial Lawyers (bd. dirs.). Democrat Avocations: piano playing; travel. Office: US Dist Ct PO Box 36060 450 Golden Gate Ave Ste 36052 San Francisco CA 94102-3482

PATERSON, RICHARD DENIS, financial executive; b. Ottawa, Ont., Can., Oct. 13, 1942; m. Antoinette Paterson; children: Christopher, Russell, Kathlyn, Victoria, Connor. B in Commerce, Concordia U., Montreal, Que., Can., 1964. Auditor Coopers & Lybrand, Montreal, 1964-67; acct. Genstar Corp., Montreal, 1967-69; dir. fin. and adminstrn. Indussa Corp. (subs. Genstar Corp.), N.Y.C., 1969-73; v.p., comptroller Genstar Corp., Montreal and San Francisco, 1973-83, sr. v.p., CFO San Francisco, 1983-87; exec. v.p. Genstar Investment Corp., San Francisco, 1987-95; mng. dir. Genstar Capital LLC, San Francisco, 1996—. Bd. dirs. Gentek Bldg. Products, Inc.; chmn. bd. dirs. Prestolite Electric Inc.; chmn. Andros Inc. Mem. Order Chartered Accts. Que. Office: Genstar Capital LLC 555 California St Ste 4850 San Francisco CA 94104-1700 E-mail: paterson@gencap.com

PATIENCE, JOHN FRANCIS, research scientist; b. Thamesford, Ont., Nov. 13, 1951; s. Alwyn Francis Patience and Ellen Sophie Rosenberg; m. Ann Valerie German, Apr. 27, 1974; children: Emily, Matthew, Michael. BSc in Agr., U. Guelph, Ont., 1974, MSc, 1976; PhD, Cornell U., 1985. Cert. profl. agrologist. Extension swine specialist Sask. Agriculture, Regina, 1975-78; nutritionist Federated Co-op Ltd., Saskatoon, Sask., 1978-82; grad rsch. asst. Cornell U., Ithaca, N.Y., 1982-85; rshc. assoc. U. Sask., Saskatoon, 1987-89, assoc. prof., 1989-91; pres. and CEO Prairie Swine Ctr. Inc., Saskatoon, 1991—, PSC Elstow Rsch. Farm Inc., 1999—. Vis. fellow Animal Rsch. Ctr., Ottawa, Ont., 1985-87; dir. Ag-West Biotech, Inc.; dir. Agricoll Rsch. Investments Inc. Co-author: Swine Nutrition Guide, 1989, 95. Mem. Am. Inst. Nutrition, Am. Soc. Animal Sci., Can. Soc. Animal Sci. (pres. 1993-94). Office: Prairie Swine Centre Inc 2105 8th St E PO Box 21057 Saskatoon SK Canada S7H 5N9

PATINO, DOUGLAS XAVIER, foundation, government agency, and university administrator; b. Calexico, Calif., Apr. 11, 1939; s. Jose Luis and Maria Teresa (Seymour) P.; m. Barbel Wilma Hoyer, Aug. 13, 1970; 1 child, Viktor Xavier. AA, Imperial Valley Coll., 1960; BA, Calif. State U., San Diego, 1962, MA, 1966; PhD, U.S. Internat. U., 1972. Deputy dir. Sacramento (Calif.) Concilio, Inc., 1968-69; v.p. student affairs U. So. Colo., Pueblo, 1973-75; dep. dir. for planning and [illegible] Employment Devel. Dept., dir.; sec. Calif. Health & Welfare Agy., 1975-83; dir. Ariz. Dept. of Econ. Security, Phoenix, 1983-87; pres., chief exec. officer Marin Community Found., Larkspur, Calif., 1987-91; pres. New Partnership Found. and Patino Group, San Rafael, 1991-93; vice chancellor Calif. State U. Sys., Long Beach, 1993—. Commr. Wm. T. Grand Found., 1986-88, Enterprize for the Ams., Washington, 1994—; trustee C.S. Mott Found., Flint, Mich., 1995—, Calif. Wellness Found., Woodland Hills, Calif., 1997—; chair/treas. Hispanics in Philanthropy, 1994-97. Mem. Sec. of U.S. Dept. of Labor Task Force, Ariz., 1985-86, Staff Adv. Com. of the Human Resource Com., Nat. Gov. Assn., Washington, 1983-86; bd. dirs. Calif. Leadershp, Santa Cruz, Calif., 1985-95, No. Calif. Grantmakers, 1990-91, Ariz. Assn. Bus., 1984; chair U.S. Savs. Bond Dr. for State of Calif., 1982; trustee Nat. Hispanic U., Oakland, Calif., 1987-90, Hispanic Community Fund, San Francisco, 1989-95, bd. dirs. Calif. Sch. Profl. Psychology, 1989-94, Coun. on Found., Washington, 1990-96, Found. Ctr., N.Y., 1993; pres. Calif. State U. Found. Recipient The Monty Disting. Alumni award San Diego State U., 1997, Simon Bolivar award for cmty. leadership award Hispanic Cmty. Found. and Bay Area United Way, 1996, Azteca award Human Devel. Corp., 1991, Leadership award Nat. Concilors of Am. and United Way of Bay Area, 1990, Disting. Performance award, Nat. Alliance of Bus., Washington, 1985, Superior Svc. Mgmt. award, Am. Soc. Pub. Adminstrn., 1985, Humanitarian award, Los Padrinos, Inc., 1981, Small and Minority Bus. award for the State of Calif. 1982, Disting. Alumni award, Calif. Jr. Community Coll. Assn., Sacramento, 1982, Silver Spur award, Nat. Fedn. of Charros in Guadalajaro, Jalisco, Mex., 1974, Calif. Community Svc. award, Former Gov. Ronald Reagan, Sacramento, 1973; named to 100 Most Influential Hispanics, Hispanic Bus., 1995, 97. Mem. Am. Pub. Welfare Assn. (bd. dirs., Leadership award 1987), Rotary, 1987-93. Office: Calif State U 401 Golden Shore St Ste 635 Long Beach CA 90802-4275

PATKAU, JOHN, architect; b. Winnipeg, Man., Can., Aug. 18, 1947; s. Abe John and Bertha (Klassen) P.; m. Patricia Frances Gargett, Aug. 10, 1974. BA, BA in Environ. Studies, U. Manitoba, 1969, MArch, 1972. Registered architect, B.C., Ont., Pa. Prin. John Patkau Architect Ltd., Edmonton, Can., 1977-83; ptnr. Patkau Archs. Inc., Vancouver, B.C., Can., 1984—. Chmn. edn. com. Alta. Assn. Architects, 1981; vis. critic U. Calgary, 1981, 92, U. Waterloo, 1987, 89, U. Pa., 1987, Tech. U. N.S., 1987, U. B.C., 1988, 89, UCLA, 1989; design critic U. B.C., 1985-86; urban design panel Vancouver, 1990-92; vis. prof. William Lyon Somerville Lectureship U. Calgary, 1994; Eliot Noyes vis. design critic Harvard U., 1995. Recipient Progressive Architecture citation, 1981, 99, Progressive Architecture award, 1993, 95, Can. Architects award, 1983, 84, 86, 87, 89, 90, 92, 94, 98, 99, Wood Coun. First award, 1984, Gov. Gen. medal, 1986, 90, 92, 94, 97, Gov. Gen. award, 1990, 97, Lt. Gov. Archtl. medal, 1992, Honor award, 1992. Fellow AIA (hon.), Royal Archtl. Inst. Can. (chmn. design com. 1987); mem. Archtl. Inst. B.C., Royal Can. Coll. Art, Ont. Assn. Architects. Office: Patkau Architects 1564 W 6th Ave Vancouver BC Canada V6J 1R2 also: Patkau Archs 1564 W 6th Ave Vancouver BC Canada V6J 1R2 E-mail: jpatkau@patkau.ca

PATKAU, PATRICIA FRANCES, architect, architecture educator; b. Winnipeg, Manitoba, Can., Feb. 25, 1950; d. John Frederick and Aileen Constance (Emmett) Gargett; m. John Robert Patkau, Aug. 10, 1974. BA in Interior Design, U. Manitoba, 1973; MA in Architecture, Yale, New Haven, Conn., 1978. Ptnr. Patkau Archs., Vancouver, B.C., Can., 1983—; asst. prof. Sch. Architecture UCLA, U.S.A., 1988-90; assoc. prof. Sch. Architecture U. B.C., Can., 1992—. Vis. critic U. Calgary, 1981, 87, U. Waterloo, 1987, U. Pa., U.S.A., 1987, U. Toronto, 1988, Southern Calif. Inst. Architecture, U.S.A., 1990, UCLA, 1991, U. Oreg., U.S.A., 1992, MIT, U.S.A., 1993, Yale U., 1993; design critic U. B.C., 1984-87; vis. prof. Harvard U., 1993, Eliot Noyes prof., 1995; vis. prof. U. Calgary, 1994; mem. archtl. commn. U. Wash., 1996—. Ctrl. Mortgage and Housing fellow, 1977, 78; recipient Manitoba Gold medal, 1973, Progressive Architecture citation, 1981, 93, Can. Architect Excellence award, 1983, 86, 87, 89, 90, 92, 94, Can. Wood Coun. First award, 1984, Honor award, 1992, Gov. Gen. Architecture medal, 1986, 90, 92, 94, 97, Gov. Gen. Architecture award, 1990, 97, Lt. Gov. Architecture medal, 1992, Can. Wood Coun. award, 1991, Progressive Arch. award Arch. Mag., 1995. Fellow AIA (hon.), Royal Archtl. Inst. Can.; mem. Archtl. Inst. B.C. (Honor award 1988). Office: Patkau Archs 1564 W 6th Ave Vancouver BC Canada V6J 1R2

PATMORE, KIMBERLY S. financial services executive; BBA, U. Toledo. CPA, Colo. With Ernst & Young; joined First Data Corp., Inglewood, Colo., 1992, exec. v.p., CFO, 2000—. Mem. Gov.'s Commn. on Sci. and Tech., Colo. Bd. dirs. Coors Tek, Girls Scouts, Family Tree Found. Office: First Date Corp 6200 S Qubec St Inglewood CO

PATNAUDE, WILLIAM EUGENE, architect, writer; b. Sanger, Calif., Sept. 24, 1937; s. Eugene Joseph Patnaude and Vera Mae (Giles) Patnaude Fagan; m. Mary Esther Simerly, Aug. 22, 1971 (div. 1987); children: Nathaniel, Matthew BArch, U. Calif., Berkeley, 1961; postgrad., Calif. State U., Fresno, 1968-72. Registered arch., Calif., Oreg., Wash., Idaho, Nev., N.Mex., Colo., Utah, Ariz., Mont., Ind., Iowa, Nebr., Ohio, N.Y., N.J. Draftsman, arch. Robert Stevens Assoc., Santa Cruz, Calif., 1963-66; arch. Llewelyn Davies, Weeks & Ptnrs., London, 1966, Allen Y. Lew, Fresno, Calif., 1967-69, assoc., 1969-74; v.p., arch. Lew & Patnaude, Inc., Fresno, 1978-84, pres., 1985—. Instr. Calif. State U., Fresno, 1968-81 Constn. arbitrator Am. Arbitration Assn., 1976-96; chair ctrl. area plan citizen's adv. com. City of Fresno, 1991-93, chair gen. plan update com., 1994-97; bd. dirs. Fresno Arts Ctr., 1971-74, Fresno County Alliance for the Arts, 1986-88, 91-94. With USNR, 1961-63. Recipient Award of Merit, Calif. Hist. Preservation Conf., Orange County, 1983; Award of Excellence, Woodwork Inst. Calif., 1982 Fellow AIA (nat. dir. 1983-85, pres. Calif. Coun. 1982, San Joaquin chpt. 1978, Awards of Excellence, 1972-95); mem. Constrn. Specifications Inst. (pres. Fresno chpt. 1977). Democrat. Avocations: photography, fine wines. Home: 4190 N Van Ness Blvd Fresno CA 93704-4213 Office: Lew & Patnaude Inc 1050 S St Fresno CA 93721-1497 E-mail: wparch@pacbell.net

PATRICK, DONALD LEE, social scientist, health services researcher; b. Eugene, Oreg., Sept. 23, 1944; s. Lawrence Leonard and Marie Esther (Bell) P.; m. Shirley Anne Alexander Beresford, May 31, 1980; children: Alistair Lawrence Beresford, Mira Yvonne Bell. AB with distinction, Northwestern U., 1966; MSPH, Columbia U., 1968, PhD, 1972. Rsch. assoc. U. Calif., San Diego, 1970-72; lectr. Yale U., New Haven, 1972-76; sr. lectr. U. London, 1976-82; assoc. prof. U. N.C., Chapel Hill, 1982-87; prof. and dir. social and behavioral scis. program U. Wash., Seattle, 1987—. Adj. prof. sociology, U. Wash., 1988—, dept. rehab. medicine, 1987—. Author: Health Status and Health Policy, 1993; editor: Sociology as Applied to Medicine, 1976, Disablement in Community, 1989. Mem. APHA (mem. coun. 1993-96), Spina Bifida Assn. Am. (chair profl. adv. bd. 1990-93, Pres.' award 1995), Internat. Soc. for Quality of Life Rsch. (pres. 1994-96), Inst. Medicine. Democrat. Unitarian. Avocations: gardening, music, travel. Home: 5427 43rd Ave W Seattle WA 98199-1061 Office: U Wash PO Box 357660 Seattle WA 98195-7660

PATRICK, H. HUNTER, judge; b. Gasville, Ark., Aug. 19, 1939; s. H. Hunter Sr. and Nelle Frances (Robinson) P.; m. Charlotte Anne Wilson, July 9, 1966; children: Michael Hunter, Colleen Annette. BA, U. Wyo., 1961, JD, 1966. Bar: Wyo. 1966, U.S. Dist. Ct. Wyo. 1966, Colo. 1967, U.S. Supreme Ct. 1975. Mcpl. judge City of Powell (Wyo.), 1967-68; sole practice law Powell, 1966-88; atty. City of Powell, 1969-88; justice of the peace County of Park, Wyo., 1971-88; bus. law instr. Northwest Community [illegible] 5th Jud. Dist. 1988—. Mem. Wyo. Dist. Judges Conf., sec.-treas., 1993-94, vice chair, 1994-95, chair, 1995-96. Editor: Bench Book for Judges of Courts of Limited Jurisdiction in the State of Wyoming, 1980-90. Dir. cts. Wyo. Girls State, Powell, 1982-85, 89-99; elder, deacon, moderator of deacons Powell Presbyn. Ch., 1997; mem. Wyo. Commn. Jud. Conduct & Ethics, 1997—. Recipient Wyo. Crime Victims Compensation Commn. Judicial award, 1995. Fellow Am. Bar Found., Wyo. Jud. Adv. Coun.; mem. ABA (Wyo. state del. to ho. of dels. 1994-2001, Wyo. del. judicial adminstrn. divsn., exec. com. nat. conf. trial ct. judges representing Wyo., Colo., Kans., Nebr., N.Mex. 1996-2000, bd. govs. 2001—, Pub. Svc. award for ct.-sponsored Law Day programs 1990, 92), Wyo. Bar Assn. (Cmty. Svc. award 1999, Ann. Pub. Svc. award 1999), Colo. Bar Assn., Park County Bar Assn. (sec. 1969-70, pres. 1970-71), Wyo. Assn. Cts. Ltd. Jurisdiction (pres. 1973-80), Am. Judicature Soc. Avocations: photography, travel, fishing, camping, bicycling. Home: PO Box 941 Powell WY 82435-0941 Office: PO Box 1868 Cody WY 82414-1868 E-mail: hpatrick@parkco.wtp.net

PATRICK, LYNN ALLEN, lawyer, corporate governance and land development; b. Stettler, Alta., Can., Dec. 7, 1935; s. Allen Russell and Florence Lorene (Lynn) P.; m. Roberta Colleen Hughes, May 9, 1959; children: Diane Elizabeth, Ross Gordon. BSc, U. Alta., Edmonton, Can., 1957, LLB, 1960. Bar: Alta. Ptnr. Cormie Kennedy, Edmonton, Alta., Can., 1961-83; sr. v.p., gen. counsel Mutual Fund Group, Edmonton, Can., 1983-88; pres. Stuart Olson Constrn., Inc., Edmonton, Can., 1989-92; v.p., corp. counsel, sec. The Churchill Corp., 1992-98. Dir. Sparta Water Corp., SNG Telecom, Inc., Red Oak Trail Corp. (now Innovative Sewage Systems Inc.); sec. mem. subdivsn. and devel. appeal bd. City of Edmonton; bd. dirs. Home Bank Techs., Inc. Past pres., trustee Minerva Found., Edmonton; adv. coun. mem. Minister of Edn., Alta.; gov. Banff Ctr. Mem. Can. Bar Assn., Edmonton Bar Assn., Law Soc. Alta., Real Estate Coun. Alta., Royal Glenora Club (Edmonton). Progressive. Home: 64 Quesnell Rd Edmonton AB Canada T5R 5N2 Office: 2500 10104 103rd Ave Edmonton AB Canada T5J 1V3 E-mail: lpatrick@telusplanet.net

PATRON, SUSAN HALL, librarian, writer; b. San Gabriel, Calif., Mar. 18, 1948; d. George Thomas and Rubye Denver Hall; m. René Albert Patron, July 27, 1969. BA, Pitzer Coll., 1969; MLS, Immaculate Heart Coll., 1972. Children's libr. LA Pub. Libr., 1972-79, sr. children's libr., 1980—. Reviewer Sch. Libr. Jour., 1980-90, Pubs. Weekly, 1986-91, The Five Owls, 1987-95. Author: (with Christopher Weiman) Marbled Papers, 1979, Burgoo Stew, 1991, Five Bad Boys, Billy Que, and the Dustdobbin, 1992, Maybe Yes, Maybe No, Maybe Maybe, 1993 (ALA Notable Book 1994), Bobbin Dustdobbin, 1993, Dark Cloud Strong Breeze, 1994. Mem. ALA (Caldecott award com. 1988, Laura Ingalls Wilder award com. 2001—), PEN (mem. West Lit. awards jury 1997), Calif. Libr. Assn. (Patricia Beatty award com. 1987-89, 91-92), Internat. Bd. on Books for Young Children, Soc. Children's Book Writers and Illustrators, So. Calif. Coun. on Lit. for Children and Young People (awards com. 1985), Authors Guild, Friends of Children and Lit. (mem. award com. 1984). Office: LA Pub Libr Childrens Svcs 630 W 5th St Los Angeles CA 90071-2002

PATTEN, BEBE HARRISON, minister, chancellor; b. Waverly, Tenn., Sept. 3, 1913; d. Newton Felix and Mattie Priscilla (Whitson) Harrison; m. Carl Thomas Patten, Oct. 23, 1935; children: Priscilla Carla and Bebe Rebecca (twins), Carl Thomas. D.D., McKinley-Roosevelt Coll., 1941; D.Litt., Temple Hall Coll. and Sem., 1943. Ordained to ministry Ministerial Assn. of Evangelism, 1935; evangelist in various cities of U.S., 1933-50; founder, pres. Christian Evang. Chs. Am., Inc., Oakland, Calif., 1944—, Patten Acad. Christian Edn., Oakland, 1944—, Patten Bible Coll., Oakland, 1944-83; chancellor Patten Coll., Oakland, 1983—; founder, pastor Christian Cathedral of Oakland, 1950—. Held pvt. interviews with David Ben-Gurion, 1972, Menachim Begin, 1977, Yitzhak Shamir, 1991; condr. Sta. KUSW world-wide radio ministry, 70 countries around the world, 1989-90, Stas. WHRI and WWCR world coverage short wave, 1990— Founder, condr.: radio program The Shepherd Hour, 1934— ; daily TV, 1976— , nationwide telecast, 1979— ; Author: Give Me Back My Soul, 1973; Editor: Trumpet Call, 1953— ; composer 20 gospel and religious songs, 1945— . Mem. exec. bd. Bar-Ilan U. Assn., Israel, 1983; mem. global bd. trustees Bar-Ilan U., 1991. Recipient numerous awards including medallion Ministry of Religious Affairs, Israel, 1969; medal Govt. Press Office, Jerusalem, 1971; Christian honoree of yr. Jewish Nat. Fund of No. Calif., 1975; Hidden Heroine award San Francisco Bay coun. Girl Scouts U.S.A., 1976, Golden State award Who's Who Hist. Soc., 1988; Ben-Gurion medallion Ben-Gurion Rsch. Inst., 1977; Resolutions of Commendation, Calif. Senate Rules Com., 1978, 94, Disting. Leadership award Ch. of God Sch. of Theology, 1996; hon. fellow Bar-Ilan U., Israel, 1981; Dr. Bebe Patten Social Action chair established Bar-Ilan U., 1982. Mem. Am. Assn. for Higher Edn., Religious Edn. Assn., Am. Acad. Religion and Soc. Bibl. Lit., Zionist Orgn. Am., Am. Assn. Pres. of Ind. Colls. and Univs., Am. Jewish Hist. Soc., Am.-Isreal Pub. Affairs Com. Address: 2433 Coolidge Ave Oakland CA 94601-2630

PATTEN, DUNCAN THEUNISSEN, ecologist educator; b. Detroit, Oct. 13, 1934; s. Marc T. and Doris (Miller) P.; m. Eva Chittenden, July 27, 1957; children: Michael, Marc, Robin, Scott. BA, Amherst Coll., 1956; MS, U. Mass., Amherst, 1959; PhD, Duke U., 1962. Asst. prof. ecology Va. Poly. Inst., Blacksburg, 1962-65, Ariz. State U., Tempe, 1965-67, assoc. prof., 1967-73, prof., 1973-95, prof. emeritus, 1995—, dir. ctr. environ. studies, 1980-95. Rsch. prof. Mont. State U., 1995—. Contbr. articles to profl. jours. Fellow AAAS, Ariz.-Nev. Acad. Sci.; mem. Ecol. Soc. Am. (bus. mgr. 1979-95), Brit. Ecol. Soc., Soc. Range Mgmt., Am. Inst. Biol. Scis., Soc. Wetland Scientists (pres. 1996-97), Am. Water Resource Assn., Am. Geophys. Union, Soc. Conservation Biology, Sigma Xi. Office: Mont State U Mountain Rsch Ctr Box 173490 Bozeman MT 59717-3490 E-mail: dtpatten@starband.net

PATTEN, THOMAS HENRY, JR. management, human resources educator; b. Cambridge, Mass., Mar. 24, 1929; s. Thomas Henry and Lydia Mildred (Lindgren) P.; m. Jule Ann Miller, Aug. 27, 1972; children—Laurie Kathryn, Rhonda Josephine, Jenny Lydia. A.B., Brown U., 1953; M.S., Cornell U., 1955, Ph.D., 1959. Dir. program planning Ford Motor Co., Dearborn, Mich., 1957-65; prof. mgmt. and sociology U. Detroit, 1965-67; prof. orgnl. behavior and personnel mgmt. Sch. Labor and Indsl. Relations, Mich. State U., E. Lansing, 1967-84; prof. mgmt. and human resources Calif. State Poly. U., Pomona, 1984—. Cons. in field. Author: The Foreman: The Forgotten Man of Management, 1968, Manpower Planning and the Development of Human Resources, 1971, OD-Emerging Dimensions and Concepts, 1973, A Bibliography of Compensation Planning and Administration, 1960-1974, 2d rev. edit., 1981, 3d rev. edit., 1987, Pay: Employee Compensation and Incentive Plans, 1977, Classics of Personnel Management, 1979, Organizational Development Through Teambuilding, 1981, A Manager's Guide to Performance Appraisal, 1982, Fair Pay: The Managerial Challenge of Comparable Job Worth and Job Evaluation, 1988, Exercises for Developing Human Resources Management Skills, 1996. Served with USMC, 1946-51. Mem. ASTD (chmn. orgn. devel. div. 1972), Indsl. Rels. Rsch. Assn. (chpt. pres. 1970-71), Am. Sociol. Assn., Internat. Pers. Mgmt. Assn., Internat. Indsl. Rels. Assn., Inst. Applied Behavioral Sic., Am. Compensation Assn. Home: 2540 King Way Claremont CA 91711-1719 Office: Calif State Poly U Dept Mgmt & Human Resources 3801 W Temple Ave Pomona CA 91768-2557 E-mail: thpatten@csupomona.edu

PATTERSON, DANIEL WILLIAM, dentist; b. Minot, N.D., Aug. 12, 1948; s. Girdell William and Fern Lemay Patterson. DDS, Northwestern U., 1972; Alumnus degree (hon.), U. Colo., 1977; BS in Biology, U.N.Y., 1993; M in Healthcare, U. Denver, 1994. Cert. health industry orgn. ops, U.Denver, 1993, cert. gerontology, 1996. Dentist Dan L. Hansen, DDS, P.C., Lakewood, Colo., 1974-75; pvt. practice dentistry Littleton, 1975-88; clin. instr. dept. applied dentistry U. Colo., Denver, 1981-83, lectr., 1983, clin. asst. prof. depts. restorative and applied dentistry, 1989-91, dir. advanced dentistry program, 1989-90, asst. prof. clin. track dept. restorative dentistry, 1991—. Mem. editorial adv. panel Dental Econs. Jour., 1981; also articles. Active Chatfield Jaycees, Littleton, 1976-81; vocal soloist, mem. Denver Concert Chorale, 1978-82. Lt. USN, 1968-74. Fellow Acad. Gen. Dentistry; bd. eligible Am. Bd. Gen. Dentistry; mem. ADA, Met. Denver Dental Soc., Colo. Dental Assn. (Pres.'s Honor Roll 1982-84), Mensa, Sedalia Wild Game Club. Lutheran. Avocations: reading, fishing, photography. Home: 6984 N Fargo Trl Littleton CO 80125-9270 Office: U Colo Health Scis Ctr Sch Dentistry Box C 284 4200 E 9th Ave Denver CO 80262-0284

PATTERSON, DAVID ANDREW, computer scientist, educator, consultant; b. Evergreen Park, Ill., Nov. 16, 1947; s. David Dwight and Lucie Jeanette (Ekstrom) P.; m. Linda Ann Crandall, Sept. 4, 1967; children: David Adam, Michael Andrew. BS in Math., UCLA, 1969, MS in Computer Sci., 1970, PhD, 1976. Mem. tech. staff Hughes Aircraft Co., L.A., 1972-76, Thinking Machines Corp., Cambridge, Mass., 1979; prof. computer sci. div. U. Calif., Berkeley, 1977—, chmn., 1990-93, Pardee chair, 1992—. Cons. Sun Microsystems, Inc., Mountain View, Calif., 1984—. Author: A Taste of Smalltalk, 1986, Computing Unbound, 1989, Computer Architecture: A Quantative Approach, 2nd edit., 1996, Computer Organization & Design: The Hardware/Software Interface, 2nd edit., 1998. Recipient Disting. Teaching award U. Calif., Berkeley, 1982, Outstanding Alumnus award UCLA Computer Sci. Dept. Fellow IEEE (undergrad. tchg. award 1996, tech. achievement award 1996, Reynold B. Johnson Info. Storage award, John Von Neumann medal 2000, James H. Mulligan Edn. medal 2000), ACM (Karl V. Karlstrom Outstanding Educator award 1991, Sigmod Test of Time award 1998); mem. NAE, Computing Rsch. Assn. (bd. dirs. Washington 1991—, chair 1993-97), Spl. Interest Group on Computer Architecture of ACM (bd. dirs. 1987-90, chair 1993-95). Avocations: biking, soccer, weight lifting, body surfing. Office: U Calif Computer Sci 635 Soda Hl Berkeley CA 94720-0001

PATTERSON, DENNIS JOSEPH, management consultant; b. Honolulu, Apr. 13, 1948; s. Joseph John and Dorothy Elizabeth (Snajkowski) P.; m. Susan Tyra Pedlow, Dec. 31, 1981; children: Valerie Jean, Christina Elizabeth. BA, Elmhurst (Ill.) Coll., 1970; MA, George Washington U., 1973. Asst. dir. Vancouver (B.C.) Gen. Hosp., 1973-76, dir., 1975-76; v.p. Shaugnessy Hosp., Vancouver, 1976-79; pres. Westcare, Vancouver, 1979-84; mgr. Ernst & Whinney, Chgo., 1984-86, sr. mgr., 1986-88, ptnr., 1988-93; pres. FHP Internat. Cons. Group, Inc., Fountain Valley, Calif., 1993-95; ptnr. KPMG Peat Marwick, 1996-97; sr. cons. Hay Group, 1997-98; chmn., CEO IMC Rsch. Inst. (now Healthcare Net); ptnr. Wellspring Ptnrs. Author: Indexing Managed Care, 1997; contbr. articles to profl. jours. Fin. mgr. Electoral Action Movement, Vancouver, 1978; trustee George Washington U., 1992-96, Calif. Sch. Profl. Psychology, 1993-96, Alliant U., 1999—. Fellow Am. Coll. Healthcare Execs.; mem. Royal Vancouver Yacht Club, East India Club, Phi Gamma Mu. Republican. Anglican. Avocation: sailboat racing, golf. E-mail: djp@wp-ltd.com

PATTERSON, JAMES, mayor; b. San Mateo, Calif., Feb. 18, 1948; m. Sharon LeTourneau, 1968; children: B.J., Jason, Lindsay. BA in Polit. Sci. summa cum laude, Calif. State U., Fresno, 1992. Radio broadcasting exec. Sta. KIRV-AM, Fresno, Calif., 1968—; mayor City of Fresno, 1993—. Mem. San Joaquin River Conservancy, Calif. Ten Largest Cities Mayor's Coalition, 1993—; vice chair Fresno County Transp. Authority; bd. mem. Fresno County Coun. Govts.; chmn. NO on Measure H Com., 1989, Criminal Justice and Law Enforcement Commn., 1990-91; vice chmn. YES on Measure E Com., 1988; mem. Human Rels. Commn., City of Fresno, 1987-91; bd. dirs. Leadership Fresno Alumni Assn., 1989-91, Fresno County YFC/Campus Life, 1984-88. Mem. Fresno City and County C. of C. (chmn. local govt. affairs com. 1990-91, bd. dirs. FRESPAC 1990-91, city budget rev. com. 1989-91, privatization task force 1988-89, charter sect. 809 rev. task force 1987-88). Office: Office Mayor 2600 Fresno St Fresno CA 93721

PATTERSON, JAMES RANDOLPH, physician; b. Lancaster, Pa., Jan. 30, 1942; m. Linda Lewis Patterson, Nov. 22, 1969. AB, U. Pa., 1964; MD, Columbia U., 1968. Diplomate Nat. Bd. Med. Examiners, Am. Bd. Internal Medicine, Subspecialty of Pulmonary Disease. Pulmonary and critical care specialist The Oregon Clinic, Portland, 1975—; clin. prof. medicine Oreg. health Scis. U., Portland, 1978—. Mem. Am. Bd. Internal Medicine, Phila., 1995—; trustee Collins Med. Trust, Portland, Oreg., 1992—, chair subsplty. bd. pulmonary disease, 1998—. Contbr. numerous articles to profl. jours. Recipient Class of 1964 award U. Pa., Van Loan award Am. Lung Assn. Oreg., 1990, Meritorious Achievement award Oreg. Health Scis. U., 1991; named Class Pres. Coll. Physicians and Surgeons of Columbia U., 1968, Tchr. of Yr. Providence Med. Ctr., Portland, Oreg., 1976, Internist of Yr., 1983, Best Doctors in Am., 1992—. Mem. AMA, Am. Thoracic Soc., Am. Coll. Chest Physicians, Oreg. Lung Assn., North Pacific Soc. of Internal Medicine, Pacific Interurban Clin. Club, Multnomah County Med. Soc., Oreg. Med. Assn., Oreg. Soc. Ctirical Care Medicine. Office: The Oregon Clinic 507 NE 47th Ave Ste 103 Portland OR 97213-2236 E-mail: jpatterson@orclinic.com

PATTERSON, JULIA, state legislator; m. Pat Patterson; children: Alex, Erin, Caitlin. BS in Soc. and Justice, Wash. State U.; BA in English cum laude, U. Wash. Mem. Wash. Legislature, Olympia, 1997—, chair mem. state and local govt. com., mem. human svcs. and corrections com., mem. transp. com., mem. Gov.'s com. on alcohol, tobacco and drug prevention, mem. substance abuse adv. com., mem. Gov.'s Coun. on Substance Abuse, mem. substance abuse prevention adv. com. Mem. Wash. Coun. for the Prevention of Child Abuse and Neglect; bd. dirs. Judson Park Ret. Cmty.; past mem. King County Human Svcs. Roundtable; vol. Highline Sch. Dist.; mem. Valley View PTA. Mem. LVW, Wash. Coun. on Aging, Audubon Soc. Democrat. Office: 422 John Cherberg Bldg Olympia WA 98504-0001

PATTERSON, LLOYD CLIFFORD, retired psychiatrist; b. Toronto, Ont., Can., Jan. 16, 1917; came to U.S., 1942; s. William Henry and Florence May (Sonley) P.; m. Gloria May Patterson, Nov. 12, 1943; children: Diane Meisenheimer, Pamela DeBarr. MD, U. Western Ont., London, 1942. Diplomate Am. Bd. Psychiatry; cert. Am. Psychoanalytic Assn. Intern Hollywood Presybn. Hosp., L.A., 1942-43; fellow in intern medicine U. Calif. Hosp., San Francisco, 1943-44; resident in psychiatry Langley Porter Neuropsychiat. Inst., San Francisco, 1944-48; cons. psychiatrist student health U. Calif., Berkeley, 1960-70; assoc. clin. prof. U. Calif. Med. Sch., San Francisco, 1972-2000; dir. med. edn. Alta Bates Med. Ctr., Berkeley, 1988-97; ret. Program chair Western Divisional Psychoanalytic meetings, San Francisco, 1966. Mem. East Bay Psychiat. Assn. (pres. 1962), No. Calif. Psychiat. Assn. (pres. 1968-69), San Francisco Psychoanalytic Soc. (pres. 1972-73), Am. Psychiat. Soc., Am. Psychoanalytic Soc., Calif. Med. Assn. (hosp. surveyor, mem. continuing med. edn. com. 1985-91, cons. CME com. 1992), Alameda Contra Costa Med. Assn. Avocations: tennis, golf. Home: 409 Cola Ballena Alameda CA 94501-3608

PATTERSON, ROBERT EDWARD, lawyer; b. Los Angeles, Sept. 14, 1942; s. Ellis Elwood and Helen (Hjelte) P.; m. Christina Balboni, Oct. 2, 1971; 1 child, Victor Ellis. BA, UCLA, 1964; JD, Stanford U., 1972, grad. bus. exec. program, 1986; vis. scholar, Amos Tuck School Dartmouth Coll., 1998. Bar: Calif. 1972. Ptnr. Squire Sanders & Dempsey LLP, Palo Alto, Calif., 1972—. Bd. dirs. Procyte Corp., Thompson Clive (Venture Capital), Foster Ctr. for Pvt. Equity, Amos Tuck Sch., Dartmouth Coll., Sumida Corp., InPro Biotech. LLC, Wealth Cycle Inc., Acuity Ventures; mem. adv. bd. Borealis Ventures. Served to lt. comdr. USN, 1964-69. Mem. Rotary, Palo Alto Club, Menlo Circus Club, Bohemian Club, Band of Angels. Democrat. Office: Squire Sanders & Dempsey 600 Hansen Way Ste 100 Palo Alto CA 94304-1043 E-mail: rpatterson@ssd.com

PATTON, CARL ELLIOTT, physics educator; b. San Antonio, Sept. 14, 1941; s. Carl Elliott and Geraldine Barnett (Perry) P. BS, MIT, 1963; MS, Calif. Inst. Tech., 1964, PhD, 1967. Sr. scientist Raytheon Co., Waltham, Mass., 1967-71; assoc. prof. physics Colo. State U., Ft. Collins, 1971-75, prof., 1975—. IEEE Magnetics Soc. Disting. lectr., 1993; chair Am. Phys. Soc. Topical Group on Magnetism and its Applications, 1998-99. Editor-in-chief IEEE Transactions on Magnetics, 1987-91. Fellow IEEE (Third Millenium medal 2000), Am. Phys. Soc. Office: Colo State Univ Dept Physics Fort Collins CO 80523-0001

PATTON, JACK THOMAS, family practice physician; b. Rogers, Ark., Feb. 18, 1941; s. Jack Marcus and Jewell Selah (Pense) P.; m. Lynette Anne Carr, Sept. 2, 1960; children: Robert, John, Mark, Christopher. BA in History, Calif. State U., Long Beach, 1963; MD in Medicine, U. So. Calif., L.A., 1967; MA in Bib. Studies, Mennonite Brethren Bib. Sem., Fresno, Calif., 1980; MA in History, Calif. State U., Fresno, 1993. Cert. Bd. Med. Examiners, Calif., Hawaii. Intern Tripler Army Med. Ctr., Honolulu, 1967-68; resident in gen. practice Walson Army Hosp., Ft. Dix, N.J., 1968-70; med. supt. Nazarene Hosp., Papua New Guinea, 1973-80; chmn. family practice dept. Sharp Rees-Stealy, San Diego, 1981-86; chmn. occupational medicine Kaiser Permanente, Fresno, 1986-87; assoc. med. dir. Sharp Rees-Stealy, San Diego, 1987-92; med. dir. Summer Inst. Linguistics, Papua New Guinea, 1993-94; with family practice dept. Sharp Rees-Stealy Med. Group, San Diego, 1994-97, Northwest Med. Group, Fresno, Calif., 1997—. Family practice residency liaison Tripler Army Med. Ctr., Honolulu, 1972-73; chief medicine, dep. commr. Schofield Army Med. Clinics, Wahiawa, Hawaii, 1970-72; lectr. Calif. State U., Fresno, 1978-79, Pt. Loma Nazarene Coll., 1982-85, San Jose Christian Coll., 1997—. Mem. med. sch. support Salerni Collegium, U. So. Calif. Sch. Medicine, 1967-85; lectr. Ch.-Mission Inst., Mennonite Brethren Bib. Sem., 1984-92; sec. S.E. Asian task force Mennonite Brethren Ch. Fresno, 1990-93. Maj. U.S. Army, 1966-73. Mackenzie scholar U. So. Calif. Sch. Medicine, 1966-67. Fellow Am. Acad. Family Physicians; mem. Am. Bd. Family Practice (diplomate), Calif. Acad. Family Physicians, Royal Soc. Medicine (assoc., London). Avocations: history, travel, hiking. Home: 1566 S Adler Ave Fresno CA 93727-5101 Office: 4770 W Herndon Ave Fresno CA 93722-8401

PATTON, RICHARD WESTON, retired mortgage company executive; b. Evanston, Ill., Sept. 26, 1931; s. Robert Ferry and Sue Buckley P.; m. Lynda A. Kruse, Feb. 2, 1971; 1 child, Robert Weston B.A., Amherst Coll., 1954. Sales engr. Thermo Fax Sales Corp., Chgo., 1958-60; account exec. Nat. Mortgage Investors, Inc., Chgo., 1960-61, sales mgr. Pasadena, Calif., 1962-66, asst. v.p., 1966-67, v.p., 1967-69, exec. v.p., 1969-73, pres., chief exec. officer, dir., 1973-84, vice-chmn. bd., 1984-90; pres. Richard W. Patton Enterprises, Pasadena, 1990—. Pres., chmn. exec. com., dir. Ocean Park Restaurant Corp., Santa Monica, Calif., 1977-88; dir. Cenfed Bank, Cenfed Fin. Corp. Bd. dirs. Pasadena Boys' Club, 1963-66, Opera Assocs., 1984-90; mem. steering com. Amherst Coll. Capital Fund Drive, 1963-66. 1st lt. USMCR, 1955-58. Mem. Amherst Coll. Alumni Assn. (bd. dirs. 1963—, pres. 1977-79, 86-89), Overland Club (sec., bd. dirs.), Kroenstadt Ski Club (past pres.). Office: Rich W Patton Enterprises 3644 San Pasqual St Pasadena CA 91107-5419

PATTON, STUART, biochemist, educator; b. Ebenezer, N.Y., Nov. 2, 1920; s. George and Ina (Neher) P.; m. Colleen Cecelia Lavelle, May 17, 1945; children— John, Richard, Gail, Thomas, Mary Catherine, Patricia, Joseph. BS, Pa. State U., 1943; MS, Ohio State U., 1947, PhD, 1948. Chemist Borden Co., 1943-44; rsch. fellow Ohio State U., Columbus, 1946-48; faculty Pa. State U., University Park, 1949-80, prof., 1959-80, Evan Pugh rsch. prof. agr., 1966-80; adj. prof. neuroscis. Sch. Medicine U. Calif., San Diego, 1981—. Vis. scientist Scripps Instn. Oceanography; cons. in field. Author: (with Robert Jenness) Principles of Dairy Chemistry, 1959; (with Robert G. Jensen) Biomedical Aspects of Lactation, 1975. Lt. (j.g.) USNR, 1944-46. Recipient Borden award chemistry milk Am. Chem. Soc., 1957, Agrl. and Food Chemistry award, 1975, Alexander von Humboldt sr. scientist award, 1981, Macy-Gyorgy award Internat. Soc. for Rsch. on Human Milk and Lactation, 1997, Distinguished Alumnus award Coll. of Agrl. Sci. Pa. State U., 1999, Distinguished Svc. award Am. Dairy Sci. Assn., 1999. Fellow Am. Dairy Sci. Assn.; mem. Am. Chem. Soc., Am. Soc. Biochemistry and Molecular Biology, Am. Soc. Cell Biology. Home and Office: 6208 Avenida Cresta La Jolla CA 92037-6510 E-mail: spatton@ucsd.edu

PAUL, AMY, lawyer; b. Santa Monica, Calif. d. Philip and Elaine P.; m. Mark A. Czepiel. Student, UCLA, 1990; JD cum laude, U. San Diego Law Sch., 1993. Bar: Calif.; U.S. Ct. Appeals (9th cir.). Assoc. bus. and tech. group Brobeck Phleger & Harrison LLP, 1993-95; dir. contracts and legal affairs Advanced Fibre Comm., Inc., Petaluma, Calif., 1995-99, v.p., gen. counsel, corp. sec., 1999—. Office: Advanced Fibre Comm Inc 1 Willowbrook Ct Petaluma CA 94954-6507

PAUL, BENJAMIN DAVID, anthropologist, educator; b. N.Y.C., Jan. 25, 1911; s. Phillip and Esther (Kranz) P.; m. Lois Fleischman, Jan. 4, 1936; children: Robert Allen, Janice Carol. Student, U. Wis., 1928-29; AB, U. Chgo., 1938, PhD in Anthropology, 1942. Lectr., rsch. dir. Yale U., 1942-44; community orgn. expert Inter-Am. Ednl. Found., 1946; from lectr. to assoc. prof. anthropology Harvard U., 1946-62, dir. social sci. program Sch. Pub. Health, 1951-62; prof. anthropology Stanford (Calif.) U., 1963—, chmn. dept., 1967-71, dir. program in medicine and behavioral sci., 1963-70. Cons. NIH, 1957—. Editor: Health, Culture and Community: Case Studies of Public Reactions to Health Programs, 1955, Changing Marriage Patterns in a Highland Guatemalan Community, 1963, The Maya Midwife as Sacred Professional, 1975, Mayan Migrants in Guatemala City, 1981, The Operation of a Death Squad in San Pedro la Laguna, 1988. 2d lt. AUS, 1944-46. Travelling fellow Social Sci. Rsch. Coun., 1940-41, Ctr. Advanced Study Behavioral Scis. fellow, 1962-63. Mem. Am. Anthropol. Assn. (Disting. Svc. award 1994), Phi Beta Kappa, Sigma Xi. Achievements include ethnographic field rsch. in Guatemala, 1941, 62, 64-65, 68-69, 73-79, 83-95, 97-98. Home: 622 Salvatierra St Palo Alto CA 94305-8538 Office: Stanford U Dept Anthropology Stanford CA 94305

PAUL, CHARLES S. motion picture and television company executive; b. 1949; BA, Stanford U., 1971; JD, U. Santa Clara, 1975. Law clk. U.S. Supreme Ct., 1975-76; with Cooley Castro Huddleson & Tatum, 1976-79, Atari Inc., 1979-85, sr. v.p., gen. counsel, pres. coin-operated games div., 1983-85; with MCA, Inc., Universal City, Calif., 1985-96, v.p., pres. MCA Enterprises div., 1986-89, exec. v.p., 1989, also bd. dirs., 1985-96; chmn., founder Sega Game Works, Universal City, 1996—. Office: Universal Studios MCA 1024 N Orange Dr Los Angeles CA 90038-2318

PAULSEN, VIVIAN, magazine editor; b. Salt Lake City, May 10, 1942; d. Paul Herman and Martha Oline (Blattman) P. B.A., Brigham Young U., 1964, postgrad., 1965, U. Grenoble, France, 1966. Cert. tchr., Utah. Tchr. French Granite Sch. Dist., Salt Lake City, 1966-67; assoc. editor New Era mag., Salt Lake City, 1970-82; mng. editor Friend mag., Salt Lake City, 1982—. Am. Field Service scholar, 1959; grad. fellow Brigham Young U., 1964-66 Mem. Soc. Children's Book Writers Republican. Mem. Ch. of Jesus Christ of Latter-day Saints Office: The Friend 50 E North Temple # F23 Salt Lake City UT 84150-0002

PAULSON, BOYD COLTON, JR. civil engineering educator; b. Providence, Mar. 1, 1946; s. Boyd Colton and Barbara (McKinstry) P.; m. Jane Margaret Kingdon, Feb. 12, 1970; children: Jeffrey Boyd, Laura Jane. BS, Stanford U., 1967, MS, 1969, PhD, 1971. Asst. prof. U. Ill., Urbana, 1972-73; asst. prof., assoc. prof. civil engring. Stanford (Calif.) U., 1974, prof., 1984-89, Ohbayashi prof. engring., 1989-91, Charles Leavell prof. civil engring., 1991—. Mem. civil engring. adv. com. NSF, 1983-84; mem. U.S. Nat. Com. on Tunneling, 1986-89; mem. com. on constrn. superconducting supercollider in Tex., NAS, 1988-89; presenter in field. Author: Computer Applications in Construction, 1995; co-author: Professional Construction Management, 1978, 2d edit., 1984, 3d edit., 1992; also articles. Bd. dirs. Peninsula Habitat for Humanity, 1996—, Mid-Peninsula Housing, 1999—. Fellow Humboldt Found., Munich, 1983, Brit. Coun., Glasgow, Scotland, 1990-91, Fulbright fellow, 1990-91. Mem. ASCE (chmn. constrn. divsn. 1986-87, Huber Rsch. prize 1980, Constrn. Mgmt. award 1984, Peurifoy Rsch. award 1993), Am. Soc. for Engring. Edn., Urban Land Inst., Nat. Acad. Constrn. Achievements include research on human-computer systems for project management, in analytical modeling and simulation of construction operations, in tunneling in urban environments, in low-cost housing. Office: Stanford U 4020 Civil Engring Stanford CA 94305-4020

PAULSON, DONALD ROBERT, chemistry educator; b. Oak Park, Ill., Sept. 6, 1943; s. Robert Smith and Florence Teresa (Beese) P.; m. Elizabeth Anne Goodwin, Aug. 20, 1966; children: Matthew, Andrew. BA, Monmouth Coll., 1965; PhD, Ind. U., 1968. Asst. prof. chemistry Calif. State U., Los Angeles, 1970-74, assoc. prof., 1974-78, prof., 1979—, chmn. dept., 1982-90. Vis. prof. U. B.C., Vancouver, Can., 1977-78, U. Sussex, Brighton, Eng., 1984-85. Author: Alicyclic Chemistry, 1976; contbr. articles to profl. jours. Named Outstanding Prof., Calif. State U., Los Angeles, 1978, 84, 96. Mem. Am. Chem. Soc., Chem. Soc. (London), InterAm. Photochem. Soc., Nat. Assn. Sci. Tchrs., Sigma Xi. Democrat. Episcopalian. Avocations: photography, hiking, soccer. Home: 497 E California Blvd Apt 203 Pasadena CA 91106-3789 Office: Calif State U Dept Chemistry 5151 State University Dr Los Angeles CA 90032-4226 E-mail: dpaulso@calstatela.edu

PAULSON, RICHARD L. paper and wood products executive; Joined Potlatch Corp., Spokane, Wash., 1960, v.p. mfg. N.W. Paper divsn., v.p. consumer products divsn., 1993, v.p. Minn. pulp and paper divsn., pres., COO, 1999—. Office: Potlatch Corp Ste 1100 601 W Riverside Ave Spokane WA 99201

PAULUS, NORMA JEAN PETERSEN, lawyer; b. Belgrade, Nebr., Mar. 13, 1933; d. Paul Emil adn Ella Marie (Hellbusch) Petersen; m. William G. Paulus, Aug. 16, 1958; children: Elizabeth, William Frederick. LL.B., Willamette Law Sch., 1962; LL.D. (hon.), Linfield Coll., 1985; LittD (hon.), Whitman Coll., 1990; LHD (hon.), Lewis & Clark Coll., 1996. Bar: Oreg. 1962. Sec. to Harney County Dist. Atty., 1950-53; legal sec. Salem, Oreg., 1953-55; sec. to chief justice Oreg. Supreme Ct., 1955-61; of counsel Paulus and Callaghan, Salem; mem. Oreg. Ho. of Reps., 1971-77; sec. State of Oreg., Salem, 1977-85; supt. pub. instrn., 1990-99; of counsel Paulus, Rhoten & Lien, 1985-86. Mem. Oreg. exec. bd. U.S. West, 1985-97; adj. prof. Willamette U. Grad. Sch., 1985, mem. N.W. Power Planning Com., 1986-89. Mem. adv. com. Def. Adv. Com. for Women in the Svc., 1986, Nat. Trust for Hist. Preservation, 1988-90; trustee Willamette U., 1978—; bd. dirs. Oreg. Grade Instn. Sci. and Tech., 1985-2001, Edn. Commn. States, 1991-99, Coun. Chief State Sch. Officers, 1995-98, Nat. Assessment Governing Bd., 1996-99, Oreg. Garden Found., 1997—, Oreg. Coast Aquarium, 1999—; bd. dirs., adv. bd. World Affairs Coun. Oreg., 1997—; overseer Whitman Coll., 1985—; bd. cons. Marion-Polk Boundary Commn., 1970-71; mem. Presdl. Commn. to Monitor Philippines Election, 1986; dir. Oreg. Hist. Soc., 2001—. Recipient Disting. Svc. award City of Salem, 1971, LWV, 1995, Path Breaker award Oreg. Women's Polit. Caucus, 1976; named One of 10 Women of Future, Ladies Home Jour., 1979, Woman of Yr. Oreg. Inst. Managerial and Profl. Women, 1982, Oreg. Women Lawyers, 1982, Woman Who Made a Difference award Nat. Women's Forum, 1985; Eagleton Inst. Politics fellow Rutgers U. Mem. Oreg. State Bar, Nat. Order Women Legislators, Women Execs. in State Govt., Women's Polit. Caucus Bus. and Profl. Women's Club (Golden Torch award 1971), Delta Kappa Gamma. E-mail: normap@ohs.org

PAUP, MARTIN ARNOLD, real estate and securities investor; b. Seattle, Aug. 30, 1930; s. Clarence Jacob and Emaline Ethel (Lodestein) P.; m. Mary Jean Iske, Apr. 4, 1959; children: Barbara Ann Paup Soriano, Jennifer Marie, Elizabeth Paup-Byrnes. BS, U. Wash., 1952. Indsl. engr. Boeing Airplane Co., Seattle, 1954-60; owner Coopers Unfinished Furniture, Seattle, 1960-63; claims rep. Unigard Ins., Seattle, 1963-66; asst. benefits mgr. Equitable Life Assurance, Seattle, 1966-85; owner Paup Ventures, Seattle, 1974—, Paup Investment Co., Seattle, 1963—, Ella Paup Properties, Seattle, 1963—. Bd. dirs. Denny Regrade Property Owners' Assn., Seattle, Denny Regrade Bus. Assn., Seattle, First Ave. Assn., Seattle. Seattle Dept. Community Devel. grantee, 1980. Mem. Greenwood C. of C., Seattle Opera Guild. Democrat. Roman Catholic. Avocations: opera, travel, lit., history.

PAUSA, CLEMENTS EDWARD, electronics company executive; b. South Gate, Calif., Oct. 18, 1930; s. Oscar Clements and Kathleen Patricia (O'Toole) P.; m. Janice Mary Hanson, Jan. 22, 1955; children: Geoffrey Clements, Ronald Edward. Student, UCLA, 1948-50; BS, U. Calif., Berkeley, 1953, MS, 1954, cert. in bus., 1960. Product mgr. Fairchild Semiconductor Corp., 1959-62, mgr. plant, 1962-64; gen. mgr. Fairchild Hong Kong Ltd., 1964-67, dir. plant group, 1967-68; dir. internat. mfg. Nat. Semiconductor Corp., Santa Clara, Calif., 1968-70, gen. mgr. Far East ops., 1970-73, v.p. internat. mfg., 1973-86, corp. v.p. internat. mfg., 1986-90, corp. v.p. internat. mfg. emeritus, 1991—. Dir. Price Waterhouse Coopers MCS; v.p. ops. Power Integrations, Inc., 1997-99; bd. dirs. 8 subs. cos., 2 J.V. cos. Mem. internat. adv. bd. U. Santa Clara, 1984—. Capt. USNR, 1952-81. Mem. Naval Res. Assn., Res. Officer's Assn., Calif. Alumni Assn., Delta Chi Alumni Assn. (v.p., pres. 1978-86). Republican. Roman Catholic. Office: Price Waterhouse Coopers 68 Willow Rd Menlo Park CA 94085-3653 E-mail: clements.e.pausa@us.pwcglobal.com

PAVLATH, ATTILA ENDRE, research chemist; b. Budapest, Hungary, Mar. 11, 1930; came to U.S., 1958; s. Eugene Rudolph and Yolanda Elizabeth (Hortobagyi) P.; m. Katalin Wappel, July 27, 1951; children: George, Grace. Diploma in chem. engring., Tech. U., Budapest, 1952; D in Chemistry, Hungarian Acad. of Sci., Budapest, 1955. Asst. prof. Tech. U., Budapest, 1952-56; group leader Cen. Chem. Rsch. Inst., Budapest, 1954-56; rsch. fellow McGill U., Montreal, Can., 1957-58; sr. group leader Stauffer Chem. Co., Richmond, Calif., 1958-67; project leader Western regional rsch. ctr. USDA, Albany, 1967-78, rsch. leader Western regional rsch. ctr., 1979—. Author three books; contbr. articles to profl. jours; patentee in field. Fellow Am. Inst. Chemists (councilor 1985-95, dir.

1993-95); mem. Am. Chem. Soc. (councilor 1973-90, dir. 1991-99, pres.-elect 2000, pres. 2001), Royal Chem. Soc. Great Britain, N.Am. Thermonalysis Soc., Internat. Union of Pure and Applied Chemistry. Avocations: flying, tournament bridge, tennis, table tennis, computers. Office: USDA Western Regional Rsch Ctr 800 Buchanan St Berkeley CA 94710-1105

PAYNE, ANCIL HORACE, retired broadcasting executive; b. Mitchell, Oreg., Sept. 5, 1921; s. Leslie L. and Pearl A. (Brown) P.; m. Valerie Dorrance Davies, Apr. 6, 1959; children: Anne Sparrow, Alison Louise, Lucinda Catherine. Student, Willamette U., 1939-41, U. Oreg., 1941, U. Notre Dame, Ohio State U., 1943; B.A., U. Wash., 1947; postgrad., Am. U., 1950-51; hon. PhD, Willamette Univ., 1991. Adminstrv. asst. to congressman, Washington, 1949-52; gen. mgr. Martin Van Lines, Anchorage, 1952-56; mgr. Frontiers-Oreg. Ltd., Portland, Oreg., 1956-59; asst. v.p. bus. div. King Broadcasting Co., Seattle, 1959-63, v.p., 1963-70, exec. v.p., 1970-71, pres., 1971-87. Chmn. bd. affiliates NBC, 1975-80. Mem. Oreg. Bd. Higher Edn., 1966-70; bd. trustees Whitman Coll,. 1985-90; bd. dirs. Ceasefire. Lt. (j.g.) USNR, 1942-45, PTO. Fellow Phi Beta Kappa; mem. Monday Club, Rainier Club, Alpha Delta Sigma. Episcopalian. Office: Ancil H Payne & Assocs 1107 1st Ave Apt 606 Seattle WA 98101-2944

PAYNE, ANITA HART, reproductive endocrinologist, researcher; b. Karlsruhe, Baden, Germany, Nov. 24, 1926; came to U.S., 1938; d. Frederick Michael and Erna Rose (Hirsch) Hart; widowed; children: Gregory Steven, Teresa Payne-Lyons. BA, U. Calif., Berkeley, 1949, PhD, 1952. From rsch. assoc. to prof. U. Mich., Ann Arbor, 1961-96, prof. emeritus, 1996—; assoc. dir. U. Mich. Ctr. for Study Reprodn., Ann Arbor, 1989-94; sr. rsch. scientist Stanford (Calif.) U. Med. Ctr., 1995—. Vis. scholar Stanford U., 1987-88; mem. reproductive biology study sect. NIH, Bethesda, Md., 1978-79, biochem. endocrinology study sect., 1979-83, population rsch. com. Nat. Inst. Child Health and Human Devel., 1989-93. Assoc. editor Steroids, 1987-93; contbr. book chpts., articles to profl. jours. Recipient award for cancer rsch. Calif. Inst. for Cancer Rsch., 1953, Acad. Women's Caucus award U. Mich., 1986, Mentor award Women in Endocrinology, 1999. Mem. Endocrine Soc. (chmn. awards com. 1983-84, mem. nominating com. 1985-87, coun. 1988-91), Am. Soc. Andrology (exec. coun. 1980-83), Soc. for Study of Reprodn. (bd. dirs. 1982-85, sec. 1986-89, pres. 1990-91, Carl G. Hartman award 1998). Office: Stanford U Med Ctr Dept OB GYN Divsn Reproductive Biology Stanford CA 94305-5317

PAYNE, DAVID L. bank executive; Chmn., pres., CEO Westamerica Bancorporation; gen. mgr. Gibson Publs. Office: 1108 5th Ave San Rafael CA 94901-2916

PAYNE, WILLIAM H. state legislator, lawyer; b. San Francisco, July 18, 1951; BA, MA, JD, U. N.Mex.; MA in Govt., Georgetown U. Mem. N.Mex. Senate, Dist. 20, Santa Fe, 1996—; mem. conservation com. N.Mex. Senate, Santa Fe, mem. jud. com. Republican. Office: PO Box 14823 Albuquerque NM 87191-4823

PAYTON, GARY DWAYNE, professional basketball player; b. Oakland, Calif., July 23, 1968; m. Monique Payton; children: Raquel, Gary Dwayne. Grad., Oreg. State U., 1990. Drafted NBA, 1990; guard Seattle Supersonics, 1990—. Named mem. All-Am. First Team, The Sporting News, 1990, Pacific-10 Conf. Player of Yr., 1990, NBA All-Star, 1994, 95, NBA Player of the Week; named to NBA All-Def. 1st Team, 1994, 95. Office: Seattle Supersonics 351 Elliott Ave W Seattle WA 98119-4101

PAZOUR, DON, publishing executive; Pres. Miller Freeman, Inc., San Francisco. Office: c/o Miller Freeman Inc 600 Harrison St San Francisco CA 94107-1387

PEACE, STEVE, state legislator; b. San Diego; m. Cheryl Peace, 1974; children: Clint, Bret, Chad. Degree in Polit. Sci., U. Calif., San Diego. CFO, co-founder Four Square Prodns., National City, Calif., 1972; mem. Calif. State Assembly, 1982-93, chair fin., ins. and pub. investment com., 1993; mem. Calif. State Senate, 1993—, chair com. on energy, utilities and comm., mem. and chair budget and fiscal rev. com. Coach Pony and Little League; pres. Homeowner's Assn.; co-chair Citizens for Clean Water. Democrat. Office: State Capitol Rm 3060 Sacramento CA 94814 also: 7877 Parkway Dr Ste 1B La Mesa CA 91942-2000 also: 430 Davidson St # E Chula Vista CA 91910-2411

PEALE, STANTON JERROLD, physics educator; b. Indpls., Jan. 23, 1937; s. Robert Frederick and Edith May (Murphy) P.; m. Priscilla Laing Cobb; June 25, 1960; children: Robert Edwin, Douglas Andrew. BSE, Purdue U., 1959; MS in Engring. Physics, Cornell U., 1962, PhD in Engring. Physics, 1965. Research asst. Cornell U., Ithaca, N.Y., 1962-64, research assoc., 1964-65; asst. research geophysicist, asst. prof. astronomy UCLA, 1965-68; asst. prof. physics U. Calif., Santa Barbara, 1968-70, assoc. prof., 1970-76, prof., 1976-94, prof. emeritus, rsch. prof., 1994—. Mem. com. lunar and planetary exploration NAS-NRC, Washington, 1980-84, lunar and planetary geosci. rev. panel, 1979-80, 86-89, 94-96, Planetary Sys. Sci. Working Group, 1988-93, Lunar and Planetary Sci. Coun., 1984-87, mem. com. astronomy and astrophysics, 1997—; lunar sci. adv. group NASA-JPL, Pasadena, Calif., 1970-72; mem. Keck time allocation com. NASA, 1996-98. Assoc. editor: Jour. Geophys. Research, 1987; contbr. articles to profl. jours. Recipient Exceptional Scientific Achievement medal NASA, 1980, James Craig Watson award Nat. Acad. Scis., 1982; vis. fellowships U. Colo., Boulder, 1972-73, 1979-80. Fellow AAAS (Newcomb Cleveland prize 1979), Am. Geophys. Union; mem. Am. Astron. Soc. (divsns. planet sci. and dynamic astronomy, Dirk Brouwer award 1992, chair dynamical astronomy 1999-2000), Internat. Astron. Union. Avocation: gardening. Office: U Calif Santa Barbara Dept Physics Santa Barbara CA 93106

PEARCE, DRUE, state legislator; b. Fairfield, Ill., Apr. 2, 1951; d. H. Phil and Julia Detroy (Bannister) P.; m. Michael F.G. Williams; 1 child, Tate Hanna Pearce-Williams. BA in Biol. Scis., Ind. U., 1973; MPA, Harvard U., 1984; cert. exec. program Darden Sch. Bus., U. Va., 1989. Sch. tchr., Clark County, Ind., 1973-74; curator of edn. Louisville Zoo, 1974-77; dir. Summerscene, Louisville, 1974-77; asst. v.p., br. mgr. Alaska Nat. Bank of the North, 1977-82; legis. aide to Rep. John Ringstad Alaska Ho. of Reps., Juneau, 1983, mem., 1984-88, minority whip, 1986; mem. Alaska Senate, Dist. F, Juneau, 1988—; chmn. com. oil and gas, mem. exec. com. energy coun., 1989-90; chmn. com. labor and commerce, mem. exec. coms. western state conf., coun. state govts., energy coun., 1991-92; co-chmn. senate fin., chmn. energy coun., vice chmn. com. energy, nat. coun. state govts., 1993-94; mem. select com. legis. ethics and legis. coun., 1993—; pres. senate, mem. exec. com. energy coun., vice chmn. senate coms. resources and rules, 1995-96; co-chmn. com. senate fin., mem. exec. com. energy coun., vice chmn. com. senate judiciary, 1997—. Senate pres., 1999-2000, 1995-96, fin. cons. Bowman and Miller, Anchorage, 1983; ptnr. 4150 Co., Anchorage and Kotzebue, Alaska, 1983—, Cloverland N., Anchorage, 1993—; investor, bd. dirs. Wave Energy Corp., Anchorage; resources cons. Arctic Slope Regional Corp., Anchorage, 1987-91, [illegible] Bd. dirs. Alaska Women's Aid in Crisis, Anchorage Econ. Devel. Coun., Alaska Aerospace Devel. Corp., Alaska Spl. Olympics, Gov.'s Bd.; mem. Alaska Resource Devel. Coun., Alaska Women's Polit. Caucus. Mem. DAR, Commonwealth North, Resource Devel. Counc., Alaska Support Industry Alliance, Alaska Miners Assn., Alaska Fedn. of Republican Women, Aircraft owners & Pilots Assn., United States Trotting Assn., Alaska C. of C. Republican. Home: 716 W 4th Ave Ste 500 Anchorage AK 99501-2107 Office: Office State Senate State Capitol St Juneau AK 99801-1182

PEARL, JUDEA, computer scientist, educator; b. Tel-Aviv, Sept. 4, 1936; U.S. citizen; married; 3 children. BSc, Israel Inst. Tech., 1960; MSc, Newark Coll. Engring., 1961; PhD in Elec. Engring., Poly. Inst. Bklyn., 1965. Rsch. engr. Dental Sch., NYU, 1960-61; mem. tech. staff RCA Rsch. Labs., 1961-65; dir. advanced memory devices Electronic Memories, Inc., Calif., 1966-69; prof. Sch. of Engring./Dept. Computer Scis. UCLA, 1969—. Instr. Newark Coll. Engring., 1961; cons. Rand Corp., 1972, Integrated Sci. Corp., 1975, Hughes Aircraft, 1989. Recipient Outstanding Achievement award RCA Labs., 1965. Fellow IEEE, Am. Assn. Artificial Intelligence; mem. Nat. Acad. Engring. Office: UCLA Dept Computer Sci 4532 Boelter Hl Los Angeles CA 90095-0001

PEARSON, RICHARD JOSEPH, archaeologist, educator; b. Kitchener, Ont., Can., May 2, 1938; s. John Cecil and Henrietta Anne (Wallwin) P.; m. Kazue Miyazaki, Dec. 12, 1964; 1 child, Sarina Riye. B.A. in Anthropology with honours, U. Toronto, 1960; Ph.D., Yale U., 1966. Asst. prof., then assoc. prof. archaeology U. Hawaii, 1966-71; mem. faculty U. B.C., Vancouver, 1971-2000. Author: The Archaeology of the Ryukyu Islands, 1969, Higashi Ajia no Kodai Shakai to Kokogaku, 1984, Windows on the Japanese Past, Studies in Archaeology and Prehistory, 1986, Ancient Japan, 1992; contbr. articles to profl. jours. Guggenheim fellow. E-mail: pearsonrj@home.com

PEARSON, ROBERT GREENLEES, writing services company executive; b. Kansas City, Mo., Feb. 19, 1917; s. Ridley Stillson and Agnes (Greenlees) P.; m. Laura Gray Betsy Dodge, Jan. 3, 1945; children—Bradbury, Wendy, Robert Ridley. AB with honors, U. Kans., 1938. Mgr. corp. pub. rels. Shell Oil Co. (N.Y. Head Office), 1938-71; v.p. pub. rels. Council Better Bus. Bur. (N.Y. Hdqrs.), 1971-73; writer pub. affairs dept. Mobil Oil Corp., N.Y.C., 1973-74; sr. advisor Alcoholics Anonymous World Services, Inc., N.Y.C., 1974-85; pres. Robert Pearson Assocs., Writing Svcs., Riverside, Conn., 1985—. Bd. dirs. Nat. Safety Council; pres. Fairfield County (Conn.) Council on Alcoholism, 1962 Author: Oil for Victory, 1946, The J.C. Nichols Chronicle, 1994; contbr. articles to profl. jours. Served to lt. comdr. USNR, 1941-45. Congregationalist. Clubs: Riverside (Conn.); Yacht, Dutch Treat. Home and Office: 38 Fox Hollow Rd Bellevue ID 83313

PEARSON, ROGER LEE, library director; b. Galesburg, Ill., Dec. 7, 1940; s. Clifford Emmanuel and Lillian Louise (Fisher) P. B.A., Knox Coll., 1963; M.A. in Sociology, U. Nebr.-Omaha, 1968; M.A. in Library Sci., Rosary Coll., 1974. Vol. U.S. Peace Corps, Brazil, 1964-66; extension service supr. Brown County Libr., Green Bay, Wis., 1974-75; system adminstr. Nicolet Libr. System, Green Bay, 1976-77; exec. dir. South Central Libr. System, Madison, Wis., 1977-81; dir. Corpus Christi Pub. Librs., Tex., 1981-84, Naperville (Ill.) Pub. Librs., 1984-95, Sonoma County Libr., Santa Rosa, Calif., 1996-2001; interm dir. Spokane (Wash.) Pub. Libr., summer 2001. Lectr. Grad. Sch. Libr. and Info. Sci., Rosary Coll., River Forest, Ill., 1991-95. Mem. ALA, Train Riders Assn. Calif., Am. Assn. Ret. People, Calif. Libr. Assn., Wine Libr. Assocs. Sonoma County. Avocations: power walking, travel research, train travel. Home: 1451 Country Manor Dr Santa Rosa CA 95401 Office: Sonoma County Libr 3d 8 E Santa Rosa CA 95404-4700

PEASE, GERALD, state legislator; b. Hardin, Mont., July 21, 1954; m. Maria Pease. Cert., Missoula VoTech. Rancher; hwy. constrn. worker; Dem. rep. dist. 6 Mont. Ho. of Reps., 1997-98. Trustee Lodge Grass Sch. Bd.; mem. Ptnrs. in Policy Making, Parents Lets Unite for Kids. Office: PO Box T Lodge Grass MT 59050-0556

PEASE, ROGER FABIAN WEDGWOOD, electrical engineering educator; b. Cambridge, Eng., Oct. 24, 1936; came to U.S., 1964; s. Michael Stewart and Helen Bowen (Wedgwood) P.; m. Caroline Ann Bowring, Sept. 17, 1960; children: Emma Ruth, Joseph Henry Bowring, James Edward. BA, Cambridge U., Eng., 1960, MA, PhD, Cambridge U., 1964. Rsch. fellow Trinity Coll., Cambridge, 1963-64; asst. prof. U. Calif., Berkeley, 1964-67; mem. tech. staff AT&T Bell Labs., Murray Hill, N.J., 1967-78; prof. elec. engring. Stanford (Calif.) U., 1978—. Cons. IBM, San Jose, Calif., 1964-67, Xerox Corp., Palo Alto, Calif., 1978-84, Perkin Elmer Co., Hayward, Calif., 1979-90, Lawrence Livermore (Calif.) Labs., 1984-92, Affymax Rsch. Inst., 1989-93, Affymetrix, 1993—; mem. tech. adv. bd. Ultratech. Stepper, 1993—; with Dept. of Def. Advanced Rsch. Project Agy., 1996-98. Contbr. more than 200 articles to profl. jours. Patentee (8) in field. Scoutmaster Boy Scouts Am., Holmdel, N.J., 1977-78. Pilot officer RAF, 1955-57. Fellow IEEE (Rappaport award 1982); mem. Nat. Acad. Engring., San Jose Sailing Club. Avocations: sailboat racing, windsurfing. Home: 119 Peter Coutts Circle Stanford CA 94305-2519 Office: Stanford U Dept Elec Engring Stanford CA 94305

PECK, AUSTIN H., JR. lawyer; b. Pomona, Calif., Dec. 25, 1913; s. Austin H. and Helen (Templeton) P.; m. Jean Albertson, Nov. 9, 1939 (dec. Aug. 1997); children: Julie (dec.), Francesca, Lisa; m. Janice Galloway, Apr. 3, 1998 (dec. May 2001). A.B. with distinction, Stanford, 1935, J.D., 1938. Bar: Calif. 1938. Practiced in, L.A., from 1938; mem. Latham & Watkins, 1946-76, of counsel, 1976-92. Mem. nat. coun. House Ear Inst. Mem. ABA, Calif. Bar Assn., L.A. Bar Assn., Calif. Club, L.A. Country Club, Birnam Wood Club (Montecito, Calif.), Valley Club (Montecito), Zeta Psi, Phi Delta Phi. Home: 2159 Boundary Dr Santa Barbara CA 93108-2262 Office: 633 W 5th St Los Angeles CA 90071-2005

PECK, CHARLES, hotel executive; Pres., COO Destination Hotels and Resorts, Inc., Englewood, Colo., 1998—. Office: Destination Hotels & Resorts Inc 10333 E Dry Creek Rd Ste 450 Englewood CO 80112-1562

PECK, CHRISTOPHER, newspaper editor; b. Wyo., Aug. 2, 1950; m. Kate Duignan Peck; children: Sarah, Cody. Degree in comms., Standord U., 1972. Editor The Wood River Jour., Sun Valley, Idaho; city editor, edtl. oage editor, mng. editor Times-News, Twin Falls, 1975-79; columnist, 1979; editor The Spokesman Rev., Spokane, Wash., 1982—. Dir. Nat. Assn. Press Mng. Editors Assn.; mem. Soc. Am. Soc. Newspaper Editors; Pulitzer prize nominating judge. Office: The Spokesman Review Cowles Pub Co Western Farmer Stockman PO Box 2160 Spokane WA 99210-2160

PECK, GAILLARD RAY, JR. defense contractor, aerospace and business consultant, business owner; b. San Antonio, Oct. 31, 1940; s. Gaillard Ray and Lois (Manning) P.; 1 child, Scott; m. Jean Adair Hilger, Dec. 23, 1962 (div. Oct. 1969); children: Gaillard III, Katherine Adair; m. Peggy Ann Lundt, July 3, 1975; children: Jennifer Caroline, Elizabeth Ann. BS, Air Force Acad., 1962; MA, Cen. Mich. U., 1976; postgrad., Nat. War Coll., Washington, 1982-83; MBA, U. Nev., Las Vegas, 1990. Lic. comml. pilot, flight instr. Commd. 2d lt. USAF, 1962, advanced through grades to col., 1983, ret., 1988, air force instr. pilot, fighter pilot, 1963-72, instr. Fighter Weapons Sch., 1972-75; fighter tactics officer Pentagon, Washington, 1975-78; aggressor pilot, comdr. 4477th Test & Evaluation Squadron, Nellis AFB, Nev., 1978-80, mil. advisor Royal Saudi Air Force, Saudi Arabia, 1980-82; dir. ops., vice comdr. Kadena Air Base, Japan, 1983-85; wing comdr. Zweibrucken Air Base, Germany, 1985-87; dep. dir. aerospace safety directorate USAF, Norton AFB, Calif., 1987-88; rsch. asst. U. Nev., Las Vegas, 1988-90; mktg. cons. Ctr. for Bus. & Econ. Rsch. U. Nev., Las Vegas, 1990; adminstr. Lung Ctr. of Nev., Las Vegas, 1991-93; bus. owner, cons. Las Vegas, 1993—; owner Great Western Aircraft Parts, LLC. Acad. instr. USAF. Author: The Enemy, 1973, As Best I Recall, 1994. Recipient Silver Star, Legion of Merit (2), DFC (3), Air Medal (11). Mem. Phi Kappa Phi Nat. Honor Soc., Order of Daedalians, Red River Fighter Pilots Assn., Air Force Assn., U. Nev. Las Vegas Alumni Assn., Air Force Acad. Alumni Assn., The Ret. Officers Assn. Avocations: flying, auto restoration, computer sci., hiking, camping, family activities. E-mail: gaillard.peck@nellis.af.mil; gtwestern@aolcom. Home: 1775 Sheree Cir Las Vegas NV 89119-2716 E-mail: gaillard.peck@nellis.af.mil

PECK, PAUL LACHLAN, minister; b. Glens Falls, N.Y., Sept. 11, 1928; s. Paul Lee and Caroline Jeannette (Stanton) Peck; children: Paul Barrett, Kathryn Elizabeth, Gretchen, Kole W. BS, U. Conn., 1952; ThD, Bernadean U., 1976; MEd, Westfield State Coll., 1983. Ordained to ministry Truth Ctr., 1972. With Proctor and Gamble Co., Watertown, N.Y., 1956-60; dir. deferred giving programs Syracuse (N.Y.) U., 1960-68, v.p., 1968-70, Fairleigh-Dickinson U., N.J., 1970-71, Manhattan Coll., Bronx, N.Y., 1971-75; founder, pastor Arete' Truth Cr., San Diego, 1975—. Author: Footsteps Along the Path, 1978, Inherit the Kingdom, 1978, Milestones of the Way, 1978, Freeway to Health, 1980, Freeway to Work and Wealth, 1981, Freeway to Human Love, 1982, Freeway to Personal Growth, 1982, Your Dreams Count, 1990, Heroic Love Poems, 1990. Bd. dirs. Girl Scouts U.S.A., Syracuse, 1967-70; trustee, bd. dirs. Erickson Ednl. Found., 1970-75; vol. chaplain Auburn (N.Y.) State Prison, 1967-68; mem. chaplains' coun. Syracuse U., 1960-70; co-founder suicide and drug abuse prevention program Syracuse U., 1968-71, Fairleigh-Dickinson U., 1970-71, Manhattan Coll., 1971-75. Staff sgt. USNG, 1947-50. Mem. Internat. New Thought Alliance, SAR, Rotary, Knights of Malta (svc. award 1973), Masons, Shriners, Spiritual Frontiers Fellowship. Avocations: golf, book collecting.

PECK, RALPH, state agency administrator; b. Lewistown, Mont. m. Julie Peck; 4 children. B in Bus. Mgmt. Fin. and Mktg., M of Agrl. Bus. and Econs., U. Utah. Program mgr. Rural Devel. divsn. Mont. Dept. Agr., adminstr. centralized svcs. divsn.; comptr., asst. v.p. Econ. Inc.; now dir. Mont. Dept. Agr., 1995—. Mem. Mont. Capital Fin. Adv. Coun.; mem. Water Pollution Control Adv. Coun. Recipient Mont. Gov.;s award of excellence. Mem. Western Assn. Depts. Agr. (pres.), Nat. Assn. Depts. Agr. (bd. dirs.). Office: Mont Dept Agr PO Box 200201 Helena MT 59620-0201

PECK, RAYMOND CHARLES, SR. driver behavior research specialist and research consultant; b. Sacramento, Nov. 18, 1937; s. Emory Earl and Margaret Helen (Fiebiger) P.; m. Ellie ruth Enriquez, sept. 5, 1957; children: Teresa M. Pack Montijo, Linda M. Peck Heisler, margaret V. Peck Henley, Raymond C., Christina M. Peck Reich. BA in Exptl. Psychology, Calif. State U., Sacramento, 1961, MA in Exptl. Psychology, 1968. Rsch. analyst Calif. Dept. Motor Vehicles, Sacramento, 1962-71, sr. rsch. analyst, program mgr., 1971-80, rsch. program splst. II, 1980, 81-84, acting, chief rsch., 1980-81, chief rsch., 1984-2000; pres. R.C. Peck & Assocs. Statis. cons. to pvt. and pub. orgns., 1970—; chmn. com. on operator regulation Transp. Rsch. Bd., NAS, 1976-82. Past edtl. adv. bds. Traffic Safety Evaln. Rsch. Review, Alcohol, Drugs and Driving; mem. edtl. bd. Jour. Safety Rsch., Accident Analysis and Prevention; contbr. articles to profl. jours. Recipient Met. Life award of Honor., Nat. Safety Coun., 1970, Met. Life cert. of comendation Nat. Safety Coun., 1972, A.R. Lauer award Human Factor Soc., 1981, Award of Honor, Award of Merit, Nat. Hwy. Traffic Safety Adminstrn., 1982. Mem. APHA, AAAS, Am. Statis. Assn. Am. Assn. Automotive Medicine, Internat. Coun. Alcohol, Drugs and Traffic Safety, Human Factors Soc., Soc. Epidemiologic Rsch. Democrat. Home and Office: 1200 Lakeshore Ave Apt 16D Oakland CA 94606

PECK, ROBERT A. newspaper publisher, state legislator; b. Riverton, Wyo., Oct. 7, 1924; s. LeRoy E. and Elvira Eugenia (Sostrom) P.; m. Cordelia S. Peck, Oct. 5, 1949 (dec. Feb. 1996); children: Christopher, George, Steven. BA, U. Wyo., 1949. Pub. The Riverton Ranger, 1949—; mem. Wyo. Senate, Dist. 26, Cheyenne, 1991—. Pres. Central Wyo. Coll. Bd., Riverton, 1966-81; sec. CWC Found., Riverton, 1968—. Staff sgt. U.S. Army, 1943-46, ETO. Mem. Soc. Profl. Journalists, Masons, Phi Beta Kappa. Republican. Methodist. Office: The Riverton Ranger 421 E Main PO Box 993 Riverton WY 82501-0993 E-mail: bpeck@wyoming.com, ranger@wyoming.com

PECK, ROBERT DAVID, educational foundation administrator; b. Devil's Lake, N.D., June 1, 1929; s. Lester David and Bernice Marie (Peterson) P.; m. Lylia June Smith, Sept. 6, 1953; children: David Allan, Kathleen Marie. BA, Whitworth Coll., 1951; MDiv, Berkeley (Calif.) Bapt. Div. Sch., 1958; ThD, Pacific Sch. Religion, 1964; postgrad., U. Calif., Berkeley, 1959-60, 62-63, Wadham Coll., Oxford U., Eng., 1963. Music tchr. pub. schs., Bridgeport, Wash., 1954-55; prof., registrar Linfield Coll., McMinnville, Oreg., 1963-69; asst. dir. Ednl. Coordinating Coun., Salem, 1969-75; assoc. prof. Pacific Luth. U., Tacoma, 1976-79, U. Puget Sound, Tacoma, 1977; v.p. John Minter Assocs., Boulder, Colo., 1979-81, Coun. Ind. Colls., Washington, 1981-84; adminstrv. v.p. Alaska Pacific U., Anchorage, 1984-88; pres. Phillips U., Enid, Okla., 1988-94, chancellor, 1994-95; chmn. The Pres. Found. for Support of Higher Edn., Washington, 1995—; sr. assoc. InterEd, Phoenix, 1998—. Pres. Phillips U. Ednl. Enterprises Inc., 1994-95; cons. Higher Edn. Exec. Assocs., Denver, 1984—; owner Tyee Marina, Tacoma, 1975-77; yacht broker Seattle, 1977-79. Author: Future Focusing: An Alternative to Strategic Planning, 1983, also articles. Dem. county chmn., McMinnville, 1968, Dem. candidate for state Ho. of Reps., McMinnville, 1969; pres. McMinnville Kiwanis, 1965-69. Cpl. Signal Corps, U.S. Army, 1952-54. Carnegie Corp. grantee, 1982, 84. Mem. Okla. Ind. Coll. Assn. (sec. 1989—). Mem. Christian Ch. Avocation: sailing, sculpting. E-mail: robertpeckb@cs.com

PEDEN, LYNN ELLEN, marketing executive; b. L.A., Mar. 1, 1946; d. Orlan Sidney and Erna Lou (Harris) Friedman; m. Ernest Peden, Aug. 1994. Student, UCLA, 1963-65, 71-72, Willis Bus. Coll., 1965-66, Fin. Schs. Am., 1982, Viewpoints Inst., 1970-71. Office mgr. Harleigh Sandler Co., L.A., 1965-67; customer svc. Investors Diversified Svcs., West L.A., Calif., 1968-76; exec. sec. McCulloch Oil Corp., West L.A., 1976; mgr. publs. Security 1st Group, Century City, Calif., 1976-80; office mgr. Morehead & Co., Century City, 1980-81; dir. mktg., mgr. customer svc. Inst. Mktg. Svcs., Santa Monica, Calif., 1981-82; v.p. Decatur Petroleum Corp., Santa Monica, 1982-83; asst. v.p., broker svcs., dir. Angeles Corp., L.A., 1984-87; asst. to pres. Pacific Ventures, Santa Monica, 1988-90, La Grange Group, West L.A., 1990-95; property mgmt. asst. Desert Resort Mgmt., Palm Desert, Calif., 1997-99, bus. mgr., 1999—. Fin. and ins. writer; contbr. poetry to UCLA Literacy Mag., 1964. Mem. Migi Car Am. Club (sec., newsletter editor). Home: 78580 Villeta Dr La Quinta CA 92253-3856

PEDERSEN, NORMAN A. lawyer; b. Modesto, Calif., Dec. 29, 1946; s. Melvin R. and Hilda R. (Akenhead) P. BA, U. Calif., Berkeley, 1970, MA, 1972; JD, UCLA, 1975. Bar: Calif., D.C. Trial atty. Fed. Power Commn., Washington, 1975-77; asst. to commr. Fed. Regulatory Commn., Washington, 1977-79; ptnr. [illegible], Washington, 1979-87, Graham & James, Washington, 1987-88, Jones, Day, Reavis & Pogue, Washington, 1988—. Office: Jones Day Reavis & Pogue 555 W 5th St Ste 4600 Los Angeles CA 90013-1025

PEDERSON, CON, animator; Grad., UCLA. Former writer, animator Walt Disney; animator Graphic Films Corp.; co-founder Abel & Assocs.; sr. animator MetroLight Studios, L.A., 1987—. Animator for Redstone rocket project, also Explorer Satellite program, 1958. Spl. effects supr., animated models designer (film) 2001: A Space Odyssey. Office: Metro-Light Studios 5724 W 3rd St Ste 400 Los Angeles CA 90036-3084

PEDERSON, DONALD OSCAR, electrical engineering educator; b. Hallock, Minn., Sept. 30, 1925; s. Oscar Jorgan and Beda Emelia (Dahlof) P.; m. Karen T.; children: John Jay, Katharine Dresden, Margaret Claire, Emily Mariko. Student, Iowa State U., 1943; B.S., N.D. State U., 1948; M.S., Stanford U., 1949, Ph.D., 1951; D.Applied Sci. (hon.), Katholieke U., Leuven, Belgium, 1979. Research asso. Stanford U., 1951-53; mem. tech. staff Bell Telephone Labs., Murray Hill, N.J., 1953-55; mem. faculty U. Calif., Berkeley, 1955—, now prof. elec. engring. and computer sci., dir. electronics research lab., 1960-64, prof. emeritus, 1985—, chmn. dept. elec. engring. and computer sci., 1983-85. Disting. Fulbright lectr. to Ireland, 1988; cons. in field. Contbr. numerous publs. in field. Served with U.S. Army, 1943-46. Guggenheim fellow. Fellow IEEE (Edn. medal 1969, chmn. San Francisco sect. 1971), Am. Acad. Arts. and Scis.; mem. NAS, NAE, Sigma Xi, Eta Kappa Nu. Office: U Calif Dept Elec Engring & Computer Berkeley CA 94720-0001

PEDERSON, JEROLD P. diversified utilities executive; BA in Acctg., Gonzaga U. Jr. auditor Mont. Power Co., Butte, 1965, various positions, 1965-82, contr., 1982-90, v.p. corp. fin., contr., 1990—. Office: Mont Power Co 40 E Broadway Butte MT 59701

PEDHIRNEY, GAYLAND, food products company executive; Pres., CEO, Wash. Beef Inc., Toppenish, 1996—. Bd. dirs. United Way Yakima County. Mem. Nat. Meat Assn. (bd. dirs.).

PEELER, STUART THORNE, petroleum industry executive and independent oil operator; b. Los Angeles, Oct. 28, 1929; s. Joseph David and Elizabeth Fiske (Boggess) P.; m. Sylvia Frances Townley, Nov. 5, 1985. BA, Stanford U., 1950, JD, 1953. Bar: Calif. 1953. Ptnr. Musick, Peeler & Garrett, L.A., 1958-73; with Santa Fe Internat. Corp., Orange, Calif., 1973-81, v.p., sec., assoc. gen. counsel, 1973-74, sr. v.p., gen. counsel, dir., 1975-81; vice-chmn. bd., chmn. exec. com. Supron Energy Corp., 1978-82; chmn. bd., CEO Statex Petroleum, Inc., 1982-89; chmn., pres., CEO Putumayo Prodn. Co., Tucson, 1989—. Bd. dirs. Chieftain Internat. Inc. Trustee J. Paul Getty Trust, 1963-99; mem. U.S. Tuna Team, 1957-67, capt., 1966. Served with U.S. Army, 1953-55. Decorated Army Commendation medal. Mem. AIME, State Bar Calif., Am. Judicature Soc., Theta Chi, Phi Delta Phi, Skyline Country Club. Republican. Congregationalist. Office: PO Box 35852 Tucson AZ 85740-5852 Fax: 520-544-0632

PEETS, TERRY R. retail executive; Chmn. bd. dirs. Bruno's Supermarkets, Inc., Birmingham, Ala., 1999—. Office: Brunos Supermarkets Inc 327 Coral Ave Newport Beach CA 92662

PEKELIS, ROSSELLE, judge; Former judge Wash. Superior Ct. King County; now chief judge divsn. I Wash. Ct. Appeals, Seattle; founding ptnr. Jud. Dispute Resolution, Seattle. Office: Jud Dispute Resolution 1411 4th Ave Ste 200 Seattle WA 98101-2244

PELLEGRINI, ROBERT J. psychology educator; b. Worcester, Mass., Oct. 21, 1941; s. Felix and Teresa (Di Muro) P.; 1 child, Robert Jerome. BA in Psychology, Clark U., 1963; MA in Psychology, U. Denver, 1966, PhD in Social Psychology, 1968. Prof. San Jose (Calif.) State U., 1967—. Rsch. assoc. U. Calif., Santa Cruz, 1989-90; pres. Western Inst. for Human Devel., San Jose, 1985 . Author: Psychology for Correctional Education, Bringing Psychology to Life; contbr. articles to profl. jours. Recipient Warburton award for scholarly excellence, 1995, Disting. Tchr. of Yr. award Western Psychol. Assn., 1996. Mem. Phi Beta Kappa. Office: San Jose State U Dept Psychology 1 Washington Sq San Jose CA 95192-0001

PELOSI, NANCY, congresswoman; b. Balt., Mar. 26, 1941; d. Thomas J. D'Alesandro Jr.; m. Paul Pelosi; children: Nancy Corinne, Christine, Jacqueline, Paul, Alexandra. Grad., Trinity Coll. Former chmn. Calif. State Dem. Com., 1981; committeewoman Dem. Nat. Com., 1976, 80, 84; fin. chmn. Dem. Senatorial Campaign Com., 1987; mem. U.S. Congress from 5th Calif. dist., 1987-93, U.S. Congress from 8th Calif. dist., 1993—; mem. appropriations com., intelligence com. Office: US House Reps 2457 Rayburn Bldg Washington DC 20515-0508*

PELOTTE, DONALD EDMOND, bishop; b. Waterville, Maine, Apr. 13, 1945; s. Norris Albert and Margaret Yvonne (LaBrie) P. AA, Eymard Sem. and Jr. Coll., Hyde Park, N.Y., 1965; BA, John Carroll U., 1969; MA, Fordham U., 1971, PhD, 1975. Ordained priest Roman Cath. Ch., 1972. Provincial superior Blessed Sacrament, Cleve., from 1978; ordained coadjutor bishop Diocese of Gallup, N.Mex., 1986-90, bishop, 1990—. Nat. bd. dirs. Maj. Superiors of Men, Silver Spring, Md., 1981-86, Tekakwitha Conf., Great Falls, Mont., 1981—. Author: John Courtney Murray: Theologian in Conflict, 1976. 1st native Am. bishop. Mem. Cath. Theol. Soc. Am., Am. Cath. Hist. Soc.

PELTASON, JACK WALTER, foundation executive, educator; b. St. Louis, Aug. 29, 1923; s. Walter B. and Emma (Hartman) P.; m. Suzanne Toll, Dec. 21,1946; children: Nancy Hartman, Timothy Walter H., Jill K. BA, U. Mo., 1943, MA, 1944, LLD (hon.), 1978; AM, Princeton U., 1946, PhD, 1947; LLD (hon.), U. Md., 1979, Ill. Coll., 1979, Gannon U., 1980, U. Maine, 1980, Union Coll., 1981, Moorehead (N.D.) State U., 1980; LHD (hon.), 1980, Ohio State U., 1980, Mont. Coll. Mineral Scis. and Tech., 1982, Buena Vista Coll., 1982, Assumption Coll., 1983, Chapman Coll., 1986, U. Ill., 1989. Asst. prof. Smith Coll., Mass., 1947-51; asst. prof. polit. sci. U. Ill., Urbana, 1951-52, assoc. prof., 1953-59, dean Coll. Liberal Arts and Scis., 1960-64, chancellor, 1967-77; vice chancellor acad. affairs U. Calif., Irvine, 1964-67, chancellor, 1984-92; pres. U. Calif. System, Oakland, 1992-95, Am. Coun. Edn., Washington, 1977-84; prof. emeritus dept. politics and soc. U. Calif., Irvine, 1995—; pres. Bren Found., 1997—. Cons. Mass. Little Hoover Commn., 1950 Author: The Missouri Plan for the Selection of Judges, 1947, Federal Courts and the Political Process, 1957, Fifty-eight Lonely Men, 1961, Understanding the Constitution, 15th edit., 2000, orig. edition, 1949, (with James M. Burns) Government By the People, 18th edit., 2000, orig. edit., 1952; contbr. articles and revs. to profl. jours. Recipient James Madison medal Princeton U., 1982 Fellow Am. Acad. Arts and Scis.; mem. Am. Polit. Sci. Assn. (council 1952-54), Phi Beta Kappa, Phi Kappa Phi, Omicron Delta Kappa, Alpha Phi Omega, Beta Gamma Sigma. Home: 18 Whistler Ct Irvine CA 92612-4069 Office: U Calif Dept Politics & Society Social Sci Plz Irvine CA 92697-0001 E-mail: jwpeltas@uci.edu

PELTON, HAROLD MARCEL, mortgage broker; b. Montreal, Que., Can., Jan. 24, 1922; s. Grover Cleveland and Denise (Pigeon) P.; m. Frances Farley, June 1947 (div. 1968); children: Mary Virginia Joyner, Diane Jean Slagowski; m. Virginia L. King, July 11, 1970. Student, L.A. City Coll., 1948-49, Anthony Schs., Van Nuys, Calif., 1966. Lic. real estate real broker, Calif. Stockbroker, agt. Mitchum, Jones, Templeton Assurance Co., L.A., 1957-60; owner Assurance Investment Co., Van Nuys, Calif., 1960-65; sales syndicator TSI Investment Co., L.A., 1965-69; pres., owner Univest Co., Beverly Hills, Calif., 1970-72, Am. Oil Recovery, L.A., 1973-79; v.p. Newport Pacific Funding Co., Newport Beach, Calif., 1979-81; chmn. bd. dirs. TD Publs., El Toro, 1981-83; pres., broker HP Fin., Inc., Laguna Hills, 1983--. Contbg. editor Am. Oil Recovery newspaper, 1973-79; editor Trust Deed Jour., 1981-83. Served with U.S. Army, 1942-46, PTO. Mem. L. A. Mus. Art, Laguna Hills C. of C., Kiwanis, Toastmasters. Republican. Avocations: photography, travel, reading, computers. Office: HP Fin Inc 24942 Georgia Sue Laguna Hills CA 92653-4323

PEÑA, FEDERICO FABIAN, retired federal official; b. Laredo, Tex., Mar. 15, 1947; s. Gustavo J. and Lucille P.; m. Ellen Hart, May 1988. BA, U. Tex., Austin, 1969, JD, 1972. Bar: Colo. 1973. Ptnr. Pena & Pena, Denver, 1973-83; mayor City and County of Denver, 1983-91; pres. Peña Investment Advisors, Inc., Denver, 1991-93; sec. U.S. Dept. of Energy, Washington, 1993-98, U.S. Dept. Transp., Washington, 1993-97, U.S. Dept. Energy, Washington, 1997-98; sr. advisor Vestar Capital Ptnrs., Denver, 1998-00; mng. dir. Vestar Capital Partners, Denver, 2000—. Assoc. Harvard U. Ctr. for Law and Edn., Cambridge, Mass.; mem. Colo. Bd. Law Examiners. Mem. Colo. Ho. of Reps., 1979-83, Dem. leader, 1981. Named Outstanding House Dem. Legislator, Colo. Gen. Assembly, 1981. Roman Catholic.

PEÑA, JUAN JOSÉ, interpreter; b. Hagerman, N.Mex., Dec. 13, 1945; s. Rosa Peña; m. Petra Cervantes, Dec. 22, 1974 (div. 1982); children: Federico Ezequiel, Margarita María Blea. BA, N.Mex. Highlands U., 1968, MA, 1972, postgrad. With Albert Garcia Gen. Contr., Las Vegas, N.Mex., 1955-67; teaching asst. N.Mex. Highlands U., Las Vegas, 1971-72, prof. Spanish, Chicano studies, 1972-78; teaching asst. U. N.Mex., Albuquerque, 1978-79; attendant N.Mex. State Mental Hosp., Las Vegas, 1982-83; staff and supervisory interpreter U.S. Dist. Ct. N.Mex., Albquerque, 1983—. Head Raza Unida del to PLO in Lebanon, 1981, head negotiator with Iranians for release of 2 Chicanos and 1 Indian; supr ct. interpreters and reporters sect. U.S. Dist. Ct. N.Mex.; co-chmn. Cuatro-Centennial Com., Inc.; mem. exec. com. N.Mex. Human Rights Coalition. Author collection of poetry: Angustias y Remembranzas; contbr. articles to profl. jours.; author play: Canto a La Raza, 1978. Pres. Dads Against Discrimination, Albuquerque, 1993—; chmn. bd. trustees No. N.Mex. Legal Svcs., Las Vegas, 1972-81; mem. exec. com. Ind. Socialist Parties of Latin Am.; exec. commn. N.Mex. Human Rights Coalition; vice chmn. Barelas Cmty. Devel. Corp.; Barelas rep. Hist. Neighborhoods Alliance; mem. cmty. coun. on equity Albuquerque Pub. Schs.; mem. N.Mex. Cmty. Loan Fund; bd. dirs. Albuquerque Downtown Action Team, N.Mex. Land Grant Forum; mem. textbook rev. commn. N.Mex. Dept. Edn., mem. bilingual edn. adv. com.; commr. N.Mex. Textbook Selection Commn., 2001—; nat. sec. Am. GI Forum of U.S., 2000-01. Decorated Bronze Star; recipient Human Rights award City of Albuquerque Human Rights Bd., N.Mex. State Coun. Profile of Courage award Vietnam Vets. Am., 1995, N.Mex. Nat. Guard Cinco de Mayo award, 1995, Hispanics for U N.Mex. Achievement award, 1999, Human Rights award Albuquerque Human Rights Bd., 2000. Bd. dirs. Albuquerque Downtown Action Team; mem. N.Mex. Translator and Interpreters Assn. (pres. 1984-86), Nat. Assn. Judiciary Interpreters (sec. 1986-88), Nat. Partido Raza Unida (pres. 1976-81), N.Mex. Partido Raza Unida (pres. 1972-75, 77-78), Vietnam Vets. Am. (vice chmn. chpt. 1993—), Vietnam Vets. N.Mex., Am. GI Forum (Albuquerque chpt. 1 comdr. 1993—, vice comdr. 1997-98, sec.), N.Mex. GI Forum (comdr. 1996), Nat. Assn. Chicano Studies (founding mem.), N.Mex. Chicano Studies Assn. (pres. 1972-78), Hispanic Round Table of N.Mex. (chmn. 1995, 98), Barelas Neighborhood Assn. (pres.), Historic Neighborhoods Assn., Barelas Cmty. Devel. Corp. (rep.), Phi Sigma Iota. Democrat. Roman Catholic. Avocations: weight lifting, swimming, ice skating, hiking, camping. office), (home). Home: 1115 9th St SW Albuquerque NM 87102-4027 Office: US Dist Ct Dist NMex 333 Lomas Blvd NW Albuquerque NM 87102-2272 Fax: 505-242-1603. . E-mail: jpena@nmcourtfed.us, jjpena@uswest.net

PENCE, MARTIN, retired federal judge; b. Sterling, Kans., Nov. 18, 1904; m. Eleanor Fisher, Apr. 12, 1975. Bar: Calif. 1928, Hawaii 1933. Practice law, Hilo, Hawaii, 1936-45, 50-61; judge 3d Circuit Ct., 1945-50; chief judge U.S. Dist. Ct., 1961-74, sr. judge, 1974—. Office: US Dist Ct 300 Alamonana Blvd Rm C423 Honolulu HI 96850-0423

PENDERECKI, KRZYSZTOF, composer, conductor; b. Debica, Poland, Nov. 23, 1933; s. Tadeusz and Zofia P.; m. Elzbieta Solecka; children: Lukasz, Dominique. Grad., State Acad. Music, Krakow, 1958; student, Arthur Malawski and Stanislaw Wiechowicz; Dr. honoris causa, U. Rochester, St. Olaf Coll., Northfield, Minn., Cath U., Leuven, Belgium, U. Bordeaux, France, Georgetown U., Belgrade U., Madrid U., Spain, Adam Mickiewicz U., Warsaw U., Poland, 1993, U. Catolica Argentina, Buenos Aires, 1994, Acad. Music, Cracow, 1994, Acad. Music, Warsaw, 1994, U. Glasgow, , 1995, Beijiung Conservatory, 1998, U. Pitts., 1999. Prof. composition Krakow State Sch. Music, 1959-65, Folkwang Hochschule für Musik, Essen, Fed. Republic Germany, 1966-68; composer-in-residence Sch. Music, Yale U., alternate years; guest condr. London Symphony Orch., Polish Radio Orch., Berlin Philharm. Orch. Composer: Psalms of David for chorus and percussion, 1958, Emanations for 2 string orchs., 1959, Strophes for soprano, narrator and 10 instruments, 1959, Dimensions of time and silence, 1959-61, Anaklasis, 1959-60, Threnody for the Victims of Hiroshima, 1960, Psalmus for tape, 1961, Polymorphia, 1961; Fluorescences, 1961, Stabat Mater, 1962, Canon, 1962, Sonata for cello and orch., 1964, St. Luke Passion, 1965, De Natura Sonoris I, 1966, Dies Irae, 1967, Capriccio for violin and orch., 1967, Capriccio for cello Solo, 1968; opera The Devils of Loudun, 1968-69; Utrenja for double chorus, soloists and orch., 1969-71, Cosmogony, 1970, Utrenja II-Resurrection, 1971, Actions for jazz ensemble, 1971, Partita for harpsichord, 4 solo instruments and orch., 1971-72, Cello Concerto, 1967-72; for double chorus, soloists and orchestra Ecloga VIII for 6 male voices, 1972; Symphony 1, 1972-73, Canticum Canticorum Salomonis for 16 voices and chamber orch., 1970-73, Magnificat, 1973-74, When Jacob Awoke for orch., 1974, Violin Concerto, 1976-77, Paradise Lost (rappresentazione), 1976-78, (Christmas) Symphony No. 2, 1980, Te Deum, 1979-80, Lacrimosa, 1980, Agnus Dei for a cappella chorus, 1981, Cello Concerto No. 2, 1982, Requiem, 1983, Concerto per Viola, 1983, Polish Requiem, 1983-84, The Black Mask, 1986, Der Unterbrochene Gedanke, 1987, Adagio, 1989, Ubu Rex, 1991, Sinfonietta for orchestra, 1990-91, Symphony No. 5 for orchestra, 1991-92, Partita for orchestra, rev. edit., 1991, Flute concerto, 1992-93, Quartet for Clarinet and String Trio, 1993, Divertimento per Cello solo, 1994, Violin Concerto No. 2, 1992-95, Agnus Dei, 1995, Symphony No. 3, Seven Gates of Jerusalem, 1997, Hymn to St. Daniel, 1997, Hymn to St. Adalbert, 1997, Credo, 1998, Sonata No. 2 for violin and piano, 2000, Sextet for violin, viola, piano, clarinet, and french horn, 2000, also other works; prin. guest condr. NDR Symphony Orch., Hamburg, and MDR Symphony Orch., Leipzig; artistic dir. Casals Festival, PR. Recipient 1st prize for Strophes Polish Composers Assn., 1959, UNESCO award, Fitelberg prize and Polish Ministry Culture award all for Threnody, 1960, Krakow composition prize for Canon, 1961, grand prize State N. Rhine-Westphalia for St. Luke Passion, 1966, Pax prize Poland, 1966, Jurzykowski prize Polish Inst. Arts and Scis., 1966, Sibelius award, 1967, Prix d'Italia, 1967-68, Polish 1st Class State award, 1968, Gottfried von Herder prize, 1977, prix Arthur Honegger, 1978, Sibelius prize Wihouri Found., 1983, Wolf Found. prize, 1987, 3 Grammy awards, Gamma prize Acad. Rec. Arts and Scis., 1988, Manuel de Falla Gold medal Accademia de Bellas Artes, Granada, 1989, Das Grosse Verdienstkreuz des Verdienstordens der Bundesrepublik Deutschland, 1990, 2 Grammy nominations, 1992, Grawermeyer Music award, 1992, Österreichische Ehrenzeichen für Wissenschaft und Kunst, 1994, 2 Primetime Emmy awards, 1995, 96, Crystall award, Davos, 1997, 2 Grammy awards, 1999, Musikpreis Duisburg, 1999, Cannes Classical award Composer of Yr., 2000, Principe de Asturias, 2001; grantee several founds., govts., insts. Mem. AAAL (hon.), Royal Acad. Mus. London (hon.), Nat. Acad. of Santa Cecilia (Rome) (hon.), Royal Swedish Acad. Music, Acad. of Kuenste West Berlin (extraord. mem.), Nat. Acad. of Bellas Artes (Buenos Aires) (corr.), Internat. Acad. Philosophy and Art (Berne), Nat. Acad. Scis., Belles-lettres et Arts (Bordeaux), Acad. Scientiarium et Artium Europaea (Salzburg), L'Ordre de Saint Georges de Bourgogne (officer, Brussels), Am. Acad. Arts and Letters, Bay. Acad. des Schönen Künste. Achievements include creating original notational system allowing aleatory freedom for performer within sects. of precise duration. Home: ul Cisowa 22 30229 Cracow Poland Office: ICM Artists Ltd c/o Jenny Vogel 8942 Wilshire Blvd Beverly Hills CA 90211-1934 also: Panstwowa Wyzsza Szkola Muzyczna ul Starowislna 31 038 Cracow Poland also: Am Daubhaus 6 D 55276 Oppenheim Germany Fax: 49-6133/92 63 56

PENDERGHAST, THOMAS FREDERICK, business educator; b. Cin., Apr. 23, 1936; s. Elmer T. and Dolores C. (Huber) P.; m. Marjorie Craig, Aug. 12, 1983; children: Brian, Shawna, Steven, Dean, Maria. BS, Marquette U., 1958; MBA, Calif. State U., Long Beach, 1967; D in Bus. Adminstrn., Nova U., 1987. Cert. in data processing. Sci. programmer Autonetics, Inc., Anaheim, Calif., 1960-64; bus. programmer Douglas Missile & Space Ctr., Huntington Beach, 1964-66; computer specialist N.Am. Rockwell Co., Huntington Beach, 1966-69; asst. prof. Calif. State U., Huntington Beach, 1969-72; prof. Sch. Bus. and Mgmt. Pepperdine U., L.A., 1972—; spl. adviser Commn. on Engring. Edn., 1968; v.p. Visual Computing Co., 1969-71; founder, pres. Scoreboard Animation Systems, 1971-77; exec. v.p. Microfilm Identification Systems, 1977-79; pres. Data Processing Auditors, Inc., 1981—. Data processing cons. designing computer system for fin. health and mfg. orgns., 1972—; mem. Orange County Blue Ribbon Com. on Data Processing, 1973; mem. Orange County TEC Policy Bd., 1982-87; mgmt. and organization devel. cons. Assn. Psychological Type, 1993—. Author: Entrepreneurial Simulation Program, 1988, Journey to Couples' Conflict Resolution Using Game Theory, 1999. Served to lt. USNR, 1958-60. Mem. Users of Automatic Info. Display Equipment (pres. 1966). Home: 17867 Bay St Fountain Valley CA 92708-4443 E-mail: tpenderg@pepperdine.edu

PENDLETON, OTHNIEL ALSOP, fundraiser, clergyman; b. Washington, Aug. 22, 1911; s. Othniel Alsop and Ingeborg (Berg) P.; m. Flordora Mellquist, May 15, 1935; children: John, James (dec.), Thomas, Ann, Susan. AB, Union Coll., Schenectady, N.Y., 1933; BD, Eastern Bapt. Theol. Sem., 1936; MA, U. Pa., 1936, PhD, 1945; postgrad., Columbia U., 1937-38. Ordained to ministry Bapt. Ch., 1936. Pastor chs., Jersey City, 1935-39, Phila., 1939-43; dean Sioux Falls Coll., S.D., 1943-45; fund raiser Am. Bapt. Ch., N.Y.C., 1945-47; fund-raiser Mass. Bapt. Ch., Boston, 1947-54, Seattle, Chgo., Boston, Washington, N.Y.C. and Paris, France, 1955-64, Westwood, Mass., 1971-84; staff mem. Marts & Lundy, Inc., N.Y.C., 1964-71. Lectr. Andover-Newton (Mass.) Sem., 1958, Boston U. Sch. Theology, 1958, Harvard U., Cambridge, Mass., 1977-84; cons. Grant MacEwan Coll., Edmonton, Alta., Can. Author: New Techniques for Church Fund Raising, 1955, Fund Raising: A Guide to Non-Profit Organizations, 1981; contbr. articles in field to profl. jours. Address: 627 Leyden Ln Claremont CA 91711-4236

PENDLETON, YVONNE, astrophysicist; m. Dale Cruikshank; two children. Astrophysicist Ames Rsch. Ctr., Moffett Field, Calif. Avocations: reading, scuba diving, tennis, piano playing. Office: Ames Rsch Ctr Moffett Field CA 94035

PENHOET, EDWARD, biochemicals company executive; b. Oakland, Calif., Dec. 11, 1940; AB, Stanford U., 1963; PhD, U. Wash., 1968. Dean Sch. Pub. Health U. Calif., Berkeley, 1998—. Bd. dirs., sr. adv. to CEO Chiron Corp. Office: Chiron Corp 4560 Horton St Emeryville CA 94608-2900

PENIKETT, ANTONY DAVID JOHN, Canadian government official; b. Nov. 14, 1945; s. Erik John Keith and Sarah Ann (Colwell) P.; m. Lula Mary Johns, 1974; children— John Tahmoh, Sarah Lahlil, Stephanie Yahsan Exec. asst. to nat. leader New Dem. Party, Ottawa, Ont., Canada, 1975-76, nat. pres. Canada, 1981-85, fed. councillor Canada, 1973—, leader Whitehorse, Y.T., Canada, 1980—, campaign mgr. N.W.T., Canada, 1972; city councillor City of Whitehorse, Y.T., Canada, 1977-79; elected mem. Yukon Legis. Assembly, 1978-95, opposition leader Y.T., Canada, 1982-85, 92-95, elected govt. leader Yukon Terr., 1985-92; sr. policy advisor, exec. coun. Govt. of Saskatchewan, 1995-97; dep. min. negotiations Ministry of Fin. and Corp. Rels., Govt. of B.C., Victoria, 1997-2000, dep. min. labor, 2000—. Author (film): The Mad Trapper, 1972; La Patrouille Perdue, 1974. Mem. Christian Socialist Ch. Office: Govt BC Min Fin Corp Rel PO Box 9409 Stn Prov Govt Victoria BC Canada V8W 9V1

PENNER, STANFORD SOLOMON, engineering educator; b. Unna, Germany, July 5, 1921; came to U.S., 1936, naturalized, 1943; s. Heinrich and Regina (Saal) P.; m. Beverly Preston, Dec. 28, 1942; children: Merilynn Jean, Robert Clark. BS, Union Coll., 1942; MS, U. Wis., 1943, PhD, 1946; Dr. rer. nat. (hon.), Technische Hochschule Aachen, Germany, 1981. Research asso. Allegany Ballistics Lab., Cumberland, Md., 1944-45; research scientist Standard Oil Devel. Co., Esso Labs., Linden, N.J., 1946; sr. research engr. Jet Propulsion Lab., Pasadena, Calif., 1947-50; mem. faculty Calif. Inst. Tech., 1950-63, prof. div. engring., jet propulsion, 1957-63; dir. research engring. div. Inst. Def. Analyses, Washington, 1962-64; prof. engring. physics, chmn. dept. aerospace and mech. engring. U. Calif. at San Diego, 1964-68, vice chancellor for acad. affairs, 1968-69, dir. Inst. for Pure and Applied Phys. Scis., 1968-71, dir. Energy Ctr., 1973-91. Bd. dirs. Optodyne Corp.; U.S. mem. adv. group aero. rsch. and devel. NATO, 1952-68, chmn. combustion and propulsion panel, 1958-60; mem. adv. com. engring. scis. USAF-Office Sci. Rsch., 1961-65; mem. subcom. on combustion NACA, 1954-58; mem. rsch. adv. com. on air-breathing engines NASA, 1962-64; mem. coms. on gas dynamics and edn. Internat. Acad. Astronautics, 1969-80; nat. lectr. Sigma Xi, 1977-79; chmn. fossil energy rsch. working group Dept. Energy, 1978-82, chmn. advanced fuel cell commercialization working group, 1993-95; mem. assembly engring. NAE, 1978-82; chmn. NAS-NRC U.S. Nat. Com. IIASA, 1978-82; mem. commn. engring. tech. sys. NRC, 1982-84; spl. guest Internat. Coal Sci. Confs., 1983, 85, 87, 89, 91; mentor Def. Sci. Studies Group, 1985-93; chmn. studies mcpl. waste incineration NSF, 1988-89, Calif. Coun. Sci. Tech., 1992; pub. info. adv. com. Nat. Acad. Engring., 1994-98, Independent Commn. on Environ. Edn., 1995-97, Environ. Literacy Coun., 1998—; sci. adv. bd., San Diego County, 1997—; divsn. advisor, bds. of the divsn. on engring. and phys. scis. The Nat. Acads., 2001—. Author: Chemical Reactions in Flow Systems, 1955, Chemistry Problems in Jet Propulsion, 1957, Quantitative Molecular Spectroscopy and Gas Emissivities, 1959, Chemical Rocket Propulsion and Combustion Research, 1962, Thermodynamics, 1968, Radiation and Reentry, 1968; sr. author: Energy, Vol. I (Demands, Resources, Impact, Technology and Policy), 1974, 81, Energy, Vol. II (Non-nuclear Energy Technologies), 1975, 77, 84, Energy, Vol. III (Nuclear Energy and Energy Policies), 1976; editor: Chemistry of Propellants, 1960, Advanced Propulsion Techniques, 1961, Detonations and Two-Phase Flow, 1962, Combustion and Propulsion, 1963, Advances in Tactical Rocket Propulsion, 1968, In Situ Shale Oil Recovery, 1975, New Sources of Oil and Gas, 1982, Coal Combustion and Applications, 1984, Advanced Fuel Cells, 1986, Coal Gasification: Direct Applications and Syntheses of Chemicals and Fuels, 1987, CO2 Emissions and Climate Change, 1991, Commercialization of Fuel Cells, 1995, Advanced Nuclear Techs., 1998; assoc. editor Jour. Chem. Physics, 1953-56; founding editor Jour. Quantitative Spectroscopy and Radiative Transfer, 1960-92, Jour. Def. Rsch., 1963-67, Energy-The Internat. Jour., 1975-98; sect. editor Energy and Power Systems, Ency.

Phys. Sci. and Tech., 1998—. Recipient spl. award People-to-People Program, pub. svc. award U. Calif., Sn Diego, N. Manson medal Internat. Colloquia on Gasdynamics of Explosions and Reactive Systems, 1979, internat. Columbus award Internat. Inst. Comm., Genoa, Italy, 1981, disting. assoc. award U.S. Dept. Energy, 1990, Edward Teller award for def. of freedom, 1997. Fellow Am. Phys. Soc., Optical Soc. Am., AAAS, N.Y. Acad. Scis., AIAA (dir. 1964-66, past chmn. com., G. Edward Pendray award 1975, Thermophysics award 1983, Energy Systems award 1983), Am. Acad. Arts and Scis.; mem. Nat. Acad. Engring., Internat. Acad. Astronautics, Am. Chem. Soc., Sigma Xi. Home: 5912 Avenida Chamnez La Jolla CA 92037-7402 Office: U Calif San Diego 9500 Gilman Dr La Jolla CA 92093-0411

PENNIMAN, RICHARD WAYNE See LITTLE RICHARD

PENSKAR, MARK HOWARD, lawyer; b. Detroit, Mar. 4, 1953; s. Sol Leonard and Frances (Rosenthal) P.; m. Carol Ann Stewart, Aug. 7, 1977; children: David, Rebecca. BA, U. Mich., 1974, M in Pub. Policy, 1975, JD cum laude, 1977. Bar: Calif. 1977, U.S. Dist. Ct. (no. dist.) Calif. 1977, (ea. and cen. dists.) Calif. 1983, (so. dist.) 1988, U.S. Ct. Appeals (9th cir.) 1987, U.S. Tax Ct. 1993. Assoc. Pillsbury, Madison and Sutro, San Francisco, 1977-84, ptnr., 1985-96; sr. bus. litigation atty. Pacific Gas and Electric Co., San Francisco, 1996—, acting sect. head comml. litigation I, 2001—. Mediator Superior Court early settlement program, San Francisco. Mem. bd. dirs. Orindawoods Assn. Mem. ABA, San Francisco Bar Assn., Commonwealth Club, Phi Gamma Delta (past pres. Bay Area grad. chpt.). Avocations: camping, golf, wine collecting. Home: 29 E Altarinda Dr Orinda CA 94563-2415 Office: Pacific Gas & Electric Co Law Dept B30A PO Box 7442 San Francisco CA 94120-7442 E-mail: MHPS@pge.com

PENZIAS, ARNO ALLAN, astrophysicist, technology consultant, research scientist, information systems specialist; b. Munich, Germany, Apr. 26, 1933; came to U.S., 1940, naturalized, 1946; s. Karl and Justine (Eisenreich) P.; m. Sherry Chamove Levit, Aug. 2, 1996; children: David Simon, Mindy Gail, Laurie Shifra. BS in Physics, CCNY, 1954; MA in Physics, Columbia U., 1958, PhD in Physics, 1962; Dr. honoris causa, Observatoire de Paris, 1976; ScD (hon.), Rutgers U., 1979, Wilkes Coll., 1979, CCNY, 1979, Yeshiva U., 1979, Bar Ilan U., 1983, Monmouth Coll., 1984, Technion-Israel Inst. Tech., 1986, U. Pitts., 1986, Ball State U., 1986, Kean Coll., 1986, U. Pa., 1992, Ohio State U., 1988, Iona Coll., 1988, Drew U., 1989, Lafayette Coll., 1990, Columbia U., 1990, George Washington U., 1992, Rensselaer Univ., 1992, U. Pa., 1992, Bloomfield Coll., 1994, Rankin Tech. U., 1997, Hebrew Union Coll., 1997. Mem. tech. staff Bell Labs., Holmdel, N.J., 1961-72, head radiophysics rsch. dept., 1972-76, dir. radio research lab., 1976-79, exec. dir. rsch., communications scis. div., 1979-81, v.p. rsch., 1981-95; v.p., chief scientist Lucent Technologies, 1995-98, sen. tech. adv., 1998—; venture ptnr. New Enterprise Assocs., 1998—. Bd. dirs. A.D. Little, LCC Internat., Alien Tech. Corp.; sr. advisor New Enterprise Assoc., 1997-98, adj. prof. earth and scis. SUNY, Stony Brook, 1974-84, Univ. Disting. lectr., 1990; lectr. dept. astrophys. scis. Princeton U., 1967-72, vis. prof., 1972-85; rsch. assoc. Harvard Coll. Obs., 1968-80; Edison lectr. U.S. Naval Rsch. Lab., 1979; Kompfner lectr. Stanford U., 1979; Gamow lectr. U. Colo., 1980; Jansky lectr. Nat. Radio Astronomy Obs., 1983; Michelson Meml. lectr., 1985; Grace Adams Tanner lectr., 1987; Klopsteg lectr. Northwestern U., 1987; grad. faculties alumni Columbia U., 1987-89; Regents' lectr. U. Calif., Berkeley, 1990; Lee Kuan Yew Disting. vis. Nat. U. Singapore, 1991; mem. astronomy adv. panel NSF, 1978-79, mem. indsl. panel on sci. and tech., 1982-92, disting. lectr., 1987, affiliate Max-Planck Inst. for Radioastronomy, 1978-85, chmn. Fachbeirat, 1981-83; rschr. in astrophysics, info. tech., its applications and impacts. Author: Ideas and Information Managing in a High-Tech World, 1989 (pub. in 10 langs.), Harmony-Business, Technology and Life After Paperwork, 1995; mem. editl. bd. Ann. Rev. Astronomy and Astrophysics, 1974-78; mem. editl. bd. AT&T Bell Labs. Tech. Jour., 1978-84, chmn., 1981-84; assoc. editor Astrophys. Jour., 1978-82; contbr. over 100 articles to tech. jours.; several patents in field. Trustee Trenton (N.J.) State Coll., 1977-79; mem. bd. overseers U. Pa. Sch. Engring. and Applied Sci., 1983-86; mem. vis. com. Calif. Inst. Tech., 1977-79; mem. Com. Concerned Scientists, 1975—, vice chmn., 1976—; mem. adv. bd. Union of Couns. for Soviet Jews, 1983—; bd. dirs. Coun. on Competitiveness, 1989-92. With U.S. Army, 1954-56. Named to N.J Lit, Hall of Fame, 1991; recipient Herschel medal Royal Astron. Soc, 1977, Nobel prize in Physics, 1978, Townsend Harris medal CCNY, 1979, Newman award, 1983, Joseph Handleman prize in the scis., 1983, Grad. Faculties Alumni award Columbia U., 1984, Achievement in Science award Big Brothers Inc., N.Y.C., 1985, Priestly award Dickinson Coll., 1989, Pender award U. Pa., 1992, NJ Sci. and Tech. Medal, 1996, Internat. Eng. Cons. Fell. Award, 1997, Industrial Res. Inst. Medalist, 1998, patents for: auction-based selection of telecom. carriers, participant tracking in conference call, remote card game using ordinary playing cards, computer-based transportation system, fraud prevention in calling cards, identifying telephone extensions in residence environment, double-encrypted identity verification sys. Mem. NAE, NAS (Henry Draper medal 1977), AAAS, IEEE (hon.), Am. Astron. Soc., Am. Phys. Soc. (Pake prize 1990), Internat. Astron. Union, World Acad. Arts and Sci. Office: New Enterprises Assocs 2490 Sand Hill Rd Menlo Park CA 94025-6940

PENZIEN, JOSEPH, structural engineering educator; b. Philip, S.D., Nov. 27, 1924; s. John Chris and Ella (Stebbins) P.; m. Jeanne Ellen Hunson, Apr. 29, 1950 (dec. 1985); children: Robert Joseph, Karen Estelle, Donna Marie, Charlene May; m. Mi-jung Park, June 16, 1988. Student, Coll. Idaho, 1942-43; B.S., U. Wash., 1945; Sc.D., Mass. Inst. Tech., 1950. Mem. staff Sandia Corp., 1950-51; sr. structures engr. Consol. Vultee Aircraft Corp., Fort Worth, 1951-53; asst. prof. U. Calif. at Berkeley, 1953-57, asso. prof., 1957-62, prof. structual engring., 1962-88, prof. emeritus, 1988—; dir. Earthquake Engring. Research Center, 1968-73, 77-80. Cons. engring. firms; chief tech. adv. Internat. Inst. of Seismology and Earthquake Engring., Tokyo, Japan, 1964-65; chmn. bd. Ea. Internat. Engrs., Inc., 1980-90, Internat. Civil Engring. Cons., Inc., 1990—. NATO Sr. Sci. fellow., 1969 Fellow Am. Acad. Mechanics; hon. mem. ASCE (Walter Huber Rsch. award, Alfred M. Freudenthal medal, Nathan M. Newmark medal, Ernest E. Howard award), Earthquake Engring. Rsch. Inst. (hon., Hausner medal), IAEE (hon.), EERI (Alfred E. Alquist award, Dist. Lectr. 2000); mem. Am. Concrete Inst., Structural Engrs. Assn. Calif., Seismol. Soc. Am., Nat. Acad. Engring. Home: 800 Solana Dr Lafayette CA 94549-5004 Office: Int Civil Engr Cons Inc 1995 University Ave Berkeley CA 94704

PEOPLES, DONALD R. research scientist; b. 1939; Athletic dir. Butte (Mont.) Ctrl. High Sch., 1967-69; dir. info. and evaluation Butte Model Cities Program, 1969-70; dir. pub. works, model cities and cmty. devel. Butte, 1970-77; dir. pub. works dept. Butte-Silver Bow City-County Govt., 1977-79, CEO, 1979-89; with Mont. Tech. Cos., Butte, 1989—, now pres., CEO. Office: Montana Tech Companies 220 N Alaska St Butte MT 59701-9212

PEPE, STEPHEN PHILLIP, lawyer; b. Paterson, N.J., Oct. 30, 1943; s. Vincent Attilio and Emma (Opletal) P.; m. Catherine B. Hagen, Dec. 8, 1990. BA, Montclair (N.J.) State U., 1965; JD, Duke U., 1968. Bar: Calif. 1969, J.S. Dist. Ct. (no., so., ea. and cen. dists.) Calif. 1975, U.S. Ct. Appeals (9th cir.) 1975, U.S. Sup. Ct. 1978. Assoc. O'Melveny & Myers, L.A., 1968-75, ptnr., 1976—, chmn. lab. and employment law dept., 1989-92. Co-author: Avoiding and Defending Wrongful Discharge Claims, 1987, Privacy in the Work Place, 1993, Corporate Compliance Series: Designing an Effective Fair Hiring and Termination Compliance Program, 1993, The Law of Libel & Slander, 1994; co-editor: Guide to Acquiring and Managing a U.S. Business, 1992, Calif. Employment Law Letter, 1990-94. Bd. visitors Duke Law Sch., 1992-96; bd. trustees Montclair State U. Found., 1991; bd. govs. Coll. of Labor and Employment Law, 1996—, treas., 1999—; pres. Inst. Indsl. Rels. Assn., 1989-91. With USAR, 1969-75. Fellow Coll. of Labor and Employment Law, 1996—. Mem. Am. Hosp. Assn. (labor adv. com. 1975-90), The Employers Group (bd. dirs., chmn. legal com. 1989-93), Calif. Club (chmn. employee rels. com. 1980—). Democrat. Roman Catholic. Avocations: wine collecting, wine making, wine judging, vineyard owner. Office: O Melveny & Myers 610 Newport Center Dr Newport Beach CA 92660-6419

PEPPER, DAVID M. physicist, educator, writer, inventor; b. L.A., Mar. 9, 1949; s. Harold and Edith (Kleinplatz) P.; m. Denise Danyelle Koster, Mar. 19, 1992. BS in Physics summa cum laude, UCLA, 1971; MS in Applied Physics, Calif. Inst. Tech., 1974, PhD in Applied Physics, 1980. Mem. tech. staff Hughes Rsch. Labs., Malibu, Calif., 1973-87, sr. staff physicist, 1987-91, head nonlinear and electro-optic devices sect., 1989-91, sr. scientist, 1991-94; sr. rsch. scientist HRL Labs. (formerly Hughes Rsch. Labs.), Malibu, 1994—. Adj. prof. math. and physics Pepperdine U., Malibu, 1981—; mem. adv. panel NSF, Washington, 1997, mem. U. Va. panel on advanced signal processing, 1999; mem. DARPA Def. Scis. Rsch. Coun., U.S. Govt., Washington, 1999; presenter in field. Co-author: Optical Phase Conjugation, 1983, Laser Handbook, Vol. 4, 1985, Optical Phase Conjugation, 1995, Spatial Light Modulator Technology, 1995, CRC Handbook of Laser Science and Technology, 1995; tech. referee profl. jours.; contbr. articles to tech. jours. including Sci. Am.; holder 24 patents. Mem. Sons and Daughters of 1939 Club, 2d Generation of Martyrs Meml., Mus. Holocaust. Recipient Rudolf Kingslake award Soc. Photo-Optical Instrumentation Engrs., 1982, Publ. of Yr. award Hughes Rsch. Lab., 1986, Patent award of excellence HRL Labs., 1997, 98, 99; NSF trainee Calif. Inst. Tech., 1971; Howard Hughes fellow Hughes Aircraft Co., 1973-80. Fellow Optical Soc. Am. (conf. session chair 1996, 97, 98, 99, 2000, 2001, mem. adv. bd. topical conf. on nonlinear optics, Hawaii 1996, 98, 2000, invited tutorial annual meeting laser ultrasound 2001); mem. AAAS, IEEE (guest editor, assoc. editor, mem. program com. lasers and electro-optics 1997—, instr. laser tech. 1994-2000, invited tutorial laser tech 2001), SPIE (guest editor, conf. co-chmn. 1998, 99, 2000), N.Y. Acad. Scis., Am. Phys. Soc., Laser Inst. Am., Internat. Coun. Sci. Unions (com. on sci. and tech. in developing countries), Sigma Xi (v.p. 1986-87, chpt. pres. 1987-88, 90-91, 91-92), Sigma Pi Sigma. Jewish. Avocations: classical music, travel, sports, astronomy, nature. Office: HRL Labs 3011 Malibu Canyon Rd Malibu CA 90265-4797 E-mail: dmpepper@hrl.com

PERATA, DON, state legislator; Tchr. Alameda County Pub. Schs., 1966-81; supr. Alameda County, 1986-94; mem. Calif. State Assembly, 1997-98, chmn. rules com., 1997, chmn. pub. safety com., 1998, majority leader, 1998; mem. Calif. State Senate, 1998—. Democrat. Office: State Capitol Rm 4061 Sacramento CA 95814 also: 1515 Clay St # 2002 Oakland CA 94612-1499

PERDUE, KAREN, state agency administrator; BA in Biology, Stanford U., 1978. Reporter, photographer Fairbanks (Alaska) Daily News-Miner, 1969-74; editor River Times, Fairbanks, 1974-75; foreman, expeditor Teamsters Union, Alaska Pipeline, 1975-76; health planner Tanana Chiefs Conf., Fairfanks, 1977; instr., counselor Stanford (Calif) Med. Ctr., 1978; rsch. dir. Fairbanks Town and Village Assn., 1978-79; legis. aide/press sec. U.S. Senator Ted Stevens, Washington, 1979-80; spl. asst. to lt. gov. Terry Miller State of Alaska, 1980-82; dir. Divsn. of Cmty. Devel., Dept. of Cmty. and Regional Affairs, Juneau, 1982-85; dep. commr. Dept. of Health and Social Svcs., Juneau, 1985-90; cons., ptrn. Northern Rsch. and Planning, 1991—; commr. Alaska Dept. of Health and Social Svcs., 1995—. Office: Health & Social Svcs Dept Office Commr PO Box 110601 Juneau AK 99811-0601 E-mail: karen_perdue@health.state.ak.us

PERENCHIO, ANDREW JERROLD, film and television executive; b. Fresno, Calif., Dec. 20, 1930; s. Andrew Joseph and Dorothea (Harvey) P.; m. Robin Green, July 16, 1954 (div.); children: Candace L., Catherine M., John Gardner; m. Jacquelyn Claire, Nov. 14, 1969. BS, UCLA, 1954. V.p. Music Corp. Am., 1958-62, Gen. Artists Corp., 1962-64; pres., owner theatrical agy. Chartwell Artists, Ltd., L.A., from 1964; chmn. bd. Tandem Prodns., Inc. and TAT Communications Co., L.A., 1973-83; pres., CEO Embassy Pictures, L.A., from 1983; now pres. Chartwell Partnerships Group, L.A. Promoter Muhammad Ali-Joe Frazier heavyweight fight, 1971, Bobby Riggs-Billie Jean King tennis match, 1973. Served to 1st lt. USAF, 1954-57. Clubs: Bel-Air Country (Los Angeles); Westchester (N.Y.) Country; Friars (N.Y.C.). Office: Chartwell Partnerships Group 1999 Ave Of Stars Ste 3050 Los Angeles CA 90067-4611

PEREZ, DANIEL, electronics company executive; BS in Polit. Sci., MBA, UCLA. Former sr. mgr. supply and demand/disk storage bus. IBM Corp.; dir. of materials to v.p. materials, to gen. mgr. Solectron Corp., Fremont, Calif., 1991-98, corp. v.p., chief adminstrv. officer Milpitas, 1998—. Bd. dirs. Tech. Mus. of Innovation, Calif. State Ctr. for Quality Edn. and Devel., Mexican Heritage Corp., Ctr. for Tng. and Careers, San Jose, Calif., El Teatro Campesino. Office: Solectron Corp 847 Gibraltar Dr Milpitas CA 95035

PEREZ, JEAN-YVES, engineering company executive; b. 1945; Ingenieur Civil Engring., Ecole Centrale des Arts et Manufactures, Paris, 1967; MS, U. Ill., 1970. With Soletanche Enterprise, 1971-72; pres., CEO Woodward-Clyde Group, Inc., Denver, 1967-70, 73-97; exec. v.p. URS Greiner Woodward Clyde, Denver, 1998—. With French Air Force, 1970-71. Office: URS 4582 S Ulster St Ste 600 Denver CO 80237-2635

PEREZ, REINALDO JOSEPH, electrical engineer; b. Palm River, Cuba, July 25, 1957; came to U.S., 1975; s. Reinaldo I. and Palminia Ulloa (Rodriguez) P.; m. Madeline Kelly Reilly, Mar. 11, 1989; children: Alexander, Laura-Marie, Richard Kelly, Ella-Dean. BSc in Physics, U. Fla., 1979, MSc in Physics, 1981; MScEE, Fla. Atlantic U., 1983, PhD, 1989. Comms. engr. Kennedy Space Ctr., NASA, Cape Canaveral, Fla., 1983-84; chief reliability engr. jet propulsion lab. JPL Calif. Inst. Tech., Pasadena, 1988—, chief engr. Mars surveyor program, 1994—. Instr. engring. UCLA, 1990-94; owner M.R. Rsch. Inc., a telecomm. and aerospace cons. co.; mem. U.S. Engring. Accreditation Com. for Computer Engring. Author, editor: Handbook of Electromagnetic Compatibility, 1994, Noise and Interference Issues in Wireless Communications, 3 vols., Wireless Communications Handbook, 1998; contbr. articles to profl. publs. Mem. AAAS, IEEE (sr. mem., book rev. editor 1990—), NSPE, Electromagnetic Compatibility Soc. (assoc. editor jour.), Am. Soc. Physics Tchrs., N.Y. Acad. Scis., Applied Computational Electromagnetic Soc. (assoc. editor jour., chief editor newsletter, bd. dirs., v.p.), Phi Kappa Phi. Republican. Baptist. Avocations: flying, skiing, fishing. Office: JPL Calif Inst Tech 4800 Oak Grove Dr # 301460 Pasadena CA 91109-8099

PEREZ, ROSIE, actress; b. Bklyn. d. Ismael Serrano and Lydia Perez. Dramatic appearances include: (TV) 21 Jump Street, WIOU, Rosie Perez Presents Society's Ride, 1993, Happily Ever After: Fairy Tales for Every Child, 1995, Subway Stories: Tales From The Underground, 1997, (film) Do the Right Thing, 1989, White Men Can't Jump, 1992, Night on Earth, 1992, Untamed Heart, 1993, Fearless, 1993 (Acad. award nom. Best Supporting Actress 1994), It Could Happen To You, 1994, Somebody to Love, 1995, A Brother's Kiss, 1997, Perdita Durango, 1997, 24-Hour Woman, 1998, Louis and Frank, 1998, The Road to El Dorado, 2000, (TV series) House of Buggin, 1995. Office: Parks Palmer Turner & Yemenidjian c/o Diane Schroeder 1990 S Bundy Dr Ste 600 Los Angeles CA 90025-5291

PEREZ-MENDEZ, VICTOR, physics educator; b. Guatemala, Aug. 8, 1923; came to U.S., 1946; m. 1949; 2 children MS, Hebrew U., Israel, 1947; PhD, Columbia U., 1951. Rsch. assoc. Columbia U., N.Y.C., 1951-53, staff physicist, 1953-61; sr. scientist Lawrence Berkeley Lab., U. Calif., Berkeley, 1960—. Vis. lectr. Hebrew U., 1959—; prof. physics dept. radiology U. Calif., San Francisco, 1968— Fellow IEEE, AAAS, Am. Phys. Soc., N.Y. Acad. Sci.; mem. Soc. Photo Instrumentation Engrs. Office: U Calif Lawrence Berkeley Lab Berkeley CA 94720-0001 E-mail: vpm@lbl.gov

PERHAM, LEN, communications executive; BSEE, Northeastern U., 1968. Various mgmt. positions AMD, Western Digital; pres., CEO Optical Info. Systems, Inc. (divsn. Exxon Enterprise), IDT, Santa Clara, Calif., 1983-99, also bd. dirs. Bd. dirs. IDT. Office: 2975 Stender Way Santa Clara CA 95054-3214

PERINGTON, PHILIP, management investment company executive; BA, U. Colo., 1976, cert. paralegal, 1989. Pres. Restaurant Devel. Corp., Denver, 1968-73, Harrington-Miller Co., Denver, 1973—. Regional task officer Clinton-Gore Regional Issues, 1996; chmn. Colo. State Dem. Party. Recipient Gov.'s award State of Wyo., 1991. Mem. Assn. State Dem. Chairs (chmn. 1996—). Office: Harrington Miller Co 731 Sherman ST Denver CO 80203

PERKIN, GORDON WESLEY, international health executive; b. Toronto, Ont., Can., Apr. 25, 1935; came to U.S., 1962; s. Irvine Boyer and Jean (Laing) P.; m. Elizabeth Scott, Dec. 21, 1957; children: Scott, Stuart. MD, U. Toronto, 1959. Asst. dir. clin. rsch. Ortho Rsch. Found., Raritan, N.J., 1962-64; assoc. med. dir. Planned Parenthood Fedn. Am., N.Y.C., 1964-66; program advisor Ford Found., N.Y.C., 1966-67, regional program advisor Bangkok, 1967-69, Rio de Janeiro, 1973-76, program officer Mexico City, 1976-80; project specialist Ministry Fin. and Econ. Planning, Accra, Ghana, 1969-70; cons. WHO, Geneva, 1971-73; pres. Program for Appropriate Tech. in Health, Seattle, 1980-99; dir. global health program Bill and Melinda Gates Found., 1999—. Affiliate prof. pub. health, U. Wash., Seattle. Contbr. numerous articles to profl. jours. APHA fellow, 1970. Mem. Planned Parenthood Fedn. Am. (bd. dirs. 1983-89), Planned Parenthood Seattle-King County (bd. dirs. 1982-96, mem. exec. com. 1983-86), Planned Parenthood Western Wash. (bd. dirs. 1996—), Nat. Coun. for Internat. Health (mem. bd. govs. 1984-95), NAS (com. mem. 1987-90), Alan Guttmacher Inst. (bd. dirs. 1985-90), Assn. Reproductive Health Profls., Alpha Omega Alpha. Office: Bill & Melinda Gates Found PO Box 23350 Seattle WA 98102-0650

PERKINS, FLOYD JERRY, retired theology educator; b. Bertha, Minn., May 9, 1924; s. Ray Lester and Nancy Emily (Kelley) P.; m. Mary Elizabeth Owen, Sept. 21, 1947 (dec. June 1982); children: Douglas Jerry, David Floyd, Sheryl Pauline; m. Phyllis Genevra Hartley, July 14, 1984. AB, BTh, N.W. Nazarene Coll., 1949; MA, U. Mo., 1952; MDiv, Nazarene Theol. Sem., 1952; ThM, Burton Sem., 1964; PhD, U. Witwatersrand, Johannesburg, South Africa, 1974; ThD, Internat. Sem., 1994. Ordained to Christian ministry, 1951. Pres. South African Nazarene Theol. Sem., Florida Transvaal, Africa, 1955-67, Nazarene Bible Sem., Lourenzo Marques, Mozambique, 1967-73, Campinas, Brazil, 1974-76; prof. missions N.W. Nazarene Coll., Nampa, Idaho, 1976; prof. theology Nazarene Bible Coll., Colorado Springs, Colo., 1976-97. Chmn., founder com. higher theol. edn. Ch. of Nazarene in Africa, 1967-74; sec. All African Nazarene Mission Exec., 1967-74; ofcl. Christian Council Mozambique, 1952-74. Author: A History of the Christian Church in Swaziland, 1974. Served with USN, 1944-46. Mem. Soc. Christian Philosophers, Evang. Theol. Soc., Am. Schs. Orientan Rsch., Am. Soc. Missiology, Assn. Evang. Missions Profs. Republican. Avocation: golf. Home: 6355 Oak Ave Apt 21 Temple City CA 91780-1300

PERKINS, FRANK OVERTON, university official, marine scientist; b. Fork Union, Va., Feb. 14, 1938; s. Frank Otie and Mary Ella (Hughes) P.; m. Beverly Anne Weeks. BA, U. Va., 1960; MS, Fla. State U., Tallahassee, 1962, PhD, 1966. Marine scientist Va. Inst. Marine Sci., Coll. William and Mary, Gloucester Point, 1966-69, sr. marine scientist, 1969-77, asst. dir., 1977-81, dir., dean Sch. Marine Sci., 1981-91, prof. marine sci., 1991-97; asst. v.p. rsch. and grad. edn. U. Hawaii, Honolulu, 1997—. Baptist. Home: 7519 Olowalu Pl Honolulu HI 96825-2950 Office: U Hawaii 105 Bachman Hall Honolulu HI 96822

PERKINS, HERBERT ASA, hematologist, educator; b. Boston, Oct. 5, 1918; s. Louis and Anna (Robinson) P.; m. Frances Snyder, Sept. 2, 1942; children: Susan, Deborah, Dale, Karen, Ronnie. AB cum laude, Harvard U., 1940; MD summa cum laude, Tufts U., 1943. Intern Boston City Hosp., 1944, resident, 1947-48; practice medicine specializing in transfusion medicine; clin. instr. Stanford Med. Sch., 1953-57, asst. clin. prof., 1957-58; hematologist Open Heart Surgery Team, Stanford Hosp., San Francisco, 1955-58, Jewish Hosp., St. Louis, 1958-59; dir. rsch. Irwin Meml. Blood Ctrs. (now Blood Ctrs. of the Pacific), San Francisco, 1959-78, med. and sci. dir., 1978-90, exec. dir., 1987-91, pres., 1991-93, sr. med. scientist, 1993—. Asst. prof. medicine Washington U., St. Louis, 1958-59, U. Calif., San Francisco, 1959-66, assoc. prof., 1966-71, clin. prof., 1971—. Co-editor: Hepatitis and Blood Transfusion, 1972. Maj. M.C., U.S. Army, 1944-47. Mem. AAAS, Am. Assn. Blood Banks (chmn. sci. adv. com. 1972-73, chmn. stds. com. 1968-71, chmn. com. on organ transplantation and tissue typing 1970-80, bd. dirs. 1982-86), Am. Soc. Hematology, Internat. Transfusion Soc., Am. Soc. Histocompatibility and Immunogenetics (pres. 1985-86), Nat. Marrow Donor Program (chair bd. dirs. 1995-96, chmn. com. on stds. 1987-94, chmn. fin. com. 1987-94). Home: 520 Berkeley Ave Menlo Park CA 94025-2323 Office: Blood Ctrs of the Pacific 270 Masonic Ave San Francisco CA 94118-4417 E-mail: hperkins@bloodcenters.org

PERKINS, JAN, municipal official; BA in sociology, U. Kans., 1974, MPA, 1976. Cert. Program for Sr. Execs. in State and Local Govt., John F. Kennedy Sch. Govt., Harvard U., 1987. Adminstrv. asst. City of Grand Rapids (Mich.), 1975-79, dep. city mgr., 1982-84; asst. city mgr. City of Adrian (Mich.), 1979 82; dep. city mgr. City of Santa Ana (Calif.), 1984-90; city mgr. City of Morgan Hill (Calif.), 1990-92; asst. city mgr. City of Fremont (Calif.), 1992-93, city mgr., 1993—. Mem. Internat. City/County Mgmt. Assn. (internat., awards, innovations adv., conf. planning coms.), City Mgr.'s Dept. League of Calif. Cities (exec. com., com. on the profession), Calif. Redevel. Assn., Pub. Adminstrn. Grad. Program Alumni Assn., Niles (Fremont) Rotary Club. Office: Office City Mgr City Fremont 39100 Liberty St Fremont CA 94538-1502

PERKINS, THOMAS JAMES, venture capital company executive; b. Oak Park, Ill., Jan. 7, 1932; s. Harry H. and Elizabeth P.; m. Gerd Thune-Ellefsen, Dec. 9, 1961; children: Tor Kristian, Elizabeth Siri. B.S.E.E., M.I.T., 1953; M.B.A., Harvard U., 1957. Gen. mgr. computer div. Hewlett Packard Co., Cupertino, Calif., 1963-70, dir. corp. devel., 1970-72, gen. partner Kleiner & Perkins, San Francisco, 1972-80; sr. ptnr. Kleiner Perkins Caufield & Byers, San Francisco, from 1980; chmn. bd. Tandem Computers, Inc., Cupertino, Calif. Chmn. bd. Tandem Computers, Genentech; dir. Spectra Physics., Corning Glass Works, Collagen Corp., LSI Logic Corp., Hybritech Inc., Econics Corp., Vitalink Communications Corp. Author: Classic Supercharged Sports Cars, 1984. Trustee San Francisco Ballet, 1980— . Mem. Nat. Venture Capital Assn. (chmn. 1981-82, pres. 1980-81) Clubs: N.Y. Yacht, Links, Am. Bugatti (pres. 1983—). also: Genentech Inc 460 Point San Bruno Blvd South San Francisco CA 94080-4918

PERKINS, WILLIAM CLINTON, company executive; b. Decatur, Ill., Mar. 7, 1920; s. Glen Rupert and Frances Lola (Clinton) P.; m. Eunice Cagle, Sept. 7, 1939 (div. 1954); stepchildren: William Rea Cagle, Howard Christy Cagle; 1 child, Clinton Colcord; m. Lillian Wuollet, Sept. 7, 1955 (div. 1965); m. Shirley Thomas, Oct. 24, 1969. BS Mil. Sci. and Meteorology, U. Md., 1954; MS in Bus. and Pub. Adminstrn., Sussex Coll., Eng., 1975. Commd. USAF, 1943-73, advanced through grades to col.; with Ship Systems div. Litton Ind., Culver City, Calif., 1973-75; dir. material Hughes Aircraft Co., Tehran, Iran, 1974-78; mgr. internat. s/c Northrop Corp., Dahran, Saudi Arabia, 1978-81; dir. materiel CRS, Riyadh, Saudi Arabia, 1981-83; head major subcontracts Lear Ziegler Corp., Santa Monica, Calif., 1984-88; pres., chmn. bd., CEO Snowtech, Inc., L.A., 1984—. Bd. dirs. Ice Village Ctrs., Inc., L.A., Forefront Industries, Maywood, Calif. Bd. dirs. World Children's Transplant Fund, L.A., 1987-95; mem. Mayor's Space Adv. Com., L.A., 1970-74; mem. aerospace hist. com. Mus. Sci. and Industry, L.A., 1988-98, Mus. of Flying, 1998—. Mem. AIAA (sec. chmn. 1970), Ret. Officers Assn. (pres. 1992-95), Soc. for Non-destructive Testing (program chmn. 1973), Aerospace Hist. Soc., Am. Soc. Quality Control, Am. Meterol. Soc., Sigma Alpha Epsilon (alumni chpt. pres. 1974-76). Avocations: golf, scuba diving, sailing, flying, gardening. Home: 8027 Hollywood Blvd Los Angeles CA 90046-2510 E-mail: snowtech@pacbell.net

PERKOWITZ, SIMON, architect; AA in Architecture, L.A. City Coll., 1968; BS in Architecture, Calif. Polytech. State U., 1971. Registered architect Oreg., Nev., Ga.; lic. architect Calif., profl. engr., Calif. V.p. Mackel Assocs., L.A., 1966-79; prin., exec. v.p. Musil Perkowitz Ruth, Inc., 1979—, pres., CEO, 1998—. Mem. AIA, Internat. Coun. Shopping Ctrs., NSPE, Nat. Soc. Archtl. Engrs. Office: Perkowitz & Ruth Architects Inc 111 W Ocean Blvd Ste 2100 Long Beach CA 90802-4653

PERKOWSKI, MAREK ANDRZEJ, electrical engineering educator; b. Warsaw, Poland, Oct. 6, 1946; came to U.S., 1981; s. Adam Perkowski and Hanna (Zielinska) Mystkowska; m. Ewa Kaja Wilkowska, Oct. 26, 1974; 1 child, Mateusz Jan. MS in Electronics with distinction, Tech. U. Warsaw, 1970, PhD in Automatics with distinction, 1980. Sr. asst. Inst. Automatics, Tech. U. Warsaw, 1973-80, asst. prof., 1980-81; vis. asst. prof. dept. elec. engrng. U. Minn., Mpls., 1981-83; assoc. prof. elec. engrng. Portland (Oreg.) State U., 1983-94, prof., 1994—. Co-author: Theory of Automata, 3d edit., 1976, Problems in Theory of Logic Circuits, 4th edit., 1986, Theory of Logic Circuits-Selected Problems, 3d edit., 1984; contbr. 134 articles to profl. jours., 11 chpts. to books. Mem. Solidarity, Warsaw, 1980-81. Recipient Design Automation award SIGDA/ACM/DATC IEEE, 1986-91; Rsch. grantee NSF, 1991, 94, Commn. for Familites Roman Cath. Ch., Vatican, 1981, Air Force Office Sci. Rsch., 1995. Mem. IEEE (Computer Soc.), Polish Nat. Alliance, Assn. for Computing Machinery, Am. Soc. for Engrng. Edn. Roman Catholic. Avocations: tourism, philosophy, woodcarving. Home: 15720 NW Perimeter Dr Beaverton OR 97006-5391 Office: Portland State U Dept Elec & Comp Engring PO Box 751 Portland OR 97207-0751 E-mail: mperkows@ece.pdx.edu

PERL, MARTIN LEWIS, physicist, engineer, educator; b. N.Y.C., June 24, 1927; children: Jed, Anne, Matthew, Joseph. B.Chem. Engring., Poly. Inst. Bklyn., 1948; Ph.D., Columbia U., 1955; ScD (hon.), U. Chgo., 1990. Chem. engr. Gen. Electric Co., 1948-50; asst. prof. physics U. Mich., 1955-58, asso. prof., 1958-63; prof. Stanford, 1963—. Author: High Energy Hadron Physics, 1975, Reflections on Experimental Science, 1996; contbr. articles on high energy physics and on relation of sci. to soc. to profl. jours. With U.S. Mcht. Marine, 1944-45; with AUS, 1946-47. Recipient Wolf prize in physics, 1982, Nobel Prize in Physics, 1995. Fellow Am. Phys. Soc.; mem. Nat. Acad. Scis., Am. Acad. Arts & Scis. Home: 3737 El Centro Ave Palo Alto CA 94306-2642 Office: Stanford U Stanford Linear Accelerator Ctr Stanford CA 94305 E-mail: martin@slac.stanford.edu

PERLEGOS, GEORGE, electronic executive; Pres., CEO, chmn. Atmel Inc., San Jose. Office: Atmel Inc 2325 Orchard Pkwy San Jose CA 95131-1034

PERLIS, MICHAEL FREDRICK, lawyer; b. N.Y.C., June 3, 1947; s. Leo and Betty F. (Gantz) P.; children: Amy Hannah, David Matthew; m. Angela M. Rinaldi, Dec. 23, 1988. BS in Fgn. Svc. , Georgetown U., 1968, JD, 1971. Bar: D.C. 1971, N.Y. 1993, U.S. Dist. Ct. D.C. 1971, U.S. Ct. Appeals 1971, D.C. Ct. Appeals 1971, Calif. 1980, U.S. Dist. Ct. (no. dist.) Calif. 1980, U.S Dist. Ct. (cen. dist.) Calif. 1985, U.S. Ct. Appeals (9th cir.) 1980, U.S. Supreme Ct., 1980, N.Y. 1993. Law clerk D.C. Ct. Appeals, Washington, 1971-72; asst. corp. counsel D.C., Washington, 1972-74; counsel U.S. SEC, div. enforcement, Washington, 1974-75, br. chief, 1975-77, asst. dir., 1977-80; ptnr. Pettit & Martin, San Francisco, 1980-89, Stroock & Stroock & Lavan, L.A., 1989—; adj. prof. Cath. U. Am., 1979-80. Mem. ABA (co-chmn. subcom. securities and commodities litigation 1982-83), D.C. Bar Assn., Calif. State Bar Assn. Office: Stroock & Stroock & Lavan 2029 Century Park E Ste 1800 Los Angeles CA 90067-3086

PERLMAN, DAVID, science editor, journalist; b. Balt., Dec. 30, 1918; s. Jess and Sara P.; m. Anne Salz, Oct. 15, 1941; children: Katherine, Eric, Thomas. AB, Columbia U., 1939, MS, 1940. Reporter Bismarck (N.D.) Capital, 1940; reporter San Francisco Chronicle, 1940-41, reporter, sci. editor, 1952-77, city editor, 1977-79, assoc. editor, sci. editor, 1979—; reporter New York Herald Tribune, Paris, N.Y.C., 1945-49; European corr. Colliers mag. and New York Post, 1949-51. Regents prof. human biology U. Calif., San Francisco 1974; vis. lectr. China Assn. Sci. and Tech., Beijing, Chengdu and Shanghai, 1983; sci. writer-in-residence U. Wis., 1989. Contbr. articles to major mags. Founding dir. Squaw Valley (Calif.) Community of Writers; dir. Alan Guttmacher Inst., 1990-99; trustee Scientists Inst. for Pub. Info., 1986-94; chmn. pub. svc. award com. Nat. Sci. Bd., 1998—. Served with inf. USAAF, 1941-45. Recipient Atomic Indsl. Forum award, 1975, AAAS Sci. Writing award, 1976, Ralph Coates Roe medal ASME, 1978, Margaret Sanger Cmty. Svc. award, 1981, Fellows' medal Calif. Acad. Scis., 1984, Career Achievement award Soc. Profl. Journalists, 1989, Glenn T. Seaborg award Internat. Platform Assn., 1993, Sustained Achievement award for sci. journalism Am. Geophys. Union, 1997, U. Calif. San Francisco medal, 2000, Columbia U. Journalism award, 2000, San Francisco Med. Soc. award for disting. med. reporting, 2000, Grady-Stack award for sci. journalism Am. Chem. Soc., 2001; Poynter Inst. fellow Yale U., 1984, Carnegie Corp. fellow Stanford U., 1987. Fellow Calif. Acad. Scis.; mem. AAAS (adv. bd. Science-81-86 mag., com. Pub. Understanding of Sci. 1985-90), Coun. for Advancement Sci. Writing (pres. 1976-80), Nat. Assn. Sci. Writers (pres. 1970-71, Disting. Sci. Journalism award 1994), Astron. Soc. Pacific (dir. 1976-78), Sigma Xi. Office: San Francisco Chronicle 901 Mission St San Francisco CA 94103-2905 E-mail: dperlman@sfchronicle.com

PERLMUTTER, EDWIN GEORGE (ED), state legislator; b. Denver, May 1, 1953; m. Deana M. Perlmutter; children: Alexis, Abbey, Zoey. BA, U. Colo., 1975, JD, 1978. Atty. Berenbaum, Weinshienk & Eason, P.C., 1978—; mem. Colo. Senate, Dist. 20, Denver, 1994—; mem. pub., policy and planning com., joint legal svcs. com. Trustee First Jud. and Jud. Performance Commn., 1989-91, chair, 1991-93. Mem. Maple Grove Elem. Sch. PTA. Mem. ABA, Am. Bankruptcy Inst., Colo. Bar Assn. (bd. govs.), Colo. Trial Lawyers Assn., Associated Gen. Contractors Colo., Colo. Oil and Gas Assn., Denver Bar Assn., Applewood Bus. Assn., Golden C. of C., N.W. Met. C. of C., West C. of C., U. Colo. Alumni Assn. (former dir.). Democrat. Office: State Capitol 200 E Colfax Ave Ste 274 Denver CO 80203-1716 also: 370 17th St Ste 2600 Denver CO 80202-5677 Fax: 303-866-4543

PERLOFF, MARJORIE GABRIELLE, English and comparative literature educator; b. Vienna, Austria, Sept. 28, 1931; d. Maximilian and Ilse (Schueller) Mintz; m. Joseph K. Perloff, July 31, 1953; children— Nancy Lynn, Carey Elizabeth. AB, Barnard Coll., 1953; MA, Cath. U., 1956, PhD, 1965. Asst. prof. English and comparative lit. Cath. U., Washington, 1966-68, asso. prof., 1969-71, U. Md., 1971-73, prof., 1973-76; Florence R. Scott prof. English U. So. Calif., Los Angeles, 1976—; prof. English and comparative lit. Stanford U., Calif., 1986—, Sadie Dernham prof. humanities, 1990—, prof. emerita, 2000. Author: Rhyme and Meaning in the Poetry of Yeats, 1970, The Poetic Art of Robert Lowell, 1973, Frank O'Hara, Poet Among Painters, 1977, 2nd edit., 1998, The Poetics of Indeterminacy: Rimbaud to Cage, 1981, 2d edit., 1999, The Dance of the Intellect: Studies in the Poetry of the Pound Tradition, 1985, 2d edit., 1996, The Futurist Moment: Avant-Garde, Avant-Guerre and the Language of Rupture, 1986, Poetic License: Essays in Modern and Postmodern Lyric, 1990, Radical Artifice: Writing Poetry in the Age of Media, 1991, Wittgenstein's Ladder: Poetic Language and the Strangeness of the Ordinary, 1996, Frank O'Hara, 2d edit., 1998, Poetry On and Off the Page: Essays for Emergent Occasions, 1998, Twenty-first Century Modernism, 2001; editor: Postmodern Genres, 1990; co-editor: John Cage: Composed in America, 1994; contbg. editor: Columbia Literary History of the U.S., 1987; contbr. preface to Contemporary Poets, 1980, A John Cage Reader, 1983. Guggenheim fellow, 1981-82, NEA fellow, 1985; Phi Beta Kappa scholar, 1994-95. Fellow Am. Acad. Arts and Scis.; mem. MLA (exec. coun. 1977-81, Am. lit. sect. 1993—), Comparative Lit. Assn. (pres. 1993-94, mem. adv. bd. Libr. of Am.), Lit. Studies Acad. Home: 1467 Amalfi Dr Pacific Palisades CA 90272-2752 Office: Stanford U Dept English Stanford CA 94305 E-mail: mperloff@earthlink.net

PEROCK, WAYNE R. state agency administrator; Adminstr. Conservation and Natural Resources Dept. State of Nev., divsn. State Parks, Carson City, 1995—. Office: State Nevada Conservation & Nat Res Dept 1300 S Curry St Carson City NV 89703-5202

PERRAULT, JACQUES, educator; b. Montreal, Quebec, Can., June 25, 1944; s. Jean-Paul and Irene (Girard) P.; m. Katherine Hampton Rhodes, May 4, 1996; 1 child, Juliette. BSc, McGill U., 1964; PhD, U. Calif., San Diego, 1972. Asst. prof. dept. microbiology and immunology Washington U. Sch. Medicine, St. Louis, 1977-84; assoc. prof. biology San Diego State U., 1984-87; prof. dept. of biology prof., 1987—. Contbr. articles to profl. jours. Recipient Research Career Devel. award, NIH, 1980-85; grantee, NIH, NSF, March of Dimes Defects Found., 1977—. Mem. AAAS, Am. Soc. Microbiology, Am. Soc. Virology, Gen. Soc. for Microbiology. Avocations: karate (Shotokan Japanese style). Office: San Diego State U Dept Biology San Diego CA 92182 E-mail: jperrault@sunstroke.sdsu.edu

PERRIN, EDWARD BURTON, health services researcher, biostatistician, public health educator; b. Greensboro, Vt., Sept. 19, 1931; s. J. Newton and Dorothy E. (Willey) P.; m. Carol Anne Hendricks, Aug. 18, 1956; children: Jenifer, Scott. BA, Middlebury Coll., 1953; postgrad. (Fulbright scholar) in stats, Edinburgh (Scotland) U., 1953-54; MA in Math. Stats., Columbia U., 1956; PhD, Stanford U., 1960. Asst. prof. dept. biostats. U. Pitts., 1959-62; asst. prof. dept. preventive medicine U. Wash., Seattle, 1962-65, assoc. prof., 1965-69, prof., 1969-70, prof., chmn. dept. biostats., 1970-72, prof. dept. health svcs., adj. prof. dept. biostats., 1975-98, chmn. dept., 1983-94, prof. emeritus, 1999—; prof. (hon.) West China U. of Med. Scis., Szechwan, Peoples Republic of China, 1988-98; overseas fellow Churchill Coll., Cambridge U., 1991-92; sr. scientist Seattle Vets. Affairs Med. Ctr., 1994—. Clin. prof. dept. cmty. medicine and internat. health Sch. Medicine, Georgetown U., Washington, 1972-75; dep. dir. Nat. Ctr. for Health Stats., HEW, 1972-73, dir., 1973-75; rsch. scientist Health Care Study Ctr., Battelle Human Affairs Rsch. Ctrs., Seattle, 1975-76, dir., 1976-78; dir. Health and Population Study Ctr. Batelle Human Affairs Rsch. Ctrs., Seattle, 1978-83; sr. cons. biostats. Wash./Alaska regional med. programs, 1967-72; biometrician VA Co-op Study on Treatment of Esopageal Varices, 1961-73; mem. Epidemiology and Disease Control Study Sect., NIH, 1969-73; chmn. health svcs. rsch. study sect., HEW, 1976-79; chmn. health svcs. R&D field program rev. panel, VA, 1988-91; chmn. health svcs. info. steering com. State of Washington, 1993-94; mem. nat. adv. coun. Agy. for Health Care Policy and Rsch. Dept. Health and Human Svcs., U.S. Govt., 1994-97; mem. com. on nat. stats. NRC, NAS, 1994-2000; chmn. scientific adv. com. Med. Outcomes Trust, 1994-99. Contbr. articles on biostats., health services and population studies to profl. publs.; mem. editorial bd.: Jour. Family Practice, 1978-90, Public Health Nursing, 1992-98. Mem. tech. bd. Milbank Meml. Fund, 1974-76. Recipient Outstanding Service citation HEW, 1975 Fellow AAAS, Am. Pub. Health Assn. (Spiegelman Health Stats. award 1970, program devel. bd. 1971, chmn. stats. sect. 1978-80, governing coun. 1983-85, stats. sect. recognition award 1989), Am. Statis. Assn. (mem. adv. com. to divsn. statis. policy 1975-77); mem. Assn. Health Svcs. Rsch. (pres. 1994-95, bd. dirs. 1997-2000), Inst. Medicine of Nat. Acad. Sci. (chmn. membership com. 1984-86, mem. bd. on health care svcs. 1987-96, forum health stats. 1994-95, chmn. com. on clin. evaluation 1990-93), Biometrics Soc. (pres. Western N.Am. Region 1971), Inst. Math. Stats., Internat. Epidemiologic Assn., Sigma Xi, Phi Beta Kappa. Home: 4900 NE 39th St Seattle WA 98105-5209 Office: U Wash Dept Health Svcs PO Box 358853 Seattle WA 98195-8853 E-mail: perrin@u.washington.edu

PERRINE, RICHARD LEROY, environmental engineering educator; b. Mountain View, Calif., May 15, 1924; s. George Alexander and Marie (Axelson) P.; m. Barbara Jean Gale, Apr. 12, 1945; children: Cynthia Gale, Jeffrey Richard. A.B., San Jose State Coll., 1949; M.S., Stanford U., 1950, Ph.D. in Chemistry, 1953. Cert. environ. profl., 1987. Research chemist Calif. Research Corp., La Habra, 1953-59; assoc. prof. UCLA, 1959-63, prof. engrng. and applied sci., 1963-92, prof. emeritus, 1992—, chmn. environ. sci. and engring., 1971-82; prin. Aspen Environ. Group, 1990-93. V.p. Sage Resources, 1988-91; cons. environ. sci. and engring., energy resources, flow in porous media; mem. Los Angeles County Energy Commn., 1973-81; mem. adv. council South Coast Air Quality Mgmt. Dist., 1977-82; mem. air conservation com. Los Angeles County Lung Assn., 1970-84; mem. adv. com. energy div. Oak Ridge Nat. Lab., 1987-90; mem. policy bd. Inst. Environ. and Natural Resource Rsch. and Policy U. Wyo., 1994—. Editor in chief The Environ. Profl., 1985-90. Served with AUS, 1943-46. Recipient Outstanding Engr. Merit award in environ. engring. Inst. Advancement Engring., 1975; ACT-SO award in field of chemistry West Coast region NAACP, 1984. Fellow AAAS; mem. Am. Chem. Soc., Soc. Petroleum Engrs., Am. Inst. Chem. Engrs., Can. Inst. Mining and Metallurgy, N.Am. Assn. Environ. Edn., Nat. Assn. Environ. Profls. (cert.), Air and Waste Mgmt. Assn., Assn. Environ. Engring. Profs., Sierra Club, Wilderness Soc., Audubon Soc., Sigma Xi, Tau Beta Pi, Phi Lambda Upsilon. Home: 22611 Kittridge St West Hills CA 91307-3609 Office: Univ Calif Engring Bldg I Rm 3066A Los Angeles CA 90095-0001 E-mail: rperrine@ucla.edu

PERRISH, ALBERT, retired steel company executive; b. Vancouver, B.C., Can., Nov. 18, 1914; came to U.S., 1920; s. Sam and Nettie (Prezant) P.; m. Leora Claire Quiat, Jan. 12, 1962 (dec. 1984); m. Helen Ann Frazin, June 11, 1985; children: Peggy, Kathleen. BSBA, UCLA, 1938. Commr. City of L.A. Harbor Dept., 1961-64, pres., 1964; exec. Ferro Union Inc., Torrance, Calif., 1964-99; ret., 1999. Mem. adv. bd. U.S. Dept. Commerce, Washington, 1946-50, Small Bus. Adminstrn., Washington, 1955-56. Capt. USAAF, 1942-46. Recipient Star of Solidarity, Pres. of Italy, 1954, Order of Leopold, King of Belgium, 1962, Order of Merit, Govt. of France, 1962. Mem. Am. Inst. Internat. Steel (founder, pres. West Coast chpt. 1959—).

PERRY, DALE LYNN, chemist; b. Greenville, Tex., May 12, 1947; s. Francis Leon and Violet (Inabinette) P. BS, Midwestern U., 1969; MS, Lamar U., 1972; PhD, U. Houston, 1974. NSF fellow dept. chemistry Rice U., Houston, 1976-77; Miller Research fellow dept. chemistry U. Calif.-Berkeley, 1977-79; prin. investigator solid state chemistry and spectroscopy Lawrence Berkeley Lab. U. Calif., 1979—, sr. scientist, 1987—. Lectr. Ana G. Mendez Ednl. Found., 1988; rsch. mem. G.T. Seaborg Inst. for Transactinium Sci. Author, editor: Instrumental Surface Analysis of Geologic Materials, 1990, Applications of Analytical Techniques to the Characterization of Materials, 1992, Applications of Synchrotron Radiation Techniques to Materials Science, 1993, II, 1995, III, 1996, IV, 1998, Handbook of Inorganic Compounds, 1995, Materials Synthesis and Characterization, 1997; contbr. articles to profl. jours. Fellow Royal Soc. Chemistry (London); mem. Am. Chem. Soc. (chmn. materials chemistry and engrng. subdivsn., indsl. and engrng. chemistry divsn., 1992-96), Soc. Applied Spectroscopy, Coblentz Soc., Materials Rsch. Soc. (corp. participation com. 1991-96), Sigma Xi (nat. rsch. award 1974). Office: U Calif Lawrence Berkeley Nat Lab Mail Stop 70A 1150 Berkeley CA 94720-0001

PERRY, JACQUELIN, orthopedic surgeon; b. Denver, May 31, 1918; d. John F. and Tirzah (Kuruptkat) P. B.E., U. Calif., Los Angeles, 1940; M.D., U. Calif., San Francisco, 1950; DSc (hon.), U. So. Calif., 1996. Intern Children's Hosp., San Francisco, 1950-57; resident in orthopedic surgery U. Calif., San Francisco, 1951-55; orthopedic surgeon Rancho Los Amigos Hosp., Downey, Calif., 1955—; chief pathokinesiology Rancho Los Amigos Med. Ctr., 1961—; chief stroke service Rancho Los Amigos Hosp., 1972-75; mem. faculty U. Calif. Med. Sch., San Francisco, 1966—, clin. prof., 1973—; mem. faculty U. So. Calif. Med. Sch., 1969—, prof. orthopedic surgery, 1972—, dir. polio and gait clinic, 1972—. Disting. lectr. for hosp. for spl. surgery and Cornell U. Med. Coll., N.Y.C., 1977-78; Packard Meml. lectr. U. Colo. Med. Sch., 1970; Osgood lectr. Harvard Med. Sch., 1978; Summer lectr., Portland, 1977; Shands lectr.; cons. USAF; guest speaker symposia; cons. Biomechanics Lab. Centinela Hosp., 1979—. Served as phys. therapist U.S. Army, 1941-46. Recipient Disting. Svc. award Calif., Assn. Rehab. Facilities, 1981, Pres.'s award, 1984, Milton Cohen award Nat. Assn. Rehab., 1993, Isabelle and Lenard Goldensen award for tech. United Cerebral Palsy Assn., 1981, Jow Dowling award, 1985, Profl. Achievement award UCLA, 1988, Amistad award Rancho Las Amigos Med. Ctr., Calif. 1990, Shands award Orthop. Rsch. Soc., 1998; named Woman of Yr. for Medicine in So. Calif., L.A. Times, 1959, Alumnus of Yr., U. Calif. Med. Sch., 1980, Physician of Yr. Calif. Employment Devel. Dept., 1994; Jacquelin Perry Neuro Trauma Inst. Rancho Clin. Bldg. named in her honor, 1996. Mem. AMA, Am. Acad. Orthop. Surgeons (Kappa Delta award for rsch. 1977), Am. Orthop. Assn. (Shands lectr. 1988), Western Orthop. Assn., Calif. Med. Soc., L.A. County Med. Soc., Am. Phys. Therapy Assn. (hon. Golden Pen award 1965), Am. Acad. Orthotists and Prosthetists (hon.), Scoliosis Rsch. Soc., LeRoy Abbott Soc., Am. Acad. Cerebral Palsy, Gait & Clin. Movement Analysis Soc. (mem. emeritus, Lifetime Achievement award 2000), Orthop. Rsch. Soc. (Shands award 1998). Home: 12319 Brock Ave Downey CA 90242-3503 Office: Rancho Los Amigos Med Ctr 7601 Imperial Hwy Downey CA 90242-3456

PERRY, JEAN LOUISE, dean; b. Richland, Wash., May 13, 1950; d. Russell S. and Sue W. Perry. BS, Miami U., Oxford, Ohio, 1972; MS, U. Ill., Urbana, 1973, PhD, 1976. Cons. ednl. placement office U. Ill., 1973-75; adminstrv. intern Coll. Applied Life Studies, 1975-76, asst. dean, 1976-77, assoc. dean, 1978-81, asst. prof. dept. phys. edn., 1976-81; assoc. prof. phys. edn. San Francisco State U., 1981-84, prof., 1984-90, chair, 1981-90; dean Coll. of Human and Community Scis. U. Nev., Reno, 1990—. Named to excellent tchr. list U. Ill., 1973-79. Mem. AAHPERD (fellow research consortium, pres. 1988-89), Am. Assn. Higher Edn., Am. Ednl. Research Assn., Nat. Assn. Phys. Edn. in Higher Edn., Nat. Assn. Girls and Women in Sports (guide coordinator, pres.), Delta Psi Kappa, Phi Delta Kappa. Home: 3713 Ranchview Ct Reno NV 89509-7437 Office: U Nev Coll Human Cmty Scis 136 Reno NV 89557-0001

PERRY, JOHN RICHARD, philosophy educator; b. Lincoln, Nebr., Jan. 16, 1943; s. Ralph Robert and Ann (Roscow) P.; m. Louise Elizabeth French, Mar. 31, 1962; children: James Merton, Sarah Louise, Joseph Glenn. BA, Doane Coll., Crete, Nebr., 1964; PhD, Cornell U., Ithaca, N.Y., 1968; DLitt (hon.), Doane Coll., 1982. Asst. prof. philosophy UCLA, 1968-72; vis. asst. prof. U. Mich., Ann Arbor, 1971-72; assoc. prof. UCLA, 1972-74, Stanford (Calif.) U., 1974-77; prof. Stanford U., 1977-85, Henry Waldgrave Stuart prof., 1985—, chmn. dept. philosophy, 1976-82, 90-91, 2000-01, dir. ctr. study lang. and info., 1985-86, 93-99, resident fellow Soto House, 1985-91. Author: Dialogue on Identity and Immortality, 1978, (with Jon Barwise) Situations and Attitudes, 1983, The Problem of the Essential Indexical, 1993, Dialogue on Good, Evil and the Existence of God, 1999, Knowledge, Possibility and Consciousness, 2001, Reference and Reflexivity, 2001. Pres. Santa Monica Dem. Club, Calif., 1972-74. Woodrow Wilson fellow, 1964-65, Danforth fellow, 1964-68, Guggenheim fellow, 1975-76, NEH fellow, 1980-81. Mem. Am. Philos. Assn. (v.p. Pacific divsn. 1992-93, pres. 1993-94). Office: Stanford U Dept Philosophy Bldg 90 Inner Quad Stanford CA 94305 E-mail: john@csli.stanford.edu

PERRY, L. TOM, religious organization administrator, merchant. s. Tom and Nora Sonne Perry, m. Virginia Lee (dec. 1974), three children; m. Barbara Dayton, 1976; BS, Utah State U. Ass. to the Twelve, 1972-74, Mem. Quorum of the Twelve,1974— The Ch. of Jesus Christ of LDS, Salt Lake City; chmn. ZCMI, Salt Lake City; Marine, Pacific Theater, WW2. Office: LDS Ch 50 E North Temple Salt Lake City UT 84150-0002

PERRY, MARK L. medical products executive; b. 1955; AB, U. Calif.; JD, U. Calif., Davis. Bar: Calif. 1980. Assoc. Cooley Godward, San Francisco, 1981-87, ptnr., 1987-94; sec., v.p., gen. counsel Gilead Scis., Inc., Foster City, Calif., 1994-96, CFO, v.p., gen. counsel, sec., 1996-98, sr. v.p., 1998-2000, sr. v.p. ops., 2000—. Office: Gilead Scis Inc 333 Lakeside Dr Foster City CA 94404-1146 Fax: (650) 574-4800

PERRY, MICHAEL C. theatre publisher, educator; b. Denver, Nov. 20, 1953; s. Maurice L. and Maryann Jane (Champlin) P.; m. Sharon Yvonne Perry, June 26, 1981; children: Jessica, Janalynn, Joelle, Jon-Christopher. BA, Brigham Young U., 1982. Cert. tchr., Utah. Technician Osmond Studios, Orem, Utah, 1977-84; educator Pleasant Grove (Utah) H.S., 1986-87, Spanish Fork (Utah) H.S., 1989—; pres. Encore Performance Pub., Orem, 1979—. Author, composer (musical play) Tom Sawyer, 1987;

composer (musical play) Turn the Gas Back On, 1989, Onstage, 1992; editor (scene books) For Teens and Child Actors, 1992. Recipient Best of West award Rocky Mountain Pub. Broadcasting, 1977, Emmy award Acad. of TV, 1977. Mem. Am. Soc. Composers, Authors and Pubs., Am. Alliance for Theatre and Edn. (Disting Play award 1995), Ednl. Theatre Assn., Christians In Theatre Arts, Utah Theatre Assn., Rocky Mountain Theatre Assn. Office: Encore Performance Pub PO Box 692 Orem UT 84059-0692

PERRY, RALPH BARTON, III, lawyer; b. N.Y.C., Mar. 17, 1936; s. Ralph Barton Jr. and Harriet Armington (Seelye) P.; m. Mary Elizabeth Colburn, Sept. 2, 1961; children: Katherine Suzanne, Daniel Berenson. A.B., Harvard U., 1958; LL.B., Stanford U., 1963. Bar: Calif. 1964. Assoc. and mem. Keatinge & Sterling, Los Angeles, 1963-68; mem. firm Graven Perry Block Brody & Qualls, Los Angeles, 1968—. Bd. dirs. Planning and Conservation League, 1968—, Coalition for Clean Air, 1961—, pres. 1972-80, 85-88. Served with U.S. Army, 1956-58. Mem. ABA (ho. of dels. 1975-95), State Bar Calif., L.A. County Bar Assn., Lawyers Club L.A. County (gov. 1968-82), Keep Tahoe Blue, Nat. Wildlife Fedn., Internat. Wildlife Fedn., Sierra Club, L.A. Athletic. Home: 296 Redwood Dr Pasadena CA 91105-1339 Office: Graven Perry 523 W 6th St Ste 723 Los Angeles CA 90014-1223 E-mail: rbp3@earthlink.net

PERRY, TROY D. clergyman, religious organization administrator; divorced; 2 children. Student, Midwest Bible Sch.; D in Ministry (hon.), Samaritan Coll., L.A.; D in Human Svcs., Sierra U., Santa Monica, Calif. Former pastor Ch. of God of Prophecy, Santa Ana, Calif.; founder, moderator Universal Fellowship Met. Community Chs., L.A. Rep. Met. Community Chs. and gay and lesbian rights movement numerous TV shows including 60 Minutes, Phil Donahue, The Mike Douglas Show; author: The Lord is My Shepherd and Knows I'm Gay, Don't Be Afraid Anymore, 1991, (video) God, Gays and The Gospel: This is Our Story; contbg. editor Is Gay Good? Mem. Los Angeles County Commn. Human Rels. Recipient Humanitarian award Gay Press Assn., Equality award Human Rights Campaign, 1996. Office: Universal Fellowship Met Comm Chs 8704 Santa Monica Blvd Fl 2 West Hollywood CA 90069-4548 E-mail: revtperry@ufmcchq.com

PERRY, WILLIAM JAMES, educator, former federal official; b. Vandergrift, Pa., Oct. 11, 1927; s. Edward Martin and Mabelle Estelle (Dunlap) P.; m. Leonilla Green, Dec. 29, 1947; children: David, William, Rebecca, Robin, Mark. BS in Math, Stanford U., 1949, MS, 1950; PhD, Pa. State U., 1957. Instr. math. Pa. State U., 1951-54; sr. mathematician HRB-Singer Co., State College, Pa., 1952-54; dir. electronic def. labs. GTE Sylvania Co., Mountain View, Calif., 1954-64; pres. ESL, Inc., Sunnyvale, 1964-77; tech. cons. Dept. Def., Washington, 1967-77, under sec. def. for research and engring., 1977-81; mng. dir. Hambrecht & Quist (investment bankers), San Francisco, 1981-85; chmn. Tech. Strategies & Alliances, Menlo Park, Calif., 1985-93; prof., co-dir. Ctr. for Internat. Security and Arms Control Stanford U., 1989-93; apptd. Dep. Sec. Def. Pentagon, Washington, 1993-94, appt. sec. Def., 1994-97; prof. engring.-econ. sys. and ops. rsch. Stanford (Calif.) U., 1997—. Served with U.S. Army, 1946-47. Recipient Def. Disting. Svc. medal U.S. Govt., 1980, 81, Achievement medal Am. Electronics Assn., 1980, Forrestal Medal, 1994, Henry Stimson medal, 1994, Arthur Bueche medal NAE, 1996, Eisenhower award, 1996, Presdl. Medal Freedom, 1997, Outstanding Civilian Svc. medals U.S. Army, 1997, USN, 1997, USAF, 1997, USCG, 1997, NASA, 1997, Def. Intelligence Agy., 1997; Sr. fellow Inst. Internat. Studies, Stanford U., 1997—. Fax: 650-725-0920. E-mail: wjperry@stanford.edu

PERSCHBACHER, REX ROBERT, dean, law educator; b. Chgo., Aug. 31, 1946; s. Robert Ray and Nancy Ellen (Beach) P.; children: Julie Ann, Nancy Beatrice. AB in Philosophy, Stanford U., 1968; JD, U. Calif., Berkeley, 1972. Bar: Calif. 1972, U.S. Dist. Ct. (no. dist.) Calif. 1973, U.S. Dist. Ct. (so. dist.) Calif. 1979, U.S. Ct. Appeals (9th cir.) 1980, U.S. Dist. ct. (ea. dist.) Calif. 1985. Law clk. to judge U.S. Dist. Ct. (no. dist.) Calif., San Francisco, 1973-74; asst. prof. law U. Tex., Austin, 1974-75; assoc. Heller, Ehrman, White & McAuliffe, San Francisco, 1975-78; asst. prof. law U. San Diego, 1978-79, assoc. prof. law, 1980-81; mem. faculty Inst. on Internat. and Comparative Law, London, 1984—; acting prof. law U. Calif., Davis, 1981-85, prof., 1988—, assoc. dean, 1993-98, dean Law Sch., 1998—. Dir. clin. edn. Univ. Calif., Davis, 1981-93, acad. senate, law sch. rep., 1989-91; vis. prof. law Univ. Santa Clara (Calif.), summer 1986. Co-author: California Civil Procedure and Practice, 1996, California Legal Ethics, 2nd edit., 1997, Problems in Legal Ethics, 4th edit., 1997, Cases and Materials on Civil Procedure, 3d edit., 1998; contbr. articles to legal jours. Bd. dirs. Legal Svcs. of No. Calif., 1990-96. Mem. ABA, Calif. Bar Assn., Am. Assn. Law Schs., Inn of Ct. Democrat. Avocations: travel. Office: U Calif Sch Law King Hall Davis CA 95616

PERSHING, DAVID WALTER, chemical engineering educator, researcher; b. Anderson, Ind., Oct. 2, 1948; s. Walter L. and Treva B. (Crane) P.; m. Lynn Marie Kennard, Apr. 9, 1977; 1 child, Nicole. BSChemE, Purdue U., 1970; PhDChemE, U. Ariz., 1976. Rsch. asst. Exxon Prodn. Rsch., Houston, 1969; project engr. EPA, 1970-73; asst. prof. chem. engring. U. Utah, Salt Lake City, 1977-82, assoc. prof., 1982-85, prof., 1985—, assoc. dean Grad. Sch., 1983-87, dean Coll. Engring., 1987-98, v.p., 1998-99, sr. v.p. acad. affairs, 2000—; asst. to pres. Reaction Engring. Inc., Salt Lake City, 1990—. Vis. scientist Internat. Flame Rsch. Found., Ijmuiden, The Netherlands, 1972-73; vis. assoc. prof. chem. engring. U. Ariz., Tuscon, 1976-77; cons. Energy and Environ. Rsch. Ctr., Irvine, Calif., 1974-90, Acurex Corp., Mountain View, Calif., 1974-79, Kennecott Corp., Salt Lake City, 1979-81, Nat. Bur. Standards, Washington, 1976-78, Geneva Steel, 1989-95; assoc. dir. Engring. Rsch. Ctr., NSF, 1986-97. Contbr. articles to profl. publs.; patentee in field. Maj. USPHS, 1970-73. Recipient Disting. Teaching award U. Utah, 1982, Disting. Rsch. award U. Utah, 1990; grantee NSF, PYI, 1984-90. Mem. Am. Inst. Chem. Engrs., Combustion Inst. Methodist. Office: U Utah Coll Engring 201 Presidents Cir Rm 205 Salt Lake City UT 84112-9007 E-mail: david.pershing@utah.edu

PERSON, EVERT BERTIL, newspaper and radio executive; b. Berkeley, Calif., Apr. 6, 1914; s. Emil P. and Elida (Swanson) P.; m. Ruth Finley, Jan. 26, 1944 (dec. May 1985); m. 2d, Norma Joan Betz, Mar. 12, 1986. Student, U. Calif., Berkeley, 1937; LHD, Calif. State Univs., 1983, Sonoma State U., 1993. Co-publisher, sec.-treas. Press Democrat Pub. Co., Santa Rosa, Calif., 1945-72, editor, 1972-73, pres., pub., editor-in-chief, 1973-85; sec.-treas. Finley Broadcasting Co., Santa Rosa, 1945-72, pres., 1972-89, Kawana Pubs., 1975-85; pub. Healdsburg Tribune, 1975-85; prin. Evert B. Person Investments, Santa Rosa, 1985—. Pres. Person Properties Co., Santa Rosa, 1945-70; v.p. Finley Ranch & Land Co., Santa Rosa, 1947-72, pres., 1972-79; pres. Baker Pub. Co., Oreg., 1957-67, Sebastopol (Calif.) Times, 1978-81, Russian River News, Guerneville, Calif., 1978-81; pres. publ. Kawana Pubs., 1978-85; mem. nominating com. AP, 1982-84, [illegible] Sonoma County Taxpayers Assn., 1966-69, San Francisco Spring Opera Assn., 1974-79; bd. dirs. San Francisco Opera, 1986—, v.p., 1988—; pres. Calif. Newspaperboy Found., 1957-58; chmn. Santa Rosa Civic Arts Commn., 1961-62; pres. Santa Rosa Sonoma County Symphony Assn., 1966-68, Luther Burbank Meml. Found., 1979, Santa Rosa Symphony Found., 1967-77; adv. bd. Santa Rosa Salvation Army, 1959-67, commodore 12th Coast Guard Dist. Aux., 1969-70; trustee Desert Mus., Palm Springs, 1987-92, v.p. Nat. Bd. Canine Companions, Inc., 1989-92. Decorated Knight of the Holy Sepulchre. Mem. Calif. Newspaper Pubs. Assn. (pres. 1981-82), Internat. Newspaper Fin. Execs. (pres. 1961-62), Bohemian Club, Sonoma County Press Club, Santa Rosa Golf and Country club, The Springs Club, Santa Rosa Rotary (past pres.), Masons (33 degree, Legion of Merit), Shriners. Roman Catholic. Home: 775 White Oak Dr Santa Rosa CA 95409-6155 Office: The Oaks 1400 N Dutton Ave Ste 12 Santa Rosa CA 95401-4644

PERTH, ROD, network entertainment executive; b. L.A. s. Milford (Robert) Martinson and Phyllis (Hove) Perth; m. JIll Sunderland, Apr. 27, 1974; children: Chelseah, Lauren, Erica. BS in Mgmt., San Jose State U., 1966. V.p., gen. mgr. spot sales CBS TV, N.Y.C., 1974-86; v.p., station mgr. WBBM-TV, Chgo., 1986-89; sr. v.p. late night non-network programming CBS-TV, L.A., 1989-94; pres. entertainment USA Network, L.A., 1994-95; pres. HRTS, L.A., 1995-99, Jim Henson T.V. Account exec. KNXT, L.A., 1968-71; ea. mgr. spot sales CBS, N.Y.C., 1971-74; dir. midwest spot sales, CBS, Chgo., 1974-76; dir. sales KMOX-TV, St. Louis, 1976-79, bd. dirs. HRTS. Bd. mem. State St. Coun., Chgo., 1988; contbr. L.E.A.R.N. program, L.A., 1995, Alliance for Children, L.A., 1996. Lt.j.g., U.S. Navy, 1968-74. Named Man of Yr., Alliance for Children, L.A., 1996. Mem. Hollywood (Calif.) Radio and TV Soc. (pres. 1995—). Avocations: skiing, mororcycling, photography. Office: Jim Henson Television 1416 N Labrea Ave Hollywood CA 90068

PERU, RAMIRO G. metal products executive; BS in Bus. Adminstrn., U. Ariz.; postgrad., Duke U. Acct. western contrs. dept. Phelps Dodge Corp., 1979, various positions in acctg. and fin., 1979-87, contr. Phelpd Dodge Minign Co., 1987, asst. contr., v.p. Phelps Dodge Mining Co., 1993, v.p., treas., 1995, sr. v.p., 1997, sr. v.p. orgn. devel. and info. tech., CFO, 1999—. Office: Phelps Dodge Corp 2600 N Central Ave Phoenix AZ 85004-3014

PESHKIN, SAMUEL DAVID, lawyer; b. Des Moines, Oct. 6, 1925; s. Louis and Mary (Grund) P.; m. Shirley R. Isenberg, Aug. 17, 1947; children: Lawrence Allen, Linda Ann. BA, State U. Iowa, 1948, JD, 1951. Bar: Iowa 1951. Ptnr. Bridges & Peshkin, Des Moines, 1953-66, Peshkin & Robinson, Des Moines, 1966-82. Mem. Iowa Bd. Law Examiners, 1970—. Bd. dirs. State U. Iowa Found., 1957—, Old Gold Devel. Fund, 1956—, Sch. Religion U. Iowa, 1966—. Fellow Am. Bar Found., Internat. Soc. Barristers; mem. ABA (chmn. standing com. membership 1959— , ho. of dels. 1968— , bd. govs. 1973—), Iowa Bar Assn. (bd. govs. 1958— , pres. jr. bar sect. 1958-59, award of merit 1974), Inter-Am. Bar Assn., Internat. Bar Assn., Am. Judicature Soc., State U. Iowa Alumni Assn. (dir., pres. 1957) Home: 6445 E Winchcomb Dr Scottsdale AZ 85254-3356

PETAK, WILLIAM JOHN, systems management educator; b. Johnstown, Pa., June 23, 1932; s. Val Andrew and Lola Agatha (Boroski) P.; m. Ramona Janet Cayuela, Dec. 28, 1957; children: Elizabeth Ann Petak-Aaron, William Matthew, Michael David. BS in Mech. Engring., U. Pitts., 1956; MBA, U. So. Calif., 1963, DPA, 1969. Engr. Northrop Corp., Hawthorne, Calif., 1956-59; test engr. Wyle Labs., El Segundo, 1959-63; we. regional mgr. Instrument div. Budd Co., Phoenixville, Pa., 1963-69; v.p., dir. J.H. Wiggins Co., Redondo Beach, Calif., 1969-81; prof. systems mgmt. U. So. Calif., L.A., 1982-98, exec. dir. Inst. Safety and Sys. Mgmt., 1987-98, prof. policy, planning and devel., 1998—. Chmn. earthquake mitigation com. Nat. Com. on Property Ins., Boston, 1990-92; mem. com. on natural disasters NRC, Washington, 1985-91, mem. U.S. nat. com. for the decade for natural disaster reduction, 1989-92. Co-author: Natural Hazard Risk Assessment and Public Policy, 1982, Politics and Economics of Earthquake Hazard Reduction, 1986, Disabled Persons and Earthquake Hazards, 1988; editor spl. issue Pub. Adminstrn. Rev., 1985. Commr. County of Los Angeles, 1994—; mem. policy bd. So. Calif. Earthquake Prep. Project, L.A., 1986-92; trustee Marymount Coll., Palos Verdes, Calif., 1974—. Sgt. U.S. Army, 1950-52. Mem. Soc. for Risk Analysis, Earthquake Engring. Rsch. Inst., Am. Soc. for Pub. Adminstrn., Sigma Xi. Republican. Roman Catholic. Avocations: skiing, fishing, hiking. Office: U So Calif MC 0626 Sch Policy Planning & Devel Los Angeles CA 90089-0001

PETER, RICHARD ECTOR, zoology educator; b. Medicine Hat, Alta., Can., Mar. 7, 1943; s. Arthur E. and Josephine (Wrobleski) P.; m. Leona L. Booth, Dec. 27, 1965; children: Jason E., Matthew T.B. BSc with honors, U. Atla., 1965; PhD, U. Wash., 1969. Postdoctoral fellow U. Bristol, Eng., 1969-70; asst. prof. U. Alta., Edmonton, 1971-74, assoc. prof., 1974-79, prof., 1979—, chmn. dept. zoology, 1983-89, 90-92, dean of sci., 1992—. Contbr. over 300 papers to sci. publs. Recipient Outstanding Leadership in Alberta Sci. award Alberta Sci. and Tech. Leadership Awards Found., 1998; named Disting. Biologist, Can. Coun. Univ. Biology Chairmen. Fellow AAAS, Royal Soc. Can.; mem. Can. Soc. Zoology (pres. 1991-92), Endocrine Soc., Soc. for Study of Reprodn., Internat. Soc. Neuroendocrinology, Can. Coun. of Univ. Biology Chmn. (pres. 1986-87), Internat. Fedn. Comparative Endocrinol. Socs. (pres. 1989-93, Pickford medal 1985), Canadian Conf. of Deans of Sci., 1995-96 (pres.), Western Can. Univs. Marine Scis. Soc. (pres. 2001—).

PETERS, AULANA LOUISE, lawyer, former government agency commissioner; b. Shreveport, La., Nov. 30, 1941; d. Clyde A. and Eula Mae (Faulkner) Pharis; m. Bruce F. Peters, Oct. 6, 1967. BA in Philosophy, Coll. New Rochelle, 1963; JD, U. So. Calif., 1973. Bar: Calif., 1974. Sec., English corr. Publimondial, Spa, Milan, Italy, 1963-64, Fibramianto, Spa, Milan, 1964-65, Turkish del. to Office for Econ. Cooperation & Devel., Paris, 1965-66; adminstrv. asst. Office for Econ. Cooperation & Devel., Paris, 1966-67; assoc. Gibson, Dunn & Crutcher, L.A., 1973-80, ptnr., 1980-84, 88—; commr. SEC, Washington, 1984-88. Bd. dirs. 3M Corp., Merrill Lynch & Co., Mobil Corp., Northrop Grumman, Callaway Golf Co. Recipient Disting. Alumnus award Econs. Club So. Calif., 1984, Washington Achiever award Nat. Assn. Bank Women, 1986, Critics Choice award nat. Women's Econ. Alliance, 1994, Women in Bus. award H0llywood C. of C., 1995. Mem. ABA, State Bar of Calif. (civil litigation cons. group 1983-84), Los Angeles County Bar Assn., Black Women Lawyers Assn. L.A., Assn. Bus. Trial Lawyers (panelist L.A. 1982), Women's Forum, Washington. Office: Gibson Dunn & Crutcher 333 S Grand Ave Ste 4400 Los Angeles CA 90071-3197

PETERS, CHARLES WILLIAM, research and development company manager; b. Pierceton, Ind., Dec. 9, 1927; s. Charles Frederick and Zelda May (Line) P.; m. Katharine Louise Schuman, May 29, 1953; 1 child, Susan Kay; m. 2d, Patricia Ann Miles, Jan. 2, 1981; children: Bruce Miles Merkle, Leslie Ann Merkle Sanaie, Philip Frank Merkle, William Macneil Merkle. AB, Ind. U., 1950; postgrad. U. Md., 1952-58. Supervisory rsch. physicist Naval Rsch. Lab., Washington, 1950-71; physicist EPA, Washington, 1971-76; mgr. advanced systems EATON-Consol. Controls Corp., Springfield, Va., 1976-89, v.p. Nuclear Diagnostic Systems, Inc., Springfield, Va, 1989-92, cons. Am. Tech. Inst., 1993—. With U.S. Army, 1945-47. Mem. IEEE, AAAS, Am. Phys. Soc. Home and Office: 5235 N Whispering Hills Ln Tucson AZ 85704-2510

PETERS, DOUGLAS CAMERON, mining engineer, geologist; b. Pitts., June 19, 1955; s. Donald Cameron and Twila (Bingel) P. BS in Earth and Planetary Sci., U. Pitts., 1977; MS in Geology, Colo. Sch. Mines, 1981, MS in Mining Engring., 1983. Technician, inspector Engring. Mechanics Inc., Pitts., 1973-77; rsch. asst. Potential Gas Agy., Golden, Colo., 1977-78; [illegible] Co., Golden, 1981-82, Golden, 1982-84; mining engr., prin. investigator U.S. Bur. Mines, Denver, 1984-96; owner Peters Geoscis., Golden, 1996—. Bur. rep. to Geosat Com., 1984-95; program chmn. GeoTech Conf., Denver, 1984-88, mem. long range planning subcom., 1989-92, gen. chmn., 1991; engr. in tng. #11800, Colo., profl. geologist, Wyo., #367, Pa., 2365. Author: Physical Modeling of Draw of Broken Rock in Caving, 1984, bur. mines articles and reports; editor COGS computer contbns., 1986-90, Geology in Coal Resource Utilization, 1988-91, Atlas of Coal Geology, 1999, Remote Sensing for Site Characterization, 2000; assoc. editor: Computers & Geosciences, 1991-2000; contbr. articles to profl. jours.; guest editor various jours.; dep. editor: Natural Resources Research, 1999—. Recipient award Am. Inst. Profl. Geologists, 1984, 85, 86, Appreciation award, 1987, Spl. award Denver Geotech Com., 1988, Appreciation award, 1989. Mem. Am. Inst. Profl. geologists (cert. profl. geologist # 8274, sec. Colo. sect. 1997, pres. elect 1998, pres. 1999), Am. Assn. Petroleum Geologists (astrogeology com. 1984-2000, pub. com. 1995—, Energy Mineral divsn. v.p. 1990-91, pres. 1991-92, chmn. pubs. com. 1990-98, remote sensing com. 1990—, Cert. Merit 1992, 93, 99, Pres.'s award 1993, Disting. Svc. award 1994, assoc. editor Search and Discovery 2000—), Am. Soc. Photogrammetry and Remote Sensing, Nat. Space Soc., Computer Oriented Geol. Soc. (charter, com. chmn. 1983-95, pres. 1985, dir. 1986, contbg. editor newsletter 1985-96), Assn. Exploration Geochemists, Geol. Soc. Am., Rocky Mountain Assn. Geologists, Soc. Mining Metallurgy and Exploration, Planetary Soc., Space Studies Inst., Denver Mining Club. Republican. E-mail: petersdc@petersgeo.com

PETERS, JANICE C. cable company executive; b. Harlan, Ky., Apr. 23, 1951; m. Mike Peters; 2 children. BS, Wayne State U., 1972; MBA in Mgmt., Stanford U., 1989. Customer svc. rep. Mich. Bell, 1973-78; with AT&T Corp., Chgo., 1978-85, U.S. West, Denver, Seattle, London, from 1985, MediaOne, Englewood, Colo., CEO, pres., 1997—. Bd. dirs. Primus. Office: c/o MediaOne 188 Inverness Dr W Englewood CO 80112

PETERS, JOSEPH DONALD, filmmaker; b. Montebello, Calif., Mar. 7, 1958; s. Donald Harry and Anna Lucia (Suarez) P. BA in Comm., U. So. Calif., L.A., 1982. Filmmaker Renaissance Prodns., Ltd., San Dimas, Calif., 1986—. Writer, prodr., dir. films, TV, Seniors and Alcohol Abuse, 1986, Eskimo Ice Cream Shoes, 1990 (Gold award 1991), Rachel, 1994 (Silver and Bronze award 1995), The Adventures of Sam and Kathy, 1998, Emotions, 1999 (Gold and Honorable Mention award 1999); dir. stage All's Fair in Love and ..., 2001. Nominated Internat. Man. of Yr. Internat. Biog. Ctr., 2000. Mem. Am. Film Inst., Film Artists Network, Cinewomen. Avocations: reading film books, collecting videos, sporting events. Office: Renaissance Prodns Ltd Ste 48 301 N San Dimas Canyon Rd San Dimas CA 91773-2734 E-mail: jpeters@directorsnet.com

PETERS, LEROY RICHARD, materials management consulting company executive; b. Milw., June 26, 1943; s. LeRoy Edwin and Eleanor Hedwig (Bensing) Peters; m. Barbara Jean Hackney, Nov. 18, 1964 (div. July 1970); 1 child, Neal; m. Nancy Elizabeth Till, July 17, 1971; children: Richard, Brenda, Eric, Linda. BS, U. Wis., 1966; Grad., U.S. Army/Command and, Gen. Staff Coll., Ft. Leavenworth, Kans., 1977. Cert. fellow in prodn. and inventory mgmt. Inventory supr. Bucyrus Erie, Erie, Pa. and Pocatello, Idaho, ach3-76; inventory mgr. Am. Microsystems, Pocatello, 1976-78; prodn. mgr. Worthington Compressor, Buffalo, 1978-80; mfg. mgr. St. Regis WPM Div., Denver, 1980-82; materials mgr. Robinson Brick Co., Denver, 1982-86; prodn. mgr. Merritt Equipment Co., Denver, 1986-89; instructional designer Martin Marietta, Denver, 1989-90; sr. cons. J.D. Edwards, Denver, 1990-93; sr. cons. mgr. AMX Internat., 1993-97; v.p. The Thompson Group, 1997-98; CEO, Enterprise Resource Mgmt., Inc., 1998—. Editoral com.: Aerospace and Defense Dictionary, 1990; contbr. articles to profl. jours. Scoutmaster Boy Scouts Am., Denver, 1989, cubmaster, 1988, outdoor chmn., Denver, 1990; dist. capt. Adams County Colo. Reps., Denver, 1986. Col. U.S. Army, 1966-94, Vietnam, Desert Storm. Decorated Legion of Merit, Bronze Star, Meritorious Svc. medal, Army Commendation medal. Fellow Am. Prodn. and Inventory Control Soc. (bd. dirs. region VI 1990—, pres. Colo. chpt. 1989-90); mem. Am. Def. Preparedness Assn., Moose. Lutheran. Avocations: fishing, reading, music, photography, geology. Home: 1468 W 111th Ave Northglenn CO 80234-3397

PETERS, RICHARD T. lawyer; b. La Mesa, Calif., Sept. 24, 1946; BA, Santa Clara U., 1968; JD, UCLA, 1971. Bar: Calif. 1972. Ptnr. Sidley & Austin, L.A., 1995—. Mem. Am. Coll. Bankruptcy (regent; chair 9th civic admissions coun.), State Bar Calif. (mem. debtor-creditor rels. and bankruptcy subcom. bus. law sect. 1979-81, chmn. 1981-82, mem. exec. com. bus. law sect. 1982-85, vice chmn. 1984-85), Calif. Continuing Edn. Bar (cons. 1984, 95), L.A. Fin. Lawyers Conf. (bd. govs. 1976-80), L.A. County Bar Assn. (comml. law and bankruptcy sect., bankruptcy com. 1996—). Office: Sidley & Austin 555 W 5th St Fl 40 Los Angeles CA 90013-1010

PETERS, ROBERT WOOLSEY, architect; b. Mpls., Mar. 24, 1935; s. John Eugene and Adelaide Elizabeth (Woolsey) P. BArch., U. Minn., 1958; MArch., Yale U., 1964. Registered architect, N.Mex. Participating assoc. Skidmore Owings & Merrill, Chgo., 1961-74; dir. design Schaefer & Assocs., Wichita, Kans., 1975-76; ptnr. Addy & Peters, Albuquerque, 1979-82; owner, sole proprietor Robert W. Peters AIA Architect, Albuquerque, 1985—. Exhibited work Centre Georges Pompidou, Paris, 1980, U. Art Mus., Albuquerque, 1982, 92, Albuquerque Mus., 1988; contbr. articles to Century Mag., Progressive Architecture, House & Garden, House Beautiful, also others. Recipient honor awards N.Mex. Soc. Architects, 1980-83, 86, 87, 92, HUD, 1980; 5th Nat. Passive Solar Conf., Amherst, Mass., 1981. Fellow AIA; mem. Contemporary Art Soc. N.Mex. (bd. dirs., pres.), Yale N.Mex. Democrat. Roman Catholic. Fax: (505) 898-4689

PETERSDORF, ROBERT GEORGE, physician, medical educator, academic administrator; b. Berlin, Feb. 14, 1926; s. Hans H. and Sonja P.; m. Patricia Horton Qua, June 2, 1951; children: Stephen Hans, John Eric. BA, Brown U., 1948, DMS (hon.), 1983; MD cum laude, Yale U., 1952; ScD (hon.), Albany Med. Coll., 1979; MA (hon.), Harvard U., 1980; DMS (hon.), Med. Coll. Pa., 1982, Brown U., 1983; DMS, Bowman-Gray Sch. Medicine, 1986; LHD (hon.), N.Y. Med. Coll., 1986; DSc (hon.), SUNY, Bklyn., 1987, Med. Coll. Ohio, , 1987, Univ. Health Scis., The Chgo. Med. Sch., 1987, St. Louis U., 1988; LHD (hon.), Ea. Va. Med. Sch., 1988; DSc (hon.), Sch. Medicine, Georgetown U., 1991, Emory U., 1992, Tufts U., 1993, Mt. Sinai Sch. Medicine, 1993, George Washington U., 1994; other hon. degrees. Diplomate Am. Bd. Internal Medicine. Intern, asst. resident Yale U., New Haven, 1952-54; sr. asst. resident Peter Bent Brigham Hosp., Boston, 1954-55; fellow Johns Hopkins Hosp., Balt., 1955-59; chief resident, instr. medicine Yale U., 1957-58; asst. prof. medicine Johns Hopkins U., 1958-60, physician, 1958-60; assoc. prof. medicine U. Wash., Seattle, 1960-62, prof., 1962-79, chmn. dept. medicine, 1964-79; physician-in-chief U. Wash. Hosp., 1964-79; pres. Brigham and Women's Hosp., Boston, 1979-81; prof. medicine Harvard U. Med. Sch., Boston, 1979-81; dean, vice chancellor health scis. U. Calif.-San Diego Sch. Medicine, 1981-86; clin. prof. infectious diseases Sch. Medicine Georgetown U., 1986-94; pres. Assn. Am. Med. Colls., Washington, 1986-94, pres. emeritus, 1994—; prof. medicine U. Wash., 1994—, disting. prof., sr. advisor to dean, 1998—; disting. physician Vets. Health Adminstrn., Seattle, 1993-98, sr. physician, 1998—. Cons. to surgeon gen. USPHS, 1960-79; cons. USPHS Hosp., Seattle, 1962-79; mem. spl. med. adv. group VA, 1987-94. Editor: Harrison's Priciples of Internal Medicine, 1968-90; contbr. numerous articles to profl. jours. Served with USAAF, 1944-46. Recipient Lilly medal Royal Coll. Physicians, London, 1978, Wiggers [illegible] Med. Coll., 1979, Robert H. Williams award Assn. Profs Medicine, 1983, Keen award Brown U., 1980, Disting. Svc. award Baylor Coll. Medicine, 1989, Scroll of Merit Nat. Med. Assn., 1990, 2d Ann. Founder's award Assn. Program Dirs. in Internal Medicine, 1991, Flexner award Assn. Amer. Med. Coll., 1994; named Disting. Internist of 1987, Am. Soc. Internal Medicine. Master: ACP (pres. 1975-76, Stengel award 1980, Disting. Tchr. award 1993, Laureate award Wash. chpt.), fellow: AAAS, Execs. Assn. (hon.); mem. Inst. Medicine of NAS (councillor 1977-80), Assn. Am. Physicians (pres. 1976-77, Kober medal 1996), Cosmos Club, Rainier Club. Home and Office: 1219 Parkside Dr E Seattle WA 98112-3717

PETERSEN, DAVID A. state legislator, financial advisor; b. Mesa, Ariz., Sept. 20, 1950; m. Patti Briggs; 8 children. Student, Ariz. State U., 1971-73, U. Phoenix, 1993. Fin. svcs. advisor, 1976—; mem. Ariz. Senate, Dist. 29, Phoenix, 1994—; mem. edn. com., family svcs. com., Rep. whip Ariz. State Senate. Leader Boy Scouts Am. Republican. Mem. LDS Ch. Office: State Capitol Bldg 1700 W Washington St # 213 Phoenix AZ 85007-2812 also: 623 N Miller St Mesa AZ 85203-7229 E-mail: dpeterse@azleg.state.az.us

PETERSEN, FINN BO, oncologist, educator; b. Copenhagen, Mar. 26, 1951; came to U.S., 1983; s. Jorgen and Ebba Gjeding (Jorgensen) P.; m. Merete Secher Lund, Mar. 7, 1979; children: Lars Secher, Thomas Secher, Andreas Secher. BA, Niels Steensen, Copenhagen, 1971; MD, U. Copenhagen, 1978. Intern U. Copenhagen, Copenhagen, 1978-79, resident in hematology, 1980-83; fellow oncology Fred Hutchinson Cancer Rsch. Ctr. U. Wash., Seattle, 1983-85, assoc. rschr. oncology, 1985-87, asst. mem. in clin. rsch., 1987-91, asst. prof., 1988-91, prof. medicine, 1992—; program dir. U. Utah Blood and Marrow Transplant, 1992—; med. dir. bone marrow transplant program LDS Hosp., 1997—. Author: Hematology, 1977; contbr. articles to profl. jours. Mem. AMA, AAAS, Internat. Soc. Exptl. Hematology, Am. Soc. Clin. Oncology, Am. Soc. Hematology, Assn. Gnotobiology. Office: U Utah Bone Marrow Transplant Program Div Hematology & Oncology Salt Lake City UT 84132-0001

PETERSEN, MARTIN EUGENE, curator; b. Grafton, Iowa, Apr. 21, 1931; s. Martin S. and Martha Dorothea (Paulsen) P. B.A., State U. Iowa, 1951, M.A., 1957; postgrad., The Hague (Netherlands), 1964. Curator San Diego Mus. Art, 1957-96; advisor Olaf Wieghorst Mus., El Cajon, Calif., 1996—. Extension instr. U. Calif., 1958, lectr., 1960 Author art catalogues, books, articles in field. Served with AUS, 1952-54. Mem. So. Calif. Art Historians. Home: 2003 Bayview Heights Dr Spc 138 San Diego CA 92105-5537

PETERSEN, RICHARD HERMAN, federal agency administrator, aeronautical engineer; b. Quincy, Ill., Oct. 9, 1934; s. Herman Hiese and Nancy (Getty) P.; m. Joandra Windsor Shenk, Sept. 15, 1959; children: Eric Norman, Kristin. BS in Aero. Engring., Purdue U., 1956, Dr. Engring. (hon.), 1986; MS in Aeronautics, Calif. Inst. Tech., 1957; D in Pub. Service (hon.), George Washington U., 1987; DSc (hon.), Coll. of William and Mary, 1992. Rsch. engr. NASA Ames Rsch. Ctr., Moffett Field, Calif., 1957-63, aerospace engr., 1963-65, 66-70, br. chief, 1970-73, div. chief, 1975-80; aerospace engr. NASA, Washington, 1965-66; exec. Nielsen Engring. & Rsch. Inc., Mountain View, Calif., 1973-75; dep. dir. NASA Langley Research Ctr., Hampton, Va., 1980-85, dir., 1985-91; assoc. adminstr. Aeronautics and Space Tech. NASA Hdqrs., Washington, 1991-93, retired, 1993; aerospace cons., 1993—. 1st lt. USAF, 1957-60. Recipient Disting. Alumnus award Purdue U., 1980, Meritorious Exec. award U.S. Pres., 1982, Disting. Exec. award U.S. Pres., 1989; Sloan exec. fellow Stanford U., 1973. Fellow AIAA (bd. dirs. 1984-90, Sylvanus A. Reed Aeronautics award 1991), Nat. Acad. Engring. Republican. Avocations: golf, skiing. Home and Office: 352 Dunemere Dr La Jolla CA 92037-5311

PETERSEN, ROBERT E. magazine publishing executives; b. Los Angeles, Calif., Sept. 10, 1926; s. Einar and Bertha (Putera) P.; m. Margie McNally, Jan. 26, 1963. Founder, chmn. bd. emeritus Petersen Pub. Co. (pubs. Hot Rod, Motor Trend, Car Craft, Motorcyclist, Photog., Skin Diver, Teen, Hunting, Guns & Ammo, Circle Track, Dirt Rider, Los Angeles, 1948-2000; owner, chmn. bd. Petersen Properties, L.A., 1996—; owner Petersen Aviation, Van Nuys, Calif., 1996—, Sports Afield mag. Mem. Los Angeles Library Commn., 1963-64; Bd. dirs. Boys Club Am., past pres. Hollywood br.; bd. dirs. Thalians; founder Petersen Automotive Mus., L.A. Served with USAF. Clubs: So. Calif Safari, Confrerie de la Chaine des Rotisseurs, Chevaliers du Tastevin. Office: Petersen Pub Co 6420 Wilshire Blvd Los Angeles CA 90048-5502

PETERSON, ANDREA LENORE, law educator; b. L.A., July 21, 1952; d. Vincent Zetterberg and Elisabeth (Karlsson) P.; m. Michael Rubin, May 29, 1983; children: Peter Rubin, Eric Rubin, Emily Rubin. AB, Stanford U., 1974; JD, U. Calif., Berkeley, 1978. Bar: Calif., 1979, U.S. Dist. Ct. (no. dist.) Calif., 1979. Law clk. to Judge Charles B. Renfrew U.S. Dist. Ct. (no. dist.) Calif., San Francisco, 1978-79; lawyer Cooley, Godward, Castro, Huddleson & Tatum, San Francisco, 1979-80; law clk. to Justice Byron R. White U.S. Supreme Ct., Washington, 1980-81; lawyer Heller, Ehrman, White & McAuliffe, San Francisco, 1981-83; prof. law Boalt Hall U. Calif., Berkeley, 1983—. Contbr. articles to profl. jours. Office: U Calif Sch Law Boalt Hall Berkeley CA 94720

PETERSON, BARBARA ANN BENNETT, history educator, television personality; b. Portland, Oreg., Sept. 6, 1942; d. George Wright and Hope (Chatfield) Bennett; m. Frank Lynn Peterson, July 1, 1967. BA, BS, Oreg. State U., 1964; MA, Stanford U., 1965; PhD, U. Hawaii, 1978; PhD (hon.), London Inst. Applied Rsch., 1991, Australian Inst. Coordinated R, 1995. Prof. history U. Hawaii, 1967-95, prof. emeritus history, 1995—, chmn. social scis. divsn., 1971-73, 75-76, asst. dean, 1973-74, prof. emeritus, 1995—; prof. history Oreg. State U., 2000—. Prof. Asian history and European colonial history and world problems Chapman Coll. World Campus Afloat Semester At Sea, 1974, European overseas exploration, expansion and colonialism U. Colo., Boulder, 1978, Modern China, Modern East Asia, The West in the World U. Pitts., 1999; assoc. prof. U. Hawaii-Manoa Coll. Continuing Edn., 1981; Fulbright prof. history Wuhan (China) U., 1988-89; Fulbright rsch. prof. Sophia U., Japan, 1978; rsch. assoc. Bishop Mus., 1995-98; lectr. Capital Spkrs., Washington, 1987—; prof. Hawaii State Ednl. Channel, 1993-97; adj. fellow East-West Ctr., Honolulu, 1998—; prof. history U. Pitts. Semester at Sea, fall 1999; adj. prof. Hawaii Pacific U. Co-author: Women's Place is in the History Books, Her Story, 1962-1980: A Curriculum Guide for American History Teachers, 1980; author: America in British Eyes, 1988, John Bull's Eye on America, 1995; editor: Notable Women of Hawaii, 1984, (with W. Solheim) The Pacific Region, 1990, 91, American History: 17th, 18th and 19th Centuries, 1993, America: 19th and 20th Centuries, 1993, Notable Women of China, 2000 (nominated for Pulitzer Prize 2001), Hawaii in the World, 2000; assoc. editor Am. Nat. Biography, 1998 (Dartmouth medal); contbr. articles to profl. publs. Participant People-to-People Program, Eng., 1964, Expt. in Internat. Living Program, Nigeria, 1966; chmn. 1st Nat. Women's History Week, Hawaii, 1982; pres. Bishop Mus. Coun., 1993-94; active mem. Hawaii Commn. on Status of Women; fundraiser local mus. and children's activities. Fulbright scholar, Japan, 1967, sr. tchg. Fulbright scholar, China, 1988-89; NEH-Woodrow Wilson fellow Princeton U., 1980; recipient state proclamations Gov. of Hawaii, 1982, City of Honolulu and Hawaii State Legis., 1982, Outstanding Tchr. of Yr. award Wuhan (China), U., 1988, Medallion of Excellence award Am. Biog. Assn., 1989, Woman of Yr. award, 1991; inducted into the Women's Hall of Fame, Seneca Falls, N.Y., 1991; co-champion Hawaii State Husband and Wife Mixed Doubles Tennis Championship, 1985. Fellow World Lit. Acad. (Eng.); mem. AAUW, Am. Hist. Assn. (mem. numerous coms.), Am. Studies Assn. (pres. 1984-85), Fulbright Assn. (founding pres. Hawaii chpt. 1984-88, mem. nat. steering com. chairwomen ann. conf. 1990), Am. Coun. on Edn., Maison Internat. des Intellectuals, France, Hawaii Found. History and Humanities (mem. editl. bd. 1972-73), Hawaii Hist. Assn., Women in Acad. Adminstrn., Pi Beta Phi, Phi Kappa Phi. Avocation: writing, cooking, fund raising for charity and children's organizations and museums, gardening, travel. Office: East West Ctr Burns Hall 1601 East West Rd Honolulu HI 96848-1601 also: Oreg State U History Dept 306 Milam Hill Corvallis OR 97331

PETERSON, CHASE N. university president; b. Logan, Utah, Dec. 27, 1929; s. E.G. and Phebe (Nebeker) P.; m. Grethe Ballif, 1956; children: Erika Elizabeth, Stuart Ballif, Edward Chase. A.B., Harvard U., 1952, M.D., 1956. Diplomate: Am. Bd. Internal Medicine. Asst. prof. medicine U. Utah Med. Sch., 1965-67; assoc. Salt Lake Clinic; dean admissions and fin. aids to students Harvard U., 1967-72, v.p. univ., 1972-78; v.p. health scis. U. Utah, Salt Lake City, 1978-83, prof. medicine, 1983—, pres., 1983-91, clin. prof. medicine, 1991—. Pres. emeritus U. Utah, Salt Lake City, 1992—; bd. dirs. First Security Corp., Utah Power & Light Co., D.C. Tanner Co., OEC Med. Systems. Mem. Nat. Assn. State Univs. and Land-Grant Colls. (chmn. 1988-89, chair U.S. Ofc. Tech. Assessment adv. bd. 1990-92). Home: 66 Thaynes Canyon Dr Park City UT 84060-6711 Office: U Utah Sch Medicine 50 N Medical Dr Rm 1c26 Salt Lake City UT 84132-0001

PETERSON, COURTLAND HARRY, law educator; b. Denver, June 28, 1930; s. Harry James and Courtney (Caple) P.; m. Susan Schwab, Gisvold, Jan. 28, 1966; children: Brooke, Linda, Patrick. B.A., U. Colo., 1951, LL.B., 1953; M.C.L., U. Chgo., 1959; J.D., U. Freiburg, Ger., 1964. Bar: Colo. 1953. Mem. faculty U. Colo. Law Sch., 1959—, prof., 1963—, dean, 1974-79, Nicholas Rosenbaum prof., 1991-94, Nicholas Doman prof. emeritus, 1995—. Vis. prof. U. Calif. Law Sch., Los Angeles, 1965, Max Planck Inst., Hamburg, Ger., 1969-70, U. Tex. Law Sch., Austin, 1973-74, Summer Program, Tulane U., Rodos, Greece, 1993, Summer Program, La. State U., Aix-en-Provence, France, 1996; bd. dirs. Continuing Legal Edn. in Colo., 1974-77 Author: Die Anerkennung Auslaendischer Urteile, 1964; Translator: (Bauer) An Introduction to German Law, 1965. Served to 1st lt. USAF, 1954-56. Fgn. Law fellow U. Chgo., 1957-59; Ford Found. Law Faculty fellow, 1964; Alexander von Humboldt Stiftun fellow, 1969-70 Mem. ABA, Colo. Bar Assn. (bd. govs. 1974-79), Boulder County Bar Assn., Am. Soc. Comparative Law (dir., bd. editors, treas. 1978-89, hon. pres. 1996-98), Internat. Acad. Comparative Law, Am. Law Inst., Boulder County Bar Found. (trustee 1995-2000). Home: 205 Camden Pl Boulder CO 80302-8032 Office: U Colo Law Sch Boulder CO 80309-0001

PETERSON, CRAIG ANTON, former state legislator; b. Salt Lake City, May 23, 1947; m. Annette Langford, Nov. 15, 1972; 5 children. BS Mfg. Engring. Tech., Weber State U., 1966; postgrad., Tex. A&M U., Corpus Christi, 1968-72. Pres. Craig A. Peterson Cons. LLC, Orem, Utah; mem. Utah Ho. of Reps., 1986-88, Utah State Senate, 1988-98, majority whip, 1993-94, majority leader, 1995-98; owner Craig Peterson Cons., Orem, Utah, 1998—. Mem. various coms. including mgmt., retirement, and human svcs. Republican. Office: Craig Peterson Cons 1687 N 200 W Orem UT 84057-8505

PETERSON, EDWIN J. retired supreme court justice, law educator; b. Gilmanton, Wis., Mar. 30, 1930; s. Edwin A. and Leora Grace (Kitelinger) P.; m. Anna Chadwick, Feb. 7, 1971; children: Patricia, Andrew, Sherry. B.S., U. Oreg., 1951, LL.B., 1957. Bar: Oreg. 1957. Assoc. firm Tooze, Kerr, Peterson, Marshall & Shenker, Portland, 1957-61, mem. firm, 1961-79; assoc. justice Supreme Ct. Oreg., Salem, 1979-83, 91-93, chief justice, 1983-91; ret., 1993; disting. jurist-in-residence, adj. instr. Willamette Coll. of Law, Salem, Oreg., 1994—. Chmn. Supreme Ct. Task Force on Racial Issues, 1992-94; mem. standing com. on fed. rules of practice and procedure, 1987-93; bd. dirs. Conf. Chief Justices, 1985-87, 88-91. Chmn. Portland Citizens Sch. Com., 1968-70; vice chmn. Young Republican Fedn. Orgn., 1951; bd. visitors U. Oreg. Law Sch., 1978-83, 87-93, chmn. bd. visitors, 1981-83; pres. Understanding Racism Found., 1999—. Served to 1st lt. USAF, 1952-54. Mem. Oreg. State Bar (bd. examiners 1963-66, gov. 1973-76, vice chmn. profl. liability fund 1977-78), Multnomah County Bar Assn. (pres. 1972-73), Phi Alpha Delta, Lambda Chi Alpha. Episcopalian. Home: 3365 Sunridge Dr S Salem OR 97302-5950 Office: Willamette Univ Coll Law 245 Winter St SE Salem OR 97301-3916 E-mail: epeterso@willamette.edu

PETERSON, ERLE VIDAILLET, retired metallurgical engineer; b. Idaho Falls, Idaho, Apr. 29, 1915; s. Vier P. and Marie (Vidaillet) P.; m. Rosemary Sherwood, June 3, 1955; children: Kent Sherwood, Pamela Jo. BS in Mining Engring., U. Idaho, 1940; MS in Mining Engring., U. Utah, 1941. Tech. advisor Remington Arms Co., Salt Lake City, 1941-43; constrn. engr. plutonium plant duPont, Hanford, Wash., 1943-44, R & D engr. exptl. sta. Wilmington, Del., 1944-51, plant metallurgist heavy water plant Newport, Ind., 1951-57, rsch. metallurgist metals program Balt., 1957-62, prin. project engr. USAF contracts, 1962-68, devel. engr. Wilmington, 1969-80; ret., 1980. Patentee in field; contbr. articles to profl. jours. Candidate for State Senate-Am. Party, Wilmington, 1974; com. chmn. Boy Scouts Am., Wilmington, 1975-78; treas. Local Civic Assn., Wilmington, 1977-79. Rsch. fellow U. Utah, 1940. Mem. Am. Soc. Metallurgists Internat., Del. Assn. Profl. Engrs. Republican. Avocations: lapidary, jewelry making, photography, prospecting, gardening. Home: PO Box 74 Rigby ID 83442-0074

PETERSON, GARY ANDREW, agronomics researcher; b. Holdrege, Nebr., Apr. 30, 1940; s. Walter Andrew and Evelyn Christine (Johnson) P.; m. Jacquelyn Charlene Flick, June 18, 1965; children: Kerstin, Ingrid. BS, U. Nebr., 1963, MS, 1965; PhD, Iowa State U., 1967. Research assoc. agronomy Iowa State U., Ames, 1964-67; prof. U. Nebr., Lincoln, 1967-84; prof. soil and crop scis. Colo. State U., Ft. Collins, 1984—. Assoc. editor AGronomy Jour., 1979-81, tech. editor, 1981-83, editor, 1984-89, editor-in-chief, 1991-96; contbr. articles to profl. jours. Fellow Am. Soc. Agronomy (Ciba-Geigy Agr. Achievement award 1974, Agronomic Achievement award-Soils 1990), Soil Sci. Soc. Am. (Applied Rsch. award 1987); mem. Soil Conservation Soc. Am. Republican. Avocations: reading, hiking, skiing. Office: Colo State U Dept Soil Crop Scis Fort Collins CO 80523-0001 E-mail: gpeterso@lamar.colostate.edu

PETERSON, JANE WHITE, nursing educator, anthropologist; b. San Juan, P.R., Feb. 15, 1941; d. Jerome Sidney and Vera (Joseph) Peterson; 1 child, Claire Marie. BS, Boston U., 1968; M in Nursing, U. Wash., 1969, PhD, 1981. Staff nurse Visiting Nurse Assn., Boston, 1964-66; prof. Seattle U., 1969—, dir. nursing home project, 1990-92, chair pers. com., 1988-90; chair dept. Community Health and Psychiat. Mental Health Nursing, 1987-89. Sec. Coun. on Nursing and Anthropology, 1984-86; pres. Wash. League Nursing, Seattle, 1988-90; pres. bd. Vis. Nurses Svcs., Seattle, 1988-90; contbg. cons. CSI Prodn., Okla., 1987; cons. in nursing WHO/U. Indonesia, Jakarta, fall 1989, Myanmar (Burma), Yangon, winter 1995, Beijing, 1995. Contbr. articles to profl. jours., chptrs. to books. Co-owner (with Robert Colley) North End Train Ctr., Seattle; mem. Seattle Art Mus., 1986—. Fellow: Soc. for Applied Anthropology; mem. Am. Anthropological Assn., Soc. for Med. Anthropology, Nat. League for Nursing, Am. Ethological Soc. Office: Seattle U Sch Nursing Broadway and Madison Seattle WA 98122

PETERSON, JOHN LEONARD, lawyer, judge; b. Butte, Mont., Sept. 11, 1933; s. Roy victor and Lena Pauline (Umhang) P.; m. Jean Marie Hollingsworth, June 10, 1957; children: Michael R., John Robert, Carol Jean. BA in Bus., JD, U. Mont., 1957. Bar: Mont. 1957, U.S. Supreme Ct. 1964, U.S. Ct. Appeals (9th cir.) 1974, U.S. Tax Ct. 1978. Assoc. McCaffery, Roe, Kiely & Joyce, 1957-63; ptnr. McCaffery & Peterson, 1963-79; sole practice Butte, 1979-85. Part-time U.S. bankruptcy judge, 1963-85; U.S. bankruptcy judge, Mont., 1985—; bd. govs. Nat. Conf. Bankruptcy Judges, 1989-92. Mem. Mont. Bd. Regents Higher Edn., 1975-82; del. Dem. Nat. Conv., 1968. Mem. Nat. Conf. Bankruptcy Judges, Mont. Bar Assn., Silver bow County Bar Assn., Butte Country Club. Democrat. Lutheran. Office: US Dist Ct Chief Bankruptcy Judge 215 Fed Bldg Butte MT 59701

PETERSON, KEVIN BRUCE, newspaper editor, publishing executive; b. Kitchener, Ont., Can., Feb. 11, 1948; s. Bruce Russell and Marguerite Elizabeth (Hammond) P.; m. Constance Maureen Bailey, Feb. 11, 1975 (dec. May 1975); m. Sheila Helen O'Brien, Jan. 9, 1981 B.A., U. Calgary, Alta., Can., 1968. Chief bur. Calgary Herald, 1972-75, city editor, 1976-77, news editor, 1977-78, bus. editor, 1978, mng. editor, 1978-86, editor, asst. pub., 1986-87, gen. mgr., 1987-88, pub., 1989-96; sr. counsel GPC Comms., 1999—. Pres. Canadian Univ. Press, Ottawa, Ont., Can., 1968-69; dir. New Directions for News. Harry Brittain Meml. fellow Commonwealth Press Union, London, 1979 Mem. Can. Mng. Editors (bd. dirs. 1983-87), Am. Soc. Newspaper Editors, Horsemen's Benevolent and Protective Assn., Alta. Legis. Press Gallery Assn. (v.p. 1971-76), Can. Daily Newspaper Assn. (bd. dirs. 1990-96, vice chmn. , treas 1992, chmn. 1993-96), Alta. Theatre Projects (bd. dirs. 1996—, v.p. 1998—), Calgary Ctr. for Non-Profit Mgmt. (bd. dirs. 1998—), Calgary Petroleum Club, Ranchmen's Club, 100-t-1 Club, (Arcadia, Calif.) Avocations: thoroughbred horse racing; art collecting.

PETERSON, LAURENCE E. physics educator; b. Grantsburg, Wis., July 26, 1931; m. Joelle Dallancon, 1956; children: Mark L., Daniel F., Lynn M., Julianne. BS, U. Minn., 1954, PhD, 1960. Rsch. assoc. in physics U. Minn., Mpls., 1960-62; from resident physicist to prof. physics U. Calif., San Diego, 1962—. Physics subcom. NASA Space Sci. Steering Com., 1964—, assoc. dir. sci. astrophysics divsn., 1986-88; dir. Ctr. Astrophysics & Space Sci., U. Calif., San Diego, 1988—. Fellow NSF, 1958-59, Guggenheim Found., 1973-74. Fellow Am. Phys. Soc.; mem. AIAA (space sci. award 1978), AAAS, Am. Astron. Soc., Internat. Astronomical Union. Office: U Calif San Diego Ctr Astrophysics & Space Scis MC 0424 9500 Gilman Dr La Jolla CA 92093

PETERSON, LEROY, retired secondary education educator; b. Fairfield, Ala., Feb. 15, 1930; s. Leroy and Ludie Pearl (Henderson) P.; m. Theresa Petite, Apr. 6, 1968 (div. Oct. 1984); children: Leroy III, Monica Teresa; m. Ruby Willodine Hopkins, July 21, 1985 (div. Mar. 1996). Cert. in piano, Bavarian State Acad., Wuerzburg, Fed. Republic Germany, 1954; BS in Music Edn., Miami U., Oxford, Ohio, 1957. Life credential music tchr., Calif. Tchr. music Cleve. Pub. Schs., 1957-62, L.A. Unified Schs., 1963-94; retired, 1994. Song composer. With U.S. Army, 1952-54. Mem. Alpha Phi Alpha, Phi Mu Alpha Sinfonia. Republican. Avocations: amateur concert pianist, composing, photography. Home: 13005 Spelman Dr Victorville CA 92392-7239 E-mail: nosretep@bigplanet.com

PETERSON, LESLIE RAYMOND, barrister; b. Viking, Alta., Can., Oct. 6, 1923; s. Herman S. and Margaret (Karen) P.; m. Agnes Rose Hine, June 24, 1950; children: Raymond Erik, Karen Isabelle. Student, Camrose Luth. Coll., Alta., McGill. U., Can., London U., Eng.; LLB, U. B.C., Can., 1949; LLD, Simon Fraser U., Can., 1965, U. B.C., , 1993; EdD, Notre Dame U., Nelson, Can., 1966; hon. diploma tech., B.C. Inst. Tech., 1994. Bar: B.C. 1949; called to Queens Counsel, 1960. Pvt. practice barrister, Vancouver, B.C., 1949-52; with Peterson & Anderson, 1952; then with Boughton & Co. (now Boughton Peterson Yang Anderson).; mem. B.C. Legislature for Vancouver Centre, 1956-63, Vancouver-Little Mountain, 1966; min. of edn., 1956-68; min. of labour, 1960-71; atty. gen., 1968-72; bd. govs. U. B.C., Vancouver, 1979-83, chancellor, 1987-93. Bd. dirs. Can. Found. Econ. Edn., Inst. Corp. Dirs. Can., West Vancouver Found., Inst. for Pacific Ocean Sci. and Tech., Karay Holdings Ltd.; trustee Peter Wall Inst. for Advanced Studies; chmn. U. B.C. Found., 1990 96. Bd. dirs. Portland unit Shriners Hosp. for Crippled Children, 1994-96; past bd. dirs. Western Soc. of Rehab., YMCA, Victoria B.C.; past pres. Twenty Club; hon. mem. Vancouver Jr. C. of C.; former v.p. Normanna Old People's Home; founding mem. Convocation, Simon Fraser U. and U. Victoria; hon. dep. French Nat. Assembly, Paris; hon. commr. labor State of Okla.; gov. Downtown Vancouver Assn. With Can. Army, 1942-46, ETO. Recipient Disting. Alumnus award Camrose Luth. Coll., 1980. Fellow Royal Soc. Arts; mem. Vancouver Bar Assn., Law Soc. B.C., Internat. Assn. of Govt. Labour Ofcls. (chmn. standing com., Can. mins. of edn. 1965-66), Terminal City Club (pres. 1991—), Scandinavian Bus. Men's Club (past pres.), Hazelmere Golf and Tennis Club (bd. dirs.), Union Club (Victoria), Wesbrook Soc. of U. B.C. (chmn. 1987), Order of St. Lazarus (knight comdr.), Freemason (potentate Gizeh Temple Shrine 1988), Order of Can., Order of B.C., Venerable Order of Saint John (comdr.), Order of Can. Avocations: skiing, golf, fishing, hunting. Home: 814 Highland West Vancouver BC Canada V7S 2G5 Office: Boughton Peterson Yang Anderson 595 Burrard St Ste 1000 Ste 2500 Vancouver BC Canada V7X 1S8 Fax: 604-693-5317. E-mail: lpeterson@bpya.com

PETERSON, MARY L. state agency official; BA in English, Carleton Coll., 1972; MA in Tchg. in Edn. and English, Duke U., 1974; postgrad., U. Utah, 1977-80. Tchr. English, New Canaan (Conn.) Sch. Dist., from 1973, Brighton Ctrl. Sch. Dist., Rochester, N.Y., Davis County Sch. Dist., Kaysville, Utah, until 1977; rsch. asst. in cultural founds. and ednl. adminstrn. U. Utah, Salt Lake City, 1977-79; prin. St. Nicholas Elem. Sch., Rupert, Idaho, 1979-81; cons. Nev. Dept. Edn., Carson City, 1981-92, dep. supt. instrnl., rsch. and evaluative svcs., 1992-94, supt. pub. instrn., 1994—. Assessor Nev. Assessment Ctr., Nat. Assn. Secondary Sch. Prins.; mem. accreditation team N.W. Assn. Schs. and Colls.; trainer Tchr. Effectiveness for Student Achievement, Correlates Effective Schs.; facilitator Assisting Change in Edn.; mem. state team Nat. Coun. for Accreditation Tchr. Edn. Asst. editor: Work, Family and Careers (C. Brooklyn Derr), 1980; contbr. to profl. publs. Scholar Carleton Coll., Duke U. Mem. Phi Kappa Phi, Delta Kappa Gamma. Office: Nev Dept Edn Capitol Complex 700 E 5th St Carson City NV 89701-5096

PETERSON, MILLIE M. state senator; b. Merced, Calif., June 11, 1944; BS, U. Utah, 1979, MSW, 1984. Mem. Utah Senate, Dist. 12, Salt Lake City, 1991—. Susa Young Gates Award, 1998. Mem. NASW. Democrat. Address: 7131 W 3800 S West Valley City UT 84128-3416 Office: Senate House 319 State Capitol Salt Lake City UT 84114 E-mail: mpeter7131@aol.com

PETERSON, RALPH R. engineering executive; b. 1944; BS in Civil Engring., Oreg. State U., 1969; MS in Environ. Engring., Stanford U., 1970; AMP, Harvard Bus. Sch., 1991. Engring. aide Johnson, Underkofler & Briggs, Boise, 1962-63; surveyor Smith, Keyes & Blakely, Caldwell, Idaho, 1963-64; with Chronic & Assocs., Boise, 1964-65, CH2M Hill Cos., Ltd., 1965—, sr. v.p., dir. tech., 1988, pres., CEO, 1990. Office: CH2M Hill Cos Ltd 6060 S Willow Dr Greenwood Village CO 80111-5142

PETERSON, RICHARD HERMANN, history educator, retired; b. Berkeley, Calif., Jan. 16, 1942; s. William Martin and Dorothy Jean (Heyne) P.; m. Nora Ann Lorenzo, June 21, 1970; 1 child, Nina Elizabeth. AB, U. Calif., Berkeley, 1963; MA, San Francisco State U., 1966; PhD, U. Calif., Davis, 1971. Calif. community coll. teaching credential. Asst. prof. history Ind. U., Kokomo, 1971-76; instr. social studies Coll. of Redwoods, Ft. Bragg, Calif., 1976-78; assoc. prof. history San Diego State U., 1978-82, prof. history, 1982-96, prof. emeritus, 1996—; freelance writer, 1996—. Author: Manifest Destiny in the Mines, 1975, The Bonanza Kings, 1977, 91, Bonanza Rich, 1991; book rev. editor Jour. of San Diego History, 1978-82, editl. cons., 1980-82; contbr. articles to profl. jours., websites, newspapers. Judge for papers Internat. History Fair, San Diego, Tijuana, Mex., 1983-88. Faculty Summer fellow Ind. U., 1975, 76, San Diego State U., 1980, Meritorious Performance and Prof. Promise award, 1989; rsch. grantee Sourisseau Acad., 1977, Am. Assn. State/Local History, 1988; named Golden Poet of Yr., World of Poetry, 1987-89. Mem. Am. Hist. Assn., Calif. Hist. Soc., Western History Assn., Calif. Studies Assn. Avocations: golf, gardening, writing poetry, travel. Home: 7956 Lake Adlon Dr San Diego CA 92119-3117

PETERSON, ROBIN TUCKER, marketing educator; b. Casper, Wyo., July 31, 1937; s. Walfred Arthur and Mary Lurene Peterson; m. Marjorie K. Greenwald, June 25, 1963; children: Timothy, Kimberly. BS, U. Wyo., 1959, MS in Bus., 1961; Ph.D., U. Wash., 1967. Mem. faculty Idaho State U., Pocatello, 1963-73; prof. mktg., head mktg. dept. St. Cloud (Minn.) State U., 1973-76, N.Mex. State U., Las Cruces, 1976—. Fulbright lectr., Yugoslavia, 1973; vis. scholar Ea. Mont. State Coll., 1985; Sunwest Fin. Svcs. Disting. Centennial prof. N.Mex. State U., 1991, 92; Norwest Disting. prof. N.Mex. State U., 1999; vis. lectr. Nirma Inst. Ahmedabad, India, 1999, Chiang Moi U., Thailand, 2000; Fulbright lectr. Kathmandu U., Nepal, 2001. Author: Marketing-A Contemporary Introduction, 1976, Forecasting, 1976, edit., 1983, Personal Selling, 1977, Marketing in Action, 1977, Lernbook Marketing, 1984, Marketing: Concepts and Decision Making, 1987, Principles of Marketing, 1989, Argentina, 1990, Managing the Distributor Sales Network, 1990, Business Forecasting, 1992, Getting New Products to Market Rapidly, 1994; exec. editor Bus. Forecaster, 1993-94; editor Jour. Bus. and Entrepreneurship, 1994-98; also contbr. articles to profl. publs. Served with USAR, 1962-63. Fellow Assn. Small Bus. Entrepreneurship; mem. Am. Mktg. Assn., Sales and Mktg. Execs. Internat., Acad. Mktg. Sci. (pres. 1977-78, 80-82), Am. Arbitration Assn. (Outstanding Educators Am. award), S.W. Small Bus. Assn. (pres. 1983-84, Outstanding Mktg. Educators award), S.W. Mktg. Assn., Western Mktg. Educators, Las Cruces C. of C., Las Cruces Sales and Mktg. Club, Beta Gamma Sigma, Phi Kappa Psi, Alpha Kappa Psi, Alpha Mu Alpha. Republican. Presbyterian. Home: 4350 Diamondback Dr Las Cruces NM 88011-7539 Office: NMex State U PO Box 5280 Las Cruces NM 88003-5280

PETERSON, ROY JEROME, physics educator; b. Everett, Wash., Oct. 18, 1939; married; four children. BS, U. Wash., 1961, PHD, 1966. Instr. physics Princeton (N.J.) U., 1966-68; rsch. assoc. Yale U., New Haven, 1968-70; from rsch. assoc. to prof. physics U. Colo., Boulder, 1970—, asst. vice chancellor rsch., 1996—. Program dir. Intermediate Energy Physics NSF, 1978-79. Fellow Am. Phys. Soc.; mem. Pakistan Acad. Scis. Office: U Colo Box 446 Nuclear Physics Lab Boulder CO 80309

PETERSON, RUDOLPH A. banker; b. Svenljunga, Sweden, Dec. 6, 1904; s. Aaron and Anna (Johannson) P.; m. Patricia Price, 1927 (dec. 1960); children: Linnea Peterson Bennett, R. Price; m. Barbara Welser Lindsay, Dec. 25, 1962; stepchildren: Robert I. Lindsay, Lorna Lindsay, Anne Lindsay, Margaret Lindsay. BS in Commerce, U. Calif., 1925, LLD, 1968; LHD, U. Redlands, 1967. With Comml. Credit Co., 1925-36, successively asst. mgr., v.p., gen. mgr. Mexico City, div. operations mgr. Chgo.; dist. mgr. Bank Am. Nat. Trust & Savs. Assn., Fresno, Calif., 1936-41, v.p. San Francisco, 1941-46; pres., chief exec. officer Allied Bldg. Credits, 1946-52; v.p. Transam. Corp., San Francisco, 1952-55; pres., chief exec. officer Bank of Hawaii, Honolulu, 1956-61; pres., CEO BankAm. Corp., San Francisco, 1961-70, chmn. exec. com., 1970-76, also dir., 1968-98; adminstr. UN Devel. Programme, 1971-76. Bd. dirs. Alza Corp., Asia Found.; chmn. Euro Can. Bank, 1982-94; adminstr. UN Devel. Programme, 1972-76. Mem. adv. coun. Calif. Acad. Scis. Decorated Grand Cross of Civil Merit Spain; Order of Merit Italy; named Swedish-Am. of Year Vasa Order, 1965; U. Calif. Alumnus of Year, 1968; recipient Capt. Robert Dollar Meml. award for contbn. to advancement Am. fgn. trade, 1970, Chancellor's award U. Calif., 1992, Great Swedish Heritage award, 1996. Clubs: Bohemian (San Francisco), Pacific-Union (San Francisco). Home: 86 Sea View Ave Piedmont CA 94611-3519 Office: Bank Am Ctr Mailcode CA5 705-11-01 555 California St Fl 11 San Francisco CA 94104-1502

PETERSON, WAYNE TURNER, composer, pianist; b. Albert Sea, Minn., Sept. 3, 1927; s. Leslie Jules and Irma Thelma (Turner) P.; m. Harriet Christiansen, 1948 (div. 1978); children: Alan, Craig, Drew, Grant. BA, U. Minn., 1951, MA, 1953; postgrad., Royal Acad. Music, London, 1953-54; PhD, U. Minn. Instr. music U. Minn., 1955-59; asst. prof. music Chico (Calif.) State U., 1959-60; prof. music San Francisco State U., 1960-91, prof. emeritus, 1991—. Vis. prof. composition U. Ind., Bloomington, 1992, Stanford U., 1992-94; artist in residence Briarcombe Found., Bolinas, Calif., 1983; vis. artist Am. Acad. in Rome, 1990. Composer: Allegro for String Quartet, 1952, Introduction and Allegro, 1953, Free Variations for Orch., 1954-58, Can Death Be Sleep, 1955, Earth, Sweet Earth, 1956, (cappella chorus) Cape Ann, 1957, Three Songs for Soprano and Piano, 1957, (cappella chorus) Psalm 56, 1959, Exaltation, Dithyramb and Caprice, full orchestra, 1959-60, (cappella chorus) An e e Cummings Triptych, 1962, Tangents for flute, clarinet, horn and violin, 1963, An e e Cummings Cantata, 1964, Fantasy Concertante for violin and piano, 1965, Reflections, ballet, full orchestra, 1965, Metamorphosis for Wind Quintet, 1967, Phantasmagoria for flute, clarinet, double bass, 1968, Cataclysms, full orchestra, 1968, Clusters and Fragments for string orch., 1969, Ceremony After a Fire Raid, Soprano and piano, 1969, Sinfonia and Canticle for baritone voice and organ, 1969, Capriccio for Flute and Piano, 1973, Transformations for String Quartet, 1974, Trialogue for violin, cello and piano, 1975, Diatribe for violin and piano, 1975, Encounters mixed ensemble of mini instrument, 1976, Rhapsody for Cello and Piano, 1976, An Interrupted Serenade for flute, harp and cello, 1978, Dark Reflections (cycle of four songs for high voice, violin and piano), 1980, Mallets Aforethought (symphony for percussion ensemble), 1981, Sextet for flute, clarinet, percussion, harp, violin and cello, 1982, Doubles for 2 flutes and 2 clarinets, 1982, Debussy Song Cycle transcribe for voice and small orchestra, 1983, String Quartet, 1983-84, Ariadne's Thread for harp, flute, clarinet, horn, percussion and violin, 1985, Transformations for chamber orch., 1986, Duo for viola and cello, 1986-87, Trilogy for Orch., 1987, Labyrinth for flute, clarinet, violin and piano, 1987, The Widening Gyre for full orch., 1991, The Face of the Night, the Heart of the Dark for full orch., 1991 (Pulitzer prize for music 1992), Mallets Aforthought percussion symphony revision, 1991, String Quartet # 2, 1992, Diptych, fl, cl, pec., po, rn,vc, 1992, Janus, mixed ensemble of ten instrument, 1993, Duo for Violin and Piano, 1993, And the Winds Shall Blow, a fantasy for saxophone quartet, symphony winds, brass and percussion, 1994; Theseus for smaller orchestra, Vicissiyude (fl, cl, perc, po, vn, vc, 1995, A Robert Herrick Motley (five a capella Choruses) Windup Saxaphone Quartet, Peregrinations (solo clarinet) 1996; recs. with Mercury Records, Desto Records, [illegible] Centur, San Francisco Chamber Singers; Recordings commd. Am. Music Ctr., 1959, Virtuosi of San Francisco, 1968, Unitarian Ch., 1969, Paul Mason, Inc., 1974, 87, NEA Consortium Commn., 1982, Charles Wuorinen and San Francisco Symphony, 1985, Am. Composers Symphony, Inc., 1987, San Francisco Symphony, 1991, Gerbode Found., 1990, Koussevitzky Found., 1990, Fromm Music Found., 1992, Philharmonic Orch. of Freiburg in Breisgau, Germany, 1993, U. Minn., 1995, Neel the Composer (Consortium, Comm.) 1996, Allen Blustine, 1996. Recipient 11th Ann. Norman Fromm Composer's award, 1982, Meritorious Svc. award Calif. State U. System, 1984, Top award Am. Harp Soc., 1985, Composer's award Am. Acad. and Inst. Arts and Letters, 1986, Pulitzer Prize for music, 1992; Fulbright scholar, Royal Acad. Music, 1953-54; NEA grantee, 1976; Guggenheim fellow, 1989-90, Djerassi Found. fellow, 1989-91. Home: 140 S Lake Merced Hls San Francisco CA 94132-2935 Office: San Francisco State U Dept Mus 1600 Holloway Ave San Francisco CA 94132-1722

PETICOLAS, WARNER LELAND, retired physical chemistry educator; b. Lubbock, Tex., July 29, 1929; s. Warner Marion and Beulah Francis (Lowe) P.; m. Virginia Marie Wolf, June 30, 1969; children— Laura M., Alicia B.; children by previous marriage— Cynthia M., Nina P., Phillip W. B.S., Tex. Technol. Coll., 1950; Ph.D., Northwestern U., 1954; D (honoris causa), U. Lille, France, 1997. Research asso. DuPont Co., Wilmington, Del., 1954-60; research div. IBM, San Jose, Calif., 1960-67, cons., 1967-69, mgr. chem. physics group, 1965-67; prof. phys. chemistry U. Oreg., 1967-98; ret., 1998. Vis. prof. U. Paris-Pierre and Marie Curie, 1980-81; vis. prof. Weizmann Inst. Sci., Rahovat, Israel, 1991, vis. prof. U. Reims, 1996. Committeeman Democratic party, Eugene, Oreg., 1967-70. Served with USPHS, 1955-57. Recipient Alexander von Humboldt award, W. Ger., 1984-85. Guggenheim fellow Max von Laue-Paul Langevin Inst., Grenoble, France, 1973-74 Fellow Am. Phys. Soc.; mem. Am. Chem. Soc., Am. Phys. Soc., Sigma Xi, Alpha Chi Sigma, Tau Beta Pi. Episcopalian. Home: 2829 Arline Way Eugene OR 97403-2527 E-mail: peticola@oregon.uroegon.edu

PETRAKIS, NICHOLAS LOUIS, edidemiologist, medical researcher, educator; b. San Francisco, Feb. 6, 1922; s. Louis Nicholas and Stamatina (Boosalis) P.; m. Patricia Elizabeth Kelly, June 24, 1947; children: Steven John, Susan Lynn, Sandra Kay. BA, Augustana Coll., 1943; BS in Medicine, U. S.D., 1944; MD, Washington U., St. Louis, 1946. Intern Mpls. Gen. Hosp., 1946-47; physician, researcher U.S. Naval Radiol. Def. Lab., San Francisco, 1947-49; resident physician Mpls. Gen. Hosp., 1949-50; sr. asst. surgeon Nat. Cancer Inst., USPHS, San Francisco, 1950-54; asst. research physician Cancer Research Inst., U. Calif., San Francisco, 1954-56; asst. prof. preventive medicine U. Calif. Sch. Medicine, San Francisco, 1956-60, assoc. prof., 1960-66, prof., 1966-91, chmn. dept. epidemiology and internat. health, 1978-88, prof. emeritus, 1991—; prof. epidemiology U. Calif. Sch. Pub. Health, Berkeley, 1981-91. Assoc. dir. G.W. Hooper Edn., U. Calif., San Francisco, 1970-74, acting dir., 1974-77, chmn. dept. epidemiology and internat. health, 1979-89; co-dir. Breast Screening Ctr. of No. Calif., Oakland, 1976-81; cons. Breast Cancer Task Force, Nat. Cancer Inst., Bethesda, Md., 1972-76; chmn. Biometry & Epidemiology Contract Rev. Com., Bethesda, 1977-81; mem. bd. sci. counselors, div. cancer etiology Nat. Cancer Inst., Bethesda, 1982-86; mem. scientific adv. com. Calif. State Tobacco-Related Disease Rsch. Program, 1991-93; cons. U. Crete Sch. Medicine, Heraklion, Greece, 1984; bd. dirs. No. Calif. Cancer Ctr., 1991. Contbr. over 200 research papers on breast cancer, med. oncology and hematology. Eleanor Roosevelt Internat. Cancer fellow Am. Cancer Soc., Comitato Reserche Nucleari, Cassacia, Italy, 1962; U.S. Pub. Health Service Spl. fellow Galton Lab., U. London, 1969-70; recipient Alumni Achievement award Augustana Coll., Sioux Falls, S.D., 1979, Axion award Hellenic-Am. Profl. Soc. of Calif., San Francisco, 1984, Lewis C. Robbins award Soc. for Prospective Medicine, Indpls., 1985, Otto W. Sartorius, MD, award from Susan Love MD Breast Cancer Found., 2001. Mem. Am. Soc. Preventive Oncology (founding, pres. 1984-85, Disting. Achievement award 1992), Soc. for Prospective Medicine (founding), Am. Assn. Cancer Rsch., Am. Epidemiol. Soc., Am. Soc. Clin. Investigation, Am. Bd. Preventive Medicine (cert.). Home: 335 Juanita Way San Francisco CA 94127-1657 Office: U Calif Sch Medicine Dept Epidemiology & Biostats 1699 Hsw San Francisco CA 94143-0001 E-mail: petrakis@ix.netcom.com

PETRICK, ALFRED, JR. mineral economics educator, consultant; b. Mt. Vernon, N.Y., Dec. 30, 1926; s. Alfred and Ruth (Updike) P.; m. Ruth Goodridge, Jan. 2, 1956; children: Elizabeth, Andrew Wayne. B.S., B.A., Columbia U., 1952, M.S., 1962; M.B.A., Denver U., 1966; Ph.D., U. Colo., 1969. Registered profl. engr., Colo. Sales engr. Ingersoll Rand Co., N.Y.C., 1953-54; project engr. U.S. AEC, Grand Junction, Colo., 1954-57; mining engr. Reynolds Metals Co., Bauxite, Ark., 1957-61, Guyana, 1957-61; mineral economist U.S. Bur. Mines, Denver, 1963-70; Coulter prof. Colo. Sch. Mines, Golden, 1970-84, emeritus prof., 1984—; dir. Petrick Assocs., Evergreen, Colo. Author: Economics International Development, 1977, Economics of Minerals, 1980, Preparacion y Evaluacion, 1982. Mem. com. tech. aspects strategic materials Nat. Acad. Sci., Washington, 1973-76, mem. com. surface mining and reclamation, 1979. Served with USAF, 1945-47, PTO. Fulbright research scholar U. Otago, Dunedin, New Zealand, 1986; recipient Edn. award Instituto Para Funcionarios De Las Industrias Minera y Siderurgica, Mexico City, 1981; recipient Service award Office Tech. Assessment, U.S. Congress, 1981. Mem. AIME (chmn. council econs. 1977-78, Henry Krumb lectr. 1986, service award), Profl. Engrs. Colo. Presbyterian. Home: 5544 S Hatch Dr Evergreen CO 80439-7233 Office: Colo Sch Mines Golden CO 80401

PETRIE, GEOFF, professional basketball team executive; Grad., Princeton U., 1970. Guard Portland Trail Blazers, 1970-76, exec., 1976-93; v.p. basketball ops. Sacramento Kings, 1994—. Named NBA Rookie of the Yr., 1970; selected to NBA All-Star Team, 1971, 74. Avocations: working out, golfing. Office: Sacramento Kings One Sports Parkway Sacramento CA 95834

PETRIE, GREGORY STEVEN, lawyer; b. Seattle, Feb. 25, 1951; s. George C. and Pauline P.; m. Margaret Fuhrman, Oct. 6, 1979; children: Kathryn Jean, Thomas George. AB in Polit. Sci and Econs., UCLA, 1973; JD, Boston U., 1976. Bar: Wash. 1976, U.S. Dist. Ct. (we. dist.) Wash. 1976. Adminstr. Action/Peace Corps, Washington, 1973, Fed. Power Commn., Washington, 1974; assoc. Oles Morrison et al, Seattle, 1976-80; ptnr. Schwabe Williamson Ferguson & Burdell, Seattle, 1981-94; mng. shareholder Krutch Lindell Bingham Jones & Petrie, Seattle, 1994—. Mem. Seattle-King County Bar Assn., Profl. Liability Architects and Engrs., Wash. Athletic Club. Avocations: woodworking, skiing. Office: Krutch Lindell Bingham Jones & Petrie 1201 3rd Ave Ste 3100 Seattle WA 98101-3079 E-mail: gsp@nwlink.com

PETRINI, DAVID J. banking executive; Audit mgr. Providian Fin. Corp., 1986-88, controller, 1988-90, v.p., 1990-94, sr. v.p., Sr. Fin. Officer, 1994-97, sr. v.p., CFO, 1997-98, exec. v.p., CFO, 1998—. Office: Providian 201 Mission St San Francisco CA 94105

PETRINOVICH, LEWIS FRANKLIN, psychology educator; b. Wallace, Idaho, June 12, 1930; s. John F. and Ollie (Steward) P. BS, U. Idaho, 1952; PhD, U. Calif., Berkeley, 1962. Asst. prof. San Francisco State Coll., 1957-63; from assoc. to prof. SUNY, Stony Brook, 1963-68; prof. U. Calif., Riverside, 1968-91, chmn. psychology, 1968-71, 86-89, prof. emeritus, 1991—. Author: Understanding Research in Social Sciences, 1975, Introduction to Statistics, 1976, Human Evolution, Reproduction and Morality, 1995, Living and Dying Well, 1996, Darwinian Dominion: Animal Welfare [illegible] Development, 1981, Habituation, Sensitization and Behavior, 1984; cons. editor Behavioral and Neural Biology, 1972-90, Jour. Physiol. and Comparative Psychology, 1980-82, Jour. Comparative Psychology, 1983-90. Fellow Am. Psychol. Assn., Am. Psychol. Soc., Calif. Acad. Scis., Human Behavior and Evolution Soc., Western Psychol. Assn.; mem. Am. Ornithological Union (elected), Animal Behavior Soc., Sigma Xi. Home: 415 Boynton Ave Berkeley CA 94707-1701 Office: U Calif Riverside Psychology Dept Riverside CA 92521-0001

PETROS, RAYMOND LOUIS, JR. lawyer; b. Pueblo, Colo., Sept. 19, 1950; BS, Colo. Coll., 1972; JD, U. Colo., 1975. Bar: Colo. 1975. Jud. clk. to Justice Paul V. Hodges Colo. Supreme Ct., Denver, 1975-77; assoc. Bermingham, White, Burke & Ipsen, Denver, 1977-78; from assoc. to ptnr. Hall & Evans, Denver, 1978-81; ptnr. Kirkland & Ellis, Denver, 1981-86; mem. Holme, Roberts & Owen, Denver, 1986-96, Petros & White, LLC, 1996—. Contbr. articles to profl. jours. Bd. dirs. Rocky Mountain Poison Control Found., Denver, 1988-94. Office: Petros & White LLC 730 Seventeenth St Ste 820 Denver CO 80202-3518

PETTIBON, RAYMOND, video artist; b. Tucson, June 10, 1957; BA, UCLA, 1977. One-man shows include Semaphore Gallery, N.Y.C., 1986, Feature Gallery, N.Y.C., 1989, 90, 93, Richard/Bennett Gallery, L.A., 1990, 91, Robert Berman Gallery, L.A., 1991, Galerie Rudiger Schottle, Munich, 1991, Massimo de Carlo Arte Contempranea, Milan, Italy, 1991, N.A.M.E. Gallery, Chgo., 1991, Feature Gallery, N.Y.C., 1991, Galerie Marc Jancou, Zurich, Switzerland, 1992, Galerie Metropol, Vienna, Austria, 1992, 94, Esther Schipper Galerie, Cologne, Germany, 1992, Matrix Gallery, U. Calif. Berkeley, 1992, Air de Paris, Nice, France, 1992, Univ. Galleries, Ill. State U., Normal, 1993, Regen Projects, L.A., 1993, 95, 98, Jack Hanley Gallery, San Francisco, 1993, Galerie Beaumont, Luxembourg, 1994, Galeria Ramis Barquet, Garza, Mex., 1994, Ynglingagatan, Stockholm, Sweden, 1995, 14/16 Verneuil, Paris, 1995, Contemporary Fine Arts, Berlin, 1995, 98, Galeria Massimo De Carlo, Milan, 1995, Kunsthalle Bern, Switzerland, 1995, David Zwirner Gallery, N.Y.C., 1995, 97, Tramway, Glasgow, Scotland, 1996, Taka Ishii Gallery, Tokyo, 1996, Meyer Kainer, Vienna, 1998, The Renaissance Soc., Chgo., 1998, The Drawing Ctr., N.Y.C., 1999, Phila. Mus. Art, 1999, Galerie Meyer Kainer, Vienna, 1999; exhibited in group shows at Whitney Mus. Am. Art, N.Y.C., 1997-98, 98-99, Sudwestdeutsche Landesbank, Stuttgart, Germany, 1997, Galerie Tanya Rumpff, Haarlem, The Netherlands, 1998, 11 Duke Street Ltd., London, 1998, The Parrish Art Mus., Southampton, N.Y., 1998, Laguna Art Mus., 1999, Austin Mus. Art, 1999, David Swirner, N.Y., 2000, numerous others. Office: Stuart Regen Gallery c/o Regen Projects 629 N Almont Dr Los Angeles CA 90069

PETTIGREW, EDWARD W. lawyer; b. Aurora, Ill., July 16, 1943; AB, Kenyon Coll., 1965; JD, U. Mich., 1968. Bar: Wash. 1970, Mich. 1971, U.S. Ct. Appeals (9th cir.) 1971, U.S. Dist. Ct. (we. and ea. dists.) Wash. 1971. Shareholder Graham & Dunn, Seattle, 1970—. Mem. Fed. Bar Assn. (pres. western dist. Wash. 1987-88). Office: Graham & Dunn 1420 5th Ave Fl 33 Seattle WA 98101-4087

PETTIS-ROBERSON, SHIRLEY MCCUMBER, former congresswoman; b. Mountain View, Calif. d. Harold Oliver and Dorothy Susan (O'Neil) McCumber; m. John J. McNulty (dec.); m. Jerry L. Pettis (dec. Feb. 1975); m. Ben Roberson, Feb. 6, 1988; children: Peter Dwight Pettis, Deborah Neil Pettis Moyer. Student, Andrews U., U. Calif., Berkeley. Mgr. Audio-Digest Found., L.A., Glendale; sec.-treas. Pettis, Inc., Hollywood, 1958-68; mem. 94th-95th Congresses from 37th Calif. Dist., mem. coms. on interior, internat. rels., edn. and labor. Pres. Women's Rsch. and Edn. Inst., 1979-80; bd. dirs. Kemper Nat. Ins. Cos., 1979-97, Lumbermens Mut. Ins. Co. Mem. Pres.'s Commn. on Arms Control and Disarmament, 1980-83, Commn. on Presdl. Scholars, 1990-93; trustee U. Redlands, Calif., 1980-83, Loma Linda (Calif.) U. and Med. Ctr., 1990-95; chair Loma Linda U. Children's Hosp. Found.; mem. Former Mems. Congress, 1988—. Mem. Morningside Country Club (Rancho Mirage, Calif.).

PETTIT, GEORGE ROBERT, chemistry educator, cancer researcher; b. Long Branch, N.J., June 8, 1929; s. George Robert and Florence Elizabeth (Seymour) P.; m. Margaret Jean Benger, June 20, 1953; children: William Edward, Margaret Sharon, Robin Kathleen, Lynn Benger, George Robert III. BS, Wash. State U., 1952; MS, Wayne State U., 1954, PhD, 1956. Tchg. asst. Wash. State U., 1950-52, lecture demonstrator, 1952; rsch. chemist E.I. duPont de Nemours and Co., 1953; grad. tchg. asst. Wayne State U., 1952-53, rsch. fellow, 1954-56; sr. rsch. chemist Norwich Eaton Pharms., Inc., 1956-57; asst. prof. chemistry U. Maine, 1957-61, assoc. prof. chemistry, 1961-65, prof. chemistry, 1965; vis. prof. chemistry Stanford U., 1965; prof. chemistry Ariz. State U., 1965—, chmn. organic chemistry divsn., 1966-68, Disting. Rsch. prof., 1978-79. Vis. prof. So. African, Univs., 1978; dir. Cancer Rsch. Lab., 1974-75, Cancer Rsch. Inst., 1975—; lectr. various colls. and univs.; cons. in field. Contbr. articles to profl. jours. Mem. adv. bd. Wash. State U. Found., 1981-85. With USAFR, 1951-54. Recipient Alumni Achievement award Wash. State U., 1984, Rsch. Achievement award Am. Soc. Pharmacognosy, 1995; named Dalton prof. medicinal chemistry and rsch., 1986—, Regents prof. chemistry, 1990—. Fellow Am. Inst. Chemists (Pioneer award 1989, Ariz. Gov.'s Excellence award 1993); mem. Am. Chem. Soc. (awards com. 1968-71, 78-81, Guenther award in Chemistry of Natural Products 1998), Chem. Soc. (London), Pharmacognosy Soc., Am. Assn. Cancer Rsch., Sigma Xi, Phi Lambda Upsilon. Office: Ariz State U Cancer Rsch Inst Tempe AZ 85287

PETTIT, GHERY ST. JOHN, electronics engineer; b. Woodland, Calif., Apr. 6, 1952; s. Ghery DeWitt and Frances Marie (Seitz) P.; m. Marilyn Jo Van Hoose, July 28, 1973; children: Ghery Christopher, Heather Kathleen. BS in Electrical Engring., Wash. State U., 1975. Nuclear engr. Mare Island Naval Shipyard, Vallejo, Calif., 1975-76; electronics engr. Naval Electronic Systems Engring. Ctr., Vallejo, 1976-79; sr. engr. Martin Marietta Denver Aerospace, 1979-83; staff engr. Tandem Computers Inc., Santa Clara, Calif., 1983-90, mgr. electromagnetic capability Cupertino, 1990-91, electromagnetic compatibility lead engr., 1991-95; electromagnetic compatibility engr. Intel Corp., Hillsboro, Oreg., 1995-96, Dupont, Wash., 1996—. Mem. U.S. tech. adv. group subcom. I, Spl. Com. on Radio Frequency Interferences subcom. Internat. Electrotechnical Commn.; mem. CISPR SC I, WE2, WG3 and WG4. Asst. cubmaster Boy Scouts Am., San Jose, Calif., 1985-86, cubmaster, 1986-88, ast. scoutmaster, 1988-90, scoutmaster, 1990-93. Mem. IEEE (sr.), Nat. Rsch. Coun. (bd. assessment of NIST programs 1999—), EMC Soc. (bd. dirs. 1999—), Electromagnetic Capability Soc. (sec.-treas. Littleton, Colo. chpt. 1983, sec. Santa Clara Valley chpt. 1985-87, vice chmn. 1987-89, chmn. 1989-91, sec. Santa Clara Valley sect. 1991-92, treas. 1992-93, vice chmn. 1993-94, chmn. 1994-95), IEEE Electromagetic Capability Soc. (chmn. Seattle chpt. 1997-2000). Republican. Presbyterian. Avocations: flying, amateur radio, sailing. Office: Intel Corp 2800 Center Dr Dupont WA 98327-9773 E-mail: ghery.pettit@intel.com

PETTIT, JOHN W. administrator; b. Detroit, Mar. 6, 1942; s. John W. and Clara (Schartz) P.; m. Kathleen Endres, Aug. 8, 1970; children: Julie, Andrew, Michael. BBA, U. Notre Dame, 1964; MBA, Mich. State U., 1974. CPA, Mich.; CFP, 2001. Acct. Ernst & Ernst, Detroit, 1964-67; chief acct. Detroit Inst. Tech., Detroit, 1967-69; controller, dir. adminstrn. & fin. Mich. Cancer Found., Detroit, 1969-80; chief adminstrv. officer Dana-Farber Cancer Inst., Boston, 1980-94; exec. v.p., chief oper. officer John Wayne Cancer Inst., Santa Monica, Calif., 1995-97; fin. cons. L.A., 1998—. Grant reviewer Nat. Cancer Inst., Bethesda, Md., 1979-94. Pres. advanced mgmt. program Mich. State U., 1978-79; mem. adv. bd. Arthritis [illegible] 1991-94. Mem. AICPA, Fin. Planning Assn. Avocations: sailing, woodworking, photography, music. Office: 21031 Ventura Blvd Ste 705 Woodland Hills CA 91364 E-mail: jwpettit@yahoo.com

PETTLE, CECILE, city official; BA in Acctg., Ariz. State U., 1978; MA in Bus. Adminstrn., Grand Canyon U., 1994. Dir. budget, rsch. City Hall, Pheonix, 1996—. Office: Budget & Rsch Dept City Hall 14th Fl 200 W Washington St Phoenix AZ 85009-1611

PETTY, GEORGE KIBBE, communications executive; b. Albuquerque, Nov. 26, 1941; s. George Kibbe and Annabelle (Deeter) P.; m. Margaret Catherine Pobar, Feb. 6, 1965; children: Jennifer, Lisa. BSEE, N.Mex. State U., 1965. Various positions ending with v.p. global bus. svcs. AT&T, San Francisco, 1969-94; pres., CEO TELUS Corp., Edmonton, Alta., Can., 1994—. Bd. dirs. CAE Inc.; mem. econ. coun. Alta. Econ. Devel. Authority. Mem. Mayor of San Francisco Blue Ribbon Com., 1987—; mem. Chester Twp. Sch. Bd., Va., 1984-85; bd. dirs. Edmonton Opera Assn. Capt. USAF, 1965-69. Mem. Moraga (Calif.) Country Club. Republican. Presbyterian.

PETTY, GEORGE OLIVER, lawyer; b. L.A., Mar. 31, 1939; s. Hugh Morton and May (Johnson) P.; m. Sandra Diane Kilpatrick, July 14, 1962; children: Ross Morton, Alison Lee, Christopher Henry. AB, U. Calif., Berkeley, 1961; LLB, U. Calif., 1964. Bar: Calif. 1965, Eng. and Wales 1986, U.S. Supreme Ct. 1976. Atty. Huovinen & White, Oakland, Calif., 1967-69; counsel Bechtel Power Corp., San Francisco, 1969-83; prin. counsel Bechtel Ltd., London, 1983-86; gen. counsel Sun-Diamond Growers of Calif., Pleasanton, Calif., 1987-95; pvt. practice, 1995—. Capt. U.S. Army, 1965-67. Mem. Calif. State Bar Assn., Alameda County Bar Assn., Eng. and Wales Bar Assn., Bar Assn. for Commerce, Fin. & Industry (Eng.), Middle Temple Inn. Office: 843 Arlington Ave Berkeley CA 94707-1926 E-mail: 80petty@aol.com

PETTY, THOMAS LEE, physician, educator; b. Boulder, Colo., Dec. 24, 1932; s. Roy Stone and and Eleanor Marie (Kudrna) P.; m. Carol Lee Piepho, Aug. 7, 1954; children: Caryn, Thomas, John. BA, U. Colo., 1955, MD, 1958. Intern Phila. Gen. Hosp., 1958-59; resident U. Mich., 1959-60, U. Colo., Denver, 1960-62, pulmonary fellow, 1962-63, chief resident medicine, 1963-64, instr. medicine, 1962-64, asst. prof., 1964-68, assoc. prof., 1968-74, prof. medicine, 1974—; pres. Presbyn./St. Luke's Ctr. for Health Scis. Edn., 1989-95; practice medicine, specializing in internal medicine, pulmonary medicine Denver, 1962—; prof. medicine Rush Univ., 1992—. Cons. Vencor Hosp., 1991—; chmn. Nat. Lung Health Edn. Program, 1995—. Author: For Those Who Live and Breathe, 1967, 2d edit., 1972, Intensive and Rehabilitative Respiratory Care, 1971, 3d edit., 1982, Chronic Obstructive Pulmonary Disease, 1978, 2d edit., 1985, Principles and Practice of Pulmonary Rehabilitation, 1993, Enjoying Life With COPD, 1995, 3d edit., others; contbr. articles to profl. jours. NIH and Found. grantee, 1966-88. Master ACP, Am. Coll. Chest Physicians (master, pres. 1982); mem. Assn. Am. Physicians, Assn. of Pulmonary Program Dirs. (founding pres. 1983-84, chmn. nat. lung health edn. program 1995—), Am. Bd. Internal Medicine (bd. govs. 1986-92), Am. Thoracic Soc. (Disting. Achievement award 1995), Phi Beta Kappa, Phi Delta Theta, Alpha Omega Alpha, Phi Rho Sigma (pres. 1976-78). Home: 1940 Grape St Denver CO 80220-1353 Office: Presbyn Hosp Dept Internal Medicine Denver CO 80218 E-mail: nlhep@aol.com

PETTY, TOM, rock guitarist, band leader, composer; b. Gainesville, Fla., Oct. 20, 1950; s. Earl Petty. Rock guitarist, 1969—; leader Tom Petty and the Heartbreakers, 1975—. Played in local bands The Epics, Mudcrutch while in Gainesville; songwriter, musician for Leon Russell, 1974; rec. and touring artist with the Heartbreakers, albums include Tom Petty and the Heartbreakers, 1976, You're Gonna Get It, 1978, Damn the Torpedoes, 1979, Hard Promises, 1981, Long After Dark, 1982, Southern Accents, 1985, Pack Up the Plantation, 1986, Let Me Up (I've Had Enough), 1987, Full Moon Fever, 1989, Into the Great Wide Open, 1991, Tom Petty and the Heartbreakers' Greatest Hits, 1993, Wildflowers, 1994, Songs & Music from the Motion Picture She's The One, 1996, Echo, 1999; (with The Traveling Wilburys) Traveling Wilburys Vol. 1, 1989, Traveling Wilburys Vol. 3, 1990; hit singles include Breakdown, 1978, Here Comes My Girl, 1979, Refugee, 1979, The Waiting, 1981, You Got Lucky, 1982, Don't Come Around Here No More, 1985, Jammin' Me, 1987, Free Fallin', 1989 (solo album), Playback, 1994, Wildflowers, 1995; toured the world with Bob Dylan, 1986, toured America with Georgia Satellites and Del Fuegos (Rock 'n' Roll Caravan tour), 1987; film composer She's the One, 1996. Grammy nomination (Best Rock Duo or Group Performance, 1994) for My Back Pages (with Bob Dylan, Roger McGuinn, Neil Young, Eric Clapton, and George Harrison); MTV Best Male Video (with the Heartbreakers) for Mary Jane's Last Dance; recipient MTV Video Vanguard award, CLIO Award, 1995, Grammy Best Male Rock Vocal, 1995, MTV award for Best Male Video, 1995, Nat. Veteran's Foundation Special Award of Recognition, 1995, UCLA George & Ira Gershwin Award, 1996, CA Music Awards: Billy Graham Lifetime Acheivement Award, 1998, Hollywood Walk of Fame Star, 1999. Office: Warner Bros Records 3300 Warner Blvd Burbank CA 91505-4694

PFAELZER, MARIANA R. federal judge; b. L.A., Feb. 4, 1926; AB, U. Calif., 1947; LLB, UCLA, 1957. Bar: Calif. 1958. Assoc. Wyman, Bautzer, Rothman & Kuchel, 1957-69, ptnr., 1969-78; judge U.S. Dist. Ct. (ctrl. dist.) Calif., 1978—. Mem. Jud. Conf. Adv. Com. on Fed. Rules of Civil Procedure. Pres., v.p., dir. Bd. Police Commrs. City of L.A., 1974-78. UCLA Alumnus award for Profl. Achievement, 1979, named Alumna of Yr., UCLA Law Sch., 1980, U. Calif. Santa Barbara Disting. Alumnus award, 1983. Mem. ABA, Calif. Bar Assn. (local adminstrv. com., spl. com. study rules procedure 1972, joint subcom. profl. ethics and computers and the law coms. 1972, profl. ethics com. 1972-74, spl. com. juvenile justice, women's rights subcom. human rights sect.), L.A. County Bar Assn. (spl. com. study rules procedure state bar 1974), Ninth Cir. Dist. Judges Assn. (pres.). Office: US Dist Ct 312 N Spring St Ste 152 Los Angeles CA 90012-4703

PFAU, GEORGE HAROLD, JR. stockbroker; b. Milw., May 7, 1924; s. George Harold and Elisabeth C. (Hunter) P.; m. Anne Elizabeth Mayhew (dec.); 1 child, George Harold III; children by previous marriage: Mary D., Peter W., Elizabeth C. B.S., Yale U., 1948. Tchr., 1948-49; with Fleishhacker Paper Box Co., San Francisco, 1952-54; salesman A.G. Becker & Co., San Francisco, 1954-55; v.p., sec., dir. Carl W. Stern & Co., San Francisco, 1955-57; with White Weld & Co. Inc., San Francisco, 1957-78; 1st v.p. corp. fin. dept. Blyth Eastman Dillon, San Francisco, 1978-79; sr. v.p. UBS Paine Webber, San Francisco, 1979—. Bd. dirs. 1 A Dist. Argl. Assn. Bd. dirs. The Guardsmen, 1966-67, Pathfinder Fund, 1974-82, San Francisco Zool. Soc., 1979-80; trustee Thacher Sch., Ojai, Calif., 1967-76, Town Sch., San Francisco, 1966-70; pres. Planned Parenthood San Francisco-Alameda County, 1968-69, bd. dirs., 1965—; chmn. Lincoln Club of No. Calif, 1993-95, mem., 1982—; chmn. Citizens for Better San Francisco. With C.E. AUS, 1942-44; with Am. Field Svc., 1944-45. Mem. Kappa Beta Phi, San Francisco Bond Club, Bohemian Club (San Francisco), Calif. Tennis Club, Villa Taverna. Office: UBS Paine Webber 555 California St Fl 32D San Francisco CA 94104-1502 E-mail: george.pfau@painewebber.com

PFEFFER, JEFFREY, business educator; b. St. Louis, July 23, 1946; s. Newton Stuart and Shirlee (Krisman) P.; m. Kathleen Frances Fowler, July 23, 1986. BS, MS, Carnegie Mellon U., 1968; PhD, Stanford U., 1972. Tech. staff Research Analysis Corp., McLean, Va., 1968-69; asst. prof. U. Ill., Champaign, 1971-73; from asst. prof. to assoc. prof. U. Calif., Berkeley, 1973-79; prof. Grad. Sch. Bus., Stanford U., Calif., 1979—. Vis. prof. Harvard U. Sch. Bus., Boston, 1981-82; dir., mem. compensation com. Portola Packaging, Inc.; dir. SonoSite, Inc., Audible Magic, Inc., Actify, Inc., Unicru, Inc. Author: The External Control of Organizations, 1978, Organizational Design, 1978, Power in Organizations, 1981, Organizations and Organization Theory, 1982 (Terry Book award 1984), Managing with Power, 1992, Competitive Advantage Through People, 1994, New Directions for Organization Theory, 1997, The Human Equation, 1998, The Knowing-Doing Gap, 1999, Hidden Value, 2000. Fellow Acad. Mgmt. (bd. govs. 1984-86, New Concept award 1979, Richard D. Irwin award for scholarly contbns. to mgmt. 1989); mem. Indsl. Rels. Rsch. Assn. Jewish. Avocations: cooking, music. Home: 425 Moseley Rd Hillsborough CA 94010-6715 Office: Stanford U Grad Sch Bus Stanford CA 94305 E-mail: pfeffer_jeffrey@gsb.stanford.edu

PFEIFER, LARRY ALAN, public health service coordinator; b. Rock Springs, Wyo., July 20, 1958; s. Jack Albert and Betty Lee (Ethington) P.; m. Sandra Lynn, June 20, 1986. BS cum laude, So. Oreg. State Coll., 1983, MS in Health Edn., 1989; paramedic diploma, Rogue Community Coll., 1984; postgrad., Columbia Pacific U. Cert. paramedic, Oreg. Cpt., paramedic Tualatin Valley Fire and Rescue, Portland, Oreg., 1991—. Adj. faculty Oreg. Health Scis. U. Sch. of Medicine, Dept. of Emergency Medicine, 1995; lectr. in field. Author (text) Non-Verbal Pre-Hospital Assessment of the Trauma Patient. Mem. Oreg. Paramedic Assn., Phi Kappa Phi, Kappa Delta Pi. Home: 10026 NW Priscilla Ct Portland OR 97229-5273

PFEIFFER, PHYLLIS KRAMER, publishing executive; b. N.Y.C., Feb. 11, 1949; d. Jacob N. and Estelle G. Rosenbaum-Pfeiffer; m. Stephen M. Pfeiffer, Dec. 21, 1969; children: Andrew Kramer, Elise Kramer. BS, Cornell U., 1970; postgrad., U. San Diego, 1976-78. Instr. Miss Porter's Sch., Farmington, Conn., 1970; tchr. Dewey Jr. H.S. N.Y.C. Bd. Edn., 1970-73; rschr. Hunter Coll., N.Y.C., 1971-72; account exec. La Jolla (Calif.) Light, 1973-75, advt. dir., 1975-77, gen. mgr., 1977-78, pub., 1978-87; exec. v.p. Harte Hanks So. Calif. Newspapers, 1985-87; gen. mgr. San Diego edit. L.A. Times, 1987-93; pres., pub. Marin Ind. Jour., Novato, Calif., 1993-2000; v.p. advt. and mktg. Contra Costa Times, 2000—. Dir. comm. ctr. San Diego State U., 1980-93. Bd. dirs. La Jolla Cancer Rsch. Found., 1979-82, YMCA, San Diego Ballet, 1980, Dominican Coll., San Rafael, Calif, 1994—, Marin Theater Co., Alvarado Hosp., 1981-88, chmn. fin. com., 1986, sec. bd., 1986; co-chmn. Operation USS La Jolla, USN, 1980—; mem. mktg. com. United Way, 1979-81, chmn., 1983; trustee La Jollan's Inc., 1975-78; mem. Conv. and Visitors Bur. Blue Ribbon Com. on Future, 1983; mem. resource panel Child Abuse Prevention Found., 1983—; bd. overseers U. Calif., San Diego; mem. violent crimes task force San Diego Police Dept.; trustee Nat. Pk. Trust, 2000—. Grantee N.Y. Bd. Edn., 1971-72; named Pub. of Yr., Gannet Co., Inc., 1995. Mem. Newspaper Assn. Am., Calif. Newspaper Pubs. Assn. (bd. dirs., exec. com.), Chancellor's Assn. U. Calif.-San Diego, Tiburon Peninsula Club. Office: Contra Costa Times 2640 Shadelands Dr Walnut Creek CA 94598 E-mail: ppfeiffer@cctimes.com

PFEIFFER, ROBERT JOHN, business executive; b. Suva, Fiji Islands, Mar. 7, 1920; came to U.S., 1921, naturalized, 1927; s. William Albert and Nina (MacDonald) P.; m. Mary Elizabeth Worts, Nov. 29, 1945; children—Elizabeth Pfeiffer Tumbas, Margaret Pfeiffer Hughes, George, Kathleen. Grad. high sch., Honolulu, 1937; DSc (hon.), Maine Maritime Acad.; HHD (hon.), U. Hawaii; DHL (hon.), Hawaii Loa Coll. With Inter-Island Steam Navigation Co., Ltd., Honolulu, (re-organized to Overseas Terminal Ltd. 1950), (merged into Oahu Ry. & Land Co. 1954), 1937-55, v.p., gen. mgr., 1950-54, mgr. ship agy. dept., 1954-55; v.p., gen. mgr. Pacific Cut Stone & Granite Co., Inc., Alhambra, Calif., 1955-56, Matcinal Corp., Alameda, 1956-58; mgr. div. Pacific Far East Line, Inc., San Francisco, 1958-60; with Matson Nav. Co., San Francisco, 1960—, v.p., 1966-70, sr. v.p., 1970-71; pres. The Matson Co., 1970-82; exec. v.p. Matson Nav. Co., San Francisco, 1971-73, pres., 1973-79, 84-85, 89-90, CEO, 1973-92, chmn. bd., bd.dirs., 1978-95, chmn. emeritus, 1995-98, chmn., 1998-99; chmn. emeritus, 1999—; v.p., gen. mgr. Matson Terminals, Inc., San Francisco, 1960-62, pres., 1962-70, chmn. bd., 1970-79, Matson Svcs. Co., 1973-79, Matson Agys., Inc., 1973-78; sr. v.p. Alexander & Baldwin, Inc., Honolulu, 1973-77, exec. v.p., 1977-79, chmn. bd., 1980-95, chmn. emeritus, 1995-98, 99—, chmn., pres., CEO, 1998, chmn. bd. dirs., 1998-99, CEO, 1980-92, pres., 1979-84, 89-91, chmn. emeritus, 1999—; chmn. bd., pres., dir. A&B-Hawaii, Inc., 1988-89, chmn. bd., 1989-95, chmn. emeritus, 1995-98, chmn. bd. dirs., 1998-99. Former mem. Gov.'s commn. on exec. salaries State of Hawaii, com. on jud. salaries. Past chmn. maritime transp. rsch. bd. NAS; former mem. select com. for Am. Mcht. Marine Seamanship Trophy Award; mem. commn. sociotech. systems NRC; mem. adv. com. Joint Maritime Congress; Pacific Aerospace Mus., also bd. dirs.; vice-chmn. Hawaii Maritime Ctr.; former chmn. A. Com. on Excellence (ACE), Hawaii; bd. govs. Japanese Cultural Ctr. Hawaii; hon. co-chmn. McKinley H.S. Found. Lt. USNR, WWII; comdr. Res. ret. Mem. VFW (life), Nat. Assn. Stevedores (past pres.), Internat. Cargo Handling Coord. Assn. (past pres. U.S. Com.), Propeller Club U.S. (past pres. Honolulu chpt.), Nat. Def. Transp. Assn., Containerization & Intermodal Inst. (hon. bd. advisors), 200 Club, Aircraft Owners and Pilots Assn., Pacific Club, Outrigger Club, Oahu Country Club, Maui Country Club, Pacific Union Club, Bohemian Club, World Trade Club (San Francisco), Masons, Shriners. Republican. Home: 535 Miner Rd Orinda CA 94563-1429 Office: Alexander & Baldwin Inc 822 Bishop St Honolulu HI 96813-3925

PFENNINGER, KARL H. cell biology and neuroscience educator; b. Stafa, Switzerland, Dec. 17, 1944; came to U.S., 1971, naturalized, 1993; s. Hans Rudolf and Delie Maria (Zahn) P.; m. Marie-France Maylié, July 12, 1974; children: Jan Patrick, Alexandra Christina MD, U. Zurich, 1971. Rsch. instr. dept. anatomy Washington U., St. Louis, 1971-73; rsch. assoc. sect. cell biology Yale U., New Haven, 1973-76; assoc. prof. dept. anatomy and cell biology Columbia U., N.Y.C., 1976-81, prof., 1981-86; prof., chmn. dept. cellular and structural biology U. Colo. Sch. Medicine, Denver, 1986—. Dir. interdeptmental program in cell and molecular biology Columbia U. Coll. Physicians and Surgeons, N.Y.C., 1980-85; chmn. Given Biomed. Inst., Aspen, Colo., 1992-93. Author: Essential Cell Biology, 1990, The Origins of Creativity, 2001; contbr. articles to profl. jours. Recipient C.J. Herrick award Am. Assn. Anatomists, 1977; I.T. Hirschl Career Scientist award, 1977; Javits neurosci. investigator awards NIH, 1984, 91. Mem. AAAS, Am. Soc. for Cell Biology, Am. Soc. for Biochemistry and Molecular Biology, Toxicology Forum (bd. dirs. 1995—), Assn. Anatomy, Cell Biology and Neurosci. Chairpersons (pres. 1998), Harvey Soc., Soc. for Neurosci., Internat. Brain Rsch. Orgn., Internat. Soc. for Neurochemistry. Office: U Colo Health Scis Ctr Dept Cellular & Structural Biology B 111 4200 E 9th Ave Denver CO 80262-0001 E-mail: Karl.pfenninger@uchsc.edu

PFISTER, TERRI, city official; Grad. high sch., Redfield, S.D., 1984; cert. stenographer, Stenotype Inst. of S.D., 1986. Police pension sec. City of Spokane, Wash., 1991-96, city clk., 1996—. Office: 808 W Spokane Falls Blvd Spokane WA 99201-3342

PFLAUMER, KATRINA C. lawyer; BA in English Lit. cum laude, Smith Coll.; MA in Tchg. English, Columbia U.; JD, NYU. Tchr. English and Am. Lit. Westtown Sch., Pa., 1970-72; staff atty. Seattle King County Defender Assn., 1975-77, Fed. Pub. Defender's Office, Seattle, 1977-80; pvt. practice, 1980-93; U.S. atty. Dept. Justice (we. dist.) Washington, 1993-01. Pro tem judge King County Superior Ct.; adj. prof. U. Puget Sound Sch. Law; guest lectr. U. Washington, Hastings, Cardozo, Nat. Inst. Trial Advocacy programs; lawyer rep. 9th Cir. Jud. Conf.; named to Atty. Gen. Adv. Com., 1994-95. Mem. Fire Brigade Emergency Response Team. Mem. FBA (pres. we. dist. Washington 1991, chair implementation of gender task force report com.), Nat. Assn. Criminal Def. Lawyers (mem. nominating com.), U.S. Sentencing Commn. (practitioners adv. group), Am. Civil Liberties Union (mem. legal com.), Seattle-King County Bar Assn. (mem. jud. conf. com.), Washington Assn. Criminal Def. Lawyers (pres. 1988-89), State Bench Bar (mem. press com.), Phi Beta Kappa. Office: US Dept Justice 601 Union St Ste 5100 Seattle WA 98101

PHAIR, JOSEPH BASCHON, lawyer; b. N.Y.C., Apr. 29, 1947; s. James Francis and Mary Elizabeth (Baschon) P.; m. Bonnie Jean Hobbs, Sept. 04, 1971; children: Kelly I., Joseph B., Sean P. BA, U. San Francisco, 1970, JD, 1973. Bar: Calif., U.S. Dist. Ct. (no. dist.) Calif., U.S. Ct. Appeals (9th cir.). Assoc. Berry, Davis & McInerney, Oakland, Calif., 1974-76, Bronson, Bronson & McKinnon, San Francisco, 1976-79; staff atty. Varian Assocs., Inc., Palo Alto, Calif., 1979-83, corp. counsel, 1983-86, sr. corp. counsel, 1986-87, assoc. gen. counsel, 1987-90, v.p., gen. counsel, 1990-91, v.p., gen. counsel, sec., 1991-99; v.p. adminstrn., gen. counsel, sec. Varian Med. Sys., Inc., Palo Alto, 1999—. Mem. devel. bd. St. Vincent de Paul Devel. Coun., San Francisco, 1992—. Mem. Bay Area Gen. Counsel, Silicon Valley Assn. Gen. Counsel, The Olympic Culb. Roman Catholic. Office: Varian Med Sys Inc M S V 250 3100 Hansen Way Palo Alto CA 94304-1030

PHALEN, ROBERT FRANKLYNN, environmental scientist; b. Fairview, Okla., Oct. 18, 1940; married, 1966; 2 children. B in Physics, San Diego State U., 1964, M in Physics, 1966; PhD in Biophysics, U. Rochester, 1971. Engring. aide advanced space systems dept. Gen. Dynamics/Astronautics, San Diego, 1962-63; asst. to radiation safety officer, lab. teaching asst. San Diego State U., 1964-66, instr. physics dept., 1966; mem. summer faculty biology dept. Rochester (N.Y.) Inst. Tech., 1970-72; rsch. assoc. aerosol physics dept. Lovelace Found. for Med. Edn. and Rsch., Albuquerque, 1972-74; from adj. asst. prof. to assoc. prof. in residence dept. community and environ. medicine U. Calif., Irvine, 1974-84, prof., dir. Air Pollution Health Effects Lab., 1985—, faculty Ctr. for Occupl. Environ. Health, 1985—. Reviewer Aerosol Sci. and Tech., Am. Rev. Respiratory Disease, Applied Indsl. Hygiene, Bull. Math. Biology, Exptl. Lung Rsch., Jour. Toxicology and Environ. Health, Jour. Toxicology and Applied Pharmacology, Jour. Aerosol Sci., Sci.; reviewer, mem. editl. bd. Fundamental and Applied Toxicology, 1986-92, Inhalation Toxicology, Jour. Aerosol Medicine; mem. safety and occupl. health study sect. NIH, 1988-99, mem. spl. study sects., 1980, 81, chmn. spl. study sects., 1982-84, 87, 88, 92, mem. site visit teams, 1980-2000; mem. expert panel on sulfur oxides EPA, mem. inhalation toxicology divsn. peer rev. panel, 1982, session chmn., 1983, participant workshop on non-oncogenic lung disease, 1984, mem. grants rsch. sci. rev. panel on health rsch., EPA advisor, 1985-88, 93-98; mem. task group on respiratory tract kinetic model Nat. Coun. Radiation Protection, 1978-97; mem. adv. panel on asbestos APHA, 1978; chmn. atmospheric sampling com. Am. Coun. Govtl. Indsl. Hygienists, 1982-92; chmn. NIOSH spl. study sect., 1983; panelist workshop Nat. Heart, Lung and Blood Inst., 1982; sci. advisor Prentice Day Sch., 1986-98. Author: Inhalation Studies: Foundations and Techniques, 1984, (with others) Advances in Air Sampling, 1988, Concepts in Inhalation Toxicology, 1989, Deposition, Retention and Dosimetry of Inhaled Radioactive Substances, 1997; editor: Methods in Inhalation Toxicology, 1997; contbr. numerous articles to profl. jours. Am. Legion scholar. Mem. AAAS, Am. Assn. Aerosol Rsch. (charter, chmn. ann. meeting 1985), Am. Conf. Govtl. Indsl. Hygienists, Am. Indsl. Hygiene Assn. (jour. reviewer, chmn. ann. conf. 1981, 85, 86), Brit. Occupl. Hygiene Soc., Internat. Soc. Aerosols in Medicine, So. Calif. Acad. Scis., Soc. for Aerosol Rsch., Health Physics Soc., Soc. Toxicology (chmn. 20th ann. meeting 1981, dir. 3 internat. confs. on health effects of particulate air pollution, Career Achievement award 2000). Achievements include research in nasal, tracheobronchial and pulmonary transport of inhaled deposited particles and effects of pollutant exposure on transport kinetcs, laboratory simulation and characterization of airborne environmental pollutants, respiratory tract deposition and clearance models for inhaled particles, including species comparisons and body size effects, behavior of highly-concentrated aerosols with respect to deposition in the respiratory tract. Office: U Calif Air Pollution Health Effects Lab Cmty & Environ Medicine Irvine CA 92697-1825 E-mail: rfphalen@uci.edu

PHAM, KINH DINH, electrical engineer, educator, administrator; b. Saigon, Republic of Vietnam, Oct. 6, 1956; came to U.S., 1974; s. Nhuong D. (dec.) and Phuong T. (Tran) P.; m. Ngan-Lien T. Nguyen, May 27, 1985; children: Larissa, Galen. BS with honors, Portland State U., 1979; MSEE, U. Portland, 1982; postgrad., Portland State U., 1988-90. Registered profl. engr., Oreg., Calif., Ariz., Fla., Wash., Mass., Conn., R.I. Elec. engr. Irvington-Moore, Tigard, Oreg., 1979-80, Elcon Assocs., Inc., Beaverton, 1980-87, from sr. elec. engr., assoc. ptnr., 1987-96, v.p., 1996—. Adj. prof. Portland (Oreg.) Community Coll., 1982—; mem. adv. bd. Mass Transit System Compatibility, 1994. Co-author: FE/EIT Exam: Electrical Engineering Review and Study Guide, 2000, Electrical Engineering Professional Engineer License Exam Review Handbook, 2001, pub.: Research and Education and Association, 2000; cons. tech. editor Rsch. and Edn. Assn., 1998—; contbr. articles to profl. jours. Recipient Cert. Appreciation Am. Pub. Transit Assn. and Transit Industry, 1987. Sr. mem. IEEE, Industry Applications, Power Engring. and Vehicular Tech. Soc.; mem N.Y. Acad. Scis., Mass Transit Sys. Compatibility Adv. Bd, Eta Kappa Nu. Buddhist. Avocations: reading, teaching; profl. interests include traction power systems simulation, analysis and design, computer systems simulations, other computer-related systems. Office: Elcon Assocs Inc 12670 NW Barnes Rd Portland OR 97229-9001 E-mail: kinhlien@aol.com, kpham@elconasoc.com

PHANSTIEL, HOWARD G. health care system executive; BA in Political Sci., M in Pub. Adminstrn., Syracuse U. Exec./mgmt. Prudential Bache Internat. Bank/Securities, Marine Midland Banks, Sallie Mae; exec. v.p. fin./info. svcs. WellPoint Health Networks, Inc., Woodland Hills, Calif.; chmn., CEO ARV Assisted Living, Inc., Costa Mesa; exec. v.p., CFO PacifiCare Health Sys., Santa Anna, 2000, pres., CEO, 2000. Office: PacifiCare Health Sys 3120 W Lake Ctr Dr Santa Ana CA 92704

PHELPS, ARTHUR VAN RENSSELAER, physicist, consultant; b. Dover, N.H., July 20, 1923; s. George Osborne and Helen (Ketchum) P.; m. Gertrude Kanzius, July 21, 1956; children: Wayne Edward, Joan Susan. ScD in Physics, MIT, 1951. Cons. physicist rsch. labs. Westinghouse Elec. Corp., Pitts., 1951-70; sr. rsch. scientist Nat. Bur. Standards, Boulder, Colo., 1970-88; fellow Joint Inst. Lab. Astrophysics U. Colo., Boulder, 1970-88, adjoint fellow, 1988—, chmn., 1979-81. Chmn. Gordon Rsch. Conf., Plasma Chemistry, 1990. Recipient Silver Medal award Dept. Commerce, 1978. Fellow Am. Phys. Soc. (Will Allis prize 1990). Achievements include patent for Schulz-Phelps ionization gauge; research on electron and atomic collision processes involving low energy electrons, molecules, ions, metastable atoms and resonance radiation; on laser processes and modeling; on gaseous electronics. Home: 3405 Endicott Dr Boulder CO 80305-6908 Office: U Colo Joint Inst Lab Astrophysics PO Box 440 Boulder CO 80309-0440

PHELPS, BARTON CHASE, architect, educator; b. Bklyn., June 27, 1946; s. Julian Orville and Elizabeth Willis (Faulk) P.; m. Karen Joy Simonson; 1 child, Charlotte Simonson Phelps. BA in Art with honors, Williams Coll., 1968; MArch, Yale U., 1973. Registered architect, Calif. With Colin St. John Wilson & Ptnrs., London, 1972-73, Frank O. Gehry and Assocs., Inc., Santa Monica, Calif., 1973-76, Charles Moore/Urban Innovations Group, L.A., 1976-78; dir. architecture Urban Innovations Group, L.A., 1980-84; prin. Barton Phelps & Assocs., L.A., 1984—; asst. prof. architecture Rice U. Sch. of Architecture, Houston, 1977-79; asst. dean Grad. Sch. Architecture and Urban Planning, UCLA, 1980-83; former prof. architecture Sch. Arts and Architecture UCLA. Faculty mem. Nat. Endowment Arts, Mayors Inst. for City Design, 1990, 92. Author, editor: Architecture California, 1988-92, 98; editor: Views From the River, 1998; mem. editl. bd. Archtl. Record, 1998—. Fellow Graham Found. for Advanced Studies in the Fine Arts, 1989, 96, Nat. Endowment for the Arts, 1990, 98. Mem. AIA (Coll. of Fellows, chair nat. com. on design, design excellence program USGSA, recipient design awards for L.A. Pub. Libr., Los Feliz, Royce Hall at UCLA, Arroyo House, Kranz House, North Range Clark Libr. UCLA, L.A. Dept. Water and Power Ctrl. Dist. Hdqrs., No. Hollywood Pump Sta., East Bldg. Seeds U. Elem. Sch., UCLA, Inst. Honor for Collaborative Design, Games XXIII Olympiad L.A. 1984), L.A. Conservancy. Democrat. Home: 10256 Lelia Ln Los Angeles CA 90077-3144 Office: Barton Phelps & Assocs 5514 Wilshire Blvd Los Angeles CA 90036-3829

PHELPS, MICHAEL EDWARD, biophysics educator; b. Cleve., Aug. 24, 1939; s. Earl E. and Regina Bridget (Hines) P.; m. Patricia Emory, May 15, 1969; children: Patrick, Kaitlin. B.A., Western Wash. State U., 1965; Ph.D., Washington U., St. Louis, 1970. Asst. prof. Washington U. Sch. Medicine and Engrng., 1970-73, assoc. prof., 1973-75; assoc. prof. dept. radiology U. Pa., Phila., 1975-76; prof. biomath. UCLA, 1976—, prof., chief div. nuclear medicine, 1980—, dir. Crump Inst. for Biol. Imaging, 1990—, chair molecular and med. pharmacology, 1992; assoc. dir. UCLA/DOE Lab. Structural Biology and Molecular Medicine. Mem. study sect. NIH, Bethesda, Md., 1974-78. Author: Reconstruction Tomography in Diagnostic Radiology and Nuclear Medicine, 1977, Physics in Nuclear Medicine, 1980, Principles of Tracer Kinetics, 1983; contbr. articles to profl. jours. Recipient Von Hevesy Found. award, 1975, Von Hevesy Found. award, 1982, Von Hevesy prize Von Hevesy Found., Zurich, 1978, 82, E.O. Lawrence award Dept. Energy, 1983, Pasarow Found. award, 1992, Enrico Fermi Presdl. award, 1999; holder Jennifer Jones Simon endowed chair, 1983; named Disting. Alumnus Western Wash. State U., 1980 Fellow Am. Heart Assn.; mem. ACP (Rosenthal award 1987), Inst. Medicine NAS (elected), Soc. Nuclear Medicine (Aebersold award 1983), Internat. Soc. Cerebral Blood Flow and Metabolism (Excellence award 1979), N.Y. Acad. Scis. (Sarah L. Poiley award 1984), Soc. Neuroscis. Roman Catholic. Home: 16720 Huerta Rd Encino CA 91436-3544

PHELPS, MICHAEL EVERETT JOSEPH, energy company executive; b. Montreal, Que., Can., June 27, 1947; s. Arthur A. and Hendrina (Von De Roer) P.; m. Joy Slimmon, Aug. 8, 1970; children: Erica, Julia, Lindsay. BA, U. Man., Winnipeg, Can., 1967, LLB, 1970; LLM, London Sch. Econs., 1971; LLD (hon.), U. Winnipeg, 1992, Simon Frasier U., 1994. Crown atty. Province of Man., Winnipeg, 1972-73; ptnr. Christie, Degraves, Winnipeg, 1973-76; spl. advisor to min. justice Ministry of Justice, Ottawa, Ont., 1977-79; exec. asst. Minister of Energy, Mines & Resources, Ottawa, 1980-82; sr. advisor to pres. & chief exec. officer Westcoast Transmission Co. Ltd., Vancouver, B.C., 1982-83, v.p. strategic planning, 1983-87, sr. v.p., 1987, exec. v.p., chief fin. officer, 1987-88; pres., chief exec. officer Westcoast Energy, Inc. (formerly Westcoast Transmission Co Ltd.), Vancouver, 1988-92, now chmn., CEO, 1992—, also bd. dirs., 1992—. Bd. dirs. Canadian Imperial Bank Commerce, Canfor Corp., Canadian Pacific, Westcoast Energy Internat. Inc.; mem. adv. coun. faculty commerce and bus. administrn. U. B.C.; mem. adv. bd. Team Can., Inc.; lectr. Man. Bar Admission Course, 1973, 74, 79; lectr. dept. law. Carleton U., 1977-79. Chmn. bd. dirs. Asia Pacific Found. Can.; trustee Simon fraser U. Found.; chmn. com. to nominate Can. Pension Plan Investment Bd.; mem. policy com. Bus. Coun. on Nat. Issues. Mem. Interstate Natural Gas Assn. Am. (bd. dirs., vice-chmn.). Office: Westcoast Energy Inc 1333 W Georgia St Vancouver BC Canada V6E 3K9

PHIBBS, HARRY ALBERT, interior designer, professional speaker, lecturer; b. Denver, Jan. 9, 1933; s. Harry Andrew and Mary May (Perriam) P.; m. Alice Conners Glynn, Oct. 23, 1957 (div. Jan. 1988); children: Kathleen Ann Phibbs Pierz, Paul Robert, Mary Alice Phibbs Hettle, Michael John, Peter James, Daniel Edward; m. Nevelle Haley Jones, Feb. 1988. B.A., U. Colo., 1954, B.F.A., 1957. Interior designer Howard Lorton, Inc., Denver, 1957-68; interior designer, v.p. Ronald Ansay Inc., Wheatridge, Colo., 1969-71; interior designer, pres. Phibbs Design Assos., Inc., Denver, 1972-78; interior designer, mgr. Howard Lorton, Inc., Colorado Springs, Colo., 1979-93; prin. Phibbs Design, Colorado Springs, 1993—. Pres. Interior Designers Housing Devel. Corp., 1969-72; chmn. adv. com. interior design program Pikes Peak C.C., 1998—; adj. faculty, Pike's Peak C.C., 2000—. V.p. Arvada (Colo.) Hist. Soc., 1973; bd. dirs. Colo. Opera Festival, also pres., 1986; bd. dirs. Downtown Colorado Springs, Inc., also pres., 1984; chmn. bd. trustees Interior Design Internship Denver, 1991-94. With U.S. Army, 1954-56. Fellow Am. Soc. Interior Designers (nat. pres. 1977); mem. Am. Arbitration Assn., Theta Xi (pres. Denver Area alumni club 1958-64) Democrat. Roman Catholic. Home: 91 W Boulder St Colorado Springs CO 80903-3371 Office: 10 Boulder Crescent St Colorado Springs CO 80903-3344

PHILBIN, ANN M. art facility director; b. Boston, Mar. 21, 1952; d. Richard Moore and Ann Theresa (Muller) P. BA, BFA, U. N.H.; MA, NYU, 1982. Rschr. Frick Art Reference Libr., N.Y.C., 1977-79; asst. to dir., program coord. Artists Space, N.Y.C., 1979-80; asst. curatorial coord. The New Mus., N.Y.C., 1980-81; curator Ian Woodner Family Collection, N.Y.C., 1981-83; asst. dir. Grace Borgenicht Gallery, N.Y.C., 1983-85; dir. Curt Marcus Gallery, N.Y.C., 1985-88; account dir., dir. Art Against AIDS Livet Reichard Inc., N.Y.C., 1988-90; dir. The Drawing Ctr., N.Y.C., 1990, UCLA Hammer Museum, Los Angeles. Bd. dirs. Elizabeth Streb, Ringside, N.Y., 1990, HIV Law Project, N.Y.C., 1993; founding mem. Women's Action Coalition, N.Y.C., 1991. Address: UCLA Hammer Museum 10899 Wilshire Blvd Los Angeles CA 90024

PHILIPS, CHUCK, journalist; Journalist L.A. Times, 1990—. Recipient Pulitzer prize for Beat Reporting, 1999. Office: c/o LA Times Bus Sect Times Mirror Sq Los Angeles CA 90053 E-mail: chuck.philips@latimes.com

PHILIPS, SUZANNE MARGUERITE See CASEY, SUE

PHILLIPS, ANTHONY GEORGE, neurobiology educator; b. Barrow, Cumbria, Eng., Jan. 30, 1943; came to Can., 1953; s. George William and Mabel Lilian (Wood) P. BA (hon.), U. Western Ont., London, Can., 1966, MA, 1967, PhD, 1970. Asst. prof. psychobiology U. British Columbia, Vancouver, Can., 1970-75, assoc. prof. Can., 1975-80, prof. Can., 1980—, prof. dept. psychiatry, 1994—, head dept. psychology, 1994-99. Founder Quadra Logic Tech., Inc., Vancouver. Contbr. numerous papers to sci. jours. Chmn. Can.-India Village Aid, Vancouver, 1981-86, bd. dirs. 1987—; bd. dirs. Tibetian Refuge Aid Soc., Vancouver, 1980—. Recipient Killam rsch. prize Can. Coun., 1977, Killam Rsch. prize U. B.C., 1986, D.O. Hebb award Can. Psychol. Assn.; Steacie fellow Nat. Scis. and Engrng. Rsch. Coun. (Can.), 1980. Fellow Royal Soc. Can.; mem. Soc. Neurosci., Can. Soc. for Neurosci., Can. Coll. Neuropsychopharmacology. Office: U BC Dept Psychology 2136 W Mall Vancouver BC Canada V6T 1Z4

PHILLIPS, GAIL, state legislator; b. Juneau, Alaska; m. Walt Phillips; children: Robin, Kim. BA in Bus. Edn., U. Alaska. Mem. Homer (Alaska) City Coun., 1981-84, Kenai Peninsula Borough Assembly, 1986-87; chmn. [illegible] house majority leader, 1993-94, spkr., 1995-98. Former owner, mgr. Quiet Sports; ptnr. Lindphil Mining Co.; pub. rels. cons. Active Homer United Meth. Ch., Rep. Ctrl. Com. Alaska, Kenai Peninsula Coll. Coun.; past mem. com. bd. and race coord. Iditarod Trail Dog Sled Race. Mem. Western States Legis. Coun. (exec. com.), Am. Legis Exch. Coun. (former state chmn.), Resource Devel. Coun. Alaska, Western Legis. Conf. (exec. bd.), Western States Coalition (exec. bd.), The Energy Coun. (exec. bd.). Home: PO Box 3304 Homer AK 99603-3304 also: Alaska Ho Reps State Capitol Juneau AK 99801-1182

PHILLIPS, GENEVA FICKER, academic editor; b. Staunton, Ill., Aug. 1, 1920; d. Arthur Edwin and Lillian Agnes (Woods) Ficker; m. James Emerson Phillips, Jr., June 6, 1955 (dec. 1979). BS in Journalism, U. Ill., 1942; MA in English Lit., UCLA, 1953. Copy desk Chgo. Jour. Commerce, 1942-43; editl. asst. patents Radio Rsch. Lab. Harvard U., Cambridge, Mass., 1943-45; asst. editor adminstrv. publs. U. Ill., Urbana, 1946-47; editl. asst. Quar. of Film, Radio and TV UCLA, 1952-53; mng. editor The Works of John Dryden, Dept. English UCLA, 1964—. Bd. dirs. Univ. Religious Conf., L.A., 1979— . UCLA teaching fellow, 1950-53, grad. fellow 1954-55. Mem. Assn. Acad. Women UCLA, Friends of Huntington Libr., Friends of UCLA Libr., Friends of Ctr. for Medieval and Renaissance Studies, Samuel Johnson Soc. So. Calif., Assocs. U. Calif. Press, Conf. Christianity and Lit., Soc. Mayflower Descendants. Lutheran. Home: 213 First Anita Dr Los Angeles CA 90049-3815 Office: UCLA Dept English 2225 Rolfe Hall Los Angeles CA 90024

PHILLIPS, JILL META, novelist, critic, astrologer; b. Detroit, Oct. 22, 1952; d. Leyson Kirk and Leona Anna (Rasmussen) P. Student pub. schs., Calif. Lit. counselor Book Builders, Charter Oak, Calif., 1966-77; pres. Moon Dance Astro Graphics, Covina, 1994—. Author: (with Leona Phillips) A Directory of American Film Scholars, 1975, The Good Morning Cookbook, 1976, G.B. Shaw: A Review of the Literature, 1976, T.E. Lawrence: Portrait of the Artist as Hero, 1977, The Archaeology of the Collective East, 1977, The Occult, 1977, D.H. Lawrence: A Review of the Literature and Biographies, 1978, Film Appreciation: A College Guide Book, 1979, Annus Mirabilis: Europe in the Dark and Middle Centuries, 1979, (with Leona Rasmussen Phillips) The Dark Frame: Occult Cinema, 1979, Misfit: The Films of Montgomery Clift, 1979, Butterflies in the Mind: A Précis of Dreams and Dreamers, 1980; The Rain Maiden: A Novel of History, 1987, Walford's Oak: A Novel, 1990, The Fate Weaver: A Novel in Two Centuries, 1991, Saturn Falls: A Novel of the Apocalypse, 1993, Birthday Secrets, 1998, Your Luck is in the Stars, 2000; columnist Horoscope Guide Monthly; contbr. book revs. to New Guard mag., 1974-76; contbr. numerous articles to profl. jours. including Dell Horoscope, Midnight Horoscope, Astrology-Your Daily Horoscope, Am. Astrology. Mem. Young Ams. for Freedom, Am. Conservative Union, Elmer Bernstein's Film Music Collection, Ghost Club London, Count Dracula Soc., Dracula Soc. London, Richard III Soc. Republican. Home: 515 Claraday St Apt 8 Glendora CA 91740-6043 Office: Moon Dancer Astro Graphics 425 E Arrow Hwy Ste 252 Glendora CA 91740-5607

PHILLIPS, JOHN EDWARD, zoologist, educator; b. Montréal, Que., Can., Dec. 20, 1934; s. William Charles and Violet Mildred (Lewis) P.; m. Eleanor Mae Richardson, Sept. 8, 1956; children: Heather Anne, Jayne Elizabeth, Jonathan David, Catherine Melinda, Wendy Susannah. BSc with honors, Dalhousie U., Halifax, N.S., 1956, MSc, 1957; PhD, Cambridge U., Eng., 1961. Asst. prof. Dalhousie U., Halifax, N.S., 1960-64; assoc. prof. U. B.C., Vancouver, Can., 1964-71, prof. Can., 1971—, head dept. zoology Can., 1991-96. Vis. rschr. Cambridge (Eng.) U., 1972, 76, 81; chair grant selection com. Nat. Rsch. Coun. Can., Ottawa, Ont., 1969-71; mem. coun. Nat. Sci. and Engrng. Rsch. Coun., Ottawa, 1983-87. Mem. editorial bd.: Can. Jour. Zoology, 1971-75, Am. Jour. Physiology, 1978-93, Jour. Experimental Biology, 1981-85, Am. Zool., 1996-01; contbr. articles to profl. jours. Mem. grant selection com. Can. Cystic Fibrosis Found., Toronto, 1989-91; active Vancouver Bach Choir. Named to James chair St. Francis Xavier U., Antigonish, N.S., 1993; recipient Killam Rsch. prize U. B.C. Fellow Royal Soc. Can.; mem. Can. Soc. Zoologists (sec. 1972-76, v.p. 1976-78, pres. 1979, Fry medal 2000), Am. Soc. Zoologists (exec. 1983-85, chair divsn. comp. physiol. biochemistry 1983-85). Avocations: music, choir. Home: 12908 22 B Ave White Rock BC Canada V4A 6Z3 Office: U BC Dept Zoology Vancouver BC Canada V6T 1Z4

PHILLIPS, KAREN, secondary education educator; Physical edn. tchr., adminstr. Walter D. Johnson Jr. H.S., Las Vegas, 1993-97; asst. prin. Lied Mid. Sch., Las Vegas, 1997-99; prin. Clifford J. Lawrence Jr. High Sch., 1999—. Recipient Middle Sch. Physical Edn. Tchr. of the Yr. Nat. Assn. for Sport and Physical Edn., 1993. Office: Clifford J Lawrence Jr High Sch 4410 S Juliano Rd Las Vegas NV 89147-8691

PHILLIPS, KEITH ANTHONY (TONY), professional baseball player; b. Atlanta, Apr. 25, 1959; m. Debi Vosburg; children: Victoria, Selina. Student, N.Mex. Mil. Inst. Infielder Montreal (Can.) Expos farm sys., 1978-80, San Diego Padres farm sys., 1980-81, Oakland (Calif.) Athletics farm sys., 1981-82, Oakland Athletics, 1982-89, Detroit Tigers, 1990-94; infielder, outfielder Calif. Angels, Anaheim, 1995, Chgo. White Sox., 1996-97, Anaheim Angels, 1997-98, Toronto (Ont., Can.) Blue Jays, 1998, Oakland (Calif.) Athletics, 1998—. Played in chanmpionship series, Oakland, 1988, 89; played in World Series, Oakland, 1988, 89; shares major league single-game record (9 innings) for most assists by 2d baseman, 1986. Office: c/o Oakland Athletics 7677 Oakport St Ste 200 Oakland CA 94621-1933

PHILLIPS, KEITH WENDALL, minister; b. Portland, Oreg., Oct. 21, 1946; s. Frank Clark and Velma Georgina (Black) P.; m. Mary Katherine Garland, July 16, 1973; children: Joshua, Paul, David. BA, UCLA, 1968; MDiv, Fuller Theology Sem., 1971, D. of Ministries, 1972; LHD (hon.), John Brown U., 1990. Dir. Youth For Christ Clubs, L.A., 1965-71; pres. World Impact, L.A., 1971—. Commencement speaker Tabor Coll., 1969, 91, John Brown U., 1990. Author: Everybody's Afraid in the Ghetto, 1973, They Dare to Love the Ghetto, 1975, The Making of a Disciple, 1981, No Quick Fix, 1985, Out of Ashes, 1996. Chmn. L.A. Mayor's Prayer Breakfast Com., 1985—; bd. dirs. Christian Cmty. Devel. Assn., 1992—; founder/coord. Crowns of Beauty Confs.; spkr. Promise Keeper. Named Disting. Staley lectr., 1969. Mem. Evangelistic Com. of Newark (pres. 1976—), World Impact of Can. (pres. 1978—), The Oaks (pres. 1985—), Faith Works (pres. 1987—) Baptist. Office: World Impact 2001 S Vermont Ave Los Angeles CA 90007-1279

PHILLIPS, LAYN R. lawyer; b. Oklahoma City, Jan. 2, 1952; s. James Arthur Cole and Eloise (Gulick) P.; m. Kathryn Hale, Aug. 17, 1986; children: Amanda, Parker, Graham. BS, U. Tulsa, 1974, JD, 1977; postgrad., Georgetown U., 1978-79. Bar: Okla. 1977, D.C. 1978, Calif. 1981, Tex. 1991. Asst. U.S. atty., Miami, 1980-81, L.A., 1980-83; trial atty. Bur. of Competition, Washington, 1977-80; U.S. atty. U.S. Dist. Ct. (no. dist.) Okla., Tulsa, 1983-87; judge U.S. Dist. Ct. (we. dist.) Okla., Oklahoma City, 1987-91; litigation ptnr. Irell & Manella, Newport Beach, Calif., 1991—. Tchr. trial practice U. Tulsa Coll. Law, Okla. City U. Law Sch.; lectr. Attys. Gen's. Adv. Inst., Washington. Pres. Am. Inn of Ct. XXIII, Sch. Law, Okla. U., 1989-90; pres. Am. Inn. of Ct. CVIII, Sch. Law., Okla. City U. 1990-91. Named one of Outstanding Young Ams., U.S. Jaycees, 1989. Office: Irell & Manella 840 Newport Center Dr Ste 400 Newport Beach CA 92660-6323

PHILLIPS, MICHELLE GILLIAM, actress, author; b. Long Beach, [illegible] m. John Phillips, Dec. 31, 1962 (div. 1970); children: Gilliam Chynna Phillips, Austin D. Hines, Aron S. Wilson. Grad. high sch., Ft. Jones, Calif. Model Francis Gill Agy., N.Y.C., 1962-64; singer Mamas and Papas, 1965-69. Guest appearances in TV shows include Vega$, 1980, The Fall Guy, 1983, Santa Barbara, 1984, Murder, She Wrote, 1984, Scene of the Crime, 1985, Alfred Hitchcock Presents, 1985, T.J. Hooker, 1985, Star Trek: The Next Generation, 1988, Herman's Head, 1994, Diagnsos Murder, 1994, 99, Burke's Law, 1994, Lois & Clark: The New Adventures of Superman, 1995, Too Something, 1996, Beverly Hills, 90210, 1997, 98, Pauly, 1997, The Magnificent Seven, 1998, 99, 2000, The Love Boat: The Next Wave, 1998, Rude Awakening, 1999, Providence, 1999, Twice in a Lifetime, 2000; appeared in tv movies The Death Squad, 1974, The California Kid, 1974, The Useres, 1978, Moonlight, 1982, Murder Me, Murder You, 1983, Secrets of a Married Man, 1984, Covenant, 1985, Paint Me a Murder, 1985, Stark: Mirror Image, 1986, Assault and Matrimony, 1987, Mike Hammer: Murder Takes All, 1989, Trenchcoat in Paradise, 1989, Appearances, 1990, Rubdown, 1993, Rock 'n' Roll Revolution: The British Invade America, 1995, 919 Fifth Avenue, 1995, No One Would Tell, 1996, Pretty Poison, 1996, Sweetwater, 1999; appeared in feature films Monterey Pop, 1969, The Last Movie, 1971, Dillinger, 1973, Valentino, 1977, Bloodline, 1979, The Man with Bogart's Face, 1980, Savage Harvest, 1981, American Anthem, 1986, Let It Ride, 1989, Flashing on the Sixties: A Tribal Document, 1990, Scissors, 1991, Army of One, 1993, Anna Petrovic, You Rock!, 1998, Lost in the Pershing Point Hotel, 2000, TV series Aspen, 1977, The French Atlantic Affair, 1979, Hotel, 1983, Knots Landing, 1979, Second Chances, 1993, Malibu Shores, 1996, Knots Landing: Back to the Cul-de-Sac, 1997; author: California Dreamin', 1986, Monday Monday (Grammy award). Recipient medal of Honor for Stop War Toys Campaign Alliance for Survival, 1987, Soap Opera Awards for Best Villainess, 1990.

PHILLIPS, RANDY, state legislator, marketing professional; b. Seattle, Aug. 30, 1950; m. Norma Banta; children: Christopher, Matthew. BA in Polit. Sci. and History, Alaska Meth. U., 1973. Contract adminstrv. asst.; mktg. rschr. Gamel Homes, 1982-84; pres., mng. ptnr. No. Family Home Video, 1985-87; pvt. practice mktg. and rsch., 1988—; mem. Alaska Ho. of Reps., 1976-92, Alaska Senate, Dist. L, Juneau, 1992—. Chmn. senate labor & commerce com., senate state affairs com., senate rules com., senate cmty. & regional affairs com., legis. budget & audit com., Alaska Senate, Anchorage. Named Outstanding Freshman Legislator, Tenth Legislature, 1977-78, Outstanding Rep., Standing Together Against Rape, 1987. Mem. Eagle River Fine Arts Acad., Elks. Republican. Avocations: family cabin, hockey, classic cars, coin collecting. Office: State Capitol 120 4th St Rm 103 Juneau AK 99801-1182 also: PO Box 142 Eagle River AK 99577 Fax: 907-465-4979. E-mail: senator_randy_phillips@legis.state.ak.us

PHILLIPS, ROGER, steel company executive; b. Ottawa, Ont., Can., Dec. 17, 1939; s. Norman William Frederick and Elizabeth (Marshall) P.; m. Katherine Ann Wilson, June 9, 1962; 1 child, Andrée Claire. B.Sc., McGill U., Montreal, 1960. Vice pres. mill products Alcan Can. Products Ltd., Toronto, Ont., Can., 1969-70, exec. v.p. Can., 1971-75; pres. Alcan Smelters and Chems. Ltd., Montreal, Que., Can., 1976-79; v.p. tech. Alcan Aluminium Ltd., Montreal, Can., 1980-81; pres. Alcan Internat. Ltd., Montreal, Can., 1980-81; pres., chief exec. officer IPSCO Inc., Regina, Sask., Can., 1982—. Sr. mem. Conf. Bd. Inc., N.Y., 1987—; bd. dirs. Toronto Dominion Bank, Canadian Pacific Limited. Bd. dirs. Conf. Bd. of Can., 1984-87; chmn. Coun. for Can. Unity, 1987-88. Named Officer of Order of Can., 1999. Fellow Inst. of Physics U.K. (chartered physicist); mem. Can. Assn. Physicists, Bus. Coun. on Nat. Issues, Am. Iron and Steel Inst. (bd. dirs. 1984—), Sask. C. of C. (bd. dirs. 1984—), Que. C. of C. (pres. 1981), Order of Can. (officer), Assiniboia Club (Regina), St. Denis Club, Univ. Club (Montreal). Home: 3220 Albert St Regina SK Canada S4S 3N9 Office: IPSCO Inc Armour Rd Regina SK Canada S4P 3C7 E-mail: rphillips@ipsco.com

PHILLIPS, RONALD FRANK, retired academic administrator; b. Houston, Nov. 25, 1934; s. Franklin Jackson and Maudie Ethel (Merrill) P.; m. Jamie Jo Bottoms, Apr. 5, 1957 (dec. Sept. 1996); children: Barbara Celeste Phillips Oliveira, Joel Jackson, Phil Edward. BS, Abilene Christian U., 1955; JD, U. Tex., 1965. Bar: Tex. 1965, Calif. 1972. Bldg. contractor Phillips Homes, Abilene, Tex., 1955-56; br. mgr. Phillips Weatherstripping Co., Midland and Austin, 1957-65; corp. staff atty. McWood Corp., Abilene, 1965-67; sole practice law Abilene, 1967-70; mem. adj. faculty Abilene Christian U., 1967-70; prof. law Pepperdine U., Malibu, Calif., 1970—, dean Sch. Law, 1970-97, dean emeritus, 1997—, vice chancellor, 1995—. Deacon North A and Tenn. Ch. of Christ, Midland, 1959-62; deacon Highland Ch. of Christ, Abilene, 1965-70; elder Malibu Ch. of Christ, 1978-95; mgr., coach Little League Baseball, Abilene, Huntington Beach and Malibu, 1968-78, 90-95; coach Youth Soccer, Huntington Beach, Westlake Village and Malibu, 1972-80, 85-86, 91. Recipient Alumni citation Abilene Christian U., 1974 Fellow Am. Bar Found. (life); mem. ABA, State Bar Tex., State Bar Calif., Christian Legal Soc., L.A. Bar Assn., Assn. Am. Law Schs. (chmn. sect. on adminstrn. law schs. 1982, com. on cts. 1985-87), Am. Law Inst., Nat. Conf. Commrs. on Uniform State Laws. Republican. Office: Pepperdine U 24255 Pacific Coast Hwy Malibu CA 90263-0002 E-mail: rphillip@pepperdine.edu, ronald.phillips@pepperdine.edu

PHILLIPS, STEVE, lawyer, school system administrator, columnist; b. 1964; BA, Stanford U.; JD, Hastings Coll. of Law. Lawyer, San Francisco; columnist Cleveland Plain Dealer, San Jose Mercury News; pres. San Francisco Bd. of Edn., 1992—, also bd. dirs., 1992—. Columnist, journalist, author: Justice and Hope: Past Reflections and Future Visions of Stanford Black Student Union. Past chmn. Calif. Black Student Alliance. Office: Bd Edn Office 555 Franklin St Rm 106 San Francisco CA 94102-4456

PHILLIPS, TERRY, state legislator; b. Louisville; m. Sally Phillips. Appraiser, Louisville; mem. Colo. Senate, Dist. 17, Denver, 1996—; mem. agr., natural resources and energy com.; mem. appropriations com.; mem. bus. affairs and labor com.; mem. joint capital devel. com. Democrat. Office: State Capitol 200 E Colfax Ave Denver CO 80203-1776

PHILLIPS, THEODORE LOCKE, radiation oncologist, educator; b. Phila., June 4, 1933; s. Harry Webster and Margaret Amy (Locke) P.; m. Joan Cappello, June 23, 1956; children: Margaret, John, Sally. BSc, Dickinson Coll., 1955; MD, U. Pa., 1959. Intern Western Res. U., Cleve., 1960; resident in therapeutic radiology U. Calif., San Francisco, 1963, clin. instr., 1963-65, asst. prof. radiation oncology, 1965-68, assoc. prof., 1968-70, prof., 1970—, chmn. dept. radiation oncology, 1973-98. Rsch. radiobiologist U.S. Naval Radiologic Def. Lab., San Francisco, 1963-65; rsch. physician Lawrence Berkeley Lab. Contbr. numerous articles to profl. publs. With USNR, 1963-65. Nat. Cancer Inst. grantee, 1970-99. Mem. Am. Soc. Therapeutic Radiologists (pres. 1984), Am. Soc. Clin. Oncology, Radiol. Soc. N.Am., N.Am. Hyperthermia Soc. (pres. 1994), Am. Assn. Cancer Rsch., Calif. Med. Assn., Am. Coll. Radiology, Radiation Rsch. Soc. (pres. 1977), Radium Soc., No. Calif. Radiation Oncology Assn., Inst. Medicine, Phi Beta Kappa, Alpha Omega Alpha. Democrat. Office: U Calif San Francisco Dept Radiation Oncology L 75 San Francisco CA 94143-0226

PHILLIPS, VIRGINIA A. judge; BA, U. Calif., Riverside, 1979; JD Boalt Hall, 1982. Ct. commr. Calif. Superior Ct., Riverside, 1991-95; magistrate judge U.S. Dist. Ct., L.A., 1995-99, judge, 1999—. Office: US Courthouse 3470 Twelfth St Riverside CA 92501 Fax: 213-894-0561

PHILLIPS, WILLIAM ROBERT, physician; b. Wash., Apr. 26, 1950; BA, U. Wash., 1971, MD, MPH, U. Wash., 1975. Diplomate Nat. Bd. Med. Examiners, Am. Bd. Family Practice, Am. Bd. Preventive Medicine; lic. physician and surgeon, Wash. Resident family practice Providence Med. Ctr., Seattle, 1975-78; resident preventive medicine U. Wash. Sch. Pub. Health & Cmty. Medicine, Seattle, 1976-79; vis. prof. U. Auckland, New Zealand, 1979, U. Tasmania, Hobart, Australia, 1979, U. Zimbabwe, Harare, 1993; clin. prof. family medicine U. Wash., Seattle, 1994—. Chief staff Ballard Cmty. Hosp., Seattle, 1985, chief family practice, 1984. Contbr. articles to profl. jours. Bd. trustees Ballard Cmty. Hosp., Seattle, 1985. Recipient USPHS primary care policy fellowship, 1995; named Family Physician of the Yr. Wash. Acad. Family Physicians, 1999. Fellow Am. Acad. Family Physicians (Mead Johnson award 1976, Warner-Chilcott award 1979), Wash. Acad. Family Physicians (Family Physician of Yr. 1999), Am. Coll. Preventive Medicine; mem. N.Am. Primary Care Rsch. Group (pres., rsch. awards), Soc. Tchrs. of Family Medicine. Office: Univ Washington Dept Family Medicine Box 356390 Seattle WA 98195-6390

PHILLIPS, ZAIGA ALKSNIS, pediatrician; b. Riga, Latvia, Sept. 13, 1934; came to U.S., 1949; d. Adolfs and Alma (Ozols) Alksnis; (div. 1972); children: Albert L., Lisa K., Sintija. BS, U. Wash., 1956, MD, 1959. Fellow Colo. Med. Ctr., Denver, 1961-62; sch. physician Bellevue and Issaquah (Wash.) Sch. Dists., 1970-77; pvt. practice Bellevue, 1977—; staff pediatrician Overlake Med. Ctr., 1977—, Childrens Hosp. and Med. Ctr., Seattle, 1977—, Evergreen Med. Ctr., 1977—. Attending physician Allergy Clinic, Childrens Hosp., Seattle, 1988—; cons. and contact to pediatricians in Latvia, 1988—; team mem. to Latvia, Healing the Children Contact with Latvia, 1993-97; bd. mem. Bellevue's Stay in Sch. Program, 1994-97. Mem. Am. Latvian Assn., 1972—, Wash. Latvian Assn., Seattle, 1972—; pres. Latvian Sorority Gundega, Seattle, 1990-93; bd. dirs. Sister Cities Assn., Bellevue, 1992-98, Wash. Asthma Allergy Found. Am., 1992-99. Fellow Am. Acad. Pediat.; mem. Am. Latvian Physicians Assn. (bd. dirs. 1998—), Wash. State and Puget Sound Pediatric Assn. Office: Pediatric Assn 2700 Northup Way Bellevue WA 98004-1463 E-mail: zap@u.washington.edu

PHILLIPSON, DONALD E. lawyer; b. Denver, July 22, 1942; BS, Stanford U., 1964, JD, 1968; MS, U. Calif., Berkeley, 1965. Former mem. Davis, Graham & Stubbs, Denver; now cons., writer. Mem. Nat. Soccer Hall of Fame (adminstr.). Office: 14325 Braun Rd Golden CO 80401-1431

PHILPOTT, LARRY LA FAYETTE, horn player; b. Alma, Ark., Apr. 5, 1937; s. Lester and Rena (Owens) P.; m. Elise Robichaud, Nov. 24, 1962 (div. June 1975); children: Daniel, Stacy; m. Anne Sokol, Feb. 14, 1984. B.S., Ga. So. Coll., 1962; Mus.M., Butler U., 1972. Instr. in horn Butler U., De Pauw U.; dir. music Cedarcrest Sch., Marysville, Wash., 1991—; instr. horn Western Wash. U., Dept Music, Bellingham, 1995-98. Mem., N.C. Symphony, 1960, Savannah (Ga.) Symphony, L'Orchestre Symphonique de Quebec, Que., Can., 1962-64, prin. horn player, Indpls. Symphony Orch., 1964-89, Flagstaff Summer Festival, 1968— ; artist in-residence Ind.-Purdue Indpls.; appeared with, Am. Shakespeare Theatre, summer 1965, Charlottetown Festival, summers 1967-68, Flagstaff Summer Festival, 1968-85, Marrowstone Music Festival, 1985—. Served with USN, 1956-60. Mem. Music Educators Nat. Conf., Am. Fedn. Musicians, Internat. Conf. Symphony and Opera Musicians, Internat. Horn Soc., Coll. Music Soc., Phi Mu Alpha Sinfonia. Home: 14925 63d Ave SE Snohomish WA 98296-5277 also: Western Wash U Dept Music Bellingham WA 98225-9107

PHILPOTT, LINDSEY, civil engineer, researcher, educator; b. Bridestowe, Devonshire, Eng., Aug. 2, 1948; came to U.S., 1983; s. George Anthony and Joyce Thirza (Teeling) P.; m. Christine May Pembury, Aug. 20, 1974 (div.); children: David, Elizabeth; m. Kathleen Linda Matson, Feb. 17, 1982 (div.); children: Nicholas, Benjamin; m. Kim Elaine Moore, Nov. 24, 1991. Higher Nat. Cert. in Civil Engring., Bristol (Eng.) Poly., 1973; BSCE, U. Ariz., 1986, MSCE, 1987. Registered profl. engr., Calif.; lic. water treatment plant operator, Calif.; USCG lic. operator 100 ton master. Area structural engr. Dept. Environment (Property Svcs. Agy.), Bristol, 1971-73; civil engr. Webco Civil Engring., Exeter, Eng., 1973-75; tech. mgr. Devon & Cornwall Housing Assn., Plymouth, Eng., 1975-79; prin., architect S.W. Design, Plymouth, 1979-81; archtl. engr. United Bldg. Factories, Bahrain, 1981-83, jr. engr. Cheyne Owen, Tucson, 1983-87; civil engr. Engring. Sci. Inc., Pasadena, Calif., 1987-89; project engr. Black & Veatch, Santa Ana, 1989-90; sr. engr. Brown & Caldwell, Irvine, 1990-91; environ. engr. Met. Water Dist. So. Calif., San Dimas, 1991—; instr. USCG and marlinespike seamanship Orange Coast Coll. Sailing Ctr., Newport Beach, Calif., 1999—. Adj. prof. hydraulics and instrumentation, San Antonio Coll., Walnut, Calif., 1995—. Foster parent Foster Parents Plan, Tucson, 1985-87; vol. reader tech. books Recording for the Blind, Hollywood, Calif., 1988-89, South Bay, Calif., 1990-91, Pomona, Calif., 1991—; vol. sailor/tchr. L.A. Maritime Inst. Topsail Youth Program, 1994—, Ocean Inst., 1998—. Mem. ASCE, Am. Water Works Assn., Am. Water Resources Assn. (water quality com. 1990—), Water Environment Fedn., Engrs. Soc. (pres. 1985-96), Mensa, South Bay Yacht Racing Club (Marina del Rey, Calif., commodore 1996), Marina Venice Yacht Club (Marina del Rey, commodore 1999), Internat. Guild of Knot Tyers (pres. Pacific Am. br. 2000), Santa Monica Bay Power Fleet (sec. Marine del Rey chpt. 2000—). Avocations: hiking, cycling, sailing, crosswords, knot-tying. Office: Met Water Dist Environ Compliance Divsn PO Box 54153 Los Angeles CA 90054-0153 E-mail: lphilpott@mwdh20.com

PHINNEY, BERNARD O. research scientist, educator; b. July 29, 1917; s. Bernard Orrin and Frank Maude (Lawrence) P.; m. Sally Ball Bush; children: Scott, Katcha; m. Isabelle Jean Swift, Dec. 11, 1965; children: Peter, David. BA cum laude, U. Minn., 1940, PhD, 1946; DSc (hon.), U. Bristol, 1991. Teaching and rsch. asst. Dept. Botany U. Minn., Mpls., 1940-46; postdoctoral scholar Calif. Inst. Tech., Pasadena, 1946-48; from instr. to prof. U. Calif., L.A., 1947-88, prof. emeritus, 1988—. NSF sr. postdoctoral fellow Copenhagen U., 1959-60; NSF-U.S.-Japan rsch. sci. Internat. Christian U., Mitaka, Tokyo, 1966-67; vis. prof. Dept. Chem. U. Bristol, U.K., 1973, 83. Elected mem. Nat. Acad. Scis., Washington, 1985. Rsch. grantee NSF, Dept. Energy, 1956—. Mem. AAAS, Am. Soc. Plant Physiologists (pres. 1989-90), Am. Inst. Biol. Scis., Am. Chem. Soc., Botanical Soc. Am., Genetics Soc. Am., Japanese Soc. Plant Physiologists, Internat. Soc. Plant Molecular Biologists, Phytochem. Soc. Am. Democrat. Avocations: skiing, hiking, fishing, classical music. Home: 257 Beloit Ave Los Angeles CA 90049-3009 E-mail: bop@ucla.edu

PHINNEY, E. STERL, III, astrophysicist; b. Berkeley, Calif., Jan. 27, 1960; s. Edward Sterl Jr. and Mary Catherine (Davis) P.; m. Lin Yan, June 20, 1993; 1 child, Isabelle. BS, Calif. Inst. Tech., 1980; PhD, Cambridge U., U.K., 1983. Mem. Inst. Advanced Study, Princeton, N.J., 1983-85; asst. prof. Calif. Inst. Tech., Pasadena, 1985-90, assoc. prof., 1991-94, prof., 1995—. Adv. bd., steering com. NSF Inst. for Theoretical Physics, Santa Barbara, Calif., 1990-93; chair mission definition team Laser Interferometer Space Antenna, 1997—. Contbr. articles to profl. jours.; co-author: Pulsars as Physics Laboratories, 1993. Marshall scholar Marshall Aid Commemoration Comm., 1980-83; Presdl. Young Investigator, NSF, 1985-91; fellow A.P. Sloan Found., 1990-94. Fellow Royal Astron. Soc. (U.K.), Am. Phys. Soc.; mem. Am. Astron. Soc. (Helen B. Warner prize 1995). Achievements include contbn. to theory of: black hole magnetohydrodynamics, radiation from active galactic nuclei, and the physics of binary pulsars. Office: Theoretical Astrophysics 130 33 Caltech Pasadena CA 91125-0001

PHINNEY, JEAN SWIFT, psychology educator; b. Princeton, N.J., Mar. 12, 1933; d. Emerson H. and Anne (Davis) Swift; m. Bernard O. Phinney, Dec. 11, 1965; children: Peter, David. BA, Mass. Wellesley Coll., 1955; MA, UCLA, 1969, PhD, 1973. Asst. prof. psychology Calif. State U., L.A., 1977-81, assoc. prof. psychology, 1981-86, prof. psychology, 1986—. Editor: Children's Ethnic Socialization, 1987; asst. editor Jour. Adolescence; contbr. articles to profl. jours. NIH and NSF grantee. Fellow APA; mem. Soc. for Rsch. in Child Devel., Soc. for Rsch. in Adolescence, Internat. Assn. Cross-Cultural Psychology. Avocations: skiing, hiking, travel, chamber music. Office: Calif State U Dept Psychology 5151 State University Dr Los Angeles CA 90032-4226

PHIPPS, ALLEN MAYHEW, management consultant; b. Seattle, Oct. 3, 1938; s. Donald Mayhew and Virginia (McGinn) P.; m. Joyce Elisabeth Alberti, Aug. 21, 1971; children: Ramsey Mayhew, Justin Beckwith. BA in Econs., U. Calif., Berkeley, 1961; MBA with honors, Stanford U., 1969. Security analyst Morgan Guaranty Trust Co., 1968; with Boston Cons. Group, Inc., 1969—, mgr., 1971-74; mem. sr. team Calif., 1974-77; corp. v.p., dir., 1975—. Mgr. Boston Cons. Group, G.mb.H, Munich. W. Ger., 1978-82, partner-in-charge West Coast client devel., Menlo Park, Calif., 1982-84; pres. Techno Digital Systems, Inc., 1984-86; pres., chief exec. officer, Techno Digital System (Sellectek, Inc.), 1984-85; exec. v.p., Regis McKenna Inc., Palo Alto, Calif., 1985-87; pvt. practice mgmt. cons., Menlo Pk., 1987-95; chief exec. officer Bio Electro Systems, Palo Alto, 1989-92; mng. dir., Bus. Engring. Inc., Menlo Park, Calif., 1992-95; sr. v.p. bus. and policy group SRI Internat., Menlo Park, Calif., 1995-96; pres., CEO SRI Consulting, Menlo Park, 1996-2000, ret., 2000; cons. Allen M. Phipps Mgmt. Consulting, Atherton, Calif., 2000—. Served to capt. U.S. Army, 1961-67. Decorated Bronze Star, Army Commendation medal with 2 oak leaf clusters. Mem. Alpha Delta Phi. Republican. Presbyterian. Clubs: Bohemian (San Francisco); Sharon Heights Golf and Country (Menlo Park). Home: 33 Prado Secoya St Atherton CA 94027-4126 Office: Allen M Phipps Mgmt Consulting 33 Prado Secoya Atherton CA 94027 E-mail: aphippsmc@ispchannel.com

PIANKO, THEODORE A. lawyer; b. Denville, N.J., Sept. 5, 1955; s. Theodore and Pasqualina (Liguori) P.; m. Beatriz Maria Olivera (div. Dec. 1985); m. Kathryn Anne Lindley, Feb. 18, 1990; children: Matthew James, Samuel Wahoo, Zoe Wahoo. BA, SUNY, 1975; JD, U. Mich., 1978. Bar: Mich. 1978, Ill. 1979, Calif. 1980. Atty. Ford Motor Co., Dearborn, Mich., 1978-80; assoc. Lillick McHose & Charles, L.A., 1980-83; ptnr. Sidley & Austin, L.A., 1983-94, Christie, Parker & Hale, Pasadena, Calif., 1994—. E-mail: ted@pianko.com

PICCININI, ROBERT M. grocery store chain executive; CEO, chmn., pres. Save Mart Supermarkets, Modesto, Calif., 1952—. Office: Save Mart Supermarkets PO Box 4278 Modesto CA 95352-4278

PICCIOTTO, CHARLES EDWARD, astronomer, educator; b. Buenos Aires, July 1, 1942; AB, U. Calif., Berkeley, 1964; MA, U. Calif., Santa Barbara, 1966, PhD in Physics, 1968. Prof., dept. chair physics and astronomy U. Victoria, Can. Mem. Am. Phys. Soc. Achievements include research on particle physics. Office: U Victoria Dept Physics PO Box 3055 Victoria BC Canada V8W 3P6

PICCOLO, RICHARD ANDREW, artist, educator; b. Hartford, Conn., Sept. 17, 1943; s. John D. and Lenore (Pasqual) P. BID, Pratt Inst., 1966; MFA, Bklyn. Coll., 1968. Instr. Pratt Inst., Bklyn., 1966-68, Rome, 1969—, dir., 1980—; instr. U. Notre Dame Rome Program, 1984—. Artist: solo exhibitions include: Robert Schoelkopf Gallery, N.Y.C., 1975, 79, 83, 89, Suffolk C.C., Long Island, N.Y., 1976, Am. Acad. in Rome, 1977, Galleria Temple, Rome 1979, Galleria Il Gabbiano, Rome. 1985, Contemporary Realist Gallery, San Francisco, 1989, 95; exhibited in group shows Six Americans in Italy, 1973, Metaphor in Painting, Fed. Hall Meml., N.Y., 1978, Realism and Metaphor, U. S. Fla. (traveling), 1980, Contemporary Figure Drawings, Robert Schoelkopf Gallery, 1981, Contemporary Arcadian Painting, 1982, Moravian Coll. Invitational, Bethlehem, Pa., 1981, Art on Paper , Weatherspoon Gallery of Art, N.C., 1981, Out of N.Y., Hamilton Coll., Clinton, N.Y., 1981, Galleria Gabbiano, Rome, FIAC, Paris, 1982, Contemporary Arts Mus., Houston, 1984, Umbria: Americans Painting in Italy, Gallery North, Setauket, N.Y., 1985, Storytellers, Contemporary Realist Gallery, San Francisco, Painted from Life, Bayly Mus., Charlottesville, Va., 1987; work in permanent collections Crown Am. Corp., Johnstown, Pa., Grosvenor Internat., Sacramento, Calif., Mrs. Lillian Cole, Sherman Oaks, Calif., Mr and Mrs. Robert Emery, San Francisco, Mr. Graham Gund, Boston, Dr. Robert Gutterman, San Francisco, Mr and Mrs. Joseph Jennings, San Francisco, Dr. and Mrs. Donald Innes, Jr., Charlottesville, Va., Mr. and Mrs. Alan Ovson, San Francisco, Mr. Frank Pasquerilla, Johnstown, Pa., Mr. Jon Roberts and Mr. John Boccardo, L.A. Recipient E. A. Abbey Meml. scholarship for mural painting, 1973-75; grantee NEA, 1989; mural commn. Simplicity Inspiring Invention: An Allegory of the Arts, Crown Am. Corp., Johnstown, Pa., 1989, Aer, Ignis, Terra, Aqua, U.S. Bank Plaz., Sacramento, Calif., 1991-94. Home: Piazza S Apollonia 3 Rome 00153 Italy Office: Hacket Freedman Gallery 250 Sutter St Fl 4 San Francisco CA 94108-4451

PICK, MICHAEL CLAUDE, international exploration consultant; b. Stuttgart, Fed. Republic Germany, Sept. 17, 1931; came to Can., 1963; s. Manfred and Berti (Baer) P.; m. Jeanette Patrucia Zaharko, Mar. 13, 1965; children— David, Christopher B.A., U. New Zealand, Wellington, 1952, M.A. with honors, 1954; Ph.D., U. Bristol, Eng., 1963. Sr. geologist Todd Bros. Ltd., Wellington, 1954-58; research assoc. Stanford U., Calif., 1958-60; geologist Chevron Standard Ltd., Calgary, Alta., Can., 1963-68; regional geologist BP Oil & Gas Ltd., Calgary, 1968-71; chief geologist, acting exploration mgr. Columbia Gas, Calgary, 1971-80; sr. v.p. Asamera, Inc., Calgary, 1980—; pres. Torwood Assocs. Ltd., 1988-95, Terrenex Ventures Inc., Calgary, 1988-94. Contbr. articles to profl. jours. Mem. Am. Assn. Petroleum Geologists, Can. Soc. Petroleum Geologists. Avocations: music, reading, model railroading. Home and Office: 3359 Varna Crescent NW Calgary AB Canada T3A 0E4

PICKETT, DONN PHILIP, lawyer; b. Chgo., May 3, 1952; s. Philip Gordon and Gloria Joan (Hansen) P.; m. Janet Benson, Aug. 25, 1973; children: Jessica Kelly, William Benson. BA, Carleton Coll., Minn., 1973; JD, Yale U., 1976. Bar: Calif. 1976, U.S. Dist. Ct. (no. dist.) Calif. 1976, (ctrl. dist.) Calif. 1980, (ea. dist.) Calif. 1983, U.S. Ct. Appeals (9th cir.) Calif. 1979, U.S. Ct. Appeals (5th cir.) Tex. 1994, U.S. Supreme Ct. 1991, U.S. Dist. Ct. Ariz. 1997, U.S. Dist. Ct. Colo. 1997, U.S. Ct. Appeals (fed. cir.) 1997, U.S. Ct. Appeals (11th cir.) 1998. Assoc. McCutchen, Doyle, Brown & Enersen, San Francisco, 1976-83, ptnr., 1983—. Mem. U.S. Dist. Ct. Civil Justice Reform Act adv. group, 1995—). Mem. ABA (vice chmn. civil practice com. antitrust sect. 1998), State Bar Calif. (com. on adminstrn. of justice 1988-91, vice chmn. 1992-93, chmn. 1993-94, legis. chmn. 1994-96), San Francisco Bar Assn. (judiciary com. 1988-92, exec. com. conf. of dels. 1993-96, bd. dirs. 1997—), Phi Beta Kappa. Home: 25 Meadow Hill Dr Tiburon CA 94920-1638 Office: McCutchen Doyle Brown & Enersen Three Embarcadero Ctr San Francisco CA 94111

PICKETT, WILSON, vocalist, composer; b. Prattville, Ala., Mar. 18, 1941; Albums include If You Want Me, 1974, I Want You, 1979, The Right Track, 1981, Best of Wilson Pickett, 1985; singles include In the Midnight Hour, 1965, Land of 1000 Dances, 1966, Funky Broadway, 1967, She's lookin' Good, 1968, Engine Number 9, 1970, Don't Let the Green Grass Fool You, 1971; songwriter I Found A Love, 1962, (with others) If You Need Me, 1963, It's Too Late, 1963, (with others) In the Midnight Hour, 1966, I'm a Midnight Mover, 1968, Don't Knock My Love, 1971. Inducted into Rock and Roll Hall of Fame, 1991, The Alabama Music Hall of Fame, 1999. Office: Motown Record Corp 6255 W Sunset Blvd Los Angeles CA 90028-7403

PICRAUX, SAMUEL THOMAS, applied science and physics researcher; b. St. Charles, Mo., Mar. 3, 1943; s. Samuel F. and Jeannette D. Picraux; m. Danice R. Kent, July 12, 1970; children: Jeanine, Laura, Samantha. BS in Elec. Engring., U. Mo., 1965; postgrad., Cambridge (Eng.) U., 1965-66; MS in Engring. Sci., Calif. Inst. Tech., 1967, PhD in Engring. Sci. and Physics, 1969. Mem. tech. staff Sandia Nat. Labs., Albuquerque, 1969-72, div. supr., 1972-86, dept. mgr., 1986-96, dir., 1996-2001; prof. materials engring., exec. dir. materials rsch. Ariz. State U., 2001—. Mem. solid state scis. com. NRC, 1996-98; vis. scientist dept. physics Aarhus U., Denmark, 1975; NATO lectr., 1979, 81, 83, 86.; NSF lectr. 1976, 81. Author: Materials Analysis by Ion Channeling, 1982; editor: Applications of Ion Beams to Metals, 1974, Metastable Materials Formation by Ion Implantation, 1982, Surface Alloying by Ion Electron and Laser Beams, 1986, Beam-Solid Interactions and Transient Processes, 1987; editor Nuclear Instruments and Methods International Jour., 1983-91; contbr. numerous articles to profl. jours. Recipient Ernest Orlando Lawrence Meml. award U.S. Dept. Energy, 1990, 3 Basic Energy Scis. Outstanding Rsch. awards U.S. Dept. Energy, 1985, 92, 94; Fulbright fellow, 1965-66. Fellow AAAS, Am. Phys. Soc. (chmn. materials physics divsn. 1990); mem. IEEE (sr.), Am. Vacuum Soc., Materials Rsch. Soc. (pres. 1993). Office: Ariz State U PO Box 876006 Tempe AZ 85287-6006 E-mail: picraux@asu.edu

PIEL, CAROLYN FORMAN, pediatrician, educator; b. Birmingham, Ala., Oct. 18, 1918; d. James R. and Mary Elizabeth (Dortch) Forman; m. John Joseph Piel, Aug. 3, 1951; children: John Joseph, Mary Dortch, Elizabeth Forman, William Scott. BA, Agnes Scott Coll., 1940; MS, Emory U., 1943; MD, Washington U., St. Louis, 1946. Diplomate Am. Bd. Pediatrics (examiner 1973-88, pres. 1986-87); diplomate Am. Bd. Pediatric Nephrology. Intern Phila. Gen. Hosp., 1946-47; resident Phila. Children's Hosp., 1947-49; fellow Cornell U. Med. Sch., N.Y.C., 1949-51; from instr. to assoc. clin. prof. Stanford U. Sch. Medicine, San Francisco, 1951-59; from asst. prof. to prof. Sch. Medicine, U. Calif., San Francisco, 1959-89, emeritus prof., 1989—. Author, co-author research articles in field. Bd. mem. San Francisco Home Health Service, 1977-83. Emeritus mem. Soc. for Pediatric Research, Am. Pediatric Soc., Am. Soc. for Pediatric Nephrology, Am. Soc. Nephrology, Western Soc. for Pediatric Nephrology (pres. 1960). Democrat. Presbyterian. Home: 2164 Hyde St San Francisco CA 94109-1788 Office: U Calif PO Box 748 San Francisco CA 94143-0001

PIEPER, DAROLD D. lawyer; b. Vallejo, Calif., Dec. 30, 1944; s. Walter A. H. and Vera Mae (Ellis) P.; m. Barbara Gillis, Dec. 20, 1969; 1 child, Christopher Radcliffe. AB, UCLA, 1967; JD, USC, 1970. Bar: Calif. 1971. Ops. rsch. analyst Naval Weapons Ctr., China Lake, Calif., 1966-69; assoc. Richards, Watson & Gershon, L.A., 1970-76, ptnr., 1976—; gen. counsel Foothill Transit, 2000—; spl. counsel L.A. Unified Sch. Dist., 2000—. Spl. counsel L.A. County Transp. Commn., 1984-93, L.A. County Met. Transp. Authority, 1993-94; commr. L.A. County Delinquency and Crime Commn., 1983-94, pres., 1987-94; chmn. L.A. County Delinquency Prevention Planning Coun., 1987-90. Contbr. articles to profl. jours. Peace officer Pasadena (Calif.) Police Res. Unit, 1972-87, dep. comdr., 1979-81, comdr., 1982-84; chmn. pub. safety commn. City of La Canada Flintridge, Calif., 1977-82, commr. 1977-88; bd. dirs. La Canada Flintridge Coordinating Council, 1975-82, pres. 1977-78; exec. dir. Cityhood Action Com., 1975-76; chmn. Youth Opportunities United, Inc., 1990-96, vice-chmn. 1988-89, bd. dirs. 1988-96; mem. L.A. County Justice Systems Adv. Group, 1987-92; trustee Lanterman Hist. Mus. Found., 1989-94, Calif. City Mgmt. Found., 1992—. Recipient commendation for Community Service, L.A. County Bd. Suprs., 1978, Commendation for Svc. to Youth, 1996. Mem. La Canada Flintridge C. of C. and Cmty. Assn. (pres. 1981, bd. dirs. 1976-83), Navy League U.S., Peace Officers Assn., L.A. County, UCLA Alumni Assn. (life), L.A. County Bar Assn., Calif. Bar Assn., ABA, U. So. Calif. Law Alumni Assn. Office: Richards Watson & Gershon 333 S Hope St Fl 38 Los Angeles CA 90071-1406

PIERCE, DANNY PARCEL, artist, educator; b. Woodlake, Calif., Sept. 10, 1920; s. Frank Lester and Letitia Frances (Parcel) P.; m. Julia Ann Rasmussen, July 19, 1943; children: Julia Ann, Mary L., Danny L., Duane Nels. Student, Art Ctr. Sch., L.A., 1939, Chouinards Art Inst., 1940-41, 46-47, Am. Art Sch., N.Y.C., 1947-48, Bklyn. Mus. Art Sch., , 1950-53; BFA, U. Alaska, 1963. Instr. Hunter Coll., N.Y.C., 1952-53, Burnley Sch. Art, Seattle, 1954-58, Seattle U., 1956-59; publ. Red Door Studio Press, Kent, Wash., 1959—; artist-in-res. U. Alaska, College, 1959-63; asst. prof. U. Wisc., Milw., 1964; head art dept. Cornish Sch. Allied Arts, Seattle, 1964-65; prof. art U. Wisc., Milw., 1965-84, prof. emeritus, 1984—. One-man shows include Contemporaries Gallery, N.Y.C., 1953, Handforth Gallery, Tacoma, Washington, 1958, U. Alaska, College, 1959, 63, 73, 74, Gonzaga U., Bradley Galleries, Milw., 1966, 68, 70, 72, 74, 76, 78-80, 82, Martin-Zambito Gallery, Seattle, 1997, Apple Blossom Time, 2000; father/son exhbn. Martin-Zambito Gallery, 1999; represented in permanent collections Bibliothèque Nationale, Paris, Mus. Modern Art, N.Y.C., Libr. Congress, Washington, Smithsonian Instn., Washington, Seattle Art Mus., U. Washington Henry Art Gallery, Bklyn. Mus., Princeton U., U. Alaska, U. So. Calif., William and Mary Coll., Oostduinkerke (Belgium) Nat. Fishing Mus., Nat. Mus. Sweden, Stockholm, Johnson Wax Found., Racine, Wisc., Gen. Mills Collection Art, Mpls., Huntington Libr., San Marino, Calif., various pvt. collections; pub. 23 limited edition books, 1959-98. Recipient Best Oil Landscape award Conn. Acad. Fine Arts, Hartford, 1st Prize oil Kohler Gallery, Seattle, 1974, others; chosen one of twelve artists to represent State Wash. Expo 70, Osaka, Japan, rep. U.S. Internat. São Paulo Biennial Art Exhbn.; established archives at Golda Meier Libr., U. Wis.-Mils. Mem. Artist Equity Assn. (charter, pres. Seattle chpt. 1958), Am. Colorprint Soc., Internat. Arts and Letters (life). Office: Red Door Studio 404 Summit Ave N Kent WA 98031-4712

PIERCE, ROBERT LORNE, petrochemical, oil and gas company executive; Chmn. and chief exec. officer Foothills Pipe Lines Ltd., Calgary, Alta., Can., chmn. Bd. dirs. NOVA Chems. Corp. Mem. Interstate Natural Gas Assn. Am. (bd. dirs.).

PIERCE, SUSAN RESNECK, academic administrator, English language educator; b. Janesville, Wis., Feb. 6, 1943; d. Elliott Jack and Dory (Block) Resneck; m. Kenneth H. Pierce; 1 child, Alexandra Siegel. AB, Wellesley Coll., 1965; MA, U. Chgo., 1966; PhD, U. Wis., 1972. Lectr. U. Wis., Rock County, 1970-71; from asst. prof. to prof. English Ithaca (N.Y.) Coll., 1973-82, chmn. dept., 1976-79; program officer Nat. Endowment for Humanities, 1982-83, asst. dir., 1983-84; dean Henry Kendall Coll. Arts and Scis. U. Tulsa, 1984-90; v.p. acad. affairs, prof. English Lewis and Clark Coll., Portland, Oreg., 1990-92; pres. U. Puget Sound, Tacoma, 1992—. Vis. assoc. prof. Princeton (N.J.) U., 1979; bd. dirs. Janet Elson Scholarship Fund, 1984-1990, Tulsa Edn. Fund, Phillips Petroleum Scholarship Fund, 1985-90, Okla. Math. & Sci. High Sch., 1984-90, Hillcrest Med. Ctr., 1988-90, Portland Opera, 1990-92, St. Joseph's Hosp., 1992—, Seattle Symphony, 1993—; cons. U. Oreg., 1985, Drury Coll., Springfield, Mo., 1986; mem. Middle States and N. Cen. Accreditation Bds.; mem. adv. com. Fed. Women's Program, NEH, 1982-83; participant Summit Meeting on Higher Edn., Dept. Edn., Washington, 1985; speaker, participant numerous ednl. meetings, sems., commencements; chair Frederick Ness Book Award Com. Assn. Am. Colls., 1986; mem. award selection com. Dana Found., 1986, 87; mem. Acad. Affairs Council, Univ. Senate, dir. tchr.

edn., chmn. adv. group for tchr. preparation, ex-officio mem. all Coll. Arts and Scis. coms. and Faculty Council on Internat. Studies, all U. Tulsa; bd. dirs. Am. Conf. Acad. Deans; bd. trustees Hillcrest Med. Ctr.; participant Aspen Inst. Md. 1999, Annapolis Group Media Roundtable, 1996, Harvard Seminar, 1992; former bd. dirs. Assn. Am. Colls. and Univs., 1989-92, Am. Conf. of Academic Deans, 1988-91, Am. Assn. Colls., 1989-92. Author: The Moral of the Story, 1982, also numerous essays, jour. articles, book sects., book revs.; co-editor: Approaches to Teaching "Invisible Man"; reader profl. jours. Bd. dirs. Arts and Humanities Coun., Tulsa, 1984-90; trustee Hillcrest Hosp., Tulsa, 1986-90; mem. cultural series com., community rels. com. Jewish Fedn., Tulsa, 1986-90; bd. dirs. Tulsa chpt. NCCJ, 1986-90, Kemper Mus. 1996—, Seattle Symphony, 1993-96, St. Joseph Hosp., 1992-93, Portland Opera, 1990-92. Recipient Best Essay award Arix. Quar., 1979, Excellence in Teaching award N.Y. State Edn. Council, 1982, Superior Group Service award NEH, 1984, other teaching awards; Dana scholar, Ithaca Coll., 1980-81; Dana Research fellow, Ithaca Coll., 82-83; grantee Inst. for Ednl. Affairs, 1980, Ford Found., 1987, NEH, 1989. Mem. MLA (adv. com. on job market 1973-74), South Ctrl. MLA, NIH (subcom. on college drinking), Assn. Governing Bds. (coun. of pres.), Nat. Inst. on Alcohol Abuse (presl. advisory group), Soc. for Values in Higher Edn., Assn. Am. Colls. (bd. dirs.), Am. Conf. Acad. Deans (bd. dirs. 1988-91), Coun. of Presidents, Assn. Governing Bds., Phi Beta Kappa, Phi Kappa Phi, Phi Gamma Kappa. Office: U Puget Sound 1500 N Warner St Tacoma WA 98416-0001

PIERIK, MARILYN ANNE, retired librarian, piano teacher; b. Bellingham, Wash., Nov. 12, 1939; d. Estell Leslie and Anna Margarethe (Onigkeit) Bowers; m. Robert Vincent Pierik, July 25, 1964; children: David Vincent, Donald Lesley. AA, Chaffey Jr. Coll., Ontario, Calif., 1959; BA, Upland (Calif.) Coll., 1962; cert. in teaching, Claremont (Calif.) Coll., 1963; MSLS, U. So. Calif., L.A., 1973. Tchr. elem. Christ Episcopal Day Sch., Ontario, 1959-60; tchr. Bonita High Sch., La Verne, Calif., 1962-63; tchr., libr. Kettle Valley Sch. Dist. 14, Greenwood, Can., 1963-64; libr. asst. Monrovia (Calif.) Pub. Libr., 1964-67; with Mt. Hood C.C., Gresham, Oreg., 1972-98, reference libr., 1983-98, chair faculty scholarship com., 1987-98, campus archivist, 1994-98; ret., 1998; pvt. piano tchr. Gresham, 1998—. Pvt. piano tchr., 1998; mem. site selection com. Multnomah County (Oreg.) Libr., New Gresham br., 1987, adv. com. Multnomah County Libr., Portland, Oreg., 1988-89; bd. dirs. Oreg. Episcopal Conf. of Deaf, 1985-92. Bd. dirs. East County Arts Alliance, Gresham, 1987-91; vestry person, jr. warden St. Luke's Episc. Ch., 1989-92; vestry person St. Aidan's Episcopal. Ch., 2000—; founding pres. Mt. Hood Pops, 1983-88, orch. mgr., 1983-91, 93—, bd. dirs., 1983-88, 91—. Recipient Jeanette Parkhill Meml. award Chaffey Jr. Coll., 1959, Svc. award St. Luke's Episcopal Ch., 1983, 87, Edn. Svc. award Soroptimists, 1989. Mem. AAUW, NEA, Oreg. Edn. Assn., Oreg. Libr. Assn., ALA, Gresham Hist. Soc. Avocations: music, reading. E-mail: pierikm@teleport.com

PIERNO, ANTHONY ROBERT, lawyer; b. Uniontown, Pa., Apr. 28, 1932; s. Anthony M. and Mary Jane (Saporita) P.; m. Beverly Jean Kohn, June 20, 1954; children: Kathryn Ann Pierno, Robert Lawrence Pierno, Linda Jean Pierno, Diane Marie Leonard. BA with highest honors, Whittier Coll., 1954; JD, Stanford U., 1959; LLD (hon.), Whittier Coll., 2000. Bar: Calif. 1960, D.C. 1979, Tex. 1994. Assoc. Adams, Duque & Hazeltine, L.A.; ptnr. Poindexter & Barger, L.A.; chief dep. commr. State of Calif., 1967-69, commr. of corps., 1969-71; ptnr. Wyman, Bautzer, Rothman & Kuchel, Beverly Hills, Calif.; sr. ptnr. Memel, Jacobs, Pierno & Gersh, L.A., 1976-86; ptnr. Pillsbury, Madison & Sutro, L.A., 1986-89; sr. v.p., gen. counsel MAXXAM, Inc., L.A. and Houston, 1989-97. Author: Corporate Disaggregation, 1982; editor Stanford U. Law Rev. Trustee Whittier Coll., 1977-2000, chmn. bd. trustees, 1994-2000, chmn. presdl. selection com., 1989-90; chmn. Marymount Coll., Palos Verdes, Calif., 1989-92, trustee, 1976-93; past mem. Los Angeles County Children's Svcs. Commn. With U.S. Army, 1954-56. Recipient Emcalian award Marymount Palos Verdes Coll., 1983. Mem. ABA, Los Angeles County Bar Assn., State Bar Calif. (chmn. com. on corps. 1971-75, advisor to com. on corps. 1975-76, mem. exec. com. bus. law sect. 1976-80, chmn. spl. com. on franchise law), Calif. Club (L.A.). Republican. Roman Catholic. Office: 418 Malaga Ln Palos Verdes Estates CA 90274 also: 74361 Highway 111 Ste 1 Palm Desert CA 92260-4125

PIERSKALLA, WILLIAM PETER, university dean, management-engineering educator; b. St. Cloud, Minn., Oct. 22, 1934; s. Aloys R. and Hilda A. Pierskalla; m. Carol Spargo, Children: Nicholas, William, Michael. AB in Econs., Harvard U., 1956, MBA, 1958; MS in Math., U. Pitts., 1962; PhD in Ops. Rsch., Stanford U., 1965; MA, U. Pa., 1978. Assoc. prof. Case Western Res. U., Cleve., 1965-68, So. Meth. U., Dallas, 1968-70; prof. dept. indsl. engring. and mgmt. scis. Northwestern U., Evanston, Ill., 1970-78; exec. dir. Leonard Davis Inst., U. Pa., Phila., 1978-83; prof., chmn. health care sys. dept. U. Pa., Phila., 1982-90, prof. decision sci. and systems engring., dep. dean acad. affairs Wharton Sch., 1983-89, Ronald A. Rosenfield prof., 1986-93; dir. Huntsman Ctr. Global Competition and Leadership U. Pa. Wharton Sch., 1989-91; John E. Anderson prof. UCLA, 1993—, dean John E. Anderson Grad Sch. Mgmt., 1993-97. Cons. HHS, Bethesda, Md., 1974-87, MDAX, Chgo., 1985-91, MEDICUS, Evanston, 1970-75, Sisters of Charity, Dayton, Ohio, 1982-83, Project Hope, 1990—; bd. dirs. The Bush Found., No. Wilderness Adventures, Office Tenants Network, iRise. Contbr. articles to various publs. Mem. adv. bd. Lehigh U., 1986-93, U. So. Calif. Bus. Sch., 1987-93; regent St. Mary's Coll., 1998—, Hong Kong U. Sci. and Tech., 1992—. Recipient Harold Larnder Meml. prize Can. Oper. Rsch. Soc., 1993; grantee NSF, 1970-83, HHS, Washington, 1973-82, Office Naval Rsch., Arlington, Va., 1974-77. Mem. Ops. Rsch. Soc. Am. (pres. 1982-83, editor 1979-82, Kimball Disting. Svc. medal 1989), Inst. Mgmt. Scis. (assoc. editor 1970-77), Internat. Fedn. Operational Rsch. Socs. (pres. 1989-91), Inst. for Ops. Rsch. and Mgmt. Scis. (v.p. for publs. 2000—), Omega Rho. Office: UCLA Anderson Grad Sch Mgmt 110 Westwood Plz Box 951481 Los Angeles CA 90095-1481

PIERSON, ALBERT CHADWICK, business management educator; b. Pierson, Ill., Jan. 3, 1914; s. Charles Clevel and Gertrude Fannie (Gale) P.; 1 stepchild, Jay F. Lynch. BA in Liberal Arts and Scis, U. Ill., 1935; MBA with distinction, Harvard U., 1947; PhD, Columbia U., 1963. Merchandiser Montgomery Ward & Co., Chgo., 1935-41; mgmt. cons. N.Y.C., 1947-53; prof. mgmt. San Diego State U., San Diego State U., 1954—. Cons. in field; pub. accountant, Calif.; research editor Jour. Travel Research, 1967—. Author: Trends in Lodging Enterprises, 1939-1963, 1963. Chmn. bd. Nat. Arts Found., N.Y.C.; mem. accreditation vis. teams Am. Assembly Collegiate Schs. Bus., 1977— . Served to col. AUS, 1941-46. Decorated Bronze Star. Fellow Soc. Applied Anthropology; mem. Acad. Mgmt. (pres. Western div. 1974-75), Western Council Travel Research (dir. 1965-67), Acad. Internat. Mgmt., Mil. Logistics Soc., James Joyce Soc., Beta Gamma Sigma, Sigma Iota Epsilon, Tau Sigma. Democrat. Methodist. Clubs: Harvard (Chgo.); Columbia (N.Y.C.); Marine Corps Officers (San Diego). Home: 1245 Park Row La Jolla CA 92037-3706 Office: San Diego State U Coll Bus San Diego CA 92182-0096

PIERSON, RODNEY, insurance company executive; CFO Safeco Corp., Seattle. Office: Safeco Corp Safeco Plaza Seattle WA 98185

PIERSON, THOMAS, scientific institute administrator; BBA in Mgmt. and Acctg., U. Okla., 1973; grad., Sr. Univ. Officers Mgmt. Inst., 1975; [illegible] Okla., Norman, 1971-74; bus. mgr. Sonoma State U. Found., Inc., Rohnert Park, Calif., 1974-76; assoc. dir. rsch. adminstrn. San Francisco State U. Found., Inc., 1976-84; founder, exec. dir., sec.-treas., bd. dirs. Search for Extraterrestrial Intelligence Inst., Mountain View, Calif., 1984—. Cons. in R & D and high-tech. environments, 1984—; mem. adv. bd. Sierra Nevada Field Rsch. Campus, San Francisco State U., 1978-84, guest lectr. rsch. theory and proposal writing, 1976-84; bd. dirs. Molecular Rsch. Inst., Social Tech., Inc.; instr. Nat. Coun. Univ. Rsch. Adminstrs., 1979-81; participant numerous panels on sponsored program devel. and adminstrn., human resources mgmt., gen. orgnl. mgmt. Mem. sys.-wide cost sharing com. Calif. State U., 1976, mem. sys.-wide effort reporting com., 1976-77, wys.-side task force re auditor gen. rev. of state sys., 1982-83. Recipient Russell R. Meyers award as outstanding profl. employee U. Okla., 1973, Pub. Svc. medal NASA, 1993; scholar U. Okla. Mem. AIAA, AAAS, Soc. Rsch. Adminstrs., Am. Astron. Soc., Astron. Soc. Pacific (adv. coun. 1991—), Planetary Soc., Internat. Soc. for Study Origin of Life, Am. Mgmt. Assn., Nat. Space Soc., Calif. Acad. Scis., No. Calif. Golf Assn. (tournament com.), Shoreline Golf Club (bd. dirs. 1987-88, pres. 1988). Office: SETI Inst 2035 Landings Dr Mountain View CA 94043-0818

PIES, RONALD E. retired city official; b. Rochester, N.Y., Mar. 21, 1940; s. Herman S. and Sylvia Pies; m. Bernita Orloff, Aug. 27, 1964; children: Cara Jean Tracy, David Paul. BS, Ariz. State U., 1963. Recreation leader City of Phoenix, Ariz., 1962-64; head recreation divsn. City of Scottsdale (Ariz.) Parks and Recreation Dept., 1964-69; dir. parks and recreation City of Tempe, Ariz., 1969-84, cmty. svcs. dir., 1984-98. Guest lectr. Ariz. State U.; spl. projects coord. Ariz. Lottery, 1999—. Mem., pres. Kyrene Sch. Dist. Governing Bd., 1979-82; chmn., bd. regents Pacific Revenue Sources Mgmt. Sch. NRPA; gen. chmn. Fiesta Bowl Soccer Classic, 1982-98; founding mem. Tempe YMCA bd. mgrs.; apptd. mem. Ariz. State Parks Bd., 1987-93, chair, 1991. Named Outstanding Young Man, Jaycees; recipient Superior Svc. Mgmt. award ASPA, Ariz. chpt., 1988; named to Hall of Fame, Ariz. State U. Alumni for Coll. Pub. Programs, 1996, Hall of Fame, Tempe Elem. Sch. Dist., 1996. Mem. Tempe C. of C., Ariz. Parks and Recreation Assn. (bd. dirs. 1986-98, pres. adminstrs., Disting. Fellow award 1983, Life Mem. award 1998, L.E.G.E.N.D. award 2000), Nat. Recreation and Parks Assn. (Outstanding Profl. 1991), Cactus League Baseball Assn. (pres. 1993-94, apptd. mem. Ariz. baseball commn. by Gov. Symington 1994—, chair 1995-2000), Tempe Diablos Club, Sigma Alpha Epsilon. E-mail: ronandbernita@earthlink.net

PIGFORD, THOMAS HARRINGTON, nuclear engineering educator; b. Meridian, Miss., Apr. 21, 1922; s. Lamar and Zula Vivian (Harrington) P.; m. Catherine Kennedy Cathey, Dec. 31, 1948 (dec. 1992); children: Cynthia Pigford Naylor, Julie Pigford Brink; m. Elizabeth Hood Weekes, Nov. 12, 1994. B.S. in Chem. Engring., Ga. Inst. Tech., 1943; S.M. in Chem. Engring., M.I.T., 1948, Sc.D. in Chem. Engring., 1952. Asst. prof. chem. engring., dir. Sch. Engring. Practice, M.I.T., 1950-52, asst. prof. nuclear and chem. engring., 1952-55, assoc. prof., 1955-57; head engring., dir. nuclear reactor projects and asst. dir. research lab. Gen. Atomic Co., La Jolla, Calif., 1957-59; prof. nuclear engring., chmn. dept. nuclear engring. U. Calif., Berkeley, 1959—; sr. rsch. scientist Lawrence Berkeley Lab., 1959—. Mem. panel Nat. Atomic Safety Licensing Bd. AEC-Nuclear Regulatory Commn., 1963-77; mem. Pres.'s Commn. on accident at 3-Mile Island, 1979; mem. bd. radioactive waste mgmt. and energy engring. bd., NAS-NAE, chmn. waste isolation systems panel, waste isolation pilot plant panel, fusion hybrid panel, separations and transmutations panel, transmutation of military plutonium panel, panel on health standard for radioactive waste disposal, chmn. adv. coun. Inst. Nuclear Power Op.; mem. Sec. of Energy's expert cons. group on Chernobyl accident; chmn. nuclear oversight com. Sacramento Mcpl. Utility Dist.; chmn. nuclear safety com. Gulf States Utilities Co.; mem. expert cons. group Swedish Nuclear Power Inspectorate; mem. peer rev. group for waste isolation pilot plant; mem. corp. rev. com. Oak Ridge Nat. Lab; lectr. Taiwan Nat. Sci. Found., 1990; vis. prof. Kyoto U., 1975, Kuwait U., 1976; cons. in field. Author: (with Manson Benedict) Nuclear Chemical Engineering, 1958, 2d edit., 1981; contbr. numerous articles to profl. jours.; patentee in field. Served with USNR, 1944-46. Recipient John Wesley Powell award U.S. Geol. Survey, 1981; named Outstanding Young Man of Greater Boston, Boston Jaycees, 1955; E. I. DuPont DeNemours rsch. fellow, 1948-50; Berkeley citation U. Calif., 1987; Japan Soc. for Promotion Sci. fellow, 1974-75; grantee NSF, 1960-75, EPA, 1973-78, Dept. Energy, 1979-92, Ford Found., 1974-75, Electric Power Rsch. Inst., 1974-75, Mitsubishi Metals Corp., 1989-90; named to Ga. Tech. Hall of Fame, 1995. Fellow Am. Nuclear Soc. (bd. dirs., Arthur H. Compton award 1971); mem. AIME, NAE, Am. Chem. Soc., Am. Inst. Chem. Engrs. (Robert E. Wilson award 1980, Service to Society award 1985), Atomic Indsl. Forum (dir.), Sigma Xi, Phi Kappa Phi, Tau Beta Pi. Home: 166 Alpine Ter Oakland CA 94618-1823 Office: U Calif Dept Nuclear Engring Berkeley CA 94720-0001 E-mail: pigford@nuc.berkeley.edu

PIGOTT, CHARLES MCGEE, transportation equipment manufacturing executive; b. Seattle, Apr. 21, 1929; s. Paul and Theiline (McGee) P.; m. Yvonne Flood, Apr. 18, 1953. B.S., Stanford U., 1951. With PACCAR Inc, Seattle, 1959—, exec. v.p., 1962-65, pres., 1965-86, chmn., pres., 1986-87, chmn., chief exec. officer, 1987-97, also bd. dirs., chmn. emeritus, 1997—. Dir. The Seattle Times, Chevron Corp., The Boeing Co. Pres. Nat. Boy Scouts Am., 1986-88, mem. exec. bd. Mem. Bus. Council. Office: Paccar Inc 777 106th Ave NE Bellevue WA 98004-5017

PIGOTT, MARK C. automotive executive; CEO PACCAR, Bellevue, Wash., 1997—. Office: PACCAR PO Box 1518 777 106th Ave NE Bellevue WA 98009

PIIPPO, STEVE, educator; Dir. material sci. tech. program Richland (Wash.) High Sch. Creator, author Materials Sci.Tech. Recipient A+ Sites Recognition award U.S. Dept. Edn. Office: Richland High Sch Math Sci Tech Program 930 Long Ave Richland WA 99352-3399

PIKE, MALCOLM CECIL, preventive medicine educator; b. Johannesburg, Republic of South Africa, May 2, 1935; m. Anne; 1 child. BS in Math. with honors, Witwatersrand U., Republic of South Africa, 1956; postgrad., London U., 1956; D Math. Stats., Cambridge (Eng.) U., 1958; PhD in Math. Stats., Aberdeen (Scotland) U., 1963. Asst. lectr., lectr. stats. U. Aberdeen, 1959-62; mem. sci. staff statis. rsch. unit Med. Rsch. Coun., London, 1963-69; 1st asst. Regius dept. medicine U. Oxford, Eng., 1969-73, dir. ICRF Cancer Epidemiology and Clin. Trials Units Eng., 1983-87; prof. preventive medicine U. So. Calif. Sch. Medicine, L.A., 1973-83, L.A., 1987—, chair preventive medicine, 1989-99. Mem. coun. Royal Statis. Soc., 1972-73, chmn. med. sect., 1984-86; mem. devel. rsch. segment virus cancer program NCI, 1971-78; mem. pres.' biomed. rsch. panel Interdisciplinary Cluster in Epidemiology, Biostats. and Bioengring., 1976; mem. rev. group on analysis of case-control studies Internat. Agy. Cancer Rsch., 1977; mem. safe drinking water com. NAS, 1977-83, cons. to Radiation Effects Rsch. Found., Hiroshima, Japan, 1979, 81, mem. com. on Pyrenes, 1981-83, mem. commn. on life scis., 1992-95; mem. rev. com. Internat. Agy. Cancer Rsch., 1979; mem. adv. com. on breast cancer screening Internat. Union Against Cancer, 1982; mem. faculty Internat. Agy. for Cancer Rsch., 1985; mem. U.K. Coord. Com. on Cancer Rsch., 1985-86; mem. com. on immunology of leprosy WHO, 1986-87, mem. bd. sci. counselors tropical diseases rsch., 1989-93; mem. med. rsch. del. to USSR U.K. Dept. Health and Social Security, 1986; mem. adv. panel Nat. [illegible] mem. sci. adv. com. Tobacco-Related Disease Rsch. program State of Calif., 1993-96. Assoc. editlr Med. Stats. and Epidemiology of Biometrics, 1972-76; editl. bd. Brit. Jour. Haematology, 1972-73, Brit. Jour. Cancer, 1972-73; contbr. articles to profl. publs. Recipient Guy Bronze medal Royal Statis. Soc., 1968, Brinker Internat. award of the Susan G. Komen Breast Cancer Found., 1994. Mem. NAS (mem. inst. medicine). Office: USC Norris Cancer Ctr Mail Stop 44 1441 Eastlake Ave Los Angeles CA 90033-1048 E-mail: mcpike@hsc.usc.edu

PILAND, NEILL FINNES, health services economist, researcher; b. Pomona, Calif., Nov. 6, 1943; s. Finnes Elmer and Sylvia Beatrice (Renick) PiL.; m. Diane Lynn Fiedor, Aug. 12, 1977; children: Evan Neill, Spencer Lowell, Arden Geneva. BA, UCLA, 1965, MPH, 1970, DrPH, 1979; MA, U. Calif., Davis, 1966. Rsch. assoc. Sch. Pub. Health UCLA, 1971-73, sr. rsch. assoc., 1973; health economist Stanford Rsch. Inst., Menlo Pk., Calif., 1973-77, asst. mgr. health svcs. rsch., 1974-77; dir. health ctr. study Jicarilla Apache Tribe, Dulce, N.Mex., 1978-82; dir. health systems evaluation program Lovelace Med. Found., Albuquerque, 1982-83, dir. health svcs. rsch. and edn., 1983-91; dir. Ctr. Health & Population Rsch., Albuquerque, 1991-94, Lovelace Inst. for Health and Population Rsch., Albuquerque, 1994-96; rsch. dir. Ctr. Rsch. Med. Group Mgmt. Assn., Englewood, Colo., 1996—; clin. assoc. prof. U. Colo. Sch. Medicine; rsch. prof. U. Denver. Clin. asst. prof. medicine U. N.Mex., Albuquerque, 1981, clin. assoc. prof., 1994—; vis. prof. U. N.H., Durham, 1989-90. Co-author: Strategic Nursing Management: Power and Responsibility in a New Era; mem. editorial bd. Jour. Managerial Issues, 1991—; co-editor: Physician Profiling: A Sourcebook for Adminstrators, Chart Accounts for Healthcare Organizations; contbr. over 90 articles to profl. jours. Mem. rsch. com. N.Mex. HealthNet, 1986-88; chair econ. issues N.Mex. Com. on Pub. Health Impact of Smoking, 1988; bd. dirs. Am. Geriatrics and Gerontology, 1984-87, Healthcare for Homeless, 1988-92; mem. exec. coun. N.Mex. ASSIST Com., 1992—, sci. adv. com. N.Mex. ASSIST Project, 1992—; mem. steering com. Group Practice Improvement Network, 1996—; mem. workgroup smoking control Colo. Dept. Health and Environment, 1999—. Recipient traineeship, USPHS, 1968-70. Mem. APHA, Am. Econ. Assn., Soc. Rsch. Adminstrs., Assn. Health Svcs. Rsch. Avocations: tennis, hockey, hiking, biking. Home: 8762 E Mineral Cir Englewood CO 80112-2748 Office: Med Group Mmgt Assn 104 Inverness Ter E Englewood CO 80112-5313 E-mail: npiland@mgma.com

PILGERAM, LAURENCE OSCAR, biochemist; b. Great Falls, Mont., June 23, 1924; s. John Rudolph and Bertha Roslyn (Phillips) P.; m. Cynthia Ann Moore, Apr. 16, 1971; children: Karl Erich, Kurt John. AA, U. Calif., Berkeley, 1948, BA, 1949, PhD, 1953. Instr. dept. physiology U. Ill. Profl. Coll., Chgo., 1954-55; asst. prof. dept. biochemistry Stanford (Calif.) U. Sch. Medicine, 1955-57; dir. arteriosclerosis research lab. U. Minn. Sch. Medicine, Mpls., 1957-65, Santa Barbara, Calif., 1965-71; dir. coagulation lab., assoc. dir. Cerebrovascular Research Ctr., Baylor Coll. Medicine, Tex. Med. Ctr., Houston, 1971-75; dir. Thrombosis Control Labs., Palo Alto, Calif., 1975-79, Santa Barbara, 1979—. Cons. NIH, Bio-Sci. Labs., FDA; del. Council on Thrombosis and Council on Strokes, Am. Heart Assn. Assembly. Co-editor: Nutrition and Thrombosis for the Nat. Dairy Council, 1973; contbr. sci. articles to profl. jours. Recipient CIBA award, London, 1958, Karl Thomae award, Germany, 1973; NIH grantee, 1954-75; LIfe Ins. Med. Research Fund fellow, 1952-54. Mem. Am. Soc. for Biochemistry and Molecular Biology. Office: PO Box 1583 Goleta PO Santa Barbara CA 93116

PILISUK, MARC, community psychology educator; b. N.Y.C., Jan. 19, 1934; s. Louis and Charlotte (Feferholtz) P.; m. Phyllis E. Kamen, June 16, 1956; children: Tammy, Jeff. BA, Queens Coll., 1955; MA, U. Mich., 1956, PhD, 1961. Asst. prof., assoc. rsch. psychologist U. Mich., Ann Arbor, 1961-65, founder teach-in, 1965; assoc. prof. Purdue U., West Lafayette, Ind., 1965-67; prof.-in-residence U. Calif., Berkeley, 1967-77, prof. cmty. psychology Davis, 1977—. Vis. prof. U. Calif., Wright Inst., 1991—93; cons. Ctr. for Self Help Rsch., Berkeley, Calif., 1991—93; prof. psychology Saybrook Inst. and Grad. Ctr., San Francisco, 1993—. Author: (novels) International Conflict and Social Policy, 1972, The Healing Web: Social Networks and Human Survival, 1986; editor The Triple Revolution , 1969, Poor Americans, 1970, Triple Revolution Emerging, 1972, How We Lost the War on Poverty, 1973. Fellow, NIMH, 1959—60; grantee, NSF, 1962—66, tng. grantee, Nat. Inst. Alcoholism and Drug Abuse , 1973—77. Fellow: APA (pres. divsn. peace psychology 1996—97, cadre exports violence), Soc. for Cmty. Rsch. and Action, Am. Orthopsychiat. Assn., Soc. for Psychol. Study Social Issues (coun.); mem.: APHA, ACLU, Am. Soc. on Aging, Psychologists for Social Responsibility (steering com., Disting. Svc. award 2001), Faculty for Human Rights in C.Am. E-mail: mpilisuk@saybrook.edu

PILOT, KEN, retail apparel company executive; Assoc. mdse. mgr. Gap Inc., 1989, exec. v.p. Internat. divsn., 1998-99, pres. Internat. divsn., 1999—. Office: Gap Inc 1 Harrison St San Francisco CA 94105-1602

PIMBLE, TONI, artistic director, choreographer, educator; b. Eng. Student, Elmhurst Sch. Ballet and Dramatic Arts, Royal Acad. Dancing, London. Resident choreographer Dance Aspen Co. Project; artistic dir., resident choreographer Eugene (Oreg.) Ballet Co., 1978—; artistic dir. Ballet Idaho, Boise. Past mem. faculty Dance Aspen Summer Dance Sch. Choreographer (festival) Carlisle Choreographer's Showcase, Pa. and Colo., (ballets) Two's Company, N.Y.C., Common Ground, Atlanta, 1994, Playing Field, Indlps., Borderline, Alice in Wonderland, Nebr., 1994, Wash., 1996, Quartet in Blue, Oreg., 1994, Petrushka, Nev., 1994, 95, Children of the Raven, India, Bangladesh, Sri Lanka, Syria, Jordan, Tunisia, 1995, 96, A Midsummer Night's Dream, Nev., 1997, numerous tours and sch. performances; choreographer, tchr. U. Iowa, Interlochen Sch. Arts; resident choreographer Dance On Tour Nat. Endowment Arts; artistic dir. Ballet Idaho. Active outreach programs Young Audiences Oreg., Wash. State Cultural Enrichment Program. Oreg. Arts Commn. artist fellow, Nat. Endowment Arts grantee; co-recipient Gov.'s Arts award, Oreg., 1996. Office: Ballet Idaho 501 S 8th St Ste A Boise ID 83702-7108

PINCKERT, WARREN, II, pharmaceutical executive; CEO, pres. Cholestech Corp., Hayward, Calif. Office: Cholestech Corp 3347 Investment Blvd Hayward CA 94545-3808

PINCOCK, RICHARD EARL, chemistry educator; b. Ogden, Utah, Sept. 14, 1935; s. Earl Samuel and Virginia (Christenson) P.; m. Elke Gertrud Hermann, Aug. 20, 1960; children— Christina, Gordon, Jennifer. B.S., U. Utah, 1956; A.M., Harvard U., 1957, Ph.D., 1960. Postdoctoral research fellow Calif. Inst. Tech., 1959-60; faculty U. B.C., Vancouver, Can., 1960—, prof., 1969—. Mem. Phi Beta Kappa, Sigma Pi. Office: U BC Chemistry Dept Vancouver BC Canada V6T 1Y6 E-mail: pincock@chem.ubc.ca

PINCUS, HOWARD JONAH, geologist, engineer, educator; b. N.Y.C., June 24, 1922; s. Otto Max and Gertrude (Jankowsky) P.; m. Maud Lydia Roback, Sept. 6, 1953; children: Glenn David, Philip E. BS, CCNY, 1942; PhD, Columbia U., 1949. Faculty Ohio State U., 1949-67, from instr. to assoc. prof., 1949-59, prof., 1959-67, chmn. dept. geology, 1960-65; rsch. geologist U. S. Bur. Mines, summers 1963-67; geologist, rsch. supr. U.S. Bur. Mines, 1967-68; prof. geol. sci. and civil engring. U. Wis., Milw., 1968-87, prof. emeritus, 1987—, dean Coll. Letters and Sci., 1969-72; rsch. assoc. Lamont Geol. Obs., Columbia, 1949-51; geologist Ohio Dept. Natural Resources, summers 1950-61; cons. geology and rock mechanics, [illegible] com. on rock mechanics NAS/NAE, 1975-78, 80-89, chmn., 1985-87; U.S. com. Internat. Assn. Engring. Geology/NAS, chmn., 1987-90; sr. postdoctoral fellow NSF 1962, Tech. editor Geotech. Testing Jour., 1992-95, mem.

edit. bd., 1996—. 1st lt. C.E. AUS, 1942-46. Recipient award for teaching excellence U. Wis.-Milw. Alumni Assn., 1978. Fellow ASTM (Reinhart award 1987, Award of Merit 1989), AAAS, Geol. Soc. Am.; mem. ASCE, NSPE, AAUP (pres. Ohio State U. chpt. 1955-56, mem. coun. 1965-67, pres. U. Wis.-Milw. chpt 1976-77), Am. Geophys. Union, Geol. Soc. Am. (chmn. engring. geology divsn. 1973-74), Soc. Mining Engrs., Internat. Assn. Engring. Geology, Internat. Soc. Rock Mechanics, Am. Rock Mechanics Assn., Assn. Engring. Geologists, Am. Inst. Profl. Geologists (pres. Ohio sect. 1965-66), Phi Beta Kappa (pres. Ohio State U. chpt. 1959-60, pres. U. Wis.-Milw. chpt. 1976-77), Sigma Xi. Home: 17523 Plaza Marlena San Diego CA 92128-1807 Office: PO Box 27598 San Diego CA 92198-1598

PINCUS, ROBERT LAWRENCE, art critic, cultural historian; b. Bridgeport, Conn., June 5, 1953; s. Jules Robert and Carol Sylvia (Rosen) P.; m. Georgianna Manly, June 20, 1981; 1 child, Matthew Manly. BA, U. Calif., Irvine, 1976; MA, U. So. Calif., 1980, PhD, 1987. Instr. U. So. Calif., L.A., 1978-83; art critic L.A. Times, 1981-85, San Diego Union, 1985-92, San Diego Union-Tribune, 1992—. Vis. prof. San Diego State U., 1985-86, 92. Author: On A Scale That Competes with the World: The Art of Edward and Nancy Reddin Kienholz, 1990, (with others) West Coast Duchamp, 1991, But Is It Art: The Spirit of Art as Activism, 1994, Paradise, 1994; author introduction to W.D.'s Midnight Carnival, 1988, Manuel Neri Early Work, 1953-78, 97. Recipient Chem. Bank award, 1994, Best Critical Writing award San Diego Press Club, 1994. Mem. Internat. Assn. Art Critics, Coll. Art Assn. Democrat. Office: San Diego Union Tribune PO Box 191 350 Camino De La Reina San Diego CA 92108-3003

PINES, ALEXANDER, chemistry educator, researcher, consultant; b. Tel Aviv, June 22, 1945; came to U.S., 1968. s. Michael and Neima (Ratner) P.; m. Ayala Malach, Aug. 31, 1967 (div. 1983); children: Itai, Shani; m. Ditsa Kafry, May 5, 1983; children: Noami, Jonathan, Talia. BS, Hebrew U., Jerusalem, 1967; PhD, MIT, 1972; D (hon.), U. Paris, 1999, U. Rome "La Sapienza", 2001. Asst. prof. chemistry U. Calif., Berkeley, 1972-75, assoc. prof., 1975-80, prof., 1980—, Pres.'s chair, 1993-97, Chandellor's rsch. prof., 1997-99, Miller rsch. prof., 1998-99, Glenn T. Seaborg chair chemistry, 1999—. Faculty sr. scientist materials scis. div. Lawrence Berkeley Nat. Lab., 1975—; cons. Mobil Oil Co., Princeton, N.J., 1980-84, Shell Oil Co., Houston, 1981—; chmn. Bytel Corp., Berkeley, Calif., 1981-85; vis. prof. Weizmann Inst. Sci., 1982; adv. prof. East China Normal U., Shanghai, People's Rep. of China, 1985; sci. dir. Nalorac, Martinez, Calif., 1986-92; Joliot-Curie prof. Ecole Superieure de Physique et Chemie, Paris, 1987; Walter J. Chute Disting. lectr. Dalhousie U., 1989, Charles A. McDowell lectr. U. B.C., 1989, E. Leon Watkins lectr. Wichita State U., 1990; Hinshelwood lectr., U. Oxford, 1990, A.R. Gordon Disting. lectr. U. Toronto, 1990, Venable lectr. U. N.C., 1990, Max Born lectr. Hebrew U. of Jerusalem, 1990; William Draper Harkins lectr. U. Chgo., 1991, Kolthoff lectr. U. Minn., 1991; Md.-Grace lectr. U. Md., 1992; mem. adv bd. Nat. High Magnetic Field Lab., Inst. Theoretical Physics, U. Calif. Santa Barbara, Ctr. Pure and Applied Math. U. Calif., Berkeley; mem. adv. panel chem. Nat. Sci. Found.; Randolph T. Major Disting. Lectr. U. Conn., 1992; mem. bd. sci. govs. Weizemann Inst. Sci., 1997—; Peter Smith lectr. Duke U., 1993, Arthur William Davidson lect. U. Kansas, 1992, Arthur Birch lect. Australian Nat. U., 1993, Richard C. Lord Meml. lectr. MIT, 1993, Steacie lectr. Nat. Rsch. Coun. Can., 1993, Centenary lectr. Royal Soc. Chemistry, 1994, Morris Loeb lectr. Harvard U., 1994, Jesse Boot Found. lectr., U. Nottingham, 1994, Frontiers in Chemistry lectr. Tex. A&M U., 1995, Bergman lectr. Weizmann Inst. Sci., 1995, faculty rsch. lectr. U. Calif., Berkeley, 1996, Raymond & Beverly Sackler lectr. Tel Aviv U., 1996; Priestley lectr. Pa. State U., 1997; Amy Mellon lectr. Purdue U., 1997; Rsch. frontiers chemistry lectr. U. Iowa, 1998, Moses Gomberg lectr. U. Mich., 1998, J and N Max T. Rogers, Mich. State U., 1998, Frontiers in Chemistry lectr., Wayne State U., 1998, Abbot lectr., U. N.D., 2000, John D. Roberts lectr., Calif. Tech. U., 2000, Willard lectr., U. Wis., 2000, Cliford lectr., U. Pitts., 2000, William Lloyd Evan lectr. Ohio State U., 2000, Jacob Bigeleisen lectr. Stony Brook U., 2001, Laird lectr. U. B.C., 2001; Alan S. Tetelman fellow Yale U., 2001, Regitze Vold Meml. lectr. U. Calif., San Diego, 2001, Sammet guest prof. Goëethe U., Frankfurt, 2001. Editor Molecular Physics, 1987-91; mem. bd. editors Chem. Physics, Chem. Physics Letters, Nmr: Basic Principles and Progress, Advances in Magnetic Resonance, Accounts Chemistry Research, Concepts in Magnetic Reson; adv. editor Oxford U. Press; contbr. articles to profl. jours.; patentee in field. Recipient Strait award North Calif. Spectroscopy Soc., Outstanding Achievement award U.S. Dept. of Energy, 1983, 87, 89, 97, 98, R & D 100 awards, 1987, 89, Disting. Teaching award U. Calif., E.O. Lawrence award, 1988, Pitts. Spectroscopy award, 1989, Wolf Prize for chemistry, 1991, Donald Noyce Undergrad. Teaching award U. Calif., 1992, Robert Foster Cherry award for Great Tchrs. Baylor U., Pres.'s Chair for undergrad. edn. U. Calif., 1993-97, Dickson prize Carnegie Mellon U., 2001; Guggenheim fellow, 1988, Christensen fellow St. Catherine's Coll., Oxford, 1990. Fellow Am. Phys. Soc. (chmn. divsn. chem. physics), Inst. Physics; mem. NAS, Am. Chem. Soc. (mem. exec. com. divsn. phys. chemistry, Signature award, Baekeland medal, Harrison Howe award 1991, Irving Langmuir award 1998, ACS Remsen award 2000, Dickson prize 2001), Royal Soc. Chemistry (Bourke lectr.), Internat. Soc. Magnetic Resonance (v.p., pres. 1993-96), Lawrence Hall Sci. Outreach Com. Office: U Calif Chemistry Dept D 64 Hildebrand Hill Berkeley CA 94720-0001

PINGS, CORNELIUS JOHN, educational consultant, director; b. Conrad, Mont., Mar. 15, 1929; s. Cornelius John and Marjorie (O'Loughlin) P.; m. Marjorie Anna Cheney, June 25, 1960; children: John, Anne, Mary. B.S., Calif. Inst. Tech., 1951, M.S., 1952, Ph.D., 1955. Inst. chem. engring. Stanford U., 1955-56, asst. prof., 1956-59; assoc. prof. chem. engring. Calif. Inst. Tech., 1959-64, prof., 1964-81, exec. officer chem. engring., 1969-73, vice-provost, dean grad. studies, 1970-81; provost, sr. v.p. acad. affairs U. So. Calif., 1981-93; pres. Assn. Am. Univs., Washington, 1993-98. Mem., dir. Nat. Commn. on Rsch., 1978-80; mem. bd. mgmt. Coun. on Govtl. Rels., 1980-83; bd. dirs. Nations Funds; bd. dirs. Edelback, Inc., L.A.; pres. Assn. Grad. Schs., 1977-78; pres. Western Coll. Assn., 1988-90; mem. sci. engring. and pub. policy com. NAS, 1987-92, chmn., 1988-92. Contbr. articles to tech. jours. Mem., chmn. bd. trustees Mayfield Sr. Sch. Bd., 1979-85; mem. Pasadena Redevel. Agy., 1968-81, chmn., 1974-81; bd. dirs. Huntington Meml. Hosp., Pasadena, 1986-92; chmn. L.A. Ctrl. City Assn., 1992. Recipient Arthur Nobel medal, City of Pasadena, 1981, Disting. Alumni award Calif. Inst. Tech., 1989, Presdl. medallion U. So. Calif., 1993. Fellow AIChE, Am. Acad. Arts and Scis.; mem. NAE, Calif. Club, Twilight Club, Bohemian Club, Cosmos Club, Valley Hunt Club. Roman Catholic. Office: 480 S Orange Grove Blvd # 6 Pasadena CA 91105-1736 E-mail: cjpings@usc.edu

PINIELLA, LOUIS VICTOR, professional baseball team manager; b. Tampa, Fla., Aug. 28, 1943; m. Anita Garcia, Apr. 12, 1967; children: Lou, Kristi, Derrick. Student, U. Tampa. Baseball player various minor-league teams, 1962-68, Cleve. Indians, 1968, Kansas City Royals, 1969-73, N.Y. Yankees, 1974-84, coach, 1984-85, mgr., 1985-87, 1988, gen. mgr., 1987-88, spl. advisor, TV announcer, 1989; mgr. Cin. Reds, 1990-92, Seattle Mariners, 1992—. Named to Am. League All-Star Team, 1972; recipient Ellis Island Medal of Honor, 1990; Named A.L. Rookie of the Yr Baseball Writers Assoc of Amer, 1969, Named A.L. Manager of the Yr, 1995. Office: Seattle Mariners PO Box 4100 1st Ave South & Atlantic Seattle WA 98104

PINKERTON, JOHN N. plant pathologist; Rsch. plant pathologist USDA-ARS Hort. Crops Rsch. Lab., Corvallis, Oreg. Contbr. articles to profl. publs. Recipient Lee M. Hutchins award Am. Phytopathol. Soc., 1998. Office: Hort Crops Rsch Lab 3420 NW Orchard Ave Corvallis OR 97330-5014 Fax: 541-750-8764

PINKERTON, RICHARD LADOYT, retired management educator; b. Huron, S.D., Mar. 5, 1933; s. Abner Pyle and Orral Claudine (Arneson) P.; m. Sandra Louise Lee, Aug. 28, 1965 (div. 1992); children— Elizabeth, Patricia. B.A. (La Verne Noyes scholar 1952-55), U. Mich., 1955; M.B.A., Case Western Res. U., 1962; Ph.D. (Nat. Assn. Purchasing Mgmt. fellow 1967-68), U. Wis., 1969. Sr. market research analyst Harris-Intertype Corp., Cleve., 1957-61; mgr. sales devel. Triax Corp., Cleve., 1962-64; coord. mktg. program Mgmt. Inst., U. Wis., 1964-67; dir. exec. programs Mgmt. Inst., U. Wis. (Grad. Sch. Bus.), also asst. prof. mktg., 1969-74; prof. mgmt., dean Grad. Sch. Adminstrn., Capital U., Columbus, Ohio, 1974-86; prof. mgmt., dir. Univ. Bus. Ctr., Craig Sch. Bus.. Calif. State U., Fresno, 1986-89, prof. mktg., 1989-2000, chmn. mktg. and logistics dept., 1996-2000, dir. London semester, prof. emeritus, mem. bd., 2000—. Trustee Ohio Coun. Econ. Edn., 1976-87; bd. dirs. Univ. Bus. Ctr.; cons. to govt. and industry, 1960—. Co-author: The Purchasing Manager's Guide to Strategic Proactive Procurement, 1996; contbr. articles to profl. jours. Bd. dirs. The Fresno Townhouse Assn.; bd. govs. Hannah Neil Home for Children, Columbus, 1975-78. Served as officer USAF, 1955-57, lt. col. USAFR, 1957-78. Mem. Nat. Assn. Contract Mgmt. (chmn. validation cert. com. 1990), Nat. Assn. Purchasing Mgmt. (chmn. acad. planning 1979-84, rsch. symposium 1992), Am. Mktg. Assn. (chpt. pres. 1972-73), Res. Officers Assn., Air Forces Assn., Ft. Washington Golf and Country Club, Marines Meml. Club, Cleve. Athletic Club, Beta Gamma Sigma, Alpha Kappa Psi, Phi Gamma Delta, Rotary (Paul Harris fellow). Home: 4721 N Cedar Ave Apt 111 Fresno CA 93726-1007

PINKERTON, STEVEN JAMES, city official; b. Madison, Wis., Jan. 21, 1960; BA, U. Mo., 1983; MPI in Urban Planning, MA in Econs., U. So. Calif., 1988. Mem. staff Econ. Devel. Assn. City of Redondo Beach, Calif., 1984-91; mem. redevel. adminstrn. City of Long Beach, 1991-94; dir. housing and redevel. City of Stockton, 1994—. Mem. Am. Planning Assn. (cert. city planner). Office: City Stockton 305 N El Dorado St Ste 200 Stockton CA 95202-2306

PINNELL, ROBERT PEYTON, chemistry educator; b. Fresno, Calif., Dec. 5, 1938; s. Paul Peyton and Iris Ione (Shepherd) P.; m. Sharron Lyne Gregory, Aug. 18, 1962; children: Jason Peyton, Sabrina Lyne. BS, Calif. State U., Fresno, 1960; PhD, U. Kansas, 1964. Postdoctoral fellow U. Tex., Austin, 1964-66; asst. prof. chemistry Claremont (Calif.) McKenna Coll., Scripps Coll. and Pitzer Coll., 1966-72, assoc. prof., 1972-78, prof., 1978—, chmn. joint sci. dept., 1974-77, 97—. Rsch. affilate Jet Propulsion Lab., 1986-88, vis. assoc. prof. chemistry Calif. Inst. Tech., 1973-74. Postdoctoral fellow U. Calif. at Santa Barbara, 1980-81; NASA-Am. Soc. for Engring. fellow, 1982, 83, 86, 87. Mem. Nat. Sci. Tchrs. Assn., Am. Chem. Soc., Calif. Assn. Chemistry Tchrs., Sigma Xi. Democrat. Avocation: reading. Office: Claremont McKenna Scripps & Pitzer Colls 925 N Mills Ave Claremont CA 91711-5916

PINNEY, THOMAS CLIVE, retired English language educator; b. Ottawa, Kans., Apr. 23, 1932; s. John James and Lorene Maude (Owen) P.; m. Sherrill Marie Ohman, Sept. 1, 1956; children— Anne, Jane, Sarah. B.A., Beloit Coll., Wis., 1954; Ph.D., Yale U., New Haven, 1960. Instr. Hamilton Coll., Clinton, N.Y., 1957-61; instr. English Yale U., New Haven, 1961-62; asst. prof. to prof., chmn. dept. English Pomona Coll., Claremont, Calif., 1962-97; ret., 1997. Editor: Essays of George Eliot, 1963, Selected Writings of Thomas Babington Macaulay, 1972, Letters of Macaulay, 1974-81, Kipling's India, 1986, A History of Wine in America, 1989, Kipling's Something of Myself, 1990, Letters of Rudyard Kipling, 1990, The Vineyards and Wine Cellars of California, 1994, The Wine of Santa Cruz Island, 1994. Guggenheim fellow, 1966, 84,Recipient Disting. Svc. citation Beloit Coll., 1984; fellow NEH, 1980; grantee Am. Coun. Learned Socs., 1974, 84, Am. Philos. Soc., 1968, 82, 94. Mem. MLA, Elizabethan Club (New Haven), Zamorano Club (L.A.), Phi Beta Kappa. Home: 228 W Harrison Ave Claremont CA 91711-4323 Office: Pomona Coll Dept English Claremont CA 91711

PINSON, LARRY LEE, pharmacist; b. Van Nuys, Calif., Dec. 5, 1947; s. Leland J. and Audrey M. (Frett) P.; m. Margaret K. Pinson, Mar. 18, 1972; children: Scott C., Kelly E. Student, U. Calif., Davis, 1967-69; AA, Am. River Coll., Sacramento, 1969; PharmD, U. Calif., San Francisco, 1973. Staff pharmacist/asst. dir. pharm. svcs. St. Mary's Hosp., Reno, 1973-77; chief pharmacist May Ang Base USAF, 1973-77; owner/chief pharmacist Silverada Pharmacy, Reno, 1979-2001; adj. prof. Idaho State U., Pocatello, 1989—; chief pharmacist Scolar's Food & Drug, Sak-N-Save Pharmacy, Reno, 2001—. Cons. pharmacist Physicians Hosp., 1974-93, Reno Med. Plaza, 1973—; pharmacist coordinator Intensive Pharm. Svcs., 1986-87; cons. Calif. Dept. Health & Corrections, Susanville, 1975-76, Nev. Med. Care Adv. Bd., Carson City, 1984-87; provider and reviewer Nev. State Bd. Pharmacy, Reno, 1975-84; instr. we. Nev. Cmty. Coll., 1974-76; cons. Rural Calif. Hosp. Assn., 1973-74. Co-author: Care of Hickman Catheter, 1984. Apptd. by Gov. Bob Miller, Nev. State Bd. Pharmacy, 1995—, pres., 1996—; mem. Nev. Arthritis Found.; bd. dirs. Am. Cancer Soc., 1986—; softball coach Reno/Sparks Recreation Dept., 1973—; cubmaster Pack 153, Verdi, nev.; scoutmaster com. chmn. Reno troop 1, Boy Scouts Am., 1988-92. Recipient Bowl of Hygeia award (Pharmacist of the Year), Nev. Pharmacists Assn. and A.H. Robbins Co., 1984, named Pharmacist of the Year, Nevada Pharm. Alliance, 1999. Mem. Nat. Assn. Bds. of Pharmacy, Am. Pharm. Assn., Nev. Pharmacists Assn. (pres. 1981-82), Nev. Profl. Stds. Rev. Orgn., Greater Nev. Health Sys. Agy., Kappa Psi. Avocations: skiing, fishing, backpacking, softball, golf. Home: PO Box 478 Verdi NV 89439-0478 Office: Sak-N-Save Pharmacy 1901 Silverada Blvd Reno NV 89512-5032 E-mail: rx2005@aol.com

PINTO, JOHN, state legislator, educator; b. Apache County, Ariz., Dec. 15, 1924; BS in Elem. Edn., U. N.Mex., 1962, MA in Elem. Edn., 1970. Mem. N.Mex. Senate, Dist. 3, Santa Fe, 1976—, mem. edn. com., mem. Indian cultural affairs com., mem. energy coun. Mem. McKinley County Commn., chmn. bd. commrs. With USMC, 1945-46. Democrat. Office: PO Box 163 Tohatchi NM 87325-0163

PIPES, SALLY C. think-tank executive; Asst. dir. Fraser Inst., Vancouver, B.C., Can.; pres., CEO Pacific Rsch. Inst. for Pub. Policy, San Francisco. Co-author (with Spencer Star): Income and Taxation in Canada, (with Michael Walker) 7 editions of Tax Facts; has appeared nationally on TV programs such as 20/20 and Politically Incorrect, Dateline, Inside Politics and PBS's Think Tank; regularly asked to comment on timely issues by radio and print journalists; opinion editls. have been published in various newspapers including San Francisco Chronicle, L.A. Times, Investor's Business Daily, L.A. Daily News, The Orange County Register; writes a bi-monthly column in Chief Executive mag. Bd. dirs. Fin. Instns. Commn. (B.C.), 1982— (chmn. 1989—); mem. Vancouver City Planning Commn.; trustee St. Luke's Hosp. Found. in San Francisco; bd. dirs. Ind. Women's Forum; mem. bd. advisors Western Jour. Ctr. and Citizens for Term Limits, San Francisco Lawyers chpt. of the Federalist Soc.; commr. Calif. Commn. on Transp. Investment, 1996; bd. govs. Donner-Can. Found. Mem. Mont Pelerin Soc., Nat. Assn. Bus. Economists, Can. Assn. for Bus. Econs. (pres. 2 terms), Assn. Profl. Economists of B.C. Office: Pacific Rsch Inst Pub Policy 755 Sansome St Ste 450 San Francisco CA 94111-1709

PIPPEN, SCOTTIE, professional basketball player; b. Hamburg, Ark., Sept. 25, 1965; Student, U. Ctrl. Ark., 1983-87. With Seattle Super Sonics, 1987; guard/forward Chgo. Bulls, 1987-98, Houston Rockets, 1998-99, Portland Trailblazers, 1999—. Player NBA Championship Team, 1991, 92, 93, U.S. Olympic Basketball Team, 1992. Named to All-Star team, 1990, 92-93, NBA All-Defensive First team, 1992, 93, 94, All-Defensive second team, 1991, NBA All-Star Team, 1992-94, NBA All-Star MVP, 1994, All-NBA First Team, 1994; mem. NBA championship team, 1991-93, 96. Office: Portland Trailblazers One Ctr Ct Ste 200 Portland OR 97227

PIPPIN, DONALD FERRELL, musician, director, conductor; b. Raleigh, N.C., Dec. 8, 1925; s. Raymond Edward and Dorothy (Law) Pippin. Pianist, producer Sunday Night Concerts, San Francisco, 1954-78; artistic dir. Pocket Opera, San Francisco, 1978. Translator, condr. over 60 operas including Marriage of Figaro, 1981, Belle Helene, 1981, Merry Wives, 1983, Merry Widow, 1987, Barber of Seville, 1991 among others. Democrat. Home: 39 Romain St San Francisco CA 94114-2733 Office: Pocket Opera 44 Page St Ste 404A San Francisco CA 94102-5975

PIRAINO, JAMES V. construction executive; BS in Mech. Engring., Tufts U. Various mgmt. positions WW. Grainger, Allied Signal, WESCO Internat., Inc., exec. officer, v.p. mktg.; pres., CEO Buildpoint.com, 2000—. Office: 2200 Bridge Pkwy Ste 103 Redwood City CA 94065-1186

PIRCHER, LEO JOSEPH, lawyer, director; b. Berkeley, Calif., Jan. 4, 1933; s. Leo Charles and Christine (Moore) P.; m. Phyllis McConnell, Aug. 04, 1956 (div. Apr. 1981); children: Christopher, David, Eric; m. Nina Silverman, June 14, 1987. BS, U. Calif., Berkeley, 1954, JD, 1957. Bar: Calif. 1958, (N.Y.) 1985, cert.: Calif. Bd. Legal Specialization (cert. specialist taxation law). Assoc. Lawler, Felix & Hall, L.A., 1957-62, ptnr., 1962-65, sr. ptnr., 1965-83, Pircher, Nichols & Meeks, L.A., 1983—. Adj. prof. Loyola U. Law Sch., L.A., 1959—61; corp. sec. Am. Metal Bearing Co., Gardena, Calif., 1975—; dir. Valco Internat., Inc., Orange, Calif.; spkr. various law schs. and bar assns. edn. programs. Author (with others): (novels) Definition and Utility of Leases, 1968. Chmn. pub. fin. and taxation sect. Calif. Town Hall, L.A., 1970—71. Mem.: ABA, Regency (L.A.), Calif. State Bar, N.Y. State Bar, Nat. Assn. Real Estate Investment Trusts Inc. (cert. specialist taxation law), L.A. County Bar Assn. (exec. com. comml. law sect.). Republican. Office: Pircher Nichols & Meeks Ste 1700 1925 Century Park E Los Angeles CA 90067-6022 E-mail: lpircher@pircher.com

PISANO, A. ROBERT, entertainment company executive, lawyer; b. San Jose, Calif., Mar. 3, 1943; s. Anthony Edward and Carmen Jeanne (Morisoli) P.; m. Carolyn Joan Pollock, May 5, 1979; children: Catherine J., Anthony Daniel, Elizabeth A., Alexandra N. B.A. in Pub. Administrn., San Jose State U., 1965; J.D., U. Calif.-Berkeley, 1968. Bar: Calif. Assoc. O'Melveny & Myers, Los Angeles, 1968-75, ptnr., 1976-85, 92-93; exec. v.p. office of chmn., gen. counsel Paramount Pictures, Los Angeles, 1985-91; exec. v.p. Metro-Goldwyn-Mayer Inc., Santa Monica, Calif., 1993-96; vice chmn. Metro-Goldwyn-Mayer, Inc., Santa Monica, 1997-99; bus. cons., 1999—. Bd. dirs. Coppola Group, NetFlix.com Bd. dirs. Info. for Pub. Affairs, Sacramento, 1983—; trustee Performing Arts Ctr., Los Angeles County, 1997—. Mem. Motion Picture Assn. Am. (bd. dirs. 1989-91, 93-99), Acad. Motion Picture Arts and Scis., Ctr. for Russian and Eurasian Studies (bd. overseers 1996-2001). Office: 2500 Broadway Ste B-201 Santa Monica CA 90404-3065

PISTER, KARL STARK, engineering educator; b. Stockton, Calif., June 27, 1925; s. Edwin LeRoy and Mary Kimball (Smith) P.; m. Rita Olsen, Nov. 18, 1950; children: Francis, Therese, Anita, Jacinta, Claire, Kristofer. BS with honors, U. Calif., Berkeley, 1945, MS, 1948; PhD, U. Ill., 1952. Instr. theoretical and applied mechanics U. Ill., 1949-52, faculty U. Calif., Berkeley, 1952-62, prof. engring. scis., 1962-96, Roy W. Carlson prof. engring., 1985-90, dean Coll. Engring., 1980-90, chancellor Santa Cruz, 1991-96, pres., chancellor emeritus, Roy W. Carlson prof. emeritus Berkeley, sr. assoc. to pres. Oakland, 1996-99, v.p. ednl. outreach, 1999-2000. Richard Merton guest prof. U. Stuttgart, W. Ger., 1978; cons. to govt. and industry; bd. dirs. Monterey Bay Aquarium Rsch. Inst.; trustee Monterey Inst. Internat. Studies, Am. U. of Armenia; chmn. bd. Calif. Coun. Sci. and Tech. Contbr. articles to profl. jours.; mem. editl. bd. Computer Methods in Applied Mechanics and Engring, 1972, Jour. Optimization Theory and Applications, 1982, Encyclopedia Phys. Sci. and Tech. With USNR, WWII. Fulbright scholar, Ireland, 1965, West Germany, 1973; recipient Wason Rsch. medal Am. Concrete Inst., 1960, Vincent Bendix Minorities in Engring. award Am. Soc. for Engring. Edn., 1988, Lamme medal, 1993, Alumni Honor award U. Ill. Coll. Engring., 1982, Disting. Engring. Alumnus award U. Calif. Berkeley Coll. Engring., 1992, Berkeley medal, 1996, U. Calif. Presdl. medal, 2000. Fellow ASME, AAAS, Am. Acad. Mechanics, Am. Acad. Arts and Scis., Calif. Acad. Scis. (hon.); mem. NAE, ASCE, Soc. Engring. Sci. Office: U Calif Dept Civil & Environ Engr Berkeley CA 94720 E-mail: pister@ce.berkeley.edu

PITCHER, HELEN IONE, advertising director; b. Colorado Springs, Colo., Aug. 6, 1931; d. William Forest Medlock and Frankie La Vone (Hamilton) Tweed; m. Richard Edwin Pitcher, Sept. 16, 1949; children: Dushka Myers, Suzanne, Marc. Student, U. Colo., 1962-64, Ariz. State U., 1966, Maricopa Tech. Coll., 1967, Scottsdale C.C., 1979-81. Design draftsman Sundstrand Aviation, Denver, 1962-65; tech. illustrator Sperry, Phoenix, 1966-68; art dir. Integrated Circuit Engring., Scottsdale, Ariz., 1968-71, dir. advt., 1981-92; advt. artist Motorola Inc., Phoenix, 1971-74; pres. Pitcher Tech. Pubs., Scottsdale, 1974-81; retired, 1996. Profl. advisor Paradise Valley Sch. Dist., Phoenix, 1984—; mem. bd. advisors graphic arts dept. Ariz. State U., Tempe. Mem. Nat. Audio Visual Assn., Bus. Profl. Advt. Assn. (treas. 1982-86), Direct Mktg. Club. Democrat. Mem. Ch. Christ. Avocations: raising and showing Arabian horses and Hackney ponies. Home: 13681 N 88th Pl Scottsdale AZ 85260-7655

PITCHER, TONY JOHN, fishery science educator, writer; b. Banbury, Eng., Oct. 23, 1944; arrived in Can., 1994; s. Ernest William and Winifred Nellie (Harris) P.; m. Marguerite Elizabeth Tinsey; children: Susannah Jane, Tamsin Charlotte Lucy; m. Valerie Marie Gray, May 20, 1994. BA, Oxford (Eng.) U., 1966, DPhil, MA (hon.), 1970. Lectr. biology U. Ulster, Coleraine, Ireland, 1970-78; lectr. zoology U. Wales, Bangor, 1978-84, sr. lectr., 1984-87, reader, 1988-90; prof. fisheries Inst. fü4 Meereskunde, Kiel, Germany, 1987; spl. rsch. fellow renewal resources assessment group Imperial Coll., London, 1990-93; prof., dir. Fisheries Ctr., U. B.C., Vancouver, Can., 1994—. Cons. Marine Resources Assessment Ltd., London, 1990-93; hon. prof. U. Concepcion, Chile, 1994—; participant internat. devel. aid projects in fisheries in Angola, Cameroon, Chile, Ecuador, Hong Kong, Shana, Indonesia, Kenya, Malawi, Mex., The Philippines, Sri Lanka, Tanzania, Thailand, Uganda, Zambia, Zimbabwe, Australia, Iceland, Italy, Norway, U.K., South Africa. Co-author: Fisheries Ecology, 1982; co-editor: Control Processes in Fish Physiology, 1983, The Behavior of Fishes, 1986, Collected Reports on Fisheries Research in Malawi, vol. 1, 1990, Hake: Fisheries Ecology and Markets, 1994, Molecular Genetics in Fisheries, 1994, The Impact of Species Changes in the African Lakes, 1995, 1998 Reinventing Fisheries Management; editor: The Behaviour of Teleost Fishes, 1986, 2d edit., 1992; asst. editor Jour. Fish Biology, 1981-87; series editor Fish and Fisheries, 1990-98, Fish and Aquatic Resources; founding editor Revs. in Fish Biology and Fisheries, 1991-99, Fish and Fisheries, 2000—; contbr. more than 200 articles to sci. jours. Achievements include laboratory field and theoretical research on schooling behavior of fishes and its implications for human harvest. Office: U BC Fisheries Ctr Vancouver BC Canada V6T 1Z4

PITKIN, ROY MACBETH, obstetrician, educator, retired; b. Anthon, Iowa, May 24, 1934; s. Roy and Pauline Allie (McBeath) P.; m. Marcia Alice Jenkins, Aug. 17, 1957; children: Barbara, Robert Macbeth, Kathryn, William Charles. B.A. with highest distinction, U. Iowa, 1956, M.D., 1959. Diplomate Am. Bd. Obstetrics & Gynecology, 1967. Intern King County Hosp., Seattle, 1959-60; resident in ob-gyn U. Iowa Hosps. and Clinics, Iowa City, 1960-63; asst. prof. ob-gyn U. Ill., 1965-68; assoc. prof. ob-gyn U. Iowa, Iowa City, 1968-72, prof., 1972-87, head dept. ob-gyn, 1977-87; prof. UCLA, 1987-97, head dept. ob-gyn., 1987-95, prof. emeritus, 1997—. Mem. residency rev. com. ob-gyn, 1981-87, chmn. 1985-87. Editor-in-chief: Year Book of Obstetrics and Gynecology, 1975-86; editor-in-chief: Clinical Obstetrics and Gynecology, 1979-2000; editor: Obstetrics and Gynecology, 1985-2001, editor emeritus 2001. Contbr. articles to med. jours. Served to lt. comdr. M.C. USNR, 1963-65. NIH career awardee, 1972-77 Fellow Royal Obstetricians and Gynecologists (ad eundem); mem. AMA (Goldberger award in clin. nutrition 1982), Am. Coll. Obstetricians and Gynecologists, Am. Gynecol. and Obstet. Soc. (pres. 1994-95), German Soc. Gynecology and Obstetrics (hon. 1992), Ctrl. Assn. Obstetricians and Gynecologists, Soc. Gynecologic Investigation (pres. 1985-86), Soc. Perinatal Obstetricians (pres. 1978-79), NAS, Inst. of Medicine. Presbyterian. Home: 78900 Rancho La Quinta Dr La Quinta CA 92253-6252 E-mail: rpitkin@greenjournal.org

PITMAN, BONNIE LOUISE, museum director; b. Stamford, Conn. d. Benjamin and Margaret (Hackett) P.; m. George Gelles (div. 1985); 1 child, David Gelles. AA, Pine Manor Coll., 1966; BA, Sweet Briar Coll., 1968; MA, Tulane U., 1972. Curator of edn. Winnipeg Art Gallery, Can., 1968-71, New Orleans Mus. Art, 1971-75; cons. NEA, NEH, Washington, 1976-80; assoc. dir. Seattle Art Mus., 1981-89, dir. acting, 1985-86; dep. dir. Univ. Art Mus. U. Calif., Berkeley, 1990-95; exec. dir. Bay Area Discovery Mus., Sausalito, Calif., 1995—. Cons. Parker Bros. Games, Salem, Mass., 1980, Lincoln Ctr., N.Y.C., 1980-81; program dir. The Pew Charitable Trusts, Phila., 1994—; adv. com. San Francisco Art Inst., 1996. Author: Watermelon, 1972, Museums, Magic & Children, 1981, Taking a Closer Look: Evaluation in Art Museums, 1992, Excellence and Equity: Education & The Public Dimension of Museums. Recipient leadership tomorrow award United Way of King County, Seattle, 1984-85. Mem. Am. Assn. Mus. (chair nat. taskforce on edn. 1989-94, mus. educators award 1983, v.p. 1976-80, 88-92, chair accreditation com. 1985—), Sausalito C. of C., Nat. Hist. Trust, Western Mus. Assn. (dir.'s chair award 1992). Democrat. Episcopal. Avocation: sailing. Office: Bay Area Discovery Mus 557 Fort Baker Sausalito CA 94965-2614

PITT, WILLIAM ALEXANDER, cardiologist; b. July 17, 1942; came to U.S., 1970; s. Reginald William and Una Sylvia (Alexander) P.; m. Judith Mae Wilson, May 21, 1965; children: William Matthew, Joanne Katharine. MD, U. B.C., Vancouver, 1967. Diplomate Royal Coll. Physicians Can. Intern Mercy Hosp., San Diego, 1967-68, resident, 1970-71, assoc. dir. cardiology, 1972-92; resident Vancouver Gen. Hosp., 1968-70, U. Calif., San Diego, 1971-72; with So. Calif. Cardiology Med. Group, San Diego, 1984—; pvt. practice Clin. Cons. Cardiology. Bd. trustees San Diego Found. for Med. Care, 1983-89, 91—, pres., chmn. bd. trustees, 1986-88, med. dir., 1991-96; trustee Pacific Found. for Med. Care, 1996—, med. dir., 1996—; bd. dirs. Mut. Assn. for Profl. Services, Phila., 1984-92; pres. Alternet Med. Svcs., Inc., 1992-95; pres. and med. dir. San Diego IPA, 1995—. Fellow Royal Coll. Physicians Can., Am. Coll. Cardiology (assoc.); mem. AMA, Am. Heart Assn., Calif. Med. Assn., San Diego County Med. Soc., San Diego County Heart Assn. (bd. dirs. 1982-88). Episcopalian. Office: So Calif Cardiology Med Group 6386 Alvarado Ct Ste 101 San Diego CA 92120-4906 E-mail: wmapitt@aol.com

PITTARD, WILLIAM BLACKBURN (BILLY PITTARD), television graphic designer; b. Murfreesboro, Tenn., May 8, 1954; s. Samuel G. and Annette (Batey) P.; 1 child, Colby. BS, Middle Tenn. State U., 1978. Art dir. Sta. WKRN-TV, Nashville, 1978-84; design mgr. Sta. KCBS-TV, Los Angeles, 1984-86; CEO Pittard Sullivan, Culver City, Calif., 1986—. Mem. Broadcast Designer's Assn. (bd. dirs. 1984-89, Outstanding Service award, 1986), Nat. Acad. TV Arts and Scis. (4 Emmys). Office: Pittard Sullivan 3535 Hayden Ave Culver City CA 90232-2412

PIVA, GARY, retail grocery executive; CFO WinCo Foods, Boise. Office: WinCo Foods PO Box 5756 Boise ID 83705-5756 Office Fax: (208) 377-0474

PIVEN, PETER ANTHONY, architect, management consultant; b. Bklyn., Jan. 3, 1939; s. William Meyer and Sylvia Lee (Greenberg) P.; m. Caroline Cooper, July 9, 1961; children: Leslie Ann, Joshua Lawrence. AB, Colgate U., 1960; MArch, U. Pa., 1963; MS, Columbia U., 1964. Diplomate: cert. Nat. Council Archtl. Registration Bds.; registered architect, N.Y., Pa., N.J. Architect Westermann-Miller Assocs., N.Y.C., 1964-66, Bernard Rothzeid, A.I.A., N.Y.C., 1967-68; v.p. Caudill Rowlett Scott, N.Y.C., 1968-72; prin. Geddes Brecher Qualls Cunningham, Phila., 1972-87; pres. The Coxe Group, Inc., Phila., 1980-90, dir., prin. cons., 1980—. Adj. prof. U. Pa. Grad. Sch. Fine Arts, 1989—, Rensselaer Poly. Inst. Sch. Architecture, 1994—; vis. instr. Harvard U. Grad. Sch. Design. Author: Compensation Management: A Guideline for Small Firms, 1982; co-author: Success Strategies for Design Professionals, 1987; contbr. editor Archtl. Record and Design Intelligence; contbg. author: Architects Handbook of Professional Practice, 1994. Mem. N.Y.C. Community Planning Bd., 1969-72. Fellow AIA (chmn. fin. mgmt. com. 1976-80, chmn. Fellows Jury 1998, mem. conv. task force 1998, mem. nat. ethics coun. 1999—, pres. Phila. chpt. 1980); mem. Phila. C. of C. (dir. 1980-81), The Carpenters Co. of City and County of Phila. (mng. com. 1989-91). Home: 112 N Lambert St Philadelphia PA 19103-1107 Office: The Coxe Group Inc 1218 3rd Ave Seattle WA 98101-3097

PLAISANCE, MELISSA, retail executive; b. Feb. 12, 1960; BSBA cum laude, Bucknell U., 1982; MBA, UCLA, 1990. Sr. v.p. fin. investor rels. Safeway Inc., Pleasanton, Calif.; v.p. Bankers Trust Co. Corp. Fin., L.A. Office: Safeway Inc PO Box 99 5918 Stoneridge Mall Rd Pleasanton CA 94566-0009

PLAMANN, ALFRED A. wholesale distribution executive; Pres., CEO Cert. Grocers Calif., Unified We. Grocers Inc., Commerce, Calif., 2000—. Office: Unified Western Grocers Inc 5200 Sheila St Commerce CA 90040

PLANCHON, HARRY PETER, JR. research development manager; b. Aurora, Mo., Aug. 28, 1941; s. Harry P. and Ruth Arminta (Eden) P.; m. Virginia Grace Sapp, June 13, 1964; children: Benjamin John, Matthew Brian. BSME, U. Mo., 1964; MS in Nuclear Engring., U. Ill., 1971, PhD in Nuclear Engring., 1974; MBA, U. Chgo., 1990. Cert. profl. engr. Rsch. assoc., asst. prof. U. Ill. Nuclear Engring. Dept., Urbana, 1970-74; sr. engr., mgr. Clinch River Breeder Reactor Plant Systems Westinghouse Advanced Reaction Div., Madison, Pa., 1974-84; mgr. reactor analysis Exptl. Breeder Reacter Div., Argonne (Ill.) Nat. Lab., 1984-90; assoc. dir. Reacter Analysis Div., Argonne Nat. Lab., 1990-91; assoc. dir. ENG divsn. Argonne Nat. Lab., Idaho Falls, Idaho, 1991-2000, dir. nuclear tech. divsn., 2000—. Contbr. articles to profl. jours. Lt. USN, 1964-70. Fellow Am. Nuc. Soc. (Seaborg medal 1990), mem. Am. Soc. Mech. Engrs., Beta Gamma Sigma, Tau Beta Pi, Pi Mu Epsilon, Pi Tau Sigma. Presbyterian. Avocations: hiking, skiing, photography, golf, reading. Office: Argonne Nat Lab West PO Box 2528 Idaho Falls ID 83403-2528

PLANTS, WALTER DALE, elementary education educator, minister; b. Middlefield, Ohio, June 8, 1942; s. William E. and Hazel A. Plants; m. Sarah A. Gaddis, July 5, 1962; children: Dale Anthony, Jeanette Marie. BD, Azusa Pacific U., 1967; MEd, U. Nev., 1970. Cert. elem. tchr., ednl. adminstr. Elem. tchr. Churchill County Sch. Dist., Fallon, Nev., 1967-69, 70-72, 81—; grad. asst. U. Nev., Reno, 1969-70; tchr. Kingman (Ariz.) Elem. Sch. Dist. #4, 1972-77; head sci. program E. C. Best Elem. Sch., Fallon, 1988—. Adj. instr. Ariz. State U., Tempe, 1973-77; cons. sci. Ariz. State Dept. Edn., 1975-77. Bd. dirs. Solar Energy Commn. Mohave County, Ariz., 1974; coord. County Sci. Fair, 1988-93; active Western Regional Sci. Fair Com.; sci. fair coord. Churchill County, 1989-94; mem. com. Regional Sci. Fair, 1992-94. HEW fellow, 1969; NSF grantee, 1973; AIMS Found. scholar, 1988; recipient Ariz. State PTA award, 1977, Ruth Neldon award Ariz. State Dept., 1977, Conservation award Big Sandy Natural Resources Conservation Dist. Ariz., 1976, Community Builder Svc. award Masons, Fallon, 1991, Disting. Leadership award, 1991, 92, 93; named State Tchr. of Yr. Nev. PTA, 1991, Conservation Tchr. of Yr., 1991; named to Congl. Select Edn. panel U.S. Congress, 1993. Mem. NEA, AAAS, Nat. Sci. Tchrs. Assn., Nat. Coun. Tchrs. Math., Internat. Reading Assn., Churchill County Edn. Assn. (Tchr. of Yr. 1989), Internat. Platform Assn., Nat. Arbor Day Found., World Wildlife Fund, Nat. Parks and Conservation Assn., Nat. Audubon Soc., Nev. State Tchrs. of Yr. Assn. (pres. 1994-96, pres. 1996-97), Phi Delta Kappa. Office: EC Best Elem Sch 750 E Williams Ave Fallon NV 89406-3022

PLATE, THOMAS GORDON, newspaper columnist, educator; b. N.Y.C., May 17, 1944; s. John William and Irene (Henry) P.; m. Andrea I. Margolis, Sept. 22, 1979; 1 child, Ashley Alexandra. AB, Amherst Coll., 1966; MPA, Princeton U., 1968. Writer Newsweek, N.Y.C., 1968-70; editor Newsday, L.I., N.Y., 1970-72; sr. editor N.Y. Mag., N.Y.C., 1972-75; editor edit. page L.A. Herald Examiner, 1978-82; sr. editor Time Mag., N.Y.C., 1982-83; editor in chief Family Weekly, N.Y.C., 1984-85; editor edit. pages N.Y. Newsday, N.Y.C., 1986-89, L.A. Times, 1989-95, Times Op-Ed Page columnist, contbg. editor, 1995—. Adj. prof. UCLA Pub. Policy Sch. and Letters and Scis.; mem. founders bd. UCLA Sch. Pub. Policy; founder Asia Pacific Media Network; participant World Econ. Forum, Davos. Author: Understanding Doomsday, 1971, Crime Pays!, 1975, Secret Police, 1981; co-author: Commissioner, 1978. Recipient Best Deadline Writing award Am. Soc. Newspaper Editors, 1981, Best Edit. awards L.A. Press Club, 1979, 80, 81, Best Edit. award Calif. Newspaper Pubs. Assn., 1991, 92, 94; media fellow Stanford U. Mem. Pacific Coun. on Internat. Rels., Century Assn. (N.Y.C.), Phi Beta Kappa. Avocations: tennis, photography, travel to Asia. Office: LA Times 405 Hilgard Ave Los Angeles CA 90095-9000

PLATT, JOSEPH BEAVEN, former college president; b. Portland, Oreg., Aug. 12, 1915; s. William Bradbury and Mary (Beaven) P.; m. Jean Ferguson Rusk, Feb. 9, 1946; children: Ann Ferguson Walker, Elizabeth Beaven Garrow. BA, U. Rochester, 1937; PhD, Cornell U., 1942; LLD, U. So. Calif., 1969, Claremont McKenna Coll., 1982; DSc, Harvey Mudd Coll., 1981. Instr. physics U. Rochester, N.Y., 1941-43, from asst. prof. to prof., 1946-56, assoc. chmn. dept. physics, 1954-56; staff mem. radiation lab. MIT, Cambridge, 1943-46; founding pres. Harvey Mudd Coll., Claremont, Calif., 1956-76, now part-time sr. prof. physics; pres. Claremont U. Ctr., 1976-81. Trustee Aerospace Corp., 1972-85, Consortium for Advancement of Pvt. Higher Edn., 1985-92; chief physics br. AEC, 1949-51; cons. U.S. Office Ordnance Rsch., NSF, 1953-56; mem. com. on sci. in UNESCO, NAS-NRC, 1960-62, mem. com. on internat. orgns. and programs, 1962-64, sci. advisor U.S. Del., UNESCO Gen. Conf., Paris, 1960, alt. del., 1962, chmn. Subcom. on Sino-Am. Sci. Cooperation, 1965-79; mem. panel on internat. sci. Pres.'s Sci. Adv. Com., 1961; trustee Analytic Svcs., Inc., 1958-89, chmn., 1961-89; mem. adv. com. on sci. edn. NSF, 1965-70, 72-76, chmn., 1969-70, 73-74, 74-75; bd. dirs. Lincoln Found., 1979-85, Bell & Howell Corp., 1978-88, Am. Mut. Fund, 1981-88, DeVry, Inc., 1984-87, Sigma Rsch., 1983-87, Jacobs Engring. Co., 1978-86. Author: Harvey Mudd College: The First Twenty YEars, 1994. Trustee China Found. for Promotion of Edn. and Culture, 1966—, Carnegie Found. for Advancement Tchg., 1970-78, Ancient Bibl. Manuscript Ctr., 1980—; chmn. select com. Master Plan for Higher Edn. Calif., 1971-73; mem. Carnegie Coun. for Policy Studies in Higher Edn., 1975-80. Fellow Am. Phys. Soc.; mem. IEEE, Automobile Club So. Calif. (bd. dirs. 1973-90, chmn. bd. dirs. 1986-87), Calif. Club, Sunset Club, Twilight Club, Cosmos Club, Bohemian Club, Phi Beta Kappa, Sigma Xi, Phi Kappa Phi. Home: 452 W 11th St Claremont CA 91711-3833 E-mail: joseph_platt@hmc.edu

PLATT, LEWIS EMMETT, retired electronics company executive; b. Johnson City, N.Y., Apr. 11, 1941; s. Norval Lewis and Margaret Dora (Williams) P.; m. Joan Ellen Redmund, Jan. 15, 1983; children: Caryn, Laura, Amanda, Hillary. BME, Cornell U., 1964; MBA, U. Pa., 1966. With Hewlett Packard, Waltham, Mass., 1966-71, engring. mgr., 1971-74, ops. mgr., 1976-77, div. gen. mgr., 1974-80, group gen. mgr., Palo Alto, Calif., 1980-84, v.p., 1983-85, exec. v.p., 1987-92, pres., CEO, chmn., 1993-99; ret.; Trustee Waltham Hosp., 1978-80, Wharton Sch. Bd. Overseers, 1993; mem. Mid-Peninsula YMCA, 1980—, bd. couns. YMCA-USA, 1993—, Cornell U. Coun., 1992—, Computer Sys. Policy Project, 1993—, Calif. Bus. Roundtable, 1993-95, Bus. Coun., 1993—, Bay Area Coun., 1993—, Bus. Roundtable, 1993—; vice chmn. Y Coun., 1989, mem. bd. dirs. Joint Venture, Silicon Valley, 1996. Recipient Red Triangle award Min-Peninsula YMCA, 1992, Internat. Citizens award World Forum Silicon Valley, San Jose, Calif., 1994, outstanding alumnus, Wharton Alumni Honor Roll, Wharton Schl. Business, Univ. Pa., 1994-95, award for bus. excellence U. Calif. Sch. Bus. Adminstrn., 1996, Tree of Life award Jewish Nat. Fund, 1996, Leadership and Vision award San Francisco Chpt. French-Am. C. of C., 1997. Mem. IEEE, Sci. Apparatus Mfg. Assn. (dir. 1978-80).

PLATT, WARREN E. lawyer; b. McNary, Ariz., Aug. 5, 1943; BA, Mich. State U., 1965; JD, U. Ariz., 1969. Bar: Ariz. 1969, Calif. 1991, Texas 1993. Atty. Snell & Wilmer, Phoenix. Mng. editor: Ariz. Law Rev., 1968-69. Fellow Am. Coll. Trial Lawyers; mem. Blue Key, Order of Coif, Phi Alpha Delta Office: Snell & Wilmer One Arizona Ctr Phoenix AZ 85004-0001

PLETSCH, MARIE ELEANOR, plastic surgeon; b. Walkerton, Ont., Can., May 3, 1938; came to U.S. 1962; d. Ernest John and Olive Wilhemina (Hossfeld) P.; m. Ludwig Philip Breiling, Aug. 25, 1967; children: John, Michael, Anne. MD, U. Toronto, 1962. Diplomate Am. Bd. Plastic Surgery. Intern Cook County Hosp., Chgo., 1962-63, resident, gen. surgery, 1963-64, St. Mary's Hosp., San Francisco, 1964-66; resident in plastic surgery St. Francis Hosp., San Francisco, 1966-69; practice med. specializing in plastic surgery Santa Cruz, Calif., 1969—; Monterey, 1990—; adminstr. Plasticenter, Inc., Santa Cruz, 1976-88, med. dir., 1987-88. Mem. AMA, Am. Soc. Plastic and Reconstructive Surgeons, Calif. Soc. Plastic Surgeons (mem. coun. 1986-89, sec. 1989-93, v.p. 1994-95, pres. elect 1995-96, pres. 1996-97), Am. Soc. Anesthetic Plastic Surgeons, Calif. Med. Assn., Assn. Calif. Surgery Ctrs. (pres. 1988-92), Santa Cruz County Med. Soc. (bd. govs. 1983-88, 1992-94), Santa Cruz Surgery Ctr. (bd. dirs. 1988-93). Roman Catholic. Office: Santa Cruz Can Am Med Group 1669 Dominican Way Santa Cruz CA 95065-1523 E-mail: pletsch@pacbell.net

PLISKOW, VITA SARI, anesthesiologist; b. Tel Aviv, Sept. 13, 1942; arrived in Can., 1951; came to U.S., 1967; d. Henry Norman and Renee [illegible] Sahl, m. Raymond Joel Pliskow, June 30, 1960; children: [illegible], Kami. MD, U. B.C., Vancouver, 1967. Diplomate Am. Bd. Anesthesiology. Ptnr. Olympic Anesthesia, Bremerton, Wash., 1971-84, pres., anesthesiologist, 1974-84; co-founder Olympic Ambulatory Surgery Ctr., Bremerton, 1977-83; ptnr., anesthesiologist Allenmore Anesthesia Assocs., Tacoma, 1983—. Staff anesthesiologist Harrison Meml. Hosp., Bremerton, 1971-95, Allenmore Hosp., Tacoma, 1983—. Trustee Tacoma Youth Symphony Assn., 1994—; active Nat. Coun. Jewish Women, 1972—. Fellow Am. Coll. Anesthesiologists, Am. Coll. Chest Physicians; mem. Am. Soc. Anesthesiologists (del. Wash. State 1987—), Wash. State Med. Assn. (del. Pierce County 1993-94), Wash. State Soc. Anesthesiologists (pres. 1985-87), Pierce County Med. Soc. (sec.-treas. 1992). Avocations: classical music, opera, singing (mezzo soprano). Office: Ctrl Billing PO Box 640 Tracyton WA 98393-0640

PLOMP, TEUNIS (TONY PLOMP), minister; b. Rotterdam, The Netherlands, Jan. 28, 1938; arrived in Can., 1951; s. Teunis and Cornelia (Pietersma) P.; m. Margaret Louise Bone, July 21, 1962; children: Jennifer Anne, Deborah Adele. BA, U. B.C. (Can.), Vancouver, 1960; BD, Knox Coll., Toronto, Ont., Can., 1963, DD (hon.), 1988. Ordained to ministry Presbyn. Ch., 1963. Minister Goforth Meml. Presbyn. Ch., Saskatoon, Sask., Can., 1963-68, Richmond (B.C.) Presbyn. Ch., 1968—. Clerk Presbytery of Westminster, Vancouver, 1969—; moderator 113th Gen. Assembly Presbyn. Ch. Can., 1987-88, dep. clk., 1988—; chaplain New Haven Correctional Centre, Burnaby, B.C., 1973-99 Contbr. mag. column You Were Asking, 1982—. Avocations: record collecting, audiophile, biking, swimming. Office: Richmond Presbyn Ch 7111 # 2 Rd Richmond BC Canada V7C 3L7 E-mail: tony_plomp@telus.net

PLOPPER, CHARLES GEORGE, anatomist, cell biologist; b. Oakland, Calif., June 16, 1944; s. George Eli and Josephine Viola (Gates) P.; m. Suzanne May, Nov. 9, 1969. AB, U. Calif., Davis, 1967, PhD, 1972. Chief. electron microscopy br. U.S. Army Med. Research Nutrition Lab., Denver, 1972-73; vis. scientist Calif. Primate Research Ctr., Davis, 1974-75; chief. electron microscopy div. Letterman Army Inst. Research, San Francisco, 1974-75; asst. prof. U. Hawaii Sch. Medicine, Honolulu, 1975-77; assoc. prof. Kuwait U. Sch. Medicine, 1977-78; sr. staff fellow Nat. Inst. Environ. Health Sci. Research, Triangle Park, N.C., 1978-79; from asst. to assoc. prof. U. Calif. Sch. Vet. Medicine, Davis, 1979-86, dept. chmn., 1984-88, 96—; prof. anatomy, physiology and cell biology, Sch. Vet. Medicine U. Calif., Davis, 1986—. Mem. study sect. NIH div. Research Grants, Bethesda, Md., 1986-90; Paley vis. prof. Boston U. Sch. Medicine, 1985; vis. pulmonary scholar Duke U., U. N.C., N.C. State U., 1991. Served to capt. U.S. Army, 1972-75. Recipient Norden Teaching award, Faculty Rsch. award. Mem. Am. Soc. Cell Biology, Am. Thoracic Soc., Am. Assn. Antomists, Am. Assn. Pathologists, Anat. Soc. Great Britain and Ireland, Davis Aquatic Masters (bd. dirs. 1993-95). Democrat. Avocations: swimming, hiking, tennis. Home: 511 Hubble St Davis CA 95616-2720 Office: Univ Calif Sch Vet Medicine Dept Anatomy Physiol Cell Biology Davis CA 95616

PLOTNICK, ROBERT DAVID, educator, economic consultant; b. Washington, Aug. 3, 1949; s. Theodore and Jean (Hirshfeld) P.; m. Gay Lee Jensen, Dec. 22, 1972. BA, Princeton U., 1971; MA, U. Calif., Berkeley, 1973, PhD, 1976. Rsch. assoc. Inst. Rsch. on Poverty, Madison, Wis., 1973-75; asst. prof. Bates Coll., Lewiston, Maine, 1975-77, Dartmouth Coll., Hanover, N.H., 1977-84; assoc. prof. U. Wash., Seattle, 1984-90, prof., 1990—, assoc. dean, 1990-95; acting dean, 1994-95. Vis. scholar Russell Sage Found., 1990, U. New South Wales, 1997; rsch. affiliate Inst. for Rsch. on Poverty, 1989—; dir. Ctr. for Studies in Demography and Ecology, 1997—; adj. fellow Pub. Policy Inst. Calif., 1998-2000; cons. Wash. Dept. Social and Health Svcs., Olympia, 1984-86, 90-96, 2000; cons. in field. Author: Progress Against Poverty, 1975; contbr. articles to profl. jours. Recipient Teaching Excellence award U. Wash., 1985, 89. Mem. Am. Econ. Assn., Assn. Policy Analysis and Mgmt., Population Assn. Am. Avocations: tennis, hiking, bird watching, scuba. Office: U Wash Evans Sch Pub Affairs PO Box 353055 Seattle WA 98195-3055 E-mail: plotnick@u.washington.edu

PLOTT, CHARLES RAYMOND, economics educator; b. Frederick, Okla., July 8, 1938; s. James Charles and Flossie Ann (Bowman) P.; m. Marianna Brown Cloninger, May 30, 1961; children: Rebecca Ann, Charles Hugh. BS, Okla. State U., 1961, MS, 1964; PhD, U. Va., 1965; hon. doctorate, Purdue U., 1995; D (hon.), U. Pierre Mendès France, Grenoble, 1996. Asst. prof. econs. Purdue U., 1965-68, assoc. prof., 1968-70; vis. prof. econs. Stanford U., 1968-69; Edward S. Harkness prof. econs. and polit. sci. Calif. Inst. Tech., Pasadena, 1970—, dir. Program for Study of Enterprise and Pub. Policy, 1979—, dir. Lab. for Exptl. Econs. and Polit. Sci., 1987—. Vis. prof. law U. So. Calif. Law Ctr., 1976; vis. prof. U. Chgo., 1980. Author works in fields of econs., polit. sci., philosophy, exptl. methods, math. methods; contbr. articles to profl. jours.; mem. bd. editors: Social Sci. Rsch., 1976-77, Pub. Choice, 1973-90, Jour. Econ. Behavior, 1983-85, Econ. Theory, 1990—. Named to Coll. Bus. Hall of Fame Okla. State U.; Ford Found. fellow, 1968, Guggenheim fellow, 1981, fellow Ctr. for Advanced Studies in Behavioral Scis., 1981; NSF grantee, 1972, 74, 78, 79, 80, 83, 86, 88, 92, 95, 98, 2000. Fellow Am. Acad. Arts and Scis., Econometric Soc.; mem. Am. Econ. Assn., Econ. Sci. Assn. (pres. 1987), So. Econ. Assn. (mem. exec. com. 1978-79, v.p. 1985-87, pres. 1989-90), Pub. Choice Soc. (pres. 1977-78), Western Econ. Assn. (v.p. 1996-97, pres. 1998-99), Royal Econ. Assn., Am. Polit. Sci. Assn., Econs. Sci. Assn. (pres. 1987-88), Mont Pelerin Soc. Home: 881 El Campo Dr Pasadena CA 91107-5565 Office: Calif Inst Tech Divsn Humanities & Social Sc Pasadena CA 91125-0001

PLOUGH, CHARLES TOBIAS, JR. retired electronics engineering executive; b. Oakland, Calif., Sept. 7, 1926; s. Charles Tobias Sr. and Miriam Lucille (Miller) P.; m. Jean Elizabeth Rose, June 13, 1950 (div. May 1969); children: Charles III, Cathleen, Mark, Barbara; m. Janet Mary Ansell Lumley, July 5, 1969; children: Mark Ansell Lumley, Simon John Lumley. AB with honors, Amherst Coll., 1950; BSEE with honors, U. Calif., Berkeley, 1953. Mgr. tech. devel. Fairchild Semiconductor, Palo Alto, Calif., 1958-71; v.p. Multi-State Devices, Montreal, Can., 1971-78; mgr. research and devel. Dale Electronics, Norfolk, Nebr., 1978-89, ret., 1989. Patentee in field. Treas. First Unitarian Ch., 1996-99. Mem. Lions (sec. Norfolk 1982-86; pres. Albuquerque chpt. 1999-2000); Leader Albuquerque Interfaith 1993—. Avocation: golf. Home: 2030 Quail Run Dr NE Albuquerque NM 87122-1100

PLUMMER, JASON STEVEN (JAKE), professional football player; b. Boise, Idaho, Dec. 19, 1974; Student, Ariz. State U. Quarterback Ariz. Cardinals, Phoenix, 1997—; mem. NFC wildcard team, 1998-99. Named quarterback The Sporting News col. All-Am. 2d team, 1996. Holder regular-season record as starting NFL quarterback. Office: c/o Arizona Cardinals PO Box 888 Phoenix AZ 85001-0888

PLUMMER, STEVEN TSOSIE, SR. bishop; b. Coalmine, N. Mex., Aug. 14, 1944; m. Catherine B. Tso; children: Brian Tso, Byron Tso, Steven, Jr., Cathlena. Student, San Juan C.C., Farmington, N.Mex., Phoenix Jr. Coll., Ch. Divinity Sch. the Pacific, Berekely, Calif., Cook Christian Tng. Sch., Tempe, Ariz., 1966-68. Ordained to ministry Episcopal Ch. as deacon, 1975, priest, 1976. Deacon, priest Good Shepherd Mission, Ft. Defiance, Ariz., 1976-77; vicar St. John the Baptizer, Montezuma Creek, Utah, 1977-83; regional vicar for Utah Bluff, from 1983; consecrated bishop Episc. Ch. in Navajoland, Window Rock, Ariz., 1990. Mem. Episc. Council Indian Ministries, N.Y.C. Office: The Episcopal Ch Navajoland Area Mission PO Box 720 Farmington NM 87499-0720 also: PO Box 40 Bluff UT 84512-0040

POCKER, YESHAYAU, chemistry, biochemistry educator; b. Kishinev, Romania, Oct. 10, 1928; came to U.S., 1961; naturalized, 1967. s. Benzion Israel and Esther Sarah (Sudit) P.; m. Anna Goldenberg, Aug. 8, 1950; children: Rona, Elon I. MSc, Hebrew U., Jerusalem, 1949; PhD, Univ. Coll., London, Eng., 1953; DSc, U. London, 1960. Rsch. assoc. Weizmann Inst. Sci., Rehovot, Israel, 1949-50; humanitarian trust fellow Univ. Coll., 1951-52, asst. lectr., 1952-54, lectr., 1954-61; vis. assoc. prof. Ind. U., Bloomington, 1960-61; prof. U. Washington, Seattle, 1961—. Bicentennial lectr. Mont. State U., Bozeman, 1976; Horizons in Chemistry lectr. U. N.C., Chapel Hill, 1977, guest lectr. U. Kyoto, Japan, 1984; Edward A. Doisy vis. prof. biochemistry St. Louis U. Med. Sch., 1990; plenary lectr. N.Y. Acad. Sci., 1983, Fast Reactions in Biol. Systems, Kyoto, Japan, 1984, NATO, 1989, Consiglio nat. delle Richerche, U. Bari, Italy, 1989, Sigma Tau, Spoleto, Italy, 1990; Internat. lectr. Purdue U., 1990; cons. NIH, 1984, 86, 88; Spl. Topic lectr. on photosynthesis, Leibniz House, Hanover, Fed. Republic Germany, 1991; enzymology, molecular biology lectr., Dublin, Ireland, 1992; 3M lectr., St. Paul, 1996; enzymology, molecular biology, retinal metabolism lectr., Deadwood, S.D., 1996, fast reactions in solutions and Bronsted symposium lectr., Copenhagen, 1997, self assembly kinetics of Alzheimer beta-amyloid peptides, ultrafast studies of insulin-insulin and insulin-receptor interactions; 1st Bannan invited lectr. Seattle U., spring, 1999; invited Bannan lectr. Seattle U., 2000, Alzheimer and Prion Proteins; internat. conf. Port Townsend, Wash., 2000, lectr. water sensing mechanisms, internat. symposium, Taos, N. Mex., 2000, internat. lectr. enzymology, molecular biology. Mem. editorial adv. bd. Inorganica Chimica Acta-Bioinorganic Chemistry, 1981-89; bd. reviewing editors Sci., 1985-2000; contbr. numerous articles to profl. jours.; pub. over 220 papers and 12 revs. Numerous awards worldwide, 1983-97. Mem. Royal Soc. Chemistry, Am. Chem. Soc. (nat. spkr. 1970, 74, 84, chmn. Pauling award com. 1978, plaque awards 1970, 74, 84, Outstanding Svc. award 1979, chmn. selection com. Pauling award 1996), Soc. Exptl. Biology, Am. Soc. Biol. Chemists, N.Y. Acad. Scis., Sigma Xi (nat. lectr. 1971). Avocations: Aramaic, etymology, history, philology, poetry. Office: U Wash Dept Chemistry PO Box 351700 Seattle WA 98195-1700

PODBOY, JOHN WATTS, clinical, forensic psychologist; b. York, Pa., Sept. 27, 1943; s. August John and Harriett Virginia (Watts) P.; 1 son, Matthew John. B.A., Dickinson Coll., 1966; M.S., San Diego State Coll., 1971; Ph.D., U. Ariz., 1973. Dir., Vets. Counseling Center, U. Ariz., Tucson, 1972-73; project dir. San Mateo County (Calif.) Human Relations Dept., Redwood City, 1974; staff psychologist Sonoma State Hosp., Eldridge, Calif., 1975-81; cons. clin. psychologist Comprehensive Care Corp., Newport Beach, Calif., 1974-75, Sonoma County (Calif.) Probation Dept., 1976-88; pvt. practice, Kenwood, Calif., 1982—; cons. to No. Calif. Superior Cts., 1983-85; asst. prof. Sonoma State U., 1977-81; dir. Sonoma Diagnostic and Remedial Center, 1979-82. Chmn. San Mateo County Diabetes Assn., 1975. Served to lt. USNR, 1966-69. Fellow Am. Coll. Forensic Psychology, Am. Bd. Med. Psychotherapists (fellow); mem. APA, Western Psychol. Assn., Redwood Psychol. Assn. (pres. 1983), Nat. Council Alcoholism, Nat. Rehab. Assn. Home: PO Box 488 Kenwood CA 95452-0488

PODESTO, GARY, mayor; b. 1941; Mayor City of Stockton, Calif., 1996—. Office: Office Mayor & City Coun 425 N El Dorado St Stockton CA 95202-1951

POE, JERRY B. financial educator; b. Springfield, Mo., Oct. 3, 1931; s. Carlyle and Eunice P.; m. Carol J. Mussler, Sept. 9, 1959; children: Cheryl Marie, Jennifer Brenna. A.B., Drury Coll., 1953; M.B.A. (Weinheimer fellow), Washington U., St. Louis, 1957; D.B.A. (Ford Found. fellow), Harvard U., 1963. Instr. U. Ark., spring 1957; indsl. engr. McDonnell Aircraft Corp., St. Louis, 1957; lectr. on fin. Boston U., 1959-61; asst. prof. bus. adminstrn. Drury Coll., 1961-64, assoc. prof., 1964-68, prof., 1968-74; dir. Breech Sch. Bus. Adminstrn., 1968-74; prof. fin. Ariz. State U., 1974—, chmn. dept. fin., 1974-82. Vis. prof. Fla. Tech. U., 1971; examiner, commr. North Central Assn. Colls. and Schs.; dir. NDEA Inst. Econs.; cons. in field Author: Essentials of Finance: An Integrated Approach, 1995, An Introduction to the American Business Enterprise, 1969, 7th rev. edit., 1989, Cases in Financial Management, 1977, 3d rev. edit., 1987. Mem. Regional Manpower Adv. Com.; mem. bus. and profl. adv. council Empire Bank. Served to lt. comdr. USNR, 1953-55. Mem. Fin. Mgmt. Assn., Kappa Alpha, Beta Gamma Sigma, Omicron Delta Kappa. Methodist. Office: Ariz State U Coll Bus Dept Fin Tempe AZ 85287-3906

POE, LAURA, nursing educator, administrator; b. Salt Lake City, July 20, 1962; d. William D. and Laree Jardine (Birch) P. Grad., Utah Tech. Coll., 1980; assoc. degree, Brigham Young U., 1984, B., 1986, MS, 1988. Bur. mgr., exec. dir. Utah Bd. Nursing. Author: (with others) Geri-Assistant Care Manual; contbr. articles to profl. jours. Mem. Utah Nurses Assn. (del., chair govt. rels. com.), Nightingale Soc., Phi Kappa Phi, Sigma Theta Tau.

POE, ROBERT ALAN, lawyer; b. Bracken County, Ky., Apr. 25, 1951; Student, U. Ky.; BA, Centre Coll., 1973; JD, U. Va., 1976. Bar: Colo. 1976. Mem. Holland & Hart, Denver, 1976—. Adj. prof. taxation U. Denver, 1986-88. Articles editor Va. Law Review, 1974-76. Mem. ABA, Order Coif, Phi Beta Kappa. Office: Holland & Hart 8390 E Crescent Pkwy Ste 400 Greenwood Vlg CO 80111-2822

POHL, ELIZABETH, contracting company executive; b. Dec. 15, 1957; CEO TC Enterprises, Inc., Albuquerque, 1986—. Office: TC Enterprises Inc 6000 Indian School Rd NE Albuquerque NM 87110-4178 Fax: 505-883-6275

POINDEXTER, WILLIAM MERSEREAU, lawyer; b. Los Angeles, June 16, 1925; s. Robert Wade and Irene M. Poindexter; m. Jani Jennifer Wohlgemuth, Feb. 14, 2000; children: James Wade, David Graham, Honour Hélenê, Timothy John, Cory Christenson, Greg Christenson. B.A., Yale U., 1946; postgrad., U. Chgo., 1946-47; LL.B., U. Calif., Berkeley, 1949. Bar: Calif. 1952. Practiced in, San Francisco, 1952-54, Los Angeles, 1954—; mem. firm Poindexter & Doutre, Inc., 1964—. Pres. Consol. Brazing & Mfg. Co., Riverside, Calif., 1949-52. Pres. South Pasadena-San Marino (Calif.) YMCA, 1963; Mem. San Marino Sch. Bd., 1965-69, pres., 1967; pres. Conf. of Ins. Counsel, 1975. Served with USMCR, 1943. Fellow Am. Coll. Trust and Probate Counsel; mem. ABA, L.A. County Bar Assn., State Bar Calif., Yale Club (pres. So. Calif. chpt. 1961), Calif. Lincoln Clubs (L.A. downtown chpt. chmn. 1997—). Republican. Presbyterian. Office: 1 Wilshire Bldg Ste 2420 Los Angeles CA 90017

POIROT, JAMES WESLEY, engineering company executive; b. Douglas, Wyo., 1931; m. Raeda Poirot. BCE, Oreg. State U., 1953. With various constrn. firms, Alaska and Oreg., CH2M Hill Inc., 1955, v.p., Seattle and Atlanta, from 1967; chmn. bd. CH2M Hill Ltd., Englewood, Colo., 1983-93. Former chmn. Western Regional Coun., Design Profls. Coalition, Accreditation Bd. Engring. and Tech., Indsl. Adv. Coun.; former mem. Oreg. Joint Grad. Schs. Engring., Engring. Coun.; mem. U.S. delegation UN Gen. Assembly, 1997; mem. internat. adv. bd. NRC, 1998—, chmn. com. truck size and weight, 1998—. Trustee Oreg. State U. Fedn., 1992—. Named ENR Constrn. Man of Yr., 1988. Fellow ASCE (pres. 1993-94), Am. Cons. Engrs. Coun. (life; pres. 1989-90), Am. Acad. Environ. Engrs. (diplomate), Am. Assn. Engring Socs. (vice chmn. 1995); mem. Nat. Acad. Engring. (nat. chmn. engrs. week 1994), Japan Soc. Civil Engrs. (hon. mem., 2001), World Partnership for Sustainable Devel. (founding dir.), World Fedn. Engring. Orgns. (com. on tech. transfer, pres. 1995—, v.p. 1997—), U.S. Earth Charter Commn. Office: CH2M Hill Inc PO Box 22508 Denver CO 80222-0508

POLAK, ELIJAH, engineering educator, computer scientist; b. Bialystok, Poland, Aug. 11, 1931; came to U.S., 1957, naturalized, 1977; s. Isaac and Fruma (Friedman) P.; m. Virginia Ann Gray, June 11, 1961; children: Oren, Sharon. B.S.E.E., U. Melbourne, Australia, 1957; M.S.E.E., U. Calif., Berkeley, 1959, Ph.D., 1961. Instrument engr. ICIANZ, Melbourne, Australia, 1956-57; summer student IBM Research Labs., San Jose, Calif., 1959-60; vis. asst. prof. M.I.T., fall 1964; asso. dept elec. engring. and computer scis. U. Calif., Berkeley, 1958-61, asst. prof. elec. engring. and computer scis., 1961-66, asso. prof., 1966-69, prof., 1969-94, prof. Grad. Sch., 1994—. Author: (with L.A. Zadeh) System Theory, 1969, (with E. Wong) Notes for a First Course on Linear Systems, 1970, (with others) Theory of Optimal Control and Mathematical Programming, 1970, Computational Methods in Optimization, 1971, Optimization: Algorithms and Consistent Approximations, 1997. Guggenheim fellow, 1968; U.K. Sci. Research Council sr. fellow, 1972, 76, 79, 82 Fellow IEEE; mem. Soc. Indsl. and Applied Math. (asso. editor Jour. Theory and Applications Optimization 1972—), Soc. Math. Programming. Home: 38 Fairlawn Dr Berkeley CA 94708-2106 Office: U Calif Dept Elec Engring Cp S Berkeley CA 94720-0001 E-mail: polak@eecs.berkeley.edu

POLAN, MARY LAKE, obstetrics and gynecology educator; b. Las Vegas, N.Mex., July 17, 1943; Student, Smith Coll., Paris, 1963-64; BA cum laude, Conn. Coll., 1965; PhD in Biophysics and Biochemistry, Yale U., 1970, MD, 1975. Diplomate Am. Bd. Ob-Gyn., Am. Bd. Reproductive Endocrinology, Nat. Bd. Med. Examiners. Postdoctoral fellow dept. biology, NIH postdoctoral fellow Yale U., New Haven, 1970-72, resident dept. ob-gyn. Sch. Medicine, 1975-78, fellow in oncology, then fellow in endocrinology-infertility, 1978-80, asst. instr., then lectr. molecular biophysics-biochemistry, 1970-72, instr., then asst. prof. ob-gyn., 1978-79, 80-85, assoc. prof., 1985-90; clin. clk. in ob-gyn. and pediat. Radcliffe Infirmary, Oxford (Eng.) U. Med. Sch., 1974; instr. Pahlavi U., Shiraz, Iran, 1978; Katharine Dexter McCormick and Stanley McCormick Meml. prof. Stanford (Calif.) Sch. Medicine, 1990—, chmn. dept. gynecology and obstetrics, 1990—. Vis. prof. Hunan Med. Coll., Changsha, China, 1986; mem. med. bd. Yale-China Assn., 1987-90; liaison com. on ethics in modern world Conn. Coll., New London, 1988-90; mem. med. adv. bd. Ova-Med Corp., Palo Alto, Calif., 1992-95, Vivus, Menlo Park, Calif., 1993—; bd. dirs. Metra Biosys., Mountain View, Quidel, San Diego, Stanford Health Svcs., 1994-96, Am. Home Products, Madison, N.J., 1994—; mem. reproductive endocrinology study sect. NIH, 1989-90, co-chmn. task force on opportunities for rsch. on woman's health, 1991. Author: Second Seed, 1987; guest editor: Seminars in Reproductive Endocrinology, 1984, Infertility and Reproductive Medicine Clinics of North America: GnRH Analogues, Vol. 4, 1993; editor; (with A.H. DeCherney) Surgery in Reproductive Endocrinology, 1987, (with DeCherney, S. Boyers and R. Lee) Decision Making in Infertility; ad hoc reviewer Jour. Clin. Endocrinology and Metabolism, Fertility and Sterility, Ob-Gyn., also others; contbr. numerous articles to med. jours., chpts. to books. Fellow NRSA, 1981-82; grantee NIRA, 1082-85, HD, 1985-90, NRSA, 1987-88, Johnson & Johnson, 1993-96; scholar Assn. Acad. Health Ctrs., 1993-96. Fellow ACOG (PROLOG task force for reproductive endocrinology and infertility 1988-89, rep. to CREOG coun. 1994-97); mem. Am. Fertility Soc., Soc. for Gynecologic Investigation, Soc. for Reproductive Endocrinologists, Am. Gynecologic and Obstetric Soc., Inst. Medicine (com. on rsch. capabilities of acad. depts. ob-gyn. 1990-91, bd. on health scis. policy 1992-96), San Francisco Gynecologic Soc., Bay Area Reproductive Endocrine Soc., Phi Beta Kappa. Home: 4251 Manuela Ct Palo Alto CA 94306-3731 Office: Stanford U Sch Medicine Dept Gyn OB 300 Pasteur Dr Stanford CA 94305-5317

POLANCO, RICHARD G. state senator; m. Olivia Polanco; children: Richard Jr., Gabriel, Liana. Student, East L.A. Coll., U. Redlands, U. Mexico. Mem Calif. State Assembly, 1986-94; mem. Calif. State Senate, 1994—, majority leader. Active Jr. Optimist Club; founder Eastside Assn.; co-founder Arroyo Vista Family Health Ctr., Mujeres Recovery Home, Para Los Ninos Day Care Ctr. Democrat. Office: Calif State Senate State Capitol Rm 313 Sacramento CA 95814 also: 300 S Spring St Ste 8710 Los Angeles CA 90013-1233

POLEDOURIS, BASIL K. composer; b. Kansas City, Mo., Aug. 21, 1945; s. Konstantine John and Helen Poledouris; m. Barbara Renée Godfrey, Aug. 15, 1969; children: Zoë Renée, Alexis Elene. BA in Music and Cinema, U. So. Calif., 1967, postgrad., 1967-69. Intern Am. Film Inst., L.A., 1969; freelance composer Hollywood, Calif., 1970—; pres. Basil Poledouris, Inc., Encino, 1987—. Bd. dirs. Blowtorch Flats, Venice, Calif.; mem. adv. bd. Soc. for Preservation Film Music, L.A., 1985—. Composer (film music) 90028, 1971, Extreme Close-Up, 1973, Tintorerra, 1977, Big Wednesday, 1979, Defiance, 1979, The Blue Lagoon, 1981, The House of God, 1988, Conan the Barbarian, 1981, Summer Lovers, 1982, Making the Grade, 1984, Conan the Destroyer, 1984, Red Dawn, 1984, Protocol, 1984, Flesh and Blood, 1985, Cherry 2000, 1986, Iron Eagle, 1986, Robocop, 1987 (BMI award 1988), No Man's Land, 1987, Split Decisions, 1988, Spellbinder, 1988, Farewell to the King, 1989, Wired, 1989, Hunt for Red October, 1990 (BMI award 1991), Quigley Down Under, 1990, Flight of the Intruder, 1991, White Fang, 1992, Return to the Blue Lagoon, 1991, Harley Davidson and the Marlboro Man, 1991, Robocop III, 1992, Free Willy, 1992 (BMI award 1994, gold record 1994), Hot Shots! Part Deux, 1993, Serial Mom, 1993, On Deadly Ground, 1994, Lassie, 1994, Jungle Book, 1994, Free Willy II, 1995, Under Seige II, 1995, It's My Party, 1995, Celtic Pride, 1996, Amanda, 1996, The War at Home, 1996, Switchback, 1996, Breakdown, 1997, Starship Troopers, 1997, Les Miserables, 1998, Mickey Blue Eyes, 1999, For Love of the Game, 1999, Cecil B DeMented, 2000, (TV film music) Congratulations It's A Boy, 1973, A Whale for the Killing, 1981, Fire on the Mountain, 1981, Amazons, 1984, Single Women, Single Bars, 1984, Amerika, 1987, Intrigue, 1988, Lonesome Dove, 1989 (Emmy award 1988, BMI award 1989), Nasty Boys, 1989, Lone Justice, 1990, Return to Lonesome Dove, 1993, TV pilots Alfred Hitchcock Presents, 1985, Misfits of Science, 1986, Island Sons, 1987, Murphy's Law, L.A. Takedown, 1989, Life and Times of Ned Blessing, 1991, Zoya, 1995, Tradition of Games Opening Ceremonies, 1996 Olympics, If These Walls Could Talk II, 2000, Dark Targets, 2001. Recipient resolution Calif. Legislature, 1990, Orange County Bd. Suprs., 1990, Key to City, Garden Grove City Coun., 1990, Disting. Artist award Calif. State U., Long Beach, 1992. Mem. NARAS, BMI, Am. Fedn. Musicians, Acad. Motion Picture Arts and Scis., Soc. Lyricists and Composers. Avocations: sailing, surfing.

POLESE, KIM, software company executive; BS, U. Calif., Berkeley; student, U. Wash. Product mgr. Sun Microsys., 1988-95; pres., CEO, co-founder Marimba, Inc., 1996—. Named one of Time Mags. Most Influential Ams. Office: Marimba Inc 440 Clyde Ave Mountain View CA 94043-2232

POLITAN, NICHOLAS, energy company executive; b. Belleville, N.J, 1961; BS, Duke U., 1983; JD, Stanford U., 1986. bd. dirs. Bally's Grand, Inc. V.p., CFO Kenetech Corp., San Francisco. Office: 500 Sansome St San Francisco CA 94111 Fax: (415) 391-7740

POLLACE, PAMELA L. public relations executive; b. San Jose, Calif., May 1953; BA, U. Santa Clara, 1975. Acct. mgr. mktg. comm. Oxbridge, Inc.; acct. supr. Burson Marsteller; spokesperson, mgr., dir. Intel Corp, Santa Clara, Calif., 1987-96, v.p., dir. worldwide press rels., 1996—. Office: Intel Corp Worldwide Press Rels PO Box 58119 Santa Clara CA 95052-8119

POLLARD, HENRY, mediator, arbitrator; b. N.Y.C., Jan. 10, 1931; s. Charles and Sarah (Lanster) P.; m. Adele Ruth Brodie, June 16, 1954; children: Paul A., Lydia S. AB, CCNY, 1953; JD, Columbia U., 1954. Bar: N.Y. 1954, Calif. 1962. Assoc. Sullivan & Cromwell, N.Y.C., 1954, 56-61; ptnr. Kaplan, LIvingston, Goodwin, Berkowitz & Selvin, Beverly Hills, 1962-81, Pollard, Bauman, Slome & McIntosh, Beverly Hills, Calif., 1981-87, Seyfarth, Shaw, Fairweather & Geraldson, L.A., 1987-95; of counsel Oberstein, Kibre & Horwitz, L.A., 1995-99. Judge pro tem L.A. County Mcpl. Ct.; arbitrator/mediator, mem. large complex case program Am. Arbitration Assn.; arbitrator/mediator Nat. Assn. Securities Dealers, N.Y. Stock Exch., Am. Stock Exch., Pacific Stick Exch., L.A. County Dispute Resolution Svcs.; settlement officer Beverly Hills Mcpl. Ct., L.A. County Superior Ct. Editor Columbia U. Law Rev., 1953-54. Served with U.S. Army, 1954-56. Harlan Fiske Stone scholar, 1953-54. Mem. ABA, Calif. Bar Assn., Beverly Hills Bar Assn Fax: 310-457-1713. E-mail: adrpolllard@aol.com

POLLEY, TERRY LEE, lawyer; b. Long Beach, Calif., June 2, 1947; s. Frederick F. and Geraldine E. (Davis) P.; m. Patricia Yamanoha, Aug. 4, 1973; children: Todd, Matthew. AB, UCLA, 1970; JD, Coll. William and Mary, 1973. Bar: Calif. 1973, U.S. Tax Ct. 1974, U.S. Supreme Ct. 1987. Assoc. Loeb & Loeb, L.A., 1973-78; ptnr. Ajalat, Polley & Ayoob, L.A., 1978—. Lectr. taxation law U. So.Calif., 1978-94. Author (with Charles R. Ajalat) California's Water's Edge Legislation, 1987; contbr. articles to profl. jours., legal jours.; editorial bd. William and Mary Law Rev. Chmn. bd. dirs. Greater Long Beach Christian Schs., 1988-92, sec., 1994-99; elder Grace Brethren Ch., Long Beach, 1988—. Mem. ABA (state and local tax com. 1973-92), Calif. Bar Assn. (chmn. taxation sect. 1990-91, exec. com. 1987-92, state and local tax com. 1975—, taxation sect., recipient V. Judson Klein award 1993), L.A. County Bar Assn. (exec. com. 1980-87, chmn. exec. com. 1985-86, taxation sect.), Nat. Assn. State Bar Tax Sects. (exec. com. 1990—, chmn. 1995-96, treas. 1998—). Republican. Office: Ajalat Polley & Ayoob 643 S Olive St Ste 200 Los Angeles CA 90014-1651

POLLNOW, C. lumber company executive; CFO Simpson Investment Co., Seattle. Office: Simpson Investment Co 1201 3d Ave Ste 4900 Seattle WA 98101-3045

POLLOCK, JOHN PHLEGER, lawyer; b. Sacramento, Apr. 28, 1920; s. George Gordon and Irma (Phleger) P.; m. Juanita Irene Gossman, Oct. 26, 1945; children: Linda Pollock Harrison, Madeline Pollock Chiotti, John, Gordon. A.B., Stanford U., 1942; J.D., Harvard U., 1948. Bar: Calif. 1949, U.S. Supreme Ct. 1954. Ptnr. Musick, Peeler & Garrett, L.A., 1953-60, Pollock, Williams & Berwanger, L.A., 1960-80, Rodi, Pollock, Pettker, Galbraith & Cahill, L.A., 1980-89, of counsel, 1989—. Contbr. articles to profl. publs. Active Boy Scouts Am.; trustee Pitzer Coll., Claremont, Calif., 1968-76, Pacific Legal Found., 1981-91, Fletcher Jones Found., 1969—, Good Hope Med. Found., 1980—. Fellow Am. Coll. Trial Lawyers; mem. ABA, Los Angeles County Bar Assn. (trustee 1964-66). Home: 30602 Paseo Del Valle Laguna Niguel CA 92677-2317 Office: 444 S Flower St Ste 1700 Los Angeles CA 90071-2918 E-mail: Phleger1@msn.com

POLLOCK, RICHARD EDWIN, former county official; b. Phila., Aug. 27, 1928; s. Ernest Edwin and Evelyn Marie (Scarlett) P. Student Armstrong Coll., 1947, U. Calif., Berkeley, 1949-51, 55; BA in Recreation, San Jose State U., 1961; postgrad. San Fernando Valley State U., 1969-70, U. Calif., Davis, 1963-77, UCLA, 1964, U. Calif., Santa Barbara, 1970, U. Redlands, 1979; m. Yvonne May Graves, Oct. 11, 1952 (div. Aug. 1989); children: Colleen May, Karen Marie, Richard Irvin, Annette Yvonne, Mary Ann. Swim pool mgr. and instr. Berkley Tennis Club, 1955-56; police officer City of Berkeley, 1956; recreation and aquatic supr. Pleasant Hill (Calif.) Recreation and Park Dist., 1956-62; gen. mgr. Pleasant Valley Recreation and Park Dist., Camarillo, Calif., 1962-68; bldg. insp. Ventura County (Calif.), 1969-71; adminstr. Sacramento County-Carmichael Recreation and Park Dist., 1971-73; dir. parks and recreation Imperial County (Calif.), 1973-81; ret.; mem. faculty Imperial Valley Jr. Coll., 1974-94, aquatic cons., 1957—; real estate investor, 1984-97; chmn. San Francisco Bay Area Conf. for Cooperation in Aquatics, 1958-59. Adviser/scoutmaster Desert Trails council Boy Scouts Am.; bd. dirs., instr. ARC; work with devel. disabled and handicapped children and adults; res. dep. Sheriff, 1981-97, Served from pvt. to lt. U.S. Army, 1951-55; Korea. Recipient recognition for 52 years vol. service ARC, 1989; registered recreator and park mgr.; cert. elem., secondary and community coll. tchr., Calif.; reg. hypnotherapist. Mem. Nat. Recreation and Park Assn., AAHPER, Calif. Park and Recreation Soc., Calif. County Dirs. Parks and Recreation Assn., Calif. Boating Safety Officers Assn., Aircraft Owners and Pilots Assn., Nat. Assn. Emergency Med. Technicians. Democrat. Mormon. Author: Bibliography: A Pool of Aquatic Sources, 1960. Home: 961 S Sunshine Ave Apt 5 El Cajon CA 92020-5947

POLON, LINDA BETH, elementary school educator, writer, illustrator; b. Balt., Oct. 7, 1943; d. Harold Bernard and Edith Judith Wolff; m. Marty I. Polon, Dec. 18, 1966 (div. Aug. 1983). BA in History, UCLA, 1966. Elem. tchr. L.A. Bd. Edn., 1967—; writer, illustrator Scott, Foresman Pub. Co., Glenview Ill., 1979—, Frank Schaffer Pub. Co., Torrance, Calif., 1981-82, Learning Works, Santa Barbara, 1981-82, Harper Row Co.; edtl. reviewer Prentice Hall Pub. Co., Santa Monica, Calif., 1982-83; with Addison Wesley, N.J.; writer, graphic designer, tutor. Writer-illustrator Scott Foresman Pub. Co., Glenview, Ill., 1979—, Frank Schaffer Pub. Co., Torrance, Calif., 1981-82, Learning Works, Santa Barbara, Calif., 1981-82, Harper Row Co.; editorial reviewer Prentice Hall Pub. Co., Santa Monica, Calif., 1982-83. Author: (juvenile books) Creative Teaching Games, 1974, Teaching Games for Fun, 1976, Making Kids Click, 1979, Write Up a Storm, 1979, Stir Up a Story, 1981, Paragraph Production, 1981, Using Words Correctly, 3d-4th grades, 1981, 5th-6th grades, 1981, Whole Earth Holiday Book, 1983, Writing Whirlwind, 1986, Magic Story Starters, 1987, (teacher's resource guides) Just Good Books, 1991, Kids Choice/Libraries, 1991, Write a Story-Grades 4-6, 1977, Story Starters-Grade 4-6, 1999, Grades 1-3 Storywriting, 1999, Grades 4-6 Storywriting, 1999. Mem. Soc. Children's Book Writers. Democrat. Home: 11645 Gorham Ave # 105 Los Angeles CA 90049-4753 E-mail: motey@earthlink.net

POLUMBUS, GARY M. lawyer; b. Tulsa, 1941; BS, U. Colo., 1964; JD, U. Denver, 1967. Bar: Colo. 1967, D.C. 1968. Mem. Dorsey & Whitney, Denver, 1996—. Mem. ABA, Am. Intellectual Property Law Assn. Office: Dorsey & Whitney 370 17th St Ste 4400 Denver CO 80202-5644

POLYNICE, OLDEN, professional basketball player; b. Port-au-Prince, Haiti, Nov. 21, 1964; s. Jean-Lester and Suzanne P.; children: Nikolas Justin, Tiara Alysha. Grad., U. Va., 1986. Center Seattle Seahawks, 1987-91, L.A. Clippers, 1991-92, Detroit Pistons, 1992-93, Sacramento Kings, 1993-98, Seattle Supersonics, 1998-99, Utah Jazz, 1999—. Appeared in Fox TV's Totally Hidden Videos, 1991, (movie) Eddie, 1995. Office: Utah Jazz 301 W South Temple Salt Lake City UT 84101-1216

POMBO, RICHARD, congressman, rancher, farmer; b. Tracy, Calif., 1961; m. Annette, 1983; children: Richard Jr., Rena, Rachael. Student, Calif. State U., Pomona, 1981-83. Councilman City of Tracy, 1991-92; mayor pro-tem Tracy City Coun., 1992; mem. U.S. Congress from 11th Calif. dist., 1993—; mem. agrl. com., chmn. subcom. on livestock and horticulture; mem. resources com., transp. and infrastructure com. Chmn. Pvt. Property Rights Task Force, 1993-94, Endangered Species Act Task Force, 1995-96; co-chmn. Spkr.'s Environ. Task Force, 1996. Co-founder

San Joaquin County Citizen's Land Alliance, Calif., 1986—; active San Joaquin County Econ. Devel. Assn., Tracy Bus. Improvement Dist., City Coun. (vice chmn. Cmty. Devel. Agy., Cmty. Parks Com., and Waste Mgmt. Com.), San Joaquin County Rep. Ctrl. Com. Mem. Rotary Club. Roman Catholic. Office: US Ho Reps 2411 Rayburn HOB Washington DC 20515*

POMERANTZ, MARVIN, thoracic surgeon; b. Suffern, N.Y., June 16, 1934; s. Julius and Sophie (Luksin) P.; m. Margaret Twigg, Feb. 26, 1966; children: Ben, Julie. AB, Colgate U., 1955; MD, U. Rochester, 1959. Diplomate Nat. Bd. Med. Examiners, Am. Bd. Surgery, Am. Bd. Thoracic Surgery (bd. dirs. 1989-95). Intern Duke U. Med. Ctr., Durham, N.C., 1959-60, resident, 1960-61, 63-67, instr. surgery, 1966-67; asst. prof. surgery U. Colo. Med. Sch., Denver, 1967-71, assoc. prof. surgery, 1971-74, assoc. clin. prof. surgery, 1974-93, prof. surgery, chief gen. thoracic surgery, 1992—; chief thoracic and cardiovascular surgery Denver Gen. Hosp., 1967-73, asst. dir. surgery, 1967-70, assoc.dir. surgery, 1970-73; pvt. practice Arapahoe CV Assocs., Denver, 1974-92; prof., chief gen. thoracic surgery sect. U. Colo. Health Sci. Ctr., 1992—. Clin. assoc. surgery br. Nat. Cancer Inst., 1961-63; mem.staff Univ. Hosp., Denver, Denver Gen. Hosp., Rose Med. Ctr., Denver, Denver VA Med. Ctr., Children's Hosp., Denver, U. Coll. Health Sci. Ctr., 1992—, bd. dirs., 1990-96; vice-chmn. Am. Bd. Thoracic Surgery, 1995-97, chmn., 1997-99. Guest editor Chest Surgery Clinics N.Am., 1993; contbr. numerous articles to profl. publs., chpts. to books. Fellow ACS, Am. Coll. Chest Surgeons; mem. AMA, Western Thoracic Surg. Assn. (v.p. 1992, pres. 1993-94, counselor-at-large 1988-90), Am. Assn. Thoracic Surgeons (program com. 1991), Am. Heart Assn. (bd. dirs. Colo. chpt. 1993), Colo. Med. Soc., Denver Acad. Surgery (pres. 1980), Internat. Cardiovascular Soc., Rocky Mtn. Cardiac Surgery Soc., Rocky Mtn. Traumatologic Soc., Soc. Thoracic Surgeons (nomenclature/coding com. 1991-95, standards and ethics com., govt. rels. com., chmn. program com. 1994-95), Soc. Vascular Surgeons. Office: UCHSC Divsn CTS 4200 E 9th Ave # C310 Denver CO 80262-0001

POMEROY, HORACE BURTON, III, accountant, corporate executive; b. Bronxville, N.Y., July 11, 1937; s. Horace Burton Jr. and Juhn P.; m. Margarita Maria Benavidez, July 14, 1973; children: Josephine, Emily. BS in Bus Adminstrn., U. Ariz., 1964; MBA, Boise State U., 1982. Comml. bank officer Continental Bank, Chgo., 1964-67; cons. Morgan Olmstead Kennedy Gardner, L.A., 1967-74; mgr. cash and banking Morrison Knudsen Corp., Boise, Idaho, 1974-88. Rep. Idaho State Legislature Dist. 16, 1988—. With U.S. Army, 1959-60. Mem. NRA, Nat. Corp. Cash Mgrs. Assn., Nat. Philat. Assn., Rotary. Republican. Episcopalian. Avocations: stamp collecting, fishing, golf, tennis. Home: 6822 Kingsdale Dr Boise ID 83704-7343 Office: Statehouse Boise ID 83720-0001 E-mail: hodp@aol.com

PONDEL, ROGER S. public relations executive; BA in Pub. Rels., Calif. State U., San Jose. Pub. rels. dir. Cordon Internat. Corp., Cordura Corp., Bekins Co.; pres. Pondel/Wilkinson Group, L.A., 1977—. Adj. faculty Pepperdine U., Malibu, Calif.; spkr. Reporter San Jose Mercury News. Mem. Nat. Investor Rels. Inst., Pub. Rels. Soc. Am., L.A. Soc. Fin. Analysts. Office: Pondel Wilkinson Group 12100 Wilshire Blvd Ste 400 Los Angeles CA 90025-7107 Fax: 310-207-5444

POOCHIGIAN, CHARLES, state legislator; b. Fresno, Calif., 1949; m. Debbie Poochigian; three children. BBA, Calif. State U., Fresno, 1972; JD, U. Santa Clara, 1975. Lawyer, 1975-88; chief dep. appointments sec. Gov. George Deukmejians Office, 1988-91; appointments sec. Gov. Pete Wilsons Office, 1991-94; mem. Calif. State Assembly, 1994-98, mem. appropriations, transp., budget and other coms., chmn. appropriations com., mem. Rep. caucus leadership, 1995-97, mem. budget conf. com., 1995, 96; mem. Calif. State Senate, 1998—, mem. budget and fiscal rev. com., vice chmn. revenue and taxation com., mem. agr. and water com., elections com., others. Apptd. mem. Calif. Fair Employment and Housing Commn., 1985-87. With Calif. Air Nat. Guard. Named Assembly Rep. Rookie of the Yr., Calif. Jour. mag., 1996, Legislator of Yr., Calif. Bus. Properties Assn., Calif. Citizens Against Lawsuit Abuse, Calif. Bldg. Industry Assn. Republican. Mem. Armenian Ch. Office: State Capitol Rm 2054 Sacramento CA 95814 also: 4974 E Clinton Way Ste 100 Fresno CA 93727-1520 also: 841 Mohawk St Ste 190 Bakersfield CA 93309-1547

POOL, DAVID, software executive; BA, Wash. State U. Product mgr. Clouston LTD; prin. SPRY Inc. (acquired by CompuServe 1995), 1989-95; v.p. Compuserve, 1995-96; prin. DataChannel, 1996-99; founder XML Fund, Bellevue, Wash., 1999—. Office: XML Fund 777 108th Ave NE Ste 1800 Bellevue WA 98004

POOLE, CHRISTOPHER K. computer company executive; b. 1958; Exec. dir. Latham & Watkins, Los Angeles; COO Elite Information Sys., Los Angeles, 1995-97, pres., 1997—. Office: Elite Information Sys 5100 W Gold Leaf Cir Ste 50 Los Angeles CA 90056

POOLE, HENRY JOE, JR. business executive; b. Rocky Point, N.C., July 5, 1957; s. Henry Joe Sr. and Marjorie (Morse) P.; m. Loretta Lynn Scott, Sept. 12, 1981; children: Robert Howard, Amanda Lynn. AA, Cypress Coll., 1977; student, San Diego State U., 1978, Calif. State U., Fullerton, 1978-79. Pres. Poole Ventura Inc., Ventura, Calif., 1979-92; gen. mgr. W.I.C. PVI systems divsn., Ventura, 1992-94; pres. PVI, Oxnard, 1995—. Inventor in field. Mem. ASME, Soc. Mfg. Engrs., Am. Vacuum Soc., Am. Welding Soc., Soc. Vacuum Coaters. Office: PVI PO Box 5023 Oxnard CA 93031-5023 E-mail: pvi@vcnet.com

POOLE, ROBERT ANTHONY, journalist; b. St. Austell, Cornwall, Eng., Dec. 17, 1944; arrived in Can., 1977; m. Valerie Avril Taggart, Apr. 14, 1973; children: Claire Lucy, Emma Louise. Irish editor Press Assn., Belfast, Northern Ireland, 1970-77; gen. reporter Calgary Herlat, Alta., Can., 1977-79; city editor Calgary Albertan, 1979-80, Calgary Sun, 1980-81, mng. editor, 1981-84, editor-in-chief, 1984-86, Times Colonist, Victoria, 1997—. Journalist; b. St. Austell, Cornwall, Eng., Dec. 17, 1944; arrived in Can., 1977; m. Valerie Avril Taggart, Apr. 14, 1973; children—Claire Lucy, Emma Louise. Irish editor Press Assn., Belfast, Northern Ireland, 1970-77; gen. reporter Calgary Herald, Alta., Can., 1977-79; city editor Calgary Albertan, 1979-80; city editor Calgary Sun, 1980-81, mng. editor, 1981-84, editor-in-chief, 1984-96; editor-in-chief Times Colonist, Victoria, 1997—. Office: Times Colonist 2621 Douglas St Victoria BC Canada V8W 2N4

POOLE, ROBERT WILLIAM, JR. foundation executive; b. Englewood, N.J., July 4, 1944; s. Robert William and Frances Ann (Giese) P.; m. Lou Villadsen, May 28, 1983; m. Marilyn V. Kinsky, June 1968 (div. 1974). BS, MIT, 1966, MS, 1967. Systems analyst Sikorsky Aircraft, Stratford, Conn., 1967-70; criminal justice analyst Gen. Rsch. Co., Santa Barbara, Calif., 1970-74; cons. local govt. mgmt. Santa Barbara, 1974-76; pres. Local Govt. Ctr., Santa Barbara, 1976-78, Reason Found., Santa Monica, Calif., 1978—. Author: Cutting Back City Hall, 1980; editor: Instead of Regulation, 1982, Defending a Free Society, 1984, Unnatural Monopolies, 1985; editor, pub. mag. Reason, 1971—. Bd. dirs. Mission Canyon Assn., Santa Barbara, 1984-85, Santa Barbara Futures Found., 1982-83. Fellow NSF, 1966-67. Mem. AAAS, Sigma Xi. Libertarian. Office: Reason Found 3415 S Sepulveda Blvd Ste 400 Los Angeles CA 90034-6014

POON, PETER TIN-YAU, engineer, physicist; b. Hengyang, Hunan, China, May 31, 1944; came to U.S., 1967; s. Sam. Chak-Kwong and Lai (Yiu) P.; m. Mable Tsang, Apr. 13, 1974; children: Amy Wei-Ling, Brian Wing-Yan. BS, U. Hong Kong, 1965; MA, Calif. State U., Long Beach, 1969; PhD, U. So. Calif., L.A., 1974. Tech. mgr., sr. engr. Jet Propulsion Lab./Calif. Inst. Tech., Pasadena, 1974-83; advisor Space Sta. Ada Task, task leader software mgmt. and assurance program NASA, 1984-85, software mgmt. stds., element mgr. software info. sys., 1986-88; systems mgr. for missions to Mars, Comet/Asteroid/Saturn, flight projects interface office Jet Propulsion Lab./Calif. Inst. Tech., Pasadena, 1988-91, multimission ground systems office mgr. Mission to Mars, 1991-93, telecomm. and mission systems mgr. Cassini Mission to Saturn, 1993-98, radio astronomy, French, German, Italian, and U.S. Mars space missions, 1998—. U.S. chmn., program mgmt. com., panel chair Internat. Software Engring. Stds. Symposium, Eng., 1992-93, Can., 1994-95, U.S., 1995-97, 2000—, Brazil, 1998-99; 5th Internat. Software Engring. Stds. Symposium, US, 2000—; session chair, mem. program com. IEEE Internat. Conf. on Engring. of Complex Computer Systems, Montreal, 1995-96, Como, Italy, 1996-97, Monterey, 1997-98, Tokyo, 1999-2000, Skövde, Sweden, 2000-01; mem. Internat. Orgn. for Standardization in Info. Tech. Subcom. and U.S. Tech. Adv. Group, 1995-2001; U.S. del., Prague, Czech Republic, 1996, Paris, 1996, Walnut Creek, U.S., 1997, Brisbane, Australia, 1997, Melbourne, Fla., 1998, Curitiba, Brazil, 1998; program chmn. Software Engring. Stds. Symposium, 1998—; 2nd World Congress on Software Quality, Tokyo, 2000—; program co-chmn. 5th Internat. Software Engring. Stds. Symposium, 2000—. Mem. editl. bd. Software Quality Profl., Am. Soc. for Quality, 1998—; contbr. articles to profl. jours. Active steering com. United Way, Jet Propulsion Laboratory, 1998—. Recipient Group awards NASA, 1977-2001, Recognition cert., Inventions and Contbns. Bd. Mem. IEEE (exec. com. software engring. stds. 1993-2000), Arcadia Music Club (pres. 1994-95), Sigma Xi, Eta Kappa Nu, Phi Kappa Phi, Athenaeum. Avocations: music appreciation, hiking, theatre arts. Office: Jet Propulsion Lab Calif Inst Tech 4800 Oak Grove Dr Pasadena CA 91109-8001 E-mail: Petertpoon@yahoo.com

POPE, CARL, professional society administrator; BA summa cum laude, Harvard U., 1967. Vol. Peace Corps, Barhi Barhi, India, 1967-69; with Sierra Club, San Francisco, assoc. conservation dir., polit. dir., conservation dir., exec. dir., 1992—. Bd. dirs. Calif. League of Conservation Voters, 1986-87, exec. dir., 1973-83; bd. dirs. Pub. Voice, 1989-92, Nat. Clean Air Coalition, Calif. Common Cause, 1976-78, Pub. Interest Econs., Inc., 1973-76; bd. dirs. Zero Population Growth, 1972-90, also polit. dir., 1970-73. Address: Sierra Club 85 2nd St Fl 2 San Francisco CA 94105-3456

POPE, CHARLES C. data processing executive; BS in Acctg., U. Utah; MBA, Brigham Young U. With Hewlett Packard Co., Diasonics Corp.; dir. budgets and analysis Seagate Technology, Scotts Valley, Calif., 1985, dir. fin. for Thailand ops., v.p. fin. Far East ops., v.p. fin., treas.; v.p., gen. mgr. Seagate Magnetics; sr. v.p. storage products Seagate Technologies, sr. v.p. fin., CFO, 1998—. Office: Seagate Technology Inc PO Box 66360 Scotts Valley CA 95067-0360

POPE, NORRIS, publishing executive; BA, Stanford U., 1968; PhD, Oxford U., 1976. Asst. editor Stanford (Calif.) U. Press, 1978-80, assoc. editor, 1980-83, CFO, 1983-85, editor-in-chief, 1985-96, dir., 1993—. Author: Dickens and Charity, 1978. Office: Stanford U Press 521 Lomita Dr Stanford CA 94305-2208

POPEK, GERALD JOHN, computer software company executive, educator; b. Passaic, N.J., Sept. 22, 1946; s. Joseph John Popek; m. Paulene Bunker; children: Sarah, Darren. BS, NYU, 1968; SM, Harvard U., 1970, PhD, 1972. V.p. Palyn Assocs., San Jose, Calif., 1978-83; dir. Ctr. for Exptl. Computer Sci., UCLA, 1981-84; prof. computer sci. UCLA, from 1973; chief exec. officer Locus Computing Corp., Santa Monica, Calif., 1982-87, chmn., 1982-95; chief tech. officer Platinum Tech. Inc., 1995-99, CarsDirect.com, 1999-2000, NetZero, 2000—. Bd. dirs. Palyn Assocs., San Jose. Author, editor: The Locus Distributed System Architecture, 1985. Served to capt. USAF, 1972-78. Republican. Roman Catholic. Home: 1716 Roscomare Rd Los Angeles CA 90077-2213 Office: NetZero Inc 2555 Townsgate Rd Westlake Village CA 91361-2650

POPKIN, DAVID RICHARD, academic dean, obstetrician, gynecologist; m. Linda Popkin, 1964; 4 children BSc in Agr., McGill, 1962, MD, CM, 1966. Head divsn. gynecology and gynecologic oncology Royal Victoria Hosp., Montreal, Can., 1976-82; head dept. ob-gyn. Royal Univ. Hosp. U. Saskatchewan, Saskatoon, Can., 1982-91, assoc. dean postgrad. med. edn. and clin. affairs Can., 1991-93, dean Coll. Medicine Can., 1993—. Office: Coll Medicine Health Scis 107 Wiggins Rd Saskatoon SK Canada S7N 5E5

POPOFSKY, MELVIN LAURENCE, lawyer; b. Oskaloosa, Iowa, Feb. 16, 1936; s. Samuel and Fannye Charlotte (Rosenthal) P.; m. Linda Jane Seltzer, Nov. 25, 1962; children: Mark Samuel, Kaye Sylvia. BA in History summa cum laude, U. Iowa, 1958; BA in Jurisprudence (first class honors), Oxford U., Eng., 1960; LLB cum laude, Harvard U., 1962. Bar: Calif. 1962. Assoc. Heller, Ehrman, White & McAuliffe, San Francisco, 1962-69, ptnr., 1969—, mem. exec. com., 1980-93, co-chair, 1988-93. Contbr. articles to law jours. Bd. dirs. Mt. Zion Hosp., San Francisco, 1982-88, U.S. Dist. Ct. (no. dist.) Calif. Hist. Soc., 1988—, Jewish Home for Aged, San Francisco, 1989-96, Golden Gate U., 1997-2000, Jewish Cmty. Fedn., 1997-2001. Recipient Anti-Defamation League's Disting. Jurisprudence award, 2000; named State Bar of Calif. Antitrust Lawyer of the Yr., 2000; Rhodes scholar, 1958. Fellow Am. Bar Found., Am. Coll. Trial Lawyers; mem. ABA, Calif. Bar Assn., San Francisco Bar Assn., Bur. Nat. Affairs (adv. bd. antitrust sect.), Calif. Acad. Appellate Lawyers. Democrat. Jewish. Home: 1940 Broadway Apt 10 San Francisco CA 94109-2216 Office: Heller Ehrman 333 Bush St Ste 3000 San Francisco CA 94104-2834

POPOV, EGOR PAUL, retired engineering educator; b. Kiev, Russia, Feb. 19, 1913; s. Paul T. and Zoe (Derabin) P.; m. Irene Zofia Jozefowski, Feb. 18, 1939; children: Katherine, Alexander. BS with honors, U. Calif., 1933; MS, MIT, 1934; PhD in Civil Engring./Applied Mechs., Stanford U., 1946. Registered civil, structural and mech. engr., Calif. Structural engr., bldg. designer, L.A., 1935-39; asst. prodn. engr. Southwestern Portland Cement Co., L.A., 1939-42; machine designer Goodyear Tire & Rubber Co., L.A., 1942-43; design engr. Aerojet Corp., Calif., 1943-45; asst. prof. civil engring. U. Calif. at Berkeley, 1946-48, assoc. prof., 1948-53, prof., 1953-83, prof. emeritus, 1983—, chmn. structural engring. and structural mechanics div., dir. structural engring. lab., 1956-60. Miller rsch. prof. Miller Inst. Basic Rsch. in Sci., 1968-69. Author: Mechanics of Materials, 1952, 2d edit., 1976, Introduction to Mechanics of Solids, 1968, Engineering Mechanics of Solids, 1990, 2d edit., 1999; contbr. articles profl. jours. Recipient Disting. Tchr. award U. Calif.-Berkeley, 1976-77, Berkeley citation U. Calif.-Berkeley, 1983, Disting. Lectr. award Earthquake Engring. Rsch. Inst., 1993, George W. Housner medal Earthquake Engring. Rsch. Inst., 1999. Fellow AAAS (assoc.), Am. Concrete Inst.; mem. NAE, Am. Soc. Metals, Internat. Assn. Shell Structures (hon. mem.), ASCE (hon. mem., Ernest E. Howard award 1976, J. James R. Croes medal 1979, 82, Nathan M. Newmark medal 1981, Raymond C. Reese rsch. prize 1986, Norman medal 1987, von Karman medal 1989), Soc. Exptl. Stress Analysis (Hetenyi award 1967, William M. Murray medallion 1986), Am. Soc. Engring. Edn. (Western Electric Fund award 1976-77, Disting. Educator award 1979), Soc. Engring. Sci., Internat. Assn. Bridge and Structural Engring., Am. Inst. Steel Constrn. (adv. com. specifications, Lifetime Achievement award 1999), Ukrainian Acad. Constrn. (fgn. mem.), Sigma Xi, Chi Epsilon, Tau Beta Pi. Home: 2600 Virginia St # 9 Berkeley CA 94709-1045 Office: Davis Hall Univ Calif Berkeley CA 94720 E-mail: epp@uclinkA.berkeley.edu

PORCELLO, LEONARD JOSEPH, engineering research and development executive; b. N.Y.C., Mar. 1, 1934; s. Savior James and Mary Josephine (Bacchi) P.; m. Patricia Lucille Berger, July 7, 1962 (dec. Sept. 1991); children— John Joseph, Thomas Gregory; m. Victoria Roberta Smith, June 21, 1996. B.A. in Physics, Cornell U., 1955; M.S. in Physics, U. Mich., 1957, M.S. in Elec. Engring, 1959, Ph.D. in Elec. Engring, 1963. Research asst. U. Mich., Ann Arbor, 1955-58, instr. elec. engring., 1958-61; research engr. Radar & Optics Lab., 1968-72; asso. dir. Willow Run Labs., 1970-72, asso. prof., 1969-72, prof., 1972-73, adj. prof., 1973-75. Dir. radar and optics divsn. Environ. Rsch. Inst. of Mich., Ann Arbor, 1973-76, v.p., 1973-76, trustee, 1975; asst. v.p., mgr. sensor sys. operation Sci. Applications Internat. Corp., Tucson, 1976-79, v.p., 1979-85, corp. v.p., 1985-87, mgr. def. sys. group, 1986-95, sr. v.p., 1987—, dep. mgr. tech. and advanced sys. sector, 1993-97, mgr. applied sys. group, 1995-2000, dep. mgr. space and tech. solutions sector, 1997-99. Bd. dirs. Tucson Jr. Strings, 1977-79, chmn., 1978-79 Fellow IEEE; mem. Optical Soc. Am., AAAS, Sigma Xi, Eta Kappa Nu. Roman Catholic. Achievements include research on imaging radar, synthetic aperture radar systems and radar remote sensing. Home: 5072 Grandview Ave Yorba Linda CA 92886-4216 Office: Sci Applications Internat Corp Attn LJ Porcello PO Box 820 Yorba Linda CA 92885-0820 E-mail: Leonard.J.Porcello@saic.com

PORFILIO, JOHN CARBONE, federal judge; b. Denver, Oct. 14, 1934; s. Edward Alphonso Porfilio and Caroline (Carbone) Moore; m. Joan West, Aug. 1, 1959 (div. 1983); children: Edward Miles, Joseph Arthur, Jeanne Kathrine; m. Theresa Louise Berger, Dec. 28, 1983; 1 stepchild, Katrina Ann Smith Student, Stanford U., 1952-54; BA, U. Denver, 1956, LLB, 1959, LLD (hon.), 2000. Bar: Colo. 1959, U.S. Supreme Ct. 1965. Asst. atty. gen. State of Colo., Denver, 1962-68, dep. atty. gen., 1968-72, atty. gen., 1972-74; U.S. bankruptcy judge Dist. of Colo., Denver, 1975-82; judge U.S. Dist. Ct. Colo., Denver, 1982-85, U.S. Ct. Appeals (10th cir.), Denver, 1985—. Instr. Colo. Law Enforcement Acad., Denver, 1965-70, State Patrol Acad., Denver, 1968-70; guest lectr. U. Denver Coll. Law, 1978 Committeeman Arapahoe County Republican Com., Aurora, Colo., 1968; mgr. Dunbar for Atty. Gen., Denver, 1970 Mem. ABA. Roman Catholic Office: US Ct Appeals Byron White US Courthouse 1823 Stout St Denver CO 80257-1823

PORPER, MARY, comptroller; V.p., comptroller Suissa Miller, L.A. Office: Suissa Miller 11601 Wilshire Blvd Fl 16 Los Angeles CA 90025-1770 Fax: 310-392-2625

PORT, SIDNEY CHARLES, mathematician, educator; b. Chgo., Nov. 27, 1935; s. Isadore and Sarah (Landy) P.; m. Idelle Jackson, Mar. 24, 1957; children— Ethan, Jonathan, Daniel. A.B., Northwestern U., 1957, M.S., 1958, Ph.D., 1962. Staff mathematician Rand Corp., 1962-66; assoc. prof. math. U. Calif. at Los Angeles, 1966-69, prof., 1969—. Author: (with P. Hoel and C. Stone) Probability, Statistics and Stochastic Processes, 1971, (with C. Stone) Brownian Motion and Classical Potential Theory, 1978, Theoretical Probability for Applications, 1993; contbr. articles to profl. jours. Fellow Inst. Math. Statistics; mem. Am. Math. Soc. Home: 680 Kingman Ave Santa Monica CA 90402-1334 Office: UCLA Dept Math Los Angeles CA 90024 E-mail: sport@ucla.edu

PORTER, BLAINE ROBERT MILTON, sociology and psychology educator; b. Morgan, Utah, Feb. 24, 1922; s. Brigham Ernest and Edna (Brough) P.; m. Elizabeth Taylor, Sept 27, 1943 (dec.); children: Claudia Black, Roger B., David T., Patricia A. Hintze, Corinna; m. Myrna Katherine Kennedy, Feb. 26, 1988. Student, Utah State U., 1940-41; BS, Brigham Young U., 1947, MA, 1949; PhD (Grant Found. fellow family life edn. 1951-52), Cornell U., 1952. Instr. sociology Iowa State Coll., 1949-51; asst. prof. sociology and child devel. Iowa State U., 1952-55; prof., chmn. dept. human devel. and family relationships Brigham Young U., 1955-65, dean Coll. Family Living, 1966-80, Univ. prof., 1980-87. Vis. prof. Fulbright rsch. scholar U. London, 1965-66; vis. prof. U. Wurzberg, 1980, 81, 83; facilitator human rels. workshops for the Human Devel. Inst., Denver, 1988-90. Editor: The Latter-day Saint Family, 1963, rev. edit., 1966; editor quar. jour.: Family Perspective, 1966-82; contbr. articles to profl. jours. Pres. elect Iowa Coun. Family Rels., 1954-55; pres. Utah Coun. Family Rels., 1957-58; chmn. sect. marriage counseling Nat. Coun. Family Rels., 1958-59, bd. dirs., 1957-60, exec. com., 1958-72, pres., 1963-64; bd. dirs. Am. Family Soc., 1975-85. Pilot USAAF, 1942-45. Recipient Prof. of Yr. award Brigham Young U., 1964. Mem. Am. Home Econs. Assn. (vice chmn. sect. family relations and child devel. 1955-56), Am. Sociol. Assn. (sec. sect. on family 1964-67), Am. Assn. Marriage and Family Therapy, Am. Psychol. Assn., Soc. Research in Child Devel., Sigma Xi, Phi Kappa Phi (chpt. pres. 1969-71) Home: 1675 Pine Ln Provo UT 84604-2163 Office: 4505 HBLL Brigham Young U Provo UT 84602

PORTER, BRIAN STANLEY, state legislator; b. May 2, 1938; s. Jack D. and Margaret I. (Tuter) P.; m. Bette K. WSchakohl, Apr. 26, 1958; children: Kelle, Kerry, Kory. Grad., U. Alaska, 1970, Northwestern U. Traffic Inst., 1970-71, FBI Nat. Exec. Inst., 1981. With Anchorage Police Dept., 1960-87, chief of police, 1980-87; mem. Alaska Ho. of Reps., 1987—. Chmn. Alaska Police Stds. Coun., 1978-80; chmn. Ho. Jud. com. Served with U.S. Army, 1957-58. Office: Alaska State Legis 716 W 4th Ave Ste 300 Anchorage AK 99501-2107

PORTER, BRUCE DOUGLAS, federal agency administrator, educator, writer; b. Albuquerque, Sept. 18, 1952; s. Lyle Kay and Wilma (Holmes) P.; m. Susan Elizabeth Holland, Feb. 2, 1977; children: David William, Christopher Jonathan, Lisa Jeanette, Jennifer Rachel. BA in History, Brigham Young U., 1976; AM in Soviet Studies, Harvard U., 1978, PhD in Polit. Sci., 1979. Sr. rsch. analyst Radio Free Europe/Radio Liberty, Inc., Munich, 1980-83; profl. staff mem. armed svcs. com. U.S. Senate, Washington, 1983-84; sr. analyst Northrop Corp. Analysis Ctr., Washington, 1984-86; exec. dir. Bd. for Internat. Broadcasting, Washington, 1986-90; Bradley sr. rsch. assoc. Harvard U., Cambridge, Mass., 1990-93; assoc. prof. Brigham Young U., Provo, Utah, 1993-95; min. LDS Ch., 1995—. Author: The USSR in Third World Conflicts, 1976, Red Armies in Crisis, 1991, War and the Rise of the State, 1994; co-author: The Polish Drama: 1980-82, 1983; contbr. articles to profl. jours. Lay min. Ch. Jesus Christ Latter-day Saints, bishop, 1985-90, missionary, Düsseldorf, Fed. Republic Germany, 1971-73. Post doctoral fellow Harvard Ctr. for Internat. Affairs, 1979-80, Danforth fellow, 1976-79, David O. McKay scholar Brigham Young U., 1970-71, 74-76; recipient Meritorious Svc. award Pres. of U.S., 1990. Mem. Am. Polit. Sci. Assn., Am. Assn. Advancement Slavic Studies, Internat. Studies Assn. Avocations: swimming, creative writing. Office: Quorum 70 47 E South Temple Salt Lake City UT 84150-0001

PORTER, DIXIE LEE, insurance company executive, consultant; b. Bountiful, Utah, June 7, 1931; d. John Lloyd and Ida May (Robinson) Mathis. BS, U. Calif., Berkeley, 1956; MBA, U. Calif., 1957. CLU. Personnel aide City of Berkeley, 1957-59; employment supr. Kaiser Health Found., L.A., 1959-60; personnel analyst UCLA, 1961-63; personnel mgr. Reuben H. Donnelley, Santa Monica, Calif., 1963-64; personnel officer Good Samaritan Hosp., San Jose, 1965-67; fgn. svc. officer AID, Saigon, Vietnam, 1967-71; gen. agt. Charter Life Ins. Co., L.A., 1972-77, [illegible] saw Life Ins. Co., Atlanta, 1978—, Phila. Life Ins. Co., San Francisco, 1978—; pres. Womens Ins. Enterprises, Ltd., 1976—. Cons. in field. Co-chair Comprehensive Health Planning Commn. Santa Clara County, Calif., 1973-76; bd. dirs. Family Care, 1978-80, Aegis Health Corp., 1977-92, U. Calif. Sch. Bus. Adminstrn., Berkeley, 1974-76; task force on equal access to econ. power U.S. Nat. Womens Agenda, 1977—, Lake County Transp. Coun., 2000—. With USMC, 1950-52. Mem. AAUW, CLU Soc., U. Calif. Alumni Assn., U. Calif. Sch. Bus. Adminstrn. Alumni Assn., Bus. and Profl. Women, Prytanean Alumni, The Animal Soc. Los Gatos/Saratoga (pres. 1987-90), Beta Gamma Sigma, Phi Chi Theta. Republican. Episcopalian.

PORTER, JOHN PAUL, artist, educator; b. Alturas, Calif., Nov. 26, 1935; s. Carlton Lewis and Bernice (Smith-Schulz) P.; m. Carol Lynn Jones, Apr. 20, 1957 (div. Apr. 1978); children: Sean Michal, Sheryl Lynn. BA in Art, Calif. State U., Chico, 1958; MA in Art, UCLA, 1962; postgrad., Calif. State U., Chico, 1958, Calif. State U., Sacramento, 1959-67, Calif. State U., Northridge, 1958-63, Calif. State U., San Jose, 1978, Stanford U., , 1986. Cert. secondary tchr., Calif. Prof. art, chair dept., coord. dist. Antelope County Unified Sch. Dist. & Jr. Coll., Lancaster, Calif., 1958-67; prof. art Gavilan Coll., 1967-2000, chair fine arts and humanities, 1969-75. Vis. prof. U. London, 1988. Exhbns. and one-man shows include Chico State Libr., 1958, Benny Bario Gallery, Carmichael, Calif., 1959,. Greenlee-Porter Show, Allied Arts Gallery, Lancaster, 1961, Aldous Huxley Show Porter Show Allied Arts, 1962, Charles Parker Estates, Quartz Hill, Calif., 1963, Chic Sale Art Competition, Lancaster, 1964, Tumbleweed Gallery, Pearblossom, Calif., 1964, 65, 66, Edwards AFB, 1965, Oldfield Studio, Lancaster, 1967, Hollister Art League, 1967, 70, Gilroy Mus., 1972, 78, 80, Faye Dixon's Mariposa House, 1973, El Cerrito Open Studio Show, Gilroy, Calif., 1975, De Saisset Gallery, 1978, Oaktree Allied Arts Gallery, 1978-80, Spring Art-Music Fesitval, 1970-78, San Jose Art League, 1980, Children's Home Soc. Benefit, 1981, Friendly Inn Art and Flower Show, Morgan Hill, 1979, 80, 82, Vacaville State Art Competition, 1982, Am. Greeting Card Print Nat. Convention, 1983, Union Street Gallery, 1984, Russian River STate Festival, Forestville, Calif., 1984-85, Bay Area Fine Arts Exhbn., San Francisco, 1985, Steinbeck Gallery, 1986, Glen Loma Estates, 1987, Thackery House, London, 1988, Santa Clara County Fair, 1989, Avina Gallery, Sao Paolo, Brazil, 1991, Carlton House, London, 1992, Skyline Coll, 1993, San Jose Art League, 1994, Beaux Artes Show, Reno, Nev., 1995, Willows Mansion, 1996, So. Valley Symphony Benefit, 1997, Growth and Opportunity Exec. Offices, Morgan Hill, Calif., 1997, 98; editorial Bd. Collegiate Press, 1990-94; contbr. articles to profl. jours., chpts. to books; represented in over 1200 pvt. collections. Cofounder Mushroom Fesival, Morgan Hill, 1990—. Recipient Nat. AVIP Tchr. of Yr. award, 1964, award Nat. Neighborhood Youth Corp., 1967, Mayoral Citation Svc. City of Gilroy, 1978, 96; named Man of Yr. Lancaster C. of C., 1967. Mem. Commonwealth Club, South Bay Scottish Soc. (acting chief, bd. govs.), Hearaldry Soc. Great Britain, Clan Cian Soc., Nat. Thespians (award 1965). Democrat. Congregationalist. Avocations: dancing, swimming, tennis, crafts. Home: 4002 San Ysidro Way San Jose CA 95111 E-mail: art-e-facts@webtv.net

PORTER, JON CHRISTOPHER, state legislator; b. Fort Dodge, Iowa, May 16, 1955; m. Laurie Porter; children: J. Christopher, Nicole. Student, Briar Cliff Coll. Formerly dist. mgr. ins. co.; mem. Nev. Senate, Dist. 1, 1994—. Mem. Western Ins. Info. Svc./Nev. Ins. Coun.; mem. Inst. for Ins. and Risk Mgmt., U. Nev., Las Vegas. Mem. City Coun., City of Boulder City, 1983-93, mayor, 1987-91; chair bd. dirs. Las Vegas Events, pres., 1993-95; charter bd. dirs. So. Nev. Water Authority; bd. dirs. Las Vegas Conv. and Visitors Authority; bd. dirs. Nev. League of Cities; mem. civilian mil. coun. Nellis AFB. Republican. Home: 601 Whitney Ranch Dr Ste 16 Henderson NV 89014-2642

PORTER, LOUISA S. federal judge; Apptd. presiding magistrate judge so. dist. U.S. Dist. Ct. Calif., 1991. Office: 1140 US Courthouse 940 Front St San Diego CA 92101-8994 Fax: (619) 702-9925

PORTER, STEPHEN CUMMINGS, geologist, educator; b. Santa Barbara, Calif., Apr. 18, 1934; s. Lawrence Johnson Porter Jr. and Frances (Cummings) Seger; m. Anne Mary Higgins, Apr. 2, 1959; children: John, Maria, Susannah. BS, Yale U., 1955, MS, 1958, PhD, 1962. Asst. prof. geology U. Wash., Seattle, 1962-66, assoc. prof., 1966-71, prof., 1971—, dir. Quaternary Research Ctr., 1982-98. Mem. bd. earth scis. Nat. Acad. Sci., Washington, 1983-85; mem. adv. com. divsn. polar programs NSF, Washington, 1983-84; vis. fellow Clare Hall Cambridge (Eng.) U., 1980-81; guest prof. Academia Sinica, People's Republic of China, 1987—; v.p. Internat. Union Quaternary Rsch., 1992-95, pres., 1995-99. Co-author: Physical Geology, 1987, The Dynamic Earth, 1989, 92, 95, 99, The Blue Planet, 1995, 99, Environmental Geology, 1996, Dangerous Earth, 1997; editor: Late Quaternary Environments of the United States, 1983; editor Quaternary Rsch., 1976-2000; assoc. editor Radiocarbon, 1982-89, Am. Jour. Sci., 1997—; mem. editl. bd. Quaternary Sci. Revs., 1988—, Quaternary Internat., 1989—. Served to lt. USNR, 1955-57. Recipient Benjamin Silliman prize Yale U., 1962; Willis M. Tale lectr. So. Meth. U., 1984, S.F. Emmons lectr. Colo. Sci. Soc., 1996; Fulbright Hays sr. rsch. fellow, New Zealand, 1973-74. Fellow Geol. Soc. Am., Arctic Inst. N.Am. (bd. govs.), AAAS; mem. Am. Quaternary Assn. (coun., pres. 1992-94). Avocations: photography, mountaineering. Home: 18034 15th Ave NW Seattle WA 98177-3305 Office: U Wash Dept Earth and Space Scis PO Box 351360 Seattle WA 98195-1310

PORTERFIELD, JAMES TEMPLE STARKE, business administration educator; b. Annapolis, Md., July 7, 1920; s. Lewis Broughton and Maud Paxton (Starke) P.; m. Betty Gold, Apr. 23, 1949 (dec. 1985); m. Janet Patricia Gardiner Roggeveen, Oct. 5, 1986. AB, U. Calif., Berkeley, 1942; MBA, Stanford U., 1948, PhD, 1955. From asst. to assoc. prof. Harvard U. Bus. Sch., Boston, 1955-59; prof. fin. Stanford (Calif.) U. Grad. Sch. Bus., 1959-79, James Irvin Miller Prof. fin., 1979-90, prof. emeritus, 1990—; prof. IMEDE Mgmt. Devel. Inst., Lausanne, Switzerland, 1962-63. Author: Life Insurance Stocks as Investments, 1955, Investment Decisions and Capital Costs, 1965; co-author: Case Problems in Finance, 1959. Served as lt. USNR, 1941-46. Recipient Salgo Noren award Stanford U., 1966, Richard W. Lyman award Stanford U. Alumni Assn., 1995. Home: 295 Golden Oak Dr Portola Vally CA 94028-7730 Office: Stanford U Grad Sch Bus Stanford CA 94305

PORTERFIELD, RICHARD B. career officer; Grad., U.S. Naval Acad., 1972; MS in Mgmt., Salve Regina Coll.; MS in Nat. Resource Strategy, Indsl. Coll. of Armed Forces, Washington. Commd. ensign USN, 1972; advanced through ranks to rear adm. USNR; various assignments to dir. for intelligence Nat. Mil. Joint Intelligence Ctr., 1991; dir. for requirements, plans, policy and programs (N20) OPNAV, 1994-95; dir. for intelligence J2 U.S. Pacific Command. Office: PO Box 64010 Camp H M Smith HI 96861-4010

PORTIS, ALAN MARK, physicist, educator; b. Chgo., July 17, 1926; s. Lyon and Ruth (Libman) P.; m. Beverly Portis, Sept. 5, 1948; children: Jonathan, Stephen, Sara, Eliyahu. Ph.B., U. Chgo., 1948; A.B., U. Calif., Berkeley, 1949, Ph.D., 1953. Mem. faculty U. Pitts., 1953-56, U. Calif.-Berkeley, 1956—, prof. physics, 1964-95, prof. emeritus, 1995—, asst. to chancellor for research, 1966-67, asso. dean grad. div., 1967-68, dir. Lawrence Hall Sci., 1969-72, univ. ombudsman, 1981-83, 92-94, assoc. dean Coll. Engring., 1983-87, 94-95. Author: Electromagnetic Fields/Sources and Media, 1978, Electrodynamics of High-Temperature Superconductors, 1993; contbg. author: Berkeley Physics Laboratory, 1964, 65, 66, 71. Fulbright fellow, 1961, 67, Guggenheim fellow, 1965, SERC sr. fellow, U.K., 1991-92. Fellow Am. Phys. Soc.; mem. Am. Assn. Physics Tchrs. (Robert Andrews Millikan award 1966). E-mail: portis@socrates.berkeley.edu

PORTNOY, DANIEL, microbiology educator; b. Sept. 3, 1956; married; 1 child. BA in Bacteriology, UCLA, 1978; PhD in Microbiology and Immunology, U. Washington, St. Louis, 1983; postgrad., Stanford U., 1981-83. Postdoctoral fellow Zanvil Cohn Lab. Rockefeller U., 1983-85; from instr. to asst. prof. dept. microbiology and immunology U. Washington Sch. Medicine, 1986-88; asst. prof. dept. microbiology U. Pa. Sch. Medicine, Phila., 1988-92, assoc. prof. dept. microbiology, 1992—. Lectr. in field. Author numerous chpts. to books, reviews and books; mem. editl. bd. Infection and Immunity, 1990—, Jour. Exptl. Medicine, 1992—; reviewer NIH, 1989, 90, 93; contbr. over 40 articles to profl. jours. Am. Soc. for Microbiology Found. lectr., 1990; recipient Nat. Rsch. Svc. award NIAID, 1985-86, Merit award NIAID, NIH, 1995, Rsch. award in microbiology and immunology Eli Lilly and Co., 1996, grants NIH-NIAID, 1993—. Office: U Calif Molecular Cell Biology 401 Barker Hall Spc 3202 Berkeley CA 94720-3202

PORTUESI, DONNA RAE, psychotherapist, consultant; b. Easton, Pa., Nov. 19, 1949; d. Peter and Alice Lorraine (Hull) Stagnito; m. Sebastian Portuesi, Jr., Nov. 22, 1972 (div. Sept. 1986); 1 child, Christi Noel Buck. AA, No. Seattle C.C., 1987; BA magna cum laude, Western Wash. U., 1989; MSW cum laude, U. Wash., 1992. Registered counselor, Wash. Sec. for Sen. Harry Byrd, Jr. U.S. Senate, Washington, 1970-72; founder Denver chpt. Nat. Found. for Crohn's and Colitis, 1975-79; counselor Mental Health Svcs., Everett, Wash., 1982-84; co-founder Adoption Search and Counseling Cons., Seattle, 1990-96; psychotherapist, cons. ASCC Svcs., Seattle, 1992—. Press and speech asst. U.S. Senate, Washington, 1970-72; post adoption cons., Seattle, 1992-96; workshop developer, leader Adoption Search and Counseling, Seattle, 1992-96, exec. dir., 1990-96; ind. search cons. Reunite Adoptees and Birth Parents, 1991—. Contbr. articles to profl. jours. Mem. NASW, Am. Counseling Assn., Am. Adoption Congress. Democrat. Avocations: piano, travel, pets, reading, arts and crafts. Home and Office: 12718 12th Ave NW Seattle WA 98177-4322 E-mail: ASCCARC@aol.com

PORZAK, GLENN E. lawyer; b. Ill., Aug. 22, 1948; m. Judy Lea McGinnis, Dec. 19, 1970; children: Lindsay and Austin. BA with distinction, U. Colo., 1970, JD, 1973. Bar: Colo. 1973. Assoc. Holme Roberts & Owen, Denver, 1973-80, ptnr., 1980-85, mng. ptnr. Boulder office, 1985-95; mng. ptnr. Porzak Browning & Bushong LLP, Boulder, 1996—. Bd. dirs. Wells Fargo Bank Boulder, 1993—. Contbr. articles to profl. jours. 1st Lt. U.S. Army, 1970-78. Named Disting. Alumnus U. Colo., 1991. Fellow Explorers Club (bd. dirs. 1995-96, Citation of Merit 1998); mem. Am. Alpine Club (pres. 1988-91), Colo. Mtn. Club (pres. 1983, hon. mem. 1983—), Colo. Outward Bound (trustee 1992—, vice chmn. 1997-99, chmn. 1999-2001), Phi Beta Kappa. Achievements include reaching summit of Mt. Everest, climbing highest peak on all seven continents. Home: 771 7th St Boulder CO 80302-7402 Office: Porzak Browning & Bushong 929 Pearl St Ste 300 Boulder CO 80302-5108

POST, ROBERT CHARLES, law educator; b. Bklyn., Oct. 17, 1947; s. Ted and Thelma (Feifel) P.; m. Fran Layton, Jan. 22, 1981; children: Alexander, Amelia. AB, Harvard U., 1969, PhD, 1980; JD, Yale U., 1977. Bar: D.C. 1979, Calif. 1983. Law clk. to chief judge U.S. Ct. Appeals (D.C. cir.), 1977-78; law clk. to justice William Brennen Jr. U.S. Supreme Ct. D.C., 1978-79; assoc. Williams & Connelly, Washington, 1980-82; acting prof. law U. Calif., Berkeley, 1983-87, prof. law, 1987-94, Alexander F. and May T. Morrison prof. law, 1994—. Author: Constitutional Domains, 1995; editor: Law and the Order of Culture, 1991, Censorship and Silencing: Practices of Cultural Regulation, 1998; co-editor: Race and Representation: Affirmative Action, 1998, Human Rights in Political Transistions: Gettysburg to Bosnia, 1999. Gen. counsel AAUP, 1992-94. Fellow Guggenheim Found., 1990-91, Am. Coun. Gen. Socs., 1990-91. Mem. AAUP, Am. Acad. Arts and Scis. Office: U Calif Sch Law Boalt Hall Berkeley CA 94720

POST, WILLIAM JOSEPH, utility executive; b. Salem, Ohio, Oct. 13, 1950; s. John Joseph and Barbara Louise (Walton) P.; m. Mary Kay Lane, May 2, 1987; children: Kathryn Leigh, Carly Nancy. BS, Ariz. State U., 1972. Budget mgr. Ariz. Pub. Svc., Phoenix, 1978-82, contr., 1982-85, v.p., contr., 1985-87, v.p. fin. and rates, 1987—. Bd. dir. Tumbleweed, Phoenix, Tempe Leadership, 1987, YMCA, Phoenix, 1989. Staff sgt. U.S. Army, 1969-75. Republican. Presbyterian. Home: 4824 E Crystal Ln Paradise Valley AZ 85253-2955 Office: Pinnacle West Capital 400 N. Fifth St Phoenix AZ 85004

POSTAER, LARRY, advertising executive; b. Chgo. Grad., U. Mo. Sch. Journalism, 1959. Catalog copywriter Sears; with Stern, Walters & Simmons, Chgo., 1962-64, creative dir., 1964-76; sr. v.p., group creative dir. Needham Harper & Steers, Chgo., 1976-81, exec. v.p., dir. creative svcs. L.A., 1981-86; co-founder, exec. v.p., dir. creative svcs. Rubin Postaer and Assoc., Santa Monica, 1986—. Named Co-leader of Yr. for 1990, Western States Advt. Agys. Assn., 1991. Office: 1333 2d St Santa Monica CA 90401-1100

POSTEL, MITCHELL PAUL, association administrator; b. Chgo., May 27, 1952; s. Bernard and Rosalin P.; m. Kristie McCune, Mar. 29, 1981. BA, U. Calif.-Berkeley, 1974; MA, U. Calif.-Santa Barbara, 1977. Devel. officer San Mateo County Hist. Mus., San Mateo, Calif., 1977-81; exec. dir. Fort Point and Army Mus. Assn., San Francisco, 1981-84, San Mateo County Hist. Assn., 1984—. Faculty Coll. of San Mateo. Author: History of the Burlingame Country Club, 1982, Peninsula Portrait: A Pictorial History of San Mateo County, San Mateo: A Centennial History; Seventy-five Years in San Francisco, History of Rotary Club No. 2. Mem. San Mateo County Historic Resources, Presidio Hist. Soc. (bd. dirs.). Office: San Mateo County Hist Assn 777 Hamilton St Redwood City CA 94063-1618

POSTER, STEVEN BARRY, cinematographer, photographer, publisher, digital imaging consultant; b. Chgo., Mar. 1, 1944; s. David and Lillian Violet (Diamondstone) P. Student, So. Ill. U., 1962-64, L.A. Art Ctr. Coll. Design, 1964-66; BS, Ill. Inst. Tech., 1967. Pres. Posters Internat. Ltd., L.A., 1980. Dir. photography (films) Strange Brew, 1983, Testament, 1984, Heavenly Kid, 1985, Blue City, 1986, The Boy Who Could Fly, 1986, Someone to Watch Over Me, 1986, (Am. Soc. Cinematographers nomination 1987), Big Top Pee Wee, 1987, Next of Kin, 1988, Opportunity Knocks, 1989, Rocky V, 1990, Life Stinks, 1991, Cemetery Club, 1993, Roswell, 1994, Strangers on a Train, 1996, The Color of Justice, 1996, Rocket Man, 1997, UN Chance Sur Deux, 1997, Donnie Darko, 2000, Stuart Little II, 2001. Mem. Am. Soc. Cinematographers (bd. dirs., pub. chair), Leica Hist. Soc. Am., Acad. Motion Picture Arts and Scis., Can. Soc. Cinematographers, Internat. Assn. Panoramic Photographers, Internat. Alliance of Theatrical and Stage Employees (bd. dirs.). Democrat. Jewish. Avocations: still photography, computers, bicycles.

POTASH, JEREMY WARNER, public relations executive; b. Monrovia, Calif., June 30, 1946; d. Fenwick Bryson and Joan Antony (Blair) Warner; m. Stephen Jon Potash; 1 son, Aaron Warner. AA, Citrus Coll., 1965; BA, Pomona Coll., 1967. With Forbes Mag., N.Y.C., 1967-69, Japan External Trade Orgn., San Francisco, 1970-75; v.p., co-founder Potash & Co. Pub. Rels., Oakland, Calif., 1980-87. Founding exec. dir. Calif.-Asia Bus. Coun., Oakland, 1991—; exec. dir. Customs Brokers and Forwarders Assn., San Francisco, 1990—; adv. bd. Asia Pacific Econ. Rev., 1996—; mem. No. Calif. Dist. Export Coun., 2000—, Pacific Coun. Internat. Policy, 2000—. Editor: Southeast Asia Environmental Directory, 1994; editor: Southeast Asia Infrastructure Directory, 1995-96. Bd. dirs. Judah L. Magnes Mus., Berkeley, 1981-94, co-founder docent program, 1980, pres. Women's Guild, 1980-81; bd. dirs. Temple Sinai, Oakland, 1984-86; pres. East Bay region Women's Am. Orgn. for Rehab. Through Tng., 1985-86. Recipient Export Citizen of Yr. award No. Calif. Export Coun., U.S. Dept. Commerce, 1998. Mem. World Trade Club San Francisco, Oakland Women's Lit. Soc., Book Club Calif. Office: Potash & Co Pub Rels 1946 Embarcadero Oakland CA 94606-5213

POTEMPA, KATHLEEN, dean, nursing educator; Diploma in nursing, Providence Hosp. Sch. Nursing, Southfield, Mich., 1970; BA in Psychology summa cum laude, U. Detroit, 1974; MS in Nursing, Rush U., 1978, D of Nursing Sci., 1986. Charge nurse coronary ICU Holy Cross Hosp., Ft. Lauderdale, Fla., 1970-71; staff nurse, charge nurse cardiovasc. ICU Henry Ford Hosp., Detroit, 1971-74; nurse practitioner Rush-Presbyn.-St. Luke's Med. Ctr., Chgo., 1974-75; nursing edn. coord. dept. nursing Michael Reese Hosp. and Med. Ctr., Chgo., 1975-77, nursing supr., 1977-78; asst. unit leader dept. gerontol. nursing Rush U. Coll. Nursing, Chgo., 1978-79, asst. chmn., 1979-80, assoc. chmn., asst. prof. gerontol. nursing, 1980-85, asst. prof. gerontol. nursing, 1985-86; asst. prof. nursing, dept. internal medicine, practitioner Rush Med. Coll., Rush U., 1987-88; asst. then assoc. prof. dept. med.-surg. nursing Coll. Nursing, U. Ill., Chgo., 1988—, dir. tng., pre and postdoctoral fellowship instnl. rsch., 1992—, exec. assoc. dean Coll. Nursing, 1994-95, interim dean Coll. Nursing, 1995-96; prof., dean Sch. Nursing Oreg. Health Scis. U., Portland, 1996—. Rsch. assoc. Robert Wood Johnson Tchg. Nursing Home Project, VA Edward Hines Jr. Hosp., Hines, Ill., 1985-86, co-dir. Exercise Rsch. Lab., 1985-86; dir. nursing Johnston R. Bowman Health Ctr. for Elderly, Rush Presbyn. St. Luke's Med. Ctr., Chgo., 1980-85. Contbr. articles to profl. jours. Fellow Am. Acad. Nursing; mem. ANA (coun. nurse rschrs.), Am. Soc. Hypertension, Gerontol. Soc. Am., Midwest Nursing Rsch. Soc., Heart Assn. Met. Chgo., Am. Heart Assn. Oreg., Ill. Coun. Nurse Rschrs., Am. Heart Assn. (coun. cardiovasc. nursing, coun. hypertension, coun. on strokes), Sigma Theta Tau. Office: SN ADM Oreg Health Scis U Sch Nursing 3181 SW Sam Jackson Park Rd Portland OR 97201-3011

POTTENGER, MARK MCCLELLAND, computer programmer; b. Tucson, Feb. 9, 1955; s. Henry Farmer and Zipporah Herrick (Pottenger) Dobyns. BA, UCLA, 1976, DDiv (hon.), 1998. Data entry operator Astro Computing, Pelham, N.Y., 1976-77; programmer/analyst LA-CCRS, L.A., 1977-80; programmer/analyst cons. L.A. and San Diego, 1977—, R. Gonzalez Mgmt., L.A., 1980—. Rsch. dir. Internat. Soc. for Astrol. Rsch., L.A., 1985-95. Editor: Astrological Research Methods, 1995; co-author: Tables for Aspect Research, 1986; editor The Mutable Dilemma, 1977-99; author: (computer programs) CCRS Horoscope program, 1977-92, Frequencies for Aspect Rsch., 1986-92. Recipient Jansky award Aquarius Workshops, L.A., 1989. Mem. Internat. Soc. for Astrol. Rsch., Nat. Coun. for Geocosmic Rsch. Democrat. Mem. Religious Sci. Ch. Avocations: reading science fiction and regencies. Home and Office: 3808 49th St San Diego CA 92105-2101 E-mail: markpott@pacbell.net

POTTRUCK, DAVID STEVEN, brokerage house executive; b. 1948; BA, U. Pa., 1970, MBA, 1972. Now pres., CEO U.S. Govt., 1972-74; with Arthur Young & Co., 1974 76, sr. cons.; with Citibank N.Am., 1976-81, v.p.; with Shearson/Am. Express, 1981-84, sr. v.p. consumer mktg. and advt.; with Charles Schwab & Co., San Francisco, 1984—; exec. v.p. mktg., br. adminstr. Charles Schwab and Co., Inc.; pres., co-CEO The Charles Schwab and Co., Inc; pres., CEO Charles Schwab & Co.; pres., COO The Charles Schwab Corp., pres., co-CEO. Office: Charles Schwab & Co Inc 101 Montgomery St Ste 200 San Francisco CA 94104-4175

POTTS, ERWIN REA, newspaper executive; b. Pineville, N.C., Apr. 20, 1932; s. Jennings Bryan and Edith Maxine (Matthews) P.; m. Silvia Antuna Montalbo, Feb. 18, 1961; children: Matthew Kingsley, Jeffrey Manuel, Bryan Erwin (dec.). Student, Mars Hill (N.C.) Jr. Coll., 1950-52; A.B. in Journalism, U. N.C., 1954. Reporter Charlotte News, 1954; reporter, state editor Miami Herald, Miami, Fla., 1958-64; editor, pub. North Dade (Fla.) Jour., 1964-67, asst. mng. editor, city editor Miami Herald, 1967-70; v.p., gen. mgr. Tallahassee Democrat, 1970-73, Charlotte (N.C.) Observer, 1973-75; dir. newspaper ops. McClatchy Co., 1975-79, v.p. newspaper ops., 1979-97; v.p. corp. McLatchey Co., 1997—, exec. v.p., 1985, pres., 1987, pres., CEO, 1989, chmn., CEO, 1995, chmn., 1996-2001, also bd. dirs. Bd. dirs. Stanford U. Knight Fellwoships. With USMC, 1955-58. Mem. Newspaper Assn. Am. (bd. dirs., nominating com.), Sacramento Regional Found. (bd. dirs.). Office: The McClatchy Co PO Box 15779 Sacramento CA 95852-0779

POTVIN, FELIX, professional hockey player; b. Anjou, Que., Canada, July 23, 1971; Goalie Chicoutimi, QMJHL, 1988-91, St. John's, AHL, 1991-92, Toronto Maple Leafs, 1991-99, N.Y. Islanders, 1999, Vancouver Canucks, 1999—. Recipient Goaltender of the Year Award, Can. Hockey League, 1990-91, Hap Emms Mem. Trophy, 1990-91, Jacques Plante Trophy, 1990-91, Shell Cup, 1990-91, Guy Lafleur Trophy, 1990-91, Baz Bastien Trophy, 1991-92, Dudley Garrett Mem. Trophy, 1991-92. Achievements include All-Star first team goalie, QMJHL, 1990-91, All-Star first team goalie, AHL, 1991-92, All-Rookie Team, NHL, 1992-93. Office: NY Islanders Vancouver Canucks GM Pl 800 Griffiths Way Vancouver BC Canada V6B 6G1

POULOS-WOOLLEY, PAIGE M. public relations executive; b. Woodland, Calif., Apr. 26, 1958; d. Paul William Jr. and Frances Marie (Gibson) Poulos; m. John Stuart Woolley, Jr., Feb. 3, 1990. Student, U. Calif., Davis, 1977-80. Mgr. pub. rels. Somerset Wine Co., N.Y.C. and San Martin, Calif., 1982-88; dir. comm. The Beverage Source, San Francisco, 1988-89, Rutherford (Calif.) Hill Winery, 1989-90; pres. Paige Poulos Comm., Berkeley, Calif., 1990—. Founder, chmn. WINECOM, 1992—. Pub. rels. editor: Practical Winery & Vineyards, 1994—; wine, epicurean travel editor Focus Mag. Mem. Pub. Rels. Soc. Am. (bd. dirs. 1993—, sec. 1994, pres. East Bay chpt. 1994-96, editor newsletter food and beverage sect. 1993-95, chmn. food and beverage sect. 1996-97), Women in Comm., Acad. Wine Comm. (program chair 1994, sec. 1998, pres. 2000), Internat. Assn. Bus. Communicators, Am. Inst. Wine and Food, Internat. Assn. Culinary Profls., San Francisco Profl. Food Soc., Sonoma Culinary Guild (bd. dirs. 1998-99), Assn. Epicurean Edn. of Children. Republican. Episcopalian. Avocations: horseback riding, diving, skiing, wine collecting. Office: Paige Poulos Comm PO Box 8087 Berkeley CA 94707-8087

POULTER, CHARLES DALE, chemist, educator, consultant; b. Monroe, La., Aug. 29, 1942; s. Erwin and Mary Helen Poulter; m. Susan Raetzsch, Aug. 24, 1964; children: Mary Christa, Gregory Thomas. BS, La. State U., Baton Rouge, 1964; PhD, U. Calif., Berkeley, 1967. NIH postdoctoral fellow UCLA, 1967-68; asst. prof. chemistry U. Utah, Salt Lake City, 1969-75, assoc. prof., 1975-78, prof., 1978-94, John A. Widtsoe prof. chemistry, 1994—, chair dept. chemistry, 1995-2000. Cons. Amoco Rsch. Ctr., Naperville, Ill., 1985-90, Merck Sharp & Dohme, Rahway, N.J., 1986-90, Bristol-Myers Squibb, Princeton, N.J., 1989-93, Zeneca Ag

Products, Richmond, Calif., 1993-95. Fellow AAAS; mem. Am. Chem. Soc. (organic exec. com. 1983-86, biol. divsn. councillor 1993, chair organic divsn. 1998, Ernest Guenther award 1991, Utah award 1992, Arthur C. Cope scholar 1998). Office: U Utah Dept Chemistry Salt Lake City UT 84112-0850

POULTON, L. STEVEN, state legislator; b. Salt Lake City, Jan. 10, 1950; m. Andrea Robins. BA in Bus. Mgmt., U. Utah. Lic. property and casualty ins. agt./broker, Utah; cert. ins. counselor. Formerly in ins. bus.; mem. Utah Senate, Dist. 9, Salt Lake City, 1994—; mem. bus., labor and econ. devel. com., human svcs. com.; mem. health and human svcs. appropriations; chair rules com., asst. majority whip. Treas., Salt Lake County Rep. Party. Mem. Salt Lake C. of C., Salt Lake Rotary Club. Republican. Home: 4524 Briarcreek Dr Salt Lake City UT 84117-4573 Fax: 801-486-7541

POUND, JOHN BENNETT, lawyer; b. Champaign, Ill., Nov. 17, 1946; s. William R. and Louise Catherine (Kelly) P.; m. Mary Ann Hanson, June 19, 1971; children: Meghan Elizabeth, Matthew Fitzgerald. BA, U. N.Mex., 1968; JD, Boston Coll., 1971. Bar: N. Mex. 1971, U.S. Dist. Ct. N. Mex. 1971, U.S. Ct. Appeals (10th cir.) 1972, U.S. Supreme Ct., 1993. Law clk. to Hon. Oliver Seth, U.S. Ct. Appeals, 10th Cir., Santa Fe, 1971-72. Asst. counsel Supreme Ct. Disciplinary Bd., 1977-83, dist. rev. officer, 1984—; mem. Supreme Ct. Com. on Jud. Performance Evaluation, 1983-85; bd. dirs. Archdiocese Santa Fe Cath. Social Svcs., 1995—. Contbr. articles to profl. jours. Pres. bd. dirs. N.Mex. Ind. Coll. Fund, Santa Fe; chmn. N.Mex. Dem. Leadership Coun., 1991—; bd. dirs. Santa Fe Boys Club, 1989-92; rules com. N.Mex. Dem. Party, 1982—; v.p. Los Alamos Nat. Lab. Comm. Coun., 1985-90; fin. chmn. N.Mex. Clinton for Pres. campaign, 1992; co-chmn. Clinton-Gore Re-election Campaign, N.Mex., 1996, 2000 Fellow Am. Bar Found., Am. Coll. Trial Lawyers, N.Mex. Bar Found.; mem. ABA, Am. Bd. Trial Advocates, N.Mex. Bar Assn. (health law sect. 1987—), Santa Fe County Bar Assn. Democrat. Roman Catholic. Avocations: history, foreign language, literature, swimming, baseball. Office: Herrera Long Pound Komer PA PO Box 5098 2200 Brothers Rd Santa Fe NM 87505-6903 E-mail: HLPLaw@aol.com

POWELL, JAMES LAWRENCE, museum director; b. Berea, Ky., July 17, 1936; s. Robert Lain and Lizena (Davis) P.; m. Joan Hartmann; children: Marla, Dirk, Joanna. AB, Berea Coll., 1958; PhD, MIT, 1962; DSc (hon.), Oberlin Coll., 1983; LHD (hon.), Tohoku Gakuin U., 1986; DSc (hon.), Beaver Coll., 1992. Mem. faculty Oberlin Coll., Ohio, 1962-83, also prof. geology, asso. dean, 1973-75, v.p., provost, 1976-83; pres. Franklin and Marshall Coll., Lancaster, Pa., 1983-88, Reed Coll., Portland, Oreg., 1988-91; pres., chief exec. officer The Franklin Inst., Phila., 1991-94; pres., dir. Los Angeles County Mus. Natural History, L.A., 1994—. Mem. Nat. Sci. Bd., 1986-98. Author: Strontium Isotope Geology, 1972, Pathways to Leadership: Achieving and Sustaining Success: A Guide for Nonprofit Executives, 1995, Night Comes to the Coctzcems; Dinosaur Extinction and the Transformation of Modern Geology, 1998. Fellow Geol. Soc. Am. Office: LA County Mus Nat Hist 900 Exposition Blvd Los Angeles CA 90007-4057

POWELL, RICHARD C. physicist, educator, researcher; b. Lincoln, Nebr., Dec. 20, 1939; s. William Charles and Allis (Conger) P.; m. Gwendolyn Cline Powell, June 24, 1962; children: Douglas W., David M. BS in Engring., U.S. Naval Acad., 1962; MS in Physics, Arizona State U., 1964, PhD in Physics, 1967. Staff scientist Air Force Cambridge Rsch. Labs., Bedford, Mass., 1964-68, Sandia Nat. Lab., Albuquerque, 1968-71; prof. Okla. State U., 1971-92; prof. dir. optical sci. ctr. U. Ariz., Tucson, 1992-98, v.p. rsch. and grad. studies, 1999—. Reviewer numerous physics jours. and funding agys.; cons. laser rsch. with several indsl. and govt. agys. Editor-in-chief Jour. Optical Materials, 1992-98; patents include Holographic Gratings in Rare Earth Doped Glasses and pump wavelength tuning of optical parometric oscillators with Okla. State U., 1988; contbr. numerous articles to profl. jours. Recipient over 40 grants for rsch. support, 1971—. Fellow Am. Phys. Soc. (co-chmn. Internat. Laser Sci. Conf. 1985, chmn. 1986, vice chmn. Topical Group on Laser Sci., 1986, chmn. 1987, APS rep. Joint Coun. on Quantum Electronics, 1986-90), Optical Soc. Am. (mem. bd. dirs. 1993-95, v.p. 1999, pres. 2001, mem. program com. OSA Photoacoustic Spectroscopy Mtg., 1979, mem. nom. com. 1982, organizer Laser Tech. Group Session 1985, com. mem. Meggers award, 1986, 89, 90, chmn. program com. CLEO, 1988, mem. book pub. com., 1992—, mem. awards com., 1994—, mem. organizing com. Adv. Solid State Laser Conf., 1992—, OSA rep. Internat. Coun. on Optics, 1994—, v.p. 1999; mem. IEEE (mem. solid state lasers adv. com., 1987—, program com. mem. Nonlinear Optical Materials Mtg., 1994), Sigma Xi (hon. lectr. 1983-84). Episcopalian. Avocations: skiing, fishing, softball, jogging, hiking. Office: U Ariz Rsch & Grad Studies Tucson AZ 85721-0001

POWELL, SANDY, costume designer; b. London, England, Jan. 12, 1959; Costumer designer for films including Caravaggio, 1986; The Last of England, 1987; Stormy Monday, 1988; Venus Peter, 1989; Killing Dad, 1989; For Queen and Country, 1989; Shadow of China, 1991; The Pope Must Die, 1991; Edward II 1991; The Miracle, 1991; Orlando, 1992 (Nominated BAFTA Award, Academy Award; Best Costume Design, 1994); The Crying Game, 1992; Wittgenstein, 1993; Being Human, 1993; Interview with a Vampire, 1994 (Nominated BAFTA Award, Best Costume Design, 1995); Rob Roy, 1995; Michael Collins, 1996; The Wings of a Dove, 1997 (Nominated Golden Satellite Award, BAFTA Award; Best Costume Design, 1998); The Butcher Boy, 1997; Velvet Goldmine, 1998 (Nominated Academy Award, Best Costume Design; Won Best Costume Design, British Academy Awards, 1998); Hilary and Jackie, 1998; Shakespeare in Love, 1998 (Won Academy Award, Best Costume Design; Nominated BAFTA Award, Best Costume Design, 1998). Office: c/o Costume Designers Guild 13949 Ventura Blvd Ste 309 Sherman Oaks CA 91423-3570

POWELL, TREVOR JOHN DAVID, archivist; b. Hamilton, Ont., Can., Feb. 3, 1948; s. David Albert and Morvydd Ann May (Williams) P.; m. Marian Jean McKillop, May 1, 1976. BA, U. Sask., Regina, 1971; MA, U. Regina, Sask., Can., 1980. Staff archivist Sask. Archives Bd., Regina, Sask., 1973-80, dir., 1980-86, acting provincial archivist, 1986-87, provincial archivist, 1988—. Co-author: Living Faith: A Pictorial History of Diocese of Qu'Appelle; author: From Tent to Cathedral: A History of St. Paul's Cathedral, Regina. Archivist Diocese of Qu'Appelle, Regina, Sask., 1971—, registrar, 1979—; archivist, eccles. Province of Rupert's Land, Winnipeg, Man., 1988—; mem. adv. coun. Sask. Order of Merit, 1988-95, Sask Honours, 1995—; chair selection com. Sask Vol. medal, 1995-96, Can. 125 medal, 1992. Mem. Soc. Am. Archivists, Can. Hist. Assn., Commonwealth Archivists Assn., Sask. Coun. Archives (sec.-treas. 1987-88, 90-92, pres. 1994-96, Can. Coun. Archives rep. 1994-96), Assn. Can. Archivists (bd. dirs. 1979-81). Anglican. Avocations: gardening, walking, reading, music, bird watching. Home: 241 Orchard Cres Regina SK Canada S4S 5B9 Office: Sask Archives Bd 3303 Hillsdale St Univ Regina Regina SK Canada S4S 0A2 E-mail: tpowell@archives.gov.sk.ca

POWER, DENNIS MICHAEL, museum director; b. Pasadena, Calif., Feb. 18, 1941; s. John Dennis and Ruth Augusta (Mott) P.; m. Kristine Moneva Fisher, Feb. 14, 1965 (div. Aug. 1984); children: Michael Lawrence, Matthew David; m. Leslie Gabrielle Baldwin, July 6, 1985; 1 stepchild, Katherine G. Petrosky. BA, Occidental Coll., 1962, MA, 1964; PhD, U. Kans., 1967. Asst. curator ornithology Royal Ont. Mus., Toronto, Can., assoc. curator Can., 1971-72, asst. prof. zoology U. Toronto, 1967-72; exec. dir. Santa Barbara (Calif.) Mus. Natural History, 1972-94, Oakland Mus. of Calif., 1994—. Biol. rschr.; cons. ecology. Editor: The California Islands: Proceedings of a Multidisciplinary Symposium, 1980, Current Ornithology, vol. 6, 1989, vol. 7, 1990, vol. 8, 1991, vol. 9, 1992, vol. 10, 1993, vol. 11, 1993, vol. 12, 1995; contbr. articles to sci. jours. Bd. dirs. Univ. Club Santa Barbara, 1989-92, v.p., 1991-92; bd. dirs. Santa Barbara Chamber Orch., 1990-94, v.p., 1991-94; mem. adv. coun. Santa Cruz Island Found., 1989—; mem. discipline adv. com. for museology Coun. for Internat. Exch. of Scholars, 1991-95; mem. Cultural Affairs Commn., City of Oakland, 1999—. NSF fellow U. Kans., 1967; NRC grantee, 1968-72, 74-78. Fellow Am. Ornithologists Union (life, sec. 1981-83, v.p. 1988-89), Am. Assn. Mus. (mem. coun. 1980-83), Calif. Acad. Scis.; mem. AAAS, Cooper Ornithol. Soc. (bd. dirs. 1976-79, pres. 1978-81, hon. mem. 1993), Calif. Assn. Mus. (bd. dirs. 1981-92, chmn. 1987-89), Western Mus. Conf. (bd. dirs. 1977-83, pres. 1981-83), Am. Soc. Naturalists, Assn. Sci. Mus. Dirs., Ecol. Soc., Am. Soc. Study of Evolution, Soc. Systematic Zoology, Bohemian Club, Sigma Xi. Office: Oakland Mus Calif 1000 Oak St Oakland CA 94607-4820

POWER, FRANCIS WILLIAM, newspaper publisher; b. Webster, S.D., Aug. 12, 1925; s. Frank B. and Esther C. (Fowler) P.; m. Margaret Jean Atkinson, Mar. 24, 1951; children: Patricia Ann, John Michael, Kerry Jean. B.B.A., U. N.Mex., 1948. Display advt. sales rep. The Register, Santa Ana, Calif., 1948-51; advt. mgr. Valley Morning Star, Harlingen, Tex., 1951-62; gen. mgr. Pampa (Tex.) Daily News, 1962-69; bus. mgr. Brownsville (Tex.) Herald, 1969-75; pub. The Lima (Ohio) News, 1975-91; v.p. Freedom Comm., Inc., until 1991; ret., 1991. Served with USNR, 1943-46. Roman Catholic. Clubs: Shawnee Country, Rotary, Elks. Office: Freedom Comm Inc 17666 Fitch Irvine CA 92614-6022

POWER, JOHN BRUCE, lawyer; b. Glendale, Calif., Nov. 11, 1936; m. Sandra Garfield, Apr. 27, 1998; children by previous marriage: Grant, Mark, Boyd. AB magna cum laude, Occidental Coll., 1958; JD, NYU, 1961; postdoctoral, Columbia U., 1972. Bar: Calif. 1962. Assoc. O'Melveny & Myers, L.A., 1961-70, ptnr., 1970-97, resident ptnr. Paris, 1973-75; Sheffelman disting. lectr. Sch. Law, U. Wash., Seattle, 1997. Mem. Social Svcs. Commn. City of L.A., 1993, pres., 1993; pres. circle, exec. com. Occidental Coll., 1979-82, 91-94, chair, 1993-94. Contbr. articles to jours. Bd. dirs. Met. L.A. YMCA, 1988—, treas., 1998—; mem. bd. mgrs. Stuart Ketchum Downtown YMCA, 1985-92, pres., 1989-90; mem. Los Angeles County Rep. Ctrl. Com., 1962-63; trustee Occidental Coll., 1992—, vice-chmn., 1998-2001, chmn., 2001—. Root Tilden scholar. Fellow Am. Coll. Comml. Fin. Lawyers (bd. regents 1999—); mem. ABA (comml. fin. svcs. com., com. 3d party legal opinions, UCC com., bus. law sect.), Am. Bar Found. (life), Calif. Bar Assn. (chmn. partnerships and unincorporated assns. com. 1982-83, chmn. uniform commn. code com. 1984-85, exec. com. 1987-91, chmn. bus. law sect. 1990-91, chmn. coun. sect. chairs 1992-93, liaison to state bar commn. on future of legal profession and state bar 1993-95), L.A. County Bar Assn. (exec. com. comml. law and bankruptcy sect. 1970-73, 86-89), Internat. Bar Assn., Fin. Lawyers Conf. (bd. govs. 1982—, pres. 1984-85), Exec. Svc. Corps (sec. 1985-2000, vice-chmn. 2000—, dir. 1994—), Occidental Coll. Alumni Assn. (pres. 1967-68), Phi Beta Kappa (councilor So. Calif. 1982—, pres. 1990-92). Office: O Melveny & Myers 400 S Hope St Los Angeles CA 90071-2899

POWER, THOMAS MICHAEL, economist, educator; b. Milw., May 12, 1940; s. Paul C. and Edith (Thomas) P.; m. Pamela Shore, June 13, 1977; children: Donovan, Kate. BA, Lehigh U., 1962; MA, Princeton U., 1965, PhD, 1971. Instr. Lehigh U., Bethlehem, Pa., 1966-67, Princeton (N.J.) U., 1967-68; from asst. to assoc. prof. U. Mont., Missoula, 1968-78, prof. econ., chmn., 1978—. Author: Economic Value of Quality of Life, 1980, The Economic Pursuit of Quality, 1987, Lost Landscapes and Failed Economies: The Search for an Economic Value of Place, 1996, Environmental Protection and Local Economic Well-Being: The Economic Pursuit of Quality, 1996, Post-Cowboy Economics: Pay and Prosperity in the New American West, 2001. Chmn. bd. dirs. Sussex Sch. Bd., Missoula, 1984-93. Woodrow Wilson Nat. fellow, 1963. Mem. Phi Beta Kappa. Avocations: mountaineering, mountain biking, skiing. Office: U Montana Dept Econs Missoula MT 59812-0001 E-mail: tmpower@selway.umt.edu

POWERS, J. D., III, marketing executive; Pres. J.D. Powers & Assocs., Calif., chmn. Office: J D Powers & Assocs 30401 Agoura Rd Agoura Hills CA 91301-2084

POWERS, MELVIN, publishing executive; BS, Boston Coll. Pres. Wilshire Book Co., North Hollywood, Calif., 1947—. Office: Wilshire Book Co 12015 Sherman Rd North Hollywood CA 91605-3781

POWERS, RAY LLOYD, state legislator, dairy farmer, rancher; b. Colorado Springs, June 27, 1929; s. Guy and Cora (Hill) P.; m. Dorothy Parrish, Dec. 14, 1975; 1 child, Janet. Student, Pub. Schs. Dairy farmer, Colo. Springs, 1947—. Mem. Colo. Ho. of Reps., 1978-80; mem. Colo. Senate, 1981—, senate pres., 1998—; bd. dirs. Mountain Empire Dairymen's Coop., Denver, 1967-81. Mem. Colo. Cattlemen, Republican Men's Club, Lions. Home: 5 N Marksheffel Rd Colorado Springs CO 80929-9302 Office: State Capitol 200 E Colfax Ave Ste 257 Denver CO 80203-1716

POWERS, REBECCA ANN, psychiatrist, health facility administrator; b. Portland, Oreg., Sept. 28, 1955; m. Gary A. Gusewitch. B in Tech. and Med. Tech., Oreg. Inst. Tech., 1977; M in Pub. Health, Loma Linda U., 1983, MD, 1990. Cert. Am. Bd. Psychiatry and Neurology. Receptionist and vet. asst. Gresham (Oreg.) Vet. Clinic, 1969-77; micobiologist clin. lab. Portland Adventist Med. Ctr., 1977-86; rsch. asst. dept. microbiology Loma Linda (Calif.) U. Med. Ctr., 1987, residency gen. psychiatry, 1990-93; cons. psychiatrist arrowhead home Geriatric Psychiat. Home, San Bernardino, Calif., 1992-93; gen. psychiat. review instr. nat. med. bds. Arc Ventures, Pasadena, 1992-93; fellowship child and adolescent psychiatry Stanford (Calif.) U. Hosp., 1993-95; psychiat. disability evaluations state Calif. Sunnybrook, Amberstone and Stanford Med. Groups, 1994-95; cons. child and adolescent psychiatry Seneca Ctr. Day Treatment, Fremont, Calif., 1994—; attending staff physician comprehensive pediatric care unit, med. psychiat. unit Stanford U. Hosp., 1995-97, developer and med. dir. clin. faculty co. Terminus Adolescent Alcohol and Drug Treatment Program, 1995-96; pvt. practice physician Child, Adolescent, Adult and Family Psychiatry, Los Gatos, Calif., 1995—; attending for eating disorders clin., clin. faculty co. Terminus Lucile Salter Packard Children's Hosp. at Stanford, 1995—. Founder and pres. Art Soc., 1976-77; planning com. Portland Adventist Med. Ctr., 1982-83, team capt. fund raising program, 1984, cmty svc., 1983-86, instr. clin. lab, 1977-86; cons. pub. health Clackamas County Health Dept., 1983; pub. rels. officer Med. Sch. Class 1990, 1987-90; PULSE rep. Loma Linda U. Sch. Med., 1988-90; rsch. aid, schizophrenia dopamine receptor rsch. Jerry L. Pettis VA Meml. Hosp., Loma Linda, 1991; lecturer Am. Lupus Soc., 1991, Loma Linda U. Med. Ctr., 1992; mem. com. Treatment Improvement Group for anxiety and personality disorders Behavioral Medicine Ctr. Loma Linda U. Med. Ctr., 1991-92;psychiat. evaluations smoking cessation Wellburtin Study Jerry L. Pettis Va Meml. Hosp., Loma Linda, 1992-93; co-founder, pres. elect L.A. Preventive Psychiatry Tak Force So. Calif. Psychiat. Soc., 1992-93; del. Calif. Med. Assn. Calif. House Officer Med. Soc.; developer and coord. Pediatric Psychiatry Lecture Series for pediatricians and other primary care physicians Lucile Salter Packard Children's Hosp. at Stanford, 1994-95; com. Forensic Cmty. Project for Oakland Neighborhood Steering and Oakland Planning Commn., 1994; dir. Pediatric Psychiatry Screening Stanford U., 1994; appointment prevention com. Am. Acad. Child and Adolescent Psychiatry, 1991-97; com. Well Being Physicians Calif. Med. Assn., 1995—, adv. bd. Adult and Adolescent Alcohol and Drug Treatment Program, Stanford U. Hosp, 1995-96; assoc. mem. Consortium Med. Educators in Substance Abuse, 1994; program development adolescent alcohol and drug treatment Stanford U. Med. Ctr., 1995-96; vol. clin. instr. and supervisor Stanford U. Hosp., 1995—. Asst. editor newsletter Lab Lines, 1984-86; planned and presented symposium Everything you always wanted to know about Mediacl Practice, San Bernardino County Med. Soc., 1989; contbr. chpts. to books. Recipient Janssen Clin. Scholar award U.S. Psychiat. and Mental Health Congress, 1994, Presdl. Scholar award Am. Acad. Child and Adolescent Psychiatry, 1995. Mem. AMA, Am. Acad. Child and Adolescent Psychiatry, Am. Assn. Orthopsychiatry, Am. Lupus Soc., Am. Psychiatric Assn., Calif. Acad. Preventive Medicine, Calif. Med. Assn. (com. for Well Being of Physicians), Calif. Soc. Addiction Medicine, Healthy Young 2000, No. Calif. Psychiat. Soc., No. Calif. Region Child and Adolescent Psychiat. Home: 36275 Easterday Way Fremont CA 94536-1671 Office: Stanford U Child Psychiatry 401 Quarry Rd MC 5540 Stanford CA 94305-5540 also: 14651 S Bascom Ave Ste 225 Los Gatos CA 95032-2005

POWLICK, GEORGE, shoe and clothing manufacturing executive; b. 1944; CFO, v.p. fin., sec., and dir. K-Swiss, Inc., Westlake Village, Calif., 1988—. Office: K-Swiss Inc 31248 Oak Crest Dr Westlake Village CA 91361-4643

PRAGER, ELLIOT DAVID, surgeon, educator; b. N.Y.C., Sept. 10, 1941; s. Benjamin and Sadye Zelda (Newman) P.; m. Phyllis Damon Warner, July 1, 1967; children: Rebecca, Sarah, Katherine. AB, Dartmouth Coll., 1962; MD, Harvard U., 1966. Diplomate Am. Bd. Surgery, Am. Bd. Colon and Rectal Surgery. Surg. resident Roosevelt Hosp., N.Y.C., 1966-71; colon-rectal fellow Lahey Clinic, Boston, 1971-72; staff surgeon Sansum Clinic, Santa Barbara, Calif., 1974—, dir. colorectal fellowship, 1982-97, chief of surgery, 1986-94; dir. surg. edn. Cottage Hosp., Santa Barbara, 1994-96. Mem., vice chair Residency Rev. Com., 1992—. Author: (with others) Operative Colorectal Surgery, 1994, Current Therapy in Colon and Rectal Surgery, 1990; contbr. articles to profl. jours. Lt. comdr. USN, 1972-74. Fellow Am. Coll. Surgeons (adv. coun. 1992—), Am. Soc. of Colon and Rectal Surgeons (v.p. 1992, sec. of program dirs., 1990—). Achievements include 5 patents for colostomy control devices. Office: Sansum Clinic 317 W Pueblo St Santa Barbara CA 93105-4365

PRATT, DAVID TERRY, engineering consultant; b. Shelley, Idaho, Sept. 14, 1934; s. Eugene Francis and Bernice (Montague) P.; m. Marilyn Jean Thackston, Dec. 22, 1956; children: Douglas Montague, Elizabeth Joann, Brian Stephens. BSc in Mech. Engring., U. Wash., 1956; MSc, U. Calif., Berkeley, 1962, PhD, 1968. Asst. prof. marine engring. U.S. Naval Acad., Annapolis, Md., 1961-64; prof. mech. engring., asst. dean Wash. State U., Pullman, 1968-76; prof. mech. engring. U. Utah, Salt Lake City, 1976-78; prof., chmn. mech. engring. and applied mechanics U. Mich., Ann Arbor, 1978-81; prof., chmn. mech. engring. U. Wash., Seattle, 1981-86, prof. mech. engring., 1987-96, prof. emeritus; engring. cons. Rsch. dir. supercomputing Aerojet Propulsion Rsch. Inst., Sacramento, 1986-87. Author (with W.H. Heiser) Hypersonic Airbreathing Propulsion, 1994; editor (with L.D. Smoot) Combustion and Gasification of Pulverized Coal, 1976; contbr. articles to profl. jours. Served to 1st lt. USMC, 1956-60. NSF sci. faculty fellow, 1965-66; Fulbright-Hays sr. research fellow Imperial Coll., 1974-75; David Pierpont Gardner faculty fellow U. Utah, 1976 Fellow AIAA (assoc.; Summerfield award 1999); mem. ASME, Combustion Inst. Lutheran. E-mail: pratt@combustion.com

PRATT, GEORGE JANES, JR. psychologist, author; b. Mpls., May 3, 1948; s. George Janes and Sally Elvina (Hanson) P.; m. Vonda Pratt; 1 child, Whitney Beth. BA cum laude, U. Minn., 1970, MA, 1973; PhD with spl. commendation, Calif. Sch. Profl. Psychology, San Diego, 1976. Diplomate Am. Bd. Med. Psychotherapists, Am. Acad. Pain Mgmt., Am. Coll. Forensic Examiners; lic. psychologist, Calif., 1976. Psychology trainee Ctr. for Behavior Modification, Mpls., 1971-72, U.Minn. Student Counseling Bur., 1972-73; predoctoral clin. psychology intern San Bernardino County (Calif.) Mental Health Svcs., 1973-74, San Diego County Mental Health Services, 1974-76; mem. staff San Louis Rey Hosp., 1977-78; postdoctoral clin. psychology intern Mesa Vista Hosp., San Diego, 1976; clin psychologist, dir. Psychology and Cons. Assocs. of San Diego, 1976-90; chmn. Psychology and Cons. Assocs. Press, 1977-94. Bd. dirs. Optimax, Inc., 1985-94; pres. George Pratt Ph.D., Psychol. Corp., 1979—; chmn. Pratt, Korn & Assocs., Inc., 1984-94; mem. staff Scripps Meml. Hosp., La Jolla, Calif., 1986—, chmn. psychology, 1993-95, 2000—; founder La Jolla Profl. Workshops, 1977-81; clin. psychologist El Camino Psychology Ctr., San Clemente, Calif., 1977-78; grad. teaching asst. U. Minn. Psychology and Family Studies divsn., 1971; teaching assoc. U. Minn. Psychology and Family Studies divsn., Mpls., 1972-73; instr. U. Minn. Extension divsn., Mpls., 1971-73; faculty Calif. Sch. Profl. Psychology, 1974-83, San Diego Evening Coll., 1975-77, Nat. U., 1978-79, Chapman Coll., 1978, San Diego State U., 1979-80; vis. prof. Pepperdine U., L.A., 1976-78; cons. U. Calif. at San Diego Med. Sch., 1976-78, also instr. univ., 1978—; psychology chmn. Workshops in Clin. Hypnosis, 1980-84; cons. Calif. Health Dept., 1974, Naval Regional Med. Ctr., 1978-82, ABC-TV; also speaker. Author: Sensory/Progressive Relaxation, 1979, Effective Stress Management, 1979, A Clinical Hypnosis Primer, 1984, 88, Clinical Hypnosis: Techniques and Applications, 1985, Rx for Stress, 1994; co-author: HyperPerformance, 1987, Release Your Business Potential, 1988, Instant Emotional Healing, 2000, Emotional Self-Management, 2000; contbr.: Hypnosis: Questions and Answers, 1986, Handbook for Hypnotic Suggestions and Metaphors, 1990, Imagery in Sports and Physical Performance, 1994. With USAR, 1970-76. Fellow Am. Soc. Clin. Hypnosis (cert., approved cons.); mem. Am. Psychological Assn., Nat. Register of Health Svc. Providers in Psychology, Internat. Soc. Hypnosis, Am. Assn. Sex Educators, Counselors and Therapists (cert.), San Diego Soc. Sex. Therapy and Edn. (past pres.), San Diego Soc. Clin. Hypnosis (past pres.), San Diego Psychol. Assn., Soc. Clin. and Exptl. Hypnosis, U. Minn. Alumni Assn., Beta Theta Pi. Office: Scripps Meml Hosp Campus 9834 Genesee Ave Ste 321 La Jolla CA 92037-1216

PRAUSNITZ, JOHN MICHAEL, chemical engineer, educator; b. Berlin, Jan. 7, 1928; came to U.S., 1937, naturalized, 1944; s. Paul Georg and Susi Prausnitz; m. Susan Prausnitz, June 10, 1956; children: Stephanie, Mark Robert. B Chem. Engring., Cornell U., 1950; MS, U. Rochester, 1951; Ph.D., Princeton, 1955; Dr. Ing., U. L'Aquila, 1983, Tech. U. Berlin, 1989; DSc, Princeton U., 1995. Mem. faculty U. Calif., Berkeley, 1955—, prof. chem. engring., 1963—. Cons. to cryogenic, polymer, petroleum and petrochem. industries; lectr. Danckwerts Royal Acad. Engring., London, 2000. Author: (with others) Computer Calculations for Multicomponent Vapor-Liquid Equilibria, 1967, (with P.L. Chueh) Computer Calculations for High-Pressure Vapor-Liquid Equilibria, 1968, Molecular Thermodynamics of Fluid-Phase Equilibria, 1969, 2d edit., 1986, 3rd edit., 1999, (with others) Regular and Related Solutions, 1970, Properties of Gases and Liquids, 3d edit., 1977, 4th edit., 1987, 5th edit., 2000, Computer Calculations for Multicomponent Vapor-Liquid and Liquid-Liquid Equilibria, 1980; contbr. to profl. jours. Recipient Alexander von Humboldt Sr. Scientist award, 1976, Carl von Linde Gold Meml. medal German Inst. for Cryogenics, 1987, Solvay prize Solvay Found. for Chem. Scis., 1990, Corcoran award Am. Soc. for Engring. Edn., 1991, 99, D.L. Katz award Gas Processors Assn., 1992, Waterman award Tech. U. Delft, 1998, Rossini award Internat. Union of Pure and Applied Chemistry, 2002; named W.K. [illegible] lectr. Royal Acad. Engring., London, 2000, hon. prof. Tech. U. Shanghai, 2001; Guggenheim fellow, 1962, 73, fellow Inst. Advanced Study, Berlin, 1985; Miller rsch. prof., 1966, 78; Christensen fellow St. Catherine's Coll.

Oxford U., 1994, Erskine fellow U. Canterbury, Christchurch, New Zealand, 1996. Mem. AIChE (Colburn award 1962, Walker award 1967, Inst. Lectr. award 1994), Am. Chem. Soc. (E.V. Murphree award 1979, Petroleum Chemistry Rsch. award 1995), NAE, NAS, Am. Acad. Arts and Scis. Office: U Calif 308 Gilman Hl Berkeley CA 94720-1462 E-mail: prausnit@socrates.berkeley.edu

PRAY, DONALD EUGENE, lawyer; b. Tulsa, Jan. 16, 1932; s. Clyde Elmer and Ruth Annette (Frank) P.; m. Margaret Morrow, June 12, 1953; children: Melissa, Susan; m. Lana J. Dobson, Nov. 18, 1985. BS n Petroleum Engring., U. Tulsa, 1955; LLB with honors, U. Okla., 1963. Bar: Okla. 1963, U.S. Dist. Ct. (no. dist.) Okla. 1965, U.S. Supreme Ct. 1965. Assoc. firm Fuller, Smith, Mosberg, Davis & Bowen, Tulsa, 1963-65; ptnr. firm Schuman, Deas, Pray & Doyle, Tulsa, 1965-68, Pray, Scott & Livingston, and predecessor firm, Tulsa, 1968-79; chmn., mem. exec. com. firm Pray Walker, Jackman, Williamson & Marlar (merger), Tulsa, 1979-95; exec. dir. Donald W. Reynolds Found., Tulsa, 1993-99, trustee, 2000—. Bd. dirs. Grace and Franklin Bernsen Found., U. Tulsa, St. Johns Med. Ctr., Philbrook Art Mus.; bd. dirs., exec. v.p. Tulsa Ballet Theater. Served to capt. USAF, 1955-57. Fellow Am. Bar Found.; mem. ABA (econs. com.), Tulsa Estate Planning Forum (pres.), Tulsa Mineral Lawyers Sect. (pres.), Summit Club (pres.). Republican. Presbyterian. Office: 1701 Village Center Cir Las Vegas NV 89134-6303

PRAY, RALPH MARBLE, III, lawyer; b. San Diego, June 7, 1938; s. Ralph Marble Jr. and Doris (Thomson) P.; m. Karen L. Pray (div. May 1988); children: Matthew Thomson, Kristen Leigh; m. Sandra Anne Shaw, June 7, 1988. BS, U. Redlands, 1960; JD, U. Calif., San Francisco, 1967. Bar: Calif. 1967, U.S. Dist. Ct. (so. dist.) Calif. 1968, U.S. Supreme Ct. 1972, U.S. Dist. Ct. (ea. dist.) Calif. 1985, U.S. Dist. Ct. (ctrl. dist.) Calif. 1989, U.S. Dist. Ct. (no. dist.) Calif. 1992. Assoc. Gray, Cary, Ware & Friedenrich and predecessor, San Diego, 1967-73, ptnr., 1973—; mem. mgmt. com. Gary, Cary, Ames & Frye, San Diego, 1975-80. Arbiter Superior Ct., San. Diego, 1984—. Lt. USN, 1960-64. Mem. ABA, SAR, NRA, Calif. Bar Assn., Am. Arbitration Soc. (arbiter), San Diego Zool. Soc., Ducks Unltd., Thurston Soc., Rotary Club of Coronado, Calif., Order of Coif. Republican. Episcopalian. Home: 535 C Ave Coronado CA 92118-1824 Office: Gray Cary Ware & Friedenrich 1700 Wells Fargo Plz 401 B St San Diego CA 92101-4223

PREBLE, LAURENCE GEORGE, lawyer; b. Denver, Apr. 24, 1939; s. George Enos and Ruth (Jewett) P.; m. Deborah Joan Horton, Aug. 24, 1963; children— Robin Lee, Randall Laurence B in Petroleum Refining Engring., Colo. Sch. Mines, 1961; J.D. cum laude, Loyola U., Los Angeles, 1968. Bar: Calif. 1969, N.Y. 1987, U.S. Dist. Ct. (cen. dist.) Calif. 1969, D.C. 1983. Assoc. firm O'Melveny & Myers, Los Angeles, 1968-76, ptnr. L.A., 1976—. Adj. prof. law Southwestern U., 1970-75, Loyola U. of L.A. Sch. Law, 1984-92, 99—, Fordham U. Sch. Law, 1992-98, Calif. Continuing Edn. of the Bar; lectr., author Practicing Law Inst. Trustee Harvey Mudd Coll., 1991-94, Citizens Bidget Commn. N.Y.C., 1994-98, Ho. Ear Inst., 1998—. Recipient Disting. Achievement medal Colo. Sch. Mines, 1998. Mem. Los Angeles County Bar Assn. (chmn. real property sect. 1979-80, Outstanding Leadership award 1999), Assn. Bar City of N.Y. (real property sect. exec. com. 1993-96), N.Y. State Bar Assn. (exec. com. real property sect. 1996—), Calif. Bar Assn. (mem. exec. com. real property sect.), ABA, Am. Coll. Real Estate Lawyers (bd. govs. 1986—), Anglo-Am. Real Property Inst., La Canada-Flintridge C. of C. (pres. 1974-75), Loyola Law Sch. Alumni Assn. (pres. 1978). Office: O Melveny & Myers 400 S Hope St Los Angeles CA 90071-2899

PREGERSON, HARRY, federal judge; b. L.A., Oct. 13, 1923; s. Abraham and Bessie (Rubin) P.; m. Bernardine Seyma Chapkis, June 28, 1947; children: Dean Douglas, Kathryn Ann. B.A., UCLA, 1947; LL.B., U. Calif.-Berkeley, 1950. Bar: Calif. 1951. Pvt. practice, Los Angeles, 1951-52; Assoc. Morris D. Coppersmith, 1952; ptnr. Pregerson & Costley, Van Nuys, 1953-65; judge Los Angeles Mcpl. Ct., 1965-66, Los Angeles Superior Ct., 1966-67, U.S. Dist. Ct. Central Dist. Calif., 1967-79, U.S. Ct. Appeals for 9th Circuit, Woodland Hills, 1979—. Faculty mem., seminar for newly appointed distr. Judges Fed. Jud. Center, Washington, 1970-72; mem. faculty Am. Soc. Pub. Adminstrn., Inst. for Ct. Mgmt., Denver, 1973—; panelist Fed. Bar Assn., L.A. chpt., 1989, Calif. Continuing Edn. of Bar, 9th Ann. Fed. Practice Inst., San Francisco, 1986, Internat. Acad. Trial Lawyers, L.A., 1983; lect. seminars for newly-appointed Fed. judges, 1970-71. Author over 450 published legal opinions. Mem. Community Rels. Com., Jewish Fedn. Coun., 1984—, Temple Judea, Encino, 1955—; bd. dirs. Marine Corps Res. Toys for Tots Program, 1965—, Greater Los Angeles Partnership for the Homeless, 1988—; bd. trustees Devil Pups Inc., 1988—; adv. bd. Internat. Orphans Inc., 1966—, Jewish Big Brothers Assn., 1970—, Salvation Army, Los Angeles Met. area, 1988—; worked with U.S. Govt. Gen. Svcs. to establish the Bell Shelter for the homeless, the Child Day Care Ctr., the Food Partnership and Westwood Transitional Village, 1988. 1st lt. USMCR, 1944-46. Decorated Purple Heart, Medal of Valor Apache Tribe, 1989; recipient Promotion of Justice Civic award, City of San Fernando, 1965, award San Fernando Valley Jewish Fedn. Coun., 1966, Profl. Achievement award Los Angeles Athletic Club, 1980, Profl. Achievement award UCLA Alumni Assn., 1985, Louis D. Brandeis award Am. Friends of Hebrew U., 1987, award of merit Inner City Law Ctr., 1987, Appreciation award Navajo Nation and USMC for Toys for Tots program, 1987, Humanitarian award Los Angeles Fed. Exec. Bd., 1987-88, Grateful Acknowledgement award Bet Tzedek Legal Svcs., 1988, Commendation award Bd. Suprs. Los Angeles County, 1988, Others award Salvation Army, 1988, numerous others. Mem. ABA (vice-chmn., com. on fed. rules of criminal procedure and evidence sect. of criminal 1972—, panelist Advocacy Inst., Phoenix, 1988), L.A. County Bar Assn., San Fernando Valley Bar Assn. (program chmn. 1964-65), State Bar Calif., Marines Corps Res. Officers Assn. (pres. San Fernando Valley 1966—), DAV (Birmingham chpt.), Am. Legion (Van Nuys Post), Office: US Ct Appeals 9th Cir 21800 Oxnard St Ste 1140 Woodland Hills CA 91367-7919*

PREMO, PAUL MARK, oil company executive; b. Syracuse, N.Y., Nov. 20, 1942; s. Matthias George and Kathryn (Whitbread) P.; m. Mary Catherine Hennessy, June 19, 1965; children— Deborah, Mark B.S. in Chem. Engring., Manhattan Coll., Riverdale, N.Y., 1964; S.M. in Chem. Engring., MIT, 1965. Chem. engr. Chevron Research, Richmond, Calif., 1965-69; fin. analyst Chevron Corp., San Francisco, 1969-72, coordinator, mgr. supply and distbn., 1972-79; mgr. petroleum regulations Chevron USA, San Francisco, 1979-81, sec.-treas., 1981-85, mgr. property tax adminstrn., 1985-86, mgr. natural gas regulatory affairs, 1986-92; exec. cons. Resource Mgmt. Internat., San Rafael, Calif., 1992-95; v.p. Foster Assoc., Inc., San Francisco, 1996-98; prin. Energy Econs. Consulting, Mill Valley, Calif., 1998—. Dir. Ky. Agrl. Energy Corp., Franklin Trustee Calif. Tax Found., 1985— Mem. Calif. State C. of C. (tax com.), Western Oil and Gas Assn., Am. Petroleum Inst. (property tax com.), Natural Gas Supply Assn., Inst. Property Taxation, Calif. Taxpayers Assn. (bd. dirs. 1985—), MIT Alumni Assn., Commonwealth (San Francisco), Sigma Xi, Tau Beta Pi. Avocations: sailing, investments. Home: 310 Hazel Ave Mill Valley CA 94941-5054 E-mail: paulpremo@msn.com

PRENDERGAST, WILLIAM JOHN, ophthalmologist; b. Portland, Oreg., June 12, 1942; s. William John and Marjorie (Scott) P.; m. Carolyn Grace Perkins, Aug. 17, 1963 (div. 1990); children: William John, Scott; m. Sherryl Irene Guenther, Aug. 25, 1991. BS, U. Oreg., Eugene, 1964; MD, U. Oreg., Portland, 1967. Diplomate Am. Bd. Ophthalmology. Resident in ophthalmology U. Oreg., Portland, 1970-73; pvt. practice specializing in ophthalmology Portland, 1973-82; physician, founder, ptnr. Eye Health NW (formerly Oreg. Med. Eye Clinic), Portland, 1983—; also bd. dirs.; founder, pres. (Focus Group) Inc. Focus Group Inc., Ophthalmic Clinic Networking Venture, Portland, 1992—. Clin. asst. prof. ophthalmology Oreg. Health Sci. U., 1985—; dir. Eye Health Ptnrs. Med. Optometric Managed Eye Care Venture, 1998. Vol. surgeon, Hosp. de la Familia, Nuevo Progreso, Guatamala, 2001, vol. surgeon N.W. Med. Teams, Oaxaca, Mexico, 1989, 90. With USPHS, 1968-70. Fellow Am. Acad. Ophthalmology; mem. Met. Bus. Assn., Multnomah Athletic Club, Mazamas Mountaineering Club, Portland Yacht Club, Phi Beta Kappa, Alpha Omega Alpha. Avocations: yacht racing, mountaineering. Office: Eye Health NW 1955 NW Northrup St Portland OR 97209-1614 E-mail: prenderw@omce.ehnpc.com

PRENTICE, MARGARITA, state legislator, nurse; Student, Phoenix Coll., Youngstown U.; RN, St. Joseph's Hosp. Sch.; student, U. Wash. RN, Wash. Nurse, Wash.; mem. Wash. Senate, Dist. 11, Olympia, 1988—; majority caucus vice chair Wash. Senate, Olympia, 1993-94; mem. agr. and rural econ. devel. com. Wash. Legislature, Olympia, mem. transp. com. Mem. Dem. Nat. Com. Recipient Legislator of Yr. Retail Assn. and Mortgage Bankers Assn., Wash. Health Care Assn., Wash. State Labor Coun., Wash. State Nurses Assn., Home Health Care Assn., King County Nurse of Yr., Champion of Health Care award Valley Med. Ctr., Disting. Svc. award Wash. Assn. Homes for Aging, Legislator of Yr. Wash. State Dental Hygienists Assn. Mem. ACLU, Amnesty Internat., Wash. State Nurses Assn. (1st v.p. 1968-72, labor officer 1974-78), Sierra Club, Renton Hist. Soc., Audubon Soc., Humane Soc. U.S. Democrat. Office: 419 John Cherberg Bldg Olympia WA 98504-0001

PRENTKE, RICHARD OTTESEN, lawyer; b. Cleve., Sept. 8, 1945; s. Herbert E. and Melva B. (Horbury) P.; m. Susan Ottesen, June 9, 1974; children: Catherine, Elizabeth. BSE, Princeton U., 1967; JD, Harvard U., 1974. Assoc. Perkins Coie, Seattle, 1974-80, ptnr., 1981—, CFO, 1989-94. Author: School Construction Law Deskbook, 1989, rev. 2d edit. 1998; contbr. articles to profl. jours. Pres., trustee Seattle County Day Sch., 1990-95; trustee Pocock Rowing Found., 1996—. With USN, 1967-70. Fellow Leadership Tomorrow, Seattle, 1985-86. Mem. ABA, Wash. State Bar Assn. (mem. jud. screening com. 1985-91, chmn. 1987-91), Seattle-King County Bar Assn. (chmn. jud. task force 1990-93), Am. Arbitration Assn. (arbitrator 1988—), Princeton U. Rowing Assn. (pres. 1993—, trustee 1976—), Rainier Club, Princeton Club Wash. (trustee 1986—, pres. 1990-92), Seattle Tennis Club. Avocations: art, carpentry, travel, rowing, sports. Office: Perkins Coie 1201 3rd Ave Fl 40 Seattle WA 98101-3029

PREONAS, GEORGE ELIAS, lawyer; b. Dayton, Ohio, Oct. 5, 1943; s. Louis D. and Mary (Drakos) P.; m. Aileen Strike, June 1, 1944; children: Annemarie, Michael, Stephen. BA, Stanford U., 1965; JD, U. Mich., 1968. Bar: Ill. 1968, Nev. 1969, Calif. 1974. Ptnr. Seyfarth, Shaw, Fairweather & Geraldson, L.A., 1968—. Mem. ABA, L.A. County Bar Assn., Calif. Bar Assn., Ill. Bar Assn., Nev. Bar Assn. Office: Seyfarth Shaw 2029 Century Park E Ste 3300 Los Angeles CA 90067-3019

PRESANT, SANFORD CALVIN, lawyer, educator, writer; b. Buffalo, Nov. 15, 1952; s. Allen and Reeta Presant; children: Jarrett, Danny, Lauren. BA, Cornell U., 1973; JD cum laude, SUNY, Buffalo, 1976; LLM in Taxation, Georgetown U., NYU, 1981. Bar: N.Y. 1977, D.C. 1977, U.S. Tax Ct. 1977, U.S. Ct. Claims 1978, Calif. 1992, U.S. Supreme Ct. 1982. Staff atty. SEC Options Task Force, Washington, 1976-78; assoc. Barrett Smith Schapiro, N.Y.C., 1978-80, Trubin Sillcocks, N.Y.C., 1980-81; ptnr. Carro, Spanbock, Fass, Geller, Kaster, N.Y.C., 1981 86, Finley, Kumble, Wagner, Heine, Underberg, Manley, Myerson & Casey, N.Y.C., 1987, Kaye, Scholer, Fierman, Hays & Handler, N.Y.C., 1987-95, Battle Fowler LLP, L.A., 1995-2000, Ernst & Young, L.A., 2000—; nat. dir. real estate tax strategies, opportunity funds Ernst & Young LLP, L.A., 2000—. Adj. assoc. prof. real estate NYU, 1984—; frequest lectr. in tax law; regular TV appearances on Nightly Business Report, Pub. Broadcasting System, 1986-88; co-chmn. NYU Conf. Fed. Taxation of Real Estate Transactions, 1987, PLI Advanced Tax Planning for Real Estate, 1987, PLI Real Estate Tax Forum, 1999—; conf. chmn. various confs. in field. Author: (with others) Tax Aspects of Real Investments, 1999, Understanding Estate Partnership Tax Allocations, 1987, Realty Joint Ventures, 1980-86, Tax Sheltered Investments Handbook-Special Update on Tax Reform Act of 1984, Real Estate Syndication Handbook, 1986, Real Estate Syndication Tax Handbook, 1987, The Tax Reform Act of 1986, 1987, The Final Partnership Nonrecourse Debt Allocation Regulations, 1987, Taxation of Real Estate Investments, 1987, Understanding Partnership Tax Allocations, 1987, Tax Aspects of Environmental (Superfund) Settlements, 1994, The Proposed Publicly Traded Partnership Regulations, 1995, others. Kripke Securities Law fellow NYU, 1976. Mem. ABA (nat. chmn. audit subcom. of tax sect. partnership com. 1984-86, partnership tax allocation subcom. chmn. 1986-90, nat. chmn. partnership com. 1992-94, chmn. task force publicly traded partnerships 1995—, others), N.Y. State Bar Assn. (tax sect. partnership com. 1980—), Assn. of Bar of City of N.Y. Republican. Jewish. Office: Ernst & Young LLP Ste 1800 2049 Century Park E Los Angeles CA 90067-3119 Fax: 310-284-7970. E-mail: sanford.presant@ey.com

PRESCOTT, DAVID MARSHALL, biology educator; b. Clearwater, Fla., Aug. 3, 1926; s. Clifford Raymond and Lillian (Moore) P.; m. Gayle Edna Demery; children: Lavonne, Jason, Ryan. BA, Wesleyan U., 1950; PhD, U. Calif., Berkeley, 1954. Asst. prof. UCLA Med. Sch., 1955-59; biologist Oak Ridge (Tenn.) Nat. Lab., 1959-63; prof. U. Colo. Sch. Medicine, Denver, 1963-66; prof. molecular, cell and devel. biology U. Colo., Boulder, 1966-80, Disting. prof. molecular, cell and devel. biology, 1980—. Pres. Am. Soc. Cell Biology, 1966. Author: Cell Reproduction, 1976, Cancer: The Misguided Cell, 1986, Cells, 1988; also numerous rsch. reports; editor: Methods in Cell Biology, 15 vols., 1963-78. Adv. com. March of Dimes, 1979-90. Recipient von Humboldt prize Fed. Republic Germany, 1979; grantee NIH, 1985-95, 97-2001, Nat. Found. Cancer Rsch., 1985-89, NSF, 1990-91, 95—; John Simon Guggenheim Meml. Found. fellow, 1990-91. Fellow Am. Acad. Arts and Scis.; mem. NAS, Soc. Protozoologists (pres. 1995—). Avocations: numismatics, gardening. Home: 285 Brook Pl Boulder CO 80302-8031 Office: Univ Colo Campus Box 347 MCDB Biology Boulder CO 80309-0347

PRESCOTT, LAWRENCE MALCOLM, medical and health science writer; b. Boston, July 31, 1934; s. Benjamin and Lillian (Stein) P.; m. Ellen Gay Kober, Feb. 19, 1961 (dec. Sept. 1981); children: Jennifer Maya, Adam Barrett; m. Sharon Lynn Kirshen, May 16, 1982; children: Gary Leon Kirshen, Marc Paul Kirshen. BA, Harvard U., 1957; MSc, George Washington U., 1959, PhD, 1966. Nat. Acad. Scis. postdoctoral fellow U.A. Army Rsch., Ft. Detrick, Md., 1965-66; microbiologist/scientist WHO, India, 1967-70, Indonesia, 1970-72, Thailand, 1972-78; with pub. rels. GCI, Hill & Knowlton, Aventis, Astra Zeneza, others, 1984—; cons. to internat. orgns. San Diego, 1978—. Author manuals; contbr. articles in diarrheal diseases and lab. scis. to profl. jours., numerous articles, stories, poems to mags., newspapers, including Living in Thailand, Jack and Jill, Strawberry, Bangkok Times, Spring, 1977-81; mng. editor Caduceus, 1981-82; pub., editor: Teenage Scene, 1982-83; pres. Prescott Pub. Co., 1982-83; med. writer numerous jours. including Modern Medicine, Dermatology Times, Drug and Market Devel., P&T, Clinical Cancer Letter, Anesthesiology News, Arzte Zeitong, Australian Doctor, Inpharma Weekly, Chronicle of Cardiovascular and Internal Medicine, Ophthalmology Times, Pharmacy Practice News, Body Positive, AIDS Update, Medical Allert, Infectious Diseases, Urology Times, Genetic Engineering News, Medical Week, Gastroenterology and Endoscopy News; author: Curry Every Sunday, 1984. Home and Office: 18264 Verano Dr San Diego CA 92128-1262

PRESECAN, NICHOLAS LEE, environmental and civil engineer, consultant; b. Indpls., Sept. 4, 1940; s. Nicholas Eli and Dorothy Lee (Moore) P.; m. Joan Westin, Nov. 11, 1940; children: Julie Marie, Mary Lee, Anne Westin. BSCE, Purdue U., 1963; MS in Engring., U. Calif., Berkeley, 1967. Cert. profl. engr., 35 states, value specialist. Project engr. San Bernardino County (Calif.) Flood Control, 1963, Engring. Sci. Inc., Arcadia, Calif., 1968-70, office mgr. Cleve., 1970-72, v.p., chief engr., 1972-81, v.p. internat. divsn. Arcadia, 1981-84, group v.p., 1984-87; sr. v.p. Parsons Engring. Sci. Inc., Pasadena, Calif., 1987—. Industry adv. bd. Sch. Engring. and Tech. Calif. State U., L.A., 1986-99. Contbr. articles to profl. jours. Commr. Archtl. Commn., Claremont, Calif., 1980-86; councilman Claremont City Coun., 1986-94; mayor City of Claremont, 1989-92; mem. Pasadena Tournament of Roses Assn., 1980-96, L.A. 2000 Environ. Com., 1987-88; pres. Claremont Hills Conservation Corp., 1997—. With USMC, 1963-67. Recipient Disting. Engring. Achievement award Inst. for Advancement of Engring., 1993. Fellow ASCE (mem. internat. adv. com. 1987-90); mem. NSPE, Am. Acad. Environ. Engrs., Am. Water Works Assn. (life), Water Environ. Fedn., Soc. Am. Value Engrs., Rotary. Republican. Avocations: skiing, hiking, fishing, boating, writing. Home: 727 E Alamosa Dr Claremont CA 91711-2008 Office: Parsons Engring Sci Inc 100 W Walnut St Pasadena CA 91124-0001

PRESLEY, PRISCILLA, actress; b. Bklyn., May 24, 1945; m. Elvis Presley, 1967 (div. 1973); 1 child, Lisa Marie. Studied with Milton Katselas; student, Steven Peck Theatre Art Sch., Chuck Norris Karate Sch. Co-owner Bis and Beau Boutique; co-executor, pres. Elvis Presley Enterprise, Memphis. Launched internat. fragnance line. Appearances include (films) The Naked Gun, 1988, The Adventures of Ford Fairlaine, 1990, The Naked Gun 2 1/2, 1991, The Naked Gun 33 1/3, 1994, (TV series) Those Amazing Animals, 1980-81, Dallas, 1983-88, (TV movies) Love Is Forever, 1983, Breakfast With Einstein, 1998; prodr. (TV movie) Elvis and Me, 1988; exec. prodr. The Road to Graceland, 1998; author: Elvis and Me, 1989. Office: Michelle Bega c/o Rogers & Cowan 1888 Century Park E Los Angeles CA 90067-1702

PRESNIAKOV, ALEXANDER, painter, sculptor, inventor; b. San Francisco, June 28, 1963; s. Alexander Alexandervich and Nina (Hanova) P. Student, Acad. of Art Coll., San Francisco, 1979-82. Curator Gen. Svcs. Adminstrn., Washington, 1983; artist Washington, 1984-85, San Francisco, 1986—. Songwriter Hilltop Records, L.A., 1996—, Amerecord, L.A., 1996—, Premier Melodies, N.Y.C. Commd. to paint life-size portraits of Prince Charles, Princess Diana, Miss Dame Barbara Cartland, 1982, Amb. Gerald Posner Carmen, 1983, life-size portraits of presdl. candidates for 1985 Polit. Conservative Action Conf., Sheraton Hotel, Washington; series Women in Love Cycle, 1986—; inventor Manshield Deflector, 1983; commissioned to paint life-size portrait of Pres. Ronald Reagan, 1983; author 3 novels, including Eagle's Nest, 2001; screenwriter. Recipient Literary Excellence award Iliad Press, 1995; named Prof. and Corr. Academician Dept. Arts Accademia Internazionale, Italy. Mem. Internat. Soc. Poets (disting. mem., Hall of Fame 1997-98), Legion of Honor Mus., De Young Mus., Gallery Marabella (hon.). Republican. Russian Orthodox. Achievements include creation of artistic ideal, Ultrafictorilization, utilized in all U.S. gov. Agys., 1983. Avocations: tennis, golf, equestrian. Home: 775 42d Ave San Francisco CA 94121

PRESS, BETH, publishing executive; Sr. account mgr. Conde Nast's GQ, 1998-99; dir. advt. Teen Magazine, 1999-2000, group pub., 2000—. Office: EMAP USA 6420 Wilshire Blvd Los Angeles CA 90048-5502

PRESS, WILLIAM HENRY, astrophysicist, computer scientist; b. N.Y.C., N.Y., May 23, 1948; s. Frank and Billie (Kallick) P.; m. Margaret Ann Lauritsen, 1969 (div. 1982); 1 dau., Sara Linda; m. Jeffrey Foden Howell, Apr. 19, 1991; 1 son, James Howell. AB, Harvard Coll., 1969; MS, Calif. Inst. Tech., 1971, PhD, 1972. Asst. prof. theoretical physics Calif. Inst. Tech., 1973-74; asst. prof. physics Princeton (N.J.) U., 1974-76; prof. astronomy and physics Harvard U., Cambridge, Mass., 1976-98, chmn. dept. astronomy, 1982-85; dep. lab. dir. Los Alamos Nat. Lab., 1998—. Mem. numerous adv. coms. and panels NSF, NASA, NRC; vis. mem. Inst. Advanced Study, 1983-94; mem. Def. Sci. Bd., 1985-89, sci. adv. com. Packard Found., 1988—, program com. Sloan Found., 1985-91; chmn. adv. bd. NSF Inst. Theoretical Physics, 1986-87; mem. Computer Sci. and Telecomm. Bd., 1991-96; U.S. del. IUPAP Gen. Assembly, 1996; cons. MITRE Corp., 1977—; trustee Inst. Def. Analysis, 1988—, exec. com., 1990—; chief naval ops. Exec. Panel, 1994-2000. Author: Numerical Recipes, 1986; contbr. articles to profl. jours. Sloan Found. research fellow, 1974-78 Fellow Am. Acad. Arts and Scis., Am. Phys. Soc.; mem. NAS, Am. Astron. Soc. (Helen B. Warner prize 1981), Internat. Astron. Union, Internat. Soc. Relativity and Gravitation, Assn. for Computing Machinery. Office: Los Alamos Nat Lab # Ms-a100 Los Alamos NM 87545-0001

PRESSLY, THOMAS JAMES, history educator; b. Troy, Tenn., Jan. 18, 1919; s. James Wallace and Martha Belle (Bittick) P.; m. Lillian Cameron, Apr. 30, 1943; children: Thomas James II, Stephanie Suzuki. AB, Harvard U., 1940, AM, 1941, PhD, 1950; LLD (hon.), Whitman Coll., 1981. Instr. history Princeton U., 1946-49; asst. prof. U. Wash., 1949-54, assoc. prof., 1954-60, prof., 1960-87, prof. emeritus, 1987—. Vis. assoc. prof. Princeton U., 1953-54, Johns Hopkins U., 1969-70 Author: Americans Interpret Their Civil War, 1954; editor: (with W. H. Scofield) Farm Real Estate Values in the United States, 1965, (with others) American Political Behavior, 1974, Diary of George Templeton Strong (abridged), 1988, (with Glenn M. Linden) Voices From the House Divided, 1995, (with Maclyn P. Burg) The Great War At Home and Abroad, 1999. Served with AUS, 1941-45. Ford Found. Faculty fellow, 1951-52; Center for Advanced Study in Behavioral Scis. fellow, 1955-56 Mem. Am. Hist. Assn., So. Hist. Assn. (editorial bd. Jour. So. History 1973-77), Orgn. Am. Historians. Home: 4545 E Laurel Dr NE Seattle WA 98105-3838 Office: U Wash Dept History PO Box 353560 Seattle WA 98195-3560

PRESTON, JOHN ELWOOD, lawyer; b. Celina, Ohio, Sept. 15, 1941; s. Homer Harlan and Nancy Alice (Boroff) P.; m. Alexandra Learned, Aug. 7, 1965. BA, Ohio U., 1962; LLB, George Washington U., Washington, 1965. Bar: D.C. 1967, Calif. 1973, U.S. Dist. Ct. D.C. 1967, U.S. Dist. Ct. (cen. dist.) Calif. 1984. Staff asst. Office of U.S. Senator Thomas H. Kuchel, Washington, 1964-66; atty., advisor Office of Gen. Counsel, GAO, Washington, 1966-71; mem. regulations study group Commn. on Govt. Procurement, Washington, 1970-71; div. counsel Litton Industries, Beverly Hills, Calif., 1971-79, group v.p., 1979-88, asst. gen. counsel, 1988-89, assoc. gen. counsel, 1989-90, v.p., assoc. gen. counsel, 1990-93, sr. v.p., gen. counsel, 1993—. Bd. dirs. Parks Jaeger Aerospace, Orlando, Fla., 1988-92; arbitrator Am. Arbitration Assn., L.A., 1986—. Contbr. articles to profl. jours. Mem. ABA (chmn. various coms.), Soc. Internat. Lawyers, Fed. Bar Assn., Nat. Contract Mgmt. Assn., Phi Alpha Delta. Avocations: golf, tennis, music, theatre. Office: Litton Industries Inc 21240 Burbank Blvd Woodland Hills CA 91367-6675

PRESZLER, SHARON MARIE, psychiatric home health nurse; b. L.A. d. Rudolph Edward Wirth and Bertha Marie (Thornton) Paddock; m. Alan Preszler, Aug. 31, 1966; children: Brent, Alison. BS in Nursing, Loma Linda (Calif.) U., 1963, MS in Marriage and Family Counseling, 1978. RN, Calif., Idaho; cert. pub. health nurse. Team leader med. fl. Loma Linda U. Hosp., 1963-64; office nurse Dr. Lowell Johnson, Redlands, Calif., 1964-65, Dr. H. Glenn Stevens, Loma Linda, 1965-72; team leader women's oncology Loma Linda U. Hosp., 1974-75; pub. health nurse Riverside County Pub. Health, Hemet, Calif., 1975-78; nurse, staff psychologist Dept. Health and Welfare, Idaho Falls, Idaho, 1989-91, Boise, 1991-92; psychiat. nurse Cmty. Home Health, Boise, 1992-94, Mercy Home Health

& Hospice, Nampa, Idaho, 1995-99; hospice nurse, home health nurse Mercy Med. Ctr., 1995-99, personal care supr. nurse for medicaid, 1996—. Instr. YWCA, Bartlesville, Okla., 1984-88; tchr. Bartlesville Pub. Sch., 1984-88, Heritage Retirement, Boise, 1994. Contbr. to Focus, 1986. Mem. Am. Assn. Marriage and Family Therapy, Sigma Theta Tau. Avocations: reading, tennis.

PREUSS, CHARLES FREDERICK, lawyer; b. Santa Barbara, Calif., Feb. 27, 1941; BA, Dartmouth Coll., 1962; JD, Stanford U., 1969. Bar: Calif. 1970. Ptnr. Preuss Walker & Shanagher, San Francisco, 1993-98, Preuss, Shanagher, Zvoleff & Zimmer, San Francisco, 1998—. Mem. Product Liability Adv. Coun., Inc. Mem. Am. Bd. Trial Advocates, Internat. Assn. Def. Counsel. Office: Preuss Shanagher Zvoleff & Zimmer 225 Bush St # 15f1 San Francisco CA 94104-4207

PREVITTI, JAMES P. real estate executive; Founder Forecast Group, Rancho Cucamonga, Calif., 1971—, pres., CEO, 1989—. Recipient Fair Housing award L.A. Times; named Builder of Yr., Real Estate Entrepreneur of Yr. Mem. Calif. Bldg. Industry Assn. (pres., Medal of Honor). Office: Forecast Group 10670 Civic Center Dr Rancho Cucamonga CA 91730-3803

PRICE, B. BYRON, historian; BS, U.S. Mil. Acad., 1970; MA in Mus. Sci., Tex. Tech. U., 1977; postgrad., Am. U., Washington, 1975. Tchg. asst. Tex. Tech. U., Lubbock, 1975, rsch. coord. Ranching Heritage Ctr./Mus., 1976-77; curator of history Panhandle-Plains Hist. Mus., Canyon, Tex., 1977-82, exec. dir., 1982-86, Nat. Cowboy Hall of Fame and Western Heritage Ctr., Oklahoma City, 1987-96, Buffalo Bill Hist. Ctr., Cody, Wyo., 1996—. Lectr. in field; condr. seminars in field; cons. in field. Advisory editor: The Handbook of Texas, 1986-96; editl. bd. N.Mex. Hist. Rev., 1990-93, Jour. Ariz. History, 1993-95; assoc. editor The Ency. of the West, 1996; author: Cowboys of the American West, 1996, Crafting a Southwestern Masterpiece, 1986, Imagining the Open Range: Erwin E. Smith, Cowboy Photographer, 1997, Longheed: A Painter's Painter, 1991, The National Cowboy Hall of Fame Chuck Wagon Cook Book, 1995, She Doesn't Write Like a Woman: Mari Sandoz and the Cattlemen, 1996; co-author: The Golden Spread: An Illustrated History of Amarillo and the Texas Panhandle, 1986; co-editor: Cowboy Justice, 1997, Adventuring with the Old-Timers: Trails Traveled and Tales Told, 1979; contbr. articles to profl. jours. Mem. tourism task force Okla. Dept. Commerce, 1987; mem. Okla. Film Adv. Commn., 1988-90; bd. dirs. Okla. Ctr. for the Book, 1990—; judge Arts for the Parks Ann. Exhbn., 1992-93; mem. cultural opportunities work group Okla. Futures, 1993; mem. Oklahoma City Conv. and Visitors Commn., 1996—. Recipient Gov.'s Arts award State of Okla., 1994. Mem. Tex. Assn. Mus. (exec. coun. 1985-86), Okla. Mus. Assn. (v.p. 1993-95), Mus. West Consortium (pres. 1996—), Western History Assn. (mem. program com. 1997), Am. Assn. Mus., Tex. State Hist. Assn., Western Writers of Am., Panhandle Plains Hist. Soc. Office: Buffalo Bill Hist Ctr 720 Sheridan Ave Cody WY 82414-3428

PRICE, CLIFFORD WARREN, retired metallurgist, researcher; b. Denver, Apr. 22, 1935; s. Warren Wilson and Vivian Fredricka (Cady) P.; m. Carole Joyce Waterman, June 14, 1969; children: Carla Beth, Krista Lynn Price. MetE, Colo. Sch. Mines, 1957; MS, Ohio State U., 1970, PhD, 1975. Design engr. Sundstrand Aviation-Denver, 1957-60; materials specialist Denver Rsch. Inst., 1960-63; sr. metallurgist Rocky Flats div. Dow Chem. Co., Golden, Colo., 1963-66; staff metallurgist Battelle Columbus (Ohio) Labs., 1966-75; sr. scientist Owens-Corning Fiberglas, Granville, Ohio, 1975-80; metallurgist Lawrence Livermore (Calif.) Nat. Lab., 1980-93; retired, 1993. Contbr. articles to profl. jours. Battelle Columbus Labs. fellow, 1974-75. Mem. Metall. Soc. AIME, Microscopy Soc. Am. (treas. Denver 1961-62), Am. Soc. for Metals Internat. Achievements include research on electron, scanning probe and optical microscopy, secondary ion mass spectroscopy, deformation, fracture and recrystallization mechanisms in metals, recrystallization kinetics. E-mail: cwprice@home.com

PRICE, DAVID, golf courses facilities executive; b. 1933; With Am. Golf Corp., Santa Monica, Calif., 1972—, now chmn.; chmn. Nat. Golf Properties, Santa Monica, 1993—. Office: Am Golf Corp 2951 28th St Santa Monica CA 90405-2961

PRICE, FRANK, motion picture and television company executive; b. Decatur, Ill., May 17, 1930; s. William F. and Winifred A. (Moran) P.; m. Katherine Huggins, May 15, 1965; children: Stephen, David, Roy, Frank. Student, Mich. State U., 1949-51. Writer, story editor CBS-TV, N.Y.C., 1951-53, Columbia Pictures, Hollywood, Calif., 1953-57, NBC-TV, Hollywood, Calif., 1957-58; producer, writer ZIV-TV, Hollywood, 1958, Universal Television, Universal City, 1959-64, v.p., 1964-71, sr. v.p., 1971-73, exec. v.p. in charge of production, 1973-74, pres., 1974-78; v.p., dir. MCA, Inc., 1976-78; pres. Columbia Pictures Prodn., 1978-79; chmn., chief exec. officer Columbia Pictures, 1979-84, also bd. dirs.; chmn. MCA Motion Picture Group, 1984-86; chmn., chief exec. officer Price Entertainment Inc., 1987-90; chmn. Columbia Pictures, 1990-91; chmn., chief exec. officer Price Entertainment, 1991—; prodr. The Tuskegee Airmen, 1996. With USN, 1948-49. Recipient Peabody award, 1996, NAACP Image award, 1996. Mem. Writers Guild Am., West. Office: Price Entertainment Inc 527 Spoleto Dr Pacific Palisades CA 90272-4517

PRICE, HUMPHREY WALLACE, aerospace engineer; b. San Antonio, Sept. 25, 1954; s. Humphrey Rodes and Ruth (Wallace) P. BS in Engring., U. Tex., 1976, MS in Engring., 1978. Rsch. asst. nuclear reactor lab. U. Tex., Austin, 1976; nuclear engr. EDS Nuclear, Inc., San Francisco, 1977-78; engr. Jet Propulsion Lab., Pasadena, Calif., 1978-82; rsch. engr. SW Rsch. Inst., San Antonio, 1982-84; tech. group leader Jet Propulsion Lab., Pasadena, Calif., 1984-89; configuration engr. Cassini spacecraft NASA, 1989-93; system engr. Pluto Spacecraft, 1994-97; sys. engr. Mars Sample Return Mission, 1998-2000; mgr. Solar Sail Tech. Devel. Cons. Am. Rocket Co., Camarillo, Calif., 1986-87; mem. tech. staff World Space Found., Pasadena, 1980-97. Patentee in field; contbr. to tech. papers in field. Mem. AIAA (sr.). Avocations: wind surfing, skiing, scuba diving. Office: HW Price Cons PO Box 454 La Canada Flintridge CA 91012-0454 E-mail: hoppyprice@netscape.net

PRICE, JOHN, real estate executive; Grad., U. Utah. Founder John Price Assocs., Inc., 1952, Fairfax Realty, Inc., 1972; CEO, JP Realty, Inc., Salt Lake City, 1993—, also bd. dirs. Bd. dirs. Alta Industries-Utah, Inc.; mem. adv. bd. 1st Security Bank, N.Am. Bd. trustees U. Utah; bd. dirs. Utah State Fairpark Corp. Office: JP Realty Inc 35 Century Park Way Salt Lake City UT 84115-3507

PRICE, JOHN RICHARD, lawyer, law educator; b. Indpls., Nov. 28, 1934; s. Carl Lee and Agnes I. P.; m. Suzanne A. Leslie, June 22, 1963; children: John D., Steven V. B.A. with high honors, U. Fla., 1958; LL.B. with honors, NYU, 1961. Bar: Calif. 1962, Wash. 1977, U.S. Ct. Appeals (9th cir.), U.S. Dist. Ct. (we. dist.) Wash. Assoc. McCutchen, Doyle, Brown & Enersen, San Francisco, 1961-69; prof. law U. Wash., Seattle, 1969-97, dean, 1982-88; of counsel Perkins Coie, Seattle, 1976—. Author: Contemporary Estate Planning, 1983, Price on Contemporary Estate Planning, 1992, 2d edit., 2000, Conflicts, Confidentiality and Other Ethical Issues, 2000. Served with U.S. Army, 1953-55 Root-Tilden fellow NYU Sch. Law, 1958-61 Fellow Am. Coll. Trust and Estate Counsel (former regent); mem. ABA, Am. Law Inst., Internat. Acad. of Estate and Trust Law, Order of Coif, Phi Beta Kappa. Congregationalist Home: 3794 NE 97th St Seattle WA 98115-2564 Office: 1201 3rd Ave Ste 4800 Seattle WA 98101-3029 E-mail: prici@perkinscole.com

PRICE, JONATHAN G. geologist; b. Danville, Pa., Feb. 1, 1950; s. A. Barney and Flora (Best) P.; m. Elisabeth McKinley, June 3, 1972; children: Alexander D., Argenta M. BA in Geology and German, Lehigh U., 1972; MA, U. Calif., Berkeley, 1975, PhD, 1977. Cert. profl. geologist. Geologist Anaconda Copper Co., Yerington, Nev., 1974-75, U.S. Steel Corp., Salt Lake City, 1977, Corpus Christi, 1978-81; rsch. assoc. Bur. Econ. Geology, U. Tex., Austin, 1981-85, rsch. sci., 1984-88, program dir., 1987-88; dir. Tex. Mining & Mineral Resources Rsch. Inst., Austin, 1984-88; dir., state geologist Nev. Bur. Mines & Geology, U. Nev., Reno, 1988-92, 95—. Staff dir. Bd. on Earth Scis. & Resources Nat. Rsch. Coun., Washington, 1993-95; asst. prof. Bucknell U., Lewisburg, 1977-78. Author, editor: Igneous Geology of Trans-Pecos Texas, 1986. Vol. instr. CPR and first aid ARC, 1983-95, bd. dirs. Sierra Nev. chpt., 1991-92. German Acad. Exch. Svc. fellow U. Heidelberg, 1972-73; recipient Explorer award Am. Geol. Inst., 1995. Fellow Geol. Soc. Am., Soc. Econ. Geologists; mem. Am. Inst. Profl. Geologists (Nev. sect. pres. 1992, nat. pres. 1997, John T. Galey Sr. Meml. pub. Svc. award 1999), Assn. Am. State Geologists (pres. 2000-01), Mineral. Soc. Am., Phi Beta Kappa. Office: Nev Bur Mines & Geology Unr Ms 178 Reno NV 89557-0001 E-mail: jprice@unr.edu

PRICE, KATHLEEN MCCORMICK, book editor, writer; b. Topeka, Dec. 25, 1932; d. Raymond Chesley and Kathleen (Shoffner) McCormick; m. William Faulkner Black, Aug. 25, 1956 (div. 1961); 1 child, Kathleen Serena; m. William Hillard Price, Aug. 13, 1976. BA, U. Colo., Denver, 1971. Book reviewer Denver Post, 1971-78; book editor San Diego Mag., 1978-92. Cons. editor St. John's Cathedral, Denver, 1985-95. Author: There's a Dactyl Under My Foot, 1986, The Lady and the Unicorn, 1994, From Vision to Vestment, 2001. Dir. Colo. Episcopal Vestment Guild. Fellow Phi Beta Kappa; mem. PEN, Denver Women's Press Club, Denver County Club, La Garita Club. Episcopalian. Home: 27 Crestmoor Dr Denver CO 80220-5853

PRICE, LEW PAXTON, writer, engineer, scientist; b. Takoma Park, Md., Dec. 19, 1938; s. Raymond Miller and Clarene Pearl (Morris) P.; m. Sherrie Darlene Sellers, June 25, 1960 (div. Apr. 1979); children: Terilyn Ann, Heather Rae, Crystal Alene. BS, U.S. Air Force Acad., Colorado Springs, Colo., 1960. Hon. Ho-O Ryu Bushido 6th Dan Master. Electronics engr. Pacific Telephone, Sacramento, 1965-66, engring. coord., bldgs., 1966-85; pres., design engr. Condor Aeroplane Works, Ltd., Sacramento, 1983-85; engring. coord. Tuttle Engring. and Constrn. Consultants, El Dorado Hills, Calif., 1989-92; scientist, flute design cons., writer, flutemaker Fair Oaks, Garden Valley, 1977—. Cons. flute design. Author: The Cosmic Stradivarius, 1974, Aquarian Anastasis, 1975, The Music of Life, 1984, Dimensions in Astrology, 1986, Native North American Flutes, 1990, Secrets of the Flute (Math, Physics & Design), 1991, Creating & Using the Native American Love Flute, 1994, Creating & Using Grandfather's Flute, 1995, The Oldest Magic (Prehistory & Influence of Music), 1995, Creating & Using Older Native American Flutes, 1995, Creating & Using Smaller Native American Flutes, 1995, Creating & Using the Native American Concert Flute, 1996, More Secrets of the Flute, 1997, Creating and Using Larger Native American Flutes, 1998, Creating and Using the Largest Native American Flutes, 1998, Creating and Using Very Small Native American Flutes, 1998, Behind Light's Illusion (5 book series), 1999, 2000; author, programmer: (computer program) Flute Design (Native American), 1996. Co-advisor Aviation Explorers, archery/space/sci. merit badge instr./examiner, Boy Scouts Am., North Highlands, Calif., 1968-70; panelist United Crusade, Sacramento, Calif., 1971; rifle/pistol/shotgun safety instr. NRA, Fair Oaks, Calif., 1970-72. Capt. USAF, 1960-65. Mem. No. Calif. Flute Circle (co-organizer 1996), Oreg. Native Am. Flute Circle (hon.). Avocations: flying, singing, flute playing, hiking, archery. Home and Office: PO Box 88 Garden Valley CA 95633-0088

PRICE, PETER WILFRID, ecology educator, researcher; b. London, Apr. 17, 1938; came to U.S., 1966; BSc with honors, U. Wales, Bangor, 1958-62; MSc, U. New Brunswick, Fredericton, 1964; PhD, Cornell U., 1970. Asst. prof. U. Ill., Urbana, 1971-75, assoc. prof., 1975-79; research ecologist Mus. No. Ariz., Flagstaff, 1979-80; assoc. prof. No. Ariz. U., Flagstaff, 1980-85, prof. ecology, 1985-94, Regents' prof., 1994—. Author: Evolutionary Biology of Parasites, 1980, Biological Evolution, 1996, Insect Ecology, 3d edit., 1997; editor: A New Ecology, 1984, Evolutionary Strategies of Parasitic Insects, 1975, Plant-Animal Interactions, 1991, Population Dynamics, 1995. Guggenheim fellow, 1977-78; Fulbright Sr. scholar, 1993-94. Fellow Royal Entomol. Soc. (hon.); mem. NSF (panel mem. 1978-81, 91-93), Am. Soc. Naturalists, Ecol. Soc. Am. (bd. editors 1973-76), Brit. Ecol. Soc., Entomol. Soc. Am. (Founders Award, 1993). Office: No Ariz U PO Box 5640 Flagstaff AZ 86011-5640

PRICE, ROBERT E. manufacturing company executive; b. 1942; BA, Pomona Coll., 1964. V.p. Fed-Mart Corp., 1964-75; pres., chief exec. officer Price Corp., San Diego, 1976-89; pres., chmn. bd., chief exec. officer Price Enterprises, San Diego, 1989-91, chmn. bd., chief exec. officer, 1991—, also bd. dirs. Office: EXCEL LEGACY CORP. 17140 BERNADO CENTER Dr. San Diego CA 92128

PRICE, ROBERT OTIS, mayor; b. Abilene, Kans., Jan. 4, 1932; s. Iru Paul and Irene Isabel (Parrish) P.; m. Dorothy Faye Price, Jan. 26, 1951 (dec. 1996); m. Sondra Boyd, Mar. 28, 1997; children: Fred Dennis, Donald Eugene. BA, U. Redlands, 1978. Patrolman, sgt., lt., capt. Bakersfield Police Dept., 1956-73, chief police, 1973-88; cons., troubleshooter, various cities, 1988-92; mayor City of Bakersfield, 1993—. Pres. Secret Witness Bd., 1980-83. Mem. Calif. Coun. on Criminal Justice, Sacramento, 1983-93; chmn. State Adv. Group on Juvenile Justice, Sacramento, 1988-93, Citizens Adv. Com., Fresno, Calif., 1993—, Youth Devel. Coalition, Bakersfield, 1993—, Econ. Devel. Discussion Group, Bakersfield, 1993—; chmn. western region Nat. Coalition Juvenile Justice and Delinquency Prevention, 1988-93; founder, cons. Youth Adv. Coun., Bakersfield, 1993—; founder Bakersfield Action Team, 1994. Sgt. U.S. Army, 1952-54. Recipient John W. Doubenmier award Am. Soc. Pub. Admins., 1978, Califf Morris award Calif. Probation, Parole and Corrections Officers Assn., 1982. Mem. Internat. Assn. Chiefs Police, Calif. Police Chiefs Assn., Calif. Peace Officers Assn., Calif. Council Criminal Justice, Kern County Police Chiefs Assn. (pres. 1979), Kern County Law Enforcement Admin. Assn. (pres. 1974). Republican. Avocations: photography, fishing, travel. Office: City of Bakersfield 1501 Truxtun Ave Bakersfield CA 93301-5201

PRICE, ROBERT WILLIAM, school superintendent, consultant; b. Ogden, Utah, May 13, 1950; s. William Robert and Eileen Louise (Rabe) P.; m. Sally Sandman, Sept. 20, 1975; children: Geoffrey Thomas, Caitlin Elizabeth. BS in Child Devel., Calif. State U., Hayward, 1973, MS in Sch. Adminstrn., 1986; EdD, U. Pacific, 1998. Cert. elem. tchr., Calif. Tchr. Turlock (Calif.) Sch. Dist., 1974-81; asst. prin. Monte Vista Mid. Sch., Tracy, Calif., 1981-82, prin., 1982-87; asst. supt. instrn. Tracy Pub. Schs., 1987-90, 91-93, interim supt., 1990-91; supt. Empire Union Sch. Dist., Modesto, Calif., 1993—. Cons. Campfire, Tracy, 1983; founding mem. Tracy Exch. Club, 1985; co-founder Project Bus. & Edn. Together, Tracy, 1985; bd. dirs. Boys and Girls Club of Tracy, 1987-93. Recipient Adminstrv. Leadership award Calif. Media & Libr. Educators Assn., 1994. Mem. Assn. Calif. Sch. Adminstrs. (planning com. supts. symposium 1995—, v.p. programs Region 7 1994—), Calif. League Mid. Schs. (adv. panel Region 6 1993—, chair legis. action 1994-95, Region 6 Educator of Yr. 1991). Democrat. Office: Empire Union Sch Dist 116 N Mcclure Rd Modesto CA 95357-1329 E-mail: bprice@empire.k12.ca.us

PRICE, THOMAS MUNRO, computer consultant; b. Madison, Wis., Oct. 2, 1937; s. John Edward and Georgia Winifred (Day) P.; m. Judith Ann Holm, Aug. 8, 1959; children: Scott Michael, Andrea Lynn. BS, Carroll Coll., Waukesha, Wis., 1959; MS, U. Wis., 1961, PhD, 1964. Prof. math. U. Iowa, 1964-77, U. Wyo., Laramie, 1978-79, computer user cons., 1979-85, MIS prof., 1985-89; computer cons., 1989—; home rebuilder Pecos, N.Mex., 1994-97; historic home renovator Yerington, Nev., 1997—. Contbr. articles to profl. jours. Home: Nordyke House 727 State Rt 339 Yerington NV 89447

PRICE, TOM, automotive sales executive; Founder Tom Price Dealership, Colma, Calif., 1976; mgr. corp. growth including franchising, other acquisitions FirstAm. Automotive Inc. (formerly Tom Price Dealership), San Francisco, 1997, CEO, pres.

PRICKETT, DAVID CLINTON, physician; b. Fairmont, W.Va., Nov. 26, 1918; s. Clinton Everett and Mary Anna (Gottschalk) P.; m. Mary Ellen Holt, June 29, 1940; children: David C., Rebecca Ellen, William Radcliffe, Mary Anne, James Thomas, Sara Elizabeth; m. Pamela S. Blackstone, Nov. 17, 1991. Student, Fairmont State Coll., 1940-42; AB, W.Va. U., 1944; MD, U. Louisville, 1946; MPH, U. Pitts., 1955. Pres. Prickett Chem. Co., 1938-43; acct. W.Va. Conservation Commn. Fed. Works Agy., 1941, 42; lab. asst., instr. chemistry W.Va. U., 1943; intern Louisville Gen. Hosp., 1947; surg. resident St. Joseph's Hosp., Parkersburg, W.Va., 1948-49; gen. practice, 1948-50, 55-61; physician USAF, N.Mex. and Calif., 1961-62, U.S. Army, Calif., 1963-64, San Luis Obispo County Hosp., 1965-66, So. Calif. Edison Co., 1981-84; assoc. physician indsl. and gen. practice Los Angeles County, Calif., 1967—; mem. staff Fairmont (W.V.) Gen. Hosp., 1955-60, Fairmont (W.V.) Emergency Hosp., 1955-60, St. Francis Hosp., L.A., 1970-71. Physician Bethlehem Mines Corp., Idamay, W.Va., 1956; resident physician Sedgwick County Hosp., Wichita, Kans., 1964-65; med. dir. South Gate plant GM, 1969-71; staff physician City of L.A., 1971-76; relief med. practice Appalachia summer seasons, 1977, 86, 88-97. Author: The Newer Epidemiology, 1962, rev., 1990, Public Health, A Science Resolvable by Mathematics, 1965; contbr. to publ. Med. officer USPHS, Navajo Indian Reservation, Tohatchi (N.Mex.) Health Ctr., 1953-55, surgeon, res. officer, 1957-59; pres. W.Va. Pub. Health Assn., 1951-52; sec. indsl. and pub. health sect. W. Va. Med. Assn., 1956; local and dist. health officer, W.Va., 1951-53; dist. health officer Allegheny County, Pa., 1957; med. adv. Boy Scouts Am., W.V., N. Mex. Served to 2d lt. AUS, 1943-46. Dr. Thomas Parran fellow U. Pitts. Sch. Pub. Health, 1955; named to Hon. Order Ky. Cols. Fellow Am. Pub. Health Assn; mem. AMA, Sons of Revolution, Am. Occupl. Med. Assn., Am. Acad. Family Physicians, Western Occupl. Med. Assn., Calif. Med. Assn., L.A. County Med. Assn., Am. Legion, Elks, Phi Chi. Address: PO Box 4032 Whittier CA 90607-4032

PRINCE, JOHN LUTHER, III, engineering educator; b. Austin, Tex., Nov. 13, 1941; s. John Luther and Glynda (Chollett) P.; m. Martha Ann Hight, Mar. 4, 1960; children: Cynthia Kay, John Luther IV, Alan Douglas, David William. BSEE, So. Meth. U., 1965; MEE, N.C. State U., 1968, PhD, 1969. Research engr. RTI, Res. Tri. Park, N.C., 1968-70; mem. tech. staff Tex. Instruments, Dallas, 1970-75; from assoc. prof. to prof. Clemson (S.C.) U., 1975-80; dir. R.A. Intermedics, Inc., Freeport, Tex., 1980-83; prof. U. Ariz., Tucson, 1983—. Acting dir. packaging scis. Semiconductor Rsch. Corp., 1991-92; cons. numerous semi-conductor and electronics cos., 1983—; dir. Electronic Packaging Lab., 1984-91, Ctr. for Electronic Packaging Rsch., 1991—, SEMATECH Ctr. of Excellence for Contamination and Defect Control, 1988-90. Contbr. articles to profl. jours. Named Ariz. Innovator of the Yr., 1992; NSF fellow, 1965-68. Fellow IEEE; mem. Am. Philatelic Soc. Lutheran. Avocations: stamp collecting, classic cars, motorcycles. Home: 7542 N San Lorenzo Dr Tucson AZ 85704-3141 Office: U Ariz Dept Engineering Tucson AZ 85721-0001 E-mail: prince@ece.arizona.edu, jlpmhp@aol.com

PRINDLE, WILLIAM ROSCOE, retired glass company executive, consultant; b. San Francisco, Dec. 19, 1926; s. Vivian Arthur and Harriette Alnora (Nickerson) P.; m. June Laverne Anderson, June 20, 1947; children— Carol Susan, William Alastair. B.S., U. Calif., Berkeley, 1948, M.S., 1950; Sc.D., M.I.T., 1955. Asst. tech. dir. Hazel-Atlas Glass Co., 1954-56; mgr. research Hazel-Atlas Glass div. Continental Can Co., Wheeling, W.Va., 1956-58, gen. mgr. research and devel., 1959-62; mgr. materials research Am. Optical Co., Southbridge, Mass., 1962-65; v.p. research Southbridge and Framingham, 1971-76; dir. research Ferro Corp., Cleve., 1966-67, v.p. research, 1967-71; exec. dir. Nat. Materials Adv. Bd., NRC-NAS, Washington, 1976-80; dir. adminstrv. and tech. svcs. R & D div. Corning Glass Works, N.Y., 1980-85, dir. materials rsch., 1985-87; assoc. dir. R & D, Engring. div. Corning Glass Works (now Corning, Inc.), 1987-90; div. v.p., assoc. dir. tech. group Corning Inc., 1990-92; ret. Pres. XII Internat. Glass Congress, 1980, Internat. Commn. on Glass, 1985-88. Served with U.S. Navy, 1944-46. Named Disting. Ceramist of New Eng., New Eng. sect. Am. Ceramic Soc., 1974, Toledo Glass and Ceramic award NW Ohio sect., 1986, Albert Victor Bleininger Meml. award Pitts. sect., 1989; Friedberg Meml. lecture Nat. Inst. Ceramic Engrs., 1990. Fellow Am. Ceramic Soc. (disting. life, pres. 1980-81), Soc. Glass Tech., Am. Soc. for Metals Internat.; mem. NAE, AAAS, Cosmos Club (Washington), Sigma Xi, Phi Gamma Delta. Home and Office: 1556 Crestline Dr Santa Barbara CA 93105-4611 E-mail: wprindle@aol.com

PRINGLE, EDWARD E. law educator, former state supreme court chief justice; b. Chgo., Apr. 12, 1914; s. Abraham J. and Lena (Oher) P.; m. Pauline Judd, Aug. 17, 1941; children: Bruce, Eric. LL.B., U. Colo., 1936, LL.D., 1976, U. Denver, 1979. Bar: Colo. Practiced in, Denver, 1936-42, 47-57; with fed. govt. service Washington, 1943-47; dist. judge Colo. Dist. Ct., Denver, 1957-61; justice Supreme Ct. Colo., Denver, 1961-79, chief justice, 1970-78; dir. research and writing program U. Denver Coll. Law, 1979-90, prof. emeritus, 1990—. Contbr. articles to profl. jours. Bd. dirs. Am. Med. Center, Denver; mem. Nat. Commn. for Establishment of Nat. Inst. Justice. Served with USAAF, 1942. Recipient William Lee Knous award U. Colo. Law Sch., 1975. Mem. Am., Colo., Denver bar assns., Conf. Chief Justices (chmn. 1973-74), Am. Judicature Soc. (Herbert Lincoln Harley award 1973, chmn. bd. 1974-76), Nat. Center State Cts. (pres. 1977-79) Jewish. Club: Masons (33 deg.). Office: U Denver Coll Law 1900 Olive St Denver CO 80220-1857

PRINS, DAVID, speech pathologist, educator; b. Herkimer, N.Y., Oct. 4, 1930; s. Tunis W. and Harriet Z. (Baker) P.; m. Gloria B. Fleming, June 4, 1955; children: Leslie, Steven, Douglas, Michael. BA, Central Coll. Iowa, 1952; MA, U. Mich., 1957, PhD, 1961. Tchr. Denison (Iowa) H.S., 1954-55; instr. U. Mich., 1960-63, asst. prof., 1963-66, assoc. prof., 1966-69; asst. dir. U. Mich. Speech and Hearing Camp, 1960-64, dir., 1964-69; dir. program in speech and hearing scis. U. Wash., 1974-75, assoc. prof., 1969-72, prof., 1973-92, chmn. dept. speech and hearing scis., 1975-79, assoc. dean Coll. Arts & Scis., 1979-88, prof. emeritus, 1992—. Vis. prof. U. Va. Contbr. articles in field of stuttering and articulation disorders to profl. jours. Served with U.S. Army, 1952-54. Mem. AAAS, Am. Speech and Hearing Assn., Wash. Speech and Hearing Assn., Mich. Speech and Hearing Assn. (past pres.), Phi Beta Kappa, Phi Kappa Phi. Office: U Wash Dept Speech Scis Seattle WA 98105-0240

PRISBREY, REX PRINCE, retired insurance agent, underwriter, consultant; b. Washington, Mar. 18, 1922; s. Hyrum William and Susan (Prince) P.; m. Erika Julieta Lucero, Nov. 10, 1945; children: Karol Sue Prisbey Lewallen, Pamela Blanche Prisbrey Ebert, Michael Rex. BA in Acctg., Denver U., 1949. CLU. Ptnr. Allen Stamm & Assocs., home builders, Farmington, N.Mex., 1949-52; acct. Linder Burke & Stevenson,

Santa Fe, 1949-52; agt. State Farm Ins. Cos., Farmington, 1952-56, mgr. Phoenix, 1956-60, contractor, agt. Scottsdale, Ariz., 1960—. V.p., treas. Original Curio Store Inc., Santa Fe. Pres. Farmington Jr. C. of C., 1952; v.p. N.Mex. Jr. C. of C., 1953. 1st lt. USAAF, 1941-46, CBI. Decorated DFC, Air medal with oak leaf cluster; recipient Disting. Life Underwriter award Cen. Ariz. Mgrs. Assn., 1979. Mem. Am. Soc. CLU's, Scottsdale Assn. Life Underwriters (pres. 1980-81), Airplane Owners and Pilots Assn., Hump Pilots Assn. (life, speaker at meml. of Hump Flyers, Kunming, China 1993), Pinewood Country Club (bd. dirs., treas., v.p. 1985—), Civitans (pres. Scottsdale 1962-63). Avocations: flying, golf, photography. Home: 11859 N 80th Pl Scottsdale AZ 85260-5645

PRISELAC, THOMAS M. health facility administrator; Pres., CEO Cedars-Sinai Med. Ctr., L.A., 1991—. Office: Cedars Sinai Med Ctr 8700 Beverly Blvd Rm 2622 Los Angeles CA 90048

PRITCHARD, LLEWELYN G. lawyer; b. N.Y.C., Aug. 13, 1937; s. Llewelyn and Anne Mary (Streib) P.; m. Joan Ashby, June 20, 1959; children: David Ashby, Jennifer Pritchard Vick, Andrew Harrison, William Llewellyn. AB with honors, Drew U., 1958; LLB, Duke U., 1961. Ptnr. Helsell & Fetterman, Seattle. Trustee, corp. counsel Allied Arts Found.; pres. Allied Arts Seattle, 1974-76; trustee Meth. Ednl. Found., 1970-85, pres., 1991-92; life trustee Patrons of Pacific N.W. Civil, Cultural and Charitable Orgns., 1969—, pres., 1972-73; bd. dirs. Planned Parenthood of Seattle/King County, 1972-78; trustee Seattle Symphony Orch., 1979-83, chmn. bd., 1980-82, hon. trustee; trustee U. Puget Sound., 1972-99, mem. exec. com., chmn. bd. visitors to Law Sch., 1984-88; trustee Mus. of Glass, 2000—; chancellor Pacific N.W. Ann. conf. United Meth. Ch., 1969—. Fellow Am. Bar Found. (life, state chmn. 1988-98); mem. ABA (bd. govs. 1986-89, chmn. program com. 1988-89, exec. com. 1988-89, Ho. of Dels. 1979—, nat. dir. young lawyers divsn. 1971, chmn. sect. of individual rights and responsibilities 1975-76, exec. coun. family law sect. 1992-98, chair standing com. on legal aid and indigent defendants 1973-75, chair legal needs study 1995-98, chair adv. com. to pro bono immigration project 1995—), Wash. State Bar Assn. (bd. govs. King County 1972-75), King County Bar Assn. (chair young lawyers sect. 1970). Avocations: reading, art collector. Home: 5229 140th Ave NE Bellevue WA 98005-1024 Office: Helsell & Fetterman 1500 Puget Sound Plz Seattle WA 98101 E-mail: lpritchard@helsell.com

PRITT, FRANK W. computer company executive; Founder, chmn., CEO Attachmate Corp., Bellevue, Wash., 1982—. Address: PO Box 90026 Bellevue WA 98009-9026

PRO, PHILIP MARTIN, judge; b. Richmond, Calif., Dec. 12, 1946; s. Leo Martin and Mildred Louise (Beck) P.; m. Dori Sue Hallas, Nov. 13, 1982; 1 child, Brenda Kay. BA, San Francisco State U., 1968; JD, Golden Gate U., 1972. Bar: Calif. 1972, Nev. 1973, U.S. Ct. Appeals (9th cir.) 1973, U.S. Dist. Ct. Nev. 1973, U.S. Supreme Ct. 1976. Pub. defender, Las Vegas, 1973-75; asst. U.S. atty. Dist. Nev., Las Vegas, 1975-78; dep. atty. gen. State of Nev., Carson City, 1979-80; U.S. magistrate U.S. Dist. Ct. Nev., Las Vegas, 1980-87, U.S. dist. judge, 1987—. Instr. Atty. Gen.'s Advocacy Inst., Nat. Inst. Trial Advocacy, 1992; chmn. com. adminstrn. of magistrate judge system Jud. Conf. U.S., 1993—. Bd. dirs. NCCJ, Las Vegas, 1982—, mem. program com. and issues in justice com. Mem. ABA, Fed. Judges Assn. (bd. dirs. 1992—, v.p. 1997-2001), Nev. State Bar Assn., Calif. State Bar Assn., Nev. Judges Assn. (instr.), Assn. Trial Lawyers Am., Nev. Am. Inn Ct. (pres. 1989-91), Ninth Cir. Jury (instructions com.), Nat. Conf. U.S. Magistrates (sec.). Republican. Episcopalian. Office: US Dist Ct 7015 Fed Bldg 300 Las Vegas Blvd S Ste 4650 Las Vegas NV 89101-5883

PROBASCO, CALVIN HENRY CHARLES, clergyman, college administrator; b. Petaluma, Calif., Apr. 5, 1926; s. Calvin Warren and Ruth Charlene (Winans) P.; m. Nixie June Farnsworth, Feb. 14, 1947; children— Calvin, Carol, David, Ruth B.A. cum laude, Biola Bible Coll., La Mirada, Calif., 1953; D.D. (hon.), Talbot Theol. Sem., La Mirada, 1983. Ordained to ministry, 1950. Pastor Sharon Baptist Ch., El Monte, Calif., 1951-58, Carmichael Bible Ch., 1958-97, pastor emeritus, 1997—; pres. Sacramento Bible Inst., Carmichael, 1968—. Mem. Ind. Fundamental Chs. Am. (rec. sec. 1978-81, pres. 1981-84, 1st v.p. 1987-88), Delta Epsilon Chi. Republican

PROBERT, COLIN, advertising executive; Ptnr., pres. Goodby, Silverstein & Ptnrs., San Francisco. Office: Goodby Silverstein & Ptnrs 720 California St San Francisco CA 94108-2404

PROBERT, WILLIAM B. sales executive; BA in Pschology, Sociology, Santa Cruz. V.p., sales mktg. Hearthside Homes, Koll Communities; exec. v.p., sales, mktg. Brookfield Davidson Homes; v.p., sales, mktg. Presley, San Diego; exec. v.p., sales, mktg. WL Homes, Inc., 1998—. Speaker nat. building industry events; tchr. real estate, U. Ca., San Diego. Recipient Southern's Ca. Mktg. Dir. Year, Nat. Assn. Home Builders; Major Achievement award Mktg. Excellence, Prof. Builder Mag. Office: WL Homes LLC 19600 Fairchild Ste 150 Irvine CA 92612-2516

PROCHNOW, JAMES R. lawyer; b. Hutchinson, Minn., Sept. 22, 1943; BA, Hamline U., 1965; JD, William Mitchell Law Sch., 1969. Bar: Minn. 1969, U.S. Supreme Ct. 1973, Colo. 1975. Staff civil divsn. Dept. Justice, Washington, 1973-74; legal counsel to Pres. The White House, Washington, 1974; ptnr. Baker & Hostetler, Denver, Patton Boggs, 1995—. Mem. Denver Bar Assn., Colo. Bar Assn. Office: Patton Boggs 1660 Lincoln St Ste 1900 Denver CO 80264-1601

PROCTOR, GEORGANNE C. company executive; b. 1957; m. Robert Proctor. BS in Bus. Mgmt., U. S.D.; MBA in Fin., Calif. State U., Hayward. From fin. analyst Bechtel Financing Svcs. (now part of Bechtel Enterprises), 1982-89; mgr. Bechtel Info. Tech. Group., 1989-91, mgr. project cost controls for Disney MGM Studio project, 1991; dir. fin. and acctg. Internat. Home Video divsn. Disney Co., 1991-93; dir. fin. Walt Disney Imagineering, 1993-94; CFO Bechtel Enterprises, 1994-97; sr. v.p., CFO Bechtel Group, Inc., San Francisco, 1997-1998. Office: Bechtel Group Inc PO Box 193965 San Francisco CA 94119-3965

PROCTOR, RICHARD J. geologist, consultant; b. L.A., Aug. 2, 1931; s. George Arthur and Margaret Y. (Goodman) P.; m. Ena McLaren, Feb. 12, 1955; children: Mitchell, Jill, Randall. BA, Calif. State U., L.A., 1954; MA, UCLA, 1958. Engring. geologist, Calif.; cert. profl. geologist Am. Inst. Profl. Geologists. Chief geologist Met. Water Dist., L.A., 1958-80; pres., cons. geologist Richard J. Proctor, Inc., Arcadia, Calif., 1980-95. Vis. assoc. prof. Calif. Inst. Tech., Pasadena, 1975-78. Co-author: Citizens Guide to Geologic Hazards, 1993; editor: Professional Practice Guidelines, 1985, Engineering Geology Practice in Southern California, 1992. Pres., dir. Arcadia Hist. Soc., 1993-96. Fellow Geol. Soc. Am. (Burwell Meml. award 1972); mem. Assn. Engring. Geologists (pres. 1979), Am. Inst. Profl. Geologists (pres. 1989, Van Couvering Meml. award 1990, hon. mem. 1992), Am. Geol. Inst. (sec.-treas. 1979-83).

PRONZINI, BILL JOHN (WILLIAM PRONZINI), writer; b. Petaluma, Calif., Apr. 13, 1943; s. Joseph and Helene (Guder) P.; m. Marcia Muller. Coll. student, 2 years. Author: 60 novels (including under pseudonyms), 4 books of non-fiction, 10 collections of short stories, 1971—; first novel, The Stalker, 1971; editor 80 anthologies; contbr. numerous short stories to publs. Recipient 6 scroll awards Mystery Writers Am., Life Achievement award Pvt. Eye Writers Am., 1987. Office: PO Box 2536 Petaluma CA 94953-2536 E-mail: pronhack@aol.com

PROPER, MARY, advertising executive; Controller Suissa Miller Advt., L.A. Office: Suissa Miller Advt 11601 Wilshire Blvd Fl 16 Los Angeles CA 90025-1770

PROTZMAN, GRANT DALE, university administrator, state legislator; b. Ogden, Utah, May 3, 1950; s. Paul L. and Maxine E. (Nelson) P.; m. Linda Sue Gerasta, Mar. 30, 1985; children: Heather Sue, Kristen Marie, Erin Elizabeth. BA, Utah. State U., 1976; MS, Calif. Am. U., 1979; MA, U. No. Colo., 1987, EdD, 1988. Coord. student activities Weber State U., Ogden, 1976-81, coord. student govt., 1981-82, assoc. dir. student life, 1982-84, dir. co-curricular learning, 1984-87, planning and devel. officer, dir. drug and alcohol program, 1987-91, asst. to v.p., 1991—; mem., asst. minority whip Utah State Ho. of Reps., Salt Lake City, 1986-97. Sr. cons. Inst. for Leadership Devel., Ogden, 1978—. Author: An Examination of Select Motivational Variables of Members in Three Different Types of Volunteer Organizations in a Collegiate Setting, 1988, An Investigation of the State of Motivation Management and Assessment in Volunteer Organizations, 1988; contbr. articles to profl. jours. Mem. adv. bd. Wasatch Care Ctr., Ogden, 1986-93, Families in Edn., 1992, Weber Sch. Dist., 1992; mem. Weber Area Emergency Planning Com., Ogden, 1988-93, critical workplace skills adv. bd. Applied Tech. Ctr., 1991—, mem. adv. bd. Pvt. Industry Coun./Local Community Coun., 1994—, State of Utah Region II Dept. Corrections, 1992—; mem. bd. dirs. Hospice No. Utah, 1994—. Named Outstanding Young Man of the Year, Jay Cees; Recipient Ptnrs. in Edn. Recognition award Weber Sch. Dist., 1987, Appreciation award Utah Vocat. Leadership Orgns., 1987, Extended Svc. award Ogden Sch. Dist., 1988, Outstanding Legislator award Utah Democratic Party Chmn's. award, 1988, Utah Sch. Employees Assn. Scroll of Honor award as Outstanding legislator, 1990, Weber State U. Student Svcs. Soar award, 1991, Utah Edn. Assn. Honor Roll award as Outstanding legislator, 1991, Utah Ednl. Libr. Media Assn. award for Outstanding Dedication and Svc. to Utah Lib. Media programs, 1992, Utah Assn. of Rehabilitative Facilities award for Svc. to Persons with disabilities, 1992, U.B.A.T.C. award for Support of Vocational Edn., 1992, Golden Key award, 1993, Utah Govt. Coun. for People with Disabilities award State Legis. Coalition, 1994. Mem. Nat. Assn. Campus Activities (regional coord. 1982-85, conf. educator 1980-83, Nat. Outstanding Unit of Yr. 1986, Regional Outstanding Unit of Yr. 1985), Utah Edn. Assn. (honor roll award 1991), Rotary (pres. Ogden chpt.), Kappa Delta Pi, Phi Sigma Alpha, Phi Delta Kappa. Democrat. Mormon. Avocations: auto restoration, waterskiing, hiking. Home: 3073 N 575 E Ogden UT 84414-2077 Office: Weber State U 3750 Harrison Blvd Ogden UT 84408-0001

PRUITT, GARY B. newspaper executive; m. Abby Pruitt; children: Katherine, Allison. Bachelor Degree summa cum laude, U. Fla.; M in Pub. Policy with high honors, JD, U. Calif. Gen. counsel The McClatchy Co., 1984-91, pub. The Fresno Bee, 1991-94, v.p. ops. and tech., 1994-95, pres., COO, 1995-96, CEO, 1996—. Mem. chancellors com. U. Calif., Berkeley, mem. bd. advisors Goldman Sch. Pub. Policy. Mem. AP (auditing com.), Calif. Newspaper Pubs. Assn. (various coms.), James Irvine Found. (bd. dirs.), Newspaper Assn. Am. (bd. dirs.), Phi Beta Kappa. Office: The McClatchy Co 2100 Q St Sacramento CA 95816-6816

PRUNES, FERNANDO, plastic surgeon, educator; b. Chihuahua, Mex. m. Linda R. Underwood; children: Alexander, Ariadne, Anthony. MD, U. Chihuahua, Mex., 1968. Surg. intern Booth Meml. Med. Ctr., Flushing, N.Y., 1971-72; resident in gen. surgery Tucson Hosps. Med. Edn. Program, 1972-76; resident in plastic surgery Mayo Grad. Sch. Medicine, 1979-81; chief divsn. plastic surgery Kern Med. Ctr., Bakersfield, Calif., 1983—. Asst. clin. prof. surgery U. Calif., San Diego, 1983-98. Mem. Am. Soc. Plastic Surgeons, Mayo Alumni Assn. Avocations: golf, computers. Office: Kern Med Ctr 1830 Flower St Bakersfield CA 93305-4186

PRUSINER, STANLEY BEN, neurology and biochemistry educator, researcher; b. Des Moines, May 28, 1942; s. Lawrence Albert and Miriam (Spigel) P.; children: Helen Chloe, Leah Anne. AB cum laude, U. Pa., 1964, MD, 1968; PhD (hon.), Hebrew U., Jerusalem, 1995, René Descartes U., Paris, 1996; DS (hon.), U. Pa., 1998, Dartmouth Coll., 1999; MD (hon.), U. Bologna, Italy, 2000, U. Liege, Belgium, 2000; DSc (hon.), Pa. State U., 2001. Diplomate Am. Bd. Neurology. Intern in medicine U. Calif., San Francisco, 1968-69, resident in neurology, 1972-74, asst. prof. neurology, 1974-80, assoc. prof., 1980-84, prof., 1984—, prof. biochemistry, 1988—, acad. senate faculty rsch. lectr., 1989-90, prof. virology Berkeley, 1984—, dir. Inst. for Neurodegenerative Diseases, 1999—; founder, chmn. bd. dirs. Info Biotech. LLC, South San Francisco, Calif., 2001—. Mem. neurology rev. com. Nat. Inst. for Neurodegenerative Diseases, NIH, Bethesda, Md., 1982—86, Bethesda, 1990—92; mem. Coun. Nat. Inst. Aging, NIH, Bethesda, Md., 2001—; mem. sci. adv. bd. French Found., L.A., 1985—, chmn. sci. adv. bd., 1996—; mem. sci. rev. com. Alzheimer's Disease Diagnostic Ctr. & Rsch Grant Program, State of Calif., 1985—89; chmn. sci. adv. bd. Am. Health Assistance Found., Rockville, Md., 1986—2000, hon. mem. bd. dirs., Md., 2001—; mem. spongiform encephalopathy adv. com. FDA, 1997—2001; mem. adv. bd.Family Survival Project for Adults with Chronic Brain Disorders, San Francisco, 1982—90; mem. adv. bd. San Francisco chpt. Alzheimer's Disease and Related Disorders Found., 1985—91. Editor: The Enzymes of Glutamine Metabolism, 1973, Slow Transmissible Diseases of the Nervous System, 2 vols., 1979, Prions—Novel Infectious Pathogens Causing Scrapie and CJD, 1987, Prion Diseases of Humans and Animals, 1992, Molecular and Genetic Basis of Neurologic Disease, 2d edit., 1997, Prions Prions Prions, 1996, Prion Biology and Diseases, 1999;contbr. . Trustee U. Pa., 2000—, Congregation Sherith Israel, San Francisco, 1999. Recipient Leadership and Excellence for Alzheimer's Disease award NIH, 1990-97, Potamkin prize for Alzheimer's Disease Rsch., 1991, Presl. award, 1993, Med. Rsch. award Met. Life Found., 1992, Christopher Columbus Discovery award NIH and Med. Soc. Genoa, Italy, 1992, Charles A. Dana award for pioneering achievements in health, 1992, Dickson prize for outstanding contbns. to medicine U. Pitts., 1992, Max Planck Rsch. award Alexander von Humboldt Found. and Max Planck Soc., 1992, Gairdner Found. Internat. award, 1993, Disting. Achievement in Neurosci. Rsch. award Bristol-Myers Squibb, 1994, Albert Lasker award for Basic Med. Rsch., 1994, Caledonian Rsch. Found. prize Royal Soc. Edinburgh, 1995, Paul Ehrlich and Ludwig Darmstaedter award Germany, 1995, Paul Hoch award Am. Psychopathol. Assn., 1995, Wolf prize in medicine, 1996, ICN Virology prize, 1996, Victor and Clara Soriano award World Fedn. Neurology, 1996, Pasarow Found. prize in neurosci., 1996, Charles Leopold Mayer prize French Acad. Scis., 1996, Keio Internat. prize for med. rsch., 1996, Baxter award Am. Assn. Med. Colls., 1996, Louisa Gross Horwitz prize Columbia U., 1997, Nobel prize in medicine, 1997, K.J. Zulch prize Gertrude Reemtsma Found., 1997, Benjamin Franklin medal Franklin Inst., 1998, Jubilee medal Swedish Med. Soc., 1998, Prize Lecture medal U. Coll. London, 1999, Sir Hans Krebs medal Fedn. European Biochemical Socs., 1999, Ellen Browning Scripps medal, 2000; Alfred P. Sloan Rsch. fellow U. Calif., 1976-78; Med. Investigator grantee Howard Hughes Med. Inst., 1976-81; grantee for excellence in neurosci. Senator Jacob Javits Ctr., NIH, 1985-90. Fellow: AAAS, Am. Soc. Microbiology, Am. Acad. Arts & Scis., Royal Coll. Physicians; mem.: NAS Inst. Medicine, Richard Lounsbery award for extraordinary achievements in biology and medicine 1993, Concordia Argonaut Club (bd. dirs. 1997—), Am. Acad. Neurology, Am. Assn. Physicians, Am. Soc. Neurochemistry, Am. Soc. Neurochemistry, Am. Soc. Virology, Am. Neurol. Assn., Am. Soc. Clin. Investigation, Am. Soc. Biochemistry and Molecular Biology, Am. Chem. Soc., Soc. Neurosci., Am. Soc. Human Genetics, Genetics Soc. Am., Am. Soc. Cell Biology, Am. Soc. Cellular Biology, Am. Soc. Molecular Biol. Biochemistry, Am. Philos. Soc., Royal Soc. London, Protein Soc.

PTAK, JOHN, talent agent; b. San Diego, Sept. 23, 1942; s. John and Doris Elizabeth P.; m. Margaret Elizabeth Black, May 21, 1981; 1 child, Hillary Elizabeth. BA, UCLA, 1967. Theatre mgr., booker Walter Reade Orgn., Beverly Hills, Calif., 1967-69; adminstrv. exec. Am. Film Inst., Beverly Hills, 1968-70; talent agent Internat. Famous Agy. (now ICM), L.A., 1971-75, William Morris Agy., Beverly Hills, 1976-91, Creative Artists Agy., Beverly Hills, 1991—. Co-chmn. Am. Film Inst. Ctr. for Film & Video Preservation, L.A., 1991—; mem. Nat. Film Preservation Bd., Washington, 1992—. Bd. dirs. Motion Pictures and T.V. Fund Found., 1996—, Nat. Film Preservation Found., 1997—. Avocations: tennis, travel. Office: Creative Artists Agy 9830 Wilshire Blvd Beverly Hills CA 90212-1825

PTASYNSKI, HARRY, geologist, oil producer; b. Milw., May 26, 1926; s. Stanley S. and Frances V. (Stawicki) P.; m. Nola G. Whitestine, Sept. 15, 1951; children: Ross F., Lisa Joy. BS, Stanford U., 1950. Cert. profl. geologist; cert. petroleum geologist. Dist. geologist Pure Oil Co., Amarillo, Tex., 1951-55, Casper, Wyo., 1955-58; ind. geologist, oil prodr. Casper, 1958—. With USN, 1943-46, PTO. Mem. Am. Assn. Petroleum Geologists, Am. Inst. Profl. Geologists, Ind. Petroleum Assn. Am. (v.p., bd. dirs. 1976-85), Ind. Petroleum Assn. Mountain States (v.p., bd. dirs. 1976-80, Rocky Mountain Oil and Gas Assn. (bd. dirs., exec. com. 1980-96). Republican. Episcopalian. Avocations: tennis, trout and salmon fishing, western history, golfing. Home: 1515 Brookview Dr Casper WY 82604-4895 Office: 123 W 1st St Ste 560 Casper WY 82601-2483 E-mail: hptasyn@trib.com

PUCCINELLI, ANDREW JAMES, lawyer; b. Elko, Nev., July 21, 1935; BA cum laude, U. of the Pacific, 1975, JD, 1978. Bar: Nev. 1978. Ptnr. Puccinelli & Puccinelli, Elko, Nev., 1978—. Bus. law adj. prof. No. Nev. C.C., 1982-93; legal advisor Nev. Home Health Svcs., 1980-88. Bd. dirs. Nev. Legal Svcs., 1986-93. Mem. ATLA, Nev. Trial Lawyers Assn., Nev. State Bar Assn. (bd. govs. 1993-2000, v.p. 1996-97, pres.-elect 1997-98, pres. 1998-99, No. Nev. disciplinary bd. 1988-93, CLE com. 1981-85), Elko County Bar Assn. (pres. 1985-86), Phi Delta Phi. Office: Puccinelli & Puccinelli 700 Idaho St Elko NV 89801-3824

PUCK, THEODORE THOMAS, geneticist, biophysicist, educator; b. Chgo., Sept. 24, 1916; s. Joseph and Bessie (Shapiro) Puckowitz; m. Mary Hill, Apr. 17, 1946; children: Stirling, Jennifer, Laurel. B.S., U. Chgo., 1937, Ph.D., 1940. Mem. commn. airborne infections Office Surgeon Gen., Army Epidemiol. Bd., 1944-46; asst. prof. depts. medicine and biochemistry U. Chgo., 1945-47; sr. fellow Am. Cancer Soc., Calif. Inst. Tech., Pasadena, 1947-48; prof. biophysics U. Colo. Med. Sch., 1948—, chmn. dept., 1948-67, disting. prof. dept. medicine, 1986—; founder, dir. Eleanor Roosevelt Inst. Cancer Research, 1962-95; Disting. rsch. prof. Am. Cancer Soc., 1966—. Nat. lectr. Sigma Xi, 1975-76 Author: The Mammalian Cell as a Microorganism: Genetic and Biochemical Studies in Vitro, 1972. Mem. Commn. on Physicians for the Future. Recipient Albert Lasker award, 1958, Borden award med. rsch., 1959, Louisa Gross Horwitz prize, 1973, Gordon Wilson medal Am. Clin. and Climatol. Assn., 1977, award Environ. Mutagen Soc., 1981, E.B. Wilson medal Am. Soc. Cell Biology, 1984, Bonfils-Stanton award in sci., 1984, U. Colo. Disting. Prof. award, 1987, Henry M. Porter medal, 1992; named to The Colo. 100, Historic Denver, 1992; Heritage Found. scholar, 1983; Phi Beta Kappa scholar, 1985; Fogarty Internat. scholar NIH, 1997. Fellow Am. Acad. Arts and Scis.; mem. Am. Soc. Human Genetics, Am. Chem. Soc., Soc. Exptl. Biology and Medicine, AAAS (Phi Beta Kappa award and lectr. 1983), Am. Assn. Immunologists, Radiation Research Soc., Biophys. Soc., Genetics Soc. Am., Nat. Acad. Sci., Tissue Culture Assn. (Hon. award 1987), Paideia Group, Santa Fe Inst. Sci. Bd., Phi Beta Kappa, Sigma Xi. Achievements include pioneering contributions to establishment of somatic cell approaches to mammalian cell genetics, to the identification and classification of the human chromosomes; measurement of mutation in mammalian cells; demonstration of the camp-induced reverse transformation reaction and the genome exposure defect in cancer; development of quantitative approaches to mammalian cell radiobiology. Office: Eleanor Roosevelt Inst Cancer Rsch 1899 Gaylord St Denver CO 80206-1210

PUCK, WOLFGANG, executive chef; b. St. Veit, Austria, July 8, 1949; married; two children. Chef, part owner Ma Maison, L.A., 1973; exec. chef, ptnr. Spago's, 1982, Chinois on Main, Santa Monica, 1983, Postrio, San Francisco, 1989, Granita, Malibu, Calif., 1991. Fund raising Meals on Wheels, A. Cancer Soc. L.A. Author: Modern French Cooking for the American Kitchen, 1982, The Wolfgang Puck Cookbook: Recipes from Spago and Chinois, 1986, Adventures in the Kitchen with Wolfgang Puck, 1991; producer (instructional cooking video) Spago Cooking with Wolfgang Puck. Office: Eolfgang Puck Cafe 8000 W Sunset Blvd Los Angeles CA 90046-2439

PUCKETT, W. GREER, engineer; b. Oak Ridge, Tenn., Apr. 20, 1952; s. James Beverly and Jane (Greer) P. BS, U.S. Naval Acad., 1975. Design engr. Ford Motor Co., Dearborn, Mich., 1979-80; field engr. Westinghouse, Groton, Conn., 1980-84, Dunoon, Scotland, 1984-85, Westinghouse/Northrop Grumman, Groton, 1985-96; project mgr. Northrop Grumman, Sunnyvale, Calif., 1996-99, field engr. Bangor, Wash., 1999-2000, sr. field engr. Sunnyvale, Calif., 2000—. Bd. dirs. Southeastern Conn. AIDS Project, New London, 1989-93, 1995-96, Concern Inc., New London, 1994-96, Kitsap Human Rights Network, Silverdale, Wash., 1999-2000; contbg. mem. Human Rights Campaign, Washington, 1991-98, Dem. Nat. Com., Washington, 1996—. Served U.S. Navy 1975-78. Recipient Appreciation award Southeastern Conn. AIDS Project, 1996, Westinghouse Marine Divsn. Quality Ach. award, 1989. Democrat. Presbyterian. Avocations: collecting art and antiques, playing bridge, walking, reading, doing volunteer work. Home: 4661 Albany Cir Apt 112 San Jose CA 95129 Office: Northrop Grumman Marine Sys 401 E Hendy Ave Sunnyvale CA 94088 E-mail: greerp1975@aol.com

PUERNER, JOHN P. newspaper publishing executive; BA, U. of Mich., 1958, MBA, 1959. V.p., dir. mktg. and devel. Chgo. Tribune; pres., pub. The Orlando Sentinel, Fla., 1993-99, Los Angeles Times, Calif., 2000—. Office: Los Angeles Times The Times Mirror Co Times Mirror Sq Los Angeles CA 90053-0001

PUGH, DONALD E. industry executive; Pres. Cummins Northwest, Inc. Office: Cummins Northwest Inc 811 SW Grady Way Renton WA 98055-2900

PUGH, JOHN ROBERT, chancellor, former state health administrator; b. New Orleans, Dec. 20, 1945; s. Edward Nicholls and Yvonne Marie (Duplantier) P.; m. Margaret Louise McMullen, Aug. 26, 1975; children— Margaret Elizabeth, John Robert. B.A. in Philosophy, Baylor U., 1967; M. in Social Work, U. Tex.-Austin, 1970. Program dir. McLaughlin Youth Ctr., Anchorage, 1973-78; dep. dir. Alaska Div. Social Services, Juneau, 1978-80; dir. Alaska Family and Youth Services, Juneau, 1980-83; dep. commr. Alaska Dept. Health and Social Services, Juneau, 1983, commr., 1983-86; dean, Sch. of Education Univ. Alaska Southeast, Juneau, 1986-95, chancellor, 1995—. Cons., lectr. in field Mem., Blue Ribbon Commn. for Revision of Children's Code, 1975-77; supt. Sunday Sch., No. Light United Ch., Juneau, 1979— ; mem. Gov.'s Council for Handicapped and Gifted, 1980-84; mem. precinct com. Greater Juneau Democratic Com., 1983— ; bd. dirs. Alaska State Fin. Corp., 1985— ; coach Juneau Little

League, 1984— . Served to capt. USAF, 1969-73 Mem. Nat. Assn. Social Workers (pres. 1975-76), Am. Pub. Welfare Assn., Am. Correctional Assn., Alaska Pub. Employees Assn. (pres. 1977-79), Acad. Cert. Social Workers (cert.) Methodist Avocations: fishing; outdoor sports. Office: U Alaska Southeast 11120 Glacier Hwy Juneau AK 99801

PUGH, KYLE MITCHELL, JR. musician, retired music educator; b. Spokane, Wash., Jan. 6, 1937; s. Kyle Mitchel, Sr. and Lenore Fae (Johnson) P.; m. Susan Deane Waite, July 16, 1961; children: Jeffray, Kari. BA in Edu., East Wash. U., 1975. Cert. tchr., Wash. Tuba player Spokane Symphony Orch., 1958-63; rec. assoc. Century Records, Spokane, 1965-73; tuba player World's Fair Expo '74, Spokane, 1974; bass player Russ Carlyle Orch., Las Vegas, 1976, Many Sounds of Nine Orch., northwest area, 1969-81; band tchr. Garry Jr. High School, Spokane, 1976-79, Elementary Band Program, Spokane, 1979-96; bass player Doug Scott Cabaret Band, Spokane, 1982-91. Dept. head Elem. Band Dept., Spokane, 1984-89. Editor (newsletter) The Repeater, 1987 (Amateur Radio News Svc. award 1987); extra in movie Always, 1989. Active in communications Lilac Bloomsday Assn., Spokane, 1977. Served to E-5 USNR, 1955-63 Recipient Disting. Service award Wash. State Commn., 1974, Nev. Hollerin' Champ Carl Hayden Scribe, 1979. Mem. Am. Fedn. Musicians (life), Spokane Edn. Assn. (rec. sec. 1987), Music Educator's Nat. Conf., Am. Radio Relay League (asst. dir. 1987), Ea. Wash. Music Educator's Assn. (pres. 1978-79), Dial Twisters Club (pres. 1979-80), VHF Radio Amateurs (dir. 1980-83), Elks. Avocations: ham radio operator, model railroading, photography. Home: 5006 W Houston Ave Spokane WA 99208-3728

PUGH, RICHARD CRAWFORD, lawyer; b. Phila., Apr. 28, 1929; s. William and Myrtle P.; m. Nanette Bannen, Feb. 27, 1954; children: Richard Crawford, Andrew Lembert, Catherine Elizabeth. AB summa cum laude, Dartmouth Coll., 1951; BA in Jurisprudence, Oxford (Eng.) U., 1953; LLB, Columbia U., 1958. Bar: N.Y. 1958. Assoc. firm Cleary, Gottlieb, Steen & Hamilton, N.Y.C., 1958-61, ptnr., 1969-89, counsel, 1989—; disting. prof. law U. San Diego, 1989—, univ. prof., 1998-99. Mem. faculty Law Sch. Columbia U., 1961-89, prof., 1964-69, adj. prof., 1969-89; lectr. Columbia-Amsterdam-Leyden (Netherlands) summer program Am. law, 1963, 79; dep. asst. atty. gen. tax div. U.S. Dept. Justice, 1966-68; Cons. fiscal and fin. br. UN Secretariat, 1962, 64. Editor: Columbia Law Rev., 1957-58; editor: (with W. Friedmann) Legal Aspects of Foreign Investment, 1959, Taxation of Business Enterprises, 1998, (with others) International Law, 2001, Taxation of International Transactions, 2001, International Income Taxation: Code and Regulations 2001-02. Served with USNR, 1954-56. Rhodes scholar, 1953. Mem. ABA, Am. Law Inst., Am. Coll. Tax Counsel, Am. Soc. Internat. Law, Internat. Fiscal Assn. (pres. U.S. br. 1978-79). Home: 7335 Encelia Dr La Jolla CA 92037-5729 Office: U San Diego Sch Law Alcala Park San Diego CA 92110-2429 E-mail: rpugh@acusd.edu

PUGLISI, RICHARD LAWRENCE, federal judge; BA, U. N.Mex., 1975, JD, 1979. Bar: N.Mex. 1980, Hawaii, 1981. U.S. Navy judge adv. gen. corp., 1979-82; asst. U.S. atty. Honolulu, 1982-84; with Montgomery & Andrews, P.A., 1984-91, Madison, Harbour, Mroz & Puglisi, P.A., 1991-96; magistrate judge for N.Mex. U.S. Dist. Ct., Albuquerque, 1996—. Office: US Magistrate Judge US Courthouse 333 Lomas Blvd NW Albuquerque NM 87102-2272

PUGSLEY, ROBERT ADRIAN, law educator; b. Mineola, N.Y., Dec. 27, 1946; s. Irvin Harold and Mary Catherine (Brusselars) P. BA, SUNY-Stony Brook, 1968; JD, NYU, 1975, LLM in Criminal Justice, 1977. Instr. sociology New Sch. Social Rsch., N.Y.C., 1969-71; coord. Peace Edn. programs The Christophers, N.Y.C., 1971-78; assoc. prof. law Southwestern U., L.A., 1978-81, prof., 1981—, Paul E. Treusch prof. law, 2000-01. Adj. asst. prof. criminology and criminal justice Southampton Coll.-Long Island U., 1975-76; acting dep. dir. Criminal Law Edn. and Rsch. Ctr., NYU, 1983-86; bd. advisors Ctr. Legal Edn. CCNY-CUNY, 1978, Sta. KPFK-FM, 1985-86; founder, coord. The Wednesday Evening Soc., L.A., 1979-86; vis. prof. Jacob D. Fuchsberg Law Ctr. Touro Coll., L.I., N.Y., summers, 1988, 89; lectr. in criminal law and procedure Legal Edn. Conf. Ctr., L.A., 1982-96; prof., dir. Comparative Criminal Law and Procedure Program U. B.C., Vancouver, summers, 1994, 98, 99, 2000, 01; chair pub. interest law com. Southwestern U., 1990-2001; lectr. legal profl. responsibility West Bar Rev. Faculty, Calif., 1996-98; legal analyst/commentator for print and electronic media, 1992—. Creative advisor Christopher Closeup (nationally syndicated pub. svc. TV program), 1975-83; host Earth Alert, Cable TV, 1983-87; prodr., moderator (pub. affairs discussion program) Inside L.A., Sta. KPFK-FM, 1979-86, Open Jour. program, Sta. KPFK-FM, 1991-94; contbr. articles to legal jours. Founding mem. Southwestern U. Pub. Interest Law com., 1992—; mem. L.A. County Bar Assn. Adv. Com. on Alcohol & Drug Abuse, 1991-95, co-chair, 1993-95; mem. exec. com. non-govtl. orgns. UN Office Pub. Info., 1977; mem. issues task force L.A. Conservancy, 1980-81, seminar for law tchrs. NEH UCLA, 1979; co-convenor So. Calif. Coalition Against Death Penalty, 1981-83, convener, 1983-84; mem. death penalty com. Lawyer's Support Group, Amnesty Internat., U.S.A.; founding mem. Ch.-State Coun., L.A., 1984-88; bd. dirs. Equal Rights Sentencing Found., 1983-85, Earth Alert, Inc., 1984-87; mem. adv. bd. First Amendment Info. Resources Ctr., Grad. Sch. Libr. and Info. Scis., UCLA, 1990—; mem. coun. Friends UCLA Libr., 1993—, pres., 1996—; mem. adv. bd. Children Requiring a Caring Kommunity, 1998—. Robert Marshall fellow Criminal Law Edn. and Rsch. Ctr., NYU Sch. Law, 1976-78. Mem. Am. Legal Studies Assn., Am. Soc. Polit. and Legal Philosophy, Assn. Am. Law Schs., Inst. Soc. Ethics and Life Scis., Soc. Am. Law Tchrs., Internat. Platform Assn., Internat. Soc. Reform of Criminal Law, The Scribes. Roman Catholic. Office: Southwestern U Sch Law 675 S Westmoreland Ave Los Angeles CA 90005-3905 E-mail: rpugsley@swlaw.edu

PULATIE, DAVID L. metal products executive; BS in Psychology and Personnel Mgmt., Ariz. State U.; MEd, No. Ariz. U. Sr. v.p., corp. dir. change mgmt. Motorola Inc., sr. v.p., dir. human resources semiconductor products sector, v.p., regional dir. Europe, Mid. E., S. Africa, sr. v.p., corp. dir. govt. rels. human resources; sr. v.p. human resources Phelps Dodge Corp., Phoenix, 1999—. Office: Phelps Dodge Corp 2600 N Central Ave Phoenix AZ 85004-3050

PULIDO, MARK A. pharmaceutical and cosmetics company executive; b. 1952; McKesson Drug Co., 1975-88; exec. v.p. FoxMeyer Drug Co., 1988-89; chmn., pres., CEO, Red Line Healthcare Corp., 1989-96; pres., CEO, Sandoz Pharmaceuticals Corp., 1994-95; pres., chmn., CEO, dir. McKesson Corp., 1996-99; chmn., CEO, pres. BenefitPoint, San Francisco, 2000—. Office: BenefitPoint 801 Montgomery St San Francisco CA 94133-5164

PULIDO, MIGUEL ANGEL, mayor; b. Mexico City, Mex., 19[illegible]; m. Laura Pulido; children: Miguel Robert, David. BSME, Calif. State U., Fullerton. Dir. computer program McCaughey & Smith Energy Assocs., v.p.; mem. Santa Ana (Calif.) City Coun., 1986—; mayor City of Santa Ana, 1994—. Mem. Santa Ana Redevel. Agy., Downtown Santa Ana Bus. Assn.; mem. 1st dist. Orange County Transp. Authority. Avocations: chess, backgammon, tennis, music, guitar. Office: Office Mayor & City Coun 20 Civic Ctr Plaza PO Box 1988 Santa Ana CA 92702-1988 E-mail: mpulido@ci.santa-ana.ca.us

PULLIAM, FRANCINE SARNO, real estate broker, real estate developer; b. San Francisco, Sept. 14, 1937; d. Ralph C. Stevens and Frances I. (Wilson) Sarno; m. John Donald Pulliam, Aug. 14, 1957 (div. Mar. 1965); 1 child, Wendy; m. Terry Kent Graves, Dec. 14, 1974. Student, U. Ariz., 1955-56, U. Nev., Las Vegas, 1957. Airline stewardess Bonanza Airlines, Las Vegas, 1957; real estate agt. The Pulliam Co., Las Vegas, 1958-68, Levy Realty, Las Vegas, 1976-76; real estate broker, owner Prestige Properties, Las Vegas, 1976—. Importer, exporter Exports Internat., Las Vegas, 1984—; bd. dirs. Citicorp Bank of Nev.; mem. adv. bd. to Amb. to Bahamas Chic Hect.; property mgr. Prestigo Properties, 1992—. Bd. dirs. Las Vegas Bd. Realtors, Fedn. Internat. Realtors, Nat. Kidney Found., Assistance League, Cancer Soc., Easter Seals, Econ. Rsch. Bd., Children's Discovery Mus., New Horizons Ctr. for Children with Learning Disabilities, Girl Scouts, Home of the Good Shepard, St. Jude's Ranch for Homeless Children; pres., bd. dirs. Better Bus. Bur.; chmn. Las Vegas Taxi Cab Authority; pres. Citizens for Pvt. Enterprises. Mem. Las Vegas C. of C. (bd. dirs., developer). Republican. Roman Catholic. Office: 2340 Paseo Del Prado Ste D202 Las Vegas NV 89102-4341

PURCELL, JOHN F. lawyer; b. Bellingham, Wash., Apr. 25, 1954; AB with honors, Stanford U., 1976; JD, Lewis and Clark Coll., 1980. Bar: Oreg. 1980. Ptnr. Miller Nash LLP, Portland, 1987—. Mem. Oreg. State Bar. Office: Miller Nash LLP 111 SW 5th Ave Ste 3500 Portland OR 97204-3638

PURCELL, KENNETH, psychology educator, university dean; b. N.Y.C., Oct. 21, 1928; s. Herman and Ann (Bulkin) P.; m. Claire Dickson Kepler, Dec. 17, 1949 (div. Dec. 1986); children: Kathleen Ann, Andrew Kepler; m. Marjorie Bayes, Jan. 17, 1987. B.A., Ph.D., U. Nebr. Asst. prof. U. Ky., 1956-58; dir. behavior sci. div. Children's Asthma Research Inst.; asst. prof. U. Colo. Med. Center, 1958-68; prof., dir. clin. tng. psychology U. Mass., 1968-69, chmn. dept. psychology, 1969-70; prof. psychology U. Denver, 1970—, dean Coll. Arts and Scis., 1976-84, prof. psychology, 1984-98, prof. emeritus, 1994. Author papers in field. Served to 2d lt. AUS, 1953-56. Fellow Am. Psychol. Assn., Soc. Research Child Devel., AAAS, Colo. Psychol. Assn. (dir. 1962-64) Home: 3254 S Heather Gardens Way Aurora CO 80014-3666 Office: U Denver Coll Arts & Scis Denver CO 80208-0001

PURDY, ALAN HARRIS, biomedical engineer; b. Mt. Clemens, Mich., Dec. 13, 1923; s. Harry Martin and Elinor (Harris) P.; m. Anna Elizabeth Sohn, Aug. 16, 1968 (dec.); children: Catherine, Charles, Susan, Harry; m. Margaret Josephine Kelley, Mar. 5, 1997. BSME, U. Miami, 1954; MS in Physiology, UCLA, 1967; PhD in Engring., U. Mo., 1970. Cert. clin. engr., Washington. Project engr. in acoustics Arvin Industries, Columbus, Ind., 1954-56, AC Spark Plug Co., Flint, Mich., 1956-60; asst. prof. engring. Calif. Poly. U., Pomona, 1960-62; assoc. dir. biomed. engring. U. Mo., Columbia, 1967-71; dep. assoc. dir., assoc. dir. Nat. Inst. for Occupational Safety and Health, Rockville, Md., 1971-81, scientist, biomed. engr. Cin., 1983-86; asst. dir. Fla. Inst. Oceanography, St. Petersburg, 1981-83; pres. Alpha Beta R & D Corp., San Marcos, Calif., 1986—. Cons. Smithy Muffler Corp., L.A., 1961-62, Statham Instruments, L.A., 1966; cons. faculty, Tex. Tech. U., Lubbock, 1972-73; lectr. U. Cin., 1980. Patentee in diving, acoustical and occupational safety fields. Pilot CG Aux., 1989-98. With USAF, 1942-43. Nat. Heart Inst. spl. fellow, 1963-67; Fulbright scholar, Yugoslavia, 1984. Mem. Acoustical Soc. Am., Biomed. Engring. Soc., Am. Inst. Physics, Exptl. Aircraft Assn., Aircraft Owners and Pilots Assn., DAV. Democrat. Home and Office: 941 Cycad Dr San Marcos CA 92078-5013 E-mail: ahpurdy@nethere.com

PURDY, ALAN MACGREGOR, financial executive; b. Iowa City, Apr. 23, 1940; s. Rob Roy MacGregor and Frances Norrine (Edwards) P.; m. Sarah Lane Robins, June 13, 1964; children— William Wallace, John Alan, Tammi Ann. A.B., Duke U., 1962; M.B.A., Wharton Sch. Fin. and Commerce, U. Pa., 1968. Bus. analyst Gen. Mills, Inc., Mpls., 1968-71; sr. fin. analyst Dayton Hudson Corp. (now Target Corp.), Mpls., 1972-73; mgr. capital expenditure analysis Dayton Hudson Corp., Mpls., 1973, dir. corp. analysis, 1973-75, dir. planning and analysis, 1975-77; v.p., treas. Fleming Cos., Inc., Oklahoma City, 1977-81; v.p. fin., chief fin. officer John A. Brown Co. (subs. Target Corp.), Oklahoma City, 1981-83; sr. v.p., chief fin. officer B. Dalton Co. (subs. Target Corp.), Mpls., 1983-86, Robinson's of Fla.(subs. May Co.), St. Petersburg, 1986-87, Miller's Outpost (subs. Am. Retail Group), Ontario, Calif., 1988-92, Builders Emporium (subs. Collins and Aikman Group), Irvine, 1993; RemedyTemp, Aliso Viejo, 1994—. Served with USN, 1962-66. Home: 2190 Hillview Dr Laguna Beach CA 92651-2211 Office: Remedy Temp 101 Enterprise Aliso Viejo CA 92656-2604 E-mail: alanp@remedystaff.com

PURDY, LESLIE, community college president; b. Downey, Calif., Aug. 18, 1943; d. Hubert C. and Janice M. (Harker) Noble; m. Ralph Purdy, Aug. 23, 1969; children: Christopher Hugh, George Colin. BA cum laude, Occidental Coll., L.A., 1965; MAT, Oberlin (Ohio) Coll., 1966; EdD, UCLA, 1973. Tchr. Parma (Ohio) Sr. H.S., 1966; ombudsman/instr. social sci. Raymond Coll., U. of Pacific, Stockton, Calif., 1967-69; coord. spl. svcs. ERIC Clearinghouse for C.C.'s, L.A., 1970-74; sr. instrnl. designer Coastline C.C., Fountain Valley, Calif., 1974-84, adminstrv. dean, 1984-94, pres., 1994—. Bd. dirs. Intelecom, Pasadena, Calif.; bd. dirs., pres. Instrnl. Telecom. Coun., Washington, 1987-94; adv. bd. PBS "Going the Distance" program, Washington, 1993-96; cons. Commn. on Innovation, Calif. Colls. Chancellor's Office, 1993-94. Editor: Reaching New Students Through New Technologies, 1983; instrnl. designer Psychology: The Study of Human Behavior, 1989 (Emmy 1990); exec. prodr. (telecourses): Universe: The Infinite Frontier, 1994 (Emmy 1994), Time to Grow, 1992 (Emmy 1992); contbr. articles to profl. jours. Mem. Orange County Forum, 1994—, Ctr. for Studies of Media and Values, L.A., 1990-95, Bread for the World, Washington, 1980—; bd. mem. West County Family YMCA, 1993-2000; bd. mem. Garden Grove Renaissance Found., 1998—; bd. mem. Orange County Nat. Conf. of Cmty. and Justice, 1997—, Orange County Workforce Investment Bd., 2000—. Recipient Emmy awards Am. Acad. TV Arts and Scis., 1987, 90, 92,. 95, Western Region award Instrn. Telecom. Coun., 1995; named one of Women of Distinction City of Garden Grove, 2001. Mem. Assn. of calif. C.C. Adminstrs., Assn. Ednl. Comms. and Tech., Am. Assn. of Women in C.C.'s, UCLA Alumni Assn. (Doctoral Award in Edn. 1973). Presbyterian. Avocations: backpacking, gardening, conservation, choral singing. Office: Coastline Cmty Coll Office of Pres 11460 Warner Ave Fountain Valley CA 92708 E-mail: lpurdy@cccd.edu

PURKIS, LEONARD C. media executive; b. Cardiff, Wales; Grad., Inst. Chartered Accts., Eng., Wales. Audit mgr. Coopers & Lybrand; sr. v.p. fin. GE Capital Fleet Svcs.; CFO Iomega Corp., 1995-98; CFO, exec. v.p. fin. and adminstrn. E Trade Group Inc., Palo Alto, Calif., 1998—. Office: E Trade Group Inc 4500 Bohannon Dr. Menlo Park CA 94025

PURSGLOVE, BETTY MERLE, computer software quality assurance tester; b. Pitts., Sept. 15, 1923; d. Earle E. and Merle A. (Smith) Duer; m. Larry A. Pursglove, June 30, 1944; children: Diana, Kathleen, Merry, Tanya, Yvonne. BS in Physics, U. Pitts., 1944; postgrad., Minn. U., 1945-47, Carnegie-Mellon U., 1947-49, W.Va. U., 1949-51, Mich. State U., 1968-69. Micro-pilot plant operator Minn. Mining and Mfg., St. Paul, 1944-46; [illegible] rsch. chemist Food Mach Co., Pitts., 1947-49; computer coder Dow Chem. Co., Midland, Mich., 1954; asst. entomologist pvt. collections, Midland, 1955-56; instr. chemistry Cen. Mich. U., Midland, 1958; head chem. dept. Midland Hosp., 1958-64; tchr. chemistry and physics parochial schs., Bay City, Mich., 1964; prin., chief exec. officer Crypticlear, Inc., Applegate, Oreg., 1965—. Leader Midland troup Girl Scout U.S., 1953-63. Mem. AAUW, Sigma Xi, Sigma Pi Sigma. Avocations: creative writing, performing in marching and concert bands, photography, genealogy, gardening. Home and Office: PO Box 3125 Applegate OR 97530-3125

PURVES, WILLIAM KIRKWOOD, biologist, educator; b. Sacramento, Oct. 28, 1934; s. William Kirkwood and Dorothy (Brandenburger) P.; m. Jean McCauley, June 9, 1959; 1 son, David William. B.S., Calif. Inst. Tech., 1956; M.S., Yale U., 1957, Ph.D., 1959. NSF postdoctoral fellow U. Tubingen, Fed. Republic Germany, 1959-60; Nat. Cancer Inst. postdoctoral fellow UCLA, 1960-61; asst. prof. botany U. Calif., Santa Barbara, 1961-65, assoc. prof. biochemistry, 1965-70, prof. biology, 1970-73, chmn. dept. biol. scis., 1972-73; prof. biology, head biol. sci. group U. Conn., Storrs, 1973-77; Stuart Mudd prof. biology Harvey Mudd Coll., Claremont, Calif., 1977-95, prof. emeritus, 1996—, chmn. dept. biol., 1985-95, chmn. dept. computer sci., 1985-90; adj. prof. plant physiology U. Calif., Riverside, 1979-85. V.p., sci. dir. The Mona Group LLC, 1996—. Author: Life, the Science of Biology, 1983, 6th edit., 2001. NSF sr. postdoctoral fellow U. London, 1967, Harvard U., 1968; vis. fellow computer sci. Yale U., 1983-84; vis. scholar Northwestern U., 1991; NSF rsch. grantee, 1962-83, 97-2001. Fellow AAAS; mem. Sigma Xi. Office: The Mona Group LLC 2817 N Mountain Ave Claremont CA 91711-1550 Fax: 909-626-7030. E-mail: purves@monagroup.com

PURVIS, JOHN ANDERSON, lawyer, educator; b. Aug. 31, 1942; s. Virgil J. and Emma Lou (Anderson) P.; m. Charlotte Johnson, Apr. 3, 1976; 1 child, Whitney; children by previous marriage: Jennifer, Matt. BA cum laude, Harvard U., 1965; JD, U. Colo., 1968. Bar: Colo. 1968, U.S. Dist. Ct. Colo. 1968, U.S. Ct. Appeals (10th cir.) 1978. Dep. dist. atty., Boulder, Colo., 1968-69; asst. dir., dir. legal aid U. Colo. Sch. Law, 1969; assoc. Williams, Taussig & Trine, Boulder, 1969; head Boulder office Colo. Pub. Defender Sys., 1970-72; assoc., ptnr. Hutchinson, Black, Hill, Buchanan & Cook, Boulder, 1972-85; ptnr. Purvis, Gray, Schuetze and Gordon, 1985-98, Purvis, Gray & Gordon, LLP, 1999—. Acting Colo. State Pub. Defender, 1978; adj. prof. law U. Colo., 1981, 84-88, 94, others; lectr. in field; chmn. Colo. Pub. Defender Commn., 1979-89; mem. nominating commn. Colo. Supreme Ct., 1984-90; mem. com. on conduct U.S. Dist. Ct., 1991-97, chmn., 1996-97; chmn. Boulder County Criminal Justice Com., 1975-81. Recipient Ames award Harvard U., 1964, Outstanding Young Lawyer award Colo. Bar Assn., 1978, Dist. Achievement award U. Colo. Law Sch. Alumni Assn., 1997. Mem. Internat. Soc. Barristers, Internat. Acad. Trial Lawyers, Am. Bd. Trial Advocates, Am. Coll. of Trial Lawyers (state chmn. 1998-2000), Colo. Bar Assn. (chair litigation sect. 1994-95), Boulder County Bar Assn., Colo. Trial Lawyers Assn., Am. Trial Lawyers Assn., Trial Lawyers for Pub. Justice, Colo. Bar Found., Am. Bar Found., Supreme Ct. Hist. Soc. (state chmn. 1998—), Faculty of Fed. Advocates (bd. dirs. 1999—). Democrat. Address: 1050 Walnut St Ste 501 Boulder CO 80302-5144

PUTMAN, ROBERT DEAN, retired golf course architect; b. Wallace, Idaho, Dec. 18, 1924; m. Sally Harmon, 1945; 3 children. Grad., Fresno State Coll. Art dir. Sta. KJEO-TV, Fresno, Calif., 1950's; ret., 2000. Prin. works include Arvin Mcpl. Golf Course, Wasco, Calif., Madera (Calif.) Mcpl. Golf Course, Rancho Canada Golf Course, Carmel Valley, Calif., La Manga Golf Course, Costa Blanca, Spain, Monterey (Calif.) Country Club Shore Course, San Joaquin Country Club, Fresno, Visalia (Calif.) Mcpl. Golf Course, River Island Golf Course, Poterville, Calif., Kings River Country Club, Kingsburg, Calif. Office: Robert Dean Putman GCA 5644 N Briarwood Ave Fresno CA 93711-2501

PUZDER, ANDREW F. restaurant executive, lawyer; b. Cleve., July 11, 1950; s. Andrew F. and Winifried M. Puzder; m. Deanna L. Descher, Sept. 26, 1987. BA, Cleve. State U., 1975; JD, Washington U., 1978. Gen. counsel, exec. v.p. Fidelity Nat. Fin., Inc., 1978-96, CKE Restaurants, Inc., 1997-99; pres., chief exec. ofcr. Hardee's Food Systems, Inc., 1997—, CKE Restaurants, Inc., Anaheim, Calif., 2000—. Editor Washington U. Law Quarterly, 1977-78. Author of law upheld by U.S. Supreme Ct. in Webster v. Reproductive Health Svcs., 1989; founding dir. Common Ground Network for Life and Choice, 1993. Mem. State Bar Nev., The Mo. Bar, State Bar Calif., Phi Alpha Theta. Address: CKE Restaurants 401 W Karcher Way Anaheim CA 92801

PYKE, RONALD, mathematics educator; b. Hamilton, Ont., Can., Nov. 24, 1931; s. Harold and Grace Carter (Digby) P.; m. Gladys Mary Davey, Dec. 19, 1953; children: Darlene, Brian, Ronald, Gordon. BA (hon.), McMaster U., 1953; MS, U. Wash., 1955, PhD, 1956. Asst. prof. Stanford U., Calif., 1956-58; asst. prof. Columbia U., N.Y.C., 1958-60; prof. math. U. Wash., Seattle, 1960-98, prof. emeritus, 1998—. Vis. prof. U. Cambridge, Eng., 1964-65, Imperial Coll., London, 1970-71, Colo. State U., Ft. Collins, 1979, Technion, Israel, 1988, 90, 92; pres. Inst. Math. Stats., 1986-87; mem. bd. math. scis. NRC/NAS, 1984-88, chmn. com. applications and theoretical stats., 1985-88. Editor Ann. Prob., 1972-75; contbr. articles to profl. jours. NSF grantee, 1961-91. Fellow Internat. Statis. Inst. (v.p. 1989-91), Am. Statis. Assn., Inst. Math. Stats. (pres. 1986-87); mem. Bernoulli Soc., Statis. Soc. of Can. Office: U Washington PO Box 354350 Seattle WA 98195-4350

PYLE, DAVID, elementary education educator; Elem. tchr. Carson Valley Mid. Sch., Nev., until 1994, vice prin., 1999—; staff trainer Douglas County (Nev.) Sch. Dist., 1994-99. Recipient Tchr. Excellence award Internat. Tech. Edn. Assn., 1992. Office: Carson Valley Middle Sch PO Box 1888 Minden NV 89423-1888

PYLE, KENNETH BIRGER, historian, educator; b. Bellefonte, Pa., Apr. 20, 1936; s. Hugh Gillespie and Beatrice Ingeborg (Petterson) P.; m. Anne Hamilton Henszey, Dec. 22, 1960; children: William Henszey, Anne Hamilton. AB magna cum laude, Harvard U., 1958; PhD, Johns Hopkins U., 1965. Asst. prof. U. Wash., 1965-69, assoc. prof., 1969-75, prof. history and Asian studies, 1975—, dir. Henry M. Jackson Sch. Internat. Studies, 1978-88; pres. Nat. Bur. Asian Rsch., 1988—; vice chmn. Japan-U.S. Friendship Commn., 1989-92, chmn., 1992-95. Co-chmn. Joint Com. on U.S.-Japan Cultural and Ednl. Coop., 1992-95; vis. lectr. history Stanford U., 1964-65; vis. assoc. prof. history Yale U., 1969-70, Edwin O. Reischauer Meml. Lectr., 1997. Author: The New Generation in Meiji, Japan, 1969, The Making of Modern Japan, 1978, rev. edit., 1996; editor: The Trade Crisis: How Will Japan Respond?, 1987, The Japanese Question: Power and Purpose in a New Era, 1992, rev. edit., 1996, From APEC to Xanadu, 1997; founding editor Jour. Japanese Studies, 1974-86, chmn. editl. bd., 1987-89, assoc. editor, 1989—. Bd. dirs. Maure and Mike Mansfield Found., 1970-88; bd. govs. Henry M. Jackson Found., 1983—; adv. bd. Japan Found., 1989-99, Japan-Am. Student Conf., 1991—. Recipient Japanese Imperial award 3d Class, Order of Rising Sun, 1999, The Henry M. Jackson award for disting. pub. svc., 2000; Ford Found. fellow, 1961-64; Fulbright-Hays fellow, 1970-71; Social Sci. Research Council-Am. Council Learned Socs. fellow, 1970-73, 77, 83-84 Mem. Assn. Asian Studies, Am. Hist. Assn., Coun. Fgn. Rels. Presbyterian. Home: 8416 Midland Rd Medina WA 98039-5336 Office: Henry M Jackson Sch Internat Studies U Wash Seattle WA 98195-0001

PYM, BRUCE MICHAEL, lawyer; b. Alameda, Calif., Sept. 29, 1942; s. Leonard A. and Willamay (Strandberg) P. B.B.A., U. Wash., 1964, J.D., 1967. Bar: Wash. 1967, U.S. Dist. Ct. (we. dist.) Wash. 1968, U.S. Ct. Appeals (9th cir.) 1968, U.S. Tax Ct. 1969, U.S. Supreme Ct. 1971. Law clk. Wash. State Supreme Ct., Olympia, 1967-68; assoc. Graham & Dunn, Seattle, 1968-73, shareholder, 1973-92; ptnr. Heller, Ehrman, White & McAuliffe, Seattle, 1992—; mng. ptnr. Northwest Offices, 1994-99. Bd. dirs. United Way of King County, 1986-92, chmn., 1990. Mem. ABA, Wash. State Bar Assn., King County Bar Assn. (pres. 1984-85). Office: Heller Ehrman White & McAuliffe 701 5th Ave Ste 6100 Seattle WA 98104-7098

PYNN, ROGER, physicist; b. Maidstone, Kent, Eng., Feb. 15, 1945; s. Herbert John and Kathleen (Coleman) P. MA, Trinity Coll., Cambridge, Eng., 1966; PhD, U. Cambridge, 1969. Postdoctoral fellow AB Atomenergi, Studsvik, Sweden, 1970-71; rsch. fellow Inst. for Atomenergi, Kjeller, Norway, 1971-73; assoc. physicist Brookhaven Nat. Lab., Upton, N.Y., 1973-75; staff scientist Inst. Laue-Langevin, Grenoble, France, 1975-87; dir. Manuel Lujan Jr. Neutron Scatterin Ctr. Los Alamos (N.Mex.) Nat. Lab., 1987-93; dep. program dir. LANSCE and Energy Rsch. Program, Los Alamos, N.Mex., 1993-97; dir. neutron sci. ctr. Los Alamos (N. Mex.) Nat. Lab., 1997—. Fellow AAAS, Am. Phys. Soc.; mem. Norwegian Phys. Soc., Materials Rsch. Soc.sssssssss Office: Los Alamos Nat Lab Los Alamos Sci Ctr Ms H845 Ctr Los Alamos NM 87545-0001

PYOTT, DAVID EDMUND IAN, pharmaceutical executive; married; 4 children. Diploma in German and European Law, U. Amsterdam; MA, U. Edinburgh; MBA, London Bus. Sch. Numerous positions Sandoz Nutrition, Barcelona, Spain, 1980-90, gen. mgr., 1990-92; pres., CEO Sandoz Nutrition Corp., Mpls., 1992-95; head divsn. nutrition Sandoz Internat. AG, 1995-96, Novartis AG (merger Sandoz and Ciba), 1997; pres., CEO Allergan, Inc., Irvine, Calif., 1998—. Bd. dirs. PhRMA, Avery Dennison Corp., Edwards Lifescis. Corp.; dir. Calif. Healthcare Inst.; mem. dirs.' bd., mem. exec. com. U. Calif. (Irvine) Grad. Sch. Mgmt. Mem. Pharm. Rsch. and Mfrs. Am. (bd. dirs., Allergan rep.), Pan Am. Assn. Ophthalmology (bd. dirs.), L.A. Bus. Advisors. Office: Allergan Inc 2525 Dupont Dr Irvine CA 92715

QUACKENBUSH, CHUCK, state commissioner; Commr. of ins. State of Calif., Sacramento. Office: Dept Ins 300 Capitol Mall Ste 1700 Sacramento CA 95814-4339

QUACKENBUSH, JUSTIN LOWE, federal judge; b. Spokane, Wash., Oct. 3, 1929; s. Carl Clifford and Marian Huldah (Lowe) Q.; m. Marie McAtee; children: Karl Justin, Kathleen Marie, Robert Craig. Student, U. Ill., 1947-49; BA, U. Idaho, 1951; LLB, Gonzaga U., Spokane, 1957. Bar: Wash. 1957. Dep. pros. atty., Spokane County, 1957-59; ptnr. Quackenbush, Dean, Bailey & Henderson, Spokane, 1959-80; dist. judge U.S. Dist. Ct. (ea. dist.) Wash., Spokane, 1980—, now sr. judge. Part-time instr. Gonzaga U. Law Sch., 1960-67 Chmn. Spokane County Planning Commn., 1969-73. Served with USN, 1951-54. Mem. Wash. Bar Assn., Spokane County Bar Assn. (trustee 1976-78), Internat. Footprint Assn. (nat. pres. 1967), Shriners. Episcopalian. Office: US Dist Ct PO Box 1432 Spokane WA 99210-1432

QUADT, RAYMOND ADOLPH, metallurgist, cement company executive; b. Perth Amboy, N.J., Apr. 16, 1916; s. Adolph and Florence (MacCracken) Q.; 1 child, Brian. B.S., Rutgers U., 1939; M.A., Columbia U., 1943; M.S., Stevens Inst. Tech., 1948. Tchr. high sch., Plainfield, N.J., 1939-42; research metallurgist Am. Smelting & Refining Co., Barber, 1942-48, dir. aluminum devel., 1948-50; v.p. Hunter Douglas Corp., Riverside, Calif., 1950-57; v.p. research and devel. Bridgeport Brass Co., 1958-60, v.p. spl. metals, 1962-63; v.p. Nat. Distillers and Chem. Corp., N.Y.C., 1963—; chmn. bd. Loud Co., Pomona, Calif., 1963—; pres., gen. mgr. Reactive Metals Inc., 1960-62; v.p., gen. mgr. Pascoe Steel Corp., Pomona, 1965-73; pres. Phoenix Cement Co., 1973-80, cons., 1980-83; chmn. bd. Trendex, Inc., Phoenix, 1983-87, Mesco, Phoenix, 1983-88. Vice chmn. Sunstate Bancshares Inc., Casa Grande, Ariz., 1982; bd. dirs. Republic Nat. Bank, Phoenix, 1982-98, Dimensional Visions, Inc., Phoenix; chmn. Express Delivery, Phoenix, 1991-94, Mariah Internat., Inc., Phoenix, 1992-93; v.p., sec. Ariz. Custom Motorcoaches, Mesa, Ariz., 1995-96. Mem. Am. Soc. Metals, Pomona C. of C. (pres. 1970), Phi Beta Kappa. Home and Office: 6454 S Willow Dr Tempe AZ 85283-3968

QUALLEY, CHARLES ALBERT, art educator, educator; b. Creston, Iowa, Mar. 19, 1930; s. Albert Olaf and Cleora (Dietrick) Q.; m. Betty Jean Griffith, Nov. 26, 1954; children: Janet Lynn, John Stuart. B.F.A., Drake U., 1952; M.A., U. Iowa, 1956, M.F.A., 1958; Ed.D., Ill. State U., 1967. Art tchr. Des Moines Pub. Schs., 1952, 54-55; critic art tchr. U. Iowa, 1955-57; prof. fine arts U. Colo., Boulder, 1958-90, prof. emeritus, 1990—, chmn. dept. fine arts, 1968-71, assoc. chmn., 1981-82. Vis. prof. Inst. for Shipboard Edn., semester at sea, 1979, Ill. State U., 1985 Author: Safety in the Art Room, 1986; contbg. editor Sch. Arts, 1978-85, mem. editorial adv. bd., 1985-87; author column Safetypoint, 1981-85. Served with AUS, 1952-54, Korea. Mem. Nat. Art Edn. Assn. (v.p. 1980-82, pres. 1987-89, dir. conv. svcs. 1990-99, fellow 1990—, Art Educator of Yr. 1993), Nat. Art Edn. Found. (trustee 1987—, chair bd. trustees 1996-2000), Colo. Art Edn. Assn. (editor 1965-67, 75, pres. 1976- 78), Delta Phi Delta, Omicron Delta Kappa, Pi Kappa Delta. Home: 2172 Monterrey Rd NE Rio Rancho NM 87124

QUALSET, CALVIN O. plant genetics and agronomy educator; b. Newman Grove, Nebr., Apr. 24, 1937; s. Herman Qualset and Adeline (Hanson) Vakoc; m. Kathleen Boehler; children: Douglas, Cheryl, Gary. BS, U. Nebr., 1958; MS, U. Calif., Davis, 1960, PhD, 1964. Asst. prof. U. Tenn., Knoxville, 1964-67; from asst. prof. to assoc. prof. U. Calif., Davis, 1967, prof., 1973-94, prof. emeritus, 1994—, chmn. dept. agronomy and range sci., 1975-81, 91-94, assoc. dean coll. agrl. and environ. sci., 1981-86; dir. Genetic Resources Conservation Program, Davis, 1985—. Sci, liaison officer U.S. Agy. Internat. Devel., Washington, 1985-93, mem. rsch. adv. com., 1989-92; mem. nat. plant genetic resources bd. USDA, Washington, 1982-88; bd. trustees Am. Type Culture Collection, 1993-99, Internat. Rice Rsch. Inst., 1999—. Contbr. over 200 articles to profl. jours. Fulbright fellow, Australia, 1976, Yugoslavia, 1984. Fellow AAAS (chmn. agr. sect. 1992), Am. Soc. Agronomy (pres. 1994), Crop Sci. Soc. Am. (pres. 1989); mem. Soc. Conservation Biology, Soc. Econ. Botany, Genetic Soc. Am., Internat. Union Biol. Scis. (mem. U.S. nat. com. 2000—). Achievements include development of more than 15 cultivars of wheat, oat, triticale. Office: U Calif Genetic Res Conserv Prog One Shields Ave Davis CA 95616

QUATE, CALVIN FORREST, engineering educator; b. Baker, Nev., Dec. 7, 1923; s. Graham Shepard and Margie (Lake) Q.; m. Dorothy Marshall, June 28, 1945 (div. 1985); children: Robin, Claudia, Holly, Rhodalee; m. Arnice Streit, Jan., 1987. B.S. in Elec. Engring, U. Utah, 1944; Ph.D., Stanford U., 1950. Mem. tech. staff Bell Telephone Labs., Murray Hill, N.J., 1949-58; dir. research Sandia Corp., Albuquerque, 1959-60, v.p. research, 1960-61; prof. dept. applied physics and elec. engring. Stanford (Calif.) U., 1961-95, chmn. applied physics, 1969-72, 78-81, Leland T. Edwards prof. engring., 1986—, assoc. dean Sch. Humanities and Scis., 1972-74, 82-83, rsch. prof. dept. elec. engring., 1995—. Sr. rsch. fellow Xerox Rsch. Ctr., Palo Alto, Calif., 1984-94. Served as lt. (j.g.) USNR, 1944-46. Recipient Rank prize for Opto-electronics, 1982, Pres.'s Nat. medal of Sci. 1992. Fellow IEEE (medal of honor 1988), Am. Acad. Arts and Scis., Acoustical Soc.; mem. NAE, NAS, Am. Phys. Soc., Royal Microscop. Soc. (hon.), Royal Soc. (fgn. mem.), Sigma Xi, Tau Beta Pi. Office: Stanford U E L Ginzton Lab Palo Alto CA 94305-4085

QUAYLE, DAN (JAMES DANFORTH QUAYLE), former vice president United States, entrepreneur; b. Indpls., Feb. 4, 1947; s. James C. and Corinne (Pulliam) Q.; m. Marilyn Tucker, Nov. 18, 1972; children: Tucker Danforth, Benjamin Eugene, Mary Corinne. BS in Polit. Sci., DePauw U., Greencastle, Ind., 1969; JD, Ind. U., 1974. Bar: Ind. 1974. Ct. reporter, pressman Huntington (Ind.) Herald-Press, 1965-69, assoc. pub., gen. mgr., 1974-76; with consumer protection divn. Office Atty. Gen., State of Ind., 1970-71; adminstrv. asst. to gov. State of Ind., 1971-73; dir. Ind. Inheritance Tax Div., 1973-74; tchr. bus. law Huntington Coll., 1975; mem. 95th-96th Congresses from 4th Dist. Ind., Washington; U.S. Senator from Ind. U.S. Senate, Washington, 1981-89; v.p. served under Pres. George Bush U.S., Washington, 1989-93; founder BTC, 1994. Internat. advisor to investment bankers; author, speaker, corp. bds.; disting. vis. prof. Am. Grad. Sch. Internat. Mgmt., 1997-99. Author: Standing Firm, 1994, The American Family, 1996, Worth Fighting For, 1999. Chmn. Campaign Am., 1995-99. With Ind. Army N.G., 1970-76. Mem. Huntington Bar Assn., Hoosier State Press Assn., Huntington C. of C. Club: Rotary. Republican. Office: 2425 E Camelback Rd Ste 1080 Phoenix AZ 85016

QUAYLE, MARILYN TUCKER, lawyer, wife of former vice president of United States; b. 1949; d. Warren and Mary Alice Tucker; m. J. Danforth Quayle, Nov. 18, 1972; children: Tucker, Benjamin, Corinne. BA in Polit. Sci., Purdue U., 1971; JD, Ind. U., 1974. Pvt. practice atty., Huntington, Ind., 1974-77; ptnr. Krieg, DeVault, Alexander & Capehart, Indpls., 1993-2001; pres. BTC Inc., Phoenix, 2001—. Author: (with Nancy T. Northcott) Embrace the Serpent, 1992, The Campaign, 1996.

QUEEN, DOROTHY, distribution company executive; b. Carlsbad, N.Mex., Jan. 23, 1946; m. Bill Queen (dec.); 1 child. BS in Biology, N.Mex. State U.; med. tech., Tex. Tech. Co-founder Queen Oil & Gas Co., Inc., Carlsbad, 1972—, pres. Vol. 4H, Future Farmers of Am. Avocations: being outdoors, snow skiing, nature, raising horses, bird watcher. Office: Queen Oil & Gas 3202 S Canal St Carlsbad NM 88220 Fax: 505-887-6485

QUEHL, GARY HOWARD, consultant, association executive; b. Green Bay, Wis., Mar. 25, 1938; s. Howard and Virginia Babcock (Dunning) Q.; children: Scott Boyer, Catherine Mary. BA, Carroll Coll., 1960; MS, Ind. U., 1962, EdD, 1965; LHD, Buena Vista Coll., 1977, Davis and Elkins Coll., 1979; EdD (hon.), Columbia Coll., S.C., 1987. Asst. dean students Wis. State U., 1962; asst. dean coll. Wittenberg U., 1965-67; v.p., dean coll. Lindenwood Colls., St. Charles, Mo., 1967-70; exec. dir. Coll. Ctr. of the Finger Lakes, Corning, N.Y., 1970-74; pres. Coun. of Ind. Colls., Washington, 1974-86, Coun. for Advancement and Support of Edn., Washington, 1986-90, Quehl Assocs., 1990—. Cons. in field, 1990—. Editor, author books in field. Mem. secretariat Nat. Ctr. for Higher Edn.; bd. dirs. St. Norbert Coll., Carroll Coll., Muskingum Coll., Elmira Coll., Nat. Assn. Ind. Colls. and Univs., ind. sector, Cornell Coll. Mem. Am. Coun. Edn., Am. Conf. Acad. Deans, Nat. Panel for Women in Higher Edn., North Ctrl. Assn. Acad. Deans (past pres.) Mem. United Ch. Christ. E-mial. E-mail: quehl@queasso.com

QUENNEVILLE, KATHLEEN, lawyer; b. Mt. Clemens, Mich., July 31, 1953; d. Marcel J. and Patricia (Armstrong) Q. BA, Mich. State U., 1975; JD, Golden Gate U., 1979. Bar: Calif. 1980. Atty. Wells Fargo Bank, San Francisco, 1980-81; staff counsel Calif. State Banking Dept., San Francisco, 1981-83; assoc. Manatt, Phelps, Rothenburg & Tunney, Los Angeles, 1983-84; v.p., assoc. gen. counsel Bank of Calif., San Francisco, 1984-96; sr. v.p., gen. counsel The Mechanics Bank, Richmond, Calif., 1996—. Asst treas. AIDS Legal Referral Panel of the San Francisco Bay Area, 1986-92. Mem. Calif. State Bar Assn. (bus. law sect. corp. law depts. com. 1988-90), Calif. Bankers Assn. (chair regulatory compliance com. 1994-96, legal affairs com. 1996—). Office: The Mechanics Bank 3170 Hilltop Mall Rd Richmond CA 94806-5231

QUESNEL, GREGORY L. transportation company executive; b. Woodburn, Oreg., May 24, 1948; BA in Finance, U. Oregon; MA in Bus. Adminstrn., U. Portland; grad. Exec. Program in Bus. Adminstrn., Columbia U. Dir. fin. acctg. Consolidated Freightways, Portland, 1975-78, dir. mgmt. and cost acctg., 1978-86; fin. officer CF MotorFreight, Consolidated Freightways, Portland, 1986-89; v.p. acctg. Emery Worldwide, Consolidated Freightways, Scranton, Pa., 1989-91; exec. v.p., CFO CNF Transp. Inc., Palo Alto, Calif., 1991-97, pres., CEO, 1997—. Mem. Fin. Exec. Inst., Chief Fin. Execs. (conf. bds. coun., conf. bds. coun. of fin. execs.). E-mail: colvert.nancy@cnf.com

QUIAT, GERALD M. lawyer; b. Denver, Jan. 9, 1924; s. Ira L. and Esther (Greenblatt) Q.; m. Roberta M. Nicholson, Sept. 26, 1962; children: James M., Audrey R., Melinda A., Daniel P., Ilana L., Leonard E. AA, U. Calif., Berkeley, 1942; AB, LLB, U. Denver, 1948, changed to JD, 1970. Bar: Colo. 1948, Fed. Ct. 1948, U.S. Dist. Ct. Colo. 1948, U.S. Ct. Appeals (10th cir.) 1948, U.S. Surpeme Ct. 1970. Dep. dist. atty. City and Co. of Denver, Colo., 1949-52; partner firm Quiat, Seeman & Quiat, Denver, 1952-67, Quiat & Quiat (later changed to Quiat, Bucholtz & Bull, P.C.), 1968; pres. Quiat, Bucholtz & Bull & Laff, P.C. (and predecessors), Denver, 1968-85; pvt. practice Denver, 1985—. Bd. dirs., chmn. audit com. Guaranty Bank & Trust Co., Denver. Past trustee Holding Co., Rose Med. Ctr., Denver, pres., chmn. bd. dirs., 1976-79; mem. Colo. Civil Rights Com., 1963-71, chmn., 1966-67, 69-70, hearing officer, 1963-71; bd. dirs. Am. Cancer Rsch. Ctr., Denver, chmn. bd., 1991-93, sec. of treas., 2000—; chmn. bd. Am. Med. Ctr., 1993-95; mem. nat. civil rights com., hon. mem. nat. exec. com., hon. nat. commr. Anti-Defamation League, B'nai B'rith, mem. exec. com., chmn. bd. Mountain States region, 1980-82. With inf. U.S. Army, 1942-45. Decorated Combat Infantry Badge, Bronze Star. Mem. ABA, Colo. Bar Assn., Colo. Trial Lawyers Assn. (pres. 1970-71), Am. Legion (comdr. Leyden-Chiles-Wickersham post 1 1955-56, past judge adv. Colo. dept.). Home: 5361 Nassau Cir E Englewood CO 80110-5100 Office: Penthouse Suite 1720 S Bellaire St Denver CO 80222-4304 E-mail: gqph@aol.com

QUICK, JAMES S. geneticist, plant breeder; b. Devils Lake, N.D., Oct. 20, 1940; s. James R. and Anne (Sather) Q.; children: Alissa, Kathryn, Jeanette; m. Jacklynn Panuska, June 13, 1994. BS, N.D. State U., 1962; MS, Purdue U., 1965, PhD, 1966. Asst. geneticist Rockefeller Found. India, N.Y.C., 1966-69; from assoc. prof. to prof. N.D State U., Fargo, 1969-81; prof. Colo. State U., Ft. Collins, 1981—, head, 1998—. Cons. USDA, ARS, Spain, 1977-81, Morocco, 1985—; advisor Australian Wheat Rsch. Coun., Toowoomba, Queensland, 1987-88. Editor Annual Wheat Newsletter, 1983-94; contbr. articles to profl. jours. Recipient Achievement award U.S. Durum Growers, 1978, Disting. Toastmaster award Toastmasters Internat., 1985; grantee U.S. Pasta Industry, 1977-78. Fellow Am. Soc. Agronomy (Achievement award-crops 1996), Crop Sci. Soc. Am.; mem. Coun. Agrl. Sci. and Technology, Sigma Xi. Achievements include development of 13 durum wheat cultivars, 13 hard red winter wheat cultivars, 1 soft white spring wheat cultivar; discovered new resistance to Russian wheat aphid. Office: Colo State U Dept Agronomy Fort Collins CO 80523-0001

QUICK, MICHAEL, civil engineering educator, researcher; Prof. civil engineering U. B.C., Vancouver, Can.; prof. emeritus. Recipient Camille A Dagenais award Can. Soc. Civil Engring., 1996. Office: U BC Dept Civil Engring 2010-2324 Main Mall Vancouver BC Canada V6T 1Z4

QUIGLEY, JOHN MICHAEL, economist, educator; b. N.Y.C., Feb. 12, 1942; BS with distinction, U.S. Air Force Acad., 1964; MSc with honors, U. Stockholm, Sweden, 1965; AM, Harvard U., 1971, PhD, 1972. Commd. 2d lt. USAF, 1964, advanced through grades to capt., 1968; asst. prof. econs. Yale U., 1972-74, assoc. prof., 1974-81; prof. pub. policy U. Calif., Berkeley, 1979—, prof. econs., 1981—, Chancellor's prof., 1997—, I. Donald Terner prof., 1999—, chmn. dept. econs., 1992-95; vis. prof. econs. and stats. U. Gothenberg, 1978. Cons. numerous govt. agys. and pvt. firms; econometrician Hdqrs. U.S. Air Force, Pentagon, 1965-68; research assoc. Nat. Bur. Econ. Research, N.Y.C., 1968-78; mem. com. on nat. urban policy NAS, 1985-93. Author, editor, contbr. articles to profl. jours.; editor in chief Reg. Sci. and Urban Econs., 1987—; mem. editl. bd. many sci. and sholarly jours. Fulbright scholar, 1964-65; fellow NSF, 1968-69, Woodrow Wilson, 1968-71, Harvard IBM, 1969-71, NDEA, 1969-71, Thord-Gray Am. Scandinavian Found. 1971-72, Social Sci. Research Council, 1971-72. Mem. Am. Econ. Assn., Econometric Soc., Regional Sci. Assn. (bd. dirs. 1986—), Nat. Tax Assn., Assn. for Pub. Policy and Mgmt. (bd. dirs. 1986-89, v.p. 1987-89), Am. Real Estate and Urban Econs. Assn. (bd. dirs. 1987-2001, pres. 1995-97). Home: 875 Hilldale Ave Berkeley CA 94708-1319 Office: U Calif 2607 Hearst Ave Berkeley CA 94720-7305 E-mail: quigley@econ.berkeley.edu

QUIGLEY, KEVIN WALSH, former state legislator, lawyer; b. Everett, Wash., Feb. 23, 1961; s. David W. Quigley and Mary (Cernetig) Thoreson; m. Suzanne Marion Bakke. BA with spl. honors, George Washington U., 1983; JD cum laude, NYU, 1986; LLM, Harvard U., 1992. Bar: Wash. 1988. Jr. fellow ctr. internat. studies NYU Law Sch., N.Y.C., 1986; assoc. Perkins Coie, Seattle, 1987-94; of counsel Perkins Cole, Seattle, 1995-97; mem. Wash. State Senate, Olympia, 1993-97. Chmn. health and long-term care com., mem., vice chmn. ways and means com.; dir. bus. affairs Teledesic Corp. Grad. fellow Harvard Law Sch., 1987. Mem. Rotary, Phi Beta Kappa. Democrat. Avocations: mountain climbing, architecture, carpentry. Home: 1029 Springbrook Rd Lake Stevens WA 98258-9425

QUIGLEY, PHILIP J. retired telecommunications industry executive; b. 1943; With Advanced Mobile Phone Svc. Inc., 1982-84, v.p., gen. mgr., Pacific region; with Pac Tel Mobile Access, 1984-86, pres., chief exec. officer; with Pac Tel Personal Communications, 1986-87, pres., chief exec. officer; exec. v.p., chief oper. officer Pac Tel Corp., 1987; ret. chmn., pres., chief exec. officer Pacific Telesis Group, San Francisco, 1997—; pres. Pacific Bell, 1987-94; bd. dirs. SRI Internat., Menlo Park, Calif., 1998—. Address: 801 Lombardi Ln Hillsborough CA 94010-7043

QUILLIGAN, EDWARD JAMES, obstetrician, gynecologist, educator; b. Cleve., June 18, 1925; s. James Joseph and Maude Elvira (Ryan) Q.; m. Betty Jane Cleaton, Dec. 14, 1946; children: Bruce, Jay, Carol, Christopher, Linda, Ted. B.A., M.D., Ohio State U., 1951; M.A. (hon.), Yale, 1967. Intern Ohio State U. Hosp., 1951-52, resident, 1952-54, Western Res. U. Hosps., 1954-56; asst. prof. obstetrics and gynecology Western Res. U., 1957-63, prof., 1963-65; prof. obstetrics and gynecology UCLA, 1965-66; prof., chmn. dept. Ob-Gyn Yale U., 1966-69, U. So. Calif., 1969-78, asso. v.p. med. affairs, 1978-79; prof. Ob-Gyn. U. Calif., Irvine, 1980-83, vice chancellor health affairs, dean Sch. Medicine, 1987-89; prof., chmn. ob.-gyn. dept. U. Wis., 1983-85; prof., chmn. Ob-Gyn Davis Med. Ctr. U. Calif., Sacramento, 1985-87, vice chancellor Health Scis., dean Coll. Med. Irvine, 1987-89, prof. ob-gyn, 1987-94, prof. emeritus ob-gyn., 1994; exec. dir. med. edn. Long Beach (Calif.) Meml. Health Svcs., 1995—. Contbr. articles to med. jours.; co-editor-in-chief: Am. Jour. Obstetrics and Gynecology. Served to 2d lt. AUS, 1944-46. Recipient Centennial award Ohio State U., 1970 Mem. Soc. Gynecologic Investigation, Am. Gynecol. Soc., Am. Coll. Obstetics and Gynecology, Sigma Xi. Home: 24 Urey Ct Irvine CA 92612-4077 E-mail: equilligan@home.com

QUINBY, WILLIAM ALBERT, lawyer, mediator, arbitrator; b. Oakland, Calif., May 28, 1941; s. George W. and Marge (Diaz) Q.; m. Marion Bach, Nov. 27, 1964; 1 child, Michelle Kathleen. BA, Harvard U., 1963; JD, U. Calif., San Francisco, 1967. Bar: Calif. 1967. V.p., dir., shareholder Crosby, Heafey, Roach & May, Oakland, Calif., 1967-96; mediator, arbitrator Am. Arbitration Assn. and AAA Ctr. for Mediation, San Francisco, 1996—. Bd. dirs. Haws Drinking Faucet Co., Berkeley, Calif.; mem. faculty Hastings Coll. Advocacy, San Francisco, 1980, instr. Boalt Hall Sch. Law, 1997; co-moderator Counsel Connect's Calif. ADR Discussion Group; lectr. currents devels. in banking arbitration and mediation; mem. fellowship rev. com. HEW; mem. panel disting. neutrals Ctr. for Pub. Resources, Inc.; mem. mediation panel Nat. Assn. Securities Dealers; trustee Nat. Pre-Suit Mediation Program; adj. prof. Hastings Coll. of the Law, U. Calif., 1998, 99. Author: Six Reasons--Besides Time and Money--to Mediate Rather Than Litigate, Why Health Care Parties Should Mediate Rather Than Litigate, Starting an ADR Practice Group in a Law Firm, Mediation Process Can Amicably Solve Business Disputes and Not a Gold Rush (But Silver, Maybe), ADR Practice in a Large Law Firm Produces No Overnight Bonanzas, Making The Most of Mediation (Effective Mediation Advocacy). Bd. dirs. Big Bros. East Bay, Oakland, 1983-87, Easter Seals Soc. East Bay, 1973, Oakland East Bay Symphony; chmn. bd. dirs. Bay Area Tumor Inst. Scholar Harvard U., 1962-63. Mem. ABA (sect. on dispute resolution, chair programs, mediation coms.), ATLA, Calif. Bar Assn., Alameda County Bar Assn., Calif. Bus. Trial Lawyers Assn., Am. Arbitration Assn. (large, complex case panel, comml. mediation and arbitration panels), Oakland C. of C. (bd. dirs., exec. com.), Alameda County Barristers Club (bd. dirs., pres. 1972), Harvard Club, San Francisco Calimari Club, Lakeview Club, Bohemian Club. Republican. Avocations: running, skiing, tennis, travel, gardening. Office: Wulff Quinby & Sochynsky Dispute Resolution 1901 Harrison St Ste 1420 Oakland CA 94612-3582 E-mail: wquinby@aol.com

QUINN, EDWARD J. broadcasting company executive; BS in Speech, U. Wis. Gen. sales mgr. WTMJ-TV, Milw.; v.p., gen. mgr. KTNV-TV, Las Vegas, WVUE-TV, New Orleans; gen. mgr. KGTV, v.p. McGraw-Hill Broadcasting Co., San Diego, 1986-96, pres., 1996—. Bd. govs. ABC TV Affiliates Assn.; pres.'s adv. bd. San Diego State U.; chmn. San Diego Baha Comms. Coun. Recipient George Walker Smith humanitarian award San Diego Coalition for Equality, medal of honor DAR, disting. svc. award Soc. Profl. Journalists, golden mike award Radio and TV News Dirs. Assn. So. Calif., Emmy award NATAS. Office: McGraw Hill Broadcasting Co PO Box 85347 San Diego CA 92186-5347

QUINN, FRANCIS A. bishop; b. L.A., Sept. 11, 1921; Ed., St. Joseph's Coll., Mountain View, Calif., St. Patrick's Sem., Menlo Park, Calif., Cath. U., Washington, U. Calif., Berkeley. Ordained priest Roman Cath. Ch., 1946; ordained titular bishop of Numana and aux. bishop of San Francisco, 1978; bishop Diocese of Sacramento, 1979-94, bishop emeritus, 1994—. Office: 2110 Broadway Sacramento CA 95818-2518

QUINN, MARK T. medical educator; b. San Jose, Calif., June 11, 1958; BA in Biology and Chemistry, Point Loma Coll., 1982; PhD in Physiology and Pharmacology, U. Calif., San Diego, 1987. Postdoctoral rsch. assoc. Rsch. Inst. Scripps Clinic, La Jolla, Calif., 1988-89; sr. rsch. assoc. Mont. State U., Bozeman, 1989-90, asst., assoc. rsch. prof., 1991-95, asst. prof., 1995—, assoc. prof., 1998. Contbr. articles to profl. jours. Recipient Investigator award Arthritis Found., 1991, Health FIRST award NIH,

1992—, Charles and Nora Wiley Meritorious Rsch. award, 1993; grantee Am. Cancer Soc., 1989, Am. Lung Assn., 1991-93, Arthritis Found., 1994—, USDA, 1995—; U. Calif. Regents fellow, 1981, Point Loma Coll. Rsch. Assocs. fellow, 1981, San Diego & Grad. Opportunity Rsch. fellow, 1986-87, Arthritis Found. Postdoctoral fellow, 1989-91. Mem. Am. Soc. Cell Biology, Am. Heart Assn. (coun. basic rsch., Established Investigator award 1996—), Soc. Leukocyte Biology. Office: Mont State U Dept Vet Molecular Biology Bozeman MT 59717-0001

QUINN, PATRICIA K. literary agent; b. Chico, Calif. d. Donald Joseph and Kathleen (Alexander) Q. BA, Bennington Coll., 1971; MFA in Drama, Yale U., 1976. Producer, devel. exec. various Off-Broadway and regional theatres, 1976-84; devel. cons. Sundance Film Inst., Utah, 1984-85; theatrical agt. I.C.M., L.A., 1985-90; v.p. comedy devel. Warner Bros. TV, Burbank, Calif., 1990-92; lit. and packaging agt. Met. Talent Agy., L.A., 1995—. Instr. UCLA Ext., 1995—; spkr., lectr. Nat. Assn. of TV Programming Execs., Fla. Bar, NATAS, Media Xchange (Internat.). Founding mem. N.Y. Theatre Workshop, N.Y.C., 1980-86; mem. PEN Ctr. USA West; mem. steering com. Calif. Gov.'s Conf. for Women, 1999. Mem. Women in Film (v.p. bd. dirs. 1995—). Office: Paradigm Talent and Lit Agy 4526 Wilshire Blvd Los Angeles CA 90010-3801

QUINN, WILLIAM FRANCIS, lawyer, director; b. Rochester, N.Y., July 13, 1919; s. Charles Alvin and Elizabeth (Dorrity) Q.; m. Nancy Ellen Witbeck, July 11, 1942; children: William Francis, Stephen Desford, Timothy Charles, Christopher Thomas, Ann Cecily, Mary Kaiulani, Gregory Anthony. B.S. summa cum laude, St. Louis U., 194O; LL.B. cum laude, Harvard U., 1947. Bar: Hawaii 1948. Ptnr. Robertson, Castle & Anthony, Honolulu, 1947-57; gov. Ter. of Hawaii, Honolulu, 1957-59, State of Hawaii, Honolulu, 1959-62; ptnr. Quinn & Moore, Honolulu, 1962-64; exec. v.p. Dole Co., Honolulu., 1964-65, pres., 1965-72; ptnr. Jenks, Kidwell, Goodsill & Anderson, Honolulu, 1972-73, Goodsill Anderson & Quinn, 1973-82, Goodsill Anderson Quinn & Stifel, 1982-91; ret., 1991. Mem. sr. adv. bd. 9th Cir. Jud. Coun. Served with USNR, 1942-46. Decorated knight of Holy Sepulchre Order. Mem. Pacific Club (Honolulu). Republican. Roman Catholic. Home: 4340 Pahoa Ave Apt 13C Honolulu HI 96816-5023

QUINTANA, ANNETTE, information systems company executive; b. Colorado Springs; 2 children. BS in Chem Engring., Colo. State U. Mktg. rep. IBM Corp.; pres. Excel Profl. Svcs., Inc., Greenwood Village, Colo., 1990—, Quest Database Cons. LLC sub. Excel, 1992—, Q2 Professional Svcs, Dallas, 1997—, Nova Internat., 1999—. Office: Excel Profl Svcs Inc 5600 S Quebec St Ste 310D Greenwood Vlg CO 80111-2205 Fax: 303-771-1984

QUINTANA, VICTORIA, information systems company executive; b. Colorado Springs; married; 2 children. Grad. in bus. mgmt., Colo. State U. With MCI; v.p., part owner Excel Profl. Svcs., Inc., Greenwood Village, Colo., 1990—. Past chair Colo. Children's Campaign, bd. dirs.; orgnl. liaison Colo. Indian C. of C.; active Hispanic Inst. Office: Excel Profl Svcs Inc 5600 S Quebec St Ste 310D Greenwood Vlg CO 80111-2205 Fax: 303-771-1984

QUREISHI, A. SALAM, computer software and services company executive; b. Aligarh, India, July 1, 1936; s. M.A. Jabbar and Saira (Sattar) Q.; m. Naheed Fatima; children: Lubna, Leila. BS in Physics and Math., Aligarth U., India, 1954; MS in Stats., Patna U., India, 1957. Mgr. applications IBM Corp., Palo Alto, Calif., 1961-67; founder, pres., chmn. bd. Optimum Sys., Inc., Palo Alto, 1967-71; CEO Sysorex Internat., Inc., Mountain View, 1972—. Republican. Home: PO Box 620025 Woodside CA 94062-0025 Office: Sysorex Internat Inc 335 E Middlefield Rd Mountain View CA 94043-4028

QUTUB, EILEEN, state legislator, real estate appraiser; b. York, Nebr., Mar. 2, 1948; m. Abe Qutub. BS in Mgmt. Human Resources, George Fox Coll. Mem. Oreg. Legislature, Salem, 1996—, mem. jud. com., mem. pub. affairs ocm., dep. co-chair ways and means com., mem. subcom. on transp. and econ. devel. com., asst. majority leader. Precinct Com., alt. del. Oreg. Rep. Orgn.; facilitator engring. dept.-real estate divsn. City of Charlotte, N.C. Republican. Home: 11135 Sw Patridge Loop Beaverton OR 97007 Office: S 210 State Capitol Salem OR 97310 E-mail: qutub.sen@state.or.us

RABBAT, GUY, electronics company executive, inventor; b. Cairo, Jan. 30, 1943; came to U.S., 1972; s. Victor and Alice R.; m. Elfriede Freitag, Aug. 3, 1968; children: Ralph, Shirley; m. Nadia Kobinger, Feb. 8, 1992; children: Richard, Jacques, Laurent. Baccalaureate, France; BS, Queens U., Eng., 1967, MS, 1969, PhD in Elec. Engring. with honors, 1971. Design supr. Siemens AG, Germany, 1964-68; asst. lectr. Queens U., Eng., 1968-72; dir. ops. IBM, 1972-84; v.p. Austin ops., CAE system div. Tektronix, 1984-86; head elec. engring. GM Corp., Mich., 1986-87; pres., chief exec. officer Modular Computer Systems, Inc. (MODCOMP), Ft. Lauderdale, Fla., 1987-92; mng. dir., exec. bd. dirs. Rank Xerox, Ltd., Welwyn Garden City, Herts, England, 1992-96; corp. v.p. Gen. Elec. Co., Milw., 1996-98; chief tech. officer, chief info. officer Gen. Elec. Med. Sys., Milw., 1996-98; sr. v.p. Solectron Corp., 1998—; chmn., gen. ptnr. Corcica Tech. Ventures, 2001—. Chmn. Internat. IEEE Conf. on Cirs. and Computers, 1980, Internat. IEEE Conf. on Computer Design, 1983; bd. dirs. indsl. affiliates Mich. State U., 1986-88; pres. Am. Automation Assn., 1984-86; chmn., founder High Tech. Consortium Yr. 2000 and Beyond, 1998—. Author: Hardware and Software Concepts in VLSI, 1983, Advanced Semiconductor Technology and Computer Systems, 1988; contbr. numerous scis. tech. papers; patentee in field. Fellow: IEEE (Eng. chpt., editor-in-chief, chmn. editl. bd. Circuits and Devices Mag. 1984—86, invention and outstanding contbn. awards), Royal Engring. Coun. (London). Avocations: history, archeology, poetry, jogging. Home: 16134 Rose Ave Monte Sereno CA 95030-4221 Office: Solectron Corp 847 Gibraltar Dr Bldg 5 Milpitas CA 95035-6332 E-mail: rabbat@corcica.com

RABENSTEIN, DALLAS LEROY, chemistry educator; b. Portland, Oreg., June 13, 1942; 8. Melvin Leroy and Rose Marie (Nelson) R.; m. Gloria Carolyn Duncan, Aug. 30, 1964; children: Mark, Lisa. BS, U. Wash., 1964; PhD, U. Wis., 1968. Lectr. U. Wis., Madison, 1967-68; research chemist Chevron Research Co., Richmond, Calif., 1968-69; from asst. prof. to prof. chemistry U. Alta., Edmonton, Can., 1969-85; prof. U. Calif., Riverside, 1985-97, chmn. chemistry dept., 1989-92, 98-00, dean Coll. Natural and Agrl. Scis., 1993-94, disting. prof. chemistry, 1997—. Vis. prof. U. Oxford, 1976-77, U. Western Ont., 1982; McElvain lectr. U. Wis., 1981; Dow lectr. U. B.C., 1988; Eli Lilly lectr., Ind. U., 1993; faculty rsch. lectr. U. Calif., Riverside, 2000. Contbr. articles to profl. jours. NIH and NSF grantee. Fellow AAAS, Chem. Inst. Can. (Fisher Sci. Lecture award 1984); mem. Am. Chem. Soc., Internat. Soc. Magnetic Resource. Avocations: reading, gardening, music. Home: 5162 Palisade Cir Riverside CA 92506-1621 Office: U Calif Dept Chemistry Riverside CA 92521-0001 E-mail: dallas.rabenstein@ucr.edu

RABINOVITZ, JOEL, lawyer, educator; b. 1939. A.B., Cornell U., 1960; LL.B., Harvard U., 1963. Bar: N.Y. 1963, Calif. 1981. Asst. prof. U. Fla., Gainesville, 1966-68; vis. assoc. prof. UCLA, 1968-69, acting prof., 1969-72, prof., 1972-79; vis. prof., NYU, 1976; dep. internat. Tax Counsel, Dept. Treasury, 1980-81; ptnr. with Irell & Manella, L.A., 1981—. E-mail: jrabinovitz@irell.com. Office: Irell & Manella 1800 Avenue Of The Stars Los Angeles CA 90067-1212

RABOW, MICHAEL WARREN, physician, educator; b. June 30, 1965; BA, Harvard U., 1987; MD, U. Calif., San Francisco, 1993. Diplomate Am. Bd. Internal Medicine. Resident in primary care U. Calif., San Francisco, 1993-96, fellow in gen. medicine, 1996-97, asst. prof. medicine, 1997—. Author: (with others) Current Medical Diagnosis and Treatment, 1998; contbr. articles to profl. jours. Office: U Calif San Francisco 1701 Divisadero St Ste 500 San Francisco CA 94115-3011

RABY, WILLIAM LOUIS, writer, consultant; b. Chgo., July 16, 1927; s. Gustave E. and Helen (Burgess) R.; m. Norma Claire Schreiner, Sept. 8, 1956; children: Burgess, Marianne, Marlene. BSBA, Northwestern U., 1949; MBA, U. Ariz., 1961, PhD, 1971. Ptnr. VAR CPA Firms, 1950-76, Touche Ross & Co., N.Y.C., 1977-87. Pres. Ariz. State Bd. Accountancy, 1993-94; mem. Ariz. State Bd. Tax Appeals, 1994—, chmn., 1997-99; prof. acctg. emeritus Ariz. State U.; columnist Tax Notes mag., Arlington, Va., 1990—; cons. on video and audio tax edn. tapes Bisk Pub. Co., 1992—. Author: The Income Tax and Business Decisions, 1964, Building and Maintaining a Successful Tax Practice, 1964, The Reluctant Taxpayer, 1970, Tax Practice Management, 1974, Introduction to Federal Taxation, annually, 1980-91, Tax Practice Management: Client Servicing, 1986; editor: Raby Report on Tax Practice, 1986-96, PPC Guide To Successful Tax Practice, 1991; mem. editorial adv. bd. Practical Tax Strategies; contbr. articles to profl. jours. Mem. AICPA (chmn. fed. tax divsn. 1980-83, v.p. 1983-84, coun. 1983-90), Tax Ct. Bar. Presbyterian (elder, chmn. adv. coun. on ch. and soc. 1979-81). Office: PO Box 26846 Tempe AZ 85285-6846 E-mail: wlraby@cs.com

RACHELEFSKY, GARY STUART, medical educator; b. N.Y.C., 1942; BS, Columbia Coll., 1963. Intern Bellevue Hosp. Ctr., N.Y.C., 1967-68; resident in pediatrics Johns Hopkins Hosp., 1968-70, Ctr. Disease Control, 1970-72; fellow UCLA Med. Ctr., 1972-74; clin. prof., assoc. dir. A/I Tng. Program UCLA. Fellow Am. Acad. Allergy, Asthma and Immunology (bd. dirs., past pres.). Office: 11620 Wilshire Blvd Ste 200 Los Angeles CA 90025-1767 E-mail: rachruss@ix.netcom.com

RACHINS, ALAN, actor, screenwriter; b. Cambridge, Mass., 10 Oct. m. Joanna Frank; 1 child, Robbie. Student, U. Pa.; studied with William Ball, others, N.Y.C.; student, Am. Film Inst., L.A., 1972-74. Theater roles include After the Rain, John Golden Theatre, N.Y.C., 1967, Hadrian the Seventh, Helen Hayes Theatre, N.Y.C., 1969, Oh, Calcutta!, Eden Theatre, N.Y.C., 1969; film appearances in Always, 1985, Thunder Run, 1986, North, 1994, Starquest, 1995, Showgirls, 1995, Meet Wally Sparks, 1997, Leave It to Beaver, 1997; appeared in various TV series episodes including L.A. Law, Dharma & Greg, 1997; screenwriter episodes Hill Street Blues, The Fall Guy, Hart to Hart, Knight Rider, Quincy; appeared in TV movies including The Stepsister, 1997, Unwed Father, 1997. Address: c/o Ensemble Ent 10474 Santa Monica Blvd #380 Los Angeles CA 90025

RACITI, CHERIE, artist; b. Chgo., June 17, 1942; d. Russell J. and Jacque (Crimmins) R. Student, Memphis Coll. Art, 1963-65; B.A. in Art, San Francisco State U., 1968; M.F.A., Mills Coll., 1979. Assoc. prof. art San Francisco State U., 1984-89, prof., 1989—. Lectr. Calif. State U., Hayward, 1974, San Francisco Art Inst., 1978; mem. artist com. San Francisco Art Inst., 1974-85, sec., 1980-81. One woman shows include U. Calif., Berkeley, 1972, Nicholas Wilder Gallery, Los Angeles, 1975, San Francisco Art Inst., 1977, Marianne Deson Gallery, Chgo., 1980, Site 375, San Francisco, 1989, Reese Bullen Gallery, Humboldt State U., Arcata, Calif., 1990, Mills Coll. Art Mus., Oakland, Calif., 1998; group shows include Whitney Mus. Art, 1975, San Francisco Sci. Fiction, The Clocktower, N.Y.C., Otis-Parsons Gallery, Los Angeles, 1984-85, San Francisco Art Inst., 1985, Artists Space, N.Y.C., 1988, Angles Gallery, Santa Monica, 1987, Terrain Gallery, San Francisco, 1992, Ctr. for the Arts, San Francisco, 1993, Santa Monica Coll., 1998, 25/25 25th Anniversary Exhbn., So. Exposure Gallery, San Francisco, 1999. Bd. dirs. New Langton Arts, 1988-92. Eureka fellow Fleishhacker Found., San Francisco; recipient Adaline Kent award San Francisco Art Inst., 1976, Djerassi resident, 1994, Tyrone Guthrie Ctr. resident, Ireland, 1995, Millay Colony for Arts resident 1999, Juror's award Art Coun. Inc. San Francisco. Office: San Francisco State U Art Dept 1600 Holloway Ave San Francisco CA 94132-1722 E-mail: craciti@sfsu.edu

RADA, ALEXANDER, university official; b. Kvasy, Czechoslovakia, Mar. 28, 1923; s. Frantisek and Anna (Tonnkova) R.; came to U.S., 1954, naturalized, 1959; M.S., U. Tech. Coll. of Prague, 1948; postgrad. Va. Poly. Inst., 1956-59, St. Clara U., 1966-67; Ed.D., U. Pacific, 1975; m. Ingeborg Solveig Blakstad, Aug. 8, 1953; children: Alexander Sverre, Frank Thore, David Harald. Head prodn. planning dept. Mine & Iron Corp., Kolin, Czechoslovakia, 1941-42; mgr. experimenting and testing dept. Avia Aircraft, Prague, 1943-45; sec.-gen. Central Bldg. Office, Prague, 1948; head metal courses dept. Internat. Tech. Sch. of UN, Grafenaschau, W.Ger., 1949-50; works mgr. Igref A/S, Oslo, 1950-51; cons. engr., chief sect. machines Steel Products Ltd., Oslo, 1951-54; chief engr., plant supr. Nelson J. Pepin & Co., Lowell, Mass., 1954-55; sr. project engr., mfg. supt. Celanese Corp. Am., Narrows, Va., 1955-60; mgr. mfg., facilities and maint. FMC Corp., San Jose, Calif., 1960-62; mgr. adminstrn. Sylvania Electronic Systems, Santa Cruz, Calif., 1962-72; asst. to pres., devel. officer Napa (Calif.) Coll., 1972-88; chief exec. officer NAVCO Pacific Devel. Corp., Napa, 1984-91; pres. NAVCO Calif. Co., 1991—; prof. indsl. mgmt. Cabrillo Coll., Aptos, Calif., 1963-72; mgmt. and engring. cons., 1972—. Pres. ARC, Santa Cruz, 1965-72, bd. dirs., pres., Napa, 1977-88; mem. Nat. Def. Exec. Res., U.S. Dept. Commerce, Washington, 1966—, chmn. No. Calif. region 9, 1981-88; mem. President's Export Council-DEC, San Francisco, 1982—. Recipient Meritorious Service citation ARC, 1972, Etoile Civique l'Ordre de l'Etoile Civique, French Acad., 1985; registered profl. engr., Calif. Mem. NSPE, Calif. Soc. Profl. Engrs., Am. Def. Preparedness Assn., Assn. Calif. Community Coll. Adminstrs., Nat. Assn. Corp. Dirs., World Affairs Council No. Calif., Czechoslovak Foreign Inst., Praha, 1993—, Phi Delta Kappa, Editor-in-chief Our Youth, 1945-48; co-editor (with P. Boulden) Innovative Management Concepts, 1967. Home and Office: 1019 Ross Cir Napa CA 94558-2118

RADANOVICH, GEORGE P. congressman; b. Mariposa, Calif., 1955; s. Joan and George F.; m. Ethie Weaver; 1 child, George King. BS in Agr. Bus. Mgmt., Calif. State Polytechnic U., 1978. Pres. Radanovich Winery, Mariposa, Calif., 1982—; chair County Planning Comm., 1986-87, county supr., 1988-92; mem. U.S. Congress from Calif. 19th dist., Washington, 1995—; mem. energy and com. com., resources com. Mem. Calif. Agrl. Leadership Program Class XXI, Rotary (Paul Harris Fellowship). Republican. Office: US Ho Reps 123 Cannon HOB Washington DC 20515*

RADCLIFFE, ALBERT E. judge; b. 1947; BA in History, U. Oreg., 1969, JD, 1972. Bar: Oreg. 1972, U.S. Dist. Ct. Oreg. 1973, U.S. Ct. Appeals (9th cir.) 1983. Pvt. practice, 1973-86; judge U.S. Bankruptcy Ct. Oreg., Eugene, 1986—. Vis. bankruptcy judge We. Dist. Wash., 1992; spkr. in field. Mem. Fed. Bar Assn. (hon.), N.W. Bankruptcy Inst. Planning Com., Lane County Bar Assn. (bankruptcy subcom. chmn. 1993-94), Tau Kappa Epsilon. Office: US Bankruptcy Ct Oreg 151 W 7th Ave Ste 300 Eugene OR 97401-2676

RADEN, GARY, business executive; Pres., CEO G. Rayden & Sons, Inc., Renton, WA. Office: G Rayden & Sons Inc 3215 Lind Ave SW Renton WA 98055-4020

RADER, PAUL ALEXANDER, minister, religious organization administrator; b. N.Y.C., Mar. 4, 1934; s. Lyell M. and Gladys Mina (Damon) R.; m. Kay Fuller, May 29, 1956; children: Edith Jeanne, James Paul, Jennifer Kay. BA, Asbury Coll., Wilmore, Ky., 1956; BD, Asbury Theol. Sem., 1959; LLD (hon.), Asbury Coll., Wilmore, Ky., 1984; ThM, So. Bapt. Theol. Sem., Louisville, 1961; D Missiology, Fuller Theol. Sem., 1973; DD (hon.), Asbury Theol. Sem., 1995. Ordained to ministry Salvation Army, 1961. Tng. prin. The Salvation Army, Seoul, 1973-74, edn. sec., 1974-77, chief sec., 1979-83, tng. prin. Suffern, N.Y., 1983-86, divisional comdr. for Ea. Pa. and Del. Phila., 1986-88, chief sec. ea. ter. N.Y.C., 1988, territorial comdr. U.S.A. western ter. Rancho Palos Verdes, Calif., 1989-94, gen., 1994-99; pres. Asbury Coll., 2000—. Adj. prof. Seoul Theol. Sem., 1980-82; trustee Asian Ctr. for Theol. Studies and Mission, 1980-83, Asbury Coll., 1988—; pres. The Salvation Army Calif. Corp., Rancho Palos Verdes, 1989-94. Recipient Alumnus A award Asbury Coll., 1982, Disting. Alumni award Asbury Theol. Sem., 1989; Paul Harris fellow Rotary Internat., 1989. Mem. Am. Soc. Missiology, Internat. Assn. Mission Studies. Address: Asbury Coll 1 Macklem Dr Wilmore KY 40390-1152 also: Salvation Army Internat Hdq 101 Queen Victoria St London EC4P 4EP England

RADKE, JAN RODGER, pulmonologist, physician executive; b. Detroit, Nov. 16, 1942; s. Edward V. and Dorothy M. Radke; m. Julith Hogan, June 20, 1987; children: Jennifer, John, Colin, Cameron. BS, Mich. State U., 1965; MD, U. Wis., 1969. Diplomate Am. Bd. Internal Medicine, Am. Bd. Pulmonary Disease. Intern Henry Food Hosp., 1969-70, resident internal medicine, 1970-71, resident, 1974-75, chief med. resident internal medicine, 1975-76, fellow pulmonary/critical care, 1977-78; v.p. satellite program Henry Ford Health Systems, Detroit, 1989; assoc. v.p. ambulatory program, assoc. prof. medicine Loyola U. Med. Ctr., Maywood, Ill., 1990-93, v.p. health care svcs., 1993-96; pres., CEO Univ. Care Plus, 1996-99; exec. dir. med. svcs. R & D plan and ambulatory care U. Tex. Med. Sch. and Hermann Hosp., Houston, 1996—, assoc. dean clin. affairs, 1997—, assoc. prof. medicine, 1996—; chief med. officer U. Calif., San Diego, 1999—. Lt. comdr. USNR, 1971-73. Fellow ACP, Am. Coll. Chest Physicians; mem. Am. Coll. Physician Execs. Avocation: birding. Office: USCD Healthcare 402 Dickinson St San Diego CA 92103-6902

RADUEGE, HARRY DALE, JR. career officer; b. Columbus, Ohio, Jan. 9, 1947; s. Harry Dale and Ruth Pauline (Roederer) R.; m. Julee Lydia Hux, Oct. 17, 1970; children: Chad Dale, Rian Elise, Ashley Jean. BS in Edn., Capital U., 1970; MS in Bus. Mgmt., Troy State U., 1976; MS in Telecommunications, U. So. Miss., 1978. Commd. 2d lt. USAF, 1970, advanced through grades to maj. gen., 1998, exec. officer tactical communications area Va., 1978-80, comdr. communications detachment Pirinclik, Turkey, 1980-81, chief readiness div. hdqrs. communications command Scott AFB, Ill., 1981-84, chief C3 engring. div. hdqrs. space command Colorado Springs, Colo., 1984-88; chief strategic info. warning systems staff of Chmn. Joint Chiefs of Staff, Washington, 1989-90, chief satellite communications div., 1990-91, exec. asst. to dir. command control, communications and computer systems staff, 1991-92; asst. deputy chief staff comm. computer systems Hdqs. Air Combat Command, Langley AFB, Va., 1992-93; comdr. Air Force C4 Agy., Scott AFB, Ill., 1993-95; dir. C4 Sys. U.S. Ctrl. Command, MacDill AFB, Fla., 1995-98; chief info. officer, dir. C2 sys. N.Am. Aerospace Def. Command, U.S. Space Command, Peterson AFB, Colo., 1998—, Air Force Space Command, Peterson AFB, 1998—. Asst. scoutmaster Boy Scouts Am., USAF Acad., Colo., 1985-86, scoutmaster, 1987-88; youth group leader Burke (Va.) Community Ch., 1990-92. Named one of Outstanding Young Men Am., 1979. Mem. Armed Forces Communications-Electronics Assn. (bd. dirs. 1986-87, v.p. programs 1987-88, profl. achievement award, meritorious svc. award 1985, medal of merit 1988), AIAA (sr. mem. tech. com. 1991-92). Home: 29 Westover Ave SW Washington DC 20336-5409 Office: Hdqs US Space Command J6 250 S Peterson Blvd Ste 116 Peterson AFB CO 80914

RAEBER, JOHN ARTHUR, architect, construction consultant; b. St. Louis, Nov. 24, 1947; s. Arthur William and Marie (Laux) R. AA, Jefferson Coll., 1968; AB, Washington U., 1970, MArch, 1973. Registered architect, Calif., Mo.; cert. constrn. specifier; cert. Nat. Coun. Arch. Specification writer Hellmuth, Obata & Kassabaum, St. Louis, 1973-78, constrn. administr., 1978-79; mgr. of specifications Gensler & Assocs., San Francisco, 1979-82; ind. constrn. specifier San Francisco, 1982—. Adj. prof. architecture Calif. Coll. Arts and Crafts, San Francisco, 1986—; access code advisor Constrn. Industry & Owners, 1982—; spkr., instr. seminars orgns., univs., 1982—; mem. Calif. State Bldg. Standards Commn. Accessibility Adv. Panel, Sacramento, 1981, Calif. Subcom. Rights of Disabled Adv. Panel, Sacramento, 1993; cons. Nat. Inst. Bldg. Scis., 1996—. Author: CAL/ABL: Interpretative Manual to California's Access Barriers Laws, 1982; co-author: (with Peter S. Hopf) Access for the Handicapped, 1984; columnist Constrn. Specifier Mag., 1988-95. Vol. Calif. Office Emergency Svcs. Safety Assessment, Sacramento, 1991—. Fellow AIA (San Francisco chpt. codes com., Calif. coun. codes and standards com., nat. masterspec rev. com. 1982-84, nat. codes com. corr.), Contrns. Specifications Inst. (cert., columnist newsletter San Francisco chpt. 1984-95, Ben John Small award for Outstanding Stature as practicing specifications writer 1994, pres. St. Louis chpt. 1978-79, pres. San Francisco chpt. 1993-94, tech. com., edn. com., publs. com., Specifications Proficiency award San Francisco chpt. 1989, Tech. Commendation award 1987); mem. Specifications Cons. in Ind. Practice (nat. pres. 1990-92, nat. sec./treas. 1988-90), Internat. Conf. Bldg. Officials, Phi Theta Kappa. Avocations: history, anthropology, sci. fiction. Home and Office: 75 Seward St San Francisco CA 94114-2336

RAEBURN, ANDREW HARVEY, performing arts association executive, record producer; b. London, July 22, 1933; arrived in U.S., 1964, Can., 1993; s. Walter Augustus Leopold and Dora Adelaide Harvey (Williams) R. BA in History, King's Coll., Cambridge U., Eng., 1958; MA, King's Coll., Camridge U., Eng., 1962; diploma (hon.) in music performance, Mt. Royal Coll., Calgary, Can., 1998. Mus. dir. Argo Record Co., London, 1959-64; asst. to music dir., program editor Boston Symphony Orch., 1964-73; dir. artists and repertory New World Records, N.Y.C., 1975-79; artistic adminstr. Detroit Symphony Orch., 1979-82; exec. dir. Van Cliburn Found. Inc., Ft. Worth, 1982-85; performing arts cons., 1985-93; exec. v.p. The Peter Pan Children's Fund, 1990-91; exec. dir. Esther Honens Internat. Piano Competition Found., 1993-95, pres., 1995-99, vice chmn., artistic dir., 1999-2001, pres., artistic dir., 2001—. Cons. music; radio and TV commentator; mem. faculty Boston U., 1966-67; condr. New World String Orch., 1978 Author record liner notes, Argo, RCA, Time-Life records, 1960-79, program notes, Boston Symphony Orch., 1968-73. Served with Royal Arty. Brit. Army, 1952-55; founding dean Prague Mozart Acad. 1992-93. Home: 702 235 Fifteenth Ave SW Calgary AB Canada T2R OP6 Office: 134 11th Ave SE 3rd Fl Calgary AB Canada T2G OX5 E-mail: raeburn@honens.com, ahr@cadvision.com

RAEDER, MYRNA SHARON, lawyer, educator; b. N.Y.C., Feb. 4, 1947; d. Samuel and Estelle (Auslander) R.; m. Terry Oliver Kelly, July 13, 1975; children: Thomas Oliver, Michael Lawrence. BA, Hunter Coll., 1968; JD, NYU, 1971; LLM, Georgetown U., 1975. Bar: N.Y. 1972, D.C. 1972, Calif. 1972. Spl. asst. U.S. atty. U.S. Atty's Office, Washington, 1972-73; asst. prof. U. San Fransisco Sch. Law, 1973-75; assoc. O'Melveny & Myers, L.A., 1975-79; assoc. prof. Southwestern U. Sch. Law., L.A., 1979-82, prof., 1983—, Irwin R. Buchalter prof. law, 1990; mem. faculty Nat. Judicial Coll., 1993—. Prettyman fellow Georgetown Law Ctr., Washington, 1971-73. Author: Federal Pretrial Practice, 3d edit., 2000; co-author: Evidence, State and Federal Rules in a Nutshell, 3d edit., 1997, Evidence, Cases, Materials and Problems, 2d edit., 1998, Fellow Am. Bar

Found.; mem. ABA (trial evidence com. litigation sect. 1980—, criminal justice sect. 1994-97, vice-chair planning 1997-98, chair elect 1997-98, chair 1998-99, mem. mag. bd., 2000—, adv. to nat. conf. commrs. uniform state laws drafting com. uniform rules of evidence 1996-1999), Assn. Am. Law Schs. (chair women in legal edn. sect. 1982, com. on sects. 1984-87, chair elect evidence sect. 1996, chair 1997), Nat. Assn. Women Lawyers (bd. dirs. 1991-98, pres.-elect 1993, pres. 1994-96), Women Lawyers Assn. L.A. (bd. dirs., coord. mothers support group 1987-96), Order of Coif, Phi Beta Kappa. Office: Southwestern U Sch Law 675 S Westmoreland Ave Los Angeles CA 90005-3905

RAEL, HENRY SYLVESTER, SR. retired health administrator, financial and management consultant; b. Pueblo, Colo., Oct. 2, 1928; s. Daniel and Grace (Abeyta) R.; m. Helen Warner Loring Brace, June 30, 1956 (dec. Aug. 1980); children: Henry Sylvester Jr., Loring Victoria, Thomas Warner Bush. AB, U. So. Colo., 1955; BA in Bus. Adminstrn., U. Denver, 1957, MBA, 1958. Sr. boys counselor Denver Juvenile Hall, 1955-58; adminstrv. asst. to pres. Stanley Aviation Corp., Denver, 1958-61; Titan III budget and fin. control supr. Martin Marietta Corp., Denver, 1961-65; mgmt. adv. services officer U. Colo. Med. Center, Denver, 1965-72; v.p. fin., treas. Loretto Heights Coll., Denver, 1972-73; dir. fin. and adminstrn. Colo. Found. for Med. Care, 1973-86, Tri-County Health Dept., Denver, 1986-96; fin. cons. Denver, 1996—. Cons. Clayton Found.-Denver Headstart, 1996, Colo. Dept. Pub. Health and Environ., 1997, Hosp. Shared Svcs., 1997-98, U.S. Dept. Commerce Census, 2000, Census Enumerator, 2000, Fin. Planning Assn., 2000-01; instr. fin. mgmt., mem. fin. com. am. Assn. Profl. Standards Rev. orgn., 1980-85; speaker systems devel., design assns., univs., 1967-71. Mem. budget lay adv. com. Park Hill Elem. Sch., Denver, 1967-68, chmn., 1968-69; vol. worker Boy and Girl Scouts, 1967-73; bd. dirs. Community Arts Symphony, 1981-83, 85-87; controller St. John's Episcopal Cathedral, 1982-83; charter mem. Pueblo (Colo.) Coll. Young Democrats, 1954-55; block worker Republican Party, Denver, 1965-68, precinct committeeman, 1978-84; trustee Van Nattan Scholarship Fund, 1974-96; bd. dirs. Vis. Nurse Assn., 1977-84, treas., 1982-84. Served with USAF, 1947-53, res., 1954-61. Recipient Disting. Service award Denver Astron. Soc., 1968, Citation Chamberlin Obs., 1985; Stanley Aviation masters scholar, 1957; Ballard scholar, 1956. Mem. Assn. Systems Mgmt. (pres. 1971-72), Hosp. Systems Mgmt. Soc., Budget Execs. Inst. (v.p. chpt. 1964-65, sec. 1963-64), Colo. Pub. Employees Retirement Assn. (bd. dirs. 1993), Denver Astron. Soc. (pres. 1965-66, bd. dirs. 1982-94), Am. Assn. Founds. for Med. Care (fin. com. 1981-82), Nat. Astronomers Assn. (exec. bd. 1965-97), Brandy Chase Homeowners Assn. (bd. dirs. 1997), Whispering Pines of Denver Homeowners Assn. (pres. 2001, bd. dirs., 1998), Epsilon Xi, Delta Psi Omega. Home: 7755 E Quincy Ave Apt 57 Denver CO 80237-2312

RAEL, LAWRENCE, city official; b. Mar. 26, 1959; BS in Sociology and Econs., MPA and Pub. Fin., U. N.Mex.; postgrad., Harvard U. Acting dep. sec. N.Mex. Transp. Dept., Albuquerque, 1986-87; legis. asst. U.S. Sen. Jeff Bingaman, Washington, 1987-90; dep. chief adminstrv. officer City of Albuquerque, 1991-94, chief adminstrv. officer, 1994—. Office: Office Chief Adminstrv Officer City County Bldg 11th Fl PO Box 1293 Albuquerque NM 87103-1293

RAFEEDIE, EDWARD, senior federal judge; b. Orange, N.J., Jan. 6, 1929; s. Fred and Nabeeha (Hishmeh) R.; m. Ruth Alice Horton, Oct. 8, 1961; children: Fredrick Alexander, Jennifer Ann. BS in Law, U. So. Calif., 1957, JD, 1959; LLD (hon.), Pepperdine U., 1978. Bar: Calif. 1960. Pvt. practice, Santa Monica, Calif., 1960-69; mcpl. ct. judge Santa Monica Jud. Dist., 1969-71; judge Superior Ct. State of Calif., L.A., 1971-82; dist. judge U.S. Dist. Court (cen. dist.) Calif., L.A., 1982-96, sr. judge, 1996—. With U.S. Army, 1950-52, Korea. Office: US Dist Ct 312 N Spring St Ste 244P Los Angeles CA 90012-4704

RAFFI, (RAFFI CAVOUKIAN), folksinger, children's entertainer; b. Cairo, July 8, 1948; Attended, U. Toronto. Singer, songwriter, 1970—. Recordings include: Singable Songs for the Very Young, 1976, More Singable Songs for the Very Young, 1977, The Corner Grocery Store, 1979, Baby Beluga, 1980, Rise and Sun, 1982, Raffi's Christmas Album, 1983, One Light One Sun, 1985, Everything Grows, 1987, Raffi in Concert with the Rise and Shine Band, 1989, Evergreen, Everblue: An Ecology Album for the '90's, 1990, Bananaphone, 1994 (Grammy award nom.), Raffi Radio, 1995 (Juno award nom.), Singable Song Collection, 1996; Broadway appearances: Raffi on Broadway, 1993, Bananaphone, 1994, Raffi Radio, 1995; videos: A Young Children's Concert with Raffi, 1984, Raffi and the Rise and Shine Band, 1988; author: Down By the Bay, 1988, Shake My Sillies Out, 1988, Baby Beluga, 1990, Like Me and You, 1994, The Life of a Children's Troubadour, An Qutobiography, 1998. Recipient Order of Can., 1983, Parents' Choice award Parents' Choice Mag., Best Children's Album Juno award, 1994. Office: Troubadour Records Ltd 1075 Cambie St Vancouver BC Canada V6B 5L7

RAFFIN, THOMAS A. physician; b. San Francisco, Jan. 25, 1947; s. Bennett L. and Carolyn M. Raffin; m. Michele Raffin, June 19, 1987; children: Elizabeth S., Ross Daniel, Jake Bennett, Nicholas Ethan. AB in Biol. Sci., Stanford Med. Sch., 1968, MD, 1973. Diplomate Am. Bd. Pulmonary Medicine, Am. Bd. Internal Medicine (also in Critical Care Medicine). Intern Peter Bent Brigham Hosp., 1973-75; fellow in respiratory medicine sch. medicine Stanford U., Stanford, Calif., 1975-78, med. fiberoptic bronchoscopy service dir. med. ctr., 1978—, acting asst. prof. sch. medicine, 1978-80, assoc. dir. med. ctr. intensive care units, med. dir. dept. respiratory therapy hosp., 1978—, assoc. prof. medicine sch. medicine, 1986-95, acting chief div. respiratory medicine, 1988—, chief div. pulmonary and critical care, 1990—, prof. medicine sch. of medicine, 1995—, Colleen and Robert Haas professorship in medicine/biomed. ethics, 1999—; co-dir. Stanford U. Ctr. for Biomed. Ethics, 1989—; co-founder Rigel Pharms., Inc., 1996—. Chmn. ethics com. Stanford U. Med. Ctr., 1987—. Author: Intensive Care: Facing the Critical Choices, 1988; contbr. articles to profl. jours. V.p. lung cancer com., No. Calif. Oncology Group, 1983-85; com. mem. NIH Workshop, 1984. Recipient Henry J. Kaiser Found. award, 1981, 84, 88, 97, Arthur L. Bloomfield award, 1981. Fellow ACP (rep. coun. subsplty. socs. 1986), Am. Coll. Chest Physicians (program com. mem. 1985-86); mem. AAAS, Am. Fedn. for Clin. Rsch., Am. Thoracic Soc., Santa Clara County Lung Assn. and Med. Soc., Calif. Med. Assn. (chmn. sect. chest diseases 1984-85), Soc. for Critical Care Medicine, Calif. Thoracic Soc. Jewish. Avocations: painting, gardening. Home: 13468 Three Forks Ln Los Altos CA 94022-2432 Office: Stanford U Med Ctr Dept Medicine Div Pul & Crit Care Med # H3151 Stanford CA 94305

RAFKIN, ALAN, television and film director; b. N.Y.C., July 23, 1928; s. Victor and Til (Bernstein) R.; children— Dru, Leigh Ann. B.S., Syracuse U., 1950. Guest lectr. Bowling Green State U., 1975 Actor Robert Q. Lewis TV Show, 1955, daytime shows, CBS-TV; dir. Verdict is Yours, 1960, Mary Tyler Moore Show, 1970-71, Sanford and Son, 1972, Bob Newhart Show, 1972-73, Rhoda, 1973, Let's Switch, 1975, MASH, 1976-77, Love, American Style, 1970-71, Laverne & Shirley, 1977-83; TV movie: One Day at a Time: Barbara's Crisis, 1981-82; films include Ski Party, 1965, The Ghost and Mr. Chicken, 1966, The Ride to Hangman's Tree, 1967, Nobody's Perfect, 1968, The Shakiest Gun in the West, 1968, Angel in my Pocket, 1969, How to Frame a Figg, 1971. Served with U.S. Army, 1950-52. Democrat. Jewish. also: Grey Entertainment 9150 Wilshire Blvd Beverly Hills CA 90212-3427

RAGAN, CHARLES RANSOM, lawyer; b. N.Y.C., Aug. 13, 1947; s. Charles Alexander Jr. and Josephine Forbes (Parker) R.; m. Barbara Thiel McMahon, Aug. 30, 1969; children: Alexandra Watson, Madeline McCue. AB, Princeton U., 1969; JD, Fordham U., 1974. Bar: N.Y. 1975, U.S. Ct. Appeals (3d cir.) 1975, Calif. 1976, U.S. Ct. Appeals (9th cir.) 1976, U.S. Dist. Ct. (no. dist.) Calif. 1976, U.S. Supreme Ct. 1981, U.S. Dist. Ct. (so. dist.) N.Y. 1982, U.S. Ct. Appeals (2d cir.) 1984. Law clk. to Hon. R.J. Aldisert U.S. Ct. Appeals (3rd cir.), 1974-76; assoc. Pillsbury, Madison & Sutro, San Francisco, 1976-81, ptnr., 1982-97, Palo Alto, 1997-2000, Pillsbury Winthrop, Palo Alto, 2001—. Mem. exec. com. 9th Cir. Judicial Conf., 1987-91; mem. Civil Justice Reform Act Adv. Group, No. Dist. Calif., 1995-99. Contbr. articles to profl. jours. Mem. San Francisco Bar Assn. (chair feds. cts. 1982-89). Avocations: biking, swimming, spectator sports. Office: Pillsbury Winthrop LLP 50 Fremont St San Francisco CA 94105

RAGAN, JAMES THOMAS, communications executive; b. San Diego, Mar. 15, 1929; m. Susan Held, Nov. 9, 1957; children: James, Maria, Carey, Andrew. BA, Oxford U., Eng., 1951; vocat. cert., U. State of N.Y., 1954; MA, Oxford U., Eng., 1955; vocat. cert., U. State of N.Y., 1954. With Gen. Electric Co., 1954-69; pres., chief operating officer Athena Communications Corp. subs. Gulf & Western Industries, Inc., N.Y.C., 1969-74; v.p. broadcast services Western Union Telegraph Co., 1974-76, v.p. satellite services, 1976-82, pres. Western Union personal communications corp., v.p. communication systems group, 1982-85; pres. Associated Info. Services Corp., 1985-86, Bunting, Inc., 1985-88; ptnr. Pierce Kennedy Hearth, 1988-91; CEO Nat. Lang. Assocs. Lanarea Pub., Guilford, Conn., 1990—. Patentee recreational sports equipment; author: The Ultimate Diet, The First Alaskans, A Guide to the Geography of the Native Languages, Cultures, Their Communities, and Populations, 1996. Pres. Wilton Pop Warner Football League, Wilton, Conn., 1972—73. Major USMC, 1952—54, Korea. Mem.: Sachem's Head Yacht Club, Madison Winter Club, Racquet and Tennis Club NYC, Sachem's Head Assn. (v.p., pres., treas.). Clubs: Racquet and Tennis (N.Y.C.); Sachem's Head Yacht (Guilford, Conn.); Madison Winter Club. Home: PO Box 1112 Green Valley AZ 85622 Office: Nat Lang Assocs PO Box 1112 Green Valley AZ 85622 E-mail: jtrnla@aol.com

RAGENT, BORIS, physicist; b. Cleve., Mar. 2, 1924; s. Samuel and Bertha (Lev) R.; m. Dorothy Kohn, Sept. 11, 1949; children— David Stefan, Lawrence Stanton, Jesse Ron. Student, Ohio State U., 1941-44; B.S.E.E., Marquette U., 1944; Ph.D. in Physics, U. Calif., Berkeley, 1953. Registered profl. engr., Calif. Engr. Victoreen Instrument Co., Cleve., 1946-48; engr., physicist Radiation Lab., U. Calif., Berkeley, 1948-53; physicist Livermore, 1953-56, Broadview Research Corp., Burlingame, Calif., 1956-59, Vidya div. Itek Corp., Palo Alto, 1959-66, Ames Research Ctr., NASA, Moffett Field, 1966-87, San Jose (Calif.) State U. Found., 1987-98. Lectr. Stanford U., U. Calif. Extension. Served in USNR, 1944-46. Mem. AAAS, Am. Phys. Soc., Optical Soc. Am., Am. Geophys. Union, Sigma Xi. Office: Ames Research Ctr NASA Mail Stop 245-1 Moffett Field CA 94035 E-mail: ragent@ssa1.arc.nasa.gov

RAGGIO, WILLIAM JOHN, state legislator; b. Reno, Oct. 30, 1926; s. William John and Clara M. (Cardelli) R.; m. Dorothy Brigman, August 15, 1948 (dec. Apr. 1998); children: Leslie Ann, Tracy Lynn, Mark William. Student, La. Poly. Inst., 1944-45, U. Okla., 1945-46; BA, U. Nev., 1948; JD, U. Calif. at Hastings, 1951. Bar: Nev. 1951, U.S. Supreme Ct. 1959. Atty., Reno and Las Vegas; asst. dist. atty. Washoe County, Nev., 1952-58; dist. atty., 1958-71; ptnr. firm Wiener, Goldwater, Galatz & Raggio, Ltd., 1971-72, Raggio, Walker & Wooster, Reno and Las Vegas, 1974-78, Raggio, Wooster & Lindell, 1978-92; sr. ptnr. Vargas & Bartlett, 1992-98; then Jones-Vargas (formerly Vargas & Bartlett), 1998—; mem. Nev. Senate, Washoe Dist. 3, Carson City, 1973—. Mem. Nev. Senate, 1973—, minority floor leader, 1977-81, 82-87, 91, majority flr. leader, 1987—; mem. legis. commn., vice chmn. criminal law and adminstrn. com. council State Govts., 1972-75; bd. dirs. Am. Savs. & Loan Assn.; v.p., dir Santa Fe Gaming Corp., Venotian Hotel, Las Vegas Sands, Inc. Adv. bd. Salvation Army, Reno; mem. Nev. Am. Revolutionary Bicentennial Commn., 1975-81; mem. Republican State Cen. Com. Bd. dirs. YMCA, Reno chpt. NCCJ, Salvation Army; past nat. chmn., current dir. Am. Legislative Exchange Council, dir. Sierra Health Svcs.; trustee Nat. Dist. Attys. Found. (vice chmn. 1962-65); trustee Community Action Program Washoe County. Republican candidate for U.S. Senate, 1970. Served with USNR, 1944-46; to 2d lt. USMCR, 1946-47. Named Young Man of Yr., Reno-Sparks Jr. C. of C., 1959; recipient Disting. Nevadan award, 1968, Fellows award The Salvation Army, Torch of Liberty award The Anti-Defamation League, SIR award Assoc. Gen. Contractors, 1995. Fellow Am. Bd. Criminal Lawyers; mem. ABA (state chmn. jr. bar conf. 1957-60, ho. dels.) Am. Judicature Soc., Navy Leaague, Air Force Assn., Nat. (nat. pres. 1967-68; named Outstanding Prosecutor 1965), Nev. State (sec. 1959, pres. 1960-63) Dist. Attys. Assn., NCJ (Brotherhood award 1965), Nev. Peace Officers Assn., Internat. Assn. Chiefs Police, Am. Leg. Exch. Coun. (nat. chmn. 1991-92), Am. Legion, Elks, Lion Club, Prospectors Club, Alpha Tau Omega, Phi Alpha Delta. Republican. Roman Catholic. Home: PO Box 281 Reno NV 89504-0281

RAGHAVAN, ASURI, executive; BSEE, U. Madras; MS in Computer Sci., Temple U. Sr. v.p., pres. equipment divsn. Kulicke & Soffa, until 1998; pres., CEO Gasonics, San Jose, Calif., 1998—. Office: Gasonics Intl 2730 Junction Ave San Jose CA 95134-1909

RAGINSKY, NINA, artist; b. Montreal, Apr. 14, 1941; d. Bernard Boris and Helen Theresa R.; 1 child, Sofia Katrina. BA, Rutgers U., 1962; studied painting with, Roy Lichtenstein; studied sculpture with, George Segal; studied Art History with Allan Kaprow, Rutgers U. Freelance photographer Nat. Film Bd., Ottawa, Ont., Can., 1963-81; instr. metaphysics Emily Car Coll. Art, Vancouver, B.C., Can., 1973-81; painter Salt Spring Island, 1989—. Sr. artist, jury Can. Coun.; selected Can. rep. in Sweden for Sweden Now Mag., 1979; tchr., lectr. in field, 1973—. One woman shows include Vancouver Art Gallery, Victoria Art Gallery, Edmonton Art Gallery, Art Gallery Ont., San Francisco Mus. Art, Acadia U., Nancy Hoffman Gallery, N.Y.C., Meml. U. Newfoundland Art Gallery; exhibited in group shows at Rutgers U., 1962, Montreal Mus. Fine Arts, 1963, Nat. Film Bd., Ottawa, 1964, 65, 67, 70, 71, 76, 77, Internat. Salon Photography, Bordeaux, France, 1968, Nat. Gallery Ottawa, 1968, Eastman House Rochester, N.Y., 1969, Vancouver Art Gallery, 1973, 80, Mural for Conf. Ctr. Ottawa, 1973, Field Mus., Chgo., 1976, Edmonton Art Gallery, 1978, 79, Walter Philips Gallery, 1979, Glenbow Mus. Gallery, 1979, Harbour Front Community Gallery, 1980, Hamilton Art Gallery, 1980, Musée Maisil de St. Lambert, 1981, Mendel Art Gallery, 1981, Dunlop Art Gallery, Regina, Can., 1981; represented in permanent collections Nat. Film Bd. Stills divsn., Ottawa, Ont., Banff (Alta.) Sch. Fine Arts, Nat Gallery Ottawa, Can., George Eastman House, Wadsworth Atheneum, Edmonton Art Gallery, U. Victoria, B.C., various pvt. collections. Bd. dirs. Island Watch, Salt Spring Island, B.C., 1993; founder, coord. Salt Spring Island Ecosys. Stewardship Project, 1993; founder, coord. Salt Spring Island Waterbird Watch Collective, 1994—. Decorated officer Order of Can.; recipient Kees Vermeer award for edn. and conservation, 1997. Mem. Royal Can. Acad. Arts. Avocations: gardening, birding, subject of numerous publs. Home and Office: 272 Beddis Rd Salt Spring Island BC VOS IE O Canada V8K 2J1

RAICHLEN, FREDRIC, civil engineering educator, consultant; b. Balt., Oct. 12, 1932; s. Samuel Israel and Ethel Lee (Fribush) R.; m. Judith Kurschner, May 29, 1968; children: Robert, David. B of Engring., Johns Hopkins U., 1953; MSc, MIT, 1955, DSc, 1962. Registered profl. engr., Calif., N.J. Asst. prof., assoc. prof. civil engring. Calif. Inst. Tech., Pasadena, 1962-72, prof. civil engring., 1972—. Fellow, asst. prof. civil engring. MIT, 1962; consulting engr., Pasadena, 1962—. 1st lt. USAF, 1956-59. Fellow ASCE (recipient John C. Moffatt and Frank E. Nichol Harbor and Coastal Engring. award 1994); mem. NAE, Internat. Assn. Hydraluic Rschrs., Sigma Xi. Home: 2157 Homet Rd San Marino CA 91108-1325 Office: Calif Inst Tech Dept Civil Engring 138-78 1200 E California Blvd Pasadena CA 91125-0001

RAINALDI, LIDIO G. state senator; Magistrate; Dem. senator dist. 4 N.Mex. State Senate. Mem. judiciary com. N.Mex. State Senate, vice chair Indian and cultural affairs. Home: 1101 Martinelli Gallup NM 87301 Office: NMex State Senate State Capitol Mail Rm Dept Santa Fe NM 87503 E-mail: senate@state.nm.us

RAINER, WILLIAM GERALD, cardiac surgeon; b. Gordo, Ala., Nov. 13, 1927; s. Jamie Flournoy and Lula (Davis) R.; m. Lois Sayre, Oct. 7, 1950; children: Vickie, Bill, Julia, Leslie. Student, Emory U., Atlanta, Ga., 1943-44, U. Ala., , 1944-45; MD, U. Tenn., Memphis, 1948; MS in Surgery, U. Colo., Denver, 1958. Diplomate Am. Bd. Surgery, Am. Bd. Thoracic Surgery. Intern Wesley Hosp., Chgo., 1949; gen. practice medicine Blue Island, Ill., 1950-52; resident Denver VA Hosp., 1954-59; practice medicine specializing in cardiac surgery Denver, 1960—. Bd. dirs. St. Joseph Hosp. Found., Denver; dinsting. clin. prof. surgery U. Colo. Health Sci. Ctr. Contbr. articles to profl. jours. Active Colo. Symphony Assn., Bonfils Blood Ctr.; dir. emeritus St. Joseph Hosp. Found. Bd. Lt. U.S. Army, 1952-54. Decorated Bronze Star; recipient Disting. Alumnus award U. Tenn. Health Sci. Ctr., 1992, Florence Sabin award U. Colo. Health Sci. Ctr., 1998. Mem. Soc. Thoracic Surgeons (sec. 1980-85, pres. 1989, historian 1996—, Disting. Svc. award 1998), Colo. Med. Soc. (pres. 1984-85), Denver Med. Soc. (pres. 1984), Denver Clin. & Pathology Soc., Am. Coll. Chest Physicians (pres. 1984), Am. Bd. Thoracic Surgeons (bd. dirs. 1982-88), Am. Surg. Assn., Am. Assn. Thoracic Surgery, Societé Internationale de Chirugie, Cactus Club. Avocations: photography, traveling. Office: 2005 Franklin St Ste 380 Denver CO 80205-5411 E-mail: wrainersjh828@pol.net

RAINEY, RICHARD K. state legislator; b. Medford, Oreg. m. Sue McNulty; seven children. B in Adminstrn. of Justice, Calif. State U., Sacramento; MPA, Golden Gate U. Police officer City of Compton, 1962; various positions ending with sheriff Contra Costa County Sheriff's Dept., 1978-92; mem. Calif. State Assembly, 1992-96, Calif. State Senate, 1996—, mem. local govt. com., vice chair pub. safety com. With USN. Recipient Policy award Calif. Child Devel. Adv. Com., Cornucopia award for legis. excellence Calif. Women for Agr., 1997, award for outstanding achievement in policy for children and youth Calif. Child Devel. Adv. Com., 1998; named Legislator of Yr., Calif. Probation, Parole and Correctional Assn., 1995, Legislator of Yr. award Calif. Child Devel. Adminstrs. Assn., 1997. Republican. Office: State Capitol Sacramento CA 95814 also: 1948 Mt Diablo Blvd Walnut Creek CA 94596-4412 also: Antioch City Hall 3rd and H Sts Antioch CA 94509 Fax: 925-280-0299

RAISBECK, JAMES DAVID, engineering company executive; b. Milw., Sept. 29, 1936; m. Sherry Raisbeck; 1 child, Jennifer Lee; stepchildren: Eric Valpey, Laura Valpey. BS in Aerodynamics, Purdue U., 1961. Rsch. aerodynamist Boeing Comml. Airplane Co., Seattle, 1961-66; new airplane and rsch. outplant mgr. Boeing Airplane Co., Wright-Patterson AFB, Ohio, 1966-68; program mgr. comml. STOL airplane programs Boeing Co., 1968-69; pres., CEO Robertson Aircraft Corp., Seattle, 1969-73; v.p. tech. Am. Jet Industries, Van Nuys, Calif., 1973-74; CEO Raisbeck Group, San Antonio and Seattle, 1974-80, Raisbeck Engring., Inc., Seattle, 1980—, Raisbeck Comml. Air Grp., Inc., Seattle, 1996—. Recipient Outstanding Engr. award Purdue U., 1999; named Disting. Engring. Alumnus 1979, Purdue U. Fellow AIAA (assoc.); mem. Soc. Automotive Engrs., NBAA, Purdue U. Alumni Assn., Tau Beta Pi, Phi Eta Sigma, Sigma Gamma Tau. Achievements include numerous patents in aircraft design. Office: Raisbeck Engring Inc 4411 S Ryan Way Seattle WA 98178-2021 Fax: 206-722-1892

RAISIAN, JOHN, academic administrator, economist; b. Conneaut, Ohio, July 30, 1949; s. Ernest James and Ruby Lee (Owens) R.; m. Joyce Ann Klak, Aug. 17, 1984; children: Alison Kathleen, Sarah Elizabeth. BA, Ohio U., 1971; PhD, UCLA, 1978; LLD (hon.), Albertson Coll. Idaho, 1995. Rsch. assoc. Human Resources Rsch. Ctr., U. So. Calif., L.A., 1972-73; cons. Rand Corp., Santa Monica, Calif., 1974-75, 76; vis. asst. prof. econs. U. Wash., Seattle, 1975-76; asst. prof. econs. U. Houston, 1976-80; sr. economist Office Rsch. and Evaluation, U.S. Bur. Labor Stats., Washington, 1980-81; spl. asst. for econ. policy Office Asst. Sc. for Policy, U.S. Dept. Labor, Washington, 1981-83, dir. rsch. and tech. support, 1981-84; pres. Unicon Rsch. Corp., L.A., 1984-86; sr. fellow Hoover Instn., Stanford, Calif., 1986—, assoc. dir., dep. dir., 1986-90, dir., 1990—. Exec. dir. Presdl. Task Force on Food Assistance, Washington, 1983-84. Mem. editorial bd. Jour. Labor Rsch., 1983—; contbr. articles to profl. jours. Advisor Nat. Coun. on Handicapped, Washington, 1985-86, Nat. Commn. on Employment Policy, Washington, 1987-88; chmn. minimum wage bd. Calif. Indsl. Welfare Commn., 1987; mem. nat. adv.com. Student Fin. Assistance, Washington, 1987-89; corp. mem. Blue Shield Calif., 1994-96; bd. dirs. Sentinel Groups Fund, Inc., 1997—; mem. Pacific Coun. Internat. Policy, nat. adv. bd. City Innovation. Recipient Best Publ. of Yr. award Econ. Inquiry, Western Econ. Assn., 1979, Disting. Teaching award U. Houston Coll. Social Scis., 1980, Disting. Svc. award U.S. Dept. Labor, 1983; predoctoral fellow Rand Corp., 1976. Mem. Am. Econs. Assn., Western Econ. Assn. (chmn. nominating com. 1992), Commonwealth Club of Calif., World Affairs Coun., Mont Pelerin Soc., Coun. on Fgn. Rels., Nat. Assn. Scholars, Phi Beta Kappa. Republican. Avocations: wine collecting, sports enthusiast. Office: Stanford U Hoover Hoover Inst War-Rev & Peace Stanford CA 94305-6010

RAJOTTE, RAY V. biomedical engineer, researcher; b. Wainwright, Alta., Can., Dec. 5, 1942; s. Sam and Bernadette (Tremblay) R.; m. Gloria A. Yackimetz, Aug. 20, 1966; children: Brian, Michael, Monique. RT, No. Alta. Inst. Tech., 1965; BSc in Elec. Engring., U. Alta., 1971, MSc in Elec. Engring., 1973, PhD in Biomed. Engring., 1975. Postdoctoral fellow U. Alta. Dept. Medicine, Edmonton, 1975-76, Oak Ridge (Tenn.) Nat. Lab., 1976-77, Washington U., St. Louis, 1977, UCLA, 1977; rsch. assoc. dept. medicine U. Alta., Edmonton, 1977-79, asst. prof. dept. medicine, 1979-82, asst. prof. dept. medicine & surgery, 1983-84, assoc. prof., 1984-88, prof., 1988—. Dir. Islet Cel Transplant Lab. U. Alta., 1982—, Divsn. Exptl. Surgery U. Alta., 1988-96; assoc. dir. Surg.-Med. Rsch. Inst. U. Alta., 1984-87, dir., 1987—; co-dir. Juvenile Diabetes Fund Diabetes Interdisciplinary Rsch. Program U. Alta., 1992-97. Co-editor: The Immunology of Diabetes Mellitus, 1986; mem. adv. bd. Diabetologia jour., 1993—; author over 350 publs. in field; contbr. 18 chpts. to books. Mem. Cell Transplantation Soc. (founding mem., councillor 1991—), Internat. Pancreas and Islet Transplant Assn. (founding mem., treas. 1991—), Can. Transplantation Soc. (Western councillor 1992-93), European Assn. for Study of Diabetes, Assn. Profl. Engrs., Geologists & Geophysicists Alta., Soc. Cryobiology, Am. Diabetes Assn., Can. Soc. Clin. Investigation, Transplantation Soc., Can. Diabetes Assn., Acad. Surg. Rsch., Internat. Diabetes Fedn. Achievements include patent for glucose sensor. Office: U Alta Surg-Med Rsch Inst Edmonton AB Canada T6G 2N8

RAKOVE, JACK NORMAN, history educator; b. Chgo., June 4, 1947; s. Milton Leon and Shirley (Bloom) R.; m. Helen Scharf, June 22, 1969; children: Robert, Daniel. AB, Haverford Coll., 1968; PhD, Harvard U., 1975. Asst. prof. history Colgate U., Hamilton, N.Y., 1975-80; from asst. to assoc. prof. history Stanford (Calif.) U., 1980-90, prof., 1990—, Coe prof. history and Am. studies, 1996—, prof. polit. sci., 1999—. Author: Beginnings of National Politics, 1979, James Madison and The Creation of the American Republic, 1990, Original Meanings, 1996 (Pulitzer prize for History, 1997), Declaring Rights, 1997; editor: Interpreting the Consitution, 1990, James Madison Writings, 1999. Commr. Calif. Bicentennial Commn., 1986-87. With USAR, 1968-74. NEH fellow, 1985-86, Stanford Humanities Ctr. fellow, 1988-89, 2000-01. Mem. Am. Hist. Assn., Orgn. Am. Historians, Soc. Am. Historians, Am. Polit. Sci. Assn., Am. Acad. Arts & Scis., Am. Antiquarian Soc. Office: Stanford U Dept History Stanford CA 94305-2024 E-mail: rakove@stanford.edu

RALEIGH, CECIL BARING, geophysicist; b. Little Rock, Aug. 11, 1934; s. Cecil Baring and Lucile Nell (Stewart) R.; m. Diane Lauster, July 17, 1982; children: Alison, Marianne, Lawrence, David. B.A., Pomona (Calif.) Coll., 1956; M.A., Claremont (Calif.) Grad. Sch., 1958; Ph.D., UCLA, 1963. Fellow Research Sch. Phys. Sci., Australian Nat. U., Canberra, 1963-66; geophysicist U.S. Geol. Survey, Menlo Park, Calif., 1966-80, program mgr. for earthquake prediction research program, 1980-81; dir. Lamont-Doherty Geol. Obs. and prof. geol. scis. Columbia U., Palisades, N.Y., 1981-89; dean Sch. Ocean and Earth Sci. and Tech. U. Hawaii, Honolulu, 1989—. CEO Ctr. for a Sustainable Future, Inc., 1996—; mem. Gov.'s Task Force on Sci. Tech., 1996-98; mem. NAS/NRC Ocean Studies Bd.; chmn. NAS/NRC Yucca Mountain Panel, High Tech. Devel. Corp.; bd. dirs. JOI, Inc. Author papers control earthquakes, rheology of the mantle, mechanics of faulting, crystal plasticity. Trustee Bishop Mus., 1997—. Recipient Interdisciplinary award U.S. Nat. Com. Rock Mechanics, 1969, 74; Meritorious Service award Dept. Interior, 1974; Barrows Dist. Alumnus award Pomona Coll. Fellow Am. Geophys. Union, Geol. Soc. Am. Democrat. Inventor formation fracturing method. Office: U Hawaii Sch Ocean Earth Sci & Tech Honolulu HI 96822

RALSTON, HENRY JAMES, III, neurobiologist, anatomist, educator; b. Berkeley, Calif., Mar. 12, 1935; s. Henry James and Sue Harris (Mahnke) R.; m. Diane Cornelia Daly, Oct. 29, 1960; children: Rachel Anne, Amy Sue. BA, U. Calif., Berkeley, 1956, MD, 1959. Intern Mt. Sinai Hosp., N.Y.C., 1959-60; resident in medicine U. Calif., San Francisco, 1960-61, prof., 1973—, chmn. dept. anatomy, 1973-97, chmn. acad. senate, 1986-88; spl. postdoctoral fellow U. Coll., London, 1963-65, lectr., 1981; asst. prof. anatomy Stanford (Calif.) U., 1965-69; assoc. prof. U. Wis., Madison, 1969-73; prof. anatomy U. Calif., San Francisco, 1976—. Cons. NIH; mem. com. for future of anat. scis., Macy Found., 1977-80; vis. prof. French Med. Rsch. Inst.-INSERM, Paris, 1981-82; chair step I U.S. med. lic. examination com. Nat. Bd. Med. Examiners, 1992-96. With M.C. U.S. Army, 1961-63. Recipient Henry J. Kaiser award for excellence in tchg., 1978, Jacob Javits Neurosci. Investigator award NIH, 1988-95; USPHS grant, 1966—. Mem. AAAS, Soc. Neurosci., Soc. Study Pain, Am. Pain Soc., Am. Assn. Anatomists (pres. 1987-88, chmn. publs. com. 1989-91, Henry Gray award 1997), Am. Assn. Med. Colls. (adv. panel on biomed. rsch. 1996-99), Anat. Assn. Gt. Britain, Alpha Omega Alpha. Achievements include research in field of organization of mammalian nervous system studied by electron microscopy, mechanisms subserving pain in animals and humans. Office: U Calif Dept Anatomy PO Box 0452 San Francisco CA 94143-0452 E-mail: hjr@phy.ucsf.edu

RALSTON, JOANNE SMOOT, public relations counseling firm executive; b. Phoenix, May 13, 1939; d. A. Glen and Viriginia (Lee) Smoot; m. W. Hamilton Weigelt, Aug. 15, 1991. BA in Journalism, Ariz. State U., 1960. Reporter The Ariz. Rep., Phoenix, 1960-62; co-owner, pub. rels. dir. The Patton Agy., Phoenix, 1962-71; founder, pres., owner Joanne Ralston & Assocs., Inc., Phoenix, 1971-87, 92—. Pres. Nelson Ralston Robb Comm., Phoenix, 1987-91, Joanne Ralston & Assoc., Inc., Scottsdale, Ariz., 1992—. Contbr. articles to profl. jours. Bd. dirs. Ariz. Parklands Found,. 1984-86, Gov.'s Coun. on Health, Phys. Fitness and Sports, 1984-86; mem. task force Water and Natural Resources Coun., Phoenix, 1984-86; mem. Ariz. Rep. Caucus, 1984—, others. Recipient Lulu awards (36) L.A. Advt. Women, 1964—, Gold Quill (2) Internat. Assn. Bus. Communicators, Excellence awards Fin. World mag., 1982-93, others; named to Walter Cronkite Sch. Journalism Hall of Fame, Coll. Pub. Programs Ariz. State U., 1987; named one of 25 Most Influential Arizonians, Phoenix Mag., 1991. Mem. Pub. Rels. Soc. Am. (counselor sect.), Internat. Assn. Bus. Communicators, Phoenix Press Club (pres. bd.), Investor Rels. Inst., Phoenix Met. C. of C. (bd. dirs. 1977-84, 85-91). Republican. Avocations: horses, skiing. Address: PO Box 808 Kapaau HI 96755-0808

RALSTON, LENORE DALE, academic policy and program analyst; b. Oakland, Calif., Feb. 21, 1949; d. Leonard Earnest and Emily Allison (Hudnut) R. BA in Anthropology, U. Calif., Berkeley, 1971, MPH in Behavioral Sci., 1981; MA in Anthropology, Bryn Mawr Coll., 1973, PhD in Anthropology, 1980. Asst. rschr. anthropology inst. internat. studies U. Calif., Berkeley, 1979-82, rsch. assoc. Latin Am. Study Ctr., 1982-83, acad. asst. to dean Sch. of Optometry, 1990-95, prin. policy analyst, chancellor's office, 1995—; assoc. scientist, rsch. adminstr. Med. Rsch. Inst., San Francisco, 1982-85; cons. health sci. Berkeley, 1986-90. Mem. fin. bd. Med. Rsch. Inst., 1983-84; speaker in field. Co-author: Voluntary Effects in Decentralized Management, 1983; contbr. articles to profl. jours. Commr. Cmty. Health Adv. Com., Berkeley, 1988-90; vice chair, commr. Cmty. Health Commn., Berkeley, 1990-93; mem. bd. safety com. Miles, Inc., Berkeley, 1992-94. Grantee Nat. Rsch. Svc. Award, WHO, NIMH, NSF. Fellow Applied Anthropology Assn.; mem. APHA, Am. Anthropology Assn., Sigma Xi. Home: 1232 Carlotta Ave Berkeley CA 94707-2707 E-mail: ralston@uclink4.berkeley.edu

RAMER, BRUCE M. lawyer; b. Teaneck, N.J., Aug. 2, 1933; s. Sidney and Anne S. (Strassman) R.; children: Gregg B., Marc K., Neal I. BA, Princeton U., 1955; LLB, Harvard U., 1958. Bar: Calif. 1963, N.J. 1958. Assoc., Morrison, Lloyd & Griggs, Hackensack, N.J., 1959-60; ptnr. Gang, Tyre, Ramer & Brown, Inc., L.A., 1963—. Exec. dir. Entertainment Law Inst., Law Ctr. of U. So. Calif.; bd. of councilors Law Ctr. U. So. Calif.; chmn., nat. bd. govs. Am. Jewish Com., 1995-98, nat. v.p., 1982-88, pres., 1998—, L.A. chpt., 1980-83, chair Western region, 1984-86, comty. svc. award, 1987, nat. pres., 1998—, adv. bd. Skirball Inst. on Am. Values, 1998—; chmn. Asia Pacific Rim Inst., 1989-98; trustee Loyola Marymount U., L.A. Children's Mus., 1986-89; vice chair United Way, 1991-93, corp. bd. dirs., 1981-93, chair coun. pres. 1989-90, mem. cmty. issues coun., 1989-90, chair discretionary fund distbn. com., 1987-89; bd. dirs., chair Geffen Playhouse, 1995-98, founding chair, 1998—; bd. dirs. L.A. Urban League, 1987-93, 96—, Jewish Fedn. Coun. of Greater L.A. (mem. Cmty. Rels. com., bd. dirs., exec. com.), Jewish TV Network, Sta. KCET-TV; mem., bd. dirs. Rebuild L.A., 1992-96; mem. bd. govs. Calif. Cmty. Found., 1988-98; recipient Ann. Brotherhood award NCCJs, 1990; mem. Fellows of Am. Bar Found.; mem. econ. strategy panel State Calif., 1997—; bd. dirs. Shoah Visual History Found., Righteous Persons Found., L.A. 2012 Bid Com. for the So. Calif. Olympic Games; bd. dirs. Jewish Fedn. Coun. Greater L.A., mem. exec. com., cmty. rels. com. Pvt. U.S. Army, 1958-59, 2d lt., 1961-62. Mem. ABA (mem. spl. com. jud. ind.), L.A. County Bar Assn., Calif. Bar Assn., Beverly Hills Bar Assn. (Exec. Dirs. award [illegible], Entertainment Lawyer of Yr. award [illegible]), [illegible] Copyright Soc. (pres. 1974-75), Calif. Copyright Conf. (pres. 1973-74), Princeton Club (pres. 1975-78). Office: Gang Tyre Ramer & Brown Inc 132 S Rodeo Dr Beverly Hills CA 90212-2415

RAMER, LAWRENCE JEROME, corporation executive; b. Bayonne, N.J., July 29, 1928; s. Sidney and Anne (Strassman) R.; m. Ina Lee Brown, June 30, 1957; children: Stephanie Beryl, Susan Meredith, Douglas Strassman. B.A. in Econs, Lafayette Coll., 1950; M.B.A., Harvard U., 1957; LLD (hon.), Lafayette Coll., 1992. Sales rep., then v.p. United Sheet Metal Co., Bayonne, 1953-55; with Am. Cement Corp., 1957-64; v.p. mktg. dir. Riverside Cement Co., 1960-62, v.p. mktg. parent co., 1962-64; vice chmn. bd., chief exec. officer Clavier Corp., N.Y.C., 1965-66; exec. v.p., vice chmn. bd. Pacific Western Industries, Los Angeles, 1966-70; pres., chief exec. officer Nat. Portland Cement Co. Fla., 1975-89; chmn. bd. Sutro Partners, Inc., Los Angeles, 1977-89, Somerset Mgmt. Group, 1975-92, Luminall Paints Inc., Los Angeles, 1972-95; chmn. bd., chief exec. officer Bruning Paint Co., Balt., 1979—, Pacific Coast Cement Co., Los Angeles, 1979-90; pres., chief exec. officer Ramer Equities, Inc., 1990—. Chmn. Lee and Lawrence J. Ramer Family Found., 1986—; bd. dirs. Orbis Internat., N.Y.C., The Music Ctr., L.A., Canyon Ranch, Tucson, Music Ctr. Found., L.A.; bd. dirs. Ctr. Theatre Group-Mark Taper Ahmanson Theatres, L.A., pres. and chmn., 1987-97. Chmn. bd. trustees Lafayette Coll., Easton, Pa.; trustee, chmn. bd. trustees Calif. Inst. Arts, Valencia, Calif.; bd. dirs. Non-Traditional Casting Project, N.Y.; nat. bd. govs. Am. Jewish Com., N.Y., assoc. chmn. bd. trustees; trustee Facing History and Ourselves; bd. dirs. United Friends of Children. Office: Ramer Equities Inc 1999 Ave Of Stars Ste 1090 Los Angeles CA 90067-4612 E-mail: ljramer@pacbell.com

RAMEY, DRUCILLA STENDER, legal association executive; b. 1946; BA, Radcliffe Coll.; JD, Yale U. Bar: Calif. 1972. Exec. dir., gen. counsel Bar Assn. San Francisco, 1985—. Office: Bar Assn San Francisco 465 California St Ste 1100 San Francisco CA 94104-1804

RAMIL, MARIO R. state supreme court justice; b. Quezon City, The Philippines, June 21, 1946; came to U.S., 1956; s. Quintin A. and Fausta M. (Reyes) R.; m. Judy E. Wong, Nov. 6, 1971; children: Jonathan, Bradley. BA in Polit. Sci., Calif. State U., Hayward, 1972; JD, U. Calif., San Francisco, 1975. Bar: Calif. 1976, Hawaii 1976, U.S. Dist. Ct. Hawaii, U.S. Dist. Ct. (no. dist.) Calif., U.S. Ct. Appeals (9th cir.). Law clk. San Francisco Neighborhood Legal Aid Found., 1973-75; legal counsel Sandigan-Newcomers Svcs., Inc., San Francisco, 1975-76; dep. atty. gen. Dept. Labor and Indsl. Rels., 1976-79; dep. atty. gen. adminstrn. U. Hawaii, 1979-80; staff atty. house majority atty.'s office Hawaii Ho. of Reps., 1980; pvt. practice, 1980-82; dep. atty. gen. adminstrv. div. State of Hawaii, 1982-84, ins. commr., 1984-86; dir. Hawaii State Dept. Labor and Indsl. Rels., Honolulu, 1986-91; of counsel Lyons, Brandt, Cook and Hiramatsu, 1991-93; assoc. justice Hawaii Supreme Ct., Honolulu, 1993—. Bd. dirs. Hawaii Youth-At-Risk, 1989; co-chair state conv. Dem. Party State of Hawaii, 1984; mem. Adv. Coun. on Housing and Constrn., State of Hawaii, 1981; pres., bd. dirs. Hawaii Non-Profit Housing Corp.; exec. sec., chmn. adminstrv. budget com. Oahu Filipino Community Coun.; bd. dirs, legal advisor Oahu Filipino Jaycees, 1978-81. Office: Ali'iolani Hale Hawaii Supreme Ct 417 S Kinga St Honolulu HI 96813-2902 Address: PO Box 2560 Honolulu HI 96804-2560 Fax: 808-539-4855

RAMIREZ, MICHAEL P. editorial cartoonist; b. Tokyo; s. Ireneo Edward and Fumiko Maria R. Syndicated cartoonist Copley News Svc., 1986—; cartoonist The Comml. Appeal, Memphis, 1990-98. Recipient Pulitzer Prize for editorial cartooning, 1994. Office: The LA Times Times Mirror Square Los Angeles CA 90053

RAMIREZ, RICARDO, bishop; b. Bay City, Tex., Sept. 12, 1936; s. Natividad and Maria (Espinosa) R. B.A., U. St. Thomas, Houston, 1959; M.A., U. Detroit, 1968; Diploma in Pastoral Studies, East Asian Pastoral Inst., Manila, 1973-74. Ordained priest Roman Catholic Ch., 1966; missionary Basilian Fathers, Mex., 1968-76; exec. v.p. Mexican Am. Cultural Ctr., San Antonio, 1976-81; aux. bishop Archdiocese of San Antonio, 1981-82; bishop Diocese of Las Cruces, N.M., 1982—; cons. U.S. Bishop's Com. on Liturgy, from 1981; advisor U.S. Bishop's Com. on Hispanic Affairs, from 1981. Author: Fiesta, Worship and Family, 1981. Mem. N.Am. Acad. on Liturgy, Hispanic Liturgical Inst., Padres Asociada Derechos Religiosos Educativos y Sociales Lodges: K.C; Holy Order Knights of Holy Sepulcher. Office: Diocese Las Cruces 1280 Med Park Dr Las Cruces NM 88005-3239

RAMO, SIMON, retired engineering executive; b. Salt Lake City, May 7, 1913; s. Benjamin and Clara (Trestman) R.; m. Virginia Smith, July 25, 1937; children: James Brian, Alan Martin. BS, U. Utah, 1933, DSc (hon.), 1961; PhD, Calif. Inst. Tech., 1936; DEng (hon.), Case Western Res. U., 1960, U. Mich., 1966, Poly. Inst. N.Y., 1971; DSc (hon.), Union Coll., 1963, Worcester Polytechnic Inst., 1968, U. Akron, 1969, Cleve. State U., 1976; LLD (hon.), Carnegie-Mellon U., 1970, U. So. Calif., 1972, Gonzaga U., 1983, Occidental Coll., 1984, Claremont U., 1985. With Gen. Electric Co., 1936-46; v.p. ops. Hughes Aircraft Co., 1946-53; with Ramo-Woolridge Corp., 1953-58; dir. U.S. Intercontinental Ballistic Missile Program, 1954-58, TRW Inc., 1954-85, exec. v.p., 1958-61, vice chmn. bd., 1961-78, chmn. exec. com., 1969-78, cons., 1978—; pres. The Bunker-Ramo Corp., 1964-66; chmn. bd. TRW-Fujitsu Co., 1980-83. Bd. dirs. Arco Power Techs.; vis. prof. mgmt. sci. Calif. Inst. Tech., 1978—; Regents lectr. UCLA, 1981-82, U. Calif. at Santa Cruz, 1978-79; chmn. Center for Study Am. Experience, U. So. Calif., 1978-80; Faculty fellow John F. Kennedy Sch. Govt., Harvard U., 1980-84; mem. White House Energy Research and Devel. Adv. Council, 1973-75; mem. adv. com. on sci. and fgn. affairs U.S. State Dept., 1973-75; chmn. Pres.'s Com. on Sci. and Tech., 1976-77; mem. adv. council to Sec. Commerce, 1976-77, Gen. Atomics Corp., 1988—, Aurora Capital Ptnrs., 1991—, Chartwell Investments, 1992—; co-chmn. Transition Task Force on Sci. and Tech. for Pres.-elect Reagan; mem. roster consultants to adminstr. ERDA, 1976-77; bd. advisors for sci. and tech. Republic of China, 1981-84; chmn. bd. Aetna, Jacobs & Ramo Venture Capital, 1987-90, Allenwood Ventures Inc., 1987—; advisor Axiom Venture Ptnrs., 1997—. Author: The Business of Science, 1988, other sci., engring. and mgmt. books. Bd. dirs. L.A. World Affairs Coun. 1973-85, Mus. Ctr. Found., L.A., L.A. Philharm. Assn., 1981-84; life trustee Calif. Inst. Tech., Nat. Symphony Orch. Assn., 1973-83; trustee emeritus Calif. State Univs.; bd. visitors UCLA Sch. Medicine, 1980—; bd. dirs. W.M. Keck Found., 1983—; bd. govs. Performing Arts Coun. Mus. Ctr. L.A., pres., 1976-77; co-chair Bd. of Overseers Keck Sch. Medicine U. So. Calif., 1999—. Recipient award IAS, 1956; award Am. Inst. Elec. Engrs., 1959; award Arnold Air Soc., 1960; award Am. Acad. Achievement award, 1964; award Am. Iron and Steel Inst., 1968; Disting. Svc. medal Armed Forces Communication and Electronics Assn., 1970; medal of achievement WEMA, 1970; awards U. So. Calif., 1971, 79; Kayan medal Columbia U., 1972; award Am. Cons. Engrs. Coun., 1974; medal Franklin Inst., 1978; award Harvard Bus. Sch. Assn., 1979; award Nat. Medal Sci., 1979; Disting. Alumnus award U. Utah, 1981; UCLA medal, 1982; Presdl. Medal of Freedom, 1983; named to Bus. Hall of Fame, 1984; recipient Aesculapian award UCLA, 1984, Durand medal AAIA, 1984, John Fritz medal, 1986, Henry Townley Heald award Ill. Inst. Tech., 1988, Nat. Engring. award Am. Assn. Engring. Socs., 1988, Franklin-Jefferson medal, 1988, Howard Hughes Meml. award, 1989, Air Force Space and Missile Pioneers award, 1989, Pioneer award Internat. Coun. on Sys. Engring., 1997, Disting. Pub. Svc. medal NASA, 1999, Lifetime Achievement trophy Smithsonian Inst., 1999, John F. Kennedy Astronautics award Am. Astro- [illegible] Assn., 2000. Fellow IEEE (Electronic Achievement award 1953, Golden Omega award 1975, Founders medal 1980, Centennial medal 1984), Am. Acad. Arts and Scis., Am. Acad. Polit. Sci.; mem. N.Y. Acad. Scis., Nat. Acad. Engring. (founder, coun. mem. Bueche award), Nat. Acad. Scis., Am. Phys. Soc., Am. Philos. Soc., Inst. Advancement Engring., Coun. Fgn. Rels., Pacific Coun. Internat. Policy, Internat. Acad. Astronautics, Eta Kappa Nu (eminent mem. award 1966), Theta Tau (Hall of Fame laureate). Office: 9200 W Sunset Blvd Ste 801 Los Angeles CA 90069-3603

RAMO, VIRGINIA M. SMITH, civic worker; b. Yonkers, N.Y. d. Abraham Harold and Freda (Kasnetz) Smith; m. Simon Ramo; children: James Brian, Alan Martin. BS in Edn., U. So. Calif., DHL (hon.), 1978. Nat. co-chmn., ann. giving U. So. Calif., 1968-70, vice chmn., trustee, 1971—, co-chmn. bd. councilors Sch. Performing Arts, 1975-76, co-chmn. bd. councillors Schs. Med. and Engring. Vice-chmn. bd. overseers Hebrew Union Coll., 1972-75; bd. dirs. The Muses of Calif. Mus. Sci. and Industry, UCLA Affiliates, Estelle Doheny Eye Found., U. So. Calif. Sch. Medicine; mem. adv. coun. L.A. County Heart Assn., chmn. com. to endow Chair in cardiology at U. So. Calif.; vice chmn., bd. dirs. Friends of Libr. U. So. Calif.; bd. dirs., nat. pres. Achievement Rewards for Coll. Scientists Found., 1975-77; bd. dirs. Les Dames L.A., Cmty. TV So. Calif.; bd. dirs., v.p. Founders L.A. Music Ctr.; v.p. L.A. Music Ctr. Opera Assn.; v.p. corp. bd. United Way; v.p. Blue Ribbon-400 Performing Arts Coun.; chmn. com. to endow chair in gerontology U. So. Calif.; vice chmn. campaign Doheny Eye Inst,. 1986; co-chair, bd. overseers Keck Sch. Medicine U. So. Calif., 1999—. Recipient Svc. award Friends of Librs., 1974, Nat. Cmty. Svc. award Alpha Epsilon Phi, 1975, Disting. Svc. award Am. Heart Assn., 1978, Svc. award U. So. Calif., Spl. award U. So. Calif. Music Alumni Assn., 1979, Life Achievement award Mannequins of L.A. Assistance League, 1979, Woman of Yr. award Pan Hellenic Assn., 1981, Disting. Svc. award U. So. Calif. Sch. Medicine, 1981, U. So. Calif. Town and Gown Recognition award, 1986, Asa V. Call Achievement award U. So. Calif., 1986, Phi Kappa Phi scholarship award U. So. Calif., 1986, Vision award Luminaires of Doheny Eye Inst., 1994. Mem. UCLA Med. Aux., U. So. Calif. Pres.'s Cir., Commerce Assocs. U. So. Calif., Cedars of Lebanon Hosp. Women's Guild (dir. 1967-68), Blue Key, Skull and Dagger.

RAMOS, ALBERT A. electrical engineer; b. L.A., Feb. 28, 1927; s. Jesus D. and Carmen F. (Fontes) R.; B.S. in Elec. Engring., U. So. Calif., 1950, M.S. in Systems Mgmt., 1972; Ph.D., U.S. Internat. U., 1975; m. Joan C. Pailing, Sept. 23, 1950; children— Albert A., Richard R., James J., Katherine. With guided missile test group Hughes Aircraft Co., 1950-60; with TRW DSG, 1960-91, sr. staff engr. Norton AFB, San Bernardino, Calif., 1969-91, ret., 1991. Served with USNR, 1945-46. Registered profl. engr., Calif. Mem. IEEE, NSPE, Air Force Assn., Mexican-Am. Engring. Soc., Mexican-Am. Profl. Mgmt. Assn. (mem. administering commn. dept. community svcs.), Sigma Phi Delta, Eta Kappa Nu, Tau Beta Pi. Home: 8937 Napoli Dr Las Vegas NV 89117-1182

RAMPINO, LOUIS J. bank executive; Pres., CEO Fremont Gen. Corp., 1998—. Office: Ste 600 2020 Santa Monica Blvd Santa Monica CA 90404

RAMSEY, JOHN ARTHUR, lawyer; b. Apr. 1, 1942; s. Wilbert Lewis and Lillian (Anderson) R.; m. Nikki Ann Ramsey, Feb. 9, 1943; children: John William, Bret Anderson, Heather Nicole. AB, San Diego State U., 1965; JD, Calif. Western Sch. Law, 1969. Bar: Colo. 1969, Tex. 1978. Assoc. Henry, Cockrell, Quinn & Creighton, 1969-72; atty. Texaco Inc., 1972-80; asst. to pres. Texaco U.S.A., 1980-81, asst. to divsn. v.p., 1981-82, divsn. atty. Denver, 1982-88; ptnr. Holland & Hart, 1989—. Editor-in-chief: Calif. Western Law Rev., 1969. Bd. dirs. Selective Svc., Englewood, Colo., 1972-76; chmn. coun. Bethany Luth. Ch., Englewood, 1976; mem. exec. bd. Denver Area coun. Boy Scouts Am., 1999—. Mem. ABA (vice-chmn. oil, natural gas exploration and prodn. com. sect. natural resource law 1983-88, chmn. 1989—, coun. sect. natural resources, energy and environ. law 1993). Republican. Office: Holland & Hart 8390 E Crescent Pkwy Ste 400 Greenwood Vlg CO 80111-2822

RAMSEY, PAUL GLENN, internist, dean; b. Pitts., 1949; MD, Harvard U., 1975. Diplomate Am. Bd. Internal Medicine. Intern Cambridge Hosp., 1975-76; resident in medicine Mass. Gen. Hosp., Boston, 1976-78, U. Wash., Seattle, 1980-81, fellow infectious diseases, 1978-80, prof., 1991—, chmn. dept. medicine, 1992-97; physician-in-chief U. Wash. Med. Ctr., 1992-97; v.p. for med. affairs, dean Sch. Medicine U. Wash., Seattle, 1997—. Mem. ACP, AFCR, AAP, AAAS, SGIM. Office: U Wash Sch Medicine PO Box 356350 Seattle WA 98195-6350

RANCE, QUENTIN E. interior designer; b. St. Albans, Eng., Mar. 22, 1935; came to U.S., 1981. s. Herbert Leonard and Irene Ann (Haynes) R.; m. India Adams, May 17, 1974. Grad., Eastbourne (Eng.) Sch. Art, 1960. Soft furnishings buyer Dickeson & French Ltd., Eastbourne, 1960-61, outside sales mgr., 1961-62; design dir. Laszlo Hoenig, Ltd., London, 1962-73; mng. dir. Quentin Rance Interiors Ltd., London, 1973-81; pres. Quentin Rance Enterprises, Inc., Encino, Calif., 1981—. Works featured in Designers West, 1983, Design House Rev., 1983, Profiles mag., 1987, Nat. Assn. Mirror Mfrs. Jour., 1988, Designer Specifier, 1990. Mem. Founders for Diabetic Research/City of Hope. Served with RAF, 1953-55. Recipient Hon. Mention award Nat. Assn. Mirror Mfrs., 1987, 1st Pl. Nat. Pub. Svc. award, Designer Specifier, 1990. Fellow Chartered Soc. Designers (Eng.); mem. Am. Soc. Interior Designers (profl., chpt. bd. dirs. 1983-87, 89-91, chmn. Avanti 1983-85, admissions chmn. 1985—, Presdl. citations 1984, 87, 91, 95, 97), Knights of Vine. Avocations: bicycling, antiques, fine wines, philately, theatre. Home and Office: 18005 Rancho St Encino CA 91316-4214 Fax: 818-705-8111. E-mail: gerca@earthlink.net

RANCK, BRUCE E. waste management executive; Pres., CEO Browning-Ferris Industries, Inc., Houston, 1995-99; chmn. Venturi Techs, Commerce City, Colo. Office: MPI Venturi Techs 6295 East 56th Ave Commerce City CO 80022-3926

RAND, DUNCAN DAWSON, librarian, retired; b. Biggar, Sask., Can., Oct. 28, 1940; s. Dawson Ellis and Elizabeth Edna (Gabie) R.; m. Nancy Jean Daugherty, Sept. 7, 1963; children: Jacqueline Nancy, Duncan Dawson, Thomas Nelson, John David, Jennifer Nancy. B.A., U. Sask., 1963; B.L.S., McGill U., 1964. Young adult librarian Regina Pub. Library, Sask., 1964-65; coordinator library services Regina Separate Sch. Bd., 1965-68; asst. chief librarian Regina Pub. Library, 1968-71; dep. dir. London Pub. Library and Art Mus., 1971-73, acting dir., 1973-74; chief librarian Lethbridge Pub. Library, Alta., 1974-2000, ret., 2001. Dir. So. Alta. Art Gallery, Alberta Libr., 1996—. Editor: Sask. Geneal. Soc. Bull, 1968-71. Vice pres. Alta. council Boy Scouts. Mem. Libr. Assn. Alta (dir., pres. 1986-87), Can. Libr. Assn. (dir.), Can. Assn. Pub. Librs. (chair 1976-77), Sask. Geneal. Soc. (pres.), Assn. Profl. Librs. of Lethbridge (chmn. 1982-84), So. Alta. Regional Info. Network (chmn. 1996-2000), Samaritans (pres. 1998-2001), Allied Arts Coun. (bd. dirs. 1993-98), Southern Alberta Regional Info. Network (chmn.), Rotary, Ipalosh (archivist, sec. 1980-94). Office: 810 5th Ave S Lethbridge AB Canada T1J 4C4

RANDALL, CHANDLER CORYDON, church rector; b. Ann Arbor, Mich., Jan. 22, 1935; s. Frederick Stewart and Madeline Leta (Snow) R.; m. Marian Archias Montgomery, July 2, 1960; children: Sarah Archais, Elizabeth Leggett, Rebekah Stewart. AB in History, U. Mich., 1957; S.T.B. in Theology, Berkeley Divinity at Yale U., 1960; PhD in Hebraic Studies, Hebrew Union Coll., 1969; D.D. (honoris causa), Berkeley Divinity at Yale U., 1985. Rector St. Paul's Episcopal Ch., Richmond, Ind., 1967-71; rector Trinity Episcopal Ch., Ft. Wayne, 1971-88, St. Peter's Episcopal Ch., Del Mar, Calif., 1988-00. Bd. dirs. Living Ch. Found., Milw.; bibl. theologian Episcopal Ch. Stewardship, N.Y.C., 1985; alumni coun. Berkeley Divinity at Yale, New Haven, Conn., 1981-87; bishop's cabinet Diocese of No. Ind.,

South Bend, 1983-87. Author: Satire in the Bible, 1969, An Approach to Biblical Satire, 1990; contbr. articles to profl. jours. Founder Canterbury Sch., Ft. Wayne, 1977; commr. Ind. Jud. Qualifications Commn., Indpls., 1981-87; pres. Ft. Wayne Plan Commn., 1977; bd. dirs. Ft. Wayne Park Found., 1983-88; platform com. Ind. Republican Party, Indpls., 1974. Recipient Disting. Svc. medal U. Mich., 1981, Scheuer scholar Hebrew Union Coll., 1963-66, Liberty Bell award Ft. Wayne Bar Assn., 1988; named Sagamore of the Wabash, Gov. Ind., 1987. Mem. Am. Schs. Oriental Research, Yale U. Alumni Club (pres. 1982-88), Quest Club (pres.), Rotary Club, Chi Psi (nat. chaplain 1982). Republican. Avocations: college recruiting, genealogy. Office: St Peters Episcopal Church PO Box 336 Del Mar CA 92014-0336

RANDALL, DAVID JOHN, physiologist, zoologist, educator; b. London, Sept. 15, 1938; BSc, U. Southampton, 1960, PhD, 1963, FRSC, 1981. From asst. to assoc. prof. U. B.C., 1963-73, prof. zoology, 1973—, assoc. dean grad. studies, 1990-96, 2000; head biology and chemistry City U. Hong Kong, 2000-01. Vis. lectr. Bristol U., 1968-69; vis. sci. Marine Labs U. Tex., 1970, Zool. Sta., Naples, Italy, 1973; NATO vis. sci. Acadia U., 1975, Marine Lab U. Tex., 1977; chief sci. Alpha Helix Amazon Expedition, 1976; mem. adv. bd. J. Comp Physiology, 1977-92, J. Exp. Biol., 1981-84; chmn. animal biol. comt. Nat. Res. Coun., Can., 1974; vis. prof. U. Nairobi, 1988, George Washington U., 1988-89, City U. Hong Kong, 1997; concurrent prof. Nanjing U., China, 1993—; external examiner U. Singapore, 1990-91, 2000-02; mem. UGC, Hong Kong, 2001-02. Assoc. editor: Marine Behavior Physiology. Recipient Award of Excellence Am. Fisheries Soc., 1994. Fellow Royal Soc. Can.; mem. Can. Soc. Zoologists (Fry medal 1993), Soc. Exp. Biologists. Office: City U Hong Kong Biol Chem Tat Chee Ave Kowloon Hong Kong Fax: 2788 7406. E-mail: bhrand@cityu.edu.hk

RANDALL, WILLIAM B. manufacturing company executive; b. Phila., Jan. 8, 1921; s. Albert and Ann (Fine) R.; m. Geraldine Kempson, Aug. 10, 1943; children: Robert, Erica Lynn, Lisa. Student, Rider Coll., Trenton, N.J., 1940-41. Gen. Sales mgr. Lowres Optical Mfg. Co., Newark, 1946-49; pres., founder Rand Sales Co., N.Y.C., 1949-58; gen. mgr. Sea & Ski Co. div. Botany Industries, Inc., Millbrae, Calif., 1958-61, pres., dir., 1961-66, v.p., 1961-65; pres. Renauld of France, Reno, 1967-68; chmn. bd. Renauld Internat., Reading, Pa., 1963-65; pres., chief operating officer Renauld Internat., Ltd., Burlingame and Reno, 1966-67; pres., chmn. bd. Randall Internat., Ltd., 1967-68; sr. exec. v.p. Forty-two Prods. Ltd., 1969-71; pres. Exec. Products Internat. Ltd., 1969-71, New Product Devel. Ctr., Carlsbad, Calif., 1971—; pres. Internat. Concept Ctr. Exec. Products Internat. Ltd., Irvine, 1971—, pres. Sun Research Ctr., 1974—; pres. La Costa Products Internat., 1975-86; mng. dir. merchandising La Costa Hotel and Spa, 1986-88; pres., chief exec. officer Randall Internat., Carlsbad, 1989—. Bd. dirs. Bank of La Costa, Garden Botanika. Served to 1st lt., navigator USAAF, 1942-45. Mem. Am. Mgmt. Assn., Nat. Wholesale Druggists Assn., Nat. Assn. Chain Drug Stores, Hon. Order Ky. Cols., Baja Beach and Tennis Club (bd. dirs.). Home: 7150 Arenal Ln Carlsbad CA 92009-6701 E-mail: billr@randallinternational.com

RANDHAWA, BIKKAR SINGH, psychologist, educator; b. Jullundur, India, June 14, 1933; came to Can., 1961, naturalized, 1966; s. Pritam S. and Sawaran K. (Basakhi) R.; m. Leona Emily Bujnowski, Oct. 8, 1966; children— Jason, Lisa. BA in Math., Panjab U., 1954, BT in Edn., 1955, MA in History, 1959; BEd, U. Alta., Can., 1963; MEd in Measurement and Evaluation, U Toronto, 1967, PhD, 1969. Registered psychologist. Tchr. secondary sch. math., Panjab, 1955-61; asst. headmaster, then headmaster, 1955-61; tchr. high sch. math. and sci. Beaver County, Riley, Alta., 1964-65, Camrose County, 1961-64, Edmonton (Alta.) Public Schs., 1965-67; tutor in math. for social sci. Ont. Inst. Studies in Edn., Toronto, 1968-69; mem. faculty U. Sask., Saskatoon, 1969-76, 77—, prof. ednl. psychology, 1977-2000, prof. emeritus, 2000—, asst. dean research and field services, 1982-87. Prof., coord. Visual Scholars' Program, U. Iowa, 1976-77; cons. in field. Contbr. articles profl. jours. Fellow APA, Am. Psychol. Soc. (charter), Can. Psychol. Assn.; mem. Am. Ednl. Rsch. Assn., Can. Ednl. Rsch. Assn. (pres. 1997-99), Can. Soc. Study Edn., Sask. Psychol. Assn., Phi Delta Kappa (pres. Saskatoon chpt. 1971, 85). Home: 14 Harwood Dr St Albert AB Canada T8N 5V5 Office: U Sask 3117 Edn Bldg 28 Campus Dr Saskatoon SK Canada S7N OX1 E-mail: randy.randhawa@home.com

RANDISI, ELAINE MARIE, accountant, educator, writer; b. Racine, Wis., Dec. 19, 1926; d. John Dewey and Alveta Irene (Raffety) Fehd; m. John Paul Randisi, Oct. 12, 1946 (div. July 1972); children: Jeanine Randisi Manson, Martha Randisi Chaney (dec.), Joseph, Paula, Catherine Randisi Carvalho, George, Anthony (dec.); m. John R. Woodfin, June 18, 1994. AA, Pasadena Jr. Coll., 1946; BS cum laude (Giannini scholar), Golden Gate U., 1978. With Raymond Kaiser Engrs., Inc., Oakland, Calif., 1969-75, 77-86, corp. acct., 1978-79, sr. corp. acct., 1979-82, sr. payroll acct., 1983-86; acting mgr. Lilli Ann Corp., San Francisco, 1986-89, Crosby, Heafey, Roach & May, Oakland, 1990-98. Initiated Minority Vendor Purchasing Program for Kaiser Engrs., Inc., 1975-76; corp. buyer Kaiser Industries Corp., Oakland, 1975-77; lectr. on astrology Theosophical Soc., San Francisco, 1979-99; mem. faculty Am. Fedn. Astrologers Internat. Conv., Chgo., 1982, 84. Mem. Speakers Bur., Calif. Assn. for Neurologically Handicapped Children, 1964-70, v.p., 1969; bd. dirs. Ravenwood Homeowners Assn., 1979-82, v.p., 1979-80, sec., 1980-81, mem. organizing com. Minority Bus. Fair, San Francisco, 1976; pres., bd. dirs. Lakewood Condominium Assn., 1984-87; mem. trustee Ch. of Religious Sci., 1992-95; treas. First Ch. Religious Sci., 1994-98, lic. practitioner, pres., 1990-91, sec., 1989-90. Mem. Am. Fedn. Astrologers, Calif. Scholarship Fedn. (life), Alpha Gamma Sigma (life). Home: 742 Wesley Way Apt 1C Oakland CA 94610-2339

RANDLE, ELLEN EUGENIA FOSTER, opera and classical singer, educator; b. New Haven, Oct. 2, 1948; d. Richard A.G. and Thelma Lousie (Brooks) Foster; m. Ira James William, 1967 (div. 1972); m. John Willis Randle, Dec. 24, 1983. Student, Calif. State Coll., Sonoma, 1970; studied with Boris Goldovsky, 1970; student, Grad. Sch. Fine Arts, Florence, Italy, 1974; studied with Tito Gobbi, Florence, 1974; student, U. Calif., Berkeley, 1977; BA in World History, Lone Mountain Coll., 1976, MA in Performing Arts, 1978; studied with Madam Eleanor Steber, Graz, Austria, 1979; studied with Patricia Goehl, Munich, Fed. Republic Germany, 1979; MA in Counseling and Psychology, U. San Francisco, 1990, MA in Marriage and Family Therapy, 1994, EdD in Internat. Multicultural Edn., 1998. Asst. artistic dir. Opera Piccola, Oakland, Calif., 1990-92; instr. African Am. culture and humanities Mission C.C., Santa Clara, 1997—; instr. Peralta C.C. Dist., Oakland, 1998—; psychotherapy intern, sr. peer counseling program City of Fremont, Calif., 1999-2000; psychotherapist, marriage family therapist intern Portia Bell Human Behavioral Health and Tng. Ctr., Concord, 2000—01. Instr. East Bay Performing Art Ctr., Richmond, Calif., 1986, Chapman Coll., 1986, Las Positas C.C., Livermore, Calif., 1999—; adj. prof. U. Phoenix, 1999-2000, adj. prof. U. Pheonix, Northern Calif., 2001-. Singer opera prodns. Porgy & Bess, Oakland, Calif., 1980-81, LaTraviata, Oakland, Calif., 1981-82, Aida, Oakland, 1981-82, Madame Butterfly, Oakland, 1982-83, The Magic Flute, Oakland, 1984, numerous others; performances include TV specials, religous concerts, musicals; music dir. Natural Man, Berkeley, 1986; asst. artistic dir. Opera Piccola, Oakland, Calif., 1990—. Art commr. City of Richmond, Calif. Recipient Bk. Am. Achievement award. Mem. Music Tchrs. Assn., Internat. Black Writers and Artists Inc. (life mem., local #5), Nat. Coun. Negro Women, Nat. Assn. Negro Musicians, Calif. Arts Fedn., Calif. Assn. for Counseling and Devel. (mem. black caucus), Nat. Black Child Devel. Inst., The Calif.-Nebraskan Orgn., Inc., Calif. Marital & Family Therapist Assn. (San Francisco chpt.), Black Psychotherapist of San Francisco and East Bay Area, San Francisco Commonwealth Club, Gamma Phi Delta. Democrat. Mem. A.M.E. Zion Ch. Avocations: cooking, entertaining. Home: 5314 Boyd Ave Oakland CA 94618-1112

RANEY, DENNIS R. computer hardware company executive; BChemE, S.D. Sch. Mines and Tech.; MBA, U. Chgo. Various fin., mfg. and real estate positions Hewlett Packard, head fin. and adminstrv. mgmt. intercontinental ops., head fin. and adminstrn.; sr. v.p., CFO Bristol-Meyers Squibb Pharm. Group; CFO pub. tech. cos.; sr. v.p., CFO Novell, Inc., Provo, Utah, 1998—. Bd. dirs. ADAC Labs., W. R. Hambrect & Co., Redleaf. Capt. U.S. Army. Office: Novell Inc 122 E 1700 S Provo UT 84606

RANK, LARRY GENE, retired banker; b. Auburn, Ind., July 14, 1935; s. Lloyd R. Rank and Elizabeth M. (Williamson) Jackson; m. Bette Whitehurst, May 2, 1959; children: Kevin, Karen Grad., Am. Inst. Banking, 1962, U. Balt., 1969, Grad. Sch. Banking, Brown U., 1975, Nat. Council Savs. Instns., 1985. Exec. v.p. Provident Bank Md., Balt., 1982-85, pres., chief operating officer, 1985-90, dir., 1984-90; mng. dir. Jannotta, Bray & Assocs. Inc., Balt., 1991-92; exec. dir. Big Bros. and Big Sisters Ctrl. Md. Inc., 1993-96. Assoc. cons. Drake, Beam, Morin, 1997-98. Bd. dirs. ARC, Ctrl. Md. chpt., 1984-98, chmn. bd., 1990-92, bd. dirs. Ctrl. Ariz. chpt., 1998—, nat. com. on nominations; bd. dirs. United Way of Ctrl. Md., Balt., 1990-92; chair Gov.'s Vol. Awards Selection com., 1989; chmn. Am. Heart Assn.-Heart Ball, 1989, bd. dirs. Am. Heart Assn.; chmn. bd. Neighborhood Housing Svcs.; bd. dirs. Goodwill Industries, 1989-98; vol. Valley Big Bros./Big Sisters, Phoenix; bd. dirs. N.W. Hosp. Ctr., 1985-98, chair sys. bd., 1997-98; bd. dirs. Big Bros./Big Sisters Ctrl. Md. Mem. Deacon Club, Wake Forest Wildcat Club, Villanova Club. Lutheran. Avocations: golf, sports, books, travel. Fax: (480) 753-9437. E-mail: lrank@USWest.net

RANKAITIS, SUSAN, artist; b. Cambridge, Mass., Sept. 10, 1949; d. Alfred Edward and Isabel (Shimkus) Rankaitis; m. Robbert Flick, June 5, 1976 BFA in Painting, U. Ill., 1971; MFA in Visual Arts, U. So. Calif., 1977. Rsch. asst., art dir. Plato Lab., U. Ill., Urbana, 1971-75; art instr. Orange Coast Coll., Costa Mesa, Calif., 1977-83; chair dept. art Chapman Coll., Orange, 1983-90; Fletcher Jones chair in art Scripps Coll., Claremont, 1990—. Represented by Robert Mann Gallery, N.Y.C.; overview panelist visual arts Nat. Endowment for Arts, 1983, 84; selector Bingham Ednl. Trust, 1997—. One-woman shows include Los Angeles County Mus. Art, 1983, Internat. Mus. Photography, George Eastman House, 1983, Gallery Min. Tokyo, 1988, Ruth Bloom Gallery, Santa Monica, 1989, 90, 92, Schneider Mus., Portland, Ore., 1990; Ctr. for Creative Photography, 1991, Robert Mann Gallery, N.Y.C., 1994, 97, Mus. Contemporary Photography, Chgo., 1994, Mus. of Photographic Arts, 2000; represented in permanent collections MOCA, L.A., U. N.Mex. Art, Ctr. for Creative Photography, Mus. Contemporary Photography, Chgo., Santa Barbara Mus. Art, Los Angeles County Mus. Art, Mpls. Inst. Arts, San Francisco Mus. Modern Art, Art Inst. Chgo., Mus. Modern Art, Lodz, Poland, Princeton U. Art Mus., Stanford U. Art Mus., Contemporary Art Mus., Honolulu, Mus. Contemporary Photography, Art Inst. Chgo., others. Active art auction Venice Family Clinic, 1980—. Recipient Graves award in Humanities, 1985; Nat. Endowment for Arts fellow, 1980, 88, U.S./France fellow, 1989, Agnes Bourne fellow in painting and photography Djerassi Found., 1989; Durfee Chinese/Am. grantee, 2000—; City of L.A. Cultural Affairs grantee, 2000—. Mem. Coll. Art Assn., Los Angeles County Mus. Art, Santa Monica Mus. Art. Studio: Studio 5 1403 S Santa Fe Ave Los Angeles CA 90021-2500 Home: 3117 N Lansbury Ave Claremont CA 91711-4146 E-mail: srankait@scrippscol.edu

RANNEY, AUSTIN (JOSEPH RANNEY), political science educator; b. Cortland, N.Y., Sept. 23, 1920; s. Frank Addison and Florence Edith (Ranney) R.; m. Elizabeth Mackay (div. Oct. 1975); m. Nancy Boland; children: Joseph, Douglas, Gordon, David. BS, Northwestern U., 1941, LLD (hon.), 1995; MA, U. Oreg., 1943; PhD, Yale U., 1948, DSS (hon.), 1985; LLD (hon.), SUNY, 1986, Northwestern U., 1995. Statistician Douglas Aircraft Corp., Chgo., 1942-44; instr. Yale U., New Haven, 1945-47; from instr. to prof. U. Ill., Urbana, 1947-63; prof. U. Wis., Madison, 1963-76; resident scholar Am. Enterprise Inst., Washington, 1976-86; prof. U. Calif., Berkeley, 1986-91, prof. emeritus, 1991—, chmn. dept. polit. sci., 1987-90. Author: The Doctrine of Responsible Party Government, 1954, Governing, 1958, Curing the Mischiefs of Faction, 1975, Channels of Power, 1983. Mem. Presdl.-Congl. Commn. on Polit. Activity Govtl. Employees, Washington, 1967-68, Dem. Nat. Com. Commn. on Party Structure, Washington, 1969-72, Commn. on Presdl. Debates, Washington, 1980-88; chmn. Gov.'s Commn. on Registration and Voting Participation, Madison, Wis., 1964, social sci. rsch. coun. Com. on Govtl. Processes, 1964-71, coun. on social scis. policy Yale U., 1983-88. Recipient Wilbur Lucius Cross medal Yale U. Grad. Sch., 1977; sr. rsch. fellow NSF, 1970, John Simon Guggenheim fellow, 1974, fellow Ctr. for Advanced Study in Behavioral Scis., 1978. Mem. Am. Polit. Sci. Assn. (pres. 1975-76), Am. Acad. Arts and Scis. (v.p. 1981-84). Home: 990 Regal Rd Berkeley CA 94708-1430 Office: Univ Calif Dept Polit Sci Berkeley CA 94720-0001 E-mail: ranney@socrates.berkeley.edu

RANNEY, HELEN MARGARET, physician, educator; b. Summer Hill, N.Y., Apr. 12, 1920; d. Arthur C. and Alesia (Toolan) R. AB, Barnard Coll., 1941; MD, Columbia U., 1947; ScD, U. S.C., 1979, SUNY, Buffalo, 1996. Diplomate: Am. Bd. Internal Medicine. Intern Presbyn. Hosp., N.Y.C., 1947-48, resident, 1948-50, asst. physician, 1954-60; practice medicine specializing in internal medicine, hematology N.Y.C., 1954-70; instr. Coll. Phys. and Surg. Columbia, N.Y.C., 1954-60; assoc. prof. medicine Albert Einstein Coll. Medicine, N.Y.C., 1960-64, prof. medicine, 1965-70, SUNY, Buffalo, 1970-73, U. Calif., San Diego, 1973-90, chmn. dept. medicine, 1973-86, Disting. physician vet. adminstr., 1986-91; cons. Alliance Pharm. Corp., San Diego, 1991-2000. Master ACP; fellow AAAS; mem. NAS, Inst. Medicine, Am. Soc. for Clin. Investigation, Am. Soc. Hematology, Harvey Soc., Am. Assn. Physicians, Am. Acad. Arts and Scis., Phi Beta Kappa, Sigma Xi, Alpha Omega Alpha. E-mail: hranney@ucsd.edu

RAPKE, JACK, agent; Co-head of motion picture divsn., then co-chmn. Creative Artists Agy., Beverly Hills, Calif.; prodr. Image Movers, Universal City. Office: Image Movers 100 Universal City Plz Bldg 484 Universal Cty CA 91608-1002

RAPPAPORT, LAWRENCE, plant physiology and horticulture educator; b. N.Y.C., May 28, 1928; s. Aaron and Elsie R.; m. Norma, Nov. 21, 1953; children: Meryl, Debra Kramer, Craig. BS in Horticulture, U. Idaho, 1950; MS in Horticulture, Mich. State Coll., 1951; PhD in Horticulture, Mich. State U., 1956. Lectr. U. Calif., Davis, 1956-67, jr. olericulturist dept. vegetable crops, 1956-58, asst. olericulturist, 1958-63, assoc. olericulturist, 1963-67, prof., 1968—, prof. emeritus, 1991—, dir. plant growth lab., 1975-78, chairperson dept. vegetable crops, 1978-84. Vis. scientist Calif. Inst. Tech., 1958; co-dir. Horticulture Subproject, Calif./Egypt project, 1978-82. Contbr. articles to profl. jours. 1st pres. Davis Human Rels. Coun., 1964-66; v.p. Jewish Fedn. Sacramento, 1969; pres. Jewish Fellowship, Davis, 1985-89; founder, 1st dir. Hillel Counselership at Davis, 1965-76. Decorated Bronze star; Guggenheim Found. fellow, 1963, Fulbright fellow, 1964, USPHS Spl. fellow, 1970, Am. Soc. Horticulture Sci. fellow, 1987, Sir Frederick McMaster fellow, 1991. Achievements include discovery of evidence for gibberellin-binding protein in plants; evidence for the signal hypothesis operating in plants, positive evidence for phytochrome-mediated gibberellin metabolism and stem growth; isolation of somaclonal variants of celery bearing stable resistance to Fusarium oxysporum f. sp. apii. Home: 637 Elmwood Dr Davis CA 95616-3514 Office: U Calif Dept Vegetable Crops Asmundson Hall Rm 237 One Shields Ave Davis CA 95616 E-mail: rappaport@vegmail.ucdavis.edu

RAPPEPORT, IRA J. lawyer; b. Phila., Jan. 13, 1954; BA with honors, Washington U., 1975; JD with honors, Villanova U., 1978. Bar: Calif. 1978. Assoc. Pillsbury Madison & Sutro, 1978-83, Memel, Jacobs, Pietro & Gersh, 1983-85, ptnr., 1985-87, McDermott, Will & Emery, L.A., 1987—. Mng. editor Villanova Law Rev., 1977-78. Recipient Scribes award Villanova Sch. Law, 1978. Mem. Am. Acad. Hosp. Attys., L.A. County Bar Assn. (mem. healthcare law sect.), Beverly Hills Bar Assn. (mem. healthcare law sect.), Century City Bar Assn. (mem. healthcare law sect.), Nat. Health Lawyers Assn., Calif. Soc. Healthcare Attys. Office: McDermott Will & Emery 2049 Century Park E Fl 34 Los Angeles CA 90067-3101

RAPSON, RICHARD L. history educator; b. N.Y.C., Mar. 8, 1937; s. Louis and Grace Lillian (Levenkind) R.; m. Susan Burns, Feb. 22, 1975 (div. June 1981); m. Elaine Catherine Hatfield, June 15, 1982; 1 child, Kim Elizabeth. BA, Amherst Coll., 1958; PhD, Columbia U., 1966. Asst. prof. Amherst (Mass.) Coll., 1960-61, Stanford (Calif.) U., 1961-65, U. Calif., Santa Barbara, 1965-66; from assoc. prof. to prof. history U. Hawaii, Honolulu, 1966—, founder, dir. New Coll., 1968-73. Bd. dirs. Semester at Sea, U. Pittsburgh, 1979—; psychotherapist, Honolulu, 1982—. Author: Individualism and Conformity in the American Character, 1967, Britons View America, 1971, The Cult of Youth, 1972, Major Interpretations of the American Past, 1978, Denials of Doubt, 1980, Cultural Pluralism in Hawaii, 1981, American Yearnings, 1989; co-author: (with Elaine Hatfield) Love, Sex and Intimacy: Their Psychology, Biology and History, 1993, Emotional Contagion, 1994, Love and Sex: Cross-Cultural Perspectives, 1995, Rosie, 2000; mem. editl. bd. Univ. Press Am., 1981—. Woodrow Wilson fellow, Wilson Found., Princeton, 1960; Edward Perkins scholar, Columbia U., 1961; Danforth tchr., Danforth Found., St. Louis, 1965; recipient E. Harris Harbison for Gifted Teaching award, Danforth Found., 1973, Outstanding Tchr. award Stanford U. 25th Reunion Class, 1992. Mem. Am. Hist. Assn., Orgn. Am. Hist., Nat. Womens Hist. Project, Phi Beta Kappa, Outrigger Canoe Club, Honolulu Club. Avocations: squash, travel, classical music. Office: U Hawaii Dept History 2530 Dole St Honolulu HI 96822-2303

RASCÓN, ARMANDO, artist; b. Calexico, Calif., Dec. 9, 1956; s. Reynoldo and Maria (Herrera) R. BFA Coll. Creative Studies, U. Calif., Santa Barbara, 1979. Owner Terrain Gallery, San Francisco, 1988—. Guest faculty dept. art U. Calif., Davis, 1988, Calif. Coll. Arts and Crafts, Oakland, 1991, dept. art practice U. Calif., Berkeley, 1995; juror, panelist Artist Trust Fellowship Grants, Visual Arts, Seattle, 1994; lectr. N.Y. Mus. Modern Art, 1995; panelist LEF Found. Orgn. Grants, Cambridge, Mass., 1996, Nev. State Coun. on the Arts Grants, Carson City, 1996, 97; v.p. San Francisco Art Commn., 1996-97; presenter various lectrs., panels, workshops, confs. One-man shows include Randolph Street Gallery, Chgo., 1991, INTAR, N.Y., 1994, San Diego Mus. Contemporary Art, 1997, Blue Star Art Space, San Antonio, 1998. Bd. dirs. New Langton Arts, San Francisco, 1988-92; vice-chair Art Commn. City of San Francisco, 1997. Recipient Hazel S. Lagerson scholarship U. Calif., Santa Barbara, 1975, fellowship grant in painting Nat. Endowment for Arts, Washington, 1987, Adaline Kent award San Francisco Art Inst., 1994, Goldie award in visual art San Francisco Bay Guardian, 1994; U.S. Mexico Fund for Culture grantee, 1999; Calif. Arts Coun. Artist fellow, 1999. Home and Office: 165 Jessie St Fl 2 San Francisco CA 94105-4010

RASMUSON, BRENT (JACOBSEN), photographer, graphic artist, lithographer; b. Logan, Utah, Nov. 28, 1950; s. Eleroy West and Fae (Jacobsen) R.; m. Tess Bullen, Sept. 30, 1981; children: John, Mark, Lisa. Grad. auto repair and painting sch., Utah State U. Pre-press supr. Herald Printing Co., Logan, 1969-79; profl. drummer, 1971-75; owner, builder auto racing engines Valley Automotive Specialties, 1971-76; exec. sec. Herald Printing Co., 1979-89; owner Brent Rasmuson Photography, Smithfield, Utah, 1986—, Temple Picture Classics, Smithfield, 1996—. Author photo prints of LDS temples: Logan, 1987, 95, 98, 2000, Manti, 1989, 2000, Jordan River, 1989, 96, 98, 2000, Provo, 1990, Mesa, Ariz., 1990, 96, Boise, Idaho, 1990, 96, 2000, Salt Lake LDS Temple, 1990, 96, Idaho Falls, 1991, 94, 2000, St. George, 1991, 93, 2000, Portland, Oreg., 1991, 96, 97, 2000, L.A., 1991, 96, 97, 2000, Las Vegas, Nev., 1991, Seattle, 1992, Oakland, Calif., 1993, 94, Ogden, 1992; author photo print: Statue of Angel Moroni, 1994; author photos used to make neckties and watch dials of LDS temples: Salt Lake, Manti, Logan, L.A., Oakland, Seattle, Las Vegas, Mesa, Portland, St. George, Jordan River, scenic tie Mammoth Hot Springs in Yellowstone Park, 1995; landscape scenic photographs featured in Best of Photography Ann., 1987, 88, 89, also in calendars and book covers; author photo print of Harris Rsch., Inc. Internat. Hdqrs. (recipient 1st prize nat. archtl. photo competition); designer several bus. logos. Mem. Internat. Platform Assn., Assoc. Photographers Internat., Internat. Freelance Photographers Orgn., Nat. Trust Hist. Preservation, Nat. Air and Space Soc. Republican. Mem. Ch. Jesus Christ. Avocations: landscape design, travel, reading, numismatics, philately. Home and Office: 40 N 200 E Smithfield UT 84335-1543

RASMUSON, EDWARD BERNARD, banker; b. Houston, Aug 27, 1940; s. Elmer Edwin and Lile Vivian R.; m. Cathryn Elaine Robertson, Sept. 11, 1969; children: Natasha Ann, Laura Lile, David Edward. BA, Harvard U., 1962. Mgmt. trainee Brown Brothers Harriman, 1963, Chem. N.Y., 1964; asst. cashier Nat. Bank Alaska, Anchorage, 1964-66, asst. v.p., 1966-68, v.p., 1968-73, pres., 1973-85, chmn. bd. dirs. 1986—. Bd. regents U. Alaska, 1975-89; mem. Rasmuson Found., 1973—; past trustee Sheldon Jackson Coll.; past pres. Anchorage United Way; Hon. Consul of Sweden, State of Alaska. Mem. Young Pres.'s Orgn., World Bus. Coun. Republican. Presbyterian. Clubs: Explorers, Pioneers of Alaska; Wash. Athletic, Seattle Yacht, Rainier (Seattle); Metropolitan, Harvard (N.Y.C.). Lodges: Rotary, Elks. Office: Nat Bank Alaska PO Box 100600 Anchorage AK 99510-0600

RASMUSSEN, CRAIG P. career officer; BA in Internat. Rels. and Econs., Colo. State U., 1972; MBA in Econs. and Fin., Hardin-Simmons U., 1975; M in Nat. Security Policy, Naval War Coll., 1991. Commd. 2d lt. USAF, 1972, advanced through grades to maj. gen., 2000; KC-135 aircraft comdr. 917th Air Refueling Squadron, Dyess AFB, Tex., 1973-78; air staff tng. officer The Pentagon, Washington, 1978-79; various assignments Plattsburgh AFB, N.Y., 1979-83; dep. chief plans and ops. divsn. The Cols. Group, AF Mil. Pers. Ctr., Randolph AFB, Tex., 1983-86; FB-111 instr. pilot 393rd Bomb Squadron, Pease AFB, N.H., 1986-90; ops. officer to comdr. 715th Bomb Squadron, Pease AFB, 1986-90; asst. dep. comdr. for ops. 509th Bomb Wing, Pease AFB, 1986-90; chief nuclear treaties br. Strategic Plans and Policy Directorate, the Joint Staff, Washington, 1991-93; comdr. 60th Ops. Group, Travis AFB, Calif., 1993-95, 62nd Airlift Wing, McChord AFB, Wash., 1995-96, 305th Air Mobility Wing, McGuire AFB, NJ, Turkey, 1996-98; vice comdr. 15th Air Force, Travis AFB, Calif., 1998-2000; chief Office of Def. Cooperation, Turkey, 2000—. Decorated Legion of Merit, Combat Readiness Medal with oak leaf cluster, Aerial achievement medal, AF Achievement medal, DSM, others. Office: HQ ODC Turkey PSC 90 Unit 7025 APO AE 09822-7025 E-mail: rasmussen@odc-t.ankara.af.mil

RASMUSSEN, HARRY PAUL, horticulture and landscape educator; b. Tremonton, Utah, July 18, 1939; s. Peter Y. and Lorna (Nielsen) R.; m. Mary Jane Dalley, Sept. 4, 1959; children: Randy Paul, Lorianne, Trent Dalley, Rachelle. AS, Coll. of So. Utah, 1959; BS, Utah State U., 1961;

MS, Mich. State U., 1962, PhD, 1965. Rsch. scientist Conn. Agr. Expt. Sta., New Haven, 1965-66; rschr., instr. Mich. State U., East Lansing, 1966-81; chmn. dept. horticulture and landscape architecture Wash. State U., Pullman, 1981-88; dir. Utah Agrl. Expt. Sta. Utah State U., 1988—. Assoc. v.p. Utah State U., Logan, 1992-99. Contbr. articles to profl. jours., chpts. to books. Mem. bd. control YMCA, Lansing, Mich., 1976; mem. coun. Boy Scouts Am., Lansing, 1980; stake pres. Ch. of Jesus Christ of Latter Day Saints, Lansing, 1973-81. NDEA fellow, 1961-65. Fellow Am. Soc. Horticulture Sci.; mem. AAAS, Scanning Electron Microscopy (chmn. plant sect. 1976-83, chmn. exptl. sta. com. on orgn. and policy 1996-97). Home: 1949 N 950 E Logan UT 84341-1813 Office: Utah State U 225 Agr Sci Bldg Logan UT 84322-0001

RASMUSSEN, JOHN OSCAR, nuclear scientist, researcher; b. St. Petersburg, Fla., Aug. 8, 1926; s. John Oscar and Hazel (Ormsby) R.; m. Louise Brooks, Aug. 27, 1950; children— Nancy, Jane, David, Stephen. B.S., Calif. Inst. Tech., 1948; Ph.D., U. Calif. at Berkeley, 1952; M.A. (hon.), Yale U., 1969. Mem. faculty dept. chemistry U. Calif., Berkeley, 1952-68, 73-91, prof. chemistry, 1971-91, ret., 1991, mem. research staff, 1952-68; sr. rsch. assoc. Lawrence Berkeley Nat. Lab., 1972—. Prof. chemistry Yale U. 1969-73; asso. dir. Yale Heavy Ion Accelerator Lab., 1970-73; vis. research prof. Nobel Inst. Physics, Stockholm, 1953; vis. prof. Inst. Nuclear Sci. U. Tokyo, 1974, Fudan U., Shanghai, 1979, hon. prof., 1984. Contbr. articles on radioactivity, nuclear models, heavy ion reactions. Served with USN, 1944-46. Recipient E.O. Lawrence Meml. award AEC, 1967; NSF sr. postdoctoral fellow Niels Bohr Inst., Copenhagen, 1961-62, NORDITA fellow, 1979, Guggenheim Meml. fellow, 1973, Alexander von Humboldt sr. rsch. fellow Tech. U. Munich, 1991. Fellow Am. Phys. Soc., AAAS; mem. Am. Chem. Soc. (Nuclear Applications in Chemistry award 1976), Fedn. Am. Scientists (chmn. 1969). Office: Lawrence Berkeley Nat Lab Ms 50A 1148 Berkeley CA 94720-0001

RASMUSSEN, MARILYN, state legislator; b. Seattle; m. Don Rasmussen; 7 children. Livestock and timber farmer; mem. Wash. Senate, Dist. 2, Olympia, 1992—; chair agr. and rural econ. devel. com. Wash. Senate, mem. commerce, trade, housing and fin. instns. com.; mem. edn. com. Wash. Legislature, Olympia, mem. ways and means capital subcom., mem. vets. and mil. affairs com., mem. Agy. Coun. on Coord. Transp., mem. Nat. Conf. State Legislatures. Mem. Eatonville Sch. Bd., 1980-87; bd. dirs. Marymount Assn. for Sr. Housing, Nisqually River Interpretive Ctr. Found.; mem. Rocky Mountain Elk Found.; mem. adv. com. Women of Vision; mem. Gov.'s Prayer Breakfast Com.; mem. adv. com. Harborview Vis.; past bd. dirs. Good Samaritan Mental Health Bd.; eucharistic min. Our Lady of Good Counsel. Mem. Wash. State Dairy Fedn., Kiwanis (Spanaway-Parkland), Am. Agri-Women, Wash. Women for the Survival Agr., Wash. Cattlemen's Assn., Wash. Cattlewomen's Assn., South Pierce County C. of C., Vladivostok Sister City Assn., Am. Tree Farm Sys., Tacoma Sportsmen's Club, Delta Kappa Gamma. Democrat. Office: 409 Legislative Bldg Olympia WA 98504-0001

RASMUSSEN, THOMAS VAL, JR. lawyer, small business owner; b. Salt Lake City, Aug. 11, 1954; s. Thomas Val and Georgia (Smedley) R.; m. Donita Gubler, Aug. 15, 1978; children: James, Katherine, Kristin. BA magna cum laude, U. Utah, 1978, JD, 1981. Bar: Utah 1981, U.S. Dist. Ct. Utah 1981, U.S. Supreme Ct. 1985, U.S. Ct. Appeals (10th cir.) 1999. Atty. Salt Lake Legal Defender Assn., Salt Lake City, 1981-83, Utah Power and Light Co., Salt Lake City, 1983-89; of counsel Hatch, Morton & Skeen, Salt Lake City, 1989-90; ptnr. Morton, Skeen & Rasmussen, Salt Lake City, 1991-94, Skeen & Rasmussen, Salt Lake City, 1994-97; pvt. practice, Salt Lake City, 1997—. Co-owner, developer Handi Self-Storage, Kaysville, Utah, 1984-93; instr. bus. law Brigham Young U., Salt Lake City, 1988-90. Adminstrv. editor Jour. Contemporary Law, 1980-81, Jour. Energy Law and Policy, 1980-81. Missionary Ch. of Jesus Christ of Latter-Day Sts., Brazil, 1973-75. Mem. Utah, Salt Lake County Bar Assn., Intermountain Miniature Horse Club (pres. 1989, 2d v.p. 1990), Phi Eta Sigma, Phi Kappa Phi, Beta Gamma Sigma. Avocations: tennis, scuba diving, showing horses, travel, collecting art. Home: 3094 Whitewater Dr Salt Lake City UT 84121-1561 Office: 4659 Highland Dr Salt Lake City UT 84117-5137

RASOR, DINA LYNN, investigator, journalist; b. Downey, Calif., Mar. 21, 1956; d. Ned Shaurer and Genevieve Mercia (Eads) R.; m. Thomas Taylor Lawson, Oct. 4, 1980. BA in Polit. Sci., U. Calif., Berkeley, 1978. Editorial asst. ABC News, Washington, 1978-79; researcher Pres.'s Commn. on Coal, Washington, 1979; legis. asst. Nat. Taxpayers Union, Washington, 1979-81; founder, dir. Project on Mil. Procurement, Washington, 1981-89; investigative reporter Lawson-Rasor Assocs., El Cerrito, Calif., 1990-92; pres., CEO, investigator Bauman & Rasor Group, El Cerrito, 1993—. Author: The Pentagon Underground, 1985; editor: More Bucks, Less Bang, 1983; contbr. articles to profl. jours. Recipient Sigma Delta Chi Outstanding Leadership award Soc. Profl. Journalists, 1986; named to register Esquire Mag., 1986, Nat. Jour., 1986. Mem. United Ch. Christ.

RASPORICH, ANTHONY WALTER, university dean; b. Port Arthur, Ont., Can., Jan. 9, 1940; s. Milan and Sophia (Grgurich) R.; m. Beverly Jean Matson. BA, Queen's U., Kingston, Ontario, 1962, MA, 1965; PhD, U. Man., Winnipeg, 1970. Tchr. Kingston Bd. Edn., 1962-63; prof. history U. of Calgary, Alta., 1966-97, prof. emeritus, 1997—, dean social scis. faculty Alta., 1986-94. Author: For a Better Life, 1982, Oil and Gas in Western Canada 1900-80, 1985; editor: The Making of the Modern West, 1984; co-editor: Canadian Ethnic Studies, 1980-00, Sports in the West, 1990. C.D. Howe postdoctoral fellow, fellow Assn. Univs. Colls. Can., Thunder Bay, Ontario, 1970, Vis. Can. Studies, Sussex, Eng., 1979, Killam Found., Calgary, 1979, Social Scis. Human Rsch. Coun., Ottawa, Can., 1981. Mem. Canada Ethnic Studies Assn. Office: U Calgary Dept History Calgary AB Canada T2N 1N4

RASUL, FIROZ, business executive; B in Indsl. Engring., U. Hertfordshire, U.K.; MBA, McGill U., Montreal. With Gen. Foods Corp., Europe, Black & Decker; v.p. mktg. and sales MDI Mobile Data Internat., 1981-88; pres., CEO, Ballard Power Sys., Burnaby, B.C., Can., 1988-99, CEO Can., 1999—, also bd. dirs. Can. Chmn. Focus Humanitarian Assistance Can.; mem. nat. com. Aga Khan Found. Can.; bd. dirs. Ismaili Coun. Can. Office: Ballard Power Sys 9000 Glenlyon Pkwy Burnaby BC Canada V5J 5J9

RATH, ALAN T. sculptor; b. Cin., Nov. 25, 1959; s. George and Carolyn R. BSEE, MIT, 1982. One-man exhbns. include San Jose (Calif.) Art Mus., 1990, Dorothy Goldeen Gallery, Santa Monica, Calif., 1990, 92, Walker Art Ctr., Mpls., 1991, Mus. Contemporary Art, Chgo., 1991, Carl Solway Gallery, Cin., 1991, Inst. Contemporary Mus., Honolulu, 1992, Ctr. Fine Art, Miami, Fla., 1992, Galerie Hans Mayer, Dusseldorf, Germany, 1992, Hiroshima (Japan) City Mus. Contemporary Art, 1994, Worcester (Mass.) Art Mus., 1994, John Weber Gallery, N.Y.C., 1994, Haines Gallery, San Francisco, 1995, 96, 98, Contemporary Art Mus., Houston, 1995, Aspen Art Mus., Colo., 1996, Dorfman Projects, N.Y.C., 1998, Yerba Buena Ctr. for the Arts, San Francisco, 1998, Site Santa Fe (N.Mex.), 1998, Mus. of Art, Austin, Tex., 1999, Scottsdale Mus. of Contemporary Art, 1999; group exhbns. include Visiona, Zurich, 1989, Ars Electronica, Linz, Austria, 1989, L.A. Contemporary Exhbns., 1989, Mus. Folkwang, Essen, Germany, 1989, Cite des Arts et des Nouvelles Technologies, Montreal, 1990, Stadtmuseum Siegburg, Siegburg, Germany, 1990, San Francisco Mus. Modern Art, 1990, 95, 98, Denver ArtMus., 1991, Whitney Am. Art, N.Y.C., 1991, Alvar Alto Mus., Jyvaskyla, Finland, 1992, Internat. Ctr. Photography, N.Y.C., 1992, Padigilione d'Arte Contemporanea, Ferrara, Italy, 1992, John Weber Gallery, N.Y.C., 1993, Spiral Art Ctr., Tokyo, 1994, Aldrich Mus. of Contemporary Art, Ridgefield, Conn., 1995, Otso Gallery, Espo Finland, 1996, LaLonja, Palma de Malloren, Spain, 1996, Kunsthalle, Vienna, 1998, L.A. Mus. Contemporary Art, 1999, Taipei ICA, Taiwan, 2001, Bienal de Valencia, Spain, 2001. Grantee NEA, 1988; Guggenheim fellow, 1994. Office: IKON 830 E 15th St Oakland CA 94606-3631

RATH, HOWARD GRANT, JR. lawyer; b. L.A., Sept. 2, 1931; s. Howard Grant and Helen (Cowell) R.; m. Peyton McComb, Sept. 13, 1958 (dec. Apr. 1984); children: Parthenia Peyton, Francis Cowell; m. Dorothy Moser, Aug. 29, 1986. BS, U. Calif., 1953; JD, U. So. Calif., 1958. Bar: Calif. 1959, U.S. Dist. Ct. (cen. dist.) Calif., 1959, U.S. Ct. Claims 1974, U.S. Tax Ct. 1960. Assoc. O'Melveny & Myers, L.A., 1959-66; tax counsel, dir. tax adminstrn., asst. treas. Northrop Corp. L.A., 1966-74; sr. tax ptnr. Macdonald, Halsted & Laybourne, L.A., 1974-86, Hill & Weiss, L.A., 1986-90; ptnr. Lewis, D'Amato, Brisbois & Bisgaard, L.A., 1990—; dir. Rath Packing Co., Waterloo, Iowa, 1966-81. 1st lt. U.S. Army, 1953-55. Mem. State Bar Calif., L.A. County Bar Assn., L.A. Yacht Club, Valley Hunt Club (pres. 1981-82), Order of Coif, Phi Beta Kappa. Republican. Episcopalian. E-mail: rath@ldbb.com. Office: Lewis D'Amato Brisbois & Bisgaard 221 N Figueroa St Ste 1200 Los Angeles CA 90012-2646

RATHBUN, JOHN WILBERT, American studies educator; b. Sioux City, Iowa, Oct. 24, 1924; s. Wilbert W. and Paulina Amanda (Baldes) R.; m. Mary Regina Walsh, Aug. 2, 1947 (div. Sept. 19, 1985); children: Mary Walsh, John Philip. Ph.B., Marquette U., Milw., 1951, M.A., 1952; Ph.D., U. Wis., 1956. Mem. faculty Calif. State U., Los Angeles, 1956—, prof. English/Am. studies, 1959—, chmn. dept. Am. studies, 1969-75, prof. emeritus, 1991—. Author: American Literary Criticism, 1800-1860, vol. 1, 1979, (with Harry Hayden Clark) American Literary Criticism, 1860-1905, vol. 2, 1979, Literature and Literary Analysis, 1983; (with Monica Grecu) American Literary Critics and Scholars, 1800-1850, vol. 1, 1987, 1850-1880, vol. 2, 1880-1900, 1988, vol. 3, 1988; contbr. articles to profl. jours. Served with AUS, 1943-46. Recipient Service citation Calif. State U., Los Angeles, 1977, Univ. Meritorious Achievement award, 1986; Fulbright fellow Romania, 1979-81. Mem. Am. Studies Assn. (council 1974), So. Calif. Am. Studies Assn. (pres. 1973), Coll. English Assn. So. Calif. (pres. 1966-67), MLA. Democrat. Office: 5151 State University Dr Los Angeles CA 90032-4226

RATHWELL, PETER JOHN, lawyer; b. Windsor, Ont., Can., Aug. 20, 1943; came to U.S., 1947; s. Harold Wilfred and Jean Isabel (Lucas) R.; m. Ann Wickstrom Williams, Sept. 10, 1977; 1 child, James Michael BA, U. Ariz., 1965, JD, 1968. Bar: Ariz. 1968. Assoc. Boettcher, Crowder & Schoolitz, Scottsdale, Ariz., 1972-73; ptnr. Snell & Wilmer, Phoenix, 1973—. Seminar lectr. Nat. Bus. Inst. Inc., 1987-90, Ariz. Ann. Bankruptcy Symposium, 1995, 97, Am. Agrl. Lawyers Assn., 1997, 99, Lormans Bus. Seminars, 2000—. Mem. exec. com. Jr. Achievement Ariz., Phoenix, 1980-92, 2000—, bd. advisors, 1980—; chmn. scholarship fund St. Mary H.S., 1982-91; mem., chmn. Phoenix Parks Bd., 1982-87; trustee Orme Sch., 1991—, chair devel. com., 1994—; treas., trustee Smith Scholarship Trust U. Ariz. Law Sch., 1985—. Capt. JAGC, USAF, 1969-72. Fellow State Bar Ariz. Found. (founding mem.), Maricopa County Bar Found. (founding mem.); mem. Am. Bankruptcy Inst., Ariz. Bar Assn. (bar counsel 1982-87, 97, chmn. discipline hearing com. 1987-93, mem. bankruptcy sect.), S.W. Bankruptcy Conf. (bd. advisors 1995—), Maricopa County Bar Assn. (seminar lectr. 1987), Comml. Law League Am., Phoenix Zoo Wildest Club in Town (founding mem. 1972). Republican. Avocations: fishing, raising cattle. Home: 4523 E Mountain View Rd Phoenix AZ 85028-5213 Office: Snell & Wilmer 1 Arizona Ctr Phoenix AZ 85004

RATKOWSKI, DONALD J. mechanical engineer, consultant; b. Cleve., July 29, 1938; m. Joyce Ellen Kotlarczyk, July 15, 1961; children: Rhonda, Tamyra, Cheryl, Randall. Student, Ariz. State U.; AAS, Alliance Coll., 1959, DSc (hon.), 1986. Sr. project engr. semiconductor products div. Motorola, 1960-70, 75-77; v.p. engring. Danker & Wohlk, 1970-75; founder, pres. Paragon Optical Inc., 1976-90; exec. v.p. Pilkinton Vision Care, 1987-90, cons., 1990-91; pres. DJR Resources Inc., Chandler, Ariz., 1990—. Mem. adv. bd. Am. Sec. Coun., 1988-89; mem. steering com. Optometry Coll., Marcinkowski Acad. Medicine, Poland, 1989-91; founder Rigid Gas Permeable Lens Inst., 1985; speaker Nat. Contact Lens Examiners, 1984-91. Contbr. articles to profl. jours.; patentee in field. Sustaining mem. Rep. Nat. Com., 1983-90; mem. U.S. Congl. Adv. Bd., 1990. Recipient Alumnus of Yr. award Alliance Coll., 1985. Mem. Opticians Assn. Am. (assoc. mem. adv. coun. 1987-88), Contact Lens Soc. Am. (bd. dirs. 1986-88, founder scholarship program 1988, hon. chmn. steering com. edn. fund 1989-91), Contact Lens Mfrs. Assn. chmn. external communication com. 1981-90, bd. dirs. 1982-84, Trailblazer award 1987, program chmn. 1989-90, Leonardo DaVinci award 1990), Ariz. Soc. Plastic Engrs. bd. dirs. 1976-78, 83, v.p. 1980-81, pres. 1981-82), Sigma Tau Gamma (Outstanding Alumni award 1985). Home and Office: DJR Resources Inc 8105 N 47th St Paradise Valley AZ 85253

RATLIFF, LOUIS JACKSON, JR. mathematics educator; b. Cedar Rapids, Iowa, Sept. 1, 1931; s. Louis Jackson and Ruth Sara (Sidlinger) R.; m. Georgia Lee Smith, May 9, 1996. BA, State U. Iowa, 1953, MA, 1958, PhD, 1961. Lectr. Ind. U., Bloomington, 1961-63, U. Calif., Riverside, 1963-64, asst. prof. math., 1964-67, assoc. prof., 1967-69, prof., 1969—. Author: Chain Conjectures in Ring Theory, 1978; assoc. editor Procs. of AMS, 1987-92, Comm. in Algebra, 1990-95; contbr. articles to profl. jours. 1st lt. USAF, 1953-57. NSF fellow, 1960-62, grantee, 1965-69, 71-88; recipient Disting. Teaching award, U. Calif.-Riverside, 1983. Mem. Am. Math. Soc., Phi Beta Kappa. Democrat. Seventh Day Adventist. Home: 22344 San Joaquin Dr W Canyon Lake CA 92587-7849 Office: U Calif Dept Math Riverside CA 92521-0001 E-mail: ratliff@math.ucr.edu

RATNATHICAM, CHUTTA, transportation company executive; married; 3 children. Grad., Royal Coll., Sri Lanka, 1967; MBA, U. Portland, 1973. Corp. auditor CNF Transp. Inc., Palo Alto, Calif., 1977-78, various positions, 1978-91, v.p. Emery Subs., 1991-97, sr. v.p., CFO, from 1998, now CEO. Mem. Am. Inst. Cert. Mgmt. Accts., Srk Land Inst. Chartered Accts., Fin. Execs. Inst. (San Francisco chpt.). Office: 3240 Hillview Ave Palo Alto CA 94304-1201

RATNER, BUDDY DENNIS, bioengineer, educator; b. Bklyn., Jan. 19, 1947; s. Philip and Ruth Ratner; m. Cheryl Cromer; 1 child, Daniel Martin. BS in Chemistry, Bklyn. Coll., 1967; PhD in Polymer Chemistry, Polytech. Inst. Bklyn., 1972. Fellow U. Wash., Seattle, 1972-73, from rsch. assoc. to assoc. prof., 1973-86, prof., 1986—, Wash. Rsch. Found. Endowed Prof. Bioengring., 2001—. Bd. dirs. U. Washington Engineered Biomaterials NSF Engring. Rsch. Ctr.; founder Asemblon, Inc.; prof. bioengring. Washington Rsch. Found., 2001. Editor: Surface Characterization of Biomaterials, 1989, Plasmas and Polymers, 1994-99, Biomaterials Science: An Introduction to Materials in Medicine, 1996, Characterization of Polymeric Biomaterials, 1997; mem. editl. bds. 9 jours. and book series; editor Jour. Undergrad. Rsch. in Bioengring., 1998—; contbr. over 300 articles to profl. jours. Recipient Faculty Achievement/Outstanding Rsch. award Burlington Resources Found., 1990, Perkin Elmer Phys. Electronics award for excellence in surface sci. Fellow Internat. Acad. Med. and Biol. Engring., Am. Inst. Med. Biol. Engring. (founder, pres.-elect), Am. Vacuum Soc.; mem. AAAS, AIChE (C.M.A. Stine award 1998), Am. Chem. Soc., Internat. Soc. Contact Lens Rsch., Materials Rsch. Soc., Soc. for Biomaterials (pres. 1991-92, Clemson award 1989, fellow 1994), Biomed. Engring. Soc. Achievements include 15 patents in field. Office: U Wash Dept Bioengring PO Box 351720 Seattle WA 98195-1720 E-mail: ratner@uweb.engr.washington.edu

RATNER, DAVID LOUIS, retired law educator; b. London, Sept. 2, 1931; AB magna cum laude, Harvard U., 1952, LLB magna cum laude, 1955. Bar: N.Y. 1955. Assoc. Sullivan & Cromwell, N.Y.C., 1955-64; assoc. prof. Cornell Law Sch., Ithaca, N.Y., 1964-68, prof., 1968-82; prof. law U. San Francisco Law Sch., 1982-99, dean, 1982-89, prof. emeritus, 1999—. Exec. asst. to chmn. SEC, Washington, 1966-68; chief counsel Securities Industry Study, Senate Banking Com., Washington, 1971-73; vis. prof. Stanford (Calif.) U., 1974, Ariz. State U., Tempe, 1974, U. San Francisco, 1980, Georgetown U., Washington, 1989-90, U. Calif., Hastings, San Francisco, 1992; mem. Larkspur (Calif.) Planning Commn., 1992—. Author: Securities Regulation; Cases and Materials, 5th edit., 1998, Securities Regulation in a Nutshell, 6th edit., 1998, Institutional Investors: Teaching Materials, 1978. Fulbright scholar Monash U., Australia, 1981. Mem. Cosmos Club (Washington), Harvard Club of San Francisco (pres. 1999-2000), Phi Beta Kappa. Home and Office: 84 Polhemus Way Larkspur CA 94939-1928 E-mail: dlratner@aol.com

RATNER, MARINA, mathematician, educator, researcher; b. Moscow, 30 Oct. MA, PhD, Moscow State U. Asst. High Tech. Engring. Sch., Moscow, 1969-71; lectr. Hebrew U., Jerusalem, 1971-74, sr. tchr. pre-acad. sch., 1974-75; from acting asst. prof. to assoc. prof. U. Calif., Berkeley, 1975-82, prof., 1982—. Alfred P. Sloan rsch. fellow, 1977-79, Miller rsch. prof., 1985-86, John Simon Guggenheim fellow, 1987-88; recipient John J. Carty medal for the Advancement of Science Nat. Acad. of Sciences, 1994. Mem. NAS (John J. Carty Medal for the Advancement of Science, 1994), AAAS. Office: Univ Calif Berkeley Dept Math 970 Evans Hall Berkeley CA 94720-3841

RATTO, DOUGLAS C. protective services official; b. Feb. 19, 1939; m. Katty Ratto; children: Brian, Chris, Julie. With Lincoln Fire Dist., North Stockton, Calif., 1961-65; firefighter City of Stockton, 1965-73, capt., 1973-80, bn. chief, 1980-82, dep. fire chief, 1982-88, fire chief, 1988—. Mem. Local 1229 (pres.). Office: City of Stockton Fire Dept 425 N Eldorado St Stockton CA 95202-1997

RAU, DAVID EDWARD, real estate company executive; b. Lincoln, Nebr., Sept. 27, 1956; s. Leo George and Anne Marie (Pavel) R.; divorced; children: Andrew David, Peter Nicholas, Victoria Anne. BBA, U. Ariz., 1978. CPA, Ariz., N.Mex. Sr. Peat Marwick Main, Albuquerque, 1978-82, supervising sr. Phoenix, 1982-83; asst. treas. Kroy Inc., Scottsdale, Ariz., 1983-85; acct. Zolondek & Blumenthal, Phoenix, 1985; v.p., controller Del Webb Corp., Phoenix, 1985—. Bd. dirs. Ariz. Tax Rsch. Assn. Chmn. Phoenix chpt. walk Juvenile Diabetes Found., 1990, pres. 1992, 93, 94; mem. Ariz. Town Hall; advisor Phoenix Sky Harbour Ctr. Tech. Adv. Panel, 1987; treas. Drugs Don's Work in Ariz., 1994—. Mem. Ariz. Soc. CPAs, Albuquerque Jaycees (treas. 1981-82), Nat. Assn. Real Estate Cos. (tax com.), Ariz. C. of C. (bd. dirs.), Beta Alpha Psi. Republican. Roman Catholic. Avocations: skiing, fishing, family. Office: Del E Webb Corp 2231 E Camelback Rd Phoenix AZ 85016-3453

RAUCH, IRMENGARD, linguist, educator; b. Dayton, Ohio, Apr. 17, 1933; d. Konrad and Elsa (Knott) R.; m. Gerald F. Carr, June 12, 1965; children: Christopher, Gregory. Student, Nat. U. Mex., summer 1954; BS with honors, U. Dayton, 1955; MA, Ohio State U., 1957; postgrad. (Fulbright fellow), U. Munich, Fed. Republic Germany, 1957-58; PhD, U. Mich., 1962. Instr., German and linguistics U. Wis., Madison, 1962-63, asst. prof., 1963-66; assoc. prof. German U. Pitts., 1966-68; assoc. prof. German and linguistics U. Ill., Urbana, 1968-72, prof., 1972-79, U. Calif., Berkeley, 1979—. Author: The Old High German Diphthongization: A Description of a Phonemic Change, 1967, The Old Saxon Language: Grammar, Epic Narrative, Linguistic Interference, 1992, Semiotic Insights: The Data Do the Talking, 1998; editor: (with others) Approaches in Linguistic Methodology, 1967, Spanish edit., 1974, Der Heliand, 1974, Linguistic Method: Essays in Honor of Herbert Penzl, 1979, The Signifying Animal: The Grammar of Language and Experience, 1980, Language Change, 1983, The Semiotic Bridge: Trends From California, 1989, On Germanic Linguistics: Issues and Methods, 1992, Insights in Germanic Linguistics I: Methodology in Transition, 1995, Across the Oceans: Studies from East to West in Honor of Richard K. Seymour, 1995, Insights in Germanic Linguistics II: Classic and Contemporary, 1996, Synthesis in Diversity: Semiotics Around the World, 1997, New Insights in Germanic Liguistics I, 1999; editor of three series: Berkeley Insights in Linguistics and Semiotics, Berkeley Models of Grammars, Studies in Old Germanic Languages and Literatures. founder, co-editor Interdisciplinary J. for Germanic Linguistics and Semiotic Anaylsis; contributor articles to profl. jours. Named outstanding woman on campus U. Ill. Sta. WILL, 1975; recipient Disting. Alumnus award U. Dayton, 1985; research grantee U. Wis., summer 1966, U. Ill., 1975-79, Eastern Ill. U., 1976, Nat. Endowment Humanities, 1978, U. Calif., Berkeley, 1979— ; travel grantee NSF, Linguistics Soc. Am., 1972; Guggenheim fellow, 1982-83; IBM Distributed Acad. Computing Environment, 1986; NEH grantee, 1988; Festschrift: Interdigitations: Essays for Irmengard Rauch, 1999. Mem. Linguistics Soc. Am., MLA, Am. Assn. Tchrs. German (hon.), Society for Germanic Philogy, Philogical Assn. of the West Coast, Phonetics Assn., Semiotic Soc. Am. (pres. 1982-83), Semiotic Circle of Calif. (founder), Internat. Assn. for Semiotic Studies (pres., dir. 5th congress 1994), Alpha Sigma Tau, Delta Phi Alpha. Home: 862 Camden Ct Benicia CA 94510-3633 Office: U Calif Dept German Berkeley CA 94720-0001

RAUE, JORG EMIL, electrical engineer; b. Stettin, Germany, June 13, 1936; came to U.S., 1952; s. Ludwig and Liselotte (Barth) R.; m. Anke Volkmann, June 29, 1957; children: Monika Kay, Jennifer Faye. BSEE, Milw. Sch. Engring., 1961; MSEE, Marquette U., 1965, PhDEE, 1968. Mem. faculty Milw. Sch. Engring., 1961-68, chmn. dept., 1968-69; research engr. TRW Systems, Redondo Beach, Calif., 1969-76, mgr. dept., 1976-79; sr. research scientist TRW Electronic Systems, Rendondo Beach, Calif., advanced systems mgr., 1980-93; tech. cons., 1993—; chmn. dept. elec. engring. Calif. Polytech State U., San Luis Opispo, 1979-80. Mem. faculty Marquette U., Milw., 1968-69, Loyola U., Los Angeles, 1970-72, U. So. Calif., Los Angeles, 1983—. Contbr. articles to profl. jours. Served with U.S. Army, 1955-58. Recipient Disting. Tchr. award Milw. Sch. Engring., 1968; named Outstanding Alumnus Milw. Sch. Engring., 1985. Fellow IEEE; mem. Microwave Soc. of IEEE (sec. adminstrn. com. 1985—), Sigma Xi. Avocations: tennis, bicycling, flying. Home and Office: 28813 Rothrock Dr Rancho Palos Verdes CA 90275-3060

RAUGHTON, JIMMIE LEONARD, education consultant, public administrator, urban planner; b. Knoxville, Tenn., Oct. 9, 1943; s. George L. and Ann (Simotes) R. BA in Urban and Regional Planning, U. No. Colo., 1974, MA, 1976; PhD, U. Colo., 1993. Mgr. Flexitran divsn. Gathers, De Vilbliss Archs. and Planners, 1966-68; asst. dir. planning City of Aurora, Colo., 1968-71; planner City of Lakewood, 1971-73, City of Boulder, 1973-74; instr. urban planning C.C. of Denver, 1974-76, divsn. dir. human resources and svcs., 1976-81, divsn. dir. sci. and tech., 1981-85; v.p. State of Colo. C.C., 1985—. Chmn. profl. adv. com. to Colo. Gov.'s Land Use Adviser, 1973; cons. Denver Regional Coun. of Govts. for Model Sign Code, 1973, City of Boulder Transp. Dept., 1975—; coord. devel. Rocky Mountain Energy and Environ. Tech. Ctr., 1980; exec. dir. Edn. Found. Colo., 1989-98; spkr. in field. Mem. exec. bd. Civic Ctr. Assn., Denver, 1973-75; supervisory com. Colo. State Employees Credit Union, 1986—; mem. bd. Support Sys. Consol., 1984, Bridge Industry, 1984-85; candidate

Denver City Coun., 1975; bd. dirs. Plan Metro Denver, 1975-76, Four Corner Art Collection, 1973—. Recipient Citizen award of honor Assn. Beautiful Colo. Roads, 1972. Mem. ASTD, Am. Inst. Planners (mem. exec. bd. Colo. 1970-75, treas. 1972-73), Am. Soc. Planning Ofcls., Am. Vocat. Assn., Pi Alpha Alpha, Colo. City Mgrs. Assn. Home: 2501 High St Denver CO 80205-5565

RAULINAITIS, PRANAS ALGIS, electronics executive, consultant; b. Kaunas, Lithuania, May 13, 1927; came to U.S., 1954, naturalized, 1960; s. Pranas Viktoras and Paulina (Gervaite) R.; m. Angele Staugaityte, Oct. 4, 1952; 1 son, Pranas Darius. With Commonwealth Rys. of Australia, Melbourne, 1949-53; asst. to fin. acct. Kitchen & Sons, Pty. Ltd., Melbourne, 1953-54; v.p. photo divsn. Interphoto Corp., L.A, 1954-71; sr. v.p., sec. Craig Corp., L.A., 1971-87; pres. PAR Enterprises, Burbank, Calif., 1987—. Adviser Ministry Fgn. Affairs Republic of Lithuania, 1992. Former pres. Lithuanian Am. Coun., Inc. of Calif.; bd. dirs. Lithuanian-Am. assns.; founder, dir., v.p. Baltic Am. Freedom League; former mem. Am. Soc. Internat. Law. E-mial. Home and Office: PAR Enterprises 1501 W Riverside Dr Burbank CA 91506-3027 E-mail: raulalgis@juno.com

RAUSSER, GORDON C(LYDE), agricultural and resource economics educator; b. Lodi, Calif., July 21, 1943; s. Elmer A. and Doyve Ester (Meyers) R.; children: Sloan, Stephanie, Paige. BS summa cum laude, Calif. State U., 1965; MS with highest honors, U. Calif., Davis, 1968, PhD with highest honors, 1971. Prof. econs. and agrl. econs. U. Calif., Davis, 1969-74; vis. prof. U. Chgo., 1972-74; prof. econs. and stats. Iowa State U., 1974-75; prof. bus. adminstrn. Harvard U., 1975-78; prof., chmn. dept. agrl. and resource econs. U. Calif., Berkeley, 1979-85, 93-94, Robert Gordon Sproul disting. prof., 1985—; dir. Giannini Found., Berkeley, 1984-86; dean nat. resources U. Calif., 1994-2000. Vis. prof. Hebrew U. and Ben-Gurion U., Israel, 1978; Ford Found. vis. prof., Argentina, 1972; spl. cons. and sr. economist Council Econ. Advisors, 1986-87; chief economist Agy. for Internat. Devel., 1988-90; advisor econ. research service U.S. Dept. Agriculture, 1978-80, 86-88, Agriculture Can., 1977-79, Bur. Agrl. Econs., Australia, 1987, U.S. Office Mgmt. and Budget, 1986; mem., chmn. planning com. Sch. Bus. Adminstrn. U. Calif., Berkeley, 1986-87, mem. adv. com. Agrl. Issues Ctr., 1984-85, mem. planning com. Agrl. and Natural Resources Program, 1986, mem. econs. programs evaluation com., 1987-88; mem. Citrus Planning Commn., Brazil, 1984; pres. Inst. for Policy Reform, Washington, 1989-94; prin., founder Law & Econ. Cons. Group, Berkeley, Calif., Washington, Chgo., N.Y.C., 1988-2000; co-founder Law and Econs. Cons. Group, 1990-2000; sr. cons. Charles River Assocs., 2000—. Author numerous books including Macroeconomic Environment for U.S. Agricultural Policy, Alternative Agricultural and Food Policies and the 1985 Farm Bill, The Emergence of Market Economies in Eastern Europe, New Directions in Econometric Modeling and Forecasting in U.S. Agriculture, Dynamics of Agricultural Systems: Economic Prediction and Control, Quantitative Methods in Agricultural Economics, GATT Negotiations and the Political Economy of Policy Reform; editor: Decision-Making in Business and Economics, 1977-79, Am. Jour. Agrl. Econs., 1983-86. Mem. western nutrition ctr. coordinating com. U.S. Dept. Agr., 1980-83; mem. Arab-Am. Council for Cultural and Econ. Exchange, 1979-81; bd. dirs. Giannini Found. Agrl. Econs., 1979-84, mem. exec. com., 1979-84 ; mem. planning com. Berkeley Food Coop., 1980-83, planning com. for agrl. and food policy Resources for the Future, 1984-85; mem. adv. com. Calif. State Dept. Agriculture, 1982-84; bd. dirs. Am. Agrl. Econs. Awards. Grantee U.S. Dept. Agr., NSF, World Bank, Chgo. Merc. Exch., U.S. Bur. Mines; Fulbright scholar, Australia, 1987; Sr. fellow Resources for Future, 1984-85. Fellow AAAS, Am. Statis. Assn., Am. Agrl. Econs. Assn. (agrl. policy planning com. 1984-86, outstanding enduring rsch. contbn. com. 1982-84, outstanding PhD dissertation com. 1974-76, chmn. outstanding article com. 1983-86, Pub. Enduring Quality award 1993, Disting. Policy Contbn. award 1993, rsch. awards of merit 1976, 78, 80, 82, 86, 89, 92, 93, 94, 2000, 01); mem. Am. Econ. Assn., Am. Acad. Polit. and Social Sci., Econometric Soc., Math. Assn. Am., Ops. Rsch. Soc., Western Agrl. Econ. Assn. (Best Pub. Rsch. award 1978, 94, Outstanding Pub. Rsch. award 1994), Alpha Gamma Rho, Alpha Zeta. Club: Commonwealth (dir. agriculture study group 1983-84). Home: 661 San Luis Rd Berkeley CA 94707-1725 Office: U Calif Berkeley ARE 207 Giannini Hall Berkeley CA 94720-3310

RAUWERDINK, WILLIAM JAY, accountant; b. Sheboygan, Wis., Mar. 3, 1950; s. Harvard M. and Dorothy M. (Duenk) R.; m. Ann Catherine Geske, July 14, 1979; 1 child, Margaret Allene. BBA, U. Wis., 1972; MBA, Harvard U., 1974. CPA, N.Y., Mich., Mass. Ptnr. Deloitte & Touche, Detroit, 1993-95; exec. v.p., CFO, treas., sec. The MEDSTAT Group, Inc., Ann Arbor, 1994—95, Lason, Inc., Troy, 1996—2000. Bd. dirs. Trinity Health Svcs., Novi, Mich., 1998—. Mem. Wis. Bus. Alumni Assn. (bd. dirs. 1980-89, pres. 1984-85), Rennaisance Club (Detroit), Harvard Club (Boston). Club: Rennaisance (Detroit); Harvard (Boston).

RAVEN, BERTRAM H(ERBERT), psychology educator; b. Youngstown, Ohio, Sept. 26, 1926; s. Morris and Lillian R.; m. Celia Cutler, Jan. 21, 1961; children: Michelle G., Jonathan H. BA, Ohio State U., 1948, MA, 1949; PhD, U. Mich., 1953. Rsch. assoc. Rsch. Ctr. for Group Dynamics, Ann Arbor, Mich., 1952-54; lectr. psychology U. Mich., Ann Arbor, 1953-54; vis. prof. U. Nijmegen, U. Utrecht, The Netherlands, 1954-55; psychologist RAND Corp., Santa Monica, Calif., 1955-56; prof. UCLA, 1956—, chair dept. psychology, 1983-88. Vis. prof. Hebrew U., Jerusalem, 1962-63, U. Wash., Seattle, U. Hawaii, Honolulu, 1968, London Sch. Econs. and Polit. Sci., London, 1969-70; external examiner U. of the W.I., Trinidad and Jamaica, 1980—, rsch. assoc. Psychol. Rsch. Ctr., 1993—; participant Internat. Expert Conf. on Health Psychology, Tilburg, The Netherlands, 1986; cons., expert witness in field, 1979—. Co-dir. Tng. Program in Health Psychology, UCLA, 1979-88; cons. World Health Orgn., Manila, 1985-86; cons., expert witness various Calif. cts., 1978—. Author: (with others) People in Groups, 1976, Discovering Psychology, 1977, Social Psychology, 1983, Social Psychology: People in Groups (Chinese edition), 1994; editor: (with others) Contemporary Health Services, 1982, Policy Studies Rev. Ann., 1980; editor: Jour. Social Issues, 1969-74; contbr. articles to profl. jours. Guggenheim fellow, Israel, 1962-63; Fulbright scholar The Netherlands, 1954-55, Israel, 1962-63, Britain, 1969-70; recipient Citation from Los Angeles City Council, 1966, Rsch. on Soc. power by Calif. Sch. of profl. psychology, L.A., 1991; NATO sr. fellow, Italy, 1989. Fellow APA (chair bd. social and ethical responsibility 1978-82), Am. Psychol. Soc., Soc. for Psychol. Study of Social Issues (pres. 1973-74, coun. 1995-97, Kurt Lewin award 1998); mem. AAAS, Am. Sociol. Assn., Internat. Assn. Applied Psychology, Soc. Exptl. Social Psychology, Assn. Advancement of Psychology (founding, bd. dirs. 1974-81), Internat. Soc. Polit. Psychology (governing coun. 1996-98), Interam. Psychol. Soc., Am. Psychology-Law Soc. Avocations: guitar, travel, international studies. Home: 2212 Camden Ave Los Angeles CA 90064-1906 Office: UCLA Dept Psychology Los Angeles CA 90095-1563 E-mail: raven@ucla.edu

RAVEN, ROBERT DUNBAR, lawyer; b. Cadillac, Mich., Sept. 26, 1923; s. Christian and Gladys L. (Dunbar) R.; m. Leslie Kay Erickson, June 21, 1947; children: Marta Ellen, Matt Robert, Brett Lincoln. AB with honors, Mich. State U., 1949; LLB, U. Calif., Berkeley, 1952. Bar: Calif. 1953. Assoc. Morrison & Foerster and predecessor, San Francisco, 1952-56, ptnr., 1956-94, sr. of counsel, 1994—; chmn. Morrison & Foerster (and predecessor), San Francisco, 1974-82. Mem. Jud. Coun. of Calif., 1983-87. Bd. dirs. Bay Area USO, 1964-73, pres., 1968-70; mem. San Francisco Mayor's Criminal Justice Coun., 1971-72; co-chmn. San Francisco Lawyer's Com. for Urban Affairs, 1976-78; bd. dirs. Lawyers Com. for Civil Rights Under Law, 1976-96. With USAAF, 1942-45. Decorated Air medal with oak leaf cluster. Mem. ABA (pres. 1989, mem. standing com. fed. judiciary 1975-80, chmn. 1978-80, chmn. standing com. on legal aid and indigent defendants 1981-83, chair standing com. dispute resolution 1991-93, chair sect. dispute resolution 1993-94), FBA, Am. Arbitration Assn. (bd. dirs. 1988-96), CPR Inst. for Dispute Resolution (mem. exec. com.), Internat. Acad. Trial Lawyers, State Bar Calif. (gov. 1978-81, pres. 1981), Bar Assn. San Francisco (pres. 1971), Am. Law Inst., Am. Bar Found., Am. Judicature Soc., Boalt Hall Alumni Assn. (pres. 1972-73), World Trade Club (San Francisco), Order of Coif. Democrat. Home: 1064 Via Alta Lafayette CA 94549-2916 Office: Morrison & Foerster 425 Market St San Francisco CA 94105-2482

RAVENHOLT, REIMERT THOROLF, epidemiologist, researcher; b. Milltown, Wis., Mar. 9, 1925; s. Ansgar Benedikt and Kristine Henriette (Petersen) R.; divorced; children: Janna, Mark, Lisa, Dane; m. Betty Butler Howell, Sept. 26, 1981. BS, U. Minn., 1948, MB, 1951, MD, 1952; MPH, U. Calif., Berkeley, 1956. Bd. cert. preventive medicine. Intern USPHS Hosp., San Francisco, 1951-52; epidemic intelligence service officer USPHS Communicable Disease Ctr., Atlanta, 1952-54; dir. epidemiology and communicable disease div. Seattle-King County Health Dept., 1954-61; epidemiology cons. European area USPHS, Paris, 1961-63; assoc. prof. preventive medicine U. Wash. Med. Sch., Seattle, 1963-66; dir. Office of Population, AID, Washington, 1966-79, World Health Surveys, Ctrs. for Disease Control, 1980-82; asst. dir. epidemiology and research Nat. Inst. Drug Abuse, Rockville, Md., 1982-84; chief epidemiology br. FDA, Rockville, Md., 1984-87; dir. World Health Surveys, Inc., Seattle, 1987-93; pres. Population Health Imperatives, Seattle, 1993—. Author/designer website dealing with epidemiology. Served with USPHS, 1951-54, 61-63. Recipient Disting Honor award AID, 1973, Hugh Moore Meml. award IPPF and Population Crisis Com., 1974. Fellow Am. Coll. Epidemiology, APHA (Carl Schultz award 1978), mem. Am. Coun. on Sci. and Health (bd. dirs.); mem. Cosmos Club (Washington). Independent. Home: 3156 E Laurelhurst Dr NE Seattle WA 98105-5333 E-mail: ravenrt@oz.net

RAVENTOS, ANTOLIN, radiology educator; b. Wilmette, Ill., June 3, 1925; s. Enrique Antolin and Juanita (Gillespie) R.; m. Anne Patricia Gray, 1976 Student, Northwestern U., 1941-44; S.B., U. Chgo., 1945, M.D., 1947; M.Sc., U. Pa., 1954. From instr. to prof. radiology Sch. Medicine U. Pa., Phila., 1950-70; prof. radiology Sch. Medicine, U. Calif.-Davis, 1970-91, chmn. dept., 1970-77, prof. emeritus, 1991—. Assoc. editor: Cancer, 1964-91. Served with AUS, 1944-46, 52-54. Fellow Am. Coll. Radiology (chancellor 1964-70), Am. Radium Soc. (pres. 1972-73) Home: PO Box 3136 El Macero CA 95618-0736 Office: 44434 Country Club Dr El Macero CA 95618-1043

RAVISHANKARA, AKKIHEBAL R. chemist; PhD, U. Fla., 1975. Chief atmospheric chem. kinetics group NOAA, Boulder, Colo. Adj. prof. dept. chemistry U. Colo., Boulder; postdoctoral rsch. assoc. U. Md., 1976. Named Robertson Meml. lectr., NAS, 1999. Office: DSRC Rm 1A123 325 Broadway Boulder CO 80305-3328

RAWITCH, ROBERT JOE, journalist, educator; b. L.A., Oct. 11, 1945; s. Sam and Jean (Reifman) R.; m. Cynthia Z. Knee, Oct. 27, 1968; children: Dana Leigh, Jeremy Aaron, Joshua Eric. BA in Journalism, Calif. State U., Northridge, 1967; MS in Journalism, Northwestern U., 1968. Reporter L.A. Times, 1968-80, asst. met. editor, 1980-82, editor Valley sect., 1982-83, suburban editor, 1983-89, exec. editor Valley and Ventura County edits., 1989-93; dir. editorial ops. Valley and Ventura County edits., 1993-95; v.p. Winner and Assocs., 1996—. Lectr. Calif. State U., Northridge, 1971-83, 95-96. Co-author: Adat Ari El, The First Fifty Years, 1988. Chmn. Calif. Freedom of Info. Com., 1978-79; pres. Calif. First Amendment coalition, 1991 93; found. bd. dirs. Temple Adat Ari El, 1987 92; bd. dirs. Calif. State U. Northridge Found., 1998—. Recipient Greater L.A. Press Club award, 1973, 75, 79, L.A. Jewish Youth of Yr. award United Jewish Fund, 1963, Clarence Darrow Found. award, 1979. Mem. Soc. Profl. Journalists (nat. bd. dirs. 1979-82), Calif. Soc. Newspaper Editors (pres. 1995-96), Medill Alumni Assn. (bd. dirs. 1994—). Office: Winner & Assocs 16501 Ventura Blvd Encino CA 91436-2007

RAWLINGS, ROBERT HOAG, newspaper publisher; b. Pueblo, Colo., Aug. 3, 1924; s. John W. and Dorothy (Hoag) R.; m. Mary Alexandra Graham, Oct. 18, 1947; children: Jane Louise, John Graham, Carolyn Anne, Robert Hoag II. Student, Colo. U., 1943-44; BA, Colo. Coll., 1947. Reporter Pueblo Chieftain and Pueblo Star-Jour., 1947-51, advt. rep., 1951-62, gen. mgr., 1962-79, pub., editor, 1980—. Sec. Star-Jour. Pub. Corp., 1962-84, pres., 1984—; past chmn. bd. dirs. Colo. Nat. Bank, Pueblo; me. adv. bd. U.S. Bank. Bd. dirs. U.S. Air Force Acad. Found., U. So. Colo. Found.; pres. Robert Hoag Rawlings Found., So. Colo. Cmty. Found., Medal of Honor Meml. Com.; mem. Colo. Chem. Demilitarzation Citizens Adv. Commn. With USNR, 1942-46. Named Colo. Newspaper Person of Yr., 1989, Disting. Univ. Fellow Pres. Club U. So. Colo., 1993, Outstanding Citizen of Yr. Pueblo C. of C. 1994, Colo. Bus. Leader of Yr., Colo. Assn. of Commerce and Industry, 1994; recipient Outstanding Svc. to Univ. award U. So. Colo. Alumni Assn., 1993, Colo. Corp. Philanthropy award Nat. Philanthropy Assn., 1993, Louis T. Benezet award Colo. Coll. Alumni Assn., 1996, Living Legend award U. Colo., 1997, Outstanding Am. Achievement award U. So. Colo., 1997, Outstanding Svc. to Hispanic Cmty. award, U. So. Colo. and Pueblo Hispanic Edn. Found., 1999; named Donor of Yr. Nat. Assn. Univ. Athletic Devel. dirs., 1995, Creative Spirit award Pueblo United Way, 1998, Lifetime Svc. award Colo. Bd. Vet. Affaris, 2000, Medal of Valor, Congl. Medal Honor Soc., 2000; named to Pueblo Hall of Fame, 1999, The Pueblo Greater Sports Assn. Hall of Fame, 1999. Mem. Colo. Press Assn. (dir. 1963-66, 76-78, pres. 1985, chmn. bd. dirs. 1986, Golden rule Makeup awrd 1998), Rocky Mountain Ad Mgrs. (past pres.), Colo. AP (past pres.) Colo. forum, U. So. Colo. Found., Colo. Mental Health Inst., Rotary. Presbyterian. Home: 1401 Rancho Del Sol Pueblo CO 81008-2043 Office: The Pueblo Cheiftain Star Jour Pub Corp PO Box 4040 Pueblo CO 81003-0040

RAWLINS, V. LANE, university president; b. Rigby, Idaho, Nov. 30, 1937; m. Mary Jo Rawlins, three children. BA in Economics, Brigham Young U., 1963; MA in Economics, U of Calif., Berkeley, 1969. Faculty Wash. State U., Pullman, 1968-86, chair. economics, 1977-82, vice provost, 1981-86; vice chancellor, academic affairs U. of Alabama, 1986-91; pres. Memphis St. U., Memphis, 1991-00, Wash. State U., Pullman, Wa., 2000—. Office: Washington State U Office Pres PO Box 641048 Pullman WA 99164-1048

RAWLINSON, DENNIS PATRICK, lawyer; b. Portland, Oreg., Mar. 1, 1947; s. Thomas F. and Betty (Price) R.; m. M. Diane Schatz, Apr. 26, 1980. BA, U. Notre Dame, 1969; MBA, JD, Cornell U., 1976. Bar: Oreg. 1976, U.S. Dist. Ct. Oreg. 1976; cert. civil trial lawyer Nat. Inst. Trial Advocacy. Assoc. Miller, Nash, Wiener, Hager & Carlsen, Portland, Oreg., 1976-82, ptnr., 1982—. Contbr. articles to profl. jours. Pres., bd. dirs. Portland Opera Assn., 1990-96. 1st lt. Army Med. Svc. Corps, 1970-72, Korea. Mem. ABA (chair creditor's rights subsection and task force on discovery guidelines litigation sect.), Oreg. State Bar Assn. (mem. exec. com. debtor/creditor sect. 1988-91, chair-elect and mem. exec. com. litigation sect. 1992—, mng. editor litigation jour. 1992—, mng. editor Oreg. Comml. Practice manual 1988—), Owen Panner Inn of Ct. (master), Arlington Club Toastmasters (pres.), Rotary Club Portland (pres., bd. dirs.), Multnomah Athletic Club (pres., trustee). Avocations: running, backpacking, white water rafting, wine collecting. Office: Miller Nash Wiener Hager & Carlsen 111 SW 5th Ave Ste 3500 Portland OR 97204-3699

RAWLINSON, JOSEPH ELI, foundation executive, lawyer; b. Delta, Utah, May 9, 1915; s. Eli Wilford and Dora Pearl (Day) R.; m. Elaine Millicent Andersen, June 2, 1947; children: James, Jolene, Nancy, Rex, Anina, Cheryl, Mark, Lisa, David. BS, U. Utah, 1936; JD, Loyola U., 1958. Bar: Calif. 1959; CPA, Calif. Agt. IRS, Wichita, 1938-52; acct. Serene Koster, Barbour, Calif., 1952-62; lawyer in pvt. practice, 1959; pres., CEO Fritz B. Burns Found., Burbank, 1980—. Recipient Silver medal Am. Inst. Accts., 1942. Office: Fritz B Burns Found 4001 W Alameda Ave Ste 203 Burbank CA 91505-4338 E-mail: josepheli@aol.com

RAWSON, ERIC GORDON, optical engineer; b. Saskatoon, Sask., Can., Mar. 4, 1937; s. Donald Strathern and Hildred Iantha (Patton) R.; m. Zivile Anne Nalivaika, May 5, 1966; children: Carol, Dalia, Cliff. BA, U. Saskatchewan, 1959, MA, 1960; PhD, U. Toronto, Ont., 1966. Mem. tech. staff Bell Telephone Labs., Murray Hill, N.J., 1966-73; mem. rsch. staff Xerox PARC, Palo Alto, Calif., 1973-78, area mgr., 1978-94; prin. Rawson Optics, Inc., Brentwood, 1994-99, pres., CEO, 1999—. Bd. dirs., sec. Alamed. Corp., Palo Alto, 1991—. Editor: Book of Milestones Fiber Optics Local Area Networks, 1994; contbr. over 65 articles to profl. jours. Fellow Optical Soc. Am. (mem. engrng. coun. 1995—, Engrng. Excellence award 1990), Soc. Photo-Instrumentation Engrs.; mem. IEEE (sr.). Achievements include over 30 patents for optics and biomedical monitoring. Office: 763 Franklin Dr Brentwood CA 94513-6463 E-mail: ericrawson@rawsonoptics.com

RAWSON, LEONARD LEE, state legislator, business executive; b. Dona Ana, N.Mex., Oct. 19, 1954; BA in Mgmt., N.Mex. State U. Mem. N.Mex. Senate, Dist. 37, Santa Fe, 1992—; mem. corps. and transp. com. N.Mex. Senate, mem. ways and means. Republican. Office: Rep Caucus PO Box 996 Las Cruces NM 88004-0996

RAWSON, RAYMOND D. dentist, state legislator; b. Sandy, Utah, Nov. 2, 1940; s. James D. and Mable (Beckstead) R.; m. Linda Downey, July 23, 1959; children: Raymond Blaine, Mark Daniel, Pamela Ann, David James, Kristi Lynn, Kenneth Glenn, Richard Allen. BS, U. Nev. at Las Vegas, 1964; DDS, Loma Linda U., 1968; MA, U. Nev., 1978. Diplomate Am. Bd. Forensic Odontology (pres. 1984), Am. Bd. Oral Medicine. Gen. practice dentistry, Las Vegas, 1968—. Instr. dental hygiene, dental dir. Clark County Community Coll., 1977—, dep. coroner, chief dental examiner, 1977—; adj. prof. U. Nev., 1977—, adj. assoc. prof. oral diagnosis and forensic dentistry Northwestern U., Chgo., 1985—. Contbr. articles to profl. jours. Active Boy Scouts Am., 1968—; chmn. youth and family health comm. assembly on fed. issues, Nat. Conf. State Legislators, mem. steering comm. Reforming STates Group, coun. of State Govts.; pres. Red Rock Stake; bishop Ch. Jesus Christ Latter-day Saints, 1978-84; asst. majority leader Nev. State senator. Recipient Cmty. Heroes award Nat. Conf. Christians and Jews, Las Vegas, 1994. Fellowo Am. Acad. Forensic Scis. (pres., chmn.), ADA (editl. rev. bd. jour.), Fedn. Dentaire Internat., Omicron Kappa Upsilon (commr. edn. commn. of the states). Republican. Office: 6375 W Charleston Blvd Las Vegas NV 89146-1139 Address: Nev Senate 401 S Carson St Rm 213A Carson City NV 89701-4747

RAY, ALBERT, family physician; b. N.Y.C., Aug. 8, 1948; s. Herman and Stella (Meritz) R.; m. Cheryl Antecol, Oct. 8, 1977; children: Heather, Erin, Samantha. BA, Bklyn. Coll., 1969; MD, Cath. U. Louvain, Belgium, 1976. Diplomate Am. Bd. Family Practice, Can. Coll. Family Physicians. Intern Meml. U. of Nfld., St. John's, Can., 1976; resident McGill U., Montreal, 1978; family physician SCPMG, San Diego, 1978—. Clin. prof. U. Calif., San Diego, 1978—; mem. cmty. faculty UCLA, USD, U. Calif., Davis, USC; mem. clerkship cmty. adv. bd. U. Calif., San Diego, 1995—; pres. profl. staff Kaiser Found. Hosp.; bd. dirs. So. Calif. Permanente Med Group; asst. chief family medicine Kaiser Permanente, San Diego. Author: Lecons d'Histologie, 1973; contbr. to profl. jours. Program chair adult edn. Congregation Beth Israel, 1995; bd. dirs. Temple Emanuel, San Diego, 1990, Agy. for Jewish Edn.; expert reviewer Med. Bd. Calif., 1995; spl. med. cons. Calif. Dept. of Corps., 1996. Fellow Am. Acad. Family Physicians; mem. AMA, Calif. Med. Assn., San Diego County Med. Soc. (mem. profl. conduct com. 1994), San Diego Acad. Family Physicians (pres.), Calif. Acad. Family Phyicians (chair sci. program com.). Avocations: golf, tennis, travel, antiques. Office: Kaiser Permanente 4405 Vandever Ave San Diego CA 92120-3315

RAY, GENE WELLS, industrial executive; b. Murray, Ky., Apr. 23, 1938; s. Terry Lee and Loreen (Lovett) R.; m. Becky Huie, Mar. 5, 1956 (dec. 1976); m. Taffin Ray; children: Don Dickerson, Kathy Pratt, Nancy Solomon. BS in Math., Physics and Chemistry, Murray State U., 1956; MS in Physics, U. Tenn., 1962, PhD in Theoretical Physics, 1965. With tech. staff Aerospace Corp., San Bernardino, Calif., 1965-68; mgr. strategic div. USAF (OA), Washington, 1968-70; scientist, sr. v.p., systems group mgr. Sci. Applications Inc., La Jolla, Calif., 1970-81, also bd. dirs.; pres., chief exec. officer Titan Systems Inc., San Diego, 1981-85, CEO, 1985—, CEO, pres., chmn.; assoc. prof. Carson Newman Coll., Tenn., 1964-65. Inventor mass flow meter. 1st lt. USAR, 1963-68. Republican. Avocations: tennis, wine collecting. Home: PO Box 2464 Rancho Santa Fe CA 92067-2464 Office: Titan Corp 3033 Science Park Rd San Diego CA 92121-1199

RAY, GILBERT T. lawyer; b. Mansfield, Ohio, Sept. 18, 1944; s. Robert Lee Ray and Renatha (Goldie) Washington; m. Valerie J. Reynolds, June 14, 1969; children: Tanika, Tarlin. BA, Ashland Coll., 1966; MBA, U. Toledo, 1968; JD, Howard U., 1972. Assoc. O'Melveny & Myers, L.A., 1972-79, ptnr., 1980-2000, ret. ptnr., 2000—. Bd. dirs. Host Marriott Svcs. Corp., Sierra Monolithins, Inc., Automobile Club of So. Calif., Haynes Found., Watson, Wyatt & Co. Mem. The Calif. Club, L.A. Country Club. Democrat. Office: O'Melveny & Myers 400 S Hope St Los Angeles CA 90071-2899

RAYMOND, DOROTHY GILL, lawyer; b. Greeley, Colo., June 2, 1954; d. Robert Marshall and Roberta (McClure) Gill; m. Peter J. Raymond, June 8, 1974. BA summa cum laude, U. Denver, 1975; JD, U. Colo., 1978. Bar: Conn. 1978, Colo. 1981. Assoc. Dworkin, Minogue & Bucci, Bridgeport, Conn., 1978-80; counsel Tele-Communications, Inc., Englewood, Colo., 1981-88; v.p., gen. counsel WestMarc Communications, Inc., Denver, 1988-91, Cable Television Labs., Inc., Boulder, Colo., 1991-96, sr. v.p., gen. counsel, 1996—. Mem. Am. Corp. Counsel Assn. (pres. 1990-91, Colo. chpt. dir. 1988-94), Colo. Assn. Corp. Counsel (pres. 1987), Sports Car Club Am. (nat. champion ladies stock competition 1981, 85, 86, 88). Avocations: sewing, reading, outdoor activities. Office: Cable Television Labs Inc 400 Centennial Pkwy Louisville CO 80027-1266

RAYMOND, KENNETH NORMAN, chemistry educator, research chemist; b. Astoria, Oreg., Jan. 7, 1942; s. George Norman and Helen May (Dunn) R.; m. Jane Galbraith Shell, June 19, 1965 (div. 1976); children: Mary Katherine, Alan Norman; m. Barbara Gabriele Sternitzke, June 17, 1977; children: Gabriella Petra, Christopher Norman. B.A., Reed Coll., 1964; Ph.D., Northwestern U., 1968. Asst. prof. chemistry U. Calif.-Berkeley, 1967-74, assoc. prof., 1974-78, prof., 1978—; vice chmn. dept. U. Calif. Berkeley, 1982-84, chmn., 1993-96. Mem. study sect. NIH, 1983; mem. chemistry adv. com. NSF, 1985-87; co-chair bd. chem. scis. & technology NRC, 2000—.awd Editor: Bioinorganic Chemistry II, 1977; assoc. editor Biology of Metals, 1987-91; editl. bd. Inorganic Chemistry, 1976-86, Accounts Chem. Rsch., 1982-90, Inorganica Chemica Acta f-Block Elements, 1984-90, Jour. Coordination Chemistry, 1981—, Jour. Inorganic and Nuclear Chemistry, 1974-81, Jour. Am. Chem. Soc., 1983-95, Topics in Current Chemistry, 1981-97, Metals in Biology, 1993—, Jour. Supramolecular Chemistry, 1992—, Jour. Biol. Inorganic Chemistry,

1996—; U.S. editl. advisor Springer-Verlag in Chemistry, 1972-91; contbr. articles to profl. jours.; author more than 400 papers, 11 patents in field. Alfred P. Sloan rsch. fellow, 1971-73; Miller rsch. prof., 1977-78, 96; Guggenheim fellow, 1980-81; recipient E.O. Lawrence award, Dept. Energy, 1984, Humboldt Rsch. award for U.S. Scientists, 1992, 2000, Alfred R. Bader award Am. Chem. Soc., 1994. Mem. NAS, Am. Acad. Arts and Scis., Am. Chem. Soc. (chair divsn. inorganic chemistry 1996), Am. Crystallographic Soc., Sigma Xi. Democrat. Office: U Calif Berkeley Dept Chemistry Berkeley CA 94720-1460 E-mail: raymond@socrates.berkeley.edu

REA, WILLIAM J. judge; b. 1920; BA, Loyola U., 1942; LLB, U. Colo., 1949. With U.S. Census Bur., Denver, 1949-50; adjuster Farmers Ins. Group, L.A., 1950; pvt. practice law L.A., 1950-64, Santa Ana, Calif., 1964-68; judge Superior Ct., L.A., 1968-84, U.S. Dist. Ct. (cen. dist.) Calif., L.A., 1984—, sr. judge. Past pres. L.A. chpt. Nat. Exec. Com.; chmn. Constrn. and By-Law Com. With USN, WWII. Mem. L.A. County Bar Assn. (Outstanding Jurist award 1985), So. Calif. Def. Counsel Assn. Disting. Svc. award 1982), Internat. Acad. Trial Lawyers (Trial Judge of Yr. 1982), L.A. Trial Lawyers Assn., Am. Bd. Trial Advs. (nat. pres.), L.A. County Bar Assn. (Trial Judge of Yr. 1985). Office: US Dist Ct 312 N Spring St Los Angeles CA 90012-4701

READ, RICHARD EATON, newspaper reporter; b. St. Andrews, Scotland, Sept. 3, 1957; s. Arthur H. and Katharine (Eaton) R.; m. Kim R. Kunkle, July 26, 1986; 1 child, Nehalem Kunkle-Read. BA in English, Amherst Coll., 1980; postgrad., Harvard U., 1996-97. Press sec. Mass. Commn. on State and County Bldgs., 1980; staff writer The Oregonian, 1981-86; fellow The Henry Luce Found./The Nation, Bangkok, Thailand, 1986-87; freelance writer Tokyo, 1987-89; Asia bur. chief The Oregonian, Tokyo, 1989-94; sec., 1st dir., 1st v.p. Fgn. Corrs. Club of Japan, 1990-93; internat. bus. writer The Oregonian, Portland, 1994-99, sr. writer internat. affairs, 1999—. Recipient Pulitzer prize for explanatory reporting, 1999, Overseas Press Club award for bus. reporting from abroad, 1999, Scripps Howard Found. award for bus. reporting, 1999, Blethen award for enterprise reporting Pacific Northwest Newspaper Assn., 1999, Oreg. Gov.'s award for achievement in internat. bus., 2000, Pulitzer prize for pub. svc., 2001, Bruce Baer award, 2001, Media Leadership award Am. Immigration Lawyers Assn., 2001; named Internat. Citizen of Yr. 1999 World Affairs Coun. Oreg.; Eisenhower Exch. fellow, Peru, 1997; Nieman fellow, 1996-97.

REAGAN, GARY DON, state legislator, lawyer; b. Amarillo, Tex., Aug. 23, 1941; s. Hester and Lois Irene (Marcum) R.; m. Nedra Ann Nash, Sept. 12, 1964; children: Marc Kristi, Kari, Brent. BA, Stanford U., 1963, JD, 1965. Bar: N.Mex. 1965, U.S. Dist. Ct. N.Mex. 1965, U.S. Supreme Ct. 1986. Assoc. Smith & Ransom, Albuquerque, 1965-67; ptnr. Smith, Ransom, Deaton & Reagan, Albuquerque, 1967-68, Williams, Johnson, Houston, Reagan & Porter, Hobbs, 1968-77, Williams, Johnson, Reagan, Porter & Love, Hobbs, 1977-82; pvt. practice pvt. practice, Hobbs, 1982—; city atty. City of Hobbs, 1978-80, 97—, City of Eunice, N.Mex., 1980—; mem. N.Mex. State Senate, 1993-96. Instr. N.Mex. Jr. Coll. and Coll. of S.W., Hobbs, 1978-84; N.Mex. commr. Nat. Conf. Commrs. Uniform State Laws, 1993-96; adv. mem. N.Mex. Constl. Revision Commn., 1993-95. Mayor City of Hobbs, 1972-73, 76-77, city commr., 1970-78; pres., dir. Jr. Achievement of Hobbs, 1974-85; pres., trustee Landsun Homes, Inc., Carlsbad, N.Mex., 1972-84; trustee Lydia Patterson Inst., El Paso, Tex., 1972-84, N.Mex. Conf. United Meth. Ch., 1988—, Coll. S.W. Hobbs, 1989-2001; chmn. County Dem. Com., 1983-85. Mem. ABA, State Bar N.Mex. (coms. 1989-96, v.p. 1992-93, pres. 1994-95), Lea County Bar Assn. (pres. 1976-77), Hobbs C. of C. (pres. 1989-90), Rotary (pres. Hobbs 1985-86), Hobbs Tennis Club (pres. 1974-75). Home: 200 E Eagle Dr Hobbs NM 88240-5323 Office: 1819 N Turner Ste G Hobbs NM 88240-3834 E-mail: lglregan@nm.net

REAGAN, HARRY EDWIN, III, lawyer; b. Wichita, Kans., Sept. 9, 1940; s. Harry E. II and Mary Elizabeth (O'Steen) R.; m. Marvene R. Rogers, June 17, 1965; children: Kathleen, Leigh, Mairen. BS, U. Pa., 1962, JD, 1965. Bar: Pa. 1965, U.S. Dist. Ct. (ea. dist.) Pa. 1965, U.S. Ct. Appeals (3d cir.) 1965. From assoc. to ptnr. Morgan, Lewis & Bockius, Phila., 1965-98. Chmn. Northhampton Twp. Planning Commn., Bucks County, Pa., 1974-79; mem. Warwick Twp. Planning Commn., 1980-95, chmn., 1994; supr. Warwick Twp., 1996-98; chmn. San Miguel County (Colo.) Open Space Commn., 1998—, chmn., 2001—, Town of Telluride Open Space Commn., 1999—. Mem. ABA (labor sect.), Pa. Bar Assn. (labor sect.), Phila. Bar Assn. (labor sect.), Indsl. Rels. Assn. (pres. Phila. chpt. 1990-91). Republican. Presbyterian. Avocations: coaching rugby, skiing, raising horses, bicycling. Home and Office: 12350 McKenzie Springs Rd Placerville CO 81430

REAGAN, JANET THOMPSON, psychologist, educator; b. Sept. 15, 1945; d. Virgil Joe and Carrie mae (Alexander) Thompson; children: Natalia Alexandria, Robert Barry. BA in Psychology, Berea Coll., 1967; PhD in Psychology, Vanderbilt U., 1972. Mgr. rsch. and eval. Nashville Mental Health Ctr., 1971-72; mgr. eval. Family Health Found., New Orleans, 1973-74; asst. prof. dept. health systems mgmt. Tulane U., New Orleans, 1974-77; dir. eval. Project Heavy West, L.A., 1977-78; asst. prof. health adminstrn. Calif. State U.-Northridge, 1978-83; assoc. prof., dir. health adminstrn., 1983-87; prof., dir. health adminstrn., 1987—. Cons. in field. Contbr. to books, articles to profl. jours., papers to profl. assns. Mem. edtl. adv. bd. Jour. of Long Term Care Adminstrn. Mem. Am. Pub. Health Assn., Am. Coll. Health Care Adminstrn., Assn. Health Svcs. Rsch., Am. Coll. Health Care Execs. (com. on higher edn. 1987, chmn. 1991), Assn. Univ. Programs in Health Adminstrn. (task force on undergrad. edn. 1985-90, chmn. 1988-90, mem. bd. dirs. 1995, chmn. bd. dirs. 1998-99), Psi Chi, Phi Kappa Phi. Home: 9354 Encino Ave Northridge CA 91325-2414 Office: Calif State U Dept Health Sci Northridge CA 91330-0001 E-mail: janet.reagan@csun.edu

REAGAN, JOSEPH BERNARD, retired aerospace executive, management consultant; b. Somerville, Mass., Nov. 26, 1934; s. Joseph B. and Helen Lowry R.; m. Dorothy Hughes; children: Patrick, Michael, Kevin, Kathleen, Brian, John, Maureen. BS in Physics, Boston Coll., 1956, MS in Physics, 1959; PhD in Space Sci., Stanford U., 1975; postgrad. exec. mgmt., Pa. State U., State College, 1981. Staff scientist, rsch. scientist, sr. scientist, scientist Lockheed Rsch. & Devel. Div., Palo Alto, Calif., 1959-75, mgr., 1975-84, dir., 1984-86, dep. gen. mgr., 1986-88, v.p., asst. gen. mgr., 1988-90; v.p. gen. mgr. Lockheed Missle and Space Co., 1991-96. Bd. dirs. Southwall Technologies Inc., Palo Alto. Contbr. articles to profl. jours. Bd. dirs. Tech. Mus., San Jose. Capt. U.S. Army, 1956-64. Recipient Career Achievement in Sci. award Boston Coll. Alumni Assn., 1993. Fellow AIAA (outstanding engr. San Francisco chpt. 1988); mem. Am. Geophys. Union, Nat. Acad. of Engring., Nat. Rsch. Coun. (mem. naval studies bd.). Republican. Roman Catholic. Avocations: computer and woodworking hobbies. Home and Office: 13554 Mandarin Way Saratoga CA 95070-4847 E-mail: jbr733@aol.com

REAGAN, NANCY DAVIS (ANNE FRANCIS ROBBINS), volunteer, wife of former President of United States; b. N.Y.C., July 6, 1923; d. Kenneth and Edith (Luckett) Robbins; step dau. Loyal Davis; m. Ronald Reagan, Mar. 4, 1952; children: Patricia Ann, Ronald Prescott; stepchildren: Maureen, Michael. BA, Smith Coll.; LLD (hon.), Pepperdine U., 1983; LHD (hon.), Georgetown U., 1987. Contract actress, MGM, 1949-56; films include The Next Voice You Hear, 1950, Donovan's Brain, 1953, Hellcats of the Navy, 1957; Author: Nancy, 1980; formerly author syndicated column on prisoner of war and missing in action soldiers and their families; author: (with Jane Wilkie) To Love a Child, (with William Novak) My Turn: The Memoirs of Nancy Reagan, 1989. Civic worker, visited wounded Viet Nam vets., sr. citizens, hosps. and schs. for physically and emotionally handicapped children, active in furthering foster grandparents for handicapped children program; hon. nat. chmn. Aid to Adoption of Spl. Kids, 1977; spl. interest in fighting alcohol and drug abuse among youth: hosted first ladies from around the world for 2d Internat. Drug Conf., 1985; hon. chmn. Just Say No Found., Nat. Fedn. of Parents for Drug-Free Youth, Nat. Child Watch Campaign, President's Com. on the Arts and Humanities, Wolf Trap Found. bd. of trustees, Nat. Trust for Historic Preservation, Cystic Fibrosis Found., Nat. Republican Women's Club; hon. pres. Girl Scouts of Am. Named one of Ten Most Admired Am. Women, Good Housekeeping mag., ranking #1 in poll, 1984, 85, 86; Woman of Yr. Los Angeles Times, 1977; permanent mem. Hall of Fame of Ten Best Dressed Women in U.S.; recipient humanitarian awards from Am. Camping Assn., Nat. Council on Alcoholism, United Cerebral Palsy Assn., Internat. Ctr. for Disabled; Boys Town Father Flanagan award; 1986 Kiwanis World Service medal; Variety Clubs Internat. Lifeline award; numerous awards for her role in fight against drug abuse. Address: 2121 Avenue Of The Stars Fl 34 Los Angeles CA 90067-5062

REAGAN, RONALD WILSON, Fourtieth President of the United States; b. Tampico, Ill., Feb. 6, 1911; s. John Edward and Nelle (Wilson) R.; m. Jane Wyman, Jan. 25, 1940 (div. 1948); children: Maureen E., Michael E.; m. Nancy Davis, Mar. 4, 1952; children: Patricia, Ronald. AB, Eureka Coll., 1932, MA (hon.), 1957. Actor GE Theatre, 1954-62; host TV series Death Valley Days, 1962-66; gov. State of Calif., 1967-74; businessman, rancher, commentator on public policy, 1975-80; Pres. of U.S., 1981-89. Sports announcer, motion picture and TV actor, 1932-66. Author: Where's The Rest of Me?, Speaking My Mind: Selected Speeches, 1989, An American Life: The Autobiography, 1990. Mem. Calif. State Rep. Ctrl. Com., 1964-66; del. Rep. Nat. Conv., 1968, 72; chmn. Rep. Gov. Assn., 1968-73; mem. presdl. Commn. CIA Activities Within U.S., 1975; bd. dirs. Com. Present Danger, Washington, 1977—; cand. for Rep. nomination for Pres., 1976. Served as capt. USAAF, 1942-45. Recipient Great Am. of Decade award, Va. Young Am. for Freedom, Man of Yr. Free Enterprise award, San Fernando Valley Bus. & Profl. award, 1964, Am. Legion award, 1965, Horation Alger award, 1969, George Washington Honor medal, Freedoms Found. Valley Forge award, 1971, Disting. Am. award; inducted into Nat. Football Found. Hall of Fame, Am. Patriots Hall of Fame. Mem. SAG (pres. 1947-52, 59), Am. Fedn. Radio & TV Artists, Lions, Friars, Tau Kappa Epsilon. Republican. Address: 11000 Wilshire Blvd Fl 34 Los Angeles CA 90067

REAL, MANUEL LAWRENCE, federal judge; b. San Pedro, Calif., Jan. 27, 1924; s. Francisco Jose and Maria (Mansano) R.; m. Stella Emilia Michalik, Oct. 15, 1955; children: Michael, Melanie Marie, Timothy, John Robert. B.S., U. So. Calif., 1944, student fgn. trade, 1946-48; LL.B., Loyola Sch. Law, Los Angeles, 1951. Bar: Calif. 1952. Asst. U.S. Atty.'s Office, Los Angeles, 1952-55; pvt. practice law San Pedro, Calif., 1955-64; U.S. atty. So. Dist. Calif., 1964-66; judge U.S. Dist. Ct. (cen. dist.) Calif., L.A., 1966—. Served to ensign USNR, 1943-46. Mem. Am., Fed., Los Angeles County bar assns., State Bar Calif., Am. Judicature Soc., Chief Spl. Agts. Assn., Phi Delta Phi, Sigma Chi. Roman Catholic. Club: Anchor (Los Angeles). Office: US Dist Ct 312 N Spring St Ste 217P Los Angeles CA 90012-4704

REAM, BOB, political organization administrator; Chmn. Mont. Dem. Party, Helena. Office: Mont Dem Party PO Box 802 Helena MT 59624-0802 Fax: 406-442-9534

REAM, JAMES TERRILL, architect, sculptor; b. Summit, N.J., Sept. 8, 1929; s. Merrill Jay and Catherine Ada (Terrill) R.; m. Joyce Kimball Johnson, June 9, 1953 (div. Dec. 1976); children— Claudia, Sarah, Benjamin, m. Nancy Ann Buford, Jan. 1, 1980; stepchildren— Kathleen, Ann Maguire BArch, Cornell U., 1953; postgrad., Pratt Inst., 1953-54, U. Rome, 1956-57. Registered architect. Assoc. W. C. Muchow Assocs., Denver, 1959-62; prin. Ream, Quinn & Assocs., Denver, 1962-66; v.p. design John Carl Warnecke & Assocs., San Francisco, 1966-69; prin., pres. James Ream & Assocs., Inc., San Francisco, 1969-78, Robbins and Ream Inc., San Francisco, 1978-83; prin. James Ream Architect, San Francisco, 1983—. Prin. archtl. works include Denver Convention Ctr., Currigan Hall, Pasadena Conf. Ctr., Stapleton Plaza Hotel, Vail Transp. Ctr. Bd. dirs. San Francisco Planning and Urban Rsch. Assn., 1977—; chmn. bd. dirs. San Francisco Heritage, 1984-91, pres., 1983-84. Served to 1st lt. USAF, 1954-56. Recipient citation for design in steel Am. Iron and Steel Inst., 1975; Honor award Am. Concrete Inst., 1975; Nat. Design award Prestressed Concrete Inst., 1983; Honor award for design in steel Am. Inst. Steel Constrn., 1970 Fellow AIA (honor award western region 1969, fellowship in design 1979, honor award for design excellence 1983, design cons. San Jose Arena). Democrat. Avocations: opera, theater, hiking, tennis. Office: 3385 Clay St San Francisco CA 94118-2006

REARDEN, CAROLE ANN, clinical pathologist, educator; b. Belleville, Ont., Can., June 11, 1946; d. Joseph Brady and Honora Patricia (O'Halloran) R. BSc, McGill U., 1969, MSc, MDCM, 1971. Diplomate Am. Bd. Pathology, Am. Bd. Immunohematology and Blood Banking, Am. Bd. HIstocompatibility and Immunogenetics. Resident and fellow Children's Meml. Hosp., Chgo., 1971-73; resident in pediatrics U. Calif., San Diego, 1974, resident then fellow, 1975-79, asst. prof. pathology, 1979-86, dir. histocompatability and immunogenetics lab., 1979-94, assoc. prof., 1986-92, prof., 1992—, head divsn. lab. medicine, 1989-94; dir. med. ctr. U. Calif. Thornton Hosp. Clin. Labs., San Diego, 1993—. Prin. investigator devel. monoclonal antibodies to erythroid antigens, recombinant autoantigens; dir. lab. exam. com. Am. Bd. Histocompatibility and Immunogenetics. Contbr. articles to profl. jours.; patentee autoantigen pinch. Mem. Mayor's Task Force on AIDS, San Diego, 1983. Recipient Young Investigator Rsch. award NIH, 1979; grantee U. Calif. Cancer Rsch. Coordinating Com., 1982, NIH, 1983; scholar Nat. Blood Found. Mem. Am. Soc. Investigative Pathology, Am. Soc. Hematology, Am. Assn. Blood Banks (com. organ transplantation and tissue typing 1982-87, tech. com. 13 edit. tech. manual 1996—), Am. Soc. Histocompatibility and Immunogenetics. Office: U Calif San Diego Dept Pathology 0612 9500 Gilman Dr La Jolla CA 92093-0612 E-mail: arearden@ucsd.edu

REARDON, JOHN E. broadcast executive; BA in Bus. Adminstrn. and Fin., Loyola U., 1977. Gen. mgr. Sta. KTLA-TV, L.A., 1999—. Office: Sta KTLA TV 5800 W Sunset Blvd Los Angeles CA 90028-6607

REBEK, JULIUS, JR. chemistry educator, consultant; b. Beregszasz, Hungary, Apr. 11, 1944; came to U.S., 1949; s. Julius and Eva (Racz) R.; divorced; children: Eva Louise, Anna Elizabeth. BA, U. Kans., 1966; PhD, MIT, 1970. Asst. prof. chemistry UCLA, 1970-76; assoc. prof. U. Pitts., 1976-80, prof., 1980-89, MIT, Cambridge, 1989-96; dir. Skaggs Inst. for Chem. Biol. Scripps Rsch. Inst., 1996—. Cons. Cubist, Inc., Cambridge, Mass., Darwin, Seattle. Contbr. over 150 articles to rsch. publs. NSF fellow 1967-70, A. P. Sloane fellow, 1977, A. V. Humboldt fellow, 1981, Guggenheim fellow, 1986; recipient James Flack Norris award in physical chemistry, 1997. Fellow Am. Acad. Arts and Sci.; mem. Am. Chem. Soc. (A.C. Cope scholar 1991), Nat. Acad. Sci. Achievements include discoveries in reaction mechanisms, molecular recognition and a self-replicating system. Office: Scripps Rsch Inst 10550 N Torrey Pines Rd La Jolla CA 92037-1000

REBER, DAVID JAMES, lawyer; b. Las Vegas, Nev., Mar. 1, 1944; s. James Rice and Helen Ruth (Cusick) R.; m. Jacqueline Yee, Aug. 31, 1968; children: Emily, Brad, Cecily. BA, Occidental Coll., L.A., 1965; JD, Harvard U., 1968. Bar: Calif. 1969, Hawaii 1975, U.S. Dist. Ct. Hawaii, U.S. Ct. Appeals (9th cir.), U.S. Supreme Ct. Asst. prof. law U. Iowa, Iowa City, 1968-70; assoc. Sheppard Mullin Richter & Hampton, L.A., 1970-75, Goodsill Anderson Quinn & Stifel, Honolulu, 1975-76, ptnr., 1976—. Dir. Oahu Econ. Devel. Bd., Honolulu, Hawaii Appleseed Pub. Interest Law Ctr., Honolulu, Legal Aid Soc.; dir., pres. Legal A.d Soc. Hawaii. Mem. ABA (bus., antitrust and pub. utilities sects.), Hawaii Bar Assn. Avocations: golf, tennis, softball, travel. Office: Goodsill Anderson Et Al 1099 Alakea St Ste 1800 Honolulu HI 96813-4511 E-mail: dreber@goodsill.com

REBHUN, JOSEPH, allergist, immunologist, medical educator; b. Przemysl, Poland, Oct. 7, 1921; came to U.S., 1950; s. Baruch and Serel R.; m. Maria Birkenhejm, Aug. 10, 1945; children: Lillian Friedland, Richard B.R., Donald. MD, U. Innsbruck, Austria, 1950; MS in Medicine, Northwestern U., 1954. Diplomate Am. Bd. Allergy and Immunology. Intern Barnert Meml. Hosp., Patterson, N.J.; resident in internal medicine Tompkins County Meml. Hosp. and Cornell U., N.Y., 1951-52; fellow in allergy Northwestern U. Med. Sch./Chidlren's Meml. Hosp., Chgo., 1952-54; fellow instr. Northwestern U. Med. Sch., 1954; asst. clin. prof. medicine Loma Linda U., 1957-93; clin. prof. medicine U. So. Calif., L.A., 1965-91, ret., 1998. Chief allergy Chgo. Eye, Ear, Nose and Throat Hosp., 1953-55; cons. Pacific State Hosp., Spadra Pomona Valley Cmty. Hosp., Pomona Casa Colina Hosp. Author: SOS, 1946, The Cry of Democracy for Help, God and Man in Two Worlds, 1985, The Embers of Michael, 1993, Crisis of Morality and Reaction to the Holocaust, 1998, Leap to Life: Triumph Over Nazi Evil, 2000; contbr. numerous articles to med. jours. Pres. Am. Congress Jews from Poland, 1969-70. Capt., U.S. Mil., San Francisco. Recipient honors City and County of L.A., L.A. Office Dist. Atty., Senate of State of Calif., all 1985. Fellow Am. Acad. Allergy (rsch. coun. 1960-65), Am. Coll. Allergy, Assn. Clin. Allergy and Immunology; mem. West Coast Allergy Soc., Calif. Allergy Assn., L.A. Soc. Allergy, L.A. Med. Assn., Calif. Med. Assn. E-mail: joerebhun@aol.com

RECHARD, PAUL ALBERT, retired civil engineering company executive, consultant; b. Laramie, Wyo., June 4, 1927; s. Ottis H. and Mary R. (Bird) R.; m. Mary Lou Roper, June 26, 1949; children: Robert Paul, Karen Ann. BS, U. Wyo., 1948, MS, 1949, CE, 1955. Registered land surveyor, Wyo.; registered profl. engr., Wyo., Utah, Mont., Colo., Calif., Nebr., S.D., N.Mex.; cert. profl. hydrologist Am. Inst. Hydrology; diplomate Am. Acad. Environ. Engrs. Hydraulic engr. U.S. Bur. Reclamation, Cody, Wyo. and Billings, Mont., 1949-54; dir. water resources Natural Resource Bd., Cheyenne, Wyo., 1954-58; prin. hydraulic engr. Upper Colorado River Commn., Salt Lake City, 1958-64; dir. Water Resources Rsch. Inst. U. Wyo., Laramie, 1964-81, mem. faculty dept. civil engring., 1964-82, prof., 1964-82; pres. Western Water Cons., Laramie, 1980-2001, Hydrology Assocs., Laramie, 1978-80; ret. Western Water Consults., Inc., 2001. Owner Paul A. Rechard, P.E., Laramie, 1964-78. Editor: Compacts, Treaties and Court Decrees Affecting Wyoming Water, 1956; contbr. articles to tech. publs. Pres., Thayer Sch. PTA, Laramie, 1965; mem. Laramie City Planning Commn., 1974-80. Served with USNR, 1945-46. Recipient Wyo. Eminent Engr. award Tau Beta Pi, 1993; named Disting. Alumnus U. Wyo., 1998; named Outstanding Engr. Wyo. Engring. Soc., 1999. Fellow ASCE (life mem., pres. Wyo. sect. 1968); mem. Am. Soc. Testing Materials, NSPE, Am. Geophys. Union, Nat. Water Well Assn., Wyo. Engring. Soc. (pres. 1976, hon.), Am. Water Works Assn., Am. Water Resources Assn., U.S. Com. on Large Dams, Lions (pres. Laramie 1968), Masons, Sigma Xi (pres. Wyo. chpt. 1973), Phi Kappa Phi (pres. Wyo. chpt. 1969), Gamma Sima Delta, Sigma Tau (pres. Wyo. chpt. 1948, selected Wyo. Eminent Engr. 1993). Republican. Presbyterian. Home: 316 Stuart St Laramie WY 82070-4866 Office: Western Water Cons Inc 611 Skyline Rd Laramie WY 82070-8909

REDD, F. BENNION, federal magistrate; b. 1921; BS, U. Utah, 1949, JD, 1951. County atty. Office of County Atty., 1951-78; magistrate judge U.S. Dist. Ct. Utah, Monticello, 1979—. Served with U.S. Army, 1944-46. Office: PO Box 157 132 S Main St Monticello UT 84535 Fax: 435-587-2244

REDDEN, JAMES ANTHONY, federal judge; b. Springfield, Mass., Mar. 13, 1929; s. James A. and Alma (Cheek) R.; m. Joan Ida Johnson, July 13, 1950; children: James A., William F. Student, Boston U., 1951; LL.B., Boston Coll., 1954. Bar: Mass., 1954, Oreg., 1955. Pvt. practice, Mass., 1954-55; title examiner Title & Trust Ins. Co., Oreg., 1955; claims adjuster Allstate Ins. Co., 1956; mem. firm Collins, Redden, Ferris & Velure, Medford, Oreg., 1957-73; treas. State of Oreg., 1973-77; atty. gen., 1977-80; U.S. dist. judge, now sr. judge U.S. Dist. Ct. Oreg., Portland, 1980—. Chmn. Oreg. Pub. Employee Relations Bd.; mem. Oreg. Ho. of Reps., 1963-69, minority leader, 1967-69. With AUS, 1946-48. Mem. ABA, Mass. Bar Assn., Oreg. State Bar. Office: US Dist Ct 1527 US Courthouse 1000 SW 3d Ave Portland OR 97204-2902

REDGRAVE, LYNN, actress; b. London, Mar. 8, 1943; d. Michael Scudemore and Rachel (Kempson) R.; m. John Clark, Apr. 2, 1967; children: Benjamin, Kelly, Annabel. Ed., Queensgate Sch., London, Central Sch. Speech and Drama. Stage debut as Helena in Midsummer Night's Dream, 1962; theatrical appearances include The Tulip Tree, Andorra, Hayfever, Much Ado About Nothing, Mother Courage, Love for Love, Zoo, Zoo, Widdershins Zoo, Edinburgh Festival, 1969, The Two of Us, London, 1970, Slag, London, 1971, A Better Place, Dublin, 1972, Born Yesterday, Greenwich, 1973, Hellzapoppin, N.Y., 1976, California Suite, 1977, Twelfth Night, Stratford Conn. Shakespeare Festival, 1978, The King and I, St. Louis, 1983, Les Liaisons Dangereuses, L.A., 1989, The Cherry Orchard, L.A., 1990, Three Sisters, London, 1990, Notebook of Trigorin, U.S., 1996; Broadway appearances include Black Comedy, 1967, My Fat Friend, 1974, Mrs. Warren's Profession (Tony award nomination), 1975, Knock, Knock, 1976, St. Joan, 1977, Sister Mary Ignatius Explains It All, 1985, Aren't We All?, 1985, Sweet Sue, 1987, A Little Hotel on the Side, 1992, The Masterbuilder, 1992, Shakespeare For My Father (Tony and Drama Desk nominations, Elliot Norton award 1993), 1993, also nat. tour, 1996, West End, 1996, Moon over Buffalo, 1996, The Mandrake Root, 2001, Noises Off, 2001; film appearances include Tom Jones, Girl With Green Eyes, Georgy Girl (Recipient N.Y. Film Critics award, Golden Globe award, Oscar nomination for best actress 1967), The Deadly Affair, Smashing Time, The Virgin Soldiers, Last of the Mobile Hotshots, Don't Turn the Other Cheek, Every Little Crook and Nanny, Everything You Always Wanted to Know About Sex, The National Health, The Happy Hooker, The Big Bus, Sunday Lovers, Morgan Stuart's Coming Home, Getting It Right, Shine, 1996, Gods and Monsters, 1998 (Recipient Golden Globe award for best performance by an actress in a supporting role in a motion picture 1998), Strike, 1998, The Annihilation of Fish, 1999, The Simian Line, 2000, The Next Best Thing, 2000, How to Kill Your Neighbor's Dog, 2000, My Kingdom, 2001, Unconditional Love, 2001; TV appearances include: The Turn of the Screw, Centennial, 1978, The Muppets, Gauguin the Savage, Beggarman Thief, The Seduction of Miss Leona, Rehearsal for Murder, 1982, Walking On Air, The Fainthearted Feminist (BBC-TV), 1984, My Two Loves, 1986, The Old Reliable, 1988, Jury Duty 1989, Whatever Happened to Baby Jane, 1990, Fighting Back (BBC-TV), 1992, Calling the Shots (Masterpiece Theatre), 1993, Toothless, 1997, Indefensible: The Truth About Edward Brannigan, 1997, Different, 1999, White Lies, 1998, A Season for Miracles, 1999, AFI's 100 Years...100 Stars, 1999, Varian's War, 2000, Lion of Oz and the Badge of Courage (voice), 2000; guest appearances include Carol Burnett Show, Evening at the Improv and Steve Martin's Best show Ever, Circus of the

Stars; co-host nat. TV syndication Not for Women Only, 1977—; nat., TV spokesperson Weightwatchers, 1984-92; TV series include House Calls, 1981, Teachers Only, 1982, Chicken Soup, 1989; Rude Awakening, 1998, albums: Make Mine Manhattan, 1978, Cole Porter Revisited, 1979; video: (for children) Meet Your Animal Friends, Off We Go, Off We Go Again: audio book readings include, Pride and Prejudice, The Shell Seekers, The Blue Bedroom, The Anastasia Syndrome, The Women in His Life, Snow In April, Gone With The Wind, 1994, The World of Philosophy, 1996; author: This is Living, 1990, Shakespeare For My Father, 1993. Named Runner-up Actress, All Am. Favorites, Box Office Barometer 1975; recipient Sarah Siddons award as Chgo.'s best stage actress of 1976, 94. Mem. The Players (pres. 1994).

REDING, JOHN ANTHONY, lawyer; b. Orange, Calif., May 26, 1944; AB, U. Calif., Berkeley, 1966, JD, 1969. Bar: Calif. 1970, U.S. Dist. Ct. (no., ctrl., ea. and so. dists.) Calif., U.S. Claims Ct., U.S. Supreme Ct. Formerly mem. Crosby, Heafey, Roach & May P.C., Oakland, Calif.; now ptnr. Paul, Hastings, Janofsky & Walker, LLP, San Francisco, nat. chmn. litigation dept. Mem. ABA (sects. on litigation, intellectual property, and natural resources, energy and eviron. law, coms. on bus. torts, internat. law, trial practice and torts and insurance), Am. Intellectual Property Law Assn., State Bar Calif. (sect. on litigation), Bar Assn. San Francisco, Assn. Bus. Trial Lawyers. Office: Paul Hastings Janofsky & Walker LLP 345 California St San Francisco CA 94104-2606 E-mail: jackreding@paulhastings.com

REDMAN, ERIC, lawyer; b. Palo Alto, Calif., June 3, 1948; s. M. Chandler and Marjorie Jane (Sachs) R.; children: Ian Michael, Graham James; m. Heather Bell, 1996. AB, Harvard U., 1970, JD, 1975; BA, Oxford U., 1972, MA, 1980. Bar: Wash. 1975, U.S. Dist. Ct. (we. dist.) Wash. 1975, D.C. 1979, U.S. Ct. Appeals (9th cir.) 1981, U.S. Supreme Ct. 1983. Asst. U.S. senator W.G. Magnuson, Washington and Seattle, 1968-71, 74-75; assoc. Preston, Thorgrimson et al, Seattle, 1975-78, ptnr., 1979-82, Heller, Ehrman, White & McAuliffe, Seattle, 1983—. Author: Dance of Legislation, 1973; also book revs., articles. Office: Heller Ehrman White & McAuliffe 6100 Columbia Ctr 701 5th Ave Ste 6100 Seattle WA 98104-7098

REDMAN, KEN, zoo officer; Exec. dir. Honolulu Zoo. Office: Honolulu Zoo 151 Kapahulu Ave Honolulu HI 96815-4096

REDMOND, BILL, former congressman, minister; m. Shirley Raye Robertson; children: Bethany Joy, Jordan Andrew. BA in Ministry and Administrn., Lincoln Christian Coll., 1979, MDiv, 1988. Spl. edn. instr., 1980-83; past tchr. and administr. handicapped adults; past min. Santa Fe Christian Ch.; mem. Ho. of Reps. from N.Mex. 3d congl. dist., 1997-98, mem. nat. security com., mem. banking and fin svcs. com., mem. vet. affairs com. Past instr. adulty basic edn. U. N.Mex. Active Boy Scouts Am., numerous youth drug prevention programs, Big Brother program; past foster parent. Served USAR. Office: PO Box 1226 Los Alamos NM 87544-1226 Fax: 202-226-1331*

REDMOND, JOHN T. hotel and recreational facility executive; Sr. agt. audit divsn. Nev. Gaming Control Bd., 1980-85; with Caesars Palace, 1985-95, sr. v.p., CFO, 1995-96; with MGM Grand Devel., 1996-99; pres., COO Primadonna Resorts, 1999—; co-CEO MGM Grand, Inc., 1999—. Office: MGM Grand 3799 Las Vegas Blvd S Las Vegas NV 89109

REECE, PARIS G. chief financial officer home building company; V.p. Richmond Amer Home, 1988-90, sect., 1990-96, CFO, 1990-93, treas., 1993-96, sr. v.p., 1994-99, exec. v.p., 1999—. Office: Richmond Amer Home 3600 S Yosemite St Denver CO 80237-1812

REED, CHARLES BASS, chief academic administrator; b. Harrisburg, Pa., Sept. 29, 1941; s. Samuel Ross and Elizabeth (Johnson) R.; m. Catherine A. Sayers, Aug. 22, 1964; children: Charles B. Jr., Susan Allison. BS, George Washington U., 1963, MA, 1964, EdD, 1970; postgrad. Summer Inst. for Chief State Sch. Officers, Harvard U. Grad Sch. Edn., 1977; D of Pub. Svc. (hon.), George Washington U., 1987; LLD (hon.), Stetson U., 1987; LHD (hon.), St. Thomas U., 1988; LittD (hon.), Waynesburg Coll., 1990. From asst. prof. to assoc. prof. George Washington U., Washington, 1963-70; asst. dir. Nat. Performance-Based Tchr. Edn. Project, Am. Assn. Colls. for Tchr. Edn., Washington, 1970-71; assoc. for planning and coordination Fla. Dept. Edn., Tallahassee, 1971-75, dir. Office Ednl. Planning, Budgeting, and Evaluation, 1975-79; edn. policy coord. Exec. Office of Gov., Tallahassee, 1979-80, dir. legis. affairs, 1980-81, dep. chief of staff, 1981-84, chief of staff, 1984-85; chancellor State Univ. System Fla., Tallahassee, 1985-98, Calif. State U. Sys., Long Beach, 1998—. Mem. Nat. Commn. on H.S. Sr. Yr.; mem. Rand Edn. Adv. Bd. Mem. Coun. for Advancement and Support of Edn., Coun. on Fgn. Rels., Bus.-Higher Edn. Forum. Disting. fellow,Fullbright Commn. 50th Anniversary, Peru, 1996. Mem. Am. Assn. State Colls. and Univs., Am. Assn. for Higher Edn., Am. Coun. on Edn., Assn. Governing Bds. of Univs. and Colls., Nat. Assn. State Univs. and Land-Grant Colls., Nat. Assn. Sys. Heads, Internat. Assn. Univ. Presidents, Hispanic Assn. Colls. and Univs. Democrat. Roman Catholic Office: Calif State U Office Chancellor 401 Golden Shore St Fl 6 Long Beach CA 90802-4210 E-mail: creed@calstate.edu

REED, DAVID ANDREW, foundation executive; b. Butler, Pa., Feb. 24, 1933; s. Sherman W. and Caroline (Janner) R.; m. Virginia Rogers, Dec. 1, 1956; children: Kristine Lynn, Katherine Louise, Elizabeth Anne, Amy Janner. A.B., Allegheny Coll., 1955; M.S., U. Pitts., 1961. Adminstrv. resident Titusville (Pa.) Hosp., 1959, Cin. Gen. Hosp., 1960-61; asst. adminstr. Warren (Pa.) Gen. Hosp., 1961-62, Western Pa. Gen. Hosp., Pitts., 1962-63; with Cin. Gen. Hosp., 1963-69, adminstr., 1964-69; asso. prof. hosp. adminstrn. U. Cin. Coll. Medicine, 1966-69; preceptor program med. and hosp. adminstrn. U. Pitts. Grad. Sch. Pub. Health, 1966-69; pres. Lenox Hill Hosp., N.Y.C., 1969-78; v.p., chief exec. officer Good Samaritan Hosp., Phoenix, 1978-82; pres. SamCor/Samaritan Health Service, Phoenix, 1982-89; pres., chief exec. officer The Samaritan Found., Phoenix, 1989, St. Joseph Health System, Orange, Calif., 1990-95; pres. DAR Consulting Group, Dana Point, 1995—; chmn. PacifiCare Health Sysytems Inc, Santa Ana, Calif., 1999—. Instr.; past pres. Greater Cin. Hosp. Council, Phoenix Regional Hosp. Council; bd. govs. Greater N.Y. Hosp. Assn.; chmn. Am. Hosp. Assn., also trustee; cons. Hosp. Devel. and Research Inst. Contbr. articles to profl. jours. Bd. dirs. Urban League Cin. Served with AUS, 1955-57. Fellow Am. Coll. Hosp. Adminstrs. (life); mem. Catalina Island Yacht Club, Dana West Yacht Club, Marbella Country Club, Ctr. Club, Phi Gamma Delta. Presbyterian. Office: PacifiCare Health Sysytems Inc 3120 Late Ctr Dr Santa Ana CA 92704 E-mail: consultdar@aol.com

REED, EDWARD CORNELIUS, JR. federal judge; b. Mason, Nev., July 8, 1924; s. Edward Cornelius Sr. and Evelyn (Walker) R.; m. Sally Torrance, June 14, 1952; children: Edward T., William W., John A., Mary E. BA, U. Nev., 1949; JD, Harvard U., 1952. Bar: Nev. 1952, U.S. Dist Ct. Nev. 1957, U.S. Supreme Ct. 1974. Atty. Arthur Andersen & Co., 1952-53; spl. dep. atty. gen. State of Nev., 1967-79; judge U.S. Dist. Ct. Nev., Reno, 1979—, chief judge, now sr. judge. Former vol. atty. Girl Scouts Am., Sierra Nevada Council, U. Nev., Nev. Agrl. Found., Nev. State Sch. Adminstrs. Assn., Nev. Congress of Parents and Teachers; mem. Washoe County Sch. Bd., 1956-72, pres. 1959, 63, 69; chmn. Gov.'s Sch. Survey Com., 1958-61; mem. Washoe County Bd. Tax Equalization, 1957-58, Washoe County Annexation Commn., 1968-72, Washoe County Personnel Com., 1973-77, chmn. 1973; mem. citizens adv. com. Washoe County Sch. Bond Issue, 1977-78, Sun Valley, Nev., Swimming Pool Com., 1978, Washoe County Blue Ribbon Task Force Com. on Growth, Nev. PTA (life); chmn. profl. div. United Way, 1978; bd. dirs. Reno Siver Sox, 1962-65. Served as staff sgt. U.S. Army, 1943-46, ETO, PTO. Mem. ABA (jud. adminstrn. sect.), Nev. State Bar Assn. (adminstrv. com. dist. 5, 1967-79, lien law com. 1965-78, chmn. 1965-72, probate law com. 1963-66, tax law com. 1962-65), Am. Judicature Soc. Democrat. Baptist. Named in his honor Edward C. Reed H.S., Sparks, Nev., 1972. Office: US Dist Ct 400 S Virginia St Ste 606 Reno NV 89501-2182

REED, IRVING S. electrical engineer; BS in Math., Cal. Inst. Tech., 1944, PhD in Math., 1949. With Northrop Aircraft Co., 1949-50, Computer Rsch. Corp., 1950-51; with Lincoln Lab. MIT, 1951-60; with Rand Corp., 1960-63; prof. dept. elec. engring. and computer sci. U. So. Calif., L.A., 1963—. Cons. Jet Propulsion Lab., Hughes Aircraft Co., Rand Corp., Mitre Corp.; Shannon lectr. Internat. Symposium Info. Theory, Les Arcs, France, 1982. Co-author: Theory and Design of Digital Machines, 1962, Error—Control Coding for Data Networks, 1994; contbr. articles to profl. jours. Recipient Roy Carlton award for Outstanding Paper 1985, Disting. Alumni award Calif. Inst. Tech., 1992. Fellow IEEE (life, Charles Babbage Outstanding Sci. award 1986, Richard W. Hamming medal 1989, Masaru Ibuka Consumer Electronics award 1995, Warren White Radar medal 2001); mem. NAE. Office: U So Calif Dept Elec Engring Sys Los Angeles CA 90089-2560

REED, JAMES EARL, protective services official; b. San Francisco, Mar. 21, 1957; s. Arlen Earl and Louise (Gibbs) R.; m. Jody Lynn Bales, Feb. 14, 1976 (div. Aug. 1978); 1 child, Darci Lynn; m. Donna Kaye Lewis, June 25, 1994. A in fire sci., Casper Coll., 1995. State cert. fire fighter I, II, III, state cert. fire svc. instr. I, state cert. fire prevention officer I. Shop worker, shop foreman, salesman Becker Fire Equipment, Casper, Wyo., 1975-78; safety equipment maintance Bell H2S Safety and Oilind Safety Engring., Casper, 1978-80; tchr. outreach program Casper Coll., 1988-90; owner operator J.R.'s Custom Hand Planted Signs, 1980-93; capt. Casper (Wyo.) Fire Dept., 1978-93, comdr., 1993—; artist Images Studio, Casper, 1991—. Instr. CPR courses Am. Heart Soc., ARC, 1980—; instr. SCBA courses, 1983-85. Active fund raisers City/County Fire Fighters Burn Fund, 1982, 84—, fund raisers Muscular Dystrophy Assn., 1981, 82, 85-89, fund raisers March of Dimes, 1984, 85, 87, fund raisers Casper Mountain Racers Youth Olympics, 1985-87, Casper Event Ctr.'s "Spl. Christmas for Spl. Kids," 1984-87; mem. Wyo. chpt. Multiple Sclerosis Soc., 1994—. Named Firefighter of Yr. Casper Fire Dept., Casper Ladies Auxiliary, Am. Legion Regional and Post 2, 1984, Man in Blue, Casper Fire Dept., 1994. Mem. Casper Fire Fighters Assn. (entertainment com. 1980—, exec. com. 1988-90), City County Fire Fighters Burn Fund (trustee 1985-86, treas. 1986-89, sec. 1989-91, pres. 1992—). Republican. Seventh-day Adventist. Avocations: painting, alpine and water skiing, weight lifting, racquetball. Home: PO Box 2297 Casper WY 82602-2297

REED, JOHN THEODORE, writer, publisher; b. Camden, N.J., July 5, 1946; s. Theodore and Marion Theresa (Simonsick) R.; m. Margaret Ogden Tunnell, May 31, 1975; children: Daniel Tunnell, Steven Tunnell, Michael Tunnell. BS, U.S. Mil. Acad., West Point, N.Y., 1968; MBA, Harvard U., 1977. Salesman Pritchett & Co., Pine Hill and Collingswood, N.J., 1972-74; property mgr. Fox & Lazo Inc., Cherry Hill, 1974-75; writer Harcourt Brace Jovanovich, Boston, 1976-86; bank exec. Crocker Nat. Bank, San Francisco, 1977-78; writer, pub. Danville, Calif., 1977—. Author, pub.: Apartment Investing Check Lists, 1978, Aggressive Tax Avoidance for Real Estate Investors, 1981, 16th edit., 1998, How to Manage Residential Property for Maximum Cash Flow and Resale Value, 1995, 5th edit., 1998, How to Use Leverage to Maximize Your Real Estate Investment Return, 1984, 86, How to Increase the Value of Real Estate, 1986, Office Building Acquisition Handbook, 1982, 85, 87, Residential Property Acquisition Handbook, 1991, How To Buy Real Estate for at Least 20% Below Market Value, 1993, 2d edit., 1996; Coaching Youth Football Defense, 1994, 2d edit., 1996; John T. Reed's Real Estate Investor's Monthly Newsletter, 1986—, Coaching Youth Football, 1995, 3d edit., 2000, Football Clock Management, 1997, 2d edit., 2001, Aggressive Tax Avoidance for Real Estate Investors, 17th edit., 2001, Youth Baseball Coaching, 2000, How to Get Started in Real Estate Investment, 2000, Gap-Air-Mirror Defense for Youth Football, 2000, How to Buy Real Estate for Little of No Money Down, 2001. Coach, Youth Flag Football, 1999. 1st lt. U.S. Army, 1968-72, Vietnam. Mem. Nat. Assn. Real Estate Editors, Am. Baseball Coaches Assn., Am. Football Coaches Assn., Nat. Youth Sports Coaches Assn., Nat. Fedn. Interscholastic Coaches Assn., Calif. Coaches Assn., Football Writers Assn., Profl. Football Rschrs. Assn. Avocations: reading, activities with family. Home and Office: 342 Bryan Dr Alamo CA 94507-2858

REED, KENNETH G. petroleum company executive; b. 1917; married. Ed., U. Tex. With Amerada Petroleum Corp., Tulsa, 1948-70, sr. v.p., 1967-70; exec. v.p. internat. operations Amerada Hess Corp., N.Y.C., 1970; pres., chief exec. officer APEXCO, Inc., Tulsa, 1971-77, Natomas Internat. Corp., 1977, also dir.; exec. v.p. energy, dir. Natomas Co., San Francisco, 1977-83, vice chmn., pres., 1983—; pres., dir. Natomas Energy Co., 1979—; chmn., chief exec. officer Overseas Petroleum Ltd., San Francisco, 1984—. Dir. Natomas N.Am. Inc., 1st Nat. Bank & Trust Co., Tulsa, Oneok Inc., Tulsa. Home: 1210 Mission Ridge 3840 Rimrock Rd Billings MT 59102-0100 Office: 3840 Rimrock Rd Apt 1210 Billings MT 59102-0153

REED, RICHARD JOHN, retired meteorology educator; b. Braintree, Mass., June 18, 1922; s. William Amber and Gertrude Helen (Volk) R.; m. Joan Murray, June 10, 1950; children: Ralph Murray, Richard Cobden, Elizabeth Ann. Student, Boston Coll., 1940-41, Dartmouth Coll., 1943-44; BS, Calif. Inst. Tech., 1945; ScD, MIT, 1949. Research staff mem. MIT, Cambridge, 1950-54; asst. prof. dept. atmospheric scis. U. Wash., Seattle, 1954-58, assoc. prof., 1958-63, prof., 1963-91, prof. emeritus, 1991—. Cons. U.S. Weather Service, Suitland, Md., 1961-62, European Ctr. for Medium Range Weather Forecasts, Reading, Eng., 1985-86; exec. scientist NRC, Washington, 1968-69; trustee Univ. Corp. for Atmospheric Research, Boulder, Colo., 1987-92. Served to lt. (j.g.) USN, 1942-46. Fellow AAAS, Am. Meteorol. Soc. (pres. 1972, Meisinger award 1964, Second Half Century award 1972, Charles Franklin Brooks award 1983, Carl-Gustaf Rossby Rsch. medal 1989, hon. mem. 1999), Royal Meteorol. Soc. (hon. mem.), Am. Geophys. Union; mem. NAS. Democrat. Unitarian. Office: U Wash Box 351640 Dept Atmospheric Scis Seattle WA 98195-1640 E-mail: reed@atmos.washington.edu, richardjreed@aol.com

REED, SANDY, former magazine editor; m. Bob Ingle. B Journalism, Kans. State U. Reporting and sr. editing positions San Jose (Calif.) Mercury News, Miami (Fla.) Herald, Billings (Mont.) Gazette, Oakland (Calif.) Tribune; exec. editor news ops. InfoWorld, San Francisco, 1984-90, exec. editor Pers. Computing mag., 1985-90, editor-in-chief, 1990-00, exec. editor PC/Computing, 1991-00. Founding editor Macintosh Bus. Rev.; founding editl. dir. New Media Age mag. (now NewMedia mag). Named one of most influential journalists covering computer industry Mktd. Computers mag. Avocations: surfing the web, reading, travel. Office: Infoworld 155 Bovet Rd Ste 800 San Mateo CA 94402-3150

REED, WALLACE ALLISON, anesthesiologist; b. Covina, Calif., May 19, 1916; s. Wallace Allison and Mary Julia (Birdsall) R.; m. Maria Eva Wiemers, Jan. 20, 1938; children: Ellen E., Barbara R. (Mrs. David Maurice Knize), Wallace J., Michael E., Kathryn L., Vikki T. A.B., UCLA, Los Angeles, 1937; postgrad., U. Cologne, 1937-38; U. Freiburg, Breisgau, 1938-39; M.D., U. So. Calif., 1944. Diplomate: Am. Bd. Anesthesiology. Intern Santa Fe Coast Lines Hosp., Los Angeles, 1943-44; resident Los Angeles County Gen. Hosp., 1946-47, asst. to head dept. anesthesiology, 1946-47; clin. instr. surgery U. So. Calif. Sch. Medicine, 1946-47; practice medicine, specializing in anesthesiology Phoenix, 1948-89. Hon. staff mem. Good Samaritan Hosp., St. Joseph Hosp., Maricopa County Gen. Hosp.; mem. hon. staff Children's Hosp.; co-founder John L. Ford, M.D., Surgicenter, 1970; vice pres. Maricopa Found. for Med. Care, 1970-74, pres., 1975-76; mem. House Ways and Means Adv. Com.; adv. coun. Nat. Health Inst., 1975-76; mem. accreditation coun. for ambulatory health care Joint Commn. on Accreditation of Hosps., 1975-79; vice-chmn. Accreditation Assn. for Ambulatory Health Care, 1979-81, pres., 1981-83; mem. panel for study Nat. Health Ins., Congl. GAO; chmn. bd. Alterna Care Corp., 1984-87, now chmn. bd. emeritus; mem. adv. bd. Kino Inst., 1994-95. Bd. dirs. South Phoenix Montessori Sch., pres. bd., 1971-75, Alzheimer's Assn., Greater Phoenix chpt. 1998-2000, co-v.p. 2000; bd. dirs. Ctrl. Ariz. Health Sys. Agy., 1975-78; exec. dir. Surgictr. of Phoenix, 1987-97. Capt. M.C., AUS, 1944-46. Recipient Pinal award Ariz. Psychiat. Soc., 1967-68, Gerard B. Lambert Merit award for innovative ideas that improve patient care; John L. Ford M.D., 1972; recipient spirit of philanthropy award Alzheimer's Assn., 1996, Samba Disting. Svc. award, 2000. Fellow Am. Coll. Anesthesiologists; mem. Am. Soc. Anesthesiologists, Ariz., Maricopa County socs. anesthesiologists, AMA, Acad. Anesthesiology (pres. 1969, dir. 1966-72), Federated Amb. Surgery Assn. (pres. 1974-75, dir.), Soc. for Ambulatory Anesthesia (bd. dirs. 1985-87), Ariz. Med. Assn. (dir. 1972-78), Maricopa County Med. Soc. (pres. 1964, dir., Salsbury medal 1967, 71, Thomas Dooley medal 1970), Central Ariz. Physicians Service Assn. (pres. 1982-83), Am. Assn. Founds. for Med. Care (dir. 1970-74), Guedel Assn. (pres. 1972), Seed Money for Growth Found. (pres. 1984—), Internat. Assn. for Amb. Surgery (hon.), mem. Warmer Rsch. Found. (1992—). Methodist. Home: 4716 N Dromedary Rd Phoenix AZ 85018-2939 Office: 1040 E Mcdowell Rd Phoenix AZ 85006-2622 E-mail: somnus4@home.com

REEDER, CLINTON BRUCE, economist, public policy consultant, farmer; b. Pendleton, Oreg., Apr. 22, 1939; s. O. Howard and Rachel B. (Porter) R.; n. Karen J. Durham, June 19, 1960; childre: Jeffrey T., Lori J., Paul D. BS, Oreg. State U., 1961, MS, 1963; PhD, Purdue U., 1966; postgrad., U. Oreg. Instr. agrl. econs. Purdue U., West Lafayette, 1963-66; contract mgmt. trainer Nat. Food Mfg. Corp., 1972-78; farmer Pendleton, Oreg., 1978—; mgmt. cons., 1968-2001; mktg. economist, bus. mgmt. specialist Dept. Agrl., Econs. & Extension Svc, Oreg. State U., Corvallis, 1966-78; econ. & pub. policy cons. Clinton B. Reeder & Assocs., 1968—; dir. Northwest Wheat Policy Project, 1992—, WestFork Natural Resources Rsch. Ctr., 1995—. Ombudsman Oreg. Agrl. Water Quality Mgmt. Program, 2000. Recipient Disting. Svc. award Oreg. Wheat Growers League, 1998, County Points of Light award Nat. Assn. Counties, 1992, Voice of Industry award, 1989, OFS Unity award, 1988; inducted into Hall of Fame, Coll. Agr., Oreg. State U., 1998. Republican. Avocations: reading, public service, writing, research. Home and Office: 47647 Reeder Rd Pendleton OR 97801-9226

REEDER, F. ROBERT, lawyer; b. Brigham City, Utah, Jan. 23, 1943; s. Frank O. and Helen H. (Heninger) R.; m. Joannie Anderson, May 4, 1974; children: David, Kristina, Adam. JD, U. Utah, 1967. Bar: Utah 1967, U.S. Ct. Appeals (1oth cir.) 1967, U.S. Ct. Appeals (D.C. and 5th cirs.) 1979, U.S. Ct. Mil. Appeals 1968, U.S. Supreme Ct. 1972. Shareholder Parsons, Behle & Latimer, Salt Lake City, 1968—. Bd. dirs. Holy Cross Found., 1981-90, chmn., 1987-90; bd. dirs. Holy Cross Hosp., 1990-93, treas., 1986-87, vice chmn., 1987-93; bd. dirs. Holy Cross Health Svcs. Utah, 1993-94, treas., 1993-94; bd. dirs. Sale Lake Regional Med. Ctr., 1995—, vice chmn., 1995-2000, chmn., 2000—; trustee Univ. Hosp. Found.; hon. col. Sale Lake City Police, Salt Lake County Sheriff. Served with USAF, 1967 73. Mem. ABA, Utah State Bar, Salt Lake County Bar (ethics adv. com. 1989-94), Cottonwood Country Club (bd. dirs. 1978-82, 83-86, pres. 1981-82), Rotary. Office: Parsons Behle & Latimer PO Box 45898 Salt Lake City UT 84145-0898

REED-GRAHAM, LOIS L. administrator, secondary education educator; b. Muscogee, Okla., Jan. 19, 1933; d. Louis G. and Bonnie (Hill) Reed; children: Harold Gibson, Kathryn Ann Graham. RN, San Diego County Hosp., 1957; BA, Calif. State U., Sacramento, 1972, MPA, 1978; postgrad., Calif. State U., Sacremento; EdD, U. Laverne. Tchr., adminstr., job developer CETA, Sacramento, 1972-78; bus. instr. Los Rios Community Coll., Sacramento, 1978-84; tchr. grade 6 Mark Hopkins Sch., Sacramento, 1984-89; acting adminstr. Fern Bacon Sch., Sacramento; adminstr. Sacramento City Schs.; tchr. grades 7,8, mentor tchr. Fern Bacon Sch., Sacramento, asst. prin. secondary edn. Sacramento City Schs., 1989 93; elem. sch. prin. Theodore Judah Elem. Sch., Sacramento, 1993—; asst. supt. secondary, middle and K-8 schs. Sacramento City Unified Sch.; prin. Hubert Bancroft Elem. Sch., Sacramento. Cons. Prentice Hall Pub. Co. Contbr. articles to profl. publs. Mem. Calif. State Fair Employment and Housing Commn. Mem. AAUW (bd. dirs., pres. Sacramento chpt. 1990), Nat. Assn. Univ. Women (pres.) Home: 7408 Toulon Ln Sacramento CA 95828-4641

REES, NORMA S. academic administrator; b. N.Y.C., Dec. 27, 1929; d. Benjamin and Lottie (Schwartz) D.; m. Raymond R. Rees, Mar. 19, 1960; children— Evan Lloyd, Raymond Arthur BA, Queens Coll., 1952; Ma, Bklyn. Coll., 1954; PhD, NYU, 1959; D of Arts and Letters honoris causa, John F. Kennedy U., 2001. Cert. speech-language pathology, audiology. Prof. communicative disorders Hunter Coll., N.Y.C., 1967-72; exec. officer, speech and hearing scis. grad. sch. CUNY, N.Y.C., 1972-74, assoc. dean for grad. studies, 1974-76, dean grad. studies, 1976-82; vice chancellor for acad. affairs U. Wis., Milw., 1982-85, from 1986, acting chancellor, 1985-86; vice chancellor for acad. policy and planning Mass. Bd. Regents for Higher Edn., Boston, 1987-90; pres. Calif. State U., Hayward, 1990—. Chmn. Commn. Recognition of Postsecondary Accreditation, 1994-96; mem. adv. com. quality and integrity U.S. Dept. Edn. Contbr. articles to profl. jours. Trustee Citizens Govtl. Rsch. Bur., Milw., 1985-87; active Task Force on Wis. World Trade Ctr., 1985-87; bd. dirs. Am. Assn. State Colls. and Univs., 1995-97, Coun. of Postsecondary Accreditation, Washington, 1985-94, Greater Boston YWCA, 1987-90; mem. Calif. Sch. to Career Coun.; mem. Oakland Edn. Cabinet; mem. steering com. Econ. Devel. Alliance for Bus., Alameda County, 1995—; mem. Gov.'s Sch. Career Coun., Calif., 1998—; mem., sec. edn. Nat. Adv. Com. Institutional Quality and Integrity, 1998—; bd. dirs. Bay Area World Trade Ctr., 2001—. Fellow Am. Speech-Lang-Hearing Assn. (honors); mem. Am. Coun. Edn. (com. internat. edn. 1991-93), Am. Assn. Colls. and Univs. (chair task force on quality assessment 1991-92, mem. steering com. of coun. of urban met. colls. & univs. 1992—), Nat. Assn. State Univs. and Land Grant Colls. (exec. com. divsn. urban affairs 1985-87, com. accreditation 1987-90), Hayward C. of C. (bd. dirs. 1995—), Oakland C. of C. (bd. dirs. 1997—). Office: Calif State Univ Hayward 25800 Carlos Bee Blvd Hayward CA 94542-3001 E-mail: nrees@csuhayward.edu

REESE, DELLA (DELOREESE PATRICIA EARLY), singer, actress; b. Detroit, July 6, 1931; d. Richard and Nellie Early; m. Vermont Adolphus Bon Taliaferro (div.); m. Leroy Basil Gray (div.); m. Franklin Thomas Lett, Jr. Student, Wayne U. Ordained to ministry Ch. Understanding Principles for Better Living Inc., April, 1987. Choir singer, 1938—, with Mahalia Jackson troupe, 1945-49, Erskine Hawkins, N.Y.C.; solo artist, 1957—; organized gospel group at Wayne U.; appearances include: (radio shows) with Robert Q. Lewis; (TV shows) Della, 1969, The Voyage of the Yes, 1972, Twice in a Lifetime, 1974, Cop on the Beat, 1975, Chico and the Man, 1974, 76-78, Nightmare in Badham County, 1976 (Emmy nomination), Roots: The Next Generation, 1979, It Takes Two, 1982, Charlie & Co., 1985, 86, The Kid Who Loved Christmas, 1990, The Royal Family, 1991, You Must Remember This, 1992, Touched By an Angel, 1994—, A Match Made in Heaven, 1997, Miracle in the Woods, 1997, Emma's Wish, 1998, The Secret Path, 1999, Having Our Say: The Delany Sisters' First 100 Years, 1999; spl. appearances with Jackie Gleason, Ed Sullivan, McCloud, 1971, Sanford and Son, 1972, Welcome Back, Kotter, 1975, The A-Team, 1983, Night Court, 1984, MacGyver, 1985, Designing Women, 1986, L.A. Law, 1986, Married People, 1990, Dream On, 1990, Picket Fences, 1992, Promised Land, 1996, Anya's Bell, 1999; guest host The Tonight Show; actress (films) Let's Rock, 1958, Psychic Killer, 1975, Harlem Nights, 1989, A Thin Line Between Love and Hate, 1996, (plays) Same Time Next Year, Ain't Misbehavin, Blues in the Night, The Last Minstrel Show; recs. for Jubilee, RCA Victor Records, ABC Paramount Records, Jazz Ala Carte, AIR Co. (Grammy nomination 1987); author: Angels Along the Way, 1997, (voice) Dinosaur, 2000. Voted Most Promising Singer of Yr. 1957; recipient Image awards, 1996, 98-2000, Star on Walk of Fame, 1994. Office: William Morris Agy c/o Norman Brokaw 151 S El Camino Dr Beverly Hills CA 90212-2775

REESE, JOHN ROBERT, lawyer; b. Salt Lake City, Nov. 3, 1939; s. Robert McCann and Glade (Stauffer) R.; m. Francesca Marroquin Gardner, Sept. 5, 1964 (div.); children— Jennifer Marie, Justine Francesca; m. Robin Ann Gunsul, June 18, 1988. AB cum laude, Harvard U., 1962; LLB, Stanford U., 1965. Bar: Calif. 1966, U.S. Dist. Ct. (no. dist.) Calif. 1966, U.S. Ct. Appeals (9th cir.) 1966, U.S. Dist. Ct. (cen. dist.) Calif. 1974, U.S. Supreme Ct. 1976, U.S. Dist. Ct. (ea. dist.) Calif. 1977, U.S. Ct. Appeals (6th cir.) 1982, U.S. Ct. Appeals (8th cir.) 1985, U.S. Ct. Appeals (10th cir.) 1992, U.S. Ct. Appeals (Fed. cir.) 1994. Assoc. McCutchen, Doyle, Brown & Enersen, San Francisco, 1965-74, ptnr., 1974—. Adj. asst. prof. law Hastings Coll. of Law, 1991; lectr. U. Calif., Berkeley, 1987, 92. Mem. editorial, adv. bds. Antitrust Bull., Jour. Reprints for Antitrust Law and Econs. Bd. dirs. Friends of San Francisco Pub. Libr., 1981-87; bd. vis. Stanford U. Law Sch., 1983-86. Capt. U.S. Army, 1966-68 Decorated Bronze Star Mem. ABA, State Bar Calif., San Francisco Bar Assn., U.S. Supreme Ct. Hist. Soc., Ninth Jud. Cir. Hist. Soc., Calif. Acad. Appellate Lawyers, Order of the Coif. Avocations: aviculture, gardening. Home: 9 Morning Sun Dr Petaluma CA 94952-4780 Office: McCutchen Doyle Brown & Enersen 3 Embarcadero Ctr San Francisco CA 94111-4003

REESE, MONTE NELSON, agricultural association executive; b. Mooreland, Okla., Mar. 31, 1947; s. James Nelson and Ruby Edith (Bond) R.; m. Treisa Lou Bartow, May 25, 1968; children: Bartow Allan, Monica Lynnelle. BS in Agrl. Econs., Okla. State U., 1969. Staff asst. Wilson Cert. Foods, Oklahoma City, 1969-71; assoc. farm dir. Sta. WKY Radio and TV, Oklahoma City, 1971-73; radio-TV specialist Tex. A&M U., College Station, 1973; dir. agrl. devel. Oklahoma City C. of C., 1973-76; asst. exec. dir. Am. Morgan Horse Assn., Westmoreland, N.Y., 1976-77; v.p. pub. affairs Farm Credit Banks of Wichita, Kans., 1977-87; exec. dir. Coffey County Econ. Devel., Burlington, 1987-88; farm dir. Mid-Am. Ag Network, Wichita, 1988-89; CEO Cattlemen's Beef Promotion and Rsch. Bd., Englewood, Colo., 1989-96; exec. dir. Cattlemen's Beef Promotion & Rsch. Bd., Englewood, CO, 1996-98, COO, 1998—. Lt. col. USAR, 1969—. Office: Cattlemens Beef Promotion Rsch Bd 5520 S Quebec Englewood CO 80111

REEVES, BARBARA ANN, lawyer; b. Buffalo, Mar. 29, 1949; d. Prentice W. and Doris Reeves; m. Richard C. Neal; children: Timothy R. Neal, Stephen S. Neal (dec.), Robert S. Neal, Richard R. Neal. Student, Wellesley Coll., 1967-68; B.A. (NSF fellow, Lehman fellow), New Coll., Sarasota, Fla., 1970; J.D. cum laude, Harvard U., 1973. Bar: Calif. 1973, D.C. 1977. Law clk. U.S. Ct. Appeals, 9th Circuit, Portland, Oreg., 1973-74; assoc. firm Munger, Tolles and Rickershauser, L.A., 1977-78; trial atty. spl. trial sect. Dept. Justice (Antitrust div.), 1974-75; spl. asst. to asst. atty. gen. Antitrust div. Dept. Justice, Washington, 1976-77; chief antitrust div. L.A. field office, 1978-81; ptnr. Morrison & Foerster, L.A., 1981-94, Fried, Frank, Harris, Shriver & Jacobson, L.A., 1995-97, Paul, Hastings, Janofsky & Walker, L.A., 1997—. Mem. exec. com. state bar conf. of dels. L.A. Delegation, 1982-91; del. 9th Cir. Jud. Conf., 1984-88; mem. Fed. Ct. Magistrate Selection Com., 1989; bd. dirs. Pub. Counsel, 1988-92, Western Ctr. Law and Poverty, 1992-98; lectr. in field. Editor: Federal Criminal Litigation, 1994; contbg. author: World Antitrust Law, 1995; contbr. articles to profl. jours. Mem. ABA (litigation sect., antitrust sect.), Fed. Bar Assn. (officer 1998—), Assn. Bus. Trial Lawyers (officer 1997—), Am. Arbitration Assn. (arbitrator, mediator, mem. adv. panel large complex case program), L.A. County Bar Assn. (antitrust sect. officer 1980-81, litigation sect. officer 1988-93 trustee 1990-92, chair alternative dispute resolution sec. 1992-95, L.A. County Ct. ADR com.). Home: 1410 Hillcrest Ave Pasadena CA 91106-4503 Office: Paul Hastings Janofsky & Walker 555 S Flower St Fl 23D Los Angeles CA 90071-2300

REEVES, JAMES N. lawyer; b. Albert Lea, Minn., Oct. 14, 1945; AB, Dartmouth Coll., 1967; student, George Washington U.; JD, U. Minn., 1970. Bar: Minn. 1970, Alaska 1972, U.S. Ct. Appeals (9th cir.), U.S. Supreme Ct. Law clk. U.S. Dist. Ct. Minn., 1970-71; asst. atty. gen. State of Alaska, 1971-78; mem. Bogle & Gates (name now Dorsey & Whitney), Anchorage. Sr. fellow East-West Ctr., Honolulu, 1977. Mem. ABA, Alaska Bar Assn. Office: Dorsey & Whitney 1031 W 4th Ave Ste 600 Anchorage AK 99501-5907

REEVES, PEGGY, state legislator; b. Macon, Feb. 20, 1941; m. F. Brent Reeves. BS, Dominican Coll., 1963. Neurophysiology rsch. technician, 1963-64; sci. tchr., 1964-65; sales and broker-assoc. Bartran Homes, 1978-80; broker-assoc. Wheeler Realty, 1983—; mem. Colo. Ho. of Reps., Denver, 1982-84, 87-96, Colo. Senate, Dist. 14, Denver, 1996—; mem. appropriations com., mem. legis. audit com.; mem. health, environment, welfare and instns. com.; mem. local govt. com. Mem. Ft. Collins City Coun., 1973-77, 79-82, Ft. Collins Water Bd., 1977-79; mem. Women's Econ. Devel. Coun., 1988X; mem. One West Art Ctr., Ft. Collins Cmty. Found., Alliance for Children with Disabilities; mem. adv. bd. Colo. Mcpl. Bond Supervision, Vet. Medicine. Mem. AAUW, Colo. State U. Women's Assn., Nat. Assn. Realtors, Colo. Assn. Realtors, Ft. Collins Bd. Realtors. Office: State Capitol 200 E Colfax Ave Ste 274 Denver CO 80203-1716

REFO, PATRICIA LEE, lawyer; b. Alexandria, Va., Dec. 31, 1958; BA with high honors and high distinction, U. Mich., 1980, JD cum laude, 1983. Bar: Ill. 1983, Ariz. 1996, U.S. Dist. Ct. (no. dist.) Ill. 1988, U.S. Ct. Appeals (7th cir.) 1989, U.S. Ct. Appeals (11th cir.) 1990, U.S. Ct. Appeals (5th cir.) 1992, U.S. Ct. Appeals (9th cir.) 1998, Fed. Trial Bar (no. dist.) Ill. 1993, U.S. Dist. Ct. Ariz. 1996. Ptnr. Jenner & Block, Chgo., 1991-96, Snell & Wilmer L.L.P., Phoenix, 1996—. Mem. evidence rules adv. com., U.S. Jus. Conf. 2000—; mem. faculty Nat. Inst. Trial Advocacy, 1989—; bd. advisors Comml. Lending Liability News; lectr. ALI/ABA and Practicing Law Inst. on Various subjects including trial advocacy and lender liability [illegible] of the Class, IICLE Class Actions Handbook, 1986, Closing Argument: A String of Pearls, Litigation, 1998. Dir. Ariz. Found. for Women, 1999—, Ariz. Acad. Decathlon Assn., 1998—, Legal Clinic for the Disabled, 1994-96, Chgo. Lawyers' Com. Civil Rights Under Law, 1987-91, Cabrini Green Legal Aid Clinic, 1987-91. Mem. ABA (chair sect. litigation 1990 annual meeting, co-chair sect. litigation Pro Bono com. 1990-93, dir. divsns. sect. litigation 1993-94, sec. sect. litigation 1994-98, mem. Ho. of Dels. 1998—). Office: Snell & Wilmer LLP One Arizona Ctr Phoenix AZ 85004-2202

REGALA, DEBBIE, state senator; b. Tacoma, Apr. 27, 1945; m. Leo Regala; children: Alisa, Tim, Jonathan. BA in Fgn. Lang., Edn., U. Puget Sound. Dem. rep. dist. 27 Wash. Ho. of Reps., 1994-2000; Dem. senator dist. 27 Wash. State Senate, 2000—. Mem. edn., labor, commerce and fin. instns. and ways and means coms. Wash. State Senate, vice chair environ., energy and water com.; mem. Joint Legis. Audit and Review Com. Mem. bd. dirs. Nature Conservancy, Point Defiance Zool. Soc.; mem. exec. com. Wash. Cmty. Forestry Coun., Puyallup River Watershed Coun.; parent vol. McCarver Elem.; mem. activities coun. Tacoma Art Mus., docent; lector St. Patrick's Cath. Ch., mem. Parish Coun. Marriage Preparation Team; work site supr. 4 environ. restoration projects; commr. Met. Pk. Sits. Tacoma, 1986-92, pres., 1989, 91. Office: PO Box 40427 405 John A Cherberg Bldg Olympia WA 98504-0427 Fax: 360 786-1999. E-mail: regala_de@leg.wa.gov

REGAN, MURIEL, librarian; b. N.Y.C., July 15, 1930; d. William and Matilda (Riebel) Blome; m. Robert Regan, 1966 (div. 1976); 1 child, Jeanne Booth. BA, Hunter Coll., N.Y.C., 1950; MLS, Columbia U., 1952; MBA, Pace U., N.Y.C., 1982. Post libr. US Army, Okinawa, 1952-53; researcher P.F. Collier, N.Y.C., 1953-57; asst. libr. to libr. Rockefeller Found., N.Y.C., 1957-67; dep. chief libr. Manhattan Community Coll., N.Y.C., 1967-68; libr. Booz Allen & Hamilton, N.Y.C., 1968-69, Rockefeller Found., N.Y.C., 1969-82; prin. Gossage Regan Assocs., Inc., N.Y.C., 1980-95; pub. svcs. libr. Carlsbad (N.Mex.) Pub. Libr., 1995-2000. Dir. N.Y. Met. Reference and Rsch. Libr. Agy., 1988-95, Coun. Nat. Libr. and Info. Assns., 1991-95; cons. Librs. Info. Ctrs., Gossage Sager Assocs., 2001—. Elder First Presbyn. Ch. of Carlsbad, 1997-99, Stephan min., 2000—. Mem. ALA, Spl. Librs. Assn. pres. 1989-90), Archons of Colophon, Altrusa. Avocations: cats, reading, playing piano, traveling. Home: 604 N Lake St Carlsbad NM 88220-5014 E-mail: murielregan@hotmail.com

REGAN, WILLIAM JOSEPH, JR. energy company executive; b. Bronx, N.Y., Mar. 7, 1946; s. William Joseph and Eleanor F. (Malone) R.; m. Mary Lee Wynn; children— Katrina Lee, Thomas Wynn, James William B.S., U.S. Air Force Acad., 1967; M.B.A., U. Wis.-Madison, 1969, Ph.D., 1972. Asst. prof. Wayne State U., Detroit, 1971-75; with Nat. Bank Detroit, 1975-77; sr. bus. planner Am. Natural Resources Co., Detroit, 1977-78, dir. fin. planning, 1978-82, v.p., treas., 1982-85; v.p. corp. fin. United Svcs. Automobile Assn., San Antonio, 1986-88, sr. v.p., treas., 1988-95; v.p., treas. Entergy Corp., New Orleans, 1995-99; CFO Calif. Ind. Sys. Operator Corp., Folsom, Calif., 1999—. Home: 15181 De La Pena Cir Rncho Murieta CA 95683-9798 Office: 151 Blue Ravine Rd Folsom CA 95630 E-mail: wregan@calweb.com, wregan37@earthlink.net

REGGIO, GODFREY, film director; b. New Orleans, 1940; Pres. St. Petersburg Film Festival, 2000. Dir. (films) Koyaanisqatsi, 1983, Powaqqatsi, 1988 (Best Film, Sao Paolo Film festival), Anima Mundi, 1992, Evidence, 1995. Mem. Christian Bros., 1954-68; founder Inst. for Regional Edn., Santa Fe, N.Mex., 1972. Home: care Inst for Regional Edn PO Box 2404 Santa Fe NM 87504-2404

REGINALD, ROBERT, administrator, writer, university librarian; b. Fukuoka, Kyushu, Japan, Feb. 11, 1948; came to U.S., 1949; s. Roy Walter and Betty Jane (Kapel) Burgess; m. Mary Alice Wickizer, Oct. 15, 1976; step children: Richard Albert Rogers, (Mary) Louise Reynnells. AB (honors) cum laude, Gonzaga U., 1969; MS in Libr. Sci., U. So. Calif., L.A., 1970. Periodicals libr. Calif. State U., San Bernardino, 1970-78, 80-81, asst. bibliographer, 1976-83, chief cataloger with rank of prof., 1984-1994, head tech. services and collection development, 1994—; editor Newcastle Pub. Co., North Hollywood, Calif., 1970-94; pub. The Borgo Press, San Bernardino, 1975-99; owner Millefleurs Info. Svcs., 2000—. As author, editor or pub. directly or indirectly involved in publ. over 1200 vols.; author 92 books including: Contemporary Science Fiction Authors, 1975, Science Fiction and Fanatasy Literature, 2 vols., 1979 (Book of Yr. Choice mag. 1980), Science Fiction and Fantasy Awards, 1981, (with Jeffrey M. Elliot) If J.F.K. Had Lived, 1982, (with Kevin Hancer) The Paperback Price Guide No. 2, 1982, (with T.E. Dikty) The Work of Julian May, 1985, (with J. Elliot) The Work of George Zebrowski, 1986, (with J. Elliot and Mary Burgess) The Arms Control, Disarmament and Military Security Dictionary, 1989; outside reader: Anatomy of Wonder, 1981, Horror Literature: A Critical Guide, 1989, Fantasy Literature: A Critical Guide, 1989; adv. editor (with others) Science Fiction, 62 books, 1975, Supernatural & Occult Fiction, 63 books, 1976, Lost Race and Adult Fantasy Fiction, 69 books, 1978, others; pub., co-editor: Science Fiction & Fantasy Book Rev., 12 nos., 1979-80; cons. editor: Survey of Modern Fantasy Literature, 5 vols., 1983; editor LTF Newletter, Calif. Faculty Assn., 1987-89, also numerous monographic series; author numerous articles, revs., pubs.' catalogues, state documents; designer, prodn. mgr. over 100 pub. vols. Recipient Meritorious Performance and Profl. Promise award Calif. State U., San Bernardino, 1987; U. So. Calif., fellow, 1969-70. Mem. AAUP, NEA, Calif. Tchrs. Assn., Calif. Faculty Assn. (libr. task force 1987-91, 94—), Sci. Fiction Writers Am., Horror Writers Am., Mystery Writers Am., Sci. Fiction Rsch. Assn., Ky. Hist. Soc., Blue Earth County Hist. Soc., Upper Cumberland Valley Hist. Soc., Geneal. Soc., Internat PEN West. Democrat. Avocations: genealogical and historical research, films, travel. Office: Millefleurs PO Box 2845 San Bernardino CA 92406-2845 also: Calif State Univ Pfau Libr 5500 University Pkwy San Bernardino CA 92407-2318

REGNIER, JAMES, state supreme court justice; b. Aurora, Ill. m. Linda Regnier; 3 children. BS, Marquette U., 1966; JD, U. Ill., 1973. Judicial Fellow ACTL, Internat. Soc. Barristers; completed atty. mediator tng., Atty.-Mediator Tng. Inst., Dallas, 1993. Lawyer pvt. practice, Rochelle, Ill., 1973-78; co-founder, ptnr. Regnier, Lewis and Boland, Great Falls, Mont., 1979-91; lawyer pvt. practice, Missoula, 1991-97; justice Mont. Supreme Ct., Helena, 1997—. Appt. Mont. Supreme Ct. Commn. on Civil Jury Instrn.; appt. lawyer-rep. to 9th Cir. Judicial Confs., 1987, 88, 89, chair Mont. lawyer delegation, 1989; lectr. U. Mont. Sch. Law, numerous continuing legal edn. seminars. Contbr. Mont. Pattern Jury Instrns. for Civil Cases, 1985. Co-founder Mont. chpt. Am. Bd. Trial Advocates, 1989—, pres. Officer USN, Vietnam. Office: Montana Supreme Ct Justice Bldg 215 N Sanders St Helena MT 59601-4522

REHBERG, DENNIS R. congressman; b. Billings, Mont., Oct. 5, 1955; m. Janice; 1 child. Student, Mont. State U., Wash. State U. Rancher and businessman; legis. aide, 1977; fin. dir. Congl. Campaigns, 1980-82; Mont. state rep. Dist. 88, 1985-89; lt. gov. Mont., 1991-96; mem. U.S. Congress from Mont. at large, Washington, 2001—; mem. agr. com., resources com., transp. and infrastructure com. Office: US Ho Reps 516 Cannon Ho Office Bldg Washington DC 20515*

REHMUS, CHARLES MARTIN, law educator, arbitrator; b. Ann Arbor, Mich., June [illegible], 1926, s. Paul A. and Amy B. (Martin) R., m. Carolyn Brown, Dec. 21, 1948 (div. July 1982); children— Paul, James, Jon, David; m. Laura Carlson, Sept. 4, 1982 AB, Kenyon Coll., 1947; MA, Stanford U., 1951, PhD, 1955. Commr. Fed. Mediation and Conciliation Service, San Francisco, 1952-58; staff dir. Presdl. R.R. Commn., Washington, 1959-61; prof. polit. sci. U. Mich. Ann Arbor, 1962-80, dir. Inst. Labor and Indsl. Relations, 1962-76; chmn. Mich. Employment Relations Commn., Detroit, 1976-80; dean N.Y. State Sch. Indsl. and Labor Relations, Cornell U., Ithaca, 1980-86; prof. law U. San Diego, 1988-97. Author: Final-Offer Arbitration, 1975, The Railway Labor Act at Fifty, 1977, Labor and American Politics, 1967, rev. edit., 1978, The National Mediation Board, 1984, Emergency Strikes Revisited, 1990. Chmn. 4 Presdl. emergency bds. at various times. Served to lt. USNR, 1943-45; PTO Mem. Internat. Inst. Labor Studies (bd. govs. 1984-92), Indsl. Rels. Rsch. Assn. (exec. bd. 1984-88), Nat. Acad. Arbitrators (bd. govs. 1979-82, v.p. 1993-95).

REHORN, LOIS M(ARIE), nursing administrator; b. Larned, Kans., Apr. 15, 1919; d. Charles and Ethel L. (Canaday) Williamson; m. C. Howard Smith, Feb. 15, 1946 (dec. Aug. 1980); 1 child, Cynthia A. Huddleston; m. Harlan W. Rehorn, Aug. 25, 1981. RN, Bethany Hosp. Sch. Nursing, Kansas City, Kans., 1943; BS, Ft. Hays Kans. State U., Hays, 1968, MS, 1970. RN, N.Mex.; lic. pvt. pilot. Office nurse, surg. asst. Dr. John H. Luke, Kansas City, Kans., 1943-47; supr. nursing unit Larned (Kans.) State Hosp., 1949-68, dir. nursing edn., 1968-71, dir. nursing, 1972-81, ret., 1981. Recipient Order of the Blue Key, 1942-43; named Nurse of Yr. DNA-4, 1986. Mem. Am. Nurses Assn., Kans. Nurses Assn. (dist. treas.), N.Mex. Nurses Assn. (dist. pres. 1982-86, dist. bd. dirs. 1986-88). Avocation: flying (pilot). Home: 1436 Brentwood Dr Clovis NM 88101-4602

REIBER, GREGORY DUANE, forensic pathologist; b. Loma Linda, Calif., May 25, 1955; s. Clifford D. and Anna M. (Field) R.; m. Faustina Mae Davis, Feb. 10, 1980; children: Jenessa Anne, Zachary Duane. BS magna cum laude, Andrews U., Berrien Springs, Mich., 1977; MD, Loma Linda (Calif.) U., 1981. Diplomate Am. Bd. Pathology. Resident in pathology Loma Linda U. Med. Ctr., 1981-85; fellow in forensic pathology Root Pathology Lab., San Bernardino, Calif., 1985-86, assoc. pathologist, 1986-90, No. Calif. Forensic Pathology, Sacramento, 1990—. Asst. clin. prof. pathology Loma Linda U. Sch. Medicine, 1987-90, U. Calif., Davis, 1990—; program dir., forensic pathology fellowship NCFP/U. Calif. Davis, 1994—; apptd. Calif. SIDS Autopsy Protocol Com. Contbr. articles to profl. jours. Fellow Am. Soc. Clin. Pathologists, Am. Coll. Forensic Examiners; mem. Am. Bd. Forensic Examiners, AMA, Internat. Wound Ballistics Assn., Nat. Assn. Med. Examiners, Am. Acad. Forensic Scis., Calif. Med. Assn., Sacramento-El Dorado Med. Soc., Alpha Omega Alpha. Republican. Seventh-day Adventist. Avocations: early music, biking, photography, tropical fish. Office: No Calif Forensic Pathology 2443 Fair Oaks Blvd Ste 311 Sacramento CA 95825-7684

REICH, KENNETH IRVIN, journalist; b. Los Angeles, Mar. 7, 1938; s. Herman and Ruth Alberta (Nussbaum) R.; children: Kathleen, David. B.A., Dartmouth Coll., 1960; M.A. (Woodrow Wilson fellow), U. Calif., Berkeley, 1962. With UPI, Sacramento, 1962-63, Life mag., 1963-65; with Los Angeles Times, 1965—, polit. writer, 1972-77, 1984 Olympics writer, 1977-84, investigative reporter ins. law, ins. politics & fin. sports, 1985-92. Covering earthquakes, volcanoes, and other issues relating to geology, 1987—; columnist of consumer affairs, 1998-2001; lectr. in field. Author: Making it Happen, Peter Ueberroth and the 1984 Olympics, 1985; contbr. articles to mags. Meml. chmn. Dartmouth Class of 1960, 1993-95, class sec. 1995—. Daniel Webster Nat. Honor scholar Dartmouth Coll., 1956-60 Office: Times Mirror Sq Los Angeles CA 90053 E-mail: ken.reich@latimes.com

REICHARDT, PAUL BERNARD, provost, chemistry educator; b. St. Louis, Aug. 15, 1943; s. Bernard George and Elaine Charlotte (Schmudde) R.; m. Cordelia Morris Hufnagel, Apr. 27, 1968; children: Laura, Rebecca, Daniel. BS, Davidson Coll., 1965; PhD in Organic Chemistry, U. Wis., 1969. Post-doctoral rsch. assoc. Yale U., New Haven, 1969-71, instr., 1971; asst. prof. Ohio State U., Columbus, 1971-72; asst. prof. chemistry U. Alaska, Fairbanks, 1972-75, assoc. prof. chemistry, 1975-81, prof. chemistry, 1981—, dean coll. natural scis., 1991-96, dean coll. sci., engrng. & math., 1996-98, provost, 1998—. Head dept. chemistry U. Alaska, Fairbanks, 1978-82, 88-90, interim dean coll. natural scis., 1990-91, interim provost, 1993-94; interim dir. U. Alaska Mus., 1992-93; mem. Gov.'s Sci. & Engring. Adv. Com., 1986-90, Alaska 2000 Sci. Standards Com., 1992-93. Contbr. articles to profl. jours., chpts. to books and monographs. Named one of Outstanding Young Men of Am., Jaycees, 1980; recipient Inspirational Tchr. award U. Alaska at Fairbanks Alumni Assn., 1982. Mem. AAAS, Am. Chem. Soc., Phi Beta Kappa, Sigma Xi (pres. local chpt. 1994-95), Phi Kappa Phi. Presbyterian. Avocations: fishing, camping, hiking. Office: U Alaska Office Provost Signers Hall Fairbanks AK 99775-7580 E-mail: fnpbr@uaf.edu

REID, BELMONT MERVYN, brokerage house executive; b. San Jose, Calif., May 17, 1927; s. C. Belmont and Mary Irene (Kilfoyl) R. BS in Engring., San Jose State U., 1950, postgrad.; m. Evangeline Joan Rogers, June 1, 1952. Pres., Lifetime Realty Corp., San Jose, 1969-77, Lifetime Fin. Planning Corp., San Jose, 1967-77; founder, chmn. bd. Belmont Reid & Co., Inc., San Jose, 1960-77; pres., registered investment advisor JOBEL Fin. Inc., Carson City, Nev., 1980—; pres., chmn. bd. Data-West Systems, Inc., 1984-85. County chmn. 1982-85, Carson City Rep. Cen. Com., treas., 1979-81; chmn. Carson City Debt. Mgmt. Commn., 1986-99; rural county chmn. Nev. Rep. Cen. Com., 1984-88; mem. Carson City Charter Rev. Com., 1986-91, chmn., 1988-91; bd. dirs. Carson City Coun. No. 347, Navy League of U.S., 1987—. With USN, 1945-46, 51-55. Decorated Air medals. Mem. Nat. Assn. Securities Dealers, Mcpl. Securities Rulemaking Bd., Carson City C. of C. (pres. 1986-87, bd. dir. 1982-88), Capital Club of Carson City, Rotary (chpt. sec. 1983-84, 86-87, pres. 1988-89, Paul Harris fellow). Home: 610 Bonanza Dr Carson City NV 89706 Office: 711 E Washington St Carson City NV 89701-4063

REID, FRANCES EVELYN KROLL, cinematographer, director, film company executive; b. Oakland, Calif., Mar. 25, 1944; d. William Farnham and Marion Storm (Teller) Kroll. BA, U. Oreg., 1966. Tchr. secondary sch., Los Angeles, 1968-69; sound recordist Churchill Films, Los Angeles, 1971; freelance sound recordist Los Angeles, 1972-75; freelance producer, dir. Los Angeles, 1975-78; freelance cinematographer Berkeley, Calif., 1978—; pres. Iris Films, Berkeley, 1977—. Vol. Peace Corps, Malawi, Africa, 1969-70. Producer/dir. Long Night's Journey Into Day, 2000 (Grand Jury award Sundance 2000); dir. (film) In The Best Interests of the Children, 1977 (Blue Ribbon Am. Film Festival 1978), The Changer: A Record of the Times, 1991, Skin Deep, 1995, Talking About Race, 1994, Straight from the Heart, 1994 (Acad. award nominee 1995); cinematographer: (film) The Times of Harvey Milk, 1984 (Oscar 1985), Living with AIDS, 1986 (Student Acad. award 1987), Common Threads: Stories from the Quilt, 1989 (Oscar award 1990), Complaints of a Dutiful Daughter, 1994 (Acad. award nominee 1995). Mem. Film Arts Found., Assn. Ind. Video and Filmmakers, Acad. Motion Picture Arts and Scis. Office: Iris Films 2600 10th St # 413 Berkeley CA 94710-2522

REID, HARRY, senator; b. Searchlight, Nev., Dec. 2, 1939; s. Harry and Inez Reid; m. Landra Joy Gould; children— Lana, Rory, Leif, Josh, Key AS, Southern Utah State U., 1959; LLD (hon.), U. So. Utah, 1984; BA, Utah State U., 1961; JD, George Washington U., 1964. Senator from Nev. U.S. Senate, Washington, asst. dem. leader. Mem. appropriations, [illegible] environ. pub. works.

REID, ROBERT TILDEN, medical association administrator, internist; b. Dallas, Feb. 20, 1931; s. Robert Tilden and Gldays Tressy (King) R.; divorced; children: Robert Tilden, Richard Thomas, Annette Marie, Randolph Young. BS, So. Meth. U., Dallas, 1957; MD, U. Tex.-Southwestern, Dallas, 1959. Diplomate Am. Bd. Internal Medicine, Am. Bd. Rheumatology, Am. Bd. Allergy and Immunology. Intern Parkland Meml. Hosp., Dallas, [illegible]

Jollla, Calif., 1963-70; pvt. practice La Jollla, 1970—; chief staff Scripps Meml. Hosp., La Jollla, 1976-78; scientific dir. Erik and Ese Banck Clinical Rsch. Ctr., San Diego, 1994—. Mem. San Diego County Med. Soc. (pres. 1991), Calif. Med. Assn. (trustee 1992-95). Office: Erik & Ese Banck Clinical Rsch 12395 El Camino Real Ste 117 San Diego CA 92130-3083 Address: 9850 Genebee Ave La Jolla CA 92037

REID, RORY, political organization administrator; Sr. v.p., gen. counsel Lady Luck Gaming Corp., Nev.; state chmn. Nev. Dem. Party, 1999—. Mem. Dem. Nat. Com. 1999—. Office: Nev Dem Party 1785 E Sahara Ave Ste 496 Las Vegas NV 89104-3712 also: 3790 Paradise Rd Ste 130 Las Vegas NV 89109-4648

REID, TIM, actor, producer; b. Norfolk, Va., Dec. 19, 1944; s. William Lee and Augustine (Wilkins) R.; m. Daphne Maxwell, 1982; children: Tim II, Tori LeAnn, Christopher Tubbs. BBA in Bus. and Mktg., Norfolk State Coll., 1968. Sales rep. DuPont Corp., 1968-71; comedian Chgo., 1971-75; founder Imagequest, Timalove Enterprises, 1979; co-founder New Millennium Studios, 1997. Appeared in numerous TV programs, including Easy Does It, 1976, The Marily McCoo and Billy Davis, Jr. Show, 1977, The Richard Pryor Show, 1977, WKRP in Cincinnati, 1977, Simon and Simon, 1982-83, Teachers Only, 1983, CBS Summer Playhouse, 1987, Frank's Place, 1987-88 (Critics Choice award, Image award, Best Actor award Viewers for Quality TV), Snoops, 1989, Sister, Sister, 1994-98, Linc's, 1999-2000, also various TV spls., episodes, in films Uptown Saturday Night, 1984, Mother, Jugs, and Speed, 1976, Dead Bang, 1989, The Fourth War, 1990, Color Adjustment, 1991, The Union, Out-of-Sync, 1995, Simon & Simon: In Trouble Again, 1995, Intimate Portrait: Pam Grier, 1999, Intimate Portrait: Loni Anderson, 1999, Alley Cats Strike, 2000; exec. prodr. Frank's Place, 1987-88, The Snoops, 1989; creator, prodr. The Tim and Daphne Show, 1991; writer (TV) WKRP in Cincinnati, 1978-82; author (poems) As I Feel It, 1982. Organizer, sponsor Ann. Tim Reid Celebrity Weekend; bd. dirs. Nat. Acad. Cable Programming. Recipient Emmy award nomination, 1988; named to Nat. Black Coll. Alumni Hall of Fame, 1991. Mem. SAG, AFTRA, NAACP (life, Best Actor award), Writers Guild Am. Office: Met Talent 4526 Wilshire Blvd Los Angeles CA 90010-3801 E-mail: timr@nmstudios.com

REID-BILLS, MAE, magazine editor, historian; b. Shreveport, La. d. Dayton Taylor and Bessie Oline (Boles) Reid; m. Frederick Gurdon Bills (div.); children: Marjorie Reid, Nancy Hawkins, Frederick Taylor, Virginia Thomas, Elizabeth Sharples. AB, Stanford U., 1942, MA, 1965; PhD, U Denver, 1977. Mng. editor Am. West mag., Tucson, 1979-89, cons. editor, 1989—. Gen. Electric fellow, 1963; William Robertson Coe fellow, 1964. Mem. Orgn. Am. Historians, Am. Hist. Assn., Phi Beta Kappa, Pi Alpha Delta.

REIDY, MIKE, food products executive; CFO LePrino Foods, Denver. Office: LePrino Foods 1830 W 38th Ave Denver CO 80211-2200

REIDY, RICHARD ROBERT, publishing company executive; b. Patchogue, N.Y., May 9, 1947; s. Joseph Robert and Irene (Jennings) R.; m. Carolyn Alyce Armstrong, Mar. 21, 1970; children: Dawn Patricia, Shawn Patrick, Christopher Keith. Student, Suffolk County Community Coll., 1966-68, L.I. Tech. Sch., 1969-70, Scottsdale Community Coll., 1983-84, 85-86. Lic. real estate agt., Ariz. Restaurant owner Reidy's, Patchogue, 1973-77; design draftsman Sverdrop & Parcel, Tempe, Ariz., 1978-79, Sullivan & Masson, Phoenix, 1979-81; pres. Success Pub. Co., Scottsdale, 1983 90; with U.S. Postal Dept., 1980—. Editor, owner, pub.: Who's Who in Arizona, 1984-85, 89-90, Success Properties LLC, 2000-. Chief Scottsdale YMCA, 1983-84; eucharistic minister St. Daniel the Prophet Cath. Ch., Scottsdale, 1985—; mem. World Wide Marriage Encounter, 1986—; pres. Coronado High Sch. Band Boosters, 1988-89. Mem. Scottsdale C. of C., Phoenix Better Bus. Bur. Office: Success Pub Co PO Box 3431 Scottsdale AZ 85271-3431

REIF, DAVID (FRANK DAVID REIF), artist, educator; b. Cin., Dec. 14, 1941; s. Carl A. and Rachel L. (Clifton) R.; m. Ilona Jekabsons, July 30, 1966; 1 child, Megan Elizabeth. BFA, Art Inst. Chgo., 1968; MFA, Yale U., 1970. Asst. prof. art U. Wyo., Laramie, 1970-74, assoc. prof., 1974-81, prof., 1981—; assoc. prof. U. Mich., Ann Arbor, 1980-81; acting head dept. art U. Wyo., Laramie, 1986-87. Selection cons. Ucross Found. Residency Program, Wyo., 1983—; exhibit juror Artwest Nat., Jackson, Wyo., 1986; panelist Colo. State U., Ft. Collins, 1981; lectr. U. Mich., 1980; apptd. Wyo. Arts Coun., 1993-96; vis. artist lectr. Colo. State U., 1996; vis. artist Colo. State U., Ft. Collins, 1996; 3-D juror, art exhbn. Colo. State Fair, Pueblo, 2001. One-man shows include U. Wyo. Art Mus., 1993, Dorsky Galleries, N.Y.C., 1980, No. Ariz. U., 1977, 87, U. Mich., 1980, 81, One West Ctr. Contemporary Art, Ft. Collins, 1991, West Wyo. C.C., Rock Springs, 1999; exhibited in group shows at First, Second and Third Wyo. Biennial Tour, 1984-88, U.S. Olympics Art Exhbn., L.A., 1984, Miss. Mus. Art and NEA Tour, 1981-83, L.A. Invitational Sculpture Tour Exhbn., 1991-92, Nicolaysen Art Mus., Casper, Wyo., 1994. Apptd. chair Wyo. Arts Coun., 1995-96. With USAR, 1963-69. Recipient F.D. Pardee award Yale U., 1970; Best Sculpture award Joslyn Art Mus. Omaha, 1978; grantee Nat. Endowment Arts, 1978-79, Wyo. Basic Rsch., 1983-84, 86-87; Tchg. Excellence grantee U. Wyo., 1996-97. Mem. Coll. Art Assn., Internat. Sculpture Ctr. Democrat. Home: 3340 Aspen Ln Laramie WY 82070-5702 Office: U Wyo Dept Art PO Box 3138 Laramie WY 82071-3138

REIF, JOHN STEVEN, epidemiologist, veterinarian; b. N.Y.C., Sept. 18, 1940; s. Hans V. and Anne (Marie) R. DVM, Cornell U., 1963; MSc in Epidemiology, U. Pa., 1966. NIH postdoctoral fellow U. Pa., Phila., 1966-68, asst. prof., 1969-73, assoc. prof., 1974-78; prof., chief comparative medicine sect. Inst. Rural Environ. Colo. State U., Ft. Collins, 1979-95, chmn. dept. environ. health, 1995—. Prof. U. Otago Sch. Medicine, Wellington, N.Z., 1987-88. Contbr. numerous articles to profl. jours. Mem., pres. Larimer County Bd. Health, Ft. Collins, 1980-85; mem. Colo. Bd. Health, Denver, 1982-87. Fogarty fellow NIH, 1987-88; recipient Recognition award Tchrs. Preventive Medicine, 1989. Fellow Am. Coll. Epidemiology; mem. Internat. Epidemiology Assn., Internat. Soc. Environ. Epidemiology, Soc. for Epidemiologic Rsch. Office: Colo State U Dept Environ Health Fort Collins CO 80523-0001 E-mail: jreif@cvmbs.colostate.edu

REILLY, PAUL V. printing company executive; CPA. Various positions Polychorme Corp.; with Saddle River Capital, 1994-95; sr. v.p. fin., CFO Mail-Well Inc., Englewood, Colo., 1995-98, pres., COO, 1998—, also bd. dirs. Office: Mail Well Inc 23 Inverness Way E Ste 160 Englewood CO 80112-5713

REILLY, WILLIAM KANE, former government official, educator, lawyer, conservationist; b. Decatur, Ill., Jan. 26, 1940; s. George P. and Margaret (Kane) M.; m. Elizabeth Buxton; children: Katherine, Megan. B.A. in History, Yale U., 1962; J.D., Harvard U., 1965; M.S. in Urban Planning, Columbia U., 1971. Bar: Ill., Mass. 1965. Atty. firm Ross & Hardies, Chgo., 1965; assoc. dir. Urban Policy Center, Urban Am., Inc., also Nat. Urban Coalition, Washington, 1969-70; sr. staff mem. Pres.'s Council Environ. Quality, 1970-72; exec. dir. Task Force Land Use and Urban Growth, 1972-73; pres. Conservation Found., Washington, 1973-89, World Wildlife Fund, Washington, 1985-89; adminstr. U.S. EPA, Washington, 1989-93; Payne vis. prof. Stanford U., 1993-94, vis. prof., 1994-97; CEO Aqua Internat. Ptnrs., Tex. Pacific Group, San Francisco, 1997—. Chmn. Natural Resources Coun. Am., 1982-83; head U.S. del. Earth Summit, 1992; head U.S. del. to negotiate Amendments to Montreal Protocol on the Ozone Layer, 1990, 92; bd. dirs. E.I. DuPont de Nemours and Co., Am. Acad. in Rome, Evergreen Holdings, Inc., Ionics Inc., Nat. Geog. Soc., World Wildlife Fund, Presidio Trust; mem. internat. adv. bd., Lafarge; chair adv. bd. Goldman Sch. Pub. Policy U. Calif. at Berkeley. Editor: The Use of Land, 1973, Environment Strategy America, 1994-96; author articles in field, chpts. in books. Served to capt., CIC U.S. Army, 1966-67. Clubs: University (Washington), Univ. (N.Y.C.). Office: Aqua Internat Ptnrs 345 California St Ste 1770 San Francisco CA 94104-2606

REINGLASS, MICHELLE ANNETTE, lawyer; b. L.A., Dec. 9, 1954; d. Darwin and Shirley (Steiner) R. Student, U. Calif., Irvine, 1972-75; BSL, Western State U., 1977, JD, 1978. Bar: Calif. 1979, U.S. Dist. Ct. (ctrl. dist.) Calif. 1979, U.S. Ct. Appeals (9th cir.) 1981, U.S. Dist. Ct. (so. dist.) Calif. 1989. Pvt. practice employee litig., Laguna Hills, Calif., 1979—. Instr. Calif. Continuing Edn. of Bar, 1990—, Western State Coll., 1991, Rutter Group, 1994—; chmn. magistrate selection com. U.S. Dist. Ct. (ctrl. dist.) Calif., L.A., 1991, 93, 94, 95, mem. commn., 1997; lectr. in field. Contbr. articles to profl. jours. Pres. Child or Parental Emergency Svcs., Santa Ana, Calif., 1982-92; bd. dirs. Pub. Law Ctr., Santa Ana, Coalition for Justice; mem. exec. com. CHOC Follies. Recipient Jurisprudence award Anti-Defamation League, 1997; named to Hall of Fame, Western State U., 1993; named one of Best Lawyers, bestlawyers.com, 2001. Mem. State Bar Calif., Orange County Bar Assn. (del. to state conv. 1980-94, bd. dirs. 1983-94, chmn. bus. litigation sect. 1989, sec. 1990, treas. 1991, pres.-elect 1992, pres. 1993), Orange County Trial Lawyers Assn. (bd. dirs. 1987-89, Bus. Trial Lawyer of Yr. award 1995), Orange County Women Lawyers (Lawyer of Yr. award 1996), Vols. in Parole (chmn. adv. com. 1990-91), Peter Elliot Inns Ct. (master), Am. Bd. of Trial Advocates. Avocations: distance running, skiing. Office: 23161 Mill Creek Dr Ste 170 Laguna Hills CA 92653-1650

REINHARD, CHRISTOPHER JOHN, merchant banking, venture capital executive; b. Bridgeport, Conn., Nov. 11, 1953; s. Warren John and Marian Louise (Dutter) R.; m. Maureen Francis, Sept. 24, 1977; 1 child, Griffin John. BS, Babson Coll., 1976, MBA, 1977. Sr. fin. analyst Gen. Motors Corp., Detroit and N.Y.C., 1977-81; asst. sec. Wheelabrator-Frye Inc., N.H., 1981-83; asst. sec., asst. treas. The Signal Cos., Inc., La Jolla, Calif., 1983-86; mng. dir., v.p. The Henley Group, Inc., La Jolla, 1986-90; mng. dir. Fisher Sci. Group, Inc., La Jolla, 1986-90; mng. dir., v.p. Wheelabrator Tech. Inc., Henley Mfg. Corp., 1987-90; founder, pres. Colony Group Inc., Rancho Santa Fe, 1990—, Reinhard Assocs., Rancho Santa Fe, 1990-95; founder, v.p., CFO Advanced Access, Inc., San Diego, 1995-97. Pres. Direct Feedback, Inc., 1990, Dairy Queen Ventures, 1990-94, Winsor Sport Fencing, 1993—; founder, pres. and COO, Collateral Therapeutics Inc., 1995—; gen. ptnr. Cabrillo Ventures, 1995—; founder, pres. ihumon, 2000—. Mem. Boston Athenaeum, N.Y. Athletic Club, San Diego Polo Club, Rancho Santa Fe Polo Club, Duquesne Club. Office: Collateral Therapeutics 11622 El Camino Real San Diego CA 92130-2049

REINHARDT, STEPHEN ROY, federal judge; b. N.Y.C., Mar. 27, 1931; s. Gottfried and Silvia (Hanlon) R.; children: Mark, Justin, Dana. B.A. cum laude, Pomona Coll., 1951; LL.B., Yale, 1954. Bar: Calif. 1958. Law clk. to U.S. Dist. Judge Luther W. Youngdahl, Washington, 1956-57; atty. O'Melveny & Myers, L.A., 1957-59; partner Fogel Julber Reinhardt Rothschild & Feldman (L.C.), L.A., 1959-80; judge U.S. Ct. Appeals (9th cir.), L.A., 1980—. Mem. exec. com. Dem. Nat. Com., 1969-72, nat. dem. committeeman for Calif., 1976-80; pres. L.A. Recreation an dParks Commn., 1974-75; mem. Coliseum Commn., 1974-75; mem. L.A. Police Commn., 1974-78, pres., 1978-80, sec., mem. exec. com. L.A. Olympic Organizing com., 1980-84; bd. dirs. Amateur Athletic Found. of L.A., 1984-92; adj. prof. Loyola Law Sch., L.A., 1988-90. Served to 1st lt. USAF, 1954-56. Mem. ABA (labor law com. 1975-77).*

REINHARDT, WILLIAM PARKER, chemical physicist, educator; b. San Francisco, May 22, 1942; s. William Oscar and Elizabeth Ellen (Parker) R.; m. Katrina Hawley Currens, Mar. 14, 1979; children: James William, Alexander Hawley. BS in Basic Chemistry, U. Calif., Berkeley, 1964; AM in Chemistry, Harvard U., 1966, PhD in Chem. Physics, 1968; MA (hon.), U. Pa., 1985. Instr. chemistry Harvard U., 1967-69, asst. prof. chemistry, 1969-72, assoc. prof., 1972-74; prof. U. Colo., Boulder, 1974-84, chmn. dept. chemistry, 1977-80; prof. chemistry U. Pa., Phila., 1984-91, chmn. dept., 1985-88, D. Michael Crow prof., 1987-91; prof. chemistry U.Wash., Seattle, 1991—, assoc. chmn. undergrad. program, 1993-96. Adj. prof. physics U. Wash., Seattle, 1998—; vis. fellow Joint Inst. for Lab. Astrophysics of Nat. Bur. Stds. and U. Colo., 1972, 74, fellow, 1974-84; dir. Telluride Summer Rsch. Ctr., 1986-89, treas., 1989-93; com. on atomic, molecular and optical scis. NRC, 1988-90; vis. scientist Nat. Inst. Stds. and Tech., summers 1993—; vis. prof. chemistry U. Melbourne, Australia, 1997, Harvard U., 1998, Davidson Lctr., u. Kansas, 2000. Mem. editl. bd. Phys. Rev. A., 1979-81, Chem. Physics, 1985-94, Jour. Chem. Physics, 1987-89, Jour. Physics B (U.K.), 1992—, Internat. Jour. Quantum Chemistry, 1994—; rschr. theoretical chem. physics, theoretical atomic and molecular physics for numerous publs. Recipient Camille and Henry Dreyfus Tchr. Scholar award, 1972; Alfred P. Sloan fellow, 1972; J.S. Guggenheim Meml. fellow, 1978; Coun. on Rsch. and Creative Work faculty fellow, 1978; Wilsmore fellow U. Melbourne (Australia), 1997; J.W. Fulbright sr. scholar, Australia, 1997. Fellow AAAS, Am. Phys. Soc., Phi Beta Kappa; mem. Am. Chem. Soc., Sigma Xi (nat. lectr. 1980-82), Phi Lambda Upsilon (Fresenius award 1977). Office: U Wash Dept Chemistry PO Box 351700 Seattle WA 98195-1700 E-mail: rein@chem.washington.edu

REINMUTH, OSCAR MACNAUGHTON, physician, educator; b. Lincoln, Nebr., Oct. 23, 1927; s. Oscar William and Catharine Anne (MacNaughton) R.; m. Patricia Dixon, June 19, 1951 (div. Jan. 1977); children— David Dixon, Diane MacNaughton, Douglas Stewart; m. Audrey Longridge Holland, June 26, 1980. B.S., U. Tex., Austin, 1948; M.D. (F.B. Hanes research fellow 1950-51), Duke U., 1952. Intern Duke Hosp., 1952-53; asst. resident in medicine Yale U. Med. Ctr., 1953-54, NIH research trainee, 1954-55; asst. resident in neurology Boston City Hosp., 1955-56, chief resident, teaching fellow in neurology Harvard U. Neurol. unit, 1956-57; NIH spl. trainee, clin. asst. Nat. Hosp., London, 1957-58; from asst. prof. to prof. neurology U. Miami (Fla.) Med. Sch., 1958-77; prof. neurology and behavioral neuroscience, chmn. dept. U. Pitts. Med. Sch., 1977-93, prof. emeritus, 1994—; prof. neurology U. Ariz. Coll. Medicine, Tucson, 1993—. Mem. research tng. com. A, B, and C NIH, 1966-73 Served with AUS, 1946-47. Recipient Mosby award, 1952. Fellow ACP, Am. Acad. Neurology (1st v.p. 1973-76), Am. Neurol. Assn. (1st v.p. 1977-78, 2d v.p. 1976-77), Am. Heart Assn. (fellow stroke coun., vice chmn. 1978-79, chmn. 1980-82, editor publs. 1975-78, editor-in-chief Stroke jour. 1987-91, Award of Merit 1992). Home: 5545 N Entrada Quince Tucson AZ 85718-4709 Office: U Med Ctr Dept Neurology 1501 N Campbell Ave Tucson AZ 85724-0001 E-mail: oreinmuth@aol.com

REIS, C. DALE, company executive; Bachelor's Degree, Grove City Coll.; Master's Degree, MIT. With Raytheon, 1967—, program mgr. large phased-array radar sys., dir. data acquisition sys., mgr. submarine signal divsn. and equipment devel. labs., gen. mgr. equipment divsn.; dep. gen. mgr. electronic sys.; v.p.; sr. v.p.

REISER, PAUL, actor, comedian; b. N.Y.C., Mar. 30, 1957; m. Paula Reiser. BFA in Music, SUNY, Binghampton, 1977. Comedian various nightclubs and venues including Catch a Rising Star, N.Y.C., The Comic Strip, N.Y.C., The Improv, N.Y.C., 1979—. Performances include (feature films) Diner, 1982, Beverly Hills Cop, 1984, Aliens, 1986, Beverly Hills Cop II, 1987, Cross My Heart, 1987, Crazy People, 1990, The Marrying Man, 1991, Bye Bye, Love, 1995, The Story of Us, 1999; (TV series) The Investigator, HBO, The Comedy Zone, (TV spls.) Paul Reiser: Out on a Whim, HBO, 1987, (TV pilots) Diner, CBS, Just Married, ABC, (TV movies) Sunset Limousine, 1987, You Ruined My Life, 1987, The Tower, 1993; regular (TV series) My Two Dads, NBC, 1987-1991, Mad About You, NBC, 1992-99 (Emmy nomination, Lead Actor - Comedy Series, 1994); guest star various talk shows including The Tonight Show, Late Night with David Letterman; author: Couplehood, 1994, Babyhood. Office: care William Morris Agency 151 S El Camino Dr Beverly Hills CA 90212-2704

REISS, HOWARD, chemistry educator; b. N.Y.C., Apr. 5, 1922; s. Isidor and Jean (Goldstein) R.; m. Phyllis Kohn, July 25, 1945; children: Gloria, Steven. AB in Chemistry, NYU, 1943; PhD in Chemistry, Columbia U., 1949. With Manhattan Project, 1944-46; instr., then asst. prof. chemistry Boston U., 1949-51; with Ctrl. Rsch. Lab., Celanese Corp. Am., 1951-52, Edgar C. Bain Lab. Fundamental Rsch., U.S. Steel Corp., 1957, Bell Telephone Labs., 1952-60; asso. dir., then dir. rsch. div. Atomics Internat., div. N.Am. Aviation, Inc., 1960-62; dir. N.Am. Aviation Sci. Ctr., 1962-67, v.p. co., 1963-67; v.p. rsch. aerospace systems group N.Am. Rockwell Corp., 1967-68; vis. lectr. chemistry U. Calif. at Berkeley, summer 1957; vis. prof. chemistry UCLA, 1961, 62, 64, 67, prof., 1968-91, prof. emeritus, 1991—; vis. prof. U. Louis Pasteur, Strasbourg, France, 1986, U. Pa., 1989; vis. fellow Victoria U., Wellington, New Zealand, 1989. Vis. fellow Princeton (N.J.) Materials Inst., 1996; cons. to chem.-physics program USAF Cambridge Rsch. Labs., 1950-52; chmn. editor Procs. Internat. Conf. Nucleation and Interfacial Phenomena, Boston; mem. USAF Office Sci. Rsch. Physics and Chemistry Rsch. Evaluation Groups, 1966—, Oak Ridge Nat. Lab. Reactor Chemistry Adv. Com., 1966-68; adv. com. math. and phys. scis. NSF, 1970-72, ARPA Materials Rsch. Coun., 1968—; chmn. site rev. com. NRC Associateships Program, Naval Rsch. Lab., 1989. Author: Methods of Thermodynamics, 1965; author articles; editor in field.; editor: Progress in Solid State Chemistry, 1962-71, Jour. Statis. Physics, 1968-75, Jour. Colloid Interface Sci; mem. editorial adv. bd. Internat. Jour. Physics and Chemistry of Solids, 1955, Progress in Solid State Chemistry, 1962-73, Jour. Solid State Chemistry, 1969, Jour. Phys. Chemistry, 1970-73, Ency. of Solid State, 1970, Jour. Nonmetals, 1971—, Jour. Colloid and Interface Sci., 1976-79, Langmuir, 1985—. Guggenheim Meml. fellow, 1978; Howard Reiss chair in chemistry and biochemistry established named in his honor, UCLA, 1999. Fellow AAAS, Am. Phys. Soc. (exec. com. div. chem. physics 1966-69); mem. NAS, Am. Chem. Soc. (chmn. phys. chemistry sect. N.J. sect. 1957, Richard C. Tolman medal 1973, Kendall award in colloid and surface chemistry 1980, J.H. Hildebrand award in theoretical and exptl. phys. chemistry of liquids 1991, Van Arkel hon. chair in chemistry U. Leiden, The Netherlands, 1994), Am. Assn. for Aerosol Rsch. (David Sinclair award 1997), Phi Beta Kappa, Sigma Xi, Phi Lambda Upsilon. Office: U Calif Dept Chemistry And Biochemis Los Angeles CA 90095-0001

REITAN, HAROLD THEODORE, management consultant; b. Max, N.D., Nov. 3, 1928; s. Walter Rudolph and Anna Helga (Glesne) R.; m. Margaret Lucille Bonsac, Dec. 29, 1954 (div.); children: Eric, Karen, Chris, Jon. BA, St. Olaf Coll., 1950; MA in Social Psychology, U. Fla., 1962, PhD, 1967. Commd. officer USAF, 1951, advanced through grades to col., 1971; comdr. USAF Spl. Treatment Ctr., Lackland, Tex., 1971-74, USAF Corrections and Rehab. Group, Lowry, Colo., 1974-76, USAF Tech. Tng. Wing, 1976-78; ret., 1978; mgr. health svcs. Coors Industries, Golden, Colo., 1978-84, mgr. tng. and orgnl. devel., 1984-89, cons. mgmt. assessment, tng. and devel., 1989—. Contbr. articles to profl. jours. Decorated D.F.C. with oak leaf cluster, Bronze Star, Legion of Merit with oak leaf cluster, Air medal with 5 oak leaf clusters. Mem. APA, Phi Kappa Phi. Republican. Lutheran. Home and Office: 116 S Nome St Aurora CO 80012-1242 E-mail: htr1@earthlink.net

REITEN, RICHARD G. natural gas industry executive; b. 1939; BA, U. Wash., 1962. With Simpson Timber Co., Seattle, 1962-64, St. Regis Paper Co., Tacoma, 1964-66, Hearin Products, Inc., Portland, Oreg., 1966-71, Di Giorgio Corp., San Francisco, 1971-79, pres. bldg. material group; with Nicoli Co., Portland, 1979-87; dir. Oreg. Econ. Devel. Dept., Salem, 1987-89; pres. Portland Gen. Corp., 1989-92, Portland Gen. Electric Co., 1992-95, pres., COO, 1996-97, pres., CEO, 1997—. Office: Northwest Natural Gas Co One Pacific Square 13th Fl 220 NW 2nd Ave Portland OR 97209-3943

REITSEMA, HAROLD JAMES, aerospace engineer; b. Kalamazoo, Jan. 19, 1948; s. Robert Harold and Bernice Jean (Hoogsteen) R.; m. Mary Jo Gunnink, Aug. 6, 1970; children: Ellen Celeste, Laurie Jean. BA, Calvin Coll., 1972; PhD, N.Mex. State U., 1977. Rsch. assoc. U. Ariz., Tucson, 1977-79, sr. rsch. assoc., 1979-82, vis. scientist, 1987—; sr. mem. tech. staff Ball Aerospace, Boulder, Colo., 1982-85, prin. systems engr., 1985-88, program mgr., 1988-89, staff cons., 1989-96, dir., 1996—. Cons. Aerospace Tech., 1987—. Contbr. articles to Astrophys. Jour., Aston. Jour., Nature, Sci., Icarus. Bd. dirs. EE Barnard Obs., Golden, Colo., 1984-91. Fellow AIAA (assoc., tech. com. chair 1991, Engr. of Yr. Colo. region 1990); mem. Am. Astron. Soc. (planetary sci. com. 1991-94), Internat. Astron. Union. Achievements include discovery of Larissa, fifth satellite of Neptune; co-discovery of Telesto, seventeenth satellite of Saturn; patents for Optically-coupled Shaft Angle Encoder. Home: 4795 Hancock Dr Boulder CO 80303-1103 Office: Ball Aerospace 1600 Commerce St Boulder CO 80301-2734 E-mail: hreitsema@ball.com

REITZ, BRUCE ARNOLD, cardiac surgeon, educator; b. Seattle, Sept. 14, 1944; BS, Stanford U., 1966; MD, Yale U., 1970. Diplomate: Am. Bd. Surgery, Am. Bd. Thoracic Surgery. Intern Johns Hopkins Hosp., Balt., 1970-71, cardiac surgeon-in-charge, 1982-92; resident Stanford U. Hosp., (Calif.), 1971-72, 74-78; clin. assoc. Nat. Heart Lung Blood Inst., NIH, Bethesda, Md., 1972-74; asst. prof. Stanford U. Sch. Medicine, 1977-81, assoc. prof., 1981-82; prof. surgery Johns Hopkins U. Sch. Medicine, Balt., 1982-92; prof., chmn. Sch Medicine Stanford (Calif.) U., 1992—. Developer heart-lung transplant technique, 1981. Office: Stanford U Sch Medicine Dept Cardiothoracic Surgery Stanford CA 94305 E-mail: breitz@stanford.edu

REMBE, TONI, lawyer, director; b. Seattle, Apr. 23, 1936; d. Armin and Doris (McVay) R.; m. Arthur Rock, July 19, 1975. Cert. in French Studies, U. Geneva, 1956; LL.B., U. Wash., 1960; LLM in Taxation, NYU, 1961. Bar: N.Y., Wash., Calif. Assoc. Chadbourne, Parke, Whiteside & Wolff, N.Y.C., 1961-63, Pillsbury, Madison & Sutro, San Francisco, 1964-71, ptnr., 1971—. Bd dirs. Aegon N.V., The Netherlands, Potlatch Corp., Spokane, Wash., SBC Comms., Inc., San Antonio. Pres. Van Loben Sels Charitable Found., San Francisco; bd. trustees Am. Conservatory Theatre, San Francisco. Fellow Am. Bar Found.; mem. ABA, Am. Judicature Soc., State Bar Calif., Bar Assn. San Francisco, Commonwealth Club of Calif. Office: Pillsbury Winthrop LLP 50 Fremont St San Francisco CA 94105-2230

REMER, DONALD SHERWOOD, engineering educator, economist, consultant; b. Detroit, Feb. 16, 1943; s. Nathan and Harriet R.; m. Louise Collen, Dec. 21, 1969; children: Tanya, Candace, Miles. BS, U. Mich., 1965; MS, Calif. Inst. Tech., 1966, PhD, 1970. Registered profl. engr., Calif., Mich., La. Tech. service engr., chem. raw materials div. coordinator, sr. running plan coordinator, task team mgr. Exxon, Baton Rouge, 1970-75; assoc. prof. engring. Harvey Mudd Coll., Claremont, Calif., 1975-79, prof., 1980—, Oliver C. Field prof. engring., dir. Energy Inst., 1981-83; cons., mem. tech. staff, mgr. planning analysis Jet Propulsion Lab., Calif. Inst.

Tech., 1976-98; co-founder, ptnr. Claremont Cons. Group, 1979—; mem. adv. council Nat. Energy Found., N.Y.C., 1981-85. Mem. Inst. Mgmt. Cons., 1988-89; presenter short courses Calif. Inst. Tech. Indsl. Rels. Ctr. and UCLA engring. and mgmt. program, 1994—, also to industry and vogt. on cost estimation of projects, econ. evaluation of projects, software devel., cost and schedule estimation, and project mgmt. for software intensive sys. Case study editor Am. Soc. Engring. Edn., Inst. Indsl. Engrs., Engring. Economist, 1977-89; mem. editorial bd. Jour. Engring. Costs and Prodn. Econs., 1985-91, Internat. Jour. Prodn. Econs., 1992—; contbr. articles to profl. jours. Shelter mgr. ARC, Baton Rouge, 1965-70. Recipient Outstanding Chem. Engr. award U. Mich., 1965, First Place Pub. Relations award Am. Inst. Chem. Engring., 1975, Outstanding Alumni Fund Achievement award Calif. Inst. Tech., 1976, Outstanding Young Man of Am. award, 1976, NASA award, 1983, Best Paper of the Year in Jour. Parametrics, Internat. Soc. Parametric Analysts, 1991-92, Centennial award certificate Am. Soc. Engring. Edn., 1993; named Outstanding Research Seminar Speaker Occidental Research Corp., 1976. Mem. Am. Soc. Engring. Mgmt. (bd. dirs. 1981-83), Toastmasters Club (pres. Claremont-Pomona chpt. 1978).

REMINGTON, BRUCE A. physics researcher; Hydrodynamics group leader Lawrence Livermore Nat. Lab., 1986—. Recipient Excellence in Plasma Physics award Am. Phys. Soc., 1995. Fellow Am. Physical Soc. (pub. rels. coord. divsn. plasma physics). Office: Lawrence Livermore Nat Lab PO Box 808 Livermore CA 94551-0808

REMSING, DENNIS, advertising agency executive; Exec. v.p., gen. mgr. Rubin Postaer and Assocs., Santa Monica, Calif. Office: Rubin Postaer and Assocs 1333 2d St Santa Monica CA 90401

RENARD, RONALD LEE, allergist; b. Chgo., July 31, 1949; s. Robert James and Dorothy Mae (Fruik) R.; m. Maureen Ann Gilmore, Aug. 5, 1972 (div. Mar. 1992); children: Jeffrey, Stephen, Justin, Leigh Ellen; m. Catherine L. Walker, Apr. 1, 1992; children: Morgan, Michal, Luke. 1 & 2 Degre de la Langue, U. de Montepellier, France, 1970; BS in French, U. San Francisco, 1971; MD, Creighton U., 1976. Dir. med. ICU, lt. U.S. Army Hosp., Ft. Leonard Wood, Md., 1980-81; dir. respiratory therapy, asst. chief allergy svc. Walter Reed Med. Ctr., Washington, 1981-84; staff allergist Chico (Calif.) Med. Group, 1984-86; allergist pvt. practice Redding, Calif., 1986—. Dir. ACLS program Enloe Hosp., Chico, 1988-91; bd. dirs. Am. Lung Assn. Calif., 1989-91, med. dir. asthma camp, Chico, Redding, 1986-95; asst. prof. medicine USPHS, Bethesda, Md., 1982-84; asst. prof. family medicine U. Calif. Davis Med. Sch., Redding, 1990-94; Shasta County Planning Commr., 1994-95. Contbr. articles to profl. jours. Fellow Am. Acad. Allergy & Immunology, Am. Coll. Allergists; mem. Alpha Omega Alpha Nat. Honor Med. Soc., Assn. Mil. Allergists, Calif. Thoracic Soc. Republican. Roman Catholic. Avocations: hunting, biking. Office: 2632 Edith Ave Ste B Redding CA 96001-3043 Fax: 530-246-8856. E-mail: rrenard@juno.com

RENDELL-BAKER, LESLIE, anesthesiologist, educator; b. St. Helens, Eng., Mar. 27, 1917; came to U.S., 1957, naturalized, 1963; s. Frank Nelder and Ada (Gill) Rendell-B.; m. Rosemary Carr Hogg, Aug. 17, 1946; children: Sheila Diane, Helen Rosemary, Frances Nelda. BS, MB, London U. Guys Hosp. Med. Sch., 1941. Diplomate: Am. Bd. Anesthesiology. Resident in anesthesiology Brit. Army of Rhine Hosps., 1945-46, Guy's Hosp., London, 1946-48; sr. asst. (assoc. prof.) anesthesiology Welsh Nat. Sch. Medicine, Cardiff, 1948-57; Fulbright asst. prof. anesthesiology U. Pitts., 1955-56; from asst. prof. to assoc. prof. Sch. Medicine Case Western Res. U., Cleve., 1957-62; dir. dept. anesthesiology Mt. Sinai Hosp., N.Y.C., 1962-79; prof., chmn. dept. anesthesiology Mt. Sinai Sch. Medicine, CUNY, 1966-79; prof. dept. anesthesiology Sch. Medicine Loma Linda (Calif.) U., 1979-97, prof. emeritus, 1998—. Chmn. sect. com. Z79 standards for anesthesia and respiratory equipment Am. Nat. Stds. Instn., 1962-68, vice chmn., 1969-81, mem. exec. com. med. devices stds. mgmt. bd., 1973-79, bd. dirs., 1976-79; chmn. classification panel on anesthesiology devices FDA, 1972-76 Author: (with W.W. Mushin) Principles of Thoracic Anesthesia, 1953, (with W.W. Mushin and Thompson) Automatic Ventilation of the Lungs, 3rd edit., 1980, The Origins of Thoracic Anesthesia, 1991, (with others) The Care of Anesthesia Equipment, 1992; editor: Problems with Anesthetic and Respiratory Therapy Equipment, 1982, The History and Evolution of Pediatric Anesthesia Equipment, 1992, Maintenance, Cleaning and Sterilization of Anesthetic Equipment, 1998, Future Directions in Anesthesia Apparatus, 1998. Served to capt. Royal Army Med. Corps, 1942-46. Fellow Royal Coll. Anaesthetists; fellow Royal Soc. Medicine, Assn. Anaesthetists Gt. Britain and Ireland; mem. Am. Soc. Anesthesiologists (chmn. com. equipment and standardization 1962-68), Am. Soc. for Testing and Materials (chmn. subcom. D10-34 1981-91), Assn. Advancement Med. Instrumentation , AAAS. Achievements include invention of baby endotracheal connector, pediatric face masks and equipment. Home: 630 Beauregard Crest Redlands CA 92373-5602 Office: Loma Linda U Sch Medicine Dept Anesthesiology 11234 Anderson St Loma Linda CA 92354-2804

RENDU, JEAN-MICHEL MARIE, mining executive; b. Tunis, Tunisia, Feb. 25, 1944; s. Paul C. and Solange M. (Krebs) R.; m. Karla M. Meyer, Aug. 18, 1973; children: Yannick P., Mikaël P. Ingénieur des Mines, Ecole des Mines St. Etienne, France, 1966; MS, Columbia U., 1968, D. Engring. Sci., 1971. Mgr. ops. rsch. Anglovaal, Johannesburg, Republic of South Africa, 1972-76; assoc. prof. U. Wis., Madison, 1976-79; assoc. Golder Assocs., Denver, 1979-84; dir. tech. and sci. systems Newmont Mining Corp., Danbury, Conn., 1984-88; v.p. Newmont Gold Co., Denver, 1988-93, Newmont Mining Corp., Denver, 1993-2001; ind. cons. Denver, 2001—. Author: An Introduction to Geostatistical Methods of Mineral Evaluation, 1978, 81; contbr. tech. papers to profl. jours. Recipient Jackling award Soc. Mining, Metallurgy and Exploration, 1994, Pres.'s citation, 1993. Fellow South African Inst. of Mining and Metallurgy (corr. mem. of coun.); mem. NAE, N.Y. Acad. Sci., Internat. Assn. for Math. Geology, Soc. Mining, Metallurgy and Exploration, Sigma Xi. Roman Catholic. Fax: 720-49384643. E-mail: JMRendu@aol.com

RENEHAN, ROBERT FRANCIS XAVIER, Greek and Latin educator; b. Boston, Apr. 25, 1935; s. Francis Xavier and Ethel Mary (Sullivan) R.; m. Joan Lee Axtell-Damerow, Sept. 9, 1966; children— Martin, Sharon, Stephen, Judith, John. A.B., Boston Coll., Chestnut Hill, Mass., 1956; A.M., Harvard, 1958, Ph.D., 1963. Instr. Greek and Latin U. Calif. at Berkeley, 1963-64; instr. Harvard U., 1964-65; asst. prof. Boston Coll., 1966-69, assoc. prof., 1969-71, prof., 1971-77, chmn. dept. classical studies, 1969-77; prof. Greek and Latin U. Calif. at Santa Barbara, 1976—, chmn. dept., 1984-88, 93-200. Author: Greek Textual Criticism, 1969, Leo Medicus, 1969, Greek Lexicographical Notes, 1975, 2d series, 1982, Studies in Greek Texts, 1975; assoc. editor Classical Philology, 1976—, Am. Jour. Philology, 1987-95; sr. mem. editl. bd. Classical Antiquity, 1980-87, Revised Supplement to Liddell-Scott-Jones Greek-English Lexicon, 1987-96; contbr. articles to profl. jours. Nat. Endowment for Humanities Sr. fellow, 1972-73 Mem. Am. Philol. Assn., Soc. for Ancient Medicine. Office: U Calif Dept Classics Santa Barbara CA 93106 E-mail: renehan@classics.ucsb.edu

RENEKER, MAXINE HOHMAN, librarian; b. Chgo., Dec. 2, 1942; d. Roy Max and Helen Anna Christina (Anacker) Hohman; m. David Lee Reneker, June 20, 1964 (dec. Dec. 1979); children: Sarah Roeder, Amy Johannah, Benjamin Congdon. BA, Carleton Coll., 1964; MA, U. Chgo., 1970; DLS, Columbia U., 1992. Asst. reference libr. U. Chgo. Libraries, 1965-66; classics libr. U. Chgo. Libr., 1967-70, asst. head acquisitions, 1970-71, personnel libr., 1971-72, personnel/bus. libr. U. Colo. Libr., Boulder, 1978-80; asst. dir. sci. and engring. div. Columbia U., N.Y.C., 1981-85; assoc. dean of univ. librs. for pub. svcs. Ariz. State U. Libr., Tempe, 1985-89; dir. instrnl. and rsch. svcs. Stanford (Calif.) Univ. Librs., 1989-90; assoc. provost for libr. and info. resources Naval Postgrad. Sch., Monterey, Calif., 1993—. Acad. libr. mgmt. intern Coun. on Libr. Resources, 1980-81; chmn. univ. librs. sect. Assn. Coll. and Rsch. Librs., 1989-90. Contbr. articles to profl. jours. Rsch. grantee Coun. on Library Resources, Columbia U., 1970-71, fellow, 1990-92. Mem. ALA, Am. Soc. Info. Sci., Sherlockian Scion Soc., Phi Beta Kappa, Beta Phi Mu. Home: 740 Dry Creek Rd Monterey CA 93940-4208 Office: Naval Postgrad Sch Dudley Knox Libr 411 Dyer Rd Monterey CA 93943-5198 E-mail: mreneker@nps.navy.mil

RENFREW, CHARLES BYRON, lawyer; b. Detroit, Oct. 31, 1928; s. Charles Warren and Louise (McGuire) R.; m. Susan Wheelock, June 28, 1952 (div. June 1984); children: Taylor Allison Ingham, Charles Robin, Todd Wheelock, James Bartlett; m. Barbara Jones Orser, Oct. 6, 1984; 5 stepchildren. AB, Princeton U., 1952; JD, U. Mich., 1956. Bar: Calif. 1956. Assoc. Pillsbury, Madison & Sutro, San Francisco, 1956-65, ptnr., 1965-72, 81-82; U.S. dist. judge No. Dist. Calif., San Francisco, 1972-80; dep. atty. gen. U.S. Washington, 1980-81; instr. U. Calif. Boalt Hall Sch. Law, 1977-80; v.p. law Chevron Corp. (formerly Standard Oil Co. Calif.), San Francisco, 1983-93, also bd. dirs.; ptnr. LeBoeuf, Lamb, Greene & McRae, San Francisco, 1994-97; pvt. practice San Francisco, 1998—. Mem. exec. com. 9th Cir. Jud. Conf., 1976-78, congl. liaison com. 9th Cir. Jud. Council, 1976-79, spl. com. to propose standards for admission to practice in fed. cts. U.S. Jud. Conf., 1976-79; chmn. spl. com. to study problems of discovery Fed. Jud. Ctr., 1978-79; mem. council on role of cts. U.S. Dept. Justice, 1978-83; mem. jud. panel Ctr. for Pub. Resources, 1981—; head U.S. del. to 6th UN Congress on Prevention of Crime and Treatment of Offenders, 1980; co-chmn. San Francisco Lawyers Com. for Urban Affairs, 1971-72, mem., 1983—; bd. dirs. Internat. Hospitality Ctr., 1961-74, pres., 1967-70; mem. adv. bd. Internat. Comparative Law Ctr., Southwestern Legal Found., 1983-93; trustee World Affairs Council No. Calif., 1984-87, 94—, Nat. Jud. Coll., 1985-91, Grace Cathedral, 1986-89. Contbr. articles to profl. jours. Bd. fellow Claremont U., 1986-94; bd. dirs. San Francisco Symphony Found., 1964-80, pres., 1971-72; bd. dirs. Coun. Civic Unity, 1962-73, pres., 1971-72; bd. dirs. Opportunity Through Ownership, 1969-72, Marin County Day Sch., 1972-74, No. Calif. Svc. League, 1975-76, Am. Petroleum Inst., 1984—, Nat. Crime Prevention Coun., 1982—; alumni trustee Princeton U., 1976-80; mem. vis. com. u. chgo. Law Sch., 1977-79, u.Mich. Law Sch., 1977-81; bd. visitors J. Reuben Clark Law Sch., Brigham Young U., 1981-83, Stanford Law Sch., 1983-86; trustee Town Sch. for Boys, 1972-80,pres. 1975-80; gov. San Fransciso Symphony Assn., 1974—; mem. nat. adv. bd. Ctr. for Nat. Policy, 1982—; bd. dirs. Nat. Coun. Crime and Deliquency, 1981-82,NAACP Legal Def. and Edn. Fund, 1982—; parish chancellor St. Luke's Episcopal Ch., 1968-71, sr. warden, 1974-76; mem. exec. coun. San Francisco Deanery, 1969-70; mem. diocesan coun. Episcopal Diocese of Calif., 1970; chmn. Diocesan Conv., 1977, 78, 79. Served with USN, 1946-48, 1st lt. U.S. Army, 1952-53. Fellow Am. Bar Found.; mem. ABA (coun. mem. sect. antitrust law 19778-82, vice c hmn. sect. antitrust law 1982-83), San Francisco Bar Assn. (past bd. dirs.), Assn. Gen. Counsel, State Bar Calif., Am. Judicature Soc., Am. Coll. Trial Lawyers (pres. 1995-96), Am. Law Inst., Coun. Fgn. Rels., Order of Coif, Phi Beta Kappa, Phi Delta Phi. Office: 710 Sansome St San Francisco CA 94111-1704

RENGER, MARILYN HANSON, elementary education educator; b. Shelly, Idaho, July 17, 1949; d. Merril H. and Betty Jean (Hendricksen) Hanson; m. Robert Carl Renger, Sept. 11, 1971; children: Katherine, James. BA in History, U. Calif., Santa Barbara, 1971; postgrad., Calif. Luth. U., 1973-74. Tchr. Ventura (Calif.) Unified Schs., 1974-79, 85-98, asst. prin., 1998—. Cons. State of Calif., 1989-93. Recipient Disting. Tchr. K-12 award Nat. Coun. for Geog. Edn., 1992. Mem. Nat. Coun. Geographic Edn. (Nat. Disting. Teaching award 1992), Calif. Geographic Soc. (steering com. 1989-93, co-dir. summer inst. 1992), Nat. Coun. Social Studies. Office: Balboa Mid Sch 247 S Hill Rd Ventura CA 93003-4401

RENNER, ANDREW IHOR, surgeon; b. Buenos Aires, Aug. 1, 1951; came to U.S., 1956; s. Vladimir and Emelia R.; m. Cristina Sasyk, Apr. 17, 1982. MD, Albert Einstein Coll. Medicine, 1975. Diplomate Am. Bd. Surgery. Pvt. practice gen. surgery, Burbank, Calif. Chmn. dept. surgery St. Joseph Hosp., Burbank, 1995-97. Fellow ACS, Internat. Coll. Surgeons; mem. Am. Soc. Gen. Surgeons, L.A. Surg. Soc. Office: 2701 W Alameda Ave Ste 300 Burbank CA 91505-4408 Fax: 818-843-5283

RENNIE, I. DRUMMOND, periodical editor, medical educator; Dep. editor Jour. AMA; nephrologist Rush-Presbyn. St. Lukes Hosp. and Rush Med. Sch., Chgo., 1967-77; assoc. prof. medicine Harvard (Brigham and Women's Hosp.); dep. editor New England Jour. of Medicine. Adv. com. on scientific integrity to Pub. Health Svc.; adj. prof. of medicine U. Calif. San Francisco; co-dir. San Francisco Cochrane Ctr.; proposal rev. adv. team Nat. Sci. Found.; founder CONSORT, QUOROM coms. Contbr. numerous articles to profl. publs. Fellow ACP; mem. New World Assn. of Med. Editors (pres. coun. of biology editors, past pres., exec. bd.). Office: Stanford U UCSF Stanford U Evidence based Practice Ctrwood Bldg T246 Stanford CA 94305-5405 E-mail: rennie@itsa.ucsf.edu

RENNIE, PAUL STEVEN, research scientist; b. Toronto, Ont., Can., Feb. 9, 1946; m. Carol Andrews, 1968; 1 child, Jan. BSc, U. Western Ont., 1969; PhD in Biochemistry, U. Alta., 1973. Rsch. assoc. U. Alta., 1975-76, asst. prof. medicine, 1976-79, assoc. prof., 1979; rsch. scientist B.C. Cancer Agy., 1979-92, dir. rsch., 1992-97; prof. surgery U. B.C., 1986—, dir. prostate rsch. lab., 1998—. Med. Rsch. Coun. rsch. fellow Imperial Cancer Rsch. Fund, 1973-75; rsch. scholar Nat. Cancer Inst. Can., 1976-79. Mem. Can. Soc. Clin. Investigation, Biochem. Soc., Endocrine Soc. Achievements include research on biochemical control of growth in androgen responsive organs and neoplasms; genetic markers in prostate cancer. Office: Prostate Ctr Jack Bell Rsch Ctr 2660 Oak St Vancouver BC Canada V6H 3Z6 E-mail: prennie@interchange.ubc.ca

RENO, JOSEPH HARRY, retired orthopedic surgeon; b. Allentown, Pa., Mar. 5, 1915; s. Harvey Luther and Olive May (Wilson) R.; m. Maude Olivia Mutchler, June 27, 1942; children: Joseph David, Sally Jo, Diana Jane, Deborah Marion. Student, Temple U., 1934-37, MD, 1941. Intern. Chester (Pa.) Hosp., 1941-42; resident Tex. Scottish Rite Hosp. for Crippled Children, Dallas, 1942-43, 44-45, Robert Packer Hosp., Sayre, Pa., 1943-44; assoc. Homer Stryker, M.D., Kalamazoo, 1945-46; pvt. practice Bethlehem, Pa., 1946-71, Flagstaff, Ariz., 1971-93; team physician Lehigh U., Bethlehem, 1946-70, No. Ariz. U., Flagstaff, 1971-77, Ariz. State U., Tempe, 1977-84. Chief surg. staff Flagstaff Hosp., 1975. Contbr. articles to profl. jours.; prodr. surg. films for Am. Acad. Ortho. Surgeons and others, 1952-70. Pres. Coconino County Easter Seal Soc., 1973; bd. dirs., med. advisor Ariz. Easter Seal Soc., 1974-84. Recipient Pioneer award Ariz. Med. Assn., 1981, Cert. of Appreciation, Pa. Dept. Health Crippled Children's Div., 1971; Dr. Joseph Reno Sports Medicine award named in honor, No. Ariz. State U. and Blue Cross Blue Shield, 1986. Fellow Am. Acad. Ortho. Surgeons, Am. Assn. for Surgery of Trauma, Am. Coll. Sports Med., Am. Coll. Surgeons (chmn. Lehigh Valley subcom. on trauma 1954-66, Ea. Pa. chpt. pres. 1969); mem. NRA, Am. Bd. Ortho. Surgery (cert., diplomate 1948), Coconino County Med. Soc. (pres. 1976), Western Ortho. Assn., Babcock Surg. Soc., Mason, Phi Chi, Alpha Tau Omega. Home: 405 Jacks Canyon Rd Apt 105 Sedona AZ 86351-9222

RENSE, PAIGE, editor, publishing company executive; b. Iowa, 04 May; m. Kenneth Noland, Apr. 10, 1924. Editor-in-chief Architectural Digest, L.A., 1970—. Appeared on Good Morning Am., The Today Show, Entertainment Tonight. Recipient Nat. Headliner award Women in Communications, 1983, Pacifica award So. Calif. Resources Coun., 1978, editl. award Dallas Market Ctr., 1978, golden award Chgo. Design Resources Svc., 1982, Agora award, 1982, outstanding profl. incomms. award, 1982, trailblazers award, 1983, disting. svcs. award Resources Coun., Inc., 1988, Spirit of Achievement award, 1995, Pratt Inst. Founders award, 1997; named woman of yr. L.A. Times, 1976, Muses, 1986, woman of internat. accomplishment, 1991, Spirit of Achievement award, 1995, The Pratt Inst. Founders award, 1997; named to Interior Design Hall of Fame. Office: Archtl Digest The Conde Nast Publ Inc 6300 Wilshire Blvd Fl 11 Los Angeles CA 90048-5204

RENSON, JEAN FELIX, retired psychiatry educator; b. Liège, Belgium, Nov. 9, 1930; came to U.S., 1960; s. Louis and Laurence (Crahai) R.; m. Gisèle Bouillenne, Sept. 8, 1956; children: Marc, Dominique, Jean-Luc. MD, U. Liege, 1959; PhD in Biochemistry, George Washington U., 1971. Diplomate Am. Bd. Psychiatry. Asst. prof. U. Liège, 1957-60; rsch. fellow U. Liege, 1966-72; clin. assoc. prof. dept. psychiatry U. Calif., San Francisco, 1978—; ret. 1994. Vis. asst. prof. Stanford U., Palo Alto, Calif., 1972-77. Assoc. editor: Fundamentals of Biochemical Pharmacology, 1971. NIH fellow, 1960-66. Avocations: neurosciences, music. E-mail: grenson@inreach.com

RENWICK, EDWARD S. lawyer; b. L.A., May 10, 1934; AB, Stanford U., 1956, LLB, 1958. Bar: Calif. 1959, U.S. Dist. Ct. (cen. dist.) Calif. 1959, U.S. Ct. Appeals (9th cir.) 1963, U.S. Dist. Ct. (so. dist.) Calif. 1973, U.S. Dist. Ct. (no. dist.) Calif. 1977, U.S. Dist. Ct. (ea. dist.) Calif. 1981, U.S. Supreme Ct. 1985. Ptnr. Hanna and Morton LLP, L.A. Mem., bd. vis. Stanford Law Sch., 1967-69; mem. environ. and natural resources adv. bd. Stanford Law Sch. Bd. dirs. Calif. Supreme Ct. Hist. Soc. Fellow Am. Coll. Trial Lawyers, Am. Bar Found.; mem. ABA (mem. sect. on litigation, antitrust law, bus. law, chmn. sect. of nat. resources, energy and environ. law 1987-88, mem. at large coord. group energy law 1989-92, sect. rep. coord. group energy law 1995-97, Calif. del. legal com., interstate oil compact com.), Calif. Arboretum Assn. (trustee 1986-92), L.A. County Bar Assn. (chmn. natural resources law sect. 1974-75), The State Bar of Calif., Chancery Club (pres. 1992-93), Phi Delta Phi. Office: Hanna and Morton LLP 444 S Flower St Ste 2050 Los Angeles CA 90071-2922 E-mail: erenwick@hanmor.com

RENZETTI, ATTILIO DAVID, JR. physician; b. N.Y.C., Nov. 11, 1920; s. Attilio and Anna (Accardi) R.; m. Mabel Lucille Woodruff, May 24, 1947; children: Patricia Ann, Laurence, Pamela Sorensen, David. AB, Columbia Coll., 1941, MD, 1944. Diplomate: Am. Bd. Internal Medicine (chmn. subsplty. bd. pulmonary disease 1970-72). Intern, resident Bellevue Hosp., N.Y.C., 1944-45, 47-49, 51-52, fellow cardiopulmonary physiology, 1949-51; asst. prof. medicine U. Utah, 1952-53, State U. N.Y., Syracuse, 1953-57; assoc. prof. SUNY, 1957-60; asst. prof. Johns Hopkins U., 1960-61; assoc. prof. U. Md., 1960-61, U. Utah, Salt Lake City, 1961-67, prof., 1967-90, emeritus, 1990—. Editorial bd.: Am. Rev. Respiratory Disease, 1964-67; Contbr. articles to med. jours. Pres. Utah TB and Health Assn., 1965-66; bd. dirs. Am. Lung Assn., 1965-74, 78-81. With M.C. AUS, 1945-47. Mem. Am. Thoracic Soc. (pres. 1975-76) Home and Office: 1801 London Plane Rd Salt Lake City UT 84124-3531

REPASS, RANDY, electrical company executive; Chmn., CEO West Marine, Watsonville, Calif. Office: West Marine PO Box 50050 500 Westridge Dr Watsonville CA 95077-5050

REPINE, JOHN EDWARD, internist, educator; b. Rock Island, Ill., Dec. 26, 1944; married, 1969, 88; 6 children. BS, U. Wis., 1967; MD, U. Minn., 1971. Instr., then assoc. prof. internal medicine U. Minn., Mpls., 1974-79; asst. dir divsn. exptl. medicine Webb-Waring Inst. Biomedical Rsch., Denver, 1979-89; prof. medicine, pres. and dir. Webb-Waring Inst. Cancer, Aging & Antioxidant Rsch., Denver, 1989—; prof. medicine U. Colo., Denver, 1979—, James J. Waring prof. medicine, 1996—, prof. pediatrics, 1981-96. Mem. rsch. com., co-chmn. steering com. Aspen Lung Conf., 1980, chmn., 1981; assoc. dean for student advocacy Nat. Heart and Lung Inst., 1990—. Young Pulmonary Investigator grantee Nat. Heart & Lung Inst., 1974-75; recipient Basil O'Connor Starter Rsch. award Nat. Found. March of Dimes, 1975-77. Mem. AAAS, Am. Assn. Immunologists, Am. Soc. Clin. Investigation, Am. Heart Assn. (established investigator award 1976-81), Am. Thoracic Soc., Assn. Am. Physicians. Achievements include research in role of phagocytes and oxygen radicals in lung injury and host defense (ARDS). Office: Webb Waring Inst Cancer Aging & Antioxidant Rsch Box C322 4200 E 9th Ave Denver CO 80220-3706

RESCH, CHARLOTTE SUSANNA, plastic surgeon; b. Charlottesville, Va., Sept. 24, 1957; d. Johann Heinrich and Eleonore Susanne (Stenzel) R.; m. John Arthur Niero, Jan. 31, 1990. Student, Dalhousie U., Halifax, Nova Scotia, Can., 1974-76; MD with distinction, Dalhousie U. Med. Sch., Halifax, Nova Scotia, Can., 1980. Diplomate Dalhousie U., Am. Bd. Plastic Surgery; licentiate Med. Coun. Can.; cert. Bd. Med. Quality Assurance Calif. Intern Ottawa Gen. Hosp., Ont., Can., 1980-81; gen. surgery resident Dalhousie U., Halifax, Nova Scotia, Can., 1981-85; plastic surgery resident Wayne State U., Detroit, 1985-87; pvt. practice San Francisco, 1988-89; pre-ptnr. Southern Calif. Permanente Physicians Group, Fontana, 1989-92, ptnr., 1992—. Contbr. articles to profl. jours. Fellow ACS; mem. Am. Soc. Plastic and Reconstructive Surgeons, Calif. Med. Soc., San Bernardino Med. Soc., Alpha Omega Alpha. Avocations: travel, skiing, bicycling, gardening, gourmet cooking. Office: Kaiser Found Hosp Dept Plastic Surgery 9985 Sierra Ave Fontana CA 92335-6720

RESCOE, MICHAEL E. computer company executive; b. 1953; BA, Tulane U.; MBA, U. Tex. Sr. v.p. corp. fin. Kidder, Peabody & Co.; sr. mng. dir. Bear, Stearns & Co. Inc.; CFO, ENSERCH Corp., Dallas, until 1997; sr. v.p., CFO, PG&E Corp., San Francisco, from 1997; now v.p. fin. 3Com Corp., Santa Clara, Calif. Office: 3Com Corp PO Box 58145 Santa Clara CA 95052

RESNICK, JEFFREY I. plastic surgeon; b. Jersey City, Mar. 2, 1954; s. Victor and Regina (Bistritz) R.; m. Michele Gail Zinger, July 12, 1981; children: Andrew Gregory, Daniel Zachary. BS, Yale U., 1975; MD, U. Pa., 1980. Diplomate Am. Bd. Surgery, Am. Bd. Plastic Surgery. Resident in surgery Mass. Gen. Hosp., Boston, 1980-85, resident in plastic surgery, 1985-87; fellow in craniofacial surgery UCLA, 1987-88; pvt. practice plastic surgery Santa Monica, Calif., 1989—. Asst. clin. prof. plastic surgery UCLA, 1987—, U. So. Calif., 1998—. Contbr. articles to profl. jours. Surgeon Interplast, Vietnam, Nepal. Mem. Am. Soc. Plastic Surgeons, Am. Soc. Maxillofacial Surgeons, Am. Cleft Palate-Craniofacial Assn., Plastic Surgery Ednl. Found., Sigma Xi, Alpha Omega Alpha. Office: 1301 20th St Ste 470 Santa Monica CA 90404-2082

RESNICK, LYNDA, art company executive; Co-owner, vice chmn. Franklin Mint; co-owner Roll Internat. Chmn. Teleflora. Chmn. mktg. com. Conservation Internat., bd. dirs. Assn. for Cure of Cancer of the Prostate, CaP CURE, Milken Family Found.; mem. exec. com., trustee, chmn. acquisitions com. L.A. County Mus. Art; mem. com. on sculpture and decorative arts Met. Mus. Art; trustee Phila. Mus. Art; bd. overseers U. Pa.;

mem. acquisition com. Nat. Gallery Art, Washington. Recipient Gold Effie award, 1983; named one of Top 50 U.S. Women Bus. Owners, Working Women, #1 L.A.-based woman Bus. Owner, L.A. bus. Jour., one of top 100 U.S. art collectors Art & Antiques mag. Office: Roll Internat Corp 11444 W Olympic Blvd Los Angeles CA 90064-1549

RESNIK, ROBERT, medical educator; b. New Haven, Dec. 7, 1938; s. Nathan Alfred and Elsie (Hershman) R.; m. Lauren Brahms, Oct. 29, 1966; children: Andrew Scott, Jamie Layne. BA, Yale U., 1960; MD, Case Western Res. U., 1965. Intern in internal medicine Mt. Sinai Hosp., Cleve., 1965-66; resident in ob-gyn. Yale U. Sch. Medicine, 1966-70; asst. prof. Sch. Medicine U. Calif., San Diego, 1974-78, assoc. prof., 1978-82, prof. reproductive medicine, 1982—, chmn. dept., 1982-95, dean clin. affairs, 1988-90, dean admissions, 1995—. Cons. Nat. Heart, Lung and Blood Inst. NIH, Washington, 1987; mem. exec. com. Coun. Residency Edn. Ob-Gyn, Washington, 1988-94, residency rev. com., 1988-94. Editor: (textbook) Maternal-Fetal Medicine: Principles and Practice, 1984, 4th edit., 1999; contbr. numerous articles to profl. jours. Major U.S. Army, 1970-72. Rsch. grantee Nat. Found., NIH. Fellow Am. Coll. Obstetrics and Gynecology (vice chmn. obs. practice com. 1998-2000), Pacific Coast Obstet. and Gynecol. Soc.; mem. Soc. Gynecologic Investigation (coun. 1983-88), Perinatal Rsch. Soc. (pres. 1985), Am. Gynecologic and Obstet. Soc. (coun.), Am. Gynecol. Club (sec., treas.), San Diego Gynecol. Soc. (pres. 1982), Yale Club. Office: U Calif Sch Medicine 9500 Gilman Dr Dept 0621 La Jolla CA 92093-0621

RESTER, GEORGE G. architect, designer, painter, sculptor, showman; b. Ponchatoula, La., Oct. 5, 1923; s. Kelly Caldwell Rester and Myra Vira (Adams) Smith; m. Virginia Wilhelmena, June 25, 1955; children: Gina Louise, Taira Elizabeth, Licia Therese. Student, U.S. Army Engring. Sch., Ft. Belvoir, Va., 1943, Soulé Coll., 1945-48, Delgado Tech. Inst., 1949-50, Art Ctr. Coll. Design, 1961-62. Registered architect, La., Calif., Fla., Colo., N.Y., Ariz., Tex., N.J., Mich., Minn., Wash., N.Mex.; cert. Nat. Coun. Archtl. Registration Bds. Architect, designer, draftsman various firms, New Orleans, 1953-60; pvt. practice architecture Culver City, Calif., 1960-61; project architect Welton Beckett Architect, Beverly Hills, 1961-64; dir. archtl. design and prodn. (chief architect) Walt Disney Imagineers, Glendale, 1965-71, 76-87; sr. prin. engr. Ralph M. Parsons Engring. Co., Pasadena, 1973-76; prin. George G. Rester Architect, AIA, 1987—. Prin. works as designer/planner with Walt Disney Imagineers design team include New Orleans Sq., Space Mountain at Disneyland, Calif., 1965; as master planner, concepts designer, Walt Disney World, Fla., 1967 (Internat. accolades 1987), Resort Community (internat. accolades 1987), E.P.C.O.T. at World Disney World, Fla., 1982, New Fantasyland at Disneyland, Calif., 1983 (internat. accolades); concepts designer Theme Park, Tokyo Disneyland, 1983 Served with combat engrs., U.S. Army, 1943-45, ETO, Africa, Mid. East. Mem. AIA, Internat. Platform Assn., Nat. Trust for Hist. Preservation, New Orleans Amateur Artists Soc. (founding pres. 1940-42). Home and Office: 26337 Dunwood Rd Palos Verdes Peninsula CA 90274-2371

RETALLACK, GREGORY JOHN, geologist, educator; b. Hobart, Australia, Nov. 8, 1951; came to U.S., 1977; s. Kenneth John Retallack and Moira Wynn (Dean) Gollan; m. Diane Alice Johnson, May 31, 1981; children: Nicholas John, Jeremy Douglas. B.A., Macquarie U., Sydney, 1973; B.Sc. with honors, U. New Eng., 1974, Ph.D., 1978. Vis. asst. prof. Northern Ill. U., Dekalb, 1977-78; vis. scholar Ind. U., Bloomington, 1978-81; asst. prof. U. Oreg., Eugene, 1981-86, assoc. prof., 1986-92, prof., 1992—. Author: Geological Excursion Guide to the Sea Cliffs North of Sydney, 1978, Late Eocene and Oligocene Paleosols from Badlands National Park, South Dakota, 1983, Soils of the Past, 1990, Miocene Paleosols and Ape Habitats in Pakistan and Kenya, 1991, Colour Guide to Paleosols, 1997; contbr. numerous articles in field to profl. jours. Grantee NSF, 1979—, Wenner-Gren Found., 1983. Fellow AAAS, Geol. Soc. Am.; mem. Geol. Soc. Australia, Bot. Soc. Am., Paleontol. Soc. (pres. Pacific sect. 1986), Oreg. Acad. Sci. (pres. 1986), Soc. Econ. Paleontologists and Mineralogists, Sigma Xi (pres. U. Oreg. chpt. 1983-84). Home: 2715 Elinor St Eugene OR 97403-2513

RETHORE, BERNARD GABRIEL, retired manufacturing and mining company executive; b. May 22, 1941; s. Francis Joseph and Katharine Eunice (MacDwyer) R.; m. Marilyn Irene Watt, Dec. 1, 1962; children: Bernard Michael, Tara Jean, Kevin Watt, Alexandra Marie, Rebecca Ann, Christopher Philip, Abigail Lyn. BA, Yale U., 1962; MBA, U. Pa., 1967. Assoc. McKinsey & Co., Inc., Washington, 1967-73, sr. assoc., 1973; v.p., gen. mgr. Greer div. Microdot, Inc., Darien, Conn., 1973-77, v.p. ops. connector group, 1977-78, pres. bus. devel. group, 1978-82, pres. fastening sys. and sealing devices groups, 1982-84; pres. Microdot Industries, Darien, 1984-87, pres., CEO, 1988; pres. Microdot Europe Ltd., Darien, 1984-88; sr. v.p. Phelps Dodge Corp., Phoenix, 1989-95; group exec. Phelps Dodge Industries, Phoenix, 1989-90, pres., 1990-95; pres., CEO, bd. dirs. BW/IP Internat., Inc., Phoenix, 1995-97, chmn., 1997; CEO, chmn. bd. dirs. Flowserve Corp., Phoenix, 1997-2000, ret., 2000. Bd. dirs. Maytag Corp., Belden, Inc., Amcast Indsl. Corp.; cons. U.S. Govt., UN; mem. Thunderbird Global Bus. Coun., Am. Grad. Sch. Internat. Mgmt., 1990—, chmn., 1991-94. Mem. dean's adv. bd. Wharton Sch. Bus., U. Pa., 1972-80 Elected mem. bd. fin. Town of Westport, Conn., 1986-90; trustee Ballet Ariz., 1989-95, vice chmn., 1991-95; bd. dirs. Boys Hope of Phoenix, 1989-95; trustee Phoenix Country Day Sch., 1992—, Thunderbird, Am. Grad. Sch. Internat. Mgmt., 1994—. Served to Capt., inf., AUS, 1962-65. Decorated Bronze Star. Mem. Nat. Assn. Mfrs. (bd. dirs. 1994-95, 96-99), Yale Club (N.Y.C.), Union League (Chgo.), La Cima (Dallas), Wharton Bus. Sch. Alumni Assn., Nat. Assn. Corp. Dirs. (blue ribbon com. on bd. role in strategic plan 2000), Gainey Ranch Club (Scottsdale, Ariz.). Home: 6533 E Maverick Rd Paradise Valley AZ 85253 Office: McDyre & Spendgey Ltd Ste 300 7702 E Doubletree Ranch Rd Scottsdale AZ 85258 E-mail: brethore@msltd.cc

REULING, MICHAEL FREDERICK, supermarket company, real estate executive; b. Peoria, Ill., May 11, 1946; s. F.H. and Doris (Salzenstein) R.; m. Susan Ruth Morgan, Aug. 10, 1968; children— Jessica Sue, Jeremy Michael B.A. in Econs., Carleton Coll.; J.D., U. Mich. Bar: Utah, Idaho, Tex., Fla. Assoc. Van Cott, Bagley, Cornwall & McCarthy, Salt Lake City, 1971-73; assoc. real estate Skaggs-Albertson's, Richardson, Tex., 1974-78; assoc. contracts Albertson's, Inc., Boise, Idaho, 1973-74, sr. v.p., gen. counsel, 1978-81, sr. v.p. real estate, 1981-86, exec. v.p. store devel., 1986-99, vice chmn., 1999—. Mem. Idaho State Bar Assn., Utah State Bar Assn., Fla. State Bar Assn., Tex. State Bar Assn. Office: Albertsons Inc 250 Parkcenter Blvd PO Box 20 Boise ID 83726-0020

REUTHER, RONALD THEODORE, museum director; b. Dec. 29, 1929; s. Frederick and Grace (Roehll) R.; m. Mary B. Howard, 1956; children: Catherine Virginia, Paul Douglas, Jon Frederick, Victoria Grace. BA, U. Calif., 1951, postgrad., 1953, U. Ariz., 1952. Mgr. Micke Grove Zoo, 1957-62; gen. curator Cleve. Zoo, 1958-62; asst. dir., 1964-66; dir. Indpls. Zoo, 1962-64, San Francisco Zoo, 1966-73; pres., exec. dir. Phila. Zoo, 1973-78; dir. corp. devel. Exploratorium, San Francisco, 1980-81; founder We. Aerospace Mus., Oakland, Calif., 1980, exec. dir., 1995-99; field rep. Bell & Howell Edn. Corp./DeVry Inst. Tech., 1983-88; exec. dir. Whale Ctr., Oakland, Calif., 1988-89; edn. cons. Sierra Acad. Aeronautics, Oakland, 1989-92; lectr. Golden State U., San Francisco, 1992. Co-founder Pt. Reyes Bird Observatory, Calif., 1968-70; v.p. Del. Valley Mus. Coun., 1976-78. Author zoo guidebooks, Wings Over San Francisco Bay, 1997, Mem. exec. com. Greater Phila. Cultural Alliance, 1976-78. 1st lt. USAF, 1953-57; with USARNG, 1958-66; lt. col. USAR, 1966-81, ret. Mem. The Explorers Club (chmn. No. Calif. chpt. 1990-95), Tamalpais Conservation Club (life mem.), Ox-5 Pioneers (bd. govs. Golden Gate chpt. 1996—). E-mail: reuther@itilink.com

REVEAL, ERNEST IRA, III, lawyer; b. Chgo., Oct. 19, 1948; s. Ernest Ira Jr. and Hazel (Holt) R.; m. Katherine Trennerry, Nov. 24, 1979; children: Genevieve, Adrienne, Danielle. BA, Cornell U., 1970; JD, U. Mich., 1973. Bar: Minn. 1973, U.S. Dist. Ct. Minn. 1973, U.S. Ct. Appeals (8th cir.) 1974, U.S. Dist. Ct. S.D. 1976, U.S. Ct. Claims 1976, U.S. Ct. Appeals (7th cir.) 1984, U.S. Dist. Ct. (so. dist.) Calif. 1991, U.S. Ct. Appeals (9th cir.) 1991, U.S. Supreme Ct., 1991. Assoc. Robins, Kaplan, Miller & Ciresi, Mpls., 1973-79, ptnr., 1979—. Author: Public Sector Labor Law, 1983. Mem. Civil Svc. Commn., St. Paul, Minn., 1976. Mem. ABA, Minn. Bar Assn. (past chair labor law and employment law sect.), Calif. Bar Assn. (exec. com. antitrust and unfair competition sect.), Cornell Club of Minn. (past pres.). Democrat. Presbyterian. Avocations: sports, reading. Office: Robins Kaplan Miller & Ciresi 600 Anton Blvd Ste 1600 Costa Mesa CA 92626-7652 E-mail: eireveal@rkmc.com

REVEL, JEAN-PAUL, biology educator; b. Strasbourg, France, Dec. 7, 1930; came to U.S., 1953; s. Gaston Benjamin and Suzanne (Neher) R.; m. Helen Ruth Bowser, July 27, 1957 (div. 1986); children: David, Daniel Neher, Steven Robert; m. Galina Avdeeva Moller, Dec. 24, 1986; 1 stepchild, Karen. BS, U. Strasbourg, 1949; PhD, Harvard U., 1957. Rsch. fellow Cornell U. Med. Sch., N.Y.C., 1958-59; from instr. to prof. Harvard Med. Sch., Boston, 1959-71; prof. Calif. Inst. Tech., Pasadena, 1971—, AB Ruddock chair in biology, 1978—, dean of students, 1996—. Mem. sch. advisors bd. Nat. Insts. Aging, Balt., 1977-80; mem. ad hoc adv. biology NSF, Washington, 1982-83; mem. Nat. High Voltage Microscopy Adv. Group, Bethesda, Md., 1983, Nat. Rsch. Resources Adv. Coun., 1986-90. Author: (with E.D. Hay) Fine Structure of Developing Avian Cornea, 1969; editor: Cell Shape and Surface Architecture, 1977, Science of Biological Specimen Preparation, 1986; mem. editl. bd. Jour. Cell Biology, 1969-72, Internat. Rev. Cytology, 1970, Cell and Tissue Rsch., 1979—, Molecular and Cell Biology, 1983-91; editor in chief Jour. Microscopy Soc. Am., 1994-96. Fellow AAAS (leader biol. scis. sect. 1991-92, Gordon conf. cell adhesion); mem. Am. Soc. Cell Biology (pres. 1972-73), Electron Micros. Soc. Am. (pres. 1988, Disting. Scientist award 1993), Soc. Devel. Biology. Avocations: watercolors, photography. Office: Calif Inst Tech # 156-29 Pasadena CA 91125-0001 E-mail: revelj@caltech.edu

REW, LAWRENCE BOYD, lawyer; b. Eugene, Oreg., June 22, 1936; BA, Whitman Coll., 1958; JD, Willamette U., 1961. Bar: Oreg. 1961. Ptnr. Corey, Byler, Rew, Lorenzen & Hojem, LLP, Pendleton, Oreg., 1965—. Mem. ABA, Oreg. State Bar Assn. (pres. 2000, Pub. Svc. award 1991, bd. bar examiners 1975-79, bd. govs. 1996-2000). Office: Corey Byler Rew Lorenzen & Hojem LLP PO Box 218 222 SE Dorion Ave Pendleton OR 97801-2553

REWCASTLE, NEILL BARRY, neuropathology educator; b. Sunderland, Eng., Dec. 12, 1931; arrived in Can., 1955; s. William Alexander and Eva (Coapes) R.; m. Eleanor Elizabeth Barton Boyd, Sept. 27, 1958 (dec. Jan. 1999); 4 children. MB, ChB in Medicine cum laude, U. St. Andrews, Scotland, 1955; M.A., FRCPC in gen. pathology, U. Toronto, 1962, FRCPC in neuropathology, 1968. Licentiate Med. Coun., Can. Rotating intern U. Vancouver, 1955-56; resident in pathology Shaughnessy Hosp., Vancouver, 1956-57, U. Toronto, Ont., Can., 1957-60; fellow Med. Rsch. Coun. Can., 1960-64; demonstrator dept. pathology U. Toronto, Ont., Can., 1964-65, lectr., acting head neuropathology Can., 1965-69, assoc. prof. Can., 1969-70, prof. div. neuropathology Can., 1970-81, head div. neuropathology Can., 1969-81; prof., head dept. pathology U. Calgary, Alta., Can., 1981-91, prof. Can., 1981-2000, prof. emeritus pathology, lab. medicine, clin. neuroscis. Can., 2000—. Dir. dept. histopathology Foothills Hosp., Calgary, 1981-91, pathologist, 1981—, cons. neuropathology, 1981—; spl. acad. adv. to dean faculty medicine U. Calgary, 1995-97. Recipient Queen Elizabeth Silver Jubilee medal, 1977. Fellow: Royal Coll. Physicians (cert.); mem. Can. Assn. Neuropathologists (sec. 1965-69, pres. 1976-79).

REYNDERS, JOHN VAN WICHEREN, computational physicist; b. N.Y.C., May 24, 1964; s. Charlton Jr. and Knowlton (Ames) R.; m. Mary Frances Neven, Oct. 8, 1994; 1 child, Rebecca. BS, Rensselaer Poly. Inst., 1986; PhD, Princeton U., 1992. Team leader Los Alamos (N.Mex.) Nat. Lab., 1992-93, mem. staff, 1993-94, postdoctoral rsch. assoc., 1994—. Mem. Am. Phys. Soc. Methodist. Home: General Delivery Burlington MA 01803-9999 Office: Los Alamos Nat Lab Mail Stop B287 Los Alamos NM 87545-0001

REYNOLDS, CLARK WINTON, economist, educator; b. Chgo., Mar. 13, 1934; m. Nydia O'Connor Viales; children: Rebecca, C. Winton III, Matthew, Camila. AB, Claremont (Calif.) Men's Coll., 1956; student, MIT, 1956-57, 58; student divinity sch., Harvard U., 1957-58; MA, U. Calif., Berkeley, 1961, PhD in Econs., 1962. Asst. prof. Occidental Coll., L.A., 1961-62; from asst. to assoc. prof. dept. edn. and econ. growth Yale U., New Haven, 1962-67; sr. fellow The Brookings Inst., Washington, 1975-76; prof. econs., prin. investigator, founding dir. Ams. program Stanford (Calif.) U., sr. fellow Inst. Internat. Studies, 1996—, prof. emeritus econs., 1996—. Vis. prof. Nat. U. Mex., Chapingo, 1966, El Colegio de Mex., Mexico City, 1964, 65, 79, Hopkins-Nanjing Ctr. for Chinese and Am. Studies, Nanjing, China, 1999—; vis. lectr. in econs. Stockholm U. Econs., 1968; fellow St. Antony's Coll., Oxford, 1975; vis. rsch. scholar Internat. Inst. for Applied Systems Analysis, Laxenburg, Austria, 1978. Author: The Mexican Economy, 1970; co-author: Essays on the Chilean Economy, 1965, (with C. Tello) U.S.-Mexican Relations: Economic and Social Aspects, Las Relaciones Mexico Estados Unidos, 1983, Dynamics of North American Trade, 1991, North American Labor Market Interdependence, 1992, Open Regionalism in the Andes, 1996. Dir. Monticello West Found., 1980—. Woodrow Wilson Found. fellow, 1956-57, Rockefeller Found. fellow, 1957-58, Doherty Found. fellow, 1960-61, Inst. Internat. Studies fellow Stanford U., 1990—; grantee Social Sci. Rsch. Coun., Ford Found., Hewlett Found., Rockefeller Found., Mellon Found., MacArthur Found., Tinker Found. Mem. Am. Econ. Assn., Cosmos Club (Washington). Office: Stanford U Inst Internat Studies Encina Hall W Rm 305 306 Stanford CA 94305-6084

REYNOLDS, JAMES FRANCIS, JR. physician; b. St. Albans, Vt., June 20, 1947; s. James F. Sr. and Eleanor (Paquette) R.; married; children: Matthew, Katelyn, Aaron. BS, U.S. Mil. Acad., West Point, N.Y., 1969; MD, U. Louisville, 1978. Diplomate Am. Bd. Pediatrics, Am. Bd. Med. Genetics. Commd. U.S. Army, 1969, advanced through grades to col., 1974; pediatrics resident U. Va., Charlottesville, 1978-81, genetics fellow, 1981-83; clin. geneticist dept. med. genetics Shodair Hosp., Helena, Mont., 1983—. Assoc. editor Am. Jour. Med. Genetics, 1983-95; editor various books on med. genetics; contbr. articles to profl. jours. Mem. health profl. adv. com. Mont. March of Dimes, 1987—; mem. Mont. Coun. for Maternal and Child Health, 1987—. Fellow Am. Acad. Pediatrics, Am. Coll. Med. Genetics; mem. Am. Soc. Human Genetics. Avocations: hiking, snow skiing, stained glass craft. Office: Shodair Hosp PO Box 5539 Helena MT 59604-5539

REYNOLDS, JERRY OWEN, sports team executive; b. French Lick, Ind., Jan. 29, 1944; Student, Vincennes U., Oakland City Coll., Ind. U., Ind. State U. Coach Rockhurst Coll., Kansas City, Mo., 1975-84, Pittsburg (Kans.) State U., 1984-85; asst. coach Sacramento Kings, 1985-86, 86-87, 87-88, head coach, 1988-89, dir. player personnel, 1989-92, gen. mgr., 1992-94; gen. mgr, v.p. Sacramento Monarchs, (WNBA), 1998—. Office: Sacramento Monarchs 1 Sports Pkwy Sacramento CA 95834-2300

REYNOLDS, RICHARD V. career officer; BS in Aeronautical Engring., USAF Acad., 1971; MSME, Calif. State U., Fresno, 1984; MA in Nat. Security/Strategic Studies, Coll. of Naval Warfare, 1987. Commd. 2d lt. USAF, 1971, advanced through grades to brig. gen., 1996; T-38 instr., check pilot 25th Flying Tng. Squadron, Vance AFB, Okla., 1972-75; B-52G aircraft comdr., instr. pilot, flight examiner 325th Bombardment Squadron, Fairchild AFB, Wash., 1975-79; exptl. test pilot 6512th Test Squadron, 1980-82; project pilot B-1 Combined Test Force, Edwards AFB, Calif., 1980-82, project test pilot, ops. officer, 1983-86; comdr. 4952nd Test Squadron, Wright-Patterson AFB, Ohio, 1987-89; dir. bomber and tanker programs Aeronautical Systems Divsn., Wright-Patterson AFB, 1989-90, dir. of advanced tactical aircraft programs, 1989-90; dep. program dir. B-2 Systems Program Office, Wright-Patterson AFB, 1990-92; dep. dir. Office of Asst. Sec. of the AF for Acquisition, the Pentagon, Washington, 1992-94; program dir. B-2 System Program Office, Wright-Patterson AFB, 1994-96; program exec. officer for airlift and trainers the Pentagon, Washington, 1996-98; comdr. Air Force Flight Test Ctr., Edwards AFB, 1988-98. 2-star gen. Air Force Flight Test Ctr., Edwards AFB, 1998—. Decorated Legion of Merit with oak leaf cluster. Office: 1 S Rosamond Blvd Edwards CA 93524-1001

REYNOLDS, ROBERT HARRISON, retired export company executive; b. Mpls., Sept. 6, 1913; s. Clarence H. and Helen (Doyle) R.; m. Gladys Marie Gaster, Apr. 7, 1934 (dec.); 1 child, Shirley Anne Reynolds Potestio (dec.); m. Viola E. Shimel, June 26, 1982. Export sales mgr., rolled products sales mgr. Colo. Fule & Iron Corp., Denver, 1938=46; pres. Rocky Mountain Export Co., Inc., Denver, 1941-93. Mem.: Denver Club (life). Home: 13850 E Marina Dr Aurora CO 80014-5509 Office: 12331 E Cornell Ave Aurora CO 80014-3323

REYNOLDS, ROGER LEE, composer, educator; b. Detroit, July 18, 1934; s. George Arthur and Katherine Adelaide (Butler) R.; m. Karen Jeanne Hill, Apr. 11, 1964; children: Erika Lynn, Wendy Claire. BSE in Physics, U. Mich., 1957, MusB in Music Lit., 1960, MusM in Composition, 1961. Assoc. prof. U. Calif. San Diego, La Jolla, 1969-73, founding dir. Ctr. Music Expt. and Related Rsch., 1972-77, prof., 1973—; George Miller prof. U. Ill., 1971—. Vis. prof. Yale U., New Haven, 1981; sr. rsch. fellow ISAM, Bklyn. Coll., 1985; Valentine prof. Amherst (Mass.) Coll., 1988; Rothschild composer in residence Peabody Conservatory of Music, 1992-93. Author: MIND MODELS: New Forms of Musical Experience, 1975, A Searcher's Path: A Composer's Ways, 1987, A Jostled Silence: Contemporary Japanese Musical Thought, 1992-93; first Dolby Digital 5.1 DVD release of custom-designed, multichannel classical compositions: WATERSHED, Mode Records, 1998; contbr. numerous articles and revs. to profl. jours. Bd. dirs. Am. Music. Ctr., Meet the Composer, Fromm Found. Harvard U.; mem. bd. govs. Inst. Current World Affairs; co-founder ONCE festivals, 1960. Recipient Koussevitzky Internat. Rec. award, 1970, citation Nat. Inst. Arts and Letters, 1971, NEA awards, 1975, 78, 79, 86, Pulitzer prize for music, 1989; sr. fellow Inst. Studies in Am. Music, 1985, fellow Inst. Current World Affairs, Rockefeller Found., Guggenheim Found.; Fulbright scholar. Office: U Calif San Diego Dept Music 0326 La Jolla CA 92093

REYNOLDS, WILLIAM CRAIG, mechanical engineer, educator; b. Berkeley, Calif., Mar. 16, 1933; s. Merrill and Patricia Pope (Galt) R.; m. Janice Erma Reynolds, Sept. 18, 1953; children: Russell, Peter, Margery. B.S. in Mech. Engring., Stanford U., 1954, M.S. in Mech. Engring., 1955, Ph.D. in Mech. Engring., 1957; D in Engring. (hon.), UMIST, U.K., 2000. Faculty mech. engring. Stanford U., 1957—, chmn. dept. mech. engring., 1972-82, 89-93, Donald Whittier prof. mech. engring., 1986—, chmn. Inst. for Energy Studies, 1974-81; staff scientist NASA/Ames Rsch. Ctr., 1987—; dir. Ctr. for Integrated Turbulence Simulations, 1997—. Author: books, including Engineering Thermodynamics, 2d edit, 1976; contbr. numerous articles to profl. jours. NSF sr. scientist fellow Eng., 1964, Otto Laporte awd., Am. Physical Soc., 1992. Fellow ASME (Fluids Engring. award 1989) Am. Phys. Soc.; mem. AIAA (Fluid Dynamic award), Stanford Integrated Mfg. Assn. (co-chmn. 1990-94), Nat. Acad. of Engrs., Am. Acad. Arts Scis., Tau Beta Pi. Achievements include research in fluid mechanics and applied thermodynamics. Office: Stanford U Dept Mech Engring Stanford CA 94305-3030

REYNOSO, CRUZ, lawyer, educator; b. Brea, Calif., May 2, 1931; m. Jeannene Reynoso; children: Trina Heter, Ranene Royer, Len Reid-Reynoso, Rondy. AA, Fullerton Jr. Coll., 1951; AB, Pomona Coll., 1953; postgrad., George Washington U., 1954-55; LLB, U. Calif., Berkeley, 1958; postgrad., Nat. U. Mexico, Mexico City, 1958-59; hon. degree, U. Santa Clara, 1981, Lincoln U., 1984, DePaul U., 1986, U. San Diego, 1991, Thomas Jefferson Law Sch., 1997, others. Legis. asst. State Senator from Imperial County, Calif., 1959-60; pvt. law practice El Centro, 1959-68; asst. chief div. fair employment practices Dept. Indsl. Rels., San Francisco, 1965-66; staff sec. Gov. Edmund G. Brown, Sacramento, 1966; assoc. gen. counsel EEOC, Washington, 1967-68; from dep. dir. to dir. Calif. Rural Legal Assistance, San Francisco, 1968-72; prof. law U. N.Mex. Sch. Law, Albuquerque, 1972-76; assoc. justice 3d Dist. Ct. Appeal, Sacramento, 1976-82, Calif. Supreme Ct., San Francisco, 1982-87; of counsel O'Donnell & Gordon, L.A. and Sacramento, 1987-88; spl. counsel Kaye, Scholer, Fierman, Hays & Handler, 1988-90; prof. law UCLA Sch. Law, 1991—. Vice chmn. U.S. Commn. Civil Rights, 1993—. Bd. dirs. Rosenberg Found., 1977-93, pres., 1989; bd. dirs. Mex. Am. Legal Def. Ednl. Fund, The Cmty. Bd. Program, 1977-90, Children Now, 1990—, Coun. on Founds., 1991-92, Natural Resources Def. Coun., 1987—; bd. dirs. Latino Issues Forum, 1987—, chair, 1987-93. With U.S. Army, 1953-55. Recipient Loren Miller Legal Svcs. award Calif. State Bar. Mem. ABA (com. on lawyer referral and info. svc. 1989-91), L.A. Bar Assn., Am. Judicature Soc. (bd. dirs. 1992-96), Calif. Judges Assn., La Raza Lawyers Assn., Mex. Am. Bar Assn., Nat. Hispanic Bar Assn., Nat. Assn. Latino Elected and Apptd. Ofcls. Office: UCLA Sch Law 405 Hilgard Ave Los Angeles CA 90095-9000

REZNICK, RICHARD HOWARD, pediatrician; b. Chgo., Oct. 31, 1939; s. Louis and Mae Reznick; m. Barbara Ann Glantz, June 20, 1965; children: Steven L., Alicia T., Scott M., Stacey R. BS, U. Ill., 1961; MD, Loyola U., Chgo., 1965. Diplomate Am. Bd. Pediatrics. Resident in pediat. Michael Reese Hosp., Chgo., 1966-68; pediatrician USAF, Homestead AFB, Fla., 1968-70; pediatrician pvt. practice Winnetka, Ill., 1970-71, Scottsdale, Ariz., 1971—. Pres. med. staff Phoenix Children's Hosp., 1990-93, bd. dirs. 1990-94. Capt. USAF, 1968-70. Fellow Am. Acad. Pediatrics (treas. Ariz. chpt. 1982-84); mem. AMA, Ariz. Med. Assn., Phoenix Pediatric Soc. (treas. 1976-77), Maricopa County Med. Soc. Avocations: aerobics, bicycling, gardening, classical music, collecting stamps. Office: Papago Buttes Pediatric Ctr 8573 E San Alberto Ste E100 Scottsdale AZ 85258-4318

RHEIN, TIMOTHY J. retired transportation company executive; b. 1941; BS, U. Santa Clara, 1962. Mil. contract and revenue analyst Am. Pres. Lines Ltd., Oakland, Calif., 1967-71, sr. analyst, 1971-72, mgr. mktg. planning, 1972-73, dir. traffic systems and adminstrn., 1973-75, dir. mktg. adminstrn., 1975-76, dir. worldwide sales, 1976-78, v.p. N.Am., 1978-80, v.p. traffic, 1980-84, sr. v.p., 1984-87, pres., also chief oper. officer, 1987-90; pres., chief exec. officer APL Ltd., Oakland, 1990-2000, retired, 2000. With U.S. Army, 1962-67. Office: APL Ltd 1111 Broadway Fl 25 Oakland CA 94607-4036

RHEINISH, ROBERT KENT, university administrator; b. Mt. Vernon, N.Y., Oct. 27, 1934; s. Walter Washington and Doris Elizabeth (Standard) R.; m. Dorothy Ellen Steadman, May 3, 1957 (div. 1976); children: Robert Scott, Joel Nelson; m. Shirley Marie Suter, Aug. 1, 1976. BA, U. South Fla., 1963; MS, Ind. U., 1969, EdD, 1971. Staff engr. Armed Forces Radio & TV Svc., Anchorage, 1960-61; trainee Nat. Park Svc. Tng. Ctr., Grand Canyon, Ariz., 1965; historian Home of F.D.R., Nat. Historic Site, Hyde Park, N.Y., 1964-65, Sagamore Hill Nat. Hist. Site, Oyster Bay, 1965-66; asst. coord. nat. environ. edn. devel. program Dept. of Interior, Washington, 1968; supervisory historian Lincoln Boyhood Nat. Meml., Lincoln City, Ind., 1966-68; dir. learning resources ctr. Whittier (Calif.) Coll., 1971-73; dir. media and learning resources Calif. State U., Long Beach, 1973-88. Chmn. media dirs. The Calif. State Univs., Long Beach, 1975-76; radio announcer Sta. WTCX-FM, St. Petersburg, Fla., 1961-63; co-host with David Horowitz (2 broadcasts) On Campus, Sta. KNBC-TV, L.A., 1972-73; guest lectr. 6th Army Intelligence Sch., Los Alamitos Armed Forces Res. Ctr., 1987; founder Rheino Ltd., 1997. Coord. multi-media program: In Search of Yourself, 1975 (Silver award Internat. Film and TV Festival of N.Y.), The House that Memory Built, 1981 (Cindy award Info. Film Producers of Am.), The Indochinese and Their Cultures, 1985 (Silver award Internat. Film & TV Festival of N.Y.); holder 2 patents. With RCAF, 1954-55, USAF, 1957-61. U.S. Office of Edn. grad. fellow, 1969-71; recipient Learning Resources Ctr. Devel. Fund award Pepsico, Sears, Prentice-Hall, et al, 1973; Nat. Def. Edn. Act grantee, 1974-76. Mem. NRA, Am. Legion. Republican. Avocations: collecting militaria, boating, political writing. Home: 380 Long Br W Prescott AZ 86303-5306 E-mail: rheino@commspeed.net

RHINES, MARIE LOUISE, composer, violinist; b. Boston; BA in History and Polit. Sci., Northeastern U.; postgrad., Yale U.; MusM, New Eng. Conservatory, Boston. Dir. chamber music Groton (Mass.) Sch. for Boys; prof. of violin King's Coll. Choir Sch., Cambridge, Eng.; concert-master, asst. conductor Cape Cod Symphony, Hyannis, Mass.; producer, announcer, founder The Folk Heritage program Nat. Pub. Radio, Sta. WGBH-FM, Boston; guest faculty U. Colo., Boulder; conductor, Mozart Orch. Harvard U., Cambridge, Mass., 1985-86; panelist Mass. Coun. on Art and Humanities, Boston, 1986; pub., pres., founder Sedona (Ariz.) Music Pub. Co., 1988—; composer, guest soloist USAF Concert Band, Southwestern States, 1990—; guest soloist, composer in residence U.S. Command Band of Air Force Res., Warner Robins AFB, Ga., 1991; artist Ariz. Commn. on Arts and Humanities, Phoenix, 1990—; guest solo violin artist Holland Am. Cruise Lines, 1996. Artist-in-residence U. Calif., LaJolla; composer-artist-in-residence State of Tenn., Nashville; guest poet, musician Ariz. Cowboy Poets Gathering, Prescott, 1990-91; mem. violin faculty No. Ariz. U. 1993. Composer, publisher numerous works for solo violin, voice, chamber orchestra, full symphony orch. and opera chorus; solo violin concert appearances at major concert halls and as soloist with symphony orchs. throughout U.S., Can., Europe; numerous radio and TV interviews and documentaries; recording artist, N.Y., Nashville, 1996, RCA Studios. Cmty. Speakers Bureau Lect. Ariz. Humanities Council, 2000-01. Recipient Music Composition award, Artist Found.; Rockefeller grantee Am. Music Ctr. Mem. ASCAP (22 composing and performing awards), Nashville Assn. of Musicians, Meet the Composer. Avocations: mountain climbing, gourmet cooking, gardening, psychology, philosophy. Home and Office: Sedona Music 2255 Corral Rd Sedona AZ 86336-3272 E-mail: marierhines@hotmail.com

RHINES, PETER BROOMELL, oceanographer, atmospheric scientist; b. Hartford, Conn., July 23, 1942; s. Thomas B. and Olive (Symonds) R.; m. Marie Louise Lenos, Oct. 12, 1968; (div. 1983); m. Linda Jean Mattson; 1 child, Andrew Nelson B.S., M.S., M.I.T., Cambridge U., 1964; Ph.D., Trinity Coll., Cambridge U., Eng., 1967. Asst. prof. oceanography M.I.T., Cambridge, 1968-71; rsch. asst. dept. applied math. and theoretical physics Cambridge U., Eng., 1971-72; scientist Woods Hole Oceanographic Inst., Woods Hole, Mass., 1972-84; prof. oceanography and atmospheric scis. U. Wash., Seattle, 1984—. Vis. fellow Christ's Coll., Cambridge, Eng., 1979-80, 1983 Recipient de Florez research award MIT, 1963; NSF fellow, 1963-64; Guggenheim fellow, 1979-80; Queen's fellow in marine scis., Australia, 1988; A.E. Sloan Research scholar MIT, 1960-63; Marshall scholar Cambridge, 1964-67; Green scholar U. Calif., San Diego, 1981. Fellow Am. Geophys. Union, Am. Meteorol. Soc. (Henry Stommel award 1999); mem. Am. Acad. Arts and Scis., Nat. Acad. Scis. Avocations: classical guitar, walking, studying the global environment, developing laboratory-based teaching resources. Home: 5753 61st Ave NE Seattle WA 98105-2037 Office: U Wash Sch Oceanography Dept Oceanography Seattle WA 98195-0001

RHOADES, JOHN SKYLSTEAD, SR. federal judge; b. 1925; m. Carmel Rhoades; children: Mark, John, Matthew, Peter, Christopher. AB, Stanford U., 1948; JD, U. Calif., San Francisco, 1951. Prosecuting atty. City of San Diego, 1955-56, dep. city atty., 1956-57; pvt. practice San Diego, 1957-60; ptnr. Rhoades, Hollywood & Neil, San Diego, 1960-85; judge U.S. Dist. Ct. (so. dist.) Calif., San Diego, 1985—. With USN, 1943-46. Office: US Dist Ct 940 Front St San Diego CA 92101-8994

RHOADS, DEAN ALLAN, state legislator, cattle rancher; b. Tonasket, Wash., Oct. 5, 1935; s. Clyde Chester and Mamie Katerine (Kennedy) R.; m. Sharon Lois Packer, Jan. 8, 1964; children: Shamria, Chandra. BS in Agrl. Bus. Mgmt., Calif. State Poly. Coll., San Luis Obispo, 1963. Mgr. Calif. Livestock Mktg. Assn., Visalia, 1963-66; cow-calf operator Tuscarora, Nev., 1966—; mem. Nev. Assembly, 1976-82, Nev. Senate, Northern Nev., Carson City, 1988—. Past pres., bd. dirs. Pub. Lands Coun., Washington, 1970-91. Mem. Nev. Tax Payers Assn. (bd. dirs. 1982-91), Nev. Cattlemen's Assn. (bd. dirs. 1968-91, Cattleman of Yr. 1980), Rotary. Republican. Presbyterian. Avocations: skiing, golf. Address: PO Box 8 Tuscarora NV 89834-0008 Office: Nev Senate 401 S Carson St Rm 245 Carson City NV 89701-4747

RHODE, DEBORAH LYNN, law educator; b. Jan. 29, 1952; BA, Yale U., 1974, JD, 1977. Bar: D.C. 1977, Calif. 1981. Law clk. to judge U.S. Ct. Appeals (2d cir.), N.Y.C., 1977-78; law clk. to Hon. Justice Thurgood Marshall U.S. Supreme Ct., D.C., 1978-79; asst. prof. law Stanford (Calif.) U., 1979-82, assoc. prof., 1982-85, prof., 1985—; dir. Inst. for Rsch. on Women and Gender, 1986-90, Keck Ctr. of Legal Ethics and The Legal Profession, 1994—; sr. counsel jud. com. Ho. of Reps., Washington, 1998. Trustee Yale U., 1983-89; pres. Assn. Am. Law Schs., 1998; Ernest W. McFarland prof. Stanford Law Sch., 1997—; sr. counsel com. on the jud. U.S. Ho. of Reps., 1998. Author: Justice and Gender, 1989, (with Geoffrey Hazard) the Legal Profession: Responsibility and Regulation, 3d edit., 1993, (with Annette Lawson) The Politics of Pregnancy: Adolescent [illegible] (with Barbara Allen Babcock, Ann E. Freedman, Susan Deller Ross, Wendy Webster Williams, Rhonda Copelon, and Nadine H. Taub) Sex Discrimination and the Law, 1997, Speaking of Sex, 1997, Professional Responsibility: Ethics by the Pervasive Method, 1998, In the Interests of Justice, 2000; editor: Theoretical Perspectives on Sexual Difference, 1990, Ethics in Practice, 2000; contbr. articles to profl. jours. Mem. ABA (chair commn. on women and the profession 2000—). Office: Stanford U Law Sch Crown Quadrangle Stanford CA 94305

RHODE, EDWARD ALBERT, veterinary medicine educator, veterinary cardiologist; b. Amsterdam, N.Y., July 25, 1926; s. Edward A. and Katherine (Webb) R.; m. Dolores Bangert, 1955; children: David E., Peter R., Paul W., Robert M., Catherine E. DVM, Cornell U., 1947. Diplomate Am. Coll. Veterinary Internal Medicine. Prof. emeritus vet. medicine U. Calif., Davis, 1964—, chmn. dept. vet. medicine, 1968-71; assoc. dean instrn. U. Calif. Sch. Vet. Medicine, Davis, 1971-81, dean, 1982-91. Mem. AAAS, Nat. Acad. Practices, Am. Coll. Vet. Internal Medicine, Am. Vet. Medicine Assn., Basic Sci. Coun., Am. Heart Assn., Am. Acad. Vet. Cardiology, Am. Physiol. Soc., Calif. Vet. Medicine Assn. Office: U Calif Sch Vet Med Davis CA 95616

RHODY, RONALD EDWARD, banker, communications executive; b. Frankfort, Ky., Jan. 27, 1932; s. James B. and Mary M. (Clark) R.; m. Patricia Schupp, Apr. 23, 1955; children: Leslie K., Mary M., Virginia K., Ronald C. Student, Georgetown (Ky.) Coll., 1950-52, U. Ky., 1953-55. Pub. rels. dir. Kaiser Aluminum & Chem. Corp., Ravenswood, W.Va., 1959-62, N.Y.C., 1962-67, corp. v.p. Oakland, Calif., 1967-83; sr. v.p. corp comm. Bank of Am. NT&SA, San Francisco, 1983—, exec. v.p., 1992-94; CEO Rhody, Inc., 1994—. Author: The CEO's Playbook, 1999; contbr. articles to profl. jours. Founding chmn. adv. bd. San Francisco Acad.; mem. Global Pub. Affairs Inst., N.Y.C. Named Pub. Rels. Profl. of Yr., Pub. Rels. News, 1981; recipient Hall of Fame award Page Soc., 1997. Mem. Pub. Rels. Soc. Am. (accredited, pres.'s adv. coun. Rex Harlow award), Internat. Assn. Bus. Communicators (Gold Quill award 1980), Pub. Rels. Roundtable San Francisco (mem. bd. govs., awards 1980, 85). Clubs: San Francisco Press; International (Washington); Nat. Press (Washington). Home: 2725 Pontiac Dr Walnut Creek CA 94598-4437 Office: Rhody Inc 2725 Pontiac Dr Walnut Creek CA 94598-4437 E-mail: ronrhody@msn.com

RIASANOVSKY, NICHOLAS VALENTINE, historian, educator; b. Harbin, China, Dec. 21, 1923; came to U.S., 1938, naturalized, 1943; m. Arlene Ruth Schlegel, Feb. 15, 1955; children— John, Nicholas, Maria. BA, U. Oreg., 1942; AM, Harvard U., 1947; DPhil, Oxford (Eng.) U., 1949. Mem. faculty U. Iowa, 1949-57, U. Calif., Berkeley, 1957—, prof. history, 1961—, Sidney Hellman Ehrman prof. European history, 1969—; trustee Nat. Council Soviet and E. European Research, 1978-82; mem. Kennan Inst. Acad. Council, 1986-89. Vis. research prof. USSR Acad. Scis., Moscow, 1969, Moscow and Leningrad, 1974, 79 Author: Russia and the West in Teaching of the Slavophiles: A Study of Romantic Ideology, 1952, Nicholas I and Official Nationality in Russia, 1825-1855, 1959, A History of Russia, 1963, 6th edit., 1999, The Teaching of Charles Fourier, 1969, A Parting of Ways: Government and the Educated Public in Russia, 1801-1855, 1976, The Image of Peter the Great in Russian History and Thought, 1985, The Emergence of Romanticism, 1992, Collected Writings 1947-94, 1993; co-editor: California Slavic Studies, 1960—; editl. bd. Russian rev., Zarubezhnaia Periodicheskaia Pechat' na Russkom Iazyke, Simvol; contbr. articles to profl. jours. Served to 2d lt. AUS, 1943-46. Decorated Bronze Star; recipient Silver medal Commonwealth Club Calif., 1964; Rhodes scholar, 1947-49; Fulbright grantee, 1954-55, 74, 79; Guggenheim fellow, 1969; sr. fellow Nat. Endowment Humanities, 1975; Fulbright sr. scholar, sr. fellow Ctr. Advanced Studies in Behavioral Scis., 1984-85; sr. fellow Woodrow Wilson Internat. Ctr. for Scholars, 1989-90. Mem. AAAS, Am. Assn. Advancement Slavic Studies (pres. 1973-76, Disting. Contbr. award 1993), Am. Hist. Assn. (award for Scholarly Distinction 1995), Am. Acad. Arts and Scis.

RICARDI, LEON JOSEPH, electrical engineer, researcher; b. Brockton, Mass., Mar. 21, 1924; s. Philip Julius and Eva Isabel (DuBois) R.; m. Angelena Marie Giorgio, Jan. 19, 1947; children: Eva Marie, John Philip, Richard Christopher. B.S. in Elec. Engring, Northeastern U., 1949, M.S., 1952, Ph.D., 1969. Engr. Andrew Alford Cons. Engrs., Boston, 1950-51; project engr. Gabirel Labs., Needham, Mass., 1951-54; group leader, head Tech. Adv. Office, MIT-Lincoln Lab., Lexington, 1954-84; pres. L.J. Ricardi, Inc., El Segundo, Calif., 1984-95, Creative Engring., Manhattan Beach, 1996—. Part-time tchr. Northeastern U., Boston, 1969-80; cons. U.S. Air Force, 1965-85. Served with USAF, 1943-45. Fellow IEEE. Roman Catholic. Office: Creative Engring 1525 Curtis Ave Manhattan Beach CA 90266-7020 E-mail: lricardi@juno.com

RICCARDI, VINCENT MICHAEL, pediatrician, researcher, educator, entrepreneur; b. Bklyn., Oct. 14, 1940; s. Gabriel John and Frances Mary (Novak) R.; m. Susan Leona Bogda, July 27, 1967; children: Angela M., Ursula M., Mikah F. AB, UCLA, 1962; MD, Georgetown U., 1966; MBA, U. LaVerne, 1993. Intern, resident in medicine U. Pitts., 1966-68; fellow in genetics Harvard Med. Sch., Boston, 1968-70, 72; asst. prof. medicine U. Colo. Med. Ctr., Denver, 1973-75; assoc. prof. medicine, pediatrics Med. Coll. Wis., Milw., 1975-77; prof. medicine, pediatrics Baylor Coll. Medicine, Houston, 1977-90; med. dir. The Genetics Inst., Pasadena, Calif., 1990-92; clin. prof. pediatrics UCLA, 1991—; founder, CEO Am. Med. Consumers, La Crescenta, 1992. Dir. The Neurofibromatosis Inst., La Crescenta, Calif., 1985—. Author: Genetic Approach to Human Disease, 1977, Communication and Counseling in Health Care, 1983, Neurofibromatosis, 1986, rev. edit., 1992, 99. Maj. U.S. Army, 1970-71. Fellow ACP, AAAS, Am. Coll. Med. Genetics; mem. Am. Soc. Human Genetics, Am. Coll. Physician Execs. Avocation: writing poetry and screenplays, acting in movies. Office: Am Med Consumers 5415 Briggs Ave La Crescenta CA 91214-2205 E-mail: riccardi@medcomsumer.com

RICCITIELLO, JOHN S. interactive software/gaming executive; Pres., CEO Wilson Sporting Goods Co.; pres., CEO bakery divsn. Sara Lee Corp.; pres., COO Electronic Arts, Redwood City, Calif., 1997—. Office: Electronic Arts Inc 209 Redwood Shores Pkwy Redwood City CA 94065

RICE, CONDOLEEZZA, academic administrator, political scientist; b. Birmingham, Ala., 1955; BA cum laude, U. Denver, 1974, PhD, 1981; MA, U. Notre Dame. Asst. prof. dept. polit. sci. to assoc. prof. Stanford (Calif.) U., 1981-93, prof., 1993—, provost, 1993-99; spl. asst. to U.S. President Nat. Security Affairs, Washington, 1989-91; dir. Soviet and East European Affairs, Washington; sr. fellow Hoover Inst., Stanford, Calif. Cons. ABC News, Washington; mem. spl. advisory panel to comdr. and chief strategic air commd.; mem. gov. ind. advisory redistricting the state of Calif.; mem. U.S. Delegation to 2+4 Talks on German Unification. Author: The Soviet Union and the Czechoslovak Army, (with Alexander Dallin) THe Gorbachev Era. Recipient Walter J. Gores award, 1984. Mem. Coun. Fgn. Rels. Office: Stanford U Hoover Inst Stanford CA 94305-6010

RICE, DONALD BLESSING, business executive, former secretary of air force; b. Frederick, Md., June 4, 1939; s. Donald Blessing and Mary Celia (Santangelo) R.; m. Susan Fitzgerald, Aug. 25, 1962; children: Donald Blessing III, Joseph John, Matthew Fitzgerald. BSChemE, U. Notre Dame, 1961, DEng (hon.), 1975; MS in Indsl. Adminstrn., Purdue U., 1962, PhD in Mgmt. and Econs., 1965, D. Mgmt. (hon.), 1985; LLD (hon.), Pepperdine U., 1989; LHD (hon.), West Coast U., 1993; D in Pub. Policy (hon.), [illegible] 1967-69, dep. asst. sec. def. resource analysis, 1969-70; asst. dir. Office Mgmt. and Budget, Exec. Office Pres., 1970-72; pres., CEO The Rand Corp., Calif., 1972-89; sec. USAF, 1989-93; pres., COO Teledyne, Inc., L.A., 1993-96; pres., CEO Agensys, Inc., Santa Monica, Calif., 1996—, also bd. dirs. Bd. dirs. Vulcan Materials Co., Wells Fargo & Co.; chmn. Scios Inc., Pilkington Aerospace, Unocal Corp., Amgen Inc.; mem. Nat. Sci. Bd., 1974-86; chmn. Nat. Commn. Supplies and Shortages, 1975-77; mem. nat. adv. com. oceans and atmosphere Dept. Commerce, 1972-75; mem. adv. panel Office Tech. Assessment, 1976-79; adv. council Coll. Engring., U. Notre Dame, 1974-88; mem. Def. Sci. Bd., 1977-83, sr. cons., 1984-88; mem. U.S. Commn. Nat. Security/21st Century, 1998-2001; dir. for sec. def. and Pres. Def. Resource Mgmt. Study, 1977-79; trustee RAND, 2001, chmn. grad. sch. bd. govs., 1999—. Author articles. Served to capt. AUS, 1965-67. Recipient Sec. Def. Meritorious Civilian Service medal, 1970, Def. Exceptional Civilian Svc. medal, 1993, Forrestal award, 1992; Ford Found. fellow, 1962-65 Fellow AAAS, Nat. Acad. of Pub. Adminstrn.; mem. Inst. Mgmt. Scis. (past pres.), Tau Beta Pi. Office: UroGenesys Inc 1701 Colorado Ave Santa Monica CA 90404-3436 E-mail: drice@urogenesys.com

RICE, DOROTHY PECHMAN (MRS. JOHN DONALD RICE), medical economist; b. Bklyn., June 11, 1922; d. Gershon and Lena (Schiff) Pechman; m. John Donald Rice, Apr. 3, 1943; children: Kenneth D., Donald B., Thomas H. Student, Bklyn. Coll., 1938-39; BA, U. Wis., 1941; DSc (hon.), Coll. Medicine and Dentistry N.J., 1979. With hosp., and med. facilities USPHS, Washington, 1960-61; med. econs. studies Social Security Adminstrn., 1962-63; health econs. br. Community Health Svc., USPHS, 1964-65; chief health ins. rsch. br. Social Security Adminstrn., 1966-72, dep. asst. commr. for rsch. and statistics, 1972-75; dir. Nat. Ctr. for Health Stats., Rockville, Md., 1976-82; prof. Inst. Health & Aging U. Calif., San Francisco, 1982-94, prof. emeritus, 1994—. Developer, mgr. nationwide health info. svcs.; expert on aging, health care costs, disability, and cost-of-illness. Contbr. articles to profl. jours. Recipient Social Security Adminstrn. citation, 1968, Disting. Service medal HEW, 1974, Jack C. Massey Found. award, 1978 Fellow Am. Public Health Assn. (domestic award for excellence 1978, Sedgwick Meml. medal, 1988), Am. Statis. Assn.; mem. Inst. Medicine, Assn. Health Scvs. Rsch. (President's award 1988), LWV. Home: 13895 Campus Dr Oakland CA 94605-3831 Office: U Calif Sch Nursing Calif San Francisco CA 94143-0646

RICE, EARLE (WILMONT), JR. writer; b. Lynn, Mass., Oct. 21, 1928; s. Earle Wilmont and Grace Elizabeth (Nottingham) Rice; m. Georgia Joy Black Wood, Nov. 1, 1958; children: Ellen Jean, Earle Wilmont, III. Student, Sch. Practical Art, Boston, 1947, San Jose (Calif.) City Coll., , 1959, Foothill Coll., Los Altos, Calif., 1971. Product engr. ISS/Sperry Univac, Cupertino, Calif., 1973-74; sr. design specialist GTE/Sylvania, Mountain View, 1974; sr. design checker Westinghouse Corp., Sunnyvale, 1974; tech. writer Nuclear Svcs. Corp., Campbell, 1974; lead checker, tech. writer ESL, Inc., Sunnyvale, 1975; sr. E/M designer Finnigan Corp., Sunnyvale, 1975-76, Advanced Devices Labs., Inc., Santa Clara, Calif., 1976, Argosys., Inc., Palo Alto, 1976; equipment designer Raytheon Co., Goleta, 1976-78; sr. staff specialist Vitro Labs./Automation Ind., Oxnard, 1978-79; engring. drawing checker Gen. Dynamics, San Diego, 1979, 87-89; sr. E/M designer GE Co., Lompoc, Calif., 1980; sr. field engr. Martin Marietta Corp., Vandenberg AFB, 1980-84; engring. pub. specialist Lockheed Austin Divsn., Austin, Tex., 1984-85; design engr. Sundstrand Turbomach, San Diego, 1985-87; sr. design engr. ROHR, INC., Chula Vista, 1989-93. Author: (fiction) Tiger, Lion, Hawk, 1977, The Animals, 1979, Fear on Ice, 1981, More Than Macho, 1981, Death Angel, 1981, The Gringo Dies at Dawn, 1993, (chpt.) The Secret of Barking Dog Bayou, 1993 (Second Place award Fla. Freelance Writers Assn.), White Sun and Blue Sky, 1994 (Third Place award Fla. Freelance Writers Assn.), So Long, Slimeball!, 1994, (non-fiction) The Cuban Revolution, 1995, The Battle of Britain, 1996, The Battle of Midway, 1996, The Inchon Invasion, 1996, The Battle of Belleau Wood, 1996, The Attack on Pearl Harbor, 1996, The Tet Offensive, 1996, The Nuremberg Trials, 1996, The Salem Witch Trials, 1996, The O.J. Simpson Trial, 1996, The Final Solution, 1997, Nazi War Criminals, 1997, The Battle of the Little Bighorn, 1997, Life Among the Great Plains Indians, 1997, Life During the Crusades, 1997, Life During the Middle Ages, 1998, Kamikazes, 1999, The Third Reich, 2000, The Bombing of Pearl Harbor, 2000, The Cold War, 2000, Strategic Battles in the Pacific, 2000, Strategic Battles in Europe, 2000; adaptor: Dracula, 1995, All Quiet on the Western Front, 1995, The Grapes of Wrath, 1996; contbr. articles to mags. With USMC, 1948-57. Mem. U.S. Naval Inst., Soc. Children's Book Writers and Illustrators, League WW I Aviation Historians, Cross & Cockade Internat., Air Force Assn. Republican. Avocations: reading, spectator sports. Home and Office: PO Box 2131 Julian CA 92036-2131 E-mail: ericejr@julian-ca.com

RICE, EDWARD EARL, former government official, author; b. Saginaw, Mich., Feb. 6, 1909; s. William Edward and Katherine Marie (Meyer) R.; m. Mary June Kellogg, Oct. 26, 1942. Student. U. Wis., 1926-28; BS, U. Ill., 1930, postgrad., 1934-35, U. Mex., 1931, Coll. Chinese Studies, also pvt. tutors, Beijing, 1935-37. Joined Fgn. Svc., Dept. State, 1935; lang. attache Beijing, 1935-37; vice consul Canton, China, 1938-40; consul Foochow, China, 1940-42; 2d sec. Am. Embassy, Chungking, China, 1942-45; asst. chief div. Chinese affairs Dept. State, 1946-48, asst. chief div. Philippine affairs, 1948-49; 1st sec., consul Am. Embassy, Manila, 1949-51; consul gen. Stuttgart, Fed. Republic Germany, 1952-56; fgn. svc. insp. Dept. State, 1956-58, dep. dir. pers., 1959, mem. plicy planning coun., 1959-61, dep. asst. sec. of state for Far Ea. affairs, 1962-63; consul gen., min. Hong Kong, 1964-67; diplomat in residence with rank of prof. U. Calif., Berkeley, 1968-69, rsch. assoc. Ctr. for Chinese Studies, 1969—. Vis. prof. Marquette U., 1973; advisor U.S. del. 3d, 4th and 5th sessions Econ. Commn. for Asia Far East, 1948-49. Author: Mao's Way, 1972, Wars of the Third Kind, 1988. Recipient Gold medal for non-fiction Commonwealth Club, 1973. Mem. Beta Gamma Sigma. Home: 1819 Lagoon View Dr Belvedere Tiburon CA 94920-1807 Office: U Calif Ctr for Chinese Studies Berkeley CA 94720

RICE, GLEN ANTHONY, professional basketball player; b. Flint, Mich., May 28, 1967; Grad., U. Mich., 1989. Player Miami Heat, 1989-95, Charlotte Hornets, 1995-99, L.A. Lakers, 1999—. Named to NBA All-Rookie Second Team, 1990, All-NBA Second Team, 1996-97, All-NBA Third Team, 1997-98; named NBA All-Star, 1996, 97, recipient All Star MVP award, 1997; recipient MVP award Miami Heat, 1993-94, 94-95, named capt., 1994. Office: c/o LA Lakers 3900 W Manchester Blvd Inglewood CA 90305-2200

RICE, JERRY LEE, professional football player; b. Starkville, Miss., Oct. 13, 1962; m. Jackie Rice; children, Jaqui, Jerry Jr. Student, Miss. State Valley U. Football player San Francisco 49ers, 1985—; Sports Illustrated Player of the Year, 1986, 90; NFL MVP, 1987; AP/NFL/Sports Illustrated Offensive Player of the Year, 1993. MVP in Blue-Gray Game. Named MVP, Super Bowl XXIII, 1989, Sporting News NFL Player of Yr., 1987, 90; named to Sporting News Coll. All-Am. team, 1984, Sporting News All-Pro team, 1986-92, Pro Bowl team, 1986-96, 95, Pro Bowl MVP, 1995. Achievements include being a holder of NFL career records for most touchdown receptions (131), most touchdowns (139); most consecutive games with one or more touchdowns (13), 1987; NFL single-season record for most touchdown receptions (22), 1987; shares NFL single-game record for most touchdown receptions (5), 1990. Office: c/o San Francisco 49ers 4949 Centennial Blvd Santa Clara CA 95054-1229

RICE, JULIAN CASAVANT, lawyer; b. Miami, Fla., Dec. 31, 1923; s. [illegible] 1958; children— Scott B., Craig M. (dec.), Julianne C., Linda D., Janette M. Student, U. San Francisco, 1941-43; JD cum laude, Gonzaga U., 1950. Bar: Wash. 1950, Alaska 1959, U.S. Tax Ct. 1988. Pvt. practice law,

Spokane, 1950-56, Fairbanks, Alaska, 1959—; prin. Law Office Julian C. Rice (and predecessor firms), Fairbanks, 1959, Salcha, Alaska, 1999. Founder, gen. counsel Mt. McKinley Mut. Savs. Bank, Fairbanks, 1965-99, chmn. bd., 1979-80; v.p., bd. dirs., gen. counsel Skimmers, Inc., Anchorage, 1966-67; gen. counsel Alaska Carriers Assn., Anchorage, 1960-71, Alaska Transp. Conf., 1960-67. Mayor City of Fairbanks, 1970-72. Served to maj. USNG and USAR, 1943-58. Decorated Bronze Star, Combat Infantryman's Badge. Fellow Am. Bar Found. (life); mem. ABA, Wash. State Bar Assn. (50-Yr. mem. award 2000), Alaska Bar Assn., Transp. Lawyers Assn., Alternative Dispute Resolution Com., Am. Arbitration Assn., Spokane Exchange Club (pres. 1956). E-moial. Office: 10104 Salcha Dr Salcha AK 99714-9624 E-mail: salcha@earthlink.net

RICE, NANCY E. state supreme court justice; b. Denver, June 2, 1950; 1 child. BA cum laude, Tufts U., 1972; JD, U. Utah, 1975. Law clerk U.S. Dist. Ct. of Colo., 1975-76, dep. state pub. defender, appellate divn., 1976-77; asst. U.S. atty. Dist. of Colo., 1977-87; dep. chief civil divn. U.S. Attorney's Office, 1985-88; judge Denver Dist. Ct., 1988-98; apptd. judge Colo. Supreme Ct., 1998—. Contbr. articles to profl. jours. Mem. Denver Bar Assn., Colo. Bar Assn. (bd. govs. 1990-92, exec. coun., 1991-92), Women's Bar Assn., Rhone-Brackett Inn of Ct. (master 1993-97), Women Judges Assn. (co-chair nat. conf. 1990). Office: Colo Supreme Ct Colo State Jud Bldg 2 E 14th Ave Fl 4 Denver CO 80203-2115

RICE, NORMAN B. bank executive, former mayor; b. Denver, May 4, 1943; m. Constance Rice; 1 child, Mian. BA in Comm., MPA, U. Wash. Past mgr. corp. contbns. and soc. policy Rainier Nat. Bank; past dir. govt. svcs. Puget Sound Coun. Govts.; past asst. dir. Seattle Urban League; past reporter KIXI Radio; past editor, writer KOMO TV; with govt. City of Seattle, 1978—, city councilman, 1978-89, mayor, 1990-97; pres., chief exec. officer Fed. Home Loan Bank of Seattle, 1999—. Pres. U.S. Conf. of Mayors, 1995; bd. dirs. Safeco Corp., Regence Blue Shield. Office: Fed Home Loan Bank 1501 4th Ave Ste 1900 Seattle WA 98101-1693

RICE, REGINA KELLY, marketing executive; b. Yonkers, N.Y., July 11, 1955; d. Howard Adrian and Lucy Virginia (Butler) Kelly; m. Mark Christopher Rice, Sept. 11, 1981; children: Amanda Kelly, Jaime Brannen. BS in Community Nutrition, Cornell U., 1978. Account exec. J. Walter Thompson Co., N.Y.C., 1978-79; sr. account exec. Ketchum, MacLeod & Grove, N.Y.C., 1979-80; supr. Burson Marstellar, Hong Kong, 1981-83; v.p., dep. dir. food and beverage unit, creative dir. N.Y. office Hill and Knowlton, N.Y.C., 1983-91; mktg. cons. Rice & Rohr, N.Y.C., 1991-93; sr. v.p., dir. consumer mktg. practice Manning, Selvage & Lee, N.Y.C., 1993-97, sr. v.p. global tng. dir., 1999—; chief inspiration officer, dir. corp. devel. Internat. Pub. Rels. Assn., 1999-2001. Writer Fast and Healthy Mag., 1991-2000. Mem. Pub. Rels. Soc. Am. Roman Catholic. Avocation: provence pottery. Home: 3635 Patrick Henry Pl Agoura Hills CA 91301-3636 Office: Pondel Wilkinson/MS&L 12100 Wilshire Blvd Ste 400 Los Angeles CA 90025 E-mail: Kelly.Rice@MSLPR.com

RICE, ROD W. corporate executive; b. 1964; BSBA in Acctg. and Econs., Portland State U. CPA. Former acct. Deloitte & Touche; controller Direct Focus Inc., Vancouver, Wash., 1994-95, chief fin. officer, treas., sec., 1995—. E-mail: www.directfocusinc.com. Office: Direct Focus Inc 2220 NE 65th Ave Vancouver WA 98661

RICE, SUSAN F. fundraising consultant; b. Chgo., Dec. 10, 1939; BA, St. Mary's Coll., 1961; MPA, UCLA, 1976; EdD, Pepperdine U., 1986. Pres. YWCA, Santa Monica, Calif., 1978, League of Women Voters Calif., San Francisco, 1979-81; sr. fundraising profl. adminstr., instr. Santa Monica (Calif.) Coll., 1978-81; dir. govtl. rels. UCLA Alumni Assn., 1981-82; dir. devel. UCLA Grad. Sch. Mgmt., 1982-89; dep. dir. mktg. and devel., dir. major gifts Spl. Olympics Internat., Washington, 1989-90; v.p. devel. Bus. Exec. Nat. Security, Washington, 1991-92; pres., CEO Greater L.A. Zoo Assn., 1992-96; prin. SFR Consulting, L.A., 1996—. Co-author: Women, Money and Political Clout in Women as Donors, Woman as Philanthropists, 1994, Fund Raising in Crisis Mode in Advancing Philanthropy, 1997. Bd. dirs. St. Mary's Coll. Alumnae Assn., Notre Dame, Ind., 1982-84, Santa Monica Coll. Assocs., 1984-94, Internat. Human Rights Law Group, 1990-92; trustee, chair pers. compensation com. L.A. Mus. Nat. History Found., 1982-89; treas. Women's Commn. Refugee Women, 1990-96; vice chmn. pers. commn. Santa Monica Coll. Dist., 1985-89. Recipient Disting. Alumna award St. Mary's Coll., 1986, Humanitarian award, NCCJ-L.A., 1995. Mem. Nat. Soc. Fundraising Execs. (bd. dirs. 1995-97, v.p. Greater L.A. chpt.).

RICE, WALLACE WILLIAM, secondary education educator; b. Basin, Wyo., May 3, 1936; s. William Peace Jr. and Emma Anna (Wahl) R.; m. Rozella Peterson, June 23, 1962 (div. 1998); children: Steven C., Kevin E. BS in Geology, U. Wyo., 1959, MS in Natural Sci., 1967. Oil well logger Anders Well Logging, Fort Collins, Colo., 1959-61; office mgr. Wyo. Hwy Dept., Cheyenne, Wyo., 1962; adminstrv. asst. Sch. Dist. #1, Cheyenne, 1962-63; sci. tchr. Johnson H.S., Cheyenne, 1963-65; earth sci. tchr. Ctrl. H.S., Cheyenne, 1966-96; ret., 1996. Athletic ticket mgr. Ctrl. H.S., Cheyenne, 1968-96, asst. wrestling coach, 1962-63, 67—. Sec.-treas. Laramie County Rheumatic Fever Prevention Soc., Cheyenne, 1962—; leader Boy Scouts Am.; v.p. Trinity Luth. Ch., 1978-79, King of Glory Luth. Ch., 1989-91. With USNG, 1954-62. Recipient Silver Beaver award Boy Scouts Am., 1985, Commr. award, 1988, Dist. award of Merit, 1994, Founder's award Order of Arrow, 1996. Mem. Nat. Sci. Tchr. Assn. (regional meeting dir. 1972), Wyo. Math. Sci. Assn., Am. Fedn. Tchrs. (pres. 1978-79, 82, sec. 1982-96). Home: 222 E 2nd Ave Cheyenne WY 82001-1406

RICH, ANDREA LOUISE, museum administrator; BA, UCLA, 1965, MA, 1966, PhD, 1968. Asst. prof. comms. studies UCLA, L.A., 1976, asst. dir. office learning resources, 1976, acting dir. Media Ctr., 1977, dir. office of instructional devel., 1978-80, asst. vice chancellor office of instructional devel., 1980-86, asst. exec. vice chancellor, 1986-87, vice chancellor acad. adminstrn., 1987-91, exec. vice chancellor, 1991-95; pres., CEO L.A. County Mus. of Art, L.A., 1995—, pres., dir. Office: L A County Mus Art 5905 Wilshire Blvd Los Angeles CA 90036-4597

RICH, BEN ARTHUR, lawyer, educator; b. Springfield, Ill., Mar. 27, 1947; s. Ben Morris and Betty Lorraine (Ingalls) R.; m. Caroline Rose Castle, Oct. 4, 1984 (div. Nov. 1988); m. Kathleen Mills, Aug. 17, 1991. Student, U. St. Andrews, Scotland, 1967-68; BA, DePauw U., 1969; JD, Washington U., 1973; PhD, U. Colo., 1995. Bar: Ill. 1973, N.C. 1975, Colo. 1984. Rsch. assoc. U. Ill. Coll. Law, Urbana, 1973-74; staff atty. Nat. Assn. Attys. Gen., Raleigh, N.C., 1974-76; prin. Hollowell, Silverstein, Rich & Brady, Raleigh, 1976-80; dep. commr. N.C. Indsl. Commn., Raleigh, 1980-81; counsel N.C. Meml. Hosp., Chapel Hill, 1981-84; assoc. univ. counsel U. Colo. Health Scis. Ctr., Denver, 1984-86; gen. counsel U. Colo., Boulder, 1986-89, spl. counsel to the regents, 1989-90; asst. clin. prof. U. Colo. Sch. Medicine, 1992-94; asst. prof. U. Colo. Health Scis. Ctr., 1995-99, asst. dir. program in healthcare ethics, humanities and law, 1995-99; assoc. prof. bioethics program U. Calif.-Davis Med. Ctr., Sacramento, 2000—. Asst. prof. attendent U. Colo. Sch. Medicine, 1986-91, adj. instr. Sch. Law, 1988-95, adj. prof., 1996—; vis. assoc. prof., 1990-91; lectr. U. Denver Coll. Law; vis. prof. U. Calif. Davis Sch. Law. Contbr. articles to jours., chpts. to books. Mem. Am. Coll. Legal Medicine (assoc.-in-law 1987), Am. Philos. Assn., Am. Soc. Bioethics and Humanities, Am. Soc. Law, Medicine and Ethics (health law tchrs. sect.), Toastmasters Internat. (pres. Raleigh chpt. 1978). Unitarian. Avocations: sailing, jogging, tennis. Home: 4905 Ridgeline Ln Fair Oaks CA 95628-6585 Office: U Calif Davis Med Ctr Bioethics Program 4150 V St Ste 2400 Sacramento CA 95817

RICH, CLAYTON, retired university official and educator; b. N.Y.C., May 21, 1924; s. Clayton Eugene and Leonore (Elliot) R.; m. Mary Bell Hodgkinson, Dec. 19, 1953 (div. May 2, 1974); 1 son, Clayton Greig; m. Rosalind Rich, Apr. 6, 1987. Grad., Putney Sch., 1942; student, Swarthmore Coll., 1942-44; M.D., Cornell U., 1948. Diplomate Am. Bd. Internal Medicine. Intern Albany (N.Y.) Hosp., 1948-49, asst. resident, 1950-51; research asst. Cornell U. Med. Coll., 1949-50; asst. Rockefeller U., 1953-58, asst. prof., 1958-60; asst. prof. medicine U. Wash. Sch. Medicine, 1960-62, assoc. prof., 1962-67, prof., 1967-71, assoc. dean, 1968-71; chief radioisotope service VA Hosp., Seattle, 1960-70, assoc. chief staff, 1962-71, chief staff, 1968-70; v.p. med. affairs, dean Sch. Medicine; prof. medicine Stanford U., 1971-79, Carl and Elizabeth Naumann prof., 1977-79; chief staff Stanford U. Hosp., 1971-77, chief exec. officer, 1977-79. Sr. scholar Inst. Medicine, Nat. Acad. Sci., Washington, 1979-80; Mem. gen. medicine B study sect. NIH, 1969-73, chmn., 1972-73; mem. spl. med. adv. group VA, 1977-81; provost U. Okla. Health Scis. Ctr., Oklahoma City, 1980-92—, v.p. for healh scis., 1983-92; also exec. dean, prof. U. Okla. Coll. Medicine, 1980-83, emeritus Regents prof. and provost U. Okla., 1993—. Editorial bd.: Calcified Tissue Research, 1966-72, Clin. Orthopedics, 1967-72, Jour. Clin. Endocrinology and Metabolism, 1971-72; Contbr. numerous articles to med. jours. Bd. dirs. Children's Hosp. at Stanford, Stanford U. Hosp., 1974-79; chmn. Gordon Research Conf. Chemistry, Physiology and Structure of Bones and Teeth, 1967; bd. dirs. Okla. Med. Research Found.; bd. dirs. Leadership Oklahoma City, 1981-92, v.p., 1985-92; bd. dirs. Okla. Blood Inst., 1982-92, Oklahoma City chpt. ARC, 1983-92. Lt. USNR, 1951-53. Fellow ACP, AAAS; mem. Assn. Am. Physicians, Western Assn. Physicians, Am. Soc. Mineral and Bone Research (adv. bd. 1977-80), Am. Soc. Clin. Investigation, Assn. Am. Med. Colls. (exec. council 1975-79), Inst. of Medicine, Western Soc. Clin. Research (v.p. 1967-68), Endocrine Soc., Assn. Acad. Health Ctrs. (bd. dirs. 1984-88, chmn. 1987-88), Sigma Xi, Alpha Omega Alpha. Office: 13450 64th Ter NE Kirkland WA 98034-1656 E-mail: claytrich@aol.com

RICH, MICHAEL DAVID, research corporation executive, lawyer; b. L.A., Jan. 23, 1953; s. Ben Robert and Faye (Mayer) R.; m. Debra Paige Granfield, Jan. 12, 1980; children: Matthew, William. AB, U. Calif., Berkeley, 1973; JD, UCLA, 1976. Bar: Calif., 1976. Extern law clk. to judge U.S. Dist. Ct., Boston, 1975; staff mem. RAND, Santa Monica, Calif., 1976-85, dir. resource mgmt. program, 1980-85, dep. v.p., 1986, v.p. nat. security rsch. and dir. Nat. Def. Rsch. Inst., 1986-93, sr. v.p., 1993-95, exec. v.p., 1995—. Chmn. bd. dirs. Coun. for Aid to Edn., 1996—. Author numerous classified and unclassified reports and articles. Bd. dirs. WISE Sr. Svcs.; mem. bd. councillors UCLA Found., 2000—; chmn. fin. oversight com., Santa Monica-Malibu Unified Sch. Dist., 2000—; mem. acad. adv. bd. Fathom, 2000—. Mem. Council Fgn. Relations. Office: RAND PO Box 2138 1700 Main St Santa Monica CA 90401-3297 E-mail: mrich@rand.org

RICH, ROBERT STEPHEN, lawyer; b. N.Y.C., Apr. 30, 1938; s. Maurice H. and Natalie (Priess) R.; m. Myra N. Lakoff, May 31, 1964; children: David, Rebecca, Sarah. AB, Cornell U., 1959; JD, Yale U., 1963. Bar: N.Y. 1964, Colo. 1973, U.S. Tax Ct. 1966, U.S. Supreme Ct. 1967, U.S. Ct. Claims 1968, U.S. Dist. Ct. (so. dist.) N.Y. 1965, U.S. Dist. Ct. (ea. dist.) N.Y. 1965, U.S. Dist. Ct. Colo. 1980, U.S. Ct. Appeals (10th cir.) 1978; conseil juridique, Paris, 1968. Assoc. Shearman & Sterling, N.Y.C., Paris, London, 1963-72; ptnr. Davis, Graham & Stubbs, Denver, 1973—. Adj. faculty U. Denver Law Sch., 1977—; mem. adv. bd. U. Denver Ann. Tax Inst., 1985—, global bus. and culture divsn., U. Denver, 1992—, Denver World Affairs Coun., 1993—, Coll. Arts & Scis., U. Colo., Denver, 2000—; mem. Colo. Internat. Trade Coun., 1985—; mem. Rocky Mt. Dist. Export Coun., U.S. Dept. Commerce, 1993—; tax adv. com. U.S. Senator Hank Brown; bd. dirs. Clos du Val Wine Co. Ltd., Danskin Cattle Co., Ouray Ranch, Areti Wines, Ltd., Taltarni Vineyards, Christy Sports, others. Author treatises on internat. taxation; contbr. articles to profl. jours. Bd. dirs. Alliance Francaise, 1977—, Denver Internat. Film Festival, 1978-79, Copper Valley Assn.; actor, musician N.Y. Shakespeare Festival, 1960; sponosr Am. Tax Policy Inst., 1991—; trustee, sec. Denver Art Mus., 1982—; mem. adv. bd. Denver World Affairs Coun., 1993—; pres. So. Boulder Park Ecol. Assn., 1999—, dir. Anschutz Family Found.; mem. adv. bd. Coll. Arts and Sci., U. Colo., Denver, 2000—. Capt. U.S. Army, 1959-60; pres. & dir. Ouray Ranch, Colo., 2001-. Fellow Am. Coll. Tax Coun. (bd. regents 10th cir. 1992—), Soc. Fellows Aspen Inst.; mem. ABA, Internat. Bar Assn., Colo. Bar Assn., N.Y. State Bar Assn., Assn. Bar City of N.Y., Asia-Pacific Lawyers Assn., Union Internat. des Avocats, Internat. Fiscal Assn. (pres. Rocky Mt. br. 1992—, U.S. regional v.p. 1988—), Japan-Am. Soc. Colo. (bd. dirs. 1989—, pres. 1991-93), Confrerie des Chavaliers du Tastevin, Rocky Mt. Wine and Food Soc., Meadowood Club, Denver Club, Mile High Club, Cactus Club Denver, Yale Club, Denver Tennis Club. Office: Cherry Creek Sta PO Box 61429 Denver CO 80206-8429 also: Antelope Co 555 17th St Ste 2400 Denver CO 80202-3941 E-mail: robertrich@aya.yale.edu

RICHARD, EDWARD H. manufacturing company executive, former municipal government official; b. Mar. 15, 1937; s. Henry and Ida Richard. BA, Antioch Coll., 1959. Pres., chmn., bd. dirs. Magnetics Internat. Inc., Maple Heights, Ohio, 1967-86; exec. v.p. Stearns Magnetics S.A., Brussels, Belgium, 1974-77; prin. Edward H. Richard & Assocs., Cleve., 1967-96; pres., treas. David Round & Son, Inc., Cleve. Chmn. Cleve. dist. adv. council Small Bus. Adminstrn., 1975-79; former mem. nat. adv. council Dept. Treasury; cons. and advisor in field; del. world trade fairs. Former trustee Regional Econ. Devel. Coun., Met. Cleve. Jobs. Coun., Cleve. Devel. Found., Cleve. BBB; former trustee Hiram House, Antioch U., former treas., 1972-77; N.E. Ohio Regional Sewer Dist., Greater Cleve. Domed Stadium Corp., Greater Cleve. Conv. and Visitor Bur.; former trustee, vice-chmn. Cleve. Ctr. Econ. Edn.; former pres. Bratenahl Condominium Assn.; mem., chmn. fin. com. Bratenahl Bd. Edn., 1971-75; mem., bd. trustees, treas., chair fin. com. La Jolla Playhouse; CEO, pres. Mainly Mozart Festival, 1998—. E-mail: dj0975@aol.com

RICHARD, ROBERT CARTER, psychologist; b. Waterloo, Iowa, Apr. 4, 1938; s. Quentin Leroy and Adeline Pauline (Halverson) R.; m. Shirley Ruth Jones, Aug. 25, 1962 (div. Mar. 1999); children: David, John; m. Jacqueline J. Mendes, Feb. 19, 2000. BA Wheaton (Ill.) Coll., 1960; BD, Fuller Theol. Sem., 1963, PhD, 1973; STM, Andover Newton Theol. Sch., 1964. Ordained to ministry Am. Bapt. Conv., 1963; lic. psychologist, Calif. Pastor Peninsula Bapt. Ch., Gig Harbor, Wash., 1965-68; marriage and family counselor Glendale (Calif.) Family Svc., 1970-71; psychol. asst. Oakland and Pleasant Hill, Calif., 1972-71; psychologist Rafa Counseling Ctr., Pleasant Hill, 1974—. Mem. faculty John f. Kennedy U., Orinda, Calif., 1975-78; adj. faculty mem. New Coll., Berkeley, Calif, 1986; co-founder, bd. dirs. New Directions Counseling Ctr., 1974-81; rschr. assertiveness tng., lay counselor tng., psychotherapy and religious experience, treatment of adults abused as children. Author: (with Deacon Anderson) The Way Back: A Christian's Journey to Mental Wholeness, 1989; contbr. articles to profl. publs. Recipient Integration of Psychology and Theology award, 1973. Am. Calif. Contra Costra (past pres.) psychol. assns., Christian ASsn. Psychol. Studies. Republican. Baptist. Office: Rafa Counseling Ctr 101 Gregory Ln Ste 33 Pleasant Hill CA 94523-4915 E-mail: robertcrichard@cs.com

RICHARD, ROBERT JOHN, library director; b. Oakland, Calif., Sept. 20, 1947; s. John Argyle and Vern Elizabeth (Bauer) R.; m. Anne Elizabeth Terrell, June 8, 1968 (div. 1982); children: Jennifer Lynn, Laura Ellen, Constance Anne, Andrea Lee. Student, Fullerton Coll., 1965-67; B.A. in Biology, Chapman Coll., Orange (Calif.), 1972; M.S.L.S., Calif. State U.-Fullerton, 1973. Cert. county librarian, Calif. Audiovisual specialist Fullerton Pub. Libr., 1969-72, asst. to city librarian, 1972-73, librarian, 1973-76; br. librarian Orange County Pub. Libr., Orange, 1976-78, regional adminstr., 1979-80; assoc. dir. Long Beach Pub. Libr., Calif., 1980-81; dir. Sacramento Pub. Libr., 1981-86, Santa Ana (Calif.) Pub. Libr., 1986—. Mem. ALA, Pub. Library Execs. Assn So. Calif., Calif. Library Assn., Library Adminstrn. and Mgmt. Assn., Library Info. and Tech. Assn., Pub. Library Assn. Office: Santa Ana Pub Libr 26 Civic Center Plz Santa Ana CA 92701-4078

RICHARDS, HERBERT EAST, minister emeritus, commentator; b. Hazleton, Pa., Dec. 30, 1919; s. Herbert E. and Mabel Richards; m. Lois Marcey, Jan. 1, 1942; children: Herbert Charles, Marcey Lynn, Robyn Lois, Fredrick East, Mark Allen. AB, Dickinson Coll., 1941; BD, Drew U., 1944; MA, Columbia, 1944; DD, Coll. of Idaho, 1953; postgrad., Union Theol. Sem., 1941-48, Bucknell U., 1943-44. Accredited news reporter Nat. Assn. Broadcasters. Ordained to ministry Methodist Ch., 1944; pastor in Boiling Springs, Pa., 1937-40, West Chester, 1940-41, Basking Ridge, N.J., 1941-47; mem. faculty Drew U. and Theol. Sem., 1944-51, assoc. prof. homiletics and Christian criticism, chmn. dept., asst. dean, 1947-51; spl. lectr. religion Howard U., 1947; minister 1st Meth. Cathedral, Boise, Idaho, 1951-69, 1st United Meth. Ch., Eugene, Oreg., 1969-78, Tabor Heights United Meth. Ch., Portland, 1978-86, minister emeritus, 1986—. Weekly radio broadcaster Sta. KBOI, Sta. KIDO, 1941— ; weekly TV broadcaster CBS, 1945— , ABC, 1969— , NBC, 1973; pres. Inspiration, Inc., TV Found., 1965— , TV Ecology, 1973; producer Life TV series ABC, 1974-85, PBS TV, 1968-85, also BBC, Eng., Suise Romande, Geneva; chmn. Idaho bd. ministerial tng. Meth. Conf., 1954-60, TV, Radio and Film Commn., 1954-62, Oreg. Coun. Public Broadcasting, 1973; del. Idaho Conf. Meth. Gen. Conf., 1956, Jurisdictional Conf., 1956, World Meth. Coun., 1957, 81, World Meth. Conf., 1981, mem. Gen. Conf., 1956-60, Jurisdictional Conf., 1956, 60; meml. chaplain Idaho Supreme Ct., 1960; chaplain Idaho Senate, 1960-68; mem. Task Force on TV and Ch., 1983 Author: In Time of Need, 1986, Faith and the Pursuit of Healing, 1996; contbr. articles to religious publs.; composer: oratorios Prophet Unwilling, 1966, Meet Martin Luther, 1968, Dear Jesus Boy, 1973. Mem. Commn. on Centennial Celebration for Idaho, 1962-63; committeeman Boy Scouts Am.; bd. dirs. Eugene chpt. ARC, 1954-73; trustee Willamette U., Cascade Manor Homes; adv. bd. Medic-Alert Found. Recipient Alumni citation in religious edn. Dickinson Coll., 1948, Golden Plate award Am. Acad. Achievement, 1965, Jason Lee Mass Media TV award, 1983, Disting. Citizen award Idaho Statesman Newspaper, 1964, Disting. Alumnus award Drew U., 1965, disting. Eagle award Boy Scouts Am. ; named Clergyman of Yr., Religious Heritage Am., 1964. Mem. AAUP, CAP (chaplain Idaho wing, lt. col.), Am. Acad. Achievement (bd. govs. 1967—), Am. Found. Religion and Psychiatry (charter gov.), Idaho Found. Medicine and Biology (charter), Greater Boise Ministerial Assn. (pres.), Eugene Ministerial Assn. (pres. 1978), Masons (33 degree, editor Pike's Peak Albert That Is), Shriners, Elks, Rotary (editor Key and Cog, pres. dist. 510 Pioneer Club), Kappa Sigma (Grand Master of Beta Pi). Home: 10172 SE 99th Dr Portland OR 97266-7227 Office: Tabor Heights United Meth Ch 6161 SE Stark St Portland OR 97215-1935

RICHARDS, LAURA, government researcher; Dir. dept. fisheries and oceans Inst. Ocean Scis., Sidney, B.C., Can. Office: Inst Ocean Scis PO Box 6000 Sidney BC Canada V8L 4B2

RICHARDS, NORMAN BLANCHARD, lawyer; b. Melrose, Mass., May 27, 1924; s. Henry Edward and Annie Jane (Blanchard) R.; m. Diane Maionchi, July 9, 1977; children— Terri, Jeffrey. B.S., Bowdoin Coll., 1945; J.D., Stanford U., 1951. Bar: Calif. bar 1951. Mem. firm McCutchen Doyle Brown & Enersen, San Francisco, 1951—, partner, 1960—. Mem. faculty Tulane Admiralty Law Inst., Hastings Coll. Advocacy. Bd. visitors Stanford Law Sch. With USN, 1943-46. Fellow Am. Coll. Trial Lawyers; mem. ABA, Calif. State Bar, San Francisco Bar ASsn., Maritime Law Assn. U.S. Home: 85 Platt Ave Sausalito CA 94965-1897 Office: McCutchen Doyle Brown & Enerson 3 Embarcadero Ctr San Francisco CA 94111-4003

RICHARDS, PAUL LINFORD, physics educator, researcher; b. Ithaca, N.Y., June 4, 1934; s. Lorenzo Adolph and Zilla (Linford) R.; m. Audrey Jarratt , Aug. 24, 1965; children: Elizabeth Anne, Mary-Ann. AB, Harvard U., 1956; PhD, U. Calif., Berkeley, 1960. Postdoctoral fellow U. Cambridge (Eng.), 1959-60; mem. tech. staff Bell Telephone Labs., Murray Hill, N.J., 1960-66; prof. physics U. Calif., Berkeley, 1966—. Faculty sr. scientist Lawrence Berkeley Lab., 1966-2001; advisor NASA, 1975-92, 98—; hon. prof. Miller Inst. Rsch. in Phys. Scis., Berkeley, 1969-70, 87-88, 2001; vis. prof. Ecole Normale Superieure, Paris, 1984, 92; vis. astronomer Paris Obs., 1984. Contbr. over 300 articles to profl. jours. Guggenheim Meml. Found. fellow, Cambridge, Eng., 1973-74; named Calif. Scientist of Yr. Mus. Sci., L.A., 1981; recipient sr. scientist award Alexander von Humboldt Found., Stuttgart, Fed. Republic Germany, 1982, Button medal, 1997; Berkeley Faculty Rsch. lectr. 1991. Fellow NAS, Am. Phys. Soc. (Isakson prize 2000), Am. Acad. Arts and Scis. Avocations: vineyardist, wine making.

RICHARDS, STEPHEN C. corporate development executive; BA in Stats. and Econs., U. Calif., Davis; MBA in Fin., U. Calif., L.A. CPA, Calif. V.p., contr. Jefferies and Co., Inc.; v.p., dep. contr. Becker Paribas; mng. dir., CFO corr. clearing Bear Stearns and Co.; sr. v.p. corp. devel. and new ventures E*TRADE, Palo Alto, Calif., 1996—, chief online trading officer Menlo Park. Office: E*Trade Group Inc 4500 Bohannon Dr Menlo Park CA 94025

RICHARDS, VINCENT PHILIP HASLEWOOD, retired librarian; b. Sutton Bonington, Nottinghamshire, Eng., Aug. 1, 1933; emigrated to Can., 1956, naturalized, 1961; s. Philip Haslewood and Alice Hilda (Moore) R.; m. Ann Beardshall, Apr. 3, 1961; children: Mark, Christopher, Erika. A.L.A., Ealing Coll., London, 1954; B.L.S. with distinction, U. Okla., 1966. Cert. profl. librarian, B.C. Joined Third Order Mt. Carmel, Roman Catholic Ch., 1976; with Brentford and Chiswick Pub. Libraries, London, 1949-56; asst. librarian B.C. (Can.) Pub. Library Commn., Dawson Creek, 1956-57; asst. dir. Fraser Valley Regional Library, Abbotsford, B.C., 1957-67; chief librarian Red Deer (Alta., Can.) Coll., 1967-77; dir. libraries Edmonton (Alta.) Pub. Library, 1977-89; libr. and book industry cons. Victoria, Can., 1990—. Pres. Faculty Assn. Red Deer Coll., 1971-72, bd. govs., 1972-73 Contbr. articles to profl. jours., 1954— . Vice pres. Jeunesses Musicales, Red Deer, 1969-70; bd. dirs. Red Deer TV Authority, 1975-76, Alta. Found. Lit. Arts, 1984-86. Served with Royal Army Ednl. Corps, 1951-53. Home and Office: 105 1049 Costin Ave Victoria BC Canada V9B 2T4 E-mail: varichards@pacificcoast.net

RICHARDSON, A(RTHUR) LESLIE, former medical group consultant; b. Feb. 21, 1910; came to U.S., 1930, naturalized, 1937; s. John William and Emily Lilian (Wilkins) R.; m. B. Kathleen Sargent, Oct. 15, 1937. Student spl. courses, U. So. Calif., 1933-35. Mgr. Tower Theater, L.A., 1931-33; acct. Felix-Krueper Co., L.A., 1933-35; indsl. engr. Pettengill, Inc., L.A., 1935-57; purchasing agt. Gen. Petroleum Corp., L.A., 1937-46; adminstr. Beaver Med. Clinic, Redlands, Calif., 1946-72, exec. cons., 1972-75, 85; sec.-treas. Fern Properties, Inc., Redlands, 1955-75, Redelco, Inc., Redlands, 1960-67; pres. Buinco, Inc., Redlands, 1956-65; vice-chmn. Redlands adv. bd. Bank of Am., 1973-80; exec. cons. Med. Adminstrs.

Calif., 1975-83. Pres. Redlands Area Cmty. Chest, 1953; vol. exec. Internat. Exec. Svc. Corps, Jakarta, 1977, Singapore, 1979; mem. San Bernardino County (Calif.) Grand Jury, 1952-53; bd. dirs. Beaver Med. Clinic Found., Redlands, 1961-2000, sec.-treas., 1961-74, pres., 1974-75, chmn. bd. dirs., 1992-2000. Lt. Med. Adminstrv. Corps, AUS, 1942-45. Recipient Redlands Civic award Elks, 1953. Fellow Am. Coll. Med. Practice Execs. (life, disting. fellow 1980, pres. 1965-66, dir.); mem. Med. Group Mgmt. Assn. (hon. life; mem. nat. long range planning com. 1963-68, pres. western sect. 1960), Kiwanis (pres. 1951), Masons. Episcopalian. Home: 1 Verlie Dr Redlands CA 92373-6943

RICHARDSON, ARTHUR WILHELM, lawyer; b. Glendale, Calif., Apr. 3, 1963; s. Douglas Fielding and Leni (Tempelaar-Lietz) R.; m. Noriko Satake, Nov. 14, 1998. AB, Occidental Coll., 1985; student, London Sch. Econs., 1983; JD, Harvard U., 1988. Bar: Calif. 1989. Assoc. Morgan, Lewis and Bockius, L.A., 1988-90; staff lawyer U.S. SEC, L.A., 1990-92, br. chief, 1992-96, sr. counsel, 1996—2001. Mem. ABA, Calif. Bar Assn., L.A. County Bar Assn., Harvard/Radcliffe Club So. Calif., Town Hall Calif., L.A. World Affairs Coun., Sierra Club, Phi Beta Kappa. Presbyterian. Home: 2328 Mallard Ln #6 Beavercreek OH 45431

RICHARDSON, BETTY H. prosecutor; b. Oct. 3, 1953; BA, U. Idaho, 1976; JD, Hastings Coll. Law, 1982. Staff aid U.S. Senator Frank Church, 1976-77; teaching asst. Hastings Coll. Law, 1980-82, tchg. asst., 1980-82; legal rsch. asst. criminal divsn. San Francisco Superior Ct., 1982-84; jud. law clk. Chamber of Idaho Supreme Ct. Justice Robert C. Huntley Jr., 1984-86; atty. U.S. Dept. Justice, Boise, Idaho, 1993-2001, Richardson & O'Leary, Eagle, 2001—. Instr. Boise State U., 1987, 89; mem. U.S. Atty. Gen.'s Adv. Com. subcoms. on environ., civil rights and native Am. issues, others; mem. hon. adv. bd. for Crime Victims Amendment in Idaho, 1994; mem. Dist. of Idaho Judges and Lawyer Reps. com., gender fairness com., Civil Justice Reform Act com. and criminal adv. com. Mem. Idaho Indsl. Commn., 1991-93, chmn., 1993; mem. adv. bd. Family and Workplace Consortium; mem. Assistance League of Boise. Recipient Harold E. Hughes Exceptional Svc. award Nat. Rural Inst. on Alcohol and Drug Abuse, 1999; Tony Patino fellow Hastings Coll. Law, 1982. Mem. Idaho Bar Assn. (governing coun. govt. and pub. sectors lawyers sect., Pro Bono Svc. award 1988—), Idaho Pros. Attys. Assn., Assistance league of Boise, YMCA. Office: Richardson & O'Leary 99 E State St Eagle ID 83616 also: 5796 N Dalspring Boise ID 83713

RICHARDSON, CAMPBELL, retired lawyer; b. Woodland, Calif., June 18, 1930; s. George Arthur and Mary (Hall) R.; m. Patricia Packwood, Sept. 3, 1957 (dec. Oct. 1971); children: Catherine, Sarah, Thomas; m. Carol Tamblyn, June 1975 (div. Dec. 1977); m. Susan J. Lienhart, May 3, 1980; 1 child, Laura. AB, Dartmouth Coll., 1952; JD, NYU, 1955. Bar: Oreg. 1955, U.S. Dist. Ct. Oreg. 1957. Ptnr. Stoel Rives LLP, Portland, 1964-2000; ret., 2000—. Co-author: Contemporary Trust and Will Forms for Oregon Attorneys and for Idaho Attorneys; contbr. articles to profl. jours. Mem. Portland/Metro Govt. Boundary Commn., 1976; mem. Oreg. Adv. Com. to U.S. Commn. on Civil Rights, 1976-84; bd. dirs. Ctr. for Urban Edn., Portland, 1980-84, Dorchester Conf., Inc., 1982, Oreg. Zoo Found., 1993—; chmn. planned giving com. St. Vincent Med. Found., 1988-98; mem. planned giving coun. Oreg. Health Scis. Found., 1994—; trustee Met. Family Svc. Found., 1990-98; bd. dirs. Elders in Action, Portland, 2000—. Served with U.S. Army, 1955-57. Mem. ABA, Oreg. Bar Assn., Multnomah County Bar Assn., Estate Planning Coun. Portland (pres. 1978), Am. Coll. Trust and Estate Counsel, City Club, Multnomah Athletic Club (Portland). Republican. Home: 1500 SW 5th Ave Unit 1701 Portland OR 97201-5430 Office: Stoel Rives LLP 900 SW 5th Ave Ste 2300 Portland OR 97204-1229 E-mail: crichardson@stoel.com

RICHARDSON, CHARLES H. lawyer; b. Sept. 25, 1951; Student, Univ. Calif., 1973; LLB, Denver Coll. Law, 1976. City atty., Aurora, Colo., 1986—. Office: City Attys Office 1470 S Havana St Aurora CO 80012-4014

RICHARDSON, ELAINE, state legislator; Student, Bryant Coll., Pima Coll.; U. Ariz.; D (hon.), Tucson U. Comml. real estate broker, Ariz.; small bus. owner; mem. Ariz. Senate, Dist. 11, Phoenix, 1996—. Mem. West Univ. Neighborhood Assn., real estate rev. com. on Edn. Initiatives; precinct com. person legis. dist. #11, Ariz.; mem. adv. bd. Emergency Med. Svcs. for Children, U. Ariz. Health Scis. Ctr.; bd. dirs., community substance abuse adv. coun. Altar Valley Sch. Dist.; del. Jt. Protocol Session, Ariz.-Mex. Commn.; bd. mem. La Frontera Ctr., Inc.; regional dir. Nat. Order of Women Legislators. Recipient Women on the Move award, 1997. Mem. Dems. of Greater Tucson, Ariz. Women's Polit. Caucus, Nat. Conf. of State Legislatures (vice chair energy and transp. com.), Toastmasters, Plateau Club, Sierra Club. Office: PO Box 962 Tucson AZ 85702-0962

RICHARDSON, EVERETT VERN, hydraulic engineer, educator, administrator, consultant; b. Scottsbluff, Nebr., Jan. 5, 1924; s. Thomas Otis and Jean Marie (Everett) R.; m. Billie Ann Kleckner, June 23, 1948; children: Gail Lee, Thomas Everett, Jerry Ray B.S., Colo. State U., 1949, M.S., 1960, Ph.D., 1965. Registered profl. engr., Colo. Hydraulic engr. U.S. Geol. Survey, Wyo., 1949-52, hydraulic engr. Iowa, 1953-56, rsch. hydraulic engr. Colo., 1956-63, project chief, 1963-68; prof. civil engring., adminstr. engring. rsch. ctr. Colo. State U., Ft. Collins, 1968-82, prof. in charge of hydraulic program, 1982-88, prof. civil engring., 1988-94, prof. emeritus, 1994—, dir. hydraulic lab. engring. rsch. ctr., 1982-88, dir. Egypt water use project, 1977-84, dir. Egypt irrigation improvement project, 1985-90; dir. Egypt Water Rsch. Ctr. Egypt Water Rsch. Ctr. Project, Ft. Collins, 1988-89; sr. assoc. Ayers Assocs. Inc. (formerly Resource Cons./Engrs., Inc.), Ft. Collins, Colo., 1989-93, Ayres Assocs., Ft. Collins, 1994—. Dir. Consortium for Internat. Devel., Tucson, Ariz., 1972-87; developer, instr. stream stability and scour at hwy. bridges course for State Dept. Transps. for NHI, FHWA; investigator for NTSB of 1987 I-90 bridge failure, N.Y., 1997, railroad bridge failure, Ariz., CALTRAN of 1995 I-5 bridge failure; cons. in field. Sr. author: Highways in the River Environment, Fed. Hwy. Adminstrn., 1975, 90, 2001, Evaluating Scour at Bridges, Fed. Hwy. Adminstrn., 1991, 93, 95, 2001; contbr. to Engring. and Civil Engring. Handbook, 1995, Handbook of Fluid Dynamics and Fluid Machinery, 1996, Water Resources-Environmental Planning, Management, and Development, 1996; contbr. articles to profl. jours., chpts. in books. Mem. Ft. Collins Water Bd., 1969-84; mem. N.Y. State Bridge Safety Assurance Task Force, 1988-91. Decorated Bronze Star, Purple Heart; Combat Infantry Badge, U.S. Govt. fellow MIT, 1962-63. Fellow ASCE (J.S. Stevens award 1961, chair task com., bridge scour rsch. 1990-96, vice chair 1997—, hydraulics divsn. task com. excellence award, 1993, Hans Albert Einstein award 1996, editor Compendium of Stream Stability and Scour Papers, 1991-98); mem. Internat. Congress for Irrigation and Drainage (bd. dirs.), Sigma Xi, Chi Epsilon, Sigma Tau. Home: 824 Gregory Rd Fort Collins CO 80524-1504 Office: Ayres Assocs PO Box 270460 Fort Collins CO 80527-0460

RICHARDSON, JOHN EDMON, marketing educator; b. Whittier, Calif., Oct. 22, 1942; s. John Edmon and Mildred Alice (Miller) R.; m. Dianne Elaine Ewald, July 15, 1967; 1 child, Sara Beth. BS, Calif. State U., Long Beach, 1964; MBA, U. So. Calif., 1966; MDiv, Fuller Theol. Sem., 1969, D of Ministry, 1981. Prof. mktg. Sch. Bus. and Mgmt. Pepperdine U., Malibu, Calif., 1969—. Author: (leader's guides) Caring Enough to Confront, 1984, The Measure of a Man, 1985; editor: Ann. Editions: Marketing, 1987—, Bus. Ethics, 1990—. Mem. Am. Mgmt. Assn., Soc. Bus. Ethics, Christian Writers Guild, Fuller Sem. Alumni Cabinet (pres. 1982-85), Am. Mktg. Assn., Beta Gamma Sigma. Avocations: fishing, woodworking, golf, photography. Office: Pepperdine U Sch Bus and Mgmt 400 Corporate Pointe Fl 4 Culver City CA 90230-7627

RICHARDSON, JOHN VINSON, JR. library and information science educator; b. Columbus, Ohio, Dec. 27, 1949; s. John Vinson Sr. and Hope Irene (Smith) R.; m. Nancy Lee Brown, Aug. 22, 1971. BA, Ohio State U., 1971; MLS, Peabody Coll., 1972; PhD, Ind. U., 1978. Asst. prof. UCLA, 1978-83, assoc. prof., 1983-98, editor The Libr. Quar., 1994—, prof., 1998—. Faculty coord. UCLA-St. Petersburg State Acad. of Culture Exch. Program, 1996—; fellow advanced rsch. Inst. U. Ill., 1991; pres. Info. Transfer, Inglewood, Calif., 1988—; mem. editl. bd. Ref. Svcs. Rev., Ann Arbor, Mich., 1991—, Jour. Govt. Info., Oxford, Eng., 1975—, Index to Current Urban Documents, Westport, Conn., 1987—, U. Calif. Press Catalogues and Bibliographies series, 1994-97; vis. fellow Charles Stuart U. NSW Australia, 1990; vis. scholar ALISE Russia Project, St. Petersburg and Moscow, 1996; vis. disting. scholar OCLC Inc., Dublin, Ohio, 1996-97; chmn. Calif. Pacific Ann. Conf. Com. on Archives and History, 1992-96; Henderson lectr. U. N.C., Chapel Hill, 1997; mem. UCLA Privilege and Tenure, 1999-2000, chair, 2000—. Author: Spirit of Inquiry, 1982, Gospel of Scholarship, 1992, Knowledge-based Systems for General Reference Work, 1995. Mem. UCLA Grad. Coun., 1992-96, chair, 1995-96; mem. U. Calif. systemwide coord. com. on grad. affairs, 1993-96; pres. Wesley Found., L.A., 1981-87; lay del. Cal-Pac Conf. United Meth. Ch., 1985, 86, 92-96, chair conf. commn. on archives and history, 1992—96. Rsch. grantee Coun. on Libr. Resources, 1985, 90, Assn. Libr. and Info. Sci. Educators rsch. grantee, 1984, 87, 98, Online Computer Libr. Ctr. Libr. and Info. Sci. rsch. grantee, 1999; Harold Lancour scholar Beta Phi Mu, 1986, 99, Kaliper Sr. scholar U. Mich., 1998-99; recipient Louise Maxwell award Ind. U. Alumni Assn., 1995. Mem. ALA (Justin Winsor prize 1990, Ref. and Adult Svcs. divsn. Outstanding Paper award 1992), AAAS, Assn. Libr. and Info. Sci. Educators (rsch. paper prize 1986, 91, rsch. grants 1984, 87, 98), Am. Soc. for Info. Sci. (Best Info. Sci. book 1995), Am. Assn. Adv. Slavic Studies, Sigma Xi. Democrat. Avocations: wine tastin-g,reading, fgn. travel, lilac point Siamese. Office: UCLA GSE&IS DIS Campus Box 951520 Los Angeles CA 90095-1520 E-mail: jrichard@ucla.edu

RICHARDSON, JUDY MCEWEN, education administrator, consultant, cartoonist; b. Appleton, Wis., June 3, 1947; d. John Mitchell and Isabel Annette (Ruble) McEwen; m. Larry Leroy Richardson, Mar. 19, 1972 (div. Oct. 1983). BA in English, Stanford U., 1968, MA in Edn., 1969; PhD in Higher Edn., U. Wash., 1975. Dir. ednl. rsch. St. Olaf Coll., Northfield, Minn., 1975-79; evaluation specialist Northwest Regional Ednl. Laboratory, Portland, 1980-82; legis. rsch. analyst Ariz. State Sen., Phoenix, 1982-87; dir. sch. fin. Ariz. Dept. Edn., Phoenix, 1987-92, assoc. superintendent, 1992-94; ednl. cons. Scottsdale, Ariz., 1994-96; exec. dir. Ariz. State Bd. for Sch. Capital Facilities, Phoenix, 1996-98; sch. fin. cons. Peacock, Hislop, Staley & Given, Phoenix, 1998—. Cartoonist for the Ariz. Capitol Times, 1995-96. Office: Peacock Hislop Staley & Given Inc 2999 N 44th St Ste 100 Phoenix AZ 85018-7261 E-mail: jrichardson@phsg.com

RICHARDSON, MELVIN MARK, state legislator, broadcast executive; b. Salt Lake City, Apr. 29, 1928; s. Mark and Mary (Lundquist) R.; m. Dixie Joyce Gordon, 1952; children: Pamela, Mark, Lance, Todd, Kristi. Grad., Radio Operational Engring. Sch., Burbank, Calif., 1951. Radio announcer, program dir. Sta. KBUH, Brigham City, Utah, 1951-54; mgr. Sta. KLGN, Logan, 1954-58; announcer, sports dir. Sta. KID Radio/TV, Idaho Falls, Idaho, 1958-86; mgr., program dir. Sta. KID-FM/AM, Idaho Falls, 1986; mem. Idaho Ho. of Reps., 1988-92, Idaho Senate, Dist. 32, Boise, 1992—. Cons., dir. INEL Scholastic Tournament, Idaho Nat. Engring. Lab.; speaker in field. Host: Mel's Sports Scene, Thirty Minutes, Channel Three Reports, Probes, Probing America. Dir. Assn. Idaho Cities, Ricks Coll. Booster Club, Bonneville County Crime Stoppers, Idaho Falls Child Devel. Ctr.; active Idaho Centennial Commn., Anti-Lottery Com., Gov.'s Conf. on Children; commr. Bonneville County Parks and Recreation Commn.; mayor City of Ammon, Idaho, 1966-72; candidate from Idaho Dist. # 2 for U.S. Congress. Sgt. USAR, 1951-57. Named Man of Yr., Ricks Coll., 1980. Mem. Idaho Broadcasters Assn. (bd. dirs.). Republican. Mem. LDS Ch. Home and Office: 3725 Brookfield Ln Idaho Falls ID 83406-6803 Address: State Capitol PO Box 83720 Boise ID 83720-3720

RICHARDSON, WALTER JOHN, architect; b. Long Beach, Calif., Nov. 14, 1926; s. Walter Francis and Ava Elizabeth (Brown) R.; m. Marilyn Joyce Brown, June 26, 1949 (div. 1982); children: Mark Steven, Glenn Stewart; m. Mary Sue Sutton, Dec. 4, 1982. Student, UCLA, 1944-45, Long Beach City Coll., 1946; BA, U. Calif., Berkeley, 1950. Registered architect, Ala., Ariz., Calif., Colo., Fla., Hawaii, Ill., Kans., Md., Mass., Nev., N.J., N.Y., Okla., Oreg., Tex., Utah, Vt., Va., Wash. Draftsman Wurster, Bernardi, Emmons, San Francisco, 1950-51, Skidmore, Owings & Merrill, San Francisco, 1951; designer Hugh Gibbs Architect, Long Beach, 1952-58; ptnr. Thomas & Richardson Architects, Long Beach, Costa Mesa, 1958-70; pres. Walter Richardson Assocs. Architects, Newport Beach, Calif., 1970-74; chmn. bd. Richardson, Nagy, Martin Architects and Planners, Newport Beach, 1974—. Co-author: The Architect and the Shelter Industry, 1975. Chmn. Planning Commn., City of Orange, Calif., 1967-68. With USAF, 1945. Recipient over 200 Gold Nugget Design awards Pacific Coast Builders Conf., San Francisco, 1969-96, 12 Builders Choice Design awards Builder Mag.; named Architect of Yr. Profl. Builder mag., 1986. Fellow AIA (pres. Orange County chpt. 1970, chmn. nat. housing com. 1976, 7 design awards); mem. Nat. Assn. Home Builders, Nat. Coun. Archtl. Registration Bds., Urban Land Inst., Alpha Tau Omega. Republican. Avocations: photography, downhill skiing, travel. Office: RNM Archs Planners 4611 Teller Ave Ste 100 Newport Beach CA 92660-2104

RICHENS, MURIEL WHITTAKER, marriage and family therapist, educator; b. Prineville, Oreg. d. John Reginald and Victoria Cecilia (Pascale) Whittaker; children: Karen, John, Candice, Stephanie, Rebecca. BS, Oreg. State U.; MA, San Francisco State U., 1962; postgrad., U. Calif., Berkeley, 1967-69, U. Birmingham, Eng., 1973, U. Soria, Spain, 1981. Lic. sch. adminstr., tchr. 7-12, pupil pers. specialist, Calif.; lic. marriage and family therapist, Calif. Tchr. Springfield (Oreg.) High Sch.; instr. San Francisco State U.; instr., counselor Coll. San Mateo, Calif., San Mateo High Sch. Dist., 1963-86; therapist AIDS Health Project U. Calif., San Francisco, 1988—; marriage and family therapist, pvt. practice San Mateo. Guest West German-European Acad. seminar, Berlin, 1975. Lifeguard, ARC. Postgrad. student Ctr. for Human Communications, Los Gatos, Calif., 1974, U. P.R., 1977, U. Guadalajara (Mex.), 1978, U. Durango (Mex.), 1980, U. Guanajuato (Mex.) 1982. Mem. U. Calif. Berkeley Alumni Assn., Am. Contract Bridge League (Diamond Life Master, cert. instr., cert. dir.), Women in Comm., Computer-Using Educators, Commonwealth Club, Pi Lambda Theta, Delta Pi Epsilon. Republican. Roman Catholic. Home and Office: 847 N Humboldt St Apt 309 San Mateo CA 94401-1451

RICHEY, EVERETT ELDON, religious studies educator; b. Claremont, Ill., Nov. 1, 1923; s. Hugh Arthur and Elosia Emma (Longnecker) R.; m. Mary Elizabeth Reynolds, Apr. 9, 1944; children: Eldon Arthur, Clive Everett, Loretta Arlene, Charles Estel. ThB, Anderson U., 1946; MDiv, Sch. Theology, Anderson, Ind., 1956, ThD, Iliff Sch. of Theology, Denver, 1960. Pastor Ch. of God, Bremen, Ind., 1946-47, Laurel, Miss., 1947-48, First Ch. of God, Fordyce, Ark., 1948-52; prof. Arlington Coll., Long Beach, Calif., 1961-68; pastor Cherry Ave. Ch. of God, Long Beach, 1964-68; prof. Azusa (Calif.) Pacific U., 1968-93. Mem. Christian Ministries Tng. Assn., 1968; mem., chmn. Commn. on Christian Higher Edn./Ch. of God, 1982-93; pres. Ch. Growth Investors, Inc., 1981-98. Author: ednl. manual Church Periodical--Curriculum, 1971-83, 97. Mem. Assn. Profs. and Rschrs. Religious Edn., Christian Ministries Tng. Assn. Republican. Avocation: gardening. Home and Office: 413 N Valencia St Glendora CA 91741-2418 E-mail: eerichey@juno.com

RICHMAN, ANTHONY E. textile rental industry association executive; b. Dec. 13, 1941; s. Irving M. and Helen V. (Muchnic) R.; Judy Harriet Richman, Dec. 19, 1964; children: Lisa Michele, Jennifer Beth. BS, U. So. Calif., 1964. With Reliable Textile Rental Svcs., L.A., 1964—; svc. mgr., 1969; sales and svc. mgr., 1970-73; plant mgr., 1973-75; gen. mgr., bd. dirs., 1975-78; v.p., sec.-treas., 1975-82; exec. v.p., CEO, 1982-84; pres., CEO, 1984—. Bd. dirs. Guild for Children, 1979—, Valley Guild for Cystic Fibrosis, 1974—, Cystic Fibrosis Found. of L.A. and Orange Counties, 1989—; pres. Textile Rental/Svc. Assn. Am., 1993-95; exec. dir. Western Textile Svcs. Assn., Studio City, Calif., 1996—. Office: Western Textile Svcs Assn 12444 Ventura Blvd Ste 204 Studio City CA 91604-2409

RICHMAN, DAVID PAUL, neurologist, educator, researcher; b. Boston, June 9, 1943; s. Harry S. and Anne (Goodkin) R.; m. Carol Mae von Bastian, Aug. 31, 1969; children: Sarah Ann, Jacob Charles. AB, Princeton U., 1965; MD, Johns Hopkins U., 1969. Diplomate Am. Bd. Psychiatry and Neurology. Intern, then asst. resident in medicine Albert Einstein Coll. Medicine, N.Y.C., 1969-71; resident in neurology Mass. Gen. Hosp., Boston, 1971-73, chief resident, 1973-74; instr. neurology Harvard U. Med. Sch., Boston, 1975-76; assoc. prof. neurology U. Chgo., 1976-80, assoc. prof., 1981-85, prof., 1985-91, Straus prof. neurol. Scis., 1988-91; prof. neurology U. Calif., Davis, 1991—, chmn. dept., 1991-97. Mem. com. Nat. Inst. Aging, NIH, 1984-85, mem. immunogical scis. study sect., 1986-90. Mem. AAAS, Am. Assn. Immunologists, Am. Acad. Neurology, Am. Neurol. Assn., Phi Beta Kappa, Sigma Xi. Office: U Calif Davis Dept Neurology 1515 Newton Ct Davis CA 95616-4859

RICHMAN, DOUGLAS DANIEL, medical virologist, educator, internist; b. N.Y.C., Feb. 15, 1943; s. Daniel Powell and Louise Kohnstamm (Woolf) R.; m. Eva Acquino, June 21, 1965; children: Sara, Matthew. AB cum laude, Dartmouth Coll., 1965; MD, Stanford U., 1970. Diplomate, Am. Bd. Internal Medicine, diplomate Am. Bd. Infectious Diseases; diplomate Am. Bd. Med. Examiners. Intern Stanford (Calif.) Med. Sch., 1970-71, resident, 1971-72; rsch. assoc. LID/NIAID NIH, Bethesda, Md., 1972-75; fellow Beth Israel and Children's Hosps., Harvard Med. Ctr., Boston, 1975-76; asst. prof. depts. pathology and medicine U. Calif., San Diego, 1976-82, assoc. prof., 1982-88, prof., 1988—. Vis. prof. Hubei Med. Coll., Wuhan, People's Republic of China, 1987, Tokyo Med. and Dental U., Kumamoto U. Sch. Medicine, Inst. for Virus Rsch. at Kyoto U., St. Marianna U., Tokyo, Inst. Med. Rsch., Tokyo, Fukishima Prefecture Med. Sch., Japan, 1990; mem. U. Calif. President's Cancer Rsch. Coord. Com., 1984-89, NIH AIDS Rsch. Review Com., 1987-90; cons. FDA Ctr. for Drugs and Biologics, 1986-89; pubs. com. Infectious Disease Soc. Am., 1987-90, and other national committees; dir. U. Calif.-San Diego Ctr. for AIDS Rsch., AIDS Rsch. Inst. Contbr. over 430 articles to profl. jours. including JAMA, New Eng. Jour. of Medicine, Current Therapy, Jour. Clin. Microbiology; author (with others) Internat. Textbook of Medicine, Vol. II; contbr. over 300 abstracts to profl. jours. and sci. meetings; mem. editorial bds.: Diagnostic Microbiology and Infectious Diseases, 1982—, Antimicrobial Agts. and Chemotherapy, 1987—, Jour. of AIDS, 1988—, Antiviral Agts., 1988—, Serodiagnosis and Immunotherapy, 1988—, AIDS, 1990—, AIDS Alert, 1990—, Antiviral Drug Resistance, 1996—, Clin. Virology, 1997—, others. Recipient Lowell Rantz award in infectious diseases, 1970, AMA Physicians Recgonition award, 1976, 79, 82, 85, 88, John Simon Guggenheim fellowship, 1984, Visiting Fellowship, Clare Hall, U. Cambridge, 1984-85. Fellow AAAS, Am. Coll. Physicians, Infectious Diseases Soc. Am., Am. Soc. for Microbiology, Am. Fed. for Clin. Rsch., Pan Am. Group for Rapid Viral Diagnosis, Am. Soc. for Virology, Am. Venereal Disease Assn., Soc. for Gen. Microbiology, Internat. Soc. of Antiviral Rsch., Internat. AIDS Soc., VA Soc. for Physicians in Infectious Diseases. Office: U Calif San Diego Dept Pathology & Medicine 9500 Gilman Dr La Jolla CA 92093-0679 E-mail: drichman@ucsd.edu

RICHMAN, PETER MARK, actor, painter, writer, producer; b. Phila., Apr. 16, 1927; s. Benjamin and Yetta Dora (Peck) R.; m. Theodora Helen Landess, May 10, 1953; children: Howard Bennett, Kelly Allyn, Lucas Dion, Orien, Roger Lloyd. BS in Pharmacy, Phila. Coll. Pharmacy and Sci., 1951; student of Lee Strasberg, N.Y.C., 1952-54; mem., Actors' Studio, N.Y.C., 1954—. Registered pharmacist, Pa., N.Y. Appeared in little theater, Phila., 1946-51, on stage radio and in live TV, Phila., N.Y.C., and Los Angeles, 1948-65, including Have I Got a Girl for You (pre-Broadway tryout), Biltmore Theater, L.A., 1962, The Deputy, Ctr. Theater Group, L.A., 1965; appeared at Grove Theater, Nuangola, Pa., 1952, Westchester Playhouse, 1953, Drury Lane, Chicago, 1957, Strand, N.J., 1957, Capri, 1959, Ogonquit (Maine) Playhouse, 1955-62, Matunuck, R.I., 1955, Falmouth, Mass., 1953-55, Westport, Conn., 1955, Harrison, Maine, 1962, Dennis, Mass., 1955-62, Phila. Playhouse in the Park, 1962-63; Broadway plays include End as a Man, 1953, Hatful of Rain,Broadway and Nat. Tour, 1956-57, Masquerade, 1959; off-Broadway plays include End as a Man, 1953, The Dybbuk, 1954, The Zoo Story (400 performances), 1960-61; Rainmaker, Private Lives, Angel Street, Arms and the Man, Rose Tattoo, Liliom, Funny Girl, Owl and the Pussycat, Hold Me, Equus, Night of the Iguana, Blithe Spirit, Twelve Angry Men, Henry Fonda Theatre, L.A., 1985, Babes in Toyland, Calif. Mus. Theater, 1988, Ray Bradbury's Next in Line, L.A., 1992, and numerous others; writer, performer (one man show) 4 Faces, L.A., 1995, N.Y.C., 1996, The Actors Studio, N.Y.C., 1996, and others; motion pictures include Friendly Persuasion, 1956, The Strange One, 1956, Black Orchid, 1958, The Dark Intruder, 1965, Agent for HARM, 1965, For Singles Only, 1967, Judgement Day (formerly The Third Hand), 1988, Friday the 13th, Part 8 (Jason Takes Manhattan), 1989, Naked Gun 2 1/2 (The Smell of Fear), 1991, Pool Hall Junkies, 2001; prodr., writer, actor 4 Faces (film), 2000; appeared on TV series as Nick Cain in Cain's Hundred, 1961-62, as David in David Chapter III for CBC, 1966, as Duke Page in series Longstreet, 1971-72, as Reverend Snow in series Three's Company, 1978-79, as Andrew Laird in series Dynasty, 1981-84, as Channing Capwell in series Santa Barbara, 1984, voice of God series Heroes of the Bible, 1979, voice of the Phantom in animated series Defenders of the Earth, 1986, as Madros in Berlin series My Secret Summer (formerly Mystery of the Keys), 1991; guest star over 500 TV shows, including Hotel, Dallas, Hart to Hart, Fantasy Island, Murder She Wrote, Nothing Sacred, Three's Company, Knight Rider, Star Trek: The Next Generation, Matlock, Beverly Hills 90210, others; starred in TV movies House on Greenapple Road, 1968, McCloud, 1969, Yuma, 1970, Nightmare at 43 Hillcrest (Wide World of Entertainment), 1974, Mallory, 1975, The Islander, 1978, Greatest Heroes of the Bible, 1979, Blind Ambition, 1979, The PSI Factor, 1981, Dynasty, 1981, Dempsey, 1983, City Killer, 1984, Bonanza, The Next Generation, 1988; one-man shows (paintings) Am. Masters Gallery, L.A., 1967, Orlando Gallery, L.A., 1966, McKenzie Gallery, L.A., 1969, 73, Hopkins Gallery, L.A., 1971, Goldfield Gallery, L.A., 1979, Galerie des Stars, L.A., 1988, Crocker Mus., Sacramento, Calif., 1967, Parkhurst Gallery, Seal Beach, Calif., 1991, 1996 March thru July, inaugural exhibition of the Henley Gallery Chapman U., Orange, Calif. (a 30 yr. retrospective, A life in Art); group shows include Bednarz Gallery, L.A., 1968, Dohan Gallery, L.A., 1966, Celebrity Art Exhibits, 55-city tour, 1964-65, represented in permanent collections U.S. and abroad; playwright: Heavy, Heavy What Hangs Over? , 1971, a Medal for Murray, 1991 4 Faces, 1995; dir. plays Apple of His Eye, 1954, Glass Menagerie, 1954; author: (novels) Hollander's Deal, 2000, (stories) The

Rebirth of Ira Masters, 2001; featured in book Actor as Artists, 1992, Guide to Artists in Southern California, 1994. Trustee Motion Picture and TV Fund. Served with USN, 1945-46. Recipient silver medallion Motion Picture TV Fund, 1990, Sybil Brand Humanitarian award Jeffrey Found., 1990, Spl. award, 1997, Drama-Logue critics performance award for 4 Faces, 1996, Golden Halo Eagle award, So. Calif. Motion Picture Coun., 1997. Mem. SAG, AFTRA, Actors Equity Assn., Assn. Can. TV and Radio Artists, Acad. Motion Picture Arts and Scis., Acad. TV Arts and Scis. Office: c/o Spencer Kazarian Assoc 11365 Ventura Blvd PO Box 7403 Studio City CA 91604 E-mail: pmri@petermarkrichman.com

RICHTER, BURTON, physicist, educator; b. N.Y.C., Mar. 22, 1931; s. Abraham and Fanny (Pollack) R.; m. Laurose Becker, July 1, 1960; children: Elizabeth, Matthew. B.S., MIT, 1952, Ph.D., 1956. Research assoc. Stanford U., 1956-60, asst. prof. physics, 1960-63, assoc. prof., 1963-67, prof., 1967—, Paul Pigott prof. phys. sci., 1980—, tech. dir. Linear Accelerator Ctr., 1982-84, dir. Linear Accelerator Ctr., 1984-99; dir. emeritus, 1999—. Cons. NSF; sec. Energy Adv. Bd.; bd. dirs. Varian Med. Systems, Litel Instruments; Loeb lectr. Harvard U., 1974; DeShalit lectr. Weizmann Inst., 1975; pres. Internat. Union of Pure and Applied Physics, 1997. Contbr. over 300 articles to profl. publs. Recipient E.O. Lawrence medal Dept. Energy, 1975; Nobel prize in physics, 1976 Fellow Am. Phys. Soc. (pres. 1994), AAAS; mem. NAS, Am. Acad. Arts and Scis. Achievements include research in elementary particle physics. Office: Stanford Linear Accel Ctr PO Box 20450 Stanford CA 94309-0450

RICHTER, PETER CHRISTIAN, lawyer; b. Opava, Czechoslovakia, June 13, 1944; came to U.S., 1951; s. Hanus and Alzbeta (Kindlarova) R.; m. Leslie Diane Rousseau, Nov. 25, 1967; children: Timothy Jason, Lindsey Berta. BS, U. Oreg., 1967, JD, 1971. Bar: Oreg. 1971, U.S. Dist. Ct. 1972, U.S. Ct. Appeals (9th cir.) 1972, U.S. Supreme Ct. 1983. Assoc. Veatch, Lovett & Stiner, Portland, Oreg., 1971-73; ptnr. Miller, Nash, Wiener, Hager & Carlsen, Portland, 1978—. Adj. prof. law trial advocacy Northwestern Sch. of Law, Lewis and Clark Coll., Portland, 1986—; pro tempore judge Multnomah County Cir. Ct., Portland, 1985—, Oreg. State Bar Trial Advocacy Seminars, 1988—; trial advocacy coll. planner, instr. Oreg. State Bar, 1998—. Author: (handbook) Oregon State Bar, 1987, 88, 89; co-author: (chpt. in book) Oregon State Bar Damage Manual, 1985, 90; editor, program planner Sales: The Oregon Experience, 1989. Trustee, bd. dirs. Parry Ctr. for Children, Portland, 1990; former bd. dir. Boy Scouts of Am., Columbia Pacific Coun., Portland, Nat. Conf. Christians and Jews, Portland, 1983; bd. advisers Pacific Crest Outward Bound, 2000—. With Oreg. Army N.G., 1967-75. Recipient Cert. of Appreciation Northwestern Sch. of Law, 1990; named one of ten Best Litigators in Oreg, Nat. Bar Jour. Fellow Am. Bar Found.; mem. ABA (trial techniques com.), Fed. Bar Assn. (Oreg. chpt.), Am. Bd. Trial Advocates (advocate), Oreg. Bar Assn. (lectr. trial advocacy seminars 1988—, mem. jud. adminstn. com, bus. lit. sec. exec. comm.), Multnomah Bar Assn. (former bd dirs.), Oreg. Assn. Def. Counsel (cert. of appreciation 1987, 89) Inns of Ct., Multnomah Athletic Club (trustee), Arlington Club. Avocations: squash, tennis, skiing, golf, reading, motorcycling riding. Office: Miller Nash Wiener Hager & Carlsen 111 SW 5th Ave Ste 3500 Portland OR 97204-3699 E-mail: richter@millernash.com

RICK, CHARLES MADEIRA, JR. geneticist, educator; b. Reading, Pa., Apr. 30, 1915; s. Charles Madeira and Miriam Charlotte (Yeager) R.; m. Martha Elizabeth Overholts, Sept. 3, 1938 (dec.); children: Susan Charlotte Rick Baldi, John Winfield. BS, Pa. State U., 1937; AM, Harvard U., 1938, PhD, 1940. Asst. plant breeder W. Atlee Burpee Co., Lompoc, Calif., 1936, 37; instr., jr. geneticist U. Calif., Davis, 1940-44, asst. prof., asst. geneticist, 1944-49, assoc. prof., asso. geneticist, 1949-55, prof., geneticist, 1955—; chmn. coordinating com. Tomato Genetics Coop., 1950-82; dir. CMR Tomato Genetics Resource Ctr., 1975—; mem. genetics study sect. NIH, 1958-62; mem. Galapagos Internat. Sci. Project, 1964; mem. genetic biology panel NSF, 1971-72; mem. nat. plant genetics resources bd. USDA, 1975-82. Gen. Edn. Bd. vis. lectr. N.C. State U., 1956; Faculty Research lectr. U. Calif., 1961; Carnegie vis. prof. U. Hawaii, 1963; vis. prof. Universidade São Paulo, Brazil, 1965; vis. scientist U. P.R., 1968; centennial lectr. Ont. Agr. Coll. U. Guelph, Ont., Can., 1974; adj. prof. Univ. de Rosario, Argentina, 1980; univ. lectr. Cornell U., 1987; Daniel F. Dayton meml. lectr. U. Ill., 1998; mem. Plant Breeding Research Forum, 1982-84, Century of Genetics symposium Brigham Young U., 2000. Contbr. numerous articles in field to books and sci. jours. Recipient award of distinction Coll. Agr. and Environ. Scis., U. Calif., Davis, 1991, Disting. Svc. award Calif. League Food Processors, 1993, Alexander von Humboldt award Alexander von Humboldt Found., 1993; grantee NSF, USPHS/NIH, Rockefeller Found., 1953-83; Guggenheim fellow, 1948, 50, Pa. State U. Alumni fellow, 1991; C.M. Rick Tomato Genetics Resource Ctr. at U. Calif., Davis named in his honor, 1990, Presdl. award, Crop Sci. Soc. Am., 1997, Filippo Maseri Florio World prize, 1997. Fellow Am. Soc. Hort. Sci. (M.A. Black award 1974, Vaughan rsch. award 1946, Hall of Fame 1998), Calif. Acad. Sci., AAAS (Campbell award 1959), Indian Soc. Genetics and Plant Breeding (hon.); mem. NAS, Bot. Soc. Am. (Merit award 1976), Mass. Hort. Soc. (Thomas Roland medal 1983), Soc. Econ. Botany (named Disting. Econ. Botanist 1987), Nat. Coun. Comml. Plant Breeders (Genetic and Plant Breeding award 1987), Am. Genetics Assn. (Frank N. Meyer medal 1982). Office: U Calif Davis CA 95616-1845 E-mail: rick@vegmail.ucdavis.edu

RICKARD, MARGARET LYNN, library and grants consultant, former library director; b. Detroit, July 31, 1944; d. Frank Mathias and Betty Louise (Lee) Sieger; m. Cyriac Thannikary, Nov. 13, 1965 (div. Feb. 1973); 1 child, Luke Anthony; m. Marcos T. Perez, Mar. 1973 (dec. Oct. 1973); m. Lui Gotti, Dec. 23, 1984 (dec. Aug. 1997); m. William A. Rickard, Aug. 22, 1998. AB, U. Detroit, 1968; MLS, Pratt Inst., 1969; postgrad., NYU, 1976-77. Cert. libr., N.Y. Sr. libr. Queens Pub. Libr., Jamaica, N.Y., 1969-77; libr. dir. El Centro (Calif.) Pub. Libr., 1977-99; ret., 1999. County libr./cons. Imperial County Free Libr., 1993-99; vice chmn., chmn. Serra Coop. Libr. Sys., San Diego, 1980-82; libr. cons., 1998—. Pres. Hist. Site Found., El Centro, 1988-99, 92, sec., 1989, trustee, 1989-99, v.p., 1991-92; fin. sec. St. Elizabeth Luth. Ch., El Centro, 1988; mem. Downtown El Centro Assn., mem. arches bus. improvement dist.; active numerous civic coms., fundraising events; mem. comm. and arts task force Imperial County Arts Coun.; coord. arts and culture com. City of El Centro Strategic Plan. Title IIB fellow Pratt Inst., 1968-69. Mem. ALA, AAUW (v.p. El Centro 1988), Calif. Libr. Assn., Calif. County Librs. Assn., El Centro C. of C., Toastmasters, Soroptimist Internat. of El Centro (v.p. El Centro 1978, corr. sec. 1990-91, 1st v.p. 1991-92, pres. 1992-93, 2d v.p. 1995-96, 98-99, recording sec. 1997-98, life mem.), Women of Moose (sr. regent El Centro 1988-89, ednl. advancement chmn. 1999-2000). Democrat. Lutheran. Home and Office: 5827 Ritz Rd PO Box 232 Pollock Pines CA 95726-0232

RICKLES, DONALD JAY, comedian, actor; b. L.I., N.Y., May 8, 1926; s. Max S. and Etta (Feldman) R.; m. Barbara Sklar, Mar. 14, 1965; children: Mindy Beth, Lawrence Corey. Grad., Am. Acad. Dramatic Arts, N.Y.C. Appeared in TV shows The Don Rickles Show, 1971-72, C.P.O. Sharkey, 1976-77, Foul-Ups, Bleeps and Blunders, 1984, Daddy Dearest, 1993; appeared in movies Run Silent, Run Deep, 1958, The Rat Race, 1960, Kelly's Heroes, 1992, Casino, 1995, Toy Story, 1995, Quest for Camelot, 1998, Toy Story 2, 1999, others; appeared as comedian at Stardust Hotel, Las Vegas, Nev., Harrah's Club, Reno and Lake Tahoe, Nev., Caesar's, Atlantic City, numerous other nightclubs; numerous appearances TV variety shows; rec. albums include Don Rickles Speaks and Hello Dummy. Served with USN, 1943-45. Named Entertainer of Yr., Friars Club, 1974; awarded star on Hollywood Walk of Fame, 2000. Jewish. Office: care Shefrin Co 808 S Ridgeley Dr Los Angeles CA 90036-4727

RICKS, MARY F(RANCES), archaeologist, anthropologist, consultant; b. Portland, Oreg., July 6, 1939; d. Leo and Frances Helen (Corcoran) Samuel; m. Robert Stanley Ricks, Jan. 7, 1961; children: Michael Stanley, Allen Gilbert. BA, Whitman Coll., 1961; MA, Portland State U., 1977, MPA, 1981, PhD, 1995. Asst. to dir. auxiliary services Portland State U., 1975-79, instnl. researcher, 1979-85, dir. instnl. research and planning, 1985-97, rsch. assoc. prof., 1994-97, rsch. assoc. prof. emerita, 1997—. Contbr. articles and presentations to profl. socs. Vol. archeologist BLM-USDI, Lakeview, Oreg., 1975—. Fellow Soc. Applied Anthropology; mem. Soc. Am. Archaeology, Pacific N.W. Assn. Instnl. Rsch. and Planning (pres. 1990-91), Assn. Oreg. Archaeologists (v.p. 1988-90), Assn. Instl. Rsch., City Club of Portland, Sigma Xi. Home: 8106 SW 187th Ave Beaverton OR 97007-5697 E-mail: ricksm@pdx.edu

RIDDER, PAUL ANTHONY, newspaper executive; b. Duluth, Minn., Sept. 22, 1940; s. Bernard H. and Jane (Delano) R.; m. Constance Louise Meach, Nov. 6, 1960; children: Katherine Lee Pennoyer, Linda Jane, Susan Delano Cobb, Paul Anthony, Jr. B.A. in Econs., U. Mich., 1962. With Aberdeen (S.D.) Am. News, 1962-63; With Pasadena (Calif.) Star News, 1963-64; with San Jose (Calif.) Mercury News, 1964-86, bus. mgr., 1968-75, gen. mgr., 1975-77, pub., 1977-86, pres., 1979-86, Knight-Ridder Newspaper Div., Miami, Fla., 1986—; pres., chmn., CEO Knight-Ridder, Miami, 1989—, also bd. dirs. Bd. dirs. Seattle Times, Knight-Ridder, Inc., Newspaper First. Bd. dirs. United Way; mem. adv. bd. Ctr. for Econ. Policy Devel. Stanford U., U. Mich.; mem. pres.' adv. bd. U. Mich. Named Calif. Pub. of Yr., 1983, Newspaper Exec. of Yr., Ad Week, 1991. Mem. Fla. C. of C. (bd. dirs., coun. of 100), Cypress Point Club, Indian Creek Club, Pine Valley Golf Club.

RIDDIFORD, LYNN MOORHEAD, zoologist, educator; b. Knoxville, Tenn., Oct. 18, 1936; d. James Eli and Virginia Amalia (Berry) Moorhead; m. Alan Wistar Riddiford, June 20, 1959 (div. 1966); m. James William Truman, July 28, 1970. AB magna cum laude, Radcliffe Coll., 1958; PhD, Cornell U., 1961. Rsch. fellow in biology Harvard U., Cambridge, Mass., 1961-63, 65-66, asst. prof. biology, 1966-71, assoc. prof., 1971-73; instr. biology Wellesley (Mass.) Coll., 1963-65; assoc. prof. zoology U. Wash., Seattle, 1972-75, prof., 1975—, Virginia and Prentice Bloedel Univ. prof., 2000—. Mem. study sect. tropical medicine and parasitology NIH, Bethesda, Md., 1974-78, 97; mem. Competitive Grants panel USDA, Arlington, Va., 1979, 89, 95; mem. regulatory biology panel NSF, Washington, 1984-88; mem. governing coun. Internat. Ctr. for Insect Physiology and Ecology, 1985-91, chmn. program com., 1989-91; chmn. adv. com. SeriBiotech, Bangalore, India, 1989; mem. biol. adv. com. NSF, 1992-95. Mem. editl. bd. profl. jours.; contbr. articles to profl. jours. Bd. dirs. Entomol. Found., 1998—, pres. 2001; bd. dirs. Whitney Lab., 2000—. Recipient Gregor J. Mendel award Czech Republic Acad. Scis., 1998; NSF fellow, 1958-63; grantee NSF, 1964—, NIH, 1975—, Rockefeller Found., 1970-79, USDA, 1978-82, 89—; John S. Guggenheim fellow, 1979-90; NIH fellow, 1986-87. Fellow AAAS, Am. Acad. Arts and Scis., Royal Entomol. Soc., Entomol. Soc. Am. (Recognition award in insect physiology, biochemistry and toxicology); mem. Soc. Integrative and Comparative Biology (pres. 1991), Am. Soc. Biochem. and Molecular Biology, Entomol. Soc. Am., Am. Soc. Cell Biology, Soc. Devel. Biology. Methodist. Home: 16324 51st Ave SE Bothell WA 98012-6138 Office: U Wash Dept Zoology PO Box 351800 Seattle WA 98195-1800 E-mail: lmr@u.washington.edu

RIDE, SALLY KRISTEN, physics educator, scientist, former astronaut; b. L.A., May 26, 1951; d. Dale Burdell and Carol Joyce (Anderson) R.; m. Steven Alan Hawley, July 26, 1982 (div.). BA in English, BS in Physics, Stanford U., 1973, PhD in Physics, 1978. Teaching asst. Stanford U., Palo Alto, Calif., researcher dept. physics; astronaut candidate, trainee NASA, 1978-79, astronaut, 1979-87, on-orbit capsule communicator STS-2 mission Johnson Space Ctr., on-orbit capsule communicator STS-3 mission, mission specialist STS-7, 1983, mission specialist STS-41G, 1984; sci. fellow Stanford (Calif.) U., 1987-89; dir. Calif. Space Inst. of U. Calif. San Diego, La Jolla, 1989-96, pres. space com., 1999-2000; prof. Physics U. Calif. San Diego, La Jolla, 1989—. Mem. Presdl. Commn. on Space Shuttle, 1986, Presdl. Com. of Advisors on Sci. and Tech., 1994—. Author: (with Susan Okie) To Space and Back, 1986, (with T.O'Shaughnessy) Voyager: An Adventure to the Edge of the Solar System, 1992, The Third Planet: Exploring the Earth From Space, 1994, The Mystery of Mars, 1999. Office: U Calif San Diego Calif Space Inst 0426 La Jolla CA 92093-0426

RIDGE, MARTIN, historian, educator; b. Chgo., May 7, 1923; s. John and Ann (Lew) R.; m. Marcella Jane VerHoef, Mar. 17, 1948; children: John Andrew, Judith Lee, Curtis Cordell, Wallace Karsten. AB, Chgo. State U., 1943; AM, Northwestern U., 1949, PhD, 1951. Asst. prof. history Westminster Coll., New Wilmington, Pa., 1951-55; from asst. prof. to prof. San Diego State Coll., 1955-66; prof. history Ind. U., Bloomington, 1966-79, Calif. Inst. Tech., 1980-95; prof. emeritus, 1995. Vis. prof. UCLA, summer 1963, Northwestern U., summer 1959; editor Jour. Am. History, 1966-77; sr. research assoc. Huntington Library, 1977—; bd. dirs. Calif. Hist. Landmarks Commn., 1954-64; cons. in field; Tanner lectr. Mormon Hist. Assn., 1991; Whitsett Meml. lectr., Calif. State U., 1992. Author: (book) Ignatius Donnelly: Portrait of a Politician, 1962, Ignatius Donnelly: Portrait of a Politician, 2d edit., 1991, The New Bilingualism: An American Dilemma, 1981, Frederick Jackson Turner: Wisconsin's Historian of the Frontier, 1986, My Life East and West, 1994; co-author: California Work and Workers, 1963, The American Adventure, 1964, America's Frontier Story, 1969, Liberty and Union, 1973, American History after 1865, 1981, Westward Expansion, 1982, Westward Expansion, 6th edit., 2001; editor: Children of Ol'Man River, 1988, Westward Journeys, 1989, History, Frontier and Section, 1993, The American West: The Reader, 1999. Served with U.S. Maritime Service, 1943-45. William Randolph Hearst fellow, 1950; fellow Social Sci. Research Council, 1952; fellow Guggenheim Found., 1965; fellow Am. Council Learned Socs., 1960; Newberry fellow, 1964; Huntington fellow, 1974; Annenberg scholar U. So. Calif., 1979-80; recipient Best Book award Phi Alpha Theta, 1963, Gilberto Espinos prize N.Mex. Historical Review, 1989, Ray Allan Billington prize Western History Assn., 1991. Mem. Am. Hist. Assn. (v.p. Pacific Coast br. 1994, pres. 1995, Best Book award 1963), Orgn. Am. Historians, Western History Assn. (v.p. 1985-86, pres. 1986-87), So. History Assn., Agrl. History Soc., Social Sci. History Soc., Hist. Soc. So. Calif. (pres. 1994-99). Democrat. E-mail. Office: Huntington Library San Marino CA 91108 E-mail: mridge@huntington.org

RIDLEY-THOMAS, MARK, city official; m. Avis Ridley-Thomas; children (twins) Sebastian, Sinclair. BA, MA, Immaculate Heart Coll.; PhD, U. So. Calif. City councilman 8th dist. L.A. City Coun., 1991—; past mem. L.A. County Met. Transit Authority. Exec. dir. So. Christian Leadership Conf. of Greater L.A., 1981-91; chmn. Black Leadership Coalition on Edn.; co-founder, mem. Black-Asian Dialogue; co-chmn. Latino-Black Roundtable; co-convener New Majority Working Group; chmn. info. tech. and gen. svcs. com., ad hoc com. on gangs and juvenile justice, L.A. City Coun.

RIECKE, HANS HEINRICH, architect; b. Münster, Westfalia, Germany, Mar. 30, 1929; came to U.S., 1955; s. Hans Joachim and Hildegard (Schwarze) R.; m. Elvira Maria Magdalena Kaatz, Nov. 30, 1954; children: Christine, Annette, Monica, Ralph, Heidi. Student architecture, Technische Hochschule, Hannover, Fed. Republic. Germany, 1953; BA in Architecture, U. Calif., Berkeley, 1957. Registered architect, Calif., Hawaii, Ind. Draftsman Orinoco Mining Co., Puerto Ordaz, Venezuela, 1954-55, H.K. Ferguson Co., San Francisco, 1956-57; architect, ptnr. Hammarberg and Herman, Oakland, Calif., 1957-74; prin. Hans Riecke, Architect Inc., Kahului, Maui, Hawaii, 1974-78, Riecke Sunnland Kono Architects Ltd, Kahului, Maui, 1978-96; pres. HR Architect Inc., Maui, 1996—. Bd. dirs. Kihei Community Assn., Maui, Hawaii, 1975-77, Seabury Hall, Makawao, Maui, 1980-82; chmn. Mayor's Com. on Housing, County of Maui, 1984. Recipient Merit award Pacific Coast Builders Con., Kahului, Hawaii, 1990. Fellow AIA (pres. Maui chpt. 1990); mem. Am. Arbitration Assn. (panel of arbitrators 1980). Avocations: biking, gardening. Office: HR Arch Inc 77 Apalapani Ln Haiku HI 96708-5625

RIEDEL, BERNARD EDWARD, retired pharmaceutical sciences educator; b. Provost, Alta., Can., Sept. 25, 1919; s. Martin and Naomi E. (Klingaman) R.; m. Julia C. McClurg, Mar. 5, 1944 (dec. Mar. 1992); children: Gail Lynne, Dwain Edward, Barry Robert; m. Della Williams, Sept. 2, 2000. BS in Pharmacy, U. Alta., Edmonton, 1943, MS in Pharmacology, 1949; PhD in Biochemistry, U. Western Ont., 1953; DSc (hon.), U. Alta., 1990. Lectr., asst. prof. Faculty of Pharmacy U. Alta., Edmonton, 1946-49, asst. prof. then assoc. prof., 1953-58, prof., 1959-67, exec. asst. to v.p., 1961-67; dean, prof. Faculty Pharm. Scis. U. B.C., Vancouver, 1967-84, coordinator Health Scis. Centre, 1977-84. Mem. sci. adv. com. Health Rsch. Found. of B.C., 1991-95. Contbr. numerous articles on pharmacology to profl. jours. Elder Ryerson United Ch.; mem. exec. bd. Boy Scouts Can., Edmonton Region, Alta.; mem. Cancer Control Agy. of B.C., trustee 1979-86, v.p., 1984, pres. 1985-86; bd. dirs. B.C. Lung Assn., 1988-2000, v.p., 1989, pres., 1990-91; chmn., bd. dirs. B.C. Organ Transplant Soc., 1986-89, hon. bd. dirs., 2000. Wing comdr. RCAF, 1943-46, 49-67. Decorated mem. Order of Can.; recipient Gold medal in Pharmacy, 1943; Centennial medal, 1967, 75th Anniversary medal U. B.C., 1990; Can Forces decoration, 1965; Commemorative medal for 125th Anniversary of the Confedn. of Can., 1992, Spl. Svcs. award Assn. Faculties of Pharmacy of Can., 2001. Mem. Alta. Pharm. Assn. (hon. life), Can. Pharm. Assn. (hon. life), Assn. of Faculties of Pharmacy of Can. (hon. life, chmn. 1959, 69, special svc. award 2001), Can. Biochem. Soc., Pharmacol. Soc. Can., Can. Assn. of Univ. Tchrs., Can. Soc. Hosp. Pharmacists, B.C. Coll. Pharmacists (hon. life), U. B.C. Profs. Emeriti Divsn. Alumni Assn. (pres. 1993-95). Home: 8394 Angus Dr Vancouver BC Canada V6P 5L2 E-mail: briedel@interchange.ubc.ca

RIEDY, MARK JOSEPH, finance educator; b. Aurora, Ill., July 9, 1942; s. Paul Bernard and Kathryn Veronica R.; m. Erin Jeanne Lynch, Aug. 29, 1964; children: Jennifer Erin, John Mark. BA in Econs. maxima cum laude, Loras Coll., 1964; MBA, Washington U., St. Louis, 1966; PhD, U. Mich., 1971. Asst. prof. bus. adminstrn. U. Colo., Boulder, 1969-71; sr. staff economist Council of Econ. Advisers, Washington, 1971-72; spl. asst. to chmn. Fed. Home Loan Bank Bd., Washington, 1972; v.p., dir. research PMI Investment Corp., San Francisco, 1973; v.p., chief economist Fed. Home Loan Bank of San Francisco, 1973-77; exec. v.p., chief operating officer Mortgage Bankers Assn. of Am., Washington, 1978-84; pres., chief operating officer Fed. Nat. Mortgage Assn., Washington, 1985-86, cons., 1986-87; pres., chief operating officer J.E. Robert Cos., Alexandria, Va., 1987-88; pres., chief exec. officer Nat. Coun. Community Bankers, Washington, 1988-92, also bd. dirs.; Ernest W. Hahn prof. real estate fin. U. San Diego, 1993—, dir. Real Estate Inst. Mem. adv. coun. Credit Rsch. Ctr., Purdue U., 1981-82, Trellion Technologies; bd. dirs. Fed. Nat. Mortgage Assn., Am. Residential Mortgage Corp., Continental Savs. Bank, AccuBanc Mortgage Corp., Pan Pacific Retail Properties, Inc., Am. Residential Investment Trust, Noble Broadcast Group, Drayton Ins. Cos., Perpetual Savs. Bank, Ctr. for Fin. Studies, TeoMedia, Inc.; bd. dirs., chmn. bd. Neighborhood Bancorp; mem. San Diego Mayor's Renaissance Commn. Chmn. St. Vincent De Paul Village; bd. dirs. Lambda Alpha Internat.; mem. bd. govs. San Diego Regional Policy Inst. Woodrow Wilson scholar, 1964; Nat. Def. scholar, 1964-66; U.S. Steel Found. fellow, 1966-68; Robert G. Rodkey Found. fellow, 1966-69; Earhart Found. fellow, 1968-69 Mem. Am. Econ. Assn., Am. Fin. Assn., Nat. Assn. Bus. Economists, Am. Soc. Assn. Execs., Urban Land Inst. Office: U San Diego Sch Bus Adminstrn 5998 Alcala Park San Diego CA 92110-2492 E-mail: mriedy@sandiego.edu

RIEGEL, BYRON WILLIAM, ophthalmologist, educator; b. Evanston, Ill., Jan. 19, 1938; s. Byron and Belle Mae (Huot) Riegel; m. Marilyn Jills, May 18, 1968; children: Marc William, Ryan Marie, Andrea Elizabeth. BS, Stanford U., 1960; MD, Cornell U., 1964. Diplomate Am Bd Ophthalmology, Nat Bd Med Examiners. Intern King County Hosp., Seattle, 1964-65; asst. resident in surgery U. Wash., Seattle, 1965; resident in ophthalmology U. Fla., Visalia, Calif., 1968-71; pvt. practice medicine specializing in ophthalmology Sierra Eye Med. Group, Inc., Visalia, 1972—. Mem staff Kaweah Delta Dist Hosp, chief staff, 1978—79, bd dirs, asst secy, 1983—90; mem staff St Agnes Hosp, Fresno, Calif.; asst med dir Sierra Ambulatory Surg Ctr, 2000—. Flight surgeon USN, 1966—68. Co-recipient Fight-for-Sight Citation for research in rentinal dystrophy, 1970. Fellow: ACS, Am Acad Ophthalmology; mem.: Rotary (Visalia), Calif Med Asn (del 1978—79), Tulare County Med Asn, Calif Asn Ophthalmology (vpres 3d party liaison 1994—96, dir 1996—98), Am Soc Cataract and Refractive Surg, Int Pacoemulsification and Cataract Methodology, Phacoemulsification and Cataract Methodology Soc. Roman Catholic. Home: 3027 Keogh Ct Visalia CA 93291-4228 Office: 2830 W Main St Visalia CA 93291-4300 E-mail: briegel@sierraeye.com

RIEKE, PAUL VICTOR, lawyer; b. Seattle, Apr. 1, 1949; s. Luvern Victor and Anna Jane (Bierstedt) R.; m. Judy Vivian Farr, Jan. 24, 1974; children: anna Katharina, Peter Johann. BA, Oberlin Coll., 1971; postgrad., U. Wash., 1971, Shoreline C.C., 1972-73; JD, Case Western Res. U., 1976. Bar: Wash. 1976, U.S. Dist. Ct. (we. dist.) Wash. 1976, U.S. Tax Ct. 1978. Assoc. Hatch & Leslie, Seattle, 1976-82, ptnr., 1982-91, Foster, Pepper & Shefelman, PLLC, 1991—. Exec. notes editor Case Western Res. U. Law Rev., 1975-76. Mem. exec. bd. dist. coun. N. Pacific dist. Am. Luth Ch., Seattle, 1978-83, coun. pres., 1983, Am. Luth. Ch. pub. bd., 1984-87; v.p. Northwest Wash. Synod of Evangelical Luth. Ch. Am., Seattle, 1988-90, mem. Synod Coun., 1990-92, del. ELCA Nat. Assembly, 1991, ELCA Northwest Synod Regional Rep., 1992-96, region one coun. pres., 1994-96. Mem. ABA, Wash. State Bar Assn., Seattle-King County Bar Assn., Order of Coif. Democrat. Lodge: Seattle Downtown Central Lions. Home: 321 NE 161st St Shoreline WA 98155-5741 Office: Foster Pepper & Shefelman PLLC 34th Fl 1111 3rd Ave Seattle WA 98101 E-mail: RiekP@Foster.com

RIEKE, WILLIAM OLIVER, foundation director, medical educator, former university president; b. Odessa, Wash., Apr. 26, 1931; s. Henry William and Hutoka S. (Smith) R.; m. Joanne Elynor Schief, Aug. 22, 1954; children: Susan Ruth, Stephen Harold, Marcus Henry. B.A. summa cum laude, Pacific Luth. U., 1953; M.D. with honors, U. Wash., 1958. Instr. anatomy U. Wash. Sch. Medicine, Seattle, 1958, asst. prof., 1961-64, adminstrv. officer, 1963-66, assoc. prof., 1964-66; prof., head dept. anatomy Coll. Medicine U. Iowa, Iowa City, 1966-71; dean protem Coll. Medicine U. Iowa (Coll. Medicine), 1969-70, chmn. exec. com., 1969-70; vice chancellor for health affairs, prof. anatomy U. Kans. Med. Center, Kansas City, 1971-73, exec. vice chancellor, prof. anatomy, 1973-75; affiliate prof. biol. structure U. Wash. Sch. Medicine, Seattle, 1975-96; pres. Pacific Lutheran U., Parkland, Wash., 1975-92; pres. emeritus, 1992—; exec. dir. Ben B. Cheney Found., 1992—. Mem. interdisciplinary gen. basic sci. test com. Nat. Bd. Med. Examiners, 1968-72, chmn. anatomy test com., 1972-75, mem. at large, 1975-79; spl. coms. NIH, 1970-72; mem. adv. com. Inst. Medicine, Nat. Acad. Scis., 1974-76; mem.

Commn. on Colls., NW Assn. Schs. and Colls., 1979-84 Editor: Procs. 3d Ann. Leucocyte Culture Conf, 1969; editorial bd.: Am. Jour. Anatomy, 1968-71. Bd. dirs. Luth. Ednl. Council N. Am., 1980-83, pres., 1982-83; chmn. Wash. Friends Higher Edn., 1983-91. Named one of Most Effective Coll. or Univ. Pres., Bowling Green State U. Rsch. Study, 1986, Disting. Alumnus Pacific Luth. U., 1970, Disting. Alumnus Pi Kappa Delta, 1977, Disting. Alumnus U. of Washington Med. Alumni, 1989; decorated Knight First Class Royal Norwegian Order of Merit, 1989; named to Cashmere H.S. Wall of Fame, 1995. Lutheran (mem. ch. council 1967-70). Home: 13905 18th Ave S Tacoma WA 98444-1006 Office: Ben B Cheney Found 1201 Pacific Ave Ste 1600 Tacoma WA 98402-4379 E-mail: cheneyfndn@aol.com

RIEMKE, RICHARD ALLAN, mechanical engineer; b. Vallejo, Calif., Oct. 11, 1944; s. Allan Frederick and Frances Jewell (O'Brien) R. BA in Physiology, U. Calif., Berkeley, 1967, MA in Physiology, 1971, PhD in Engring. Sci., 1977. Postdoctoral fellow U. So. Calif., Los Angeles, 1977-78; rsch. engr. Del Mar Avionics, Irvine, Calif., 1979; staff fellow NIH, Bethesda, Md., 1980; cons. engr. Idaho Nat. Engring. and Environ. Lab., Idaho Falls, 1980—. Served with U.S. Army Res. 1969-75. Mem. AAAS, ANS, Am. Soc. Mech. Engrs., Biomed. Engring. Soc., Soc. Computer Simulation, Soc. Math. Biology, Soc. Engring. Sci., Order of Golden Bear, Alpha Sigma Phi. Republican. Roman Catholic. Avocations: swimming, surfing. Home: 1727 Grandview Dr # 4 Idaho Falls ID 83402-5016 Office: Bechtel BWXT Idaho Idaho Nat Engring Envir Lab Idaho Falls ID 83415-3890

RIENNER, LYNNE CAROL, publishing executive; b. Pitts., Aug. 3, 1945; d. David and Molly (Rice) R. BA, U. Pa., 1967. Exec. v.p., assoc. publisher, editorial dir. Westview Press Inc., Boulder, Colo., 1975-84; pub., owner Lynne Rienner Pub. Inc., Boulder, 1984—. Pub. cons. various orgns.; lectr. U. Denver Pub. Inst., 1981-84, 93—; panelist nat. meetings Bd. dirs. Boulder Breast Cancer Coalition, 1993-95. Mem. Assn. Am. Pubs. (bd. dirs. 1992-96, 99—, exec. coun. of profl. and scholarly pub. divsn. 1996—). Office: Lynne Rienner Pub Inc 1800 30th St Ste 314 Boulder CO 80301-1026

RIESENBECK, RONALD, supermarket executive; CFO Save Mart Supermarkets, Modesto, Calif. Office: Save Mart Supermarkets PO Box 4278 Modesto CA 95352-4278

RIESS, GORDON SANDERSON, management consultant; b. Thessaloniki, Greece, Feb. 25, 1928; came to U.S., 1932; s. Lewis William and Dorothy Onward (Sanderson) R.; m. Priscilla Rich, June 2, 1951; children: Mark C., Kimberly A., Blake G. AB with highest honors, Whitman Coll., 1949; MBA cum laude, Harvard U., 1951. Cert. mgmt. cons.; registered profl. cons.; accredited profl. cons. With Ford Internat. Div., N.Y.C., 1951-53; asst. fin. mgr. Ford Motor Co., Mid. East, Alexandria, Egypt, 1953-57; gen. sales mgr. Ford Motor Co., Rome, Italy, 1957-60; regional fin. mgr. Ford Motor Co., Scandinavia, Copenhagen, Denmark, 1960-62; gen. mgr. Ford Motor Co., European, Brussels, Belgium, 1962-67; v.p. Internat. Paper Co., Zurich, Switzerland, 1967-71; exec. v.p. Cinema Internat. Corp., London, 1971-75; chmn., pres. Stewart-Riess Labs. Inc., Tarzana, Calif., 1976-83; pres., CEO Intercontinental Enterprises Ltd., Beverly Hills, 1983—. Chmn. Vis. Nurse Found., L.A., 1985-87; bd. dirs., chmn. Vis. Nurse Assn., L.A., 1976-97; bd. dirs. Beverly Found., Pasadena, Calif., 1990-97; vice-chmn. of bd. Witman Coll., Walla Walla, Wash., 1985-96. Author: Confessions of a Corporate Centurion-Tales of International Adventures, From Communism to Capitalism; inventor/patentee pre-fillable hypodermic syringe. Chmn. Inter-Community Sch. Zurich, 1968-71; trustee Am. Sch. London, 1972-75; vice chmn. Krafterliner Mfgs. Assn., Zurich, 1968-71; bd. dirs. Vols. in Tech. Assistance, Arlington, Va., 1986-93; bd. overseers Muhlenberg Coll., 1993—; internat. bd. Czechoslovak Mgmt. Ctr., 1992—. Sgt. U.S. Army, 1946-47. R.H. Macy scholar, Harvard Bus. Sch., 1949. Mem. Am. Assn. Profl. Cons., Am. Cons. League, Asia Acad. Mgmt., Hollywood Radio & Television Soc., Inst. Mgmt. Cons., Lic. Execs. Soc. Avocations: skiing, scuba diving. Office: Intercontinental Ent Ltd # 3194 256 S Robertson Blvd Beverly Hills CA 90211-2898 E-mail: gsr@mindspring.com

RIFKIN, ARNOLD, film company executive; b. Bklyn. m. Rita George; two children. BA, U. Cin. Founder Rifkin-David, 1974-80; merged to form Rifkin/David/Kimble/Parseghian, 1980-81, DHKPR, 1981-84; head motion picture dept. Triad Artists, Inc., 1984-92, founding ptnr.; exec. v.p., worldwide head motion picture divsn. William Morris Agy., Beverly Hills, Calif., 1992-96; pres. William Morris Talent and Lit. Agy., Beverly Hills, 1996-2000; CEO Cheyenne Enterprises, LLC, Santa Monica, 2000—. Lectr. UCLA; bd. dirs. Am. Cinematape. Bd. councillors U. So. Calif. Office: Cheyenne Enterprises 406 Wilshire Blvd Santa Monica CA 90401-1410

RIGGS, GEORGE E. newspaper publishing executive; Pub., CEO Contra Costa (Calif.) Times.

RIGGS, HENRY EARLE, academic administrator, engineering management educator; b. Chgo., Feb. 25, 1935; s. Joseph Agnew and Gretchen (Walser) R.; m. Gayle Carson, May 17, 1958; children: Elizabeth, Peter, Catharine. BS, Stanford U., 1957; MBA, Harvard U., 1960. Indsl. economist SRI Internat., Menlo Park, Calif., 1960-63; v.p. Icore Industries, Sunnyvale, 1963-67, pres., 1967-70; v.p. fin. Measurex Corp., Cupertino, 1970-74; prof. engring. mgmt. Stanford U., 1974-88, Ford prof., 1986-88, Ford prof. emeritus, 1990—, v.p. for devel., 1983-88; pres. Harvey Mudd Coll., Claremont, 1988-97, pres. emeritus, 1997—; pres. Keck Grad. Inst., Claremont, 1997—. Bd. dirs. Mutual Funds of capital Rsch. Group. Author: Accounting: A Survey, 1981, Managing High-Tech Companies, 1983, Financial and Cost Analysis, 1994; contbr. articles to Harvard Bus. Rev. Bd. dirs. Mt. Baldy Coun. Boy Scouts Am., 1993—. Baker scholar Harvard Bus. Sch., Boston, 1959; recipient Gores Teaching award Stanford U., 1980. Mem. Stanford U. Alumni Assn. (bd. dirs. 1990-94, chmn. 1993), Calif. Club, Sunset Club, Twilight Club, Phi Beta Kappa, Tau Beta Pi. Congregationalist. Office: Keck Grad Inst 535 Watson Dr Claremont CA 91711-4817 E-mail: henry_riggs@kgi.edu

RIGGS, JACK TIMOTHY, lt governor, emergency physician; b. Coeur d'Alene, Idaho, Oct. 1, 1954; m. Rachel, children, Shannon, Peter, Jennifer. BS summa cum laude, U. Idaho, 1976; MD, U. Wash., 1980. Diplomate Am. Bd. Emergency Medicine. Intern Deaconess Med. Ctr., Spokane, Wash., 1980-81; mem. Idaho Senate, Dist. 4, Boise, 1996-2000; owner North Idaho Immediate Car Ctrs., 1985—; lt. gov. State of Idaho, 2001—. Fellow Am. Coll. Emergency Physicians; mem. AMA, Am. Coll. Physician Execs., Idaho Med. Assn., Am. Coll. Occupl. and Environ. Medicine. Address: 1701 Lincoln Way Coeur D Alene ID 83814-2537 Office: Office of Lt Gov State Capitol PO Box 83720 Boise ID 83720-3720

RIGGS, R. WILLIAM, state supreme court judge; Grad., Portland State U., 1961; JD, U. Oreg., 1968. Atty. Willner Bennett & Leonard, 1968-78; judge circuit ct. 4th Jud. Dist., 1978-88; judge Oreg. Ct. of Appeals, 1988-98, Oreg. Supreme Ct., 1998—. Active mem. Cmty. Law Poject; founder Integra Corp. Capt. USNR. Office: Supreme Ct Bldg 1163 State St Salem OR 97310-0260 E-mail: r.william.riggs@ojd.state.or.us

RIKER, WILLIAM KAY, pharmacologist, educator; b. N.Y.C., Aug. 31, 1925; s. Walter Franklin and Eleanore Louise (Scafard) R.; m. Carmela Louise DePamphilis, Dec. 21, 1947 (dec. 1981); children: Eleanor Louise, Gainor, Victoria; m. Leena Mela, Aug. 13, 1983. B.A., Columbia U., 1949; M.D., Cornell U., 1953. Intern 2d Cornell med. div., Bellevue Hosp., 1953-54; practice medicine, specializing in pharmacology Phila., 1954-69, Portland, Oreg., 1969—. Instr., asst. prof. dept. pharmacology U. Pa. Sch. Medicine, 1954-61; spl. fellow dept. physiology U. Utah Sch. Medicine, 1961-64; assoc. prof., prof., chmn. dept. pharmacology Woman's Med. Coll., Phila., 1964-69; prof., chmn. dept. pharmacology U. Oreg. Sch. Medicine, U. Oreg. Health Scis. Center, 1969-91, prof., 1991-98, prof. emeritus, 1998—, asst. dean. for admissions, 1986-89; mem. neurol. disorders program project com. NIH, 1975-79. Editor: Jour. Pharmacology and Exptl. Therapeutics, 1969-72; contbr. articles to biomed. jours. Served with USNR, 1943-46. Recipient Christian R. and Mary F. Lindback Found. award for disting. teaching, 1968; Pa. Plan scholar, 1957-61; Nat. Inst. Neurol. Diseases and Blindness spl. fellow, 1961-64; USPHS-NIH research grantee, 1958-83 Mem. Am. Soc. Pharmacology and Exptl. Therapeutics (sec.-treas. 1978-81, pres. 1985-86), Western Pharmacol. Soc. (pres. 1976), Japanese Pharmacol. Soc., Assn. Med. Sch. Pharmacologists (sec. 1976-78), Epilepsy Assn. Am., Pharm. Mfrs. Assn. Found. (chmn. pharmacology-morphology adv. com., sci. adv. com. 1976-92), Cosmos Club.

RILEY, CARROLL LAVERN, anthropology educator; b. Summersville, Mo., Apr. 18, 1923; s. Benjamin F. and Minnie B. (Smith) R.; m. Brent Robinson Locke, Mar. 25, 1948; children: Benjamin Locke, Victoria Smith Evans, Cynthia Winningham A.B., U. N.Mex., 1948, Ph.D., 1952; M.A., UCLA, 1950. Instr. U. Colo., Boulder, 1953-54; asst. prof. U. N.C., Chapel Hill, 1954-55, So. Ill. U., Carbondale, 1955-60, assoc. prof., 1960-67, prof., 1967-86, Disting. prof., 1986-87, Disting. prof. emeritus, 1987—, chmn. dept., 1979-82, dir. mus., 1972-74; rsch. assoc. lab. anthropology Mus. N.Mex., 1987—. Rsch. collaborator Smithsonian Instn., 1988—; adj. prof. N.Mex. Highlands U., 1989—. Author: The Origins of Civilization, 1969, The Frontier People, 1982, expanded edit., 1987, Rio del Norte, 1995, Bandelier, 1996, The Kachina and Cross, 1999; editor: American Historical Anthropology, 1967, Man Across the Sea, 1971, Southwestern Journals of Adolph F. Bandelier, 4 vols., 1966, 70, 75, 84, Across the Chichimec Sea, 1978, A Zuni Life, 1998, The Casas Grandes World, 1999, others; contbr. numerous articles to profl. jours. Served in USAAF, 1942-45 Decorated 4 battle stars; grantee Social Sci. Research Council, NIH, Am. Philos. Soc., Am. Council Learned Socs., NEH, others Home and Office: 1106 6th St Las Vegas NM 87701 E-mail: criley@newmexico.com

RILEY, GRANNAN, performing company executive; Studied with Doreen gilday, Eugene, Oreg.; BFA, U.S. Internat. U., San Diego; postgrad., Academie des Grand Ballets Canadiens, Montreal. Co-founder Eugene (Oreg.) Ballet Co, 1978—, mng. dir., 1984—. Mem. dance touring panel Western States Arts Found.; mem. selection panel Arts N.W., Individual Artist Fellowship, Oreg. and Idaho. Dancer (ballets) Petrushka, the Firebird, Coppelia, others, worldwide tours. Active outreach programs Young Audiences Oreg., Wash. State Cultural Enrichment Program. Co-recipient Gov.'s Arts award, 1996. Office: Eugene Ballet Co PO Box 11200 Eugene OR 97440-3400

RILEY, JACK, actor, writer; b. Cleve., Dec. 30, 1935; s. John A. and Agnes C. (Corrigan) R.; m. Ginger Lawrence, May 18, 1975; children: Jamie, Bryan. BS in English, John Carroll U., 1961. Mem.: Rolling Along of 1960, Dept. Army Travelling Show; co-host: Baxter & Riley, Sta.-WERE, Cleve., 1961-65; numerous TV appearances, including: as Mr. Carlin on Bob Newhart Show, CBS-TV, 1972-78; Occasional Wife, 1966, Mary Tyler Moore, 1972, Barney Miller, 1979, Diff'rent Strokes, 1979, Hart to Hart, 1980, Love Boat, 1984, Night Court, 1985-91, St. Elsewhere, 1986, Evening Shade, 1992, Family Matters, 1993, Married with Children, 1994, Coach, 1996, The Drew Carey Show, 1996, Seinfeld, 1997, Working, 1998, numerous appearances on Tonight Show with Jay Leno, 1997-99; appeared in feature films including Catch-22, 1969, McCabe and Mrs. Miller, 1970, Long Goodbye, 1972, Calif. Split, 1974, World's Greatest Lover, 1978, High Anxiety, 1978, Butch and Sundance: The Early Years, 1979, History of the World, Part I, 1981, Frances, 1983, To Be or Not To Be, 1983, Finders Keepers, 1984, Spaceballs, 1987, Rented Lips, 1987, Gleaming the Cube, 1988, C.H.U.D. II, 1988, The Player, 1992, T-Rex, 1995, (voice) The Rugrat's Movie, 1998, Boogie Nights, 1997; plays West Coast premier of Small Craft Warnings, 1975, Los Angeles revival of 12 Angry Men, 1985, Zeitgeist, 1990, House of Blue Leaves, at Cleve. Playhouse and tour Ea. Europe, 1993, The Odd Couple, Beck Ctr., Cleve., 1999, Do I Hear a Waltz? at Pasadena playhouse, 2001; TV writer: Don Rickles Show, 1968, Mort Sahl Show, 19667; writer commls. for, Blore & Richman Inc., Los Angeles, 1966-84; numerous radio commls. and TV voice-overs, Rugrats (cartoon series), 1993. Served with U.S. Army, 1958-61. Mem. Screen Actors Guild, Actor's Equity, AFTRA, Writers Guild Am., Acad. Motion Picture Arts and Scis., Acad. TV Arts and Scis. Office: c/o Ho Reps 400 S Beverly Dr Beverly Hills CA 90212-4424

RILEY, MICHAEL (MIKE RILEY), professional football coach; b. Wallace, Idaho, July 6, 1953; m. Dee Riley; children: Matthew, Kate. BS in Soc. Sci., U. Ala., 1975; MS, Whitworth Coll., 1976. Defensive back Crimson Tide U. Ala., 1971-74; grad. asst. coach U. Calif., 1975; def. coord., secondary coach, asst. athletic dir. Linfield Coll., McMinnville, Oreg., 1977-82; secondary coach Winnipeg Blue Bombers CFL, 1983-84, winner 2 Grey Cup Winnepeg Blue Bombers, head coach Winnipeg Blue Bombers, 1987-90; defensive coord., sec. coach No. Colo. U., 1986; head coach San Antonio Riders World League Am. Football, 1991-92; asst. head coach, offensive coord./quarterbacks coach U. So. Calif., 1993-96; head coach Oreg. State U., 1997-98; head coach San Diego Chargers NFL, 1998—. Office: care San Diego Chargers PO Box 609609 San Diego CA 92160-9609

RILEY, VICTOR J., JR. financial services company executive; b. Buffalo, Aug. 29, 1931; s. Victor J. and Gwenevieve Riley; m. Marilyn A. Felrath, Aug. 8, 1954; children: Victor J. III, Karen, Patricia, Kevin, Shawn, Mary Katherine BA in Econs., U. Notre Dame; LLD, Coll. St. Rose, 1983. With trust div. 1st Nat. Bank Miami, Fla., 1955-62; mgr. Miami office Bowles, Andrews & Towne, 1962-64; trust officer Nat. Comml. Bank (now Key Bank N.A.), Albany, N.Y., 1964-73; pres., chief exec. officer KeyCorp (formerly Key Banks Inc.), Albany, 1973-96, chmn. emeritus, 1996—; ret., 1996. Also dir.; chmn. bd. Key Bank N.A., Albany, 1984—, Ctr. Econ. Growth; dir. Albany Med. Ctr., Interstate Banking Commn. for State of N.Y., 1986—. Hon. chmn. Capital Dist. Cerebral Palsy Telethon, Albany, 1981-87; bd. dirs. Pop Warner Football League; chmn. various fund raising drives. Served with U.S. Army, 1953-55. Apptd. civilian aide to Sec. Army, 1985—. Decorated Knight of Malta Mem. N.Y. State Bankers Assn. (long-range planning com.), Interstate Banking Com. State N.Y. Republican. Roman Catholic Avocations: travel, fishing, cooking. Home: PO Box 2414 Cody WY 82414-2414 Office: KeyCorp 1130 Sheridan Ave Cody WY 82414-3647

RILEY, WILLIAM L. lawyer; b. Bay Shore, N.Y., 1942; BA, Williams Coll., 1964; JD, Duke U., 1967. Bar: N.Y. 1967, Calif. 1970. Mem. Orrick, Herrington & Sutcliffe, San Francisco, 1972-95, ptr., 1975—. Contbr. to profl. jours. Office: Orrick Herrington & Sutcliffe Fed Res Bank Bldg 400 Sansome St San Francisco CA 94111-3143

RIMEL, WHITNEY, federal judge; Apptd. bankruptcy judge ea. dist. U.S. Bankruptcy Ct. Calif., 1998. Office: 1130 O St Rm 2656 Fresno CA 93721-2201

RIMOIN, DAVID LAWRENCE, physician, geneticist; b. Montreal, Nov. 9, 1936; s. Michael and Fay (Lecker) R.; m. Mary Ann Singleton, 1962 (div. 1979); 1 child, Anne; m. Ann Piilani Garber, July 27, 1980; children: Michael, Lauren. BSc, McGill U., Montreal, 1957, MSc, MD, CM, 1961; PhD, Johns Hopkins U., 1967; LHD (hon.), Finch U., 1997. Asst. prof. medicine, pediat. Washington U., St. Louis, 1967-70; assoc. prof. UCLA, 1970-73, prof., 1973—, chief med. genetics, Harbor-UCLA Med. Ctr., 1970-86; dir. dept. pediat., dir. Med. Genetics and Birth Defects Ctr., 1986—; Steven Spielberg chmn. pediat. Cedars-Sinai Med. Ctr., L.A., 1989—. Chmn. coun. Med. Genetics Orgn., 1993. Co-author: Principles and Practice of Medical Genetics, 1983, 90, 96, 01; contbr. articles to profl. jours., chpts. to books. Recipient E. Mead Johnson award Am. Acad. Pediat., 1976, Col. Harland Saunders award March of Dimes, 1997. Fellow ACP, AAAS, Am. Coll. Med. Genetics (pres. 1991-96, bd. dirs. 1996-98), Am. Coll. Med. Genetics Found. (pres. 1999—); mem. Am. Fedn. Clin. Rsch. (sec.-treas. 1972-75), Western Soc. Clin. Rsch. (pres. 1978), Western Soc. Pediat. Rsch. (pres. 1995, Ross Outstanding Young Investigator award 1976), Am. Bd. Med. Genetics (pres. 1979-83), Am. Soc. Human Genetics (pres. 1984), Am. Pediat. Soc., Soc. Pediat. Rsch., Am. Soc. Clin. Investigation, Assn. Am. Physicians, Johns Hopkins Soc. Scholars, Inst. Medicine. Office: Cedars Sinai Med Ctr 8700 Beverly Blvd Los Angeles CA 90048-1865 E-mail: david.rimoin@cshs.org

RIMSZA, SKIP, mayor; b. Chgo. m. Kim Gill; children: Brian, Jenny, Alexander, Taylor, Nicole. Mem. Phoenix City Coun., 1990-94; vice mayor City of Phoenix, 1993, mayor, 1994—. Former pres. Bd. Realtors. Mem. several cmty. bds. Office: Office Mayor 200 W Washington St Fl 11 Phoenix AZ 85003-1611

RINDONE, JOSEPH PATRICK, clinical pharmacist, educator; b. Santa Fe, Oct. 4, 1954; s. Guido Salvatore and Elizabeth Ann (Murphy) R.; m. Diane Marie Rollins, June 11, 1991; children: Jacqueline, Alexandra. BS, U. Nebr., 1977; PharmD, Creighton U., 1978. Lic. pharmacist, Nebr., Calif. Staff pharmacist Bergan Mercy Hosp., Omaha, 1978, Phoenix (Ariz.) VA Med. Ctr., 1978-81, clin. resident, 1981; clin. pharmacist Tucson VA Med. Ctr., 1982-93; assoc. prof. U. Ariz., Tucson, 1982—; clin. pharmacist Prescott (Ariz.) VA Med. Ctr., 1993—, rsch. coord., 1994—. Author: Therapeutic Monitoring of Antibiotics, 1991; contbr. articles to Arch. Internal Medicine, Pharmacotherapy, Clin. Therapeutics, Am. Jour. Cardiology, Am. Jour. Therapeutics, Chest, West Jour. Medicine, Am. Jour. Health Sys. Pharm., Jour. AMA. Regents scholar U. Nebr., 1976. Mem. Ariz. Soc. Hosp. Pharmacists. Avocations: sports, photography, bridge, astronomy. E-mail: JosephRindone@med.va.gov

RINEARSON, PETER MARK, journalist, writer, software developer; b. Seattle, Aug. 4, 1954; s. Peter Morley and Jeannette Irene (Love) R.; m. Jill Chan, Sept. 15, 1991. Student, U. Wash., 1972-78. Editor Sammamish Valley News, Redmond, Wash., 1975-76; reporter Seattle Times, 1976-78, govt. and polit. reporter, 1979-81, aerospace reporter, 1982-84, Asian corr., 1985-86; pres. Alki Software Corp., Seattle, 1990—, Raster Ranch, Ltd., 1995-99; sr. v.p. Oxygen Media, 1999-2000. Mem. vis. com. Sch. Comm., U. Wash., 1996—; mem. nat. adv. bd. Poynter Inst. for Media Studies, 2000—. Author: Word Processing Power with Microsoft Word, 4th edit., 1991, Microsoft Word Style Sheets, 1987, Quick Reference Guide to Microsoft Word, 1988, Microsoft Word Companion Disk, 1988, Masterword, 1990, 91, 92, (with Bill Gates and Nathan Myhrvold) The Road Ahead, 1995, rev. edit., 1996, Babynamer.com, 2977-79. Recipient Spl. Paul Myhre award-series Penney-Mo. Newspaper awards, 1983, Disting. Writing award Am. Soc. Newspaper Editors, 1984, Pulitzer prize for feature writing, 1984, Lowell Thomas Travel Writing award, 1984, John Hancock award,1985, semi-finalist NASA Journalist-in-Space Project, 1986; U.S.-Japan Leadership Program fellow Japan Soc., 1988. Office: Alki Software Corp 300 Queen Anne Ave N # 410 Seattle WA 98109-4512

RINEHART, FREDERICK ROBERTS, publishing executive; b. N.Y.C., Sept. 30, 1953; s. George Henry Doran R. and Sharon Kerley (Bonner) Caulfield; m. Kim Bennett, Aug. 28, 1976; children: Alexander Vaughan, Coney Cutamora. BA with highest honors, U. Calif., Santa Barbara, 1977. Asst. dir. U. Press of Colo., Boulder, 1977-87; pres. Roberts Rinehart Pubs., Niwot, Colo., 1987—; mng. dir. Charterhouse Publ., Dublin, Ireland, 1994—. Pubs. bd. mem. Denver Mus. Natural History, 1989—. Editor: Chronicles of Colorado, 1984. Bd. dirs. Colo. Ctr. for the Book, 1994—. Recipient Design awards Rocky Mountain Book Pubs. Assn., 1987, 88, 90, 91, 92, Merit award Am. Soc. of Landscape Architects, 1992. Mem. Kent Sch. Boat Club. Avocations: running, rowing, reading, range management. Office: Roberts Rinehart Pubs 5455 Spine Rd Mezzanine W Boulder CO 80301-3345

RINEY, HAL PATRICK, advertising executive; b. Seattle, July 17, 1932; s. Hal Patrick and Inez Marie R.; children: Benjamin Kennedy, Samantha Elizabeth; m. Edith Caldwell. BA, U. Wash., Seattle, 1954. From art dir./writer to v.p., creative dir. BBDO, Inc., San Francisco, 1956-72; exec. v.p., creative dir. Botsford Ketchum, San Francisco, 1972-76; sr. v.p., mng. dir., creative dir. Ogilvy & Mather, San Francisco, 1976-81; exec. v.p. Ogilvy & Mather West, 1981-86; chmn., CEO, Hal Riney & Ptnrs., Inc., San Francisco, 1986-98, Publicis & Hal Riney, San Francisco, 1998—. Recipient 5 Lion d'Or du Cannes awards, 18 Clio awards, 15 Addy awards, Grand Prix du Cannes; named to Creative Hall of Fame. Mem. Am. Assn. Advt. Agys., San Francisco Advt. Club, San Francisco Soc. Communicating Arts, Wild Goose Club, Meadow Club, St. Francis Yacht Club. Home: 1 Los Pinos Nicasio CA 94946-9701 Office: Publicis & Hal Riney 2001 The Embarcadero San Francisco CA 94133-5200

RING, ALICE RUTH BISHOP, retired physician; b. Ft. Collins, Oct. 11, 1931; d. Ernest Otto and Mary Frances (Drohan) Bishop; m. Wallace Harold Ring, July 26, 1956 (div. 1969); children: Rebecca, Eric, Mark; m. Robert Charles Diefenbach, Sept. 10, 1977. BS, Colo. State U., 1953; MD, U. Colo., 1956; MPH, U. Calif., Berkeley, 1971. Diplomate Am. Bd. Preventive Medicine. Physician cons. Utah State Divsn. Health, Salt Lake City, 1960-65; med. dir., project head start Salt Lake City Cmty. Action Program, 1965-70; resident Utah State Divsn. Health, 1969-71; asst. assoc. reg. health dir. USPHS, San Francisco, 1971-75, med. cons. Atlanta, 1975-77, dir. primary care, 1977-84; dir. divsn. diabetes control Ctrs. Disease Control, Atlanta, 1984-88; dir. WHO Collabor Ctr., Atlanta, 1986-91; dir. preventive medicine residency Ctrs. Disease Control, Atlanta, 1988-93; exec. dir. Am. Bd. Preventive Medicine, 1993-98. Trustee Am. Bd. Preventive Medicine, 1990-92; lectr. Emory U. Sch. Pub. Health, 1988-94; bd. dirs. Redwood Coast Med. Svcs., v.p., 1994—; mem. adv. com. Shemli Hospice, Gualala, Calif. Co-author: Clinical Diabetes, 1991. Bd. dirs. Diabetes Assn. Atlanta, 1985-90, med. adv. com., 1990-94. Fellow Am. Coll. Preventive Medicine (bd. dirs. 1990-94, Spl. Recognition award 1998); mem. AMA (grad. med. edn. adv. com. 1993-97), Assn. Tchrs. Preventive Medicine, Am. Acad. Pediatrics. Office: PO Box 364 Gualala CA 95445-0364 E-mail: ard@mcn.org

RING, MICHAEL WILSON, lawyer; b. Phoenix, Feb. 14, 1943; s. Clifton A. and Leona (Wilson) R. BA, U Wash., 1964; JD, U. Calif., Berkeley, 1968. Bar: Calif. 1969. Assoc. Sheppard, Mullin, Richter & Hampton, L.A., 1968-76, ptnr., 1976-87, Mayer, Brown & Platt, L.A., 1987-92, Sonnenschein Nath & Rosenthal, L.A., 1992—. Mem. ABA, L.A. County Bar Assn., Am. Coll. Real Estate Lawyers, Urban Land Inst. (assoc.), Internat. Coun. Shopping Ctrs. (assoc.). Home: 3030 Mountain View Ave Los Angeles CA 90066-3129 Office: Sonnenschein Nath & Rosenthal 601 S Figueroa St Ste 1500 Los Angeles CA 90017-5720 E-mail: mwr@sonnenschein.com

RING, TERRY WILLIAM, company executive, environmentalist; b. Lewiston, Idaho, Nov. 11, 1955; s. Robert L. and Irene M. (Sullivan) R. BA, Boise State U., 1979. Pres. Silver Creek Outfitters, Inc., Ketchum, Idaho, 1980—. Bd. dirs. Idaho Nature Conservancy, Ketchum, 1982—, chmn., 1986-2; bd. dirs. The Peregrine Fund, Boise, Idaho, 1994—. Mem. Nature Conservancy (Oak Leaf Awd. 1993) Home: PO Box 1096 Sun Valley ID 83353-1096

RINSCH, CHARLES EMIL, retired insurance company executive; b. Vincennes, Ind., June 28, 1932; s. Emil and Vera Pearl (White) R.; m. Maryann Elizabeth Hitchcock, June 18, 1964; children: Christopher, Daniel, Carl. BS in Stats., Ind. U., 1953; MS in Bus., Butler U., 1959; MBA, Stanford U., 1960. Budget analyst Chrysler Corp., Indpls., 1955-57; sr. fin. analyst Ford Motor Co., Indpls., 1957-59; budget dir. Nat. Forge Co., Warren, Pa., 1960-61; div. controller and asst. to v.p., fin. Norris Industries, L.A., 1961-65; v.p., treas., sec. Teledyne Inc, L.A., 1965-88; pres., chief exec. officer, dir. Argonaut Group Inc., L.A., 1988-2000, ret. Cubmaster Pack 721, Boy Scouts Am., L.A., 1987-88, treas. 1981-87; mem. dean's adv. coun. Ind. U. Sch. Bus. 1st lt. U.S. Army, 1953-55. Mem. Acad. Alumni Fellows Ind. U. Sch. Bus. Avocations: photography, travel. Home: 19849 Greenbriar Dr Tarzana CA 91356-5428

RINSKY, ARTHUR C. lawyer; b. Cin., July 10, 1944; AB with honors, U. Cin., 1966; JD cum laude, U. Mich., 1969; LLM in Taxation, NYU, 1974. Bar: Fla. 1969, Calif. 1975, U.S. Tax Ct. 1974; cert. tax specialist. Ptr. Gray, Cary, Ware & Freidenrich, P.C., Palo Alto, Calif., 1975—. Mem. ABA, State Bar Calif., Phi Beta Kappa, Phi Eta Sigma. Office: Gray Cary Ware & FreidenrichPC 400 Hamilton Ave Palo Alto CA 94301-1833

RIORDAN, GEORGE NICKERSON, investment banker; b. Patchogue, N.Y., May 16, 1933; s. E. Arthur and Constance E. (Whelden) R.; m. Ann Wiggins, Jan. 4, 1958; children— Susan M., Peter G. B.S., Cornell U., 1955; M.B.A., Harvard U., 1960. Vice-pres. Lehman Bros., N.Y.C., 1960-71; mng. dir. Blyth Eastman Paine Webber, Los Angeles and N.Y.C., 1971-81, Prudential-Bache Securities, Los Angeles, 1981-88, Bear Stearns & Co., Inc., L.A., 1988-89, Dean Witter Reynolds Inc., 1989-91. Chmn. bd. MSC Software, Inc., 1997-99; bd. dirs. Pancho's Mexican Buffet, Inc., Ft. Worth, MSC Software, Inc., L.A. Served to capt. USAF, 1955-57 Mem. Calif. Club, Quoque Field Club (L.I., N.Y.), Athenaeum Club, Valley Hunt Club (Pasadena, Calif.). Office: 815 Colorado Blvd Ste 104 Los Angeles CA 90041-1720 E-mail: george.riordan@mscsoftware.com

RIORDAN, RICHARD J. mayor; b. Flushing, N.Y., 1930; m. Eugenia Riordan; 6 children (2 dec.); m. Jill Riordan. Attended, U. Calif., Santa Clara; grad., Princeton U., 1952; JD, U. Mich., 1956. With O'Melveny & Myers, L.A.; owner, operator Original Pantry Cafe; founder Total Pharmaceutical Care, Tetra Tech; mayor L.A., 1993—. Co-founder LEARN, 1991; sponsor Writing to Read computer labs Riordan Found.; active Eastside Boys and Girls Club. 1st Lt. U.S. Army, Korea. Office: Los Angeles City Hall 200 N Main St Rm 800 Los Angeles CA 90012

RIOS, PETER, state legislator, counselor; b. Hayden, Ariz. m. Gloria Rios; children: Rebecca, Danita Jelani, Peter Anthony. AA, Phoenix Coll., 1971; BA, Ariz. State U., 1974, MA, 1976. Minority project counselor Ariz. State U.; eligibility worker Food Stamp Program, Ariz.; employment specialist Phoenix; counselor Native Ams. Indian H.S. and Salt River Indian Reservation, Phoenix; worker Child Protective Svcs.; supr. children adoptions program State Ariz., 1978-80; owner Tia Maria's Grocery and Grill, 1982-88; mem. Ariz. Senate, Dist. 7, Phoenix, 1982-94, 97—; mem. appropriations com., mem. judiciary com.; mem. commerce, agr. and natural resources com. Part-time family and youth counselor Maricopa Juvenile Ct., 1993—. Active Valley Big Bros., Phoenix. Democrat. Roman Catholic. Office: State Capitol Bldg 1700 W Washington St Ofc 316 Phoenix AZ 85007-2812 E-mail: prios@azleg.state.az.us

RIPLEY, STUART MCKINNON, real estate consultant; b. July 28, 1930; s. Rob Roy and Nina Pearl (Young) R.; m. Marilyn Haerr MacDiarmid, Dec. 28, 1964; children: Jill, Bruce, Kent. BA, U. Redlands, 1952; MBA, U. Calif., Berkeley, 1959. V.p., dir. J.H. Hedrick & Co., Santa Barbara/San Diego, 1958-63; v.p. mktg. Cavanaugh Devel. Co., San Gabriel, Calif., 1963-65; v.p. mktg. dir. Calabasas Park, Bechtel Corp., Calabasas, 1967-69; v.p. mktg. Avco Cmty. Developers, Inc., La Jolla, 1969-74; mktg. dir. U.S. Home Corp., Fla. Divsn., Clearwater, 1974-75; pres., dir. Howard's Camper Country, Inc., National City, Calif., 1975-77; v.p., mktg. dir. Valcas Internat. Corp., San Diego, 1976-77, pres., 1977-79, Stuart M. Ripley, Inc., 1977-79, Sunview Realty, Inc., a Watt Industries Co., Santa Monica, Calif., 1979-80; owner Everett Stunz Co., Ltd., La Jolla, 1981—. Exec. v.p. Harriman-Ripley Co., Fallbrook, Calif.; avocado/floraculture rancher, subdivider, Fallbrook, 1978—; lectr. UCLA, 1961; pres. Century 21 Coastal, Century 21 Bajamar, Baja California, Mex., 1994-97. Comdr. USNR, 1952-55, ret. U. Redlands fellow, 1960—. Mem. Nat. Assn. Homebuilders, Sales and Mktg. Coun., Sales and Mktg. Execs., Elks, Pi Chi. Republican. Episcopalian. Home: 2085 Via Ladeta La Jolla CA 92037-6905 Office: 7624 Girard Ave La Jolla CA 92037-4420

RIPPEL, CLARENCE W. academic administrator; Acting pres. Lincoln U., to 1998, pres., 1998—. Office: Lincoln U Office of President 401 15th St Oakland CA 94612-2801

RIPPEN, HELGA EDITH, pharmaceutical company administrator; b. Tripoli, Libya, Mar. 10, 1959; BSME, Fla. Atlantic U., 1981; PhD, Duke U., 1986; MD, U. Fla.; MPH, Johns Hopkins U., Baltimore. Diplomate in pub. health and gen. preventive medicine Am. Bd. Preventive Medicine. DAAD postdoctoral fellow Max Planck Inst. for Biochemistry, Martinsried, Fed. Republic Germany, 1986-87; NATO postoctoral fellow U. B.C., Vancouver, Can., 1987-88; AAAS sci. engring. diplomacy fellow U.S. AID, Arlington, Va., 1991-96; residency preventive medicine Johns Hopkins U., 1996; dir. Health Info. Tech. Inst., 1996-99; chmn. Internet Healthcare Coalition, 1998—; co-chmn. eHeath Ethics Initiative, 2000; dir. med. informatics Pfizer Health Solutions, Santa Monica, Calif., 2001—. Chair IEEE-USA Med. Tech. Policy Com., 1998-2000. Co-creator, initiator Equal Access Student Run Clinic, Gainesville, Fla., 1991. Wimberly scholar, 1980; Am. Heart Assn. grantee, 1985-86. Mem. AMA, AAAS, Am. Coll. Preventive Medicine, Am. Tchrs. Preventive Medicine, Sigma Xi, Phi Kappa Phi, Tau Beta Pi. Avocations: painting, bicycling, hiking, cooking, travel. E-mail: helga.rippen@pfizer.com

RIPPER, RITA JO (JODY RIPPER), strategic planner, researcher; b. Goldfield, Iowa, May 8, 1950; d. Carl Phillip and Lucille Mae (Stewart) Ripper. BA, U. Iowa, 1972; MBA, NYU, 1978. Fin. and credit specialist Control Data Corp., Mpls., 1974-78; regional mgr. Raytheon Corp., Irvine, Calif., 1978-83; v.p. Caljo Corp., Des Moines, 1980-84; asst. v.p. Bank of Am., San Francisco, 1984-88; pres. The Northhaven Co., San Francisco, 1988—, The Boardroom Adv. Group, San Francisco, 1990-93; v.p. project mgr. Imperial Bank, 1998-99. Am. United. Vol. Cancer, Heart, Lung Assns., Edina, N.Y.C., Calif., 1974-78, 84—. Mem. Amnesty Internat., Ams. United for Separation of Ch. and State, ACLU, Peoples for the Am. Way, Internat. Mktg. Assn., World Trade Ctr. Assn., Acctg. Soc. (pres. 1975-76), World Trade Club, Intertel, Mensa, Beta Alpha Psi (chmn. 1977-78), Phi Gamma Nu (v.p. 1971-72), Corinthian Yacht Club. Presbyterian. E-mail: jodyripper@aol.com

RIPPON, THOMAS MICHAEL, art educator, artist; b. Sacramento, Apr. 1, 1954; s. Samuel Joseph Jr. and June Evelyn (Garnet) R.; m. Sarah Sterrett, Dec. 22, 1980; children: Adam Michael, Peter Thomas. MFA, Art Inst. Chgo., 1979. Instr. Columbia Coll., Chgo., 1978-79; asst. prof. Montana State U., Bozeman, 1980, Calif. State U., Sacramento, 1981; assoc. prof. Tenn. Tech. U., Cookeville, 1982-87; asst. prof. U. Nev., Reno, 1987-89; assoc. prof. U. Montana, Missoula, 1989—, chair dept. art, 1990-96. Artist in residence U. Nevada, Reno, 1988; vis. prof. U. Calif., Davis, 1989; lectr. in field, 1973—. Solo exhbns. include Quay Gallery, San Francisco, 1975, 77, 81, 85, Rochester (Minn.) Art Ctr., 1979, Betsy Rosenfield Gallery, Chgo., 1980, 82, 84, Drake U., Des Moine, Iowa, 1985, Cross Creek Gallery, Malibu, Calif., 1987, 88, Judith Weintraub Gallery, Sacramento, 1990, 91, Huntington (W.Va.) Mus. Art, 1991, Kohler Art Ctr., Sheboygan, Wis., 1992, Yellowstone Art Ctr., Billings, Mont., 1993, Missoula Mus. Arts, 1994, Holter Mus. Art, Helena, Mont., 1995, John Natsovlas Gallery, 1995, 97, Mobila Gallery, Cambridge, Mass., 1999, others; group exhbns. include San Francisco Mus. Modern Art, 1972, Davis (Calif.) Art Ctr., 1973, Oakland Mus., 1974, Evanston (Ill.) Art Ctr., 1974, Fendrick Gallery, Washington, 1975, Campbell Mus., Camden, N.J., 1976, Montana State U., Bozeman, 1976, De Young Mus., San Francisco, 1978, Am. Craft Mus., N.Y.C., 1978, 81, Phila. Mus. Modern Art, 1980, Craft and Folk Mus., L.A., 1980, Indpls. Mus. Art, 1982, Impressions Today Gallery, Boston, 1982, Elements Gallery, N.Y.C., 1983, Tampa (Fla.) Mus., 1983, Hyde Park Art Ctr., Chgo., 1983, 85, Traver-Sutton Gallery, Seattle, 1984, Erie (Pa.) Art Mus., 1985, Fay Gold Gallery, Atlanta, 1986, Seattle Art Mus., 1987, Candy Store Art Gallery, Folsom, Calif., 1987, Crocker Art Mus., Sacramento, 1988, Lang Gallery Scripps Coll., Claremont, Calif., 1988, Sherley Koteen & Assoc., Washington, 1989, 90, Eve Mannes Gallery, Atlanta, 1989, Art Gallery Western Australia, 1989, Joanne Rapp Gallery, Scottsdale, 1990, Missoula Mus. of Arts, 1991, 92, Sutton West Gallery, Missoula, 1992, Yellowstone Art Ctr., 1992, Natsoulas Gallery, Davis, Calif., 1993, Mus. Internat. del Ceramiche, Faenza, Italy, 1997, John Elder Gallery, N.Y.C., 1998, M.H. De Young Mus., San Francisco, 1999, many others; represented in pvt. collections; pub. collections include San Francisco Mus. Art, L.A. County Mus. Art, Sheldon Meml. Collection U. Nebr., Mus. Fine Arts, Salt Lake City, Ch. Fine Arts Collection U. Nev., Reno, Kanzawa-Shi, Hokkoku Shinbun, Kyoto, Japan, Renwick Gallery Smithsonian Institution, Contemporary Art Mus., Honolulu, J.B. Speed Art Mus., Louisville, Ky., U. Iowa, Ames, Missoula Mus. Arts, others. Recipient Kingsley Art Club award Crocker Art Mus., Sacramento, 1971, Crocker-Kingsley award, 1972; NEA fellow, 1974, 81, Nelson Raymond fellow Art Inst. Chgo., 1979. Office: U Montana Dept Art Missoula MT 59812-0001

RIS, WILLIAM KRAKOW, lawyer; b. Dubuque, Iowa, June 11, 1915; s. Rinehart F. and Anna W. (Krakow) R.; m. Patty S. Nash, Dec. 28, 1940; children: Frederic N., William Krakow Jr. AB, U. Colo., 1945, LLB, 1939. Bar: Colo. 1939. Practice in, Denver, 1939-43, 46-86; with firm Wood, Ris & Hames, P.C., 1948-86, of counsel, 1986—. Mem. Commn. on Jud. Qualifications, 1973-77, chmn., 1977 Served with AUS, 1943-46. Fellow Am. Bar Found., Am. Coll. Trial Lawyers (bd. regents 1982-83); mem. Colo. Bar Assn. (pres. 1962-63), Denver Law Club (pres. 1956-57), Order of Coif. Episcopalian. Home: 2800 S University Blvd Unit 114 Denver CO 80210-6072 Office: 1775 Sherman St Ste 1600 Denver CO 80203-4317

RISCH, JAMES E. lawyer, state legislator; b. Milw., May 3, 1943; s. Elroy A. and Helen B. (Levi) R.; m. Vicki L. Choborda, June 8, 1968; children— James E., Jason S., Jordan D. B.S. in Forestry, U. Idaho, 1965, J.D., 1968. Dep. pros. atty. Ada County, Idaho, 1968-69, chief dep. pros. atty., 1969-70, pros. atty., 1971-75; mem. Idaho Senate, Dist. 18, Boise, 1974-88, 95—; majority leader Idaho Senate, 1977-82, 97—, pres. pro tem, 1983-88, asst. majority leader, 1996; ind. counsel to Gov. of Idaho, 1996; ptnr. Risch Goss & Insinger, Boise, Idaho, 1975—. Prof. law Boise State U., 1972-75. Bd. dirs. Nat. Dist. Attys. Assn., 1973,, Idaho Co., 1992-94; chmn. bd. dris. Am. Trailer Mfg. Co., 1995—; pres. Idaho Prosecuting Attys., 1970-74; chmn. George Bush Presdl. Campaign, Idaho, 1988; gen. counsel Idaho Rep. Party, 1991—. Mem. ABA, Idaho Bar Assn., Boise Bar Assn., Ducks Unlimited, Nat. Rifle Assn., Nat. Cattlemens Assn., Idaho Cattlemans Assn., Am. Angus Assn., Idaho Angus Assn., Am. Legis. Exch. Coun., Boise Valley Angus Assn., Phi Delta Theta, Xi Sigma Pi Republican. Roman Catholic Avocations: hunting, fishing, skiing. Home: 5400 S Cole Rd Boise ID 83709-6401 Office: Risch Goss & Insinger 407 W Jefferson St Boise ID 83702-6012

RISLEY, TODD ROBERT, psychologist, educator; b. Palmer, Alaska, Sept. 8, 1937; s. Robert and Eva Lou (Todd) R.; 1 child, Todd Michael; m. Cheryl Thomas, Mar. 30, 1996. A.B. with distinction in Psychology, San Diego State Coll., 1960; M.S., U. Wash., 1963, Ph.D., 1966. Asst. prof. psychology Fla. State U., Tallahassee, 1964-65; research assoc. Bur. Child Research, U. Kans., Lawrence, 1965-77, sr. scientist, 1977—, asst. prof. dept. human devel., 1967-69, assoc. prof., 1969-73, prof., 1973-84; prof. psychology U. Alaska, Anchorage, 1982—. Pres. Ctr. for Applied Behavior Analysis, 1970-82; dir. Johnny Cake Child Study Ctr., Mansfield, Ark., 1973-74; vis. prof. U. Auckland (N.Z.), 1978; acting dir. Western Carolina Ctr., Morgantown, N.C., 1981; dir. Alaska Div. Mental Health and Devel. Disabilities, 1988-91; cons. in field to numerous orgns. and instns. Co-author: The Infant Center, 1977, Shopping with Children: Advice for parents, 1978, The Toddler Center, 1979, Meaningful Differences, 1995, The Social World of Children, 1999; editor: Jour. Applied Behavior Analysis, 1971-74; mng. editor: Behavior Therapy, The Behavior Therapist, Behavioral Asessment, 1977-80; mem. editl. bds. of numerous profl. jours.; contbr. revs. and numerous articles. Co-chmn. Fla. task force on use of behavioral procedures in state programs for retarded, 1974— ; mem. resident abuse investigating com. div. retardation Fla. Dept. Health and Rehab. Services, 1972— ; mem. adv. com. Social Research Inst., U. Utah, 1977— ; mem. Alaska Gov.'s Council on Handicapped and Gifted, 1983-88, NIH Mental Retardation Research Com., 1987-88, Alaska Mental Health Bd., 1988. Grantee NIMH, 1971-72, 72-73; research grantee Nat. Ctr. Health Services, 1976-79; grantee Nat. Inst. Edn., 1973, NIH, 1967— Fellow APA (coun. of reps. 1982-85, pres. div. 25, 1989, Edgar Doll award 2000), Am. Psychol. Soc.; mem. AAAS, Am. Assn. Mental Deficiency (Rsch. award 2000), Assn. Advancement of Behavior Therapy (dir. 1975-80, pres. 1976-77, chmn. profl. rev. com. 1977—, series editor Readings in Behavior Therapy 1977—), Soc. Behavioral Medicine, Assn. Behavior Analysis, Sigma Xi. E-mail: risley@alaska.net

RISSE, GUENTER BERNHARD, physician, historian, educator; b. Buenos Aires, Argentina, Apr. 28, 1932; s. Francisco B. and Kaete A. R.; m. Alexandra G. Paradzinski, Oct. 14, 1961; children— Heidi, Monica, Alisa. MD, U. Buenos Aires, 1958; PhD, U. Chgo., 1971. Intern Mercy Hosp., Buffalo, 1958-59; resident in medicine Henry Ford Hosp., Detroit, 1960-61, Mt. Carmel Hosp., Columbus, Ohio, 1962-63; asst. dept. medicine U. Chgo., 1963-67; asst. prof. dept. history of medicine U. Minn., 1969-71; asso. prof. dept. history of medicine and dept. history of sci. U. Wis., Madison, 1971-76, prof., 1976-85, chmn. dept. history of medicine, 1971-77; prof. dept. history health scis. U. Calif., San Francisco, 1985-99, prof. dept. anthropology, history and social medicine, 1999-2001, prof. emeritus, 2001—. Dept. chair, 1985-99; mem. project com. Ctr. for Photog. Images in Medicine and Health Care; Karl Sudholf Meml. lectr., Germany, 2000. Author: Paleopathology of Ancient Egypt, 1964, Hospital Life in Enlightenment Scotland, 1986, Mending Bodies—Saving Souls: A History of Hospitals, 1999; editor: Modern China and Traditional Chinese Medicine, 1973, History of Physiology, 1973, Medicine Without Doctors, 1977, AIDS and the Historian, 1991, Culture, Knowledge and Healing, Historical Perspectives of Homeopathic Medicine in Europe and North America, 1998; mem. editl. bd. Jour. History of Medicine, 1971-74, 90-93, Clio Medica, 1973-88, Bull. History of Medicine, 1980-94, Medizinhistorisches Jour., 1981—, Med. History, 1989-95, NTM Internat. Jour. of History, Ethics, Medicine, 1992—, History of Philos. Life Scis., 1993—, Asclepio, 1995—, Health and History, 1998—. Served with Argentine Armed Forces, 1955. Recipient NIH grants, 1971-73, 82-84, WHO grant, 1979, named Logan Campbell Disting. Lectr., New Zealand, 1994. Mem. Am. Assn. History of Medicine (pres. 1988-90, William H. Welch medal 1988), History Sci. Soc., Deutsche Gesellschaft fur Geschichte der Medizin, European Assn. History of Medicine and Health, Internat. Network for History of Pub. Health, Mex. Soc. History and Philosophy of Medicine, Peruvian Assn. Med. Ethnology and History, Brit. Soc. for Social History of Medicine, Argentine Ateneo de Historia de la Medicina, AIDS History Group (co-chair 1988-94), Internat. Network for History of Hosps. (convenor 1995—), Bay Area Med. Hist. Club (pres. 1994-96). Home: 933 NW Richmond Beach Rd Seattle WA 98177-3219 E-mail: profgbr@aol.com

RISSER, ARTHUR CRANE, JR. zoo administrator; b. July 8, 1938; s. Arthur Crane and Mary Winn (Stevenson) R.; children: Michelle W., Stephen C., Michael R. BA, Grinnell Coll., Iowa, 1960; MA, U. Ariz., Tucson, 1963; PhD, U. Calif., Davis, 1970. Mus. technician Smithsonian Instn., Washington, 1963-64; rsch. assoc. Sch. Medicine U. Md., Balt., 1964-65; grad. teaching asst. U. Calif., Davis, 1965-70; asst. prof. biology U. Nev., Reno, 1970-74; asst. curator birds Zool. Soc., San Diego, 1974-76, curator birds, 1976-81, gen. curator birds, 1981-86; gen. mgr. San Diego Zoo, 1986—. Co-chmn. Calif. Condor Working Group on Captive Breeding and Reintroduction, 1983-85; mem. Calif. Condor Recovery Team, 1984-86; bd. dirs. Internat. Found. Conservation Birds, 1979-88, Rsch. and Conservation Found. of Papua New Guinea, 1991—. Treas. Planned Parenthood, Reno, 1972; bd. dirs. Chinese Hist. Soc. Greater San Diego & Baja, Calif., 1995-99. Fellow Am. Assn. Zool. Parks and Aquariums. Office: San Diego Zoo PO Box 120551 San Diego CA 92112-0551 E-mail: arisser@sandiegozoo.org

RISSER, PAUL GILLAN, academic administrator, botanist; b. Blackwell, Okla., Sept. 14, 1939; s. Paul Crane and Jean (McCluskey) R.; children: David, Mark, Stephen, Scott. BA, Grinnell Coll., 1961; MS in Botany, U. Wis., 1965, PhD in Botany and Soils, 1967. From asst. prof. to prof. botany U. Okla., 1967-81, also asst. dir. biol. sta., chmn. dept. botany and microbiology, 1977-81; dir. Okla. Biol. Survey, 1971-77; chief Ill. Natural History Survey, 1981-86; program dir., ecosystem studies NSF; provost and v.p. acad. affairs U. N.Mex., 1989-92; former pres. Miami U., Oxford, Ohio; pres. Oreg. State U., 1996—. Author: (with Kathy Cornelison) Man and the Biosphere, 1979, (with others) The True Prairie Ecosystem, 1981; research, numerous publs. in field. Trustee Pioneer Multi-County Library Bd. Mem. Am. Acad. Arts and Scis., Ecol. Soc. Am. (pres.), Brit. Ecol. Soc., Soc. Range Mgmt., Southwestern Assn. Naturalists (pres.), Am. Inst. Biol. Sci. (pres.), Torrey Bot. Club. Presbyterian. Office: Oregon State U Kerr Adminstrn Bldg Office of the Pres Corvallis OR 97331-8507

RISTAU, KENNETH EUGENE, JR. lawyer; b. Knoxville, Tenn., Feb. 14, 1939; s. Kenneth E. and Frances (Besch) R.; m. Mary Emily George, Nov. 27, 1967 (div. Apr. 1985); children: Heidi, Mary Robin, Kenny, Michael, Robert; m. Emily Pettis, Mar. 31, 1990; 1 child, James Patrick. BA, Colgate U., 1961; JD, NYU, 1964. Bar: U.S. Ct. Appeals (9th cir.) 1968, U.S. Ct. Appeals (D.C. cir.) 1974, U.S. Supreme Ct. 1974, U.S. Dist. Ct., Southern Dist. of Calif., 1993. Assoc. Gibson, Dunn & Crutcher, L.A., 1964-69, ptnr. Irvine, Calif., 1969-2000, adv. ptnr., 2000—. Fellow Coll. Labor and Employment Lawyers (charter); mem. Employers Group (adv. bd.), Orange County Indsl. Rels. Rsch. Assn. (pres. 1992-93), Big Canyon Country Club, Rancho Las Palmas Country Club, Orange County Health Club, Santa Fe Hunt Club. Office: Gibson Dunn & Crutcher LLP Jamboree Ctr 4 Park Plz Irvine CA 92614-8557

RITCHEY, SAMUEL DONLEY, JR. retired retail store executive; b. Derry Twp., Pa., July 16, 1933; s. Samuel Donley and Florence Catherine (Litsch) R.; m. Sharon Marie Anderson, Apr. 6, 1956; children: Michael Donley, Tamara Louise, Shawn Christopher. BS, San Diego State U., 1955, MS, 1963; postgrad., Stanford U., 1964. With Lucky Stores Inc., 1951-61, 64-86, pres., chief operating officer, 1978-80, pres., chief exec. officer, 1980-81, chmn., chief exec. officer, 1981-85, chmn. bd., 1981-86. Bd. dirs. SBC Comms. The McClatchey Co., De La Salle Inst., John Muir/Mt. Diablo Health Sys.; grad. mgr. San Diego State U., 1961-63; lectr. in field; past chmn. Calif. Power Exchange, mem. adv. coun. Grad. Sch. Bus., Stanford U. Sloan Found. fellow. Mem. Mex. Am. Legal Def. and Edn. Fund, Western Assn. Food Chains (bd. dirs., pres.), Food Mktg. Inst. (bd. dirs., vice chmn.), Sloan Alumni Assn. (adv. bd., pres.). Office: 485 Hartz Ave Ste 105 Danville CA 94526-3803

RITCHIE, DANIEL LEE, academic administrator; b. Springfield, Ill., Sept. 19, 1931; s. Daniel Felix and Jessie Dee (Binney) R. B.A., Harvard U., 1954, M.B.A., 1956. Exec. v.p. MCA, Inc., Los Angeles, 1967-70; pres. Archon Pure Products Co., Los Angeles, 1970-73; exec. v.p. Westinghouse Electric Corp., Pitts., 1975-78; pres. corp. staff and strategic planning Westinghouse Broadcasting Co., 1978-79, pres., chief exec. officer, 1979-81, chmn., chief exec. officer, Westinghouse Broadcasting & Cable, Inc., 1981-87; owner Rancho Cielo, Montecito, Calif., 1977—; chancellor U. Denver, 1989—. With U.S. Army, 1956-58. Office: U Denver Office of Chancellor University Park Denver CO 80208-0001 E-mail: dritchie@du.edu

RITCHIE, JAMES L. cardiologist; BA, Yale U., 1963. Chief divsn. of cardiology U. Wash. Sch. Medicine. Recipient Disting. Achievement award Am. Heart Assn., 1996. Office: U Wash Sch Medicine Box 356422 1959 NE Pacific St Seattle WA 98195-0001

RITCHIE, ROBERT OLIVER, materials science educator; b. Plymouth, Devon, U.K., Jan. 2, 1948; came to U.S., 1974; s. Kenneth Ian and Kathleen Joyce (Sims) R.; m. Connie Olesen (div. 1978); 1 child, James Oliver; m. HaiYing Song, 1991. BA with honors, U. Cambridge, Eng., 1969, MA, PhD, 1973, ScD, 1990. Cert. engr., U.K. Goldsmith's rsch. fellow Churchill Coll. U. Cambridge, 1972-74; Miller fellow in basic rsch. sci. U. Calif., Berkeley, 1974-76; assoc. prof. mech. engring. MIT, Cambridge, 1977-81; prof. U. Calif., Berkeley, 1981—; dep. dir. Materials Scis. Divsn. Lawrence Berkeley Nat. Lab., Cambridge, 1990-94, dir. Ctr. for Advanced Materials, 1987-95, head Structural Materials Dept., Materials Scis. Divsn., 1995—. Cons. Alcan, Allison, Applied Materials, Boeing, Chevron, Exxon, GE, GM, Grumman, Guidant, Instron, Northrop, Rockwell, Westinghouse, Baxter, Carbomedics, Med. Inc., Shiley, St. Jude Med.; Van Horn Disting. lectr. Case Western U., 1997. Editor 11 books; contbr. more than 400 articles to profl. jours. Recipient Curtis W. McGraw Rsch. award Am. Soc. Engring. Educators, 1987, Rosenhain medal Inst. Materials London, 1992, G.R. Irwin medal ASTM, 1985, Mathewson gold medal TMS-AME, 1985, Van Horn Disting. Lectr. award Case Western Res. U., 1997; named one of Top 100 Scientists, Sci. Digest mag., 1984. Fellow Inst. Materials (London), Am. Soc. Metals Internat., Internat. Congress on Fracture (hon. fellow, 1989, pres. 1997—); mem. ASME, NAE, Am. Soc. Materials, Materials Rsch. Soc., Minerals, Materials and Metals Soc. (Mathewson Gold medal 1985, Disting. Structural Materials Scientist/Engr. award 1996), Nat. Acad. Engring. Avocations: skiing, antiques, orchids, tennis. Home: 590 Grizzly Peak Blvd Berkeley CA 94708-1238 Office: U Calif Dept Materials Sci and Engring Berkeley CA 94720-1760 E-mail: RORitchie@LBL.gov

RITONDARO, GARY H. printing company executive; With Diamond Shamrock Corp.; v.p., CFO Ferro Corp.; sr. v.p. fin., CFO Mail-Well Inc, Englewood, Colo., 1999—. Office: Mail-Well Inc Ste 160 23 Inverness Way Englewood CO 80112

RITSEMA, FREDRIC A. lawyer; b. Kansas City, Mo., Feb. 12, 1951; AB, Calvin Coll., 1973; JD, U. Colo., 1976. Bar: Colo. 1976. Ptnr. Ritsema & Lyon PC, 1993—. Subcoms. Workers' Compensation. Mem. Denver Bar Assn., Colo. Def. Lawyers Assn. Office: Ritsema & Lyon PC 999 18th St Ste 3100 Denver CO 80202-2499

RITTER, DANIEL BENJAMIN, lawyer; b. Wilmington, Del., Apr. 6, 1937; s. David Moore and Bernice Elizabeth (Carlson) R.; m. Shirley F. Sether, Jan. 29, 1971 (dec. Jan. 1998); 1 child, Roxane Elise. AB with honors, U. Chgo., 1957; LLB, U. Wash., 1963. Bar: Wash. 1963, U.S. Dist. Ct. (we. dist.) Wash. 1963, U.S. Tax Ct. 1965, U.S. Ct. Appeals (9th cir.) 1963. Assoc. Davis, Wright Tremaine (formerly Davis, Wright and Jones), 1963-69, ptnr., 1969—. Lectr. Bar Rev. Assocs. Wash., Seattle, 1964-86; chmn. internat. dept. Davis, Wright and Jones, Seattle, 1984-85, chmn. banking dept., 1986-89. Casenote editor U. Wash. Law Rev., 1962-63; contbg. author: Washington Commercial Law Desk Book, 1982, rev. edit., 1987, Washington Community Property Desk Book, 1977. Trustee Cathedral Assoc., Seattle, 1980-86; legal counsel Wash. State Reps., Bellevue, 1983-92; bd. dirs. U. Chgo. Club Puget Sound, Seattle, 1982—, pres., 1984-86; bd. dirs. Am. Lung Assn. Wash., Seattle, 1983-92; mem. vis. com. U. Wash. Law Sch., 1984-88; trustee U. Wash. Law Sch. Found., 1989-92; chmn. alumni rels. coun. U. Chgo., 1986-88; mem. statute law com. State of Wash., 1978-87; bd. dirs. Seattle Camerata, 1991-93; bd. dirs. Early Music Guild, Seattle, 1993-96. Mem. ABA (bus. law sect.), Wash. State Bar Assn. (chmn. bus. law sect. 1988-89, uniform comml. code com. 1980—, chmn. 1980-86, chmn. internat. law com. 1979-81, judicial recommendations com. 1991-93), Seattle-King County Bar Assn. (chmn. internat. and comparative law sect. 1980-82), Rainier Club, Order of Coif. Republican. Lutheran. Avocation: reading, theater, early music. Home: 907 Warren Ave N Apt 202 Seattle WA 98109-5635 Office: Davis Wright Tremaine 2600 Century Sq 1501 4th Ave Seattle WA 98101-1688

RITTER, RUSSELL JOSEPH, mayor, college official; b. July 22, 1932; s. Walter A. and Sally C. (Mellen) R.; m. Linaire Wells, Aug. 4, 1956; children: Michael, Leslie, Teresa, Gregory, Daniel. Student, Carroll Coll., Helena, 1950-53; AB in History, U. Mont.-Missoula, 1957, MA in History and Polit. Sci., 1962, postgrad. in History, 1963. Salesman Capital Ford, 1953-54, 56-57; tchr., coach Billings (Mont.) Central H.S., 1957-58, Loyola H.S., Missoula, 1958-62, Flathead H.S., kalispell, Mont., 1962-69; dir. devel. and comty. rels. Carroll Coll., Helena, 1969-76, v.p. for coll. rels., 1976-91; dir. corp. & govt. rels. Washington Corp., Helena, 1991—. Pres. Dennis & Phyllis Washington Found., Helena; commr. City of Helena, 1977-80, mayor pro-tem, 1980, mayor, 1981—; exec. sec.-treas. Carroll Coll. Foun., Inc.; owner Danny's Drive In, Kalispell, 1965-69; ptnr. R-B Enterprises, Inc., Kalispell, 1967-71; dir. Mont. Taxpayers Assn., 2000—, Mountain States Legal Found., 2000—; v.p. Capital Investment, Inc. (KMTX Radio), Helena, 1973-80; pres. Swinging Door Art Gallery, Inc., Helena, 1973—. Bd. dirs. Brubaker & Assocs., Inc., Kalispell, 1971-74, Norwest Bank of Helena, All Am. Indian Hall of Fame, 1972-78, Jr. Achievement, 1975-79, Mont. Physicians Svc., 1984-86, Blue Cross/Blue Shield Mont., 1986—, Mont. C. of C., chmn. Mont. Cmty. Fin. Corp., 1986; bd. govs. Mont. Spl. Olympics, 1984-86; mem. Citizen's Adv. Council, 1975-76; chmn. City-County Bldg., Inc., 1978; mem. Mont. Friendship Forc; co-chmn. Mont. Centenial Celebration. Served with USMC, 1953-56. Mem. Helena C. of C. (dir. 1972-75, v.p. 1973, pres. 1974, Ambassador's Club 1976—, chmn. 1978), Mont. Ofcls. Assn., Mont. Abassadors (Ambassador of Yr. 1986, bd. dirs. 1989, 2d v.p. 1989, pres. 1991). Club: Montana. Lodge: K.C. (4th degree).

RITVO, EDWARD ROSS, psychiatrist; b. Boston, June 1, 1930; s. Max Ritvo; m. Riva Golan, Sept. 11, 1989; children: Deborah, Eva, Anne, Matthew, Victoria, Skylre, Max. BA, Harvard U., 1951; MD, Boston U. Sch. Medicine, 1955. Diplomate Am. Bd. Psychiatry and Neurology, Am. Bd. Child Psychiatry. Prof. UCLA Sch. Medicine, 1963—. Author 4 books; contbr. over 150 articles to profl. jours. Capt. U.S. Army, 1959-61. Recipient Blanche F. Ittleson award Am. Psychiat. Assn., 1990. Mem. Nat. Soc. for Autistic Children, Profl. Adv. Bd. (chmn.). Office: UCLA Sch Medicine Dept Psychiatry 760 Westwood Plz Los Angeles CA 90095-8353

RITZ, RICHARD ELLISON, architect, architectural historian, writer; b. Colfax, Wash., Dec. 8, 1919; s. Henry Clay and Katharine Fredericka (Failing) R.; m. Evelyn R. Robinson, Sept. 21, 1940; children: Margaret Karen Ritz Barss, Susan Elizabeth Ritz Williams. Student, Whitman Coll., 1936-37. Registered architect, Oreg. Draftsman, job capt. Pietro Belluschi, Architect, Portland, Oreg., 1946-51; project mgr., chief prodn. Belluschi and Skidmore, Owings & Merrill, Portland, 1951-56; project mgr., then gen. mgr. Skidmore, Owings & Merrill, Portland, 1956-82; pvt. practice architecture Portland, 1982-94; founder Greenhills Press, 1991. Author: A History of the Reed College Campus, 1990, An Architect Looks at Downtown Portland, 1991, The Central Library Portland's Crown Jewel, 1998; editor: A Guide to Portland Architecture, 1968; contbr. articles to profl. jours. Bd. dirs. Architecture Found., Portland, 1982-85; mem. Portland Hist. Landmarks Commn., 1987-98. Sgt. USAF, 1942-45. Fellow AIA (bd. dirs. Portland chpt. 1975-79, pres. 1978, mem. handbook com. Fin. Mgmt. for Architects 1980); mem. Soc. Archtl. Historians, Oreg. Coun. Architects (del. 1975-79), Portland Art Mus., Oreg. Hist. Soc., Lang Syne Soc., City Club Portland, Univ. Club (Portland), Multnomah Athletic Club. Presbyterian. Home and Office: 4550 SW Greenhills Way Portland OR 97221-3214

RIVARA, FREDERICK PETER, pediatrician, educator; b. Far Rockaway, N.Y., May 17, 1949; s. Frederick P. and Mary Lillian (Caparelli) R.; m. J'May Bertrand, May 17, 1975; children: Matthew, Maggie. BA, Holy Cross Coll., 1970; MD, U. Pa., 1974; MPH, U. Wash., 1980. Diplomate Am. Bd. Pediatrics. Intern Children's Hosp. and Med. Ctr., Boston, 1974-75, resident, 1975-76, Seattle, 1978-80; RWJ clin. scholar U. Wash., Seattle, 1978-80, assoc. prof. pediatrics, 1984-89, prof. pediatrics, head divsn. gen. pediatrics, 1990—; mem. staff Nat. Health Svc. Corps, Hazard, Ky., 1976-78; asst. prof. pediatrics U. Tenn., Memphis, 1981-84. Editor Archives of Pedatrics and Adolescent Medicine. Fellow Am. Acad. Pediatrics; mem. Ambulatory Pediatrics Assn., Internat. Assn. Child, Adolescent and Injury Prevention (pres. 1993-2000). Office: Harborview Med Ctr 325 9th Ave PO Box 359960 Seattle WA 98195-9960

RIVELUNI, TOMASSO P. engineer; Engr. Jet Propulsion Lab., Pasadena, Calif. Recipient Engring. of Yr. award, 1998. Mem. AIAA. Office: Jet Propulsion Lab 4800 Oak Grove Dr Bldg 180 Pasadena CA 91109-8001

[illegible] Rivera; 5 children. BA, No. Ariz. U.; JD, Ariz. State U. Atty. civil rights divsn. Dept. of Justice, 1976-77; asst. U.S. atty. Dist. Ariz., 1977-81; with Langerman, Beam, Lewis and Marks, 1981-84; ptnr. Rivera, Scales and Kizer, 1984-98; atty. City of El Mirage, U.S. Dept. Justice, Ariz., 1998-2001; with Haralson, Miller, Pitt & McAnally PLC, Phoenix, 2001—. Vice-chair adv. com. civil rights Atty. Gen. Ariz. dist., 1998-2001, adv. com. native Am. issues, domestic terrorism subcom., 1998-2001, chair subcom. no Mem. com. Los Abogados; bd. dirs. Inst. for Cmty. Initiatives, 1996-98; coach Little League. With N.G. Mem. Ariz. State Bar. (bd. govs. 1995-98, bd. officer, sec. treas. 1996, 2d v.p. 1997-98, exec. dir. search com. 1996-97, chair appointments com. 1997-98), Hispanic Bar Assn., Los Abogados Bar Assn. (bd. dirs. 1981-83). Democrat. Avocation: reading. Office: Haralson Miller Pitt & McAnally PLC 3003 N Central Ave Ste 1400 Phoenix AZ 85012 E-mail: jrivera@hmpmlaw.com

RIVERS, JOAN, entertainer; b. N.Y.C., June 8, 1937; d. Meyer C. Molinsky; m. Edgar Rosenberg, July 15, 1965 (dec.); 1 child, Melissa. BA, Barnard Coll., 1958. Formerly fashion coordinator Bond Clothing Stores. Debut entertaining, 1960; mem. From Second City, 1961-62; TV debut Tonight Show, 1965; Las Vegas debut, 1969; nat. syndicated columnist Chgo. Tribune, 1973-76; creator: CBS TV series Husbands and Wives, 1976-77; host: Emmy Awards, 1983; guest hostess: Tonight Show, 1983-86; hostess The Late Show Starring Joan Rivers, 1986-87, Hollywood Squares, 1987—, (morning talk show) Joan Rivers (Daytime Emmy award 1990), 1989-93, Can We Shop? Home Shopping Network, 1994, (radio) The Joan Rivers Show, 1997—, E! Pre-awards Show, 1995—; originator, screenwriter TV movie The Girl Most Likely To, ABC, 1973; other TV movies include: How to Murder A Millionaire, 1990, Jackie Collins' Lady Boss, 1992, Tears and Laughter: The Joan and Melissa Rivers Story, 1994; cable TV spl. Joan Rivers and Friends Salute Heidi Abromowitz, 1985; film appearances include The Swimmer, 1968, Uncle Sam, The Muppets Take Manhattan, 1984; co-author, dir.: (films) Rabbit Test, 1978 (also acted), Spaceballs, 1987, Serial Mom, 1994; actress: theatre prodn. Broadway Bound, 1988, Sally Marr...and her escorts, 1994; recs. include: comedy album What Becomes a Semi-Legend Most, 1983; author: Having a Baby Can be a Scream, 1974, The Life and Hard Times of Heidi Abromowitz, 1984, (autobiography with Richard Meryman) Enter Talking, 1986, (with Richard Meryman) Still Talking, 1991; debuted on Broadway (play) Broadway Bound, 1988, creator Seminar You Deserve To Be happy, 1995; (books) From Mother to Daughter: Thoughts and Advice on Life, Love and Marriage, 1998, Don't Count the Candle, Just Keep the Fire Lit, 1999. Nat. chmn. Cystic Fibrosis, 1982—, benefit performer for AIDS, 1984. Recipient Cleo awards for commls., 1976, 82, Jimmy award for best comedian, 1981; named Hadassah Woman of Yr., 1983, Harvard Hasty Pudding Soc. Woman of Yr., 1984. Mem. Phi Beta Kappa. Office: William Morris Agy 151 S El Camino Dr Beverly Hills CA 90212-2775 also: JR Worldwide 150 E 58th St New York NY 10155-0002

RIVETTE, GERARD BERTRAM, manufacturing company executive; b. Syracuse, N.Y., May 18, 1932; s. George Francis and Helen (McCarthy) R.; m. Patricia Anne Yates, June 20, 1953; children: Kevin Gerard, Brian Yates. AB, Syracuse U., 1954; postgrad., U. Buffalo, 1957-59, Rutgers U., 1962-65; DHL, Monterey Inst. Intl. Studies, 1998. Owner-mgr. Rivette Sales and Svc., Syracuse, 1950-54; sales rep. Sperry-Rand, Inc., Elmira, N.Y., 1954-55; with Hewitt-Robins Inc., Buffalo, 1955-62, mgr. conveyor equipment sales Passaic, N.J., 1962-65; pres. Hewitt-Robins (Can.) Ltd., Montreal, 1965-69, also dir.; Can. regional mgr. Hewitt-Robins Inc., 1965-69; pres. Conergics Corp., Kansas City, Kans., 1970-86, Mid-West Conveyer Co., 1970-86, Alpine Metals Co., Salt Lake City, Con Cal Corp., Orange, Calif.; chmn. bd. Versa Corp., Mt. Sterling, Ohio, 1972-86, Baker Erection Co., Kansas City, Mo., 1971-86, Arrowhead Conveyer Corp., Oshkosh, Wis., 1979-86, Conveyer Sales and Mfg., Seattle, 1983-86; chmn. bd., pres. Conveyer Corp. Am., Ft. Worth, 1978-86, Mayfran Internat. Inc., Cleve., 1984-86, Mayfran Limburg B.V., The Netherlands, 1984-86, Guardian Resources Ltd., Palo Alto, Calif., 1982—; chmn. bd. Jeffrey Chain Co., Morristown, Tenn., 1985-96, Whitney Chain Corp., Morristown, 1985-96; chmn. bd., pres. Guardian Resources Ltd., Redwood City, 1966-91, Jeffrey Chain Can. Inc., Toronto, 1987-96; chmn. bd. Intelligent Software Internat. Inc., Redwood City, 1985-96, Tsubakimoto Mayfran, Osaka, Japan, 1984-86, Greaves Midwest Engring. Ltd., Bangalore, India, 1977-86. Bd. dirs. Jeffrey Chain Can., Toronto. Trustee U. Kansas City, 1983-95, Midwest Rsch., Inst., 1983-93; bd. dirs. Monterey Inst. Internat. Studies, 1989—. Office: PO Box 205 Pebble Beach CA 93953-0205

ROACH, CHARLES T. real estate company executive; Sr. v.p., gen. mgr. Sun City West and Sun City Grand Del Webb Corp., Phoenix, 1998—. Office: Del Webb Corp PO Box 29040 Phoenix AZ 85038-9040

ROACH, PAM, state legislator; m. Jim Roach; 5 children. BA in History, Brigham Young U., 1970. Mem. Wash. Legislature, Olympia, 1990—, mem. econ. devel. fin. authority com., mem. energy, tech., and telecom. com., mem. jud. com., mem. waysn and means com., mem. sentencing guidelines commn., mem. joint com. on pension policy, mem. statute law com. Guardian mem. Boy Scouts Am.; bd. dirs. Auburn Food Bank; past mem. Gov.'s Juvenile Issues Task Force; mem. local coun. Boy Scouts Am.; past mem. adv. com. Soos Creek Cmty. Plan Tech., Maple Valley Cmty. Summit. Mem. Am. Legis. Exch. Coun., Nat. Conf. State Legislatures, Auburn C. of C. Republican. Office: 202 Irving Newhouse Ofc Olympia WA 98504-0001

ROARK, TERRY PAUL, astronomer, educator; b. Okeene, Okla., June 11, 1938; s. Paul J. and Erma K. (Morrison) R.; m. Beverly Brown, Sept. 7, 1963; 1 child, David. C. BA in Physics, Oklahoma City U., 1960; MS in Astronomy, Rensselaer Poly. Inst., 1962, PhD in Astronomy, 1966. Asst. provost for curricula Ohio State U., Columbus, 1977-79, assoc. provost for instrn., 1979-83; prof. physics Kent (Ohio) State U., 1983-87, v.p. acad. and student affairs, 1983-87, provost, 1985-87; pres. U. Wyo., Laramie, 1987-97, prof. physics and astronomy, 1987-2001; interim pres. Mont. State U., Bozeman, 2000. Bd. dirs. Rocky Mountain Fed. Savs. Bank, chmn. audit com., 1989-93; commr. Western Interstate Commn. for Higher Edn., 1987-97, chmn., 1991; bd. dirs. Associated Western Univs., 1987-94, chmn., 1991, bd. trustees, 1994-97, chmn. 1996; adv. bd. Wyo. Geol. Survey, 1987-97; mem. Warren AFB Civilian Adv. Coun., 1987-97; bd. dirs. First Interstate Bank of Wyo. Mem., treas. Ctr. for Pub. Edn., Columbus, 1980-83; mem. fin. adv. com. LWV, Kent, 1986; mem. long range planning com. Cleve. Urban League, 1985-86; mem. adv. com. Battelle youth sci. program Columbus and Ohio Pub. Schs., 1982; bd. dirs. Ivinson Hosp. Found., 1987-97. Mem. Am. Astron. Soc., Internat. Astron. Union, Nat. Assn. State Univs. and Land Grant Colls. (bd. dirs. 1994-96, chair commn. on intenat. affairs 1995), Astron. Soc. Pacific, Sigma Xi, Phi Kappa Phi, Omicron Delta Kappa. Avocations: photography, music, hiking. Office: U Wyo Dept Physics & Astronomy PO Box 3905 Laramie WY 82071-3905

ROATH, STEPHEN D. pharmaceutical company executive; b. 1941; With Long's Drug Stores Corp., 1964—, exec. v.p. store ops., 1988-91, pres., CEO, 1991—. Office: Longs Drug Stores Corp 141 N Civic Dr Walnut Creek CA 94596-3858

ROBBINS, ANNE FRANCIS See REAGAN, NANCY DAVIS

ROBBINS, JAMES EDWARD, electrical engineer; b. Renovo, Pa., May 11, 1931; s. James Edward and Marguerite Neva (Cleary) R.; m. Elizabeth [illegible] Dorothy Raye Bell, July 23, 1971; stepchildren: Mark, Lori. BEE, Pa. State U., 1958; MS in Math., San Diego State U., 1961. Registered profl. engr., Calif., Ariz. Rsch. engr. Astronautics divsn. Gen. Dynamics Co., San Diego, 1961-62; sr. engr. Kearfott divsn. Gen. Precision Co., San Marcos, Calif., 1962-65; sys. engring. specialist Teledyne Ryan Aerospace Co., San Diego, 1965-76; mgr. tech. ops. Electronics divsn. Gen. Dynamics Co., Yuma, Ariz., 1965-76; v.p. Cibola Info. Sys., Yuma, 1982-84; cons. engr. Robbins Engring. Co., Yuma, 1984-85; sr. engring. specialist Gen. Dynamics Svcs. Co., Yuma, Ariz., 1985-90; sys. engr. Trimble Navigation, Sunnyvale, Calif., 1990—. Contbr. articles to profl. jours. With USN, 1951-55, Korea. Mem. Inst. Navigation, Nat. Soc. Profl. Engrs., Ariz. Soc. Profl. Engrs. (pres. we. divsn. 1986), Am. Legion, VFW (post comdr. 1963-65), Tau Beta Pi. Home: PO Box 1728 430 Ave Portola El Granada CA 94018-1728 Office: Trimble Navigation 645 N Mary Ave Sunnyvale CA 94085-2933 E-mail: jim_robbins@trimble.com, jim_robbins@earthlink.com

ROBBINS, NANCY LOUISE See MANN, NANCY LOUISE

ROBBINS, STEPHEN J. M. lawyer; b. Seattle, Apr. 13, 1942; s. Robert Mads and Aneita Elberta (West) R.; m. Nina Winifred Tanner, Aug. 11, 1967; children: Sarah E.T., Alicia S.T. AB, UCLA, 1964; JD, Yale U., 1971. Bar: D.C. 1973, U.S. Dist. Ct. D.C. 1973, U.S. Ct. Appeals (D.C. cir.) 1973, U.S. Ct. Appeals (3d cir.) 1973, U.S. Dist. Ct. (ea. and no. dists.) Calif. 1982, U.S. Dist. Ct. (cen. dist.) Calif. 1983, Supreme Ct. of Republic of Palau, 1994. Pres. U.S. Nat. Student Assn., Washington, 1964-65; dir. scheduling McGovern for Pres., Washington, 1971-72; assoc. Steptoe & Johnson, Washington, 1972-75; chief counsel spl. inquiry on food prices, com. on nutrition and human needs U.S. Senate, Washington, 1975; v.p., gen. counsel Straight Arrow Pubs., San Francisco, 1975-77; dep. dist. atty. City and County of San Francisco, 1977-78; regional counsel U.S. SBA, San Francisco, 1978-80; spl. counsel Warner-Amex Cable Communications, Sacramento, 1981-82; ptnr. McDonough, Holland and Allen, Sacramento, 1982-84; v.p. Straight Arrow Pubs., N.Y.C., 1984-86; gen. legal counsel Govt. State of Koror, Rep. of Palau, Western Caroline Islands, 1994-95; pvt. practice law, 1986—. Adj. prof. govt. Calif. State U., Sacramento, 1999—. Staff sgt. U.S. Army, 1966-68. Mem. ABA (sect. urban, state and local govt. sect. real property, probate and trust law, sect. natural resources energy, environ. law, forum com. on affordable housing and cmty. devel.), D.C. Bar, State Bar of Calif., Urban Land Inst., Am. Hist. Assn., Supreme Ct. Hist. Soc., Acad. Polit. Sci., Chamber Music Soc. of Sacramento, Oreg. Shakespeare Festival, Shaw Island Hist. Soc. Democrat. Unitarian. Avocations: theatre, art, hiking. Office: 2150 3rd Ave Sacramento CA 95818-3102

ROBBINS, THOMAS EUGENE, writer; b. Blowing Rock, N.C., 1936; m. Terrie Hemingway (div.); m. Alexa d'Avalon, 1995; 1 child, Fleetwood Starr. Student, Washington and Lee U., 1954-56, U. Wash., 1963; degree in social sci., Va. Commonwealth U., 1959. Former copy editor Richmond (Va.) Times-Dispatch, Seattle Post-Intelligencer; art critic Seattle Times. Author: Guy Anderson, 1965, Another Roadside Attraction, 1971, Even Cowgirls Get the Blues, 1976 (Best Am. Short Story 1977), Still Life with Woodpecker, 1980, Jitterbug Perfume, 1984, Skinny Legs and All, 1990, Half Asleep in Frog Pajamas, 1994, Fierce Invalids Home from Hot Climates, 2000. With USAF. Office: PO Box 338 La Conner WA 98257-0338

ROBERTS, ALAN SILVERMAN, orthopedic surgeon; b. Apr. 20, 1939; s. Joseph William and Fannie (Margolies) S.; children: Michael Eric, Daniel Ian. BA, Conn. Wesleyan U., 1960; MD, Jefferson Med. Coll., 1966. Rotating intern Lankenau Hosp., Phila., 1966-67; resident in orthoaedics Tulane U. Med. Coll., 1967-71; pvt. practice specializing in orthopaedics and hand surgery L.A., 1971—. Mem. clin. faculty UCLA Med. Coll., 1971-76. Contbr. articles to profl. jours. With AUS, 1961. Riordan Hand fellow, 1969, Boyes Hand fellow, 1971. Mem. AMA, ACS, Am. Acad. Orthopaedic Surgeons, Calif. Med. Assn., L.A. County Med. Assn., Western Orthopaedic Assn., Riordan Hand Soc. Republican. Jewish.

ROBERTS, DELAINE, state legislator; b. Afton, Wyo., Jan. 15, 1933; m. Nelda Roberts. Student, Brigham Young U., U. Wyo. Sheriff Lincoln County, Wyo.; apptd. U.S. Marshall; mem. Wyo. Senate, Dist. 16, Cheyenne, 1996—; mem. rev. com. Wyo. Senate, Cheyenne, mem. travel, recreation, wildlife, and cultural resources com. Mem. Sch. Bd. Lincoln County Sch. Dist. # 9. Mem. NRA, Peace Officers Assn., Rotary, Lions. Republican. Office: PO Box 5173 Etna WY 83118-0173 also: Wyo Senate State Capitol Cheyenne WY 82002-0001

ROBERTS, DONALD FRANK, JR. communications educator, educator; b. Seattle, Mar. 30, 1939; s. Donald Frank Sr. and Ruth Amalia (Geiger) R.; m. Karlene Hahn, 1963 (div. 1981): 1 child, Donald Brett; m. Wendy G. Roberts, Aug. 26, 1983; stepchildren: Richard L., David L., Katherine M. AB, Columbia U., 1961; MA, U. Calif., Berkeley, 1963; PhD, Stanford U., 1968. Instr., dept. English U. Hawaii, Honolulu, 1963-64; asst. dir. ednl. svc. bur. The Wall Street Jour., Princeton, N.J., 1964-65; asst. prof., rsch. assoc. dept. Comm., Inst. Comm. Rsch. Stanford (Calif.) U., 1970-76, assoc. prof., 1976-84, prof. Comm., 1984—, dir. Inst. Comm. Rsch., 1985-90, chmn. dept. Comm., 1990-96, Thomas More Storke Prof., 1991—. Cons. NIMH, 1970-71, Rand Corp., 1972-74, Sta. KQED-TV, 1975-77, Far West Lab. Ednl. Rsch. and Devel., 1978-79, FTC, 1978-80, Westinghouse Broadcasting, 1983-86, Soc. Nutrition Edn., 1984-86, The Disney Channel, 1986-87, WHO, 1988-89, SRI Internat., 1988-89, Carnegie Coun. Adolescence, 1989-90, NBC, 1992, Ctr. Disease Control, 1992, Children Now, 1992—, Software Pubs. Assn., 1994, Nickelodeon, 1994, JP Kids, 1995-97, MGM Animation, 1996—, DIC Entertainment, 1997—, Planet Lingo, 1997-2001, Sunbow Entertainment, 1999—, ABC/Disney TV Animation, 2000—, Disney Online, 2000—, Nelvana, Ltd., 2000—; bd. advisors Media Scope, 1992-94; bd. dirs. Recreational Software Adv. Coun., 1994-98; proposal reviewer NIMH, NSF, U.S. Agy. Internat. Devel., Can. Coun., John and Mary R. Markle Found., W.T. Grant Found.; spkr. numerous seminars, confs., symposia. Co-author: Process and Effects of Mass Communication, 1971, Television and Human Behavior, 1978, It's Not ONLY Rock and Roll, 1998, Kids & Media @ the New Millennium, 1999; mem. editl. bd. Jour. Broadcasting, 1980-88, Pub. Opinion Quarterly, 1981-86, Communicare, 1986—; editl. reviewer Commn. Rsch., Comm. Monograph, Comm. Yearbrook, Human Comm. Rsch., Jour. Comm., Jour. Quarterly, Child Devel., Jour. Applied Psychology, Jour. Ednl. Psychology, Psychology Bull., Jour. Adolescent Health; contbr. articles to profl. jours, also monographs and book chpts. Fellow Human Scis. Rsch. Coun., Pretoria. South Africa, 1985, 1987, Fullbright Teaching fellow Inst. for Unterrichtstechnologie Und Medienpadagogic, Austria, 1987. Mem. APA, Internat. Comm. Assn., Assn. Edn. in Journalism and Mass Comm., Soc. Rsch. Child Devel., Soc. Personality and Soc. Psychology. Office: Stanford U Dept Comm McClatchy Hall Stanford CA 94305-2050 E-mail: droberts@stanford.edu

ROBERTS, DONALD JOHN, economics and business educator, consultant; b. Winnipeg, Man., Can., Feb. 11, 1945; came to U.S., 1967; s. Donald Victor and Margaret Mabel (Riddell) R.; m. Kathleen Eleanor Taylor, Aug. 26, 1967. BA with honors, U. Man., 1967; PhD, U. Minn., 1972. Instr. dept. managerial econs. and decision scis. J.L. Kellogg Grad. Sch. Mgmt., Northwestern U., Evanston, Ill., 1971-72, asst. prof., 1972-74; assoc. prof. J. L. Kellogg Grad. Sch. Mgmt., Northwestern U., Evanston, 1974-77; prof. J.L. Kellogg Grad. Sch. Mgmt., Northwestern U., Evanston, 1977-80, Grad. Sch. Bus., Stanford (Calif.) U., 1980, Jonathan B. Lovelace prof., 1980-2001, assoc. dean, dir. rsch., 1987-90, dir. exec. program in strategy [illegible] 2000—, John H. and Irene S. Scully prof., 2001—. Prof. (by courtesy) dept. econs. Stanford U., 1986—; vis. rsch. faculty U. Catholique de Louvain, Belgium, 1974-75; inaugural Clarendon lectr. mgmt. studies Oxford U., 1997; cons. bus., econs. and antitrust, 1976—; vis. fellow All Souls Coll., Oxford U., 1995, Nuffield Coll., Oxford U., 1999-00; vis. acad. fellow in leadership and orgn. McKinsey & Co., London, 1999-00. Co-author: Economics, Organization and Management, 1992;; assoc. editor Jour. Econ. Theory, 1977-92, Econometrica, 1985-87, Games and Economics Behavior, 1988—; mem. editl. bd. Am. Econ. Rev., 1991-95, Jour.

Econs. and Mgmt. Strategy, 1991-98, Orgns. and Markets Abstracts, 1996—; contbr. articles to profl. jours. NSF grantee, 1973-93; rsch. fellow Ctr. Ops. Rsch. and Econometrics, Heverlee, Belgium, 1974, fellow Ctr. for Advanced Study in the Behavioral Scis., 1991-92. Fellow Econometric Soc. (coun. 1994-96); mem. Am. Econ. Assn., Beta Gamma Sigma. Home: 835 Santa Fe Ave Stanford CA 94305-1022 Office: Stanford U Grad Sch Bus Stanford CA 94305-5015 E-mail: roberts_john@gsb.stanford.edu

ROBERTS, DWIGHT LOREN, engineering consultant, writer; b. San Diego, June 3, 1949; s. James Albert and Cleva Lorraine (Conn) R.; B.A., U. San Diego, 1976, M.A., 1979; m. Phyllis Ann Adair, Mar. 29, 1969; children: Aimee Renee, Michael Loren, Daniel Alexandr. Engring. aide Benton Engring. Inc., San Diego, 1968-73; pres. Robert's Tech. Research Co., also subs. Marine Technique Ltd., San Diego, 1973-76; pres. Research Technique Internat., 1978—; freelance writer, 1979—; owner Agrl. Analysis, 1985-88; constrn. mgr. Homestead Land Devel. Corp., 1988-92; sr. engr. cons. Morrison Knudson, 1992-95; sr. soils analyst Geotechnics, Inc., 1995-98; offsite field supt. coastal divsn. Kaufman and Broad, 1998—. Served with U.S. Army, 1969-71. Mem. ASTM, AAAS, Nat. Inst. Sci., N.Y. Acad. Scis., Nat. Inst. Cert. in Engring. Techs., Soil and Found. Engr. Assn., Phi Alpha Theta. Baptist. Author: Geological Exploration of Alaska, 1898-1924, Alfred Hulse Brooks, Alaskan Trailblazer, Papaveraceae of the World, Demarchism, Arid Regions Gardening, Visions of Dame Kind: Dreams, Imagination and Reality, Antal's Theory of the Solar System, Science Fair-A Teacher's Manual, Common Ground: Similarities of the World Religions, Black Sheep-Scientific Discoveries From the Fringe, After Manhattan, The Christofilos Effect; and others; contbr. articles to profl. jours. Office: 3111 E Victoria Dr Alpine CA 91901-3679

ROBERTS, GEORGE P. computer company executive; Chmn., CEO P-Com, Campbell, Calif. Office: P Com 3175 Winchester Blvd Campbell CA 95008-6557

ROBERTS, GEORGE R. investment banking company executive; married; 3 children. JD, U. Calif., San Francisco. With Bears, Stearns, New York, until 1976; founding ptnr. Kohlberg, Kravis, Roberts, San Francisco. Dir. Beatrice Co., Chgo., Houdaille Industries Inc., Northbrook, Ill., Malone and Hyde, Memphis, Union Tex. Petroleum Holdings Inc., Houston. Office: Kohlberg Kravis Roberts & Co 2800 Sand Hill Rd Ste 200 Menlo Park CA 94025-7055

ROBERTS, JACK EARL, lawyer, ski resort operator, wood products company executive, real estate developer; b. L.A., Nov. 5, 1928; s. James Earle and Illa Ann (Morgan) R.; m. Marilyn Humphreys, Sept. 13, 1954; children: Ronda, Cyndi, Scott, Robynne, Craig. BS in Acctg. and Bus. Adminstrn., Brigham Young U., 1952; JD, George Washington U., 1955, LLM in Taxation (Teaching fellow), 1956. Bar: Calif. 1957; CPA, Ariz. Pvt. practice, L.A.; atty. Office Chief Counsel, IRS, L.A., 1956-60; mem. firm Roberts, Carmack, Johnson, Poulson & Harmer, L.A., 1961-78; pres. Park West Ski Resort, Park City, Utah, 1975-88; pres., dir. Accudyne Corp., Los Angeles, 1972-89, Richmark Corp., Los Angeles, 1972-77; chmn., dir. Comml. Wood Products Co., Los Angeles, 1968—; pres., dir. Snyderville Devel. Co., Inc., Utah, 1978-94, Community Water Co., Salt Lake City, 1987-2000, Roberts Mgmt. Corp., Salt Lake City, 1988—, Ste. Vacations, Inc., Salt Lake City, 1989—. Contbr. articles on legal subjects to tech. jours. Pres. Westwood Rep. Club, 1968; mem. cen. coms. Calif. State, L.A. County Rep. Party, 1974-77; mem. Utah State Cen. and Exec. Coms., 1981-96, Summit County Rep. cen. and exec. coms., 1978-84; chmn. Summit County, 1981-83; chmn. Utah State Rep. Com., 1988-89, state sec., 1986-88. Mem. Calif. Bar Assn., D.C. Bar Assn. Office: 2726 E Wasatch Dr Salt Lake City UT 84108-1929

ROBERTS, JAMES E. civil engineer; b. Jameson, Mo., Nov. 24, 1930; BS, U. Calif. Berkeley, 1953; MS, U. So. Calif., 1966. Registered profl. engr., Calif. Mgr. Bridges Design Sect. Calif. Dept. Transp., 1968-72; chief Engring. Equipment Divsn., 1976-81, project dir., 1981-85, chief bridge design engr., 1985-87, chief bridge engr., 1987-93, dept. dir. engring., 1993-94, dir. engring. svc. dept., chief structural engr., 1994-99, chief dep. dir. ops. and engring., 1999—. Fellow ASCE (Constrn. Mgmt. award 1996); mem. Nat. Acad. Engring., Am. Concrete Inst., Am. Welding Soc., Am. Assn. State Hwy. & Transp. Ofcls. Home: 1960 Tudor Ct Carmichael CA 95608-5742 Office: Calif Dept Transp Engring Svc Dept PO Box 942874 Sacramento CA 94274-0001

ROBERTS, JANICE, marketing professional; Honors degree in Econs. Dir. mktg. and bus. devel. BICC Techs. Group BICC PLC, 1989, pres. BICC Comm., mng. dir. Data Networking, 1989; v.p., gen. mgr. 3Com Corp., Santa Clara, Calif., Eng., 1992, sr. v.p. bus. devel., pres. 3Com Vemtures. Mem. Chartered Inst. Mktg. Office: 3Com 5400 Bayfront Plz PO Box 58145 Santa Clara CA 95052-8145

ROBERTS, JERRY, newspaper editor; Polit. editor city desk San Francisco Chronicle, editl. pg. editor, 1995-98, mng. editor, 1998—. Office: San Francisco Chronicle 901 Mission St San Francisco CA 94103-2905

ROBERTS, JOHN D. chemist, educator; b. L.A., June 8, 1918; s. Allen Andrew and Flora (Dombrowski) R.; m. Edith Mary Johnson, July 11, 1942; children: Anne Christine, Donald William, John Paul, Allen Walter. AB, UCLA, 1941, PhD, 1944; D in Natural Scis. (hon.), U. Munich, 1962; D.Sc. (hon.), Temple U., 1964, Notre Dame U., 1993, U. Wales, 1993; DS (hon.), Scripps Rsch. Inst., 1996. Instr. chemistry UCLA, 1944-45; NRC fellow chemistry Harvard U., 1945-46, instr. chemistry, 1946, MIT, 1946, asst. prof., 1947-50, assoc. prof., 1950-52; vis. prof. Ohio State U., 1952, Stanford U., 1973-74; prof. organic chemistry Calif. Inst. Tech., 1953-72, inst. prof. chemistry, 1972-88, inst. prof. chemistry emeritus, lectr., 1988—, dean of faculty, v.p., provost, 1980-83, lectr., 1988—, chmn. divsn. chemistry and chem. engring., 1963-68, acting chmn., 1972-73. Robert Noyce vis. prof. sci. Grinnell Coll., 2001. Author: Basic Organic Chemistry, Part I, 1955, Nuclear Magnetic Resonance, 1958, Spin-Spin Splitting in High-Resolution Nuclear Magnetic Resonance Spectra, 1961, Molecular Orbital Calculations, 1961, (with M.C. Caserio) Basic Principles of Organic Chemistry, 1964, 2d edit., 1977, Modern Organic Chemistry, 1967, (with R. Stewart and M.C. Caserio) Organic Chemistry-Methane To Macromolecules, 1971; (autobiography) At The Right Place at the Right Time, 1990; cons. editor: McGraw-Hill Series in Advanced Chemistry, 1957-60; editor in chief Organic Syntheses, vol. 41; mem. editorial bd. Spectroscopy, Organic Magnetic Resonance in Chemistry, Asymmetry, Tetrahedron Computer Methodology. Trustee L.S.B. Leakey Found., 1983-92; bd. dirs. Huntington Med. Rsch. Insts., Organic Syntheses Inc., Coleman Chamber Music Assn.; mem. Calif. Competitive Tech. adv. com., 1989—. Guggenheim fellow, 1952-53, 55-56; recipient Am. Chem. Soc. award pure chemistry, 1954, Harrison Howe award, 1957, Roger Adams award in organic chemistry, 1967, Alumni Profl. Achievement award UCLA, 1967, Nichols medal, 1972, Tolman medal, 1975, Michelson-Morley award, 1976, Norris award, 1978, Pauling award, 1980, Theodore Wm. Richards medal, 1982, Willard Gibbs Gold medal, 1983, Golden Plate award Am. Acad. Achievement, 1983, Priestley medal, 1987, Madison Marshall award, 1989, (with W. V.E. Doering) Robert A. Welch award, 1990, Nat. Medal Sci. NSF, 1990, Glenn T. Seaborg medal, 1991, Award in nuclear magnetic resource, 1991, Svc. to Chemistry award, 1991, Arthur C. Cope award Am. Chem. Soc. 1994, Chem. Pioneer award, 1994, History Maker award from Pasadena Hist. Soc., 1994; named hon. alumnus Calif. Inst. Tech., 1990, SURF dedicatee, 1992, Most Influential Chemists of Last 75 yrs. Chem. and Engring. News, 1998, Chem. Scis. award Nat. Acad. Scis., 1999. Mem. NAS (councillor 1980-83, mem. com. on sci. and engring. pub. policy 1983-87, Chem. Scis. award 1999), AAAS (councillor 1992-95), Am. Chem. Soc. (chmn. organic chemistry divsn. 1956-57, Nakanishi prize 2001), Am. Philos. Soc. (mem. coun. 1983-86), Am. Acad. Arts and Scis., Sigma Xi, Phi Lambda Upsilon, Alpha Chi. Sigma. Office: Calif Inst Tech Crellin Lab Pasadena CA 91125-0001

ROBERTS, JOHN DERHAM, lawyer; b. Orlando, Fla., Nov. 1, 1942; s. Junius P. and Mary E. Roberts; m. Malinda K. Swineford, June 11, 1965; 1 child, Kimberlyn Amanda. Cert., Richmond (Va.) Bus. Coll., 1960; BS, Hampden-Sydney (Va.) Coll., 1964; LLB, Washington & Lee U., 1968. Bar: Va. 1968, Fla. 1969, U.S. Supreme Ct. 1969, U.S. Ct. Customs and Patent Appeals 1970, U.S. Tax Ct. 1970, U.S. Ct. Appeals (5th cir.) 1970, U.S. Ct. Appeals (9th cir.) 1974, U.S. Supreme Ct. 1969. Law clk. U.S. Dist. Ct., Jacksonville, Fla., 1968-69; assoc. Phillips, Kendrick, Gearhart & Aylor, Arlington, Va., 1969-70; asst. U.S. Atty. mid. dist. Fla. U.S. Dept. Justice, Jacksonville, 1970-74, Dist. of Alaska, Anchorage, 1974-77, U.S. magistrate judge, 1977—. Bd. dirs. Teen Challenge Alaska, Anchorage, 1984-93; chmn. Eagle Scout Rev. Bd., 1993—; bd. dirs. Alaska Youth for Christ, 1993-96; govs.'s Prayer Breakfast Com., 1994—, vice-chair, 1998—. Recipient Citizenship award DAR, Anchorage, 1984, plaque, U.S. Navy, Citizen Day, Adak, Alaska, 1980. Mem. ABA, Nat. Conf. Spl. Ct. Judges (exec. bd. 1985-92), 9th Cir. Conf. Magistrates (exec. bd. 1982-85, chmn. 1984-85), Alaska Bar Assn., Anchorage Bar Assn., Chi Phi, Psi Chi, Phi Alpha Delta. Republican. Office: US Magistrate Judge 222 W 7th Ave Unit 46 Anchorage AK 99513-7504

ROBERTS, JOHN PETER LEE, cultural advisor, administrator, educator, writer; b. Sydney, Australia, Oct. 21, 1930; s. Noel Lee and Myrtle Winifred (Reid) R.; m. Christina Van Oordt, July 28, 1962; children—Noel, Christina, Olga. Student, State Conservatorium Music, New South Wales; MA, Carleton U., 1988; DFA (hon.), U. Victoria, 1992; LLD (hon.), U. Man., 1997. With CBC Radio, Toronto, Can., 1955—, producer, 1955—, head music and variety, 1971—, spl. adv. music and arts, 1975; sr. advisor cultural devel., head office Ottawa, 1983-87; mem. exec. bd. Internat. Music Centre, Vienna, 1968-80, first chmn. radio and comml. rec. group, 1969-70, hon. mem., 1980; mem. exec. bd. Internat. Inst. Music Dance and Theatre, Vienna, 1969-75; bd. govs. Can. Conf. Arts, 1970-76; exec. bd. Internat. Music Coun., Paris, 1973-79; v.p. Internat. Music Council, 1975, pres., 1978-79, Can. Music Centre, Toronto, 1971-77, dir. gen., 1977-81; pres. Can. Music Council, 1968-71, 75-77; dir. Festival Singers of Can., 1965-78, Elmer Iseler Singers, 1979-81, Toronto Mendelssohn Choir, 1969-81, Nat. Youth Orch. Can., 1973-80; chmn. 1st World Music Week, 1975, Internat. Music Day, 1975-82; v.p. Internat. Inst. Audio-Visual Communication and Cultural Devel. (Mediacult), Vienna, 1976-87, pres., 1987-93, Internat. Rsch. Inst. for Media, Communication, Cultural Devel., Vienna, 1993-95. V.p. Musicians Internat. Mus. Aid Fund., Geneva, 1978, 79; pres. Les Jeunesses Musicales du Can., 1979-83; chmn. jury Internat. Vocal Competition, Rio de Janeiro, 1979, Esther Honen's Calgary Internat. Piano Competition, 1996; spl. advisor to chmn. Can. Radio-TV and Telecomms. Commn., 1981-83; sr. advisor cultural devel. CBC, 1983-87; dean of faculty of fine arts U. Calgary, 1987-95; vis. fellow McGill Inst. for Study of Can. McGill U., Montreal, 1995-96; adj. prof. U. Calgary, 1995—; bd. dirs. Nickle Arts Mus., 1987-95, Calgary Philharm. Orch., 1988-94, Esther Honen's Internat. Piano Competition, 1994. Mem. editorial bd. Can. Music Book, 1970-77 Mem. exec. bd. dirs. Can. Nat. Commn. for UNESCO, 1976-80; founding pres. Glenn Gould Found., Toronto, 1983—. Decorated Order of Can. (mem., 1983, officer, 1996); Cross of Honour for Sci. and the Arts (Austria). Mem. Can. assn. Fine Arts Deans (chmn. 1989-93), Internat. Coun. Fine Arts Deans (bd. dirs. 1992-94). Office: U Calgary Faculty Fine Arts 2500 University Dr NW Calgary AB Canada T2N 1N4

ROBERTS, KEVIN, recreational facility executive; Pres. American Golf Corp., Santa Monica, Calif., 1981; pres. golf ops. Golf Ops., Santa Monica. Office: Am Golf Corp 2951 28th St Santa Monica CA 90405-2961

ROBERTS, LAWRENCE GILMAN, telecommunications company executive; b. Dec. 21, 1937; s. Elliott John and Elizabeth (Gilman) R.; m. June Ellen Stuller, 1959 (div. 1973); children: Paul, Kenny. BS, MIT, 1959, MS, 1960, PhD, 1963. Dir. info. proc. Advanced Rsch. Projects Agy. U.S. Dept. Def., Arlington, Va., 1969-73; pres., CEO, GTE Telenet Corp., Vienna, 1973-82; pres. DHL, Redwood City, Calif., 1982-83; chmn., CEO, NetExpress, Inc., Foster City, 1983-93; pres. ATM Systems, Santa Clara, 1993-98; chmn., CEO, Caspian Networks, Palo Alto, 1998—. Recipient L.M. Ericsson award for comms. Mem. NAE, IEEE (internet award, 2000), IEEE Computer Soc., Am. Fedn. Info. Processing (Harry Goode award, W. Wallace McDowell award), Assn. Computing Machinery (SIGCOM award), Sigma Xi. Office: Caspian Networks 170 Baytech Dr San Jose CA 95134 E-mail: lroberts@caspiannetworks.com

ROBERTS, LINDA, truck transportation services company executive; With Profit Freight Sys.; co-founder Profl. Sales Group Ltd., sales and mtkg. co., 1990, Profl. Transp. Group, Ltd., 1990; with Truck, Net, Inc., 1991, Timely Transp., Inc., 1992, Rapid Transit, Inc., 1995; pres. Profl. Transp. Group, Ltd., Inc., Newport Beach, Calif., 1997—.

ROBERTS, MICHAEL FOSTER, biology educator; b. Guatemala City, Guatemala, Aug. 8, 1943; s. Ralph Jackson and Arleda (Allen) R.; m. Mary Sherill Noe, Dec. 27, 1966; children: Rosemary, Amelia. BA, U. Calif., Berkeley, 1966; MA, U. Wis. (Madison), 1968, PhD, 1972. Fellow John B. Pierce Found. Lab., Yale U., New Haven, 1972-76; asst. prof. Yale U., New Haven, 1976-81, Linfield Coll., McMinnville, oreg., 1981-84, assoc. prof., 1984-90, prof. biology, 1990—. Guest referee editor Am. Physiol. Soc., Bethesda, Md., 1974—; peer rev. com. Am. Heart Assn., Portland, Oreg., 1982-87. Contbr. articles to profl. jours. Program dir. Murdock Trust. Named NIH Predoctoral Fellow, 1969-72, Postdoctoral fellow, 1972-76; recipient NIH Rsch. grant, 1982-85, Am. Heart Assn. rsch. grant, 1985-86, 99—; grantee Murdock Trust. Mem. Am. Physiol. Soc., Sigma Xi. Office: Linfield Coll Dept Biology Mcminnville OR 97128 Business E-Mail: mrobert@linfield.edu

ROBERTS, PAUL HARRY, mathematics educator; b. Aberystwyth, Wales, Eng., Sept. 13, 1929; s. Percy Harry and Ethel Frances (Mann) R.; m. Maureen Frances Tabrett, Dec. 16, 1989. BA, Cambridge U., Eng., 1951, MA, PhD, 1954, ScD, 1966. Rsch. assoc. U. Chgo., 1954-55, assoc. prof., 1961-63; scientific officer Atomic Weapons Rsch. Establisment, Aldermaston, U.K., 1955-56; rsch. fellow U. Durham, Newcastle, U.K., 1956-59, lectr. U.K., 1959-61; prof. math. U. Newcastle upon Tyne, Eng., 1963-86; prof. math. and geophysical scis. U. Calif., L.A., 1986—. Author: (book) An Introduction to Magnetohydrodynamics, 1967; co-editor: (book) Rotating Fluids in Geophysics, 1979; editor: Geophysical and Astrophysical Fluid Dynamics, 1976—. Mem. Royal Astronomical Soc., Royal Soc. London, Am. Geophysical Union (John Adam Fleming medal, 1999. Office: UCLA Inst of Geophysics & Planetary Physics Los Angeles CA 90095-1567

ROBERTS, PAUL V. civil and environmental engineering educator; BS, Princeton U., 1960; PhD in Chem. Engring., Cornell U., 1966; MS, Stanford U., 1971. Process engr. Chevron Rsch. Co., 1966-68; rsch. engr. Stanford (Calif.) Rsch. Inst., 1968-71; sr. rsch. scientist and group leader process engring. Swiss Fed. Inst. Water Supply and Water Pollution Control, Dubendorf, Switzerland, 1972, head engring. dept., 1973-76; from adj. prof. to assoc. prof. Stanford (Calif.) U., 1976-84, assoc. dept. chmn., 1985-90, prof. environ. engring. dept. civil engring., 1984—, C.L. Peck prof. engring., 1989—. Prin. investigator 25 sponsored projects at Stanford U., 1976— Mem. Nat. Acad. Engring., Am. Water Works Assn. (Rsch. Achievement award 1983, 85-87, 91). Achievements include rsch. projects including chemical process and environmental engineering with emphasis on trace contaminants, water reuse, unit operations of water treatment and advanced waste treatment; transfer of volatile organic pollutants to the atmosphere; transformation and fates of trace contaminants in the groundwater environment; hazardous waste remediation, sorption and mass transfer phenomena. Office: Stanford U Dept Civil & Environ Engrg Stanford CA 94305-4020

ROBERTS, PETER CHRISTOPHER TUDOR, engineering executive; b. Georgetown, Demerara, Brit. Guiana, Oct. 12, 1945; came to U.S., 1979; s. Albert Edward and Dorothy Jean (Innis) R.; m. Julia Elizabeth Warner, Nov. 10, 1984; children: Kirsta Anne, Serena Amanda, Angelee Julia, Zephanie Elizabeth, Fiona Ann, Emrys Tudor, Peter Christopher Tudor Roberts II. BSc with honors, Southampton (Eng.) U., 1969, PhD in Microelectronics, 1975. Rsch. fellow dept. electronics Southampton U., 1974-77; prof. microcircuit dept. electronics INAOE, Tonantzintla, Mexico, 1977-79; staff scientist Honeywell Sys. & Rsch. Ctr., Mpls., 1979-84; dir. advanced tech. Q-Dot Inc. R&D, Colorado Springs, Colo., 1984-86; program mgr. Honeywell Opto-Electronics, Richardson, Tex., 1986; vis. prof. U. N.Mex. CHTM, Albuquerque, 1987; supr. engring. Loral Inc. (formerly Honeywell), Lexington, Mass., 1988-90; mgr. engring. Litton Sys. Inc., Tempe, Ariz., 1990-96; staff scientist Motorola Corp. Rsch. Labs., Tempe, 1996—; dir. Pi-Rho Technics Internat., Inc., Gilbert, Ariz., 1996—. Cons. engr. Q-Dot, Inc. R&D, Colorado Springs, 1982—, pvt. stockholder, 1984—. Author: (with P.C.T. Roberts) Charge-Coupled Devices and Their Applications, 1980; contbr. articles to Boletin del INAGE, IEEE Transactions on Electron Devices, Procs. of the IEE (UK), Procs. of the INTERNEPCON, Internat. Jour. Electronics,IEEE Electron Device Letters, Electronics Letters, Solid State and Electron Devices, IEEE Jour. Solid State Circuits, others. Republican. Achievements include patent for VHSIC bipolar ROM and RAM ciruits; patents pending for GaAs 2 GHz by 16-Bit Digital Active Backplane; random access image readout, others. Home: 639 N Sunway Dr Gilbert AZ 85233-3504 Office: Motorola Labs Ceramics Tech Ctr 7700 S River Pkwy Tempe AZ 85284-1808

ROBERTS, RICHARD N. psychologist; AB in Govt., Columbia U., 1968; MSW, U. Hawaii, 1974, PhD in Psychology, 1977. Asst. prof. dept. psychology U. N.C., Greensboro, 1978-82; dir. pre-kindergarten ednl. program Ctr. Devel. Early Edn. Kamehameha Schs., Honolulu, 1983-89; assoc. prof. dept. psychology Utah State U., Logan, 1989—, co-dir. Early Intervention Rsch. Inst., 1989—, dir. rsch. and evaluation Ctr. for Persons with Disabilities, 1989—. Cons. to Hawaii State Hosp., 1977, Hawaii Job Corps, 1977, USAF, 1976, others. Editor: Coming home to preschool: The sociocultural context of early education, 1993; author monograph and workbook; contbr. chpts. to books, articles to profl. jours.; presenter in field. Served as lt. USN, 1968-72. Recipient numerous grants. Mem. APA, APHA, Utah Pub. Health Assn., Assn. Maternal and Child Health Programs, Soc. for Rsch. in Child Devel., Coun. for Exceptional Children. Office: Utah State U Early Intervention Rsch Logan UT 84322-0001

ROBERTS, ROBERT WINSTON, social work educator, dean; b. Balt., July 23, 1932; s. Kelmer Swan Roberts and Lettie Mae (Collins) Johnston; m. Helen Elizabeth Perpich, Mar. 4, 1964 (div. Apr. 1997). BA with high honors, San Francisco State U., 1957; MSW, U. Calif., Berkeley, 1959; D in Social Welfare, Columbia U., 1970. Caseworker Edgewood Protestant Orphanage, San Francisco, 1959-62, Jewish Family Service, San Francisco, 1962-63; research assoc. U. Calif., Berkeley, 1963-65; research analyst Family Service Assn. Am., N.Y.C., 1965-69; asst. prof. U. Chgo., 1967-70; prof. U. So. Calif., Los Angeles, 1970-90, dean sch. social work, 1980-88, dean emeritus, prof. emeritus, 1990—. Vis. prof. Western Australia Inst. Tech. (now Curtin U.), Perth, 1976-77, Chinese U. Hong Kong and U. Hong Kong, 1980; cons. Crittenton Services, Los Angeles, 1970-72, James Weldon Johnson Community Ctr., N.Y., 1966-67; bd. dirs. El Centro, Los Angeles. Editor: The Unwed Mother, 1966; co-editor: Theories of Social Casework, 1970, Child Caring: Social Policy and the Institution, 1973, Theories of Social Work with Groups, 1976, Theory and Practice of Community Social Work, 1980; editorial bd. Social Work Jour.; contbr. articles to profl. jours. Staff sgt. USAF, 1950-54; sgt. 1st class USAR, 1956-59. Fellow NIMH, 1957-58, 65-67, Crown Zellerbach Found., 1958-59; recipient Outstanding Educator award Los Amigos de la Humanidad, 1979; named Disting. Assoc., Nat. Acad. Practice in Social Work, 1985. Mem. ACLU, NASW (chmn. social action com. 1960-61), Council on Social Work Edn. (bd. dirs. 1970-73, del. to assembly 1971-72, commn. minority groups 1972-73). Avocations: cooking, reading, travel, photography. Office: U So Calif Montgomery Ross Fisher Rm 21 Los Angeles CA 90089-0001

ROBERTS, RON, county official; b. 1942; BA, San Diego State U.; MA, U. Calif., Berkeley, 1968. Chmn. county dist. 4 Office of Bd. of Suprs., San Diego, 1994—. Office: Office Bd Suprs County Adminstrn Ctr 1600 Pacific Hwy Ste 335 San Diego CA 92101-2470

ROBERTS, SIDNEY, biological chemist; b. Boston, Mar. 11, 1918; s. Samuel Richard and Elizabeth (Gilbert) R.; m. Clara Marian Szego, Sept. 14, 1943. B.S., MIT, 1939; postgrad., Harvard U., 1939-41; M.S., U. Minn., 1942, Ph.D., 1943. Instr. physiology U. Minn. Med. Sch., 1943-44, George Washington U. Med. Sch., 1944-45; rsch. assoc. Worcester Found. Exptl. Biology, Shrewsbury, Mass., 1945-47; asst. prof. physiol. chemistry Yale U. Med. Sch., 1947-48; mem. faculty U. Calif. Med. Sch., Los Angeles, 1948—, prof. biol. chemistry, 1957—; chmn. acad. senate UCLA, 1989-90; mem. adv. panel regulatory biology NSF, 1955-57, adv. panel metabolic biology, 1957-59; mem. metabolism study sect. NIH, 1960-63; basic sci. study sect. Los Angeles County Heart Assn., 1958-63. Cons. VA Hosp., Long Beach, Calif., 1951-55, Los Angeles, 1958-62; air conservation tech. adv. com. Los Angeles County Lung Assn., 1972-76 Author articles, revs.; editor med. jours. Served to 2d lt. AUS, 1944-48. MIT Nat. Entrance scholar, 1935; Guggenheim fellow, 1957-58. Fellow AAAS; mem. Am. Physiol. Soc., Endocrine Soc. (v.p. 1968-69, Ciba award 1953), Brit. Biochem. Soc., Soc. Neurosci., Am. Chem. Soc. (exec. com. div. biol. chemistry 1956-59), Am. Soc. Biol. Chemists, Am. Soc. Neurochemistry, Internat. Soc. Neurochemistry, Phi Beta Kappa, Sigma Xi (pres. UCLA chpt. 1959-60). Home: 1371 Marinette Rd Pacific Palisades CA 90272-2627 Office: UCLA Sch Med Dept Biol Chemistry Los Angeles CA 90095-1737 E-mail: sr@ucla.edu

ROBERTS, WALTER HERBERT BEATTY, anatomist, educator; b. Field, B.C., Can., Jan. 24, 1915; came to U.S., 1956, naturalized, 1965; s. Walter McWilliam and Sarah Caroline (Orr) R.; m. Olive Louise O'Neal, Sept. 1, 1937; children: Gayle, Sharon, David. M.D., Coll. Med. Evangelists (later Loma Linda U.), 1939. Intern St. Paul's Hosp., Vancouver, B.C., 1938-40; med. dir. Rest Haven Hosp. Sanitarium and Hosp., Sidney, Vancouver Island, 1940-53; post doctoral trg. White Meml. Hosp., Los Angeles, 1946-47, hosp., Edinburgh, Scotland, 1953-55; instr. in anatomy Loma Linda U., 1955-58, asst. prof. anatomy, 1959-62, asso. prof., 1962-70, prof., 1971—, chmn. dept. anatomy, 1974-81; prof. emeritus. Mem. Am. Assn. Anatomists, Sigma Xi, Alpha Omega Alpha. Adventist. Home: 11366 Campus St Loma Linda CA 92354-3302 Office: Loma Linda Univ Dept Path & Human Anatomy Divsn Human Anatomy Loma Linda CA 92350-0001

ROBERTS-DEMPSEY, PATRICIA E. secondary school educator; Tchr. Challenger High Sch., Spanaway, Wash., 1969—. Recipient Wash. State Tchr. of Yr. award, 1991-91. Office: Challenger HS 18020 B St E Spanaway WA 98387-8316

ROBERTSON, ARMAND JAMES, II, judge; b. San Diego, Sept. 23, 1937; s. Armand James and Muriel H. R.; m. Marion Sperry, Aug. 11, 1962; children: Armand James, Laura Marie. A.M. in Econs, Stanford U., 1960; LL.B., Harvard U., 1965. Bar: Calif. 1966. Law clk. to Charles M. Merrill, U.S. Ct. Appeals (9th cir.), 1965-66; assoc. firm Howard, Prim, Rice, Nemerovski, Canady & Pollak, San Francisco, 1966-71, ptnr., 1971-77; dir. Howard, Rice, Nemerovski, Canady, Robertson & Falk (P.C.), San Francisco, 1977-95; judge of the Superior Ct. City and County of San Francisco, 1995—. Bd. dirs. St. Francis Found., 1996—, chmn., 1999—. Lt. (j.g.) USN, 1960-62. Mem. Am. Law Inst., ABA (antitrust sect.), CPR Inst. for Dispute Resolution, Phi Beta Kappa. Home: Edgewood Ave San Francisco CA 94117-3713 Office: San Francisco Superior Ct 400 Mcallister St Rm 210 San Francisco CA 94102-4512

ROBERTSON, CAREY JANE, musician, educator; b. Culver City, Calif., Apr. 18, 1955; d. Robert Bruce and Marjorie Ellen (Greenleaf) Coker;l m. Brian Collins Robertson, June 28, 1975 (div. July 1985); 1 child, Sean Kalen. BMus, Calif. State U., Northridge, 1977; MMus, U. So. Calif., L.A., 1979, PhD of Mus. Arts, 1987. Organist/choir dir. Village Meth. Ch., North Hollywood, Calif., 1972-75, St. Bede's Episcopal Ch., Mar Vista, 1975-79; organist interim St. Alban's Episcopal Ch., Westwood, 1985; organist Covenant Presbyn. Ch., Westchester, 1985-90; organist/choir dir. St. David's United Ch., West Vancouver, B.C., Can., 1990-91; prin. organist Claremont (Calif.) United Ch. of Christ, 1991—. Prof. organ Claremont Grad. U., 1991—, Benjamin U., Buena Park, Calif.; concert organist Am. Guild of Organists, throughout U.S. and Can., 1974—; cons. Sch. Theology, U. B.C., 1990. Bd. dirs. Ruth and Clarence Mader Found., Pasadena, Calif., 1993—. Recipient Music Tchrs. Nat. Assn. Wurlitzer Collegiate Artist award, 1980; Irene Robertson scholar, 1977, 78. Mem. Am. Guild Organists (historian, sec. 1985-92, exec. com. 1983-85, sub-dean Pasadena chpt., 1998-99), Pi Kappa Lambda (Scholastic award 1987). Avocations: scuba diving, water skiing. Home: 633 Maple Way Upland CA 91786-4511

ROBERTSON, HUGH DUFF, lawyer; b. Grosse Pointe, Mich., Mar. 14, 1957; s. Hugh Robertson and Louise (Grey) Bollinger; m. Mercedes Dano, May 3, 1997. BBA in Fin., U. Wis., Whitewater, 1978; JD, Whittier Coll., 1982. Bar: Calif. 1983, U.S. Tax Ct. 1984. Pres., CEO, A. Morgan Maree Jr. & Assocs., Inc., L.A., 1979—. Mem. ABA (forum com. on entertainment 1982—), State Calif., L.A. County Bar Assn., Beverly Hills Bar Assn., Acad. TV Arts and Scis., Am. Film Inst., Phi Alpha Delta. Republican. Episcopalian. Avocations: sports, swimming. Office: A Morgan Maree Jr & Assocs 1125 Gayley Ave Los Angeles CA 90024-3403

ROBERTSON, JOSEPH E., JR. ophthalmologist, educator; b. Jackson County, Ind., July 24, 1952; s. Joseph E. and Virginia Faye (Baxter) R.; children: Kathryn Faye, Charles Joseph. BS cum laude, Yale U., 1974; MD, Ind. U., 1978; MBA, U. Oreg., 1997. Diplomate Am. Bd. Ophthalmology. Intern Bapt. Med. Ctr., Birmingham, Ala., 1978-79; resident Oreg. Health Sci. U., Portland, 1979-82; pvt. practice Vancouver, Wash., 1982-83; fellow Oreg. Health Sci. U./Devers Hosp./Good Samaritan Hosp., Portland, 1983-84; vitreous surgery fellow Steve Charles, M.D., Memphis, 1984-85; asst. prof. Oreg. Health Sci. U., Portland, 1985-92, assoc. prof., 1992-97, prof., chmn. dept. opthalmology, 1997—. Contbr. articles to profl. jours., chpts. to books; editor videotapes. Apptd. mem. Oreg. Commn. for the Blind, 1988-94. Mem. Am. Acad. Ophthalmology (Oreg. rep. to coun. 1992-95, COVE com. 1988-93, skills transfer adv. com. 1994-98, nat. chair and state coord. Diabetes 2000), Oreg. Acad. Ophthalmology (pres. 1990-91), U. Medical Group (exec. com. 1997—; v.p. 1998—), Oreg. Med. Assn. Democrat. Presbyterian. Avocations: snow skiing, windsurfing, snowboarding, hiking, jogging. Office: Casey Eye Inst OHSU 3375 SW Terwilliger Blvd Portland OR 97201-4197

ROBERTSON, MARY LOUISE, archivist, historian; b. L.A., May 19, 1945; d. Snell and Dorothy (Tregoning) R. BA, UCLA, 1966, MA, 1968, PhD, 1975. Teaching asst. dept. history UCLA, 1967-70; acting instr. UCLA Extension, 1973-74; acting instr. dept. history Pepperdine U., L.A., 1970, Calif. State U., Northridge, 1972-73; asst. curator manuscripts Huntington Libr., San Marino, Calif., 1975, assoc. curator, 1977, chief curator, 1979—. Adj. prof. English Claremont Grad. Sch., 1994. Author: Guide to British Historical Manuscripts in the Huntington Library, 1982; co-author, editor: Guide to American Historical Manuscripts in the Huntington Library, 1979; co-editor: State, Sovereigns & Society in Early Modern England, 1998; contbr. articles on Tudor history to profl. jours. Mabel Wilson Richards dissertation fellow, 1970-72. Mem. Am. Hist. Assn., Soc. Calif. Archivists, N.Am. Conf. on Brit. Studies, Pacific Coast Conf. on Brit. Studies (treas. 1986-88, pres. 1988-90), Phi Beta Kappa. Office: Huntington Libr 1151 Oxford Rd San Marino CA 91108-1299

ROBERTSON, MONROE WAYNE, JR. oil company executive; b. Oklahoma City, Jan. 8, 1950; s. Monroe Wanye Sr. and Virginia Lee (Barker) R.; m. Marilyn Louise Robertson, June 1, 1973; children: Tiffany Lee, Randall Monroe. BSME in Mech. Engring., MS in Mech. Engring., MS in Nuclear Engring., MIT, 1973. Engr. Gen. Atomic, San Diego, 1973-74, sr. engr., 1974-76, sr. bus. analyst, 1976-77; staff bus. analyst, 1977-79; sr. assoc. corp. planning Gulf Oil Co., Pitts., 1979-80, mgr. corp. planning, 1980-83; mgr. fin. analyst Gulf Oil Internat., Houston, 1983-85, Gotco, Inc., Houston, 1985-86; dir. planning Terra Resources, Tulsa, 1986-88; dir. corp. planning Apache Corp., Denver, 1988—. Mem. Planning Forum. Mem. Am. Petroleum Inst., Petroleum Club (Tulsa). Republican. Methodist. Avocations: golf, fishing, gardening. Home: 7633 S Waco St Aurora CO 80016-1879 Office: Apache Corp 1700 Lincoln St Ste 1900 Denver CO 80203-4519

ROBERTSON, PAUL B. dean, dental educator; Dean dentistry U. Wash., Seattle. Office: U Wash Sch Dentistry PO Box 356365 Seattle WA 98195-6365

ROBERTSON, PETER JAMES, oil company executive; b. Edinburgh, Scotland, Jan. 31, 1947; came to U.S., 1969; s. James Donald and Evelyn Patricia (McNaughton) R.; m. Candace Povey, Dec. 29, 1971; children: James Darrell, Nicole Povey, Emily Jemma. BS in Mech. Engring., Edinburgh U., 1969; MBA, U. Pa., 1971. Refinery engr. Union Oil Co. of Calif., Chgo., 1971-72; mcht. banker Noble Grossart Ltd., Edinburgh, 1972-73; fin. analyst Standard Oil Co. of Calif. (Chevron), San Francisco, 1973-78, audit mgr. Europe London, 1978-80; comptr. Chevron Oil Europe, London, 1980-83; asst. comptr. Chevron U.S.A., Inc., San Francisco, 1983-86, comptr., 1987-89, v.p. fin., 1989-91; asst. comptr. Chevron Corp., San Francisco, 1986-87; pres. Warren Petroleum Co., Tulsa, 1991—; now pres. Chevron Overseas Petroleum Co., San Ramon, Calif. Bd. dirs. Okla. chpt. The Nature Conservancy, Tulsa area United Way, Indian Nations coun. Boy Scouts Am., Tulsa, 1991—. Recipient Thouron award Thouron Scholarship Found., U. Pa., 1969-71. Mem. Met. Tulsa C. of C., U.S. Hispanic C. of C. (sr. exec. adv. com. 1990-92), Midcontinent Oil and Gas Assn. Avocations: travel, map collecting (antique), skiing. Office: Chevron Corp 6001 Bollinger Canyon Rd San Ramon CA 94583

ROBERTSON, PIEDAD F. college president; Pres. Bunker Hill C.C., [illegible] 1991-95; [illegible] Santa Monica (Calif.) Coll., 1995—. Named Woman of Yr. Santa Monica YMCA, 1999. Office: Santa Monica Coll Office of President 1900 Pico Blvd Santa Monica CA 90405-1628

ROBERTSON, RICHARD TRAFTON, entertainment company executive; b. Tacoma Park, Md., Aug. 23, 1945; s. Collins Trafton and Sigrid (Bergman) R.; m. Beverly Wise, Dec. 20, 1969 (div. Jan. 1984). BS, Va. Commonwealth U., 1967. Field rep. D. Van Nostrand Pub. Co., Princeton, N.J., 1968-69; account exec., sales mgr. NBC, Washington, San Francisco, Cleve. and N.Y.C., 1969-73; account exec., v.p. sports mktg. CBS TV Network, Chgo. and N.Y.C., 1973-78; exec. v.p., v.p. mktg. Office of Pres., Lorimar Telepictures, Culver City, Calif., 1978—; now pres. domestic TV distbn. Warner Bros., Burbank. Lutheran. Clubs: Bel-Air (Calif.) Country; Monterrey Country (Palm Desert, Calif). Avocations: golf, skiing, tennis. Office: Warner Bros Domestic TV Distbn 4001 W Olive Ave Burbank CA 91505-4272

ROBERTSON, ROBERT GRAHAM HAMISH, physicist; b. Ottawa, Ont., Can., Oct. 3, 1943; came to U.S., 1971; s. Hugh Douglas and Alice Madeleine (Bell) R.; m. Peggy Lynn Dyer, July 4, 1980; 1 child, Ian. BA, MA, Oxford (Eng.) U., 1965; PhD, McMaster U., Hamilton, Ont., Can., 1971. Rsch. assoc. Mich. State U., East Lansing, 1971-72, asst. rsch. prof., 1972-73, asst. prof., 1973-78, assoc. prof., 1978-81, prof., 1981-82; mem. staff Los Alamos (N.Mex.) Nat. Lab., 1981—, fellow, 1988—; prof. U. Washington, Seattle, 1994—; scientific dir. Ctr. for Exptl. Nuclear Physics and Astrophysics, 2000—. Rsch. assoc. Princeton (N.J.) U., 1975-76; vis. scientist Argonne (Ill.) Nat. Lab., 1979, Chalk River (Ont., Can.) Nuclear Lab., 1980. Contbr. over 50 articles to profl. jours. Alfred P. Sloan Found. fellow Mich. State U., 1976; Trevelyan scholar Eng., 1962-65, NRC scholar McMaster U., 1965-69, Oriel Coll. scholar, 1962-65. Fellow Am. Phys. Soc. (chair divsn. nuclear physics 2000, Tom W. Bonner prize 1997), Inst. Physics of Eng.; mem. Can. Assn. Physicists. Achievements include first observation of nuclear isobaric quintet; development of technique for precise measurement of neutrino mass, determination of Lithium-6 synthesis in early universe. Office: Dept Physics U Washington Seattle WA 98195-0001 E-mail: rghr@u.washington.edu

ROBINO, DAVID J. computer company executive; b. Ft. Collins, Colo., Nov. 16, 1959; BS, Graceland Coll.; MS in Indsl. Rels., Iowa State U. With Maytag Co., Iowa, Pepsi-Cola., N.Y. and Ind., AC Nielsen, sr. v.p. internat. bus., 1993; v.p. bus. markets divsn. AT&T; with Gateway, Inc., San Diego, 1998—, vice chmn., 2000—. Bd. dirs. San Diego Regional Econ. Devel. Corp. Bd. dirs. San Diego Sci. and Tech. Commn., U. Calif. San Diego Found.; chmn. bd. trustees Graceland U., Lamoni, Iowa; exec. com. bd. dirs. Iowa Coll. Found. Office: Gateway Inc 4545 Towne Centre Ct San Diego CA 92121

ROBINSON, BERNARD LEO, retired lawyer; b. Kalamazoo, Feb. 13, 1924; s. Louis Harvey and Sue Mary (Starr) R.; m. Betsy Nadell, May 30, 1947; children: Robert Bruce, Patricia Anne, Jean Carol. BS, U. Ill., 1947, MS, 1958; JD, U. N.Mex., 1973. Bar: N.Mex. 1973, U.S. Supreme Ct. 1976. Rsch. engr. Assn. Am. Railroads, 1947-49; instr. arch. Rensselaer Poly. Inst., 1949-51; commd. 2d lt. U.S. Army, 1945, advanced through grades to lt. col., 1965, ret., 1968; engr. Nuclear Def. Rsch. Corp., Albuquerque, 1968-71; lawyer Albuquerque, 1973-85, Silver City, N.Mex., 1985-89, Green Valley, Ariz., 1989-90, Sierra Vista, 1990-91; pres. Robinson Fin. Svcs., Tucson, 1993-95. Dist. commr. Boy Scouts Am., 1960-62. Decorated Air medal. Mem. ASCE, ABA, Ret. Officers Assn., DAV, Assn. U.S. Army, VFW. Home: 11821 N Pyramid Point Dr Tucson AZ 85737-3726

ROBINSON, CHARLES PAUL, nuclear physicist, diplomat, business executive; b. Detroit, Oct. 9, 1941; s. Edward Leonard and Mary Opal (Edmondson) R.; m. Barbara Thomas Woodard; children by previous marriage: Paula S., Colin C. BS in Physics, Christian Bros. U., 1963; PhD in Physics, Fla. State U., 1967. Mem. nuclear test staff Los Alamos (N.Mex.) Nat. Lab., 1967-69, chief test operator, 1969-70, mem. advanced concepts staff, 1971-72, assoc. div. leader, lasers, 1972-76, div. leader, 1976-79, assoc. dir., 1980-85; sr. v.p., bd. dirs. Ebasco Services Inc. subs. Enserch Corp., N.Y.C., 1985-88; ambass. to nuclear testing talks U.S. Dept. State, Geneva, 1988-90; v.p. Sandia Nat. Labs., Albuquerque, 1990-95, pres., 1995—. Instr. U. N.Mex., Los Alamos, 1974-76; mem. sci. adv. group Def. Nuclear Agy., Washington, 1981-86; mem. nat. security bd. Los Alamos Nat. Lab., 1985-88; chmn. Presdl. Tech. Adv. Bd., 1991; mem. U.S. Strategic Command Adv. Bd. Pres. Student Concerts Inc., Los Alamos, 1972-74; exec. bd. Boy Scouts of N.Mex. Recipient Outstanding Pub. Svc. medal Joint Chiefs of Staff, 1996. Mem. Am. Phys. Soc., Am. Nuclear Soc., NAE. Avocation: choral singing. Office: Sandia Nat Labs PO Box 5800 Albuquerque NM 87185-0100

ROBINSON, CHARLES WESLEY, energy company executive; b. Long Beach, Calif., Sept. 7, 1919; s. Franklin Willard and Anna Hope (Gould) R.; m. Tamara Lindovna, Mar. 8, 1957; children: Heather Lynne, Lisa Anne, Wendy Paige. BA in Econs. cum laude, U. Calif., Berkeley, 1941; MBA, Stanford U., 1947. Asst. mgr. mfg. Golden State Dairy Products Co., San Francisco, 1947-49; v.p., then pres. Marcona Corp., San Francisco, 1952-74; undersec. of state for econ. affairs Dept. State, Washington, 1974-75; dep. sec. of state, 1976-77; sr. mng. ptnr. Kuhn Loeb & Co., N.Y.C., 1977-78; vice chmn. blyth Eastman Dillon & Co., N.Y.C., 1978-79; chmn. Energy Transition Corp., Santa Fe and Washington, 1979-82; pres. Robinson & Assocs., Inc., Santa Fe, 1982—. Pres. Dyna-Yacht, Inc., San Diego, 1992—, Mangia Onda Co., San Diego, 1992—; bd. dirs. The Allen Telecom, Inc., NIKE, Inc. Patentee slurry transport and boat designs, boat engr. Brookings Instn., Washington, 1977—. Lt. USN, 1941-46. Recipient Disting. Honor award Dept. State, 1977. Republican. Methodist. Office: Robinson & Assocs Inc PO Box 2224 Santa Fe NM 87504-2224

ROBINSON, CLEO PARKER, artistic director; Degree in Dance Edn. Psychology, Denver U., DFA (hon.), 1991. Founder, exec. artistic dir., choreographer Cleo Parker Robinson Dance Ensemble, Denver. Mem. dance, expansion arts and inter-arts panels NEA; bd. dirs. Denver Ctr. Performing Arts; tchr. in workshops. Co-creator (documentary) African-Americans at Festae, Run Sister Run, (film) Black Women in the Arts, (music video) Borderline. Recipient Thelma Hill Ctr. for the Performing Arts award, 1986; Choreography fellow NEA; named one of Colo. 100, 1992; named to Blacks in Colo. Hall of Fame, 1994. Mem. Internat. Assn. Blacks in Dance (2nd v.p.). Office: Cleo Parker Robinson Dance Ensemble 119 Parker Ave W Denver CO 80205

ROBINSON, CURTIS JOHN, educator, writer, marketer, consultant; b. N.Y.C., Dec. 13, 1951; s. Herschel Edward and Delores Viola (Westberg) R.; m. Robin Gail Elton, July 14, 1989; children: Thomas Samuel, William Frederick. BA in History with honors, U. Calif., Davis, 1974, MA in Geography, 1981. Editor in chief The Calif. Aggie, Davis, 1973-74; teaching asst. U. Tex., Austin, 1974-75; acct., auditor Internat. Telephone, Fairbanks, Alaska, 1975-76; asst. to dean Cosumnes River Coll., Sacramento, 1976-77; editor, asst. editor U. Calif., Davis, 1977-80, mgr. data processing, 1982-85, mgr. promotional comm., 1980-85, dir. mktg., 1985-94; editor in chief Calif. Dept. Edn. Press, Sacramento, 1994—. Dir. alumni assn. bd. U. Calif., Davis, 1986-90. Author, editor: Handbook Small and Specialty Crops, 1991, Market Share, 1994, (video) Bringing the World to UC Davis, 1992; author articles. Mem. Cmty. Cable TV Bd., Davis, 1984-86; chair Cmty. Devel. Block Grant, Davis, 1980-84; [illegible] Yolo County Devel. Com., Davis, 1983-85. Mem. Nat. Univ. Continuing Edn. Assn. (chair Region VI Profl. Devel. 1991-94, mem. nat. mktg. adv. com. 1992-95, mem. Region VI exec. com. 1993-94, Silver award for Mktd. Excellence 1994, Gold award 1994), Assn. Am. Geographers, Assn. Pacific Coast Geographers (Pres.'s award 1991). Democrat. Methodist. Avocations: herb gardening, guitar, writing, travel, maps. Office: Dept Edn Publs 515 L St Ste 250 Sacramento CA 95814-3321

ROBINSON, GAIL PATRICIA, retired mental health counselor; b. Medford, Oreg., Dec. 31, 1936; d. Ivan T. and Evelyn H. (Hamilton) Skyrman; m. Douglas L. Smith; children: Shauna J., James D. BS in Edn., Oreg. State U., 1958, PhD in Counseling, 1978; MS in Counseling, Western Oreg. State Coll., 1974. Lic. profl. counselor, Oreg. Tchr. Monterey (Calif.) Pub. Schs., 1958-59, Corvallis (Oreg.) Pub. Schs., 1959-62, 69-75, counselor, 1977-81; pvt. practice Corvallis, 1977-95. Vol. therapist Children's Svcs. divsn., Linn and Benton Counties, 1982-83; asst. prof. Western Oreg. State coll., 1977, counselor, 1982-83; mem. grad. faculty Oreg. State U., Corvallis, 1978-95; presenter workshops, lectr. in field. Contbr. articles to profl. jours. Mem. Benton County Mental Helath Citizens Adv. Bd., 1979-85, chair, 1982-83; trustee WCTU Children's Farm Home, 1978-84, chair child welfare com., 1982-83, pres., 1984; mem. Old Mill Sch. Adv. Bd., 1979-85, chair, 1979-81; bd. dirs. Cmty. Outreach, 1979-83; mem. Benton Com. for Prevention of Child Abuse, 1979-85, v.p., 1982; mem. Oreg. Bd. Lic. Profl. Counselors and Therapists, 1989-95, chair, 1989-90. Mem. ACA (govt. rels. com. 1988-91, professionalization com. 1988-92, pres. 1996-97), Am. Mental Health Counselors Assn. (chair consumer and pub. rels. com. 1988-91, bd. dirs. Western region 1989-91, chair strategic planning com. 1994-95, pres. 1992-93), Oreg. Counseling Assn. (chair licensure liaison com. 1985-91, exec. bd. 1985-88, steering com. 1986-87, register editorial com. 1985-86, Disting. Svc. award 1985, 87, Leona Tyler award 1989), Oreg. Mental Health Counselors Assn.

ROBINSON, HERBERT HENRY, III, educator, psychotherapist; b. Leavenworth, Wash., Mar. 31, 1933; s. Herbert Henry II and Alberta (Sperber) R.; m. Georgia Murial Jones, Nov. 24, 1954 (div. 1974); children: Cheri Dean Asbury, David Keith, Peri Elizabeth Layton, Tanda Rene Graff, Gaila Daire. Grad. of Theology, Bapt. Bible Coll., 1959; BA in Philosophy/Greek, Whitworth Coll., 1968; MA in Coll. Teaching, Ea. Wash. U., 1976; postgrad., Gonzaga U., 1980—. Cert. psychotherapist, perpetrator treatment program supervision; nat. bd. cert. counselor. Choir dir. Twin City Bapt. Temple, Mishawaka, Ind., 1959-61; min. Inland Empire Bapt. Ch., Spokane, 1961-73; tchr. philosophy Spokane (Wash.) C.C., 1969-72; dir. Alternatives to Violence, Women in Crisis, Fairbanks, Alaska, 1985-87; tchr. pub. rels. U. Alaska, Fairbanks, 1986-87; dir. Alternatives to Violence Men Inc., Juneau, 1988-89; tchr. leadership mgmt. U. Alaska S.E., Juneau, 1988-89; min. Sci. of Mind Ctr., Sandpoint, Idaho, 1989-92; dir., therapist Tapio Counseling Ctr., Spokane, 1991—; cert. psychotherapist, supr. perpetrator treatment program Wash. Cons. Lilac Blind/Alpha Inc./Marshall Coll., Spokane, 1975-85, Alaska Placer Mining Co., Fairbanks, 1987; tchr. Spokane Falls C.C., Spokane, 1979-85; seminar, presenter Human Resource Devel., Spokane and Seattle, Wash., Pa., 1980; guest trainer United Way/Kellogg Found. Inst. for Volunteerism, Spokane, 1983. 1st trombone San Diego Marine Band, 1953-56, Spokane Symphony, 1961; bd. dirs. Tanani Learning Ctr., Fairbanks, 1987; mem. consensus bldg. team Sci. of Mind Ctr., Sandpoint, 1989-92. Cpl. USMC, 1953-56. Mem. ACA, Assn. for Humanistic Edn. and Devel., Assn. for Religious Values in Counseling, Internat. Assn. Addictions and Offender Counselors, Internat. Assn. Marriage and Family Counselors, Am. Assn. Profl. Hypnotherapists, Masterson Inst. Office: Tapio Counseling 5325 E Sprague Ave Spokane WA 99212-0820

ROBINSON, JAMES WILLIAM, retired management consultant; b. Bklyn., Feb. 22, 1919; s. Charles Edward and Adelaide (Reimer) R.; m. Dorothy L. Luckow, July 5, 1946; 1 child, Joan Barbara. AB, Cornell U., 1940, LLB, 1942. Bar: N.Y. 1942. Assoc. atty. Whitman, Ransom & Coulson, 1946-57; with Westvaco Corp., N.Y.C., 1957-69, sec., 1966-69; prin., mng. dir. Georgeson & Co. Inc., N.Y.C., 1969-82; mng. dir. Morrow & Co., N.Y.C., 1982-90; pres. J.W. Robinson Assocs., Inc., Gig Harbor, Wash., 1990—. Mem. adv. com. shareholder comms. SEC; com. on shareowner comms. N.Y. Stock Exch., 1986-92. Editor: Tender Offers Handbook, Proxy Rules Handbook. Capt. AUS, 1942-46. Decorated Bronze (V) Star medal. Mem. ABA, N.Y. State Bar Assn., Assn. Bar City N.Y., Am. Soc. Corp. Secs., Canterwood Country Club, Phi Delta Phi, Lambda Chi Alpha. Home and Office: 4820 Old Stump Dr NW Gig Harbor WA 98332-8899

ROBINSON, JOHN LEWIS, geography educator; b. Leamington, Ont., Can., July 9, 1918; s. William John and Emily Laverne (Dunphy) R.; m. Josephine Rowan, Oct. 14, 1944; children: David, Jo-Anne, Patricia. B.A., Western Ont. U., 1940; M.A., Syracuse U., 1942; Ph.D., Clark U., 1946; LLD (hon.), Western Ont. U., 1984; DSc (hon.), U. B.C., 1994. Geographer N.W.T. Adminstrn., Ottawa, Ont., 1943-46; prof., head dept. geography U. B.C., Vancouver, 1946-68, prof. geography, 1968-85, prof. emeritus, 1985—. Author 14 books on aspects of regional geography of Can., including British Columbia: 100 Years of Geographical Change, 1973, Themes in the Regional Geography of Canada, 1983, 2d edit., 1989; contbr. articles to profl. jours. Recipient citation of merit Assn. Am. Geographers, 1966; Massey medal Canadian Geog. Soc., 1971 Mem. Canadian Assn. Geographers (pres. 1956, citation for service to profession 1976) Office: U BC Dept Geography Vancouver BC Canada V6T 1Z2

ROBINSON, JOHN MINOR, lawyer, retired business executive; b. Uniontown, Pa., Mar. 18, 1910; s. John M. and Martha (Downs) R. A.B., Harvard U., 1932, LL.B, 1935. Bar: Calif. 1936. Assoc. firm Macdonald & Pettit, 1935-41; partner firm Musick, Peeler & Garrett, 1947-77; v.p., sec. Consol. Western Steel div. U.S. Steel Corp. (and predecessors), 1941-57. Mem. Calif. Club (past pres. L.A.), Pacific Union Club (San Francisco), Cypress Point Club (Pebble Beach, Calif.), Royal and Ancient Golf Club of St. Andrews (Fife, Scotland). Office: 9500 Center St Carmel CA 93923-8552

ROBINSON, MARK LEIGHTON, oil company executive, petroleum geologist, horse farm owner; b. San Bernardino, Calif., Aug. 4, 1927; s. Ernest Guy and Florence Iola)Lemmon) R.; m. Jean Marie Ries, Feb. 8, 1954; children; Francis Willis, Mark Ries, Paul Leighton. AB cum laude in Geology, Princeton U., 1950; postgrad., Stanford U., 1950-51. Geologist Shell Oil Co., Billings, Mont., Rapid City, S.D., Denver, Midland, Tex., dist. geologist Roswell, N.Mex., 1957-60, divsn. mgr., 1961-63, Jackson, Miss., 1964-65, Bakersfield, Calif., 1967-68, mgr. exploration econs. N.Y.C., 1969; ctrl. office staff BIPM (Royal Dutch Shell Oil Co.), The Hague, The Netherlands, 1966; pres., chmn. bd. dirs. Robinson Resource Devel. Co., Inc., Roswell, 1970—. Chmn., pres. Como Petroleum Corp., Roswell, 1994—. Campaign chmn. Chaves County Rep. Com., Roswell, 1962; mem. alumni schs. com. Princeton U., 1980—; vestry St. Andrew's Episcopal Ch., Roswell, N.Mex., 1999—. With USNR, 1945-46. Mem. Assn. Petroleum Geologists, Stanford U. Earth Scientists Assn., Yellowstone Bighorn Rsch. Assn., Am. Horse Show Assn., SAR, Sigma Xi. Episcopalian. Achievements include discovery of Lake Como oil field, Miss., 1971, McNeal oil field, Miss., 1973, North Deer Creek gas field, Mont., 1983, Bloomfield East oil field, Mont., 1986, West Cat Claw Draw gas field, N.Mex., 1991; [illegible] Home: 2003 Southridge Rd Roswell NM 88203-9346 Office: Robinson Resource Devel Co Inc PO Box 1227 Roswell NM 88202-1227

ROBINSON, MICHAEL R. aeronautical engineer; Dir. bus. devel. The Boeing Co. (formerly Rockwell Internat. Corp.), Long Beach, Calif. Co-originator and first program manager of the X-31 enhanced maneuverability fighter demonstrator and originator of the international team to conduct the program. Recipient DGLR Team award in recognition of exceptional achievements in the field of Aeronautics, 1996. Fellow Am. Inst. Aeronautics & Astronautics (aircraft design award 1994). Office: The Boeing Co Mail Stop C078-0600 2401 E Wardlow Rd Long Beach CA 90807-5309 E-mail: michael.r.robinson2@boeing.com

ROBINSON, PAUL ARNOLD, historian, educator, writer; b. San Diego, Oct. 1, 1940; s. Joseph Cook and Beryl Marie (Lippincott) R.; m. Ute Brosche, Aug. 3, 1964 (div. Aug. 1967); 1 child, Susan Marie. B.A., Yale U., 1962; postgrad., Free U. Berlin, 1962-63; PhD, Harvard U., 1968. Asst. prof. history Stanford U. (Calif.), 1967-73, assoc. prof., 1973-80, prof. history, 1980—, Richard W. Lyman prof. in the humanities, 1994—. Author: The Freudian Left, 1969, The Modernization of Sex, 1976, Opera and Ideas: From Mozart to Strauss, 1985, Freud and His Critics, 1993, Ludwig van Beethoven: Fidelio, 1996, Gay Lives: Homosexual Autobiography from John Addington Symonds to Paul Monette, 1999; editor: Social Thought in America and Europe, 1970; contbg. editor The New Republic, 1979-85. Guggenheim fellow, 1970-71, Stanford Humanities Ctr. fellow, 1984-85, 96-97, Inst. for Advanced Study fellow, 1990-91. Mem. Am. Acad. Arts and Scis., Am. Hist. Assn. Home: 671 Santa Ynez St Palo Alto CA 94305-8542 Office: Stanford Univ Dept History Stanford CA 94305 E-mail: paul.robinson@forsythe.stanford.edu

ROBINSON, PETER, paleontology educator, consultant; b. N.Y.C., N.Y., July 19, 1932; s. Edward and Carol Nye (Rhoades) R.; m. Patricia Ellen Fisher, Sept. 11, 1954 (div. Mar. 1980); children: Diane Elizabeth, Nathan; m. Paola D'Amelio Villa, Dec. 8, 1984 BS, Yale U., 1954, MS, 1958, PhD, 1960. Instr. Harpur Coll. SUNY, Binghamton, 1955-57; rsch. assoc. Yale Peabody Mus., New Haven, 1960-61; curator geology U. Colo. Mus., Boulder, 1961—, asst. prof. natural history, 1961-67, assoc. prof., 1967-71, prof., 1971—, dir. mus., 1971-82, prof. geol. sci., 1971—. Geologist Colo. Nubian Expdn., Sudan, 1962-66; chief Colo. Paleontol. Expdn., Tunisia, 1967-81 ; mem. geol. adv. group Colo. Bur. Land Mgmt., Denver, 1983-91. Mem. AAAS, Soc. Vertebrate Paleontology (pres. 1977-78), Australian Mammal Soc., Soc. Española Paleontologia, Sigma Xi Democrat. Home: 912 Hover Ridge Cir Longmont CO 80501-4141 Office: Mus U Colo Campus Box 265 Boulder CO 80309 E-mail: peter.robinson@colorado.edu

ROBINSON, RICHARD ALLEN, JR. human resources development trainer, consultant; b. Ellensburg, Wash., Aug. 21, 1936; s. Richard Allen and Rosa Adele (Oswald) R.; m. R. Elaine Whitham, Sept. 8, 1956; children: Sharon E. Robinson Losey, Richard Allen, René L. Rivera. BA, U. Wash., 1958; postgrad., U.S. Army Command and Gen. Staff Coll., 1969-70; MA, U. Mo., 1971. Commd. 2d lt. U.S. Army, 1958, advanced through grades to lt. col., 1972, various infantry assignments including command, 1958-72, R&D assignments including dep. dir. test of behavioral sci., 1975-77, ret., 1979; chief office orgn. and employee devel. Wash. Dept. Social and Health Svcs., Olympia, 1979—; pvt. practice orgn. and mgmt. devel. cons./trainer, 1979—. Contbg. author: Games Trainers Play, vol. II, 1983. Decorated Legion of Merit with oak leaf cluster, Bronze Star. Mem. ASTD. Office: DSHS Mail 8425 27th St W Tacoma WA 98466-2722 E-mail: robbyr@msn.com

ROBINSON, ROBERT BLACQUE, foundation administrator; b. Long Beach, Calif., Apr. 24, 1927; s. Joseph LeRoi and Frances Hansel R.; m. Susan Amelia Thomas, Jan. 21, 1960; children: Victoria, Shelly, Blake, Sarah. Student, Oreg. State Coll., 1946; BA, UCLA, 1950; student, U. Hawaii. Partner, Pritchard Assocs. (Mgmt. Cons.), Honolulu, 1956-58; asst. dir. Econ. Planning and Coordination Authority, Hawaii, 1959; dep. dir. dept. econ. devel. State of Hawaii, 1960-63; asst. mgr. Pacific Concrete and Rock Co., Ltd., Honolulu, 1963-66, exec. v.p. and gen. mgr., 1966-68, pres. and gen. mgr., 1968-75, chmn., 1976-77; pres. C. of C. of Hawaii, Honolulu, 1977—. Bd. govs. Hawaii Employers Coun., 1969-74, mem. exec. com., 1969-74, vice chmn., 1973-74; bd. dirs. Pacific Aerospace Mus., 1982-86; mem. Hawaii Tourism Conf., 1977, chmn., 1981-82; bd. dirs. Aloha United Fund, 1970-76, sec., 1972, v.p., 1973-76; bd. dirs. Oahu Devel. Conf., 1970-75; treas., bd. dirs. Crime Stoppers Hawaii, 1981—; mem. Hawaii Joint Coun. on Econ. Edn., 1985 ; bd. dirs. Jr. Achievement Hawaii, 1967-73, pres., 1969; bd. dirs. Hawaii Ednl. Coun., 1974-75, Health and Community Services Coun. Hawaii, 1982-84; mem. exec. com. Hawaii Conv. Ctr. Coun., 1984—, Interagency Energy Conservation Coun., State of Hawaii, 1978—; trustee Cen. Union Ch., 1983-86; bd. dirs. Waikiki Improvement Assn. Inc., 1986—; mem. Ctr. for Tropical and Subtropical Aquacultute industry Adv. Coun., 1987—; chmn. Mayor's Adv. Com. on Pacific Nations Ctr., 1988-89. Lt. comdr. USNR, 1945-46, ret. Mem. Japan-Am. Conf. of Mayors and C. of C. Pres. (mem. Am. exec. com. 1974—), Am. Soc. Assn. Execs. (past dir. Hawaii chpt.), Hawaii Execs. Coun. (found. , Young Pres. Assn. (past mem.), Aloha Soc. Assn. Execs., C. of C. Hawaii (dir. 1972-75, chmn. 1975), Coun. of Profit Sharing Industries (past dir. Hawaii sect.), Cement and Concrete Products Industry of Hawaii (pres. 1968), Hawaii Mfrs. Assn. (past dir.), Navy League of U.S. (Hawaii council), Engring. Assn. Hawaii, Pacific Club, Rotary, Sigma Chi. Home: 1437 Kalaepohaku St Honolulu HI 96816-1804 Office: C of C Hawaii 735 Bishop St Ste 220 Honolulu HI 96813-4816

ROBINSON, SHANNON, state legislator; b. Coronado, Calif., 1948; BA, JD, U. N.Mex. Atty.; mem. N.Mex. Senate, Dist. 17, Sante Fe, 1988—. Democrat. Home: 716 Indiana St SE Albuquerque NM 87108-3813

ROBINSON, THEODORE GOULD, landscape and golf course architect; b. Long Beach, Calif., May 17, 1923; s. Franklin Willard and Hope (Gould) R.; m. Barbara Henderson, Oct. 28, 1949; children: Theodore G. Jr., Kristine Robinson Monroe, Leigha Robinson Ramsey. BA, U. Calif., Berkeley, 1944; MS, U. So. Calif., 1948. With Gordon Whitnall & Assocs., L.A., 1941-51; prin. Robinson Golf Design, Dana Point, Calif., 1951—. Designer 170 golf courses throughout world. Ensign USN, 1943-46. Recipient awards for best new courses Golf Digest. Mem. Am Soc. Golf Course Architects (pres. 1983). Office: Robinson Golf Designs Inc 30131 Town Center Dr Ste 268 Laguna Niguel CA 92677-2082

ROBINSON, WILLIAM P. academic administrator, consultant, speaker; b. Elmhurst, Ill., Sept. 30, 1949; s. Paul Frederick and Lillian (Horton) R.; m. Bonnie Van Laan, Aug. 10, 1974; children: Brenna Kay, Benjamin Paul, Bailley Kay. Student, Moody Bible Inst., Chgo., 1967-70; AB, U. No. Iowa, 1972; postgrad., Princeton (N.J.) Theol. Sem., 1972-73; MA, Wheaton Coll., 1975; PhD, U. Pitts., 1979. Assoc. minister First Presbyn. Ch., Pitts., 1975-77; instr. U. Pitts., 1977-79; asst. prof. sch. continuing studies Nat. Coll. Edn., Evanston, Ill., 1979-80, dean sch. continuing studies, 1980-84, sr. v.p., 1984-86; pres. Manchester Coll., North Manchester, Ind., 1986-93, Whitworth Coll., Spokane, Wash., 1993—. Bd. dirs. Coun. Indep. Colls., Ind. Colls. Wash., Whitworth Coll.; cons., speaker for U.S. corps. and svc. orgns. Bd. dirs. Wash. Friends of Higher Edn., Spokane Symphony; vol. various orgns., especially prion work and hunger projects. Recipient various acad. awards. Mem. Nat. Assn. Ind. Colls. and Univs., Coun. Ind. Colls., Spokane Country Club, Spokane Club. Presyterian. Avocation: sports. Office: Whitworth Coll Office of Pres 300 W Hawthorne Rd Spokane WA 99218-2515

ROBITAILLE, LUC, professional hockey player; b. Montreal, P.Q., Can., Feb. 17, 1966; With Hull Olympiques Major Jr. Hockey League, Que., 1983-84, L.A. Kings, 1984-94, Pitts. Penguins, 1994-95, N.Y. Rangers, 1995-97, L.A. Kings, 1997—. Scored winning goal for nat. team of Can. at 1994 World Hockey Championship. Recipient Guy LaFleur trophy, 1985-86, Can. Hockey Player of Yr. award, 1985-86, Calder Meml. trophy, NHL Rookie of Yr., 1986-87; named to NHL All-Star team, 1987, 88, 90-91, 92-93. Office: Los Angeles Kings 1111 S Figueroa St Los Angeles CA 90015-1300

ROBLE, RAYMOND GERALD, science administrator; b. Mar. 14, 1935; BS in Engring. Physics, BS in Engring. Math., U. Mich., 1957, MSME, 1961, PhD in Aeronomy, 1969. Engr. Bendix Rsch. Labs., Southfield, Mich., 1961-64; rsch. sci. Space Physics Rsch. Lab., U. Mich., 1964-69; postdoctoral fellow advanced study program Nat. Ctr. Atmospheric Rsch., 1969-70, scientist lab. for atmospheric scis., 1970-73, scientist atmospheric quality and modification div., 1973-77, project leader thermospheric dynamics and aeronomy project atmosphericchem. and aeronomy div., 1977-81, sr. scientist atmospheric chem. and aeronomy div., 1978-84, sr. scientist high altitude obs., 1984—, head, terrestrial impact of solar output sect. high altitude obs., 1986—, dep. dir. high altitude obs., 1993-95, acting dir. high altitude obs., 1995-98. Commn. URSI III Working Group 8 Incoherent Scatter, 1975-77; guest investigator OSO-8 Satellite Team Occultation Studes, 1975-79, NASA Atmospheric Explorer Satelite Team, 1975-80; panel mem. USRA Sci. Definition for Atmosphere, Magnetosphere and Plasmas in Space Payload, 1976-78, Upper Atmoshpere Geophysics, Geophysics Study com., Geophysical Rsch. bd., NAS, 1976-77, USRA Computer Simulation in Space Physics, 1977-79, NASA Sci. Definition Panel UARS Satellite Program, 1977-78, Sun, Weather and Climate Geophysics Study com., Geophysical Rsch. bd., NAS, 1977-82, Survey on Solar-Terrestrial Rsch. in the 1980's, com. on Solar-Terrstrial Rsch. Geophysical Rsch. bd., NAS program, 1979-81, Mid. Atmosphere Program Panel, NAS, 1981-86; theoretician NASA Dynamics Explorer Satellite Team, 1977—; mem. AGU com. for Pub., 1977-84, Atmospheric and Space Physics Mgmt. Ops. Working Group, NASA Solar-Terrestrial Physics Program, 1978-81, Space Power Sys. Overviewcom. Inst. Telecomms., 1978-82; lecturer Dept. Astrophysical, Planetary and Atmospheric Scis. U. Colo., 1978—; com. Solar and Space Physics, Space Sci. bd. NAS, 1980-83, Geophysics Study com. Geophysical Rsch. bd. NAS, 1980-84, IUGG on Atmospheric Electricity, 1981—, AGU for Pub. Affairs, 1982-84, IUGG com. Solar-Terrestrial film Planet earth, 1984-86; sec. Aeronomy Div. Solar-Planetary Relationships Sect. AGU, 1982-84; mem. Earth Scis. Task Group Study Major Dirs. for Space Scis.: 1995-2015, Space Sci. bd., 1984-88; chmn. Am. Geophysical U. com. on Atmospheric and Space Electricity, 1984-88; co-investigator, prin. investigator, NASA. Contbr. over 250 articles to profl. jours. With USN, 1957-60. Recipient CEDAR Prize Lecture, 1994; fellow Am. Geophysical Union., 1986. Mem. NAS (Arctowski medal, 1996), Am. Geophysical Union, Am. Inst. Aeronautics and Astronautics. Office: Nat Ctr Atmospheric Rsch High Altitude Obs PO Box 3000 Boulder CO 80307-3000

ROBLES, ERNEST, federal judge; b. 1956; BA, U. Calif., Berkeley, 1978; JD, U. Mich., 1981. With Musick, Peeler & Garrett, L.A., 1981-82, Hancock, Rothert & Bunshoft, San Francisco, 1982-87, Kornblum & Ferry, San Francisco, 1987-88; asst. U.S. trustee San Jose, Calif., 1988-93; apptd. bankruptcy judge ctrl. dist. U.S. Dist. Ct. Calif., 1993. Editl. advisor Calif. Bankruptcy Jour. Mem. Am. Bankruptcy Inst., Nat. Conf. Bankruptcy Judges (ethics com. nat. conf.), Mex.-Am. Bar Assn., L.A. County Bar Assn. (exec. com. comml. law and bankruptcy sect.). Office: Roybal Federal Bldg 255 E Temple St Los Angeles CA 90012-3332 Fax: 213-894-1536

ROCHA, GUY LOUIS, archivist, historian; b. Long Beach, Calif., Sept. 23, 1951; s. Ernest Louis and Charlotte (Sobus) R. BA in Social Studies and Edn., Syracuse U., 1973; MA in Am. Studies, San Diego State U., 1975; postgrad., U. Nev., 1975—. Cert. archivist Am. Acad. Cert. Archivists. Tchr. Washoe County Sch. Dist., Reno, 1975-76; history instr. Western Nev. C.C., Carson City, 1976; curator manuscripts Nev. Hist. Soc., Reno, 1976-81, interim asst. dir., 1980, interim dir., 1980-81; state adminstr. archives and records Nev. State Libr. and Archives, Carson City, 1981—. Hist. cons. Janus Assocs., Tempe, Ariz., 1980, Rainshadow Assocs., Carson City, 1983—; mem. State Bd. Geog. Names. Co-author: The Ignoble Conspiracy: Radicalism on Trial in Nevada, 1986, The Earp's Last Frontier: Wyatt and Virgil Earp in Nevada 1902-1905, 1988; contbr. to books and govt. study; host weekly radio talk show Sta. KPTL, Carson City, 1988-2000; hist. cons. to film Las Vegas, 1996. Mem. Washoe Heritage Coun., Reno, 1983-85; editl. bd. Nev. Hist. Soc., Reno, 1983—; mem. Washoe County Dem. Ctrl. Com., Reno, 1984-87; ex-officio mem. Nev. Commn. Bicentennial U.S. Constn., 1986-91. Mem. Conf. Intermountain Archivists (coun. mem. 1979-87, v.p. 1984-85, pres. 1985-86), No. Nev. Pub. Adminstrs. Group (pres. 1986-87), S.W. Labor Studies Assn., State Hist. Records Adv. Bd. (dep. coord. 1984-86, coord. 1986—), Westerners Internat. Nev. Corral (dep. sheriff 1980-81, sheriff 1984-85, mem. state coords. steering com. 1985-87, vice chmn. 1986-87), Soc. Am. Archivists, Western History Assn., Nat. Assn. Govt. Archives and Records Adminstrs., Orgn. Am. Historians. Home: 1824 Pyrenees St Carson City NV 89703-2331 Office: Nev State Libr & Archives 100 N Stewart St Carson City NV 89701-4285

ROCHE, JAMES G. electronics executive; Capt. U.S. Navy, 1960-83; Office Sect. Defense, 1975-79; sr. profl. staff mem. Senate Select Com. Intelligence, 1979-81; princ. dep. dir. policy planning staff U.S. Dept. State, 1981-83; staff dir. U.S. Senate Com. on Armed Svcs.; v.p., dir. analysis ctr. Northrop Grumman, 1984-89, v.p., special asst. to chmn., pres., CEO, 1989-91, v.p., adv. devel. planning, 1991-; corp. v.p., pres. Northrop Grumman's Elec. Sensors, Systems Sector, 1998—. Office: Northrop Grumman Corp 1840 Century Park E Los Angeles CA 90067-2101

ROCHELEAU, JAMES ROMIG, retired university president; b. Anchorage, Mar. 21, 1940; s. James Albert and Sophia (Rivord) R.; m. Margaret Anne Sheehan, Nov. 28, 1981; children from previous marriage: Renee, Tanya, Andrea. BA, U. Idaho, 1968, MA, 1969; PhD, Wash. State U., Pullman, 1975. Account exec. Spokesman Rev., Spokane, Wash., 1963; sales rep. RJR Nabisco, Inc., Spokane, 1963-66; grad. asst. U. Idaho, Moscow and Wash. State U., Pullman, 1967-70; instr. history Wash. State U., 1970-71; asst. prof. history Buena Vista Coll., Storm Lake, Iowa, 1971-76, dir., 1976-81, dean continuing edn., 1981-84; pres. Upper Iowa U., Fayette, 1984-94, pres. emeritus, 1994—. Cons. North Ctrl. Assn., Chgo., 1981—, Kellogg Found., 1994-99, Univ. Pres., 1994—. Active N.E.-Midwest Leadership Coun. Served with U.S. Army, 1958-61. Mem. Nat. Assn. Ind. Colls. and Univs., Iowa Assn. Ind. Colls. Univs., Coun. Ind. Colls., Iowa Coordinating Coun. for Post-High Sch. Edn., C. of C. Home and Office: PO Box 5361 Lynnwood WA 98046

ROCHETTE, EDWARD CHARLES, association executive; b. Worcester, Mass., Feb. 17, 1927; s. Edward Charles and Lilia (Viau) R.; m. Mary Ann Ruland, July 29, 1978; children by previous marriage— Edward Charles, Paul, Philip. Student, Washington U., St. Louis, Clark U. Exec. editor Krause Publs., Iola, Wis., 1960-66; acting exec. dir. Am. Numismatic Assn., Colorado Springs, Colo., 1967-68, exec. v.p., 1972-87, ret., 1987; editor jour. The Numismatist, Colorado Springs, 1968-72; exec. dir. Am. Numismatic Assn., Colorado Springs, 1998-02. Bd. overseers Inst. Philatelic and Numismatic Studies, Adelphi U., Garden City, N.Y., 1979-81; chmn. medals com. Colo. Centennial Bicentennial Commn., 1976; mem. adv. panel Carson City Silver Dollar program Gen. Services Adminstrn., 1979-80; numismatic cons. U.S. Olympic Com. USOC, 1995—; mem. U.S. Assay Commn., 1965. Served with USN, 1944-46. Recipient Gold medal for syndicated column Numismatic Lit. Guild, 1980, 86-88; inducted to Numismatic Hall of Fame, 2000. Mem. Am. Numis. Assn. (life, medal of merit 1972, Numismatic Hall of Fame 2000), Am. Soc. Assn. Execs., Colo. Soc. Assn. Execs. (pres. 1988-89). Democrat. Roman Catholic. Lodge: Pikes Peak Kiwanis (pres. 1987-88) Office: Am Numis Assn 818 N Cascade Ave Colorado Springs CO 80903-3208 E-mail: rochette@money.org

ROCK, ARTHUR, venture capitalist; b. Rochester, N.Y., Aug. 19, 1926; s. Hyman A. and Reva (Cohen) R.; m. Toni Rembe, July 19, 1975. BS, Syracuse U., 1948; MBA, Harvard U., 1951. Gen. ptnr. Davis & Rock, San Francisco, 1961-68, Arthur Rock & Assocs., San Francisco, 1969-80. Mem. exec. com. Teledyne, Inc., L.A., 1961-94; dir. emeritus, founder, past chmn., chmn. exec. com., lead dir. Intel Corp., Santa Clara, Calif.; bd. dirs. Echelon Corp., San Jose, Calif.; bd. govs. Nasdaq Stock Market, Inc. Trustee Calif. Inst. Tech.; pres. Basic Fund; bd. dirs. San Francisco Opera Assn., 1970-92, San Francisco Mus. Modern Art; mem. vis. com. Harvard U. Bus. Sch., 1982-88. Recipient Medal of Achievement Am. Electronics Assn., 1987, Am. Acad. Achievement, 1989, Lifetime Achievement in Entrepreneurship and Innovation award U. Calif., 1999; named to Jr. Achievement Hall of Fame, 1990, Calif. Bus. Hall of Fame, 1990, Bay Area Bus. Coun. Hall of Fame, 1995, Arents Pioneer medal Syracuse U., 1997, Outstanding Dir., Corp. Am., 1999, SDForum Visionary award, 2001. Mem. NASD (bd. govs.). Office: 1 Maritime Plz Ste 1220 San Francisco CA 94111-3502

ROCKFORD, MARV, television executive; b. Chgo., Mar. 1, 1950; BS in Journalism, Northwestern U., 1972, MA in Sci. Journalism, 1973. News dir. KCNC TV, 1987-95, v.p., gen. mgr., 1995—. Bd. dirs. Denver Meml. C. of C., Colo. Bus. Com. Arts. Mem. RTNDA. Office: KCNC TV 1044 Lincoln St Denver CO 80203-2717

ROCKSTROH, DENNIS JOHN, journalist, screenwriter; b. Hermosa Beach, Calif., Feb. 1, 1942; s. Philip Herman and Alicia (Rubio) R.; m. Le Thi Que Huong, May 2, 1970; children: Bryan Benjamin, Paula Kim-Mai. Student, San Luis Rey Coll., 1960-61, El Camino Coll., 1961-62, San Fernando Valley State Coll., 1965-67. Reporter Thousand Oaks (Calif.) News Chronicle, 1966-67; tchr. Girls' High Sch., Qui Nhon, Vietnam, 1967-70; instr. Dalat U./Vietnamese Mil. Acad., 1970-71, Ohlone Coll., Fremont, Calif., 1984—; freelance war corr. Dispatch News Svc., Vietnam, 1967-71; city editor Santa Paula (Calif.) Daily Chronicle, 1972-73; reporter San Jose (Calif.) Mercury News, 1973-90, columnist, 1990—. Guest lectr. U. Calif., Berkeley, 1987-91. Vol. Internat. Vol. Svcs., Vietnam, 1967-71; bd. dirs. San Jose unit ARC, 1978, Hope Rehab., San Jose, 1976-77. With U.S. Army, 1962-65, Vietnam. Co-recipient Pulitzer prize for Loma Prieta earthquake coverage, 1989; decorated Army Commendation Medal for Valor, 1965. Mem. Soc. Profl. Journalists, St. Anthony's Sem. Alumni Assn., Nat. Soc. Newspaper Columnists. Roman Catholic. Home: 3573 Tankerland Ct San Jose CA 95121-1244 Office: San Jose Mercury News 3890 Mowry Ave Ste 202 Fremont CA 94538-1447 E-mail: drockstroh@sjmercury.com, drockstroh@yahoo.com

RODARTE, ARTHUR H. state legislator; b. Ojo Caliente, N.Mex., May 2, 1948; BBA, N.Mex. State U. Owner Oliver's Grocery Store; mem. N.Mex. Legislature, Santa Fe, 1996—, mem. conservation com., mem. rules com. Democrat. Office: PO Box 132 Ojo Caliente NM 87549-0132

RODEKOHR, DIANE E. state official; A in Bus. Mgmt., Nat. Bus. Inst., 1958. Asst. exec. dir. Associated Gen. Contractors of Wyo., 1963-78; field rep. to Sen. Alan Simpson Wyo., 1978-84; state dir. to Sen. Alan Simpson, 1984-96; state dir. to Sen. Michael Enzi, 1997—. Mem. PEO, Cheyenne C. of C., Rotary (sec. 1995-99). Office: Office Sen Michael Enzi 2120 Capitol Ave Ste 2007 Cheyenne WY 82001-3631

RODES, DAVID STUART, college program director; b. 1939; BA in Comparative Lit. summa cum laude, So. Meth. U., 1961; PhD in English, Stanford U., 1968. Asst. prof. English UCLA, 1966-74, lectr., 1974-79, sr. lectr. in English, 1980—, acting dir. Grunwald Ctr. for the Graphic Arts, 1989-92, dir. Grunwald Ctr. for the Graphic Arts, 1992—. Founder chancellor's adv. com. Office of Instrnl. Devel., 1974, chair, 1980-89; acad. advisor BBC-TV Shakespeare series, 1978-84; artistic dir. Shakespeare Santa Cruz, 1981—. Gen. editor Augustan Reprint Soc. Clark Libr., 1969-91; contbr. articles to profl. jours. Mem. Phi Beta Kappa (sec. 1979-72, treas. 1978-80). Office: Armand Hammer Mus Art Culture Ctr Grunwald Ctr Graphic Arts UCLA 10899 Wilshire Blvd Fl 3 Los Angeles CA 90024-4201

RODGERS, FREDERIC BARKER, judge; b. Albany, N.Y., Sept. 29, 1940; s. Prentice Johnson and Jane (Weed) R.; m. Valerie McNaughton, Oct. 8, 1988; 1 child: Gabriel Moore. AB, Amherst Coll., 1963; JD, Union U., 1966. Bar: N.Y. 1966, U.S. Ct. Mil. Appeals 1968, Colo. 1972, U.S. Supreme Ct. 1974, U.S. Ct. Appeals (10th cir.) 1981, U.S. Ct. Appeals (fed. cir.) 2001. Chief dep. dist. atty., Denver, 1972-73; commr. Denver Juvenile Ct., 1973-79; mem. Mulligan Reeves Teasley & Joyce, P.C., Denver, 1979-80; pres. Frederic B. Rodgers, P.C., Breckenridge, Colo., 1980-89; ptnr. McNaughton & Rodgers, Central City, 1989-91; county ct. judge Gilpin County Combined Cts., 1987—. Presiding mcpl. judge cities of Breckenridge, Blue River, Black Hawk, Central City, Edgewater, Empire, Idaho Springs, Silver Plume and Westminster, Colo., 1978-96; chmn. com. on mcpl. ct. rules of procedure Colo. Supreme Ct., 1984-96; mem. gen faculty Nat. Jud. Coll. U. Nev., Reno, 1990—, elected to faculty coun., 1993-99 (chair 1999). Author: (with Dilweg, Fretz, Murphy and Wicker) Modern Judicial Ethics, 1992; contbr. articles to profl. jours. Mem. Colo. Commn. on Children, 1982-85, Colo. Youth Devel. Coun., 1989-98, Colo. Family Peace Task Force, 1994-96. Served with JAGC, U.S. Army, 1967-72; to maj. USAR, 1972-88. Decorated Bronze Star with oak leaf cluster, Air medal. Recipient Outstanding County Judge award Colo. 17th Judicial Dist. Victim Adv. Coalition, 1991; Spl. Community Svc. award Colo. Am. Legion, 1979. Fellow Am. Bar Found., Colo. Bar. Found. (life); mem. ABA (jud. div. exec. coun. 1989-2000, vice-chair 1996-97, chair-elect 1997, chair 1998-99, mem. Ho. of Dels. 1993—, jud. divsn. del. to ABA nominating com. 2000—, bd. govs. Dist. 11 2001—), Colo. Bar Assn. (bd. govs. 1986-88, 90-92, 93-99), Continental Divide Bar Assn., Denver Bar Assn. (bd. trustees 1979-82), First Jud. dist. Bar Assn. (trustee 2000—), Nat. Conf. Spl. Ct. Judges (chmn. 1989-90), Colo. County Judges Assn. (pres. 1995-96), Colo. Mcpl. Judges Assn. (pres. 1986-87), Colo. Trial Judges Coun. (v.p. 1994-95, sec. 1996-97), Denver Law Club (pres. 1981-82), Colo. Women's Bar Assn., Am. Judicature Soc., Nat. Coun. Juvenile and Family Ct. Judges, Federalist Soc. for Law and Pub. Policy Studies, Judge Advs. Assn., Univ. Club (Denver), Arlberg Club (Winter Park), Marines Meml. Club (San Francisco), Rotary (charter pres. Peak to Peak 2000—, Paul Harris fellow 1996). Episcopalian. Office: Gilpin County Justice Ctr Central City CO 80427-0398 E-mail: frederic.rodgers@judicial.state.co.us

RODGERS, JANET AHALT, nursing educator, dean; b. Hershey, Pa. d. Harold A. and Margaret L. (Bittle) Ahalt; m. Terry C. Rodgers. BSN, Wagner Coll., 1957; MA in Psychiat.-Mental Health Nursing, NYU, 1964, PhD Nursing, 1971; cert., N.Y. Med. Coll., 1973. RN, N.Y. Staff N.Y. State Psychiat. Inst., N.Y.C., 1957-59, head nurse, 1959-61; asst. DON Psychiat. Treatment Ctr., N.Y.C., 1961-62; group therapist Creedmoor State Hosp., Queens, N.Y., 1963; instr. Wagner Coll., S.I., 1964-66, asst. prof., 1966-68, lectr. psychiat. nursing, 1969-70; asst. prof. psychiat. nursing Lehman Coll.

CUNY, 1971-74, coord. psychiat. nursing Lehman Coll., 1971-76, assoc. prof., dep. chmn., 1974-77; prof., chairperson dept. nursing Old Dominion U., Norfolk, Va., 1977-79; cons., 1979-81; prof., chair dept. nursing Lycoming Coll., Williamsport, Pa., 1981-87; dean., prof. Philip Y. Hahn Sch. Nursing U. San Diego, 1987—. Vis. assoc. prof. Sch. Nursing U. Pa., 1981; presenter in field. Contbr. articles to profl. jours. Mem. adv. bd. Lee Hawkins Endowment Fund, Norfolk, Va., 1978-83, N.Y.C. Com. for Children, 1973-77, Bronx Health Manpower Consortium Bd., 1975-76, Ea. Va. Health Edn. Consortium, 1977-79; mem. health adv. bd. Divine Providence Hosp.-Cmty. Mental Health Ctr., 1985-87; bd. dirs. Regional Home Health Svcs., Williamsport, Pa., 1982-87, Divine Providence Hosp., Williamsport, 1986-87, San Diego Hospice, 1989-92, Am. Lung Assn. San Diego and Imperial Counties, 1994-96, Am. Heart Assn., 1996-2000, Assn. Calif. Nurse Leaders, 1996-98; bd. trustees Scripps Health, San Diego, 1998—, The Whittier Inst. for Diabetes, 2001; exec. ptnr. Cmty. Health Improvement Ptnrs., San Diego County, 1999—. Fellow Am. Orthopsychiat. Assn., Am. Acad. Nursing; mem. ANA, Am. Assn. Colls. Nursing (bd. dirs. 1987-94, pres.-elect 1990-92, pres. 1992-94, Wagner Coll. Alumni Assn. Achievement award 1977), Wagner Coll. Nat. Alumni Assn. (bd. dirs. 1999—), NYU Alumni Assn. (v.p. 1970-72, Mary Barr Alumni award Sch. Nursing 1993), Pi Lambda Theta, Kappa Delta Pi, Phi Kappa Phi, Sigma Theta Tau (Beta Upsilon and Zeta Mu chpts.). Office: U San Diego Hahn Sch Nurs & Health Svcs 5998 Alcala Park San Diego CA 92110-2492 E-mail: rodgers@acosd.edu

RODGERS, THOMAS J. electronics executive; Pres., CEO Cypress Semiconductor Corp., San Jose, Calif. Office: Cypress Semiconductor Corp 3901 N 1st St San Jose CA 95134-1599

RODIN, MIKE, lawyer; b. Norwalk, Conn., Sept. 18, 1954; AB with honors, U. Chgo., 1975; JD cum laude, NYU, 1979. Bar: Pa. 1979, U.S. Dist. Ct. (mid. dist.) Pa. 1979, Wash. 1981, U.S. Dist. Ct. (mid. dist.) Wash. 1981. Law clk. to Hon. Malcolm Muir U.S. Dist. (mid. dist.) Pa., 1979-81; assoc. Preston Gates & Ellis LLP, Seattle, 1981-86; ptnr. Preston Thorgrimson, Seattle, 1987-90; gen. counsel Puget Sound Bancorp, Tacoma, 1990-93, Key Bank of Washington, Tacoma, 1993-97; regional gen. counsel/N.W. region Key Corp, 1995-98; gen. counsel SkyTeller, LLC, Greenwood Village, Colo., 1998—; assoc. gen. counsel First Data Corp., Greenwood Village, 2001—; sr. counsel 1st Data Corp., Greenwood Village, 1998-2000. Speaker in field. Author: (with others) Washington Practice Manual, 1986-89. Fellow Securities Inst., NYU, 1979. Mem. Wash. State Bar Assn. (chair ad hoc securities com. bus. law sect. 1997, mem. opinion letter com. 1991-97), Seattle-King County Bar Assn. Office: First Data Corp 6200 S Quebec St Ste 350 Greenwood Village CO 80111-4729 E-mail: mike.rodin@firstdatacorp.com

RODKIN, LOREE, jewelry artist; Studied film making, art history, design, N.Y.C. Hollywood actors mgr., interior designer; jewelry maker Loree Rodkin Gothic Jewelry, Beverly Hills, Calif. Designer of In Memory Ring to honor friend, lover, or family mem. proceeds donated to Elton John AIDS Found. Office: Loree Rodkin Gothic Jewelry 453 Rodeo Dr Beverly Hills CA 90209 Fax: 310-276-8104. E-mail: lrodkin@instanet.com

RODMAN, ALPINE C. arts and crafts company executive; b. Roswell, N.Mex., June 23, 1952; s. Robert Elsworth and Verna Mae (Means) R.; m. Sue Arlene Lawson, Dec. 13, 1970; 1 child, Connie Lynn. Student, Colo. State U., 1970-71, U. No. Colo. Ptnr. Pinel Silver Shop, Loveland, Colo., 1965-68, salesman, 1968-71; real estate salesman Loveland, 1971-73; mgr. Traveling Traders, Phoenix, 1974-75; co-owner Deer Track Traders, Loveland, 1975-85; pres. Deer Track Traders, Ltd., 1985—. Author: The Vanishing Indian: Fact or Fiction?, 1985. Mem. Civil Air Patrol, 1965-72, 87-92, dep. comdr. for cadets, 1988-90; cadet comdr. Ft. Collins, Colo., 1968, 70, Colo. rep. to youth tng. program, 1969, U.S. youth rep. to Japan, 1970. Mem. Bur. Wholesale Sales Reps., Western and English Salesmen's Assn. (bd. dirs. 1990), Internat. Platform Assn., Indian Arts and Crafts Assn. (bd. dirs. 1988-94, exec. com. 1989-92, v.p. 1990, pres. 1991, market chmn. 1992), Crazy Horse Grass Roots Club. Republican. Office: Deer Track Traders Ltd PO Box 448 Loveland CO 80539-0448

RODMAN, SUE A. wholesale company executive, artist, writer; b. Ft. Collins, Colo., Oct. 1, 1951; d. Marvin F. Lawson and Barbara I. (Miller) Lawson Shue; m. Alpine C. Rodman, Dec. 13, 1970; 1 child, Connie, Lynn. Student, Colo. State U., 1970-73. Silversmith Pinel Silver Shop, Loveland, Colo., 1970-71; asst. mgr. Traveling Traders, Phoenix, 1974-75; co-owner, co-mgr. Deer Track Traders, Loveland, 1975-85; v.p. Deer Track Traders, Ltd., Loveland, 1985—. Author: The Book of Contemporary Indian Arts and Crafts, 1985. Mem. U.S. Senatorial Club, 1982-87, Rep. Presdl. Task Force, 1984-90; mem. CAP, 1969-73, 87-90, pers. officer, 1988-90. Mem. Internat. Platform Assn., Indian Arts and Crafts Assn., Western and English Sales Assn., Crazy Horse Grass Roots Club. Mem. Am. Baptist Ch. Avocations: museums, piano, recreation research, fashion design. Office: Deer Track Traders Ltd PO Box 448 Loveland CO 80539-0448

RODRIGUE, GEORGE P. newspaper editor; Exec. editor, v.p. news The Press Enterprise, Riverside, Calif., 1998—. Office: The Press Enterprise 3512 14th St Riverside CA 92501-3878

RODRIGUEZ, ALEXANDER EMMANUEL, professional baseball player; b. N.Y.C., July 27, 1975; Grad. high sch., Miami. Baseball player Seattle Mariners, 1995—. Named Winner Am. League Batting Title, 1996; 3rd player in major league history 40 home runs and 40 stolen bases in one season; 2nd consecutive all star game.

RODRIGUEZ, ARTURO SALVADOR, labor union official; b. San Antonio, June 23, 1949; s. Arthur Salvador and Felice (Quintero) R.; m. Linda Fabela Chavez, Mar. 30, 1974; children: Olivia, Julie, Arthur. BA in Sociology, St. Mary's U., 1971; MSW, U. Mich., 1973. Various positions United Farm Workers of Am., Keene, Calif., 1973-90, v.p., 1981-93, organizer, 1990-92; pres. United Farm Workers Am. AFL-CIO, Keene, 1993—. Chief instr. UFW Sch., Keene, 1978-79; coord. Edward Kennedy Presdl. Dr., San Antonio, 1980. Office: United Farm Workers Am AFL CIO PO Box 62 La Paz 29700 Woodford Tehachapi Rd Keene CA 93531

RODRIGUEZ, JUAN ALFONSO, technology corporation executive; b. Santiago, Cuba, Feb. 10, 1941; came to U.S., 1953; s. Alfonso and Marie Madeleine (Hourcadette) R. BEE, CCNY, 1962; MEE, NYU, 1963. Engr. IBM, Poughkeepsie, N.Y. and Boulder, Colo., 1963-68, engring. mgr., 1968-69; dir. tech. Storage Tech. Corp., Louisville, 1969-74, v.p. engring., 1974-77, v.p., gen. mgr. disk, 1977-79, v.p., gen. mgr. optical disk Longmont, 1979-85; pres., CEO Exabyte Corp., Boulder, 1985-87, CEO, 1987-90; chmn., 1987-92; pres. Sweetwater Corp., 1992-93, chmn., 1992-95, also bd. dirs.; prof. elec. and computer engring. and engring. mgmt. U. Colo., 1992—, co-exec. dir. Ctr. for Entrepreneurship, 1994-2000; chmn. Datasonix, 1992-96, Vixel, 1995-99; chmn., CEO Ecrix Corp., 1996—. Mem. devel. coun. Coll. Engring. U. Colo., 1990-92; Decisionism Corp.; mem. engring. adv. bd. CCNY, bd. dirs. Colo. Advanced Tech. Enterprise, 1994-98; Robert J. Appel Disting. lectr. law and tech. Law Sch. U. Denver, 1990. Patentee in field. Bd. dirs. Boulder YMCA, 1982-87, U. Colo. Artist Series, 1988-92; mem. bd. govs. Boulder County United Way, 1989-93, chairperson campaign, 1992; commr. Colo. Advance Tech. Inst., 1988-92. Recipient Ind. Quality award Rocky Mountain sect. Am. Soc. Quality Control, 1990, Gen. Palmer award for Outstanding Engr. in Industry The Am. Cons. Engrs. Coun. of Colo., 1995; named Boulder Spirit Entrepreneur of Yr., 1989, Entrepreneur of the Decade Boulder C. of C., 1994, Hispanic Engr. of Yr., Entrepreneur Hispanic Engr. Nat. Achievement Awards Coun., 1995; finalist Entrepreneur of Yr., Arthur Young & Inc Mag., 1989. Fellow IEEE; mem. Computer Soc. of IEEE (mem. steering com. on mass storage 1981-93), Soc. Photo-Optical Instrumentation Engrs., Boulder C. of C. (chmn. entrepreneurs support program 1989), Greater Denver C. of C. (bd. dirs. 1990-91). Office: Univ Colo PO Box 425 Boulder CO 80309-0425

RODRIGUEZ, LEONARD, foundation administrator; b. Phoenix, Jan. 27, 1944; s. Jesus H. and Manuela (Razo) R.; m. Jo Ann Gama, Jan. 16, 1965 ; 1 child, Lena Teresa. BS in Mktg., Ariz. State U., 1981, MPA, 1995. Cert. tchr., Ariz. Adminstrv. svcs. officer Title XX Adminstrn., Phoenix, 1979-81, Block Grants Adminstrn., Phoenix, 1981-84; property mgmt. mgr. State of Ariz., Phoenix, 1984-86; pres. LTR Mgmt. Svcs., Phoenix, 1986-93; dir. PALS computer literacy program N.W. Resources and Learning Ctr., 1989-91; program cons. City of El Mirage, 1989-91; master tchr. Rio Salado C.C., 1989-91; project dir., exec. dir. Westside Coalition for Substance Abuse Prevention, 1990-91; mem. chpt. svcs. Make-A-Wish Found. of Am., 1993-97; found. adminstn., 1997—. Adj. clin. instr., faculty assoc. Ariz. State U., 1979-89; cons. Applied Econs. Curriculum, Jr. Achievement of Cen. Ariz., Inc., 1987; nat. tng. cons. Ctr. Substance Abuse Prevention, Housing & Urban Devel., Macro Internat., Washington, 1992-93. Chmn. community rels. minority recruitment program Ariz. State U., Tempe, 1985-86; bd. dirs. Concilio Latino de Salud, Inc., pres. 1993-94, Friendly House, Inc., Phoenix, 1985-87, pres., 1987; mem. community problem solving coordinating com. Valley of the Sun United Way, 1988; alliance chmn. Gov.'s Office of Drug Policy, mem. statewide exec. com., 1991; program cons. Cada Uno, Inc., 1990-91; adult literacy coord. Chandler Pub. Libr., 1992-93; tng. cons. Phoenix Fight Back Program, 1992-93; outreach coord. Hemophilia Assn., Ariz., 1992-93. Mem. Am. Soc. Public Adminstrn., Ariz. Adminstrs. Assn., Counterparts (founder 1986), Hispanic C. of C., Vesta Club (chmn. scholarship com. 1983), Rotary (pres. 1987-88, voting del. internat. conv. 1987). Avocations: painting, sculpture, late 19th century art. Home: 6225 N 30th Way Phoenix AZ 85016-2212

RODRIGUEZ, NANCY, state legislator; b. San Luis, Colo., Mar. 18, 1953; BBA, MBA. Mem. N.Mex. Senate, Dist. 24, Santa Fe, 1996—; mem. edn. com.; mem. fin. com. Democrat. Office: 1838 Camino La Canada Santa Fe NM 87501

RODSTEIN, RICHARD M. apparel executive; b. 1955; m. Leslie Rodstein. BA in Econs., UCLA, 1976, MBA, 1978. Exec. Ernst & Young, 1978-83; v.p. fin. K2, Inc. (formerly Anthony Industries, Inc.), L.A., 1983-85, sr. v.p. fin., 1985-88, exec. v.p., 1988-90, pres., COO, 1990—, CEO, 1995—, also bd. dirs. Office: K2 Inc 4900 S Eastern Ave Los Angeles CA 90040 Fax: 323-724-2800

ROE, CHARLES RICHARD, baritone; b. Cleve., May 24, 1940; s. Andrews Rogers and Margaret (Dalton) R.; children by previous marriage— Charles Andrews, Richard Nevins, Robert Arthur; m. Jo Ann Marie Belli, May 21, 1988. B.Mus., Baldwin-Wallace Coll., 1963; M.Mus., U. Ill., 1964. Instr. in music Tex. Tech. U., 1964-68; asst. prof. music Eastern Mich. U., 1968-74; vis. assoc. prof. U. So. Calif., L.A., 1976-77, assoc. prof., 1979-84, prof., 1984-89, U. Ariz., Tucson, 1989—. Vis. prof. and artist in residence Western Mich. U., 1978-79; faculty Music Acad. of the West, 1981, 82 Leading singer, N.Y.C. Opera, 1974-81; appeared in leading roles with, Mich. Opera Theater, Sacramento Opera, San Antonio Opera, Ft. Worth Opera, Ky. Opera, Conn. Opera, Utah Opera, Cleve. Opera, Miss. Opera, Lake George Opera, Shreveport Opera, Toledo Opera; appeared with, symphonies: Phila., Cleve., Detroit, Toledo, Wichita, Duluth. Mem. Am. Guild Musical Artists, Actors Equity, Nat. Assn. Tchrs. Singing (S.W. region Singer of Year 1966), AAUP. Office: U Ariz Sch Music PO Box 210004 Tucson AZ 85721-0004

ROE, THOMAS LEROY WILLIS, pediatrician; b. Bend, Oreg., Sept. 1, 1936; MD, U. Oregon Health Scis. U., Portland, 1961. Diplomate Am. Bd. Pediatrics. Intern U. Calif., San Francisco, 1961-62, resident, 1962-64; physician Sacred Heart Med. Ctr., Eugene, Oreg.; pvt. practice Peace Health Med. Group, Eugene, 1969—; clin prof. pediatrics U. Oreg., Portland, 1985—. Fellow Am. Acad. Pediatricians; mem. AMA, North Pacific Pediatrics Soc. E-mial. Office: Peace Health Med Clinic 1162 Willamette St Eugene OR 97401-3568 E-mail: troe@peacehealth.org

ROEDER, RICHARD KENNETH, business owner, lawyer; b. Phila., Oct. 11, 1948; s. Walter August and Gloria (Miller) R.; 1 child, William Frederick. AB, Amherst Coll., 1970; JD, U. Calif., Berkeley, 1973, Cambridge U., , 1973-74. Assoc. Paul, Hastings, Janofky & Walker, L.A., 1974-81, ptnr., 1981-90; founding ptnr. Aurora Capital Group, L.A., 1990—. Office: Aurora Capital Group Ste 2100 10877 Wilshire Blvd Los Angeles CA 90024-4341

ROEDERER, JUAN GUALTERIO, physics educator; b. Trieste, Italy, Sept. 2, 1929; came to U.S., 1967, naturalized, 1972; s. Ludwig Alexander and Anna Rafaela (Lohr) R.; m. Beatriz Susana Cougnet, Dec. 20, 1952; children: Ernesto, Irene, Silvia, Mario. Ph.D., U. Buenos Aires, 1952. Research scientist Max Planck Inst., Gottingen, W.Ger., 1952-55; group leader Argentine Atomic Energy Commn., Buenos Aires, 1953-59; prof. physics U. Buenos Aires, 1959-66, U. Denver, 1967-77, U. Alaska, Fairbanks, 1977-93, prof. emeritus, 1993—, dir. Geophys. Inst., 1977-86, dean Coll. Environ. Scis., 1978-82. Vis. staff Los Alamos Nat. Lab., 1969-81; chmn. U.S. Arctic Research Com., 1987-91; sr. adviser Internat. Ctr. Theoretical Physics, Trieste, Italy, 1998—. Author: Dynamics of Geomagnetically Trapped Radiation, 1970, Physics and Psychophysics of Music, 1973, 3d edit., 1995; contbr. articles to profl. jours. Nat. Acad. Sci. NASA sr. research fellow, 1964-66 Fellow AAAS, Am. Geophys. Union (Edward A. Flinn III award, 2000); mem. Assn. Argentina de Geodestas y Geofisicos (hon.), Nat. Acad. Sci. Argentina (corr.), Nat. Acad. Sci. Austria (corr.), Third World Acad. Scis. (assoc.), Internat. Assn. Geomagnetism and Aeronomy (hon.). Lutheran. Achievements include research on plasma and energetic particles in earth's and Jupiter's magnetosphere, policy issues for Arctic, perception of music. Home: 105 Concordia Dr Fairbanks AK 99709-3029 Office: U Alaska Geophys Inst Fairbanks AK 99775-7320 E-mail: jgr@gi.alaska.edu

ROEHL, JERRALD J. lawyer; b. Austin, Tex., Dec. 6, 1945; s. Joseph E. and Jeanne Foster (Scott) R.; m. Nancy J. Meyers, Jan. 15, 1977; children: Daniel J., Katherine C., J. Ryan, J. Taylor. BA, U. N.Mex., 1968; JD, Washington and Lee U., 1971. Bar: N.Mex. 1972, U.S. Ct. Appeals (10th cir.) 1972, U.S. Supreme Ct. 1977. Practice of law, Albuquerque, 1972—; pres. Roehl Law Firm P.C. and predecessors, Albuquerque, 1976—. Lectr. to profl. groups; real estate developer, Albuquerque. Bd. advs. ABA Jour. 1981-83; bd. editors Washington and Lee Law Rev., 1970-71. Bd. dirs. Rehab. Ctr. of Albuquerque, 1974-78; mem. assocs. Presbyn. Hosp. Ctr., Albuquerque, 1974-82; incorporator, then treas. exec. com. Ctr. City Coun., 1991— Recipient award of recognition State Bar N.Mex., 1975, 76, 77. Mem. ABA (award of achievement Young Lawyers div. 1975, council econs. of law practice sect. 1978-80, exec. council Young Lawyers div. 1979-81, fellow div. 1984—, council tort and ins. practice sect. 1981-83), N.Mex. Bar Assn. (pres. young lawyers sect. 1975-76), Albuquerque Bar Assn. (bd. dirs. 1976-79), N.Mex. Def. Lawyers Assn. (pres. 1983-84), Sigma Alpha Epsilon, Sigma Delta Chi, Phi Delta Phi. Roman Catholic. Clubs: Albuquerque County, Albuquerque Petroleum. Home: 4411 Constitution Ave NE Albuquerque NM 87110-5721 Office: Roehl Law Firm PC 300 Central Ave SW Albuquerque NM 87102-3298 E-mail: lawyer@roehl.com

ROEHRIG, JOHN T. immunologist, educator; BS in Microbiology, U. Ill., 1973; PhD in Microbiology, U. Mo.-Columbia, 1977. Rsch. microbiologist divsn. vector-borne infectious diseases Ctr. Disease Control and Prevention, Fort Collins, Colo., 1981-84, supervisory rsch. microbiologist, 1984—, chief immunochemistry br./sect., 1985-98; chief arbovirus diseases br. Colo. State U., Fort Collins, 1981—, biosafety com. mem., 1981—, affiliate faculty mem. dept. microbiology, 1981—. Presenter in field. Ad hoc reviewer Am. Jour. of Tropical Medicine and Hygiene, Archives of Virology, Infectio and Immunity, Jour. of Gen. Virology, Jour. of Infectious Diseases, Jour. of Med. Virology, Jour. of Virology, Virology and Virus Rsch.; contbr. chpts. to books and numerous articles to profl. jours. Grantee U.S. Army, 1987-90, NATO, 1987-90, WHO, 1989-91. Mem. AAAS, Am. Soc. for Virology, Am. Soc. for Microbiology, Am. Com. for Arthropod-Bone Viruses, Protein Soc., Am. Peptide Soc., Am. Soc. for Tropical Medicine and Hygiene, U. Ill. Alumni Assn., U. Mo. Alumni Assn., Sigma Xi. Office: Divsn Vector Borne Infectious Diseases Ctrs Disease Control PO Box 2087 Fort Collins CO 80522-2087

ROELANDTS, WILLEM P. computer company executive; came to U.S., 1982; B of Elec. Engring., Rihks Hogere Tech. Sch., Anderlecht, Belgium. Svc. engr. Hewlett-Packard, Belgium, 1967, various mgmt. positions in engring., rsch. & devel. France, until 1982, mgr. rsch. & devel. Cupertino, Calif., 1983-85, gen. mgr. info. nteworks group, 1985-88, v.p., gen. mgr., 1988-90, gen. mgr. networked systems group, 1990-92, gen. mgr. computer systems orfn., 1992-93, sr. v.p., 1993-96; CEO Xilinx, Inc., San Jose, 1996—. Office: 2100 Logic Dr San Jose CA 95124-3450

ROELLER, HERBERT ALFRED, biology and medical scientist, educator; b. Magdeburg, Germany, Aug. 2, 1927; came to U.S., 1962; s. Alfred H. and Elfriede (Wartner) R.; m. Manuela R. Buresch, Dec. 20, 1957. Abiturium, Christian Thomasius Schule, Halle/Saale, 1946; PhD, Georg August U., Goettingen, 1962; MD, U. Muenster, 1955. Project assoc. zoology U. Wis., Madison, 1962-65, asst. prof. pharmacology, 1965-66, rsch. assoc. zoology, 1966-67, assoc. prof. zoology, 1967-68; prof. biology Tex. A&M U., 1968-83, prof. biochemistry and biophysics, 1974-83, dir. Inst. Devel. Biology, 1973-83, Disting. prof., 1977—, Alumni prof., 1980-85. V.p. rsch. Zoecon Corp., Palo Alto, Calif., 1968-72, sci. adv., 1972-85, chief scientist, Zoecon Rsch. Inst., Palo Alto, 1985-88; sci. advisor Syntex Rsch., Palo Alto, 1966-68, European Cmty., 1988—, Affymax Rsch. Inst., Palo Alto, 1989-96; corp. advisor Symyx Techs., Sunnyvale, Calif., 1996—; mem. adv. panel regulatory biology, divsn. biol. and med. scis. NSF, 1969-72; mem. Internat. Centre Insect Physiology and Ecology, Nairobi, Kenya, 1970—, dir. rsch., 1970-75. Mem. editl. bd. Jour. Chem. Ecology, 1974—; Contbr. articles to profl. jours. Recipient Disting. Achievement award for research Tex. A&M U., 1976. Fellow Tex. Acad. Sci.; mem. German Acad. Naturforscher Leopoldina, AAAS, Am. Soc. Zoologists, Entomol. Soc. Am., Am. Soc. Devel. Biology, Sigma Xi.

ROELLIG, LEONARD OSCAR, physics educator; b. Detroit, May 17, 1927; s. Oscar Otto and Laura K. (Rutz) R.; m. B. Pauline Cowdin, June 20, 1952; children: Thomas Leonard, Mark Douglas, Paul David. A.B., U. Mich., 1950, M.S., 1956, Ph.D., 1959. From asst. prof. to prof. physics Wayne State U., Detroit, 1958-78, dean, 1971-72, asso. provost, 1972-76; pres. Central Solar Energy Research Corp., Detroit, 1977; prof. physics CCNY, 1978-96, prof. emeritus, 1996—; vice chancellor acad. affairs CUNY, 1978-83. Vis. prof. Univ. Coll., London, 1968-69, Tata Inst. Fundamental Rsch., Bombay, India, 1973, Paul Scherrer Inst., Villigen, Switzerland, 1991-92; chmn. bd. advisers Midwest Regional Solar Energy Planning Venture, 1977. Co-author: Positron Annihilation, 1967; contbr. articles to profl. jours. Bd. dirs. Luth. Publicity Bur., 1981-91, v.p., 1984-85, pres., 1985-89; v.p. Grosse Pointe (Mich.) Human Rels. Coun., 1969-70. With USN, 1945-46, U.S. Army, 1950-52. Recipient Wayne State U. Fund Research Recognition award, 1963, Probus Club award for acad. achievement, 1968, Probus Club award for acad. leadership, 1977 Mem. Am. Phys. Soc. Home: 4520 Sioux Dr Boulder CO 80303-3733 Office: U Colo Dept Physics Boulder CO 80302 E-mail: loroellig@aol.com

ROELLIG, MARK D. telecommunications industry executive, lawyer; BS in Applied Maths. with highest distinction, U. Mich., 1976; JD, George Washington U., 1979; MBA, U. Washington, 1988. Assoc. Perry & Smity, Seattle, Reed, McClure, Moceri & Thonn, Seattle; litigation and regulator atty. law dept. U S West, Seattle, 1983-92, v.p. law and litigation sect. Denver, 1992-95, v.p. law and human resources, asst. sec. corp. sect., 1995, exec. v.p. pub. policy and regulatory law, 1996-97, exec. v.p. pub. policy, human resources, law, gen. counsel, 1997—. Mem. Beta Gamma Sigma. Office: US West Inc 1801 California St Ste 4750 Denver CO 80202-2658

ROELLIG, RICHARD H. career officer; BS in Mgmt., Miami U., Oxford, Ohio, 1966; MBA in Govt. Contracting, George Washington U., 1970; grad., Armed Forces Staff Coll., 1977, Def. Sys. Mgmt. Coll., 1977; MS in Sys. Mgmt., U. So. Calif., L.A., 1978; grad., Indsl. Coll. of Armed Forces, 1981. Commd. 2d lt. USAF, 1966, advanced through grades to maj. gen., 1997; dep. base contracting officer Eglin AFB, Fla., 1970-72; air staff tng. officer Air Force Procurement Policy Office, Washington, 1972-73; adminstrv. contracting officer DCAS-Litton, L.A., 1973-74; officer in charge Teledyne Ryan Plant, DCAS, San Diego, 1974-76; weapon sys. acquisition staff officer Hdqs. Air Force Sys. Command, Andrews AFB, Md., 1977-80; exec. officer Electronic Sys. Divsn., Hanscom AFB, Mass., 1981-82, dir. pers., 1982-83; vice comdr. Air Force Contract Mgmt. Divsn., Kirtland AFB, N.Mex., 1984-87; dep. contracting and mfg. Aero. Sys. Divsn., Wright-Patterson AFB, Ohio, 1987-89; comdr. Arnold Engring. Devel. Ctr., Arnold AFB, Tenn., 1989-91; program dir. Tri-Svc. Standoff Attack Missile Sys. Program Office, Wright-Patterson AFB, 1991-95; dir. contracting Air Force Materiel Command, Wright-Patterson AFB, 1995-97; comdr. Ogden Air Logistics Ctr., Hill AFB, Utah, 1997—. Decorated Disting. Svc. medal, Def. Superior Svc. medal, Legion of Merit with 2 oak leaf clusters. Office: OOALC/CC 7981 Georgia St Hill Air Force Base UT 84056

ROEMER, ELIZABETH, astronomer, educator; b. Calif., Sept. 4, 1929; d. Richard Quirin and Elsie Roemer. BA with honors, U. Calif., Berkeley, 1950, PhD (Lick Obs. fellow), 1955. Tchr. adult class Oakland pub. schs., 1950-52; lab technician U. Calif. at Mt. Hamilton, 1954-55; grad. research astronomer U. Calif. at Berkeley, 1955-56; research asso. Yerkes Obs. U. Chgo., 1956; astronomer U.S. Naval Obs., Flagstaff, Ariz., 1957-66; asso. prof. dept. astronomy, also in lunar and planetary lab. U. Ariz., Tucson, 1966-69, prof., 1969-97; prof. emerita, 1997—; astronomer Steward Obs., 1980-97, astronomer emerita, 1997—. Chmn. working group on orbits and ephemerides of comets commn. 20 Internat. Astron. Union, 1964-79, 85-88, v.p. comm. 20, 1979-82, pres., 1982-85, v.p. commn. 6, 1973-76, 85-88, pres., 1976-79, 88-91; mem. adv. panels Office Naval Research, Nat. Acad. Scis.-NRC, NASA; researcher and author numerous publs. on astrometry and astrophysics of comets and minor planets including 79 recoveries of returning periodic comets, visual and spectroscopic binary stars, computation of orbits of comets and minor planets. Recipient Dorothea Klumpke Roberts prize U. Calif. at Berkeley, 1950, Mademoiselle Merit award, 1959; asteroid (1657) named Roemera, 1965; Benjamin Apthorp Gould prize Nat. Acad. Scis., 1971; NASA Spl. award, 1986. Fellow AAAS (council 1966-69, 72-73), Royal Astron. Soc. (London); mem. Am. Astron. Soc. (program vis. profs. astronomy 1960-75, council 1967-70, chmn. div. dynamical astronomy 1974), Astron. Soc. Pacific (publs. com. 1962-73, Comet medal com. 1968-74, Donohoe lectr. 1962), Internat. Astron. Union, Am. Geophys. Union, Brit. Astron. Assn., Phi Beta Kappa, Sigma Xi. Office: U Ariz PO Box 210092 Lunar & Planetary Lab Tucson AZ 85721-0092

ROENICK, JEREMY, professional hockey player; b. Boston, Jan. 17, 1970; Center Chgo. Blackhawks, 1988-96, Phoenix Coyotes, 1996—. Named The Sporting News NHL Rookie of the Yr., 1989-90. Played in NHL All-Star Games, 1991-94. Office: Phoenix Coyotes One Renaissance Sq 9375 E Bell Rd Scottsdale AZ 85260-1500

ROESNER, LARRY AUGUST, civil engineer; b. Denver, Mar. 14, 1941; s. Walter George and Sarah Jane (Merrick) R.; m. Kathleen Ann Fahrenbruch, Dec. 13, 1964; children: David John, Kevin Walter, Nathan August, Melissa Jane. BS, Valparaiso (Ind.) U., 1963; MS, Colo. State U., 1965; PhD, U. Wash., Seattle, 1969. Registered profl. engr., Calif., Fla., Colo. From assoc. engr. to prin. engr. Water Resources Engrs., Inc., Walnut Creek, Calif., 1968-77; from assoc. to v.p. Camp Dresser & McKee Inc., Annandale, Va., 1977-85, sr. v.p., dir. water resources Maitland, Fla., 1985-92, chief tech. officer, 1992-98; dean Camp Dressert & McKee Corp. U., 1998-99; Harold H. Short prof. civil infrastructure systems Colo. State U., Ft. Collins, 1999—, interim head deptl civil engring., 2000—. Guest lectr., cons. urban hydrology and surface water quality; NRC exec. com. Wastewater Mgmt. in Urban Coastal Areas, 1992; chair Engring. Found. Conf. Stormwater Mgmt.-Sustainable Urban Water Resources in the 21st Century, 1997; urban wet weather adv. com. Water Environ. Rsch. Fedn.; U.S. del. to joint IHR/IAWQ com. on urban drainage. Contbr. articles to profl. jours. Recipient Water Resource Planning and Mfmg. Divsn. Svc. to the Profession award 1999. Fellow ASCE (chmn. 1995 water resources planning and mgmt. div. splty. conf., nat. Walter L. Huber civil engring. rsch. prize 1975); mem. NAE, Am. Acad. Environ. Engrs. (diplomate), Am. Water Resources Assn., Am. Cons. Engrs. Assn., Water Environ. Fedn. (chmn. urban quality runoff task force), Tau Beta Pi (eminent engr.). Republican. Lutheran. Achievements include development of mathematical models for U.S. government agencies including QUAL-II stream quality model for the EPA; an urban stormwater management model, dynamic hydraulics model for storm drainage and sewer systems. Home: 5926 Huntington Hills Dr Fort Collins CO 80525-7118 Office: Colo State U Dept Civil Engring Fort Collins CO 80523-0001 E-mail: roesner@engr.colostate.edu

ROETHE, JAMES NORTON, lawyer; b. Milw., Jan. 27, 1942; s. Arthur Frantz and Bess Irma (Norton) R.; m. Nita May Dorris, July 15, 1967; children: Melissa Dorris, Sarah Rebacca. BBA, U. Wis., Madison, 1964, JD, 1967. Bar: Wis. 1967, Calif. 1968, U.S. Dist. Ct. (we. dist.) Wis. 1967, U.S. Dist. Ct. (no. dist.) Calif. 1972, U.S. Ct. Claims 1975, U.S. Ct. Appeals (9th cir.) 1980, U.S. Dist. Ct. (ea. dist.) Calif. 1982, U.S. Dist. Ct. (ctrl. dist.) Calif. 1986). U.S. Ct. Appeals (4th cir.) 1988, U.S. Ct. Appeals (2d cir.) 1989. Assoc. Pillsbury, Madison & Sutro, San Francisco, 1971-77, ptnr., 1978-92; sr. v.p., dir. litigation Bank of Am., San Francisco, 1992-96, exec. v.p., gen. counsel, 1996-98, dep. gen. counsel, 1998-99; ptnr. Pillsbury Winthrop LLP, 2000—. Staff atty. Commn. on CIA Activities within U.S., Washington, 1975. Editor: Africa, 1967; editor-in-chief Wis. Law Rev., 1966-67. Bd. dirs. Orinda (Calif.) Assn., 1984-85, pres., 1986; mem. City of Orinda Planning Commn., 1988-94, chmn., 1990, 93; bd. dirs. Calif. Shakespeare Festival, 1993—, pres., 2001; bd. visitors U. Wis. Law Sch., 1994-99. Served to lt. USNR, 1967-71. Fellow Am. Bar Found.; mem. ABA, Wis. Bar Assn., Calif. Bar Assn., Bar Assn. San Francisco, Wis. Law Alumni Assn. (bd. dirs. 2000—), Orinda Country Club, Order of Coif, Phi Kappa Phi. office e-mail: roethe. Home: 36 Fallen Leaf Ter Orinda CA 94563-1209 E-mail: jimroethe@aol.com, jn@pillsburywinthrop.com

ROFFMAN, HOWARD, motion picture company executive; b. Phila. Student, U. Pa.; JD, U. Fla. Assoc. Morgan, Lewis & Bockius, Washington; from legal counsel to gen. counsel Lucasfilm, Ltd., San Rafael, Calif., 1980-84, acting COO, 1984-85, v.p. licensing, 1986-99; pres. Lucas Licensing, San Rafael, 1999—. Author: Presumed Guilty, 1974, Understanding the Cold War, 1976, The Edge of Desire, 1995, Three, 1996, Tales, 1997, Pictures of Fred, 1998, Jagged Youth, 2000, Johan Paulik, 2001. Mem. Calif. Bar Assn., Washington Bar Assn., Licensing Industry Merchandising Assn. Office: Lucas Licensing Ltd PO Box 10148 San Rafael CA 94912-0148

ROGAN, JAMES E. lawyer, former congressman; m. Christine Apffel; children: Dana and Claire (twins). BA in Polit. Sci., U. Calif., Berkeley, 1979; JD, UCLA, 1983. Past atty. Lillick McHose and Charles (now Pillsbury, Madison and Sutro), L.A.; past dep. dist. atty L.A County; judge Glendale (Calif.) Mcpl. Ct., 1990-93, presiding judge, 1993-94; past mem. Calif. Assembly, 1994-96, assembly majority leader, 1996; mem. U.S. Congress from 27th Calif. dist., 1996-2001; mem. house jud. com., mem. commerce com., asst. minority whip; ptnr. Venable, Baetjer, Howard & Civiletti, Washington, 2001—. Adj. prof. trial advocacy Sch. Law Southwestern U.; adj. prof. criminal law Coll. Law Glendale U.; past adj. prof. criminal law Glendale C.C.; mem. Selective Svc. Sys. U.S. Govt., 1981—. Office: Venable Baetjer Howard & Civiletti 1201 New York Ave NW Ste 1000 Washington DC 20005 Fax: 202-225-5828*

ROGAN, RICHARD A. lawyer; b. L.A., Sept. 6, 1950; AB with honors, Hamilton Coll., 1972; JD, U. Calif., 1975. Bar: Calif. 1975. Ptnr. Broad, Schulz, Larson & Wineberg, 1978-94, chmn., 1991-93; ptnr. Jeffer, Mangels, Butler & Marmaro, San Francisco, 1994—. Editorial assoc. Hastings Law Jour., 1974-75. Trustee Bentley Sch., 1989-92. Mem. ABA (mem. corp., banking, and bus. sect.), Bar Assn. of San Francisco (mem. comml. law and bankruptcy sect.), Calif. Receivers Forum (bd. dirs. Bay Area chpt.), Delta Sigma Rho. Office: Jeffer Mangels Butler One Sansome St Fl 12 San Francisco CA 94104

ROGEL, STEVEN R. forest products company executive; BS in Chem. Engring., U. Wash., 1965. With St. Regis Paper Co., 1965-70; asst. mgr. St. Anne-Nackawic Pulp and Paper, Nackawic, N.B., Can., 1970-72; tech. dir. Willamette Industries, Inc., Albany, Oreg., 1972-95, pres., CEO, 1995-97, Weyerhaeuser Co., Tacoma, 1997—, chmn., 1999—. Bd. dirs. Kroger Co. Trustee Pacific U.; bd. dirs. Pacific Harbors coun. Boy Scouts Am. Mem. Am. Forest and Paper Assn. (bd. dirs.). Office: Weyerhaeuser Co 33663 Weyerhaeuser Way S Federal Way WA 98003

ROGERS, DAVID HUGHES, finance executive; b. Chgo., May 21, 1947; s. Joseph Gordon and Viola Winifred (Hughes) R.; Bonnie Hope Sinai, 1997; children: Kirsten Morgan, Loren Avery, Daniel Jay. BA, U. Mich., 1968; PhD, Columbia U., 1975. Economist Fed. Res. Bank of Cleve., 1974-75; asst. treas. B.F. Goodrich Co., Akron, Ohio, 1975-82; exec. v.p., chief fin. officer First Tex. Savs. Assn., Dallas, 1982-83; sr. exec. v.p., chief operating officer PriMerit Bank, Las Vegas, 1984-87, pres., dir., 1987-91, vice chmn., 1991-92; COO, The Baird Cos., Las Vegas, 1992-99; v.p., chief fin. officer Norall Labs., Las Vegas, 1999—. Adj. prof. econs. C.C. of So. Nev., 1998—. Author: Consumer Banking in New York, 1975; also articles. Bd. dirs. Boulder Dam area coun. Boy Scouts Am., 1986—; bd. dirs. Nev. Sch. Arts, 1988-98; chmn. Las Vegas Bus. Bank, 1995-99. Office: Norall Labs 8440 W Lake Mead Blvd Las Vegas NV 89128-7648 E-mail: DrRogers75@aol.com

ROGERS, GARTH WINFIELD, lawyer; b. Fort Collins, Colo., Nov. 4, 1938; s. Harlan Winfield and Helen Marie (Orr) R.; m. Joanne Kathleen Rapp, June 16, 1962; children: Todd Winfield, Christopher Jay, Gregory Lynn, Clay Charles. BS, U. Colo., 1958, LLB, 1962. Bar: Colo. 1962; U.S. Dist. Ct. Colo. 1962. Law clk. to presiding justice U.S. Dist. Ct., Denver, 1962-63; assoc. Allen, Stover & Mitchell, Ft. Collins, 1963-68; ptnr. Allen, Rogers & Vahrenwald, Ft. Collins, 1968-97; ret., 1997. Articles editor Rocky Mountain Law Rev., 1961-62. Past bd. dirs. Salvation Army, Ft. Collins, Ft. Collins C. of C., United Way of Ft. Collins, Trinity Luth. Ch., Ft. Collins, others; bd. dirs. Poudre Sch. Dist. Bd. Edn. Mem. ABA, Colo. Bar Assn., Larimer County Bar Assn. Avocations: Nicaragua projects, participative sports, amateur writing, reading. Office: 215 W Oak St Ste 202 Fort Collins CO 80521-2734

ROGERS, HOWARD H. chemist; b. N.Y.C., Dec. 26, 1926; s. Julian Herbert and Minnie (Jaffa) R.; m. Barbara Kniaz, Mar. 27, 1954 (div. 1978); children: Lynne, Mark David, Susan; m. Maureen Dohn, Dec. 28, 1978. BS in Chemistry, U. Ill., 1949; PhD in Inorganic Chemistry, MIT, 1953. Research group leader Allis-Chalmers Mfg. Co., West Allis, Wis., 1952-61; sr. tech. specialist Rocketdyne div., Rockwell, Canoga Park, Calif., 1961-70; chief research scientist Martek Instruments, Newport Beach, 1970-73; scientist Boeing Satellite Systems, Torrance, 1973—. Developer nickel-hydrogen battery; patentee; contbr. sci. papers to profl. publs. in field. Served with USN, 1944-46. Recipient Lawrence A. Hyland Patent award Hughes Aircraft Co., 1987. Mem. Electrochem. Soc. (chmn. So. Calif./Nev. sect. 1976-78), Am. Chem. Soc., Sigma Xi. Home: 18361 Van Ness Ave Torrance CA 90504-5309 Office: Boeing Satellite Systems B231/2019 PO Box 2999 Torrance CA 90509-2999 E-mail: howard.rogers@alum.mit.edu

ROGERS, JACK DAVID, plant pathologist, educator; b. Point Pleasant, W.Va., Sept. 3, 1937; s. Jack and Thelma Grace R.; m. Belle C. Spencer, June 7, 1958. BS in Biology, Davis and Elkins Coll., 1960; MF, Duke U., 1960; PhD, U. Wis., 1963. From asst. prof. to prof. Wash. State U., Pullman, 1963-72, chmn. dept. plant pathology, 1986-99. Contbr. articles to profl. jours. Recipient William H. Weston Teaching Excellence award Mycological Soc. Am., 1992. Mem. Mycological Soc. of Am. (pres., 1977-78), Am. Phytopathol. Soc., Botanical Soc. Am., British Mycological Soc.

ROGERS, JERRY L. federal agency administrator; b. Tex., Dec. 22, 1938; s. Ancell Robert and Grace Evalena (Coin) R.; m. Peggy Floretta Sifford, Apr. 6, 1963; children: Tiana Lynne Conklin, Elvin Houston, Jeffrey Martin. BA in History, Tex. Tech, 1962, MA, 1965. Historian Nat. Park Svc., Ft. Davis, Tex., 1965-66, historian Nat. Register Washington, 1967-69, chief registration, 1972-73, chief grants divsn., 1973-75, chief archeology and hist. preservation, 1975-79, assoc. dir. cultural programs, 1981-83, assoc. dir. cultural resources, 1983-94; regional dir. S.W. region, 1994-95; supt. S.W. office, 1995-99; dir. Ranching Heritage Ctr. Tex. Tech Mus., Lubbock, 1969-72; dep. assoc. dir. Heritage Conservation Svc., Washington, 1979-81; nat. conf. chairperson NPS, 1998—. Internat. cons. in hist. preservation to Italy, Russia, Spain, China, India, Egypt. Contbr. articles to prof. jours. Mem. adv. com. on cemeteries and memls. VA, Washington, 1987-94. Recipient Meritorious Svc. award Dept. Interior, 1992. Mem. AIA (mem. com. hist. resources, ex-officio mem. 1979-94), Nat. Trust Hist. Preservation (trustee 1981-94), Civil War Trust. N.Mex. Heritage Preservation Alliance (bd. dirs. 1996—), Coun. on Am.'s Mil. Past (bd. dirs. 1997—). Avocations: geneology, classic automobiles. Home: 29 Bosque Loop Santa Fe NM 87505-2231 Office: Nat Park Svc 1100 Old Santa Fe Trail PO Box 728 Santa Fe NM 87504-0728

ROGERS, JOE, lieutenant governor; m. Juanita Kay; children: Trent, Jordan, Haley. Degree in bus., Colo. State U.; JD, Ariz. State U. Past law clk. to Hon. Robert Broomfield U.S. Dist. Ct.; assoc. Davis, Graham & Stubbs, Colo., 1989-93; staff counsel to Sen. Hank Brown U.S. Congress, Washington, 1993-95; lt. gov. State of Colo., 1998—. Past atty. Lend-A-Lawyer Program, Colo. Mem. Denver Bar Assn. (bd. dirs. credit union 1990-93), Colo. Bar Assn., Sam Carey Bar Assn. Office: Lt Govs Office 136 State Capitol Denver CO 80203-1792

ROGERS, RONALD, public relations executive; Pres., CEO Rodgers & Assocs., L.A. Office: 1875 Century Park E Ste 300 Los Angeles CA 90067-2504

ROGERS, SAMUEL SHEPARD See SHEPARD, SAM

ROGERS, T. GARY, food products company executive; b. 1943; BSME, U. Calif., 1963; MBA, Harvard U., 1968. Assoc. McKinsey & Co., San Francisco; founder, pres. Vintage Ho. Restaurants, Calif. and Tex.; chmn. bd., CEO Dreyer's Grand Ice Cream, Inc., Oakland, Calif., 1977—. Dir. Levi Strauss & Co., Stanislaus Food Products, Gardenjiin Farms, The Friends of Calif. Crew. Mem. Bay Area Coun. Mem. Internat. Dairy Foods Assn. (bd. dirs.). Office: Dreyers Grand Ice Cream Inc 5929 College Ave Oakland CA 94618

ROGGER, HANS JACK, history educator; b. Herford, Germany, Sept. 9, 1923; s. Max and Berni (Heilbronn) R.; m. Claire Ryan, Jan. 2, 1955; 1 son, Alexander. B.A., Sarah Lawrence Coll., 1948; Ph.D., Harvard U., 1956. Asst. prof. Sarah Lawrence Coll., Bronxville, N.Y., 1953-58, asso. prof., 1958-61, UCLA, 1961-66, prof. history, 1966-92, chmn. dept., 1978-83, dir. Russian and East European Studies Center, 1962-66, prof. emeritus, 1992—. Fellow Russian Rsch. Ctr., Harvard U., 1962; sr. mem. St. Antony's Coll., Oxford U., 1972; vis. scholar George Kennan Ctr. Advanced Russian Studies, 1975, mem. acad. coun., 1984-88; sr. assoc. fellow Oxford Ctr. Postgrad. Hebrew Studies, 1984—; co-dir. Rand/UCLA Ctr. Soviet Studies, 1989-93. Author: (with E. Weber) The European Right, 1965, 66, 74, (with H. Hyman) Heard Round the World, 1969, National Consciousness in 18th Century Russia, 1960, 70, Russia in Modernization and Revolution, 1881-1917, 1983, Jewish Policies and Right-Wing Politics in Imperial Russia, 1985; contbr. chpts. to book: Shared Destiny: Fifty Years of Soviet-American Relations, 1985, Pogroms: Anti-Jewish Violence in Modern Russia History, 1991, Hostages of Modernization, 1993, Guerre et Culture, 1994; mem. editl. bd.: Am. Hist. Rev., 1982-85, Slavic Rev., 1985-91, Contention, 1992-96, also assoc. editor, 1993-96. Served with USN, 1943-46. Recipient Guggenheim fellowship, 1964-65; Am. Council Learned Socs. fellow, 1962; Nat. Endowment Humanities fellow, 1975-76 Mem. AAUP, Am. Assn. Advancement Slavic Studies (bd. dirs. 1982-85), Am. Hist. Assn. Office: UCLA Dept History Los Angeles CA 90024

ROHDE, JAMES VINCENT, software systems company executive; b. O'Neill, Nebr., Jan. 25, 1939; s. Ambrose Vincent and Loretta Cecilia R.; m. Tatiana Rohde; children: Maria, Sonja, Daniele, Olga. B of Comml. Sci., Seattle U., 1962. Chmn. bd. dirs., pres. Applied Telephone Tech., Oakland, Calif., 1974; v.p. sales and mktg. Automation Electronics Corp., Oakland, 1975-82; pres., CEO, founder Am. Telecorp, Inc., Redwood City, Calif., 1982-99; founder, vice-chmn., bd. dirs. Ceon Corp., Redwood City, 1999—. Chmn. exec. com., chmn. emeritus Pres.'s Coun. Heritage Coll., Toppenish, Wash., 1985—; chmn. bd. dirs. Calif. chpt. Coun. of Growing Cos., 1990-93. Bd. dirs. Ind. Colls. No. Calif., 1991-93. Named U.S. Dept. Commerce Export Exec. Yr. No. Calif., 1993. Mem. Am. Electronics Assn. (bd. dirs. 1992-94, vice-chmn. No. Calif. coun. 1992-93, chmn. 1993-94). Republican. Roman Catholic. Office: Ceon Corp 720 Bay Rd Redwood City CA 94063-2469 E-mail: jrohde@ceon.com

ROHLFING, FREDERICK WILLIAM, lawyer, political consultant, retired judge; b. Honolulu, Nov. 2, 1928; s. Romayne Raymond and Kathryn (Coe) R.; m. Joan Halford, July 15, 1952 (div. Sept. 1982); children: Frederick W., Karl A., Brad (dec.); m. Patricia Ann Santos, Aug. 23, 1983. BA, Yale U., 1950; JD, George Washington U., 1955. Bar: Hawaii 1955, Am. Samoa 1978. Assoc. Moore, Torkildson & Rice, Honolulu, 1955-60; ptnr. Rohlfing, Nakamura & Low, Honolulu, 1963-68, Hughes, Steiner & Rohlfing, Honolulu, 1968-71, Rohlfing, Smith & Coates, Honolulu, 1981-84; sole practice Honolulu, 1960-63, 71-81, Maui County, 1988—; dep. corp. counsel County of Maui, Wailuku, Hawaii, 1984-87, corp. counsel, 1987-88; land and legal counsel Maui Open Space Trust, 1992-97, also bd. dirs. Polit. cons., 1996, 98; magistrate judge U.S. Dist. Ct. Hawaii, 1991-96. Active Hawaii Ho. Reps., 1959-65, 80-84, Hawaii State Senate, 1966-75; U.S. alt. rep. So. Pacific Commn., Noumea, New Caledonia, 1975-77, 1982-84; Maui adv. coun. State Reappointment Commn., 2001; hon. chmn. Maui coms. George W. Bush for Pres. Capt. USNR, 1951-87. Mem. Hawaii Bar Assn., Maui Country Club, Naval Intelligence Profls. Avocations: ocean swimming, golf. Home and Office: RR 1 Box 398 Kekaulike Ave Kula HI 96790

ROHRABACHER, DANA, congressman; b. Coronado, Calif., June 21, 1947; s. Donald and Doris Rohrabacher; m. Rhonda Carmont, Aug. 1997. Student, L.A. Harbor Coll., 1965-67; BA in History, Long Beach State Coll., 1969; MA in Am. Studies, U. So. Calif., 1976. Reporter City News Svc./Radio West, L.A.; editorial writer Orange County Register, 1979-80; asst. press. sec. Reagan for Pres. Campaign, 1976, 80; speechwriter, spl. asst. to Pres. Reagan White House, Washington, 1981-88; mem. 101st-102nd Congresses from Calif. dist., 1989-93, 103d-106th Congress from 45th dist. Calif., 1993—. U.S. del. Young Polit. Leaders Conf., USSR; disting. lectr. Internat. Terrorism Conf., Paris, 1985; mem. Internat. Rels. com.; chmn. sci. subcom. on space and aeroratics. Recipient Disting. Alumnus award L.A. Harbor Coll., 1987. Avocations: surfing, white water rafting. Office: US Ho Reps 2338 Rayburn HOB Washington DC 20515

ROHWER, WILLIAM D., JR. university dean; b. Denver, Oct. 2, 1937; AB, Harvard U., 1959; PhD, U. Calif., Berkeley, 1964. Asst. prof. education U. Calif., Berkeley, 1964-68, assoc. prof., 1968-70, prof., 1970-95, acting assoc. dean grad. div., 1969-70, assoc. dean, 1970, acting dir. Inst. Human Learning, 1971, chmn. div. ednl. psychology, vice-chmn. dept. edn., 1982, assoc. dean edn., 1983-86, acting dean, 1989-90, dean, 1990-95, prof. emeritus, dean emeritus, 1996—; acting dir. Inst. Human Devel., Berkeley, 1996-98. Vis. lectr. psychology U. Wis., Madison, 1967; rsch. psychologist U.S. Naval Pers. Rsch. Activity, San Diego, 1964. Contbr. articles to profl. jours.; ad hoc reviewer Child Develop., Devel. Psychology, Jour. Ednl. Psychology, Jour. Exptl. Child Psychology, Psychol. Rev., Sci. Recipient Palmer O. Johnson Meml. award Am. Ednl. Rsch. Assn., 1972; fellow Van Leer Jerusalem Found., 1974-75, Ctr. Advanced Study Behavioral Scis. Stanford U., 1979-80; scientific adviser Bernard Van Leer Found., 1974-75; grantee U.S. Office Edn., OEO, NSF, Nat. Inst. Child Health and Human Devel. E-mail: wdr@socrates.berkeley.edu

ROITBERG, BERNARD DAVID, biology educator; b. Windsor, Ont., Can., June 24, 1953; s. Harry and Jeanette Roitberg; m. Carol Ann Hubbard, July 8, 1977; 1 child, Gabriela. BS, Simon Fraser U., 1975; MS, U. B.C., 1977; PhD, U. Mass., 1982. Rsch. assoc. U. Mass., Amherst, 1982; from asst. prof. to assoc. prof. Simon Fraser U., Burnaby, Can., 1982-93, prof. Can., 1993—. Guest prof. German Rsch. Coun., U. Kiel, 1993, U. Tel Aviv, 1995; mem. grant panel NSERC, 1996—, chair panel, 1999. Editor: Chemical Ecology of Insects, 1992; assoc. editor jours. Can. Entomologist, 1989-93, Am. Naturalist, 1996—. Mem. Entomol. Soc. Can. (dir. 1989-91, C. Gordon Hewitt award 1990), Entomol. Soc. B.C. (pres. 1988), Brit. Ecol. Soc., Animal Behavior Soc. Achievements include demonstration of pheromone learning in insects, a new mimicry form, suicide in insects, new theory for mosquito feeding; development and confirmation of new theory on life expectancy and reproduction. Office: Simon Fraser U Dept Bioscis Burnaby BC Canada V5A 1S6

ROLL, JOHN MCCARTHY, judge; b. Pitts., Feb. 8, 1947; s. Paul Herbert and Esther Marie (McCarthy) R.; m. Maureen O'Connor, Jan. 24, 1970; children: Robert McCarthy, Patrick Michael, Christopher John. BA, U. Ariz., 1969, JD, 1972; LLM, U. Va., 1990. Bar: Ariz. 1972, U.S. Dist. Ct. Ariz. 1974, U.S. Ct. Appeals (9th cir.) 1980, U.S. Supreme Ct. 1977. Asst. pros. atty. City of Tucson, 1973; dep. county atty. Pima County (Ariz.), 1973-80; asst. U.S. Atty. U.S. Attys. Office, Tucson, 1980-87; judge Ariz. Ct. Appeals, 1987-91, U.S. Dist. Ct. Ariz., 1991—. Mem. criminal justice mental health standards project ABA, 1980-83, mem. com. model jury instrns. 9th circuit, 1994—, chair, 1998—, mem. panel workshop criminal law CEELI program, Moscow, 1997; mem. U.S. Jud. Conf. Adv. Com. Criminal Rules, 1997—. Contbr. Merit Selection: the Arizona Experience, Ariz. State Law Jour., 1991, The Rules Have Changed: Amendments ot the Rules of Civil procedure, Defense Law Jour., 1994, Ninth Cir. Judges' Benchbook on Pretrial Proceedings, 1998, 2000. Coach Frontier Baseball Little League, Tucson, 1979-84; mem. parish coun. Sts. Peter and Paul Roman Cath. Ch., Tucson, 1983-91, chmn., 1986-91; mem. Roman Cath. Dioceses Tucson Sch. Bd., 1986-90. Recipient Disting. Faculty award Nat. Coll. Dist. Attys., U. Houston, 1979, Outstanding Alumnus award U. Ariz. Coll. Law, 1992. Mem. Fed. Judges Assn., KC (adv. coun. 1991). Republican. Office: US Dist Ct 405 W Congress Tucson AZ 85701

ROLLANS, JAMES O. service company executive; b. Glendale, Calif., July 7, 1942; s. Henry Leo and Geraldine Ada (Berg) R.; children: Jodie Helene, Thomas James, Daniel Joseph. BS, Calif. State U., Northridge, 1967. Vice pres., dir. Chase Manhattan Bank, 1976-78; v.p. corp. communications Dart Industries, Los Angeles, 1978-80; v.p. bus. analysis and investor relations Dart & Kraft, Chgo., 1980-82; sr. v.p., CFO Fluor Corp., Irvine, Calif., 1982-99, also bd. dirs., 1998—; pres., group exec. Bus. Svcs., Aliso Viejo, 1999. Bd. dirs. Cupertino Elec.; mem. Flowserve Corp. Bd. dirs. Irvine Med. Ctr. Episcopalian. Avocations: boating; skiing; fishing; hunting. Office: Fluor Corp One Enterprise Dr Aliso Viejo CA 92656

ROLLE, ANDREW F. historian, writer; b. Providence, Apr. 12, 1922; m. Frances Squires, Dec. 1945 (div.); children: John Warren, Alexander Frederick, Julia Elisabeth.; m. Myra Moss, Nov. 1983. BA, Occidental Coll., 1943; MA, UCLA, 1949, PhD, 1953; grad., So. Calif. Psychoanalytic Inst., 1976. Am. vice consul, Genoa, Italy, 1945-48; editorial asso. Pacific Hist. Rev., 1952-53; from asst. prof. to Cleland prof. history Occidental Coll., 1953-88; rsch. scholar Huntington Libr., San Marino, Calif., 1988—. Author: Riviera Path, 1946, An American in California, 1956, reprinted, 1982, The Road to Virginia City, 1960, reprinted, 1989, Lincoln: A Contemporary Portrait, 1961, (with Allan Nevins, Irving Stone) California: A History, 1963, rev. edits., 1963, 69, 78, 87, 98, Occidental College: The First Seventy-Five Years, 1963, The Lost Cause: Confederate Exiles in Mexico, 1965, 1992, The Golden State, 1967, rev. edit., 1978, 1989, 2000, California, A Student Guide, 1965, Los Angeles, A Student Guide, 1965; Editor: A Century of Dishonor (Helen Hunt Jackson), 1964, Life in California (Alfred Robinson), 1971, Voyage to California (Jour. of Lucy Herrick), 1998; The Immigrant Upraised, 1968, The American Italians: Their History and Culture, 1972, Gli Emigrati Vittoriosi, 1973; (with George Knoles others) Essays and Assays, 1973, (with others) Studies in Italian American Social History, 1975, (with others) Los Angeles: The Biography of a City, 1976, 2d edit., 1991, (with Allan Weinstein and others) Crisis in America, 1977, The Italian Americans: Troubled Roots, 1980, 2d edit. 1985, Los Angeles: From Pueblo to Tomorrow's City, 1981, 2nd edit., 1995, Occidental College: A Centennial History, 1986, John Charles Frémont: Character as Destiny, 1991, Henry Mayo Newhall and His Times, 1992, Westward the Immigrants, 1999. Served to 1st lt. M.I. AUS, 1943-45, 51-52. Decorated Cavaliere Ordine Merito Italy; recipient silver medal Italian Ministry Fgn. Affairs; Commonwealth award for non-fiction; Huntington Library-Rockefeller Found. fellow; resident scholar Rockefeller Found. Center, Bellagio, Italy Fellow Calif. Hist. Soc.; mem. Phi Beta Kappa. Office: Huntington Libr Rsch Div San Marino CA 91108

ROLLE, MYRA MOSS See MOSS, MYRA ELLEN

ROLLINS, ALDEN MILTON, documents librarian; b. Billerica, Mass., July 31, 1946; s. Alden Milton and Agnes Morgan (Simpson) R. BA, Am. U., 1968; MLS, U. R.I., 1973. Cert. geneal. record specialist, Bd. for Certification of Genealogists., Vt., N.H. Documents libr. U. Alaska Libr., Anchorage, 1973—. Author: The Fall of Rome: A Reference Guide, 1983, Rome in the Fourth Century A.D., 1991, Vermont Warnings Out, 1995. With U.S. Army, 1969-71. Mem. Nat. Geneal. Soc., Geneal. Soc. Vt., N.H. Geneal. Soc., New Eng. Hist. Geneal. Soc., N.H. Hist. Soc., Vt. Hist. Soc. (life), Piscataqua Pioneers (life). Avocation: genealogy. Home: 221 E 7th Ave Apt 114 Anchorage AK 99501-3639 Office: U Alaska Libr Govt Documents 3211 Providence Dr Anchorage AK 99508-4614

ROLLO, F. DAVID, hospital management company executive, health care educator; b. Endicott, N.Y., Apr. 15, 1939; s. Frank C. and Augustine L. (Dumont) R.; m. Linda Wood, June 1, 1991; children : Mindee, Alex. BA, Harpur Coll., 1959; MS, U. Miami, 1965; PhD, Johns Hopkins U., 1968; MD, Upstate Med. Ctr., Syracuse, N.Y., 1972. Diplomate Am. Bd. Nuclear Medicine. Asst. chief nuclear medicine services VA Hosp., San Francisco, 1974-77, chief nuclear medicine Nashville, 1977-79; sr. v.p. med. affairs Humana Inc., Louisville, 1980-92; dir. nuclear medicine div. Vanderbilt U. Med. Ctr., Nashville, 1977-81; prof. radiology Vanderbilt U., Nashville, 1979—; pres., CEO Metricor Inc., Louisville, 1992-95; sr. v.p. med. affairs HCIA, Louisville, 1995-96; sr. v.p. med. affairs, med. dir. Raytel Med. Corp., San Mateo, Calif., 1996-99; chief med. officer ADAC Labs., Milpitas, 1999—. Mem. med. adv. com. IBT, Washington, 1984—; mem. pvt. sector liaison panel Inst. of Medicine, Washington, 1983—; bd. dirs. ADAC Labs. Editor: Nuclear Medicine Physics, Instruments and Agents, 1977; co-editor: Physical Basis of Medical Imaging, 1980, Digital Radiology: Focus on Clinical Utility, 1982, Nuclear Medicine Resonance Imaging, 1983; mem. editorial adv. bd. ECRI, 1981—. Pres. bd. dirs. Youth Performing Arts Coun., Louisville, 1984-85; bd. dirs. Louisville-Jefferson County Youth Orch., 1983-85; sr. v.p., exec. com. USA Internat. Harp Competition, 1992-94, chmn., 1994—. Fellow Am. Coll. Cardiology, Am. Coll. Nuclear Physicians (profl. Am. Coll. Radiology com. 1982-84, chmn. 1984); mem. AMA, Soc. Nuclear Medicine (trustee 1979-83, 84—, Cassen Meml. lectr. western region 1980, 84), Radiol. Soc. N.Am., Am. Coll. Radiology, Ky. Sci. Tech. Coun. (exec. bd. 1987—), Advancement Med. Instrumentation (bd. dirs. 1986—), Louisville C. of C. (chmn. MIC com. 1987—). Avocations: racquetball, squash, golf. Home: 15735 Peach Hill Rd Saratoga CA 95070-6447 Office: 2755 Campus Dr San Mateo CA 94403-2513

ROLSTON, HOLMES, III, theologian, educator, philosopher; b. Staunton, Va., Nov. 19, 1932; s. Holmes and Mary Winifred (Long) R.; m. Jane Irving Wilson, June 1, 1956; children: Shonny Hunter, Giles Campbell. BS, Davidson Coll., 1953; BD, Union Theol. Sem., Richmond, Va., 1956; MA in Philosophy of Sci., U. Pitts., 1968; PhD in Theology, U. Edinburgh, Scotland, 1958. Ordained to ministry Presbyn. Ch. (USA), 1956. Asst. prof. philosophy Colo. State U., Ft. Collins, 1968-71, assoc. prof., 1971-76, prof., 1976—. Vis. scholar Ctr. Study of World Religions, Harvard U., 1974-75; official observer UNCED, Rio de Janiero, 1992. Author: Religious Inquiry: Participation and Detachment, 1985, Philosophy Gone Wild, 1986, Science and Religion: A Critical Survey, 1987, Environmental Ethics, 1988, Conserving Natural Value, 1994, Genes, Genesis and God, 1999; assoc. editor Environ. Ethics, 1979—; mem. editorial bd. Oxford Series in Environ. Philosophy and Pub. Policy, Zygon: Jour. of Religion and Sci.; contbr. chpts. to books, articles to profl. jours. Recipient Oliver P. Penock Disting. Svc. award Colo. State U., 1983, Coll. award for Excellence, 1991, Univ. Disting. Prof., 1992; Disting. Russell fellow Grad. Theol. Union, 1991, Disting. Lectr., Chinese Acad. of Social Scis., 1991, Disting. Lectr., Nobel Conf. XXVII, Gifford Lectr., U. Edinburgh, 1997; featured in Fifty Key Thinkers on the Environment, 2001. Mem. AAAS, Am. Acad. Religion, Soc. Bibl. Lit. (pres. Rocky Mountain-Gt. Plains region), Am. Philos. Assn., Internat. Soc. for Environ. Ethics (pres. 1989-94), Phi Beta Kappa. Avocation: bryology. Home: 1712 Concord Dr Fort Collins CO 80526-1602 Office: Colo State U Dept Philosophy Fort Collins CO 80523-0001

ROMAN, STAN G. lawyer; b. Athens, Ga., Dec. 31, 1954; s. Costic and Marilyn (Gracey) R.; m. Elizabeth Ann Whelan, Sept. 18, 1982; 3 children. BA, U. N.C., 1976; JD with honors, U. Tex., 1979. Bar: Calif. 1979, U.S. Dist. Ct. (no., so., ctrl. and ea.) Calif. 1979, , U.S. Ct. Appeals (9th cir.) 1979. Congl. intern Honorable John Buchanan, Washington, 1977; summer assoc. Bradley, Arant, Rose & White, Birmingham, Ala., 1978; assoc. Bronson, Bronson & McKinnon, San Francisco, 1979-85, ptnr., 1985-99, Krieg, Keller, Sloan, Reilley & Roman, San Francisco, 1999—. Judge pro tem, arbitrator, mediator Calif. Superior Ct., San Francisco, 1989—. Mem. ABA, Assn. Bus. Trial Lawyers, Def. Rsch. Inst., Calif. Bar Assn., San Francisco Bar Assn. San Francisco Com. Urban Affairs, Phi Beta Kappa, Phi Eta Sigma. Avocations: running, golf, skiing, swimming. Office: Krieg Keller Sloan Reilley & Roman LLP 114 Sansome St Fl 7 San Francisco CA 94104-3803 E-mail: sroman@kksrr.com

ROMANOW, ROY JOHN, provincial government official, barrister, solicitor; b. 1939; s. Michael and Tekla R.; m. Eleanore Boykowich, 1967. Arts and Laws degrees, U. Sask. Mem. Sask. Legislative Assembly, 1967-82, 1986—; provincial sec., 1971-72; atty. gen. of province, 1971-82; minister of intergovernmental affairs, 1979-82; leader, Sask. New Dem. Party, 1987—; leader of the opposition, 1987-91; leader of the majority, 1991-2000; premier, 1991-2001; mem. Commn. on Future of Health Care in Can., 2001—. Opposition house leader for New Dem. Party Caucus, 1986. Co-author: Canada Notwithstanding, 1984. Office: PO Box 160 Sta Main Saskatoon SK Canada S7K 3K4

ROMER, ROY R. former governor; b. Garden City, Kans., Oct. 31, 1928; s. Irving Rudolph and Margaret Elizabeth (Snyder) R.; m. Beatrice Miller, June 10, 1952; children: Paul, Mark, Mary, Christopher, Timothy, Thomas, Elizabeth B.S. in Agrl. Econs., Colo. State U., 1950; LL.B., U. Colo., 1952; postgrad., Yale U. Bar: Colo. 1952. Engaged in farming in Colo., 1942-52; ind. practice law Denver, 1955-66; mem. Colo. Ho. of Reps., 1958-62, Colo. Senate, 1962-66; owner, operator Arapahoe Aviation Co., Colo. Flying Acad., Geneva Basin Ski Area; engaged in home site devel.; owner chain farm implement and indsl. equipment stores Colo.; commr. agr. state of Colo., 1975, chief staff, exec. asst. to gov., 1975-77, 83-84, state treas., 1977-86, gov., 1987-98. Chmn. Gov. Colo. Blue Ribbon Panel, Gov. Colo. Small Bus. Council; mem. agrl. adv. com. Colo. Bd. Agr. Bd. editors Colo. U. Law Rev., 1960-62. Past trustee Iliff Sch. Theology, Denver; mem., past chmn. Nat. Edn. Goals Panel; co-chmn. Nat. Coun. on Standards and Testing; mem. adv. bd. Ad Coun.; former chair Dem. Nat. Com., now chair Dem. Nat. Conv. Com. With USAF, 1952-53. Mem. Dem. Gov.'s Assn. (chmn.), Nat. Gov.'s Assn. (former chmn.), Colo. Bar Assn., Order of the Coif. Democrat. Presbyterian. Office: PO Box 6949 Denver CO 80206-0949*

ROMERO, GLORIA, state senator; 1 child, Soledad. Degree, Barstow Cmty. Coll., Calif. State U., Long Beach; PhD in Psychology, U. Calif., Riverside. Prof. Calif. Coll. Sys., 1980-98; majority whip Calif. State Assembly, Sacramento, 1998—2001; mem. Calif. State Senate, 2001—. Com. mem. 1999-00; v.p. L.A. Cmty. Coll. Bd. Trustees, 1995-97; chair L.A. Elected Charter Reform Commn., 1997; rschr. in field of HIV/AIDS [illegible] Contbr. articles to profl. jours. Chair Hispanic Adv. Coun. to L.A. Police Commn.; co-founder Women's Adv. Coun. L.A. Police Commn.; mem. Domestic Violence Task Force, L.A. Recipient Comision Femenil Cmty. Svc. award, Cmty. Svc. award Mexican-Am. L.A. County Bar Assn., Latin Am. Advancement Edn. and Cmty. award Labor Coun., Cmty. Svc. award San Gabriel Valley League of United Latin-Am. Citizens, Incredible Women Making History award YWCA. Mem. ACLU, Nat. Orgn. Women, Nat. Women's Political Caucus, Nat. Latina Alliance, Calif. Faculty Assn./AFL-CIO, Sierra Club. Office: State Capital Room 4062 Sacramento CA 95814 also: 1000 San Gabriel Blvd Ste 201 Rosemead CA 91770 E-mail: gloria.romero@assembly.ca.gov

ROMERO, RICHARD M. state legislator, educator; b. Oakland, July 21, 1944; divorced. BS in Edn., U. Albuquerque, 1967; MA in Edn. Adminstrn., N.Mex. State U., 1971. Ednl. adminstr.; mem. N. Mex. Senate, Dist. 12, Santa Fe, 1992—; mem. rules com.; vice chair ways and means com. Mem. Metro bd. YMCA. With USAF, 1968-69. Democrat. Office: 907 Silver Ave SW Albuquerque NM 87102-3002

ROMESBURG, KERRY D. university president, former state education administrator; b. Akron, Ohio, Mar. 12, 1945; s. Bert Lewis and Edna (Bartlett) R.; m. Judy Kaye Land, July 2, 1965; children: Rod A., Donald A. BA, Ariz. State U., 1967, MA, 1968, PhD, 1972. Tchr. math. East H.S., Phoenix, 1969-70; asst. dir. instl. rsch. Ariz. State U., Tempe, 1972-73; planning analyst Ariz. Bd. Regents, Phoenix, 1973-74; exec. dir. Ariz. Commn. Post Secondary Edn., Phoenix, 1974-75, Alaska Commn. Postsecondary Edn., Juneau, 1975; pres. Utah Valley St. Coll., Orem, Utah, 1996—. Mem. Western Interstate Commn. on Higher Edn., Boulder, Colo., 1977—, chmn., 1981-82; mem. Western Tech. Manpower Coun., 1982—; mem. Nat. Adv. Coun. for United Student Aid Funds, N.Y.C., 1978—. Recipient Outstanding Alumnus award Ariz. State U., 1982; NDEA fellow, 1972. Mem. State Higher Edn. Exec. Officers, Nat. Adv. Coun. State Postsecondary Planning Commns., Am. Assn. Higher Edn., NEA. Office: Utah Valley State College 800 W University Pkwy Orem UT 84058-0001

ROMIG, ALTON DALE, JR. materials scientist, educator; b. Bethlehem, Pa., Oct. 6, 1953; s. Alton Dale and Christine (Groh) R.; m. Julie H. Romig. BS, Lehigh U., 1975, MS, 1977, PhD, 1979. Metallurgist, tech. staff Sandia Nat. Labs., Albuquerque, 1979-87, supr. phys. metallurgy, 1987-90, mgr. metallurgy, 1990-92, dir. materials and process scis., 1992-95; dir. Microelectronics and Photonics, 1995-98, Microsys. Sci., Tech. and Components, 1998-99; v.p. Sci. Tech. and Components, 1999—. Part time full prof. N.Mex. Inst. Mining and Tech., Socorro, 1981—; Acta/Scripta Metallurgica Lectr., 1993. Author: Principles of Analytical Electron Mecroscopy, 1986, Scanning Electron Microscopy, X-ray Microanalysis and Analytical Electron Microscopy, 1991, Scanning Electron Microscopy and Microanalysis, 1992; editor numerous procs. in phys. metallurgy and electron microscopy; contbr. over 160 articles to sci. jours. Fellow Am. Soc. Metals Internat. (trustee 1992-95, v.p. 1996-97, pres. 1997-98, Outstanding Rsch. award 1992); mem. TMS, Electron Microscopy Soc. Am. (Burton Outstanding Young Sci. medal 1988), Microbeam Analysis Soc. (pres. 1990, Heinrich award for Outstanding Young Sci. 1991), Materials Rsch. Soc., Sigma Xi, Tau Beta Pi. Home: 304 Big Horn Ridge Pl NE Albuquerque NM 87122-1446 Office: Sandia Nat Labs M/S 0513 Divsn 1000 Albuquerque NM 87185 E-mail: adromi@sandia.gov

RONDEAU, ANN E. career officer; b. San Antonio; Diploma in History, Eisenhower Coll., 1973; Grad., Officer Candidate Sch., 1974. Commd. 2d lt. USN, 1974, advanced through grades to rear adm.; various assignments to exec. officer Fast Sealift Squad. One, New Orleans, 1987-89; asst. for polit.-mil. analysis Chief of Naval Operation (CNO), 1989-90; various to mil. asst. to Prin. Deputy Under Sec. of Def. for Policy, 1995-96; assigned to Navy's Quadrenniel Def. Rev. Support Office, 1997—; dep. chief of staff Shore Base Mgmt. N46/U.S. Pacific Fleet. Decorated Def. Superior Svc. medal, Legion of Merit, Def. meritorious Svc. medal (2 times), Navy Meritorious Svc. medal (2 times), Navy Commendation medal (3 times); recipient Groben award for Leadership Eisenhower Coll.

RONEY, JOHN HARVEY, lawyer, consultant; b. L.A., June 12, 1932; s. Harvey and Mildred Puckett (Cargill) R.; m. Joan Ruth Allen, Dec. 27, 1954; children: Pam Roney Peterson, J. Harvey, Karen Louise Hanke, Cynthia Allen Harmon. Student, Pomona Coll., 1950-51; BA, Occidental Coll., 1954; LLB, UCLA, 1959. Bar: Calif. 1960, D.C. 1976. Assoc. O'Melveny & Myers, L.A., 1959-67, ptnr., 1967-94, of counsel, 1994—; gen. counsel Pa. Co., 1970-78, Baldwin United Corp., 1983-84; dir. Coldwell Banker & Co., 1969-81, Brentwood Savs. & Loan Assn., 1968-80. Spl. advisor Rehab. of Mut. Benefit Life Ins. Co., 1991-94; cons., advisor to Rehab. of Confederation Life Ins. Co., 1994-95; mem. policy adv. bd. Calif. Ins. Commn., 1991-95. Served to 1st lt. USMCR, 1954-56. Mem. ABA, Calif. Bar Assn. (ins. law com. 1991-95, chmn. 1993-94), L.A. County Bar Assn., D.C. Bar Assn., N.Y. Coun. Fgn. Rels., Pacific Coun. on Internat. Policy, Conf. Ins. Counsel, Calif. Club, Sky Club (N.Y.), Gainey Ranch Golf Club (Scottsdale), L.A. Country Club. Republican. Home: The Strand Hermosa Beach CA 90254 Office: 400 S Hope St Ste 1665 Los Angeles CA 90071-2801 E-mail: jroney@omm.com

RONEY, RAYMOND G. educator, publisher; b. Phila., July 26, 1941; s. Wallace and Rosezell (Harris) R.; m. Ruth Agnes Westgaph, May 2, 1970; 1 child, Andre. BA in Polit. Sci., Cen. State U., Wilberforce, Ohio, 1963; MLS, Pratt Inst., Bklyn., 1965. Head reference dept. Howard U., Washington, 1965-66; dir. libr. and info. svcs. Nat. League of Cities/U.S. Conf. Mayors, Washington, 1967-70; dir. libr. svcs. Washington Tech. Inst., 1970-78; deputy dir. learning resources U. D.C., 1978-84; dean instrnl. svcs. El Camino Coll., Torrance, Calif., 1984—; pub. Libr. Mosaics Mag., Culver City, 1989—. Pres. Yenor, Inc., Culver City, Calif., 1989—. Author: (books) Introduction to AV for Technical Assistants, 1981, AV Tech. Primer, 1988. Pres. Shepard Park Citizens Assn., Washington, 1973-83; chmn. Friends of Libr., L.A. Southwest Coll., 1993—. Recipient Adminstrv. Excellence award INTELECOM, Pasadena, Calif., 1993, Outstanding Adminstr. of Yr. award Calif. Assn. Postsecondary Adminstrs., 1997. Mem. ALA, Coun. on Libr. Media Technology (officer, bd. dirs., Outstanding Leadership award 1994), Calif. Acad. and Rsch. Librs. (program chmn.), Learning Resources Assn. of Calif. C.C. (bd. dirs.). Avocations: music, reading, travel. Office: El Camino Coll 16007 Crenshaw Blvd Torrance CA 90506-0001

ROOD, DAVID S. linguistics educator; b. Albany, N.Y., Sept. 14, 1940; s. J. Henry and Pearl B. (Stanley) R.; m. Juliette A. Victor; 1 child, Jennifer. AB, Cornell U., 1963; MA, U. Calif., Berkeley, 1965; PhD, U. Calif., 1969. Instr. U. Colo., Boulder, 1967-69, asst. prof., 1969-77, assoc. prof., 1977-82, prof., 1982—; vis. prof. U. Köln, Germany, 1998-99. Author: Wichita Grammar, 1975, Siouan Languages Archive, 1982; (with others) Beginning Lakhota, 1976; editor Internat. Jour. of Am. Linguistics, 1981-2001; contbr. numerous articles to profl. jours. NSF grantee, 1972-96, NEH grantee, 1972-96, Volkswagen Stiftung grantee, 2000—. Mem. Linguistic Soc. Am., Soc. for Study Indigenous Langs. Am., Soc. for Linguistic Anthropology, Tchrs. of English to Speakers Other Langs. Office: U Colo Dept Linguistics 295 UCB Boulder CO 80309-2747 E-mail: rood@colorado.edu

ROOKS, CHARLES S. foundation administrator; b. Whiteville, N.C., June 29, 1937; BA in English, Wake Forest Coll., 1959; Rockefeller Brothers fellow, Harvard U., 1959-60; MA in Polit. Sci., Duke U., 1964, PhD in Polit. Sci., 1968. Rsch. assoc. Voter Edn. Project, Atlanta, 1969-70, dir. tech. assistance programs, 1970-71, dep. dir., 1971-72; exec. dir. Southeastern Coun. of Founds., Atlanta, 1972-78; dir. mem. svcs. Coun. on Founds., Washington, 1979-80, v.p., 1981-82, acting CEO, 1981-82; exec. dir. Meyer Meml. Trust, Portland, Oreg., 1982—. Instr. polit. sci. Duke U., Durham, N.C., 1963, 65-67; asst. prof. of govt. Lake Forest Coll., Ill., 1967-69; asst. prof. polit. sci. Clark Coll., Atlanta, 1969-71; bd. dirs. Pacific Northwest Grantmakers Forum, Forum of Regional Assns. of Grantmakers; mem. adv. bd. Neighborhood Partnership Fund (Oreg. Cmty. Found.); mem. adv. bd. Giving in Oreg. Coun.; co-chair Northwest Giving Project. Contbr. articles to profl. jours. Home: 2706 SW English Ct Portland OR 97201-1622 Office: Meyer Memorial Trust 1515 SW 5th Ave Ste 500 Portland OR 97201-5450

ROOKS, JUDITH PENCE, midwifery, public health consultant; b. Spokane, Wash., Aug. 18, 1941; d. Lawrence Cyrus and Christine Atrice (Snow) Pence; m. Peter Geoffrey Bourne, Mar. 1972 (div.); m. Charles Stanley Rooks, Sept. 21, 1975; 1 child, Christopher Robert. BS, U. Wash., 1963; MS, Cath. U. Am., 1967; MPH, Johns Hopkins U., 1974. Cert. edpidemiologist, nursing, nurse-midwifery, mediation. Staff nurse The Clin. Ctr., NIH, Bethesda, Md., 1965; asst. prof. nursing dept. San Jose (Calif.) State Coll., 1967-69; epidemiologist Ctrs. for Disease Control, Atlanta, 1970-78; asst. prof. dept. ob-gyn. Oreg. Health Sci. U., Portland, 1978-79; expert Office of the Surgeon Gen., Dept. HHS, Washington, 1979-80; project officer U.S. AID, Washington, 1980-82; prin. investigator Sch. Pub. Health Columbia U., N.Y.C., 1988-89, assoc. Pacific Inst. for Women's Health, 1993-2001; cons. Portland, 1982—. Mem. tech. adv. com. Family Health Internat., Research Triangle Park, N.C., 1986-97; mem. midwifery adv. com. Frontier Nursing Svc., Hyden, Ky., 1997—; mem. com. Inst. of Medicine NAS, Washington, 1983-85; academic faculty cmty.-base nurse-midwifery edn. program Frontier Sch. Midwifery and Family Nursing, Hyden, Ky., 1993-95; dir. N.Y. Acad. Medicine/Maternity Ctr. Assn. evidence-based symposium on The Nature and Management of Labor Pain, 1999-01. Author: Midwifery and Childbirth in America, 1997; co-author: Nurse-Midwifery in America, 1986, Reproductive Risk in Maternity Care and Family Planning Services, 1992; mem. editl. bd. Birth, 1996—; editl. cons. Jour. Nurse Midwifery, 1992-2000; contbr. articles to profl. jours. Mem bd. advisors World Affairs Coun. Oreg., Portland, 1987-90; bd. dirs. Planned Parenthood of the Columbia/Willamette, Portland, 1987-90; chm. Ga. Citizens for Hosp. Abortion, Atlanta, 1969-70; assoc. Pacific Coun. on Internat. Policy, 1995-97. Recipient nat. award Nat. Perintal Assn., 1999. Mem. APHA (chair com. on women's rights 1982-83, mem. governing coun. 1976-77, 79-82, Martha May Eliot award for svc. to mothers and children 1993, Hattie Hemschemeyer award for cont. outstanding contbns. to nurse-midwifery and maternal and child health care 1998), Am. Coll. Nurse-Midwives (life, pres. 1983-85). Avocations: gardening, walking, reading, traveling, cooking. Home and Office: 2706 SW English Ct Portland OR 97201-1622 E-mail: jprooks1@home.com

ROOP, JOSEPH MCLEOD, economist; b. Montgomery, Ala., Sept. 29, 1941; s. Joseph Ezra and Mae Elizabeth (McLeod) R.; m. Betty Jane Reed, Sept. 4, 1965; 1 dau., Elizabeth Rachael. BS, Ctrl. Mo. State U., Warrensburg, 1963; PhD, Wash. State U., Pullman, 1973. Economist Econ. Rsch. Svc., U.S. Dept. Agr., Washington, 1975-79; sr. economist Evans Econs., Inc., Washington, 1979-81; staff scientist Battelle Pacific N.W. Nat. Lab., Richland, Wash., 1981—. Adj. prof. dept. econs. Wash. State U., 1999—; with Internat. Energy Agy., Paris, 1990-91. Contbr. tech. articles to profl. jours. Served with U.S. Army, 1966-68. Dept. Agr. Coop. State Rsch. Svc. rsch. grantee, 1971-73. Mem. Am. Econ. Assn., Econometric Soc., Internat. Assn. Energy Econs., Am. Statis. Assn. Home: 715 S Taft St Kennewick WA 99336-9587 Office: PO Box 999 MSIN K6-05 Richland WA 99352-0999 E-mail: joe.roop@pnl.gov, jroop715@worldnet.att.net

ROOS, ERIC EUGENE, plant physiologist; b. Charleroi, Pa., May 23, 1941; s. Carl F. and Isabelle (McPherson) R.; m. Lois Bonita Bruno, Aug. 24, 1964; children: Michael, Erin. BS, Waynesburg Coll., 1963; PhD, W.Va. U., 1967. Supr. plant physiologist, rsch. leader Nat. Seed Storage Lab, Agrl. Research Service of USDA, Ft. Collins, Colo., 1967—, now asst. area dir. Fellow Am. Soc. Agronomy, Am. Soc. Hort. Sci., Crop Sci. Soc. Am.; mem. Sigma Xi, Gamma Sigma Delta. Office: USDA Agrl Rsch Svc 1201 Oakridge Dr Ste 150 Fort Collins CO 80525-6266

ROOSEVELT, MICHAEL A. lawyer; b. L.A., Dec. 7, 1946; BA, Harvard U., 1969; JD, Columbia U., 1972. Bar: Calif. 1973. Shareholder Friedman, Olive, mcCabbin, Spalding, Bilter Roosevelt et al, San Franciso, 1996—. Mem. ABA. Office: Friedman McCubbin Spalding 425 California St Fl 22 San Francisco CA 94104-2102

ROOT, CHARLES JOSEPH, JR. finance executive, consultant; b. Pierre, S.D., July 26, 1940; s. Charles Joseph and Hazel Ann (Messenger) R.; 1 child from previous marriage, Roseann Marie; m. Sharon Lee, June 24, 1995; stepchildren: Nichole Marie Marcillac, Monique Marie Marcillac. Student, San Francisco Jr. Coll., 1963-65, La Salle Extension U., 1970-71, Coll. of Marin, 1971-72, Am. Coll. Life Underwriters, 1978-82. Registered investment advisor; charter fin. cons.; cert. fin. planner. Estate planner Bankers Life Co., San Francisco, 1966-78; fin. planner Planned Estates Assocs., Corte Madera, Calif., 1978-81; mng. dir. Double Eagle Fin. Corp., Santa Rosa, 1981—; investment advisor, 1983—; personal bus. mgr., 1987—. V.p. Big Bros. of Am., San Rafael, Calif., 1976-80; treas. com. to elect William Filante, San Rafael, 1978, Cmty. Health Ctrs. of Marin, Fairfax, Calif., 1982-83, Wellspring Found., Philo, Calif., 1981-85; treas., bd. dirs. Ctr. for Attitudinal Healing, Tiburon, Calif., 1989-92; bd. dirs. Pickle Family Circus, San Francisco, 1988, United Way Sonoma Lake, Mendocino Counties, 1993—; bd. dirs. Redwood Empire Estate Planning Coun., Santa Rosa, Calif., 1992—, v.p. programs, 1993, pres. 1995-96). Mem. Internat. Assn. Fin. Planners, Coll. Fin. Planning (cert. fin. planner 1988), Registry of fin. Planning, Nat. Assn. Life Underwriters, Marin County Assn. Life Underwriters (v.p. 1971-76, editor newsletter 1976-80), Rotary (Paul Harris Fellow 1980). Republican. Avocations: pilot, downhill skiing, scuba diving, golf. Office: Double Eagle Fin Corp PO Box 2790 Santa Rosa CA 95405-0790

ROOT, GEORGE L., JR. lawyer; b. 1947; BA, Syracuse U.; JD cum laude, U. San Diego. Ptnr. Foley & Lardner, San Diego. Guest lectr. Nat. U., San Diego, U. Calif., San Diego; adj. prof. San Diego State U. Mem. San Diego County Bar Assn. (chmn. mental health com. 1983, task force on children at risk 1995), Assn. Calif. Hosp. Dists. (legis. com. 1995), Calif. Soc. Healthcare Attys., Healthcare Fin. Mgmt. Assn., Nat. Health Lawyers Assn. Office: Foley & Lardner 402 W Broadway Fl 23 San Diego CA 92101-3542

ROOTMAN, JACK, ophthalmologist, surgeon, pathologist, oncologist, artist; b. Calgary, Alta., Can., June 22, 1944; s. Abraham S. and Lillian (Walman) R.; m. Jenny Puterman, June 20, 1965; children: Russel Mark, Kathryn Anne, Daniel Benson. MD, U. Alta., 1968. Res. ophthalmology U. Alta., Edmonton, 1973, clin. asst. prof. ophthalmology and pathology, 1973-75; from asst. prof. to assoc. prof. ophthalmology & pathology U. B.C., Vancouver, 1976-84, prof. ophthalmology & pathology, 1985—, chmn. ophthalmology, 1990—. Cons. pathologist Vancouver Gen. Hosp., 1989; pathology cons. Can. Reference Ctr. Cancer Pathology, Ottawa, Ont., 1989; chmn. ocular & orb tumor group B.C. Cancer Agy., 1980—. Author: Diseases of the Orbit: A Multidisciplinary Approach, 1988, Orbital Surgery: A Conceptual Approach, 1995; contbr. chpts. to books, numerous articles to profl. jours.; inventor Rootman Orbital Surgery Set, numerous orbital surgical procedures; reviewer Can. Jour. Ophthalmology, 1981—, Survey Ophthalmology, 1990—, Am. Jour. Ophthalmology, 1992, Brit. Jour. Ophthalmology, 1993, others in field; paintings exhibited in group shows Vancouver Gen. Hosp. Gallery, 1988, Zack Gallery, Vancouver, 1989, N.W. Watercolor Soc. Nat. Exhibition, 1994, Can. Fed. Artists, 1997-98, Western Fed. Watercolor Socs., 1998; one-man shows include Taylor Gallery, Mayne Island, B.C., 1989, U. B.C. Faculty Club, 1990, C.J. Herman Galleries, Vancouver, 1991, 92, 93, Greenhill Galleries, Adelaide,

Australia, 1997. Chmn. Vancouver Talmud Torah, 1982-84; bd. dirs. Contemporary Art Gallery, Vancouver, 1991; v.p. Emily Carr Found., Emily Carr Inst. Art and Design. Recipient 1st Prize (tied) Can. Fed. Artists 50th Anniversary Show, 1991; Can. Cancer Soc. fellow, 1974, Med. Rsch. Coun. fellow, 1977-78, E.A. Baker Found. fellow, 1978, 82, 91; Vancouver Found. grantee, 1978, B.C. Cancer Found. grantee, 1978, McLean Fund grantee, 1979, B.C. Health Care Rsch. Found. grantee 1979-81, 83-85, 87-89, 92, B.C. Med. Svcs. Found. grantee 1982-83, Med. Rsch. Coun. grantee, 1982-88, others. Fellow Royal College Surgeons; mem. Am. Bd. Ophthalmology (cert., diplomate), Royal Coll. Physicians and Surgeons (specialty com. ophthalmology, accrediation surveys), Am. Acad. of Ophthalmology, B.C. Med. Assn., Can. Ocular Pathology Study Group, Can. Oculoplastic Study Group, Can. Ophthalmol. Soc., Hogan Soc., Internat. Orbit Soc., N.Am. Skull Base Soc. (charter), Am. Assn. Ophthalmic Pathologists, others. Office: Univ BC Dept Ophthalmology 2550 Willow St Vancouver BC Canada V5Z 3N9

ROPER, WILLIAM ALFORD, JR. diversified technology services company executive; b. Birmingham, Ala., Mar. 14, 1946; BA in Math., U. Miss., 1968; grad. in banking, So. Meth. U., 1974; grad. fin. mgmt. program, Stanford U., 1986. Owner, gen. mgr. real estate devel. and wholesale distbn. cos.; loan officer, br. mgr. Deposit Guaranty Nt. Bank, until 1981; various positions, including corp. v.p., treas. Bell & Howell Co., 1981-87; exec. v.p., CFO, Intelogic Trace, Inc., 1987-90; sr. v.p., CFO, Sci. Applications Internat. Corp., San Diego, 1990-2000, corp. exec. v.p., 2000—. Mem. adv. bd. Allendale Mut. Ins. Co., Johnston, R.I.; mng. dir. Carlisle Enterprises, LLC, La Jolla, Calif.; bd. dirs. Cush Automotive Group, San Diego, Network Solutions, Inc., Herndon, Va., Holiday Bowl, San Diego. Chmn. bd. ACCION San Diego; bd. dirs. Alvarado Hosp. Med. Ctr., San Diego; vice chmn. bd. San Diego Conv. Ctr. Corp. Mem. CEO Roundtable, Greater San Diego C. of C. (bd. dirs., exec. com., chmn. fin. com.). Office: Sci Applications International 10260 Campus Point Dr San Diego CA 92121

ROSA, FREDRIC DAVID, construction company executive; b. Monroe, Wis., Oct. 31, 1946; s. Fredric Carl Rosa and Irene (Sommers) Rosa Figi; m. Melanie A. Downs, May 31, 1986; children: Mark, Katherine. BBA in Mktg., U. Wis., 1968. Dir. mktg. Swiss Colony Stores, Inc., Monroe, 1968-80; pres. Videotape Indsl. Prodns., Inc., Madison, Wis., 1980-82; agt. VR Bus. Brokers, Colorado Springs, Colo., 1982-83; sales rep. NCR Corp., Denver, 1983-85; prin. F. D. Rosa & Assocs., Denver, Aspen and Eagle, Colo., 1985-89; pres. Peak Benefit Cons., Colorado Springs, 1989-95; registered prin. Nexus Fin. Programs, Inc., Colorado Springs, Colo., 1990-92, Nutmeg Securities Ltd., Colorado Springs, 1992-94; sales staff Am. Airlines, Colorado Springs, Colo., 1993-95. Cons. Kolb-Lena Cheese Co., Lena, Ill., 1983-85; instr. The Am. Coll., Bryn Mawr, Pa., 1990-91, A.D. Banker & Co., Overland Park, Kans., 1995-97; owner Fred Rosa Constrn., Colorado Springs, 1990-94, Lakewood, Colo., 1995—. Contbr. articles to trade publs. and newspapers. Mem. Am. Soc. CLU and Chartered Fin. Cons., Mensa, Internat. Legion of Intelligence, Delta Sigma Pi (life). Methodist. Avocations: big game hunting, skiing, camping, travel. Home and Office: Fred Rosa Constrn 1270 Cody St Lakewood CO 80215-4897 E-mail: roosa1660@iwon.com

ROSA, RICHARD JOHN, mechanical engineer, educator; b. Detroit, Mar. 19, 1927; s. Richard Kellock and Beatrice (Boleau) R.; m. Jane Norton, Sept. 2, 1950 (div. 1970); children: Katrina, Richard Scott, Cynthia; m. Marion Hogarty, Sept. 16, 1978. BEP, Cornell U., 1953, PhD, 1956. Prin. research scientist AVCO Research Lab., Everett, Mass., 1956-75; prof. mech. engring. Mont. State U., Bozeman, 1975—. Cons. in field; vis. scholar U. Sydney, Australia, 1977; vis. prof. Tokyo Inst. Tech., 1981; U.S. coordinator U.S.-Japan Coop. Program in Magnetohydrodynamics, 1982-86. Author: MHD Energy Conversion, 1968, 2d edit., 1987; contbr. articles to profl jours.; patentee in field. Served to lt. (j.g.) USN, 1945-49. NSF grantee, 1982-87, Dept. Edn. grantee, 1988—. Mem. IEEE (sr.), AIAA (sr., com. mem.), ASME, AAAS. Avocations: skiing, sailing, hiking.

ROSALDO, RENATO IGNACIO, JR. cultural anthropology educator; b. Champaign, Ill., Apr. 15, 1941; s. Renato Ignacio and Mary Elizabeth (Potter) R.; m. Michelle Sharon Zimbalist, June 12, 1966 (dec. Oct. 1981); children: Samuel Mario, Manuel Zimbalist; m. Mary Louise Pratt, Nov. 26, 1983; 1 child, Olivia Emilia Rosaldo-Pratt. AB, Harvard U., 1963, PhD, 1971. Asst. prof. cultural anthropology Stanford (Calif.) U., 1970-76, assoc. prof., 1976-85, prof., 1985—, Mellon prof. interdisciplinary studies, 1987-90, dir. Ctr. for Chicano Rsch., 1985-90, chair anthropology, 1994-96, Lucie Stern prof. social scis., 1993—. Author: Ilongot Headhunting 1883-1974, 1980, Culture and Truth, 1989. Recipient Harry Benda prize Assn. for Asian Studies, 1983; Guggenheim fellow, 1993. Fellow Am. Acad. Arts and Scis. Avocations: poetry, swimming, drawing, dancing. Home: 2520 Cowper St Palo Alto CA 94301-4218 Office: Stanford U Dept Anthropology Palo Alto CA 94305-2145

ROSCH, JOHN THOMAS, lawyer; b. Council Bluffs, Iowa, Oct. 4, 1939; s. H.P. and Phebe Florence (Jamison) R.; m. Carolyn Lee, Aug. 18, 1961; children: Thomas Lee, Laura Lee. BA, Harvard U., 1961, LLB, 1965. Bar: Calif. 1966, U.S. Dist. Ct. (no. dist.) Calif. 1966, U.S. Dist. Ct. (ea. dist.) Calif. 1967, U.S. Ct. Appeals (9th cir.) 1966. Assoc. McCutchen, Doyle, Brown & Enersen, San Francisco, 1965-72, ptnr., 1972-73, 75-93; office mng. ptnr. Latham & Watkins, San Francisco, 1994—. Dir. Bur. Consumer Protection, FTC, Washington, 1973-75 Contbr. articles profl. jours. Fellow Am. Bar Found., Am. Coll. Trial Lawyers; mem. ABA (past chmn. antitrust sect.), State Bar Calif., San Francisco Bar Assn., Calif. State and Antitrust and Trade Regulation Sect. (past sect. chair). Republican. Episcopalian. Office: Latham & Watkins 505 Montgomery St Fl 19th San Francisco CA 94111-2552

ROSCOE, STANLEY NELSON, psychologist, aeronautical engineer; b. Eureka, Calif., Nov. 4, 1920; s. Stanley Boughton and Martha Emma (Beer) R.; m. Margaret Hazel Brookins, Dec. 21, 1948 (dec.); children: Lee Marin Roscoe Bragg, Jack; m. Elizabeth Frances Lage, Mar. 12, 1977 (dec.); 1 child, Catherine Marie; m. Gayle Buchanan Karshner, Mar. 15, 1990. AB in Speech and English, Humboldt State U., 1943; postgrad., U. Calif., Berkeley, 1942, 46; MA in Psychology, U. Ill., 1947, PhD in Psychology, 1950. Cert. psychologist, Calif. Research asst. U. Ill., Urbana-Champaign, 1946-50, research assoc., 1950-51, asst. prof., 1951-52; assoc. dir. Inst. Aviation, head aviation research lab., Champaign, 1969-75, prof. aviation psychology and astronautical engring., 1969-79, prof. emeritus, 1979—; prof. psychology N.Mex. State U., Las Cruces, 1979-86, prof. emeritus, 1986—; with Hughes Aircraft Co., Culver City, Calif., 1952-69, 75-77, dept. mgr., 1962-69, sr. scientist, 1975-77; tech. adviser, cons. in field. Pres. Illiana Aviation Scis. Ltd., Las Cruces, N.Mex., 1976—; v.p. Aero Innovation, Inc., Montreal. Author: Aviation Psychology, 1980, Flightdeck Performance: The Human Factor, 1990,, Heydays in Mattole, 1996, Predicting Human Performance, 1997, Keeping the Picture: The Measurement of Flow Control, 1999; editor: Aviation Research Monographs, 1971-72, Heydays in Humboldt, 1991, From Humboldt to Kodiak, 1992; assoc. cons. editor: Human Factors Jour., 1982—, Internat. Jour. Aviation Psychology, 1991—; contbr. more than 200 articles to profl. jours.; patentee, inventor in field. 1st lt. AC, U.S. Army, 1943-46. Fellow APA (divsn. of applied and engring. psychology, Franklin V. Taylor award 1976), Human Factors and Ergonomics Soc. (pres. 1960-61, Jerome H. Ely award 1968, 73, 89, 91, Alexander C. Williams award 1973, Paul M. Fitts award 1974, Pres.'s award 1990), Royal Aero Soc. (Eng.); mem. IEEE, AIAA, Inst. Navigation, Assn. Aviation Psychologists (ann. career award 1978), Aerospace Human Factors Assn. (Paul T. Hansen award 1994), Sigma Xi, Phi Kappa Phi, Phi Sigma, Chi Sigma Epsilon. Home: 2750 Sunnygrove Ave Mckinleyville CA 95519-7912 Office: PO Box 4498 Las Cruces NM 88003-4498 E-mail: roscoe@aero.ca

ROSE, DOYLE, broadcast executive; Pres. Radio emmis Comm., Encino, Calif., 1998—. Office: KPWR MS Broadcasting 15821 Ventura Blvd Ste 685 Encino CA 91436-4796

ROSE, MARGARETE ERIKA, pathologist; b. Esslingen, Germany, Feb. 12, 1945; came to U.S., 1967; d. Wilhelm Ernst and Lina (Schurr) Pfisterer; m. Arthur Caughey Rose, Feb. 3, 1967; children: Victoria Anne, Alexandra Julia, Frederica Isabella. MD, U. So. Calif., L.A., 1972. Diplomate Am. Bd. Anatomic and Clin. Pathology. Pathologist St. Joseph Med. Ctr., Burbank, Calif., 1977-78, Glenview Pathology Med. Group, Culver City, 1979—. Dir. anatomic pathology Glenview Meml. Pathology, Culver City, 1988—; dir. Life Chem. Lab., Woodland Hills, Calif.; co-dir., lab. Holy Cross Med. Ctr., Mission Hills, Calif., 1994-95; bd. dirs. Women in Recovery, Inc. Mem. Because I Love You, L.A., 1994. Fellow Am. Soc. Pathology, Coll. Am. Pathology. Avocations: cross-stitching, gardening, traveling. Office: Brotman Med Ctr Dept Pathology 3828 Hughes Ave Culver City CA 90232-2716

ROSE, MARK ALLEN, humanities educator, educator; b. N.Y.C., Aug. 4, 1939; s. Sydney Aaron and Rose (Shapiro) R.; m. Ann Bermingham; 1 son, Edward Gordon. AB summa cum laude, Princeton, 1961; LittB, Merton Coll., Oxford (Eng.) U., 1963; PhD, Harvard, 1967. From instr. to assoc. prof. English Yale U., 1967-74; prof. English U. Ill., Urbana, 1974-77; prof. U. Calif., Santa Barbara, 1977—, chmn. dept. English, 1987-89; dir. U. Calif. Humanities Rsch. Inst., 1989-94, chmn. dept. English, 1997—. Author: Heroic Love, 1968, (fiction) Golding's Tale, 1972, Shakespearean Design, 1972, Spenser's Art, 1975, Alien Encounters, 1981, Authors and Owners, 1993; editor: Twentieth Century Views of Science Fiction, 1976, Twentieth Century Interpretations of Antony and Cleopatra, 1977, (with Slusser and Guffey) Bridges to Science Fiction, 1980, Shakespeare's Early Tragedies, 1994, (CD-ROM) Norton Shakespeare Workshops. Woodrow Wilson fellow, 1961, Henry fellow, 1961-62, Dexter fellow, 1966, Morse fellow, 1970-71, NEH fellow, 1979-80, 90-91. Mem. MLA, Renaissance Soc. Am., Shakespeare Soc. Am., Phi Beta Kappa. Home: 1135 Oriole Rd Montecito CA 93108-2438 Office: English Dept U Calif Santa Barbara CA 93106

ROSE, PETER J. delivery service executive; V.p. air divsn. The Harper Group, San Francisco, 1969-81; exec. v.p. Expeditors Internat. Wash. Inc., Seattle, 1981-88, pres., CEO, 1988—, chmn., 1996—. Office: Expeditors Internat Wash Inc 1015 3rd Ave Seattle WA 98104

ROSE, ROBERT E(DGAR), state supreme court chief justice; b. Orange, N.J., Oct. 7, 1939; B.A., Juniata Coll., Huntingdon, Pa., 1961; LL.B., NYU, 1964. Bar: Nev. 1965. Dist. atty. Washoe County, 1971-75; lt. gov. State of Nev., 1975-79; judge Nev. Dist. Ct., 8th Jud. Dist., Las Vegas, 1986-88; justice Nev. Supreme Ct., Carson City, 1989—, chief justice, 1993-94, Carson City, 1999-2000. Office: Nev Supreme Ct Capitol Complex 201 S Carson St Carson City NV 89701-4702

ROSE, SCOTT A. lawyer; b. Flint, Mich., Feb. 10, 1953; BS with distinction, Ariz. State U., 1975, JD cum laude, 1979. Bar: Ariz. 1979. Chmn. bd. The Cavanagh Law Firm, Phoenix. Articles editor Ariz. State Law Jour., 1978-79. Ariz. Govt. Affairs chmn. Internat. Coun. Shopping Ctrs. Mem. ABA, State Bar Ariz., Maricopa County Bar Assn., Downtown Phoenix Rotary Club 100 (bd. dirs.). Office: The Cavanagh Law Firm 1850 N Central Ave Ste 2400 Phoenix AZ 85004

ROSEANNE, (ROSEANNE BARR), actress, comedienne, producer, writer; b. Salt Lake City, Nov. 3, 1952; d. Jerry and Helen Barr; m. Bill Pentland, 1974 (div. 1989); children: Jessica, Jennifer, Brandi, Buck, Jake; m. Tom Arnold, 1990 (div. 1994); m. Ben Thomas, 1994. Former window dresser, cocktail waitress; prin. Full Moon & High Tide Prodns., Inc. As comic, worked in bars, church coffeehouse, Denver; produced showcase for women performers Take Back the Mike, U. Boulder (Colo.); performer The Comedy Store, L.A.; showcased on TV special Funny, 1986, also The Tonight Show; featured in HBO-TV spl. On Location: The Roseanne Barr Show, 1987 (Am. comedy award Funniest Female Performer in TV spl., 1987, Ace award Funniest Female in Comedy, 1987, Ace award Best Comedy Spl. 1987); star of TV series Roseanne ABC, 1988-97 (U.S. Mag. 2nd Ann. Readers Poll Best Actress in Comedy Series, 1989, Golden Globe nomination Outstanding Lead Actress in Comedy Series 1988, Emmy award Outstanding Lead Actress in Comedy Series, 1993); actress: (motion pictures) She-Devil, 1989, Look Who's Talking Too (voice), 1990, Freddy's Dead, 1991, Even Cowgirls Get the Blues, 1994, Blue in the Face, 1995, Unzipped, 1995, Meet Wally Sparks, 1997; TV movies: Backfield in Motion, The Woman Who Loved Elvis, 1993; appeared in TV spl. Sinatra: 80 Years My Way, 1995; exec. prodr. Saturday Night Spl., Fox-TV; author: Roseanne: My Life as a Woman, 1989, My Lives, 1994; (host) Roseanne Show, 1998—, I am Your Child, 1997 (TV), Get Bruce, 1999. Active various child advocate orgns. Recipient Peabody award, People's Choice award (4), Golden Globe award (2), Am. Comedy award, Humanitas award, Nickelodeon Kids Choice award, 1990, Eleanor Roosevelt award for Outstanding Am. Women, Emmy award, 1993.

ROSELL, SHARON LYNN, physics and chemistry educator, researcher; b. Wichita, Kans., Jan. 6, 1948; d. John E. and Mildred C. (Binder) R. BA, Loretto Heights Coll., 1970; postgrad., Marshall U., 1973; MS in Edn., Ind. U., 1977; MS, U. Wash., 1988. Cert. profl. educator, Wash. Assoc. instr. Ind. U., Bloomington, 1973-74; instr. Pierce Coll. (name formerly Ft. Steilacoom (Wash.) Community Coll.), 1976-79, 82, Olympic Coll., Bremerton, Wash., 1977-78; instr. physics, math. and chemistry Tacoma (Wash.) Community Coll., 1979-89; instr. physics and chemistry Green River Community Coll., Auburn, Wash., 1983-86; researcher Nuclear Physics Lab., U. Wash., Seattle, 1986-88; asst. prof. physics Cen. Wash. U., Ellensburg, 1989—. Mem. faculty senate Ctrl. Washington U., 1992-98. Lector and dir. Rite of Christian Initiation of Adults, St. Andrew's Ch., Ellensburg, Wash., 1993—, mem. parish coun., 1995-2000. Mem. Am. Phys. Soc., Am. Assn. Physics Tchrs. (rep. com. on physics for 2-yr. colls. Wash. chpt. 1986-87, v.p. 1987-88, 94-95, pres. 1988-89, 95-96, past pres. 1996-97), Am. Chem. Soc., Internat. Union Pure and Applied Chemistry (affiliate), Pacific Northwest Assn. Coll. Physics (bd. dirs. 1997-99, 2001—), Soc. Physics Students (councilor zone 17 1998—). Democrat. Roman Catholic. Avocations: leading scripture discussion groups, reading, writing poetry, needlework. Home: 1100 N B St Apt 2 Ellensburg WA 98926-2570 Office: Cen Wash U Physics Dept Ellensburg WA 98926 E-mail: rosells@cwu.edu

ROSEN, CHARLES ABRAHAM, electrical engineer, consultant; b. Toronto, Ont., Can., Dec. 7, 1917; came to U.S., 1950; s. Morris and Ida (Muscet) R.; m. Blanche Jacobson, May 15, 1941; children: Hal, Steven, Naomi, Sema. BEE, Cooper Union, 1940; M in Engring., McGill U., 1950; PhD, Syracuse U., 1957. Founder, CEO Electrolabs Registered, Montreal, Can., 1946-50; semiconductor designer GE, Syracuse, N.Y., 1950-52, mgr. dielectrics group, 1952-57; mgr. applied physics SRI Internat., Menlo Park, Calif., 1957-62, dir. artificial intelligence, 1962-78; founder, chmn. Machine Intelligence Corp., Sunnyvale, 1980-85; co-founder, dir. Ridge Vineyards, Cupertino, 1962-87; CEO Cultured Foods Corp., San Francisco, 1988-92, also bd. dirs.; pvt. practice cons. Atherton, Calif., 1988—. Cons. Ricoh Rsch., Menlo Park, 1989—, Food Machinery, Sunnyvale, 1989—; adv. com. Nat. Rsch. Coun., Washington, 1990-92; dir. Techniquip Corp., Livermore, Calif., 1995—, Electric Mobility Sys., Los Altos, Calif., 1996-2000. Co-author Principles of Transistor Circuits, 1953, Solid State Dielectric Design, 1959; contbr. articles to profl. jours.; patentee in field. P.O. Air Force, Can., 1944-45. Recipient Engelberger award Robot Inst. Am., 1982. Fellow IEEE (Taylor award 1975), Am. Assn. Artificial Intelligence; mem. AAAS, Am. Physical Soc. Avocations: winemaking, horticulture, hydroponics, inventions. Home: 139 Tuscaloosa Ave Atherton CA 94027-4016 Office: Molecular Delivery Corprp Ste 415 6900 Koll Centery Pkwy Pleasanton CA 94566 E-mail: rosenca@attglobal.net

ROSEN, JUDAH BEN, computer scientist; b. Phila., May 5, 1922; s. Benjamin and Susan (Hurwich) R.; children— Susan Beth, Lynn Ruth. BSEE, Johns Hopkins U., 1943; PhD in Applied Math., Columbia U., 1952. Rsch. assoc. Princeton (N.J.) U., 1952-54; head applied math. dept. Shell Devel. Co., 1954-62; vis. prof. computer sci. dept. Stanford (Calif.) U., 1962-64; prof. dept. computer sci. and math. rsch. ctr. U. Wis., Madison, 1964-71; prof., head dept. computer sci. U. Minn., Mpls., 1971-92, fellow Supercomputer Inst., 1985—; sr. fellow Supercomputer Ctr., San Diego, 1993—; adj. rsch. prof. dept. computer sci. and engrin. U. Calif. San Diego, La Jolla, 1992—. Fulbright prof. Technion, Israel, 1968-69, Davis vis. prof. 1980; invited lectr. Chinese Acad. Sci., Peking, 1980, Guilin, 1996, Samos, Greece, 2000; lectr., cons. Argonne (Ill.) Nat. Lab.; mem. Nat. Computer Sci. Bd. Author: Topics in Parallel Computing, 1992; editor: Nonlinear Programming, 1970, Supercomputers and Large-Scale Optimization, 1988; assoc. editor Global Optimization, 1990—, Annals of Ops. Rsch., 1984—; contbr. articles to profl. jours. and procs. Grantee NSF, 1995—, ARPA/NIST, 1994-97. Mem. Assn. Computing Machinery, Soc. Indsl. and Applied Math., Math. Programming Soc. Achievements include research in supercomputers and parallel algorithms for optimization, computation of molecular structure and drug design by energy minimization and homology models, algorithms for structured approximation in signal processing. Home: 4771 Caminito Impersado San Diego CA 92130-2470 Office: U Calif San Diego Dept Computer Sci Engring 9500 Gilman Dr La Jolla CA 92093-0114 E-mail: jbrosen@cs.ucsd.edu

ROSEN, LOUIS, physicist; b. N.Y.C., June 10, 1918; s. Jacob and Rose (Lipionski) R.; m. Mary Terry, Sept. 4, 1941; 1 son, Terry Leon. BA, U. Ala., 1939, MS, 1941; PhD, Pa. State U., 1944; DSc (hon.), U. N.Mex., 1979, U. Colo., 1987. Instr. physics U. Ala., 1940-41, Pa. State U., 1943-44; mem. staff Los Alamos Sci. Lab., 1944-90, group leader nuclear plate lab., 1949-65, alt. div. leader exptl. physics div., 1962-65, dir. meson physics facility, 1965-85, div. leader medium energy physics div., 1965-86, sr. lab. fellow, 1985-90, sr. fellow emeritus, 1990—; Sesquicentennial hon. prof. U. Ala., 1981. Mem. panel on future of nuclear sci., chmn. subpanel on accelerators NRC of NAS, 1976, mem. panel on instnl. arrangements for orbiting space telescope, 1976; mem. U.S.A.-USSR Coordinating Com. on Fundamental Properties of Matter, 1971-90. Author papers in nuclear sci. and applications of particle accelerators.; bd. editors: Applications of Nuclear Physics; co-editor Climate Change and Energy Policy, 1992. Mem. Los Alamos Town Planning Bd., 1962-64; mem. Gov.'s Com. on Tech. Excellence in N.Mex.; mem. N.Mex. Cancer Control Bd., 1976-80, v.p., 1979-81; co-chmn. Los Alamos Vols. for Stevenson, 1956; Dem. candidate for county commr., 1962; bd. dirs. Los Alamos Med. Ctr., 1977-83, chmn., 1983; bd. govs. Tel Aviv U., 1986. Recipient E.O. Lawrence award AEC, 1963, Golden Plate award Am. Acad. Achievement, 1964, N.Mex. Disting. Pub. Svc. award, 1978; named Citizen of Yr., N.Mex. Realtors Assn., 1973; Guggenheim fellow, 1959-60; alumni fellow Pa. State U., 1978; Louis Rosen prize established in his honor by bd. dirs. Meson Facility Users Group, 1984; Louis Rosen Auditorium dedicated, 1995. Fellow AAAS (coun. 1989), Am. Phys. Soc. (coun. 1975-78, chmn. panel on pub. affairs 1980, div. nuclear physics 1985, mem. subcom. on internat. sci. affairs 1988). Home: 1170 41st St Los Alamos NM 87544-1913 Office: Los Alamos Sci Lab PO Box 1663 Los Alamos NM 87544-0600

ROSEN, MOISHE, religious organization founder; b. Kansas City, Mo., Apr. 12, 1932; s. Ben and Rose (Baker) R.; m. Ceil Starr, Aug. 18, 1950; children: Lyn Rosen Bond, Ruth. Diploma, Northeastern Bible Coll., 1957; DD, Western Conservative Bapt. Sem., 1986. Ordained to ministry Bapt. Ch., 1957. Missionary Am. Bd. Missions to the Jews, N.Y.C., 1956, minister in charge Beth Sar Shalom Los Angeles, 1957-67, dir. recruiting and tng. N.Y.C., 1967-70; leader Jews for Jesus Movement, San Francisco, 1970-73, exec. dir., 1973-96, founder, 1973—. Speaker in field. Author: Saying of Chairman Moishe, 1972, Jews for Jesus, 1974, Share the New Life with a Jew, 1976, Christ in the Passover, 1977, Y'shua, The Jewish Way to Say Jesus, 1982, Overture to Armageddon, 1991, The Universe is Broken: Who on Earth Can Fix It?, 1991, Demystifying Personal Evangelism, 1992, Witnessing to Jews, 1998. Trustee Western Conservative Bapt. Sem., Portland, Oreg., 1979-85, 86-91, Bibl. Internat. Coun. on Bibl. Inerrancy, Oakland, Calif., 1979-89; bd. dirs. Christian Advs. Serving Evangelism, 1987-91. Named Hero of the Faith, Conservative Bapt. Assn. Am., 1997. Office: Jews for Jesus 90 Miraloma Dr San Francisco CA 94127-1641 E-mail: MityMo@aol.com

ROSEN, PETER, health facility administrator, emergency physician, educator; b. Bklyn., Aug. 3, 1935; s. Isadore Theodore and Jessie Olga (Solomon) R.; m. Ann Helen Rosen, May 16, 1959; children: Henry, Monte, Curt, Ted. BA, U. Chgo., 1955; MD, Washington U., St. Louis, 1960. Diplomate Am. Bd. Surgery, Nat. Bd. Med. Examiners, Am. Bd. Emergency Medicine; cert. Advanced Cardiac Life Support Instr., Advanced Trauma Life Support Provider. Intern U. Chgo. Hosps. & Clinics, 1960-61; resident Highland County Hosp., Oakland, Calif., 1961-65; assoc. prof. divsn. emergency medicine U. Chgo. Hosps. & Clinics, 1971-73, prof. divsn. emergency medicine, 1973-77; dir. divsn. emergency medicine Denver City Health & Hosps., 1977-86, 87-89; asst. dir. dept. emergency medicine U. Calif., San Diego Med. Ctr., 1989—, dir. edn. dept. emergency medicine, 1989—, dir. emergency medicine residency program, 1991-2000, dir. emeritus, 2000—. Attending physician Hot Springs Meml. Hosp., Thermopolis, Wyo., Worland (Wyo.) County Hosp., Basin-Graybull Hosp., Basin, Wyo., 1968-71, U. Chgo. Hosps. & Clinics, 1971-77; dir. emergency medicine residency program, divsn. emergency medicine U. Chgo. Hosps. & Clinics, 1971-77; emergency medicine med. advisor State of Colo., 1977-85; dir. emergency medicine residency program Denver Gen. Hosp., St. Anthony Hosp. Systems, St. Joseph Hosp., 1977-88; clin. prof. divsn. emergency medicine Oreg. Health Scis. U., Portland, 1978-89; prof. sect. emergency medicine, dept. surgery U. Colo. Health Scis. Ctr., 1984-89; dep. mgr. med. affairs Denver Dept. Health & Hosps., 1986-87; med. dir. life flight air med. svc. U. Calif., San Diego Med. Ctr., 1989-91; mem. hosp. staff U. Calif., San Diego Med. Ctr., Tri-City Med. Ctr., Oceanside, Calif., 1989—; base hosp. physician, adj. prof. medicine & surgery U. Calif., San Diego Med. Ctr., 1989—; chair med. ethics com., mem. ethics consult team U. Calif., San Diego Med. Ctr., 1990—, mem. recruitment and admissions com., 1992—; lectr. in field; cons. in field. Author: (with others) Case Reports in Emergency Medicine: 1974-76, 1977, Encyclopedia Brittannica, 1978, 85, Principles and Practice of Emergency Medicine, 1978, 86, Protocols for Prehospital Emergency Care, 1980, 84, Cardiopulmonary Resuscitation, 1982, An Atlas of Emergency Medicine Procedures, 1984, Critical Decisions in Trauma, 1984, Emergency Pediatrics, 1984, 86, 90, Controversies in Trauma Management, 1985, Standardized Nursing Care Plans for Emergency Department, 1986, Emergency Medicine: Concepts and Clinical Practice, 1988, 92, The Clinical Practice of Emergency Medicine, 1991, Essentials of Emergency Medicine, 1991, Current Practice of Emergency Medicine, 1991, Care of the Surgical Patient, 1991, Diagnostic Radiology in Emergency Medicine,

1992, Pediatric Emergency Care Systems: Planning and Management, 1992, The Airway: Emergency Management, 1992; contbg. editor, editor abstracts sect. Jour. Am. Coll. Emergency Physicians, Annals of Emergency Medicine, 1976-83; mem. editorial bd. Topics in Emergency Medicine, 1979-82, ER Reports, 1981-83; consulting editor Emergindex Microindex, 1980—; editor in chief Jour. Emergency Medicine, 1983—; contbr. articles to profl. jours. Capt. USMC, 1965-68, lt. col. Res. inactive. Recipient AMA award, 1970, Am. Hosp. Assn. award, 1973. Fellow Am. Coll. Surgeons, Am. Burn Assn., Am. Coll. Emergency Physicians (chmn. edn. com. 1977-79, bd. dirs. Colo. chpt. 1977-80, pres. Colo. chpt. 1981-82, N.C. chpt. award 1976, Outstanding Contbns. and Leadership in Emergency Medicine award 1977, Silver Tongue Debater award 1980, John. D. Mills Outstanding Contbn. to Emergency Medicine award 1984); mem. Am. Trauma Soc. (founding), Soc. Acad. Emergency Medicine (Leadership award 1990), Alpha Omega Alpha Honor Med. Soc. (grad.), Coun. Emergency Medicine Dirs. Office: U Calif 200 W Arbor Dr San Diego CA 92103-1911

ROSEN, STEVEN O. lawyer; b. N.Y.C., Jan. 11, 1949; s. Albert I. and Yvette (Sterenbuch) R.; m. Martha M., July 10, 1983; 1 child, Melissa L. BS Aerospace Engring., SUNY, 1970; MS System and Control Engring., Case Western Reserve, 1975; JD, Lewis & Clark Coll., 1977. Bar: Ill. 1977, Oreg. 1978. Assoc. Lord, Bissell & Brook, Chgo., 1977-79, Miller, Nash, Wiener, Hager & Carlsen, Portland, Oreg., 1979-84, ptnr., 1984-97; pvt. practice Portland and Salem, 1997—. Disting. adj. prof. Lewis & Clark Law Sch., 1986. Mem. ABA (dir. divsns. sect. of litigation 1996-97, chair aviation litigation com. 1990-93), Oreg. State Bar Assn. (exec. com. aviation sect. 1984—, chair 1994-95). Avocation: skiing. Address: The Rosen Law Firm 620 SW Main St Ste 702 Portland OR 97205-3030 E-mail: rosen@rosenlawfirm.com

ROSENBAUM, LOIS OMENN, lawyer; b. Newark, Apr. 10, 1950; d. Edward and Ruth (Peretz) Omenn; m. Richard B. Rosenbaum, Apr. 4, 1971; children: Steven, Laura. AB, Wellesley Coll., 1971; JD, Stanford U., 1974. Bar: Calif. 1974, Oreg. 1977, D.C. 1974, U.S. Supreme Ct. 1990, Wash. 2001. Assoc. Fried, Frank, Harris, Shriver & Kampelman, Washington, 1974-75, Orrick, Herrington, Rowley & Sutcliffe, San Francisco, 1975-77, Stoel Rives LLP (formerly Stoel, Rives, Boley, Jones & Grey), Portland, Oreg., 1977-81, ptnr., 1981—. Mem. U.S. Dist. Ct. Mediation Panel. Bd. dirs. Providence Med. Found., 1990-95, Robison Jewish Home, 1994-97, Jewish Family & Child Svc., 1997-2000, Am. Jewish Commn., 2000—; past mem. Nat. Legal Com. Am. Jewish Com. Wellesley Coll. scholar, 1971. Mem. ABA, Multnomah County Bar Assn. (arbitration panel), Am. Arbitration Assn. (panel mem.), Multnomah Athletic Clubs, Wellesley Club (pres. 1987-88). Office: Stoel Rives LLP 900 SW 5th Ave Ste 2600 Portland OR 97204-1268

ROSENBERG, CLAUDE NEWMAN, JR. investment adviser; b. San Francisco, Apr. 10, 1928; s. Claude Newman and Elza (Wolff) R.; m. Louise Jankelson, Dec. 19, 1968; children: Linda Kay, Douglas Claude. BA, Stanford U., 1950, MBA, 1952. Research analyst J. Barth & Co., San Francisco, 1955-62, partner charge research, 1962-70; investment adviser, pres. Rosenberg Capital Mgmt., San Francisco, 1970-96. Lectr. and mem. adv. council Grad. Sch. Bus., Stanford; adv. bd. mem. Entrepreneur's Found., Hauser Ctr., Kennedy Sch. Govt., Harvard U.; founding chmn. The Philanthropic Rsch. Inst., 1997; founder, chmn. The Newtithing Group, 1997. Author: Stock Market Primer, 1962, rev., 1970, 76, 81, 87, The Common Sense Way to Stock Market Profit, 1968, rev., 1978, Psycho-Cybernetics and the Stock Market, 1970, Investing with the Best, 1986, rev., 1993, Wealthy and Wise, 1994. Bd. dirs. Jewish Welfare Fedn., Presbyn. Children's Cancer Research Center, Internat. Hospitality Center, Jewish Community Center; trustee San Francisco Ballet Assn., Univ. High Sch., San Francisco.; chmn. adv. council Stanford U. Sch. Bus.; chmn., founder Newtithing Group, 1997. Served with USNR, 1951-53. Recipient Arbuckle award Stanford U. Grad. Sch. Bus., 1984, Daniel I. Forrestal Leadership award Assn. of Investment and Mgmt. Rsch. 1992, Lilywhite award Employee Benefit Rsch. Inst., 1994, Bus. Statesman award Harvard Bus. Sch. Assn. of No. Calif., 1995, Lifetime Achievement award San Francisco C. of C., 1997, Fishes and Loaves Philanthropist award Cath. Charities, 1998. Mem. Fin. Analysts San Francisco, Alumni Assn. Stanford U. Grad. Sch. Bus. (pres.) Republican. Jewish religion. Clubs: Family (San Francisco), Concordia-Argonaut (San Francisco), Calif. Tennis (San Francisco), Family (San Francisco). Home: 2465 Pacific Ave San Francisco CA 94115-1237 Office: Four Embarcadero Center Fl 37 San Francisco CA 94111

ROSENBERG, HOWARD ANTHONY, journalist; b. Kansas City, Mo., June 10, 1942; s. Sherman Rosenberg and Claire (Kanchuk) Rosenberg Magady; m. Carol Finkel; 1 child, Kirsten. Journalist Los Angeles Times, TV critic, columnist, 1988—. Recipient Editorial award Los Angeles Times, 1981; Headliner award Atlantic City Press Club, 1984; Pulitzer prize Columbia U., 1985. Office: Los Angeles Times Times Mirror Sq Los Angeles CA 90053

ROSENBERG, PHILIP, production designer; Prodn. designer: (films) The Anderson Tapes, 1971, Child's Play, 1972, The Gambler, 1974, Network, 1976, Next Stop, Greenwich Village, 1976, The Sentinel, 1977, (with Tony Walton) The Wiz, 1978 (Academy award nomination best art direction 1978), (with Tony Walton) All the Jazz, 1979 (Academy award best art direction 1979), Eyewitness, 1981, Soup for One, 1982, Lovesick, 1983, Daniel, 1983, Garbo Talks, 1984, The Manhattan Project, 1986, Moonstruck, 1987, Running on Empty, 1988, The January Man, 1989, Family Business, 1989, Q & A, 1990, Other People's Money, 1992, A Stranger Among Us, 1993, Guilty as Sin, 1993, The Pelican Brief, 1993, Night Falls on Manhattan, 1995, Critical Care, 1996, A Perfect Murder, 1997, The Hurricane, 1998. Office: c/o ICM 8942 Wilshire Blvd Beverly Hills CA 90211-1934

ROSENBERG, RICHARD MORRIS, banker; b. Fall River, Mass., Apr. 21, 1930; s. Charles and Betty (Peck) R.; m. Barbara K. Cohen, Oct. 21, 1956; children: Michael, Peter. BS, Suffolk U., 1952; MBA, Golden Gate U., 1962; LLB, Golden Gate Coll., 1966. Publicity asst. Crocker-Anglo Bank, San Francisco, 1959-62; banking services officer Wells Fargo Bank, N.A., San Francisco, 1962-65, asst. v.p., 1965-68, v.p. mktg. dept., 1968, v.p., dir. mktg., 1969, sr. v.p. mktg. and advt. div., 1970-75, exec. v.p., from 1975, vice chmn., 1980-83, Crocker Nat. Corp., 1983-85; pres., chief operating officer Seafirst Corp., 1986-87, also dir.; pres., chief operating officer, also bd. dirs. Seattle First Nat. Bank, 1985-87; vice chmn. bd. BankAm. Corp., San Francisco, 1987-90, chmn., CEO, 1990-96. Bd. dirs. Airborne Express, Pacific Life, MiFund; past chmn. Mastercard Internat.; past. pres. Fed. Res. Adv. Coun. Bd. dirs. San Francisco Symphony, United Way; trustee Calif. Inst. Tech.; bd. dirs. Am. Ctr. for Wine, Food and the Arts. Jewish. Office: Bank of Am CA5-705-11-01 555 California St San Francisco CA 94104- E-mail: richard.rosenberg@bankofamerica.com

ROSENBERG, SAUL ALLEN, oncologist, educator; b. Cleve., Aug. 2, 1927; BS, Western Res. U., 1948, MD, 1953. Diplomate Am. Bd. Internal Medicine, Am. Bd. Oncology. Intern Univ. Hosp., Cleve., 1953-54; resident in internal medicine Peter Bent Brigham Hosp., Boston, 1954-61; research asst. toxicology AEC Med. Research Project, Western Res. U., 1948-53; asst. prof. medicine and radiology Stanford (Calif.) U., 1961-65, assoc. prof., 1965-79, chief div. oncology, 1965-93, prof., 1970-95; prof. [illegible] assoc. dean, 1989-92. Chmn. bd. No. Calif. Cancer Program, 1974-80. Contbr. articles to profl. jours. Served to lt. M.C. USNR, 1954-56. Master ACP; mem. Am. Assn. Cancer Research, Inst. Medicine Nat. Acad. Sci., Am. Fedn. Clin. Research, Am. Soc. Clin. Oncology (pres. 1982-83), Assn. Am. Physicians, Calif. Acad. Medicine, Radiation Research Soc., Western Soc. Clin. Research, Western Assn. Physicians. Office: Stanford U Sch Medicine Div Oncology 269 Campus Dr Stanford CA 94305

ROSENBLATT, GERD MATTHEW, chemist; b. Leipzig, Germany, July 6, 1933; came to U.S., 1935, naturalized, 1940; s. Edgar Fritz and Herta (Fisher) R.; m. Nancy Ann Kaltreider, June 29, 1957 (dec. Jan. 1982); children: Rachel, Paul; m. Susan Frances Barnett, Nov. 23, 1990. BA, Swarthmore Coll., 1955; PhD, Princeton U., 1960; Doctorate in Physics (hon.), Vrije U. Brussel, 1989. Chemist Lawrence Radiation Lab., U. Calif., 1960-63, cons., guest scientist, 1968-84; from asst. to assoc. prof. chemistry Pa. State U., University Park, 1963-70, prof., 1970-81; assoc. div. leader Los Alamos (N.Mex.) Nat. Lab., 1981-82, chemistry div. leader, 1982-85; dep. dir. Lawrence Berkeley (Calif.) Lab., 1985-89, sr. chemist, 1985—. Lectr. U. Calif., Berkeley, 1962-63; vis. prof. Vrije U. Brussels, 1973; vis. fellow Southampton U., 1980, King's Coll., Cambridge, 1980; adj. prof. chemistry U. N.Mex., 1981-85; cons. Aerospace Corp., 1979-85, Solar Energy Rsch. Inst., 1980-81, Xerox Corp., 1977-78, Hooker Chem. Co., 1976-78, Los Alamos Nat. Lab., 1978, 1996—; mem. external adv. com. Ctr. for Materials Sci., Los Alamos Nat. Lab. 1985-93; mem. rev. com. chemistry divsn., 1985; mem. rev. com. for chem. engring. divsn. Arbonne Univ. Assn., 1974-80, chmn., 1977-78; mem. rev. com. for chem. sci. Lawrence Berkeley Lab., 1984; chmn. rev. com. for chem. and materials sci. Lawrence Livermore Nat. Lab., 1984-91; mem. bd. advs. Combustion Rsch. Facility, Sandia Nat. Lab., 1985-89; mem. bd. advs. R&D divsn. Lockheed Missiles & Space Co., 1985-87; chmn. chemistry III panel Nat. Com., Com. on Date for Sci. and Tech., 1986-92, Internat. Union of Pure and Applied Chemistry, 1986-92; mem. basic scis. lab. program panel energy, 1985-89; sec. IUPAC Commn. on High Temperature and Solid State Chemistry, 1992-95, chmn., 1996-97. Editor: (jour.) Progress in Solid State Chemistry, 1977—; mem. editorial bd. High Temperature Sci., 1979—; contbr. articles to profl. jours. Du Pont grad. fellow, Princeton U., 1957-58; fellow Solvay Inst., 1973, U.K. Rsch. Coun., 1980. Fellow AAAS; mem. Am. Chem. Soc., Am. Phys. Soc., Electrochem. Soc., Nat. Rsch. Coun. (chmn. high temperature sci. and tech. com. 1977-79, 84-85, panel on exploration of materials sci. and tech. for nat. welfare 1986-88, sci. and tech. info. bd. 1990-91, chmn. numerical data adv. bd. 1986-90, solid state scis. com. 1988-91, chmn. western regional materials sci. and engring. meeting 1990, panel on long-term retention of selected sci. and tech. records of fed. govt. 1993). Achievements include first use of imaging detectors to obtain Raman compositional profiles and two-dimensional maps of chemical compositions, of rotational Raman scattering as a temperature and state-population probe in high temperature and combustion systems; elucidation of role of crystal defects and molecular structure in the evaporation of solid materials; first experimental determination of how molecular polarizability anisotrophies change with internuclear distance; estimation of thermodynamic properties and molecular structures for gaseous molecules. Home: 1177 Miller Ave Berkeley CA 94708-1754 Office: Lawrence Berkely Nat Lab Berkeley CA 94720-0001

ROSENBLATT, MURRAY, mathematics educator; b. N.Y.C., Sept. 7, 1926; s. Hyman and Esther R.; m. Adylin Lipson, 1949; children: Karin, Daniel B.S., CCNY, 1946; M.S., Cornell U., 1947, Ph.D. in Math., 1949. Asst. prof. statistics U. Chgo., 1950-55; assoc. prof. math. Ind. U., 1956-59; prof. probability and statistics Brown U., 1959-64; prof. math. U. Calif., San Diego, 1964—. Vis. fellow U. Stockholm, 1953; vis. asst. prof. Columbia U., 1955; guest scientist Brookhaven Nat. Lab., 1959; vis. fellow U. Coll., London, 1965-66, Imperial Coll. and Univ. Coll., London, 1972-73, Australian Nat. U., 1976, 79; overseas fellow Churchill Coll., Cambridge U., Eng., 1979; Wald lectr., 1970; vis. scholar Stanford U., 1982 Author: Statistical Analysis of Stationary Time Series, 1957, Random Processes, 1962, (2d edit), 1974, Markov Processes, Structure and Asymptotic Behavior, 1971, Studies in Probability Theory, 1978, Stationary Sequences and Random Fields, 1985, Stochastic Curve Estimation, 1991, Gaussian and Non-Gaussian Linear Time Series and Random Fields, 2000; mem. editl. bd. Jour. Theoretical Probability. Recipient Bronze medal U. Helsinki, 1978; Guggenheim fellow, 1965-66, 71-72 Fellow Inst. Math Statistics, AAAS; mem. Internat. Statis. Inst., Nat. Acad. Scis. Office: U Calif Dept Math La Jolla CA 92093 also: PO Box 2066 La Jolla CA 92038-2066 E-mail: mrosenblatt@ucsd.edu

ROSENBLATT, PAUL GERHARDT, judge; b. 1928; AB, U. Ariz., 1958, JD, 1963. Asst. atty. gen. State of Ariz., 1963-66; adminstrv. asst. to U.S. Rep., 1967-72; soel practice Prescott, Ariz., 1971-73; judge Yavapai County Superior Ct., Prescott, 1973-84, U.S. Dist. Ct. Ariz., Phoenix, 1984—. Office: US Dist Ct 230 N 1st Ave Phoenix AZ 85025-0230 also: 401 W Washington St Phoenix AZ 85003-2117

ROSENBLATT, ROGER ALAN, physician, educator; b. Denver, Aug. 8, 1945; s. Alfred Dreyfus and Judith Ann (Ginsburg) R.; m. Fernne Schnitzer, Sept. 23, 1942; children: Eli Samuel, Benjamin. BA magna cum laude, Harvard U., 1967, MD cum laude, M in Pub. Health, 1971. Diplomate Am. Bd. Family Practice, Nat. Bd. Med. Examiners. Intern internal medicine U. Wash., Seattle, 1971-72, resident in family medicine, 1974; regional med. cons. region X Pub. Health Service, Seattle, 1974-76, dir. Nat. Health Services Corps., 1976-77; asst. prof. dept. family medicine U. Wash., Seattle, 1977-81, assoc. prof. dept. family medicine, 1981-85, prof., vice chmn. dept. family medicine, 1985—. Cons. U.S. Agy. for Internat. Devel., 1978, Western Interstate Commn. Higher Edn., 1981-82; vis. prof. medicine U. Auckland, New Zealand, 1983-84, Royal Australia Coll. Gen. Practitioners, Victoria, 1984, U. Calgary, 1988, U. Mo., 1988; vis. prof., Fogarty Ctr. Sr. Internat. fellow dept. ob-gyn. NIH, Coll. Medicine, U. Wales, Cardiff, 1992-93. Author: Rural Health Care, 1982; contbr. numerous articles on healthcare to profl. jours. Mem. Beyond War, Physicians for Social Responsiblity. Served with USPHS, 1974-77. Recipient Hanes Rsch. award North Am. Primary Care Rsch. Group, 1996. Mem. Am. Acad. Family Physicians (Hanes Rsch. award 1996), Am. Pub. Health Assn., Soc. Tchrs. Family Medicine (Hanes Rsch. award 1996), Nat. Rural Health Assn., Nat. Council Internat. Health, Nat. Acad. Sci. (elected inst. medicine 1987), Am. Rural Health Assn. (Research award 1985), Phi Beta Kappa. Office: U Wash Dept Family Medicine PO Box 354696 Seattle WA 98195-4696

ROSENBLUTH, MARSHALL NICHOLAS, physicist, educator; b. Albany, N.Y., Feb. 5, 1927; s. Robert and Margaret (Sondhein) R.; m. Sara Unger, Feb. 6, 1979; children by previous marriage— Alan Edward, Robin Ann, Mary Louise, Jean Pamela. BA, Harvard, 1945; MS, U. Chgo., 1947, PhD, 1949. Inst. Stanford U., 1949-50; staff mem. Los Alamos Sci. Lab., 1950-56; sr. research adviser Gen. Atomic Corp., San Diego, 1956-67; prof. U. Calif., San Diego, 1960-67, Inst. for Advanced Study, Princeton U., N.J., 1967-80; dir. Inst. for Fusion Studies, U. Tex., 1980-87; prof. U. Calif., San Diego, 1987-92, chief U.S. scientist Internat. Thermonuclear Engring. Reactor, 1992—. Lectr. with rank prof. in astrophys. scis. Princeton U.; also vis. sr. research physicist Princeton U. (Plasma Physics Lab.), 1967-80; Andrew D. White vis. prof. Cornell U., 1976; cons. AEC, NASA, Inst. Def. Analysis. Served with USNR, 1944-46. Recipient E.O. Lawrence award, 1964, Albert Einstein award, 1967, Maxwell prize, 1976, Enrico Fermi award Dept. Energy, 1985, Nat. Medal of Sci., Pres. of the [illegible] humanitarian svc. 2000), Nat. Acad. Sci., Am. Acad. Arts and Scis. Home: 2311 Via Siena La Jolla CA 92037-3933 Office: U Calif San Diego Dept Physics 9500 Gilman Dr La Jolla CA 92093-0319

ROSENDIN, RAYMOND JOSEPH, electrical contracting company executive; b. San Jose, Calif., Feb. 14, 1929; s. Moses Louis and Bertha C. (Pinedo) R.; m. Jeanette Marie Bucher, June 30, 1951 (dec. Feb. 1967); children: Mark R., Patricia A., Debra M., Cynthia C., David R.; m. Nancy Ann Burke, July 6, 1984; children: Raymond M., Callie R., Blake W. Student engring., San Jose State U., 1947-48; B.S.E.E., Heald's Engring. Coll., San Francisco, 1950. V.p., CEO Rosendin Electric, Inc., San Jose, Calif., 1953-59, exec. v.p., CEO, 1969-75, pres., CEO, 1975-94, chmn., CEO, 1995-2000, chmn., 2000—, former dir. Former dir. Community Bank, San Jose Bd. fellows U. Santa Clara, Calif., 1966-93, pres. bd., 1969-72, bd. regents, 1972-82; bd. dirs. United Way, Santa Clara, 1970-74; O'Connor's Hosp., San Jose, 1979-85, Community Hosp., Los Gatos, Calif., 1968-74. Recipient Man of Yr. award Santa Clara Valley Youth Village, 1963, Optimist of Yr. award Optimist Club, San Jose, 1970 Mem. C. of C. Greater San Jose (past dir.), Nat. Elec. Contractors Assn. (past pres., gov., dir.) Republican. Roman Catholic. Club: St. Claire (San Jose) Avocation: boating. Office: Rosendin Electric Inc 880 Mabury Rd San Jose CA 95133-1021

ROSENFELD, ARTHUR H. physics educator, research director; b. Birmingham, Ala., June 22, 1926; BS in Physics, Va. Poly. Inst., 1944; PhD in Physics, U. Chgo., 1954; DSc (hon.), U. Durham, Eng., 1983. Rsch. assoc. Inst. Nuclear Studies U. Chgo., 1954-55; rsch. assoc. Lawrence Berkeley Lab. U. Calif., Berkeley, 1955-57; asst. prof. to assoc. prof. U. Chgo., 1957-63; prof. physics U. Calif., Berkeley, 1963-94, dir. particle data group Lawrence Berkeley Lab., 1964-75, acting chmn. dept. computer sci., 1967-68, leader rsch. group A Lawrence Berkeley Lab., 1971-73, leader energy-efficient bldgs. rsch program Lawrence Berkeley Lab., 1975-83, vice chmn. energy and resources grad. program, 1986-94, dir. Ctr. Bldg. Sci. Lawrence Berkeley Lab., 1986-94, founder, acting dir. Calif. Inst. for Energy Efficiency, 1988-90, prof. emeritus, 1994—; sr. advisor to asst. sec. energy efficiency U.S. Dept. Energy, Washington, 1994-99; commr. Calif. Energy Commn., Sacramento, 2000—. Vis. prof. Coll. de France, Paris, 1978; co-founder Am. Coun. Energy-Efficient Econ., 1979, chmn., 1981-83, pres., 1984-90, bd. dirs., 1990-94; mem. steering com. advanced customer tech. test maximum energy efficiency Pacific Gas & Electric Co., 1989-98; mem. tech. adv. panel joint com. on energy regulation and environ. State of Calif., 1990-91; mem. Nat. Sci. and Tech. Coun., 1994—, civilian indsl. tech. com, 1994—, co-chmn. subcom. constrn. and bldg., 1994—. Author: (with E. Fermi and others) Nuclear Physics, 1949, Experimental Meson Spectroscopy, 1968, 3d edit., 1972, Supplying Energy Through Greater Efficiency: The Potential for Conservation in California's Residential Sector, 1983, A New Prosperity: The SERI Solar/Conservation Study, 1991, Scenarios of U.S. Carbon Reductions, Interlaboratory Working Group, 1997; contbr. articles, seminars to profl. jours., confs.; assoc. editor Jour. Computational Physics, 1964-73, Energy and Bldgs., 1979—, Energy, the Internat. Jour., 1985-91; editl. cons. Ency. of Applied Physics, 1988—. Mem. governing bd. Am. Inst. Physics, 1974-77; co-founder Am. Coun. for an Energy Efficient Economy, 1979; chmn. 1981-83, pres. 1984—, mem. adv. com. Calif. Legis. Joint Com. on Energy Regulation and Environ., 1989—. Recipient Sadi Carnot award US Dept. of Energy, 1993, Star Energy Efficiency for outstanding contbn. in promoting energy efficiency Alliance to Save Energy, 1995. Fellow Am. Physical Soc. (sec., treas. divsn. particles and fields 1967-71, Leo Szilard award for physics in the pub. interest 1986); mem. NAS (panel on policy implications of greenhouse warm 1990—), Fedn. Am. Sci. (coun. 1964-72, 77-81, 83-87, 94-98), Am. Inst. Physics (mem. governing bd. 1974-77). Achievements include co-developement of Ultra-Violet Water Works to purify water in villages and slums, 1996; studied under Enrico Fermi at U. Chgo. Office: Calif Energy Commn 1516 9th St Sacramento CA 95814 E-mail: AHRosenfeld@LBL.gov

ROSENFELD, MICHAEL G. medical educator; Prof. dept. medicine U. Calif. Med. Sch., La Jolla, 1996—. Mem. NAS. Office: U Calif San Diego Sch Medicine Howard Hughes Med Inst 9500 Gilman Dr Dept 345 La Jolla CA 92093-0345

ROSENFIELD, GENE, construction executive; CEO, mng. ptnr. Western Pacific Housing, El Segundo, Calif., 1989—. Office: Western Pacific Housing 300 Continental Blvd Ste 390 El Segundo CA 90245

ROSENFIELD, RUTH, advertising executive; b. Santa Monica, Calif., Nov. 24, 1962; m. Thomas Andrew Rosenfield, 1989; children: Charlotte Elyse, Oliver Cole. Student, UCLA, 1980-82; BFA with honors, Art Ctr. Coll. Design, 1985. Art dir. Oglivy & Mather, N.Y.C., 1985-86, Chiat/Day, N.Y.C., 1986-88, Venice, Calif., 1988-91; v.p., assoc. creative dir. Hill Holliday, L.A., 1991-93; freelance art dir. San Francisco and L.A., 1993-95; v.p., creative dir. Publicus & Hal Riney (formerly Hal Riney & Ptnrs.), San Francisco, 1995—. Recipient Comm. Arts award, Cannes awards, Obie awards, Belding awards, Andy awards. Office: Publicus & Hal Riney 2001 The Embarcadero San Francisco CA 94133-5200

ROSENHEIM, DANIEL EDWARD, journalist, television news director; b. Chgo., Aug. 12, 1949; s. Edward W. and Margaret Morton (Keeney) R.; m. Christina J. Adachi, May 10, 1974 (div. 1979); m. Cindy Catherine Salans, June 20, 1980; children: Joseph Michael, James Salans, Nicholas Edward. BA, Wesleyan U., 1971. Factory worker, Pitts. and Chgo., 1972-77; reporter Sun-Jour., Lansing, Ill., 1977; bus./labor editor Hammond (Ind.) Times, 1977-80; bus. writer Chgo. Sun Times, 1980-82, spl. writer, 1982-84; bus. writer Chgo. Tribune, 1984-85; econs. editor San Francisco Chronicle, 1985-87, city editor, 1987-94, mng. editor, 1994-96; news dir. KRON-TV, San Francisco, 1996-2000, KPIX-TV, San Francisco, 2000—. Mem. adv. bd. News Lab, Project for Excellence in Journalism. Mem. Soc. Profl. Journalists, Radio and TV News Dirs. Assn., San Francisco Tennis Club. Avocations: tennis, golf, fly fishing. Office: KRON TV 1001 Van Ness Ave San Francisco CA 94109-6982

ROSENKILDE, CARL EDWARD, physicist; b. Yakima, Wash., Mar. 16, 1937; s. Elmer Edward and Doris Edith R.; m. Bernadine Doris Blumenstine, June 22, 1963 (div. Apr. 1991); children: Karen Louise, Paul Eric; m. Wendy Maureen Ellison, May 24, 1992. BS in Physics, Wash. State Coll., 1959; MS in Physics, U. Chgo., 1960, PhD in Physics, 1966. Fellow Argonne (Ill.) Nat. Lab., 1966-68; asst. prof. math. NYU, 1968-70; asst. prof. physics Kans. State U., Manhattan, 1970-76, assoc. prof., 1976-79; physicist Lawrence Livermore (Calif.) Nat. Lab., 1979-93, lab. assoc., 1994-95, participating guest, 1995-97, cons., 1974-79; chief scientist C.R. Sci., 1993-98. Astronomy instr. Los Positas Coll., 1997; part-time instr. physics Bellarmine Coll. Prep., 1999-2000; full-time instr., 2000—. Contbr. articles to profl. jours. Woodrow Wilson fellow, 1959-60. Mem. Am. Phys. Soc., Am. Assn. Physics Tchrs., Calif. Math. Coun. C.C., Am. Astron. Soc., Soc. for Indsl. and Applied Math., Am. Geophys. Union, Accoustical Soc. Am., Math. Assn., Am., Tubists Universal Brotherhood Assn., Phi Beta Kappa, Phi Kappa Phi, Phi Eta Sigma, Sigma Xi. Republican. Presbyterian. Achievements include rsch. in nonlinear wave propagation in complex media, theoretical physics, fluid dynamics. E-mail: crosenkilde@bcp.org

ROSENTHAL, HERBERT MARSHALL, lawyer; BA, UCLA; JD, Hasting Coll. Law, U. Calif., San Francisco. Bar: Calif. 1962. Formerly exec. dir. State Bar Calif., San Francisco; pvt. practice Millbrae, Calif. Office: PO Box 507 Millbrae CA 94030-0507

ROSENTHAL, ROBERT, psychology educator; b. Giessen, Germany, Mar. 2, 1933; came to U.S., 1940, naturalized, 1946; s. Julius and Hermine (Kahn) R.; m. Mary Lu Clayton, Apr. 20, 1951; children: Roberta, David C., Virginia. A.B., UCLA, 1953, Ph.D., 1956. Diplomate: clin. psychology Am. Bd. Examiners Profl. Psychology. Clin. psychology trainee Los Angeles Area VA, 1954-57; lectr. U. So. Calif., 1956-57; acting instr. UCLA, 1957; from asst. to assoc. prof., coordinator clin. tng. U. N.D., 1957-62; vis. assoc. prof. Ohio State U., 1960-61; lectr. Boston U., 1965-66; lectr. clin. psychology Harvard U., Cambridge, Mass., 1962-67, prof. social psychology, 1967-95, chmn. dept. psychology, 1992-95, Edgar Pierce prof. psychology, 1995-99, Edgar Pierce prof. emeritus, 1999—; disting. prof. U. Calif., Riverside, 1999—. Author: Experimenter Effects in Behavioral Research, 1966, enlarged edit., 1976; (with Lenore Jacobson) Pygmalion in the Classroom, 1968, expanded edit., 1992, Meta-analytic Procedures for Social Research, 1984, rev. edit., 1991, Judgment Studies, 1987; (with others) New Directions in Psychology 4, 1970, Sensitivity to Nonverbal Communication: The Pons Test, 1979; (with Ralph L. Rosnow) The Volunteer Subject, 1975, Primer of Methods for the Behavioral Sciences, 1975, Essentials of Behavioral Research, 1984, 2d edit., 1991, Understanding Behavioral Science, 1984, Contrast Analysis, 1985, Beginning Behavioral Research, 1993, 3rd edit., 1999, People Studying People: Artifact and Ethics in Behavioral Research, 1997, (with Ralph L. Rosnow and Donald B. Rubin) Contrasts and Effect Sizes in Behavioral Research: A Correlational Approach, 2000; (with Brian Mullen) BASIC Meta-analysis, 1985; editor: (with Ralph L. Rosnow) Artifact in Behavioral Research, 1969, Skill in Nonverbal Communication, 1979, Quantitative Assessment of Research Domains, 1980, (with Thomas A. Sebeok) The Clever Hans Phenomenon: Communication With Horses, Whales, Apes and People, 1981; (with Blanck and Buck) Nonverbal Communication in the Clinical Context, 1986; (with Gheorghiu, Netter and Eysenck) Suggestion and Suggestibility: Theory and Research, 1989. Recipient Donald Campbell award Soc. for Personality and Social Psychology, 1988, James McKeen Cattell Sabbatical award, 1995-96; co-recipient Golden Anniversary Monograph award Speech Comm. Assn., 1996; named Watson lectr. U. N.H., Lanzetta Meml. lectr. Dartmouth Coll., Bayer lectr. Yale Sch. Medicine, Foa lectr. Temple U., Disting. Alumni lectr. UCLA; Guggenheim fellow, 1973-74, fellow Ctr. for Advanced Study in Behavioral Scis., 1988-89; sr. Fulbright scholar, 1972. Fellow AAAS (co-recipient Sociopsychol. prize 1960, co-recipient Behavioral Sci. Rsch. prize 1993), APA (co-recipient Cattell Fund award 1967, co-chmn. Task Force on Statis. Inference), Am. Psychol. Soc. (charter, James McKeen Cattell award 2001); mem. Soc. Exptl. Social Psychology (Disting. Scientist award 1996), Ea. Psychol. Assn. (Disting. lectr. 1989), Mid-western Psychol. Assn., Mass. Psychol. Assn. (Disting. Career Contbn. award 1979), Soc. Projective Techniques (past treas.), Phi Beta Kappa, Sigma Xi. Home: 6985 Withers Rd Riverside CA 92506-5621 Office: U Calif Ls-p Riverside CA 92521-0001

ROSENTHAL, SOL, lawyer; b. Balt., Oct. 17, 1934; s. Louis and Hattie (Getz) R.; m. Diane Myra Sackler, June 11, 1961; children: Karen Abby, Pamela Margaret, Robert Joel. AB, Princeton U., 1956; JD, Harvard U., 1959. Bar: Md. 1959, Calif. 1961. Law clk. to chief judge U.S. Ct. Appeals, 4th cir., Balt., 1959-60; assoc. Kaplan, Livingston, Goodwin, Berkowitz & Selvin, Beverly Hills, Calif., 1960-66, ptnr., 1966-74, Buchalter, Nemer, Fields & Younger, L.A., 1974-96; of counsel Blanc, Williams, Johnston & Kronstadt, L.A., 1996-2000, Arnold & Porter, 2000—. Bd. dirs. Playboy Enterprises, Inc., Chgo.; arbitrator Dirs. Guild Am., L.A., 1976—, Writers Guild Am., L.A., 1976—, Am. Film Mktg. Assn., 1989—; negotiator Writers Guild-Assn. Talent Agts., L.A., 1978—; mem. entertainment panel Am. Arbitration Assn., 1997—. Founder Camp Ronald McDonald for Good Times, L.A., 1985; charter founder Mus. Contemporary Art, L.A., 1988. Fellow Am. Bar Found.; mem. ABA, Calif. Bar Assn., L.A. County Bar Assn. (trustee 1981-82), L.A. Copyright Soc. (pres. 1973-74), Acad. TV Arts and Scis. (bd. govs. 1990-92), Beverly Hills Bar Assn. (pres. 1982-83), Phi Beta Kappa. Office: Arnold & Porter 1900 Ave Of Stars Ste 1700 Los Angeles CA 90067-4408

ROSENWASSER, LANNY JEFFREY, allergist, immunologist; b. N.Y.C., Mar. 3, 1948; MD, NYU, 1972. Cert. in allergy and immunology; cert. in internal medicine. Intern U. Calif.-HC Moffitt Hosp., San Francisco, 1972-73; resident U. Calif. Affiliated Hosps., San Francisco, 1973-74; head Allergy Immunology Nat. Jewish Med. Rsch. Ctr., Denver, 1998—. Mem. Alpha Omega Alpha, Sigma Xi. Office: Nat Jewish Med & Rsch Ctr 1400 Jackson St Denver CO 80206-2761

ROSENZWEIG, FRED, desktop publishing executive; b. 1956; BS in Engring., Pa. State U.; MBA, U. Calif., Berkeley. Former plant mgr. Tandem Computers; dir. mfg. Electronics for Imaging, Inc., Foster City, Calif., 1993-95, v.p., 1995-2000, pres., 2000—. Office: Electronics for Imaging Inc 303 Velocity Way Foster City CA 94404

ROSENZWEIG, MARK RICHARD, psychology educator; b. Rochester, N.Y., Sept. 12, 1922; s. Jacob and Pearl (Grossman) R.; m. Janine S.A. Chappat, Aug. 1, 1947; children: Anne Janine, Suzanne Jacqueline, Philip Mark. BA, U. Rochester, 1943, MA, 1944; PhD, Harvard U., 1949; hon. doctorate, U. René Descartes, Sorbonne, 1980, U. Louis Pasteur, Strasbourg, France, 1998. Postdoctoral rsch. fellow Harvard U., 1949-51; asst. prof. U. Calif., Berkeley, 1951-56, assoc. prof., 1956-60, prof. psychology, 1960-91, assoc. rsch. prof., 1958-59, rsch. prof., 1965-66, prof. emeritus, 1991—, prof. grad. studies, 1994—. Vis. prof. biology U. Sorbonne, Paris, 1973-74. Author: Biologie de la Mémoire, 1976, (with A.L. Leiman) Physiological Psychology, 1982, 2nd edit., 1989, (with M.J. Renner) Enriched and Impoverished Environments: Effects on Brain and Behavior, 1987, (with D. Sinha) La Recherche en Psychologie Scientifique, 1988, (with W.H. Holtzman, M. Sabourin and D. Bélanger) History of the International Union of Psychological Service, 2000; editor: (with P. Mussen) Psychology: An Introduction, 1973, 2nd edit., 1977, (with E.L. Bennett) Neural Mechanisms of Learning and Memory, 1976, International Psychological Science: Progress, Problems, and Prospects, 1992, (with A.L. Leiman and S.M. Breedlove) Biological Psychology, 1996, 3d edit., 2001; co-editor: (with L. Porter) Ann. Rev. of Psychology, 1968-94, (with K. Pawlik) International Handbook of Psychology, 2000; contbr. articles to profl. jours. Served with USN, 1944-46. Recipient Disting. Alumnus award U. Rochester; Fulbright rsch. fellow; faculty rsch. fellow Social Sci. Rsch. Coun., 1960-61; rsch. grantee NSF, USPHS, Easter Seal Found., Nat. Inst. Drug Abuse. Fellow AAAS, APA (Disting. Sci. Contbn. award 1982, Disting. Contbn. award for Internat. Advancement of Psychology 1997), Am. Psychol. Soc.; mem. NAS, NAACP (life), Am. Physiol. Soc., Am. Psychol. Soc., Internat. Union Psychol. Sci. (hon. life, mem. exec. com. 1996—, v.p. 1980-84, pres. 1988-92, past pres. 1992-96, mem. U.S. nat. com. for Internat. Union Psychol. Sci., NRC and NAS 1984-96), Internat. Brain Rsch. Orgn., Soc. Exptl. Psychologists, Soc. for Neurosci., Société Française de Psychologie, Sierra Club (life), Common Cause, Fulbright Assn. (life), Phi Beta Kappa, Sigma Xi. Office: U Calif Dept Psychology 3210 Tolman Hall Berkeley CA 94720-1650

ROSENZWEIG, RICHARD STUART, publishing company executive; b. Appleton, Wis., Aug. 8, 1935; s. Walter J. and Rose (Bahcall) R. B.S., Northwestern U., 1957; Advanced Mgmt. Program, Harvard U., 1975. Credit rep. Dun & Bradstreet, Inc., 1958; with Playboy Enterprises, Inc., 1958—, exec. asst. to pres., 1963-73, sr. v.p., dir., 1973-82, dir. mktg., 1974-82, exec. v.p. publs. group, 1975-77, exec. v.p., head West Coast ops., 1977-80, exec. v.p. corp. affairs, 1980-82, exec. v.p., chmn. emeritus, 1982—; pres. Playboy Jazz Festivals, 1989—. Dir. I. Bahcall Industries, Appleton. Trustee L.A. Film Expn.; mem. 2d decade coun. Am. Film Inst.; bd. dirs. Mus. Contemporary Art, Chgo., Periodical and Book Assn. Am., Internat. Inst. Kidney Diseases of UCLA, Children of Night, Maple Ctr. Beverly Hills; mem., chmn. bd. UCLA Legis. Network, Town Hall of Calif.; adv. bd. West Hollywood Mktg. Corp., 1985—; bd. dirs. So. Calif. ACLU, 1985—; mem. Los Angeles County Mus.; apptd. to blue ribbon com. project West Coast Gateway. With AUS, 1957. Recipient Do-ers award, 1988, Beverly Hills medal Beverly Hills City Coun., 1993. Mem. Am. Mktg. Aslsn., L.A. Pub. Affairs Officers Assn., UCLA Chancellor's Assocs., Pres.'s Cir., Beverly Hills C. of C. (bd. dirs., visitors' bur., v.p.), Beverly Hills Fine Art Commn. (chmn.), Beverly Hills Econ. Devel. Coun., Founders Circle of Music Ctr., Pub. Affairs Coun., Craft and Folk Art Mus., Pres.' Coun. and Contemporary ARts Coun. L.A. Mus. Contemporary Art, The Am. Cinematheque (groundbreaker), Variety Club So. Calif. (bd. dirs.). Office: Playboy Enterprises Inc 9242 Beverly Blvd Beverly Hills CA 90210-3732

ROSER, STEVEN A. retired career officer; BA in Polit. Sci., SUNY, Plattsburgh, 1971; M in Internat. Rels., Webster U., 1984. Commd. 2d lt. USAF, advanced through grades to brig. gen.; instr. CH-3 instr. pilot 350th Strategic Reconnaissance Squadron, Davis-Monthan AFB, Ariz., 1972-75; mission airlift dir. 437th Mil. Airlift Wing, Charleston AFB, S.C., 1977-82; civil res. air fleet mgmt. officer Dep. Chief of Staff for Plans, Mil. Airlift Command, Scott AFB, Ill., 1982-84; chief strategic airlift programming Hdqrs. USAF, the Pentagon, Washington, 1985-87; comdr. 14th Mil. Airlift Squadron, Norton AFB, Calif., 1987-89; dep. inspector gen. U.S. Atlantic Command, Norfolk, Va., 1990-93; comdr. 62nd Ops. Group, McChord AFB, Wash., 1993-94, 11th Wing, Bolling AFB, D.C., 1994-96, 437th Airlift Wing, Charleston AFB, S.C., 1996-98, 60th Air Mobility Wing, Travis AFB, Calif., 1998-2000, ret., 2000. Decorated D.F.C., Legion of Merit with oak leaf cluster, Aeiral Achievement medal, Combat Readiness medal with oak leaf cluster, Vietnam Svc. medal with silver star. Office: 400 Brennan Cir Travis AFB CA 94535-5001

ROSETT, ARTHUR IRWIN, lawyer, educator; b. N.Y.C., July 5, 1934; s. Milton B. and Bertha (Werner) R.; m. Rhonda K. Lawrence; children: David Benjamin, Martha Jean, Daniel Joseph. A.B., Columbia U., 1955, LL.B., 1959. Bar: Calif. 1968, N.Y. State 1960, U.S. Supreme Ct. 1963. Law clk. U.S. Supreme Ct., 1959-60; asst. U.S. atty. So. Dist. N.Y., 1960-63; practice law N.Y.C., 1963-65; assoc. dir. Pres.'s Commn. on Law Enforcement and Adminstrn. Justice, 1965-67; acting prof. law UCLA, 1967-70, prof., 1970—. Author: Contract Law and Its Application, 1971, 6th edit. (with D.J. Bussell), 1999, (with D. Cressey) Justice by Consent, 1976, (with E. Dorff) A Living Tree, 1987. Served with USN, 1956-58. Mem. Am. Law Inst. Home: 641 S Saltair Ave Los Angeles CA 90049-4134 Office: UCLA Law Sch 405 Hilgard Ave Los Angeles CA 90095-1476

ROSHKO, ANATOL, aeronautic engineer; b. Bellevue, Alta, July 15, 1923; came to the U.S., 1950; married, 1957; 2 children. BS, U. Alta, 1945; MS, Calif. Inst. Tech., 1947, PhD in Aero. Engring., 1952. Instr. math. U. Alta, 1945-46, lectr. engring., 1949-50; rsch. fellow Calif. Inst. Tech., Pasadena, 1952-55, asst. prof. to prof., 1955-85; acting. dir. Grad Aero. Labs, Pasadena, 1985-87; Theodore Von Karman prof. aeronautics Calif. Inst. Tech., Pasadena, 1985—, prof. emeritus, 1994—. Sci. liaison officer Office Naval Rsch., London, 1961-62; cons. McDonnell Douglas Corp., 1954-90, Rocketdyne Corp. Divsn., Rockwell Internat., 1984-90; founding dir. Wind Engring. Rsch. Inc., 1970; mem. Aero. & Space Engring. Bd., 1988-93. Recipient Timoshenko medal ASME, 1999; named to U. Alta. Alumni Wall of Recognition, 1998. Fellow AAAS, AIAA (Dryden Rsch. lectr. 1976, Fluid Dynamics award 1998), Am. Phys. Soc. (Fluid Dynamics prize 1987), Indian Acad. Scis. (hon.); mem. ASME, Nat. Acad. Engring. Office: Calif Inst Tech Mail Sta 105-50 1201 E California Blvd Pasadena CA 91125-0001

ROSKI, EDWARD P., JR. professional sports team executive; s. Edward P. Roski, III; m. Gayle Roski. BS in Fin. and Real Estate, U. So. Calif., 1962. Pres. So. Calif.-based Majestic Realty Co.; owner L.A. Kings, 1995—. Dir. Big Bros. of Greater L.A.; bd. govs. Natural History Mus. of L.A. County; bd. dirs. Comerica Bank, Calif. With USMC, 1962-66. Mem. Explorers Club, Soc. Indsl. Realtors. Avocations: cycling, mountain climbing. Office: Los Angeles Kings 3900 W Manchester Blvd PO Box 10 Inglewood CA 90306-0010

ROSKY, BURTON SEYMOUR, lawyer; b. Chgo., May 28, 1927; s. David T. and Mary W. (Zelkin) R.; m. Leatrice J. Darrow, June 16, 1951; children: David Scott, Bruce Alan. Student, Ill. Inst. Tech., 1944-45; BS, UCLA, 1948; JD, Loyola U., L.A., 1953. Bar: Calif. 1954, U.S. Supreme Ct 1964, U.S. Tax Ct 1964; C.P.A., Calif. Auditor City of L.A., 1948- 51; with Beidner, Temkin & Ziskin (C.P.A.s), L.A., 1951-52; supervising auditor Army Audit Agy., 1952-53; practiced law L.A., Beverly Hills, 1954—; ptnr. Duskin & Rosky, 1972-82, Rosky, Landau & Fox, 1982-93, Rosky, Landau & Stahl, Beverly Hills, 1993-99; pvt. practice Beverly Hills, 1999—. Lectr. on tax and bus. problems; judge pro tem Beverly Hills Mcpl. Ct., L.A. Superior Ct.; mem. L.A. Mayor's Community Adv. Council. Contbr. profl. publs. Charter supporting mem. Los Angeles County Mus. Arts; contbg. mem. Assocs. of Smithsonian Instn.; charter mem. Air and Space Mus; mem. Am. Mus. Natural History, L.A. Zoo; supporting mem. L.A. Mus. Natural History; mem. exec. bd. So. Calif. coun. Nat. Fedn. Temple Brotherhoods, mem. nat. exec. bd.; mem. bd. govs. Loyola Sch. Law, L.A. With USNR, 1945-46. Walter Henry Cook fellow Loyola Law Sch. Bd. Govs. Fellow Jewish Chautauqua Soc. (life mem.); mem. Am. Arbitration Assn. (nat. panel arbitrators), Am. Assn. Attys.-CPAs (charter mem. pres. 1968), Calif. Assn. Attys.-CPAs (charter mem., pres. 1963), Calif. Soc. CPAs, Calif., Beverly Hills, Century City, Los Angeles County bar assns., Am. Judicature Soc., Chancellors Assocs. UCLA, Tau Delta Phi, Phi Alpha Delta.; mem. B'nai B'rith. Jewish (mem. exec. bd., pres. temple, pres. brotherhood). Club: Mason. Office: 8383 Wilshire Blvd Beverly Hills CA 90211-2410

ROSS, CHARLOTTE PACK, social services administrator; b. Oklahoma City, Oct. 21, 1932; d. Joseph and Rose P. (Traibich) Pack; m. Roland S. Ross, May 6, 1951 (div. July 1964); children: Beverly Jo, Sandra Gail; m. Stanley Fisher, Mar. 17, 1991. Student U. Okla., 1949-52, New Sch. Social Rsch., 1953. Cert. tchr. Exec. dir. Suicide Prevention and Crisis Ctr. San Mateo County, Burlingame, Calif., 1966-88; pres., exec. dir. Youth Suicide Nat. Ctr., Washington, 1985-93; exec. dir. Death with Dignity Edn. Ctr., San Mateo, Calif., 1994—; pres. Calif. Senate Adv. Com. Youth Suicide Prevention, 1982-84; speaker Menninger Found., 1983, 84; instr. San Francisco State U., 1981-83; conf. coord. U. Calif., San Francisco, 1971—; cons. univs. and health svcs. throughout world. Contbg. author: Group Counseling for Suicidal Adolescents, 1984, Teaching Children the Facts of Life and Death, 1985; mem. editorial bd. Suicide and Life Threatening Behavior, 1976-89. Mem. regional selection panel Pres.'s Commn. on White House Fellows, 1975-78; mem. CIRCLON Svc. Club, 1979—, Com. on Child Abuse, 1981-85; founding mem. Women for Responsible Govt., co-chmn., 1974-79. Recipient Outstanding Exec. award San Mateo County Coordinating Com., 1971, Koshland award San Francisco Found., 1984. Fellow Wash. Acad. Scis.; mem. Internat. Assn. Suicide Prevention (v.p. 1985—), Am. Assn. Suicidology (sec. 1972-74, svc. award 1990), bd. govs. 1976-78, accreditation com. 1975—, chair region IX, 1975-82), Assn. United Way Agy. Execs. (pres. 1974), Assn. County Contract Agys. (pres. 1982), Peninsula Press Club.

ROSS, DAVID A. art museum director; b. Malverne, N.Y., Apr. 26, 1949; s. Joshua and Grayce R.; m. Margaret Gronner; children: Lindsay, Emily. B.A., Syracuse U.; postgrad., Grad. Sch. Fine Arts, Syracuse. Curator video art Everson Mus. Art, Syracuse, N.Y., 1971-74; dep. dir. program devel. and TV Long Beach Mus. Art, Calif., 1974-77; chief curator Univ. Art Mus., Berkeley, 1977-82; dir. Inst. of Contemporary Art, Boston, 1982-91; dir., CEO Whitney Mus. Am. Art, 1991-98; dir. San Francisco Mus. Modern Art, 1998—. Active Fed. Adv. Com. om Internat. Exbns., 1990—. Contbr. articles to profl. jours. Mem. Assn. Art Mus. Dirs. Office: San Francisco Mus Modern Art 151 3rd St San Francisco CA 94103-3107

ROSS, DELMER GERRARD, historian, educator; b. Los Banos, Calif., Nov. 5, 1942; s. Elmer G. and Orva Beth (Dickinson) R.; m. Karen Ann Gibson, June 17, 1977; children: Michelle, Richard. BA, Pacific Union Coll., 1965; MA, U. Calif., Santa Barbara, 1967, PhD, 1970. Instr. Pacific Union Coll., Angwin, Calif., 1968-69; from asst. to assoc. prof. Oakwood Coll., Huntsville, Ala., 1970-76; from assoc. prof. to prof. history Loma Linda U., Riverside, Calif., 1976-91, chmn. dept. history and polit. sci., 1986-90; prof. history and polit. sci. La Sierra U., Riverside, 1991—. Author: Visionaries and Swindlers, 1975, Rails Across Costa Rica, 1976, Rails in Paradise, 1991, Gold Road to La Paz, 1992, Development of Railroads in Guatemala and El Salvador, 1849-1929, 2001; mem. editl. bd. Adventist Heritage mag., 1987-90. Bd. dirs. Inst. for Research in Latin Am., Mobile, Ala., 1968-82. Mem. Am. Hist. Assn., Assn. 7th Day Adventist Historians (exec. sec. 1973-74, sec.-treas. 1974-75, pres. 1981-82), Assn. Western Adventist Historians, Nat. Railway Hist. Soc., Colo. Railroad Hist. Found. (life), Railway and Locomotive Hist. Soc. Republican. Office: La Sierra U Dept History Riverside CA 92515 E-mail: dross@lasierra.edu

ROSS, HUGH COURTNEY, electrical engineer; b. Dec. 31, 1923; s. Clare W. and Jeanne F. Ross; m. Sarah A. Gordon (dec.); m. Patricia A. Malloy; children: John C., James G., Robert W. Student, Calif. Inst. Tech., 1942, San Jose State U., 1946-47; BSEE, Stanford U., 1950, postgrad., 1954. Registered profl. elec. engr., Calif. Instr. San Benito (Calif.) High Sch. and Jr. Coll., 1950-51; chief engr. vacuum power switches Jennings Radio Mfg. Corp., San Jose, Calif., 1951-62; chief engr. ITT Jennings, San Jose, 1962-64; pres. Ross Engring. Corp., Campbell, 1964—. Contbr. articles to tech. jours.; patentee in field. Fellow IEEE (life) (chmn. Santa Clara Valley subsect. 1960-61); mem. Am. Vacuum Soc., Am. Soc. Metals. Avocations: electronics, electric autos, camping, ranching, solar power. Office: 540 Westchester Dr Campbell CA 95008-5012

ROSS, JOHN, physical chemist, educator; b. Vienna, Austria, Oct. 2, 1926; came to U.S., 1940; s. Mark and Anna (Krecmar) R.; m. Virginia Franklin (div.); children: Elizabeth A., Robert K.; m. Eva Madarasz. BS, Queens Coll., 1948; PhD, MIT, 1951; D (hon.), Weizmann Inst. Sci., Rehovot, Israel, 1984, Queens Coll., SUNY, , 1987, U. Bordeaux, France, 1987. Prof. chemistry Brown U., Providence, 1953-66, MIT, Cambridge, 1966-80, chmn. dept., 1966-71, chmn. faculty of Inst., 1975-77; prof. Stanford (Calif.) U., 1980—, chmn. dept., 1983-89. Cons. to industries, 1979—; mem. bd. govs. Weizmann Inst., 1971—. Author: Physical Chemistry, 1980, 2d edit., 2000; editor Molecular Beams, 1966; contbr. articles to profl. jours. 2nd lt. U.S. Army, 1944-46. Recipient medal Coll. de France, Paris, Presdl. Nat. Med. of Sci., 1999. Fellow AAAS, Am. Phys. Soc.; mem. NAS, Am. Acad. Arts and Scis., Am. Chem. Soc. (Irving Langmuir Chem. Physics prize 1992, Peter Debye award in phys. chemistry 2001). Home: 738 Mayfield Ave Palo Alto CA 94305-1044 Office: Stanford U Dept Chemistry Stanford CA 94305-5080

ROSS, JOHN, JR. cardiologist, educator; b. N.Y.C., Dec. 1, 1928; s. John and Janet (Moulder) R.; children: Sydnie, John, Duncan; m. Lola Romanucci, Aug. 26, 1972; children: Adan, Deborah Lee. A.B., Dartmouth Coll., 1951; M.D., Cornell U., 1955. Intern Johns Hopkins Hosp., 1955-56; resident Columbia-Presbyn. Med. Center, N.Y.C., 1960-61, N.Y. Hosp.-Cornell U. Med. center, 1961-62; chief sect. cardiovascular diagnosis cardiology br. Nat. Heart Inst., Bethesda, Md., 1962-68; prof. medicine U. Calif., San Diego, 1968—, also dir. cardiovascular div., 1968-91; prof. cardiovascular research Am. Heart Assn. San Diego Co. Affiliate, San Diego, 1985—. Mem. cardiology adv. com. Nat. Heart, Lung and Blood Inst., 1975-78, task force on arteriosclerosis, 1978-80, adv. council, 1980-84; bd. dirs. San Diego Heart Assn.; vis. prof. Brit. Heart Assn., 1990. Author: Mechanisms of Contraction of the Normal and Failing Heart, 1968, 76, Understanding the Heart and Its Diseases, 1976; mem. editorial bd. Circulation, 1967-75, 80-88, editor in chief 1988-93, Circulation Research, 1971-75, Am. Jour. Physiology, 1968-73, Annals of Internal Medicine, 1974-78, Am. Jour. Cardiology, 1974-79, 83-88; cons. editor Circulation, 1993 ; contbr. chpts. to books, sci. articles to profl. jours. Served as surgeon USPHS, 1956-63. Recipient Ing. Enzo Ferrari prize Organizing Com. for Enzo Ferrari, Modena, Italy, 1989, James B. Herrick award Coun. Clin. Cardiology Am. Heart Assn., 1990, Grande Ufficiale Order of Merit Republic of Italy, 1998. Fellow Am. Coll. Cardiology (master 1998—, v.p. trustee, pres. 1986-87, Disting. Scientist award 1990), ACP; mem. Am. Soc. Clin. Investigation (councillor), Am. Physiol. Soc., Assn. Am. Physicians, Cardiac Muscle Soc., Assn. Univ. Cardiologists, Assn. West. Physicians (councillor). Home: 8599 Prestwick Dr La Jolla CA 92037-2025 Office: U Calif Dept Med M # 0613B San Diego CA 92093 E-mail: jross@ucsd.edu

ROSS, JUNE ROSA PITT, biologist, educator; b. Taree, New South Wales, Australia, May 2, 1931; came to U.S., 1957; d. Bernard and Adeline Phillips; m. Charles Alexander, June 27, 1959. BSc with honors, U. Sydney, New S. Wales, Australia, 1953, PhD, 1959, DSc, 1974. Research assoc. Yale U., New Haven, 1959-60, U. Ill., Urbana, 1960-65, Western Wash. U., Bellingham, 1965-67, assoc. prof., 1967-70, prof. biology, 1970—, chair dept. biology, 1989-90. Pres. Western Wash. U. Faculty Senate, Bellingham, 1984-85; conf. host Internat. Bryozoology Assn., 1986. Author: (with others) A Textbook of Entomology, 1982, Geology of Coal, 1984; editor (assoc.) Palaios, 1985-89; contbr. articles 120 to profl. jours. Recipient J. Wolfensohn Award of Excellence Sydney U. Grads. Union of N.Am., 1995, P. and R. Olscamp Outstanding Rsch. award Western Wash. U., 1986; NSF grantee. Mem. Australian Marine Scis. Assn., The Paleontol. Soc. (councillor 1984-86, treas. 1987-93), U.K. Marine Biol. Assn. (life), Microscopy Soc. of Am., Internat. Bryozoology Assn. (pres. 1992-95). Avocations: hiking, classical music. Office: Western Wash U Dept Biology Bellingham WA 98225-9160 E-mail: ross@biol.wwu.edu

ROSS, KATHLEEN ANNE, college president; b. Palo Alto, Calif., July 1, 1941; d. William Andrew and Mary Alberta (Wilburn) R. BA, Ft. Wright Coll., 1964; MA, Georgetown U., 1971; PhD, Claremont Grad. U., 1979; LLD (hon.), Alverno Coll. Milw., 1990, Dartmouth Coll., 1991, Seattle U., 1992; LHD (hon.), Whitworth Coll., 1992; LLD (hon.), Pomona Coll., 1993; LHD (hon.), Coll. of New Rochelle, 1998; LLD (hon.), U. Notre Dame, 1999, Gonzaga U., 1999. Cert. tchr., Wash. Secondary tchr. Holy Names Acad., Spokane, Wash., 1964-70; dir. rsch. and planning Province Holy Names, Wash. State, 1972-73; v.p. acads. Ft. Wright Coll., Spokane, 1973-81; rsch. asst. to dean Claremont Grad. Sch., Calif., 1977-78; assoc. faculty mem. Harvard U., Cambridge, Mass., 1981; pres. Heritage Coll., Toppenish, Wash., 1981—. Cons. Wash. State Holy Names Schs., 1971-73; coll. accrediting assn. evaluator N.W. Assn. Schs. and Colls., Seattle, 1975—; dir. Holy Names Coll., Oakland, Calif., 1979—; cons. Yakama Indian Nation, Toppenish, 1975—; speaker, cons. in field. Author: (with others) Multicultural Pre-School Curriculum, 1977, A Crucial Agenda: Improving Minority Student Success, 1989; Cultural Factors in Success of American Indian Students in Higher Education, 1978. Chmn. Internat. 5-Yr. Convocation of Sisters of Holy Names, Montreal, Que., Can., 1981, 96; TV Talk show host Spokane Council of Chs., 1974-76. Recipient E.K. and Lillian F. Bishop Founds. Youth Leader of Yr. award, 1986, Disting. Citizenship Alumna award Claremont Grad. Sch., 1986, Golden Aztec award Washington Human Devel., 1989, Harold W. McGraw Edn. prize, 1989, John Carroll award Georgetown U., 1991, Holy Names medal Ft. Wright Coll., 1981, Pres. medal Eastern Washington U., 1994; named Yakima Herald Rep. Person of Yr. 1987, First Annual Leadership award Region VIII Coun. Advancement and Support Edn., 1993; Wash. State Medal of Merit, 1995; MacArthur fellow, 1997; numerous grants for projects in multicultural higher edn., 1974—. Mem. Nat. Assn. Ind. Colls. and Univs., Soc. Intercultural Edn., Tng. and Rsch., Sisters of Holy Names of Jesus and Mary-SNJM. Roman Catholic. Office: Heritage Coll Office of Pres 3240 Fort Rd Toppenish WA 98948-9562

ROSS, LANSON CLIFFORD, JR. religious studies educator, writer; b. Killdeer, N.D., June 23, 1936; s. Lanson Charles and Mabel (Smith) R.; children: David F., Lanson III. BA in Biblical Studies, Seattle Pacific U., 1960; M. Sacred Theology, Internat. Coll., 1984; D of Ministries, 1986. founder Planned Living Seminars; pres. Viet/Aid. Author: Total Life Prosperity, 1983; Give Your Children a Target, 1985, Take Charge of Your Life, 1986, The Bubble Burst, 1987; producer 5 vol. video seminar A Planned Life Style, 1986, and film A Time to Grow (J.C. Mc Pheeters award 1988). Mem. Seattle Yacht Club. E-mail: lanson@casagrande.com. Office: PO Box 1354 Arizona City AZ 85223-1354

ROSS, MICHAEL CHARLES, lawyer; BA, U. Va., 1970, JD, 1977. Assoc. Latham & Watkins, 1977-85, ptnr., 1985-93; sr. v.p., gen. counsel, sec. Safeway Inc., Oakland, 1993-2000. Office: Safeway Inc 5918 Stoneridge Mall Rd Pleasanton CA 94588-3229

ROSS, ROBERT, health agency administrator; Exec. dir., sr. v.p. Muscular Dystrophy Assn., Tucson. Office: Muscular Dystrophy Assn 3300 E Sunrise Dr Tucson AZ 85718-3299

ROSS, RUSSELL, pathologist, educator; b. St. Augustine, Fla., May 25, 1929; s. Samuel and Minnie (DuBoff) R.; m. Jean Long Teller, Feb. 22, 1956; children: Valerie Regina, Douglas Teller. A.B., Cornell U., 1951; D.D.S., Columbia U., 1955; Ph.D., U. Wash., 1962; DSc (hon.P, Med. Coll. of Pa., 1987. Intern Columbia-Presbyn. Med. Ctr., 1955-56, USPHS Hosp., Seattle, 1956-58; spl. research fellow pathology sch. medicine U. Wash., Seattle, 1958-62, asst. prof. pathology and oral biology sch. medicine and dentistry, 1962-65, assoc. prof. pathology Sch. Medicine, 1965-69, prof. Sch. Medicine, 1969—, adj. prof. biochemistry Sch. Medicine, 1978—, assoc. dean for sci. affairs sch. medicine, 1971-78, chmn. dept. pathology sch. medicine, 1982-94; dir. Ctr. for Vascular Biology, 1991—. Vis. scientist Strangeways Rsch. Lab., Cambridge, Eng.; mem. rsch. com. Am. Heart Assn.; mem. adv. bd. Found. Cardiologique Princess Liliane, Brussels, Belgium; life fellow Clare Hall, Cambridge U.; mem. adv. coun. Nat. Heart, Lung and Blood Inst., NIH, 1978-81; vis. prof. Royal Soc. Medicine, U.K., 1987, 95. Editl. bd. Procs. Exptl. Biology and Medicine, 1971-86, Jours. Cell Biology, 1972-74, Exptl. Cell Rsch., 1982-92, Jour. Exptl. Medicine, Growth Factors, Am. Jours. Pathology, Internat. Cell Biology Jour., Circulation, Arteriosclerosis & Thrombosis, Growth Regulation; assoc. editor Arteriosclerosis, 1982-92, Jours. Cellular Physiology, Jours. Cellular Biochemistry; exec. editor Trends in Cariovascular Medicine; reviewing editl. bd. Sci. mag., 1987-90; contbr. articles to profl. jours. Trustee Seattle Symphony Orch. Recipient Birnberg Rsch. award Columbia U., 1972, Nat. Rsch. Achievement award Am. Heart Assn., 1990, Rous-Whiple award Am. Assn. Pathologists, 1992, Glorney-Raisbeck award N.Y. Acad. Medicine, 1995, Gordon Wilson medal Am. Clin. and Climatol. Assn., 1981, Disting. Achievement award Soc. Cardiovascular Pathology, 1998, Lucien prize McGill U., 1998, Internat. Okamoto award Japan Vascular Disease Rsch. Found., 1998; named to Inst. Medicine, Nat. Acad. Scis.; Japan Soc. Promotion of Sci. fellow, 1985, Guggenhem fellow, 1966-67. Fellow AAAS, Am. Acad. Arts and Scis.; mem. Am. Soc. Cell Biology, Tissue Culture Assn., Am. Assn. Pathologists (Rous-Whipple award 1992), Internat. Soc. Cell Biology, Electron Microscope Soc. Am., Am. Soc. for Investigative Pathology (pres. 1994-95), Am. Heart Assn. (fellow Coun. on Arteriosclerosis, Nat. Rsch. Achievement award 1990), Royal Micros. Soc., Harvey Soc. (hon.), Am. Soc. Biochemistry and Molecular Biology, Romanian Acad. Med. Scis. (hon.), Royal Belgian Acad. Scis. (fgn. corr. mem.), Brazilian Acad. Medicine (hon. fgn.), Sigma Xi.

ROSS, STAN, accounting firm executive; b. 1939; With Kenneth Leventhal & Co., L.A., 1964—, now mng. ptnr.; now vice chmn., mng. ptnr. real estate Ernst & Young, LLP, L.A., 1995—. Vice chmn., spl. cons. Kenneth Consultant Kenneth Leevnthal & Co.; chmn. bd. USC Lusk Ctr. Real Estate. Office: Kenneth Leventhal & Co 2049 Century Park E Ste 1700 Los Angeles CA 90067-3174

ROSS, STEVEN CHARLES, business administration educator, consultant; b. Salem, Oreg., Jan. 14, 1947; s. Charles Reed and Edythe Marie (Calvin) R.; m. Meredith Lynn Buholts, June 15, 1969; children: Kelly Lynn, Shannon Marie. BS, Oreg. State U., 1969; MS, U. Utah, 1976, PhD, 1980. Cons. IRS Tng. Staff, Ogden, Utah, 1977-80; asst. prof. Marquette U., Milw., 1980-88; assoc. prof. Mont. State U., Bozeman, 1988-89; assoc. prof. bus. adminstrn. Western Wash. U., Bellingham, 1989—. Chmn. acad. coord. commn., Western Wash. U., 1997—, mem. faculty senate 2000—; govt. and industry cons.; cons. editor microcomputing series West Pub. Co. Author 30 books and several articles in computer systems field. Mem. adv. com. Milwaukee County Mgmt., 1981-85, Port of Bellingham, 1990-2000; chmn. 1998 U.S. Sailing Jr. Championships. Capt. U.S. Army, 1969-75. Rsch. fellow U. Utah, 1977-79, Marquette U., 1981-84, Western Wash. U., 1998. Mem. Acad. Mgmt., Decision Scis. Inst., Inst. Mgmt. Scis., Assn. for Computing Machinery, Assn. Computer Educators, Bellingham Yacht Club (trustee 1992-93, sec. 1993-94, rear commodore, 1994-95, vice commodore 1995-96, commodore 1996-97). Office: Western Wash U Coll Bus and Econs Bellingham WA 98225

ROSS, SUE, entrepreneur, author, fundraising executive; b. Chgo., Feb. 2, 1948; d. Irving and Rose (Stein) R. BA in Secondary Edn., Western Mich. U., 1971; postgrad., Northwestern U., Chgo. State U., U. Ill. Dir. youth employment Ill. Youth Svcs. Bur., Maywood, 1978-79; exec. dir. Edn. Resource Ctr., Chgo., 1979-82; asst. dir. devel. Art Inst. Chgo., 1982-83, mgr. govt. affair, 1983-84, dir. govt. affairs, 1984-85; v.p. devel. Spertus Inst. of Judaica, Chgo., 1985-90; mgmt. and fundraising consultant Sue Ross Enterprises, Chgo. and San Francisco, 1990—; founder, pres. Kid Angels Internat., San Francisco, 1994—. Lectr. Sch. Art Inst., Chgo., 1982-85, Episcopalian Archdioceses, Chgo., 1984, Nat. Soc. Fund Raising Execs., Chgo., 1984-90; instr. DePaul U. Sch. for New Learning, 1987-88, Columbia Coll., Chgo., 1980-91; dep. dir. devel. Lead Internat., 2000-01. Resident counsel for devel. The Joffrey Ballet, 1990-91; resident counsel for devel. The 1995 Children's World Peace Festival; adv. panelist Chgo. Office Fine Arts, 1981-82; v.p., bd. dirs. Lines Contemporary Ballet, 1995—; mem. adv. bd. Silkworm Peace Inst., 1996—; mem. Marin Coun. Agys., dev. dirs. Roundtable 1998—; co-chair Marin Estate Planning Seminar, 1999—; mem. adv. coun. Greater Chgo. Food Depository, 1984-85; exec. com. Chgo. Coalition Arts in Edn., 1981-82; mem. info. svcs. com. Donors' Forum Chgo., 1986-88; mem. Marin Devel. Dirs. roundtable, 1999-2001; mem. internationally renowned Gospel Choir of Glide Meml., 1991-93, San Francisco City Chorus, 1994; mem. com. Congregation Sherith Israel, 1996, San Francisco Angel Club, 1994; dir. devel. and comm. Osher Marin Jewish Cmty. Ctr., 1998-2001. Mem. Am. Fund Raising Profls. (Golden Gate chpt.)), World Affairs Coun. Democrat. Jewish. Avocations: community service, singing. Home and Office: 18 Arcangel Ct Fairfax CA 94930-1102

ROSS, TERRY D. lawyer; b. Glendale, Calif., Aug. 12, 1943; BA, U. Calif., Santa Barbara, 1965; JD, Hasting Coll. Law, San Francisco, 1968. Bar: Calif. 1969, U.S. Dist. Ct. (so. dist.) Calif. 1969, U.S. Dist. Ct. (ctrl. dist.) Calif. 1992, U.S. Dist. Ct. (no. dist.) Calif. 1999, U.S. Ct. Appeals (9th cir.) 1977, U.S. Supreme Ct. 1983. Ptnr. Gray, Cary, Ware & Freidenrich, San Diego. Mem. panel arbitrators Am. Arbitration Assn. Note and comment editor Hastings Law Jour., 1967-68. Bd. dirs., mem. exec. bd., 1st v.p. E. San Diego Co. YMCA. Mem. ABA (sect. litigation), State Bar Calif., San Diego County Bar Assn. (mem. arbitration panel, superior ct. com.), S.D. Marlin Club, SDMB Boat and Ski Club, Phi Delta Phi. Office: Gray Cary Ware & Freidenrich 401 B St Ste 1700 San Diego CA 92101-4297 E-mail: tross@graycary.com

ROSSER, EDWIN MICHAEL, mortgage company executive; b. Denver, Oct. 11, 1940; s. Edwin Michael and Anne (Ratliff) R.; m. Keren Call, July 17, 1969; children: Kevin, William. BS, Colo. State U., 1964; MA, U. No. Colo., 1974. Cert. mortgage banker. Mktg. officer United Bank Mortgage, Denver, 1968-74; dir. nat. accounts PMI Mortgage Ins. Co., Denver, 1974-85; v.p. Moore Mortgage Co., Denver, 1985-87, Pacific First Mortgage Corp., Englewood, Colo., 1987-89; 1st v.p. 1st Nat. Bank, San Francisco, 1990-93; v.p. nat. accounts United Guaranty Corp., 1993—. Bd. dirs. Rocky Mtn. Women's Inst. Photographer represented in Denver Art Mus., The Buffalo in Winter, (1st place award 1981). Steering com. Blueprint for Colo., Govs. Unified Housing Task Force; mem. Colo. Housing Coun. (chmn. 1986-87); bd. dirs. Colo. State Found.; mem. adv. bd. Arapahoe County Open Space and Trails, 1999—; mem. Colo. Land Use Commn., 1999. Mem. Am. Planning Assn., Mortgage Bankers Assn. Am. (cert., bd. govs. 1986-90, state and local achievement award 1986, Ernest P. Schumacher award 1988, membership achievement award 1995, Burton Wood Legis. Svc. award), Colo. Mortgage Bankers Assn. (bd. dirs. 1979-88, pres. 1986, E.C. Spelman award 1978, Lifetime Achievement award 1998), Colo. Assn. Commerce and Industry, Denver Nat. Soc. Real Estate Fin., Mus. Natural History, Denver C. of C., Colo. State U. Alumni Assn. (nat. pres. 1985, bd. dirs. 1979-87, mem. found. bd. 1987-91, 93-2000, Honor Alumnus 1984, ha Sasso award Dept. Athletics 1993), City Club Denver, Commonwealth Club. Calif., Nat. Soc. for Real Estate Fin. (CRF designation 1997), Societas Internat. Real Estate Fin. Found. (adv. bd.), Colo. State U. Henry Alumni (Svc. award 2000), Alpha Sigma Gamma. Republican. Roman Catholic. Avocations: competitive swimming, photography. Home: 12478 E Amherst Cir Aurora CO 80014-3306 Office: United Guaranty Residential Ins Co 6312 S Fiddlers Green Cir Englewood CO 80111-4943 E-mail: emrcmb@aol.com

ROSSER, JAMES MILTON, academic administrator; b. East St. Louis, Ill., Apr. 16, 1939; s. William M. and Mary E. (Bass) R.; 1 child, Terrence. BA, So. Ill. U., 1962, MA, 1963, PhD, 1969. Diagnostic bacteriologist Holden Hosp., Carbondale, Ill., 1961-63; rsch. bacteriologist Eli Lilly & Co., Indpls., 1963-66; coordinator Black Am. studies, instr. health edn. So. Ill. U., Carbondale, 1968-69, asst. prof. Black Am. studies dir., 1969-70, asst. to chancellor, 1970; assoc. vice chancellor for acad. affairs U. Kans., Lawrence, 1970-74, assoc. prof. edn., pharmacology and toxicology, 1971-74; vice chancellor dept. higher edn. State of N.J., Trenton, 1974-79, acting chancellor, 1977; pres., prof. health care mgmt. Calif. State U., Los Angeles, 1979—. Tech. resource panel Ctr. for Research and Devel. in Higher Edn., U. Calif., Berkeley, 1974-76; health maintenance orgn. com. Health Planning Coun., State of N.J., 1975-79; standing com. on R & D bd. trustees Ednl. Testing Service, 1976-77; steering com. and task force on retention of minorities in engring. Assembly of Engring. NRC, 1975-78; mem. Bd. Med. Examiners, State of N.J., 1978-79; vis. faculty Inst. Mgmt. of Lifelong Edn., Grad. Sch. Edn., Harvard U., 1979; mem. Calif. State U. Trustees Spl. Long Range Fin. Planning Com., 1982-87; mem. Am. Coun. on Edn., 1979—, AFL/CIO Labor Higher Edn. Coun., 1983—, Nat. Commn. Higher Edn. Issues, 1981-82; mem. The Calif. Achievement Coun., 1983-89, strategic adv. counc. Coll. and Univs. Systems Exchange, 1988-91; bd. dirs. Am. Humanities Coun., So. Calif. Am. Humanics, Inc. Coun., Sanwa Bank Calif., Edison Internat., Fedco, Inc.; task force on equality and fairness Texaco, 1999—. Author: An Analysis of Health Care Delivery, 1977. Exec. bd., chmn. varsity scouting program L.A. area coun. Boy Scouts Am., 1980—; bd. dirs. Hispanic Urban Ctr., L.A., 1979—, L.A. Urban League, 1982-95, Cmty. TV of So. Calif., Sta. KCET, 1980-89, 98—, United Way, L.A., 1980-91, Orthopaedic Hosp., 1983-86, L.A. Philharm. Assn., 1986-99, Nat. Health Found., 1990—, Calif. C. of C., 1993—; mem. Citizen's Adv. Coun. Congl. Caucus Sci. and Tech., 1983—; mem. performing arts coun./edn. coun. Music Ctr., 1984—; minority bus. task force Pacific Bell, 1985-86; bd. govs. Nat. ARC, 1986-91, Mayor's Blue Ribbon Task Force on Drugs, City of L.A., 1988, L.A. Annenberg Met. Project, 1994—; Nat. Adv. Coun. on Aging, 1989-93; bd. trustees Woodrow Wilson Nat. Fellowship Found., 1993—; bd. advisors Historically Black Colls. and Univs. and Minority Insts., Dept. Air Force, 1997—; bd. dirs. Ams. for the Arts, 1991—; mem. L.A. Adv. Alliance, Pasadena Tournament of Roses, 2000—; mem. Action Forum on Diversity in the Engring. Workforce, Nat. Acad. Engring., 2000—. NSF fellow, 1961; NDEA fellow, 1967-68; recipient award of recognition in Edn. Involvement for Young Achievers, 1981, Pioneer of Black Hist. Achievement award Brotherhood Crusade, 1981, Alumni Achievement award So. Ill. U., 1982, Friend of Youth award Am. Humanics, Inc., 1985, Leadership award Dept. Higher Edn. Ednl. Equal Opportunity Fund Program, 1989, Medal of Excellence Gold State Minority Found., 1990, Take Charge of Learning Success award Inst. for Redesign of Learning. Mem. Calif. C. of C. (bd. dirs. 1993—), Alhambra C. of C. (bd. dirs. 1979—), Los Angeles C. of C. (bd. dirs. 1985-90), Am. Assn. State Colls. and Univs., Kappa Delta Pi, Phi Kappa Phi. Roman Catholic. Office: Calif State U Office of Pres 5151 State University Dr Los Angeles CA 90032-4226

ROSSI, DINO J. state legislator, real estate broker; b. Seattle, Oct. 15, 1959; m. Terry Rossi; children: Juliauna, Jake, Joseph. BA in Bus. Mgmtr., Seattle U., 1982. Mem. Wash. Senate, Dist. 5, Olympia, 1996—; mem. energy, tech., and telecom. com. Wash. Senate; mem. natural resources, parks and recreation com.; mem. ways and means com.; mem. capital budget subcom.; mem. joint com. on pension policy. Vol. Sr. Ctr.; co-founder Operation Homefront; past bd. dirs. Boys and Girls Club, Mountains to Sound Greenway Bd. Mem. Rotary (Issaquah). Republican. Office: 109A Irving Newhouse Ofc Olympia WA 98504-0001

ROSSI, MARIO ALEXANDER, architect; b. Chgo., Apr. 9, 1931; s. Gastone J. and Irma (Giorgi) R.; m. Jo Ann Therese Kneip, Apr. 12, 1958; children: John Vincent, Lyn Ann, Paul Alexander, Mara Ann. BArch, Ill. Inst. Tech., 1955. Architect Omnimetrics, L.A., 1967-78; pvt. practice Seal Beach, Calif., 1975—. Prin. works include fin. models for Calif. Fed. Bank, L.A., First Nat. City Bank, N.Y.C., Glendale (Calif.) Fed. Bank, Wailea, Alexander and Baldwin, Hawaii. Lt. (j.g.) USN, 1955-58. Achievements include research computerized techniques in architecture and economic feasibility land development. Home and Office: 1721 Catalina Ave Seal Beach CA 90740-5710

ROSSI, STEVEN R. newspaper publishing company executive; m. Rosemary; four children. BA, Ursinus Coll.; MBA, U. Pa. Gen. mgr., corp. controller IU Internat. Corp.; v.p., gen. mgr. Amerigas Indsl. Gases, 1988-91; v.p., chief fin. officer Knight Ridder, San Jose, Calif., 1987-88, sr. v.p., 1988-91, exec. v.p., 1991-96, sr. v.p. ops., 1996— [illegible] Am. Music Theater Festival; bd. dirs. Univ. Arts. Mem. Pa. Newspapers Publ.'s Assn. (bd. dirs.). Office: Knight Ridder 50 W San Fernando St San Jose CA 95113-2429

ROSSITER, BRYANT WILLIAM, chemistry consultant; b. Ogden, Utah, Mar. 10, 1931; s. Bryant B. and Christine (Peterson) R.; m. Betty Jean Anderson, Apr. 16, 1951; children: Bryant, Mark, Diane, Steven, Linda, Karen, Matthew, Gregory. BA, U. Utah, 1954, PhD, 1957. Researcher Eastman-Kodak Co., Rochester, N.Y., 1957-63, head color phys. chem. lab., 1963-70, dir. chemistry div., 1970-84, dir. sci., tech. devel., 1984-86; pres. Viratek Inc., Costa Mesa, Calif., 1986-89; sr. v.p. ICN Pharms., Costa Mesa, 1989-90; ret., 1990; pres., CEO WRECON, Inc., Laguna Hills, Calif., 1991-96, ret., 1996. Sr. editor John Wiley & Sons, N.Y.C., 1970—; chmn. bd. Nucleic Acid Rsch. Inst., Costa Mesa, 1987-88; trustee Eastman Dental Ctr., Rochester, 1973-93 (bd. pres. 1982-85); bd. dirs. Verax & Corp. Editor: (chem. treatises) Physical Methods of Chemistry (11 vols.), 1970-76, Physical Methods, (12 vols.), 1986—, Chemical Experimentation Under Extreme Conditions, 1979. Mem. rsch. adv. com. U.S. Agy. for Internat. Devel., Washington, chmn. rsch. adv. com., 1989-92; mem. panel on biosci. Pres.' Coun. Advisors on Sci. and Tech., 1991; mem. adv com. Cornell Internat. Inst. for Food, Agr. and Devel., 1991; presiding officer Ch. Jesus Christ Latter Day Saints, Ea. U.S. and Can., 1959-86, counselor presidency San Diego temple, 1998—. 1st lt. USAFR, 1951-58. Named Hon. Alumni Brigham Young U., Provo, Utah, 1982. Fellow AAAS, Am. Inst. Chemists (lectr., Fellows award 1988, Will Judy award Juanita Coll. 1978); mem. Internat. Union Pure and Applied Chemistry (chmn. U.S. nat. com., orignator, chmn. Chemical Rsch. Applied to World Needs com. 1975-87, chmn. Chemical Rsch. Applied to World Needs II The Internat. Conf. on Chemistry and World Food Supplies, 1982), Am. Chem. Soc. (chmn. internat. activities). Avocations: horseback riding, reading, fishing. Home and Office: 25662 Dillon Rd Laguna Hills CA 92653-5800 E-mail: bwr@Ni.Net

ROSSUM, RALPH ARTHUR, political science educator; b. Alexandria, Minn., Dec. 17, 1946; s. Floyd Arthur and June Marion (Carlson) R.; m. Constance Mary Brazina, Aug. 19, 1972; children: Kristin, Brent, Pierce. BA summa cum laude, Concordia Coll., 1968; MA, U. Chgo., 1971, PhD, 1973. Instr. Grinnell (Iowa) Coll., 1972-73; asst. prof. Memphis State U., 1973-77, assoc. prof., 1977-80, Loyola U., Chgo., 1980-83, assoc. dean grad. sch., 1981-82; dep. dir. bur. justice stats. U.S. Dept. Justice, Washington, 1983-84; Alice Tweed Tuohy prof. govt. Claremont (Calif.) McKenna Coll., 1984-88, v.p. and dean of faculty, 1988-91; pres. Hampden-Sydney (Va.) Coll., 1991-92; Salvatori Vis. prof. Claremont (Calif.) McKenna Coll., 1992-93, Salvatori prof. Am. Constitutionalism, 1994—; Fletcher Jones Prof. of Am. Politics U. Redlands, Redlands, Calif., 1993-94. Mem. adv. bd. Nat. Inst. Corrections, U.S. Dept. Justice, 1988-91; mem. Robert Presley Inst. Corrections Rsch. and Tng., State of Calif., 1988-91; dir. Rose Inst. of State and Local Govt., 2000—. Author: Federalism, the Supreme Court and the Seventeenth Amendment, 2001, others; co-author: The American Founding, 1981, American Constitutional Law, 1983, 5th edit., 1999, others; sr. editor Benchmark, 1983-86, book rev. editor, 1986—; contbr. 55 articles to profl. jours. and chpts. to books. Trustee Episcopal Theol. Sch., Claremont, 1987-91. Ford Found. fellow, 1968-72. Mem. Am. Polit. Sci. Assn. Episcopalian. Office: Claremont McKenna Coll Dept Govt 850 Columbia Ave Claremont CA 91711-3901 E-mail: ralph.rossum@claremontmckenna.edu

ROST, THOMAS LOWELL, plant biology educator; b. St. Paul, Dec. 28, 1941; s. Lowell Henry Rost and Agnes Marie (Wojtowicz) Jurek; m. Ann Marie Ruhland, Aug. 31, 1963; children: Christopher, Timothy, Jacquelyn. BS, St. John's U., Collegeville, Minn., 1963; MA, Mankato State U., 1965; PhD, Iowa State U., 1971. Postdoctoral fellow Brookhaven Nat. Lab., Upton, N.Y., 1970-72; asst. to full prof. dept. botany U. Calif., Davis, 1972-82, faculty asst. to chancellor, 1982-83, prof., chmn. plant biology sect., 1994-96, assoc. dean divsn. biol. sci., 1996—. Cons. faculty of agronomy U. Uruguay, 1979, 89; vis. fellow Rsch. Soc. Biol. Sci., Canberra, Australia, 1979-80; vis. prof. U. Wroclaw, Poland, 1987, U. Exeter, Eng., 1993. Co-author: Botany: A Brief Introduction to Plant Biology, 1979, Botany: An Introduction on Plant Biology, 1982; co-editor: Mechanisms and Control of Cell Division, 1977, Plant Biology, 1998; also numerous articles to profl. jours. Served to capt. U.S. Army, 1965-67. Fellow Japan Soc. Promotion of Sci.; mem. Bot. Soc. Am., Soc. Exptl. Biology, Am. Inst. Biol. Sci. Democrat. Roman Catholic. Avocation: community theatre. Office: U Calif Sect Plant Biology Davis CA 95616-8537

ROSTER, MICHAEL, lawyer; b. Chgo., May 7, 1945; AB, Stanford U., 1967, JD, 1973. Bar: Calif. 1973, D.C. 1980. Ptnr. McKenna, Conner & Cuneo, L.A. and Washington, 1973-87, Morrison & Foerster, L.A. and Washington, 1987-93; gen. counsel Stanford (Calif.) U., 1993-2000; exec. v.p., gen. counsel Golden West Fin. Corp., 2000—. Bd. dirs. Silicon Valley Bancshares, vice chmn., 1995-98; chmn. Encirq, 1998—, Insert Therapeutics, 2000—. Contbr. articles to profl. jours. Bd. dirs. pasadena Heritage, 1986-87. Lt. (j.g.) USN, 1969-71. Mem. ABA (chmn. com. on savs. instns. 1985-89, fin. svcs. com. 1981—, banking com. 1989—), Calif. Bar Assn. (chmn. banking com. 1978-79), Am. Corp. Counsel Assn. (chmn. 2000-01), Stanford U. Alumni Assn. (chmn. 1992), Univ. Club (Washington), L.A. Athletic Club. Home: 1321 Fairlawn Way Pasadena CA 91105-1002 Office: Golden West Fin Corp 1901 Harrison Oakland CA 94612

ROSTOKER, GORDON, physicist, educator; b. Toronto, Ont., Can., July 15, 1940; s. Louis and Fanny (Silbert) R.; m. Gillian Patricia Farr, June 29, 1966; children: Gary David, Susan Birgitta, Daniel Mark. BSc in Physics, U. Toronto, 1962, MA in Physics, 1963; PhD in Geophysics, U. B.C., Can., 1966. Postdoctoral fellow Royal Inst. Tech., Stockholm, 1966-68; asst. prof. physics U. Alta., B.C., 1968-73, assoc. prof., 1973-79, prof., 1979-97, McCalla Rsch. Prof., 1983-84, prof. emeritus, 1997—, ann. Killam prof. B.C., 1991-92, dir. Inst. Earth and Planetary Physics, 1985-91. Assoc. chmn. dept. physics U. Alta., 1976-79, univ. rep. to bd. dirs. Can. Network for Space Rsch., 1992-94, mem. univ. rsch. policy com., 1987-91; cons. TRW Sys. Group, 1973, Dome Petroleum Ltd., 1981, U. Western Ont., 1983, York U., 1986; contract rschr. Energy, Mines and Resources, Can., Hydro-Québec; mem. assoc. com. space rsch. Nat. Rsch. Coun. Can., 1975-80, mem. com. on internat. sci. exchgs., 1977-79, others; mem. physics and astronomy com. Natural Scis. and Engring. Rsch. Coun., 1979-82, mem. spl. ad hoc com. on physics and astronomy, 1987-91, mem. grant selection com. for sci. publs., 1988-92; prin. investigator CANOPUS, 1989—; chmn. divsn. III Internat. Assn. Geomagnetism and Aeronomy, 1979-83; chmn. working group on data analysis phase of Internat. Magnetospheric Study Sci. Com. on Solar Terrestrial Physics of Internat. Coun. Sci. Unions, 1980-86, co-chmn. steering com. for Solar-Terrestrial Energy Program, 1987-89, chmn., 1989-97/ Editor Can. Jour. Physics, 1980-86, mem. editl. adv. bd., 1986-96; assoc. editor Jour. Geomagnetism and Geoelectricity, 1993-96; contbr. over 250 articles to profl. publs. Mem. pub. adv. com. Govtl. Environ. Conservation Authority of Province of Alta., Edmonton, 1973-74. Recipient Steacie prize EWR Steacie Meml. Fund, 1979, Geophys. Centenary medal Acad. Scis. USSR, 1984. Fellow Royal Soc. Can.; mem. Am. Geophys. Union (assoc. editor Jour. Geophys. Rsch. 1976-79, 92-94, internat. sec. 1998—), Can. Assn. Physicists (sec.-treas. Can. Geophys. Union 1973-74, chmn. divsn. aeronomy and space physics 1977-78, publs. com. 1980-86), Internat. Assn. Geomagnetism and Aeronomy (v.p. 1995—). Achievements include use of ground magnetometer arrays to [illegible] systems which flow in the ionosphere and magnetosphere during episodes of strong auroral disturbance. Office: U Alta Dept Physics Edmonton AB Canada T6G 2J1

ROSTOKER, MICHAEL DAVID, former micro-electronics company executive, lawyer; b. Quincy, Mass., Mar. 15, 1958; s. David and E. Louise (Berleue) R. Student, Carnegie-Mellon U., 1976-78; BS in Indsl. Engring., U. Pitts., 1980; JD, Franklin Pierce Law Ctr., 1984; PhD in Indsl. Engring., City U., L.A., 1992; JSM, Stanford U., 1997; PhD in Econs., Moscow State U., 1999. Bar: U.S. Patent and Trademark Office 1983, N.H. 1984, U.S. Dist. Ct. N.H. 1984, Mass. 1985, Pa. 1985, U.S. Dist. Ct. D.C. 1985, U.S. Ct. Appeals (D.C. cir.) 1985. Lectr. in computer sci. Point Park Coll., Pitts., 1979-80; sys. analyst GE, Fitchburg, Mass., 1980-81; patent atty. Rines and Rines, Boston and Concord, N.H., 1983-85; patent counsel Schlumberger Well Svcs., Houston, 1985-87; sr. counsel intellectual property Intel Corp., Santa Clara, Calif., 1987-88; v.p. strategic alliances LSI Logic Corp., Milpitas, 1988-96; pres., CEO Microelectronics Rsch. Inc. subs. Kawasaki, San Jose, 1996-99; ret., 1999. Cons. in field, Concord, 1981-85; mem. faculty computer sci. and math. Franklin Pierce Coll., Rindge, N.H., 1981-85; mem. adj. faculty law Franklin Pierce Law Ctr., 1983-85; edtl. bd. Software Protection Reporter, 1984-94; lectr. seminars in field. Author: Computer Jurisprudence: Legal Responses to the Information Revolution, 1985, Technology Management: Licensing and Protection for Computers in the World Market, 1993; contbr. articles to profl. jours.; patentee in field. Mem. ABA (patents, sci. and tech., litigation sects.), Am. Trial Lawyers Assn., Am. Intellectual Property Assn. Republican. Jewish. Avocations: volleyball, racquetball, weightlifting, theater, music. Home: 108 Mcpherson Ct Boulder Creek CA 95006-9203 Office: Microelectronics Rsch Inc 2570 N 1st St Ste 301 San Jose CA 95131-1018

ROTENBERG, MANUEL, physics educator; b. Toronto, Ont., Can., Mar. 12, 1930; came to U.S., 1946; s. Peter and Rose (Plonzker) R.; m. Paula Weissbrod, June 23, 1952; children: Joel, Victor. BS, MIT, 1952, PhD, 1956. Staff Los Alamos (N.Mex.) Nat. Lab., 1955-58; instr. physics Princeton (N.J.) U., 1958-59; asst. prof. U. Chgo., 1959-61; prof. applied physics U. Calif., San Diego, 1961-93, dean grad. studies and research, 1975-84, chmn. dept. elec. engring. and computer sci., 1988-93, rsch. prof., 1993—. Author: The 3-j and 6-j Symbols, 1959; founding editor: Methods of Computational Physics, 1963, Jour. of Computational Physics, 1962; editor: Biomathematics and Cell Kinetics, 1981. Fellow Am. Phys. Soc.; mem. AAAS, Sigma Xi. Office: U Calif San Diego La Jolla CA 92093-0407

ROTH, DUANE J. pharmaceutical executive; With Ortho Diagnostic Systems, Inc.; pres. Analytab Products Inc.; CEO Alliance Pharm. Corp., San Diego, 1985—, chmn., 1989—. Chmn. San Diego Regional Econ. Devel. Corp.; mem. bd. dir. Biotechnology Industry Org., CA Healthcare Inst. Office: Alliance Pharm Corp 3040 Science Park Rd San Diego CA 92121-1102

ROTH, JOE, motion picture company executive; b. N.Y.C., June 13, 1948; Prodn. assistant various commls. and feature films, San Francisco; also lighting dir. Pitchel Players, San Francisco, then producer L.A.; co-founder Morgan Creek Prodns., L.A., 1987-89; chmn. 20th Century Fox Film Corp., L.A., 1989-92; founder Caravan Pictures, L.A., 1992-94; chmn. Walt Disney Motion Pictures Group, Burbank, 1994-97, Walt Disney Studios, Burbank, 1997-2000; founder Revolution Pictures, 2000—. Bd. dirs. Pixar Studios, 2000—. Prodr. numerous films including Tunnelvision, Cracking Up, Americathon, Our Winning Season, The Final Terror, The Stone Boy, Where the River Runs Black, Bachelor Party, Off Beat, Streets of Gold (dir. debut), Revenge of the Nerds II (also dir.); exec. prodr. Young Guns, Dead Ringers, Skin Deep, Major League, Renegades, Coupe de Ville (also dir.), Enemies: A Love Story: Caravan Pictures releases include Walt Disney's The Three Musketeers, Angie, Angels in the Outfield, I Love Trouble, A Low Down Dirty Shame, Houseguest, The Jerky Boys, Heavyweights, Tall Tale, While You Were Sleeping. Office: Walt Disney Studio 500 S Buena Vista Team Disney Bldg Rm 606 Burbank CA 91521-0004

ROTH, JOHN KING, philosopher, educator; b. Grand Haven, Mich., Sept. 3, 1940; s. Josiah V. and Doris Irene (King) R.; m. Evelyn Lillian Austin, June 25, 1964; children: Andrew Lee, Sarah Austin. BA, Pomona Coll., 1962; student, Yale U., 1962-63, MA, 1965, PhD, 1966; LHD, Ind. U., 1990, Grand Valley State U., 1998, Hebrew Union Coll., 1999, We. U. Health Scis., 1999. Asst. prof. philosophy Claremont McKenna Coll., Calif., 1966-71, assoc. prof., 1971-76, Russell K. Pitzer prof. philosophy, 1976—; vis. prof. philosophy Franklin Coll., Lugano, Switzerland, 1973. Fulbright lectr. in Am. studies U. Innsbruck, Austria, 1973-74, Royal Norwegian Ministry of Edn., Oslo, Norway, 1995-96; vis. prof. philosophy Doshisha U., Kyoto, Japan, 1981-82; vis. prof. Holocaust studies U. Haifa, Israel, 1982. Author: Freedom and the Moral Life, 1969, Problems of the Philosophy of Religion, 1971, American Dreams, 1976, A Consuming Fire, 1979; (with Richard L. Rubenstein) Approaches to Auschwitz, 1987; (with Frederick Sontag) The American Religious Experience, 1972, The Questions of Philosophy, 1988; (with Robert H. Fossum) The American Dream, 1981, American Ground, 1988; (with Rubenstein) The Politics of Latin American Liberation Theology, 1988; (with Michael Berenbaum) Holocaust: Religious and Philosophical Implications, 1989, Ethics, 1991; (with Carol Rittner) Memory Offended, 1991; (with Creighton Peden) Rights, Justice, and Community, 1992; (with Carol Rittner) Different Voices, 1993, American Diversity, American Identity, 1995, Inspiring Teaching, 1997, From the Unthinkable to the Unavoidable, 1997, Encyclopedia of Social Issues, 1997, Private Needs, Public Selves: Talk About Religion in American, 1997, (with Stephen R. Haynes) The Death of God Movement and the Holocaust, 1999, Ethics After the Holocaust, 1999. Spl. advisor U.S. Holocaust Meml. Coun., Washington, 1980-85, mem., 1995-98. Danforth grad. fellow, 1962-66; Graves fellow, 1970-71; NEH fellow, 1976-77, Koerner fellow Oxford Ctr. for Hebrew and Jewish Studies, Eng.; Faculty Pairing grantee Japan-U.S. Friendship Commn., 1981-83; named U.S. Prof. of Yr. Coun. Advancement and Support of Edn. and Carnegie Found. Advancement of Tchg., 1988. Mem Am. Philos. Assn., Am. Acad. Religion, Am. Studies Assn., Calif. Coun. for Humanities, Phi Beta Kappa. Presbyterian. Home: 1458 Augusta Dr Upland CA 91786-2446 Office: Claremont McKenna Coll 850 Columbia Ave Claremont CA 91711-3901 E-mail: John.Roth@claremontmckenna.edu

ROTH, JOHN ROGER, geneticist, biology educator; b. Winona, Minn., Mar. 14, 1939; s. Frederick Daniel and Louise Mae (Wirt) R.; m. Uta Goetz (div.); children: Katherine Louise, Frederick Phillip; m. Sherylynne Harris, Jan. 4, 1986. BA, Harvard U., 1961; PhD, John Hopkins U., 1965. From asst. prof. molecular biology to prof. molecular biology U. Calif., Berkeley, 1967-76; disting. prof. biology U. Utah, Salt Lake City, 1976—. Recipient Disting. Prof. award, 1990, Rosenblatt award, 1990. Mem. NAS, Am. Soc. for Microbiology, Genetics Soc. Am. Office: U Utah Dept Biology 257 S 1400 E Salt Lake City UT 84112-0840

ROTH, PAUL B. emergency medicine physician; b. Glen Ridge, N.J., Oct. 7, 1947; s. Jerome M. and Selma (Leitner) R. BS, Fairleigh Dickinson U., 1969, MS, 1972; MD, George Washington U., 1976; postgrad., U. N.Mex., 1976-79. Owner, pres. EMS of N.Mex., Albuquerque, 1978-82; owner, mem. of bd. Heights Urgent Care Ctr., Albuquerque, 1980-82; dir. divsn. emergency medicine U. N.Mex. Sch. Medicine, Albuquerque, 1982-91, chair dept. emergency medicine, 1991-93; interim chief med. officer U. N.Mex. Med. Ctr., Albuquerque, 1992-93, now dean medicine, 1995—; prof. emerg. med. U. N. Mex. Med. Ctr., Albuquerque, 1991—. Dir. Ctr. for Disaster Medicine U. N.Mex. Sch. Medicine, Albuquerque, 1990—; co-chair NDMS-Med. Response Steering Com., Rockville, Mass., 1991—; chair sect. on disaster medicine Nat. ACEP, Dallas, 1991—. Contbr. articles to Annals of EM, Current Practice of EM-Disaster Medicine, Jour. of AMA. Recipient Outstanding Individual Svc. award Nat. Disaster Med. System, 1986. Fellow Am. Coll. Emergency Physicians; mem. AMA, Soc. for Acad. Emergency Medicine, Am. Coll. Physician Execs., Am. Acad. Family Physicians. Office: U NMex Sch Medicine Dean Basic Med Scis Bldg Rm 177 Albuquerque NM 87131-0001

ROTH, PETER, broadcast executive; b. Larchmont, N.Y. m. Andrea Roth; 2 children. Student, U. Pa.; grad., Tufts U., 1972. From mgr. to dir. children's programs ABC TV Network, 1976, dir. current programs, 1979, v.p. current prime-time series, 1981; past pres. Stephen J. Cannell Prodns.; pres. prodn. Twentieth Network TV, 1992, pres., 1993, 20th Century Fox TV, 1994, Fox Entertainment Group, L.A., 1996-98, Warner Bros. Television, Burbank, Calif., 1998—. Office: Warner Bros Television 300 Television Plz Bldg 140 Burbank CA 91522-0001

ROTH, RANDALL W. lawyer; b. Ellinwood, Kans., May 14, 1948; BS summa cum laude, Regis Coll., 1970; LLM, U. Miami, 1975. Bar: Colo. 1975, Kans. 1980, Hawaii 1983. Of counsel Goodsill Anderson Quinn & Stifel, Honolulu. Prof. law U. Hawaii, 1982—. Mem. ABA, Am. Coll. Trust and Estate Counsel, Hawaii State Bar Assn. (pres. 1999), Alpha Sigma Nu. Office: Goodsill Anderson Quinn & Stifel 1099 Alakea St Honolulu HI 96813-4511 E-mail: rroth@hawaii.edu

ROTHBLATT, DONALD NOAH, urban and regional planner, educator; b. N.Y.C., Apr. 28, 1935; s. Harry and Sophie (Chernofsky) R.; m. Ann S. Vogel, June 16, 1957; children: Joel Michael, Steven Saul. BCE, CUNY, 1957; MS in Urban Planning, Columbia U., 1963; Diploma in Comprehensive Planning, Inst. Social Studies, The Hague, 1964; PhD in City and Regional Planning, Harvard U., 1969. Registered profl. engr. N.Y. Planner N.Y.C. Planning Commn., 1960-62, N.Y. Housing and Redevel. Bd., 1963-66; research fellow Ctr. for Environ. Design Studies, Harvard U., Cambridge, Mass., 1965-71; teaching fellow, instr., then asst. prof. city and regional planning Harvard U., 1967-71; prof. urban and regional planning, chmn. dept. San Jose State U., Calif., 1971—. Lady Davis vis. prof. urban and regional planning Hebrew U., Jerusalem and Tel Aviv U., 1978; vis. scholar Indian Inst. Architects, 1979, Shandong Province, China, 1996, U. Lodz, Poland, 2000; vis. scholar, rsch. assoc. Inst. Govtl. Studies, U. Calif., Berkeley, 1980—; cons. to pvt. industry and govt. agys. Author: Human Needs and Public Housing, 1964, Thailand's Northeast, 1967, Regional Planning: The Appalachian Experience, 1971, Allocation of Resources for Regional Planning, 1972, The Suburban Environment and Women, 1979, Regional-Local Development Policy Making, 1981, Planning the Metropolis: The Multiple Advocacy Approach, 1982, Comparative Suburban Data, 1983, Suburbia: An International Assessment, 1986, Metropolitan Dispute Resolution in Silicon Valley, 1989, Good Practices for the Congestion Management Program, 1994, Activity-Based Travel Survey and Analysis of Responses to Increased Congestion, 1995, An Experiment in Sub-Regional Planning: California's Congestion Management Policy, 1995, Estimating the Origins and Destinations of Transit Passengers from On/Off Counts, 1995, Changes in Property Values Induced by Light Transit, 1996, Comparitive Study of Statewide Transportation Planning Under ISTEA, 1997, North American Metropolitan Planning Reexamined, 1999, Government Performance Measures Linking Urban Mass Transportation With Land Use and Accessibility Factors, 2000, Best Practices in Developing Regional Transportation Plans, 2001; editor: National policy for Urban and Regional Development, 1974, Regional Advocacy Planning: Expanding Air Transport Facilities for the San Jose Metropolitan Area, 1975, Metropolitan-wide Advocacy Planning; Dispersion of Low and Moderate Cost Housing in the San Jose Metropolitan Area, 1976, Multiple Advocacy Planning: Public Surface Transportation in the San Jose Metropolitan Area, 1977, A Multiple Advocacy Approach to Regional Planning: Open Space and Recreational Facilities for the San Jose Metropolitan Area, 1979, Regional Transpotation Planning for the San Jose Metropolitan Area, 1981, Planning for Open Space and Recreational Facilities in the San Jose Metropolitan Area, 1982, Regional Economic Development Planning for the San Jose Metropolitan Area, 1984, Planning for Surface Transportation in the San Jose Metropolitan Area, 1986, Expansion of Air Transportation Facilities in the San Jose Metropolitan Area, 1987, Provision of Economic Development in the San Jose Met. Area, 1988, Metropolitan Governance: American/Canadian Intergovernmental Perspectives, 1993, Metropolitan Governance Revisited, 1998; contbr. numerous articles to profl. jours.; dir.: Pub. TV series Sta. KTEH, 1976. Mem. adv. coun. Bay Area Met. Transp. Commn., 1995—. Served to 1st lt. C.E., U.S. Army, 1957-59. Rsch. fellow John F. Kennedy Sch. Govt. Harvard U., 1967-69; William F. Milton rsch. fellow, 1970-71; faculty rsch. grantee, NSF, 1972-82, Calif. State U., 1977-78; grantee Nat. Inst. Dispute Resolution, 1987-88, Can. Studies Enrichment Program, 1989-90, Can. Studies Rsch. Program, 1992-93, Univ. Rsch. and Tng. Program grantee Calif. Dept. Transp., 1993-97; recipient Innovative Teaching award Calif. State U. and Coll., 1975-79; co-recipient Best of West award Western Ednl. Soc. for Telecommunication, 1976; recipient award Internat. Festival of Films on Architecture and Planning, 1983, Meritorious Performance award San Jose State U., 1986, 88, 90. Mem. Assn. Collegiate Schs. of Planning (pres. 1975-76), Am. Inst. Cert. Planners, Am. Planning Assn., Planners for Equal Opportunity, Internat. Fedn. Housing and Planning, AAUP, Calif. Edn. Com. on Architecture and Landscape, Architecture and Urban and Regional Planning (chmn. 1973-75) Office: San Jose State U Dept Urban & Regional Planni San Jose CA 95192-0185

ROTHENBERG, ALAN I. lawyer, professional sports association executive; b. Detroit, Apr. 10, 1939; m. Georgina Rothenberg; 3 children B.A., U. Mich., 1960, J.D., 1963. Bar: Calif. 1964. Assoc. O'Melveny & Myers, L.A., 1963-66; ptnr. Manatt Phelps Rothenberg & Phillips, L.A., 1968-90, Latham & Watkins, L.A., 1990—; instr. sports law U. So. Calif., 1969, 76, 84, Whittier Coll. Law, 1980, 84; pres., gen. counsel L.A. Lakers and L.A. Kings, 1967-79, L.A. Clippers Basketball Team, 1982-89; pres. U.S. Soccer Fedn., Chgo., 1990-98; chmn., founder Maj. League Soccer, N.Y.C., 1995. Soccer commr. 1984 Olympic Games; chmn., pres., CEO 1994 World Cup Organizing Com., 1990-94; founder, chmn. Major League Soccer, 1994—; bd. dirs., pres. Constl. Rights Found., 1987-90. Mem. aBA, State Bar Calif. (pres. 1989-90), Los Angeles County Bar Assn., L.A. Bar Assn., Nat. Basketball Assn. (bd. govs. 1971-79, 82-89), N.Am. Soccer League (bd. govs. 1977-80, Major League Soccer mgmt. com. 1994—), Order of Coif. Office: Latham & Watkins 633 W 5th St Ste 4000 Los Angeles CA 90071-2005

ROTHENBERG, HARVEY DAVID, educational administrator; b. May 31, 1937; s. Max and Cecelia Rothenberg; m. Audrey Darlynne Roseman, July 5, 1964; children: David Michael, Mark Daniel. BBA, State U. Iowa, 1960; MA, U. No. Colo., 1961; postgrad., Harris Tchrs. Coll., 1962-63; PhD, Colo. State U., 1972. Distributive edn. tchr. Roosevelt H.S., St. Louis, 1961-63, Proviso West H.S., Hillside, Ill., 1963-64, Longmont (Colo.) Sr. H.S., 1964-69, 70-71; supr. rsch. and spl. programs St. Vrain Valley Sch. Dist., Longmont, 1971-72; chmn. bus. divsn. Arapahoe C.C., Littleton, Colo., 1972-75; dir. vocat., career and adult edn. Arapahoe County Sch. Dist. 6, Littleton, 1975-96; part-time instr. Met. State Coll., Denver, 1975-85, Arapahoe C.C., Littleton, 1975-80, Regis U., 1980—. Dir. faculty, curriculum Sch. Profl. Studies, Regis U., 1996-98, instr., facilitator, 1998—; owner HDR Bus. and Ednl. Consulting, 1988—; owner Shreveport Bombers Indoor Football Team of Indoor Profl. Football League, 1999—; vis. prof. U . Ala., Tuscaloosa, summer 1972; dir. Chatfield Bank, Littleton, 1974-83, Yaak River Mines Ltd., Amusement Personified Inc.; pres. Kuytia Inc., Littleton, 1975—; co-owner Albuquerque Lasers. Author: Conducting Successful Business Research, 1996. Mem. City of Longmont Long-Range Planning Commn., 1971-72, pres. Homeowners Bd., 1978-80. Recipient Outstanding Young Educator award St. Vrain Valley Sch. Dist., 1967, Outstanding Vocat. Educator, Colo., 1992, Western Region U.S., 1993. Mem. Am. Vocat. Assn., Nat. Assn. Local Sch. Adminstrs., Colo. Vocat. Assn. (mem. exec. com. 1966-68, treas. 1972-73), Littleton C. of C., Colo. Assn. Vocat. Adminstrs., Colo. Educators for and About Bus., Elks, Masons, Delta Sigma Pi, Delta Pi Epsilon. Home: 7461 S Sheridan Ct Littleton CO 80128-7084 E-mail: rothenbergs@msn.com

ROTHERHAM, LARRY CHARLES, insurance executive; b. Council Bluffs, Iowa, Oct. 22, 1940; s. Charles Sylvester and Edna Mary (Sylvanus) R.; m. Florene F. Black, May 29, 1965; children: Christopher Charles, Phillip Larry, Kathleen Florene. Student, Creighton U., 1959-61; BSBA, U. Nebr., 1965; postgrad., Am. Coll., Bryn Mawr, Pa., 1985, 87. CPCU, CLU, ARM. Claims rep. and underwriter Safeco Ins. Co., Albuquerque, 1965-69; br. mgr. Ohio Casualty Group, Albuquerque, 1969-99, resident v.p. Denver, 1997-99. Assoc. in risk mgmt. Ins. Inst. Am., 1976—. Mem. PTA Collet Park Elem. Sch., Albuquerque, 1963-82, Freedom H.S., Albuquerque, 1982-86; bd. chmn. N.Mex. Property Ins. Program; mem. N.Mex. Workers compensation Appeals Bd. Mem. New Mex. Soc. Chartered Property & Casualty Underwriters (charter mem., pres. 1975-77), New Mex. Soc. Chartered Life Underwriters, New Mex. Ins. Assn. Democrat. Roman Catholic. Avocations: race walking, swimming, hiking, camping. Home: 10677 W Parkhill Pl Littleton CO 80127-5547

ROTHMAN, PAUL ALAN, publishing executive; b. Bklyn., June 26, 1940; s. Fred B. and Dorothy (Regosin) R.; m. Mary Ann Dalson, July 28, 1966 (div. 1992); m. Carol Ann Liske, Sept. 17, 1999; children: Deborah, Diana. BA, Swarthmore Coll., 1962; JD, U. Mich., 1965; LLM in Taxation, NYU, 1967. Bar: N.Y. 1965. Assoc. Dewey, Ballentine, Busby, Palmer & Wood, N.Y.C., 1965-67; v.p. Fred B. Rothman & Co., Littleton, Colo., 1967-85, pres., 1985-2000; chmn. bd. Colo. Plasticard, Littleton, 1983-95; owner LoDo Law Books, Denver, 1998—. Editor Mich. Law Rev., 1963-65. Home: 1801 Wynkoop St Apt 708 Denver CO 80202-1196 Office: LoDo Law Books 1701 Wynkoop St Union Sta # 300 Denver CO 80202 E-mail: parothman@yahoo.com

ROTHMAN, THOMAS EDGAR, production executive; b. Balt., Nov. 21, 1954; s. Donald and Elizabeth (Davidson) R.; m. Jessica Randolph Harper, Mar. 11, 1989; children: Elizabeth, Eleanor. BA, Brown U., 1976; JD, Columbia U., 1980. Ptnr. Frankfurt, Garbus, Klein, N.Y.C., 1982-87; exec. v.p. prodn. Columbia Pictures, Burbank, Calif., 1987-89; sr. v.p. prodn. Samuel Goldwyn Co., L.A., 1989-91, pres. worldwide prodn., 1991—; pres. domestic dist. Twentieth Century Fox Film Group, pres. worldwide prodn. Trustee Sundance (Utah) Inst. Office: Twentieth Century Fox PO Box 900 Beverly Hills CA 90213-0900

ROTHSTEIN, BARBARA JACOBS, federal judge; b. Bklyn., Feb. 3, 1939; d. Solomon and Pauline Jacobs; m. Ted L. Rothstein, Dec. 28, 1968; 1 child, Daniel. B.A., Cornell U., 1960; LL.B., Harvard U., 1966. Bar: Mass. 1966, Wash. 1969, U.S. Ct. Appeals (9th cir.) 1977, U.S. Dist. Ct. (we. dist.) Wash. 1971, U.S. Supreme Ct. 1975. Pvt. practice law, Boston, 1966-68; asst. atty. gen. State of Wash., 1968-77; judge Superior Ct., Seattle, 1977-80, Fed. Dist. Ct. Western Wash., Seattle, 1980—, chief judge, 1987-94. Faculty Law Sch. U. Wash., 1975-77, Hastings Inst. Trial Advocacy, 1977, N.W. Inst. Trial Advocacy, 1979—; mem. state-fed. com. U.S. Jud. Conf., chair subcom. on health reform. Recipient Matrix Table Women of Yr. award Women in Communication, Judge of the Yr. award Fed. Bar Assn., 1989; King County Wash. Women Lawyers Vanguard Honor, 1995. Mem. ABA (jud. sect.), Am. Judicature Soc., Nat. Assn. Women Judges, Fellows of the Am. Bar, Wash. State Bar Assn., U.S. Jud. Conf. (state-fed. com., health reform subcom.), Phi Beta Kappa, Phi Kappa Phi. Office: US Dist Ct 705 US Courthouse 1010 5th Ave Ste 215 Seattle WA 98104-1189

ROTTER, JEROME ISRAEL, medical geneticist; b. L.A., Feb. 24, 1949; s. Leonard L. and Jeanette (Kronenfeld) R.; m. Deborah Tofield, July 14, 1970; children: Jonathan Moshe, Amy Esther, Samuel Alexander. BS, UCLA, 1969, MD, 1973. Intern Harbor-UCLA Med. Ctr., Torrance, Calif., 1973-74, fellow in med. genetics, 1975-78, asst. research pediatrician, 1978-79, faculty div. med. genetics, 1978-86; resident in medicine Wadsworth VA Hosp., Los Angeles, 1974-75; asst. prof. medicine and pediatrics Sch. Medicine UCLA, 1979-83, assoc. prof. Sch. Medicine, 1983-87, prof. Sch. Medicine, 1987—; dir. divsn. med. genetics and co. dir. med. genetics birth defect ctr. Cedars-Sinai Med. Ctr., 1986—, assoc. dir. hypertension ctr., 1996—. Key investigator Ctr. for Ulcer Rsch. and Edn., L.A., 1980-89; dir. genetic epidemiology core Ctr. for Study of Inflammatory Bowel Disease, Torrance, 1985-91; assoc. dir. Cedars-Sinai Inflammatory Bowel Disease Ctr., L.A., 1992—; dir. Stuart Found. CSMC Common Disease Risk Assessment Ctr., 1986-96; dir. genetic epidemiology core project molecular biology of arteriosclerosis UCLA, 1987—. Bd. govs. Cedars-Sinai, chair med. genetics, 1990—. Recipient Regents scholarship UCLA, 1966-73; recipient Richard Weitzman award Harbor-UCLA, 1983, Ross award Western Soc. for Pediatric Rsch., 1985. Mem. Am. Heart Assn., Am. Soc. Human Genetics, Am. Gastroent. Assn., Am. Diabetes Assn., Soc. for Pediatric Research, Western Soc. for Clin. Investigation (mem. council 1985-88), Am. Fedn. for Med. Rsch., Western Assn. Physicians, Am. Soc. for Clin. Investigation, Am. Assn. Physicians. Jewish. Avocations: reading, racquetball. Office: Cedars Sinai Med Ctr Divsn Med Genetics 8700 Beverly Blvd Los Angeles CA 90048-1865

ROULAC, STEPHEN E. real estate consultant; b. San Francisco, Aug. 15, 1945; s. Phil Williams and Elizabeth (Young) R.; children: Arthur, Fiona. BA, Pomona Coll., 1967; MBA with distinction, Harvard Grad. Sch. Bus. Administrn., 1970; JD, U. Calif., Berkeley, 1976; PhD, Stanford U., 1978. CPA, Hawaii. Asst. constrn. supt., foreman, adminstr. Roulac Constrn. Co., Pasadena, Calif., 1963-66; rsch. asst. Econs. Rsch. Assocs., L.A., 1966-67; assoc. economist Urbanomics Rsch. Assocs., Claremont, Calif., 1967; acquisition auditor Litton Industries Inc., Chgo., Beverly Hills, 1967-68; tax cons. Lybrand, Ross Bros. and Montgomery, L.A., 1968; cons. to constrn. group and corp. planning dept. Owens-Corning Fiberglas Corp., Toledo, 1969-70; CEO Questor Assocs., San Francisco, 1972-83; chmn. nat. mgmt. adv. svcs. Kenneth Leventhal & Co., 1983-84; pres. Stephen E. Roulac & Co., 1985-86; mng. ptnr. Roulac Group of Deloitte Haskins & Sells (Deloitte & Touche), 1987-91; CEO The Roulac Group, Larkspur, Calif., 1992—. Strategic fin. econ. and transactions cons. Roulac Capitol Mkt. Strategies, Roulac Capitol Flows; expert witness, preparer econ. analyses for legal matters including civil trial of Irvine Co., Jewell et. al. vs. Bank of Am., Tchrs. vs. Olympia & York, Calif. Legis., Calif. Corps. Dept., Midwest Securities Commrs. Assn., Nat. Assn. Securities Dealers, SEC, Dept. of Labor, HUD; advisor to investment arm of Asian country, Calif. Pub. Employees Retirement System, U.S. Dept. Labor, numerous others; adj. prof. Tex. A&M U., 1986, U. Chgo., 1985, UCLA, 1983-84, Stanford Grad. Sch. Bus., 1970-79, Pacific Coast Banking Sch., 1978, Hastings Coll. Law, 1977-78, U. Calif., Berkeley, 1972-77, Calif. State U., 1970-71, Northeastern U., 1969-70; keynote speaker, instr. continuing edn. sessions, program chmn., corps., orgns. Author: Real Estate Syndications Digest: Principles and Applications, 1972, Case Studies in Property Development, 1973, Syndication Landmarks, 1974, Tax Shelter Sale-Leaseback Financing: The Economic Realities, 1976, Modern Real Estate Investment: An Institutional Approach, 1976, (with Sherman Maisel) Real Estate Investment and Finance, 1976 (1976 Bus. Book of Yr. The Libr. Jour.); editor-in-chief, pub. Calif. Bicyclist, 1988-95, Tex. Bicyclist, 1989-94, Roulac's Strategic Real Estate, 1979-89; columnist Forbes, 1983, 84, 87, 92, 93, Intuition Network, Ctr Real Estate Rsch. Northwestern U., Nat. Bureau Real Estate Rsch., New Leaders, World 2000, NACORE/ARES Corp. Rsch. Found., Mystery Sch.; mem. editorial adv. bd. Am. Real Estate and Urban Econs. Assn. Jour., 1977-81, Housing

Devel. Reporter, 1978-80, Fin. Edn. Jour., 1976-70, Jour. Housing Rsch., 1996—, Jour. Real Estated Edn. and Practice, 1996—, Jour. Real Estate Lit., 1996—, Jour. Property Valuation and Investment, 1992—, Real Estate Workouts and Asset Mgmt., 1992—; assoc. editor Real Estate Rev., 1993—; editor Jour. Real Estate Rsch., 1992—; contbg. editor Real Estate Law Jour., 1973-78, Real Estate Rev., 1973-75; spl. issue editor Calif. Mgmt. Rev., 1976; editor: Real Estate Syndication Digest, 1971-72, Notable Syndications Sourcebook, 1972, Real Estate Securities and Syndication: A Workbook, 1973, Due Diligence in Real Estate Transactions, 1974, Real Estate Venture Analysis, 1974, Real Estate Securities Regulation Sourcebook, 1975, Questor Real Estate Investment Manager Profiles, 1982, Questor Real Estate Securities Yearbook, 1980-85, Retail Giants and Real Estate, 1986, Roulac's Top Real Estate Brokers, 1984-88, (monograph) Ethics in Real Estate; contbr. articles to profl. jours., newspapers; cassettes; frequent appearer on TV shows including MacNeil/Lehrer Newshour, 1986, Cable News Network, 1987, ABC TV, 1987, KCBS Radio, 1986, WABC Radio, Dallas, 1986. Mem. real estate adv. com. to Calif. Commr. Corps., 1973, Calif. Corp. Commr.'s Blue Ribbon Com. on Projections and Track Records, 1973-74; mem. adv. bd. Nat. Bicycle Month, League of Am. Wheelmen, Ctr. for Real Estate Rsch. Kellogg Grad. Sch. Mgmt., Northwestern U. Named Highest Instr. Student Teaching Evaluations, Schs. Bus. Adminstrn., U. Calif., Berkeley, 1975-76; named to Pomona Coll. Athletic Hall of Fame, 1981; W.T. Grant fellow Harvard U., 1969-70,; George F. Baker scholar Harvard Grad. Sch. Bus. Adminstrn., 1970; Stanford U. Grad. Sch. Bus. fellow, 1970-71. Mem. Strategic Mgmt. Soc., Am. Acad. Mgmt., Am. Fin. Assn., Am. Planning Assn, European Real Estate Soc., Internat. Real Estate Soc., Inst. Mgmt. Cons., ISSSEEM, Soc. Sci. Exploration, Am. Real Estate and Urban Econs. Assn., Intuition Network (bd. dirs.), World Future Soc. (exec. com. and adv. bd. World 2000), Am. Econ. Assn., Am. Real Estate Soc. (pres. 1995-96, award for best paper presented in ann. meeting, 1995, 96), Noetic Soc., Nat. Bur. Real Estate Rsch. (founder, bd. dirs.), Harvard Club N.Y., L.A. Adventures Club. Avocations: arts, antiquarian books, reading, bicycle racing (U.S. team 1990), outdoor activities. Office: The Roulac Group 709 5th Ave San Rafael CA 94901-3202

ROUNDS, BARBARA LYNN, psychiatrist; b. L.A., Mar. 17, 1934; d. Ralph Arthur and Florene V. (Heyer) Behrend; divorced 1962; children: Steve, Mike, Pamela, Ronald, Thomas. BA, Stanford U., 1964, MD, 1966; postgrad., San Francisco Psychoanalytic, 1973-81. Diplomate Am. Bd. Psychiatry and Neurology; cert. psychoanalyst. Intern New Orleans Pub. Health Svc., 1966-67; resident psychiat. Mendocino State Hosp., 1967-69, U. Calif. Davis, 1969-70; staff psychiatrist U. Calif. Davis Med. Sch., Sacramento, 1970-77, clin. instr., 1970-76; psychiatrist pvt. practice, Sacramento, 1971—; asst. clin. prof. U. Calif. Davis, Sacramento, 1976-84, assoc. clin. prof., 1984-94. Mem. Am. Psychiat. Assn., Am. Psychoanalytic Assn., AMA, Cen. Calif. Psychiat. Soc. (pres.-elect 1990-91, pres. 1991-92). Democrat. Home: 8910 Leatham Ave Fair Oaks CA 95628-6506 Office: 1317 H St Sacramento CA 95814-1928

ROUNSAVILLE, GUY, JR. lawyer; b. 1943; BA, Stanford U., 1965; JD, U. Calif., San Francisco, 1968. Bar: Calif. 1969. Atty. Wells Fargo, 1969-73, v.p., counsel, 1974-77, v.p., chief counsel, 1977-78, sr. v.p., chief counsel, sec., 1980-85, exec. v.p., chief counsel, sec., 1985-98; ptnr. Allen, Matkins, Leck, Gamble & Mallory, San Francisco, 1999—.

ROUSE, RICHARD HUNTER, historian, educator; b. Boston, Aug. 14, 1933; s. Hunter and Dorothee (Hüsmert) R.; m. Mary L. Ames, Sept. 7, 1959; children: Thomas, Andrew, Jonathan. BA, State U. Iowa, 1955; MA, U. Chgo., 1957; PhD, Cornell U., 1963. Mem. faculty UCLA, 1963—, prof. history, 1975—. Assoc. dir. Ctr. Medieval and Renaissance Studies, 1966-67, acting dir., 1967-68; dir. Summer Inst. in Paleography, 1978, chair grad. coun., 1989-90; adv. bd. Hill Monastic Microfilm Libr., St. John's U., Collegeville, Minn., Ambrosiana Microfilm Library, Notre Dame (Ind.) U., Corpus of Brit. Medieval Libr. Catalogues, Brit. Acad. Author: Serial Bibliographies for Medieval Studies, 1969, (with M.A. Rouse) Preachers, Florilegia and Sermons: Studies on the Manipulus Florum of Thomas of Ireland, 1979; (with others) Texts and Transmission, 1983; (with C.W. Dutschke) Medieval and Renaissance Manuscripts in the Claremont Libraries, 1986; (with M.A. Rouse) Cartolai, Illuminators and Printers in Fifteenth-Century Italy, 1988; (with L. Bataillon and B. Guyot) La Production du livre universitaire au moyen age, exemplar et pecia, 1988, (with others) Guide to Medieval and Renaissance Manuscripts in the Huntington Library, 1989, (with M. Ferrari) Medieval and Renaissance Manuscripts at the University of California, Los Angeles, 1991, (with M.A. Rouse and R.A.B. Mynors) Registrum de libris doctorum et auctorum veterum, 1991, (with M.A. Rouse) Authentic Witnesses: Approaches to Medieval Texts and Manuscripts, 1991, (with M.A. Rouse) Manuscripts and Their Makers: Commercial Book Producers in Medieval Paris 1200-1500, 2 vols., 2000; co-editor: Viator: Medieval and Renaissance Studies, 1970—; mem. editorial bd. Medieval and renaissance manuscripts in Calif. libraries, Medieval Texts, Toronto; Medieval Texts, Binghamton, Library Quar., 1984-88, Speculum, 1981-85, Revue d'histoire des Textes, 1986—, Cambridge Studies in Paleography and Codicology, 1990—, Catalogue of Medieval and Renaissance Manuscripts in the Beinecke Rare Book and Manuscript Library Yale University, 1984—, Filologia MedioLatina, 1994—. Am. Coun. Learned Socs. fellow, 1972-73, vis. fellow All Souls Coll., Oxford, 1978-79, Guggenheim fellow, 1975-76, Rosenbach fellow in bibliogrpahy U. Pa., 1976, NEH fellow, 1981-82, 84-85, 94-96, Inst. for Advanced Studies fellow Jerusalem, 1991; J.R. Lyell reader in bibliogrpahy U. Oxford, 1991-92; vis. fellow Pembroke Coll., U. Oxford, 1992, 2000-01. Fellow Royal Hist. Soc., Medieval Acad. Am.; mem. Medieval Assn. Pacific (councillor 1965-68, pres. 1968-70), Medieval Acad. Am. (councillor 1977-80), Comité international de paléographie (treas. 1985-90), Comité international du vocabulaire des institutions et de la communication intellectuelles au moyen age, 1987—, Societa internazionale per lo studio del medioevo latino, 1988—. Home: 11444 Berwick St Los Angeles CA 90049-3416 Office: U Calif Dept History Los Angeles CA 90024 E-mail: rouse@history.ucla.edu

ROUSH, GLENN A. state senator; m. Ardith Roush. Ret. Mont. Power Co.; Dem. senator dist. 43 Mont. State Senate, 1998—, mem. bus. and industry com., mem. hwys. and transp. com., mem. natural resources com. Democrat. Home: PO Box 185 Cut Bank MT 59427-0185

ROUSS, RUTH, lawyer; b. Des Moines, May 21, 1914; d. Simon Jacob and Dora (Goldin) R.; m. Dennis O'Rourke, Jan. 21, 1940; children: Susan Jerene, Kathleen Frances, Brian Jay, Dennis Robert, Ruth Elizabeth, Dolores Ann. B.A., Drake U., 1934, J.D., 1937. Bar: Iowa bar 1937, U.S. Supreme Ct. bar 1945, Colo. bar 1946, D.C. bar 1971. Legal counsel to Jay N. Darling, Des Moines, 1937-38; atty. Office of Solicitor, Dept. Agr., 1938-45, asst. to solicitor, 1940-45; practice law Colorado Springs, Colo., 1946—; mem. firm Williams & Rouss, 1946-50, individual practice law, 1950-69; of counsel firm Sutton, Shull & O'Rourke, Colorado Springs and Washington, 1969-72; mem. firm Rouss & O'Rourke, Colorado Springs and Washington, 1972-99, Colorado Springs, 2000—. Dir., sec.-treas. ManExec., Inc. Mem. cast chorus, Colo. Opera Festival, 1976, 78; mem., Colorado Springs Chorale, 1976— . Bd. dirs. Human Relations Commn. City Colorado Springs, 1968-73, chmn., 1971-72; bd. dirs., sec. Colorado Springs Community Planning and Research Council, 1972-78; bd. dirs. Logos, Inc., Colorado Springs, 1972-78, sec., 1976-77, v.p., 1977-78; bd. dirs. Colorado Springs Opera Festival, Colorado Springs World Affairs Council, Urban League of Pikes Peak Region; mem. com. protection human rights Penrose Hosp., adv. council Am. Lung Assn. of Colo., Pikes Peak region; dir., pres., Joseph Henry Edmondson Found.; adv. bd. Care Castle Divsn. Pikes Peak Seniors,El Paso County, Colo. Mem. El Paso County (Colo.) Bar Assn., Colo. Bar Assn., D.C. Bar Assn., Am. Law Inst. (life), Internat. Fedn. Women Lawyers, Women's Forum Colo., Phi Beta Kappa. Home: 8 Heather Dr Colorado Springs CO 80906-3114 Office: Box 572 231 E Vermijo Ave Colorado Springs CO 80903-2113

ROVEN, ALFRED NATHAN, surgeon; b. Czechoslovakia, Apr. 6, 1947; came to the U.S., 1949. BA in Psychology, Calif. State U., Northridge, 1969; MD, U. So. Calif., 1977. Diplomate Am. Bd. Plastic and Reconstructive Surgery, Am. Bd. Otolaryngology. Resident in otolaryngology U. So. Calif., 1977-82; clin. chief plastic surgery Cedars Sinai Med. Ctr., L.A., 1989-91; resident in plastic and reconstructive surgery U. N.C., 1982-84; clin. chief burns Cedars Sinai Med. Ctr., L.A., 1990-92, clin. chief hands, 1990-92. Qualified med. examiner State of Calif., 1985. Contbr. articles to profl. jours. Physician L.A. Free Clinic, 1995—. Avocation: reading. Office: 444 S San Vicente Blvd Ste 600 Los Angeles CA 90048-4166

ROVIRA, LUIS DARIO, state supreme court justice; b. San Juan, P.R., Sept. 8, 1923; s. Peter S. and Mae (Morris) R.; m. Lois Ann Thau, June 25, 1966; children— Douglas, Merilyn. B.A., U. Colo., 1948, LL.B., 1950. Bar: Colo. 1950. Justice Colo. Supreme Ct., Denver, 1979-95, chief justice, 1990-95, ret., 1995. Mem. Pres.'s Com. on Mental Retardation, 1970-71; chmn. State Health Facilities Council, 1967-76; arbiter and mediator Jud. Arbiter Group, Denver. Bd. dirs Children's Hosp.; trustee Temple Buell Found., Denver Found., Harry S. Truman Scholarship Found. With AUS, 1943-46. Mem. ABA, Colo. Bar Assn., Denver Bar Assn. (pres. 1970-71), Colo. Assn. Retarded Children (pres. 1968-70), Alpha Tau Omega, Phi Alpha Delta. Clubs: Athletic (Denver), Country (Denver). Home: 4810 E 6th Ave Denver CO 80220-5137 Office: Judicial Arbiter Group 1601 Blake St Denver CO 80202

ROWE, KATHERINE L. computer company executive; BSME, Purdue U.; MS in Mgmt. Tech., MIT. Engring. mgr. ELDEC Corp.; mfg. mgr., project mgr. Physio-Control Corp.; dir. mfg. Tera Computer Co., Seattle, 1994-96, v.p. mfg., 1996—. Office: Tera Computer Co 411 1st Ave S Ste 600 Seattle WA 98104-3847

ROWE, MARY SUE, accounting executive; b. Melrose, Kans., Aug. 31, 1940; d. Gene and Carmen (Glidewell) Woffard; m. Edward Rowe, Nov. 27, 1985; children from previous marriage: Denise, Dynell, Dalene, Denette. Student, MTI Bus. Coll., 1968, Calif. State U., Fullerton, 1969, Broome (N.Y.) Community Coll., , 1974-76; cert. Sch. Bus. Mgmt., Calif. State U., San Bernardino, 1986. Variou bookkeeping and secretarial, 1968-76; asst. mgr., acct. RM Dean Contracting, Chenango Forks, N.Y., 1976-80; acctg. asst. Hemet (Calif.) Unified Sch. Dist., 1981-86; dir. acctg. Desert Sands Unified Sch. Dist., Indio, Calif., 1986-91; bus. svcs. cons. ednl. div. Vicenti, Lloyd & Stutzman, CPA, La Verne, 1991-97; sch. bus. cons., computer trainer Hemet, 1997—. Bd. dirs. Family Svcs. Assn., Hemet, 1982-83, PTA Officer, 1993-95. Mem. NAFE, Calif. Assn. Sch. Bus. Ofcls. (acctg. com., R*D com., vice chmn. 1988-90, chmn. 1990-91, state acctg. adv. com. 1990-92), Riverside Assn. Chief Accts. (co-chmn. 1986-88), Coalition for Adequate Sch. Housing. Republican. Home and Office: 4981 Vailwood Dr Hemet CA 92544-7819

ROWE, PETER A. newspaper columnist; b. Walnut Creek, Calif., Sept. 7, 1955; s. Raymond Alan and Marion (Green) R.; m. Lynn Hanson, Aug. 13, 1977; children: Kyle, Reid, Alec. BA in History, BA in Journalism, U. Calif., 1977; MSJ, Northwestern U., 1981. Reporter Argus, Fremont, Calif., 1977-80, Va.-Pilot, Norfolk, 1981-84, San Diego Union, 1984-87, asst. features editor, 1987-88, features editor, 1988-92; columnist San Diego Union-Tribune, 1992—. Gannett fellow Northwestern U., 1980-81. Mem. Nat. Soc. Newspaper Columnists (pres. 2000—). Roman Catholic. Office: San Diego Union Tribune PO Box 120191 San Diego CA 92112-0191 E-mail: peter.rowe@uniontrib.com

ROWE, SANDRA MIMS, newspaper editor; b. Charlotte, N.C., May 26, 1948; d. David Lathan and Shirley (Stovall) Mims; m. Gerard Paul Rowe, June 5, 1971; children: Mims Elizabeth, Sarah Stovall. BA, East Carolina U., Greenville, N.C., 1970; postgrad., Harvard U., 1991. Reporter to asst. mng. editor The Ledger-Star, Norfolk, Va., 1971-80, mng. editor, 1980-82, The Virginian-Pilot and The Ledger Star, Norfolk, 1982-84, exec. editor, 1984-86, v.p., exec. editor, 1986-93; editor The Oregonian, Portland, 1993—. Mem. Pulitzer Prize Bd., 1994—. Bd. visitors James Madison U., Harrisonburg, VA., 1991-95; chmn. adv. bd. The Knight Found.; mem. adv. bd. The Poynter Inst., Medill Sch. Journalism, Northwestern U. Named Woman of Yr. Outstanding Profl. Women of Hampton Rds., 1987; inducted into Va. Journalism Hall of Fame, 2000. Mem. Am. Soc. Newspaper Editors (pres., bd. dirs. 1992-99), Va. Press Assn. (bd. dirs. 1985-93). Episcopalian. Office: The Oregonian 1320 SW Broadway Portland OR 97201-3499

ROWE, TINA L. government official; b. Griffin, Ga., July 22, 1946; 1 child. Student, FBI Nat. Acad., 1981; AA, Aurora (Colo.) C.C., 1991; BA, Colo. Christian U., 1999. From patrol officer to comdr. patrol dist. 2 Denver Police Dept., 1969-94; U.S. marshal for Dist. Colo., U.S. Marshals Svc., Dept. Justice, Denver, 1994—. Trainer, spkr. cons. operational planning, motivation, leadership. Recipient various awards, including Woman of Yr. award Bus. and Profl. Women's Club, 1994; named Outstanding Law Enforcement officer, Am. Legion, 1999. Mem. FBI Nat. Acad. Assocs., Nat. Sheriffs Assn., Colo. Assn. Chiefs Police, Intenat. Assn. Chiefs of Police, Am. Coll. Forensic Examiners, Am. Bd. Law Enforcement Experts. Baptist. Office: US Marshals Svc Dept Justice 1929 Stout St Rm 324C Denver CO 80294-1929

ROWEN, HENRY STANISLAUS, economics educator; b. Boston, Oct. 11, 1925; s. Henry S. and Margaret Isabelle (Maher) R.; m. Beverly Camille Griffiths, Apr. 18, 1951; children: Hilary, Michael, Christopher, Sheila Jennifer, Diana Louise, Nicholas. BS, MIT, 1949; M in Philosophy, Oxford (Eng.) U., 1955. Economist Rand Corp., Santa Monica, Calif., 1950-61, pres., 1967-72; dep. asst. sec. internat. security affairs Dept. Def., Washington, 1961-64; asst. dir. Bur. Budget, Washington, 1965-66; prof. pub. policy Stanford (Calif.) U., 1972-95, dir. pub. policy program, 1972-75; sr. fellow Hoover Inst., Stanford, Calif., 1983—; Edwin B. Rust prof. pub. policy Stanford (Calif.) U., 1986-95, dir. Asia/Pacific Rsch. Ctr., 1997-2001; asst. sec. internat. security affairs Dept. Def., Washington, 1989-91. Chmn. nat. intelligence coun. CIA, Washington, 1981-83. Co-author: (with R. Imai) Nuclear Energy and Nuclear Proliferation, 1980, (with C. Wolf Jr.) The Future of the Soviet Empire, 1987; editor: Options for U.S. Energy Policy, 1977, Behind East Asian Growth, 1998; co-editor: (with C. Wolf Jr.) The Impoverished Superpower, 1990, (with C. Lee, W. Miller, M. Hancock) The Silicon Valley Edge, 2001; contbr. numerous articles to profl. jours. Chmn. chief naval ops. exec. panel USN, Washignton, 1972-81, mem., 1983-89, 91-93; mem. def. sci. bd. Dept. Def., Washington, 1983 89, chmn. Def. Policy Bd., 1991-94. With USN, 1943-46, PTO. Mem. Internat. Inst. Strategic Studies. Republican. Roman Catholic. Office: Hoover Inst Hoover Tower Rm 1005 Stanford CA 94305-5015

ROWHANI, ADIB, plant pathologist; BS in Plant Protection, Pahlavi U., Shiraz, Iran, 1970; MS in Plant Pathology, McGill U., Montreal, Can., 1977, [illegible] Plant pathology specialist U. Calif., Davis. Contbr. articles to profl. jours. Recipient Lee M. Hutchins award Am. Phytopathol. Soc., 1999. Achievements include development of molecular methodologies for the detection and elimination of viruses that attack grapevines, fruit and nut trees and strawberries; characterization of viruses to better understand their biology and epidemiology in order to be able to develop more efficient methodologies for their detection and control. Office: U Calif Found Plant Materials Svc One Shields Ave Davis CA 95616-8600 Fax: 530-752-2132

ROWLAND, FRANK SHERWOOD, chemistry educator; b. Delaware, Ohio, June 28, 1927; m. Joan Lundberg, 1952; children: Ingrid Drake, Jeffrey Sherwood. AB, Ohio Wesleyan U., 1948; MS, U. Chgo., 1951, PhD, 1952, DSc (hon.), 1989, Duke U., 1989, Whittier Coll., 1989, Princeton U., 1990, Haverford Coll., 1992, Clark U., 1996, U. East Anglia, 1996; LLD (hon.), Ohio Wesleyan U., 1989, Simon Fraser U., 1991, U. Calgary, 1997; laurea honoris causa, U. Urbino (Italy), 1998; DSc, Carleton Coll., 1998, Gustavus Adolphus Coll., 1997, Occidental Coll., 1998, Kanagawa Univ., Japan, 1999. Instr. chemistry Princeton (N.J.) U., 1952-56; asst. prof. chemistry U. Kans., 1956-58, assoc. prof. chemistry, 1958-63, prof. chemistry, 1963-64, U. Calif., Irvine, 1964—, dept. chmn., 1964-70, Aldrich prof. chemistry, 1985-89, Bren prof. chemistry, 1989-94, Bren rsch. prof., 1994—. Humboldt sr. scientist, Fed. Republic of Germany, 1981; chmn. Dahlem (Fed. Republic of Germany) Conf. on Changing Atmosphere, 1987; vis. scientist Japan Soc. for Promotion Sci., 1980; co-dir. western region Nat. Inst. Global Environ. Changes, 1989-93; del. Internat. Coun. Sci. Unions, 1993-98; fgn. sec. NAS, 1994—, Korean Acad. Sci. Tech.; lectr., cons. in field. Contbr. numerous articles to profl. jours. Mem. ozone commn. Internat. Assn. Meteorology and Atmospheric Physics, 1980-88, hon. life mem., 1996, mem. commn. on atmospheric chemistry and global pollution, 1979-91; mem. acid rain peer rev. panel U.S. Office of Sci. and Tech., Exec. Office of White House, 1982-84; mem. vis. com. Max Planck Insts., Heidelberg and Mainz, Fed. Republic Germany, 1982-96; ozone trends panel mem. NASA, 1986-88; chmn. Gordon Conf. Environ. Scis.-Air, 1987; mem. Calif. Coun. Sci. Tech., 1989-95, Exec. Com. Tyler Prize, 1992—. Recipient numerous awards including John Wiley Jones award Rochester Inst. of Tech., 1975, Disting. Faculty Rsch. award U. Calif., Irvine, 1976, Profl. Achievement award U. Chgo., 1977, Billard award N.Y. Acad. Sci., 1977, Tyler World Prize in Environment Achievement, 1983, Global 500 Roll of Honor for Environ. Achievement UN Environment Program, 1988, Dana award for Pioneering Achievements in Health, 1987, Silver medal Royal Inst. Chemistry, U.K., 1989, Wadsworth award N.Y. State Dept. Health, 1989, medal U. Calif., Irvine, 1989, Japan prize in Environ. Sci., 1989, Dickson prize Carnegie-Mellon U., 1991, Albert Einstein prize of World Cultural Coun., 1994, Nobel Prize in Chemistry, 1995, Alumni medal U. Chgo., 1997, Nevada medal, 1997; Guggenheim fellow, 1962, 74. Fellow AAAS (pres. elect 1991, pres. 1992, chmn. bd. dirs. 1993), Am. Phys. Soc. (Leo Szilard award for Physics in Pub. Interest 1979), Am. Geophys. Union (Roger Revelle medal 1994); mem. NAS (bd. environ. studies and toxicology 1986-91, com. on atmospheric chemistry 1987-89, com. atmospheric scis., solar-terrestial com. 1979-83, co-DATA com. 1977-82, sci. com. on problems environment 1986-89, Infinite Voyage film com. 1988-92, Robertson Meml. lectr. 1993, chmn. com. on internat. orgns. and programs 1993—, chmn. office of internat. affairs 1994—, co-chmn. interacad. panel 1995-2000, mem. exec. com. 2000—), Am. Acad. Arts and Scis., Am. Chem. Soc. (chmn. divsn. nuclear sci. and tech. 1973-74, chmn. divsn. phys. chemistry 1974-75, Orange County award 1975, Tolman medal 1976, Zimmerman award 1980, E.F. Smith lectureship 1980, Environ. Sci. and Tech. award 1983, Esselen award 1987, Peter Debye Phys. Chem. award 1993), Am. Meteorological Soc. (hon.), European Acad. Arts, Scis. and Humanities, Korean Acad. Sci. Tech., Phi Beta Kappa, Sigma Xi. Home: 4807 Dorchester Rd Corona Del Mar CA 92625-2718 Office: U Calif Irvine Dept of Chemistry 571 Rowland Hall Irvine CA 92697-0001 E-mail: rowland@uci.edu

ROWLEY, BEVERLEY DAVIES, medical sociologist; b. Antioch, Calif., July 28, 1941; d. George M. and Eloise (DeWhitt) Davies; m. Richard B. Rowley, Apr. 1, 1966 (div. 1983). BS, Colo. State U., 1963; MA, U. Nev., 1975; PhD, Union Inst., 1983. Social worker Nev. Dept. Pub. Welfare, Reno, 1963-65, Santa Clara County Dept. Welfare, San Jose, Calif., 1965-66; field dir. Sierra Sage coun. Camp Fire Girls, Sparks, Nev., 1966-70; program coord. div. health scis. sch. medicine U. Nev., 1976-78, program coord., health analyst office rural health, 1978-84, acting dir. office rural health, 1982-84; exec. asst. to pres. Med. Coll. of Hampton Rds., Norfolk, Va., 1984-87; rsch. mgr. Office Med. Edn. Info. AMA, Chgo., 1987-88, dir. dept. data systems, 1988-91; dir. med. edn. Maricopa Med. Ctr., Phoenix, 1991-99; pres. Med. Edn. and Rsch. Assocs., Inc., Phoenix, Chgo., 1999—, Med. Edn. & Rsch. Assocs., Tempe, Ariz., 1999—; vis. prof. Ariz. State U. East, Mesa, 1999-2000. Various positions as adj. prof. and lectr. in health scis. U. Nev. Sch. of Medicine, 1972-75; lectr. dept. family and cmty. medicine U. Nev., 1978-84, asst. dir., evaluator Health Careers for Am. Indians Programs, 1978-84; cons. Nev. Statewide Health Survey, 1979-84; interim dir. Health Max, 1985-86; asst. prof. dept. family and cmty. medicine Med. Coll. of Hampton Rds., Norfolk, Va., 1985-87. Editor of five books; contbr. numerous articles to profl. jours; developer three computer systems including AMA-FREIDA. Mem. Am. Sociol. Assn., Nat. Rural Health Assn. (bd. dirs. 1986-88), Assn. Behavioral Sci. and Med. Edn. (pres. 1986), Assn. Am. Med. Colls. (exec. coun. 1993-95), Coun. Acad. Scis. (adminstrv. bd. 1992-97), Assn. Hosp. Med. Edn. (bd. dirs. 1997—), Delta, Delta, Delta. Avocations: hiking, skiing, gardening, sewing, ceramics. Office: MERA Inc 8850 S Los Feliz Dr Tempe AZ 85284-3430 E-mail: BRowley@MERAInc.com

ROY, CHUNILAL, psychiatrist; b. Digboi, India, Jan. 1, 1935; came to Can., 1967, naturalized, 1975; s. Atikay Bandhu and Nirupama (Devi) R.; m. Elizabeth Ainscow, Apr. 15, 1967; children: Nicholas, Phillip, Charles. MB, BS, Calcutta Med. Coll., India, 1959; diploma in psychol. medicine, Kings Coll., Newcastle-upon-Tyne, Eng., 1963. Intern Middlesborough Gen. Hosp., Eng., 1960-61; jr. hosp. officer St. Luke's Hosp., Middlesborough, Eng., 1961-64, sr. registrar Eng., 1964; sr. hosp. med. officer Parkside Hosp., Macclesfield, Eng., 1964-66; sr. registrar Moorehaven Hosp., Ivybridge, Eng., 1966; reader, head dept. psychiatry Maulana Azad Med. Coll., New Delhi, 1966; sr. med. officer Republic of Ireland, County Louth, 1966; sr. psychiatrist Sask. Dept. Psychiat. Services, Can., 1967-68; regional dir. Swift Current, Can., 1968-71; practice medicine specializing in psychiatry Regina, Sask., Can., 1971-72; founding dir., med. dir. Regional Psychiat. Ctr., Abbotsford, B.C., Can., 1972-82. With dept. psychiatry Vancouver Gen. Hosp., 1983—; cons. to prison adminstrs.; hon. lectr. psychology and clin. prof. dept. psychiatry U. B.C., clin. prof. emeritus, 2000; ex-officio mem. Nat. Adv. Com. on Health Care of Prisoners in Can.; cons. (hon.) psychiatrist Vancouver Hosp.; advisor Asian chpt. Psychosomatic Medicine, World Congress of Law and Medicine, New Delhi, 1985; appointed hon. consul for Burkina Faso, 1997; appointed auditor Med. Svcs. Com. B.C., 1997; appointed advisor mental health Govt. West Bengal, India, 1999; pres. organizing com. World Mental Health Assembly, 1999, clinical prof. emeritus, Dept. of Psychiatry, UBC, 2000-. Author: (with D.J. West and F.L. Nichols) Understanding Sexual Attacks, 1978, Hospital or Prison Memories; co-author: Oath of Athens, 1979; ; assoc. editor Internat. Jour. Offender Therapy and Comparative Criminology, 1978—; field editor Jour. of Medicine and Law; corr. editor Internat. Jour. Medicine; mem. bd. Internat. Law Medicine, 1979—; mem. editl. rev. bd. Evaluation, 1977—; contbr. articles to profl. jours. Recipient merit awards Dept. Health, Republic of Ireland, 1966, Can. Penitentiary Svc., 1974, Correctional Svcs. Can., 1983, citation by pres. U. B.C., 1983, Letten Saugstad Found. prize, Holland, 1995; knighted by Order of St. John Beaumont Found., 1995; Awarded Order of Francisco Fajardo Gov. of Caracas, 1998, Legacy award Vancouver Travel and Conv. Ctr., 1998. Fellow Royal Coll. Psychiatry (Can.), Royal Coll. Psychiatry (Eng.), Pacific Rim Coll. Psychiatrists (founder); mem. World Psychiat. Assn.

(sec., vice chmn. forensic psychiatry 1983), World Fedn. Mental Health, Internat. Coun. Prison Med. Svcs. (founding sec.-gen. 1977), Can. Med. Assn., Can. Psychiat. Assn., Internat. Acad. Legal Medicine and Social Medicine, Indian Psychiat. Assn. (life), Assn. Physicians and Surgeons Who Work in Can. Prisons (founding pres. 1974), Internat. Found. for Tng. in Penitentiary Medicine and Forensic Psychiatry (founding pres. 1980), World Psychiatry Assn., Australian Acad. Forensic Sci. (corr.), Can. Physicians Interested in South Asia (v.p. 1989, pres. 1990), Internat. Coll. Psychosomatic Medicine (adv. Asian chpt.), Internat. Conf. on Health, Culture and Contemporary Soc. (chief advisor Bombay 1989), World Psyciat. Assn. (vice chmn. forensic psychiat. sect. 1989), World Assn. Health, Culture and Environ. (sec.-gen. 1995, award 1995), World Assembly for Mental Health (pres. 2001), Order of St. John (knight 1992), Vancouver MultiCultural Soc. (bd. dirs. 1992-93), B.C. Psychiat. Assn. (pres. 1995-96). Home: 2439 Trinity St Vancouver BC Canada V5K 1C9 Office: 1417-750 W Broadway Vancouver BC Canada V5Z 1J4 Fax: (604) 872-0302

ROY, PATRICK, professional hockey player; b. Quebec City, Que., Can., Oct. 5, 1965; Goaltender Montreal Canadiens, 1984-95, Colo. Avalanche, 1995—. Mem. Stanley Cup Championship teams, 1986, 93, 96. Recipient Conn Smythe trophy as playoff MVP, 1986, William M. Jennings trophy 1986-89, 91-92, Trico Goaltender award, 1988-89, 89-90, Georges Vezina trophy, 1988-89, 89-90, 91-92; named to NHL All-Rookie Team, 1985-86, NHL All-Star Second Team, 1987-88, 90-91, NHL All-Star First Team, 1988-89, 89-90, 91-92., Sporting News All-Star Team, 1988-89, 89-90, 91-92. Achievements include playing in Stanley Cup Championships, 1986, 93. Office: Colo Avalanche 100 Chopper Pl Denver CO 80204

ROYBAL-ALLARD, LUCILLE, congresswoman; b. Boyle Heights, Calif., June 12, 1941; d. Edward Roybal; m. Edward T. Allard; 4 children. BA, Calif. State U., L.A. Former mem. Calif. State Assembly; mem. U.S. Congress from 33rd Calif. dist., 1993—; mem. appropriationscom. Democrat. Office: Ho of Reps 2435 Rayburn Bldg Washington DC 20515-0533*

ROYCE, EDWARD R. (ED ROYCE), congressman; b. Los Angeles, Oct. 12, 1951; m. Marie Porter. BA, Calif. State U., Fullerton. Tax mgr. Southwestern Portland Cement Co.; mem. Calif. Senate, 1983-93, U.S. Congress from 39th Calif. dist., 1993—; mem. banking and fin. svcs. com., internat. rels. com. Vice chmn. Public Employment and Retirement Com.; mem. Bus. and Profs. com., Indsl. Rels. com.; legis. author, campaign co-chmn. Proposition 15 Crime Victims/Speedy Trial Initiative; author nation's 1st felony stalking law, bill creating Foster Family Home Ins. Fund, legis. creating foster parent recruitment and tng. program; mem. Banking and Fin. Svcs. Com., Internat. Rels. Com. Named Legis. of Yr. Orange County Rep. Com., 1986, Child Adv. of Yr. Calif. Assn. Svc. for Children, 1987. Mem. Anaheim C. of C. Republican. Office: US Ho Reps 2202 Rayburn Ho Office Bldg Washington DC 20515*

RUBELI, PAUL E. gaming company executive; b. 1943; married. BS, U. Notre Dame; MBA, Columbia U., 1967. Assoc. A.T. Kearney Inc., Chgo., 1969-73; v.p., gen. mgr. Bunker-Ramo Corp., 1973-76; group v.p. Baker Industries, Parsippany, N.J., 1976-79; exec. v.p. and pres. Ramada Inns Inc., Phoenix, 1979-89; pres., CEO Aztar Corp., Phoenix, 1989—, chmn., 1991—. Served to 1st lt. AUS, 1967-69. Office: Aztar Corp 2390 E Camelback Rd Ste 400 Phoenix AZ 85016-3479

RUBENSTEIN, BERNARD, orchestra conductor; b. Springfield, Mo., Oct. 30, 1937; s. Milton and Evelyn Marion (Friedman) R.; m. Ann Warren Little, Aug. 28, 1961; children: Tanya, Stefan Alexei. B.Mus. with distinction, Eastman Sch. Music, U. Rochester, 1958; M.Mus., Yale U., 1961. Assoc. prof. conducting, dir. orch. orgns. Northwestern U., Evanston, Ill., 1968-80; music dir. San Juan Symphony, Durango, Colo., 1997—, Farmington, N.Mex., 1997—. Asst. condr. R.I. Philharm. Orch., 1961-62; condr. music dir. Santa Fe Symphony Orch., 1962-64; condr. Greenwood Chamber Orch., Cummington, Mass., 1968-79; asst. condr. Stuttgart Opera, 1966-68; condr., music dir. Music for Youth, Milw., 1970-80; assoc. condr. Cin. Symphony Orch., 1980-86; music dir. Tulsa Philharm., 1984-96, condr. laureate, 1996—, condr. laureate, 1996—; music dir. San Juan Symphony, 1997—; guest condr. numerous orchs. including Milw. Symphony Orch., St. Paul Chamber Orch., Guadalajara Symphony Orch., Berlin Radio Orch., Frankfurt Radio Orch., Grant Park Orch., Chgo., die reihe, Vienna, Austrian Radio Orch., Eastman Philharm., Halle Symphony Orch., E. Ger., Warsaw Philharm., St. Louis Little Symphony, W. German Radio Orch., Palazzo Pitti Orch. Florence, Italy, Frankfurt Opera, Tonkuenstler Orch., Vienna, S.W. German Radio Orch., Baden-Baden, Jerusalem Symphony, Anchorage, Hamilton, Ont., Hartford Conn., L.A. Chamber Orch., Austin (Tex.) Symphony, Am. Composers Orch. N.Y.C., Nat. Opera of Mongolia. Winner internat. conducting competition Serate Musicale Fiorentine, 1965; Fulbright scholar, 1964-66; recipient Charles Ditson award Yale U., 1961, Martha Baird Rockefeller award, 1966-68 Mem. Am. Symphony Orch. League, Condrs. Guild. Office: 1070 Governor Dempsey Dr Santa Fe NM 87501-1078 E-mail: baton@ix.netcom.com

RUBENSTEIN, EDWARD, physician, educator; b. Cin., Dec. 5, 1924; s. Louis and Nettie R.; m. Nancy Ellen Millman, June 20, 1954; children: John, William, James. MD, U. Cin., 1947. House staff Cin. Gen. Hosp., 1947-50; fellow May Inst., Cin., 1950; sr. asst. resident Ward Med. Service, Barnes Hosp., St. Louis, 1953-54; chief of medicine San Mateo County Hosp., Calif., 1960-70; assoc. dean postgrad. med. edn., prof. medicine Stanford (Calif.) U., 1971—, emeritus, active. Mem. faculty Stanford Photon Research Lab.; affiliated faculty mem. Stanford Synchortron Radiation Lab., 1971—; mem. maj. materials facilities com. Nat. Research Council, 1984-85, Nat. Steering Com. 6 GeV Electron Storage Ring., 1986—. Author: (textbook) Intensive Medical Care; editor-in-chief: (textbook) Sci. Am. Medicine, 1978-94; editor: Synchotron Radiation Handbook, 1988, vol. 4, 1991; editor Synchotron Radiation in the Biosciences, Molecular Medicine; mem. editorial adv. bd. Sci. Am., Inc., 1991-94; series editor: Molecular Cardiovascular Disease, 1995, Molecular Oncology, 1996, Molecular Neuroscience, 1998. Served with USAF, 1950-52. Recipient Kaiser award for outstanding and innovative contbns. to med. edn., 1989, Albion Walter Hewlett Award, 1993. Fellow AAAS, Royal Soc. Medicine; mem. APS, ACP (master), Inst. Medicine, Calif. Acad. Medicine, Western Assn. Physicians, Soc. Photo-Optical Engrs., Am. Clin. and Climatol. Assn., Alpha Omega Alpha. Achievements include research on mechanisms of autoimmunity, dysfunction of the choroid plexus and cerebrospinal fluid circulatory system, snychrotron radiation and molecular chivality. Office: Stanford Med Ctr Dept of Medicine Stanford CA 94305

RUBENSTEIN, LEONARD SAMUEL, communications executive, ceramist, painter, sculptor, photographer; b. Rochester, N.Y., Sept. 22, 1918; s. Jacob S. and Zelda H. (Gordon) R.; m. (dec. 1983); children: Carolinda, Eric, Harley. Student, Case Western Res. U., 1938; BFA cum laude, Alfred U., 1939; postgrad., U. Rochester, 1940-41. Creative dir. Henry Hempstead Advt. Agy., Chgo., 1949-55; v.p., exec. art dir. Clinton E. Frank Advt. Agy., Chgo., 1955-63; v.p., nat. creative dir. Foster & Kleiser divsn. Metromedia, Inc., L.A., 1967-73; ret. Metromedia, Inc., L.A., 1984, v.p. corp. creative cons., 1984-88. Guest lectr. U. Chgo.; instr. Columbia Coll., Chgo., Fashion Inst., L.A.; creator Smithsonian exhibition Images of China: East and West, 1982; lectr. in field. Author: (with Charles Hardison) Outdoor Advertising, 1967; contbr. articles to profl. jours.; one-man show at Calif. Mus. Sci. and Industry, 1970; two-person shows at Palos Verdes Art Ctr., 1987, one-man show, 1998; exhibited in group shows; writer, prodr.: (video) Paul Soldner, Thoughts on Creativity, 1989, High-Tech/Low-Tech: The Sci. and Art of Ceramics, 1994; represented in permenant collections Smithsonian Instn. Renwick Gallery, Am. Ceramic Soc. Ross C. Purdy Ceramic Mus., Internat. Mus. Ceramic Art Alfred U., Laguna Mus. Art, Calif. Past pres. Art Dirs. Club Chgo. Recipient Spl. Citation, Art Dirs. Club Chgo. Mem. Soc. Typog. Arts (past dir.), Am. Ceramic Soc. (bd. dirs. So. Calif. design chpt. 1998), Am. Craft Coun., Inst. Outdoor Advt. (past plans bd.), L.A. County Mus. Art, Mus. Contemporary Art L.A. (charter), Palos Verdes (Calif.) Art Ctr., B'nai B'rith, Phi Epsilon Pi. Home and Office: 30616 Ganado Dr Rancho Palos Verdes CA 90275

RUBENSTEIN, STEVEN PAUL, newspaper columnist; b. L.A., Oct. 31, 1951; s. Victor Gerald and Florence (Fox) R.; m. Caroline Moira Grannan, Jan. 1, 1989; children: William Laurence, Anna Katherine. BA, U. Calif., Berkeley, 1977. Reporter L.A. Herald Examiner, 1974-76, San Francisco Chronicle, 1976-81, columnist, 1981—. Office: San Francisco Chronicle 901 Mission St San Francisco CA 94103-2905

RUBIN, BRUCE ALAN, lawyer; b. Pitts., Sept. 12, 1951; s. Stanley and Elaine (Roth) R.; m. Suzanne Kay Boss, Aug. 23, 1975; children: Daniel, Jay. BA, Yale U., 1973; JD, Stanford U., 1976. Bar: Oreg. 1976, U.S. Dist. Ct. Oreg. 1976, U.S. Ct. Appeals (9th cir.) 1976. Atty. Miller, Nash LLP, Portland, 1976—, chair corp. governance litigation dept. Exec. com. Oreg. Task Force on Close Corps. and Shareholder Rights, 1999-2000. Author: Wrongful Discharge in Oregon, 1988. Mem. ABA (com. on corp. counsel, subcom. chair), Oreg. State Bar (disciplinary coun. 1990—), Multnomah Bar Assn. (ct. liaison com.). Avocation: competitive long distance running. Office: Miller Nash LLP 111 SW 5th Ave Ste 3500 Portland OR 97204-3638

RUBIN, BRUCE JOEL, screenwriter, director, producer; b. Detroit, Mar. 10, 1943; s. Jim and Sondra R.; m. Blanche Mallins; children: Joshua, Ari. Student, Wayne State U., 1960-62; grad. film sch., NYU, 1965; MA, Ind. U., 1980. Former asst. film editor NBC News; mem. film dept. Whitney Mus., assoc. curator; screenwrtier Sanford-Gross, L.A. Screenwriter: (with Robert Statzel and Phillip Frank Messina) Brainstorm, 1983, Deadly Friend, 1986, Ghost, 1990 (Academy award best original screenplay 1990), Jacob's Ladder, 1990; writer, dir., prodr. My Life, 1993; filmmaker (with Brian de Palma and Robert Fiore) Dionysus in '69, 1970; screenwriter (with Michael Tolkin) Deep Impact, 1998. Office: care Geoffrey Sanford 1015 Gayley Ave Ste 301 Los Angeles CA 90024-3424

RUBIN, GERALD MAYER, molecular biologist, biochemistry educator; b. Boston, Mar. 31, 1950; s. Benjamin H. and Edith (Weisberg) R.; m. Lynn S. Mastalir, May 7, 1978; 1 child, Alan F. B.S., MIT, 1971; Ph.D., Cambridge U., Eng., 1974. Helen Hay Whitney Found. fellow Stanford U. Sch. Medicine, Calif., 1974-76; asst. prof. biol. chemistry Sidney Farber Cancer Inst.-Harvard U. Med. Sch., Boston, 1977-80; staff mem. Carnegie Instn. of Washington, Balt., 1980-83; John D. MacArthur prof. genetics U. Calif., Berkeley, 1983—. Investigator Howard Hughes Med. Inst., 1987—, v.p. biomedical rsch., 2000—. Recipient Young Scientist award Passano Found., 1983, U.S. Steel Found. award Nat. Acad. Scis., 1985, Eli Lilly award in biochemistry Am. Chem. Soc., 1985, Genetics Soc. Am. medal, 1986. Mem. Nat. Acad. Scis. Office: Howard Hughes Med Inst 4000 Jones Bridge Rd Bethesda MD 20815-6789 E-mail: rubing@hhmi.org

RUBIN, GERROLD ROBERT, advertising executive; b. Evanston, Ill., Mar. 31, 1940; s. Bennie George and Anita (Perich) R.; m. Barbara Ann Nieman, Sept. 5, 1962; children: John, Ann. B.S. in Radio, TV, Film, Northwestern U., 1962. Account exec. Leo Burnett Advt., Chgo., 1962-67, account supr. Toronto, Ont., 1967-68, Needham, Harper Steers, Chgo., 1968-73, account dir. Los Angeles, 1973-78; mgmt. rep. Needham, Harper & Steers, Chgo., 1978-81, pres., CEO Los Angeles, 1981-86, Rubin, Postaer & Assocs., Santa Monica, Calif., 1986—. Bd. dirs. Country Music Assn., Nashville, 1983— . Presbyterian. Office: Rubin Postaer & Assocs 1333 2nd St Santa Monica CA 90401-1100

RUBIN, KARL COOPER, mathematics educator; b. Urbana, Ill., Jan. 27, 1956; s. Robert J. and Vera (Cooper) R. AB, Princeton U., 1976; MA, Harvard U., 1977, PhD, 1981. Instr. Princeton (N.J.) U., 1982-83; mem. Inst. Advanced Study, Princeton, 1983-84; prof. Columbia U., N.Y.C., 1988-89; asst. prof. math. Ohio State U., Columbus, 1984-87, prof., 1987-97; prof. math. Stanford (Calif.) U., 1997—. Contbr. articles to Inventiones Math. Recipient Presdl. Young Investigator award NSF, 1988; NSF postdoctoral fellow, 1981, Sloan fellow, 1985, Guggenheim fellow, 1994. Mem. Am. Math. Soc. (recipient Cole Prize, 1992), Phi Beta Kappa. Achievements include rsch. on elliptic curves, Tate-Shafarevich groups, Birch and Swinnerton-Dyer conjecture, Iwasawa theory and p-adic L-functions. Office: Stanford U Dept Math Stanford CA 94305-2125

RUBIN, MICHAEL, lawyer; b. Boston, July 19, 1952; m. Andrea L. Peterson, May 29, 1983; children: Peter, Eric, Emily. AB, Brandeis U., 1973; JD, Georgetown U., 1977. Bar: Calif. 1978, U.S. Dist. Ct. (no. dist.) Calif. 1978, U.S. Ct. Appeals (9th cir.) 1978, U.S. Ct. Appeals (5th, 7th, 10th cirs.) 1982, U.S. Supreme Ct. 1984, U.S. Ct. Appeals (D.C. cir.) 1984, U.S. Ct. Appeals (11th cir.) 1987. Teaching fellow Law Sch. Stanford (Calif.) U., 1977-78; law clerk to Hon. Charles B. Renfrew U.S. Dist. Ct. (no. dist.) Calif., San Francisco, 1978-79; law clerk to Hon. James R. Browning U.S. Ct. Appeals (9th cir.), San Francisco, 1979-80; law clerk to Hon. William J. Brennan, Jr. U.S. Supreme Ct., Washington, 1980-81; assoc. Altshuler & Berzon, San Francisco, 1981-85, ptnr., 1985-89, Altshuler, Berzon, Nussbaum, Berzon & Rubin, San Francisco, 1989-2000, Altshuler, Berzon, Nussbaum, Rubin & Demain, San Francisco, 2000—. Office: Altshuler Berzon Nussbaum Rubin & Demain 177 Post St Ste 300 San Francisco CA 94108-4700 E-mail: mrubin@altshulerberzon.com

RUBINSTEIN, JONATHAN, computer company executive; BSEE, MSEE, Cornell U.; MS in Computer Sci., Colo. State U. Arch. HP 9000 series, mem. design team HP 9836 workstation Hewlett-Packard; mgr. processor devel. Titan graphics supercomputer family Stardent Computer, designer, arch. 3000 and 2000 computer sys.; v.p., gen. mgr. hardware, v.p. hardware engring. NeXT Computer; exec. v.p., COO FirePower Sys.; sr. v.p. hardware engring. Apple Computer, Inc., Cupertino, Calif., 1997—. Patentee in field; contbr. articles to profl. jours. Mem. IEEE, Assn. for Computing Machinery. Office: 1 Infinite Loop Cupertino CA 95014-2083

RUBINSTEIN, MOSHE FAJWEL, engineering educator; b. Miechow, Poland, Aug. 13, 1930; came to U.S., 1950, naturalized, 1965; s. Shlomo and Sarah (Rosen) R.; m. Zafrira Gorstein, Feb. 3, 1953; children: Iris, Dorit. BS, UCLA, 1954, MS, 1957, PhD, 1961. Designer Murray Erick Assos. (engrs. and archs.), L.A., 1954-56; structural designer Victor Gruen Assos., L.A., 1956-61; asst. prof. UCLA, 1961-64, assoc. prof. dept. engring., 1964-69, prof., 1969—, chmn. engring. sys. dept., 1970-75, program dir. modern engring. for execs. program, 1965-70. Cons. Pacific Power & Light Co., Portland, Oreg., Northrop Corp., U.S. Army, NASA Rsch. Ctr., Langley, Tex. Instruments Co., Hughes Space System Divsn., U.S. Army Sci. Adv. Com., Kaiser Aluminum and Chem. Corp., IBM Corp., TRW. Author: (with W.C. Hurty) Dynamics of Structures, 1964 (Yugoslavian transl. 1973), Matrix Computer Analysis of Structures, 1966 (Japanese transl. 1974), Structural Systems, Statics Dynamics and Stability, 1970 (Japanese transl. 1979), Patterns of Problem Solving, 1975, (with K. Pfeiffer) Concepts in Problem Solving, 1980, Tools for Thinking and Problem Solving, 1986; IEEE Press Videotapes; Models for People Driven Quality, 1991, Quality through Innovation, 1991, Creativity for Ongoing Total Quality, 1993, Relentless Improvement, 1993, (with I.R. Firstenberg) Patterns of Problem Solving, 2d edit., 1995, (with I.R. Firstenberg) The Minding Organization, 1999 (Portuguese/Japanese transl. 2000, Spanish/Chinese/Russian transls. 2001). Recipient Disting. Tchr. award UCLA Acad. Senate, 1964, Western Electric Fund award Am. Soc. Engring. Edn., 1965, Disting. Tchr. trophy Engring. Student Soc., UCLA, 1966; Sussman prof. for disting. visitor Technion-Israel Inst. Tech., 1967-68; named Outstanding Faculty Mem., UCLA Engring. Alumni award, 1979, Outstanding UCLA Civil Engring. Alumni award, 1990, Outstanding Faculty Mem., State of Calif. Command Coll., 1987, 88, 89, 94, 95; Fulbright-Hays fellow, Yugoslavia and Eng., 1975-76; voted one of UCLA's Top 20 Profs. of the Century. Mem. ASCE, Am. Soc. Engring. Edn., Seismol. Soc. Am., Sigma Xi, Tau Beta Phi. Achievements include research in use of computers in structural systems, analysis and synthesis; problem solving and decision theory; creativity and innovation in the organization. Home: 10488 Charing Cross Rd Los Angeles CA 90024-2646 Office: UCLA Sch Engring & Applied Sci Los Angeles CA 90024 E-mail: mrubinst@ucla.edu

RUCH, CHARLES P. academic administrator; b. Longbranch, N.J., Mar. 25, 1938; s. Claud C. and Marcella (Pierce) R.; m. Sally Joan Brandenburg, June 18, 1960; children: Cheryl, Charles, Christopher, Cathleen. BA, Coll. of Wooster, 1959; MA, Northwestern U., 1960, PhD, 1966. Counselor, tchr. Evanston (Ill.) Twp. High Sch., 1960-66; asst. prof. U. Pitts., 1966-70, assoc. prof., dept. chmn., 1970-74; assoc. dean sch. edn. Va. Commonwealth U., Richmond, 1974-76, dean sch. edn., 1976-85, interim provost, v.p., 1985-86, provost, v.p., 1986-93; pres. Boise (Idaho) State U., 1993—. Cons. various univs., govtl. agys., ednl. founds. Author or co-author over 50 articles, revs., tech. reports. Mem. Am. Psychol. Assn., Am. Ednl. Research Assn., Phi Delta Kappa. Office: Boise State U 1910 University Dr Boise ID 83725-0399 E-mail: cruch@boisestate.edu

RUCKELSHAUS, WILLIAM DOYLE, investment group executive; b. Indpls., July 24, 1932; s. John K. and Marion (Doyle) R.; m. Jill Elizabeth Strickland, May 11, 1962; children: Catherine Kiley, Mary Hughes, Jennifer Lea, William Justice, Robin Elizabeth. B.A. cum laude, Princeton U., 1957; LL.B., Harvard U., 1960. Bar: Ind. 1960. Atty. Ruckelshaus, Bobbitt & O'Connor, Indpls., 1960-68; dep. atty.-gen. Ind., 1960-65; chief counsel office atty.-gen. Ind., 1963-65; minority atty. Ind. Senate, 1965-67; mem. Ind. Ho. of Reps., 1967-69, majority leader, 1967-69; asst. atty.-gen. charge civil div. Dept. Justice, 1969-70; adminstr. EPA, Washington, 1970-73; acting dir. FBI, 1973; dep. atty. gen. U.S., 1973; mem. firm Ruckelshaus, Beveridge, Fairbanks & Diamond, Washington, 1974-76; sr. v.p. law and corp. affairs Weyerhaeuser Co., Tacoma, 1976-83; adminstr. EPA, Washington, 1983-85; pres. William D. Ruckelshaus Assocs., 1985-88; mem. firm Perkins Coie, Seattle, 1985-88; chmn. bd., CEO Browning-Ferris Industries, Inc., Houston, 1988-95, chmn., 1988-99; founder, prin., also bd. dirs. Madrona Investment Group, LLC, 1996—; chmn. World Resources Inst., Washington D.C., 1999—. Bd. dirs. Cummins Engine Co., Monsanto Co., Nordstrom, Inc., Weyerhaeuser Co., Inc., Gargoyles, Inc., Coinstar, Inc., Solutia, Inc. Rep. nominee for U.S. Senate, Ind., 1968; appointed by Pres. Clinton to serve as U.S. envoy to Pacific Salmon Treaty with Can., 1997-98. Mem. World Resource Inst. (chmn. 1998—), Fed. Bar Assn., Ind. Bar Assn., D.C. Bar Assn., Indpls. Bar Assn. Office: Madrona Investment Group LLC 1000 2nd Ave Ste 3700 Seattle WA 98104-1053

RUDD, ELDON, retired congressman, political consultant; b. Camp Verde, Ariz. m. Ann Merritt. BA, Ariz. State U., 1947; JD, U. Ariz., 1950. Bar: Ariz. 1949, U.S. Supreme Ct. 1953. Pvt. practice, Tucson, 1950; spl. agt.-diplomatic assignment principally Latin Am. FBI, 1950-70; mem. Maricopa County (Ariz.) Bd. Suprs., 1972-76; bd. dirs. Ariz.-Mex. Commn., 1972-92; with U.S.-Mex. Interparliamentary Com., 1976-84; mem. 95th-99th Congresses from 4th Dist. Ariz., 1976-87; of counsel Shimmel, Hill, Bishop & Gruender, P.C., Phoenix, 1987-93; pres. Eldon Rudd Consultancy, Scottsdale, Ariz., 1993—. Chmn. Phoenix chpt. Soc. Former Spl. Agts. FBI, 1995-96, western regional v.p., 1974. Author: World Communism-Threat to Freedom, 1987. Mem. numerous pub. svc. orgns., including energy and water, mil. and internat. affairs. Fighter pilot USMCR, 1942-46. Mem. Fed. Bar Assn. (chpt. pres. 1976), Ariz. Bar Assn., Maricopa County Bar Assn., Scottsdale Bar Assn., Paradise Valley Country Club (bd. dirs. 1989-92), Phi Delta Phi, Blue Key. Republican. Roman Catholic. Home: PO Box 873 Scottsdale AZ 85252-0873 Fax: 480-947-4677

RUDDY, JAMES W. lawyer; b. 1949; AB, U. Mich., 1971; JD, Wayne State U., 1973. Bar: Wash. 1974, Mich. 1974. Assoc. gen. counsel Safeco Corp., 1984-89, v.p., gen. counsel, 1989—, now sr. v.p. , gen. counsel. Office: Safeco Corp Safeco Plz T 22 Seattle WA 98185-0001

RUDEE, MERVYN LEA, engineering educator, researcher; b. Palo Alto, Calif., Oct. 4, 1935; s. Mervyn C. and Hannah (Mathews) R.; m. Elizabeth Eager, June 20, 1958; children: Elizabeth Diane, David Benjamin. BS, Stanford U., 1958, MS, 1962, PhD, 1965. Asst. prof. materials sci. Rice U., Houston, 1964-68, assoc. prof., 1968-72, prof. materials sci., 1972-74; prof. U. Calif. San Diego, La Jolla, 1974—, founding provost Warren Coll., 1974-82, founding dean Sch. Engring., 1982-93, coord. grad. program on materials sci., 1994-99, faculty athletic rep., 1999—; interim dean engring. U. Calif., Riverside, 1995-97. Vis. scholar Corpus Christi Coll., Cambridge, Eng., 1971-72; CFO, prin. Univ. Planning Assocs., Inc.; vis. scientist IBM Thomas J. Watson Rsch. Ctr., Yorktown Heights, N.Y., 1987; dir. fellows program Calif. Coun. on Sci. and Tech., 1999-2000. Pres., bd. trustees Mus. Photographic Art, San Diego, 1995-96; trustee The Burnham Inst., 1998—, The Glen Canyon Inst., 1999—. Lt. (j.g.) USN, 1958-61. Guggenheim fellow, 1971-72 Fellow AAAS; mem. Microscopy Soc. Am., Materials Rsch. Soc., Am. Physics Soc., Tex. Soc. Electron Microscopy (hon., pres. 1966), Sigma Xi, Tau Beta Pi. Home: 1745 Kearsarge Rd La Jolla CA 92037-3829 Office: U Calif San Diego Dept Elec & Cptr Engring La Jolla CA 92093-0407 E-mail: rudee@ucsd.edu

RUDER, MELVIN HARVEY, retired newspaper editor; b. Manning, N.D., Jan. 19, 1915; s. Moris M. and Rebecca (Friedman) R.; m. Ruth Bergan, Feb. 10, 1950; 1 dau., Patricia E. Morton. BA, U. N.D., 1937, MA, 1941; postgrad., Northwestern U., 1940; LLD (hon.), U. Mont., 1998. Asst. prof. journalism U. N.D., 1940; indsl. relations specialist Westinghouse Electric Co., Sharon, Pa., 1940-41; pub. relations with Am. Machine & Foundry Co., N.Y.C., 1946; founder, editor Hungry Horse News, Columbia Falls, Mont., 1946-78, editor emeritus, 1978—. Chmn. adv. coun. Flathead Nat. Forest, Dist. 6 Sch. Bd., 1967-70; pres. Buffalo Hill Terr. Resident Coun., 1997. Served to lt. (s.g.) USNR, 1942-45. Recipient Pulitzer prize for gen. local reporting, 1965 Mem. Mont. Press Assn. (pres. 1957), Flathead Associated C. of C. (pres. 1971), Glacier Natural History Assn. (pres. 1983). Home: Buffalo Hill Terr 203 Somerset Dr Kalispell MT 59901

RUDIN, ANNE NOTO, former mayor, nurse; b. Passaic, N.J., Jan. 27, 1924; m. Edward Rudin, June 6, 1948; 4 children BS in Edn., Temple U., 1945, RN, 1946; MPA, U. So. Calif., 1983; LLD (hon.), Golden Gate U., 1990. RN, Calif. Mem. faculty Temple U. Sch. Nursing, Phila., 1946-48; mem. nursing faculty Mt. Zion Hosp., San Francisco, 1948-49; mem. Sacramento City Council, 1971-83; mayor City of Sacramento, 1983-92; ind. pub. policy cons. Pres. LWV, Riverside, 1957, Sacramento, 1961, Calif., 1969-71, Calif. Elected Women's Assn., 1973-97; trustee Golden Gate U., 1993-96; mem. adv. bd. U. So. Calif., Army Depot Reuse Commn., 1992-94; bd. dirs. Sacramento Theatre Co., 1992-99, Japan Soc. No. Calif., Sacramento Symphony, 1993-96, Calif. Common Cause, 1993 -96, Sacramento Edn. Found.; v.p. Sacramento Traditional Jazz Soc. Found.; pres. bd. dirs. Natomas Basin Conservancy; foreman Sacramento County Grand Jury, 2000-01. Recipient Women in Govt. award U.S. Jaycee Women, 1984, Woman of Distinction award Sacramento Area Soroptimist Clubs, 1985, Civic Contbn. award LWV Sacramento, 1989, Woman of

Courage award Sacramento History Ctr., 1989, Peacemaker of Yr. award Sacramento Mediation Ctr., 1992, Regional Pride award Sacramento Mag., 1993, Humanitarian award Japanese Am. Citizen's League, 1993, Outstanding Pub. Svc. award Am. Soc. Pub. Adminstrn., 1994; named Girl Scouts Am. Role model, 1989, Cmty. Svc. Recognition award, Japanese Am. Citizens League, 1999, Sacramento Traditional Jazz Soc. Hall of Fame, 2000.

RUDOLPH, ABRAHAM MORRIS, pediatrician, educator; b. Johannesburg, Republic of South Africa, Feb. 3, 1924; s. Chone and Sarah (Feinstein) R.; m. Rhona Sax, Nov. 2, 1949; children: Linda, Colin, Jeffrey. MBBCh summa cum laude, U. Witwatersrand, Johannesburg, 1946, MD, 1951; D (hon.), Rene Descartes U., Paris, 1996. Instr. Harvard Med. Sch., 1955-57, assoc. pediatrics, 1957-60; assoc. cardiologist in charge cardiopulmonary lab. Children's Hosp., Boston, 1955-60; dir. pediatric cardiology Albert Einstein Coll. Medicine, 1960-66, prof. pediatrics, assoc. prof. physiology, 1962-66; vis. pediatrician Bronx Mcpl. Hosp. Ctr., N.Y.C., 1960-66; prof. pediatrics U. Calif., San Francisco, 1966-94, prof. physiology, 1974-88, Neider prof. pediatric cardiology, prof. ob-gyn and reproductive scis., 1974-94, chmn. dept. pediatrics, 1987-91, prof. pediatrics emeritus, 1994—; practice medicine, specializing in pediatric cardiology San Francisco. Mem. cardiovascular study sect. NIH, 1961-65, mem. nat. adv. heart council, 1968-72; established investigator Am. Heart Assn., 1958-62; career scientist Health Research Council, City N.Y., 1962-66; Harvey lectr., Oxford, Eng., 1984; inaugural lectr. 1st Nat. Congress Italian Soc. Perinatal Medicine, 1985. Mem. editl. bd. Pediatrics, 1964-70, Circulation, 1966-74, 83-88; assoc. editor Circulation Rsch., 1-70; Am. assoc. editor Pediatric Rsch., 1970-97; editor Rudolph's Pediatrics, Rudolph's Fundamentals of Pediatrics; contbr. articles profl. jours. Recipient Merit award Nat. Heart, Lung and Blood Inst., 1986, Arvo Yllpo medal Helsinki U., Finland, 1987, Jonxis medal Children's Hosp. Groningen, 1993, Nils Rosen von Rosenstein award Swedish Pediat. Soc., 1999. Fellow AAAS, Royal Coll. Physicians (Edinburgh), Royal Coll. Physicians (London); mem. NAS Inst. Medicine, Am. Acad. Pediatrics (E. Mead Johnson award for research in pediatrics 1964, Borden award 1979, past chmn. sect. on cardiology, Lifetime Med. Edn. award 1992, Joseph St. Geme leadership award Pediatrics 1993), Am. Phys. Soc., Soc. for Clin. Investigation, Soc. for Pediatric Research (coun. 1961-64), Am. Pediatric Soc. (coun. 1985-92, v.p. 1992-93, pres. 1993-94, Howland award 1999), Am. Heart Assn. (Rsch. Achievement award 1991). Office: U Calif Cardiovascular Rsch Inst Calif Rm M1331 San Francisco CA 94143-0001

RUDOLPH, GILBERT LAWRENCE, lawyer; b. L.A., Aug. 23, 1946; s. Martin Muttel and Marion (Perlman) R.; Susan Ilene Fellenbaum, Sept. 18, 1983; children: Samara Lisa, Felicia Beth. BA, Ariz. State U., 1967; postgrad., Am. U., Washington, 1967-69; JD, U. Cin., 1973. Bar: D.C. 1973, U.S. Dist. Ct. D.C. 1974, U.S. Ct. Appeals (D.C. cir.) 1974, Ariz. 1975, U.S. Dist. Ct. Ariz. 1975, Calif. 1979. Assoc. Streich, Lang, Weeks & Cardon, P.A., Phoenix, 1975-78; ptnr. Gilbert L. Rudolph, P.C., Phoenix, 1978-87; sr. mem. O'Connor, Cavanagh, Anderson, Killingsworth & Beshears, P.A., Phoenix, 1987-99; shareholder Greenberg Traurig LLP, Phoenix, 1999—. Lectr. on lending issues. Bd. dirs. Make-A-Wish Found. of Am., 1984-89, Aid to Adoption of Spl. Kids, Ariz., 1995—. Mem. ABA (com. on consumer fin. svcs. bus. law sect. 1981—, com. on comml. fin. svcs. 1989—, mem. com. on uniform comml. code 1992—), Conf. on Consumer Fin. Law (governing com. 1986—), Ariz. Consumer Fin. Assn. (regulatory counsel 1996—). Republican. Jewish. Office: Greenberg Traurig LLP Ste 700 2375 E Camelback Rd Phoenix AZ 85016 E-mail: rudolphG@gtlaw.com

RUDOLPH, JEFFREY N. museum director; Exec. dir. Calif. Sci. Ctr., L.A. Office: Calif Sci Ctr 700 State Dr Expn Pk Los Angeles CA 90037-1210

RUDOLPH, JOHN, construction executive; MS, U. Santa Clara. Exec. v.p. Rudolph & Sletten, Inc., Foster City, Calif., president, 1997—, chief exec. officer, 1998—. Office: Rudolph & Sletten Inc 989 E Hillsdale Blvd Foster City CA 94404-2113

RUDOLPH, RONALD ALVIN, human resources executive; b. Berwyn, Ill., May 12, 1949; s. Alvin J. and Gloria S. (Nicoletti) R. BA, U. Calif., Santa Cruz, 1971. Sr. cons. De Anza Assocs., San Jose, Calif., 1971-73; pers. adminstr. McDonnell Douglas Corp., Cupertino, 1974-75; employment rep. Fairchild Semiconductor, Mountain View, 1973-74, 75; compensation analyst Sperry Univac, Santa Clara, 1975-78; mgr. exempt compensation div. Intel Corp., Santa Clara, 1978-79, compensation mgr., 1979-82, dir. corp. compensation, 1982-85; v.p. human resources UNISYS Corp., San Jose, 1985-91, ASK Group Inc., Mountain View, Calif., 1991-94, 3 Com Corp., Santa Clara, 1994-98; v.p. adminstrn. Wyse Tech. Inc., San Jose, Calif., 1999—. Cons. Rudolph Assocs., Cupertino, 1982—; bd. dirs. Dynamic Temp. Svcs., Sunnyvale, Calif. Mem. Spl. Com. for Parolee Employment, Sacramento, 1973-75; bd. dirs. Jr. Achievement, San Jose, 1987-88. Mem. Am. Soc. Pers. Adminstrs., Am. Compensation Assn., No. Calif. Human Resources Coun. Avocations: sailing, reading, running, camping. Office: 3 Com Corp Santa Clara CA 95050

RUDOLPH, WALTER PAUL, engineering research company executive; b. Binghamton, N.Y., Aug. 17, 1937; s. Walter Paul and Frieda Lena (Hennemann) R.; m. Leila Ortencia Romero, Dec. 18, 1960; children: Jonathan, Jana, Catherine. BEE, Rensselaer Poly. Inst., 1959; MSBA, San Diego State U., 1964. Elec. engr. Gen. Dynamics/Astronautics, San Diego, 1959-62; ops. research analyst Navy Electronics Lab., San Diego, 1962-64; mem. profl. staff Gen. Electric Tempo, Honolulu, 1964-70, Ctr. for Naval Analysis, Arlington, Va., 1970-77; pres. La Jolla (Calif.) Rsch. Corp., 1977—. Served to Capt. USNR, 1959-92. Republican. Presbyterian. Home: 1559 El Paso Real La Jolla CA 92037-6303 Office: La Jolla Rsch Corp PO Box 1207 La Jolla CA 92038-1207

RUFF, DOYLE C. airport manager; b. Orlando, Fla., Apr. 26, 1938; m. Lu R., 5 children. BS, Fla. State U., 1959. cert. airport exec. Commd. 2d. lt. USAF, 1959; advanced through grades to Col., 1980; retired, 1980; airport mgr. Fairbanks (AK) Internat. Airport, 1983-87; airport dir. Anchorage (AK) Internat. Airport, 1987-89; dir. of airports City of Redding (Calif.), 1989-93; airport mgr. Fairbanks (AK) Internat. Airport, 1993—. Mem. Rotary Club of Fairbanks. Recipient Airport Mgr. of the Year for Calif. and the Southwestern U.S. 1992-93. Mem. Am. Assn. of Airpot Execs., Airports Coun. Internat., Aircraft Owners and Pilots Assn., USAF Assn., USAF thunderbird Alumni Assn. Office: Fairbanks Internat Airport 6450 Airport Way Ste 1 Fairbanks AK 99709-4671

RUGGE, HENRY FERDINAND, medical products executive; b. South San Francisco, Oct. 28, 1936; s. Hugo Heinrich and Marie Mathilde (Breiholz) R.; m. Sue Callow, Dec. 29, 1967. BS in Physics, U. Calif., Berkeley, 1958, PhD in Physics, 1963. Sr. physicist Physics Internat. Co., San Leandro, 1963-68; dir. adminstrn. and fin. Arkon Sci. Labs., Berkeley, Calif., 1969-71; v.p. Norse Systems, Inc., Hayward, 1972-74, Rasor Assocs., Inc., Sunnyvale, 1974-81, v.p., gen. mgr., 1983-87, exec. v.p. fin., 1988-89, pres., chief exec. officer, 1990—; chmn. UltraVision Inc., Calgary, Alta., Can., 1993-96, also bd. dirs. Can., 1993—; pres., CEO Mission Med., Inc., Fremont, Calif., 1997-99. Pres. Berlinscan, Inc., [illegible], 1991-92; cons. The Rugge Group, Berkeley, 1987-90, bd. dirs. Rasor Assocs., Inc., Space Power Inc., Analatom, Inc. Patentee in area med. devices. U. Calif. scholar, 1954-58. Mem. Am. Heart Assn., Berkeley Bicycle (treas. 1983-84), Phi Beta Kappa. Avocations: bicycle racing, wine, food. Home: 46 Hiller Dr Oakland CA 94618-2302 Office: Mission Med Inc 5670 Stewart Ave Fremont CA 94538-3174 E-mail: hrugge@missionmed.com

RUIZ, VICKI LYNN, history educator; b. Atlanta, May 21, 1955; d. Robert Paul and Erminia Pablita (Ruiz) Mercer; m. Jerry Joseph Ruiz, Sept. 1, 1979 (div. Jan. 1990); children: Miguel, Daniel; m. Victor Becerra, Aug. 14, 1992. AS in Social Studies, Gulf Coast Community Coll., 1975; BA in Social Sci., Fla. State, 1977; MA in History, Stanford U., 1978, PhD in History, 1982. Asst. prof. U. Tex., El Paso, 1982-85, U. Calif., Davis, 1985-87, assoc. prof., 1987-92; Andrew W. Mellon prof. Claremont (Calif.) Grad. Sch., 1992-95, chmn. history dept., 1993-95; prof. history Ariz. State U., Tempe, 1995—, chair dept. Chicano studies, 1997—. Dir. Inst. of Oral History, U. Tex., El Paso, 1983-85, minority undergrad. rsch. program U. Calif., Davis, 1988-92. Author: Cannery Women, Cannery Lives, 1987, From Out of the Shadows, 1998 (Choice Outstanding Book of 1998); editor: Chicana Politics of Work and Family, 2000; co-editor: Women on U.S.-Mexican Border, 1987, Western Women, 1988, Unequal Sisters, 1990, 3d edit., 1999. Mem. Calif. Coun. for Humanities, 1990-94, vice chmn., 1991-93. Fellow Univ. Calif. Davis Humanities Inst., 1990-91, Am. Coun. of Learned Socs., 1986, Danforth Found., 1977. Mem. Orgn. Am. Historians (chmn. com. on status of minority history 1989-91, nominating com. 1987-88, exec. bd. 1995-98), Immigration History Soc. (exec. bd. 1989-91, Am. Hist. Assn. (nat. coun. 1999—), Am. Studies Assn. (nominating bd. 1992-94, nat. coun. 1996-99), Western History (nominating bd. 1993-95). Democrat. Roman Catholic. Avocations: walking, needlework. Office: Ariz State U History Dept Tempe AZ 85287

RUMBOLZ, MICHAEL DAVID, gaming control board chairman, lawyer; b. Biloxi, Miss., Mar. 20, 1954; s. Richard Henry Rumbolz and Nikki (Sirginson) Brown; m. Carol Rumbolz, June 4, 1983. BA in Polit. Sci., U. Nev., Las Vegas, 1976; JD, U. So. Calif., 1980. Bar: Nev., U.S. Dist. Ct. Nev., U.S. Ct. Appeals (9th cir.), U.S. Tax Ct. Assoc. Jones, Jones, Bell, Close & Brown Cht., Las Vegas, 1980-83; chief, dep. atty. gen. State of Nev., Las Vegas, 1983-84, chief, dep. atty. gen. gaming div., 1984-85; mem. Nev. Gaming Control Bd., Las Vegas, 1985-87; chmn., Carson City, Nev., 1987—. Mem. Internat. Assn. Gaming Attys. (com. chmn. 1986—), ABA (gen. practice sect., mem. gaming law com.), Nev. Bar Assn. (mem. exec. com.). Democrat. Avocations: golf, tennis. Home: 4498 Farmcrest Dr Las Vegas NV 89121-4906 Office: Anchor Gaming 815 Pilot Rd Las Vegas NV 89119

RUMMAGE, STEPHEN MICHAEL, lawyer; b. Massillon, Ohio, Dec. 27, 1955; s. Robert Everett and Kathleen Patricia (Newman) R.; m. Elizabeth Anne Seivert, Mar. 24, 1979; children: Everett Martin, Carter Kevin. BA in History and English, Stanford U., 1977; JD, U. Calif., Berkeley, 1980. Bar: Wash. 1980, U.S. Dist. Ct. (we. dist.) 1980, U.S. Ct. Appeals (9th cir.) 1983, U.S. Supreme Ct. 1985. Assoc. Davis, Wright et al, Seattle, 1980-85; ptnr. Davis Wright Tremaine, Seattle, 1986—. Co-author: Employer's Guide to Strike Planning and Prevention, 1985. Mem. Wash. Athletic Club. Democrat. Roman Catholic. Office: Davis Wright Tremaine 1501 4th Ave Ste 2600 Seattle WA 98101-1688 E-mail: steverummage@dwt.com

RUMMEL, ROBERT WILAND, aeronautical engineer, writer; b. Dakota, Ill., Aug. 4, 1915; s. William Howard and Dora (Ely) R.; m. Marjorie B. Cox, Sept. 30, 1939; children— Linda Kay, Sharon Lee, Marjorie Susan, Robert Wiland, Diana Beth. Diploma aeronautical engrng., Curtiss Wright Tech. Inst. Aeros., 1935. Stress analyst Hughes Aircraft Co., Burbank, Calif., 1935-36, Lockheed Aircraft Corp., Burbank, 1936; draftsman Aero Engrng. Corp., Long Beach, Calif., 1936, Nat. Aircraft Co., Alhambra, 1936-37; chief engr. Rearwin A/C & Engines, Inc., Kansas City, Kans., 1937-42; chief design engr. Commonwealth A/C, Inc., Kansas City, 1942-43; v.p. engrng. Trans World Airlines, Inc., Kansas City, Mo., 1943-59, v.p. planning and research, 1959-69, v.p. tech. devel., 1969-78; pres. Robert W. Rummel Assos., Inc., Mesa, Ariz., 1978-87; aerospace cons., 1987—. Commnr. Presdl. Commn. Space Shuttle Challenger Accident, 1986; chmn. nat. rsch. coun. Aero Space Engrng. Bd. Fellow Inst. Aero. Scis., Soc. Automotive Engrs.; mem. NAE, Masons (32 deg.), Shriners. Home and Office: 1189 Leisure World Mesa AZ 85206-3067 E-mail: RWRummel@aol.com

RUNNER, GEORGE CYRIL, JR. minister, educational administrator; b. Scotia, N.Y., Mar. 25, 1952; s. George Cyril and Kay Carol (Cooper) R.; m. Sharon Yvonne Oden, Jan. 13, 1973; children: Micah Stephen, Rebekah Kay. Student, Antelope Valley Coll., Lancaster, Calif., 1970-88; grad. mgmt. cert., Azusa Pacific U., 1988; student, U. Redlands. Lic. to ministry Am. Bapt. Chs. in USA, 1977. Exec. pastor 1st Bapt. Ch. Lancaster, 1973—; founder, exec. dir. Desert Christian Schs., Lancaster, 1977—; founder, internat. dir. Supporting Ptnrs. in Christian Edn., Lancaster, Guatemala City, Guatemala, 1989—. Seminar leader Internat. Ctr. for Learning, Ventura, Calif., 1972-82; curriculum cons. Gospel Light Pubs., Glendale, Calif., 1974-80; bd. dirs. Greater L.A. Sunday Sch. Assn., 1978-79. Assemblyman State of Calif., 36th Dist., Lancaster, 1996; bd. dirs. Lancaster Econ. Devel. Corp.; mem. Salvation Army, Lancaster. Mem. Internat. Fellowship Ch. Sch. Adminstrs., Assn. Christian Schs. Internat., Christian Mgmt. Assn., Lancaster Ministerial Assn. Republican. Office: Desert Christian Schs 1st Bapt Ch 44648 15th St W Lancaster CA 93534-2806

RUNNICLES, DONALD, conductor; b. Edinburgh, Scotland, Nov. 16, 1954; Student, Edinburgh U., Cambridge U., London Opera Ctr.; DMus (hon.), U. Edinburgh, 1995. Music dir. San Francisco Opera, 1992—. Repetiteur Mannheim, Germany, Nat. theatre, from 1980, Kapellmeister, from 1984; prin. condr. Hanover, from 1987; numerous appearances with Hamburg Staatsoper; former gen. music dir. Stadtische Buhnen, Freiburg/Breisgau; mus. dir. San Francisco Opera, 1992—; appearances with Met. Opera include Lulu, 1988, The Flying Dutchman, 1990, The Magic Flute; condr. Vienna Staatsoper, 1990-91, Sonome, 1996; debut at Glyndebourne with Don Giovanni, 1991, Salzburg Festival with Don Giovanni, 1996, also numerous symphonic engagements; condr. London Symphony Orch., La Scale Milan Freischütz, Orch. de Paris, Israel Philharm., Rotterdam Philharm., Seattle Symphony, Pitts. Symphony, St. Louis Symphony, Chgo. Symphony, San Francisco Symphony, Cleve. Orch., New World Symphony, Bavarian Radio Symphony Orch., 2 complete ring cycles with Wiener Staatsoper; rec. Hansel and Gretel (Humperdinck), Gluck's Orphée with San Francisco Opera Orch., 1995, Tannhäuser-Bayreuth Festspick, 1995, Harvey Milk with San Francisco Opera, 1996; opened Edinburgh Festival, 1994, 96. Office: San Francisco Opera War Meml Opera House 301 Van Ness Ave San Francisco CA 94102-4509

RUNQUIST, LISA A. lawyer; b. Mpls., Sept. 22, 1952; d. Ralf E. and Violet R. BA, Hamline U., 1973; JD, U. Minn., 1976. Bar: Minn. 1977, Calif. 1978, U.S. Dist. Ct. (ctrl. dist.) Calif. 1985, U.S. Supreme Ct. 1995. Assoc. Caldwell & Toms, L.A., 1978-82; ptnr. Runquist & Flagg, L.A., 1982-85; pvt. practice Runquist & Assocs., L.A., 1985-99, Runquist & Zybach LLP, L.A., 1999—. Mem. adv. bd. Exempt Orgn. Tax Rev., 1990—, Calif. State U. L.A. Continuing Edn. Acctg. and Tax Program, 1995—. Mem. editorial bd. ABA Bus. Law Today 1995—. Author articles to profl. jours. Mem. ABA (bus. law sect. coun. 1995-99, com. on nonprofit corps. 1986—, chair 1991-95, subcom. current devels. in nonprofit corp. law 1989—, chair 1989-91, subcom. rels. orgns. 1989—, chair 1987-91, 95-98, subcom. legal guidebook for dirs. 1986—, ad hoc com. on info. tech., 1997—, chair 1997-98, co-chair, 1998—, sect. liaison to ABA tech. coun. 1997-2000, subcom. model nonprofit corp. act, partnerships and unincorp. bus. orgns. com. 1987—, state regulation of securities com. 1988-99, tax law sect. exempt orgns. com. 1987—, subcom. religious orgns. 1989—, co-chair 1995-97, subcom. non (c) (3) orgns. 1997—, co-chair 1997—, corp. laws com. 1999—, subcom. guidebook for dirs. of closely held corps. chair 2000—), Calif. Bar Assn. (bus. law sect., nonprofit and unincorp. orgns. com. 1985-92, 93-96, 97—, chair 1989-91), Christian Legal Soc., Ctr. Law and Religious Freedom, Christian Mgmt. Assn. (dir. 1983-89). Office: 10618 Woodbridge St Toluca Lake CA 91602-2717 E-mail: lisa@runquist.com

RUOSLAHTI, ERKKI, medical research administrator; b. Puumala, Finland; B.Medicine, U. Helsinki, Finland, 1961, MD, 1965, Dr.Medicine, 1967; Dr.Medicine (hon.), U. Lund, Sweden, 1991. Rsch./teaching asst. dept. serology and bacteriology U. Helsinki, 1964-66; head blood group dept. State Serum Inst., Helsinki, 1966-68; NIH rsch. fellow Calif. Inst. Tech., 1968-70; asst. prof., acting assoc. prof. dept. serology U. Helsinki, 1970-75; prof. bacteriology and serology U. Turku, Finland, 1975-76; sr. rsch. scientist dept. immunology City of Hope, Duarte, Calif., 1976; dir. immunobiology divsn. immunology City of Hope Nat. Med. Ctr., Duarte, 1978-79; assoc. sci. dir. La Jolla (Calif.) Cancer Rsch. Found., 1979-80, v.p., COO, 1982-89; sci. dir. La Jolla (Calif.) Cancer Rsch. Found. (now The Burnham Inst) 1980—, pres., CEO and dir. Cancer Ctr., 1989—. Adj. prof. dept. pathology U. Calif., San Diego, 1980—; mem. sci. adv. bd. Helen Keller Eye Rsch. Found., Birmingham, Ala., 1989—; mem. pathobiochemistry study sect. Nat. Cancer Inst., 1981-85; Robert and Estelle Stadtler lectr. U. Tex., Sys. Cancer Ctr., 1984, Burton L. Baker Meml. lectr. U. Mich., Ann Arbor, 1987, Harvey Soc. lectr., 1988, Jeanette Piperno Meml. lectr. Temple U., Phila., 1989, G.H.A. Clowes award and lectr. Am. Assn. Cancer Rsch., 1990, Karl H. Beyer lectr. U. Wis., 1990, Walter Hubert lectr. 33d Ann. Meeting, Brit. Assn. for Cancer Rsch., 1992. Contbr. over 300 articles to profl. jours.; editl. bd. mem. Matrix, 1991—, Internat. Jour. Cancer, 1979—, Ann. Rev. of Cell Biology, 1987-90, Jour. Cell Biology, 1987-89, Jour. Biol. Chemistry, 1985-88, Cancer Rsch., 1979-82; reviewing editor Science, 1989—; editor-in-chief Cell Regulation, 1989-91. Recipient Barbara Robert Meml. medal French Soc. of Connective Tissue, 1988, Outstanding Investigator award Nat. Cancer Inst., 1986-93, Robert J. and Claire Pasarow Found. award, 1991, Lella Gruber Cancer Rsch. award Am. Acad. Dermatology, 1993, Abbott award Internat. Soc. for Oncodevelopmental Biology and Medicine, 1995, Gairdner Found. Internat. award Gairdner Found., 1997. Fellow Am. Acad. Arts and Scis.; mem. Finnish Acad. Scis. Office: The Burnham Inst 10901 N Torrey Pines Rd La Jolla CA 92037-1062

RUPERT, DOROTHY, state legislator; b. Meadow Grove, Nebr., Oct. 20, 1926; m. Richard Rupert. BA, Nebr. Wesleyan U., 1948; MA, U. Colo., 1967; postgrad., Harvard U., 1993. Tchr., counselor various high schs., 1948-96; dir. counseling svcs. statewide Colo., 1977-78; developer, dir. Displaced Homemaker Program, 1979-80; mem. Colo. Ho. of Reps., Denver, 1986-94, Colo. Senate, Denver, 1994—, mem. health, environment, welfare and instns. com., mem. jud. com., mem. state local govt. com. Attendee UN Beijing Conf., 1995, Peace & Justice Internat. Conf., Bolivia, 1992, Helsinki, 1995. Mem. Thornton City Coun., 1958-61. Mem. Colo. Counselors Assn. (past pres.), Nat. Human Rights Commn. for Counselors, Nat. Order Women Legislators (bd. dirs.), NOW, Nat. Abortion Rights Action League, AAUW, Amnesty Internat., World Internat. League for Peace and Freedom. Democrat. Office: State Capitol 200 E Colfax Ave Ste 274 Denver CO 80203-1716

RUPPERT, JOHN LAWRENCE, lawyer; b. Chgo., Oct. 7, 1953; s. Merle Arvin and Loretta Marie (Ford) R.; m. Katharine Marie Tarbox, June 5, 1976. BA, Northwestern U., 1975; JD, U. Denver, 1978; LLM in Taxation, NYU, 1979. Bar: Colo. 1978, U.S. Dist. Ct. Colo. 1978, Ill. 1979, U.S. Tax Ct. 1981. Assoc. Kirkland & Ellis, Denver, 1979-84, ptnr., 1984-88, Ballard, Spahr, Andrews & Ingersoll, Denver, 1988-96; shareholder Brownstein Hyatt Farber & Strickland, P.C., Denver, 1996—. Lectr. U. Denver Coll. Law, fall 1984-92; adj. prof. law grad. tax program, 1993-94; sec. Capital Assocs., Inc., 1989-96; sec. Brothers Gourmet Coffees, Inc., 1995-2000; asst. sec. Renaissance Cosmetics, Inc., 1996-98, Rhythms Net Connections Inc., 2000-2001; sec. Skillset Software, Inc., 2000-01; asst. sec. Rhythms NetConnections Inc., 2000-01. Contbr. articles to profl. jours. Mem. ABA, Colo. Bar Assn. (mem. exec. coun. tax sect. 1985-89), Denver Bar Assn. Office: Brownstein Hyatt Farber & Strickland PC 410 17th St Fl 22D Denver CO 80202-4402 E-mail: jruppert@bhfs.com, ruppert53@aol.com

RUSCONI, LOUIS JOSEPH, marine engineer; b. San Diego, Oct. 10, 1926; s. Louis Edward and Laura Ethelyn (Salazar) R.; m. Virginia Caroline Bruce, Jan. 1, 1972. BA in Engrng. Tech., Pacific Western U., 1981, MA in Marine Engrng. Tech., 1982; PhD in Marine Engrng. Mgmt., Clayton U., 1986. Cert. nuclear ship propulsion plant operator, surface and submarine; diplomate naval ship nuclear propulsion system. Enlisted USN, 1944, electrician's mate chief, 1944-65, retired, 1965; marine electrician planner U.S. Naval Shipyard, Vallejo, Calif., 1965-72; marine elec. technician Imperial Iranian Navy, Bandar Abbas, Iran, 1974-79; marine shipyard planner Royal Saudi Navy, Al-Jubail, Saudi Arabia, 1980-86. Cons. in marine engrng., 1986—. Author: Shipyards Operations manual, 1980, poetry (Golden Poet award 1989, Silver Poet award 1990). Mem. Rep. Presdl. Task Force, Washington, 1989-90, trustee, 1991. Mem. IEEE, U.S. Naval Inst., Soc. of Naval Architects and Marine Engrs. (assoc. mem.), Fleet Res., Nat. Geographic Soc. Avocations: creative writing, poetry, martial arts. Home: 949 Myra Ave Chula Vista CA 91911-2315

RUSH, DOMENICA MARIE, health facilities administrator; b. Gallup, N.Mex., Apr. 10, 1937; d. Bernardo G. and Guadalupe (Milan) Iorio; m. W. E. Rush, Jan. 5, 1967. Diploma, Regina Sch. Nursing, Albuquerque, 1958. RN N.Mex.; lic. nursing home adminstr. Charge nurse, house supr. St. Joseph Hosp., Albuquerque, 1958-63; dir. nursing Cibola Hosp., Grants, 1960-64; supr. operating room, dir. med. seminars Carrie Tingley Crippled Children's Hosp., Truth or Consequences, N.Mex., 1964-73; adminstr. Sierra Vista Hosp., Truth or Consequences, 1974-88, pres., 1980-89; clin. nursing mgr. U. N.Mex. Hosp., 1989-90; adminstr. Nor-Lea Hosp., Lovington, N.Mex., 1990-94; with regional ops. divsn. Presbyn. Healthcare Svcs., Albuquerque, 1994—, regional ops., 1994—; adminstr. Sierra Vista Hosp., Truth or Consequences, N.Mex., 1995—. Bd. dirs. N.Mex. Blue Cross/Blue Shield, 1977-88, chmn. hosp. relations com., 1983-85, exec. com. 1983—; bd. dirs. Region II Emergency Med. Svcs. Originating bd. SW Mental Health Ctr., Sierra County, N.Mex., 1975; chmn. Sierra County Personnel Bd., 1983—. Named Lea County Outstanding Woman, N.Mex. Commn. on Status of Women; Woman of Yr. for Lea County, N.Mex., 1993. Mem. Am. Coll. Health Care Adminstrs., Sierra County C. of C. (bd. dirs. 1972, 75-76, svc. award 1973, Businesswoman of the Yr. 1973-74), N.Mex. Hosp. Assn. (bd. dirs., sec.-treas., pres.-elect, com. chmn., 1977-88, pres. 1980-81, exec. com., 1980-83, 84-85, recipient meritorius svc. award 1988), N.Mex. So. Hosp. Coun. (sec. 1980-81, pres. 1981-82), Am. Hosp. Assn. (N.Mex. del. 1984-88, regional adv. bd. 1984-88). Republican. Roman Catholic. Avocations: raising thoroughbred horses, cooking. Home: 1100 N Riverside Dr Truth Or Consequences NM 87901-9789 Office: 800 E 9th Ave Truth Or Consequences NM 87901-1934

RUSH, HERMAN E. television executive; b. Phila., June 20, 1929; s. Eugene and Bella (Sacks) R.; m. Joan Silberman, Mar. 18, 1951; children: James Harrison, Mandie Susan. BBA, Temple U., 1950. With Ofcl. Films, 1951-57; owner Flamingo Films, 1957-60; with Creative Mgmt. Assos., N.Y.C., 1960-71, pres. TV divsn., 1964-71, exec. v.p. parent co., dir., 1964-71; ind. prodr., 1971-75; prodr. Wolper Orgn., 1975-76; pres. Herman Rush Assos., Inc. (Rush-Flaherty Agy. subs.), 1977-78, Marble Arch TV, Los Angeles, 1979-80, Columbia Pictures TV, Burbank, Calif., 1980-87; chmn., CEO, Coca-Cola Telecom., 1987-88, Rush Assocs., Inc., Burbank, 1988—, Katz/Rush Entertainment, Beverly Hills, Calif., 1990-96, New Tech Entertainment, LLC, Beverly Hills, 1996—; chmn., CEO internet content provider Entertainment Internat., Inc. CEO Infotainment Internat., Inc.; chmn. Entertainment Industries Coun.; pres., chmn. Royal Animated Art, Inc.; chmn. bd. dirs. E Capital Fin. Corp. Trustee Sugar Ray Robinson Youth Found., 1967-75; pres. Retarded Infant Services, N.Y.C., 1957-63; bd. dirs. U.S. Marshall's Service Found., Just Say No Found.; conferee White House Conf. for a Drug Free America, 1987, 88. Mem. Acad. TV Arts and Scis., Hollywood Radio and TV Soc., Producers Caucus. Clubs: Friars, Filmex. Office: Rush Entertainment Group # 3045 3340 Ocean Park Blvd Santa Monica CA 90405 E-mail: hermanrush@aol.com

RUSHER, WILLIAM ALLEN, writer, commentator; b. Chgo., July 19, 1923; s. Evan Singleton and Verna (Self) R. AB, Princeton, 1943; JD, Harvard U., 1948; DLitt (hon.), Nathaniel Hawthorne Coll., 1973. Bar: N.Y. bar 1949. Assoc. Shearman & Sterling & Wright, N.Y.C., 1948-56; spl. counsel fin. com. N.Y. Senate, 1955; assoc. counsel internal security subcom. U.S. Senate, 1956-57; pub., v.p. Nat. Review mag., N.Y.C., 1957-88, also bd. dirs.; Disting. fellow The Claremont Inst, 1989—. Mem. Adv. Task Force on Civil Disorders, 1972 Author: Special Counsel, 1968, (with Mark Hatfield and Arlie Schardt) Amnesty?, 1973, The Making of the New Majority Party, 1975, How to Win Arguments, 1981, The Rise of the Right, 1984, The Coming Battle for the Media, 1988; editor: The Ambiguous Legacy of the Enlightenment, 1995; columnist Universal Press Syndicate, 1973-82, Newspaper Enterprise Assn., 1982—; played role of Advocate in TV program The Advocates, 1970-74. Chmn., bd. dirs. Media Rsch. Ctr., Washington, 2001—, Nat. Rev. Bd., 1957-88, 90—; bd. advisors Ashbrook Ctr., Ashland, Ohio, past chmn.; past vice chmn. Am. Conservative Union; past trustee Pacific Legal Found., Sacramento. Served as 2d lt. to capt., USAAF, 1943-45, India-Burma Theater. Recipient Disting. Citizen award NYU Sch. Law, 1973. Mem. ABA, U. Club (N.Y.C. and San Francisco), Met. Club (Washington). Anglican. Home and Office: 850 Powell St San Francisco CA 94108-2051

RUSS, CHARLES PAUL, III, lawyer, corporate executive; b. N.Y.C., Aug. 24, 1944; s. Charles Paul Jr. and Dorothea (von Frieling) R.; m. Dianne P. McLaughlin, June 24, 1969; children: Alexander Peter, Andrew William. B.A., Amherst Coll., 1966; J.D., Columbia U., 1969. Bar: N.Y. 1970, Ga. 1973. Assoc. Sullivan & Cromwell, N.Y.C., 1969-72, Gambrell & Mobley, Atlanta, 1972-74, ptnr., 1974; sr. atty. Stauffer Chem. Co., Westport, Conn., 1975-78; asst. gen. counsel Geo Internat. Corp., Stamford, 1978-80, v.p., gen. counsel, 1980-84; v.p., sec., gen. counsel NCR Corp., Dayton, Ohio, 1984-92; exec. v.p., sec., gen. counsel U.S. West, Inc., Englewood, Colo., 1992-98. Bd. dirs. U.S. West, MediaOne Group Harlan Fiske Stone scholar Columbia U., 1969 Mem. ABA, Am. Corp. Counsel Assn., Ohio State Bar Assn., Assn. Gen. Counsel. Clubs: Dayton Country, Miami Valley Hunt and Polo, NCR Country, Seabrook Island Ocean. Home: 122 Pulehu Rd Kula HI 96790-9787 Office: US West Inc Ste 230 3200 Cherry Creek South Dr Denver CO 80209-3246

RUSSELL, BARRY, federal judge; b. 1940; BS, UCLA, 1962, JD, 1966. Estate and gift tax examiner U.S. Treasury Dept., 1966-67; dep. pub. defender L.A. County, 1967-70; asst. U.S. atty. L.A., 1970-74; apptd. bankruptcy judge cen. dist. U.S. Dist. Ct. Calif., 1974; apptd. to Ninth Cir. Bankruptcy Appellate Panel, 1988—, presiding judge, 1999—. Author: Bankruptcy Evidence Manual, 1987—. Recipient So. Calif. Mediation Assn. Judges award, 1997. Fellow Am. Coll. Bankruptcy; mem. ABA (Franklin N. Flaschner Jud. award as outstanding judge 1987), FBA (nat. pres. 1990-91), Nat. Conf. Bankruptcy Judges, L.A. County Bar Assn. (Dispute Resolution Svcs. Emil Gumpert Jud. ADR award), Phi Alpha Delta. Office: Roybal Federal Bldg 255 E Temple St Los Angeles CA 90012-3334

RUSSELL, BILL, professional baseball coach; b. Pittsburg, Kans., Oct. 21, 1948; m. Susan, Jan. 25, 1997; children: Amy lynn, Cynthia Ann. Outfielder, shorstop L.A. Dodgers, 1973-86, infield mgr., bench coach, 1987-91, 94-96; mgr. Triple-A, Albuquerque, 1992-93, Mesa Seguaros, Ariz., 1993; head coach L.A. Dodgers, 1997-2000. Named shrotstop to All-Star Team, 1973, 76, 80. Avocations: hunting, fishing, collecting antiques. Office: c/o LA Dodgers 1000 Elysian Park Ave Los Angeles CA 90012-1112

RUSSELL, BRYON, basketball player; b. Dec. 31, 1970; m. Kimberly; 1 child, Kajun. Grad., Long Beach State U. Forward Utah Jazz, Salt Lake City, 1993—. Office: Utah Jazz 301 W South Temple Salt Lake City UT 84101-1216

RUSSELL, CAROL ANN, personnel service company executive; b. Detroit, Dec. 14, 1943; d. Billy and Iris Koud; m. Victor Rojas (div.). BA in English, CUNY-Hunter Coll., 1993. Registered employment cons. Various positions in temp. help cos., N.Y.C., 1964-74; v.p. Wollborg-Michelson, San Francisco, 1974-82; co-owner, pres. Russell Staffing Resources, Inc., San Francisco and Sonoma, 1983-98; ret.; co-founder Workplacecentral.com, 1999—. Media guest, spkr., workshop and seminar leader in field; host/cmty. prodr. Job Net program for TCI Cable T.V. Pub. Checkpoint Newsletter; feature writer/columnist The Slant; contbr. articles to profl. publs. Founding v.p. The Friends of the Frank Lloyd Wright Civic Ctr. Libr. Marin County. Named to the Inc. 500, 1989, 90. Mem. Am. Women in Radio and TV, Soc. to Preserve and Encourage Radio Drama Variety and Comedy, No. Calif. Human Resources Coun., Soc. Human Resource Mgmt., Calif. Assn. Pers. Cons. (pres. Golden State chpt. 1984-85), Calif. Assn. Temp. Svcs., Bay Area Pers. Assn. (pres. 1983-84), Pers. Assn. Sonoma County, Profl. Resume Writers Am., Am. Jewish Congress. E-mail: nastypumps@hotmail.com

RUSSELL, CHARLES ROBERTS, chemical engineer; b. Spokane, Wash., July 13, 1914; s. Marvin Alvin and Dessie Corselia (Price) R.; m. Dolores Kopriva, May 17, 1943; children: Ann E., John C., David F., Thomas R. B.S. in Chem. Engring, Wash. State U., 1936; Ph.D. in Chem. Engring. (Procter and Gamble Co. fellow 1940-41), U. Wis., 1941. Egr. div. reactor devel. AEC, Washington, 1950-56; engr. Gen. Motors Tech. Center, Warren, Mich. and Santa Barbara, Calif., 1956-68; assoc. dean engring. Calif. Poly. State U., San Luis Obispo, 1968-73, prof. mech. engring., 1973-80. Mem. nuclear standards bd. Am. Nat. Standards Inst., 1956-78; cons., 1980—; sec. adv. com. reactor safeguards AEC, 1950-55 Author: Reactor Safeguards, 1962, Elements of Energy Conversion, 1967, Energy Sources, Ency. Britannica. Served with USNR, 1944-46. Mem. Am. Chem. Soc. Republican. Roman Catholic. Club: Channel City (Santa Barbara). Home and Office: 3071 Marilyn Way Santa Barbara CA 93105-2040 E-mail: crrus1@aol.com

RUSSELL, DAVID E. judge; b. Chicago Heights, Ill., Mar. 19, 1935; s. Robert W. and Nellie Russell; m. Denise A. Hurst, Apr. 1, 1968 (div. 1978); children: Dirk, Kent, Laura, Rachel; m. Sandra M. Niemeyer, Oct. 31, 1982. BS in Acctg., U. Calif., Berkeley, 1957, LLB, 1960. Bar: Calif. 1961, U.S. Dist. Ct. (no. dist.) Calif. 1961, U.S. Tax Ct. 1967; CPA, Calif. Staff acct. Lybrand, Ross Bros. & Montgomery, San Francisco, 1960-64; assoc. Robert C. Burnstein, Esquire, Oakland, Calif., 1964-65; ptnr. Russell & Humphreys, Sacramento, 1965, Russell, Humphreys & Estabrook, Sacramento, 1966-70, prin., 1971-73; shareholder Russell, Jarvis, Estabrook & Dashiell, Sacramento, 1974-86; bankruptcy judge U.S. Bankruptcy Ct. for Ea. Dist. Calif., Sacramento, 1986—. Office: US Bankruptcy Ct 501 I St Sacramento CA 95814-7300

RUSSELL, FRANCIA, ballet director, educator; b. Los Angeles, Jan. 10, 1938; d. W. Frank and Marion (Whitney) R.; m. Kent Stowell, Nov. 19, 1965; children: Christopher, Darren, Ethan. Studies with, George Balanchine, Vera Volkova, Felia Doubrouska, Antonina Tumkovsky, Benjamin Harkarvy; student, NYU, Columbia U. Dancer, soloist N.Y.C. Ballet, 1956-62, ballet mistress, 1965-70; dancer Ballets USA/Jerome Robbins, N.Y.C., 1962; tchr. ballet Sch. Am. Ballet, N.Y.C., 1963-64; co-dir. Frankfurt (Fed. Republic Germany) Opera Ballet, 1976-77; dir., co-artistic dir. Pacific N.W. Ballet, Seattle, 1977—; dir. Pacific N.W. Ballet Sch., Seattle. Affiliate prof. of dance U. Wash. Dir. staging over 100 George Balanchine ballet prodns. throughout world, including Russia and China, 1964—. Named Woman of Achievement, Matrix Table, Women in Comm., Seattle, 1987, Gov.'s Arts award, 1989, Dance Mag. award, 1996. Mem. Internat. Women's Forum. Home: 2833 Broadway E Seattle WA 98102-3935 Office: Pacific NW Ballet 301 Mercer St Seattle WA 98109-4600

RUSSELL, IRWIN EMANUEL, lawyer; b. N.Y.C., Jan. 24, 1926; m. Suzanne Russell, Nov. 15, 1968. BS in Econs., U. Pa., 1947; JD, Harvard U., 1949. Bar: N.Y. 1949, Calif. 1971. Atty. office chief counsel Wage Stabilization Bd., Washington, 1951-53; pvt. practice N.Y.C., 1954-71; founder, chmn., dir. RAI Rsch. Corp., Hauppage, N.Y., 1954-91; exec. v.p., treas., dir. The Wolper Orgn., Inc., L.A., 1971-76; pvt. practice Beverly Hills, Calif., 1977—. Dir. Walt Disney Co., Burbank, Calif., The Lipper Fund, Inc., N.Y.C. With USAAF, 1944-45. Home: 10590 Wilshire Blvd Apt 1402 Los Angeles CA 90024-4563 Office: 9401 Wilshire Blvd Ste 760 Beverly Hills CA 90212-2933

RUSSELL, JAMES BRIAN, broadcast executive, media consultant; b. Hartford, Conn., Jan. 30, 1946; s. Seymour and Marian (Kamins) R.; m. Kathleen Anne Schardt, Dec. 28, 1968; children: Theodore, Jennifer, Kimberly. BA in Journalism, Am. U., 1968; postgrad. Wharton Sch. Bus., U. Pa.; postgrad., Stanford U. News dir. Sta. WPIK-AM, Arlington, Va., 1965-66; editor, anchorman Sta. WAVA-AM/FM, Washington, 1966-68; editor, corr. UPI, Washington, Cambodia and, Vietnam, 1968-71; from reporter to exec. prodr. All Things Considered Nat. Pub. Radio, Washington, 1971-78; sta. dir., sr. v.p. programming Stas. KTCA/KTCI-TV, Mpls./St. Paul, 1978-88; v.p. nat. prodns., exec. prodr. Marketplace U. So. Calif., L.A., 1988-97; v.p. USC Radio and GM Marketplace Prodns., L.A., 1997-99; sr. v.p. nat. programming Minn. Pub. Radio and GM Marketplace Prodns., L.A., St. Paul, 2000—. Cons. Corp. Pub. Broadcasting, Nat. Endowment Arts, Sta. WNET-TV, N.Y.C., Sta. WGBH-TV, Boston, Nat. Pub. Radio, Am. Pub. Radio, Pub. Radio Internat., Am. Documentary Consortium, The Learning Channel, The Pacific Rim Consortium, Internat. Pub. TV Conf., Audible, Inc. Columnist pub. broadcasting's Current newspaper. Mem. prison visitor program AMICUS, St. Paul, 1984-85. Postgrad. fellow in journalism U. Mich.; recipient Nat. Headliner award 1972, 74, Ohio State award, 1973, 75, duPont Columbia awards Columbia U., 1979, 81, 97, Peabody award 2001, Nat. TV Emmy award Acad. TV Arts and Scis., 1989, William Kling award for Innovation and Entrepreneurship, 1998, Mo. Honor medal for disting. svc. in journalism, 2000. Home: 3820 Gundry Ave Long Beach CA 90807-4227 Office: Marketplace Prodns 261 S Figueroa Ave #200 Los Angeles CA 90012 E-mail: jrussell@marketplace.org

RUSSELL, JEFFREY BURTON, historian, educator; b. Fresno, Calif., Aug. 1, 1934; s. Lewis Henry and Ieda Velma (Ogborn) R.; m. Diana Emily Mansfield, June 30, 1956; children: Jennifer, Mark, William, Penelope. A.B., U. Calif., Berkeley, 1955, A.M., 1957; Ph.D., Emory U., 1960. Asst. prof. U. N.Mex., Albuquerque, 1960-61; jr. fellow Soc. of Fellows, Harvard U., Cambridge, Mass., 1961-62; mem. faculty U. Calif., Riverside, 1962-75, prof. dept. history, 1969-75, assoc. dean grad. div., 1967-72; dir. Medieval Inst.; Michael P. Grace prof. medieval studies U. Notre Dame, South Bend, Ind., 1975-77; dean grad. studies Calif. State U., Sacramento, 1977-79; prof. history U. Calif., Santa Barbara, 1979—, prof. religious studies, 1994—. Author: Dissent and Reform in the Early Middle Ages, 1965, Medieval Civilization, 1968, A History of Medieval Christianity: Prophecy and Order, 1968, Religious Dissent in the Middle Ages, 1971, Witchcraft in the Middle Ages, 1972, The Devil: Perceptions of Evil from Antiquity to Primitive Christianity, 1977, A History of Witchcraft: Sorcerers, Heretics, and Pagans, 1980, Medieval Heresies: a Bibliography, 1981, Satan: The Early Christian Tradition, 1981, Lucifer: The Devil in the Middle Ages, 1984, Mephistopheles: The Devil in the Modern World, 1986, The Prince of Darkness, 1988, Ruga in Aevis, 1990, Inventing the Flat Earth: Columbus and the Historians, 1991, Dissent and Order in the Middle Ages, 1992, A History of Heaven: The Singing Silence, 1997, Essays in Honor of Jeffrey B. Russell, 1998; contbr. articles in field to profl. jours. Fulbright fellow, 1959-60; Am. Council Learned Socs. grantee, 1965, 70; Social Sci. Research Council grantee, 1968; Guggenheim fellow, 1968-69; Nat. Endowment for Humanities sr. fellow, 1972-73 Fellow Medieval Acad. Am.; mem. Medieval Assn. Pacific, Am. Soc. Ch. Histor Am. Acad. Religion, Astron. Soc. Pacific, Sierra Club. Home: 4796 Calle Camarada Santa Barbara CA 93110-2053 Office: U Calif Dept History Santa Barbara CA 93106 E-mail: russell@humanitas.ucsb.edu

RUSSELL, KEN (HENRY KENNETH ALFRED RUSSELL), film and theatre director; b. Southampton, Eng., July 3, 1927; s. Henry and Ethel (Smith) R.; m. Shirley Kingdon, Feb. 3, 1957 (div.); 5 children; m. Vivian Jolly, June 10, 1984; children: Molly, Rupert. Student, Walthamstow Art Sch., Internat. Ballet Sch. Formerly dancer, actor, still photographer, BBC documentary film maker; feature film dir.; feature films include French Dressing, 1964, Billion Dollar Brain, 1967,Women in Love, 1970, The Music Lovers, 1970, The Boy Friend, 1971, The Devils, 1971, Savage Messiah, 1972, Mahler, 1975, Tommy, 1975, Lizstomania, 1975, Altered States, 1980, Crimes of Passion, 1984, Gothic, 1986, Salome's Last Dance, 1986, Aria, 1987, The Lair of the White Worm, 1988, The Rainbow, 1989, Whore, 1991, Lady Chatterly, 1993; dir., writer: film Valentino, 1977; actor, The Russia House, 1990; dir.: operas Rakes Progres, 1982, Die Soldaten, 1983, Madame Butterfly, Spoleto and Melbourne; La Boheme, Macenata; Faust, Vienna; Mephisto, Rhodes and Genoa. Served with Mcht. Navy, 1945; Served with also RAF. Recipient Screen writers Guild award for TV films Elgar, Debussy, Isadora, Dante's Inferno; Delius award (Merit Scroll); award Guild TV Producers and Dirs., 1966; Desmond Davis award, 1968 Office: c/o Peter Rawley Internat Creative Mgmt 8942 Wilshire Blvd Beverly Hills CA 90211-1934 Home: 16 Salisbury Pl London W1H 1FH England

RUSSELL, MARJORIE ROSE, manufacturing company executive; b. Welcome, Minn., Sept. 3, 1925; d. Emil Frederick and Ella Magdalene (Sothman) Wohlenhaus; m. Kenneth Kollmann Russell, Sept. 15, 1947 (div. May 1973); children: Jennie Rose, Richard Lowell, Laura Eloise, James Wesley. Student, Northwestern Sch., Mpls., 1944-45, St. Paul Bible Inst., , 1946-47. Cook U. Minn., Mpls., 1943-45; maintenance person U. Farm Campus/N.W. Schs., St. Paul, 1945-46; clk. Kresge Corp., Mpls., 1945; cook, waitress, mgr. Union City Mission Bible Camp, Mpls., 1944-47; caterer for v.p. Gt. No. R.R., St. Paul, 1947; custodian Old Soldiers Home, St. Paul, 1946; nurse Sister Elizabeth Kenney Polio Hosp., St. Paul, 1946; seamstress Hirsch, Weis, White Stag, Pendleton, Mayfair, Portland, Oreg., 1960-72; owner, operator, contract mgr., creative designer The Brass Needle, Portland, 1972—. Contractor Forrester's Sanderson Safety, Scotsco, Nero & Assocs., Gara Gear, Portland, 1972—, Columbia Sportswear; tchr. Indo Chinese Cultural Ctr., Portland, 1982; mfr. of protective chaps and vests for the Pacific Northwest hogging industry. Designer, producer Kisn Bridal Fair, 1969; composer: He Liveth in Me, 1968; prodr. Safety Chaps for Loggers. Sec. Model Cities Com., Portland, 1969; com. mem. Neighborhood Black Christmas Parade, Portland, 1970; custume designer Local Miss Jr. Black Beauty Contest, Portland, 1973; nominating com. Nat. Contract Mgmt. Assn., Portland, 1978; mem. nominating com. Multi-Cultural Sr. Adv. Com., 1988-91. Mem. NAFE, Urban League, Urban League Guild (historian 1991-92), Am. Assn. Ret. Persons, Nat. Contract Mgmt. Assn. Democrat. Mem. United Ch. of Christ. Avocations: music, swimming, painting, gardening, arts. Home and Office: The Brass Needle 2809 NE 12th Ave Portland OR 97212-3219

RUSSELL, NEWTON REQUA, retired state legislator; b. L.A., June 25, 1927; s. John Henry and Amy (Requa) R.; m. Diane Henderson, Feb. 12, 1953; children: Stephen, Sharon, Julia. BS, U. So. Calif., 1951; postgrad., UCLA, Georgetown U. Spl. agt. Northwestern Mut. Life Ins. Co., Calif., 1954-64; mem. Calif. State Assembly, 1964-74, Calif. Senate, 1974-96, ret., 1996. Vice-chmn. com. on energy, utilities and comm., mem. com. on local govt., mem. com. on fin. and investment, internat. trade, mem. com. on transp., com. ins., joint com. on rules, select com. on Calif.'s wine industry, mem. Com. on Legis. Ethics, Joint Oversight Com. on Lowering the Cost of Electric Svcs, chmn. senate select com. mediation. Mem. Rep. State Ctrl. Com. Served with USN, 1945-46. Recipient Outstanding Legislator award Calif. Rep. Assembly, 1968, 76, 81, Mayor's commendation City of Burbank, 1978, Disting. Svc. awrad County Suprs. Assn. Calif., 1980, Nat. Rep. Legislator of Yr., 1981, Legislator of Yr. award Los Angeles County Fedn. Rep. Women, 1982, Legislator of Yr. award Calif. Credit Union League, 1983, Paul Harris Fellow award Rotary Found. Rotary Internat., numerous honors from cmty. orgns. and instns. Mem. Rotary Internat., Am. Legion, Delta Tau Delta, Alpha Kappa Phi. Mem. Church on the Way.

RUSSELL, PATRICK JAMES, priest; b. Boise, Idaho, May 10, 1959; s. Glenn Edward and Doralea (Trumble) R. BA, Boise U., 1982; MDiv, St. Patrick's Sem., 1986. Ordained priest Roman Catholic Ch., 1986. Assoc. pastor St. Marks Cath. Ch., Boise, 1986-91; chaplain Chateau de Boise, 1991—, Bishop Kelly H.S., 1993—. Active Nat. Cath. Office for Persons With Disabilities, 1991—, Idaho Vocations Bd., 1992-95; founder, dir. Father Russell Charity Golf Scramble for Persons with Chronic Illnesses, 1986—; apptd. tribunal advocate Office of Canonical Affairs, Idaho, 1996—; apptd. priest mem. bioethics com. St. Alphonsus Regional Med. Ctr., 1999. Named Idaho Handicapped Student of Yr., 1974, Best Actor, Boise Little Theatre, 1979-80, Outstanding Young Man of Am., 1983, 84, 86, 87, Outstanding Youth in Achievement, Cambridge, U.K., Internat. Man of Yr., Cambridge, 1995. Mem. Osteogenesis Imperfecta Fdn., Am. Film Inst., Amnesty Internat., Nat. Theatre Comm. Group (charter), Internat. Soc. Poets (life, award), Right to Life/Spl. Olympics, Sigma Phi Epsilon. Democrat. Avocations: writing, painting, music, public speaking, acting. E-mail: patrick7@micron.net

RUSSELL, PAUL EDGAR, electrical engineering educator; b. Roswell, N.Mex., Oct. 10, 1924; s. Rueben Matthias and Mary (Parsons) R.; m. Lorna Margaret Clayshulte, Aug. 29, 1943; children: Carol Potter, Janice Russell Cook, Gregory. BSEE, N.Mex. State U., 1946, BSME, 1947; MSEE, U. Wis., 1950, PhDEE, 1951. Registered elec. engr., Ariz. From instr. to asst. prof. elec. engring. U. Wis., Madison, 1947-52; sr. engr., design specialist Gen. Dynamics Corp., San Diego, 1952-54; from prof. to chmn. elec. engring. dept. U. Ariz., Tucson, 1954-63; dean engring. Kans. State U., Manhattan, 1963-67; prof. Ariz. State U., Tempe, 1967-90; dir. engring. Ariz. State U. West, Phoenix, 1985-88; dir. Sch. Constrn. and Tech. Ariz. State U., Tempe, 1988-90. Cons. in field, 1954—; programs evaluator, mem. engring. commn. Accreditation Bd. for Engring. and Tech., N.Y.C., 1968-81. Contbr. articles to jours. and chpts. to books. Served as sgt. U.S. Army, 1944-46. Recipient Disting. Service award N.Mex. State U., 1965. Fellow IEEE (life, chmn. Ariz. sect. 1960), Accreditation Bd. Engring. and Tech.; mem. Am. Soc. Engring. Educators. Home: 5902 E Caballo Ln Paradise Valley AZ 85253

RUSSELL, RICHARD DONCASTER, geophysicist, educator, geoscientist; b. Toronto, Ont., Can., Feb. 27, 1929; s. Richard Douglas and Ada Gwennola (Doncaster) R.; m. Virginia Ann Reid Clippingdale, Aug. 11, 1951; children: Linda Jean, Morna Ann, Mary Joyce. BA, U. Toronto, 1951, MA, 1952, PhD, 1954. Asst. prof. physics U. Toronto, 1956-58, prof., 1962-63; asso. prof. physics U. B.C., Vancouver, 1958-62, prof. geophysics, 1963-91, prof. emeritus, 1991—, head dept. geophysics, 1968-72, head dept. geophysics and astronomy, 1972-79, bd. govs., 1978-81, assoc. dean sci., 1980-83, assoc. v.p. acad., 1983-86. Sec.-gen. Inter-Union Commn. on Geodynamics, 1976-80; profl. geoscientist. Author textbooks.; Contbr. articles to profl. jours. Fellow Royal Soc. Can.; mem. Am. Geophys. Union, Can. Geophys. Union (J. Tuzo Wilson medal 1992). Home: 226-4955 River Rd Delta BC Canada V4K 4V9 Office: U BC Dept Earth & Ocean Scis Vancouver BC Canada V6T 1Z4 E-mail: russell@geop.ubc.ca

RUSSELL, THOMAS PAUL, physicist; b. Boston, Nov. 18, 1952; s. Robert Boyd and Catherine (Connelly) R.; m. Catherine Ciulla, Aug. 4, 1978. B.S., Boston State Coll., 1974; M.S., U. Mass., 1976, Ph.D., 1979. Postdoctoral fellow U. Mainz (W.Ger.), 1979--81; mem. research staff IBM Research Lab., San Jose, Calif., 1981— . Contbr. articles to sci. jours. Mem. Am. Phys. Soc., Am. Chem. Soc. (A.K. Doolittle award 1984), Am. Crystallographic Soc., AAAS. Roman Catholic. Office: IBM Almaden Rsch Ctr 650 Harry Rd San Jose CA 95120-6001

RUSSIANO, JOHN See MILES, JACK

RUSSIN, ROBERT ISAIAH, sculptor, educator; b. N.Y.C., Aug. 26, 1914; s. Uriel and Olga (Winnett) R.; m. Adele Mutchnick, May 21, 1937; children: Joseph Mark, Lincoln David, Uriel Robin. BA, CCNY, 1933, MS, 1935; postgrad. (Inst. fellow), Beaux Arts Inst. Design, 1935-36. Tchr. sculpture Copper Union Art Inst., N.Y.C., 1944-47; prof. art U. Wyo., Laramie, 1947-86, prof., artist-in-residence, 1976-85, Disting. prof. emeritus, 1985—. One-man shows Tucson Fine Arts Ctr., 1966, Colorado Springs (Colo.) Fine Arts Ctr., 1967, Palm Springs (Calif.) Desert Mus., Chas. G. Bowers Meml. Mus., Judah L. Magnes Meml. Mus., Berkeley, Calif.; retrospective one-man exhbn. Nat. Gallery Modern Art, Santo Domingo, Dominican Republic, 1976, Tubac Ctr. of the Arts, Ariz., 1987, Old Town Gallery-Park City, Ut., Riggins Gallery, Scottsdale, Ariz., 1989, Fine Arts Mus., U. Wyo., 1991; sculpture commns. include 2 8-foot metal figures, Evanston (Ill.) Post Office, 1939, three life-size carved figures, Conshohocken (Pa.) Post Office, 1940, Benjamin Franklin Monument, U. Wyo., 1957, Bust of Lincoln, Lincoln Mus., Washington, (now in Gettysburg Mus.), 1959, Lincoln Monument atop summit Lincoln Hwy., (now U.S. Interstate 80), Wyo, 1959, monumental bas-relief bronze Cheyenne (Wyo.) Fed. Bldg, 1966, two carved wood walls, Denver Fed. Bldg., 1966, monumental fountain, City of Hope Med. Ctr., Los Angeles, 1966-67, statue, Brookhaven (N.Y.) Nat. Lab., 1968, life-size bronze sculpture fountain, City of Hope, 1969, Pomona Coll., 1973, monumental bronze sculpture Prometheus Natrona County (Wyo.) Pub. Library, 1974, Man and Energy, Casper (Wyo.) C. of C., 1974, 12-foot marble carving Menorah Med. Ctr., Kansas City, Mo., 1975, Einstein and Gershwin medals Magnes Meml. Mus, Berkeley, Nat. Mus. Art, Santo Domingo, Dominican Republic, 1975, monumental fountain, Galleria d'Arte Moderna, Santo Domingo, 1977, Duarte Monument, Santo Domingo, 1977, 30 foot steel and water fountain monument City Hall, Casper, 1980, marble and bronze monument, Lincoln Centre, Dallas, 1982, acrylic steel and bronze monument, Herschler State Office Bldg., Cheyenne, 1984, marble monument, U. Wyo., Laramie, 1985, portrait head Charles Bluhdorn, chmn. Gulf & Western, 1975, portrait bust Pres. J. Balaguer of Dominican Republic, 1975, portrait head G. Wilson Knight, Shakespearean actor and scholar, 1975, 2 12-foot bronze figures The Greeting and the Gift for Bicentennial Commn., Cheyenne, 1976, monumental marble head of Juan Pablo Duarte liberator Dominican Republic, Santo Domingo, 1976, monumental marble, Pan Am. Family, Dominican Republic, 1977, marble sculpture Trio, U. Wyo., 1985, Isaac B. Singer medal for Magnes Mus., 1983, monumental Holocaust Figure Tucson Jewish Community Ctr., 1989, granite monument Chthonodynamis, Dept. Energy Bldg., Washington, 1992, bust Hon. Milward Simpson, 1993, bust James Forest U. Wyo., 1993, bronze statue Univ. Med. Ctr., Tuscon, Head, Gov. Stanley Hathway, Cheyenne, Wy. 1995; contbr. articles to profl. jours.Head, Pres. Franklin D. Roosevelt, Rotunda (pres.hosp. Bethsda, Md.). Recipient awards sec. fine arts U.S. Treasury, 1939, 40, Lincoln medal U.S. Congress, 1959, Alfred G.B. Steel award Pa. Acad. Fine Arts, 1961, medal of Order of Duarte Sanchez y Mella, Dominican Republic, 1977; Ford Found. fellow, 1953. Mem. Nat. Sculpture Conf. (exec. bd.), Sculptors Guild, Nat. Sculpture Soc., AIA, AAUP, Coll. Art Internat. Inst. Arts and Letters, Phi Beta Kappa (hon.) Home: 61 N Fork Rd Centennial WY 82055 also: 1160 W Placita Salubre Green Valley AZ 85614-1334 E-mail: adbo@webtv.net

RUSSON, LEONARD H. state supreme court justice; b. Salt Lake City, May 15, 1933; JD, Utah Coll., 1962. Pvt. practice, Salt Lake City, 1962-84; judge Utah Dist. Ct. (3d dist.), Utah Ct. Appeals; justice Utah Supreme Ct., Salt Lake City, chief justice. Vice chair Utah Bd. Dist. Ct. Judges; mem. Jud. Conduct Commn., Utah Supreme Ct. Adv. Com. on Code of Profl. Conduct. Office: Utah Supreme Ct PO Box 140210 450 S State St Salt Lake City UT 84114-0210

RUSSONIELLO, JOSEPH PASCAL, lawyer; b. Jersey City, Oct. 12, 1941; s. Sabin G. and Justine B. (Terraciano) R.; m. Moira F. Ward, Aug. 29, 1969. B in Social Sci., Fairfield U., 1963; JD, NYU, 1966. Bar: N.J. 1967, Calif. 1969. Spl. agt. FBI, Washington, 1966-67; dep. dist. atty. City and County San Francisco (Calif.) Dist. Atty. Offices, 1969-75; assoc. Cooley Godward Castro Huddleson & Tatum, San Francisco, 1975-78; U.S. atty. U.S. Dept. Justice (no. dist.) Calif., San Francisco, 1982-90; ptnr. Cooley Godward L.L.P., San Francisco, 1978-82, 90—. Pres., bd. dirs. San Francisco (Calif.) Law Sch., 1996—; analyst KTVU-Ch. 2, Oakland, Calif., 1994—. Pres. Northgate Cottages, Napa, Calif., 1988—; chmn. Catholics for Truth and Justice, San Francisco, 1991—; v.p. Mid-Pacific region Nat. Italian Am. Fedn., 1996-99. Recipient Man of Yr. award NIAF, 1986, Man of Yr. award St. Thomas More Soc., San Francisco, 2000, Assumpta award Trustees St. Mary's Cathedral, 2000, Papal Pro Ecclesia medal, 2000; named Alumni of Yr.-Pub. Sector, NYU Law Sch., 1991. Fellow Am. Coll. Trial Lawyers; mem. Am. bd. Trial Lawyers (adv.), McFetridge Inn of Ct. (barrister). Republican. Avocations: tennis, golf, reading, playing the saxophone. Home: 2850 Jackson St San Francisco CA 94115-1146 Office: Cooley Godward LLP 1 Maritime Plz San Francisco CA 94111-3404 E-mail: Russonielloj@cooley.com

RUSZKIEWICZ, CAROLYN MAE, newspaper editor; b. Tucson, Nov. 10, 1946; d. Robert Frank and Charlotte Ruth (Hadley) Knapton; m. Joseph Charles Ruszkiewicz, July 11, 1969. BA, Calif. State U., Long Beach, 1971, MA, 1973. Reporter Long Beach (Calif.) Press-Telegram, 1968-85, consumer editor, 1985-86, lifestyle editor, 1986-89, regional news editor, 1989-91, city editor, 1991-95, asst. mng. editor, 1995-97, mng. editor, 1997—. Avocations: swimming, walking, reading. Office: Long Beach Press Telegram 604 Pine Ave Long Beach CA 90844-0003

RUTES, WALTER ALAN, architect; b. N.Y.C., Sept. 21, 1928; s. Jack and Sarah (Ogur) R.; m. Helene Darville, Apr. 2, 1952; children: Daniel J., Linda Lee. B.Arch. (Sands Meml. medal 1950), Cornell U., 1950; fellow city planning, MIT, 1951; postgrad., Harvard U. Grad. Sch. Design, 1978. Cert. Nat. Council Archtl. Registration Bds. Assoc. ptnr. Skidmore, Owings & Merrill, N.Y.C., 1951-72; v.p. John Carl Warnecke & Assocs., N.Y.C., 1972-74; staff v.p. Intercontinental Hotels Corp., N.Y.C., 1974-80; dir. architecture Holiday Inns, Inc., Memphis, 1980-83; dir. design The Sheraton Corp., Boston, 1983-85; chmn 9 Tek Ltd. Devel. Cons., 1985—. Chmn. adv. bd. Hult Fellowships for Constrn. Industry, 1968-75, Architects and Engrs. Com. New Bldg. Code, 1968; mem. zoning adv. com. N.Y.C. Planning Commn., 1970; lectr. in field, 1968—; mem. steering com. UNESCO Council Tall Bldgs. and Urban Habitat, 1980—; vis. prof. Cornell-Essec Grad. Program; vis. prof. Nova U. Author: Hotel Planning and Design, 1985, Hotel Design, Planning and Development, 2001; (software) SHAPE, Megatrends and Marketecture; contbr. articles to profl. jours.; prin. works include Lincoln Center Library for Performing Arts, N.Y.C., 1967, Am. Republic Ins. Co. Nat. Hdqrs., Des Moines, 1967, HUD Apts., Jersey City, 1972, Merrill Lynch Bldg., N.Y.C., 1973, Tour Fiat, Paris, 1974, Aid Assn. for Luths. Nat. Hdqrs., Appleton, Wis., 1976, Semiramis Intercontinental Hotel, Cairo, 1985, Intercontinental, Jeddah, 1983, Embassy Suites Internat., 1985, Universal City Hotel Complex, L.A., 1986, TechWorld Conv. Hotel, Washington, 1986, Sheraton Fairplex Conv. Ctr., L.A., 1992, Orlando Conv. Ctr. Hotel, 1993, Winter Olympiad Media Complex, Norway, 1993, Ephesus Resort Complex, Turkey, 1986, Royal Christiania Hotel, Oslo, Norway, 1991, EuroFrance Leisure Park Complex, Cannes, 1993, Kuna Hills Multi Resort, Guam, 1994. Recipient Platinum Circle award Hotel Design Industry, 1988. Fellow AIA; mem. Ethical Culture Soc. Office: 8501 N 84th Pl Scottsdale AZ 85258-2419 also: 25 Richbell Rd White Plains NY 10605-4110

RUTH, CRAIG, business executive; b. July 18, 1930; s. Clarence Miller and Kathryn Dorothy (Buch) R.; m. Marion Nelson, Apr. 19, 1958; children: Robert Nelson, Lee Kathryn, William Walter, Ann Alva. BA, Muskingum Coll., 1952; postgrad., Northwestern U., 1956. Tchr., coach, N.Y.C. and Chgo., 1955-66; dir. mktg. Great Lakes Carbon Co., Los Angeles, 1966-68; exec. v.p. Ketchum, Peck & Tooley, Los Angeles, 1968-75; pres. Tooley & Co., Los Angeles, 1975—. Mgr. Two Rodeo Dr., Beverly Hills; bd. dirs. Los Angeles Internat. Bus. Ctr.; council mem. Urban Land Inst., 1982—. Bd. dirs. Bldg. Owner & Mgrs. Assn.; chmn. Elgin Baylor & Jerry West Nights Los Angeles Lakers, Ed Sherman Night, Muskingum Coll., Los Angeles, Muskingum Coll. Reunion Com.; vice chmn. USMC Scholarship Ball. Capt. USMC, 1953-55. Named one of Outstanding Men of Am. C. of C., 1965; recipient Humanitarian award Nat. Conf. Christians and Jews, 1988. Mem. Internat. Assn. Corp. Real Estate Execs., Spinal Cord Soc., 3rd Marine Divsn. (life), Japan Am. Cultural Coun., Beverly Hills Econ. Devel. Coun., Bus. Devel. Coun. (beverly Hills chpt.), Big Ten Club. Republican. Presbyterian. Avocations: tennis, playing trumpet, skiing, flying, boating. Home: 2 Hummingbird Ln Rolling Hills CA 90274-5229 Office: Tooley & Co 11150 Santa Monica Blvd Ste 20 Los Angeles CA 90025-3380

RUTHERFORD, ROBERT BARRY, vascular surgeon; b. Edmonton, Alta., Can., July 29, 1931; s. Robert Lyon and Kathleen Emily (Gunn) R.; m. Beulah Kay Folk, Aug. 20, 1955; children: Robert Scott, Lori Jayne, Holly Anne, Trudy Kaye, Jay Wilson. BA in Biology, Johns Hopkins U., [illegible] surgeon U. Colo. Health Sci. Ctr., Denver, emeritus prof. surgery U. Colo., Denver, 1996—. Editor: (texts) Management of Trauma, 1968, 5 edits., Vascular Surgery, 1978, 5th edition, 2000, An Atlas of Vascular Surgery, Vol. 1, 1993, Vol. 2, 1998, Decision Making in Vascular Surgery, 2001; editor quar. rev. Seminars in Vascular Surgery; sr. editor Jour. Vascular Surgery. Fellow ACS, Royal Coll. Surgeons of Glasgow; mem. Am. assn. for Vascular Surgery, Phi Beta Kappa, Alpha Omega Alpha. Republican. Unitarian. Avocations: skiing, biking, wind surfing, sailing. Office: PO Box 680 Silverthorne CO 80498-0680

RUTHERFORD, WILLIAM DRAKE, investment executive; b. Marshalltown, Iowa, Jan. 14, 1939; s. William Donald and Lois Esther (Drake) R.; m. Janice W. Rutherford, Feb. 4, 1965 (div. Mar. 1982); children: Wayne Donald, Melissa Drake; m. Karen Anderegg, Jan. 2, 1994. BS, U. Oreg., 1961; LLB, Harvard U., 1964. Bar: Oreg. 1964, U.S. Dist. Ct. Oreg. 1966. Assoc. Maguire, Kester & Cosgrave, Portland, Oreg., 1966-69; house counsel May & Co., Portland, 1969-70, pvt. practice, 1970-71, McMinnville, Oreg., 1971-84; mem. Oreg. Ho. of Reps., Salem, 1977-84; state treas. State of Oreg., Salem, 1984-87; chmn. Oreg. Investment Coun., Salem, 1986-87; exec. v.p., dir. U.S. and Australia ops. ABD Internat. Mgmt. Corp., N.Y.C., 1987-88, pres., chief exec. officer, bd. dirs., 1988-89; pres., bd. dirs. Societé Gen. Touche Remnant, 1990-93; dir. spl. projects Metallgesellschaft Corp., N.Y.C., 1994-95; mng. dir. Macadam Capital Ptnrs., Portland, 1995-96; CEO Fiberboard Asbestos Compensation Trust, Portland, 1997; prin. Rutherford Investment Mgmt. LLC, 1998—. Chmn. bd. dirs. Metro One Telecomms. Bd. dirs. Portland Opera Assn., 1995-99. Recipient Contbn. to Individual Freedom award ACLU, 1981 Mem. Nat. Assn. State Treas. (exec. v.p. 1985, 86, pres. western region 1985, 86), Nat. Assn. State Auditors, Comptr. and Treas. (exec. com. 1987), Nat. Assn. Corp. Dirs. Republican. E-mail: WRutherford!rutherfordinvestment.com. Home: 6978 SW Foxfield Ct Portland OR 97225-6054 Office: 10300 S W Greenburg Rd Ste 115 Portland OR 97223

RUTSALA, VERN A. poet, English language educator, writer; b. Feb. 5, 1934; s. Ray Edwin and Virginia Mae (Brady) R.; m. Joan Merle Colby, Apr. 6, 1957; children: Matthew, David, Kirsten. BA, Reed Coll., 1956; MFA, U. Iowa, 1960. Instr. Lewis and Clark Coll., Portland, 1961-64, asst. prof., 1964-69, assoc. prof., 1969-76, prof., 1976—. Vis. prof. U. Minn., Mpls., 1968-69, Bowling Green (Ohio) State U., 1970; writer-in-residence U. Idaho, Moscow, 1988, Redlands (Calif.) U., 1979; chair English dept. Lewis and Clark, Portland, 1986-89. Author: The Window, 1964, Laments, 1975, The Journey Begins, 1976, Paragraphs, 1978, Walking Home from the Icehouse, 1981, Backtracking, 1985, Ruined Cities, 1987, Selected Poems, 1991, Little-Known Sports, 1994. With U.S. Army, 1956-58. GUggenheim Found. fellow, 1982-83, NEA fellow, 1975, 79, Masters fellow Oreg. Arts Commn., 1990; recipient Carolyn Kizer prize Western Oreg. State Coll., 1988, N.W. Poets prize N.W. Rev., 1975, Hazel Hall award Oreg. Inst. Lit. Arts, 1992, Juniper prize U. Mass. Press, 1993, Duncan Lawrie prize Arvon Found., 1994, Carolyn Kizer prize, 1997. Mem. AAUP, AWP, PEN, Poetry Soc. Am. Avocations: drawing, painting, watching the ocean, sports. Office: Lewis & Clark Coll Dept English Portland OR 97219

RUTTER, NATHANIEL WESTLUND, geologist, educator; b. Omaha, Nov. 22, 1932; s. John Elliot and Karleen (Ludden) R.; m. Mary Marie Munson, Sept. 11, 1961; children: Todd, Christopher. BS, Tufts U., 1955; MS, U. Alaska, 1962; PhD, U. Alta., 1965, DSc honoris causa, 2001. Geologist Venezuelan Atlantic Refining Co., 1955-58; research scientist Geol. Survey Can., Calgary, Alta., 1965-74, head urban projects sect Ottawa, Ont., 1974; environ. advisor Nat. Energy Bd., Ottawa, 1974-75; assoc. prof. dept. geology U. Alta., Edmonton, 1975-77, 77-80, prof., chmn. dept., 1980-89, 77-96; pres. Can. nat. com. Internat. Geol. Correlation Program, UNESCO, 1996-97; prof. dept. atmospheric scis. U. Alta. (Can.), Edmonton, 1996-97, univ. prof., 1997—, assoc. dean. faculty sci. Pres. Internat. Union Quaternary Rsch. Congress, 1982-87; mem. Internat. Geosphere-Biosphere Program: A Study of Global Change, 1988-94; mem. rsch. com. Can. Global Change Program, 1992-94; chmn. global change com. INUQA, 1991-95; hon. prof. Chinese Acad. Sci., Beijing, 1994—; disting. lectr. Sigma Xi, 1995-97; mem. scientific bd. Internat. Union of Geol. Scis.-UNESCO, 1997—. Contbr. numerous articles to profl. jours.; assoc. editor Arctic, Geosci. Can. Quaternary Rsch.; mem. editorial bd. Quaternary Sci. Revs.; editor in chief Quaternary Internat. Grantee Natural Scis. and Engring. Research Council of Can.; grantee Energy, Mines and Resources Fellow Royal Soc. Can.; mem. Assn. Profl. Engrs., Geologists and Geophysicists of Alta., Internat. Union Quaternary Rsch. (v.p. 1982-87, pres. 1987-91, hon. 1999), Can. Quaternary Assn. (v.p. 1981-82, Johnston medal 1997), Geol. Soc. Am. (mgmt. bd. dirs. quaternary geol. and geomorphology div. 1982-84), Geol. Assn. of Can. (J. Willis Ambrose medal 1998), Internat. Assn. Quaternary Rsch. (hon.). Clubs: Explorer's, Cosmos. Home: Rural Route 3 Stony Plain AB Canada T7Z 1X3 Office: U Alta Dept Earth & Atmospheric Scis Edmonton AB Canada T6G 2E3 E-mail: nat.rutter@ualberta.ca

RUYTER, NANCY LEE CHALFA, dance educator; b. Phila., May 23, 1933; d. Andrew Benedict Chalfa and Lois Elizabeth (Strode) McClary; m. Ralph Markson (div.); m. Hans C. Ruyter, Dec. 7, 1968 (dec. Jan. 1998). BA in History, U. Calif., Riverside, 1964; PhD in History, Claremont Grad. Sch., 1970. Tchr. theater dept. Pomona Coll., 1965-72; instr. dance program U. Calif., Riverside, 1972-76, acting chair dance program, 1974-75; instr. dance dept. UCLA, 1976; instr. phys. edn. dept. Orange Coast Coll., 1976-77; asst. prof. dept. phys. edn. and dance Tufts U., 1977-78; asst. prof. phys. edn. dept. Calif. State U., Northridge, 1978-82; from asst. prof. to full prof. dance dept. U. Calif., Irvine, 1982—, assoc. dean Sch. Fine Arts, 1984-88, 95-96, chair dept. dance, 1989-91. Presenter in field. Appeared with Jasna Planina Folk Ensemble, 1972-77, 78-79, Di Falco and Co., 1955-57; choreographer, dir. numerous coll. dance prodns.; contbr. articles, revs. to profl. publs.; author: Reformers and Visionaries: The Americanization of the Art of Dance, 1979, The Cultivation of Body and Mind in Nineteenth-Century American Delsartism, 1999. Mem. Am. Soc. Theatre Rsch., Bulgarian Studies Assn., Congress on Rsch. in Dance (bd. dirs. 1977-80, pres. 1981-85), Folk Dance Fedn., Internat. Fedn. Theatre Rsch., Soc. Dance Rsch., Soc. Ethnomusicology, Soc. Dance History Scholars (steering com. 1980-81), Spanish Dance Soc., Theatre Libr. Assn. Office: U Calif-Irvine Dept Dance Irvine CA 92697-0001 E-mail: nlruyter@uci.edu

RYAN, CLARENCE AUGUSTINE, JR. biochemistry educator; b. Butte, Mont., Sept. 29, 1931; s. Clarence A. Sr. and Agnes L. (Duckham) R.; m. Patricia Louise Meunier, Feb. 8, 1936; children: Jamie Arlette, Steven Michael (dec.), Janice Marie, Joseph Patrick (dec.). BA in Chemistry, Carroll Coll., 1953; MS in Chemistry, Mont. State U., 1956, PhD in Chemistry, 1959. Postdoctoral fellow in biochemistry Oreg. State U., Corvallis, 1959-61, U.S. Western Regional Lab., Albany, Calif., 1961-63, chemist Berkeley, 1963-64; asst. prof. biochemistry Wash. State U., Pullman, 1964-68, assoc. prof., 1968-72, prof., 1972—, Charlotte Y. Martin disting. prof., 1991—, chmn. dept. agrl. chemistry, 1977-80, fellow Inst. Biol. Chemistry, 1980—. Faculty athletics rep. to PAC-10 & NCAA Wash. State U., 1991-94, 96-97; vis. scientist dept. biochemistry U. Wash., 1981, Harvard U. Med. Sch., 1982, Bert and Natalie Vallee vis. prof., 1997; res. adv. bd. Kemin Industries, Des Moines, 1981—, Plant Genetics, Davis, Calif., 1987-89; research adv. bd. Frito-Lay, Inc., Dallas, 1982, Plant Genetic Engring. Lab., N.M. State U., Las Cruces, 1986-89, Noble Found., 1996—; mem. NRC rev. bd. Plant Gene Exptl. Ctr., Albany, Calif., 1990-93; mgr. biol. stress program USDA Competitve Grants Program, Washington, 1983-84; former mem. adv. panels for H. McKnight Found., Internat. Potato Ctr., Lima, Peru, Internat. Ctr. Genetic Engring. and Biotech., New Delhi, Internat. Ctr. Tropical Agr., Cali, Columbia, Internat. Tropical Agr., Ibandan, Africa; mem. grant rev. panels NSF, USDA, DOE, NIH; co-organizer Internat. Telecomms. Symposium on Plant Biotech.; mem. adv. bd. Bert and Natalie Vallee Found., Harvard Med. Sch., 1997-2000. Mem. editl. bd. several biochem. and plant physiology jours.; contbr. articles to profl. publs., chpts. to books; co-editor 2 books. Trustee Carroll Coll., Helena, Mont., 1998—; mem. rsch. bd. Danforth Plant Sci. Ctr., Washington U., 1998—. Grantee USDA, NSF, NIH, Rockefeller Found., McKnight Found.; recipient Merck award for grad. rsch. Mont. State U., 1959, career devel. awards NIH, 1964-74, Alumni Achievement award Carroll Coll., 1986, Pres.'s Faculty Excellence award in rsch. Wash. State U., 1986; named to Carroll Coll. Alumni Hall of Fame, 1981, Carroll Coll. Basketball Hall of Fame, 1982; named 1 of 100 centennial disting. alumni Mont. State. U., 1993; non-resident fellow Noble Found., 1996—. Mem. AAAS, Nat. Acad. Scis. (elected 1986), Am. Chem. Soc. (Kenneth A. Spencer award 1992), Am. Soc. Plant Physiologists (Steven Hales Prize 1992), Am. Soc. Exptl. Biology, Biochem. Soc., Am. Peptide Soc., Internat. Soc. Chem. Ecology (Silverstein-Simione award 1997), Internat. Soc. Plant Molecular Biology (bd. dirs.), Phytochem. Soc. N.Am., Nat. U. Continuing Assn. (Creative Programming award 1991), Phi Kappa Phi (Recognition award 1976). Democrat. Avocations: fishing, basketball, golf. Office: Wash State Univ Inst Biol Chemistry Pullman WA 99164-0001

RYAN, DON, state legislator; b. Great Falls, Mont., Dec. 21, 1951; m. Terri Ryan; children: Bill, Annie, Sean. BA, U. Mont., 1976. Eligibility technician Mont. Social and Rehab. Svc., 1985-89; tchr., coach Stevensville, Mont., 1989-94; clk., recorder Cascade County, 1993-95; daycare owner Lil-Pals and Playmates, 1995—. Mem. Lincoln Sch. PTA, 1999-2000; past pres. Ancient Order Hibernians, 1990—; campaign worker Friends of Pat Williams, 1991-92; trustee Great Falls Pub. Schs., 1995—, mem. transp. subcom., 1998, chair long-range bldg. planning com., 1998—. Mem. Nat. Sch. Bds. Assn. (del. Fed. Rels. Network 1993-95), Mont. Sch. Bds. Assn. Roman Catholic. Office: 2101 Seventh Ave S Great Falls MT 59405 E-mail: donterryan@aol.com

RYAN, JANE FRANCES, corporate communications executive; b. Bronxville, N.Y., Nov. 1, 1950; d. Bernard M. and Margaret M. (Griffith) R.; m. Kevin Horan, Dec. 26, 1982; 1 child, Kevin. BS in Journalism, Ohio U., 1972; MBA in Mktg., Golden Gate U., 1990. Asst. promotion mgr. Fawcett Publs., Greenwich, Conn., 1972-75; mktg. coordinator Fawcett Mktg. Services div. CBS, Greenwich, 1975-78; dist. sales mgr. CBS Publs., San Francisco, 1978; prodn. mgr. Cato Inst., San Francisco, 1979-81; account supr. Bus. Media Resources, Mill Valley, Calif., 1981-90, dir. mktg. svcs., 1990-93; dir. publs. RAND Corp., Santa Monica, 1993—. Bd. dirs. Daybreak, Santa Monica, Calif. Office: RAND 1700 Main St Santa Monica CA 90401-3297

RYAN, JOHN DUNCAN, lawyer; b. Portland, Oreg., Dec. 20, 1920; s. Thomas Gough and Virgian Abigail (Hadley) R.; m. Florence A. Ryan, Jan. 30, 1970 (dec. 1987); m. Virginia Kane Wilson, June 15, 1996. BS, Fordham U., 1943; JD, Lewis & Clark Coll., Portland, 1950. Bar: Oreg. 1950. Pvt. practice, Portland, 1950—. Adj. instr. Northwestern Sch. Law Lewis & Clark Coll., 1953-70. Author: (poems) Expressions, 1993, Expressions II, 1995, Expressions III, 1998-99. Sgt. Air Corps, U.S. Army, 1942-46, ETO. Recipient St. Thomas More award Catholic Lawyers for Social Justice, 1993. Mem. ABA (Oreg. delegate 1985-93, chmn. spl. com. on law & literacy 1991-93), Am. Coll. Trial Lawyers, Am. Trial Lawyers Assn., Oreg. State Bar (bd. govs. 1963-67), Oreg. Trial Lawyers Assn. (Trial Lawyer of Yr. 1993), Multnomah County Bar Assn. (Professionalism award 1997), Washington County Bar Assn. Home and Office: 1206 Circulo Aguilar Rio Rico AZ 85648-3355 and: 503 SW Colony Dr Portland OR 97219-7763 E-mail: ryan98@theriver.com

RYAN, JOHN EDWARD, federal judge; b. Boston, Jan. 22, 1941; s. Howard Frederick and Mary (Burke) R.; m. Terri Reynolds; children: Valerie, Jennifer, Keely. BSEE, U.S. Naval Acad., 1963; LLB, Georgetown U., 1972; MS, Pacific Christian U., 1979. Assoc. Hale and Dorr, Boston, 1972-76, C.F. Braun, Alhambra, Calif., 1976-77; gen. counsel Altec Corp., Anaheim, 1977-79; v.p., sr. atty. Oak Industries, San Diego, 1979-82; sr. v.p. Oak Media, San Diego, 1982-84; ptnr. Dale and Lloyd, La Jolla, Calif., 1984-85, Jennings, Engstrand and Henrikson, San Diego, 1985-86; bankruptcy judge U.S. Bankruptcy Ct., Santa Ana, Calif., 1986—. Ex officio dir. Orange County Bankruptcy Forum; mem. Calif. State-Fed. Jud. Coun., 1998—; Ninth Cir. Bankruptcy Appellate Panel, 1996—. With USN, 1963-69. Fellow Am. Coll. Bankruptcy; mem. Mass. Bar Assn., Calif. Bar Assn., Orange County Bar Assn., Bankruptcy Judges Assn. Roman Catholic. Avocations: tennis, camping, kayaking. Home: 3155 Summit Dr Escondido CA 92025-7529 Office: US Bankruptcy Ct PO Box 22026 Santa Ana CA 92702-2026

RYAN, MARY GENE, career officer, occupational health nurse; b. Corona, Calif., Sept. 11, 1953; d. Robert James and Genevieve Louise (Kubilis) Guzinski; m. Robert Eldon Ryan III, June 9, 1979; children: Michael Warren, Jessica Gene, Matthew James. BSN, So. Conn. State Coll., 1975; MPH, U. Tex., 1980. Commd. 2d lt. USAF, 1976, advanced through grades to lt. col., 1995; staff nurse obstetrics U. Conn. Med. Ctr., Farmington, 1975-76; med.-surgical staff nurse Williams AFB (Ariz.) Hosp., 1976-77; flight nurse instr. 2d Aeromed. Evacuation Squadron, Rhein Main, Fed. Republic of Germany, 1977-79; officer in charge environ. health Wilford Hall Med. Ctr., Lackland AFB, Tex., 1980-84; chief environ. health AFSC Hosp., Edwards AFB, Calif., 1984-88; dir. occupational health Peterson Med. Clinic, Oxnard, 1988-89; mgr. health and safety County of Ventura (Calif.)/Gen. Svcs. Agy., 1989-96; chief operating officer 2SCO Ltd., 1996-97; exec. dir. MG Ryan & Co., Inc., 1997—. Cons. environ. health L.A. AFB, 1984-88; exec. officer Calif. Air Nat. Guard 146 Med. Sqd., 2000—. Contbr. articles to profl. jours. Mem. choir, soloist, lay eucharistic min. Edwards AFB Cath. Chapel, 1984-88, mem. religious edn. com., 1984-85, lectr., commentator, 1986-87, marriage encounter counselor, 1991—; team mom for various sports, 1989—; AIDS educator, Edwards AFB, 1986-88. Recipient Meritorious Svc. medals USAF, Clin. award Am. Assn. Occupational Health Nurses, 1991. Mem. APHA (occupational health sect.), Am. Assn. Occupational Health Nurses, Claif. Assn. Occupational Health Nurses, Calif. Ctrl. Coast Occupational Health Nurses Assn. (pres. 1993-97, bd. dirs. 1998—), Ventura County Med. Aux. Avocations: sailing, sewing, skiing, swimming. E-mail: ryanfive@emhhospital.com maci6224@aol.com

RYAN, STEPHEN JOSEPH, JR. ophthalmology educator, university dean; b. Honolulu, Mar. 20, 1940; s. S.J. and Mildred Elizabeth (Farrer) F.; m. Anne Christine Mullady, Sept. 25, 1965; 1 dau., Patricia Anne. A.B., Providence Coll., 1961; M.D., Johns Hopkins U., 1965. Intern Bellevue Hosp., N.Y.C., 1965-66; resident Wilmer Inst. Ophthalmology, Johns Hopkins Hosp., Balt., 1966-69, chief resident, 1969-70; fellow Armed Force Inst. Pathology, Washington, 1970-71; instr. ophthalmology Johns Hopkins U., Balt., 1970-71, asst. prof., 1971-72, assoc. prof., 1972-74; prof. ophthalmology Keck Sch. Medicine U. So. Calif., L.A., 1974—, chmn. dept. ophthalmology Sch. Medicine, 1974-95, dean Keck Sch. Medicine, 1991—; acting head ophthalmology div., dept. surgery Children's Hosp., L.A., 1975-77; med. dir. Doheny Eye Inst. (formerly Estelle Doheny Eye Found.), L.A., 1977-86; chief of staff Doheny Eye Hosp., L.A., 1985-88. Mem. advisory panel Calif. Med. Assn., 1975—. Editor: (with M.D. Andrews) A Survey of Ophthalmology--Manual for Medical Students, 1970, (with R.E. Smith) Selected Topics on the Eye in Systemic Disease, 1974, (with Dawson and Little) Retinal Diseases, 1985, (with others) Retina, 1989, 2000; assoc. editor: Ophthalmol. Surgery, 1974-85; mem. editl. bd. Am. Jour. Ophthalmology, 1981—, Internat. Ophthalmology, 1982—, Retina, 1983—, Graefes Archives, 1984—; contbr. articles to med. jours. Recipient cert. of merit AMA, 1971; Louis B. Mayer Scholar award Research to Prevent Blindness, 1973; Rear Adm. William Campbell Chambliss USN award, 1982. Mem. Wilmer Ophthal. Inst. Residents Assn.

Am. Acad. Ophthalmology and Otolaryngology (award of Merit 1975), Am. Ophthal. Soc., Pan-Am. Assn. Ophthalmology, Assn. Univ. Profs. of Ophthalmology, L.A. Soc. Ophthalmology, AMA, Calif. Med. Assn., Los Angeles County Med. Assn., Pacific Coast Oto-Ophthal. Soc., L.A. Acad. Medicine, Pan Am. Assn. Microsurgery, Macula Soc, Retina Soc., Nat. Eye Care Project, Rsch. Study Club, Jules Gonin Club, Soc. Scholars of Johns Hopkins U. (life). Office: Keck Sch Medicine Univ So Calif 1450 San Pablo St Los Angeles CA 90033-1042

RYAN, SYLVESTER D. bishop; b. Catalina Island, Calif., Sept. 3, 1930; Grad., St. John's Sem., Camarillo, Calif. Ordained priest Roman Cath. Ch., 1957, titular bishop of Remesiana. Aux. bishop, L.A., 1990-92; bishop Monterey, Calif., 1992—. Office: Chancery Office PO Box 2048 631 Abrego St Monterey CA 93940-3203

RYAN, WILLIAM, executive; B of Psychology, MEd. Ptnr. Neuhaus Ryan Wong, South San Francisco. Office: 601 Gateway Blvd Ste 900 South San Francisco CA 94080-7006

RYCHNOVSKY, SCOTT DOUGLAS, chemist, educator; b. Albuquerque, May 26, 1959; s. Raymond E. and Sheila Lee (Irish) R. BS, U. Calif., Berkeley, 1981; PhD, Columbia U., 1986; postgrad., Harvard U., 1986-87, Yale U., 1987-88. Asst. prof. U. Minn., 1988-94, assoc. prof., 1994-95; prof. U. Calif., Irvine, 1995-96. Contbr. articles to Jour. Am. Chem. Soc. Recipient Research award Pfizer Inc., 1992, Pres. Young Investigator award NSF, 1991; scholar Searle Found., 1989. Mem. Am. Chem. Soc. Achievements include research in new synthetic methods, and studies with ent-cholesterol.

RYLES, GERALD FAY, private investor, business executive; b. Walla Walla, Wash., Apr. 3, 1936; s. L. F. and Janie Geraldine (Bassett) R.; m. Ann Jane Birkenmeyer, June 12, 1959; children— Grant, Mark, Kelly. B.A., U. Wash., 1958; M.B.A., Harvard U., 1962. With Gen. Foods Corp., White Plains, N.Y., 1962-65, Purex Corp., Ltd., Lakewood, Calif., 1966-68; cons. McKinsey & Co., Inc., Los Angeles, 1968-71; with Fibreboard Corp., San Francisco, 1971-79, v.p., 1973-75, group v.p., 1975-79; with Consol. Fibres, Inc., San Francisco, 1979-88, exec. v.p., 1979-81, pres., dir., 1981-86, chief exec. officer, 1986-88; cons. Orinda, 1988-90; with Interchecks Inc., 1990-92, pres., CEO, 1990-92; bus. exec., pvt. investor, 1992-94; chmn. bd., CEO Microserv, Inc., Kirkland, Wash., 1994—2001, chmn. bd., 2001—. Bd. dirs. Aculight, Bothell, WA. Mem. adv. com. entrepreneur and innovation program U. Wash. Bus. Sch. Served to capt. U.S. Army, 1958-66. Mem. Harvard Bus. Sch. Assn., Univ. Wash. Alumni Assn., World Trade Club (San Francisco), Harbor Club (Bellevue, Seattle). Republican. Episcopalian. Home: 127 3rd Ave Apt 301 Kirkland WA 98033-6177 E-mail: geraldr@msvine.com

RYMER, ILONA SUTO, artist, retired educator; b. N.Y.C., Dec. 1, 1921; d. Alexander and Elizabeth (Komaromy) Suto; m. Robert Hamilton Rymer, Mar. 27, 1944 (dec. Dec. 1999); children: Thomas Parker, Shelley Ilona. BA, Long Beach State U., 1953, MA, 1954. Tchr., cons. Long Beach (Calif.) Sch. Dist., 1953-56; tchr. Orange (Calif.) Sch. Dist., 1956-58; tchr., cons. Brea (Calif.)-Olinda Sch. Dist., 1958-80; ind. artist, designer Graphic Ho. Studio, Santa Ynez, Calif., 1980—, Stampa-Barbara, Santa Barbara, 1990—. Author: (instrn. book) Folk Art U.S.A., 1975 (proclamation City of Brea 1975); art editor, feature writer, illustrator Arabian Connection mag., Santa Ynez, 1985-86; needlepoint designer Backstitch Store, Solvang, Calif., 1982-83; Pres. Reagan's portrait on his stallion (now housed in the Reagan Libr., Simi Valley, Calif.; illustrator back cover: Khemosabi and Ruth, 1995; paintings exhibited Dennas Mus. Ctr., Northwestern Mich. Coll., 2001. Co-founder, mem. Gallery los Olivos, pres., 1993—; lectr. folk art Brea Sch. Dist., 1975-80. Recipient 1st pl. Seminar award Rex Brandt, Corona del Mar, Calif., 1961, Affiliate award Laguna Art Mus., Laguna Beach, Calif., 1967, Best of Watercolor award Orange County Fair, Orange, 1969, Bicentennial trip to France, Air France, Brea, 1975, Proclamation for Tchg., City of Brea, 1980, Theme award Santa Barbara County Fair, 1991. Mem. Calif. Gold Coast Watercolor Soc. (signature), Santa Barbara Art Assn., Ctrl. Coast Art Assn., Artist Guild Santa Ynez Valley, Calif. Presbyterian. Avocation: showing family's Arabian horses. Studio: PO Box 822 Santa Ynez CA 93460-0822 E-mail: ilonar@silcom.com

RYMER, PAMELA ANN, federal judge; b. Knoxville, Tenn., Jan. 6, 1941; AB, Vassar Coll., 1961; LLB, Stanford U., 1964; LLD (hon.), Pepperdine U., 1988. Bar: Calif. 1966, U.S. Ct. Appeals (9th cir.) 1966, U.S. Ct. Appeals (10th cir.), U.S. Supreme Ct. V.p. Rus Walton & Assoc., Los Altos, Calif., 1965-66; Assoc. Lillick McHose & Charles, L.A., 1966-75, ptnr., 1973-75, Toy and Rymer, L.A., 1975-83; judge U.S. Dist. Ct. (cen. dist.) Calif., L.A., 1983-89, U.S. Ct. Appeals (9th cir.), L.A., 1989—. Faculty The Nat. Jud. Coll., 1986-88; mem. com. summer ednl. programs Fed. Jud. Ctr., 1987-88, mem. com. appellate judge edn., 1996-99; chair exec. com. 9th Cir. Jud. Conf., 1990; mem. com. criminal law Jud. Conf. U.S., 1988-93, Ad Hoc com. gender-based violence, 1991-94, fed.-state jurisdiction com., 1993-96; mem. commn. on structural alternatives Fed. Cts. Appeals, 1997-98. Mem. editorial bd. The Judges' jour., 1989-91; contbr. articles to profl. jours. and newsletters. Mem. Calif. Postsecondary Edn. Commn., 1974-84, chmn., 1980-84; mem. L.A. Olympic Citizens Adv. Commn.; bd. visitors Stanford U. Law Sch., 1986-99, trustee, 1991—, chair, 1993-96, exec. com., chmn. bd. trustees com. acad. policy, planning and mgmt. and its ad. hoc. com. athletics., chmn. bd. visitors Sch. Law, 1987—; bd. visitors Pepperdine U. Law Sch., 1987—; mem. Edn. Commn. of States Task Force on State Policy and Ind. Higher Edn., 1987-89, Carnegie Commn. Task Force Sci. and Tech. Jud. and Regulatory Decisionmaking, 1990-93, Commn. Substance Abuse Coll. and Univ. Campuses, 1992-94, commn. substance abuse high schs. Ctr. Addiction and Substance Abube Columbia U.; bd. dirs. Constnl. Rights Found., 1985-97, Pacific Coun. Internat. Policy, 1995—, Calif. Higher Edn. Policy Ctr., 1992-97; Jud. Conf. U.S. Com. Fed.-State Jurisdiction, 1993, Com. Criminal Law, 1988-93, ad hoc com. gender based violence, 1991-94; chair exec. com. 9th cir. jud. conf., 1990-94. Recipient Outstanding Trial Jurist award L.A. County Bar Assn., 1988; named David T. Lewis Disting. Jurist-in-Residence U. Utah, 1992. Mem. ABA (task force on civil justice reform 1991-93, mem. coord. com. agenda civil justice reform in Am. 1991), State Bar Calif. (antitrust and trade regulation sect., exec. com. 1990-92), L.A. County Bar Assn. (chmn. antitrust sect. 1981-82, mem. editl. bd. The Judges Jour. 1989-91, mem. com. professionalism 1988—, numerous other coms.), Assn. of Bus. Trial Lawyers (bd. govs. 1990-92), Stanford Alumni Assn., Stanford Law Soc. Soc. Calif., Vassar Club So. Calif. (past pres.). Office: US Ct Appeals 9th Cir US Court of Appeals Bldg 125 S Grand Ave Rm 600 Pasadena CA 91105-1621*

RYNN, NATHAN, physics educator, consultant; b. N.Y.C., Dec. 2, 1923; s. Meyer and Rose (Wolkerwiczer) Rynkowsky; m. Glenda Brown, June 24, 1989; children by previous marriage: Jonathan, Margaret, David. BSEE, CCNY, 1944; MS, U. Ill., 1947; PhD, Stanford U., 1956. Rsch. engr. RCA Labs., Princeton, N.J., 1947-52; rsch. asst. Stanford U., Palo Alto, Calif., 1952-56, rsch. assoc., 1958; mem. tech. staff Ramo-Woolridge, L.A., 1956-57; supr. Huggins Labs., Menlo Park, Calif., 1957-58; rsch. staff physicist Princeton U., 1958-65; prof. physics U. Calif.-Irvine, 1965-94, prof. physics emeritus, rsch. prof. physics, 1994—. Vis. prof. Ecole Polytechnique Fed. of Lausanne, Switzerland, 1984-90, Ecole Polytechnique, Paris, and other European univs. and labs., 1973-80; indsl. sci. advisor/cons., 1964—; com. mem. Plasma Sci. Com. Nat. Rsch. Coun.; founder and leader plasma physics rsch. facility. Contbr. articles and revs. to profl. jours. With USN, 1944-46. Grantee NSF, U.S. Dept. Energy, Air Force Geophys. Lab.; Fulbright sr. fellow, 1978. Fellow Am. Phys. Soc., IEEE, AAAS; mem. Am. Geophys. Union, Sigma Xi. Office: U Calif Dept Physics & Astronomy Irvine CA 92697-4575 E-mail: nrynn@uci.edu

SA, JULIE, councilwoman; b. Korea, Dec. 15, 1950; came to U.S., 1973, naturalized, 1982; married. Degree in Polit. Sci., Dong-A U., Korea. Owner restaurant chain; councilwoman City of Fullerton, Calif., 1992-94, 96-99, mayor, 1994-95. Rep. bd. Orange County Sanitation Dists.; rep. to Tri-City Park Authority, City of Fullerton. Mem. Fullerton C. of C., Orange County Korean C. of C., Orange County Chinese C. of C. Office: Office of City Council 303 W Commonwealth Ave Fullerton CA 92832-1710

SAARI, DONALD GENE, mathematician, economist; b. Ironwood, Mich., Mar. 9, 1940; s. Gene August and Martha Mary (Jackson) S.; m. Lillian Joy Kalinen, June 11, 1966; children: Katri, Anneli. BS, Mich. Technol. U., 1962; PhD, Purdue U., 1967, DSc (hon.), 1989, U. Caen, France, 1998, Mich. Tech. U., , 1999. Research astronomer Yale U., New Haven, 1967-68; prof. dept. math. Northwestern U., Evanston, Ill., 1968-2000, prof. econs., 1988-2000, Pancoe prof. math., 1995-2000, chmn. dept., 1981-84; prof. U. Nanjing (China), 1995; disting. prof. econ., prof. math. U. Calif., Irvine, 2000—. Cons. Nat. Bur. Standards, Gaithersburg, Md., 1979-86, Commn. 9, Internat. Astron. Union, 1985-91; mem. nat. com. math. Nat. Rsch. Coun., 1997—, chair 2001—. Assoc. editor Jour. Econ. Behavior and Orgn., 1988-94, Celestial Mechanics and Dynamical Astronomy. 1989-97, Econ. Theory, 1990—, Social Choice and Welfare, 1997—, Qualitative Theory of Dynamical Sys., 1999—, Positivity, 2000—. Recipient Duncan Black award, Pub. Choice Soc., 1991, Chauvenet prize Mathematical Assn. of Am., 1995; Guggenheim fellow, 1988-89. Mem. NAS, Am. Math. Soc. (chief editor bull. 1999—, mem. coun. 1999—), Math. Assn. Am. (Ford prize 1985, Chauvenet prize 1995, Allendoerfer award 1999), Am. Astron. Soc., Soc. Indsl. and Applied Math. (editor jour. 1981-88), Econometric Soc. Office: U Calif Dept Econs Dept Math Irvine CA 92697-0001 E-mail: dsaari@uci.edu

SABATINI, WILLIAM QUINN, architect; b. Pitts. s. William L. and Lydia M. (Contento) S.; m. Carol Anne Christoffel, Feb. 26, 1972; children: Quinn, Jay, Jillian. BA, Franklin & Marshall Coll., 1971; MArch, U. N.Mex., 1978. Registered arch., N.Mex., Nev.; cert. Nat. Coun. Archtl. Registration Bds. Intern Jess Holmes, Arch., Albuquerque, 1974-78; project mgr. Jack Miller & Assocs., Las Vegas, 1978-81; sr. design arch. HNTB, Kansas City, Mo., 1981-84; prin. Holmes Sabatini Assocs. Arch. (now Dekker Perich Sabatini), Albuquerque, 1984—. Prin. works include Ctrl. Campus Bookstore U. N.Mex. (Merit award N.Mex. Soc. Archs. 1977), Luna County Courthouse, Deming, N.Mex. (Honor award N.Mex. Hist. Preservation Soc. 1978), James R. Dickinson Libr. U. Nev., Las Vegas (Merit award AIA 1981, Honor award Nev. Soc. Arch. 1981), Reno Conv. Ctr. (Merit award Nev. Soc. Archs. 1983), Corp. Hdqs. Nev. Power Co., Las Vegas (Honor award Nev. Soc. Archs. 1983), YMCA, Las Vegas (Honor award Nev. Soc. Archs. 1983), Sanctuary Remodel St. Johns United Meth. Ch., Albuquerque (Best Interiors award N.Mex. Bus. Jour. 1986), The Presidio Office Bldg., Albuquerque (Best Bldgs. award and Best Interiors award N.Mex. Bus. Jour. 1987, Project of Yr. award Assoc. Gen. Contractors N.Mex. 1987), Suarez Residence, Albuquerque (Merit award N.Mex. Soc. Am. 1988), Fire Sta. Number 13 and Fire Marshall's Office, Albuquerque (Merit award Albuquerque Conservation Soc. 1987, Best Bldgs. award N.Mex. Bus. Jour. 1988), Santa Fe Imaging Ctr. (Citation of Excellence, Modern Health Care Mag., AIA com. on healthcare 1989, Best Bldgs. award N.Mex. Bus. Jour. 1989), Health Scis. Bldg. U. N.Mex. (Best Bldgs. award N.Mex. Bus. Jour. 1989), U.S. Port of Entry, Columbus, N.Mex. (Best Bldgs. award N.Mex. Bus. Jour. 1989, Honor award N.Mex. Soc. Archs. 1990, GSA Design award U.S. Gen. Svcs. Adminstrn. 1990), Student Svcs. Bldg., Albuquerque TVI (Best Bldgs. award N.Mex. Bus. Jour. 1989, Merit award Albuquerque Conservation Soc. 1990), Expansion and Renovation Albuquerque Conv. Ctr. (Best Bldgs. award N.Mex. Bus. Jour. 1990), Lovelace Multi-Specialty Clinic Facility, Albuquerque (Merit award N.Mex. Soc. Archs. 1991), Pete's Playground U. N.Mex. Hosp. (Honor award N.Mex. Soc. Archs. 1992, Best Bldgs. Spl. award N.Mex. Bus. Jour. 1993), Nursing Unit Remodel U. N.Mex. Hosp. (Excellence award Am. Soc. Interior Designers 1992), 3.5 Meter Telescope Kirtland AFB, N.Mex. (Honor award AIA 1993). Bd. dirs. Albuquerque Chamber Orch., 1988, Hospice Rio Grande, 1992-94; mem. adv. bd. Balloon Mus., 1989-91; mem. adv. bd. St. Pius High Sch., 1993-96. With USAR, 1971-78. Mem. AIA (bd. dirs. Albuquerque chpt. 1986-87). Roman Catholic. Office: Dekker Perich Sabatini 6801 Jefferson St NE Albuquerque NM 87109-4379

SABATINO, CARMEN, mayor; Former tchr. Modesto City Sch. Dist., Calif.; restaurant owner; mayor City of Modesto, Calif., 1999—. Former tchr. Modesto City Sch. Dist. Office: City Hall PO Box 642 Modesto CA 95353-0642 E-mail: csabatino@ci.modesto.ca.us

SABEAN, BRIAN R. professional baseball team executive; m. Barbara Sabean; childrne: Colin, Sean, Brendan, Darren. Grad., Eckerd Coll., St. Petersburg, Fla., 1978. Asst. baseball coach St. Leo (Fla.) Coll., 1978-79, Tampa (Fla.) U., 1980-82, head baseball coach, 1983-85; dir. scouting N.Y. Yankees farm sys., 1986-90, v.p. player devel./scouting, 1990-92; asst. to gen. mgr., v.p. scouting/player pers. San Francisco Giants, 1993-95, sr. v.p., player pers., 1995-96, sr. v.p., gen. mgr., 1996—. Achievement: San Francisco Giants won divisional flag in 1997. Office: c/o San Francisco Giants 24 Willie Mays Plz San Francisco CA 94107-2134

SABERSKY, ROLF HEINRICH, mechanical engineer; b. Berlin, Germany, Oct. 20, 1920; came to U.S., 1938, naturalized, 1944; s. Fritz and Berta (Eisner) S.; m. Bettina Sofie Schuster, June 16, 1946; children— Carol, Sandra. B.S., Calif. Inst. Tech., 1942, M.S., 1943, Ph.D., 1949. Devel. engr. Aerojet Gen. Co., 1943-46, regular cons., 1949-70; asst. prof. Calif. Inst. Tech., Pasadena, 1949-55, asso. prof., 1955-61, prof. mech. engring., 1961-88, prof. emeritus, 1988—. Cons. various indsl. orgns. Author: Engineering Thermodynamics, 1957, Fluid Flow, 4th edit., 1999; contbr. articles to profl. jours. Fellow ASME (Heat Transfer Meml. award 1977, 50th anniversary award Heat Transfer Div 1988); mem. Sigma Xi, Tau Beta Pi. Home: Valle Verde EG 117 900 Calle De Los Amigos Santa Barbara CA 93105-4435 Office: Calif Inst Tech Divsn Engring & Applied Sci Pasadena CA 91125-0001 E-mail: sabersky@silcom.com

SABEY, J(OHN) WAYNE, academic administrator, consultant; b. Murray, Utah, Dec. 10, 1939; s. Alfred John and Bertha (Lind) S.; m. Marie Bringhurst, Sept. 10, 1964; children: Clark Wayne, Colleen, Carolyn, Natasha Lynne. BA in Asian Studies, Brigham Young U., 1964, MA in Asian History, 1965; PhD in East Asian History, U. Mich., 1972. Teaching asst. Brigham Young U., Provo, 1964-65, rsch. asst., 1965, adj. prof. history, 1988-89; rsch. asst. U. Mich., Ann Arbor, 1966; from instr. to asst. prof. history U. Utah, Salt Lake City, 1970-80; v.p. Western Am. Lang. Inst., Salt Lake City, 1980-84, dir., 1984-86, pres., 1986—; exec. v.p. Pacific Rim Bus. Coords., Salt Lake City, 1993—, also bd. dirs., 1993—; dir. Japan Ops. E'OLA Products, Inc., St. George, Utah, 1996-99; MBA program dir. Walden U., Mpls., 1999—. Assoc. dir. exch. program between U. Utah and Nagoya Broadcasting Network of Japan, 1973-79; lectr. in field, Superior award in extemporaneous speaking, 1956. Author essay, contbr. articles to ency. Chmn. bd. trustees Western Am. Lang. Inst., 1986—, sec. to bd. trustees, 1980-86; chmn. bd. trustees Found. for Internat. Understanding, 1982—; mem. internat. adv. coun. Salt Lake C.C., 1988-94; mem. bd. advisors Consortium for Internat. Edn., 1972-77. Horace H. Rackham Sch. grad. studies fellow, 1969-70, Fulbright-Hays rsch. fellow (Japan), 1968-69, U.S. Nat. Def. fgn. lang. fellow, 1965-68. Mem. Assn. for Asian Studies (gen. chairperson, chairperson local arrangements western conf. 1970-72), Phi Kappa Phi. Avocations: piano, hiking, basketball, stamp collecting, tennis. Home and Office: 8710 Oakwood Park Cir Sandy UT 84094-1800 E-mail: wmnsabey@inconnect.com

SABHARWAL, RANJIT SINGH, mathematician; b. Dhudial, India, Dec. 11, 1925; came to U.S., 1958, naturalized, 1981; s. Krishan Ch and Devti (An) S.; m. Pritam Kaur Chadha, Mar. 5, 1948; children— Rajinderpal, Amarjit, Jasbir. B.A. with honors, Punjab U., 1944, M.A., 1948; M.A. U. Calif, Berkeley, 1962; Ph.D., Wash. State U., 1966. Lectr. math. Khalsa Coll., Bombay, India, 1951-58; teaching asst. U. Calif., Berkeley, 1958-62; instr. math. Portland (Oreg.) State U., 1962-62, Wash. State U., 1963-66; asst. prof. Kans. State U., 1966-68; assoc. prof. math. Calif. State U., Hayward, 1968-74, prof. math., 1974-92, prof. emeritus math., 1992—. Author papers on non-Desarguesian planes. Mem. Am. Math. Soc., Math. Assn. Am., Sigma Xi. Address: 25179 Old Fairview Ave Hayward CA 94542-1355

SABIN, GARY B. real estate executive; b. Provo, Utah, 1954; Degree, Brigham Young U., 1977, Stanford U., 1985. Chmn. bd. dirs., CEO, pres. Excel Legacy Corp., San Diego. Office: Excel Legacy Corp Ste 300 17140 Bernardo Center Dr San Diego CA 92128

SABIN, GARY BYRON, financial company executive, investment advisor; b. Provo, Utah, Apr. 7, 1954; s. Marvin Elmer and Sylvia (Wall) S.; m. Valerie Purdy, Aug. 18, 1976; children: Kimberly, Justin, Spencer, Jennifer. AA in Lang., Brigham Young U., 1976, BS in Fin., 1977; CFP, Coll. Fin. Planning, 1981; postgrad. (Sloan fellow) Stanford U. Grad. Sch. Bus., 1984-85. Regional gen. mgr. Investors/N.Am. Mgmt., Orem, Utah, 1975-77; pres., chief exec. officer Excel Interfin. Corp., San Diego, 1977—; chmn. Warner Beck, Inc., San Diego, 1983-88; gen. ptnr. various cos., San Diego, 1979—. Recipient Outstanding Young Man of Am. award U.S. Jaycees, 1983. Mem. Inst. Cert. Fin. Planners, Nat. Assn. Securities Dealers (registered prin. 1982—), Young Pres.'s Orgn. Republican. Mormon. Home: 18540 Wild Horse Crk Poway CA 92064-6610 Office: Excel Interfin Corp 16955 Via Del Campo San Diego CA 92127-1718

SABIN, JACK CHARLES, engineering and construction firm executive; b. Phoenix, June 29, 1921; s. Jack Byron and Rena (Lewis) S.; BS, U. Ariz., 1943; BSChemE, U. Minn., 1947; m. Frances Jane McIntyre, Mar. 27, 1950; children— Karen Lee, Robert William, Dorothy Ann, Tracy Ellen. With Standard Oil Co. of Calif., 1947-66, sr. engr., 1966— ; pres., dir. Indsl. Control & Engring., Inc., Redondo Beach, Calif., 1966— ; owner/mgr. Jack C. Sabin, Engr.-Contractor, Redondo Beach, 1968— ; staff engr. Pacific Molasses Co., San Francisco, 1975-77; project mgr. E & L Assocs., Long Beach, Calif., 1977-79; dir. Alaska Pacific Petroleum, Inc., 1968— , Marlex Petroleum, Inc., 1970, 71— , Served with U.S. Army, 1942-46; capt. Chem. Corps, Res., 1949-56. Registered profl. engr., Calif., Alaska; lic. gen. engring. contractor, Ariz., Calif. Mem. Nat. Soc. Profl. Engrs., Ind. Liquid Terminals Assn., Conservative Caucus, Calif. Tax Reduction Com., Tau Beta Pi, Phi Lambda Upsilon, Phi Sigma Kappa. Republican. Clubs: Elks; Town Hall of Calif. Address: 151 Camino De Las Colinas Redondo Beach CA 90277-5828

SABLE, BARBARA KINSEY, former music educator; b. Astoria, L.I., N.Y., Oct. 6, 1927; d. Albert and Verna (Rowe) Kinsey; m. Arthur J. Sable, Nov. 03, 1973. BA, Coll. Wooster, 1949; MA, Tchrs. Coll. Columbia U., N.Y.C., 1950; DMus, U. Ind., 1966. Office mgr., music dir. Sta. WCAX, Burlington, Vt., 1954; instr. Cottey Coll., 1959-60; asst. prof. N.E. Mo. State U., Kirksville, 1962-64, U. Calif., Santa Barbara, 1964-69; prof. music U. Colo., Boulder, 1969—, prof. emeritus, 1992—. Author: (novels) The Vocal Sound, 1982;contbr. poetry and short stories. Mem.: Nat. Assn. Tchrs. Singing (past state gov., assoc. editor bull.), AAUP, Colo. Music Tchrs. Assn. Democrat. Avocation: poetry. Home: 3430 Ash Ave Boulder CO 80305-3432 Office: U Colo PO Box 301 Boulder CO 80309-0301 E-mail: bks@sable-boulder.com

SABSAY, DAVID, library consultant; b. Waltham, Mass., Sept. 12, 1931; s. Wiegard Isaac and Ruth (Weinstein) S.; m. Helen Glenna Tolliver, Sept. 24,1 966. AB, Harvard U., 1953; BLS, U. Calif., Berkeley, 1955. Circulation dept. supr. Richmond (Calif.) Pub. Library, 1955-56; city libr. Santa Rosa (Calif.) Pub. Library, 1956-65; dir. Sonoma County Library, Santa Rosa, 1965-92; libr. cons., 1992—. Coordinator North Bay Coop. Library System, Santa Rosa, 1960-64; cons. in field, Sebastopol, Calif., 1968—. Contbr. articles to profl. jours. Commendation, Calif. Assn. Library Trustees and Commrs., 1984. Mem. Calif. Library Assn. (pres. 1971, cert. appreciation 1971, 80), ALA. Club: Harvard (San Francisco). Home and Office: 667 Montgomery Rd Sebastopol CA 95472-3020 E-mail: dsabsay@sonic.net

SACK, EDGAR ALBERT, electronics company executive; b. Pitts., Jan. 31, 1930; s. Edgar Albert and Margaret Valentine (Engelmohr) S.; m. Eugenia Ferris, June 7, 1952; children: Elaine Kimberley, Richard Warren. BS, Carnegie-Mellon U., 1951, MS, 1952, PhD, 1954. Dept. mgr. Westinghouse Research Lab., Pitts., 1960-63; engring. mgr. Westinghouse Microelectronics, Balt., 1963-65, operations mgr., 1965-67, div. mgr., 1967-69; div. v.p. Gen. Instrument Corp., Hicksville, N.Y., 1969-73, group v.p., 1973-77, sr. v.p., 1977-84; pres., chief exec. officer Zilog Inc., Campbell, Calif., 1984-98, also chmn. bd. dirs.; pres. Productivity Assocs., Coronado; founder, chmn. CDT, Inc., San Jose, 1998-99. Bd. dirs. Enfo-Web, Inc., Mountainview, Calif., LXi, Inc., Mountainview; vis. com. elec. engring. dept. Carnegie-Mellon U., 1969-74; mem. indsl. adv. coun. SUNY, Stony Brook, 1979-83; mem. adv. com. on solid state electronics Poly. Inst. Tech., 1981-83. Author: Forward Controllership Business Management System, 1989, 2nd edit., 1993; patentee in field. Mem. Action Com. Long Island, 1982-84; bd. dirs. Coronado Shores Assn. # 7; mem. Sharp Coronado Hosp. Aux. Recipient 2nd Ann. Hammerschlag Disting. Lectr. award Carnegie Mellon U., 1995. Fellow IEEE, Poly. Inst. Tech.; mem. Semicondr. Industry Assn. (dir. 1982-85); mem. Carnegie Mellon Alumni Assn. (Merit award 1981), Eta Kappa Nu (Outstanding Young Elec. Engr. 1959), Huntington Yacht Club (vice comdr. 1977), Tau Beta Pi (finalist San Francisco Entrepreneur of Yr. award 1991), Phi Kappa Phi. Home and Office: 1780 Avenida Del Mundo Unit 404 Coronado CA 92118-4011 E-mail: esack@pacbell.net

SACKETT, JOHN IRVIN, nuclear engineer; b. Spokane, Wash., May 5, 1943; s. Melvin and Mary Sackett; m. Karen King, June 15, 1965; children: Brent, Erik. BSME, U. Idaho, 1965; PhD in Nuclear Engring., U. Ariz., 1970. Registered profl. engr., Idaho. Asst. nuclear engr. EBR-II ops. Argonne Nat. Lab., Idaho Falls, Idaho, 1970-72, nuclear engr., 1973-74, sect. mgr. EBR-II ops. analysis, 1974-82, assoc. divsn. dir., 1982-89, sr. nuclear engr., 1983, mgr. EBR-II plant testing in support of IFR program, 1986, IFR divsn. dir., 1989-91, dep. assoc. lab. dir., 1991—. Bd. dirs. United Way, Bonneville County, Idaho, CHC Found., 1996; past squadron comdr. Civil Air Patrol. Recipient U. Chgo. award for Disting. Performance at Argonne Nat. Lab., 1976, 78, U. Idaho Outstanding Alumni award "Silver and Gold," 1996, ANA Spl. award for Pioneering Work in Passive Reactor Safety, Am. Nuclear Soc., 1991, Walker Cisler award for Disting. Work in Breeder Reactor Design and Operation, 1996. Fellow Am. Nuc. Soc. (asst. to nat. pres. 1989-90, chmn. Idaho sect. 1986-87, nat. bd. dirs. 1986-88, nat. chmn. profl. divsns. com. 1988-89, nat. chmn. planning com. 1987-88). Home: PO Box 1826 Idaho Falls ID 83403-1826 Office: Argonne Nat Lab PO Box 2528 Idaho Falls ID 83403-2528

SACKETT, SUSAN DEANNA, film and television production associate, writer; b. N.Y.C., Dec. 18, 1943; adopted d. Maxwell and Gertrude Selma (Kugel) S. BA in Edn., U. Fla., 1964, MEd, 1965. Tchr. Dade County Schs., Miami, Fla., 1966-68, L.A. City Schs., 1968-69; asst. publicist, comml. coord. NBC-TV, Burbank, Calif., 1970-73; asst. to Gene Roddenberry creater Star Trek, 1974-91; prodn. assoc. TV series Star Trek: The Next Generation, 1987-91, writer, 1990-91. Lectr. and guest speaker Star Trek convs. in U.S., Eng., Australia, 1974-93. Author, editor: Letters to Star Trek, 1977; co-author: Star Trek Speaks, 1979, The Making of Star Trek--The Motion Picture, 1979; You Can Be a Game Show Contestant and Win, 1982, Say Goodnight Gracie, 1986; author: The Hollywood Reporter Book of Box Office Hits, 1990, 2d edit., 1996, Prime Time Hits, 1993, Hollywood Sings, 1995, Website and Memoir: Insidetrek.com, 1999. Mem. ACLU, Writers Guild Am., Am. Humanist Assn., Humanist Soc. Greater Phoenix (pres. 2000—), Mensa, Sierra Club. Democrat. E-mail: Susan@insidetrek.com

SACKMAN, DAVE, marketing executive; married; 3 children. BA in Anthropology, U. Calif. Pres., CEO Lieberman Rsch. Worldwide, L.A.; dir. rsch. Columbia Pictures; dir. mktg. Winchell's; dir. mktg. dept. group health svcs. Am. Med. Internat. Active Young Pres. Orgn. Mem. Mktg. Rsch. Assn. (mem. strategic planning com., mem. exec. forum on rsch. quality, mem. exec. com. nat. bd. dirs.). Avocations: basketball, tennis. Office: Liberman Rsch Worldwide 1900 Ave Of Stars Los Angeles CA 90067-4301

SADUN, ALFREDO ARRIGO, neuro-ophthalmologist, scientist, educator; b. New Orleans, Oct. 23, 1950; s. Elvio H. and Lina (Ottoleghi) S.; m. Debra Leigh Rice, Mar. 18, 1978; children: Rebecca Eli, Elvio Aaron, Benjamin Maxwell. BS, MIT, 1972; PhD, Albert Einstein Med. Sch., Bronx, N.Y., 1976, MD, 1978. Intern Huntington Meml. Hosp. U. So. Calif., Pasadena, 1978-79; resident Harvard U. Med. Sch., Boston, 1979-82, HEED Found. fellow in neuro-ophthalmology Mass. Eye and Ear Inst., 1982-83, instr. ophthalmology, 1983, asst. prof. ophthalmology, 1984; dir. residential tng. U. So. Calif. Dept. Ophthalmology, L.A., 1984-85, 90—; asst. prof. ophthalmology and neurosurgery U. So. Calif., L.A., 1984-87, assoc. prof., 1987-90, full prof., 1990—, mem. internal review bd., F. thornton endowed chair, prof. vision rsch., 2000—. Prin. investigator Howe Lab. Harvard U., Boston, 1981-84, E. Doheny Eye Inst., L.A., 1984—; examiner Am. Bd. Ophthalmology; mem. Nat. Residency Rev. Com. for Accreditations, 1993—, chmn., 1998—; mem. internal rev. bd. U. So. Calif.; mem. sci. exec. bd. K. Rasmussen Found.; mem. sci. adv. bd. Internat. Found. for Optic Nerve Diseases. Author: Optics for Ophthalmologists, 1988, New Methods of Sensory Visual Testing, 1989; editor: Ophthalmology; contbr. articles to profl. jours. and chpts. to books. James Adams scholar, 1990-91; recipient Pecan D. award, 1988-92, Rsch. to Prevent Blindness Sr. Investigator award, 1996-97, Rsch. to Prevent Blindness Sr. Investigator award, 1996, Lighthouse Internat. Pisort award 1999. Fellow Am. Acad. Ophthalmology Neuro-Ophthalmologists; mem. NIH (Med. Scientists Tng. award 1972-78), Am. Assn. Anatomists, Assn. Univ. Prof. Ophthalmology (assoc.), Am. Bd. Ophthalmology (rep. to residency rev. com. 1994—), Soc. to Prevent Blindness, Nat. Eye Inst. (New Investigator Rsch. award 1983-86, rsch. grants 1988-91, 93—), Soc. Neuroscis., Assn. Rsch. in Vision and Ophthalmology, N.Am. Neuro-Ophthal. Soc. (chmn. membership com. 1990—, v.p. 1994—). Avocation: writing. Home: 2478 Adair St San Marino CA 91108-2610

SAFFMAN, PHILIP G. mathematician, educator; b. Leeds, Eng., Mar. 19, 1931; s. Sam Ralph and Sarah (Rebecca) S.; m. Ruth Arion, Sept. 2, 1954; children: Louise J., Mark E., Emma E. B.A., Trinity Coll., Cambridge U., 1953, M.A., Ph.D., Cambridge U., 1956. Asst. lectr. applied math. Cambridge U., 1958-60; reader in applied math. Kings Coll., London U., 1960-64; prof. fluid mechanics Calif. Inst. Tech., Pasadena, 1964-69, prof. applied math., 1969-95, Theodore von Kármán prof. applied math. and aeros., 1995—. Contbr. articles to profl. jours. Trinity Coll. fellow, 1955-59; recipient Otto Laporte award, Am. Physical Soc., 1994, Fluid Dynamics Award, Am. Inst. Aeronautics and Astronautics, 1995. Fellow Am. Acad. Arts and Scis., Royal Soc. London. Office: 217-50 Firestone Calif Inst Tech Pasadena CA 91125

SAFFO, PAUL, communications executive; BA, Harvard Coll.; LLB, Cambridge U.; JD, Stanford U. Bar: N.Y., Calif. Dir. Inst. For The Future, Menlo Park, Calif., 1985—. Author: Dreams in Silicon Valley; contbr. columns to Wired; contbr. essays to profl. jours. including L.A. Times, N.Y. Times, Fortune, Byte, PC Computing, Infoworld. Office: Inst For The Future 2744 Sand Hill Rd Menlo Park CA 94025-7020

SAFONOV, MICHAEL GEORGE, electrical engineering educator, consultant; b. Pasadena, Calif., Nov. 1, 1948; s. George Michael and Ruth Garnet (Ware) S.; m. Nancy Kelshaw Schorn, Aug. 31, 1968 (div. Oct. 1983); 1 child, Alexander; m. Janet Sunderland, Feb. 25, 1985; 1 child, Peter. BSEE, MSEE, MIT, 1971, EE, 1976, PhDEE, 1977. Electronic engr. Air Force Cambridge Rsch. Lab., Hanscom AFB, Mass., 1968-71; rsch. asst. MIT, Cambridge, 1975-77; prof. elec. engring. U. So. Calif., L.A., 1977—, assoc. chmn. dept., 1989-93. Vis. scholar Cambridge (Eng.) U., 1983-84, Imperial Coll., London, 1987, Calif. Inst. Tech., Pasadena, 1990-91; cons. Honeywell Systems and Rsch. Ctr., Mpls., 1978-83, Space Systems div. TRW, Redondo Beach, Calif., 1984, Northrop Aircraft, Hawthorne, Calif., 1985-91, also numerous others. Author: Stability and Robustness of Multivariable Feedback Systems (hon. mention Phi Beta Kappa 1981); co-author: (book and software) Robust-Control Toolbox, 1988; assoc. editor IEEE Trans. on Automatic Control, 1985-87, Internat. Jour. Robust and Nonlinear Control, 1989-93, Sys. and Control Letters, 1995—. Awards com. chair Am. Automatic Control Coun., 1993-95. Lt. (j.g.) USNR, 1972-75. Rsch. grantee Air Force Office Sci. Rsch., 1978—, NSF, 1982-84. Fellow IEEE; mem. AIAA (sr.), Common Cause. Republican. Office: U So Calif Dept EE Sys MC 2563 3740 McClintock Ave # 310 Los Angeles CA 90089-2563 E-mail: safanov@usc.edu

SAGAWA, YONEO, horticulturist, educator; b. Olaa, Hawaii, Oct. 11, 1926; s. Chikatada and Mume (Kuno) S.; m. Masayo Yamamoto, May 24, 1962 (dec. Apr. 1988); children: Penelope Toshiko, Irene Teruko. AB, Washington U., St. Louis, 1950, MS, 1952; PhD, U. Conn., 1956. Postdoctoral research assoc. biology Brookhaven Nat. Lab., Upton, N.Y., 1955-57, guest in biology, 1958; asst. prof., then assoc. prof. U. Fla., 1957-64; dir. undergrad. sci. ednl. research participation program NSF, 1964; cons. biosatellite project NASA, 1966-67; prof. horticulture U. Hawaii, 1964—; dir. Lyon Arboretum, 1967-91; assoc. dir. Hawaiian Sci. Fair, 1966-67, dir., 1967-68; research assoc. in biology U. Calif., Berkeley, 1970-71; rsch. assoc. Bishop Mus., Honolulu, 1992—, Botanical Rsch. Inst. of Tex., 1993—, Hawaii Tropical Botanical Garden, 1995—; external assessor U. Pertanian, Malaysia, 1994—. Mem. Internat. Orchid Commn. on Classification, Nomenclature and Registration; fellow Inst. voor Toepassing van Atoomenergie in de Landbouw, U. Agr., Wageningen, The Netherlands, 1979-80; mem. sci. adv. bd. Nat. Tropical Bot. Garden, Kauai, Hawaii; councilor Las Cruces Bot. Garden, Costa Rica; cons. FAO, Singapore, 1971, USAID-Agribus. Assistance Program, Vols. in Overseas Coop. Assistance, UN Devel. Program-UN Internat. Short Term Adv. Resources; dir. Hawaii Tropical Bot. Garden; hon. scientist Rural Devel. Adminstrn., Republic of Korea, 1998—; cons. Fiji-N.Z. Bus. Coun., 1996, 97, 98, 99, 2000; cons. IRETA, Western Samoa, 1997, 98; cons. Nat. Hort. Rsch. Inst., Suwon, Republic of Korea, 1998, 2000. Editor: Hawaii Orchid Jour., 1972-99, Pacific Orchid Soc. Bull., 1960-71, mem. edit. bd.. Allertonia, 1976; contbr. numerous articles to profl. jours. Trustee Friends of Honolulu Bot. Gardens, 1973-99 Recipient Disting. Svc. award South Fla. Orchid Soc., 1968, Cert. of Achievement Garden Club Am., 1995, Gold award Hawaii Orchid Growers Assn., 1996; grantee Am. Orchid Soc., Atomic Energy Commn., NIH, HEW, Inst. Mus. Svcs., Stanley Smith Hort. Trust, Honolulu Orchid Soc. Fellow Am. Orchid Soc. (hon. life, Gold medal for outstanding contbns. and svcs. 1999); mem. AAAS, Internat. Assn. Hort. Sci., Am. Assn. Hort. Sci., Am. Inst. for Biol. Scis., Bot. Soc. Am., Hawn Bot. Soc. (past v.p.), Internat. Assn. Plant Tissue Culture, Internat. Palm Soc., Am. Anthurium Soc. (hon. life), Pacific Orchid Soc. (trustee 1994), Kaimuki Orchid Soc. (hon. life), Honolulu Orchid Soc. (hon., life), Lyon Arboretum Assn. (trustee 1974-91), Garden Club Honolulu (hon., life), Aloha Bonsai Club, Sigma Xi, Gamma Sigma Delta, Phi Kappa Phi (past pres., v.p., councillor U. Hawaii chpt.). Democrat. Office: U Hawaii TPSS St John Rm 102 3190 Maile Way Honolulu HI 96822-2279 Fax: 808-956-3894. E-mail: yoneo@hawaii.edu

SAGER, PHILIP TRAVIS, academic physician, cardiac electrophysiologist; b. N.Y.C., Jan. 23, 1956; s. Clifford Julius nad Ruth (Levy) S. BS in Chemistry and Biology, MIT, Cambridge, Mass., 1977; MD, Yale U., New Haven, Conn., 1982, resident, cardiology fellow, 1982-88. Diplomate Am. Bd. Internal Medicine, Am. Bd. Cardiology, AM. Bd. Cardiac Electrophysiology. Asst. prof. medicine Sch. Medicine, U. So. Calif., L.A., 1988-90, asst. dir. electrophysiology, 1988-90, dir. Pacemaker Ctr., 1988-90; asst. prof. medicine Sch. Medicine, UCLA, 1990-96, assoc. prof. of medicine, 1996—; dir. cardiac electrophysiology West L.A. VA Med. Ctr., 1990-96. Mem. cardiology adv. com. VA Adminstrn., Washington, 1990-94; cons. electrophysiology ACGME, Chgo., 1995—; vis. prof. Kern Med. Ctr., Bakersfield, Calif., 1991, 94, U. Iowa Sch. Medicine, 1994, Northwestern U. Sch. Medicine, 1994, Yale U. Sch. Medicine, 1995, U. Calif., San Francisco, 1996; co-chair NASPE EPS Fellowship Dirs. com., 1997—; invited lectr. major med. instns. and symposiums; cons. pharm. cos. Contbr. chpts. to books, numerous rsch. articles to profl. jours. of innovative rsch.; reviewer many scientific jours. Recipient many rsch. grants, including Am. Heart Assn., 1996. Fellow Am. Heart Assn. (coun. on clin. cardiology 1997—), Am. Coll. Cardiology, Am. Coll. Physicians; mem. Am. Fedn. Clin. Rsch., Nat. Assn. Pacing and Electrophysiology (program dirs. com. 1992—, govt. com. 1994—, assoc. chair program dirs. com. 1997—), Phi Beta Kappa, Alpha Omega Alpha. Avocations: bicycling, scuba diving, reading history, movies. Office: W LA VAMC-UCLA Dept 111E 11301 Wilshire Blvd Dept 111E Los Angeles CA 90073-1003 Fax: 310-470-0954. E-mail: PSAGER@UCLA.edu

SAGNESS, RICHARD LEE, education educator, former academic dean; b. Rock Rapids, Iowa, Jan. 9, 1937; s. David Harold and Joyce Morrow (Carlson) S.; m. Donna Jayne Lanxon, Feb. 18, 1956; children: Debbi Van Vooren, Becky Hardy, Beth Sagness Higbee. BA, U. No. Iowa, 1961; MS, Emporia State U., 1965; PhD, Ohio State U., 1970; grad. Inst. for Higher Edn. Mgmt., Harvard U., 1977. Tchr. biology Cen. High Sch., Sioux City, Iowa, 1961-66; lectr. biology Emporia (Kans.) State U., 1966-67; info. analyst Ohio State U., 1967-70; asst. prof. sci. edn. U. S.D., Vermillion, 1970-72, assoc. prof., 1972-75, coord. sci. edn., 1970-75; prof. sci. edn., assoc. dean Sch. Edn. U. S.D., Vermillion, 1975-79; prof. edn. Coll. Edn. Idaho State U., Pocatello, 1979-99, dean Coll. Edn., 1979-89, dir. clin. experiences and student svcs., 1993-99, prof. emeritus, 1999—. Past mem. Idaho Profl. Stds. Commn.; faculty rep. to bd. dirs. Idaho State U. Found., 1992-97; mem. Idaho Sch.-to-Work Collaborative Team, 1994-97. Contbr. articles to profl. jours. Bd. dirs. Vermillion Devel. Corp., 1974-78, pres., 1976-77; bd. dirs. Pocatello United Fund, 1976-79, 82-83, v.p., 1982-83, pres., 1985-86, Bannock Meml. Hosp. Found., v. chmn. 1999—. With U.S. Army, 1955-57. Mem. Idaho Assn. Colls. Tchr. Edn. (pres. 1984-88), Am. Assn. Colls. of Tchr. Edn. (rep., chairperson govtl. rels. com. 1988-89, bd. dirs. 1988-92), Pocatello C. of C. (bd. dirs. 1983-89, pres. 1987-88), Tchr. Edn. Coun. State Colls. and Univs. (exec. coun. 1988-90), N.W. Assn. Schs. and Colls. (commn. on schs. 1995—, bd. trustees 1997—), Rotary (bd. dirs. local club 1988-89, team leader study exch. team to Sweden 1991, pres.-elect 1997-98), Masons, Order Eastern Star (past patron), Rotary (pres. Pocatello club 1998-99, dist. 5400 found. scholarship com. 1997—), Phi Delta Kappa (past pres.). Office: Idaho State U PO Box 8059 Pocatello ID 83209-0001

SAHATJIAN, MANIK, nurse, psychologist; b. Tabris, Iran, July 24, 1921; came to U.S., 1951; d. Dicran and Shushanig (Der-Galustian) Mnatzaganian; m. George Sahatjian, Jan. 21, 1954; children: Robert, Edwin. Nursing Cert., Am. Mission Hosps.-Boston U., 1954; BA in Psychology, San Jose State U., 1974, MA in Psychology, 1979. RN, Calif. Head nurse Am. Mission Hosp., Tabris, 1945-46; charge nurse Banke-Melli Hosp., Tehran, 1946-51; vis. nurse Vis. Nurse Assn., Oakland, Calif., 1956-57; research asst. Stanford U., 1979-81, Palo Alto (Calif.) Med. Research Found., 1981-84; documentation supr. Bethesda Convalescent Ctr., Los Gatos, Calif., 1985-86; sr. outreach worker City of Fremont (Calif.) Human Svcs., 1987-90, case mgr., 1990-97; ret., 1997. Guest rsch. asst. NASA Ames Lab., Mountain View, Calif., summers 1978, 79. Author (with others) psychol. research reports. Mentor elem. sch. children., pro bono tchg./counseling for srs. who are home bound, Fremont, Calif., 1999—; pro bono tchr. peer counseling trainers for srs. Armenian Cmty. Santa Clara, Calif., St. Andrew Ch. Fulbright scholar, 1951; Iran Found. scholar, 1953. Mem. AAUW, Western Psychol. Assn., Am. Assn. Sr. Counseling. Democrat. Mem. St. Andrew Armenian Church. Avocations: oil painting, classic dance. Home: 339 Starlite Way Fremont CA 94539-7642

SAIFER, MARK GARY PIERCE, pharmaceutical executive; b. Phila., Sept. 16, 1938; s. Albert and Sylvia (Jolles) S.; m. Phyllis Lynne Trommer, Jan. 28, 1961 (dec.); children: Scott David, Alandria Gail; m. Merry R. Sherman, June 26, 1994. AB, U. Pa., 1960; PhD, U. Calif., Berkeley, 1966. Acting asst. prof. zoology U. Calif., Berkeley, 1966, fellow, 1967-68; sr. cancer rsch. scientist Roswell Park Meml. Inst., Buffalo, 1968-70; lab. dir. Diagnostic Data Inc., Palo Alto, Calif., 1970-78; v.p. DDI Pharms., Inc., Mountain View, 1978-94, Oxis Internat., Inc., 1994-95; sci. dir. Mountain View Pharms., Inc., Menlo Park, Calif., 1996—, also bd. dirs. Author, patentee in field. Mem. AAAS (life), Am. Assn. Pharm. Scientists, Parenteral Drug Assn. Home: 1114 Royal Ln San Carlos CA 94070-4277 Office: Mountain View Pharms Inc 3475 Edison Way Ste S Menlo Park CA 94025-1821 E-mail: saifer@mvpharm.com

ST. ARNAUD, ROLAND, soil scientist; Soil scientist U. Saskatchewan, Saskatoon, Can. Office: Coll Agrl 308001 U Saskatchewan Saskatoon SK Canada S7N 0W0

ST. CLAIR, CARL, conductor, music director; Music dir. Pacific Symphony Orch., Santa Ana, Calif., 1990—, Ann Arbor (Mich.) Symphony Orch., 1985-92, Cayuga Chamber Orch., 1986-92. Albums include Fire Water Paper: A Vietnam Oratorio, 1995, Corigliano Piano Concerto. Recipient NEA/Seaver Condrs. award, 1990. Office: Pacific Symphony Orch 1231 E Dyer Rd Ste 200 Santa Ana CA 92705-5606

ST. GEORGE, WILLIAM ROSS, lawyer, retired naval officer, consultant; b. Southport, N.C., Nov. 19, 1924; s. William B. and Ila (Ross) St. G.; m. Emma Louise Bridger, June 10, 1950; children— Victoria Butler, William Ross, Susan Bridger. B.S., U.S. Naval Acad., 1946; J.D., George Washington U., 1953. Bar: D.C. 1953, U.S. Supreme Ct. 1964, Calif. 1980. Commd. ensign U.S. Navy, 1946, advanced through grades to vice adm., 1973; comdg. officer U.S.S. Josephus Daniels, 1969-70; comdr. Cruiser-Destroyer Flotilla 11, also comdr. Cruiser-Destroyer Flotilla 3, 1973; dep. and chief staff to comdr.-in-chief U.S. Pacific Fleet, 1973-76; comdr. Naval Surface Force, U.S. Pacific Fleet, 1976-79, ret., 1979; sole practice San Diego, 1980—. Decorated D.S.M. with oak leaf cluster, Legion of Merit, Bronze Star. Presbyterian. Home: 862 San Antonio Pl San Diego CA 92106-3057 E-mail: williamstgeorge@aol.com

SAINT-JACQUES, BERNARD, linguistics educator; b. Montreal, Que., Can., Apr. 26, 1928; s. Albert and Germaine (Lefebvre) Saint-J.; m. Marguerite Fauquenoy. M.A., Sophia U., Tokyo, 1962; M.S., Georgetown U., 1964; Doctorat es Lettres and Scis. Humaines, Paris U., 1975. Asst. prof. linguistics U. B.C., Vancouver, 1967-69, assoc. prof., 1969-78, prof., 1978-90, prof. emeritus, 1991—; prof. Aichi U., Japan, 1990—. Mem. U.S. Citizen Amb. Program. Author: Structural Analysis of Modern Japanese, 1971, Aspects sociolinguistiques du bilinguisme canadien, 1976, Language and Ethnic Relations, 1979, Japanese Studies in Canada, 1985, Studies in Language and Culture, 1995; editor: Intercultural Communication Studies, 1998; co-editor: Contrasting Political Institutions, 1997, (with M. Iwasaki) Democratic Viability in Politics, 2000. Leave fellow Can. Council, 1974; profl. fellow Japan Found., 1981; research fellow French Govt., 1982, Ohira Programme, Japan, 1983 Fellow Royal Soc. Can. Acad., Internat. Acad. Intercultural Rsch.; mem. Linguistic Soc. Am., Can. Soc. Asian Studies, Can. Linguistics Assn., Sietar Japan. Office: U BC Dept Linguistics Vancouver BC Canada V6T 1Z1 also: Aichi ShuKutoKu U Katahira NagaKute NagaKute-cho Aichi-gun 480-1197 Japan E-mail: saintj@asu.aasa.ac.jp

ST. JEAN, GARRY, professional basketball coach; m. Mary Jane St. Jean; children: Emily, Gregory. B in Phys. Edn., Springfield (Mass.) Coll., 1973, M in Phys. Edn., postgrad. cert., Springfield (Mass.) Coll. Head coach Chicopee (Mass.) High Sch., 1973-80; coll. scout, asst. bench coach, asst. dir. player pers. Milw. Bucks, 1980-86; asst. coach, asst. player pers. dir. N.J. Nets, 1986-88; asst. coach Golden State Warriors, 1988-92; head coach Sacramento Kings, 1992-95; gen. mgr. Golden State Warriors, 1996—. Office: Golden State Warriors 1011 Broadway Oakland CA 94607-4027

SAJAK, PAT, television game show host; b. Chgo., Oct. 26, 1947; m. Lesly Brown, Dec. 31, 1990. Newscaster WEDC-Radio, Chicago, IL; disk jockey WNBS-Radio, Murray, KY; staff announcer, public affairs program host, weatherman WSM-TV, Nashville; weatherman, host The Sunday Show, 1977-81; host Wheel of Fortune, 1981—, The Pat Sajak Show, 1989-90. Film appearances include: Airplane II: The Sequel, 1982, Jack Paar is Alive and Well, 1987; NBC television specials, host, The Thanksgiving Day Parade, The Rose Parade. Served with U.S. Army, Vietnam. Office: Wheel of Fortune 3400 W Riverside Dr Burbank CA 91505-4669

SAKAMOTO, GORDON, newspaper editor; Bur. chief AP, 1993—. Office: PO Box 2956 Honolulu HI 96802-2956

SAKAMOTO, KATSUYUKI, retired college chancellor, psychology educator; b. L.A., Oct. 24, 1938; m. Edna Christine Sakamoto; children: David Katsu, Bryce Yoshio. BA in Psychology, Calif. State U., Fresno, 1961, MA in Psychology, 1968; PhD in Exptl. Social Psychology, So. Ill. U., Carbondale, 1971; postgrad., Carnegie Mellon U., 1984. Acting dir. Army Edn. Ctr., Munich, 1962-63; dir. social svcs. Salvation Army, Fresno, Calif., 1964-66; assoc. prof. psychology Keuka Coll., Keyka Park, N.Y., 1971-78; prof. social psychology Ea. Oreg. State Coll., La Grande, 1978-85, assoc. dean, then acting dean, 1980-82, 84, assoc. dean acad. affairs, 1982-85; prof. psychology Ind. U. East, Richmond, 1985-91, vice chancellor for acad. affairs, 1985-90, spl. asst. to chancellor, 1990-91; prof., chancellor Calif. Sch. Profl. Psychology, Alameda, 1991-98, ret., 1998. Lectr. So. Ill. U., 1970-71; vis. prof. SUNY, Binghamton, 1973; adj. prof. Alfred (N.Y.) U., 1972-76, Nazareth Coll. Rochester, N.Y., 1975-78, Eisenhower Coll., Seneca Falls, N.Y., 1975-77; evaluator Western Assn. Schs. and Colls., 1991—; commr.-at-large North Ctrl. Assn. Colls. and Schs., 1989-91, educator, cons., 1986-91; mem. exec. bd. for study ctrs. in Japan, China and Korea, campus dir. Oreg. Sys. Higher Edn., 1980-85; bd. visitors Newark (N.Y.) Devel. Ctr., 1975-77; presenter in field. Contbr. articles to profl. jours. Bd. dirs. troop 119 Boy Scouts Am., Richmond, 1986-91, Project 100001, Townsend Cmty. Ctr., Richmond, 1987-89, Alameda Girls Club, Inc., 1992—, Asian Cmty. Mental Health Svcs., 1991—, Found. for Edni. Excellence, Alameda, 1993—; pres., bd. dirs. Whitewater Opera Co., Richmond, 1987-91, Leadership Wayne County, Richmond, 1988-91; cons. teaching mini-grant program Richmond Cmty. Schs., 1988-91; mem. citizens adv. bd. Wayne County Sheriff's Dept., 1989-91. Mem. APA, Am. Assn. for Higher Edn., Am. Assn. State Colls. and Univs., Am. Assn. Univ. Adminstrs. (nat. v.p. 1990-92, bd. dirs. Found. 1991—), Am. Assn. for Higher Edn. (founding mem. Asian Am. caucus), Asian Am. Psychol. Assn. (treas., membership officer 1983-91, pres. 1988-91), Calif. Psychol. Assn., Nat. Assn. Acad. Affairs Adminstrs., Nat. Coun. Schs. Profl. Psychology, Rotary (bd. dirs. Alameda 1993—). Home: 620 W Wilson Ave Unit A Glendale CA 91203-2476 Office: Calif Sch Profl Psychology 1005 Atlantic Ave Alameda CA 94501-1148

SAKAMOTO, NORMAN LLOYD, state legislator, civil engineer; b. Honolulu, May 22, 1947; s. Shuichi and Fusa (Hayashi) S.; m. Penelope A. Hayasaka, July 12, 1970; children: David H., Gregory F., Katherine E. BSCE, U. Hawaii, 1969; MSCE, U. Ill., 1970. Registered profl. engr., Calif., Hawaii; lic. spl. inspector, Hawaii; lic. contractor, Hawaii. Engr. storm drain City of L.A., 1970-71, engr. streets and frwys., 1972-73; engr. hydrology C.E., 1971-72; v.p. S & M Sakamoto, Inc., Honolulu, 1973-85; pres. SC Pacific Corp., Kapolei, 1985—; mem. Hawaii Senate, Dist. 16, Honolulu, 1996—. Bd. dirs. Bldg. Industry Assn., Honolulu, spl. appointee, 1991-92, pres.-elect, 1993, pres., 1994; bd. dirs. City Contractors Assn., Honolulu; trustee Home Builders Inst., 1993-96; del. White House Conf. on Small Bus., 1995; co-chair Hawaii Congress on Small Bus. Scoutmaster Honolulu area Boy Scouts Am., 1989-92, 93-; elected to Hawaii State Senate, Dist. 16, 1996—; Aliamanu Clubhouse adv. bd. Boys and Girls Club. Named Remodeler of Month Bldg. Industry Assn., 1990, 91, 96, Remodeler of Yr., 1991. Mem. ASCE, Nat. Assn. Home Builders (dir. 1992—), Internat. Fellowship Christian Businessmen, Contrs. Industry Legis. Assn., C. of C. Evangelical. Office: SC Pacific Corp 91-178 Kalaeloa Blvd Kapolei HI 96707-1819

SAKIC, JOSEPH STEVE, professional hockey player; b. Burnaby, B.C., Canada, July 7, 1969; Capt. Quebec Nordiques, 1991-95; with Colo. Avalanche, 1995—. Won WHL East Most Valuable Player Trophy, 1986-87, WHL Stewart (Butch) Paul Meml. Trophy, 1986-87, Four Broncos Meml. Trophy, 1987-88, Bob Clarke Trophy, 1987-88, Conn Smythe Trophy NHL, 1996; named to WHL All-Star Second Team, 1986-87, Can. Hockey League Player of Yr., 1987-88, WHL Player of Yr., 1987-88; played in NHL All-Star Game, 1990-94, 96. Office: c/o Colo Avalanche 1000 Chopper Cir Denver CO 80204-5809

SAKOGUCHI, BEN, artist, retired art educator; b. San Bernardino, Calif., 1938; Student, San Bernardino Valley Coll., 1956-58; BA, UCLA, 1960, MFA, 1964; postgrad., Calif. State U., L.A., 1982-83. Prof. art Pasadena (Calif.) City Coll., 1964-97, retired, 1997. Solo exhbns. include Ceeje Gallery, L.A., 1964, 65, 67, La Jolla (Calif.) Mus., 1965, U. Calif. Santa Cruz, 1967, L.A. City Coll., 1968, 81, Santa Barbara (Calif.) Mus. Art, 1968, Brand Art Ctr., Glendale, Calif., 1971, Zara Gallery, San Francisco, 1973, Compton (Calif.) Coll., 1977, Works, San Jose, Calif., 1978, Mira Costa Coll., Oceanside, Calif., 1983, Roberts Art Gallery, Santa Monica H.S., Calif., 1985, Mount St. Mary's Coll., L.A., 1988, Aljira Ctr. Contemporary Art, Newark, 1992, Alternative Mus., N.Y.C., Rancho Santiago Coll., Santa Ana, 1995, Space, L.A., 1998, El Camino Coll., Torrance, Calif., 1998; 2 person exhbns. Santa Ana Coll., 1978, Aarnun Gallery, Pasadena, 1980, San Francisco Fine Arts Mus., 1980, Gorman Mus. U. Calif. Davis, 1981, [illegible], 1997, group exhbns. include Alternative Mus., 1982, 89, 91, 92, 95, NYU Stony Brook, 1983, Triton Mus., Santa Clara, 1984, ARCO Ctr. Visual Arts, L.A., 1984, L.A. Mcpl. Art Gallery, 1985, Watts Towers Art Ctr., L.A., 1986, Whatcom

Mus. History and Art, Bellingham, Wash., 1989 (circulated various museums nationwide, 1992), New Mus. Contemporary Art, N.Y.C., 1990, Peace Mus., Chgo., 1995, Fort Mason Ctr., San Francisco, 1995, Mus. Modern Art, N.Y.C., 1995, Nat. Japanese Am. Hist. Soc., 1999, San Francisco, Pacific Asia Mus., 2000, L.A. County Mus. Art, 2000, Corcoran Gallery Art, Washington, 2000, others; represented permanent collections Am. Express Co., N.Y.C., Atlantic Richfield Corp., L.A., Bklyn. Mus., Chgo. Art Inst., Mus. Modern Art, N.Y.C., Phila. Mus. Art, Nat. Mus. Am. Art, Smithsonian Instn., Fogg Art Mus., Harvard U., numerous others; subject numerous articles, publs., exhbn. catalogs and revs., 1965—. NEA fellow 1980, 95, Pasadena Arts Commn. fellow 1991, Calif. Cmty. Found. J. Paul Getty Trust Fund for Visual Arts fellow, 1997, Lila Wallace-Reader's Digest Fund Artists Giverny fellow, 1997. Home: 1183 Avoca Ave Pasadena CA 91105-3450

SALAMON, MIKLOS DEZSO GYORGY, mining engineer, educator; b. Balkany, Hungary, May 20, 1933; came to U.S., 1986; naturalized, 1993; s. Miklos and Sarolta (Obetko) S.; m. Agota Maria Meszaros, July 11, 1953; children: Miklos, Gabor. Diploma in Engring., Polytech U., Sopron, Hungary, 1956; PhD, U. Durham, Newcastle, England, 1962; doctorem honoris causa, U. Miskolc, Hungary, 1990. Rsch. asst. dept. mining engring. U. Durham, 1959-63; dir. rsch. Coal Mining Rsch. Controlling Coun., Johannesburg, South Africa, 1963-66; dir. collieries rsch. lab. Chamber of Mines of South Africa, Johannesburg, 1966-74, dir. gen. rsch. orgn., 1974-86; disting. prof. Colo. Sch. Mines, Golden, 1986-98, disting. prof. emeritus, 1998—, head dept. mining engring., 1986-90; dir. Colo. Mining and Mineral Resources Rsch. Inst., 1990-94; pres. Salamon Cons. Inc., Arvada, Colo., 1995—. 22d Sir Julius Wernher Meml. lectr., 1988; hon. prof. U. Witwatersrand, Johannesburg, 1979-86; vis. prof. U. Minn., Mpls., 1981, U. Tex., Austin, 1982, U. NSW, Sydney, Australia, 1990, 91-96; mem. Presdl. Commn. of Inquiry into Safety and Health in South African Mining Industry, 1994-95. Co-author: Rock Mechanics Applied to the Study of Rockbursts, 1966, Rock Mechanics in Coal Mining, 1976; contbr. articles to profl. jours. Mem. Pres.'s Sci. Adv. Council, Cape Town, South Africa, 1984-86, Nat. Sci. Priorities Com., Pretoria, South Africa, 1984-86. Recipient Nat. award Assn. Scis. and Tech. Socs., South Africa, 1971. Fellow South African Inst. Mining and Metallurgy (hon. life, v.p. 1974-76, pres. 1976-77, gold medal 1964, 85, Stokes award 1986, silver medal 1991, 99), Inst. Mining and Metallurgy (London), Hungarian Acad. Scis. (external), 1998; mem. AIME, Internat. Soc. Rock Mechanics. Roman Catholic. E-mail: mdg_salamon@msn.com

SALAMONE, GARY P. (PIKE), newspaper editor-in-chief, cartoonist; b. Rochester, N.Y., Aug. 26, 1950; BA, St. John Fisher Coll., 1972; MA, San Diego State U., 1979. Editor, pub. Inkslinger's Review, San Diego, 1981—; founder, news dir. Continental News Svc., San Diego, 1985—; pub., columnist Continental Newstime, San Diego, 1987—; founder, editor-in-chief Continental Features/Continental News Svc., San Diego, 1988—; pub., cartoonist Kids' Newstime, San Diego, 1992—. Author: An Examination of Alexander Hamilton's Views on Civil Liberty, 1979, Valley in the Hollow of His Hand, 1999, 2d edit., 2000. Vol. radio announcer, reader Nat. Pub. Radio Affiliate Sta. KPBS, San Diego, 1976-81; founder Fisher Recycling, Rochester, N.Y., 1971; pres. Young People's Conservation Com., Webster-Penfield, N.Y., 1971; high sch. coord. Ecology Centre, San Diego, 1976; vol. pub. info. asst. Cleve. Nat. Forest, San Diego. Mem. Phi Alpha Theta, Pi Sigma Alpha. Democrat. Office: Continental Features/News Svc PMB 265 501 W Broadway Plaza A San Diego CA 92101-3562

SALAND, LINDA CAROL, anatomy educator, neuroscience researcher; b. N.Y.C., Oct. 24, 1942; d. Charles and Esther (Weingarten) Gewirtz; m. Joel S. Saland, Aug. 16, 1964; children: Kenneth, Jeffrey. BS, CCNY, 1963, PhD in Biology, 1968; MA in Zoology, Columbia U., 1965. Rsch. assoc. dept. anatomy Columbia U. Coll. Physicians and Surgeons, N.Y.C., 1968-69; sr. rsch. assoc. dept. anatomy Sch. Medicine U. N.Mex., Albuquerque, 1971-78, asst. prof. anatomy, 1978-83, assoc. prof., 1983-89, prof., 1989-97, prof. dept. neuroscis., 1997—. Ad hoc reviewer study sect. NIH, 1994, 95, 97, 2000, mem. site visit team. Mem. editl. bd. Anat. Record, 1980-98; contbr. articles to profl. jours. Predoctoral fellow NDEA, 1966-68; rsch. grantee Nat. Inst. on Drug Abuse, 1979-83, NIH Minority Biomed. Rsch. Support Program, 1980-2000, NIH, 1986-95. Mem. AAAS, Am. Assn. Anatomists, Soc. for Neurosci., Women in Neurosci. (chmn. steering com. 1991-93), Am. Soc. Cell Biology. Office: U NMex Sch Medicine Dept Neuroscis Basic Med Sci Bldg Albuquerque NM 87131-0001 E-mail: lsaland@salud.unm.edu

SALAT, CRISTINA, writer; b. N.Y.C. Student, L.I. U. Freelance editor, 1987—; author, editor, manuscript cons., workshop facilitator, 1985—. Author: Living in Secret, 1993, Alias Diamond Jones, 1993, Min Mors Koereste hedder Janey, 1995, Defending the Dreamcatchers, 1999, Robin, Romeo & Juliette, 1999, Peanut's Emergency, 1999; contbr. to anthologies including Sister/Stranger, 1993, Am I Blue, 1994, Once Upon A Time, 1996; contbr. to popular publ. Home: PO Box 13214 Pahoa HI 96778

SALAZAR, KENNETH L. state attorney general; b. Mar. 2, 1955; s. Henry and Emma Salazar; m. Hope Hernandez; children: Melinda, Andrea. BA in Polit. Sci., Colo. Coll., 1977, LLD (hon.), 1993; JD, U. Mich., 1981. Bar: Colo. 1981, U.S. Dist. Ct. Colo. 1981, U.S. Ct. Appeals (10th cir.) 1981, U.S. Supreme Ct. 1999. Farmer, rancher, Conejos County, Colo.; law clk. Colo. Atty. Gen., summer 1979; assoc. Sherman & Howard, Denver, 1981-86; chief legal counsel Office of Gov., Denver, 1986-90; exec. dir. Colo. Dept. Natural Resources, Denver, 1990-94; dir. Parcel, Mauro, Hultin & Spaanstra, Denver, 1994-98; atty. gen. State of Colo., 1999—. Gov.'s rep. State Bd. Equalization, Denver, 1990. Chair Great Outdoors Colo., Denver, 1993-94, Rio Grande Compact Commn., 1995-97, Sangre de Cristo Land Grant Commn., 1993-95; mem. Colo. Water Conservation Bd., Denver, 1990—; mem. City and County of Denver Ethics Panel, 1993; bd. dirs. Denver Cmty. Leadership Forum, 1988; gov.'s rep. State Bd. on Property Tax Equalization, 1987-91; del. Soviet-Am. Young Leadership Dialogue, 1984; bd. dirs. Servicios de la Raza HUD 202 Project, 1985-89, chair, 1986; mem. Am. Israel Friendship League, 1986-89. mem. adv. com. Colo. U. Law Sch. Natural Resources Law Ctr., 1989-92; mem. Western Water Policy Rev. Adv. Commn., 1995-97. Juan Tienda scholar. Mem. ABA, Colo. Bar Assn. (bd. govs. 1989-90, task force to assess the legal profession 1986), Denver Bar Assn. (2d v.p. 1989, chair policy-cmty. rels. subcoms. 1982-84), Hispanic Bar Assn. (ABA task force on opptys. for minorities in legal profession, bd. dirs. 1986-87), Am. Judicature Soc. Avocations: basketball, outdoor activities, politics. Office: State Colo Dept Law 1525 Sherman St Fl 5 Denver CO 80203-1700 E-mail: attorney.general@state.co.us

SALCUDEAN, MARTHA EVA, mechanical engineer, educator; b. Cluj, Romania, Feb. 26, 1934; arrived in Can., 1976, naturalized, 1979; d. Edmund and Sarolta (Hirsch) Abel; m. George Salcudean, May 28, 1955; 1 child, Septimiu E. BEng, U. Cluj, 1956, postgrad., 1962; PhD, U. Brasov, Romania, 1969; PhD (hon.), DSc (hon.), U. B.C., 2001. Mech. engr. Armatura, Cluj, 1956-63; sr. rsch. officer Nat. Rsch. Inst. Metallurgy, Bucharest, 1963-75; part-time lectr. Inst. Poly., Bucharest, 1967-75; sessional lectr. U. Ottawa, 1976-77, from asst. prof. to assoc. prof., 1977-85; prof., head dept. mech. engring. U. B.C., Vancouver, Can., 1985-93, assoc. v.p. rsch. Can., 1993-96, acting v.p. rsch. pro-tem Can., 1995, Weyerhausen Indsl. Rsch. chair computational fluid dynamics Can., 1996—. Mem. grant selection com. for mech. engring. Natural Scis. and Engring. Rsch. Coun. Can.; mem. Nat. Adv. Panel to Min. Sci. and Tech. on advanced indsl. materials, Can., 1990; mem. governing coun. Nat. Rsch. Coun.; mem. defense science adv. bd. Dept. Nat. Def.; chair Sci. Coun. B.C. Contbr. numerous articles to profl. jours. Decorated Order of B.C., 1998; recipient Gold medal B.C. Sci. Coun., Killam Rsch. prize U. B.C. Rsch. Coun. Can. grantee, 1978—, Commemorative medal 125th anniversary Can. Confederation, 1993, Julian C. Smith medal Engring. Inst. Can., 1994-95, Meritorious Achievement award Assn. Profl. Engrs. & Geoscientists B.C., 1996, Killam Meml. prize engring., 1998, Order of B.C., 1998. Fellow CSME, Can. Acad. Engring., Royal Soc. Can.; mem. ASME, Assn. Profl. Engrs. Ont. Home: 1938 Western Pkwy Vancouver BC Canada V6T 1W5

SALDICH, ROBERT JOSEPH, electronics company executive; b. N.Y.C., June 7, 1933; s. Alexander and Bertha (Kasakove) S.; m. Anne Rawley, July 21, 1963 (div. Nov. 1979); 1 child, Alan; m. Virginia Vaughan, Sept. 4, 1983; stepchildren: Tad Thomas, Stan Thomas, Melinda Thomas, Margaret Thomas Dudley. BSChemE, Rice U., 1956; MBA, Harvard U., 1961. Mfg. mgr. Procter & Gamble Mfg. Co., Dallas, Kansas City, Kans., 1956-59; rsch. asst. Harvard Bus. Sch., Boston, 1961-62; asst. to pres. Kaiser Aluminum & Chem. Corp., Oakland, Calif., 1962-64; mgr. fin. and pers., then gen. mgr. various divsns. Raychem Corp., Menlo Park, 1964-83, with office of pres., 1983-87, pres. Raynet Corp. subs., 1987-88, sr. v.p. telecomms. and tech., 1988-90, pres., CEO, 1990-95; ret. Raynet Corp. subs. Raychem Corp., 1995. Bd. dirs. Am. Leadership Forum. Mem. NCCJ (bd. dirs. Silicon Valley chpt.), Calif. Roundtable (dir. Bay Area Coun.), San Francisco Com. on Fgn. Rels., Commonwealth Club (bd. dirs.). Jewish. Avocations: sailing, skiing. Office: 27 Crescent Dr Palo Alto CA 94301-3106

SALDIN, THOMAS R. consumer products company executive, lawyer; b. 1946; BA, Carleton Coll., 1968; JD, Cin. Coll. Law, 1974. Law clk. to presiding justice U.S. Dist. Ct. (so. dist.) Ohio, 1974-76; assoc. Benjamin, Faulkner & Tepe & Sach, Cin., 1976-78; asst. gen. counsel Albertson's Inc., Boise, Idaho, 1978-81, v.p., gen. counsel, 1981-83, exec. v.p., adminstrv. gen. counsel, 1983—. Office: Albertson's Inc 250 E Parkcenter Blvd Boise ID 83706-3999

SALESKY, WILLIAM JEFFREY, corporate executive; b. Boston, June 12, 1957; s. Harry Michael Salesky and Eleanor Faith (Stutman) Spater; m. Cherri Lynne DeGreek, Nov. 27, 1982; 1 child, Joshua Steven. BS, U. Calif., Davis, 1978; MS, U. Calif., Berkeley, 1980, PhD, 1982. Co-op engr. Bechtel Corp. Inc., San Francisco, 1977-78; engr. U. Calif., Davis, 1978-79; rsch. assoc. Lawrence Berkeley Lab., 1979-82; project mgr. Smith Internat., Irvine, Calif., 1982-89; dir. engring. & quality assurance Mark Controls, Long Beach, 1989-94; v.p. engring. Stamet Inc., Gardena, 1994-97; pres., founder Skytron Corp., Irvine, 1997—; founder Skytron Mall TV Network, 1999—. Cons. Printnoix Corp., Irvine, Calif., 1988, Metal Alloys Inc., Irvine, 1986-88, Ceracon Inc., Irvine, 1984-86; chmn. L.A. Conf. on Fugitive Emissions from Valves, 1993. Patentee in field. Mgr. Irvine Baseball Assn., 1990; grad. asssembly rep. U. Calif., Berkeley, 1980-81; mem. race com. Internat. Am.'s Cup Class World Championship; mem. San Diego Crew Classic Race Com., 1992—; mem. Am.'s Cup Race Com., 1992, 95. Recipient Meritorious award Petroleum Engr. mag., 1988, award for outstanding contbns. Valve Mfrs. Assn. Am., 1993. Mem. ASTM, Am. Soc. Metals Internat. (bd. dirs. 1988-90, Earl Parker fellow 1981), Soc. Petroleum Engrs., Am. Petroleum Inst., South Shore Yacht Club (CFO 1989-91, bd. dirs. 1991-93). Avocation: yacht racing, golf. Office: Skytron Corp 16 Technology Dr Ste 169 Irvine CA 92618-2328 E-mail: bill@skytron.com

SALIBA, JACOB, manufacturing executive; b. East Broughton, Que., Can., June 10, 1913; s. Said and Nazira (David) S.; m. Adla Mudarri, May 31, 1942; children: John, Thomas, Barbara. BS, Boston U., 1941. Sr. supervising engr. Thompson and Lichtner Co., Boston, 1944-49; pres. Kingston Dress Co., Boston, 1949-51, Indsl. & Mgmt. Assocs., Inc., Boston, 1951-54, Maine Dress Co., Cornish, 1948-61; exec. v.p., mem. exec. com. Cortland Corp., Inc. (formerly Brockway Motor Co., Inc.), N.Y.C., 1954-59; exec. v.p. Sawyer-Tower, Inc., Boston, 1955-56, pres., 1956-59; v.p. Farrington Mfg. Co.; exec. v.p. Farrington Packaging Corp., 1959-61, Farrington Instruments Corp.; pres. N.E. Industries, Inc., from 1961, also bd. dirs.; pres. Fanny Farmer Candy Shops, Inc., 1963-66, W.F. Schrafft & Sons Corp., 1967-68; pres. frozen foods div. W.R. Grace & Co., 1966-68; pres. Katy Industries, Inc., Elgin, Ill., 1969-88, chmn., CEO, 1988-94. Chmn. bd. dirs. Schon & Cie; bd. dirs. Dresdner RCM Europe Fund NYSE, Katy Industries, NYSE; spl. cons. Air Material Commmand, USAF, Dayton, Ohio, 1942-43; cons. to chief air staff USAF, 1952-54; co-chmn. Air Force Spare Study Group, 1953. Mem. corp. Mass. Gen. Hosp., Mus. Sci. Mem. Union League Club, Bridgton Club, Highlands Country Club, Palm Beach Yacht Club. Methodist. Office: Katy Industries Inc 6300 S Syracuse Way Englewood CO 80111-6720 E-mail: salibagido@aol.com

SALINGER, CHARLES, dermatologist; b. N.Y.C. s. Ernest and Mae (Brenner) S.; m. Donna Marcia Gafford, May 14, 1974 (div. 1992); children: Jennifer, Jeffrey. BS, U. Wis., 1965; MD, SUNY, Syracuse, 1968. Lic. M.D., Calif. Intern Charity Hosp., La. State U., New Orleans, 1968-69, resident in dermatology, 1969-72; chief of dermatology USAF Maxwell Hosp., Montgomery, Ala., 1972-74; pvt. practice, dermatology La Mirada, Calif., 1974—. Chief med. staff La Mirada (Calif.) Cmty. Hosp., 1987-88; clin. assoc. prof. dermatology, Coll. Osteo. Medicine, Pomona, Calif., 1977—; trustee Med. Ctr. La Mirada, 1985-90. Major USAF, 1972-74. Fellow Am. Acad. Dermatology, Am. Soc. Dermatologic Surgery, Internat. Soc. Dermatologic Surgery, Pacific Dermatologic Assn., L.A. Met. Dermatologic Soc. (pres. 1994-95, bd. dirs. 1987-90); mem. AMA, Calif. Med. Assn., L.A. County Med. Assn. Jewish. Avocations: downhill skiing, Little League baseball (mgr.), quarterhorses, billfishing. Home: 5440 Emerywood Dr Buena Park CA 90621-1635 Office: 12675 La Mirada Blvd La Mirada CA 90638-2200

SALMON, BETH ANN, magazine editor in chief; b. Syracuse, N.Y., Oct. 1, 1969; d. Richard George and Sharon Dian (Clark) S. BFA, Emerson Coll., 1991. Editl. asst. Let's Live mag., L.A., 1994, asst. editor, 1994-95, editor in chief, 1995—. Author: (screenplays) Postcards, 1994, Watch Me, 1995. Office: Lets Live Magazine 11050 Santa Monica Blvd Los Angeles CA 90025-3594

SALMON, MATT, former congressman, communications company executive; b. Salt Lake City, Jan. 21, 1958; s. Robert James and Gloria (Aagard) S.; m. Nancy Huish, June, 1979; children: Lara, Jacob, Katie, Matthew. BA in English Lit., Ariz. State U., 1981; MA in Pub. Adminstrn., Brigham Young U., 1986. Mgr. pub. affairs U.S. West, Phoenix, 1988-94; mem. Ariz. State Senate, Mesa, 1990-94, U.S. Congress from 1st Ariz. dist., Washington, 1995-2001; mem. internat. rels. and sci. coms., asst. major whip; exec. v.p. APCO Worldwide, Scottsdale, Ariz., 2001—. Bd. dirs. Mesa United Way, 1990—, Ariz. Sci. Mus., 1992—. Recipient Outstanding Svc. award Ariz. Citizens with Disabilities, 1991, Excellence in Govt. award Tempe Ctr. for Handicapped, 1992; named Outstanding Young Phoenician, Phelps Dodge/Phoenix Jaycees, 1990, Outstanding Legislator, Mesa United Way, 1991. Republican. Mormon. Avocations: tennis, racquetball, cycling. Office: APCO Worldwide 6991 E Camelback Rd Ste D216 Scottsdale AZ 85251*

SALMON, TIMOTHY JAMES, professional baseball player; b. Long Beach, Calif., Aug. 24, 1968; Outfielder Anaheim Angels (formerly Calif. Angels), Anaheim, 1992—. Named Minor League Player of Yr. The Sporting News, 1992, Am. League Rookie of Yr., 1993, Pacific Coast League MVP, 1992, Am. League Rookie of Yr. Baseball Writer's Assn. of Am., 1993. Office: Anaheim Angels 2000 Gene Autry Way Anaheim CA 92806-6100

SALOMON, DARRELL JOSEPH, lawyer; b. Feb. 16, 1939; s. Joseph and Rosalie Rita (Pool) S.; m. Christine Mariscal, Apr. 25, 1992; 1 child, Camilla Lind. Student, Georgetown U., 1957-59; BS, U. San Francisco, 1964, JD, 1966. Bar: Calif. 1970, U.S. Dist. Ct. (cen. and no. dists.) Calif. 1970, U.S. Supreme Ct. 1971. Assoc. Offices of Joseph L. Alioto, San Francisco, 1970, 72, 73; dep. city atty. City of San Francisco, 1972; assoc. Salomon & Costello, 1981; ptnr. Hill, Farrer & Burrill, L.A., 1984-87, Arter & Hadden, L.A., 1987-94; assoc. Keck, Mahin & Cate, San Francisco, 1994-96; chmn. Commerce Law Group A Profl. Corp., 1996-99; chief asst. dist. atty. City of San Francisco, 2000; gen. counsel San Francisco Examiner, 2000—. Lectr. law Santa Clara U. Mem. Human Rights Commn. City and County of San Francisco, 1975; mem., past pres. Civil Svc. Commn., San Francisco, 1976-84; trustee San Francisco War Meml. and Performing Arts Ctr., 1984-88; bd. dirs. L.A. Symphony Master Chorale, 1985-87, Marin Symphony Assn., 1995-97. Recipient Disting. Svc. citation United Negro Coll. Fund, 1975; D'alton-Power scholar Georgetown U., 1957. Mem. ABA, Consumer Attys. of Calif. (bd. govs. 1977), Soc. Calif. Pioneers, L.A. Bar Assn., Chit Chat Club, San Francisco Lawyers Club. Office: San Francisco Examiner 988 Market St San Francisco CA 94124 E-mail: dsalomon@s.f.examiner.com

SALONER, GARTH, management educator; b. Johannesburg, South Africa, Jan. 18, 1955; came to U.S. 1978; s. Max and Rachel (Aronowitz) S.; m. Marlene Shoolman, Dec. 26, 1978; children: Amber, Romy, Kim. BCom, U. Witwatersrand, S. Africa, 1976; MBA, U. Witwatersrand, 1977; MS in Statistics, Stanford U., 1981, MA in Econs., PhD, 1982. Asst. lectr. U. Witwatersrand, 1977-78; asst. prof. econs. MIT, Cambridge, 1982-86, assoc. prof. econs. and mgmt., 1986-89, prof., 1990; vis. assoc. prof. bus. adminstrn. Harvard Bus. Sch., Boston, 1989-90; vis. asst. prof. Stanford (Calif.) U., 1986-87, prof. strategic mgmt. and econs. Grad. Sch. Bus., 1990—, Robert A Magowan prof., 1993-99, dir. rsch. and curriculum devel., 1993-96, assoc. dean for acad. affairs, 1994-96, co-dir. Ctr. Elec. Bus. & Commerce, 1999—, Jeffrey S. Skoll prof., 2000—. Bd. dirs. Brilliant Digital Entertainment, Next Stage Entertainment, Quick Response Svcs., Inc., Syntheon; rsch. assoc. Nat. Bur. Econ. Rsch., 1991—; mem. adv. bd. Voxeo, Talkie, eOneGlobal. Author: Strategic Management, 2001; assoc. editor Rand Jour. Econs., 1986-88, co-editor, 1988-95; assoc. editor Internat. Jour. Indsl. Orgn., 1988-95, Econs. of Innovation and New Tech., 1988-95, Strategic Mgmt. Jour., 1991-94; contbr. articles to profl. jours. Nat. fellow, Hoover Inst., 1986-87, Sloan fellow, 1987-89; grantee, NSF, 1982, 85, 88. Mem. Am. Econ. Assn., Acad. Mgmt. Jewish. Avocations: bicycling, photography. Home: 4151 Amaranta Ave Palo Alto CA 94306-3903 Office: Stanford U Grad Sch Bus Stanford CA 94305

SALTZ, HOWARD JOEL, newspaper editor; b. Bronx, N.Y., Apr. 11, 1960; s. Fred Raymond and Sheila Lois (Goldberg) S. BA in Liberal Arts, SUNY, Stony Brook, 1983. Reporter Greenwich Time, So. Conn. Newspapers divsn. Times Mirror, 1983-85; with MediaNews Group, 1985—, N.J. Advance, Dover, 1985-87, editor, 1987-88, Hamilton (Ohio) Jour.-News, 1988-89, Fremont (Calif.) Argus, 1989-91; editor Johnstown (Pa.) Tribune-Democrat MediaNews Group, 1991-96; dep. bus. editor Denver Post, 1996-98, dep. mng. editor features, 1998-2000, multimedia editor, 2000—. Adv. com. dept. journalism Ohlone Coll., Fremont, Calif., 1990-91. Bd. dirs. YMCA, Fremont-Newark, Calif., 1990-91, Johnstown Area Heritage Assn., 1991-93. Mem. Greater Johnstown C. of C. (bd. dirs. 1991 96), Soc. Profl. Journalists (bd. dirs. Northern Calif. chpt. 1990-91). Avocations: skiing, travel, scuba. Address: 535 Garfield St Denver CO 80206-4513 Office: Denver Post 1560 Broadway Denver CO 80202-5177 E-mail: hsaltz@denverpost.com

SALTZMAN, JOSEPH, journalist, producer, educator; b. L.A., Oct. 28, 1939; s. Morris and Ruth (Weiss) S.; m. Barbara Dale Epstein, July 1, 1962; children: Michael Stephen Ulysses, David Charles Laertes. BA, U. So. Calif., 1961; MS, Columbia U., 1962. Freelance writer, reporter, prodr., 1960—; reporter Valley Times Today, L.A., 1962-64; editor Pacific Palisades Palisadian Post, 1964; sr. writer-prodr. CBS-KNXT TV, L.A., 1964-74; freelance broadcast cons. L.A., 1974—; sr. prodr. investigative unit Entertainment Tonight, 1983; prof. journalism U. So. Calif., L.A., 1974—; assoc. dir. Sch. Journalism U. So. Calif. Annenberg, L.A., 1996-99, assoc. dean Annenberg Sch. for Comm., 1999—; sr. prodr. investigative unit Entertainment Tonight, 1983; dir. Image of the Journalist in Popular Culture project Norman Lear Ctr., Annenberg Sch. Comm., U. So. Calif., 2001—. CFO THe Jester & Pharley Phund. Documentaries include Black on Black, 1968, The Unhappy Hunting Ground, 1971, The Junior High School, 1971, The Very Personal Death of Elizabeth Schell-Holt-Hartford, 1972, Rape, 1972, Why Me?, 1974; spl. producer: Entertainment Tonight, 1983; supervising producer med. films, video, audio, 1984-93; assoc. mass media editor, columnist USA Today, 1983— ; syndicated columnist: King Features Syndicate, 1983-92; contbg. editor Emmy Mag., 1986-90, Roberts Reviewing Svc., 1964-95; others. Recipient AP certificates of excellence and merit, 1968, 72, 73, 74, 75, Edward R. Murrow awards for distinguished achievements in broadcast journalism, 1969, 72, Alfred I. duPont-Columbia U. award in broadcast journalism, 1973-74, Silver Gavel award Am. Bar Assn., 1973, Ohio State award Am. Exhbn. Ednl. Radio-Television Programs and Inst. for Edn. by Radio-TV Telecom. Ctr., 1974, Broadcast Media awards San Francisco State U., 1974, 75, Media award for excellence in comm. Am. Cancer Soc., 1976, Disting. Alumni award U. So. Calif., 1992; Seymour Berkson fellow, 1961; Robert E. Sherwood fellow, 1962; alt. Pulitzer traveling fellow, 1962-63. Mem. NATAS (regional Emmy awards 1965, 68, 74, 75), Radio-TV News Assn. (Golden Mike awards 1969, 71, 73, 75), Writers Guild Am., Greater Los Angeles Press Club (awards 1968, 74, 75), Columbia U., U. So. Calif. alumni assns., Skull and Dagger, Blue Key, Phi Beta Kappa, Sigma Delta Chi, Pi Sigma Alpha, Alpha Epsilon Rho. Home: 2116 Via Estudillo Palos Verdes Peninsula CA 90274-1931 Office: U So Calif Annenberg Sch Journalism Univ Park Los Angeles CA 90089-0001 E-mail: saltzman@usc.edu

SALVADORE, TONY, broadcast executive; V.p., gen. mgr, Sta. KNBR, San Francisco. Office: Sta KNBR 55 Hawthorne St San Francisco CA 94105-3906

SALZMAN, DAVID ELLIOT, entertainment industry executive; b. Bklyn., Dec. 1, 1943; s. Benjamin and Rose Harriet (Touby) S.; m. Sonia Camelia Gonsalves, Oct. 19, 1968; children: Daniel Mark, Andrea Jessica, Adam Gabriel. B.A., Bklyn. Coll., 1965; M.A., Wayne State U., 1967. Dir. TV ops. Wayne State U., 1966-67; producer Lou Gordon Program, 1967-70; program mgr. Sta. WKBD-TV, Detroit, 1970-71, Sta. KDKA-TV, Pitts., 1971-72, gen. mgr., 1973-75; program mgr. Sta. KYW-TV, Phila., 1972-73; chmn. bd. Group W Prodns., N.Y.C and Los Angeles, 1975—; founder, pres. United Software Assocs., 1980-81; creator News Info. Weekly Service, 1981; exec. v.p. Telepictures Corp., 1980-84, vice chmn., 1984; pres. Lorimar Telepictures Corp. (merger Telepictures and Lorimar, Inc.), 1985-90, Lorimar TV, 1986-90; creator Newscope: Nat. TV News Cooperative, 1983; pres., CEO David Salzman Entertainment, Burbank, Calif., 1990-93; co-CEO Quincy Jones-David Salzman Entertainment (QDE), 1993—; exec. prodr. Jenny Jones Show, 1991—. Exec. prodr. Mad-TV, In the House, 68th Ann. Acad. awards, Concert of the Americas,

1995, Vibe-TV, 1997-98, Steel, 1997; CEO David Salzman Enterprises, 1998—; co-owner Vibe Mag., 1995—, Spin Mag., 1995—, Sta. WNOL-TV, 1995—, Sta. WATL-TV, 1995—, Sta. KCWE-TV, 1995, Sta. WGRB-TV, 1998; bd. dirs. 411.com, Broadwave USA, Event in Radio, eMaiMai; guest lectr. at schs.; bd. govs. Films of Coll. and Univ. Students. Contbr. articles to Variety and numerous comms. trade publs. Bd. dirs. Pitts. Civic Light Opera, Am. Blood Bank, Pitts., Hebrew Inst., Jewish Community Ctr., Harrison, N.Y., Temple Etz Chaim, USC Sch. Cinema-TV, Emory U. Ctr. for Leadership, Emory Bus. Sch., Bklyn. Coll. Found., HELP group. Recipient award Detroit chpt. Am. Women in Radio and TV, 1969, award Golden Quill, 1971, award Golden Gavel, 1971, local Emmy award, 1972, award AP, 1974, Gold medal Broadcast Promotion Assn., 1983, Lifetime Achievement award Bklyn. Coll., 1990, Disting. Alumnus award, Golden Plate award Am. Acad. Achievement, 1995; BPME Gold medal San Francisco Film Festival, 1984, N.Y., 1985, Chgo., 1986, Tree of Life award Jewish Nat. Fund, 1988. Mem. Acad. TV Arts and Scis., Nat. Assn. TV Program Execs., Radio-TV News Dirs. Assn., Am. Mgmt. Assn., Am. Film Inst., Brooklyn Coll. Found. Office: Mad TV Hollywood Ctr Studios 2d Fl 1040 N Las Palmas Bldg 2 Hollywood CA 90038 E-mail: davvids@madtv.com

SAM, DAVID, federal judge; b. Hobart, Ind., Aug. 12, 1933; s. Andrew and Flora (Toma) S.; m. Betty Jean Brennan, Feb. 1, 1957; children: Betty Jean, David Dwight, Daniel Scott, Tamara Lynn, Pamela Rae, Daryl Paul, Angie, Sheyla. BS, Brigham Young U., 1957; JD, Utah U., 1960. Bar: Utah 1960, U.S. Dist. Ct. Utah 1966. Sole practice and ptnr., Duchesne, Utah, 1963-76; dist. judge State of Utah, 1976-85; judge U.S. Dist. Ct. Utah, Salt Lake City, 1985-97; chief judge U.S. Dist. Ct., Salt Lake City, 1997, sr. judge, 1999—. Atty. City of Duchesne, 1963-72; Duchesne County atty., 1966-72; commr. Duchesne, 1972-74; mem. adv. com. Codes of Conduct of Jud. Conf. U.S., 1987-91, Jud. Coun. of 10th Cir., 1991-93; mem. U.S. Del. to Romania, Aug. 1991. Chmn. Jud. Nomination Com. for Cir. Ct. Judge, Provo, Utah, 1983; bd. dirs. Water Resources, Salt Lake City, 1973-76. Served to capt. JAGC, USAF, 1961-63. Named Judge of Yr., Utah State Bar, 1999. Mem. Utah Bar Assn., Supreme Ct. Hist. Soc., Am. Inns of Ct. VII (counselor 1986-89), A. Sherman Christensen Am. Inn of Ct. I (counselor 1989-98), Utah Jud. Conf. (chmn. 1982), Utah Dist. Judges Assn. (pres. 1982-83), Order of Coif (hon. Brigham Young U. chpt.). Mem. LDS Ch. Avocations: beekeeping, reading, sports, cooking chinese food. E-mail: david. Office: US Dist Ct 148 US Courthouse 350 S Main St Ste 150 Salt Lake City UT 84101-2180 E-mail: sam@utd.uscourts.gov

SAMET, DEE-DEE, lawyer; b. Greensboro, N.C., Sept. 18, 1940; BA, U. Ariz., 1962, JD, 1963. Bar: Ariz. 1964. Ptnr. Samet & Gage, P.C., Tucson, 2001; pvt. practice Tucson, 2001—. Arbitrator U.S. Dist. Ct. Ariz., Gender Equality Task Force, 1993; judge pro tem Pima County Superior Ct., 1985—; Ninth Cir. Lawyer rep., 1990-93; mem. Jud. Performance Rev. Commn., 1996-99. Mem. State Bar Ariz. (family law sect., workers compensation sect., trial law sect., co-chair worker's compensation sect. 1988-89, gender bias task force, bd. govs. 1994-97, pres.-elect, pres. 1999-2000), Nat. Panel Arbitrators, Am. Arbitration Assn. (com. on exams., supreme ct. state Ariz. 1984-91), Pima County Bar Assn. (bd. dirs. 1994—), Nat. Assn. Coun. for Children, Ariz. Assn. Coun. for Children, So. Ariz. Fed. Bar Assn. (exec. com. 1995—), So. Ariz. Women Lawyers Assn. (bd. dirs. 1990, pres. 1994-95), Nat. Orgn. Social Security Claimants' Reps. Office: Dee-Dee Samet PC 717 N 6th Ave Tucson AZ 85705-8304

SAMET, JACK I. lawyer; b. N.Y.C., Aug. 6, 1940; s. William and Tillie (Katz) S.; m. Helen Ray, Feb. 12, 1967; 1 son, Peter Lawrence. BA, Columbia U., 1961; JD, Harvard U., 1964. Bar: N.Y. 1964, Calif. 1973. Assoc. Whitman & Ransom, N.Y.C., 1966-69, Hall, Casey, Dickler & Howley, N.Y.C., 1969-73; ptnr. Ball, Hunt, Hart, Brown & Baerwitz, L.A., 1973-81, Buchalter, Nemer, Fields & Younger, L.A., 1981-94, Baker & Hostetler, L.A., 1994—, mem. policy com., 1997-98; ptnr.-in-charge L.A., 1997-98. Arbitrator Nat. Assn. Securities Dealers, L.A., 1976—; speaker, panelist Calif. Continuing Edn. of Bar, 1988. Mem. ABA, Sports Club/L.A., Million Dollar Advocates Forum, Am. Bd. Trial Advocates. Avocations: exercise, reading. Home: 2741 Aqua Verde Cir Los Angeles CA 90077-1502 Office: Baker & Hostetler 333 S Grand Los Angeles CA 90017-3212 E-mail: jsamet@bakerlaw.com

SAMPLE, JOSEPH SCANLON, foundation executive; b. Chgo., Mar. 15, 1923; s. John Glen and Helen (Scanlon) S.; m. Patricia M. Law, Dec. 22, 1942 (div.); children: Michael Scanlon, David Forrest, Patrick Glen; m. Miriam Tyler Willing, Nov. 19, 1965. B.A., Yale U., 1947. Trainee, media analyst, media dir. Dancer-Fitzgerald-Sample, Inc., advt. agy., Chgo., 1947-50, v.p., media dir., 1952-53; pres. Mont. Television Network KTVQ, Billings, KXLF-AM-TV, Butte, Mont., KRTV, Great Falls, KPAX-TV, Missoula, 1955-84; dir., prodr. Yellowstone Pub. Radio KEMC, Billings, 1993—. Pres. Greater Mont. Found., 1986—; chmn. Wheeler Ctr. Mont State U., 1988—. Served with AUS, 1943-46. With U.S. Army, 1950-52. Mem. Rotary, Yellowstone Country Club, Port Royal Club, Hole in The Wall Golf Club, Hilands Golf Club, Naples Yacht Club. Home: 606 Highland Park Dr Billings MT 59102-1909 Office: 14 N 24th St Billings MT 59101-2422 E-mail: scatman01@msn.com

SAMPLE, STEVEN BROWNING, university executive; b. St. Louis, Nov. 29, 1940; s. Howard and Dorothy (Cunningham) S.; m. Kathryn Brunkow, Jan. 28, 1961; children: Michelle Sample Smith, Elizabeth Ann. BS, U. Ill., 1962, MS, 1963, PhD, 1965; DHULL (hon.), Canisius Coll., 1989; LLD (hon.), U. Sheffield, Eng., 1991; EdD (hon.), Purdue U., 1994; DHL (hon.), Hebrew Union Coll., 1994; DL (hon.), U. Nebr., 1995. Sr. scientist Melpar Inc., Falls Church, Va., 1965-66; assoc. prof. elec. engring. Purdue U., Lafayette, Ind., 1966-73; dep. dir. Ill. Bd. Higher Edn., Springfield, 1971-74; exec. v.p. acad. affairs, dean Grad. Coll., prof. elec. eng. U. Nebr., Lincoln, 1974-82; prof. elec. and computer engring. SUNY, Buffalo, 1982-91; pres. U. So. Calif., L.A., 1991—, prof. elec. engring., 1991—, Robert C. Packard pres.'s chair, 1995—. Bd. dirs. Santa Catalina Island Co., UNOVA, William Wrigley Jr. Co., Advanced Bionics, AMCAP/AMF; vice chmn., bd. dirs. Western N.Y. Tech. Devel. Ctr., Buffalo, 1982-91; chmn. bd. dirs. Calspan-UB Rsch. Ctr., Inc., Buffalo, 1983-91; mem. Calif. Coun. Sci. and Tech., Irvine, Calif., L.A. Bus. Advisors, Nat. Acad. of Engring., 1998—; cons. in field; bd. trustees U. So. Calif., 1991—, bd. overseers Keck Sch. Medicine. Contbr. articles to profl. jours.; patentee in field. Timpanist St. Louis Philharm. Orch., 1955-58; chmn. Western N.Y. Regional Econ. Devel. Coun., 1984-91; trustee U. at Buffalo Found., 1982-91, Studio Arena Theatre, Buffalo, 1983-91, Western N.Y. Pub. Broadcasting Assn., 1985-91; bd. dirs. Buffalo Philharm. Orch., 1982-91, Regenstrief Med. Found., Indpls., 1982—, Rsch. Found. SUNY, 1987-91; chmn. Gov.'s Conf. on Sci. and Engring. Edn., Rsch. and Devel., 1989-91; bd. dirs. L.A. chpt. World Affairs Coun., Hughes Galaxy Inst. Edn., L.A., 1991-94, Rebuild L.A. Com., L.A. Annenberg Metro Project, Coalition of 100 Club of L.A. Recipient Disting. Alumnus award Dept. Elec. Engring. U. Ill., 1980, citation award Buffalo Coun. on World Affairs, 1986, Engr. of Yr. award N.Y. State Soc. Profl. Engrs., 1985, Alumni Honor award Coll. Engring., U. Ill., 1985, Outstanding Elec. Engr. award Purdue U., 1993, Humanitarian award Nat. Conf. Christians and Jews, L.A., 1994, Hollzer Meml. award Jewish Fedn. Coun. Greater L.A., 1994, Eddy award L.A. County Econ. Devel. Corp., 2000; Sloan Found. fellow, 1962-63, NSF grad. fellow, 1963-65, Am. Coun. Edn. fellow Purdue U., 1970-71, NSF [illegible] IEEE (Outstanding Paper award 1976), Nat. Assn. State Univs. and Land-Grant Colls. (ednl. telecommunications com., 1982-83, chmn. coun. of pres. 1985-86, edn. and tech. com. 1986-87, exec. com. 1987-89), Coun. on Fgn. Rels., Assn. Pacific Rim Univs. (chmn., co-founder 1997—), Assn. Am. Univs. (vice chmn. 1997-98, chmn. 1998-99, exec. com. 1995—, tenure com. 1997—, assessing quality of univ. edn. and rsch. com. 2000—, co-chair task force on rsch. accountability 2001—), NAE. Episcopalian. Office: U So Calif Office of Pres University Park Adm 110 Los Angeles CA 90089-0012

SAMS, JOHN B., JR. career officer; BA, The Citadel, 1967; MA in Personnel Mgmt., Ctrl. Mich. U., 1977. Commd. 2d. lt. USAF, 1967, advanced through grades to lt. gen., 1996; pilot Mather AFB, 1969-71; squadron ops. officer Cam Ranh Bay Air Base, South Vietnam, 1971-72; instr. pilot Kincheloe AFB, Mich., 1972-74; inspection plans officer Norton AFB, Calif., 1974-76; various assignments Offutt AFB, Nebr., 1977-80, 82-84, Offutt AFB, 1987-88, The Pentagon, Washington, 1981-82, 94-95; asst. dep. comdr. Minot AFB, N.C., 1985-87; comdr. Carswell AFB, Tex., 1988-90, Maxwell AFB, Ala., 1990-91, Travis AFB, Calif., 1991-93, 98—, Scott AFB, Ill., 1993-94, 96-98; dir. plans and policy U.S. Atlantic Command, Norfolk, Va., 1995-96. Decorated DFC, Legion of Merit with two oak leaf clusters, Meritorious Svc. medal with oak leaf cluster, Air Medal with two oak leaf clusters.

SAMSON, ALVIN, former distributing company executive, consultant; b. N.Y.C., May 2, 1917; s. Morris and Jennie (Buitekant) S.; m. Ann Carol Furmansky, Aug. 15, 1942; children: Leslie Joan, Marla Adriane. Br. mgr. U.S. Hardware and Paper Co., 1947-51; mdse. mgr. U.S. Servateria, 1951-57; dir. purchasing U.S. Consumer Products, Los Angeles, 1959-64, v.p. ops., 1964-66, pres., 1966-72, San Diego, Bakersfield, Las Vegas, Phoenix, 1966-72, Zelman Co., Los Angeles, San Francisco and Las Vegas, 1968-72, Triple A Corp., Los Angeles, 1966-72, U.S. Consumer Products-Wesco Mdse., Los Angeles, 1972-74; v.p. APL Corp., N.Y.C., 1967-74; pres. USCP-WESCO, 1974-85; cons. A. Samson Cons., Beverly Hills, 1985-92; retired, 1992. Active USCG Aux., 1981—, divsn. capt., 1992—. With USAAF, 1942-45. Named Man of Year Housewares Club So. Calif., 1965 Mem. Nat. Assn. Service Merchandisers (dir. 1982-85)

SAMUELI, HENRY, electrical engineering educator, entrepreneur; b. Buffalo, Sept. 20, 1954; s. Aron and Sala (Traubman) S.; m. Susan Faye Eisenberg, Aug. 22, 1982; children: Leslie Pamela, Jillian Meryl, Erin Sydney. BS, UCLA, 1975, MS, 1976, PhD, 1980. Staff engr. TRW Inc., Redondo Beach, Calif., 1980-83, section mgr., 1983-85; asst. prof. UCLA, 1985-90, assoc. prof., 1990-94, prof., 1994—. Cons. TRW, Inc., Redondo Beach, 1985-89; co-founder, chief scientist PairGain Techs., Inc., Tustin, Calif., 1989-94; co-founder, chief tech. officer Broadcom Corp., Irvine, Calif., 1991—. Named one of Top 20 Entrepreneurs of 1997, The Red Herring Mag., 1997, one of Top 50 Cyber Elite, Time Digital Mag., 1997. Mem. IEEE, Sigma Xi, Tau Beta Pi. Republican. Jewish. Avocations: skiing, basketball. Office: Broadcom Corp PO Box 57013 Irvine CA 92619-7013

SAMUELS, DONALD L. lawyer; b. Washington, May 8, 1961; s. Jack Donald Samuels and Francis Diane (Katcher) Yeoman; m. Linda Marie Tveidt, Aug. 17, 1986. AB, Brown U., 1983; JD, Columbia U., 1986. Bar: Calif. 1986, U.S. Dist. Ct. (cen., no., ea. and so. dists.) Calif. 1988, U.S. Ct. Appeals (9th cir.) 1989, Colo. 1996, U.S. Ct. Appeals (7th cir.) 1996, U.S. Dist. Ct. Colo. 1997, U.S. Ct. Appeals (10th cir.) 1997, Tex. 1998. Law clk., L.A., 1986-87; assoc. Sidley & Austin, L.A., 1987-94, ptnr., 1994-95, Samuels & Samuels, L.A., 1995-97; officer, dir., shareholder Ireland & Stapleton, Denver, 1997—. Mem. ABA, Calif. Bar Assn., Colo. Bar Assn., Phi Beta Kappa. Home: 9931 E Progress Cir Greenwood Vlg CO 80111-3673 Office: Ireland & Stapleton Pryor & Pascoe PC 1675 Broadway Ste 2600 Denver CO 80202-4685 E-mail: dsamuels@irelandstapleton.com

SAMUELS, JOSEPH, JR. protective services official; b. 1949; m. Sabrina Samuels; 1 child, Joseph. BA in Psychology, Lincoln U.; MPA, Calif. State U., Hayward, 1988; student, Nat. Exec. Inst. Br. mgr. Household Fin. Corp.; with Oakland (Calif.) Police Dept., 1974-91, capt. patrol divsn., chief police, 1993-99, Fresno (Calif.) Police Dept., 1991-93, Richmond (Calif.) Police Dept., 1999—. Chair regional citizens adv. com. Calif. Youth Authority, 1986-91; former mem. Calif. State Commn. Crime, Juvenile Justice and Delinquency Prevention. Active YMCA, Oakland, East Oakland Youth Devel. Ctr., Oakland Citizens Com. Urban Renewal; mem. Fight Crime Invest in Kids, 1997. Mem. Nat. Orgn. Black Law Enforcement Execs., Calif. Peace Officers Assn., Calif. Police Chiefs Assn., Internat. Assn. Chiefs Police, Police Exec. Rsch. Forum. Office: Police Headquarters 401 27th St Richmond CA 94804-1769

SAMUELSON, DERRICK WILLIAM, lawyer; b. Mpls., July 24, 1929; s. Oscar W. and Ruth (Hill) S.; m. Diana L. Webster, Aug. 10, 1957; children: David W., Deirdre S. Columbia. B.S., U.S. Mil. Acad., 1951; LL.B., Harvard U., 1957. Bar: N.Y. 1958. Assoc. firm Lowenstein, Pitcher, Hotchkiss, Amann & Parr, N.Y.C., 1957-60; staff atty. internat. div. Warner-Lambert Pharm. Co., Morris Plains, N.J., 1960-63; counsel internat. div. Olin Mathieson Chem. Corp., N.Y.C., 1964-65; v.p., gen. counsel ITT World Communications Inc., N.Y.C., 1965-70, ITT Asia Pacific, Inc., N.Y.C., 1970-81; sr. counsel ITT Corp., N.Y.C., 1981-87, asst. gen. counsel, asst. sec., 1987-92; of counsel Mulvaney, Kahan & Barry, San Diego, 1993—. Mem. panel neutrals and internat. panel Am. Arbitration Assn., 1995—; mem. bd. arbitrators Nat. Assn. Securities Dealers, Inc., 1996—. Pres. Am-Indonesian C. of C., 1976-79, Smoke Rise Club, 1976-77, 88-89; chmn. Am. ASEAN Trade Coun., Inc., 1978-92. With U.S. Army, 1951-54. Home: 2940 Via Asoleado Alpine CA 91901-3182 Office: First Nat Bank Bldg 401 W A St San Diego CA 92101-7901 E-mail: dsamuelson@prodigy.net

SAMUELSON, PAMELA ANN, law educator; b. Seattle, Aug. 4, 1948; d. Peter David and Margaret Susanne (Green) S.; m. Robert J. Glushko, May 7, 1988; 1 child, Robert M. BA in History, U. Hawaii, 1971, MA in Polit. Sci., 1972; JD, Yale U., 1976. Bar: N.Y. 1977, U.S. Dist. Ct. (so. dist.) N.Y. 1977. Rsch. assoc. Vera Inst. of Justice, N.Y.C., 1976-77; assoc. Willkie Farr & Gallagher, N.Y.C., 1977-81; prin. investigator Software Engring. Inst., Pitts., 1985-86; asst. prof. Law Sch. U. Pitts., 1981-84, assoc. prof. Law Sch., 1984-87, prof. Law Sch., 1987-96; prof. law and info. mgmt. U. Calif. Law Sch./Sch. Info. Mgmt. and Sys., Berkeley, 1996—. Bd. dirs. Berkeley Ctr. for Law and Tech./U. Calif., Berkeley; vis. prof. Emory Law Sch., Atlanta, 1989-90, Cornell Law Sch., Ithaca, 1995-96; mem. Nat. Rsch. Coun. Study Com. on Intellectual Property Rights and Info. Infrastructure, 1998-2000. Contbr. articles to profl. jours. Bd. dirs. ACLU Greater Pitts., 1983-88, Electronic Frontier Found., 2000—. John D. and Catherine T. MacArthur Found. fellow, 1997, Pub. Policy fellow Electronic Frontier Found., 1997—; recipient Disting. Alumni award U. Hawaii, 2000. Mem. ABA (sci. and tech. sect.), Am. Intellectual Property Law Assn. (subcom. chair 1988-89), Assn. Am. Law Schs. (intellectual property sect.). Democrat. Avocations: gardening, reading. Office: U Calif Berkeley Sch Info Mgmt and Sys 102 South Hall #4600 Berkeley CA 94720-4600 E-mail: pam@sims.berkeley.edu

SANCHEZ, BERNADETTE M. state senator; Dem. senator dist. 26 [illegible] chair corps. and transp. Home: 7712 Ranchwood NW Albuquerque NM 87120 Office: NMex State Senate State Capitol Mail Rm Dept Santa Fe NM 87503 E-mail: senate@state.nm.us

SANCHEZ, GILBERT, retired academic administrator, microbiologist, researcher; b. Belen, N.Mex., May 7, 1938; s. Macedonio C. and Josephine H. Sanchez; m. Lorena T. Tabet, Aug. 26, 1961; children— Elizabeth, Phillip, Katherine B.S. in Biology, N.Mex. State U., 1961; Ph.D. in Microbiology, U. Kans., 1967. Research asst. U. Kans., Lawrence, 1963-67; research assoc., postdoctoral fellow Rice U., Houston, 1967-68; prof. N.Mex. Inst. Tech., Socorro, 1968-79; dean grad. studies Eastern N.Mex. U., Portales, 1979-83; v.p. acad. affairs U. So. Colo., Pueblo, 1983-85; pres. N.Mex. Highlands U., Las Vegas, 1985-95. Cons. NIH, NSF, Solvex Corp., Albuquerque, 1979-83; bd. dirs. Fed. Res. Bank, Denver. Contbr. numerous articles to profl. jours. Patentee in field Pres. Socorro Sch. Bd., 1974-79, Presbyn. Hosp. Bd., Socorro, 1977-79 Research grantee Dept. Army, 1976-79, N.Mex. Dept. Energy, 1979-83, NSF, 1979 Mem. Am. Soc. Microbiology, Am. Soc. Indsl. Microbiology, AAAS, Am. Assn. Univs. and Colls. (bd. dirs. 1988-90), Hispanic Assn. Univs. and Colls. (pres. 1986-89). Roman Catholic. Lodge: Rotary Avocations: auto mechanics; welding; woodworking; golf.

SANCHEZ, LEONEDES MONARRIZE WORTHINGTON (HIS ROYAL HIGHNESS DUKE DE LEONEDES OF SPAIN SICILY GREECE), fashion designer; b. Flagstaff, Ariz., Mar. 15, 1951; s. Rafael Leonedes and Margaret (Monarrize) S. BS, No. Ariz. U., 1974; studied, Fashion Inst. Tech., N.Y.C., 1974-75; AA, Fashion Inst. D&M, L.A., 1975; lic., La Ecole de la Chambre Syndical de la Couture Parisian, Paris, 1976-78; certificate, La Mason de Couture, Paris, 2000. Lic. in designing. Contract designer/asst. to head designer House of Bonnet, Paris, 1976—; dress designer-in-residence Flagstaff, 1978—; mem. faculty No. Ariz. U., Flagstaff, 1978-80; designer Ambiance, Inc., L.A., 1985—; designer Interiors by Leonedes subs. Studio of Leonedes Couturier, Ariz., 1977, Calif., 1978, London, Paris, 1978, Rome, 1987, Milan, Spain, 1989, Palazzo de Leonedes, 1998, designer Liturgical Vesture subs.; CEO Leonedes Internat., Design Consortium, Leonedes Internat. Ltd., 1999—; designer El Casillo de Nuevo Espana, Santa Fe, La Maison de Couture, Paris, 2000, La Maison de Couture de Leonedes Internat., Paris, 2001. Owner, CEO, designer Leonedes Internat., Ltd., London, Milan, Paris, Spain, Ambian Ariz, Calif., Appolonian Costuming, Ariz., London, Milan, Paris, El Castillo de Leonedes, Sevilla, Spain, Villa Apollonian de Leonedes, Mykonos, Greece, Palazzo de Leonedes Internat., Sicily; cons. House of Bonnet, Paris, 1976—, Bob Mackie, Studio City, Calif., 1974-75; CEO, designer artistical dir., Leonedes internat.; appointee commn. on religious antiquities Congregation on the Arts, The Vatican, Italy, 1998. Bd. dirs. Roman Cath. Social Svcs., 1985-86, Northland Crisis Nursery, 1985—; bd. dirs., chmn. Pine Country Transit, 1986-88; pres. Chicanos for Edn.; active master's swim program ARC, Ariz., 1979—; eucharistic min., mem. art and environ. com., designer liturgical vesture St. Pius X Cath. Ch.; vol. art tchr., instr. St. Mary's Regional Sch., Flagstaff, 1987-90, vol. art dir.; mem. Flagstaff Parks and Recreation Commn., 1994-96, citizens' adv. com. master plan, 1994-96; mem. cmty. bd. adv. com. Flagstaff Unified Sch. Dist., 1995; active Duke de Leonedes Found. de Nuevo Espana, Santa Fe, Duke de Leonedes Found. de Neuvo Espana, Santa Fe; prin. chair Duke de Leonedes Found., The Netherlands, 1995; de neuvo espana Duke de Leuedes Found., Santa Fe, N.Mex., 1996. Decorated Duke de Leonedes (Spain), 1994, His Royal Highness (Spain, Greece, Sicily), 1998; recipient Camellian Design award 1988, Atlanta. Mem. AAU (life, chairperson swimming Ariz. 1995, vice chairperson physique, mem. citizen adv. bd. parks and recreation, chairperson state of Ariz. physique, swimming, adv. to Olympic inquiry com., advisor to internat. Olympic com. on physique), Am. Film Inst., Am. Assn. Hist. Preservation, Costume Soc., Am. Nat. Physique Com., Internat. Consortium Fashion Designers, Nat. Cath. Ednl. Assn., La Legion de Honour de la Mode Parisienne, Social Register Assn., Phi Alpha Theta (historian 1972-73, pres. 1973-74), Pi Kappa Delta (pres. 1972-73, historian 1973-74). Republican. Avocations: body building, swimming. Office: El Castillo de Leonedes Seville Spain also: El Castillo de Nuevo Espana Santa Fe NM 87501 also: Villa de Apollonian de Leonedes Mykonos Greece

SANCHEZ, LORETTA, congresswoman; b. Anaheim, Calif., Jan. 7, 1960; BA, Chapman U., 1982; MBA, Am. U., 1984. With Orange County Transp. Authority, 1984-87, Fieldman Rolapp & Assocs., 1987-90; strategic mgmt. cons. Booz Allen & Hamilton; owner, operator AMIGA Advisors Inc.; mem. U.S. Congress from 46th Calif. dist., 1997—; mem. edn. and the workforce com., mem. armed svcs. com. Mem. Anaheim Rotary Club. Democrat. Office: US Ho of Reps 1230 Longworth Ho Office Bldg Washington DC 20515-0001*

SANCHEZ, MICHAEL STEVEN, state legislator, lawyer; b. Belen, N.Mex., Aug. 3, 1950; BA, JD, U. N.Mex., 1973. Pvt. practice, Loshunas, N.Mex., 1978—; mem. N.Mex. Senate, Dist. 29, Santa Fe, 1992—; mem. conservation com. N.Mex. Senate, Santa Fe, mem. jud. com. Dem. County chmn., 1986-92; bd. dirs. La Vida Felicidad, U. N.Mex. Oncology Bd. Mem. ATLA, N.Mex. Bar Assn., Valencia County Bar Assn., U. N.Mex. Alumni Assn., Moose, Elks. Democrat. Home: 3 Bunton Rd Belen NM 87002-8293

SANCHEZ, RAYMOND G. state legislator; b. Albuquerque, Sept. 22, 1941; s. Gillie and Priscilla S.; 1 child, Raymond Michael. BA, U. N.Mex., 1964, JD, 1967. Bar: N. Mex. 1967. Practice law, Albuquerque; mem. N.Mex. Ho. of Reps., 1970—; speaker N. Mex. Ho. of Reps., 1983-84, 87-88, 92—; mem. judiciary com., rules and order of bus. com., voters and elections com.; interim mem. workers compensation, legis. reform study coms., legis. coun. Bd. dirs. New Mex. Amigos, N.Mex. Diamond Jubilee/U.S. Constl. Bicentennial Commn., New Mex. First, Albuquerque Com. Fgn. Rels., N. Valley Neighborhood Assn. Mem. Nat. Assn. Latino Elected and Apptd. Ofcls. (bd. dirs.), Alameda Optimist Club (bd. dirs., charter mem.), U. N.Mex. Sch. Law Alumni Assn. (bd. dirs.), Elks Club, Sigma Xi. Democrat. Avocations: handball, scuba diving, swimming, spectator sports. Office: State Capitol House of Reps Office of Speaker Santa Fe NM 87501 also: PO Box 1966 Albuquerque NM 87103-1966

SAND, THOMAS CHARLES, lawyer; b. Portland, Oreg., June 4, 1952; s. Harold Eugene and Marian Anette (Thomas) S.; m. Rhonda Diane Laycoe, June 15, 1974; children: Kendall, Taylor, Justin. Student, Centro des Artes y Lenguas, Cuernavaca, Mex., 1972; BA in English, U. Oreg., 1974; JD, Lewis and Clark Coll., 1977. Bar: Oreg. 1977, U.S. Dist. Ct. Oreg. 1977, U.S. Ct. Appeals (9th cir.) 1984. Assoc. Miller, Nash, LLP, Portland, 1977-84, ptnr., 1984—, mng. ptnr., 1999—. Mem. Oreg. State Bar Com. on Professionalism, 1989, chmn., 1990; dir. young lawyers divsn. Multnomah County Bar Assn., 1980; spl. asst. atty. gen. Wasco County 1983 Gen. Election; speaker in field. Contbr. articles to legal jours. Mem. U.S. Dist. Ct. of Oreg. Hist. Soc., 1990—; bd. dirs. Portland Area coun. Camp Fire, Inc., 1978-90,pres., 1984-86; bd. dirs. Oreg. Indoor Invitational Track Meet, Inc., 1982-84. Recipient Boss of the Yr. award Portland Legal Secs. Assn., 1989. Mem. ABA (securities litigation com., subcom. on broker-dealer litigation), Oreg. Bar Assn., Multnomah Bar Assn. (bd. dirs. task force on structure and orgn. 1989, chmn. com. on professionalism 1988, nominating com. 1986, participating atty. in N.E. legal clin. Vol Lawyers project, award of merit for svc. to profession 1988), Securities Industry Assn. (compliance and legal divsn.), Northwestern Sch. of Law, Lewis and Clark Coll. Alumni Assn. (bd. dirs. 1992, pres. 1997), Valley Comm. Presbyterian Ch., Multnomah Athletic Club, Portland Golf Club. Avocations: golf, guitar, camping, river rafting, children's sports. Office: Miller Nash LLP 111 SW 5th Ave Ste 3500 Portland OR 97204-3699

SANDAGE, ALLAN REX, astronomer; b. Iowa City, June 18, 1926; s. Charles Harold and Dorothy (Briggs) S.; m. Mary Lois Connelley, June 8, 1959; children: David Allan, John Howard. AB, U. Ill., 1948, DSc (hon.), 1967; PhD, Calif. Inst. Tech., 1953; DSc (hon.), Yale U., 1966, U. Chgo., 1967, Miami U., Oxford, Ohio, 1974, Graceland Coll., Iowa, 1985; LLD (hon.), U. So. Calif., 1971; D (hon.), U. Chile, 1992. Astronomer Mt. Wilson Obs., Palomar Obs., Carnegie Instn., Washington, 1952—; Peyton fellow Princeton U., 1952; asst. astronomer Hale Obs., Pasadena, Calif., 1952-56; astronomer Obs. Carnegie Instn., Pasadena, 1956—; sr. rsch. astronomer Space Telescope Sci. Inst. NASA, Balt., 1986—; Homewood Prof. of physics Johns Hopkins U., Balt., 1987-89. Vis. lectr. Harvard U., 1957; mem. astron. expdn. to South Africa, 1958; cons. NSF, 1961-64; Sigma Xi nat. lectr., 1966; vis. prof. Mt. Stromlo Obs., Australian Nat. U., 1968-69; vis. rsch. astronomer U. Basel, 1985, 92, vis. prof., 1994; vis. rsch. astronomer U. Calif., San Diego, 1985-86; vis. astronomer U. Hawaii, 1986; Lindsey lectr. NASA Goddard Space Flight Ctr., 1989; Jansky lectr. Nat. Radio Astron. Obs., 1991; Grubb-Parsons lectr. U. Durham, Eng., 1992. Assoc. edit. Ann. Rev. Astronomy and Astrophysics, 1990—. With USNR, 1944-45. Recipient Helen Warner prize Am. Astron. Soc., 1960, Russell prize, 1973, Pope Pius XI Gold medal Pontifical Acad. Sci., 1966, Rittenhouse medal, 1968, Presdl. Nat. Medal of Sci., 1971, Adon medal Obs. Nice, 1988, Crafoord prize Swedish Royal Acad. Scis., 1991, Tomalla Gravity prize Swiss Phys. Soc., 1993, Peter Gruber Found. prize for cosmology, 2000; Fulbright-Hays scholar, 1972. Mem. Lincei Nat. Acad. (Rome), Royal Astron. Soc. (Eddington medal 1963, Gold medal 1967), Astron. Soc. Pacific (Gold medal 1975), Royal Astron. Soc. Can., Franklin Inst. (Elliott Cresson medal 1973, Gruber Cosmology prize 2000), Am. Philos. Soc., Royal Soc. London (fgn.), Phi Beta Kappa. Home: 8319 Josard Rd San Gabriel CA 91775-1003 Office: 813 Santa Barbara St Pasadena CA 91101-1232

SANDERS, ADRIAN LIONEL, educational consultant; b. Paragould, Ark., Aug. 3, 1938; s. Herbert Charles and Florence Theresa (Becherer) S.; m. Molly Jean Zecher, Dec. 20, 1961. AA, Bakersfield Coll., 1959; BA, San Francisco State U., 1961; MA, San Jose State U., 1967. 7th grade tchr. Sharp Park Sch., Pacifica, Calif., 1961-62; 5th grade tchr. Mowry Sch., Fremont, 1962-64; sci. tchr. Blacow Sch., Fremont, 1964-76; 5th grade tchr. Warm Springs Sch., Fremont, 1977-87, 5th grade gifted and talented edn. tchr., 1987-94; edn. cons., 1994—. Mem. San Diego Hist. Soc., 1999, Nat. Geog. Soc., Washington, 1976—, Alzheimer's Family Relief Program, Rockville, Md., 1986; vol. 7 km. Race for Alzheimer's Disease Willow Glen Founders Day, San Jose, 1988-92. Named Outstanding Young Educator, Jr. C. of C., Fremont, Calif., 1965. Mem. Zoolog. Soc. San Diego, Calif. Ctr. for the Arts (Escondido). Avocations: photography, travelling, visiting presidents' birthplaces, collecting license plates, collecting matchbooks worldwide. Home and Office: 1437 Stoneridge Cir Escondido CA 92029-5514

SANDERS, AUGUSTA SWANN, retired nurse; b. Alexandria, La., July 22, 1932; d. James and Elizabeth (Thompson) Swann; m. James Robert Sanders, Jan. 12, 1962 (div. 1969). Student, Morgan State U., 1956. RN. Pub. health nurse USPHS, Washington, 1963-64; mental health counselor Los Angeles County Sheriff's Dept., 1972-79; program coordinator Los Angeles County Dept. Mental Health, 1979-88; program dir. L.A. County Dept. Health Svcs., 1989-92; ret., 1992. Apptd. by Calif. Gov. Jerry Brown to 11th Dist. Bd. Med. Quality Assurance, 1979-85; health cons., legal, 1994—; motivational spkr. Mem. Assemblyman Mike Roo's Commn. on Women's Issues, 1981-86, Senator Diane Watson's Commn. on Health Issues, 1979-85; chmn. Commn. Sex Equity L.A. Unified Sch. Dist., 1984-90; bd. dirs., sec. High Desert chpt. ARC, 1998. Named Woman of Yr., Crenshaw-Latijera Local Orgn., 1988, Wilshire Local Orgn., 1990, Victor Valley Local Orgn., 1994. Mem. NAFE, Los Angeles County Employees Assn. (v.p. 1971-72), So. Calif. Black Nurses Assn. (founding mem.), Internat. Fedn. Bus. and Profl. Women (pres. L.A. Sunset dist. 1988-89, dist. officer 1982-89, Calif. v.p. membership and mktg. 1995-96), Internat. Assn. Chem. Dependency Nurses (treas. 1990-92), Victor Valley Bus. and Profl. Women (pres. 1997-98), High Desert LWV (founder), High Desert Intercoun. Women's Orgns., Nat. Coun. of Negro Women, Am. C. of C. (adminstrn.-ednl. chmn.), Victor Valley African Am. C. of C. (edn. com.), Apple Valley C. of C., High Desert Investment Club (chmn. 1998-99), Chi Eta Phi. Democrat. Methodist. Avocations: travelling, crocheting, movies, concerts, plays.

SANDERS, CHARLES FRANKLIN, management and engineering consultant; b. Louisville, Dec. 22, 1931; s. Charles Franklin and Maragret Rhea (Timmons) S.; m. Marie Audrey Galuppo, Dec. 29, 1956; children: Karen Lynn, Craig Joseph, Keith Franklin. B.Chem. Engring., U. Louisville, 1954, M.Chem. Engring., 1958; Ph.D., U. So. Calif., 1970. Research engr. Exxon Research and Engring. Co., Linden, N.J., 1955-62; asst. prof. engring. Calif. State U., Northridge, 1962-68, assoc. prof., 1968-71, prof., 1971-82, chmn. dept., 1969-72, dean Sch. Engring. and Computer Sci., 1972-81; pres., chief exec. officer, dir. Rusco Industries, Los Angeles, 1981-82; exec. v.p. Energy Systems Assocs., Tustin, Calif, 1982-89, Energeo, San Francisco, 1989-95, also bd. dirs.; v.p. tech. Smith-Bellingham Capital, San Francisco, 1989-91. Bd. dirs. Clean-Air Technology, Inc., L.A., 1997-99, Applied Tech. Solutions, Inc., Costa Mesa, Calif. Bd. dirs. San Fernando Valley Child Guidance Clinic, 1979-81. Served to 1st lt. U.S. Army, 1956-57. NSF fellow, 1965-67 Mem. AIChE, NSPE, SAE, Calif. Soc. Profl. Engrs., Am. Soc. for Engring. Edn. Republican. E-mail: cfs@home.com, cfs@atsusa.net

SANDERS, ELIZABETH ANNE WEAVER (BETSY SANDERS), management consultant; b. Gettysburg, Pa., July 25, 1945; Student, Gettysburg (Pa.) Coll., 1963-65; BA in German Lang. and Linguistics, Wayne State U., 1967; MEd, Boston U., 1970; postgrad., U. Wash., 1976-78. Prin. The Sanders Partnership, Sutter Creek, Calif., 1971-90; founder, dir. Nat. Bank So. Calif., 1971-90; v.p., gen. mgr. Nordstrom Inc.; prin. The Sanders Partnership, Sutter Creek, Calif. Bd. dirs. Wal Mart Stores, Inc., Washington Mut., Wellpoint Health Sys., Inc., Wolverine Worldwide, Inc., Advantica Restaurant Group, H.F. Ahmanson Co., Carl Karcher Enterprises, Sport Chalet, St. Joseph Health Sys. Trustee Gettysburg Coll. Recipient Woman of Achievement in Bus. award YWCA South Orange County, Director's Choice award, 1997; named Woman of Yr. Bus. and Industry YWCA North Orange County, Humanitarian of Yr. NCCJ, Author of Yr., 1996. Mem. Internat. Women's Forum. Office: The Sanders Partnership PO Box 14 Sutter Creek CA 95685-0014

SANDERS, JACK THOMAS, religious studies educator; b. Grand Prairie, Tex., Feb. 28, 1935; s. Eula Thomas and Mildred Madge (Parish) S.; m. M. Patricia Chism, Aug. 9, 1959 (dec. Oct. 1973); 1 son, Collin Thomas; m. Susan Elizabeth Plass, Mar. 3, 1979. B.A., Tex. Wesleyan Coll., 1956; M.Div., Emory U., 1960; Ph.D., Claremont Grad. Sch., 1963; postgrad., Eberhard-Karls U., Tuebingen, Germany, 1963-64. Asst. prof. Emory U., Atlanta, 1964-67, Garrett Theol Sem., Evanston, Ill., 1967-68, McCormick Theol. Sem., Chgo., 1968-69; assoc. prof. U. Oreg., Eugene, 1969-75, prof., 1975-97, head dept. religious studies, 1973-80, 85-90, prof. emeritus, 1997—. Author: The New Testament Christological Hymns, 1971, Ethics in the New Testament, 1975, 2d edit., 1986, Ben Sira and Demotic Wisdom, 1983, The Jews in Luke-Acts, 1987, Schismatics, Sectarians, Dissidents, Deviants: The First One Hundred Years of Jewish-Christian Relations, 1993, Charisma, Converts, Competitors: Societal and Sociological Factors in the Success of Early Christianity, 2000; editor: Gospel Origins and Christian Beginnings, 1990, Gnosticism and the Early Christian World, 1990; mem. edit. bd. Jour. Bibl. Lit., 1977-83. Mem. policy bd. Dept. Higher Edn. Nat. Council Chs., N.Y.C., 1971-73. NDEA grad. study fellow, 1960-63; Fulbright Commn. fellow, 1963-64; Am. Council Learned Socs. travel grantee, 1981; NEH fellow, 1983-84 Mem. AAUP (chpt. pres. 1981-82), Studiorum Novi Testamenti Soc., World Union Jewish Studies, Assn. for Jewish Studies, Soc. Bibl. Lit. (regional sec. 1969-76, sabbatical rsch. award 1976-77), Archeol. Inst. Am. (chpt. pres. 1988-89), Soc. for Sci. Study of Religion, Assn. for Sociology Religion. Democrat. Home: 2555 Birch Ln Eugene OR 97403-2191 Office: U Oregon Dept Religious Studies Eugene OR 97403 E-mail: jsanders@uoregon.edu

SANDERS, JAMES ALVIN, minister, religious studies educator; b. Memphis, Nov. 28, 1927; s. Robert E. and Sue (Black) S.; m. Dora Cargille, June 30, 1951; 1 son, Robin David. BA magna cum laude, Vanderbilt U., 1948, BD with honors, 1951; student, U. Paris, 1950-51; PhD, Hebrew Union Coll., 1955; DLitt, Acadia U., 1973; STD, U. Glasgow, 1975; DHL, Coe Coll., 1988, Hebrew Union Coll., 1988, Hastings Coll., 1996, Calif. Luth. U., 2000. Ordained teacher Presbyn. Ch., 1955; instr. French Vanderbilt U., 1948-49; faculty Colgate Rochester Div. Sch., 1954-65, assoc. prof., 1957-60, Joseph B. Hoyt prof. O.T. interpretation, 1960-65; prof. O.T. Union Theol. Sem., N.Y.C., 1965-70, Auburn prof. Bibl. studies, 1970-77; adj. prof. Columbia, N.Y.C., 1966-77; prof. Bibl. studies Sch. Theology and Grad. Sch., Claremont, Calif., 1977-97; vis. prof. Union Theol. Seminary and Columbia U., 1997-98, Yale Divinity Sch., 1998, Jewish Theol. Seminary, 2001. Ann. prof. Jerusalem Sch. of Am. Schs. Oriental Rsch., 1961-62; fellow Ecumenical Isnt., Jerusalem, 1972-73, 85; Ayer lectr., 1971, 79, Shaffer lectr., 1972, Fondren lectr., 1975, Currie lectr., 1976, McFadin lectr., 1979, Colwell lectr., 1979; guest lectr. U. Fribourg, Switzerland, 1981, 90, Hebrew Union Coll., 1982, 88, Oral Roberts U., 1982, Tulsa U., 1982, Ind. U., 1982, Coe Coll., 1983, Garrett Sem., 1984, Pepperdine U., 1985, Western Sem., 1985, Bethany Sem., 1986; lectr. Union Sem. Sesquicentennial, 1987, U. Wis., 1987, U. Chgo., 1987; Gray lectr. Duke U., 1988; guest lectr. Notre Dame U., Georgetown U., Tex. Christian U., 1989, Alexander Robertson lectr. U. Glasgow, 1990-91, Gustavson lectr. United Theol. sem., 1991; assoc. program lectr. Smithsonian, 1990, Am. Bible Soc. Sesquicentennial, 1991, U. N.Mex., 1992, 94, 97, Am. Interfaith Inst., 1992, Georgetown U., 1992; Lily Rosmen lectr. Skirball Mus., 1992; vis. prof. U. N.Mex., 1992, Southwestern U., 1992, Calif. Luth. U., 1992, 94, Willamette U., 1993, Peter Craigie lectr. U. Calgary, 1993, U. So. Ariz., 1993; Samuel Iwry lectr. John Hopkins U., 1993; lectr. San Diego State U., 1994, Creighton U., 1995, The Mercantile Libr., N.Y.C., 1995, U. Heidelberg, Germany, 1995, U. Mich., 1995; session chair, Internat. Congress for Fiftieth Anniversary of Dead Sea Scrolls, Jerusalem, 1997; Womack lectr. The Methodist Coll., 1996; Purcell lectr. Barton Coll., 1997, Vatican Symposium, 1999, Temple Emanu-El, 1999; mem. internat. O.T. text critical com. United Bible Socs., 1969—; mem. nat. adv. acad. bd. Hebrew Union Coll., 1997—; bd. dirs. Mobilization for the Human Family, 1998—; exec. officer Ancient Bibl. Manuscript Ctr. for Preservation and Rsch., 1977-80, pres., 1980—, VIS. PROF., Jewish Theological Seminary, 2001—. Author: Suffering as Divine Discipline in the Old Testament and Post-Biblical Judaism, 1955, The Old Testament in the Cross, 1961, The Psalms Scroll of Qumran Cave 11, 1965, The Dead Sea Psalms Scroll, 1967, Near Eastern Archaeology in the Twentieth Century, 1970, Torah and Canon, 1972, 74, Identité de la Bible, 1975, God Has a Story Too, 1979, Canon and Community, 1984, From Sacred Story to Sacred Text, 1987, Luke and Scripture, 1993; editor: Paul and the Scriptures of Israel, 1993, Early Christian Interpretation of the Scriptures of Israel, 1997, The Function of Scripture in Early Jewish and Christian Tradition, 1998; contbr. over 250 articles to profl. jours.; mem. editorial bd. Jour. Bibl. Lit., 1970-76, Jour. for Study Judaism, Bibl. Theology Bull., Interpretation, 1973-78, New Rev. Standard Version Bible Com.; 2 vols. of essays: A Gift of God in Due Season, 1996, The Quest for Context and Meaning, 1997 pub. in honor of Sanders' retirement. Trustee Am. Schs. Oriental Research. Fulbright grantee, 1950-51, Lilly Endowment grantee, 1981, NEH grantee, 1980, 91-92; Lefkowitz and Rabinowitz interfaith fellow, 1951-53, Rockefeller fellow, 1953-54, 85, Guggenheim fellow, 1961-62, 72-73, Human Scis. Rsch. fellow, 1989. Mem. Soc. Bibl. Lit. and Exegesis (pres. 1977-78), Phi Beta Kappa, Phi Sigma Iota, Theta Chi Beta. Home: PO Box 593 Claremont CA 91711-0593 Office: Ancient Bible Manuscript Ctr 1325 N College Ave Claremont CA 91711-3154 E-mail: SandersJA@aol.com

SANDERS, JERRY, social services executive; b. San Pedro, Calif., July 14, 1950; m. Rana Sampson; children: Jamie, Lisa. AA, Long Beach City Coll., 1970; BA in Pub. Adminstrn., Nat. U., 1988; student, San Diego State U. Cert. P.O.S.T mgmt. Police officer San Diego Police Dept., 1973-93, chief of police, 1993-99; pres. United Way San Diego, 1999—. Bd. dirs. The Nat. Conf., San Diego State U. Cmty. Adv. Bd., Children's Initiative, Youth Econ. Enterprise Zones; mem. cmty. leaders adv. bd. ElderHelp of San Diego. Recipient Headliner of Yr. award San Diego Press Club, 1984, 93, Exceptional Performance citation for SWAT leadership, 1986. Office: United Way 4699 Murphy Canyon Rd San Diego CA 92123-5371

SANDERS, NANCY IDA, writer; b. Everett, Pa., May 17, 1960; d. Richard J. and Phyllis (Harden) Hershberger; m. Jeffrey L. Sanders, May 23, 1982; children: Daniel M., Benjamin L. Freelance writer, 1985—. Editor TCC Manuscript Svc.; contbg. editor The Christian Communicator, 1992-2000; leader Chino Hills Writers Critique Group. Author: Favorite Bible Heroes: Activities for Ages 4 and 5, 1993, Bible Crafts on a Shoestring Budget for Grades 3 and 4, 1993, Amazing Bible Puzzles: Old Testament, 1993, Amazing Bible Puzzles: New Testament, 1993, Jumbo Bible Bulletin Boards: More Bible Stories for Preschool and Primary, 1994, Jumbo Bible Bulletin Boards: Fall and Winter, Preschool and Primary, 1994, Jonah: Six Fun Surprises, 1994, Moses: Six Fun Surprises, 1994, My Book About Ben and Me, 1994, My Book About Sara and Me, 1994, Cents-ible Bible Crafts, 1995, The Fall into Sin, 1995, Jesus Walks on the Water, 1995, WA-A-A-AY COOL Bible Puzzles, 1996, Red Hot Bible Puzzles, 1996, Marshal Matt and the Slippery Snacks Mystery, 1996, Marshal Matt and the Case of the Secret Code, 1996, Marshal Matt and the Topsy-Turvy Trail Mystery, 1996, Marshal Matt and the Puzzling Prints Mystery, Marshall Matt and the Case of the Freezing Fingers, 1997, Archy's Adventures with Colors, 1998, Archy's Adventure with Numbers, 1998, Archy's Alphabet Adventure, 1998, Unforgettable Edible Bible Crafts, 1999, Old Testament Days, 1999, Bible Crafts and More, 1999, Lost and Found, 2000, Hidden Treasure, 2000, Comet Campout, 2000, Moon Rocks and Dinosaur Bones, 2000, IS Irrestible Mini-Plays for Teaching Math, 2000, Can't Catch Me!, 2000, Off the Fair, 2000, Cooks, Cakes, and Chocolate Milkshakes, 2000, The Super Duper Seed Surprise, 2000, A Kid's Guide to African American History, 2000, Just Right Science Plays for Emergent Readers, 2001, (with Jeff Sanders) American History Mini-Books, 2001, Word Family Mini-Books, 2001, Fresh and Fun, 2001, The Pet I'll Get, 2001, My Many Hats, 2001, Kingdon Kidz: Noah, 2001, Kingdom Kidz: King Solomon, 2001, Kingdom Kidz: Zacchaeus, 2001, Kingdom Kidz, Martha and Mary, 2001; asst. editor: Trails 'N' Treasure, Christian Magazine for Kids, 1998-99. Mem. Soc. Children's Book Writers and Illustrators. Home: 15212 Mariposa Ave Chino Hills CA 91709-2703

SANDERS, RICHARD BROWNING, state supreme court justice; b. Tacoma; 1 child: Laura. BA, U. Wash., 1966, JD, 1969. Assoc. Murray, Scott, McGavick & Graves, Tacoma, 1969, Caplinger & Munn, Seattle, 1971; hearing examiner State Wash., Olympia, 1970; pvt. practice Wash., 1971-95; justice Wash. Supreme Ct., Olympia, 1995—. Adj. prof. U. Wash. Sch. Law; lectr. in field. Contbr. articles to profl. jours. Office: Supreme Court of Washington Temple Justice PO Box 40929 Olympia WA 98504-0929 Fax: (360) 357-2092. E-mail: j_r.sanders@courts.wa.gov

SANDERSON, DAVID R. physician; b. South Bend, Ind., Dec. 26, 1933; s. Robert Burns and Alpha (Rodenberger) S.; divorced, 1978; children: David, Kathryn, Robert, Lisa; m. Evelyn Louise Klunder, Sept. 20, 1980. BA, Northwestern U., 1955, MD, 1958. Cons. in medicine Mayo Clinic, Rochester, Minn., 1965-87, chmn. dept. thoracic disease, 1977-87, cons. in medicine Scottsdale, Ariz., 1987—, chmn. dept. internal medicine, 1988-96, vice chmn. bd. govs., 1987-94. Assoc. dir. Mayo Lung Project, Nat. Cancer Inst., Rochester. Contbr. articles to profl. jours. Recipient Noble award Mayo Found., Rochester, Chevalier Jackson award Am. Bronchoesophagologic Assn., 1990. Fellow ACP, Am. Coll. Chest Physicians (gov. for Minn. 1981-87); mem. Am. Bronchoesophagologic Assn., World Assn. for Bronchology, Internat. Bronchoesophagologic Assn., Internat. Assn. Study of Lung Cancer, AMA, Sigma Xi, Sigma Chi (Significant Sig award 1989). Presbyterian. Home: 10676 E Bella Vista Dr Scottsdale AZ 85258-6086 Office: Mayo Clinic Scottsdale 13400 E Shea Blvd Scottsdale AZ 85259-5499 E-mail: dsanderson958@md.nwu.edu

SANDLER, HERBERT M. retired savings and loan association executive; b. N.Y.C., Nov. 16, 1931; s. William B. and Hilda (Schattan) S.; m. Marion Osher, Mar. 26, 1961. BSS, CCNY, 1951; JD, Columbia U., 1954. Bar: N.Y. 1956. Asst. counsel Waterfront Commn. N.Y. Harbor, 1956-59; ptnr. firm Sandler & Sandler, N.Y.C., 1960-62; pres., dir., mem. exec. com. Golden West Savs. & Loan Assn. and Golden West Fin. Corp., Oakland, Calif., 1963-75; co-chmn. bd., co-CEO, dir., mem. exec. com. World Savs. & Loan Assn. and Golden West Fin. Corp., Oakland, 1975—. Charter mem. Thrift Instns. Adv. Coun., to Fed. Res. Bd., 1980-81; former chmn. Legis. and Regulation Com. Calif. Savs. and Loan League; former mem. bd. dirs. Fed. Home Loan Bank, San Francisco. Pres., trustee Calif. Neighborhood Services Found.; chmn. Urban Housing Inst.; mem. policy adv. bd. Ctr. for Real Estate and Urban Econs. U. Calif., Berkeley. With U.S. Army, 1954-56. Office: Golden West Fin Corp 1901 Harrison St Oakland CA 94612-3588

SANDLER, MARION OSHER, retired savings and loan association executive; b. Biddeford, Maine, Oct. 17, 1930; d. Samuel and Leah (Lowe) Osher; m. Herbert M. Sandler, Mar. 26, 1961. BA, Wellesley Coll., 1952; postgrad., Harvard U.-Radcliffe Coll., 1953; MBA, NYU, 1958; LLD (hon.), Golden Gate U., 1987. Asst. buyer Bloomingdale's (dept. store), N.Y.C., 1953-55; security analyst Dominick & Dominick, N.Y.C., 1955-61; sr. fin. analyst Oppenheimer & Co., N.Y.C., 1961-63; sr. v.p., dir. Golden West Fin. Corp. and World Savs. & Loan Assn., Oakland, Calif., 1963-75, vice chmn. bd. dirs., CEO, mem. exec. com., dir., 1975-80, pres., co- chief exec. officer, dir., mem. exec. com., 1980-93, chmn. bd. dirs., CEO, mem. exec. com., 1993—; pres., chmn. bd. dirs., CEO Atlas Assets, Inc., Oakland, 1987—, Atlas Advisers, Inc., Oakland, 1987—, Atlas Securities, Inc., Oakland, 1987—. Mem. adv. com. Fed. Nat. Mortgage Assn., 1983-84. Mem. Pres.'s Mgmt. Improvement Coun., 1980, Thrift Insts. Adv. Coun. to Fed. Res. Bd., 1989-91, v.p., 1990, pres., 1991; mem. policy adv. bd. Ctr. for Real Estate and Urban Econs. U. Calif., Berkeley, 1981—, mem. exec. com. policy adv. bd., 1985—; mem. ad hoc com. to rev. Schs. Bus. Adminstrn. U. Calif., 1984-85; vice chmn. industry adv. com. Fed. Savs. and Loan Ins. Corp., 1987-88, Ins. Corp., 1987-88; bd. overseers NYU Schs. Bus., 1987-89; mem. Glass Ceiling Commn., 1992-93. Mem. Phi Beta Kappa, Beta Gamma Sigma. Office: Golden W Fin Corp 1901 Harrison St Fl 6 Oakland CA 94612-3588

SANDLER, MICHAEL DAVID, lawyer; b. Los Angeles, Feb. 27, 1946; AB, Stanford U., 1967; JD, Yale U., 1972. Bar: Calif. 1973, D.C. 1973, Wash. 1985. Assoc. Steptoe & Johnson, Washington, 1972-75, 77-79, ptnr., 1980-85; spl. asst. to legal adviser Dept. of State, Washington, 1975-77; ptnr. Foster, Pepper & Shefelman, Seattle, 1985-97, Sandler Ahern & McConaughy PLLC, Seattle, 1997—. Adj. prof. law Georgetown U., Washington, 1979, 81-82, U. Wash., Seattle, 1985-92. Vol. Peace Corps, Ethiopia and Ghana, 1968-70. Mem. ABA (chair 1995-96 sect. internat. law and practice). Office: Sandler Ahern & McConaughy PLLC 1200 5th Ave Ste 1900 Seattle WA 98101-3135 E-mail: mike@sandler.com

SANDLER, THOMAS R. accountant; b. Mt. Kisco, N.Y., Dec. 16, 1946; s. Louis and Susan (Rosen) S.; m. Alison G. Corneau, Aug. 26, 1972; children— Justin C., Shawn A. B.S. summa cum laude, Ithaca Coll., 1968; M.S., SUNY-Binghamton, 1972. C.P.A., N.Y., Colo. 1982. Asst. acct. KPMG Peat Marwick, White Plains, N.Y., 1972, mgr. Phoenix, 1975, sr. mgr. N.Y.C., 1978, ptnr. Denver, 1981-92, ptnr. in-charge corp. recovery svcs. N.Y.C., 1993-94; mng. ptnr. BDO Seidman, Denver, 1994-95; CFO, treas., sec. Samsonite Corp., Denver, 1995-98; pres. Samsonite Am., Denver, 1998—. Contbr. articles to profl. jours. Past trustee, past pres. Colo. Children's Chorale; treas., past pres., gov., mem. exec. com., committeeman Colo. Golf Assn.; committeeman U.S. Golf Assn. bd. dirs. Pacific Coast GOlf Assn.; chair-elect Travel Goods Assn. Mem. AICPA, Colo. Soc. CPAs (chmn. real estate and govt. acctg. com.), Bear Creek Golf Club, Country Club at Castle Pines. E-mail: Tom. Home: 896 Anaconda Ct Castle Rock CO 80104-9044 Office: Samsonite Corp Corp Bldg 11200 E 45th Ave Denver CO 80239-3000 E-mail: Sandler@Samsonite.com

SANDMAN, IRVIN W(ILLIS), lawyer; b. Seattle, Mar. 19, 1954; BA summa cum laude, U. Wash., 1976; JD, UCLA, 1980. Bar: U.S. Dist. Ct. (we. and ea. dists.) Wash. 1980. Prin. Graham & Dunn, Seattle, 1980—. Staff mem. UCLA Law Review. Mem. ABA (vice chair resort and tourism com. 1996-2001, co-chair 2001—), Acad. Hospitality Attys. (charter), Wash. State Hotel and Motel Assn. (govtl. affairs key contact), Wash. State Bar Assn. (chmn. creditor/debtor sect. 1988-90, editor newsletter 1984—, speaker continuing legal edn.). Office: Graham & Dunn 1420 5th Ave Fl 33 Seattle WA 98101-4087

SANDMEYER, E. E. toxicologist, consultant; b. Winterthur, Zurich, Switzerland, Aug. 9, 1929; came to U.S., 1955; d. Fritz Henry and Aline (Schoch) S. BSChemE, Technikum, Winterthur, 1951; MS in Organic Chemistry, Ohio State U., 1960, PhD in Biochemistry, 1965. Cert. civil svc. chemist II, Nev., biochemist II, Pa., clin. lab. dir. Ctrs. for Disease Control. Asst. prof. sci., gen. chemistry, organic chemistry Friends U., Wichita, 1965-66; asst. prof. biochemistry, labs., and rsch. U. Nev., Reno, 1966-71; head corp. toxicology Gulf Oil Corp., Pitts., 1971-76; divsn. head organic analysis Barringer Labs., Denver, 1987-88; pres., toxicologist, owner Transcontec, Inc., Kelseyville, Calif., 1976—. Div. head organic analysis Barringer Labs., Denver, 1986-88. Contbg. author: Patty's Industrial Hygiene and Toxicology, 1981, A Guide to General Toxicology, 1983. Mem. AAAS, Am. Chem. Soc., Soc. Environ. Health, Sigma Xi, Sigma Delta Epsilon. Office: Transcontec 7305 Live Oak Dr Kelseyville CA 95451-7862

SANDQUIST, GARY MARLIN, engineering educator, researcher, consultant, writer; b. Salt Lake City, Apr. 19, 1936; s. Donald August Sandquist and Lillian (Evaline) Dunn; m. Kristine Powell, Jan. 17, 1992; children from previous marriage: Titia, Julia, Taunia, Cynthia, Carl; stepchildren: David, Michael, Scott, Diane, Jeff. BSME, U. Utah, 1960; MS in Engring. Sci., U. Calif., Berkeley, 1961; PhD in Mech. Engring., U. Utah, 1964, MBA, MBA, U. Utah, 1995. Registered profl. engr., Utah, N.Y., Minn., Calif.; cert health physicist, quality auditor; diplomate in environ. engring. Staff mem. Los Alamos (N.Mex.) Sci. Lab., 1966; postdoctoral fellow MIT, 1969-70; rsch. prof. surgery Med. Sch., U. Utah, Salt Lake City, 1974—, prof., dir. nuc. engring. dept. mech. engring., 1975—, acting chmn. dept., 1984-85; expert in nuc. sci. Internat. Atomic Energy Agy., UN, 1980—; chief scientist Rogers and Assocs. Engring. Corp., Salt Lake City, 1980—; mgr., owner Applied Sci. Profls., LLC, Salt Lake City, 1999—. Vis. scientist MIT, Cambridge, Mass., 1969-70; vis. prof. Ben Gurion U., Israel; advisor rocket design Hercules, Inc., Bachus,

Utah, 1962; sr. nuc. engr. Idaho Nat. Engring. Lab., Idaho Falls, 1963-65; cons. nuc. sci. State of Utah, 1982—; vis. prof. Ben Gurion U., Beer Sheva, Israel, 1985; cons. various cos.; spkr. Nuc. Energy Inst., 1990—. Author: Geothermal Energy, 1973, Introduction to System Science, 1985. Comdr. USNR, 1954-56, Korea; ret. Recipient Glen Murphy award in nuc. engring. Am. Soc. Engring. Edn., 1984. Fellow ASME, Am. Nuc. Soc.; mem. Am. Soc. Quality (sr.), Am. Health Physics Soc., Alpha Nu Sigma, Sigma Xi, Tau Beta Pi, Pi Tau Sigma. Republican. Mormon. Home: 2564 Neffs Cir Salt Lake City UT 84109-4055 Office: U Utah 2116 Merrill Engring Bldg Salt Lake City UT 84112 E-mail: gms@asp-llc.com

SANDRICH, JAY H. television director; b. L.A., Feb. 24, 1932; s. Mark R. and Freda (Wirtschafter) S.; m. Nina Kramer, Feb. 11, 1952 (div.); children: Eric, Tony, Wendy; m. Linda Green Silverstein, Oct. 4, 1984. BA, UCLA, 1953. Producer (TV show) Get Smart, 1965; dir. (TV shows) He and She, 1967, Mary Tyler Moore Show, 1970-88, Soap, 1977-79, Cosby Show, 1984-92; dir. (films) Seems Like Old Times, 1980, For Richer, For Poorer (HBO), 1992, Neil Simon's London Suite (NBC), 1996. Served to 1st lt. Signal Corps U.S. Army, 1952-55. Mem. Dirs. Guild Am. (award 1975, 85, 86), TV Acad. Arts and Scis. (Emmy award 1971, 73, 85, 86).

SANDY, JOHN A. state legislator; b. Twin Falls, Idaho, June 8, 1948; m. Robin Sandy; 1 child, Alex McConnell. BS in Agr., U. Idaho. Farmer; apptd. senator, dist. 22 Idaho Senate, Boise, 1995-98, elected senator, dist. 22, 1998—. Mem. agrl. affairs, state affairs, edn., and transp. coms. Idaho state Rep. 1st vice chair. Republican. Methodist. Office: State Capitol PO Box 83720 Boise ID 83720-3720

SANGUINETTI, EUGENE FRANK, art museum administrator, educator; b. Yuma, Ariz., May 12, 1917; s. Eugene F. and Lilah (Balsz) S.; children: Leslie, Gregory. BA, U. Santa Clara, 1939; postgrad., U. Ariz., 1960-62. Instr. art history U. Ariz., Tucson, 1960-64; dir. Tucson Mus. and Art Ctr., 1964-67, Utah Mus. Fine Arts, Salt Lake City, 1967—; adj. prof. art history U. Utah, Salt Lake City, 1967—. Contbr. articles to profl. jours. Served with USAAF, 1942-44, to capt. M.I., U.S. Army, 1944-46. Mem. Am. Assn. Museums, Am. Assn. Mus. Dirs., Am. Fedn. of Arts, Coll. Art Assn., Western Assn. Art Museums, Salt Lake City C. of C. Home: 30 S St Salt Lake City UT 84103-4133

SANI, ROBERT LEROY, chemical engineering educator; b. Antioch, Calif., Apr. 20, 1935; m. Martha Jo Marr, May 28, 1966; children: Cynthia Kay, Elizabeth Ann, Jeffrey Paul. B.S., U. Calif.-Berkeley, 1958, M.S., 1960; Ph.D., U. Minn., 1963. Postdoctoral researcher dept. math Rensselaer Poly. Inst., Troy, N.Y., 1963-64; asst. prof. U. Ill., Urbana, 1964-70, assoc. prof., 1970-76; prof. chem. engring. U. Colo., Boulder, 1976—; co-dir. Ctr. for Low-g Fluid Mechanics and Transport Phenomena, U. Colo., Boulder, 1986-89, dir., 1989—. Assoc. prof. French Ministry Edn., 1982, 84, 86, 92, 94, 95, 96, 97; cons. Lawrence Livermore Nat. Lab., Calif., 1974-84. Contbr. numerous chpts. to profl. publs.; co-author three books; mem. editorial bd. Internat. Jour. Numerical Methods in Fluids, 1981—, Revue Européenne des Éléments Finis, 1990—, Internat. Jour. Computational Engring. Sci., 1998—. Guggenheim fellow, 1970 Mem. AICE, Soc. for Applied and Indsl. Math., World User Assn. in Applied Computational Fluid Dynamics (bd. dirs.). Democrat. Office: U Colo Dept Chem Engring PO Box 424 Boulder CO 80309-0424 E-mail: sani@pastis.colorado.edu

SANKS, ROBERT LELAND, environmental engineer, emeritus educator; b. Pomona, Calif., Feb. 19, 1916; s. John B. and Nellie G. (Church) S.; m. Mary Louise Clement, May 16, 1946 (dec. Oct. 1994); children: Margaret Nadine, John Clement; m. Edith Millen Harrington, Dec. 2, 1999. Registered profl. engr., Mont. Draftsman City of La Habra Calif., 1940; asst. engr. Alex Morrison cons. engr., Fullerton, Calif., 1941; jr. engr. U.S. Army Engrs., Los Angeles, 1941-42; asst. research engr. dept. civil engring. U. Calif.-Berkeley, 1942-45; structural engr. The Austin Co., Oakland, Calif., 1945-46; instr. dept. civil engring. U. Utah, Salt Lake city, 1946-49, asst. prof. Salt Lake City, 1949-55, assoc. prof., 1955-58; structural engr. The Lang Co., Salt Lake City, 1950; instrument man Patti McDonald Co., Anchorage, 1951; checker Western Steel Co., Salt Lake City, 1952; structural engr. Moran, Proctor, Meuser and Rutledge, N.Y.C., 1953, F.C. Torkelson Co., Salt Lake City, 1955; soils engr. R.L. Sloane & Assocs., Salt Lake City, 1956; prof., chmn. dept. civil engring. Gonzaga U., Spokane, Wash., 1958-61; prof. dept. civil engring.-engring. mechanics Mont. State U., Bozeman, 1966-82, prof. emeritus, 1982—; vis. prof. U. Tex.-Austin, 1974-75; part-time sr. engr. Christian, Spring, Sielbach & Assoc., Billings, Mont., 1974-82. Cons. engr., 1945—; lectr. at pumping sta. design workshops, 1988—; assoc. specialist San. Engring. Research Lab., 1963-65, research engr., 1966. Author: Statically Indeterminate Structural Analysis, 1961; co-author: (with Takashi Assano) Land Treatment and Disposal of Municipal and Industrial Wastewaters, 1976, Water Treatment Plant Design for the Practicing Engineer, 1978; editor-in-chief: Pumping Station Design, 1989 (award Excellence profl. & scholarly pub. div. Assn. Am. Pubs. 1989), 2d edit., 1998; contbr. articles on civil engring. to profl. publs. Mem. Wall of Fame, Fullerton High Sch., 1987; NSF fellow, 1961-63 Mem. ASCE (life, chmn. local qualifications com. intermountain sect. 1950-56, pres. intermountain sect. 1957-58), Am. Water Works Assn. (pres. Mont. sect. 1981-82, George Warren Fuller award), Mont. Water Environ. Fedn., Assn. Environ. Engring. Profs., Rotary, Sigma Xi, Chi Epsilon. Home: 411 W Dickerson St Bozeman MT 59715-4538 Office: Mont State U Dept Civil Engring Bozeman MT 59717-0001 E-mail: sanks@mcn.net

SANNWALD, WILLIAM WALTER, librarian; b. Chgo., Sept. 12, 1940; s. William Frederick and Irene Virginia (Stanish) S.; children: Sara Ann, William Howard. B.A., Beloit Coll., 1963; M.A.L.S., Rosary Coll., River Forest, Ill., 1966; M.B.A., Loyola U., Chgo., 1974. Mktg. mgr. Xerox Univ. Microfilms, 1972-75; assoc. dir. Detroit Public Library, 1975-77; dir. Ventura (Calif.) County Library, 1977-79; city libr. San Diego Public Libr., 1979-97; asst. to city mgr. for libr. design and devel. City of San Diego, 1997—. Vis. instr. mktg. San Diego State U. Author: Checklist of Library Building Design Considerations, 3d edit., 1997; chairperson editorial adv. bd. Pub. Librs. Pres. Met. Libraries Sect., 1989. Recipient Outstanding Prof. award and Outstanding Mktg. Prof. award, 1985; Award of Merit AIA San Diego chpt., 1988, Irving Gill award for Architecture and Mgmt., 1995. Mem. ALA, Online Computer Libr. Ctr. (mem. users coun. 1996), Calif. Library Authority for Systems and Services (pres. congress of mems. 1980), Calif. Library Assn., Libr. Admintrn. and Mgmt. Assn. (pres. 1995-96). Roman Catholic. Home: 3538 Paseo Salamoner La Mesa CA 91941-7329 Office: San Diego Pub Libr 820 E St San Diego CA 92101-6478

SANO, EMILY JOY, museum director; b. Santa Ana, Calif., Feb. 17, 1942; d. Masao and Lois Kikue (Inokuchi) S. BA, Ind. U., 1967; MA, Columbia U., 1970, MPhil, 1976, PhD, 1983. Lectr. Oriental Art Vassar Coll., Poughkeepsie, N.Y., 1974-79; curator Asian Art, asst. dir. programs Kimbell Art Mus., Ft. Worth, 1979-89; dep. dir. collections and exhbns. Dallas Mus. Art, 1989-92; dep. dir., chief curator Asian Art Mus., San Francisco, 1993-95, dir., 1995—. Author: Great Age of Japanese Buddhist Sculpture, 1982; editor: The Blood of Kings, 1986, Weavers, Merchants and Kings, 1984, Painters of the Great Ming, 1993. Active Assn. Art Mus. [illegible] grantee Carnegie, 1963-64, Fulbright-Hays, 1977-78. Office: Asian Art Mus Golden Gate Park San Francisco CA 94118 E-mail: esano@asianart.org

SANO, ROY I. bishop; Ordained to ministry United Meth. Ch., later consecrated bishop. Appointed Bishop Rocky Mountain Conf. United Meth. Ch., Denver, now bishop L.A. area; with Calif.-Pacific Ann. Conf., 1992—. Bishop. Ordained to ministry United Meth. Ch., later consecrated bishop; appointed Bishop Rocky Mountain Conf., United Meth. Ch., Denver; now bishop United Meth. Ch. in L.A. area; with Calif.-Pacific Ann. Conf., 1992—. Office: Bishop United Meth Ch LA Area PO Box 6006 Pasadena CA 91102-6006

SANSWEET, STEPHEN JAY, journalist, author, marketing executive; b. Phila., June 14, 1945; s. Jack Morris and Fannie (Axelrod) S. BS, Temple U., 1966. Reporter Phila. Inquirer, 1966-69; reporter Wall Street Jour., Phila., 1969-71, Montreal, Que, Can., 1971-73, L.A., 1973-84, dep. bur. chief, 1984-87, bur. chief, 1987-96; dir. speciality mktg. Lucasfilm Ltd., San Rafael, Calif., 1996-97, dir. content mgmt. and fan rels., 1997—; sr. editor Star Wars Galaxy Mag., 1996-2000. Lectr. bus. journalism U. So. Calif., L.A., 1984-87. Author: The Punishment Cure, 1976, Science Fiction Toys and Models, 1981, Star Wars: From Concept to Screen to Collectible, 1992, Tomart's Price Guide to Worldwide Star Wars Collectibles, 1994, 2d edit., 1997, The Quotable Star Wars, 1996, Star Wars Scrapbook: The Essential Collection, 1998, Star Wars Encyclopedia, 1998, Star Wars Collectibles: A Pocket Manual, 1998, Anakin Skywalker: The Story of Darth Vader, 1998, Star Wars: The Action Figure Archive, 1999; cons. editor: Star Wars Galaxy, 1993, 2d series, 1994, 3d series, 1995; editor: Star Wars Trilogy Spl. Edn. card sets, 1997. Recipient award for best fire story Phila. Fire Dept., 1968, Pub. Svc.-Team Mem. award Sigma Delta Chi, 1977; finalist Loeb award, 1990. Mem. Soc. Profl. Journalists. Avocation: collecting toys and movie memorabilia. Office: Lucasfilm Ltd PO Box 2009 San Rafael CA 94912-2009

SANTA, RICHARD A. materials company executive; b. 1951; MBA in Fin., Rutgers U. Pub. acct. Price Waterhouse; CFO Scott U.S.A.; corp. contr. Scott Sports Group, Inc.; CFO Dynamic Materials Corp., Lafayette, Colo., 2000—. Office: 551 Aspen Ridge Dr Lafayette CO 80026 Office Fax: 303-604-1897

SANTER, BENJAMIN, atmospheric scientist, meteorologist; b. Washington, June 3, 1955; BS Environ. Scis. with 1st class honors, U. East Anglia, Norwich, Eng., 1976; NATO Rsch. Studentship, U. East Anglia, 1977, PhD in Climatology, 1987. Jr. rsch. assoc. Sch. Environ. Scis. U. East Anglia, Norwich, Eng., 1978-79, rsch. assoc. climatic rsch. unit, 1983-87; project engr. dept. new techs., air pollution and Dornier Sys. GmbH, Friedrichshafen, Germany, 1980-83; postdoct., rsch. scientist Max-Planck Inst. Meteorologie, Hamburg, Germany, 1987-92; physicist earth and environ. scis. directorate Lawrence Livermore Nat. Lab., Livermore, Calif., 1992—. Expert witness German Bundestag Enquete Commn. Hearings on Greenhouse-Gas-Induced Climate Change, Bonn, Germany, 1992; cons. Battelle Pacific Northwest Lab., 1992-93, mem. sci. adv. panel climate change, data and detection program NOAA, 1995—; mem. Climate Variability and Predictability Numerical Experimentation Group, 1995—; participant numerous confs., workshops; lectr. in field. Co-author: Proceedings of NATO Advanced Study Institute on Physically-Based Modelling and Simulation of Climate and Climatic Change, 1988, Science and Engineering on Supercomputers, 1990, Supercomputer '90, Greenhouse-Gas-Induced Climate Change: A Critical Appraisal of Simulations and Observations, 1991, Global Warming: Concern for Tomorrow, 1993, Agricultural Dimensions of Global Climate Change, 1993, Dahlem Workshop on Global Changes in the Perspective of the Past, 1993, Climate Change int the Intra-American Sea, 1993, Communicating About Climate: the Story of the Model Evaluation Consortium for Climate Assessment, 1997; mem. editl. bd. Climatic Change, 1996—; contbr. numerous articles to profl. jours., chpts. to books. MacArthur fellow John D. and Catherine T. MacArthur Found., 1998; Ford Travel scholar, 1974; recipient Outstanding Scientific Paper award U.S. Dept. Commerce Environ. Rsch. Lab. Nat. Oceanic and Atmospheric Adminstrn., 1997, Norbert Gerbier-MUMM Internat. award World Meteorol. Orgn., 1998. Mem. Am. Geophys. Union. Achievements include research in climate modeling and greenhouse-gas effects supporting the hypothesis that human activity contributes to global warming. Avocations: rock-climbing, mountaineering, poetry. Office: Lawrence Livermore Nat Lab PCMDI PO Box 808 L-264 Livermore CA 94551-0808 Fax: (925) 422-7675. E-mail: santer1@llnl.gov

SANTIAGO, MIKE, communications executive; Pres. Creators Syndicate, L.A., 1997—. Office: Creators Syndicate 5777 W Century Blvd Ste 700 Los Angeles CA 90045-5675

SANTILLAN, ANTONIO, financial company executive; b. Buenos Aires, May 8, 1936; naturalized, 1966; s. Guillermo Spika and Raphaella C. (Abaladejo) S.; children: Andrea, Miguel, Marcos. Grad., Morgan Park Mil. Acad., Chgo., 1954; BS in Psychology, Coll. of William and Mary, 1958. Cert. real estate broker. Asst. in charge of prodn. Wilding Studios, Chgo., 1964; pres. Adams Fin. Services, Los Angeles, 1965—. Writer, producer, dir. (motion pictures) The Glass Cage, co-writer Dirty Mary/Crazy Harry, Viva Knievel; contbg. writer Once Upon a Time in America; TV panelist Window on Wall Street; contbr. articles to profl. fin. and real estate jours. Served with USNR, 1959. Recipient Am. Rep. award San Francisco Film Festival, Cork Ireland Film Fest, 1961. Mem. Writer's Guild Am., L.A. Bd. Realtors, Beverly Hills Bd. Realtors (income/investment divsn. steering com.), Westside Realty Bd. (bd. dirs.), L.A. Ventures Assn. (bd. dirs.), Jonathan Club (L.A.), Rotary, Roundtable, Toastmasters Internat. Avocations: golf, tennis, skiing. Office: Adams Fin Svcs Inc 425 N Alfred St West Hollywood CA 90048-2504

SAPP, DONALD GENE, retired minister; b. Phoenix, Feb. 27, 1927; s. Guerry Byron and Lydia Elmeda (Snyder) S.; m. Anna Maydean Nevitt, July 10, 1952 (dec.); m. Joann Herrin Mountz, May 1, 1976; children: Gregory, Paula, Jeffrey, Mark, Melody, Cristine. AB in Edn., Ariz. State U., 1949; MDiv, Boston U., 1952, STM, 1960; D Ministry, Calif. Grad. Sch. Theology, 1975. Ordained to ministry Meth. Ch., 1950. Dir. youth activities Hyde Park (Mass.) Meth. Ch., 1950-52; minister 1st Meth. Ch., Peabody, Mass., 1952-54, Balboa Island (Calif.) Cmty. Meth. Ch., 1954-57, Ch. of the Foothills Meth., Duarte, Calif., 1957-63; sr. minister Aldersgate United Meth. Ch., Tustin, 1963-70, Paradise Valley (Ariz.) United Meth. Ch., 1970-83; dist. supt. Cen. West Dist. of Desert S.W. Conf. United Meth. Ctr., Phoenix, 1983-89. Editor Wide Horizons, 1983-89; contbr. articles to profl. jours. Chaplain City of Hope Med. Ctr., Duarte, 1957-63; trustee Plaza Community Ctr., L.A., 1967-70; corp. mem. Sch. Theology at Claremont, Calif., 1972-80; pres. Met. Phoenix Commn., 1983-85; del. Western Jurisdictional Conf. United Meth. Ch., 1984, 88; bd. dirs. Coun. Chs., L.A., 1963-67, Orange County (Calif.) Human Rels. Coun., 1967-70, Interfaith Counseling Svc. Found., 1982-89, Wesley Cmty. Ctr., Phoenix, 1983-89; gen. conf. United Meth. Ch., 1988. With USN, 1945-46. Mem. Ariz. Ecumenical Coun., Bishops and Exec. Roundtable, Rotary (pres.), Kappa Delta Pi, Tau Kappa Epsilon. Democrat. Avocation: overseas travel. Home: 5225 E Road Runner Rd Paradise Valley AZ 85253-3306

SAPSOWITZ, SIDNEY H. entertainment and media company executive; b. N.Y.C., June 29, 1936; s. Max and Annette (Rothstein) Sapsowitz; m. Phyllis Skopp, Nov. 27, 1957; children: Donna Dawn Chazen, Gloria Lynn Aaron, Marsha Helene Gleit. BBA summa cum laude, Paterson State U. (N.J.), 1980. Various fin. and oper. systems positions Metro Goldwyn Mayer, Inc., N.Y.C., 1957-68; exec. v.p., dir. Penta Computer Assoc. Inc., [illegible] CFO Am. Film. Theatre, N.Y.C., 1973-76, Cinema Shares Internat Dristb. Corp., N.Y.C., 1976-79; sr. cons. Solomon, Finger & Newman, N.Y.C., 1979-80; exec. v.p., CFO Met. Goldwyn Mayer, L.A., 1980-82; various positions leading to exec. v.p. fin. and adminstrn., CFO MGM/UA Entertainment Co., Culver City, Calif., 1982-86, also bd. dirs. L.A.; fin. v.p.; chief bus. and ops. officer, Office of Pres., dir. United Artists Corp., Beverly Hills, Calif., 1986-87; chmn. bd., CEO MGA/UA Telecommunications Corp., Beverly Hills, 1986-89; sr. exec. v.p., dir., mem. exec. com. MGA/UA Communications Co., 1986-89; chmn., CEO Sid Sapsowitz & Assocs., Inc., 1989—. Pres., Wayne Conservative Congregation, N.J., 1970-77. Mem. Am. Mgmt. Assn., Am. Film Inst., Acad. Motion Picture Arts and Scis., Fin. Exec. Inst., TV Acad. Arts and Scis., KP (chancellor comdr.).

SARDELLA, EDWARD JOSEPH, television news anchor; b. Buffalo, June 2, 1940; s. Joseph Edward and Josephine Jenny (D'Amico) S.; m. Sandra K. Lorenzen, Jan. 17, 1975. BA in Speech Arts, Occidental Coll., L.A., 1962. Radio disc jockey, newsman KWIN/KTIL/KERG, Ashland/Tillamook/Eugene, Oreg., 1966-69; reporter KVAL-TV, Eugene, 1969-70; reporter/anchor KOIN-TV, Portland, Oreg., 1970-72, KMGH-TV, Denver, 1972-74; news anchor/sr. editor KUSA-TV, Denver, 1974—. Adj. instr. journalism U. Colo., Boulder, 1984-92. Author: Write Like You Talk, 1984; co-author: The Producing Strategy, 1995. Olympic torchbearer, 1996. Capt. USMC, 1962-66. Recipient Emmy award Nat. Assn. TV Arts and Scis., 1992, 93, 94, 95, 96, also Silver Circle Career Achievement award, 1999; named Colo. Broadcaster of Yr., 1997, Journalist of Yr. Colo. chpt. Soc. Profl. Journalists, 2000. Office: KUSA TV 500 E Speer Blvd Denver CO 80203-4187

SARGENT, JOSEPH DANIEL, motion picture and television director; b. Jersey City, July 22, 1925; s. Domenico and Maria (Noviello) Sargente; student theatre arts New Sch. for Social Research, 1946-49; m. Carolyn Nelson, Nov. 22, 1970; children by previous marriage— Athena, Lia. Dir. films: Street-Fighter, 1959, Spy in the Green Hat, 1966, One Spy too Many, 1966, Girl from U.N.C.L.E., 1966, The Hell With Heros, 1968, The Sunshin Patriot, 1968, Colosses, The Forbin Project, feature, 1969, The Immortal, 1969, Tribes (Outstanding Directorial Achievement award Dirs. Guild Am.), ABC, 1969, Wheeler and Murdoch, 1970, (also prodr.) Maybe I'll Come Home in the Spring, ABC, 1970, (also prodr.) Longstreet, 1970, Man on a String, 1971, The Man, feature, 1972, White Lightning, feature, 1972, The Marcus-Nelson Murders (Emmy award, Dirs. Guild Am. award), CBS, 1973, Sunshine, CBS, 1973, The Man Who Died Twice, 1973, The Taking of Pelham 1-2-3 (Best Dir. award San Sebastian Film Festival), feature, 1974, Hustling, ABC-TV, 1975, Friendly Persuasion, ABC-TV, 1975, The Night That Panicked America (also prodr., Fantasy Film Fans Internat. award), ABC-TV, 1975, MacArthur, 1977, Goldengirl, 1979, Playing for Time, 1979, Amber Waves, ABC-TV, 1979, 80, Playing for Time,1980, Coast To Coast, 1980, Freedom, ABC-TV, 1981, The Manions of America ABC-TV, 1981, Tomorrow's Child, 1982, Memorial Day, 1983, Choices of the Heart, 1983, Nightmares, 1983, Terrible Joe Moran, 1984, Love Is Never Silent, 1985 (Emmy award), James A. Michner's Space, 1985, Passion Flower, 1986, There Must Be a Pony, 1986, (also prodr.) Of Pure Blood, 1986, (also prodr.) Jaws 4: The Revenge, 1987, The Karen Carpenter Story, 1989, Day One, 1989, (also actor) Ivory Hunters (The Last Elephant), 1990, (also actor) Caroline?, 1990, Incident at Lincoln Bluff, 1990, (also actor) Love She Sought (A Green Journey, Last Chance for Romance), 1990, Never Forget, 1991, Miss Rose White, 1992, (also prodr.) Somebody's Daughter, 1992, (also prodr.) Skylark, 1993, WWII: When Lions Roared, 1994, Abraham, 1994, Larry McMurty's Streets of Laredo, 1995, Miss Evers' Boys, 1997, Mandela and de Klerk, 1997, Long Island Incident, 1998, The Wall, 1998, (also prodr.) Dostoevsky's Crime and Punishment, 1998, Vola Sciusciù, 1999, Lesson Before Dying, 1999; dir. TV series Gunsmoke (TV series), 1955, The Fugitive (TV series) 1963, The Man from U.N.C.L.E. (TV series), 1964, Star Trek (TV series), 1966, The Invaders (TV series), 1967, Garrison's Gorillas, 1967, It Takes a Thief, 1967; actor Tobruk, 1967; guest appearances include: Gunsmoke, 1957, 59, Zane Grey Theater, 1958, 60, The Twilight Zone, 1961, pres. Joseph Sargent Prodns., Inc. Served with U.S. Army, 1943-46. Recipient Best TV Film award Monte Carlo TV Film Festival, 1975 for The Night That Panicked America. Mem. Dirs Guild Am., Screen Actors Guild, AFTRA, Actors Equity Assn. Office: c/o Shapiro Lichtman 8827 Beverly Blvd Los Angeles CA 90048-2405

SARGENT, WALLACE LESLIE WILLIAM, astronomer, educator; b. Elsham, Eng., Feb. 15, 1935; s. Leslie William and Eleanor (Denniss) S.; m. Anneila Isabel Cassells, Aug. 5, 1964; children: Lindsay Eleanor, Alison Clare. B.Sc., Manchester U., 1956, M.Sc., 1957, Ph.D., 1959. Research fellow Calif. Inst. Tech., Pasadena, 1959-62; sr. research fellow Royal Greenwich Obs., 1962-64; asst. prof. physics U. Calif., San Diego, 1964-66; mem. faculty dept. astronomy Calif. Inst. Tech., 1966—, prof., 1971-81, Ira S. Bowen prof. astronomy, 1981—, dir. Palomar Obs., 1997-2000. Miller Prof. U. Calif., Berkeley, 1993; Thomas Gold lectr. Cornell U., Ithaca, N.Y., 1994-95; Sackler lectr. Harvard U., Cambridge, Mass., 1995, U. Calif., Berkeley, 1996. Contbr. articles to profl. jours. Alfred P. Sloan fellow, 1968-70. Fellow Am. Acad. Arts and Scis., Royal Soc. (London); mem Am. Astron. Soc. (Helen B. Warner prize 1969, Dannie Heineman prize 1991, Henry Norris Russell lectr. 2001), Royal Astron. Soc. (George Darwin lectr. 1987, assoc. 1998), Astron. Soc. Pacific (Bruce Gold medal 1994), Internat. Astron. Union. Club: Athenaeum (Pasadena). Home: 400 S Berkeley Ave Pasadena CA 91107-5062 Office: Calif Inst Tech Astronomy Dept 105-24 Pasadena CA 91125-0001

SARICH, VINCENT M. anthropologist, educator; b. Chicago, Ill., Dec. 13, 1934; s. Matt and Manda Saric; m. Jorjan Snyder; children: Kevin, Tamsin. BS, Ill. Inst. Tech., 1955; PhD, U. Calif., Berkeley, 1967. Instr. anthropology Stanford U., Berkeley, Calif., 1965; from asst. prof. to assoc. prof. anthropology U. Calif., Berkeley, 1967-81, prof., 1981-94, prof. emeritus, 1994—; vis. faculty U. Auckland, New Zealand, 1999—. Office: U Calif Dept Anthropology 232 Kroeber Hall Berkeley CA 94720-3710 also: U Auckland Private Bag 92019 Auckland New Zealand

SARKISIAN, CHERILYN **See CHER**

SARLAT, GLADYS, public relations consultant; b. Elizabeth, N.J., July 22, 1923; d. Max and Dora (Levin) S. BS, U. Wash., 1946. Asst. Kay Sullivan Assocs., N.Y.C., 1949-50; fashion dir. Warsaw & Co., N.Y.C., 1950-54; asst. fashion coord. Emporium Dept. Store, San Francisco, 1955-56; prodn. mgr. Cunningham & Walsh Advt., San Francisco, 1957-58; v.p., pub. rels. dir. Harwood Advt. Inc., Tucson and Phoenix, 1959-68; v.p., dir. Waller & Sarlat Advt. Inc., Tucson, 1968-69; pres. Godwin & Sarlat Pub. Rels., Inc., Tucson, 1970-87, cons., 1988—; of counsel Liess Peck & Godwin, LP&G, Tucson, 1993—. Cons. in field. Mem. adv. com. Downtown Devel. Corp., 1979-85, Festival in the Sun; bd. dirs. Tucson Conv. and Vis. Bur., 1993-95, Greater Tucson Devel. Com., 1999—. Named Woman of Yr. for Bus., Ariz. Daily Star, 1963; recipient Lulu award L.A. Woman in Advt., 1962. Mem. Pub. Rels. Soc. Am. (past bd. dirs., counselors acad., bd. UA presents), Fashion Group, Tucson Met. C. of C. (v.p., dir. 1976-85, chmn. bd. 1986-87, Tucson Woman of Yr. 1990). Republican. Jewish. Home: 5530 N Camino Arenosa Tucson AZ 85718-5417 Office: 177 N Church Ave Ste 315 Tucson AZ 85701-1154 E-mail: gspr@azmindset.com

SARNOFF, THOMAS WARREN, television executive; b. N.Y.C., Feb. 23, 1927; s. David and Lizette (Hermant) S.; m. Janyce Lundon, May 21, 1955; children: Daniel, Timothy, Cynthia. Grad., Phillips Acad., 1939-43; [illegible] postgrad. Sch. Bus. Adminstrn., 1948-49; D.H.L., Columbia Coll. Engaged in prodn. and sales with ABC, Inc., 1949-51; prodn. Metro-Goldwyn-Mayer, 1951-52; with NBC, 1952-77; v.p. prodn. and bus. affairs NBC

(Pacific div.), 1956-60, v.p. adminstrn. West Coast, 1960-62, v.p. charge West Coast, 1962-65, staff exec. v.p. West Coast, 1965-77; pres. NBC Entertainment Corp., 1972-77, Sarnoff Internat. Enterprises, 1977-81, Sarnoff Entertainment Corp., 1981—; exec. v.p. Venturetainment Corp., 1981-87, pres., 1987—. Bd. dirs. Multimedia Games, Inc., 1998—. Exec. producer Bonanza: The Next Generation, 1987, Bonanza: The Return, 1993, Back to Bonanza Retrospective, 1993, Bonanza: Under Attack, 1995. Mem. Calif. Commn. for Reform Intermediate and Secondary Edn. Pres., Research Found., St. Joseph Hosp., Burbank, 1965-73, Permanant Charities Com. of Entertainment Industries, 1971-72; nat. trustee Nat. Conf. Christians and Jews. Served with Signal Corps AUS, World War II. Mem. Acad. TV Arts and Scis. (chmn. bd. trustees 1972-74, chmn. past pres.'s coun. 1989-92), Acad. TV Arts and Scis. Found. (pres. 1990-99, chmn., CEO 1999—), The Caucus for Prodrs., Writers and Dirs. Office: 2451 Century Hl Los Angeles CA 90067-3510

SARPKAYA, TURGUT, mechanical engineering educator; b. Aydin, Turkey, May 7, 1928; came to U.S., 1951, naturalized, 1962; s. Hasip and Huriye (Fetil) S.; m. Gunel Ataisik, Aug. 26, 1963. B.S. in Mech. Engring, Tech. U. Istanbul, 1950, M.S., 1951; Ph.D. in Engring, U. Iowa, 1954. Research engr. MIT, Cambridge, 1954-55; asst. prof. U. Nebr., 1957-59, assoc. prof., 1959-62, prof. mech. engring., 1962, distinguished prof., 1962-66; research prof. U. Manchester, Eng., 1966-67, U. Gottingen, Fed. Republic of Germany, 1971-72; prof. mech. engring., chmn. dept. mech. engring. U.S. Naval Postgrad. Sch., Monterey, Calif., 1967-71, 72—, Disting. prof. mech. engring., 1975—. Cons. aerospace industry, 1967—, petroleum industry, 1976— Author: Mechanics of Wave Forces on Offshore Structures, 1981; mem. editorial bd.; Zentralbaltt fur Mathematik; editor: Procs. Heat Transfer and FLuid Mechanics Inst., 1970; contbr. chpts. to many books and over 200 papers on fluid dynamics. Served with C.E. AUS, 1955-57. Fellow Royal Instn. Naval Architects, AIAA, ASME (Lewis F. Moody award 1967, exec. bd. fluids engring. fivsn., chmn. review com., Freeman Scholar award 1988, Engring. award 1991, Fluids Engring. award 1990); mem. ACME (Collingwood prize 1957, Offshore Mechanics and Arctic Engring. award 1993), Heat Transfer and Fluid Mechanics Inst. (chmn., Am. Inst. Aeros. and Astronautics, Am. Soc. Engring. Edn. Achievements include patent for fluidic elements. Home: 25330 Vista Del Pinos Carmel CA 93923-8804 Office: Naval Postgrad Sch Mech Engring Code ME SL 1 University Cir Monterey CA 93943-5000 E-mail: sarp@nps.navy.mil

SARSON, JOHN CHRISTOPHER, television producer, director, writer; b. London, Jan. 19, 1935; s. Arnold Wilfred and Annie Elizabeth (Wright) S.; m. Evelyn Patricia Kaye, Mar. 25, 1963; children: Katrina May, David Arnold BA with honors, Trinity Coll., Cambridge, Eng., 1960, MA, 1963. Dir. Granada TV, Manchester, Eng., 1960-63; producer, dir. Sta. WGBH-TV, Boston, 1963-73; pres. Blue Penguin, Inc., Boulder, Colo., 1974—; v.p. TV programming Sta. WYNC-TV, N.Y.C., 1989-90. Dir. Pub. Broadcasting Assocs., Newton, Mass.; cons. to numerous pub. TV stations Creator, producer MAsterpiece Theatre, PBS, 1970-73, Zoom, PBS, 1971-73; producer Live From the Met, PBS, 1977-79, Kid's Writes, Nickelodeon, 1982-83, American Treasure, a Smithsonian Journey, 1986, Spotlight Colorado, 1991, Parenting Works, 1993, 95-97, Club 303, 1994. Served with Royal Navy, 1956-57 Recipient Emmy award, 1973, 74, Peabody award Ohio State U., 1978, Internat. Emmy award, 1983, Nat. Acad. TV Arts and Scis. Gov.'s award, 1991. Mem. Dirs. Guild Am., Nat. acad. TV Arts and Scis. (gov. Heartland chpt.), Windows on the Rockies User Group (pres.). Avocations: music, cooking, gardening, travel, computers. Home and Office: 3031 5th St Boulder CO 80304-2501 E-mail: csarson123@hotmail.com

SASAKI, TSUTOMU (TOM SASAKI), real estate company executive, international trading company executive, consultant; b. Tokyo, July 28, 1945; came to U.S., 1979; s. Tsuneshiro and Kimiko (Fujiwara) S.; m. Yoko Katsura, Feb. 21, 1971; children: Mari, Tomoko. BA, Sophia U., Tokyo, 1969. Plant export adminstrn. Ataka & Co., Ltd., Osaka, Japan, 1969-76; officer Seattle-First Nat. Bank, Tokyo, 1976-79, AVP bus. mgr., 1982-84, AVP Japan mgr. Seattle, 1979-82, v.p. Japan mgr., 1984-90; owner, pres. BBS Internat., Inc., Seattle, 1990—. Bd. dirs. Wired, Inc., Seattle, InterPac Devel. Inc., InterPac Mgmt., Inc., Riverplace Mgmt., Inc., BBS Bus. Svc., Inc., N.W. Club Mgmt., Inc. Bd. dirs. Adopt-a-Stream Found., Everett, Wash., 1987X; bd. trustees N.W. Sch., Seattle. Am. Field Svc. scholar, 1963-64. Mem. Japan Am. Soc. Wash. (chmn. membership com. 1988, bd. dirs. 1997X), British Am. Bus. Coun., Fairwood Golf & Country Club, Wash. Athletic Club. Avocations: golf, gardening, music, photography. Home: 4625 136th Ave SE Bellevue WA 98006-3007 Office: BBS Internat Inc 720 Olive Way Ste 1025 Seattle WA 98101-1880

SASAKI, Y(ASUNAGA) TITO, engineering executive; b. Tokyo, Feb. 6, 1938; came to U.S., 1967; s. Yoshinaga and Chiyoko S.; m. Janet L. Cline; 1 child, Heather N. Diploma in Indsl. Design, Royal Coll. Art, London, 1962; MS in Ekistics, Athens (Greece) Tech. Inst., 1965. Cert. planner Am. Inst. Cert. Planners. Tech. officer London County Coun., 1962-63; sr. rschr. Inst. Battelle, Geneva, Switzerland, 1965-67; planning dir. Golden Gate Bridge, San Francisco, 1970-74; pres. Visio Internat., Inc., San Francisco, 1974-85, Quantum Mechanics Corp., Sonoma, Calif., 1981—. Mem. ASME, AIAA, Am. Vacuum Soc., Am. Welding Soc. Achievements: co-developer of the world's most sensitive helium leak detector and the world's lowest out-gasing stainless steel. Home: PO Box 200 Vineburg CA 95487-0200 Office: Quantum Mechanics Corp 21885 8th St E Sonoma CA 95476-9797 E-mail: TitoSasaki@attglobal.net

SASENICK, JOSEPH ANTHONY, animal health and food safety company executive; b. Chgo., May 18, 1940; s. Anthony E. and Caroline E. (Smicklas) S.; m. Barbara Ellen Barr, Aug. 18, 1962; children: Richard Allen, Susan Marie, Michael Joseph. BA, DePaul U., 1962; MA, U. Okla., 1966. With Miles Labs., Inc., Elkhart, Ind., 1963-70; product mgr. Alka-Seltzer, 1966-68, dir. mktg. grocery products divsn., 1968-70; with Gillette Corp., Boston, 1970-79, dir. new products/new ventures, personal care divsn., 1977; v.p. diversified cos. and pres. Jafra Cosmetics Worldwide, 1977-79; mktg. dir. Braun AG, Kronberg, W. Ger., 1970-73; chmn. mng. dir. Braun U.K. Ltd., 1973-77; with Abbott Labs., North Chicago, 1979-84, corp. v.p., pres. consumer products divsn., 1979-84; pres., CEO, Moxie Industries, 1984-87; pres., CEO Personal Monitoring Technologies, Rochester, N.Y., 1987; pres. Bioline Labs., Ft. Lauderdale, Fla., 1988; mng. dir., ptnr. Vista Resource Group, Newport Beach, Calif., 1988-90; pres., CEO, Alcide Corp., Redmond, Wash., 1991-92, chmn., CEO, 1992—, 2001—. Mem. Columbia Tower Club, El Niguel Club, Wash. Athletic Club, Tech. Alliance. Home: 1301 Spring St Apt 24J Seattle WA 98104-1353 Office: Alcide Corp 8561 154th Ave NE Redmond WA 98052-3557

SATA, LINDBERGH SABURO, psychiatrist, educator; b. Portland, Oreg., Jan. 6, 1928; s. Charles Kazuo and Ito (Kojima) S.; m. Yuriko Kodama, Aug. 19, 1956; children: Roberta, Camille, Holly, John. BS, U. Utah, 1951, MD, 1958, MS, 1964. Intern U. Utah Coll. Medicine, Salt Lake Gen. Hosp., 1958-59, resident in psychiatry, 1959-62, chief resident in psychiatry, 1961-62; adminstrv. chief resident neurology U. Utah Coll. Medicine, VA Hosp., Salt Lake City, 1960-61; fellow Inst. for Mental Retardation, Letchworth Village, Thiells, N.Y., 1962; intern Behavioral Sci. Intern Program Nat. Tng. Labs., Bethel, Maine, 1966; instr. U. Utah, 1962-64; asst. prof. The Psychiat. Inst. U. Md., Balt., 1964-67, assoc. prof., 1967-68, U. Wash., Seattle, 1968-77, asst. dean, 1969-70, prof., 1977-78; prof., chmn. St. Louis U. Sch. Medicine, 1978-94, prof. emeritus, chmn. emeritus, 1994—. Fellow Am. Coll. Psychiatrists, Am. Psychiat. Assn., Pacific Rim Coll. Psychiatrists (founding); mem. Am. Assn. for Social Psychiatry. Office: 1606 Riverview Dr NE Auburn WA 98002-3054

SATHER, GLEN CAMERON, professional hockey team executive, coach; b. High River, Alta., Canada, Sept. 2, 1943; Former professional hockey player; pres., gen. mgr. Edmonton Oilers, Nat. Hockey League, Alta., Can., coach, 1977-89, now alt. gov. Coach winning team in Stanley Cup competition, 1987. Recipient Jack Adams Award for NHL Coach of the Yr., 1986. Office: c/o Edmonton Oilers 11230 110th St 2nd Flr Edmonton AB Canada T5B 4M9

SATO, RICHARD MICHIO, consulting engineering company executive; b. Paia, Maui, Hawaii, Dec. 30, 1934; s. Shinichi and Namie (Hanazawa) S.; m. Althea Reiko Ouye; children: Janice Muraoka, Kelvin. BSCE, U. Hawaii, 1956. Registered civil/structural engr., Calif., Hawaii, Guam. Civil and structural engr. Dalton Dalton Assocs., L.A., 1960-62; structural engr. William M. Taggart, SE, L.A., 1962-67; project coord. Office of Univ. Planning U. Hawaii, Honolulu, 1967-69; project engr. T.Y. Lin Hawaii, Honolulu, 1969; pres. Sato & Assocs., Inc. (formerly Richard M. Sato & Assoc. & Sato & Kuniyoshi, Inc.), Honolulu, 1969—. 1st lt. U.S. Army, 1957-59. Mem. Am. Concrete Inst., Prestressed Concrete Inst., Structural Engrs. Assn. Hawaii (pres. 1976), Consulting Engrs. Coun. Hawaii, Hui Kokua Kinipopo (pres. 1993—), U. Hawaii Pres.'s Club, U. Hawaii Alumni Assn., Chi Epsilon. Avocations: golf, sports fan. Office: Sato & Assocs Inc 2046 S King St Honolulu HI 96826-2219

SATO, TADASHI, artist; b. Maui, Hawaii, Feb. 6, 1923; Student, Honolulu Sch. Art, Bklyn. Mus. Art Sch., New Sch. Soc. Rsch. One man shows include First Hawaiian Ctr., Honolulu, 1997-98, The Contemporary Museum at First Hawaiian Bank, 1997; exhbns. include Guggenheim Mus., N.Y.C., 1954, Honolulu Acad. Arts, 1957, Pacific Heritage Exhibit, L.A., 1963, McRoberts and Tunnard Ltd., London, 1964, White House Festival Arts, Washington, 1965, Berlin Art Festival, 1967, Japanese C. of C., Honolulu, 1993-94, Maui Cmty. and Cultural Assn., 1994, Loa Gallery, Honolulu, 2000; represented in permanent collections Albright-Knox Art Gallery, Buffalo, Guggenheim Mus., Whitney Mus. Am. Art, N.Y.C., Honolulu Acad. Arts, U. Art Gallery, Tucson, (mosaic) Hawaii State Capitol Bldg., State Libr. Aina Haina, Oahu, Wailulu War Meml. Gymnasium, Maui, Krannert Art Mus., Ill., U. Nebr.; murals executed Halekulani Hotel, Honolulu, (mosaic) West Maui Recreation Ctr., (oil) Bay Club, Kapalua, Maui, (oil) ballroom of Hawaii Conv. Ctr., Honolulu; retrospective exhbn. Hui No Eau, Makawao, Maui, 1992. Office: PO Box 476 Lahaina HI 96767-0476

SATRE, PHILIP GLEN, casino entertainment executive, lawyer; b. Palo Alto, Calif., Apr. 30, 1949; s. Selmer Kenneth and Georgia June (Sterling) S.; m. Jennifer Patricia Arnold, June 30, 1973; children: Malena Anne, Allison Neal, Jessica Lilly, Peter Sterling. BA, Stanford U., 1971; JD, U. Calif.-Davis, 1975; postgrad. sr. exec. program, MIT, 1982. Bar: Nev. 1975, Calif. 1976. Assoc. Vargas & Bartlett, Reno, 1975-79; v.p., gen. counsel, sec. Harrah's, Reno, 1980-83, sr. v.p., 1983-84; pres. Harrah's East, Atlantic City, 1984; pres., CEO Harrah's Hotels and Casinos, Reno, 1984-91; dir., sr. v.p. Gaming Group The Promus Cos., Inc., Memphis, 1988-91, dir., pres., COO, 1991-94, dir., pres. CEO, 1994-95; pres., CEO Harrah's Entertainment, Inc., Memphis, 1995—, chmn., pres., CEO, 1997—; dir. JDN Realty Co., Memphis, 1999—. Dir., treas. Nat. Jud. Coll., Reno. Active The Stanford Athletic Bd., 1996—. Mem. ABA, Nev. Bar Assn., Calif. Bar Assn., Order of Coif, Phi Kappa Phi, Stanford Alumni Assn. (pres. Reno chpt. 1976-77), Young Pres. Orgn., The Bus. Roundtable. Office: PO Box 29526 Las Vegas NV 89126-9526 also: 5100 W Sahara Ave Las Vegas NV 89146

SATTERFIELD, BUDDY, real estate development executive; Pres. Ariz. divsn. Shea Homes, Walnut, Calif., 1994—. Office: J F Shea Co Inc PO Box 489 Walnut CA 91788-0489

SATTLER, BRUCE WEIMER, lawyer; b. South Gate, Calif., July 30, 1944; s. LeRoy Edward and Mary Beth (Weimer) S.; m. Earle Martha Ross, July 22, 1972. BA, Stanford U., 1966, JD, 1969. Bar: Colo. 1969, U.S. Dist. Ct. Colo. 1969, U.S. Dist. Ct. Mont. 1982, U.S. Dist. Ct. (no. dist.) Tex. 1989, U.S. Ct. Appeals (10th cir.) 1969, U.S. Ct. Appeals (9th cir.) 1984, U.S. Ct. Appeals (5th cir.) 1972. Assoc. Holland & Hart, Denver, 1969-75, ptnr., 1975-87; assoc. Equal Employment Opportunity Commn., Denver, 1973, Morris, Lower & Sattler, Denver, 1987-90; ptnr. Faegre & Benson, Denver, 1990—. Bd. dirs. ACLU of Colo., Denver, 1975-80, 88-94, Legal Aid Soc. of Metro Denver, 1976—, Colo. Lawyers Com., Denver, 1990-94, Children's Legal Clinic, Denver, 1989-91, Colo. Women's Employment and Edn., Denver, 1986-89. Fellow Am. Coll. Trial Lawyers; mem. ABA, Denver Bar Assn., Colo. Bar Assn. Office: Faegre & Benson 370 17th St Ste 2400 Denver CO 80202-5665

SATZ, LOUIS K. publishing executive; b. Chgo., Apr. 28, 1927; s. Harry Addison and Faye (Pollen) S.; m. Janet Maas, Jan. 2, 1952 children: Jay, Jonathan. B.S. in Mktg, U. Ill., 1949. Circulation dir. Pubs. Devel. Corp., Chgo., 1953, Guns mag., Jr. Arts and Activities, 1961; wholesaler sales mgr., then v.p., dir. sales Bantam Books, Inc., N.Y.C., 1962-80, sr. v.p., dir. diversified markets, 1980-84; pub. Passport Books, Lincolnwood, Ill., 1985-88; pres. Louis K. Satz Assocs., Pub. Cons., N.Y.C., 1988-91; ptnr. Scott/Satz Group, Pub. Cons., Walnut Creek, Calif., 1991—. Guest lectr. Sarah Lawrence Coll.Pub. Sch., Pace U.; faculty Hofstra U., Denver Pub. Inst.; cons. World Book Encyclopedia, 1995—; bd. dirs. N.Y. is Book Country, Brandeis U. Pub. Scholarship Fund, Oscar Dystel Fellowship NYU. Served with AUS, World War II, ETO. Mem. Am. Assn. Pubs. (chmn. small books mktg. div. 1975) Office: Scott Satz Group 558 Monarch Ridge Dr Walnut Creek CA 94596-2956

SAUCIER, BONNIE L. dean, pediatrics nurse; b. Alton, Ill., Oct. 12, 1945; d. Robert E. and Laura L. (Rice) Powers; children: Michelle Marie, Kent Lawrence. Diploma, St. Johns Hosp. Sch. Nursing, Springfield, Ill., 1966; BA, Stephens Coll., 1976; MEd, U. Mo., 1977; MSN, U. Mo., Kansas City, 1983; PhD in nursing, Tex. Womans U., 1986. RN, Calif., Tex. Pediatric staff nurse St. Johns Hosp., St Louis, 1966-69; asst. head nurse pediatrics North Kansas City (Mo.) Meml. Hosp., 1969-71; instr. nursing Trenton (Mo.) Jr. Coll., 1974-81; asst. prof. Mo. Western State Coll., St. Joseph, Mo., 1981-84; Inst. Cook County Coll., Gainesville, Tex., 1984-85; dir. health scis. Midwestern State U., Wichita Falls, 1986-92; prof., chair dept. nursing Calif. State U., Bakersfield, 1992—. Adj. inst. U. Tex., Arlington, 1985-86; bd. dirs. ARC. Wichita Falls, 1988-92; adv. bd., cons. Vernon (Tex.) Regional Jr. Coll., 1987-92; trustee Red River Hosp. Wichita Falls, 1989-92. Contbr. articles to profl. jours. Adv. bd. Care Team Healtha Care Svcs. Wichita Falls, 1991-92; bd. dirs. March of Dimes, 1989, Nat. Kidney Found., 1989-90; mem. Midwestern Div. Tex. Hosp., 1987-92; Tex. Orgn. of Baccalaureate Nursing Programs, 1989-92, Tex. Outstanding Rural Scholars Adv., 1989-92, Tex. Nurses Edn. Adv., 1989-90. Profl. Nursing Shortage grant, Office of Gov., 1991, Profl. Nursing Retention grantee Coordinating Bd., 1991; named to Women's Hall of Fame, Mayors Commn., 1991. Mem. Tex. Nurses Assn. (coun. edn. 1991-92), Tex. Nurses Assn. #11 (pres. 1990-91, bd. dirs. 1991-92), Calif. Nurses Assn. (state adv. com. for nursing manpower study 1992), Calif. Assn. Colls. of Nursing (health care adv. com., MSA program 1992-93, acad. senator), Tex. League for Nursing (bd. dirs. 1985-92), So. Coun. on Collegiate Edn., Sigma Theta Tau. Republican. Roman Catholic. Avocations: walking, travel, racquetball, reading. Office: Calif State U 9001 Stockdale Hwy Bakersfield CA 93311-1022

SAUER, DAVID ANDREW, writer, computer consultant; b. Urbana, Ill., Feb. 25, 1948; s. Elmer Louis and Frances (Hill) S. BA, Northwestern U., 1970; MS, Simmons Coll., 1975. Reference libr. Boston U., 1976-78, bibliographer, 1978-84, sci. bibliographer, 1984-88, head Stone Sci. Libr., 1988-94; v.p. info. svcs. CyberHelp, Inc., 1995-98; sr. tech. editor Qualcomm., Inc., 1997-2000; tech. pubs. supr. QCP Inc., 2000—. Co-author: Internet for Windows, 1994, WinComm Pro: The Visual Learning Guide, 1995, ProComm Plus V2 for Windows: The Visual Learning Guide, 1995, Access for Windows 95: The Visual Learning Guide, 1995, Cruising America Online 2.5, 1995, Internet for Windows: The America Online 2.5 Edition, 1995, Internet for Windows: The Microsoft Network, 1996, Cruising CompuServe, 1996, WinFax Pro 7 for Windows: The Visual Learning Guide, 1996, Windows NT 4.0 Visual Desk Reference, 1997, Discover Internet Explorer 4, 1997, Discover Netscape Communicator, 1997. Mem. S.W. Corridor Project, Boston, 1977-87, Forest Hills Neighborhood Improvement Assn., Boston, 1977-90, Forest Hills/Woodbourne Neighorhood Group, 1991-94. Mem. ALA, Spl. Librs. Assn., Soc. Tech. Comm., Hillside Colony Homeowners Assn. Democrat. Home: 1802 Mckee St Unit C4 San Diego CA 92110-1964 Office: 10300 Campus Point Dr San Diego CA 92121-1511

SAUNDERS, DEBRA J. columnist; b. Newton, Mass., Dec. 8, 1954; BA in Latin and Greek, U. Mass., Boston, 1980. Asst. dir. Arnold Zenker Assocs., 1982-83; writer/rschr., account exec. Todd Domke Assocs., Sacramento, 1983-84, Russo Watts & Rollins, Sacramento, 1985-86; asst. to Rep. Leader Calif. Assembly, Sacramento, 1987-88; columnist, editl. writer L.A. Daily News, 1988-92; columnist San Francisco Chronicle, 1992—. Leader study group on polit. speechmaking Harvard U., Cambridge, Mass., 1984; tchr. editl. and column writing UCLA Ext., 1992. Published in Wall St. Jour., Nat. Review, Weekly Std., Reason mag.; syndicated nationally via Creators Syndicate; appeared on Politically Incorrect, CNN and BBC radio. Office: San Francisco Chronicle 901 Mission St San Francisco CA 94103-2905

SAUNDERS, JAMES, management and training consultant; b. Chgo., Sept. 22, 1924; s. James Windam and Carrie Evelyn (Cox) S.; m. Gwendolyn Haithcox, Oct. 21, 1945 (dec. May 1971); children: Patricia Ann, Kathryn Lynn; m. Anita Joanne Laster, Sept. 16, 1972 (div. Oct. 1977); m. Bettye Jean Ricks, Apr. 18, 1981. BS in Math., Roosevelt U., 1953. Quality assurance rep. Dept. Army and Signal Corps., Chgo., 1945-63; dep. dir. quality assurance U.S. Naval Ordnance Plant, Forest Park, Ill., 1963-70; quality systems mgr. Gen. Foods Corp., Chgo., 1970-82; pres. Saunders and Assocs., Peoria, Ariz., 1982-91; councilman, vice mayor City of Peoria, 1985-91. Examiner Ariz. Govs. Alliance for Quality, 1995. Bd. dirs., sec. Ariz. Retirement Ctrs., Peoria, 1984-85; pres., chmn., bd. dirs., founder Peoria Econ. Devel. Group, 1987-91, dir. emeritus, 1991—; mem. Peoria Personnel Bd., 1984-85, Maricopa County Pvt. Industry Coun., 1984-89, chmn., 1988-89, exec. com. Westside Transp. Coalition, Peoria, 1988-89. Recipient Black Achiever of Industry award Chgo. YMCA, 1977, Image Govt. award NAACP, 1989, also various other awards. Mem. Peoria C. of C. (v.p., bd. dirs. 1985), Westside Coalition Chambers Commerce, Lions (sec., v.p. Peoria chpt. 1983-86), Kiwanis, Masons, Alpha Phi Alpha. Avocations: travel, golf, photography, reading. Home: 18847 N 88th Dr Peoria AZ 85382-8528

SAUNDERS, JAMES HARWOOD, accountant; b. Carlsbad, N.Mex., Apr. 2, 1948; s. Eugene C. and Ruth (Powelson)S.; m. Kathleen Sue Matson, Jan. 26, 1974 (div. Apr. 1982); m. Bette Kim McCutcheon, Sept. 4, 1982 (div. Oct. 1997); children: James C., Carl J., William K. AA in Adminstrn. Justice, Glendale Coll., Glendale, Ariz., 1975; BSBA, Ariz. State U., 1978. CPA, N.M., Ariz., Colo., Nev., Utah; lic. funeral dir. and embalmer; cert. fraud examiner; lic. pvt. investigator. Embalmer Denton Funeral Home, Carlsbad, 1964-69; clk., trainee Sears & Roebuck Co., Dallas and Albuquerque, 1969-71, Phoenix, 1971-73; police sgt. spl. ops. Phoenix Police Dept., 1973-80; staff acct. various CPA firms, Carlsbad, 1980-83; owner James H. Saunders Acctg., Carlsbad, 1983-86; pvt. practice acctg. Eagar, Ariz., 1987—. Auditor, mgmt. advisor to several Ariz. municipalities, 1987—. Vol. fireman Carlsbad Fire Dept., 1965-68; reserve dep. Bermallio County Sheriff Dept., Albuquerque, 1969-70. Mem. AICPA, Ariz. Soc. CPAs, N.Mex. Soc. CPAs, N.Mex. Assn. Funeral Dirs., Lions (sec. Carlsbad chpt. 1985-87, pres. Springerville, Ariz. chpt. 1987-91). Avocations: coin collecting, hunting, fishing, old movies, reading. E-mail: jamesH49@aol.com

SAUNDERS, PETER PAUL, investor; b. Budapest, Hungary, July 21, 1928; emigrated to Can., 1941, naturalized, 1946; s. Peter Paul and Elizabeth (Halom) Szende; m. Nancy Louise McDonald, Feb. 11, 1956; children: Christine Elizabeth McBride, Paula Marie. Student, Vancouver Coll., 1941-44; B.Com., U. B.C., 1948. Acct. Canadian Pacific Rly. Co., 1948-50; founder, pres. Laurentide Fin. Corp., Ltd., 1950-66, vice chmn., 1966-67; chmn., pres. Coronation Credit Corp. Ltd., Vancouver, B.C., Can., 1968-78, Versatile Corp. (formerly Coronation Credit Corp. and Cornat Industries Ltd.), Vancouver, Can., 1978-87; prin., pres. Saunders Investment Ltd., Vancouver, 1987—. Bd. dirs. Computrol Security Sys. Ltd., Greene Valley Concessions.; chmn., dir. Harlan Fairbanks Co. Ltd. Past pres. Vancouver Symphony Soc., 1968-70, Can. Cancer Soc., B.C. and Yukon Rdgion, 1975-77, Vancouver Art Gallery Assn., 1981-83; chmn. Vancouver Opera Round Table, 1984-92. Mem. Vancouver Club, Shaughnessy Golf and Country Club, Royal Vancouver Yacht Club, Thunderbird Country Club (Rancho Mirage, Calif.). Avocations: golf, skiing, hunting, boating. Home: 3620 Alexandra St Vancouver BC Canada V6J 4B9 Office: Saunders Investment Ltd PO Box 49352 Bentall Ctr Vancouver BC Canada V7X 1L4

SAUSMAN, KAREN, zoological park administrator; b. Chgo., Nov. 26, 1945; d. William and Annabell (Lofaso) S. BS, Loyola U., 1966; student, Redlands U., 1968. Keeper Lincoln Park Zoo, Chgo., 1964-66; tchr. Palm Springs (Calif.) Unified Sch., 1968-70; ranger Nat. Park Svc., Joshua Tree, Calif., 1968-70; zoo dir. The Living Desert, Palm Desert, 1970—. Natural history study tour leader internat., 1974—; part-time instr. Coll. Desert Natural History Calif. Desert, 1975-78; field reviewer conservation grants Inst. Mus. Svcs., 1987—, MAP cons., 1987—, panelist, 1992—; internat. studbook keeper for Sand Cats, 1988-2001, for Cuvier's Gazelle, Mhorr Gazelle, 1990-2000; co-chair Arabian Oryx species survival plan propogation group, 1986-95; spkr. in field. Author Survival Captive Bighorn Sheep, 1982, Small Facilities- Opportunities and Obligations, 1983; wildlife illustrator books, mags, 1970—; editor Fox Paws newsletter Living Desert, 1970—, ann. reports, 1976—; natural sci. editor Desert Mag., 1979-82; compiler Conservation and Management Plan for Antelope, 1992; contbr. articles to profl. jours. Past bd. dirs., sec. Desert Protective Coun.; adv. coun. Desert Bighorn Rsch. Inst., 1981-85; bd. dirs. Palm Springs Desert Resorts Convention and Visitors Bur., 1988-94; bd. dirs., treas. Coachella Valley Mountain Trust, 1989-92. Named Woman Making a Difference Soroptimist Internat., 1989, 93, 97, Woman of Distinction, Riverside Bus. Press, 2000. Fellow Am. Assn. Zool. Parks and Aquariums (bd. dirs., accredation field reviewer, desert antelope taxon adv. group, caprid taxon adv. group, felid taxon adv. group, small population mgmt. adv. group, wildlife conservation and mgmt. com., chmn. ethics com. 1987, mem. com., internat. rels. com., ethics task force, pres'. award 1972-77, outstanding svc. award 1983, 88, editor newsletter, Zool. Parks and Aquarium Fundamentals 1982); mem. Internat. Species Inventory System (mgmt. com., policy adv. group 1980-96), Calif. Assn. Mus. (v.p. 1992-96), Calif. Assn. Zoos and Aquariums, Internat. Union Dirs. Zool. Gardens, Western Interpretive Assn. (so. Calif. chpt.), Am. Assn. Mus., Arboreta and Botanical Gardens So. Calif. (coun. dirs.), Soc. Conservation Biology, Nat. Audubon. Soc., Jersey Wildlife Preservation Trust Internat.,

Nature Conservancy, East African Wildlife Soc., African Wildlife Found., Kennel Club Palm Springs (past bd. dirs., treas. 1978-80), Scottish Deerhound Club Am. (editor Scottish Deerhounds in N.A., 1983, life mem. U.K. chpt.), Internat. Bengal Cat Soc. (pres. 1994-96). Avocations: pure bred dogs, cats, dressage, painting, photography. Office: The Living Desert 47 900 Portola Ave Palm Desert CA 92260 E-mail: kastld@aol.com

SAUTE, ROBERT EMILE, drug and cosmetic consultant; b. West Warwick, R.I., Aug. 18, 1929; s. Camille T. and Lea E. (Goffinet) S.; m. Arda T. Darnell, May 18, 1957; children: Richard R., Steven N., Allen K. BS, R.I. Coll. Pharmacy, 1950; MS, Purdue U., 1952, PhD, 1953. Registered pharmacist. Tech. asst. to pres. Lafayette (Ind.) Pharmacal, 1955-56; sr. rsch. and devel. chemist H.K. Wampole Denver Chem. Co., Phila., 1956-57; supt. Murray Hill (N.J.) plant Strong Cobb Arner Inc., 1957-60; adminstrv. dir. rsch. and devel. Avon Products Inc., Suffern, N.Y., 1960-68; dir. rsch. and devel. toiletries div. Gillette Co., Boston, 1968-71; group v.p. Dart Industries, L.A., 1972-75; pres. Saute Cons., Inc., L.A., 1975—. Bd. dirs. Joico Labs., Inc., Cosmetics Enterprises, Ltd. Contbr. to books; patentee in field. With U.S. Army, 1953-55. Fellow Soc. Cosmetic Chemists (bd. dirs. 1987-89, 94-96, chmn. Calif. chpt. 1986); mem. AAAS, N.Y. Acad. Scis., Soc. Investigative Dermatology, Am. Assn. Pharm. Scientists, Sigma Xi, Rho Chi. Avocations: travel, art, music, cooking, wine.

SAUVEY, RAYMOND ANDREW, museum director; b. Green Bay, Wisc., Aug. 6, 1953; s. Raymond Norbert and Joan Florence (Smits) S. BA Comm., U. Wisc., Green Bay, 1980. Gen. mgr. Nat. R.R. Museum, Green Bay, Wis., 1990; dir. Calif. St. Railroad Museum, Sacramento. With U.S. Army, 1971-74, USN, 1984-89. Mem. Nat. Railway Hist. Soc., Railway and Locomotive Hist. Soc., Rotary.

SAVAGE, ELDON PAUL, retired environmental health educator; b. Bedford, Iowa, Apr. 4, 1926; s. Paul and Nora (Arthur) S.; m. Ella May, June 5, 1948; children: Steven P., Michael D. BS, U. Kans., 1950; MPH, Tulane U., 1958; PhD, Okla. U., 1968. Coord. environ. sanitation demonstration projects USPHS, Kans., Iowa and Pa., 1950-64; chief state aids sect. pesticide ctr. Ctr. for Disease Control, Atlanta, 1964-70; chief chem. epidemiology sect. Inst. Rural Environ. Health, Colo. State U., Ft. Collins, 1970-84, prof., dir. environ. health divsn., 1984-85, head dept. environ. health, 1985-90, dir. environ. health svcs., 1987-93, prof. emeritus, 1993—. Contbr. articles to profl. jours. Mem. Am. Acad. Sanitarians (sec., treas., diplomate), Nat. Environ. Health Assn., Sigma Xi, Gamma Sigma Delta. Home: Savage EE Arabian Horses 5220 Apple Dr Fort Collins CO 80526-4302 Office: Colo State U Inst Rural Envrion Health Fort Collins CO 80523-0001

SAVAGE, NEVE RICHARD, marketing executive; b. Harrow, Eng., Nov. 18, 1944; came to U.S., 1970, naturalized, 1983; s. Richard Marshall and Joan Muriel (Eperon) S.; m. Ann Elizabeth Freeman, Apr. 29, 1972; children: Sarah-Jane, Megan, Truan. B.A., U. Oxford (Eng.), 1966, M.A., 1968. Account supr. Garland-Compton Advt., London, 1966-70; sr. v.p. Compton Advt., N.Y.C., 1970-77, dir., 1980-83; exec. v.p. Cadwell Davis Savage Advt., N.Y.C., 1977-82; exec. v.p. internat. Wells, Rich, Greene, Inc., N.Y.C., 1983-86; vice chmn. Kornhauser & Calene Inc., 1986-88; exec. group dir. Ogilvy & Mather, 1988-94; v.p. mktg. AT&T Wireless Svcs., Kirkland, Wash., 1994-98; v.p. client results Ave. A Internet Media, Seattle, 1998-2000; pres. Avenue A Internat., London, 2000—.

SAVAGE, STEPHEN MICHAEL, lawyer; b. Norwich, Conn., Apr. 23, 1946; s. Alfred and Iva (Allen) S.; m. Lois Palestine, July 4, 1968; children: Meredith, William, Sam. BA, U. Pa., 1968; JD, Harvard U., 1973. Bar: Ariz. 1973, U.S. Dist. Ct. Ariz. 1973. With Fennemore Craig, Phoenix, 1973—, chmn. mgmt. com., 1988—. Mem. Greater Phoenix Leadership; bd. dirs. Ariz. Diabetes Assn., Phoenix, 1983-87, Ariz. Sci. Ctr., Phoenix, 1992—; chmn. bd. dirs. All Saints' Episcopal Day Sch., Phoenix, 1988; comdr., pres. Mounted Sheriff's Posse Maricopa County, Phoenix, 1992-93. Mem. ABA, State Bar Ariz. (chmn. sect. corp., banking and bus. law 1983-84), Maricopa County Bar Assn., Assn. Corp. Growth, Phoenix Country Club. Avocations: team roping, golf. Office: Fennemore Craig 3003 N Central Ave Ste 2600 Phoenix AZ 85012-2913

SAVAGE, TERRY RICHARD, information systems executive; b. St. Louis, Oct. 21, 1930; s. Terry Barco and Ada Vanetta (Cochran) S.; m. Gretchen Susan Wood, Sept. 26, 1964; children: Terry Curtis, Christopher William, Richard Theodore. AB, Washington U., St. Louis, 1951, MA, 1952; PhD, U. Pa., 1954. Mgr. system software IBM Rsch., Yorktown Heights, N.Y., 1956-63; dir. data processing Documentation Inc., Bethesda, Md., 1963-64; mgr. info. systems Control Data Corp., Rockville, 1964-67; dir. rsch. Share Rsch. Corp., Santa Barbara, Calif., 1967-68; computer-aided acquisition and logistic support program mgr. TRW, Redondo Beach, 1968-92; ret., ind. cons. pvt. practice, 1992—. Expert witness for various coms. U.S. Congress, 1981, 84, 88, 89. Contbr. articles to profl. jours. Bd. dirs. ABC-Clio Press, Santa Barbara, 1970-75, Help the Homeless Help Themselves, Rancho Palos Verdes, Calif., 1988-94, ChorusLiners, Rancho Palos Verdes, 1983—, Savage Info. Svcs., Inc., Torrance, Calif., 1992—. Mem. Cosmos Club. Home and Office: 30000 Cachan Pl Rancho Palos Verdes CA 90275-5412 E-mail: terrysavage@home.com

SAVERY, MATTHEW, music conductor, director, educator; b. Berkshire County, Mass. MusB, New Eng. Conservatory Music; MusM, U. Mich.; studied with Gustav Meier, Pascal Verrot, Frank Battisti. Music dir., conductor Symphonic Choir, 1994—, Butte Symphony Orch., 1994-99, Bozeman (Mont.) Symphony Orch., 1994—. Lectr. schs. Mont.; clincian Music Ekucators N.W. Conf., 1997; chmn. young artist competition Mont. Assn. Symphony Orch., 1997—. Music dir., conductor (theater) Damn Yankees, Guys and Dolls, Annie; past music dir. Comic Opera Guild, Ann Arbor, Mich., Stockbridge (Mass.) Sinfonia, Tecumseh (Mich.) Orch.; past conductor orch. festivals Mont. AA H.S.; appeared in , conductor Tchaikovsky's Nutcracker, 1995, 96, Tchaikovsky's Sleeping Beauty, The Magic Toy Shop. U. Mich. fellow; recipient Eugene and Sadie Power award for performing arts. Office: Bozeman Symphony Orch PO Box 1174 Bozeman MT 59771-1174

SAVITZ, MAXINE LAZARUS, aerospace company executive; b. Balt., Feb. 13, 1937; d. Samuel and Harriette (Miller) Lazarus; m. Sumner Alan Savitz, Jan. 1, 1961; children: Adam Jonathan, Alison Carrie. BA in Chemistry magna cum laude, Bryn Mawr Coll., 1958; PhD in Organic Chemistry, MIT, 1961. Instr. chemistry Hunter Coll., N.Y.C., 1962-63; sr. electrochemist Mobility Equipment Rsch. and Devel. Ctr., Ft. Belvoir, Va., 1963-68; prof. chemistry Federal City Coll., Washington, 1968-72; program mgr. NSF, Washington, 1972-74; dir. FEA Office Bldgs. Policy Rshc. U.S. Dept. Energy, Washington, 1974-75, dir. div. indsl. conservation, 1975-76, from dir. div. bldgs. and community systems to dep asst sec., 1975-83; pres. Lighting Rsch. Inst., 1983-85; asst. to v.p. engring. Ceramic Components div. The Garrett Corp., 1985-87; gen. mgr. ceramic components divsn. AlliedSignal Inc., Torrance, Calif., 1987-99; gen. mgr. tech. partnerships Honeywell, Torrance, 1999—. Bd. dirs. Am. Coun. for Energy Efficient Economy, Energy Found., EPRI; cons. State Mich. Dept. Commerce, 1983, N.C. Alternative Energy Corp., 1983, Garrett Corp., 1983, Energy Engring. Bd., Nat. Rsch. Bd., 1986-93, Office Tech. Assessment, U.S. Congress Energy Demand Panel, 1987-91, nat. materials adv. bd. NRC, 1989-94; bd. dirs. U.S. Advanced Ceramic Assn., 1989-98, chmn., 1992; adv. com. div. ceramics/materials ORNL, 1989-92, adv. com. dir., 1992-96; mem. lab. adv. com. Pacific N.W. Nat. Lab., 2000—; adv. bd. Sec. Energy, 1992—; mem. Def. Sci. Bd., 1993-96; vis. com. adv. tech. Nat. Inst. Standards and Tech., 1993-98, Nat. Sci. Bd., 1999—. Editor Energy and Bldgs.; contbr. articles to profl. jours. Mem. policy com. NAE, 1994-98. NSF postdoctoral fellow, 1961, 62, NIH predoctoral fellow, 1960, 61. Mem. Nat. Acad. Engring. Office: Honeywell Tech Partnerships 2525 W 190th St Torrance CA 90504-6002 E-mail: maxine.savitz@honeywell.com

SAVOIA, MARIA CHRISTINA, associate dean; BA with highest honors, Wellesley Coll., 1972; MD, Harvard U., 1976. Diplomate Am. Bd. Internal Medicine. Med. intern U. Calif., San Diego, 1976-77, med. resident, 1977-79, fellow divsn. infectious diseases, 1980-84, clin. instr. medicine, 1980-84, asst. adj. prof. medicine, 1984-90, acting vice-chair dept. medicine, 1987-89, assoc. prof. clin. medicine, 1990-96, assoc. dean curriculum and student affairs sch. medicine, 1990—, acting dir. office learning resources sch. medicine, 1991-95, acting assoc. dean admissions sch. medicine, 1991, chief acad. officer sch. medicine, 1994—, prof. clin. medicine, 1996—; sr. fellow in med. edn. Harvard Macy Inst., Boston, 1996-97; assoc. investigator VA Med. Ctr., San Diego, 1981-84, asst. chief to acting chief med. svc., 1984-90, 87-89. Author: (with others) Medical Microbiology and Infectious Diseases, 1986, Infectious Disease, 1986, Principles and Practice of Infectious Diseases, 1989, Infections in Urology, 1990, Medical Complications During Pregnancy, 1995, and others; contbr. numerous articles and abstracts to profl. jours. Recipient Calif. Women in Govt. award, 1987; NSF grantee, 1972; Durant scholar Wellesley (Mass.) Coll., 1968-72. Fellow Infectious Diseases Soc. Am.; mem. Am. Soc. Microbiology. Office: Univ Calif Sch Medicine Assoc Dean Student Affairs 9500 Gilman Dr La Jolla CA 92093-0606

SAVOY, DOUGLAS EUGENE, bishop, religious studies educator, explorer, writer; b. Bellingham, Wash., May 11, 1927; s. Lewis Dell and Maymie (Janett) S.; m. Elvira Clarke, Dec. 5, 1957 (div.); 1 son, Jamil Sean (dec.); m. Sylvia Ontaneda, July 7, 1971; children: Douglas Eugene, Christopher Sean, Sylvia Jamila. Student, U. Portland, 1947-8; DST, D Canon and Sacred Law, Jamilian U. of the Ordained, 1980. Ordained to ministry Internat. Community of Christ Ch., 1962, bishop, 1971. Head bishop Internat. Community of Christ Ch., 1971—; lectr. in ministerial tng. studies, 1972—; pastor Univ. Chapel, Reno, 1979—; founder Jamilian Parochial Sch., 1976; chancellor, founder Sacred Coll. of Jamilian Theology; pres., founder Jamilian U. of the Ordained, 1980; pres. Advs. for Religious Rights and Freedoms; chmn. World Coun. for Human Spiritual Rights, 1984—; head Jamilian Order of Patriarchs, 1990—; engaged in newspaper pub. West Coast, 1949-56; began explorations in jungles east of Andes in Peru to prove his theory that high civilizations of Peru may have had their origin in jungles, 1957; pres., founder Andean Explorers Found & Ocean Sailing Club, Reno. Expedition dir. Grand Ophir Sea Expedition; capt. Feathered Serpent III-Ophir, 1997-98. Author: Antisuyo, The Search for Lost Cities of the High Amazon, 1970, Vilcabamba, Last City of the Incas, 1970, The Cosolargy Papers, vol. 1, 1970, vol. 2-3, 1972, The Child Christ, 1973, Arabic edit., 1976, Japanese edit., 1981, The Decoded New Testament, 1974, Arabic edit., 1981, Millenium Edition, 1983, On The Trail of The Feathered Serpent, 1974, Code Book and Community Manual for Overseers, 1975, Prophecies of Jamil, First Prophecy to the Americas, vol. 1, 1976, Second Prophecy to the Americas, 1976, The Secret Sayings of Jamil, The Image and the Word, vol. 1, 1976, vol. 2, 1977, Project X—The Search For the Secrets of Immortality, 1977, Prophecy to the Races of Man, Vol. 2, 1977, Solar Cultures of The Americas, 1977, Dream Analysis, 1977, Vision Analysis, 1977, Christoanalysis, 1978, The Essaei Document: Secrets of an Eternal Race, 1978, Millennium edit., 1983, The Lost Gospel of Jesus: Hidden Teachings of Christ, 1978, Millennium edit., 1983, Secret Sayings of Jamil, vol. 3., 1978, vol. 4, 1979, Prophecy to The Christian Churches, vol. 3, 1978, The Sayings, vol. 4, 1979, Solar Cultures of Oceania, 1979, Prophecy of The End Times, vol. 4, 1980, Solar Cultures of Israel, vols. 1 and 2, 1980, Solar Cultures of China, 1980, Christotherapy, 1980, Christophysics, 1980, Christodynamics, 1980, Code Book of Prophecy, 1980, The Sayings, vol. 5, 1980, vol. 6, 1981, Solar Cultures of India, 1981, Prophecy on the Golden Age of Light and the Nation of Nations, Vol. 5, 1981, Solar Cultures of Israel, vol. 3, 1981, The Counsels, 1982, Prophecy of the Universal Theocracy, vol. 6, 1982, Prophecy of the New Covenant, vol. 7, 1982, The Book of God's Revelation, 1983, Miracle of the Second Advent, 1984, Clerical Studies in Theology, Book I, Book II, Book III, Book IV, Transformative Theology: The School of Revelation, Transformative Theology: The School of Prophecy, Liturgical Theology: Preparation for Advanced Degrees, 1993; over 400 audio tape rec. lectures, 1974—, numerous others.; dir. documentary film Adventure: Trail of the Feathered Serpent, 1970, Lost City of the Andes, 1987; wrote, dir. videos Royal Roads to Discovery, Mystery of the Essenes of Old Israel, Secrets From the High Andes of Peru, 1993, The Gran Vilaya Expeditions, 1996; contbr. articles on Peruvian cultures to mags., also articles on philosophy and religion; discoverer lost city of Incas at Vilcabamba Cuzco, numerous ancient cities in Amazonia including Gran Pajaten, Gran Vilaya, Monte Peruvia, Twelve Cities of the Condor, Gran Saposoa. Trustee in Trust Head Bishop Internat. Community of Christ. Served with AS USNR, 1944-46. Decorated Order of the Grand Cross Senate of Peru, 1989; recipient Participant's medallion Seawanhaka Yacht Club, 1977; Gold medal Ministry Industry and Tourism Peru, Silver Hummingbird, 1987; Silver medal and scroll City of Ica, Peru; honored with Gene Savoy Day by City of Reno, 1996, numerous exploring awards. Mem. Geog. Soc. Lima, Andean Explorers Found., Ocean Sailing Club (Explorer of the Century 1989, Flag awards), World Coun. for Human Spiritual Rights, Advs. for Religious Rights and Freedoms, Authors Guild, Explorers Club (N.Y.C., Flag awards), L.A. Yacht Club. Home: 2025 La Fond Dr Reno NV 89509-3025 Office: 643 Ralston St Reno NV 89503-4436 E-mail: gene@savoy.reno.nv.us

SAVRUN, ENDER, engineering executive, researcher, engineer; b. Adana, Turkey, July 29, 1953; came to U.S., 1978; s. Yusuf and Nemide Savrun; m. Canan Erdamar, Oct. 23, 1979; children: Altay, Seray. BS, Istanbul (Turkey) Tech. U., 1976, MS, 1978; PhD, U. Wash., 1986. Rsch. engr. Charlton Industries, Redmond, Wash., 1984-85; rsch. scientist Flow Industries, Kent, 1985-87, Photon Scis., Bothell, 1987-88; mgr. rsch. Keramont Rsch. Corp., Tucson, 1988-89; v.p. R & D Keramont Corp., Tucson, 1989-92; founder, pres. Sienna Rsch., Inc., Tucson, 1992—. Contbr. articles to profl. jours.; patentee in field. Turkish Govt. scholar, 1979. Mem. Materials Rsch. Soc., Am. Soc. for Metals, Am. Ceramic Soc. Avocations: cross-country skiing, camping, travel.

SAWDEI, MILAN A. lawyer; b. Bakersfield, Calif., Aug. 23, 1946; BA, U. Calif., Long Beach, 1969; JD, W.S.U., 1975. Bar: Calif. 1975, U.S. Dist. Ct. (ctrl. dist.) Calif. 1975. House counsel Sanyo Electric, Inc., 1975-77; assoc. counsel Brown Co. (Gulf & Western), 1978-80; divsn. counsel Petrolane, Inc., 1980-83; sr. counsel Bergen Brunswig Corp., Orange, Calif., 1983-90, v.p., chief legal officer, 1990-92, exec. v.p., chief legal officer, sec., 1992—. Mem. ABA, Am. Corp. Counsel Assn., Am. Soc. Corp. Secs., L.A. County Bar Assn. Office: Bergen Brunswig Corp 4000 Metropolitan Dr Orange CA 92868-3510

SAWYER, CHARLES HENRY, anatomist, educator; b. Ludlow, Vt., Jan. 24, 1915; s. John Guy and Edith Mabel (Morgan) S.; m. Ruth Eleanor Schaeffer, Aug. 23, 1941; 1 dau., Joan Eleanor. BA, Middlebury Coll., 1937, DSc honoris causa, 1975; student, Cambridge U., Eng., 1937-38; Ph.D., Yale, 1941. Instr. anatomy Stanford, 1941-44; assoc., asst. prof., assoc. prof., prof. anatomy Duke U., 1944-51; prof. anatomy UCLA, Los Angeles, 1951-85, prof. emeritus, 1985—, chmn. dept., 1955-63, acting chmn., 1966-69, faculty research lectr., 1966 [illegible] Endocrinology, 1955-59, Proc. Soc. Exptl. Biology and Medicine, 1959-63, Am. Jour. Physiology, 1972-75; Author papers on neuroendocrinology. Mem. Internat. Brain Research Orgn. (council 1964-68), AAAS, Am. Assn. Anatomists (v.p. 1969-70, Henry Gray award 1984), Am. Physiol. Soc., Am. Zool. Soc., Neurosci. Soc., Endocrine Soc. (council 1968-70, Koch award 1973), Am. Acad. Arts and Scis., Nat. Acad. Scis., Soc. Exptl. Biology and Medicine, Soc. Study Reprodn. (dir. 1969-71, Hartman award 1977), Internat. Neuroendocrine Soc. (council 1972-76), Hungarian Soc. Endocrinology and Metabolism (hon.), Japan Endocrin Soc. (hon.), Phi Beta Kappa, Sigma Xi. Home: 466 Tuallitan Rd Los Angeles CA 90049-1941 Office: U Calif Sch Medicine Dept Neurobiology Los Angeles CA 90095-0001

SAWYER, THOMAS WILLIAM, career officer; b. Turlock, Calif., Nov. 19, 1933; s. Everett Edward and Marie Georgine (Gunderson) S.; m. Faith Barry Martin, Feb. 16, 1957; children: William Everet, John Martin, Susan Quincy BS in Mil. Sci., U. Nebr., 1965; MS in Internat. Rels., George Washington U., 1974. Enlisted U.S. Air Force, 1952, commd. and advanced through grades to maj. gen., 1983; comdr. 57th Fighter Squadron, Keflavik, Iceland, 1971-73; chief internat. relations div. Hdqrs. U.S. Air Force, Washington, 1974-77; vice comdr. 20th Air Div., Fort Lee, Va., 1977-78; mil. asst. to Sec. Air Force, 1978-80; comdr. 26th Air Div., Luke AFB, Ariz., 1980-82; dep. ops. NORAD and Space Command, Colorado Springs, Colo., 1982-86; retired USAF, 1986; founder, pres. Aerospace Network Inc., 1986-98; pres. Pathfinder Tech., Inc., 1998—. Bd. dirs. Pikes Peak chpt. ARC, Colo./Wyo. chpt. Am. Def. Preparedness Assn. Decorated Disting. Service medal, Def. Disting. Service medal, Legion of Merit with 2 oak leaf clusters, Silver Star (2) Mem. Phoenix C. of C. (bd. dirs. 1980-82), Colorado Springs C. of C. Avocations: nat. security affairs, woodworking, automobile bldg. Office: Pathfinder Tech Inc 10 W Cheyenne Mountain Blvd Colorado Springs CO 80906-4335

SAX, JOSEPH LAWRENCE, lawyer, educator; b. Chgo., Feb. 3, 1936; s. Benjamin Harry and Mary (Silverman) S.; m. Eleanor Charlotte Gettes, June 17, 1958; children: Katherine Elaine Dennett, Valerie Beth, Amber Sax Rosen. AB, Harvard U., 1957; JD, U. Chgo., 1959; LLD (hon.), Ill. Inst. Tech., 1992. Bar: D.C. 1960, Mich., 1966, U.S. Supreme Ct. 1969. Atty. U.S. Dept. Justice, Washington, 1959-60; pvt. practice law Washington, 1960-62; prof. U. Colo., 1962-65, U. Mich., Ann Arbor, 1966-86; dep. asst. sec. and counselor U.S. Sec. Interior, Washington, 1994-96; prof. U. Calif. Law Sch., Berkeley, 1986—. Fellow Ctr. Advanced Study in Behavioral Scis., 1977-78. Author: Waters and Water Rights, 1967, Water Law, Planning and Policy, 1968, Defending the Environment, 1971, Mountains Without Handrails, 1980, Legal Control of Water Resources, 1991, Playing Darts with a Rembrandt, 1999. Bd. dirs. Environ. Law Inst., Washington, 1970-75; trustee Center for Law and Social Policy, 1970-76; gov.'s rep. Gt. Lakes Task Force, 1984-85. With USAF, 1960. Fellow AAAS; mem. University Club (San Francisco). E-mail: saxj@law.berkeley.edu

SAXBERG, BORJE OSVALD, management educator; b. Helsinki, Finland, Jan. 25, 1928; came to U.S., 1950, naturalized, 1966; s. Oskar Valdemar and Martha (Granberg) S.; m. A. Margrete Haug; children: Bo Erland Haug, Bror Valdemar Haug. BA, Swedish Sch. Bus. and Econs., 1950; BS, Oreg. State U., 1952; MS, U. Ill., 1953, PhD, 1958. Teaching asst., instr. U. Ill., 1953-57; prof. dept. mgmt. and orgn. U. Wash., 1957—; asso. dean U. Wash. (Bus. Sch.), 1967-70, chmn. dept. mgmt. and orgn., 1972-76, chmn. faculty senate, 1980-81, chmn. dept. mgmt. and orgn., 1989-93; dir. program in entrepreneurship and innovation, 1989-95. Cons. in field. Author: (with R. Joseph Monsen) The Business World, 1967, (with H.P. Knowles) Personality and Leadership Behavior, 1971, (with R.A. Johnson) Management, Systems and Society, 1976, (with B. Mar) Managing High Technology, 1985. Ford Found. fellow, 1960-61 Mem. Am. Sociol. Assn., Rainier Club, Swedish Club (Seattle). Home: 7336 58th Ave NE Seattle WA 98115-6257 Office: Univ Wash Grad Sch Bus 353200 Seattle WA 98195-0001

SAXE, DEBORAH CRANDALL, lawyer; b. Lima, Ohio, July 23, 1949; d. Robert Gordon and Lois Barker (Taylor) Crandall; m. Robert Saxe, June 3, 1989; children: Elizabeth Sara, Emily Jane. BA, Pa. State U., 1971; MA, UCLA, 1973, JD, 1978. Bar: Calif. 1978, D.C. 1979, U.S. Dist. Ct. D.C. 1979, U.S. Dist. Ct. (ea. dist.) Calif. 1981, U.S. Dist. Ct. (ctrl. dist.) Calif. 1982, U.S. Dist. Ct. (no. and so. dists.) Calif. 1987, U.S. Ct. Appeals (4th and D.C. cirs.) 1979, U.S. Ct. Appeals (6th cir.) 1985, U.S. Ct. Appeals (8th and 9th cirs.) 1987, U.S. Ct. Appeals (2nd cir.) 1990, U.S. Supreme Ct. 1982, U.S. Dist. Ct. (no. dist.) Ill. 2001, U.S. Ct. Appeals (7th cir.) 2001. Assoc. Seyfarth, Shaw, Fairweather & Geraldson, Washington, 1978-83, Jones, Day, Reavis & Pogue, Washington, 1983-85, L.A., 1985-87, ptnr., 1988-97; shareholder Heller Ehrman White & McAuliffe, 1997—. Judge pro tem, Small Claims Ct., L.A., 1985-88. Co-author: Advising California Employers, 1990, 2d edit., 1995; contbg. editor Employment Discrimination Law, 1989. Bd. dirs. Eisner Pediatric and Family Med. Ctr., L.A., 1990—, chair, 1996-98; bd. dirs. Constitutional Rights Found., 1997—, L.A. County Bar Found., 1999—. Mem. ABA (labor law sect. 1978—), Calif. Bar Assn. (labor law sect. 1985—), L.A. County Bar Assn. (labor and employment law sect. 1985—, mem. exec. com. 1988—, vice chair 2001—, sec. 1999-2000, treas. 2000-01), Pi Lambda Theta, Phi Beta Kappa. Office: Heller Ehrman White & McAuliffe 601 S Figueroa St Fl 40 Los Angeles CA 90017-5704 Fax: 213-614-1868. E-mail: dse@hewm.com

SAXE, STEVEN LOUIS, lawyer; b. San Francisco, May 28, 1942; s. Jules Irving and Marian (Adams) S.; m. Joanne Saxe, July 12, 1964; children: Julie Ann, Jeffrey Scott. BS, U. Calif., Berkeley, 1964; JD, U. San Francisco, 1967. Bar: Calif. 1967, U.S. Dist. Ct. (no. and ea. dist.) Calif. 1967. Clk. Calif. Ct. Appeals, San Francisco, 1967-68; assoc. Farella, Brown & Martel, San Francisco, 1968-69; sr. counsel Bank Am., San Francisco, 1969-80; ptnr. Boyden, Cooluris, Hauser & Saxe, San Francisco, 1980-91, Pillsbury, Madison & Sutro, San Francisco, 1991-2000, Boyden Cooluris Livingston & Saxe PC, Larkspur, Calif., 2000—. Dir. Ecumenical Assn. Housing, San Rafael, Calif., 1985-92; pres. Congregation Rodef Sholom, San Rafael, 1992-94; dir., pres. Fair Housing Marin, San Rafael, 1995—. Mem. ABA, Consumer Bankers Assn., Coll. Am. Coll. Fin. Svcs. Lawyers. Office: Boyden Cooluris Livingston & Saxe PC 900 Larkspur Landing Cir Larkspur CA 94939-1723 E-mail: ssaxe@bclslaw.com

SAXTON, LLOYD, psychologist, writer; b. Loveland, Colo., Sept. 28, 1929; s. Oliver George and Alice Augusta (Andersen) S.; m. Nancy Alison Roberts, Dec. 17, 1955; children: Perry Brent, Jay Ronald, Barbara Jean. AB in English, U. Calif., Berkeley, 1950, BS in Psychology, 1954; MS in Psychology, San Francisco State U., 1955; PhD in Psychology, U. of the Pacific, Stockton, Calif., 1957. Diplomate Am. Bd. Forensic Examiners (cert. 1996); lic. psychologist, Calif. Intern in clin. psychology Children's Hosp., San Francisco, 1955-56; teaching fellow U. Pacific, San Francisco, 1955-57, instr. psychology, 1957-58, asst. prof. psychology, 1958-60; assoc. prof. psychology Am. Acad. of Asian Studies, San Francisco, 1960-62, prof. psychology, 1962-65; chmn. dept. psychology Coll. of San Mateo, Calif., 1965-75, prof. psychology, 1975-92; pvt. practice San Francisco/Larkspur, 1958—; emeritus, 1995. Author: Individual, Marriage and the Family, 1968, Individual, 9th edit., 1996; author/editor: A Marriage Reader, 1970, The American Scene, 1970. Mem. APA, AAAS, AAUP, Am. Assn. Marriage and Family Therapists, Western Psychol. Assn., Am. Coll. [illegible] Chess Fedn. Democrat. Avocations: chess, sailing, music, ballet, opera. Home and Office: 57 Hatzic Ct Larkspur CA 94939-1992

SAY, CALVIN, state official; b. Feb. 1, 1952; m. Cora Say; children: Geoffrey, Jared. BEd, U. Hawaii at Manoa. Mem. state house State of Hawaii, 1976—; mgr. Kotake Shokai Ltd. Chmn. fin. com. Staste of Hawaii, mem. labor mgmt. com. Mem. Palolo Little League, Pop Warner, Hawaii Youth Symphony, Hawaii Sports Hall of Fame and Mus., Palolo Cmty. Coun., Honolulu Symphony Soc., Gov.'s Com. Commemorating the Chinese Bicentennial,; dir. Pacific Rim Found. Democrat. Office: Hawaii Ho Reps Hawaii State Capitol Rm 431 415 S Beretania St Honolulu HI 96813-2407

SAYKALLY, RICHARD JAMES, chemistry educator; b. Rhinelander, Wis., Sept. 10, 1947; s. Edwin L. and Helen M. S. BS, U. Wis., Eau Claire, 1970; PhD, U. Wis., Madison, 1977. Postdoctoral Nat. Bur. Standards, Boulder, Colo., 1977-79; asst. prof. U. Calif., Berkeley, 1979-83, assoc. prof., 1983-86, prof., 1986—, vice chmn. dept. chemistry, 1988-91, Miller Rsch. Prof., 1996. Bergman lectr. Yale U., 1987; Merck-Frost lectr. U. B.C., 1988; Bourke lectr. Royal Soc. Chemistry, 1992; Samuel M. McElvain lectr. U. Wis., Madison, 1995; Harry Emmett Gunning lectr. U. Alta., 1995; U. Calif., Berkley, Miller Rsch. prof., 1997-98; Bryce Crawford lectr., U. Minn., 1999; prin. investigator Lawrence Berkeley Lab., 1983-91; prin. investigator Sci. for Sci. Tchrs., NSF; mem. Laser Sci. Topical Group Fellowship Com., 1993—; mem. internat. steering com. 12th Internat. Conf. on Laser Spectroscopy, 1995; mem. exec. com. Divsn. Chem. Physics, 1995—; vis. prof. U. Nijmegen, 1991, Max-Planck Inst. for Fluid Dynamics, Göttingen, 1991, Cambridge U., 1995, U. Montpellier, 1996, Tech. U. Munich, 1996-97. Contbr. over 200 articles to profl. jours.; editl. rev. bd. Jour. Chem. Physics, 1993-95, Molecular Physics, 1983—, Chem. Physics Letters, 1987—, Spectroscopy Mag., 1986—, Rev. of Sci. Instruments, 1987-90, Jour. Molecular Spectroscopy, 1995—. Recipient Disting. Alumnus award U. Wis., Eau Claire, 1987, Bomen Michelson prize for spectroscopy, 1989, E.K. Plyler prize for molecular spectroscopy, 1989, E.R. Lippincott medal OSA, SAS, 1992, Disting. Tchg. award U. Calif., 1992, Humboldt sr. scientist award, 1995; fellow Dreyfuss Found., 1979, Churchill fellow Cambridge U., 1995; Presdl. Young Investigator NSF, 1984-88. Fellow Am. Phys. Soc., Royal Soc. Chemistry, Am. Acad. Arts and Scis.; mem. NAS, AAAS, AAUP, Optical Soc. Am., Am. Chem. Soc. (Harrison Howe award 1992, Irving Langmuir award 1999). Office: U Calif Dept Chemistry 419 Latimer Hall # 1460 Berkeley CA 94720-1460

SAYLES, JOHN THOMAS, film director, writer, actor; b. Schenectady, N.Y., Sept. 28, 1950; s. Donald John and Mary (Rausch) S. BS, Williams Coll., 1972. Film dir., writer, actor Paradigm, L.A., 1994—. Author: Pride of the Bimbos, 1975, Union Dues, 1979, Thinking in Pictures: The Making of the Movie "Matewan," 1987, The Anarchists Convention, 1979, Los Gusanos, 1991; short stories I-80 Nebraska, M.490 - M.205, 1975 (O Henry award), Breed, Golden State, 1977 (O Henry award), Hoop; writer, dir. plays: New Hope for the Dead, 1981, Turnbuckle; screenwriter: Piranha, 1978, The Lady in Red, 1979, Battle Beyond the Stars, 1980, Alligator, 1981, The Challenge, 1982, Enormous Changes at the Last Minute, 1985, Wild Thing, 1987, The Clan of the Cave Bear, 1988, Breaking In, 1989; screenwriter, actor: The Howling, 1981; dir., screenwriter, actor: Return of the Secaucus Seven, 1980 (Los Angeles Film Critcs award, 1980), Lianna, 1983, The Brother From Another Planet, 1984, Matewan, 1987, Eight Men Out, 1988, City of Hope, 1991; dir., screenwriter: Baby, It's You, 1983, Passion Fish, 1992; actor: Hard Choices, 1986, Something Wild, 1986, Little Vegas, 1990, Straight Talk, 1992, Malcolm X, 1992, Matinee, 1993, My Life's in Turnaround, 1994; dir. Bruce Springsteen music videos Born in the U.S.A., I'm on Fire, Glory Days; TV work includes A Perfect Match, Unnatural Causes, Shannon's Deal, spl. Mountain View. MacArthur Found. grantee. Office: Paradigm c/o Stuart Robinson 10100 Santa Monica Blvd Los Angeles CA 90067-4003

SAYLOR, MARK JULIAN, newspaper editor; b. Wellsville, N.Y., Mar. 19, 1954; s. Richard Samuel and Naomi (Roth) S.; children: Samuel, Benjamin, Katie. BA cum laude, Harvard Coll., 1976. Staff writer Ark. Democrat, Little Rock, 1976-77, San Jose (Calif.) Mercury News, 1977-81, asst. met. editor, 1981-82, govt. and politics editor, 1982-85; asst. city editor San Diego County edit. LA Times, L.A., 1985-89, city editor San Diego edit., 1989-91, Calif. polit. editor, 1991-95; entertainment editor Business, 1995—. Avocation: chess master. Office: LA Times Times Mirror Sq Los Angeles CA 90053

SAYRE, JOHN MARSHALL, lawyer, former government official; b. Boulder, Colo., Nov. 9, 1921; s. Henry Marshall and Lulu M. (Cooper) S.; m. Jean Miller, Aug. 22, 1943; children: Henry M., Charles Franklin, John Marshall Jr., Ann Elizabeth Sayre Taggart (dec.). BA, U. Colo., 1943, JD, 1948. Bar: Colo. 1948, U.S. Dist. Ct. Colo. 1952, U.S. Ct. Appeals (10th cir.) 1964. Law clk. trust dept. Denver Nat. Bank, 1948-49; asst. cashier, trust officer Nat. State Bank of Boulder, 1949-50; ptnr. Ryan, Sayre, Martin, Brotzman, Boulder, 1950-66, Davis, Graham & Stubbs, Denver, 1966-89, of counsel, 1993—; asst. sec. of the Interior for Water and Sci., 1989-93. Bd. dirs. Boulder Sch. Dist. 3, 1951-57; city atty. City of Boulder, 1952-55; gen. counsel Colo. Mcpl. League, 1959-63; prin. counsel No. Colo. Water Conservancy Dist. and mcpl. subdist., 1964-87, spl. counsel, 1987, bd. dirs. dist., 1960-64; former legal counsel Colo. Assn. Commerce and Industry. Lt. (j.g.) USNR, 1943-46, ret. Decorated Purple Heart; recipient William Lee Knous award U. Colo. Law Sch., 1999. Fellow Am. Bar Found. (life), Colo. Bar Found. (life); mem. ABA, Colo. Bar Assn., Boulder County Bar Assn. (pres. 1959), Denver Bar Assn., Nat. Water Resources Assn. (Colo. dir. 1980-89, 93-95, pres. 1984-86), Denver Country Club, Univ. Club, Phi Beta Kappa, Phi Gamma Delta, Phi Delta Phi. Home: 355 Ivanhoe St Denver CO 80220-5841 Office: Davis Graham & Stubbs 1550-17th St Ste 500 Denver CO 80202 E-mail: john.sayre@dgslaw.com

SAYWELL, WILLIAM GEORGE GABRIEL, business development and management consultant; b. Regina, Sask., Can., Dec. 1, 1936; s. John Ferdinand Tupper and Vera Marguerite S.; m. Helen Jane Larmer; children: Shelley Jayne, William James Tupper, Patricia Lynn. BA, U. Toronto, 1960, MA, 1961, PhD, 1968; LLD (hon.), U. B.C., 1994, Simon Fraser U., 1997. Asst. prof. dept. East Asian studies U. Toronto, 1963-69, asst. prof., 1969-71, assoc. prof. RDt., 1971-82, prof., 1982-83, chmn. dept., 1971-76; prof. dept. history, pres., vice chancellor Simon Fraser U., Burnaby, B.C., Can., 1983-93; pres., chief exec. officer Asia Pacific Found. of Can., Vancouver, 1993-99; vice chmn. Intercedent Ltd., 1999—; chmn. Intercedent Ventures Ltd.; ptnr. Acad. Search Can. Ltd.; pres. William Saywell & Assocs., Vancouver, 1999—. Cons. in higher edn.; ptnr. Acad. Search Can.; sinologist and 1st sec. Can. Embassy, Beijing, 1972-73; dir. U. Toronto-York U. Ctr. Modern East Asia, 1974-75; prin. Innis Coll., 1976-79; vice provost U. Toronto, 1979-83; dir. Westcoast Energy, Western Garnet Internat., Tokyo-Mitsubishi Bank (Can.). Author articles and revs. on Chinese affairs to profl. jours. Decorated Order of Can. Order of B.C. Office: 701 2095 Beach Ave Vancouver BC Canada V6G 1Z3

SCAGLIONE, CECIL FRANK, marketing executive, publisher; b. North Bay, Ont., Can., Dec. 2, 1934; came to U.S., 1967, naturalized, 1982; s. Frank and Rose (Aubin) S.; m. Mary Margaret Stewart, Nov. 11, 1954 (div. 1982); children: Cris Ann, Michael Andrew, Patrick Andrew (dec.); m. Beverly Louise Rahn, Mar. 25, 1983. Student, North Bay Coll., 1947-52, Ryerson Tech. Inst., Toronto, Ont., 1955-56, San Diego State U., , 1979. Accredited Pub. Rels. Soc. Am. Fin. Writer Toronto Telegram, 1955; reporter Sarnia (Ont.) Observer, 1956-57; reporter, editor Kitchener-Waterloo (Ont.) Record, 1957-61; reporter, editor, analyst Windsor (Ont.) Star, 1961-67; writer, editor, photo editor Detroit News, 1967-71; reporter, assoc. bus. editor San Diego Union, 1971-80; mgr. corp. comm. Pacific Southwest Airlines, San Diego, 1981-83; sr. v.p. media rels. Berkman & Daniels, Inc., San Diego, 1984-87; prin. Scaglione Mktg. Comm., 1987—. Pres., CEO, editor in chief Mature Life Features, 1990—. Founding editor-in-chief Aeromexico Mag., 1973; contbr. articles, columns and photographs to various publs. Mem. San Diego County Crime Commn. Recipient award B. F. Goodrich Can., Ltd., 1962, 66, San Diego Pub. Rels. Profl. of the Yr., 1995, Spl. Achievement award Nat. Assn. Recycling Industries, 1978; named Nat. Media Adv. SBA, 1980; Herbert J. Davenport fellow, 1977 U. Mo.; Can. Centennial grantee, 1966. Mem. San Diego Press Club (hon. life, past pres., awards 1978, 80, 84), Airline Editors Forum (awards 1982, 83), Soc. Profl. Journalists. Roman Catholic.

SCALA, JAMES, health care industry consultant, writer; b. Ramsey, N.J., Sept. 16, 1934; s. Edvigi and Lorene (Hendricksen) S.; m. Nancy Peters, June 15, 1957; children: James, Gregory, Nancy, Kimberly. BA, Columbia U., 1960; PhD, Cornell U., 1964; postgrad., Harvard U., 1968; LHD (hon.), Hofstra U., 1998. Cert. nutrition specialist. Staff scientist Miami Valley Labs., Procter and Gamble Co., 1964-66; head life scis., dir. fundamental rsch. Owens Ill. Corp., 1966-71; dir. nutrition T.J. Lipton Inc., 1971-75; dir. health scis. Gen. Foods Corp., 1975-78; v.p. sci. and tech. Shaklee Corp., San Francisco, 1978-85, sr. v.p. sci. affairs, 1986-87. Cons. Georgetown U. Med. Sch., U. Calif.-Berkeley extension. Author: Making the Vitamin Connection, 1985, The Arthritis Relief Diet, 1987, 89, Eating Right for a Bad Gut, 1990, 92, new edit., 1999, The High Blood Pressure Relief Diet, 1988, 90, Look 10 Years Younger, Feel 10 Years Better, 1991, 93, Prescription for Longevity, 1992, 94, If You Can't/Won't Stop Smoking, 1993, The New Arthritis Relief Diet, 1998, 25 Natural Ways to Manage Stress and Avoid Burnout, 2000, 25 Natural Ways to Relieve Irritable Bowel Syndrome, 2000; editor: Nutritional Determinants in Athletic Performance, 1981, New Protective Roles for Selected Nutrients, 1989; columnist Dance mag.; contbr. articles to profl. publs. With USAF, 1953-56. Disting. scholar U. Miami, Fla., 1977, Fla. Atlantic U., 1977. Mem. AAAS, Am. Inst. Nutrition, Am. Coll. Nutrition, Brit. Nutrition Soc., Sports Medicine Coun., Am. Soc. Cell Biology, Inst. Food Technologists, Astron. Soc. Pacific (bd. dirs., chmn. devel. coun.), Am. Dietetic Assn., Olympic Club (San Francisco), Oakland Yacht Club, Sigma Xi. Republican. E-mail: jscala2@home.com

SCALAPINO, DOUGLAS JAMES, physics educator; b. San Francisco, Dec. 10, 1933; s. John and Marie Constance (Pederson) S.; m. Diane Holmes Lappe, June 19, 1955; children: Lisa, Leigh, Kenneth, Lynne, Anne. BS, Yale U., 1955; PhD, Stanford U., 1961. Rsch. assoc. Washington U., St. Louis, 1961-62, U. Pa., Phila., 1962-64, asst. prof., 1964-66, assoc. prof., 1966-68, prof., 1968-69; vis. prof. U. Calif., Santa Barbara, 1968-69, prof. physics, 1969—; prin. investigator Inst. for Theoretical Physics, Santa Barbara, 1979—. Cons. E.I. Du Pont De Nemours & Co. Inc., Wilmington, Del., 1963-88; Faculty Rsch. lectr., U. Calif., Santa Barbara, 1983; IBM Almaden Rsch. Ctr., San Jose, Calif., 1989—; mem. sci. adv. bd. Superconductor Techs.Inc., Santa Barbara, 1987—; fellow Los Alamos Nat. Lab., 1992—. Contbr. articles to profl. jours. Fellow Alfred P. Sloan Found., 1964-66, fellowship, Guggenheim Found., 1976-77.; grantee NSF, U.S. Dept. Energy, pvt. corps., 1965—. Fellow Am. Phys. Soc. (Julius Edgar Lilienfeld prize 1998); mem. NAS, Am. Acad. Arts and Scis., Phi Beta Kappa, Sigma Xi. Office: U Calif Santa Barbara Dept Physics 552 University Ave Santa Barbara CA 93106-0002

SCANLON, JOHN M. (JACK), fiber optics company executive; BSEE, U. Toronto; MSEE, Cornell U. Group v.p. AT&T and Bell Labs, until 1990; v.p. cellular infrastructure group Motorola; chief oper. officer Cambridge Tech. Group; CEO Global Crossings Ltd., Beverly Hills, Calif., vice chair, CEO Asia. Pres. emeritus Cornell U. Engring. Bd. Patentee in field. Bd. dirs. Outward Bound. Mem. IEEE (sr.), Nat. Acad. Scis. Office: Global Crossings Ltd 360 N Crescent Dr Beverly Hills CA 90210-4802

SCARBOROUGH, DEAN A. consumer product company executive; b. Chester, Pa., Oct. 14, 1955; BA, Hiram Coll., 1977; MBA, U. Chgo., 1979. Mktg. mgr. Avery Dennison, Pasadena, Calif., 1985, v.p., gen. mgr. Follson Roll. divsn., 1990-95, mgr. Fosson Roll Europe The Netherlands, 1995-97, group v.p. Fosson Roll Worldwide Calif., 1999-2000, pres., COO, 2000—. Bd. dirs. United Way, Lake County, Ohio; mem. adv. com. Greater Western Res. coun. Boy Scouts Am., Ohio; bd. visitors Hiram Coll. Office: Avery Dennison Corp 150 N Orange Grove Blvd Pasadena CA 91103

SCARBOROUGH, STEPHEN J. construction executive; Pres. Std. Pacific Corp., Costa Mesa, Calif., 1965—. Office: Std Pacific Corp 1565 W McCartha Blvd Costa Mesa CA 92626

SCATES, ALLEN EDWARD, professional volleyball coach; BA, UCLA, 1961, MS, 1962. Coach volleyball UCLA, 1970—. Coached UCLA to 18 NCAA championships. Recipient All Time Great Coach awrd USA Volleyball, 1995; inducted Volleyball Hall of Fame, 1993, Calif. Beach Volleyball Hall of Fame, 1998; named AVCA Coach of Yr., 5 times, U.S. Olympic Com. Coach Yr., 1998. Office: UCLA Morgan Ctr PO Box 24044 Los Angeles CA 90024-0044 E-mail: ascates@athletics.ucla.edu

SCHACHMAN, HOWARD KAPNEK, molecular biologist, educator; b. Phila., Dec. 5, 1918; s. Morris H. and Rose (Kapnek) S.; m. Ethel H. Lazarus, Oct. 20, 1945; children— Marc, David. BSChemE, Mass. Inst. Tech., 1939; PhD in Phys. Chemistry, Princeton, 1948; DSc (hon.), Northwestern U., 1974; MD (hon.), U. Naples, 1990. Fellow NIH, 1946-48; from instr. to asst. prof. U. Calif., Berkeley, 1948-54, assoc. prof. biochemistry, 1954-59, prof. biochemistry and molecular biology, 1959-91, chmn. dept. molecular biology, dir. virus lab., 1969-76, prof. emeritus, dept. molecular and cell biology, 1991-94, prof. grad. sch., 1994—. Mem. sci. coun. and sci. adv. bd. Stazione Zoologica, Naples, Italy, 1988—; cons. bd. sci. Meml. Sloan-Kettering Cancer Ctr., 1988-97; mem. sci. adv. com. Rsch. ! Am., 1990—; William Lloyd Evans lectr. Ohio State U., 1988, Carl and Gerty Cori lectr., Washington U. Sch. Medicine, 1993; faculty rsch. lectr. U. Calif., Berkeley, 1994; Alta. Heritage Found. for Med. Rsch. vis. prof. U. Alta., 1996; Wellcome vis. prof. in basic med. scis., 1999-00. Author: Ultracentrifugation in Biochemistry, 1959. Mem. bd. sci. counselors Cancer Biology and Diagnosis divsn. Nat. Cancer Inst., 1989-92; ombudsman in basic scis. NIH, 1994—. Lt. USNR, 1945-47. Recipient John Scott award, 1964, Warren Triennial prize Mass. Gen. Hosp., 1965, Alexander von Humboldt award, 1990, Berkeley citation for disting. achievement and notable svc. U. Calif., 1993, Theodor Svedberg award, 1998; Guggenheim Meml. fellow, 1956. Mem. AAAS (mem. com. on sci. freedom and responsibility 1998—, Sci. Freedom and Responsibility award 2000), NAS (chmn. biochemistry sect. 1990-93, panelist sci. responsibility and conduct of rsch. 1990-92), Am. Chem. Soc. (award in chem. instrumentation 1962, Calif. sect. award 1958), Am. Soc. Biochemistry and Molecular Biology (pres. 1987-88, chmn. pub. affairs com. 1989—, Merck award 1986, Herbert A. Sober award 1994), Fedn. Am. Socs. for Exptl. Biology (pres. 1988-89, pub. affairs exec. com. 1989—, pub. svc. award 1994), Acad. Nat. Dei Lincei (fgn. mem.). Achievements include development of the ultracentrifuge as a tool for studying macromolecules of biological interest; studies on structure and function of a regulatory enzyme: Aspartate transcarbamylase. Office: U Calif Berkeley Dept Molecular Cell Bio 229 Stanley Hall # 3206 Berkeley CA 94720-3206

SCHADE, WILBERT CURTIS, education administrator; b. St. Louis, Jan. 4, 1945; s. Wilbert Curtis and Florence Mary (Allen) S.; m. Jacqueline Siewert, May 14, 1977; children: Benjamin Allen Siewert, Timothy Knorr Siewert. BA, U. Pa., 1967; AM, Washington U., St. Louis, 1970; PhD, Ind. U., 1986. Tchg. asst. dept. romance lang. Washington U., St. Louis, 1967-68; tchr. French St. Louis Priory Sch., 1970-71; assoc. instr. dept. French and Italian Ind. U., Bloomington, 1972-74, 76-80; tchr. French Webster Groves (Mo.) H.S., 1975-76; asst. dir. admissions Beloit (Wis.) Coll., 1980-83, assoc. dir. admissions, 1983-84; dir. coll. placement and dir. admissions Westover Sch., Middlebury, Conn., 1984-90; head upper sch. The Key Sch., Annapolis, Md., 1990-94, interim dir. devel., 1994-95; tchr. French, head lang. dept. Wasatch Acad., Mt. Pleasant, Utah, 1995-96, asst. headmaster for acad. affairs, 1996-2000; tchr., dir. of studies Internat. Seminar Series, Paris, 1999—. Lectr. in field. Co-editor: African Literature in its Social and Political Dimensions, 1983; mem. editl. bd. Jour. Coll. Admission, 2000—; contbr. articles to profl. jours. including World Lit. Written in English, Studies in 20th Century Lit. Active Anne Arundel County (Md.) Task Force on Year Round Edn., 1994-95, Utah State Office of Edn.'s Fgn. Lang. Instrl. Materials and Texbook Adv. Com., 1996-98. NEH Summer Inst. on African Am. Lit. and Film grant, 1994. Mem. Nat. Assn. Coll. Admission Counseling (presenter nat. conf. 1985), Rocky Mountain Assn. for Coll. Admission Counseling (exec. bd., chief assembly del. to Nat. Assn.), African Lit. Assn. (exec. com. 1979), Phi Delta Kappa. Soc. of Friends. Avocation: tennis. Home: PO Box 3549 20 Malheur Ln Sunriver OR 97707

SCHAECHTER, MOSELIO, microbiology educator; b. Apr. 26, 1928; children: Judy, John. Student, Cen. U., Ecuador, 1947-49; MA, U. Kans., 1952; PhD, U. Pa., 1954. Postdoctoral fellow State Serum Inst., Copenhagen, 1956-58; from instr. to asst. prof. to assoc. prof. U. Fla., Gainesville, 1958-62; from assoc. prof. to disting. prof. dept. microbiology Tufts U., Boston, 1962-95, prof. emeritus, 1995—. Adj. prof. San Diego State U., 1995—. Editor: Molecular Biology Bacterial Growth, 1985, Escherichia coli and Salmonella Typhimurium, 1987, 95, Mechanisms of Microbiol. Disease, 1989, 92; author: In the Company of Mushrooms, 1997. Mem. Am. Soc. Microbiology (pres. 1985-86, chmn. internat. activities), Am. Soc. Med. Sch. Microbiology Chmn. (pres. 1984-85, chair internat. activities 1986-94), Soc. Gen. Microbiology, Boston Mycol. Club, Sigma Xi. Avocations: field mycology, hiking. Office: San Diego State U Dept Biology San Diego CA 92182 E-mail: mschaech@sunstroke.sdsu.edu

SCHAEFER, JOHN PAUL, chemist, corporate executive; b. N.Y.C., Sept. 17, 1934; s. Conrad and Meta (Rekelkamm) S.; m. Helen Marie Schwarz, May 18, 1958; children— Ann Marie, Susan Margaret. B.S., Poly. Inst. Bklyn., 1955; Ph.D. in Chemistry, U. Ill., 1958; fellow, Calif. Inst. Tech., 1958-59. Asst. prof. U. Calif. at Berkeley, 1959-60; mem. faculty U. Ariz., 1960—, prof. chemistry, head dept., 1968-70; dean Coll. Liberal Arts U. Ariz., 1970-71, pres., 1971-82, Rsch. Corp., 1982—, also bd. dirs.; chmn. bd. Rsch. Corp. Techs. Inc., 1988—. Bd. dirs. Olin Corp., Rsch. Corp. Techs. Bd. dirs. Tucson Airport Authority; bd. govs. U.S.-Israel Binat. Sci. Found., 1972-77. Mem. AAAS, Nat. Audubon Soc., Tucson Audubon Soc. (pres. 1961-65), Am. Chem. Soc., Ariz. Acad., Nature Conservancy, Newcomen Soc., Sigma Xi, Phi Lambda Upsilon, Phi Kappa Phi. Office: Rsch Corp 101 N Wilmot Rd Ste 250 Tucson AZ 85711-3361

SCHAEFER, WILLIAM DAVID, English language educator; b. Dighton, Mass., May 11, 1928; s. Louis and Elsie K. (Otterbein) S.; m. Josephine R. Lamprecht, Aug. 8, 1958; 1 dau., Kimberly. B.A., NYU, 1957; M.S., U. Wis., 1958, Ph.D., 1962. Mem. faculty UCLA, 1962-90, prof. English, 1970-90, chmn. dept., 1969-71, exec. vice chancellor, 1978-87. Author: James (BV) Thomson: Beyond the City, 1965, Speedy Extinction of Evil and Misery, 1967, Education Without Compromise: From Chaos to Coherence in Higher Education, 1990; contbr. articles to profl. jours., short stories to literary mags. Served with AUS, 1954-56. Fulbright fellow Eng., 1961-62 Mem. MLA (exec. dir. 1971-78). Home: 164 Stagecoach Rd Bell Canyon CA 91307-1044 Office: UCLA 405 Hilgard Ave Los Angeles CA 90095-9000 E-mail: wschae444@aol.com

SCHAEFFER, GLENN WILLIAM, casino corporate financial executive; b. Pomona, Calif., Oct. 11, 1953; s. William Donald and Mary Louise (Miller) S.; m. Deborah Lynn Helfer, Sept. 6, 1974 (div. Apr. 1981); m. Renee Sue Riebel, May 25, 1985 AB summa cum laude, U. Calif., Irvine, 1974, MA, 1975; MFA, U. Iowa, 1977. Fin. cons. Dean Witter, Los Angeles, 1977-78; assoc. Hill and Knowlton, Inc., Los Angeles, 1978-81; v.p. Ramada Inns, Inc., Phoenix, 1981-84; exec. v.p., chief fin. officer Circus Circus Enterprises, Inc., Las Vegas, Nev., 1984-91, pres., 1991-93, also bd. dirs.; ptnr. Gold Strike Resorts, Jean, Nev., 1993-95; pres. Mandalay Resort Group, 1995—. Wine grower and estate bottler, N.Z. Founder and patron Internat. Inst. Modern Letters. Pres. Hitch fellow U. Calif.-Irvine, 1973-74 Mem. Phi Beta Kappa. Avocations: reading, bicycling. Office: Mandalay Resort Group 3950 Las Vegas Blvd S Las Vegas NV 89119

SCHAEFFER, LEONARD DAVID, healthcare executive; b. Chgo., July 28, 1945; s. David and Sarah (Levin) S.; m. Pamela Lee Sidford, Aug. 11, 1968; children: David, Jacqueline. BA, Princeton U., 1969. Mgmt. cons. Arthur Andersen & Co., 1969-73; dep. dir. mgmt. Ill. Mental Health/Devel. Disability, Springfield, 1973-75; dir. Ill. Bur. of Budget, Springfield, 1975-76; v.p. Citibank, N.A., N.Y.C., 1976-78; asst. sec. mgmt. and budget HHS, Washington, 1978, adminstr. HCFA, 1978-80; exec. v.p., COO Student Loan Mktg. Assn., Washington, 1980-82; pres., CEO Group Health, Inc., Mpls., 1983-86; chmn., CEO Blue Cross of Calif., Woodland Hills, 1986—, WellPoint Health Networks Inc., 1992—. Bd. dir. Allergan, Inc., Irvine, Calif.; bd. councilors U. So. Calif. Sch. Policy, Planning & Devel., 1988—; bd. dir. exec. com. Blue Cross-Blue Shield Assn., Chgo., 1986—; mem. Congl. Prospective Payment Assessment Commn., 1987—93; mem. Pew Health Professions Com., Phila., 1990—93; chmn. bd. trustees Nat. Health Found., LA, 1992—2001; chmn. bd. dir. Nat. Health Care Mgmt., 1993—; mem. Coun. on the Econ. Impact of Health Sys. Change, 1996—; co-chair adv. coun. dept. of health care policy Harvard Med. Sch., 1998—; founding chmn. Coalition for Affordable and Quality Healthcare, 2000. Bd. gov. Town Hall of Calif., LA, 1989; bd. trustees The Brookings Inst., Nat. Health Mus., 2000—. Kellogg Found. fellow, 1981-89, Internat. fellow King's Fund Coll., London, 1990—; recipient Citation-Outstanding Svc., Am. Acad. Pediats., 1981, Disting. Pub. Svc. award HEW, Washington, 1980. Mem. NAS, Inst. of Medicine, Health Ins. Assn. Am. (chmn. 1999), Cosmos Club, Princeton Club, Regency Club. Office: Wellpoint Health Networks Inc 1 Wellpoint Way Thousand Oaks CA 91362-3893

SCHAEFFER, REINER HORST, military officer, foreign language professional; b. Berlin, Fed. Republic Germany, Jan. 13, 1938; came to U.S., 1958; s. Immanuel Emil and Wilhelmine (Fahrni) Frei-S.; m. Cathy Anne Cormack, Apr. 6, 1966; 1 child, Brian Reiner Nat. cert., Bus. Sch., Thun, Switzerland, 1957; BGS in Bus., U. Nebr., 1970; MPA in Orgnl. Behavior, U. Mo., 1972; PhD in Fgn. Lang. Edn., Ohio State U., 1979. Commd. officer USAF, 1958, advanced through grades to lt. col.; instr. German, French USAF Acad., Colorado Springs, Colo., 1975-77, assoc. prof., 1979-81, chmn. German, 1981, dir. librs., 1982-86, prof., 1986-92, dir. Acad. Librs., 1986-92. Bd. dirs. Friends of AF Acad. Librs.; pres. Fgn. Lang. Ctr., Inc., 1999-2001. Named Disting. Grad. Air Force Inst. Tech, Wright-Patterson AFB, Ohio, 1979; recipient 5 Meritorious Service medals, 5 Air Force Commendation medals Mem. Am. Assn. Tchrs. of German, Swiss Club (pres. Colorado Springs chpt. 1990-96, chmn.), Pi Alpha Alpha, Alpha Sigma Alpha. Republican. Avocations: skiing; golfing; hiking; soccer. Home: 751 Babbling Brook Prescott AZ 86303 E-mail: swiss13@juno.com

SCHAFER, GLENNS, insurance company executive; b. St. Johns, Mich., Sept. 6, 1949; BS in Acctg. magna cum laude, Mich. State U., 1971; MBA in Fin. summa cum laude, U. Detroit, 1976. CPA, Mich.; registered fin. prin. With Peat Marwick Mitchell and Co., 1971-74; from asst. contr. to sr. v.p., CFO Alexander Hamilton Life Ins. Co., 1974-82; sr. v.p., CFO E.F. Hutton Life, 1982-86; v.p. corp. fin. Pacific Life, 1986-87, sr. v.p., CFO, 1987-91, exec. v.p., CFO, 1991-95, pres., 1995—, also bd. dirs. Bd. dirs. PIMCO Advisor L.P., Mich. State U. Grad. Sch. Bus. Adv. Bd., Ct. Apptd. Spl. Advs. Sgt. USAR, 1968-74. Fellow Life Mgmt. Inst.; mem. AICPA, Fin. Execs. Inst. Office: Pacific Life Ins Co PO Box 9000 Newport Beach CA 92658-9030

SCHAFFER, JEFFREY L. lawyer; b. L.A., Aug. 21, 1952; AB, U. Calif., Berkeley, 1974; JD, U. Calif., 1979. Bar: Calif. 1979, U.S. Dist. Ct. (no. dist.) Calif., U.S. Ct. Appeals (9th cir.) 1985. Mem. Howard, Rice, Nemerovski, Canady, Falk & Rabkin, San Francisco, 1988—. Panelist Continuing Edn. Bar, 1983-92, computer law inst. U. So. Calif., 1986. Assoc. editor Calif. Law REv., 1977-79. Mem. ABA (bus. law sect.), Am. Bankruptcy Inst., State Bar Calif. (bus. law sect., mem. debtor/creditor and bankruptcy com. 1987-90, 96-98, UCC com. 1998—), Bar Assn. San Francisco (comml. law and bankruptcy sect., co-chair barristers club's bankruptcy and comml. law com. 1984-85), Berkeley Law Found., Order of Coif, Phi Beta Kappa. Office: Howard Rice Nemerovski Canady Falk & Rabkin 3 Embarcadero Ctr Fl 7 San Francisco CA 94111-4074

SCHAFFER, JOEL LANCE, dentist; b. Bklyn., Oct. 18, 1945; s. Martin Alter and Irene Natalie (Shore) S.; m. Susan Anne Swearingen, Feb. 14, 1980 (div.); 1 child, Jericho Katherine. BS, L.I. U., 1967; DDS, Howard U., 1971. Dental intern Eastman Dental Ctr., Rochester, N.Y., 1971-72; gen. practice dentistry, Boulder, Colo., 1973—; evaluator Clin. Rsch. Assocs.; lectr. in field, 1972—. Contbr. articles to dental jours; patentee in field. Advisor Boulder Meals on Wheels; mem. Boulder County Com. for Persons with Disabilities. Named outstanding clinician Boulder County Dental Forum, 1979. Fellow Am. Soc. Dental Aesthetics; mem. ADA, Am. Acad. Oral Implantology, Boulder County Dental Soc., Tau Epsilon Phi, Alpha Omega. Jewish. Home: 4171 S Hampton Cir Boulder CO 80301-6017 Office: 2880 Folsom St Boulder CO 80304-3739

SCHAFFER, ROBERT (BOB SCHAFFER), congressman; b. Cin., July 24, 1962; s. Robert James and Florence Ann (Bednar) S.; m. Maureen Elizabeth Menke, Feb. 8, 1986; children: Jenniffer and Emily (twins), Justin, Sarah. BA in Polit. Sci., U. Dayton, 1984; hon. doctorate in mgmt., Colo. Tech. U. Speechwriter republican caucus Ohio Gen. Assembly, 1984-85; legis. asst. State of Ohio, Columbus, 1985; majority adminstrv. asst. Colo. State Senate, Denver, 1985-87, mem., 1987-96, U.S. Congress from 4th Colo. dist., Washington, 1997—; mem. agr. com., edn. and workforce com., resources com. Mem. Rep. Policy Com., GOP Theme Team; commr. Colo. Advanced Tech. Inst., 1988—; proprietor No. Front Range Mktg. and Distbn., Inc. Mem. Mental Health Bd. Larimer County, 1986-87; mem. com. on human svcs. Nat. Conf. State Legislatures; campain co-chmn. Arnold for Lt. Gov.; Republican candidate for Lt. Gov. of Colo., 1994. Named Nat. Legislator of Yr., Rep. Nat. Legislators Assn., 1995, Taxpayer Champion, Colo. Union of Taxpayers, 1995, Bus. Legislator of the Yr. Colo. Assn. Commerce and Industry, Named Guardina Small Bus. Nat. Fedn. Ind. Bus.; recipient Spirit of Enterprise award U.S. C. of C. Mem. Jaycees (Mover and Shaker award 1989), KC. Roman Catholic. Avocations: backpacking, skiing, baseball, painting, reading. Home: 5027 Alder Ct Fort Collins CO 80525-5588 Office: US Ho Reps 212 Cannon Ho Office Bldg Washington DC 20515-0001*

SCHAFFNER-IRVIN, KRISTEN, oil executive; Owner Team Petroleum, Huntington Beach, Calif. Office: Team Petroleum PO Box 659 Huntington Beach CA 92648-0659

SCHANDER, MARY LEA, protective services official; b. June 11, 1947; d. Gerald John Lea and Marian Lea Coffman; m. Edwin Schander, July 3, 1971. BA, Calif. Luth. Coll., 1969; MA, UCLA, 1970. Staff aide City of Anaheim (Calif.) Police Dept., 1970-72, staff asst., 1972-78, sr. staff asst., 1978-80; with Resource Mgmt. Dept. City of Anaheim, 1980-82; asst. to dir. Pub. Safety Agy. City of Pasadena Police Dept., 1982-85, spl. asst. to police chief, 1985-88, adminstrv. comdr., 1988-92, police comdr., 1992—. Freelance musician; publisher Australian Traditional Songs, 1985, Songs in the Air of Early California, 1994; lectr. Calif. Luth. Coll.; instr. Calif. State U., Northridge, Pasadena City Coll., 2000-01; cons. City of Lodz, Poland, Internat. Assn. Chiefs of Police; speaker, panelist League of Calif. Cities, Pasadena Commn. on Status of Women; mcpl. mgmt. asst. CLEARS. Prodr.: (cable TV program) Traditional Music Showcase; contbr. articles in field to profl. jours. Bd. dirs. ARC, Rotary Club Pasadena, S.W. Chamber Music; instr. Bd. Corrections. Recipient Police Chief's Spl. award City of Pasadena, 1987, Women at Work Medal of Excellence, 1988, 2d Century Leadership award YWCA, 1998; Augustana fellow Calif. Luth. Coll., 1969. Mem. Internat. Assn. Chiefs of Police, Pasadena Arts Coun., L.A. Coun. Peace Officers, S.W. Chamber Music Soc. Home: PO Box 50151 Pasadena CA 91115-0151 Office: Pasadena Police Dept 207 N Garfield Ave Pasadena CA 91101-1791 E-mail: mschander@ci.pasadena.ca.us

SCHAPIRO, GEORGE A. electronics company executive; b. Richmond, Va., Mar. 21, 1946; s. Irwin Abraham and Jeanne (Goldman) S.; m. Jo Ann Katzman, Aug. 6, 1978; children: Rebecca Jeanne, Amy Elizabeth. BA, U. Va., 1967; MS in Indsl. Adminstrn., Carnegie-Mellon U., 1969. Fin. analyst data processing group IBM, Harrison, N.Y., 1968; product mktg. mgr. data sys. divns. Hewlett-Packard Co., Cupertino, Calif., 1969-74, med. electronics divsn. Waltham, Mass., 1974-76; pres., CEO Andros Inc., Berkeley, Calif., 1976-80, 90-91, Andros Analyzers, Inc., Berkeley, 1979-90, chmn. profl. bd. dirs., 1991—. Pres., CEO Hepatix Inc., Houston, Tex., 1992-93; pres., CEO U.S. Med. Instruments, Inc., San Diego, Calif., 1992-93; CEO Sonic Force, LLC, Burlingame, Calif., 1993-98; CEO Megabios, Inc., Burlingame, 1994; pres. Cardiac Mariners, Inc., Los Gatos, Calif., 1999-2000; guest lectr. Stanford U. Sch. Bus., U. Calif. at Berkeley Coll. Engring. and Extension Sch., Am. Mgmt. Assn. Seminar Series. Bd. dirs. Anesthesia Patient Safety Found. Mem. Assn. Computing Machinery, Assn. Advancement Med. Instrumentation, World Pres.'s Orgn. Democrat. Jewish. Home and Office: 3880 Ralston Ave Hillsborough CA 94010-6743

SCHAPP, REBECCA MARIA, museum director; b. Stuttgart, Fed. Republic Germany, Dec. 12, 1956; came to U.S., 1957; d. Randall Todd and Elfriede Carolina (Scheppan) Spradlin; m. Thomas James Schapp, May 29, 1979. AA, DeAnza Coll., 1977; BA in Art, San Jose State U., 1979, MA in Art Adminstrn., 1985. Adminstrv. dir. Union Gallery, San Jose, Calif., 1979-82; from mus. coordinator to dep. dir. de Saisset Mus. Santa Clara (Calif.) U., 1982-92, dir., 1993—. Mem. San Francisco Mus. Modern Art; bd. dirs. Works of San Jose, v.p. 1983-85. Mem. Non-Profit Gallery Assn. (bd. dirs.). Democrat. Avocations: racquetball, walking, bicycling, camping. Office: De Saisset Mus Santa Clara U 500 El Camino Real Santa Clara CA 95050-4345

SCHATT, PAUL, newspaper editor; b. N.Y.C., Aug. 31, 1945; divorced; children: Suzannah, Andrew. BA with distinction Polit. Sci., English, Ariz. State U., 1967. Editor Ariz. Republic, 1964-66, reporter, 1965-74, urban affairs editor, 1974-75, asst. city editor, 1975-79, chief asst. city editor, 1979-82, asst. met. editor, 1985-86, met. editor, 1986-88, editor edit. pages, 1993—, asst. editor Ariz. Mag., 1981-82, editor, 1982-85; editor edit. pages Phoenix Gazette, 1988-93, The Ariz. Republic, 1993-97, assoc. editor, 1998—. Pres. 1st amendment coalition of Az., 1999; vis. lectr. Pub. Affairs Journalism, Ariz. State U., 1976—, instr. Mass. Comm. Dept., 1974-76; dir. Eugene C. Pulliam Fellowship. Phoenix program, 1990—; writing coach, 1989; del. Pre White House Conf. Librs., 1991, pres., Arizona Newspapers Assn., 2000—. V.p. Crisis Nursery, 1984-87, bd. dirs. 1980-87; exec. bd. Hospice of the Valley, 1980-87; pres. Friends of Phoenix Pub. Libr., 1985-86, bd. dirs. 1986—; bd. trustees 1st Amendment Congress, 1989—; bd. dirs. Ariz. Humanities Coun., 1999—; Dean's adv. bd., Arizona State U. Honors Coll., 1999—, adv. bd., Northern Arizona U. Sch. of Communications, 1999—, bd. dirs. Camelback Hosps. 1982-89, chmn. bd. dirs. 1986-87, Cactus Pine Coun. Girl Scouts Am., 1988-89, Sun Sounds Inc., 1982-89, Valley Leadership Inc., 1991—, alum. assn., 1985-89, Ariz. Zool. Soc., 1991—, Barrow Neurol. Found., 1991—, Kids Voting, 1991-93, Barry Goldwater Inst., 1991-93, Ariz. Club, 1991—. With Ariz. Nat. Guard, 1966-79. Recipient Montgomery award Outstanding Svc. to Community Friends of Phoenix Pub. Libr., 1989; profl. Journalism fellow Stanford U., 1970-71. Mem. Am. Soc. Newspaper Editors, Soc. Profl. Journalists (pres. Valley of Sun chpt. 1974-75, 83-84, exec. bd. 1988-92), Sigma Delta Chi (co-chair nat. convention 1974). Office: The Ariz Republic Editorial Dept 200 E Van Buren St Phoenix AZ 85004-2238 E-mail: paul.schatt@pni.com

SCHATZ, IRWIN JACOB, cardiologist, educator; b. St. Boniface, Man., Can., Oct. 16, 1931; came to U.S., 1956, naturalized, 1966; s. Jacob and Reva S.; m. Barbara Jane Binder, Nov. 12, 1967; children: Jacob, Edward, Stephen and Brian (twins). Student, U. Man., Can.), Winnipeg, 1951, M.D. with honors, 1956. Diplomate: Am. Bd. Internal Medicine. Intern Vancouver (B.C.) Gen. Hosp., 1955-56; resident Hammersmith Hosp., U. London, 1957, Mayo Clinic, Rochester, Minn., 1958-61; head sec. peripheral vascular disease Henry Ford Hosp., Detroit, 1961-68; asso. prof. medicine Wayne State U., 1968-71, chief sect. cardiovascular disease, 1969-71; assoc. prof., asso. dir. sect. cardiology U. Mich., 1972-73, prof. internal medicine, 1973-75; prof. medicine John A. Burns Sch. Medicine, U. Hawaii, 1975—, chmn. dept. medicine, 1975-90. Author: Orthostatic Hypotension, 1986; contbr. numerous articles to med. jours. Rockefeller Found. scholar, 1991. Master ACP (bd. govs. 1984-89, Laureate award Hawaii chpt. 1992); fellow Am. Coll. Cardiology (bd. govs. 1980-84), Am. Autonomic Soc. (hon.); mem. Am. Heart Assn. (fellow couns. cardiology and circulation), Am. Fedn. Clin. Rsch., Asian-Pacific Soc. Cardiology (v.p. 1987-91), Accreditation Coun. for Grad. Med. Edn. (chmn. residence rev. com. internal medicine 1993-95), Hawaii Heart Assn. (pres.), Western Assn. Physicians, Am. Autonomic Soc. (chmn. bd. govs., pres. 1996-98), Pacific Interurban Club, Oahu Country Club. Jewish. Home: 4983 Kolohala St Honolulu HI 96816-5126 Office: 1356 Lusitana St Honolulu HI 96813-2421 E-mail: schatzi@hawaii.edu

SCHATZ, MONA CLAIRE STRUHSAKER, social worker, educator, consultant, researcher; b. Phila., Jan. 4, 1950; d. Milton and Josephine (Kivo) S.; m. James Fredrick Struhsaker, Dec. 31, 1979 (div.); 1 child, Thain Mackenzie. BA, Metro State Coll., 1976; postgrad., U. Minn., 1976; MSW, U. Denver, 1979; D in Social Work/Social Welfare, U. Pa., 1986. Teaching fellow U. Pa., Phila., 1981-82; asst. prof. S.W. Mo. State U., Springfield, 1982-85; prof. Colo. State U., Ft. Collins, 1985—, field coord., 1986-88, dir. non-profit agy. adminstrn. program, 1995-97, project dir. Edn. and Rsch. Inst. for Fostering Families, 1987—, dir. youth agy. adminstrn. program Am. Humanics, 1988-90; mem. coun. foster care cert. program Western Gov.'s U., 1998—. Cons. Mgmt. and Behavioral Sci. Ctr., The Wharton Sch. U. Pa., 1981-82; resource specialist So. N.J. Health Sys. Agy., 1982; adj. faculty mem. U. Mo., Springfield, 1994; med. social worker Rehab. and Vis. Nurse Assn., 1985-90; mem. Colo. Child Welfare Adv. Com., Family Conservation Initiative; internat. cons. and trainer Inst. for Internat. Connections, Russia, Latvia, Albania, U.S., Hungary, Ukraine, Romania, 1992—. Contbr. articles to profl. jours. including Jour. Social Work Edn., New Social Worker, Chosen Child: Internat. Adoption Mag., others. Cons., field rep. Big Bros./Big Sisters of Am., Phila., 1979-83; acting dir., asst. dir. Big Sisters of Colo., 1971-78; owner Polit. Cons. in Colo., Denver, 1978-79; active Food Co-op, Ft. Collins, Foster Parent, Denver, Capital Hill United Neighbors, Adams County (Denver) Social Planning Coun., Co., Colo. Justice Coun., Denver, Regional Girls Shelter, Springfield; bd. dirs. Crisis Helpline and Info. Svc. Scholar Lilly Endowment, Inc., 1976, Piton Found., 1978; recipient Spl. Recognition award Big Bros./Big Sisters of Am., 1983, Recognition award Am. Humanics Mgmt. Inst., 1990, Innovative Tchg. award Ctr. for Tchg. and Learning/Colo. State U. Mem. Inst. Internat. Connections (bd. dirs., mem. adv. bd.), Coun. Social Work Edn., Group for Study of Generalist Social Work, Social Welfare History Group, Nat. Assn. Social Workers (nominating com. Springfield chpt., state bd. dirs., No. Colo. rep.), Student Social Work Assn. Colo. State U. (adv. 1986-89), Permanency Planning Coun. for Children and Youth, NOW (treas. Springfield chpt. 1984-85), Student Nuclear Awareness Group (advisor), Student Social Work Assn. (advisor), Har Shalom (tchg. in youth edn. program), Alpha Delta Mu. Democrat. Avocations: cooking, travel, reading, biking, sewing. Office: Colo State U Social Work Dept Fort Collins CO 80523-0001 E-mail: schatz@cahs.colostate.edu

SCHATZBERG, ALAN FREDERIC, psychiatrist, researcher; b. N.Y.C., Oct. 17, 1944; s. Emanuel and Cila (Diamand) S.; m. Nancy R. Silverman, Aug. 27, 1972; children: Melissa Ann, Lindsey Diamand. BS, NYU, 1965, MD, 1968; MA (hon.), Harvard U., 1989. Diplomate Nat. Bd. Med. Examiners, Am. Bd. Psychiatry and Neurology. Intern Lenox Hill Hosp., N.Y.C., 1968-69; resident in psychiatry Mass. Mental Health Ctr., Boston, 1969-72; clin. fellow in psychiatry Harvard Med. Sch., Boston, 1969-72, asst. prof. psychiatry, 1977-82, assoc. prof., 1982-88, prof., 1988-91; interim psychiatrist-in-chief McLean Hosp., Belmont, Mass., 1984-86, dir. depression rsch. facility, 1985—, svc. chief, 1982-84, 86-88; psychiatrist adv. panel Eli Lilly & Co., Indpls., 1986-93; clin. dir. Mass. Mental Health Ctr., Boston, 1988-91; Kenneth T. Norris, Jr. prof. psychiatry and behavioral scis. Stanford U., 1991—, chmn. dept. psychiatry and behavioral scis. Sch. Medicine, 1991—. Cons. AMA Videoclinics, Chgo., 1979-83; mem. AMA/FAA panel on health regulations, Chgo., 1984-86; mem. NIH Biol. Psycholathology and Clin. Neuroscis. Intitial Rev. Group, 1991-95, chmn., 1993-94. Co-author: Manual of Clinical Psychopharmacology, 1986, 3d edit., 1997; contbr. more than 200 articles to profl. publs., chpts. to books; co-editor: Depression: Biology, Psychodynamics and Treatment, 1978, Hypothalamic-Pituitary-Adrenal Axis, 1988, Textbook of Psychopharmacology, 1995, 2d edit., 1998; mem. editl. bd. McLean Hosp. Jour., 1975-88, Jour. Psychiat. Rsch., 1986—, co-editor in chief, 2000—; mem. editl. bd. Integrative Psychiatry, 1990—, Harvard Rev. Psychiatry, 1992—, Archives of Gen. Psychiatry, 1995—, Psychoneuroendocrinology, 1995—, Annals Psychiatry, 1992—, Anxiety, 1993, Jour. Clin. Psychopharmacology, 1993—; assoc. editor-in-chief Depression, 1992—. Maj. USAF, 1972-74. Rsch. grantee NIMH, 1984-87, 94—, Poitras Charitable Found., 1985-93. Fellow APA, Am. Coll. Neuropsychopharmacology (coun. 1994-97, pres. 1999—), Am. Psychopath. Assn.; mem. Am. Coll. Psychiatrists, Mass. Psychiat. Soc. (coun. 1987-90), No. Calif. Psychiat. Soc. (v.p. 1997-99). Avocations: travel, theater, tennis, swimming, fine arts. Office: Stanford U Sch Medicine 401 Quarry Rd Rm 300 Stanford CA 94305-5717

SCHATZKI, GEORGE, law educator; b. 1933; AB, Harvard U., 1955, LL.B. 1958, LL.M. 1965. Prof. law U. Tex., Austin, 1965-79; dean U. Wash. Sch. Law, Seattle, 1979-82, prof., 1979-84; dean U. Conn. Sch. Law, Hartford, 1984-90, prof., 1994-2000; prof. law Ariz. State U., Tempe, 2000—. Vis. prof. law U. Pa., Phila., 1973-74, Harvard U., Cambridge, Mass., 1977-78; vis. lectr. law Yale U., New Haven, 1993, 96. Co-author: Labor Relations and Social Problems: Collective Bargaining in Private Employment, 1978, Labor and Employment Law, 1988, 2d edit., 1995. Teaching fellow Harvard U., Cambridge, Mass., 1963-65. Office: Ariz State U Coll Law PO Box 877906 Tempe AZ 85287-7906 E-mail: george.schatzki@asu.edu

SCHAUER, RONALD L. executive; BSEE, S.D. State U. Pres., CEO Magnetic Data, Inc.; founder, corp. v.p., gen. mgt. Stolle Corp.; mgr. lab. engring., mfg., product/process devel. 3M; chmn., pres. CEO HMT Tech., Fremont, Calif., 1994—. Office: HMT Technology Corp 1055 Page Ave Fremont CA 94538-7342

SCHAUF, VICTORIA, pediatrician, educator, infectious diseases consultant; b. N.Y.C., Feb. 17, 1943; d. Maurice J. and Ruth H. (Baker) Bisson; m. Michael Delaney; 2 children. BS with honors in Microbiology, U. Chgo., 1965, MD with honors, 1969. Intern pediatrics U. Chgo. Hosp., 1969-70; resident pediatrics Sinai Hosp. of Balt., 1970-71; chief resident pediatrics Children's Hosp. Nat. Med. Ctr., Washington, 1971-72; rsch. trainee NIH, Bethesda, Md., 1972; asst. prof. microbiology Rush Med. Coll., Chgo., 1972-74; prof. pediatrics, head pediatric infectious diseases U. Ill., Chgo., 1974-84; med. officer FDA, Rockville, Md., 1984-86; chmn. dept. pediatrics Nassau County Med. Ctr., East Meadow, N.Y., 1986-90; prof. pediatrics SUNY, Stony Brook, 1987-94. Vis. prof. Rockefeller U., 1990-92; mem. vis. faculty Chiang Mai (Thailand) U., 1978; mem. ad hoc com. study sects. NIH, Bethesda, 1981-82; bd. dirs. Pearl Stetler Rsch. Found., Chgo., 1982-84; cons. FDA, 1987-88, 93-95, Can. Bur. Human Prescription Drugs, Ottawa, 1990—, Biotech. Investors, 1993-95; course dir. pediat. infectious diseases rev. course Cornell U. Med. Coll., N.Y.C., 1994, faculty, 1995. Co-author: Pediatric Infectious Diseases: A Comprehensive Guide to the Subspecialty, 1997; prodr. radio and TV programs in field; contbr. articles to profl. jours., chpts. to books. Vol. physician Cook County Hosp., Chgo., 1974-84; mem. adv. com. Nat. Hansen's Disease Ctr., La., 1986, Nassau County Day Care Coun., N.Y., 1988-90; mem. adv. bd. Surg. Aid to Children of World, N.Y., 1986-90; commr., sec. Kern County Children and Families Commn., 1999—. Am. Lung Assn. grantee U. Ill., 1977; recipient contract NIH, U. Ill., 1978-81, grantee, 1979-84. Fellow Infectious Diseases Soc. Am.; mem. Pediatric Infectious Diseases Soc. (exec. bd.), Soc. Pediatric Rsch., Am. Pediatric Soc., AAAS, Am. Soc. Microbiology, Am. Acad. Pediatrics, Phi Beta Kappa, Alpha Omega Alpha. Avocation: walking.

SCHEERER, ERNEST WILLIAM, dentist; b. Wabash, Ind., May 18, 1932; s. Ernest William and Anna Lucille (Bahler) S.; m. Ingrid Elvy Yvonne, Sept. 28, 1973. BS, Purdue U., 1954; DDS, Ind. U., 1961. Intern The Queen's Hosp., Honolulu, 1961-62; assoc. Pvt. Dental Practice, Honolulu, 1963-65; owner Pvt. Solo Dental Practice, Honolulu, 1965-75; ptnr. Dental Adminstrn., Honolulu, 1975-78; v.p. Scheerer & West Dental Corp., Honolulu, 1978—. Chief Dept. Dentistry Queen's Hosp., Honolulu. Contbr. various clin. articles to profl. jours. Mem. Big Bros., Hawaii, 1968-74. Mem. Master Acad. Gen. Dentistry, Hawaii Acad. Gen. Dentistry (past pres.), Am. Coll. Dentists, ADA, Hawaii Dental Assn. (treas.), Internat. Acad. Gnathology, Pierre Fauchard Soc., Fedn. Dental Internat., Am. Equilibration Soc., Acad. of Osseointegration, Am. Acad. Esthetic Dentistry, Am. Coll. Dentists O.K.U., Hawaii Med. Libr. (sec.), Elks. Mem. United Ch. of Christ. Club: Pacific. Avocations: tennis, travel, Hawaiian music. Office: Scheerer & West Inc 735 Bishop St Ste 211 Honolulu HI 96813-4884 E-mail: ewscheerer@aol.com

SCHEIBEL, ARNOLD BERNARD, psychiatrist, educator, research director; b. N.Y.C., Jan. 18, 1923; s. William and Ethel (Greenberg) S.; m. Madge Mila Ragland, Mar. 3, 1950 (dec. Jan. 1977); m. Marian Diamond, Sept. 1982. BA, Columbia U., 1944, MD, 1946; MS, U. Ill., 1952. Intern Mt. Sinai Hosp., N.Y.C., 1946-47; resident in psychiatry Barnes and McMillan Hosp., St. Louis, 1947-48, Ill. Neuropsychiat. Inst., Chgo., 1950-52; asst. prof. psychiatry and anatomy U. Tenn. Med. Sch., 1952-53, assoc. prof., 1953-55, UCLA Med. Ctr., 1955-67, prof., 1967—, mem. Brain Rsch. Inst., 1960—, acting dir. Brain Rsch. Inst., 1987-90, dir., 1990-95. Cons. VA hosps., L.A., 1956—. Contbr. numerous articles to tech. jours, chpts. to books.; mem. editl. bd. Brain Rsch., 1967-77, Developmental Psychobiology, 1968—, Internat. Jour. Neurosci., 1969—, Jour. Biol. Psychiatry, 1968—, Jour. Theoretical Biology, 1980—; assoc. editor News Report, 1989—. Mem. Pres.'s Commn. on Aging, Nat. Inst. Aging, 1980—. Served with AUS, 1943-46; from lt. to capt. M.C. AUS, 1948-50. Guggenheim fellow (with wife), 1953-54, 59; recipient Disting. Svc. award Calif. Soc. Biomed. Rsch., 1998. Fellow Am. Acad. Arts and Scis., Norwegian Acad. Scis., Am. Psychiat. Assn. (life, Harriet and Charles Luckman Disting. Tchg. award 1997) AAAS; mem. Am. Neurol. Assn., Soc. Neuorosci., Pyschiat. Rsch. Assn., Soc. Biol. Psychiatry, So. Calif. Psychiat. Assn. Home: 16231 Morrison St Encino CA 91436-1331 Office: UCLA Dept Neurobiology Los Angeles CA 90024 E-mail: scheibel@ucla.edu

SCHEIBER, HARRY N. law educator; b. 1935; BA, Columbia U., 1955; MA, Cornell U., 1957, PhD, 1961; MA (hon.), Dartmouth Coll., 1965; D.Jur.Hon., Uppsala U., Sweden, 1998. Instr. to assoc. prof. history Dartmouth Coll., 1960-68, prof., 1968-71; prof. Am. history U. Calif., San Diego, 1971-80; prof. law Boalt Hall, U. Calif., Berkeley, 1980—. Chmn. jurisprudence and social policy program, 1982-84, 90-93, assoc. dean, 1990-93, 96-99; The Stefan Riesenfeld prof., 1991—; vice chair Univ. Academic Senate, 1993-94, chair 1994-95; Fulbright disting. sr. lectr., Australia, 1983, marine affairs coord. Calif. Sea Grant Coll. Program, 1989-2000; vis. rsch. prof. Law Inst. U. Uppsala, Sweden, 1995, hon. prof. DiTella U., Buenos Aires, 1999; cons. Calif. Jud. Coun., 1992-93; acting dir. Ctr. for Study of Law and Soc., 1999—. Co-author, co-author((with L. Friedman)): American Law and the Constitutional Order, 1978co-author: The State and Freedom of Contract, 1998, Law of the Sea: The Common Heritage and Emerging Challenges , 2000, Inter-Allied Conflicts and Ocean Law (1945-1953), 2001, numerous others; editor: Yearbook of the California Supreme Court Historical Society, 1994—;contbr. articles to law revs. and social sci.jours. Chmn. Littleton Griswold Prize Legal History, 1985-88; pres. N.H. Civil Liberties Union, 1969-70; chmn. Project '87 Task Force on Pub. Programs, Washington, 1982-85; dir. Berkeley Seminar on Federalism, 1986-95; cons. judiciary study U.S. Adv. Commn. Intergovernmental Rels., 1985-88; dir. NEH Inst. on Constitutionalism, U. Calif., Berkeley, 1986-87, 88-91. Recipient Sea Grant Colls. award, 1981-83, 84-85, 86—; fellow Ctr. Advanced Study in Behavioral Scis., Stanford Calif., 1967, 71; Guggenheim fellow, 1971, 88; Rockefeller Found. humanities fellow, 1979, NEH fellow, 1985-86; NSF grantee 1979, 80, 88-89. Fellow U. Calif. Humanities Rsch. Inst., Am. Soc. for Legal History (hon.), Japan Soc. for Promotion of Sci.; mem. Am. Hist. Assn., Orgn. Am. Historians, Agrl. History Soc. (pres. 1978), Econ. History Assn. (trustee 1978-80), Law and Soc. Assn. (trustee 1979-81, 96-99), Nat. Assessment History and Citizenship Edn. (chmn. nat. acad. bd. 1986-87), Marine Affairs and Policy Assn. (bd. dirs. 1991-96), Ocean Governance Study Group (steering com. 1991—), Internat. Coun. Environ. Law, Calif. Supreme Ct. Hist. Soc. (bd. dirs. 1993—, v.p. 1997-98). Office: U Calif Berkeley Law Sch Boalt Hall Berkeley CA 94720-2150 E-mail: scheiber@law.berkeley.edu

SCHEID, STEVEN L. investment company executive; Exec. v.p. mutual funds, fin. vice-chmn. The Charles Schwab Corp., San Francisco, 1999—. Office: The Charles Schwab Corp 101 Montgomery St Ste 200 San Francisco CA 94104-4175

SCHEINMAN, DANIEL, lawyer; b. 1963; BA, Brandeis U.; JD, Duke U. Bar: Calif. 1990. V.p. of legal govt. affairs Cisco Systems, Inc., San Jose, Calif. Office: Cisco Systems Inc 170 W Tasman Dr San Jose CA 95134-1700

SCHEKMAN, RANDY W. molecular biology administrator, biochemist; b. St. Paul, Dec. 30, 1948; married, 1973; 1 child. BA, UCLA, 1970; PhD in Biochemistry, Stanford U., 1975. Fellow U. Calif., San Diego, 1974-76, from asst. to assoc. prof. Berkeley, 1976-83, prof., 1983—, head divsn. biochemistry and molecular biology, 1990-97, co-chair dept. molecular and cellular biology, 1997—. Fellow Cystic Fibrosis Found., 1974, Sabbatical fellow John S. Guggenheim Found., 1982; recipient Gairdner Found. Internat. award, 1996. Mem. Am. Soc. Microbiology, Am. Soc. Biochemists & Molecular Biologists. Achievements include research on molecular mechanism of secretion and membrane assembly in eucaryotic cells. Office: U Calif Dept Molecular Cell Bio 401 Barker Hall Spc 3202 Berkeley CA 94720-3202

SCHELBERT, HEINRICH RUEDIGER, nuclear medicine physician; b. Wuerzberg, Germany, Nov. 5, 1939; MD, U. Würzburg (Germany), 1964. Diplomate Am. Bd. Nuclear Medicine. Intern Mercy Med. Ctr., Phila., 1966-67, resident, 1967-68, 70-71; resident in cardiology U. Dusseldorf, Germany, 1971-72; fellow in cardiology, resident in nuclear medicine U. Calif., San Diego, 1968-69, asst. rsch. cardiologist, 1972-75, assoc. rsch. radiologist, 1975-76; hosp. assoc. UCLA Med. Ctr., 1977—; prof. radiol. scis. UCLA Sch. Medicine, 1980-90, prof. pharmacol. and radiol. scis., 1993—. Recipient Georg von Hevesy prize 2d Internat. Congress World Fedn. Nuclear Medicine and Radiation Biology, 1978, 3d Internat. Congress World Fedn. Nuclear Medicine and Radiation Biology, 1982. Fellow Am. Coll. Cardiology; mem. Am. Heart Assn. (disting. scientific achievement award 1989), Soc. Nuclear Medicine (Herrman L. Blumgart pioneer lectr. award 1989, George De Hevesy Nuclear Medicine Pioneer award 1998), German Soc. Nuc. Med. (hon.). Office: UCLA Sch Medicine Dept Molecular Med B2-985J Box 956948 Los Angeles CA 90095-0001

SCHELL, ORVILLE, dean; BA magna cum laude, Harvard Univ., 1964; MA, Univ. Calif., 1967, PhD, 1968. Co-producer WGBH-TV, Boston, 1984; rsch. assoc. Univ. Calif., Berkeley, 1986; con. NBC Nightly News, 1987; cons. CBS 60 Minutes, 1991; dean grad. sch. journalism Univ. Calif., 1996—. Co-dir. The Bay Area Inst., 1968-71; founder, editor-in-chief Pacific News Svc., 1970-96; corespondent New Yorker Mag., 1975, WGBH-TV Boston Frontline, 1994; rsch. assoc. Ctr. for Chinese Studies Univ. Calif,; cons. in field. Editorial bd. mem. Frontline, 1996. Bd. dirs. Yale-China Assn., Nat. Com. on U.S. China Rels., vice chmn. Human Rights Watch/Asia, 1989; pres. China Symposium, 1988-89; mem. coun. on fgn. rels. Recipient Best Magazine Article on Fgn. Subject award, 1992, Alfred I. Dupont-Columbia Univ. Silver Baton award, 1993, Emmy award, 1992, Page One award Bay Area Book Reviewers Assn., 1985; numerous rsch. grants; Guggenheim Found. fellow, 1981. Mem. Author's Guild, PEN, Coun. on Fgn. Rels. Office: Univ Calif Sch Journalism 121 Northgate Hall Berkeley CA 94720-5860

SCHELL, PAUL E. S. mayor; b. Fort Dodge, Iowa, Oct. 8, 1937; m. Pam Schell. BA, U. Iowa, 1960; JD, Columbia U., 1963. Pvt. practice, 1963-74; dir. dept. cmty. devel. City of Seattle, 1974-77, mayor, 1998—; pres., founder Cornerstone Columbia Devel. Co., 1979-87; commr. Port of Seattle, 1989-99, pres. commn., 1995-99; dean Architecture and Urban Planning U. Wash., 1992-95. Past bd. dirs. Intiman Theatre, A Contemporary Theater; past pres. Allied Arts; founder, active Cascadia Project; bd. dirs. Trade Devel. Alliance; mem. Friends of the Pike Place Market. Office: Office Mayor Municipal Bldg 600 4th Ave Fl 12 Seattle WA 98104-1850

SCHELLER, RICHARD H. molecular and cellular physiology educator; b. Milw., Oct. 30, 1953; BA in Biochemistry with honors, U. Wis., 1975; PhD in Chemistry, Calif. Inst. Tech., 1980. Postdoctoral fellow divsn. biology Calif. Inst. Tech., 1980-81; postdoctoral fellow in molecular neurobiology Columbia U. Coll. Physicians and Surgeons, 1981-82; asst. prof. dept. biol. scis. Stanford (Calif.) U., 1982-87, assoc. prof. dept. biol. scis., 1987-90, assoc. prof. dept. molecular and cellular physiology, 1990-93, assoc. prof. dept. biol. scis. by courtesy, 1990-93, prof. dept. molecular and cellular physiology, 1993—, prof. dept. biol. scis., 1993; assoc. investigator Howard Hughes Med. Inst., Stanford U. Med. Ctr., 1990-94, investigator, 1994—. Mem. molecular, cellular and devel. neurobiology rev. com. NIMH, 1993-96; mem. sci. adv. bd. Hereditary Disease Found., 1995-96; mem. neurobiology adv. bd. Cold Spring Harbor Lab., 1995; mem. sr. rev. com. McKnight Endowment Fund, 1995; mem. Nat. Adv. Mental Health Coun., 1996. Mem. editl. bd. Jour. Neurosci., 1984-90, DNA, 1984—, Ann. Rev. Neurosci., 1985-90, Molecular Brain Rsch., 1985, Cellular and Molecular Neurobiology, 1986, Synapse, 1989-91, Neuron, 1990, Current Opinion in Neurobiology, 1990; sect. editor Jour. Neurosci., 1991-95; monitoring editor Jour. Cell Biology, 1991; assoc. editor Genes to Cells, 1995; contbr. articles to profl. publs. Recipient Basil O'Connor award March of Dimes Found., 1983, Presdl. Young Investigator award, 1985, Alan T. Waterman award NSF, 1989, Merit award NIMH, 1992, W. Alden Spencer award Columbia U., 1993, award in molecular biology NAS, 1997; fellow NIH, 1976-80, 81-82, Alfred P. Sloan Found., 1984, Klingstein fellow in Neuroscis., 1985; scholar McKnight Found., 1983, Pew scholar in biomed. scis., 1986; Camile and Henry Dreyfus Tchr. scholar, 1986. Mem. Soc. for Neurosci. (young investigator award selection com. 1996). Office: Stanford U Med Ctr Mailcode 5428 B 155 Beckman Ctr Stanford CA 94305-5345*

SCHELLMAN, JOHN A. chemistry educator; b. Phila., Oct. 24, 1924; s. John and Mary (Mason) S.; m. Charlotte Green, Feb. 10, 1954; children: Heidi M., Lise C. AB, Temple U., 1948; MS, Princeton U., 1949, PhD, 1951; PhD (hon.), Chalmers U., Sweden, 1983, U. Padua, Italy, 1990. USPHS postdoctoral fellow U. Utah, 1951-52, Carlsberg Lab., Copenhagen, 1953-55; DuPont fellow U. Minn., Mpls., 1955-56, asst. prof. chemistry, 1956-58; assoc. prof. chemistry Inst. Molecular Biology, U. Oreg., Eugene, 1958-63, prof. chemistry, rsch. assoc., 1963—. Vis. Lab. Chem. Physics, Nat. Inst. Arthritis and Metabolic Diseases, NIH, Bethesda, Md., 1980; vis. prof. Chalmers U., Sweden, 1986, U. Padua, Italy, 1987. Contbr. articles to profl. jours. Served with U.S. Army, 1943-46 Fellow Rask-Oersted Found., 1954, Sloan Found., 1959-63, Guggenheim Found., 1969-70 Fellow Am. Phys. Soc.; mem. NAS, Am. Chem. Soc., Am. Soc. Biochemistry and Molecular Biology, Am. Acad. Arts and Scis., Biophys. Soc., Phi Beta Kappa, Sigma Xi. Democrat Home: 780 Lorane Hwy Eugene OR 97405-2340 Office: Univ Oreg Inst Molecular Biology Eugene OR 97403 E-mail: john@molbio.uoregon.edu

SCHENDEL, STEPHEN ALFRED, plastic surgery educator, craniofacial surgeon; b. Mpls., Oct. 10, 1947; s. Alfred Reck and Jeanne Shirley (Hagquist) S.; children: Elliott, Mélisande. BA, St. Olaf Coll., Northfield, Minn., 1969; BS with high distinction, U. Minn., 1971, DDS, 1973; diplome asst. etranger with high honors, U. Nantes, France, 1980; MD, U. Hawaii, 1983. Diplomate Am. Bd. Plastic Surgery, Nat. Bd. Med. Examiners, Nat. Bd. Dental Examiners, Am. Bd. Oral and Maxillofacial Surgery (adv. com., bd. examiner 1991-95). Intern, then resident in oral and maxillofacial surgery Parkland Meml. Hosp., Dallas, 1975-79; resident in gen. surgery Baylor U. Med. Ctr., Dallas, 1983-84, Stanford (Calif.) U. Med. Ctr., 1984-86, resident in plastic surgery, 1986-89, acting assoc. prof. surgery, 1989-91, assoc. prof., 1991-95, head div. plastic and reconstructive surgery, 1992—, dir. residency tng., 1992-98, chmn. dept. functional restoration, 1994—, prof., 1995—; head plastic surgery, dir. Craniofacial Ctr. Lucile Salter Packard Children's Hosp., Stanford, chief pediat. surgery, 1997—. Asst. to Dr. Paul Tessier, Paris, 1987-88; asst. dept. stomatology and maxillofacial surgery Centre Hospitalier Regional Nantes, 1979-80; mem. med. bd. Lucile Salter Packard Children's Hosp. at Stanford, 1991—. Assoc. editor Selected Readings in Oral and Maxillofacial Surgery, 1989—; mem. edtl. bd. Jour. Cranio-Maxillofacial Surgery; contbr. articles and abstracts to med. and dental jours., chpts. to books. Recipient Disting. Alumnus award St. Olaf Coll., 1993; Fulbright fellow, Nantes, 1979-80, Chateaubriand fellow Govt. of France, 1987-88. Fellow ACS, Am. Acad. Pediat.; mem. European Assn. Cranio-Maxillofacial Surgeons, Am. Soc. Pediat. Plastic Surgeons, Am. Assn. Plastic Surgery, Soc. Baylor Surgeons (founding), French Assn. Maxillofacial Surgeons (fgn.), Am. Cleft Palate-Craniofacial Assn., Am. Soc. Plastic and Reconstructive Surgeons (sec. 1996—), Am. Soc. Maxillofacial Surgeons (sec.), Assn. Acad. Chairmen Plastic Surgery, Zedplast (bd. dirs. 1993—), Omicron Kappa Upsilon. Avocations: fly fishing, painting and sculpture. Office: Stanford U Med Ctr NC 104 Divsn Plastic Reconstr Surg Stanford CA 94305

SCHENDEL, WILLIAM BURNETT, lawyer; b. 1948; BA, Swarthmore Coll., 1970; JD, Boston U., 1974. Bar: Alaska 1976, U.S. Dist Ct. Alaska (9th cir.), U.S. Supreme Ct. Ptnr. Schendel & Callahan, Fairbanks, Alaska, 1981—. Pres. Alaska Bar Assn. Mem. ABA, Alaska Bar Assn. (pres. 1998-99). Office: Schendel & Callahan 613 Cushman St Ste 200 Fairbanks AK 99701-4655

SCHENDEL, WINFRIED GEORGE, insurance company executive; b. June 19, 1931; came to U.S., 1952, naturalized, 1956; s. Willi Rudolf Max and Anna Margarete (Sassen) S.; m. Joanne Wiiest, Aug. 24, 1953; children: Victor Winfried, Bruce Lawrence, Rachelle Laureen. BS in Elec. and Indsl. Engring., Hannover-Stadthagen U., Hannover, Fed. Republic of Germany, 1952. Elec. draftsman Houston Lighting & Power Co., 1954-57; elec. draftsman, corrosion technician Transcontinental Gas Pipeline Co., Houston, 1957-59; elec. engr. Ken R. White Cons. Engrs., Denver, 1959-61; sales engr. Weco divsn. Food Machinery & Chem. Corp., various locations, 1961-64; ins. field underwriter N.Y. Life Ins. Co., Denver, 1964-66, asst. mgr., 1966-70, mgmt. asst., 1970-71, gen. mgr., 1971-77, mgr., 1979-85, field underwriter, 1985—; gen. agt. Woodmen Accident and Life Ins. Co., Ft. Collins, Colo., 1998—. Ind. gen. agt., Denver, 1978-79; ins. broker and adviser, 1979—. Instnl. rep., advancement chmn. Denver Area coun. Boy Scouts Am., Lakewood, Colo., 1968-72; precinct chmn. Rep. party, Jefferson County, Colo., 1976, 78; founder, life mem. Sister City Program, Lakewood, Colo.; chmn. adv. bd. ARC, Jefferson County, Colo., 1987-89; elder Presbyn. ch. Recipient Centurion award, 1966, Northwestern Region Leader Manpower Devel. award N.Y. Life Ins. Co., 1968, Salesman of Yr. award Jefferson County Salesman with a Purpose Club, 1983, Top awards ARC, 1988-89. Mem. Nat. Assn. Life Underwriters, Gen. Agts. and Mgrs. Assn. (Conf. Nat. Mgmt. award 1975), Colo. Life Underwriters Assn. (reg. v.p. Denver met. area 1989-90), Mile High Assn. Life Underwriters (pres. 1986-87, nat. com. 1988, 91), Lakewood C. of C. (pres. people-to-people, Trailblazer of Yr. award 1982, 83, Trail Boss of Yr. 1983), Lions, Edelweiss Club, Internat. Order Rocky Mountain Goats, N.Y. Life Star, Masons, Rotary (bd. dirs. Ft. Collins chpt., Paul Harris award 1995), Shriners. Home and Office: 925 Deerhurst Cir Fort Collins CO 80525-6919 Fax: (970) 206-9082

SCHENKER, MARC BENET, preventive medicine educator; b. L.A., Aug. 25, 1947; s. Steve and Dosella Schenker; m. Heath Massey; children: Yael, Phoebe, Hilary. BA, U. Calif., Berkeley, 1969; MD, U. Calif., San Francisco, 1973; MPH, Harvard U., Boston, 1980. Instr. medicine Harvard U., Boston, 1980-82; asst. prof. medicine U. Calif., Davis, 1982-86, assoc. prof., 1986-92, prof., 1992—, chmn. dept. epidemiology and preventive medicine, 1995—. Fellow ACP; mem. Am. Thoracic Soc., Am. Pub. Health Assn., Soc. Epidemiologic Rsch., Am. Coll. Epidemiology, Soc. Occupl. Environ. Health, Internat. Commn. Occupl. Health, Assn. Tchrs. Preventive Medicine, Phi Beta Kappa, Alpha Omega Alpha. Office: Dept Epidemiology and Preventive Medicine TB 168 One Shields Ave Davis CA 95616-8638

SCHENKKAN, ROBERT FREDERIC, writer, actor; b. Chapel Hill, N.C., Mar. 19, 1953; s. Robert Frederic Sr. and Jean (McKenzie) S.; children: Sarah Victoria, Joshua McHenry. BA in Theatre Arts, U. Tex., 1975; MFA in Acting, Cornell U., 1977. Author: (plays) Final Passages, 1981, The Survivalist, 1982 (best of the fringe award Edinburgh Festival 1984), Tachinoki, 1987, Tall Tales, 1988 (Playwrights Forum award 1988, Best One Act Plays 1993), Heaven on Earth, 1989 (Julie Harris Playwright award Beverly Hills Theatre Guild 1989), The Kentucky Cycle, 1991 (Pulitzer prize for drama 1992, L.A. Drama Critics Circle Best Play award 1992, Penn Ctr. West award 1993, Best Play Tony award nominee 1993, Best Play Drama Desk award nominee 1993), Conversations with the Spanish Lady and Other One-Act Plays, 1993, The Dream Thief, 1998, Handler, 1999, (films) Crazy Horse, 1996, The Quiet American, 2001. Grantee Vogelstein Found., 1982, Arthur Found., 1988, Fund for New Am. Plays grantee 1990, Calif. Arts Coun. grantee, 1991. Mem. Writers Guild, Dramatists Guild, Actors Equity, SAG, Ensemble Studio Theatre.

SCHER, LAURA SUSAN, financial company executive; b. Passaic, N.J., Jan. 18, 1959; d. Alan E. and Frances Scher; m. Ian H. Altman, May 28, 1984. BA in Econs., Yale U., 1980; MBA, Harvard U., 1985. Assoc. cons. Bain & Co., Boston, 1981-83; chief exec. officer Working Assets Funding Service, San Francisco, 1985—. Named Baker Scholar, Harvard U., 1985.

SCHERF, DIETMAR (ALEC DONZI), publishing executive, artist, agent; b. Graz, Austria, June 12, 1961; came to U.S., 1990; s. Friedrich and Maria (Rosenberger) S.; m. Patricia Michaela Rech, Apr. 9, 1987; children: Alexander, Deborah, Daniel, David. Diploma, trade sch., Graz, 1979. CEO Handelshaus D. Scherf, Vienna, Austria, 1987-90; CEO, pres. Scherf, Inc., Las Vegas, Nev., 1990-2000, creative dir., 2001—. Author: Short Term Trading, 1990, (booklet) Ross Perot, 1992, I Love Me: Avoiding and Overcoming Depressions, 1998, The Consultant, 2000; composer, performer (CD) Nice to Meet Ya!, 1994. Avocations: swimming, movies, reading, contemporary art, Bible studies. Office: Scherf Inc PO Box 80180 Las Vegas NV 89180-0180 E-mail: ds@scherf.com

SCHERGER, JOSEPH E. family physician, educator; b. Delphos, Ohio, Aug. 29, 1950; m. Carol M. Wintermute, Aug. 7, 1973; children: Adrian, Gabriel. BS summa cum laude, U. Dayton, 1971; MD, UCLA, 1975. Family practice residency U. Wash., Seattle, 1975-78; clin. instr. U. Calif. Sch. Medicine, Davis, 1978-80, asst. clin. prof., 1980-84, assoc. clin. prof., 1984-90, clin. prof., 1990—, dir. predoctoral program, 1991-92; med. dir. family practice and community medicine Sharp Healthcare, San Diego, 1992-96; assoc. dean primary care, chair dept. family medicine U. Calif., Irvine, 1996—, [r]of. dept. family medicine, 1996—. Recipeient Hippocratic Oath award UCLA, Calif. Physician of Yr. award Am. Acad. Family Physicians. Mem. NAS (mem. Inst. Medicine), Am. Acad. Family Physicians, Soc. Tchrs. Family Medicine. Home: 13407 Wyngate Pt San Diego CA 92130-1347

SCHERICH, ERWIN THOMAS, civil engineer, consultant; b. Inland, Nebr., Dec. 6, 1918; s. Harry Erwin and Ella (Peterson) S.; student Hastings Coll., 1937-39, N.C. State Coll., 1943-44; B.S., U. Nebr., 1946-48; M.S., U. Colo., 1948-51; m. Jessie Mae Funk, Jan. 1, 1947; children— Janna Rae Scherich Thornton, Jerilyn Mae Scherich Dobson, Mark Thomas. Civil and design engr. U.S. Bur. Reclamation, Denver, 1948-84, chief spillways and outlets sect., 1974-75, chief dams br., div. design, 1975-78, chief tech. rev. staff, 1978-79, chief div. tech. rev. Office of Asst. Commr. Engring. and Rsch. Ctr., 1980-84; cons. civil engr., 1984— . Mem. U.S. Com. Internat. Commn. on Large Dams. Served with AUS, 1941-45. Registered profl. engr., Colo. Fellow ASCE; mem. NSPE (nat. dir. 1981-87, v.p. southwestern region 1991-93), Profl. Engrs. Colo. (pres. 1977-78), Jefferson County West C. of C. Republican. Methodist. Home and Office: 3915 Balsam St Wheat Ridge CO 80033-4449

SCHERMAN, CAROL E. human resources professional; married; three children. BS in Orgnl. Behavior, U. San Francisco. With Bergen Brunswig Corp., exec. v.p. human resources. CEO Medi-Mail, Inc. subs. Bergen Brunswig Corp., Las Vegas. Active Human Resources Exec. Forum of Orange County; mem. human resources adv. com. Chapman U., Orange. Office: Bergen Brunswig Corp 4000 W Metropolitan Dr Orange CA 92868-3510

SCHERR, JAMES EDWIN, sports association executive; m. April Vigil; 1 child, Evan. BS, U. Nebr.; MBA, Northwestern U. Exec. dir., treas. USA Wrestling, Colorado Springs, Colo., 1990—. Bd. dirs. USA Wrestling, Athlete Adv. Com., U.S. Olympic Com.; trustee U.S. Olympic Found.; mem. TV and mktg. commn. Internat. Fedn. Assoc. Wrestling Styles. Placed 5th in freestyle wrestling, Seoul Olympics, 1988; recipient silver medal World Championship, 1987, 89, bronze medal 1986 World meet, three U.S. Nationals titles, 2 World Cup gold medals, NCAA Championship, Outstanding Freestyle Wrestler, U.S. Nationals, 1989. Mem. USOC (exec. com.). Office: USA Wrestling 6155 Lehman Dr Colorado Springs CO 80918-3439

SCHEUER, PAUL JOSEF, chemistry educator; b. Heilbronn, Germany, May 25, 1915; came to U.S., 1938; s. Albert and Emma (Neu) S.; m. Alice Elizabeth Dash, Sept. 5, 1950; children: Elizabeth E., Deborah A., David A., Jonathan L.L. BS with honors, Northeastern U., Boston, 1943; MA, Harvard U., 1947, PhD, 1950. Asst. prof. chemistry U. Hawaii, Honolulu, 1950-55, assoc. prof. chemistry, 1956-61, prof. chemistry, 1961-85, prof. chemistry emeritus, 1985—. Vis. prof. Orsted Inst., U. Copenhagen, 1977, 89; Toyo Suisan vis. prof. U. Tokyo, 1992. Author: Chemistry of Marine Natural Products, 1973, editor 12 series, 1978-93; contbr. over 290 articles to profl. jours. Spl. agt. U.S. Army, 1944-46, ETO. Recipient Rsch. Achievement award Am. Soc. Pharmacognosy, 1994, Regents award for rsch. excellence U. Hawaii, 1972; named P.J. Scheuer award Marine Chemists, 1992; NATO fellow, 1975. Fellow AAAS, Royal Soc. Chemistry; mem. Am. Chem. Soc. (sect. chair 1956, 87, Hawaii sect. award 1996, Ernest Guenther award 1994), Northeastern U. Alumni Assn. (Disting. Alumni award 1984). Office: U Hawaii Chemistry Dept 2545 The Mall Honolulu HI 96822-2275 E-mail: Scheuer@gold.chpia.Hawaii.edu

SCHIELE, PAUL ELLSWORTH, JR. education business owner, writer; b. Phila., Nov. 20, 1924; s. Paul Ellsworth Sr. and Maud (Barclay) S.; m. Sarah Irene Knauss, Aug. 20, 1946; children: Patricia Schiele Sommers, Sandra Schiele Kicklighter, Deborah Schiele Hartigan. AT, Temple U., 1949; BA, LaVerne U., 1955; MA, Claremont Grad. U., 1961; PhD, U.S. Internat. U., San Diego, 1970. Cert. sec. tchr., Calif. 1961. Tchr. sci. and math. Lincoln High Sch., Phila., 1956-57, Ontario (Calif.) Sch. Dist., 1957-65; math. and sci. cons. Hacienda La Puente U. Sch. Dist., Calif., 1965-75; asst. prof. Calif. State U., Fullerton, 1975-83; pres., owner Creative Learning Environments and Resources, Glendora, Calif., 1983—, cons. sci. curriculum, 1985—. Dir. title III project ESEA, 1974-75, cons. for project, 1975-77; cons. in field. Author: (student workbook) Beyond the Earth, 1969, Primary Science, 1972, 2d edit., 1976, (novel) Under Cover of Night, 1995, Chasing the Wild Geese, 1996, Deceptive Appearances, 1997; editor: A Living World, 1974, 2d edit., 1986; writer 9 sound filmstrips, model units for sci. and math. activity books, 10 sci. activities for L.A. Outdoor Edn. Program, 1980; editor 21 sci. and math. activity books, 1975-76; writer, co-dir. (TV) Marine Biology Series, 1970-71; contbr. munerous articles to profl. mags., 1960-85; writer and designer of 2 sci. ednl. games; designer in field. Apptd. adv. com. Sci. and Humanities Symposium Calif. Mus. Sci. and Industry, 1974; mem. State Sci. Permit Com., Tide Pools of Calif. Coast, 1974-75; mem. Friends of Libr., Friends Libr. Found. Mem. Internat. Platform Assn., Internat. Soc. Photographers, Glendora Hist. Soc., ABI Rsch. Assn. (bd. govs.), Calif. Elem. Edn. Assn. (hon.), Nat. PTA (hon.), Calif. Inter-Sci. Coun. (pres., chmn. 1971, 72), Elem Sch. Scis. Assn. (past pres., bd. dirs.), Paddlewheel Steamboating Soc. of Am., Phi Delta Kappa (chartered). Republican. Lutheran. Avocations: travel, etchings, art collecting, fencing. Home: 231 Catherine Park Dr Glendora CA 91741-3018

SCHIFF, ADAM BENNETT, congressman, lawyer; b. Framingham, Mass., June 22, 1960; s. Edward Maurice and Sherrill Ann (Glovsky) S.; m. Eve Schiff; 1 child, Alexa Marion BA, Stanford U., 1982; JD, Harvard U., 1985. Bar: Calif. 1986. Assoc. Gibson, Dunn & Crutcher, L.A., 1986; asst. U.S. atty. U.S. Atty.'s Office, L.A., 1987-93; mem. Calif. Senate, 1996-2000, U.S. Congress from 27th Calif. dist., Washington, 2001—; mem. judiciary com., internat. rels. com. Spl. assignment to Czechoslovakia, Justice Dept., Bratislava, 1992. Democrat. Avocation: writing fiction. Office: 437 Cannon HOB Washington DC 20515-0527*

SCHIFF, DONALD WILFRED, pediatrician, educator; b. Detroit, Sept. 11, 1925; s. Henry and Kate (Boesky) S.; m. Rosalie Pergament; children: Stephen, Jeffrey, Susan, Douglas. Student, Wayne State U., 1943-44, Oberlin Coll., 1944-45; MD, Wayne State U., 1949. Diplomate Am. Bd. Pediatrics. Intern Detroit Receiving Hosp., 1949-50; resident in pediatrics U. Colo., 1954-55, chief resident in pediatrics, 1955-56; instr. U. Colo. Health Scis. Ctr., Denver, 1956-59, asst. clin. prof., 1959-69, assoc. clin. prof., 1969-78, clin. prof., 1978-87, prof., 1987—; pvt. practice Littleton (Colo.) Clinic, 1956-86, chmn. bd., 1973-79; med. dir. HMO Colo., Denver, 1980-86; med. dir. Child Health Clinic The Children's Hosp., Denver. Contbr. articles to profl. jours. Bd. dirs. Sch. Dist. VI, Colo., 1962; pres. Arapahoe Mental Health Clinic, Denver, 1968-70, bd. dirs., 1964-70; adv. coun. State of Colo. Medicaid, Denver, 1981—. With USN, 1944-46, USPHS, 1952-54, Turtle Mountain Indian Reservation, N.D. Recipient 25 Yrs. Teaching award U. Colo. Sch. Medicine, 1981. Mem. Am. Acad. Pediatrics (chmn. Colo. chpt. 1973-79, alternate dist. chmn. 1977-81, chmn. dist. 8 1981-86, nat. pres. 1988-89), Rocky Mountain Pediatric Soc., Colo. Med. Soc. Home: 600 Front Range Rd Littleton CO 80120-4052 Office: The Childrens Hosp Child Health Clinic Box BO32 1056 E 19th Ave Denver CO 80218-1088

SCHIFF, GUNTHER HANS, lawyer; b. Cologne, Germany, Aug. 19, 1927; came to U.S., 1936; s. Hans and Alice (Goldstein) S.; m. Katharine MacMillan, Jan. 27, 1950 (div. 1957); children: Eric Alan, Mary Alice; m. JoAnn R. Schiff; children: Jage, Hans Judson. B.S.F.S., Georgetown U., 1949, J.D., 1952. Bar: D.C. 1952, Calif. 1953. Assoc., ptnr., of counsel various firms, Beverly Hills, Calif., 1954-94; pvt. practice Beverly Hills, 1994—. Sec. Los Angeles Copyright Soc., Beverly Hills, 1975-76 Contbr. articles to profl. jours. Pres. Beverly Hills Civil Svc. Commn., 1984-85, 88-89; pres. Free Arts for Abused Children, 1993-94, dir.; chmn. Rent Control Rev. Bd., Beverly Hills, 1980-84; trustee Young Musicians Found. With USNR, 1945-46. Mem. ABA, Beverly Hills Bar Assn. (chmn. Resolutions Com. 1977-78), Los Angeles County Bar Assn., Los Angeles Copyright Soc., Calif. Yacht Club. Avocations: sailing; skiing; golfing. Office: 9430 W Olympic Blvd Beverly Hills CA 90212-4552 E-mail: hgschiff@pacbell.net

SCHIFF, MARTIN, physician, surgeon; b. Phila., July 16, 1922; s. Isidore and Cecelia (Miller) S.; m. Mildred Tepley, Jan. 5, 1946; children: Denise Schiff Simon, Michael, David BS, Pa. State U., 1943; MD, U. Calif.-Irvine, 1951. Intern L.A. County Gen. Hosp., 1950-51; gen. practice medicine specializing in bariatrics L.A., 1951—. Mem. staff Brotman Meml. Hosp.; lectr. L.A. area community colls. Author: Eat & Stay Slim, 1972, Miracle Weight-Loss Guide, 1976, One-Day-At-A-Time Weight Loss Plan, 1980, (5 tapes) Weight Loss Plan for Health, Happiness & A Longer Life Span, 1982, The Thin Connection, 1986, Lose Unwanted Pounds Permanently Without Dieting/Trying/Playing Games, 1998, Weight Control-Fact or Fiction?, 1999, The Power of Your Will, 1999, Connections: Feelings and Emotions, 2000. Lt. USN, 1943-45, PTO Mem. AMA, Calif. Med. Assn., L.A. Med. Assn., Am. Soc. Weight Control Specialists Home: 1220 Corsica Dr Pacific Palisades CA 90272-4016 Office: 12900 Venice Blvd Los Angeles CA 90066-3510

SCHIFFER, JOHN C. state legislator; b. Chadron, Nebr., Aug. 17, 1945; m. Nancy Schiffer. BA, Colo. Coll. Mem. Wyo. Senate, Dist. 22, Cheyenne, 1993—; mem. appropriations com. Wyo. Senate, Cheyenne. Mem. North Fork Water Users, Jackson County Sch. Bd. Mem. Wyo. Stockgrowers, Nat. Stockgrowers Assn., Wyo. Environ. Quality Coun. Republican. Home: 561 Sussex Rd Kaycee WY 82639-9616 Office: Wyo Senate State Capitol Cheyenne WY 82002-0001 E-mail: jschiffe@senate.wyoming.com

SCHIFFNER, CHARLES ROBERT, architect; b. Reno, Sept. 2, 1948; Robert Charles and Evelyn (Keck) S.; m. Iovanna Lloyd Wright, Nov. 1971 (div. Sept. 1981); m. Adrienne Anita McAndrews, Jan. 22, 1983. Student, Sacramento Jr. Coll., 1967-68, Frank Lloyd Wright Sch. Architecture, 1968-77. Registered architect, Ariz., Nev., Wis. Architect Taliesin Associated Architects, Scottsdale, Ariz., 1977-83; pvt. practice architecture Phoenix, 1983—. Lectr. The Frank Lloyd Wright Sch. of Architecture, 1994, 95. Named one of 25 Most Promising Young Americans Under 35, U.S. mag., 1979; recipient AIA Honor award Western Mountain Region, 1993, Western Home awards Sunset Mag., 1989, 91, AIA Ariz. Merit award, 1993 and numerous others. Home: 5202 E Osborn Rd Phoenix AZ 85018-6137 Office: Camelhead Office Ctr 2944 N 44th St Phoenix AZ 85018-7257

SCHILE, WAYNE, newspaper publishing executive; Pub. Billings (Mont.) Gazette, 1984-98. Address: PO Box 36300 Billings MT 59107-6300 Office: 401 N Broadway Billings MT 59101-1243

SCHILLING, CURTIS MONTAGUE, professional baseball player; b. Anchorage, Nov. 14, 1966; m. Shonda Schilling; 1 child, Gehrig. Student, Yavapai Coll., Ariz. Selected by Boston Red Sox, 1986-88; traded Balt. Orioles, 1988-91, Houston Astros, 1991-92; pitcher Phila. Phillies, 1992-2000, Arizona Diamondbacks, 2000—. Recipient Lou Gehrig award Phi Delta Theta, 1996. Office: c/o Ariz Diamondbacks Bank One Ballpark 401 E Jefferson St Phoenix AZ 85004-2438

SCHILLING, FREDERICK AUGUSTUS, JR. geologist, consultant; b. Phila., Apr. 12, 1931; s. Frederick Augustus and Emma Hope (Christoffer) S.; m. Ardis Ione Dovre, June 12, 1957 (div. 1987); children: Frederick Christopher, Jennifer Dovre. BS in Geology, Wash. State U., 1953; PhD in Geology, Stanford U., 1962. Registered geologist, Calif.; cert. engring. geologist, Calif.; registered environ. assessor, Calif. Computer geophysicist United Geophys. Corp., Pasadena, Calif., 1955-56; geologist various orgns., 1956-61, U.S. Geol. Survey, 1961-64; underground engr. Climax (Colo.) Molybdenum Co., 1966-68; geologist Keradamex Inc., Anaconda Co., M.P. Grace, Ranchers Exploration & Devel. Corp., Albuquerque and Grants, N.Mex., 1968-84, Hecla Mining Co., Coeur d'Alene, Idaho, 1984-86, various engring. and environ. firms, Calif., 1986-91; prin. F. Schilling Cons., Canyon Lake, 1991—. Author: Bibliography of Uranium, 1976. Del. citizen amb. program People to People Internat., USSR, 1990-91. With U.S. Army, 1953-55. Fellow The Explorers Club; mem. Geol. Soc. Am., Am. Assn. Petroleum Geologists, Soc. Mining Engrs., Internat. Platform Assn., Adventurers' Club L.A., Masons, Kiwanis, Sigma Xi, Sigma Gamma Epsilon. Republican. Presbyterian. Avocation: track and field. Office: F Schilling Cons 30037 Steel Head Dr Canyon Lake CA 92587-7460 also: 14661 Myford Rd Ste C Tustin CA 92780-7205 E-mail: faschill@pacbell.net

SCHIMMEL, PAUL REINHARD, biochemist, biophysicist, educator; b. Hartford, Conn., Aug. 4, 1940; s. Alfred E. and Doris (Hudson) S.; m. Judith F. Ritz, Dec. 30, 1961; children: Kirsten, Katherine. A.B., Ohio Wesleyan U., 1962; postgrad., Tufts U. Sch. Medicine, 1962-63, Mass. Inst. Tech., 1963-65, Cornell U., 1965-66, Stanford U., 1966-67, U. Calif., Santa Barbara, 1975-76; Ph.D., Mass. Inst. Tech., 1966; DSc (hon.), Ohio Wesleyan U., 1996. Asst. prof. biology and chemistry MIT, 1967-71, assoc. prof., 1971-76, prof. biochemistry and biophysics, 1976-92, John D. and Catherine T. MacArthur prof. biochemistry and biophysics, 1992-97; prof. Scripps Rsch. Inst. and The Skaggs Inst. for Chem. Biology, 1997-2001, Ernest and Jean Hahn prof. molecular biology and chemistry, 2001—. Mem. study sect. on physiol. chemistry NIH, 1975-79; indsl. cons. on enzymes and recombinant DNA; bd. dirs. Repligen Corp., Alkermes, Inc., Cubist Pharms., Inc. Author: (with C. Cantor) Biophysical Chemistry, 3 vols., 1980; mem. editl. bd. Archives Biochemistry, Biophysics, 1976-80, Nucleic Acids Rsch., 1976-80, Jour. Biol. Chemistry, 1977-82, Biopolymers, 1979-88, Internat. Jour. Biol. Macromolecules, 1983-89, Trends in Biochem. Scis., 1984—, Biochemistry, 1989—, Accounts of Chem. Rsch., 1989-94, European Jour. Biochemistry, 1991-96, Protein Sci., 1991-94, Proc. Nat. Acad. Scis., 1993-99. Alfred P. Sloan fellow, 1970-72; recipient Emily M. Gray award Biophys. Soc., 2000. Fellow AAAS, Am. Acad. Arts and Scis. (chmn. Amory prize com. 1995-96); mem. NAS (class II biochemistry sect. rep. 1995-96), Am. Philos. Soc., Am. Chem. Soc. (Pfizer award 1978, chmn. divsn. biol. chemistry 1984-85) Am. Soc. for Biochemistry and Molecular Biology (chmn. nominating com. 1990, awards com. 1995-97), Ribonucleic Acid Soc. Office: The Scripps Rsch Inst 10550 N Torrey Pines Rd La Jolla CA 92037-1000

SCHINDLER, DAVID WILLIAM, research scientist, educator; b. Fargo, N.D., Aug. 3, 1940; s. Edward William and Angeline Evelyn (Havel) S.; m. Suzanne Bayley, Apr. 24, 1979; children by previous marriage: Eva, Daniel, Rachel BS, N.D. State U., 1962, DS (hon.), 1978; DPhil, Oxford U., Eng., 1966; DSc (hon.), U. Victoria, B.C., Can., 1990. Asst. prof. Trent U., Peterborough, Ont., Can., 1966-68; project leader Freshwater Inst., Winnipeg, Man., Can., 1968-89; Killam meml. prof. ecology U. Alta., Edmonton, 1989—. Rhodes scholar, 1962; NIH spl. fellow, 1965; recipient Miroslaw Romanowski medalRoyal Society of Canada, 1994 Fellow Royal Soc. Can. (Miroslaw Romanowski Medal, 1994); mem. Internat. Limnological Soc. (nat. rep. 1974-78, Naumann-Thienemann medal 1989), Am. Geophys. Union, Am. Inst. Biol. Scis., Am. Soc. Limnology and Oceanography (pres 1982-83, G.E. Hutchinson medal 1984), Can. Soc. Limnologists (F.N. Rigler award 1984), Ecol. Soc. Am., Can. Zool. Soc. Home: Box 178 Wildwood AB Canada T0E 2M0 Office: U Alta Dept Biological Scis Edmonton AB Canada T6G 2E9

SCHIRMER, HOWARD AUGUST, JR. civil engineer; b. Oakland, Calif., Apr. 21, 1942; s. Howard August and Amy (Freuler) S.; m. Leslie May Mecum, Jan. 29, 1965; children: Christine Nani, Amy Kiana, Patricia Leolani. B.S., U. Calif., Berkeley, 1964, M.S., 1965. Registered profl. engr., Hawaii, Guam. Engr. in tng. materials and research dept. Calif. Div. Hwys., Sacramento, 1960-64; engring. analyst Dames & Moore, San Francisco, 1964-67, asst. staff engr., 1967-68, chief engr., 1969-72, asso., 1972-75, partner, mng. prin. in charge, 1975-78, regional mgr. Pacific Far East and Australia, 1978-81, chief operating officer, 1981-83; mng. dir. Dames & Moore Internat., Los Angeles, 1983-89; mgr.-dir. CH2M Hill Internat. Ltd., Denver, 1989-90, pres., 1991-96; president Transnational Assocs., Englewood, Colo., 1996—. Chmn. geotech. engring. com. Am. Cons. Engrs. Council, 1976-78, prof. liability com. 1984—; past chmn. adv. com. for engring. tech. Honolulu Community Coll. Important works include AFDM Berthing Wharf, Pearl Harbor, Aloha Stadium, Hawaii, Century Ctr., Honolulu, Manila Internat. Airport, Philippines. Past mem. intable UCLA Grad. Sch. Mgmt.; chmn. engring. sect., mem. budget com. Aloha United Way, 1974; founder Mauna Kea Ski Patrol, 1969. Fellow ASCE (Past chmn. engring. mgmt. exec. com. 1986-87, Edmund Friedman Young Engr. award for profl. achievement 1974, pres. Hawaii sect., internat. actifities com., internat. dir. 1989-92; mem. Fedn. Internationale des Ingenieures-Conseils (chmn. standing com. on profl. liability 1986-89, U.S. rep to com.., mem. task com. on constrn. ins. and law Environmental com., 1994—; Cons. Engrs. Coun. Hawaii (pres. 1972), Engring. Assn. Hawaii (past dir., 2d v.p.), Internat. Soc. Soil Mechanics and Found. Engring., Am. Public Works Assn. (sec. 1977-78, dir. 1979-0), Soc. Am. Mil. Engrs., Environmental Technologies Trade Advisory com. (vice chmn, 1994—), Market Access Subcom. (chmn. 1998), adv. com. to Internat. Trade Office, State of Colo., 1994-1998, Outrigger Canoe Club, Met. Club (Denver), Chi Epsilon (Hon. mem. U. Hawaii), Sigma Phi Epsilon. Republican. Episcopalian. Office: TransNational Assocs Inc 4100 E Quincy Ave Englewood CO 80110-5051 Fax: 303-221-0359. E-mail: schirmerha@aol.com

SCHIRRA, WALTER MARTY, JR. business consultant, former astronaut; b. Hackensack, N.J., Mar. 12, 1923; s. Walter Marty and Florence (Leach) S.; m. Josephine Cook Fraser, Feb. 23, 1946; children: Walter Marty III, Suzanne Karen. Student, Newark Coll. Engring., 1940-42; B.S., U.S. Naval Acad., 1945; D. Astronautics (hon.), Lafayette Coll., U. So. Calif., N.J. Inst. Tech. Commd. ensign U.S. Navy, 1945, advanced through grades to capt., 1965; designated naval aviator, 1948; service aboard battle cruiser Alaska, 1945-46; service with 7th Fleet, 1946; assigned Fighter Squadron 71, 1948-51; exchange pilot 154th USAF Fighter Bomber Squadron, 1951; engaged in devel. Sidewinder missile China Lake, Calif., 1952-54; project pilot F7U-3 Cutlass; also instr. pilot F7U-3 Cutlass and FJ3 Fury, 1954-56; ops. officer Fighter Squadron 124, U.S.S. Lexington, 1956-57; assigned Naval Air Safety Officer Sch., 1957, Naval Air Test Ctr., 1958-59; engaged in suitability devel. work F4H, 1958-59; joined Project Mercury, man-in-space, NASA, 1959; pilot spacecraft Sigma 7 in 6 orbital flight, Oct. 1962; in charge operations and tng. Astronaut Office, 1964-69; command pilot Gemini 6 which made rendezvous with target, Gemini 7, Dec. 1965; comdr. 11 day flight Apollo 7, 1968; ret., 1969; pres. Regency Investors, Inc., Denver, 1969-70; chmn., chief exec. officer ECCO Corp., Englewood, Colo., 1970-73; chmn. Sernco, Inc., 1973-74; with Johns-Manville Corp., Denver, 1974-77; v.p. devel. Goodwin Cos., Inc., Littleton, Colo., 1978-79; ind. cons., 1979-80. Dir. Kimberly Clark, 1983-91. Decorated D.F.C.(3), Air medal (2), Navy D.S.M.; recipient Distinguished Service medal (2) NASA, Exceptional Service medal. Fellow Am. Astronautical Soc., Soc. Exptl. Test Pilots. Home and Office: PO Box 73 Rancho Santa Fe CA 92067-0073

SCHLATTER, O. EDWARD, judge; m. Patricia Schlatter; 2 children. BA, So. Ill. U., 1964; JD, U. Denver, 1970. Dist. and chief judge 11th jud. dist. U.S. Dist. Ct. State of Colo., Denver, 1981-92, magistrate judge, 1992—. Mem. Colo. Bar Assn. (exec. coun. criminal law sect 1984-86, bd. govs. 1987-92, sr. v.p. 1991-92), 11th Jud. Dist. Bar Assn. (v.p. 1985-87, pres. 1987-89). Office: US Dist Ct State Colo 1929 Stout St Rm C 162 Denver CO 80294-1929

SCHLEI, NORBERT ANTHONY, lawyer; b. Dayton, Ohio, June 14, 1929; s. William Frank and Norma (Lindsley) S.; m. Jane Moore, Aug. 26, 1950 (div. 1963); children: Anne C. Buczynski, William K., Andrew M.; m. Barbara Lindemann, Mar. 7, 1965 (div. 1981); children: Bradford L., Graham L. (dec. 1995), Norbert L. (dec. 1996), Blake Lindsley, Elizabeth Eldridge; m. Joan Masson, Dec. 29, 1995. BA, Ohio State U., 1950; LLB magna cum laude, Yale U., 1956. Bar: Ohio 1956, Calif. 1958, D.C. 1963, U.S. Supreme Ct. 1963. Law clk. to Justice Harlan U.S. Supreme Ct., 1956-57; assoc. atty. O'Melveny & Myers, L.A., 1957-59; ptnr. Greenberg, Shafton & Schlei, L.A., 1959-62; asst. atty. gen. U.S. Dept. Justice, Washington, 1962-66; ptnr. Munger, Tolles, Hills & Rickershauser, 1968-70, Kane, Shulman & Schlei, Washington, 1968-70; ptnr.-in-charge Hughes Hubbard & Reed, L.A., 1972-89; pres., CEO Kahala Capital Corp., Santa Monica, Calif., 1983—; pvt. practice Santa Monica, 1989—. Author: (with M.S. McDougal and others) Studies in World Public Order, 1961 (Am. Soc. Internat. Law ann. book award); State Regulation of Corporate Financial Practices, 1962; editor-in-chief Yale Law Jour., 1955-56. Dem. nominee for Calif. Assembly, 1962, for sec. of state Calif., 1966. Mem. Riviera Country Club (Pacific Palisades, Calif.). Avocations: tennis, golf, skiing, sailing. E-mail: nas@usinter.net

SCHLESINGER, DEBORAH LEE, librarian; b. Cambridge, Mass., Sept. 13, 1937; d. Edward M. and Edith D. (Schneider) Hershoff; divorced; children: Suzanne, Richard. BA, U. Mass., 1961; MS, Simmons Coll., 1974; postgrad., U. Pitts., 1983. Reference librarian Bently Coll., Waltham, Mass., 1964-65; dir. Carnegie Library, Swissvale, Pa., 1973-77, South Park Twp. Library, Library, 1977-81, Monessen (Pa.) Library, 1981-82, Lewis & Clark Library, Helena, Mont., 1983-88, 89—; state librarian Mont. State Library, Helena, 1988-89. Vis. scholar Pitts. Regional Library Ctr., 1982-83. Editor Pa. Union List, 1982-83. Mem. exec. bd. Mont. Cultural Advocacy, 1983—. Mem. Mont. Library Assn. (chmn. legis. com. 1984-92, MLA lobbyist 1992—), Mont. Assn. Female Execs. (fin. com. 1986—), AAUW (exec. com. 1985-86). Democrat. Club: Montana (Helena). Avocations: flying, painting, reading, rafting, travel. Home: 2 Washington Pl Helena MT 59601-6283 Office: Lewis & Clark Libr 120 S Last Chance Gulch St Helena MT 59601-4165

SCHLESSINGER, LAURA, radio talk show host; married; 1 child, Deryk. PhD in Physiology, Columbia U. Lic. in marriage and family therapy. Nat. syndicated radio talk show host The Dr. Laura Schlessinger Program. Past mem. faculty U. So. Calif., Pepperdine U. Author: Ten Stupid Things Women Do to Mess Up Their Lives, 1994, How Could You Do That, 1996, The Abdication of Character, Courage and Conscience, Ten Stupid Things Men Do To Mess Up Their Lives, 1997, The Ten Commandments: The Significance of God's Law in Everyday Life, 1998, Why Do You Love Me? for Children, 1999. Office: Premire Radio Networks 15260 Ventura Blvd Ste 300 Sherman Oaks CA 91403-5337

SCHLOSSER, ANNE GRIFFIN, librarian; b. N.Y.C., Dec. 28, 1939; d. C. Russell and Gertrude (Taylor) Griffin; m. Gary J. Schlosser, Dec. 28, 1965. BA in History, Wheaton Coll., Norton, Mass., 1962; MLS, Simmons Coll., 1964; cert. archives adminstrn., Am. U., 1970. Head UCLA Theater arts Libr., 1964-69; dir. Louis B. Mayer Libr., Am. Film Inst., L.A., 1969-88, dir. film/TV documentation workshop, 1977-87; head Cinema-TV Libr. and Archives of the Performing Arts, U. So. Calif., L.A., 1988-91; dir. Entertainment Resources Seminar, 1990; dir. rsch. libr. Warner Bros., 1991—. Project dir. Motion Pictures, Television, Radio: A Union Catalogue of Manuscript and Special Collections in the Western U.S., 1977. Active Hollywood Dog Obedience Club, Calif. Recipient numerous grants for script indexing, manuscript cataloging, libr. automation. Mem. Soc. Calif. Archivists (pres. 1982-83), Theater Libr. Assn (exec. bd. 1983-86), Spl. Librs. Assn. Democrat. Episcopalian. Avocations: running, swimming, reading, dog obedience training. Office: Warner Bros Rsch Libr 5200 Lankershim Blvd Ste 100 North Hollywood CA 91601-3100

SCHMALE, NEAL E. utilites company executive; BS in Petroleum Engring., Colo. Sch. Mines; LLD, Loyola U. With UNOCAL, sr. v.p., pres. petroleum products and chem. divsn., CFO; exec. v.p., CFO Sempra Energy, San Diego, 1997—. Office: Sempra Energy 101 Ash St San Diego CA 92101-3017

SCHMALENBERGER, JERRY LEW, pastor, religious studies educator; b. Greenville, Ohio, Jan. 23, 1934; s. Harry Henry and Lima Marie (Hormel) S.; m. Carol Ann Walthall, June 8, 1956; children: Stephen, Bethany Allison, Sarah Layton. BA, Wittenberg U., 1956, DDiv (hon.), 1984; MDiv, Hamma Sch. Theology, Springfield, Ohio, 1959, D of Ministry, 1976. Ordained to ministry Luth. Ch., 1959. Dir. Camp Mowana, Mansfield, Ohio, 1958-59; pastor 3d Luth. Ch., Springfield, 1959-61, 1st Luth. Ch., Bellefontaine, Ohio, 1961-66, sr. pastor Tiffin, 1966-70, Mansfield, 1970-79, St. John's Luth. Ch., Des Moines, 1979-88; pres. Pacific Luth. Theol. Sem., Berkeley, Calif., 1988-96, prof. parish ministry, 1988-99. Co-dir. Iowa Luth. Hosp. Min. of Health Program, Des Moines, 1986—88; Roland Payne lectr. Gbarnga Sch. Theology, Liberia, 1987; lectr. Luth. Theol. Sem., Hong Kong, 1994, Luth. Theol. Sem. , 1999—2001, The United Theol. Coll., Kingston, Jamaica, 1994, HKBP Sem., Sumatra, 1997; guest prof. The Augustana Hochschule, Germany, 1996, 99, 2001; guest lectr. Inst. Superior Evangelical Theol. Studies, Theol. Seminary, Argentina, 1998, Ecumenical Ctr., Montevideo, Uruguay, 1998; vis. faculty Moravian Theol. Seminary, Paramararibo, Surinam, 1998. Author: Lutheran Christians' Beliefs Book One, 1984, Book Two, 1987, Iowa Parables and Iowa Psalms, 1984, Saints Who Shaped the Church, 1986, Stewards of Creation, 1987, Nights Worth Remembering, 1989, The Vine and the Branches, 1992, Call to Witness, 1993, Plane Thoughts on Parish Ministry, 1994, Invitation to Discipleship, 1995, The Preacher's Edge, 1996, Preparation for Discipleship, 1998, These Will Preach, 1999, The Parables of Jesus and Their Flip Side, 2000, The Miracles of Jesus and Their Flip Side, 2001, Dear Friends and Family, 2001, The Preacher's Workbook, Cycle A, 2001; columnist Rite Ideas, 1987-88. Bd. dirs. Grand View Coll., Des Moines, 1980-88, Wittenberg U., Springfield, Ohio, 1974-87, Luth. Social Services of Iowa, 1980-87, chmn. pre fund drive, 1988; bd. dirs. Planned Parenthood of Mid-Iowa, Des Moines, 1987-88; dir. Evang. Outreach/Luth. Ch. Am., 1983-85; mem. Iowa Luth. Hosp. Charitable Trust, 1986-88; chair Com. for Homeless Fund, Des Moines, 1986. Named Outstanding Alumni Wittenberg U., 1965, Young Man of Yr. Tiffin Jaycees, 1965, Man of Yr. Bellefontaine Jaycees, Disting. Alumni award Trinty Sem., Columbus, 1989. Mem. NAACP, Acad. Preachers, Acad. Evangelists (organizer 1986—), Kiwanis, Rotary. Avocations: historical research and writing, travel, boating. Home and Office: 162 Pelican Loop Pittsburg CA 94565-2004 E-mail: jlschmalen@aol.com

SCHMID, RUDI (RUDOLF SCHMID), internist, educator, scientist; b. Switzerland, May 2, 1922; came to U.S., 1948, naturalized, 1954; s. Rudolf and Bertha (Schiesser) S.; m. Sonja D. Wild, Sept. 17, 1949; children: Isabelle S., Peter R. BS, Gymnasium Zurich, 1941; MD, U. Zurich, 1947; PhD, U. Minn., 1954. Intern U. Calif. Med. Center, San Francisco, 1948-49; resident medicine U. Minn., 1949-52, instr., 1952-54; research fellow biochemistry Columbia U., 1954-55; investigator NIH, Bethesda, Md., 1955-57; assoc. medicine Harvard Med. Sch., 1957-59; asst. prof. Harvard U., 1959-62; prof. medicine U. Chgo., 1962-66, U. Calif., San Francisco, 1966-91, prof. emeritus, 1991—, dean Sch. Medicine, 1983-89, assoc. dean internat. rels., 1989-95. Cons. to U.S. Army surgeon gen., USPHS, VA; hon. prof. Peking Union Med. Coll., Shanghai Second Med. U., Xian U. of Med. Sci., Jillin U. Mem. editl. bd. Jour. Clin. Investigation, 1965-70, Blood, 1962-75, Gastroenterology, 1965-70, Jour. Investigative Dermatology, 1968-72, Annals Internal Medicine, 1975-79, Procs. Soc. Exptl. Biology and Medicine, 1974-84, Chinese Jour. Clin. Scis., Jour. Lab. Clin. Medicine, 1991—, Hepatology Rsch. (Japan), 1993—; hon. editor-in-chief World Jour. Gastroenterology, China, 1996—; cons. editor Gastroenterology, 1981-86. Served with Swiss Army, 1943-48. Master ACP; fellow AAAS, N.Y. Acad. Scis., Royal Coll. Physicians; mem. NAS, Am. Acad. Arts and Scis., Assn. Am. Physicians (pres. 1986), Am. Soc. Clin. Investigation, Am. Soc. Biol. Chemistry and Molecular Biology, Am. Soc. Hematology, Am. Gastroenterol. Assn., Am. Assn. Study Liver Disease (pres. 1965), Internat. Assn. Study Liver (pres. 1980), Swiss Acad. Med. Scis. (mem. senate), Leopoldina, German-Am. Acad. Coun. (exec. com.). Achievements include research in biochemistry, metabolism of hemoglobin, heme, prophyrins, bile pigments, liver and muscle. Home: 211 Woodland Rd Kentfield CA 94904-2631 Office: U Calif Med Sch Office Dean PO Box 0410 San Francisco CA 94143-0410 E-mail: schmidr@medsch.ucsf.edu

SCHMID, SIGI, professional soccer coach; b. Tuebingen, West Germany, Mar. 20, 1953; came to U.S., 1962; children: Erik, Kurt, Kyle. BS in Econs., UCLA, 1976; MA in Bus. Adminstrn., U. So. Calif. CPA, Calif. Coach UCLA Bruins, 1980-99; head coach L.A. Galaxy, 1999—. Office: c/o LA Galaxy 1010 Rose Bowl Dr Pasadena CA 91103

SCHMID-SCHOENBEIN, GEERT WILFRIED, biomedical engineer, educator; b. Albstadt, Baden-Wurttemberg, Germany, Jan. 1, 1948; came to U.S., 1971; s. Ernst and Ursula Schmid; m. Renate Schmid-Schoenbein, July 3, 1976; children: Philip, Mark, Peter. Vordiplom, Liebig U., Giessen, Germany, 1971; PhD in Bioengring., U. Calif., San Diego, 1976. Staff assoc. dept. physiology Columbia U., N.Y.C., 1976-77, sr. assoc., 1977-79; asst. prof. dept. applied mechs. & engring. scis. U. Calif., San Diego, 1979-84, assoc. prof., 1984-89, prof., 1989-94, prof. dept. bioengring., 1994—. Editor: Frontiers in Biomechanics, 1986, Physiology and Pathophysiology of Leukocyte Adhesion, 1994; author more than 220 rsch. reports. Recipient Melville medal ASME, 1990, Ratschow medal European Soc. Phlebology, 1999. Fellow Am. Inst. for Med. and Biol. Engring., Am. Heart Assn.; mem. Biomed. Engring. Soc. (pres. 1991-92), Am. Microcirculatory Soc., European Microcirculatory Soc., Am. Physiol. Soc. Achievements include bioengineering research on cardiovascular disease, microcirulation, and lymphology. Office: U Calif San Diego Dept Bioengineering La Jolla CA 92093-0412

SCHMIDT, ARTHUR, film editor; Editor: (films) (with Jim Clark) The Last Remake of Beau Geste, 1977, Coal Miner's Daughter, 1980 (Academy award nomination best film editing 1980), The Escape Artist, 1982, Firstborn, 1984, The Buddy System, 1984, (with Harry Keramidas) Back to the Future, 1985, Fandango, 1985, (with Gib Jaffe) Ruthless People, 1986, Who Framed Roger Rabbit?, 1988 (Academy award best film editing 1988), (with Keramidas) Back to the Future II, 1989, (with Keramidas) Back to the Future III, 1990, (with Dov Hoenig) The Last of the Mohicans, 1992, Death Becomes Her, 1992, (with Jim Miller) Addams Family Values, 1993, Forrest Gump, 1994 (Academy award best film editing 1994), The Birdcage, 1996. Office: Motion Picture & Video Editors Guild Local 776 7715 W Sunset Blvd Ste 220 Los Angeles CA 90046-3912

SCHMIDT, CHAUNCEY EVERETT, banker; b. Oxford, Ia., June 7, 1931; s. Walter Frederick and Vilda (Saxton) S.; m. Anne Garrett McWilliams, Mar. 3, 1954; children: Carla, Julia, Chauncey Everett. B.S., U.S. Naval Acad., 1953; M.B.A., Harvard U., 1959. With First Nat. Bank, Chgo., 1959-76, v.p., gen. mgr. br. London, Eng., 1965-68, v.p. for Europe,

Middle East, Africa, 1968-69, sr. v.p., 1969-72, exec. v.p., 1972, vice chmn. bd., 1973, pres., 1974-76; chmn. bd., chief exec. officer, dir. Bank of Calif. N.A., San Francisco, 1976—; chmn. bd., pres., chief exec. officer, dir. BanCal Tri-State Corp., 1976—. Dir. Amfac, Inc., Honolulu; mem. Adv. Council Japan-U.S. Econ. Relations; adv. bd. Pacific Rim Bankers Program. Exec. bd. and pres. San Francisco Bay Area council Boy Scouts Am.; council SRI Internat.; bd. dirs. Bay Area Council; bd. govs. San Francisco Symphony; trustee U.S. Naval War Coll. Fedn., Newport, R.I. Served with USAF, 1953-56. Mem. Assn. Res. City Bankers, Am. Bankers Assn., Internat. Monetary Conf., Calif. Bankers Clearing House Assn. (dir.), Calif. Roundtable (dir.), Japan-Calif. Assn. Clubs: Comml. (Chgo.); Bankers (San Francisco), Bohemian (San Francisco). Home: 40 Why Worry Ln Woodside CA 94062-3654 Office: Ste 140 525 Middlefield Rd Menlo Park CA 94025

SCHMIDT, CYRIL JAMES, librarian; b. Flint, Mich., June 27, 1939; s. Cyril August and Elizabeth Josephine S.; m. Martha Joe Meadows, May 22, 1965; children: Susan, Emily. BA, Cath. U. Am., 1962; MSLS, Columbia U., 1963; Ph.D., Fla. State U., 1974. Asst. bus. and industry dept. Flint Pub. Library, 1963-65; reference librarian Gen. Motors Inst., Flint, 1965; asso. librarian S.W. Tex. State U., San Marcos, 1965-67; head undergrad. libraries, asst. prof. Ohio State U., 1967-70; dir. libraries SUNY, Albany, 1972-79; also mem. faculty SUNY (Sch. Library and Info. Sci.); univ. librarian Brown U., Providence, 1979-81; exec. v.p. Rsch. Libraries Group, Stanford, Calif., 1981-89; prin. cons. Schmidt & Assocs., Palo Alto, 1989—; univ. prof. San Jose (Calif.) State U., 1992—. Author papers in field. Libr. Svcs. Act fellow, 1962-63, Higher Edn. Act fellow, 1970-72 Mem. ALA, ACLU, Pi Sigma Alpha, Beta Phi Mu. Home: 244 Forest Ave Palo Alto CA 94301-2510 Office: San Jose State U 1 Washington Sq San Jose CA 95192-0001 E-mail: schmidtc@sjsuvm1.sjsu.edu

SCHMIDT, JAMES CRAIG, retired bank executive; b. Peoria, Ill., Sept. 27, 1927; s. Walter Henry and Clara (Wolfenbarger) S.; m. Jerrie Louise Bond, Dec. 6, 1958; children: Julie, Sandra, Suzanne. Student, Ill. Wesleyan U., 1945, 48-50, Ph.B. in Bus. Adminstrn, 1952; postgrad., U. Ill. Coll. Law, 1950-52; J.D., DePaul U., 1953. Spl. agt. Fidelity & Deposit Co., Chgo., 1956-58; with Home Fed. Savs. & Loan Assn., San Diego, 1958-67; asst. sec. bus. and transp. State of Calif., 1967-69; vice-chmn., pres. Gt. Am. Bank, San Diego, 1969-88. Pres. Conf. Fed. Savs. and Loans of Calif., 1974-75; mem. Calif. Toll Bridge Authority, 1969-74; mem. Calif. State Transp. Bd., 1972-78; past chmn. San Diego Bal. Commn. Task Force. Pres. San Diego Holiday Bowl Football Game, 1986; bd. dirs. San Diego Internat. Sports Coun., San Diego Hwy. Devel. Assn., San Diego County Taxpayers Assn. Mem. Calif. Bar Assn., Ill. Bar Assn., Calif. League Savs. Instns. (chmn. 1986-87), Calif. C. of C. (bd. dirs. 1987-90), U.S. Savs. Instn. League (exec. com. 1983-86), Catfish Club, Sigma Chi, Phi Delta Phi. Office: 8383 Center Dr Ste J La Mesa CA 91942-2913 Fax: 619-469-5927

SCHMIDT, JOSEPH DAVID, urologist; b. Chgo., July 29, 1937; s. Louis and Marian (Fleigel) S.; m. Andrea Maxine Herman, Oct. 28, 1962. BS in Medicine, U. Ill., 1959, MD, 1961. Diplomate Am. Bd. Urology. Rotating intern Presbyn. St. Luke's Hosp., Chgo., 1961-62, resident in surgery, 1962-63; resident in urology The Johns Hopkins Hosp., Balt., 1963-67; faculty U. Iowa Coll. Medicine, Iowa City, 1969-76, U. Calif., San Diego, 1976—, prof., head div. urology, 1976—, vice-chmn. dept. surgery, 1985-97. Cons. U.S. Dept. Navy, San Diego, 1976—; attending urologist Vets. Affairs Dept., San Diego, 1976—; assoc. dir. for clin. rsch. U. Calif. San Diego Cancer Ctr., 1997-98. Author, editor: Gynecological and Obstetric Urology, 1978, 82, 93. Capt. USAF, 1967-69. Recipient Francis Senear award. U. Ill., 1961 Fellow Am. Coll. of Surgeons; mem. AMA, Am. Urol. Assn. Inc., Alpha Omega Alpha. Avocations: collecting antique medical books, manuscripts. Office: U Calif Med Ctr Divsn Urology 200 W Arbor Dr San Diego CA 92103-8897 Fax: 619-543-6573

SCHMIDT, KARL A. lawyer; b. Stockton, Calif., Sept. 18, 1947; BS, U. Calif., Berkeley, 1969, JD, 1974. Bar: Calif. 1974. Mem. Parker, Milliken, Clark, O'Hara & Samuelian, L.A. Contbr. Retaliation Matters, to L.A. Daily Jour. Ann. Employment Update, 1997. Mem. ABA. Office: Parker Milliken Clark O Hara & Samuelian 333 S Hope St Ste 2700 Los Angeles CA 90071-1449

SCHMIDT, MAARTEN, astronomy educator; b. Groningen, Netherlands, Dec. 28, 1929; came to U.S., 1959; s. Wilhelm and Antje (Haringhuizen) S.; m. Cornelia Johanna Tom, Sept. 16, 1955; children: Elizabeth Tjimkje, Maryke Antje, Anne Wilhelmina. BSc, U. Groningen, 1949; PhD, Leiden U., Netherlands, 1956; ScD, Yale U., 1966. Sci. officer Leiden Obs., The Netherlands, 1953-59; postdoctoral fellow Mt. Wilson Obs., Pasadena, Calif., 1956-58; mem. faculty Calif. Inst. Tech., 1959-95, prof. astronomy, 1964-95, exec. officer for astronomy, 1972-75, chmn. div. physics, math. and astronomy, 1975-78, mem. staff Hale Obs., 1959-80, dir. Hale Obs., 1978-80, emeritus prof. astronomy, 1996—. Co-winner Calif. Scientist of Yr. award, 1964 Fellow Am. Acad. Arts and Scis. (Rumford award 1968); mem. Am. Astron. Soc. (Helen B. Warner prize 1964, Russell lecture award 1978), NAS (fgn. assoc., recip. James Craig Watson Medal, 1991), Internat. Astron. Union, Royal Astron. Soc. (assoc., Gold medal 1980) Office: Calif Inst Tech 105 24 Robinson Lab Pasadena CA 91125-0001

SCHMIDT, PETER GUSTAV, shipbuilding industry executive; b. Tumwater, Wash., Dec. 3, 1921; s. Peter G. and Clara Louise (Muench) S.; m. Elva Mary Ingalls, Dec. 3, 1945; children: Mimi Schmidt Fielding, Jill Schmidt Crowson, Janet Schmidt Mano, Hans. BSME, U. Wash., 1948; MS in Naval Architecture and Marine Engring., U. Mich., 1950. Naval architect Nat. Steel Shipbldg. Corp., San Diego, 1950-52, Carl J. Nordstrom/P. Spaulding, Seattle, 1952-53; pres. Marine Constrn. & Design Co., Seattle, 1953—, Astilleros Marco Chilena Ltd., Santiago, Chile, 1960—, Marco Peruana S.A., Lima, Peru, 1965—, Campbell Industries, San Diego, 1979-99, Campbell Ship Design & Engring., Seattle, 2000—. Author papers on fishing gear and vessels. Served to lt (j.g.) USN, 1942-45, PTO. Recipient Puget Sound's Maritime Man of Yr. award Puget Sound Press Assn., 1975, Naval Arch. and Marine Engring. Merit award U. Mich., 1996. Mem. Soc. Naval Architects and Marine Engrs., Wash. State Boatbuilders Assn. (pres. 1956-58), Alpha Delta Phi. Avocations: competitive sailing, classical music. Office: Marine Constrn & Design 2300 W Commodore Way Seattle WA 98199-1226

SCHMIDT, ROBERT MILTON, physician, scientist, educator, administrator; b. Milw., May 7, 1944; s. Milton W. and Edith J. (Martinek) S.; children Eric Whitney, Edward Huntington. AB, Northwestern U., 1966; MD, Columbia U., 1970; MPH, Harvard U., 1975; PhD in Law, Medicine and Pub. Policy, Emory U., 1982; MA, San Francisco State U., 1999. Diplomate Am. Bd. Preventive Medicine. Resident in internal medicine Univ. Hosp. U. Calif.-San Diego, 1970-71; resident in preventive medicine Ctrs. Disease Control, Atlanta, 1971-74; commd. med. officer USPHS, 1971; advanced through grades to comdr., 1973; dir. hematology div. Nat. Ctr. for Disease Control, Atlanta, 1971-78, spl. asst. to dir., 1978-79, inactive res., 1979—; clin. asst. prof. pediatrics Tufts U. Med. Sch., 1974-86; clin. asst. prof. medicine Emory U. Med. Sch., 1971-81, clin. assoc. prof. community health, 1976-86; clin. assoc. prof. humanities in medicine Morehouse Med. Sch., 1977-79; attending physician dept. medicine Wilcox Meml. Hosp., Lihue, Hawaii, 1979-82, Calif. Pacific Med. Ctr., San Francisco, 1983—; dir. Ctr. Preventive Medicine and Health Research, 1983—, dir. Health Watch, 1983—; sr. scientist Inst. Epidemiology and Behavioral Medicine, Inst. Cancer Research, Calif. Pacific Med. Ctr., San Francisco, 1983-88; prof. hematology and gerontology, dir. Ctr. Preventive Medicine and Health Rsch., chair health professions program San Francisco State U., 1983-99, prof. medicine, 1983—, prof. emeritus, 1999—; dir. Health Watch Internat., 1997—. Cons. WHO, FDA, Washington, NIH, Bethesda, Md., Govt. of China, Mayo Clinic, Rochester, Minn., Northwestern U., Evanston, Ill., Chgo., U. R.I., Kingston, Pan Am. Health Orgn., Inst. Pub. Health, Italy, Nat. Inst. Aging Rsch. Ctr., Balt., U. Calif., San Diego, U. Ill., Chgo., Columbia U., N.Y.C., Harvard U., Johns Hopkins U., U. Chgo., UCLA, U. Calif. Berkeley, Brown U., Providence, UCLA, U. Calif., San Francisco, Harvard U., Stanford U., Boston, U. Chgo., Emory U., Atlanta, Duke U., N.C., U. Tex., Houston, Ariz. State U., U. Hawaii, Honolulu, U. Paris, U. Geneva, U. Munich, Heidelberg U., U. Frankfurt, U. Berlin, Cambridge (Eng.) U., U. Singapore, others; vis. rsch. prof. gerontology Ariz. State U., 1989-90; mem. numerous sci. and profl. adv. bds., panels, coms. Mem. editorial bd. Am. Jour. Clin. Pathology, 1976-82, The Advisor, 1988—, Generations, 1989—, Contemporary Gerontology, 1994—, Alternative Therapies in Health and Medicine, 1995—, Aging Today, 1997—; book and film reviewer Sci. Books and Films, 1988—, many other jours.; author: 17 books and manuals including Hematology Laboratory Series, 4 vols., 1979-86, CRC Handbook Series in Clinical Laboratory Science, 1976—; assoc. editor: Contemporary Gerontology, 1993—; contbr. more than 300 articles to sci. jours. Alumni regent Columbia U. Coll. Physicians and Surgeons, 1980—. Northwestern U. scholar, 1964-66; NSF fellow, 1964-66; Health Professions scholar, 1966-70; USPHS fellow, 1967-70; Microbiology, Urology, Upjohn Achievement, Borden Rsch. and Virginia Kneeland Frantz scholar awards Columbia U., 1970; recipient Am. Soc. Pharmacol. and Exptl. Therapy award in pharmacology, 1970, Commendation medal USPHS, 1973, Meritorious Performance and Profl. Promise award, 1989, Student Disting. Teaching and Svc. award Pre-Health Professions Student Alliance, 1992, Leadership Recognition awards San Francisco State U., 1984-89, 91-96, Meritorious Svc. award, 1992. Fellow ACP (commentator ACP Jour. Club/Annals of Internal Medicine 1993—), AAAS (med. scis. sect.), Royal Soc. Medicine (London), Gerontol. Soc. Am., Am. Geriatrics Soc., Am. Coll. Preventive Medicine (sci. com.), Am. Soc. Clin. Pathology, Internat. Soc. Hematology; mem. AMA, APHA, Am. Med. Informatics, Internat. Commn. for Standardization in Hematology, Am. Soc. Hematology, Internat. Soc. Thrombosis and Hemostasis, Acad. Clin. Lab. Physicians and Scientists, Am. Assn. Blood Banks, Nat. Assn. Advisors for Health Professions (bd. dirs.), Am. Assn. Med. Informatics (chair prevention and health evaluation informatics WG), Calif. Coun. Gerontology and Geriatrics, Am. Coll. Occupl. and Environ. Medicine, Assn. Tchrs. Preventive Medicine (edn. com., rsch. com.), Am. Soc. Microbiology, Am. Soc. Aging (editl. bd. 1990—, Dychtwald Pub. Speaking award 1991), N.Y. Acad. Scis., San Francisco Med. Soc., Calif. Med. Assn., Internat. Health Evaluation Assn. (v.p. for Ams. 1992-94, bd. dirs. 1992—, pres. 1994-96), Cosmos Club (mem. art com. 1997—), Golden Key (hon. faculty mem.), Army and Navy Club (Washington), Harvard Club (N.Y.), Havard Club (San Francisco), Circle Club, Nat. Gallery of Art (Washington), Knight of Malta, Sigma Xi, Phi Beta Kappa, others. Home: Whaleship Plaza 25 Hinckley Walk San Francisco CA 94111-2303 Office: Health Watch Med Ctr PO Box 7999 San Francisco CA 94120 7999 Fax: 415 956 8950. E-mail: rmschmidtmd@aol.com

SCHMIDT, STEPHEN C. vice president, residential community development; Grad., U. Ca. (Davis); MS in Bus. Adminstn., Stanford U. Grad. Sch. Various exec. positions, comml., indsl. devel. The Newhall Land & Farming Co., 1976-92, sr. v.p., residential community devel., 1999—. Office: The Newhall Land & Farming Co 23823 Valencia Blvd Valencia CA 91355-2103

SCHMIDT, TERRY LANE, health care executive; b. Chgo., Nov. 28, 1943; s. LeRoy C. and Eunice P. Schmidt; children: Christie Anne, Terry Lane II. BS, Bowling Green State U., 1965; MBA in Health Care Adminstrn, George Washington U., 1971; DHA, Med. U. S.C., 2001. Resident in hosp. adminstrn. U. Pitts. Med. Center, VA Hosp., Pitts., 1968-69; adminstrv. asst. Mt. Sinai Med. Center, N.Y.C., 1969-70; asst. dir. Health Facilities Planning Council of Met. Washington, 1970-71; asst. dir. dept. govtl. relations A.M.A., Washington, 1971-74; contract lobbyist and govtl. rels. Wash. Reps. in Health, Washington, 1974-87; pres. Terry L. Schmidt Inc. Physician Svcs. Group, San Diego, 1987-99, Washington Actions on Health, 1975-79; partner Washington Coun. Medicine and Health, 1979-81; pres. Recreational Enterprises, Inc., Washington, 1977-78; v.p. Crisis Communications Corp. Ltd., 1982-90; pres. Med. Cons. Inc., 1983-84, Ambulance Corp. Am., La Jolla, Calif., 1984-87; exec. dir., chief operating officer Emergency Health Assocs. P.C., Phoenix, 1989-91, Charleston Emergency Physicians, Inc., S.C., 1990-94, Joplin Emergency Physican Assocs., 1991-92, Big Valley Med. Group, 1991-92, Blue Ridge Emergency Physicians, P.C., 1992-94, Berkeley Emergency Physicians, P.C., 1992-94; chmn., pres. Univ. Inst., 1992—; asst. dir. Dept. of Emerg. Med., Med. U.S.C., 1999—. Bd. dirs., Univ. Inst., 1997—, lectr., instr. dept. health svcs. adminstrn. George Washington U., 1969-83, preceptor, 1975-84; adj. prof. grad. sch. Pub. Health San Diego State U., 1996—, preceptor, 1989—, guest lectr. health care adminstrn. Nat. U. San Diego, 1992-93; guest lectr. Bus. Adminstrn. U.S. Internat. U., San Diego, 1994—; instr. Nat. Naval Sch. Health Care Administrn., 1971-73; faculty Civil Svc. Commn. Legis. Insts., 1972-76; fac. Am. Assn. State Colls. and U. Health Tng. Insts., 1975-78; mem. adv. com. ambulatory care standards Joint Commn. Accreditation of Hosps., 1971-72, pres., Recreational Enterprises, Inc., Wash., 1977-78, guest lectr., Coll. of Med. & dept. Health Admin. & Pol., Med. U.S.C., 1998-99, preceptor, 1999—, assoc. prof., Coll. of Health, Med. U.S.C., 1999—. Author: Congress and Health: An Introduction to the Legislative Process and the Key Participants, 1976, A Directory of Federal Health Resources and Services for the Disadvantaged, 1976, Health Care Reimbursement: A Glossary, 1983; mem. editl. adv. bd. Nation's Health, 1971-73; contbr. articles to profl. jours. Bd. dirs. Nat. Eye Found., 1976-78. Mem. Med. Group Mgmt. Assn., Health Care Fin. Mgmt. Assn., Assn. Venture Capital Groups (bd. dirs. 1984-89), Amer. Coll. of Health Execs., Amer. Coll. of Med. Prac. Exec., Soc. for Acad. Emerg. Med., Assn. of Univ. Progs. in Health Admin., San Diego Venture Group (chair 1984-87), Univ. Club (life), Natl. Rep. Club, Nat. Dem. Club (life), Capitol Hill Club (life), Alpha Phi Omega (pres. Bowling Green alumni chpt. 1967-70, sec.-treas. alumni assn. 1968-71). Office: Terry L Schmidt Inc Ste 113 PMB 611 7770 Regents Rd San Diego CA 92122-1967

SCHMIDT, WALDEMAR ADRIAN, pathologist, educator; b. L.A., Aug. 22, 1941; s. Waldemar Adrian and Mary Charlotte (Parker) S.; m. Karmen LaVer Bingham, Feb. 1, 1963; children: Rebecca, Sarah, Waldemar, Diedrich. BS, Oreg. State U., 1965; PhD, MD, U. Oreg., 1969. Intern U. Oreg. Hosps. and Clinics, Portland, 1969-70, resident, 1970-73; pathologist LDS Hosp., Salt Lake City, 1973-77; prof. pathology U. Tex. Med. Sch., Houston, 1977-91, Oreg. Health Sci. U., Portland, 1991—; chief pathology and lab. medicine svc. Oreg. Health Sci. U. and VA Med. Ctr., Portland, 1997—2001, vice chair pathology, 1997—. Author: Principles and Techniques of Surgical Pathology, 1982; editor Cytopathology Annual, 1991-94, Revs. in Pathology-Cytopathology, 1994-99. Asst. scoutmaster Boy Scouts Am., Houston, 1982-91. Maj. U.S. Army, 1970-76. Fellow Am. Soc. Clin. Pathologists, Coll. Am. Pathologists; mem. Internat. Acad. Cytology, Am. Coll. Physician Execs., Sigma Xi, Alpha Omega Alpha. Avocations: photography, silviculture, apiculture. Office: VA Med Ctr 3710 SW Us Veterans Hospital R Portland OR 97201-2964

SCHMITZ, CLARENCE T. investment company executive; Exec. v.p., CFO Jefferies Group Inc., L.A.; mng. dir. Golenberg Schmitz Capital Ptnrs., LLC, L.A., 2000—. Office: Golenberg Schmitz Capital Ptnrs LLC Ste 970 11100 Santa Monica Blvd Los Angeles CA 90025-3384

SCHNABEL, GARY A. health facility administrator, director; Compliance dir. Oreg. Bd. of Pharmacy, 1994-99, acting exec. dir., 1999, exec. dir., 1999—.

SCHNABEL, ROCKWELL ANTHONY, ambassador; b. Amsterdam, Holland, Dec. 30, 1936; s. Hans and Wilhelmina S.; m. Marna Belle Del Mar, 1964; children: Mary Darrin, Christy Ann, Everton Anthony. BS in Bus. Adminstrn., Trinity Coll., The Netherlands, 1951-56. Pres. Unilife Assurance Group S.H. Luxembourg, 1974-78, Bateman Eichler Hill Richard Group, Los Angeles, 1981-83; amb. to Finland U.S. Dept. State; under sec. for travel and tourism U.S. Dept. Commerce, Washington, 1989-91, dep. sec., 1991-92, acting sec. of commerce, 1992-93; sr. ptnr. Trident Capital LLP Inc., L.A., 1992—. Bd. dirs. Internat. Game Tech., CSGystems Inc.; chmn. La.-Inc.ääääääää; bd. trustees U. Calif. Bus. Sch. Past pres. L.A. Pension Bd., Calif., 1982; mem. L.A. Olympic Organizing Com., 1983-84. With Air N.G., 1958-64. Decorated comdr. Order of Good Hope, South Africa, Grand Cross of Lion of Finland; recipient Gold medal Dutch Govt., U.S. Dept. Commerce, medal of honor the Netherlands Olympic Com. Mem. L.A. Beach Club, Calif. Club, L.A. Country Club. Office: Trident Capital Inc 11150 Santa Monica Blvd Los Angeles CA 90025-3380

SCHNAPP, ROGER HERBERT, lawyer, consultant; b. N.Y.C., Mar. 17, 1946; s. Michael Jay and Beatrice Joan (Becker) S.; m. Candice Jacqueline Larson, Sept. 15, 1979; 1 child, Monica Alexis. BS, Cornell U., 1966; JD, Harvard U., 1969; postgrad. Pub. Utility Mgmt. Program, U. Mich., 1978. Bar: N.Y. 1970, U.S. Ct. Appeals (2d cir.) 1970, U.S. Supreme, 1974, U.S. Dist. Ct. (so. dist.) N.Y. 1975, U.S. Ct. Appeals (4th and 6th cirs.) 1976, U.S. Ct. Appeals (7th cir.) 1977, U.S. Dist. Ct. (so. dist.) N.Y. 1975, U.S. Dist. Ct. (no. dist.) Calif. 1980, U.S. Ct. Appeals (8th cir.) 1980, Calif., 1982, U.S. Dist. Ct. (cen. dist.) Calif. 1982, U.S. Ct. Dist. (ea. dist.) Calif., 1984. Atty. CAB, Washington, 1969-70; labor atty. Western Electric Co., N.Y.C., 1970-71; mgr. employee rels. Am. Airlines, N.Y.C., 1971-74; labor counsel Am. Electric Power Svc. Corp., N.Y.C., 1974-78, sr. labor counsel, 1978-80; indsl. rels. counsel Trans World Airlines, N.Y.C., 1980-81; sr. assoc. Parker, Milliken, Clark & O'Hara, L.A., 1981-82; ptnr. Rutan & Tucker, Costa Mesa, Calif., 1983-84, Memel, Jacobs, Pierno, Gersh & Ellsworth, Newport Beach, 1985-86, Memel, Jacobs & Ellsworth, Newport Beach, 1986-87; pvt. practice Newport Beach, 1987—. Bd. dirs. Dynamic Constrn., Inc., Laguna Hills, Calif., 1986—; commentator labor rels. Fin. News Network; commentator Sta. KOCN Radio, 1990-91; commentator employment law Orange County Register; lectr. Calif. Western Law Sch., Calif. State U.-Fullerton, Calif. State Conf. Small Bus.; lectr. collective bargaining Pace U., N.Y.C.; lectr. on labor law Coun. on Edn. in Mgmt.; N.E. regional coord. Pressler for Pres., 1979-80. Author: Arbitration Issues for the 1980s, 1981, A Look at Three Companies, 1982; editor-in-chief Indsl. and Labor Rels. Forum, 1964-66; columnist Orange County Bus. Jour., 1989-91; contbr. articles to profl. publs. Mem. Bus. Rsch. Adv. Coun. U.S. Dept. Labor; trustee Chapman U., 1991-95. Mem. Calif. Bar Assn. (chmn.), Labor Law Consulting Group, Calif. Bd. of Legal Specialization, Balboa Bay Club, The Ctr. Club, Club 33. Republican. Jewish. Office: PO Box 9049 Newport Beach CA 92658-1049 E-mail: rhs@schnapp.com

SCHNEEMAN, BARBARA OLDS, nutritionist, educator; b. Seattle, Oct. 3, 1948; d. William Arthur and Rose (Antush) Olds; m. Paul Schneeman, Mar. 23, 1974; 1 child, Eric. BS in Food Sci. and Tech., U. Calif., Davis, 1970; PhD in Nutrition, U. Calif., Berkeley, 1974. NIH postdoctoral fellow gastrointestinal physiology Children's Hosp., Oakland, Calif., 1974-76; asst. prof. nutrition dept. nutrition and food sci. & tech. U. Calif., Davis, 1976-82, assoc. prof. nutrition, 1982-86, prof. nutrition, nutritionist, 1986—, prof. dept. internal medicine divsn. clin. nutrition, 1986—, assoc. dean Coll. Agrl. and Environ. Scis., 1985-88, chair dept. nutrition, 1988-93, dean Coll. Agrl. and Environ. Scis., 1993-99, dir. programs. divsn. agr. and natural resources, 1993-99. Pres., bd. dirs. Dannon Inst., 1996—; vis. scientist Cardiovascular Rsch. Inst., U. Calif., San Francisco, 1991-92; lectr. women in sci. series Coll. St. Catherine, St. Paul, 1987; adv. dir. Blue Cross Calif., 1992-95; mem. dietary guidelines for Ams. adv. com. to Secs. of Agr., Health and Human Svcs., 1989-90, 94-95; mem. expert panel on food safety and nutrition Inst. Food Technologists, 1985-91; mem. external adv. bd. Post Ctr. for Nutrition and Health, 1989-90; councilor Soc. for Exptl. Biology and Medicine, 1988-91. Assoc. editor Jour. Nutrition, 1991-94; contbg. editor Nutrition Revs., 1982-90; editl. bd. Jour. Nutrition, 1982-87, Procs. for Soc. Exptl. Biology and Medicine, 1985-91, Acad. Press: Food Sci. and Nutrition, 1988—. Fellow NDEA, U. Calif., Berkeley; food sci. scholar; recipient Outstanding Cmty. Svc. award Tierra del Oro coun. Girl Scouts U.S., 1995, Future Leaders award for rsch. Nutrition Found., 1978-80, Samuel Cate Prescott award for rsch. Inst. Food Tech., 1985, Farma Food Internat. Fibre prize, Copenhagen, 1989, Ethel Austin Martin disting. lectr. on Human Nutrition, S.D. State U., 1999. Mem. AAAS, Inst. Food Technologists (sec.-treas. nutrition divsn. 1988-89), Am. Physiol. Soc., Am. Inst. Nutrition (treas. 1989-92), Am. Heart Assn. (fellow arteriosclerosis coun.). Office: U Calif Davis Dept Nutrition Davis CA 95616

SCHNEIDER, CALVIN, physician; b. N.Y.C., Oct. 23, 1924; s. Harry and Bertha (Green) S.; m. Elizabeth Gayle Thomas, Dec. 27, 1967. AB, U. So. Calif., 1951, MD, 1955; JD, LaVerne (Calif.) Coll., 1973. Intern L.A. County Gen. Hosp., 1955-56, staff physician, 1956-57; pvt. practice medicine West Covina, Calif., 1957—. Staff Inter-Community Med. Ctr., Covina, Calif. With USNR, 1943-47. Mem. AMA, Calif. Med. Assn., L.A. County Med. Assn. Republican. Lutheran.

SCHNEIDER, CHARLES IVAN, newspaper executive; b. Chgo., Apr. 6, 1923; s. Samuel Hiram and Eva (Smith) S.; m. Barbara Anne Krause, Oct. 27, 1963; children: Susan, Charles I. Jr., Kim, Karen, Traci. BS, Northwestern U., 1944. Indsl. engr., sales mgr., v.p. mktg. and sales Curtis-Electro Lighting Corp., Chgo., 1945-54, pres., 1954-62, Jefferson Electronics, Inc., Santa Barbara, Calif., 1962-64; pres. 3 sub., v.p., asst. to pres. Am. Bldg. Maintenance Industries, Los Angeles, 1964-66; group v.p. Times Mirror Co., Los Angeles, 1966-88, ret.; pvt. investor and cons., 1988—. Bd. dirs. Jeppesen Sanderson, Inc., Denver, Graphic Controls Corp., Buffalo, Regional Airports Improvement Corp. Bd. regents Northwestern U., Evanston, Ill.; trustee, past pres. Reiss-Davis Child Study Center, L.A.; bd. govs., past pres. The Music Ctr.; trustee the Menninger Found.; pres. St. John's Hosp. and Health Ctr. Found., Santa Monica, Calif. Served with AUS, 1942-44. Mem. Chief Execs. Orgn. (past pres., bd. dirs.). Clubs: Standard (Chgo.); Beverly Hills Tennis (Calif.); Big. Ten of So. Calif. Avocations: tennis, squash, music, reading. Home: 522 N Beverly Dr Beverly Hills CA 90210-3318

SCHNEIDER, EDWARD LEE, botanic garden administrator; b. Portland, Oreg., Sept. 14, 1947; s. Edward John and Elizabeth (Mathews) S.; m. Sandra Lee Alfarone, Aug. 2, 1968; children: Kenneth L., Cassandra L. BA, Ctrl. Wash. U., 1969, MS, 1971; PhD, U. Calif., Santa Barbara, 1974. From asst. to assoc. prof. botany S.W. Tex. State U., San Marcos, 1974-84, prof., 1984-94, chmn. biology dept., 1984-89, dean sci., 1989-92; pres., CEO Santa Barbara (Calif.) Botanic Garden, 1992—. Author: The Botanical World, CEOs and Trustees--Building Working Partnerships; contbr. articles to profl. jours. Bd. dirs. Ctr. for Plant Conservation. Recipient Presdl. Rsch. award S.W. Tex. State U., 1986, Disting. Alumnus award Ctrl. Wash. U., 1996; grantee NSF, 1980, 90. Fellow Tex. Acad. Sci. (pres. 1992-93); mem. Internat. Water Lily Soc. (bd. dirs., sec. 1989-96, inducted into Hall of Fame, Award of Appreciation 1997), Bot. Soc. Am. (bd. dirs.,

Award of Merit 1998), Am. Assn. Bot. Gardens and Arboreta (bd. dirs.), Internat. Pollination Congress, Nat. Coun. Deans, Am. Assn. Mus. (assessment program adv. com.). Home: 1140 Tunnel Rd Santa Barbara CA 93105-2134 Office: Santa Barbara Botanic Garden 1212 Mission Canyon Rd Santa Barbara CA 93105-2126 E-mail: eschneider@sbbg.org

SCHNEIDER, GERALD L. plastic surgeon; b. Mechanicsburg, Pa., Oct. 25, 1945; s. Gordon Henry and Pauline Emma (Rife) S.; m. Patricia Davis, July 15, 1978; 1 child, Ross Roberts. BS, No. Ariz. U., 1968; MD, U. Ariz., 1973. Intern Naval Regional Med. Ctr., San Diego, 1973-74; resident in gen. surgery U.S. Naval Hosp., San Diego, 1974-78, resident in plastic surgery Portsmouth, Va., 1978-80, staff surgeon divsn. plastic surgery San Diego, 1981-83, chief divsn. plastic surgery, 1983-84; pvt. practice Flagstaff, Ariz., 1984-90; staff surgeon La Jolla (Calif.) Cosmetic Surgery Ctr., 1990-91; surgeon Scripps Clinic & Rsch. Found., La Jolla, 1991—. Capt. USNR Fellow ACS; mem. Am. Soc. Plastic and Reconstructive Surgeons, Lipoplasty Soc. North Am. Avocation: golf. Office: Scripps Clinic & Rsch Found 10666 N Torrey Pines Rd La Jolla CA 92037-1092

SCHNEIDER, MICHAEL A. state legislator; b. McCook, Nebr., Apr. 11, 1950; m. Candice H. Hill; 1 child, Andrew. Student, U. Nev., Las Vegas, So. Nev. Sch Real Estate. In real estate devel. and sales; mem. Nev. Senate, Dist. 8, Carson City, 1996—. Bd. dirs. Opportunity Village; mem. Gleams Found.; supporter Channel 10, KNPR Pub. Broadcasting. Mem. Greater Las Vegas Assn. Realtors, Nev. Assn. Realtors, So. Nev. Homebuilders Assn. Democrat. Home: 6381 Sandpiper Way Las Vegas NV 89103-2110

SCHNEIDER, NICHOLAS MCCORD, planetary scientist, educator, textbook author; b. Appleton, Wis., Dec. 17, 1956; s. Ben Ross Jr. and Mackay (McCord) S. BA in Physics and Astronomy, Dartmouth Coll., 1979; PhD in Planetary Sci., U. Ariz., 1988. Assoc. prof. lab. for atmospheric & space physics and dept. of astrophysical & planetary scis. U. Colo., Boulder, 1990—. Recipient Presdl. Young Investigator award NSF, 1991. Mem. Am. Astron. Soc. (divsn. for planetary scis.), Am. Geophys. Union, Internat. Astron. Union, Astron. Soc. of the Pacific. Office: U Colo Lab Atmospheric Space Physics CB392 Boulder CO 80309-0001 E-mail: nick.schneider@lasp.colorado.edu

SCHNEIDER, PETER, film company executive; m. Hope Schneider; 2 children. BA in Theater, Purdue U. Mng. dir. St. Nicholas Theater, Chgo., 1976-80; gen. mgr. Apollo Theater Prodns., London, 1980-83; dir. Olympic Arts Festival, L.A., 1984; with Walt Disney Studios, 1985—; pres. Walt Disney Theatrical Prodns. Walt Disney Pictures, Burbank, Calif., 1996-2000; chmn. Walt Disney Studios, Burbank, 2000—. Dir. plays The WPA, Playwrights Horizon, Circle Repertory Theater, N.Y.C. Office: Walt Disney Pictures 500 S Buena Vista St Burbank CA 91521-0006

SCHNEIDER, STEPHEN HENRY, climatologist, environmental policy analyst, researcher; b. N.Y.C., Feb. 11, 1945; s. Samuel and Doris C. (Swarte) S.; married, 1995; 2 children from previous marriage. BS, Columbia U., 1966, MS, 1967, PhD in Mechanical Engring/Plasma Physics, 1971; DSc (hon.), N.J. Inst. Tech., 1990, Monmouth Coll., 1991. NAS, NRC rsch. assoc. Goddard Inst. Space Studies NASA, N.Y.C., 1971-72; fellow advanced study program Nat. Ctr. Atmospheric Research, Boulder, Colo., 1972-73, scientist, dep. head climate project, 1973-78, acting leader climate sensitivity group, 1978-80, head visitors program and dep. dir. advanced study program, 1980-87, sr. scientist, 1980-96, head interdisciplinary climate systems sect. Colo., 1987-92; prof. biol. scis. dept., sr. fellow Inst. Internat. Studies Stanford (Calif.) U., 1992—, prof. civil and environtl. engring. dept. (courtesy). Affiliate prof. U. Corp. Atmospheric Rsch. Lamont-Doherty Geol. Obs., Columbia, U., 1976-83; mem. Carter-Mondale Sci. Policy Task Force, 1976; Clinton-Gore sci. advisor, 1992, 96; sci. advisor, interviewee Nova Sta. WGBH-TV, Planet Earth, Sta. WQED-TV; mem. internat. sci. coms. climatic change, ecology, energy, environ. edn., food and pub. policy; expert witness congl. coms.; mem. Def. Sci. Bd. Task Force on Atmospheric Obscuration; lead author intergovernmental panel on climate change Working Group I, 1995-96; coord. lead author Working Group II, 1998—; mem. core writing team Synthesis Report, 2000—. Author: (with Lynne E. Mesirow) The Genesis Strategy: Climate and Global Survival, 1976; (with Lynne Morton) The Primordial Bond: Exploring Connections Between Man and Nature Through Humanities and Science, 1981, (with Randi S. Londer) The Coevolution of Climate and Life, 1984, Global Warming: Are We Entering the Greenhouse Century?, 1989; (with W. Bach) Interactions of Food and Climate, 1981; (with R.S. Chen and E. Boulding) Social Science Research and Climate Change: An Interdisciplinary Appraisal, 1983; (with K.C. Land) Forecasting in the Social and Natural Sciences, 1987; (with P. Boston) Scientists on Gaia, 1990; editor-in-chief: The Encyclopedia of Climate and Weather, 1996, Laboratory Earth: The Planetary Experiment We Can't Afford to Lose, 1997; editor: Climatic Change, 1976—; contbr. articles on theory of climate, influence of climate on soc., relation of climatic change to world food, population, energy, development and environ. policy issues, environ. aftereffects of nuclear war, carbon dioxide greenhouse effect, pub. understanding sci., environ. edn. Recipient Louis J. Battan Author's award Am. Meteorol. Soc., 1990, Mary B. Ansari Ref. Work award Geosci. Info. Soc., 1997; named one of 100 Outstanding Young Scientists in Am. by Sci. Digest, 1984; MacArthur Found. Prize fellow John D. and Catherine T. MacArthur Found., 1992. Fellow AAAS (Westinghouse award 1991), Scientists Inst. for Pub. Info.; mem. U.S. Assn. Club Rome, Am. Meteorological Soc., Am. Geophysical Union, Fedn. Am. Scientists, Soc. Conservation Biology, Soc. Ecol. Economics., Acad. Europae (fgn.), Ecol. Soc. Am. Office: Stanford U Dept Biol Scis Stanford CA 94305-5020

SCHNEIDLER, JON GORDON, lawyer; b. Seattle, Oct. 22, 1938; s. J. Gordon and Mary Louise (Bartholomew) S.; m. Linda Gilmore White, June 27, 1964 (div. June 1988); children: Kristina Richards, Jolie Wolcott, Andrew Schneidler, Peter Schneidler; m. Elizabeth Ann Nairn, Apr. 2, 1989; 1 stepdaughter: Jessica Albright. BA, U. Wash., 1962, JD, 1968. Bar: Wash.; U.S. Ct. Appeals (9th Cir.), U.S. Dist. Ct. (we. dist.) Wash. CEO Schneidler Industries, Inc., Seattle, 1968-70; ptnr. Cartano, Botzer & Chapman, Seattle, 1970-86; dir., CEO 4100 Assocs., Seattle, 1989—. Sec. Transiplex Internat., Inc., Seattle; mem. adv. bd. Pacific Legal Found., Sacramento; trustee Ehrlich Donnan Found., Seattle. Co-author: (book) Real Property Deskbook, 1981, 2d edit. 1986; patentee Air Structure Systems, 1969. Bd. dirs. North Kitsap Sch. Bd., Poulsbo, Wash., 1984, Friends of Youth, Renton, Wash., 1974; founder, dir. Tchr. of Yr. Found., Poulsbo, 1988—. 1st lt. USAF, 1962-66. Decorated Air Force Commendation medal; recipient Baker scholar George F. Baker Foun., 1957-60. Fellow Paul Harris Found.; mem. ABA, Wash. State Bar Assn., King County Bar Assn., Coll. Club (trustee, treas. 1998—), Rotary. Avocations: fly fishing, competitive bridge, sailing, gardening. Office: 999 3rd Ave Ste 4100 Seattle WA 98104-4084

SCHNELL, ROGER THOMAS, business owner, retired state official and career officer; b. Wabasha, Minn., Dec. 11, 1936; s. Donald William and Eva Louise (Barton) S.; m. Barbara Ann McDonald, Dec. 18, 1959 (div. Mar. 1968); children: Thomas Allen, Scott Douglas. A in Mil. Sci., Command and Gen. Staff Coll., 1975; A in Bus. Administn., Wayland Bapt. U., 1987. Commd. 2d lt. Alaska N.G., 1959, advanced through grades to col., 1975, shop supt., 1965-71, personnel mgr., 1972-74, chief of staff, 1974-87, dir. logistics, 1987; electrician Alaska R.R., Anchorage, 1955-61, also foreman, 1962-64; dir. support personnel mgmt. Joint Staff Alaska N.G., 1988-92, ret.; personnel mgr. State of Alaska, 1992, asst. commr. dept. mil. and vets. affairs, 1992-95, dep. commr. dept. mil. and vets. affairs, 1995-98; owner RTS Enterprises, Anchorage, 1999—. Ind. bus. owner internat. health and preventive healthcare corp. RTS Enterprises, 1999—. Bd. dirs. Meth. Trust Fund; chmn. pastor parish rels. com. Meth. First. Ch., 2001, Alaska NG Mus. Trust Fund, 2001—. Mem. Fed. Profl. Labor Relations Execs. (sec. 1974-75), Alaska N.G. Officers Assn. (pres. 1976-78, bd. dirs. 1988—), Assn. U.S. Army (corp.), NG Assn. U.S. (life, retiree rep. from Alaska 1993—), Am. Legion, Amvets. Republican. Methodist. Avocations: travel, photography. Home and Office: Huntwood Park Estates 6817 Queens View Cir Anchorage AK 99504-5203 E-mail: rogertschnell@gci.net, rtschnellenterprises@gci.net

SCHNELLER, EUGENE STUART, health administration and policy educator; b. Cornwall, N.Y., Apr. 9, 1943; s. Michael Nicholas and Anne Ruth (Gruner) S.; m. Ellen Stauber, Mar. 24, 1968; children: Andrew Jon, Lee Stauber. BA, L.I. U., 1967; AA, SUNY, Buffalo, 1965; PhD, NYU, 1973. Rsch. asst. dept. sociology NYU, N.Y.C., 1968-70; project dir. Montefiore Hosp. and Med. Ctr., Bronx, N.Y., 1970-72; asst. prof. Med. Ctr. and sociology Duke U., Durham, N.C., 1973-75; assoc. prof., chmn. dept. Union Coll., Schenectady, 1975-79, assoc. prof., dir. Health Studies Ctr., 1979-85; prof., dir. Sch. Health Adminstrn. and Policy, Ariz. State U., Tempe, 1985-91, assoc. dean rsch. and adminstrn. Coll. Bus., 1992-94; dir. L. William Seidman Rsch. Ctr., Tempe, 1992-94, counselor to pres. for health profl. edn., 1994-96; clin. prof. cmty. and family medicine U. Ariz., 1995-96, clin. prof. prevention, rsch., 1997—; prof., dir. Sch. Health Adminstrn. and Policy Ariz. State U., 1996—. Vis. rsch. scholar Columbia U., N.Y.C., 1983-84; chmn. Western Network for Edn. in Health Adminstrn., Berkeley, Calif., 1987-92; commr. Calif. Commn. on the Future Med. Edn., 1996-97; mem. Ariz. Medicaid Adv. Bd., 1990-92, Ariz. Data Adv. Bd., 1989-91, Ariz. Health Care Group Adv. Bd., 1989; mem. health rsch. coun. N.Y. State Dept. Health, 1977-85; fellow Accrediting Commn. on Edn. for Health Svcs. Adminstrn., 1983-84, commr., 1999—. Author: The Physician's Assistant, 1980; mem. editorial bd. Work and Occupations, 1975-93, Hosps. and Health Svcs. Adminstrn., 1989-92, Health Adminstrn. Press, 1991-94; Health Mgmt. Review, 1996, Electronic Hallway, 1999; contbr. articles to profl. jours., chpt. to book. Trustee Barrow Neurol. Inst., Phoenix, 1989-95; chair nat. adv. com. Nat. Adv. Com. of the Investigator Awards in Health Svcs. Rsch. Robert Wood Johnson Found., 1993-96. Mem. APHA, Am. Sociol. Assn., Assn. Univ. Health Programs Health Adminstrn. (bd. dirs. 1990-96, chmn. bd. dirs. 1994-95), Pharm. and Therapeutics Soc. (trustee 1999—, sec. 1999—). Home: 11843 N 114th Way Scottsdale AZ 85259-2609 Office: Ariz State U Sch Health Admin Policy Tempe AZ 85287

SCHOCK, ROBERT NORMAN, geophysicist; b. Monticello, N.Y., May 25, 1939; s. Carl Louis and Norma Elizabeth (Greenfield) S.; m. Susan Esther Benton, Nov. 28, 1959; children: Pamela Ann, Patricia Elizabeth, Christina Benton. BS, Colo. Coll., 1961; MS, Rensselaer Poly. Inst., 1963, PhD, 1966; postgrad., Northwestern U., 1963-64. Cert. Calif. state wine judge. Jr. geophys. trainee Continental Oil Co., Sheridan, Wyo., 1960; jr. geologist Texaco In., Billings, Mont., 1961; teaching asst. Rensselaer Poly. Inst., Troy, N.Y., 1961-63, research asst., 1964-66; research assoc. U. Chgo., 1966-68; sr. research scientist Lawrence Livermore Nat. Lab., U. Calif., 1968—, group leader high pressure physics, 1972-74, sect. leader geoscis. and engring., 1974-76, div. leader earth scis., 1976-81, head dept. earth scis., 1981-87, energy program leader, 1987-92, dep. assoc. dir. for energy, 1992-98, sr. fellow Ctr. Global Security Rsch., 1998—. Pres. Pressure Sys. Rsch. Inc.; mem. faculty Chabot Coll., 1969-71; dir. Alameda County Flood Control and Water Conservation Dist., 1984-86; mem. adv. panel on geoscis. U.S. Dept. Energy, 1985-87; chair adv. com. U. Calif. Energy Inst., 1992-98; mem. rsch. adv. com. Gas Rsch. Inst., Chgo., 1995—; chmn. World Energy Coun., London, Study Group Energy Tech. in 21st Century, 1999—. Mem. editl. bd. Rev. Sci. Instruments, 1975-77; assoc. editor Jour. Geophys. Rsch., 1978-80; bd. assoc. editors 11th Lunar and Planetary Sci. Conf., 1980; mem. adv. bd. Physics ans Chemistry of Minerals, 1983-97; rsch. and publs. on high pressure physics, solid state physics, physics of earth interior, rock deformation, energy R&D and energy policy. Fulbright sr. fellow U. Bonn (Germany), 1973; vis. research fellow Australian Nat. U. Canberra, 1980-81 Mem. AAAS, Am. Geophys. Union, Sigma Xi, Commonwealth of Calif. Club, Cosmos Club (Washington). Office: Lawrence Livermore Nat Lab PO Box 808 Livermore CA 94551-0808 E-mail: schock1@llnl.gov

SCHOEN, RICHARD MELVIN, mathematics educator, researcher; b. Celina, Ohio, Oct. 23, 1950; s. Arnold Peter and Rosemary (Heitkamp) S.; m. Doris Helga Fischer-Colbrie, Oct. 29, 1983; children: Alan, Lucy. B.S., U. Dayton, 1972; Ph.D., Stanford U., 1976. Lectr. U. Calif.-Berkeley, 1976-78, prof. math., 1980-85; asst. prof. Courant Inst. NYU, 1978-80; prof. math. U. Calif.-La Jolla, 1985-87, Stanford U., 1987—. Contbr. articles to profl. jours. Fellow NSF, 1972, Alfred P. Sloan Found., 1979, MacArthur Found. prize, 1983, Bôcher prize, 1989. Mem. Am. Acad. Arts and Scis., Am. Math. Soc., Nat. Acad. Sci. Democrat Office: Stanford U Mathematics Dept Stanford CA 94305

SCHOENBORN, BENNO P. biophysicist, educator; b. Basel, Switzerland, May 2, 1936; came to U.S., 1955; s. Wilhelm and Maria (Dobler) S.; m. Catherine Cowie Kay, Oct. 26, 1962. BA, UCLA, 1958; PhD, U. New South Wales, Australia, 1962; DSc (hon.), N.J. Inst. Tech., 1982. Teaching fellow U. New South Wales, Sydney, 1958-61; postdoctoral fellow U. Calif., San Francisco, 1962-63, asst. prof. dept. pharmacology, 1964-66, assoc. prof. dept. pharmacology and biochemistry, 1967; biophysicist dept. biology Brookhaven Lab., Upton, N.Y., 1968-74, sr. biophysicist dept. biology, 1974-92, assoc. chmn. dept. biology, 1984-90; head ctr. structural biology, 1984-91; sr. fellow Los Alamos (N.Mex.) Nat. Lab., 1992—; adj. prof. biochemistry Columbia U., N.Y.C., 1978-93. Vis. scientist Molecular Biology Lab., Cambridge, Eng., 1964-66; adj. scientist biophysics SUNY, Stony Brook, 1988-92; mem. editorial bd. Biophys. Jour., 1977-80; mem. Reactor Safety Com., 1972-79. Editor: Neutrons in Biology, 1976, 84, 96; contbr. articles to profl. jours.; patent in multilager monochromator, 1975. Recipient E.O. Lawrence award Dept. of Energy, 1980. Mem. Nat. Com. for Crystallography, Biophys. Soc. (coun. mem. 1976-79). Republican. Avocation: sailing. Home: 816 Stagecoach Dr Santa Fe NM 87501-1144 E-mail: schoenborn@lanl.gov

SCHOENER, THOMAS WILLIAM, zoology educator, researcher; b. Lancaster, Pa., Aug. 9, 1943; s. Harold Cloyd and Alta Marjorie (Hewitt) S.; m. Susan L. Keen, 1985. BA, Harvard Coll., 1965, PhD, 1969. Asst. prof. Harvard Coll., Cambridge, Mass., 1972-73, assoc. prof., 1973-75, U. Wash., Seattle, 1975-76, prof., 1976-80, U. Calif., Davis, 1980—, chairperson sect. evolution and ecology divsn. biol. scis., 1993-99. Mem. editl. bd. dirs. Oecologia, 1984-93; past mem. editl. bd. Evolution, Am. Naturalist, Sci., Acta Oecologia; contbr. chpts. to books, articles to profl. jours. Recipient MacArthur prize Ecol. Soc. Am., 1987; grantee NSF, 1975—, Nat. Geog. Soc.; jr. fellow Harvard U., 1969-72; Guggenheim fellow, 1992-93. Mem. NAS, Am. Acad. Arts and Scis., Am. Ornithologists Union (elective), Am. Soc. Naturalists, Ecol. Soc. Am., Am. Soc. Ichthyologists and Herpetologists, Cooper Ornithol. Soc., Wilson Ornithol. Soc., Am. Arachnological Soc., Bahamas Nat. Trust, Soc. Study of Amphibians and Reptiles. Avocations: weight lifting; reading. Office: U Calif Sect Evolution Ecology Davis CA 95616

SCHOENFELD, LAWRENCE JON, real estate developer, asset lender; b. L.A., Nov. 30, 1945; s. Donald and Trudy (Libizer) S.; m. Carol Sue Gard, Aug. 24, 1969. AA, L.A. Valley Coll., Van Nuys, Calif., 1963; BBA, Wichita State U., 1969, MSBA, 1970; grad., Army Med. Acad., 1976, US Army Command/Gen Staff Coll., Ft. Leavenworth, Kans., 1988. Cert. tchr., Calif.; life lic. jr. coll. tchg. credential, Calif.; lic. real estate broker (cert.) developer, Calif. Asst. treas. Advance Mortgage, L.A., 1970-72; v.p. ops. Unigem Internat., L.A., 1972-98; pres. C. & L. Schoenfeld Investments Inc., Manhattan Beach, Calif., 1998—. Bd. dirs. The Schoenfeld Constrn. Co., South Star Wours, Uniorr Corp., Execucentre-West, Schoenfeld & Co., Customer Ground Handling Svc. Corp.; co-developer Los-Osos Mini Storage Co., Los Osos, Calif., Bay Osos,, 1984, Bay Osos Mini Storage Co., 1984, El Mercadero World Trade Show, Guatemala, 1986, 97, Santiago, 1987, Bahai, 1988, Paraguay, 1989, El Mercado, Costa Rica, 1990, Panama City, 1995, Manaus, 1996, Guayaquil, 1998, Los Osos Mini Storage Co., Quito, 1991, Santa Cruz, 1993, Ecuador, 1998, Uruguay, 1999, Punta del Este, 1999, Fortaleza, Brazil, 2000; pres. Accents on Beverly Hills, 1991, Accents at the Biltmore, Santa Barbara, 1995, Accents on Newport Beach, 1996, Accents on San Francisco Travelers Centrury Club, 2001, The Regis, L.A. Mem. Improvement Commn., Hermosa Beach., Calif. 1976-78. Served to maj. Med. Svc. Corps, U.S. Army, 1970-72; lt. col. USAR, 1972—. Mem. South Am. Travel Assn., World Trade Assn. (assoc.), Town Hall, Wichita State U. Alumni Assn. (nat. dist. rep., mem. coun. 1992—), Res. Officers Assn., Brit. Am. C. of C., Skal Internat., Travelers Century Club, Navy Golf Club, Palos Verdes Golf Club. Jewish. Office: 224 5th St Manhattan Beach CA 90266-5710 also: 8405 Pershing Dr Ste 301 Playa Del Rey CA 90293-7861 Fax: 310-318-7106. E-mail: lccorp@earthlink.net

SCHOENFELD, WALTER EDWIN, manufacturing company executive; b. Seattle, Nov. 6, 1930; s. Max and Edna Lucille (Reinhardt) S.; m. Esther Behar, Nov. 27, 1955; children— Lea Anne, Jeffrey, Gary. B.B.A., U. Wash., 1952. Vice pres., dir. Sunshine Mining Co., Kellogg, Idaho, 1964-69, First N.W. Industries, Inc. (Seattle Super Sonics), 1968-79; chmn. bd., pres. Schoenfeld Industries, Inc. (diversified holding co.), 1968-93; vice chmn., acting pres., CEO, Vans, Inc., 1993-97, chmn., bd. dirs., 1997—. Ptnr. Seattle Mariners Baseball Club, 1977-81, Seattle Sounds Soccer Club, 1974-79; bd. dirs. Hazel Bishop Cosmetics. Bd. dirs. Wash. China Rels. Coun., 1980—, Sterling Recreation Orgn., 1985-90; chmn. Access Long Distance of Washington; bd. govs. Weizmann Inst. Sci., Rehovot, Israel, 1980—; trustee Barbara Sinatra Children's Ctr., Eisenhower Hosp., Rancho Mirage, Calif., 1990—. With AUS, 1952-55, Korea. Recipient various service awards. Mem. Chief Execs. Orgn. (v.p., bd. dirs. 1987-93), Seattle C. of C., Rainier Club, Seattle Yacht Club, Tamarisk Country Club (Rancho Mirage, Calif.), Mission Hills Country Club, Glendale Country Club (Bellevue, Wash.), Alpha Kappa Psi. Office: 999 3rd Ave Ste 3800 Seattle WA 98104-4023

SCHOENKE, MARILYN LEILANI, foundation administrator; b. Wahiawa, Hawaii; m. Donald N. Basham; children: Neil, Steven, Leilani. BB, Corpus Christi State U. Exec. dir. Moanalua Gardens Found., Hawaii, 1994—. Exec. dir. Lawyer's Care; vol. Am. Cancer Soc. Mem. Alzheimer's Assn. (support svcs. coord., vol.), Manu O Ke Kai Canoe Club, Native Hawaiian C. of C., U.S. Tennis Assn., Hawaii Pacific Tennis Assn. Office: Moanalua Gardens Found 1352 Pineapple Pl Honolulu HI 96819-1754

SCHOESLER, MARK GERALD, state legislator, farmer; b. Ritzville, Wash., Feb. 16, 1957; s. Gerald E. and Dorothy (Heinemann) S.; m. Ginger J. Van Aelst, Apr. 8, 1978; children: Veronica, Cody. AA, Spokane (Wash.) C.C., 1977. Mem. Wash. Ho. of Reps., Olympia, 1992—. House majority whip, mem. rules, agr. and ecology, chair joint adminstrv. rules rev. coms., 1995-96. Pres. Wash. Friends Farms and Forests, 1991-92; mem. Cmty. Econ. Revitalization Bd.; bd. dirs. Wheatland Cmtys. Fair. Mem. Wash. Assn. Wheat Growers (dir. 1990-92). Republican. Mem. United. Ch. Christ. Home: 1588 E Rosenoff Rd Ritzville WA 99169-8710

SCHOETTLER, GAIL SINTON, former state official; b. Los Angeles, Oct. 21, 1943; d. James and Norma (McLellan) Sinton; children: Lee, Thomas, James; m. Donald L. Stevens, June 23, 1990. BA in Econs., Stanford U., 1965; MA in History, U. Calif., Santa Barbara, 1969, PhD in History, 1975. Businesswoman, Denver, 1975-83; exec. dir. Colo. Dept. of Personnel, Denver, 1983-86; treas. State of Colo., Denver, 1987-94, lt. gov., 1995-99. U.S. amb. World Radio Comm. Conf., Istanbul, 1999-2000. Mem. Douglas County Bd. Edn., Colo., 1979-87, pres., 1983-87; trustee U. No. Colo., Greeley, 1981-87; pres. Denver Children's Mus., 1975-85; bd. dirs. Nat. Jewish Hosp. Decorated Chevalier, French Legion of Honor, 1998; recipient Disting. Alumna award U. Calif. at Santa Barbara, 1987, Trailblazer award AAUW, 1997, Childrens Advocacy award Colo. Soc. Sch. Psychologists, 1997. Mem. Nat. Women's Forum (bd. dirs. 1981-89, pres. 1983-85), Internat. Women's Forum (mem. bd. dirs. 1981-89, pres. 83-85), Women Execs. in State Govt. (bd. dirs. 1981-87, chmn. 1988), Leadership Denver Assn. (bd. dirs. 1987, named Outstanding Alumna 1985), Nat. Congress Lt. Govs., Stanford Alumni Assn. Democrat.

SCHOFIELD, ANTHONY WAYNE, judge; b. Farmington, N.Mex., Mar. 5, 1949; s. Aldred Edward and Margueriete (Knudsen) S.; m. Rebecca Ann Rosecrans, May 11, 1971; children: Josie, Matthew Paul, Peter Christian, Addie, Joshua James, M. Thomas, Jacob L., Daniel Z. BA, Brigham Young U., 1973, JD, 1976. Bar: Utah 1976, U.S. Dist. Ct. Utah 1976, U.S. Ct. Appeals (7th and 10th cirs.) 1977. Law clk. to hon. judge A. Sherman Christansen U.S. Dist. Ct. Utah, Salt Lake City, 1976-77; assoc. Ferenz, Bramhall, Williams & Gruskin, Agana, Guam, 1977-79; pvt. practice American Fork, Utah, 1979-80; assoc. Jardine, Linebaugh, Brown & Dunn, Salt Lake City, 1980-81; mem., dir. Ray, Quinney & Nebeker, Provo, Utah; judge 4th Jud. Dist. Ct., Provo, 1993—. Bishop Mormon Ch., American Fork, 1985-88; commr. American Fork City Planning Commn., 1980-85; trustee American Fork Hosp., 1984-93. Mem. Cen. Utah Bar Assn. (pres. 1987, 91). Avocations: photography, music. Office: 125 N 100 W Provo UT 84601-2849

SCHOFIELD, JAMES ROY, computer programmer; b. Reedsburg, Wis., Aug. 16, 1953; s. G. C. Schofield and Margaret (Collies) Tverberg. BA, Carleton Coll., 1976. Programmer Brandon Applied Systems, San Francisco, 1977-78, Rand Info. Systems, San Francisco, 1979-83; systems programmer IBM, San Jose, Calif., 1983-91; programmer Office of Instnl. Rsch./U. Calif., Berkeley, 1991-94, Datis Corp., San Mateo, Calif., 1994-95, Compuware Corp., Los Gatos, 1995-96, Pacific Bell, San Ramon, 1996—. Mem. Assn. for Computing Machinery, Assn. for Computing Machinery Spl. Interest Group in Computers and Soc., Phi Beta Kappa. Avocations: guitar, reading, swimming. Home: PO Box 25143 San Mateo CA 94402-5143 Office: Pacific Bell 2600 Camino Ramon San Ramon CA 94583-5099

SCHOLES, MYRON S. law educator, finance educator; b. 1941; BA, McMaster U., 1962, MBA, 1964; PhD, U. Chgo., 1969. Instr. U. Chgo. Bus. Sch., 1967-68; prof. U. Chgo., 1976-83; asst. prof. MIT Mgmt. Sch., Cambridge, 1968-72, assoc. prof., 1972-73, U. Chgo., 1973-75, prof., 1975-79, Edward Eagle Brown prof. fin., 1979-82; dir. Ctr. for Rsch. in Security Prices U. Chgo., 1975-81; prof. law Stanford (Calif.) U., 1983-96, Frank E. Buck prof. emeritus fin., 1996—; sr. rsch. fellow Hoover Instn. Stanford U., 1988—; mng. dir. Salomon Bros., 1991-93; prin. Long-Term Capital Mgmt., Greenwich, Conn., 1994-98. Co-recipient Nobel prize for econs., 1997. Office: Arbor Investors 2775 Sand Hill Rd Ste 220 Menlo Park CA 94025-7019 E-mail: mscholes@pacbell.net

SCHOLTZ, ROBERT ARNO, electrical engineering educator; b. Lebanon, Ohio, Jan. 26, 1936; s. William Paul and Erna Johanna (Weigel) S.; m. Laura Elizabeth McKeon, June 16, 1962; children: Michael William, Paul Andrew. BSEE, U. Cin., 1958; MSEE, U. So. Calif., 1960; PhD, Stanford U., 1964. Co-op student Sheffield Corp., Dayton, Ohio, 1953-58, MS and PHD fellow Hughes Aircraft Co., Culver City, Calif., 1958-63, sr. staff engr., 1963-78; prof. U. So. Calif., L.A., 1963—. Vis. prof. U. Hawaii,

1969, 78; cons. LinCom Corp., L.A., 1975-81, Axiomatix Inc., L.A., 1980-86, JPL, Pasadena, 1985, Tech. Group, 1987-89, TRW, 1989, Pulson Comm., 1992-93, Colley-Godward, Palo Alto, 1994-97, Time Domain Corp., 2000—. Co-author: Spread Spectrum Comm., 3 vols., 1984, Spread Spectrum Communications Handbook, 1994, Basic Concepts in Information Theory and Coding, 1994; contbr. numerous articles to profl. jours. (recipient Leonard G. Abraham prize paper award 1983, Donald G. Fink Prize award 1984, Signal Processing Soc. Sr. Paper award 1992, Comm. Soc. Fred Ellersick Paper award 1997). Pres. South Bay Community Concert Orgn., Redondo Beach, Calif., 1975-79. Fellow IEEE (bd. govs. info. theory group 1981-86, bd. govs. communication soc. 1981-83, chmn. fin. com. NTC 1977, program chmn. ISIT 1981). Office: U So Calif Comm Scis Inst Dept Elec Engring Los Angeles CA 90089-0001 E-mail: scholtz@usc.edu

SCHOMER, HOWARD, retired clergyman, educator, social policy consultant; b. Chgo., June 9, 1915; s. Frank Michael and Daisy (Aline) S.; m. Elsie Pauline Swenson, Mar. 23, 1942 (dec. Nov. 1996); children: Karine, Mark, Paul, Ellen. B.S. summa cum laude, Harvard U., 1937, postgrad., 1939-40; student, Chgo. Theol. Sem., 1938-39, 40-41, D.D., 1954; LL.D., Olivet Coll., 1966. Ordained to ministry Congl. Ch., 1941. Student pastor, Fitzwilliam, N.H., Oak Park, Ill.; asst. dean U. Chgo. Chapel., 1940-41; counsellor Am. history Harvard U., 1939-40; civilian pub. service Am. Friends Service Com., 1941-45; Am. Bd. Mission fellow to chs. of Europe Chambon-sur-Lignon, France, 1946-55; history tchr., work camp dir. Coll. Cevenol; founder internat. conf. center Accueil Fraternel, Permanent Conf. Protestant Chs. in Latin Countries of Europe; asst. to rapporteur UN Commn. on Human Rights, UN Econ. and Social Council, 1947-48; inter-church aid sec. for Europe World Council Chs., Geneva, 1955-58; pres., prof. ch. history Chgo. Theol. Sem., 1959-66; exec. dir. dept. specialized ministries Div. Overseas Ministries, Nat. Council Chs., N.Y.C., 1967-70; participant integration demonstrations in Ala., Ga., Washington, Chgo., SCLC, 1960-66; world issues sec. United Ch. Bd. World Ministries, 1971-80; Indochina liaison officer World Council of Chs., 1970-71; United Ch. of Christ officer for social responsibility in investments, 1972-81; founder, dir. Corp. Adv. Services, 1980-90. Founder, mem. United Ch. Christ Working Group with United Ch. in German Democratic Rep. and Fed. Rep. of Germany, 1977-86; vis. prof. religion and society Andover Newton Theol. Sch., 1981; vis. lectr. Manchester Coll., St. John's U.; Woodrow Wilson vis. fellow Drew U., 1981; pres. Internat. Fellowship of Reconciliation, 1959-63, v.p., 1963-65; participant 1st-3d assemblies World Council Chs., Amsterdam, 1948, Evanston, 1954, New Delhi, 1961; rep. UN non-govt. orgn. UNIAPAC, 1979-85; pastoral assoc. First Congl. Ch. (United Ch. Christ), Montclair, N.J., 1983-89; delegated observer Vatican Council II, 1963; v.p. Am. Friends Coll. Cevenol., 1981-89; bd. dirs. Interfaith Center for Corp. Responsibility, 1973-81; chmn. exec. com. Freedom of Faith - A Christian Com. for Religious Rights, 1978-81; mem. nat. adv. bd. N.Y. State Martin Luther King Jr. Inst. for Nonviolence, 1989-92. Translator: The Prayer of the Church Universal (Marc Boegner), 1954; editor: The Oppression of Protestants in Spain, 1955, the Role of Transnational Business in Mass Economic Development, 1975; editor-at-large Christian Century, 1959-70; contbr.; Business, Religion and Ethics-Inquiry and Encounter, 1982, Aspects of Hope, 1993; articles to religious and interdisciplinary publs.; keynote address for celebration of 50th Anniversary of universal declaration of human rights; corr. in U.S. for Évangile et Liberté, 1988—. Past co-chmn. Chgo. Com. for Sane Nuclear Policy; bd. dirs. World Conf. on Religion and Peace, 1974-84, sec. for Kampuchea issues, 1979-81; former trustee Am. Waldensian Aid Soc.; mem. internat. council Internat. Ctr. Integrative Studies, 1984-91, bd. dirs., 1987-91; trustee Internat. Inst. for Effective Communication, 1987-93; bd. dirs. Alternative Lifelong Learning, 1992-97, Cambodian Found. for Justice, Peace and Devel., 1993—. Mem. ACLU, Wider Quaker Fellowship, Fellowship Reconciliation, Ctr. for Theology and the Natural Scis., Outlook Club (Berkeley), Harvard Club San Francisco, Phi Beta Kappa. Home: 110 41st St Apt 512 Oakland CA 94611-5240 E-mail: schomer15@aol.com

SCHOMP, LISA JULIANA, automotive industry executive; b. 1951; d. Ralph and Kay S.; m. Mark Wallace; children: Aaron, Tyler, Logan. From mini-maid to pres. Ralph Schomp Automotive, Littleton, Colo., 1970-88, pres., 1988—. Named 1993 Woman of Yr. Englewood (Colo.) Bus. and Profl. Women. Office: Ralph Schomp Automotive 5700 S Broadway Littleton CO 80121-8007

SCHONFELD, WILLIAM ROST, political science educator, researcher; b. N.Y.C., Aug. 28, 1942; s. William A. and Louise R. (Rost) S.; m. Elena Beortegui, Jan. 23, 1964; children: Natalie Beortegui, Elizabeth Lynn Beortegui. Student, Cornell U., 1960-61; B.A. cum laude with honors, NYU, 1964; M.A., Princeton U., 1968, Ph.D., 1970. Research asst. Princeton U., 1966-69, research assoc., 1969-70, vis. lectr., 1970; asst. prof. polit. sci. U. Calif.-Irvine, 1970-75, assoc. prof., 1975-81, prof., 1981—, dean Sch. Social Scis., 1982—; sr. lectr. Fond. Nat. de Sci. Politique, Paris, 1973-74; researcher Centre de Sociologie des Organisations, Paris, 1976-78. Author: Youth and Authority in France, 1971, Obedience and Revolt, 1976, Ethnographie du PS et du RPR, 1985 Recipient Disting. Teaching award U. Calif.-Irvine, 1984, Disting. Faculty Lectureship award for tchg., 1998, Daniel G. Aldrich Disting. Univ. Svc. award, 2000-01; Fulbright fellow Bordeaux, France, 1964-65; Danforth grad. fellow, 1964-69; Fulbright sr. lectr. Paris, 1973-74; NSF-CNRS Exchange of Scientists fellow Paris, 1976-78; Ford Found. grantee France, Spain, 1978-79; finalist Prof. Yr. Council for Advancement and Support of Edn., 1984. Mem. Am. Polit. Sci. Assn., Assoc. Francaise de Sci. Pol., Phi Beta Kappa. Office: U Calif Sch Social Scis Irvine CA 92697-0001

SCHOONOVER, MARGARET See LEFRANC, MARGARET

SCHOPF, JAMES WILLIAM, paleobiologist; b. Urbana, Ill., Sept. 27, 1941; s. James Morton and Esther Julie (Nissen) S.; m. Julie Morgan, Aug. 7, 1965 (div. 1979); 1 child, James Christopher; m. Jane Shen, Jan. 16, 1980. A.B. with high honors, Oberlin Coll., 1963; A.M., Harvard U., 1965, Ph.D. (Harvard fellow, NSF fellow), 1968. Research chemist NASA, Ames Research Center, Calif., 1967; mem. lunar sample preliminary exam. team Manned Spacecraft Center, Tex., 1968-71; asst. prof. dept. earth and space scis. UCLA, 1968-70, assoc. prof., 1970-73, prof., 1973—, mem. Inst. Evolutionary and Environ. Biology, 1970-76, mem. Inst. Geophysics and Planetary Physics, 1973—, dean honors div. Coll. Letters and Sci., 1983-85, dir. Ctr. for Study Evolution and Origin of Life, 1985—, Sigma Xi Disting. lectr., 1976, Rubey lectr., 1976, Golden Yr. Disting. lectr., 1980, Faculty Research lectr., 1984; Sigma Xi Disting. lectr. U. Cin., 1980; Disting. lectr. Buffalo Mus. Sci., 1982; J.A. Bownocker lectr. Ohio State U., 1982. Vis. lectr. Am. Inst. Biol. Scis. Vis. Biologists Program, 1969-72; M.W. Haas vis. disting. prof. geology U. Kans., 1979; extraordinary vis. prof. exobiology U. Nijmegen, Netherlands, 1980-81; C. O'Neal lectr. Ohio Wesleyan U., 1982; Sandia disting. lectr. U. N.Mex., 1985; Sigma Xi disting. lectr. U. Oreg., 1985; Du Pont disting. lectr. U. Ill., 1985; R. Stanier disting. lectr. U. Calif.-Berkeley, 1987; H.P. Mangelsdorf disting. lectr. U. N.C., 1987; mem. Bot. Soc. Am. del., People's Republic China, 1978; Academia Sinica vis. research scientist, People's Republic China, 1981, 82; mem. NASA Terrestrial Bodies Sci. Working Group, 1975-76, space program adv. council NASA Life Scis. Com., 1976-78, NASA Working Group on Origins of Life, 1978-79, NASA Space Sci. Adv. Com., 1979-82, mem. NASA Life Scis. Strategic Planning Study Com., 1985—; Alan T. Waterman Award com. NSF, 1978-81; mem. working group on precambrian biostratigraphy Internat. Geol. Correlation Program, UNESCO, 1975—; mem. Working Group on Cambrian-Precambrian Boundary, 1976—; mem. adv. com. USSR and Eastern Europe, Commn. Internat. Relations NRC, 1981-85, mem. bd. earth sci. Commn. Phys. Scis., Math. and Resources, 1982-85, mem. space sci. bd., 1983-86; mem . com. on guidelines for paleontol. collecting, 1984-86, sub.-com. on evolution and diversity Commn. on Life Scis., 1986; mem. com. space research Internat. Council Sci. Unions Mem. editorial bd.: Origins of Life, 1973—, Precambrian Research, 1973—, Evolutionary Theory, 1973—, U. Calif. Press, 1973-82, Paleobiology, 1974-83, Geomicrobiology Jour., 1977—, Evolutionary Monographs, 1977—; contbr. articles to profl. jours. Bd. dirs. Brentwood Glen (Calif.) Assn., 1972-75; trustee UCLA Found., 1983-85. Recipient N.Y. Bot. Garden award Bot. Soc. Am., 1966; Group Achievement award NASA, 1969; Outstanding Paper award Jour. Paleontology, 1971; Charles Schuchert award Paleontol. Soc., 1974; Disting. Teaching award UCLA, 1977; Alan T. Waterman award NSF, 1977; G. Hawk award U. Kans., 1979; spl. recognition diploma NASA, 1979; Outstanding Vol. in Phys. Scis. award Am. Assn. Pubs., 1983; Mark Clark Thompson medal Nat. Acad. Scis., 1986; Guggenheim fellow, 1973; U.S. Nat. Acad. Scis. exchange scientist USSR, 1975 Fellow Geol. Soc. Am. (vice-chmn. Cordilleran sect. 1983-84, chmn. 1984-85); mem. Bot. Soc. Am. (com. on sci. liaison with People's Republic China 1978—), Paleontol. Soc. (mem. Schuchert Award com. 1978-82), Internat. Soc. Study of Origin of Life (treas. 1977-83, nat. meeting adv. com. 1980, 83, 86, councilor, 1983—), Geochem. Soc. (nominating com. 1980-82), Soc. Study of Evolution (edn. com. 1980-83), Am. Philos. Soc., Sigma Xi (treas. UCLA chpt. 1972-74, chpt. v.p. 1984-84, pres. 1984-85). Office: UCLA Dept Earth Space Scis Los Angeles CA 90095-0001

SCHORR, ALAN EDWARD, librarian, publisher; b. N.Y.C., Jan. 7, 1945; s. Herbert and Regina S.; m. Debra Genner, June 11, 1967; 1 son, Zebediah. BA, CUNY, 1966; MA, Syracuse U., 1967; postgrad., U. Iowa, 1967-71; MLS, U. Tex., 1973. Tchr., rsch. asst. dept. history U. Iowa, 1967-70; govt. publs. and map libr., asst. prof. Elmer E. Rasmuson Libr., U. Alaska, 1973-78; assoc. prof., dir. libr. U. Alaska, Juneau, 1978-84; prof., dean univ. libr. Calif. State U., Fullerton, 1984-86; pres. The Denali Press, Juneau, 1986—. Freelance indexer and bibliographer; vis. lectr. Birmingham (Eng.) Poly., 1981; mem. Alaska Ednl. Del. to China, 1975. Author: Alaska Place Names, 1974, 4th edit., 1991, Directory of Special Libraries in Alaska, 1975, Government Reference Books, 1974-75, 1976, 1976-77, 1978, Government Documents in the Library Literature 1909-1974, 1976, ALA RSBRC Manual, 1979, Federal Documents Librarianship 1879-1987, 1988, Hispanic Resource Directory, 1988, 3d edit., 1996, Refugee and Immigrant Resource Directory, 1990, 92, 94; editor: The Sourdough, 1974-75, Directory of Services for Refugees and Immigrants, 1987, 3d edit., 1993, Guide to Smithsonian serial publs., 1987 ; book reviewer, columnist: S.E. Alaska Empire, 1979-82, L.A. Times; contbr. articles to profl. jours. Mem. Auke Bay (Alaska) Vol. Fire Dept.; mem. Juneau Borough Cemetery Adv. Com., 1980-81, Juneau Borough Libr. Adv. Com., 1981-82, Am. Book Awards Com., 1980; chmn. program evaluation com. Juneau Bd. Edn., 2000—, chmn. facilities com., 1994-96, chmn. policy com., 1996-98, v.p. 1999—. Mem. ALA (mem. reference and subscription books rev. com. 1975-86, mem. reference and adult svcs. divsn. publs. com. 1975-77, Nat. Assn. Hispanic Publs., Mudge citation commn. 1977-79, 84-86, Dartmouth Coll. Medal Commn., Governing Coun. 1977-84, mem. Dewey medal com. 1984-85, Denali Press award), Alaska Libr. Assn. (mem. exec. bd. 1974-75, mem. nominating com. 1977-79), Pacific N.W. Libr. Assn. (rep. publs. com. 1973-75), Assn. Coll. and Rsch. Librs. (mem. publ. com. 1976-80), Spl. Librs. Assn. (assoc. editor geography and map divsn. bull. 1975-76), Soc. for Scholarly Pub., Internat. Assn. Ind. Pubs (bd. dirs. 1990-92), Pub. Mktg. Assn., Alaska State Employees Fed. Credit Union (bd. dirs. 1997—, treas. 2001—), PEN Ctr. USA West, Amnesty Internat., Explorers Club N.Y., Wash. Athletic Club (Seattle). Office: Denali Press PO Box 1535 Juneau AK 99802

SCHORR, S. L. lawyer; b. N.Y.C., Feb. 19, 1930; s. Charles and Clara (Lerech) S.; m. Eleanor Daru, Mar. 23, 1956; children: Lewis, Andrew, Emily, Roberta. Student, L.I. U., 1948-50; LLB, Bklyn. Law Sch., 1953. Bar: N.Y. 1955, Ariz. 1962, U.S. Dist. Ct. Ariz. 1962, U.S. Supreme Ct. 1979. Planning commr. Pima County, Tucson, 1959-62; asst. city mgr. Tucson, 1962-63; ptnr. Lewis and Roca, Tucson, 1988—. Co-chair Continuing Legal Edn. Seminar on Ballot Box Zoning, U. Ariz., 1991, Ariz. State Bar Continuing Legal Edn. Seminar on Land Use Regulation and Litigation, 1977, 86, 89, 95. Bd. dirs. Pima Coll., 1966-67, Pima County Real Estate Rsch. Coun., 1997—, So. Ariz. Leadership Coun., 1997—; mem. Commn. on Improved Govtl. Mgmt., Tucson, 1974-77, Gov.'s Econ. Planning and Devel. Adv. Bd., Phoenix, 1983-85; chmn. Gov.'s Task Force on Seriously Mentally Ill, Phoenix, 1989-91. Mem. Ariz. Bar Assn., Pima County Bar Assn. Democrat. Office: Lewis Roca 1 S Church Ave Ste 700 Tucson AZ 85701-1611

SCHOTT, STEPHEN C. professional sports team executive; b. Santa Clara, Calif. m. Patricia Schott; children: Lisa, Stephen E., Kristen. Grad., Santa Clara U., 1960. CEO, owner Citation Homes, Award Homes; co-owner, mng. ptnr. Oakland (Calif.) Athletics, 1995—. Advisor athletic dept. Bronco Bench, Santa Clara U. Active Stanford-Amdahl Read to Succeed program; dir. Santa Clara County Role Model program; founding mem. Alexis de Tocqueville Soc.; regent Bellarmine Prep; past chmn. bd. St. Francis H.S. Found.; bd. trustees Santa Clara U.; bd. dirs. Los Altos Tomorrow. Named Disting. Alumnus, Santa Clara U., 1989. Mem. Nat. Assn. Home Builders. Office: Oakland Athletics 7677 Oakport St Ste 200 Oakland CA 94621-1933

SCHOVILLE, DENNIS A(RNOLD), lawyer; b. Richland Ctr., Wis., May 31, 1945; BS, U. Wis., 1967; JD with Distinction, Ill. Inst. Tech., 1973; LLM, Northwestern U., 1974. Bar: Wis. 1973, Ill. 1973, U.S. Dist. Ct. (no. dist.) Ill. 1973, Calif. 1974, U.S. Dist. Ct. (so. dist.) Calif. 1974, U.S. Ct. Appeals (9th cir.) 1985, U.S. Ct. Claims. Ptnr. Schoville & Arnell, LLP, San Diego. Capt. U.S. Army, 1968-73. Recipient Broderick award for professionalism, integrity and ethics, 1996; named Consumer Attys. San Diego Trial Lawyer of the Yr., 1995, 99. Mem. ABA, ATLA, Am. Coll. Trial Lawyers, Am. Bd. Trial Advocates (sec. San Diego chpt.), Ill. State Bar Assn., State Bar Wis., State Bar Calif., San Diego County Bar Assn., San Diego Trial Lawyers Assn. (Outstanding Trial Advocacy award-civil 1984, 89, 94), Am. Inns of Ct. (master), Disting. Flying Cross Soc. Office: Schoville & Arnell 1230 Columbia St Ste 800 San Diego CA 92101-3571

SCHRADER, LAWRENCE EDWIN, plant physiologist, educator; b. Atchison, Kans., Oct. 22, 1941; s. Edwin Carl and Jenna Kathryn (Tobiason) S.; m. Elfriede J. Massier, Mar. 14, 1981 BS, Kans. State U., 1963; PhD, U. Ill., 1967; grad., Inst. Ednl. Mgmt., Harvard U., 1991. Asst. prof. dept. agronomy U. Wis., Madison, 1969-72, assoc. prof., 1972-76, prof., 1976-84; prof., head dept. agronomy U. Ill., Urbana, 1985-89; dean Coll. Agr. and Home Econs. Wash. State U., Pullman, 1989-94, prof. dept. horticulture, 1994—. Chief competitive rsch. grants office Dept. Agr., Washington, 1980-81; trustee, treas. Agrl. Satellite Corp., 1991-94. Contbr. chpts. to books, articles to profl. jours. Active Consortium for Internat. Devel., 1989-94, chair fin. com., vice chair exec. com., 1990-92, trustee 1989-94; mem. exec. com. Coun. Agrl. Heads of Agr., 1992-94. Capt. U.S. Army, 1967-69. Recipient Soybean Researchers Recognition award 1983, Disting. Service award in Agriculture Kansas State U., 1987; Romnes Faculty fellow U. Wis., 1979 Fellow AAAS (steering group sect. agr. 1991-95, chair-elect sect. on agr., food and renewable resources 1995-96, chmn. 1996-97, past chmn. 1997-98, coun. mem. 1997-98), Am. Soc. Agronomy, Crop Sci. Soc. Am.; mem. Internat. Soc. for Hort. Sci., Am. Soc. for Hort. Sci., Am. Soc. Plant Physiologists (sec. 1983-85, pres.-elect 1986, pres. 1987), Am. Chem. Soc., Coun. for Agrl. Sci. and Tech., Blue Key, Sigma Xi, Gamma Sigma Delta, Phi Kappa Phi, Phi Eta Sigma, Alpha Zeta (named to Centennial Honor Roll 1997). Methodist Home: 3504 Crestview Rd Wenatchee WA 98801-9668 Office: Wash State U Tree Fruit Rsch & Extension Ctr 1100 N Western Ave Wenatchee WA 98801-1230 E-mail: schrader@wsu.edu

SCHRADER, WILLIAM P. organization executive, farmer; b. Phoenix; m. Bondena; children: Alissa Schrader Urshel, William P. Jr., Larry, Travis. Student, Ariz. State U. Bd. dirs. Salt River Project, Phoenix, 1964-90, v.p. bd., 1990-94, pres., 1994—. Pres. Schrader Farms, Inc. Bd. dirs. Greater Phoenix Econ. Coun., Groundwater Users Adv. Coun.; mem. Maricopa C.C.'s Found., East Valley Partnership, Scottsdale (Ariz.) Mcpl. Corp.; former mayor and mem. city coun. City of Scottsdale; 1st chmn. Parada del Sol, Scottsdale Rodeo. Named to Scottsdale Hall of Fame; named Citizen of Yr., City of Scottsdale. Mem. Am. Pub. Power Assn., Am. Mgmt. Assn., Nat. Water Resources Assn., Colorado River Water Users Assn., Scottsdale C. of C., Scottsdale Jr. C. of C. (life, Disting. Svc. award), Scottsdale Charros (life), White Mountain Country Club, Ariz. Club, Mesa Country Club (Ariz.). Methodist. Home: 5611 E Calle Camelia Phoenix AZ 85018-4663 Office: Salt River Project 1521 N Project Dr Tempe AZ 85281

SCHRADY, DAVID ALAN, civilian military employee, educator; b. Akron, Ohio, Nov. 11, 1939; s. Marvin G. and Sheila A. (O'Neill) S.; m. Mary E. Hilt, Sept. 1, 1962; children: Peter, Patrick, Matthew. BS, Case Inst. Tech., 1961, MS, 1963, PhD, 1965. Prof., chmn. Naval Postgrad. Sch., Monterey, Calif., 1974-76, dean acad. planning, 1976-80, provost and acad. dean, 1980-87, prof. ops. rsch., 1988—, Disting. prof., ops. rsch. educator, 1995—. Vis. prof. Cranfield Inst. Tech./Royal Mil. Coll. of Sci., Shrivenham, Eng., fall 1987-spring 88. Contbr. articles to profl. jours. Recipient Goodeve medal Ops. Rsch. Soc., U.K., 1992. Fellow Mil. Ops. Rsch. Soc. (pres. 1978-79, Wanner Meml. award 1984); mem. Ops. Rsch. Soc. Am. (pres. 1983-84, Kimball medal 1994), Internat. Fedn. Ops. Rsch. Socs. (hon. treas. 1988-97), Inst. Mgmt. Scis. Avocation: guitar, motor sports. Office: Naval Postgrad Sch Dept Ops Rsch Monterey CA 93943-5000

SCHRAG, PETER, editor, writer; b. Karlsruhe, Germany, July 24, 1931; came to U.S., 1941, naturalized, 1953; s. Otto and Judith (Haas) S.; m. Melissa Jane Mowrer, June 9, 1953 (div. 1969); children: Mitzi, Erin Andrew; m. Diane Divoky, May 24, 1969 (div. 1981); children: David Divoky, Benaiah Divoky; m. Patricia Ternahan, Jan. 1, 1988. A.B. cum laude, Amherst Coll., 1953. Reporter El Paso (Tex.) Herald Post, 1953-55; asst. sec., asst. dir. publs. Amherst Coll., 1955-66, instr. Am. Studies, 1960-64; asso. edn. editor Sat. Rev., 1966-68, exec. editor, 1968-69; editor Change mag., 1969-70; editor at large Saturday Rev., 1969-72; contbg. editor Saturday Review/Education, 1972-73; editorial adv. bd. The Columbia Forum, 1972-75; editorial bd. Social Policy, 1971—; contbg. editor More, 1974-78, Inquiry, 1977-80, The Am. Prospect, 1995—; editorial page editor Sacramento Bee and McClatchy Newspapers, 1978-96, contbg. editor, 1996—. Vis. lectr. U. Mass. Sch. Edn., 1970-72; fellow in profl. journalism Stanford U., Palo Alto, Calif., 1973-74; lectr. U. Calif. at Berkeley, 1974-78, 90—; Pulitzer Prize juror, 1988-89 Author: Voices in the Classroom, 1965, Village School Downtown, 1967, Out of Place in America, 1971, The Decline of the Wasp, 1972, The End of the American Future, 1973, Test of Loyalty, 1974, (with Diane Divoky) The Myth of the Hyperactive Child, 1975, Mind Control, 1978, Paradise Lost: California's Experience, America's Future, 1998; contbr. articles. Mem. adv. com. Student Rights Project, N.Y. Civil Liberties Union, 1970-72; mem. Com. Study History, 1958-72; trustee Emma Willard Sch., 1967-69; bd. dirs. Park Sch., Oakland, Calif., 1976-77, Ctr. for Investigative Reporting, 1979-81, Ed Source, 1998—; bd. visitors Claremont Grad. Sch.; mem. bd. advisors Pub. Policy Inst. Calif. Guggenheim fellow, 1971-72; Nat. Endowment for Arts fellow, 1976-77 Office: 5835 Colton Blvd Oakland CA 94611-2204 E-mail: pschrag@sacbee.com

SCHRECK, GEORGE CHARLES, lawyer; BS, Babson Coll.; JD, MBA, Boston U. Bar: Tex. 1982, Oreg. 1988. Dir. comml. and legal activities Pacificorp. Mem. ABA. Office: Ste 1700 825 NE Multnomah St Portland OR 97232-2135

SCHREIBER, ANDREW, psychotherapist; b. Budapest, Hungary, Aug. 1, 1918; s. Alexander and Bella (Gruen) S.; m. Mona Schreiber, Aug. 6, 1950 (dec. June 1985); children: Julie, Brad, Robin. BA, CCNY, 1941, MEd, 1943; MSW, Columbia U., 1949; PhD, Heed U., 1972. Diplomate Am. Bd. Sexology, Am. Psychotherapists Assn.; lic. psychotherapist, Calif. Pvt. practice, San Mateo, Calif., 1970—; exec. dir. Pride of Judea Childrens' Home, Bklyn., 1946-49; sales mgr. vibro ceramics dir. Gulton Industries, Metuchen, N.J., 1949-57; mktg. mgr. Weldotron Corp., Newark, 1957-63; head dept. spl. edn. San Mateo (Calif.) High Sch. Dist., 1964-70. Mem. faculty Heed U., 1970-71, advisor to doctoral candidates on West Coast, 1971; lectr. spl. edn. U. Calif.-Berkeley, 1973; cons. on hypnotherapy Psoriasis Rsch. Inst., Palo Alto, Calif., 1993—. Art Students League of N.Y. scholar, 1933-35, San Francisco State U. grantee. Fellow Am. Acad. Clin. Sexology; mem. NEA, AACD, Learning Disabilities Assn., Am. Assn. Sex Educators, Counselors and Therapists, Calif. Assn. Marriage and Family Therapists, Calif. Tchrs. Assn. Home: 1658 Via Laguna San Mateo CA 94404-2452 E-mail: aschre4937@aol.com

SCHREMPF, DETLEF, professional basketball player; b. Leverkusen, Germany, Jan. 21, 1963; Student, U. Washington. Forward Dallas Mavericks, 1985-89, Indiana Pacers, 1989-93, Seattle Supersonics, 1993-99, Portland Trailblazers, 1999—. Player West German Olympic Team, 1984, 92. Recipient Sixth Man award NBA, 1991, 92; mem. NBA All-Star team, 1993.

SCHRENK, GARY DALE, foundation executive; b. San Jose, Calif., Apr. 29, 1949; s. Robert Shepard and Katherine Mildred (Grant) S.; m. Rhonda Lynn King, Oct. 9, 1981 (div. Jan. 1989); children: Stephen, Kristen, James. BA in Comm., Am. U., 1970; postgrad., Regis U., 1990—. TV dir. WTOP (now WUSA), Washington, 1971-73, KBTV (now KUSA), Denver, 1973-75; with Denver Area Boy Scouts Am., 1975-80; regional dir. St. Jude Children's Rsch. Hosp., Memphis, 1980-83; dir. devel. Denver Art Mus., 1983-85; asst. dir. devel. The Children's Hosp., Denver, 1985-87; pres. North Colo. Med. Ctr. Found., Greeley, 1987—. Dir., instr. Fast Start Course, 1985—; pres. Monfort Children's Clinic, Greeley, 1994-2001 Pres. Vision Together, Weld County, Colo., 1994-95; chmn., founding dir. Weld Citizen Action Network, 1995-98, 2000—; founding dir. First Steps Weld County, 1993-99; chmn. Weld Cmty. Health Coalition, 1992—; chmn. pub. support com. Team Colo. ARC, 1997—. Recipient Disting. Citizen award Highlanders, Denver, 1974. Mem. Assn. Fundraising Profls. (mem. nat. found. bd. 1998—, nat. assembly 1994-98, bd. dirs. Colo. chpt. 1979—, pres. 1984), Colo. Assn. Nonprofit Orgns. (founding dir. 1987-92), Rotary, Greeley Country Club, Tahosa Alumni Assn. (past pres., past chair). Methodist. Avocation: golf. Home: 4956 13th St Greeley CO 80634-2215 Office: North Colo Med Ctr Found 1801 16th St Greeley CO 80631-5154 E-mail: gary.schrenk@bannerhealth.com

SCHRIER, ROBERT WILLIAM, physician, educator; b. Indpls., Feb. 19, 1936; s. Arthur E. and Helen M. Schrier; m. Barbara Lindley, June 14, 1959; children: David, Debbie, Douglas, Derek, Denise. BA, Depauw U., 1957, DSc (hon.), 1991, U. Colo., 1996, Silesian Acad. Medicine, Katowice, Poland, 1997; MD, Ind. U., 1962. Intern Marion County (Ind.) Hosp., 1962; resident U. Wash., Seattle, 1963-65; asst. prof. U. Calif. Med. Ctr., San Francisco, 1969-72, assoc. mem., 1970-72, assoc. dir. renal divsn., 1971-72, assoc. prof., 1972; prof., head renal disease U. Colo. Sch.

Med., Denver, 1972-92, prof., chmn. Dept. Medicine, 1976—. Editor 40 textbooks in internal medicine, geriat., drug usage, and kidney disease; contbr. over 700 sci. articles to profl. jours. Pres. Nat. Kidney Found., 1984-86. With U.S. Army, 1966-69. Recipient David Hume award Nat. Kidney Found., Torchbearer award, Mayo Soley award Western Soc. Clin. Investigation, Robert H. Williams award Assn. Profs. Medicine. Mem. ACP (master, John Phillips award), Am. Soc. Nephrology (treas. 1979-81, pres. 1983, John Peters award), Internat. Soc. Nephrology (treas. 1981-90, v.p. 1990-95, pres. 1995-97), Am. Clin. and Climatol. Assn. (v.p. 1986), Assn. Am. Physicians (pres. 1994-95), Western Assn. Physicians (pres. 1982), Inst. of Medicine of NAS, Alpha Omega Alpha. Achievements include research contributions centerd on the pathogenesis of acute renal failure, genetic renal disorders, mechanisms of cell injury, diabetic nephropathy and renal and hormonal control of body fluid volume; advancement of a unifying hypothesis of sodium and water regulation in health and disease which has stimulated world-wide interest in the medical science community. Office: U Colo Health Scis Ctr Dept Medicine PO Box B178 Denver CO 80262-0001 E-mail: Robert.Schrier@uchsc.edu

SCHRIER, STANLEY LEONARD, hematologist, educator; b. N.Y.C., Jan. 2, 1929; s. Harry and Nettie (Schwartz) S.; m. Peggy Helen Pepper, June 6, 1953; children: Rachel, Leslie, David. A.B., U. Colo., 1949; M.D., Johns Hopkins U., 1954. Diplomate Am. Bd. Internal Medicine (chmn. subsplty. bd. hematology). Intern Osler Med. Service, Johns Hopkins Hosp., 1954-55; resident U. Mich., Ann Arbor, 1955-56, U. Chgo. Hosp., 1958-59; sr. asst. surgeon USPHS, 1956-58; instr. medicine Stanford Sch. Medicine, Calif., 1959-60, asst. prof. medicine, 1960-63, assoc. prof., 1963-72, prof. medicine, 1972-95, chief divsn. hematology, 1968-94. Vis. scientist Weizmann Inst., Rehovot, Israel, 1967-68; vis. prof. Oxford U., Eng., 1975-76, Hebrew U., Jerusalem, 1982-83 John and Mary Markle scholar, 1961; recipient Kaiser award Stanford U., 1972, Kaiser award Stanford U., 1974, 75, David Rytand award, 1982, Eleanor Roosevelt Union Internationale Contre le Cancer award, 1975-76, Albion Walter Hewlett award, 1996. Fellow ACP; mem. Am. Soc. Hematology, Am. Physiol. Soc., Soc. Exptl. Biology and Medicine, Am. Soc. Clin. Investigation, Western Assn. Physicians, Assn. Am. Physicians. Democrat. Jewish. Office: Stanford U Sch Medicine CCSR 1155 269 Campus Dr Palo Alto CA 94305-5156 E-mail: sschrier@leland.stanford.edu

SCHROCK, THEODORE R. surgeon; b. Berne, Ind., Oct. 21, 1939; s. N.J. and M.A. Schrock; married. AB, U. Calif., San Francisco, 1961, MD, 1964. Diplomate Am. Bd. Surgery. Intern U. Calif. Hosps., San Francisco, 1964-65, resident, 1965-67, 69-71; fellow Mass. Gen. Hosp., Boston, 1967-69; chmn. dept. surgery U. Calif. San Francisco Med. Ctr., 1993-99, J. Englebert Dunphy prof. surgery, 1998—, assoc. dean clin. svcs., chief med. officer, 1999—. Fellow ACS; mem. Am. Gastroenterological Assn., Am. Soc. Colon and Rectal Surgery, Am. Soc. Gastroenterological Endoscopy, Am. Surg. Assn., Soc. Surgery Alimentary Tract. Office: UCSF Campus Box 0296 500 Parnassus Ave San Francisco CA 94143-0001 Fax: 415-353-2765. E-mail: ted.schrock@ucsfmedctr.org

SCHRODER, DIETER KARL, electrical engineering educator; b. Lübeck, Germany, June 18, 1935; came to U.S., 1964; s. Wilhelm and Martha (Werner) S.; m. Beverley Claire Parchment, Aug. 4, 1961; children: Mark, Derek. BSc, McGill U., Montreal, Que., Can., 1962, MSc, 1964; PhD, U. Ill., 1968. Sr. engr. research and devel. sect. Westinghouse Electric Corp., Pitts., 1968-73, fellow engr., 1973-77, adv. engr., 1977-79, mgr., 1979-81; prof. elec. engring. Ariz. State U., Tempe, 1981—. Researcher Inst. Solid-State Physics, Freiburg, Fed. Republic Germany, 1978-79. Author: Advanced MOS Devices, 1987, Semiconductor Material and Device Characterization, 1998; patentee in field; contbr. articles to profl. jours. Fellow IEEE (disting. nat. lectr. 1993-94); mem. Electrochem. Soc., Sigma Xi, Eta Kappa Nu. Mem. Baha'i Faith. Home: 10572 E Firewheel Dr Scottsdale AZ 85259-8711 Office: Ariz State U Dept Elec Engring Tempe AZ 85287-5706

SCHROEDER, GARY JOSEPH, state legislator, business owner, writer; b. Columbus, Wis., Nov. 8, 1944; s. Delbert Charles and Agnes Clara (Balzer) S.; m. Sharon A. Rodhain, Mar. 20, 1982; 1 child, Barrett Von Schroeder. BS, U. Wis., Superior, 1969; MS, U. Idaho, 1972, MS. Mgr. far west Hudson's Bay & Annings, London, 1973-82; owner, mgr. Moscow (Idaho) Hide & Fur, 1973—; mem. Idaho Senate, Dist. 5, Boise, 1992—. Field editor Fur Fish Game, 1988—; pub. The Schroeder Report, 1987—. Pres. region 2 Idaho Wildlife Coun., 1991-92; mem. Black Bear Mgmt. Task Force, Idaho Dept. Fish and Game, Boise, Idaho, 1991-92; mem. consensus 2000 Moscow Sch. Dist., 1992—. With USN, 1962-65. Mem. Farm Bur., Am. Legion. Republican. Avocations: hunting, fishing, hiking, exotic poultry, politics. Office: Idaho Senate PO Box 8838 Moscow ID 83843-1338

SCHROEDER, GERALD FRANK, state supreme court justice; b. Boise, Idaho, Sept. 13, 1939; s. Frank Frederick and Josephine Ivy (Lucas) S.; m. Carole Ann McKenna, 1967; children: Karl Casteel, Erich Frank. BA magna cum laude, Coll. of Idaho (now Albertson Coll. of Idaho), 1961; JD, Harvard U., 1964. Bar: Idaho 1965. Assoc. Moffatt, Thomas, Barrett & Blanton, Boise, 1965-66; pvt. practice Boise, 1966-67; asst. U.S. atty. Dept. Justice, Boise, 1967-69; judge Ada County Probate Ct., Boise, 1969-71; magistrate State of Idaho, Boise, 1971-75; dist. judge U.S. Dist. Ct. (4th dist.) Idaho, 1975-95; justice Idaho Supreme Ct., 1995—. Instr. Boise Bar Rev., 1973—; adj. faculty law Boise State U., 1986-95; former mem. Gov. Coun. on Crime and Delinquency. Author: Idaho Probate Procedure, 1971; (novel) Triangle of the Sons-Phenomena, 1983; contbr. chpt. to history text. Bd. dirs. Boise Philharm. Assn., 1978-81; adminstrv. and dist. judge 4th dist. State of Idaho, 1985-95. Toll fellow Nat. Coun. State Govt., 1990. Mem. Idaho Bar Assn., Boise Racquet and Swim Club (pres. bd. dirs. 1991-93).

SCHROEDER, JULIAN IVAN, biology educator; b. Summit, N.J., June 11, 1958; s. Manfred Robert and Anny (Menschik) S.; m. Marion G. Spors, Aug. 9, 1991; children: Julia Sofia K., Nicola A.J. Dr. rer. nat., U. Gottingen, Max Planck Inst., 1987. Postdoctoral rschr. dept. physiology UCLA Sch. Medicine, 1988-90; from asst. to prof. dept. biology U. Calif. San Diego, La Jolla, 1990-2000, Novartis Endowed chair in plant scis., 2000—. Contbr. articles to profl. jours. Recipient Heinz Meier Leibnitz prize Deutsche Forschungs Gemeinschaft, 1984, Presdl. Young Investigator award NSF, 1991; Alexander von Humboldt fellow, 1988, 96. Mem. Biophys. Soc., Am. Assn. Plant Physiologists (Charles Albert Shull award 1997). Achievements include identification of ion channels in higher plant cells, characterization of their functions for membrane signal transduction; cloning and functional roles of mineral nutrient transporters in plant roots. Office: U Calif San Diego Div Biology Ctr Molec Gene 3500 Gilman Dr La Jolla CA 92093-0116 E-mail: JISchroeder@ucsd.edu

SCHROEDER, KENNETH L. electronics executive; b. 1946; BSEE, U. Wis.; MBA, U. Pa. Gen. mgr. constrn. sys. divsn. Spectra-Physics; ops. mgr. computer group Hewlett-Packard; pres., COO Genus, Inc.; various KLA-Tencor Corp., San Jose, Calif., pres., COO, 1991-99, CEO, 1999—. Bd. dirs. SEMI, GaSonics Internat. Office: KLA Tencor Corp 160 Rio Robles San Jose CA 95134 Fax: 408-875-3030

SCHROEDER, MARY MURPHY, federal judge; b. Boulder, Colo., Dec. 4, 1940; d. Richard and Theresa (Kahn) Murphy; m. Milton R. Schroeder, Oct. 15, 1965; children: Caroline Theresa, Katherine Emily. B.A., Swarthmore Coll., 1962; J.D., U. Chgo., 1965. Bar: Ill. 1966, D.C. 1966, Ariz. 1970. Trial atty. Dept. Justice, Washington, 1965-69; law clk. Hon. Jesse Udall, Ariz. Supreme Ct., 1970; mem. firm Lewis and Roca, Phoenix, 1971-75; judge Ariz. Ct. Appeals, Phoenix, 1975-79, U.S. Ct. Appeals (9th cir.), Phoenix, 1979-2000, chief judge, 2000—. Vis. instr. Ariz. State U. Coll. Law, 1976, 77, 78 Contbr. articles to profl. jours. Mem. ABA (Margaret Brent award 2001), Ariz. Bar Assn., Fed. Bar Assn., Am. Law Inst. (coun. mem.), Am. Judicature Soc., Soroptimists. Office: US Ct Appeals 9th Cir US Courthouse Ste 610 401 W Washington St SPC-54 Phoenix AZ 85003-2156 Fax: (602) 322-7329. E-mail: mary_schroeder@ca9.uscourts.gov

SCHROEDER, MICHAEL JOHN, lawyer; b. Grosse Pointe, Mich., Mar. 29, 1956; s. Paul James and Dessa Marie (Cheyovich) S.; 1 child, Sara. BA, Calif. State U., Fullerton, 1979; JD, U. So. Calif., Los Angeles, 1982. Bar: Calif. 1982, Hawaii 1987, U.S. Dist. Ct. (cen., ea., no. and so. dists.) Calif. 1987, U.S. Ct. Appeals (9th cir.) 1987, U.S. Dist. Ct. Hawaii 1990, U.S. Supreme Ct. 1990. Assoc. Wyman, Bautzer, Christensen, Kuchel & Silberg, Newport Beach, Calif., 1982-87; ptnr. Case, Schroeder, Knowlson, Mobley & Burnett, Newport Beach, 1987-90; of counsel Hart, King & Coldren, Santa Ana, 1991—. Bd. dirs. Legion Lex., U. So. Calif. Law Sch., Los Angeles, 1983—; gen. counsel Calif. Chiropractic Assn., Sacramento, 1983-91. Editor in chief Jour. Major Tax Planning, 1980-82, Jour. Computer/Law, 1980-82. Del. White Ho. Conf. on Productivity, San Diego, 1983; mem. George Deukmejian's Govt. Efficiency Team, Sacramento, 1982; pres. Calif. Rep. Assembly, 1991-93; mem. exec. com. Calif. Rep. Party, treas., 1993-95, vice-chmn., 1995-97, chmn., 1997-99. Mem. Calif. Bar Assn., Hawaii Bar Assn., Orange County Bar Assn. Republican. Roman Catholic. Avocations: traveling, photography, white water rafting. Office: Hart King & Coldren 200 E Sandpointe Ave Fl 4 Santa Ana CA 92707-5751

SCHROEDER, RITA MOLTHEN, retired chiropractor; b. Savanna, Ill., Oct. 25, 1922; d. Frank J. and Ruth J. (McKenzie) Molthen; m. Richard H. Schroeder, Apr. 23, 1948 (div.); children— Richard, Andrew, Barbara, Thomas, Paul, Madeline. Student, Chem. Engring., Immaculate Heart Coll., 1940-41, UCLA, 1941, Palmer Sch. of Chiropractic, 1947-49; D. Chiropractic, Cleve. Coll. of Chiropractic, 1961. Engring.-tooling design data coordinator Douglas Aircraft Co., El Segundo, Santa Monica and Long Beach, Calif., 1941-47; pres. Schroeder Chiropractic, Inc., 1982-93; dir. Pacific States Chiropractic Coll., 1978-80, pres. 1980-81. Recipient Palmer Coll. Ambassador award, 1973. Parker Chiropractic Research Found. Ambassador award, 1976, Coll. Ambassador award Life West Chiropractic Coll. Mem. Internat. Chiropractic Assn., Calif. Chiropractic Assn., Internat. Chiropractic Assn. Calif., Assn. Am. Chiropractic Coll. Presidents, Council Chiropractic Edn. (Pacific State Coll. rep.), Am. Pub. Health Assn., Royal Chiropractic Knights of the Round Table. Home: 8701 N State Highway 41 Spc 18 Fresno CA 93720-1010 Office: Schroeder Chiropractic Inc 2535 N Fresno St Fresno CA 93703-1831

SCHROEDER, WILLIAM JOHN, electronics executive; b. Havre de Grace, Md., June 9, 1944; s. William Martin and Dorothy Jeanne (McLaughlin) S.; m. Marilee Jane Alne, May 28, 1966; children: Kristen, Kari Britt, Kimberley. BSEE, Marquette U., 1967, MSEE, 1968; MBA, Harvard U., 1972. Devel. engr. Honeywell Inc., Mpls., 1968-70; mgmt. cons. McKinsey & Co., Los Angeles, 1972-76; mgr. product planning Memorex Corp., Santa Clara, Calif., 1976-78; pres. Priam Corp., San Jose, 1978-85, chmn., 1985-86; pres. Conner Peripherals, Inc., San Jose, 1986-89, vice chmn., 1989-94; CEO Arcada Software Inc., a Conner Co., 1993-94; pres., CEO Diamond Multimedia Systems, Inc., San Jose, Calif., 1994-99, CyberIQ Sys., Inc., San Jose, 2000. Bd. dirs. ShareWave Inc., El Dorado Hills, Calif., CNF, Inc., Palo Alto, Calif., AlphaSmart, Cupertino, Calif., RioPort.com, San Jose. Office: CyberIQ Sys Inc 225 Baypointe Pky San Jose CA 95134-1627 E-mail: billshradr@aol.com

SCHROEDER, WILLIAM ROBERT, graphic designer, actor, linguist; b. L.A., July 9, 1941; s. Robert Manville and Miriam Ruth (Sloop) S.; m. Marie Paule Fautrel, Sept. 7, 1963. BA, UCLA, 1964; BFA, Art Ctr. Coll. Design, Pasadena, Calif., 1971. Mailman U.S. Post Office, Santa Monica, Calif., 1967-71; art dir., prodr. N.W. Ayer/West, L.A., 1971-75; pres., gen. mgr. Advt. Ctr., L.A., 1976-77, Alouette Internat., Santa Monica, 1972—. Free-lance woodcarver, Santa Monica, 1981— ; free-lance actor, Hollywood, Calif., 1983—; real estate developer, 1989—. Appeared in feature films King of the Streets, 1983, The Forbidden Tome, 1984, The End of Innocence, 1985, Poltergeist II, 1986; prodr. TV commercials, 1972-75; author, creator computerized lang. courses Mattel Intellivision, 1980-82. Publicity mgr. Concerned Homeowners of Santa Monica, 1981-82. Recipient 1st Pl. award Belding award for Excellence in Advt., L.A., 1974; Cert. of Merit, Art Dirs. Club L.A., 1972. Mem. Am. Fedn. Radio and TV Artists, Santa Monica C. of C., Mensa (L.A.), Internat. Plastic Modelers Soc., The Planetary Soc., The Found. Brain Rsch., Astronomical Soc. Pacific, Internat. Soc. Philosophical Inquiry, Internat. Legion of Intelligence, Santa Monica Theatre Guild, The Air Mus. Libertarian. Office: Alouette Internat 1626 Montana Ave Santa Monica CA 90403-1808 E-mail: alouetteinternat@compuserve.com

SCHROETER, THOMAS G. federal government official, geologist; b. Ottawa, Can. BSc in Geology, Carleton U., 1969; MSc in Geology, U. Western Ont., 1971. Various positions Geol. Survey Can. and various mining cos., summers 1966-71; with minerals divsn. Amoco Can. Petroleum, Vancouver; dist. geologist B.C. Ministry Energy, Mines and Petroleum Resources, Smithers, 1973-86, sr. regional geologist Vancouver, 1986—. Bd. dirs. Vancouver Mining Exploration Group. Contbr. articles to profl. jours. Mem. Can Inst. Mining, Metallurgy and Petroleum (Julian Boldy Meml. award 2000), Assn. Profl. Engrs. and Geoscientists B.C., Geol. Assn. Can., Soc. Econ. Geologists. Office: Min Energy and Mines 865 Hornby St Rm 301 Vancouver BC Canada V6Z 2G3

SCHUB, CRAIG S. health science association administrator; BS in Bus. Adminstrn., Calif. State U.; postgrad., Calif State U. With Johnson & Johnson, Ethicon divsn., 1981-85; acct. supr. health care mktg., ad. agency; dir. corp. planning, devel. PacifiCare Health Systems, 1990-93, pres., Secure Horizons USA, 1993—. Bd. dirs. Orange County Chapt. Am. Red Cross; trustee Alliance Aging Rsch., Washington D.C. Office: PacifiCare Health Systems 3120 W Lake Center Dr Santa Ana CA 92704-6917

SCHUBERT, GLENDON, political scientist, educator; b. Oneida, N.Y., June 7, 1918; s. Glendon Austin and Agnes (Rogers) S.; m. Elizabeth Josephine Neal (dec. 1949); children: Frank, James; m. Elizabeth Harris (div.); children: Susan, Kathleen, Robin; m. Natalie Klavans, 1999. A.B., Syracuse U., 1940, Ph.D., 1948. Mem. faculties Syracuse U., 1946-48, UCLA, 1948-49, Howard U., 1949-50, Rutgers U., 1950-51, Franklin and Marshall Coll., 1951-52, Mich. State U., 1952-67, U. Minn., 1955; William Rand Kenan Jr. prof. polit. sci. U. N.C. at Chapel Hill, 1967-68; Univ. prof. York U., 1968-70; Univ. prof. polit. sci. U. Hawaii, 1970-2000, emeritus prof., 2000—; rsch. prof. polit. sci. So. Ill. U. at Carbondale, 1986-91. Fulbright lectr. U. Oslo, Norway, 1959-60; fellow Center for Advanced Study in Behavioral Scis., 1960-61; sr. scholar in residence Center for Cultural and Tech. Interchange Between East and West, U. Hawaii, 1963-64, 65; Fulbright-Hays research scholar, Netherlands, 1977; NSF faculty fellow U. Groningen, Netherlands, 1977-78; NATO sr. fellow, U.K.; fellow Netherlands Inst. Advanced Study Humanities and Social Sci., Wassenaar, Netherlands, 1978-79 Author 30 books; assoc. editor for biosocial behavior The Behavioral and Brain Sci., 1979—; adv. editor Jour. Social and Evolutionary Systems, 1980—; assoc. editor Politics and the Life Scis., 1980-90, contbr. articles to profl. jours. in biobehavioral and polit. sci., jud. behavior and politics, and pub. policy. Served with Signal Intelligence U.S. Army, 1942-46. Decorated Bronze Star; recipient Regents' medal and award for excellence in research U. Hawaii, 1975 Mem. Internat. Soc. Polit. Psychology, Am. Polit. Sci. Assn. (past mem. exec. coun., Career Lifetime Achievement award 1999), Assn. Polit. Life Scis. (past pres., Lifetime Career Achievement award 1994), Internat. Soc. Human Ethology, Phi Beta Kappa. E-mail: nklavans@yahoo.com

SCHUCK, CARL JOSEPH, lawyer; b. Phila., Nov. 21, 1915; s. Joseph and Christina (Schadl) S.; m. Mary Elizabeth Box, June 7, 1941; children: Mary Ann (dec.), John, James, Catherine, Christopher. BS, St. Mary's Coll., 1937; postgrad., U. So. Calif., 1937-38; JD, Georgetown U., 1941. Bar: D.C. 1940, Calif. 1943, U.S. Supreme Ct. 1952. Atty. Dept. Justice, Washington, 1940-42, Alien Property Custodian, San Francisco, 1942-44, Overton, Lyman & Prince, L.A., 1944-47, mem. firm 1947-79, profl. corp. mem. firm, 1979-85. Lectr. Practising Law Inst., 1973; Del. 9th Cir. Jud. Conf., 1963-80, chmn. lawyer-dels. com., 1972, mem. exec. com., 1976-80, chmn. exec. com., 1977-78, mem. sr. adv. bd., 1989-95; mem. disciplinary bd. State Bar Calif., 1970-71. Fellow Am. Coll. Trial Lawyers (chmn. com. on complex litigation 1979-81, regent 1981-85), L.A. County Bar Assn. (trustee 1974-76), Phi Alpha Delta. Club: Chancery (pres. 1984-85). Home and Office: 16916 Hierba Dr Apt 254 San Diego CA 92128-2679

SCHUDEL, HANSJOERG, international business consultant; b. Wald, Switzerland, Sept. 27, 1937; s. Rene and Alice S. Ed., Coll. Bus. Adminstrn., Zurich, Switzerland. With Byk-Gulden, Konstanz, Germany and Sao Paulo, Brazil, 1962-69, Hicksville, N.Y., 1964-69; pres., chief exec. officer, dir. Stinnes Corp., N.Y.C., 1971-83; exec. officer Stinnes A.G., Muelheim, Fed. Republic of Germany, 1978-83; rep. for the Americas First Arab Pacific Corp. Ltd., Chappaqua, N.Y., 1984—. Mem. German-Am. C. of C. (bd. dirs. 1976-83), Internat. World Travelers Club, Swiss Soc., Confrerie de la Chaine des Rotisseurs, Order des Coteaux de Champagne, Foothills Assn. (bd. dirs., pres.). Office: First Arab Pacific Corp Ltd PMB 307 1275 4th St Santa Rosa CA 95404-4056

SCHULER, JAMES K. construction executive; Chmn., pres., CEO Schuler Homes, Inc., Honolulu, 1973—. Office: Schuler Homes Inc 828 Fort Street Mall Ste 400 Honolulu HI 96813-4321

SCHULIAN, JOHN (NIELSEN SCHULIAN), screenwriter, author; b. L.A., Jan. 31, 1945; s. John and Estella Katherine (Nielsen) S.; m. Paula Lynn Ellis, Aug. 20, 1977 (div. Oct. 1984). BA, U. Utah, 1967; MS, Northwestern U., 1968. Copy editor Salt Lake City Tribune, 1968; reporter Balt. Evening Sun, 1970-75; sportswriter Washington Post, 1975-77; sports columnist Chgo. Daily News, 1977-78, Chgo. Sun-Times, 1978-84, Phila. Daily News, 1984-86; staff writer Miami Vice, Universal City, Calif., 1986-87, story editor, 1987, The Slap Maxwell Story, North Hollywood, 1987-88; exec. story editor TV series Wiseguy, Hollywood, 1988-89; co-producer TV series Midnight Caller, Burbank, Calif., 1989-90, supervising producer, 1990-91; co-exec. producer TV series Reasonable Doubts, Burbank, Calif., 1991-92; creative cons. TV series The Untouchables, L.A., 1992-93; co-exec. producer TV series Hercules, Universal City, Calif., 1994-96; co-creator Xena: Warrior Princess, Universal City, 1995; assoc. prodr. (documentary) Ben Johnson: Third Cowboy on the Right, 1996; co-exec. prodr. (TV series) Lawless, 1996-97; consulting prodr. (TV series) JAG, 1999-2000; exec. prodr. (TV series) The Outer Limits, Vancouver, Can., 2000-01. Spl. contbr. Sports Illustrated, 1998—. Author: Writers' Fighters and Other Sweet Scientists, 1983; contbg. editor Panorama mag., 1980-81; syndicated columnist UP Syndicate; commentator Nat. Pub. Radio, 1985-86; cons. The Reader's Catalog, 1989; contbr. articles to N.Y. Times, Playboy, Gentlemen's Quar., The National, L.A. Times; included in The Best Am. Sports Writing, 1994. Mem. Pacific Coast League Hist. Soc. With U.S. Army, 1968-70. Recipient Nat. Headliners Club award, 1980, Column Writing award AP Sports Editors, 1979, 82, Best Sports Stories award, 1983, 84, Nat Fleischer Excellence in Boxing Journalism award Boxing Writers Assn. Am., 1985. Mem. Writers Guild Am., Phi Beta Kappa. Office: Endeavor Talent Agy 9701 Wilshire Blvd 10th Fl Beverly Hills CA 90212 E-mail: jschulian@aol.com

SCHULLER, ROBERT HAROLD, clergyman, author; b. Alton, Iowa, Sept. 16, 1926; s. Anthony and Jennie (Beltman) S.; m. Arvella DeHaan, June 15, 1950; children: Sheila, Robert, Jeanne, Carol, Gretchen. B.A., Hope Coll., 1947; B.D., Western Theol. Sem., 1950; D.D., Hope Coll., 1973; LL.D., Azusa Pacific Coll., 1970, Pepperdine U., 1976; Litt.D., Barrington Coll., 1977. Ordained to ministry Reformed Ch. in Am., 1950; pastor Ivanhoe Ref. Ch., Chgo., 1950-55; founder, sr. pastor Garden Grove (Calif.) Community Ch., 1955—; founder, pres. Hour of Power TV Ministry, Garden Grove, 1970—; founder, dir. Robert H. Schuller Inst. for Successful Ch. Leadership, Garden Grove, 1970—; chmn. nat. religious sponsor program Religion in Am. Life, N.Y.C., 1975—. Bd. dirs. Freedom Found. Author: God's Way to the Good Life, 1963, Your Future Is Your Friend, 1964, Move Ahead with Possibility Thinking, 1967, Self Love, the Dynamic Force of Success, 1969, Power Ideas for a Happy Family, 1972, The Greatest Possibility Thinker That Ever Lived, 1973, Turn Your Scars into Stars, 1973, You Can Become the Person You Want To Be, 1973, Your Church Has Real Possibilities, 1974, Love or Loneliness— You Decide, 1974, Positive Prayers for Power-Filled Living, 1976, Keep on Believing, 1976, Reach Out for New Life, 1977, Peace of Mind Through Possibility Thinking, 1977, Turning Your Stress Into Strength, 1978, Daily Power Thoughts, 1978, The Peak to Peek Principle, 1981, Living Positively One Day at a Time, 1981, Self Esteem: The New Reformation, 1982, Tough Times Never Last, But, Tough People Do!, 1983, Tough Minded Faith for Tender hearted People, 1984, The Be-Happy Attitudes, 1985, Be Happy You Are Loved, 1986, Success is Never Ending, Failure is Never Final, 1988, Believe in the God Who Believes in You, 1989; co-author: The Courage of Carol, 1978. Bd. dirs. Religion in Am. Life; pres. bd. dirs. Christian Counseling Service; founder Robert H. Schuller Corr. Center for Possibility Thinkers, 1976. Recipient Disting. Alumnus award Hope Coll., 1970, Prin. award Freedoms Found., 1974; named Headliner of Year in Religion, Orange County, 1977, Clergyman of Year, Religious Heritage Am., 1977 Mem. Religious Guild Architects (hon.), AIA (bd. dirs. 1986—). Club: Rotary. Office: Religion Am Life 12141 Lewis St Garden Grove CA 92840-4627

SCHULMAN, ROBERT S. lawyer; b. N.Y.C., July 9, 1941; s. Donald Benedict and Edythe (Smythe) S.; m. Susan Jan Von Helbig, Sept. 18, 1974; children: Elizabeth Jane, Jennifer Lynn. BA, Rutgers U., New Brunswick, 1963; JD cum laude, Rutgers U., Newark, 1966. Bar: N.J. 1967, Calif. 1976, U.S. Dist. Ct. N.J. 1967, U.S. Supreme Ct. 1970, U.S. Dist. Cts. (ctrl., no., so., ea., dists.) Calif. 1976, U.S. Ct. Appeals (9th cir.) Calif. 1976. With Pitney, Hardin & Kipp, Newark, 1966-74; dept. atty. gen. Office of N.J. Atty. Gen., Trenton, 1974-75; assoc. Cox, Castle & Nicholson, L.A., 1976-80; ptnr. Zobrist, Garner & Garrett, L.A., 1980-83, Stephens, Berg, Lasater & Schulman, L.A., 1984-91, Crosby, Heafey, Roach & May, L.A., 1991—. Atty. Bd. of Edn., Fairview, N.J., 1972, Bd. of Adjustment, Fairview, N.J., 1971-73. Contbr. articles to profl. jours. Dir. Deafwest Theatre, L.A., Calif., 1991-97. Mem. State Bar of Calif., Calif. [illegible] Canada Flintridge CA 91011-3825 Office: Crosby Heafey Roach & May 700 S Flower St Los Angeles CA 90017-4101

SCHULMAN, TOM, screenwriter; BA, Vanderbilt Univ. Screenwriter CAA, Beverly Hills, Calif. Writer: (films) Dead Poets Society, 1989 (Academy award best original screenplay 1989), What About Bob?, 1991; co-writer: (films) Honey, I Shrunk the Kids, 1989, Second Sight, 1989, Medicine Man, 1992; exec. prodr.: (films) Indecent Proposal, 1993; writer, dir.: (film) Eight Heads in a Duffel Bag, 1997. Office: c/o CAA 9830 Wilshire Blvd Beverly Hills CA 90212-1804

SCHULTZ, VICTOR M. physician; b. Pitts., Aug. 14, 1932; s. Irvin and Rose (Reiss) S. BS, Kent (Ohio) State U., 1955; MD, Ohio State U., Columbus, 1958. Diplomate Am. Bd. Dermatology. Pvt. practice, Santa Monica, Calif., 1965—. Fellow Am. Acad. Dermatology, Pacific Dermatologic Assn.; mem. AMA, Am. Coll. Physicians, Calif. Med. Assn., L.A. County Med. Assn. Avocations: skiing, tennis, golf, music, swimming. Office: 2461 Santa Monica Blvd Santa Monica CA 90404-2049

SCHULZ, LAURA JANET, writer, retired secretary; b. Alba, Tex., Aug. 12, 1931; d. Joseph Clifton and Laura Oza (Carruth) English; m. Gordon Robert Schulz, Dec. 4, 1953; children: LeAnn Clarinda Schulz Barclay, Peggy Gaynell Schulz Lingbloom. Grad. h.s., Denison, Tex., 1948. Sec. history dept. Tex. Christian U., Ft. Worth, 1948-49; continuity editor Sta. KDSX, Denison, 1949-51; clk., typist Perrin AFB, Sherman, Tex., 1951-55; acctg. clk. England AFB, Alexandria, La., 1955; sec. Emile R. Jardine, CPA, Stockton, Calif., 1957-59; tchr. Little Meth. Pre-Sch., Lodi, 1968-69; sec. Heather, Sanguinetti, Caminata & Sakai, CPAs, Stockton, 1983-92; sec., feature writer, photographer Lodi (Calif.) Dist. C. of C., 1993-97. Author: Katy's Children, 1990, Little Rocky's True Adventures, 1991, Depot Days, 1999. Hon. life mem. Wesleyan Svc. Guild Trinity Meth. Ch., Denison, 1955—, Calif. Congress of PTA, 1984—; pres. PTA Needham Sch., Lodi, 1968-70; leader Camp Fire, Lodi, 1974-82; vol. advisor, tchr. Grapevine Newspaper Vinewood Sch., Lodi, 1974-82; tchr. First United Meth. Ch., Lodi, 1961-80, circle chair. Recipient Appreciation award Vinewood Sch., Lodi Unified Sch. Dist., 1974-82. Mem. Nat. League Am. Pen Women, Sierra Club. Democrat. Methodist. Avocations: photography, reading, walking, camping, nature. Home: 1910 W Tokay St Lodi CA 95242-3440

SCHULZ, RENATE ADELE, German studies and second language acquisition educator; b. Lohr am Main, Germany, Feb. 24, 1940; came to U.S., 1958; 1 child, Sigrid Diane. BS, Mankato State Coll., 1962; MA, U. Colo., 1967; PhD, Ohio State U., 1974. Edn. officer U.S. Peace Corps, Ife Ezinihitte, Nigeria, 1963-65; asst. prof. Otterbein Coll., Westerville, Ohio, 1974-76, State U. Coll. N.Y., Buffalo, 1976-77; from asst. to assoc. prof. U. Ark., Fayetteville, 1977-81; from assoc. to prof. U. Ariz., Tucson, 1981—, chair dept. German, 1984-90, chair PhD program in second lang. acquisition and teaching, 1994-97. Disting. vis. prof. USAF Acad., Colorado Springs, Colo., 1990-91. Author: Options for Undergraduate Foreign Language Programs, 1979, Lesen, Lachen, Lernen, 1983, Aktuelle Themen, 1987, Im Kontext: Lesebuch zur Landeskunde, 1990; mem. editorial bd. Modern Lang. Jour., 1985—. Recipient Creative Tchg. award U. Ariz. Found., Tucson, 1984, Stephen A. Freeman award N.W. Conf. Tchg. Fgn. Langs., 1984, Bundesverdienstkreuz, Fed. Govt. Germany, 1990. Mem. Am. Coun. Tchg. Fgn. Langs. (exec. coun. 1979-81, Florence Steiner award 1993), Am. Assn. Tchrs. German (v.p. 1988-90, pres. 1990-91, editor Die Unterrichtspraxis 1980-85), MLA (del. 1989-91), Tchrs. of ESL, Am. Assn. Applied Linguistics, Am. Assn. Tchrs. French. Office: U Ariz Dept German Studies Tucson AZ 85721-0067

SCHUMACHER, HENRY JEROLD, museum administrator, former career officer, business executive; b. Torrance, Calif., June 17, 1934; s. Henry John and Rene (Wilcox) S.; m. Barbara Howell, Aug. 24, 1958; children: Sheri Lynn, Henry Jerold II. Student, Stanford U., 1953; BS, U.S. Mil. Acad., 1957; MS, Northeastern U., Boston, 1965; MBA, Auburn U., 1977. Commd. lt. U.S. Army, 1958, advanced through grades to maj. gen., 1982; army attaché Moscow, 1969-71; chief communications ops. Vietnam, 1971-72; exec. officer Office Chief of Staff, 1972-75; comdr. U.S. Army Communications Command, Panama, 1977-79; dir. network integration, Office Asst. Chief of Staff Automation and Communications, Dept. Army, 1979-81; comdr. The White House Communications Agy., Washington, 1981-82; chief U.S. Army Signal Corps, 1981-83; ret., 1983; sr. v.p. Visa Internat., 1983-86; chief oper. officer Fuel Tech., Inc., Stamford, Conn., 1986-87; pres. IMM Systems, Phila., 1987-89; exec. v.p. Cylink Corp., Sunnyvale, Calif., 1990-95; exec. dir. Hiller Mus. of No. Calif. Aviation History, Redwood City, 1995-98; mng. gen. ptnr. Distributed Syss. Ptnrs., 1999—. Decorated Def. D.S.M., D.S.M., Legion of Merit. Home: 156 Normandy Ct San Carlos CA 94070-1519 E-mail: dspartners@excite.com

SCHUMACHER, THOMAS, film company executive; Grad., UCLA. Past mem. staff L.A. Music Ctr. Mark Taper Forum; past sr. v.p. feature animation Walt Disney Pictures, Burbank, Calif., exec. v.p. feature animation and theatrical prodns., 1996-98; pres. Walt Disney Feature Animation and Walt Disney Theatrical Prodns., 1999—. Line prodr. Olympic Arts Festival, 1984; asst. gen. mgr. L.A. Ballet; co-founder, assoc. dir. L.A. Festival of the Arts, 1987; mem. edn. coun. L.A. Music Ctr.; bd. dirs. Rachel Rosenthal Co. Prodr. film The Rescuers Down Under, 1990; exec. prodr. film The Lion King, 1994. Office: Walt Disney Pictures 500 S Buena Vista St Burbank CA 91521-0006

SCHUMAN, GERALD EUGENE, soil scientist, researcher; b. Sheridan, Wyo., July 5, 1944; s. George and Mollie (Michael) S.; m. Mabel F. Kaisler, Mar. 27, 1965; children: William G., Kara L. BS in Soil Sci., U. Wyo., 1966; MS in Soil Sci., U. Nev., 1969; PhD in Agronomy, U. Nebr., 1974. Cert. profl. soil scientist. Soil scientist USDA Agrl. Rsch. Svc., Reno, 1966-69, Lincoln, Nebr., 1969-75, Cheyenne, Wyo., 1975-77, soil scientist, rsch. leader, 1977-98, soil scientist, 1998—. Reclamation cons. HKM Assocs., Billings, Mont., 1986-88; vis. fellow U. Westrn Australia, 1996-97. Co-editor: Reclaiming Mine Soils, 1987, symposium proc. Soil and Overburgen in Reclamation, 1983; contbr. articles to profl. jours., book chpts. Mem., pres., elder, trustee Our Savior Luth. Ch., Cheyenne, 1975—. Recipient Profl. of Yr. award Orgn. Profl. Employees of USDA, 1988; named Outstanding Alumnus, Coll. Agr., U. Wyo., 2000. Fellow Soil Sci. Soc. Am., Am. Soc. Agronomy (cert.), Soil and Water Conservation Soc. (bd. dirs. 1986-89, commendation 1980), Soil Sci. Soc. Am., Soc. for Range Mgmt. (Man of the Range award Wyo. sect. 1993, Outstanding Achievement award 1995); mem. Am. Soc. Surface Mining and Reclamation (nat. exec. com. 1991-93, pres. 1992-93, Reclamation Rsch. award 1991), Internat. Soil Sci. Soc. Avocations: fishing, hunting, traveling. Office: High Plains Grasslands Rsch Sta 8408 Hildreth Rd Cheyenne WY 82009-8809

SCHURMAN, DAVID JAY, orthopedic surgeon, educator; b. Chgo., Apr. 25, 1940; s. Shepherd P. and Dorothy (Laskey) S.; m. Martha Ellen Rocker, Mar. 8, 1967; children: Hilary Sue, Theodore Shepherd. BA, Yale U., 1961; MD, Columbia U., 1965. Intern Baylor U., Houston, 1965-67; resident in gen. surgery Mt. Sinai Hosp., N.Y.C., 1966-67; resident in orthop. surgery UCLA, 1969-72; asst. rsch. surgeon UCLA Med. Sch., 1972-73; asst. prof. orthopedic surgery Stanford Med. Sch., 1973-79, assoc. prof., 1979-87, prof., 1987—. Acting chief divsn. orthop. surgery Stanford U. Med. Ctr., 1990-93, fellowship dir. total joint replacement, 1983—, fellowship dir. sports medicine, 1992-95, dir. orthop. rsch. lab., 1973—. Capt. USAF, 1967-69. Fellow NIH, 1972-73; grantee NIH, 1976-96; recipient Top Dr. award, San Francisco Mag. Mem. Am. Orthopaedic Assn. (bd. dirs. 1994-95), Clin. Orthopaedics and Related Rsch. (bd. dirs. 1994-00), Assn. Bone and Joint Surgeons (v.p. 1996-97, pres. 1997-98). Office: Stanford U Sch Medicine R144 Divsn Orthop Surgery 300 Pasteur Dr Palo Alto CA 94304-2203

SCHUSTER, PHILIP FREDERICK , II, lawyer, writer; b. Denver, Aug. 26, 1945; s. Philip Frederick and Ruth Elizabeth (Robar) S.; m. Barbara Lynn Nordquist, June 7, 1975; children: Philip Christian, Matthew Dale. BA, U. Wash., 1967; JD, Willamette U., 1972. Bar: Oreg. 1972, U.S. Dist. Ct. Oreg. 1974, U.S. Ct. Appeals (9th cir.) 1986, U.S. Supreme Ct. 1986. Dep. dist. atty. Multnomah County, Portland, Oreg., 1972; title examiner Pioneer Nat. Title Co., Portland, 1973-74; assoc. Buss, Leichner et al, Portland, 1975-76; from assoc. to ptnr. Kitson & Bond, Portland, 1976-77; pvt. practice Portland, 1977-95; ptnr. Dierking and Schuster, Portland, 1996—. Arbitrator Multnomah County Arbitration Program, 1985—; student mentor Portland Pub. Schs., 1988—. Author: The Indian Water Slide, 1999; contbg. author OSB CLE Publ., Family Law; contbr. articles to profl. jours. Organizer Legal Aid Svcs. for Community Clinics, Salem, Oreg. and Seattle, 1969-73; Dem. committeeman, Seattle, 1965-70; judge Oreg. State Bar and Classroom Law Project, H.S. Mock Trial Competition, 1988—. Mem. ABA, ATLA, NAACP (exec. bd. Portland, Oreg. chpt. 1979-98), ACLU, Multnomah Bar Assn. (Vol. Lawyers Project), Internat. Platform Assn., Alpha Phi Alpha. Avocations: river drifting, camping, swimming, walking, writing. Office: 3565 NE Broadway St Portland OR 97232-1820 E-mail: schuster@pcez.com

SCHUTZ, JOHN ADOLPH, historian, educator, former university dean; b. L.A., Apr. 10, 1919; s. Adolph J. and Augusta K. (Gluecker) S. AA, Bakersfield Coll., 1940; BA, UCLA, 1942, MA, 1943, PhD, 1945. Asst. prof. history Calif. Inst. Tech., Pasadena, 1945-53; assoc. prof. history Whittier (Calif.) Coll., 1953-56, prof., 1956-65; prof. Am. history U. So. Calif., L.A., 1965-91, chmn. dept. history, 1974-76, dean social scis. and communication, 1976-82. Author: William Shirley: King's Governor of Massachusetts, 1961, Peter Oliver's Origin and Progress of the American Rebellion, 1967, The Promise of America, 1970, The American Republic, 1978, Dawning of America, 1981, Spur of Fame: Dialogues of John Adams and Benjamin Rush, 1980, 2001, A Noble Pursuit: A Sesquicentennial History of the New England Historic Genealogical Society, 1995, Legislators of the Massachusetts General Court, 1691-1780, 1997; joint editor: Golden State Series; contbg. author: Spain's Colonial Outpost, 1985, Generations and Change: Genealogical Perspectives in Social History, 1986, Making of America: Society and Culture of the United States, 1990, rev. edit., 1992, Encyclopedia Britannica. Trustee Citizens Rsch. Found., 1985-99; mem. Neighborwatch, L.A., 1999—. NEH grantee, 1971; Sr. Faculty grantee, 1971-74; U. Calif. fellow, 1944-45. Mem. Am. Hist. Assn. (pres. Pacific Coast br. 1972-73, sec.-treas. 1951-88, 95-96), Am. Studies Assn. (pres. 1974-75), Mass. Hist. Soc. (corr.), New Eng. Hist. Geneal. Soc. (trustee 1988-2000, trustee emeritus 2001—, editor, author intro. book Boston Merchant Census of 1789, 1989, rec. sec. 1995—), Colonial Soc. Mass. (corr.). Home and Office: 1100 White Knoll Dr Los Angeles CA 90012-1353 E-mail: jschutz@rcj.usc.edu

SCHUYLER, ROBERT LEN, investment company executive; b. Burwell, Nebr., Mar. 4, 1936; s. Norman S. and Ilva M. (Hoppes) S.; m. Mary Carol Huston, June 13, 1958; children: Kylie Anne, Nina Leigh, Melynn Kae, Gwyer Lenn. BS, U. Nebr., 1958; MBA, Harvard U., 1960. Asst. to treas. Potlatch Forests, Inc., Lewiston, Idaho, 1962-64, dir. corp. planning San Francisco, 1964-66; mgr. fin. analysis Weyerhaeuser Co., Tacoma, 1966-68, mgr. investment evaluation dept., 1968-70, v.p. fin. and planning, 1970-72, sr. v.p. fin. and planning, 1972-85, exec. v.p., chief fin. officer, 1985-91; mng. ptnr. Nisqually Ptnrs., Tacoma, 1991-95; bd. dirs. Grande Alberta Paper, Ltd., 1992—. Past mem. nat. adv. bd. Chem. Bank, U. Wash. MBA program, coun. fin. exec. Conf. Bd., Pvt. Sector Coun., exec. com. Am. Paper Inst.; bd. dirs. Paragon Trade Brands Inc., Montrail, Inc. Past chmn. Santa Fe County Bd. Econ. Advs.; chmn. Santa Fe Bus. Incubator; past trustee Santa Fe Chamber Music Festival; commr. N.Mex. Dept. Econ. Devel. Mem. Anglers Club, Sangre de Cristo Flyfishers, Las Campanas Golf & Country Club, Don Quixote Club. Home and Office: 46 Hollyhock Cir Santa Fe NM 87501-8595 E-mail: skysantafe@msn.com

SCHWAB, CHARLES R. brokerage house executive; b. Sacramento, 1937; m. Helen O'Neill; 5 children. , Stanford U., 1959, postgrad., 1961. Formerly mut. fund mgr., Marin County, Calif.; founder brokerage San Francisco, 1971; now chmn., CEO Charles Schwab & Co., Inc. Author: How to be Your Own Stockbroker, 1984. Republican. Office: Charles Schwab & Co Inc 101 Montgomery St San Francisco CA 94104-4175

SCHWABE, ARTHUR DAVID, physician, educator; b. Varel, Germany, Feb. 1, 1924; came to U.S., 1938, naturalized, 1943; s. Curt and Frieda (Roseno) S. M.D., U. Chgo., 1956. Intern UCLA Med. Center, 1956-57, asst. resident, then assoc. resident medicine, 1957-59, chief resident medicine, 1960-61, USPHS fellow gastroenterology, 1959-60; now mem. staff; chief gastroenterology Harbor Gen. Hosp., Torrance, Calif., 1962-67; cons. Wadsworth VA Center, Los Angeles; mem. faculty UCLA Med. Sch., 1961—, asst. prof. medicine, 1962-67, assoc. prof., 1967-71, prof., 1971-89, chief div. gastroenterology, 1967-88, vice chmn. dept. medicine, 1971-74, emeritus prof., 1989—. Contbr. articles to profl. jours. Served with AUS, 1943-46. Recipient UCLA Golden Apple award sr. class UCLA, 1967, 70, Outstanding Tchr. award UCLA Med. House Staff, 1968, 78, Disting. Teaching award UCLA, 1971, S.M. Mellinkoff Faculty award, 1983; Edward F. Kraft scholar, 1951; Ambrose and Gladys Bowyer fellow medicine, 1958-59 Fellow ACP; mem. Am. Gastroenterol. Assn., N.Y. Acad. Sci., So. Calif. Soc. Gastroenterology (pres. 1969), Western Assn. Physicians, Western Soc. Clin. Investigation, Western Gut Club (chmn. 1969-70), Alpha Omega Alpha. Office: 10833 Le Conte Ave Los Angeles CA 90095-3075

SCHWARTZ, DONALD, chemistry educator; b. Scarsdale, N.Y., Dec. 27, 1927; s. Harry A. and Ethel S.; m. Lois Schwartz, Sept. 8, 1948; children: Leanne, Mark W., Scott B., Bradley F. B.S., U. Mo., 1949; M.S., Mont. State U., 1951; Ph.D., Pa. State U., 1955. Program dir. NSF, 1966-68; asso. dean Grad. Sch., Memphis State U., 1968-70; dean advanced studies Fla. Atlantic U., Boca Raton, 1970-71; v.p., acting pres. State U. N.Y., Buffalo, 1971-74; chancellor Ind. U.-Purdue U., Ft. Wayne, Ind., 1974-78; chancellor, prof. U. Colo., Colorado Springs, 1978-83, prof., 1983-93, prof. emeritus, 1993—. Cons. in field. Author papers structure of coal and organo-titanium compounds, also on higher edn. Bd. dirs. Colorado Springs Osteo. Found., 1985—. Served with USCG, 1945. Research fellow AEC, 1953-55; N.Y. State fellow, 1947-48 Mem. Am. Chem. Soc., AAAS, Sigma Xi, Phi Lambda Upsilon, Phi Delta Kappa. Clubs: Rotary, Shriners. Home: 21 Sanford Rd Colorado Springs CO 80906-4219

SCHWARTZ, EDWARD J. federal judge; b. 1912; Judge Mcpl. Ct. and Superior Ct., San Diego; judge U.S. Dist. Ct. for So. Dist. Calif., former chief judge, now sr. judge. Office: US Dist Ct 4134 US Courthouse 940 Front St San Diego CA 92101-8994

SCHWARTZ, LEON, foreign language educator; b. Boston, Aug. 22, 1922; s. Charles and Celia (Emer) S.; m. Jeanne Gurtat, Mar. 31, 1949; children— Eric Alan, Claire Marie. Student, Providence Coll., 1939-41; BA, UCLA, 1948; certificat de phonetique, U. Paris, 1949; MA, U. So. Cal., 1950, PhD, 1962. Tchr. English, Spanish and Latin Redlands (Calif.) Jr. High Sch., 1951-54; high sch. tchr. Spanish and French, 1954-59; prof. French Calif. State U., Los Angeles, 1959-87, chmn. dept. fgn. langs. and lit., 1970-73, prof. emeritus, 1987—. Author: Diderot and the Jews, 1981. Served as 2d lt. USAAF, 1942-45. Decorated Air medal with 5 oak leaf clusters; recipient Outstanding Prof. award Calif. State U. L.A., 1976 Mem. Am. Assn. Tchrs. French, Modern and Classical Lang. Assn. So. Calif., Am. Soc. 18th Century Studies, Société Diderot, Calif. State U. L.A. Emeriti Assn. (pres. 1998-2000), Phi Beta Kappa, Phi Kappa Phi, Pi Delta Phi, Sigma Delta Pi, Alpha Mu Gamma. Office: Calif State U Dept Modern Langs and Lit Los Angeles CA 90032 E-mail: l_schwar@pacbell.net

SCHWARTZ, LOUIS BROWN, law educator; b. Phila., Feb. 22, 1913; s. Samuel and Rose (Brown) S.; m. Berta Wilson, Mar. 29, 1937 (div. 1954); children: Johanna, Victoria; m. Miriam Robbins Humboldt, Sept. 16, 1964. B.S. in Econs, U. Pa., 1932, J.D., 1935. Bar: Pa. 1935, U.S. Supreme Ct. 1942. Atty. SEC, Washington, 1935-39; chief gen. crimes and spl. projects sect. Dept. Justice, 1939-43, chief judgment and enforcement sect. antitrust div., 1945-46; also mem. inter-departmental coms. on war crimes and status-of-forces treaties; prof. law U. Pa. Law Sch., 1946-83, Benjamin Franklin prof., 1964-83; prof. law Hastings Coll. Law, U. Calif., 1983-98, emeritus prof., 1998—. Vis. prof. Harvard U., Columbia U., U. Calif. at Berkeley, Cambridge (Eng.) U.; Ford vis. Am. prof. Inst. Advanced Legal Studies, U. London (Eng.), 1974; vis. disting. prof. Ariz. State U., 1980; mem. Atty. Gen.'s Nat. Com. Study Antitrust Laws, 1954-55, Pa. Gov.'s Commn. on Penal and Correctional Affairs, 1956-60; adv. commn. Revision Pa. Penal Code, 1963-68; nat. adv. council Nat. Defender Project, 1964-69; dir. Nat. Commn. on Reform of Fed. Criminal Laws, 1968-71; co-reporter Model Penal Code Am. Law Inst., 1962; cons. FTC, Dept. Justice, other agencies. Author: Free Enterprise and Economic Organization, 1959, 6th edit. (with John J. Flynn, Harry First) titled Antitrust and Government Regulation, 1983-85 (2 vols.), Le Système Pénal des Etats-Unis, 1964, Law Enforcement Handbook for Police, 1970, 2d edit., 1979, Proposed Federal Criminal Code, (with Comments and Working Papers), 1971; contbr. numerous articles to profl. jours. Served as lt. (j.g.) USNR, 1944-45. Mem. Ams. Democratic Action (nat. bd.), Am. Law Inst. (adv. com. pre-arraignment code), Order of Coif. Home: San Francisco Towers 1661 Pine St Apt 945 San Francisco CA 94109-0423 Office: U Calif Hastings Coll Law 200 Mcallister St San Francisco CA 94102-4707

SCHWARTZ, MILTON LEWIS, federal judge; b. Oakland, Calif., Jan. 20, 1920; s. Colman and Selma (Lavenson) S.; m. Barbara Ann Moore, May 15, 1942; children: Dirk L., Tracy Ann, Damon M., Brooke. A.B., U. Calif. at Berkeley, 1941, J.D., 1948. Bar: Calif. bar 1949. Rsch. asst. 3d Dist. Ct. Appeal, Sacramento, 1948; dep. dist. atty., 1949-51; practice in Sacramento, 1951-79; partner McDonough, Holland, Schwartz & Allen, 1953-79; U.S. dist. judge Eastern Dist. Calif., U.S. Dist. Ct., Calif., 1979-90, sr. judge, 1990—. Prof. law McGeorge Coll. Law, Sacramento, 1952-55; mem. Com. Bar Examiners Calif., 1971-75 Pres. Bd. Edn. Sacramento City Sch. Dist., 1961; v.p. Calif. Bd. Edn., 1967-68; trustee Sutterville Heights Sch. Dist. Served to maj. 40th Inf. Divsn. AUS, 1942-46, PTO. Named Sacramento County Judge of Yr., 1990; Milton L. Schwartz Am. Inn of Court named in his honor, Davis, Calif. Fellow Am. Coll. Trial Lawyers; mem. State Bar Calif., Am. Bar Assn., Am. Bd. Trial Advocates, Anthony M. Kennedy Am. Inn of Ct. (pres. 1988-90, pres. emeritus 1990—). Office: US Dist Ct Rm 15 200 501 I St Sacramento CA 95814

SCHWARTZ, ROBERT JOHN, landscape contractor, landscape designer; b. Elkhorn, Wis., June 14, 1954; s. Robert Knilans and Mary Cosella (Fleming) S. 2 BS degrees cum laude, U. Wis., Stevens Point, 1976; AA in Landscape Design ad hoc, U. Minn., 1985; AA, Calif. Poly. Inst., Pomona. Lic. landscape contractor, Calif., Nev. Real estate broker, salesman McKy-Ellis Realtors Madison Wis., Janesville, Wis., 1979-80; sole proprietor Teutonic Landscapes Co., Milw., 1982-85, Rancho Cucamonga, Calif., 1985-88, Rialto, 1989-96, Las Vegas, Nev., 1996—. Supporter St. Joseph's Indian Sch., Chamberlain, S.D., 1986—, Mercy Home for Boys and Girls, Chgo., 1986—, Asian Relief, Inc., Riverdale, Md., 1986—, So. Poverty Law Ctr., Montgomery, Ala., 1991-93; active The Heritage Found., Washington, 1992—, The Wall of Liberty Nat. Found., Washington, 1993—, Am. Conservative Union, Washington, 1993—. Recipient City Hall Coun. citations City of Claremont, Calif., 1986-87, City of Upland, Calif., 1989. Democrat. Avocations: para-sailing, traveling, ancient and medieval European Armaments collecting. Home and Office: Mission West Pools Inc 1750 S Rainbow Ave Ste 11 Las Vegas NV 89102 Address: 9709 Double Rock Dr Las Vegas NV 89134

SCHWARTZ, WILLIAM BENJAMIN, internist, educator; b. Montgomery, Ala., May 16, 1922; s. William Benjamin and Molly (Vendruff) S.; children: Eric A., Kenneth B., Laurie A. M.D., Duke U., 1945. Diplomate: Am. Bd. Internal Medicine (mem. test com. nephrology). Intern, then asst. resident medicine U. Chgo. Clinics, 1945-46; asst. medicine Peter Bent Brigham Hosp., Boston; also research fellow medicine Harvard Med. Sch., 1948-50; fellow medicine Children's Hosp., Boston, 1949-50; mem. faculty Tufts U. Sch. Medicine, 1950-96, prof. medicine, 1958-96, Endicott prof., 1975-76, Vannevar Bush Univ. prof., 1976-96, chmn. dept. medicine, 1971-76; mem. staff New Eng. Center Hosps., 1950-59, sr. physician, chief renal service, 1959-71, physician-in-chief, 1971-76; prof. medicine U. So. Calif., L.A., 1992—; disting. physician Dept. VA, 1994-97. Established investigator Am. Heart Assn., 1956-61; chmn. gen. medicine study sect. NIH, 1965-69; mem. sci. adv. bd. USAF, 1965-68, Nat. Kidney Found., 1968— , chmn., 1970—; mem. tng. com. Nat. Heart Inst., 1969-70; prin. adviser health scis. program, Rand Corp., 1977-88. Author numerous articles in field. Markle scholar med. scis., 1950-55 Mem. Inst. Medicine NAS, Am. Soc. Nephrology (pres. 1974-75), Acad. Arts and Scis., ACP, Am. Fedn. Clin. Research, Am. Physiol. Soc., Am. Soc. Clin. Investigation, Assn. Am. Physicians, Phi Beta Kappa, Sigma Xi, Alpha Omega Alpha. Office: U So Calif 1355 San Pablo St Ste 144 Los Angeles CA 90033-1026

SCHWARZ, GLENN VERNON, newspaper editor; b. Chgo., Nov. 24, 1947; s. Vernon Edward and LaVerne Louise (Schuster) S.; m. Cynthia Frances Meisenhoelder, June 17, 1984; 1 child, Chloe. BA, San Francisco State U., 1970. Sports writer San Francisco Examiner, 1970-87, sports editor, 1988—. Fundraiser San Francisco Zoological Soc., 1987—. Mem. AP Sports Editors, Baseball Writers Assn. Am. (bd. dirs. 1986-87). Avocation: nature travel. Office: San Francisco Examiner 110 5th St San Francisco CA 94103-2918

SCHWARZ, JOHN HENRY, theoretical physicist, educator; b. North Adams, Mass., Nov. 22, 1941; s. George and Madeleine (Haberfeld) S.; m. Patricia Margaret Moyle, July 11, 1986. AB, Harvard U., 1962; PhD, U. Calif., Berkeley, 1966. Instr. physics Princeton (N.J.) U., 1966-69, asst. prof., 1969-72; research assoc. Calif. Inst. Tech., Pasadena, 1972-85, Harold Brown prof. theoretical physics, 1985—. Co-author: Superstring Theory, 1987. Trustee Aspen (Colo.) Ctr. for Physics, 1982—. Recipient Dirac medal Internat. Ctr. for Theoretical Physics, 1989; Guggenheim fellow, 1978-79, MacArthur Found. fellow, 1987. Fellow NAS, Am. Phys. Soc., Phi Beta Kappa (vis. scholar 1990-91). Office: Calif Inst Tech # 452 48 Pasadena CA 91125-0001

SCHWARZ, STEVEN EMANUEL, electrical engineering educator, administrator; b. L.A., Jan. 29, 1939; s. Carl and Lillian Schwarz; m. Janet Lee Paschal, July 27, 1963. BS, Cal Tech, 1959, MS, 1961, PhD, 1964; AM, Harvard U., 1962. From asst. prof. to prof. elec. engring. U. Calif., Berkeley, 1964-99, assoc. dean Coll. Engring., 1991-96, prof. emeritus, 1999. Author: Electromagnetics for Engineers, 1990; co-author: Electrical Engineering, An Introduction, 1984, 93; contbr. articles to profl. jours. Guggenheim fellow, 1971-72. Fellow IEEE. Office: U Calif Berkeley Electrical Engring Dept 231 Cory Hall Berkeley CA 94720-1713

SCHWARZER, WILLIAM W, federal judge; b. Berlin, Apr. 30, 1925; came to U.S., 1938, naturalized, 1944; s. John F. and Edith M. (Daniel) S.; m. Anne Halbersleben, Feb. 2, 1951; children: Jane Elizabeth, Andrew William. AB cum laude, U. So. Calif., 1948; LLB cum laude, Harvard U., 1951. Bar: Calif. 1953, U.S. Supreme Ct. 1967. Teaching fellow Harvard U. Law Sch., 1951-52; asso. firm McCutchen, Doyle, Brown & Enersen, San Francisco, 1952-60, ptnr., 1960-76; judge U.S. Dist. Ct (no. dist.) Calif., San Francisco, 1976—; dir. Fed. Jud. Ctr., Washington, 1990-95. Sr. counsel Pres.'s Commn. on CIA Activities Within the U.S., 1975; chmn. U.S. Jud. Conf. Com. Fed.-State Jurisdiction, 1987-90; mem. faculty Nat. Inst. Trial Advocacy, Fed. Jud. Ctr., All-ABA, U.S.-Can. Legal Exch., 1987, Anglo-U.S. Jud. Exch., 1994-95, Salzburg Seminar on Am. Studies; disting. prof. Hastings Coll. Law U. Calif. Author: Managing Antitrust and Other Complex Litigation, 1982, Civil Discovery and Manadatory Disclosure, 1994, Federal Civil Procedure Before Trial, 1994; contbr. articles to legal publs., aviation jours. Trustee World Affairs Coun. No. Calif., 1961-88; chmn. bd. trustees Marin Country Day Sch., 1963-66; mem. Marin County Aviation Commn., 1969-76; mem. vis. com. Harvard Law Sch., 1981-86. Served with Intelligence, U.S. Army, 1943-46. Fellow Am. Coll. Trial Lawyers (S. Gates award 1992), Am. Bar Found.; mem. ABA (Meador Rosenberg award 1995), Am. Law Inst., San Francisco Bar Assn., State Bar Calif., Coun. Fgn. Rels. Office: 450 Golden Gate Ave San Francisco CA 94102-3661

SCHWENDIMAN, DAVE J. prosecutor; Asst. U.S. atty. State of Utah, Salt Lake City. Office: US Attys Office 185 S St Ste 400 Salt Lake City UT 84103-4139

SCHWERIN, KARL HENRY, anthropology educator, researcher; b. Bertha, Minn., Feb. 21, 1936; s. Henry William and Audrey Merle (Jahn) S.; m. Judith Drewanne Altermatt, Sept. 1, 1958 (div. May 1975); children: Karl Frederic, Marguerite DelValle; m. Partha Louise Hake Buell, Jan. 25, 1979; stepchildren: Tamara, Brent, Taryn. BA, U. Calif., Berkeley, 1958; PhD, UCLA, 1965. Instr. Los Angeles State Coll., 1963; asst. prof. anthropology U. N.Mex., Albuquerque, 1963-68, assoc. prof., 1968-72, prof., 1972-2001, asst. chmn. dept. anthropology, 1983-85, chmn. dept. anthropology, 1987-93, prof. emeritus, 2001—. Prof. invitado Inst. Venezolano de Investigaciones Cientificas, Caracas, 1979. Author: Oil and Steel Processes of Karinya Culture Change, 1966, Antropologia Social, 1969, Winds Across the Atlantic, 1970; editor: Food Energy in Tropical Ecosystems, 1985; contbr. articles to profl. jours. V.p. Parents without Ptnr., Albuquerque, 1976-77. Grantee Cordell Hull Found., Venezuela, 1961-62, N.Y. Zool. Soc., Honduras, 1981; Fulbright scholar Cañar, Ecuador, 1969-70, Paris, 1986; founded Karl H. Schwerin Fellowship in Ethnology. Fellow Am. Anthropol. Assn.; mem. Am. Ethnol. Soc., Am. Soc. Ethnohistory (pres. 1975), Southwestern Anthropol. Assn. (co-editor Southwestern Jour. Anthropology 1972-75), N.Mex. Cactus and Succulent Soc. (v.p. 1970-71), Internat. Congress of Americanists (35th-40th, 43d, 46th, 48th, 49th, 50th), Sigma Xi (chpt. pres. 1980-81). Avocations: photography, gardening, hiking, camping, cycling. Office: U NMex Dept Anthropology Albuquerque NM 87131-0001 E-mail: schwerin@unm.edu

SCHWICHTENBERG, DARYL ROBERT, drilling engineer; b. nr. Tulare, S.D., Nov. 8, 1929; s. Robert Carl and Lillian Rose (Hardie) S.; m. Helen M. Spencer, 1955 (div. Jan. 1971); children: Helayne, Randall, Hyalyn, Halcyon, Rustan; m. Helen Elizabeth Doehring, Nov. 11, 1971 (div. May 1982); 1 child, Suzanne. Student, U. Wyo., 1954-55; BSME, S.D. Sch. Mines and Tech., 1957; postgrad., Alexander Hamilton Inst., N.Y.C., 1962-63. Lic. pilot, rated AMEL. Office engr. Ingersoll-Rand Co., Mpls., 1957-58, sub br. mgr. Duluth, Minn., 1959-60, product engr. N.Y.C., 1960-63, devel. engr., 1964, sales mgr. Phillipsburg, N.J., 1965; pres., founder Daryl Drilling Co., Inc., Flagstaff, Ariz., 1965-82; pres. Silent Rose Mining Co., Fallon, Nev., 1982-85; sr. design engr. Nev. Test Site Fenix & Scisson, 1985-90; prin. project engr. Raytheon Svcs. Nev., 1990-95, project mgr., 1995-96; asst.project mgr. Bechtel Nev., Las Vegas, 1996—. Co-owner, mgr. Dead Shot Ranch, Bondurant, Wyo., 1977-82. Inventor electronic subtitling for opera patrons. 1st lt. U.S. Army, 1950-54, Korea. Decorated Bronze Star. Mem. ASME, NRA, VFW, Inst. Shaft Drilling Tech. (speaker, instr. 1986-96), Am. Legion, Mensa, Ducks Unlimited, The Will James Soc. Republican. Avocations: hunting, raising and training horses, flying, prospecting. Office: Bechtel Nev M S NTS 330 PO Box 98521 Las Vegas NV 89193-8521

SCHWIETZ, ROGER L. bishop; Ordained priest Roman Cath. Ch., 1967, consecrated bishop, 1990. Bishop Diocese of Duluth, Minn., 1989-99; archbishop Archdiocese of Anchorage, 1999—. Home: 7538 Stanley Anchorage AK 99518 Office: Archdiocese of Anchorage 225 Cordova St Anchorage AK 99501-2409

SCHWIMMER, SIGMUND, food enzymologist; b. Cleve., Sept. 20, 1917; s. Solomon and Sarah (Brown) S.; m. Sylvia Klein, Dec. 18, 1941; children— Susan, Elaine. Student Ohio State U., 1935-36; B.S., George Washington U., 1940; M.S., Georgetown U., 1941, Ph.D., 1943. From lab. asst. to research chemist USDA, Washington and Berkeley, Calif., 1936-62; adj. prof. biology Calif. Inst. Tech., Pasadena, 1963-65; chief research biochemist USDA, Berkeley, 1966-72, collaborator emeritus, 1975— ; adj. prof. dept. nutritional scis. U. Calif.-Berkeley, 1985-87; sr. expert biochemistry UN Indsl. Devel. Orgn., Haifa, Israel, 1973-74; cons. food enzymology, Berkeley, 1980— ; lectr. dept. biotech. food engring. Israel Inst. Tech., Haifa, 1973; vis. scientist Food Industry Rsch. and Devel. Inst., Hsinchu, Taiwan, 1992. Contbr. articles to profl. jours.; editor, Biochem. Sci. Biotech., Cambridge, Eng., 1983—, Trends in Biochemistry, Trends in Biotechnology, 1983—, Jour. Food Biochemistry, 1977-98; author: Source Book of Food Enzymology, 1982 (Jour. Assn. Coll. and Research Librarians award 1983). Fellow John S. Guggenheim, NSF; recipient Superior Service award USDA, 1949, 59, Lifetime Achievement award, 1993, Agrl. and Food Chemistry Divsn. award Am. Chem. Soc., 1996. Fellow Inst. Food Technologists; mem. Am. Soc. Biochemistry Molecular Biology, Sigma Xi. Office: Western Regional Ctr USDA 800 Buchanan St Berkeley CA 94710-1105 also: U Calif Dept Nutritional Sci Berkeley CA 94720-0001

SCIFRES, DONALD RAY, semiconductor laser, fiber optics and electronics company executive; b. Lafayette, Ind. m. Carol Scifres. B.S., Purdue U., 1968; M.S., U. Ill., 1970, Ph.D., 1972. Rsch. and tchg. asst. U. Ill., Urbana, 1968-72; rsch. fellow, area mgr. Xerox Corp., Palo Alto, Calif., 1972-83; founder, pres., CEO SDL, Inc., San Jose, 1983-2001, dir., 1983-2001, chmn., 1992-2001; co-chmn. JDS Uniphase Corp., 2001—; pes. Transmission & Amplification Bus. Group, 2001—. Nat. lectr. IEEE Quantum Electronics Soc., 1979 Bd. editors Jour. Fiber and Integrated Optics, 1978; mem. editorial adv. bd. Photonics Spectra, 1992—; contbr. articles to tech. jours.; patentee in field. Recipient Disting. Engring. Alumni award Purdue U., 1990, Outstanding Elec. Engr. award, 1992, Engring. Alumni award U. Ill., 1991, Alumni Honor award, 1993, Distinction in Photonics award Laurin Pub. Co., 1999; U. Ill. fellow, 1968; Gen. Telephone and Electronics fellow, 1970-72. Fellow IEEE (Jack Morton award 1985, 3d Millenium award 2000), IEEE Lasers and Electro-Optics Soc. (pres. 1992, Engring. Achievement award 1994), Optical Soc. Am. (Edward H. Land medal 1996); mem. Am. Phys. Soc. (George E. Pake prize 1997), Lasers and Electro-Optics Mfg. Assn. (bd. dirs. 1992—, sec. 1994, pres. 1996), Nat. Acad. Engring., Tau Beta Pi, Eta Kappa Nu, Phi Eta Sigma. Office: SDL Inc 80 Rose Orchard Way San Jose CA 95134-1356

SCIOSCIA, MIKE, professional baseball team manager; b. Nov. 27, 1958; Former catcher major league baseball/L.A. Dodgers, to 1990; catching instr. L.A. Dodgers, 1993, bench coach, 1997-98; coach Peoria Javelinas, 1997; minor league coach Albuquerque/Pacific Coast League, 1999; mgr. Anaheim (Calif.) Angels, 1999—. Career highlights include: finished second in Nat. League in on-base percentage, 1985/batted .296, hit a game-tying, ninth-inning home run in Game 4 of the 1988 Nat. League Championship Series, posted career highs of 12 home runs and 66 RBI along with a .264 average in 1990.

SCITOVSKY, ANNE AICKELIN, economist, researcher; b. Ludwigshafen, Germany, Apr. 17, 1915; came to U.S., 1931, naturalized, 1938; d. Hans W. and Gertrude Margarete Aickelin; 1 dau., Catherine Margaret. Student, Smith Coll., 1933-35; BA, Barnard Coll., 1937; postgrad., London Sch. Econs., 1937-39; MA in Econs., Columbia U., 1941. Mem. staff legis. reference svc. Libr. of Congress, 1941-44; mem. staff Social Security Bd., 1944-46; with Palo Alto (Calif.) Med. Found./Rsch. Inst., 1963—, chief health econs. div., 1973-94, sr. staff scientist, 1994—. Lectr. Inst. Health Policy Studies, U. Calif., San Francisco, 1975-94; mem. Inst. Medicine of NAS, Nat. Acad. Social Ins., Pres.'s Commn. for Study of Ethical Problems in Medicine and Biomed. and Behavioral Rsch., 1979-82, U.S. Nat. Com. on Vital and Health Stats., 1975-78, Health Resources and Svcs. Adminstrn., AIDS adv. com., 1990-94; cons. HHS, Inst. Medicine Coun. on Health Care Tech. Assessment, 1986-90. Home: 161 Erica Way Menlo Park CA 94028-7439 Office: Palo Alto Med Found Rsch Inst Ames Bldg 795 El Camino Real Palo Alto CA 94301-2302 E-mail: ascitovsky@aol.com

SCIUCHETTI, DALE, municipal official; b. Kellogg, Idaho, Feb. 15, 1940; BA, Whitworth Coll., Spokane, Wash., 1962; MBA, U. Wash., 1964. Cert. mcpl. fin. adminstr. Lead analyst Boeing, Seattle, 1962-68; asst. chief acct. Cowles Pub., Spokane, 1968-70; tchr. Gonzaga U., Spokane, 1970-73; field auditor City of Spokane, 1973-74, retirement specialist, 1974-75, retirement dir., 1975-82, treas., 1982—. Recipient Nat. Svc. award Mcpl. Treasurers of U.S. and Can., 1997. Mem. Wash. Mcpl. Treasurer's Assn. (pres. 1993), Wash. Fin. Officers Assn. (charter), Profl. Fin. Officer. Office: 808 W Spokane Falls Blvd Spokane WA 99201-3345 E-mail: dsciuchetti@spokanecity.org

SCLATER, JOHN GEORGE, geophysics educator; b. Edinburgh, Scotland, June 17, 1940; s. John George and Margaret Bennett (Glen) S.; m. Naila Gloria Sclater; children: Iain Andrew, Stuart Michael. B.Sc., Edinburgh U., 1962; Ph.D., Cambridge (Eng.) U., 1966. Research geophysicist Scripps Inst. Oceanography, La Jolla, Calif., 1965-72, prof., 1991—; asso. prof. MIT, 1972-77, prof., 1977-83; dir. Joint Program Oceanography Woods Hole Oceanographic Inst., 1981-83; Shell Cos. chair in geophysics U. Tex., Austin, 1983-91; prof. Scripps Instn. Oceanography, U. Calif., San Diego, 1991—, now prof. geophysics La Jolla. Sweeney lectr. Edinburgh U., 1976. Contbr. articles to profl. jours. Guggenheim Found. fellow, 1998-99; recipient Rosenstiel award oceanography, 1979, numerous award for publs. Fellow Geol. Soc. Am., Royal Soc. London, Am. Geophys. Union (Bucher medal 1985); mem. NAS (mem. ocean studies bd., 1985-92, chair 1988-91). Home: 5701 Skylark Pl La Jolla CA 92037-7742 Office: Scripps Instn Oceanography La Jolla CA 92093-0215

SCOLES, EUGENE FRANCIS, law educator, lawyer; b. Shelby, Iowa, June 12, 1921; s. Sam and Nola E. (Leslie) S.; m. R. Helen Glawson, Sept. 6, 1942; children— Kathleen Elizabeth, Janene Helen. AB, U. Iowa, 1943, JD, 1945; LLM, Harvard U., 1949; JSD, Columbia U., 1955. Bar: Iowa 1945, Ill. 1946. Assoc. Seyfarth-Shaw & Fairweather, Chgo., 1945-46; asst. prof. law Northeastern U., 1946-48, assoc. prof., 1948-49, U. Fla., 1949-51, prof., 1951-56, U. Ill., Champaign, 1956-68, Max Rowe prof. law, 1982-89, prof. emeritus, 1989—; vis. prof. McGeorge Law Sch. U. Pacific, Sacramento, 1989-92; prof. U. Oreg., 1968-82, dean Sch. Law, 1968-74, disting. prof. emeritus, 1982—. Vis. prof. Khartoum U., Sudan, 1964-65. Author: (with H.F. Goodrich) Conflict of Laws, 4th edit., 1964, (with R.J. Weintraub) Cases and Materials on Conflict of Laws, 2d edit., 1972, (with E.C. Halbach, Jr., R.C. Link, P.G. Roberts) Problems and Materials on Decedents' Estates and Trusts, 6th edit., 2000, Problems and Materials on Future Interests, 1977, (with P. Hay, P.J. Borchers, S.C. Symeonides) Conflict of Laws, 3d edit., 2000; contbr. articles to profl. jours.; notes and legislation editor Iowa Law Rev., 1945; reporter Uniform Probate Code Project, 1966-70; mem. joint editorial bd. Uniform Probate Code, 1972— Mem. ABA, Soc. Pub. Tchrs. Law, Am. Law Inst., Ill. Bar Assn., Assn. Am. Law Schs. (pres. 1978), Order of Coif Office: U Oreg Sch Law 1515 Agate St Eugene OR 97403-1221 E-mail: escoles@law.uoregon.edu

SCORDELIS, ALEXANDER COSTICAS, civil engineering educator; b. San Francisco, Sept. 27, 1923; s. Philip Kostas and Vasilica (Zois) S.; m. Georgia Gumas, May 9, 1948; children: Byron, Karen. B.S., U. Calif., Berkeley, 1948; M.S., M.I.T., 1949. Registered profl. engr., Calif. Structural designer Pacific Gas & Electric Co., San Francisco, 1948; engr. Bechtel Corp., San Francisco, summer 1951, 52, 53, 54; instr. civil engring. U. Calif., 1949-50, asst. prof., 1951-56, assoc. prof., 1957-61, prof., 1962-89, asst. dean Coll. Engring., 1962-65, vice chmn. div. structural engring, structural mechanics, 1970-73, Nishkian prof. emeritus, 1990—. Cons. engring. firms, govt. agys. Contbr. articles on analysis and design of complex structural systems, reinforced and prestressed concrete shell and bridge structures to profl. jours. Served to capt., C.E. U.S. Army, 1943-46, ETO. Decorated Bronze star, Purple Heart; recipient Western Electric award Am. Soc. Engring. Edn., 1978; Axion award Hellenic Am. Profl. Soc., 1979; Best paper award Canadian Soc. Civil Engring., 1982, K.B. Woods award NAS Transp. Rsch. Bd., 1983, Citation U. Calif. Berkeley, 1989, Disting. Engring. Alumnus award Berkeley Engring. ALumni Soc., 1993, Leadership award Am. Segmental Bridge Inst., 1993, Freyssinet medal Internat. Fedn. for Prestressed Concrete, 1994. Fellow ASCE (hon. mem. 1989, Moisseiff award 1976, 81, 92, Howard award 1989), Am. Concrete Inst.; mem. Internat. Assn. Shell and Spatial Structures (hon., Torroja medal 1994), Internat. Assn. Bridge and Structural Enging. (Tedesko medal 1998), Structural Engrs. Assn. Calif., Nat. Acad. Engring. Home: 724 Gelston Pl El Cerrito CA 94530-3045 Office: U Calif 729 Davis Hall Berkeley CA 94720-1711

SCORGIE, GLEN GIVEN, religious studies educator; b. Mar. 29, 1952; married; 3 children. MA, Wheaton Grad. Sch., 1974; MCS, Regent Coll., 1982; postgrad., Cambridge U., 1983; PhD, U. St. Andrews, 1986. Mktg. asst. IBM Can., Toronto, 1974-76; dir. admissions Can Bible Coll., Regina, 1976-79, asst. prof. theology, 1984-88, assoc. prof. theology, 1988-91; dean, v.p. N.Am. Bapt. Coll., 1991-96; prof. theology Bethel Seminary, San Diego, 1996—. Spkr. in field. Author: A Call for Continuity: The Theological Contribution of James Orr, 1988; contbr. articles to profl. jours. British Govt. Overseas Rsch. scholar, 1981-84. Mem. Am. Acad. Religion, Evang. Theol. Soc., Can. Evang. Theol. Assn., Conf. Faith and History, Delta Epsilon Chi. Office: Bethel Seminary 6116 Arosa St San Diego CA 92115-3999

SCORSINE, JOHN MAGNUS, lawyer; b. Rochester, N.Y., Dec. 3, 1957; s. Frank and Karin (Frennby) S.; m. Susan Nauss, May 31, 1980 (div.); m. Theresa A. Burke, Dec. 17, 1988; 1 child, Jennifer E. BS, Rochester Inst. Tech., 1980; JD, U. Wyo., 1984. Bar: Wyo. 1984, U.S. Dist. Ct. Wyo. 1984, U.S. Ct. Appeals (10th cir.) 1989, U.S. Army Ct. Criminal Appeals 1995. Part-time deputy sheriff Monroe County (N.Y.), 1978-80; police officer Casper (Wyo.) Police Dept., 1980-81; intern U.S. Atty. Office, Cheyenne, Wyo., 1983-84; pvt. practice Rock Springs, 1984-85; ptnr. Scorsine and Flynn, Rock Springs, 1986; prin. Scorsine Law Office, Rock Springs, 1986-95; commr. Dist. and County Court, 1986-95; dep. chief of staff for mil. support Wyo. Nat. Guard, 1995—. Ptnr. Sunset Advt., 1987-89; chmn. bd. dirs. Youth Home Inc., Rock Springs, 1987-88; treas. Sweetwater County Cmty. Corrections Bd., 1990-95; mem. Nat. Ski Patrol, 1976-97, Wyo. Bd. of Parole, 1998—. Leader Medicine Bow Ski Patrol, Laramie, Wyo., 1983; legal advisor Rocky Mountain divsn. Nat. Ski Patrol, 1984; asst. patrol leader White Pine Ski Area, Pinedale, Wyo., 1986; avalanche advisor Jackson Hole Snow King Ski Patrol, 1987-96, avalanche instr. 1993-96; sect. chief Teton sect. nat. Ski Patrol, 1991-94, mem. Eldore Ski Patrol, 1996-97; mem. Sweetwater County Search and Rescue, 1989-95, tng. officer, 1993-95; mem. Sweetwater County Emergency Dive Team, 1990-95, mem. Sweetwater County Fire Dept., 1992-94, Reliance Vol. Fire Dept., 1994-95; lt.k, training officer Laramie Cmty. Fire Dist. #6 and Burns Ambulance Svc., 1995-98, treas./sec. bd. dirs. 1997-98, Am. N. Peary Land expdn., 1989; scoutmaster Boy Scouts Am., 1987-93, 96-98, 4H leader, 1997—; pres. Sweetwater County Vol. Fire Assn., 1993-94; mem. Laramie County Sch. Dist. #2 accreditation panel; dir. emergency svcs. Wyo. Civil Air Patrol, 1998—, comdr. Wyo. wing, 1999—. Maj. JAG, USAR , 1991—; bd. dirs., sec. Burns Cmty. Ambulance, 1997-99. Recipient Yellow Merit star Nat. Ski Patrol, 1993, Fritch Volunteerism award, 1993, Armed Forces Outstanding Vol. Svc. medal Mem. ABA, Wyo. State Bar, Wyo. Trial Lawyers Assn., Assn. Am. Trial Lawyers, Rock Springs C. of C., Res. Officers Assn. (nat. councilman 1993—, state pres. 1994), Rotary. Democrat. Lutheran. Avocations: rock climbing, backpacking, hunting, scuba, karate. Home: 1090 State Hwy 214 Burns WY 82093 Office: Wyo Nat Guard 5500 Bishop Blvd Cheyenne WY 82009-3320 E-mail: john.scorsine@wy.ngb.ermy.mil

SCOTT, A. TIMOTHY, lawyer, business executive; b. Natchez, Miss., Feb. 16, 1952; s. John William and Patricia (O'Reilly) S.; m. Nancy E. Howard, June 7, 1976; children: Kevin Howard, Brian Howard. BA in Psychology, Stanford U., 1974, JD, 1977. Bar: Calif. 1977, U.S. Tax Ct. 1978. Assoc. then ptnr. Agnew, Miller & Carlson, L.A., 1977-83; assoc. Greenberg, Glusker, Fields, Claman & Machtinger, L.A., 1983; ptnr. Sachs & Phelps, L.A., 1983-91; mem. Heller, Ehrman White & McAuliffe, L.A., 1991-96, of counsel, 1996-99; sr. v.p., tax counsel Pub. Storage, Inc., Glendale, Calif., 1996—. Speaker in field. Note editor Stanford Law Rev., 1976-77; contbr. article to profl. publs., chpt. to book. Mem. ABA, L.A. County Bar Assn. (chmn. real estate taxation com. 1988-91, exec. com., taxation sect. 1989-91), Order of Coif. Democrat. Avocations: volleyball, gardening, Calif. wine, contemporary art, skiing. Office: Pub Storage Inc 701 Western Ave Glendale CA 91201-2349 E-mail: tscott@publicstorage.com

SCOTT, CHARLES KENNARD, state legislator, cattle rancher; b. Klamath Falls, Oregon, Aug. 19, 1945; s. Oliver Kennard and Deborah Ann (Hubbard) S.; m. Elaine Fenton, Dec. 20, 1975; children: Daniel, Abigail. AB, Harvard Coll., 1967; MBA, Harvard Univ., 1969. Analyst HEW and EPA, 1969-74; v.p., mgr. Bates Creek Cattle Co., Casper, Wyo., 1974—. Mem. Wyo. Senate, 1982—; chmn. Labor, Health and Social Svc. com.

SCOTT, DEBORAH L. costume designer; Costume designer: (films) E.T. The Extra-Terrestrial, 1982, Twilight Zone-The Movie ("Kick the Can", "Nightmare at 20,000 Feet"), 1983, Back to the Future, 1985, About Last Night..., 1986, Armed and Dangerous, 1986, Who's That Girl?, 1987, Moving, 1988, Coupe de Ville, 1990, Defending Your Life, 1991, Eve of Destruction, 1991, Sliver, 1993, Jack the Bear, 1993, Legends of the Fall, 1994, Indian in the Cupboard, 1995, To Gillian on Her 37th Birthday, 1996, Titanic, 1997 (Acad. award 1998), Wild Wild West, 1999, The Patriot, 2000, Minority Report, 2001. Recipient Academy award, 1998.

SCOTT, DONALD MICHAEL, educator; b. L.A., Sept. 26, 1943; s. Bernard Hendry and Barbara (Lannin) S.; m. Patricia Ilene Pancoast, Oct. 24, 1964 (div. June 1971); children: William Bernard, Kenneth George. BA, San Francisco State U., 1965, MA, 1986. Cert. tchr. Calif. Tchr. Mercy High Sch., San Francisco, 1968-71; park ranger Calif. State Park System, Half Moon Bay, 1968-77; tchr. adult div. Jefferson Union High Sch. Dist., Daly City, Calif., 1973-87; dir. NASA-NPS Project Wider Focus, Daly City, 1983-90; dir. Geo.S. Spl. Projects Wider Focus, San Francisco, 1990—, also bd. dirs. Daly City; nat. park ranger/naturalist Grant-Kohrs Ranch Nat. Hist. Site, Deer Lodge, Mont., 1987-88; nat. park ranger pub. affairs fire team Yellowstone Nat. Park, 1988; nat. park ranger Golden Gate Recreation Area, 1988-92. Rsch. subject NASA, Mountain View, Calif., 1986-90; guest artist Yosemite (Calif.) Nat. Park, 1986; nat. park ranger Golden Gate Nat. Recreation Area, Nat. Park Svc., San Francisco, 1986, nat. park svc. history cons. to Bay Dist., 1988-94; adj. asst. prof. Skyline Coll., 1989-94, Coll. San Mateo, 1992-94; aerospace edn. specialist NASA/OSU/AESP, 1994; cons. Friends of Ea. State Penitentiary Project, Phila., 1993. Contbr. articles, photographs to profl. jours., mags., chpts. to books. Pres. Youth for Kennedy, Lafayette, Calif., 1960; panelist Community Bds. of San Francisco, 1978-87; city chair Yes on A com., So. San Francisco, San Mateo County, Calif., 1986; active CONTACT Orgn., 1991—, bd. dirs. 1995—; mem. edn. working group Case for Mars VI, Boulder, 1996; state rep. Mont., Nev., 1999—. Mem. Nat. Assn. for Interpretation (founding mem.), Yosemite Assn. (life), Wider Focus, Friends of George R. Stewart, Nat. Sci. Tchrs. Assn., Nat. Coun. of Tchrs. of Math., Internat. Tech. Edn. Assn., Smithsonian Planetary Soc. (charter mem.), Mars Soc. (founding), Orange County Space Soc., Mars Soc. Ednl. Task Force. Avocations: photography, hiking, camping, travel. Home and Office: NASA Ames Rsch Ctr MS 253 2 Moffett Field CA 94035-1000

SCOTT, DOUGLAS EDWARD, lawyer; b. Evanston, Ill., Jan. 20, 1957; BA magna cum laude, U. Ill., 1979, MBA, 1981; JD, UCLA, 1984. Bar: Calif., 1984; U.S. Dist. Ct. (cen. dist.) Calif.; CPA, Ill. Assoc. O'Melveny & Myers, 1984-87; sr. v.p., gen. counsel, asst. sec. Sci. Applications Internat. Corp., San Diego, 1987—. James scholar. Mem. ABA, State Bar of Calif. (sr. v.p., gen. counsel and asst. sec.), Phi Beta Kappa. Office: Sci Applications Internat Corp Mail Stop F 3 10260 Campus Point Dr San Diego CA 92121

SCOTT, EDWARD WILLIAM, JR. computer software company executive; b. Panama City, Panama, May 25, 1938; s. Edward William and Janice Gertrude (Grimison) S.; m. Cheryl S. Gilliland, apr. 23, 1988; children: Edward William, Heather Yolanda Deirdre, Reece Donald. BA, Mich. State U., 1959, MA, 1963; BA, Oxford (Eng.) U., 1962. Personnel specialist Panama Canal Co., 1962-64, staff asst. to dir. personnel, 1964-66; personnel officer IRS, Detroit, 1966-68; staff personnel mgmt. specialist U.S. Dept. Justice, Washington, 1968-69, chief personnel systems and evaluation sect., 1970-72; dir. U.S. Dept. Justice (Office Mgmt. Programs), 1972-74; asso. dep. commr. planning and evaluation U.S. Dept. Justice (U.S. Immigration and Naturalization Service), 1974-75, dep. asst. atty. gen. adminstrn., 1972-75; asst. sec. for adminstrn. (Transp. Dept.), 1977-80; pres. Office Power, Inc., Washington, 1980-81; dir. mktg. Computer Consoles Inc., 1981-84; v.p. mktg. Dest Systems, 1984-85; dir. govt. mktg. Sun Microsystems, Mountain View, Calif., 1985-88; exec. v.p. Pyramid Tech., Mountain View, 1988-95; founder, pres. BEA Sys., Inc., San Jose, Calif., 1995—. Founder Ctr. for Global Devel., Washington; founder, pres.

escottVentures, Inc.; pres. U.S. Dept. Justice Fed. Credit Union, 1970-73. Recipient Presdl. Mgmt. Improvement certificate, 1971; Spl. Commendation award Dept. Justice, 1973; also Spl. Achievement award, 1976; William A. Jump Meml. award, 1974; presdl. sr. exec. service rank of Disting. Exec., 1980; Mich. State U. scholar, 1957-60. Mem. Phi Eta Sigma, Phi Kappa Phi. Democrat. Office: BEA Sys Inc 2315 N 1st St San Jose CA 95131-1010 E-mail: ed@escottventures.com

SCOTT, GREGORY KELLAM, judge trial referee, former state supreme court justice, lawyer; b. San Francisco, July 30, 1943; s. Robert and Althea Delores Scott; m. Carolyn Weatherly, Apr. 10, 1971; children: Joshua Weatherly, Elijah Kellam. BS in Environ. Sci., Rutgers U., 1970, EdM in Urban Studies, 1971; JD cum laude, Ind. U., Indpls., 1977. Asst. dean resident instrn. Cook Coll. Rutgers U., 1972-75; trial atty. U.S. SEC, Denver, 1977-79; gen. counsel Blinder, Robinson & Co., Inc., Denver, 1979-80; asst. prof. coll. law U. Denver, 1980-85, assoc. prof., 1985-93, prof. emeritus, 1993—, chair bus. planning program, 1986-89, 92-93; justice Colo. Supreme Ct., Denver, 1993-2000; gen. counselor Kaiser-Hill Co., Golden, 2000—; judge trial referee Colo. Supreme Ct., 2000. Of counsel Moore, Smith & Bryant, Indpls., 1987-90; v.p., gen. counsel Comml. Energies, Inc., 1990-91; presenter in field. Author: (with others) Structuring Mergers and Acquisitions in Colorado, 1985, Airport Law and Regulation, 1991, Racism and Underclass in America, 1991; contbr. articles to profl. jours. Mem. ABA, Nat. Bar Assn., Nat. Assn. Securities Dealers, Inc., Nat. Arbitration Panel (arbitrator), Colo. Bar Found., Sam Cary Bar Assn., Am. Inn Ct. (founding mem. Judge Alfred A. Arraj inn). Avocations: golfing, reading, traveling. Office: Kaiser-Hill Co LLC Rocky Flats Environ Tech Site 10808 Hwy 93 Unit B Golden CO 80403-8200

SCOTT, GREGORY W. health care company executive; B in Math. Econ., Colgate U.; MS, U. Mich. cert. CLU. Sr. v.p. Prudential Capital Corp.; gen. ptnr. RRY Ptnrs.; v.p. corp. fin. Salomon Brothers, Inc.; COO, CFO Medsite, 1999-01; exec. v.p., CFO PacifiCare, Santa Ana, Calif., 2001—. Office: PacifiCare Health Sys 3120 W Lake Ctr Dr Santa Anna CA 92704

SCOTT, JACK A. state senator; b. Sweetwater, Tex., Aug. 24, 1933; m. Lacreta Isbell Scott; 5 children. BA, Abilene Christian U., 1954; MA in Divinity, Yale U., 1962; MBA, Claremont U., 1967, PhD, 1970; D (hon.), Pepperdine U., 1991. Mem. faculty Pepperdine U., 1962-72, provost, 1970-73; dean Orange Coast Coll., 1973-78; pres. Cypress Coll., 1978-87, Pasadena City Coll., 1987-95; prof. higher edn. Pepperdine U., 1995—; Dem. rep. dist. 44 Calif. Ho. of Reps., 1996-2000; Dem. senator dist. 44 Calif. State Senate, 2000—. Bd. trustees Pacific Oaks Coll.; past chair Accreditation Commn. of Western Assn. of Schs.; mem. budget, edn., higher edn. and transp. coms. Calif. Ho. of Reps., chair gun violence, ins. Mem. bd. dirs. Coalition for a Non-Violent City; past chair Am. Heart Assn. Mem. Assn. Calif. C.C. Adminstrs. (past pres.), Rubio Canon Land and Water Assn. (bd. dirs.), Pasadena Rotary (bd. dirs.). Mem. Ch. of Christ. Office: 215 N Marengo Ave Ste 185 Pasadena CA 91101 also: Calif State Senate State Capitol Rm 4146 PO Box 942849 Sacramento CA 94249-0001 E-mail: jackscott4senate@earthlink.net, Jack.Scott@assembly.ca.gov

SCOTT, JAMES MICHAEL, research biologist; b. San Diego, Sept. 20, 1941; m. 1966; 2 children. BS, San Diego State U., 1966, MA, 1970; PhD in Zoology, Oreg. State U., 1973. Biol. aide U.S. Bur. Comml. Fisheries, 1966-68; asst. curator vertebrates Nat. Hist. Mus., Oreg. State U., 1969-73; rschr. Dept. Fisheries & Wildlife, 1973-74; biologist in charge Mauna Loa Field Sta. U.S. Fish & Wildlife Svc., 1974-84, dir. Condor Field Sta., 1984-86; instr. ornithology Malheur Environ. Field Sta., Pacific U., 1972, 73, leader Fish & Wildlife Rsch. Unit U. Idaho, Moscow, 1986—. Leader Maui Forest Bird Recovery Team, 1975-79, Hawaii Forest Bird Recovery Team, 1975; mem. Palila Recovery Team, 1975; mem. Am. Ornithologists Union Conservation Com., 1974-75, 75-76, sci. adv. bd. Nature Conservancy Hawaii Forest Bird Project, 1981; Richard M. Nixon scholar Whittier Coll. Fellow Am. Ornithologists Union; mem. Nature Conservancy, Ecol. Soc. Am., The Wildlife Soc., Soc. Conservation Biology, Inst. Biol. Sci., Cooper Ornithol. Soc. (pres. 1997—). Office: U Idaho Fish & Wildlife Rsch Unit 1130 Kamiaken St Moscow ID 83843-3855

SCOTT, JOHN D. pharmacologist; b. Edinburgh, Scotland, Apr. 13, 1958; married; 2 children. BSc in Biochemistry with honors, Herriot-Watt U., Edinburgh, 1980; PhD in Biochemistry, U. Aberdeen, 1983. NIH postdoctoral fellow dept. pharmacology U. Wash., Seattle, 1983-86, rsch. asst. prof. dept. biochemistry, 1986-88; asst. prof. dept. physiology & biophysics, dept. biol. chemistry U. Calif., Irvine, 1988-89; asst. scientist Ctr. Rsch. Occupl. & Environ. Toxicology Oreg. Health Scis. U., 1989-90, asst. scientist Vollum Inst. Advanced Biomed. Rsch., dept. biochemistry & molecular biology, 1990-92, scientist, 1993-97, sr. scientist, 1997—; investigator Howard Hughes Med. Ctr. (known as Vollum Inst.), 1997—. Spkr. in field. Editl. bd. Jour. Biol. Chemistry; contbr. articles to profl. jours. Recipient John J. Abel award Am. Soc. Pharmacology & Exptl. Therapeutics, 1996; Med. Endowments Honorary scholar U. Aberdeen, 1980-83. Mem. ASBMB, Biochem. Soc., Protein Soc. Office: Vollum Inst Oreg Health Scis U 3181 SW Sam Jackson Park Rd Portland OR 97201-3011

SCOTT, JOYCE ALAINE, university official; b. Long Beach, Calif., May 21, 1943; d. Emmett Emery Scott and Grace (Evans) Wedum B.A., U. Conn., 1964; M.A., U. Va., 1966; Ph.D., Duke U., 1973. From instr. to assoc. prof. U. Wyo., Laramie, 1971-74, asst. dean, 1974-78, asst. v.p. acad. affairs, 1976-81, assoc. v.p. acad. affairs, 1981-84; provost, v.p. SUNY-Potsdam, 1984-86; exec. v.p. Wichita State U., Kans., 1986-90, v.p. on spl. assignment, 1990-91; sr. cons. Am. Assn. State Colls. and Univs., 1991-92, v.p. acad. and internat. programs, 1992-97; deputy commr. Mont. U. System, Helena, 1998—. Mem. Commn. on Ednl. Credit and Credentials of Am. Council on Edn., Washington, 1982-87; cons. faculty Am. Open U., Lincoln, Nebr., 1981-82. Contbr. articles to profl. jours. Trustee Jones Internat. U. Mem. MLA, AAHE, Am. Assn. Tchrs. French, Phi Beta Kappa, Phi Sigma Iota. Republican. Presbyterian Office: Office Commr Higher Edn Box 59620-3101 Helena MT 59620-3101 E-mail: jscott@oche.montana.edu

SCOTT, KELLY, newspaper editor; Sunday Calendar editor The L.A. Times. Office: LA Times Times Mirror Sq Los Angeles CA 90053

SCOTT, KENNETH EUGENE, lawyer, educator; b. Western Springs, Ill., Nov. 21, 1928; s. Kenneth L. and Bernice (Albright) S.; m. Viviane H. May, Sept. 22, 1956 (dec. Feb. 1982); children: Clifton, Jeffrey, Linda; m. Priscilla Gay, July 30, 1989; children: Ashley, Shaler. BA in Econs., Coll. William and Mary, 1949; MA in Polit. Sci., Princeton U., 1953; LLB, Stanford U., 1956. Bar: N.Y. 1957, Calif. 1957, D.C. 1967. Assoc. Sullivan & Cromwell, N.Y.C., 1956-59, Musick, Peeler & Garrett, L.A., 1959-61; chief dep. savs. and loan commr. State of Calif., L.A., 1961-63; gen. counsel Fed. Home Loan Bank Bd., Washington, 1963-67; Parsons prof. law and bus. Stanford (Calif.) Law Sch., 1968-95, emeritus, 1995—; sr. rsch. fellow Hoover Instn., 1978-95, emeritus, 1995—. Mem. Shadow Fin. Regulatory Com., 1986—, Fin. Economists Roundtable, 1991—; bd. dirs. Am. Century Mut. Funds, Mountain View, Calif., Dresdner RCM Global Funds, San Francisco. Author: (with others) Retail Banking in the Electronic Age, 1977; co-editor: The Economics of Corporation Law and Securities Regulation, 1980. Mem. ABA, Calif. Bar Assn., Phi Beta Kappa, Order of Coif, Pi Kappa Alpha, Omicron Delta Kappa. Home: 610 Gerona Rd Stanford CA 94305-8453 Office: Stanford Law Sch Stanford CA 94305-8610 E-mail: kenscott@stanford.edu

SCOTT, MATTHEW PETER, biology educator; b. Boston, Jan. 30, 1953; s. Peter Robert and Duscha (Schmid) S.; m. Margaret Tatnall Fuller, May 13, 1990; children: Lincoln Fuller, Julia Fuller. BS, MIT, 1975, PhD, 1980. Postdoctoral tng. Ind. U., Bloomington, 1980-83; from asst. prof. to assoc. prof. U. Colo., Boulder, 1983-90; prof. Stanford (Calif.) U., 1990—, chmn. dept. devel. biology, 1997-98, assoc. chmn. dept. devel. biology, 1999—; assoc. investigator Howard Hughes Med. Inst., 1989-90, investigator, 1993—. Vis. prof. genetics Harvard Med. Sch., 1994-95. Recipient Passano Young Investigator award Passano Found., 1990. Mem. NAS, Am. Acad. Arts and Scis. Achievements include research in developmental genetics, in particular, homeotic genes, signaling systems, and cancer biology. Office: Stanford U Sch Med Dept Devel Biology 279 Campus Dr Beckman B300 Stanford CA 94305-5329

SCOTT, MICHAEL DENNIS, lawyer; b. Mpls., Nov. 6, 1945; s. Frank Walton and Donna Julia (Howard) S.; m. Blanca Josefina Palacios, Dec. 12, 1981; children: Michael Dennis, Cindal Marie, Derek Walton. BS, MIT, 1967; JD, UCLA, 1974. Bar: Calif. 1974, U.S. Dist. Ct. (no., so. and cen. dists.) Calif. 1974, U.S. Patent Office 1974, U.S. Ct. Appeals (9th cir.) 1974, U.S. Supreme Ct. 1978, U.S. Ct. Appeals (fed. cir.) 1989. Systems programmer NASA Electronics Research Lab., Cambridge, Mass., 1967-69, Computer Sciences Corp., El Segundo, Calif., 1969-71, Univac, Valencia, 1971; from assoc. to ptnr. Smaltz & Neelley, Los Angeles, 1974-81; exec. dir. Ctr. for Computer/Law, Los Angeles, 1977-94; pvt. practice Los Angeles, 1981-86, 88-89; pres. Law and Tech. Press, 1981-94; ptnr. Scott & Roxborough, Los Angeles, 1986-88, Graham & James, 1989-93; v.p., gen. counsel Sanctuary Woods Multimedia, Inc., San Mateo, Calif., 1993-94; of counsel Steinhart & Falconer, San Francisco, 1995-97; ptnr. Hosie Wes Sacks & Brelsford, Menlo Park, Calif., 1997-98, Perkins Coie LLP, 1998—. Adj. assoc. prof. law Southwestern U., L.A., 1975-80, 2001—Loyola U., L.A., 1997-99, Pepperdine U., L.A., 2001—; chmn. World Computer Law Congress, L.A., 1991, 93. Author: (with David S. Yen) Computer Law Bibliography, 1979, The Scott Report, 1981-86, Computer Law, 1984, Scott on Computer Law, 1991, Multimedia: Law and Practice, 1993, Scott on Multimedia Law, 1996, (with Warren S. Reid) Year 2000 Computer Crisis: Law Business Technology, 1998, Internet and Technology Law Desk Reference, 1999, 2000, Intellectual Property and Licensing Law Desk Reference; editor in chief: Computer/Law Jour., 1978-94, Software Protection, 1982-92, Software Law Jour., 1985-94, Internat. Computer Law Adviser, 1986-92, Cyberspace Lawyer, 1996—, E-Commerce Law Report, 1998—. Mem. Computer Law Assn. (bd. dirs. 1994-99), Calif. State Bar Assn. Office: 1620 26th St Santa Monica CA 90403

SCOTT, PATRICK, broadcast executive; BA in Comm., Washington State U. Floor dir. Sta. KOMO TV, 1969-70, prodr./dir., 1970-74, prodn. mgr., program mgr., 1979-82, v.p. news/programming, 1982-87, v.p., sta. mgr., 1984-87, v.p., gen. mgr., 1987-90, exec. v.p. broadcast ops., gen. mgr., 1990-92; pres., CEO Fisher Broadcasting, 1992—. Bd. dirs. MSTV, NAB TV, Fisher Broadcasting Inc.; chair NewVenco. Active cmty. projects United Way of King County, Wash., Children's Hosp. Found. Bd. Mem. Wash. Assn. Broadcasters (chair alcohol task force, Broadcaster of Yr. 1993), ABC TV Affiliates Assn. (bd. govs.), Broadcast Pioneers, Rotary Club (Seattle). Avocation: fishing. Office: Fisher Broadcasting Inc 100 4th Ave N Seattle WA 98109-4932

SCOTT, RICHARD G. religious organization administrator; b. Pocatello, Idaho, Nov. 7, 1928; s. Kenneth Leroy and Mary Whittle S.; m. Jeanen Watkins, July 16, 1953; 7 children. Degree in mech. engring., George Washington U.; postgrad. in nuclear engring. Mem. staff naval and land based power plants, 1953-65; head North Mission LDS Ch., Cordoba, Argentina, 1965-69, regional rep. in Uruguay, Paraguay, N.C., S.C., Va., Washington, 1969-77, mem. 1st Quorum of Seventy, 1977-83, mem. presidency of 1st Quorum of Seventy, 1983-88, apostle, 1988—. Avocations: jazz and classical music, hiking, birding, painting. Office: LDS Ch 50 E North Temple Salt Lake City UT 84150-0002

SCOTT, ROBERT LANE, chemist, educator; b. Santa Rosa, Calif., Mar. 20, 1922; s. Horace Albert and Maurine (Lane) S.; m. Elizabeth Sewall Hunter, May 27, 1944; children: Joanna Ingersoll, Jonathan Armat, David St. Clair, Janet Hamilton. S.B., Harvard U., 1942; M.A., Princeton U., 1944, Ph.D., 1945. Sci. staff Los Alamos Lab., 1945-46; Frank B. Jewett fellow U. Calif., Berkeley, 1946-48; faculty UCLA, 1948—, prof. chemistry, 1960-92, prof. emeritus, 1993—, chmn. dept., 1970-75. Author: (with J.H. Hildebrand) Solubility of Nonelectrolytes, 3d edit, 1950, rev., 1964, Regular Solutions, 1962, Regular and Related Solutions, 1970; Contbr. articles to profl. jours. Guggenheim fellow, 1955; NSF sr. fellow, 1961-62; Fulbright lectr., 1968-69 Fellow AAAS, Am. Phys. Soc.; mem. Am. Chem. Soc. (Joel Henry Hildebrand award 1984), Royal Soc. Chemistry (London), Sigma Xi. Home: 11128 Montana Ave Los Angeles CA 90049-3509 E-mail: scott@chem.ucla.edu

SCOTT, SHIRLEY, city council; married; four children. BA, Drew U., 1965; MA Germanic Langs., U. Cin., 1968. Operator Scott Supply Svc. Inc.; city coun. Tucson City Coun., 1995—. Bd. dirs. Tucson Clean and Beautiful. Office: Tucson City Coun 8123 E Poinciana Dr Tucson AZ 85730-4641

SCOTT, WALTER, JR. business consultant; b. Balt., July 24, 1925; s. Walter and Margaret Catherine (Pfeiffer) S.; m. Barbara Main, July 6, 1946 (dec. 1964); children: Stephen Walter, Susan Marjorie, Cynthia Margaret, Christopher Main; m. Mary Joan Braun, Aug. 5, 1966 (dec. 1986); m. Helene Lyda Burke, May 1, 1987. AB, Duke U., 1945; MBA with distinction, Harvard U., 1949. Advtg. mgr. The Quaker Oats Co., Chgo., 1950-57; v.p. mktg. J.H. Filbert, Inc., Balt., 1957-67, pres., 1968-77; div. gen. mgr. Cen. Soya Co., Ft. Wayne, Ind., 1972-77; exec. v.p. Fairmont Foods Co., Des Plaines, Ill., 1978-81; pres. McKeon, Scott, Woolf & Assocs., Palo Alto, Calif., 1982-84; chmn. bd. Integral Cons. Group, Mill Valley, 1986-87, Scott, Woolf & Assocs., Palo Alto, 1984—, Mulford Moreland & Assocs., San Jose, Calif., 1986-89; bd. dirs. Mulford Moreland Scott & Assocs., San Jose, West Marine Products, Watsonville, Calif., 1995—2001. Chmn., speaker pres. courses, Am. Mgmt. Assn., N.Y.C., 1970-90; trustee Calif. Inst. Integral Studies, San Francisco, 1983-89. With USNR, 1943-46, PTO. Mem. Phi Beta Kappa. Home and Office: 1450 Redford Dr Palm Springs CA 92264

SCOTT, WILLIAM CORYELL, medical executive; b. Sterling, Colo., Nov. 22, 1920; s. James Franklin and Edna Ann (Schillig) S.; m. Jean Marie English, Dec. 23, 1944 (div. 1975); children: Kathryn, James, Margaret; m. Carolyn Florence Hill, June 21, 1975; children: Scott, Amy Jo, Robert. AB, Dartmouth Coll., 1942; MD, U. Colo., 1944, MS in OB/GYN, 1951. Cert. Am. Bd. Ob-Gyn., 1956, 79, Am. Bd. Med. Mgmt., 1991. Intern USN Hosp., Great Lakes, Ill., 1945-46, Denver Gen. Hosp., 1946-47; resident Ob-Gyn St. Joseph's Hosp., Colo. Gen. Hosp., Denver, 1946-51; practice medicine specializing in Ob-Gyn Tucson, 1951-71; assoc. prof. emeritus U. Ariz. Med. Sch., Tucson, 1971—; v.p. med. affairs U. Med. Ctr., Tucson, 1984-94. Contbr. articles to med. jours. and chpt. to book. Pres. United Way, Tucson, 1979-80, HSA of Southeastern Ariz., Tucson, 1985-87; chmn. Ariz. Health Facilities Authority, Phoenix, 1974-83. Served to capt. USNR, 1956-58. Recipient Man of Yr. award, Tucson, 1975. Fellow ACS, Am. Coll. Ob-Gyn, Pacific Coast Ob-Gyn Soc., Ctrl. Assn. of Ob-Gyn; mem. AMA (coun. on sci. affairs 1984-93, chmn. 1989-91), Am. Coll. Physician Execs., Ariz. Med. Assn. Republican. Roman Catholic. Avocations: golf, gardening, photography. Address: HC 1 Box 923 Sonoita AZ 85637-9705 E-mail: cbarc3@netscape.net

SCOTT, W(ILLIAM) RICHARD, sociology educator; b. Parsons, Kan., Dec. 18, 1932; s. Charles Hogue and Hildegarde (Hewit) S.; m. Joy Lee Whitney, Aug. 14, 1955; children: Jennifer Ann, Elliot Whitney, Sydney Brooke. AA, Parsons Jr. Coll., 1952; AB, U. Kans., 1954, MA, 1955; PhD, U. Chgo., 1961; D (hon.), Copenhagen Sch. Bus., 2000, Helsinki Sch. Econs., 2001. From asst. prof. to assoc. prof. sociology Stanford (Calif.) U., 1960-69, prof., 1969-99, prof. emeritus, 1999—, chair dept. sociology, 1972-75. Courtesy prof. Sch. Medicine, Stanford U., 1972—, Sch. Edn., Grad. Sch. Bus., 1977—; fellow Ctr. for Advanced Study in Behavioral Scis., 1989-90; dir. Orgns. Rsch. Tng. Program, Stanford U., 1972-89, Ctr. for Orgns. Rsch., 1988-96; mem. adv. panel Sociology Program NSF, Washington, 1982-84; mem. epidemiol. and svc. rsch. rev. panel NIMH, Washington, 1984-88; mem. Commn. on Behavioral and Social Scis. and Edn., NAS, 1990-96; vis. prof. Kellogg Grad. Sch. Mgmt., Northwestern U., winter 1997, Hong Kong U. Sci. and Tech., fall 2000. Author: (with O.D. Duncan et al) Metropolis and Region, 1960; (with P.M. Blau) Formal Organizations, 1962, Social Processes and Social Structures, 1970; (with S.M. Dornbusch) Evaluation and the Exercise of Authority, 1975, Organizations: Rational, Natural and Open Systems, 1981, rev. edit., 1998; (with J.W. Meyer) Organizational Environments: Ritual and Rationality, 1983, edit., 1992; (with A.B. Flood) Hospital Structure and Performance, 1987; (with J.W. Meyer), Institutional Environments and Organizations: Structural Complexity and Individualism, 1994, Institutions and Organizations, 1995, rev. edit., 2001; (with S. Christensen) The Institutional Construction of Organization, 1995; (with M. Ruef et al) Institutional Change and Healthcare Organizations: From Professional Dominance to Managed Care, 2000; editor Ann. Rev. of Sociology, 1986-91; (with R. Cole) The Quality Movement and Organization Theory, 1999. Fellow Woodrow Wilson, 1954-55; mem. Nat. Commn. Nursing, 1980-83; chair Consortium Orgns. Rsch. Ctrs., 1989-91; elder First Presby. Ch., Palo Alto, Calif., 1977-80, 83-86. Social Sci. Rsch. Coun. fellow, U. Chgo., 1959; named Edmund P. Learned Disting. Prof., Sch. Bus. Adminstrn., U. Kans, 1970-71; recipient Cardinal Citation for Disting. Svc. Labette C.C., Parsons, 1981, Disting. Scholar award Mgmt. and Orgn. Theory divsn. Acad. Mgmt., 1988, Richard D. Irwin award for scholarly contbns. to mgmt. Acad. Mgmt., 1996. Mem. Inst. Medicine, Am. Sociol. Assn. (chmn. sect. on orgns. 1970-71, mem. coun. 1989-92), Acad. Mgmt., Sociol. Rsch. Assn., Macro-Organizational Behavior Soc., Phi Beta Kappa. Democrat. Presbyterian. Home: 940 Lathrop Pl Stanford CA 94305-1060 Office: Stanford U Dept Sociology Bldg 120 Stanford CA 94305 E-mail: scottwr@stanford.edu

SCOTTI, JAMES VERNON, astronomer; b. Bandon, Oreg., Aug. 22, 1960; s. Paul Carl and Elizabeth Louise (Garoutte) S.; m. Karriaunna K.-R. Harlan, May 15, 1983; children: Jennifer Anne, Christopher James. BS, U. Ariz., 1983. Planetarium asst. Flandrau Planetarium, Tucson, 1979-82; student rsch. asst. Lunar and Planetary Lab., Tucson, 1982-83, rsch. asst., 1983-93, sr. rsch. specialist, 1993—. Mem. Am. Astron. Soc. (assoc.), Div. for Planetary Scis., Assn. Lunar and Planetary Observers (asst. comets recorder). Achievements include being a leading observer of faint comets, being heavily involved in observing comet P/Shoemaker-Levy 9 before and during its impact on Jupiter in July 1994. Office: U Ariz Lunar And Planetary Lab Tucson AZ 85721-0001

SCOULAR, ROBERT FRANK, lawyer; b. Del Norte, Colo., July 9, 1942; s. Duane William and Marie Josephine (Moloney) S.; m. Donna V. Scoular, June 3, 1967; children— Bryan T., Sean D., Bradley R. B.S. in Aero. Engring., St. Louis U., 1964, J.D., 1968. Bar: Mo. 1968, Colo. 1968, N.D. 1968, U.S. Supreme Ct. 1972, Calif. 1979. Law clk. to chief judge U.S. Ct. Appeals (8th cir.), 1968-69; ptnr. Bryan, Cave, McPheeters & McRoberts, St. Louis, 1969-89, mng. ptnr. Los Angeles, 1979-84, exec. com., 1984-85, sect. leader tech., computer and intellectual property law, 1985-89; ptnr. Sonnenschein, Nath, Rosenthal, Chgo., 1990—, mng. ptnr. L.A., 1990—, mem. policy and planning com., 1995—. Co-leader intellectual property practice, 1990-98; dir. Mo. Lawyers Credit Union, 1978-79. Contbr. articles to profl. jours. Bd. dirs. St. Louis Bar Found., 1975-76, 79; bd. dirs., vice chmn. L.A. Area Coun. Boy Scouts Am.; league commr. Am. Youth Soccer Orgn.; mem. alumni coun. St. Louis U., 1979-82, dean's coun. Sch. Law, 2000—; hon. dean Dubourg Soc. Recipient Nat. Disting. Eagle Scout award. Mem. ABA (nat. dir. young lawyers div. 1977-78), Am. Judicature Soc., Bar Assn. Met. St. Louis (v.p. 1978-79, sec. 1979, chmn. young lawyers sect. 1975-76), Los Angeles County Bar Assn., Assn. Bus. Trial Lawyers, Calif. Bar. Assn., Mo. Bar (chmn. young lawyers sect. 1976-77, disting. svc. award), Computer Law Assn., Fed. Bar Assn., Dubourg Soc. (hon. dean). Home: 1505 Lower Paseo La Cresta Palos Verdes Peninsula CA 90274-2066 Office: Sonnenschein Nath & Rosenthal 601 S Figueroa St Ste 1500 Los Angeles CA 90017-5720

SCOUTEN, WILLIAM HENRY, chemistry educator, academic administrator; b. Corning, N.Y., Feb. 12, 1942; s. Henry and M. Anna (Kimble) S.; m. Nancy Jane Coombs, July 16, 1965; children: Lisa, Linda, Michael, William Jr., Thomas, David. BA, Houghton Coll., 1964; PhD, U. Pitts., 1969. NIH postdoctoral fellow SUNY, Stony Brook, 1969-71; asst. prof. Bucknell U., Lewisburg, Pa., 1971-77, assoc. prof., 1977-83, prof., 1983-84; prof., chmn. dept. chemistry Baylor U., Waco, Tex., 1984-93; dir. biotech. ctr. Utah State U., Logan, 1993-2000; dean Coll. Sci. U. Tex., San Antonio, 2000—. Vis. scientist for minority inst. Fedn. Am. Socs. Exptl. Biology, Washington; adj. prof. U. of Utah, 1996, mem. Ctr. for Biopolymers at Interfaces, 1996; chmn. Coun. of Biotech. Ctrs., 1998; mem. govt. rels. coms. Coun. Chem. Rsch., 1996; bd. dirs. emerging cos. sect. Biotechnology Industry Orgn., 1997; mem. Nat. Adv. Bd. Agrl. Rsch. Author: Affinity Chromatography, 1981; editor: Solid Phase Biochem., 1983; editor-in-chief Internat. Jour. Bio-Chromatography, 1994—; mem. editl. bd. Bioconjugate Chemistry, 1994-99, Jour. Molecular Recognition, 1994-99—, Bioseparation, 1995—. Fulbright fellow, 1976; Dreyfus Tchr. scholar, Dreyfus Found., 1976; NSF Sci. Devel. NSF, 1978; Lindbach Disting. Tchr. Bucknell U., 1975. Mem. Am. Soc. Biol. Chemists, Am. Chem. Soc., Internat. Soc. for Biorecognition Tech., Coun. for Biotech. Ctrs. (bd. dirs. 1996—), Internat. Soc. for Molecular Recognition (pres. 1990-93), Assn. for Internat. Practical Tng. (bd. dirs. 1991-98), Coun. for Chem. Rsch. (governing bd. 2000—). Republican. Baptist. Office: Utah State U 4700 Old Main Hl Logan UT 84322-4700

SCOZZARI, ALBERT, portfolio manager, inventor; b. Chgo. BA, Northeastern Ill. U., 1973; MPA, Ill. Inst. Tech., 1974; PhD, Columbia Pacific U., 1986. Cons. World Bank Group, 1987-99. Adj. prof. bus. studies. Ill. Inst. Tech., 1975, Columbia Pacific U., 1986; artist-in-residence Ariz. Coun. Fine Arts, 1999. Author: Mass Communications in Politics, 1978, Managing for Effectiveness, 1986, Management in the 90s, 1990, Vietnam Faces, 1995, Field Cross, 1996, The Mountain, 1997, The Trail, 1997, A Collection of Verses and Poems, 1997. Pres. Homeowners Assn., Phoenix, 1992-96, Scozzari Meml. Scholarship Fund, 1991—. With USNR, 1961-66, ret. ANG, 1979-87. Mem. Am. Fedn. Musicians (life), Assn. Stage and Film Actors (life), Am. Poets and Writers Guild (life), Am. Mensa Assn. (life), Vietnam Vets. Am. (life), Adventurers Club. (life). Home: PMB 1004 110 Rainbow Dr Livingston TX 77399-1010 E-mail: alsmondousa@yahoo.com

SCRIPPS, ROBERT P. publishing executive; Trustee Edward W. Scripps Trust, San Diego. Office: Edward W Scripps Trust 625 Broadway Ste 625 San Diego CA 92101-5483

SCRUGGS, ELAINE M. mayor; m. Larry Scruggs; 1 child, Jennifer. Former mgmt. specialist; elected mem. Glendale (Ariz.) City Coun., 1990-93; mayor City of Glendale, 1994, re-elected, 1996, 98, 2000. Past chmn. Maricopa (Ariz.) Assn. Govts., chair youth policy adv., chmn. Regional Pub. Transp. Authority, chmn. Ariz. Mcpl. Water Users Assn., chair Maricopa Assn. Govt. Regional Aviation Systems policy com.; chair Ariz. Mcpl. Tax Code Commn. Dir. Glendale Leadership Program, 1984-89; mem. Ariz. Coalition for Tomorrow, Ariz. Women in Mcpl. Govt.; mem. youth adv. commn., Mayor's Alliance Against Drugs and Gangs. Mem. Glendale C. of C. Office: Office Mayor 5850 W Glendale Ave Glendale AZ 85301-2563

SCUDDER, RICHARD B. newspaper executive; b. Newark, May 13, 1913; s. Edward W. and Katherine (Hollifield) S.; m. Elizabeth A. Shibley, June 24, 944; children: Elizabeth H. (Mrs. Philip Difani), Charles A., Carolyn (Mrs. Peter M. Miller), Jean (Mrs. Joseph Fulmer). AB, Princeton U., 1935; LHD (hon.), Mon Coll. Reporter Newark News, 1935-37, v.p., 1941-51, pub., 1951-72; reporter Boston Herald, 1937-38; chmn. MediaNews Group, Gloucester County Times, Inc., Garden State Newspapers, Inc., Garden State Paper Co., Denver Newspapers, Inc. Trustee Riverview Hosp., N.J. Conservation Found., Monmouth County Conservation Found.; former trustee Rutgers U.; adv. com. Princeton (N.J.) Environ. Inst. Served from pvt. to maj. AUS, 1941-45. Decorated bronze star; recipient TAPPI award, 1971; Nat. Recycling award Nat. Assn. Secondary Materials Industries, 1972; Nat. Resource Recovery Man of Year award, 1978; Papermaker of Yr. award Paper Trade Jour., 1978; named to Paper Industry Hall of Fame, 1995. Mem. N.J. Audubon Soc., Rumson Country Club, Seabright Beach Club, Seabright Lawn Tennis Club, Mill Reef Club, Adirondack League Club. Office: Media News Group 1560 Broadway Ste 2100 Denver CO 80202-6000 Address: 309 S Broad St Woodbury NJ 08096-2406

SCUDDER, THAYER, anthropologist, educator; b. New Haven, Aug. 4, 1930; s. Townsend III and Virginia (Boody) S.; m. Mary Eliza Drinker, Aug. 26, 1950; children: Mary Eliza, Alice Thayer. Grad., Phillips Exeter Acad., 1948; A.B., Harvard U., 1952, Ph.D., 1960; postgrad., Yale U., 1953-54, London Sch. Econs., 1960-61. Rsch. officer Rhodes-Livingstone Inst., No. Rhodesia, 1956-57, sr. rsch. officer No. Rhodesia, 1962-63; asst. prof. Am. U., Cairo, 1961-62; rsch. fellow Ctr. Middle East Studies, Harvard U., 1963-64; asst. prof. Calif. Inst. Tech., Pasadena, 1964-66, assoc. prof., 1966-69, prof. anthropology, 1969-2000, prof. emeritus, 2000—; dir. Inst. for Devel. Anthropology, Binghamton, N.Y., 1976—; commr. World Commn. on Dams, 1998-2000. Cons. UN Devel. Program, FAO, IBRD, WHO, Ford Found., Navajo Tribal Coun., AID, World Conservation Union, Lesotho Highlands Devel. Authority, South China Electric Power Joint Venture Corp., U.S. Nat. Rsch. Coun., Que.-Hydro, Environ. Def. Fund, Ministry of Industry and Handicrafts, Lao People's Dem. Republic. Author: The Ecology of the Gwembe Tonga, 1962; co-author: Long-Term Field Research in Social Anthropology, 1979, Secondary Education and the Formation of an Elite: The Impact of Education on Gwembe District, Zambia, 1980, No Place to Go: The Impacts of Forced Relocation on Navajos, 1982, For Prayer and Profit: The Ritual, Economic and Social Importance of Beer in Gwembe District, Zambia, 1950-1982, 1988, The IUCN Review of the So. Okavango Integrated Water Development Project, 1993. John Simon Guggenheim Meml. fellow, 1975; recipient Lucy Mair medal for applied anthropology Royal Anthropol. Inst., 1998. Mem. Am. Anthrop. Assn. (1st recipient Solon T. Kimball award for pub. and applied anthropology 1984, Edward J. Lehman award 1991), Soc. Applied Anthropology (Bronislaw Malinowski award 1999), Am. Alpine Club. Office: Calif Inst Tech # 228 77 Pasadena CA 91125-0001 E-mail: tzs@hss.caltech.edu

SCULLY, MARLAN ORVIL, physics educator; b. Casper, Wyo., Aug. 3, 1939; s. Orvil O. and Thelma G. (Thoms) S.; m. Judith Bailey, Aug. 16, 1958; children: James, Robert, Steven. AS, Casper Coll., 1959; BS, U. Wyo., 1961; MS, Yale U., 1963, PhD, 1966. Instr. Yale U., New Haven, 1967-69; asst. prof. MIT, Cambridge, 1969-71, assoc. prof., 1971-72; prof. U. Ariz., Tucson, 1972-80; disting. prof. U. N.Mex., Albuquerque, 1980—. Dir., co-founder Radtech, 1984; mem. Joint counm. on Quantum Electronics, Internat. Commn. on Optics; mem. program com. VIIth and VIIIth Internat. Conf. on Quantum Electronics (co-chmn. program com.); panel mem. Internat. Conf. on Hot Electrons in Semiconductors, North Tex. State U.; co-dir. VIIth Course of NATO Internat. Sch. Quantum Electronics; mem. program com. for OSA sponsored topical meeting on Picosecons Phenomena, Hilton Head, S.C., 1978; invited lectr. U.S.-Japan Coop. Seminar on Laser Spectroscopy, Hakone, Japan, 1977 ; mem. NRC panel on electron, atomic and molecular physics; advisor to ARO Nat. Acad. Panel, Los Alamos Physics Div. Author: (with others) Laser Physics, 1974; contbr. articles to profl. jours. Recipient Elliott Cresson medal The Franklin Inst., 1990; John S. Guggenheim fellow, 1970, Alfred P. Sloan fellow, 1972. Fellow AAAS, Optical Soc. Am. (dir. at large 1978-80, publs. com. 1972, Ives medal com. 1976, chmn. Wood prize com. 1978, Adolph E. Lomb medal 1970; mem. Max Planck Soc. Avocations: cattle ranching, inventing. Home: Scully Farm Estancia NM 87016 Office: Univ N Mex Dept Physics Albuquerque NM 87131-0001

SCULLY, VINCENT EDWARD, sports broadcaster; b. Bronx, N.Y., Nov. 29, 1927; s. Vincent Aloysius and Bridget (Freehill) S.; m. Sandra Hunt, Nov. 11, 1973; children: Michael, Kevin, Todd, Erin, Kelly, Catherine Anne. B.A., Fordham U., 1949. Sports announcer Bklyn. Dodgers Profl. Baseball Team, 1950-57, L.A. Dodgers Profl. Baseball Team, 1957—, CBS-TV, 1975-82, NBC-TV, 1982-89. Served with USNR, 1944-45. Recipient TV award Look mag., 1959; named Sportscaster of Year in Calif., 1959, 60, 63, 69, 71, 73-75; Nat. Sportscaster of Year, 1966, 78, 82; named to Fordham U. Hall of Fame, 1976. Mem. AFTRA, Screen Actors Guild, Catholic Actors, TV Acad. Arts and Scis. Roman Catholic. Clubs: Lambs (N.Y.C.); Bel Air Country, Beach. Office: LA Dodgers 1000 Elysian Park Ave Los Angeles CA 90012-1112

SEABOLT, RICHARD L. lawyer; b. Chgo., Aug. 28, 1949; BGS with distinction, U. Mich., 1971; JD, U. Calif., Hastings, 1975. Bar: Calif. 1975. With Hancock, Rothert & Bunshoft, San Francisco, 1975—, ptnr., 1981—. Pres. Def. Seminar Assocs., 1992—; chair com. jury instrn. litig. sect. State Bar Calif. Frequent speaker and author profl. jours., Large Complex Case Panel-Constrn., Am. Arbitration Assn. Mem. ABA, State Bar Calif., Bar Assn. San Francisco. Office: Hancock Rothert & Bunshoft LLP Four Embarcadero Ctr San Francisco CA 94111-4106 Fax: 415-955-2599. E-mail: rlseabolt@hrblaw.com

SEADER, JUNIOR DEVERE (BOB), chemical engineering educator; b. San Francisco, Aug. 16, 1927; s. George Joseph and Eva (Burbank) S.; m. Joyce Kocher, Aug. 12, 1950 (div. 1960); m. Sylvia Bowen, Aug. 11, 1961; children: Steven Frederick, Clayton Mitchell, Gregory Randolph, Donald Jeffrey, Suzanne Marie, Robert Clark, Kathleen Michelle, Jennifer Anne. BS, U. Calif., Berkeley, 1949, MS, 1950; PhD, U. Wis., 1952. Instr. chem. engring. U. Wis., Madison, 1951-52; group supr. chem. process design Chevron Rsch. Corp., Richmond, Calif., 1952-57, group supr. engring. rsch., 1957-59; prin. scientist heat transfer and fluid dynamics rsch. Rocketdyne div. N.Am. Aviation, Canoga Park, Calif., 1959-66, vis. tech. specialist, summer 1967; prof. chem. engring. U. Idaho, 1965-66, U. Utah, Salt Lake City, 1966—, chmn. dept. chem. engring., 1975-78; tech. cons. Trustee CACHE Corp., Austin, Tex.; inst. lectr. Am. Inst. Chem. Engrs., 1983, also dir., 1983-85. Author 8 books; assoc. editor IEC Rsch. jour., 1986-99; co-author widely used vapor-liquid equilibrium correlation. Served with USNR, 1945-46. Recipient Disting. Teaching award U. Utah, 1975, Donald L. Katz lectureship, 1990, Dean's Tchg. award U. Utah, 1998. Fellow Am. Inst. Chem. Engrs. (Computing in Chem. Engring. award 1988); mem. ACS, Sigma Xi, Phi Lambda Upsilon. E-mail: j.seader@m.cc.utah.edu Heat transfer rsch. connected with the devel. of rocket engines associated with the Apollo and Space Shuttle projects, 1960-65; rsch. on tar sands, process synthesis, catalyst effective factors, bifurcation analysis. Home: 13696 Vestry Rd Draper UT 84020-7521 Office: U Utah Dept Chem Engring Rm 3290 50 S Central Campus Dr Salt Lake City UT 84112-9203 E-mail: j.seader@m.cc.utah.edu

SEAGREN, STEPHEN LINNER, oncologist; b. Mpls., Mar. 13, 1941; s. Morley Raymond and Carol Christine (Linner) S.; m. Jill Garrie; 1 child, Sean Garrie. AB, Harvard U., 1963; MD, Northwestern U., 1967. Diplomate Am. Bd. Internal Medicine, Am. Bd. Med. Oncology, Am. Bd. Radiology. From asst. prof. to assoc. prof. radiology and medicine U. Calif., San Diego, 1977-88, prof., 1988—, chief divsn. radiation oncology. Contbr. over 80 articles to profl. jours. Bd. dirs. Wellness Cmty., San Diego, 1988—, chair profl. adv. com., 1988—; chair radiol. oncology com. Cancer and Acute Leukemia Group, Chgo., 1986-98; assoc. dir. U. Calif. San Diego Cancer Ctr., 1998-2000. Lt. comdr. USNR, 1971-73. Fellow ACP. Avocations: physical fitness, bridge, skiing, golf, tennis. Office: U Calif San Diego Med Ctr 200 W Arbor Dr San Diego CA 92103-9000 E-mail: sseagren@ucsd.edu

SEALE, JOHN CLEMENT, director, cinematographer; b. Warwick, Queensland, Australia, Oct. 5, 1942; s. Eric Clement and Marjorie Lyndon (Pool) S.; m. Louise Lee Mutton, Sept. 23, 1967; children: Derin Anthony, Brianna Lee. Grad. high sch., Sydney, Australia; Doctorate (hon.), Griffith U., 1997. Camera asst. film dept. Australian Broadcasting Com., 1962-68; freelance technician, camera operator various films, series, commls., 1968-76. Dir. feature film, Till There Was You, 1989-90. Dir. photography: Goodbye Paradise (Golden Tripod 1982), Careful, He Might Hear You (Best Cinematography 1983), Witness, 1984 (Golden Tripod 1984, Oscar nomination 1986, Brit. Acad. award nomination 1986), The Hitcher, 1985, Children of a Lesser God, 1985 (Golden Tripod 1985), The Mosquito Coast, 1986, Stakeout, 1987, Gorillas in the Mist (Brit. Acad. award nomination 1989, Premier Mag. Cinematographer of the Yr. 1989), Rainman, 1988 (Acad. award nomination 1988, Artistic Achievement award 1989), Dead Poets Society, 1989, The Doctor, 1991, Lorenzo's Oil, 1992, The Firm, 1993, The Paper, 1993, Beyond Rangoon, 1994, The American President, 1995, The English Patient, 1995-96 (Best Cinematography award L.A. Film Critics Assn., Acad. award Cinematography, 1996, Brit. Acad. award 1996, Best Cinematrography award Am. Soc. Cinematographers 1996, European Best Cinematography award 1997, Chgo. Film Critics award, Fla. Film Critics award), Ghosts of Mississippi, 1996, City of Angels, 1997, At First Sight, 1998, The Talented Mr. Ripley, 1998, The Perfect Storm, 1999, Harry Potter, 2000. Recipient Film Critics Cir. Australia 1990 Tribute; named European Cinematographer of Yr., 1997. Mem. Australian Cinematographers Soc. (named Cinematographer of Yr. 1982, 84, Inaugural mem. Hall of Fame 1997), Am. Soc. Cinematographers. Avocations: building boats, sailing.

SEALE, ROBERT L. former state treasurer, political organization chairman; b. Inglewood, Calif., Oct. 4, 1941; m. Judy Seale (dec.). BSA, Calif. Poly. U. Former contr. and sr. fin. officer Rockwell Internat.; sr. accountant Ernst & Ernst, L.A.; mng. ptnr. Pangborn & Co., Ltd. CPA's, 1985-88; now state treas. State of Nev.; chair. Nev. Rep. Party. Former treas. Nev. Rep. Com. Mem. Nat. Assn. State Treas. (past pres.). Office: Nev Republican Party 528 S Decatur Las Vegas NV 89104

SEALE, ROBERT MCMILLAN, office services company executive; b. Feb. 1, 1938; s. Robert McMillan and Margaret Sutherland (Miller) S. BA, Emory U., 1959. With N.Y. Life Ins. Co., San Francisco, 1960-67, Dictaphone Office Svcs. divsn. Dictaphone Corp., San Francisco, 1967-69; pres. Am. Profl. Svc., Inc., Dictation West Miss Jones' Word Processing, various locations, 1969-93; pres. Environments West, 1980-86, Los Arcos Properties, 1980—. Founder Seale Orgn., 1993; lectr. in field. Contbr. articles in field to profl. jours. Bd. dirs. The Rose Resnic Ctr. for Blind and Handicapped, Computer Based Patient Record Inst.; med. word processing cons. to hosps., health care insts., office equipment mfrs.; chmn. San Francisco Mayor's Com. for Employment of Handicapped, 1971-73; mem. Calif. Gov.'s Planning and Adv. Com. for Vocat. Rehab. Planning, 1968-69; pres. Calif. League for Handicapped, 1968-70, bd. dirs., 1966-73, 84-89, adv. coun., 1973-77; v.p. Stebbins Found., 1980-89; pres. Stebbins Housing Corp., 1980-89; assoc. St. Francis Hosp. Found., 1990—; sec., founder Palm Springs Coalition of Neighborhoods. Recipient Spoke and Spark award U.S. Jr. C. of C., 1967, KABL Outstanding Citizen's award, 1965, 71. Mem. Am. Health Info Mgmt. Assn., Adminstrv. Mgmt. Soc., Sales and Mktg. Execs. Assn., Am. Assn. Med. Transcription (Disting. Svc. award 1985), Med. Transcription Industry Alliance, Emory U. Alumni Assn., Emory Lamplighters Soc., U.S. C. of C., Las Palmas Alliance (chmn.), Delta Tau Delta. Office: 280 W Camino Sur Palm Springs CA 92262-4303

SEAMAN, ARLENE ANNA, retired musician, educator; b. Pontiac, Mich., Jan. 21, 1918; d. Roy Russell and Mabel Louise (Heffron) S. BS, life cert., Ea. Mich. U., 1939; MMus, Wayne State U., 1951; postgrad., Colo. Coll., 1951-52, Acad. Music, Zermatt Switzerland, 1954, 58, U. Mich. Guest conductor Shepherds and Angels, Symphonie Concertante, 1951; asst. conductor Detroit Women's Symphony, 1960-68; adjudicator Mich. State Band and Orch. Festivals, Solo and Ensemble Festivals, 1950-70, Detroit Fiddler's Band Auditions, 1948-52, Mich. Fedn. Music Clubs, 1948-55; tchr. Ea. Mich. U., 1939-42, Hartland Sch. Music, 1939-42, Pontiac (Mich.) Pub. Schs., 1942-45, Detroit Pub. Schs., 1945-73, pvt. studio, 1973-90. Performer cello South Oakland Symphony, 1958-65, Detroit Women's Symphony, 1951-68, Riviera Theatre Orch., 1959, 60, Masonic Auditorium Opera, Ballet Seasons, 1959-65, Toledo Ohio Symphony, 1963-70, others; performer trumpet Detroit Brass Quartet, 1974-78; piano accompanist various auditions, recitals, solo and ensemble festivals; composer: Let There Be Music, 1949, Fantasy for French Horn and Symphonic Band, 1951. Mem. Quota Internat., Delta Omicron. Home: 14650 N Alamo Canyon Dr Tucson AZ 85737-8812

SEAMAN, DARYL KENNETH, oil company executive; b. Rouleau, Sask., Can., Apr. 28, 1922; BSME, U. Sask., 1948, LLD (hon.), 1982, U. Calgary, 1993. Cert. mech. engr. CEO Bow Valley Industries Ltd., Calgary, Alta., Can., 1962-70, 85-91, chmn., chief exec. officer Can., 1970-82; chmn. Box Valley Industries Ltd., Calgary, Can., 1982-85; pres. Bow Valley Industries Ltd., Calgary, Can., 1985-87, chmn., 1991-92. Bd. dirs. Far West Mining Ltd., CCR Techs. Ltd., Pure Techs. Ltd, E-tronics, Inc., Bow Valley Energy Ltd.; co-owner, bd. dirs. Calgary Flames Hockey Club; chmn., pres. Dox Investments, Inc. Mem. Royal Commn. Econ. Union and Devel. Prospects for Can., 1982-85; active numerous coms. for fundraising U. Sask.; hon. chmn. The Western Heritage Centre Soc.; chmn. nat. adv. com. Banff Sch. Mgmt. Served with RCAF, 1941-45, North Africa, Italy. There is no repetition since it is indicated as an award you received and as a membership. Mem. Assn. Profl. Engrs., Geologists and Geophysicists (hon. life, Frank Spragins award, 1985, McGill Mgmt. Achievement award, 1979), Order of Canada 1993, Western Heritage Centre Soc., Ranchmen's Club, RAF Club, Earl Grey Golf Club, Calgary Petroleum Club, Calgary Golf and Country Club, U. Calgary Chancellor's Club. Progressive Conservative. Mem. United Ch. Can. Avocations: ranching, golf, hunting, skiing. Home and Office: Dox Investments Inc 500 333 5th Ave SW Calgary AB Canada T2P 3B6

SEARS, DAVID O'KEEFE, psychology educator; b. Urbana, Ill., June 24, 1935; s. Robert R. and Pauline (Snedden) S.; divorced; children: Juliet, Olivia, Meredith. BA in History, Stanford U., 1957; PhD in Psychology, Yale U., 1962. Asst. prof. to prof. psychology and polit. sci. UCLA, 1961—, dean social scis., 1983-92. Dir. Inst. for Social Sci. Rsch., 1993—. Author: Public Opinion, 1964, Politics of Violence, 1973, Tax Revolt, 1985, Political Cognition, 1986, Social Psychology, 2000, Racialized Politics, 2000. Fellow Am. Acad. Arts and Scis.; mem. Soc. for Advancement Socio-Econs. (pres. 1991-92), Internat. Soc. Polit. Psychology (pres. 1994-95). Office: UCLA Psychology Dept Los Angeles CA 90095-0001 E-mail: sears@psych.ucla.edu

SEARS, WILLIAM M. aerospace transportation executive; b. St. Louis, July 15, 1947; BS in elec. engring., MS in elec. engring., Purdue U.; M in engring. mgmt., U. Mo. Rolla. Sr. engr. McDonnell Douglas, 1969, program mgr. new bus. devel., 1988, v.p., gen. mgr. new aircraft products divsn., 1990-97, pres., 1997; sr. v.p., CFO The Boeing Co, 2000—. V.p. Naval Aviation Mus. Found.; dir. March of Dimes; bd. trustees St. Louis Sci. Ctr., Washington U. Recipient Alumni Achievement award, U. Mo.-Rolla, Outstanding Elec. Engr. award, Purdue U., Disting. Alumni award, 1988, Laurel award, Aviation Week, 1995, Robert J. Collier award, Nat. Aeronautic Assn., Fleet Admiral Chester A. Nimitz award, Navy League, 2000. Fellow Am. Insts Aeronautics and Astronautics (Hap Arnold award). Office: The Boeing Co 7755 E Marginal Way Seattle WA 98108

SEARSON, DEE, retail products executive; CFO MTS, Inc., West Sacramento. Office: MTS Inc PO Box 919001 West Sacramento CA 95691-9001

SEAU, JUNIOR (TIANA SEAU JR.), professional football player; b. Samoa, Jan. 19, 1969; Student, U. So. Calif. Linebacker San Diego Chargers, 1990—. Player Super Bowl XXVIV, 1994. Named to Sporting News Coll. All-Am. Team, 1989, to Pro Bowl Team, 1991-93, 96, to Sporting News NFL All Pro Team, 1992, 93. Office: San Diego Chargers PO Box 609609 San Diego CA 92160-9609

SEAVE, PAUL L. prosecutor; AB in History, Princeton U., 1975; JD cum laude, U. Pa., 1979. Jud. clk. to Chief Justice Samuel J. Roberts Pa. Supreme Ct., 1979-80; litig. assoc. Ballard, Spahr, Andrews & Ingersoll, Phila., 1980-83; asst. U.S. atty., chief criminal complaints unit U.S. Attys. Office, L.A., 1983-87; assoc. Gibson, Dunn & Crutcher, Washington, 1988-89; chief Orange County br. U.S. Attys. Office, Santa Ana, Calif., 1989-93, first asst U.S. atty. Sacramento, 1993-97; U.S. atty. U.S. Attys. Office Ea. Dist., Sacramento, 1997—. Instr. Littleton Legal Writing; mem. FBA, 1991-93; adj. prof. Northwestern U. Sch. Law, L.A., 1986, Loyola Law Sch., L.A., 1992, McGeorge Sch. Law, Sacramento, 1996; spkr. in field. Editor: U. Pa. Law Rev.; contbr. articles to profl. jours. Vice chair, bd. dirs. Sacramento Jewish Cmty. Rels. Coun., 1994—. McConnell scholar Princeton U. Mem. ABA (co-chair white collar crime ethics subcom. 1992-93, bd. dirs. white collar crime subcom. 1992-95), Ea. Dist. Jud. Conf. (planning com. 1995, 96), Inns of Ct. Office: Office US Atty 501 I St Ste 10-100 Sacramento CA 95814-7300

SEAVEY, WILLIAM ARTHUR, lawyer, vintner; b. Los Angeles, Aug. 28, 1930; s. Arthur Jones and Dorothy (Keyes) S.; m. Mary van Beuren, June 25, 1955; children: Dorothy K., Arthur V.B., William G., Frederic A., Charles K. AB, Princeton U., 1952; LLB, Harvard U., 1955; grad. Inst. Internat. Studies, U. Geneva, Switzerland, 1956, D in Polit. Sci., 1970. Bar: Calif. 1957, U.S. Dist. Ct. (so. and no. dist.) Calif. 1957, U.S. Ct. Appeals (9th cir.) 1957. Assoc. Luce, Forward, Kunzel & Scripps, San Diego, 1956-57; asst. U.S. atty. U.S. Dist. Ct. (so. dist.) Calif., 1957-59; with Noon & Seavey, San Diego, 1959-65; lectr. in internat. law and econ., asst. to pres. Mills Coll., Oakland, Calif., 1968-74; ptnr. Richards & Seavey, San Francisco, 1974-76, Davis, Stafford, Kellman & Fenwick, San Francisco, 1976-78; of counsel Friedman, Olive, McCubbin, Spalding, Bilter, Roosevelt etal, San Francisco, 1987—. Proprietor Seavey Vineyard, Napa County, 1981—. Author: Dumping Since the War: The Gatt and National Laws, 1970. Councilman City of Coronado, Calif., 1960-62, mayor 1962-64; trustee French-Am. Internat. Sch., San Francisco, 1968-96; pres. English Speaking Union, San Francisco, 1982-85, Alliance Francaise, San Francisco, 1979-81; chair Javits Fellowship Bd., Washington, 1989-92; mem. Columbus Fellowship Found. Bd., Washington, 1993-99; dir. San Francisco Com. on Fgn. Rels., 1995-98, chmn., 1998—. Mem. ABA, Calif. Bar Assn., San Francisco Bar Assn., Am. Soc. Internat. Law. Republican. Clubs: Pacific Union, Cercle de l'Union, World Trade (San Francisco), The Met. (Washington). Avocation: skiing, jazz piano. Home: 90 Hazel Ln Piedmont CA 94611-4033 Office: 425 California St Fl 22 San Francisco CA 94104-2102 also: 1310 Conn Valley Rd Saint Helena CA 94574-9624 E-mail: waseavey@pacbell.net, info@seaveyvineyard.com

SEBASTIAN, PETER, international affairs consultant, former ambassador; b. June 19, 1926; m. Harvel Huddleston, Dec. 11, 1951; 1 child, Christopher B.A., U. Chgo., 1950; postgrad., U. d'Aix-Marseille, Nice, France, 1949, New Sch. for Social Research, N.Y.C., 1950, Nat. War Coll., , 1969-70. Dir., owner cons. co., N.Y.C., 1950-57; U.S. Fgn. Service officer Dept. State, Washington, 1957-76, dep. exec. sec., 1976-77, sr. seminar, 1977-78; U.S. consul gen. Casablanca, Morocco, 1978-80; minister, counselor Am. embassy, Rabat, Morocco, 1980-82; dir. for North Africa Dept. State, Washington, 1982-84; ambassador to Tunisia Tunis, 1984-87; ambassador-in-residence Ctr. for Strategic Internat. Studies, Georgetown U., Washington, 1987-88; cons in fgn. affairs to the public and pvt. sector, lectr., 1988—. Contbr. poems to Osmose, 1949; author studies for U.S. Dept. State and other U.S agys. Served to sgt. AUS, 1944-46 Decorated Ouissam Alaouite (Morocco), numerous U.S. mil. decorations; recipient Presdl. Meritorious Service award, 1985. Mem. Am. Fgn. Svc. Assn., Nat. Geog. Soc., Mid. East Inst. Episcopalian Avocations: painting, drawing, photography. E-mail: Batuta@aol.com

SEBRIS, ROBERT, JR. lawyer; b. N.Y.C., May 20, 1950; s. Robert and Ruth (Kagis) S.; m. S. Lawson Hollweg, Sept. 8, 1973; children: Jared Matthew, Bryan Taylor. BS in Indsl. Labor Rels., Cornell U., 1972; JD, George Washington U., 1978. Bar: D.C. 1978, Wash. 1980. Labor rels. specialist Onondaya County Office labor rels., Syracuse, N.Y., 1973-74, U.S. Dept. Labor, Washington, 1972-75; labor rels. mgr. U.S. Treasury Dept., Washington, 1975-78; employee rels. mgr. Washington, 1978-80; assoc. Davis, Wright, Todd, Riese & Jones, Seattle, 1980-84; ptnr. Davis, Wright, Tremain, Bellevue, Wash., 1985-92, Sebris Busto, P.S., Bellvue, 1992—. Expert witness T.E.A.M. Act Amendments NLRA U.S. Senate hearing, 1997. Co-Author: Employer's Guide to Strike Planning, 1985; contbr. articles to profl. jours. Mem. Bellevue C.C. Found., 1988-95, pres., 1995-96; chair employment law cert. program U. Wash. Law Sch., 1996-97. Mem. ABA (health law forum, labor and employment law sect., com. on employee rights), Wash. Bar Assn., D.C. Bar Assn., Seattle/King County Bar Assn. (chmn. labor law sect. 1991-92), Pacific Coast Labor Law Conf. (planning com. 1980-93, chmn. 1991-92), Am. Health Lawyers Assn., Soc. Human Resource Mgmt. Avocations: golf, soccer, coaching youth sports. Home: 16301 Mink Rd NE Woodinville WA 98072-9463 Office: Sebris Busto PS Ste 325 14205 SE 36th St Bellevue WA 98006 E-mail: rsebris@sebrisbusto.com

SEDILLO, ORLANDO DELANO, city official; b. Monticello, N.Y. BA in Sociology and Phys. Edn., U. Albuquerque, 1962. Supr. City of Albuquerque Pks. and Recreation Dept., 1961-66; dir. City of Albuquerque Neighborhood Youth Corps, 1967; manpower devel. specialist U.S. Dept. of Labor, Albuquerque, 1967-70; dir., model cities program City of

Albuquerque, 1971; manpower devel. specialist U.S. Dept. Labor, Dallas, 1971-74; dir. Comprehensive Employment and Tng. Program U.S. Dept. Labor/City of Albuquerque, 1974-78; dir. Pks. and Recreation Dept. City of Albuquerque Pks., 1978-86; dir. solid waste collection and disposal dept. City of Albuquerque, 1986-87; dir. state pks. and recreation divsn. State of N.Mex., 1987; dep. county mgr. Bernalillo County, Albuquerque, 1990-91; asst. dir. Human Resource Programs U.S. Forest Svc., USDA, Washington, 1991-96; dir. solid waste mgmt. dept. City of Albuquerque, 1997—. Mem. U.S. Conf. Mayors employment and tng. adv. coun., 1977-78; mem. state manpower svcs. coun. N.Mex., 1974-78; mem. gov.'s recreation priorities adv. com., 1982-86; mem. Bur. Land Mgmt.'s Albuquerque dist. adv. coun., 1986-89; mem. assessment bd., City of El Paso, Tex., for selection of dir. of pks. and recreation dept., 1982, 86; chmn. Albuquerque Bot. Garden adv. bd., 1983-86. Chmn., bd. dirs., N.Mex. Vols. for Outdoors, 1986; bd. dirs. Albuquerque Boys' Clubs, 1983-84. Recipient Outstanding Exec. award Albuquerque Hispano C. of C., 1977, N.Mex. Disting. Pub. Svc. award Gov.'s Disting. Pub. Svc. Award Coun., 1985, Washburn award Ctrl. N.Mex. Autobahn Soc., 1986, cert. of appreciation Nat. Recreation and Pks. Assn., Spl. Olympics Program of N.Mex., Nat. Alliance of Businessmen, LUCAC Nat. Edn. Svc. Ctr., Inc., N.Mex., cert. THANKS U. N.Mex., cert. appreciation dept. health, phys. edn. and recreation; cert. appreciation Albuquerque Internat. Balloon Fiesta, Open Space Task Force, Albuquerque Police Dept., N.Mex. Horse Coun. and Heights Lions Club; recipient Leadership award Keep Am. Beautiful; cert. appreciation for vol. svcs. Gov. of N.Mex.; named Individual of Yr. Albuquerque Conservation Assn., 1986. Mem. Assn. Retarded Citizens (pres. bd. dirs. 1982-83), N.Mex. Recreation and Pks. Assn. (v.p. 1985-86, pres. 1986-87, mem. profl. cert. bd. 1983-86, profl. award 1982). Office: City Albuquerque Dept Solid Waste Mgmt 4600 Edith Blvd NE Albuquerque NM 87107-4043 Fax: 505-761-8167

SEDLOCK, JOY, psychiatric social worker; b. Memphis, Jan. 23, 1958; d. George Rudolph Sedlock and Mary Robson; m. Thomas Robert Jones, Aug. 8, 1983. AA, Ventura (Calif.) Jr. Coll., 1978; BS in Psychology, Calif. Luth. U., 1980; MS in Counseling and Psychology, U. LaVerne, 1983; MSW, Calif. State U., Sacramento, 1986. Research asst. Camarillo (Calif.) State Hosp., 1981, tchr.'s aide, 1982; sub. tchr. asst. Ventura County Sch. Dist., 1981; teaching asst. Ventura Jr. Coll., 1980-82, tchr. adult edn., 1980-84; psychiatric social worker Yolo County Day Treatment Ctr., Broderick, Calif., 1986, Napa (Calif.) State Hosp., 1986—. Bd. dirs. Napa County Humane Soc. Home: PO Box 1095 Yountville CA 94599-1095 Office: Napa State Hosp Napa Vallejo Hwy Napa CA 49558

SEDWICK, JOHN W. judge; b. Kittanning, Pa., Mar. 13, 1946; s. Jack D. and Marion (Hilton) S.; m. Deborah Brown, Aug. 22, 1966; children: Jack D. II, Whitney Marie. BA summa cum laude, Dartmouth Coll., 1968; JD cum laude, Harvard U., 1972. Bar: Alaska 1972, U.S. Dist. Ct. Alaska 1972, U.S. Ct. Appeals (9th cir.) 1973. Lawyer Burr, Pease and Kurtz, Anchorage, 1972-81, 1982-92; dir. div. lands State of Alaska, Anchorage, 1981-82; judge U.S. Dist. Ct. Alaska, Anchorage, 1992—. Mem. Commonwealth North, Anchorage, 1985; bd. dirs. South Addition Alaska R.R. Com., Anchorage, 1984. Sgt. USNG, 1969-72. Mem. ABA, Alaska Bar Assn. (chmn. environ. law sect. 1984, law examiners com. 1986-89, civil rules com. 1990-92, fee arbitration com. 1991-92). Episcopalian. Office: US Dist Ct Box 32 222 W 7th Ave Unit 4 Anchorage AK 99513-7564

SEE, CAROLYN, English language educator, novelist, book critic; b. Pasadena, Calif., Jan. 13, 1934; d. George Newton Laws and Kate Louise (Sullivan) Daly; m. Richard Edward See, Feb. 18, 1955 (div. June 1959); 1 child, Lisa Lenine; m. Tom Sturak, June 11, 1959; 1 child, Clara Elizabeth Marya. BA, Calif. State U., L.A., 1958; PhD, UCLA, 1963. Prof. English, Loyola Marymount Coll., L.A., 1970-85, UCLA, L.A., 1985—; book critic L.A. Times, 1981-93, Washington Post, 1993—. Author: (novels) Rhine Maidens, 1980, Golden Days, 1986, Making History, 1991, Dreaming: Hard Luck and Good Times In America, 1995, The Handyman, 1999, also 3 others. Bd. dirs. Calif. Arts Coun., L.A., 1987-91, Day Break, for homeless, Santa Monica, Calif., 1989—, Friends of English, UCLA, 1990—; buddy for life AIDS Project Los Angeles, AIDS relief, L.A., 1990—. Recipient award Sidney Hillman Found., 1972, Robert Kirsch award L.A. Times, 1994; PEN Ctr. USA West Lifetime Achievement award 1998; grantee Nat. Endowment for Arts, 1980, Guggenheim fellow, 1990-91. Mem. Writers Guild Am., Libr. Found. Calif., PEN Ctr. USA West (pres. 1990-91), Nat. Book Critics Cir. (bd. dirs. 1986-90). Democrat. Avocations: gardening, sailing, dancing, brush clearing. Home: 17339 Tramonto Dr Pacific Palisades CA 90272-3124 Office: UCLA Dept English 405 Hilgard Ave Los Angeles CA 90095-9000

SEEBACH, LYDIA MARIE, physician; b. Red Wing, Minn., Nov. 9, 1920; d. John Henry and Marie (Gleusen) S.; m. Keith Edward Wentz, Oct. 16, 1959; children: Brooke Marie, Scott. BS, U. Minn., 1942, MB, 1943, MD, 1944, MS in Medicine, 1951. Diplomate Am. Bd. Internal Medicine. Intern Kings County Hosp., Bklyn., 1944; fellow Mayo Found., Rochester, Minn., 1945-51; pvt. practice Oakland, Calif., 1952-60, San Francisco, 1961—. Asst. clin. prof. U. Calif., San Francisco, 1981—; mem., vice chmn. Arthritis Clinic, Presbyn. Hosp., San Francisco, 1961-88, pharmacy com., 1963-78; chief St. Mary's Hosp. Arthritis Clinic, San Francisco, 1968-72; exec. bd. Pacific Med. Ctr., San Francisco, 1974-76. Contbr. articles to med. jours. Fellow ACP; mem. AMA, Am. Med. Womens Assn. (pres. Calif. chpt. 1968-70), Am. Rheumatism Assn., Am. Soc. Internal Medicine, Pan Am. Med. Womens Assn. (treas.), Calif. Acad. Medicine, Calif. Soc. Internal Medicine, Calif. Med. Assn., San Francisco Med. Soc., San Francisco Med. Assn., San Francisco Soc. Internal Medicine, No. Calif. Rheumatism Assn., Internat. Med. Women's Assn., Mayo Alumni (bd. dirs. 1983-89), Iota Sigma Pi. Republican. Lutheran. Avocations: music, cooking, gardening, needlepoint. Office: 490 Post St Ste 939 San Francisco CA 94102-1414

SEEBASS, ALFRED RICHARD, III, aerospace engineer, educator, university dean; b. Denver, Mar. 27, 1936; s. Alfred Richard Jr. and Marie Estelle (Wright) S.; m. Nancy Jane Palm, June 20, 1958; children: Erik Peter, Scott Gregory. BS in Engring. magna cum laude, Princeton U., 1958, MS in Engring., 1961; PhD, Cornell U., 1962. Asst. prof., assoc. prof. Cornell U., Ithaca, N.Y., 1962-72, prof. aerospace engring., assoc. dean engring., 1972-75; hdqrs. staff rsch. divsn. NASA, 1966-67; prof. aerospace engring., mech. engring. and math. U. Ariz., Tucson, 1975-81; dean U. Colo. Coll. Engring. and Applied Sci., Boulder, 1981-94; John R. Woodhull prof. and chair aerospace engring. scis. U. Colo., Boulder, 1993-94; faculty assoc. Boeing Sci. Rsch. Labs., 1970. Cons. in field; mem. coms. NAE, NAS, NRC, NASA, Dept. Transp., sci. adv. bd. Air Force, Aero. and Space Engring. Bd., Los Alamos Nat. Lab; grant investigator NASA, Office Naval Rsch., Air Force Office Sci. Rsch., 1966—; mem. U.S.-Israel Bi-nat. Fund; aeronautics and space engring. bd. NRC, 1977-84, vice-chmn., 1979-81, chmn., 1981-83, mem. Commn. on Engring. and Tech. Sys., 1982-83; mem. Numerical Aerodynamics Simulator Adv. Group, 1978-97; chmn. Air Force Office Scientific Rsch. rev. panel Flight Dynamics Lab., Wright-Patterson AFB, 1979; adv. coun. NASA, 1981-83; survey com. on plasma physics and fluids, subcom. on fluids NRC, 1983-84; engring. rsch. bd. Panel on Transp. Sys. Rsch., 1984-85; sci. adv. bd. USAF, 1984-88, chmn. Air Force Operational Test & Evaluation Ctr. Divsn. Adv. Group, 1986-88, mem. Arnold Engring. & Devel. Ctr. Divsn. Adv. Group, 1984-88, aerospace vehicles panel, 1984-88; adv. coun. univ. study planning group NASA, 1988-97; bd. dirs. Aerosonde, Ltd.; mech. and electronic external adv. com. Los Alamos (N.Mex.) Nat. Lab., 1991-93, chair divsn. rev. com. Engring. Scis. & Applications, Los Alamos, 1995-98; mem. NASA Adv. Coun. U. Rels. Task Force, 1991-93; mem. Commn. on Phys. Scis., Math. & Applications NRC, 1992-95; chmn. NRC Com. Air Force Hypersonics Tech., 1997-98. Editor: Sonic Boom Research, 1967, Nonlinear Waves 1974, Russian, 1977; assoc. editor: Physics of Fluids, 1978-80; mem. editl. bd. Ann. Rev. Fluid Mechanics, Phys. Fluids, AIAA Jour.; editor-in-chief (book series) Progress Astronautics and Aeronautics, 1990-95; contbg. author: Handbook of Applied Mathematics, 1974; contbr. articles to profl. jours., chpts. to books; reviewer Jour. Fluid Mechanics, Physics of Fluids, Jour. Acoustical Soc. Am., AIAA Jour., Jour. Aircraft, Jour. Applied Mechanics, NSF. Daniel and Florence Guggenheim fellow Princeton U., 1958-59, Woodrow Wilson fellow Cornell U., 1959-60; recipient Disting. Engring. Alumni award U. Colo., 1983, Meritorious Civilian Svc. award Dept. Air Force, 1988, (with H. Sobieczky) Max Planck Rsch. prize, Germany, 1991, U. Colo. medal 1994, U. Colo. Coll. of Engring. Centennial medal 1994, Frank J. Malina medal Internat. Astronautics Fedn., 1994. Fellow AAAS (mem. engring. sect. nominating com. 1987-90, chair 1990, coun. del. engring. sect. 1991-94, vice chair, chair engring. sect. 1995-97), AIAA (mem. fluid mechanics tech. com. 1977-80, tech. dir. bd. dirs. 1978-81, exec com. 1980-81, assoc. editor jour. 1981-83, Disting. lectr. 1995-98); mem. Nat. Acad. Engring. (aerospace peer com. 1987-90, 99—, chair 1990, mem. com. on membership 1991-93, vice chmn. 1991, chair 1992, acad. adv. bd. 1997-98), Am. Soc. Engring. Edn. (mem. sr. rsch. award com. 1990-93, chair 1993), Sigma Xi, Tau Beta Pi. Office: U Colo Box 429 Aerospace Engring Sci Boulder CO 80309-0429 E-mail: seebass@spot.colorado.edu

SEEGAL, JOHN FRANKLIN, lawyer; b. Newton, Mass., May 21, 1946; s. Samuel Melbourne and Martha (Lewenberg) S.; m. Barbara Ellen Wayne, Apr. 2, 1982; children: Sarah Rachel, Laura Rose. BA, Harvard U., MBA, JD, Harvard U., 1973. Assoc. Orrick, Herrington & Sutcliffe, LLP, San Francisco, 1973-78, ptnr., 1979—. Co-chmn. Inst. on Securities Regulation, 2001—. Mem. ABA, Calif. Bar Assn. Republican. Jewish. Office: Orrick Herrington & Sutcliffe LLP 400 Sansome St San Francisco CA 94111-3143

SEEGER, LEINAALA ROBINSON, law librarian, educator; b. Wailuku, Hawaii, July 2, 1944; d. John Adam and Anna Hiilani (Leong) Robinson; 1 child, Maile Lea. BA, U. Wash., 1966; JD, U. Puget Sound, 1977; M in Law Librarianship, U. Wash., 1979. Bar: Wash. 1977. Reference librarian U. Puget Sound Sch. Law., Tacoma, 1977-79, assoc. law librarian, 1981-86; asst. librarian McGeorge Sch. Law, U. of Pacific, Sacramento, 1979-81; assoc. librarian pub. svc. Harvard Law Sch., Cambridge, Mass., 1986-89; dir. law library, assoc. prof. law U. Idaho Coll. Law, Moscow, 1989-97, U. Hawaii Sch. of Law, Honolulu, 1997—. Mem. Assn. Am. Law Schs. (librs. and technol. com. 1997-99, chmn. 1998-99), Wash. state Bar Assn., Am. Assn. Law Librs. (chmn. minority com. 1990-91, v.p., pres.-elect Western Pacific chpt. 1985-86, 90-91, pres. 1991-92, vice chmn. edn. com. 1991-92, chmn. 1992-93). Avocations: scuba, snorkeling, wine education, flying, aerobics.

SEEGMILLER, JARVIS EDWIN, biochemist, educator; b. St. George, Utah, June 22, 1920; m. Roberta Eads, 1950 (dec. 1992); children: Dale S. Maudlin, Robert E., Lisa S. Taylor, Richard L.; m. Barbara A. Ellertson, 1995. AB, U. Utah, 1942; MD, U. Chgo., 1948. Asst. U.S. Bur. Mines, Utah, 1941; asst. nat. def. rsch. com. Northwestern Tech. Inst., 1942-44; asst. medicine U. Chgo., 1947-48; intern Johns Hopkins Hosp., 1948-49; biochemist Nat. Inst. Arthritis and Metabolic Diseases, 1949-51; rsch. assoc. Thorndike Meml. Lab. Harvard Med. Sch., 1952-53; vis. investigator Pub. Health Rsch. Inst., N.Y.C., 1953-54; chief sect. human biochemistry, genetics, asst. sci. dir. Nat. Inst. Arthritis and Metabolic Diseases, 1954-69; prof. dept. medicine, dir. divsn. rheumatology U. Calif., San Diego, 1969-90, founding dir. Stein Inst. Rsch. Aging, 1983-90, prof. emeritus medicine, assoc. dir. Stein Inst. Rsch. Aging, 1990—. Vis. scientist U. Coll. Hosp. Sch. Medicine, London, 1964-65; Harvey Soc. lectr., 1970. Contbr. numerous articles to profl. jours. Macy scholar Basel Inst. Immunology; Guggenheim fellow Swiss Inst. Exptl. Cancer Rsch., Lausanne, 1982-83, John Simon Guggenheim Meml. Found. fellow, 1982, Fogarty Internat. fellow Oxford U., 1989. Mem. Nat. Acad. Sci., Harvey Soc. (hon.), Am. Soc. Biol. Chemists, Am. Rheumatism Assn., Am. Fedn. Clin. Rsch., Am. Soc. Human Genetics, Am. Soc. Clin. Investigation, AAAS, Assn. Am. Physicians, Am. Acad. Arts and Sci. Office: U Calif San Diego 9500 Gilman Dr La Jolla CA 92093-0664 E-mail: jseegmiller@ucsd.edu

SEELENFREUND, ALAN, pharmaceutical company executive; b. N.Y.C., Oct. 22, 1936; s. Max and Gertrude (Roth) S.; m. Ellyn Bolt; 1 child, Eric. BME, Cornell U., 1959, M. in Indsl. Engring., 1960; PhD in Mgmt. Sci., Stanford U., 1967. Asst. prof. bus. adminstrn. Grad. Sch. Bus. Stanford U., Palo Alto, Calif., 1966-71; mgmt. cons. Strong, Wishart and Assocs., San Francisco, 1971-75; various mgmt. positions McKesson Corp., San Francisco, 1975-84, v.p., chief fin. officer, 1984-86, exec. v.p., chief fin. officer, 1986-89, chmn., CEO, 1989-97, chmn., 1997-99, also bd. dirs.; chmn. McKesson HBOC Corp., San Francisco, 1997—. Bd. dirs. Pacific Gas and Electric Co. Bd. dir. Golden Gate Nat. Park Assn. Mem. Nature Conservancy, World Wildlife Fund, St. Francis Yacht Club, Villa Taverna Club, Pacific Union Club. Avocations: sailing, skiing, hiking. Office: McKesson Corp 1 Post St Ste 3275 San Francisco CA 94104-5292

SEEMAN, MELVIN, sociologist, educator; b. Balt., Feb. 5, 1918; s. Morris and Sophie (Kostman) S.; m. Alice Ruth Zerbola, June 30, 1944; children— Teresa E., Paul D. B.A., Johns Hopkins U., 1944; Ph.D., Ohio State U., 1947. Asst. prof. sociology Ohio State U., 1947-52, assoc. prof., 1953-59; prof. UCLA, 1959-88, prof. emeritus, 1988—. Mem. Am. Sociol. Assn. Home: 21532 Paseo Serra St Malibu CA 90265-5112 Office: UCLA Dept Sociology 405 Hilgard Ave Los Angeles CA 90095-9000 E-mail: mseeman@conet.ucla.edu

SEGAL, HELENE ROSE, periodical editor; b. L.A., Jan. 31, 1955; d. Alan and Lila E. Segal. Student, Calif. State U., Fullerton, 1973-75; BA in English, U. Calif., Santa Barbara, 1978. Library asst. ABC-CLIO, Santa Barbara, 1979-80, editorial asst., 1980-81, asst. editor, 1981-83; mng. editor ABC POL SCI, ABC-CLIO, Santa Barbara, 1983-2001; project mgr. ABC-CLIO, Santa Barbara, 2001—. Mem. Am. Polit. Sci. Assn., Current World Leaders (adv. bd. 1989—). Avocations: reading, collecting, swimming. Home: 142 La Vista Grande Santa Barbara CA 93103-2817 Office: ABC CLIO 130 Cremona Dr Ste C Santa Barbara CA 93117-5505 E-mail: hsegal@abc-clio.com

SEGAL, JACK, mathematics educator; b. Phila., May 9, 1934; s. Morris and Rose (Novin) S.; m. Arlene Stern, Dec. 18, 1955; children: Gregory, Sharon. B.S., U. Miami, 1955, M.S., 1957; Ph.D., U. Ga., 1960. Instr. math. U. Wash., Seattle, 1960-61, asst. prof., 1961-65, assoc. prof., 1965-70, prof., 1970-1999, chmn. dept., 1975-78, prof. emeritus, 2000—. Author: Lecture Notes in Mathematics, 1978, Shape Theory, 1982. NSF postdoctoral fellow Inst. Advanced Study, Princeton, N.J., 1963-64; Fulbright fellow U. Zagreb, Croatia, 1969-70, U. Coll. London hon. rsch. fellow, 1988; Nat. Acad. Sci. exch. prof. U. Zagreb, Croatia, 1979-80. Mem. Am. Math. Soc. Home: 8711 25th Pl NE Seattle WA 98115-3416 Office: U Washington Dept Mathematics Seattle WA 98195-0001 E-mail: segal@math.washington.edu

SEGEL, KAREN LYNN JOSEPH, lawyer, taxation specialist; b. Youngstown, Ohio, Jan. 15, 1947; d. Samuel Dennis and Helen Anita Joseph; m. Alvin Gerald Segel, June 9, 1968 (div. Sept. 1976); 1 child, Adam James. BA in Soviet and East European Studies, Boston U., 1968; JD, Southwestern U., 1975. Bar: Calif., 1996, U.S. Tax Ct., 1996, U.S. Dist. Ct. (cen. dist.) Calif., 1996, U.S. Ct. Appeals (9th cir.), 1997. Adminstrv. asst. Olds Brunel & Co., N.Y.C., 1968-69, U.S. Banknote Corp., N.Y.C., 1969-70; tax acct. S.N. Chilkov & Co. CPA's, Beverly Hills, Calif., 1971-74; intern Calif. Corps. Commr., 1975; tax. sr. Oppenheim Appel & Dixon CPA's, L.A., 1978, Fox, Westheimer & Co. CPA's, L.A., 1978, Zebrak, Levine & Mepos CPA's, L.A., 1979; ind. cons. acctg., taxation specialist Beverly Hills, 1980—. Settlement officer L.A. County Superior Ct., 2000; law student mentor Southwestern U., 1996-2000, tax moot ct. judge, 1997; settlement officer Beverly Hills Mcpl. Ct. Editorial adv. bd. Am. Biog. Inst. High sch. amb. to Europe People-to-People Orgn., 1963. Mem. Calif. State Bar, Women's Inner Circle of Achievement, Complex Litig. Inns of Ct., L.A. County Bar Assn, Beverly Hills Tinseltown Rose Soc. Avocations: collecting seashells, lhasa apso dog breeding, art, travel, music. E-mail: kjslaw@earthlink.net

SEGERBLOM, SHARON B. social services administrator; b. Miami, Okla., Dec. 19, 1948; d. Charles L. and Doris E. (Randall) Butler; m. Richard Segerblom; children: Eva, Carl. Student, Okla. State U.; degree in nursing, U. Tulsa, 1971; BA in Polit. Sci., U. Nev. Past mgr. Neighborhood Response divsn. City of Las Vegas, past intergovtl. cmty. rels. cood., past chief asst. to the mayor, dir. Neighborhood Svcs., 1997—. Rschr. Focus on Nev.'s Children, 1987, Focus on Nev.'s Women, co-editor, video writer, prodr. Issues chairperson Gov.'s Conf. on Women, 1989-90; 1st v.p. Clark County Area Coun. PTA, 1989-90, Girl Scouts USA Frontier Coun., 1991-93; bd. dirs. WE Can, 1989-90, Martin Luther King Jr. Com., Weed and Seed Steering Com.; bd. dirs., past pres. Clark County Atty.'s Wives, 1988-89; past pres. Women's Dem. Club Clark County; mem. Clark County Dem. Ctrl. Com., 1989-90; past bd. dirs. Jr. League of Las Vegas, 1990; mem. adv. bd. REACH-OUT; fundraiser Boy Scouts Am., Boulder Dam Coun. Recipient Cmty. Svcs. award for excellence Gov.'s Conf. on Women, 1990, Heart of Gold award Focus on Nev.'s Women, Jr. League of Las Vegas, 1989-90. Mem. Assn. for Children for Enforcement of Support (bd. dirs. 1989-90). Office: Dept Neighborhood Svcs City Las Vegas City Hall 400 Stewart Ave Las Vegas NV 89101-2927

SEGGER, MARTIN JOSEPH, museum director, art history educator; b. Felixtowe, Eng., Nov. 22, 1946; s. Gerald Joseph and Lillian Joan (Barker-Emery) S.; m. Angele Cordonier, Oct. 4, 1968; children: Cara Michelle, Marie-Claire, Margaret Ellen. BA, U. Victoria, B.C. Can., 1969, diploma in edn., 1970; MPhil, U. London, 1973. Prof. art history U. Victoria, 1970-74; museologist Royal B.C. Mus., Victoria, 1974-77; dir. Maltwood Art Mus., prof. art history U. Victoria, 1977—, dir. cmty. rels., 2001—. Cons. Nat. Mus. Corp., Ottawa, 1977, UNESCO, O.E.A., Cairo, 1983. Author: exhbn. catalogue House Beautiful, 1975, Arts of the Forgotten Pioneers, 1971, Victoria: An Architectural History, 1979, (commendation Am. Assn. State and Local History 1980), This Old House, 1975, This Old Town, 1979, British Columbia Parliament Buildings, 1979, The Heritage of Canada, 1981, Samuel Maclure: In Search of Appropriate Form, 1986 (Hallmark award 1987, 98), (a guide) St. Andrew's Cathedral, 1990, The Development of Gordon Head Campus, 1988, An Introduction to Museum Studies, 1989, An Introduction to Heritage Conservation, 1990, Botswana Live, 1994, Exploring Victoria's Architecture, 1996; contbr., cons. British Columbia Encyclopedia, 2000. Bd. govs. Heritage Can. Found., 1979-83; chmn. City of Victoria Heritage Adv. Com., 1975-79; bd. dirs. Heritage Trust, 1977-86, B.C. Touring Coun., Sta. CFUV Radio, B.C. Govt. House Found., 1987-93, Royal Brit. Columbia Mus., 1996—; co-chair Brit. Columbia Arts Festival; mem. B.C. Heritage Adv. Bd., 1973-83; councillor City of Victoria, 1987-93; vice-chair Provincial Capital Commn., 1991—; pres. Assn. Vancouver Island Municipalities, 1993-94; chmn. B.C. Festival of the Arts, 1999; bd. dirs. Internat. Coun. Mus.-Can., 1999; bd. mem. Victoria Coll. Art, 2001—. Decorated knight Equestrian Order of Holy Sepulchre of Jerusalem; recipient award Heritage Can. Communications, 1976, Heritage Conservation award Lt. Gov. B.C., 1989, Harley J. McKee award Assn. Preservation Technology, 1994; named Hon. Citizen City of Victoria, 2000. Fellow Royal Soc. Arts, Can. Mus. Assn. (counsellor 1975-77), Can. Mus. Assn.; mem. Internat. Coun. Mus. (chair internat. com. for tng. of pers. 1995-98), Internat. Coun. Monuments and Sites (bd. dirs. 1980-82), Soc. Study Architecture Can. (bd. dirs. 1979-81), Authors Club (London), Can Mus. Dirs. Orgn., Carnavon Club. Roman Catholic. Avocations: travel, motor mechanics, water color painting. Home: 1035 Sutlej St Victoria BC Canada V8V 3P2 E-mail: msegger@uvic.ca

SEGIL, LARRAINE DIANE, materials company executive; b. Johannesburg, South Africa, July 15, 1948; came to U.S., 1974; d. Jack and Norma Estelle (Cohen) Wolfowitz; m. Clive Melwyn Segil, Mar. 9, 1969; 1 child, James Harris. BA, U. Witwatersrand, South Africa, 1967, BA with honours, 1969; JD, Southwestern U., L.A., 1979; MBA, Pepperdine U., 1985. Bar: Calif. 1979, U.S. Supreme Ct. 1982. Cons. in internat. transactions, L.A., 1976-79; atty. Long & Levit, L.A., 1979-81; chmn., pres. Marina Credit Corp., L.A., 1981-85; pres., chief exec. officer Electronic Space Products Internat., L.A., 1985-87; mng. ptnr. The Lared Group, L.A., 1987—; pres. Lared Presentations Inc.; keynote spkr. and expert on alliances, globalization, and leadership. Author: (novel) Belonging, 1994, Intelligent Business Alliances, 1996. Bd. govs. Cedars Sinai Med. Ctr., L.A., 1984—; bd. dirs. So. Calif. Tech. Execs. Network, 1984-86, DARE. Mem. ABA (chmn. internat. law com. young lawyers div. 1980-84), Internat. Assn. Young Lawyers (exec. coun. 1979-81, coun. internat. law and practice 1983-84), World Tech. Execs. Network (chmn.). Avocations: piano, horseback riding. Office: The Lared Group 1901 Ave of Stars Los Angeles CA 90067-6001

SEIDEL, GEORGE ELIAS, JR. animal scientist, educator; b. Reading, Pa., July 13, 1943; s. George E. Sr. and Grace Esther (Heinly) S.; m. Sarah Beth Moore, May 28, 1970; 1 child, Andrew. BS, Pa. State U., 1965; MS, Cornell U., 1968, PhD, 1970; postgrad., Harvard U. Med. Sch., Boston, 1970-71. Asst. prof. physiology Colo. State U., Ft. Collins, 1971-75, assoc. prof., 1975-83, prof., 1983-93, univ. disting. prof., 1993—. Vis. scientist Yale U., 1978-79, MIT, 1986-87; mem. bd. on agr. NRC. Co-editor: New Technologies in Animal Breeding, 1981; contbr. articles to profl. jours. Recipient Alexander Von Humboldt award, N.Y.C., 1983, Animal Breeding Research award Nat. Assn. Animal Breeders, Columbia, Mo., 1983, Clark award Colo. State U., 1982, Upjohn Physiology award, 1986; Gov's. award for Sci. and Tech., Colo., 1986. Mem. AAAS, NAS, Am. Dairy Sci. Assn., Am. Soc. Animal Sci. (Young Animal Scientist award 1983), Soc. for Study of Reprodn., Internat. Embryo Transfer Soc. (pres. 1979, disting. svc. award 2001). Home: 3101 Arrowhead Rd Laporte CO 80535-9374 Office: Colo State U Animal Repro Biotech Lab Fort Collins CO 80523-0001

SEIFF, ALVIN, planetary, atmospheric and aerodynamics scientist; b. Kansas City, Mo., Feb. 26, 1922; s. Harry Louis and Sara Dorothy (Silverstone) S.; m. Robbye Walker, Mar. 27, 1948 (div. Oct. 1959); children: David Wilson, Deborah Ellen Seiff Hedgecock; m. Julia Gwynne Hill, June 23, 1968; children: Michael Harry, Geoffrey Bernard. BS ChemE, U. Mo., 1942; postgrad., U. Tenn., 1946-48, Stanford U., 1959-60. Chem. engr. TVA, Florence, Ala., 1942-43; tech. supr. uranium isotope separ. Tenn. Eastman Corp., Oak Ridge, 1944-45; instr. physics U. Tenn., Knoxville, 1945-48; aero. rsch. scientist NACA Ames Aero. Lab., Moffett Field, Calif., 1948-57; chief supersonic free flight rsch. br. NACA, Moffett Field, 1952-63; chief vehicle environment div. NASA Ames Rsch. Ctr., Moffett Field, 1963-72, sr. staff scientist dir.'s office, 1972-77, sr. staff scientist space sci. div., 1977-86; sr. rsch. assoc. San Jose (Calif.) State U. Found., 1987—. Mem. entry sci. team Viking Mars Mission Langley Rsch. Ctr., NASA, Hampton, Va., 1972-77, mem. sci. steering group Pioneer Venus Project Ames Rsch. Ctr., Moffett Field, 1972-82, Galileo Project, sci. group Jet Propulsion Lab., Pasadena, 1979—, mem. sci. team Soviet-French Vega Venus Balloom Mission, 1984-87, chmn. sci. adv. team atmosphere structure and meteorology Mars Pathfinder Mission, 1993—;

mem. basic Rsch. Coun., NASA, Washington, 1973-76; Von Karman lectr., 1990; prin. investigator structure of Jupiter's atmosphere, Galileo entry probe, 1995. Author and editor: Ballistic Range Technology, 1972; (with others) Venus, 1983; contbr. articles to profl. jours. Recipient Exceptional Scientific Achievement medals NASA, 1978, 81, 97, H. Julian Allen award Ames Rsch. Ctr., 1982; named to Space Hall of Fame Mus., 1997. Fellow AIAA (assoc.); mem. Am. Astron. Soc. (div. planetary sci.), Am. Geophys. Union. Avocations: music, piano, gardening, home design and construction. Office: Ames Rsch Ctr Mail Stop 245 2 Moffett Field CA 94035

SEIFF, STEPHEN S. ophthalmologist; b. L.A., Sept. 30, 1925; s. Max and Minnie F. (Feldman) S.; m. Gloria Louise Holtzman, Apr. 16, 1950; children: Stuart R., Sherri Seiff Sloane, Karen Seiff Sacks. AA, UCLA, 1945; AB, U. Calif., Berkeley, 1946; MD, U. Calif., San Francisco, 1949. Diplomate Am. Bd. Ophthalmology. Intern County Gen. Hosp., L.A., 1949-50; fellow in anesthesiology Lahey Clinic, Boston, 1950-51; resident in ophthalmology U. Calif., San Francisco, 1952-55; clin. prof. dept. ophthalmology UCLA, 1956—; pvt. practice Beverly Hills, Calif., 1955—; clin. chief divsn. ophthalmology Cedars/Sinai Med. Ctr., L.A., 1957—; attending ophthalmologist Children's Hosp., L.A., 1956-94. Lectr. in field; assoc. examiner Am. Bd. Ophthalmology. Collaborating author: Clinical Anticoagulant Therapy, 1965; contbr. articles to profl. jours. Bd. dirs. That Man May See Inc., San Francisco; former exec. com. mem. UCLA Hosp. Lt. M.C. USNR, 1950-52. Recipient Sr. Honor award UCLA Dept. Ophthalmology, 1994. Fellow ACS, Am. Acad. Ophthalmology; mem. L.A. Soc. Ophthalmology (past pres.), Frederick Cordes Eye Soc. (past nat. pres.), Am. Soc. Cataract and Refractive Surgery (founding mem.). Avocation: sailing. Office: 435 N Roxbury Dr Ste 107 Beverly Hills CA 90210-5003 E-mail: sseiff@aol.com

SEILER, FRITZ ARNOLD, physicist; b. Basel, Switzerland, Dec. 20, 1931; came to U.S., 1980; s. Friedrich and Marie (Maibach) S.; m. Mary Catherine Coster, Dec. 22, 1964; children: Monica, Simone, Daniel. BA in Econs., Basel Sch. of Econs., 1951; PhD in Physics, U. Basel, 1962. Rsch. assoc. U. Wis., Madison, 1962-63; scientific assoc. U. Basel, 1963-69, privat dozent, 1969-75, dozent, 1975-80; sr. scientist Lovelace Inhalation Toxicology Inst., Albuquerque, 1980-90; sr. tech. assoc. IT Corp., Albuquerque, 1990-92, disting. tech. assoc., 1992-96; v.p. Inst. Regulatory Sci., Albuquerque, 1996-97; prin. Sigma Five Cons., Los Lunas, N.Mex., 1997—. Cons. Swiss Dept. Def., 1968-74; vis. scientist Lawrence Berkeley Labs., 1974-75. Contbr. numerous articles to profl. jours. With Swiss Army staff, 1964-75. Fellow Am. Phys. Soc., Health Physics Soc., Soc. for Risk Analysis, Fachverband fuer Strahlenschutz, Am. Nat. Stds. Inst. (mgmt. coun. 1987—, com. N14 1986—). Office: Sigma Five Consulting PO Box 1709 Los Lunas NM 87031-5193 Fax: 505-866-5197. E-mail: faseiler@nmia.com

SEILER, STEVEN LAWRENCE, health facility administrator; b. Chgo., Dec. 30, 1941; married. B, U. Ariz., 1963; M, U. Iowa, 1965. Adminstrv. resident Rush-Presbyn.-St. Luke's Med. Ctr., Chgo., 1965, adminstrv. asst., 1965-68; asst. adminstr. Lake Forest (Ill.) Hosp., 1968-71, adminstr., 1971-73, pres., 1973-86; exec. v.p Voluntary Hosps. Am., Park Ridge, Ill., 1987-89, sr. v.p., 1986-92; CEO Good Samaritan Regional Med. Ctr., Phoenix, 1992—. Adj. prof. Contbr. articles to profl. jours. Mem. AHA (svc. com.)., Ill. Hosp. Assn. (chair 1980-81). Home: 3930 E Rancho Dr Paradise Vly AZ 85253-5025 Office: Good Samaritan Regional Med Ctr 1111 E Mcdowell Rd Phoenix AZ 85006-2612

SEINFELD, JERRY, comedian; b. Bklyn., Apr. 29, 1955; s. Kal and Betty S. Grad. with degree in theatre communications, Queens (N.Y.) Coll., 1976. Former salesman. Stand-up comedian, 1976—; joke-writer (TV series) Benson, ABC, 1980; actor, co-writer, prod. (TV series) Seinfeld, NBC-TV, 1989-97 (Emmy award Outstanding Comedy Series, 1993, Emmy nomination, Lead Actor - Comedy Series, 1994), (TV movie) The Ratings Game, 1984, The Tommy Chong Roast, 1986, The Seinfeld Chronicles, 1990, I'm Telling You for the Last Time, 1999; writer Jerry Seinfeld-Stand-Up Confidential, 1987; author: Sein Language, 1993.; guest appearances The Larry Sanders Show, 1992, News Radio, 1995. Recipient Am. Comedy award funniest male comedy stand-up, 1988, funniest actor in a TV series, 1992. Jewish. Avocations: Zen, yoga.

SEINFELD, JOHN HERSH, chemical engineering educator; b. Elmira, N.Y., Aug. 3, 1942; s. Ben B. and Minna (Johnson) S. BS, U. Rochester, 1964; PhD, Princeton U., 1967. Asst. prof. chem. engring. Calif. Inst. Tech., Pasadena, 1967-70, assoc. prof., 1970-74, prof., 1974—, Louis E. Nohl prof., 1980—, exec. officer for chem. engring., 1973-90, chmn. engring. and applied sci. div., 1990-2000. Allan P. Colburn meml. lectr. U. Del., 1976; Camille and Henry Dreyfus Found. lectr. MIT, 1979; mem. coun. Gordon Rsch. Confs., 1980-83; Donald L. Katz lectr. U. Mich., 1981; Reilly lectr. U. Notre Dame, 1983; Dean's Disting. lectr. U. Rochester, 1985; Katz lectr. CUNY, 1985; McCabe lectr. N.C. State U., 1986; Lewis lectr. MIT, 1986; Union Carbide lectr. SUNY, Buffalo; Van Winkle lectr. U. Tex., 1988; Bicentennial lectr. La. State U., 1988; Ida Beam lectr. U. Iowa, 1989, David Mason lectr. Stanford U., 1989; Julian Smith lectr. Cornell U., 1990; Merck lectr. Rutgers U., 1991; Henske Disting. lectr. Yale U., 1991; lectr. AIChE, 1980; Centennial lectr. U. Pa., 1993; Miles Disting. lectr. U. Pitts., 1994; Kelly lectr. Purdue U., 1996; Disting. rsch. lectr. Carnegie Mellon U., 1998; Berkeley lectr. U. Calif., Berkeley, 1998; Sigma Xi lectr., 1998—, Merck Sharp & Dohme lectr. U. P.R., 1998; Hess lectr. U. Va., 1998; inaugural disting. lectr. U. Toledo, 1999, Priestly lectr. Commonwealth Scientific and Indsl. Rsch. Orgn., 2000. Author: Numerical Solution of Ordinary Differential Equations, 1971, Mathematical Methods in Chemical Engineering, Vol. III, Process Modeling, Estimation and Identification, 1974, Air Pollution: Physical and Chemical Fundamentals, 1975, Lectures in Atmospheric Chemistry, 1980, Atmospheric Chemistry and Physics of Air Pollution, 1986, Fundamentals of Air Pollution Engineering, 1988, Distributed Parameter Systems--Theory and Applications, 1989, Atmospheric Chemistry and Physics, 1998; assoc. editor Environ. Sci., Tech., 1981-97; mem. editorial bd. Computers, Chem. Engring, 1974-96, Jour. Colloid and Interface Sci, 1978-95, Advances in Chem. Engring, 1980—, Revs. in Chem. Engring, 1980—, Aerosol Sci. and Tech., 1981-93; assoc. editor: Atmospheric Environment, 1976—. Recipient Donald P. Eckman award Am. Automatic Control Coun., 1970, Pub. Svc. medal NASA, 1980, Disting. Alumnus award U. Rochester, 1989; Camille and Henry Dreyfus Found. Tchr. Scholar grantee, 1972. Fellow Japan Soc. Promotion Sci., AIChE (bd. dirs. 1988-91, mem. editl. bd. jours. 1985—, Allan P. Colburn award 1976, William H. Walker award 1986, Warren K. Lewis award 2000), NAE, Am. Assn. Adv. Sci.; mem. Am. Soc. Engring. Edn. (Curtis W. McGraw Rsch. award 1976, George Westinghouse award 1987), Assn. Aerosol Rsch. (bd. dirs. 1983—, v.p. 1988-90, pres. 1990-92), Am. Acad. Arts and Scis., Am. Chem. Soc. (Svc. through Chemistry award 1988, Creative Advances in Environ. Sci. and Tech. award 1993), Internat. Aerosol Rsch. Assembly (Fuchs award 1998, Nev. medal 2001), Sigma Xi, Tau Beta Pi. Home: 525 S Catalina Ave Pasadena CA 91106-3306 Office: Calif Inst Tech Divsn Engring Applied Sci Pasadena CA 91125-0001 E-mail: seinfeld@caltech.edu

SEITMAN, JOHN MICHAEL, lawyer, arbitrator, mediator; b. Bloomington, Ill., Feb. 9, 1942; BS, U. Ill., 1964, JD, 1966. Bar: Calif., U.S. Dist. Ct. (so., cen., no. and ea. dists.) Calif., U.S. Ct. Appeals (9th cir.). Prin. Lindley, Lazar & Scales, San Diego, 1966-97. Lectr. in continuing legal edn. Bd. dirs. San Diego County Bar Found., 1983-89, treas. 1983-84 pres., 1988-89, del. to 9th Cir. Jud. Conf., 1986, 88. Fellow Am. Bar Found.; mem. ABA, State Bar Calif. (pres. 1991-92), San Diego County Bar Assn. (pres. 1986). Office: PO Box 2156 Del Mar CA 92014-1456

SEJNOWSKI, TERRENCE JOSEPH, science educator; b. Cleve., Aug. 13, 1947; s. Joseph Francis and Theresa (Cudnik) S.; m. Beatrice Alexandra Golomb, Mar. 24, 1990. BS, Case Western Res. U., 1968; PhD, Princeton U., 1978. Rsch. fellow Harvard Med. Sch., Boston, 1979-82; prof. biophysics Johns Hopkins U., Balt., 1982-90; prof. U. Calif. San Diego, Salk Inst., La Jolla, 1988—. Investigator Howard Hughes Med. Inst., 1991—; bd. dirs. San Diego McDonnell-Pew Ctr. for Cognitive Neurosci., 1990-98, Inst. for Neural Computation, U. Calif. San Diego., 1990—. Editor-in-chief Neural Computation, 1989—; co-inventor: (with others) the Boltzmann machine and NET talk; mem. editl. bd. Sci. Mag., 1990—. Pres. Neural Info. Processing Sys. Found. Recipient Presdl. Young Investigator award NSF, 1984, Wright prize Harvey Mudd Coll., 1996; Sherman Fairchild Disting. scholar Calif. Inst. Tech., 1993. Fellow IEEE; mem. Soc. for Neurosci., Am. Phys. Soc., Internat. Neural Network Soc. (governing bd. 1988-92, Hebb prize 1999), Am. Math. Soc., Assn. Rsch. in Vision and Ophthalmology, Am. Assn. Artificial Intelligence, Biophys. Soc., Optical Soc. Am., Am. Psychol. Soc., Am. Psychol. Assn., N.Y. Acad. Scis., Fedn. Am. Soc. Exptl. Biophysics, Soc. Neuroscience, Internat. Soc. Neuroethology, Soc. Math. Biology. Achievements include co-invention of the Boltzmann machine, of NETtalk, a neural network for text-to-speech. Office: Salk Inst PO Box 85800 San Diego CA 92186-5800 E-mail: terry@salk.edu

SEKANINA, ZDENEK, astronomer; b. Mlada Boleslav, Czechoslovakia, June 12, 1936; came to U.S., 1969; s. Frantisek Sekanina and Hedvika (Kolarikova) Sekaninova; m. Jana Soukupova, Apr. 1, 1966; 1 child, Jason. Diploma, Charles U., Prague, Czechoslovakia, 1959, PhD in Astronomy, 1963. Astronomer Stefanik Obs., Prague, 1959-66, Ctr. for Numerical Math., Charles U., Prague, 1967-68; vis. scientist Inst. d'Astrophysique, Univ. de Liege, Cointe-Ougree, Belgium, 1968-69; physicist Smithsonian Astrophys. Obs., Cambridge, Mass., 1969-80; mem. tech. staff Jet Propulsion Lab., Pasadena, Calif., 1980-81, rsch. scientist, 1981-84, sr. rsch. scientist, 1984—. Assoc. Harvard Coll. Obs., Cambridge, 1969-80; mem. NASA Comet Sci. Working Group, 1977-80; cons. Jet Propulsion Lab., 1977-80; prin. U.S. co-investigator Particulate Impact Analyzer Experiment, Dust Impact Detector Sys. Experiment, European Space Agy.'s Giotto Mission to Comet Halley, 1980-89; mem. NASA-European Spacy Agy. Comet Halley Environ. Working Group, 1980-89; discipline specialist Near Nucleus Studies Network, Internat. Halley Watch, 1982-90; mem. imaging sci. subsys. team Comet Rendezvous Asteroid Flyby Mission, 1986-92; mem. sci. definition team ESA/NASA Comet Nucleus Sample Return Mission, 1988—; co-investigator STARDUST Discovery Mission, 1994—. Editor Comet Halley Archive, 1982-91; mem. editorial bd. Kosmicke Rozhledy, 1963-69. Recipient Exceptional Sci. Achievement medal NASA, 1985; minor planet named Sekanina, 1976. Mem. Internat. Astron. Union (mem. commns. 15, 10, 22, mem. organizing commn. 22 1976-82, organizing commn. 15 1979-85, mem. working group on comets 1988—, assoc. dir. Ctrl. Bur. for Astron. Telegrams 1970-80), COSPAR (working group 3, panel C, exec. mem. 1980-82), Learned Soc of Czech Republic (hon. 1996—), Czech Astron. Soc. (hon.). Roman Catholic. Office: Jet Propulsion Lab 4800 Oak Grove Dr Pasadena CA 91109-8001 E-mail: zs@sek.jpl.nasa.gov

SEKINE, DEBORAH KEIKO, systems analyst, programmer; b. Honolulu, Dec. 1, 1952; d. Yoshiteru and Yaeko (Matsuda) Isa; m. Andrew K. Sekine, May 8, 1993. BA in Math. with distinction, BEd with distinction, U. Hawaii, 1974, MS in Computer Sci., 1976, MBA, 1987. Data analyst, engr. in-charge Kentron, Honolulu, 1977-81; sys. analyst Am. Savs., Honolulu, 1981-82; analyst, programmer City and County of Honolulu, 1982—. Cons. Am. Savs., Honolulu, 1982. Contbr. articles to profl. jours. Vol. Hawaii Dem. Conv., Honolulu, 1984, Mayoral campaign, 1988, 92; com. co-chair Hui Makaala, Honolulu, 1989—; caregiver Makiki Christian Ch., Honolulu, 1991—. Mem. IEEE, Assn. for Computing Machinery, Am. Fedn. State County Mcpl. Employees, U. Hawaii MBA Alumni Assn., Phi Kappa Phi. Mem. United Ch. of Christ. Avocations: jogging, reading, writing, tennis, listening to gospel music. Home: 3322 George St Honolulu HI 96815-4319

SELANNE, TEEMU, professional hockey player; b. Helsinki, Finland, July 3, 1970; Hockey player Winnipeg Jets Nat. Hockey League, 1992-95, hockey player Phoenix Coyotes, 1995-97, hockey player Anaheim Mighty Ducks, 1997—. Played in All-Star Game, 1996, 94, 93. Named Rookie of Yr. Sporting News, 1992-93, All Rookie team, 1992-93; Recipient Calder Meml. Trophy, 1992-93. Office: Mighty Ducks PO Box 61077 2695 E Katella Ave Anaheim CA 92803-6177

SELBY, HUBERT, JR. writer; b. N.Y.C., July 23, 1928; s. Hubert and Adalin (Layne) S.; m. Inez Taylor, Apr. 23, 1955 (div. 1960); children: Claudia, Kyle; Suzanne Schwartzman, Dec. 26, 1969; children: Rachel, William. Student public schs., Bklyn. Author: Last Exit to Brooklyn, 1964, The Room, 1971, The Demon, 1976, Requiem for a Dream, 1978, Song of the Silent Snow, 1986, The Willow Tree, 1998; screenwriter: Day and Night, 1986, Remember the Sabath Day, 1974, Love Your Buddy Week, 1978, Solder of Fortune, 1990, Requiem for a Dream, 1998, Fear the X, 2000. Served with U.S. Mcht. Marine, 1944-46. Mem. Writers Guild Am. (West chpt.), Authors Guild.

SELDEN, ROBERT WENTWORTH, physicist, science advisor; b. Phoenix, Aug. 11, 1936; s. Edward English and Mary Priscilla (Calder) S.; m. Mary Tania Hudd, June 1958 (div. 1976); 1 child, Ian Scott; m. Marjorie Anne Harmon, Feb. 20, 1977; children: Brock, Thane, Shawna, Kirsten. BA in Physics cum laude, Pomona Coll., 1958; MS in Physics, U. Wis., 1960, PhD in Physics, 1964. Rsch. assoc. Lawrence Livermore (Calif.) Nat. Lab., 1965-67, staff mem., 1967-73, group leader, 1973-78, asst. assoc. dir., 1978-80; div. leader applied theoretical physics Los Alamos (N.Mex.) Nat. Lab., 1980-83, dep. assoc. dir. strategic def. rsch., 1983-84, assoc. dir. theoretical and computational physics, 1984-86, dir. Ctr. for Nat. Securities Studies, 1986-88, assoc. dir. for lab. devel., 1991-94; chief scientist USAF, Washington, 1988-91, panel chmn. sci. adv. bd., 1984-88, 91-96, chmn. sci. adv. bd., 1999—; cons. Los Alamos, 1994—. Chmn. study group on reactor materials and nuclear explosives U.S. Dept. Energy, 1976-78; mem. ballistic missile def. techs. adv. panel U.S. Congress Office Tech. Assessment, 1984-85, The Pres.'s Defensive Tech. Study Team, Washington, 1983; strategic adv. group U.S. Strategic Command, 1996—; jt. adv. com. Sec. Def., Sec. Energy, 1996—. Editor Rsch. Jour. Lawrence Livermore Nat. Lab., 1976-77; contbr. sci. and tech. papers to profl. jours. Pres. Livermore Cultural Arts Coun., 1969-72; chmn. Livermore Sister City Orgn., 1973, Planning Commn. City of Livermore, 1971-76; bd. dirs. Orch. of Santa Fe, 1986-88. Capt. U.S. Army, 1964-67. Grad. fellow Edward John Noble Found., 1958-62; recipient Theodore von Karman award for outstanding contbn. to def. sci., 1989, medal for outstanding pub. svc. U.S. Sec. Def., 1996; decorated for exceptional civilian svc. USAF, 1988, 91, 96. Mem. AAAS, Am. Phys. Soc., N.Y. Acad. Sci., Air Force Assn. Avocations: tennis, hiking, music. Office: 624 La Bajada Los Alamos NM 87544-3805 E-mail: selden@cybermesa.com

SELIGMAN, THOMAS KNOWLES, museum administrator; b. Santa Barbara, Calif., Jan. 1, 1944; s. Joseph L. and Peggy (Van Horne) S.; children: Christopher, Timothy, Dylan. BA, Stanford U., 1965; BFA with honors, San Francisco Acad. Art, 1967; MFA, Sch. Visual Art, N.Y.C., 1968. Tchr., mus. dir. Peace Corps, Liberia, 1968-70; curator dept. Africa, Oceania and Ams. Fine Arts Museums San Francisco, 1971-88, dep. dir. edn. and exhbns., 1972-88, dep. dir. ops. and planning, 1988-91; dir. Stanford (Calif.) U. Cantor Arts Ctr., 1991—. Mem. cultural property adv. com. USIA, 1988-92, Nat. Endowment for Art Indemnity Panel, 1992-95. Author mus. catalogues, articles in field. Trustee Internat. Coun. Mus./Am. Assn. Mus., 1990-94, Am. Fedn. Arts; mem. adv. coun. Acad. Art Coll. Grad. Program. Fellow Nat. Endowment Arts, 1974-75, 87. Mem. Assn. Art Mus. Dirs., Am. Assn. Mus., Leaky Found. Address: Cantor Ctr for Visual Arts Stanford U Lomita Dr & Museum Way Stanford CA 94305-5060

SELLAR, GEORGE L. state legislator; b. Jan. 23, 1929; m. Alma Sellar; 1 child. Student, Wenatchee Valley Coll., Harvard U. Mem. Wash. Legislature, Olympia, 1972—, mem. edn. com., mem. rules com., mem. transp. com., mem. Gov.'s Blue Ribbon Commn. on Transp., mem. dept. cmty., trade and econ. devel. tourism adv. com., mem. legis. transp. com. Recipient 100 Percent Voting Record Wash. State Farm Bur. Mem. Wash. Pub. Port Assn., Pacific N.W. Waterways Assn., Wenatchee Area C. of C. Republican. Office: 401 C Legislative Bldg Olympia WA 98504-0001

SELLER, GREGORY EROL, marketing executive, writer, consultant; b. Denver, Oct. 4, 1953; s. Otto Gustave and Dolores Louise (Crawford) S. BBA, U. Colo., 1975. Account exec. Gt.-West Life, L.A., 1975-79, asst. v.p. group devel. Denver, 1980-84; v.p. govt. mkts. and nat. accts. Great-West Life, L.A., 1988—; pres., chief exec. officer Benefits Communication Corp., Denver, 1985-87, sr. v.p. govt. mkts., 1991—. Bd. dirs. Benefits Communication Co. Editor newsletter Focus on 457, 1988—. Mem. vestry, treas. St. Thomas Episc. Ch., Hollywood, Calif., 1989-93. Mem. Delta Upsilon. Democrat. Home: 26 Pienza Laguna Niguel CA 92677-8623 Office: Great West Life 18101 Von Karman Ave Ste 1460 Irvine CA 92612-0174

SELLERS, ROBERT SCOT, real estate developer; b. L.A., Jan. 26, 1957; s. Walter DeWitt and Diolenda Teresa (Bernardes) S.; m. Gretchen Alice Geddes, June 6, 1987. BS, Lewis & Clark Coll., 1978; MBA, Stanford U., 1981. Lic. real estate broker, Calif., Colo. Loan officer The Oreg. Bank, Portland, 1978-79; controller CFI Mgmt. Svcs., Portland, 1979; cons. Boston Consulting Group, Palo Alto, Calif., 1980; asst. project mgr. Lincoln Property Co., Denver, 1981-82, v.p., 1982-83, ptnr., Colo., 1983-87, ptnr., So. Calif. San Diego, 1987-91, ptnr. Irvine, Calif., 1991-94; chmn. and CEO Archstone Communities Trust, Englewood, CO, 1994—. Real estate developer apts. and hotels, Denver and San Diego, 1985—. Chmn. bd. Christian Internat. Scholars Found., Seattle, 1988-90; founding mem., bd. advisors High Ground Assocs., San Diego, 1988-91. Mem. Bldg. Industry Assn. (president's coun. 1987—, speakers bur. 1988-91), Apt. Assn. Metro Denver (membership dir. 1987), Constrn. Industry Fedn. Republican. Avocations: tennis, bicycling, golf, cross country skiing, mountain climbing, triathlons. Office: Archstone Communities Trust 7670 S Chester St Unit 100 Englewood CO 80112-3436

SELVA, BERT, real estate development executive; Pres. Colo. divsn. Shea Homes, Walnut, Calif., 1996—. Office: J F Shea Co Inc PO Box 489 Walnut CA 91788-0489

SELVIN, NEIL, computer company executive; Pres., CEO Global Village, Sunnyvale, Calif.; PRES. & CEO ONEWORLD SYSTEMS, INC, SUNNYVALE, CA.

SELZ, PETER HOWARD, art historian, educator; b. Munich, Germany, Mar. 27, 1919; came to U.S., 1936, naturalized, 1942; s. Eugene and Edith S.; m. Thalia Cheronis, June 10, 1948 (div. 1965); children: Tanya Nicole Eugenia, Diana Gabrielle Hamlin; m. Carole Schemmerling, Dec. 18, 1983 Student, Columbia U., U. Paris; MA, U. Chgo., 1949, PhD, 1954; DFA, Calif. Coll. Arts and Crafts, 1967. Instr. U. Chgo., 1951-56; asst. prof. art history, head art edn. dept. Inst. Design, Ill. Inst. Tech., Chgo., 1949-55; chmn. art dept., dir. art gallery Pomona Coll., 1955-58; curator dept. painting and sculpture exhbns. Mus. Modern Art, 1958-65; dir. univ. art mus. U. Calif., Berkeley, 1965-73, prof. history of art, 1965—; Zaks prof. Hebrew U., Jerusalem, 1976. Vis. prof. CUNY, 1987; mem. pres.'s council on art and architecture Yale U., 1971-76. Author: German Expressionist Painting, 1957, New Images of Man, 1959, Art Nouveau, 1960, Mark Rothko, 1961, Fifteen Polish Painters, 1961, The Art of Jean Dubuffet, 1962, Emil Nolde, 1963, Max Beckmann, 1964, Alberto Giacometti, 1965, Directions in Kinetic Sculpture, 1966, Funk, 1967, Harold Paris, 1972, Ferdinand Holder, 1972, Sam Francis, 1975, The American Presidency in Political Cartoons, 1976, Art in Our Times, 1981, Art in a Turbulent Era, 1985, Chillida, 1986, Twelve Artists from the GDR, 1989, Max Beckmann: The Self Portraits, 1992, William Congdon, 1992, Beckmann, 1996, Gottfried Helnwein, 1997, Beyond the Mainstream, 1997; co-author: Theories and Documents of Contemporary Art, 1996, Beyond the Mainstream, 1998, Barbara Chase-Riboud, 1999, Nathan Oliveira, 2001; editor: Art in Am., 1967—, Art Quar., 1969-75, Arts, 1981-92, Cross-Currents in Modern Art, 2000, Nathan Oliveira, 2001; contbr. articles to art publs. Trustee Am. Crafts Coun., 1985-89, Marin Mus. Assn., 1993—; mem. acquisitions com. Fine Arts Mus. San Francisco, 1993; pres. Berkeley Art Project, 1988-93; mem. adv. coun. archives Am. Art, 1971—; project dir. Christo's Running Fence, 1973-76; commr. Alameda County Art Commn., 1990-95; bd. dirs. Richmond Art Ctr., 1998—; chair Berkeley Art Festival, 1997-2000. With OSS AUS, 1941-46. Decorated Order of Merit Fed. Republic Germany; Fulbright grantee Paris, 1949-50; fellow Belgian-Am. Ednl. Found.; sr. fellow NEH, 1972; resident Rockefeller Found. Study Ctr., Bellagio, 1994. Mem. Coll. Art Assn. Am. (dir. 1959-64, 67-71), AAUP, Internat. Art Critics Assn. Office: U Calif Dept Art History Berkeley CA 94720-0001

SEMEL, GEORGE HERBERT, plastic surgeon; b. N.Y.C., Apr. 20, 1938; s. Louis Bennett and Sara Sonja (Eutis) S. AB, Columbia U., 1959; MD, Boston U., 1963. Diplomate Am. Bd. Plastic Surgery. Intern L.A. County Gen. Hosp., 1963-64; resident gen. surgery Long Beach (Calif.) VA Hosp., 1964-67; residency in plastic surgery Mayo Clinic, Rochester, Minn., 1967-69; chief resident plastic surgery Med. U. S.C., Charleston, 1969-70; pvt. practice L.A., 1970—; staff Cedars Sinai Hosp., L.A. Founder L.A. Music Ctr., 1978, Mus. Contemporary Art, 1980. With Calif. NG, 1964-69, USNG, 1969-73. Mem. AMA, Am. Soc. Plastic Surgery, Am. Lipoplasty Soc., L.A. Soc. Plastic Surgeons, L.A. County Med. Soc., Phi Gamma Delta. Office: 450 S Beverly Dr Beverly Hills CA 90212-4402

SEMENZA, DIRK A. metal fabrication executive; b. Ft. Benton, Mont., Oct. 10, 1962; s. Lenard and Opal E. Semenza. Grad. h.s., Gr. Falls, Mont. Worked in construction; founder, project controller, sec., treas. R Squared Metal Fabrication, Inc., Gt. Falls, Mont., 1990—. FAA approval for R Squared 736 Simulator. Recipient Jay Hollingsworth Speas Airport award AIAA, 1996. Address: Hout PO Box 3293 Great Falls MT 59403-3293

SENEKER, CARL JAMES, II (KIM SENEKER), lawyer; b. San Jose, Calif., Oct. 12, 1942; s. Carl James and Beth D. (Hearn) S.; m. Julie Marie Pardee, June 17, 1967; children: Mark Gwynn, Todd Christian. AB, Stanford U., 1964; JD, U. Calif., Berkeley, 1967. Bar: Calif. 1969, U.S. Dist. Ct. (no. dist.) Calif. 1973. Law clk. to Hon. William O. Douglas U.S. Supreme Ct., Washington, 1967-68; ptnr. Morrison & Foerster, San Francisco, 1971-84, 96—, L.A., 1984-96. Adj. prof. law, lectr. law sch. Stanford U., Palo Alto, Calif., 1982-83. Co-editor: California Real Estate Law and Practice, Vols. 12 & 13, 1983-96; contbr. articles to profl. jours. Bd. dirs. L.A. Hdqs. City Assn., 1988-93. Capt. USAF, 1968-71. Mem. Am. Coll. Real Estate Lawyers [illegible] 1990-97, [illegible] 1995-97, pres. 1997-98), State Bar Calif. (real property law sect., vice-chair exec. com. 1987-90). Roman Catholic. Avocations: golf, travel, music. Office: Morrison & Foerster 425 Market St Fl 32 San Francisco CA 94105-2467

SENN, DEBORAH, insurance commissioner; m. Rudi Bertschi. BA, MA, U. Ill.; JD, Loyola U. Rep. cmty. groups, consumers, women & family groups, labor and small bus.; elected Wash. state ins. commr. Olympia, 1992-96. Avocations: hiking, outdoors. Office: Insurance Bldg PO Box 40255 Olympia WA 98504-0255

SENSIPER, SAMUEL, consulting electrical engineer; b. Elmira, N.Y., Apr. 26, 1919; s. Louis and Molly (Pedolsky) S.; m. Elaine Marie Zwick, Sept. 10, 1950; children— Martin, Sylvia, David. BSEE, MIT, 1939, ScD, 1951; EE, Stanford U., 1941. Asst. project engr. to sr. project engr., cons. Sperry Gyroscope, Garden City, Great Neck, N.Y., 1941-51; sect. head and sr. staff cons. Hughes Aircraft, Culver City, Malibu, Calif., 1951-60. Lab. div. mgr. Space Gen. Corp., Glendale, Azusa, Los Angeles, 1960-67; lab. mgr. TRW, Redondo Beach, Calif., 1967-70; cons. elec. engr., Los Angeles, 1970-73; dir. engring. Transco Products, Venice, Calif., 1973-75; cons. elec. engr. in pvt. practice, Los Angeles, 1975— ; faculty U. So. Calif., Los Angeles, 1955-56, 79-80 Contbr. articles to profl. jours.; patentee in field. Recipient Cert. of Commendation U.S. Navy, 1946; indsl. electronics fellow M.I.T., 1947-48 Fellow IEEE, AAAS; mem. Calif. Soc. Profl. Engrs., Fedn. Am. Scientists, MIT Alumni Assn., Stanford Alumni Assn., Electromagnetics Acad., Sigma Xi, Eta Kappa Nu. Home and Office: 3775 Modoc Rd #226 Santa Barbara CA 93105-4481 E-mail: sensiper1@ieee.org

SENTZ, DENNIS, chemical company executive; BBA in Acctg., U. Wisc., 1970. cert. CPA, CMA. Contoller, CFO Instrumentarium Imaging, Inc.; v.p., CFO Foster Wheeler Energy Corp., 1993-97; CFO BE&K-Bechtel Internat., 1997-99; v.p. acctg., controller Eco Soil Sys., Inc., San Diego, 1999-00, CFO, 2000—. Office: Eco Soil Sys Inc 10740 Thornmint Rd San Diego CA 92127

SEQUEIRA, JIM, city official; BS in Engring., Calif. State U., 1975. Dir. utilities dept. City of Sacramento, 1993—. Mem. Calif. Mcpl. Utilities Assn., Sacramento Area Water Works Assn. Office: City Sacramento Utilities Dept 1395 35th Ave Sacramento CA 95822

SÉQUIN, CARLO H. computer science educator; b. Winterthur, Switzerland, Oct. 30, 1941; came to U.S., 1970; s. Carl R. and Margrit (Schaeppi) S.; m. Margareta Frey, Oct. 5, 1968; children: Eveline, Andre. B.S., U. Basel, Switzerland, 1965, Ph.D., 1969. Mem. tech. staff Bell Labs., Murray Hill, N.J., 1970-76; vis. Mackay lectr. U. Calif.-Berkeley, 1976-77, prof. elec. engring. computer scis., 1977—, assoc. chmn. computer sci., 1980-83, assoc. dean capital projects, 2001—. Contbr. 200 articles to profl. jours.; author first book on charge-coupled devices; patentee integrated circuits. Fellow IEEE, Assn. Computing Machinery, Swiss Acad. Engring. Scis. Office: U Calif Dept EECS Computer Scis Divsn Berkeley CA 94720-0001

SERAFIN, ROBERT JOSEPH, science center administrator, electrical engineer; b. Chgo., Apr. 22, 1936; s. Joseph Albert and Antoinette (Gazda) S.; m. Betsy Furgerson, Mar. 4, 1961; children: Katherine, Jenifer, Robert Joseph Jr., Elizabeth. BSEE, U. Notre Dame, 1958; MSEE, Northwestern U., 1961; PhDEE, Ill. Inst. Tech., 1972. Engr. Hazeltine Rsch. Corp. Ill. Inst. Tech. Rsch. Inst., 1960-62; assoc. engr., rsch. engr., sr. rsch. engr. Nat. Ctr. for Atmospheric Rsch., Boulder, Colo., 1962-73, mgr. field observing facility, 1973-80, dir. atmospheric tech. div. Bouulder, 1981-89, dir. ctr., 1989-2000. Chair Nat. Weather Svc. Modernization Com. Author: Revised Radar Handbook, 1989; contbr. numerous articles to profl. jours.; editl. bd./com. Acta Meteorologica Sinica; editl. founder Jour. Atmospheric and Oceanic Tech.; patentee in field. Speaker various civic groups in U.S. and internationally. Fellow IEEE, Am. Meteorol. Soc. (pres.); mem. NAE, NAS (human rights com.), Boulder C. of C., Sigma Xi. Avocations: golf, fishing, skiing. Office: Nat Ctr Atmospheric Rsch 1850 Table Mesa Dr PO Box 3000 Boulder CO 80307-3000

SERNA, PATRICIO, state supreme court chief justice; b. Reserve, N.Mex., Aug. 26, 1939; m. Eloise Serna; 1 stepchild, John Herrera; children: Elena Patricia, Anna Alicia. BSBA with honors, U. Albuquerque, 1962; JD, U. Denver, 1970; LLM, Harvard U., 1971; postgrad., Nat. Jud. Coll., 1985, 90, 92, 94. Bar: N.Mex. 1970, Colo. 1971, U.S. Dist. Ct. N.Mex. 1970. Probation and parole officer State of N.Mex., Santa Fe, Las Cruces, 1966-67; spl. asst. to commn. mem. Equal Opportunity Commn., Washington, 1971-75; asst. atty. gen. State of N.Mex., Santa Fe, 1975-79; pvt. practice Santa Fe, 1979-85; dist. judge First Jud. Dist., Santa Fe, 1985-96; supreme ct. justice N.Mex. Supreme Ct., Santa Fe, 1996-01, chief justice, 2001—. Adj. prof. law Georgetown U., Washington, 1973, Cath. U., Washington, 1974-75; faculty advisor Nat. Jud. Coll., Reno, 1987. Exhibited at N.Mex. Mus. Fine Arts, Gov.'s Gallery, Santa Fe. Active Citizens Organized for Real Edn., Santa Fe, No. N.Mex. Martin Luther King Jr. State Holiday Commn., Santa Fe; past bd. dirs. Santa Fe Group Homes Inc. With U.S. Army, 1963-65. Mem. N.Mex. Bar Assn., N.Mex. Hispanic Bar Assn., Nat. Hispanic Bar Assn., Nat. Coun. Juvenile and Family Ct. Judges, No. N.Mex. Am. Inns of Ct., Santa Fe Bar Assn., Elks, Fraternal Order of Eagles, Fraternal Order of Police, Phi Alpha Delta. Avocations: hiking, fishing, ping pong, chess, painting. Office: NMex Supreme Ct PO Box 848 Santa Fe NM 87504-0848

SESONSKE, ALEXANDER, nuclear and chemical engineer; b. Gloversville, N.Y., June 20, 1921; s. Abraham and Esther (Kreitzer) S.; m. Marjorie Ann Mach, Apr. 17, 1952 (dec. Jan. 1995); children: Michael Jan, Jana Louise. B.Chem. Engring., Rensselaer Poly. Inst., 1942; M.S., U. Rochester, 1947; Ph.D., U. Del., 1950. Engr. Chem. Constrn. Corp., N.Y.C., 1942; chem. engr. Manhattan Project, 1943-45, Columbia-So. Chem. Corp., 1945-46; staff Los Alamos Sci. Lab., 1950-54, 60-61, cons., 1961-63; faculty Purdue U., Lafayette, Ind., 1954, prof. nuclear and chem. engring., 1959-86, prof. emeritus, 1986—, asst. chmn. dept. nuclear engring., 1966-73. Cons. Oak Ridge Nat. Lab., 1963-67, Electric Power Research Inst., 1974; mem. rev. com. Argonne (Ill.) Nat. Lab., 1965-67, 75-81; ind. cons. 1986—. Author: (with Samuel Glasstone) Nuclear Reactor Engineering, 1963, 4th edit., 1994, Nuclear Power Plant Design Analysis, 1973; mem. editorial bd. Advances in Nuclear Sci. and Tech., 1972—; contbr. numerous articles to profl. jours. Recipient Wall of Fame award U. Del., 1988. Fellow Am. Nuclear Soc. (Arthur H. Compton award 1987); mem. Am. Inst. Chem. Engrs., Am. Soc. Engring. Edn., Sigma Xi, Omega Chi Epsilon. Achievements include research on nuclear fuel mgmt., liquid metal heat transfer and nuclear reactor engring. Home and Office: 24441 Calle Sonora Apt 331 Laguna Woods CA 92653-7707 E-mail: alses1@cs.com

SESSIONS, DON DAVID, lawyer; BS, Brigham Young U.; JD, Loyola Law Sch., L.A., 1976. Bar: Calif. 1976. Sole practice employee rights, Mission Viejo, Calif., 1976—. Adj. prof. Western State U. Coll. Law. Mem. Calif. Bar Assn. (Labor and employment law sect.), Nat. Employment Lawyer's Assn., Calif. Employment Lawyer's Assn., Orange County Bar Assn. (labor and employment law sect.). Office: 23456 Madero Ste 170 Mission Viejo CA 92691-7901

SESSIONS, KATHRYN L. state legislator, educator; b. Jackson, Wyo., Feb. 13, 1942; widowed; 3 children. BS, Utah State U., 1970; MS, Leslie Coll., 1990. Educator, Wyo., 1970—; mem. Wyo. Ho. Reps., Cheyenne, 1992-98, Wyo. Senate, Dist. 7, Cheyenne, 1998—; mem. appropriations com. Wyo. Senate, Cheyenne, mem. rules and procedures. com. Mem. NEA, LWV, Wyo. Edn. Assn., Alpha Delta Kappa (edn. com.). Democrat. Mem. LDS Ch. Home: 930 Centennial Dr Cheyenne WY 82001-7407 Office: Wyo Senate State Capitol Cheyenne WY 82002-0001

SESSLER, ANDREW MARIENHOFF, physicist; b. Bklyn., Dec. 11, 1928; s. David and Mary (Baron) S.; m. Gladys Lerner, Sept. 23, 1951 (div. Dec. 1994); children: Daniel Ira, Jonathan Lawrence, Ruth. BA in Math. cum laude, Harvard U., 1949; MA in Theoretical Physics, Columbia U., 1951, PhD in Theoretical Physics, 1953. NSF fellow Cornell U., N.Y., 1953-54; asst. prof. Ohio State U., Columbus, 1954, assoc. prof., 1960; on leave Midwestern Univs. Research, 1955-56; vis. physicist Lawrence Radiation Lab., 1959-60, Niels Bohr Inst., Copenhagen, summer 1961; rschr. theoretical physics U. Calif. Lawrence Berkeley Lab., Berkeley, 1961-73, rschr. energy and environment, 1971-73, dir., 1973-80, sr. scientist plasma physics, 1980-94, disting. sr. staff scientist, 1994—. U.S. advisor Panjab U. Physics Inst., Chandigarh, India; mem. U.S.-India Coop. Program for Improvement Sci. Edn. in India, 1966, high energy physics adv. panel to U.S. AEC, 1969-72, adv. com. Lawrence Hall Sci., 1974-78; chmn. Stanford Synchrotron Radiation Project Sci. Policy Bd., 1974-77, EPRI Advanced Fuels Adv. Com., 1978-81, BNL External Adv. Com. on Isabelle, 1980-82; mem. sci. pol. bd. Stanford Synchrotron Radiation Lab., 1991-92; L.J. Haworth dist. scientist Brookhaven Nat. Lab., 1991-92. Mem. editl. bd. Nuclear Instruments and Methods, 1969—; correspondent Comments on Modern Physics, 1969-71; contbr. articles in field to profl. jours. Mem. hon. adv. bd. Inst. Advanced Phys. Studies, LaJolla Internat. Sch. Physics, 1991—; mem. Superconducting Super Collider Sci. Policy Com., 1991-93. Recipient E.O. Lawrence award U.S. Atomic Energy Commn., 1970, U.S. Particle Accelerator Sch. prize, 1988; fellow Japan Soc. for Promotion Sci. at KEK, 1985. Fellow AAAS (nominating com. 1984-87), Am. Phys. Soc. (chmn. com. internat. freedom scientist 1982, study of directed energy weapons panel 1985-87, chmn. panel pub. affairs 1988, chmn. divsn. physics of beams 1990, chmn. com. applications of physics 1993, divsnl. councilor for DPB 1994-97, pres.-elect 1997, pres. 1998, past pres. 1999, Nicholson medal 1994, Robert R. Wilson prize 1997); mem. NAS, IEEE, Fedn. Am. Scientists Coun. (vice chmn. 1987-88, chmn. 1988-92), N.Y. Acad. Sci., Assoc. Univ. Inc. (bd. dirs. 1991-94). Office: U Calif Lawrence Berkeley Lab 1 Cyclotron Rd MS 71 259 Berkeley CA 94720-0001 E-mail: AMSessler@lbl.gov

SESTINI, VIRGIL ANDREW, retired biology educator; b. Las Vegas, Nov. 24, 1936; s. Santi and Merceda Francesca (Borla) S. BS in Edn., U. Nev., 1959; postgrad., Oreg. State U., 1963-64; MNS, U. Idaho, 1995; postgrad., Ariz. State U., 1967, No. Ariz. U., 1969. Cert. tchr., Nev. Tchr. biology Rancho H.S., 1960-76; sci. chmn., tchr. biology Bonanza H.S., Las Vegas, 1976-90, ret., 1990. Co-founder, curator exhibits Meadows Mus. Nat. History, 1993-94; part-time tchr., sci. chmn. Meadows Sch., 1987-94; ret., 1994; edn. specialist, cell biologist SAGE Rsch., Las Vegas, 1993, ret., 1998; founder Da Vinci Enterprises, Las Vegas, 1995. Author: Lab Investigators for High School Honors Biology, 1992, Laboratory Investigations in Microbiology, 1992, Genetics Problems for High School Biology, 1995, Science Laboratory Report Data Book, 1995, Field and Museum Techniques for the Classroom Teacher, 1995, Selected Lab Investigations and Projects for Honors and AP Biology, Vol. I Microbiology, 1995, Telecommunications: A Simulation for Biology Using the Internet, 1995; co-author: A Biology Lab Manual for Cooperative Learning, 1989, Metrics and Science Methods: A Manual of Lab Experiments for Home Schoolers, 1990, Experimental Designs in Biology I: Botany and Zoology, 1993, Designs in Biology: A Lab Manual, 1993, Integrated Science Lab Manual, 1994, Supplemental Experiments and Field Studies for AP Biology, 1998; contbr. articles to profl. jours. including The Sci. Tchr., Am. Biology Tchr., Fine Scale Models, Ships in Scale, IPMS Jour. With USAR, 1959-65. Reciepient Rotary Internat. Honor Tchr. award, 1965, Region VIII Outstanding Biology Tchr. award, 1970, Nev. Outstanding Biology Tchr. award Nat. Assn. Biology Tchrs., 1970, Nat. Assn. Sci. Tchrs., Am. Gas Assn. Sci. Tchg. Achievement Recognition award, 1976, 80, Gustov Ohaus award, 1980, Presdl. Honor Sci. Tchr. award, 1983; Presdl. award excellence in math. and sci. tchg., 1984, Celebration of Excellence award Nev. Com. on Excellence in Edn., 1986, Hall of Fame award Clark County Sch. Dist., 1988, Excellence in Edn. award, 1987, 88, Spl. Edn. award 1988, NSEA Mini-grants, 1988, 89, 92, World Decoration of Excellence medallion World Inst. Achievement, 1989, Cert. Spl. Congrl. Recognition, 1989, Senatorial Recognition, 1989, mini-grant Jr. League Las Vegas, 1989, Excellence in Edn. award Clark Country Sch. Dist., 1989; named Nev. Educator of Yr., Milken Family Found./Nev. State Dept. Edn., 1989; grantee Nev. State Bd. Edn., 1988, 89, Nev. State Edn. Assn., 1988-89. Mem. AAAS, NEA, Nat. Assn. Taxidermists, Nat. Sci. Tchrs. Assn. (life, Nev. state membership chmn. 1968-70), Nat. Assn. Biology Tchrs. (life, OBTA dir. Nev. state 1991-93), Am. Soc. Microbiology, Coun. for Exceptional Children, Am. Biographic Inst. (rsch. bd. advisors 1988), Nat. Audubon Assn., Nat. Sci. Suprs. Assn., Am. Inst. Biol. Scis., Nautical Rsch. Guild, Internat. Plastic Modelers Soc., So. Nev. Scale Modelers (Las Vegas coord., Modeloberfest, 1995), Silver State Scale Modelers Guild. Avocations: scale models, military figures, scale models circus, photography. E-mail: v.sestini@aol.com

SETIAN, NERSES MIKAIL, retired bishop; b. Zara, Turkey, Oct. 18, 1918; s. Nishan and Bayzar (Deveciyan) S. B. in Philosophy, U. Gregoriana, Rome, 1937, L.Theology, 1942, J.C.D., 1945. Ordained priest Armenian Catholic Ch., 1941. Ordained titular bishop of Ancira at the Armenians and 1st exarch of the apostolic exarchate for Armenian-Rite Catholics in Can. and U.S.A. Armenian Catholic Ch., N.Y.C., 1981—; bishop Our Lady Queen of Martyrs, L.A., 1995-99. Home and Office: Our Lady Queen Martyrs 1327 Pleasant Ave Los Angeles CA 90033-2328

SETTLES, F. STAN, JR. engineering educator, manufacturing executive; b. Denver, Oct. 3, 1938; s. Frank S. and Dorothy Marie (Johnson) S.; m. Evelyn Brown, June 10, 1961; children: Frank S. III, Richard, Charles, Michael. BS in Prodn. Tech., Indsl. Engring., LeTourneau Coll., Longview, Tex., 1962; MS in Indsl. Engring., Ariz. State U., 1967, PhD in Indsl. Engring., 1969. Sr. systems analyst AiResearch Mfg. Co., Phoenix, 1968-70, project mgr., 1970-74, mgr. operational planning, 1974-80; mgr. indsl. engrs. Garrett Pneumatic Systems, Phoenix, 1980-83; mgr. indsl. mfg. engring. Garrett Turbine Engring. Co., Phoenix, 1983-85; v.p. mfg. ops. AiResearch Mfg. Co., Torrance, Calif., 1985-87; dir. indsl. mfg. engring. The Garrett Corp., Phoenix, 1987-88; dir. planning Garrett Engine Div., Phoenix, 1988-92; asst. dir. White House Office of Sci. and Tech. Policy, 1992-93; program dir. NSF, 1992-94; prof., chmn. indsl. and systems engring. dept. U. So. Calif., L.A., 1994—. Faculty assoc. Ariz. State U., Tempe, 1974-85, 90-92, rsch. prof., 1992-94. Mem. sch. bd. Tempe Elem. Sch. Dist., 1976-80; mem. YMCA Indian Guides, nat. chief, 1978-79. Fellow Inst. Indsl. Engrs. (pres. 1987-88, Ops. Rsch. award 1980); mem. Nat. Acad. Engrs., Soc. Mfg. Engrs. (sr.), Inst. Ops. Rsch. and Mgmt. Sci. (sr.), Am. Soc. Quality Control, Am. Soc. Engring. Edn. Republican. Presbyterian. Home: 1310 E Ocean Blvd Unit 1602 Long Beach CA 90802-6917 Office: U So Calif Dept Indsl Sys Engring Los Angeles CA 90089-0001

SEVIER, ERNEST YOULE, lawyer; b. Sacramento, June 20, 1932; s. Ernest and Helen Faye (McDonald) S.; m. Constance McKenna, Apr. 12, 1969; children: Carolyn Stewart, Katherine Danielle. A.B., Stanford U., 1954, J.D., 1956. Bar: Calif. 1956, U.S. Supreme Ct. 1965. Asso. mem. firm Sedgwick, Detert, Moran & Arnold, San Francisco, 1958-62; mem. firm Severson & Werson, San Francisco, 1962-99. Served with USAF, 1956-57. Fellow Am. Bar Found.; mem. ABA (chmn. tort and ins. practice sect. 1982-83, exec. coun. 1976-84, chmn. standing com. on assoc. comms. 1988-90, chmn. coord. com. on Outreach to Pub. 1989-90, chmn. standing com. on lawyers responsibility for client protection 1991-94, commn. on non-lawyer practice 1992-95), Calif. Bar Assn. Office: Severson & Werson 1 Embarcadero Ctr Fl 26 San Francisco CA 94111-3715

SEVILLA, CARLOS A. bishop; b. San Francisco, Aug. 9, 1935; Ed., Gonzaga U., Santa Clara U., Jesuiten Kolleg, Innsbruck, Austria, Cath. Inst. Paris. Ordained priest Roman Cath. Ch., 1966, bishop, 1989. Titular bishop, Mina, 1989—; aux. bishop San Francisco, 1989—. Office: Archdiocese San Francisco 445 Church St San Francisco CA 94114-1720

SEVILLA, STANLEY, lawyer; b. Cin., Apr. 3, 1920; s. Isadore and Dienna (Levy) S.; m. Lois A. Howell, July 25, 1948; children: Stanley, Susan, Donald, Carol, Elizabeth. BA in Econs. with high honors, U. Cin., 1942; JD, Harvard U., 1948. Bar: Calif. 1949. Since practiced in, Los Angeles; assoc. Williamson, Hoge & Curry, 1948-50; mem. firm Axelrod, Sevilla and Ross, 1950-75, Stanley Sevilla (P.C.), 1975—. Gen. counsel La.-Pacific Resources, Inc., 1970-90. Bd. dirs. Caesars World, Inc., 1989-95. With USAAF, 1942-46. Mem. Beverly Hills Bar Assn., Phi Beta Kappa, Tau Kappa Alpha. Home: 16606 Merrivale Ln Pacific Palisades CA 90272-2236 Office: PO Box 308 Pacific Palisades CA 90272-0308

SEWELL, ROBERT DALTON, pediatrician; b. Newman, Calif., Apr. 28, 1950; s. James Dalton and Mary Louise (Hartwell) S.; m. Laura Slinkard-Ekberg, May 21, 1998; children: Kevin, David; stepchildren: Nicole, Samantha. BA magna cum laude, Pacific Union Coll., 1972; MD, Loma Linda U., 1975. Diplomate Am. Bd. Pediatrics. Pediat. intern and resident White Meml. Med. Ctr., L.A., 1975-77; pediat. resident, chief resident Milton S. Hershey Med. Ctr., Pa. State U., Hershey, 1977-80; pediatrician Children's Med. Ctr. Asheville, N.C., 1980-81, Lincoln City (Oreg.) Med. Ctr. P.C., 1982-95; examining physician C.A.R.E.S. Ctr. Emanuel Hosp. & Health Ctr., Portland, Oreg., 1988-90; asst. prof. Loma Linda (Calif.) U. Sch. Medicine, 1995-97; with Good Shepherd Med. Group, Hemiston, Oreg., 1998-2001; physician examiner Guardian Care Ctr., Pendleton, 1999-2001. Chmn. child protection team North Lincoln Hosp., Lincoln City, 1983-89, sec. med. staff, 1990-92, pres. med. staff, 1992-94; mem. Citizens' Rev. Bd. Lincoln County, Newport, Oreg., 1986-92, Early Intervention adv. com., Newport, 1986-90. Mem. North Lincoln Local Sch. Com., Lincoln City, 1983-94, chmn., 1986-90; bd. dirs. Lincoln Shelter and Svcs., Inc., Lincoln City, 1983-89, chmn., 1987-89; mem. North Lincoln divsn. Am. Heart Assn., Lincoln City, 1986-89, v.p., 1987-89; mem. Drug and Alcohol Task Force, Lincoln City, 1988; mem., 2d vice-chmn. Yr. 2000 Plan housing com. Lincoln City Planning Commn., 1987-88; mem. AIDS task force Lincoln County Sch. Dist., 1987-89; mem. Lincoln County Children's Agenda Taskforce, 1988; mem. med. rev. com. Oreg. Med. Assn., 1990-95, mem.-at-large med. staff sect. gov. bd., 1993-95. Named Citizen of Yr. child protection com. Lincoln County, 1984, Man of Yr. Lincoln City C. of C., 1988. Mem. Am. Acad. Pediatrics (sect. on child abuse), Am. Profl. Soc. of Abuse of Children (charter mem.), Nat. Assn. Counsel for Children, Internat. Soc. for Prevention Child Abuse and Neglect, Oreg. Profl. Soc. on Abuse of Children (founding pres. 1992-94), Oreg. Med. Assn. (mem. health care fin. com. 1999-2001). Democrat. Seventh-day Adventist. Avocations: music, sports, boating, auto racing. E-mail: kidsdr@eoni.com

SEYMOUR, BRIAN RICHARD, mathematics educator, researcher; b. Chesterfield, Derby, Eng., Sept. 25, 1944; came to U.S., 1968, Can., 1973; s. Douglas and Hilda (Ball) S.; m. Rosemary Jane Pembleton, Sept. 23, 1943; children— Mark, Jane, Richard. B.Sc. with honors, U. Manchester, 1965; Ph.D., U. Nottingham, 1968. Asst. prof. Lehigh U., 1969-70, N.Y. U., 1970-73, U. B.C., 1973-76; assoc. prof. U. B.C., 1976-81, Vancouver, Can., prof. math., 1981—, dir. inst. applied math, 1986-93; vis. prof. Ctr. Water Rsch. U. Western Australia, 1993-94. Contbr. research papers to profl. jours. Sci. Research Council sr. research fellow Oxford U., 1978; Killam sr. fellow Killam Trust, Monash U., 1984. Mem. Can. Applied Math. Soc., Soc. Indsl. & Applied Math. Avocation: field hockey. Office: U BC 222 1984 Mathematics Rd Vancouver BC Canada V6T 1Z2

SEYMOUR, LISA, museum director; b. Oct. 30, 1962; m. E. David Seymour. BA in Mass Comms., U. Denver, 1984; MA in Mass Comms., 1985. Grad. teaching asst. U. Denver, 1985; records clk. typist Kingman (Ariz.) Police Dept., 1985-86; sec. First Presbyn. Ch., Elko, Nev., 1986-87; exec. dir. Elko (Nev.) County Against Domestic Violence, 1987; exec. dir. of found. Elko (Nev.) Gen. Hosp. Found., 1989-90; mgr. cmty. rels. Elko (Nev.) Gen. Hosp., 1987-90; adtg. mgr. Elko (Nev.) Ind., 1990-91, newspaper editor, reporter, photographer, 1991-94; archivist and oral historian Northeastern Nev. Mus., Elko, 1994-95; interim mus. adminstr., 1995; mus. dir., 1996-99. Grantee Newmont Gold Co., E.L. Cord Found., E.L. Wiegand Found., 1996. Office: c/o Northeastern Nev Mus 1515 Idaho St Elko NV 89801-4021

SEYMOUR, MICHAEL, production designer; Prodn. designer, L.A., 1964—. Prodn. designer: (films) Robbery, 1967, Entertaining Mr. Sloane, 1970, Gumshoe, 1971, Theatre of Blood, 1973, Rosebud, 1975, Alien, 1979 (Academy award nomination best art direction 1979), Ghost Story, 1981, Eureka, 1984, The Bride, 1985, Mr. Destiny, 1990, (with Benjamin Fernandez) Revenge, 1990, Gunmen, 1992, The Thing Called Love, 1993, Beverly Hills Cop III, 1994. Recipient Brit. Acad. award for Art Direction, 1979. Office: 1264 Ozeta Ter Apt 302 West Hollywood CA 90069-1837

SHACKELFORD, CHARLES DUANE, civil engineering educator, researcher; b. Sewickley, Pa., Sept. 9, 1954; m. Anne Marie Lynch, Apr. 2, 1984; children: Kathryn, David, Daniel. BSCE, U. Mo., Rolla, 1980; MS, U. Tex., 1983, PhD, 1988. Registered profl. engr., Calif., Colo. Civil design engr. Pacific Gas and Electric Co., San Francisco, 1980-81; geotech. engr. Ardaman and Assocs., Inc., Orlando, Fla., 1983-84; rsch. intern Oak Ridge (Tenn.) Nat. Lab., summer 1984; asst. prof. dept. civil engring. Colo. State U., Ft. Collins, 1988-93, assoc. prof. dept. civil engring., 1993-99, prof. dept. civil engring., 1999—. Cons. David E. Daniel, Austin, Tex., 1985-89, Shepard and Miller, Inc., 1990, USAF, 1991, Woodward-Clyde Cons., 1992, Dept. of Energy, 1993, 95; lectr. in field. Editor: Geotechnical News Mag. (environ. geotechnics sect.), 1988—; contbr. articles to Jour. of Contaminant Hydrology, Jour. Geotech. Engring., Jour. Engring. Geology, Nuclear and Chem. Waste Mgmt., Geotech. Testing Jour., others. Vol. sci. fair judge Long's Peak Sci. Fair, U. No. Colo., Greeley, 1988-89. With U.S. Army, 1973-76. U. Tex. Geotech. fellow, 1984-86; grantee NSF Nat., 1992-97; recipient Young Investigator award NSF, 1992. Mem. ASTM, ASCE (mem. environ. geotechnics com. 1988-92, chmn. environ. geotechnics com. 1992—, Walter L. Huber Civil Engring. prize 1995), Assn. Ground Water Scientists and Engrs., Internat. Soc. for Soil Mechanics and Found. Engring. (sec. environ. control com. 1991—), Soil Sci. Soc. of Am. Achievements include research in contaminant transport through saturated and unsaturated porous media, coupled flow processes, diffusion of contaminants in soils, electrokinetics remediation, environmental geotechnics, in situ soil washing, permeability and compatibility of fine-grained soils, permeable reactive walls, physico-chemical properties of soils, soil and waste stabilization, unsaturated flow through clay liners and cover systems. Office: Colo State U Dept Civil Engring Fort Collins CO 80523-0001

SHACKMAN, DANIEL ROBERT, psychiatrist; b. N.Y.C., Nov. 15, 1941; s. Nathan H. and Dorothy K. Shackman. BA, Columbia U., 1962, MD, 1966. Diplomate Am. Bd. Psychiatry and Neurology. Intern Mount Sinai Hosp., N.Y.C., 1966-67, resident, chief resident, fellow, 1967-70; psychiatrist USAF, Spokane, Wash., 1970-72; clin. and adminstrv. staff Brentwood VA Hosp., L.A., 1972-79; pvt. practice psychiatry L.A., 1975-87, Santa Barbara, Calif., 1984—. Asst. clin. prof. UCLA Sch. Medicine, L.A., 1975-87; psychiat. cons. Calif. Dept. Rehab., L.A., 1975-87; cons. psychiatrist Sanctuary Psychiat. Ctrs., Santa Barbara, 1984—; chmn. dept. psychiatry Santa Barbara (Calif.) Cottage Hosp., 1990-92. Bd. dirs. Family Counseling Svc., Spokane, 1971-72. Maj. USAF,

1970-72. Mem. Am. Psychiat. Assn., Am. Acad. Child/Adolescent Psychiatry, So. Calif. Psychiat. Soc. (dist. councillor 1989-92), Am. Soc. Clin. Psychopharmacology. Avocations: music appreciation and performance, computer science. Office: 924 Anacapa St Santa Barbara CA 93101-2115

SHACTER, DAVID MERVYN, lawyer; b. Toronto, Ont., Can., Jan. 17, 1941; s. Nathan and Tillie Anne (Schwartz) S. BA, U. Toronto, 1963; JD, Southwestern U., 1967. Bar: Calif. 1968, U.S. Ct. Appeals (9th cir.) 1969, U.S. Supreme Ct. 1982. Law clk., staff atty. Legal Aid Found., Long Beach, Calif., 1967-70; asst. city atty. City of Beverly Hills, 1970; ptnr. Shacter & Berg, Beverly Hills, 1971-83, Selwyn, Capalbo, Lowenthal & Shacter Profl. Law Corp., 1984-99; pvt. practice, 1999—. Del. State Bar Conf. Dels., 1976—; lectr. Calif. Continuing Edn. of Bar, 1977, 82, 83, 86; judge pro tem L.A. and Beverly Hills mcpl. cts.; arbitrator L.A. Superior Ct., 1983—, also judge pro tem; disciplinary examiner Calif. State Bar, 1986. Bd. dirs. and pres. Los Angeles Soc. Prevention Cruelty to Animals, 1979-89. Mem. Nat. Assn. of Securities Dealers / Dispute Resolution Dept. (arbitrator, 1998—), Beverly Hills Bar Assn. (bd. govs. 1985—, editor-in-chief jour., sec. 1987-88, treas. 1988-89, v.p. 1989-90, pres.-elect 1990-91, pres. 1991-92), Beverly Hills Bar Found. (pres. 1995—, bd. govs. 1998—), Am. Arbitration Assn. (nat. panel arbitrators, neutral arbitrator, panel chmn.), City of Hope Med. Ctr. Aux., Wilshire C. of C. (bd. dirs., gen. counsel 1985-87). Office: 2566 Overland Ave Ste 550 Los Angeles CA 90064-3371 E-mail: david@shacter.org

SHADE, LINDA BUNNELL, university chancellor; BA in English and Comm., Baylor U., 1964; MA in English Lang. and Lit., U. Colo., 1967, PhD in English Lit., 1970. Asst. prof. English, acting assoc. dean Coll. Humanities U. Calif., Riverside, 1970-77; dean acad. programs and policy studies Calif. State U. Sys., 1977-87; vice chancellor acad. affairs Minn. State U. Sys., St. Paul, 1987-93; chancellor U. Colo., Colorado Springs, 1993—. Active Minn. Women's Econ. Round Table, 1989-93; mem. exec. com. Nat. Coun. for Accreditation Tchr. Edn., 1996-99. Mem. St. Paul chpt. ARC; mem. cmty. bd. Norwest Bank, Colorado Springs, 1997—, mem. El Pomar awards for Excellence com., 1997—; mem. leadership commn. ACE, 1997—; mem. subcom. ROTC; mem. edn. com. U.S. Army. Recipient Disting. Alumni award Baylor U., 1995; Woodrow Wilson dissertation fellow, Univ. Colo. Avocations: gardening, baseball, cooking, Sable Burmese cats. Office: U Colo 1420 Austin Bluffs Pkwy Colorado Springs CO 80918-3733

SHADEGG, JOHN B. congressman; b. Phoenix, Oct. 22, 1950; s. Stephen and Eugenia Shadegg; m. Shirley Shadegg; children: Courtney, Stephen. BA, U. Ariz., 1972, JD, 1975. Advisor U.S. Sentencing Commn.; spl. asst. atty. gen. State of Ariz., 1983-90; spl. counsel Ariz. State Ho. Rep. Caucus, 1991-92; pvt. practice; mem. U.S. Congress from 4th Ariz. dist., 1995—; mem. commerce com., fin. svcs. com.; asst. whip U.S. Ho. Reps. Mem. Victims Bill of Rights Task Force, 1989-90; mem. Fiscal Accountability and Reform Efforts Com., 1991-92; counsel Arizonian's for Wildlife Conservation, 1992; chmn. Proposition 108-Two-Thirds Tax Limitation Initiative, 1992. Rep. Party Ballot Security chmn., 1982; active Corbin for Atty. Gen., 1982-86; Rep. Precinct committeeman; chmn. Ariz. Rep. Caucus, 1985-87; chmn. Ariz. Lawyers for Bush-Quayle, 1988; mem. steering com., surrogate spkr. Jon Kyl for Congress, 1988-92; former pres. Crime Victim Found.; founding dir. Goldwater Inst. Pub. Policy; chmn. Ariz. Juvenile Justice Adv. Coun.; mem. adv. bd. Salvation Army; mem. vestry Christ Ch. of Ascension, 1989-91; mem. class II Valley Leadership; bd. dirs. Ariz. State U. Law Soc. Office: US House Reps 432 Cannon Ho Office Bldg Washington DC 20515-0001*

SHAFER, JAMES ALBERT, health care administrator; b. Chgo., Aug. 26, 1924; s. James Earl and Kathleen (Sutterland) S.; m. Irene Jeanne Yurcega, June 20, 1948; children: Kathleen Mary, Patricia Ann. Technician Zenith Radio Corp., Chgo., 1946-47; owner, operator Eastgate Electronics, Chgo., 1947-61; applications engr. Perfection Mica Co., Bensenville, Ill., 1961-71; pres. Electronics Unltd., Northbrook, 1972-73, Ariz. Geriatric Enterprises Inc., Safford, 1974-86; sec.-treas. Saguaro Care Inc., 1988—. Republican. Roman Catholic. Avocations: computers, photography. Home: PO Drawer H 10729 W Cottonwood Wash Rd Pima AZ 85543-0630 Office: Saguaro Care Inc PO Drawer H Pima AZ 85543 E-mail: JSHAFER@EAZNET.COM

SHAFF, BEVERLY GERARD, education administrator; b. Oak Park, Ill., Aug. 16, 1925; d. Carl Tanner and Mary Frances (Gerard) Wilson; m. Maurice A. Shaff, Jr., Dec. 20, 1951 (dec. June 1967); children: Carol Maureen, David Gerrard, Mark Albert. MA, U. Ill., 1951; postgrad., Colo. Coll., 1966, 73, Lewis and Clark Coll., 1982, Portland State U., 1975-82. Tchr. Haley Sch., Berwyn, Ill., 1948-51; assoc. prof. English, Huntingdon Coll., Montgomery, Ala., 1961-62; tchr. English, William Palmer High Sch., Colorado Springs, Colo., 1964-67, 72-76, dir., 1967-72; tchr. English, Burns (Oreg.) High Sch., 1976-78; tchr. English as 2d lang. Multnomah County Ednl. Svc. Dist., Portland, Oreg., 1979-85; coord. gen. studies Portland Jewish Acad., 1984-90; with Indian Edn. Prog./Student Tng. Edn. Prog. (STEP) Portland Pub. Schs., 1990-92, 95—; tchr. St. Thomas More Sch., Portland, 1992-95; tchr. Indian Edn. Act Program Portland Pub. Schs., 1995—. Del. Colorado Springs Dem. Com., 1968, 72; active Rainbow Coalition, Portland; ct. apptd. spl. adv. CASA; mem. Lake Oswego Libr. Bd., Citizens Rev. Bd. Mem. Nat. Assn. Admnstrs., Nat. Assn. Schs. and Colls., Nat. Coun. Tchrs. Math., Nat. Coun. Tchrs. English. Home: 430 NE 16th Ave Apt 201 Portland OR 97232-2886

SHAFFER, OREN GEORGE, former manufacturing company executive; b. Sharpsville, Pa., Aug. 13, 1942; s. Oren G. and Alice Marie (Miller) S.; m. Evelyne Soussan, Oct. 2, 1965; children: Kathleen R., Oren O. BSBA, U. Calif., Berkeley, 1968; MS, MIT, 1985. Mem. internal tng. squad Goodyear Tire and Rubber Co., Akron, Ohio, 1968-69, asst. comptr., 1983-84, v.p., treas., 1985-87, exec. v.p., CFO, 1987-90; mem. fin. staff Goodyear SA, Diegem, Belgium, 1969-70, fin. mgr. Benelux Belgium, 1970-75; CFO, Goodyear France, Paris, 1975-80, pres., 1981-83; CFO, Goodyear Tyre and Rubber Co., Wolverhampton, Eng., 1980-81; exec. v.p., CFO Ameritech Corp., Chgo., 1994-2000; pres., CEO Sorrento Networks Corp., San Diego, 2000—, advisor, 2000—. Bd. dirs. Akron Priority Corp., pres. 1987. Mem. Nat. Assn. Accts., Fin. Execs. Inst., Officer's Conf. Group. Clubs: Firestone Country, Portage Country (Akron). Office: Sorrento Networks Corp 9990 Mesa Rim Rd San Diego CA 92121

SHAFFER, RAYMOND C. state legislator; b. Wilkes-Barre, Pa., Dec. 12, 1932; m. Sharon Van Allen; children: Thomas, Robin, Diane, James, Cindy. Grad., Youngstown Coll. Profl. code adminstrn. U.S. Marine Corps; mem. Nev. Senate, Dist. 2, 1984—; majority whip Nev. Senate, 1991. Mem. Western States Water Policy Com. Mem. Disabled Am. War Vets Lions, North Las Vegas Luncheon Optimist Club (pres.), Foot Printers, Internat. Conf. Bldg. Ofcls., Marine Corps League, North Las Vegas Twp. Dem. Club, Nat. Conf. State Legislatures. Democrat. Home: PO Box 337200 North Las Vegas NV 89033-0037

SHAGAN, STEVE, screenwriter, novelist, film producer; b. N.Y.C., Oct. 25, 1927; Film technician Consol. Film, Inc., N.Y.C., 1952-56, RCA, Cape Canaveral, Fla., 1956-59; asst. to publicity dir. Paramount Pictures, Hollywood, Calif., 1962-63. Prodr.: (TV series) Tarzan, 1966; prodr., writer movies for TV, Universal and CBS, Hollywood, Calif., 1968-70; writer original screenplay) Save the Tiger, 1972 (Writers Guild award, Acad. award nominee 1973); prodr. film, author screenplay: City of Angels (produced as movie Hustle), 1975, novel, screenplay The Formula, 1979, screenplay Voyage of the Damned, 1976 (Acad. award nominee); writer, prodr. film The Formula, 1980; author: (novels) Save the Tiger, 1972, City of Angels, 1975, The Formula, 1979, The Circle, 1982, The Discovery, 1985, Vendetta, 1986, Pillars of Fire, 1989, A Cast of Thousands, 1993, (screenplays) Primal Fear, 1996, Gotti, 1996 (Emmy nominee Best Screenplay). Served with USCG, 1944-46. Mem. Writers Guild Am. (bd. dirs. West chpt. 1978-82).

SHAH, AJAY, electronics company executive; Chmn., pres., CEO Smart Modular Tech., Fremont, Calif. Office: Smart Modular Tech PO Box 1757 Fremont CA 94538-0175

SHAH, GIRISH POPATLAL, information technology consultant; b. Junagadh, India, Apr. 11, 1942; came to U.S., 1963; s. Popatlal Gulabchand and Lalitaben Popatlas (Kamdar) S.; m. Devmani Manilal Jhaveri, June 18, 1968; children: Nivisha, Munjal, Bhavin. B in Tech., Indian Inst. Tech., Bombay, 1963; MS, U. Calif., Berkeley, 1965. Project analyst IBM Corp., Palo Alto, Calif., 1965-67; v.p. Optimun Systems, Inc., Palo Alto, 1967-72; pres. Banking Systems Internat. Corp., Jakarta, Indonesia and Campbell, Calif., 1972-76; dir. software services Tymshare Transactions Services, San Francisco, 1980-83; sr. scientist McDonnell Douglas Corp., Fremont, Calif., 1984-86; dir. corp. devel. Sysorex Internat., Inc., Cupertino, 1986-87, v.p. Mountain View, 1987-96; sr. v.p. Sysorex Info. Systems Inc., Mountain View, 1987-91; exec. cons. IBM Corp., Mountain View, 1996—. Mem. adv. bd. Goodwill Industries, San Francisco, 1980-82; bd. dirs. Gujarate Cultural Assn., 1982; chmn. temple bd. Jain Ctr., 1990-94; co-chmn. Jaina Conv., 1991-94; city gov. Fedn. Indo-Am. Assns., Fremont, Calif., 1991-95; mem. pres.'s coun. Fedn. Jain Assoc. N.Am., 1995—, v.p., 1999-01, treas., 2001—; mem. Jaina charitable trust, 1995—; bd. dirs. Jain Ctr. No. Calif., 1996—, mem. exec. com., 1999—. J.N. Tata Trust nat. scholar, 1963. Mem. Assn. Indians in Am. (v.p. 1980). Democrat. Home: 4048 Twyla Ln Campbell CA 95008-3721 Office: IBM Corp 1055 Joaquin Rd Mountain View CA 94043-1243 E-mail: girish@theshahs.com

SHAH, HARESH CHANDULAL, civil engineering educator; b. Godhra, Gujarat, India, Aug. 7, 1937; s. Chandulal M. and Rama Shah; m. Mary-Joan Dersjant, Dec. 27, 1965; children: Hemant, Mihir. BEngring., U. Poona, 1959; MSCE, Stanford U., 1960, PhD, 1963. From instr. to assoc. prof. U. Pa., Phila., 1962-68; assoc. prof. civil engring. Stanford (Calif.) U., 1968-73, prof., 1973—, chmn. dept. civil engring., 1985-94, John A. Blume prof. engring., 1988-91, Obayashi prof. engring., 1991-97, dir. Stanford Ctr. for Risk Analysis, 1987-94, Obayashi prof. engring. emeritus, 1998—. Trustee Geohazards Internat.; bd. dirs. Liquid Software, Inc., OYO-RMS (Japan) Inc., ERS, R.M. Software (India) Ltd., Risk Mgmt. Solutions, Inc.; cons. in field; pres. World Seismic Safety Initiative, 1994—. Author 1 book; contbr. over 250 articles to profl. jours. Mem. ASCE, Am. Concrete Inst., Earthquake Engring. Rsch. Inst., Seismol. Soc. Am., Sigma Xi, Tau Beta Pi. Avocations: hiking, climbing, travel. Office: Risk Mgmt Solutions Inc 149 Commonwealth Dr Menlo Park CA 94025-1133 E-mail: shah@cive.stanford.edu, hareshs@riskinc.com

SHAH, JAMI J. mechanical engineering educator, researcher; b. Karachi, Pakistan, July 11, 1950; came to U.S., 1975; s. Maqsood A. and Nasim K. Shah. BSME, NED Engring. Coll., Karachi, 1973; MSMetE, U. Pitts., 1976; PhDME, Ohio State U., 1984. Engr. Pakistan Steel, Karachi, 1973-75; prodn. engr. Pakistan Oxygen, Karachi, 1976-80; assoc. prof. Ariz. State U., Tempe, 1984—. Cons. rsch. area in application of artificial intelligence techniques to engring. design and mfg. automation; tchr. creativity techniques in engring. & bus. Author 2 books; contbr. articles to profl. jours. Mem. Computer Soc. of IEEE, ASME, Sigma Xi. Avocations: hiking, climbing, desert plants. Office: Ariz State U Dept Mech Engring Tempe AZ 85287

SHAHAN, SHERRY JEAN, writer, educator; b. Long Beach, Calif., Aug. 14, 1949; d. Frank Rowe Webb and Sylvia Jean (Brunner) Benedict; m. Edgar Harold Shahan, Oct. 23, 1982; children: Kristina Michelle Beal, Kyle Shannon Beal. BS in Social Scis., Calif. Poly. State U., San Luis Obispo, 1978. Lectr. Saddleback Coll. Writers Conf., Orange County, Calif., 1992, Cuesta Community Coll., San Luis Obispo, 1988—, Calif. Reading Assn., 1998—, Nat. Coun. Tchrs. English, 1999—. Author: (books) Dashing Through the Snow: The Story of the Jr. Iditarod (a photo essay, 1997), (mid. grade novel) Frozen Stiff, 1998, (photoessay) The Little Butterfly, 1998, (photoessay) Fifth Grade Crush, 1986, Barnacles Eat With Their Feet: Delicious Facts About the Tide Pool Chain, (2 photo essay), 1996, (photograph only), The Sunflower Family, 1996, Telephone Tag, 1996, Wait Until Dark: Seven Scary Sleep-Over Stories, 1996, (photo essay) Feeding Time at the Zoo, 2000, (picture book) A Jazzy Alphabet, 2002, (collection of romantic short stories), True Love, 1996, Working Dogs, 1999; contbr. articles, photographs numerous regional and nat. newspapers and mags. Mem. Am. Soc. Journalists and Authors, Soc. Am. Travel Writers, So. Calif. Children's Booksellers, Soc. Children's Book Writers, Pi Gamma Mu. Home and Office: 2603 Richard Ave Cayulos CA 93430 E-mail: Kidbooks@thegrid.net

SHAHEEN, GEORGE T. management consultant; b. 1944; Mng. ptnr.-cons. for N.Am., Andersen Worldwide Orgn., until 1989; mng. ptnr., CEO Andersen Cons., Chgo., 1989-99; chmn., CEO Webvan Group, Inc., Foster City, Calif., 1999—. Office: Webvan Group Inc 310 Lakeside Dr Foster City CA 94404

SHAM, LU JEU, physics educator; b. Hong Kong, Apr. 28, 1938; s. T.S. and Cecilia Maria (Siu) Shen; m. Georgina Bien, Apr. 25, 1965; children: Kevin Shen, Alisa Shen. GCE, Portsmouth Coll., Eng., 1957; BS, Imperial Coll., London U., Eng., 1960; PhD in Physics, Cambridge U., Eng., 1963. Asst. rsch. physicist U. Calif. at San Diego, La Jolla, 1963-66, assoc. prof., 1968-75, prof., 1975—, chair dept. physics, 1995-98, dean div. natural scis., 1985-89; asst. prof. physics U. Calif. at Irvine, 1966-67; rsch. physicist IBM Corp., Yorktown Heights, N.Y., 1974-75. Reader Queen Mary Coll., U. London, 1967-68. Assoc. editor Physics Letters A., 1992—; contbr. sci. papers to profl. jours. Recipient Churchill Coll. studentship, Eng., 1960-63, Sr. U.S. Scientist award Humboldt Found., Stuttgart, Germany, 1978, Faculty Rsch. lectr. award, 2000; fellow Guggenheim Found., 1984, Chancellor Assocs. award for Excellence in Rsch., 1995. Fellow Am. Phys. Soc.; mem. AAAS, NAS, Acad. Sinica Republic of China, Optical Soc. Am. Democrat. Avocation: tennis, folk dancing. Office: U Calif San Diego Dept Physics 0319 La Jolla CA 92093-0319 E-mail: lsham@ucsd.edu

SHAMBAUGH, STEPHEN WARD, lawyer; b. South Bend, Ind., Aug. 4, 1920; s. Marion Clyde and Anna Violet (Stephens) S.; m. Marilyn Louise Pyle (dec. 1993); children: Susan Wynne Shambaugh Hinkle (dec. 1998), Kathleen Louise Shambaugh Thompson. Student, San Jose State Tchrs. Coll., 1938-40, U. Ark., 1951; LLB, U. Tulsa, 1954. Bar: Okla. 1954, Colo. 1964. Mem. staff Reading & Bates, Inc., Tulsa, 1951-54; v.p., gen. mgr., legal counsel Reading & Bates Drilling Co. Ltd., Calgary, Alta., Can., 1954-61; sr. ptnr. Bowman, Shambaugh, Geissinger & Wright, Denver, 1964-81; sole practice Denver, 1981-97; now ret. Dir., fin. counsel various corps. Col. USAF ret. Mem. Colo. Bar Assn., Okla. Bar Assn., P-51 Mustang Pilots Assn., Masons, Elks, Phi Alpha Delta.

SHANAHAN, MIKE, professional football coach; b. Oak Park, Ill., Aug. 24, 1952; m. Peggy; children: Kyle, Krystal. BS Phys. Edn., Eastern Illinois U., Charleston, Ill., 1974; MS Phys. Edn., 1975. Student coach Eastern Illinois U.; asst. coach U. Oklahoma, 1975-76; offensive coord., No. Ariz. U., 1976-77, Ea. Ill. U., 1977-78, U. Minn., 1979-80; offensive coord., U. Fla., 1980-84, asst. head coach, 1983-84; receivers coach Denver Broncos, 1984-87; head coach Los Angeles Raiders, 1988-89; asst. coach Denver Broncos, NFL, 1989-91; offensive coordinator San Francisco 49ers, 1992-94; head coach Denver Broncos, 1995—. Avocations: golf, travel. Office: Denver Broncos 13655 Broncos Pkwy Englewood CO 80112-4150

SHANDLING, GARRY, comedian, scriptwriter, actor; b. Chgo., Nov. 29, 1949; s. Irving and Muriel S. Grad., U. Ariz. TV screenwriter: Sanford and Son, Welcome Back Kotter, Three's Company; guest host The Tonight Show, 1986-88; host Emmy Awards 1987, 88, Grammy Awards 1990, 91, 92; writer, prodr. Garry Shandling: Alone in Las Vegas, 1984; exec. prodr., writer It's Garry Shandling's Show 25th Anniversay Special, 1986, It's Garry Shandling's Show, 1986-90 (Ace award best comedy series 1989, 90, Ace award best actor in a comedy seires 1990), Garry Shandling: Stand-Up, 1991, The Larry Sanders Show, 1992— (CableAce award, Writing in a Comedy Series, 1994); actor: (film) Love Affair, 1994, Mixed Nuts, 1994. Office: Agency 9100 Wilshire Blvd # 1000 Beverly Hills CA 90212

SHANDS, HENRY LEE, plant geneticist, administrator; b. Madison, Wis., Aug. 30, 1935; s. Ruebush George and Elizabeth (Henry) S.; m. Catherine Miller, Nov. 20, 1962; children: Deborah A., Jeanne A., James L. BS, U. Wis., 1957; MS, Purdue U., 1961, PhD, 1963. NSF fellow Swedish Seed Assn., Svalov, 1962-63; asst. prof. Purdue U., West Lafayette, Ind., 1963-66, asst. prof. botany and plant pathology, 1965-66; rsch. agronomist, leader ea. wheat project Dekalb Hybrid Wheat, Inc., Lafayette, 1966-79; rsch. agronomist, dir. sunflower rsch. Dekalb Genetics and predecessor firms, Glyndon, Minn., 1979-86; nat. program leader for plant germplasm USDA Agrl. Rsch. Svc., Beltsville, Md., 1986-92, assoc. dep. adminstr. for genetic resources, 1992-97, asst. adminstr. genetic resources, 1997-2000; dir. Nat. Seed Storage Lab., Fort Collins, Colo., 2000—. Mem. AID Project, Minas Gerais, Brazil, 1963-65. 1st lt. U.S. Army, 1957-59. Recipient 1st Victor M. Bendelow Meml. Lectr. award U. Man., 1992. Fellow AAAS, Am. Soc. Agronomy, Crop Sci. Soc. Am. (Frank N. Meyer medal for plant genetic resources 1992); Am. Genetic Assn., Genetics Soc. Can., Am. Phytopath. Soc. Office: USDA-ARS 1111 S Mason St Fort Collins CO 80521-4500

SHANE, WILLIAM WHITNEY, astronomer; b. Berkeley, Calif., June 3, 1928; s. Charles Donald and Mary Lea (Heger) S.; BA, U. Calif., Berkeley, 1951, postgrad., 1953-58; ScD, Leiden (The Netherlands) U., 1971; m. Clasina van der Molen, Apr. 22, 1964; children: Johan Jacob, Charles Donald. rsch. assoc. Leiden U., 1961-71, sr. scientist, 1971-79; prof. astronomy, dir. Astron. Inst., Cath. U. Nijmegen, The Netherlands, 1979-88; guest prof. astronomy Leiden U., 1988-93; C.H. Adams fellow Monterey (Calif.) Inst. Rsch. Astronomy, 1994—. With USN, 1951-53. Fellow AAAS; mem. Internat. Astron. Union (commns. 33, 34), Am. Astron. Soc., Astron. Soc. Netherlands, Astron. Soc. of the Pacific, Phi Beta Kappa. Achievements include research on structure and dynamics of galaxies, observational astronomy. Home: 9095 Coker Rd Prunedale CA 93907-1401 Office: Monterey Inst Rsch Astronomy 200 8th St Marina CA 93933-6002

SHANK, CHARLES VERNON, science administrator, educator; b. Mt. Holly, N.J., July 12, 1943; s. Augustus Jacob and Lillian (Peterson) S.; m. Brenda Buckhold, June 16, 1969. BS, U. Calif., Berkeley, 1965, MS, PhD, 1969. Mem. tech. staff AT&T Bell Labs., Holmdel, N.J., 1969-76, head quantum physics and electronics dept., 1976-83, dir. Electronics Rsch. Lab., 1983-89; dir. Lawrence Berkeley Lab., faculty mem. chemistry, physics, elec. engring. and computer scis. U. Calif., Berkeley, 1989—. Numerous patents in field. Recipient E. Longstreth medal Franklin Inst., Phila., 1982, Morris E. Leeds award IEEE, 1982, David Sarnoff award IEEE, 1989. R.W. Wood prize. Fellow AAAS, Am. Phys. Soc. (George E. Pake prize 1996, Arthur L. Schawlow prize 1997), Optical Soc. Am. (R. W. Wood prize 1981); mem. NAS, NAE, Am. Acad. Arts and Scis. Home: 9 Ajax Pl Berkeley CA 94708-2119 Office: Lawrence Berkeley Nat Lab Ms 50A 4119 Berkeley CA 94720-0001

SHANK, MAURICE EDWIN, aerospace engineering executive, consultant; b. N.Y.C., Apr. 22, 1921; s. Edwin A. and Viola (Lewis) S.; m. Virginia Lee King, Sept. 25, 1948; children: Christopher K., Hilary L. Shank-Kuhl, Diana L. Shank. B.S. in Mech. Engring., Carnegie-Mellon U., 1942; D.Sc., MIT, 1949. Registered profl. engr., Mass. Assoc. prof. mech. engring. MIT, Cambridge, 1949-60; dir. advanced materials R&D Pratt & Whitney, East Hartford, Conn., 1960-70; mgr. materials engring. and rsch., 1971-72; dir. engring. tech., 1972-80; dir. engine design and structures engring. Pratt & Whitney, East Hartford, Conn., 1980-81, dir. engring. tech., 1981-85, dir. engring. tech. assessment, 1985-86; v.p. Pratt Whitney of China, Inc., East Hartford, 1986-87; pvt. exec. cons. to industry and govt., 1987—. Cons. editor McGraw-Hill Book Co., N.Y.C., 1960-80; adv. com. to mechanics div. Nat. Bur. Standards, Washington, 1964-69; vis. com. dept. mech. engring. Carnegie-Mellon U., Pitts., 1968-78; corp. vis. coms. depts. materials sci. and engring., dept. aeros. and astronautics MIT, 1968-74, 79-92; mem. rsch. and tech. adv. coun. com. on aero. propulsion NASA, Washington, 1973-77, mem. aero. adv. com., 1978-86; mem. aero. and space engring. bd. NRC, 1989-92; lectr. in field. Contbr. articles to profl. jours. Served to maj. U.S. Army Corps. of Engrs., Ordnance Corps, 1942-46, Middle East/North Africa. Fellow AIAA, ASME, AIME, Am. Soc. Metals; mem. Nat. Acad. Engring., Conn. Acad. Sci. and Engring. Episcopalian. Club: Cosmos Avocations: boating; fishing.

SHANKS, PATRICIA L. lawyer; b. Salt Lake City, Apr. 3, 1940; BA in Microbiology with honors, Stanford U., 1962; JD, U. Colo., 1978. Bar: Calif. 1978. Mng. ptnr. McCutchen, Doyle, Brown & Enersen, L.A., 1990-94, ptnr., 1994—. Trustee L.A. County Bar Found. Recipient West Publishing award; Stork scholar. Mem. Order of the Coif, Practice in Environ. Law. Office: McCutchen Doyle Brown & Enersen 355 S Grand Ave Ste 4400 Los Angeles CA 90071-3106

SHANNON, MARYLIN LINFOOT, state legislator, educator; b. LaGrande, Oreg., Sept. 7, 1941; BA in Edn., Ctrl. Wash. U. Mem. Oreg. Legislature, Salem, 1994—, mem. edn. com., mem. gen. govt. com., mem. health and human svcs. com., Salem, chair transp. com., mem. water and land use com. Republican. Home: 7955 Portland Rd NE Brooks OR 97305-9401 Office: S 218 State Capitol Salem OR 97310

SHANNON, RICHARD STOLL, III, financial executive; b. N.Y.C., Mar. 22, 1943; s. Richard Stoll Jr. and Margaret (Cather) S.; m. Ann Wright Schmidt, June 14, 1965; children: Clea Cather, Kathryne Baltzelle, Arianna Wright. BA, Stanford U., 1966, MA, 1969; PhD, Harvard U., 1973. Asst. prof. U. Mich., Ann Arbor, 1973-78; mgr., trustee, gen. ptnr. various family trusts, partnerships and corps. Englewood, Colo., 1978-84; pres. Shannon Mgmt. Corp., Englewood, 1985—. Author: The Arms of Achilles, 1975; editor (with others) Oral Literature and The Formula, 1976. Bd. dirs. Cherryvale Sanitation Dist., Englewood, 1984—, pres., 1986-93; regional chmn. Stanford Ann. Fund/Keystone Project, 1985-98; mem. Rackham Advancement Coun., U. Mich., 1992-97. Teaching fellow Harvard U., 1970-73. Mem. Am. Finance Assn., Denver C. of C., Cherry Creek Commerce Assn., Cherry Hills Country Club, Denver Petroleum Club, Phi Beta Kappa. Avocations: golf, fishing, reading, research. Office: Shannon Mgmt Corp # 112 2600 South Wadsworth Blvd Lakewood CO 80235

SHANNON, THOMAS FREDERIC, German language educator; b. Cambridge, Mass., Mar. 16, 1948; m. Christine D. Höner. BA in German summa cum laude, Boston Coll., 1969; MA in German Lit., SUNY, Albany, 1973; MA in Theoretical Linguistics, Ind. U., 1975, PhD in Germanic Linguistics, 1982. Instr. in German Boston Coll., 1969-70; teaching fellow in German SUNY, Albany, 1971-73; univ. fellow Ind. U., Bloomington, 1973-74, assoc. instr., 1974-76, 79-80; acting asst. prof. in Germanic linguistics U. Calif., Berkeley, 1980-82, asst. prof., 1982-87, assoc. prof., 1987-94, prof., 1994—, dir. lang. lab., 1989-92, assoc. dir. Berkeley Lang. Ctr., 1994-95, dir. edn. abroad study ctr. Germany, 2000—. Co-organizer Berkeley Confs. on Dutch Lang. and Lit., 1987, 89, 91, 93, 95, 97, 10th Interdisciplinary Conf. Netherlandic Studies, 2000; econs. presenter and spkr. in field. Contbr. articles to profl. jours.; mem. editl. adv. bd. Am. Jour. Germn Linguistics & Lit., 1998—. With USAR, 1970-76. Grantee Fulbright Found., 1976-78, U. Calif. Berkeley, 1983-84, 94-95, ACLS, 1987, Internat. Assn. Netherlandic Studies, 1988, 91, 94, 97, German Acad. Exch. Svc., summer 1996; NDEA fellow, 1969; Fulbright rsch./lectr. grantee Rijksuniversiteit Groningen, Netherlands, 1992-93; Inst. fuer deutsche Sprache summer rsch. grantee, Mannheim, Germany, 1997. Mem. MLA (exec. com. discussion group in Germanic philology 1989-94, discussion group for Netherlandic Studies 1995-99, divsn. on lang. change 1995-99), Am. Assn. Netherlandic Studies (exec. com. 1988—, editor newsletter 1989-95, series editor publs. 1994—), Am. Assn. Tchrs. German, Internat. Assn. Netherlandic Studies, Internat. Assn. Germanstik, Internat. Soc. Hist. Lingusitics, Linguistic Soc. Am., Netherlands Am. U. League, Pacific Ancient & Modern Lang. Assn., European Linguistic Soc., Soc. Germanic Philology (v.p. 1991-92, 95-99), Interna. Cognitive Linguistics Soc., Alpha Sigma Nu. Home: 770 Rose Dr Benicia CA 94510-3709 Office: U Calif Dept German 5319 Dwinelle Hall Berkeley CA 94720-2502

SHANSBY, JOHN GARY, investment banker; b. Seattle, Aug. 25, 1937; s. John Jay and Jule E. (Boyer) S.; m. Joyce Ann Dunsmore, June 21, 1959 (div.); children: Sheri Lee, Kimberly Ann, Jay Thomas; m. Barbara Anderson De Meo, Jan. 1, 1983 (div.); m. Jane Robinson Dettner, May 1, 1990. B.A., U. Wash., 1959. Sales exec. Colgate-Palmolive Co., N.Y.C., 1959-67; subs. pres. Am. Home Products Corp., N.Y.C., 1968-71; v.p. Clorox Co., Oakland, Calif., 1972-73; ptnr. Booz, Allen & Hamilton, San Francisco, 1974-75; chmn. bd., chief exec. officer, dir. Shaklee Corp., San Francisco, 1975-86; mng. gen. ptnr. The Shansby Group, San Francisco, 1986—. Bd. dirs. The Sharper Image. Chmn. Calif. State Commn. for Rev. of Master Plan Higher Edn.; founder J. Gary Shansby chair mktg. strtegy U. Calif., Berkeley; trustee Calif. State U. Mem. San Francisco C. of C. (past pres.), Villa Traverna Club, Pennask Lake Fishing Club (B.C.), Sky Club of N.Y.C., Sigma Nu. Republican. Office: The Shansby Group 250 Montgomery St San Francisco CA 94104-3406

SHANSTROM, JACK D. federal judge; b. Hewitt, Minn., Nov. 30, 1932; s. Harold A. and Willian (Wendorf) S.; m. June 22, 1957; children: Scott S., Susan K. BA in Law, U. Mont., 1956, BS in Bus., LLB, U. Mont., 1957. Atty. Park County, Livingston, Mont., 1960-65; judge 6th Jud. Dist. Livingston, 1965-82; U.S. magistrate Billings, Mont., 1983-90; U.S. Dist. judge Billings, 1990-96; chief judge U.S. Dist. Ct., 1996—. Capt. USAF, 1957-60. Office: US Dist Ct PO Box 985 Billings MT 59103-0985

SHAO, SHIU, financial executive; b. Taipei, Taiwan, Rep. of China, Nov. 13, 1951; came to U.S., 1975; s. Chi-Ching and Tintz (Yu) S.; m. Misara Chan; 1 child, G.R. BS in Physics, Chan Yuan U., 1973; MBA in Fin., U. Pitts., 1977. Programmer analyst Standard Brands, Inc., Burlingame, Calif., 1977-78; acctg. analyst Watkins Johnson Co., Palo Alto, Calif., 1978-81; controller Oromeccanica Inc., Burbank, Calif., 1981-82; v.p. fin., CFO Oroamerica, Inc., Burbank, 1982—; dir. Am. Internat. Chain Co., Emex Corp. Author: Financial Credit Line Tie to Commodity Index for Precious Metals Industries, 1982. Jr. Achievement advisor, Santa Clara County, Calif., 1979. Served to 2d lt. Chinese Marine Corps, 1973-75. Mem. Nat. Assn. Accts. Home: 1568 Scenic Dr Pasadena CA 91103-1937 Office: Oroamerica Inc 443 N Varney St Burbank CA 91502-1733

SHAPAZIAN, ROBERT MICHAEL, publishing executive; b. Fresno, Calif. s. Ara Michael and Margaret (Azhderian) S. BA, U. Calif., 1964; AM, Harvard U., 1965, PhD in Renaissance English and Fine Arts, 1970. Design assoc. Arthur Elrod Assocs., L.A., 1971-73; v.p. El Mar Corp, Fresno, Calif., 1973-87; dir., art dir. The Lapis Press, Venice, 1987—. Mem. photographic forum San Francisco Mus. Art, 1982 85, Mus. Modern Art, N.Y.C., 1985; mem. photographic com. Met. Mus. Art, N.Y.C., 1994; dir. Gagosian Gallery, L.A. Author: Metaphorics of Artificiality, 1970, Maurice Tabard, 1985; editor: Surrealists Look at Art, 1991 (AIGA award 1991, N.Y. Art Dirs. award 1991), A Witch, 1992 (AIGA award 1992, N.Y. Art Dirs. award 1992, L.A. Art Dirs. award 1992), Pacific Wall (AIGA award 1993), Albucius (We. Art Dirs. award 1993, N.Y. Art Dirs. award 1994), Sam Francis: Saturated Blue, Writings from the Notebooks, 1996. Bd. dirs. Big Brothers/Big Sisters, Fresno, Calif., 1980-82, Film Forum, L.A., 1984-86, Grunwald Ctr. for Graphic Arts, UCLA, 1996—. Recipient Individual Achievement award Lit. Market Pl., N.Y.C., 1992, 23 awards for art direction and design; named Chevalier in Order of Arts and Letters, Govt. of France. Mem. Harvard Club (N.Y.C.). Avocations: twentieth century art, illustrated books, experimental photography. Office: PO Box 36821 Los Angeles CA 90036-0821

SHAPIRO, BARRY, toy company executive; b. Bklyn., Apr. 18, 1942; s. Sidney and Anne (Sokol) S.; m.. Frances Rosenfeld, Apr. 5, 1970 (div. Mar. 1993); children: David Scott, Sean Jonathan. BA in English, Rutgers U., 1963. Asst. buyer J.C. Penney Co., N.Y.C., 1966-69; dir. product planning and internat. ops. Gabriel Industries, Inc., N.Y.C., 1969-78; exec. v.p. Lakeside Games div. Leisure Dynamics, Inc., Mpls., 1978-79, pres., 1979-80; exec. v.p. Toy Game & Hobby Group div. Leisure Dynamics, Inc., Mpls., 1980-81; exec. v.p., gen. mgr., chief exec. officer Wham-O, San Gabriel, Calif., 1981-83; exec. v.p., gen. mgr. Imagineering, Inc., Phoenix, 1984-91; pres. Packing Specialist Inc. SW, Phoenix, 1991—. Cons. to various toy cos. Vol. Jewish Big Bros., 1964-78, vice chmn. Big Bros. of N.Y., 1976-78; coach Little League, Mpls., Arcadia, Calif., 1979—; v.p. Temple Shaarei Tikvah, Arcadia, 1982-84; bd. dirs. Har Zion Synagogue, 1988-90, v.p. 1989-90. Recipient Army Commendation medal. Mem. Assn. Toy Mfg. Am. Jewish. Avocations: tennis, golfing, reading.

SHAPIRO, DAVID, newspaper editor; b. Culver City, Calif., Sept. 1, 1948; m. Maggie Shapiro; children: Treena, Jared. BA in Am. History, U. Hawaii. Editorial asst. Star-Bulletin, Hilo, Hawaii, 1968-87, mng. editor Honolulu, 1987—. Office: Star Bulletin 605 Kapiolani Blvd Honolulu HI 96813-5129

SHAPIRO, FANIA, computer company executive; CEO Setka Computer Cons., San Ramon, Calif. Office: Setka Computer Cons 3223 Crow Canyon Rd Ste 250 San Ramon CA 94583-1332 Fax: 925-824-0222

SHAPIRO, LARRY JAY, pediatrician, scientist, educator; b. Chgo., July 6, 1946; s. Philip and Phyllis (Krause) S.; m. Carol-Ann Uetake; children: Jennifer, Jessica, Brian. A.B., Washington U., St. Louis, 1968, M.D., 1971. Diplomate Am. Bd. Pediatrics, Am. Bd. Med. Examiners, Am. Bd. Med. Genetics. Intern St. Louis Children's Hosp., 1971-72, resident, 1971-73; research assoc. NIH, Bethesda, Md., 1973-75; asst. prof. Sch. Medicine, UCLA, 1975-79, assoc. prof., 1979-83, prof. pediatrics and biol. chemistry, 1983-91; investigator Howard Hughes Med. Inst., 1987-91, W.H. and marie Wattis Disting. Prof.; prof., chmn. dept. pediat. U. Calif.-San Francisco Sch. Medicine, 1991—, chief pediat. svcs. U. Calif. San Francisco Med. Ctr., 1991—. Contbr. numerous articles to profl. publs. Served to lt. comdr. USPHS, 1973-75. Fellow AAAS, Am. Acad. Pediatrics (E. Mead Johnson award in rsch. 1982); mem. Inst. Medicine-NAS, Soc. Pediatric Rsch. (coun. 1984-87, pres. 1991-92), Western Soc. for Pediatric Rsch. (coun. 1983-87, Ross award in rsch. 1981, pres. 1989-90), Soc. for Inherited Metabolic Disease (coun. 1983-88, pres. 1986-87), Assn. Am. Physicians, Am. Soc. Human Genetics (council 1985-88, pres. elect 1995, pres. 1997), Am. Soc. Clin. Investigation, Am. Pediatric Soc., Am. Acad. Arts & Scis. Office: U Calif Med Ctr 505 Parnassus Ave San Francisco CA 94143-0001

SHAPIRO, LUCILLE, molecular biology educator; b. N.Y.C., July 16, 1940; d. Philip and Yetta (Stein) Cohen; m. Roy Shapiro, Jan. 23, 1960 (div. 1977); 1 child, Peter; m. Harley H. McAdams, July 28, 1978; stepchildren: Paul, Heather. BA, Bklyn. Coll., 1961; PhD, Albert Einstein Coll. Medicine, 1966. Asst. prof. Albert Einstein Coll. Medicine, N.Y.C., 1967-72, assoc. prof., 1972-77, Kramer prof., chmn. dept. molecular biology, 1977-86, dir. biol. scis. div., 1981-86; Eugene Higgins prof., chmn. dept. microbiology, Coll. Physicians and Surgeons Columbia U., N.Y.C., 1986-89; Joseph D. Grant prof. devel. biology Stanford U. Sch. Medicine, 1989-97, chmn. dept. devel. biology, 1989-97, Virginia and D.K. Ludwig prof. of cancer rsch. dept. devel. biology, 1998—; dir. Beckman Ctr. Molecular & Genetic Medicine Stanford U., 2001—. Bd. sci. counselors NIH, Washington, 1980-84; bd. sci. advisors G.D. Searle Co., Skokie, Ill., 1984-86; sci. adv. bd. SmithKline Beecham, 1993-2000, PathoGenesis, 1995-2000, Ludwig Found., 2000—; bd. dirs. Glaxo Smith Kline; trustee Scientists Inst. for Pub. Info., 1990-94; lectr. Harvey Soc., 1993; commencement address U. Calif., Berkeley, 1994; DeWitt Stetten disting. lectr., 1989, John M. Lewis lectr. Rockefeller U., 1998, Marker lectr. Pa. State U., 1999, Lundberg lectr. Gothenburg U., Sweden, 1999; honors lectr. NYU, 1998; disting. scientist lectr. NAS, 1999; Crawford lectr. U. Iowa, 1999, Oshman lectr. Baylor U., 2000, Adam Neville lectr., U. Dundee, Scotland, 2001, Genome lectr., Harvard U., 2001. Editor: Microbiol. Devel., 1984; mem. editorial bd. Jour. Bacteriology, 1978-86, Trends in Genetics, 1987—, Genes and Development, 1987-91, Cell Regulation, 1990-92, Molecular Biology of the Cell, 1992—, Molecular Microbiology, 1991-96, Current Opinion on Genetics and Devel., 1991—; contbr. articles to profl. jours. Mem. sci. bd. Helen Hay Witney Found., N.Y.C., 1986-94, Biozentrum, Basel, 1999—, Hutchinson Cancer Ctr., Seattle, 1999; mem. grants adv. bd. Beckman Found., 1999—; co-chmn. adv. bd. NSF Biology Directorate, 1988-89; vis. com., bd. overseers Harvard U., Cambridge, Mass., 1987-90; mem. sci. bd. Whitehead Inst., MIT, Boston, 1988-93; mem. sci. rev. bd. Howard Hughes Med. Inst., 1990-94, Cancer Ctr. of Mass. Gen. Hosp., Boston, 1994; mem. Presidio Coun. City of San Francisco, 1991-94; mem. pres. coun. U. Calif., 1991-97. Recipient Hirschl Career Scientist award, 1976, Spirit of Achievement award, 1978, Alumna award of honor Bklyn. Coll., 1983, Excellence in Sci. award Fedn. Am. Soc. Exptl. Biology, 1994; Jane Coffin Child fellow, 1966; resident scholar Rockefeller Found., Bellagio, Italy, 1996. Fellow AAAS, Am. Acad. Arts and Scis., Am. Acad. Microbiology; mem. Nat. Acad. Sci., Inst. Medicine of Nat. Acad. Sci., Am. Soc. Biochemistry and Molecular Biology (nominating com. 1982, 87, coun. 1990-93), Am. Heart Assn. (sci. adv. bd. 1984-87). Avocation: watercolor painting. Office: Stanford U Sch Medicine Beckman Ctr Dept Devel Biology Stanford CA 94305

SHAPIRO, MARK HOWARD, physicist, educator, academic dean, consultant; b. Boston, Apr. 18, 1940; s. Louis and Sara Ann (Diamond) S.; m. Anita Rae Lavine, June 8, 1961; children: David Gregory, Diane Elaine, Lisa Michelle. A.B. with honors, U. Calif., Berkeley, 1962; M.S. (NSF coop. fellow), U. Pa., 1963, Ph.D., 1966. Research fellow Kellogg Radiation Lab., Calif. Inst. Tech., Pasadena, 1966-68; vis. assoc. divsn. math., physics and astronomy Calif. Inst. Tech., 1976—; research assoc. Nuclear Structure Research Lab. U. Rochester (N.Y.), 1968 70; mem. faculty Calif. State U., Fullerton, 1970—, prof. physics, 1978—, acting assoc. dean Sch. Math., Sci. and Engring., 1985-86, acting dir. Office Faculty Research and Devel., 1986-87, chmn. physics dept., 1989-96, 98-01; dir. tchr. enhancement program NSF, Washington, 1987-88. Tour speaker Am. Chem. Soc., 1983-85 Editor, publisher: The Irascible Professor, 1999; contbr. over 125 articles to profl. jours. Pres. Pasadena Young Democrats, 1967-68; mem. pub. info. and edn. com. Calif. Task Force on Earthquake Preparedness, 1981-85; bd. dirs. Calif. State U. Fullerton Found., 1982-85. Grantee Research Corp., 1971-74, Calif. Inst. Tech., 1977-78, U.S. Geol. Survey, 1978-85, Digital Equipment Corp., 1982, NSF, 1985-87, 90—. Mem. AAAS, Am. Phys. Soc., Am. Assn. Physics Tchrs. (profl. concerns com. 1990-93, chmn. 1991-93), Am. Geophys. Union, N.Y. Acad. Scis., Materials Rsch. Soc., Coun. on Undergrad. Rsch. (physics/astronomy councillor 1993—). Achievements include research in experimental nuclear physics, experimental nuclear astrophysics, geophysics and atomic collisions in solids. Office: Calif State Univ Physics Dept Fullerton CA 92834-6866 E-mail: mshapiro@fullerton.edu

SHAPIRO, MARTIN, law educator; b. 1933; BA, UCLA, 1955; PhD, Harvard U., 1961. Instr. polit. sci. Harvard U., Cambridge, Mass., 1960-62, prof., 1971-74; asst. prof. Stanford U., Calif., 1962-65; assoc. prof. U. Calif., Irvine, 1965-70, prof. Berkeley, 1970, prof. law, 1977—, prof. San Diego, 1974-77. Author: Law and Politics in the Supreme Court, 1964, Freedom of Speech, The Supreme Court and Judicial Review, 1966, Supreme Court and Administrative Agencies, 1968, Courts, 1981, Who Guards the Guardians, 1987. Mem. Law and Soc. Assn. (trustee 1992-95), Western Polit. Sci. Assn. (pres. 1978), Am. Acad. Arts and Scis., Am. Polit. Sci. Assn. (v.p. 1988). Office: U Calif Law Sch 886 Simon Hl Berkeley CA 94720-0001

SHAPIRO, MARVIN SEYMOUR, lawyer; b. N.Y.C., Oct. 26, 1936; s. Benjamin and Sally (Book) S.; m. Natalie Kover, July 12, 1959; children: Donna, Meryl. AB, Columbia U., 1957, LLB, 1959. Bar: D.C. 1959, Calif. 1962. Atty. appellate sect. Civil Div. U.S. Dept. Justice, Washington, 1959-61; ptnr. Irell & Manella, L.A., 1962-99, mng. ptnr., 1992-97. Lectr. U. So. Calif. Tax Inst., Calif. Continuing Edn. of the Bar, Practising Law Inst. Articles editor Columbia Law Rev., 1958-59. V.p., bd. dirs. Jewish Fedn. Coun., L.A., 1985-95; treas. Alan Cranston Campaign, 1974, 80, 86; chmn. credentials com. Dem. Nat. Com., 1972-76; bd. dirs. L.A. Opera Co., 1997—. Mem. Beverly Hills Barristers (pres. 1970). Avocations: travel, golf. Home: 432 N Cliffwood Ave Los Angeles CA 90049-2620

SHAPIRO, MEL, playwright, director, drama educator; b. Bklyn., Dec. 16, 1935; s. Benjamin Shapiro and Lillian (Lazarus) Bestul; m. Jeanne Elizabeth Shapiro, Feb. 23, 1963; children: Joshua, Benjamin. BFA, MFA, Carnegie-Mellon U., 1961. Resident dir. Arena Stage, Washington, 1963-65; producing dir. Tyrone Guthrie Theater, Mpls., 1968-70; master tchr. drama NYU, N.Y.C., 1970-80; guest dir. Lincoln Ctr. Repertory, N.Y.C., 1970; dir. N.Y. Shakespeare Festival, N.Y.C., 1971-77; prof. Carnegie Mellon U., Pitts., 1980-90, head. dept., 1980-87. Head acting UCLA Sch. Theater, Film and TV, 1990—. Dir. N.Y.C. prodns. The House of Blue Leaves, 1970, Bosoms and Neglect, 1978, Marco Polo Sings a Solo, 1998, Taming of the Shrew, 1999; co-adaptor mus. Two Gentlemen of Verona, 1971 (Tony award); author: (plays) The Price of Admissions, 1984 (Drama-Logue mag. award), The Lay of the Land (Joseph Kesselring award 1990), A Life of Crime, 1993; (books) An Actor Performs, 1996, The Director's Companion, 1998. With U.S. Army, 1955-57. Recipient N.Y. Drama Critics award, 1971, 72, Obie award Village Voice, 1972, Drama Desk award, 1973, Drama-logue award, 1993. Mem. Soc. Stage Dirs. and Choreographers (founder, editor The Jour. 1978). Office: UCLA Sch Theatre Film & TV 405 Hilgard Ave Los Angeles CA 90095-9000 E-mail: mshapiro@ucla.edu

SHAPIRO, RICHARD STANLEY, physician; b. Moline, Ill., June 11, 1925; s. Herbert and Esther Dian (Grant) S.; m. Arlene Blum, June 12, 1949; children: Michele Pamela, Bruce Grant, Gary Lawrence; m. Mary Lou Coook, Oct. 11, 1971. BS in Pharmacy, MS in Preventive Medicine & Environ., U. Iowa, 1951, MD, 1957. Diplomate Am. Bd. Allergy and Immunology. Pharmacist, Rock Island, Ill., 1951-53; rsch. asst. U. Iowa Coll. Medicine, Iowa City, 1950-51, 53-57; practice medicine specializing in allergy Beverly Hills, Calif., 1958-62, Lynwood, 1962—. Attending physician Good Hope Found. Allergy Clinic, Los Angeles, 1958-62, Cedars of Lebanon Hosp., Hollywood, Calif., 1959-68, U. So. Calif.-Los Angeles County Med. Center, 1962—; physician St. Francis Hosp., Lynwood, 1962—; assoc. clin. prof. medicine U. So. Calif., 1978-84, emeritus, 1984—. Contbr. articles to profl. jours. Bd. dirs. Westside Jewish Cmty. Ctr., 1961-65, Camp JCA, 1964-65. With USNR, 1943-45; PTO. Fellow Am. Geriatric Soc., Am. Coll. Allergy, Am. Assn. Clin. Immunology & Allergy; mem. AMA, AAAS, Am. Soc. Tropical Medicine and Hygiene, Am. Acad. Allergy, Am. Soc. Internal Medicine, Am. Heart Assn., West Coast Allergy Soc., Calif. Med. Assn., Calif. Soc. Internal Medicine, Calif. Soc. Allergy, L.A. County Med. Assn., L.A. Allergy Soc., Sierra Club, B'nai B'rith, Masons, Sigma Xi. Jewish. Office: 8301 Florence Ave Ste 104 Downey CA 90240-3946

SHAPIRO, ROBERT, lawyer; b. Plainfield, N.J., Sept. 2, 1942; BS in Fin., UCLA, 1965; JD, Loyola U., L.A., 1968. Bar: Calif. 1969, U.S. Ct. Appeals (9th cir.) 1972, U.S. Dist. Ct. (cen., no. & so. dists.) Calif. 1982. Dep. dist. atty. Office of Dist. Atty., L.A., 1969-72; sole practice L.A., 1972-87, 88—; of counsel Bushkin, Gaims, Gaines, Jonas, L.A., 1987-88; Christensen, Miller, Fink & Jacobs, L.A., 1988-95; ptnr. Christensen, Miller, Fink, Jacobs, Glaser, Weil & Shapiro, L.A., 1995—. Author: Search for Justice, 1996, Misconception, 2001. Recipient Am. Jurisprudence award Bancroft Whitney, 1969. Mem. Nat. Assn. Criminal Def. Lawyers, Calif. Attys. for Criminal Justice, Trial Lawyers for Pub. Justice (founder 1982), Century City Bar Assn. (Best Criminal Def. Atty. 1993). Office: 2121 Avenue Of The Stars Fl 19 Los Angeles CA 90067-5010

SHARER, KEVIN W. healthcare products company executive; b. Clinton, Iowa, Mar. 2, 1948; m. Fay M. Sharer; children: Heather, Keith. BS in Aero. Engring, U.S. Naval Acad., 1970; MS in Aero. Engring., U.S. Naval Postgrad. Sch., 1971; MBA, U. Pitts., 1982. Commd. lt. USN, 1970, advanced through grades to lt. comdr., resigned, 1978; with AT&T, 1978-82; cons. McKinsey & Co., 1982-84; pres., chief exec. officer GE Am. Communications, Princeton, N.J., 1984-89; exec. v.p. MCI Telecommunications Corp., Washington, 1989-92; pres., COO Amgen Inc., Thousand Oaks, Calif., 1992-2000, CEO, 2000—, also bd. dirs. Office: Amgen Inc 1 Amgen Ctr Dr Thousand Oaks CA 91320-1799

SHARER, WILLIAM E. state senator; Owner small bus.; Rep. senator dist. 1 N.Mex. State Senate. Mem. edn., Indian and cultural affairs coms. N.Mex. State Senate. Home: Box 203 Farmington NM 87499 Office: NMex State Senate State Capitol Mail Rm Dept Santa Fe NM 87503 E-mail: senate@state.nm.us

SHARIFF, ASGHAR J. geologist; b. Haft Kel, Iran, July 28, 1941; came to U.S., 1964, naturalized, 1978; s. Abdulwahab and Sakineh (Kamiab) S.; m. Kay L. Schoenwald, Aug. 9, 1969; 1 child, Shaun. BS, Calif. State U., Northridge, 1971, MS, 1983. Cert. prof. geologist, Who. Petroleum geologist Iranian Oil Exploration and Producing Co., Ahwaz, 1971-74; geol. cons. D.R.L., Inc., Bakersfield, Calif., 1974-76, Strata-log, Inc., Bakersfield, 1976-79, Energy Log, Inc., Sacramento, 1979-80; geologist U.S. Dept. Energy, Washington, 1980-81, Bur. Land Mgmt. Dept. Interior, Washington, 1981-89, asst. dist. mgr. Rawlins, Wyo., 1989-93, chief reservoir mgmt. group Casper, 1993—. Contbr. articles to profl. jous. Mem. Am. Assn. Petroleum Geologists, Soc. Petroleum Engrs. E-mail: asghar_shariff@blm.gov

SHARMA, ARJUN DUTTA, cardiologist; b. Bombay, June 2, 1953; came to U.S., 1981; s. Hari D. and Gudrun (Axelsson) S.; m. Carolyn D. Burleigh, May 9, 1981; chldren: Allira, Eric, Harrison. BSc, U. Waterloo, Ont., Can., 1972; MD, U. Toronto, Ont., 1976. Intern Toronto Gen. Hosp., 1976-77, resident in medicine, 1978-80, St. Michael's Hosp., Toronto, 1980-81; residency medicine Toronto Gen. Hosp., 1977-78; Rsch. assoc. Washington U., St. Louis, 1981-83; asst. prof. pharmacy and toxicology U. Western Ont., London, 1985-89, asst. prof. medicine, 1983-89, assoc. prof. medicine, 1989-90; dir. interventional electrophysiology Sutter Meml. Hosp., Sacramento, 1990-95. Abstract reviewer, faculty of ann. sci. sessions N.Am. Soc. for Pacing and Electrophysiology, 1993-97; assoc. clin. prof. U. Calif., Davis, 1990-96, clin. prof. medicine, 1997—; cons. Medtronic Inc., Mpls., 1985-2000, Telectronics Pacing Sys., Inc., 1990-94, Ela Med., 2000—, Guidant, 2000—; mem. rsch. com. Sutter Inst. Med. Rsch., 1991-97; mem. exec. com. Sutter Heart Inst., 1992; program dir. Update in Tachyarhythmia Mgmt., Palm Springs, 1996, Pacing Defibrillation and Electrophysiology, Squaw Valley, 1997; mem. atrial fibrillation adv. bd. Guidant Inc. Reviewer profl. jours., including Circulation, Am. Jour. Cardiology; contbr. articles to profl. publs. Mem. coun. for basic sci. Am. Heart Assn., chmn. ann. sci. session, 1989. Recipient John Melady award, 1972, Dr. C.S. Wainwright award, 1973-75, Rsch. prize Toronto Gen. Hosp., 1979, 80, Ont. Career Scientist award Ont. Ministry of Health, 1983-89; Med. Rsch. Coun. Can. fellow, 1981-83. Fellow ACP, Am. Coll. Cardiology; mem. Am. Fedn. Clin. Rsch., Canadian Cardiovasc. Soc., N.Y. Acad. Scis., Sacramento Eldorado Med. Soc. Avocations: skiing, tennis, philately. Office: 3941 J St Ste 260 Sacramento CA 95819-3633 E-mail: skeedud1@aol.com

SHARMA, SANTOSH DEVRAJ, obstetrician/gynecologist, educator; b. Kenya, Feb. 24, 1934; came to U.S., Jan. 1972; d. Devraj Chananram and Lakshmi (Devi) S. BS, MB, B.J. Medical Sch., Pune, India, 1960. House surgeon Sasson Hosp., Poona, India, 1960-61; resident in ob-gyn. various hospitals, England, 1961-67; house officer Maelor Gen. Hosp., Wrexham, U.K., 1961-62; asst. prof. ob-gyn. Howard U. Med. Sch., Washington, 1972-74; assoc. prof. John A. Burns Sch. Med., Honolulu, 1974-78, prof., 1978 --. Fellow Royal Coll. Ob-Gyn., Am. Coll. Ob-Gyn. Avocations: travel, photography, environmental protection. Office: 1319 Punahou St Rm 824 Honolulu HI 96826-1032

SHARMA, SHIV KUMAR, geophysicist; b. India, July 2, 1946; came to U.S., 1977; m. Madhu Malaviya, Aug. 10, 1974; 2 children. BSc, Jiwaji U., 1968; MSc, Jiwaji (India) U., 1973; PhD, Indian Inst. Tech., Delhi, 1980. Rsch. fellow IIT, Delhi, India, 1969-74; rsch. assoc. U. Leicester, 1974-77; with Geophysics Lab., Washington, 1977-80; rschr. Hawaii Inst. Geophysics & Planetology U. Hawaii, Honolulu, 1980—. Contbr. over 160 rsch. papers to profl. jours; patentee in field. Carnegie Postdoctoral fellow; rsch. grantee. Fellow Nat. Acad. Sci. (India) ; mem. Am. Geophys. Union, Am. Ceramic Soc., Am. Electrochem. Soc., Mineral Soc. Am., Optical Soc. Am., Pacific Congress, Soc. for Applied Spectroscopy. Avocations: reading, writing, travel. Office: U Hawaii Sch Ocean & Earth Sci & Tech Hawaii Inst Geophys & Planet 2525 Correa Rd Honolulu HI 96822-2219

SHARMAN, WILLIAM, professional basketball team executive; b. Abilene, Tex., May 25, 1926; m. Joyce Sharman; children from previous marriage: Jerry, Nancy, Janice, Tom. Student, U. So. Calif. Basketball player Washington Capitols, 1950-51, Boston Celtics, 1951-61; coach L.A./Utah Stars, 1968-71, L.A. Lakers, 1971-76, gen. mgr., 1976-82, pres., 1982-88, spl. cons., 1991—. Author: Sharman on Basketball Shooting, 1965. Named to All Star 1st Team, NBA, 1956-59, 2nd Team, 1953, 55 (game MVP), 60, All League Team, 7 times, named Coach of Yr., 1972,

One of Top Players in NBA History, league 50th anniversary, 1997, league leader free-throw percentage, 7 times; named to Basketball Hall of Fame, 1975, Naismith Basketball Hall of Fame, 1976; named All-Am., twice; inductee U. So. Calif. Hall of Fame, 1994; Porterville H.S. gymnasium renamed in his honor, 1997. Home: 7510 W 81st St Playa Del Rey CA 90293-8807 Office: LA Lakers 555 N Nash St El Segundo CA 90245-2818

SHARON, TIMOTHY MICHAEL, physicist; b. Portsmouth, Va., Aug. 21, 1948; s. Lester Clark and Ruth May (Banister) Sharon; m. Carla Deon Colley, Dec. 17, 1977. Student, Santa Ana Coll., 1966—68; BA, U. Calif., Irvine, 1970, MA, 1972, PhD, 1976. Jr. specialist solid state theory U. Calif., Irvine, 1976; rsch. asst. radiation physics Med. Ctr. and Sch. Medicine, 1976—77; cons. to attending staff Rsch. and Edn. Found., 1976—77; mktg. physicist Varian Assoc., Irvine, 1977—78; prin. engr., program mgr. Spectra Rsch. Sys., Newport Beach, Calif., 1977—82; v.p. Brewer-Sharon Corp., Newport Beach, 1981—86, Micor Instruments, Inc., Irvine, 1983—86; pres., CEO Medelec Instruments Co., Inc., Newport Beach, 1986—88; pres. Pacific Crest Enterprises, El Toro, 1988—91; pres., CEO Novus Group NA, El Toro, 1991—96; pres. Instafil, Lake Forest, 1995—. Adj. faculty physics and engring. Columbia Pacific U., San Rafael, Calif., 1981—87; dean Sch. Engring., Newport U., Newport Beach, Calif., 1983—87; mem. adv. panel on pub. Am. Inst. Physics, 1974—75. Editor (assoc.): (jour.) Future Oncology, 2000—;contbr. articles to profl. jours. Fellow: Brit. Interplanetary Soc. (assoc.); mem.: Smithsonian Instn., Nat. Geographic Soc., Mensa, Intertel, Club 33, Acad. Magical Arts, Festival of Arts Laguna Beach, Sigma Pi Sigma, Phi Theta Kappa, Alpha Gamma Sigma, AAAS, Am. Assn. Physicists in Medicine, Am. Film Inst., Nat. Hist. Soc., Assn. Advancement Med. Instrumentation, IEEE, Am. Phys. Soc.

SHARP, LEWIS I. museum director; Dir. Denver Art Mus. Office: Denver Art Mus 100 W 14th Avenue Pkwy Denver CO 80204-2749

SHARP, ROBERT PHILLIP, geology educator, researcher; b. Oxnard, Calif., June 24, 1911; s. Julian Hebner Sharp and Alice Sharp Darling; m. Jean Prescott Todd, Sept. 7, 1938; adopted children: Kristin Todd, Bruce Todd B.S., Calif. Inst. Tech., Pasadena, 1934, M.S., 1935; M.A., Harvard U., Cambridge, Mass., 1936, Ph.D., 1938. Asst. prof. U. Ill., Urbana, 1938-43; prof. U. Minn., Mpls., 1946-47, Calif. Inst. Tech., Pasadena, 1947-79, chmn., 1952-67, prof. emeritus, 1979—. Author: Glaciers, 1960, Field Guide-Southern California, 1972, Field Guide-Coastal Southern California, 1978, Living Ice-Understanding Glaciers and Glaciation, 1988, (with A.F. Glazner) Geology Under Foot in Southern California, 1993, Geology Underfoot in Death Valley and Owens Valley, 1997. Served to capt. USAF, 1943-46 Recipient Exceptional Sci. Achievement medal NASA, 1971, Nat. Medal Sci., 1989, Charles P. Daly medal Am. Geog. Soc., 1991; Robert P. Sharp professorship Calif. Inst. Tech., 1978. Fellow Geol. Soc. Am. (councillor, Kirk Bryan award 1964, Penrose medal 1977, G.K. Gilbert and Disting. Career award 1996), Am. Geophys. Union; hon. fellow Internat. Glaciological Soc.; mem. NAS. Republican. Avocations: flyfishing, snorkeling, camping. Home: 1901 Gibraltar Rd Santa Barbara CA 93105-2326 Office: Calif Inst Tech 1200 E California Blvd Pasadena CA 91106 E-mail: aleen@gps.caletch.edu

SHARPE, ROLAND LEONARD, engineering company executive, earthquake and structural engineering consultant; b. Shakopee, Minn., Dec. 18, 1923; s. Alfred Leonard and Ruth Helen (Carter) S.; m. Jane Esther Steele, Dec. 28, 1946; children: Douglas Rolfe, Deborah Lynn, sheryl Anne. BSCE, U. Mich., 1947, MSE, 1949. Registered civil engr. and structural engr., Calif. Designer Cummins & Barnard, Inc., Ann Arbor, Mich., 1947-48; instr. engring. U. Mich., 1948-50; exec. v.p. John A. Blume & Assocs., engrs., San Francisco, 1950-73; chmn., founder Engring. Decision Analysis Co., Inc., Cupertino, Calif., 1974-87; cons. earthquake engr., 1987—. Mng. dir. EDAC, GmbH, Frankfurt, Germany, 1974-82; dir. EDAC; pres. Calif. Devel. & Engring. Co., Inc., Las Vegas, Nev., 1973-81; mem. nat. earthquake hazard reduction program adv. com. overviewing Fed. Emergency Mgmt. Agy., U.S. Geol. Survey, NSF and Nat. Inst. Stds. and Tech., 1990-93. Author: (with J. Blume, E.G. Kost) Earthquake Engineering for Nuclear Facilities, 1971; author, co-author over 200 engring. papers and reports; author of 3 chpts.: DOE Seismic Safety Manual, 1996. Mem. Planning Commn., Palo Alto, 1955-60; mng. dir. Applied Tech. Coun., Palo Alto, 1973-83; dir. Earthquake Engring. Rsch. Inst., 1972-75, now mem.; project dir., editor Tentative Provision for Devel. of Seismic Regulations for Buildings, 1978; tech. mgr., contbr., editor Data Processing Facilities: Guidelines for Earthquake Hazard Mitigation, 1987. Served with USMC, 1942-46. Recipient citation for contbn. to constrn. industry Engring. news Record, 1978-79, 86-87; chmn. U.S. Joint Com. on Earthquake Engring., 1982-88. Fellow ASCE (hon. mem. 1994, chmn. dynamic effects com. 1978-80, exec. com. structural div. 1980-84, 89-93, chmn. 1983, mgmt. group B 1989-93, Earnest E. Howard award 1994); mem. Japan Structural Cons. Assn. (hon. mem. 1992), Structural Engrs. Assn. Calif. (dir. 1971-73, chmn. seismology com. 1972-74), Structural Engrs. No. Calif. (dir. 1969-71, life mem.), Am. Concrete Inst. (life), Structural Engrs. World Congress (pres. 1995—, chair 1998). Home: 10320 Rolly Rd Los Altos CA 94024-6568 Office: Sharpe Struct Engrs 10320 Rolly Rd Ste 1 Los Altos CA 94024-6568 E-mail: rsharpe3@mindspring.com

SHARPE, WILLIAM FORSYTH, economics educator; b. Cambridge, Mass., June 16, 1934; s. Russell Thornley Sharpe and Evelyn Forsyth (Jillson) Maloy; m. Roberta Ruth Branton, July 2, 1954 (div. Feb. 1986); children: Deborah Ann, Jonathan Forsyth; m. Kathryn Dorothy Peck, Apr. 5, 1986. AB, UCLA, 1955, MA, 1956, PhD, 1961; DHL honoris causa, DePaul U., 1997. Economist Rand Corp., 1957-61; asst. prof. econs. U. Wash., 1961-63, assoc. prof., 1963-67, prof., 1967-68, U. Calif., Irvine, 1968-70; Timken prof. fin. Stanford U., 1970-89, Timken prof. emeritus, 1989-92; prin. William F. Sharpe Assocs., 1986-92; prof.fin. Stanford U., 1993-95, STANCO 25 prof. fin., 1995-99, emeritus, 1999—; chmn. Financial Engines, Inc., 1996—. Author: The Economics of Computers, 1969, Portfolio Theory and Capital Markets, 1970; co-author: Fundamentals of Investments, 1989, 2d edit., 1993, 3d edit., 2000, Investments, 6th edit., 1999. With U.S. Army, 1956-57. Recipient Graham and Dodd award Fin Analysts' Fedn., 1972, '73, '86-88. Nicholas Molodovsky award, 1989. Nobel prize in econ. scis., 1990, UCLA medal, 1998. Mem. Am. Fin. Assn. (v.p. 1979, pres. 1980), Western Fin. Assn. (Enduring Contbn. award 1989), Ea. Fin. Assn. (Disting. Scholar award 1991), Am. Econ. Assn., Phi Beta Kappa.

SHARPLESS, K. BARRY, chemist, educator; b. Phila., Apr. 28, 1941; m. Jan Dueser, Apr. 28, 1965; children: Hannah, William, Isaac. BA, Dartmouth Coll., 1963, hon. doctorate, 1995; PhD, Stanford U., 1968; hon. doctorate, Swedish Royal Inst. Tech., 1995, Tech. U. Munich, 1995, Cath. U. Louvain, Belgium, 1996. Postdoctoral assoc. Harvard U., Stanford U., to 1970, faculty dept. chemistry, 1977-80; faculty MIT, Cambridge, 1970-77, 1980-90; W. M. Keck prof. chemistry Scripps Rsch. Inst. and Skaggs Inst. of Chem. Biology, La Jolla, Calif., 1990—. Recipient Paul Janssen Prize for Creativity in Organic Synthesis, Chem. Pioneer award Am. Inst. Chemists, 1988, Prelog medal Swiss Fed. Inst. Tech., Zurich, 1988, Scheele medal and prize Swedish Acad. Pharm. Scis.; A.P. Sloan fellow, Guggenheim fellow, 1987-88; Camille and Henry Dreyfus Tchr. scholar, Tetrahedron prize for Creativity in Organic Chemistry, 1993, King Faisal Internat. prize for sci., 1995, Microbial medal Kitasato Inst., Tokyo, [illegible] medal in chemistry, 2001, Wolf prize in chemistry, 2001. Fellow AAAS, Am. Acad. Arts and Scis., Royal Soc. Chemistry (hon.); mem. NAS (Award in Chemical Sciences, 2000), Am. Chem. Soc. (Creative Work in Synthetic Organic Chemistry award 1983, Harrison Howe award Rochester chpt. 1987, Remsen award Md. sect. 1989, Arthur C. Cope award 1992, Roger Adams award 1997, Richards medal Northeastern sec. 1998, Top 75 Contbrs. to Chem. Enterprise 1998). Office: Scripps Rsch Inst BCC 315 10550 N Torrey Pines Rd La Jolla CA 92037-1000

SHARPTON, THOMAS, physician; b. Augusta, Ga., July 15, 1949; s. Thomas and Elizabeth (Dozier) S. BA, Northwestern U., 1971; MS, Stanford U., 1973, MD, 1977. Intern Martinez (Calif.) VAMC, 1977-78, resident, 1978-80; mem. staff Kaiser Permanente Med. Group, Oakland, Calif., 1980—; asst. clin. prof. medicine U. Calif., San Francisco, 1994—. Cons. Berkeley (Calif.) Free Clinic, 1977—; chmn. peer review Kaiser Permanente Med. Group, Oakland, 1985-86; clin. mem. faculty U. Calif., San Francisco, 1992, asst. clin. prof., 1994; chair AIDS therapeutics com. No. Calif. Kaiser Hosps., 1996-2000. Mem. Alameda County Profl. Adv. Com., Oakland, 1984-88, Alameda County AIDS Task Force, Oakland, 1985-88. Fellow ACP; mem. Calif. Med. Assn., Alameda-Contra Costa Med. Assn., Am. Soc. Microbiology, Mensa, Sigma Pi Sigma, Phi Beta Kappa. Republican. Club: Phi Beta Kappa of No. Calif. Avocations: classical piano. Office: Kaiser PMG 280 W Macarthur Blvd Oakland CA 94611-5642 Business E-Mail: Thomas.Sharpton@kp.org

SHARROW, MARILYN JANE, library administrator; b. Oakland, Calif. d. Charles L. and H.Evelyn Sharrow; m. Larry J. Davis. BS in Design, U. Mich., 1967, MALS, 1969. Libr. Detroit Pub. Libr., 1968-70; head fine arts dept. Syracuse (N.Y.) U. Librs., 1970-73; dir. libr. Roseville (Mich.) Pub. Libr., 1973-75; asst. dir. librs. U. Wash., Seattle, 1975-77, assoc. dir. librs., 1978-79; dir. librs. U. Man., Winnipeg, Can., 1979-82; chief libr. U. Toronto, Can., 1982-85; libr. U. Calif., Davis, 1985—. Chair bd. North Regional Libr. Facility, 1999—. Recipient Woman of Yr. in Mgmt. award Winnipeg YWCA, 1982; named Woman of Distinction, U. Calif. Faculty Women's Rsch. Group, 1985. Mem. ALA, Assn. Rsch. Librs. (bd. dirs., v.p., pres.-elect 1989-90, pres. 1990-91, chair sci. tech. work group 1994-98, rsch. collections com. 1993-95, 2000—, preservation com. 1997-99), OCLC-Rsch. Librs. Adv. Com. (vice-chair 1992-93, chair 1993-94), Calif. State Network Resources Libr. Com., Can. Assn. Rsch. Libr. (pres. 1984-85). Office: U Calif Shields Libr 100 NW Quad Davis CA 95616-5292 E-mail: mjsharrow@ucdavis.edu

SHARTIN, STACY D. lawyer; b. Mpls., Mar. 10, 1949; AB cum laude, U. Calif., L.A., 1970, JD, 1973. Bar: Calif. 1973. Ptnr. Seyfarth, Shaw, Fairweather & Geraldson (now Syefarth Shaw), L.A., 1980—. Mem. ABA, Calif. State Bar (exec. com. labor and employment sect.), Los Angeles County Bar Assn. Office: Seyfarth Shaw 2029 Century Park E Ste 3300 Los Angeles CA 90067-3063

SHASTID, JON BARTON, wine company executive; b. Hannibal, Mo., Nov. 21, 1914; s. Jon Shepherd and Mary (Barton) S.; m. Natalie Kiliani, Dec. 16, 1944; children— Lucinda, Jon G.H., Victoria A., Thomas Bartwyn. Bar: Calif. bar 1959; C.P.A., Calif., Kans. Pub. accountant, Dodge City, Kans., 1938-42; v.p. finance Johnson Bronze Co., New Castle, Pa., 1946-54; exec. v.p., treas. E. & J. Gallo Winery, Modesto, Calif., 1954-88; pres. Gallo Wine Co. of La. at New Orleans, 1960-89. City councilman, Modesto, 1961-69. Served to capt. USAAF, 1942-46. Mem. State Bar of Calif., Am. Bar Assn., Calif. Soc. C.P.A.'s. Home and Office: 1700 Tice Blvd #444 Walnut Creek CA 94595

SHAVELSON, MELVILLE, writer, theatrical producer and director; b. N.Y.C., Apr. 1, 1917; s. Joseph and Hilda (Shalson) S.; m. Lucille T. Myers, Nov. 2, 1938; children: Richard, Carol-Lynne. AB, Cornell U., 1937. Author: How to Make a Jewish Movie, 1970, Lualda, 1975, The Great Houdinis, 1976, The Eleventh Commandment, 1977, Ike, 1979, Don't Shoot, It's Only Me, 1990; writer Bob Hope Pepsodent Show, NBC radio, 1938-43; screenwriter The Princess and the Pirate, 1944, Wonder Man, 1944, Room for One More, 1951, I'll See You in My Dreams, 1952; screenwriter, dir. The Seven Little Foys, 1954, Beau James, 1956, Houseboat, 1957, The Five Pennies, 1958, It Started in Naples, 1959, On the Double, 1960, Yours, Mine and Ours, 1968, The War Between Men and Women, 1972, The Legend of Valentino, 1975, Deceptions, 1985; screenwriter, dir., producer The Pigeon That Took Rome, 1962, A New Kind of Love, 1963, Cast a Giant Shadow, 1966, Mixed Company, 1974, The Great Houdinis, 1976, Ike, 1979; dir. The Other Woman, 1983; creator TV shows including Danny Thomas Show, ABC-TV, 1953, My World— and Welcome To It, NBC-TV, 1969; author Broadway mus. Jimmy, 1969. Recipient Screen Writers Guild award, 1959, Christopher award, 1959, Sylvania TV award, 1953, Acad. Award nominations (screenplay), 1955, 58, Screen Writers Ann. award nominations (screenplay), 1952 (2), 58, 59, 62, 68, 72, 75, Screen Writers award (best written Am. mus.), 1959, Award of Merit United Jewish Appeal, 1966. Mem. Dirs. Guild Am., Writers Guild Am. (exec. bd. dirs 1960-75, 78, pres. screen writers br. 1967, pres. found. 1975-96, pres. emeritus 1997—, v.p. 1996—), Acad. Motion Picture Arts and Scis. (mem. bd. govs.), Writer Guild Am. West (pres. 1969-70, 79-81, 85-87, Valentine Davies award 1979, Laurel award 1984, Morgan Cox award 1998), Sigma Delta Chi. Home and Office: 11947 Sunshine Ter Studio City CA 91604-3708

SHAVER, JAMES PORTER, education educator, university dean; b. Wadena, Minn., Oct. 19, 1933; BA magna cum laude, U. Wash., Seattle, 1955; MA in Teaching, Harvard U., 1957, EdD, 1961. Instr. Grad. Sch. Edn., Harvard U., 1961-62; assoc. prof., dir. Social Studies Curriculum Ctr., Ohio State U., Columbus, 1964-65; mem. faculty Utah State U. Coll. Edn., Logan, 1962-64, prof., 1965—, chmn. Bur. Rsch. Svcs., 1965-93, assoc. dean rsch., 1978-93, acting dean Sch. Grad. Studies, 1990-91, 92-93, dean, 1993-99, prof. emeritus secondary edn., 1999—. Mem. Commn. Youth Edn. for Citizenship, ABA, 1975-81; mem. edn. task force Am. Hist. Assn.-Am. Polit. Sci. Assn. Project '87, 1981-84; tech. advisor Nat. Ctr. on Effective Secondary Schs., 1988-91; mem. adv. bd. program in civic and moral edn. Inst. for Philosophy and Pub. Policy, U. Md., 1992—; mem. steering com. Nat. Assessment Ednl. Progress Civics Consensus Project, 1995-96. Co-author: Teaching Public Issues in the High School, 1966, 2d edit., 1974, Facing Value Decisions: Rationale-building For Teachers, 1976, 2d edit., 1982; editor: Building Rationales for Citizenship Education, 1977, Handbook of Research on Social Studies Teaching and Learning, 1991; co-editor: Democracy, Pluralism, and the Social Studies, 1968; also others. Recipient Outstanding Svc. and Tchg. award Utah Coun. for the Social Studies, 1975, 78, Lifetime Achievement award, 1998. Mem. AAAS, AAUP, Nat. Coun. Social Studies (pres. 1976, Exemplary Rsch. award 1977, Exemplary Rsch. Editor award 1991), Am. Ednl. Rsch. Assn., Phi Beta Kappa, Phi Kappa Phi. Home: PO Box 176 Hyrum UT 84319-0176 Office: Utah State U 2815 Old Main Hill Logan UT 84322-2815 E-mail: shaver@cc.usu.edu

SHAW, ANTHONY, physician, pediatric surgeon; b. Shanghai, China, Oct. 31, 1929; s. Bruno and Regina (Hyman) S.; m. Iris Violet Azian, Mar. 12, 1955; children: Brian Anthony, Diana Shaw Clark, Daniel Aram. BA cum laude, Harvard Coll., 1950; MD, NYU, 1954. Diplomate Am. Bd. Surgery; cert. spl. competence pediat. surgery. Intern and resident in surgery Columbia-Presbyn. Med. Ctr., N.Y.C., 1954-56, 58-62; resident in pediat. surgery Babies Hosp., N.Y.C., 1962; asst. prof. surgery Columbia U. Coll. Physicians and Surgeons, N.Y.C., 1965-70; chief pediat. surgery St. Vincent's Hosp., N.Y.C., 1963-70, Harlem Hosp. Ctr., N.Y.C., 1965-70; prof. surgery U. Va., Charlottesville, 1970-81, chief pediat. surgery Med. Ctr., 1970-81, prof. surgery UCLA, 1981-2001, emeritus prof. surgery, 2001—; chief pediat. surgery Olive View-UCLA Med. Ctr., Sylmar, 1986-2001. Expert witness on child abuse L.A. Superior Ct., 1986—; chmn. gov.'s adv. com. child abuse and neglect Commonwealth of Va., 1975-80; vis. prof. pediat. surgery People's Republic of China, 1985. Contbr. more than 220 articles to profl. jours. Mem. Gov.'s Task Force on Child Abuse Va., 1973-74. Capt. U.S. Army, 1956-58. Recipient Commrs. award Va. Dept. Social Svcs., 1980, award Gov.'s Adv. Bd., Cert. of Recognition HEW, 1978. Fellow Am. Pediat. Surg. Assn. (sec. 1982-85), ACS (v.p. 1987-89); mem. AMA, Pacific Coast Surg. Assn. (v.p. 1989-90), Am. Soc. Law, Medicine, and Ethics, Am. Profl. Soc. on Abuse of Children, Alpha Omega Alpha. Avocations: writing humor, grandchildren. Home and Office: One S Orange Grove Blvd # 9 Pasadena CA 91105 E-mail: shawpas@pacbell.net

SHAW, ARTHUR E. conductor; Studied with, Sidney Harth; degree, Wichita State U.; postgrad. in Conducting, U. Mich., 1982-85. Asst. condr. Ark. Symphony Orch., 1977-79; music dir., condr. Adrian (Mich.) Symphony Orch., 1979-87, Rogue Valley Symphony, Ashland, Oreg., 1987—. Condr. Rogue Opera, 1987-89; founding dir., guest condr. Youth Symphony So. Oreg.; guest condr. Little Rock Cmty. Theatre, 1979, Summer Music Camp No. Ariz. U., 1988, Ota (Japan) Jr. Symphony, 1990, Jalisco Philharm., Mex., 1992, Ctrl. Oreg. Symphony, 1994, Britt Festivals, 1996. James Robertson Meml. Conducting scholar, 1976-77. Office: Rogue Valley Symphony SOU Music Hall 1250 Siskiyou Blvd Ashland OR 97520-5010

SHAW, DAVID LYLE, journalist, writer; b. Dayton, Ohio, Jan. 4, 1943; s. Harry and Lillian (Walton) S.; m. Alice Louise Eck, Apr. 11, 1965 (div. Sept. 1974); m. Ellen Torgerson, July 17, 1979 (dec.); stepchildren: Christopher, Jordan; m. Lucy Stille, Apr. 14, 1988; 1 child, Lucas. BA in English, UCLA, 1965. Reporter Huntington Park Signal (Calif.), 1963-66, Long Beach Independent (Calif.), 1966-68, L.A. Times, 1968-74, media critic, 1974—. Author: WILT: Just Like Any Other 7-Foot, Black Millionare Who Lives Next Door, 1973, The Levy Caper, 1974, Journalism Today, 1977, Press Watch, 1984, The Pleasure Police, 1996; contbr. numerous articles to mags. including Gentlemen's Quar., Cigar Aficionado, Esquire, TV Guide, Bon Appetit, Food & Wine. Recipient Mellett Fund Nat. award, 1983, PEN West award, 1990, Calif. Bar Assn. Gold Medallion, 1990, Pulitzer Prize for disting. criticism, 1991, Soc. Profl. Journalists Non-Deadline Reporting award, 1999, 2000. E-mial. Office: LA Times Times Mirror Sq Los Angeles CA 90012 E-mail: david.shaw@latimes.com

SHAW, ELEANOR JANE, newspaper editor; b. Columbus, Ohio, Mar. 23, 1949; d. Joseph Cannon and Wanda Jane (Campbell) S. BA, U. Del., 1971. With News-Jour. newspapers, Wilmington, Del., 1970-82, editor HEW desk, asst. met. editor, 1977-80, bus. editor, 1980-82; topics editor USA Today, 1982-83; asst. city editor The Miami Herald, 1983-85; projects editor The Sacramento Bee, 1985-87, news editor, 1987-91, exec. bus. editor, 1991-93, editor capitol bur. news, 1993-95, state editor, 1995-99; mgr. employee comm. The McClatchy Co., Sacramento, 1999—. Bd. dirs. Del. 4-H Found., 1978-83. Mem. Calif. Soc. Newspaper Editors (bd. dirs. 1990-96), No. Calif. Wine Soc. (v.p. 1987-93, pres. 1993—). Office: The McClatchy Co PO Box 15779 Sacramento CA 95852-0779 E-mail: eshaw@mcclatchy.com

SHAW, HERBERT JOHN, physics educator emeritus; b. Seattle, June 2, 1918; s. Herbert John and Nell Grace (Cayley) S.; m. Francel Harper, Apr. 25, 1943; children: John Joseph, Kathleen, Karen. BA, U. Wash., 1941; MS, Stanford U., 1943, PhD, 1948. Test engr. GE, Schenectady, 1940-41; rsch. assoc. elec. engring. dept. Stanford (Calif.) U., 1948-50, rsch. assoc. Microwave Lab., 1950-57, sr. rsch. assoc., 1957-74, assoc. dir., 1968-77, adj. prof., 1974-83, rsch. prof. applied physics dept., 1983-88, prof. emeritus, 1989—. Liaison scientist U.S. Office Naval Rsch., London, 1968-69; cons. to numerous electronics and optics cos. and govt. agys., 1950—. Fellow IEEE (Morris N. Liebmann Meml. award 1976, achievement award group on sonics and ultrasonics 1981); mem. NAE, Tau Beta Pi. Home: 719 Alvarado Row Stanford CA 94305-1037 Office: Stanford U Edward L Ginzton Lab Stanford CA 94305-4085 E-mail: shaw@ee.stanford.edu

SHAW, JIM, JR. broadcast executive; b. Ontario, Can., July 29, 1957; m. Wanda Shaw; children: Haley Morgan, Parker James. Various mgmt. positions Shaw Comm., Inc., Calgary, Alta., Can., 1982, past pres. cable TV Can., past sr. v.p. ops. Can., pres., CEO Can., 1995—. Chmn. bd. dirs. Vision.com, Can.; bd. dirs. Microcell Telecomm., Montreal, CableLabs, Montreal; mem. adv. coun. faculty bus. U. Alberta; owner Shaw FiberLink, Shaw DBS Ventures, YTV, SEGA Channel, Digital Music Express, Microcell; operator 9 radio stas. Gov. Shawnigan Lake Sch., B.C.; active Young Pres. Orgn.; past bd. dirs. Cable TV Stds. Found. Office: Shaw Comm 630 3d Ave SW Calgary AB Canada T2P 4L4

SHAW, J.R. communications executive; b. Brigden, Ont., Can., Aug. 14, 1934; s. Francis Earl and Lottie Myrtle (Gaw) S.; m. Carol Bulman, July 21, 1956; children: Jim, Heather, Julie, Bradley. BA, Mich. State U., 1958; LLD (hon.), Graceland Coll., Lamoni, Iowa, 1993, U. (Can.) Alta., , 1993. Founder, chmn., CEO Shaw Comm., Inc., Calgary, Can., 1966-98, exec. chair Can., 1999—. Chmn. bd. govs. YTV, TreeHouse, country music video network CMT, others; bd. dirs., past chmn. Shaw Industries, Ltd., Can. and worldwide; bd. dirs. Suncor Energy Inc., Millar Western Forest Products Ltd., Winalta Shelters Inc., McKenzie Meadows Golf Corp., The Springs Resort Pres., bd. dirs. Shaw Family Found.; hon. life bd. dirs. Edmonton Northlands; gov. Can. Olympic Found.; past chmn. bd. govs. No. Alberta Inst. Tech.; past mem. bd. dirs., strategic planning com. Can. Cable TV Assn. Named to Honour List CCTA, 1992, Bus. Hall Fame Jr. Achievement No. Alta., 1993; recipient Velma Graham award contbns. Can. broadcasting sys. Ted Rogers Sr., 1992, Entrepreneur of Yr. award, 1992, Pinnacle award for bus. leadership So. Alta. Milner Fenerty, 1996, Friend Industry award Alta. Motion Picture Industries Assn., 1997; inducted into Can. Bus. Hall of Fame, Jr. Achievement Can., 1998. Mem. Calgary Golf and Country, Ranchmen's (Calgary), Sidney North Saanich Yacht Club. Protestant. Avocations: skiing, golf, boating. Office: Shaw Comm Inc Ste 900 630 3d Ave SW Calgary AB T2P 4L4 Canada

SHAW, MICHAEL, biologist, educator; b. Barbados, W.I., Feb. 11, 1924; s. Anthony and Myra (Perkins) S.; m. Jean Norah Berkinshaw, Oct. 16, 1948; children— Christopher A., Rosemary E., Nicholas R., Andrew L. BSc, McGill U., 1946, MSc, 1947, PhD, 1949, DSc, 1975. Nat. Research Council Can. postdoctoral fellow Botany Sch., Cambridge U., 1949-50; Assoc. prof. biology U. Sask., 1950-54, prof., 1954-67, prof., head dept. biology, 1961-67; dean faculty agrl. scis. U. B.C., 1967-75, v.p. acad. devel., 1975-81, acad. v.p., provost, 1981-83, univ. prof., 1983-89, univ. prof. emeritus, 1989—. Mem. Sci. Council Can., 1976-82, Natural Scis. and Engring. Research Council Can., 1978-80 Contbr. articles to profl. jours. Recipient Queen's Silver Jubilee medal, 1977, gold medal Biol. Coun. Can., 1983. Fellow Royal Soc. Can. (Flavelle medal 1976), Can. Phytopath. Soc., Am. Phytopath. Soc., N.Y. Acad. Scis.; mem. AAAS, Can. Bot. Assn., Can. Soc. Plant Physiologists (gold medal 1971), Am. Soc. Plant Physiologists. Home: 1792 Western Pky Vancouver BC Canada V6T 1V3 Office: U BC Dept Plant Sci Vancouver BC Canada V6T 1V3

SHAW, MILTON CLAYTON, mechanical engineering educator; b. Phila., May 27, 1915; s. Milton Fredic and Nellie Edith (Clayton) S.; m. Mary Jane Greeninger, Sept. 6, 1939; children: Barbara Jane, Milton Stanley. BSME, Drexel Inst. Tech., 1938; M of Engring. Sci., U. Cin., 1940, ScD, 1942; PhD (hon.), U. Louvain, Belgium, 1970; DEng (hon.), Drexel U., 1996. Rsch. engr. Cin. Milling Machine Co., 1938-42; chief materials br. NACA, 1942-46; with MIT, 1946-61, prof. mech. engring., 1953-61, head materials processing divsn., 1952-61; prof., head dept.

mech. engring. Carnegie Inst. Tech., Pitts., 1961-75; univ. prof. (hon.) Carnegie-Mellon U., 1974-77; prof. engring. Ariz. State U., Tempe, 1977-86, emeritus prof. engring., 1986—. Cons., lectr. in field; pres. Shaw Smith & Assos., Inc., Mass., 1951-61; Lucas prof. Birmingham (Eng.) U., 1961; Springer prof. U. Calif., Berkeley, 1972; Distinguished guest prof. Ariz. State U., 1977; mem. Nat. Materials Adv. Bd., 1971-74; v.p. conf. com. Engring. Found., 1976-78. Recipient Outstanding Research award Ariz. State U., 1981, Am. Machinist award, 1972, Schlesinger award German Govt., 1997; P. McKenna award, 1975; Guggenheim fellow, 1956; Fulbright lectr. Aachen T.H., Germany, 1957; OECD fellow to Europe, 1964—. Fellow Am. Acad. Arts and Scis., ASME (Hersey award 1967, Thurston lectr. 1971, Outstanding Engring. award 1975, ann. meeting theme organizer 1977, Gold medal 1985, hon. 1980), Am. Soc. Lubrication Engrs. (hon., nat. award 1964), Am. Soc. Metals (Wilson award 1971, fellow 1981); mem. Internat. Soc. Prodn. Engring. Research (pres. 1960-61, hon. mem. 1975), Am. Soc. for Engring. Edn. (G. Westinghouse award 1956), Soc. Mfg. Engrs. (hon. mem. 1970, Gold medal 1958, Internat. Edn. award 1980, M.C. Shaw award 1999), Nat. Acad. Engring., Polish Acad. Sci., Am. Soc. Precision Engrs. (hon.), Japan Soc. Precision Engrs. (Internat. award 1999), Drexel 100. Home: Unit C119 2625 E Southern Ave Tempe AZ 85282-7633 Office: Ariz State U Engring Dept Tempe AZ 85287-6106 Fax: 480-965-1384

SHAY, ROSHANI CARI, political science educator; b. Milw., Oct. 5, 1942; d. Walter John and Dorothee May (Dahnke) O'Donnell; 1 child, Mark Sather. Student, Willamette U., 1960-63; BA, U. Oreg., 1968, MA, 1971, PhD, 1974. Adminstrv. asst. Dept. of Youth Svcs., Lubbock, Tex., 1963; tchg. asst., instr. U. Oreg., Eugene, 1969-72; vis. asst. prof. Oreg. State U., Corvallis, 1973-74, Willamette U., Salem, Oreg., 1973-79, Lewis and Clark Coll., Portland, 1976, 78; from asst. prof. to prof. Western Oreg. U., Monmouth, 1979—, chair history, polit. sci., pub. adminstrn. dept., 1991-94, chair social sci. divsn., 1994-2000. Author: (with others) The People of Rajneeshpuram, 1990, Annual Yearbook in the Sociology of Religion, 1995, (simulation) European Unity Project, 1982. Co-founder, v.p., sec.-treas Ind. Opportunities Unltd., Salem, 1986—; co-founder, sec. Inst. for Justice and Human Rights, San Francisco, 1988-94; bd. dirs. Oreg. UN Assn., Portland, 1982-2000, Salem UN Assn., 1982-91; v.p., pres., bd. dirs. Garten Svcs. Inc. for Disabled, Salem, 1989—; pres. Assn. Oreg. Faculties, 1989-91; mem. adv. bd. Connections Program for Disabled Deaf, Salem, 1989-2000; pres., bd. dirs. Model UN of the Far West, San Francisco, 1981-84, 86-88, 95-2000; mem. Oreg. Women's Polit. Caucus. Danforth Found. fellow, 1968-74; named Woman of Achievement YWCA Tribute, Salem, 1990, Mem. of Yr., Oreg. Rehab. Assn., 1995. Mem. AAUW, Am. Fedn. Tchrs. (v.p., legis. officer local 2278 1982-88), Western Polit. Sci. Assn., Communal Studies Assn., Mental Health Assn. Oreg., Oreg. Acad. Sci., Soc. for Utopian Studies, Oreg. Hosp. Found., Oreg. Internat. Coun., Oreg. Mediation Assn., Phi Kappa Phi (pres., sec., treas.), Phi Alpha Delta Law Fraternity Internat. (Outstanding Faculty Advisor in USA, 2000). Democrat. Avocations: volunteer work with multiply disabled deaf, reading, meditation. Home: 348 S Main St Falls City OR 97344-9763 Office: Western Oreg U 345 Monmouth Ave N Monmouth OR 97361-1314 E-mail: shayr@wou.edu

SHAYE, ROBERT KENNETH, cinema company executive; b. Detroit, Mar. 4, 1939; s. Max Mendle and Dorothy S.; m. Eva G. Lindsten, 1970; children: Katja, Juno. B.B.A., U. Mich., 1960; postgrad., Sorbonne, 1961; J.D., Columbia U., 1964. Bar: N.Y. 1967. Chmn. of the bd., CEO New Line Cinema Corp., N.Y.C., 1967—. Trustee Neurosci. Inst., Am. Film Inst.; dir. Mind, Body Found. Bd. dirs. Legal Aid Soc., N.Y.C. Recipient 1st prize Rosenthal competition Soc. Cinematologists, 1964; recipient cert. of merit Inst. Copyrights and Patents, U. Stockholm, 1966; Recipient award ASCAP/Nathan Burkan Meml. competition, 1964; Fulbright scholar, 1964-66 Mem. Motion Picture Pioneers (bd. dirs.). Club: Friar's (N.Y.C.). Office: New Line Cinema 116 N Robertson Blvd West Hollywood CA 90048-3103 also: New Line Cinema Corp 888 7th Ave Fl 19 New York NY 10106-2599

SHEA, CHRISTINA, mayor; Mayor City of Irvine, Calif., 1996—. Office: City Hall One Civic Center Plaza Irvine CA 92606-5208

SHEA, DEBBIE BOWMAN, state legislator; b. Butte, Mont., June 26, 1951; divorced. BS in Elem. Edn., Eastern Mont. Coll., 1974; MA in Edn., U. Mont., 1989. Formerly tchr. 8th grade pub. schs.; mem. Mont. Ho. of Reps., 1994-96, Mont. Senate, Dist. 18, Helena, 1997—; mem. joint appropriations subcom. on corrections/pub. safety Mont. Senate; mem. edn. and cultural resources com. Mont. State Senate, mem. hwys. and transp. com., mem. fin. and claims com. Democrat. Home: 100 Moon Ln Butte MT 59701-3975

SHEA, DION WARREN JOSEPH, university official, fund raiser; b. New London, Conn., June 10, 1937; s. Frank Steven and Violette Marie (Dion) S.; m. Elizabeth M. Siaba, Dec. 31, 1986; children from previous marriage: Dion Warren Joseph, Nancy Wallace. AB, ScB in Physics, Brown U., 1959; MA in Physics, Boston U., 1962; PhD in Physics, U. Colo., 1968. Mem. tech. staff RCA, 1959-62; asst. prof. physics Creighton U., 1967-68; NRC/Environ. Sci. Svcs. Adminstrn. fellow, rsch. assoc. Environ. Sci. Svcs. Adminstrn., Boulder, Colo., 1968-70; exec. dir. Soc. Physics Students, Am. Inst. Physics, 1970-87, mgr. edn. div., 1972-87; cons. ednl. and computer sytems, 1988—; dir. alumni affairs U.S. Merchant Marine Acad., Kings Point, NY, 1989-93; asst. dir. devel. CUNY Grad. Sch., 1993-99. Author sci. articles. Fellow AAAS; mem. Am. Phys. Soc., Am. Assn. Physics Tchrs., Assn. Coll. Honor Socs. (exec. com. 1984-86), Am. Soc. Assn. Execs., Assn. Fundraising Profls., Planned Giving Group Greater N.Y., Coun. Advancement and Support Edn., Sigma Xi, Sigma Pi Sigma, Sigma Chi, Huntington Bicycle Club (treas. 2000-01), Appalachian Mountain Club, Port Dive Club (treas. 1980-83). Home: PO Box 1428 Golden CO 80402-1428 Office: Shea Cons PO Box 1428 Golden CO 80402-1428 E-mail: Dion_Shea@yahoo.com

SHEA, FRAN, broadcast executive; Sr. v.p. programming E! Entertainment TV, L.A., 1995-98, acting pres. LA, 1998-99, pres., 1999—. Office: E! Entertainment TV 5670 Wilshire Blvd Fl 2D Los Angeles CA 90036-5679 Fax: 213-954-2661

SHEA, JOHN F. construction executive, contractor; Pres., prin., owner J.F. Shea Co., Inc., Redding, Calif., 1968—. Office: JF Shea Co Inc 655 Brea Canyon Rd Walnut CA 91789 Fax: 530-246-9940

SHEA, KEVIN MICHAEL, lawyer; b. Indpls., Dec. 23, 1951; s. James Louis and Elizabeth (Walker) S.; children: Brendan Alkire, Maura Kathryn. BS, U. Colo., 1973; JD, U. Detroit, 1976. Bar: Colo. 1976, U.S. Dist. Ct. D.C. 1976, U.S. Ct. Appeals (10th cir. 1980), U.S. Supreme Ct. 1982. Dep. dist. atty., Boulder, Colo., 1976-79; shareholder, dir., assoc. Roath & Brega P.C., Denver, 1980-85; spl. counsel Holme Roberts & Owen, Denver, 1985-87, ptnr., 1987-94, Ballard, Sphar, Andrews & Ingersoll, Denver, 1995—. Mem. ABA (vice chair environ. crime sect. 1991—), Colo. Bar Assn. (chair criminal law sect. 1990-91), Denver Country Club (bd. dirs.). Democrat. Avocation: ranching. Office: Ballard Sphar Andrews Inger 1225 17th St Ste 2300 Denver CO 80202-5596

SHEA, PATRICK A. lawyer, educator; b. Salt Lake City, Feb. 28, 1948; s. Edward J. and Ramona (Kilpack) S.; m. Deborah Fae Kern, Sept. 1, 1980; children: Michael, Paul. BA, Stanford U., 1970; MA, Oxford U., Eng., 1972; JD, Harvard U., 1975. Bar: Utah 1976, D.C. 1979. Mem. profl. staff majority leader's office U.S. Senate, 1971, asst. staff dir. intelligence com., 1975-76; assoc. VanCott, Bagley, Salt Lake City, 1976-79, ptnr., 1980-87; counsel fgn. relations com. U.S. Senate, 1979-80; gen. counsel KUTV, Comm. Investment Corp., Standard Comm.; dir. Bur. of Land Mgmt. Dept. of Interior, 1997-98; dep., asst. sec. interior Land & Minerals Mgmt., 1998-2000; of counsel Ballard, Spahr, Andrews & Ingersoll LLP, Salt Lake City, 2000—. Cons. judiciary com. U.S. Ho. of Reps., 1972-73; adj. prof. polit. sci. U. Utah, Salt Lake City, 1981-97. Chmn. Utah Democratic Party, Salt Lake City, 1983-85; v.p. Tomorrow-Today Found., Salt Lake City, 1982-84. Mem. Am. Rhodes Scholar Assn., Utah Bar Assn., D.C. Bar Assn., Stanford Alumni Assn. (pres.-elect 1983-84). Roman Catholic. Club: Alta. Office: Ballard Spahr Andrews & Ingersoll LLP One Utah Ctr Ste 600 201 S Main St Salt Lake City UT 84111-2221 Fax: 202-208-3144. E-mail: sheap@ballardspahr.com

SHEAHAN, LARRY L. state legislator, lawyer; b. Spokane, Wash., Dec. 3, 1959; m. Lura Sheahan; 1 child, Ann. BA in Polit. Sci., Wash. State U., 1982; JD, Willamette U., 1985. Ptnr. Sheahan & Sheahan, P.S., Spokane; mem. Wash. Senate, Dist. 9, Olympia, 1999—; mem. higher edn. com.; mem. human svcs. and corrections com.; mem. transp. com. Mem. Rosalia Christian Ch. Mem. Rosalia C. of C. (past pres.), Wash. State Bar Assn., Whitman County Bar Assn., Pullman C. of C., Wash. Assn. Wheat Growers, U.S. Dry Pea and Lentil Assn., Wash. State U. Alumni Assn., Lions (Rosalia), Phi Beta Kappa. Republican. Office: 410A Legislative Bldg Olympia WA 98504-0001

SHEARER, DEREK NORCROSS, international studies educator, diplomat, administrator; b. L.A., Dec. 5, 1946; s. Lloyd and Marva (Peterson) S.; m. Ruth Y. Goldway, July 8, 1976; 1 child, Casey (dec.); stepchildren: Anthony, Julie. BA, Yale U., 1968; PhD, Union Grad. Sch., Yellow Springs, Ohio, 1977. Lectr. U. Calif., L.A., 1979-81; dir. internat. and pub. affairs ctr., prof. of pub. policy Occidental Coll., L.A., 1981-94, 98—; dep. under sec. U.S. Dept. Commerce, Washington, 1993; U.S. ambassador to Finland, U.S. Dept. State, Washington, 1994-97; prof. internat. affairs Occidental Coll., L.A., 1997—; internat. advisor Ziff Bros. Investments, 1998—. Fellow Econ. Strategy Inst., Washington, 1993; policy adv. to Presidential Candidate Bill Clinton, 1990-92; adv. on NATO peace keeping USN, 1997—; pub. policy fellow Woodrow Wilson Internat. Scholars Ctr., 1999-2000; dir. global affairs Occidental Coll., 2001—. Contbr. articles to profl. publs. Planning commr. City of Santa Monica (Calif.), 1984; bd. mem. Nat. Consumer Bank, Washington, 1991. Recipient Guggenheim Fellowship Guggenheim Found., 1984, U.S.-Japan Leadership fellow Japan Soc., 1991. Democrat. Avocations: basketball, tennis, travel, mysteries. Office: DWA Occidental Coll Los Angeles CA 90041 Fax: 323-259-2907

SHEARER, HARRY JULIUS, screenwriter, director, actor; b. Los Angeles, Dec. 23, 1943; s. Mack Shearer and Dora (Kohn) Warren; m. Penelope Joyce Nichols, Oct. 1974 (div. 1977). BA, UCLA, 1964; postgrad., Harvard U., 1964-65. Cert. secondary tchr., Calif. Reporter Newsweek mag., Los Angeles, Boston, 1964-65; legis. intern Calif. State Assembly, Sacramento, 1965-66; tchr. Compton (Calif.) Unified Sch. Dist., 1966-68; writer, actor, producer The Credibility Gap, Los Angeles, 1968-76; creative cons. TV shows Fernwood 2Night, America 2Night, Los Angeles, 1977; dir. History of White People in America, Los Angeles, 1985—; actor, writer TV show Saturday Night Live, N.Y.C., 1979-80, 84-85; creator nat. pub. radio show Sta. KCRW, Santa Monica, Calif., 1983—. Co-creator, co-producer: (recs.) A Great Gift Idea, 1974, A Star Is Bought, 1975; co-writer (films) Real Life, 1976, This is Spinal Tap, 1984 (also co-star); writer, star, dir. (TV spls.) It's Just TV, 1985, This Week Indoors, 1987, The Magic of Live, 1988; co-star The Simpsons, Fox-TV, 1989—; author weekly column Man Bites Town, L.A. Times Sunday Mag., 1990—; actor (films) The Truman Show, 1998, Godzilla, 1998; writer, dir. Teddy Bears Picnic, 2000. Recipient Emmy nominations, 1977, 80, Award for Cable Excellence Cable TV Acad., 1988. E-mail: r.murphy@mgmgt.com

SHEARER, RONALD ALEXANDER, economics educator; b. Trail, C., Can., June 15, 1932; s. James Boyd and Mary Ann (Smith) S.; m. Renate Elizabeth Selig, Dec. 20, 1956 (dec.); children: Carl, Bruce. B.A., U. B.C., 1954; M.A., Ohio State U., 1955, Ph.D., 1959. Asst. prof. econs. U. Mich., 1958-62; economist Royal Commn. Banking and Finance, Toronto, 1962-63; mem. faculty U. B.C., Vancouver, 1963—, prof. econs., 1970-98, emeritus prof., 1998—, head dept., 1972-76. Co-author: Money and Banking, 1975, The Economics of the Canadian Financial System, 1994; editor: Trade Liberalization and a Regional Economy, 1971. Mem. Am., Canadian Econs. Assns. Office: U BC Dept Econs Vancouver BC Canada E-mail: rshearer@interchange.ubc.ca

SHEARER, WILLIAM KENNEDY, lawyer, publisher; b. Marysville, Calif., Jan. 21, 1931; s. William and Eva (Kennedy) S.; m. Eileen Mary Knowland; Nov. 25, 1956; 1 child, Nancy Lorena; stepchildren: David, Douglas, Diane. BA, San Diego State U., 1955; JD, Western State U., 1975. Bar: Calif. 1975, U.S. Dist. Ct. (so. dist.) Calif. 1975, U.S. Ct. Claims 1976, U.S. Supreme Ct. 1982, U.S. Ct. Appeals (fed. cir.) 1982, U.S. Ct. Appeals (9th cir.) 1983. Legis. asst. to Congressman James Utt, 1953, 55-56; exec. dir. San Diego County Rep. Cen. Com., 1956-58; pub. Oceanside-Carlsbad Banner, Oceanside, Calif., 1958-63; adminstrv. asst. Assemblyman E.R. Barnes, Sacramento, 1963-65; polit. campaign cons. Banner Advt., San Diego, Los Angeles, 1964-75; atty. Duke, Gerstel, Shearer LLP, San Diego, 1975—. Pub. newsletters Calif. Statesman, 1962—, Legis. Survey, 1963—, Fgn. Policy Rev., 1972—, Am. Ind., 1974—. Rep. nominee for State Assembly, San Diego County, 1956, 58; state chmn. Am. Ind. Party, Calif., 1967-70, nat. chmn. 1968-71, 73-77; nat. vice chmn. U.S. Taxpayers Party, 1992-96, chmn. 1996-99; Am. Ind. nominee for Gov., 1970; adv. com. Elections Com., Calif. Legislature, Sacramento, 1971-76; mem. Blue Ribbon Task Force on Calif.'s Home Constrn. Industry, 1996-97; bd. dirs. San Diego Gilbert & Sullivan Co., 1984-90, pres. 1986-88, v.p., 1985-86, 88-90. With U.S. Army, 1953-55. Mem. Calif. Bar Assn., San Diego County Bar Assn. Avocations: ancient Near Eastern history, gardening, music. Home: 8160 Palm St Lemon Grove CA 91945-3028 Office: Duke Gerstel Shearer LLP WKS 101 W Broadway Ste 1120 San Diego CA 92101-8296

SHEARING, MIRIAM, state supreme court justice; b. Waverly, N.Y., Feb. 24, 1935; BA, Cornell U., 1956; JD, Boston Coll., 1964. Bar: Calif. 1965, Nev. 1969. Justice of peace Las Vegas Justice Ct., 1977-81; judge Nev. Dist. Ct., 1983-92, chief judge, 1986; justice Nevada Supreme Ct., Carson City, 1993-97, chief justice, 1997—. Mem. ABA, Am. Judicature Soc. (vice chair, 1999—), Nev. Judges Assn. (sec. 1978), Nev. Dist. Ct. Judges Assn. (sec. 1984-85, pres. 1986-87), State Bar Nev., State Bar Calif., Clark County Bar Assn. Democrat. E-mail: shearing@nvcourts.state.nv.us

SHEEHAN, JAMES JOHN, historian, educator; b. San Francisco, May 31, 1937; s. James B. and Sally W. (Walsh) S.; m. 1960; 1 child, Michael L.; m. Margaret L. Anderson, Sept. 2, 1989. BA, Stanford U., 1958; MA, U. Calif., Berkeley, 1959, PhD, 1964. From asst. to assoc. prof. Northwestern U., Evanston, Ill., 1964-79; prof. Stanford (Calif.) U., 1979-86, chmn. dept., 1982-89, Dickason prof. in humanities, 1986—. Author: Lujo Brentano, 1966, German Liberalism, 1978, German History 1770-1866, 1989, Der Ausklang des alten Reiches, 1994, Museums in German Artworld, 2000; editor: The Boundaries of Humanity, 1991; contbr. articles to profl. jours. Decorated officer's cross Order of Merit; fellow Am. Council Learned Socs., 1981-82, NEH, 1985-86, Wissenschaftskolleg Berlin; Guggenheim fellow, 2000—. Fellow AAAS (Humboldt Rsch. prize 1995), Am. Acad. Berlin; mem. Royal Hist. Soc. (corr.), Am. Hist. Assn. (nominating com. 1979-81, chmn. conf. group on Ctrl. European history 1985-86), Am. Philos. Soc. Office: Stanford U Dept History Stanford CA 94305

SHEEHAN, LAWRENCE JAMES, lawyer; b. San Francisco, July 23, 1932; AB, Stanford U., 1957, LLB, 1959. Bar: Calif. 1960. Law clk. to chief judge U.S. Ct. Appeals 2d Cir., N.Y.C., 1959-60; assoc. O'Melveny & Myers, L.A., 1960-68, ptnr., 1969-94, of counsel, 1995—. Bd. dirs. FPA Mut. Funds, TCW Convertible Securities Fund Inc., Source Capital, Inc. Mem. ABA, Los Angeles County Bar Assn., Calif. Bar Assn., Order of Coif. Office: O Melveny & Myers 1999 Avenue Of The Stars Los Angeles CA 90067-6035 also: 400 S Hope St Los Angeles CA 90071-2801 E-mail: lsheehan@omm.com

SHEEHAN, MICHAEL JARBOE, archbishop; b. Wichita, Kans., July 9, 1939; s. John Edward and Mildred (Jarboe) S. MST, Gregorian U., Rome, 1965; D of Canon Law, Lateran U., Rome, 1971. Ordained priest Roman Cath. Ch., 1964. Asst. gen. sec. Nat. Coun. Cath. Bishops, Washington, 1971-76; rector Holy Trinity Sem., Dallas, 1976-82; pastor Immaculate Conception Ch., Grand Prairie, Tex., 1982-83; bishop Diocese of Lubbock, 1983-93; archbishop Archdiocese of Santa Fe, Albuquerqe, N.Mex., 1993—. Past chmn. Am. Bd. Cath. Missions, 1989-91; trustee Cath. Relief Svcs., 1992—. Contbr. articles to New Cath. Ency. Trustee St. Mary Hosp., Lubbock, 1983-89; bd. dirs. Tex. Conf. of Chs. Mem. Serra Club (chaplain 1983-93, chmn. NCCB com. on Evangelization 1996-99, mem. NCCB adminstrv. com. Washington). Avocations: snow skiing, racquetball. Office: Archdiocese Santa Fe 4000 Saint Josephs Pl NW Albuquerque NM 87120-1714

SHEEN, PORTIA YUNN-LING, retired physician; b. Republic of China, Jan. 13, 1919; came to U.S., 1988; d. Y. C. and A. Y. (Chow) Sheen; m. Kuo, 1944 (dec. 1970); children: William, Ida, Alexander, David, Mimi. MD, Nat. Med. Coll. Shanghai, 1943. Intern, then resident Cen. Hosp., Chungking, Szechuan, China, 1943; with Hong Kong Govt. Med. and Health Dept., 1948-76; med. supt. Kowloon (Hong Kong) Hosp., 1948-63, Queen Elizabeth Hosp., Kowloon, 1963-73, Med. and Health Hdqrs. and Health Ctr., Kowloon, 1973-76, Yan Chai Hosp., New Territories, Hong Kong, 1976-87. Fellow Hong Kong Coll. Family Physicians; mem. AAAS, British Med. Assn., Hong Kong Med. Assn., Hong Kong Pediatric Soc., N.Y. Acad. Sci. Methodist. Avocations: reading, music. Home: 1408 Golden Rain Rd Apt 7 Entry 1 Roosmoor Walnut Creek CA 94595-2442 E-mail: pylsheen@abyssinians.org

SHEERAN, MICHAEL JOHN LEO, priest, college administrator; b. N.Y.C., Jan. 24, 1940; s. Leon John and Glenna Marie (Wright) S. AB, St. Louis U., 1963, PhL, 1964, AM in Polit. Sci., 1967, AM in Theology, STL, St. Louis U., 1971; PhD, Princeton U., 1977. Joined Soc. of Jesus, 1957; ordained priest Roman Catholic Ch., 1970. Exec. editor Catholic Mind, N.Y.C., 1971-72; assoc. editor Am. Mag., N.Y.C., 1971-72; assoc. chaplain Aquinas Inst., Princeton, N.J., 1972-75; asst. dean Regis Coll., Denver, 1975-77, dean of Coll., 1977-82, v.p. acad. affairs, 1982-92, acting pres., 1987-88, pres., 1993—. Retreat dir., cons. on governance for religious communities, 1970—. Author: Beyond Majority Rule, 1984; contbr. articles and editls. to publs. Trustee Rockhurst Coll., Kansas City, Mo., 1982-91, Creighton U., Omaha, 1985-95, U. San Francisco, 1985-94, 2001—, Loyola U., New Orleans, 1994-96, Rocky Mountain Coll. Art and Design, 1994-99, Regis Jesuit H.S., 1999—; chmn. Mile High United Way, 1999-2000. Ford Found. scholar, 1963. Democrat. Home: 3333 Regis Blvd Denver CO 80221-1154 Office: Regis U 3333 Regis Blvd Denver CO 80221-1099

SHEFFIELD, GARY ANTONIAN, professional baseball player; b. Tampa, Fla., Nov. 18, 1968; Baseball player Milw. Brewers, 1986-92, San Diego Padres, 1992-93, Florida Marlins, 1993-98; outfielder L.A. Dodgers, 1999—. Mem. Nat. League All-Star Team, 1992-93, 96; Sporting News Player of the Year, 1992; Sporting News All-Star Team, 1992; recipient Silver Slugger award, 1992; named Minor League Co-Player of the Yr. Sporting News, 1988, Comeback Player of Yr., Sporting News, 1992. Nat. Batting League Champion, 1992. Office: LA Dodgers Pro Player Stadium 1000 Elysian Park Ave Los Angeles CA 90012-1112

SHEFFIELD, NANCY, city agency administrator; b. Mpls. BA in Sociology and Psychology, U. Minn., 1969; postgrad., U. Wis., 1992. Participant City of Aurora (Colo.) Supervisory Cert. Series Program, 1988-90. Social worker LeSueur County Human Svcs. Cept., Le Centre, Minn., 1969-71; quality control reviewer Minn. Dept. Human Svcs., St. Paul, 1971-74, quality control supr., 1974-75; neighborhood planner City of Aurora, 1987, neighborhood support supr., 1987-94, acting mgr. Original Aurora Renewal, 1994-95, acting mgr. neighborhood support divsn., 1995, dir. neighborhood svcs., 1996—. Mem. PTO, vol. elem. sch. media ctr., 1980-86. E-mail. Office: City Aurora Dept Neighborhood Svcs 1470 S Havana St Aurora CO 80012-4090 E-mail: nsheffie@aurora.ci.co.us

SHEFFIELD, RICHARD LEE, physicist; b. Dayton, Ohio, Sept. 22, 1950; s. Albert H. and Pauline E. (Schutte) S.; m. Antoinette M. Mals, Oct. 28, 1978; children: Nicole, Angela, Michael. BS, Wright State U., 1972; PhD, MIT, 1978. Staff mem. high energy high density physics Los Alamos (N.Mex.) Nat. Lab., 1978-82, staff mem. free electron laser tech., 1982-85, dep. group leader, 1985-89, group leader accelerator theory & free electron laser tech., 1989-93, prin. investigator advanced FEL initiative, 1990—, now project leader advanced accelerator tech. Advisor UV/FEL adv. panel Brookhaven (N.Y.) Nat. Lab., 1991—, Project Leader Advanced Accelevator Tech., 1994—; lectr. U.S. Accelerator Summer Sch., 1989. Editorial bd. Particle Accelerators, 1991—; patentee photoinjector, high brightness electron accelerators. Pres. Los Alamos United Way, 1981-84; vice chmn. Los Alamos County Planning and Zoning Commn., 1983-86, exec. coun. for divsn. of Beams and Particles. Recipient R&D 100 award R&D 100 Mag., 1988, Strategic Def. Tech. Achievements award Strategic Def. Preparedness Assn., 1989. Fellow Am. Phys. Soc. (prize for Achievement in Accelerator Physics and Tech., 1993); mem. Sigma Pi Sigma.

SHEINFELD, DAVID, composer; b. St. Louis, Sept. 20, 1906; s. Joseph and Feige (Sandler) S.; m. Dorothy Jaffe, Apr. 12, 1942; children: Daniel, Paul. MusB, Am. Conservatory Music, Chgo., 1929; studies with Ottorino Respighi, Santa Cecilia Acad., Rome, 1929-31. Violinist, arranger various radio programs, Chgo., 1934-40; violist Pitts. Symphony, 1944-45; violinist San Francisco Symphony, 1945-71; ind. composer, tchr. San Francisco, 1971—. Composer orchestral and chamber music works including Adagio and Allegro, 1947, Patterns, 1962, Dualities, 1981, Dreams and Fantasies, 1982; commd. to compose work for San Francisco Symphony Assn. Orch.'s 60th anniversary, 1971 (Recipient Norman Fromm award for chamber music composition 1979), 2d string quartet Kronos Quartet, 1990; compositions performed by symphony orchs. in San Francisco, Chgo., Pitts., Phila., Phila. Chamber Symphony, chamber music performed, numerous cities in U.S., Can., Eng. Recipient Composer's award AAAL, 1993, award Koussevitzky Music Found., 1993; NEA grantee for orch. work, 1987-88. Mem. Broadcast Music, Inc. Avocations: astronomy, physics. Home and Office: 1458 24th Ave San Francisco CA 94122-3312

SHEKHAR, STEPHEN S. obstetrician/gynecologist; b. New Delhi, Jan. 13, 1944; came to U.S., 1972; s. S.P. Jain and Shakuntala Mithal; m. Claudette Dorita, Jan. 6, 1978; children: Sasha, Stephen. MBBS, Punjabi U., Patiala, India, 1966. Surgeon Nat. Health Svc. U.K., 1966-72; intern Roosevelt Hosp.-Columbia Coll. Physicians and Surgeons, N.Y.C., 1972-73; resident in ob-gyn. St. Clare's Hosp., N.Y. Med. Coll., N.Y.C., 1973-76, Harlem Hosp.-Columbia U., N.Y.C. and N.J., 1976-77; pvt. practice Studio City, Calif., 19777—. Mem. staff Los Angeles County-U. So. Calif. Med. Sch.; clin prof. ob-gyn. and family medicine U. So. Calif. Sch. Medicine. Fellow ACS, Am. Coll. Ob-Gyn., L.A. Soc. Ob-Gyn.; mem. AMA, Calif. Med. Assn., L.A. County Med. Assn. Home and Office: PO Box 1742 Medford OR 97501-0136

SHELDON, BETTI L. state legislator; b. Aberdeen, Wash. 5 children. Student, Gonzaga U. Mem. Wash. Senate, Dist. 23, Olympia, 1992—; majority flood leader Wash. Senate, Olympia, 1999—; mem. Dem. flood leader Wash. Legislature, Olympia, 1997-98, majority caucus vice chair, 1995, majority whip, 1995-96, majority asst. floor leader, 1993-95, mem. higher edn. com., mem. rules com., mem. ways and means com. Bd. ditrs. Small Bus. Improvement Coun., Commn. on Student Learning's K-123 Accountability Task Force., Nat. Assn. Adminstrv. Rules Rev., YMCA Youth and Govt., Gov.'s Regulatory Reform Task Force, Big Bros. and Big Sisters Kitsap County, Kitsap County Econ. Devel. Coun., Puget Sound Naval Bases Assn., West Sound Arts Coun., Bremerton Olympic Peninsula Coun. Navy League; mem. Wash. Devel. Fin. Authority; mem. adv. bd. for corp. rels. Martha & Mary Luth. Svcs.; mem. delivery plan adv. group Dept. Health Am. Indian Health Care; trustee Keyport Naval Underseas Mus. Found. Recipient Woman of Yr. Bremerton Kitsap YWCA, 1993, Strong Kids, Strong Families, Strong Cmtys. award YMCA, 1999, Dem. Woman of Yr. Wash. State Fedn. Women's Clubs, 1997. Mem. Bremerton Area C. of C. (past exec. dir.), Wash. C. of C. Execs. (v.p.). Democrat. Office: 410A Legislative Bldg Olympia WA 38504-0482

SHELDON, GARY, conductor, music director; b. Bay Shore, N.Y., Jan. 21, 1953; Student, Wash. U., St. Louis, 1972; BMus, Juilliard Sch. Music, 1974; diploma, Inst. Hautes Etudes Musicales, Montreux, Switzerland, 1975. Prin. condr. Opera Theater, Syracuse, 1976-77; asst. condr. Syracuse Symphony Orch., 1976-77, New Orleans Symphony Orch., 1977-80; assoc. condr. Columbus (Ohio) Symphony Orch., 1982-89; music dir. Lancaster (Ohio) Festival, 1988—, Marin Symphony Orch., San Rafael, Calif., 1990—. Composer: Variations on a Theme of Handel, 1984, Mississippi River (for documentary film Miss. River Mus.), Memphis; rec. performances include Beauty and the Beast (with Frank DiGiacomo), 1977, Ballet Class with Karen Hebert, 1982. Recipient New Orleans Music and Drama Found. award, 1982, 3d prize Rupert BBC Symphony Found., London, 1982, 4th prize Leopold Stokowski Conducting Competition, 1986. Mem. Am. Symphony Orch. League (youth orch. div. bd. dirs. 1980—). Office: Marin Symphony Orch 4340 Redwood Hwy San Rafael CA 94903-2121

SHELDON, TIMOTHY, state legislator; m. Linda Sheldon; 1 child, Alexandra. BS in Econs., U. Pa., 1969; MBA, U. Wash., 1972. Gen. mgr. Sheldon Properties, Olympic Peninsula, 1986—; mem. Wash. Senate, Dist. 35, Olympia, 1997—; vice chair agr. and rural econ. devel. com.; vice chair natural resources, parks and recreation com. Wash. Legislature, Olympia, mem. commerce, trade, housing and fin. instns. com., mem. transp. com., mem. joint task force on rural land use and econ. devel., mem. cmty. econ. revitalization bd. Exec. dir. Econ. Devel. Coun. Mason County; mem. Wash. State WWI Meml. fundraising com.; mem. Pacific N.W. Econ. Region Del. Coun.; mem. Mason County Hist. Soc.; mem. Olympic Coll. Shelton Bldg. Fund.; bd. govs. Boys and Girls Club, North Mason County. Mem. Wash. Farm Forestry Assn. Democrat. Office: 408 Legislative Bldg Olympia WA 98504-0001

SHELLAN, RONALD A. lawyer; b. Everett, Wash., Oct. 17, 1949; s. Henry and Sondra Ilsa (Hess) S.; m. Rebecca Rae, March 24, 1972; children: Elisabeth S., David W. BA magna cum laude, U. Wash., 1972; LLM, Willamette U., 1975. Bar: Oreg. 1975, U.S. Dist. Ct. Oreg. 1979, U.S. Tax Ct. 1982; CPA, Oreg. 1978. Law clk. Oreg. Tax Ct., Salem, 1976; tax sr. Coopers & Lybrand, Portland, 1977-79; atty. Sussman, Shank, Wapnick, Caplan & Stiles, Portland, 1979-91, Weiss, Jensen, Ellis & Botteri, Portland, 1991; ptnr. Miller, Nash, Wiener, Hager & Carlsen (name now Miller Nash LLP), Portland, 1991—. Author: G Reorganization Tax Free Acquisition of Financially Distressed Corporations; assoc. editor Willamette Law Jour., 1974-75. V.p. Nat. Multiple Sclerosis Soc. Oreg. Chapter, 1989-96, Robison Jewish Home, Portland, 1990-96. Mem. Oreg. State Bar (chair tax section), Oreg. Soc. CPA's (dir. 1978), Portland Tax Forum (pres.). Avocations: racquetball, skiing. Office: Miller Nash LLP 111 SW 5th Ave Ste 3500 Portland OR 97204-3638

SHELLEDY, JAMES EDWIN, III, newspaper editor; b. Spencer, Iowa, Nov. 11, 1942; s. James E. Jr. and Patricia L. (Cornwall) S.; m. Susan Emily Thomas, Mar. 7, 1986; 1 child, Ian Whittaker. BA, Gonzaga U., 1966. Reporter Spkesman-Rev., Spokane, Wash., 1963-66; tchr., coach Kootenai High Sch., Harrison, Idaho, 1967-71; reporter AP, Boise, 1971-72; reporter, editor Lewiston (Idaho) Morning Tribune, 1973-80; editor, pub. Idahonian, Moscow, 1981-91, Daily News, Pullman, Wash., 1981-91; editor The Salt Lake Tribune, Salt Lake City, 1991—. Juror Pulitzer Prize Com., Columbia U., 1987-88; dir. Investigative Reporters and Editors, 1978-82; bd. dirs. New Directions for News, 1989-96, Newspaper Agy. Corp., 1994-99; mem. AP audit com., N.Y.C., 1982-91. Dir. Idaho Parks Found., Boise, 1976-78, Idaho-Washington Symphony, Pullman, Wash., 1986-89; commr. Idaho Lottery Commn., Boise, 1989-91; adv. bd. Utah YWCA, 1992-97; bd. visitors La. State U. Sch. Comms., 1995—. Roman Catholic. Avocations: golf, sailing. Office: The Salt Lake Tribune 143 S Main St Ste 400 Salt Lake City UT 84111-1945

SHELLER, JOHN WILLARD, lawyer; b. L.A., Oct. 29, 1950; s. Willard Newton and Barbara (Tremaine) S.; m. Mary Elizabeth Hodor, Aug. 9, 1975; children: Matthew John, James Henry. BA, Stanford U., 1972; JD, Loyola U., L.A., 1975. Bar: Calif. 1975. Ptnr. Haight, Brown & Bonesteel, Santa Monica, Calif., 1975—; pub. Melville Press, Pacific Palisades, 1996—. Mem. Am. Bd. Trial Advs. Contbr. articles to profl. jours. Mem. Calif. State Bar Assn., Los Angeles County Bar Assn., So. Calif. Assn. Def. Counsel, Fedn. Ins. and Corp. Counsel, L.A. Country Club. Avocation: golf. Home: 15461 De Pauw St Pacific Palisades CA 90272-4370 Office: Haight Brown & Bonesteel PO Box 680 1620 26th St Santa Monica CA 90406-0680

SHELLEY, MARKE R. career officer; BArch, U. Idaho, 1971; MA in Nat. Security, Coll. of Naval Warfare, 1987. Lic. profl. architect, Wash., NSW/Australia. Commd. 2d lt. USN, 1971, advanced through ranks to rear adm.; various assignments to comdr. Maritime Def. Zone Pacific, 1988-89; comdr. Joint Task Force Mid. East in Bahrain, 1989-90; team chief for European Command's Mil. Liaison Team Bucharest, 1994; comdr. Mil. Sealift & Command Pacific and Far East; ind. architect, comml. real estate developer Seattle. Adj. prof. Naval War Coll., Seattle, 1990-94. Decorated Def. Meritorious Svc. medal, Meritorious Svc. medal, Navy and Marine Corps Commendation medal, Navy Achievement medal. Mem. Naval Res. Assn. (pres. 13th dist.), Res. Officers Assn., The Naval Inst., Navy League, Surface Navy Assn., Fleet Res. Assn., Am. Legion. Office: 11424 NE 94th St Kirkland WA 98033-5706

SHELLHORN, RUTH PATRICIA, landscape architect; b. L.A., Sept. 21, 1909; d. Arthur Lemon and Lodema (Gould) S.; m. Harry Alexander Kueser, Nov. 21, 1940. Student dept. landscape architecture, Oreg. State Coll., 1927-30; grad. landscape architecture program, Cornell U. Coll. Architecture, 1933. Pvt. practice landscape architecture, various cities, Calif., 1933—; exec. cons. landscape architect Bullocks Stores, 1945-78, Fashion Sqs. Shopping Ctrs., 1958-78, Marlborough Sch., L.A., 1968-93, El Camino Coll., Torrance, Calif., 1970-78, Harvard Sch., North Hollywood, 1974-90. Cons. landscape architect, site planner Disneyland, Anaheim, Calif., 1955, U. Calif., Riverside Campus, 1956-64, numerous others, also numerous gardens and estates; landscape architect Torrance (Calif.) City Goals Com., 1969-70; cons. landscape architect City of Rolling Hills (Calif.) Community Assn., 1973-93. Contbr. articles to garden and profl. publs.; subject of Oct. 1967 issue Landscape Design & Constrn. mag. Named Woman of Year, Los Angeles Times, 1955, Woman of Year, South Pasadena-San Marino (Calif.) Bus. Profl. Women, 1955; recipient Charles Goodwin Sands medal, 1930-33, Landscape Architecture award of merit Calif. State Garden Clubs, 1984, 86, Horticulturist of the Yr. award So. Calif. Hort. Inst., numerous nat., state, local awards for excellence. Fellow Am. Soc. Landscape Architects (past pres. So. Calif. chpt.), Phi Kappa Phi, Kappa Kappa Gamma (Alumni Achievement award 1960) Achievements include projects subject of Oct. 1967 issue of Landscape Design and Constrn. Mag. Home and Office: 362 Camino De Las Colinas Redondo Beach CA 90277-6435

SHELTON, JOEL EDWARD, clinical psychologist; b. Havre, Mont., Feb. 7, 1928; s. John Granvil and Roselma Fahy (Ervin) S.; m. Maybelle Platzek, Dec. 17, 1949; 1 child, Sophia. AB, Chico (Calif.) State Coll., 1951; MA, Ohio State U., 1958, PhD, 1960. Psychologist Sutter County Schs., Yuba City, Calif., 1952-53; tchr., vice prin. Lassen View Sch., Los Molinos, 1953-55; tchr. S.W. Licking Schs., Pataskala, Ohio, 1955-56; child psychologist Franklin Village, Grove City, 1957; clin. psychologist Marion (Ohio) Health Clinic, 1958; intern Children's Mental Health Ctr., Columbus, Ohio, 1958-59; acting chief research psychologist Children's Psychiat. Hosp., Columbus, 1959-60; cons. to supt. schs. Sacramento County, Calif., 1960-63; mem. faculty Sacramento State Coll., 1961-69; clin. psychologist DeWitt State Hosp., Auburn, Calif., 1965; exec. dir. Children's Ctr. Sacramento, Citrus Heights, 1963-64, Gold Bar Ranch, Garden Valley, 1964-72; clin. psychologist El Dorado County Mental Health Ctr., Placerville, 1968-70, Butte County Mental Health Dept., Oroville, 1970-94; dir. dept. consultation, edn. and community services Butte County Mental Health Ctr., Chico, 1974-85, outpatient supr., 1986-94. Mgmt. cons., 1972-94; advisor to pres. Protaca Industries, Chico, 1974-80; exec. sec. Protaca Agrl. Rsch., 1974-80; small bus. cons., 1983—; cons. on coll. scholarships and funding, 1991-92, computer cons., 1994—; freelance photographer, 1995—. With U.S. Army, 1946-47. Mem. APA, Western Psychol. Assn., Internat. Freelance Photographers Assn. Home: 1845 Veatch St Oroville CA 95965-4787 E-mail: joele@cheerful.com

SHEN, YUEN-RON, physics educator; b. Shanghai, Mar. 25, 1935; came to U.S. BS, Nat. Taiwan U., 1956; MS, Stanford U., 1959; PhD, Harvard U., 1963; DSc (hon.), Hong Kong U. Sci. and Tech., 1997, Nat. Chiao-Tung U., Taiwan, 1998. Rsch. asst. Hewlett-Packard Co., Palo Alto, Calif., 1959; rsch. fellow Harvard U., Cambridge, Mass., 1963-64; asst. prof. U. Calif., Berkeley, 1964-67, assoc. prof., 1967-70, prof., 1970—, chancellor's prof., 1997-2000. Prin. investigator Lawrence Berkeley Nat. Lab., 1967—. Author: The Principles of Nonlinear Optics, 1984. Recipient Charles Hard Townes award, 1986, Arthur L. Schawlow prize Am. Phys. Soc., 1992, DOE Alexander von Humboldt award, 1984, DOE Outstanding Rsch. award DOE-MRS Rsch., 1983, DOE Sustained Outstanding Rsch. award, 1987, Max Planck Rsch. award, 1996, Materials Sci. award Solid State Physics, 1997; Sloan fellow, 1966-68, Guggenheim Found. fellow, 1972-73. Fellow Am. Phys. Soc. (disting. traveling lectr. Laser Sci. Topical Group 1994-96, Frank Isakson prize 1998), Photonics Soc. Chinese-Ams., Optical Soc. Am.; mem. AAAS, NAS, Acad. Sinica, Chinese Acad. Scis. (fgn.). Achievements include research in nonlinear optics and condensed matter physics. Office: U Calif Berkeley Dept Physics Berkeley CA 94720-0001

SHENK, GEORGE H. lawyer; b. N.Y.C., Sept. 10, 1943; BA, Princeton U., 1965; M in Internat. Affairs, Columbia U., 1967; JD, Yale U., 1970. Bar: N.Y. 1971, Calif. 1985. Assoc. Coudert Bros., Paris, 1970, N.Y.C., 1970-73, Hong Kong, 1973-75, Tokyo, 1975-78, ptnr. N.Y.C., 1978-91, San Francisco, 1991-94, Heller Ehrman, White & McAuliffe, 1994—. Exec. dir. San Francisco Com. on Fgn. Rels. Contbr. articles to pubs. Mem. Bar Assn. City of N.Y., Calif. State Bar Assn., Coun. Fgn. Rels., Pacific Coun. on Internat. Policy. Office: Heller Ehrman White & McAuliffe 333 Bush St San Francisco CA 94104-2806

SHEPARD, KATHRYN IRENE, public relations executive; b. Tooele, Utah, Jan. 6, 1956; d. James Lewis and Glenda Verleen (Slaughter) Clark; m. Mark L. Shepard, June 5, 1976. BA in History, Boise State U., 1980. On-air writer Sta. KTTV, Channel 11, L.A., 1982-85; publicity dir. Hollywood (Calif.) C. of C., 1985-87; pres. Kathy Shepard Pub. Rels., Burbank and Portland, 1987-93; dir. public relations Las Vegas Hilton, 1993-94; dir. comms. Hilton Gaming, 1994-96; dir. corp. comms. Hilton Hotels Corp., 1996-97, v.p. corp. comms., 1997—. Instr. pub. rels. ext. program UCLA, 1991-92. Contbr. articles to profl. publs. Mem. Public Communicators L.A. (pres. 1991-92, bd. dirs. 1987-91), Pub. Rels. Assn. Am., Women in Comms. Avocations: genealogy, film, travel. Office: Hilton Hotels Corp PR Dept 9336 Civic Center Dr Beverly Hills CA 90210-3604 E-mail: kathy_shepard@hilton.com

SHEPARD, ROGER NEWLAND, psychologist, educator; b. Palo Alto, Calif., Jan. 30, 1929; s. Orson Cutler and Grace (Newland) S.; m. Barbaranne Bradley, Aug. 18, 1952; children: Newland Chenoweth, Todd David, Shenna Esther. BA, Stanford U., 1951; PhD, Yale U., 1955; AM (hon.), Harvard U., 1966; ScD (hon.), Rutgers U., 1992. Rsch. assoc. Naval Research Lab., 1955-56; rsch. fellow Harvard, 1956-58; mem. tech. staff Bell Telephone Labs., 1958-66, dept. head, 1963-66; prof. psychology Harvard U., 1966-68, dir. psychol. labs., 1967-68; prof. psychology Stanford U., 1968-98, Ray Lyman Wilbur prof. social sci., 1989-96, Ray Lyman Wilbur prof. emeritus social sci., 1996—. Guggenheim fellow Center for Advanced Study in Behavioral Scis., 1971-72; recipient, N.Y. Acad. Scis. award, 1987, Nat. Medal of Sci., 1995, Gold medal Am. Psychol. Found., 2000. Fellow AAAS, APA (pres. exptl. div. 1980-81, Disting. Sci. Contbn. award 1976); mem. Am. Acad. Arts and Scis., Nat. Acad. Scis., Psychometric Soc. (pres. 1973-74), Psychonomic Soc., Soc. Exptl. Psychologists (Howard Crosby Warren medal 1981), Am. Philos. Soc., Yale Grad. Sch. Alumni Assn. (Wilbur Cross medal 2001). Office: Stanford U Dept Psychology Mailcode 2130 Bldg 420 Stanford CA 94305-2130

SHEPARD, SAM (SAMUEL SHEPARD ROGERS), playwright, actor; b. Ft. Sheridan, Ill., Nov. 5, 1943; s. Samuel Shepard and Jane Elaine (Schook) Rogers; m. O-Lan Johnson Dark, Nov. 9, 1969 (div.); 1 son, Jesse Mojo; children with Jessica Lange: Hannah Jane, Samuel Walker. Student, Mt. San Antonio Jr. Coll., Walnut, Calif., 1961-62. Playwright-in-residence Magic Theatre, San Francisco. Author: (plays) Cowboys, 1964, The Rock Garden, 1964, 4-H Club, 1965, Up to Thursday, 1965, Dog, 1965, Rocking Chair, 1965, Chicago, 1965 (Obie award 1966), Icarus's Mother, 1965 (Obie award 1966), Fourteen Hundred Thousand, 1966, Red Cross, 1966 (Obie award 1966), Melodrama Play, 1966 (Obie award 1968), La Turista, 1967 (Obie award 1967), Cowboys #2, 1967, Forensic and the Navigators, 1967 (Obie award 1968), The Holy Ghostly, 1969, The Unseen Hand, 1969, Operation Sidewinder, 1970, Shaved Splits, 1970, Mad Dog Blues, 1971, Terminal, 1971, (with Patti Smith) Cowboy Mouth, 1971, Black Bog Beast Bait, 1971, The Tooth of Crime, 1972 (Obie award 1973), Blue Bitch, 1973, (with Megan Terry and Jean-Claude van Itallie) Nightwalk, 1973, Geography of a Horse Dreamer, 1974, Little Ocean, 1974, Action, 1974 (Obie award 1975), Killer's Head, 1974, Suicide in B-Flat, 1976, Angel City, 1976, Curse of the Starving Class, 1977 (Obie award 1977), Buried Child, 1978 (Pulitzer Prize in drama 1979, Obie award 1979), Tongues, 1979, Savage/Love, 1979, Seduced, 1979, True West, 1981, Fool for Love, 1983 (Obie award 1984), Superstitions, 1983, The Sad Lament of Pecos Bill on the Eve of Killing his Wife, 1983, A Lie of the Mind, 1985 (New York Drama Critics' Circle award 1986), States of Shock, 1991, Simpatico, 1993; (collections of plays) Five Plays by Sam Shepard, 1967, The Unseen Hand and Other Plays, 1971, 2nd edit., 1986, Mad Dog Blues and Other Plays, 1972, The Tooth of Crime and Geography of a Horse Dreamer, 1974, Angel City, Curse of the Starving Class and Other Plays, 1976, Buried Child, Seduced, Suicide in B-Flat, 1979, Four Two-Act Plays by Sam Shepard, 1980, Chicago and Other Plays, 1981, Seven Plays, 1981, Fool for Love and The Sad Lament of Pecos Bill on the Eve of Killing His Wife, 1983, Fool For Love and Other Plays, 1984, 1986; contbr. to Oh! Calcutta, 1976; (screenplays) Me and My Brother, 1967, (with Michelangelo Antonioni, Tonino Guerra, Fred Graham, and Clare Peploe) Zabriskie Point, 1970, (with Murray Mednick) Ringaleevio, 1971, (with others) Oh! Calcutta!, 1972, (with Bob Dylan) Renaldo and Clara, 1978, Paris, Texas, 1984 (Golden Palm award Cannes Film Festival 1984), Fool for Love, 1985; (other writings) Rolling Thunder Logbook, 1977, Hawk Moon: A Book of Short Stories, Poems and Monologues, 1981, Motel Chronicles, 1982; writer, dir.: (plays) Fool for Love, 1983, A Lie of the Mind, 1985, (screenplays) Far North, 1988, Silent Tongue, 1993; actor: (films) Renaldo and Clara, 1978, Days of Heaven, 1978, Resurrection, 1980, Raggedy Man, 1981, Frances, 1982, The Right Stuff, 1983 (Academy award nomination best supporting actor 1984), Country, 1984, Fool for Love, 1985, Crimes of the Heart, 1986, Baby Boom, 1987, Steel Magnolias, 1989, Hot Spot, 1990, Bright Angel, 1991, Defenseless, 1991, Thunderheart, 1992, The Pelican Brief, 1993, Safe Passage, 1994, The Good Old Boys, 1995, Curtain Call, 1997, The Only Thrill, 1997, (TV performances) Streets of Laredo, 1995, Lily Dale, 1996, Purgatory, 1999, Dash & Lilly, 1999, Hamlet, 2000 (nominated for Golden Globe, Best Actor). Fellow U. Minn., 1966, Yale U., 1967; grantee Rockefeller Found., 1967, Guggenheim Found., 1968, 71; recipient Nat. Inst. and Am. Acad. Arts and Letters award for lit., 1974, Creative Arts award Brandeis U., 1975, Theater Hall of Fame, 1994. Mem. Am. Acad. and Inst. of Arts and Letters, 92. Office: Internat Creative Mgmt 8942 Wilshire Blvd Beverly Hills CA 90211-1934

SHEPARD, THOMAS HILL, physician, educator; b. Milw., May 22, 1923; s. Francis Parker and Elizabeth Rhodes (Buchner) S.; m. Alice B. Kelly, June 24, 1946; children: Donna, Elizabeth, Ann. A.B., Amherst Coll., 1945; M.D., U. Rochester, 1948. Intern Strong Meml. Hosp., Rochester, N.Y., 1948-49, resident, 1950-52, Albany (N.Y.) Med. Center, 1949-50; pediatric endocrine fellow Johns Hopkins Hosp., 1954-55; pediatrician U. Wash., Seattle, 1955-61; embryologist dept. anatomy U. Fla., 1961-62; teratologist U. Wash., 1961—, prof. pediatrics, head central lab. for human embryology, 1961-93, prof. emeritus, 1993—; rsch. assoc. dept. embryology Carnegie Inst., 1962, U. Copenhagen, 1963. Cons. NIH, FDA, EPA, 1971— ; vis. prof. pediatrics U. Geneva, 1972, 73-74. Author: A Catalog of Teratogenic Agents, 1973, 10th edit., 2001; contbr. articles to profl. jours. Served with U.S. Army, 1946-48; Served with USAF, 1952-54. Mem. Teratology Soc. (hon. mem. 1993, pres. 1968), Western Soc. Pediatric Rsch. (pres. 1970), Am. Pediatric Soc., Japanese Teratology Soc. (hon. 1998), Orgn. for Teratogen Answering Svcs. (hon.). Home: 3015 98th Ave NE Bellevue WA 98004-1818 Office: U Wash Sch Medicine Dept Pediatrics Seattle WA 98195-0001

SHEPHERD, JOHN FREDERIC, lawyer; b. Oak Park, Ill., May 22, 1954; s. James Frederic Shepherd and Margaret Joanne (Crotchett) Woollen; children: Eliza Marion, Justine Catherine. AB magna cum laude, Dartmouth Coll., Hanover, N.H., 1976; JD, U. Denver, 1979. Bar: Colo. 1979, U.S. Dist. Ct. Colo. 1979, D.C. 1981, U.S. Dist. Ct. D.C. 1981, U.S. Ct. Appeals (10th cir.) 1981, U.S. Ct. Appeals (D.C. cir.) 1982, U.S. Ct. Appeals (9th cir.) 1990, U.S. Supreme Ct. 1984. Assoc. Holland & Hart, Denver, 1979-81, Washington, 1981-85, ptnr., 1985-87, Denver, 1987—; natural resources disting. practitioner in residence U. Denver Coll. Law, 1998. Reporter Mineral Law Newsletter, 1985-92. Mem. 50 for Colo., Denver, 1989. Mem. ABA (chmn. pub. lands and land use com. 1991-93, mem. coun. for sect. of natural resources energy and environ. law 1993-96), Rocky Mountain Mineral Law Found. (mem. long-range planning com. 1988—, trustee 1993-95), Dartmouth Alumni Club (pres. Washington chpt. 1985-86, trustee Rocky Mt. chpt., 1998—), Denver Athletic Club. Avocations: flyfishing, basketball, running. Home: 320 Clermont St Pkwy Denver CO 80220-5642 Office: Holland & Hart 555 17th St Ste 3200 Denver CO 80202-3950 E-mail: JShepherd@Hollandhart.com

SHEPHERD, KAREN, former congresswoman; b. Silver City, N.Mex., July 5, 1940; m. Vincent P. Shepherd. BA, U. Utah, 1962; MA, Brigham Young U., 1963. Former instr. Brigham Young U., Am. U., Cairo; former pres. Webster Pub. Co.; former adminstr. David Eccles Sch. Bus., U. Utah; former dir. Salt Lake County Social Svcs., Utah; former dir. continuing edn. Westminster Coll.; former mem. Utah Senate; mem. 103d Congress from 2d Utah dist., Washington, 1993-95; exec. dir., U.S. rep. European Bank for Reconstruction Devel., 1996—; mem. Nat. Common Cause Governing Bd., Washington, 1995-96; exec. dir., U.S. rep. European Bank for Reconstruction Devel., 1996—; mem. exec. com., chair East West Trade and Investment Forum Am. C. of C., U.K., 1998—. Founder Karen Shepherd Fund; founding mem. Utah Women's Polit. Caucus, Project 2000; mem. Internat. Delegation to Monitor Elections in West Bank and Gaza, Israel. Former mem. United Way, Pvt. Industry Coun.; former mem. adv. bd. U.S. West Grad. Sch. Social Work; trustee Westminster Coll. Recipient Women in Bus. award U.S. Small Bus. Assn., Woman of Achievement award, Pathfinder award, YWCA Leadership award, 1st place award Nat. Assn. Journalists, Disting. Alumni award U. Utah Coll. Humanities. Fellow Inst. Politics Kennedy Sch Govt., Internat. Women's Forum; Salt Lake Area C. of C. (pub. rels. com.). Home: PO Box 1049 Salt Lake City UT 84110-1049 Office: 21 G St Salt Lake City UT 84103-2949

SHEPHERD, PAUL H. elementary school educator; b. Salt Lake City, Sept. 6, 1955; s. Richard Lawrence and Janis (Hoskings) S.; m. Marlene Wade, Aug. 31, 1978; children: Janice, Faith, Matthew, Andrew, Luke, Christian. BS in Elem. Edn., U. Utah, 1981, MEd, 1985. Cert. elem. tchr., Utah. Printer Transamerica Film Svc., Salt Lake City, 1978-81; tchr. Granite Sch. Dist., Salt Lake City, 1981—. Pres. Granite Fedn. Tchrs., 1985-87, treas., 1990-92. Active mem. State House of Reps., 1992-94; Bishop LDS Ch., West Jordan, Utah, 1988; mem. Oquivrh Shadows Community Coun., West Jordan, 1987; chmn. rels. com. Boy Scouts Am., 1972—. Recipient Outstanding Tchr. award Excel Found., 1985, Elem. Tchr. of Yr. award Utah Fedn. Tchrs., 1991. Mem. ASCD, Utah Assn Gifted Children. Democrat. Avocations: fishing, guitar. Home and Office: 6644 W 5095 S West Jordan UT 84084-7728 E-mail: shepfam@concentric.net, paul.shepherd@granite.k12.ut.us

SHEPPARD, JACK W. retired career officer; b. Parkersburg, W.Va., Aug. 8, 1931; s. James Lee and Audrey Irene (Heiney) S.; m. Norma Ann Stutler, Sept. 4, 1953; children— Bradley, Gregory BAC, U. Akron, Ohio, 1955; MA in Pub. Adminstrn., [illegible] U., 1966. [illegible] Force, 1955, advanced through grades to maj. gen.; vice comdr. 60 Mil. Airlift Wing, USAF, Travis AFB, Calif., 1977-79; comdr. 1606 Air Base Wing, USAF, Kirtland AFB, N.Mex., 1979-81; dir. internat. staff Inter Am.

Def. Bd., USAF, Washington, 1981-82; dep. chief staff for personnel USAF Mil. Airlift Command, Scott AFB, Ill., 1982-83, chief of staff, 1983-85; comdr. Twenty First Air Force, McGuire AFB, N.J., 1985-87; asst. dep. chief staff programs and resources Hdqrs. USAF, Washington, 1987-88, ret., 1988. Mem. Kirtland partnership com., pres. Albuquerque Armed Forces Adv. Assn. Mem. Albuquerque Armed Forces Adv. Assn., Order of Daedalians, Air Force Assn., Airlift Assn., USAF Order of the Sword, USAF Order of the Bayonet, Theta Chi. Presbyterian Home: PO Box 908 21 Beaver Ln Cedar Crest NM 87008-0908 E-mail: jackgenusaf@cs.com

SHER, BYRON D. state legislator, law educator; b. 1928; BSBA, Washington U., St. Louis, 1949; JD, Harvard U., 1952. Bar: Mass. 1952. Sole practice, Boston, 1952-54; teaching fellow Harvard U., Cambridge, Mass., 1954-55; asst. prof. law So. Methodist U., Dallas, 1955-57; asst. prof. Stanford (Calif.) U. Law Sch., 1957-59, assoc. prof., 1959-62, prof., 1962—; senator Calif. State Legislature, Sacramento, 1996—. Cons. Fulbright research scholar Victoria U., Wellington, N.Z., 1964; mem. Calif. State Assembly, 1980-96. Author: (with others) Law and Society, 1960, mem., Calif. Senate, 1996. Mem. Nat. Conf. Commrs. Uniform State Laws. Office: 5589 Winfield Blvd Ste 102 San Jose CA 95123-1219 Address: 260 Main St Ste 201 Redwood City CA 94063-1733 also: State Capitol Rm 2082 Sacramento CA 95814

SHER, PAUL PHILLIP, pathologist; b. Bklyn., Oct. 25, 1939; s. Louis and Lottie (Kloner) S.; m. Joan E. Zeffren, June 9, 1964; children: Matthew, Andrew, Lawrence. BS cum laude, Hobart Coll., 1961; MD, Washington U., 1965. Diplomate Am. Bd. Pathology. Intern Columbia-Presbyn. Hosp., N.Y.C., 1965-66, resident in pathology, 1966-69; instr. pathology Columbia Presbyn. Hosp., N.Y.C., 1968-70; resident in pathology Englewood (N.J.) Hosp., 1969-70; dir. clin. chemistry Frances Delafeld Hosp., N.Y.C., 1970-71; dir. blood bank Bethesda Naval Hosp., Rockville, Md., 1971-72, dir. hematology, 1973; dir. clin. chemistry NYU Med. Ctr., Tisch Hosp., 1973, dir. clin. labs., 1980-93. Editor Lab. Med.; contbr. articles to profl. jours. Lt. comdr. USN, 1971-73. Fellow Coll. Am. Pathologists, Am. Soc. Clin. Pathologists, Explorer's Club.

SHERFY, BRADLEY LLOYD, professional golfer; b. Jan. 9, 1956; m. Jeannette Meier; children: Kelli, Corinne, James. BS in Econs., UCLA, 1978. Profl. golfer, 1978—; head golf profl. Harbor Golf Practice Ctr., Wilmington, Calif., 1995—. Head profl. PGA Mulligan Golf Ctr., Torrance, Calif. Named So. Calif. PGA Player of Yr., 1993, 94, 95, SCPGA Match & Stroke Play Champion; record holder Desert Falls Country Club, Palm Valley Country Club, Hillcrest Country Club, Spanish Hills Country Club, De Bell Golf Course, Buenaventura Golf Coiurse. Office: UCLA 325 Westwood Plz Los Angeles CA 90095-8356

SHERIDAN, CHRISTOPHER FREDERICK, human resources executive; b. Syracuse, N.Y., June 7, 1953; s. Frederick John and Patricia Ann (McCormick) S.; m. Diane Marie Harman, Dec. 31, 1977; children: Ryan, Kelly. BS in Indsl. Relations, LeMoyne Coll., 1975. Employee rels. trainee Anaconda Co., Buffalo, 1975-76, employee rels. rep. Los Angeles, 1976-78; pers. mgr. HITCO, Gardena, Calif., 1978-80; labor rels. rep. Miller Brewing Co., Fulton, N.Y., 1980-82, labor rels. mgr. Los Angeles, 1982-90; employee rels. mgr. Ryder Distbn. Resources, Anaheim, Calif., 1990-91; dir. human resources Alta-Dena Cert. Dairy Inc., City of Industry, 1991-99; regional human resources dir. west/southwest Dean Foods Co., 1999—. Mem. Soc. Human Resources Mgmt., Am. Mgmt. Assn. Roman Catholic. Avocations: golf, basketball, reading, music. Email: chris. Office: Dean Foods Co 17637 Valley Blvd La Puente CA 91744-5731 E-mail: chris_sheridan@deanfoods.com

SHERK, KENNETH JOHN, lawyer; b. Ida Grove, Iowa, Feb. 27, 1933; s. John and Dorothy (Myers) Sherk; children: Karin Fulton, Katrina, Keith, Kyle. BSC, U. Iowa, 1955; JD, George Washington U., 1961. Bar: Ariz. 1962, U.S. Dist. Ct. Ariz. 1962, U.S. Ct. Appeals (9th cir.) 1966, U.S. Supreme Ct. 1974. Assoc. Moore & Romley, Phoenix, 1962-67, ptnr., 1967-79, Romley & Sherk, Phoenix, 1979-85; dir. Fennemore Craig, Phoenix, 1985—. 1st lt. U.S. Army, 1955-58, Korea. Recipient Profl. Achievement Svcs. award George Washington Law Assn., 1986, Ariz. Judges Assn., 1989, Disting. Svc. award Phoenix Assn. Def. Counsel, 1990; named Mem. of Yr. State Bar of Ariz., 1994. Fellow Am. Coll. Trial Lawyers, Am. Acad. Appellate Lawyers, Am. Bar Found., Ariz. Bar Found. (Walter E. Craig award 1999); mem. ABA (ho. of dels. 1990-93), Ariz. Bar Assn. (pres. 1985-86), Maricopa County Bar Assn. (pres. 1978-79). Republican. Congregational. Avocations: fishing, hiking, bicycling. Home: 1554 W Las Palmaritas Dr Phoenix AZ 85021-5429 Office: Fennemore Craig 3003 N Central Ave Ste 2600 Phoenix AZ 85012-2913

SHERMAN, BRAD JAMES, congressman; b. L.A., Oct. 24, 1954; s. Maurice H. and Lane (Moss) S. BA summa cum laude, UCLA, 1974; JD magna cum laude, Harvard U., 1979. Bar: Calif. 1979; CPA, Calif. Pvt. practice, L.A., 1980-91; chmn. Calif. Bd. Equalization, Sacramento, 1991-95; mem. U.S. Congress from 24th Calif. dist., 1997—; mem. banking and fin. svcs. com., internat. rels. com. Lectr. on tax law and policy; mem. Calif. Franchise Tax Bd., 1991-95. Contbr. articles to legal jours. Bd. dirs., rep. on tax issues Calif. Common Cause, 1984-89; mem. exec. com. Calif. Dem. Com., 1991—. Mem. Calif. State Bar. Jewish. E-mila. Office: US Ho Reps 1524 Longworth HOB Washington DC 20515-0524 E-mail: brad.sherman@mail.house.gov

SHERMAN, IRWIN WILLIAM, biological sciences educator; b. N.Y.C., Feb. 12, 1933; s. Morris and Anna (Ezaak) S.; m. Vilia Gay Turner, Aug. 25, 1966; children: Jonathan Turner, Alexa Joy. BS, CCNY, 1954; MS, Northwestern U., 1959, PhD, 1960. Asst. prof. U. Calif., Riverside, 1962-67, assoc. prof., 1967-70, prof. biology, 1970—, chmn. biology dept., 1974-79, dean Coll. Natural and Agrl. Scis., dir. agrl. expt. sta., 1981-88, exec. vice chancellor, 1993-94. Instr. marine biol. lab., Woods Hole, Mass., 1963-68; mem. study sect. tropical medicine NIH, 1970-73; cons. Agy. Internat. Devel., 1978-90; mem. ad hoc study group U.S. Army, 1975-78. Author: The Invertebrates: Function and Form, 1976, Biology: A Human Approach, 1989, Malaria: Parasite Biology, Pathogenesis, Protection, 1998, Chemotherapy of Malaria. Steering com. World Health Orgn., 1978-87. With U.S. Army, 1954-56. USPHS fellow Rockefeller Inst., 1960-62, Guggenheim fellow, 1967, NIH/Nat. Inst. Med. Rsch. fellow 1973-74, Walter and Eliza Hall Inst. for Med. Rsch. fellow, 1986; Wellcome Trust lectr. Brit. Soc. Parasitology, 1987, Scripps Rsch. Inst. fellow 1991. Mem. AAAS, Am. Soc. Tropical Medicine and Hygiene, Soc. Protozoology, Soc. Parasitology, Sigma Xi. Democrat. Jewish. Avocations: painting, reading. Office: U Calif Riverside Dept Biology Riverside CA 92521-0001 E-mail: sherman@mail.ucr.edu

SHERMAN, RANDOLPH, plastic and reconstructive surgeon, educator; b. St. Louis, May 27, 1951; s. Leon and Pearl (Lichtenfeld) S.; m. Sandra Lee Wackerman, May 3, 1992; 1 child, Max Lassen. BA, U. Rochester, 1973; MD, U. Mo., 1977. Diplomate Am. Bd. Surgery, Am. Bd. Plastic Surgery (cert. added qualification in hand surgery 1989). Intern in gen. medicine U. Wis., Madison, 1978; intern in surgery U. Calif., San Francisco, 1978-79, resident in surgery, 1979-81, SUNY, Syracuse, 1981-83; fellow in plastic and reconstructive surgery U. So. Calif., 1983-85, asst. prof. surger and orthopedics, 1985-91, assoc. prof. clin. surgery and orthopaedics, 1991-92, assoc. prof. clin. surgery, orthopaedics and neurol. surgery, 1992-96, chmn. divsn. plastic and reconstructive surgery, 1994—, prof. clin. surgery, orthopaedics and neurol. surgery, 1996—. Mem. cons. staff City of Hope Nat. Med. Ctr., Duarte, Calif., 1985-91, 94—, St. John's Hosp., Santa Monica, 1989—; mem. staff, med. dir. Microsurg. Ctr. Hosp. Good Samaritan, L.A., 1985-93; mem. plastic and reconstructive surgery staff Kenneth Norris Jr. Cancer Hosp., L.A., 1985—, L.A. County/U. So. Calif. Med. Ctr., L.A., 1985—; mem. staff St. Vincent Med. Ctr., L.A., 1986-92, Orthop. Hosp., L.A., 1986—; Shriner's Hosp. for Crippled Children, L.A., 1987-92, Children's Hosp. L.A., 1987—, Cedars Sinai Med. Ctr., L.A., 1987—, Estelle Doheny Eye Hosp., L.A., 1994—, numerous others; chief plastic and reconstructive surgery divsn. U. So. Calif. U. Hosp., L.A., 1991—; lectr., rschr. in field. Editor: Orthopedic Clinics, 1993; assoc. editor Surg. Rounds, 1989—, Jour. Hand Surgery, 1992-96, Am. Jour. Reconstructive Microsurgery, 1995—; contbr. articles to profl. jours., chpts. to books. Founder L.A. chpt. Operation Smile Internat., 1993—. Recipient L.A. Humanitarian award Calif. Hosp., 1994; Microsurg. Devel. grantee Hosp. Good Samaritan, 1987-92, U. So. Calif. U. Hosp., 1992—; grantee Searle R&D, 1995-97, Cohesion Corp., 1997. Fellow ACS, Am. Assn. Plastic Surgeons, Am. Assn. Hand Surgeons (bd. dirs. 1991-95), Am. Soc. Hand Surgery, Am. Soc. Reconstructive Microsurgery, Calif. Soc. Plastic Surgery; mem. Am. Soc. Plastic and Reconstructive Surgery, Am. Soc. Peripheral Nerve, Internat. Soc. Reconstructive Microsurgery, Calif. Med. Assn., Calif. Soc. Plastic Surgery, Assn. Acad. Chmn. Plastic Surgery, Plastic Surgery Rsch. Coun., Musculoskeletal Infection Soc., Undersea Med. Soc., Flying Physicians Assn., Wound Healing Soc. Avocations: flying, mountain climbing, scuba diving, jazz piano, gardening. Office: U So Calif Divsn Plastic Surgery 1450 San Pablo St Ste 2000 Los Angeles CA 90033-1042 Business E-Mail: rsherman@surgery.usc.edu

SHERMAN, SIGNE LIDFELDT, portfolio manager, former research chemist; b. Rochester, N.Y., Nov. 11, 1913; d. Carl Leonard Broström and Herta Elvira Maria (Tern) Lidfeldt; m. Joseph V. Sherman, Nov. 18, 1944 (dec. Oct. 1984). BA, U. Rochester, 1935, MS, 1937. Chief chemist Lab. Indsl. Medicine and Toxicology Eastman Kodak Co., Rochester, 1937-43; chief rsch. chemist Chesebrough-Pond's Inc., Clinton, Conn., 1943-44; ptnr. Joseph V. Sherman Cons., N.Y.C., 1944-84; portfolio strategist Sherman Holdings, Troy, Mont., 1984—. Author: The New Fibers, 1946. Fellow Am. Inst. Chemists; mem. AAAS, AAUW (life), Am. Chem. Soc., Am. Econ. Assn., Am. Assn. Ind. Investors (life), Fedn. Am. Scientists (life), Union Concerned Scientists (life), Earthquake Engring. Rsch. Inst., Nat. Ctr. for Earthquake Engring. Rsch., N.Y. Acad. Scis. (life), Cabinet View Country Club. Office: Sherman Holdings Angel Island 648 Halo Dr Troy MT 59935-9415 E-mail: creative@libby.org

SHERMAN, ZACHARY, civil and aerospace engineer, consultant; b. N.Y.C., Oct. 26, 1922; s. Harry and Minnie (Schulsinger) S.; m. Bertha Leikin, Mar. 23, 1947; children: Gene Victor, Carol Beth. BCE, CCNY, 1943; MCE, Polytech. U. N.Y., Bklyn., 1953, PhD in Civil Engring. & Mechanics, 1969; MME, Stevens Inst. Tech., 1968. Registered profl. engr., N.Y., N.J. Stress analyst Gen. Dynamics, San Diego, 1943-45; sr. stress analyst Republic Aviation, Farmingdale, N.Y., 1945-47, 59-62; prof. civil engring. U. Miss., Oxford, 1954-59; lectr. civil engring. Stevens Inst. Tech., Hoboken, N.J., 1962-67, CUNY, 1967-69; assoc. prof. aerospace engring. Pa. State U., State College, 1969-73; prin. Dr. Zachary Sherman Cons. Engrs., Santa Monica, Calif., 1973—; aerospace engr. FAA, N.Y.C., N.Y., 1980-86. Designated cons. engr. rep., FAA, 1986—. Contbr. articles to profl. jours. NSF grantee, 1972. Fellow ASCE; mem. AIAA (v.p. Western Conn. chpt. 1977-78), N.Y. Acad. Scis., Sigma Xi. Achievements include development of beam/beam-column deck suspension bridge, prestressed aircraft wing. Home and Office: 2021 California Ave Apt 7 Santa Monica CA 90403-4531 Fax: 310-264-5990

SHERRATT, GERALD ROBERT, retired university president; b. Los Angeles, Nov. 6, 1931; s. Lowell Heyborne and Elva Genevieve (Lamb) S. B.S. in Edn., Utah State U., 1953, M.S. in Edn. Adminstrn., 1954; Ph.D. in Adminstrn. Higher Edn., Mich. State U., 1975. Staff assoc. U. Utah, Salt Lake City, 1961-62; dir. high sch. relations Utah State U., Logan, 1962-64, asst. to pres., 1964-77, v.p. for univ. relations, 1977-81; pres. So. Utah U., Cedar City, 1982-97. Dir. Honeyville Grain Inc., Utah; mem. coun. pres. Utah Sys. Higher Edn., 1982-97; chmn. bd. Utah Summer Games, Cedar City, 1984-97; chmn. pres.'s coun. Rocky Mountain Athletic Conf., Denver, 1984-85 Author hist. pageant: The West: America's Odyssey, 1973 (George Washington Honor medal 1973); musical review: How the West Was Won, 1998. Chmn. Festival of Am. West, Logan, Utah, 1972-82; chmn. bd. Utah Shakespearean Festival, Cedar City, 1982-86; chmn. bd. dirs. Salt Lake City Br. of the Fed. Res. Bank of San Francisco, 1996-98; bd. trustees Salt Lake Organizing Com. Winter Olympics 2002. 1st lt. USAF, 1954-57. Recipient Editing award Indsl. Editors Assn., 1962, Robins award Utah State U., 1967, Disting. Alumnus award Utah State U., 1974, So. Utah U., 1991, Total Citizen award Cedar City C. of C., 1993, Minuteman award Utah Nat. Guard, 1997; named to Utah Tourism Hall of Fame, 1989; Centennial medal So. Utah U., 1997; Imperial Order Utah Shakespearean Festival, 1997; named to Hall of Honor Utah Summer Games, 1997, Utah Educators Hall of Fame, 1999. Mem. Am. Assn. State Colls. and Univs., Cache C. of C. (bd. dirs. 1980-82), Cedar City Civic Club (pres.), Phi Kappa Phi, Phi Delta Kappa, Sigma Nu (regent 1976-78) Mem. LDS Ch.

SHERRER, CHARLES DAVID, college dean, clergyman; b. Marion, Ohio, Sept. 21, 1935; s. Harold D. and Catherine E. (Fye) S. A.B., U. Notre Dame, 1958, M.A., 1965; S.T.L., Gregorian U., 1962; Ph.D., U. N.C., 1969; HHD, King's Coll., 1997. Ordained priest Roman Cath. Ch., 1961. Instr. English U. Portland, Oreg., 1963-64, asst. prof., 1969-74, prof., 1990—, chmn. dept., 1970-74, dean Grad. Sch., 1982-87, mem. Bd. Regents, 1986-87, acad. v.p., 1987-96; pres. King's Coll., Wilkes Barre, Pa., 1974-81. Bd. trustees Stonehill Coll., 1992-98; dir. studies Holy Cross Fathers, Ind. Province, 1979-88. Office: U Portland Portland OR 97203

SHERRIFFS, RONALD EVERETT, communication and film educator; b. Salem, Oreg., Apr. 10, 1934; s. Robert William and Margaret Kathleen (Tutt) S.; m. Mary Lona West, July 9, 1960; children: Ellen, Matthew. BA, San Jose State U., 1955, MA, 1957; PhD, U. So. Calif., 1964. Instr. theater Mich. State U., East Lansing, 1960-61; asst. prof. broadcasting Tex. Tech U., Lubbock, 1964-65; asst. prof. speech U. Oreg., Eugene, 1965-70, assoc. prof., 1970-79, prof. telecomm. and film, 1979-92, chmn. dept. speech, 1978-84, 88-90, prof. journalism and comm., 1993-2000, prof. emeritus, 2000. Author: (with others) Speech Communication via Radio and TV, 1971, TV Lighting Handbook, 1977, Small Format TV Production, 1985, 3d edit., Video Field Production and Editing, 1994, 4th edit., 1996; prodr., dir. TV programs, 1965—. Mem. Oreg. Pub. Broadcasting Policy Adv. Bd., 1980-88. Served to lt. comdr. USNR, 1957-68, PTO. Faculty enrichment program grantee Can., 1984, 91. Mem. Nat. Communication Assn., AAUP, We. States Communication Assn. Clubs: Oreg. Track; McKenzie Flyfishers (Eugene). Office: U Oreg Journalism Sch Eugene OR 97403 E-mail: sherriff@oregon.uoregon.edu

SHERVHEIM, LLOYD OLIVER, insurance company executive, lawyer; b. Kensington, Minn., June 22, 1928; s. Lewis and Ruth Amanda (Thronson) S.; m. Ruth Elaine Rhodes, Oct. 29, 1950; children: Daniel, Anne, Heidi, Garold, Robette, Shanna, Bryce. Student, Gustavus Adolphus Coll., 1948-50, U. Minn., 1950-52; B.S., LL.B., William Mitchell Coll. Law, 1958. Bar: Minn. 1959. Supr., asst. to corp. sec. Investors Diversified Services, Inc., 1952-59; legal counsel Investors Syndicate Life Ins. Co., Mpls., 1959-66; gen. counsel Western Life Ins. Co., St. Paul, 1966-72; corporate sec. St. Paul Cos., Inc., 1969-82, chief legal officer, 1972-78, v.p. legal affairs, 1978-85, sr. v.p. law, corporate sec., 1985-89. Corporate sec. St. Paul Fire and Marine Ins. Co., 1969-82; dir. St. Paul Ins. Co., Tex., St. Paul Surplus Lines Ins. Co., St. Paul Mercury Ins. Co., St. Paul Guardian Ins. Co., St. Paul Ins. Co., Ill. Charter patron Minn. Theatre Co., 1958; mem. Lake Elmo City Council, 1970-78; past chmn. protection open space task force Met. Open Space Adv. Bd., 1969-70; trustee William Mitchell Coll. Law, 1981-92, vice chmn., 1983-86, chmn., 1986-89; dir. Minn. Citizens Council on Crime and Justice, 1986-89. With U.S. Army, 1946-48. Mem. ABA, Minn. Bar Assn. (chmn. ins. com. 1964-65, gov. 1980-81), Fed. Bar Assn. (pres. Minn. chpt. 1978-79), Ramsey County Bar Assn. (ethics com. 1978-80), Assn. Life Ins. Counsel, Am. Soc. Corp. Secs., Am. Life Conv. (v.p. Minn. chpt. 1969-71), Am. Judicature Soc., Corp. Counsel Assn. Minn. (dir., pres. 1979-80), Pool and Yacht Club (St. Paul). Lutheran (chmn. bd. trustees). Home and Office: 2880 Desert Trail Dr Bullhead City AZ 86429-5875

SHIDELER, ROSS PATRICK, foreign language and comparative literature educator, writer, translator, poet; b. Denver, Apr. 12, 1936; B.A., San Francisco State U., 1958; M.A., U. Stockholm, 1963; Ph.D., U. Calif., Berkeley, 1968. Instr. in comparative lit. U. Calif., Berkeley, 1967-68; asst. prof. English Hunter Coll., N.Y.C., 1968-69; asst. prof. Scandinavian lang. and comparative lit. UCLA, 1969-73, assoc. prof., 1973-79, prof., 1979—; chmn. program in comparative lit., 1979-86, 92-96. Author: (monograph) Voices Under The Ground: Themes and Images in the Poetry of Gunnar Ekelof, 1973, Per Olov Enquist-A Critical Study, 1984; translator: (play) The Night of the Tribades (Per Olov Enquist), 1977, The Hour of the Lynx, 1990 (Per Olov Enquist), 1990; co-editor: (with Kathleen L. Komar) Lyrical Symbols and Narrative Transformations. Essays in Honor of Ralph Freedman, 1998, Questioning the Father: From Darwin to Zola, Ibsen, Strindberg and Hardy, 1999; U.S. assoc. editor Swedish Book Rev., 1984—. Fellow NDFL, 1964; fellow NDEA, 1965; Fulbright-Hays fellow, 1966-67 Mem. MLA (exec. com. divsn. Scandinavian Langs. and Lits. 1993-97), Soc. Advancement Scandinavian Studies (exec. coun. 1985-89, v.p. 1997-99, pres. 1999-2001), Am. Comparative Lit. Assn., Assn. Depts. and Programs Comparative Lit. (exec. com. 1993-94, 94-98). Office: UCLA Dept Comparative Lit Los Angeles CA 90024

SHIELDS, FRANK W. state legislator; b. New Castle, Pa., Mar. 26, 1945; m. Suzanne Shields; 2 children. BA in Secondary Edn., Slippery Rock State Coll., 1967; MDiv, Eastern Bapt. Sem., 1972; DMin, Drew U., 1981. Pastor Trinity United Meth. Ch., 1973-75, Chihoquin United Meth. Ch., 1975-78, Sunnyside United Meth. Ch., 1978-98; mem. Oreg. Legislature, Salem, 1998—, mem. gen. govt. com., vice chair health and human svcs. com., mem. subcom. on human resources. Democrat. Methodist. Office: 2414 SE 143rd Ave Apt 2 Portland OR 97233-2400

SHIELDS, WILLIAM, printing company executive; Pres. Shields Bag & Printing Co., Yakima, Wash. Office: Shields Bag & Printing Co 1009 Rock Ave Yakima WA 98902-4629

SHIERSHKE, NANCY FAY, artist, educator, property manager; b. St. Helens, Oreg., May 10, 1935; d. David Cline and Matilda Ruth (Pearce) Morrison; m. H. McNeal Kavanagh, Sept. 4. 1955 (dec. Dec. 1978); children: Marjorie L. Wood, David M. Kavanagh, Katherine F. Fiske; m. Richard M. Shiershke, Nov. 29, 1980. AA, Pasadena (Calif.) City Coll., 1956; BA, UCLA, 1965. Substitute elem. sch. tchr., Buena Park, Calif., 1967-69; property mgr. Pky. Cts., Arcadia, 1977—; libr. Reading Rm., Arcadia, 1979-87; freelance artist Kavanagh-Shiershke Art St., Arcadia, Calif., 1985—; art gallery hostess Descanso Gardens, La Canada, Flintridge, 1990—; display and sales person Village Fine Arts Gallery, Arcadia, 1991-92; art instr. Tri Cmty. Adult Edn., Covina, Calif., 1994—, Claremont (Calif.) Art Edn., 1998—. Art instr. Claremont (Claif.) Adult Edn. Group shows include Pasadena Presbyn. Ch., 1985—, Hillcrest Ch., 1992—, Descanso Gardens, 1994—, San Gabriel Fine Arts, 1994—. Named Artist of the Yr. Mid Valley art League, 1990; Recipient Best of Show San Gabriel Fine Arts, 1991, Hulsebus award Pasadena Prebyn. Ch., 1996. Mem. Nat. Watercolor Soc., San Gabriel Fine Arts, Mid Valley Arts League (Artist of Yr. 1998), East Valley Art Assn., Valley Watercolor Soc., Foothill Creative Arts Group, Water Color West. Home: 505 Vaquero Rd Arcadia CA 91007-6045 Office: 614 E Vine Ave West Covina CA 91791

SHIFFMAN, MICHAEL A. lawyer; b. Newark, July 23, 1941; LLB magna cum laude, Lincoln U., 1973. Bar: Calif. 1973, U.S. Dist. Ct. (no. dist.) Calif. 1973; lic. real estate broker. Atty. Lanahan & Reilley, San Francisco. Editor: Lincoln U. Law Rev., 1972-73. Mem. ABA, Internat. Bar Assn., State Bar Calif. Office: Lanahan & Reilley 120 Howard St G/F San Francisco CA 94105-1615 E-mail: shifflaw@aol.com

SHILLINGTON, EDWARD BLAIN, consultant diversified financial services company; b. Grayburn, Sask., Can., Aug. 28, 1944; s. Sterling Arthur and Dorathy Jessie (Henry) S.; m. Sonia Shirley Koroscil, Aug. 15, 1970; children: Ryan Sterling, Tara Dawn. BA, LLB, U. Sask., 1967. Mem. Sask. Legis. (Regina N.E.), 1975-99, minister of coop. and coop. devel., 1975-77, minister of consumer affairs, 1975-76, minister of govt. svcs., 1976-78, minister of culture and youth, 1977-80, minister of edn., 1978-79, assoc. minister of fin., 1992, minister of labour, 1992-95, assoc. minister fin. and minister of crown investments, 1995, minister of justice and atty. gen., 1995, minister of intergovtl. affairs and provincial sec., 1995-97, govt. house leader, 1995-97; ptnr. Shillington-Doré Law Office, 1980-92; provincial sec., dep. govt. house leader Govt. Sask., Regina, 1997-98; sr. cons. PriceWaterhouseCoopers, Regina, 1999—. Avocations: reading, boating, fishing, flying. Office: PriceWaterhouseCoopers Rm 204 Legislative Bldg Regina SK Canada S4P 0J3

SHIMODA, JERRY YASUTAKA, retired national historic park manager; b. Haleiwa, Hawaii, Mar. 21, 1930; s. Tamotsu and Sasai Shimoda; m. Clara H. Segawa, Aug. 7, 1954; children: Karen Marie K., Randall T., Shaun T., Teri Ellen H., Jacqueline Y., David Y. BA in Govt., U. Hawaii, 1952, MA in Far Ea. Area Studies, 1957; postgrad., St. Louis U., 1957-59. Historian Jefferson Nat. Expansion Meml. Nat. Hist. Site, St. Louis, 1957-60; chief historian, in charge hist. rsch. and visitor svcs. Saratoga Nat. Hist. Park, Stillwater, N.Y., 1960-66; chief historian Home of Franklin D. Roosevelt Nat. Hist. Site and, Frederick Vanderbilt Nat. Hist. Site, Hyde Park, N.Y., 1966-69; instr. Nat. Park Svc. Stephen T. Mather Tng. Ctr., Harpers Ferry, W.Va., 1969-72; supt. Pu'uhonua o Honaunau (Hawaii) Nat. Hist. Park, 1972-96, Puukohola Heiau Nat. Hist. Site, Kawaihae, 1972-96; ret., 1996. Lectr. environ. edn. Pa. State U., U. W.Va., Shepard Coll., 1969-72; acting supr. Kaloko-Honokohau Nat. Hist. Park, 1988-90; instr. environ. edn., interpretive and basic instructing techniques U. Hawaii, Hilo, Kapiolani C.C.; instr. Japanese culture U. Hawaii, Hilo, 1994; U.S. del. U.S.-Japan Panel on Nat. Parks and Equivalent Res., 1968-97, World Conf. on Marine Parks, Tokyo, 1975; Japanese translator U.S. Nat. Park Svc.; mem. internat. bd. dirs. Heritage Interpretation Internat., 1989-98; presenter in field. Author booklets on nat. parks, mgmt. and history; contbr. numerous articles to profl. publs., mags. and newspapers. Bd. dirs. Volcano Art Ctr.; mem. adv. com. Wailoa State Ctr.; mem. Hawaii Gov.'s Task Force on Ocean and Recreation; chmn. restoration com. St. Benedict's Ch., Honaunau, 1982-95; chmn. bd. dirs. Kahua Na'au 'Ao, 1996-97; vol. trainer in leadership, interpretation and environ. edn. Nat. Pk. Svc., 1996—. Recipient Spl. Achievement award Nat. Park Svc., 1964, 68, 70, resolution W.Va. Senate, 1971, Hawaii Ho. of Reps., 1982, sec.'s cert. Dept. Interior, 1971, Exec. of Yr. award West Hawaii chpt. Profl. Secs. Internat., 1981, cert. Govt. of Japan, 1981, staff plaque Pu'uhonua o Honaunau Nat. Hist. Park, Puukohola Heiau Nat. Hist. Site and Kaloko-Honokohau Nat. Hist. Park, 1988, cert. Japan Nat. Parks Assn., 1989, cert. of appreciation South Kona Aloha Lions Club, 1990, Meritorious Svc.

award Sec. Interior, 1996, others. Mem. Hawaii Mus. Assn. (bd. dirs. 1988-92), Kona Hist. Soc. (bd. dirs. 1988-92), Big Island Ocean Recreation and Tourism Assn. (exec. com.), Kona Judo Club (pres. 1977-96), Rotary (pres. Kona Mauka 1978-79, co-founder Volcano chpt. 2001, Paul Harris fellow 1991, Disting. Svc. award 1992). Avocations: writing, reading, travel, teaching.

SHIMPFKY, RICHARD LESTER, bishop; b. Albuquerque, Oct. 18, 1940; m. Jamel Shimpfky, 1966; children: Trevor, Allison, Joshua. Grad., U. Colo., 1963, Va. Theol. Seminary, 1970. Ordained to diaconate Episc. Ch., 1970. With William L. Philips Found., Richmond, Va., 1963-67; curate St. Peter's Ch., Arlington, 1970-72; vicar All Saints' Sharon Chapel, Alexandria, Va., 1972-73, rector, 1973-77, Christ Ch., Ridgewood, N.J., 1977-90; bishop Diocese El Camino Real, Monterey, Calif., 1990—. Avocations: reading, traveling. Office: Diocese El Camino Real PO Box 1903 Monterey CA 93942-1903

SHIN, PAULL HOBOM, investment company executive, state legislator; b. Kumchon, Korea, Sept. 27, 1935; came to U.S., 1955; adopted s. Ray and Eloise (Siddoway) Paull; m. Donna June Skaggs, June 12, 1963; children: Paull Y., Alisa M. BA, Brigham Young U., 1962; MPIA, U. Pitts., 1964; MA, U. Wash., 1972, PhD, 1978. Asst. prof. Brigham Young U., Laie, Hawaii, 1964-67; prof. Shoreline Coll., Seattle, 1969-72; pres. A.P.S. Investment Co., Seattle, 1982—; chmn. T.T.I. Telecom. Inc., Bellevue, Wash., 1992—; mem. Wash. Ho. of Reps., Olympia, 1992-94, Wash. Senate, Dist. 21, Olympia, 1998—. Commr., chmn. Office of Pres. Korea, Seoul, 1985-88. Mission pres. LDS Ch., Seoul, 1988-91; bd. dirs. Asian-Ams. for Political Action, Seattle, 1982-84, United Way, Snohomish County, 1992—; advisor internat. trade Office Gov., Wash. State, 1983-88, Boy Scouts Am., 1986-88. With U.S. Army, 1958-60. Recipient Outstanding Svc. award Pres. Korea, 1985. Mem. Wash. State Korean Assn. (pres. 1983-84, Community Svc. award 1983), Rotary Club. Avocations: reading, travel, fishing, youth activities. Home: 8910 189th Pl SW Edmonds WA 98026-5929 Office: 405 John Obrien Bldg Olympia WA 98504-0001 Address: Legis Bldg Rm 412B Olympia WA 98504-0001 E-mail: shin_pa@leg.wa.gov

SHINDLER, MERRILL KARSH, writer, radio personality; b. N.Y.C., July 2, 1948; s. Joseph and Miriam (Karsh) S. BA, CCNY, 1970; MFA, NYU, 1971. Entertainment editor San Francisco Bay Guardian, 1972-75; music editor Rolling Stone mag., San Francisco, 1976-79; film critic Los Angeles mag., 1979-89; restaurant critic L.A. Examiner, 1979-88; editor Zagat Los Angeles Restaurant Survey, 1986—; restaurant critic L.A. Reader, 1990-96, Daily Breeze, 1990—, Daily News, 1989-94, San Gabriel Valley Newspapers, 1994—. Author: Best Restaurants of L.A., 1989, Zagat, L.A. Restaurant Survey, 1986—, American Dish, 1996, El Cholo: A History, 1998; writer (radio shows) Am. Top 40, 1979-89, 98—, Casey's Top 40, 1989—, Casey's Biggest Hits, 1990—, USA Top 20, 1990—, (TV shows) Am. Top 10, 1980-93, Cinemattractions, 1990—, USA Music Today, 1990—; host radio show Feed Your Face with Merrill Shindler, KLSX-FM, 1988—; contr. to Gault-Millau Best of Los Angeles, 1988, Gault-Millau Best of Hong Kong, 1989; contbr. articles to jours. Avocations: restaurants, cooking, jogging, travel.

SHINEFIELD, HENRY ROBERT, pediatrician; b. Paterson, N.J., Oct. 11, 1925; s. Louis and Sarah (Kaplan) S.; m. Jacqueline Marilyn Walker; children: Jill, Michael, Kimberley Strome, Melissa Strome. B.A., Columbia U., 1945, M.D., 1948. Diplomate: Am. Bd. Pediatrics (examiner, 1975— , bd. dirs., 1979-84, v.p., 1981-84). Rotating intern Mt. Sinai Hosp., N.Y.C., 1948-49; pediatric intern Duke Hosp., Durham, N.C., 1949-50; asst. resident pediatrician N.Y. Hosp. (Cornell), 1950-51, pediatrician to outpatients, 1953-59, instr. in pediatrics, 1959-60, asst. prof., 1960-64, asso. prof., 1964-65, asst. attending pediatrician, 1959-63, asso. attending pediatrician, 1963-65; pediatrician to outpatients Children's Hosp., Oakland, Calif., 1951-53; chief of pediatrics Kaiser-Permanente Med. Center, San Francisco, 1965-89, chief emeritus, 1989—; co-dir. Kaiser-Permanente Pediat4ric Vaccine Study Ctr., San Francisco, 1984—; asso. clin. prof. pediatrics Sch. Medicine U. Calif., 1966-68, clin. prof. pediatrics, 1968—, clin. prof. dermatology, 1970—; asso. attending pediatrician Paterson (N.J.) Gen. Hosp., 1955-59; chief of pediatrics Kaiser Found. Hosp., San Francisco, 1965-86; attending Moffitt Hosp., San Francisco, 1967-88; practice medicine specializing in pediatrics Paterson, 1953-59. Cons. San Francisco Gen. Hosp., 1967-88, Childrens Hosp., San Francisco, 1970-88, Mt. Zion Hosp., San Francisco, 1970-88; mem. research grants rev. br. NIH, HEW, 1970-74; med. dir. USPHSR, 1969—; bd. dirs. San Francisco Peer Rev. Orgn., 1975-81, sec., exec. com., 1976-81; chmn. Calif. State Child Health Disability Bd., 1973-82; mem. Inst. of Medicine, Nat. Acad. Scis., 1980—; cons. Bur. Drugs FDA, 1970, NIH, HEW, 1974—. Editorial bds. Western Jour. of Medicine, 1968-80, American Jour. of Diseases of Children, 1970-82; contbr. writings to profl. publs. Chmn. San Francisco Med. Adv. Com. Nat. Found. March of Dimes, 1969-80. Served with USPHS, 1951-53. Fellow Am. Acad. Pediatrics (com. of fetus and newborn 1969-76, mem. com. on drugs 1978-82); mem. AMA, Soc. Pediatric Research, Infectious Diseases Soc. Am., Western Pediatric Soc., Western Soc. Clin. Research, Am. Pediatric Soc., Phi Beta Kappa. Home: 2705 Larkin St San Francisco CA 94109-1117 Office: Kaiser Permanente 4131 Geary Blvd San Francisco CA 94118-3101 E-mail: henry.shinefield@kp.org

SHINOZUKA, MASANOBU, civil engineer, educator; b. Tokyo, Dec. 23, 1930; came to U.S., 1957, naturalized, 1971; s. Akira and Kiyo S.; m. Fujiko Sakamoto, Oct. 25, 1954; children: Rei, Naomi, Megumi. BS, Kyoto (Japan) U., 1953, MS, 1955; PhD, Columbia U., 1960. Rsch. asst. civil engring. Columbia U., N.Y.C., 1958-61, asst. prof., 1961-65, assoc. prof., 1965-69, prof., 1969-88, Renwick prof., 1977-88; prof. Princeton U., 1988-94, Sollenberger prof. civil engring., 1989-94, on leave, 1990—; dir. Nat. Ctr. for Earthquake Engring. Rsch. SUNY, Buffalo, 1990-94; prof. civil engring. U. So. Calif., L.A., 1994—. Vis. Capen prof. structural engring., dept. civil engring., 1990—; vis. scholar N.C. State U., Raleigh, 1967-68; pres. Modern Analysis Inc., Princeton, N.J., 1972— ; co-chmn. 2d Internat. Conf. on Structural Safety and Reliability, 1978, 3d, 1981, 4th, 1985, 5th, 1989, also co-editor Proc. of 2d, 3d and 4th confs.; mem. steering com. U.S. Panel on Structural Control Rsch., 1990—; cons. in field. Editor: Probabilistic Engineering Mechanics, 1987—, Reliability Approach in Structural Engineering, 1975; co-editor Proc. ASCE Symposium on Probabilistic Methods in Structural Engring., 1981. Recipient Wessex Inst. Tech. medal, 1991; NSF grantee, 1968—. Mem. NAE, ASCE (Walter L. Huber prize 1972, State of the Art of Civil Engring. award 1973, Alfred M. Freudenthal medal 1978, Nathan M. Newmark medal 1985, Moisseiff award 1988, C. Martin Duke award 1991, Theodore Von Karman medal 1994), ASME, AIAA, Japan Soc. Civil Engrs., Sigma Xi. Home: 7 Sea Ter Newport Beach CA 92657-1018 Office: U So Calif Dept Civil Engring 3620 S Vermont Ave Los Angeles CA 90089-0082

SHIPPEY, SANDRA LEE, lawyer; b. Casper, Wyo., June 24, 1957; d. Virgil Carr and Doris Louise (Conklin) McClintock; m. Ojars Herberts Ozols, Sept. 2, 1978 (div.); children: Michael Ojars, Sara Ann, Brian Christopher; m. James Robert Shippey, Jan. 13, 1991; 1 child, Matthew James. BA with distinction, U. Colo., 1978; JD magna cum laude, Boston U., 1982. Bar: Colo. 1982, U.S. Dist. Ct. Colo. 1985. Assoc. Cohen, Brame & Smith, Denver, 1983-84, Parcel, Meyer, Schwartz, Ruttum & Mauro, Denver, 1984-85, Mayer, Brown & Platt, Denver, 1985-87; counsel western ops. GE Capital Corp., San Diego, 1987-94; assoc. Page, Polin, Busch & Boatwright, San Diego, 1994-95, v.p., gen. counsel First Comml. Corp., San Diego, 1995-96; legal counsel NextWave Telecom Inc., San Diego, 1996-98; ptnr. Procopio, Cory, Hargreaves and Savitch, LLP, 1998—. Active Pop Warner football and cheerleading; bd. dirs. San Diego Christian Found., 2001—. Mem. Phi Beta Kappa, Phi Delta Phi. Republican. Mem. Ch. of Christ. Avocations: tennis, golf, photography. Home: 15839 Big Springs Way San Diego CA 92127-2034 Office: Procopio Cory Et Al 530 B St Ste 2100 San Diego CA 92101-4496 E-mail: sls@procopio.com

SHIRE, HAROLD RAYMOND, law educator, writer, scientist; b. Denver, Nov. 23, 1910; s. Samuel Newport and Rose Betty (Herman) S.; m. Cecilia Goldhaar, May 9, 1973; children: David, Darcy, Esti. MBA, Pepperdine U., 1972, LLD (hon.), 1975; JD, Southwestern U., L.A., 1974; M in Liberal Arts, U. So. Calif., 1977; PhD in Human Behavior, U.S. Internat. U., San Diego, 1980. Bar: Calif. 1937, U.S. Dist. Ct. (so. dist.) Calif. 1939, U.S. Supreme Ct. 1978. Dep. dist. atty. L.A. County, Calif., 1937-38; asst. U.S. atty. So. Dist. Calif., L.A. and San Diego, 1939-42; pvt. practice L.A., 1946-56; pres., chmn. bd. Gen. Connectors Corp., U.S. and Eng., 1956-73; prof. mgmt. and law Pepperdine U., Malibu, Calif., 1974-75, U.S. Internat. U., San Diego, 1980-83; dir. Bestobell Aviation, Eng., 1970-74. Author: Cha No Yu and Symbolic Interactionism: Method of Predicting Japanese Behavior, 1980, The Tea Ceremony, 1984. Patentee aerospace pneumatics; invented flexible connectors; designed, manufactured flexible integrity systems. Advisor U. S.C. Gerontology Andrus Ctr., pre-retirement tng., 1976-80; bd. dirs. Pepperdine U., 1974-80; nat. bd. govs. Union Orthodox Jewish Congregations Am., 1973—; mem. Rep. Nat. Com.; pres. Jewish Nat. Fund Legion of Honor, 1991—; mem. Presdl. Roundtable, Washington, 1989-97; mem. Inner Cir., Pres. Regan and Bush, 1989-92; life mem. Rep. Nat. Com. With U.S. Army, 1942-46. Decorated chevalier du vieux moulin (France); companion Royal Aero. Soc. (U.K.); recipient Tea Name Grand Master Soshitsu Sen XV Urasenke Sch., Kyoto, Japan, 1976, Medal of Honor Jewish Nat. Fund, Legion of Honor, 1991, U.S. Senate Medal of Freedom. Mem. ABA, Am. Welding Soc., Soc. Material and Process Engrs., Am. Legion (svc. officer China #1 Shanghai), Calif. Symphony Soc. (pres. 1998—), Masons (32 degree, Hiram award 1994), Royal Arch, Shrine, Legion of Honor Jewish Nat. Fund (nat. chmn. bd. 1999). Achievements include design and manufacture of fluidic systems flexible integrity for Saturn IV and welding in Apollo XI landing on moon, 1969. Office: PO Box 1352 Beverly Hills CA 90213-1352

SHIREMAN, JOAN FOSTER, social work educator; b. Cleve., Oct. 28, 1933; d. Louis Omar and Genevieve (Duguid) Foster; m. Charles Howard Shireman, Mar. 18, 1967; 1 child, David Louis. BA, Radcliffe Coll., 1956; MA, U. Chgo., 1959, PhD, 1968. Caseworker N.H. Children's Aid Soc., Manchester, 1959-61; dir. research Chgo. Child Care Soc., 1968-72; assoc. prof. U. Ill., Chgo., 1972-85; prof. Portland (Oreg.) State U., 1985—, dir. PhD program, 1992-99; interim exec. dir. Partnership for Rsch., Tng. and Grad. Edn. in Child Welfare, 1994. Research cons. child welfare orgns., Ill., 1968-85, Oreg. 1985—; lectr. U. Chgo., 1968-72. Co-author: Care and Commitment: Foster Parent Adoption Decisions, 1985, Adoption: Theory, Policy and Practice, 1997; mem. editl. bd. Jour. Sch. Social Work, 1978-81, Social Work Rsch. and Abstracts, 1990-93, Children and Youth Svcs. Rev., 1990—, Jour. Social Work Edn., 1990-95; contbr. articles to profl. jours., chpts. to books. Bd. dirs. Oreg. chpt. Nat. Assn. for Prevention Child Abuse, 1985-87; bd. dirs. Friendly House, Portland, 1991-97, pres., 1995-96; mem. adv. com. children's svcs. divsn. State of Oreg., 1985-95. Grantee HEW, 1980-82, Chgo. Community Trust, 1982-86, Oreg. Children's Trust Fund, 1991-96. Mem. NASW, AAUP, Acad. Cert. Social Workers, Coun. on Social Work Edn., Phi Beta Kappa. Home: 2535 SW Sherwood Dr Portland OR 97201-1679 Office: Portland State U Grad Sch Social Work PO Box 751 Portland OR 97207-0751 E-mail: shiremj@rri.pdx.edu

SHIRES, GEORGE THOMAS, surgeon, educator; b. Waco, Tex., Nov. 22, 1925; s. George Thomas and Donna Mae (Smith) S.; m. Robbie Jo Martin, Nov. 27, 1948; children: Donna Blain, George Thomas III, Jo Ellen. MD, U. Tex., Dallas, 1948. Diplomate Am. Bd. Surgery (dir. 1968-74, chmn. 1972-74). Intern Mass. Meml. Hosp., Boston, 1948-49; resident in surgery Parkland Meml. Hosp., Dallas, 1950-53; faculty U. Tex. Southwestern Med. Sch., Dallas, 1953-60, assoc. prof. surgery, acting chmn. dept., 1960-61, prof., chmn. dept., 1961-74; surgeon in chief surg. svcs. Parkland Meml. Hosp., 1960-74; prof., chmn. dept. surgery U. Wash. Sch. Medicine, Seattle, 1974-75; chief of service Harborview Med. Center, Seattle, Univ. Hosp., Seattle, 1974-75; chmn. dept. surgery N.Y. Hosp.-Cornell U. Med. Coll., 1975-91; dean, provost for med. affairs Cornell U. Med. Coll., 1987-91, prof. emeritus, 1996—; prof., chmn. surgery Tex. Tech. U., Lubbock, 1991-95, Canizaro disting. prof. surgery, 1995-97; prof. surgery U. Nev. Sch. Medicine, Las Vegas, 1997—. Cons. Surgeon Gen., U.S. Army, 1965-75, Jamaica Hosp., 1978-91, Inst. Medicine Nat. Acad. Scis., 1975—; metabolism and truama com. Nat. Acad. Scis.-NRC, 1964-71, com. trauma, 1964-71; rsch. program evaluation com., reviewer clin. investigation applications career devel. program VA, 1972-76; gen. med. rsch. program projects com. NIH, 1965-69; mem. Surgery A study sect., 1970-74, chmn., 1976-78; mem. Nat. Adv. Gen. Med. Scis. Coun., 1980-84; cons. editl. bd. Jour. Trauma, 1968-88. Mem. editl. bd. Year Book Med. Publs., 1970-92, Annals of Surgery, 1972—, Surg. Techniques Illustrated: An International Comparative Text, 1974-75, Am. Jour. Surgery, 1968—, Contemporary Surgery, 1973-89; assoc. editor-in-chief Infections in Surgery, 1981; mem. editl. bd. Jour. Clin. Surgery, 1980-82; editor Surgery, Gynecology and Obstetrics, 1982-93. Lt. M.C. USNR, 1949-50, 53-55. Life Ins. Med. Rsch. fellow, 1947. Fellow Coll. Medicine South Africa (hon.); mem. ACS (bd. regents 1971-82, chmn. bd. regents 1978-80, pres. 1981-82), AMA, Dallas Soc. Gen. Surgeons (pres.-elect, pres. 1972-74), Am. Assn. Surgery Trauma, Am. Burn Assn., Am. Surg. Assn. (sec. 1969-74, pres. 1980), Digestive Disease Found. (founding mem.), Halsted Soc., Internat. Soc. Burn Injuries, Internat. Surg. Soc. (sec. 1978-81, v.p. 1982-83, pres. U.S. chpt. 1984-85), Am. Burn Assn., Pan-Am. Med. Assn. (surgery council 1971), Pan Pacific Surg. Assn., Soc. Clin. Surgery, Soc. Surgery Alimentary Tract, Soc. Surg. Chairmen (pres. 1972-74), Soc. Univ. Surgeons (chmn. publs. com. 1969-71), So. Surg. Assn., Surg. Biology Club (sec. 1968-70), N.Y. Surg. Soc. (pres. 1981-82), Western Surg. Assn., Allen O. Whipple Surg. Soc., James IV Assn. Surgeons (bd. dirs. 1980-81, sec. 1981-87, pres. 1987-91), Alpha Omega Alpha, Alpha Pi Alpha, Phi Beta Pi. Office: U Nev Sch Medicine 2040 W Charleston Blvd Ste 501 Las Vegas NV 89102-2207 E-mail: gtshires@nvtrauma.com

SHIRLEY, DAVID ARTHUR, chemistry educator, science administrator; b. North Conway, N.H., Mar. 30, 1934; m. Virginia Schultz, June 23, 1956 (dec. Mar. 1995); children: David N., Diane, Michael, Eric, Gail; m. Barbara Cerny, Dec. 26, 1995. BS, U. Maine, 1955, ScD (hon.), 1978; PhD in Chemistry, U. Calif.-Berkeley, 1959; D honoris causa, Free U. Berlin, 1987. With Lawrence Radiation Lab. (now Lawrence Berkeley Lab.), U. Calif., Berkeley, 1958-92, assoc. dir., head materials and molecular research div., 1975-80, dir., 1980-89, lectr. chemistry, 1959-60, asst. prof., 1960-64, assoc. prof., 1964-67, prof., 1967-92, vice chmn. dept. chemistry, 1968-71, chmn. dept. chemistry, 1971-75; sr. v.p. rsch., dean grad. sch. Pa. State U., University Park, 1992-96; dir. emeritus Lawrence Berkeley Nat. Lab., 1997—. Chair bd. overseers Fermilab. Contbr. over 400 rsch. articles. NSF fellow, 1955-58, 66-67, 70; recipient Ernest O. Lawrence award AEC, 1972, Humboldt award (sr. U.S. scientist); listed by Sci. Citation Index as one of the world's 300 most cited scientists for work published during 1965-78. Fellow Am. Phys. Soc., mem. Nat. Acad. Scis., Am. Chem. Soc., AAAS, Am. Acad. Arts and Scis., Bohemian Club, Explorers Club, Sigma Xi, Tau Beta Pi, Sigma Pi Sigma, Phi Kappa Phi.

SHIRTCLIFF, JOHN DELZELL, business owner, oil jobber; b. Roseburg, Oreg., Mar. 2, 1948; s. Henry Marion and Sheila Nell (Delzell) S.; m. Connie Lee Cantrell, June 13, 1975; children: Darcie, Danielle, Andrew. BS, Oregon State U., 1970. Pres. Shirtcliff Oil Co., Myrtle Creek, Oreg., 1971—. Engr. Myrtle Creek (Oreg.) Vol. Fire Dept., 1971—, emergency technician, 1981—; mem. Rep. Cen. Com., Roseburg, Oreg., 1982-88; chmn. Umpqua Community Coll. Budget Com., Roseburg, 1983-96; bd. dirs. Mercy Hospice, Roseburg, 1988-96. 2nd lt. U.S. Army, 1970-71. Named Citizen of Year, Myrtle Creek City, 1986, Vol. of Year, Douglas County C. of C., 1987. Mem. Petroleum Marketeers Assn. Am. (dir. Oreg. 1988), Oreg. Petroleum Marketers Assn. (v.p. legis. chmn. 1986, pres. 1987, PMAA dir. 1988), Pacific Oil Conf. (bd. dirs., v.p. 1995, gen. chmn. 1997), Lions, Elks, Masons, Shriners. Republican. Avocations: landscaping, jogging, golf. Office: Shirtcliff Oil Co 283 SW Western Ave PO Box 6003 Myrtle Creek OR 97457-0051

SHIRVANI, HAMID, architect, educator, author, administrator; b. Tehran, Iran, Oct. 20, 1950; came to U.S., 1974, naturalized, 1986; s. Majid and Taji (Granpisheh) S. Diploma in architecture, Poly. of Cen. London, 1974; MArch, Pratt Inst., 1975; MS, Rensselaer Poly. Inst., 1977; MLA, Harvard U., 1978; MA, Princeton U., 1979, PhD, 1980. Project designer London Borough of Barnet, 1973-74; asst. prof. architecture Pa. State U., 1979-82; prof., dir. grad. studies SUNY, Syracuse, 1982-85; prof., dir. Sch. Urban Planning and Devel., U. Louisville, 1985-86; prof. architecture and urban design U. Colo., Denver, 1986-92, dean Sch. of Architecture and Planning, 1986-91; prof. philosophy, dean Coll. Arts and Scis. U. Mass., Lowell, 1992-95; v.p. grad. studies and rsch., prof. urban studies CUNY Queens Coll., Flushing, 1995-2000; provost, exec. v.p., Martha Masters prof. art/architecture Chapman U., Orange, Calif., 2000—. Mem. vis. faculty So. Calif. Inst. Architecutre, U. So. Calif.; lectr. numerous universities worldwide including U. Tex., San Antonio, Lehigh U., U. Waterloo (Can.), U. Sydney (Australia), Mo. State U., Columbia U., N.Y.C., Amsterdam Acad. Art, U. Venice (Italy), Chinese U. Hong Kong, So. China Inst. U., U. Calif., Irvine, Villanova U., Rutgers U., Ariz. State U., Duke U., U. Pa., Yale U., U. Colo., U. N.C. Author: Urban Design: A Comprehensive Reference, 1981, Urban Design Review, 1981, Urban Design Process, 1985, Beyond Public Architecture, 1990; editor Urban Design Rev., 1982-85, Urban Design and Preservation Quar., 1985-88; mem. editorial bd. Jour. Archtl. Edn., 1988-94, Avant Garde, 1988-93, Jour. Planning Edn. and Rsch., 1987-93, Art and Architecture, 1974-78, Jour. Am. Planning Assn., 1982-88. Recipient Gold Medal in Architecture and Urbanism, Faculty Honor award, Acad. Leadership award, Faculty Rsch. award. Fellow Am. Soc. Landscape Archs. (recognition award), Royal Geog. Soc., Royal Soc. Arts; mem. Am. Studies Assn., Am. Inst. Cert. Planners, Am. Planning Assn. (chmn. urban design divsn. 1987-89, Disting. award 1984, Urban Design award 1985), Sigma Xi, Omicron Delta Epsilon, Tau Sigma Delta (Silver medal in archtl. edn. 1988), Tau Beta Pi, Sigma Lambda Alpha. Office: Chapman U Orange CA 92866-1099 Fax: 714-997-6801. E-mail: Ham@chapman.edu

SHMAVONIAN, GERALD S. film producer; b. L.A., June 26, 1945; s. Sarkis Neshan and Berje-Lucia (der Hareutunyan) S. Student, U. Calif., Berkeley, 1964-70. Leader archaeol. excavation team, Guatemala, Turkey, 1970-75; pub. City Mags., 1975-80; special advisor Bicentennial Commission, Washington, D.C., 1987; chmn. Am. Nationalities Coun., Stanford U., 1983-86; pres. L.A. Talent, 1986-2000, Am. Documentary Film Acad., 2001—. Recipient Intercollegiate Boxing Championship, 1965. Mem. Calif. Scholarship Fedn. (life, pres. 1963), Nat. Forensic League (pres. 1963, degree of honor). Home: 6219 N Prospect Ave Fresno CA 93711-1658

SHNEOUR, ELIE ALEXIS, biochemist, researcher; b. Neuilly-sur-Seine, France, Dec. 11, 1925; came to U.S., 1941, naturalized, 1944; s. Zalman and Salomea (Landau) S.; m. Polly H. Henderson, Sept. 7, 1990; children from previous marriage: Mark Zalman, Alan Brewster. BA, Columbia U., 1947; DSc (hon.), Bard Coll., 1969; MA, U. Calif., Berkeley, 1955; PhD, UCLA, 1958. Tchr. and rsch. fellow U. Calif., Berkeley, 1953-55, Am. Heart Assn. rsch. fellow, 1958-62, tchg. and rsch. fellow L.A., 1958; rsch. fellow Nat. Cancer Inst., 1956-57; Am. Heart Assn. rsch. fellow NYU, 1958-59; rsch. assoc. genetics Stanford U., 1962-65; assoc. prof. biology and neuroscis. U. Utah, 1965-69; rsch. neurochemist City of Hope Nat. Med. Ctr., Duarte, Calif., 1969-71. Dir. rsch. Calbiochem., 1971-75; pres. Biosystems Insts., Inc., 1975—; dir. Biosystems Rsch. Inst., 1979—; mem. steering com. Nat. Acad. Sci. Study Group on Biology and the Exploration of Mars, 1964; chmn. Western Regional coun. Rsch. in Basic Bioscis. for Manned Orbiting Missions, Am. Inst. Biol. Scis., NASA, 1966-69; fellow Com. Sci. Investigation Claims of Paranormal, 1996—. Author: Extraterrestrial Life, 1965, (with Eric A. Ottesen) National Academy of Sciences, National Rsch. Coun., 1966, (with S. Moffat) Life Beyond the Earth, 1966, The Malnourished Mind, 1974; contbr. numerous articles to sci. and lay jours. Chmn. citizens adv. coun. San Diego Pub. Schs., 1971-72; mem. adv. coun. Cousteau Soc., 1977-98; bd. dirs. Am.-Ukraine Trade Coun., 1991-96, Lunar Power System Coalition, 1993—, Transinnova S.A. France, 1990—; chmn. sci. adv. bd. County of San Diego, 1995—. With U.S. Army, 1944-45. Recipient William Lockwood prize, 1947. Mem. IEEE, AAAS (chmn. So. Calif. Skeptics soc. Pacific divsn. 1988-90), Am. Chem. Soc., N.Y. Acad. Scis., Am. Inst. Biol. Scis., Am. Soc. for Biochemistry and Molecular Biology (chmn. sci. advisors program 1973-75, mem. com. on pub. policy 1974-76, congl. liaison 1992—), Am. Soc. Neurochemistry (mem. coun. 1971-73), Soc. Neurosci., Internat. Soc. Neurochemistry, U.S. C. of C. (bd. dirs. 1993—), La Jolla Chamber Music Soc. (bd. dirs. 1994-97), Internat. Coun. for Global Health Progress (N.Am. adv. bd. 1996—), Sigma Xi, Phi Sigma. Office: Biosyss Insts Inc 700 Front St MS CDM 608 San Diego CA 92101-6085

SHOEMAKER, BILL (WILLIAM LEE SHOEMAKER), retired jockey, horse trainer; b. Fabens, Tex., Aug. 19, 1931; s. B. B. and Ruby (Call) S.; 1 child, Amanda Elisabeth. Jockey, 1949-90; ret., 1990; trainer, 1990-97. Author: Stalking Horse, 1994, Fire Horse, 1995, Dark Horse, 1996. Achievements include winning Ky. Derby, 1955, 59, 65, 86, Belmont Stakes, 1957, 59, 62, 67, 75, Preakness Stakes, 1963, 67; ret. with 8,833 wins, including over 1000 Stakes wins. Office: care Vincent Andrews Mgmt 315 S Beverly Dr Ste 208 Beverly Hills CA 90212-4310

SHOEMAKER, CAROLYN SPELLMANN, planetary astronomer; b. Gallup, N.Mex., June 24, 1929; d. Leonard Robert and Hazel Adele (Arthur) Spellmann; m. Eugene Merle Shoemaker, Aug. 18, 1951 (dec. July 1997); children: Christine Shoemaker Abanto, Patrick Gene, Linda Shoemaker Salazar. BA cum laude, Chico State Coll., 1949, MA, 1950; ScD (hon.), No. Ariz. U., 1990. Vis. scientist Br. astrogeology U.S. Geol. Survey, Flagstaff, Ariz., 1980—; rsch. asst. Calif. Inst. Tech., Pasadena, 1981-85; rsch. prof. astronomy No. Ariz. U., Flagstaff, 1989—; mem. staff Lowell Obs., Flagstaff, 1993—. Guest observer Palomar Obs., Palomar Mountain, Calif., 1982-94; Ruth Northcott Meml. lectrs. R.A.S.C., 1995; co-McGovern lectr. Cosmos Club Found., 1995. Co-recipient Rittenhouse medal Rittenhouse Astron. Soc., 1988, Scientist of Yr. award ARCS Found., 1995, James C. Watson medal NAS, 1998; recipient Woman of Distinction award Soroptimists, 1994, 20th Anniversary Internat. Women's Yr. award Zonta and 99s, 1995, NASA Exceptional Scientific Achievement medal, 1996, Woman of Distinction award Nat. Assn. Women in Edn., 1996, Shoemaker award Am. Inst. Profl. Geologists, 1997, plaque Internat. Forest Friendship, Atchison, Kans., 1997, Robert Burnham Jr. award Western Regional Astron. League, 2000; named Disting. Alumna of the Calif. State U., Chico, 1990. Fellow Am. Acad. Arts and Scis., mem. AAAS, Astron. Soc. of Pacific, Am. Geophys. Union, Meteoritical Soc. Achievements include discovery of 32 comets including Periodic Comet

Shoemaker-Levy 9 which impacted Jupiter in July 1994, more than 500 asteroids including 44 Earth approachers and approximately 68 Mars crossers, meteorites at Veevers Crater, Australia and impactites at Wolfe Creek Crater, Australia. Home: 5231 Hidden Hollow Rd Flagstaff AZ 86001-3821 Office: Lowell Obs 1400 W Mars Hill Rd Flagstaff AZ 86001-4499

SHOEN, EDWARD JOSEPH, transportation and insurance companies executive; s. Leonard and Anna (Carty) S. MBA, Harvard U. Pres., chmn. Amerco Nev. Corp., Phoenix; pres. U-Haul Internat., Inc., Phoenix. Office: Amerco 1325 Airmotive Way Reno NV 89502 also: Amerco 1325 Airmotive Way Reno NV 89502-3201

SHONK, ALBERT DAVENPORT, JR. advertising executive; b. L.A., May 23, 1932; s. Albert Davenport and Jean Spence (Stannard) S. BS in Bus. Adminstrn., U. So. Calif., 1954. Field rep. mktg. divsn. L.A. Examiner, 1954-55, asst. mgr. mktg. and field supr. mktg. divsn., 1955-56, mgr. mktg. divsn., 1956-57; account exec. Hearst Advt. Svc., L.A., 1957-59; account exec., mgr. keith H. Evans & Assocs., San Francisco, 1959-65; owner, pres. Albert D. Shonk Co., L.A., 1965-97; gen. ptnr. Shonk Land Co.LTD, Charleston, W.Va., 1989-00; dir. Shonk, LLC, Del., 2001—. Pres. Signet Cir. Corp., Inc., 1977-81, dir., 1962-81, hon. life dir., 1981—, treas., 1989—. Bd. dirs. Florence Crittenton Ctr., sec., 1978, 1st v.p., 1978-79, exec. v.p., 1979-81, pres., 1981-83, chmn. bd., 1983-85, hon. life dir.,, 1986—, treas., 1997, pres., 1997—; co-chair centennial com., founding chmn. Crittenton Assocs.; treas. Balboa Island Mus. and Hist. Soc., 1999—; bd. dirs. Balboa Island Improvement Assn., 2000—. Recipient Medallion of Merit Phi Sigma Kappa, 1976, Founders award, 1961, NIC Interfraternal award, 1989. Mem. Advt. Club L.A., Pubs. Rep. Assn. of So. Calif., Nat. Assn. Pubs. Reps. (past v.p. West Coast 1981-83), Jr. Advt. Club L.A. (hon. life, dir., treas., 1st v.p.), Trojan Club, Skull and Dagger, U. So. Calif. Alumni Assn. (bd. dirs. 2000-01), U. S.C. Marshall Sch. Bus. Alumni Assn. (nat. bd. 1991-99, treas. 1995-99), U. S.C. Assocs., Marshall Assocs. (bd. dirs. 1999—), Inter-Greek Soc. (co-founder, hon. life, dir., v.p. 1976-79, pres. 1984-86), Rotary (Paul Harris fellow), Phi Sigma Kappa (dir. grand coun. 1962-70, 77-79, grand pres. 1979-83, chancellor 1983-87, 90-91, recorder 1995—, v.p. meml. found. 1979-84, pres. 1984, trustee pres. Phi Sigma Kappa found. 1984-95, trustee emeritus 1995—), World Affairs Coun., Alpha Kappa Psi, Town Hall. Home: 225 Sapphire Ave Newport Beach CA 92662-1148

SHONTERE, JAMES G. construction executive; CFO, sec. JF Shea, Walnut, Calif. Office: JF Shea 655 Brea Canyon Rd Walnut CA 91789

SHOOTER, ERIC MANVERS, neurobiology educator, consultant; b. Mansfield, Eng., Apr. 18, 1924; came to U.S., 1964; s. Fred and Pattie (Johnson) S.; m. Elaine Staley Arnold, May 28, 1949; 1 child, Annette Elizabeth. BA, Cambridge (Eng.) U., 1945, MA, 1949, PhD, 1950, ScD, 1986; DSc, U. London, 1964. Sr. scientist biochemistry Brewing Industry Rsch. Found., 1950-53; biochemistry lectr. Univ. Coll., London, 1953-63; assoc. prof. genetics Stanford U., 1963-68, prof. genetics and biochemistry, 1968-75, prof., chmn. neurobiology dept., 1975-87, prof. neurobiology, 1987—, chmn. Neurosci. PhD Program, 1972-82. Assoc. Neurosci. Rsch. Program, N.Y.C., 1979-89; mem. tchg. staff Internat. Sch. Neurosci., Praglia, Italy, 1987-93; sr. cons. Markey Charitable Trust, Miami, Fla., 1985-97; mem. sci. adv. bd., and dir. Regeneron Pharm., Inc., Tarrytown, N.Y., 1988—. Assoc. editor: (book series) Ann. Rev. Neuroscis., 1984-2001; contbr. numerous articles to profl. jours. Recipient Wakeman award Duke U., 1988, Bristol-Myers-Squibb award for Disting. Achievement in Neurosci. Rsch., 1997; faculty scholar Josiah Macy Jr. Found., N.Y.C., 1974-75. Fellow AAAS, Royal Soc. (London), Am. Acad. Arts and Scis.; mem. Inst. Medicine of NAS (fgn. assoc.), Biochem. Soc., Am. Assn. Biol. Chemists, Soc. for Neurosci. (Ralph W. Gerard prize 1995), Am. Soc. Neurochemistry, Internat. Soc. Neurochemistry, Internat. Brain Rsch. Orgn. Avocation: travel. Home: 370 Golden Oak Dr Portola Vally CA 94028-7757 Office: Stanford U Sch Medicine Dept Neurobiology 299 Campus Dr Stanford CA 94305-5101

SHOR, SAMUEL WENDELL WILLISTON, naval engineer; b. N.Y.C., June 25, 1920; s. George Gershon and Dorothy (Williston) S.; m. Joan Bopp, June 21, 1958; children: Peter Williston, Molly Hathaway. Student, Harvard U., 1937-39; BS, U.S. Naval Acad., 1942; Naval Engr., MIT, 1949; MS in Math., NYU, 1963. Commd. ensign U.S. Navy, 1942, advanced through grades to capt., 1962; served in cruisers Chicago, St. Louis, and Quincy, Pacific and Atlantic, 1942-46; assigned San Francisco Naval Shipyard, 1949-52, naval reactors br. AEC, 1952-53; AEC rep. for initial test of submarine nuclear propulsion in U.S.S. Nautilus and U.S.S. Seawolf, 1953-57; AEC rep. for startup testing of Shippingport Atomic Power Sta., 1957-58; design supt., prodn. engring. officer N.Y. Naval Shipyard, 1958 63; dir. sonar systems office Naval Ship Systems Command, 1963-67, exec. dir. plans, 1967-69, dep. comdr. for engring., 1969-71; project mgr. electronic warfare Naval Electronic Systems Commd., 1971-73; with Bechtel Power Corp., San Francisco, 1973—. Author tech. papers. Mem. Soc. Naval Architects and Marine Engrs., Soc. Naval Engrs., Am. Math. Soc., Am. Phys. Soc., Sigma Xi. Home: 318 Montford Ave Mill Valley CA 94941-3313 Office: Bechtel Corp 50 Beale St Ste 1 San Francisco CA 94105-1895

SHORE, JAMES H(ENRY), psychiatrist; b. Winston-Salem, N.C., Apr. 6, 1940; s. James Henry and Ellen Elizabeth (Hayes) S.; m. Christine Lowenbach, Aug. 24, 1963; children— Ellen Ottilie, James Henry. M.D., Duke U., 1965. Diplomate Am. Bd. Psychiatry and Neurology. Intern U. Utah Med. Center, 1965-66; resident in psychiatry U. Wash., 1966-69; chief mental health office Portland (Oreg.) Area Indian Health Service, 1969-73; assoc. prof. psychiatry, dir. community psychiatry tng. program U. Oreg. Health Scis. Center, 1973-75, prof., chmn. dept. psychiatry, 1975-85; chmn. dept. psychiatry U. Colo. Health Scis. Ctr., Denver, 1985-99, interim chancellor, 1992-93, 98. Dir. Colo. Psychiatry Hosp., 1985-99; interim dir. U. Colo. Hosp., Denver, 1987-88, interim exec. vice chancellor, 1995-97, chancellor, 1999—; mem. exptl. and spl. edn. com. NIMH-Internal Rev. Group, 1976-80; cons. in field. Contbr. numerous articles to profl. publs. Mem. Various community bds. Served with USPHS, 1969-73. Decorated USPHS Commendation medal; various grants. Fellow Am. Psychiat. Assn., Am. Coll. Psychiatry; mem. Am. Assn. Chmn. Depts. Psychiatry (pres. 1989), Am. Bd. Psychiatry and Neurology (dir. 1987—, pres. 1994), Residency Rev. Com. for Psychiatry (chmn. 1991-92). Office: U Colo Health Scis Ctr PO Box A 095 4200 E 9th Ave Denver CO 80220-3706

SHORENSTEIN, DOUGLAS W. corporate executive; BA, U. Calif., Berkeley; JD, Hastings Coll. Chair United Way of the Bay Area, 1998—. Office: Shorenstein 555 California St Ste 4900 San Francisco CA 94104

SHORENSTEIN, ROSALIND GREENBERG, internist; b. N.Y.C., Jan. 14, 1947; d. Albert Samuel and Natalie Miriam (Sherman) Greenberg; m. Michael Lewis Shorenstein, June 18, 1967; children: Anna Irene, Claire Beth. BA in Chemistry, Wellesley Coll., 1968; MA in Biochemistry and Molecular Biology, Harvard U., 1970, PhD in Biochemistry and Molecular Biology, 1973; MD, Stanford U., 1976. Diplomate Am. Bd. Internal Medicine. Resident in internal medicine UCLA Med. Ctr., 1976-79; pvt. practice internal medicine Santa Cruz, Calif., 1979—. Mem. dept. internal medicine Dominican Hosp., Santa Cruz, 1979—; co-dir. med. svcs. Health Enhancement & Lifestyle Planning Systems, Santa Cruz, 1983—. Contbr. articles to profl. journals. Dir. Santa Cruz Chamber Players, 1993-94, pres., bd. dirs., 1994—. Recipient Charlie Parkhurst award Santa Cruz Women's Commn., 1989; NSF fellow, 1968-72, Sarah Perry Wood Med. fellow Wellesley Coll., 1972-76. Mem. Am. Soc. Internal Medicine (del. 1994, 95), Calif. Soc. Internal Medicine (trustee 1994—, sec.-treas. 1996-2000), Am. Med. Women's Assn. (Outstanding Svc. award 1987, br. #59 pres. 1986—), Calif. Med. Assn. (com. on women 1987-93), Santa Cruz County Med. Soc. (mem. bd. govs. 1993—, sec. 1997-99, pres. 2000—), Phi Beta Kappa, Sigma Xi. Jewish. Office: 700 Frederick St Ste 103 Santa Cruz CA 95062-2239

SHORENSTEIN, WALTER HERBERT, commercial real estate development company executive; b. Glen Cove, N.Y., Feb. 23, 1915; m. Phyllis J. Finley, Aug. 8, 1945 (dec.); children: Joan (Dec.), Carole, Douglas. Student, Pa. State U., 1933-34, U. Pa., 1934-36; D in Econs. (hon.), HanYang U., Seoul, Republic of Korea, 1988. With property sales mgmt. depts. Milton Meyer & Co., San Francisco, 1946-51, ptnr., 1951-60, owner, chmn. bd. dirs., 1960—, Shorenstein Group, San Francisco, Shorenstein Co., San Francisco, 1960—. Appt. by Pres. Johnson adv. del. UN Econ. Commn. for Asia and Far East, 1967, Pub. Advisory Com. U.S. Trade Policy; apptd. Pres. Carter Com. for Preservation fo White House; appt. by Pres. Clinton bd. dirs. Corp. Nat. Svc., 1994-96, adv.com. U.S. Commerce Dept. Industry, 1995-96. Past chmn. bd. trustees Hastings Law Ctr., U. Calif., San Francisco; founding mem. exec. adv. com. Hubert H. Humphrey Inst. Pub. Affairs, U. Minn.; bd. visitors; past pres., hon. life bd. dirs. San Francisco Park and Recreation Commn.; chmn. Vietnam Orphans Airlift; bd. dirs. San Francisco Performing Arts Ctr.; trustee Asia Found.; fin. chmn. Dem. Nat. Conv., 1984; founder Joan Shorenstein Ctr. on Press, Politics and Public Policy, Harvard U., 1986; apptd. by Pres. Clinton to Nat. Svc. Commn., 1994, Bd. of Americorp, founding mem. WWII Nat. Monument com., Nat. Endowment Arts, White House Endowment Fund; apptd. by Pres. Carter chair White House Preservation Fund; apptd. by Mayor Frank Jordon chair Save the San Francisco Giants com.; personal advisor Pres. Johnson, Carter, Clinton; chmn. Pacific Rim Econ. Coun., San Francisco; bd. visitors Internat. Studies Bd. Stanford U.; co-founder Orpheum, Curran and Golden Gate Theatres, San Francsico; founder Johnson Presdl. Libr., Carter Ctr.; chmn. San Francisco U. N50 nat. com., 1995, also numerous polit. activities. Maj. USAF, 1940-45. Named Leader of Tomorrow, Time mag., 1953, Calif. Dem. of Yr., 1985; recipient Nat. Brotherhood award NCCJ, 1982, Disting. Svc. award Dem. Nat. Com., 1983, Golden Plate award Am. Acad. Achievement, 1991, Svc. to Youth award Cath. Youth Orgn., 1994, Lifetime Achievement award Dem. Party, 1997; inducted Real Estate Legends Hall of Fame, 1997, Bay Area Coun. Bay Area Bus. Hall of Fame, 1998; Shorenstein award named in his honor Dem. Nat. Com., 1999. Mem. Calif. C. of C. (past bd. dirs.), San Francisco C. of C. (past chmn. bd. dirs., life bd. dirs.). Office: Shorenstein Co 555 California St Ste 4900 San Francisco CA 94104-1714

SHORS, CLAYTON MARION, cardiologist; b. Beemer, Nebr., June 10, 1925; s. Joseph Albert and Morva Edith (Clayton) S.; m. Arlene Towle, June 6, 1948; children: Susan Debra, Clayton Robert, Scott Towle B.S., U. Nebr., 1950, M.D., 1952. Diplomate Am. Bd. Internal Medicine (subspecialty cardiovascular disease). Intern Detroit Receiving Hosp., 1952-53, resident, 1953-56; practice medicine specializing in cardiology Detroit; chief cardiology St. John Hosp., Detroit. Bd. dirs. Sedona Acad.; mem. Sedona 30. Served with U.S. Army, 1943-46 Fellow Am. Coll. Cardiology, Internat. Coll. Angiology, Am. Heart Assn. Council on Clin. Cardiology; mem. Alpha Omega Alpha Home: 44 Rue De La Rose Sedona AZ 86336-5970 Office: 1785 W Highway 89A Sedona AZ 86336-5567 also: 6562 E Crested Saguaro Ln Scottsdale AZ 85262-7373

SHORT, MARTIN, actor, comedian; b. Hamilton, Ont, Canada, Mar. 26, 1950; s. Charles Patrick and Olive Short; m. Nancy Dolman; children: Katherine, Oliver, Henry. Degree in social work, McMaster U., 1972. Actor: (feature films) Three Amigos, 1986, Innerspace, 1987, Cross My Heart, 1987, Three Fugitives, 1989, The Big Picture, 1989, Pure Luck, 1991, Father of the Bride, 1991, Captain Ron, 1992, We're Back! A Dinosaur's Story, 1993 (voice), Clifford, 1994, The Pebble and the Penguin, 1995 (voice), Father of the Bride 2, 1995, Mars Attack, 1996, Jungle 2 Jungle, 1997, The Fairy Godmother, 1997, A Simple Wish, 1997, Mumford, 1998, Akbar's Adventure Tours, 1998, (voice) Prince of Egypt, 1998, Mumford, 1999; (TV series) The Associates, 1979, I'm a Big Girl Now, 1980-81, SCTV Network 90, 1982-84, Saturday Night Live, 1985-86, The Completely Mental Misadventures of Ed Grimley, 1988-89 (voice), The Martin Short Show, 1994, (miniseries) Merlin, 1998; (TV movies) The Family Man, 1979, Sunset Limousine, 1983, Alice in Wonderland, 1999, (TV spls.) Martin Short's Concert for the North Americas, 1985, Really Weird Tales, 1987, I, Martin Short Goes Hollywood, 1989, The Martin Short Show (TV series), 1999-2000; also numerous revues and cabaret appearances with Second City comedy troupe, 1977-78, appeared on Broadway in The Goodbye Girl, 1993. Won 1999 Tony Award, Best Actor-Musical, Little Me. Office: William Morris Agency care Ames Cushing 151 S El Camino Dr Beverly Hills CA 90212-2775

SHORTELL, STEPHEN MICHAEL, health services researcher; b. New London, Wis., Nov. 9, 1944; BBA, U. Notre Dame, 1966; MPH, UCLA, 1968; MBA, U. Chgo., 1970, PhD in Behavioral Sci., 1972. Rsch. asst. Nat. Opinion Rsch. Ctr., 1969; instr., rsch. assoc. Ctr. Health Adminstrv. Studies, 1970-72; acting dir. grad. program hosp. adminstrn. U. Chgo., 1973-74, from asst. prof. to assoc. prof., 1974-79; prof. dept. health svc. Sch. Pub. Health and Cmty. Medicine, U. Wash., 1979-82; A.C. Buehler Disting. prof. health svc. mgmt. Northwestern U., Evanston, Ill., 1982-98; Blue Cross disting. prof. health policy and mgmt. Sch. Pub. Health, U. Calif., Berkeley, 1998—. Cons. VA, Robert Wood Found., Henry Kaiser Found.; asst. prof. Health Svcs. Orgn., U. Chgo., 1972-74; adj. asst. prof. dept. sociology U. Wash., 1975-76, dir. doctoral program dept. health svcs. Sch. Pub. Health and Cmty. Medicine, 1976-78; prof. sociology dept. sociology Northwestern U., 1982, prof. preventive medicine Sch. Medicine. Contbr. numerous publs. to profl. jours. Recipient Baxter prize Baxter-Allegiance Found., 1995. Fellow Am. Coll. Healthcare Execs. (Gold medal 1998); mem. Inst. Med.-NAS. Office: Univ Calif Berkeley Sch Pub Health 407 Warren Hl Berkeley CA 94720-0001

SHORTZ, RICHARD ALAN, lawyer; b. Chgo., Mar. 11, 1945; s. Lyle A. and Wilma Warner (Wildes) S.; m. Jennifer A. Harrell; children: Eric, Heidi. BS, Ind. U., 1967; JD, Harvard U., 1970. Bar: Calif. 1971, U.S. Supreme Ct. 1980. Assoc. Gibson, Dunn & Crutcher, L.A., 1970-73; sr. v.p., gen. counsel, sec. Tosco Corp., L.A., 1973-83; ptnr. Jones, Day, Reavis & Pogue, L.A., 1983-95, Rogers & Wells, L.A., 1995-97, Morgan Lewis & Bockius, L.A., 1997—. Mem. L.A. World Affairs Inst., 1983—, Town Hall L.A., 1983—. 2nd lt. U.S. Army, 1970-71. Mem. ABA, L.A. Bar Assn., Calif. Bar Assn., Calif. Club, Beach Club (Santa Monica, Calif.), L.A. Country Club. Republican. Episcopalian. Home: 1343 Pavia Pl Pacific Palisades CA 90272-4047 Office: Morgan Lewis & Bockius 300 S Grand Ave Ste 2200 Los Angeles CA 90071-3132 E-mail: rshortz@morganlewis.com

SHOTTS, WAYNE J. nuclear scientist, federal agency administrator; b. Des Plaines, Ill., Mar. 20, 1945; s. Norman Russell Shotts and Winnifred Mae (Averill) Shotts Goeppinger; m. Melinda Maureen Antilla, June 24, 1967 (dec. Feb. 1975); children: Kenneth Wayne Shotts, Jeffrey Alan Shotts; m. Jacquelyn Francyle Willis, Aug. 11, 1979. BA in Physics, U. Calif., Santa Barbara, 1967; PhD, Cornell U., 1973. Rsch. physicist E.I. duPont deNemours & Co., Wilmington, Del., 1973-74; physicist U. Calif., Livermore, Calif., 1974—, Lawrence Livermore (Calif.) Nat. Lab., 1974-79; group leader, thermonuclear design divsn. Lawrence Livermore Nat. Lab., Livermore, Calif., 1979-85, divsn leader, nuclear chemistry, 1985-86, divsn. leader, prompt diagnostics, 1986-88, prin. dep. assoc. dir., military applications, 1988-92, prin. dep. assoc. dir. def. and nuclear techs., 1992-95, assoc. dir. nonproliferation arms control/internat. security, 1995—. Recipient Ernest Orlando Lawrence Meml. award U.S. Dept. Energy, Washington, 1990. Mem. Am. Phys. Soc., Am. Assn. Advancement Sci. Office: Lawrence Livermore Nat Lab PO Box 808 Livermore CA 94551-0808

SHOUP, TERRY EMERSON, university dean, engineering educator; b. Troy, Ohio, July 20, 1944; s. Dale Emerson and Betty Jean (Spoon) S.; m. Betsy Dinsomore, Dec. 18, 1966; children: Jennifer Jean, Matthew David. BME, Ohio State U., 1966, MS, 1967, PhD, 1969. Asst. prof. to assoc. prof. Rutgers U., New Brunswick, N.J., 1969-75; assoc. prof. to prof. U. Houston, 1975-80; asst. dean, prof. Tex. A&M U., College Sta., 1980-83; dean, prof. Fla. Atlantic U., Boca Raton, 1983-89; dean, Sobrato prof. Santa Clara (Calif.) U., 1989—. Cons., software specialist Numerical Methods in Engring. Author: (books) A Practical Guide to Computer Methods for Engineers, 1979, Resheniye Ingenyernikh Zadach NA EVM Prakticheskoye rukovodstvo, 1982, Narichnik Po Izchislitelni Methodi Za Ingeneri, 1983, Numerical Methods for the Personal Computer, 1983, Applied Numerical Methods for the Microcomputer, 1984, (with L.S. Fletcher) Introduction to Engineering with FORTRAN Programming, 1978, Solutions Manual for Introduction to Engineering Including FORTRAN Programming, 1978, Introduccion a la ingenieria Incluyendo programacion FORTRAN, 1980, (with L.S. Fletcher and E.V. Mochel) Introduction to Design with Graphics and Design Projects, 1981, (with S.P. Goldstein and J. Waddell) Information Sources, 1984, (with Carl Hanser Verlag) Numerische Verfahren fur Arbeitsplatzrechner, 1985, (with F. Mistree) Optimization Methods with Applications for Personal Computers, 1987; (software) Numerical Methods for the Personal Computer-Software User's Guide, Version 2, 1983, Optimization Software for the Personal Computer, 1986; editor in chief Mechanism and Machine Theory, 1977—; contbr. more than 100 articles to profl. jours. Fellow ASME (chmn. Design Engring. div. 1987-88, Mech. Engring. div. 1980-81, Centennial medal 1980, Gustus Larson award 1981); mem. Am. Soc. for Engring. Edn. (Dow Outstanding Faculty award 1974, Western Electric award 1984), Fla. Engring. Soc. Home: 440 Galleria Dr Apt 12 San Jose CA 95134-2467 Office: Santa Clara U Coll Engring Office of Dean 500 El Camino Real Santa Clara CA 95053-0001

SHOWALTER, BUCK (WILLIAM NATHANIEL SHOWALTER III), major league baseball team manager; b. DeFuniak Springs, Fla., May 23, 1956; Student, Chipola Jr. Coll., Fla., Miss. State U. Player various minor league teams N.Y. Yankee orgn., 1977-83, minor league coach, 1984, minor league mgr., 1985-89; coach N.Y. Yankees, 1990-91, mgr., 1992-95; with Ariz. Diamondbacks, 1996—. Named N.Y.-Pa. League Mgr. of Yr., 1985, Eastern League Mgr. of Yr., 1989, Am. League Mgr. of Yr., 1994. Office: Arizona Diamondbacks Bank One Ball Park 401 E Jefferson St Phoenix AZ 85004-2438

SHOWS, WINNIE M. speaker, author, consultant; b. L.A., Apr. 2, 1947; d. William Marion Arvin and Joan Catherine (Sperry) Wilson; m. George Albert Shows, Mar. 18, 1967 (div. May 1980); 1 child, Sallic; m. Michael P. Florio, Jan. 1, 1990 (div.). BA in English, UCLA, 1969; MEd, Calif. State U., Long Beach, 1976. Tchr. St. Joseph High Sch., Lakewood, Calif., 1969-71; tchr. high sch. Irvine (Calif) Unified Sch. Dist., 1972-79; freelance writer, 1979-80; mgr. pub. rels. Forth, Inc., Hermosa Beach, Calif., 1980-81; account mgr., account supr., dir. mktg. Franson & Assoc., San Jose, 1981-84; v.p., pres. Smith & Shows, Menlo Park, 1984-96; spkr., author, cons. in field; co-founder Spkrs. in the Mountains. Presenter seminar in field. Author (newsletter) Smith & Shows Letter, 1989-94, Hairbal and Other Poems of Trans Formation, 2000. Vol. Unity Palo Alto (Calif.) Cmty. Ch., 1989-99, Newcomers, Menlo Park, 1990-93, Kara, Palo Alto, 1991-98, Menlo Park Sch. Dist., 1993-95, Asistencia Para Latinos, 2000. Named Woman of Vision, Career Action Ctr., 1994. Mem. Nat. Spkrs. Assn. (treas., Mem. of Yr. No. Calif. chpt. 1999, Mem. of Yr., 1999), SRI Organon Toastmaster of the Yr. 1995, Karl Lind award 1996). Office: 1614 W Kiowa St Colorado Springs CO 80904 E-mail: winnie@wshows.com

SHREEVE, JEAN'NE MARIE, chemist, educator; b. Deer Lodge, Mont., July 2, 1933; d. Charles William and Maryfrances (Briggeman) S. BA in Chemistry, U. Mont., 1953, DSc (hon.), 1982; MS in Analytical Chemistry, U. Minn., 1956; PhD in Inorganic Chemistry, U. Wash., 1961; NSF postdoctoral fellow, U. Cambridge, Eng., 1967-68. Asst. prof. chemistry U. Idaho, Moscow, 1961-65, assoc. prof., 1965-67, prof., 1967-73, 2000—, acting chmn. dept. chemistry, 1969-70, 1973, head dept. and prof., 1973 87, v.p. rsch. and grad. studies, prof. chemistry, 1987-99. Lucy W. Pickett lectr. Mt. Holyoke Coll., 1976, George H. Cady lectr. U. Wash., 1993; mem. Nat. Com. Standards in Higher Edn., 1965-67, 69-73. Mem. editl. bd. Jour. Fluorine Chemistry, 1970—, Jour. Heteroatom Chemistry, 1988-95, Accounts Chem. Rsch., 1973-75, Inorganic Synthesis, 1976—; contbr. articles to sci. jours. Mem. bd. govs. Argonne (Ill.) Nat. Lab., 1992-98. Recipient Disting. Alumni award U. Mont., 1970; named Hon. Alumnus, U. Idaho, 1972; recipient Outstanding Achievement award U. Minn., 1975, Sr. U.S. Scientist award Alexander Von Humboldt Found., 1978, Excellence in Teaching award Chem. Mfrs. Assn., 1980; U.S. hon. Ramsay fellow, 1967-68, Alfred P. Sloan fellow, 1970-72. Mem. AAAS (bd. dirs. 1991-95), AAUW (officer Moscow chpt. 1962-69), Am. Chem. Soc. (bd. dirs. 1985-93, chmn. fluorine divsn. 1979-81, Petroleum Rsch. Fund adv. bd. 1975-77, women chemists com. 1972-77, Fluorine award 1978, Garvan medal 1972, Harry and Carol Mosher award Santa Clara Valley sect. 1992), Göttingen (Germany) Acad. Scis. (corr. mem.), Idaho Acad. Sci. (Disting. Scientist 2001), Phi Beta Kappa. Avocations: fishing, gardening. Office: U Idaho Dept Chemistry Moscow ID 83844-2343 Fax: 208-885-9146. E-mail: jshreeve@uidaho.edu

SHREVE, THEODORE NORRIS, construction company executive; b. St. Louis, Feb. 14, 1919; s. Truxtun Benbridge adn Beulah (Dyer) S.; m. Caroline Prouty, Jan. 7, 1943; children: Sara Ann Caile, Suzanne Shreve Foster, Theo Carol. BS, U. Colo., 1942. Registered profl. engr., Colo. Sec., treas. Trautman & Shreve, Inc., Denver, 1946-68, pres., 1965-86, chmn. bd., 1984—; pres. 4030 Corp., Denver, 1984—. Bd. dirs. Colo. U. Found., 1988—; rep. Country Assembly, 1962. Served with USNR, 1942-45. Mem. Colo. Soc. Profl. Engrs., Rotary, Gyro Club, Denver Country Club, Sigma Phi Epsilon. Republican. Episcopalian. Home: 420 S Marion Pkwy Apt 1403 Denver CO 80209-2549 Office: Trautman & Shreve 4406 Race St Denver CO 80216-3818 E-mail: tshreve333@aol.com

SHRIVER, MARIA OWINGS, news correspondent; b. Chgo., Nov. 6, 1955; d. Robert Sargent and Eunice Mary (Kennedy) S.; m. Arnold Schwarzenegger, Apr. 26, 1986; children: Katherine Eunice, Christina Aurelia, Patrick. BA, Georgetown U. Coll. Am. Studies, Washington, 1977. News producer Sta. KYW-TV, 1977-78; producer Sta. WJZ-TV, 1978-80; nat. reporter PM Mag., 1981-83; news reporter CBS News, Los Angeles, 1983-85; news correspondent, co-anchor CBS Morning News, N.Y.C., 1985-86; co-host Sunday Today, NBC, 1987-90; anchor Main Street, NBC, 1987; co-anchor Yesterday, Today, and Tomorrow, NBC, 1989; anchor NBC Nightly News Weekend Edition, 1989-90, Cutting Edge with Maria Shriver, NBC, 1990, First Person with Maria Shriver, NBC, 1991—. Co-anchor summer olympics, Seoul, Korea, 1988; substitute anchor NBC News at Sunrise, Today, NBC Nightly News with Tom Brokaw; contbg. anchor Dateline, NBC. Appeared in Last Action Hero, 1993; correspondent

TV series The American Parade, 1984. Recipient Christopher award for "Fatal Addictions", 1990, Exceptional Merit Media award Nat. Women's Political Caucus, first-place Commendation award Am. Women in Radio and TV, 1991, Emmy nomination. Democrat. Roman Catholic. Office: NBC News First Person with Maria Shriver 3000 W Alameda Ave Burbank CA 91523-0002

SHRONTZ, FRANK ANDERSON, airplane manufacturing executive; b. Boise, Idaho, Dec. 14, 1931; s. Thurlyn Howard and Florence Elizabeth (Anderson) S.; m. Harriet Ann Houghton, June 12, 1954; children: Craig Howard, Richard Whitaker, David Anderson. Student, George Washington U., 1953; LLB, U. Idaho, 1954; MBA, Harvard U., 1958; postgrad., Stanford U., 1969-70. Asst. contracts coordinator Boeing Co., Seattle, 1958-65, asst. dir. contract adminstrn., 1965-67, asst. to v.p. comml. airplane group, 1967-69, asst. dir. new airplane program, 1969-70, dir. comml. sales operations, 1970-73, v.p. planning and contracts, 1977-78; asst. sec. Dept. Air Force, Washington, 1973-76, Dept. Def., Washington, 1976-77; v.p., gen. mgr. 707/727/737 div. Boeing Comml. Airplane Co., Seattle, 1978-82, v.p. sales and mktg., 1982-84, pres., 1985-86; pres., chief exec. officer The Boeing Co., Seattle, 1986-96, chmn., 1988-97, chmn. emeritus, 1997—. Bd. dirs. Boise Cascade Corp., 3M Co., Chevron; mem. Boeing bd., 1985-97. Regent Smithsonian Instn. 1st lt. AUS, 1954-56. Mem. Phi Alpha Delta, Beta Theta Pi. Clubs: Overlake Golf and Country, Columbia Tower. Office: The Boeing Co PO Box 3707 Seattle WA 98124-2207

SHROPSHIRE, DONALD GRAY, hospital executive; b. Winston-Salem, N.C., Aug. 6, 1927; s. John Lee and Bess L. (Shouse) S.; m. Mary Ruth Bodenheimer, Aug. 19, 1950; children: Melanie Shropshire David, John Devin. B.S., U. N.C., 1950; Erickson fellow postgrad., U. Chgo., 1958-59; LLD (hon.), U. Ariz., 1992; EdD (hon.), Tucson U., 1994. Personnel asst. Nat. Biscuit Co., Atlanta, 1950-52, asst. personnel mgr. Chgo., 1952-54; adminstr. Eastern State Hosp., Lexington, Ky., 1954-62; assoc. dir. U. Md. Hosp., Balt., 1962-67; adminstr. Tucson Med. Ctr., 1967-82, pres., 1982-92, pres. emeritus, 1992—, bd. dirs., 1995; pres. Tucson Hosps. Med. Edn. Program, 1970-71, sec., 1971-86; pres. So. Ariz. Hosp. Council, 1968-69; bd. dirs. Ariz. Blue Cross, 1967-76, chmn. provider standards com., 1972-76; chmn. Healthways Inc., 1985-92. Mem. bd. La Posada at Park Centre, Inc., Green Valley, Ariz., 1996-2000, chmn. bd., 1996-99, mem. emeritus, 2000—. Bd. dirs. Health Planning Coun. Tucson, mem. exec. com., 1969-74; chmn. profl. divsn. United Way, Tucson, 1969-70, vice chmn. campaign, 1988, Ariz. Health Faciltities Authority, bd. dirs., 1992—; chmn. dietary svcs. com., vice chmn., 1988, Md. Hosp. Coun., 1966-67; bd. dirs. Ky. Hosp. Assn., 1961-62, chmn. coun. profl. practice, 1960-61; past pres. Blue Grass Hosp. Coun.; trustee Assn. Western Hosps., 1974-81, pres., 1979-80; mem. accreditation Coun. for Continuing Med. Edn., 1982-87, chair, 1986; bd. govs. Pima C.C., 1970-76, sec., 1973-74, chmn., 1975-76, bd. dirs. Found., 1978-82, Ariz. Bd. Regents, 1982-90, sec., 1983-86, pres., 1987-88; mem. Tucson Airport Authority, 1987—, bd. dirs., 1990-95, pres., 1995; v.p. Tucson Econ. Devel. Corp., 1977-82; bd. dirs. Vol. Hosps. Am., 1977-88, treas., 1979-82; mem. Ariz. Adv. Health Coun. Dirs., 1976-78; bd. dirs. Tucson Tomorrow, 1983-87, Tucson Downtown Devel. Corp., 1988-95, Rincon Inst., 1992-97, Sonoran Inst., 1992-97; dir. Mus. No. Ariz., 1988—; nat. bd. advisors Coll. Bus. U. Ariz., 1990—, mem. Dean's Bd. Coll. Fine Arts, 1992—, chmn., 1992-96, pres. Ariz. Coun. Econ. Edn., 1993-95; vis. panel Sch. Health Adminstrn. and Policy Ariz. State U., 1990-92; bd. dirs. Cmty. Found. So. Ariz., 1996-2001; mem. adv. bd. Steele Meml. Rsch. Ctr., U. Ariz. Coll. Medicine, 1996—. Named to Hon. Order Ky. Cols.; named Tucson Man of Yr. 1987, Tucson Father of Yr. 1997; recipient Disting. Svc. award Anti-Defamation League B'nai B'rith, 1989. Mem. Am. Hosp. Assn. (nominating com. 1983-86, trustee 1975-78, ho. dels. 1972-78, chmn. coun. profl. svc. 1973-74, regional adv. bd. 1969-78, chmn. joint com. with NASW 1963-64, Disting. Svc. award 1989), Ariz. Hosp. Assn. (Salisbury award 1982, bd. dirs. 1967-72, pres. 1970-71), Ariz. C. of C. (bd. dirs. 1988-93), Assn. Am. Med. Colls. (mem. assembly 1974-77), Tucson C. of C. (bd. dirs. 1968-69), United Comml. Travelers, Nat. League for Nursing, Ariz. Town Hall (bd. dirs. 1982-92, chmn. 1990-92, treas. 1985), Pima County Acad. Decathlon Assn. (dir. 1983-85), The Rotary Club of Tucson (pres. 1993-94), U. Ariz. Alumni Assn. Coll. Nursing (hon. alumnus 1998). Baptist (ch. moderator, chmn. finance com., deacon, ch. sch. supt., trustee, bd. dirs. ch. found.) Home: 6734 N Chapultepec Cir Tucson AZ 85750-1001 Office: Tucson Med Ctr 5301 E Grant Rd Tucson AZ 85712-2805

SHU, FRANK HSIA-SAN, astronomy educator, researcher, writer; b. Kunming, China, June 2, 1943; came to U.S., 1949; s. Shien-Siu and Irene I-Jen (Hsia) S.; m. Helen Chien-Ping Pu, June 22, 1968 B.S. in Physics, MIT, 1963; Ph.D. in Astronomy, Harvard U., 1968. Asst. prof. SUNY-Stony Brook, 1968-71, assoc. prof., 1971-73, U. Calif.-Berkeley, 1973-76, prof. astronomy, 1976—, chmn. dept. astronomy, 1984-96, chancellor's prof. astronomy, 1996—, univ. prof., 1998—. Research assoc. MIT, Cambridge, 1968, sr. research assoc., 1971; vis. scientist Kapteyn Astron. Lab., Groningen, The Netherlands, 1973; mem. Inst. Advanced Study, Princeton, N.J., 1982 Author: The Physical Universe, 1982; also numerous sci. and popular articles Pamphlet writer McGovern Campaign, Suffolk County, N.Y., 1972 Recipient Bok prize Harvard U., 1972, Dirk Brouwer award, 1996; Sloan research fellow, 1972-74 Mem. AAAS, Internat. Astron. Union, Am. Astron. Soc. (councilor 1982-85, Warner prize 1977), Astron. Soc. of Pacific (bd. dirs. 1985-86), Sigma Xi Democrat Avocations: chess; poker; bridge; sports; wine and food. Office: U Calif Berkeley Dept Astronomy 601 Campbell Hall Berkeley CA 94720-3411

SHUBB, WILLIAM BARNET, judge; b. Oakland, Calif., May 28, 1938; s. Ben and Nellie Bernice (Fruechtenicht) S.; m. Sandra Ann Talarico, July 29, 1962; children: Alisa Marie, Carissa Ann, Victoria Ann. AB, U. Calif., Berkeley, 1960, JD, 1963. Bar: Calif., 1964, U.S. Ct. Internat. Trade 1981, U.S. Customs Ct. (1980, U.S. Ct. Appeals (9th cir.) 1964, U.S. Supreme Ct. 1972. Law clk. U.S. Dist. Ct., Sacramento, 1963-65; asst. U.S. atty., Sacramento, 1965-71; chief asst. U.S. atty. (ea. dist.) Calif., 1971-74; assoc. Diepenbrock, Wulff, Plant & Hannegan, Sacramento, 1974-77, ptnr., 1977-80, 81-90; U.S. atty. Eastern Dist. Calif., 1980-81; judge U.S. Dist. Ct. (ea. dist.) Calif., 1990-96, sr. judge, 1996—; chmn. com. drafting of local criminal rules U.S. Dist. Ct. (ea. dist.) Calif., 1974, mem. speedy trial planning com., 1974-80; lawyer rep. 9th Cir. U.S. Jud. Conf., 1975-78; mem. faculty Fed. Practice Inst., 1978-80; instr. McGeorge Sch. Law, U. Pacific, 1964-66. Mem. ABA, Fed. Bar Assn. (pres. Sacramento chpt. 1977), Calif. Bar Assn., Assn. Def. Counsel, Am. Bd. Trial Advs., Sacramento County Bar Council.

SHUBERT, GUSTAVE HARRY, research executive, consultant, social scientist; b. Buffalo, Jan. 18, 1929; s. Gustave Henri and Ada Shubert (Smith) S.; m. Rhea Brickman, Mar. 29, 1952; children: Wendy J., David L. BA, Yale U., 1948; MA, NYU, 1951. Staff mem. Lincoln Lab., MIT, 1955-57; adminstr. sys. engring. Hycon Ea., Inc., Paris, 1957-59; with RAND Corp., Santa Monica, Calif., 1959—, corp. v.p. domestic programs, 1968-75, sr. corp. v.p. domestic programs, 1975-78, sr. corp. v.p., 1978-89, trustee, 1973-89, sr. fellow, corp. advisor and adv. trustee, 1989—; founding dir. Inst. Civil Justice, 1979-87; trustee mutual funds Neuberger Berman, N.Y.C., 1989—. Cons. Keene Corp., N.Y.C., 1990-92; pres. N.Y.C. Rand Inst., 1972-73, trustee, 1972-79; trustee Housing Allowance Offices Brown County, Wis. and South Bend, Ind., 1973-80; mem. adv. coun. Sch. Engring., Stanford U., 1976-79; mem. policy adv. com. clin. scholars program UCLA, 1975-88; mem. adv. group evaluation and methodology divsn. GAO, 1986-96; mem. adv. commn. on professionalism ABA, 1985-87; mem. Calif. jud. system com. Los Angeles County Bar Assn., 1984-85; mem. com. on evaluation of poverty rsch. NAS. Mem. Pacific Coun. of Fgn. Affairs, 1991; mem. U.S. adv. com. Internat. Inst. Applied Sys. Analysis, 1998—; mem. history dept. adv. bd. Carnegie Mellon U., 1995—. With USAF, 1951-55. Decorated Air medal with 3 oak leaf clusters, Commendation medal. Mem. AAAS, Am. Judicature Soc. (bd. dirs. 1987-90), Inst. Strategic Studies (London), Coun. of Fgn. Rels. Home: 13838 W Sunset Blvd Pacific Palisades CA 90272-4022 Office: RAND Corp 1700 Main St Santa Monica CA 90401-3297 E-mail: shubert@rand.org

SHUER, LAWRENCE MENDEL, neurosurgery educator; b. Toledo, Apr. 12, 1954; s. Bernard Benjamin and Estelle Rose (Drukker) S.; m. Paula Ann Elliott, Sept. 4, 1976; children: Jenna, Tammy, Nichole. BA with high distinction, U. Mich., 1975, MD cum laude, 1978. Diplomate Am. Bd. Neurol. Surgery, Nat. Bd. Med. Examiners. Fellow in neurology Inst. Neurology, London, 1979; intern in surgery Stanford (Calif.) U. Sch. Medicine, 1978-79, resident in neuropathology, 1980, resident in neurosurgery, 1980-84, clin. asst. prof. surgery and neurosurgery, 1984-90, assoc. prof., 1990—, acting chmn. dept. neurosurgery, 1992-95, 96—, assoc. dean, 1996—, chief of staff Stanford Health Sys., 1996—; chief of staff Stanford U. Hosp. and Clinics, 1971-96. Numerous presentations in field. Contbr. articles and abstracts to med. jours., chpts. to books. Recipient Kaiser tchr. award Stanford U., 1993; James B. Angell scholar. Mem. AMA, Am. Assn. Neurol. Surgeons, Congress Neurol. Surgeons, Western Neurosurg. Soc., Calif. Assn. Neurol. Surgeons (bd. dirs., treas. 1995—), Calif. Med. Assn., Am. Heart Assn. (fellow stroke coun.), Santa Clara County Med. Assn., San Francisco Neurol. Soc., Alpha Omega Alpha. Avocations: skiing, swimming, travel. Office: Stanford U Med Ctr 300 Pasteur Dr R229 Palo Alto CA 94304-2203 E-mail: lshuer@stanford.edu

SHUGART, ALAN F. retired electronic computing equipment company executive; b. L.A., Sept. 27, 1930; BS in Engring. and Physics, U. Redlands, 1951. Dir. engring. IBM, San Jose, Calif., 1952-69; v.p. Memorex Corp., Sunnyvale, 1969-73; pres. Shugart Assocs., 1973-78; chmn., pres., chief exec. officer, coo Seagate Tech., Scotts Valley, Calif., 1978-98, also bd. dirs. Office: c/o Seagate Tech 920 Disc Dr Scotts Valley CA 95066-4544

SHUGART, HOWARD ALAN, physicist, educator; b. Orange, Calif., Sept. 21, 1931; s. Howard Ancil and Bertha Elizabeth (Henderson) S.; m. Elizabeth L. Hanson, Feb. 6, 1971. B.S., Calif. Inst. Tech., 1953; M.A., U. Calif.-Berkeley, 1955, Ph.D., 1957. Teaching asst. physics U. Calif.-Berkeley, 1953-56, assoc., 1957, lectr., 1957-58, acting asst. prof., 1958-59, asst. prof., 1959-63, assoc. prof., 1963-67, prof., 1967-93, prof. emeritus, 1993—, vice chmn. 1968-70, 79-87, 89-2001, acting chmn., summer 1979, 80, 81, 83, 84,87; atomic beam group leader Lawrence Berkeley Lab. Lawrence Berkeley Nat. Lab., 1965-79. Cons. Convair divsn. Gen. Dynamics Corp., 1960-61; mem. com. nuclear constants NRC, 1960-63. Recipient Donald Sterling Noyce prize for excellence in undergrad. tchg. U. Calif., 1988, Berkeley citation, 1993. Fellow Am. Phys. Soc. (acting sec. Pacific Coast 1961-64, exec. com. div. electron and atomic physics 1972-74), Nat. Speleological Soc. (gov. 1954-56); mem. Sigma Xi. Office: U Calif Dept Physics Berkeley CA 94720-7300

SHULER, KURT EGON, chemist, educator; b. Nuremberg, Germany, July 10, 1922; came to U.S., 1937, naturalized, 1944; s. Louis and Donie (Wald) Schulherr; m. Beatrice Gwyn London, Nov. 11, 1944. BS, Ga. Inst. Tech., 1942; PhD, Cath. U. Am., 1949. Fellow Johns Hopkins U., 1949-51; sr. staff mem., asst. group supr., chem. physics group Applied Physics Lab., Johns Hopkins, 1951-55; supervisory phys. chemist Nat. Bur. Standards, 1955-58, cons. to dir., 1958-61, asst. dir., sr. research fellow, 1963-68; rsch. staff, sci. adviser to v.p. rsch. Gen. Motors Corp., 1958; spl. asst. to dir. rsch. Inst. Def. Analyses, 1961-63; vis. prof. chemistry U. Calif., San Diego, 1966-67, prof. chemistry, 1968-91, prof. emeritus, 1991—, chmn. dept., 1968-70, 84-87. Cons. in field; mem. Solvay Conf., 1962, 78; mem. adv. panel, chemistry div. NSF, 1973-75. Author, editor tech. books; assoc. editor: Jour. Math. Physics, 1963-66; bd. editors: Jour. Statis. Physics, 1968-80; mem. adv. bd.: Chem. Engring. News, 1967-70; contbr. articles to profl. jours. Served with U.S. Army, 1944-46. Recipient Distinguished Service award Nat. Bur. Standards, 1959, Gold medal award Dept. Commerce, 1968; Solvay Found. fellow, 1975 Fellow Am. Inst. Chemists, AAAS, Am. Phys. Soc., Washington Acad. Sci.; mem. Am. Chem. Soc., Washington Philos. Soc. Club: Rancho Santa Fe Golf Home: PO Box 1504 Rancho Santa Fe CA 92067-1504 Office: Univ Calif San Diego Dept Chemistry La Jolla CA 92093

SHULL, HARRISON, chemist, educator; b. Princeton, N.J., Aug. 17, 1923; s. George Harrison and Mary (Nicholl) S.; m. Jeanne Louise Johnson, 1948 (div. 1962); children: James Robert (dec.), Kathy, George Harrison, Holly; m. Wil Joyce Bentley Long, 1962; children: Warren Michael Long, Jeffery Mark Long, Stanley Martin, Sarah Ellen. A.B., Princeton U., 1943; Ph.D., U. Calif. at Berkeley, 1948. Assoc. chemist U.S. Naval Research Lab., 1943-45; asst. prof. Iowa State U., 1949-54; mem. faculty Ind. U., 1955-79, research prof., 1961-79, dean Grad. Sch., 1965-72, vice chancellor for research and devel., 1972-76, dir. Research Computing Center, 1959-63, acting chmn. chemistry dept., 1965-66, acting dean arts and scis., 1969-70, acting dean faculties, 1974; mem. faculty, provost, v.p. acad. affairs Rensselaer Poly. Inst., 1979-82; chancellor U. Colo., Boulder, 1982-85, prof. dept. chemistry, 1982-88; provost Naval Postgrad. Sch., 1988-95; asst. dir. rsch., quantum chemistry group Uppsala (Sweden) U., 1958-59; vis. prof. Washington U., St. Louis, 1960, U. Colo., 1963; founder, supr. Quantum Chemistry Program Exchange, 1962-79; chmn. subcom. molecular structure and spectroscopy NRC, 1958-63; chmn. Fulbright selection com. chemistry, 1963-67; mem. adv. com. Office Sci. Personnel, 1957-60; chmn. First Gordon Research Conf. Theoretical Chemistry, 1962; mem. com. survey chemistry Nat. Acad. Sci., 1964-65; mem. adv. panel chemistry NSF, 1964-67; mem. adv. panel Office Computer Activities, 1967-70, cons. chem. information program, 1965-71, mem. adv. com. for research, 1974-76; mem. vis. com. chemistry Brookhaven Nat. Lab., 1967-70; mem. adv. com. Chem. Abstracts Service, 1971-74. Dir. Storage Tech. Corp., 1983-99; chief of Naval Ops. Exec. Panel, 1984-88. Assoc. editor: Jour. Chem. Physics, 1952-54; editorial adv. bd.: Spectrochimica Acta, 1957-63, Internat. Jour. Quantum Chemistry, 1967— , Proc. NAS, 1976-81; contbr. articles to profl. jours. Trustee Argonne U. Assn., 1970-75, Asso. Univs., Inc., 1973-76, U. Rsch. Assn., 1984-89, Inst. Defense Analysis, 1984-96. Served as ensign USNR, 1945. NRC postdoctoral fellow phys. scis. U. Chgo., 1948-49; Guggenheim fellow U. Uppsala, 1954-55; NSF sr. postdoctoral fellow, 1968-69; Sloan research fellow, 1956-58 Fellow Am. Acad. Arts and Scis. (v.p. 1976-83, chmn. Midwest Ctr. 1976-79), Am. Phys. Soc.; mem. AAAS, Nat. Acad. Scis. (com. on sci. and pub. policy 1969-72, coun., exec. com. 1971-74, chmn. U.S.-USSR sci. policy subgroup for fundamental rsch. 1973-81, naval studies bd. 1974-79, 96—, chmn. Commn. on Human Resources, 1977-81, nominating com. 1978), Am. Chem. Soc., Royal Swedish Acad. Scis. (fgn. mem.), Royal Acad. Arts and Scis. Uppsala (corr. mem.), Cosmos Club (Washington), Old Capital Club (Monterey), Phi Beta Kappa, Sigma Xi, Phi Lambda Upsilon. Office: Naval Postgrad Sch Monterey CA 93943

SHULMAN, LEE S. foundation executive; b. Chgo., Sept. 28, 1938; BA, MA, U. Chgo., 1959, PhD, 1963; hon. doctorate, U. Judaism, 1989, Hebrew Union Coll., 1995, Mich. State U., 1996, Drury Coll., 1999, U. Aveiro Portugal, 1999, So. Ill. U., 2001. Prof. ednl. psychology and med. edn. Mich. State U., 1968-82; prof. edn. and psychology Stanford (Calif.) U., 1982-98; pres. Carnegie Found. for the Advancement of Tchg., Menlo Park, Calif., 1997—. Office: 555 Middlefield Rd Menlo Park CA 94025-3443

SHULTZ, GEORGE PRATT, former government executive, economics educator; b. N.Y.C., Dec. 13, 1920; s. Birl E. and Margaret Lennox (Pratt) S.; children: Margaret Ann Shultz Tilsworth, Kathleen Pratt Shultz Jorgensen, Peter Milton, Barbara Lennox Shultz White, Alexander George; m. Charlotte Mailliard, Aug. 15, 1997. BA in Econs., Princeton U., 1942; PhD in Indsl. Econs., MIT, 1949; Hon. degree, Yeshiva U., U. Tel Aviv, Technion-Israel Inst. Tech., Keio U., Tokyo, Brandeis U., U. Notre Dame, Princeton U., Loyola U., U. Pa., U. Rochester, Carnegie-Mellon U., Baruch Coll., Northwestern U., Tblisi State U.; Hon. degree , Columbia U. Mem. faculty M.I.T., 1949-57; assoc. prof. indsl. relations MIT, 1955-57; prof. indsl. relations Grad. Sch. Bus., U. Chgo., 1957-68; dean sch. Grad. Sch. Bus. U. Chgo., 1962-68, fellow Ctr. for Advanced Study in Behavioral Scis., 1968-69; U.S. sec. labor, 1969-70; dir. Office Mgmt. and Budget, 1970-72; U.S. sec. treasury, also asst. to Pres., 1972-74; chmn. Council on Econ. Policy, East-West Trade Policy com.; exec. v.p. Bechtel Corp., San Francisco, 1974-75, pres., 1975-81, vice chmn., 1977-81; also dir.; pres. Bechtel Group, Inc., 1981-82; prof. mgmt. and pub. policy Stanford U., 1974-82, prof. internat. econs., 1989-91, prof. emeritus, 1991—; chmn. Pres. Reagan's Econ. Policy Adv. Bd., 1981-82; U.S. sec. of state, 1982-89; disting. fellow Hoover Instn., Stanford, 1989—. Bd. dirs. Charles Schwab & Co., Bechtel Group, Inc., Infrastructureworld; mem. GM Corp. Adv. Coun., Gilead Scis. Bd., Unext.COM Bd.; chmn. J.P. Morgan Internat. Coun.; chmn. adv. coun. Inst. Internat. Studies, 1990-98, Calif. Gov.'s Econ. Policy Adv. Bd., 1995-98, Bechtel Group Inc. Author: Pressures on Wage Decisions, 1951, (with Charles A. Myers) The Dynamics of a Labor Market, 1951, (with John R. Coleman) Labor Problems: Cases and Readings, 1953, (with T.L. Whisler) Management Organization and the Computer, 1960, (with Arnold R. Weber) Strategies for the Displaced Worker, 1966, (with Robert Z. Aliber) Guidelines, Informal Controls and the Market Place, 1966, (with Albert Rees) Workers and Wages in the Urban Labor Market, 1970, Leaders and Followers in an Age of Ambiguity, 1975, (with Kenneth W. Dam) Economic Policy Beyond the Headlines, 1977, 2d edition, 1998, Turmoil and Triumph: My Years as Secetary of State, 1993; also articles, chpts. in books, reports, and essays. Served to capt. USMCR, 1942-45. Recipient medal of Freedom, 1989. Mem. Am. Econ. Assn., Indsl. Relations Research Assn. (pres. 1968), Nat. Acad. Arbitrators. Office: Stanford U Hoover Instn Stanford CA 94305-6010

SHULTZ, JOHN DAVID, lawyer; b. L.A., Oct. 9, 1939; s. Edward Patterson and Jane Elizabeth (Taylor) Schultz; m. Joanne Person, June 22, 1968; children: David Taylor Schultz, Steven Matthew Schultz. Student, Harvard Coll., 1960—61; BA, U. Ariz., 1964; JD, Boalt Hall, U. Calif., Berkeley, 1967. Bar: N.Y. 1968, Calif. 1978. Assoc. Cadwalader, Wickersham & Taft, N.Y.C., 1968—77; ptnr. Lawler, Felix & Hall, L.A., 1977—83, mem. exec. com., chmn. planning com., co-chmn. recruiting and hiring com.; ptnr. Morgan, Lewis & Bockius, L.A., 1983—, chmn. mgmt. com., mem. lateral entry com., chmn. profl. evaluation com., chmn. practice devel. com., chmn. recruiting com. Mem. adv. bd. Internat. and Comparative Law Ctr., Southwestern Legal Found., 1981—; active Practicing Law Inst. Adv. Bd., Corp. and Securities Law, 1992—; Trustee St. Thomas Ch., N.Y.C., 1969—72, Shore Acres Point Corp., Mamaroneck, NY, 1975—77. Mem.: Jonathan Club (L.A.), Phi Delta Phi, Sigma Chi, ABA, Assn. Bar City of N.Y., State Bar Calif., N.Y. State Bar Assn. Episcopalian. Office: Morgan Lewis & Bockius LLP 300 S Grand Ave Ste 22 Los Angeles CA 90071-3109

SHUMAN, THOMAS ALAN, protective services official, consultant; b. Fairmont, W.Va., Dec. 31, 1946; BA, N.Mex. State U., 1969, 73; postgrad., U. N.Mex., 1988. Mgr. Drum Appliance, Inc., Las Cruces, N.Mex., 1971-75; classification supr. N.Mex. Corrections Dept., Santa Fe, 1976-80, mgmt. analyst supr., 1981-83, dir. classification, 1983-84, dep. sec., 1984-87; pres. Correctional Data Systems, Santa Fe, 1987—; owner Desktop Publ. Co., Santa Fe, 1988—; dir. N.Mex. Corrections Tng. Acad., 1991-95, probation, parole dir., 1995—; pres. Silicon Wizard Corp., 1989—. Cons. Nat. Inst. Corrections, Washington, 1988, Am. Correctional Assn., Md., 1987—. Mem. Smithsonian Inst., U.S. Naval Inst. Served to lt. U.S. Army, 1969-71, Vietnam. Decorated Bronze Star, Presdl. Commendation. Mem. NRA, N.Mex. State U. Alumni Assn. Republican. Presbyterian. Avocations: fishing, painting, photography, writing. E-mail: talans@aol.com

SHUMWAY, NORMAN EDWARD, surgeon, educator; b. Kalamazoo, 1923; M.D., Vanderbilt U., 1949; Ph.D. in Surgery, U. Minn., 1956. Diplomate: Am. Bd. Surgery, Am. Bd. Thoracic Surgery. Intern U. Minn. Hosps., 1949-50, med. fellow surgery, 1950-51, 53-54, Nat. Heart Inst. research fellow, 1954-56, Nat. Heart Inst. spl. trainee, 1956-57; mem. surg. staff Stanford U. Hosps., 1958—, asst. prof. surgery, 1959-61, assoc. prof., 1961-65, prof., 1965—, head div. cardiovascular surgery Sch. Medicine, 1974—; Frances and Charles D. Field prof. Stanford U., 1976-2000, prof. emeritus, 2000—. Served to capt. USAF, 1951-53. Mem. AMA, Soc. Univ. Surgeons, Am. Assn. Thoracic Surgery, Am. Coll. Cardiology, Transplantation Soc., Samson Thoracic Surg. Soc., Soc. for Vascular Surgery, Alpha Omega Alpha Office: Stanford U Med Ctr Dept Cardiovascular Surgery CVRB Upper Level N Stanford CA 94305-5407

SHURTLEFF, AKIKO AOYAGI, artist, consultant; b. Tokyo, Jan. 24, 1950; d. Kinjiro and Fumiyo (Sugata) Aoyagi; m. William Roy Shurtleff, Mar. 10, 1977 (div. 1995); 1 child, Joseph Aoyagi. Grad., Women's Coll. Art, Tokyo, 1971; student, Acad. Art, San Francisco, 1991-92. Fashion designer, illustrator Marimura Co. and Hayakawa Shoji, Inc., Tokyo, 1970-72; co-founder, art dir. Soyfoods Ctr. consulting svcs., Lafayette, Calif., 1976-94; freelance illustrator, graphic designer. Lectr. U.S. Internat. Christian U., Tokyo, 1977, Japanese Tofu Mfrs. Conv., Osaka, 1978; presenter cooking demonstrations, tchr. cooking classes. Co-author, illustrator: The Book of Tofu, 1975, The Book of Miso, 1975, The Book of Kudzu, 1977, Tofu and Soymilk Prodduction, 1979, The Book of Tempeh, 1979, Miso Production, 1979, Tempeh Production, 1980; illustrator: Spirulina (L. Switzer), 1982, The Book of Shiatsu-The Healing Art of Finger Pressure (S. Goodman), 1990, Staying Healthy with Nutrition (E. Haas), 1992, Culinary Treasures of Japan (by John and Jan Belleme), 1992, Yookoso, An Invitation to Contemporary Japanese, Vols. 1 and 2 (Hasu-Hiko Tohsaku), 1994-95, Blue Collar and Beyond (Yana Parker), 1995, Damn Good Ready to Go Resumes, 1995, Homework (Peter Jeswald), 1995, Vegetarian's A to Z Guide to Fruits and Vegetables (Kathleen Robinson with Pete Luckett), 1996, Hubert Keller's Cuisine, 1996, Doctor Generic Will See You Now (Oscar London), 1996, Everyday Pediatrics for Parents (Elmer R. Grossman, M.D.), 1996, Angels in My Kitchen-Devine Dessert Recipes (Caryl Westwood), 1997. Avocations: walking, designing cpmpany logos, running, dancing. Office: PO Box 443 Lafayette CA 94549-0443 E-mail: akiko1717@aol.com

SHURTLEFF, MARK L. state attorney general; BA, Brigham Young U.; JD, U. Utah. Officer, atty. JAG USN, 1985—90; pvt. practice in law Calif., 1990—93; asst. atty. gen. State of Utah, 1993—97; dep. county atty. Salt Lake County, 1997—98; commr. Salt Lake County Commn., 1999—2000, chmn., 2000; atty. gen. State of Utah, 2001—. Leader Boy Scout troops, 1980—; anti-drug lectr., at-risk youth mentor. Office: State Capitol Bldg Rm 236 Salt Lake City UT 84114*

SHURTLIFF, MARVIN KARL, lawyer; b. Idaho Falls, Idaho, Nov. 6, 1930; s. Noah Leon and Melba Dorothy (Hunting) S.; m. Peggy L. Griffin Nov. 23, 1963; 1 dau., Jennifer Karyl. B.A., Idaho State Coll., 1962; J.D., U. Idaho, 1968. Bar: Idaho 1968. Tchr. pub. schs., Jefferson County, Idaho, 1964-65; atty. U.S. Dept. Justice, Washington, 1968-74; commr. Idaho Pub.

Utilities Commn., 1974-75, pres., 1975-76; spl. asst., legal counsel Gov. of Idaho, Boise, 1977; U.S. atty. for Dist. of Idaho, Boise, 1977-81; practice law Boise, 1981—. Mem. Idaho Ho. of Reps., 1962-64 Mem. Idaho State Bd. Edn., 1990-95. Mem. Idaho Bar Assn. Democrat. Home: 62 Horizon Dr Boise ID 83702-4419 Office: PO Box 1652 Boise ID 83701-1652

SHUSTER, ALVIN, journalist, newspaper editor; b. Washington, Jan. 25, 1930; s. Fred and Dora (Levy) S.; m. Miriam Schwartz, June 22, 1952; children: Fred, Jessica, Beth. AB, George Washington U., 1951. Reporter Washington Bur. N.Y. Times, 1952-61, asst. news editor, 1961-66, reporter London Bur., 1967-70; bur. chief Saigon, Vietnam, 1970-71, London, 1971-75, Rome, 1975-77; dep. editor editorial pages L.A. Times, 1977-83, fgn. editor, 1983-95, sr. consulting editor, 1995—. Pres. Fgn. Corrs. Assn., London, 1973-74; trustee Monterey (Calif.) Inst. Internat. Studies, 1983-99; chmn. Pulitzer Prize Jury Internat. Reporting, 1999. Editor: The Witnesses, 1964, Washington: The New York Times Guide to the Nations' Capital, 1967, International Press Institute Report, 1995—; contbg. author: The Kennedy Years, 1964; contbg. editor Columbia Journalism Rev., 1999—. Nieman fellow Harvard U., 1966-67. Mem. Reform Club (London). Office: Los Angeles Times Times Mirror Sq Los Angeles CA 90053

SHUSTER, DIANA, artistic director; Artistic dir. Am. Musical Theatre of San Jose, Calif. Office: Am Musical Theatre 1717 Technology Dr San Jose CA 95110-1305

SHUSTERMAN, NEAL DOUGLAS, writer, screenwriter; b. N.Y.C., Nov. 12, 1962; s. Milton and Charlotte Ruth (Altman) S.; m. Elaine Gale Jones, Jan. 31, 1987; children: Brendan, Jarrod, Joelle, Erin. BA in Psychology and Drama, U. Calif., Irvine, 1985. Author, screenwriter, 1987—. Author: Guy Talk, 1987, The Shadow Club, 1988 (Children's CHoice award Internat. Reading Assn. 1989), Dissidents, 1989, Speeding Bullet, 1991 (Best Book for Teens award N.Y. Pub. Libr., nominated Calif. Young Reader Medal 1995-96), Kid Heroes, 1991, What Daddy Did, 1991 (Best Book for Young Adults award ALA, Outstanding Work of Fiction award So. Calif. Coun. Lit. for Children and Young People, Children's Choice award and Young Adult Choice award Internat. Reading Assn., Pick of the List award ABA, Best Book for Teens award N.Y. Pub. Libr., Okla. Sequoyah award 1994), The Eyes of Kid Midas, 1992 (ALA Best Book for Reluctant Readers), Darkness Creeping, 1993, Piggyback Ninja, 1994, Scorpion Shards, 1995 (N.Y. Pub. Libr. Best Book for the Teenaged), Darkness Creeping II, 1995, Mindquakes, 1996 (ALA YALSA Quick Pick), Mindstorms, 1996, Mindtwisters, 1997, The Dark Side of Nowhere, 1997 (ALA Best Book, ALA Quick Pick--Top 10 Book), Thief of Souls, 1999, Downsiders, 1999 (ALA Best Book, ALA Quick Pick), MindBenders, 2000; screenwriter: Double Dragon, 1992, Evolver, 1993; dir. Heart on a Chain, 1991 (Golden Eagle award CINE), What About the Sisters, 1993 (Golden Eagle award CINE), Games: How to Host a Teen Mystery, Hot Times at Hollywood High, 1994, Barbecue with the Vampire, 1997, Roswell that Ends Well, 1999, How to Host a Murder: Roman Ruins, 1996, The Good, the Bad and the Guilty, 1997, The Tragical Mystery Tour, 1998, The Maiming of the Shrew, 2000, Saturday Night Cleaver, 2000, (TV) Goosebumps: The Werewolf of Fever Swamp, 1996, Goosebumps: Night of the Living Dummy III, 1997, Animorphs (staff writer), 1998. Mem. PEN, Writers Guild Am. West, Soc. Children's Book Writers and Illustrators. Avocations: swimming, tennis, storytelling. Office: PO Box 18516 Irvine CA 92623-8516 E-mail: NStoryman@aol.com

SHUTLER, MARY ELIZABETH, academic administrator; b. Oakland, Calif., Nov. 14, 1929; d. Hal Wilfred and Elizabeth Frances (Gimbel) Hall; m. Richard Shutler Jr., Sept. 8, 1951 (div. 1975); children: Kathryn Allice (dec.), John Hall, Richard Burnett. BA, U. Calif., Berkeley, 1951; MA, U. Ariz., 1958, PhD, 1967. Asst., assoc., full prof. anthropology, chmn. dept. San Diego State U., 1967-75; prof. anthropology, dept. chmn. Wash. State U., Pullman, 1975-80; dean Coll. Arts and Scis., prof. anthropology U. Alaska, Fairbanks, 1980-84; vice chancellor, dean of faculty, prof. anthropology U. Wis. Parkside, Kenosha, 1984-88; provost, v.p. for acad. affairs, prof. anthropology Calif. State U., L.A., 1988-94; provost West Coast U., L.A., 1994-97; dean Sch. of Arts and Scis. Nat. U., La Jolla, Calif., 1997—. Mem. core staff Lahav Rsch. Project, Miss. State U., 1975-92. Co-author: Oceanic Prehistory, 1975, Deer Creek Cave, 1964, Archaeological Survey of Southern Nevada, 1963, Stuart Rockshelter, 1962; contbr. articles to jours. in field. Mem. coun. Gamble House. Fellow Am. Anthropol. Assn.; mem. Soc. for Am. Archaeology, Am. Schs. for Oriental Rsch., Am. Coun. Edn., Am. Assn. for Higher Edn., Am. Assn. State Colls. and Univs., Delta Zeta. Republican. Roman Catholic. Avocations: travel, gardening, cats. E-mail: eshutler@nu.edu

SIAS, JOHN B. multi-media company executive, newspaper publisher, publishing executive; b. 1927; A.B., Stanford U., 1949. Group v.p. Metromedia Inc., 1962-71; with Capital Cities Communications, 1971-93; pres. Fairchild Pubs. Inc., 1971-75, exec. v.p., pres. pub. div., 1975-85; pres. ABC-TV Network Group, N.Y.C., 1986-93; also former exec. v.p. Capital Cities/ABC Inc.(parent), N.Y.C.; pres., ceo Chronicle Pub. Co., San Francisco, 1993—. Served with AUS, 1945-46. Office: Chronicle Pub Co 901 Mission St San Francisco CA 94103-2905 also: Capital Cities ABC Inc 24 E 51st St New York NY 10022-6801

SIBURG, DAN, marketing professional; Pres. Direct Mktg. Svcs., Inc., Scottsdale, AZ. Office: Direct Mktg Svc Inc 6370 E Thomas Rd Scottsdale AZ 85251-7053

SICILIAN, JAMES MICHAEL, research engineer; b. Bronx, N.Y., May 25, 1947; s. Leonard James and Veronica Patricia (Reinwald) S. BS, MIT, 1969; MS, Stanford U., 1970, PhD, 1973. Tech. editor C.S. Draper Lab., Cambridge, Mass., 1968-69; research analyst Savannah River Lab., Aiken, S.C., 1973-76; staff Los Alamos (N.Mex) Scientific Lab, 1976-79, asst. group leader, 1979-80; sr. scientist Flow Science, Inc., Los Alamos, 1980-96, sec. of corp., 1980-96, v.p., 1990-96; treas. LFD Techs., Inc., 1998—. Cons., 1996—. Mem. Cultural Ctr. adv. com., Los Alamos, 1987-89; vice chmn. Park and Recreation Bd., Los Alamos, 1989-90; treas. N.Mex. Theater Assn., 1983-85; pres. Los Alamos Little Theater, 1978-79, v.p., 1997-98; sec. Los Alamos Light Opera, 1990-91. Recipient AEC spl. fellowship, U.S. AEC, 1969-72. Mem. AAAS, AIAA, ASME, Sigma Xi. Avocations: theatrical productions, skiing. Office: Remolinos 1345 Los Pueblos St Los Alamos NM 87544-2663 E-mail: jim@lfdtech.com

SICKELS, ROBERT JUDD, political science educator; b. Nyack, N.Y., June 26, 1931; s. Robert and Dorothy (Judd) S.; m. Alice Esterer; children: Stephen Judd, Wendy. B.A., U. Chgo., 1950, M.A., 1954; Ph.D., Johns Hopkins U., 1960. Asst. staff dir. Pres.'s Commn. on Registration and Voting Participation, Washington, 1963-64; asso. dir. exec. insts. U.S. CSC, Washington, 1964-65; asso. prof. polit. sci. Purdue U., West Lafayette, Ind., 1965-68; assoc. prof. polit. sci. U. N.Mex., Albuquerque, 1968-73, prof., 1973-95, prof. emeritus, 1995—, chmn. dept., 1976-81. Author: Race, Marriage, and the Law, 1972, Presidential Transactions, 1974, The Presidency, 1980, John Paul Stevens and The Constitution: The Search for Balance, 1988; contbr. articles to profl. jours. Home: 1514 Harvard Ct NE Albuquerque NM 87106-3712

SIDDON, THOMAS EDWARD, Canadian government official, environmental consultant; b. Drumheller, Alta., Can., Nov. 9, 1941; s. Ronald Victor and Gertrude Violet (Humfrey) S.; m. Patricia Audrey Yackimetz, Sept. 1, 1962; children— Charles, David, Robert, Elizabeth, Katherine BSME with distinction, U. Alta., 1963; MS in Aerospace Engring., U. Toronto, 1965, PhD in Aerodyn Noise, 1968. Assoc. prof. mech. engring. U. B.C., 1968-79; mem. House of Commons, Ottawa, Ont., Can., 1978-93, minister of state for sci. and tech., 1984-85, minister of fisheries and oceans, 1985-90, minister Indian Affairs and Northern Devel., 1990-93, min. nat. def., 1993; mem. Queen's Privy Coun., 1984—; now dir. mkt. recycle corp., cons. Kaleden, Can. Founder acoustical engring. firm and audiometric testing bus.; acoustical cons., Can., U.S.; mem. priorities and planning com., 1988-93, environment, fed.-provincial rels. com., human rels. com., cultural affairs com.; lectr. environ. law; pres. Bonaccord Consulting Group Environ. Solutions. Alderman Twp. of Richmond, B.C., 1975-77. Recipient Assn. Profl. Engrs. award, 1978 Fellow Acoustical Soc. Am. Anglican Office: Box 118 Kaleden BC Canada V0H 1K0

SIDRAN, MARK HARRIS, lawyer; b. Seattle, July 7, 1951; married. BA in Govt. magna cum laude, Harvard U., 1973; JD, U. Wash., 1976. Bar: Wash. With King County Prosecuting Atty.'s Office, 1975-80, asst. chief criminal dep. juvenile sect., 1980-85; ptnr. McKay & Gaitan, 1986-89; city atty. City of Seattle, 1989—. Apptd. spl. counsel to Gov. Booth Gardner State of Wash., 1987—. Mem. Am. Jewish Com. Bd.; past bd. dirs. United Way King County. Office: Seattle City Atty 600 4th Ave Ste 1000 Seattle WA 98104-1877 Fax: 206-684-8284

SIEBEL, THOMAS M. executive; Various positions including group v.p., gen. mgr. Oracle Corp.; CEO Gain Tech., until 1992; chmn., CEO Siebel Systems, San Mateo, Calif., 1993—. Office: Siebel Systems Inc 1855 S Grant St San Mateo CA 94402-7016

SIEBERT, DAVE, councilman; City councilman City of Phoenix, 1995—. Office: City Council 200 W Washington St Fl 11 Phoenix AZ 85003-1611

SIEFER, STUART B. architect; b. Detroit, Nov. 28, 1942; s. Louis and Esther (Ressler) S.; m. Nancy Ann Feldman, Apr. 23, 1967; children: Eric S., Jeremy M., Ted B. BA, Wayne State U., 1965; postgrad., U. Detroit, 1965-68; BArch, Ariz. State U., 1971. Registered architect, Ariz. Designer, draftsman various firms, Detroit, 1966-68; rschr. Detroit Bd. Edn., 1967; archtl. designer Peace Corps, Tegucigalpa, Honduras, 1968-70; designer, job capt. various firms, Phoenix, 1970-73; prin. Siefer Assocs., Tempe, Ariz., 1973—. Bd. dirs. Downtown Tempe Community, Inc., 1993—; vol. bd. mem. Tempe Ctr. for Habilitation, 1993—; mem. Ariz. Town Hall, Phoenix, 1993—. Recipient 16 design awards Tempe Beautification Com., 1975—, merit & Crescordia award Valley Forward Assn. AIA Ariz., 1988, 93, Beautification award City of Mesa, Ariz., AIA Ariz. Archs. medal, 1996. Mem. AIA (pres. Rio Salado chpt.), Rio Salado Architecture Found. (exec. mem.), Tempe C. of C. (pres. 1992-93) Found. (founding bd. mem. 1995). Avocations: jogging, skiing, hiking, tennis.

SIEGAN, BERNARD HERBERT, lawyer, educator; b. Chgo., July 28, 1924; s. David and Jeannette S.; m. Sharon Goldberg, June 15, 1952 (dec. Feb. 1985); m. Shelley Zifferblatt, Nov. 19, 1995. AA, Herzl. Jr. Coll., Chgo., 1943, 46; Student, Roosevelt Coll., Chgo., 1946-47; J.D., U. Chgo., 1949. Bar: Ill. 1950. Practiced in, Chgo.; partner firm Siegan & Karlin, 1952-73; pres., sec. various small corps. and gen. partner in partnerships engaged in real estate ownership and devel., 1955-70; weekly columnist Freedom newspaper chain, other papers, 1974-79. Cons. law and econs. program U. Chgo. Law Sch., 1970-73; adj. prof. law U. San Diego Law Sch., 1973-74, Disting. prof., 1975—; adj. scholar Cato Inst., Washington, 1991—, Heritage Found., 1992—; cons. windfalls and wipeouts project HUD, 1973-74; cons. FTC, 1985-86, U.S. Justice Dept., dir. constl. bibliog. project, 1986-88; keynote speaker 5th Internat. Conf. on Urbanism, Porto Alegre, Brazil, 1989; nominated by Pres. Reagan to U.S. Ct. Appeals (9th cir.) Feb. 2, 1987, confirmation denied July 14, 1988 by party line vote Senate Judiciary Com. Author: Land Use Without Zoning, 1972, Spanish edit., 1995, Other People's Property, 1976, Economic Liberties and the Constitution, 1980, The Supreme Court's Constitution: An Inquiry Into Judicial Review and Its Impact on Society, 1987, Drafting a Constitution for a Nation or Republic Emerging into Freedom, 1992, 2d edit., 1994, Portuguese, Ukrainian, Polish and Spanish edits., 1993, Property and Freedom: The Constitution, Supreme Court and Land Use Regulation, 1997, Adapting a Constitution to Protect Freedom and Provide Abundance (in Bulgarian), 1998, Property Rights: From Magna Carta to the Fourteenth Amendment, 2001; editor: Planning without Prices, 1977, The Interaction of Economics and the Law, 1977, Regulation, Economics and the Law, 1979, Government, Regulation and the Economy, 1980. Mem. pres.-elect's Task Force on Housing, 1980-81; mem. Pres.'s Commn. on Housing, 1981-82; mem. Nat. Commn. on bicentannial of U.S. Constn., 1985-91; chmn. adv. com. Affordable Housing Conf., San Diego, 1985, Rights of Regulated Conf., Coronado, Calif., 1976; chmn. Conf. on the Taking Issue, 1976; mem. Houston Regional Urban Design Team, Study of Houston, 1990; mem. U.S. team Bulgarian Econ. Growth and Transition Project, 1990; mem. devel. bd. Mingei Internat. Mus. World Folk Art, 1981-84. Served with AUS, 1943-46. Research fellow law and econs. U. Chgo. Law Sch., 1968-69; Urban Land Inst. research fellow, 1976-86; recipient Leander J. Monks Meml. Fund award Inst. Humane Studies, 1972, George Washington medal Freedom Founds. at Valley Forge, 1981, Spl. award Liberal Inst. of Rio Grande do Sul, Porto Alegre, Brazil, 1989, Thorsnes award for outstanding legal scholarship, 1998; named Univ. Prof., U. San Diego, 1997-98. Home: 6005 Camino De La Costa La Jolla CA 92037-6519

SIEGEL, DAVID M. construction executive; CFO, sr. v.p., treas. William Lyons Homes, Newport Beach, Calif., 1991—. Office: William Lyons Homes The Presley Companies 4490 Von Karman Ave Newport Beach CA 92660-2008

SIEGEL, JAY STEVEN, chemistry educator; b. Inglewood, Calif., Aug. 16, 1959; s. Erwin and Jeanne (Strzesak) S. BS, Calif. State U., Northridge, 1980; MA, Princeton U., 1982, PhD, 1985. Researcher Princeton (N.J.) U., 1981-83, 84-85, Eidgenossische Technishche Hochschule, Zürich, Switzerland, 1983-84, U. Louis Pasteur, Strasbourg, France, 1985-86; asst. prof. U. Calif., San Diego, 1986—. Observer, mem. com. on stereochemistry Internat. Union of Pure and Applied Chemists, 1985—. Contbr. articles to sci. jours. Calif. State scholar, 1977-70; Swiss U. grantee, 1983-84, NSF-CNRS Sci. Exchange grantee, 1985-86; named Presdl. Young Investigator NSF, 1988—. Mem. Am. Chem. Soc., N.Y. Acad. Scis., Sigma Xi. Home: 8411 Cliffridge Ln La Jolla CA 92037-2119 Office: U Calif San Diego Dept Chemistry B-014 La Jolla CA 92093

SIEGEL, L. PENDLETON, paper and wood products executive; b. Richmond, Va. Grad., Dartmouth Coll. V.p., sr. analyst for forest products Drexel, Burnham, Lambert, v.p. fin., 1983, exec. v.p. pulp-based ops. and planning, 1993; mgr. strategic planning Potlatch Corp., 1979, pres., COO, CEO, chmn., 1999—. Office: Potlatch Corp Ste 1100 601 W Riverside Ave Spokane WA 99201

SIEGEL, LOUIS PENDLETON, forest products executive; b. Richmond, Va., Nov. 6, 1942; s. John Boschen Jr. and Francis Beale (Tyler) S.; m. Nancy Dicks Blanton, Apr. 10, 1974 (dec. July 1976); m. Nancy Northon, June 26, 1982; children: Kathryn Tyler. AB in Econs., Dartmouth Coll., 1967. Asst. cashier, security researcher First Nat. Citibank, N.Y.C., 1967-71; v.p. security rsch. Drexel Burnham Lambert, N.Y.C., 1971-79; with Potlatch Corp., San Francisco and Spokane, Wash., 1979—, sr. v.p. fin. and adminstrn. San Francisco, 1989, group v.p. wood products and corp. planning, 1989-92, group v.p. pulp and paperboard and corp. planning, 1992-93, exec. v.p. pulp-based ops. and corp. planning, 1993-94, pres., COO San Francisco and Spokane, Wash., 1994-99, also bd. dirs. Spokane, chair, CEO, 1999—. Bd. dirs. San Francisco Fed. Corp., 1985-96. Pres., bd. dir. Bay Area Sci. Fair, San Francisco, 1989-90. With USCG, 1964-65. Republican. Episcopalian. Avocations: golf, tennis, fishing. Office: Potlatch Corp 601 W Riverside Ave Ste 1100 Spokane WA 99201-0603

SIEGEL, MACE, company executive; Chmn. The Macerich Co., Santa Monica, Calif., 1997—. Office: 233 Wilshire Blvd Ste 700 Santa Monica CA 90401

SIEGEL, MICHAEL ELLIOT, nuclear medicine physician, educator; b. N.Y.C., May 13, 1942; s. Benjamin and Rose (Gilbert) S.; m. Marsha Rose Snower, Mar. 20, 1966; children: Herrick Jove, Meridith Ann. AB, Cornell U., 1964; MD, Chgo. Med. Sch., 1968. Diplomate Nat. Bd. Med. Examiners. Intern Cedars-Sinai Med. Ctr., L.A., 1968-69, resident in radiology, 1969-70; NIH fellow in radiology Temple U. Med. Ctr., Phila., 1970-71; NIH fellow in nuclear medicine Johns Hopkins U. Sch. Medicine, Balt., 1971-73, asst. prof. radiology, 1972-76; assoc. prof. radiology and medicine U. So. Calif., L.A., 1976—, prof. radiology, 1989—, dir. divsn. nuclear medicine, 1982-99. Dir. Sch. Nuclear Medicine, Los Angeles County-U. So. Calif. Med. Ctr., 1976-99; dir. divsn. nuclear medicine Kenneth Norris Cancer Hosp. and Rsch. Ctr., L.A., 1983-99; dir. dept. nuclear medicine Orthopaedic Hosp., L.A., 1981—, Intercmty. Hosp., Covina, Calif., 1981—, U. So. Calif. Univ. Hosp., L.A., 1993—; clin. prof. radiology U. Calif., San Diego, 2000—. Author: Textbook of Nuclear Medicine, 1978, Vascular Surgery, 1983, 88, numerous other textbooks; editor: Nuclear Cardiology, 1981, Vascular Disease: Nuclear Medicine, 1983. Mem. Maple Ctr., Beverly Hills. Served as maj. USAF, 1974-76. Recipient Outstanding Alumnus award Chgo. Med. Sch., 1991. Fellow Am. Coll. Nuclear Medicine (sci. investigator 1974, 76, nominations com. 1980, program com. 1983, trustee 1993, disting. fellow, 1993, bd. reps. 1993—, bd. dirs. 1994—, treas. 1996—, chmn. ann. sci. program 1996—, pres.'s award 1997, v.p. 1997-98, pres. 1999—); mem. Soc. Nuclear Medicine (sic. exhbn. com. 1978-79, program com. 1979-80, Silver medal 1975), Calif. Med. Assn. (sci. adv. bd. 1987—), Radiol. Soc. N.Am., Soc. Nuclear Magnetic Resonance Imaging, Friars So. Calif., Alpha Omega Alpha. Achievements include research on development of nuclear medicine techniques to evaluate cardiovascular disease and diagnose and treat cancer; clinical utilization of video digital displays in nuclear medicine development; invention of pneumatic radiologic pressure system. Office: U So Calif Med Ctr PO Box 693 1200 N State St Los Angeles CA 90033-1029

SIEGEL, SHELDON C. pediatrician, allergist, immunologist; b. Mpls., Jan. 30, 1922; s. Carl S.; m. Priscilla Rikess, Mar. 3, 1946; children—Linda, Nancy. A.A., Va. Jr. Coll., 1940; B.A., B.S., U. Minn., 1942, M.D., 1945. Intern U. Minn. Hosp., 1946, resident in pediatrics, 1947-48; fellow in pediatric allergy Rochester, N.Y., 1949-50; practice medicine specializing in pediatric allergy and pediatrics St. Paul, 1950-52, San Antonio, 1952-54, Los Angeles, 1954—; clin. instr. pediatrics U. Rochester, 1949-50, U. Minn., 1950-51; asst. prof. pediatrics U. Tex., 1952-54; asst. clin. prof. U. Calif. at Los Angeles Med. Sch., 1955, clin. asso. prof., 1957-62, clin. prof., 1963—, co-chief pediatric allergy clinic, 1957—; mem. staff Harbor Gen. Hosp., Torrance, Calif., Daniel Freeman Hosp., Inglewood, Centinela Valley Community Hosp., Inglewood, Hawthorne (Calif.) Community Hosp. Editorial bd.: Jour. Allergy, 1973-75; contbr. articles to med. jours. Fellow Am. Acad. Allergy (pres. 1974), Am. Coll. Allergists, Am. Acad. Pediatrics; mem. AMA, Allergy Found. Am. (pres. 1976), Calif., Los Angeles County med. assns., Los Angeles Pediatric Soc., Calif., Los Angeles socs. allergy, Western Pediatric Research Soc., Am. Bd. Med. Specialists, Sigma Xi. Office: 11620 Wilshire Blvd Los Angeles CA 90025-1706

SIEGMAN, ANTHONY EDWARD, electrical engineer, educator; b. Detroit, Nov. 23, 1931; s. Orra Leslie and Helen Salome (Winnie) S.; married. AB summa cum laude, Harvard U., 1952; MS, UCLA, 1954; PhD, Stanford U., 1957. Faculty Stanford (Calif.) U., 1957—, assoc. prof. elec. engring., 1960-64, prof., 1964-98, prof. engring. emeritus, 1998—. Dir. Edward L. Ginzton Lab., 1978-83; cons. Lawrence Livermore Labs., Coherent Inc., GTE; mem. Air Force Sci. Adv. Bd.; vis. prof. Harvard U., 1965 Author: Microwave Solid State Masers, 1964, An Introduction to Lasers and Masers, 1970, Lasers, 1986; contbr. over 200 articles to profl. jours. Recipient Schawlow award Laser Inst. Am., 1991; Guggenheim fellow IBM Rsch. Lab., Zurich, 1969-70; Alexander von Humboldt Found. sr. scientist Max Planck Inst. Quantum Optics, Garching, Fed. Republic Germany, 1984-85. Fellow AAAS, IEEE (W.R.G. Baker award 1971, J.J. Ebers award 1977), Am. Phys. Soc., Laser Inst. Am., Optical Soc. Am. (R.W. Wood prize 1980), IEEE Laser Electro-Optics Soc. (Quantum Electronics award 1989), Am. Acad. Arts and Scis.; mem. NAS, NAE, AAUP, Phi Beta Kappa, Sigma Xi. Achievements include patents for microwave and optical devices and lasers, including the unstable optical resonator. Office: Stanford U Ginzton Lab MC 4085 Stanford CA 94305-4085

SIGBAND, NORMAN BRUCE, management communication educator; b. Chgo., June 27, 1920; s. Max and Bessie S.; m. Joan C. Lyons, Aug. 3, 1944; children: Robin, Shelley, Betsy. BA, U. Chgo., 1940, MA, 1941, PhD, 1954; LHD (hon.), DePaul U., 1986. Asst. prof. bus. communication De Paul U., 1946-50, assoc. prof., 1950-54, prof., 1954-65; prof. mgmt. communication U. So. Calif., 1965—, chmn. dept. mktg., 1970-72; assoc. dean U. So. Calif. (Sch. Bus.), 1975-80, Disting. prof. emeritus, 1989—. Disting. Centennial lectr. U. Tex., Austin, 1986; cons. to industry; speaker, condr. workshops, seminars in field; Scholar in Residence, Va. Commonwealth U., 1987, DePaul U., 1988; Disting. emeritus prof. U. So. Calif., 1989., Author books including: Practical Communication for Everyday Use, 25th edit., 1954, Effective Report Writing for Business, Industry and Government, 1960, Communication for Management, 1970, Communicacion Para Directivos, 1972, Management Communication for Decision Making, 1972, Communication for Management and Business, 1976, Communication for Managers, 6th edit., 2001, Communicating in Business, 1987, 3d edit., 1989, Patient-Pharmacist Consultation: A Communication Skills Approach, 1993, Communication for Pharmacists and Other Health Professionals, 1995, 2d edit., 1996, (with J. Biles) The American University in the New Millennium: Problems and Opportunities, 2001; movies include: Communication Barriers and Gateways, 2d edit., 1993, Listening: A Key to Problem Solving (award winner), 2d edit., 1993, The Grapevine, The Power of a Minute, 1992; gen. editor books including: Harcourt Brace Jovanovich Bus. series; contbr. numerous articles to profl. jours., mags. Served to capt. AUS, 1942-46, ETO. Decorated Bronze Star; recipient recognition award City of L.A., 1985, hon. alumnus award U. So. Calif., 1991. Fellow Am. Bus. Communication Assn. (pres. 1964-65); mem. Internat. Communication Assn., Acad. Mgmt., Anti-Defamation League, Hadassah Assocs., Blue Key, Phi Kappa Phi, Alpha Kappa Psi, Beta Gamma Sigma. Democrat. Jewish. Home: 3109 Dona Susana Dr Studio City CA 91604-4355 Office: U So Calif Health Sci Campus 1985 Zonal Ave Los Angeles CA 90033-1039

SIGLER, MARJORIE DIANE, computer programming executive, analyst; b. Fullerton, Calif., Sept. 19, 1943; d. Earl Lawrence Whipple and Ruth Juanita (Long) Purcell; children: Stephen, Deborah; m. William A. Sigler, June 10, 1995. Grad. computer programming, LaSalle U., Chgo., 1973; BSBA, U. Phoenix, 1994, MS, 1997. Computer programmer Los Alamos (N.Mex.) Nat. Lab., 1972-81, cons. control data, 1984-89, computer tech., 1989—. Contract programmer Computer Assistance, Inc., Tulsa, 1981-82; profl. svcs. analyst Control Data Corp., Denver, 1982-84, Los Alamos, 1984-89. Mem. Order Ea. Star (past matron). Home: 90 Aspen Grv Jemez Springs NM 87025-9683

SILAK, CATHY R. former state supreme court justice; b. Astoria, N.Y., May 25, 1950; d. Michael John and Rose Marie (Janor) S.; m. Nicholas G. Miller, Aug. 9, 1980; 3 children. BA, NYU, 1971; M in City Planning, Harvard U., 1973; JD, U. Calif., 1976. Bar: Calif. 1977, U.S. Dist. Ct. (no. dist.) Calif. 1977, D.C. 1979, U.S. Ct. Appeals (D.C. cir.) 1979, U.S. Dist. Ct. (so. dist.) N.Y. 1980, Idaho 1983, U.S. Dist. Ct. Idaho 1983, U.S. Ct. Appeals (2nd cir.) 1983, U.S. Ct. Appeals (9th cir.) 1985. Law clk. to Hon. William W. Schwarzer U.S. Dist. Ct. (no dist.), Calif., 1976-77; pvt. practice San Francisco, 1977-79, Washington, 1979-80; asst. U.S. atty. So. Dist. of N.Y., 1980-83; spl. asst. U.S. atty. Dist. of Idaho, 1983-84; pvt. practice Boise, Idaho, 1984-90; judge Idaho Ct. Appeals, 1990-93; justice Idaho Supreme Ct., Boise, 1993—2000. Assoc. gen. counsel Morrison Knudsen Corp., 1989-90; mem. fairness com. Idaho Supreme Ct. and Gov.'s Task Force on Alternative Dispute Resolution; instr. and lectr. in field. Assoc. note and comment editor Calif. Law Rev., 1975-76. Land use planner Mass. Dept. Natural Resources, 1973; founder Idaho Coalition for Adult Literacy; bd. dirs. Literacy Lab., Inc.; mem. adv. bd. Boise State U. Legal Asst. Program. Recipient Jouce Stein award Boise YWCA, 1992, Women Helping Women award Soroptimist, Boise, 1993. Fellow Idaho Law Found (ann., lectr.); mem. ABA (nat. conf. state trial judges jud. adminstrn. divsn.), Nat. Assn. Women Judges, Idaho State Bar (corp./securities sect., instr.), Am. Law Inst., Fellows of the Am. Bar Found. Office: Idaho Supreme Ct Supreme Ct Bldg PO Box 83720 Boise ID 83720-3720

SILJAK, DRAGOSLAV D. engineering educator, researcher; b. Belgrade, Yugoslavia, Sept. 10, 1933; came to U.S. 1964, naturalized; s. Dobrilo T. and Ljubica Z. (Zivanovic) S.; m. Dragana T. Todorovic, Sept. 28, 1967; children— Ana, Matija. BSEE, U. Belgrade, 1958, MSEE, 1961, ScD, 1963. Docent prof. U. Belgrade, 1963-64; assoc. prof. U. Santa Clara, Calif., 1964-70, prof. engring., 1970-84, B. and M. Swig Univ. chair, 1984—. Author: Nonlinear Systems, 1969, Large Scale Systems, 1978, Decentralized Control of Complex Systems, 1991; mem. editl. bd. Jour. Difference Equations, Nonlinear World, Comm. in Applied Analysis, Internat. Jour. Computer Rsch., Theory, Methods and Applications, Dynamics of Cont., Disc. and Impulsive Systems, Math. Problems in Engring., Stability and Control: Theory and Applications. Disting. prof. Fulbright Found., 1984. Fellow IEEE (life); mem. Serbian Acad. Scis. and Arts (hon.) Mem. Christian Orthodox Ch. E-mail: dsiljak@scu.edu

SILLARS, MALCOLM OSGOOD, communication educator; b. Union City, N.J., Feb. 12, 1928; s. Malcolm Osgood and Dorothy Edna (Browning) S.; m. Charlotte Jane Grimm, June 1, 1948; children— Paul Louis, Bruce Malcolm, Alan Leslie. B.A., U. Redlands, 1948, M.A., 1949; Ph.D., U. Iowa, 1955. Asst. prof. communication Iowa State U., Ames, 1949-53; asst. prof. Calif. State U., Los Angeles, 1954-56, prof., dean Northridge, 1970-71, pres., 1969-70; prof. U. Mass., Amherst, 1971-74; prof. communication U. Utah, Salt Lake City, 1974-97, dean humanities, 1974-81, ret., 1998. Author: Speech: Content and Communications, 6th edit., 1991, Argumentation and Critical Decision Making, 5th edit., 2001, Communication Criticism, 2001; contbr. articles to profl. jours. Recipient Silver Beaver award Boy Scouts Am. Mem. ACLU, Nat. Comm. Assn. (pres.), We. States Comm. Assn. (pres.). Democrat. Home: 3508 Eastoaks Dr Salt Lake City UT 84124-3811

SILLMAN, ARNOLD JOEL, physiologist, educator; b. N.Y.C., Oct. 10, 1940; s. Philip and Anne L. (Pearlman) S.; m. Jean Fletcher Van Keuren, Sept. 26, 1969; children: Andrea Jose, Diana Van Keuren. A.B., U. Calif., Los Angeles, 1963, M.A., 1965, Ph.D., 1968. Asst. prof. U. Calif., L.A., 1969-73, Davis, 1975-78, assoc. prof., 1978-85, prof., 1985—; asst. prof. U. Pitts., 1973-75. Contbr. articles to profl. jours. USPHS trainee, UCLA, 1966-67; fellow NSF, 1967-68, Fight for Sight, Inc., 1968-69. Mem. Am. Physiol. Soc., Soc. Gen. Physiologists, Am. Soc. Zoologists, Assn. Rsch. in Vision and Ophthalmology, AAAS, N.Y. Acad. Sci. Jewish. Home: 1140 Los Robles St Davis CA 95616-4927 Office: U Calif Sect Neurobiology Physiology & Behavior Divsn Biol Scis Davis CA 95616 E-mail: ajsillman@ucdavis.edu

SILVA, ERNEST R. visual arts educator, artist; b. Providence, Dec. 11, 1948; BFA, U. R.I., 1971; MFA, Tyler Sch. Art, 1974. Instr. U. R.I., Kingston, 1977-79; lectr. dept. visual arts U. Calif. San Diego, La Jolla, 1979-87, prof. dept. visual arts, 1987—; represented by Jan Baum Gallery, L.A., Lenore Gray Gallery, Providence. Bd. dirs. Installation Gallery, San Diego, mem. arts adv. bd., 1992—, exec. com., 1993—; lectr. Phila. Coll. Art, 1973, U. R.I., 1974, 84, 91, RISD, 1977, Tyler Sch. Art, Elkins Park, Pa., 1979, U. Calif. Irvine, 1981, Southwestern Coll., Chula Vista, 1982, San Diego State U., 1985, Nat. Soc. Arts and Letters, Washington, 1986, Friends of Jung, San Diego, 1991. One-person exhbns. include Inst. Contemporary Art, Boston, 1972, Artists Space, N.Y.C., 1975, Anyart Contemporary Art Ctr., Providence, R.I., 1976, Lenore Gray Gallery, Providence, 1978, 79, 92, Roy Boyd Gallery, L.A., 1982, 84, 87, Quint Gallery, San Diego, 1982, 83, 86, Jan Baum Gallery, L.A., 1989, 91, Tuttle Gallery, McDonogh, Md., 1990, Porter Randall Gallery, La Jolla, 1994, Mus. Contemporary Art, Roskilde, Denmark, 1995, many others; group exhbns. include Mus. Phila. Civic Ctr., 1973, Cheltenham (Pa.) Art Ctr., 1973, Pratt Graphic Ctr., N.Y.C., 1975, Corcoran Art Gallery, Washington, 1975, Ft. Worth Art Mus., 1976, Baker Gallery, La Jolla, 1980, Ind. Contemporary Exhbns., L.A., 1982, Navy Pier, Chgo., 1983, 84, 85, Roy Boyd Gallery, Chgo., 1983, 85, 86, Heckscher Mus. Art, Huntington, N.Y., 1984, Indpls. Mus. Art, 1984, Forum Internat. Kunstmesse, Zurich, Switzerland, 1984, Nat. History Mus., San Diego, 1985, Visual Arts Ctr. Alaska, Anchorage, 1985, San Francisco Airport Mus., 1985, Sonrisa Gallery, L.A., 1985, Alaska State Mus., Juneau, 1986, Foire Internat. De L'Art Contemporain, Nice, France, 1986, Lyceum Theatre, San Diego, 1987, Installation Gallery, San Diego, 1986, 87, 88, Chgo. Internat. Art Exposition, 1987,L.A. Convention Ctr., 1987, Cmty. Arts, San Francisco, 1989, 90, Annex Gallery, La Jolla, 1990, Bill Bace Gallery, N.Y.C., 1991, David Lewinson Gallery, Del Mar, Calif., 1991, Southwestern Coll. Art, Chula Vista, Calif., 1992, Boehm Gallery Palomar Coll, San Marcos, Calif., 1993, Porter Randall Gallery, La Jolla, 1992, numerous others; represented in permanent collections Fogg Art Mus. Harvard U., Cambridge, Mass., Grand Rapids (Mich.) Art Mus., La Jolla Mus. Contemporary Art, Laguna Mus. Art, De Saisset Mus. U. Santa Clara, Newport Harbor Art Mus., Newport Beach, Calif., Mus. Contemporary Art, San Diego, La Jolla, San Jose Mus. Art, San Diego Mus. Art; subject reviews, articles, 1974—. Office: U Calif San Diego Visual Arts 0084 9500 Gilman Dr La Jolla CA 92093-5004

SILVA, JOSEPH, JR. dean, medical educator; Dean sch. medicine U. Calif., Davis. Office: U Calif Sch Medicine Office of Dean 2315 Stockton Blvd Rm 1501 Sacramento CA 95817

SILVA, ROBERT OWEN, retired protective service official; b. La Junta, Colo., Sept. 5, 1935; s. Owen Delbert and Gertrude H. (Kerr) S.; m. Meredith Ann Ginn, Dec. 18, 1953; children— Edward, Andrew, Colleen. Student Pueblo Jr. Coll., 1953, FBI Nat. Acad., 1975, Police Found. Exec. Program, 1979-80. Cert. peace officer, Colo. Police officer Pueblo Police Dept., Colo., 1958-66, sgt., 1966-72, capt., 1972-77, chief of police, 1977-92, ret. dir. Colo. Police Officers Standards and Tng. Bd. dirs. Salvation Army, Pueblo, Easter Seals Soc., Pueblo, Community Corrections Bd., Pueblo, Served with U.S. Army, 1955-57; apptd. by gov. Colo. Crim. Justice Comsn., 1990. Mem. Pueblo Community Coll. Criminal Justice Adv. Bd., Leadership Pueblo Steering Com., Pikes Peak Community Coll. Criminal Justice Program (chmn. adv. bd. 1981), Organized Crime Strike Force (bd. dirs. 1977-84, chmn. 1982, 83, 84); Colo. Assn. Chiefs of Police (pres. 1984-85), Rocky Mountain Info. Network (chmn. bd. dirs. 1986—), Presbyterian (elder). Lodges: Kiwanis (bd. dirs. 1982-84), Elks.

SILVER, MARY WILCOX, oceanography educator; b. San Francisco, July 13, 1941; d. Philip E. and Mary C. (Kartes) Wilcox; children: Monica, Joel. BA in Zoology, U. Calif., Berkeley, 1963; PhD in Oceanography, U. Calif., La Jolla, 1971. Asst. prof. biology San Francisco State U., 1971-72; prof. marine sci. U. Calif., Santa Cruz, 1972—, chmn. dept., 1992-95. Contbr. numerous articles on biol. oceanography to profl. jours. Grantee NSF, 1979—; recipient Bigelow medal, 1992. Mem. Am. Soc. Limnology and Oceanography, Am. Phycological Soc. Office: U Calif Dept Ocean Sci Santa Cruz CA 95064 E-mail: msilver@cats.ucsc.edu

SILVER, MICHAEL, school superintendent; b. Landsberg, Germany, Jan. 30, 1948; came to U.S., 1949; s. Norman and Esther Silver; m. Beverley Ann Moss, May 16, 1971; children: Sabina, Joseph. AB, Washington U., 1970, MEd, 1973, PhD, 1982. Cert. supt. Mo., Wash. Tchr. Normandy Sch. Dist., St. Louis, 1970-72, Parkway Sch. Dist., St. Louis, 1972-75, asst. prin., 1976-79, adminstrv. asst., 1979-83, asst. to supt., 1983-84, asst. supt., 1984-86; supt. Tukwila Sch. Dist., Seattle, 1986—. Bd. dirs. Cities in Schs., Seattle; mem. adv. bd. Sta. KCTS, Seattle, 1990—; vis. exec. Seattle U. Sch. Edn., 1995. Author: Values Education, 1976, Facing Issues of Life and Death, 1976. Pres. SeaTac Task Force, Seattle, 1989; bd. dirs. Anti-Defamation League, Seattle, 1987—; mem. City of Tukwila (Wash.) 2000 Com., 1988-90. Recipient A Plus award Wash. Coun. Econ. Edn., 1992, Excellence in Ednl. Leadership award Univ. Coun. for Ednl. Adminstrn., 1998, Art Tribute award, Wash. Art Edn. Assn., 2001; named Exec. Educator, 100 Exec. Educator Mag., 1985, 1996 Assoc. for Inst. for Ednl. Inquiry Leadership Program; named to Homework Ctrl.; 100 Most Influential People in U.S. Pub. Edn.; I/D/E/A fellow Charles F. Kettering Found., 1978, 88, Title VI fellow Washington U., 1971-73; named Supt. of Yr. Wash. Libr. Media Assn., 2000. Mem. ASCD, Am. Assn. Sch. Adminstrs., Wash. Assn. Sch. Adminstrs. (met. chpt., pres. 1989-90), King County Supts. (chmn. adv. com. 1989-90, 95-96), Southcenter Rotary Club (Paul Harris fellow 1994), Southwest King County C. of C., Phi Delta Kappa. Home: 14127 SE 50th St Bellevue WA 98006-3409 Office: Tukwila Sch Dist 4640 S 144th St Seattle WA 98168-4134 E-mail: silverm@tukwila.wednet.edu

SILVER, ROSLYN O. federal judge; b. Phoenix, Feb. 28, 1946; m. Steven J. Silver. BA, U. Calif. Santa Barbara, 1968; JD, Ariz. State U., 1971. Law clk. Hon. Lorna E. Lockwood Ariz. Supreme Ct., Phoenix, 1971-72; advisor, litigator Navajo Nation Native Am. Rights Fund, Phoenix, 1974-76; legal counsel Dial Corp., Phoenix, 1976-78; ptnr. Logan and Aguirre, Phoenix, 1978-79; legal counsel EEOC, Phoenix, 1979-80; asst. U.S. Atty. Dist. Ariz., Phoenix, 1980-84; asst. atty. gen. Ariz. Atty. Gen.'s Office, Phoenix, 1984-86; acting 1st asst., chief criminal divsn. dist. Ariz. U.S. Atty. Office, Phoenix, 1986-94; judge Dist. Ariz. U.S. Dist. Ct., Phoenix, 1994—. Chair 9th Cir. Article III judges edn. com. Named one of 100 Significant Women and Minorities in Ariz.'s Legal History, 2000. Mem. ABA, Fed. Bar Assn., Nat. Assn. Women Judges, Ariz. Bar Assn. (Pub. Lawyer of Yr.), Ariz. Women Lawyers Assn. (outstanding legal practitioner award 1999), Ariz. State U. Alumni Assn. (outstanding alumnus award 1996). Office: US Dist Ct 230 N 1st Ave Ste 6031 Phoenix AZ 85025-0005

SILVERBERG, LEWIS HENRY, legal consultant; b. L.A., Nov. 1, 1934; s. Milton Henry and Marjorie Vella (Coates) S.; children: Stephen, Richard, Donna; m. Alice Ellen Deakins, Mar. 9, 1979. BA, Pomona Coll., 1955; JD, UCLA, 1958. Bar: Calif. 1959, U.S. Supreme Ct. 1966. Pvt. practice, San Diego, 1959-89; bus. cons. San Diego, 1993—. Bd. dirs. Internet C. and C., Inc. Trustee San Diego Zool. Soc., 1989-99; active various pub., charitable and ednl. orgns. Office: 1515 Merritt Dr El Cajon CA 92020-7847 E-mail: lewberg@home.com

SILVERMAN, ALAN HENRY, lawyer; b. N.Y.C., Feb. 18, 1954; s. Melvin H. and Florence (Green) S.; m. Gretchen E. Freeman, May 25, 1986; children: Willa C.F., Gordon H.F. BA summa cum laude, Hamilton Coll., 1976; MBA, JD, U. Pa., 1980. Bar: N.Y. 1981, U.S. Dist. Ct. (so. and ea. dist.) N.Y. 1981, U.S. Ct. Internat. Trade 1981, D.C. 1986, U.S. Supreme Ct. 1990. Assoc. Hughes, Hubbard & Reed, N.Y.C., 1980-84; asst. counsel Newsweek, Inc., N.Y.C., 1984-86; v.p., gen. counsel, sec., dir. adminstrn. Cable One, Inc., Phoenix, 1986—. Contbr. articles to profl. jours. Mem. prevention adv. com. Gov. Pa. Justice Commn., 1975-79; bd. dirs. Lawyers' Alliance for N.Y., 1982-85, N.Y. Lawyers Pub. Interest, 1983-85, Nat. Assn. JD-MBA Profls., 1983-85, Bus. Vols. for Arts, Inc., Phoenix, 1989-93, Ariz. Vol. Lawyers for the Arts, Inc., 1994-97, First Amendment Coalition Ariz., Inc., 1991—; mem. Maricopa County Citizens Jud. Adv. Coun., 1990-93; mem. citizens' bond com. City of Phoenix, 2000. Mem. ABA, Assn. of Bar of City of N.Y., D.C. Bar Assn., Phi Beta Kappa. Home: 5833 N 30th St Phoenix AZ 85016-2401 Office: Cable One Inc 1314 N 3d St Phoenix AZ 85004 E-mail: alan.silverman@cableone.net

SILVERMAN, BARRY G. federal judge; b. N.Y.C., Oct. 11, 1951; 1 child, Bagel Ann. BA summa cum laude, Ariz. State U., 1973, JD, 1976. Bar: Ariz. 1976, U.S. Dist. Ct. Ariz. 1976, U.S. Ct. Appeals (9th cir.) 1976, U.S. Supreme Ct. 1980. Asst. city prosecutor, Phoenix, 1976-77; dep. atty. Maricopa County, 1977-79; ct. commr., 1979-84; judge, 1984-95, Superior Ct. Ariz. Maricopa County, 1995; apptd. magistrate judge U.S. Dist. Ct. Ariz., 1995; judge U.S. Ct. Appeals 9th cir., 1998—. Instr. constnl. law Coll. Law, Ariz. State U., spring, 1983, adj. prof. advanced criminal procedure, spring 1989; lectr. comty. property BAR/BRI Ariz., Idaho and Nev. Bar Rev. Courses , 1989—; mem. Ariz. Supreme Ct. Com. on Jud. Edn. and Tng., 1988—. Recipient Exel award Soc. Nat. Assn. Publs., 1992. Mem. ABA, State Bar Ariz., Maricopa County Bar Assn. (Henry Stevens award 1991). Avocations: magic, beagles, baseball, wine tasting. Office: 401 W Washington St SPC 78 Phoenix AZ 85003

SILVERMAN, BRUCE GARY, advertising executive; b. N.Y.C., Feb. 16, 1945; s. Edward E. and Lillian (Brill) S.; children: Jennifer, Matthew; m. Nancy Cole, 1996; children: Christen Cole, Larry Cole. BA, Adelphi U., 1965; JD, Albany Law Sch., 1967. Sr. v.p., exec. creative dir. Ogilvy & Mather Inc., N.Y.C., 1967-80; exec. v.p., exec. creative dir. Bozell & Jacobs Inc., Dallas, 1981-83, Batten, Barton, Durstine & Osborn Inc., L.A., 1984-85; exec. v.p., creative dir. Asher/Gould Advt. Inc., L.A., 1986-89, pres., chief creative officer, 1989-95, pres., COO, 1996-97; pres. Western Internat. Advocacy Group, L.A., 1997-98; exec. v.p., mng. dir. Initiative Media, L.A., 1998—; pres., CEO Initiative Ptnrs., USA, 1999—. V.p., bd. dirs. L.A. Children's Mus., 1984-88; chmn. Resource Devel. com. Starbright Pavillion Found., 1993; bd. dirs. L.A. Minority Advtg. Tng. Program. Mem. Acad. TV Arts and Scis. Home: 3168 Dona Mema Pl Studio City CA 91604-4264 Office: Initiative Media Worldwide 5700 Wilshire Blvd Los Angeles CA 90036-3659

SILVERMAN, LEONARD M. university dean, electrical engineering educator; B.S., Columbia U., 1962, M.S., 1963, Ph.D., 1966. Prof. elec. engring. U. So. Calif., Los Angeles, 1966—, dean sch. engring., 1966—. Mem. Nat. Acad. Engring. Office: U So Calif Sch Engring University Park Los Angeles CA 90089-0001

SILVERMAN, PAUL HYMAN, science administrator, former university official; b. Mpls., Oct. 8, 1924; s. Adolph and Libbie (Idlekope) S.; m. Nancy Josephs, May 20, 1945; children: Daniel Joseph, Claire. Student, U. Minn., 1942-43, 46-47; BS, Roosevelt U., 1949; MS in Biology, Northwestern U., 1951; PhD in Parasitology, U. Liverpool, Eng., 1955, DSc, 1968. Rsch. fellow Malaria Rsch. Sta., Hebrew U., Israel, 1951-53; rsch. fellow dept. entomology and parasitology Sch. Tropical Medicine, U. Liverpool, 1953-56; sr. sci. officer dept. parasitology Moredun Inst., Edinburgh, Scotland, 1956-59; head dept. immunoparasitology Glaxo, Allen & Hanbury, Ltd., Ware, Eng., 1960-62; prof. zoology and vet. pathology and hygiene U. Ill., Urbana, 1963-72, chmn., head dept. zoology, 1963-68; prof., chmn. dept. biology, v.p. for rsch. U. N.Mex., 1972-77; provost, rsch. and grad. studies Ctrl. Adminstrn. SUNY, Albany, 1977-79, pres. Rsch. Found., 1979-80; pres. U. Maine, Orono, 1980-84; biol. divsn. Lawrence Berkeley Lab. U. Calif., Berkeley, 1984-86; head biomed. divsn. Lawrence Berkeley Lab., 1986-87; adj. prof. med. parasitology Sch. Pub. Health U. Calif., Berkeley, 1986, assoc. lab. dir. for life scis., dir Donner Lab., 1987-90, dir. systemwide biotech. rsch. and edn. program, 1989-90; dir. Beckman's Scientific Affairs, Fullerton, Calif., 1990-93; assoc. chancellor Ctr. for Health Scis., adj. prof. medicine U. Calif., Irvine, 1993-96. Dir. Western Ctr., Am. Acad. Arts and Scis., 1997—; cons., Commn. Colls. and Univs., North Central Assn. Colls. and Secondary Schs., 1964—; chmn. Commn. on Instns. Higher Edn., 1974-76; Fulbright prof. zoology Australian Nat. U., Canberra, 1969; adjoint prof. biology U. Colo., Boulder, 1970-72; mem. bd. Nat. Council on Postsecondary Accreditation, Washington, 1975-77; dir. research in malaria immunology and vaccination US AID, 1965-76; bd. dirs. Inhalation Toxicology Research Inst., Lovelace Biomed. and Environ. Research Inst., Albuquerque, 1977-84, Hastings Ctr.; mem. N.Y. State Gov.'s High Tech. Opportunities Task Force; chmn. research and rev. com. N.Y. State Sci. and Tech. Found.; mem. pres.'s council New Eng. Land Grant Univs.; bd. advs. Lovelace-Bataan Med. Center, Albuquerque, 1974-77; adv. com. U.S. Army Command and Gen. Staff Coll., Ft. Leavenworth, Kans., 1983-84. Mem. editl. bd. Jour. Anti-Aging Medicine, 1997—; contbr. articles to profl. jours. Chmn. rsch. rev. com. N.Y. State Sci. and Tech. Found.; bd. dirs. Hastings Ctr., 1997—. Fellow Meridian Internat. Inst., 1992; assoc. The Hastings Ctr., 1995—. Fellow Royal Soc. Tropical Medicine and Hygiene, N.Mex. Acad. Sci.; mem. Am. Soc. Parasitologits, Am. Soc. Tropical Medicine and Hygiene, Am. Soc. Immunologists, Brit. Soc. Parasitology (coun.), Brit. Soc. Immunologists, Soc. Gen. Microbiology, Soc. Protozoologists, Am. Soc. Zoologists, Human Genome Orgn., Am. Inst. Biol. Scis., N.Y. Acad. Scis., N.Y. Soc. Tropical Medicine, World Acad. Art and Sci., B'nai B'rith, Sigma Xi, Phi Kappa Phi. Office: Am Acad Arts & Scis 3000 Berkeley Pl Irvine CA 92697-7425

SILVERMAN, TREVA, writer, producer, consultant; b. N.Y.C. d. Nathan and Janno (Harra) S. Student, U. Chgo., 1956; BA, Bennington Coll., 1958. Staff writer: (TV) The Entertainers, 1964, The Monkees, 1966, 67, 68, Captain Nice, 1968, Room 222, 1969, The Mary Tyler Moore Show, 1970-75 (Emmy award Best Comedy Writer 1974, Writer of Yr. 1974); episode writer He and She, 1968, Get Smart, 1968; writer: (TV pilots) Dates from Hell, 1991, Boy, Girl, Boy, 1991, Home Again, 1992, Ladies Night, 1992, The Rev, 1995, San Diego Presents, 1996; (features) A Nice Girl, 1980, Going All the Way, 1986, Act One, 1987; writer, prodr. children's musicals Theatre East, N.Y.C., 1960-63, Scandal, 1985, Hearts' Desire: Out of Town, 1992; contbg. writer: Julius Monk's Upstairs at the Downstairs, 1962-64; cons. Columbia pictures TV comedy programming, 1985-86, MTM Prodns., 1986, Just in Time, ABC-TV, 1987. Named one of TV Women of Yr., Ladies Home Jour., 1975. Mem. Writers Guild Am. (Best Spl./Variety Writer award 1969), Dramatists Guild, Acad. TV Arts and Scis. Democrat. Office: 8827 Beverly Blvd Los Angeles CA 90048-2405

SILVERSTEIN, JOSEPH HARRY, conductor, musician; b. Detroit, Mar. 21, 1932; s. Bernard and Ida (Katz) S.; m. Adrienne Shufro, Apr. 27; children: Bernice, Deborah, Marc. Student, Curtis Inst. Music, 1945-50; D (hon.), Tufts U., 1971, R.I. U., 1980, Boston Coll., 1981, New Eng. Conservatory, 1986, Susquehanna, 1996, Brigham Young U., 1998. Violinist Houston Symphony Orch., Phila. Orch.; concertmaster Denver Symphony Orch., Boston Symphony Orch.; formerly chmn. string dept. New Eng. Conservatory Music; also chmn. faculty Berkshire Music Sch.; mem. faculty Boston U. Sch. Music, Yale U. Sch. Music; music dir. Boston Symphony Chamber Players, Boston U. Symphony Orch., Chautauqua (N.Y.) Instn., 1987—; interim music dir. Toledo Symphony Orch.; prin. guest condr. Balt. Symphony Orch., 1981; condr. Utah Symphony, music dir., 1983—, condr. laureate, 1998—. Mem. faculty Longy Sch., Curtis Inst.; artistic advisor Winnepeg and Aartford Symphonies. Recipient Silver medal Queen Elizabeth of Belgium Internat. contest, 1959, Naumber Found. award, 1960; named one of ten outstanding young men Boston C. of C., 1962. Fellow Am. Acad. Arts and Scis.; mem. Chamber Music Soc. Lincoln Ctr. (artist). Office: Utah Symphony Orch 123 W South Temple Salt Lake City UT 84101-1496 E-mail: jogyviolin@aol.com

SILVERSTEIN, MARTIN ELLIOT, surgeon, consultant, writer; b. N.Y.C., Sept. 6, 1922; s. Louis and Ethel (Statman) S.; m. Mabelle A. Cremer, Dec. 10, 1962. AB cum laude, Columbia U., 1945; MD, N.Y. Med. Coll., 1948. Instr. bacteriology N.Y. Med. Coll., 1953-57, asst. to dean for clin. scis., 1953-58, instr. surgery, 1953-55, asst. dean, 1958; asst. vis. surgeon Bird S. Coler Hosp., N.Y.C., 1953-57, assoc. vis. surgeon, 1957-60; asst. vis. surgeon Met. Hosp., N.Y.C., 1953-57, assoc. vis. surgeon, 1957-60; asst. attending surgeon Flower and 5th Ave. Hosps., N.Y.C., 1953-57; asst. attending surgeon Monorah Med. Ctr. U. Kans. Sch. Medicine, N.Y.C., 1963-65, exec. dir. Monorah Med. Ctr. Kansas City, 1963-65, exec. dir. Danciger Inst. for Health Scis. Mo., 1963-66, chmn. dept. exptl. surgery Danciger Inst. for Health Scis., 1963-66; chmn. dept. Surgery Menorah Med. Ctr. U. Kans. Sch. Medicine Affiliate, Kansas City, 1963-66; assoc. clin. prof. surgery U. Kans. Sch. Medicine, Kansas City, 1966-67; surgeon courtesy staff N.Y. Infirmary, 1969; surgeon Grand Canyon Med. Group and Hosp., 1969-70; chief sect. on surgery of trauma, dept. surgery U. Ariz. Coll. Med., Tucson, 1974-80, adj. assoc. prof. optical scis., 1979-83, assoc. prof. surgery, 1974-83, dir. quality assurance Univ. Hosp., 1983-84, rsch. prof. family and community medicine, internat. medicine, 1984-85, rsch. prof. surgical biology, 1984-85; sr. fellow in sci. and tech. Ctr. for Strategic and Internat. Studies Georgetown U., Washington, 1983-87. Pres. Claude Gips Found. Inc., N.Y.C., 1967-93; disting. vis. prof. Uniformed Svcs. U. Health Scis., 1984, adj. prof. surgery, 1999—; clin. prof. surgery F. Edward Hebert Sch. Medicine, 1984-99; disting. vis. prof. Tulane U. Med. Sch., 1984; mem. internat. adv. bd. Univ. Microfilms Internat. Collections on Terrorism, 1987—; internat. cons. Disaster Mgmt. and Disaster Medicine, Australia, India, others, 1983—; gov. emeritus Internat. Coun. for Computer Comm., 1996—, exec. com. v.p. 1977-92; bd. rep. Am. Coll. Nuclear Med., 2001—. Author: Disaster: Your Right to Survive, 1991; mem. editorial bd. Terrorism, 1976—, Prehosp. and Disaster Medicine, 1989—; assoc. editor Jour. Prehosp. Care, 1984-85;

contbr. articles to profl. jours. With U.S. Army, 1943-45; lt. (j.g.) USNR, 1946-53. Fgn. fellow NSF, 1974. Fellow ACS (chmn. Ariz. State com. on trauma 1979-84), Am. Assn. for Surgery of Trauma, Am. Coll. Emergency Physicians, Am. Coll. Gastroenterology, Am. Coll. Nuc. Medicine (bd. reps. 2001—); mem. World Assn. for Emergency and Disaster Medicine (exec. com. 1987-92), Critical Care Soc., Internat. Coun. Computer Comm. (co-founder).

SILVERSTONE, LEON MARTIN, neuroscientist, cardiologist, educator, researcher; b. London, May 21, 1939; came to U.S., 1976; s. Jack Stanley and Sadie (Osen) S.; children from previous marriage: Samantha, Frances, Mark; m. Deborah Advani, Sept. 13, 1998. Student, U. London, 1958-59; L.D.S., U. Leeds, U.K., 1963, B.Ch.D., 1964, D.D.Sc., 1971; L.D.S., Royal Coll. Surgeons, Eng., 1964; PhD, U. Bristol, Eng., 1967; postgrad., U. London, 1969-76. House surgeon Leeds Dental Hosp., Eng., 1963-64; rsch. fellow med. rsch. coun. unit Bristol Med. and Dental Sch., 1964-67; lectr. in dental surgery U. Bristol, 1967-68; sr. lectr. child dental health Med. Coll., Royal London Hosp., 1969-75, reader in preventive and pediat. dentistry, 1975-76; cons. Royal London Hosp., 1973-76; vis. Lasby prof. Dental Sch. U. Minn., Mpls., 1974-75; prof., head divsn. cardiology Dows Inst. Dental Rsch., Coll. Dentistry, U. Iowa, Iowa City, 1976-82; assoc. dean rsch. Dental Sch. U. Colo. Health Scis. Ctr., Denver, 1982-89, dir. Oral Scis. Rsch. Inst., 1986-89; biomed. cons., 1990; v.p. R & D The Synaptic Corp., La Jolla, Calif., 1990-95; dir. R&D BioSciences Systems LLC, La Jolla, 1995—. Vis. Nicholaysen prof. U. Oslo, 1972; cons. Pan Am. Health Orgn., 1973-85, dental rsch. Va, 1978-85; mem. study sect. and program adv. com. NIH-Nat. Inst. Dental Rsch., 1976-84, chmn. subcom. on dental caries, 1982-83, chmn. program adv. com., 1983-84; pres. Neura Corp., La Jolla, Calif., 1997-98. Mem. editorial bd. Caries Rsch., 1976-86; contbr. chpts. to books, articles in field to profl. publs. Recipient Nobel-Pharma A.B. Bofors prize in child dental health, 1971, ORCA-ROLEX rsch. prize, 1973, Disting. award in child dental health, 1981; NIH/Nat. Inst. Dental Rsch. grantee, 1976-89. Mem. European Orgn. Caries Research (mem. bd., sci. councillor 1971-83, pres. 1977-79), Internat. Assn. Dental Research (pres. cariology group 1982-83, Disting. Scientist award 1984), Am. Assn. Dental Research (pres. cariology group chpt. 1982-83, chmn. publs. com. 1985-86), Brit. Dental Assn., Internat. Assn. Dentistry for Children (exec. com. 1972-79, jour. editor 1971-79), AAAS, Soc. Exptl. Biology and Medicine, Space Medicine Com., AAUP, Am. Acad. Pedodontics, Omega Kappa Upsilon, Sigma Xi. Office: 3248 Brant St San Diego CA 92103 E-mail: neuromod@home.com

SILVERTON, NANCY, food service executive; b. June 20, 1954; m. Mark Peel; three children. Student, Calif. State U., Cordon Bleu, London, Ecole Le Notre, France. Pastry chef Michael's Restaurant, Santa Monica, Calif.; 1st exec. pastry chef Spago, West Hollywood; founder LaBrea Bakery, L.A., 1989, v.p. product devel., exec. v.p. Recipient Chef of Yr. award James Beard Found., Top 10 Chefs award Food and Wine Mag. Office: Campanile Restaurant 624 S LaBrea Ave Los Angeles CA 90036

SILVESTRI, ALAN ANTHONY, film composer; b. N.Y.C., Mar. 26, 1950; s. Louis and Elizabeth (Clarke) S.; m. Sandra Dee Shue; children: Alexandra, Joseph, James. PhD in Music (hon.), Berklee Coll. Music, Boston, 1995. Film scores include The Doberman Gang, 1972, The Amazing Dobermans, Las Vegas Lady, 1976, Romancing the Stone, 1984, Par ou t'es rentre? On t'as vu sortir, 1984, Fandango, 1984, Cat's Eye, 1984, Back to the Future, 1985 (Grammy award nominations best instrumental composition and best album of original score for a motion picutre, 1985), Summer Rental, 1985, Clan of the Cave Bear, 1986, The Delta Force, 1986, American Anthem, 1986, Flight of the Navigator, 1986, No Mercy, 1986, Critical Condition, 1987, Outrageous Fortune, 1987, Predator, 1987, Overboard, 1987, Who Framed Roger Rabbit?, 1988 (Grammy award nominations best instrumental composition and best album of original score for a motion picutre, 1988), My Stepmother Is an Alien, 1988, Mac and Me, 1988, She's Out of Control, 1989, Downtown, 1989, The Abyss, 1989, Back to the Future II, 1989, Back to the Future III, 1990, Young Guns II, 1990, Predator II, 1990, Soapdish, 1991, Dutch, 1991, Ricohet, 1991, Shattered, 1991, Father of the Bride, 1991, Ferngully: The Last Rainforest, 1992, Death Becomes Her, 1992, Stop! Or My Mom Will Shoot, 1992, The Bodyguard, 1992, Cop and a Half, 1993, Sidekicks, 1993, Super Mario Bros., 1993, Judgment Night, 1993, Grumpy Old Men, 1993, Clean Slate, 1994, Blown Away, 1994, Forrest Gump, 1994 (Academy award nomination best original score 1994, Grammy award nomination best instrumental performance 1994, Golden Globe award nomination best original score 1994), Richie Rich, 1994, The Quick and the Dead, 1994, The Perez Family, 1995, Judge Dredd, 1995, Father of the Bride II, 1995, Sgt. Bilko, 1995, Grumpier Old Men, 1995, Eraser, 1996, Long Kiss Goodnight, 1996, Fools Rush In, 1996, Volcano, 1997, Contact, 1997, Mousehunt, 1997, Odd Couple II, 1998, Parent Trap, 1998, Holyman, 1998, Practical Magic, 1998, Siegfried & Roy, The Magic Box, 1999, Stuart Little, 1999, Reindeer Games, 2000, What Lies Beneath, 2000; TV themes include CHiPs, 1978-83, Manimal, 1983. Recipient ACE award Nat. Acad. Cable Programming for Tales from the Crypt - All Through the House, 1990, Saturn award Acad. Arts and Sci. for fantasy and horror film, 1987. Mem. Nat. Acad. Recording Arts and Scis., Acad. Motion Picture Arts and Scis.

SIMERVILLE, JAMES JASPER, pediatrician; b. Bend, Oreg., Sept. 15, 1939; s. George Melvin and Clara Louise (Jasper) S.; m. Carol Marie Smith, Dec. 26, 1961; children: Pamela Marie, Steven James, Jeffrey Alan. BS, Oreg. State U., 1961; MD, U. Oreg., 1965. Diplomate Am. Bd. Pediatrics; diplomate in occupational medicine Am. Bd. Preventive Medicine. Commd. 2d lt. USAF, 1964, advanced through grades to col., 1979; intern USAF Hosp. Travis, Travis AFB, Calif., 1965-66; resident USAF Hosp. Wilford Hall, Lackland AFB, Tex., 1966-68; chief pediatric svc. USAF, Westover AFB, Mass., Lakenheath, Eng., and Scott AFB, Ill., Eng., 1968-75; dir. med. edn. USAF Hosp. Scott, Scott AFB, 1975-84; cons. in pediatrics, then dep. comdr. U.S. Air Force Acad. Hosp., Colorado Springs, Colo., 1976-84; retired USAF, 1984; dir. Colorado Springs Sports Medicine Clinic, 1984-87, Colo. Ctr. Occupational Medicine, Colorado Springs, 1985-92; med. dir. Colorado Springs Health Ptnrs., 1992-96, Pacific Care, 1996—. Med. cons. sports medicine program, Chapman Coll., Colorado Springs, 1983-88. Fellow Am. Acad. Pediatrics; mem. Colo. Med. Soc., El Paso County Med. Soc. Roman Catholic. Avocations: walking, hiking, camping, golf, skiing. Office: Pacific Care 5755 Mark Dabling Blvd Ste 350 Colorado Springs CO 80919-2247

SIMKIN, PETER ANTHONY, internist, educator; b. Morgantown, W.Va., Nov. 22, 1935; s. William Edward and Ruth Helen (Commons) S.; m. Penelope Hart Payson, Aug. 9, 1958; children— Andrew, Caroline, Mary, Elizabeth. B.A., Swarthmore Coll., 1957; M.D., U. Pa., 1961. Intern N.C. Meml. Hosp., Chapel Hill, 1961-62, resident, 1962-63, Univ. Hosps. Cleve., 1965-66; fellow in medicine U. Wash., Seattle, 1966-69, asst. prof., 1969-74, assoc. prof., 1974-84, prof., 1984—. Mem. editorial bd.: Arthritis and Rheumatism, 1981-85, BIMR Rheumatology, 1980-84; contbr. articles to profl. jours. Bd. dirs. Wash. chpt. Arthritis Found., 1974-90, chmn. med. and sci. com., 1974-78. Served with U.S. Army, 1963-65. Fellow Am. Coll. Rheumatology; mem. Western Soc. Clin. Research, Am. Fedn. Clin. Investigation. Quaker. Office: U Wash Rheumatology 356428 Seattle WA 98195-0001

SIMMONS, GEOFFREY STUART, physician; b. Camp Gordon, Ga., July 28, 1943; s. Ted R. and Jane A. (Lavander) S.; m. Sherry Simmons, Sept. 7, 1985; children: Bradley, Anais. BS, U. Ill., 1965, MD, 1969. Intern U. So. Calif., L.A., 1969-70, resident, 1971-74; pvt. practice Astoria, Oreg., 1974-77, Eugene, 1977—; chmn. internal medicine dept. Peace Health Med. Group, 1996-98, 2000—. Bd. dirs. Lane County Med. Soc.; med. correspondent KUGN Radio, 1993-95. Author: The Z Papers, 1977, The Adam Experiment, 1978, Pandemic, 1980, Murdock, 1982, The Glue Factory, 1995, To Glue Or Not To Glue, 1997; med. commentator KABC Radio, 1970. Avocation: writing.

SIMMONS, GEORGE FINLAY, mathematics educator; b. Austin, Tex., Mar. 3, 1925; s. George Finlay and Armede Victoria (Hatcher) S.; m. Hope Bridgeford, Sept. 11, 1954; 1 child, Nancy Bingham. BS, Caltech, 1946; MS, U. Chgo., 1948; PhD, Yale U., 1957. Instr. U. Chgo., 1947-50, U. Maine, Orono, 1950-52, Yale U., New Haven, 1952-56; asst. prof. U. R.I., Kingston, 1956-58, Williams College, Williamstown, Mass., 1958-62; assoc. prof. math. Colo. Coll., Colorado Springs, 1962-65, prof., 1965-90, prof. emeritus, 1990—. Author: Introduction Topology and Modern Analysis, 1962, Differential Equations, 1972, 2d edit., 1991, Precalculus Mathematics in a Nutshell, 1981, Calculus with Analytic Geometry, 1985, 2d edit., 1995, Calculus Gems: Brief Lives and Memorable Mathematics, 1992. Mem. Math. Assn. Am. Avocations: travel, cooking, trout fishing, billiards. Home: 1401 Wood Ave Colorado Springs CO 80907-7348 Office: Colorado College Dept Math Colorado Springs CO 80903

SIMMONS, JANET BRYANT, writer, publisher; b. Oakland, Calif., Apr. 22, 1925; d. Howard Pelton and Janet Horn (McNab) Bryant; m. William Ellis Simmons, May 17, 1944 (div. 1979); children: William Howard, Janet Margaret Simmons McAlpine. BA, San Jose State U., 1965; MA, U. San Francisco, 1979. Social worker Santa Clara County Social Svcs., San Jose, Calif., 1965-91; editor, pub. Enlightenment Press, Santa Clara, 1994—. Author: The Mystical Child, 1996. Mem. AAUW, Am. Booksellers Assn., Pubs. Mktg. Assn., Bay Area Ind. Pubs. Assn., Audubon Soc., Jacques Cousteau Soc. Avocations: playing piano, swimming, Tai Chi, travel, gardening. Office: Enlightenment Press PO Box 3314 Santa Clara CA 95055-3314 E-mail: enlightenmentpress@home.com

SIMMONS, RAYMOND HEDELIUS, lawyer; b. Salinas, Calif., May 27, 1958; s. Raymond Hedelius and Antoinette (Lynch) S. BA magna cum laude, U. Calif., San Diego, 1979; JD magna cum laude, U. Calif., San Francisco, 1982. Bar: Calif. 1982, U.S. Dist. Ct. (no. dist.) Calif. 1982, Ga. 1987. Assoc. Farella, Braun & Martel, San Francisco, 1982-85; atty., v.p. Barnett-Range Corp., Atlanta, 1985-86; counsel Nationwide Capital Corp. subs. HomeFed. Bank, Atlanta, 1986, HomeFed. Bank, San Diego, 1987-90; gen. counsel, sr. v.p., sec. ITT Fed. Bank, San Francisco, 1990-95; also ITT Residential Capital Corp., ITT Residential Capital Servicing Corp., San Francisco; pvt. practice, Newport Beach, Calif., 1995—. Mem. ABA, Calif. Bar Assn., Ga. Bar Assn., Calif. Scholarship Fedn. (life), Order of Coif, Thurston Soc. E-mail: simmonsfirm@mindspring.com

SIMMONS, RICHARD J. lawyer; b. Brockton, Mass., Nov. 26, 1951; BA summa cum laude, U. Mass., 1973; JD, U. Calif., Berkeley, 1976. Bar: Calif. 1976. Ptnr. Sheppard, Mullin, Richter & Hampton, L.A., 1995—. Lectr. State of Calif., 1977-88; instr. UCLA, 1980-87; appointed to bd. Calif. Minimum Wage Bds. 1982, 84, 87; adv. bd. U. Calif. Boalt Hall Law Sch. Indsl. Relations Law Journal, 1985—. Reviews editor, editor in chief: Indsl. Relations Law Jour. 1975-76; Author: Wrongful Discharge and Employment Practices Manual, 1989, 2001, Employee Handbook and Personnel Policies Manual, 1983, 87, 92, Wage and Hour Manual for California Employers, 1982, 86, 88, 89, 91, 2001, Employment Discrimination and EEO Practice Manual for California Employers, 1982, 85, 91, 2000, Employer's Guide to the American with Disabilities Act, 1990, 91, 92, The Employer's Guide to the California Family Rights Act of 1991, 1992, 2000, Employer Obligations Under the Federal Plant Closing Law, 1989, The New Federal Polygraph Law, 1989, The New Federal Immigration Law: The Immigration Reform and Control Act of 1986, 1987, COBRA: The Federal Health Insurance Rules for the 1990's, 1987,90, 2001; contbr. articles to profl mags. and jours. Commonwealth scholar. Mem. ABA (labor, employment law, tax sect.), L.A. County Bar Assn. (tax, labor sect.), The State Bar Calif., Calif. Soc. Health Care Attys., Am. Soc. Health Care Attys., Phi Kappa Phi. Office: Sheppard Mullin Richter & Hampton 333 S Hope St Ste 4700 Los Angeles CA 90071-1448

SIMMONS, ROY WILLIAM, banker; b. Portland, Oreg., Jan. 24, 1916; s. Henry Clay and Ida (Mudd) S.; m. Elizabeth Ellison, Oct. 28, 1938; children— Julia Simmons Watkins, Matthew R., Laurence E., Elizabeth Jane Simmons Hoke, Harris H., David E. Asst. cashier First Nat. Bank Layton, Utah, 1944-49; Utah bank commr., 1949-51; exec. v.p. Bank of Utah, Ogden, 1951-53; pres. Lockhart Co., Salt Lake City, 1953-64, Zion's First Nat. Bank, Salt Lake City, 1964-81, chmn. bd., 1965-98. Chmn., CEO Zion's Bancorp, 1965-91, chmn. bd., 1991—; chmn. bd. Zion's Savs. & Loan Assn., 1961-69; pres. Lockhart Co., 1964-87; bd. dirs. Ellison Ranching Co. Chmn. Utah Bus. Devel. Corp., 1969-80; Mem. Utah State Bd. Regents, 1969-81. Mem. Salt Lake City C. of C. (treas. 1964-65), Sigma Pi. Republican. Mem. Ch. of Jesus Christ of Latter Day Saints. Home: 817 Crestwood Rd Kaysville UT 84037-1712 Office: Zions Bancorp 10 E South Temple Ste 1000 Salt Lake City UT 84133-1112

SIMMONS, SARAH R. lawyer; b. Ducktown, Tenn., Jan. 23, 1948; BA magna cum laude, U. Ariz., 1970, postgrad.; JD magna cum laude, U. Denver, 1973. Bar: Colo. 1974, Ariz. 1975. Mem. Molloy, Jones & Donahue, Tucson, Brown & Bain, P.A., Tucson. Trustee Tohono Club Park, 1995—, sec., 1997-99, v.p. 1999-2001, pres., 2001—; trustee Tucson Airport Authority, 1996—; mem. Law Coll. Assn. Bd., 1996—, sec. 1998—, pres. 2000-01; 4th R bd. Tucson Unified Sch., 1996—; bd. dirs. United Way of Tucson, 1995-2000, Family Advocacy Resource and Wellness Ctrs., Resources for Women, 1995-2000; bd. dirs. Ariz. Town Hall, 1998—; mem. adv. bd. Ariz. for a Drug Free Workplace, 1991—, So. Ariz. Sports Devel. Corp., U. Ariz. Social and Behavioral Scis., 1994-96; sec. So. Ariz. Minutemen, 1996-98. Recipient Tucson Woman of Yr. C. of C., 1994, Women on the Move award YWCA, 1995, Outstanding Alumni award U. Ariz. Coll. of Law, 1993; named one of 100 Women and Minorities in the Law, 2000. Fellow ABA, Ariz. Bar Assn.; mem. Nat. Assn. Bond Lawyers, State Bar Ariz. (bd. govs. 1987-95, sec.-treas. 1989-90, 2d v.p. 1990-91, 1st v.p. 1991-92, pres.-elect 1992-93, pres. 1993-94, employment law sect., profl. conduct com., fee arbitration com.), Ariz. Women Lawyers Assn. (charter), Colo. Bar Assn., Pima County Bar Assn. (bd. dirs. 1985-94), Am. Judicature Soc., So. Ariz. Legal Aid (bd. dirs. 1990-93), Lawyers Against Hunger (bd. dirs., v.p. D-M 50 1996-98, pres. 1998-2000), Order St. Ives, Phi Beta Kappa, Phi Kappa Phi, Phi Alpha Theta, Kappa Beta Pi. Office: Brown & Bain PA 1 S Church Ave Fl 19 Tucson AZ 85701-1612

SIMMONS, WILLIAM, physicist, retired aerospace research executive; b. Chgo., Apr. 24, 1932; s. Walter Garfield and Edna Dean (Winch) S.; m. Barbara Millet Haury, Oct. 4, 1954; children: Sheryl Lee, Cynthia Jane, Shelly Jean. BA in Physics, Carleton Coll., 1953; MS in Physics, U. Ill., 1955, PhD in Physics, 1960. Mem. tech. staff Space Tech. Labs., Redondo Beach, Calif., 1960-62; sr. rsch. scientist Gen. Tech., Torrance, 1962, TRW, Redondo Beach, 1962-71, dir. rsch., 1984-89, chief engr. spl. projects assigned to Lawrence Livermore (Calif.) Labs., 1989-92; engring. mgr. Lawrence Livermore Labs., 1972-84, rsch. reviewer, 1985-89; prof. engring. UCLA, 1968-72. Tech. panel mem. U. Calif., Berkeley, 1985; tech. reviewer Dept. Energy, Washington, 1986—, mem. rev. com., 1987—; cons. in field, 1992-99. Editor, reviewer 2 books, 1982, 83; contbr. numerous articles to profl. jours. 10 patents in electro-optics devices. Named Disting. Engring. Prof. of Yr. UCLA, 1972, one of Top 100 Innovators in U.S.A, Sci. Digest, 1986; George F. Baker Found. scholar Carleton Coll., 1949-53. Mem. IEEE (sr., life, gen. chmn. symposia 1988, 89, Simon Ramo Major medal 1987), Laser Inst. Am., Laser Engring. and Optical Soc., Am. Phys. Soc., Soc. of Photographic and Instrumentation Engrs., U.S. Chess Club, Phi Beta Kappa, Sigma Xi. Republican. Avocations: chess, table tennis, bridge. Office: Sys Solutions 1621 W 25th St Ste 231 San Pedro CA 90732-4300

SIMNAD, MASSOUD T. engineering educator; b. Teheran, Iran, Mar. 11, 1920; came to U.S., 1948; s. Reza an Ferhunde (Magari) S.; m. Lenora Virginia Brown, May 28, 1954; childrne: Jeffrey, Virginia. BS, London U., 1942; PhD, U. Cambridge, Eng., 1946. Rsch. fellow U. Cambridge, 1945-48; postdoctoral fellow Carnegie-Mellow U., Pitts., 1949-50, mem. faculty, 1950-56; with Gen. Atomics, San Diego, 1956-81; adj. prof., cons. in engring. U. Calif., San Diego, 1981—. Vis. prof. MIT, Cambridge, 1962-63; mem. tech. coms. U.S. Dept. Energy, 1970—; cons. in field. Author papers, monographs in field; patentee in field. Fellow Am. Nuc. Soc., Am. Soc. Metals, AAAs; mem. AIAA, NAE, Electrochem. Soc., Inst. Global Conflict and Cooperation, World Affairs Coun., UN Club, Sierra Club. Avocations: art, music, gardening, sports, travel. Home: 2393 Garth Rd Charlottesville VA 22901-5415 Office: U Calif Mail Code R-011 La Jolla CA 92093 E-mail: msimnad@aol.com

SIMON, MARVIN KENNETH, electrical engineer, consultant; b. N.Y.C., Sept. 10, 1939; s. Sidney and Belle (Cone) S.; m. Anita Joyce Sauerhof; children: Brette, Jeffrey. BEE, CCNY, 1960; MSEE, Princeton U., 1961; PhD, NYU, 1966. Mem. tech. staff Bell Telephone Labs., Holmdel, N.J., 1961-63, 66-68; sr. rsch. engr. Jet Propulsion Lab., Pasadena, Calif., 1968—. Adj. prof. Calif. Inst. Tech., Pasadena, 1986-87, 88-90. Author: Telecommunications Systems Engineering, 1973, Phase-Locked Loops and Their Application, 1978, reprinted, 1991, Spread Spectrum Communications, Vols. I, II, III, 1984, Introduction to Trellis--Coded Modulation with Application, 1990, Digital Communication Techniques, Vol. I: Signal Design and Detection, 1994, Spread Spectrum Communications Handbook, 1994, Mobile Communications Handbook, 1995, Digital Communications over Fading Channels: A Uniform Approach to Performance Analysis, 2000; also numerous articles; patentee in field. Recipient NASA Exptl. Svc. medal, 1979, NASA Exptl. Engring. Achievement medal, 1995. Fellow IEEE (Bicentennial medal 1984, Armstrong Achievement award 1997, 3d Millennium medal 2000), Inst. for Advancement Engring. Avocation: computer games. Office: Jet Propulsion Lab Mail Stop 238-343 4800 Oak Grove Dr Pasadena CA 91109-8001

SIMON, MELVIN I. molecular biologist, educator; b. N.Y.C., Feb. 8, 1937; s. Hyman and Sarah (Liebman) S.; m. Linda, Jan. 7, 1959; children— Joshua, David, Rachel B.S., CCNY, 1959; Ph.D., Brandeis U., 1963. Postdoctoral fellow Princeton U., N.J., 1963-65; prof. biology U. Calif.-San Diego, La Jolla, 1965-82, Calif. Inst. Tech., Pasadena, 1982—, chmn., 1995-2000, prof., 2000—. Pres., dir. Agouron Inst., La Jolla, 1980— Contbr. articles to profl. jours. Mem. Nat. Acad. Scis. (Selman A. Waksman microbiology award 1991), Am. Soc. Microbiology

SIMON, RALPH E. electronics executive; b. Passaic, N.J., Oct. 20, 1930; s. Paul and Sophie (Epstein) S.; m. Elena Schiffman, June 22, 1952; children: Richard L., David P., Michael A. BA, Princeton U., 1952; PhD, Cornell U., 1959. Mem. tech. staff RCA Labs., Princeton, N.J., 1958-67, dir., 1967-69; mgr. RCA Electronic Components, Lancaster, Pa., 1969-75; v.p. RCA Solid State Div., Lancaster, 1975-80; v.p. optoelectronics div. Gen. Instrument Corp., Palo Alto, Calif., 1980-84; pres. Lytel Inc., Somerville, N.J., 1984-87; pres., CEO QT Optoelectronics, Sunnyvale, Calif., 1989—. Dir. Xsirius Scientific, Inc., Marina Del Rey, Calif., 1988-91, Applied Electron Corp., Santa Clara, Calif., 1987—. Pres., mem. Lawrence Twp. Bd. Edn., Lawrenceville, N.J., 1964-69, Community Action Orgn., 1967-69. Recipient UK Zworykin prize IEEE, 1973. Office: QT Optoelectronics 610 N Mary Ave Sunnyvale CA 94085-2906

SIMON, RICHARD D. transportation executive; Chmn., pres., CEO Simon Transp. Svcs., West Valley City, Utah, 1988—. Office: Simon Transp Svcs 5175 W 2100 S West Valley City UT 84120-1252 Fax: 800-777-0004

SIMON, RONALD I. financial executive; b. Cairo, Nov. 4, 1938; came to U.S., 1942; s. David and Helene (Zilkha) S.; m. Anne Faith Hartman, June 19, 1960; children: Cheryl, Eric, Daniel. BA, Harvard U., 1960; MA, Columbia U., 1962, PhD, 1968. V.p. Harpers Internat., N.Y.C., 1959-62; fin. analyst Amerace Corp., N.Y.C., 1965-66; v.p. Am. Foresight Inc., Phila., 1966-67; asst. to pres. Avco Corp., Greenwich, Conn., 1967-70; exec. v.p. Avco Community Developers Inc., La Jolla, Calif., 1970-73; pres. Ronald I. Simon Inc., La Jolla, 1973—, Delta Data Systems Corp., Phila., 1980-81; exec. v.p. Towner Petroleum Corp., Houston, 1983-85; mng. dir., chief fin. officer The Henley Group Inc., La Jolla, 1986-90; pvt. practice fin. cons. La Jolla, 1990—. Vice-chmn. bd. dirs. Softnet Corp., San Francisco, Calif., 1998-2001, acting chmn. and CEO, 2001—; bd. dirs. Collateral Therapeutics, Inc., San Diego, Western Water Co., Point Richmond, Calif.; exec. v.p., CFO/bd. dirs. Western Water Co., San Diego, 1997-2000. Bd. dirs. San Diego Opera Co., 1988-90; bd. dirs. Univ. Art Gallery U. Calif., San Diego, 1991-95. Ford Found. fellow, 1963-65. Office: 1020 Prospect St La Jolla CA 92037-0068

SIMON, SHELDON WEISS, political science educator; b. St. Paul, Jan. 31, 1937; s. Blair S. and Jennie M. (Dim) S.; m. Charlann Lilwin Scheid, Apr. 27, 1962; 1 child, Alex Russell BA summa cum laude, U. Minn., 1958, PhD, 1964; MPA, Princeton U., 1960; postgrad., U. Geneva, 1962-63. Asst. prof., then prof. U. Ky., 1966-75; prof. polit. sci. Ariz. State U., 1975—, chmn. dept., 1975-79, dir. Ctr. Asian Studies, 1980-88. Vis. prof. George Washington U., 1965, U. B.C., Can., 1972-73, 79-80, Carleton U., 1976, Monterey Inst. Internat. Studies, 1991, 96, Am. Grad. Sch. Internat. Mgmt., 1991-92; cons. USIA Rsch. Analysis Corp., Am. Enterprise Inst. Pub. Policy Rsch., Hoover Instn., Orkand Corp.; cons., dir. S.E. Asian Projects, Nat. Bur. Asian Rsch., 1998. Author: Asian Neutralism and U.S. Policy, 1975, The ASEAN States and Regional Security, 1982, The Future of Asian-Pacific Security Collaboration, 1988; editor: The Military and Security in the Third World, 1978, East Asian Security in the Post-Cold War Era, 1993, Southeast Asian Security in the New Millenium, 1996, The Many Faces of Asian Security, 2001; also others; contbr. articles to profl. jours., chpts. to books. Mem. Com. Fgn. Relations, Phoenix, 1976— ; bd. dirs. Phoenix Little Theater, 1976-79 Grantee Am. Enterprise Inst., 1974, Earhart Found., 1979, 81, 92, 84, 88, U.S. Inst. Peace, 1994-96, 2000-01, Nat. Bur. Asian Rsch., 1998, W. Alton Jones Found., 2000; Hoover Instn. fellow, 1980, 85. Mem. Am. Polit. Sci. Assn., Assn. Asian Studies, Internat. Studies Assn. (profl. ethics com. 1987-91, v.p. 1991-93), Asia Soc. (contemporary affairs com. 1987—), U.S. Coun. for Asia-Pacific Security (exec. bd. 1998—), Phi Beta Kappa. Democrat. Jewish Avocations: acting, singing, tennis. Home: 5630 S Rocky Point Rd Tempe AZ 85283-2134 Office: Ariz State U Polit Sci Dept Tempe AZ 85287 E-mail: shells@asu.edu

SIMONDS, JOHN EDWARD, newspaper editor; b. Boston, July 4, 1935; s. Alvin E. and Ruth Angeline (Rankin) S.; m. Rose B. Muller, Nov. 16, 1968; children— Maximillian P., Malia G.; children by previous marriage— Rachel F., John B. B.A., Bowdoin Coll., 1957. Reporter Daily Tribune, Seymour, Ind., 1957-58, UPI, Columbus, Ohio, 1958-60; reporter, asst. city editor Providence Jour. Bull., 1960-65, Washington Evening Star, 1965-66; corr. Gannett News Svc., Washington, 1966-75; mng. editor Honolulu Star Bull., 1975-80, exec. editor, 1980-87, sr. editor, editorial page editor, 1987-93; exec. Hawaii Newspaper Agy., Honolulu, 1993-99; reader rep. The Honolulu Advertiser, 1999—. Served with U.S. Army, 1958. Mem. Am. Soc. Newspaper Editors, AP Mng. Editors, Soc. Profl. Journalists, Nat. Conf. Editl. Writers, Orgn. News Ombudsmen. Home: 5316 Nehu Pl Honolulu HI 96821-1941 Office: The Honolulu Advertiser 605 Kapiolani Blvd Honolulu HI 96813-5195 E-mail: jsimonds@honolulu.gannett.com

SIMONE, ROBERT M. broadcast executive; b. Springfield, Mass., Dec. 11, 1949; V.p., gen. mgr. Sta. KDVR-TV, Denver, 1997—. Office: Sta KDVR TV 100 E Speer Blvd Denver CO 80203-3437

SIMONI, ROBERT D. biology educator; married; 3 children. BA in Biology, San Jose State Coll., 1962; PhD in Biochemistry, U. Calif., Davis, 1966. Postdoct. fellow biology dept. Johns Hopkins U., Balt., 1966-68, rsch. assoc., 1968-71; asst. prof. dept. biol. scis. Stanford (Calif.) U., 1971-77, assoc. prof. dept. biol. scis., 1977-82, prof. dept. biol. scis., 1982—, chmn. dept. biol. scis., 1985-86, 89-94. Vis. scholar Max-Planck Inst. Biology, Tubingen, Germany, 1977-78; ad hoc mm. cell biology study sect. NIH, 1973, biochemistry study sect., 1975, mem. biochemistry study sect., 1976-80, mem. chmn.'s adv. com. to dir. on peer review, 1979, chmn. phys. biochemistry study sect., 1979-80, mem. cellular and molecular basis of disease rev. pcoml. Gen. Med. Scis., 1987-91; spkr., lectr. in field. Editor: Jour. Biochemistry, 1996, Jour. Biochemistry, Molecular Biology and Biophysics, 1996; assoc. editor, mem. editl. bd. Jour. Biol. Chemistry, 1987—; mem. editl. bd. Jour. Supramolecular Structure, 1978-86; developer Jour. biol. Chemistry On Line, 1994. contbr. numerous articles to profl. jours. Fellow NSF, 1966-68, Fulbright fellow, 1977-78; recipient William C. Rose award Am. Soc. Biochemistyr and Molecular Biology, 1998. Mem. Am. Cancer Soc. (biochemistry-carcinogenesis rev. panel 1979-80, chmn. 1986-87). Home: 563 Jefferson Dr Palo Alto CA 94303-2834 Office: Stanford U Biol Scis Dept Gilbert Bldg 326 B Stanford CA 94305-5020

SIMONS, LYNN OSBORN, educational consultant, federal agency official; b. Havre, Mont., June 1, 1934; d. Robert Blair and Dorothy (Briggs) Osborn; m. John Powell Simons, Jan. 19, 1957; children: Clayton Osborn, William Blair. Tchr. Midvale (Utah) Jr. H.S., 1956-57, Sweetwater county Sch. Dist. 1, Rock Springs, Wyo., 1957-58, U. Wyo., 1959-61, Natrona County Sch. Dist. 1, Casper, Wyo., 1963-64; credit mgr. Gallery 323, Casper, 1972-77; Wyo. state supt. pub. instrn. Cheyenne, 1979-91; sec.'s regional rep. region VIII U.S. Dept. Edn., Denver, 1993-95; mem. Denver Fed. Exec. Bd., 1995-2001; ednl. cons., 1993—. Mem. State Bds. Charities and Reform, Land Commrs., Farm Loan, 1979-91; mem. State Commns. Capitol Bldg., Liquor, 1979-91; Ex-officio mem. bd. trustees U. Wyo., 1979-91; ex-officio mem. Wyo. Community Coll. Commn., 1979-91; mem. steering com. Edn. Commn. of the States, 1988-90; mem. State Bd. Edn., 1971-77, chmn., 1976-77; advisor Nat. Trust for Hist. Preservation, 1980-86. Mem. LWV (pres. 1970-71). Democrat. Episcopalian Office: US Dept Edn 1244 Speer Blvd Ste 310 Denver CO 80204-3582 E-mail: siminov@worldnet.att.net

SIMONS, STEPHEN, mathematics educator, researcher; b. London, Aug. 11, 1938; came to U.S., 1965; s. Jack Isidore Simons and Ethel Esther (Littman) Harris; m. Jacqueline Mania Berchadsky, Aug. 13, 1963; 1 son, Mark. BA, Cambridge U., Eng., 1959, PhD, 1962. Instr. U. B.C., Vancouver, Can., 1962-63; asst. prof. U. BC., Vancouver, Can., 1964-65, U. Calif., Santa Barbara, 1965-67, assoc. prof., 1967-73, prof., 1973—, chmn. dept., 1975-77, 88-89. Trustee Math. Scis. Rsch. Inst., Berkeley, Calif., 1988-94. Peterhouse rsch. fellow, Cambridge U., 1963-64. Mem. Am. Math. Soc. Office: Univ Calif Dept Math Santa Barbara CA 93106

SIMONS, THOMAS W., JR. history educator; b. Crosby, Minn., Sept. 4, 1938; s. Thomas Winston and Mary Jo (Enochs) S.; m. Margaret Eleanor Quinn, Dec. 23, 1963; children: Suzanne Deirdre, Benjamin Thomas. BA, Yale U., 1958; MA, Harvard U., 1959, PhD, 1963. Joined Fgn. Svc., Dept. State, 1963; sec. del., tech. sec. U.S. Del. to 6th round trade negotiation in GATT, 1964-67; consular officer, polit. officer Am. Embassy, Warsaw, Poland, 1968-71; Coun. on Fgn. Rels. fellow Hoover Instn., Stanford, Calif., 1971-72; internat. rels. officer Bur. Politico-Mil. Affairs, 1972-74, mem. policy planning staff, 1974-75; chief external reporting unit, polit. sect. Am. Embassy, Moscow, 1975-77, dep. chief of mission Bucharest, Romania, 1977-79, counselor for polit. affairs London, 1979-81; dir. for Soviet Union affairs Dept. State, 1981-85; mem. Sr. Seminar in Fgn. Policy, 1985-86; dep. asst. sec. for European and Can. affairs Dept. State, 1986-89; diplomat-in-residence, adj. prof. history Brown U., Providence, 1989-90; amb. extraordinary and plenipotentiary Poland, 1990-93. Coord. U.S. assistance to new ind. states of former Soviet Union, Washington, 1993-95; amb. extraordinary and plenipotentiary, Pakistan, 1995-98; cons. prof. history Ctr. Internat. Security and Coop. Stanford U., 1998—. Author: The End of the Cold War?, 1990, Eastern Europe in the Postwar World, 2d edit., 1993. Office: Dept History Stanford U Stanford CA 94305-2024

SIMONSON, SUSAN KAY, hospital clinical care coordinator; b. La Porte, Ind., Dec. 5, 1946; d. George Randolph and Myrtle Lucille (Opfel) Menkes; m. Richard Bruce Simonson, Aug. 25, 1973. BA with honors, Ind. U., 1969; MA, Washington U., St. Louis, 1972. Perinatal social worker Yakima Valley Meml. Hosp., Yakima, Wash., 1979-81, dir. patient support program, 1981—, dir. social svc., 1982-98; instr. Spanish, ethnic studies, sociology Yakima Valley Coll., Yakima, 1981—. Pres. Yakima Child Abuse Council, 1983-85; developer nat. patient support program, 1981. Contbr. articles to profl. jours. Mem. adv. council Robert Wood Johnson Found. Rural Infant Health Care Project, Yakima, 1980, Pregnancy Loss and Compassionate Friends Support Groups, Yakima, 1982—, Teen Outreach Program, Yakima, 1984—. Recipient NSF award, 1967, discharge planning program of yr. regional award Nat. Glasrock Home Health Care Discharge Planning Program, 1987; research grantee Ind. U., 1968, Fulbright grantee U.S. Dept. State, 1969-70; Nat. Def. Edn. Act fellowship, 1970-73. Mem. Soc. Med. Anthropology, Soc. Hosp. Social Work Dirs. of Am. Hosp. Assn. (regional award 1989), Nat. Assn. Social Workers, Phi Beta Kappa. Office: Yakima Valley Meml Hosp 2811 Tieton Dr Yakima WA 98902-3799

SIMPSON, ALAN KOOI, former senator, lawyer; b. Cody, Wyo., Sept. 2, 1931; s. Milward Lee and Lorna (Kooi) S.; m. Ann Schroll, June 21, 1954; children— William Lloyd, Colin Mackenzie, Susan Lorna. BS, U. Wyo., 1954, JD, 1958; LLD (hon.), Calif. Western Sch. of Law, 1983, Colo. Coll., 1986, Notre Dame U., 1987; JD (hon.), Am. U., 1989, Rocky Mountain Coll., 1996, U. Wyo., 1999. Bar: Wyo. 1958, U.S. Supreme Ct. 1964. Asst. atty. gen. State of Wyo., 1959; city atty. City of Cody, 1959-69; ptnr. Simpson, Kepler, and Simpson, Cody, Wyo., 1959-78; mem. Wyo. Ho. of Reps., 1964-77, majority whip, 1973-75, majority floor leader, 1975-77, speaker pro tem, 1977; mem. U.S. Senate from Wyo., 1978-96, asst. majority or minority leader, 1984-94, chmn. vets. affairs com., chmn. fin. subcom. on Social Security and Family Policy, chmn. subcom. on immigration and refugee policy; mem. Spec. Com. on Aging; dir. Inst. Politics Kennedy Sch. Govt. Harvard U.; shareholder Burg, Simpson, Eldredge, Hersh & Jardine PC, Cody, Wyo. Guest lectr. London exchange program Regent's Coll., London, 1987; vis. lectr. Lombard chair Shorenstein Ctr. for Press, Politics and Pub. Policy, Kennedy Sch. Govt., Harvard [illegible] Synergy Techs. Corp. Chmn. bd. trustees Buffalo Bill Hist. Ctr. (trustee emeritus), Cody, Grand Teton Music Festival; mem. Smithsonian Nat. Bd., Washington; bd. trustees Folger Shakespears Libr., Washington; dir. Inst. of Politics of the Kennedy Sch. Harvard Univ., Cambridge, Mass. Recipient Nat. Assn. Land Grant Colls. Centennial Alumni award U. Wyo., 1987, Lifetime Svc. award Vietnam Vets. Am., 1993, Thomas Jefferson award in law U. Va., 1998. Mem. Wyo. Bar Assn., Park County Bar Assn., U. Wyo Alumni Assn. (pres. 1962, 63, Disting. Alumnus award 1985), VFW (life), Am. Legion, Amvets. (Silver Helmet award). Lodges: Eagles, Elks, Masons (33 deg.), Shriners, Rotary (pres. local club 1972-73). Office: Burg Simpson Eldredge Hersh & Jardine 1135 14th St PO Box 490 Cody WY 82414

SIMPSON, ALLYSON BILICH, lawyer; b. Pasadena, Calif., Feb. 5, 1951; d. John Joseph and Barbaran Rita (Bessolo) Bilich; m. Roland Gilbert Simpson, Aug. 11, 1979; children: Megan Elise, Erin Marie, Brian Patrick. BS, U. So. Calif., L.A., 1973, JD, 1976. Bar: Calif. 1976. Staff atty. Gen. Telephone Co., Thousand Oaks, Calif., 1978-79; group staff atty., dir. legis. compliance Pacific Mut. Life Ins. Co., Newport Beach, 1980-86; corp. counsel and sec. Amicare Ins. Co., Beverly Hills, 1986; assoc. Leboeuf, Lamb, Leiby & MacRae, L.A., 1986-87; from assoc. to ptnr. Musick, Peeler & Garrett, L.A., 1988-94; ptnr. Sonnenschein Nath & Rosenthal, L.A., 1994-95; sr. v.p., sec., gen. counsel Fremont Compensation Ins. Group, Glendale, Calif., 1995—. Vis. pro. bus. law U. So. Calif., L.A., 1981. Trustee St. Anne's Maternity Home Found., L.A., 1991-97; bd. dirs. St. Anne's Maternity Home, L.A., 1993-97. Mem. Western Pension and Benefits Conf., Conf. Ins. Counsel, Am. Corp. Counsel Assn. Republican. Roman Catholic. Avocations: music, reading, family. Office: Fremont Compensation Ins Group 500 N Brand Blvd Ste 1100 Glendale CA 91203-3392

SIMPSON, BARCLAY, manufacturing company executive; b. Oakland, Calif., May 25, 1921; s. Walter Chapin and Jessie B. (Smith) S.; m. Joan Devine Simpson, Oct. 10, 1945 (div. 1971); children: John, Anne, Jean; m. Sharon Elizabeth Hanley, June 8, 1984; children: Jeffrey, Julie, Amy, Elizabeth. BSBA, U. Calif., Berkeley, 1966. Chmn. Simpson Mfg. Co. Inc., Pleasanton, Calif., 1980—; owner, dir. Barclay Simpson Fine Arts Gallery, Lafayette, 1981—. Bd. dirs. Civic Bank of Commerce, Oakland, Calif., McFarland Energy Corp., Santa Fe Springs, Calif., Calender-Robinson Ins., San Francisco. Author: (exhbn. catalogue) Rembrandt, 1989. Bd. dirs. Bay Area Rapid Transit, Oakland, 1977-88, pres., 1977; trustee John Muir Hosp., Walnut Creek, 1967-75, Univ. Art Mus., Berkeley, Calif., 1988—, Calif. Coll. Arts & Crafts, Oakland, 1987—. Sr. lt. USN, 1942-46, PTO. Address: UC Berkeley Art Museum & Pacific Film Archive 2625 Durant Ave Berkeley CA 94720-2250

SIMPSON, CHARLES ROBERT, marketing professional; BS in Bus. Adminstrn., U. Tenn., 1971; MBA in Mktg., Bloomfield Coll., 1973. Gen. ptnr. Simpson Constrn. and Restoration, Paterson, N.J., 1972-79; v.p. sales and mktg. The Jim Walter Corp., Tampa, Fla., 1979-83; v.p. franchise mktg. Comml. Credit/Control Data, Mpls., 1983-84; v.p. acquisitions Equity Program Investment Corp., Falls Church, Va., 1984-85; pres., gen. mgr. Simpson Mktg. Group, Chandler, Ariz., 1985-87; v.p. mktg. and sales Hooker U.S.A., L.J. Hooker Homes, L.J. Hooker Internat., Phoenix, Atlanta, Dallas, 1987-91; cons. Resolution Trust Corp.-Oversight Bd., Phoenix, Denver, 1991—. Lectr. Ariz. State U., Tempe, Harvard U. Grad. Sch. Bus. Contbg. editor of rsch. recommendations in weekly publs. Mem. Habitat for Humanities; adv. bd. Resolution Trust Corp.; mem. Greenspeace; past mem. bd. dirs. Verde Valley Sch., Sedona, Ariz. Recipient Pacesetter award Nat. Assn. Homebuilders, 1989, MIRM designation, 1988, MAME award in a career total of 21 categories, 1987-90, Nat. MIRM award, 1988. Mem. Nat. Trust for Hist. Preservation, Nat. Park and Wildlife Fedn., Benevolent Protective Order of Elks, Univ. Club, Essex County Hist. Soc. (past pres.). Office: PO Box 31203 Phoenix AZ 85046-1203 E-mail: tfqcrs@msn.com

SIMPSON, DAVID WILLIAM, artist, educator; b. Pasadena, Calif., Jan. 20, 1928; s. Frederick and Mary Adeline (White) S.; m. Dolores D. Debus, July 30, 1954; 1 stepchild, Gregory C. Vose; 1 child, Lisa C. B.F.A., Calif. Sch. Fine Arts, 1956; M.A., San Francisco State Coll., 1958. Instr. art Am. River Jr. Coll., Sacramento, 1958-60, Contra Costa Jr. Coll., San Pablo, Calif., 1960-65; prof. art U. Calif., Berkeley, 1967-91, prof. emeritus, 1991—. Exhibited in one-man shows including Robert Elkon Gallery, N.Y.C., 1961, 63, 64, San Francisco Mus. Art, 1967, Henri Gallery, Washington, 1968, Oakland Mus., 1978, Modernism, San Francisco, 1980-81, 84, 86, 2001, Sheldon Meml. Art Gallery, Lincoln, Nebr., 1990, Mincher/Wilcox Gallery, San Francisco, 1991, 92, 93, Angles Gallery, Santa Monica, Calif., 1991, 92, 94, 99, Bemis Found., Omaha, Nebr., 1991, Anthony Ralph Gallery, N.Y.C., 1992, John Berggruen Gallery, San Francisco, 1994, Charlotte Jackson Fine Art, Santa Fe, 1995, Laguna Art Mus., Laguna Beach, Calif., 1995 Haines Gallery, San Francisco, 1997, 99, 2000, Studio La Citta, Verona, Italy, 1998, Renate Scroder Gallery, Koln, Germany, 2000, 2001; group shows include Mus. Modern Art, N.Y.C., 1963, Carnegie Internat., Pitts., 1961-62, 66-67, L.A. Mus. Art, 1964, U. Ill., 1969, Expo '70, Osaka, Japan, 1970, Josly Art Mus., Omaha, 1970, John Berggruen Gallery, San Francisco, 1979, Angles Gallery, Santa Monica, 1988, 90, John Good Gallery, N.Y., 1992, John Berggruen Gallery, San Francisco, 1993, Cheryl Haines Gallery, San Francisco, 1996, Museo di Arte Moderna e Contemporanea, Trento, Italy, 1996, Studio La Citta, Verona, Italy, 1996, Llonja, Palma De Majorca, Spain, 1997, Museo Cantonale d'Arte, Lugano, Switzerland, 1997, Studio La Citta, Verona, Italy, 1997, Haines Gallery, San Francisco, 1997, Palazzo Ducale, Gubbio, Italy, 1999; represented in permanent collections including Phila. Mus. Art, Nat. Collection Fine Arts, Washington, Seattle Art Mus., La Jolla (Calif.) Mus. Art, Mus. Modern Art, N.Y.C., San Francisco Mus. Art, Oakland (Calif.) Mus., Panza Collection, Italy, Laguna Art Mus., Laguna Beach, Calif., Univ. Art Mus., Berkeley, Calif., Museo Cantonale d'Arte Lugano, Switzerland. Home: 565 Vistamont Ave Berkeley CA 94708-1244 Office: U Calif Dept Art Berkeley CA 94720

SIMPSON, MICHAEL, talent agent; Co-head William Morris Agy., Beverly Hills, Calif. Office: William Morris Agy 151 S El Camino Dr Beverly Hills CA 90212-2775

SIMPSON, MICHAEL K. congressman; b. Burley, Idaho, 1950; m. Kathy Johnson, 1971. Student, Utah State U.; DDS, Washington U., St. Louis, 1978. Dentist, Blackfoot, Idaho, 1978—; mem. from 2d Idaho dist. U.S. Ho. Reps., Washington, 1999—. Serves on Agr., Resources, Transp. and Infrastructure and Veterans Affairs coms. Served as spkr. majority caucus chmn. and asst. majority leader in the Idaho Ho. Reps.Elected to U.S. Ho. Reps. in 1998, when 3-term Rep. Michael Crapo was elected to the U.S. Senate. Elected to Blackfoot City Coun., 1980, Idaho Ho. Reps., 1984; asst. majority leader, 1989-91; spkr. of the house, 1991-97. Mem. Idaho's Rep. Party Hall of Fame. Recipient Friend of Edn. award, 1994, Citizen of the Yr. award Idaho Family Forum, 1996, Boyd A. Martin award Assn. Idaho Cities. Mem. Idaho State Dental Assn. (Pres.'s award 1998), Am. Legis. Exch. Coun. (state chmn., nat. bd. dirs., Jefferson award 1994). Republican. Avocations: golf, chess, painting. Office: US Ho Reps 1440 Longworth Hob Washington DC 20515-0001*

SIMPSON, O. J. (ORENTHAL JAMES SIMPSON), former professional football player, actor, sports commentator; b. San Francisco, July 9, 1947; s. Jimmie and Eunice (Durton) S.; m. Marguerite Whitley, June 24, 1967 (div.); children: Arnelle, Jason; m. Nicole Brown, 1985 (div. 1992); children: Sydney, Justin. Student, U. So. Calif.; grad., City Coll. San Francisco. Halfback Buffalo Bills, 1969-78, San Francisco 49'ers, 1978-79; sports commentator ABC Sports, 1979-86; analyst ABC Monday Night Football broadcasts, 1984-1985; co-host NBC Sports NFL Live. Motion picture appearances include The Towering Inferno, 1974, The Cassandra Crossing, 1977, Killer Force, 1976, Capricorn One, 1978, Firepower, 1979, Hambone & Hillie, 1984, The Naked Gun, 1988, The Naked Gun 2 1/2: The Smell of Fear, 1991, The Naked Gun 33 1/3: The Final Insult, 1994; TV films include A Killing Affair, 1977, Goldie and the Boxer, 1979, The Golden Moment: An Olympic Love Story, 1980, Student Exchange, Cocaine and Blue Eyes; co-host "NFL" Live on NBC, 1990—; author: I Want to Tell You, 1995. Recipient Heisman trophy N.Y. Downtown Athletic Club, 1968; voted Coll. Player of Decade ABC Sports, 1970; named to Am. Football League All-Star Team, 1970, ProBowl Team, 1972, 73, 74, 75, 76; named Nat. Football League Player of Decade Pro Football Monthly, 1979; inducted into Pro Football Hall of Fame, 1985; mem. world record 440 yard relay team (38.6 seconds), 1967; former record holder for most yards rushing gained in a season, most yards rushing gained in a game. Office: care O J Simpson Enterprises 11661 San Vicente Blvd Ste 632 Los Angeles CA 90049-5114

SIMPSON, ROBERT GLENN, lawyer; b. Seattle, June 27, 1932; s. Harold Vernon and Anna Rondeau (McCabe) S.; m. Josephine Anne Heald, June 7, 1959; children: Jenifer Jane, Thomas Glenn, Mary Elizabeth. BS, U. Oreg., 1954; LLB, Willamette U., 1959. Bar: Oreg. 1959. Assoc. William B. Adams Law Office, Portland, Oreg., 1959-67; ptnr. Adams McLaughlin & Simpson, Portland, 1967-70, Schwabe Williamson & Wyatt, Portland, 1970—. Trustee, sec. Legacy Good Samaritan Hosp. and Med. Ctr., Portland, 1983-89, mem. cmty. bd., 1989-98; trustee, chancellor Episcopal Diocese of Oreg., Portland, 1988—. Mem. Oreg. State Bar (exec. com. health law sect. 1987-90), Am. Health Lawyers Assn. (program com. 1987-88), Oreg. Acad. Healthcare Attys. (pres. 1977-78, legis. com. 1989), Multnomah Athletic Club, Univ. Club. Home: 13345 SW Iron Mountain Blvd Portland OR 97219-9306 Office: Schwabe Williamson & Wyatt 1211 SW 5th Ave Ste 1800 Portland OR 97204-3713 E-mail: rsimpson@schwabe.com

SIMS, DOUGLAS D. bank executive; b. 1946; Grad., U. Ill., Urbana, 1968. With St. Louis Bank for Cooperatives, St. Louis, 1969-74; v.p. Ctrl. Bank for Coops., 1974-78; pres. St. Louis Bank for Coops., 1978-84; exec. v.p. Farm Credit Banks of St. Louis, 1984-86, pres., 1986-88, Nat. Bank for Cooperatives, Englewood, Colo., 1988-93; CEO CoBank, Englewood, 1994—. Office: CoBank 5500 S Quebec St Greenwood Village CO 80111-1914

SINAY, HERSHEL DAVID, publishing executive; b. Chgo., Mar. 15, 1938; s. Irving Paul and Gertrude (Drucker) S. BA, U. So. Calif., 1960. Telecom. and Cinema account exec. Wall St. Jour., L.A., 1961-63; account exec. R.J. Friedman Assocs., L.A., 1963-66; dir. sales Performing Arts Mag., L.A., 1966-72; pub. East, West Network, L.A., 1972-79, 85-87; pres., pub. Calif. Bus. Mag., L.A., 1979-85; pub., editor-in-chief Ranch & Coast Mag., DelMar, Calif., 1987-88; pub. Am. Film. Mag., L.A., 1988-91; pres. Project Mktg. Custom Publ. Specialists divsn. Sinay Comm., Inc., L.A., 1991—. Pub. Am. Cinema Editors Tribute Program, 1993-97, Billboard Music Awards Tribute Book, 1993, 1st Ann. Thurgood Marshall Lifetime Achievement Award Tribute Book, NAACP Legal Def. and Ednl. Fund, 1993, 96. Recipient 32 Maggie awards Western Pub. Assn., 1979-2000, Pub Am. Film Inst. Life Achievement awards Tribute Book, 1991—. Mem. Am. Film Inst., Western Pub. Assn. (v.p., bd. dirs.), L.A. Advt. Club. Avocations: yachting, jogging, gardening, photography. Office: 810 S Hauser Blvd Los Angeles CA 90036-4726 E-mail: publish@mediaone.net

SINAY, JOSEPH, retail executive; b. Chgo., Dec. 5, 1920; s. Hyman and Ella S.; m. Ruth Milman, Mar. 7, 1961; 1 dau., Elise Sinay Spilker. Student, Herzl Jr. Coll., 1939. Gen. mgr. Fanchon & Marco Theatres, L.A., 1943-54; v.p., founder Interstate United, Chgo., 1953-56; ptnr. Josam Investment Co., L.A., 1956-97, Sinay Co. L.L.C., L.A., 1997—; pres., CEO R B Industries Inc., L.A., 1956-89, also chmn. bd. dirs., cons.; chmn. bd. dirs. Gorian Sinay Land Co., Inc., L.A., 1997—. Bd. dirs. Am. Acad. Dramatic Arts; pres. Variety Clubs Internat., 1985-87; gen. chmn. United Jewish Welfare L.A., 1976; pres. We. region Am. Friends Hebrew U., 1980; Calif. fin. chmn. Muskie for Pres., 1972; trustee Idyllwild Arts Found., 1968-73; bd. dirs. Constl. Rights Found., 1973-78. Mem. Nat. Home Furnishing Assn. Jewish. Office: Sinay Co LLC 1801 Century Park E Los Angeles CA 90067-2302

SINCLAIR, ALASTAIR JAMES, geology educator; b. Hamilton, Ont., Can., Aug. 1, 1935; s. Burton Leslie and Grace (Isherwood) S.; m. Elizabeth Mary Sylvia Hill, June 13, 1964; children: Alison Trevena, Fiona Tamsin. BS, U. Toronto, 1957, MS, 1958; PhD, U. B.C., 1964. Asst. prof. U. Wash., Seattle, 1962-64, U. B.C., Vancouver, 1964-68, assoc. prof., 1968-74, prof., 1974-98, prof. emeritus, 1999—, head dept. geol. scis., 1985-90, dir. Geol. Engring., 1979-80, 81-82, 92-98. Pres. Sinclair Cons. Ltd., Vancouver, 1980—; Can. Inst. Mining and Metallurgy Disting. lectr., 1999-2000. Contbr. numerous articles to profl. jours. Killam Sr. fellow, 1990-91. Fellow Geol. Assn. Can. (treas. mineral deposits divsn. 1978-89, Disting. Svc. award 2001), Soc. Econ. Geologists; mem. Assn. Profl. Engrs. B.C., Internat. Assn. Math. Geologists, Assn. Exploration Geochemists (councillor 1992-96), Can. Inst. Mining, Metallurgy and Petroleum (life, disting. lectr. 1999-2000, Robert Elver award 1991), Geol. Soc. Brazil (hon. mem. sci.-tech. commn. geochemistry 1982), Brazilian Geochem. Soc. (hon. 1987). Avocations: classical music, skiing, golf. Home: 2972 W 44th Ave Vancouver BC Canada V6N 3K4 Office: U BC Dept Earth and Ocean Scis Vancouver BC Canada V6T 1Z4

SINCLAIR, JAMES WALTER, lawyer; b. Twin Falls, Idaho, June 17, 1953; s. James A. and Orriette (Coiner) S.; m. Jeanne L. Williams, Mar. 18, 1983. BA, Stanford U., 1975; JD, U. Idaho, 1978. Bar: Idaho 1978, U.S. Dist. Ct. Idaho 1978. Assoc. Benoit & Alexander, Twin Falls, 1978-81; ptnr. Benoit, Alexander & Sinclair, Twin Falls, 1981-85, Benoit, Alexander, Sinclair, Harwood & High, Twin Falls, 1985—. Pres. Magic Valley Regional Med. Ctr. Found., Inc., Twin Falls, 1987-89; chair ind. affiliates Am. Heart Assn., 1992-93, chair-elect Rocky Mountain com., 1993-94; chmn. profl. com. United Way, 1980, bd. dirs., 1981-83, assoc. campaign chmn., 1982, v.p., campaign chmn., 1983, loaned exec., 1989-90; mem. guidance adv. bd. Twin Falls Sch. Dist., 1989-91, incorporator and legal counsel, 1991, sec., bd. dirs. Ednl. Found., Inc., 1991—; bd. dirs. Magic Valley Regional Med. Ctr. Found., Inc., 1987-90, pres., 1989; mem. profl. adv. com. Coll. So. Idaho Estate Planning Coun., 1991—. Mem. ABA (young lawyers divsn. 1978-83, chmn. membership Idaho young lawyer divsn. 1978-80, arson project com. 1982-83, law & media com. 1982-83), Am. Heart Assn. (bd. dirs. Idaho 1987—, chmn. 1992-93, divsn. pres. 1993—, co-chair divsn. heart ball 1993—, chair North West Rocky Mountain Region heart com. 1994, chair Idaho long range/ strategic planning com. 1994—, bd. dirs. 1996—, nominating issues task force 1996, co-chair structure task force 1996, Meritorious Achievement award 1996), Internat. Assn. Def. Coun., Def. Rsch. Inst., Idaho Bar Assn. (profl. conduct review com. 1982-84, civil rules adv. bd. 1984-88, fee arbitration com. 1996, sec./treas. Ffith Jud. Dist. 1980-81, v.p. Fifth Dist. 1981), Idaho Def. Counsel Assn., Young Family Christian Assn. (bd. dirs. 1981-83, membership com. 1982-83, first v.p. 1983), Stanford Club Idaho (co-pres. 1982-83). Avocations: snow skiing, golf, tennis, jogging. Office: Benoit Alexander Sinclair Harwood & High PO Box 366 126 2d Ave N Twin Falls ID 83303-0366

SINCLITICO, DENNIS J. lawyer; b. St. Louis, Jan. 9, 1947; BA, U. San Diego, 1968; JD cum laude, U. Wis., 1971. Bar: Wis. 1971, Calif. 1972, U.S. Dist. Ct. (cen. and so. dists.) Calif. 1972. Prof. Calif. Coll. Law, 1972; ptnr. La Follette, Johnson, De Haas, Fesler & Ames, P.C., L.A. Arbitrator spl. arbitration plan Los Angeles County Superior Ct., 1975—. Mem. Am. Bd. Trial Advocates (nat. exec. com. 1978—, pres. L.A. chpt., editor newsletter), State Bar Wis., State Bar Calif., Assn. So. Calif. Def. Counsel (program chmn. 1980-81, bd. dirs. 1980—), Cal-Abota (chair 1994), Phi Alpha Delta. Office: La Follette Johnson De Haas Fesler & Ames PC 865 S Figueroa St Ste 3100 Los Angeles CA 90017-2578

SINCOFF, STEVEN LAWRENCE, chemistry educator; b. N.Y.C., Apr. 17, 1948; s. Murray B. and Lillian (Goldberg) S.; m. Marcella Seay, June 12, 1993; children by previous marriage: Kristina Lynne, Carolyn Suzanne. BSChemE, N.J. Inst. Tech., 1969, MSChemE, 1972; PhD in Analytical Chemistry, Ohio State U., 1980. Commd. 2d lt. USAF, 1969, advanced through grades to lt. col., 1987, retired, 1991, fuels mgmt. officer, 1970-74; chem. engr. Aero. Systems Div., Wright-Patterson AFB, Ohio, 1974-77; assoc. prof. chemistry USAF Acad., Colorado Springs, Colo., 1980-84, dir. continuing edn. dept. chemistry, 1982-84; chief gas analysis lab. McClellan (AFB) Cen. Lab., Calif., 1984-88; exec. officer to comdr. Tech. Ops. Div. McClellan AFB, 1988-89, chief info. officer, 1989-91; gen. mgr. ChemWest Analytical Lab., Sacramento, 1991-92; dir. ops. Barringer Labs., Inc., Golden, Colo., 1992-94; instr. chemistry C.C. Aurora, 1995-98, Butte Coll., Oroville, Calif., 1998—. Reviewer chemistry textbooks Saunders Pub., Phila., 1983-84. Mem. Am. Chem. Soc., Air Force Assn. Jewish. Avocations: microcomputers, hiking. Home and Office: 14574 Carnegie Rd Magalia CA 95954-9647 Office: Butte Coll Dept Chemistry Oroville CA 95965 E-mail: sincoffst@butte.cc.ca.us

SINEGAL, JAMES D. wholesale distribution executive; b. 1936; With Fed-Mart Corp., 1954-77, exec. v.p.; v.p. Builders Emporium, 1977-78; exec. v.p. Price Co., 1978-79; with Sinegal/Chamberlin & Assocs., 1979-83; pres., COO Costco Wholesale Corp., Issaquah, Wash., 1983—, CEO, 1988—, bd. dirs. Address: Costco Wholesale PO Box 34331 999 Lake Dr Ste 200 Issaquah WA 98027-8982

SINES, RANDY DWAIN, business executive; b. Spokane, Jan. 16, 1948; s. Myron Jones and Paula Inez (Walls) S.; m. Irene Cheng, Mar. 18, 1981. Student, Wash. State U., 1966-67, U. Wash., 1968-69. Lic. water well contractor, Wash., Mont. With Boeing Co., 1967, Winchell's Donut House, Inc., Seattle, 1968-71; owner, mgr. bakeries Wash. and Mont., 1972-78; owner, mgr. Sonsine Inc., Great Falls, Mont., 1976-79; pres. Gardian Port Corp., Oxnard, Calif., 1980-82; pres., chmn. SNS Motor Imports, Inc., Oxnard, 1982-86; chmn. Karakal Corp. of Ams., Ventura, Calif., 1986-89; CEO, chmn. Steel Stix, U.S.A., 1990—; chmn. MIT U.S.A. Corp., 1991—; mng. ptnr. Sharps Internat., 1993—. CEO Casinovations Inc., 1995-96; founder, CEO Inven Corp., Spokane, Wash., 1996-97; chmn. Digideal Corp., Las Vegas, 1998—. Holder more than 50 utility patents. Recipient alumni grant Wash. State U., 1967. Home: 4056 S Madelia St Spokane WA 99203-4227 E-mail: rsines@digideal.com, rds@mittusa.com

SINGER, ALLEN MORRIS, lawyer; b. Mpls., Dec. 30, 1923; s. William and Ida (Simenstein) S. JD, U. Chgo., 1948; LLM, Harvard U., 1958. Bar: Ill. 1948, Calif. 1949. Pvt. practice, 1950-55, 59—; v.p., sec., gen. counsel ABM Industries, San Francisco, 1969-85. Assoc. prof. law U. Oreg., 1955-59; lectr. law Stanford (Calif.) U., 1960-62; of counsel Cooper, White & Cooper, San Francisco, 1970-97. Contbr. articles to profl. jours. Mem. U. Chgo. Nat. Alumni Cabinet, 1978-80. 2nd lt., USAAF, 1943-45. Mem. ABA, San Francisco Bar Assn., Calif. Bar Assn. Office: 1070 Green St Ste 703 San Francisco CA 94133-5414

SINGER, FREDERICK RAPHAEL, medical researcher, educator; b. St. Louis, June 27, 1939; s. Meyer and Lee (Minkle) S.; m. Sandra Joy Barnes, Aug. 16, 1964; children: Stefanie, Jeffrey. Student, UCLA, 1956-59; BS, U. Calif., Berkeley, 1960; MD, U. Calif., San Francisco, 1963. Diplomate Am. Bd. Internal Medicine, Am. Bd. Endocrinology and Metabolism. Intern UCLA Affiliated Hosp., 1963-64; resident VA Hosp., L.A., 1964-65, 68-69; instr. in medicine Harvard U., Boston, 1971-72; asst. prof. medicine UCLA, 1972-73, U. So. Calif., L.A., 1973-74, assoc. prof., 1974-78, prof., 1978-89, prof. orthopaedic surgery, 1980-89; dir. Bone Ctr. Cedars-Sinai Med. Ctr., L.A., 1989-92, clin. prof. medicine, 1993—. Dir. Osteoporosis/Metabolic Bone Disease program St. Johns Hosp. and Health Ctr., Santa Monica, 1992—; dir. Skeletal Biology Lab, John Wayne Cancer Inst., Santa Monica, 1992—; mem. endocrine and metabolic drug adv. com. FDA, USPHS, Bethesda, Md., 1983-87. Author: Paget's Disease of Bone, 1977; contbr. numerous articles, revs. to profl. jours. Vice chmn. cmty. adv. com. Univ. High Sch., L.A., 1984. Capt. USAF, 1965-67. Calif. State scholar, 1956-60; clin. investigator VA, 1971-73. Mem. Endocrine Soc., Am. Soc. Clin. Investigation, Am. Soc. Bone and Mineral Rsch. (chmn. pub. affairs 1981-86, coun. 1987, pres.-elect 1989, pres. 1990), Paget's Disease Found. (chmn. bd. dirs. 1990—). Office: John Wayne Cancer Inst 2200 Santa Monica Blvd Santa Monica CA 90404-2302 E-mail: singerf@yahoo.com

SINGER, HERSH, marketing executive; Chmn. SMS Rsch. & Mktg. Svcs. Office: SMS Rsch & Mktg Svcs 1042 Fort St Mall Ste 200 Honolulu HI 96813-5698

SINGER, KURT DEUTSCH, news commentator, writer, publisher; b. Vienna, Austria, Aug. 10, 1911; came to U.S., 1940, naturalized, 1951; s. Ignaz Deutsch and Irene (Singer) S.; m. Hilda Tradelius, Dec. 23, 1932 (div. 1954); children: Marian Alice Birgit, Kenneth Walt; m. Jane Sherrod, Apr. 9, 1955 (dec. Jan. 1985); m. Katherine Han, Apr. 8, 1989. Student, U. Zürich, Switzerland, 1930, Labor Coll., Stockholm, Sweden, 1936; Ph.D., Div. Coll. Metaphysics, Indpls., 1951. Escaped to, Sweden, 1934; founder Ossietzky Com. (successful in release Ossietzky from concentration camp); corr. Swedish mag. Folket i Bild, 1935-40; founder Niemöller Com.; pub. biography Göring in Eng. (confiscated in Sweden), 1940; co-founder pro-Allied newspaper Trots Allt, 1939; corr. Swedish newspapers in, U.S., 1940; editor News Background, 1942; lectr. U. Minn., U. Kans., U. Wis., 1945-49; radio commentator WKAT, 1950; corr. N.Am. Newspaper Alliance, N.Y.C., 1953—; pres. Singer Media Corp., 1987—. Dir. Oceanic Press Service, San Clemente, Calif. Author, editor: underground weekly Mitteilungsblätter, Berlin, Germany, 1933; author: The Coming War, 1934, (biog.) Carl von Ossietzky, 1936 (Nobel Peace prize), Germany's Secret Service in Central America, 1943, Spies and Saboteurs in Argentina, 1943, Duel for the Northland, 1943, White Book of the Church of Norway, 1940, Spies and Traitors of World War II, 1945, Who are the Communists in America, 1948, 3000 Years of Espionage, 1951, World's Greatest Women Spies, 1952, Kippie the Cow; juvenile, 1952, Gentlemen Spies, 1953, The Man in the Trojan Horse, 1954, World's Best Spy Stories, 1954, Charles Laughton Story; adapted TV, motion pictures, 1954, Spies Over Asia, 1955, More Spy Stories, 1955, My Greatest Crime Story, 1956, My Most Famous Case, 1957, The Danny Kaye Saga; My Strangest Case, 1958, Spy Omnibus, 1959, Spies for Democracy, 1960, Crime Omnibus Spies Who Changed History, 1961, Hemmingway-Life and Death of a Giant, 1961, True Adventures in Crime, Dr. Albert Schweitzer, Medical Missionary, 1962, Lyndon Baines Johnson-Man of Reason, 1964, Ho-i-man; juveniles, 1965; Kurt Singer's Ghost Omnibus, 1965; juvenile Kurt Singer's Horror Omnibus; The World's Greatest Stories of the Occult, The Unearthly, 1965, Mata Hari-Goddess of Sin, 1965, Daughter of Mata Hari, 1965, Lyndon Johnson-From Kennedy to Vietnam, 1966, Weird Tales Anthology, 1966, I Can't Sleep at Night, 1966, Weird Tales of Supernatural, 1967, Tales of Terror, 1967, Famous Short Stories, 1967, Folktales of the South Pacific, 1967, Tales of The Uncanny, 1968, Gothic Reader, 1968, Bloch and Bradbury, 1969, Folktales of Mexico, 1969, Tales of the Unknown, 1970, The House in the Valley, 1970, Hablan Los Artistas, 1970, Tales of the Macabre, 1971, Three Thousand Years of Espionage, 1971, El Mundo de Hoy, 1971, Cuentos Fantasticos del Mas, 1971, Aldous Huxley, El Camino al Infierno, 1971, Ghouls and Ghosts, 1972, The Unearthly, 1972, The Gothic Reader, 1972, Satanic Omnibus, 1973, The Plague of the Living Dead, 1973, Gothic Horror Omnibus, 1974, Dictionary of Household Hints and Help, 1974, Supernatural, 1974, They are Possessed, 1976, True Adventures into the Unknown, 1980, I Spied-And Survived, 1980, Great Adventures in Crime, 1982, The Oblong Box, 1982, Shriek, 1984, First Target Book of Horror, 1984, 2d, 1984, 3d, 1985, 4th, 1985, Solve A Crime, 1994, The Ultimate Quiz Book, 1994, The Complete Guide to Career Advancement, 1994, The Sex Quiz Book, 1994, The Marriage Quiz Book, The Psychology Quiz Book, The Teenage Quiz Book, Success Secrets, 1995, Conozcase Mejor y Triunfe, 1995, The Joy of Practical Parenting, 1995; editor: UN Calendar, 1959-58; fgn. corres. German mags., 1996-2000; contbr. articles to newspapers, popular mags., U.S., fgn. countries, all his books and papers in Boston U. Library-Spl. Collections, Awd Literatur Haus, Vienna, Austria. Mem. UN Speakers Research Com., UN Children's Emergency Fund, Menninger Found. Mem. Nat. Geog. Soc., Smithsonian Assos., Internat. Platform Assn. (v.p.), United Sch. Assemblies (pres.)

SINGER, ROBERT, plastic surgeon; b. Buffalo, Oct. 22, 1942; s. Murray and Fay Singer; m. Judith Harris. Student, SUNY, Buffalo, 1960-63; MD, SUNY, 1967. Lic. physician, Calif.; diplomate Am. Bd. Plastic and Reconstructive Surgery. Resident in gen. surgery Stanford Med. Ctr., Palo Alto, Calif., 1967-69, Santa Barbara Cottage and Gen. Hosp., 1972-74; resident in plastic surgery Vanderbilt U., 1974-76; pvt. practice specializing in emergency and trauma San Diego, 1971-72; pvt. practice plastic, reconstructive and aesthetic surgery La Jolla, Calif., 1976—. Prior asst. clin. prof. plastic surgery U. Calif., San Diego; sr. staff, chief plastic surgery Scripps Meml. Hosp., La Jolla, 1980-86, vice chmn. dept. surgery, 1989-91. Contbr. articles to profl. jours. Active San Diego Opera, San Diego Mus. of Man, La Jolla Playhouse, Voices for Children, San Diego Zoo, Mus. Photog. Arts, KPBS, others; mem. exec. com. Anti-Defamation League. Fellow ACS; mem. AMA, Calif. Med. Assn., San Diego County Med. Soc., San Diego Internat. Soc. Plastic Surgeons (pres. 1988-89), Calif. Soc. Plastic Surgeons (pres. 1995), Am. Soc. Aesthetic Plastic Surgeons (pres. 1994-95), Internat. Soc. Clin. Plastic Surgeons, Am. Soc. Plastic and Reconstructive Surgeons (trustee 1996—, chmn. bd. trustees 1998-99), J.B. Lynch Soc., Royal Soc. Medicine, Am. Assn. for Accreditation of Ambulatory Surgery Facilities (v.p. 1998—), San Diego Plastic Surgery Soc. (pres. 1989-90), Aesthetic Surgery Edn. and Rsch. Found. (pres.-elect). Jewish. Avocations: tennis, travel, Pre-Columbian art. Office: 9834 Genesee Ave Ste 100 La Jolla CA 92037-1214

SINGH, LOREN CHAN, technical writing specialist; b. Palo Alto, Calif., Sept. 10, 1943; s. Shau Wing and Anna Mae Chan; m. Frances Anastasia Chow, Apr. 19, 1975 (div. Jan. 1988); children: Karen Monique Chan, Pierre Benedict Chan, Marc Henri Chan; m. Sandra Marie Miner, Mar. 14, 2000. AB, Stanford U., 1965, AM, 1966; MS, Golden Gate U., 1988; PhD, UCLA, 1971. Teaching asst. UCLA, 1968-69, teaching assoc., 1969-70; lectr. in history Calif. State U., Northridge, 1970-71, San Jose (Calif.) State U., 1971-72, asst. prof. history, 1972-76, assoc. prof. history, 1976-80; lectr. history Calif. State U., Hayward, 1980-81; prodn. test technician Nicolet Paratronics Corp., Fremont, Calif., 1982; computer svc. technician Bell-Northern Rsch., Mountain View, 1982-83; rsch. analyst Bell-No. Rsch., Mountain View, 1984-85, tech. writer, 1985-87; sr. tech. writer StrataCom, Inc., Campbell, Calif., 1987-88; tech. writer Sun Microsystems, Palo Alto, 1988-90, sr. tech. writer, 1990-2000; tech. writer Brocade Comms. Sys., Inc., San Jose, Calif., 2000—. Author: Sagebrush Statesman, 1973, SPARCstation 1 Installation Guide, 1989, Collected Technical Support Notes, 1988, SPARCstation 2 Installation Guide, 1990, Desktop Storage Pack Installation Guide, 1989-90, SPARCstation 10 Installation Guide, 1992, SPARCstation 10 Networking and Communication Guide, 1993, SPARCstation 10SX VSIMMs Installation, 1993, SPARCstation 20 HyperSPARC Module Upgrade, 1995, SPARCstation 20 SuperSPARC-II Module Upgrade, 1995, Sun Ultra 1 Reference Manual, 1995-96, Sun Ultra 2 Reference Manual, 1996, Sun Ultra 30 Installation Guide, 1997, Sun Ultra 30 Reference Manual, 1997, SPARCstorage FlexiPack Removable Storage Tray Installation Guide, 1997, Sun StorEdge Long Wave Gigabit Interface Converter Service Manual, 1999, Sun StorEdge PCI Dual Fibre Channel Host Adapter Installation, 2000; editor: Chinese-American History Reader, 1976; contbr. articles to profl. jours. Radio sta. trustee ARC, Menlo Park, Calif., 1975-80. Recipient Presdl. Sports award Pres.'s Coun. on Phys. Fitness and Sports, 1973. Mem. Nat. Geog. Soc., Am. Radio Relay League, Almaden Masters Swim Club. Democrat. Sikh. Avocations: masters swimming, amateur radio, philately. Home: 195 Blossom Hill Rd # 123 San Jose CA 95123-2348 E-mail: lsingh@brocade.com

SINGLEHURST, DONA GEISENHEYNER, horse farm owner; b. Tacoma, June 19, 1928; d. Herbert Russell and Rose Evelyn (Rubish) Geisenheyner; m. Thomas G. Singlehurst, May 16, 1959 (dec.); 1 child, Suanna Singlehurst. BA in Psychology, Whitman Coll., 1950. With pub. rels. and advt. staff Lane Wells, L.A., 1950-52; staff mem. in charge new bus. Bishop Trust Co., Honolulu, 1953-58; mgr. Town & Country Stables, Honolulu, 1958-62; co-owner, v.p. pub. rels. Carol & Mary, Ltd., Honolulu, 1964-84; owner Stanhope Farms, Waialua, Hawaii, 1969—. Internat. dressage judge, sport horse breeding judge Am. Horse Shows Assn.; sr. judge Can. Dressage Fedn. Chmn. ways and means com. The Outdoor Cir., Hawaii, 1958-64, life mem.; pres. emeritus Morris Animal Found., Englewood, Colo., 1988—, pres., 1984-88; bd. dirs., pres. Delta Soc., Renton, Wash., 1994-97, chmn. emeritus 1998—, N.Y.C.; mem. Jr. League of Honolulu. Recipient Best Friends award Honolulu Vet. Soc., 1986, Spl. Recognition award Am. Animal Hosp. Assn., 1988, Recognition award Am. Vet. Med. Assn. Mem. NAFE, AAUW, Hawaii Horse Show Assn. (Harry Hutaff award 1985, past pres., bd. dirs.), Hawaii Combined Tng. Assn. (past pres. bd. dirs.), Calif. Dressage Soc., U.S. Dressage Fedn., U.S. Equestrian Team (area chmn. 1981-85), Hawaiian Humane Soc. (life), U.S. Pony Clubs (dist. commr. 1970-75, nat. examiner 1970-75), Pacific Club, Outrigger Canoe Club. Republican. Episcopalian. Avocations: music, travel. Home and Office: Stanhope Farms PO Box 546 Waialua HI 96791

SINGLETON, FRANCIS SETH, dean; b. Phila., July 13, 1940; s. William Francis and Anna A. (Setian) S.; m. Margaret Neff, June 14, 1962 (div. 1983); children: William, Andrew; m. Charlotte T. Kennedy, Jan. 16, 1988. AB, Harvard U., 1962; MA, Yale U., 1963, PhD, 1968. Budget examiner Bur. of Budget, Washington, 1964-65; dean Pearson Coll. Yale U., New Haven, 1966-69; lectr. U. Dares Salaam, Tanzania, 1969-70; asst. prof. U. Alta., Edmonton, Can., 1970-71; from assoc. prof. to prof., chair politics and govt. Ripon (Wis.) Coll., 1972-83; rsch. assoc. Russian Ctr., Harvard U., Cambridge, Mass., 1983-84; dean arts and scis. Pacific U., Forest Grove, Oreg., 1984-91, prof. govt., 1991—; academic dean Espiritu Santo U., Guayaquil, Ecuador, 1994-97. Ampart lectr. U.S.I.A., Africa, 1983, 90; lectr. Ural U., Russia, 1991; cons. Russia Fedn. Govt., 1992; mem. Pacific Coun. on Internat. Policy, 1998—. Author: Africa in Perspective, 1968; contbr. articles to profl. publs., chpts. to books. Bd. dirs. Com. Fgn. Rels., Portland, 1989-92; mem. adv. com. Light Rail Tri-Met, Portland, Oreg., 1989-94. Grantee Rockefeller Found., 1969-70, Nat. Coun. Soviet and E. Europe Rsch., 1983-84; U.S. Fulbright scholar, Vietnam, 1999-2000. Avocations: sailing, outdoor activities. E-mial. Home: Hall Quarry Rd PO Box 185 Mount Desert ME 04660-0185 Office: Pacific U 2043 College Way Forest Grove OR 97116-1797 E-mail: ssinglet@pacificu.edu, sethsing@acadice.net

SINGLETON, JAMES KEITH, federal judge; b. Oakland, Calif., Jan. 27, 1939; s. James K. and Irene Elisabeth (Lilly) S.; m. Sandra Claire Hoskins, Oct. 15, 1966; children: Matthew David, Michael Keith. Student, U. Santa Clara, 1957-58; AB in Polit. Sci., U. Calif., Berkeley, 1961, LLB, 1964. Bar: Calif. 1965, Alaska, 1965. Assoc. Delaney Wiles Moore and Hayes, Anchorage, 1963, 65-68, Law Offices Roger Cremo, Anchorage, 1968-70; judge Alaska Superior Ct., Anchorage, 1970-80, Alaska Ct. Appeals, Anchorage, 1980-90, U.S. Dist. Ct. for Alaska, Anchorage, 1990-95, chief judge, 1995—. Chmn. Alaska Local Boundary Commn., Anchorage, 1966-69. Chmn. 3d Dist. Rep. Com., Anchorage, 1969-70. Mem. ABA, Alaska Bar Assn., Phi Delta Phi, Tau Kappa Epsilon. Office: US Dist Ct 222 W 7th Ave Unit 41 Anchorage AK 99513-7504

SINISCALCO, GARY RICHARD, lawyer; b. N.Y.C., Aug. 14, 1943; BA in Econs., Le Moyne Coll., 1965; JD, Georgetown U., 1969. Bar: Calif. Regional counsel, sr. trial atty. EEOC, San Francisco, 1969-78; ptnr. Orrick, Herrington & Sutcliffe, San Francisco, 1978—, past co-chair employment law dept. Mem. adv. bd. Nat. Employment Law Inst.; lectr. in field. Co-author: Manager's Guide to Lawful Terminations, 1991; author: (with others) Employment Discrimination Law, 1979, 3rd edit., 1996; contbr. articles to profl. jours. Mem. ABA (mem. com. on internat. labor rels. and equal employment opportunity, mgmt. co-chairperson equal employment opportunity com. 1996-98), State Bar Calif., Bar Commonwealth Va., Am. Employment Law Coun. (founder). Office: Orrick Herrington 400 Sansome St San Francisco CA 94111-3143

SINSHEIMER, ROBERT LOUIS, retired university chancellor and educator; b. Washington, Feb. 5, 1920; s. Allen S. and Rose (Davidson) S.; m. Flora Joan Hirsch, Aug. 8, 1943 (div. 1972); children: Lois June (Mrs. Wickstrom), Kathy Jean (Mrs. Vandagriff), Roger Allen; m. Kathleen Mae Reynolds, Sept. 10, 1972 (div. 1980); m. Karen Current, Aug. 1, 1981. S.B., MIT, 1941, M.S., 1942, Ph.D., 1948. Staff mem. radiation lab. MIT, Cambridge, 1942-46; assoc. prof. biophysics, physics dept. Iowa State Coll., Ames, 1949-55, prof., 1955-57; prof. biophysics Calif. Inst. Tech., Pasadena, 1957-77, chmn. div. biology, 1968-77; chancellor U. Calif., Santa Cruz, 1977-87, chancellor emeritus, 1987—, prof. Santa Barbara, 1988-90, prof. emeritus, 1990—. Editor: Jour. Molecular Biology, 1959-67, Ann. Rev. Biochemistry, 1966-72. Named Calif. Scientist of Year, 1968; recipient N.W. Beijerinck-Virologie medal Netherlands Acad. Sci., 1969 Fellow Am. Acad. Arts and Scis.; mem. Am. Soc. Biol. Chemists, Biophys. soc. (pres. 1970), AAAS, Nat. Acad. Scis. (mem. council 1970-73, chmn. bd. editors Proc. 1972-80), Inst. Medicine. Achievements include discovery of single-stranded DNA, circular DNA; co-investigator in first in vitro replication of infective DNA. Office: U Calif MCD Biology Santa Barbara CA 93106

SION, MAURICE, mathematics educator; b. Skopje, Yugoslavia, Oct. 17, 1928; came to Can., 1960; s. Max and Sarah (Alalouf) S.; m. Emilie Grace Chisholm, Sept. 15, 1957; children: Crispin, Sarah, Dirk. BA, NYU, 1947, MA, 1948; PhD, U. Calif., Berkeley, 1951. Mathematician Nat. Bur. Stds., Washington, 1951-52; instr. U. Calif., 1952-53; asst. prof. U. Calif., 1957-60; mem. Inst. for Advanced Study, Princeton, N.J., 1955-57, 62; asst. prof. U. B.C., Vancouver, Can., 1960, assoc. prof. Can., 1961, prof. Can., 1964-89, prof. emeritus Can., 1989—, head math. dept. Can., 1984-86, dir. Quadra Inst. Math. Can., 1970-89. Author: Introduction to Methods of Real Analysis, 1969, Theory Semi Group Valued Measures, 1973; contbr. articles to profl. jours. With U.S. Army, 1953-55. Mem. Am. Math. Soc., Can. Math. Soc. (v.p. 1972-74). Office: U BC Dept Math Vancouver BC Canada V6T 1Z2

SIRIGNANO, WILLIAM ALFONSO, aerospace and mechanical engineer, educator; b. Bronx, N.Y., Apr. 14, 1938; s. Anthony P. and Lucy (Caruso) S.; m. Lynn Haisfield, Nov. 26, 1977; children: Monica Ann, Jacqueline Hope, Justin Anthony. B.Aero.Engring., Rensselaer Poly. Inst., 1959; Ph.D., Princeton U., 1964. Mem. research staff Guggenheim Labs., aerospace, mech. scis. dept. Princeton U., 1964-67, asst. prof. aerospace and mech. scis., 1967-69, assoc. prof., 1969-73, prof., 1973-79, dept. dir. grad. studies, 1974-78; George Tallman Ladd prof., head dept. mech. engring. Carnegie-Mellon U., 1979-85; dean Sch. Engring., U. Calif.-Irvine, 1985-94, prof., 1994—. Cons. indsutry and govt., 1966—; lectr. and cons. NATO adv. group on aero. rsch. and devel., 1967, 75, 80; chmn. nat. and internat. tech. congs.; chmn. acad. adv. coun. Indsl. Rsch. Inst., 1985-88; mem. space sci. applications adv. com. NASA, 1985-90, chmn. combustion sci. microgravity disciplinary working group, 1987-90; chmn. com. on microgravity rsch. space studies bd. NRC, 1991-94. Assoc. editor: Combustion Sci. and Tech., 1969-70, 2000—; assoc. tech. editor Jour. Heat Transfer, 1986-92; contbr. articles to nat. and internat. profl. jours., also rsch. monographs. United Aircraft research fellow, 1973-74; Disting. Alumni Rsch. award U. Calif. Irvine, 1992. Fellow AIAA (Pendray Aerospace Lit. award 1991, Propellants and Combustion award 1992), ASME (Freeman scholar 1992), AAAS, Am. Phys. Soc.; mem. Inst. Dynamics of Explosives and Reactive Systems (v.p. 1991-95, pres. 1995-99, Oppenheim award 1993), Combustion Inst. (treas. internat. orgn., chmn. ea. sect., Alfred C. Egerton Gold medal 1996), Soc. Indsl. and Applied Math., Orange County Engring. Coun. (Excellence award 1994), Am. Electronics Assn. (recognition 1994). Office: U Calif Sch Engring S3202 Engring Gtwy Irvine CA 92697-0001 E-mail: sirignan@uci.edu

SISK, DANIEL ARTHUR, lawyer; b. Albuquerque, July 12, 1927; s. Arthur Henry and Myrl (Hope) S.; m. Katharine Banning, Nov. 27, 1954; children: John, Sarah, Thomas. B.A., Stanford U., 1950, J.D., 1954. Bar: N.Mex. 1955, Calif. 1954. Ptnr. firm Modrall, Sperling, Roehl, Harris & Sisk, Albuquerque, 1954-70, 71—; justice N.Mex. Supreme Ct., Santa Fe, 1970. Chmn. bd. Sunwest Fin. Svcs., Inc., Albuquerque, 1975-90. Pres. Legal Aid Soc., Albuquerque, 1960-61; trustee Sandia Sch., 1968-72, Albuquerque Acad., 1971-73, A.T. & S.F. Meml. Hosps., Topeka, 1966-82; bd. dirs. N.Mex. Sch. Banking Found., 1981-85. Served with USNR, 1945-46, PTO; to capt. USMCR, 1951-52, Korea. Mem. N.Mex. Bar Assn., Albuquerque Bar Assn. (dir. 1962-63), ABA, State Bar Calif. Presbyn. (elder). Office: 500 4th St NW Albuquerque NM 87102-5324

SISLEY, BECKY LYNN, physical education educator; b. Seattle, May 10, 1939; d. Leslie James and Blanche (Howe) S.; m. Jerry Newcomb, 1994. BA, U. Wash., 1961; MSPE, U. N.C., Greensboro, 1964; EdD, U. N.C., 1973. Tchr. Lake Washington H.S., Kirkland, Wash., 1961-62; instr. U. Wis., Madison, 1963-65, U. Oreg., Eugene, 1965-68, prof. phys. edn., 1968—, women's athletic dir., 1973-79, head undergrad. studies in phys. edn., 1985-92. Co-author: Softball for Girls, 1971; contbr. articles to profl. jours. Mem. athletic adv. bd. Women's Sports Found., 1993-96. Admitted to Hall of Fame, N.W. Women's Sports Found., Seattle, 1981, Honor award, N.W. Dist. Assn. for Health, Phys. Edn., Recreation and Dance, 1988, State of Oreg. Sports Hall of Fame, 1993; recipient Honor award Nat. Assn. for Girls and Women in Sports, 1995, Disting. Alumni award Sch. Health and Human Performance U. N.C., Greensboro, 1996; inducted into U. Oreg. Athletic Hall of Fame, 1998; U.S. record holder Age 50-59 Triple Jump, Javelin, High Jump, Age 55-59 Javelin, Pole Vault, Age 60-64 Javelin, Pole Vault; world record holder Age 55-59, and Age 60-64, Pole Vault. Mem. AAHPERD, Oreg. Alliance Health, Phys. Edn., Recreation and Dance (hon. life mem.), Western Soc. for Phys. Edn. of Coll. Women (exec. bd. 1982-85), Oreg. High Sch. Coaches Assn., N.W. Coll. Women's Sports Assn. (pres. 1977-78), Oreg. Women's Sports Leadership Network (dir. 1987-97), Phi Epsilon Kappa, others. Office: U Oreg Phys Activity & Recreation Svcs Eugene OR 97403

SISSEL, GEORGE ALLEN, manufacturing executive, lawyer; b. Chgo., July 30, 1936; s. William Worth and Hannah Ruth (Harlan) S.; m. Mary Ruth Runsvold, Oct. 5, 1968; children: Jenifer Ruth, Gregory Allen. B.S. in Elec. Engring., U. Colo., 1958; J.D. cum laude, U. Minn., 1966. Bar: Colo. 1966, Ind. 1973, U.S. Supreme Ct. 1981. Assoc. Sherman & Howard, Denver, 1966-70; with Ball Corp., Broomfield, Colo., 1970—, assoc. gen. counsel, 1974-78, gen. counsel, 1978-95, corp. sec., 1980-95, v.p., 1981-87, sr. v.p., 1987-95, pres., 1995-98, CEO, 1995-2001, chmn. bd., 1996—, also bd. dirs. Bd. advisors First Chgo. Equity Capital, 1995—; bd. dirs.

First Merchants Corp. Assoc. editor: U. Minn. Law Rev., 1965-66. Served with USN, 1958-63. Mem. ABA, Can. Mfrs. Inst. (bd. dirs., chmn.), Nat. Assn. Mfrs. (bd. dirs.), Colo. Bar Assn., Colo. Assn. Commerce & Industry, Order of Coif, MIT Soc. Sr. Execs., (bd. govs. 1987-95), Sigma Chi, Sigma Tau, Eta Kappa Nu. Methodist. Lodge: Rotary.

SITVER, MORTON, federal judge; b. 1936; JD, NYU, 1960. Apptd. magistrate judge U.S. Dist. Ct. Ariz., 1979. Office: 5043 US Courthouse Fed Bldg 230 N 1st Ave Phoenix AZ 85025-0230 Fax: 602-514-7096

SIZEMORE, HERMAN MASON, JR. newspaper executive; b. Halifax, Va., Apr. 15, 1941; s. Herman Mason and Hazel (Johnson) S.; m. Connie Catterton, June 22, 1963; children: Jill, Jennifer. AB in History, Coll. William and Mary, 1963; postgrad., U. Mo., 1965; MBA, U. Wash., 1985. Reporter Norfolk (Va.) Ledger-Star, summers 1961, 62, 63; copy editor Seattle Times, 1965-70, copy-desk chief, 1970-75, asst. mng. editor, 1975-77, mng. editor, 1977-81, prodn. dir., 1981-83, asst. gen. mgr., 1984, v.p., gen. mgr., 1985, pres., chief operating officer, 1985—. Vis. instr. Sch. Comms. U. Wash., 1972-78; bd. dirs. Times Comms. Co., Walla Walla Union-Bull, Inc., Yakima Herald-Republic, Blethen Maine Newspapers, Northwestern Mut. Life Ins. Co., 1993—, mem. policyowner examining com., 1985, chmn., 1986. Bd. dirs. Ctrl. Puget Sound Campfire Coun., 1985-91, pres., 1989-90; bd. dirs. Ptnrs. in Pub. Edn., 1987-88, Downtown Seattle Assn.; chmn. bd. dirs. United Way; adv. coun. Puget Sound Blood Ctr. and Program; adv. bd. USO-Puget Sound Area, U. Wash. Sch. Bus. Named Seattle Newsmaker of Tomorrow, 1978; recipient Alumni medallion Coll. William and Mary, 1998. Mem. AP Mng. Editors, Soc. Profl. Journalists, Pacific N.W. Newspaper Assn. (bd. dirs.), Newspaper Assn of Am. (vice-chair newsprint com.), Allied Daily Newspapers Washington, Coll. William and Mary Alumni Assn., Greater Seatt C. of C. (bd. dirs.), U. Wash. Exec. MBA Alumni Assn. (pres. 1988), Wash. Athletic Club (chmn. bd. dirs.), Rainier Club, Rotary. Methodist. Office: Seattle Times PO Box 70 Seattle WA 98111-0070

SIZEMORE, NICKY LEE, computer scientist; b. N.Y.C., Feb. 13, 1946; s. Ralph Lee and Edith Ann (Wangler) S.; m. Frauke Julika Hoffmann, Oct. 31, 1974; 1 child, Jennifer Lee Sizemore; 1 stepchild, Mark Anthony Miracle. BS in Computer Sci., SUNY, 1989. Sgt. first class U.S. Army, 1964-68, 70-86; computer operator UNIVAC, Washington, 1968-69, programmer, 1969-70; programmer/analyst Ultra Systems, Inc., Sierra Vista, Ariz., 1986-87; computer scientist Comarco, Inc., Sierra Vista, 1987-92, ARC, Profl. Svcs. Group, Sierra Vista, 1992-93, Computer Scis. Corp., Ft. Huachuca, Ariz., 1994; sr. cons. Inference Corp., 1995; subject matter expert Northrop Corp., Sierra Vista, Ariz., 1995—; sr. info. sys. engr. Harris Corp., Sierra Vista, 1996—. Speaker numerous confs., seminars, symposia; tech. columnist Sierra vista Herald. Mem. Computer Soc. IEEE, Am. Assn. for Artificial Intelligence (co-dir. workshop on verification, validation, and test of knowledge-based sys. 1988), Assn. for Computing Machinery. Avocations: chess, jogging/aerobics, karate. Home and Office: 880 E Charles Dr Sierra Vista AZ 85635-1611

SKAFF, ANDREW JOSEPH, lawyer, public utilities, energy and transportation executive; b. Sioux Falls, S.D., Aug. 30, 1945; s. Andrew Joseph and Alice Maxine (Skaff) S.; m. Lois Carol Phillips, Oct. 4, 1971; children— Amy Phillips, Julie Phillips. B.S. in Bus. Adminstrn, Miami U., Oxford, Ohio, 1967; J.D., U. Toledo, 1970. Bar: Calif. 1971, U.S. Supreme Ct. 1974. Prin., sr. counsel Calif. Public Utilities Commn., 1977; gen. counsel Delta Calif. Industries, Oakland, 1977-82, sec., 1978-82; mem. Silver Rosen, Fischer & Stecher, San Francisco, 1982-84; sr. ptnr. Skaff and Anderson, San Francisco, 1984-90; pvt. practice Law Office of Andrew J. Skaff, 1990-95; ptnr. Knox Ricksen LLP, Oakland, 1995-97, Crosby, Heafey Roach & May, Oakland, 1997-99, Energy Law Group LLP, Oakland, 2000—. Officer Delta Calif. Industries and subs. Contbr. articles to legal jours.; contbg. mem. law rev. U. Toledo, 1970. Mem. ABA, Calif. Bar Assn., Conf. Calif. Pub. Utilities Counsel, Calif. Cogeneration Coun., Assn. Transp. Practitioners, Alameda County Bar Assn. Office: Energy Law Group LLP Lake Merritt Plz 1999 Harrison St Ste 2700 Oakland CA 94612-3582 E-mail: Askaff@energy-law-group.com

SKAGGS, BEBE REBECCA PATTEN, college dean, clergywoman; b. Berkeley, Calif., Jan. 30, 1950; d. Carl Thomas and Bebe (Harrison) P. BS in Bible, Patten Coll., 1969; BA in Philosophy, Holy Names Coll., 1970; MA in Bibl. Studies New Testament, Wheaton Coll., 1972; PhD in Bibl. Studies New Testament, Drew U., 1976; MA in Philosophy, Dominican Sch. Philosophy & Theology, 1990; postgrad., U. Calif., Berkeley, 1991-92. Ordained to ministry Christian Evang. Ch., 1963. Co-pastor Christian Cathedral, Christian Evang. Chs. Am., Inc., 1964—; assoc. prof. Patten Coll., Oakland, Calif., 1975-82, dean, 1977—, prof. N.T., 1982—. Presenter in field. Author: Before the Times, 1980, The World of the Early Church, 1990; contbg. author: Internat. Standard Bibl. Ency., rev. edit., 1983, Women's Study Bible, Pneuma Faculty Dialogue. Active Wheaton Coll. Symphony, 1971-72, Drew U. Ensemble, 1971-75, Young Artists Symphony, N.J., 1972-75, Somerset Hill Symphony, N.J., 1973-74, Peninsula Symphony, 1977, 80-81, Madison Chamber Trio, N.J., 1973-75. Named one of Outstanding Young Women of Am., 1976, 77, 80-81, 82; St. Olaf's Coll. fellow, 1990. Mem. AAUP, Am. Acad. Religion, Soc. Bibl. Lit., Internat. Biographical Assn., Christian Evang. Chs. of Am., Inc. (bd. dirs. 1964—), Inst. for Bibl. Rsch., Soc. for Pentecostal Studies (pres. 1998-99), Phi Delta Kappa.

SKAGGS, SANFORD MERLE, lawyer; b. Berkeley, Calif., Oct. 24, 1939; s. Sherman G. and Barbara Jewel (Stinson) S.; m. Sharon Ann Barnes, Sept. 3, 1976; children: Stephen, Paula Ferry, Barbara Gallagher, Darren Peterson. BA, U. Calif., Berkeley, 1961; JD, U. Calif., 1964. Bar: Calif. 1965. Atty. Pacific Gas and Electric Co., San Francisco, 1964-73; gen. counsel Pacific Gas Transmission Co., San Francisco, 1973-75; ptnr. Van Voorhis & Skaggs, Walnut Creek, Calif., 1975-85, McCutchen, Doyle, Brown & Enersen, San Francisco and Walnut Creek, 1985—. Mem.Calif. Law Revision Commn., 1990—, chmn. 1993; dir. John Muir/Mt. Diablo Health Sys., 1996—. Councilman City of Walnut Creek, 1972-78, mayor 1974-75, 76-77; bd. dirs. East Bay Mcpl. Utility Dist., 1978-90, pres., 1982-90. Mem. Calif. State Bar Assn., Contra Costa County Bar Assn., Urban Land Inst., Lambda Alpha, Alpha Delta Phi, Phi Delta Phi. Republican. Office: McCutchen Doyle Brown & Enersen 1333 N California Blvd Ste 210 Walnut Creek CA 94596-4585

SKEEN, JOSEPH RICHARD, congressman; b. Roswell, N.Mex., June 30, 1927; s. Thomas Dudley and Ilah (Adamson) S.; m. Mary Helen Jones, Nov. 17, 1945; children: Mary Elisa, Mikell Lee. B.S., Tex. A&M U., 1950. Soil and water engr. Ramah Navajo and Zuni Indians, 1951, 1951; rancher Lincoln County, N.Mex., 1952—; mem. N.Mex. Senate, 1960-70, 97th-103rd Congresses from 2nd N.Mex. dist., Washington, 1981—; mem. appropriations com., subcom. chair Interior, agr., chmn. appropriations com., subcom. def.; mem. subcom. interior. Chmn. N.Mex. Republican Party, 1963-66. Served with USN, 1945-46; Served with USAFR, 1949-52. [illegible] Woolgrowers Assn., N.Mex. Cattle Growers Assn., N.Mex. Farm and Livestock Bur. Republican. Club: Elks. Office: House of Reps Washington DC 20515-0001

SKEFF, KELLEY MICHAEL, health facility administrator; b. Center, Colo., 1944; MD, U. Chgo., 1970. Diplomate Am. Bd. Internal Medicine. Intern Harbor Gen. Hosp., Torrance, Calif., 1970-71; resident in internal medicine U. Colo. Med. Ctr., Denver, 1974-75, Stanford (Calif.) U. Hosps., 1975-76, fellow in internal medicine, 1976; resident in internal medicine Stanford U., 1989—, assoc. prof. medicine. Recipient Alpha Omega Alpha award Assocs. Am. Med. Coll., 1994. Office: Stanford U Dept Med 300 Pasteur Dr Palo Alto CA 94304-2203

SKELTON, DOUGLAS H. architect; b. Cottage Grove, Oreg., Apr. 17, 1939; s. Harry Edward and Mary Jane (Caldwell) S.; m. Bonita L. Baker, June 17, 1961; children: Paul D., Cynthia J., Justin D. Student, Oreg. State U., 1957-59; degree in architecture, U. Oreg., 1963. Registered architect, Oreg. Draftsman Payne & Struble Architecture, Medford, Oreg., 1965-66; intern architect Wayne Struble Architect, Medford, 1966-70, assoc., 1973-78; project architect William Seibert Architect, Medford, 1970-73; ptnr. Struble & Skelton Architects, Medford, 1978-83; owner Douglas Skelton Architect, Medford, 1983-89; ptnr. Skelton, Straus & Seibert Architects, Medford, 1989—. Design bldg. renovation (911 Mag. 1991, Excellence in Sch. Architecture AS&U mag. 1987). Bd. dirs. Rogue Valley Christian Ch., 1990—; mem. hist. and archtl. review commn. City of Jacksonville, Oreg., 1993-96. Winner Design Competition, Lake Creek Learning Ctr., 1998. Mem. AIA (pres. So. Oreg. chpt. 1973), Architects Coun. Oreg. (treas. 1989), Rotary (pres. Jacksonville/Applegate chpt. 1998-99). Avocations: camping, fishing, boating. Office: Skelton Straus & Seibert Architects and Planners LLP 26 Hawthorne Ave Medford OR 97504-7114

SKIENS, WILLIAM EUGENE, electrical interconnect systems scientist, polymer engineer; b. Burns, Oreg., Feb. 21, 1928; s. William Poleman and Eugenia Glenn (Hibbard) S.; m. Vesta Lorraine Franz, Nov. 4, 1955; children: Rebecca, Beverly, Michael. Student, N.W. Nazarene U., 1946-48; BS in Chemistry, Oreg. State U., 1951; PhD in Phys. Chemistry, U. Wash., 1957. Chemist Dow Chem. Co., Pittsburg, Calif., 1951-53, rsch. chemist Midland, Mich. and Walnut Creek, Calif., 1957-58, 1958-73, E.I DuPont de Nemours, Wilmington, Del., 1955; sr. rsch. chemist Battelle Meml. Inst., Richland, Wash., 1973-84, also cons., 1984—; mgr. media system devel. Optical Data, Inc., Beaverton, Oreg., 1984-89; chief scientist Precision Interconnect, Portland, 1989—. Cons. WHO, Geneva, 1978-85, PI Med., Portland, 1991—. Contbr. chpts. to books, articles to profl. jours.; patentee in field. Com. chmn. Concord, Calif. council Boy Scouts Am., 1969-72; sec. Tri-Cities Nuclear Council, Richland, Wash., 1984. Named Alumni of Yr. N.W. Nazarene U., 1982. Mem. Am. Chem. Soc. (chmn. Richland sect. 1982), Soc. Plastic Engrs., Sigma Xi. Republican. Mem. Ch. Nazarene. Avocations: skiing, photography, backpacking, golf. Home: 31179 SW Country View Ln Wilsonville OR 97070-7479 Office: Precision Interconnect 16640 SW 72nd Ave Portland OR 97224-7298 E-mail: gene.skiens@precisionint.com

SKILES, SCOTT, professional basketball coach; b. LaPorte, Ind., Mar. 5, 1964; Profl. basketball player Milwaukee Bucks, 1986; various teams Orlando, Washington, Philadelphia, others; asst. coach Phoenix Suns, 1997-99, head coach, 1999—. Home: Phoenix Suns PO Box 515 Phoenix AZ 85001

SKILLERN, FRANK L., JR. bank executive; Gen. counsel FDIC, 1979-81; law practice Dallas and Washington; with IDS, 1983-89; pres., CEO, Acuma Unit, Am. Express, London, 1989-91; chmn., pres. Am. Express Centurion Bank, N.Y.C., 1991—; exec. v.p. Optima Card and consumer lending svcs. Am. Express Travel Related Svcs. Co., Inc., N.Y.C., 1991—.

SKINNER, G(EORGE) WILLIAM, anthropologist, educator; b. Oakland, Calif., Feb. 14, 1925; s. John James and Eunice (Engle) S.; m. Carol Bagger, Mar. 25, 1951 (div. Jan. 1970); children: Geoffrey Crane, James Lauriston, Mark Williamson, Jeremy Burr; m. Susan Mann, Apr. 26, 1980; 1 dau., Alison Jane. Student, Deep Springs (Calif.) Coll., 1942-43; B.A. with distinction in Far Eastern Studies, Cornell U., Ithaca, N.Y., 1947, Ph.D. in Cultural Anthropology, 1954; LLD (hon.), U. Hong Kong, 2001. Field dir. Cornell U. S.E. Asia program, also Cornell Research Center, Bangkok, Thailand, 1951-55; rsch. assoc. in Indonesia, 1956-58; asso. prof., then prof. anthropology Cornell U., Ithaca, N.Y., 1960-65; asst. prof. sociology Columbia, 1958-60; sr. specialist in residence East-West Ctr. Honolulu, 1965-66; prof. anthropology Stanford, 1966-89; Barbara Kimball Browning prof. humanities and scis., 1987-89; prof. anthropology U. Calif., Davis, 1990—. Vis. prof. U. Pa., 1977, Duke U., spring, 1978, Keio U., Tokyo, spring 1985, fall 1988, U. Calif.-San Diego, fall 1986; field rsch. China, 1949-50, 77, S.E. Asia, 1950-51, Thailand, 1951-53, 54-55, Java and Borneo, 1956-58, Japan, 1985, 88, 95; mem. joint com. on contemporary China Social Sci. Research Coun.-Am. Acad. Learned Socs., 1961-65, 80-81, internat. com. on Chinese studies, 1963-64, mem. joint com. on Chinese studies, 1981-83; mem. subcom. rsch. Chinese Soc. Social Sci. Rsch. Coun., 1961-70, chmn., 1963-70; dir. program on East Asian Local Systems, 1969-71; dir. Chinese Soc. Bibliography Project, 1964-73; assoc. dir. Cornell China Program, 1961-63; dir. London-Cornell Project Social Rsch., 1962-65; mem. com. on scholarly communication with People's Republic of China, Nat. Acad. Scis., 1966-70, mem. social scis. and humanities panel, 1982-83; mem. adv. com. Ctr. for Chinese Rsch. Materials, Assn. Rsch. Libraries, 1967-70; mem. policy and planning com. China in Time and Space, 1993-96. Author: Chinese Society in Thailand, 1957, Leadership and Power in the Chinese Community of Thailand, 1958; also articles; Editor: The Social Sciences and Thailand, 1956, Local, Ethnic and National Loyalties in Village Indonesia, 1959, Modern Chinese Society: An Analytical Bibliography, 3 vols, 1973, (with Mark Elvin) The Chinese City Between Two Worlds, 1974, (with A. Thomas Kirsch) Change and Persistence in Thai Society, 1975, The City in Late Imperial China, 1977, The Study of Chinese Society, 1979. Served to ensign USNR, 1943-46. Fellow Center for Advanced Study in Behavioral Scis., 1969-70; Guggenheim fellow, 1969; NIMH spl. fellow, 1970 Mem. NAS, AAAS, Am. Anthrop. Assn., Am. Sociol. Assn., Assn. Asian Studies (bd. dirs. 1962-65, chmn. nominating com. 1967-68, pres. 1983-84), Soc. for Cultural Anthropology, Internat. Union for Sci. Study of Population, Social Sci. History Assn., Am. Ethnol. Soc., Population Assn. Am., Siam Soc., Soc. Qing Studies, Soc. Econ. Anthropology, Phi Beta Kappa, Sigma Xi. Office: U Calif Dept Anthropology 1 Shields Ave Davis CA 95616-5270 E-mail: gwskinner@ucdavis.edu

SKINNER, KNUTE RUMSEY, poet, English educator; b. St. Louis, Apr. 25, 1929; s. George Rumsey and Lidi (Skjoldvig) S.; m. Jeanne Pratt; 1953; divorced 1954; 1 child, Frank; m. Linda Kuhn, Mar. 30, 1961 (div. Sept. 1977); children: Dunstan, Morgan; m. Edna Kiel, Mar. 25, 1978. Student, Culver-Stockton Coll., 1947-49; BA, U. No. Colo., 1951; MA, Middlebury Coll., 1954; PhD, U. Iowa, 1958. Instr. English U. Iowa, Iowa City, 1955-56, 57-58, 60-61; asst. prof. English Okla. Coll. for Women, 1961-62; lectr. creative writing Western Wash. U., Bellingham, 1962-71, asso. prof. English, 1971-73, prof. English, 1973-97; pres. Signpost Press Inc., nonprofit corp., 1983-95. Author: Stranger with a Watch, 1965, A Close Sky Over Killaspuglonane, 1968, 75, In Dinosaur Country, 1969, The Sorcerers: A Laotian Tale, 1972, Hearing of the Hard Times, 1981, The Flame Room, 1983, Selected Poems, 1985, Learning to Spell "Zucchini," 1988, The Bears and Other Poems, 1991, What Trudy Knows and Other Poems, 1994, The Cold Irish Earth: New and Selected Poems of Ireland, 1965-1995, 1996, An Afternoon Quiet and Other Poems, 1998; editor: [illegible] 1977 [illegible] contbr. poetry, short stories to anthologies, textbooks, periodicals. Nat. Endowment for the Arts fellow, 1975 Mem. Am. Conf. Irish Studies, Wash. Poets Assn. E-mail: kielskin@eircom.net

SKLANSKY, JACK, electrical and computer engineering educator, researcher; b. N.Y.C., Nov. 15, 1928; s. Abraham and Clara S.; m. Gloria Joy Weiss, Dec. 24, 1957; children: David Alan, Mark Steven, Jeffrey Paul. BEE, CCNY, 1950; MSEE, Purdue U., 1952; D in Engring. Sci., Columbia U., 1955. Research engr. RCA Labs., Princeton, N.J., 1955-65; mgr. Nat. Cash Register Co., Dayton, Ohio, 1965-66; prof. elec. and computer engring. U. Calif., Irvine, 1966—; pres. Scanicon Corp., Irvine, 1980-89; prof. radiology Charles R. Drew U. of Medicine and Sci., L.A., 1995—. Author: (with others) Pattern Classifiers and Trainable Machines, 1981; editor: Pattern Recognition, 1973, (with others) Biomedical Images and Computers, 1982; editor-in-chief: Machine Vision and Applications, 1987. Recipient best paper award Jour. Pattern Recognition, 1977; rsch. grantee NIH, 1971-84, Army Rsch. Office, 1984-91, NSF, 1992-96, Office of Naval Rsch., 1995-97, Naval Air Warfare Ctr., 1997-98, Calif. Breast Cancer Rsch. Program, 1997-99, U.S. Army Med. Rsch. and Material Command, 1999—, Calif. Telehealth and Telemedicine Ctr., 2000—. Fellow IEEE, Internat. Assn. for Pattern Recognition; mem. ACM. Office: U Calif Dept Elec Computer Engring Irvine CA 92697-2625 E-mail: sklansky@uci.edu

SKLAR, LOUISE MARGARET, service executive; b. L.A., Aug. 12, 1934; d. Samuel Baldwin Smith and Judith LeRoy (Boughton) Nelson; m. Edwynn Edgar Schroeder, Mar. 20, 1955 (div. July 1975); children: Neil Nelson, Leslie Louise Schroeder Grandclaudon, Samuel George; m. Martin Sklar, Oct. 17, 1983. Student, U. So. Calif., 1952-54, UCLA, 1977-79. Acct. Valentine Assocs., Northridge, Calif., 1976-78, programmer, 1978-79; contr. Western Monetary, Encino, 1979-81; pres. Automatic Computer Composition, Reno, 1984—. Mem. Am. Contract Bridge League (bd. govs. 1993-99, mem. nat. charity com. 1982, mem. nat. goodwill com. 1994—), Assn. Los Angeles County Bridge Units (bd. dirs. 1990-2000, sec. 1984-86), DAR, Conn. Soc. Genealogists, Ky. Hist. Soc., So. Calif. Asistance League, Heart of Am. Geneal. Soc., Greater L.A. Zoo Assn., Safari Club Internat., Zeta Tau Alpha. Republican. Avocations: tournament bridge, travel. Office: Automatic Computer Composition Inc Reno NV 89511

SKLAR, RICHARD LAWRENCE, political science educator; b. N.Y.C., Mar. 22, 1930; s. Kalman and Sophie (Laub) S.; m. Eva Molineux, July 14, 1962; children: Judith Anne, Katherine Elizabeth. A.B., U. Utah, 1952; M.A., Princeton U., 1957, Ph.D., 1961. Mem. faculty Brandeis U., U. Ibadan, Nigeria, U. Zambia, SUNY-Stony Brook, UCLA; now prof. emeritus polit. sci. UCLA. Mem. fgn. area fellowship program Africa Nat. Com., 1970-73; Simon vis. prof. U. Manchester, Eng., 1975, Fulbright vis. prof. U. Zimbabwe, 1984; Lester Martin fellow Harry S. Truman Rsch. Inst., Hebrew U. Jerusalem, 1979; fellow Africa Inst. of South Africa, 1994—. Author: Nigerian Political Parties: Power in an Emergent African Nation, 1963, Corporate Power in an African State, 1975; co-author: Postimperialism: International Capitalism and Development, 1987, African Politics and Problems in Development, 1991; co-editor: Postimperialism and World Politics, 1999; contbr. articles to profl. jours. Served with U.S. Army, 1952-54. Rockefeller Found. grantee, 1967 Mem. Am. Polit. Sci. Assn., African Studies Assn. (dir. 1976-78, 80-83, v.p. 1980-81, pres. 1981-82), AAUP (pres. Calif. Conf. 1980-81) Home: 1951 Holmby Ave Los Angeles CA 90025-5905

SKOGEN, HAVEN SHERMAN, investment company executive; b. Rochester, Minn., May 8, 1927; s. Joseph Harold and Elpha (Hemphill) S.; m. Beverly R. Baker, Feb. 19, 1949; 1 child, Scott H. BS, Iowa State U., 1950; MS, Rutgers U., 1954, PhD, 1955; MBA, U. Chgo., 1970. Registered profl. engr., Wis. Devel. engr. E.I. duPont, Wilmington, Del., 1955-57; prof. Elmhurst (Ill.) Coll., 1957-58; chief engr. Stackpole, St. Marys, Pa., 1958-62; plant mgr. Magnatronics, Elizabethtown, Ky., 1962-65; mgr. Allen-Bradley, Milw., 1965-70; v.p. Dill-Clithrow, Chgo., 1970-74; oil co. exec. Occidental Oil Co., Grand Junction, Colo., 1974-92; ptnr. H&B Investment CO., 1992—. Author: Synthetic Fuel Combustion, 1984; inventor radioactive retort doping, locus retorting zone. Naval Rsch. fellow, 1951-55. Fellow Am. Inst. Chemists; mem. Internat. Platform Assn., Masons, Elks, Sigma Xi, Phi Beta Kappa, Phi Lambda Upsilon. Republican. Avocations: fly fishing, travel, reading, teaching. Home: 3152 Primrose Ct Grand Junction CO 81506-4147

SKOLL, JEFFREY, Internet company executive; BSEE, U. Toronto, 1987; MBA, Stanford U., 1995. Founder Skoll Engring., 1987, Micros on the Move Ltd., 1990; mgr. distbn. channels online news info. Knight-Ridder Info.; pres. eBay Inc., San Jose, Calif., v.p. strategic planning and analysis. Office: eBay Inc 2125 Hamilton Ave San Jose CA 95125-5905

SKOOG, WILLIAM ARTHUR, former oncologist, educator; b. Culver City, Calif., Apr. 10, 1925; s. John LUndeen and Allis Rose (Gatz) S.; m. Ann Douglas, Sept. 17, 1949; children: Karen, William Arthur, James Douglas, Allison. AA, UCLA, 1944; BA with great distinction, Stanford U., 1946, MD, 1949. Intern in medicine Stanford Hosp., San Francisco, 1948-49, asst. resident in medicine, 1949-50, N.Y. Hosp., N.Y.C., 1950-51; sr. resideit in medicine Wadsworth VA Hosp., L.A., 1951, attdneing specialist in internal medicine, 1962-68; pvt. practice internal medicine Los Altos, Calif., 1959-61; pvt. practice hematology and oncology, Santa Monica, 1971-72; pvt. practice med. oncology, San Bernardino, 1972-94. Assoc. staff Palo Alto-Stanford (Calif.) Med. Ctr., San Francisco, 1959-61, U. Calif. Med. Ctr., San francisco, 1959-61; assoc. attending physician UCLA Hosp. and Clinics, 1961-78; vis. physicisn in internal medicine Harbor Gen. Hosp., Torrance, Calif., 1962-65, attending physician, 1965-71; cons. in chemistry Clin. Lab., UCLA Hosp., 1963-68; affiliate cons. staff St. John's Hosp., Santa Monica, 1967-71, courtesy staff, 1971-72; courtesy attending med. staff Santa Monica Hosp., 1967-72; staff physician St. Bernardine (Calif.) Hosp., 1972-94, hon. staff, 1994—; staff physician San Bernardino Cmty. Hosp., 1972-90, courtesy staff, 1990-94; chief sect. oncology San Bernardino County Hosp., 1972-76; cons. staff Redlands(Calif.) Cmty. Hosp., 1972-83, courtesy staff, 1983-94, hon. staff, 1994—; asst. in medicine Cornell U. Med. Coll., N.Y.C., 1950-51; jr. rsch. physician UCLA Atomic Energy Project, 1954-55; instr. medicine, asst. rsch. physician dept. medicine UCLA Med. Ctr., 1955-56, asst. prof. medicine, asst. rsch. physician, 1956-59; clin. assoc. in hematology VA Ctr., L.A., 1956-59; co-dir. metabolic rsch. unit UCLA Ctr. for Health Scis., 1955-59, 61-65; co-dir. Health Scis. Clin. Rsch. Ctr., 1965-689, dir., 1968-72; clin. instr. medicine Stanford U., 1959-61; asst. clin. prof. medicine, assoc. rsch. physician U. Calif. Med. ctr., San fRancisco, 1959-61; lectr. medicine UCLA Sch. Medicine, 1961-62, assoc. prof., 1962-734, assoc. clin. prof., 1973—. Contbr. articles to med. jours. With USNR, 1943-46, lt. M.C., 1951-53. Fellow ACP; mem. AMA, Calif. Med. Assn., So. Calif. Acad. Clin. Oncology, Western Soc. Clin. Rsch., Am. Fedn. Clin. Rschr., L.A. Acad. Medicine, San Bernardino County Med. Soc., Am. Soc. Clin. Oncology, Am. Soc. Internal Medicine, Calif. Soc. Internal Medicine, Inland Soc. Internal Medicine, Redlands Country Club, Phi Beta Kappa, Sigma Xi, Alpha Omega Alpha, Alpha Kappa Kappa. Episcopalian (vestryman 1965-70). Home: 1119 Kimberly Pl Redlands CA 92373-6786 Fax: 909-798-5016. E-mail: wasredarrow@aol.com

SKOPIL, OTTO RICHARD, JR. federal judge; b. Portland, Oreg., June 3, 1919; s. Otto Richard and Freda Martha (Boetticher) S.; m. Janet Rae Lundy, July 27, 1956; children: Otto Richard III, Casey Robert, Shannon Ida, Molly Jo. BA in Econs., Willamette U., 1941, LLB, 1946, LLD (hon.), 1983. Bar: Oreg. 1946, IRS, U.S. Treasury Dept., U.S. Dist. Ct. Oreg., U.S. Ct. Appeals (9th cir.), U.S. Supreme Ct. 1946. Assoc. Skopil & Skopil, 1946-51; ptnr. Williams Skopil, Miller & Beck (and predecessors), Salem, Oreg., 1951-72; judge U.S. Dist. Ct., Portland, 1972-79, chief judge, 1976-79; judge U.S. Ct. Appeals (9th cir.), Portland, 1979—, now sr. judge. Chmn. com. adminstrn. of fed. magistrate sys. U.S. Jud. Conf., 1980-86;

co-founder Oreg. chpt. Am. Leadership Forum; chmn. 9th cir. Jud. Coun. Magistrates Adv. Com., 1988-91; chmn. U.S. Jud. Conf. Long Range Planning Com., 1990-95. Hi-Y adviser Salem YMCA, 1951-52; appeal agt. SSS, Marion County (Oreg.) Draft Bd., 1953-66; master of ceremonies 1st Gov.'s Prayer Breakfast for State Oreg., 1959; mem. citizens adv. com., City of Salem, 1970-71; chmn. Gov.'s Com. on Staffing Mental Instns., 1969-70; pres., bd. dirs. Marion County Tb and Health Assn., 1958-61; bd. dirs. Willamette Valley Camp Fire Girls, 1946-56, Internat. Christian Leadership, 1959, Fed. Jud. Ctr., 1979; trustee Willamette U., 1969-71; elder Mt. Park Ch., 1979-81. Served to lt. USNR, 1942-46. Recipient Oreg. Legal Citizen of Yr. award, 1986, Disting. Alumni award Willamette U. Sch. Law, 1988. Mem. ABA, Oreg. Bar Assn. (bd. govs.), Marion County Bar Assn., Am. Judicature Soc., Oreg. Assn. Def. Counsel (dir.), Def. Research Inst., Assn. Ins. Attys. U.S. and Can. (Oreg. rep. 1970), Internat. Soc. Barristers, Prayer Breakfast Movement (fellowship council). Clubs: Salem, Exchange (pres. 1947), Illahe Hills Country (pres., dir. 1964-67). Office: Sr Circuit Judge 827 US Courthouse 1000 SW 3rd Ave Portland OR 97204-2930

SKOTHEIM, ROBERT ALLEN, retired museum administrator; b. Seattle, Jan. 31, 1933; s. Sivert O. and Marjorie F. (Allen) S.; m. Nadine Vail, June 14, 1953; children— Marjorie, Kris, Julia. BA, U. Wash., 1955, MA, 1958, PhD, 1962; LLD (hon.), Hobart and William Smith Colls., Geneva, N.Y., 1975; LittD (hon.), Whitman Coll., 1988; LHD (hon.), Coll. Idaho, 1988, Occidental Coll., 1989, Ill. Wesleyan U., 1990; DFA (hon.), Willamette U., 1989. Prof. history U. Wash., 1962-63; prof. history Wayne State U., Detroit, 1963-66; prof. UCLA, 1966-67, U. Colo., Boulder, 1967-72; provost, dean faculty Hobart and William Smith Colls., 1972-75; pres. Whitman Coll., Walla Walla, Wash., 1975-88, Huntington Libr., Art Collections & Bot. Gardens, San Marino, Calif., 1988-2001; ret., 2001. Author: American Intellectual Histories and Historians, 1966, Totalitarianism and American Social Thought, 1971; Editor: The Historian and the Climate of Opinion, 1969; co-editor: American Social Thought: Sources and Interpretations, 2 vols, 1972. Guggenheim fellow, 1967-68 Mem. Phi Beta Kappa (hon.)

SKURZYNSKI, GLORIA JOAN, writer; b. Duquesne, Pa., July 6, 1930; d. Aylmer Kearney and Serena Elizabeth (Decker) Flister; m. Edward Joseph Skurzynski, Dec. 1, 1951; children: Serena Nolan, Janine Skurzynski-Mahoney, Joan Alm, Alane Ferguson, Lauren Thliveris. Student, Carlow Coll., 1948-50. Author: The Magic Pumpkin, 1971, The Remarkable Journey of Gustavus Bell, 1973, The Poltergeist of Jason Morey, 1975, In a Bottle with a Cork on Top, 1976, Two Fools and a Faker, 1977, Bionic Parts for People, 1978 (Golden Kite Honor Bk. award Soc. Children's Bk. Writers), Martin by Himself, 1979, What Happened in Hamelin, 1979 (telecast on Storybreak, CBS, 1987, Christopher award, Reviewer's Choice award, Horn Bk. Honor List, ALA Booklist), Honest Andrew, 1981, Safeguarding the Land, 1981, Three Folktales, 1981, Manwolf, 1981 (Best Bks. for Young Adults award ALA, Reviewer's Choice award ALA Booklist, Bks. of Yr. award Child Study Assn., Notable Children's Trade Bk. in Field of Social Studies), Lost in the Devil's Desert, 1982 (Utah Children's Bk. award), The Tempering, 1983 (Golden Kite award Soc. Children's Bk. Writers, Best Bks. for Young Adults award ALA, Best Bks. of Yr. award Sch. Libr. Jour., Children's Bks. of Yr. award Libr. Congress, Bks. of Yr. award Child Study Assn.), Trapped in the Slickrock Canyon, 1984 (Golden Spur award Western Writers Am., Am. Booksellers Pick of the List, Jr. Lit. Guild Selection), Caught in the Moving Mountains, 1984, Swept in the Wave of Terror, 1985, The Minstrel in the Tower, 1988, Dangerous Ground, 1989, Robots, 1990 (100 Children's Bks. award N.Y. Pub. Libr. 1990, Outstanding Science Trade Bk. for Children award NSTA/CBC 1991), Almost the Real Thing, 1991 (Children's Sci. Bk. award Am. Inst. Physics 1992), Here Comes the Mail, 1992, Good-Bye, Billy Radish, 1992 (Best Bks. of Yr. award Sch. Libr. Jour., Jefferson Cup Hon. award Va. Libr. Assn., Judy Lopez Meml. Hon. Bk., Women's Nat. Bk. Assn.), Get the Message, 1993 (Outstanding Sci. Trade Bks. for Children award NSTA/CBC 1994, Bks. for the Teen Age award N.Y. Pub. Libr. 1994), Know the Score, 1994 (Bks. for the Teen Age award N.Y. Pub. Libr. 1995), Zero Gravity, 1994 (Outstanding Sci. Trade Bks. for Children award NSTA/CBC 1995, Children's Bk. of Yr., Bank Street Coll. Child Study Com.), Cyberstorm, 1995, Caitlin's Big Idea, 1995, Waves, the Electromagnetic Universe, 1996, Virtual War, 1997, (with Alane Ferguson) The Mystery of the Spooky Shadow, 1996, The Mystery of the Vanishing Creatures, 1996, Wolf Stalker, 1997, Rage of Fire, 1998, Discover Mars, 1998, Cliff-Hanger, 1999, Spider's Voice, 1999, Deadly Waters, 1999. Mem. Soc. of Children's Book Writers and Illustrators, Utah Women's Forum, Internat. Women's Forum. Home and Office: 2559 Spring Haven Dr Salt Lake City UT 84109-4032

SKYLSTAD, WILLIAM S. bishop; b. Omak, Wash., Mar. 2, 1934; s. Stephen Martin and Reneldes Elizzbeth (Danzl) S. Student, Pontifical Coll., Josephinum, Worthington, Ohio; M.Ed., Gonzaga U. Ordained priest Roman Catholic Ch., 1960; asst. pastor Pullman, Wash., 1960-62; tchr. Mater Cleri Sem., 1961-68, rector, 1968-74; pastor Assumption Parish, Spokane, 1974-76; chancellor Diocese of Spokane, 1976-77; ordained bishop, 1977; bishop of Yakima, Wash., 1977-90, Spokane, 1990—. Home: 1025 W Cleveland Ave Spokane WA 99205-3320 Office: Diocese of Spokane PO Box 1453 1023 W Riverside Ave Spokane WA 99210-1103

SLACK, DONALD CARL, agricultural engineer, educator; b. Cody, Wyo., June 25, 1942; s. Clarence Ralbon and Clara May (Beightol) S.; m. Marion Arline Kimball, Dec. 19, 1964; children: Jonel Marie, Jennifer Michelle. BS in Agrl. Engring., U. Wyo., 1965; MS in Agrl. Engring., U. Ky., 1968, PhD in Agrl. Engring., 1975. Registered profl. engr., Ky., Ariz. Asst. civil engr. City of Los Angeles, 1965; research specialist U. Ky., Lexington, 1966-70, agrl. engring. advisor Tha Phra, Thailand, 1970-73, research asst. Lexington, 1973-75; from asst. prof. to assoc. prof. agrl. engring. U. Minn., St. Paul, 1975-84; prof. U. Ariz., Tucson, 1984—, head dept. agrl. and biosystems engring., 1991—. Mem. Mid. East and Mediterranean Desert Devel. Program, 1997—; vis. prof. dept. atmospheric sci. Fed. U. Paraiba, Campina Grande, Brazil, 1997; vis. prof. dept. irrigation Chapingo Autonomous U., Mexico, 2000; tech. adv. Ariz. Dept. Water Resources, Phoenix, 1985—, Tucson active mgmt. area, 1996—; cons. Winrock Internat., Morrilton, Ark., 1984, Water Mgmt. Synthesis II, Logan, Utah, 1985, Desert Agrl. Tech. Sys., Tucson, 1985—, Portek Hermosillo, Mexico, 1989—, World Bank, Washington, 1992—, Malawi Environ. Monitoring Project, 1996, Mex. Inst. for Water Tech., 1997, Nat. Agrl. Rsch. Inst., La Serema, Chile, 1997; dep. program support mgr. Rsch. Irrigation Support Project for Asia and the Near East, Arlington, Va., 1987—94; mem. adv. team Cearan Found. for Meteorology and Hydrology, Fortaleza, Brazil, 1995—; mem. internat. adv. panel Matrou Resources Mgmt. Project, World Bank, Egypt, 1996—2000. Contbr. articles to profl. jours. Fellow ASCE (Outstanding Jour. Paper award 1988), Am. Soc. Agrl. Engrs. (Ariz. sect. Engr. of Yr. 1993); mem. Am. Geophys. Union, Am. Soc. Agronomy, Soil Sci. Soc. Am., Am. Soc. Engring. Edn., SAR, Brotherhood of Knights of the Vine (master knight), Sigma Xi, Tau Beta Pi, Alpha Epsilon, Gamma Sigma Delta. Democrat. Lutheran. Achievements include 3 patents pending; developer of infrared based irrigation scheduling device. Avocations: hunting, camping, hiking, model railroading. Home: 9230 E Visco Pl Tucson AZ 85710-3167 Office: U Ariz Agrl Biosystems Engring Tucson AZ 85721-0001 E-mail: slackd@u.arizona.edu

SLADE, COLIN L. electronics manufacturing executive; m. Marianne; 2 children. BS in Acctg., U. Oreg. CPA. Internat. svc. Price Waterhouse, London; audit mgr.; corp. controller, CFO Graphic Software; fin. mgr. info. display group Tektronix, Inc., Beaverton, Oreg., 1987; v.p. fin.; corp. controller; controller color printing and imaging divsn.; CFO, 2000—. Office: Tektronix Inc 14200 SW Karl Braun Dr Beaverton OR 97077

SLADE, LYNN HEYER, lawyer; b. Santa Fe, Jan. 29, 1948; m. Susan Zimmerman, 1 child, Benjamin, 1 child from a previous marriage, Jessica. BA in Econs., U. N.Mex., 1973, JD, 1976. Bar: N.Mex. 1976, U.S. Dist. Ct. N.Mex. 1976, U.S. Ct. Appeals (10th cir.) 1978, U.S. Ct. Appeals (D.C. cir.) 1984, U.S. Supreme Ct. 1984. Ptnr. Modrall, Sperling, Roehl, Harris & Sisk, PA, Albuquerque, 1976—. Adj. prof. U. N.Mex. Sch. Law, Albuquerque, 1990; bd. dirs. N. Mex. First. Editor N.Mex. Law Rev., 1975-76; contbr. articles to profl. jours. Trustee-at-large Rocky Mountain Min. L. Found., 1995-97; bd. dirs. N.Mex. First, 1999—, chair nominating and membership com., 2001—. Fellow N.Mex. Bar Found.; mem. ABA (sect. of environ., energy and resources, membership officer 1998-2000, chair com. on Native Am. natural resources 1991-94, coun. mem. 1995-98, mem. sects. litigation, dispute resolution, internat. law, pub. utilities and comm., and transp. law), N.Mex. State Bar (chair, bd. dirs. sect. of natural resources 1983-87, bd. dirs. Indian law sect. 1987-90). Home: 143 Olguin Rd Corrales NM 87048-6930 Office: Modrall Sperling Roehl Harris & Sisk PA 500 4th St NW Ste 1000 Albuquerque NM 87102-2186 E-mail: lslade@modrall.com

SLAGHT, KENNETH D. career officer; b. Chgo. Grad., U.S. Naval Acad., 1970; student, Def. Sys. Mgmt. Coll.; M in Computer Sys. Mgmt., Naval Postgrad. Sch. Commd. ensign USN, advanced through grades to rear adm.; divsn. dir. for automation Navy Recruiting Command; divsn. dir. automated plans and programs Jt. Chiefs of Staff; dep. dir. material profl. policy Naval Mil. Personnel Command; dep. dir. info. transfer sys. dir. Space and Naval Warfare Sys. Command; project officer Comm. Support Sys.; program mgr. Jt. Maritime Comm. Sys.; chief engr. Space and Naval Warfare Sys. Command, 1997—, vice comdr., 1999—. Decorated Legion of Merit, Def. Meritorious Svc. medal, Navy Meritorious Svc. medal with Gold star, Nat. Der. Svc. medal with Bronze star. Office: 4301 Pacific Hwy San Diego CA 92110-3127

SLATE, JOHN BUTLER, biomedical engineer; b. Schenectady, N.Y., Sept. 27, 1953; s. Herbert Butler and Violet (Perugi) S. BSEE, U. Wis., 1975, MEE, 1977, PhDEE, 1980. Spl. fellow of cardiovascular surgery U. Ala., Birmingham, 1980-81, dept. biomed. research engr., 1981-82; microbiology fellow, 1981-82; sr. research engr. IMED Corp., San Diego, 1982-83, sr. research scientist, 1983-86; sci. dir. Pacesetter Infusion Ltd. (dba MiniMed Technologies), Sylmar, Calif., 1986-87; v.p. tech. MiniMed Technologies, Sylmar, 1987-91; v.p. R & D Siemens Infusion Systems, Sylmar, 1991-93; v.p. tech. devel. Via Med., San Diego, 1993-94; pres. Slate Engring., San Diego, 1994—, Avant Drug Delivery Systems, Inc., San Diego, 1997—. Mem. IEEE (IEE Ayrton award), Sigma Xi. Office: Slate Engring 3914 Kendall St San Diego CA 92109-6129 E-mail: jslate@san.rr.com

SLATER, JAMES MUNRO, radiation oncologist; b. Salt Lake City, Jan. 7, 1929; s. Donald Munro and Leone Forestine (Fehr) S.; m. JoAnn Strout, Dec. 28, 1948; children: James, Julie, Jan, Jerry, Jon. BS in Physics, U. Utah, Utah State U., 1954; MD, Loma Linda U., 1963; PhD (hon.), Andrews U., Berrien Springs, Mich., 1996. Diplomate Am. Bd. Radiology. Intern Latter Day Saints Hosp., Salt Lake City, 1963-64, resident in radiology, 1964-65; resident in radiotherapy Loma Linda U. Med. Ctr., White Meml. Med. Center, L.A., fellow in radiotherapy, 1967-68, U. Tex.-M.D. Anderson Hosp. and Tumor Inst., Houston, 1968-69; faculty Loma Linda (Calif.) U., 1975—, prof. radiology, 1979—, chmn. radiation scis. dept., 1979-89, dir. nuclear medicine, 1975-79, dir. radiation oncology, 1970—, chmn. dept. radiation oncology, 1990—, dir. Cancer Inst., 1993—, exec. v.p. Med. Ctr., 1994-95; treas. Med. Ctr., 1995-96; founder, dir. Loma Linda U./NASA Radiation Biology Lab., 1997—. Co-dir. cmty. radiology oncology program L.A. County-U. So. Calif. Comprehensive Cancer Ctr., 1978-83; mem. cancer adv. coun. State of Calif., 1980-85; clin. prof. U. So. Calif., 1982—; founding mem. Proton Therapy Coop. Group, 1985—, chmn. 1987-91; cons. charged particle therapy program Lawrence Berkeley Lab., 1986-94; cons. R&D monoclonal antibodies Hybritech Inc., 1985-94, bd. dirs., 1985-94; cons. Berkeley lab., 1986-94; mem. panel cons. Internat. Atomic Energy Agy. UN, 1994—; cons. Sci. Applications Internat. Corp., 1979, 89-91. Bd. dirs. Am. Cancer Soc., San Bernardino/Riverside, 1976—, exec. com., 1976—; pres. Inland Empire chpt., 1981-83. NIH fellow, 1968-69; recipient exhbn. awards Radiol. Soc. N.Am., 1973, exhbn. awards European Assn. Radiology, 1975, exhbn. awards Am. Soc. Therapeutic Radiologists, 1978, Alumnus of Yr. award, 1993-94. Fellow Am. Coll. Radiology; mem. AAAS, AMA, ACS (liaison mem. to commn. on cancer 1976-84), Am. Radium Soc., Am. Soc. Clin. Oncology, Am. Soc. Therapeutics Radiologists, Assn. Univ. Radiologists, Soc. for Clinical Trials, N.Y. Acad. Scis., Calif. Med. Assn., Calif. Radiol. Soc., Gilbert H. Fletcher Soc. (pres. 1981-82), Loma Linda U. Med. Sch. Alumni Assn., Radiol. Soc. N.Am., Bernardino County Med Soc., Soc. Chairmen Of Acad. Radiation Oncology Programs, Alpha Omega Alpha. Achievements include development of world's first proton accelerator system for treating patients with cancer and some benign diseases in a hospital environment; development of world's first computer assisted radiation treatment planning system utilizing patient's digitized anatomic images with overlying radiation distribution images. Home: 181 White Horse Trl Palm Desert CA 92211-8937 Office: Loma Linda U Med Ctr Radiation Medicine 11234 Anderson St Loma Linda CA 92354-2804 E-mail: jmslater@dominion.llumc.edu

SLATER, MICHAEL, communications executive; Founder MicroDesign Resources, 1997—. Lectr. Stanford U., Santa Clara U., Nat. Technol. U.; seminars in field. Author: Microprocessor Based Design; co-author: Practical Microprocessors; editl. dir., pub. Microprocessor Report; dir. Microprocessor Forum. Office: MicroDesign Resources PMB92 708 Gravenstein Hwy N Sebastopol CA 95472-2808

SLATTERY, CHARLES WILBUR, biochemistry educator; b. La Junta, Colo., Nov. 18, 1937; s. Robert Ernest Slattery and Vrgie Belle (Chamberlain) Tobin; m. Arline Sylvia Relile, June 15, 1958; children: Scott Charles, Coleen Kay. BA, Union Coll., 1959; MS, U. Nebr., 1961; PhD, 1965. Instr. chemistry Union Coll., Lincoln, Nebr., 1961-63; asst. prof., assoc. prof. chemistry Atlantic Union Coll., South Lancaster, Mass., 1963-68; rsch. assoc. biophysics MIT, Cambridge, 1967-70; asst. prof., then prof. biochemistry Loma Linda U., Calif., 1970-80; prof. biochemistry-pediatrics, 1980—; chmn. dept., 1983-99. Vis. prof. U. So. Calif., L.A., 1978-79. Contbr. articles to profl. jours. NIH grantee, 1979-82, 86-89, AHA (Calif.), 1981-83, 83-84. Mem. AAAS, Am. Chem. Soc. (biochemistry divsn.), Am. Dairy Sci. Assn., N.Y. Acad. Scis., The Protein Soc., Am. Soc. Biochemistry and Molecular Biology, Internat. Soc. Rsch. on Human Milk and Lactation, Sigma Xi. Office: Loma Linda U Sch Medicine Dept Biochemistry Loma Linda CA 92350-0001

SLAUGHTER, JOHN BROOKS, former university administrator; b. Topeka, Mar. 16, 1934; s. Reuben Brooks and Dora (Reeves) S.; m. Ida Bernice Johnson, Aug. 31, 1956; children: John Brooks, Jacqueline Michelle. Student, Washburn U., 1951-53; BSEE, Kans. State U., 1956, DSc (hon.), 1988; MS in Engring., UCLA, 1961; PhD in Engring. Scis, U. Calif., San Diego, 1971; D Engring. (hon.), Rensselaer Poly. Inst., 1981; DSc (hon.), U. So. Calif., 1981, Tuskegee Inst., 1981, U. Md., 1982, U. Notre Dame, 1982, U. Miami, 1983, U. Mass., 1983, Tex. So. U., 1984, U. Toledo, 1985, U. Ill., 1986, SUNY, 1986; LHD (hon.), Bowie State Coll., 1987; DSc (hon.), Morehouse Coll., 1988, Kans. State U., 1988; LLD (hon.), U. Pacific, 1989; DSc (hon.), Pomona Coll., 1989; LHD (hon.), Alfred U., 1991, Calif. Luth. U., 1991, Washburn U., 1992. Registered profl. engr., Wash. Electronics engr. Gen. Dynamics Convair, San Diego, 1956-60; with Naval Electronics Lab. Center, San Diego, 1960-75, div. head, 1965-71, dept. head, 1971-75; dir. applied physics lab. U. Wash., 1975-77; asst. dir. NSF, Washington, 1977-79, dir., 1980-82; acad. v.p., provost Wash. State U., 1979-80; chancellor U. Md., College Park, 1982-88; pres. Occidental Coll., Los Angeles, 1988-99; co-chair Calif. Citizens Commn. on Higher Edn., 1996-99; ret., 1999. Res., CEO NACME, Inc., N.Y.C.; bd. dirs., vice chmn. San Diego Transit Corp., 1968-75; mem. com. on minorities in engring. Nat. Rsch. Coun., 1976-79; mem. Commn. on Pre-Coll. Edn. in Math., Sci. and Tech. Nat. Sci. Bd., 1982-83; bd. dirs. Solutia, Inc., ARCO, Avery Dennison Corp., IBM, Northrop Grumman Corp.; chmn. advancement com. Music Ctr. of L.A. County, 1989-93. Editor: Jour. Computers and Elec. Engring., 1972—. Bd. dirs. San Diego Urban League, 1962-66, pres., 1964-66; mem. Pres.'s Com. on Nat. Medal Sci., 1979-80; trustee Rensselaer Poly. Inst., 1982; chmn. Pres.'s Com. Nat. Collegiate Athletic Assn., 1986-88; bd. govs. Town Hall of Calif., 1990; bd. dirs. L.A. World Affairs Coun., 1990. Recipient Engring. Disting. Alumnus of Yr. award UCLA, 1978, UCLA medal, 1989, Roger Revelle award U. Calif.-San Diego, 1991, Disting. Svc. award NSF, 1979, Svc. in Engring. award Kans. State U., 1981, Disting. Alumnus of Yr. award U. Calif.-San Diego, 1982, Martin Luther King Jr. Nat. award, 1997; Naval Electronics Lab. Ctr. fellow, 1969-70; elected to Topeka High Sch. Hall of Fame, 1983, Hall of Fame of Am. Soc. Engring. Edn., 1993; named Kansan of Yr. by Kans. Native Sons and Daus., 1994. Fellow IEEE (chmn. com. on minority affairs 1976-80), Am. Acad. Arts and Scis.; mem. NAE, Nat. Collegiate Athletic Assn. (chmn. pres. commn.), Am. Soc. for Engring. Edn. (inducted into Hall of Fame 1993), Phi Beta Kappa (hon.), Tau Beta Pi, Eta Kappa Nu. Office: NACME Inc Empire State Bldg 350 Fifth Ave Ste 2212 New York NY 10118-2299

SLAVITT, EARL BENTON, lawyer; b. Chgo., Sept. 12, 1939; s. Harold Hal and Rose (Hoffman) S.; m. Amy Lerner, July 12, 1987; 1 child, Gabriel Harrel; children from previous marriage: Andrew Miller, Lesley Deborah. BS in Econs., U. Pa., 1961, JD, 1964. Bar: Ill. 1964, U.S. Dist. Ct. (no. dist.) Ill. 1964, U.S. Supreme Ct. 1971. Assoc. Wisch, Crane & Kravets, Chgo., 1964-67, Ressman & Tishler, Chgo., 1967-69; assoc., then ptnr. Levy & Erens, Chgo., 1969-78; ptnr. Tash & Slavitt, Chgo., 1978-81, Katten Muchin & Zavis, Chgo., 1981—. Contbr. articles to profl. jours.; author poems and plays. Vol. Hospice of Ill. Masonic Med. Ctr., Chgo., 1987-89, Pro bono Advocates, 1989, Chgo. Ho., 1991 (recipient Outstanding Vol. award), Lawyers for the Creative Arts, Bus. Vols. for the Arts, 1992—; bd. dirs. Playwrights Ctr., Chgo., 1987, Jewish Reconstructionist Congregation, Chgo., 1978, 91, 92, Legal Clinic for the Disabled, 1993-96, pres., 1995-96, Sarah's Circle, 1994-96. Mem. Ill. State Bar Assn. (mem. real estate com. 1976, recipient Pro Bono Cert. Accomplishment 1994), Chgo. Bar Assn. (mem. real estate com. 1976, real estate fin. com. 1982), Chgo. Coun. Lawyers (mem. jud. selection com. 1969), Lawyers in Mensa (bd. govs. 1983). Democrat. Jewish. Office: Katten Muchin & Zavis 1999 Ave Of Stars Ste 1400 Los Angeles CA 90067-6115 E-mail: earl.slavitt@kmz.com

SLEEP, NORMAN H. geophysics educator; BS in Math., Mich. State U., 1967; MS in Geophysics, MIT, 1969, PhD in Geophysics, 1973. Postdoc. rsch. assoc. Mass. Inst. Tech., Cambridge, 1973; asst. prof. Geophysics Northwestern U., Evanston, Ill., 1973-79; from assoc. prof. to prof. Geophysics Stanford U., Palo Alto, Calif., 1979—. Contbr. articles to profl. jours. including Earth Planetary Sci., J. Geophysical Rsch., Nature. Recipient James B. Macelwane award, 1980, George P. Woollard award, 1991. Fellow Am. Geophysical Union (Walter H. Bucher medal 1998), Geological Soc. Am., AAAS. Office: Stanford U Dept Geophysics Mitchell Bldg Rm 373A Palo Alto CA 94305-2215

SLEICHER, CHARLES ALBERT, chemical engineer; b. Albany, N.Y., Aug. 15, 1924; s. Charles Albert and Beatrice Eugena (Cole) S.; m. Janis Jorgensen, Sept. 5, 1953; children— Jeffrey Mark, Gretchen Gail. B.S., Brown U., 1946; M.S., M.I.T., 1949; Ph.D., U. Mich., 1955. Asst. dir. M.I.T. Sch. Chem. Engring.; Practice Bangor, Maine, 1949-51; research engr. Shell Devel. Co., Emeryville, Calif., 1955-59; assoc. prof. chem. engring. U. Wash., Seattle, 1960-66, prof., 1966-92, prof. emeritus, 1993—, dept. chmn., 1977-89. Cons. Westinghouse Hanford Co.; profl. photographer, 1994—. Contbr. articles on extraction, heat transfer, fluid mechanics, pesticide transport to profl. jours.; contbr. photos to mags. Served with USN, 1943-47. NSF postdoctoral fellow, 1959-60; SEED grantee, 1973 74; research grantee NSF; research grantee Chevron Research Corp.; research grantee Am. Chem. Soc. Fellow AIChE (program and awards coms.), AAAS; mem. Am. Chem. Soc., N.Am. Nature Photography Assn., Photographic Soc. Am., Sigma Xi. Achievements include holder of chem. reactor design patentee. Home: 5002 Harold Pl NE Seattle WA 98105-2809 Office: U Wash Dept Chem Engring PO Box 351750 Seattle WA 98195-1750

SLEIGHT, ARTHUR WILLIAM, chemist, educator; b. Ballston Spa, NY, Apr. 1, 1939; s. Hollis Decker and Elizabeth (Smith) S.; m. Betty F. Hilberg, Apr. 19, 1963; children: Jeffrey William, Jeannette Anne, Jason Arthur. AB, Hamilton Coll., 1960; PhD, U. Conn., 1963. Faculty U. Stockholm, Sweden, 1963-64; with E.I. du Pont de Nemours & Co., Inc., Wilmington, Del., 1965-89, rsch. mgr. solid. state/catalytic chemistry, 1981-89; Harris Chair prof. materials sci. Oreg. State U., Corvallis, 1989—; dir. Ctr. for Advanced Materials Rsch., 1995—. Adj. prof. U. Del., 1978-89. Editor: Materials Rsch. Bull., 1994—; editorial bd. Inorganic Chemistry Rev., 1979—, Jour. Catalysis, 1986—, Applied Catalysis, 1987—, Solid State Scis., 1987—, Chemistry of Materials, 1988—, Materials Chemistry and Physics, 1988—, Jour. of Solid State Chemistry, 1988—; patentee in field; contbr. articles to profl. jours. Mem. Presdl. Commn. Superconductivity, 1989. Recipient Phila. chpt. Am. Inst. Chemists award, 1988, Gold Medal award Nat. Assn. Sci. Tech. and Soc., 1994. Mem. Am. Chem. Soc. (award Del. sect. 1978, Chemistry of Materials award 1997). Home: PO Box 907 Philomath OR 97370-0907 Office: Oreg State U Dept Chemistry 153 Gilbert Hall Corvallis OR 97331-8546 E-mail: arthur.sleight@orst.edu

SLETTEN, JOHN ROBERT, construction company executive; b. Gt. Falls, Mont., Sept. 19, 1932; s. John and Hedvig Marie (Finstad) S.; m. Patricia Gail Thomas, Dec. 16, 1962; children: Leighanne, Kristen Gail, Erik John. BS in Archtl. Engring., Mont. State U., 1956, PhD (hon.), 1993. Estimator Sletten Constrn. Co., Gt. Falls, 1956-63, v.p., area mgr. Las Vegas, Nev., 1963-65, pres., chief exec. officer Gt. Falls, 1969—. Bd. dirs. 1st Banks, Gt. Falls, Blue Cross-Blue Shield, Helena, Mont. Chmn. Gt. Falls Mil. Affairs Com., 1985; pres. President's Cir., Mont. State U., Bozeman, 1986; trustee Mont. Hist. Soc., Helena, 1987. with USMC, 1950-52. Mem. Mont. Contractors Assn. (bd. dirs. 1969-75, pres. 1974), Mont. C. of C. (chmn. 1984), Pachyderm Club, Rotary (bd. dirs. Gt. Falls), Elks. Republican. Lutheran. Avocations: skiing, fishing, hunting. Office: Sletten Inc 1000 25th St N PO Box 2467 Great Falls MT 59403-2467

SLIPSAGER, HENRIK C. human resources specialist; CFO ISS Internat. Svc. Sys., Inc., 1984-85, exec. v.p., COO, 1985-88, pres., CEO, 1988-94; exec. v.p. janitorial svcs. Am. Bldg. Maintenance Industries Inc., San Francisco, 1994-99, sr. v.p., 1997-99, pres. Am. Bldg. Maintenance Co., 1999-2000, CEO, pres., 2000—. Office: ABM Industries 160 Pacific Ave San Francisco CA 94111

SLOAN, JERRY (GERALD EUGENE SLOAN), professional basketball coach; b. McLeansboro, Ill., Mar. 28, 1942; m. Bobbye; 3 children: Kathy, Brian, Holly. Student, Evansville (Ind.) Coll., 1965. Professional basketball player, Baltimore, 1965-66, Chicago Bulls, NBA, 1966-76; head coach Chicago Bulls, 1979-82; scout Utah Jazz, NBA, Salt Lake City, 1983-84, asst. coach, 1984-88, head coach, 1988—. Player 2 NBA All-Star games; named to NBA All-Defensive First Team, 1969, 72, 74, 75. Office: c/o Utah Jazz Delta Ctr 301 W South Temple Salt Lake City UT 84101-1216

SLOAN, L. LAWRENCE, publishing executive; b. N.Y.C., 1947; Grad., UCLA. Chmn. Price Stern Sloan, Inc., West Hollywood, Calif. Pres. Sloan Co. Office: 11150 W Olympic Blvd Los Angeles CA 90064-1817 Error in get_biog_sketch x28000198ORA-20101: in exception ORA-06502: PL/SQL: numeric or value error: character string buffer too small

SLOANE, ROBERT MALCOLM, university administrator; b. Boston, Feb. 11, 1933; s. Alvin and Florence (Goldberg) S.; m. Beverly LeBov, Sept. 27, 1959; 1 child, Alison Sloane Gaylin. A.B., Brown U., 1954; M.S., Columbia U., 1958. Adminstrv. resident Mt. Auburn Hosp., Cambridge, Mass., 1957-58; med. adminstr. AT&T, N.Y.C., 1959-60; asst. dir. Yale New Haven Hosp., 1961-67; assoc. adminstr. Monmouth Med. Center, Long Branch, N.J., 1967-69; adminstr. City of Hope Nat. Med. Center, Duarte, Calif., 1969-80; pres. Los Angeles Orthopedic Hosp., Los Angeles Orthopedic Found., 1980-86; pres., CEO Anaheim (Calif.) Meml. Hosp., 1986-94; pres. Vol. Hosp. Am. West, Inc., L.A., 1995; healthcare cons. Monrovia, Calif., 1996-98; v.p. Rudolph Dew and Assocs., Torrance, 1997-98; dir. health adminstrn. program U. So. Calif., L.A., 1998—2001. Mem. faculty Columbia U. Sch. Medicine, 1958-59, Yale U. Sch. Medicine, 1963-67, Quinnipac Coll., 1963-67, Pasadena City Coll., 1972-73, Calif. Inst. Tech., 1973-85, U. So. Calif., 1976-96, clin. prof. 1987-95, 98—, UCLA, 1985-87; chmn. bd. Health Data Net, 1971-73; bd. dirs. Intervalley Health Plan, 1995—; pres. Anaheim Meml. Devel. Found., 1986-94; pres., CEO InTech Health Sys., Inc., 1996—; sr. cons. APM, Inc., 1996-97. Author: (with B. L. Sloane) An Introduction to Health Care Delivery Organization: Functions and Management, 1971, 2d edit., 1977, 3d edit., 1992, (with Richard Harder) 4th edit., 1999; mem. editl. and adv. bd. Health Devices, 1972-90; contbr. articles to hosp. jours. Bd. dirs. Health Systems Agy. Los Angeles County, 1977-78, Vol. Hosps. of Am., 1986-95, chmn., 1993-94, pres., 1995; bd. dirs. Calif. Hosp. Polit. Action Com., 1979-87, vice chmn., 1980-83, chmn., 1983-85. Served to lt. (j.g.) USNR, 1954-56. Fellow Am. Coll. Healthcare Execs. (regent 1989-93, nominations com. 1994-97); mem. Am. Hosp. Assn., Healthcare Assn. So. Calif. (bd. dirs., sec. 1982, treas. 1983, chmn. elect 1984, chmn. 1985, past chmn. 1986, 89), Calif. Healthcare Assn. (bd. dirs. exec. com. 1984-86, 89), Anaheim C. of C. (bd. dirs. 1994). Home: 1301 N Santa Anita Ave Arcadia CA 91006-2419 Office: U So Calif Rgl 230 University Park Los Angeles CA 90089-0001

SLOANE, THOMAS O. speech educator; b. West Frankfort, Ill., July 12, 1929; s. Thomas Orville and Blanche (Morris) S.; m. Barbara Lee Lewis, Nov. 1, 1952; children— Elizabeth Alison, David Lewis, Emily. B.A., So. Ill. U., 1951, M.A., 1952; Ph.D., Northwestern U., 1960. Instr. English, Washington and Lee U., 1958-60; asst. prof. speech U. Ill., 1960-65, assoc. prof., 1965-70, assoc. head dept., 1967-68, asst. dean liberal arts and scis., 1966-67; prof. rhetoric, chmn. rhetoric dept. U. Calif., Berkeley, 1970-92, pres.'s chair, 1987-90. Dir. Nat. Endowment Humanities Summer Seminar for Coll. Tchrs., 1979 Editor: The Oral Study of Literature, 1966, The Passions of the Minde in Generall (Thomas Wright), 1971, (with Raymond B. Waddington) The Rhetoric of Renaissance Poetry, 1974, (with Joanna H. Maclay) Interpretation, 1972; Donne, Milton and the End of Humanist Rhetoric, 1985, On the Contrary, 1997, (with Peter Oesterreich) Rhetorica Movet, 1999; editor in chief: Encyclopedia of Rhetoric, 2001; contbr. articles to profl. jours. Served to lt. USNR, 1952-55. Faculty research fellow, 1964; U. Ill. instructional devel. awardee, 1965; Henry H. Huntington Library research awardee, 1967; U. Calif. humanities research fellow, 1974; Guggenheim fellow, 1981-82 Office: U Calif Berkeley CA 94720-0001 E-mail: tds@uclink.berkeley.edu

SLOM, SAMUEL M. state legislator; b. Allentown, Pa., Apr. 13, 1942; m. Francine Slom; children: Sam Mason, Stuart Matthew, Sid Michael, Spencer Madison. BA in Govt. and Econs., U. Hawaii, 1963, JD, 1966. Pvt. cons. economist; owner SMS Consultants, Conv. Spkrs. of Hawaii; pres., exec. dir. Small Bus. Hawaii; mem. Hawaii Senate, Dist. 8, Honolulu, 1996—; mem. commerce and consumer protection com. Hawaii Senate, Honolulu, mem. econ. devel. com., mem. edn. and tech. com., mem. labor and environ. com., mem. transp. and intergovtl. affairs com. Soccer coach AYSO Region 48; mem. Kamiloiki Elem. Sch. PTO; mem. adv. coun. SBA; mem. organizing com. Rediscover Hawaii Kai. Mem. U. Hawaii Alumni Assn. Office: State Capitol 415 S Beretania St Honolulu HI 96813-2407

SLONECKER, CHARLES EDWARD, anatomist, medical educator, writer; b. Gig Harbor, Wash., Nov. 30, 1938; s. William Mead and Helen Spencer (Henderson) S.; m. Jan Hunter, June 24, 1961; children— David Charles, Derron Scott, John Patrick. Student, Olympic Coll., 1957-58; student in Sci., U. Wash., 1958-60, DDS, 1965, PhD in Biol. Structure, 1967. Sci. asst. in pathology U. Bern, Switzerland, 1967-68; asst. prof. U. B.C., Vancouver, Canada, 1968-71, assoc. prof. Canada, 1971-76, prof. Canada, 1976, head of anatomy Canada, 1981-92, dir. ceremonies and univ. rels. Canada, 1989—, acting v.p. external affairs Canada, 1998-99, 00-01. Advisor Community Unit YMCA, Vancouver, 1981-92; group com. chmn. Boy Scouts, Can., 1976-82; mem. cabinet United Way Lower Mainland, 1997-99. With USAR, 1955-63. Recipient Award of Merit Am. Acad. Dental Medicine, 1965; recipient Award of Merit Wash. State Dental Assn., 1965, Dennis P. Duskin Meml. award U. Wash., 1965, Master Tchr. award, Cert. of Merit U. B.C., 1975-76 Fellow Am. Coll. Dentists; mem. Am. Assn. Anatomists (Centennial Gold medal 1987, program sec. 1982-90, v.p. 1991-93, pres. 1994), Can. Assn. U. Tchrs. (U. B.C. Killam Tchg. prize 1995), Sigma Xi (pres. U. B.C. 1981-82, 88-89), Omicron Kappa Upsilon (chpt. sec.). Anglican. Home: 6007 Dunbar St Vancouver BC Canada V6N 1W8 Office: Univ BC 6251 Cecil Green Park Rd V6T 1Z1 Vancouver BC Canada V6T 1W5 E-mail: csloneck@exchange.ubc.ca

SLUDIKOFF, STANLEY ROBERT, publisher, writer; b. Bronx, N.Y., July 17, 1935; s. Harry and Lillie (Elberger) S.; m. Ann Paula Blumberg, June 30, 1972; children: Lisa Beth, Jaime Dawn, Bonnie Joy. B.Arch., Pratt Inst., 1957; grad. student, U. So. Calif., 1960-62. Lic. architect, real estate broker. Project planner Robert E. Alexander, F.A.I.A. & Assos., Los Angeles, 1965-66, Daniel, Mann, Johnson & Mendenhall (City and Regional Planning Cons.), Los Angeles, 1967-70; pres., editor, pub. Gambling Times Inc., also Two Worlds Mgmt., Inc., Los Angeles, 1971—; v.p. Prima Quality Farms, Inc., P.R.; chmn. Creative Games, Inc., 1992—. Pres. Las Vegas TV Weekly, also Postal West, Las Vegas, 1975-79; founder Stanley Roberts Sch. Winning Blackjack, 1976; instr. city and regional planning program U. So. Calif., 1960-63; founding mem. Mfrs. Direct, 1996. Author: (under pen name Stanley Roberts) Winning Blackjack, 1971, How to Win at Weekend Blackjack, 1973, Gambling Times Guide to Blackjack, 1983; author: The Beginner's Guide to Winning Blackjack, 1983, Begin to Win at Blackjack, 1997, Begin to Win at Video Poker, 1997, Begin to Win at Craps, 1997; also monthly column, 1977—; inventor Daily Digit lottery game; patentee in field. Mem. Destination 90 Forum, Citizens Planning Group, San Fernando Valley, Calif., 1966-67, Rebuild L.A. land use com., 1992—. Served to lt. col. U.S. Army, now Res. ret. Recipient commendation from mayor Los Angeles for work on model cities funding, 1968 Mem. AIA, Am. Planning Assn., Am. Inst. Cert. Planners, Internat. Casino Assn. (sec. 1980—), Res. Officers Assn. (life), Mensa (life) Home: 10035 Laramie Ave Chatsworth CA 91311-3912 Office: 16140 Valerio St # B Van Nuys CA 91406-2916 E-mail: srs@gamblingtimes.com

SMALES, FRED BENSON, corporate executive; b. Keokuk, Iowa, Oct. 7, 1914; s. Fred B. and Mary Alice (Warwick) S.; m. Constance Brennan, Dec. 11, 1965; children: Fred Benson III, Catherine (Mrs. Jonathan Christensen); children by previous marriage: Patricia (Mrs. Murray Pilkington), Nancy (Mrs. Bruce Clark). Student public schs., Los Angeles. With Champion Internat., Inc., 1933-68, successively San Francisco mgr., 1938-44, Los Angeles, Western div. mgr., 1944-55, v.p. Western sales div., 1955-65, v.p., regional dir., 1965-68, pres. Lewers & Cooke, Inc. div., 1966-68; chmn. Securities of Am., Inc., 1968-70; chmn., pres., dir. Hawaiian Cement Co., 1970-84; pres. Transpacific Cons., 1984-94; owner Plywood Hawaii, 1995—. Trustee Hawaii-Pacific U., Hawaii Maritime Ctr. Recipient Disting. Citizen award Nat. Govs. Assn., 1986. Mem. C. of C. Hawaii (past chmn.), So. Calif. Yachting Assn. (sr. staff commodore), Balboa Yacht Club (Corona del Mar, Calif, sr. staff commodore), Transpacific Yacht, Waikiki Yacht (staff commodore), Pacific Club (past pres.), Royal Hawaiian Ocean Racing (dir.), Sequoia Yacht Club (Redwood City, Calif., sr. staff commodore). Home: 46-422 Hulupala Pl Kaneohe HI 96744-4243 Office: 1062 Kikowaena Pl Honolulu HI 96819-4413

SMALL, ELISABETH CHAN, psychiatrist, educator; b. Beijing, July 11, 1934; came to U.S., 1937; d. Stanley Hong and Lily Luella (Lum) Chan; m. Donald M. Small, July 8, 1957 (div. 1980); children Geoffrey Brooks, Philip Willard Stanley; m. H. Sidney Robinson, Jan. 12, 1991. Student, Immaculate Heart Coll., L.A., 1951-52; BA in Polit. Sci., UCLA, 1955, MD, 1960. Intern Newton-Wellesley Hosp., Mass., 1960-61; asst. dir. for venereal diseases Mass. Dept. Pub. Health, 1961-63; resident in psychiatry Boston State Hosp., Mattapan, Mass., 1965-66, Tufts New Eng. Med. Ctr. Hosps., 1966-69, psychiat. cons. dept. gynecology, 1973-75; asst. clin. prof. psychiatry Sch. Medicine Tufts U., 1973-75, assoc. clin. prof., 1975-82, asst. clin. prof. ob-gyn, 1977-80, assoc. clin. prof. ob-gyn, 1980-82; from assoc. prof. to prof. psychiatry U. Nev. Sch. Med., Reno, 1982-95; practice psychiatry specializing in psychological effects of bodily changes on women, 1969—; emeritus prof. psychiatry and behavioral scis. U. Nev. Sch. Medicine, Reno, 1995—, from assoc. prof. to clin. assoc. prof. ob-gyn, 1982-88; mem. staff Tufts New Eng. Med. Ctr. Hosps., 1977-82, St. Margaret's Hosps., Boston, 1977-82, Washoe Med. Ctr., Reno, Sparks (Nev.) Family Hosp., Truckee Meadows Hosp., Reno, St. Mary's Hosp., Reno; chief psychiatry svc. Reno VA Med. Ctr., 1989-94. Lectr., cons. in field; mem. psychiatry adv. panel Hosp. Satellite Network; mem. office external peer rev. NIMH, HEW; psychiat. cons. to Boston Redevelopment Authority on Relocation of Chinese Families of South Cove Area, 1968-70; mem. New Eng. Med. Ctr. Hosps. Cancer Ctr. Com., 1979-80, Pain Control Com., 1981-82; reproductive sys. curriculum com. Tufts Univ. Sch. Medicine, 1975-82. Mem. editorial bd. Psychiat. Update Am. (Psychiat. Assn. ann. rev.), 1983-85; reviewer Psychosomatics and Hosp. Community Psychiatry, New Eng. Jour. of Medicine, Am. Jour. of Psychiatry Psychosomatic Medicine; contbr. articles to profl. jours. Immaculate Heart Coll. scholar, 1951-52, Mira Hershey scholar UCLA, 1955; fellow Radcliffe Inst., 1967-70. Fellow Am. Coll. Psychiatrists (sci. program com. 1989-98); mem. AMA, Am. Psychiat. Assn. (rep. to sect. com. AAAS, chmn. ad hoc com. Asian-Am. Psychiatrists 1975, task force 1975-77, task force cost effectiveness in consultation 1984—, caucus chmn. 1981-82, sci. program com. 1982-88, courses subcom. chmn. sci. program com. 1986-88), Nev. Psychiat. Assn. (life), Assn. for Acad. Psychiatry (fellowship com. 1982), Washoe County Med. Assn., Nev. Med. Soc. Avocations: snow skiing, culinary arts. Home and Office: 825 Caughlin Xing Reno NV 89509-0647 Fax: 775-825-6860

SMALL, MARSHALL LEE, lawyer; b. Kansas City, Mo., Sept. 8, 1927; s. Phillip and Lillian Small; m. Mary Rogell, June 27, 1954; children: Daniel, Elizabeth. B.A., Stanford U., 1949, J.D., 1951. Bar: Mo. 1951, Calif. 1955, N.Y. 1990. Law clk. to Justice William O. Douglas U.S. Supreme Ct., Washington, 1951-52; assoc. Morrison & Foerster, San Francisco, 1954-60, ptnr., 1961-92, sr. of counsel, 1993—. Reporter corp. governance project Am. Law Inst., 1982-92. 1st lt. U.S. Army, 1952-54. Mem. ABA (com. corp. laws 1975-82), Phi Beta Kappa, Order of Coif Office: Morrison & Foerster LLP 425 Market St San Francisco CA 94105-2482 E-mail: msmall@mofo.com

SMARR, LARRY LEE, science administrator, educator, astrophysicist; b. Columbia, Mo., Oct. 16, 1948; s. Robert L. Jr. and Jane (Crampton) S.; m. Janet Levarie, June 3, 1973; children: Joseph Robert, Benjamin Lee. BA, MS, U. Mo., 1970; MS, Stanford U., 1972; PhD, U. Tex., 1975. Rsch. asst. in physics U. Tex., Austin, 1972-74; lectr. dept. astrophys. sci. Princeton U., 1974-75; rsch. assoc. Princeton U. Obs., 1975-76; rsch. affiliate dept. physics Yale U., New Haven, 1978-79; asst. prof. astronomy dept. U. Ill., Urbana, 1979-81, asst. prof. physics dept., 1980-81, assoc. prof. astronomy and physics dept., 1981-85, prof. astronomy and physics dept., 1985—; dir. Nat. Ctr. for Supercomputing Applications, Champaign, Ill., 1985—, Nat. Computational Sci. Alliance, 1997—. Cons. Lawrence Livermore Nat. Lab., Calif., 1976—, Los Alamos (New Nex.) Nat. Lab., 1983—; mem. Commn. on Phys. Sci., Math. and Resources, NRC, Washington, 1987-90, commn. on Geoscience, Environ. and Resources, 1990—, adv. panel on Basic Rsch. in the 90's Office Tech. Assesment, 1990—. Editor: Sources of Gravitational Radiation, 1979; mem. editoral bd. Science mag., 1986-90; contbr. over 50 sci. articles to jours. in field. Co-founder, co-dir. Ill. Alliance to Prevent Nuclear War, Champaign, 1981-84. Recipient Fahrney medal Franklin Inst., Phila., 1990; NSF fellow Stanford U., 1970-73, Woodrow Wilson fellow, 1970-71, Lane Scholar U. Tex., Austin, 1972-73, jr. fellow Harvard U., 1976-79, Alfred P. Sloan fellow, 1980-84. Fellow Am. Phys. Soc.; mem. NAE, AAAS, Am. Astron. Soc., Govt. Rsch. Roundtable U. Ind. Avocations: marine aquarium, gardening. Office: NCSA at UIUC 605 E Springfield Ave Champaign IL 61820-5518

SMARTT, BILL, air courier company executive; CFO DHL Airways Inc., Redwood City, Calif.; exec. v.p., CFO, chief administrv. officer DHL Worldwide Express, Redwood City. Office: DHL Worldwide Express 333 Twin Dolphin Dr Redwood City CA 94065-1496

SMARTT, RICHARD A. museum director; Dir., sci. chmn. N.Mex. Mus. Natural History, Albuquerque. Office: NMex Mus Natural History & Sci 1801 Mountain Rd NW Albuquerque NM 87104-1375

SMATHERS, JAMES BURTON, medical physicist, educator; b. Prairie du Chien, Wis., Aug. 26, 1935; s. James Levi and Irma Marie (Stindt) S.; m. Sylvia Lee Rath, Apr. 20, 1957; children— Kristine Kay, Kathryn Ann, James Scott, Ernest Kent. B.Nuclear Enging., N.C. State Coll., 1957, M.S., 1959; Ph.D., U. Md., 1967. Diplomate Am. Bd. Radiology, Am. Bd. Health Physics, Am. Bd. Medical Physics; cert. in radiation oncology physics; registered profl. engr., D.C., Tex., Calif. Research engr. Atomics Internat., Canoga Park, Calif., 1959, Walter Reed Army Inst. Research, Washington, 1961-67; prof. nuclear engring. Tex. A. and M. U., College Station, 1967-80, prof., head bioengring., 1976-80; prof., head med. physics, dept. radiation oncology UCLA, 1980-2001, prof. emeritus, 2001—. Cons. U.S. Army, Dept. Energy, also pvt. industry. Served with U.S. Army, 1959-61. Recipient Excellence in Teaching award Gen. Dynamics, 1971; Excellence in Research award Tex. A. and M. U. Former Students Assn., 1976 Mem. Am. Nuclear Soc., Health Physics Soc., Am. Assn. Physcists in Medicine, Am. Soc. Engring. Edn. (Outstanding Tchr. award in nuclear engring. div. 1972), Radiation Research Soc., Nat. Soc. Profl. Engrs., Calif. Soc. Profl. Engrs., Sigma Xi, Sigma Pi Sigma, Phi Kappa Phi. Home: 18229 Minnehaha St Northridge CA 91326-3427 E-mail: smathers@ucla.edu

SMEGAL, THOMAS FRANK, JR. lawyer; b. Eveleth, Minn., June 15, 1935; s. Thomas Frank and Genevieve (Andreachi) S.; m. Susan Jane Stanton, May 28, 1966; children: Thomas Frank, Elizabeth Jane. BS in Chem. Enging., Mich. Technol. U., 1957; JD, George Washington U., 1961. Bar: Va. 1961, D.C. 1961, Calif. 1964, U.S. Supreme Ct. 1976. Patent examiner U.S. Patent Office, Washington, 1957-61; staff patent atty. Shell Devel. Co., San Francisco, 1962-65; patent atty. Townsend and Townsend, San Francisco, 1965-91, mng. ptnr., 1974-89; sr. ptnr. Graham and James, San Francisco, 1992-97; pres., ptnr. Knobbe, Martens, Olson & Bear, San Francisco, 1997—. Mem. U.S. del. to Paris Conv. for Protection of Indsl. Property; mem. adv. com. Ct. of Appeals for Fed. Cir., 1992-96. Contbr. articles to profl. jours. Pres. bd. dirs. Legal Aid Soc. San Francisco, 1982-84, Youth Law Ctr., 1973-84; bd. dirs. Nat. Ctr. for Youth Law, 1978-84, San Francisco Lawyers Com. for Urban Affairs, 1972—, Legal Svcs. for Children, 1980-88; bd. dirs., presdl. nominee Legal Svcs. Corp., 1984-90, 93—. Capt. Chem. Corps, U.S. Army, 1961-62. Recipient St. Thomas More award, 1982. Mem. ABA (chmn. PTC sect. 1990-91, ho. of dels. 1988-2000, mem. standing com. Legal Aid and Indigent Defendants 1991-94, chair sect. officer conf. 1992-94, bd. govs. 1994-97, standing com. on Pro Bono and Pub. Svc. 1997-2001, standing com. on Gavel awards 2001—), Intellectual Property Law Assn. (chmn. nat. coun. 1989), Nat. Inventors Hall of Fame (pres. 1988), Calif. Bar Assn. (v.p. bd. dirs. 1986-87), Am. Patent Law Assn. (pres. 1986), Internat. Assn. Intellectual Property Lawyers (pres. 1995—), Bar Assn. San Francisco (pres. 1979), Patent Law Assn. San Francisco (pres. 1974), World Trade Club, Olympic Club, Golden Gate Breakfast Club, Claremont Club (Berkeley). Republican. Roman Catholic. Office: Knobbe Martens Olson & Bear 201 California St Ste 1150 San Francisco CA 94111-5002 E-mail: tsmegal@kmob.com

SMELSER, NEIL JOSEPH, sociologist; b. Kahoka, Mo., July 22, 1930; s. Joseph Nelson and Susie Marie (Hess) S.; m. Helen Thelma Margolis, June 10, 1954 (div. 1965); children: Eric Jonathan, Tina Rachel; m. Sharin Fateley, Dec. 20, 1967; children: Joseph Neil, Sarah Joanne. BA, Harvard U., 1952, PhD, 1958; BA, Oxford (Eng.) U., 1954, MA, 1959; grad., San Francisco Psychoanalytic Inst., 1971. Mem. faculty U. Calif., Berkeley, 1958-94, prof. sociology, 1962—, asst. chancellor ednl. devel., 1966-68; assoc. dir. Inst. of Internat. Studies, Berkeley, 1969-73, 80-89; prof. sociology U. Calif., Berkeley, 1972-94; prof. emeritus, 1994—; dir. edn. abroad program for U. Calif., Berkeley, 1977-79, spl. advisor Office of Pres., 1993-94, dir. Ctr. for Advanced Study in Behavioral Scis., 1994-2001. Bd. dirs. Social Sci. Rsch. Coun., chmn., 1971-73, com. econ. growth, 1961-65; trustee Ctr. for Advanced Study in Behavioral Scis., 1980-93, chmn., 1984-86; trustee Russell Sage Found., 1990—; subcom. humanism Am. Bd. Internal Medicine, 1981-85, 89-90, adv. com., 1992-99, chmn. adv. com., 1995-99; chmn. sociology panel Behavioral and Social Scis. survey NAS and Social Sci. Rsch. Coun., 1967-69; com. on basic rsch. in behavioral and social scis. NRC, 1980-89, chmn., 1984-86, co-chmn., 1986-89; chmn. com. of selection Guggenheim Found., 1996—; chmn. Commn. for Behavioral and Social Scis. and Edn. (NAS/NRC), 1996—, German-Am. Acad. Coun., 1999-2000. Author: (with T. Parsons) Economy and Society, 1956, Social Change in the Industrial Revolution, 1959, Theory of Collective Behavior, 1962, The Sociology of Economic Life, 1963, 2d edit., 1975, Essays in Sociological Explanation, 1968, Sociological Theory: A Contemporary View, 1971, Comparative Methods in the Social Sciences, 1976, (with Robin Content) The Changing Academic Market, 1980, Sociology, 1981, 2d edit., 1984, 3d edit., 1987, 4th edit., 1991, 5th edit., 1995, Social Paralysis and Social Change, 1991, Effective Committee Service, 1993, Sociology, 1994, Problematics of Sociology, 1997, The Social Edges of Psychoanalysis, 1998; editor: (with W.T. Smelser) Personality and Social Systems, 1963, 2d edit., 1971, (with S.M. Lipset) Social Structure and Mobility in Economic Development, 1966, Sociology, 1967, 2d edit., 1973, (with James Davis) Sociology: A Survey Report, 1969, Karl Marx on Society and Social Change, 1973, (with Gabriel Almond) Public Higher Education in California, 1974, (with Erik Erikson) Themes of Work and Love in Adulthood, 1980, (with Jeffrey Alexander et al) The Micro-Macro Link, 1987, Handbook of Sociology, 1988, (with Hans Haferkamp) Social Change and Modernity, 1992; (with Richard Munch) Theory of Culture, 1992; (with Richard Swedberg) The Handbook of Economic Sociology, 1994; (with Jeffrey Alexander) Diversity and Its Discontents, 1999; (with William Julius Wilson and Faith Mitchell) American Becoming: Racial Trends and their Consequences, 2001; editor Am. Sociol. Rev., 1962-65; adv. editor Am. Jour. Sociology, 1960-62. Rhodes scholar, 1952-54; Jr. fellow Soc. Fellows, Harvard U., 1955-58, fellow Russell Sage Found., 1989-90. Mem. Am. Sociol. Assn. (coun. 1962-65, 67-70, exec. com. 1963-65, pres. elect 1995-96, pres. 1996-97), Pacific Sociol. Assn., Internat. Sociol. Assn. (exec. com. 1986-94, v.p. 1990-94), Am. Acad. Arts and Scis. (hon.), Am. Philos. Soc. (hon.), Nat. Acad. of Scis. (hon.). E-mail: neil@casbs.stanford.edu

SMERDON, ERNEST THOMAS, engineering educator; b. Ritchey, Mo., Jan. 19, 1930; s. John Erle and Ada (Davidson) S.; m. Joanne Duck, June 9, 1951; children: Thomas, Katherine, Gary. BS in Engring., U. Mo., 1951, MS in Engring., 1956, PhD in Engring., 1959. Registered profl. engr., Ariz. Chmn. dept. agrl. engring. U. Fla., Gainesville, 1968-74, asst. dean for rsch., 1974-76; vice chancellor for acad. affairs U. Tex. System, Austin, 1976-82; dir. Ctr. for Rsch. in Water Resources U. Tex., 1982-88; dean Coll. Engring. and Mines U. Ariz., Tucson, 1988-92, vice provost, dean Engring, 1992-97; sr. edn. assoc. NSF, Arlington, Va., 1997-00; prof. civil engring. and hydrology U. Ariz., Tucson, 2000—. -mem. bd. sci. and tech. for internat. devel. NRC, 1990-94, mem. com. on plannin and remediation for irrigation-induced water quality problems, 1990-96, chair com. Yucca Mountain peer rev., 1995, mem. com. study of rsch.-doctorate programs in U.S., 1991-95, com. on Missouri River Ecosystem Sci., 1999=2001; others. Editor: Managing Water Related Conflicts: The Engineer's Role, 1989. Mem. Ariz. Gov.'s Sci. and Tech. Coun., Tucson, 1989-98; bd. dirs. Greater Tucson Econ. Coun., Tucson, 1990-95. Recipient Disting. Svc. in Engring. award U. Mo., 1982. Fellow AAAS, ASCE (hon. mem., Outstanding Svc. award irrigation and drainage divsn. 1988, Royce Tipton award 1989), NAE (peer com. 1986-90, acad. adv. bd. 1989-95, 98-99, tech. policy options co. 1990-91, chair com. on career-long edn. for engrs. 1997—), Am. Soc. Agrl. Engrs., Am. Water Resources Assn. (Icko Iben award 1989), Am. Soc. Engring. Edn. (chmn., bd. dirs. engring. dean's coun. 1995-97, pres. 1998-99), Am. Geophys. Union, Univ. Coun. on Water Resources, Ariz. Soc. Profl. Engrs. (Engr. of Yr. award 1990), Sigma Xi, Phi Kappa Phi, Tau Beta Pi, Pi Mu Epsilon. Avocations: hiking, golf, scuba diving, painting. Office: U Ariz Rm N521 Tucson AZ 85721-0001

SMILEY, RICHARD WAYNE, researcher; b. Paso Robles, Calif., Aug. 17, 1943; s. Cecil Wallace and Elenore Louise (Hamm) S.; m. Marilyn Lois Wenning, June 24, 1967; 1 child, Shawn Elizabeth. BSc in Soil Sci., Calif. State Poly. U., San Luis Obispo, 1965; MSc in Soils, Wash. State U., 1969, PhD in Plant Pathology, 1972. Asst. soil scientist Agrl. Rsch. Svc., USDA, Pullman, Wash., 1966-69; rsch. asst. dept. plant pathology Wash. State U., Pullman, 1969-72; soil microbiologist Commonwealth Sci. and Indsl. Rsch. Orgn., Adelaide, Australia, 1972-73; rsch. assoc. dept. plant pathology Cornell U., Ithaca, N.Y., 1973-74, asst. prof., 1975-80, assoc. prof., 1980-83, supt. Columbia Basin Agrl. Rsch. Ctr., 1983-2000, prof. Oreg. State U., 1985—. Vis. scientist Plant Rsch. Inst., Victoria Dept. Agr., Melbourne, Australia, 1982-83. Author: Compendium of Turfgrass Diseases, 1983, 2d edit., 1992; contbr. more than 200 articles to profl. jours.; author slide set illustrating diseases of turfgrasses. Postdoctoral fellow NATO, 1972. Fellow Am. Phytopath. Soc. (sr. editor APS Press 1984-87, editor-in-chief 1987-91); mem. Am. Soc. Agronomy, Internat. Turfgrass Soc., Am. Sod Producers Assn. (hon. life), Coun. Agrl. Sci. and Tech., Rotary (pres. Pendleton chpt. 1991-92, Paul Harris fellow 1993). Achievements include discovery of the etiology of a serious disease of turfgrasses, which led to a redefinition of studies and disease processes in turfgrasses. Office: Oreg State U Columbia Basin Agr Rsch Ctr PO Box 370 Pendleton OR 97801-0370 E-mail: richard.smiley@orst.edu

SMILEY, ROBERT HERSCHEL, university dean; b. Scottsbluff, Nebr., Mar. 17, 1943; s. Eldridge Herschel and Lucile Agnes (Kolterman) S., m. Sandra P. Mason (div. 1975); children: Peter, Michael, Robin; m. JoAnn Charlene Cannon, June 3, 1978; 1 child, Matthew. BS, UCLA, 1966, MS, 1969; PhD, Stanford U., 1973. Sr. aerospace engr. Martin Marietta Co., Littleton, Colo., 1966-67; mem. tech. staff, engr. Hughes Aircraft Co., Culver City, Calif., 1967-69; prof. econs. and policy, assoc. dean Grad. Sch. Mgmt. Cornell U., Ithaca, N.Y., 1973-89; dean, prof. mgmt. Grad. Sch. Mgmt. U. Calif., Davis, 1989—. Econ. cons. IBM, GM, Amex, SBA, Air Transport Assn., others; mem. rsch. adv. bd. NFIB, 1988—, policy adv. com. Ctr. for Coops., Davis, 1989—, adv. bd. Tech. Devel. Ctr., Davis, 1990—. Editor Sinergie, 1984—, Small Bus. Econs., 1988—; mem. editorial bd. Comstock's Mag., 1989—; contbr. articles to econs. and mgmt. jours. Bd. dirs. Sacramento Valley Forum, 1990—, Japan-Am. Conf., Sacramento, 1991—; chair sponsors com. Access '91, Sacramento, 1991; bd. govs. Capitol Club. SBA grantee, DOE grantee. Mem. Am. Econs. Assn., European Assn. for Rsch., Western Econs. Assn., Beta Gamma Sigma, Capitol Club. Avocations: skiing, tennis, swimming, biking. Office: U Calif AOB4 Dept Grad Sch Mgmt Davis CA 95616-8609

SMILEY, ROBERT WILLIAM, JR. investment banker; b. Lansing, Mich., Nov. 17, 1943; s. Robert William Sr. and Rebecca Lee (Flint) S. AB in Econs., Stanford U., 1970; postgrad., San Fernando Valley Coll. Law, 1973-75; MBA in Corp. Fin., City U. Los Angeles, 1979; LLB, LaSalle U., 1982. Bar: Calif. 1984. Sr. v.p. mktg. Actuarial Systems Inc., San Jose, Calif., 1972-73; founder, chmn. Benefit Systems Inc., L.A., and SE Nev., 1973-84, Brentwood Square Savs. and Loan, Los Angeles, 1982-84; chmn., CEO The Benefit Capital Cos. Inc., L.A. and S.E. Nev., 1984—. Lectr. U. Calif. Extension, Los Angeles and Berkeley, 1977—; instr. Am. Coll. Life Underwriters. Editor, contbg. author: Employee Stock Ownership Plans: Business Planning, Implementation, Law and Taxation, 1989, 2d edit. 1998; contbg. author: The Handbook of Employee Benefits, 1984, 6th edit., 2000; contbr. articles to profl. jours. Mem. nat. adv. coun., trustee Reason Found., L.A., 1983-91; bd. dirs. Nat. Ctr. for Employee Ownership, Oakland, Calif.; trustee The Employee Ownership Found., Washington. With USN, 1961-64, Vietnam. Recipient Spl. Achievement award Pres.' Commn. on Pension Policy, 1984. Fellow Life Mgmt. Inst.; mem. Employee Stock Ownership Plan Assn. (founder, pres., bd. dirs., lifetime dir.), Assn. for Corp. Growth, Western and SW Pension Confs., Nat. Assn. Bus. Economists, ABA, Calif. Bar Assn. Office: The Benefit Capital Cos Inc PO Box 542 Logandale NV 89021-0542

SMITH, AARON, retired research director, clinical psychologist; b. Boston, Nov. 3, 1930; s. Harry and Anne (Gilgoff) S.; m. Sept. 7, 1952 (div.); children: Naomi E., Jeffrey O., David G., Andrew H.; m. D. Sharon Casey, Jan. 7, 1972. AB, Brown U., 1952; PhD, U. Ill., 1958. Co-dir. N.E. Psychol. Clinic, Phila., 1959-75; dir. rsch. Haverford State Hosp., Pa., 1962-73, asst. hosp. dir., 1973-75; assoc. rsch. prof. U. Nev., Reno, 1975-2001; dir. rsch. VA Med. Ctr., Reno, 1975-2001; exec. dir. Sierra Biomed. Rsch. Corp., Reno, 1989-2001. Chmn. Nev. Legislature Mental Health Task Force, Carson City, 1978; sci. adviser Gov.'s Com. on Radiation Effects, Carson City, 1979-82. Co-author: Anti-depressant Drug Studies 1956-66, 1969, Medications and Emotional Illness, 1976; co-editor: Goal Attainment Scaling: Application, Theory, and Measurement, 1994; contbr. chpts. to books and articles to profl. jours. Grantee Squibb Inst. med. Rsch., 1965-69, NIMH, 1965-69, Smith Kline & French Labs., 1968-69, VA Health Svcs. Rsch., 1976-93. Mem. APA, We. Psychol. Assn., Gerontol. Soc. Am., Assn. Health Svcs. Rsch. Home: 1516 Diamond Country Dr Reno NV 89511-6149 Office: VA Med Ctr 1000 Locust St Reno NV 89502-2597

SMITH, ALAN JAY, computer science educator, consultant; b. N.Y.C., Apr. 10, 1949; s. Harry and Elsie Smith. SB, MIT, 1971; MS, Stanford (Calif.) U., 1973, PhD in Computer Sci., 1974. From asst. prof. to full prof. U. Calif., Berkeley, 1974—; assoc. editor ACM Trans. on Computers Systems, 1982-93. Vice-chmn. elec. engring. & computer sci. dept. U. Calif., Berkeley, 1982-84; nat. lectr. ACM, 1985-86; mem. editorial bd. Jour. Microprocessors and Microsystems, 1988—; subject area editor Jour. Parallel and Distbn. Computing, 1989—; mem. IFIP working group 7.3.; program chmn. Sigmetrics 89, Performance 1989, Hot Chips Symposium, 1990, 94, 97. Fellow IEEE (disting. visitor 1986-87), Assn. for Computing Machinery (chmn. spl. interest group on computer architecture 1991-93, chmn. spl. interest group on ops. systems 1983-87, bd. dirs. spl. interest group on performance evaluation 1985-89, bd. dirs. spl. interest group on computer architecture 1993—, nat. lectr. 1985-86); mem. Computer Measurement Group. Office: U Calif Dept Of Computer Sci Berkeley CA 94720-0001

SMITH, ANN DELORISE, municipal official; b. Union, S.C., June 26, 1941; 1 child. BS in Social Svc., Ea. Mich. U., 1962, postgrad., 1992-93. Planner III demonstration agy. City of L.A., 1970-75, sr. grants mgmt. specialist cmty. devel. dept., 1975-83, sr. mgmt. analyst I dept. aging, 1983-94, gen. mgr. dept. aging, 1994—. Del. White House Conf. on Aging, 1995; tchr. h.s. social studies, Flint and Ecors, Mich., 1962-63, grant cons., 1964-69, L.A./Detroit. Mem. adv. bd. Roybal Inst., Drew/RAND Ctr. on Health and Aging, KCET; mem. L.A. Urban League; mem. bd. dirs. Delta Sigma Theta HeadStart/State Presch.; involved in fed. grant programs including War on Poverty, 1960's. Mem. Am. Soc. on Aging, Nat. Ctr. and Caucus on Black Aging, Nat. Assn. of Area Agencies on Aging, Calif. Assn. of Area Agencies on Aging, Nat. Coun. on Aging, Gerontol. Soc. Am., Delta Sigma Theta. Home: 3803 S Dunsmuir Ave Los Angeles CA 90008-1016 Office: City of LA Dept Aging 2404 Wilshire Blvd Los Angeles CA 90057-3310

SMITH, ANNA DEAVERE, actor, educator, playwright; b. Balt., Sept. 18, 1950; d. Deavere Young and Anna (Young) S. BA, Beaver Coll., Pa., 1971, D hon., 1973; MFA, Am. Conservatory Theatre, 1977; D hon., U. N.C., 1995; hon. degree, Wheelock Coll., 1995, Colgate U., 1997, Sch. Visual Arts, 1997, Wesleyan U., 1997, Northwestern U., 1997, Coll. of the Holy Cross, 1997. Ann O'Day Maples prof. arts and drama Stanford U. Artist-in-residence Ford Found., 1997. Playwright, performer one-woman shows On the Road: A Search for American Character, 1983, Aye, Aye, Aye, I'm Integrated, 1984, Piano, 1991 (Drama-Logue award), Fires in the Mirror, 1989 (Obie award 1992, Drama Desk award 1992, N.Y. Drama Critics spl. citation 1993-94), Twilight: Los Angeles 1992 (Obie award, 2 Tony award nominations, Drama Critics Cir. spl. citation, Outer Critics Cir. award, Drama Desk award, Audelco award, Beverly Hills, Hollywood NAACP theatre awards), House Arrest, 1997; writer libretto for Judith Jamison, performer Hymn, 1993; appeared in (films) Dave, 1993, Philadelphia, 1993, The American President, 1995, Twilight: Los Angeles, 2000. Founding dir. The Inst. on Arts and Civic Dialogue Harvard U., 1998. Named One of Women of Yr., Glamour mag., 1993; fellow Bunting Inst., Radcliffe Coll.; genius fellow The MacArthur Found., 1996. Office: 1460 4th St Ste 212 Santa Monica CA 90401-3414 also: Stanford U Dept Drama Memorial Hall Stanford CA 94305

SMITH, ANNICK, writer, producer; b. Paris, May 11, 1936; came to U.S., 1937; d. Stephen and Helene Deutch; m. David James Smith (dec. 1974); children: Eric, Stephen, Alex, Andrew. Student, Cornell Univ., 1954-55, U. Chgo., 1955-57; BA, U. Wash., 1961. Editor U. Wash. Press, Seattle, 1961-64, Montana Bus. Quarterly, U. Montana, Missoula, 1971-72; founding bd. mem. Sundance Film Inst., Sundance, Utah, 1981-85; founding mem. Ind. Film Project, N.Y.C., 1981-84; acting dir. Montana Com. for the Humanities, Missoula, 1983-84; devel. dir. Hellgate Writers, Inc., Missoula, 1986-96; creative dir. Yellow Bay Writers Workshop, U. Montana Continuing Edn. Dept, Missoula, 1987-98. Freelance filmmaker, producer, arts administrator, writer, Mont., 1974—; past H.S. tchr., cmty. organizer, environ. worker. Exec. prodr. Heartland, 1981; co-prodr. A River Runs Through It, 1992; co-editor: (with William Kittredge) The Last Best Place; author: Homestead, 1994, Big BlueStem A Journey into the Tall Grass, 1996, In This We Are Native, 2001; contbr. to anthologies including Best Am. Short Stories, 1992. Recipient Western Heritage award Cowboy Hall of Fame, 1981; Mont. Humanites award Mont. Com. for Humanities, 1988, Okla. Book award, 1997, Bancroft Prize Denver Pub. Libr., 1998. Mem. Trout Unlimited, Blackfoot Challenge. Democrat. Office: Box 173 Star Route Bonner MT 59823

SMITH, CECILIA MAY, hospital official; b. Oakland, Calif., Feb. 18, 1933; d. Frederick Arthur and Inez Calista Small; m. Harold Joseph Smith, June 17, 1957 (dec. June 18, 1966); children: Harold Frederick, Estelle Marie. BS, Holy Name Coll., 1956; MS, U. Calif., San Francisco, 1966; postgrad., U. Calif., Berkeley, 1972. RN, Calif. Asst. prof. U. Nev., Reno, 1966-69; instr. U. Wash., Seattle, 1972-74; dir. continuing edn. Wash. State Nurses Assn., Seattle, 1974-78; pres., ptnr. World of Continuing Edn., Seattle, 1975-85; continuing edn. specialist U. Calif., San Francisco, 1979-82; asst. adminstr. Cordilleras Mental Health Ctr., Redwood City, Calif., 1984-86, adminstr., 1986-90; dir. psychiat. svcs. St. Luke's Hosp., San Francisco, 1990—. Mem. ANA Nat. Accreditation Bd., Kansas City, 1974-7; sec., workshop leader Nat. Staffing Systems, San Francisco, 1981-82; cons. WHO, New Delhi, 1985. Editor ind. study courses for nurses and nursing home adminstrs., 1975-85; author AIDS ind. study courses, 1984; contbr. articles to Jour. of Continuing Edn. Recipient Marie Durocher scholarship Coll. of Holy Name, 1952, NIMH traineeship U. Calif. San Francisco, 1963, Nursing Rsch. fellowship U. Calif. Berkeley, 1969-71. Mem. Sigma Theta Tau. Office: St Luke's Hosp 3555 Cesar Chavez San Francisco CA 94110-4403 E-mail: ceciliams33@hotmail.com

SMITH, CHARLES ANTHONY, business executive; b. Santa Fe, Sept. 16, 1939; s. Frances (Mier) Vigil; m. Paula Ann Thomas, June 26, 1965; 1 child, Charlene Danielle. Student various adminstrv. & law courses. Circulation mgr. Daily Alaska Empire, 1960-63; agt. Mut. of N.Y. Life Ins. Co., Juneau, Alaska, 1964-65; mng. ptnr. Future Investors in Alaska and Cinema Alaska, Juneau, 1961-62; SE Alaska rep. K & L Distbrs., 1966-68; mgr. SE Alaska Alaska Airlines Newspapers, 1969; dep. Alaska Retirement Sys., Juneau, 1970-71; apptd. dir. hwy. safety, gov.'s hwy. safety rep. Juneau, 1971-83; pres. Valley Svc. Ctr., I Nc., 1984-94; chmn. S.E. Alaska Employer Support of the Guard and Reserve, 1992—; pres. 3-S Corp., 1995—. Apptd. chmn. S.E. Alaska for ESGR, 1995; apptd. Alaska state dir. Selective Svc., 1996—. Author various hwy. safety manuals and plans. Alaska pres. Muscular Dystrophy Assn. Am.; pres. SE Alaska Emergency Med. Svcs. Coun., 1965-72; state dir. Selective Svc., 1996. Served to maj. Army N.G., 1964-88. Named Alaska Safety Man of Yr., 1977. Mem. Am. Assn. Motor Vehicle Adminstrs., Alaska Peace Officers Assn., Nat. Assn. Gov.'s Hwy. Safety Reps., N.G. Assn., Internat. Platform Assn., Elks (Juneau). Roman Catholic. Home: PO Box 32856 Juneau AK 99803-2856

SMITH, CHARLES CONARD, refractory company executive; b. Mexico, Mo., Feb. 10, 1936; s. Charles Adelbert and Waldine (Barnes) S.; m. Constance Nagel, Oct. 6, 1962; children: Stewart Ashley, Graham Prior. BS in Ceramic Engring., Iowa State U., 1958; MBA, Stanford U., 1962. Process engr. Kaiser Refractory divsn. Kaiser Aluminum, Moss Landing, Calif., 1962-65, materials mgr. Mexico, Mo., 1965-67, divsn. planning Oakland, Calif., 1967-69; v.p., gen. mgr. Kaiser Refractories Argentina, Buenos Aires, 1969-74; with divsn. planning Kaiser Refractories divsn. Kaiser Aluminum, Oakland, 1974-77, mktg. mgr., 1977-80, gen. mgr. mfg., 1980-82, v.p., gen. mgr. refractories divsn., 1982-85; chmn., pres., CEO Nat. Refractories and Mineral Corp., Livermore, Calif., 1985—. Patentee in refractory field. Lt. USNR, 1958 60. Mem. Refractories Inst. (past chmn., exec. com.). Republican. Avocations: fishing, biking, kite flying, photography, music.

SMITH, CHARLES LEWIS, retired career officer and association executive; b. Clarkston, Ga., Oct. 27, 1920; s. Robert Clyde and Emelyn (Bloodworth) S.; m. Mildred Lee Stilley, Sept. 5, 1947; children: Jan, Robert Eugene. Student, Ga. Sch. Tech., 1938-39. Enlisted USN, 1937, advanced through grades to comdr., 1968; various assignments including comdg. officer USS Chickasaw (ATF 83), 1962-64; leadership devel. officer Amphibious Force U.S. Pacific Fleet, 1964-66; comdg. officer USS Tioga County (LST 1158), 1966-68; dept. head Amphibious Sch. U.S. Naval Amhibious Base, Coronado, Calif., 1968-70, ret., 1970; dir. pub. rels. and fin. San Diego County Coun. Boy Scouts Am., 1971-80, dir. pub. rels., 1980-82, dir. planned giving, 1982-85, ret., 1985. Mem. nat. adv. bd. Am. Security Coun., 1994-97. Trustee God Bless Am. Week, Inc., 1972-80, pres., 1977-78, co-chmn. San Diego Bicentennial Pageant, 1976; mem. adv. bd. Commd. Officers Mess (Open) U.S. Naval Sta., 1973-89; bd. dirs. Boys Club Chula Vista, Calif., 1985-87; devel. com. Alvarado Health Found., Alvarado Hosp. Med. Ctr., 1986-87; charter rev. com. City of Chula Vista, 1986-88; mem. accolades com. City of San Diego, 1988-90; rsch. bd. advisors Am. Biog. Inst., 1988—; vol. Boy Scouts Am. 1935-71, 85—; scout commr. San Diego County coun. 1969-71, mem. internat. rels. com. 1985-92, bd. dirs., 1995-97, scoutmaster 7th Nat. Jamboree, Farragut State park, Idaho, 1969, 13th World Jamboree, Japan, 1971, mem. local staff Nat. Jamboree, Ft. A.P. Hill, Va., 1986, mem. nat. staff, 1997. Recipient svc. award Civitan Internat., 1968, Cmty. Svc. resolution Calif. Senate, 1970, Southwestern Coll., 1973, Silver Beaver award Boy Scouts Am., 1965, Svc. to Youth resolution Calif. Senate, 1985, award Armed Forces YMCA Century Club, 1988, Appreciation award United Way San Diego, 1974-82, citation for heroism Sheriff of San Diego, 1991, Recognition award San Diego Rotary Club, 1991, citation for svc. City of San Diego Accolades Com., 1992, Disting. Svc. award U.S.S. Chickasaw (ATF-83) Assn., 1993, Svc. award U.S.S. Wickes (DD578), 1995, Cert. of Appreciation, USN Meml. Found., 1997, 99, Cert. of Appreciation, Warrant Officers Assn., 1998, Nat. Commander Hero's of '76, Patroits of '76 award, 1999, 2000, Cer. of Appreciation, Nat. Sojourners, 2000, Veterans of the Vietnam War, 2001, 65 Year Verterans award, Boy SAcouts of Am. Youth, 2000, Certificate of Appreciation, Veterans of Foreign Wars, 2001; Scouter Chuck Smith Day proclaimed by City of San Diego, 1985; flagpole dedicated to Scouter Chuck Smith San Diego County Coun. Boy Scouts Am., 1992; named to Hon. Order Ky. Cols., 1985, bd. dirs., 1987—, pres., 1996. Mem. VFW (Cert. of Appreciation 1995, 96, 97, 99, 2000), Nat. Soc. Fund Raising Execs. (bd. dirs. San Diego chpt. 1975-80, 84-85, hosp. com. 1984-85), UN Assn. (bd. dirs. San Diego chpt. 1972-85), Ret. Officers Assn. (life, bd. dirs. Sweetwater chpt. 1972-92, pres. 1975, 81), Navy League U.S. (bd. dirs. 1984—, greeters 1983—, Appreciation award 1985, Cert. of Merit 1991), Mil. Order World Wars (comdr. 1989-90, nat. citations 1987, 91, 92, Outstanding Chpt. Comdr. award Dept. So. Calif. 1990, Patrick Henry medallion and medal 1996), Am. Legion, Crazy Horse Meml. Found., Clarkston Civitan Club (founding bd. dirs.), Eagle Scout Alumni Assn. (founder 1973, bd. dirs. 1986-88, life mem. 1985—), Hammer Club San Diego, Kiwanis (bd. dirs. 1984-88, chmn. fellowship com. 1983-84, boys and girls com. 1984-85, planned giving com. 1988-89), Order of the Arrow (vigil, Cross Feathers award 1968), Masons, Shriners, Order of Ea. Star (life), Nat. Sojourners (life, Cert. of Appreciation 1999). Methodist.

SMITH, CHARLES Z. state supreme court justice; b. Lakeland, Fla., Feb. 23, 1927; s. John R. and Eva (Love) S.; m. Eleanor Jane Martinez, Aug. 20, 1955; children: Carlos M., Michael O., Stephen P., Felica L. BS, Temple U., 1952; JD, U. Wash., 1955. Bar: Wash. 1955. Law clk. Wash. Supreme Ct., Olympia, 1955-56; dep. pros. atty., asst. chief criminal div. King County, Seattle, 1956-60; ptnr. Bianchi, Smith & Tobin, Seattle, 1960-61; spl. asst. to atty. gen. criminal div. U.S. Dept. Justice, Washington, 1961-64; judge criminal dept. Seattle Mcpl. Ct., 1965-66; judge Superior Ct. King County, 1966-73; former assoc. dean, prof. law U. Wash., 1973; now justice Wash. Supreme Ct., Olympia. Mem. adv. bd. NAACP, Seattle Urban League, Wash. State Literacy Coun., Boys Club, Wash. Citizens for Migrant Affairs, Medina Children's Svc., Children's Home Soc. Wash., Seattle Better Bus. Bur., Seattle Foundation, Seattle Symphony Orch., Seattle Opera Assn., Community Svc. Ctr. for Deaf and Hard of Hearing, Seattle U., Seattle Sexual Assault Ctr., Seattle Psychoanalytic Inst., The Little Sch., Linfield Coll., Japanese Am. Citizens League, Kawabe Meml. Hous, Puget Counseling Ctr, Am. Cancer Soc., Hutchinson Cancer Rsch. Ctr., Robert Chinn Found.; pres. Am. Bapt. Chs. U.S.A., 1976-77, U.S. Commn. on Internat. Religious Freedom, 1999-2000. lt. col. ret. USMCR Mem. ABA, Am. Judicature Soc., Washington Bar Assn., Seattle-King County Bar Assn., Order of Coif., Phi Alpha Delta, Alpha Phi Alpha. Office: Wash Supreme Ct Temple of Justice PO Box 40929 Olympia WA 98504-0929

SMITH, D. ADAM, congressman; b. Washington, June 15, 1965; m. Sara Bickle-Eldridge, 1993. BA, Fordham U., 1987; JD, U. Wash., 1990. Driver United Parcel Svc., 1985-87; mem. Wash. State Senate, 1990-96; atty. Cromwell Mendoza Belur, 1992-93; asst. prosecuting atty. City of Seattle, 1993-96; mem. 106th Congress from 9th dist. Wash., 1997—. Democrat. Office: 116 Canon Hob Washington DC 20515-0001

SMITH, DANIEL WALTER, engineering educator; BS in Civil Engring., Calif. State U., 1967; MS in Sanitary Engring., San Jose State U., 1968; PhD in Environ. Health Engring., U. Kans., 1970. Registered profl. engr. Alta., Can., Calif., Alaska, N.W. Territories. Tchg. asst. dept. civil engring. U. Kans., Lawrence, 1969-70; asst. prof. environ. health engring. U. Alaska, Fairbanks, 1971, asst. prof. water resources Inst. Water Resources, 1972-75, asst. prof. environ. quality engring., 1972-75; head No. Tech. Ctr. Environ. Protection Svc. Dept. of the Environment, Edmonton, Alta., Can., 1975-77; sr. environ. engr. R&M Cons., Inc., Anchorage, 1977-78; assoc. prof. civil engring. U. Alta., Edmonton, 1978-80, prof. civil engr., 1980—, chair dept. civil engring., 1990-94, dir. environ. engring. program, 1996—. Pres. Daniel W. Smith & Assocs. Ltd., Edmonton, Alta., 1979—; sr. v.p., tech. dir. TekTran Internat., Info. and Edn., Inc., Alta. and Kitchener, Ont., 1982-87; spl. cons. James F. MacLaren, Ltd., Edmonton, 1980, Barrow (Alaska) Electric and Utilities Coop, 1980—, FMS (Lavalin) Engrs., Edmonton, 1980-84, Dept. Pub. Works City of Yellowknife, 1985-88, Reid Crowher & Ptnrs., Edmonton, 1986-90, HDR Engring. (OTT Water Engrs., Inc.) Anchorage, Alaska, 1987-93, City of Edmonton, 1986—, Edmonton Bd. Health, 1988-95, Stanley Cons. Group ltd., Stanley Environ., Sentra, Edmonton, 1995 , Health Can. Med. Svcs. Br., Alta., 1998; organizer internat. symposiums on cold regions environ. engring., 1976, 79, 82, 83, 87; lead instr. faculty of extension U. Alta., Can., 1985; mem. grant selection com. NSERC, 1995-96, re-allocations steering com., 1997, organizer, co-instr., instr. numerous workshops. Co-author: Cold Climate Utilities Delivery Design Manual, 1979; editor, co-editor numerous books including Design of Water and Wastewater Services for Cold Climate Communities, 1981, Scale-Up of Water and Wastewater Treatment Processes, 1983, Cold Climate Utilities Manual, 1986; tech. editor: Cold Regions Utilities Monograph, 1996; contbr. numerous articles to profl. jours., chpts. to books. Recipient Award of Merit Soc. Tech. Comm., 1987, Profl. Award of Merit Assn. Profl. Engrs., Geologists and Geophysicists of N.W. Territories, 1993, Edmonton Amb. award Edmonton Convention Bur. Econ. Devel. Edmonton, 1997, Gold medal Polish Assn. Sanitary Engrs. and Techs. Fellow ASCE (mem. tech. affairs com. cold regions engring. splty. confs. 1978, 81, 84, 86, 89, 91, 94, chair 1984, co-chair 1994, mem. exec. com. tech. coun. on cold regions engring. 1980-85, 96—, chmn. 1983-84, 99-2000, chmn. CSCE/ASCE Environ. Engring. Conf., 1997, design and constrn. com. 1988—, edn. com. 1989—; mem. editl. com. Cold Region Engring. Jour. 1992-94, editl. bd. 1995-97, editor Jour. Environ. Engring. and Sci., assoc. editor Ozone Sci. and Engring., mem. profl. affairs com. environ. engring. divsn. 1996—, Elbert F. Rice Meml. Lectr. award 1989, Can-Am Amity Civil Engring. award 1989), Engring. Inst. Can., Canadian Soc. Civil Engring. (chmn. environ. engring. divsn. 1979-84, chair tech. activities com. 1984-86, sr. v.p. 1986-87, pres. 1987-88, invited spkr. cold regions environ. engring. Nat. Lecture Tour 1997, T.C. Keefer medal (with G.R. Finch) 1987, (with H. Mao) 1998, Albert E. Berry medal 1988), Canadian Acad. Engring.; mem. Am. Water Works Assn. (life, student mem. award 1966-67), Am. Acad. Environ. Engrs. (diplomat), Canadian Pulp and Paper Assn., Internat. Assn. Water Quality, Internat. Ozone Assn., Engring. Inst. Can. (fellow), Assn. Environ. Engrs., Instn. Water and Environ. Mgmt. (Eng., mem. profl. review com. 1995-96), Western Can. Water and Wastewater Assn. (elected to Select Soc. Sanitary Sludge Shovelers 1995), Assn. Profl. Engrs. and Geologists B.C. (mem. CCPE environ. engring. syllabus com. 1997), Chi Epsilon. Achievements include 3 patents for automated oxygen uptake rate measurement device; contribution to application of laser Doppler reserch tools for studying treatment processes fundamentals; research in ozone water and wastewater treatment, water treatment, distribution system corrosion studies, advanced wastewater treatment studies, solid waste management, freeze separation wastewater treatment, river quality and indicator organism modelling, pulp mill wastewater treatment. Office: U Alta Dept Civil & Environ Environ Engring Bldg Rm 304 Edmonton AB Canada T6G 2M8 Fax: (780) 492-8289. E-mail: dwsmith@civil.ualberta.ca

SMITH, DAVID JOHN, physicist, educator; b. Melbourne, Australia, Oct. 10, 1948; arrived in U.S., 1984; s. Arthur and Agnes Frances S.; m. Gwenneth Paula Bland, Sept. 18, 1971 (div. 1992); children: Heather F., Marion J. BSc with honors, U. Melbourne, Australia, 1970, PhD, 1978, DSc, 1988. Post-doctoral rsch. asst. Cavendish Lab. U. Cambridge, Eng., 1976-78, sr. rsch. assoc. Eng., 1979-84; assoc. prof. Ariz. State U., Tempe, 1984-87, prof., 1987—, regents prof., 2000—, dir. Ctr. for Solid State Sci., 2001—. Dir. Cambridge U. High Resolution Electron Microscope, 1979-84, NSF Ctr. for High Resolution Electron Microscopy, Tempe, 1991-96. Author 11 chpts. in books; editor 15 conf. procs.; contbr. over 340 articles to profl. jours. Recipient Faculty Achievement award Burlington Resources Found., 1990. Fellow Inst. Physics (U.K., Charles Vernon Boys prize 1985); mem. Am. Phys. Soc., Material Rsch. Soc., Microscopy Soc. Am. Office: Ariz State U Ctr Solid State Sci Tempe AZ 85287 E-mail: david.smith@asu.edu

SMITH, DAVID MICHAEL, financial planner; b. Fresno, Calif., Dec. 29, 1944; s. Ralph S. and Verla Fern (Tharp) S.; m. Barbara J. Bryson, June 27, 1964; children: Brandon, Eric. AA, Fresno City Coll., 1964; AB, Calif. State U., Fresno, 1966. Tchr. English Fresno Unified Sch. Dist., 1967-79; registered rep. TMI Equities, Inc., Fresno, 1979-82, regional mgr. Camarillo, Calif., 1982-85; fin. planner Associated Planners Securities Corp.,

Camarillo, 1985-89, David M. Smith & Assocs., Camarillo, 1989—; mayor City of Camarillo, 1991, 95. Council mem. City of Camarillo, 1988-95; pres. Fresno Dem. Coaltion, 1979. Mem. Fin. Planning Assn., Camarillo Noontime Optimists Club. Office: David M Smith & Assocs 1200 Paseo Camarillo Ste 190 Camarillo CA 93010-6085

SMITH, DAVID WAYNE, psychologist, educator; b. Ind., Apr. 16, 1927; s. Lowell Wayne and Ruth Elizabeth (Westphal) S.; m. Marcene B. Leever, Oct. 20, 1948; children: David Wayne, Laurreen Lea. B.S., Purdue U., 1949; M.S., Ind. U., 1953, Ph.D., 1955. Diplomate Am. Bd. Psychol. Specialities. Prof. rehab., dir. Rehab. Center; asso. dean, later asst. v.p. acad. affairs Ariz. Health Scis. Center, U. Ariz., Tucson, 1955-80; research prof. rehab., adj. prof. medicine, cons. in research S.W. Arthritis Center, Coll. Medicine, 1980-87; prof. rehab. and rheumatology, dept. medicine U. Ariz., 1987—, also dir. disability assessment program. Pres. allied health professions sect. Nat. Arthritis Found.; bd. dirs. Nat. Arthritis Found. (S.W. chpt.); nat. vice chmn. bd. dirs.; mem. NIH Nat. Arthritis Adv. Bd., 1977-84; also chmn. subcom. community programs and rehab.; mem. staff Ariz. Legislature Health Welfare, 1972-73; Mem. Gov.'s Council Dept. Econ. Security, 1978-85; pres., bd. dirs. Tucson Assn. for Blind, 1974-86; chmn. Gov.'s Council on Blind and Visually Impaired, 1987—; active Gov.'s Coun. on Arthritis and Musculoskeletal Disease, 1987—, Gov.'s State wide Coun. on Rehab., 1998—, Am. Bd. Forensic Examiners, 1997—. Author: Worksamples; contbr. chpts. to books and articles to profl. jours. Mem. Gov.'s State Rehab. Coun., 1998—. Recipient Gov.'s awards for leadership in rehab., 1966, 69, 72, 73; awards for sci. and vol. services Nat. Arthritis Found., 1973, 75; 1st nat. Addie Thomas award Nat. Arthritis Found., 1983, Benson award, 1989, Govt. Affairs award, 1989; Arthritis Found. fellow, 1983. Mem. Am. Psychol. Assn. (div. 17 counseling psychology), Am. Coll. Forensics, Assn. Schs. Allied Health Professions, Nat. Rehab. Assn., Ariz. Psychol. Assn. Home: 5765 N Camino Real Tucson AZ 85718-4213 Office: U Ariz Arizona Health Scis Ctr Tucson AZ 85724-0001

SMITH, DERRIN RAY, information systems company executive; b. Columbus, Ohio, Feb. 19, 1955; s. Ray Stanley Smith and Clara (Diddle) Craver; m. Catherine Marie Massey, Aug. 18, 1979; children: Shannon Cathleen, Allison Collette, Micayla Colleen, Nicole Catherine. BS, Regis U., 1981; MBA, U. Phoenix, 1984; PhD, U. Denver, 1991. Test lab. mgr. Ball Aerospace Systems, Ball Corp., Boulder, 1975-84; sr. systems engr. Martin Marietta Info. Systems, Denver, 1984-87; tech. cons. MITRE Fed. R & D Ctr., Colorado Springs, 1988-92; pres. DRS Scis., Inc., Denver, 1992—; nat. program mgr. cable/telephone/full svc. network The Nat. Program Dir. Time Warner, 1994—; chmn., CEO GETGO, Inc., 2000—. Tech. cons. U.S. Space Command-RAPIER, Colorado Springs, 1989-91, Unisys Corp., Greenwood Village, Colo., 1992; adj. prof. CIS dept. Univ. Coll., U. Denver, 1992; secretariat Corp. Planner's Roundtable, St. Louis, 1982-84; spkr. in field. Author: Evolving the Mountain; Defense Acquisition Management of Strategic Command and Control System Procurements, 1991; contbr. articles to profl. jours. Res. police officer Federal Heights (Colo.) Police Dept., 1979-82. With USMC, 1978-84. Recipient Outstanding Achievement award Rocky Mountain News, 1981, Reservist of Yr. award Navy League U.S., 1981. Mem. Assn. Former Intelligence Officers (pres. Rocky Mountain chpt.). Roman Catholic. Avocations: martial arts, skiing, sailing, creative writing, mountaineering. Home: 3746 E Easter Cir S Littleton CO 80122-2033 Office: DRS Sciences Inc PO 2091 Littleton CO 80161-2091

SMITH, DONALD E. broadcast engineer, manager; b. Salt Lake City, Sept. 10, 1930; s. Thurman A. and Louise (Cardall) S.; m. Helen B. Lacy, 1978. BA, Columbia U., 1955; BS, U. Utah, 1970; postgrad., U. So. Calif., U. Utah, Harvard U.; PhD (hon.), Columbia U., 1985. Engr. Iowa State U. (WOI-TV), 1955-56; asst. chief engr. KLRJ-TV, Las Vegas, 1956-60; studio field engr. ABC, Hollywood, Calif., 1960; chief engr. Teletape, Inc., Salt Lake City, 1961; engring. supr. KUER, U. Utah, Salt Lake City, 1962-74, gen. mgr., 1975-85. Freelance cinematographer, 1950—; cons. radio TV (mgmt. engr. and prodn.), 1965—. Mem. Soc. Motion Pictures and TV Engrs., Lambda Chi Alpha. Home: 963 Hollywood Ave Salt Lake City UT 84105-3347 E-mail: donesmith@home.com

SMITH, DONALD RICHARD, editor, publisher; b. Stockton, Calif., Aug. 20, 1932; s. Robert Gordon and Gertrude (Schweitzer) S.; m. Darlene Ruth Thomas, May 7, 1961; children: Douglas Robert, Deborah Renae. Student, Coll. Pacific, 1951, Delta Coll., 1951-52. Editor, pub. Calif. Odd Fellow & Rebekah, Linden, 1950—; editor Elk Grove (Calif.) Citizen, 1953-55; asst. dir. U.N. Pilgrimage for Youth, N.Y.C., 1956-59; editor, pub. Linden (Calif.) Herald, 1959-86, Lockeford (Calif.)-Clements Post, 1960-62, Internat. Rebekah News, Linden, 1963-86, Internat. Odd Fellow & Rebekah, Linden, 1986-97; dir. communications Sovereign Grand Lodge, Linden, 1990-92. Author: From Stagestop to Friendly Community, 1976, Leadership Manual, 1980, The Three Link Fraternity, 1993, Six Links of Fellowship, 1995. Bd. dirs. Odd Fellow-Rebekah Youth Camp, Inc., Long Barn, Calif., 1959-61; bd. dirs. The Meadows of Napa Valley, 1995—, pres. bd., 1998-99; bd. dirs., chmn., S.J. County 4-H Found., 1986—; chmn. Linden Rep. Com., 1962-66, Linden Centennial Observance, 1963, Linden Mcpl. Coun., 1981-90, sec., 1981-88, pres., 1988-90. Recipient Legion of Honor Order of Demolay, 1961, John Williams award S.J. Tchrs. Assn., 1963, 87, Golden Key award Stockton Tchrs. Assn., 1971, Achievement award County Bd. Suprs., 1970, Grand Decoration of Chivalry, 1969, Citizen of Yr. award Lions Internat., 1982, Meritorious Svc. Jewel, Ind. Order of Odd Fellows, 1992. Mem. IOOF Internat. Press Assn. (pres. 1962-63), Desktop Pub. Assn., Linden Peters C. of C. (pres. 1968-69), S.J. Hist. Soc. (trustee 1986-90), Lions, Odd Fellows Internat. (sovereign grand master 1969-70), Odd Fellows Calif. (grand master 1958-59), Internat. Coun. Ind. Order Odd Fellows (sec. 1990-96). Avocations: collecting Lionel trains, stamps, coins, historical books, research. Home: 5350 Harrison St Linden CA 95236-9523 Office: Linden Publ 19033 E Main PO Box 129 Linden CA 95236-0129 E-mail: donsioof@hotmail.com

SMITH, DWIGHT MORRELL, chemistry educator; b. Hudson, N.Y., Oct. 10, 1931; s. Elliott Monroe and Edith Helen (Hall) S.; m. Alice Beverly Bond, Aug. 27, 1955 (dec. 1990); children— Karen Elizabeth, Susan Allison, Jonathan Aaron; m. Elfi Nelson, Dec. 28, 1991. BA, Ctrl. Coll., Pella, Iowa, 1953; PhD, Pa. State U., 1957; ScD (hon.), Cen. Coll., 1986; LittD (hon.), U. Denver, 1990. Postdoctoral fellow, instr. Calif. Inst. Tech., 1957-59; sr. chemist Texaco Rsch. Ctr., Beacon, N.Y., 1959-61; asst. prof. chemistry Wesleyan U., Middletown, Conn., 1961-66; assoc. prof. Hope Coll., Holland, Mich., 1966-69, prof., 1969-72; prof. chemistry U. Denver, 1972—, chmn. dept., 1972-83, 99-01, vice chancellor for acad. affairs, 1983-84, chancellor, 1984-89; pres., bd. trustees Hawaii Loa Coll., Kaneohe, 1990-92. Mem. Registry for Interim Coll. and Univ. Pres.; mem. adv. bd. Solar Energy Rsch. Inst., 1989—91; mem. vis. com. Zettlemoyer Ctr. for Surface Studies Lehigh U., 1990—96; dept. chemistry and geochemistry Colo. Sch. Mines; mem. sci. adv. bd. Denver Rsch. Inst. Editor Revs. on Petroleum Chemistry, 1975-78; editl. adv. bd. Recent Rsch. Devels. in Applied Spectroscopy, 1998—; contbr. articles to profl. jours.; patentee selective hydrogenation. Chmn. Chs. United for Social Action, Holland, 1968-69; mem. adv. com. Holland Sch. Bd., 1969-70; bd. commrs. Colo. Adv. Tech. Inst., 1984-88, Univ. Senate, United Meth. Ch., Nashville, 1987-88, 91-93; mem. adv. bd. United Way, Inst. Internat. Edn., Japan Am. Soc. Colo., Denver Winter Games Olympics Com.; mem. bd. bds. or consistories Ref. Ch. Am., N.Y., Conn., Mich., United Meth. Ch., Colo. DuPont fellow, 1956-57, NSF fellow Scripps Inst., 1971-72; recipient grants Research Corp., Petroleum Research Fund, NSF, Solar Energy Research Inst. Mem. AAAS, Am. Assn. Aerosol Rsch., Am. Chem. Soc. (chmn. Colo. 1976, sec. western Mich. 1970-71, joint coun. and bd. com. on sci. 1997-98, award Colo. sect. 1986), Soc. Applied Spectroscopy, Mile High Club, Sigma Xi. Home: 1931 W Sanibel Ct Littleton CO 80120-8133 Office: U Denver Dept Chem & Biochem Denver CO 80208-0001

SMITH, EDGAR BENTON, dermatologist; b. Houston, June 2, 1932; s. Burt Benton and Lela Elizabeth (Grant) S.; m. Francis Elaine Newton, Aug. 1, 1953; children— Sheri Elaine Smith Dinehart, Robin Marie Smith Fredrickson. Student, Rice U., 1950-53; BA, U. Houston, 1956; MD, Baylor U., 1957; diploma clin. medicine of the tropics, U. London, 1967. Intern Walter Reed Gen. Hosp., Washington, 1957-58; resident Brooke Gen. Hosp., Ft. Sam Houston, Tex., 1960-63; asst. prof. dermatology U. Miami Sch. Medicine, 1967-68, Baylor Coll. Medicine, Houston, 1968-71; asso. prof. medicine (dermatology) U. N.Mex. Sch. Medicine, Albuquerque, 1971-75, prof., 1975-78; prof., chmn. dept. dermatology U. Tex. Med. Br., Galveston, 1978-99; prof. dermatology U. N. Mex., Albuquerque, 1999—. Contbr. articles in field to profl. jours. Served with U.S. Army, 1956-66. Recipient Khatali award U. N.Mex. Sch. Medicine, 1976; Fulbright scholar London Sch. Hygiene and Tropical Medicine, 1966-67; Alfred Stengel travelling scholar ACP, 1967 Mem. AMA, Am. Acad. Dermatology (bd. dirs. 1978-82, pres.-elect 1988, pres. 1989, Sulzberger internat. lectr. 1992), Assn. Profs. Dermatology (sec.-treas. 1979-82), Am. Dermatol. Assn. (bd. dirs. 1994—), Southwestern Dermatol. Soc. (sec. 1974-77, pres. 1978), South Ctrl. Dermatol. Congress (sec.-gen. 1973-76, pres. 1976-81), Tex. Dermatol. Soc. (trustee 1986), So. Med. Assn. (chmn. dermatology sect. 1988), Baker Street Irregulars, Alpha Omega Alpha. Democrat. Methodist. Home: 3918 Solano Pl NE Albuquerque NM 87110-5636 Office: U NMex Dept Dermatology 1021 Medical Arts Ave NE Albuquerque NM 87131-5231 E-mail: esmith@salud.unm.edu

SMITH, EDWARD JOHN, geophysicist, physicist; b. Dravosburg, Pa., Sept. 21, 1927; married, 1953; 4 children. BA, UCLA, 1951, MS, 1952, PhD in Physics, 1960. Rsch. geophysicist Inst. Geophysics UCLA, 1955-59; mem. tech. staff Space Tech. Labs., 1959-61, Jet Propulsion Lab, 1961—. Recipient medal Exceptional Sci. Achievement NASA. Mem. AAAS, Internat. Sci. Radio Union, Am. Geophys. Union, Am. Astron. Soc., Sigma Xi. Achievements include research in planetary magnetism, space physics, interplanetary physics, wave-particle interactions in plasmas, propagation of electromagnetic waves, solar-terrestrial relations. Office: Calif Inst Tech Jet Propulsion Lab 4800 Oak Grove Dr Pasadena CA 91109-8001

SMITH, EDWIN P. career officer; b. Allentown, Pa., Aug. 8, 1945; Grad., U.S. Mil. Acad., 1967; MA, U. Ky., 1976; MBA, L.I. U., 1979; grad., Command and Gen. Staff Coll., Can. Nat. Def. Coll. Commd. 2d lt. U.S. Army, 1967, advanced through grades to lt. gen., 1998, various assignments U.S. and overseas. Decorated Purple Heart.

SMITH, ELDON, cardiologist, physiology and biophysics educator; MD, Dalhousie U., Halifax, N.S. From asst. prof. to assoc. prof. medicine and physiology Dalhousie U., Halifax, N.S., Can., 1973-80; prof. medicine and physiology and biophysics U. Calgary, 1980—, chief divsn. cardiology, 1980-86, chair dept. medicine, 1985-90, assoc. dean, clin., 1990-92, dean faculty of medicine, 1992-97. Corp. dir. Biomax, Inc., Vasogen Inc., Can. Natural Resources, Ltd., Pheromone Scis. Corp. Editor-in-chief Can. Jour. Cardiology, 1997—. Fellow Royal Coll. Physicians and Surgeons Can., Am. Coll. Cardiology. Office: U Calgary Faculty Medicine 3330 Hosp Dr Calgary AB Canada T2N 4N1 E-mail: esmith@ucalgary.ca

SMITH, ELDRED GEE, church leader; b. Lehi, Utah, Jan. 9, 1907; s. Hyrum Gibbs and Martha E. (Gee) S.; m. Jeanne A. Ness, Aug. 17, 1932 (dec. June 1977); children: Miriam Smith Skeen, Eldred Gary, Audrey Gay Smith Vance, Gordon Raynor, Sylvia Dawn Smith Isom; m. Hortense H. Child, May 18, 1978; stepchildren: Carol Jane Child Burdette (dec.), Thomas Robert Child. Employed with sales div. Bennett Glass & Paint Co., Salt Lake City, 6 years; mech. design engr. Remington Arms Co., 2 years; design engr., prodn. equipment design Tenn. Eastman Corp., Oak Ridge, Tenn., 3 years; now presiding patriarch Ch. Jesus Christ of Latter-day Saints. Home: 2942 Devonshire Cir Salt Lake City UT 84108-2526 Office: 47 E South Temple Salt Lake City UT 84150-9701

SMITH, EMIL L. biochemist, consultant; b. N.Y.C., July 5, 1911; s. Abraham and Esther (Lubart) S.; m. Esther Press, Mar. 29, 1934; children— Joseph Donald, Jeffrey Bernard B.S., Columbia U., 1931, Ph.D., 1936. Instr. biophysics Columbia U., N.Y.C., 1936-38; John Simon Guggenheim fellow Cambridge U., Eng., 1938-39, Yale U., New Haven, 1939-40; fellow Rockefeller Inst., N.Y.C., 1940-42; biophysicist, biochemist E. R. Squibb & Sons, New Brunswick, N.J., 1942-46; assoc. prof. to prof. biochemistry U. Utah, Salt Lake City, 1946-63; prof. biol. chemistry Sch. Medicine UCLA, 1963-79, prof. emeritus, 1979—. Cons. NIH, Am. Cancer Soc., Office Naval Research Author: (with others) Principles of Biochemistry, 7th edit., 1983; also numerous articles Recipient Stein-Moore award Protein Soc., 1987. Mem. NAS, Am. Acad. Arts and Scis., Am. Philos. Soc., Am. Soc. Biochemistry and Molecular Biology, Am. Chem. Soc., Protein Soc., Acad. Scis. Russia (fgn.). Office: UCLA Sch Medicine Los Angeles CA 90095-1737

SMITH, EPHRAIM PHILIP, academic administrator, former university dean, educator; b. Fall River, Mass., Sept. 19, 1942; s. Jacob Max and Bertha (Horvitz) S.; m. Linda Sue Katz, Sept. 3, 1967; children: Benjamin, Rachel, Leah. B.S., Providence Coll., 1964; M.S., U. Mass., 1965; Ph.D., U. Ill., 1968. Chmn. dept. acctg. U. R.I., Kingston, 1972-73; dean Sch. Bus. Shippensburg State Coll., Pa., 1973-75; dean Coll. Bus. Adminstrn. Cleve. State U., 1975-90; dean Sch. Bus. Adminstrn. and Econ. Calif. State U., Fullerton, 1990-98, v.p. acad. affairs, 1998—. Co-author: Principles of Supervision: First and Second Level Management, 1984, Federal Taxation-Advanced Topics, 1995, Federal Taxation-Basic Principles, 2001, Federal Taxation Comprehensive Topics, 2001; contbr. articles to profl. jours. Mem. Am. Acctg. Assn., Am. Taxation Assn., Am. Inst. for Decision Scis., Fin. Execs. Inst., Beta Gamma Sigma, Beta Alpha Psi. Office: Calif State Univ VPAA Office MH-133 800 N State College Blvd Fullerton CA 92831-3599 E-mail: esmith@fullerton.edu

SMITH, ERNEST KETCHAM, electrical engineer; b. Peking, China, May 31, 1922; (parents Am. citizens); s. Ernest Ketcham and Grace (Goodrich) S.; m. Mary Louise Standish, June 23, 1950; children: Priscilla Varland, Nancy Smith Johnson, Cynthia Jackson. BA in Physics, Swarthmore Coll., 1944; MSEE, Cornell U., 1951, PhD, 1956. With Mut. Broadcasting Sys., 1946-49, chief plans and allocations engr., 1949; with radio propagation lab. Nat. Bur. Stds., Boulder, 1951-65, chief ionosphere rsch. sect. Colo., 1957-60, divsn. chief, 1960-65; dir. aeronomy lab. Environ. Sci. Svcs. Adminstrn., Boulder, 1965-67; dir. Inst. Telecom. Scis., 1968, dir. univ. rels., 1968-70; assoc. dir. Inst. Telecom. Scis. Office of Telecom., Boulder, 1970-72, cons., 1972-76; tech. staff Jet Propulsion Lab. Calif. Inst. Tech., Pasadena, 1976-87; adj. prof. dept. elec. and computer engring. U. Colo., Boulder, 1987—. Vis. fellow Coop. Inst. Rsch. on Environ. Scis., 1968; assoc. Harvard Coll. Obs., 1965-75; adj. prof. U. Colo., 1969-78; internat. vice-chmn. study group 6, Internat. Radio Consultative Com., 1958-70, chmn. U.S. study group, 1970-76; mem. U.S. nat. com. Internat. Sci. Radio Union, mem.-at-large U.S. nat. com., 1986-88; convener Boulder Catalogue to the Future, 1990. Author: Worldwide Occurrence of Sporadic E, 1957; (with S. Matsushita) Ionospheric Sporadic E, 1962. Contbr. numerous articles to profl. jours. Editor: Electromagnetic Probing of the Upper Atmosphere, 1969; assoc. editor for propagation IEEE Antennas and Propagation Mag., 1989—. Mem. 1st Congl. Ch., moderator, 1995-97. Recipient Diplôme d'honneur, Internat. Radio Consultative Com., Internat. Telecom. Union, 1978. Fellow IEEE (fellow com. 1993, 94, 95), AAAS; mem. Am. Geophys. Union, Electromagnetics Acad., Svc. Club, Kiwanis, Univ. Club, Athenaeum (Pasadena), Boulder Country Club, UN Assn. of Am. (convenor Boulder chpt. 1994), Sigma Xi (pres. U. Colo. chpt. 1994-95, v.p. 95-98). Home: 5159 Idylwild Trl Boulder CO 80301-3667 Office: U Colo Dept Elec & Computer Engring Campus Box 425 Boulder CO 80309-0425 E-mail: ernest.smith@colorado.edu, n6hqkek@aol.com

SMITH, F. D. (RICKY SMITH), rail transporation executive; Pres. Stevedoring Svcs. Am., Seattle, 1979-81, CEO, chmn., 1981—. Office: 1131 SW Klickitat Way Seattle WA 98134-1108

SMITH, FREDRICA EMRICH, rheumatologist, internist; b. Princeton, N.J., Apr. 28, 1945; d. Raymond Jay and Carolyn Sarah (Schleicher) Emrich; m. Paul David Smith, June 10, 1967. AB, Bryn Mawr Coll., 1967; MD, Duke U., 1971. Intern, resident U. N.Mex. Affiliated Hosps., 1971-73; fellow U. Va. Hosp., Charlottesville, 1974-75; pvt. practice, Los Alamos, N.Mex., 1975—. Chmn. credentials com. Los Alamos Med. Ctr., 1983—, chief staff, 1990; bd. dirs. N.Mex. Physicians Mut. Liability Ins. Co., Albuquerque. Contbr. articles to med. jours. Mem. bass sect. Los Alamos Symphony, 1975—; mem. Los Alamos County Parks and Recreation Bd., 1984-88, 92-96, Los Alamos County Med. Indigent Health Care Task Force, 1989—; mem. ops. subcom. Aquatic Ctr., Los Alamos County, 1988—. Fellow ACP, Am. Coll. Rheumatology; mem. N.Mex. Soc. Internal Medicine (pres. 1993-96), Friends of Bandelier. Democrat. Avocations: swimming, music, reading, hiking. Office: Los Alamos Med Ctr 3917 West Rd Los Alamos NM 87544-2275

SMITH, GARY, marketing executive; b. 1943; Sr. v.p., dir. mktg. Safeway, Inc., Pleasanton, Calif., 1995—. Office: Safeway Inc 5918 Stoneridge Mall Rd Pleasanton CA 94588-3229

SMITH, GEORGE FOSTER, retired aerospace company executive; b. Franklin, Ind., May 9, 1922; s. John Earl and Ruth (Foster) S.; m. Jean Arthur Farnsworth, June 3, 1950; children— David Foster, Craig Farnsworth, Sharon Windsor. BS in Physics, Calif. Inst. Tech., 1944, MS, 1948, Ph.D. magna cum laude (Standard Oil fellow 1949-50), 1952. Founding staff mem. Engring. Research Assos., St. Paul, 1946-48; teaching fellow, resident asso. Calif. Inst. Tech., 1948-52; staff Hughes Research Labs., Malibu, Calif., 1952-87, assoc. dir., 1962-69, dir., 1969-87; v.p. Hughes Aircraft Co., 1965-81, sr. v.p., 1981-87, policy bd., 1966-87. Adj. asso. prof. elec. engring. U. So. Calif., 1959-62; cons. Army Sci. Adv. Panel, 1975-78 Contbr. numerous articles to profl. jours. Adv. local Explorer post Boy Scouts Am., 1965-70; bd. mgrs. Westchester YMCA, 1974— , chmn., 1979-81; chmn. trustees Pacific Presbyn. Ch., Los Angeles, 1959-62. Served to lt. (j.g.) USNR, 1944-46. Recipient Disting. Alumnus award Calif. Inst. Tech., 1991. Fellow IEEE (pres. Sorenson fellows 1972-73, Frederick Philips award 1988), Am. Phys. Soc.; mem. AAAS, Caltech Assocs. (bd. dirs. 1990—, pres. 1993-94), Sierra Club, Sigma Xi (chpt. pres. 1957-58), Tau Beta Pi. Achievements include 6 patents in field; directed leading industrial research in electronics, lasers, and electro-optics; conducted first laser range finder experiments. Office: Hughes Elecronics Corp Rsch Labs 3011 Malibu Canyon Rd Malibu CA 90265-4737 E-mail: GEOFSMITH@aol.com

SMITH, GEORGE LARRY, analytical and environmental chemist; b. Beloit, Kans., Oct. 11, 1951; s. Richard Bailey and Vonda Ellene (Cox) S.; m. Charlene Janell Musgrove, Sept. 4, 1973; 1 child, Brian Lawrence. BA, Augustana Coll., 1973. Cert. grade 3 water treatment operator, Calif. Lab. technician Sanitary Dist. of Hammond, Ind., 1973; chemist Federated Metals Corp., Whiting, 1973-77; rsch. technician Air Pollution Technology, Inc., San Diego, 1978-80, environ. chemist, 1980-81, sr. tech. asst., 1981; staff chemist I Occidental Research Corp., Irvine, Calif., 1981-82, receiving chemist, 1982-84; processing chemist Chem. Waste Mgmt., Inc., Kettleman City, 1984-87, analytical chemist, 1987-89, wet analytical chemistry group leader, 1989-90, inorganic lab. supr., 1990-94, quality assurance/quality control specialist, 1994-96; lab. mgr. Bolsa Rsch. Assocs., Inc., Hollister, 1996—; lab. mgr., chemist Tri Cal-Bolsa Rsch. Assocs., Inc., Hollister, 1999—. Lab. analyst for published article in environ. sci. and tech., 1981. Bd. dirs. Apostolic Christian Missions, Inc., San Diego, 1978-82. Mem. Am. Chem. Soc., Nat. Geog. Soc., Assn. Ofcl. Analytical Chemists Internat., Planetary Soc., Sierra Club. Avocations: coin collecting, drawing, photography, reading about science, history and religion. Home: 991 Meridian St Hollister CA 95023-4130 Office: Bolsa Rsch Assocs Inc 8770 Hwy 25 Hollister CA 95024 E-mail: glschem@aol.com

SMITH, GLENN A. lawyer; b. Oakland, Calif., July 11, 1946; BA, Pomona Coll., 1968; JD, U. Calif., Berkeley, 1971; LLM in Taxation, NYU, 1973. Bar: Calif. 1972, D.C. 1975. Law clerk to Hon. William M. Drennen U.S. Tax Ct., 1973-75; ptnr. Heller, Ehrman, White & McAuliffe, Palo Alto, San Francisco, Calif., 1977—. Office: Heller Ehrman White & McAuliffe 525 University Ave Ste 900 Palo Alto CA 94301-1907

SMITH, GORDON, finance company executive; Sr. v.p. Am. Express Co., Phoenix, 1997—. Office: Am Express Co 20022 N 31st Ave Phoenix AZ 85027-3900

SMITH, GORDON E. publishing executive; Bureau chief Copley News Svc., L.A., 1998—. Office: Copley News Svc 500 W Temple St Rm 479 E Los Angeles CA 90012

SMITH, GORDON HAROLD, senator; b. Pendleton, Oreg., May 25, 1952; s. Milan Dale and Jessica (Udall) S.; m. Sharon Lankford; children: Brittany, Garrett, Morgan. BA in History, Brigham Young U., 1976; JD, Southwestern U., 1979. Law clk. to Justice H. Vern Payne N.Mex. Supreme Ct.; pvt. practice Ariz.; owner Smith Frozen Foods; mem. Oreg. State Senate, 1992-95, pres., 1995-96; senator from Oreg. U.S. Senate, 1997—. Mem. budget com., chair subcom. water and power, mem. subcom. forests and pub. land mgmt., mem. subcom. energy rsch., devel., prodn. and regulation, mem. energy and natural resources com., chair subcom. European affairs, mem. subcom. Near Eastern and South Asian affairs, mem. fgn. rels. com., mem. subcom. on East Asian and Pacific affairs. Office: US Senate 404 Russell Senate Ofc Bldg Washington DC 20510-0001*

SMITH, GORDON PAUL, management consulting company executive; b. Salem, Mass., Dec. 25, 1916; s. Gordon and May (Vaughan) S.; m. Daphne Miller, Nov. 23, 1943 (div. 1968); m. Ramona Chamberlain, Sept. 27, 1969; children: Randall B., Roderick F. B.S. in Econs, U. Mass., 1947; M.S. in Govt. Mgmt, U. Denver (Sloan fellow), 1948; postgrad. in polit. sci, NYU, 1948-50; DHL (hon.), Monterey Inst. Internat. Studies, 1994. Economist Tax Found., Inc., N.Y.C., 1948-50; with Booz, Allen & Hamilton, 1951-70, partner, 1959-62, v.p., 1962-67, mng. pntr. Western U.S., 1968-70; partner Harrod, Williams and Smith (real estate devel.), San Francisco, 1962-69; state dir. fin. State of Calif., 1967-68; pres. Gordon Paul Smith & Co., Mgmt. Cons., 1968—; pres., chief exec. officer Golconda Corp., 1972-74, chmn. bd., 1974-85. Pres. Cermetek Corp., 1978-80; bd. dirs. exec. com. First Calif. Co., 1970-72, Gromon Corp., 1976-85; bd. dirs. Madison Venture Capital Corp.; adviser task force def. procurement and contracting Hoover Commn., 1954-55; spl. asst. to pres. Republic Aviation Corp., 1954-55; cons., Hawaii, 1960-61, Alaska, 1963;

cons. Wash. Hwy. Adminstrn., 1964, also 10 states and fed. agys., 1951-70, Am. Baseball League and Calif. Angels, 1960-62; bd. dirs. Monterey Coll. Law; chmn. Ft. Ord Econ. Devel. Adv. Group, 1991; chmn. Coalition on Rsch. and Edn., 1993—; bd. dirs. Monterey Bay Futures Project; adv. bd. Ctr. for Non-Proliferation Studies, 1997—; over 750 TV, radio and speaking appearances on econs., mgmt. and public issues. Author articles on govt., econs. and edn. Mem. 24 bds. and commns. State of Calif., 1967-72, sr. advisor to pres., 1998—; mem. Calif. Select Com. on Master Plan for Edn., 1971-73; mem. alumni council U. Mass., 1950-54, bd. dirs. alumni assn., 1964-70; bd. dirs. Alumni Assn. Mt. Hermon Prep. Sch., 1963; bd. dirs. Stanford Med. Ctr., 1960-62, pres., chmn., 1962-66; chmn. West Coast Cancer Found., 1976-87, Coalition Rsch. and Edn., 1993—, Jim Tunney Youth Fund, 1994—; trustee, chmn. Monterey Inst. Internat. Studies, 1978-92, trustee emeritus, 1995—; trustee Northfield Mt. Hermon Sch., 1983-93, Robert Louis Stevenson Sch., 1993—; mem. devel. council Community Hosp. of Monterey Peninsula, 1983-84; bd. dirs. Friends of the Performing Arts, 1985—; bd. dirs. Monterey County Symphony Orch., 1991-96, Monterey Bay Futures Project, 1992—. Recipient spl. commendation Hoover Commn., 1955, Alumni of Yr. award U. Mass., 1963, Trustee of Yr. award Monterey-Peninsula, 1991, Monterey-Peninsula Outstanding Citizen of Yr. award, 1992, Laura Bride Powers Heritage award, 1991, U.S. Congl. award, 1992, Calif. Senate and Assembly Outstanding Citizen award, 1992, Wisdom award of honor Wisdom Soc., 1992; permanent Gordon Paul Smith Disting. Chair for Internat. Studies established at Monterey Inst. Internat. Studies; Gordon Paul Smith Scholarship Fund named in his honor Northfield Mt. Hermon Sch.; named to Honorable Order of Ky. Cols. Mem. Monterey History and Art Assn. (bd. dirs. 1987-92, pres. 1985-87, chmn. 1987-92, hon. lifetime dir. 1992—), The Stanton Heritage Ctr. (chmn. 1987-92, chmn. emeritus 1992—), Salvation Army (bd. dirs., chmn. hon. cabinet), Monterey Peninsula Mus. Art, Carmel Valley (Calif.) Country Club, Monterey Peninsula Country Club, Old Capitol Club. Home: 253 Del Mesa Carmel CA 93923

SMITH, GREGORY R. lawyer; b. Chgo., Jan. 9, 1944; BA summa cum laude, Claremont Men's Coll., 1965; JD magna cum laude, Harvard U., 1968; MS, London Sch. Econs., 1969. Bar: Calif. 1969. Ptnr. Irell & Manella, L.A. Vis. prof. U. Kansas Sch. Law, 1975. Mem. bd. editors Harvard Law Review, 1966-68. Mem. State Bar Calif., Phi Alpha Delta. Office: Irell & Manella Ste 900 1800 Avenue Of The Stars Los Angeles CA 90067-4276

SMITH, GREIG LOUIS, deputy councilman; b. South Pasadena, Calif., Nov. 26, 1948; s. John Harold and Gloria Mae (Pitre) S.; m. Christine Marie Crippen, Apr. 14, 1973; children: Krista Lynn, Matthew John. AA, Pierce Coll., 1978; cert. advt., UCLA, 1988. Area dir. Rep. Ctrl. Com., 1969-70; youth dir. Re-elect Senator Murphy, L.A., 1970-71; mktg. dir. V.I.V.A., L.A., 1971-72; exec. dir. Ams. for Agnew, Washington, 1972-73; owner Greig's Formal Wear, Northridge, Calif., 1973-81; chief dep. for Councilman Bernson City of L.A., 1979—. Govt. rels. officer L.A. Olympic Organizing Com., 1984. Vice chmn. San Fernando Valley Breakfast Forum, 1975-78, C.I.V.I.C.C., San Fernando Valley, 1976-78; pres. North Hills Jaycees, Granada Hills, Calif., 1976-77; chmn. bd. North Valley YMCA, Mission Hills, Calif., 1979-80, 92—; founding mem. North Valley Rep. Assembly, 1992., founding mem. SOLID Foundation, commd. reserve police officer City of L.A., 1993. Named Citizen of Yr. Granada Hills C. of C., 1977, Vol. of Yr. North Valley YMCA, 1988, Citizen of Yr. Internat. Order of Foresters, 1990. Mem. Jr. Chamber Internat. (senator, life), Alpha Sigma Gamma. Office: 11614 Ostrom Ave Granada Hills CA 91344

SMITH, HARVEY ALVIN, mathematics educator, consultant; b. Easton, Pa., Jan. 30, 1932; s. William Augustus and Ruth Carolyn (Krauth) S.; m. Ruth Wismer Kolb, Aug. 27, 1955; children: Deirdre Lynn, Kirsten Nadine, Brinton Averil. BS, Lehigh U., 1952; MS, U. Pa., 1955, AM, 1958, PhD, 1964. Asst. prof. math Drexel U., 1960-65; mem. tech. staff Inst. Def. Analyses, Arlington, Va., 1965-66; assoc. prof. math Oakland U., 1966-68; ops. research scientist Exec. Office of Pres., Washington, 1968-70; prof. math. Oakland U., 1970-77; prof. Ariz. State U., Tempe, 1977—; cons. Inst. Def. Analyses, 1967-69, Exec. Office Pres., 1967-73, U.S. Arms Control and Disarmament Agy, 1973-79, Los Alamos Nat. Lab., 1980-93. Author: Mathematical Foundations of Systems Analysis, 1969. NSF fellow, 1964-65; recipient Meritorious Service award Exec. Office of Pres., 1970 Mem. Soc. Indsl. and Applied Math., Am. Math. Soc., AAAS, Sigma Xi Home: 18 E Concorda Dr Tempe AZ 85282-3517 Office: Ariz State U Dept Math Tempe AZ 85287-1804 E-mail: hsmith@math.la.asu.edu

SMITH, H(OWARD) DUANE, zoology educator; b. Fillmore, Utah, June 25, 1941; s. Howard Martell and Mary Ellen (Mitchell) S.; m.. Dahnelle Bower, Dec. 18, 1961; children: Cory, Neichol. BS, Brigham Young U., 1963, MS, 1966; PhD, U. Ill., 1969. From asst. prof. to prof. Brigham Young U., Provo, Utah, 1969—; pvt. practice Orem, 1973—; dir. Monte L. Bean Life Sci. Mus., Provo. Dir. Life Sci. Mus. Co-author: Special Publications-Mammalogy, 1994; contbr. articles to profl. jours. Mem. Am. Soc. Mammalogists (sec.-treas. 1987—), Wildlife Soc., Ecol. Soc. Am., Rocky Mountain Elk Found., Sigma Xi (pres. 1996-97). Republican. Mormon. Avocations: hunting, fishing. Office: Brigham Young Univ 290 MLBM Provo UT 84602-1049 E-mail: Duane@Museum.BYU.EDU

SMITH, HOWARD RUSSELL, manufacturing company executive; b. Clark County, Ohio, Aug. 15, 1914; s. Lewis Hoskins and Eula (Elder) S.; m. Jeanne Rogers, June 27, 1942; children: Stewart Russell, Douglas Howard, Jeanne Ellen Smith James. A.B., Pomona Coll., 1936. Security analyst Kidder, Peabody & Co., N.Y.C., 1936-37; economist ILO, Geneva, 1937-40; asst. to pres. Blue Diamond Corp., Los Angeles, 1940—; v.p., gen. mgr., dir. Avery Dennison Corp., Pasadena, Calif., 1946-56, pres., 1956-75, chmn. bd., 1975-84, chmn. exec. com., 1984-95; dir. emeritus, 1995—; chmn. bd. Kinsmith Fin. Corp., San Marino, Calif., 1979—. Bd. dirs., past pres., chmn. Los Angeles Philharm. Assn.; chmn. emeritus, bd. trustees Pomona Coll., Claremont, Calif.; past chmn. bd. Children's Hosp. Los Angeles, Community TV of So. Calif. (Sta. KCET), Los Angeles. Lt. USNR, 1943-46. Home: 1458 Hillcrest Ave Pasadena CA 91106-4503 Office: Avery Dennison Corp 150 N Orange Grove Blvd Pasadena CA 91103-3534

SMITH, HYRUM WAYNE, management executive; b. Salt Lake City, Oct. 16, 1943; s. Joseph F. and Ruth (Pingree) S.; m. A. Gail Cooper, Dec. 21, 1966; Glenna, Stacie, Sharwan, Joseph, Rebecca, Jacob. BS in Bus., Brigham Young U., Provo, Utah, 1971. Ins. salesman Conn. Mut. Life, Honolulu, 1971-72; div. mgr. Nat. Inventory Control Systems, Portland, Oreg., 1972-73; v.p. sales western div. Automated Data Processing, Portland, 1973-78; mission pres. Later-Day Saints Ch., Ventura, Calif., 1978-81; owner Golden Eagle Motivation, Ventura, 1981-82; cons. Charles Hobbs, Salt Lake City, 1982-83; co-owner Hyrum Smith & Assocs., Salt Lake City, 1983-84; owner, chmn. bd. Franklin Internat. Inst., Inc., Salt Lake City, 1984—. Author: Where Eagles Rest, 1982; co-author: Excellence Through Time Management, 1985; author: Advanced Day Planner Users Guide, 1987. Bd. mem. Great Salt Lake Coun., Boy Scouts Am., 1982—, Explorers, 1982—. 1st lt. U.S. Army, 1967-69. Recipient Pub. Svc. award Assn. Fed. Investigators, Washington, 1988. Mem. Am. Soc. Tng. and Devel. Republican. Mormon. Avocations: boating, reading. Home: 38 E Hope St Saint George UT 84770-2892 Office: Franklin Covey Co. 2200 W Parkway Blvd Salt Lake City UT 84119-2099

SMITH, IRBY JAY, film producer; b. San Antonio, Apr. 17, 1938; s. Irby Jay and Virginia Lee (Algee) S.; m. Elaine Nicholson, June 8, 1956; children: Kimberly, Carrie, Jay. Student, Occidental Coll., 1955-56; BA summa cum laude, U. Calif., Berkeley, 1960. Pub. info. spcialist, tv interview host, writer U.S. Dept. Health, Edn. and Welfare, L.A., 1960-66; writer, dir. CRM/McGraw-Hill Films, L.A., 1969-70; pvt. practice asst. dir., prodn. mgr., prodr., dir., 1966—. Prodr. City Slickers, Prefontaine, Wild America, Rookie of the Year, Angels in the Outfield, Enemies a Love Story, Major League, Young Guns I and II. Recipient ALA award for writing and directing ednl. films, 1970, 2 Cine Golden Eagle awards for writing and directing ednl. films, 1970. Mem. Dirs. Guild Am., Phi Beta Kappa. Democrat. Avocation; thought.

SMITH, JAMES ALEXANDER, metal processing executive; b. Harvey, N.D., Jan. 16, 1926; s. James Kay MacKenzie and Palma Theresa (Johnson) S.; m. Cleo Lorraine, Sept. 1, 1948 (div. 1962); children: Deborah Kay Smith Hooper, Daryl Lynn Smith O'Neill, Darcey Amelia Smith Ryan; m. Louise Mae Hammer, July 21, 1979. BS, U. Minn., 1951. Ptnr., v.p. VIP, Phoenix, 1960-78; founder Therm-O-Low Inc., Phoenix, 1978-84; v.p., gen. mgr., pres. 3XKryogenics, Phoenix, 1984-86; founder, pres. Cryogenics Internat., Inc., Tempe, Ariz., 1987-90. Lectr. and speaker on cryogenics. Patentee (U.S. and fgn.) in field. Staff sgt. U.S. Army, 1943-46. Decorated Bronze star, Combat Infantryman Badge with 2 battle stars. Mem. Soc. Mfg. Engrs. (Ariz. chpt. chmn. 1983, chmn. western states zone 1985, Pres.'s award 1984), Cryogenic Soc. Am., Am. Soc. Metals, VFW (life mem.). Republican. Lutheran.

SMITH, JAMES LAWRENCE, research physicist; b. Detroit, Sept. 3, 1943; s. William Leo and Marjorie Marie (Underwood) S.; m. Carol Ann Adam, Mar. 27, 1965; children: David Adam, William Leo. BS, Wayne State U., 1965; PhD, Brown U., 1974. Mem. staff Los Alamos (N.Mex.) Nat. Lab., 1973-82, fellow, 1982-86, dir. ctr. materials sci., 1986-87, fellow, 1987—; chief scientist Superconductivity Tech. Ctr., 1988-99; N.Am. editor Philos. Mag., 1990-95; editor Philos. Mag. B., 1995—. Contbr. articles to profl. jours. Recipient E.O. Lawrence award, 1986, Disting. Alumni award Wayne State U., 1993. Fellow Am. Phys. Soc. (internat. prize for new materials 1990); mem. AAAS, Materials Rsch. Soc., Minerals Metals Materials Soc., Am. Crystallographic Assn., Brown Alumni Assn. (bd. govs. 1998-2000), Phi Beta Kappa. Achievements include patents for design of magnetic field and high-strength conductors. Office: Los Alamos Nat Lab Mail Stop G770 Los Alamos NM 87545-0001

SMITH, JAMES PATRICK, economist; b. Aug. 3, 1943; s. James P. and Winefred (Harrison) S.; m. Sandra Berry, Oct. 25, 1983; children: Gillian Clare, Lauren Theresa. BS, Fordham U., 1965; PhD, U. Chgo., 1972. Rsch. assoc. Nat. Bur. Econ. Rsch., N.Y.C., 1972-74; sr. economist Rand Corp., Santa Monica, Calif., 1974—, dir. of rsch. labor and population, 1977-93. Bd. mem. Occupl. Safety and Health Standards State Calif. Editor: Female Labor Supply, 1980, The New Americans, 1997, The Immigration Debate, 1998, Wealth, Work, and Health, 1999; bd. editors: Am. Econ. Rev., 1980-83; author articles in field. Recipient Merit award NIH, 1995—. Mem. NIA (monitoring com., health and retirement survey, chair NAS panel on emigration, prin. investigator New Immigrant Survey), Am. Econ. Assn., Phi Beta Kappa. Office: RAND PO Box 2138 Santa Monica CA 90407-2138

SMITH, JANET HUGIE, lawyer; b. Logan, Utah, Aug. 1, 1945; BA magna cum laude, Utah State U., 1967; MA cum laude, Stanford U., 1969; JD, U. Utah, 1976. Bar: Utah 1976, U.S. Supreme Ct. 1992, U.S. Ct. Appeals (10th cir.) 1977. Shareholder, exec. com. Ray, Quinney & Nebeker, Salt Lake City, 1983—. Mem. ABA (labor and employment law sect.), Utah State Bar (labor and employment law sect.), CUE (labor lawyers adv. coun.), Am. Law Coun., Am. Coll. Trial Lawyers, Aldon J. Anderson Am. Inns of Ct. E-mial. Office: Ray Quinney & Nebeker Deseret Bldg 79 S Main St Ste 600 Salt Lake City UT 84111-1901 E-mail: jhs@rqn.com

SMITH, JEFFREY L. (THE FRUGAL GOURMET), cooking expert, television personality, author; b. Seattle, Jan. 22, 1939; s. Emely S.; m. Patricia M. Dailey, 1964; children: Jason, Channing. BA, U. Puget Sound, 1962, DHL (hon.), 1987; MDiv, Drew U., 1965, DDiv (hon.), 1993. Ordained to ministry United Meth. Ch., 1965. Served Meth. chs., Hartsdale, N.Y., rural, Wash.; chaplain, asst. prof. religion U. Puget Sound, Tacoma, 1966-72; founder The Chaplain's Pantry, Tacoma, 1972-83; host Seattle Today TV program The Frugal Gourmet (formerly Cooking Fish Creatively), 1973-77; host PBS program The Frugal Gourmet, 1983—. Author: The Frugal Gourmet, 1984, The Frugal Gourmet Cooks with Wine, 1986, The Frugal Gourmet Cooks American, 1987, The Frugal Gourmet Cooks Three Ancient Cuisines: China, Greece and Rome, 1989, The Frugal Gourmet on Our Immigrant Ancestors: Recipes You Should Have Gotten From Your Grandmother, 1990, The Frugal Gourmet's Culinary Handbook, 1991, The Frugal Gourmet Celebrates Christmas, 1991, The Frugal Gourmet Whole Family Cookbook, 1992, The Frugal Gourmet Cooks Italian: Recipes from the New and Old World Simplified for the American Kitchen, 1993, The Frugal Gourmet Keeps the Feast: Past, Present and Future, 1995. Recipient Daytime Emmy nominations (5), Best of the West Edn. TV award Western Ednl. Network, 1986. Office: The Frugal Gourmet Inc 88 Virginia St Apt 2 Seattle WA 98101-1047

SMITH, JEFFRY ALAN, health administrator, physician, consultant; b. L.A., Dec. 8, 1943; s. Stanley W. and Marjorie E. S.; m. Jo Anne Hague. BA in Philosophy, UCLA, 1967, MPH, 1972; BA in Biology, Calif. State U., Northridge, 1971; MD, UACJ, 1977. Diplomate Am. Bd. Family Practice. Resident in family practice WAH, Takoma Park, Md., NIH, Bethesda, Walter Reed Army Hosp., Washington, Children's Hosp. Nat. Med. Ctr., Washington, 1977-80; occupational physician Nev. Test Site, U.S. Dept. Energy, Las Vegas, 1981-82; dir. occupational medicine and environ. health Pacific Missile Test Ctr., Point Mugu, Calif., 1982-84; dist. health officer State Hawaii Dept. Health, Kauai, 1984-86; asst. dir. health County of Riverside (Calif.) Dept. Health, 1986-87; regional med. dir. Calif. Forensic Med. Group, Monterey, Calif., 1987-94; med. dir. Cmty. Human Svcs., Monterey, 1987-94, Colstrip (Mont.) Med. Ctr., 1994-97; cons. San Bernadino County, Riverside County, Riverside, Calif., 1998—; regional med. dir. Point Loma Healthcare Med. Group, Inc., San Diego, 1997-99; med. dir., CEO So. Calif. Mobile Physician Svcs., Riverside, Calif., 1997—. Fellow Am. Acad. Family Physicians; mem. AMA, Am. Occupational Medicine Assn., Flying Physicians, Am. Pub. Health Assn. Avocations: pvt. pilot. Office: Ste 71-448 5225 Canyon Crest Dr Riverside CA 92507-6301

SMITH, JOHN ARTHUR, state legislator; b. Deming, N.Mex., 1942; BS, U. N.Mex., 1966. Real estate appraiser; mem. N.Mex. Senate, Dist. 35, Santa Fe, 1988—; mem. fin. com. N.Mex. Senate, vice chair pub. affairs com. Democrat. Office: PO Box 998 Deming NM 88031-0998

SMITH, JOSEF RILEY, internist; b. Council Bluffs, Iowa, Oct. 1, 1926; s. George William Smith and Margaret (Wood) Hill; divorced; children: Sarah L. Kratz, David L., Mary E. Loeb, John R., Ruthann P. Sherrier, Mark A.; m. Susan Frances Irwin, Feb. 9, 1973; 1 child, Christopher I. Student, Tulane U., 1944-46; BM, Northwestern U., 1950, MD, 1951; MSEE, Marquette U., 1964. Diplomate Am. Bd. Internal Medicine. Instr. internal medicine U. Miss. Med. Sch., Jackson, 1956-59; asst. prof. Marquette U. Med. Sch., Milw., 1959-63; from assoc. prof. to full prof. U. Mich. Med. Sch., Ann Arbor, 1963-72; physician Youngstown (Ohio) Hosp., 1972-79, Group Health Med. Assn., Tucson, 1979-84, Assocs. in Internal Medicine, Tucson, 1985-87; pvt. practice Tucson, 1987—. Co-author: Clinical Cardiopulmonary Physiology, 1960, Textbook of Pulmonary Disease, 1965, 2d rev. edit., 1974; contbr. articles to profl. jours. Controller Mahoning County TB Clinic, Youngstown, 1973-79. Served to lt. USNR, 1952-54. Fellow ACP, Sigma Xi; mem. Ariz. Med. Assn., Pima County Med. Assn., Am. Thoracic Soc., Ariz. Thoracic Soc., Bioengring. Med. Soc. (founder). Avocations: photography, computer programming. Office: 2224 N Craycroft Rd Ste 109 Tucson AZ 85712-2811

SMITH, KERRY CLARK, lawyer; b. Phoenix, July 12, 1935; s. Clark and Fay (Jackson) S.; m. Michael Waterman, 1958; children: Kevin, Ian. AB, Stanford U., 1957, JD, 1962. Bar: Calif. 1963, U.S. Supreme Ct. 1980. Assoc. Chickering & Gregory, San Francisco, 1962-70, ptnr., 1970-81, Pettit & Martin, San Francisco, 1981-95, Hovis, Smith, San Francisco, 1995-99; pvt. practice San Francisco, 1999—. Mem. editl. bd. Stanford Law Rev., 1961-62. Lt. USN, 1957-60. Mem. ABA (bus. law sect.), Calif. Bar Assn., San Francisco Bar Assn., Orinda County Club, Palms Golf Club, La Quinta Citrus Golf Club, San Francisco World Trade Club. Office: Smith Law Offices 601 California St Ste 1600 San Francisco CA 94108-2821 E-mail: kerrysmith50965@msn.com

SMITH, KIRK ROBERT, environmental health sciences educator, researcher; b. Calif., Jan. 19, 1947; MPH, U. Calif., Berkeley, PhD in Biomed. & Environ. Health Scis., 1977. Founder, leader energy program East-West Ctr., Honolulu, 1978-85, sr. fellow, program area coord. environ. risk, 1985—; prof. environ. health scis. U. Calif., Berkeley, 1995—; dep. dir. Inst. Global Health, 2000—. Author: 8 books; contbr. numerous articles to profl. jours. Named One of Am.'s 100 Brightest Young Scientists, Sci. Digest, 1984, Alumnus of Yr., U. Calif. Sch. Pub. Health, 1989. Mem. NAS. Achievements include research on pollution in developing countries. Office: U Calif Sch Pub Health Environ Health Scis Warren Hall Berkeley CA 94720-7360 E-mail: KRKSmith@uclink4.berkeley.edu

SMITH, LEONARD BINGLEY, musician; b. Poughkeepsie, N.Y., Sept. 5, 1915; s. Frank Roderick and Ethel (Schubert) S.; m. Helen Gladys Rowe, Apr. 20, 1940 (dec. 1993); 1 dau., Sandra Victoria. Student, N.Y. Mil. Acad., 1930-33, Ernest Williams Sch. Music, 1933-36, NYU, 1936-37, Curtis Inst. Music, 1943-45; H.H.D., Detroit Inst. Tech., 1965. Pres. Accompaniments Unltd., Inc., 1952—. Cornet soloist, Ernest Williams Band, 1933-36, The Goldman Band, summers 1936-42; 1st trumpet, Barrere Little Symphony, 1935-37, Detroit Symphony Orch., 1937-42, Ford Sunday Evening Hour, 1937-42; condr., The Leonard Smith Concert Band, 1945—, Detroit Concert Band, 1945—, U. Detroit Bands, 1949-50, Moslem AAONMS Band, 1945-57, Scandinavian Symphony Orch. of Detroit, 1959-61, guest condr., Indpls. Symphony Orch., 1967; guest condr., soloist, clinician numerous concerts, U.S., Can.; mus. dir. John Philip Sousa documentary for BBC, 1970; Sousa Am. Bicentennial Recorded Collection; record series Gems concert band, Blossom Festival Band; condr. Blossom Festival Concert Band, 1972—; The Indomitable Teddy Roosevelt; producer: Our Am. Heritage in Music, 1970; pres., Bandland, Inc., 1951-61; Author: Treasury of Scales; over 350 pub. compositions; mem. bd. advisors Instrumentalist mag. Chmn. music com. Mich. Civil War Centennial Commn., 1961-64; gov. bd. Mac Award. With USNR, 1942-45. Recipient spl. medal Mich. Polish Legion Am. Vets., Distinguished Service medal Kappa Kappa Psi; Mich. Minuteman Gov.'s award, 1973; Freedom Found. award, 1975; Gen. William Booth award, 1976, Embassy Mich. Tourism award, 1979; named Alumnus of Distinction N.Y. Mil. Acad., 1976 Mem. ASCAP, Philippine Bandsmen's Assn. (hon.), Am. Fedn. Musicians, Internat. Platform Assn., Assn. Concert Bands (pres. 1982-83). Clubs: Masons (33 deg.), Shriners, K.T, Jesters. Office: c/o Detroit Concert Band Inc 7443 E Butherus Dr Ste 100 Scottsdale AZ 85260-2459

SMITH, LESLIE C. federal judge; BA, Vanderbilt U., 1962; JD with high distinction, U. Ky.; LLM, U. Western Australia, Perth. Dist. judge 7th Jud. Dist. N.Mex., 1989-95; magistrate judge U.S. Dist. Ct. N.Mex., Las Cruces, 1995—. Office: US Courthouse 200 E Griggs Ave Las Cruces NM 88001-3523

SMITH, LESLIE ROPER, hospital and healthcare administrator; b. Stockton, Calif., June 20, 1928; s. Austin J. and Helen (Roper) S.; m. Edith Sue Fincher, June 22, 1952; children: Melinda Sue, Leslie Erin, Timothy Brian. A.B., U. Pacific, 1951; M.S. in Pub. Adminstrn, U. So. Calif., 1956. Adminstrv. asst. Ranchos Los Amigos Hosp., Downey, Calif., 1953-57; asst. adminstr. Harbor Gen. Hosp., Torrance, 1957-65; adminstr. Harbor UCLA Med. Ctr., 1966-71; acting regional dir. Los Angeles County Coastal Health Services Region, 1973; pres. San Pedro Peninsula Hosp., San Pedro, Cal., 1974-86; exec. dir. Los Angeles County/U. So. Calif. Med. Center, 1971-73; adminstr. Long Beach (Calif.) Hosp., 1965-66; asso. clin. prof. community medicine and pub. health, also emergency medicine U. So. Calif., 1968-78; instr. U. So. Calif. (Sch. Pub. Adminstrn.), 1968; preceptor hosp. adminstrn. UCLA Sch. Pub. Health, 1964—; chief exec. officer French Hosp. Med. Ctr. and Health Plan, 1986-87; dir. health care services McCormack & Farrow, 1987—. Lectr. in field, 1963— ; cons. emergency health services HEW, 1970-73; chmn. com. disaster preparedness Hosp. Council So. Calif., 1966-72, sec., 1971— , pres., 1973; mem. Calif. Assembly Com. on Emergency Med. Services, 1970, Calif. Emergency Med. Adv. Com., 1972-75, Los Angeles County Commn. on Emergency Med. Services, 1975-83, Los Angeles Health Planning and Devel. Agy. Commn., 1980-83; bd. dirs. Blue Cross of So. Calif.; mem. hosp. relations com. Blue Cross of Calif.; mem. adv. com. on emergency health services Calif. Dept. Health, 1974-75; bd. dirs., mem. exec. com. Truck Ins. Exchange of Farmers Ins. Group, 1977-82; bd. dirs. Hosp. Council of So. Calif., 1966-76, 81-86, Health Resources Inst., 1985-86; chmn. Preferred Health Network, 1983-86 Mem. goals com., Torrance, 1968— ; pres. Silver Spur Little League, Palos Verdes, 1969-70. Served with AUS, 1946-48. Recipient Silver Knight and Gold Knight award Nat. Mgmt. Assn., 1970, 85, Walker Fellowship award, 1976 Fellow Am. Coll. Health Care Execs. (life); mem. Am., Nat. mgmt. assns., Am. Hosp. Assn. (chmn. com. on community emergency health services 1973), Calif. Hosp. Assn. (chmn. com. emergency services 1965-70, trustee 1973-76, bd. dirs. Calif. Ins. Service Group 1980-82), County Suprs. Assn. Calif. (chmn. joint subcom. on emergency care 1970) Presbyn. (elder, trustee). Home: 27 Marseille Laguna Niguel CA 92677-5400 E-mail: lrs_essmith1@msn.com

SMITH, LLOYD HOLLINGSWORTH, physician; b. Easley, S.C., Mar. 27, 1924; s. Lloyd H. and Phyllis (Page) S.; m. Margaret Constance Avery, Feb. 27, 1954; children— Virginia Constance, Christopher Avery, Rebecca Anne, Charlotte Page, Elizabeth Hollingsworth, Jeffrey Hollingsworth. A.B., Washington and Lee U., 1944, D.Sc., 1969; M.D., Harvard, 1948. Intern, then resident Mass. Gen. Hosp., Boston, 1948-50, chief resident physician, 1955-56; mem. Harvard Soc. Fellows, 1952-54; asst. prof. Harvard Soc. Fellows (Med. Sch.), 1956-63; vis. investigator Karolinska Inst., Stockholm, 1954-55, Oxford (Eng.) U., 1963-64; prof. medicine, chmn. dept. U. Calif. Med. Sch., San Francisco, 1964-85, assoc dean, 1985-2000. Mem. Pres.'s Sci. Adv. Com., 1970-73 Bd. overseers Harvard, 1974-80. Served to capt., M.C. AUS, 1950-52. Mem. Am. Acad. Arts and Scis., Am. Soc. Clin. Investigation (pres. 1969-70), Western Soc. Clin. Rsch. (pres. 1969-70), Assn. Am. Physicians (pres. 1974-75), Am. Fedn. Clin. Rsch. Achievements include special research genetic and metabolic diseases. Home: 309 Evergreen Dr Kentfield CA 94904-2709 Office: U Calif San Francisco Med Ctr San Francisco CA 94143-0001 E-mail: lloydhsmith@aol.com

SMITH, LONNIE MAX, diversified industries executive; b. Twin Falls, Idaho, July 28, 1944; s. Lonnie E. and Christie (Stuart) S.; m. Cheryl Diane Smith, June 10, 1968; children: Kristen, Maryam, Rebecca, Michael, Catherine. BSEE, Utah State U., 1967; MBA, Harvard U., 1974. Engr., mgr. field services, mgr. tech. services to asst. to v.p. plans and control IBM Corp., San Francisco, Palo Alto, Calif., and White Plains, N.Y., 1967-74; mgr., corp. strategy, then cons. Boston Cons. Group, 1974-76; exec. v.p. Am. Tourister, Inc., Warren, R.I., 1978-81; sr. v.p. corp. planning Hillenbrand Industries, Inc., Batesville, Ind., 1977-78, sr. exec. v.p., 1982-97, also bd. dirs., 1997; pres., CEO Intuitive Surgs., Mountain View, Calif., 1997—. Pres. Biosite Diagnostics, Lozion Corp. Served to 1st lt. U.S. Army, 1969-72. Mormon. Avocations: tennis, skiing. Office: Intuitive Surg 1340 W Middlefield Rd Mountain View CA 94043-3061

SMITH, MALLORY S. business executive; Sr. v.p. housing group Fleetwood Enterprises, Inc., Riverside, Calif., 1998—. Office: Fleetwood Enterprises Inc PO Box 7638 3125 Myers St Riverside CA 92513-7638

SMITH, MARIE B. college president; BA, San Francisco State U.; MA in Biology, Sonoma State U.; DEdn, U. San Francisco. Biology instr. to acting pres. Indian Valley Coll., Novato, Calif., 1974; dean Coll. at Life Chiropractic Coll.-West San Lorenzo, 1985; staff to dean instrn. Coll. of Alameda, 1990, pres., 1991-94, Am. River Coll., 1995—. Chair planning team McClennan AFB Privatization and Reuse adv. com.; co-chair strategic planning teams Los Rio C.C. Dist. Mem. Grant Joint Union H.S. Dist. Vol. Integration Cmty. adv. coun.; mem. Golden Gate U. Women's Leadership Inst., Calif. Ctr. for Health Improvement, Life College West, San Lorenzo, Calif.; pres. ARC. Mem. Biol. Field Svc. Assn. Office: Am River Coll 4700 College Oak Dr Sacramento CA 95841-4217

SMITH, MARSHA H. state agency administrator, lawyer; b. Boise, Idaho, Mar. 24, 1950; d. Eugene F. and Joyce (Ross) Hatch; m. Terrell F. Smith, Aug. 29, 1970; 2 children. BS in Biology/Edn., Idaho State U., 1973; MLS, Brigham Young U., 1975; JD, U. Wash., 1980. Bar: Idaho, U.S. Dist. Ct. Idaho, U.S. Ct. Appeals (9th cir.), U.S. Ct. Appeals (D.C. cir.). Dep. atty. gen. Bus./Consumer Protection Divsn., Boise, 1980-81, Idaho Pub. Utilities Commn., Boise, 1981-89, dir. policy and external rels., 1989-91, commr., 1991—, pres., 1991-95. Mem. Harvard Electricity Policy Group, Nat. Coun. on Competition and The Electric Industry; chair com. for regional electric power coop. Western Interstate Energy Bd. Legis. dist. chair Ada County Democrats, Idaho, 1986-89. Mem. Nat. Assn. Regulatory Utility Commrs. (chair electricity com.). Office: Idaho Pub Utilities Commn PO Box 83720 Boise ID 83720-3720

SMITH, MARTIN BERNHARD, journalist; b. San Francisco, Apr. 20, 1930; s. John Edgar and Anna Sophie (Thorsen) S.; m. Joan Lovat Muller, Apr. 25, 1953; children: Catherine Joan, Karen Anne. AB, U. Calif., Berkeley, 1952, M Journalism, 1968. Reporter, city editor Modesto (Calif.) Bee, 1957-64; reporter, mng. editor Sacramento Bee, 1964-75; polit. editor, columnist McClatchy Newspapers, Sacramento, 1975-92; ret., 1992. Episcopalian.

SMITH, MAUREEN MCBRIDE, laboratory administrator; b. Santa Monica, Calif., Mar. 4, 1952; d. Clayton Laird McBride and Luella (Sullivan) Boudreau; step-father Henry A Boudreau; m. Gary Howard Cothran, July 27, 1974 (div. Apr. 1982); m. Guy Gordon Smith, Feb. 12, 1983; stepchildren: Keri Lynn, Scott Allen. BS magna cum laude, Calif. State Coll., San Bernardino, 1978, MS, 1993. Analytical chemist Chalco Engring., Edwards AFB, Calif., 1978-79, 82; microbiol. lab. tech. AVEK Water Agy., Quartz Hill, 1979-81, chemist, lab. mgr., 1982—. Instr. Antelope Valley Coll., Lancaster Calif., 1980-82. Mem. AAAS, Am. Chem. Soc. Avocations: skiing, photography, training and showing golden retrievers. Address: 6500 W Avenue N Palmdale CA 93551-2855

SMITH, MICHAEL PETER, social science educator, researcher; b. Dunkirk, N.Y., Aug. 2, 1942; s. Peter Joseph and Rosalie Barbara (Lipka) S.; m. Patricia Anne Lendway, Aug. 21, 1965. BA magna cum laude, St. Michael's Coll., 1964; MA in Polit. Sci., U. Mass., 1966, PhD in Polit. Sci., 1971. Instr., asst. prof. dept. govt. Dartmouth Coll., Hanover, N.H., 1968-71; asst. prof. dept. polit. sci. Boston U., 1971-74; assoc. prof., prof. dept. polit. sci. Tulane U., New Orleans, 1974-86; prof. community studies U. Calif., Davis, 1986—, chmn. dept. applied behavioral scis., 1986-91. Vis. prof. pub. policy U. Calif., Berkeley, 1981, city planning U. N.C., Chapel Hill, 1982, city planning U. Calif., Berkeley, 1985; vis. scholar in govt. U. Essex, Eng., 1979; vis. scholar polit. and social sci. U. Cambridge, Eng., 1982; vis. scholar Inst. Urban and Regional Devel., U. Calif., Berkeley, 1990, 94 Internat. Ctr. for Advanced Studies, NYU, 1998. Author: The City & Social Theory, 1979, City, State and Market, 1988, Transnational Urbanism, 2001; co-author: Restructuring the City, 1983, California's Changing Faces, 1993; editor: Cities in Transformation, 1984, Breaking Chains, 1991, After Modernism, 1992, Marginal Spaces, 1995, Comparative Urban & Community Research, 1986—; co-editor: The Capitalist City, 1987—, The Bubbling Cauldron, 1995, Transnationalism from Below, 1998, City and Nation: Rethinking Place and Identity, 2001; mem. editl. bd. U. Press Am., 1976—. Mem. Internat. Polit. Sci. Assn., Am. Polit. Sci. Assn., Internat. Sociol. Assn. Rsch. Coms. on Urban & Regional Devel. and Comparative Cmty. Rsch. Office: Dept Human & Cmty Devel Univ Calif Davis CA 95616

SMITH, MICHAEL ROBERT, electro-optical engineer, physicist; b. Tela, Honduras, Aug. 24, 1937; s. Ike Morgan and Edith Helen (Hudson) S.; m. Suzanne Ruth Hudgins, Aug. 20, 1960; children: Stephen, Monica, Meryl. BME, Ga. Inst. Tech., 1959, MS in Nuclear Engring., 1961; PhD, Case Inst. Tech., 1965. Mem. tech. staff Hughes Rsch. Labs., Malibu, Calif., 1965-68; v.p., dir. rsch. Britt Corp., L.A., 1968-73; sr. staff engr. Singer/Librascope divsn., Glendale, Calif., 1973-78; pres. Exocor Tech., Newbury Park, 1978-95; asst. prof., head physics program Calif. Luth. U., Thousand Oaks, 1990-96; design leader LIGO project Calif. Inst. Tech., Pasadena, 1996—. Contbr. articles to profl. jours.; inventor emergency vehicle warning and traffic control sys., emergency vehicle warning sign, flat electro-optic display panel, high power mirror, laser recording film with opaque coating, pulsed gas laser with radiation cooling, infrared laser photocautery device; 8 U.S. patents; 9 fgn. patents. Greek folk dance tchr. Arts Coun., Thousand Oaks, Calif., 1991-97. Mem. IEEE, Laser Electro-Optic Soc. (chair 1995-97), Sigma Xi, Pi Tau Sigma. Republican. Home: 680 S Marengo Ave Apt 9 Pasadena CA 91106-3659 E-mail: smith@ligo.caltech.edn

SMITH, MILTON RAY, computer company executive, lawyer; b. Idaho, 1935; AA, Long Beach (Calif.) City Coll., 1958; BS, Portland State U., 1962; MS, Oreg. State U., 1969; JD, Lewis and Clark Coll., 1970. Bar: Oreg. 1970, U.S. Dist. Ct. Oreg. 1970, U.S. Ct. Appeals (9th cir.) 1971, U.S. Supreme Ct. 1973. Tech. writer Northrop Corp., Hawthorne, Calif., 1957-58; engring. writer Tektronix Inc., Beaverton, Oreg., 1958-60, design engr., 1960-63, project engr., 1963-65, program mgr., 1966-70; asst. engring. mgr. Eldorado Electronics, Concord, Calif., 1965-66; ptnr. Acker, Underwood & Smith, Portland, Oreg., 1970-86; chmn., chief exec. officer Floating Point Systems Inc., Beaverton, 1986-88, pres., chief exec. officer, [illegible] Inc., Tigard, Oreg., 1992-94; pres., CEO Zeelan Tech., Inc., Beaverton, 1994-95; mgmt. cons., 1995—. CEO, Test Sys. Strategies, Inc., Beaverton, 1992-93; bd. dirs. ThrustMaster, Inc., Beaverton, Integrated Measurement Sys., Beaverton. Bd. dirs. Oreg. Bus. Council, Portland, 1986-88; mem. bd. visitors Northwestern Sch. Law, Portland, 1986—. With USN, 1953-56. Mem. Am. Electronics Assn. (exec. com. Oreg. coun. 1987-93, vice chmn. 1994-95, chmn. 1995-96), Oreg. State Bar, Founders Club Portland. Republican. Office: 6717 NE 126th St Vancouver WA 98686-3485

SMITH, NEIL, professional football player; b. New Orleans, Apr. 10, 1966; Student, U. Nebr. Defensive end Kansas City Chiefs, 1988-96, Denver Broncos, 1997—. Played in Pro Bowl, 1991-93; named defensive lineman The Sporting News All-America team, 1987. Office: Denver Broncos 13655 Broncos Pkwy Englewood CO 80112-4150

SMITH, NEVILLE VINCENT, physicist; b. Leeds, Eng., Apr. 21, 1942; came to U.S., 1966; s. Horace J.H. and Ethel S.; m. Elizabeth Jane Poulson, 1970; children: Katherine, Elizabeth. BA, Cambridge (Eng.) U., 1963, MA, PhD, Cambridge (Eng.) U., 1967. Rsch. assoc. Stanford (Calif.) U., 1966-68; mem. staff AT&T Bell Labs., Murray Hill, N.J., 1969-94, head condensed state physics rsch. dept., 1978-81; scientific program head Advanced Light Source Lawrence Berkeley Nat. Lab., Berkeley, Calif., 1994—. Contbr. articles to jours. in field. Fellow Am. Phys. Soc. (Davisson-Germer prize 1991). Office: Lawrence Berkeley Nat Lab 1 Cyclotron Rd Berkeley CA 94720-0001

SMITH, ORVILLE AUVERNE, physiology educator; b. Nogales, Ariz., June 16, 1927; s. Orville Auverne and Bess (Gill) S.; m. Clara Jean Smith; children— Nanette, Marcella. B.A. in Psychology, U. Ariz., 1949; M.A., Mich. State U., 1950, Ph.D., 1953. Instr. psychology Mich. State U., East Lansing, 1953-54; fellow U. Pa., Phila., 1954-56; trainee dept. physiology and biophysics U. Wash., Seattle, 1956-58, instr. physiology and biophysics, 1958-59, asst. prof., 1959-61, 62-63; asst. dir. Regional Primate Research Ctr., 1962-69, assoc. prof., 1963-67, prof., 1967-97; assoc. dir. Regional Primate Research Center, 1969-71, dir., 1971-88, prof. emeritus, 1997—. Contbr. articles to profl. jours. Mem. Am. Physiol. Soc., Am. Soc. Primatologists (pres. 1977-79), Internat. Congress Physiol. Scis., Am. Assn. Anatomists, AAAS, Pavlovian Soc. N.Am. (pres. 1977-78), Internat. Primatological Soc., AAUP, Neurosci. Soc. Home: 30311 201st Ct SE Kent WA 98042-5920 Office: U Wash Regional Primate Rsch Ctr PO Box 357330 Seattle WA 98195-7330

SMITH, PETER HOPKINSON, political scientist, consultant, writer; b. Bklyn., Jan. 17, 1940; s. Joseph Hopkinson and Mary Edna (Sullivan) S.; children: Jonathan Yeardley, Peter Hopkinson Jr, Joanna Alexandra. BA, Harvard U., 1961; MA, PhD, Columbia U., 1966. Asst. prof. Dartmouth Coll., Hanover, N.H., 1966-68; from asst. prof. to prof. U. Wis., Madison, 1968-80; prof. MIT, Cambridge, 1980-86; Simón Bolívar prof. L.Am. studies U. Calif., San Diego, 1987—, dir. Ctr. for Iberian and L.Am. studies, 1989—. Cons. Ford Found., N.Y.C., 1984—; vis. mem. Inst. for Advanced Study, Princeton, N.J., 1972-73. Author: Politics and Beef in Argentina: Patterns of Conflict and Change, 1969, Argentina and the Failure of Democracy: Conflict among Political Elites, 1904-55, 1974, Labyrinths of Power: Political Recruitment in Twentieth-Century Mexico, 1979, Mexico: The Quest for a U.S. Policy, 1980, Mexico: Neighbor in Transition, 1984; co-author: Modern Latin America, 1984, 89, 92, editor: Statistics, Epistemology, and History, 1984, Drug Policy in the Americas, 1992, The Challenge of Integration: Europe and the Americas, 1993, Talons of the Eagle, 1995; co-editor: New Approaches to Latin Am. History, 1974, The Family in Latin America, 1978; series editor: Latin America in Global Perspective, 1995—; contbr. articles to profl. jours. Guggenheim fellow, 1975-76; disting. Fulbright lectr. Mexico, 1984. Mem. Latin Am. Studies Assn. (pres. 1981), Am. Polit. Sci. Assn., Am. Hist. Assn., Coun. for Internat. Exch. Scholars, Coun. on Fgn. Rels. Office: U Calif Ctr Iberian & LAm Studies 9500 Gilman Dr La Jolla CA 92093-0528

SMITH, PHILLIP J. food products executive; V.p., controller various divsn. Cullum Cos. Inc., Dallas, 1975-84; v.p., CFO Market Basket Food Stores, Tex., 1984-87; controller Stater Bros., Colton, Calif., 1987, v.p., controller, sr. v.p., CFO, 2000—. Office: Stater Bros Markets 21700 Barton Rd Colton CA 92324

SMITH, RALPH EARL, virologist; b. Yuma, Colo., May 10, 1940; s. Robert C. and Esther C. (Schwarz) S.; m. Sheila L. Kondy, Aug. 29, 1961 (div. 1986); 1 child, Andrea Denise; m. Janet M. Keller, 1988. BS, Colo. State U., 1961; PhD, U. Colo., 1968. Registered microbiologist Am. Soc. Clin. Pathologists. Fellow Duke U. Med. Ctr., Durham, N.C., 1968-70, asst. prof., 1970-74, assoc. prof., 1974-80, prof. virology, 1980-82; prof., head dept. microbiology Colo. State U., Ft. Collins, 1983-88, prof. microbiology, assoc. v.p. rsch., 1989-99, interim v.p. rsch., 1990-91, prof. microbiology, assoc. v.p. rsch., 1991-99, interim head dept. microbiology, 1999—. Cons. Bellco Glass Co., Vineland, N.J., 1976-80, Proctor & Gamble Co., Cin., 1985-86, Schering Plough Corp., Bloomfield, N.J., 1987-89. Contbr. articles to profl. jours.; patentee in field. Bd. dirs. Colo. Ctr. for Environ. Mgmt., v.p. for rsch.; mem. pollution prevention adv. bd. Colo. Dept. Pub. Health and Environment; mem. Rocky Mountain U. Consortium on Environ. Restoration, Environ. Inst. Rocky Flats; asst. scoutmaster Boy Scouts Am., Durham, 1972-82, com. mem., Ft. Collins, 1986-91; mem. adminstrv. bd. 1st United Meth. Ch., Ft. Collins. Eleanor Roosevelt fellow Internat. Union Against Cancer 1978-79. Mem. AAAS, Am. Soc. Microbiology, N.Y. Acad. Scis., Am. Soc. Virology, Gamma Sigma Delta. Democrat. Methodist. Avocations: photography, hiking. Home: 2406 Creekwood Dr Fort Collins CO 80525-2034 Office: Colo State U Dept Microbiology Fort Collins CO 80523-0001

SMITH, RAYMOND EDWARD, retired health care administrator; b. Freeport, N.Y., June 17, 1932; s. Jerry Edward and Madelyn Holman (Jones) S.; m. Lena Kathryn Jernigan Hughes, Oct. 28, 1983; children: Douglas, Ronald, Kevin, Doris Jean, Raymond. BS in Edn., Temple U., 1953; MHA, Baylor U., 1966. Commd. 2d lt. U.S. Army, 1953, advanced through grades to lt. col., 1973, helicopter ambulance pilot, 1953-63; comdr. helicopter ambulance units Korea, 1955, Fed. Republic of Germany, 1961; various hosp. adminstrv. assignments, 1963-73; pers. dir. Valley Forge (Pa.) Gen. Hosp., 1966; adminstr. evacuation hosp. Vietnam, 1967; dep. insp. Walter Reed Gen. Hosp., Washington, 1970; dir. personnel divsn. Office of Army Surgeon Gen., Washington, 1971-73, ret., 1973; adminstr. Health Care Ctrs., Phila., Phila. Coll. Osteo. Medicine, 1974-76; dir. bur. hosps. Pa. Dept. Health, Harrisburg, 1976-79; contract mgr. Blue Cross of Calif., San Diego, 1979-88, Cmty. Care Network, San Diego, 198-95; ret., 1995. Decorated Bronze Star, Legion of Merit. Mem. Am. Hosp. Assn., Am. Legion, Ret. Officers Assn., Kappa Alpha Psi, Sigma Pi Phi. Episcopalian. Home: 7630 Lake Adlon Dr San Diego CA 92119-2518

SMITH, RICHARD ALAN, neurologist, medical association administrator; Student, Brandeis U., 1958-61; grad., U. Miami, 1965. Intern in medicine Jackson Meml. Hosp., Miami, Fla., 1965-66; resident in neurology Stanford U. Hosp., Palo Alto, Calif., 1966-69; head neurology br. Navy Neuropsychiatric Rsch. Unit, San Diego, 1969-71; mem. assoc. staff microbiology Scripps Clinic and Rsch. Found., La Jolla, Calif., 1972-79, mem. assoc. staff neurology, 1972-82; dir. Ctr. Neurologic Study, San Diego, 1979—; mem. sr. staff Scripps Meml. Hosp., La Jolla, 1982—. Mem. med. adv. bd. Multiple Sclerosis Soc., San Diego; founder neurosci. network Ams. Drs., Gurnee, Ill., 1995—; pres. Coordinated Clin. Rsch. Corp., San Diego, 1996—; vis. scholar neurosci. dept. U. Calif., San Diego, [illegible] Handbook of Amyotrophic Lateral Sclerosis, 1992; contbr. articles to profl. jours. Recipient Henry Newman award San Francisco Neurologic Soc., 1968; NIH STTR grantee, 1996-97; Skaggs Clin. scholar Scripps Rsch. Inst., 1998—. Mem. AAAS, Am. Acad. Neurology (assoc.). Achievements include 6 U.S. patents; work on methodology for enhancing the systemic delivery of Dextromethorphan for the treatment of neurological and medical disorders, including emotional lability, pain, cough. and drug addiction. Office: 9850 Genesee Ave Ste 320 La Jolla CA 92037-1208 E-mail: cns@cts.com

SMITH, RICHARD HOWARD, banker; b. Tulare, Calif., Aug. 27, 1927; s. Howard Charles and Sue Elizabeth (Cheyne) S.; B.A., Principia Coll, 1958; LL.B., LaSalle U., 1975; postgrad. Sch. Banking U. Wash., 1970-72; m. Patricia Ann Howery, Mar. 12, 1950; children— Jeffrey Howard, Holly Lee, Gregory Scott, Deborah Elaine. Prin., Aurora Elementary Sch., Tulare, 1951-53; prin. Desert Sun Sch., Idyllwild, Calif., 1953-55; trust adminstr. trainee Bank of Am., San Diego, 1955-58, asst. trust officer, Ventura, Redlands, Riverside and L.A., 1958-65; asst. trust officer Security Pacific Bank, Fresno, Calif., 1965-68; trust officer, 1968-72, v.p., mgr., 1972-88, Pasadena, 1988-94; v.p. Bank of Am., L.A., 1994-95; ret., 1995; pres. Fiduciary Svcs., Fresno, 1995—; instr. San Bernardino Valley Coll., 1962— , Fresno City Coll., 1977— . With USN, 1945-46. Home: 3222 W Dovewood Ln Fresno CA 93711-2125

SMITH, ROBERT BRUCE, former security consultant, retired career officer; b. De Quincy, La., Apr. 22, 1920; s. Malcolm Monard and Jewell (Perkins) S.; m. Gladys Opal Borel, Feb. 22, 1941; children: Susan, Richard, Bruce. B.J., La. State U., 1941; grad., Command and Gen. Staff Coll., 1951-52, Army War Coll., 1958-59. Commd. 2d lt. U.S. Army, 1941, advanced through grades to maj. gen., 1969; plans and ops. officer 83d Div. Arty., Europe, 1943-45; personnel officer Philippine-Ryukyus Command, Manila, 1947-49; prof. mil. sci. and tactics ROTC, Lanier High Sch., Macon, Ga., 1949-51; chief res. officers sect., procurement br. Dept. Army, 1952-55; chief troop info. Office Chief Info., Dept. Army, 1962-63, dep. chief info., 1968-69; comdg. officer 8th F.A. Bn., 25th Inf. Div., Hawaii, 1955-56; G-1 25th Inf. Div. and U.S. Army Hawaii, 1956-58; mem. staff, faculty Command and Gen. Staff Coll., Fort Leavenworth, Kans., 1959-62; chief Alt. Nat. Mil. Command Center, Fort Ritchie, Md., 1963-64; dep. dir. ops. Office Joint Chiefs of Staff, 1964-65; asst. div. comdr. 7th Inf. Div., Korea, 1965-66; dep. comdt. Army War Coll., Carlisle, Pa., 1966-68; dep. comdg. gen. Ryukyus Islands, 1969-72, 6th U.S. Army, Presidio of San Francisco, 1972-73; ret. active duty, 1973; reporter, news editor Lake Charles (La.), 1946-47; region adminstrv. mgr. Burns Security Service, Oakland, Calif., 1974-76; ptnr. constrn. co. Napa, 1976-77, Burns Security Service, 1978-81; now ret.; dir. 1st Am. Title Co., Napa, Calif., 1988-92. Trustee Queen of Valley Hosp. Found., 1987-89; mem. Nat. coun. Boy Scouts Am., 1969-70; pres. Silverado Property Owners Assn., Inc., 1990-95. Decorated D.S.M. with oak leaf cluster, Legion of Merit with 2 oak leaf clusters, Bronze Star with oak leaf cluster; inducted into La. State U.'s Manship Sch. of Mass Communication Hall of Fame, 1996, Disting. Leadership Cadets Ole War Skule Hall of Honor, 1998. Club: Silverado Country (Napa, Calif.). Home: 350 St Andrews Dr Napa CA 94558-1544 E-mail: robtsmith@juno.com

SMITH, ROBERT F. (BOB SMITH), rancher, congressman; b. Portland, Oreg., June 16, 1931; m. Kaye Tomlinson; children: Christopher, Matthew, Tiffany. BA in Bus. Adminstrn. and Econs., Willamette U., 1953. Mem. Oreg. Ho. of Reps., 1960-73, spkr., 1969-73; mem. Oreg. State Senate, 1973-82, leader republican caucus, 1977-83; mem. 98th-105th Congresses from 2d dist. Oreg., 1983-94; pres. Smith West Co., Portland, 1995-96, cons. Medford, Oreg., 1999—. Dir. First State Bank Oreg., Key Bank; dir. exch. bd. Farmers Ins.; dir. bd. trustee Willamette U. Named one of Harney County, Oreg.'s Leading Citizens, 1957, one of Oreg.'s Outstanding Young Men, 1961. Republican. Office: Smith West Co 843 E Main St Ste 400 Medford OR 97504-7137

SMITH, ROBERT LONDON, SR. commissioner, retired air force officer, political scientist, educator; b. Alexandria, La., Oct. 13, 1919; s. Daniel Charleston and Lillie (Roberts) S.; m. Jewel Busch, Feb. 5, 1949; children: Jewel Diane, Robert London, Karl Busch. B.A., Coll. St. Joseph, 1954; M.A., U. Okla., 1955; Ph.D., Am. U., 1964. Commd. 2d lt. USAAF, 1941; advanced through grades to lt. col. USAF, 1961; various assignments in aircraft engring., command and logistics, 1941-60; rsch. logistics Hdqs. Office Aerospace Rsch., 1960-63; project sci., adminstr. postdoctoral rsch. program, asst. dir. NAS, Hdqs. Office Sci. Rsch., 1963-65; ret., 1965; asso. prof. polit. sci., head dept. eve. classes and corr. study U. Alaska, College, 1966-68, dean Coll. Bus., Econs. and Govt., 1968-70, prof., head dept. polit. sci., 1966-84, prof. emeritus, 1984—; commr. Alaska Dept. Health and Social Services, 1983—; mem. govt. panels and planning groups. Dir. Arctic 1st Fed. Savs. & Loan Assn.; corporator Mt. McKinley Mut. Savs. Bank. Author: (with others) Squadron Adminstration, 1951; also publs. on nat. security and nat. def.; Contbr. to: (with others) The United Nations Peace University, 1965. Committeeman Western region Boy Scouts Am., 1968-73; mem. exec. bd. Midnight Sun council, 1973-74, committeeman-at-large nat. council, 1968— ; mem. Alaska Gov.'s Employment Commn.; pres. United Service Orgn. Council, Fairbanks, Alaska; mem. active corps execs. SBA. Recipient Silver Beaver award Boy Scouts Am.; named Outstanding Prof. U. Alaska, 1975 Mem. Nat. Acad. Econs. and Polit. Sci., AAAS, Air Force Hist. Found., Nat. Inst. Social and Behavioral Scis., Nat. Inst. U.S. in World Affairs, Am. Polit. Sci. Assn., Assn. U.S. Army (bd. dirs. Polar Bear chpt.), Alaska C. of C. (edn. com.), Pi Gamma Mu, Pi Sigma Alpha. Roman Catholic. Club: Rotary. Home: Smithhaven 1100 9th Ave Fairbanks AK 99701-4105 also: Costa Vida Unit # 920-921 Puerto Vallarta Jalisco Mexico E-mail: lundy@alaska.com

SMITH, ROBERT NATHANIEL, broadcasting executive, lawyer; b. Detroit, July 13, 1944; s. Melvyn Maxwell Smith and Sara Evelyn Stein; m. Anne Fuchs, Sept. 11, 1971; children: Jennifer, Michael. BA, U. Mich., 1967, JD, 1970. Bar: Mich. 1971, D.C. 1971. Lawyer FCC, Washington, 1971-74; youth dir. Dem. Nat. Com., Washington, 1974-77; nat. coord. GOTV dr. Dem. nat. Com., Washington, 1976; mem. staff White House, Washington, 1977; asst. dir. Community Svcs. Adminstrn., Washington, 1977-79; pvt. practice Birmingham, Mich., 1980-83; v.p. Heritage Broadcasting Co., Birmingham, 1983-85; pres. Smith Broadcasting Group, Inc., Santa Barbara, Calif., 1985—. CEO, bd. Sunrise TV Corp., St. Petersburg, Fla., 1996—; chmn. bd. dirs. Smith Broadcasting of Santa Barbara; pres., chmn. bd. dirs. Smith TV of N.Y., Utica, N.Y.; pres. Smith Broadcasting of Alaska, Anchorage, Smith Broadcasting of Watertown (N.Y.); CEO Smith Broadcasting of Vt., LLC. Mem. Birmingham Athletic Club. Home: 221 E Constance Ave Santa Barbara CA 93105-3517 Office: Smith Broadcasting Group Inc 127 El Paseo Santa Barbara CA 93101-2229

SMITH, RODNEY, electronics executive; b. 1941; BSEE, Southampton Coll. Advanced Tech., Eng. Various positions to v.p., gen. mgr. Fairchild Semiconductor Corp., Mountain View, Calif., 1969-83; chmn., pres., CEO Altera Corp., San Jose, 1983—. Office: Altera Corp 101 Innovation Dr San Jose CA 95134-1941

SMITH, RUBEN, mayor; BA, N.Mex. State U. Mayor City of Las Cruces (N.Mex.), 1991—; CEO Branigan Cultural Ctr., Las Cruces, N.M. Office: PO Box 20000 Las Cruces NM 88004-9002

SMITH, SAMUEL HOWARD, academic administrator, plant pathologist; b. Salinas, Calif., Feb. 4, 1940; s. Adrian Reed and Elsa (Jacop) S.; m. [illegible] in Plant Pathology, U. Calif., Berkeley, 1961, PhD, 1964; D (hon.), Nihon U., Tokyo, 1989, Far Eastern State U., Vladivostok, Russia, 1997. NATO fellow Glasshouse Crops Research Inst., Sussex, Eng., 1964-65; asst. prof.

plant pathology U. Calif., Berkeley, 1965-69; assoc. prof. Pa. State U., Arendtsville, 1969-71, University Park, 1971-74, prof., 1974-85, head dept. plant pathology, 1976-81, dean Coll. Agr., dir. Pa. Agrl. Expt. Sta. and Coop. Extension Service, 1981-85; pres. Wash. State U., Pullman, 1985-2000, ret., 2000. Bd. dirs. Assoc. Western Univs.; adv. com. Wash. Sch. Employees Credit Union, 1993-95; mem. adv. com. Battelle Pacific N.W. Lab., 1993—; chair Pacific-10 Conf. CEOs, 1993-94; bd. dirs. All-Nations Alliance for Minority Participation; mem. pres.' commn. NCAA, 1994—, divsn. I chair, 1995-96; chair Pres.'s Commn., 1996—. Bd. dirs. Forward Wash., 1986-95, The Technology Alliance, 1996—, China Rels. Coun.; mem. Wash. Coun. Internat. Trade, Western Insterstate Commn. Higher Edn.; bd. dirs. Assn. Western Univs., 1993—. Mem. AAAS, Am. Phytopath. Soc., Nat. Assn. State Univs. and Land-Grand Colls. (bd. dirs. 1994—, chair commn. info. tech. 1994-96), Gamma Sigma Delta, Alpha Zeta, Epsilon Sigma Phi, Sigma Xi, Omicron Delta Kappa, Golden Key, Pi Kappa Alpha (hon.).

SMITH, SHERWOOD PAUL, plastic surgeon; b. Sault St. Marie, Ont., Can., May 25, 1941; came to U.S., 1972; s. Irwin and Sophie Edith (Freeman) S.; m. Judith Ann Gebhard, Jan. 24, 1966; 1 child, Stephen Barclay. MD, U. Toronto, 1965; MSc, McGill U., 1969. Diplomate Am. Bd. Plastic Surgery. Plastic surgeon Olympia (Wash.) Plastic Surgeons Inc. PS, 1972—. Vol. plastic surgeon Gen. Hosp. Columbo, Sri Lanka, 1985—. Fellow ACS, Royal Coll. Physicians and Surgeons of Can.; mem. Olympia Yacht Club, South Sound Sailing Soc. Avocations: sailing, bicycling, hiking, mountaineering. Office: Olympia Plastic Surg Inc PS 300 Lilly Rd NE Ste B Olympia WA 98506-5428

SMITH, STANFORD SIDNEY, former state treasurer; b. Denver, Oct. 20, 1923; s. Frank Jay and Lelah (Beamer) S.; m. Harriet Holdrege, Feb. 7, 1947; children: Monta Smith Ramirez, Franklin Stanley. Student, Calif. Inst. Tech., 1941-42, Stanford U., 1942-43; BS, U.S. Naval Acad., 1946. Pres. Vebar Livestock Co., Thermopolis, Wyo., 1961—; mem. Wyo. Senate, 1974-76; pres. Wyo. Wool GrowersAssn., 1976-78; mem. Wyo. Ho. of Reps., Cheyenne, 1978-82; treas. State Wyo., Cheyenne, 1983-99; ret., 1999. Dir. Coun. of State Govts., 1990-92; v.p. Wyo. Wool Growers, dir., 1976-82. County commr. Hot Springs County, Wyo, 1966-74. Lt. USN, 1943-54. Decorated Bronze Star Mem. Nat. Assn. State Treas. (pres. 1990-91). Republican. Methodist.

SMITH, STEVEN DELANO, professional basketball player; b. Highland Park, Mich., Mar. 31, 1969; Student, Mich. State U. Guard Miami Heat, 1991-94, Atlanta Hawks, 1994-99, Portland Trailblazers, 1999—. Named Sporting News All-Am. First Team, 1990, 91, NBA All-Rookie Team, 1992, Dream Team II, 1994. Office: Portland Trailblazer One Center Ct Ste 200 Portland OR 97227

SMITH, STEVEN GRAYSON, career officer; b. Newark, 03 Aug. m. Kathleen Hargrave; children: Erin Kathleen, Kelly Kimberlee. Grad., Valley Forge Mil. Acad., 1964; B in Indsl. Mgmt., U. Tex., 1969; M in Nat. Security Affairs, Naval War Coll., Newport, R.I.; postgrad., Cath. U., Washington. Commd. ensign USN, 1969, advanced through grades to rear adm., 1996; officer in charge SEAL team boat detachment Naval Spl. Warfare Group; exec. officer USS Horne; comdr. USS Chandler, USS Mobile Bay, Yokosuka, Japan, 1992-94; anti-air warfare comdr. USS Independence Battle Group; asst. chief of staff for manpower and pers. Comdr. in Chief of Pacific FleeT; exec. asst. Chief Naval Pers.; sr. mil. asst. Under Sec. Def. for Pers. and Readiness; mil. asst. Under Sec. Def. for Policy, 1996—. Decorated Legions of Merit, 2 Bronze Stars, Def. Disting. Svc. medal, Def. Superior Svc. medal. Office: 3985 Cummings Rd Ste 4 San Diego CA 92136-5289

SMITH, STEVEN RAY, law educator; b. Spirit Lake, Iowa, July 8, 1946; s. Byrnard L. and Dorothy V. (Fischbeck) S.; m. Lera Baker, June 15, 1975. BA, Buena Vista Coll., 1968; JD, U. Iowa, 1971, MA, 1971. Bar: Iowa 1971, Ky. 1987, Ohio 1992. From asst. to assoc. dean Sch. Law U. Louisville, 1974-81, acting dean, 1974-75, 76, prof. law, 1971-88, assoc. in medicine Med. Sch., 1983-88; dep. dir/ Assn. Am. Law Schs., 1987-88; dean, prof. law Cleve. State U., 1988-96; pres., dean and prof. Calif. Western Sch. of Law, 1996—. Author: Law, Behavior and Mental Health: Policy and Practice, 1987; contbr. chpts. to books, articles to profl. jours. Trustee U. Louisville, 1980-82, SCRIBES, 1993—; chmn. faculty adv. com. Ky. Coun. Higher Edn., 1981-82; pres. Ky. Congress of Senate Faculty Leaders, 1982-84; bd. trustees Am. Bd. Profl. Psychology, 1994—. Recipient Grawemeyer award Innovative Teaching. Metroversity Consortium, 1983, Pres. award Cleve.-Marshall Law Alumni Assn., 1995. Fellow Ohio State Bar Found.; mem. ABA (stds. rev. com. 1991-95, govt. rels. com. 1993-95, joint commn. ABA/Assn. Am. Law Schs. financing of legal edn. 1993-94, 97-98, coun. sect. legal edn. and admission to the bar 1997—), APA (pub. mem. ethics com.), Am. Econs. Assn., Assn. Am. Law Schs. (chmn. librs. com., dep. dir. 1987-88, mem. accreditation com. 1993-96, chair accreditation com. 1994-96), Ohio State Bar Assn. (coun. of dels. 1992-96), Order of Coif, City Club of Cleve. (pres. 1994-95). Office: Calif Western Sch Law Office of Pres 225 Cedar St San Diego CA 92101-3046

SMITH, THOMAS SHORE, lawyer; b. Rock Springs, Wyo., Dec. 7, 1924; s. Thomas and Anne E. (McTee) S.; m. Jacqueline Emily Krueger, May 25, 1952; children: Carolyn Jane, Karl Thomas, David Shore. BSBA, U. Wyo., 1950, JD, 1959. Bar: U.S. Dist. Ct. Wyo. 1960, U.S. Ct. Appeals (10th cir.) 1960, U.S. Tax Ct. 1969, U.S. Supreme Ct. 1971. Of counsel Smith, Stanfield & Scott, LLC, Laramie, Wyo., 1963-94, Brown, Nagel, Waters & Hiser, LLC, Laramie, 1994—. Atty. City of Laramie, 1963-86; instr. mcpl. law U. Wyo., 1987; dir. budget and fin. Govt. of Am. Samoa, 1954-56. Bd. dirs. Bur. Land Mgmt., Rawlins, Wyo., 1984-89, chmn. bd. dirs., 1991-95; bd. dirs. Ivinson Hosp. Found., 1994-95; bd. dirs. U. Wyo. Found., 1991-99, pres., 1994-95, bd. dirs. Bank of Laramie, 1998—. Francis Warren scholar, 1958. Mem Wyo. Bar Assn. (pres. 1984-85), Albany County Bar Assn., Western States Bar Conf. (pres. 1985-86), Elks. Republican. Episcopalian. Avocation: golf. Office: Brown Nagel Waters & Hiser LLC PO Box 971 515 E Ivinson Ave Laramie WY 82070-3157

SMITH, THOMAS WINSTON, cotton marketing executive; b. Crosbyton, Tex., Mar. 16, 1935; s. Lance L. and Willie Mae (Little) S.; m. Patricia Mae Zachary, Dec. 13, 1958; children— Janna Olean, Thomas Mark. B.S., Tex. A&M U., 1957; P.M.D., Harvard U., 1964. Various positions Calcot Ltd., Bakersfield, Calif., 1957-77, exec. v.p., pres., 1977—; v.p. Amcot, Inc., Amcot Internat., Inc., Bakersfield, 1977—, also bd. dirs.; bd. mgrs. N.Y. Cotton Exchange, N.Y.C., v.p., Memphis. Bd. dir. Greater Bakersfield Meml. Hosp.; mem. pres.'s adv. commn. Calif. State Coll., Bakersfield; v.p. Nat. Cotton Coun., Memphis. Mem. Rotary.

SMITH, TOM, state legislator, educator, military officer; b. St. Paul, Mar. 16, 1927; m. Sarah Jane Smith; 7 children. BA, Roosevelt U., 1968; MA, Ariz. State U., 1973. Ret. lt. col. USMC, 1945-68; ret. educator, 1970-84; mem. Ariz. Ho. of Reps., 1991-98, Ariz. Senate, Dist. 26, Phoenix, 1998—; mem. appropriations com., mem. edn. com. Ariz. State Senate, vice-chmn. judiciary com., chmn. rules com. Active Scottdale Cultural Ctr., Phoenix Symphony; mem. Scottsdale Sch. Dist. Governing Bd., 1983-86. Mem. VFW (life), 1st Marine Divsn. Assn. (life), Ret. Officers Assn., Ret. Tchrs. Assn., Navy Mutual Aid Assn., Mustang Assn., China Marine Assn. Republican. Roman Catholic. Office: State Capitol Bldg #304 1700 W Washington St # 304 Phoenix AZ 85007-2812 also: 4204 N 57th Way Phoenix AZ 85018-4608 E-mail: tsmith@azleg.state.az.us

SMITH, VALENE, anthropology educator; b. Spokane, Wash., Feb. 14, 1926; d. Ernest Frank and Lucy (Blachly) S.; m. Edwin Chesteen Golay, June 7, 1970 (dec. June 1980); m. Stanley George McIntyre, Nov. 26, 1983 (dec. Oct. 2000). BA in Geography, U. Calif., 1946, MA in Geography, 1950; PhD in Anthropology, U. Utah, 1966. Prof. earth sci. L.A. City Coll., 1947-67; prof. anthropology Calif. State U., Chico, 1967—. Cons. World Tourism Orgn., Madrid, 1987. Editor: Hosts and Guests: The Anthrop, 1989, Tourism Alternatives: Potentials and Problems in the Development of Tourism, 1992, House and Guests Revisited, 2001. Mem. Internat. Acad. for Study Tourism, Anthrop. Soc. Wash., Cert. Travel Counselors, Am. Anthrop. Assn., AAUW, Canyon Oaks Country Club, Soroptimists. Republican. Avocations: traveling, aviation, photography. Office: U Calif Dept Anthropology Chico CA 95929-0004

SMITH, VERNON LOMAX, economist, researcher; b. Wichita, Kans., Jan. 1, 1927; s. Vernon Chessman and Lula Belle (Lomax) S.; m. Joyce Harkleroad, June 6, 1950 (div. Aug. 1975); m. Carol Breckner, Jan. 1, 1980. BSEE, Calif. Inst. Tech., 1949; MA in Econs., U. Kans., 1952; PhD in Econs., Harvard U., 1955; D of Mgmt. (hon.), Purdue U., 1990. Asst. prof. econs. Purdue U., West Lafayette, Ind., 1955-58, assoc. prof., 1958-61, prof., 1961-65, Krannert prof., 1965-67; prof. Brown U., Providence, 1967-68, U. Mass., Amherst, 1968-75, U. Ariz., Tucson, 1975—, Regents' prof., —. Contbr. articles to profl. jours. Fellow Ctr. for Advanced Study in Behavioral Scis., Stanford, Calif., 1972-73; Sherman Fairchild Disting. Scholar Calif. Inst. Tech., Pasadena, 1973-74; adj. scholar CATO Inst., Washington, 1983—. Fellow AAAS, Am. Acad. Arts and Scis., Econometric Soc., Am. Econ. Assn. (Disting. fellow); me. Pvt. Enterprise Edn. Assn. (Adam Smith award), Nat. Acad. Sci. Home: 6020 N Pontatoc Rd Tucson AZ 85718-4323 Office: U Ariz McLelland Hall PO Box 210108 Tucson AZ 85721-0108

SMITH, VIN, sports editor, business owner, novelist; b. Whittier, Calif., May 19, 1944; s. M. Clifford and Anna Eugenia (Hill) S.; m. Marthea Karen Callaham, May 15, 1969 (div. 1979); children: Jayare Smith, Eric Smith; m. Ginger Hammon, Oct. 20, 1984; children: Amy Michelle, Stacey Erin, Kellie Rae. Student, Columbia Sch. Broadcasting, San Francisco, 1967; AA, Cuesta Coll., 1974; grad., Am. Sch. of Piano Tuning, 1978. Sales mgr. Sta. KTAT, Frederick, Okla., 1967-69; announcer KOCY, Oklahoma City, 1969; owner Melmart Markets, San Luis Obispo, Calif., 1971-73, Am. Direct Sales, Grover City, 1973-79; instr. piano Valley View Acad., Arroyo Grande, 1977-78, Long Piano Co., San Luis Obispo, 1977-79, piano technician, 1978-79; owner Chocolate Piano, Yreka, Calif., 1979—; instr. piano Makah Indian Tribe, Neah Bay, Wash., 1981-82; sports editor New Words Digest, Bakersfield, Calif., 1988—. Cons., stress evaluator seminar Yreka Stress Therapy Clinic, 1986-87; founder Vinco Distbrs. (formerly Vinco Enhancement Sys.), 1998; chair piano dept. Bogus Sch., 1999—, internat. relationship counselor Ask Me com., 2000—, askdrpiano.com., 2000. Sports columnist New Words Digest, 1987-91; guest columnist Siskiyou Daily News, 1991-94; nat publicist chamber music concerts So. Oreg. State Coll., 1993—; contbr. articles to profl. jours. Chmn. heart fund Tillman County Okla., 1968; pub. co-chmn. Siskiyou County No-Prop 174, 1994; campaign worker Ken Jourdan for sheriff, Yreka, 1986; publicity dir. Gene Breceda for supr., 1993-94. Recipient Cert. of Appreciation, Siskiyou County, 1988, Achievement award, 1988; winner Golden Poet award World of Poetry, 1989. Mem. Nat. Writers Club (chmn. student com. Yreka chpt. 1988), Author's Guild, Inc., Author's League of Am., Mystery Writers Am., Soc. Children's Book Writers, Jr. C. of C. (sgt.-at-arms Frederick chpt. 1967-69), Kiwanis, Moose. Avocations: horse shoe pitching, photography, reading. Home: 710 Knapp St Yreka CA 96097-2343 Office: Chocolate Piano Svcs PO Box 447 Yreka CA 96097-0447 E-mail: drpiano@snowcrest.net

SMITH, WARREN JAMES, optical scientist, consultant, lecturer; b. Rochester, N.Y., Aug. 17, 1922; s. Warren Abrams and Jessica Madelyn (Forshay) S.; m. Mary Helen Geddes, May 18, 1944 (dec. 1999); children: David Whitney, Barbara Jamie; m. Dung My Luong, Dec. 24, 2000. BS, U. Rochester, 1944; postgrad., U. Calif., Santa Barbara, 1960. Physicist Clinton Engr. Works, Tenn. Eastman Co., Oak Ridge, 1944-46; chief optical engr. Simpson Optical Mfg. Co., Chgo., 1946-59; mgr. optical sect. Raytheon Corp., Santa Barbara, 1959-62; v.p. R & D, Infrared Industries, Santa Barbara, 1962-87; chief scientist Kaiser Electro-Optics, Inc., Carlsbad, Calif., 1987—. Lectr. U. Wis., Madison, 1972—, U. Rochester, 1988—, Genesee Computer Ctr., Rochester, 1982-93, Sinclair Optics, 1994—; cons. in field; expert witness. Author: Modern Optical Engineering, 1966, 3d edit., 2000, Modern Lens Design, 1992, Practical Optical System Layout, 1997; editor McGraw-Hill series Optical and Electro-Optical Engineering; also articles. Fellow Optical Soc. Am. (pres. 1980, organizer, chmn. tech. confs., Fraunhofer medal 2001), Soc. Photo-Optical Instrumentation Engrs. (life), Internat. Soc. Optical Engring. (pres. 1983, organizer, chmn. tech. confs., Gold medal 1985, Dirs. award 1992), Sigma Chi. Avocations: tennis, sailing. Home: 1165 Countrywood Ln Vista CA 92083-5334 Office: Kaiser Electro Optics Inc 2752 Loker Ave W Carlsbad CA 92008-6603 E-mail: wsmith@keo.com

SMITH, WILLARD GRANT, psychologist, educator; b. Sidney, N.Y., June 29, 1934; s. Frank Charles and Myrtle Belle (Empet) S.; m. Ruth Ann Dissly, Sept. 14, 1957; children: Deborah Sue Henri, Cynthia Lynn Koster, Andrea Kay Richards, John Charles. BS, U. Md., 1976; MS, U. Utah, 1978, PhD, 1981. Diplomate Am. Bd. Forensic Examiners, Am. Bd. Psychol. Specialities, Am. Bd. Disability Analysts; lic. psychologist Utah, cert. sch. psychologist nat. . Tchg. asst. dept. ednl. psychology U. Utah; rsch. asst. U. Utah Med. Ctr., 1976-78; rsch. cons. Utah Dept. Edn., 1977; program evaluator Salt Lake City Sch. Dist.; program evaluator, auditor Utah State Bd. Edn., 1978; sch. psychologist Jordan Sch. Dist., Sandy, Utah, 1978-82, tchr., 1979-80; exec. dir. Utah Ind. Living Ctr., Salt Lake City, 1982-83; spl. edn. cons. Southeastern Edn. Svc. Ctr., 1983-85; sch. psychologist Jordan Sch. Dist., Sandy, 1985-96; assoc. psychologist Don W. McBride & Assocs., Bountiful, Utah, 1989-91; pvt. practice Sandy, 1991—. Master sgt. USAF, 1953-76. Decorated Air Force Commendation medal with 2 clusters. Fellow Am. Coll. Forensic Examiners; mem. APA, Nat. Assn. Sch. Psychologists, Air Force Sgts. Assn., Ret. Enlisted Assn., Phi Kappa Phi, Alpha Sigma Lambda. Home: 8955 Quail Hollow Dr Sandy UT 84093-1903

SMITH, WILLIAM RAY, former biophysicist, former engineer; b. Lyman, Okla., June 26, 1925; s. Harry Wait and Daisy Belle (Hull) S. BA, Bethany Nazarene Coll., 1948; MA, Wichita State U., 1950; PhD, UCLA, 1967. Engr. Beech Aircraft Corp., Wichita, Kans., 1951-53; sr. group engr. McDonnell Aircraft Corp., St. Louis, 1953-60; sr. engr. Lockheed Aircraft Corp., Burbank, Calif., 1961-63; sr. engr. scientist McDonnell Douglas Corp., Long Beach, 1966-71; mem. tech. staff Rockwell Internat., L.A., 1973-86, CDI Corp.-West, Costa Mesa, Calif., 1986-88, McDonnell Douglas Aircraft Corp., Long Beach, 1988-93; ret., 1993. Tchr. math. Pasadena Nazarene Coll. (now Point Loma Nazarene Coll., San Diego), 1960-62, Glendale Coll., Calif., 1972; asst. prof. math. Mt. St. Mary's Coll., L.A., 1972-73; math. cons. L.A. Union Rescue Mission Bank of Am. Learning Ctr., 1995—, Wayfarer's Ministry 1997—. Deacon Presbyn. Ch. Recipient Recognition cert. NASA, 1982. Mem. Town Hall Calif., Yosemite Assocs., UCLA Faculty Club, Sigma Xi, Pi Mu Epsilon. Republican. Avocations: sailing, photography, teaching Sunday school first grade. Home: 2405 Roscomare Rd Los Angeles CA 90077-1839 E-mail: billsmitcom@webtv.net

SMITH, ZANNIE O. career officer; b. Columbia, S.C., Mar. 27, 1943; BA in History, U. Tampa; M in Bus. Mgmt., Webster U., St. Louis. Enlisted 82d airborne divsn. U.S. Army, 1962, commd. 2d lt., advanced through grades to brig. gen.; chief of staff U.S. Army Res. Command, Atlanta, 1995; asst. divsn. comdr. ops. 10th Mountain Divsn. and Ft. Drum, 1997; dep. comdg. gen., chief of staff I Corps and Ft. Lewis, 1998—. Decorated Legion of Merit with 4 oak leaf clusters, Bronze Star medal with V and 2 oak leaf clusters, Air medal with oak leaf cluster, Combat Infantryman's badge, others. Office: AFZH-CG I Corps and Ft Lewis Fort Lewis WA 98433-9500

SMITHSON, MICHAEL, parks director; b. Fort Sill, Okla., May 23, 1953; BS in Wildlife, Evergreen State Coll., 1975; cert. in mus. technician, U. Colo., 1977. With Rocky Mt. Nat. Park, Estes Park, Colo., 1978-88; asst. chief Olympic Park, Port Angeles, Wash., 1988-94, chief of resource edn., 1995—. Office: Olympic Nat Park 600 E Park Ave Port Angeles WA 98362-6798

SMOLENSKY, EUGENE, economics educator; b. Bklyn., Mar. 4, 1932; s. Abraham and Jennie (Miller) S.; m. Natalie Joan Rabinowitz, Aug. 16, 1952; children: Paul, Beth. B.A., Bklyn. Coll., 1952; M.A., Am. U., 1956; Ph.D., U. Pa., 1961. Prof. econs. U. Wis., Madison, 1968-88, chmn. dept., 1978-80, 86-88; dir. Inst. for Research on Poverty, U. Wis., 1980-83; dean Grad. Sch. Pub. Policy, U. Calif., Berkeley, 1988-97, prof. pub. policy, 1997—. Author: Public Expenditures, Taxation and the Distribution of Income: The U.S., 1950, 61, 70, 77. Mem. Nat. Acad. Pub. Adminstrn., 1994; mem. com. on child devel. rsch. and pub. policy NAS, Washington, 1982-87, mem. com. on status of women in labor market, 1985-87. With USN, 1952-56. Mem. Am. Econs. Assn. Democrat. Jewish. Avocation: collecting old master etchings and lithographs. E-mial. Home: 669 Woodmont Ave Berkeley CA 94708-1233 Office: U Calif Dept Pub Policy 2607 Hearst Ave Berkeley CA 94720-7305 E-mail: geno@socrates.berkeley.edu

SMOLINSKI, BRYAN, professional hockey player; b. Toledo, Dec. 27, 1971; m. Julie Smolinski, July 12. B. Broadcasting, Mich. State U. Center Boston Bruins, 1992-96, Pitts. Hockey Team, 1996, New York Islanders, 1996-98, Los Angeles Kings, 1998—. Center U.S. Nat. Jr. Team, 1990 World Jr. Championships; mem. U.S. Team which won gold medal World Cup of Hockey, 1995-96. Named 1992-93 Spartans' MVP and Outstanding Offensive Player Office: Los Angeles KIngs 3900 W Manchester Blvd Inglewood CA 90305

SMOOT, GEORGE FITZGERALD, III, astrophysicist; b. Yukon, Fla., Feb. 20, 1945; BS in math., BS in physics, MIT, 1966, Ph.D. in physics, 1970. Rsch. physicist MIT, 1970; rsch. physicist Univ. Calif., Berkeley, Calif., 1971—, prof. physics, 1994—; rsch. physicist Lawrence Berkeley Lab., 1974—. Team leader, differential microwave radiometer experiment, COBE (Cosmic Background Explorer) satellite. Author: (with Keay Davidson) Wrinkles in Time, 1993. Recipient Space/Missiles Laurels award Aviation Week & Space Technology, 1992, Lawrence award US Dept of Energy, 1994. Mem. Internat. Astron. Union, Am. Phys. Soc., Am. Astron. Soc., Sigma Xi. Office: 366 Conte Hl # 7300 Berkeley CA 94720-0001

SMOOT, LEON DOUGLAS, chemical engineering educator, former dean; b. Provo, Utah, July 26, 1934; s. Douglas Parley and Jennie (Hallam) S.; m. Marian Bird, Sept. 7, 1953; children: Analee, LaCinda, Michelle, Melinda Lee. BS, Brigham Young U., 1956, B in Engring. Sci., 1957; MS, U. Wash., 1958, PhD, 1960. Registered profl. engr., Utah. Engr. Boeing Corp., Seattle, 1956; teaching and research asst. Brigham Young U., 1954-57; engr. Phillips Petroleum Corp., Arco, Idaho, 1957; engr., cons. Hercules Powder Co., Bacchus, Utah, 1961-63; asst. prof. Brigham Young U., 1960-63; engr. Lockheed Propulsion, Redlands, Calif., 1963-67; vis. asst. prof. Calif. Inst. Tech., 1966-67; assoc. prof. to prof. Brigham Young U., 1967, chmn. dept. chem. engring., 1970-77, dean Coll. Engring. and Tech., 1977-94, dean emeritus, 1994—. Expert witness on combustion and explosions; founding dir. Advanced Combustion Engring. Research Ctr. (NSF), 1986-97; cons. Hercules, Thiokol, Lockheed, Teledyne, Atlantic Research Corp., Raytheon, Redd and Redd, Billings Energy, Ford, Bacon & Davis, Jaycor, Intel Com Radiation Tech., Phys. Dynamics, Nat. Soc. Propellants and Explosives, France, DFVLR, West Germany, Martin Marietta, Honeywell, Phillips Petroleum Co., Exxon, Nat. Bur. Standards, Eyring Research Inst., Systems, Sci. and Software., Los Alamos Nat. Lab., others. Author 5 books on coal combustion; contbr. over 200 articles and tech. jours. Mem. AIChE, Nat. Fire Protection Assn., Am. Soc. Engring. Edn., Combustion Inst., Rsch. Soc. Am., Sigma Xi, Tau Beta Pi, Phi Lambda Epsilon. Republican. Mem. LDS Ch. Office: Brigham Young U Chem Engring Dept 435 T CTB Provo UT 84602

SMOTHERS, TOM, actor, singer; b. Feb. 2, 1937; s. Thomas B. and Ruth Smothers; children: Tom, Bo, Riley Rose; m. Marcy Carriker, Sept. 9, 1990. Student, San Jose State Coll. Owner winery, Kenwood, Calif. Nightclub appearances in Reno, Lake Tahoe, Las Vegas, Nev., and various venues in the U.S.; co-star TV situation comedy Smothers Brothers Show, 1965-66, Smothers Brothers Comedy Hour, CBS-TV, 1967-69, 70, weekly variety show The Smothers Brothers Show, NBC-TV, 1975; starred in films The Silver Bears, Get To Know Your Rabbit, A Pleasure Doing Business, Serial, There Goes the Bride, Pandemonium, Speed Zone; starred on Broadway in I Love My Wife, 1978-79; appeared in TV movie Terror at Alcatraz, 1982; starred in Smothers Brothers Spl. and Series, 1988-89. Office: Knave Prodns Ste 107B 6442 Coldwater Canyon Ave North Hollywood CA 91606-1137 E-mail: SMOBRO1@AOL.COM

SMULYAN, JEFFREY, radio station executive, owner pro baseball team; children: Cari, Bradley. AB in History and Telecommunications, U. So. Calif., 1969, JD, 1972. Prin., owner, chmn. Seattle Mariners; chmn. bd. Emmis Broadcasting Corp., Indpls. Recipient Tree of Life award Jewish Nat. Fund; named Entrepreneur of Yr. Indpls. Bus. Jour., 1986. Mem. ABA, Ind. Bar Assn., Fed. Bar Assn., Communications Bar Assn. Office: Seattle Mariners PO Box 4100 Seattle WA 98104-0100

SMYSER, ADAM ALBERT, newspaper editor; b. York, Pa., Dec. 18, 1920; s. Adam Milton and Miriam (Stein) S.; m. Elizabeth Harrison Avery, Dec. 25, 1943 (dec. 1983); children: Heidi, Avery; m. Doris H. Prather, Apr. 24, 1984 B.A., Pa. State U., 1941. Rewrite man Pitts. Press, 1941-42; with Honolulu Star-Bull., 1946—, city editor, 1953-60, mng. editor, 1960-65, editor, 1966-75, editor editorial page, 1975-83, contbg. editor, 1983—. Mem. Pulitzer Journalism Awards Jury, 1970 Author: Hawaii's Future in the Pacific: Disaster, Backwater or Future State?, 1988, Hawaii as an East-West Bridge, 1990; past freelance writer McGraw-Hill mags. Chmn. temp. commn. on statewide environ. planning, 1973; bd. dirs. Corp. for Community TV; chmn. steering com. Gov.'s Congress on Hawaii's Internat. Role, 1988; mem. community adv. bd. Tokai U. Pacific Ctr.; mem. Gov.'s Blue Ribbon Panel on Living and Dying With Dignity, 1997-98. Lt. USNR, 1942-46, PTO. Recipient Disting. Alumnus award Pa. State U., 1976, Hawaii's Outstanding Journalist award, 1989, Award for Disting. Contbn. to Hawaii Journalism Honolulu Cmty.-Medic Coun., 1994, award for promotion of U.S.-Asia/Pacific rels. Pacific and Asian Affairs Coun., 1994, honoree Nat. Soc. Arts and Letters, Hawaii chpt., 1998. Mem. Hawaii Econ. Assn., Honolulu Social Sci. Assn., Honolulu Acad. Arts, Am. Soc. Newspaper Editors, Japan-Am. Soc. Hawaii, Honolulu Cmty.-Media Coun., Honolulu Press Club (named to Hall of Fame 1987), Honolulu Rotary. Home: 1052 Iiwi St Honolulu HI 96816-5111 Office: Honolulu Star Bulletin 605 Kapiolani Blvd Honolulu HI 96813-5129

SMYTH, CORNELIUS EDMONSTON, retired hotel executive; b. N.Y.C., Aug. 20, 1926; s. Cornelius Joseph and Roberta Ernestine (Anderson) S.; m. Jeanne Laura Dillingham, Nov. 25, 1950 (dec. Oct. 1996); m. Jeanette M. Hubbard, Apr. 18, 1998; children: Cornelius E. Jr., Loretta M., William D., James B., Laura I., Robert B. BS in Econs., U. Pa., Phila., 1946. Cert. Hospitality Acct. Exec. Contr. Caesars Palace Hotel and Casino, Las Vegas, Nev., 1970-73, fin. v.p., 1974, adminstrv. v.p., 1975-77, exec. v.p., 1977-81; pres. Sands Hotel and Casino, Las Vegas, 1981-83; exec. v.p. Latin Am. ops. Caesars World Internat., L.A., 1983-89, pres. Mexican ops., 1989-90; bd. dirs. Venture Catalyst, Inc., San Diego, 1994—. Cons., Coronado, Calif., 1994-2001. Co-author: A Uniform System of Accounts for Hotels, 7th rev. edit., 1977. Comdr. USNR, 1944-70. Named to U.S. Table Tennis Hall of Fame, 1996. Mem. Pi Gamma Mu, Sigma Chi. Republican. Roman Catholic. Avocations: table tennis, body surfing.

SNEED, JOSEPH DONALD, philosophy educator, writer; b. Durant, Okla., Sept. 23, 1938; s. Dabney Whitfield and Sallybelle (Atkinson) S. B.S., Rice U., 1960; M.S., U Ill., 1962; Ph.D., Stanford U., 1964. Prof. Stanford U., Palo Alto, Calif., 1966-73; policy analyst SRI Internat., Menlo Park, 1973-74; prof. U. Munich, 1974-75, U. Eindhoven, Holland, 1976-77, SUNY, Albany, 1977-79; prof. philosophy Colo. Sch. Mines, Golden, 1980—. Author: The Logical Structure of Mathematical Physics, 1971, (with W. Balzer and C. Moulines) An Architectonic for Science, 1987; editor: (with S. Waldhorn) Restructuring the Federal System, 1974. Mem. Am. Philos. Assn. Office: Colo Sch Mines Golden CO 80401 E-mail: jsneed@mines.edu

SNEED, JOSEPH TYREE, III, federal judge; b. Calvert, Tex., July 21, 1920; s. Harold Marvin and Cara (Weber) S.; m. Madelon Juergens, Mar. 15, 1944 (dec. Dec. 1998); children— Clara Hall, Cara Carleton, Joseph Tyree IV. BBA, Southwestern U., 1941; LLB, U. Tex., Austin, 1947; SJD, Harvard, 1958. Bar: Tex. bar 1948. Instr. bus. law U. Tex., Austin, 1947, asst. prof. law, 1947-51, asso. prof., 1951-54, prof., 1954-57, asst. dean, 1949-50; counsel Graves, Dougherty & Greenhill, Austin, 1954-56; prof. law Cornell U., 1957-62, Stanford Law Sch., 1962-71; dean Duke Law Sch., 1971-73; dep. atty. gen. U.S. justice dept., 1973; judge U.S. Ct. Appeals (9th cir.), San Francisco, 1973—, now sr. judge. Cons. estate and gift tax project Am. Law Inst., 1960-69 Author: The Configurations of Gross Income, 1967, Footprints on the Rocks of the Mountain, 1997; contbr. articles to profl. jours. Served with USAAF, 1942-46. Mem. ABA, State Bar Tex., Am. Law Inst., Order of Coif. Office: US Ct Appeals PO Box 193939 San Francisco CA 94119-3939

SNELL, PATRICIA POLDERVAART, librarian, consultant; b. Santa Fe, Apr. 11, 1943; d. Arie and Edna Beryl (Kerchmar) Poldervaart; m. Charles Eliot Snell, June 7, 1966. BA in Edn., U. N.M., 1965; MSLS, U. So. Calif., 1966. Asst. edn. libr. U. So. Calif., L.A., 1966-68; med. libr. Bedford (Mass.) VA Hosp., 1968-69; asst. law libr. U. Miami, Coral Gables, Fla., 1970-71; acquistions libr. U. N.Mex. Law Sch. Libr., Albuquerque, 1971-72; order libr. Los Angeles County Law Libr., 1972-76, cataloger, 1976-90; libr. Parks Coll., Albuquerque, 1990-92; records technician Technadyne Engring. Cons. to Sandia Nat. Labs., 1992-93; libr. Tireman Learning Materials Ctr. U. N.Mex., Albuquerque, 1993-96, instr. libr. sci. program Coll. Edn., 1991—; rsch. technician City of Albuquerque, 1996—. Ch. libr.. Beverly Hills Presbyn. Ch., 1974-90, ch. choir libr., 1976-90. Southwestern Library Assn. scholar 1965. Mem. ALA, N.Mex. Libr. Assn., Pi Lambda Theta. Avocations: travel, reading. Office: U N Mex Coll Edn EM/LS Program Albuquerque NM 87131-0001 E-mail: psnell@unm.edu

SNELL, RICHARD, holding company executive; b. Phoenix, Nov. 26, 1930; s. Frank L. and Elizabeth (Berlin) S.; m. Alice Cosette Wiley, Aug. 1, 1954. BA, Stanford U., 1952, JD, 1954. Bar: Ariz. Ptnr. firm Snell & Wilmer, Phoenix, 1956-81; pres., chmn., chief exec. officer Ramada Inc., Phoenix, 1981-89; chmn., chief exec. officer Aztar Corp., 1989-90, chmn., bd. dirs., 1990-92; chmn. bd. dirs. Pinnacle West Capital Corp., Phoenix, 1990—; chmn. Ariz. Pub. Svc., 1990—; bd. dirs. Pinnacle West Capital Corp., Phoenix. Adv. bd. Bank One Ariz. NA; bd. dirs. Aztar Corp., Ctrl. Newspapers Inc.; bd. dirs., chmn. Ariz. Pub. Svc. Co. Trustee Am. Grad. Sch. Internat. Mgmt., Phoenix; past pres. YMCA Met. Phoenix and Valley of Sun. With U.S. Army, 1954-56. Mem. ABA, Ariz. Bar Assn., Paradise Valley Country Club, Phoenix Country Club. Republican. Lutheran. Office: Pinnacle West Capital Corp 400 E Van Buren St Phoenix AZ 85004-2223 also: Pinnacle West PO Box 52132 Phoenix AZ 85072-2132

SNIDER, ROBERT F. chemistry educator, researcher; b. Calgary, Alta., Can., Nov. 22, 1931; s. Edward C. and Agnes S. (Klaeson) S.; children: Wendy A., Timothy J., Terry E., Geoffrey Y, Eric A. M. Burrough. B.S., U. Alta., 1953; Ph.D., U. Wis., 1958. Postdoctoral fellow Nat. Research Council Can., Ottawa, 1958; instr. II U. B.C., Vancouver, 1958-60, asst. prof., 1960-65, assoc. prof., 1965-69, prof., 1969-96, prof. emeritus, 1997—; vis. research prof. U. Leiden, Netherlands, 1973-74. Recipient gov. gen. gold medal U. Alta., 1953; U. Wis. WARF unassigned fellow, 1953-55; Izaac Walton Killam Meml. fellowship, 1985-86. Fellow Chem. Inst. Can., Royal Soc. Can.; mem. Am. Phys. Soc., Can. Assn. Physicists Home: 3952 W 29th St Vancouver BC Canada V6S 1T9 Office: U BC 2036 Main Mall Vancouver BC Canada V6T 1Z1 E-mail: snider@chem.ubc.ca

SNIDER, STACEY, film company executive; Exec. v.p. Guber-Peters Entertainment Co.; pres. prodn. TriStar Pictures, 1992-96; co-pres. prodn. Universal Pictures, Universal City, Calif., 1996-98, head prodn., 1998, pres., 1998—, chmn., CEO, 1999—. Office: Universal Pictures 100 Universal City Plz Universal Cty CA 91608-1002

SNODGRASS, LYNN, small business owner, state legislator; married; children: Jenne, Megan. BS in Elem. Edn., Oreg. State U., 1973; degree, Portland State U., 1975. Owner Drake's 7 Dees Nursery & Landscape Co., Oreg.; mem. Oreg. Ho. of Reps., 1995—; dep. majority leader, 1995-97; majority leader, 1997—; speaker of the house Oregon House of Reps, Salem, 1998. Mem. Damascus (Oreg.) Sch. Dist. Budget Com., 1985-88, Damascus Sch. Bd., 1991-94; mem. Oreg. Ho. of Reps. Human Resources and Edn. Com. (Edn. sub-com.), 1995-97, Labor Com., 1995-97, Commerce Com. (Bus. sub-com.), 1995-97, Children and Families Com., 1995-97, Emergency Bd. Com. (Edn. sub-com.), 1995-97, Interim Edn. Com., 1995-97, Legis. Adminstrn. Com., 1995—, Rules and Election Com., 1997—. Mem., past pres. Mt. Hood Med. Ctr. Found.; bd. dirs. Specialized Housing, Inc., Metro Home Builder; mem. Good Shepherd Cmty. Ch.; tchr. Jr. Achievement; classroom vol. Avocations: racquetball, reading, singing, camping, cooking. Office: Oreg Ho of Dels 269 State Capitol Salem OR 97310-0001 Fax: 503-986-1347

SNOOK, QUINTON, construction company executive; b. Atlanta, July 15, 1925; s. John Wilson and Charlotte Louise (Clayson) S.; m. Louis Mullen, Jan. 19, 1947; children: Louis Ann Snook Matteson, Quinton A., Edward M., Clayson S., Charlotte T. Student, U. Idaho, 1949-51. Rancher, Lemhi Valley, Idaho, 1942—; owner, mgr. Snook Constrn., Salmon, 1952—; owner Snook Trucking, Salmon, 1967—, Lemhi Posts and Poles, Salmon, 1980—. Construction company executive; b. Atlanta, July 15, 1925; s. John Wilson and Charlotte Louise (Clayson) S.; student U. Idaho, 1949-51; m. Lois Mullen, Jan. 19, 1947; children: Lois Ann Snook Matteson, Quinton A., Edward M., Clayson S., Charlotte T. Rancher, Lemhi Valley, Idaho, 1942—; owner, mgr. Snook Constrn., Salmon, Idaho, 1952—; owner Snook Trucking, 1967—, Lemhi Posts and Poles, 1980—. Mem. Lemhi County Commn., Dist. 2, 1980-93. Named to Idaho Agrl. Hall of Fame, 1996. Mem. Am. Quarter Horse Assn., Farm Bur., Nat. Rifleman's Assn., Idaho Assn. Commrs. and Clerks (sec. 1986, v.p. 1987, pres. 1988), Am. Hereford Assn., Idaho Cattlemen's Assn., Elks. Republican. Episcopalian. Active Lemhi County Commn., Dist. 2, 1980-93. Named to Idaho Agrl. Hall of Fame, 1996. Mem. Am. Quarter Horse Assn., Farm Bur., Nat. Riflemans Assn., Idaho Assn. Commrs. and Clerks (sec. 1986, v.p. 1987, pres. 1988), Am. Hereford Assn., Idaho Cattlemens Assn., Elks. Republican. Episcopalian. Home: RR 1 Box 49 Salmon ID 83467-9701

SNOW, MARLON O. trucking executive, state agency administrator; m. Ann; children. Gen. mgr. spl. commadities Milne Truck Lines, Phoenix, L.A., 1970-81; gen. mgr. spl. commodities, sales Motor Cargo, Salt Lake City, 1981-82; owner MST Trucking, Inc., Salt Lake City, 1982—. V.p. Utah Motor Carriers for State of Utah, 1997-98. Mem. State Bd. Edn., 1994-97, chair, 1995-97; trustee Utah Valley State Coll., 1998; mem. Ho. of Reps., Utah, 1999—; bd. regents Bd. Higher Edn. State of Utah, 2001—. Mem. Utah Valley State Coll. Found. (bd. dirs. 1991—), Alpine Sch. Dist. Found. (bd. dirs. 1990—). Office: 1247 E 430 N Orem UT 84097-5400

SNOW, THEODORE PECK, astrophysics educator; b. Seattle, Jan. 30, 1947; s. Theodore P. and Louise (Wertz) S.; s. Constance M. Snow, Aug. 23, 1969); children: McGregor A., Tyler M., Reilly A. BA, Yale U., 1969; MS, U. Wash., 1970, PhD, 1973. Mem. rsch. staff Princeton (N.J.) U., 1973-77; prof. U. Colo., Boulder, 1977—, dir. Ctr. for Astrophysics and Space Astronomy, 1986-96, dir. Fiske Planetarium, 2000—. Mem. instrument devel. teams for far Ultraviolet Spectroscopic Explorer, 1999—, Cosmic Origins Spectrograph to be installed in Hubble Space Telescope. Author: (textbook) The Dynamic Universe, 1983, 4th edit., 1991, Essentials of the Dynamic Universe 4th edit., 1993 (textbook excellence award Text and Academic Authors Assn. 1994), Physics, 1986, Universe: Origins and Evolution, 1997; contbr. over 200 articles to profl. jours. Fellow Royal Astron. Soc.; mem. Am. Astron. Soc., Astron. Soc. Pacific, Sigma Xi. Achievements include discovery, through observations in ultraviolet visible, and infrared wavelengths, and through laboratory measurement of chemical reactions, of several important processes involving interstellar gas and dust, and their roles in star formation and late stages of stellar evolution. Office: U Colo Ctr Astrophysics Space Astronomy Campus Box 389 Boulder CO 80309-0389 E-mail: tsnow@casa.colorado.edu

SNOW, TOWER CHARLES, JR. lawyer; b. Boston, Oct. 28, 1947; s. Tower Charles and Margaret (Harper) S.; m. Belinda L. Snow. AB cum laude English, Dartmouth Coll., 1969; JD, U. Calif., Berkeley, 1973. Bar: Calif. 1973, U.S. Dist. Ct. (no. dist.) Calif. 1973, U.S. Ct. Appeals (9th cir.) 1973, U.S. Supreme Ct. 1976, U.S. Dist. Ct. (ea. dist.) Calif. 1979, U.S. Ct. Appeals (fed. cir.) 1980, U.S. Ct. Claims 1980, U.S. Ct. Appeals (2d cir.) 1987, N.Y. 1988, U.S. Dist. Ct. (ea. and so. dists.) N.Y. 1988, U.S. Dist. Ct. (ctrl. dist.) Calif. 1989, U.S. Dist. Ct. (no. dist.) Tex. 1995, U.S. Dist. Ct. (so. dist.) Calif. 1996, U.S. Dist. Ct. Ariz. 1996. Ptnr., chmn. litigation dept. Orrick, Herrington & Sutcliffe, San Francisco, 1973-89; ptnr. Shearman & Sterling, San Francisco, 1989-94; ptnr., chmn. securities litigation group, mem. policy com. Brobeck, Phleger & Harrison, LLP, San Francisco, 1995-97; chmn., CEO Brobeck Phleger & Harrison, San Francisco, 1998—. Arbitrator Nat. Assn. Securities Dealers, Am. Stock Exch., N.Y. Stock Exch., Pacific Coast Stock Exch., Superior Ct. City and County San Francisco, Am. Arbitration Assn.; lectr. in field. Author numerous law handbooks and articles to prof. jours. Mem. San Francisco Mus. Soc., San Francisco Symphony, San Francisco Ballet, San Francisco Opera, Am. Conservatory Theatre. Named one of 100 Most Influential Lawyers in Am., Nat. Law Jour., 2000, one of 100 Most Influential Lawyers in Calif., Calif. Law and Bus., 2000. Mem. ABA (chmn. subcom. pub. offering litig. 1984-88, co-chair task force on securities arbitration 1988-89, vice chair securities litig. com. 1986-88), Continuing Edn. Bar (bus. law inst. planning com. 1986), Securities Industry Assn., Nat. Inst. Trial Advocacy, San Francisco Bar Assn. (pres. securities litig. sect. 1995). Democrat. Avocations: internat. travel, skiing, running, scuba diving, photography. Home: 177 Ridge Dr Napa CA 94558-9777 Office: Brobeck Phleger & Harrison LLP Spear St Tower One Market St San Francisco CA 94105 E-mail: tswow@brobeck.com

SNOWDEN, DAVID L. protective services official; BA, Calif. State U., Fullerton. Chief of police, Costa Mesa, Calif. Recipient Am.'s Star award U.S. Marshal's Office. Mem. Calif. Police Chiefs Assn. (past pres.), Orange County Chiefs and Sheriffs Assn., L.A. County Chiefs Assn. Office: 99 Fair Dr Costa Mesa CA 92626-6520

SNYDER, ALAN CARHART, financial services executive; b. N.Y.C., May 25, 1946; s. John I. and Elfrida (Bendix) S.; m. Mary Burgoyne, Feb. 9, 1974. BS, BA, Georgetown U., 1968; MBA, Harvard U., 1973. Cons. Reynolds Securities, N.Y.C., 1972-73; exec. v.p. Dean Witter Reynolds, N.Y.C., 1975-85; sole proprietor Shinnecock Ptnrs., N.Y.C., 1985-89, mng. ptnr., 1989—; pres., chief oper. officer, bd. dirs. First Exec. Corp., L.A., 1990-91; COO, Exec. Life Ins. Co., L.A., 1991-93; CEO, Aurora Nat. Life Assurance Co., LA, 1993-94, cons. L.A., 1994-95; mng. ptnr. Shinnecock Group L.L.C., L.A., 1994—; chmn., CEO, pres. Answer Fin. Inc., L.A., 1997—. Baker scholar Harvard Bus. Sch., 1973.

SNYDER, ALLEGRA FULLER, dance educator; b. Chgo., Aug. 28, 1927; d. R. Buckminster and Anne (Hewlett) Fuller; m. Robert Snyder, June 30, 1951 (div. Apr. 1975, remarried Sept. 1980); children: Alexandra, Jaime. BA in Dance, Bennington Coll., 1951; MA in Dance, UCLA, 1967. Asst. to curator, dance archives Mus. Modern Art, N.Y.C., 1945-47; dancer Ballet Soc. of N.Y.C. Ballet Co., 1945-47; mem. office and prodn. staff Internat. Film Found., N.Y.C., 1950-52; editor, dance films Film News mag., N.Y.C., 1966-72; lectr. dance and film adv., dept. dance UCLA, 1967-73, chmn. dept. dance, 1974-80, 90-91, acting chair, spring 1985, chair of faculty Sch. of the Arts, 1989-91, prof. dance and dance ethnology, 1973-91, prof. emeritus, 1991—; pres. Buckminster Fuller Inst., Santa Barbara, Calif., chairwoman bd. dirs., 1984—. Vis. lectr. Calif. Inst. Arts, Valencia, 1972; co-dir. dance and TV workshop Am. Dance Festival, Conn. Coll., New London, 1973; dir. NEH summer seminar for coll. tchrs. Asian Performing Arts, 1978, 81; coord. Ethnic Arts Intercoll. Interdisciplinary Program, 1974-73, acting chmn., 1986; vis. prof. performance studies NYU, 1982-83; hon. vis. prof. U. Surrey, Guildford, Eng., 1983-84; cons. Thyodia Found., Salt Lake City, 1973-74; mem. dance adv. panel Nat. Endowment Arts, 1968-72, Calif. Arts Commn., 1974-91; mem. adv. screening com. Coun. Internat. Exch. of Scholars, 1979-82; mem. various panels NEH, 1979-85; core cons. for Dancing, Sta. WNET-TV, 1988—. Dir. film Baroque Dance 1625-1725, in 1977; co-dir. film Gods of Bali, 1952; dir. and wrote film Bayanihan, 1962 (named Best Folkloric Documentary at Bilboa Film Festival, winner Golden Eagle award); asst. dir. and asst. editor film The Bennington Story, 1952; created films Gestures of Sand, 1968, Reflections on Choreography, 1973, When the Fire Dances Between Two Poles, 1982; created film, video loop and text Celebration: A World of Art and Ritual, 1982-83; supr. post-prodn. film Erick Hawkins, 1964, in 1973. Also contbr. articles to profl. jours. and mags. Adv. com. Pacific Asia Mus., 1980-84, Festival of the Mask, Craft and Folk Art Mus., 1979-84; adv. panel Los Angeles Dance Currents II, Mus. Ctr. Dance Assn., 1974-75; bd. dirs. Council Grove Sch. III, Compton, Calif., 1976-81; apptd. mem. Adv. Dance Com., Pasadena (Calif.) Art Mus., 1970-71, Los Angeles Festival of Performing Arts com., Studio Watts, 1970; mem. Technology and Cultural Transformation com., UNESCO, 1977. Fulbright research fellow, 1983-84; grantee Nat. Endowment Arts, 1981, Nat. Endowment Humanities, 1977, 79, 81, UCLA, 1968, 77, 80, 82, 85; recipient Amer. Dance Guild Award for Outstanding Achievement in Dance, 1992. Mem. Am. Dance Therapy Assn., Congress on Rsch. in Dance (bd. dirs. 1970-76, chmn. 1975-77, nat. conf. chmn. 1972), Coun. Dance Adminstrs., Am. Dance Guild (chmn. com. awards 1972), Soc. for Ethnomusicology, Am. Anthrop. Assn., Am. Folklore Soc., Soc. Anthropology of Visual Comm., Soc. Humanistic Anthropology, Calif. Dance Educators Assn. (conf. chmn. 1972), L.A. Area Dance Alliance (adv. bd. 1978-84, selection com. Dance Kaleidoscope project 1979-81), Fulbright Alumni Assn. Home: 15313 Whitfield Ave Pacific Palisades CA 90272-2548 Office: Buckminster Fuller Inst 111 N Main St Sebastopol CA 95472-3448

SNYDER, DANIEL J. career officer; BA in Health Svcs. Adminstrn., So. Ill. U.; MA in Health Svcs. Adminstrn., Webster U.; MA in Nat. Resource Strategy, Nat. Def. U. Diplomate Am. Bd. Healthcare Mgmt. Enlisted USN, 1975, advanced through grades to capt.; dir. hosp. adminstrn. Naval Hosp., Rota, Spain; mem. staff Office Navy Surgeon Gen., Washington, Office Chief Naval Ops., Washington, dir. Navy med. readiness reengineering task force; commdg. officer Naval Hosp., Bremerton, Wash. Decorated Legion of Merit; recipient Fed. Health Care award Am. Hosp. Assn. Fellow Am. Coll. Health Execs. (mem. bd. govs. dist. 8, regent 1993-96). Office: Exec Officer Naval Hosp Commdg Ofc Fleet Hosp 5 HP01 Boone Rd Bremerton WA 98312-1898 E-mail: snyderd@pnw.med.navy.mil

SNYDER, DAVID L. film production designer; b. Buffalo, Sept. 22, 1944; s. Albert R. and Louise M. (Passero) S.; m. Terry Finn, Aug. 1, 1990; children: David Michael, Amy Lynne, Finn Henry. Grad. high sch., Niagara Falls, N.Y. Ind. film prodn. designer, Hollywood, Calif.; pres. Snyder Bros. Prodns., Inc., Hollywood. Guest speaker Tokyo Internat. Film Festival, 1985. Art dir. (films) In God We Trust, 1980, The Idolmaker, 1980, Blade Runner, 1982 (Academy award nomination best art direction 1982), Brainstorm, 1983; prodn. designer (films) Strange Brew, 1983, Racing With the Moon, 1984, The Woman In Red, 1984, My Science Project, 1985, Armed and Dangerous, 1986, Back to School, 1986, Summer School, 1987, Moving, 1988, She's Out of Control, 1989, Bill & Ted's Bogus Journey, 1991, Class Act, 1992, Super Mario Brothers, 1993, Demolition Man, 1993, Terminal Velocity, 1994, Rainbow, 1995, Vegas Vacation, 1997, Burn, Hollywood, Burn, 1997, Soldier, 1998, The Whole Nine Yards, 1999; assoc. prodr.: (film) Cold Dog Soup, 1990; exec. prodr. (film) Rainbow, 1995. Mem. NATAS, Motion Picture Art Dirs. Guild, Acad. Motion Picture Arts and Scis., Dirs. Guild Am. Democrat. Avocation: researching history of the film industry in America. Address: 3500 W Olive Ave Ste 1470 Burbank CA 91505-5514

SNYDER, DAVID RICHARD, lawyer; b. Kalamazoo, Oct. 9, 1949; s. Richard E. and Margaret L. (Vanderplough) S.; m. Phyllis Alford, Aug. 14, 1971; children: Jason Richard, Carrie Lynn. BA with high honors, Mich. State U., 1971; JD with distinction, Cornell U., 1974. Bar: Calif. 1974. Assoc. Jenkins & Perry, San Diego, 1974-77, ptnr., 1978-83, Aylward, Kintz & Stiska, San Diego, 1983-86, Luce, Forward, Hamilton & Scripps, San Diego, 1986-93, Pillsbury Madison & Sutro LLP, San Diego, 1993—; mng. bd. Pillsbury Winthrop LLP, San Diego, 1999—. V.p., dir. San Diego Venture Group, 1989-91; adj. prof. Calif. Western Sch. Law, San Diego, 1982-84; lectr. Calif. Continuing Edn. of Bar, 1983—. Co-author: Drafting Legal Instruments, 1982; editor Cornell Law Rev., 1973-74. Bd. dirs. Boys Club Chula Vista, Calif., 1979-83; pres. Corpus Christi Parish Coun., Bonita, Calif., 1988-90; trustee Children's Hosp. Found., San Diego, 1988—, chmn., 1990-92. Mem. ABA (fed. securities law com. 1987—, vice chmn. subcom. on ann. rev. fed. securities regulation, dir. corp. dirs. forum), State Bar Calif., San Diego County Bar Assn., Am. Electronics Assn. (bd. dirs., mem. exec. com. San Diego chpt. 1991-93), Corp. Dirs. Forum (bd. dirs. 2001—), Order of Coif, Phi Beta Kappa. Republican. Roman Catholic. Office: Pillsbury Winthrop 101 W Broadway Ste 1800 San Diego CA 92101-8298

SNYDER, ESTHER, food service executive; m. Harry (dec.); children: Guy, Rich. Founder, pres. In-N-Out Burger, Baldwin Park, Calif., 1948—. Office: In-N-Out Burger 13502 Hamburger Ln Baldwin Park CA 91706-5885

SNYDER, FRANCINE, psychotherapist, registered nurse, writer; b. Balt., Mar. 13, 1947; d. Jack and Naomi (Rapoport) S. AA, C.C. Balt., 1968; BA in Psychology, Antioch Coll. W, 1973; MA in MFCC, Azusa Pacific Coll., 1975; PhD in Clin. and Ednl. Psychology, Internat. Coll., 1981. RN, Hawaii; lic. marriage, family, and child counselor diplomate in psychotherapy counselor, Calif.; instr., Calif.; counselor, Calif.; credentialed cmty. coll. counselor, Calif., cmty. coll. instr. health, phys. care svcs., related techs., nursing and psychology; doctoral addictions counselor, cert. addiction specialist, cognitive behavioral therapist; endorsed domestic violence counselor 1, 2 & 3 Nat. Bd. Cognitive Behavioral Therapists. Staff and relief nurse Midway Hosp., L.A., 1972-77; counselor So. Calif. Counseling Ctr., L.A., 1972-77; counselor, exec. bd. mem., steering com. mem. Healing Ctr. for the Whole Person, Northridge, Calif., 1974-75; counselor The Family Home, North Hollywood, 1976; pvt. practice Beverly Hills, 1975-86; asst. had nurse St. Johns Mental Health Ctr., Santa Monica, 1977-79; counselor Calif. Family Study Ctr., Burbank, 1979-80; pvt. practice Kauai, Hawaii, 1986—; clin. dir., therapist Kauai YWCA Sex Abuse Treatment Program, 1989-90; clin. cons. Iniki Ohana Project, Kapaa, 1993. Student nurse Johns Hopkins Hosp., Balt., 1965-68; head and relief nurse, team leader, 1966-70; nurse Nix Meml. Hosp., San Antonio, Tex., 1970; staff nurse, team leader Cmty. Hosp, Chandler, Ariz.; cons. Slim Bionics Med. Group, L.A., 1974-75; instr. Pierce Coll., Woodland Hills, Calif., 1977, Saint Johns Med. Ctr., Santa Monica, Calif., 1977-79, Maple Ctr., Beverly Hills, Calif., 1979-80. Speaker in field. Mem. Am. Anorexia Nervosa/Bulimia Assn., Inc., Am. Mental Affiliates for Israel (exec. bd., head of allocations com.), Am. Assn. Marriage and Family Therapists (clin.), Internat. Platform Assn., Calif. Assn. Marriage and Family Therapists (clin.), Assn. for Humanistic Psychology, Children's Coalition for TV, Ctr. for the Healing Arts, Alliance for Survival, UCLA Alumni Assn.; cons. Help Anorexia, Inc., Performance Design Syss. Office: InnerVisions Change Tech PO Box 1303 Hanalei HI 96714-1303

SNYDER, HELEN DIANE, state senator; Project/event mgr.; Rep. senator dist. 15 N.Mex. State Senate. Mem. corps. and transp., Indian and cultural affairs coms. N.Mex. State Senate. Home: 4012 Delamar Ave NE Albuquerque NM 87110 Office: NMex State Senate State Capitol Mail Rm Dept Santa Fe NM 87503 E-mail: senate@state.nm.us

SNYDER, HENRY LEONARD, history educator, bibliographer; b. Hayward, Calif., Nov. 3, 1929; s. Henry Runyon and Mary (Rosenberg) S.; m. Janette Marie Hannus, July 21, 1961; children: Michael Jesse, Christopher Henry, David Lyle. BA, U. Calif., Berkeley, 1951, MA, 1960, PhD, 1963. Sr. buyer Dohrmann Comml. Co., San Francisco, 1951-59; instr. to prof. U. Kans., Lawrence, 1963-78, assoc. dean to dean research adminstrn., 1967-78; prof. history, dean arts and scis. La. State U., Baton Rouge, 1979-86; prof. history U. Calif., Riverside, 1986—; dir. Ctr. for Bibliog. Studies, 1989—; dean humanities and social scis. U. Calif., Riverside, 1986; vis. lectr. Bedford Coll., U. London, 1965-66; Fulbright lectr., research scholar U. Hamburg, Fed. Republic Germany, 1974; dir. English Short Title Catalogue for N.Am., 1978—. Editor: The Marlborough Godolphin Correspondence, 1975; co-editor: The Scottish Heritage, 1981. Pres. Baton Rouge Opera, 1981-83, Riverside Opera, 1987-90; pres. United Way, Lawrence, 1977; bd. dirs. Arts and Humanities Com., Baton Rouge, 1981-85; Sigmund, Martin, Heller Traveling fellow U. Calif.-Berkeley, 1962-63. Am. Council Learned Soc. sr. fellow, 1969-70 Fellow Royal Hist.

Soc. Gt. Brit. Bibliog. Soc. London; mem. Am. Soc. 18th Century Studies (pres. 1980-81), Conf. Brit. Studies (exec. com. 1978-83), Am. Hist. Assn., Internat. Fed. Librs. (chair rarebooks and ms. sect. 1995—). Republican. Congregationalist. Home: 220 Trinity Ave Kensington CA 94708-1139 Office: U Calif Ctr For Bibliog Studies Riverside CA 92521-0001 E-mail: hlsnyder@earthlink.net

SNYDER, LESTER M. sports association executive; b. Red Lion, Pa. m. Audrene Snyder; children: Kim, Ky. Degree, Millersville State U.; doctorate, U. Mich. Past v.p., treas., presdl. appointee to exec. com., Pacific region v.p., sect. del., pres. southwest sect., chmn. and mem. various coms. U.S. Tennis Assn., Tempe, Ariz., pres., chmn. bd. dirs., 1995-97, past pres., 1997—. Prof. counseling psychology Ariz. State U., Tempe, 1967—; founding dir. Rio Salado Bank; pres. The Heuristic Syss., Inc.; past mem. com. mgmt. Internat. Tennis Fedn., Davis Cup and budget coms., del.; bd. dirs., exec. com. Internat. Tennis Hall of Fame; past Grand Slam com. rep. to Women's Tennis Fedn. Office: 1324 E Whalers Way Tempe AZ 85283-2148

SNYDER, PAUL, federal judge; BA, U. Wash.; JD, U. Puget Sound, 1975. Bar: Wash. Ptnr. Davies Pearson, 1980-90, McGavick Graves, 1990-96; bankruptcy judge for we. dist. Wash. Tacoma, 1996—. With USNR, 1966-74. Mem. ABA, Am. Bankruptcy Inst., Nat. Conf. Bankruptcy Judges. Office: US Ct Courtroom H 1717 Pacific Ave Rm 1425 Tacoma WA 98402-3230

SNYDER, SID, state legislator, retail executive; b. Kelso, Wash., July 30, 1926; m. Bette Kennedy, 1951; children: Sid Jr., Karen, Sally. Student, Lower Columbia C.C. Grocer, owner, operator Sid's Supermarket, Seaview, 1953—; mem. Wash. Senate, Dist. 19, Olympia, 1990—; dep. sec. senate Wash. Senate, Olympia, 1988, sec. senate, 1969-88, asst. chief clk., 1957-69; Dem. majority leader; mem. agr. and rural econ. devel. com.; mem. natural resources com.; mem. parks and recreation com.; mem. rules com.; mem. ways and means com.; mem. econ. and rev. forest coun.; mem. oral history adv. bd. Chmn. bd. dirs. Bank of the Pacific; ptnr. Westwind Manor Long Beach; bd. dirs. Columbia Bank. Hon. bd. dirs. Ilwaco Heritage Mus.; bd. dirs. Long Beach Peninsula Info. Ctr., Wash. State Hist. Soc., Columbia River Maritime Mus. With USAR, WWII. Democrat. Office: 311 Legislative Bldg Olympia WA 98504-0001

SOBELLE, RICHARD E. lawyer; b. Cleve., Mar. 18, 1935; BA, Stanford U., 1956, JD, 1960; LLM, U. So. Calif., 1967. Bar: Calif. 1961, U.S. Supreme Ct. 1969. Exec. Tracinda Corp. Mem. ABA (mem. corp., banking and bus. law sect. 1969—), State Bar Calif. (del. to conf. state bar dels. 1965-77, mem. exec. com. bus. law sect. 1977-78), L.A. County Bar Assn. (mem. exec. coun., jr. barristers 1965-68, mem. exec. com. bus. and corps. sect. 1973-75). Office: Tracinda Corp 150 S Rodeo Dr Ste 250 Beverly Hills CA 90212-2417

SOBEY, EDWIN J. C. museum director, oceanographer, consultant; b. Apr. 7, 1948; s. Edwin J. and Helen (Chapin) S.; m. Barbara Lee, May 9, 1970; children: Ted Wooddall, Andrew Chapin. BS, U. Richmond, 1969; MS, Oreg. State U., 1974, PhD, 1977. Rsch. scientist Sci. Applications, Inc., Boulder, Colo., 1977-79, divsn. mgr., 1979-81; exec. dir. Sci. Mus., West Palm Beach, Fla., 1981-88, Mus. Sci. and History, Jacksonville, 1988, Nat. Invention Ctr., Akron, Ohio, 1989-92, Fresno (Calif.) Met. Mus., 1993-95; ednl. cons., 1995—. Exec. dir. A.C. Gilbert's Discovery Village, Salem, Oreg., 1997-99; pres. Northwest Invention Ctr., 1999—; founder Nat. Toy Hall of Fame, 1998; instr. mus. mgmt. U. Wash., 1998—. Author: Complete Circuit Training Guide, 1980, Strength Training Book, 1981, (with others) Aerobic Weight Training Book, 1982, The Whole Backpacker's Catalog, 1988, Increasing Your Audience, 1989, Inventing Stuff, 1995, Wrapper Rockets and Trombone Straws-Science at Every Meal, 1996, Car Smarts, 1997, Just Plane Smart, 1998, Young Inventors at Work, 1999, How to Enter and Win an Invention Contest, 1999, Fantastic Flying Fun with Science, 2000, Wacky Water Fun with Science, 2000, Inventing Toys: Kids Having Fun Learning Science, 2001; mem. editl. adv. bd. Invent Mag., 1989-92; exec. prodr.: (TV show) Idea Factory, Sta. KFSN-30, Fresno, 1995-97; co-host: (ednl. TV show) Blow the Roof Off, 1992. Alumni v.p. Leadership Palm Beach County; expdn. leader Expdn. Tng. Inst., S.E. Alaska, 1980; mem. U.S. Antarctic Rsch. Program, 1974; founder, bd. dirs. Visually Impaired Sports Program, Boulder, 1978-81; fitness instr. YMCA Boulder, 1977-81; convener 1st Nat. Conf. Sports for the Blind, 1979; bd. dirs. Leadership Palm Beach; vice chmn. County Com. on Artificial Reefs; treas. Leadership Akron Alumni Assn., 1990-91, class pres. Leadership Akron; v.p. Ohio Mus. Assn., 1991-92, pres., 1992-93; bd. dirs. Fla. Mus. Assn., 1988-89; mem. adv. bd. Marine Sci. Inst., 1990—. Lt. USN, 1970-73. Fellow Explorers Club; mem. Marine Tech. Soc. (sect. chmn. 1982-84), Coral Reef Soc. (chpt. pres. 1982-87), Nat. Inventive Thinking Assn. (bd. dirs. 1989—). Home: 2420 178th Ave NE Redmond WA 98052-5820 E-mail: sobey@gte.net

SOBOLEWSKI, JOHN STEPHEN, computer scientist, consultant; b. Krakow, Poland, July 14, 1939; came to U.S., 1966; s. Jan Zygmund and Stefania (Zwolinska) S.; m. Helen Skipper, Dec. 17, 1965 (div. July 1969); m. Carole Straith, Apr. 6, 1974; children: Anne-Marie, Elisa, Martin. BE, U. Adelaide, Adelaide, South Australia, 1962, ME, 1966; PhD in Computer Sci., Wash. State U., 1971. Sci. officer Weapons Research Establishment, Salisbury, South Australia, 1964-66; asst. prof. computer sci. Wash. State U., Pullman, 1966-73; dir. research, assoc. prof. U. Wash., Seattle, 1973-80, dir. computer svcs., 1980-88; assoc. v.p. computing U. N.Mex., Albuquerque, 1988—. Cons. govt. and industry, Seattle, 1973—; mem. bd. trustees Fisher Found., Seattle, 1984—. Author: Computers for the Dental Office, 1986; contbr. articles to profl. jours. Served as engr. with Royal Australian Army, 1957-60. Australian govt. scholar, 1954-60, Elec. Res. Bd. scholar CSIRO, Melbourne, Australia, 1961-64. Mem. IEEE, Computer Soc. Roman Catholic. Avocation: mineral collecting. Home: 8501 Northridge Ave NE Albuquerque NM 87111-2107 Office: U NMex CIRT 2701 Campus Ave NE Albuquerque NM 87131-0001 E-mail: jssob@unm.edu

SOCHYNSKY, YAROSLAV, lawyer, mediator, arbitrator; b. Feb. 5, 1946; BA in English, Colgate U., 1967; JD, Georgetown U., 1970. Bar: Calif., N.Y. Assoc. White & Case, N.Y.C., 1970-71; law clerk to Hon. William T. Sweigert U.S. Dist. Ct. (no. dist.) Calif., 1971-73; assoc. Landels, Ripley & Diamond LLP, San Francisco, 1973-76; sr. ptnr. Landels, Ripley & Diamond, San Francisco, 1976-2000; mediator Am. Arbitration Assn., San Francisco, 2000—. Lectr. Calif. Continuing Edn. Bar, 1985, Equity Asset Mgr.'s Assn., 1987, Calif. Dept. Real Estate, 1986-89). Originator, co-author California ADR Practice Guide, 1992; co-author Real Property Practice and Litigation, 1990; case and notes editor, mem. editorial bd. Georgetown Law Jour.; contbr. articles and monographs to profl. jours. Fellow Chartered Inst. Arbitrators (London); mem. ABA (mem. exec. coun. sect. on real property, probate and trust, lectr. 1988, 89, 91), Am. Arbitration Assn. (cert. mediator, mem. pres.' panel of mediators, large and compley case panel, internat. panel, real property valuation panel, No. Calif. adv. coun., lectr. 1990, speaker various panels, No. Calif. Outstanding Mediator award 1991), San Francisco Bar Assn., San Francisco Lawyers Com. for Civil Rights under Law. Office: Am Arbitration Assn 225 Bush St Fl 18 San Francisco CA 94104-4211 E-mail: ys@landels.com

SODAL, INGVAR EDMUND, electrical engineer, scientist; b. Hemne, Norway, Feb. 12, 1934; came to U.S., 1962; s. Ingebrigt L. and Johanna (A.) Sodal; m. Sally Rollins; 1 child, Silje M. Degree in elec. engring., Trondheim Tech. Coll., Norway, 1959; BSEE, U. Colo., 1964. Engr. Fjeldseth Engring., Trondheim, 1959-61; rsch. engr. U. Norway, Trondheim, 1961-62, U. Colo. Med. Ctr., Denver, 1964-66, rsch. assoc., 1966-75, instr., lectr., 1975-79; vis. rsch. assoc. dept. engring. U. Colo., Boulder, 1974-75, lectr., 1975-76; asst. prof., div. head. Ohio State U., Columbus, 1979-82, mem. grad. faculty, 1982; pres., chief exec. officer Masstron, Inc., Boulder, Colo., 1983-87; chief scientist Paradygm, Boulder, 1987-89; pres. Pacemark, Inc., Boulder, 1989-90, Med. Physics Colo., Inc., 1991—. Contbr. articles to profl. jours., chpts. to books; holder 6 patents in field. Instr. and/or program coord. in Scandinavian folklore and folk dancing for numerous groups and instns. throughout U.S., Can., and Norway, 1959—. Grantee NIH and various pvt. orgns. Mem. Village Arts Coalition, Sons of Norway. Office: 1550 Moss Rock Pl Boulder CO 80304-1543 E-mail: sodaling@csd.net

SODEN, JOHN P. publishing executive; b. Yakima, Wash., Aug. 25, 1942; BA, U. Wash., 1964. Paperback buyer Univ. Bookstore, Seattle, 1964-66; libr. svcs. coord. Am. News Co., 1966-68; trade sales rep. Little Brown & Co., L.A., 1968-70; sales mgr. U. Wash. Press, Seattle, 1971-76, mktg. mgr., 1977-90, assoc. dir., gen. mgr., 1991-96, dir., 1996—. Bd. dirs. Wash. Ctr. for the Book. Recipient Nancy Pryor Blakenship award Wash. State Gov.'s Writers Awards, 1995. Mem. Pacific N.W. Booksellers Assn. (v.p. 1975-78, bd. dirs.). Office: U Wash Press PO Box 50096 Seattle WA 98145-5096

SOFAER, ABRAHAM DAVID, lawyer, legal advisor, federal judge, law educator; b. Bombay, India, May 6, 1938; came to U.S., 1948, naturalized, 1959; m. Marian Bea Scheuer, Oct. 23, 1977; children: Daniel E., Michael J., Helen R., Joseph S., Aaron R., Raphael J. BA in History magna cum laude, Yeshiva Coll., 1962; LLB cum laude, NYU, 1965. Bar: N.Y. 1965, D.C. 1988. Law clk. to Hon. J. Skelly Wright, U.S. Ct. Appeals (D.C. cir.), Washington, 1965-66; law clk. to Hon. William J. Brennan Jr. U.S. Supreme Ct., Washington, 1966-67; asst. U.S. atty. U.S. Dist Ct. (so. dist.) N.Y., N.Y.C., 1967-69; prof. law Columbia U., N.Y.C., 1969-79; judge U.S. Dist. Ct. (so. dist.) N.Y., 1979-85; legal advisor U.S. Dept. State, Washington, 1985-90; ptnr. Hughes Hubbard & Reed, Washington, 1991-94; George P. Shultz disting. scholar, sr. fellow Hoover Instn., Stanford U., 1994—; prof. law by courtesy Stanford U., Calif., 1996—. Hearing officer N.Y. Dept. Environ. Conservation, 1975-76. Author: War, Foreign Affairs and Constitutional Power: The Origins, 1976; contbr. articles to legal, polit., fgn. jours.; editor-in-chief: NYU Law Rev, 1964-65. Served with USAF, 1956-59. Root-Tilden scholar NYU, 1965. Mem. ABA, Fed. Bar Assn., N.Y.C. Bar Assn., N.Y. Bar Assn., Am. Law Inst. Jewish. Home: 1200 Bryant St Palo Alto CA 94301-2716 Office: Stanford Univ The Hoover Instn Stanford CA 94305-6010 Fax: 650-723-2103. E-mail: sofaer@hoover.stanford.edu

SOHN, HONG YONG, chemical and metallurgical engineering educator; b. Kaesung, Kyunggi-Do, Korea, Aug. 21, 1941; arrived U.S., 1966; s. Chong Ku and Soon Deuk (Woo) S.; m. Victoria Bee Tuan Ngo, Jan. 8, 1972; children: Berkeley Jihoon, Edward Jihyun. BS in Chem. Engring., Seoul (Korea) Nat. U., 1962; MS in Chem. Engring., U. N.B., Can., 1966; PhD in Chem. Engring., U. Calif., Berkeley, 1970. Engr. Cheil Sugar Co., Busan, Korea, 1962-64; rsch. assoc. SUNY-Buffalo, 1971-73; rsch. engr. DuPont Co., Wilmington, Del., 1973-74; prof. metall. engring., adj. prof. chem. engring. U. Utah, Salt Lake City, 1974—. Cons. Lawrence Livermore Nat. Lab., 1976—, Kennecott Co., Salt Lake City, 1976—, Cabot Corp., 1984—, DuPont Co., 1987—, Utah Power and Light Co., 1987—, H.C. Starck, 1997—. Co-author: Gas-Solid Reactions, 1976; co-editor: Rate Processes of Extractive Metallurgy, 1979, Extractive Metallurgy of Refractory Metals, 1980, Advances in Sulfide Smelting, 2 vols., 1983, Recycle and Secondary Recovery of Metals, 1985, Gas-solid Reactions in Pyrometallurgy, 1986, Flash Rection Processes, 1988, Metallurgical Processes for the Year 2000 and Beyond, 1988, Metallurgical Processes for the Early Twenty-First Century, 2 vols., 1994, Proceedings of the Julian Szekely Memorial Symposium on Materials Processing, 1997, Value-Addition Metallurgy, 1998; patentee process for treating sulfide-bearing ores, continuous solvent extraction with bottom gas injection; contbr. numerous articles to sci., tech. jours. Camille and Henry Dreyfus Found. Tchr. Scholar awardee, 1977; Fulbright Disting. lectr., 1983; Japan Soc. for the Promotion of Sci. fellow, 1990. Mem. AIME (James Douglas Gold medal 2001), The Minerals, Metals and Materials Soc. (past dir., Extractive Metallurgy Lectr. award 1990, Champion H. Mathewson Gold Medal award 1993, Extraction and Processing Sci. award 1990, 94, 99), Korean Acad. Sci. and Tech. (Fellow award 1998), Am. Inst. Chem. Engrs., Korean Inst. Chem. Engrs. Office: U Utah 135 S 1460 E Rm 412 Salt Lake City UT 84112-0114 E-mail: hysohn@mines.utah.edu

SOKOL, JAN D. lawyer; b. N.Y., May 27, 1952; BS magna cum laude, Rutgers U., 1974; JD Northwestern Sch. of Law, Lewis and Clark Coll., 1977. Bar: Oreg. 1978, U.S. Dist. Ct. (dist. Oreg.), U.S. Ct. Appeals (9th cir.) 1981, U.S. Claims Ct. 1982, U.S. Supreme Ct. 1982. Law clerk to Hon. George A. Juba U.S. Dist. Ct. (dist. Oreg.), 1978-79, law clerk to Hon. Gus J. Solomon, 1979-80, law clerk to Hon. James A. Redden, 1980; mng. mem. Stewart, Sokol & Gray, 1994. Case note and comment editor Environmental Law, 1976-77. Mem. ABA (mem. forum com. on the construction industry, fidelity and surety, forest resources com.), Multnomah County. Office: Stewart Sokol & Gray 1500 Benjamin Franklin Plz One SW Columbia Portland OR 97258

SOKOLOW, MAURICE, physician, educator; b. N.Y.C., May 19, 1911; s. Alexander and Anna (Spiegelman) S.; m. Ethel Schwabacher, June 30, 1941 (dec. 1970); children: Gail Anne, Jane Carol (dec.), Anne May. AB cum laude, U. Calif., Berkeley, 1932; MD, U. Calif., San Francisco, 1936. Intern San Francisco Gen. Hosp., 1935-36; resident U. Calif., San Francisco, 1936-37, rsch. fellow, 1939-40; resident New Eng. Med. Ctr., Boston, 1937-38; rsch. fellow Michael Reese Hosp., Chgo., 1938-39; gen. practice medicine San Francisco, 1946-62; faculty cardiovascular divsn. Sch. Medicine, U. Calif., San Francisco, 1946—, assoc. prof. medicine, 1952-58, prof., 1958-78, prof. emeritus, 1978—, chief electrocardiograph dept., chief hypertension clinic, 1946-78, chief cardiovascular divsn., 1955-73; program and founding dir. cardiology tng. grant USPHS, San Francisco, 1960-73; sr. and founding mem. Cardiovascular Rsch. Inst., 1957—. Cons. in field. Author: Clinical Cardiology, 1977; contbr. articles to profl. jours. ; mem. editorial bd. Jour. Cardiovascular Medicine, 1975—, Western Jour. Medicine, 1946-68. Bd. dirs. Fromm Inst Life Long Learning, U. San Francisco. Lt. comdr. M.C. USN, 1942-46. Rsch. fellow U. Calif., 1939-40; Nat. Heart Inst. grant, 1950-78; named U. Calif. San Francisco Alumnus of Yr., 1986. Fellow Am. Coll. Cardiology (hon.); mem. Am. Fedn. Clin. Research (v.p. 1948-49), Assn. Univ. Cardiologists, Am. Soc. Clin. Investigation, Brit. Cardiac Soc. (corr.), Am. Heart Assn., San Francisco Heart Assn. (pres. 1950-51), Menlo Circus Club. Club: Menlo Circus. Home: 3452 Jackson St San Francisco CA 94118-2021 Office: U Calif Sch Medicine San Francisco CA 94143-0001 E-mail: mssoke@aol.com

SOKOLSKY, ROBERT LAWRENCE, journalist, entertainment writer; b. Boston, May 18, 1928; s. Henry and Lillian (Gorodetzky) S.; m. Sally-Ann Moss, Aug. 11, 1955; 1 son, Andrew E. AB, Syracuse (N.Y.) U., 1950. Reporter Springfield (Mass.) Union, 1950; asst. dir. pub. info. ARC, Syracuse, 1952-54; entertainment editor Syracuse Herald-Jour., 1954-61, Buffalo Courier Express, 1961-72, Phila. Bull., 1972-82; entertainment writer Riverside (Calif.) Press-Enterprise, 1983-2000; syndicated TV columnist Ottaway News Svc., 1988-96, Scripps Howard, 1996-2000; freelance writer, radio commentator pub. radio, 2000—. Radio show host; freelance writer; guest lectr. Contbr. articles to profl. jours. Bd. dirs. Brush Hollow Civic Assn., Evesham Twp., N.J. Served with U.S. Army, 1950-52. Recipient Sigma Delta Chi award for feature writing, 1950, award for entertainment coverage Twin Counties Press Club, 1984, 87, Lifetime Achievement award Inland Theatre League, 2001. Mem. Am. Newspaper Guild (Page One award for opinion writing), Syracuse Press Club, Greater Buffalo Press Assn., TV Critics Assn., Soc. Profl. Journalists (Excellence in Journalism award 1989, 93), Pen and Pencil Club of Phila., Variety Club. Republican. Jewish. Home: 3080 Saratoga St Riverside CA 92503-5435 Office: Press Enterprise 3512 14th St Riverside CA 92501-3878

SOLANO, HENRY L. lawyer; m. Janine Solano; children: Mateo, Amalia, Guadalupe. BS in Mech. Engring., U. Denver; JD, U. Colo.; LLD (hon.), U. Denver. Asst. atty. gen. Human Resources divsn. Colo. Dept. Law, 1977-82; asst. U.S. atty. Dist. Colo., 1982-87; U.S. atty. for Colo. U.S. Dept. Justice, Denver, 1994-98; solicitor U.S. Dept. Labor, Washington, 1998-2001; ptnr. LeBoeuf, Lamb, Greene & MacRae L.L.P., Denver, 2001—. Exec. dir. Colo. Dept. Instns., 1987-91, Colo. Dept. Regulatory Agys., 1987; acting exec. dir. Colo. Dept. Corrections, 1989-90; chair Cabinet Coun. on Families and Children, 1990-91; mem. adv. com. U.S. Atty. Gen., 1994-95; lectr. Kennedy Sch. Govt. Bd. dirs. Nat. Latino Children's Inst., Mex.Am. Legal Def. Edn. Fund, Denver Housing Authority, Denver Women's Commn., Colo. Dept. Social Svcs., Colo. Transit Constrn. Authority, Regional Transit Dist. Office: LeBoeuf Lamb Greene & MacRae 633 17th St Ste 2000 Denver CO 80202

SOLARI, R. C. retired heavy construction company executive; b. 1925; married. With Granite Construction Co., 1946-97, formerly pres., now pres., chief exec. officer, dir. Calif., chmn. bd. dirs.; ret., 1997. Office: Granite Constrn Co PO Box 50085 Watsonville CA 95077-5085

SOLIS, HILDA LUCIA, congresswoman, educational administrator; b. Los Angeles, Oct. 20, 1957; d. Raul and Juana (Sequiera) S.; m. Sam H. Sayyad, June 26, 1982. BA in Polit. Sci., Calif. State Poly U., 1979; MA in Pub. Adminstrn., U. So. Calif., 1981. Interpreter Immigration and Naturalization Service, Los Angeles, 1977-79; editor in chief Office Hispanic Affairs, The White House, Washington, 1980-81; mgmt. analyst Office Mgmt. and Budget, Washington, 1981-82; field rep. Office Assemblyman Art Torres, L.A., 1982; dir. Calif. Student Opportunity and Access, Whittier, 1982—; rep. 57th assembly dist. Calif. State Assembly, Sacramento, 1992-94; mem. Calif. Senate from 24th dist., 1994-2000, U.S. Congress from Calif. 31st dist., Washington, 2001—; mem. edn. and workforce com., resources com. Cons. South Coast Consortium, L.A., 1986—; mem. South Coast Ednl. Opportunity Pers. Consortium. Bd. dirs. Calif. Commn. on Status of Women, 1993—; corr. pres. Friendly El Monte (Calif.) Dem. Club, 1986—; mem. credentials com. Calif. Dem. Com., 1987-88; trustee Rio Hondo C.C., 1985-92. Recipient Meritorious Svc. award Dept. Def., 1981, Young Careerist award El Monte Bus. and Profl. Women, 1987; fellow Nat. Edn. Inst., Kellogg Found., 1984-85. Mem. Western Assn. Ednl. Opportunity Pers. (sec. bd. dirs. 1986—), Comision Feminil de Los Angeles (bd. dirs. 1983-84, edn. chmn.), Women of Moose. Roman Catholic. Home: 5250 La Madera Ave El Monte CA 91732-1236 Office: 1641 Longworth Bldg Washington DC 20515*

SOLL, HERBERT D. attorney general of Northern Mariana Islands; b. 1936; BS, U. Denver, 1958, LLB, 1960. Dir. Peace Corps , Rio de Janeiro, Brazil, 1967-70; chief pub. defender Alaska, 1971-75; trust territory pub. defender, 1975-79; dir. criminal prosecution Alaska, 1986-90; dir. Peace Corps, Sao Tome, 1990-93; judge Superior Ct., 1979-86; atty. gen. No. Mariana Islands, Saipan, 2000—. Office: Office Atty Gen PO Box 10007 Adminstrn Bldg Saipan Northern Mariana Islands 96950 E-mail: acsoll@gtepacifica.net

SOLLENDER, JOEL DAVID, management consultant, financial executive; b. N.Y.C., Nov. 11, 1924; s. Samuel and Flora (Blumenthal) S.; m. Dorothy Leaf, Aug. 6, 1958; children: Jeffrey D., Jonathan L. B.S., N.Y. U., 1946. C.P.A., N.Y. Staff auditor Ernst & Young, N.Y.C., 1946-50; with United Mchts. & Mfrs., Inc., N.Y.C., 1950-86, corp. contr., 1977—, sr. v.p., 1980—, chief acctg. officer, 1976—, also bd. dirs., officer various subs., mem. mgmt. com. parent co., 1986-88; assoc. dir. N.Y. Hist. Soc., N.Y.C.; mem. adv. coun. to Office of Charities Registration Dept. State, N.Y. State, 1988-89; v.p. fin. Piedmont Industries, N.Y.C., 1989-90; exec. v.p., CFO Earthworm Inc., 1990-95; fin. mgmt. cons.; sr. cons. I.E.S.C. A.I.D., Kazakstan, 1996—. Mem. adv. coun. San Diego State U., 1997—, audit com. San Diego Mus. Art, 1997—. Served with U.S. Army, World War II Decorated Combat Infantry Badge, Purple Heart with cluster, Prisoner of War medal, Bronze Star. Mem. AICPA, N.Y. State Soc. CPAs (chief fin. officer com.), Am. Inst. Corp. Contrs., Rancho Bernardo (Calif.) Men's Club, Bailiwick Club (Greenwich, Conn.), Greenhaven Yacht Club (Rye).

SOLLMAN, GEORGE HENRY, venture capitalist; b. Michigan City, Ind., Nov. 2, 1941; s. Henry Charles and Margaret Elisabeth (Gockel) S.; m. Maureen Tosh, July 12, 1968; children: Jennifer, Erich. Spl. student, MIT, 1965-66; BSEE, Northwestern U., 1964; MSEE, Northeastern U., 1967. Engring. dir. Honeywell Info. systems, Waltham, Mass., 1964-73; product line mgr. Control Data, Hawthorne, Calif., 1973-76; v.p., gen. mgr. Shugart/Xerox, Sunnyvale, 1976-84; spl. ptnr. Sand Hill Venture Group, Menlo Park, 1984; pres., CEO, Centigram Corp., San Jose, 1985-97; pres., CEO AtMotion Inc. (now Phone.com.), Redwood Shores, 1997-2000; chmn., CEO, Arabesque Investments LLC, Atherton, 2000—. Chmn. nat. bd. dirs. Am. Elec. Assn.; presdl. nomination Semicondr. Tech. Coun.; co-chmn. Alexis d'Toqueville Soc.; adv. coun. Joint Venture Silicon Valley. Patentee in field. Co-chmn. United Way of Santa Clara County; mem. steering com. George Lucas Ednl. Found., Marin County. E-mail: george. Home: 242 Polhemus Ave Atherton CA 94027-5439 Office: Arabesque Investments LLC 242 Polhemus Ave Atherton CA 94027-5439 E-mail: sollman@hotmail.com

SOLLOWAY, C. ROBERT, retired forest products company executive; b. Vancouver, B.C., Can., May 19, 1935; s. Harold Eugene and Elva Merle (McAllister) S.; m. Ila Noreen Kelly. B in Commerce, U. B.C., 1959, LLB, 1960. Bar: Can., 1961. Asst. to exec v.p., asst. to pres. West Coast Transmission Co. Ltd., Vancouver, 1962-68; corp. counsel, asst. sec. Weldwood of Can. Ltd., Vancouver, 1968-73, gen. counsel, sec., 1973-75, v.p., gen. counsel, sec., 1975-2000. Mem. Law Soc. B.C., Can. Bar Assn., Vancouver Bar Assn. Anglican. Clubs: Vancouver Lawn Tennis and Badminton.

SOLMER, RICHARD, surgeon; b. South Bend, Ind., Feb. 11, 1947; MD, U. Mich., 1972. Diplomate Am. Bd. Plastic Surgery. Surgical intern Hosp. of the U. Pa., Phila., 1972-73; gen. surgical resident Calif. Hosp. Med. Ctr., L.A., 1976-80; plastic surgery resident Allentown (Pa.) Affiliated Hosp., 1980-82; pvt. practice Huntington Beach, and Newport Beach, Calif., 1982—. Fellow Am. Coll. Surgeons; mem. Am. Soc. Plastic Surgeons. Office: 307 Placentia Ave Ste 208 Newport Beach CA 92663-3308

SOLOMON, ARTHUR CHARLES, pharmacist; b. Gary, Ind., May 30, 1947; s. Laurence A. and Dorothy B. (Klippel) S.; m. Janet Evelyn Irak, Aug. 23, 1969; children: Thomas, Michael, Mark, Jill. BS in Pharmacy, Purdue U., 1970, MS in Clin. Pharmacy, 1972; PharmD. Registered pharmacist; cert. nuclear pharmacist. Clin. prof. pharmacy U. Tex., Austin, 1972-75; v.p. Nuclear Pharmacy, Inc., Atlanta, 1975-83; exec. v.p., COO Diagnostek, Inc., Albuquerque, 1983-95; pres. Health Care Svcs., Inc.,

1990-95; exec. v.p., COO Value Rx, Albuquerque, 1995-96; pres. Solomon and Assocs., Albuquerque, 1996-97; pres., CEO, dir. SP Pharmaceuticals LLC, Albuquerque, 1997—. Adj. prof. U. N.Mex., 1992—. Contbr. articles to profl. jours. Named Disting. Alumnus Purdue U., 1998. Fellow Am. Soc. Cons. Pharmacists, Parental Drug Assn.; mem. Am. Pharm. Assn., Am. Assn. Pharm. Scis., Am. Soc. Hosp. Pharmacy, Nat. Assn. Retail Druggists, Nat. Coun. Prescription Drug Programs, Am. Managed Care Pharmacy Assn. (pres., dir.), Rho Chi, Pi Kappa Phi. Republican. Roman Catholic. Avocations: golf, fishing, gardening. Home: 1504 Catron Ave SE Albuquerque NM 87123-4218 Office: SP Pharmaceuticals LLC 4272 Balloon Park Rd NE Albuquerque NM 87109-5801 E-mail: asolomon@sppharma.com

SOLOMON, DAVID HARRIS, geriatrician, educator; b. Cambridge, Mass., Mar. 7, 1923; s. Frank and Rose (Roud) S.; m. Ronda L. Markson, June 23, 1946; children: Patti Jean (Mrs. Richard E. Sinaiko), Nancy Ellen. A.B., Brown U., 1944; M.D., Harvard U., 1946. Intern Peter Bent Brigham Hosp., Boston, 1946-47, resident, 1947-48, 50-51; fellow endocrinology New Eng. Center Hosp., Boston, 1951-52; faculty UCLA Sch. Medicine, 1952—, prof. medicine, 1966-93, vice chmn. dept. medicine, 1968-71, chmn. dept., 1971-81, assoc. dir. geriatrics, 1982-89; dir. UCLA Ctr. on Aging, 1991-96; prof. emeritus UCLA, 1993—. Chief med. svc. Harbor Gen. Hosp., Torrance, Calif., 1966-71; cons. Wadsworth VA Hosp., L.A., 1952-93, Sepulveda VA Hosp., 1971-93; cons. metabolism tng. com. USPHS, 1960-64, endocrinology study sect., 1970-73; cons. RAND Corp., 1997—. Editor: Jour. Am. Geriatric Soc., 1988-93; contbr. numerous articles to profl. jours. Recipient Mayo Soley award, 1986 Master ACP; mem. Assn. Am. Physicians, Am. Soc. Clin. Investigation, Western Soc. Clin. Research (councillor 1963-65), Endocrine Soc. (Robert H. Williams award 1989), Am. Thyroid Assn. (pres. 1973-74, Disting. Service award 1986), Inst. Medicine Nat. Acad. Scis., AAAS, Assn. Profs. Medicine (pres. 1980-81), Western Assn. Physicians (councillor 1972-75, pres. 1983-84), Am. Fedn. Aging Rsch. (Irving S. Wright award), Am. Geriatrics Soc. (bd. dirs. 1985-93, Milo Leavitt award 1992, Disting. Svc. award 1993, Edward Henderson award 1999), Gerontol. Soc. Am. (Freeman award 1997), Phi Beta Kappa, Sigma Xi, Alpha Omega Alpha. Home: 2103 Ridge Dr Los Angeles CA 90049-1153 Office: Rand Corp 1700 Main St Santa Monica CA 90407-2138 E-mail: david_solomon@rand.org

SOLOMON, EZRA, economist, educator; b. Rangoon, Burma, Mar. 20, 1920; came to U.S., 1947, naturalized, 1951; s. Ezra and Emily (Rose) S.; m. Janet Lorraine Cameron, May 7, 1949; children— Catherine Shan, Janet Ming, Lorna Cameron. A.B. (hons.), U. Rangoon, 1940; Ph.D., U. Chgo., 1950. Instr. U. Chgo., 1948-51, assoc. prof. fin., 1951-55, assoc. prof., 1955-57, prof., 1957-61; Dean Witter prof. fin. Stanford U., 1961-71, 73-90; dir. Internat. Ctr. Mgmt. Edn.; mem. Coun. Econ. Advisers, 1971-73. Author: The Theory of Financial Management, 1963, Money and Banking, 5th edit, 1968, The Management of Corporate Capital, 1959, Metropolitan Chicago: An Economic Analysis, 1958, The Anxious Economy, 1975, An Introduction to Financial Management, 2d edit, 1980, Beyond the Turning Point, 1981; editor: International Patterns of Inflation— A Study in Contrasts, 1984, Jour. Bus, 1953-57; bd. editors Jour. of Finance, 1965-66, Jour. Bus. Finance, 1969-73, Jour. Quantitative and Financial Analysis, 1969-71. Served as lt., Burma div. Royal Naval Vol. Res., 1942-47. Mem. Am. Econ. Assn. Home: 775 Santa Ynez St Stanford CA 94305-8478 Office: Stanford U Grad Sch Bus Stanford CA 94305

SOLOMON, GEORGE FREEMAN, psychiatrist, educator; b. Freeport, N.Y., Nov. 25, 1931; s. Joseph C. and Ruth (Freeman) S.; children: Joshua Ben, Jared Freeman. AB, Stanford U., 1952, MD, 1955. Intern, Barnes Hosp., St. Louis, 1955-56; resident in psychiatry Langley Porter Neuropsychiat. Inst., U. Calif. Med. Sch., San Francisco, 1956-59; asst. to asso. prof. psychiatry Stanford U. Med. Sch., 1962-73; dir. med. edn. Fresno County (Calif.) Dept. Health, 1973-83; clin. prof. UCLA Med. Sch., 1974-78; clin. prof. psychiatry U. Calif. Med. Sch., San Francisco, 1976-79, prof., 1980-84, vice-chmn. dept., 1978-83; adj. prof. U. Calif., San Francisco, 1984-90; prof. psychiatry and biobehavioral sci. UCLA, 1984-95, prof. emeritus, 1995—; chief chem. dependency treatment ctr. VA Med. Ctr., Sepulveda, Calif., 1984-89; chief psychoneuroimmunology, 1989-94. Chief psychiatry Valley Med. Center, Fresno, 1974-83. Author: From Psyche to Soma and Back, 2000; co-author: The Psychology of Strength, 1975; contbr. over 160 papers, chpts. and articles on psychoneuroimmunology, violence, Vietnam and other topics to profl. jours. and various publs. Capt. USAR, 1959-61. Fellow Internat. Coll. Psychosomatic Medicine, Am. Psychiat. Assn., Acad. of Behavioral Med. Research., Royal Coll. Psychiatrists, PNI Rsch. Soc. (pres. 1997-98). Home: 10724 Wilshire Blvd Apt 602 Los Angeles CA 90024-4461 Office: UCLA Sch Med Neuropsychiat Inst C8 553 Los Angeles CA 90095-0001 E-mail: gfsolomon@pol.net

SOLOMON, JACK AVRUM, lawyer, automotive distributor, art dealer; b. Omaha, Oct. 25, 1928; s. John A. and Matilda (Bienstok) S.; m. Josephine J. Kleiman, June 1948 (div. Mar. 1971); children: Debra, Alisa, Michael, Rena; m. Carolyn Summers, Dec. 1973. B.S., U. Nebr., 1950, LL.B. cum laude, 1952; LL.M. (Cook fellow), U. Mich., 1953. Bar: Nebr. 1950, Ill. 1951. Practice law, Chgo., 1950—; with firm Stiefel, Greenberg, Burns, Baldridge & Solomon, 1953-66, ptnr., 1958-66, Solomon, Rosenfeld, Elliot & Stiefel, and predecessor, 1966—, sr. ptnr., 1966—. Dir. Amco Industries, Inc., Chgo., 1968—, chmn. bd., 1968-69, sec., gen. counsel, 1969—; sec., dir. Mogen David Wine Corp., Chgo., 1964-71; chmn. bd., dir. Arts and Leisure Corp., 1969-76; pres., chmn. bd., dir. Circle Fine Art Corp., 1968-94; chmn. bd. S2 Art Group, Ltd., 1996—, Re Society, 1997—, Art of the Movies.com, 1999—. Mem. Ill., Nebr. bar assns.; mem. Fine Art Pubs. Assn. (pres. 1982—); Mem. Order of Coif. Jewish (pres. temple 1959-61). Club: Nat. Arts (N.Y.C.). Home: 2870 Augusta Las Vegas NV 89109 E-mail: szartgroup@aol.com

SOLOMON, JOHN DAVIS, aviation executive; b. Kingfisher, Okla., Oct. 22, 1936; s. Edward Dempsey and Mary Blanche (Smith) S.; m. Mildred Oraline Brammer, July 16, 1968 (div. Mar. 1984); children: Jennifer Leigh, Jason Lewis; m. Sheila Mary McLeod, Nov. 23, 1985. BA, Okla. State U., 1958. Asst. mgr. airport City of Oklahoma City Dept. Aviation, 1963-66, City of Tulsa Airport Authority, 1966-70; dir. aviation City of Oklahoma City., 1970-77, Clark County Dept. Aviation, Las Vegas, Nev., 1977-86; dir. environ. planning Landrum & Brown, Aviation Planners, Cin., 1986-88; dep. dir. aviation City of Houston Airport System, 1988-90; dir. aviation City of Kansas City, Mo., 1990-96; asst. dir. aviation City of Phoenix, 1997—. Editor Airport Mgmt. Jour., 1975; contbr. articles to aviation jours. Mem. Am. Assn. Airport Execs. (bd. dirs., ex-officio, accredited 1965, pres. 1979, Pres.'s award 1975, Disting. Svc. award 1991), Airports Coun. Internat. (bd. dirs. 1985-86), Kappa Sigma. Avocations: art, music, collecting military miniatures. Office: Dept Aviation Sky Harbor Airport 3400 E Sky Harbor Blvd Phoenix AZ 85034-4403

SOLOMON, MARK A. lawyer; b. Cedar Rapids, Iowa, Aug. 30, 1950; BA summa cum laude, Calif. State U., San Jose, 1972; JD magna cum laude, U. Santa Clara, 1975. Bar: Calif. 1975, Nev. 1976. Mem. Lionel Sawyer & Collins, Las Vegas, Nev., 1976—. Mem. ABA, State Bar Calif., State Bar Nev., Clark County Bar Assn. Office: Lionel Sawyer & Collins 1700 Bank Am Plz 300 S 4th St Ste 1700 Las Vegas NV 89101-6053

SOLOMON, RUSSELL M. retail products executive; b. 1925; CEO MTS; chmn. bd. Tower Records, West Sacramento, Calif. Office: Tower Records PO Box 919001 West Sacramento CA 95691-9001

SOLOMON, RUTH, state legislator, teacher; b. Phila., Apr. 16, 1941; d. David and Bella (Azeff) Epstein; m. Arthur Solomon; 1 child, Barry. BA, U. Ariz., 1971. Tchr. Tucson (Ariz.) Unified Sch. Dist., 1971—; mem. Ariz. Ho. of Reps., Phoenix, 1988-94, Ariz. Senate, Dist. 14, Phoenix, 1994-. Pres. Tucson Edn. Assn., 1983-85; dir. Ariz. Edn. Assn., Phoenix, 1986—. Bd. dirs. Pima County Community Action Agy., Tucson, 1986—, Mayor's Coun. Youth Initiatives, Tucson, 1987—. Mem. Bus. and Profl. Women's Coun., Alpha Delta Kappa, Phi Kappa Phi. Avocation: swimming. Office: Ariz Senate 1700 W Washington St Rm 313 Phoenix AZ 85007-2812

SOLOMON, SUSAN, chemist, scientist; b. Chicago, Ill., Jan. 19, 1956; d. Leonard Marvin and Alice (Rutman) Solomon; m. Barry Lane Sidwell, Sept. 20, 1988. BS in Chemistry, Ill. Inst. Tech., 1977; MS in Chemistry, U. Calif., Berkeley, 1979, PhD in Chemistry, 1981. Rsch. chemist aeronomy lab. NOAA, Boulder, Colo., 1981-88, program leader middle atmosphere group aeronomy lab., 1988—; head project sci. Nat. Ozone Expedition, McMurdo Sta., Antarctica, 1986, 1987. Adj. faculty U. Colo., 1982—. Co-author: Aeronomy of the Middle Atmosphere, 1984; contbr. articles to sci. jours. Recipient Gold medal U.S. Dept. Commerce, 1989, Scientist of the Year Award, 1992, R&D Magazine, Nat. Medal Science, 1999. Fellow Royal Meteorol. Soc., Am. Meteorol. Soc., Am. Geophys. Union (J.B. McElwane award 1985); mem. NAS, Am. Acad. Arts and Scis. Avocations: creative writing, crafts, scuba diving.

SOLTERO, VICTOR, state legislator; Student, Pima C.C., Tucson, 1957. Warehouse mgr. Frontier Stamps, Inc., Tucson, 1958-63; grounds maintenance field supr. Tucson Unified Sch. Dist., 1963-91; ret.; councilman City of South Tucson, 1980-88, mayor, 1988-91; mem. Ariz. State Senate, 1991—, mem. appropriations, edn., family svcs. and govt. coms. Dem. precinct committeeman; hon. co-chair Dist. 10 Labor Day Fiesta, Pio Decimo-South Tucson Norte Festival; mem. Tucson Area Literacy Coun., Regional Comprehensive Planning Exec. Com., Tucson/South Tucson Enterprise Zone Commn., Regional Transp. Authority. With Ariz. Air Nat. Guard, 1956-62. Named Outstanding Pub. Ofcl., Ariz. Pks. and Recreation Assn., 1997. Mem. Pima Assn. Govts. (regional coun. 1988-91), Greater Tuscon Econ. Devel. Coun. Democrat. Office: State Capitol Bldg 1700 W Washington St # 312 Phoenix AZ 85007-2812 E-mail: vsoltero@azleg.state.az.us

SOLTYS, JOHN JOSEPH, lawyer; b. Portsmouth, Va., Feb. 4, 1942; children: John J. III, Amy Elaine. BS, USCG Acad., 1963; JD, Willamette U., 1970. Bar: Wash. 1970, U.S. Dist. Ct. (we. and ea. dists.) Wash. 1970. From assoc. to sr. ptnr. Karr, Tuttle, Seattle, 1970-89; sr. ptnr. Cozen & O'Connor, Seattle, 1989—. Writer, spkr. in field; editor Wash. State Bar Assn. Motor Vehicle Accident Litigation Deskbook, 2000-01. Lt. (j.g.) USCG, 1963-67. Mem. Wash. Def. Trial Lawyers (pres. 1986-87), Fedn. Ins. & Corp. Counsel. Avocations: fishing, hunting, gardening. Office: Cozen & O'Connor 1201 3rd Ave Ste 5200 Seattle WA 98101-3071 E-mail: jsoltys@cozen.com

SOMEKH, SASSON, chemical company executive; BS in Physics, Tel Aviv U.; MS in Elec. Engring., PhD in Elec. Engring., Calif. Inst. Technology. Tch. staff Bell Labs.; applied materials Dry Etch Group Intel Corp.; from project mgr. etch divsn. to sr. v.p. ops. Applied Materials, Inc.; sr. v.p. Applied Materials Inc., Santa Clara, Calif., 1998—. Office: Applied Materials 3050 Bowers Ave Santa Clara CA 95054-3201

SOMERS, DANIEL E. telecommunications industry executive; b. Detroit; m. Mary Jane Somers; five children. BS in Fin., Stonehill Coll. Investment banker and fin. analyst; CFO Imasco Ltd., Montreal, Can., Hardee's Restaurant subsidiary Imasco Ltd., Rocky Mount, N.C.; pres. Radio Atlantic Holdings Ltd., Nova Scotia; exec. v.p., CFO Bell Can. Internat., Inc., 1992-95; creator Cable & Wireless Comm., U.K.; chmn., CEO Bell Cablemedia, plc, London; sr. exec. v.p., CFO AT&T; pres., CEO AT&T Broadband, Englewood, Colo., 1999—. Bd. dirs. BCE Cable Ltd., BCI Internat. Holdings Ltd., Bell Cablemedia, plc, Videotron Holdings Ltd. Office: AT&T Broadband 188 Inverness Dr W Englewood CO 80112

SOMERSET, HAROLD RICHARD, retired business executive; b. Woodbury, Conn., Sept. 25, 1935; s. Harold Kitchener and Margaret Mary (Roche) S.; m. Marjory Deborah Ghiselin, June 22, 1957 (dec. Jan. 1984); children: Timothy Craig, Paul Alexander; m. Jean MacAlpine DesMarais, Jan. 2, 1985; stepchildren: Cheryl Lyn DesMarais, James Fenelon DesMarais. B.S., U.S. Naval Acad., 1957; B.C.E., Rensselaer Poly. Inst., Troy, N.Y., 1959; LL.B., Harvard U., 1967. Bar: Mass. 1967, Hawaii 1973. Commd. ensign U.S. Navy, 1957, advanced through grades to lt., 1961; service in U.S. and Hawaii; resigned, 1964; with firm Goodwin, Procter & Hoar, Boston, 1967-72; corp. counsel Alexander & Baldwin, Inc., Honolulu, 1972-74, v.p., gen. counsel, 1974-78, group v.p.-sugar, 1978-79, exec. v.p.-agr., 1979-84; with Calif. & Hawaiian Sugar Co., San Francisco, 1984-93, exec. v.p., chief operating officer, 1984-88, pres., chief exec. officer, 1988-93, bus. cons., 1994—. Bd. dirs. Longs Drug Stores Corp., Brown and Caldwell. Mem. adv. bd. San Francisco Nat. Maritime Mus. Mem. St. Mary's Coll. Sch. Edn. (adv. coun.). Home and Office: 19 Donald Dr Orinda CA 94563-3646

SOMERSON, PAUL, magazine editor-in-chief; V.p., editor-in-chief P.C. Computing, San Francisco. Office: PC Computing 50 Beale St Fl 13 San Francisco CA 94105-1813

SOMERVILLE, CHRIS, plant biologist, educator; BS, U. Alta., 1974, PhD, 1978. Dir. dept. plant biology Carnegie Inst. Washington, Stanford, Calif.; asst. prof. U. Alta., 1980-82; assoc. prof. Mich. State U., 1982-86, prof., 1986-94, Stanford (Calif.) U., 1994—. Chmn. Mendel Biotech. Office: Carnegie Inst Washington Dept Plant Biology 290 Panama St Stanford CA 94305-4101

SOMERVILLE, MASON HAROLD, mechanical engineering educator, university dean; b. Worcester, Mass., Dec. 21, 1941; s. Harold Mervin and Eleanor Ruth (Archibald) S.; children: Mark, Matthew, Meredith, Michael, Michelle. B.S.M.E., Worcester Polytech. Inst., 1964; M.S.M.E., Northeastern U., 1966; Ph.D. in Mech. Engring., Pa. State U., 1971. Profl. engr., N.D., Ark., Tex. Grad. teaching asst Northeastern U., Boston, 1964-66; engr. Norton Co., Worcester, Mass., 1965; instr. mech. engring. dept. Pa. State U., State College, 1966-71; sr. engr. Bettis Atomic Power Lab., West Mifflin, Pa., 1971-73; prof., dir. Engring. Expt. Sta., U. N.D., Grand Forks, 1973-80; prof., head mech. engring dept. U. Ark., Fayetteville, 1980-84; prof., dean engring. Tex. Tech U., Lubbock, TX, 1984-94; dean engring. No. Ariz. U., Flagstaff, 1994—, interim provost, 1999—. Cons. Natural Gas Pipeline, Chgo., 1974-79, Archtl. Alliance, Mpls., 1978-80; bd. dirs. Mid-Am. Solar Energy Corp., Mpls., 1978-80, Ctr. for Advanced Engring and Rsch., TTU/HSC Rsch. Found.; chmn. bd. dirs. N.D. Energy Assn., 1979-80; energy advisor State of N.D., 1978-80; mem. ABET/EAC Commn., 1987-92; speaker to pub. service groups Author: Coal Gasification Environmental Impact, Analysis of U.S. Weather, 1980; numerous tech. papers. Mem. Lubbock Bd. City Devel., 1985-87 Recipient Ralph R. Teetor award Soc. Automotive Engrs., 1974, Haliburton award; rsch. grantee. Mem. ASME, ASHRAE, Am. Soc. Engring. Edn., Sigma Xi, Pi Tau Sigma. Republican. Episcopalian. Home: # 300-285 2700 Woodlands Village Blvd Flagstaff AZ 86001-7127 Office: Northern Arizona U Coll Engring & Tech PO Box 15600 Flagstaff AZ 86011-0001

SOMERVILLE, RICHARD CHAPIN JAMES, atmospheric scientist, educator; b. Washington, May 30, 1941; s. James William and Mollie (Dorf) S.; m. Sylvia Francisca Bal, Sept. 17, 1965; children: Anatol Leon, Alexander Chapin. BS in Meteorology, Pa. State U., 1961; PhD in Meteorology, NYU, 1966. Postdoctoral fellow Nat. Ctr. Atmospheric Rsch., Boulder, Colo., 1966-67; rsch. assoc. geophysical fluid dynamics lab. NOAA, Princeton, N.J., 1967-69; rsch. scientist Courant Inst. Math. Scis., N.Y.C., 1969-71; meteorologist Goddard inst. space studies NASA, N.Y.C., 1971-74; adj. prof. Columbia U., NYU, 1971-74; head numerical weather prediction sect. Nat. Ctr. Atmospheric Rsch., Boulder, 1974-79; prof. meteorology Scripps Inst. Oceanography, U. Calif.-San Diego, La Jolla, 1979—. Chmn. bd. dirs. Aspen Global Change Inst. Author: The Forgiving Air: Understanding Environmental Change, 1996. Fellow AAAS, Am. Meterol. Soc.; mem. Am. Geophysical Union, Oceanography Soc. Office: U Calif San Diego Scripps Inst Oceanography 9500 Gilman Dr Dept 0224 La Jolla CA 92093-5004

SOMORJAI, GABOR ARPAD, chemist, educator; b. Budapest, Hungary, May 4, 1935; came to U.S., 1957, naturalized, 1962; s. Charles and Livia (Ormos) S.; m. Judith Kaldor, Sept. 2, 1957; children: Nicole, John. BS, U. Tech. Scis., Budapest, 1956; PhD, U. Calif., Berkeley, 1960; D (hon.), D (hon.), U. Manchester, 2001. Mem. research staff IBM, Yorktown Heights, N.Y., 1960-64; dir. Surface Sci. and Catalysis Program Lawrence Berkeley Lab., Calif., 1964—; mem. faculty dept. chemistry U. Calif.-Berkeley, 1964—, assoc. prof., 1967-72, prof., 1972—, Miller prof., 1978. Unilever prof. dept. chemistry U. Bristol, Eng., 1972; vis. fellow Emmanuel Coll., Cambridge, Eng., 1989; Baker lectr. Cornell U., Ithaca, N.Y., 1977; mem. editorial bds. Progress in Solid State Chemistry, 1973—, Jour. Solid State Chemistry, 1976-92, Nouveau Jour. de Chemie, 1977—, Colloid and Interface Sci., 1979—, Catalysis Revs., 1981, Jour. Phys. Chemistry, 1981-91, Langmuir, 1985—, Jour. Applied Catalysis, Molecular Physics, 1992—. Author: Principles of Surface Chemistry, 1972, Chemistry in Two Dimensions, 1981, Introduction to Surface Chemistry and Catalysis, 1994; editor-in-chief Catalysis Letters, 1988—; contbr. articles to profl. jours. Recipient Emmett award Am. Catalysis Soc., 1977, Kokes award Johns Hopkins U., 1976, Albert award Precious Metal Inst., 1986, Sr. Disting. Scientist award Alexander von Humboldt Found., 1989, E.W. Mueller award U. Wis., Chemical Pioneer award Am. Inst. of Chemists, 1995, Von Hippel award Materials Rsch. Soc., 1997; Guggenheim fellow, 1969, Wolf prize in chemistry, 1998. Fellow AAAS, Am. Phys. Soc.; mem. NAS, Am. Acad. Arts and Scis., Am. Chem. Soc. (chmn. colloid and surface chemistry 1981, Surface and Colloid Chemistry award 1981, Peter Debye award 1989, Arthur W. Adamson award 1994, award for Creative Rsch. in Homogeneous and Heterogeneous Catalysis 2000), Catalysis Soc. N.Am., Hungarian Acad. Scis. (hon. 1990, Pauling medal 2000). Home: 665 San Luis Rd Berkeley CA 94707-1725 Office: U Calif Dept Chemistry D 58 Hildebrand Hl Berkeley CA 94720-0001 E-mail: somorjai@socrates.berkeley.edu

SONNENFELD, BARRY, director, cinematographer; b. New York, NY, Apr. 1, 1953; Cinematographer (films) Blood Simple, 1984, Compromising Positions, 1985, Three O'Clock High, 1987, Raising Arizona, 1987, Throw Momma from the Train, 1987, Big, 1988, When Harry Met Sally..., 1989, Miller's Crossing, 1990, Misery, 1990, (TV movies) Out of Step, 1984 (Emmy award best cinematography 1984), Double Take, 1985, Welcome Home, Bobby, 1986, Classified Love, 1986; dir. (films) The Addams Family (uncredited cameo appearance), 1991, Addams Family Values (also actor), 1993, Get Shorty, 1995, Men In Black, 1997, Maximum Bob (TV, also exec. prodr.), 1998, Wild Wild West, 1999 (also prodr.), Chippendales, 2000; dir., co-prodr.: For Love or Money, 1993; prodr.: Out of Sight, 1998 (exec.), Fantasy Island (TV, exec.), 1998, Secret Agent Man, 2000, The Crew, 3000. Office: CAA c/o Fred Specktor 9830 Wilshire Blvd Beverly Hills CA 90212 also: United Talent Agency 9560 Wilshire Blvd Fl 5 Beverly Hills CA 90212-2401

SONNENSCHEIN, RALPH ROBERT, physiologist; b. Chgo., Aug. 14, 1923; s. Robert and Flora (Kieferstein) S.; m. Patricia W. Niddrie, June 21, 1952; children— David, Lisa, Ann. Student, Swarthmore Coll., 1940-42, U. Chgo., 1942-43; BS, Northwestern U., 1943, BM, MS, Northwestern U., 1946, MD, 1947; PhD, U. Ill., 1950. Research asst. in physiology Northwestern U. Med. Sch., 1944-46; intern Michael Reese Hosp., Chgo., 1946-47; successively research fellow clin. sci., research asst. psychiatry, research asso. psychiatry U. Ill. Med. Sch., Chgo., 1947-51; mem. faculty U. Calif. Med. Sch., Los Angeles, 1951-88, prof. physiology, 1962-88, prof. emeritus, 1988—; liaison scientist Office Naval Research, London, 1971-72. Author papers on pain, innervation of skin, peripheral circulation. Served with AUS, 1943-46. Spl. research fellow USPHS, 1957-58; fellow Swedish Med. Research Council, 1964-65; grantee USAF; grantee Office Naval Research; grantee NIH; grantee NSF. Mem. Am. Physiol. Soc., Microcirculatory Soc., Soc. Exptl. Biology and Medicine, AAAS, Hungarian Physiol. Soc. (hon.). Home: 18212 Kingsport Dr Malibu CA 90265-5636 Office: U Calif Sch Medicine Dept Physiology Los Angeles CA 90095-1751

SONNTAG, BERNARD H. agrologist, public service executive; b. Goodsoil, Sask., Can., June 27, 1940; s. Henry R. and Annie (Heesing) S.; m. Mary L. Ortman, Aug. 10, 1963; children: Calvin, Galen, Courtney Anne. BSA, Sask. U., Saskatoon, 1962, MSc, 1965; PhD, Purdue U., 1971. Economist Agriculture Can., Saskatoon, 1962-66; cons. D.W. Carr & Assoc., Ottawa, Ont., Can., 1966-68; economist Agriculture Can., Lethbridge, Alta., 1968-79, Saskatoon, 1979-80, dir. rsch. sta. Brandon, Man., 1980-86, Swiftcurrent, Sask., 1986-89, Lethbridge, 1989-95; dir. gen. Prairie Farm Rehab. Adminstrn., Regina, Sask., Can., 1996-01; pres. Sonntag Agrl. Svcs., Saskatoon, Can., 2001—. Pres. Man. Inst. Agrologists, Brandon, 1984. Recipient Leadership award Bell Can., 1993; named Disting. Agrologist, Alta. Inst. Agrologists, 1995. Fellow Agrl. Inst. Can.; mem. Rotary. Roman Catholic. Home: Sonntag Agrl Svcs 318 Collinsster Rd Saskatoon SK Canada S7N 4K7 Office: Sonntag Agrl Svcs 1800 Hamilton St Regina SK Canada S4P 4L2

SONTAG, FREDERICK EARL, philosophy educator; b. Long Beach, Calif., Oct. 2, 1924; s. M. Burnett and Cornelia (Nicholson) S.; m. Carol Furth, June 10, 1950; children: Grant Furth, Anne Burnett Karch. BA with great distinction, Stanford U., 1949; MA, Yale U., 1951, PhD, 1952; LLD (hon.), Coll. Idaho, 1971. Instr. Yale U., 1951-52; asst. prof. philosophy Pomona Coll., Claremont, Calif., 1952-55, assoc. prof., 1955-60, prof., 1970—, Robert C. Denison prof. philosophy, 1972—, chmn. dept. philosophy, 1960-67, 76-77, Claremont, 1980-84; chmn. coord. com. in philosophy Clarement Grad. Sch. and Univ. Ctr., 1962-65. Vis. prof. Union theol. Sem., N.Y.C., 1959-60, Collegio de Sant' Anselmo, Rome, 1966-67, U. Copenhagen, fall 1972; theologian-in-residence Am. Ch. in Paris, fall 1973; fulbright regional vis. prof., India, East Asia, Pacific areas, 1977-78; mem. nat. adv. coun. Kent Fellowship Program of Danforth Found., 1963-66. Author numerous books, the most recent being; Love Beyond Pain: Mysticism Within christianity, 1977, Sun Myung Moon and the Unification Church, 1977, also German, Japanese and Korean transl.; (with John K. Roth) God and America's Future, 1977, What Can God Do?, 1979, A Kierkegaard Handbook, 1979, The Elements of Philosophy, 1984, (with John K. Roth) The Questions of Philosophy, 1988, Emotion, 1989, The Return of the Gods, 1989, Willgenstein and the Mystical, 1995, Uncertain Truth, 1995, The Descent of Women, 1997, The Acts of the Trinity, 1997, Truth and Imagination, 1998, 2001; [illegible] dirs. Claremont Family Svc., 1960-64; trustee The Coro Found., L.A. and San Francisco, 1967-71; bd. dirs., chmn. ways and means com. Pilgrim Place, Claremont, 1970-77. With AUS, 1943-46. Vis. scholar Ctr. for Study

Japanese Religions, Kyoto, Japan, spring 1974; vis. fellow East-West Ctr., Honolulu, summer 1974; Wig Disting. prof. award, 1970, 76. Mem. Am. Philos. Assn., Metaphys. Soc. Am. Soc. on Religion in Higher Edn. (Kent fellow 1950-52), Am. Acad. Religion, Phi Beta Kappa. Congregationalist. Office: Pomona Coll 551 N College Ave Claremont CA 91711-4410

SONTAG, PETER MICHAEL, travel management company executive; b. Vienna, Austria, Apr. 25, 1943; came to U.S., 1960; s. Otto Schiedeck and Maria Katharina (Schmidt) Cigalle; children: Alicia Alexandra, Julie Katherine. Diploma in hotel mgmt., Schule fuer Gastgewerbe, Vienna, 1960; BS magna cum laude, West Liberty State Coll., 1969, LLD, 1991; MBA, Columbia U., 1971. Steel worker Weirton (W.Va.) Steel Co., 1965-69; fin. analyst Citicorp, N.Y.C., 1970-71; ops. staff exec. ITT, N.Y.C., 1971-73; asst. v.p. Sun Life Ins. Co. Am., Balt., 1974-75; exec. v.p. Travel Guide, Inc., Balt., 1975-76; pres. Travelwhirl, Inc., Balt., 1976-78; founder Gelco Travel Services, Mpls., 1978-83; chmn., chief exec. officer Sontag, Annis & Assocs., Washington, 1983-86, US Travel Systems, Inc., Washington, 1986-95; CEO Fast Lane Travel Inc., Washington, 1995-97, Crown Mktg. Group, Clearwater, Fla., 1997-98; chmn. Travel Industries Colo. Inc., 1999; pres., CEO 800 Travel Systems, Inc., 1999—, also bd. mem. Pub. Travel Bus. Mgr., 1983-86; speaker in field, 1983—. With Austrian Air Force, 1963-64. Named one of Twenty Five Most Influential Execs. in Travel Industry Travel Bus. News, 1985, 87, 88, 89; named Delta Sigma Pi scholar. Mem. Alpha Phi Sigma, Delta Mu Delta (charter), Lakewood Country Club. Republican. Avocations: skiing, sailing, photography, collecting antique cars. Office: THOR Inc 382 S Arthur Ave Louisville CO 80027-3010

SORBY, DONALD LLOYD, university dean; b. Fremont, Nebr., Aug. 12, 1933; s. Lloyd A. and Orpha M. (Simmons) S.; m. Jacquelyn J. Burchard, Nov. 7, 1959; children: Thomas, Sharon. B.S. in Pharmacy, U. Nebr., 1955; M.S., U. Wash., 1958, Ph.D., 1960. Dir. pharm. services U. Calif., San Francisco, 1970-72; chmn. dept. pharmacy practice Sch. Pharmacy, U. Wash., Seattle, 1972-74; dean Sch. of Pharmacy, U. Mo., Kansas City, 1974-84, Sch. of Pharmacy, U. Pacific, Stockton, Calif., 1984-95, dean emeritus, 1995—. Bd. dirs. Longs Drugstores Inc. Contbr. articles in field to profl. jours. Named Disting. Alumnus, U. Nebr. Coll. Pharmacy, 2000. Mem. Am. Pharm. Assn. (Linwood F. Tice award 1995), Am. Assn. Colls. of Pharmacy (pres. 1980-81), Calif. Pharm. Assn., Calif. Soc. Health-Sys. Pharmacists, Sigma Xi, Phi Kappa Phi, Rho Chi. Home: 4362 Yacht Harbor Dr Stockton CA 95204-1126 Office: U Pacific Sch Pharmacy Stockton CA 95211-0001 E-mail: dsorby@att.net

SOREGAROLI, A(RTHUR) E(ARL), mining company executive, geologist; b. Jan. 4, 1933; arrived in Can., 1962; s. Arthur Samuel and Margaret Alice (Teasdale) S.; m. Rosalie Ann Lawrick, Dec. 22, 1962; children: Carla Jean, Brian Arthur. BSc in Geology, Iowa State Univ., 1959; MSc in Geology, U. Idaho, 1961; PhD in Geology, U. B.C., Vancouver, Can., 1968. Geologist Idaho Bur. Mines and Geology, Moscow, 1961-62, Noranda Exploration Co. Ltd., Vancouver, 1963-68, chief geologist western dist., 1968-72; asst. prof. geology U. B.C., Vancouver, 1972-74; rsch. scientist Geol. Survey Can., Ottawa, Ont., 1974-76; v.p. exploration Westmin Resources Ltd., Vancouver, 1976-90; chief geoscientist Teck Corp., Vancouver, 1990-98; pres. AES Enterprises, Ltd., Vancouver, 1998—. Dir. Mineral. Record, 1995—, pres., 1999-2001; contbr. papers to sci. lit. Pres. Britannia Beach Hist. Soc. which operates B.C. Mus. Mining, 1995—; dir. Pacific Mineral Mus. Soc., 1998—. With U.S. Army, 1952-54. Fellow Geol. Assn. Can. (Duncan R. Derry Gold medal, 1997), Soc. Econ. Geologists (pres. 1985), Geol. Soc. Am.; mem. Assn. Exploration Geochemists (pres. 1989-90), Can. Inst. Mining and Metallurgy (chmn. geology divsn. 1978, Dist. Proficiency Gold medal 1986, Julian Boldly Mem. award 1989, hon. fellow 1990, v.p. Dist. 6 1982-84, Disting. Svc. medal 1991, A.O. Dufresne award 2000), Geol. Soc. Can., Mineral Assn. Can., Friends of Mineralogy (dir. 1997-2000). Avocations: sports, mineral collecting. Fax: 604-731-8946. E-mail: rockdoc@infinet.net

SOREN, DAVID, archaeology educator, cinema author; b. Phila., Oct. 7, 1946; s. Harry Friedman and Erma Elizabeth (Salamon) Soren; m. Noelle Louise Schattyn, Dec. 22, 1967. BA, Dartmouth Coll., 1968; MA, Harvard U., 1972, PhD, 1973. Cert. Rome Classics Ctr. Curator of coins Fogg Art Mus., Cambridge, Mass., 1972; asst. prof. U. Mo., Columbia, 1972-76, assoc. prof., dept. head, 1976-81; prof. archaeology U. Ariz., Tucson, 1982-97, Regents prof., 1997—, dept. head, 1984-89. Guest curator Am. Mus. Natural History, N.Y.C., 1983-90, lectr., 1993—; creator, dir. Kourion Excavations, Cyprus, 1982-89, Portugal, 1983-84, Am. Excavations at Lugnano, Italy, 1988-93; pot cons., field dir. Tunisia Excavations, Chgo. Oriental Inst./Smithsonian Instn., 1973-78; dir. excavations Chianciano Terme, Italy, 1995—; subject of The Learning Channel TV series Archaeology, 1995. Author: Unreal Reality, 1978, Rise and Fall of Fantasy Film, 1980, Carthage, 1990, French edit., 1994, Vera-Ellen: The Magic and the Mystery, 1999, Excavation of A Roman Villa, 1999; author: Kourion: Search for a Lost Roman City, 1988, Corpus des Mosaiques de Tunisie, 1972, 3rd rev. edit., 1986, Carthage: A Mosaic of Ancient Tunisia, 1987; editor: Excavations at Kourion I, 1987; contbg. editor: Archaeology Mag.; producer: (film) Carthage: A Mirage of Antiquity, 1987; creator and guest curator: (internat. traveling exhbn.) Carthage: A Mosaic of Ancient Tunisia, 1987-92; editor, founder Roscius, 1993-95; creative cons. TV miniseries Lost Civilizations, 1994; contbr. articles to profl. jours. Subject of National Geographic spl. Archeological Detectives, 1985, Italian TV spl. RAI 1 network, 2001; work subject of feature articles in Newsweek, Conoisseur, National Geographic, Time, N.Y. Times, and others; recipient Cine Golden Eagle, 1980, Angenieux Film award Industrial Photography mag., 1980, Outstanding American Under 40 award C. Johns Hopkins-Britain's Royal Inst. Internat. Affairs, 1985; named Outstanding American Under 40 Esquire mag., 1985, hon. Italian citizen Lugnano, Italy, 1989; grantee NEH, 1979, 87, Fulbright, Lisbon, 1983. Fellow Brit. Royal Inst. Internat. Affairs; mem. Nat. Geog. Soc. (project dir. 1983-84), Am. Sch. Oriental Rsch. (dept. rep. 1981-85), Archaeol. Inst. Tucson (pres. 1983-86), Luso-Am. Commn. (citation 1983-84), Explorer's Club. Office: U Ariz Dept Classics 371 Mlb Tucson AZ 85721-0001 E-mail: soren@u.arizona.edu

SORENSEN, LINDA, lawyer; b. Eureka, Calif., Mar. 3, 1945; BS, U. Wis., Madison, 1967; JD, U. Calif., 1976. Bar: Calif. 1976, U.S. Dist. Ct. (no. dist.) Calif. 1976, U.S. Ct. Appeals (9th cir.) 1976, U.S. Dist. Ct. (ea. dist.) Calif. 1977. Assoc. Rothschild, Phelan & Mertali, San Francisco, 1976-88; dir. Howard, Rice, Nemerovski, Canady, Falk & Rabkin, San Francisco, 1988-95; shareholder Feldman, Waldman & Kline, P.C., San Francisco, 1997-99; pvt. practice Berkeley, Calif., 1999—. Mem. ABA (mem. subcom. on avoiding powers, bus. bankruptcy com. 1983-95), Bar Assn. of San Francisco (chmn. comml. law and bankruptcy sect. 1984, editor fed. cts. com., no. dist. Calif. digest 1979-82). Office: PO Box 7997 Berkeley CA 94707-7997 Fax: 510 845 1785. E-mail: lindasorensen@earthlink.net

SORENSEN, SHEILA, state legislator; b. Chgo., Sept. 20, 1947; d. Martin Thomas Moloney and Elizabeth (Koehr) Paulus; m. Wayne B. Slaughter, May, 1969 (div. 1976); 1 child, Wayne Benjamin III; m. Dean E. Sorensen, Feb. 14, 1977; (stepchildren) Michael, Debbie, Kevin, Dean C. BS, Loretto Heights Coll., Denver, 1965; postgrad. pediatric nurse practicioner, U. Colo., Denver, 1969-70. Pediatric nurse practicioner Pub. Health Dept., Denver, 1970-71, Boise, Idaho, 1971-72, Boise (Idaho) Pediatric Group, 1972-74, Pediatric Assocs., Boise, 1974-77; mem. Idaho Ho. Reps., 1987-92, Idaho Senate, Dist. 13, Boise, 1992—; chair senate health and welfare com. Idaho Senate, 1992-94, chair senate majority caucus, 1994-96, vice chair state affairs com., 1996-98, chair state affairs, 1998—. State chair Am. Legis. Exchange Coun. Precinct committeeman Ada County Rep. Ctrl. Com., Boise, 1982-86, dist. vice chair, 1985-88; polit. chair Idaho Med. Assn. Aux., 1984-87, Ada County Med. Assocs., 1986-87; bd. dirs. Family Practice Residency Program, 1992-94, Univ./Cmty. Health Sci. Assn., Bishop Kelly Found., 1993—; chair Senate Majority Caucus, 1995-96, chair state affairs com., 1999—. Recipient AMA Nathan Davis award for Outstanding State Legislator, 1994. Mem. Nat. Conf. State Legislators, Nat. Orgn. Women Legislators (state chair), Am. Legis. Exch. Coun. (Legis of Yr. award 1999). Roman Catholic.

SORENSON, PERRY, resort facility executive; m. Sally Slagle; children: Eric, Karin, Bjorn. MBA with honors, U. Utah. Dist. dir. Holiday Inns, Hawaii, 1980-83, regional v.p., 1983-86; v.p., chief operating officer Embassy Suites, Inc., 1986-88; chief operating officer Outrigger Hotels and Resorts, 1988—. Avocations: reading, running, tennis. Office: Outrigger Hotels & Resorts 2375 Kuhio Ave Honolulu HI 96815-2992

SORRENTINO, GILBERT, English language educator, novelist, poet; b. Bklyn., Apr. 27, 1929; s. August E. and Ann Marie (Davis) S.; m. Victoria Ortiz; children: Jesse, Delia, Christopher. Student, Bklyn. Coll., 1949-51, 54-56. In various positions, 1947-70; including reins. clk. Fidelity and Casualty Co., N.Y.C., 1947-48; freight checker Ace Assembly Agy., N.Y.C., 1954-56; packer Bennett Bros. Inc., N.Y.C., 1956-57; messenger Am. Houses, Inc., N.Y.C., 1948-49; shipping-room supr. Thermo-fax Sales, Inc., Queens, N.Y., 1957-60; editor Grove Press, 1965-70; tchr. Columbia U., 1966, Aspen Writers Workshop, 1967, Sarah Lawrence Coll., 1972, The New Sch. for Social Rsch., 1976—; NEH chairperson in lit. U. Scranton, 1979; prof. English Stanford (Calif.) U., 1982—. Editorial cons. Contemporary Lit., 1989-97. Author: The Darkness Surrounds Us, 1960, Black and White, 1964, The Sky Changes, 1966, The Perfect Fiction, 1968, Steelwork, 1970, Imaginative Qualities of Actual Things, 1971, Corrosive Sublimate, 1971, Splendide-Hotel, 1972, Flawless Play Restored, 1974, A Dozen Oranges, 1976, White Sail, 1977, Sulpiciae Elegidia/Elegiacs of Sulpica, 1977, The Orangery, 1978, Mulligan Stew, 1979, Aberration of Starlight, 1980, Selected Poems, 1958-80, 1981, Crystal Vision, 1981, Blue Pastoral, 1983, Something Said: Essays, 1984, Odd Number, 1985, Rose Theatre, 1987, Misterioso, 1989, Under the Shadow, 1991, Red the Fiend, 1995, Pack of Lies: A Trilogy, 1997, Gold Fools, 2001. With U.S. Army, 1951-53. Recipient Samuel Fels award in fiction Coord. Coun. Lit. Mags., 1974, John Dos Passos prize, 1981, Am. Acad. and Inst. Arts and Letters award in lit., 1985, Lannan Lit. award for fiction, 1992; John Simon Guggenheim Meml. fellow, 1973-74, 87-88; grantee Creative Artists Pub. Svc. Program, 1974-75, Nat. Endowment for Arts, 1974-75, 78-79, 83-84. Mem. PEN Am. Ctr. Office: Stanford U Dept English Stanford CA 94305

SOUTHERN, RONALD D. diversified corporation executive; b. Calgary, Alta., Can., July 25, 1930; s. Samuel Donald and Alexandra (Cuthill) S.; m. Margaret Visser, July 30, 1954; children: Nancy, Linda. BSc, U. Alta., Edmonton, 1953; LLD (hon.), U. Calgary, 1976, U. Alberta, 1991. Chmn., CEO ATCO Ltd. and Can. Utilities Ltd., Calgary, 1994-99, ATCO Ltd., Calgary, 1994-99, Can. Utilities Ltd., Calgary, 1994-99, co-chmn., CEO, 1999—. Chmn. Akita Drilling Ltd.; bd. dirs. Royal & Sun Alliance Ins. Ltd., Atco Ltd., Can. Utilities Ltd.; co-chmn., CEO Spruce Meadows, 1999—; chmn. Spruce Meadows Round Table. Decorated Order of Can., comdr. Brit. Empire; recipient Disting. Entrepreneur award U. Man. Faculty Mgmt., 1990; inducted into Can. Bus. Hall, 1995; named Businessman of Yr. U. Alta., 1986, CEO of the Yr. Fin. Post, 1996. Mem. Ranchmen's Club. Calgary Golf and Country Club. Office: ATCO Ltd & Can Utilities 1600 909-11 Ave SW Calgary AB Canada T2R IN6

SOUTHWICK, CHARLES HENRY, zoologist, educator; b. Wooster, Ohio, Aug. 28, 1928; s. Arthur F. and Faye (Motz) S.; m. Heather Milne Beck, July 12, 1952; children: Steven, Karen. B.A., Coll. Wooster, 1949; M.S., U. Wis., 1951, Ph.D., 1953. NIH fellow, 1951-53; asst. prof. biology Hamilton Coll., 1953-54; NSF fellow Oxford (Eng.) U., 1954-55; faculty Ohio U., 1955-61; assoc. prof. pathobiology Johns Hopkins Sch. Hygiene and Pub. Health, Balt., 1961-68, prof., 1968-79; assoc. dir. Johns Hopkins Internat. Ctr. for Med. Rsch. and Tng., Calcutta, India, 1964-65; chmn. dept. environ., population and organismic biology U. Colo., Boulder, 1979-82, prof. biology, 1979—, prof. emeritus, 1993—. Researcher and author publs. on animal social behavior and population dynamics, influences animal social behavior on demographic characteristic mammal populations, primate ecology and behavior, estuarine ecology and environmental quality; mem. primate adv. com. Nat. Acad. Sci.-NRC, 1963-75, com. primate conservation, 1974-75; mem. Gov.'s Sci. Adv. Com. State of Md., 1975-78; mem. com. on rsch. and exploration Nat. Geog. Soc., 1979-2000; mem. adv. bd. Caribbean Primate Rsch. Ctr., 1987-99, Wis. Primate Rsch. Ctr., 1990-98; mem. Integrated Conservation Rsch., 1989—. Editor, author: Primate Social Behavior, 1963, Animal Aggression, 1970, Nonhuman Primates in Biomedical Research, 1975, Ecology and the Quality of Our Environment, 1976, Global Ecology, 1985; Ecology and Behavior of Food-Enhanced Primate Groups, 1988; author: Global Ecology in Human Perspective, 1996. Recipient Fulbright Rsch. award India, 1959-60, Tchg. Excellence award U. Colo., 1993. Fellow AAAS, Acad. Zoology, Animal Behavior Soc.; mem. Am. Soc. Zoologists, Ecol. Soc. Am., Am. Soc. Mammalogists, Am. Soc. Primatology (Disting. Primatologist award 1994), Internat. Primatology Soc., Am. Inst. Biol. Scis.

SOUZA, LAWRENCE M. health facility administrator; AB in Bacteriology, U. Calif., Berkeley, 1975; PhD in Molecular Biology, UCLA, 1980. With Amgen, Thousand Oaks, Calif., 1981—, v.p. molecular and cellular biology, dir. exploratory programs, sr. v.p. rsch., 1997—. Adj. prof. dept. microbiology and immunology UCLA. Office: Amgen Inc One Amgen Center Dr Mailstop 27-5-A Thousand Oaks CA 91320-1789

SOWDER, ROBERT ROBERTSON, architect; b. Kansas City, Kans., Dec. 29, 1928; s. James Robert and Agnes (Robertson) S.; m. Joan Goddard, July 26, 1954; 1 dau., Lisa Robertson Lee. B.A., U. Wash., 1953; B.Arch., U. Va., 1958; grad. diploma in Architecture, Ecole Des Beaux Arts, Fontainebleau, France, 1952. Designer Architects Collaborative, Boston, 1958-59, Peirce & Pierce (architects), Boston, 1959-63; asso. Fred. Bassetti & Co. (architects), Seattle, 1963-67; partner Naramore, Bain, Brady & Johanson (architects), Seattle, 1967-81; pres. NBBJ Internat., 1976-81; architect TRA, Seattle, 1981-83; v.p. Daniel, Mann, Johnson & Mendenhall, San Francisco, 1983-93; prin. RRS Consulting, 1993—. Archtl. design critic Boston Archtl. Ctr., 1961-62. Important works include Ridgeway III Dormitories, Bellingham, Wash. (Dept. Housing and Urban Devel. Honor award), Seattle Rapid Transit (HUD Excellence award), Safeco Ins. Co. Home Office Complex, Seattle, King County Stadium, Balt. Conv. Ctr., Oreg. Conv. Ctr., San Francisco (Moscone) Conv. Ctr. Expansion, Honolulu Conv. Ctr., Wilmington (Del.) Conv. Ctr. Mem. Redmond (Wash.) Design Rev. Bd., 1996-2000. Served with CIC U.S. Army, 1954-56. Recipient Premier Prix D'Architecture Ecole Des Beaux Arts, Fontainebleau, 1951, 52, Prix D'Remondet Fontainebleau, 1952 Mem. AIA (emeritus), Internat. Assn. Assembly Mgrs., Seattle Tennis Club, Seattle Rainier Club, Scarab, Sigma Chi. Episcopalian. Home and Office: 17032 NE 135th Ct Redmond WA 98052-1715

SPAFFORD, MICHAEL CHARLES, artist; b. Palm Springs, Calif., Nov. 6, 1935; BA, Pomona Coll., 1959; MA, Harvard U., 1960. One man shows include Seattle Art Mus., 1982, 86, Reed Coll., 1984, Whtcom county Mus., 1987, U. Puget Sound, Tacoma, Wash., 1973, Tacoma Art Mus., 1975, 86, Utah Mus. Fine Arts, Salt Lake City, 1975, Francine Seders Gallery, Seattle, 1965—, Bellevue Art Mus., 1991, Cheney-Cowles Mus., Spokane, Wash., 1994, Hallie Ford Mus. Art, Willamette U., Salem, Oreg., 1999; exhibited in group shows at Wilcox Gallery, Swarthmore Coll., Pa., 1977, Seattle Art Mus., 1977, 80, 84, Am. Acad. and Inst. Arts and Letters, N.Y.C., 1980, 83, 89, 95, Kobe, Japan, 1981, Eastern Wash. U., 1982, Henry Art Gallery, 1982, 86, Bellevue Art Mus., 1987, 95, Cheney Cowles Mus., 1988, Holter Mus. of Art, Helena, Mont. Recipient Rome Prize Am. Acad. in Rome, 1967-69, award Am. Acad. and Inst. Arts and Letters, 1983, Lifetime Achievement in Arts award Corp. Coun. Arts, Seattle, 1999; Louis Comfort Tiffany Found. grantee, 1965-66; Neddy fellow, 1996. Address: c/o Francine Seders Gallery 6701 Greenwood Ave N Seattle WA 98103-5225

SPANEL, HARRIET ROSA ALBERTSEN, state legislator; b. Audubon, Iowa, Jan. 15, 1939; m. Leslie E. Spanel, June 3, 1961; 3 children. BS in Math., Iowa State U., 1961. Mem. Wash. Ho. of Reps., 1987-93, Wash. Senate, Dist. 40, Olympia, 1993—. Home: 901 Liberty St Bellingham WA 98225-5632 Office: Wash Senate PO Box 40440 Olympia WA 98504-0440

SPANGLER, DAVID ROBERT, college administrator, engineer; b. Flint, Mich., Aug. 17, 1940; s. John Solomon and Margaret Inger (McKinley) S.; m. Sally Jeanne Henry, Aug. 28, 1965; children: Timothy David, Megan Marie. BS, U.S. Mil. Acad., 1962; MS in Engring., U. Ill., 1966, PhD in Structural Dynamics, 1977. Registered profl. engr. Commd. 2d lt. U.S. Army, 1962, advanced through grades to lt. col., 1979, prof. math. U.S. Mil. Acad. N.Y., 1968-71, engr. Korea Support Command, 1972-73, dep. dist. engr. C.E. Wash., 1973-74, research coordinator Def. Nuclear Agy. Washington, 1976-79, bn. comdr. Hawaii, 1979-81, inspector C.E., 1981-82, ret., 1982; prof. engring. St. Martin's Coll., Lacey, Wash., 1982-84, pres., 1984—. Mem. Nat. Com. for Tunnelling Tech., Washington, 1977-79; cons. Thurston County, Olympia, Wash., 1982-84. Contbr. articles to profl. jours. Bd. dirs. Econ. Devel. Coun., Thurston County, 1985-88, Wash. State Capitol Mus., 1988-91. Decorated Bronze Star with 2 oak leaf clusters, Meritorious Service medal, Def. Nuclear Agy. Joint Service medal. Mem. Soc. Mil. Engrs. (v.p. 1980-81, pres. 1973-74), Nat. Assn. Ind. Colls. and Univs. (bd. dirs. 1992-95, treas. 1994), Ind. Colls. Wash. (bd. dirs.), Assn. Benedictine Colls. and Univs. (pres. 1994-95), Rotary (mem. gov.'s oversight com. on tech. 1996—). Roman Catholic. Avocation: running. Office: St Martins Coll Office of Pres Lacey WA 98503

SPANGLER, MARY, college president; BA, Chestnut Hill Coll.; MA in English, UCLA, DEdn, 1994. Prof. English L.A. Valley Coll., assoc. dean of admissions, dean of student svcs., v.p. acad. affairs, pres., 1997—. Adj. faculty Sch. of Edn. Nat. U.; presenter in field. Co-author four textbooks; contbr. articles to profl. jours. Mem. exec. edn. coun. U. Phoenix; adv. com. edn. svcs. C.C. League of Calif.; state chancellor Calif. C.C.; adv. com. Calif. Acad. Partnership Program. Mem. Hollywood C. of C. (bd. dirs.), Am. Assn. for Higher Edn., Nat. Coun. for Rsch. and Planning, Assn. for Rsch. on Nonprofit Orgns. and Vol. Action, Assn. of Calif. C.C. Adminstrs., Pi Lambda Theta. Office: Los Angeles City Coll 855 N Vermont Ave Los Angeles CA 90029-3516

SPANGLER, NITA REIFSCHNEIDER, volunteer; b. Ukiah, Calif., Apr. 17, 1923; d. John Charles and Olga Augusta (Wuertz) Reifschneider; m. Raymond Luper Spangler, Sept. 22, 1946 (dec.); children: Jon Martin, Mary Raymond, Thor Raymond. BA, Univ. Nev., 1944. News reporter Redwood (Calif.) City Tribune, 1944-46, Country Almanac, Woodside, Calif., 1969-77. Mem. bd. dirs. San Mateo (Calif.) County Hist. Assn., 1961-68, pres., 1964-66; founder, 1st pres. Portolá Expedition Bicentennial Found., 1966-70; chmn. San Mateo County Scenic Rds. Com., 1967-76; mem. San Mateo County Hist. Resource Adv.; mem. commn. San Mateo County Parks and Recreation, 1983-97, past chmn.; cons. hwy. aesthetics Cal Trans., 1981-83; mem. sch. coms. Recipient Commendation, County Bd. Suprs., 1968, 1977, 92. Mem. Sierra Club, Western History Assn., Mormon History Assn., Nev. State Hist. Soc. (life), San Mateo County Hist. Assn. (life, Resolution of Thanks 1968, 76, 94), Friends Redwood City, Kappa Alpha Theta. Democrat. Episcopalian. Avocations: historic preservation. Home: 970 Edgewood Rd Redwood City CA 94062-1818

SPANOS, ALEXANDER GUS, construction executive, professional sports team executive; b. Stockton, Calif., Sept. 28, 1923; m. Faye Spanos; children: Dean, Dea Spanos Berberian, Alexis Spanos Ruhl, Michael. LLD (hon.), U. Pacific, 1984. Chmn. bd. dirs. A.G. Spanos Constrn. Inc., Stockton, Calif., 1960—; chmn. bd. dirs. A.G. Spanos Mgmt. Inc., Stockton, 1967—, A.G. Spanos Enterprises Inc., Stockton, 1971—, A.G. Spanos Devel. Inc., Stockton, 1973—, A.G. Spanos Realty Inc., Stockton, 1978—, A.G.S. Fin. Corp., Stockton, 1980—, A.G. Spanos Securities Corp., Stockton, 1981—, San Diego Chargers, 1984—. Former trustee Children's Hosp., San Francisco, San Francisco Fine Arts Mus.; trustee Eisenhower Med. Ctr., Rancho Mirage, Calif.; hon. regent U. Pacific, Stockton, 1972-82; gov. USO, Washington, 1982—; former gov. Ronald Reagan Presdl. Found.; chmn. U.S. chpt. U.S. Greece bus. coun. Served with USAF, 1942-46. Recipient Albert Gallatin award Zurich-Am. Ins. Co., 1973, Horatio Alger award Horatio Alger Found., 1982, medal of Honor Statue of Liberty-Ellis Islan Found., 1982. Mem. Am. Hellenic Ednl. Progressive Assn., Calif. C. of C. (bd. dirs. 1980-85). Republican. Greek Orthodox. Avocation: golfing. Office: San Diego Chargers Qualcomm Stadium PO Box 609609 San Diego CA 92160-9609 also: A G Spanos Cos Ste 1A 1341 West Robinhood Dr Stockton CA 95207 E-mail: agspr@agspanos.com

SPANOS, DEAN A. professional sports team executive, business executive; b. Stockton, Calif., May 26, 1950; s. Alex G. Spanos; m. Susan Spanos; children: Alexander Gus, John Dean. BBA, U. Pacific, 1972. Pres., vice-chmn. San Diego Chargers, 1984—; pres. Spanos corp. entities; vice-chmn. AGS Fin. Corp. Past bd. regents U. Pacific. Co-winner Bing Crosby Nat. Pro-Am. Golf Tournament, 1985; winner Bob Hope Chrysler Classic, 1990, 91, AT&T Nat. Pro-Am. Golf Tournament, 1990; recipient Most Valuable Amateur trophy; mem. winning team in Sr.'s Reunion Tournament, Dallas, 1985. Avocation: golf. Office: San Diego Chargers 4020 Murphy Canyon Rd San Diego CA 92123-4407

SPARKS, DALE BOYD, allergist, health facility administrator; b. Springfield, Mo., July 14, 1929; s. Roscoe R. and Ruby V. (Boyd) S.; divorced; children: Susan L., Laura A., Lisa M., Jennifer G.; m. Leeanna M. Molccyk Pribay, Apr. 21, 2001. AB, BS, Southwest Mo. State U., 1951; BS in Medicine, U. Mo., 1953; MD, St. Louis U., 1955. Diplomate Am. Bd. Allergy and Immunology. Intern Kansas City (Mo.) Gen. Hosp. U. Med. Ctr., 1955-56; resident U. Mo. Hosp., 1958-60; fellow in allergy and immunology Northwestern U., 1960-61; mem. cons. staff Parkview Cmty. Hosp., 1961—; mem. med. staff Riverside County Regional Med. Ctr., 1961-2000, dir. respiratory therapy, 1968-85, dir. respiratory therapy and diagnostic svcs., 1965—, chmn. dept. medicine, 1978-98, chief med. staff, 1990-98; acting dir., health officer Riverside Pub. Health Dept., 1991-93. Clin. prof. medicine Loma Linda U. Mem. editl. bd. Immunology and Allergy in Practice, 1980—. Lt. USNR. Fellow ACP (coun. subsplty. socs. 1988—), Am. Coll. Allergy and Immunology (disting., bd. regents 1989-93, pres. 1990-91, chmn. fin. com./treas. 1990-93, recert. com.), Coll. Allergy, Asthma and Immunology; mem. AMA, Am. Lung Assn. (bd. dirs. 1990-95), Am. Heart Assn. (bd. dirs. 1964-70, pres. 1966), Joint Coun. Am. Allergy and Immunology (bd. dirs. 1985-90), Calif. Med. Assn., Calif. Soc. Allergy, Inland Soc. Internal Medicine, Riverside County Med. Assn. (bd. councilors 1980-99, del. CMA 1988-99), Riverside County Found. Med. Care (sec., past pres.). E-mial. Home: 3498 Ramona Dr Riverside CA 92506-1257 Office: 4646 Brockton Ave Riverside CA 92506 E-mail: dsparksmd@aol.com

SPARKS, JOHN EDWARD, lawyer; b. Rochester, Ind., July 3, 1930; s. Russell Leo and Pauline Anna (Whittenberger) S.; m. Margaret Joan Snyder, Sept. 4, 1954; children: Thomas Edward, William Russell, Kathryn Chapman McCarthy. A.B., Ind. U., 1952; LL.B., U. Calif., Berkeley, 1957; postgrad., London Sch. Econs., 1957-58. Bar: Calif. 1958. Assoc. Brobeck, Phleger & Harrison, San Francisco, 1958-66, ptnr., 1967-95, of counsel, 1996—. Adj. prof. law U. San Francisco, 1967-69; pres. Legal Aid Soc. San Francisco, 1978-79, dir., 1971-81. Editor U. Calif. Law Rev., 1956-57. Served to 1st lt. Q.M.C. U.S. Army, 1952-54, Korea. Recipient Wheeler Oak Meritorious award U. Calif., Berkeley, 1986. Fellow Am. Bar Found., Am. Coll. Trial Lawyers; mem. State Bar Calif., Bar Assn. San Francisco (bd. dirs. 1974-75), ABA, Am. Judicature Soc., Boalt Hall Alumni Assn. (pres. 1983-84), Pacific Union Club (San Francisco), Democrat. Office: Brobeck Phleger & Harrison Spear St Tower 1 Market Plz Fl 31 San Francisco CA 94105-1100 E-mail: jsparks@brobeck.com

SPARKS, MILDRED THOMAS, state agency administrator, educator; b. Montgomery, Ala., Oct. 2, 1942; d. Leon and Annie Lee (Johnson) Thomas; m. John H. Sparks, Aug. 29, 1964; children: Melanie J. Bosak, Jennifer L. David-Gerhartz, Regina F. BS, Ala. State U., 1964; MS, Pepperdine U., 1978; postgrad., Claremont Coll., Calif. State U., Boston Coll. Cert. reading specialist, contract mgmt., U. Phoenix, U. Wyo. Tchr. Dayton (Ohio) Schs., 1964-66, Oxon Hill (Md.) Schs., 1966-70; technician Reading Lab. Grambling (La.) State U., 1972; reading lab. aide Calif. City (Calif.) Schs., 1975; reading instr. Cerro Coso So. Outreach, Edwards AFB, Calif., 1976-78; substitute tchr. San Bernardino City Schs., 1979, Aquinas H.S., San Bernardino, 1978-79; reading lab. tchr. San Bernardino H.S., 1979; instr. reading lab. San Bernardino Valley Coll., 1980-81, assoc. prof. reading, dept. head, 1981-86; contract adminstr. Hercules Missile Ordinance and Space Group, Magna, Utah, 1986, Alliant Techsys. (formerly Hercules Missile Ordinance and Space Group), 1987-97; dir. Office of Black Affairs State of Utah, 1997—. Mem. Black Adv. Coun., Office of Black Affairs; presenter workshops, cmty. events; troop vol. Girl Scouts U.S.; vol. The March of Dimes, Am. Heart Assn., Visitation of the Elderly Homebound, Am. Cancer Soc. and Marriage and Family Workshop for Teens, Cath. Cmty. Svcs.; civil rights movement participant Ala. Bus Boycott; mem. minority health adv. bd. Utah Health Dept.; mem. Cath. Women League, Black Caths. Utah, Salt Lake City, African Am. Task Force, Gov.'s Initiative on Family Today, Anti-Discrimination Com.; planning com. United Way Greater Salt Lake, vol.; past pres. Salt Lake Diocesan Pastoral Coun., vol. Mem. Calif Tchrs. Assn., Nat. Coun. Tchrs. English, Assn. Supervision and Curriculum Devel., Western Coll. Reading Assn., Bus. and Profl. Women's Club, Link's, Jack and Jill of Am. Inc., Delta Kappa Gamma, Alpha Kappa Alpha. Roman Catholic (Norton lav lector). Avocations: reading, writing, gardening, cross-country skiing. Home: 3790 Becky Cir Salt Lake City UT 84109-3302 Office: Office Black Affairs 324 S State St Ste 500 Salt Lake City UT 84111 Fax: (801) 538-8678. E-mail: msparks@dced.state.ut.us

SPARKS, ROBERT DEAN, medical administrator, physician; b. Newton, Iowa, May 6, 1932; s. Albert John and Josephine Emma (Kleinendorst) S.; children: Steven Robert, Ann Louise, John James. BA, U. Iowa, 1955, MD, 1957; D of Humanitarian Service, Creighton U., 1978. Diplomate Am. Bd. Internal Medicine. Intern Charity Hosp. of La., New Orleans, 1957-58, resident in internal medicine, 1958-59, asst. in medicine, 1958-59; fellow in gen. medicine and gastroenterology Tulane U. Sch. Medicine, 1959-62, instr. medicine, 1959-63, asst. prof., 1963-64, assoc. prof., 1964-68, prof., 1968-72, asst. dean, 1964-67, assoc. dean, acting dean, 1967-68, vice dean, 1968-69, dean, 1969-72, chief sect. gastroenterology, 1968-72; chancellor Med. Ctr. U. Nebr., 1972-76, prof. medicine, 1972-76; v.p. U. Nebr. System, 1972-76; health program dir. W.K. Kellogg Found., Battle Creek, Mich., 1976-81, v.p. programming, 1981-82, sr. v.p., 1982, pres., chief programming officer, 1982-86, pres., 1982-88, trustee, 1988, pres. emeritus, cons., 1988-92; pres., CEO, Calif. Med. Assn. Found., San Francisco, 1995-98, sr. assoc., 1998—. Cons. U. Tenn. Health Sci. Ctr., 1988-90, Boston U. Health Policy Inst., 1989-90; bd. dirs., mem. sci., compensation and trust rev. coms. Syntex Corp., Palo Alto, Calif., 1987-91, v.p. product safety and compliance, 1991-93; mem. overseers com. to visit Harvard U. Med. and Dental Schs., 1984-90; mem. vis. com. U. Miami Sch. Medicine, 1982-86; assoc. med. dir. for addiction treatment svcs., dir. for edn. and rsch., Battle Creek Adventist Hosp., 1990-91; v.p. Howe-Lewis Internat Inc., Menlo Park, N.Y., 1993-94, cons., 1994-95. Contbr. articles to profl. jours. Bd. dirs. Nat. Coun. on Alcoholism and Drug Dependence, N.Y.C., 1982-93, treas., 1986-88, chmn., 1989-90, past chmn., 1991-92; bd. dirs. Battle Creek Symphony Orch., 1981-88, Lakeview Sch. Dist., Battle Crek, 1979-83, 88-91; trustee Monsour Med. Found., Jeannette, Pa., 1976-90, interim pres. 1989, chmn. bd., pres., 1989-90; mem. President's Adv. Bd. on Pvt. Sector Initiatives, Washington, 1986-89; chmn. bd. dirs. Bard Coll. Health Policy and Practice Inst., 1988-96, Consumer Health Info. Rsch. Inst., 1990-95, Chelsea-Arbor Treatment Ctr., 1990-91; bd. dirs. Calhoun County Bd. Health, 1988-91, chmn., 1989-91; mem., bd. dirs. Mental Health and Addictions Found. Mich., Battle Creek, 1991-93. Recipient Harvard Dental award Harvard U. Sch. Dental Medicine, 1992, Disting. Alumni award for achievement U. Iowa Coll. Medicine, 1998, annual Robert D. Sparks Comty. Health Leadership Achievement award CMA Found., 2000. Fellow ACP; mem. AMA, Nat. Acad. Scis. Inst. Medicine (com. study of treatment and rehab. svcs. for alcoholism and alcohol abuse, bd. mental health and behavioral medicine), Coun. Mich. Founds. (trustee 1986-88), Assn. Am. Med. Colls. (disting. svc. mem. 1975—), Phi Eta Sigma, Alpha Omega Alpha. Republican. Presbyterian. Avocations: tennis, bridge, reading, travel. Home and Office: PO Box 4620 El Dorado Hills CA 95762-0021 E-mail: rdsparksmd@worldnet.att.net

SPARKS, THOMAS E., JR. lawyer; b. Little Rock, Jan. 11, 1942; children: Thomas Gunnar, Erik Richard, Andrew Pal. BS, Washington and Lee U., 1963; JD, U. Ark., 1968; LLM, Harvard U., 1970. Bar: Ark. 1968, Calif. 1970. Assoc. Pillsbury Madison & Sutro, San Francisco, 1970-76; ptnr. Pillsbury, Madison & Sutro, San Francisco, 1977-84, Baker & McKenzie, San Francisco, 1984-87, Pillsbury Madison & Sutro, San Francisco, 1987-2000, Pillsbury Winthrop, San Francisco, 2001—. Trustee Grace Cathedral, San Francisco. 1st lt. U.S. Army, 1965. Mem. ABA, Calif. Bar Assn., Olympic Club (San Francisco), Calif. Tennis Club (pres. 2000). Office: Pillsbury Winthrop 50 Fremont St San Francisco CA 94105-2230

SPARLING, MARY LEE, biology educator; b. Ft. Wayne, Ind., May 20, 1934; d. George Hewson and Velmah Evelyn (McClain) S.; m. Albert Alcide Barber, Sept. 1, 1956 (div. Jan. 1975); children: Bonnie Lee Barber, Bradley Paul Barber. BS, U. Miami, Coral Gables, Fla., 1955; MA, Duke U., 1958; PhD, UCLA, 1962. Lectr. UCLA, 1962-63; asst. prof. Calif. State U., Northridge, 1966-72, assoc. prof., 1972-76, prof., 1976—. Statewide acad. senator Calif. State U., 1996-98. Contbr. articles to profl. jours. NSF grantee Calif. State U., Northridge, 1971-72, 81-83, 89, NIH grantee Calif. State U., Northridge, 1987-89. Mem. AAUP (pres. 1981-82), Am. Soc. Cell Biology, Soc. for Devel. Biology, Am. Soc. Zoologists, Sigma Xi (bd. dirs. Research Triangle, N.C. 1974-91). Avocations: tennis, gardening, travel. Home: 3662 Stoner Ave Los Angeles CA 90066-2839 Office: Calif State U Biology Dept Northridge CA 91330-0001

SPARR, DANIEL BEATTIE, federal judge; b. Denver, June 8, 1931; s. Daniel John and Mary Isabel (Beattie) S.; m. Virginia Sue Long Sparr, June 28, 1952; children: Stephen Glenwood, Douglas Lloyd, Michael Christopher. BSBA, U. Denver, 1952, JD, 1966. Bar: Colo. U.S. Dist. Ct. Assoc. White & Steele, Denver, 1966-70; atty. Mountain States Telephone & Telegraph Co., Denver, 1970-71; ptnr. White & Steele, Denver, 1971-74; atty. Wesley H. Doan, Lakewood, Colo., 1974-75; prin. Law Offices of Daniel B. Sparr, Denver, 1975-77; judge 2d dist. Colo. Dist. Ct., Denver, 1977-90; judge U.S. Dist. Ct. Colo., Denver, 1990—. Mem. Denver Bar Assn. (trustee 1975-78), Denver Paralegal Inst. (bd. advs. 1976-88), William E. Doyle's/Am. Inns of Ct., Am. Bd. Trial Advs., ABA, Colo. Bar Assn. Office: US Dist Ct 1929 Stout St Denver CO 80294-1929

SPAULDING, JOHN PIERSON, public relations executive, marine consultant; b. N.Y.C., June 25, 1917; s. Forrest Brisbine and Genevieve Anderson (Pierson) S.; m. Eleanor Rita Bonner, Aug. 18, 1947; children: Anne Spaulding Balzhiser, John F., Mary T. Spaulding Calvert; m. 2d, Donna Alene Abrescia, May 15, 1966. Student Iowa State Coll., 1935-36, Grinnell Coll., 1936-38, U. Chgo., 1938-39. Reporter, Chgo. City News Bur., UPI, 1939-40; editor Cedar Falls (Iowa) Daily Record, 1940-41; picture editor Des Moines Register & Tribune, 1941-42, 47-50; pub. relations dir. Motor Club Iowa, Davenport, 1950-51; commd. 2d. lt. USAF, 1942, advanced through grades to maj., 1947, recalled, 1951, advanced through grades to lt. col.; ret., 1968; v.p. Vacations Hawaii, Honolulu, 1969-70; dir. pub. relations, mgr. pub. relations services Alexander & Baldwin, Inc., Honolulu, 1970-76; mgr. community relations Matson Navigation Co., Honolulu, 1976-81. Pres., Econ. Devel. Assn., Skagit County, Wash., 1983-85; pres., chmn. Fidalgo Island Ednl. Youth Found.; mem. Anacortes (Wash.) Sch. Bd., 1982-88; mem. Gov.'s Tourism Devel. Council, 1983-85; mem. adv. com. State Ferry System, 1982—, productivity coun., 1990—; chmn. Everett chpt. S.C.O.R.E., 1984-86, Bellingham chpt., 1991—; mem. citizens adv. com. Skagit County Transit, 1995—. Decorated Air medal. Mem. Pub. Relations Soc. Am. (pres. Hawaii chpt. 1974), Hawaii Communicators (pres. 1973), Nat. Def. Transp. Assn. (pres. Aloha chpt. 1980-81, Disting. Service award 1978-79), Air Force Assn., Can. Inst. Internat. Affairs, Anacortes C. of C., Sigma Delta Chi (life). Clubs: Propeller (pres. Port of Honolulu 1979-80), Honolulu Press, Fidelgo Yacht, Hawaii Yacht, Royal Hawaiian 400 Yacht (comdr. 1977-81), Rotary (sec. 1996-98). Home: 6002 Sands Way Anacortes WA 98221-4015

SPEAR, ROBERT CLINTON, environmental health educator, consultant; b. Los Banos, Calif., June 26, 1939; s. Clinton Wentworth Spear and Maytie Izetta (Patten) Gill; m. Patricia Warner, Dec. 15, 1962; children: Andrew Warner, Jennifer Ellen. BS, U. Calif., Berkeley, 1961, MS, 1962; PhD, Cambridge U., 1968. Registered profl. engr., Calif. Sys. engr. U.S. Naval Weapons Ctr., China Lake, Calif., 1962-65, 68-69; from asst. prof. to assoc. prof. environ. health U. Calif. Sch. Pub. Health, Berkeley, 1970-81, prof., 1981—, dir. No. Calif. Occupational Health Ctr., 1980-89, assoc. dean, 1988-91, dir. environ. engrng. and health scis. lab., 1991-96; assoc. dean U. Calif. Coll. Engrng., Berkeley, 1994-96; dir. Ctr. for Occupl. and Environ. Health U. Calif., Berkeley, 1992-2000. Vice-chair Berkeley divsn. Acad. Senate, 1998-99, chair, 1999-2000; hon. prof. Sichuan Inst. Parasitic Disease. Contbr. articles on engrng. aspects of environ. health to profl. jours. Mem. Nat. Adv. Com. on Occupational Safety and Health, U.S. Dept. Labor, 1986-88. NSF grad. fellow Cambridge U., 1965-68, sr. internat. fellow Fogarty Ctr., NIH, Australian Nat. U., 1977-78, research grantee Nat. Inst. Occupational Safety and Health NIH, State of Calif., 1971— . Mem. ASME, AAAS, Am. Indsl. Hygiene Assn., Nat. Inst. Occupl. Safety and Health (bd. scientific counselors), Assn. Univ. Programs in Occupational Health and Safety (pres. 1984-85) Democrat. Avocation: sailing. Home: 1963 Yosemite Rd Berkeley CA 94707-1631 Office: U Calif Sch Pub Health Berkeley CA 94720-0001 E-mail: spear@uclink4.berkeley.edu

SPECTOR, PHIL, record company executive; b. Bronx, N.Y., Dec. 25, 1940; m. Veronica Bennett, 1968 (div. 1974); children: Gary Phillip and Louis Phillip (twins), Donte Phillip, Nicole and Phillip (twins). Student, UCLA. Producer with Atlantic Records, 1960-61; founder Philles Records, 1962; now pres. Warner-Spector Records, Inc.; also Mother Bertha Music. Mem. mus. group: Teddy Bears, 1958-59; producer records for Gene Pitney, Ike and Tina Turner, Ben E. King, the Beatles, Righteous Bros., Checkmates, Crystals, Ronettes, John Lennon, George Harrison, The Ramones, Yoko Ono, others; producer album A Concert for Bangladesh (Grammy award); composer songs including You've Lost That Lovin' Feelin' (7 million performances; named most performed song in U.S. broadcasting history 1997), others; appeared in films Tami, Easy Rider; prod., TV documentary film A Giant Stands 5 Ft. 7 In.; prod. film That Was Rock. Named to Rock and Roll Hall of Fame, 1989; named Country Music Song of Yr. Songwriter and Pub. for To Know Him Is To Love Him, 1989; recipient lifetime achievement award U. Calif., Berkeley, 1994, Phila. award Phila. Music Alliance, 1994 (includes star on Phila.'s Walk of Fame), Trustees award (Grammy) NARAS, 2000; inducted into Songwriters Hall of Fame, 1996. Office: c/o Warner-Spector Records Inc 686 S Arroyo Pky Pasadena CA 91105-3233

SPEERS, DAVID, opera company director; b. Edmonton, Alta., Can. m. Cydney Speers; children: Robert, Cailen. BM, U. Alta., 1976, MM, 1981; postgrad., Juilliard Sch., N.Y.C., 1977. Contract opera prodn. and stage mgmt. work, Can., 1974-82; conductor more than 50 profl. main stage prodns. Can., 1980-92; gen. dir. Calgary (Can.) Opera, 1988-98, Ariz. Opera, Phoenix, 1998—. Conducted operas include Manon Lescaut, La Boheme, Donizetti, Don Pasquale, La Traviata, Rigoletto, Il Trovatore, Romeo and Juliette, others. NEA scholar; grantee Can. Coun. Adminstrv. Apprenticeship program, 1978; recipient award Aspen Music Festival, 197, Flore Shaw Grad. award in music, 1981. Avocations: opera, theater, golf, sports fan, computers and internet. Office: Ariz Opera Co 4600 N 12th St Phoenix AZ 85014-4005

SPEIDEL, JOHN JOSEPH, physician, foundation officer; b. Iowa City, Sept. 17, 1937; s. Thomas Dennis and Edna (Warweg) S.; divorced; 1 child, Sabrina Brett. A.B. cum laude, Harvard U., 1959, M.D., 1963, M.P.H., 1965. Diplomate: Nat. Bd. Med. Examiners, Am. Bd. Preventive Medicine. Intern St. Luke's Hosp., N.Y.C., 1963-64; resident N.Y.C. Dept. Health, 1965-67, dep. dir. maternal and infant care project, 1966-67; chief research div. Office of Population, AID, Dept. State, Washington, 1969-76; assoc. dir. Office of Population, 1977, dep. dir., acting dir. office, 1978-83; v.p. Population Action Internat. (formerly Population Crisis Com.), 1983-87, pres., 1987-95; program officer for population Hewlett Found., 1995—. Lectr. population and family planning Georgetown U., 1973-75 Contbr. articles to profl. jours.; Editor: (with others) Female Sterilization, 1971, Hysteroscopic Sterilization, 1974, Intrauterine Devices, 1974, Control of Male Fertility, 1975, Advances in Female Sterilization Technology, 1976, Risks, Benefits and Controversies in Fertility Control, 1978, Reversal of Sterilization, 1978, Pregnancy Termination, 1979, Vaginal Contraception, 1979. Served to maj. U.S. Army, 1967-69. Recipient Meritorious Unit citation Office of Population, 1969-71, Arthur S. Flemming award Washington Downtown Jaycees, 1972 Mem. Am. Pub. Health Assn. (Carl S. Shultz award 1982), Population Assn. Am. Office: William & Flora Hewlett Found 525 Middlefield Rd Ste 200 Menlo Park CA 94025-3448

SPEIER, JACKIE, state senator; b. San Francisco; widowed; 2 children. BA, U. Calif., Davis; JD, U. Calif., San Francisco, 1976. Legal counsel Congressman Leo J. Ryan; mem. San Mateo County Bd. Suprs., chair, 1985-86; mem. Calif. State Assembly, 1986-96, chair consumer protection com.; mem. Calif. State Senate, 1998—, chair select com. on govt. oversight, mem. transp. com., bus. and professions com., mem. agr. and water resources com., others, chair ins. com., mem. joint legis. audit com. [illegible] State Capitol Rm 2032 Sacramento CA 95814 also: 400 S El Camino Ste 630 San Mateo CA 94402 also: Hiram W Johnson State Office Bldg 455 Golden Gate Ave Ste 14200 San Francisco CA 94102-7007

SPELTS, RICHARD JOHN, lawyer; b. Yuma, Colo., July 29, 1939; s. Richard Clark and Barbara Eve (Pletcher) S.; children: Melinda, Meghan, Richard John Jr.; m. Gayle Merves, Nov. 14, 1992. BS cum laude, U. Colo., 1961, JD, 1964. Bar: Colo. 1964, U.S. Dist. Ct. Colo. 1964, U.S. Supreme Ct. 1968, U.S. Ct. Appeals (10th cir.) 1970, U.S. Dist. Ct. (ea. dist.) Mich. 1986. With Ford Motor Internat., Cologne, Germany, 1964-65; legis. counsel to U.S. Senator, 89th and 90th Congresses, 1967-68; minority counsel U.S. Senate Subcom., 90th and 91st Congresses, 1968-70; asst. U.S. atty., 1st asst. U.S. atty. Fed. Dist. of Colo., 1970-77; pvt. practice Denver, 1977-89; risk mgr. sheriff's dept. Jefferson County, Golden, Colo., 1990-91. Owner Video Prodn. for Lawyers, 1991—. Selected for Leadership Denver, 1977; recipient cert. for outstanding contbns. in drug law enforcement U.S. Drug Enforcement Adminstrn., 1977, spl. commendation for criminal prosecution U.S. Dept. Justice, 1973, spl. commendation for civil prosecution U.S. Dept. Justice, 1976. Mem. Fed. Bar Assn. (chmn. govt. torts seminar 1980), Colo. Bar Assn. (bd. govs. 1976-78), Denver Bar Assn., Colo. Trial Lawyers Assn., Denver Law Club, Order of Coif. Republican. Methodist. Home and Office: 9671 Brook Hill Ct Littleton CO 80124-5431 Fax: (303) 662-9957

SPENCE, ANDREW MICHAEL, dean, finance educator; b. Montclair, N.J., 1943; BA in Philosophy summa cum laude, Princeton U., 1966; BA, MA in Maths., Oxford U., 1968; PhD in Econs. with honors, Harvard U., 1972. Asst. prof. polit. econ. Kennedy Sch. Govt. Harvard U., Cambridge, Mass., 1971-75, prof. econs., 1977-83, prof. bus. adminstrn., 1979-83, George Gund prof. econs. and bus. adminstrn., 1983-86, vis. prof. econs. dept., 1976-77, chmn. bus. econs. PhD program, 1981-83, chmn. econs. dept., 1983-84, dean Faculty Arts and Scis., 1984-90; assoc. prof. dept. econs. Stanford (Calif.) U., 1973-75, Philip H. Knight prof., dean Grad. Sch. Bus., 1990-99, Philip H. Knight prof., dean emeritus, prof. econs., 1999—. Bd. dirs. BankAm. Corp., Gen. Mills, Inc., Nike, Inc., Siebel Syss., Sun Microsyss., VeriFone, Inc.; chmn. Nat. Rsch. Coun. Bd. on Sci., Tech. and Econ. Policy. Author: 3 books; mem. editl. bd. Am. Econs. Rev., Bell. Jour. Econs., Jour. Econ. Theory and Pub. Policy; contbr. over 50 articles to profl. jours. Mem. econs. adv. panel NSF, 1977-79; mem. econs. adv. com. Sloan Found., 1979—. Danforth fellow, 1966; Rhodes scholar, 1966; recipient J.K. Galbraith prize for excellence in tchg., 1978. Fellow AAAS, Econometric Soc.; mem. Am. Econ. Assn. (John Bates Clark medal 1981). Office: Stanford U Grad Sch Bus Bldg 350 Memorial Way Stanford CA 94305-5015

SPENCE, GERALD LEONARD, lawyer, writer; b. Laramie, Wyo., Jan. 8, 1929; s. Gerald M. and Esther Sophie (Pfleeger) S.; m. Anna Wilson, June 20, 1947; children: Kip, Kerry, Kent, Katy; m. LaNelle Hampton Peterson, Nov. 18, 1969. BSL, U. Wyo., 1949, LLB, 1952, LLD (hon.), 1990. Bar: Wyo. 1952, U.S. Ct. Claims 1952, U.S. Supreme Ct. 1982. Sole practice, Riverton, Wyo., 1952-54; county and pros. atty. Fremont County, 1954-62; ptnr. various law firms, Riverton and Casper, 1962-78; sr. ptnr. Spence, Moriarity & Schuster, Jackson, 1978—. Lectr. legal orgns. and law schs. Author: (with others) Gunning for Justice, 1982, Of Murder and Madness, 1983, Trial by Fire, 1986, With Justice for None, 1989, From Freedom to Slavery, 1993, How To Argue and Win Every Time, 1995, The Making of a Country Lawyer, 1996, O.J.: The Last Word, 1997, Give Me Liberty, 1998, A Boy's Summer, 2000, Gerry Spence's Wyoming: The Landscapes, 2000, Half Moon and Empty Stars, 2001. Mem. ABA, Wyo. Bar Assn., Wyo. Trial Lawyers Assn., Assn. Trial Lawyers Am., Nat. Assn. Criminal Def. Lawyers Office: Spence Moriarity & Schuster PO Box 548 Jackson WY 83001-0548

SPENCER, CAROLINE, library director; BA, AMLS, U. Mich. Past pres. Hawaii Libr. Assn. Office: HI State Public Lib 478 S King St Honolulu HI 96813-2901

SPENCER, JOHN ANDREW, real estate development corporation executive; b. Ft. Pierce, Fla., Sept. 26, 1948; s. Andrew Jackson and Kathryn Samantha (Gray) S.; m. Maria Ester Cascante, Sept. 29, 1979; 1 child, Sarah. BS, Fla. State U., 1970; MS, Ariz. State U., 1976. CPA, Ariz. Sr. auditor Peat, Marwick, Mitchell & Co., Phoenix, 1976-79; asst. controller, controller Sahara Hotel and Casino, Las Vegas, 1979-80; asst. treas. Del Webb Hotels, Las Vegas, 1980-82; asst. controller, controller Del E. Webb Corp., Phoenix, 1982-85, v.p., controller, 1985-98, exec. v.p., CFO, 1998—. Mem. profl. adv. bd. Ariz. State U. Acctg. Dept., Tempe, 1985—. Served with USAR, 1970-76. Mem. Am. Inst. CPA's, Ariz. State Soc. CPA's. Republican. Methodist. Office: Del E Webb Corp 6001 N 24th St Phoenix AZ 85016-2099

SPENCER, MARGARET GILLIAM, lawyer; b. Spokane, Wash., Aug. 30, 1951; d. Jackson Earl and Margaret Kathleen (Hindley) Gilliam; m. John Bernard Spencer, Feb. 21, 1993. BA in Sociology, U. Mont., 1974, MA in Sociology, 1978, JD, 1982. Bar: Mont. 1982, Colo. 1982. Assoc. Holland & Hart, Denver, 1982-84, Roath & Brega, P.C., Denver, 1984-88, shareholder, dir., 1988-89; spl. counsel Brega & Winters, P.C., Denver, 1989; corp. counsel CH2M Hill, Inc., Denver, 1989—. Democrat. Episcopalian. Avocations: skiing, scuba diving. Office: CH2M Hill Inc PO Box 22508 Denver CO 80222-0508

SPENCER, PETER SIMNER, neurotoxicologist; b. London, Nov. 30, 1946; U.S. citizen; married; 2 children. BSc, U. London, 1968, PhD in Pathology, 1971. Rsch. asst. Nat. Hosp. Nervous Disorders U. London, 1968-70, rsch. fellow Royal Free Hosp. Sch. Medicine, 1970-71; fellow pathology Albert Einstein Coll. Medicine, 1971-73, asst. prof., 1973-81, assoc. prof. neurosci., 1977-83, prof. neurosci., 1983-88, assoc. prof. pathology, dir. Inst. Neurotoxicology, 1979-88; dir., cr. scientist Ctr. Rsch. of Occupl. Environ./Toxicol. Oreg. Health Sci. U., 1988—, prof. neurology and mem. neurosci. faculty, 1988—. Cons. Nat. Inst. Occupational Safety & Health, 1976-77, EPA, 1977—; chmn. adv. bd. Jour. Neurotoxicology, 1978—; mem. adv. bd. Rutgers U. Toxicology Program, 1984, Howe & Assocs., 1985, Peripheral Nerve Repair & Regeneration, 1985; mem. bd. toxicol. and environ. health hazards NAS, 1984, Safe Drinking Water Com., 1985; sec. Third World Med. Rsch. Found., 1985—; adj. prof. Coll. Vet. Medicine Oreg. State U. Assoc. editor Jour. Neurocytology, 1977—; author: Experimental and Clin. Neurotoxicology. Fellow Joseph P. Kennedy Jr. Found., 1974-76; recipient Silvio O. Conte Nat. prize for Neuroscience contbns. relevant to environ. health, 1993, Sr. Travel award Alzheimer Assn. Mem. AAAS, Am. Assn. Neuropathologists (Weil award 1976, Moore award), Am. Soc. Cell Biologists, Am. Neurological Assn., Anatomic Soc. Gt. Britain & Ireland, Brit. Neuropathology Soc., World Fedn. Neurology, Royal Coll. Pathologists, Pan-Am. Neuroepidiology Found. (hon.). Achievements include research in cellular relationships in the nervous system and the effects of neurotoxic chemicals. Office: Oregon Health Scis U # L606 3181 SW Sam Jackson Park Rd Portland OR 97201-3079

SPENCER, ROBERT C. retired political science educator; b. Chgo., Mar. 28, 1920; m. Edith Maxham McCarthy, Sept. 13, 1941; children: Margaret, Catherine, Anne, Thomas More, David. AB, U. Chgo., 1943, MA, 1952, PhD in Polit. Sci. (Univ. fellow 1952-53), 1955. Instr. polit. sci. and sociology St. Michaels Coll., 1949-51, asst., then assoc. prof. polit. sci., 1953-60, prof. govt., 1960-63, dir. summer sessions, 1960-61, asst. to pres., 1963-65; prof. polit. sci., chmn. dept., dean summer sessions U. R.I., 1965-67; grad. dean U. R.I. (Grad. Sch.), 1967-69; founding pres. Sangamon State U., Springfield, Ill., 1969-78, prof. govt. and public affairs, 1978-80, prof. emeritus U. Ill. Springfield, 1980-93, retired, 1993—. Research assoc. Indsl. Relations Center, U. Chgo., 1952-53; extension lectr. N.Y. State Sch. Indsl. and Labor Relations, Cornell U., 1956-57; vice chmn. West Central Ill. Ednl. Telecommunications Consortium, 1975-77, chmn., 1977-78; chmn. task force personnel Vt. Little Hoover Commn., 1957-58; mem. Ill. adv. com. U.S. Commn. on Civil Rights, 1979-87; bd. mgrs. Franklin Life Variable Annuity Funds, 1974— ; vis. prof. polit. sci., sr. rsch. assoc. local govt. ctr. Mont. State U., Bozeman, 1985, 89, 90—. Author: (with Robert J. Huckshorn) The Politics of Defeat, 1971. Bd. dirs. City Day Sch., Springfield, 1979-83, Gt. Am. People Show Repertory Co., 1980-90; vice chmn. Petersburg Libr. Bd., 1982-88; chmn. Petersburg Zoning Bd. Appeals, 1984-90; mem. Vt. Senate, 1959-63; faculty fellow Ford Found.'s Nat. Ctr. for Edn. in Politics, rsch. dir. Dem. Nat. Com., 1962-63; mem. adv. bd. Landmark Preservation Coun. Ill., 1986-89; mem., treas. Gallatin County Coun. on Aging, 1993—. Roman Catholic. Home: 2303 S 3rd Ave Bozeman MT 59715-6009

SPENCER, TED M. museum director; Exec. dir. Alaska Aviation Heritage Mus., Anchorage, 1977-2000; curator Alaska Hist. Aviation Inst., Anchorage, San Diego, 2000—. Home and Office: Alaska Hist Aviation Inst 7317 Michelin Pl Apt 5 Anchorage AK 99518-2896

SPENCER, TERRY R. state legislator, lawyer; b. Logan, Utah, Mar. 19, 1960; m. Sharon Perschon; 2 children. BS in Polit. Sci., MS in Econs., PhD in Econs., Utah State U.; JD, Brigham Young U. Bar: Utah, Idaho, Calif. Atty. TR Spencer & Assocs.; mem. Utah Senate, Dist. 22, Salt Lake City, 1998—; chair judiciary com.; mem. state/local affairs com., higher edn. appropriations. Active Boy Scouts Am. Republican. Home: 1110 Kimberly Dr Layton UT 84040-2808 E-mail: vimcla@sprynet.com

SPENCER, WILLIAM FRANKLIN, SR. soil scientist, researcher; b. Carlinville, Ill., Mar. 4, 1923; s. Jesse H. and Mayme (Wohlert) S.; m. Marjorie Ann Hall, June 2, 1946; children: Barbara Annette, William Franklin Jr., Gary Alan. BS in Agr., U. Ill., 1947, MS in Chemistry, 1950, PhD in Agronomy, 1952. Asst. chemist U. Fla., Lake Alfred, 1951-54; soil scientist USDA Agrl. Rsch. Svc., Laramie, Wyo., 1954-55, Brawley, Calif., 1955-57; assoc. soil chemist U. Fla., Lake Alfred, 1957-62; rsch. leader USDA Agrl. Rsch. Svc., Riverside, Calif., 1962-95. Mem. Western Soil & Water Rsch. Com., Riverside, 1965-75; cons. Cen. U., Maracay, Venezuela, 1959. Contbr. over 105 articles to profl. jours. With U.S. Army, 1943-46, PTO. Fellow AAAS, Am. Soc. Agronomy, Soil Sci. Soc. Am.; mem. Soc. Environ. Toxicology and Chemistry, Internat. Soil Sci. Soc., Gamma Sigma Delta, Sigma Xi. Methodist. Achievements include research on behavior and fate of pesticides. Home: 2935 Arlington Ave Riverside CA 92506-4450 Office: U Calif Usda Agrl Rsch Svc Riverside CA 92521-0001

SPERBER, BURTON S. construction executive; b. 1929; Chmn., pres. Valley Crest Landscape, Inc., Calabasas, Calif., 1949—. Office: Environ Industries Inc 24121 Ventura Blvd Calabasas CA 91302-1449

SPERLING, GEORGE, cognitive scientist, educator; s. Otto and Melitta Sperling BS in Math., U. Mich., 1955; MA in Psychology, Columbia U., 1956; PhD in Psychology, Harvard U., 1959. Rsch. asst. in biophysics Brookhaven Nat. Labs., Upton, N.Y., summer 1955; rsch. asst. in psychology Harvard U., Cambridge, Mass., 1957-59; mem. tech. rsch. staff Acoustical and Behavioral Rsch. Ctr., AT&T Bell Labs., Murray Hill, N.J., 1958-86; prof. psychology and neural sci. NYU, N.Y.C., 1970-92; disting. prof. cognitive scis., neurobiology and behavior U. Calif., Irvine, 1992—. Instr. psychology Washington Sq. Coll., NYU, 1962-63; vis. assoc. prof. psychology Duke U., spring 1964; adj. assoc. prof. psychology Columbia U., 1964-65; acting assoc. prof. psychology UCLA, 1967-68; hon. rsch. assoc. Univ. Coll., U. London, 1969-70; vis. prof. psychology U. Western Australia, Perth, 1972, U. Wash., Seattle, 1977; vis. scholar Stanford (Calif.) U., 1984; mem. sci. adv. bd. USAF, 1988-92. Recipient Meritorious Civilian Svc. medal USAF, 1993; Gomberg scholar U. Mich., 1953-54; Guggenheim fellow, 1969-70. Fellow AAAS, APA (Disting. Sci. Contbn. award 1988), Am. Acad. Arts and Sci., Optical Soc. Am.; mem. NAS, Assn. for Rsch. in Vision and Ophthalmology, Ann. Interdisciplinary Conf. (founder, organizer 1975—), Eastern Psychol. Assn. (bd. dirs. 1982-85), Soc. for Computers in Psychology (steering com. 1974-78), Psychonomic Soc., Soc. Exptl. Psychologists (Warren medal 1996), Soc. for Math. Psychology (chmn. 1983-84, exec. bd. 1979-85), Phi Beta Kappa, Sigma Xi. Office: U Calif SS Plz A Dept Cognitive Scis Irvine CA 92697-5100 E-mail: sperling@uci.edu

SPERLING, IRENE R. publishing executive; Publisher Tradeshow Week, L.A. Office: Tradeshow Week 5700 Wilshire Blvd Ste 120 Los Angeles CA 90036-3644 E-mail: isperling@tsweek.com

SPEYER, JASON LEE, aeronautical engineer, educator; b. Boston, Apr. 30, 1938; s. Joseph Louis and Ruth Sylvia (Steinmetz) S.; m. Barbara Joan Sachs, Sept. 11, 1966; children— Gil, Gavriel, Rakhel, Joseph B.S., MIT, 1960; M.S., Harvard U., 1964, Ph.D., 1968. Registered profl. engr., Tex. Engr. Boeing Co., Seattle, 1960-61; sr. engr. Raytheon Co., Bedford, Mass., 1961-68; sr. analyst Analytical Mechanics Assocs., Inc., Cambridge, 1968-70; mem. research staff Charles Stark Draper Lab., Cambridge, 1970-76; Harry H. Power prof. engring. U. Tex., Austin, 1976-90; prof. engring. UCLA, 1990—. Lectr. MIT, 1971-76; vis. scientist Weizmann Inst. Sci., 1972-73; Lady Davis prof. Technion, Haifa, Israel, 1983; Hunsaker vis. prof. aeros. and astronautics MIT, 1989-90. Recipient Hocott Disting. Engring. Rsch. award Coll. Engring., U. Tex., 1985, Exceptional Civil Svc. award USAF, 1991; Raytheon fellow, 1963-67; Hugh L. Dryden lectureship Am. Inst. of Aeronautics and Astronautics, 1995 Fellow IEEE (bd. govs. Control Sys. Soc. 1982—, assoc. editor Transaction on Automatic Control), AIAA (Mechanics and Control of Flight award 1985, Dryden lectureship in rsch. 1995, assoc. editor Jour. Spacecraft and Rockets, Jour. Guidance and Control). Home: 11358 Chalon Rd Los Angeles CA 90049-1721 Office: UCLA Dept Mech Aerospace Engring 420 Westwood Plz # 951597 Los Angeles CA 90095-8357

SPICER, WILLIAM EDWARD, III, physicist, educator, engineer; b. Baton Rouge, Sept. 7, 1929; s. William Edward II and Kate Crystal (Watkins) S.; m. Cynthia Stanley, June 12, 1951 (div. 1969); children: William Edward IV, Sally Ann; m. Diane Lubarsky, Apr. 24, 1969; 1 dau., Jacqueline Kate. B.S., Coll. William and Mary, 1949, MIT, 1951; M.A., U. Mo., 1953, Ph.D., 1955; D.Tech. (hon.), U. Linköping, Sweden, 1975. Scientist RCA Labs, 1955-61, Lawrence Radiation Lab., U. Calif.-Livermore, 1961-62; mem. faculty Stanford U., 1962—, prof. elec. engring. and materials sci. engring., 1965—, prof. by courtesy applied physics, 1976—, Stanford Ascherman prof. engring., 1978—, prof. Stanford Synchrotron Radiation Lab, 1992—; dir. Acad. Skills, Inc., Los Altos, Calif., 1971-73; dep. dir. Stanford Synchrotron Radiation Lab., 1973-75, cons. dir., 1975—, prof., 1992—, Stanford Linear Accelerator Ctr., 1993—. Cons. to govt. and industry, 1962—; mem. solid state scis. panel Nat. Acad. Sci.-NRC, 1965-73; cons., lectr. Chinese Univ. devel. project World Bank-Fudan U., 1983; mem. panel atomic and molecular physics div. Nat. Bur. Standards, 1966-73, chmn., 1971-73; mem. adv. group election devices Dept. Def., 1975-82; fellow Churchill Coll., Cambridge U., Eng., 1979; mem. panel Japanese tech. evaluation program U.S. Dept. Commerce and NSF, 1983-84; co-founder, acting dir. Stanford Photon. Lab., 1972; chmn. affiliated faculty Stanford Syncrotron Radiation Lab., 1988-92. Mem. editorial bd. Jour. Crystal Growth, 1981-85; author publs. theory and experiment solid state and surface physics and chemistry, photoemission, optical properties solids, electronic structure metals, semiconductors, insulators, high temperature superconductors; patentee in field. Bd. dirs. Princeton (N.J.) YMCA, 1960-62. Recipient Achievement award RCA, 1957, 60, mentor award Nat. Conf. Black Phys. Students, 1992; named Scientist of Yr., Indsl. Research and Devel. mag., 1981; Guggenheim fellow, 1978-79 Fellow IEEE, Am. Phys. Soc. (Oliver Buckley Solid State Physics prize 1980), Am. Vacuum Soc. (chmn. electronics material div. 1978-79, dir. 1979-80, trustee 1981-82, Medard W. Welch award 1984); mem. AAAS (Mentor award for Lifetime Achievement 2001), Amer Contract Bridge League (life master 1997, bronze life master 2000), Phi Beta Kappa. Home: 785 Mayfield Ave Palo Alto CA 94305-1043 Office: Stanford U Mccullough Bldg Stanford CA 94305 E-mail: dmspicer@aol.com

SPIEGEL, HART HUNTER, retired lawyer; b. Safford, Ariz, Aug. 30, 1918; s. Jacob B. and Margaret (Hunter) S.; m. Genevieve Willson, Feb. 12, 1946; children: John Willson, Claire Margaret Spiegel Brian, Jennifer Emily Spiegel Grellman. BA, Yale U., 1940, LLB, 1946. Bar: Calif. 1946, D.C. 1960. Assoc. Brobeck, Phleger & Harrison, San Francisco, 1947-55, ptnr., 1955-90. Chief counsel IRS, Washington, 1959-61, mem. adv. group to commr., 1975. Served to lt. USMC, 1942-46, PTO. Mem. ABA (coun. mem. tax sect. 1966-68), Am. Law Inst., Bar Assn. San Francisco (pres. 1983), Pacific Union Club, Berkeley Tennis Club (pres. 1964-65). Home: 3647 Washington St San Francisco CA 94118-1832 Office: Brobeck Phleger & Harrison 1 Market Pla Spear St Tower San Francisco CA 94105

SPIEGEL, MARILYN HARRIET, real estate executive; b. Bklyn., Apr. 3, 1935; d. Harry and Sadie (Oscher) Unger; m. Murray Spiegel, June 12, 1954; children: Eric Lawrence, Dana Cheryl Mann, Jay Barry. Grad. high sch., Bklyn. Exec. sec. S & W Paper Co., N.Y.C., 1954-58; salesperson Red Carpet Realtors, Los Alamitos, Calif., 1974-75, Coll. Park Realtors, Garden Grove, 1975-79; owner, broker S & S Properties, Los Alamitos, 1979—. Named Realtor of Yr., 1989. Mem. Calif. Assn. Realtors (bd. dirs. 1984—), West Orange County Bd. Realtors (bd. dirs. 1984—, 1st v.p. 1987, pres. 1988), Million Dollar Sales Club, Long Beach C. of C., Seal Beach C. of C., Orange County C. of C., Summit Orgn., Toastmasters (pres. founders group Garden Grove, 1990). Home: 1371 Oakmont Rd Apt 150D Seal Beach CA 90740-3732 Office: S & S Properties 3502 Katella Ave Ste 208 Los Alamitos CA 90720-3130

SPIEGELBERG, HANS LEONHARD, medical educator; b. Basel, Switzerland, Jan. 8, 1933; came to U.S., 1961; s. Hans G. S.; m. Elizabeth von der Crone, May 19, 1962; children: Franzi, Daniel, Markus. MD, U. Basel, Basel, 1958. Med. diplomate, Switzerland. Intern and resident in pediatric allergy and immunology Dept. of Medicine, U. of Basel, Switzerland; intern and resident in allergy and immunology NYU, N.Y.C., 1961-63; with Scripps Rsch. Inst., La Jolla, Calif., 1963-90; prof. U. Calif., San Diego, 1990—, now prof. emeritus. Cons. VA Med. Ctr., L.A., 1966-90. Editor (jour.) Seminars in Immunopathology, 1988—. Home: 2234 Paseo Dorado La Jolla CA 92037-3208 Office: U Calif San Diego 9500 Gilman Dr La Jolla CA 92093-5004

SPIEGELMAN, ARTHUR, broadcast executive; Bureau chief Reuters America, Inc., L.A., 1994—. Office: Reuters America Inc 445 S Figueroa St Ste 2000 Los Angeles CA 90071-1650

SPIELBERG, STEVEN, motion picture director, producer; b. Cin., Dec. 18, 1946; m. Amy Irving, Nov. 27, 1985 (div.); 2 children: Max Samuel, Sasha; m. Kate Capshaw; 1 dau. BA, Calif. State Coll., Long Beach; Hon. Doctorate in Creative Arts, Brandeis U., 1986. Founder Amblin Entertainment (Universal Studios), Dreamworks SKG (with Jeffrey Katzenberg and David Geffen); directed segments of TV series Columbo; dir. TV movies Night Gallery, 1969, Duel, 1971, Savage, 1972, Something Evil, 1972; exec prodr. series: Steven Spielberg's Amazing Stories, Tiny Toon Adventures, Family Dog, seaQuest DSV; films include (dir.). The Sugarland Express, 1974 (also story), Jaws, 1975, Close Encounters of the Third Kind, 1977 (also co-writer), 1941, 1979, Raiders of the Lost Ark, 1981, Indiana Jones and the Temple of Doom, 1984, Indiana Jones and the Last Crusade, 1989, Hook, 1991, Jurassic Park, 1993, Men in Black, 1996; (dir., prodr.): E.T. The Extra-Terrestrial, 1982, The Color Purple, 1985, Empire of the Sun, 1987, Always, 1989, Schindler's List, 1993 (Best Drama & Best Dir. Golden Globe awards, Best Picture & Best Dir. Acad. awards), Saving Private Ryan (Golden Clobe award for Best Dir. 1999, Best Director Academy Award 1998, nominee Best Picture Academy award 1999); (dir., exec. prodr.): Twilight Zone: The Movie, 1983; (prodr.): Poltergeist, 1982 (also co-writer), An American Tail: Fievel Goes West, 1991, Casper, 1995; (exec. prodr.): I Wanna Hold Your Hand, 1978, Used Cars, 1980, Continental Divide, 1981, Gremlins, 1984, The Goonies, 1985, Back to the Future, 1985, Young Sherlock Holmes, 1985, The Money Pit, 1986, An American Tail, 1986, Innerspace, 1987, *batteries not included, 1987, Who Framed Roger Rabbit?, 1988, The Land Before Time, 1988, Dad, 1989, Back to the Future Part II, 1989, Joe Verses the Volcano, 1990, Back to the Future Part III, 1990, Gremlins 2: The New Batch, 1990, Arachnophobia, 1990, Cape Fear, 1991, We're Back!: A Dinosaur's Story, 1993, The Flintstones, 1994, The Little Rascals, 1994, Balto, 1995, Twister, 1996, The Lost World, 1997, Amistad, 1997, Deep Impact, 1998, The Mask of Zorro, 1998, The Last Days, 1998; (T.V. series) Steven Spielberg Presents Toonsylvania, 1998; (actor): The Blues Brothers, 1980; exec. prodr.: Flintstones in Viva Rock Vegas, 1999, Band of Brothers, 1999, (TV series) The Unfinished Journey, 1999, Semper Fi, 2000. Recipient Man of Yr. award Hasty Pudding Theater, Harvard U., 1983, Outstanding Directorial Achievement award for feature films Dirs. Guild Am., 1985, Film award Brit. Acad. Film and TV Arts, 1986, Irving Thalberg Mem. award Acad. Motion Picture Arts and Scis., 1987, Golden Lion award for career achievement Venice Film Festival, 1993, Life Achievement award Am. Film Inst., 1995. Fellow Brit. Acad. Film and TV Arts. Achievements include winning film contest with 40-minute war movie, Escape to Nowhere, at age 13; made film Firelight at age 16, and made 5 films while in coll.; became TV dir. at Universal Pictures at age 20. Office: CAA 9830 Wilshire Blvd Beverly Hills CA 90212-1804

SPIES, ALLAN, telecommunications executive; m. Karen Spies; 2 children. BS in Physics, Calif. Luth. U.; M. Mgmt., Pace U. With US West, Denver, v.p. fin., contr., exec. v.p., CFO, 1997—; v.p., CFO US West Multimedia Comm., a divsn. US West Media Group, Denver; bd. dirs. InfoNow Corp., Denver, 2000—. Office: InfoNow Corp 1875 Lawrence St Ste 1100 Denver CO 80202

SPIESS, FRED NOEL, oceanographer, educator; b. Oakland, Calif., Dec. 25, 1919; s. Fred Henry and Elva Josephine (Monck) S.; m. Sarah Scott Whitton, July 25, 1942; children: Katherine Spiess Dallaire, Mary Elizabeth Spiess DeJong, John Morgen Frederick, Helen Spiess Shamble, Margaret Josephine Deligio-Spiess. A.B., U. Calif., Berkeley, 1941, Ph.D., 1951; M.S., Harvard U., 1946. With Marine Phys. Lab., U. Calif., San Diego, 1952—, dir., 1958-80, U. Calif. Inst. Marine Resources, 1980-88, Scripps Inst. Oceanography, La Jolla, 1964-65, prof. oceanography, 1961-90, prof. emeritus, rsch. prof., 1990—; chair U. Calif. Acad. Coun. and Assembly U. Calif. Bd. Regents, 1988-90. Mem. Naval Research Adv. Commn., 1978-81; mem. com. on geodesy Nat. Acad. Scis., 1980-84; mem. Def. Sci. Bd., 1976-79; chair Acad. Senate Task Force U. Calif., Merced, 1999-2001. Capt. USNR, 1941-79. Decorated Silver Star medal, Bronze Star medal; recipient John Price Wetherill medal Franklin Inst., 1965; Compass Disting. Scientist award Marine Technol. Soc., 1971; Robert Dexter Conrad award U.S. Sec. of Navy, 1974, Navy Disting. Pub. Svc. award, 1990; Newcomb Cleveland prize AAAS, 1981 Fellow Acoustical Soc. Am. (Pioneers of Underwater Acoustics medal 1985), Am. Geophys. Union (Maurice Ewing award 1983), Marine Tech. Soc. (Lockheed award 1985); mem. Nat. Acad. Engring., Phi Beta Kappa, Sigma Xi. Home: 9450 La Jolla Shores Dr La Jolla CA 92037-1137 Office: U Calif San Diego Scripps Inst Oceanogra La Jolla CA 92093-0205 E-mail: fspiess@ucsd.edu

SPILKER, LINDA JOYCE, aerospace scientist; b. Mpls., Apr. 26, 1955; d. Arthur Elzear and Bonnie Joy (Jansen) Bies; m. John Leonard Horn, Jr., July 31, 1976 (div.); children: Jennifer, Jessica; m. Thomas Richard Spilker, 1997. BA in Physics, Calif. State U., Fullerton, 1977; MS in Physics, Calif. State U., L.A., 1983; PhD in Geophysics and Space Physics, UCLA, 1992. Rep. Voyager Infrared Radiometer and Spectrometer expt. Jet Propulsion Lab., Pasadena, Calif., 1977-90, sci. assoc. Voyager Photopolarimeter, 1984-90, sc. assoc. Voyager Infrared Radiometer and Spectrometer, 1988-90, study scientist Cassini asst., 1988-90, co-investigator Cassini Composite Infrared Spectrometer, 1990—, dep. project scientist Cassini mission, 1990—, prin. investigator planetary geology and geophysics, 1993—. Mem. planetary sci. data steering group NASA, Washington, 1991-95, adv. coun. for planetary data sys. ring node, Moffett Field, Calif., 1990—. Contbr. chpt. Van Nostrand Encyclopedia of Planetary Science, 1994; contbr. jour. articles Icarus. Pres. North San Gabriel Valley Dem. Club, Monrovia, Calif., 1992-94. Recipient Exceptional Service medal NASA, 1990; Sci. Achievement award, 1992, Distinguished Alumna award Calif. State U., 1996; named to Hall of Fame Placentia-yorba Linda Unified Sch. Dsit., 1998-99. Mem. AAAS, Divsn. of Planetary Sci. Democrat. Presbyterian. Avocations: hiking, astronomical observing, piano, jogging. Home: 457 Granite Ave Monrovia CA 91016-2324 Office: Jet Propulsion Lab MS 230-205 4800 Oak Grove Dr Pasadena CA 91109-8001

SPILLER, EBERHARD ADOLF, physicist, researcher; b. Halbendorf, Ger., Apr. 16, 1933; came to U.S., 1968; s. Walter Richard and Ruth Elfriede (Radzey) S.; m. Dietz, Dec. 18, 1964; children— Michael, Bettina. Diploma, U. Frankfurt, Ger., 1960, Ph.D., 1964. Asst. U. Frankfurt, 1960-68, mem. faculty, 1966-68; physicist IBM Research Center, Yorktown Heights, N.Y., 1968-93; emeritus physicist IBM, 1993-97. Guest prof. Tech. U. Denmark, 1994-95, U. Ctrl. Fla., 1996; vis. scientist Nat. Inst. Stds. and Tech., 1997—, Lawrence Livermore Lab., Calif., 1997—. Author: Soft X-Ray Optics, 1994. Fellow AAAS, Am. Optical Soc.; mem. German Phys. Soc., Photo-Optic Instrumentation Soc. Achievements include research in solid state physics, laser and coherence optics, nonlinear optics, thin films, soft x-rays, x-ray microscopy, lithography; inventor multilayer x-ray optics, x-ray astronomy, x-ray lithography. Office: Lawrence Livermore Nat Lab MS-L395 Livermore CA 94551 E-mail: spiller@llnl.gov, espill@attglobal.net

SPINDEL, ROBERT CHARLES, electrical engineering educator; b. N.Y.C., Sept. 5, 1944; s. Morris Tayson and Isabel (Glazer) S.; m. Barbara June Sullivan, June 12, 1966; children: Jennifer Susan, Miranda Ellen BSEE, Cooper Union, 1965; MS, Yale U., 1966, MPhil, 1968, PhD, 1971. Postdoctoral fellow Woods Hole Oceanographic Instn., Mass., 1971-72, asst. scientist, 1972-76, assoc. scientist, 1976-82, sr. scientist, 1982-87, chmn. dept. ocean engring., 1982-87; dir. applied physics lab. U. Wash., Seattle, 1987—. Mem. naval studies bd. NRC, 1987-99; mem. Naval Rsch. Adv. Com., 1998—. Contbr. articles to profl. jours.; patentee on underwater nav. Recipient A.B. Wood medal Brit. Inst. Acoustics, 1981, Gano Dunn medal The Cooper Union, 1989. Fellow IEEE (assoc. editor jour. 1982—), Acoustical Soc. Am., Marine Tech. Soc. (pres. elect 1991-93, pres. 1993-95), Oceanography Soc. (Munk award 2001). Independent. Jewish. Avocations: automobile restoration, hiking. Home: 14859 SE 51st St Bellevue WA 98006-3515 Office: U Wash Applied Physics Lab 1013 NE 40th St Seattle WA 98105-6606 E-mail: spindels@aol.com, spindel@APL.Washington.edu

SPINDLER, GEORGE DEARBORN, anthropologist, educator, writer, editor; b. Stevens Point, Wis., Feb. 28, 1920; s. Frank Nicholas and Winifred (Hatch) S.; m. Louise Schaubel, May 29, 1942; 1 dau., Sue Carol Spindler Coleman. B.S., Central State Tchrs. Coll., Wis., 1940; M.A., U. Wis., 1947; Ph.D., U. Calif. at Los Angeles, 1952. Tchr. sch. in, Wis., 1940-42; research asso. Stanford, 1950-51, mem. faculty, 1951—, prof. anthropology and edn., 1960-78, exec. head dept., 1963-67, 84; editor Am. Anthropologist, 1962-66. Cons. editor Holt, Rinehart & Winston, 1965-91, Harcourt, 1991—; vis. prof. U. Wis., 1979-85, U. Calif., Santa Barbara, 1986-91, Harvard U., 1999. Author: Menomini Acculturation, 1955, (with A. Beals and L. Spindler) Culture in Process, 1967, rev. edit., 1973, Transmission of American Culture, 1959, (with L. Spindler) Dreamers Without Power, 1971, rev. edit., 1984, Burgbach: Urbanization and Identity in a German Village, 1973, (with Louise Spindler) The American Cultural Dialogue and its Transmission, 1990; editor: Education and Anthropology, 1955, (with Louise Spindler) Case Studies in Cultural Anthropology, 1960— , Methods in Cultural Anthropology, 1965—, Case Studies in Education and Culture, 1966—, Basic Units in Anthropology, 1970; editor, contbr.: Education and Culture, 1963, Being An Anthropologist, 1970, Education and Cultural Process, 1974, rev. edit., 1987, 97, The Making of Psychological Anthropology, 1978, 2nd edit., 1994, Doing the Ethnography of Schooling, 1982, Interpretive Ethnography of Schooling at Home and Abroad, 1987, Pathways to Cultural Awareness: Cultural Therapy with Students and Teachers, 1994, Fifty Years of Anthropology and Education: A Spindler Anthology, 2000. Pres. Peninsula Sch. Bd., Menlo Park, Calif., 1954-56. Served with AUS, 1942-45. Recipient Lloyd W. Dinkelspeil award Stanford U., 1978, Disting. Svc. award Soc. Internat. Diplomacy and Third World Anthropologists, 1984, Disting. Career Contbn. award Com. on Role and Status of Minorities, Am. Edn. Rsch. Assn., Nat. Acad. Edn., 1994, Father of Ednl. Ethnography award Nat. Ednl. Ethnography Conf., 2000; fellow Ctr. Advanced Study of Behavioral Scis., 1956-57; subject of Vol. 17 Psychoanalytic Study of Soc. essays, 1992. Fellow Am. Anthrop. Assn.; mem. Southwestern Anthrop. Assn. (pres. 1962-63), Coun. for Anthropology and Edn. (pres. 1982, George and Louise Spindler award for outstanding contbns. to ednl. anthropology 1987, disting. Scholar award 1998), Nat. Acad. Edn. Office: Ethnographics 1247 Alice St Davis CA 95616-2174 E-mail: geospinner@aol.com

SPINDLER, PAUL, corporate executive, consultant; b. Chgo., May 2, 1931; s. Isaac Edward and Sophia (Stein) S.; m. Gail Klynn; children from previous marriage: Kevin, Makayla, Sydney, Jeffrey. BA in Journalism, Temple U., 1952. Reporter Akron Beacon Jour., Akron, Ohio, 1955-58, San Francisco Examiner, 1958-59; editor Santa Clara (Calif.) Daily Jour., 1959-63; dir. pub. affairs Litton Industries, Inc., Beverly Hills, Calif., 1963-68; dir. pub. relations Internat. Industries, Beverly Hills, 1968-70; pres. Paul Spindler & Co., L.A., 1970-75; exec. v.p. Manning Selvage & Lee, Inc., N.Y.C., 1975-85; pres. The Spindler Co., L.A., 1985-87; pres. Western div. GCI Group, L.A., 1987-91; pres. GCI Spindler, L.A., 1991-96; chmn. Bristol Retail Solutions, Inc., Newport Beach, Calif., 1996-98; pres. Paul Spindler Co., L.A., 1998—. Bd. dirs. Phoenix House Calif., Inc. Cpl. U.S. Army, 1952-54. Mem. Mountain Gate Country Club (L.A.). Democrat. Jewish. Office: Paul Spindler Co 1875 Century Park E Ste 800 Los Angeles CA 90067-2509 E-mail: paul@spindlercompany.com

SPINRAD, HYRON, astronomer; b. N.Y.C., Feb. 17, 1934; s. Emanuel B. and Ida (Silverman) S.; m. Bette L. Abrams, Aug. 17, 1958; children— Michael, Robert, Tracy. A.B., U. Calif. at Berkeley, 1955, M.A., 1959, Ph.D. (Lick Obs. fellow), 1961. Studied galaxies U. Calif. at Berkeley, 1960-61; planetary atmospheres work Jet Propulsion Lab., Pasadena, Calif., 1961-63; investigation atmospheres of coolest stars U. Calif. at Berkeley, 1964-70. Mem. Am. Astron. Soc., Astron. Soc. Pacific. Achievements include spl. research water vapor on Mars, molecular hydrogen on Jupiter, Saturn, Uranus and Neptune, temperature measurements on Venus atmosphere, spectra of galaxies and near-infrared observations, 71-72, location of faint radio galaxies, redshifts of galaxies, galaxy evolution and cosmology, 1973, spectroscopic observations of volatile gases in comets. Home: 7 Ketelsen Ct Moraga CA 94556-1814 Office: U Calif Dept Astronomy Berkeley CA 94720-0001

SPINWEBER, CHERYL LYNN, psychologist, sleep specialist; b. Jersey City, July 26, 1950; d. Stanley A. And Evelyn M. (Pfleger) S.; m. Michael E. Bruich, June 18, 1977; children: Sean Michael Bruich, Gregory Alan Bruich. AB with distinction, Cornell U., 1972; PhD in Exptl. Psychology, Harvard U., 1977. Lic. psychologist, Calif. Asst. prof. psychiatry Tufts U. Sch. Medicine, Medford, Mass., 1977-79; asst. dir. sleep lab. Boston State Hosp., 1973-79; dep. head dept. behavioral psychopharmacology Naval Health Research Ctr., San Diego, 1978-86, head dept. behavioral psychopharmacology, 1986-89; research asst. prof. dept. psychiatry Uniformed Svcs. U. of the Health Scis., Bethesda, Md., 1985—. Lectr. workshop instr. U. Calif. San Diego, La Jolla, 1979-81, vis. lectr. 1979-86; assoc. adj. prof. Dept. Psychology, 1989-94, adj. prof., 1994—; courtesy clin. staff appointee dept. psychiatry Naval Hosp., San Diego, 1984-89, clin. dir. Sleep Disorders Ctr. Mercy Hosp., San Diego, 1991—; pediatric sleep specialist Children's Hosp., San Diego, 1992-95. Contbr. articles to profl. jours. Scholar Cornell U., Ithaca, N.Y., 1968-72, West Essex Tuition, 1968-72, Cornell U. Fedn. Women, 1917-72, Harvard U., 1972-73, 74-76, NDEA Title IV, 1973-74; postdoctoral associateship Nat. Research Council, 1978-80, Outstanding Tchg. award U. Calif. San Diego, 1994. Fellow Am. Sleep Disorders Assn., Clin. Sleep Soc., We. Psychol. Assn. (sec.-treas. 1986—); mem. Am. Men and Women of Sci., Sleep Rsch. Soc. (exec. com. 1986-89), Calif. Sleep Soc., Sigma Xi.

SPIRO, MELFORD ELLIOT, anthropology educator; b. Cleve., Apr. 26, 1920; s. Wilbert I. and Sophie (Goodman) S.; m. Audrey Goldman, May 27, 1950; children: Michael, Jonathan. BA, U. Minn., 1941; PhD, Northwestern U., 1950. Mem. faculty Washington U., St. Louis, 1948-52, U. Conn., 1952-57, U. Wash., 1957-64; prof. anthropology U. Chgo., 1964-68; prof., chmn. dept. anthropology U. Calif., San Diego, 1968-99, prof. emeritus, 1999—. Bd. dirs. Social Sci. Rsch. Coun., 1960-62 Author: (with E.G. Burrows) An Atoll Culture, 1953, Kibbutz: Venture in Utopia, 1955, Children of Kibbutz, 1958, Burmese Supernaturalism, 1967, Buddhism and Society: A Great Tradition and Its Burmese Vicissitudes, 1971, Kinship and Marriage in Burma, 1977, Gender and Culture: Kibbutz Women Revisited, 1979, Culture and Human Nature, 1993; editor: Context and Meaning in Culture Anthropology, 1965, Oedipus in the Trobriands, 1982, Anthropological Other or Burmese Brother: Studies in Cultural Analysis, 1992, Gender Ideology and Psychological Reality, 1997. Fellow Am. Acad. Arts and Scis., Nat. Acad. Scis.; mem. Am. Anthrop. Assn., Am. Ethnol. Soc. (pres. 1967-68), AAAS, Soc. for Psychol. Anthropology (pres. 1979-80) Home: 2500 Torrey Pines Rd La Jolla CA 92037-3400 Office: U Calif-San Diego 9500 Gilman Dr La Jolla CA 92093-5004

SPIRTOS, MARIA, magazine publisher; BS, U. So. Calif., 1988; postgrad., UCLA, 1997. CPA, Calif. Mem. audit staff Ernst & Young, LLP, 1988-93; dir. fin. and adminstrn. Winsford Corp., 1993-96, v.p., CFO, 1996—; pres. Am. Collegiate Network, Inc., pub. U, The Nat. Coll. Mag., 1997—. Office: 1800 Century Park E Ste 820 Los Angeles CA 90067-1511

SPISAK, JOHN FRANCIS, environmental company executive; b. Cleve., Mar. 27, 1950; s. Ernest Lawrence and Adele Marie (Chipko) S.; m. Barbara Ann Heisman, June 10, 1972; children: John Stefan, Theresa Rose. BS in Chemistry, BS in Biology with honors, Purdue U., 1972. Rsch. engr. Anaconda Minerals, Tucson, 1972-79; chief metallurgist Fed. Am. Uranium, Riverton, Wyo., 1979-80; v.p. ops. Anschutz Mining Corp., Denver, 1980-87; chmn. bd. dirs. Warrenton Refining (subs. of Anschutz Corp.), Denver, 1987-89; dir., owner BE&K/Terranext, Inc., Denver, 1989—. Mem. Western States-U.S. Senate Coalition for Superfund Reform; CEO, Am. Purificaion Corp., Newport Beach, Calif., Smart Truck Sys., Moreno Valley, Calif. Contbr. articles to profl. publs.; patentee sequential flotation of sulfide ores. Named One of Fifty Colo. Top Bus. Leaders, Colo. Assn. Commerce and Industry. Mem. AIME, Soc. Mining, Metallurgy and Exploration, Nat. Assn. Environ. Mgrs. (co-founder, bd. dirs. Washington chpt., co-chmn. govt. liaison and advocacy com.), Denver Petroleum Club, Elks. Republican. Roman Catholic. Avocations: classical piano, cycling, model railroads. Home: 9384 Oakbrush Way Lone Tree CO 80124-3070 Office: Am Purification Inc 20101 SW Birch St Ste 140 Newport Beach CA 92660-1749 E-mail: jfsapi@aol.com

SPITZER, HUGH D. lawyer; b. Seattle, Feb. 14, 1949; s. George Frederick and Dorothy Lea (Davidson) S.; m. Ann Scales, Oct. 14, 1983; children: Johanna Spitzer, Claudia Spitzer, Jenny Spitzer. BA, Yale U., 1970; JD, U. Wash., 1974; LLM, U. Calif., 1982. Bar: Wash. 1974, U.S. Dist/ Ct. (ea. and we. dists.) Wash. 1975, U.S. Ct. Appeals (9th and D.C. cirs.) 1975, U.S. Supreme Ct. 1980. Program analyst N.Y.C. Health and Hosp. Corp., 1970-71; labor lawyer Hafer, Cassidy & Price, Seattle, 1974-76; legis. asst. Seattle City Coun., 1976-77; legal counsel to mayor City of Seattle, 1977-81; mcpl. bond lawyer Foster Pepper & Shefelman, PLLC, Seattle, 1982—. Affiliate prof. sch. law U. Wash. Contbr. articles to profl. jours. Vice chair Puget Sound Water Quality Authority Wash. State, 1989-96; chair Seattle Law Income Housing Levy Oversight com., 1988-96; chair Wash. State Affordable Housing Adv. Bd., 2000—. Mem. Nat. Assn. Bond Lawyers, Pub. Legal Edn. Working Group, Am. Judicature Soc. (mem. exec. com. Coun. on Pub. Legal Edn.). Democrat. Avocations: piano, hiking, skiing. Office: Foster Pepper & Shefelman PLLC 1111 3rd Ave Bldg Ste 3400 Seattle WA 98101-3292 E-mail: spith@foster.com

SPITZER, JACK J. banker; b. N.Y.C., Sept. 11, 1917; s. Ira I. and Jennie (Brody) S.; m. Charlotte May Braunstein, Dec. 21, 1941; children: Jil Spitzer-Fox, Robert Braunstein. BA, UCLA, 1938; LLD (hon.), Adelphi U., 1980, Ben-Gurion U.of the Negev, 1991. Pres., CEO Spitzer Co., L.A., 1951-59; pres., chief exec. officer Brentwood Savs. & Loan, L.A., 1959-66, Sterling Savs. & Loan, Riverside, Calif., 1966-72, Security Savs. & Loan, Seattle, 1972-78; chmn. bd. dirs. Cert. Reports, Kinderhook, N.Y., 1967—; chmn. bd. dirs., chief exec. officer Covenant Mortgage, Mercer Island, Wash., 1982—; chmn. Vitritek Environ., Inc., Columbia, Md., 1993—. Pres. United Way, Riverside, 1970; nat. chmn. David Ben-Gurion Centennial Com. of the U.S., Inc., 1985-87; mem. U.S. Del. to Inauguration of Pope John Paul II, apptd. by Pres. Carter, 1978; 1st v.p. Dem. County Ctrl. Com., L.A., 1953-62; Vice chmn., bd. govs. Ben-Gurion Univ. of Negev, 1984—, pres. Am. Assocs., 1985; founder, chmn. Seattle-Beer Sheva (Israel) Sister City Com., 1977, 2001; exec. committeeman Am. Jewish Joint Distbn. Com., 1985-96; v.p. Conf. on Jewish Material Claims, 1978—; vice chmn. bd. trustees Med. Edn. for South African Blacks, 1984-2001; chmn. bd. trustees B'nai B'rith Youth Orgn., 1996—; chmn. adv. coun. Cath. U. Am.-Internat. Ctr. for Global Aging.; apptd. to pub. del./amb. by Pres. Clinton 52d Session UN. Served to 2d lt. U.S. Army, 1943-46. Spitzer dept. of Social Work at Ben-Gurion Univ. named in his honor, 1986; recipient Outstanding Communal Svc. award Wurtzweiler Sch. Social Work, 1987, Gold medal for Humanitarian Svc., B'nai B'rith, 1994, Torch of Liberty award, Anti-Defamation League of B'nai B'rith, 1975. Mem. Meml. Found. for Jewish Culture (treas. 1978—, chmn. exec. com. 1990—, pres. 1994-96, hon. life pres. 1996—), Alexis de Tocqueville Soc., United Way, Rainier Club (Seattle), A.Z.A. of B'nai Brith (internat. pres. 1938-39, Harry Lapidus Communal Svc. award 1936, Sam Beber Outstanding Alumnus award 1970), B'nai Brith (west coast pres. 1968-69, internat. pres. 1978-82, hon. pres. 1982—, internat. chmn. susquicentennial celebration 1992-94), Rotary (World Cmty. Svc. award 1994). Avocation: ping pong. Home: PO Box 2008 Kirkland WA 98083-2008 Office: Covenant Mortgage Corp 9725 SE 36th St Ste 304 Mercer Island WA 98040-3896

SPITZER, MARC LEE, state legislator, lawyer; b. Pitts., Sept. 12, 1957; s. Richard A. and Edith (Brodie) S., m. Jacque, one child. BA in History and Polit. Sci. summa cum laude, Dickinson Coll., 1979; JD cum laude, U. Mich., 1982. Bar: Ariz. 1982, U.S. Dist. Ct. Ariz. 1982, U.S. Tax Ct. 1982, U.S. Ct. Appeals (9th cir.) 1985. Dir. KPMG Peat Marwick, Phoenix, 1982—; mem. Ariz. Senate, Phoenix, 1992-. State sen. dist. 18, majority leader Ariz. State Senate, 1997—; mem. joint legis. tax com. Bd. dirs. Ariz. Acad., 1990; mem. devel. com. Dickinson Coll., 1985-86; dir. Arizonans for Cultural Devel.; vice-chmn. Ariz. 18th Dist., 1986—; alternate del. 1988 Rep. Nat. Conv. GOP; legal counsel Ariz. Rep. Party. Recipeint awards for legis. svc. from 32 non-profit orgns. Mem. ABA (vice-chmn., tax legis. sect.), State Bar Ariz. (cert. specialist taxation), Ariz. Tax Research Found. (bd. dirs. 1984—), Ariz. Tax Research Assn., Maricopa County Bar Assn., Phoenix 100 Rotary, Heritage Found., Ariz. Club, Phi Beta Kappa, Sigma Alpha Epsilon. Jewish. Avocations: fishing, prospecting, classical music, racquetball. Office: Arizona State Senate 1700 W Washington St Rm 305 Phoenix AZ 85007-2812

SPITZER, ROBERT J. academic administrator; BBA, Gonzaga U.; MPhil, St. Louis U.; STB, Gregorian U., Rome; ThM, Weston Sch. Theology, Cambridge, Mass.; PhD in Philosophy, Cath. U. of Am. Tchr. Georgetown U., 1984-90, Seattle U., 1978-80, 90-98; pres. Gonzaga U. Co-founder U. Faculty for Life; founder, adv. Life Principles. Office: Gonzaga U 502 E Boone Ave Spokane WA 99258-0001

SPOFFORD, ROBERT HOUSTON, advertising agency executive; b. N.Y.C., Apr. 3, 1941; s. Robert Knowlton and Linda Prieber (Houston) S.; m. Susan Proctor Allerton; children: Margaret, Robert Christopher. B.E.E., Cornell U., 1964. Account exec. Batten, Barton, Durstine & Osborn, Inc., N.Y.C., 1964-71, v.p., 1971-84, sr. v.p., 1984-88, exec. v.p., dir. strategic planning, 1988-96; exec. v.p. BBDO Univ., Barcelona, Spain, 1997—. Contbr. articles to advt. and data processing jours. Mem. Westchester County Democratic Com. N.Y. 1974-78; ch. organist First recipient Founder's medal Batten, Barton, Durstine & Osborn, Inc., 1985 Congregationalist. Home: 61 Dunfries Ter San Rafael CA 94901-2415 Office: BBDO LA 10960 Wilshire Blvd Los Angeles CA 90024-3702 E-mail: spoffo@bbdowest.com

SPOOR, JAMES EDWARD, human resources executive, entrepreneur; b. Rockford, Ill., Feb. 19, 1936; s. Frank Kendall and Genevieve Eileen (Johnson) S.; m. Nancy E. Carlson, Sept. 8, 1962; children: Sybll K., Kendall P., Andrea K., Marcie K. BS in Psychology, U. Ill., 1958. Pers. mgr. Nat. Sugar Refining Co., N.Y.C., 1960-64; Pepsico, Inc., N.Y.C., Auburn, N.Y., 1964-67; mgr. internat. pers. Control Data Corp., Mpls., 1967-75; v.p. pers. and employee rels. Vetco, Inc., Ventura, Calif., 1975-79; v.p. employee rels. Hamilton Bros. Oil Co., Denver, 1979-84; pres., founder, CEO Spectrum Human Resource Systems Corp., Denver, 1984—. Cons., author, spkr. on human resources and entrepreneurism. Mem. adv. bd. Salvation Army, 1978-79; chmn. Spl. Commn. for Ventura County Bd. Suprs., 1978; mem. task force on human resources Colo. Sch. Mines, 1983; state chair Coun. Growing Cos., 1991-92, nat. pres., 1992-94; bd. dirs. Breckenridge Outdoor Edn. Ctr., 1994-98, chmn., 1996-98. Mem. Internat. Human Resources Mgmt. Assn. (nat. bd. dirs. 1997—).

SPRAGUE, ANN LOUISE, space scientist; b. Bellfonte, Pa., Feb. 25, 1946; d. David Carpenter and Opal (Wheat) S.; m. Donald M. Hunten, 1995. BA in Geology, Syracuse U., 1969; MA, Boston U., 1980; PhD, U. Ariz., 1990. Sci. tchr. Selinsgrove Mid. Sch., 1970-79; space scientist Lunar and Planetary Lab. U. Ariz., Tucson, 1990—. Mem. com. lunar and planetary exploration (COMPLEX) NRC, 2000—. Contbg. author: Caloris Basin: An Enhanced Source for Potassium in Mercury's Atmosphere, 1990, Sulfur at Mercury, Elemental at the Poles and Sulfides in the Regolith, 1995, Water Brought In to Jupiter's Atmosphere by Fragments R and W of Comet SL-9, 1996, Distribution and Abundance of Sodium in Mercury's Atmosphere, 1985-1988, 1997; editl. bd. ICARUS. Mem. AAAS, Internat. Astron. Union, Am. Astron. Soc., Am. Geophys. Union. Office: U Ariz Lunar & Planetary Lab Tucson AZ 85721-0001 E-mail: sprague@lpl.arizona.edu

SPRAGUE, MIKE, state legislator; b. Cut Bank, Mont., Jan. 14, 1944; m. Susie Sprague BS in Bus., Eastern Mont. Coll. Bus. developer; mem. Mont. Senate, Dist. 6, Helena, 1995—; chair local govt. com., vice chair bus. and industry com. Mont. State Senate, mem. edn. and cultural resources com. Past 1st vice chair Republican Exec. Bd.; Republican precinct committeeman. Served with U.S. Navy, Vietnam. Republican. Home: 174 Erickson Ct S Billings MT 59105-2347

SPRECHER, DAVID A. university administrator, mathematician; b. Saarbrucken, Fed. Republic Germany, Jan. 12, 1930; s. Wolfgang and Karolina (Jung) S.; children: Lorrie, Jeannie. Student, Hebrew U., 1952-54; A.B., U. Bridgeport, 1958; Ph.D., U. Md., 1963. Instr. math. U. Md., 1961-63; asst. prof. Syracuse U., 1963-66; asso. prof. math. U. Calif.-Santa Barbara, 1966-71, prof., 1971-92, prof. emeritus, 1993—, chmn. dept., 1972-75, assoc. dean Coll. of Letters and Sci., 1975-78, dean Coll. of Letters and Sci., 1978-81, provost/dean, 1981-91. Author: Elements of Real Analysis, 1970, 2nd edit., 1987, Precalculus Mathematics, 1974, Finite Mathematics, 1976; (with P. Frank and A. Yaqub) A Brief Course in Calculus With Applications, 1971, 2nd edit., 1976; (with P. Frank) Calculus, 1975; contbr. articles to profl. jours. Served with Israeli Army, 1948-50. Mem. Am. Math. Soc., Math. Assn. Am. Office: U Calif 6607 South Hall Santa Barbara CA 93106

SPRINGER, CAROL, state official; Ariz. State treas., Phoenix. Home: 1735 Oregon Ave Prescott AZ 86305-2229 Office: Arizona State Senate 1700 W Washington St Phoenix AZ 85007-2890

SPRINGER, CHARLES EDWARD, retired state supreme court chief justice; b. Reno, Feb. 20, 1928; s. Edwin and Rose Mary Cecelia (Kelly) S.; m. Jacqueline Sirkegian, Mar. 17, 1951; 1 dau., Kelli Ann. BA, U. Nev., Reno, 1950; LLB, Georgetown U., 1953; LLM, U. Va., 1984; student Grad. Program for Am. Judges, Oriel Coll., Oxford (Eng.), 1984. Bar: Nev. 1953, U.S. Dist. Ct. Nev. 1953, D.C. 1954, U.S. Supreme Ct. 1962. Pvt. practice law, Reno, 1953-80; atty. gen. State of Nev., 1962, legis. legal adv. to gov., 1958-62; legis. bill drafter Nev. Legislature, 1955-57; mem. faculty Nat. Coll. Juvenile Justice, Reno, 1978—; juvenile master 2d Jud. Dist. Nev., 1973-80; justice Nev. Suprem Ct., Carson City, 1981—; vice-chief justice Nev. Supreme Ct., Carson City, 1987, chief justice, 1998-99, ret., 1999. Mem. Jud. Selection Commn., 1981, 98, Nev. Supreme Ct. Gender Bias Task Force, 1981—; trustee Nat. Coun. Juvenile and Family Ct. Judges, 1983—; mem. faculty McGeorge Sch. Law, U. Nev., Reno, 1982—; mem. Nev. Commn. for Women, 1991-95. With AUS, 1945-47. Recipient Outstanding Contbn. to Juvenile Justice award Nat. Coun. Juvenile and Family Ct. Judges, 1989, Midby-Byron Disting. Leadership award U. Nev., 1988. Mem. ABA, Am. Judicature Soc., Am. Trial Lawyers Assn., Phi Kappa Phi. Office: Nev Supreme Ct Capitol Complex 201 S Carson St Carson City NV 89701-4702

SPRINGER, GEORGE STEPHEN, mechanical engineering educator; b. Budapest, Hungary, Dec. 12, 1933; came to U.S., 1959; s. Joseph and Susan (Grausz) S.; m. Susan Martha Flory, Sept. 15, 1963; children: Elizabeth Anne, Mary Katherine. B in Engring., U. Sydney, Australia, [illegible] (hon.), Tech. U. Budapest, 2000. Registered profl. engr., Mass. Asst. prof. mech. engring. MIT, Cambridge, Mass., 1962-67; prof. mech. engring. U. Mich., Ann Arbor, 1967-83; Paul Pigott prof., chmn. dept. aeronautics and astronautics Stanford (Calif.) U., 1983—. Author: Erosion by Liquid Impact, 1975; co-author, co-editor 12 books; contbr. over 200 articles to scholarly and profl. jours. Recipient Pub. Svc. Group Achievement award, NASA, 1988, Medal of Excellence in Composite Materials U. Del., 1999. Fellow AIAA (Engr. of Yr. 1995, Structures Structural Dynamics and Materials award 2000), ASME (Worcester Reed Warner medal 1994), Soc. Advancement Materials and Process Engring. (Delmonte award 1991); mem. Am. Phys. Soc., Soc. Automotive Engrs. (Ralph Teetor award 1978), Nat. Acad. Engring., Hungarian Nat. Acad. Sci. (fgn. mem.), Am. Soc. Composites (Outstanding Rschr. award 1997). Achievements include patent in field. Office: Stanford U Dept Aeronautics & Astronautics Stanford CA 94305

SPRINGER, PAUL DAVID, lawyer, motion picture company executive; b. N.Y.C., Apr. 27, 1942; s. William W. and Alma (Markowitz) S.; m. Mariann Frankfurt, Aug. 16, 1964; children: Robert, William. BA, U. Bridgeport, 1963; JD, Bklyn. Law Sch., 1967. Bar: N.Y. 1968, U.S. Dist. Ct. (so. and ea. dists.) N.Y. 1968, U.S. Ct. Appeals (2d cir.) 1970, U.S. Supreme Ct. 1973, Calif. 1989. Assoc. Johnson & Tannenbaum, N.Y.C., 1968-70; assoc. counsel Columbia Pictures, N.Y.C., 1970, Paramount Pictures, N.Y.C., 1970-79, v.p., theatrical distbn. counsel, 1979-85, sr. v.p., chief resident counsel East Coast, 1985-87, sr. v.p., asst. gen. counsel L.A., 1987—. Bar: N.Y. 1968, U.S. Dist. Ct. (so. and ea. dists.) N.Y. 1968, U.S. Ct. Appeals (2d cir.) 1970, U.S. Supreme Ct. 1973, Calif. 1989. Trustee West Cunningham Park Civic Assn., Fresh Meadows, N.Y., 1978—. Mem. ABA, Assn. of Bar of City of N.Y., L.A. Copyright Soc., Acad. Motion Picture Arts and Scis., Motion Picture Pioneers. E-mail: paul_springer@paramount.com

SPRINGER, WAYNE RICHARD, healthcare system official, research biochemist; b. Milw., Nov. 16, 1946; s. Richard Andrew and Irma Edna (Richter) S.; m. Jane Bradley, Aug. 19, 1972; chldren: Matthew Bradley, Katherine Jane. BA, Northwestern U., 1968; PhD, U. Calif., Berkeley, 1977. Vol. Peace Corps, Somalia, Antigua, 1969-72; postdoctoral fellow U. Calif., San Diego, 1977-79, rsch. biochemist, 1979-92; assoc. project biochemist, 1992-99; rsch. biochemist VA Med. Ctr., San Diego, 1979-99, chem. hygiene officer, 1992-94, chief environ., health and safety, 1994—. Judge Sci. Fair. Mem. Am. Biol. Safety Assn. Avocations: travel, gardening. Office: VA San Diego Healthcare Sys (138S) 3350 La Jolla Village Dr San Diego CA 92161-0002

SPRITZER, RALPH SIMON, lawyer, educator; b. N.Y.C., Apr. 27, 1917; s. Harry and Stella (Theuman) S.; m. Lorraine Nelson, Dec. 23, 1950; children: Ronald, Pamela. B.S., Columbia U., 1937, LL.B., 1940. Bar: N.Y. bar 1941, U.S. Supreme Ct. bar 1950. Atty. Office Alien Property, Dept. Justice, 1946-51; anti-trust div. Dept. Justice, 1951-54, Office Solicitor Gen., 1954-61; gen. counsel FPC, 1961-62; 1st asst. to solicitor gen. U.S., 1962-68; prof. law U. Pa., Phila., 1968-86, Ariz. State U., Tempe, 1986—; gen. counsel AAUP, 1983-84. Adj. prof. law George Washington U., 1967; cons. Adminstrv. Conf. U.S., Ford Found., Pa. Gov.'s Justice Commn. Served with AUS, 1941-46. Recipient Superior Service award Dept. Justice, 1960; Tom C. Clark award Fed. Bar. Assn., 1968 Mem. Am. Law Inst. Home: 1024 E Gemini Dr Tempe AZ 85283-3004 Office: Ariz State Univ Coll Law Tempe AZ 85287

SPROSTY, JOSEPH PATRICK, producer, writer, weapons specialist; b. Cleve., Aug. 25, 1947; s. Joseph Patrick and Anna Margret (Louchka) S. Grad., Midpark H.S., Middleburgh, Ohio, 1965; student, San Diego City Coll., 1972-73. Class 2 firearms lic. Prop builder The Goulardi Show WJW-TV8, Cleve., 1962-65; sub-agent Internat. Artists Agy., San Diego and L.A., 1982-83; casting dir. Cinemode Films, 1982; operator, owner Actors Artists Agy., L.A., 1983-87; founder, prodr., dir. Magnum Prodns., 1985; founder Sprosty Prodns., 1990. Demonstrator weapons and handling of weapons, Propmaster TV Co., Van Nuys, Calif., 1992; expert witness Laser Weapon Scam, 1984; vis. lectr. firearms safety, handling, rules and regulations governing use of firearms in motion picture, TV prodn. U. So. Calif., 1996—; animal wrangler specializing in opossums. Scripwriter: (films) Vanishing Point II, The Apartment Manager, The Big House, Rambo III (optioned), Rambo IV (revised), Boneyard, Mister Ed - Talking Again, Mister Ed - Radio Talk, Brick, Life Plus One, Gun Slave, Fixation, Last Chance (renamed Terminal Virus), You're So Beautiful, Home Dead Home, Kung Fu Cop, The Fisherman, numerous others; prodr., dir. (video) Break Disc, 1985; location mgr., armorer, weapons splst.: (film) Heat from Another Sun (retitled Maladiction), 1988; armorer, 2nd asst. dir., assoc. prodr., weapons splst.: (film) Provoked, 1989; weapons splst., armorer: (film) Big City, 1990; co-prodr., animal wrangler, weapons splst.: (film) Opossum de Oro, 1996; weapons splst.: (tv shows) Jake and the Fat Man, Black's Magic, Hill Street Blues, Murder, She Wrote, On the Edge of Death, Emerald Point N.A.S., (7 episodes) America's Most Wanted, (3 episodes) FBI: The Untold Stories, numerous others, (films) Revolt, Rocky IV, Streets of Fire, Walk in the Sun, Cloak & Dagger, One Man's Poison, Killing Zoe, Desert Storm, The Movie, Live Shot, Outer Heat, Zipperhead, Four Minute Warning, The Robbery, Spirit, Texas Payback, High Adventure, The Waterfront, The Philadelphia Experiment II, Opossum de Oro, Harlem Nights, Tango & Cash, Die Hard, Provoked, Beverly Hills Cop II, Big City, numerous others. Spkr. Veterans Day Calif. State U., Dominguez Hills, 1993. Served with USN, 1965-67 (hon. discharge). Mem. AFTRA, SAG (charter mem. San Diego br.). Home: 337 W Maple St Glendale CA 91204-2014

SPROUL, JOHN ALLAN, retired public utility executive; b. Oakland, Calif., Mar. 28, 1924; s. Robert Gordon and Ida Amelia (Wittschen) S.; m. Marjorie Ann Hauck, June 20, 1945; children: John Allan, Malcolm J., Richard O., Catherine E. A.B., U. Calif., Berkeley, 1947, LL.B., 1949. Bar: Calif. 1950. Atty. Pacific Gas & Electric Co., San Francisco, 1949-52, 56-62, sr. atty., 1962-70, asst. gen. counsel, 1970-71, v.p. gas supply, 1971-76, sr. v.p., 1976-77, exec. v.p., 1977-89; gen. counsel Pacific Gas Transmission Co., 1970-73, v.p., 1973-79, chmn. bd., 1979-89, also bd. dirs. Atty. Johnson & Stanton, San Francisco, 1952-56; bd. dirs. Oreg. Steel Mills, Inc. Bd. dirs. emeritus Hastings Coll. Law. Served to 1st lt. USAAF, 1943-46. Mem. Calif. Bar Assn. (inactive), Pacific Coast Gas Assn., Pacific-Union Club, Orinda Country Club. Home: 8413 Buckingham Dr El Cerrito CA 94530-2531 Office: Pacific Gas & Electric Co Mail Code H17F PO Box 770000 San Francisco CA 94177-0001

SPRUDE, MARGARET, credit services company executive; b. 1946; BS in Bus., MS of Accountancy, Western Ill. U. CPA. Various fin.-exec.-level positions card divsn. including CFO Bank of Am., 1986-2000, mng. dir., CFO Household Internat. Credit Card Svcs. divsn., 2000—. Office: Household Internat Inc 1441 Schilling Pl Salinas CA 93901-4543 E-mail: masprude@household.com

SPUDICH, JAMES A. biology educator; b. Collinsville, Ill., Jan. 7, 1942; married, 1964; 2 children. BS, U. Ill., 1963; PhD in Biochemistry, Stanford U., 1968. USPHS trainee Stanford (Calif.) U., 1968; asst. prof. biochemistry U. Calif., San Francisco, 1971-74, assoc. prof., 1974-76; prof., 1976; prof. biochemistry and devel. biology Beckman Ctr., Stanford U. Sch. Medicine, 1977—. Editor: Annual Rev. Cell Biology, 1994. Recipient Lewis S. Rosentiel award for disting. work in basic med. rsch., 1996, Repligen Corp. award, 1997. Mem. Am. Soc. Cell Biologists (pres. 1989). Achievements include research in molecular basis of cytokinesis amoeboid movement and other forms of cell motility. Office: Stanford U Sch Medicine Dept Biochemistry Stanford Med Ctr Beckman Ctr B400 Stanford CA 94305-5307

SQUIRES, WILLIAM RANDOLPH, III, lawyer; b. Providence, Sept. 6, 1947; s. William Randolph and Mary Louise (Gress) S.; m. Elisabeth Dale McAnulty, June 23, 1984; children: Shannon, William R. IV, Mayre Elisabeth, James Robert. BA in Econs., Stanford U., 1969; JD, U. Tex., 1972. Bar: Wash. 1973, U.S. Dist. Ct. (we. dist.) Wash. 1973, U.S. Dist. Ct. (ea. dist.) Wash. 1976, U.S. Ct. Appeals (9th cir.) 1976, U.S. Supreme Ct. 1976, U.S. Ct. Fed. Claims 1982. Assoc. Oles, Morrison, Rinker, Stanislaw & Ashbaugh, Seattle, 1973-78; ptnr., chmn. litig. group Davis Wright Tremaine, Seattle, 1978-97; mem. Summit Law Group, Seattle, 1997—. Fellow Am. Coll. Trial Lawyers; mem. ABA, Internat. Bar Assn., Wash. State Bar Assn., King County Bar Assn., Wash. Athletic Club, Rainier Club (Seattle). Episcopalian. Home: 5554 NE Penrith Rd Seattle WA 98105-2845 Office: Summit Law Group 1505 Westlake Ave N Ste 300 Seattle WA 98109-6211 E-mail: randys@summitlaw.com

SREENIVASAN, SREENIVASA RANGA, physicist, educator; b. Mysore, Karnataka, India, Oct. 20, 1933; came to U.S., 1959; s. Sreenivasachari and Alamelammal (Rangaswami) S.; m. Claire de Reineck, Nov. 16, 1963; children: Gopal, Govind, Gauri, Gayatri, Aravind. BS, U. Mysore, 1950, BS, 1952; PhD, Gujarat U., India, 1958. Lectr. St. Philomena's Coll., Mysore, 1952-54; rsch. fellow Harvard U., Cambridge, Mass., 1959-61; rsch. assoc. NASA Inst. for Space Studies, N.Y.C., 1961-64; vis. scientist Max Planck Inst. Physics and Astrophysics, Munich, Fed. Republic of Germany, 1964-66; prof. physics U. Calgary, Alta., Can., 1967—. Vis. prof. Royal Inst. Tech., Stockholm, Sweden, 1974-75. Contbr. articles to profl. jours. Chmn. Coun. South Asians, Calgary, 1981-84; pres. Calgary Interfaith Community Action Assn., 1986; pri. Sch. East Indian Langs. and Performing Arts, Calgary, 1986. Recipient Govt. of India Sr. Rsch. scholar, Ahmedabad, 1955-58. Achievements include rsch. in force-free fields, electrostatic instabilities in plasmas, evolution of massive stars, size of convective cores in rotating stellar models. Home: 2110 30 Ave SW Calgary AB Canada T2T 1R4 Office: U Calgary 2500 University Dr NW Calgary AB Canada T2N 1N4

SRINIVASAN, VENKATARAMAN, marketing and management educator; b. Pudukkottai, Tamil Nadu, India, June 5, 1944; came to U.S., 1968; s. Annaswamy and Jambagalakshmi Venkataraman; m. Sitalakshmi Subrahmanyam, June 30, 1972; children: Ramesh, Mahesh. B Tech., Indian Inst. Tech., Madras, India, 1966; MS, Carnegie-Mellon U., 1970, PhD, 1971. Asst. engr. Larsen & Toubro, Bombay, 1966-68; asst. prof. mgmt. and mktg. U. Rochester, N.Y., 1971-73, assoc. prof., 1973-74, Stanford (Calif.) U., 1974-76, prof., 1976-82, dir. PhD program in bus., 1982-85, Ernest C. Arbuckle prof. mktg. and mgmt. sci., 1982—; mktg. area coord., 1976-78, 88-93, 2000—. Cons. in field. Mem. editorial bd. Jour. Mktg. Rsch., 1988—, Mktg. Sci., 1980—, Mgmt. Sci., 1974-91; contbr. articles to profl. jours. Mem. Am. Mktg. Assn., Inst. Ops. Rsch./Mgmt. Scis. Hindu. Avocation: classical music.

STABBERT, FREDERICK JOSEPH, paper company executive; b. Seattle, Nov. 17, 1943; s. Wallace Roger and Eleanor Clarice (Joringdal) S.; m. Faith Edna Jordan, Nov. 22, 1963; children Monica, Michael B.A. in Bus. Adminstrn., U. Puget Sound, 1968. Trainee div. Zellerback Paper Co., South San Francisco, Calif., 1960-70, sales rep., 1970-71, mng., adminstr. Los Angeles, 1971-75, mgr. div. Sacramento, 1975-76, mgr. indsl. bus. unit San Francisco, 1976-79, v.p., regional mgr., 1979-80, exec. v.p., 1980-83; sr. v.p. Crown Zellerbach Corp., San Francisco, 1983—; pres. Zellerbach Paper Co., San Francisco, 1983—. Mem. Nat. Paper Trade Assn. (treas. 1984— , bd. dirs. 1983—) Republican Avocations: golfing; skiing; tennis. Home: 3550 Tripp Rd Redwood City CA 94062-3636 Office: Zellerback Paper Co 3130 Crow Canyon Pl San Ramon CA 94583-1346

STABILE, BRUCE EDWARD, surgeon; b. Monterey Park, Calif., Apr. 14, 1944; s. Edward Emilio and Angela (Cramandozzi) S.; m. Caroline Graston, Sept. 18, 1967; children: Jessica, Drew. BA, UCLA, 1966; MD, U. Calif., San Francisco, 1970. Diplomate Am. Bd. Surgery. From asst. prof. to assoc. prof. UCLA Sch. Medicine, 1977-85; from assoc. prof. to prof. surgery U. Calif. San Diego Sch. Medicine, 1985-93; prof. surgery UCLA Sch. Medicine, 1993—, vice chmn. dept. surgery, 1992—. Chmn. dept. surgery Harbor-UCLA Med. Ctr., Torrance, 1993—, acting med. dir., 1997-98; interim assoc. dean UCLA Sch. Medicine, 1997-98, vice chmn. dept. surgery, 1993—; med. expert Med. Bd. Calif., 1980—. Fellow Am. Coll. Surgeons, Am. Surg. Assn., Am. Bd. Surgery (dir.); mem. Soc. Univ. Surgeons, Assn. Acad. Surgery, Am. Gastroenterol. Assn., San Diego Soc. Gen. Surgeons (pres. 1992-93), L.A. Surg. Soc. (pres. 2000 01). Office: Harbor UCLA Med Ctr 1000 W Carson St Torrance CA 90502-2004

STACK, GEOFFREY LAWRENCE, real estate developer; b. Trinidad, British West Indies, Sept. 16, 1943; s. Gerald Francis and V. Louise (Bell) S.; m. Victoria Hammack, 1970 (div. 1986); 1 child, Kathryn; m. Nancy J. Haarer, Apr. 19, 1987; children: Alexandra, Natalie. BA, Georgetown U., 1965; MBA, U. Pa., 1972. Dir. acquisitions J.H. Snyder Co., L.A., 1972-75; from project mgr. to exec. v.p. Richards West, Newport Beach, Calif., 1975-77; pres. Regis Homes Corp., Newport Beach, 1977-93; mng. dir. Sares-Regis Group, Irvine, Calif., 1993—. Bd. dirs. Arral & Ptnrs., Hong Kong, Calif. Housing Coun., Sacramento, Tejon Ranch Co., 1998. Bd. regents Franciscan Sch. of Theology, Berkeley, Calif., 1991—; bd. dirs. Nat. Multihousing Coun., 1987—, bd. trustees Harbor Day Sch., 1996. Capt. USMC, 1967-70. Decorated 2 Bronze Stars, 21 Air medals, Navy Commendation medal, Purple Heart. Mem. Young Pres. Orgn., Big Canyon Country Club, Pacific Club, Olympic Club. Democrat. Roman Catholic. Office: Sares Regis Group 18802 Bardeen Ave Irvine CA 92612-1521 E-mail: jstack@sares-regis.com

STACK, KEVIN J. lawyer; b. N.Y.C., Aug. 12, 1951; BA cum laude, UCLA, 1973; JD cum laude, Loyola U., L.A., 1976. Bar: Calif. 1976, U.S. Dist. Ct. (ctrl. dist.) Calif. 1977. Ptnr. Knapp, Petersen & Clarke, Glendale, Calif., 1984—. Office: Knapp Petersen & Clarke 500 N Brand Blvd Fl 20 Glendale CA 91203-1923

STACY, ANGELICA M. chemistry educator; Prof. dept. chemistry U. Calif., Berkeley. Recipient Francis P. Garvan-John M. Olin medal Am. Chem. Soc., 1995. Office: U Calif Dept Chemistry 419 Latimer Hall Berkeley CA 94720-1460

STACY, RICHARD A. judge; b. Eldorado, Ark., Mar. 7, 1942; s. Jack Leonard S. and Estelle (Mabry) Carrier; m. Karen Kay King, Aug. 20, 1961; children: Mark L., Andrea L. BA, U. Wyo., 1965, JD, 1967. Bar: Wyo. 1967, Colo. 1967, U.S. Supreme Ct. 1972. Revisor Wyo. Statute Revision Com., Cheyenne, 1967-69; asst. atty. gen. State of Wyo., 1969-72; asst. U.S. atty. Dept. Justice, Cheyenne, 1972-75; U.S. atty. Dis. Wyo., Cheyenne, 1981-94; adminstrv. law judge Office of Hearing & Appeals, San Jose, Calif., 1994-99, Denver, 1999—; mem. atty. gen.'s adv. com. of U.S. attys. Dept. Justice, 1981-84. Mem. Gov.'s Statewide Drug Alcohol Adv. Bd., 1988-94. Mem. ABA, Wyo. Bar Assn., Colo. State Bar, Santa Clara County Bar Assn. (hon., com. on bench, bar, media, police relationships 1995—). Republican. Episcopalian. Club: Kiwanis (charter pres. Wheatland 1977). Office: Hearings & Appeals 1244 Speer Blvd Ste 752 Denver CO 80204-3584

STAEHELIN, LUCAS ANDREW, cell biology educator; b. Sydney, Australia, Feb. 10, 1939; came to U.S., 1969; s. Lucas Eduard and Isobel (Malloch) S.; m. Margrit Weibel, Sept. 17, 1965; children: Daniel Thomas, Philip Roland, Marcel Felix. Dipl. Natw., Swiss Fed. Inst. Tech., Zurich, 1963, Ph.D. in Biology, 1966. Research scientist N.Z. Dept. Sci. and Indsl. Research, 1966-69; research fellow in cell biology Harvard U., Cambridge, Mass., 1969-70; asst. prof. cell biology U. Colo., Boulder, 1970-73, assoc. prof., 1973-79, prof., 1979—. Vis. prof. U. Freiburg, 1978, Swiss Fed. Inst. Tech., 1984, 92, U. Melbourne, Australia, 1998; mem. cellular biology and physiology study sect. NIH, Bethesda, Md., 1980-84; mem. DOE panel on rsch. directions for the energy bioscis., 1988, 92; mem. NSF adv. panel for cellular orgn., 1994-96; mem. plant biology panel NASA. Editor Jour. Cell Biology, 1977-81, European Jour. Cell Biology, 1981-90, Plant Physiology, 1986-92, Plant Jour., 1991-97, Biology of the Cell, 1996-99; editor: (with C.J. Antzen) Encyclopedia of Plant Physiology, Vol. 19, Photosynthesis III, 1986; contbr. numerous articles to sci. jours. Recipient Humboldt award Humboldt Found., 1978, Sci. Tchr. award U. Colo., 1984, Outstanding Faculty award U. Colo.-Boulder Parents Assn., 2001; grantee NIH, 1971—, USDA, 1994—, NASA, 1997—; hon. sr. fellow U. Melbourne, Australia, 1998. Mem. AAAS, Am. Soc. Cell Biology, Am. Soc. Plant Physiology, German Acad. Natural Scis. Leopoldina. Home: 2855 Dover Dr Boulder CO 80305-5305 Office: Dept Molecular Cell U Colo 347 UCB Boulder CO 80309-0347 E-mail: staeheli@spot.colorado.edu

STAEHLE, ROBERT L. foundation executive; b. Rochester, N.Y., Apr. 22, 1955; s. Henry Carl and Isabel Montgomery S. BS in Aero. and Astronautic Engring., Purdue U., 1977. Prin. investigator Skylab Expt. ED-31 (bacteria aboard Skylab), NASA/Marshall Space Flight Center, Huntsville, Ala., 1972-74, student trainee engring., 1974-77; sci. observation analyst Caltech/Jet Propulsion Lab., Pasadena, Calif., 1977-78; engr. advanced projects group, 1978-83; mem. tech. staff system integration sect. of Space Sta., 1983-87; mem. tech. staff and space sta., user ops. team leader, 1987-88; tech. mgr. Jet Propulsion Lab., Pasadena, Calif., 1988—, mgr. space sta. Freedom support office Pasadena ops., 1990-92, Pluto team leader, 1992-93, mgr. Pluto Express preproject, 1993-96, mgr. Ice and Fire preprojects, 1996-98, dep. mgr. outer planets/solar probe project, 1998-2000, dept. mgr. Europa Orbiter project, 2000—. Prin. founder, pres. World Space Found., South Pasadena, Calif., 1979—; founding dir. So. Calif. Space Bus. Roundtable, 1987-95; bd. dirs. Altadena Foothills Conservancy, 2000—. Co-author: Project Solar Sail, New Am. Libr., 1990; contbr. articles to profl. jours. Mem. Cmty. Leaders Adv. Bd. for Irvine Scholars, Occidental Coll., L.A., 1996-97; bd. dirs. Caltech Y, 1987-93, Altadena Foothills Conservancy, 2000—. Nat. Space Club Goddard scholar, 1977; Charles A. Lindbergh Fund grantee, 1986. Fellow Brit. Interplanetary Soc.; mem. AIAA, Tau Beta Pi, Sigma Gamma Tau. Avocations: photography, hiking, mountain biking. Office: Jet Propulsion Lab Pasadena CA 91109 E-mail: robert.l.staehle@jpd.nasa.gov

STAFFORD, HELEN ADELE, retired biology educator; b. Oct. 9, 1922; BA, Wellesley U., 1944; MA, Conn. Coll., 1948; PhD, U. Pa., 1951. Rsch. assoc., instr. biochemistry, instr. botany U. Chgo., 1951-54; asst. prof. biology Reed Coll., Portland, Oreg., 1954-58, assoc. prof., 1959-65, prof., 1965-87, prof. emeritus, 1987—. Staff Yale U., 1969-70, Oreg. Grad. Ctr., 1977-78; CUEBS commr., 1968-71; panel mem. metabolic biology NSF, 1973-75; pres. Phytochemical Soc. N.Am., 1977-78. Editor Recent Advances in Phytochemistry, 1989-94; mem. editl. bd. Plant Physiology, 1964-92, Plant Sci., 1982—. Recipient C.R. Barnes award Am. Soc. Plant Physiologists, 1996; Guggenheim fellow Harvard U., 1958-59, NSF sr. postdoctoral fellow U. Calif., L.A., 1963-64. Office: Reed Coll Dept Biology 3203 SE Woodstock Blvd Portland OR 97202-8138

STAFFORD, MIKE, broadcast executive; Sr. v.p., gen. mgr., gen. sales mgr. Sta. KSON-FM, San Diego. Office: Sta KSON FM 1615 Murray Canyon Rd Ste 710 San Diego CA 92108-4321

STAFFORD, PATRICK PURCELL, poet, writer, management consultant; b. L.A., Mar. 13, 1954; s. Elsan H. Stafford and Ann (Ruelle) Lane; m. Liane Beale Stafford, Jan. 2, 1987; 1 child, David. Student, U.S. Armed Forces Inst., 1971, UCLA, 1980, 81. Head script writer Hollywood (Calif.) Radio Network, 1981-82; mgr. new bus. Harry Koff Agy., Encino, Calif., 1984-85; pres., mgr. Legal Experts, L.A., 1988-94, Creative Adminstrs., L.A., 1994—; office adminstr. Moneymaker & Kelley, L.A., 1989-90. Sales rep. Now Messenger Svc., L.A., 1993-98; staff mgr. Stafford Resume Svc., L.A., 1990—. Author: Homage to a Princess, 2000; feature writer Amateur Chef Mag.; contbr. poems, articles, short stories to profl. publs. Mem. Big Bros. of Greater L.A., 1991. With USMC, 1971-78, Vietnam. Recipient Concept/Essay award L.A. Rtd., 1990, Poetry Contest award Tradition Mag., 1991, Hon. Mention award Iliad Press, 1992, Wash. State Coll., 1990, Winner in Play-Reading Series, Altered Stage Theatre Co., 1991, 1st prize Jacobytebooks Poetry Contest, 2000. Mem. The Writer's Exch. (life), Marino's of Beverly Hills (charter). Libertarian. Avocations: classical music and films, martial arts, biking, boxing. Home and Office: 1775 Southgate Way Grants Pass OR 97527-7241 E-mail: thinksuccess@hotmail.com

STAGER, DONALD K. retired construction company executive; Chmn., pres., CEO Dillingham Constrn. Holdings Inc., Pleasanton, Calif., 1982-99; ret., 1999. Dir. Harding Lawson Assocs., Novato, Calif. Recipient, Roebling award Am. Soc. of Civil Engineers, 1995, Golden Beaver award for Mgmt Beavers, Inc., 1998. Office: 957 Wapato Way Manson WA 98831-9595

STAGGS, THOMAS, entertainment company executive; CFO The Walt Disney Co., Burbank, Calif. Office: The Walt Disney Co 500 S Buena Vista St Burbank CA 91521-0006

STAHL, FRANKLIN WILLIAM, biology educator; b. Boston, Oct. 8, 1929; AB in Biology, Harvard U., 1951; PhD in Biology, U. Rochester, 1956; DSc (hon.), Oakland U., 1966, U. Rochester, 1982. Grad. tchg. asst., rsch. asst. U. Rochester, 1951-54, predoctoral fellow NSF, 1954-55; postdoctoral fellow NSF, NRC, divsn. med. sci. Calif. Inst. Tech., 1955-57, rsch. fellow, 1957-58; assoc. prof. biology, rsch. assoc. Inst. Molecular Biology, U. Oreg., Eugene, 1959-63, prof. biology, mem., 1963—, acting dir., 1973-74. Vol. scientist divsn. molecular genetics Med. Rsch. Coun., Cambridge, Eng., 1964-65; mem. virology study sect. NIH, 1968-71; sabbatical leave MRC Unit of Molecular Genetics, U. Edinburgh, Scotland, 1969-70, Internat. Genetics and Biophysics Lab., Napoli, Italy, 1969-70; Lady Davis vis. prof. genetics dept. Hebrew U., Jerusalem, 1975-76; mem. microbial genetics study sect. NSF, 1987—. Mem. editl. bd. Virology, 1959-62, Molecular and Gen. Genetics, 1967-78, 80-82, Genetics, 1971-76, Jour. Genetics, 1986—; contbr. articles to profl. jours. Recipient Thomas Hunt Morgan medal for lifetime achievement in genetics Genetics Soc. Am., 1996; named Am. Cancer Soc. rsch. prof. molecular genetics, 1985—; Guggenheim fellow, 1975, 85, MacArthur fellow, 1985-90. Mem. NAS, European Molecular Biology Orgn., Am. Acad. Arts and Scis. Office: U Oregon Inst Molecular Biology Eugene OR 97403-1229

STAHL, JACK LELAND, real estate company executive; b. Lincoln, Ill., June 28, 1934; s. Edwin R. and Edna M. (Burns) S.; m. Carol Anne Townsend, June 23, 1956; children: Cheryl, Nancy, Kellea BS in Edn., U. N.Mex., 1957. Tchr. Albuquerque Public Schs., 1956-59; pres. House Finders, Inc., Albuquerque, 1959-65; v.p. N.Mex. Savs. & Loan Assn., Albuquerque, 1965-67; chmn. bd. Hooten-Stahl, Inc., Albuquerque, 1967-77; mem. N.Mex. Ho. of Reps., 1969-70; pres. The Jack Stahl Co., Albuquerque, 1977—; mem. N.Mex. Senate, 1981-86; lt. gov. State of N.Mex., 1987-90. Mem. N. Mex. Ho. of Reps., 1969-70, exec. bd. Gr. S.W. Coun. Boy Scouts Am, 1982-89; bd. dirs. BBB N. Mex., 1968-82, pres. 1975-76; trustee Univ Heights. Hosp.,1980-85; vice chmn. N. Mex. Bd. Fin., 1987-90, N. Mex. Cmty. Devel. Coun., 1987-90; bd. dirs. Ctr. for Entrepreneurship and Econ. Devel., 1994-96; mem. Gov.'s Bus. Adv. Coun., 1995-97. Named Realtor of Yr., Albuquerque Bd. Realtors, 1972. Mem. Nat. Assn. Realtors, Nat. Homebuilders Assn., N.Mex. Amigos, 20-30 Club (pres. 1963-64), Rotary. Republican. Methodist. Office: 1911 Wyoming Blvd NE Albuquerque NM 87112-2865 E-mail: Jstahl@webtv.net

STAHL, LOUIS A. lawyer; b. Oct. 31, 1940; s. Louis A. and Dorothy (Cox) S.; m. Mary Kathleen Quinn, Apr. 4, 1960; children: Lisa, Suzanne, Gretchen, Nicole. BA magna cum laude, Wheeling Jesuit U., 1962; postgrad., Duquesne U., 1965-66; JD summa cum laude, Notre Dame U., 1971. Bar: Ariz. 1971, U.S. Dist. Ct. Ariz. 1971, U.S. Ct. Appeals (9th cir.) 1974, U.S. Supreme Ct. 1975. Ptnr. Streich Lang P.A., Phoenix, 1971—. Mem. Maricopa County Superior Ct. Rule 26.1 Study Com., 1992—; Frances Lewis lawyer in residence Washington & Lee Univ. Law Sch., 1986; seminar panelist Ariz. Bankers Assn., 1987, Profl. Ednl. Systems, Inc., 1989; mediator, arbitrator U.S. Arbitration and Mediation of Ariz., Nev. and N. Mex., 1993—. Contbg. author: Arizona Attorneys' Fees Manual, 1987, Arizona Professionalism Manual, 1992; contbr. papers to law revs. and jours. Active Phoenix and Maricopa County Young Reps., Ariz. Rep. Party's Lawyers' Ballot Security Com., 1980, Vols. for Reagan-Bush, 1980, Re-elect Rep. Ernest Baird Fin. Com., 1992, Ariz. Rep. Caucus.; founding mem., v.p., dir., legal counsel Performing Arts Combined Talent; pres., bd. dirs. Make a Wish Found. Ctrl. & So. Ariz., 1995—. Mem. ABA (vice-chmn. health ins. com., sect. ins., negligence and compensation law 1973-79, contbg. editor The Forum 1976-79), State Bar Ariz. (mem. profl. liability com. 1979-86, chmn. 1983-86, mem. com. on rules of profl. conduct ethics com. 1981-93, com. on professionalism 1989-91, discipline task force 1991-92, co-chmn. peer rev. com. 1991—), Def. Rsch. Inst., Ariz. Assn. of Def. Counsel, Ariz. Bar Found., Phoenix C. of C. (military affairs com.), Am. Numismatic Assn., Phoenix Coin Club. Office: Streich Lang PA Renaissance One 2 N Central Ave Fl 2 Phoenix AZ 85004-2345

STAHL, RICHARD G. C. journalist, editor; b. Chgo., Feb. 22, 1934; m. Gladys C. Weisbecker; 1 child, Laura Ann. Student, Northwestern U., U. Ill., Chgo. Editor Railway Purchases and Stores Mag., Chgo., 1960-63; editor pub. rels. dept. Sears Roebuck & Co., Chgo., 1963-68; dir pub. rels. dept. St. Joseph's Hosp. Med. Ctr., Phoenix, 1968-72; v.p. pub. rels. Consultation Svcs., Inc., Phoenix, 1972-73; creative dir. Don Jackson and Assoc., Phoenix, 1973; editor, pub. rels. mgr. Maricopa County Med. Soc., Phoenix, 1974-76; sr. editor Ariz. Hwys. mag., Phoenix, 1977-99; ret., 1999. Regional editor: (travel guides) Budget Travel, 1985, USA, 1986, Arizona, 1986; free-lance writer and editor. Mem. Soc. Profl. Journalists. Avocation: woodworking. Office: Ariz Hwys Mag 2039 W Lewis Ave Phoenix AZ 85009-2819

STAHMANN, ROBERT F. education educator; b. Peoria, Ill., Nov. 26, 1939; s. Fred Soeffner and Mary Emma (Thompson) S.; m. Kathleen Cook, Dec. 21, 1965; children: Benjamin C., John C., Paul C., Mark C., Anne. BA, Macalester Coll., 1963, MS, U. Utah, 1965, PhD, 1967. Research fellow U. Utah, 1966-67; sr. counselor U. Iowa, Iowa City, 1967-71, coordinator counseling service, 1971-72, dir. counseling service, 1972-75, asst. prof. edn., 1967-71, asso. prof., 1971-75; prof. family scis. Brigham Young U., Provo, Utah, 1975—, chmn. dept. family scis., 1983-89, dir. Marriage and Family Counseling Clinic, 1976-83, coordinator program in marriage and family therapy, 1977-83. Vis. prof. sex and marital therapy clinic Coll. Medicine, U. Utah, 1980-81; mem. Utah State Marriage and Family Therapy Licensing Bd., 1982-92; mem. Commn. Accreditation for Marriage and Family Therapy Edn., 1989-94, chair, 1990-94. Co-author: Premarital Counseling, 1980, 2d edit., 1987, Dynamic Assessment in Couples Therapy, 1993, Premarital and Remarital Counseling, 1997; co-editor: Ethical and Professional Issues for Marital and Family Therapists, 1980; co-editor, contbr.; Counseling in Marital and Sexual Problems: A Clinician's Handbook, 1977, 3d edit., 1984; assoc. editor: Jour. Coll. Student Pers., 1971-77; editor: Jour. Assoc. Mormon Counselors and Psychotherapists, 1977-78; contbr. chpts. to books., articles to profl. jours. Scoutmaster Boy Scouts Am., 1969-72, 83-87, cubmaster, 1976-79; mem. Orem City Beautification Commn., 1976-77; mem. adv. bd. Ret. Sr. Vol. Program for Utah County, 1987-89. Fellow Am. Assn. Marriage and Family Therapy (bd. dirs. 1977-79); mem. ACA, Internat. Family Therapy Assn., Am. Assn. Sex Educators, Counselors and Therapists (cert.), Utah Assn. Marriage and Family Counselors (pres. 1978-80), Nat. Coun. on Family Rels., Utah Coun. on Family Rels. (pres. 1987 88), Sigma Xi, Phi Kappa Phi. Mem. LDS Ch. Office: Brigham Young Univ 240 TLRB Provo UT 84602 E-mail: robert_stahmann@byu.edu

STAKY, RICHARD, real estate development company executive; Degree, Albion Coll.; grad. degree, U. Detroit. Chief fin. officer, exec. v.p. no. Calif., divsn. pres. Pulte Homes, Tucson, Denver, regional pres. Rocky Mtn. divsn. Denver, WL Homes LLC, Greenwood Village, Colo. Office: John Laing Homes Colo 7000 E Belleview Ave Ste 2000 Greenwood Village CO 80111-1617

STALLINGS, CHARLES HENRY, physicist; b. Durham, N.C., Dec. 28, 1941; s. Henry Harroll and Dorothy (Powers) S.; m. Elizabeth Bright, Sept. 4, 1965; children: Deborah, Sharon. BS, N.C. State U., 1963, MS, 1964; PhD, U. Wis., 1970. Sr. physicist Physics Internat. Co. (now Maxwell Physics Internat.), San Leandro, Calif., 1970-73, dep. dept. mgr., 1974-76, dept. mgr., 1976-79, dir. satellite x-ray test facility office, 1979-81, dir. bus. devel., 1981-83, v.p., dir. rsch. devel., v.p., gen. mgr., 1983—. Contbr. articles to tech. jours. Mem. Gen. Plan Rev. Com., Pleasanton, Calif., 1983. Mem. Am. Phys. Soc., IEEE (mem. pulsed power sci. and tech. com. 1996—, chmn. 12th internat. pulsed power conf. 1999). Home: 1717 Courtney Ave Pleasanton CA 94588-2692 Office: Maxwell Physics Internat 2700 Merced St San Leandro CA 94577-5602 E-mail: cstallings@maxwell.com

STALLINGS, VALERIE AILEEN, retired councilwoman, consultant; b. Chgo., Dec. 23, 1939; d. Jay Sims and Mary Elizabeth (Batson) Spire; adoptive dau. Willian Mundo Spire; m. John R. Stallings, July 14, 1961 (div. 1970); children: Dana Elizabeth, Marshall Brigg. AA, Palomar (Calif.) Coll., 1978; BA, U. Calif., San Diego, 1980. Rschr., lab. mgr. Salk Inst., La Jolla, Calif., 1970-91; mem. coun. City of San Diego, 1991-2001, ret., 2001. Sabbatical rschr. Netherlands Cancer Inst., 1981; city rep. Jack Murphy Stadium Authority, San Diego, 1991-2000; chmn. pub. facilities and recreation City of San Diego, 1992-95; chmn. fiscal policy San Diego Wastewater, 1993-94; dir. San Diego Area Wastewater Mgmt. Dist., 1993—. Contbr. articles to sci. jours. Pres. Pacific Beach Dem. Club, San Diego; mem. Pacific Beach Planning Commn., San Diego. Named Legislator of Yr., SEIU Svc. Coun., 1992. Mem. Nat. Women's Polit. Caucus, Calif. Elected Women's Assn. for Edn. and Rsch., U. Calif. Alumni Assn. (bd. dirs.). Democrat. Avocations: triathlons, jogging, leading safaris in East Africa, photography. Office: Dist 6 1536 Frankfort St San Diego CA 92110

STALLKNECHT-ROBERTS, CLOIS FREDA, publisher, publicist; b. Birmingham, Ala., Dec. 31, 1934; d. August and Sadie Bell (Wisener) Anton; m. Randall Scott Roberts; children: Yvonne Denise, April O'dell, Kurt William. Publicist Ms. Clois Presents, L.A., 1968—; advt. Engineered Magic, Advt., Santa Ana, Calif., 1976, 77, 81; pub. Internat. Printing, L.A., 1981—. Editor: Nostradamus, William Bartram, Apuleious, 1990-92, Metamorphoses L.A., 1996-97. Home and Office: PO Box 165 Inyokern CA 93527-0165 Office: Engineered Magic 510 De La Estrella San Clemente CA 92672

STAMBAUGH, RONALD DENNIS, physicist, researcher; b. Milw., May 15, 1947; s. Wilbert Foster and Joyce Elaine (Miller) S.; m. Mildred Alice Considine, June 22, 1968; children: James, Emily, Claire, Margaret. BS, U. Wis., 1969; MPhil, Yale U., 1971, PhD, 1974. Computer programmer U. Wis., Madison, 1967-69; rsch. asst. Yale U., New Haven, 1970-74; sr. scientist Gen. Atomics, San Diego, 1975-77, br. mgr., 1978-79, plasma control coord., 1979-84, mgr. physics dept., 1984-91, divsn. dir., 1991—. Chmn. divertor expert group ITER, 1994—; BPX dep. physics head Princeton (N.J.) Plasma Lab., 1990-91; exec. com. APS-DPP, 1987-89, 91-92. Mem. editl. bd. Nuclear Fusion, 1991—. Recipient award for Excellence in Plasma Physics Research Am. Physical Society, 1994 Fellow Am. Phys. Soc. (Excellence in Plasma Physics 1994). Achievements include experimental verification of plasma stability theory for Tokamaks. Office: Gen Atomics PO Box 85608 San Diego CA 92186-5608

STAMES, WILLIAM ALEXANDER, realtor, cost management executive; b. Douglas, Ariz., Mar. 26, 1917; s. Alex Basil and Teresa (Ruis) S.; m. Marguerite Winifred Nelson, June 11, 1943; 1 child, Wynn Lorain. AA, Long Beach Coll., 1941; postgrad., U. Calif., Berkeley, 1962-64; cert. mgmt. practice, Naval Offices CIC Sch., Glenview, Ill., 1955; grad., Real Estate Inst., Calif. Lic. real estate assoc.; grad. Realtors Inst. Owner Stames Beverage Co., Brawley, Calif., 1945-50; liaison engr. Lockheed Missiles & Space Co., Sunnyvale, 1958-60, sr. liaison engr., 1960, adminstr., 1960-62, staff adminstr., 1962-63, sr. liaison engr., sr. design engr., 1965-70; owenr, mgr. Cost Reduction Equipment Sales & Tech., Sunnyvale, 1967-76; realtor Cornish & Carey, Palo Alto, Calif., 1988-99; real estate assoc. Coldwell Banker, Coronado, 1999—. Dir. ret. activities office Naval Amphibious Base, Coronado, Calif. Author: Polaris Electrical Subsystems Design History, 1964, Poseidon Subsystem Invention, 1971. Comdr. USNR, 1941-69, ret., World War II, Korea, Vietnam. Decorated DFC, Air medal with 4 gold stars. Mem. Am. Mgmt. Assn., Mountain View Real Estate Bd. (pres.), Calif. Assn. Realtors (bd. dirs.), Tailhook Assn., Commonwealth San Francisco. Ret. Officers Club (-past pres. Peninsula chpt.), Lions. Home: 1060 Coronado Ave Coronado CA 92118-2439

STAMEY, THOMAS ALEXANDER, urologist, educator; b. Rutherfordton, N.C., Apr. 26, 1928; s. Owen and Virginia (Link) S.; m. Kathryn Simmons Dec. 1, 1973; children: Fred M., Charline, Thomas A. III, Allison, Theron. BA, Vanderbilt U., 1948; MD, Johns Hopkins U., 1952. Diplomate Am. Bd. Urology. Intern, then resident Johns Hopkins Hosp., 1952-56; asst. prof. urology Johns Hopkins U. Sch. Medicine, Balt., 1958-60, assoc. prof., 1960-61; assoc. prof., chmn. divsn. urology Stanford (Calif.) U., 1961-64, assoc. prof., 1964-90, prof., 1991—, chmn. dept., 1964-95. Author: Renovascular Hypertension, 1967, Pathogenesis and Treatment of Urinary Tract Infections, 1980, Urinalysis and Urinary Sediment: A Practical Guide for the Health Science Professional, 1985; editor: Campbell's Urology, edits. 4-6, 1978-92, Monographs in Urology, 1980-99. Capt. M.C., USAF, 1956-58. Recipient Sheen award ACS, 1990, Ferdinand C. Valentine award N.Y. Acad. Medicine, 1991. Mem. Am. Urol. Assn. (Ramon Guiteras award 1995, John K. Lattimer award 2000, Eugene Fuller Triennial Prostate award 2001), Am. Surg. Assn. (sr.), Inst. Medicine of NAS. Avocations: fishing, astronomy. Office: Stanford U Med Ctr Dept Urology S 287 300 Pasteur Dr Stanford CA 94305-5118 E-mail: tstamey@stanford.edu

STAMM, ALAN, lawyer; b. Galesburg, Ill., Nov. 22, 1931; s. Gustave Frederick and Miriam (Simon) S.; m. Shelley Lynn Ramage, Mar. 19, 1978; 1 child, Lucinda Anne. Student, Universidad Nacional de Mex., summer 1950; AB, Yale U., 1952; JD, Harvard U., 1957. Bar: Calif. 1957, U.S. Supreme Ct. 1963. Assoc. Thelen, Marrin, Johnson & Bridges, San Francisco, 1957-60; staff atty. Litton Industries Inc., Beverly Hills, Calif., 1960-66, asst. sec., 1963-66; sec., gen. counsel Internat. Rectifier Corp., L.A., 1966-69, v.p., 1968-69; v.p., gen. counsel Republic Corp., L.A., 1969-71, also bd. dirs., 1970-71; v.p., gen. counsel Sat. Rev. Industries, N.Y.C., 1971-72, Mattel Inc., Hawthorne, Calif., 1972-74, staff cons., 1974-75; of counsel Long & Levit, L.A., 1975-82, O'Donnell & Gordon, L.A., 1983-87, Hedges, Powe & Caldwell, L.A., 1988-90; pvt. practice L.A., 1990—. Judge pro tem Mcpl. Ct. L.A. Jud. Dist., 1977—; arbitrator L.A. Superior Ct. 1979—, judge pro tem L.A. Superior Ct. 1989—, arbitrator Nat. Assn. Securities Dealers, 1981—. Founding trustee Ctr. for Law in the Pub. Interest; trustee Marlborough Sch., L.A.; bd. govs. Century City Hosp., L.A.; counsel bus. and profl. com. L.A. Philharmonic; bd. dirs. Yale Alumni Fund. Lt. (j.g.) USNR, 1952-54; lt. comdr. Res.; ret. Mem. ABA, Calif. Bar Assn., L.A. Bar Assn., Am. Jewish Com., Harvard Law Sch. Assn., L.A. County Art Mus., Am. Arbitration Assn. (nat. panel arbitrators), NAACP, Sierra Club, Nat. Assn. Yale Alumni (former bd. govs.), Yale Club of So. Calif. (former dir.), Harvard Club of So. Calif., Phi Beta Kappa. Home: 422 Denslow Ave Los Angeles CA 90049-3507 Office: Ste 810 1801 Avenue of the Stars Los Angeles CA 90067-5801

STAMM, BOB, museum official; Chmn. bd. trustees Albuquerque Mus. Office: Albuquerque Mus 2000 Mountain Rd NW Albuquerque NM 87104-1459

STAMM, ROBERT JENNE, building contractor, construction company executive; b. Albuquerque, Nov. 17, 1921; s. Roy Allen and Elizabeth C. (Baldridge) S.; m. Florence I. Bradbury, May 14, 1943; children— R. Brad, Susan Stamm Evans. BSCE, U. N.Mex., 1942; postgrad. in Naval Architecture, U.S. Naval Acad., 1943. Registered profl. engr. and surveyor, N.Mex. With Bradbury Stamm Constrn. Co., Albuquerque, 1946—, chmn., 1983—, former CEO, pres.; comdr./ret. USNR, 1943-69. Mem. U. N.Mex. Found., 1982-94, N.Mex. Commn. on Higher Edn., 1986-95; mem. centennial exec. com. U. N.Mex., chmn. devel. fund, 1984-85, 89-94; trustee Albuquerque Cmty. Found., 1983-2001; trustee Albuquerque Mus., 1993—, chmn. 1995-97, Nat. Conservancy/N.Mex., 1998—; trustee N.Mex. Mus. Natural History Found., 1995-2001; bd. dirs., pres. Albuquerque Bus.-Edn. Compact, 1987-88, Albuquerque Mus. Found., 1986-91, 96-97, Indsl. Found. Albuquerque; past bd. dirs. United Way, Girl Scouts U.S.A., Boy Scouts Am., Presbyn. Hosp. Ctr. Found., Presbyn. Heart Inst., Greater Albuquerque Cmty. Ednl. Alliance, N.Mex. First, Albuquerque Econ. Forum, Albuquerque YMCA, Anderson-Abruzzo Internat. Balloon Mus. Recipient Regents Recognition medal U. N.Mex., 1986, Zimmerman award U. N.Mex., 1988, U. N.Mex. Centennial Alumnus award Nat. Assn. State Univ. and Land Grant Colls., 1987, Disting. Pub. Svc. award State N.Mex., 1990, Award of Excellence, Presbyn. Health Fedn., 1991, Disting. Citizen award Boy Scouts-Great S.W. Coun., 1994, Disting. Alumni award Coll. Engring. U. N.Mex., 1999, United Way Lifetime Achievement award, 1999, N.Mex. Ethics in Bus. Individual award, 2000; named Most Admired Co., N.Mex. Pvt. 100, 1991, 92, 94, 95, 96, 97, 98; named to Albuquerque Sr. Citizen Hall of Fame, 1994; named for N.Mex. Outstanding Philanthropic Leadership, 1994. Mem. NSPE (Albuquerque Engr. of Yr. 1987, N.Mex. Lifetime Svc. award 1995), Assoc. Gen. Contractors N.Mex. (pres. bldg. br. 1962), Econ. Forum Albuquerque (bd. dirs. 1998—), Exec. Assn. Greater Albuquerque, Albuquerque country Club (bd. dirs. 1972-76, 87-89), Albuquerque Tennis Club (bd. dirs. 1978-80). Avocations: tennis, golf. Home: 1524 Las Lomas Rd NE Albuquerque NM 87106-4532 Office: Bradbury Stamm Constrn Co PO Box 10850 Albuquerque NM 87184-0850 E-mail: rstamm@bradburystamm.com

STAMPER, MALCOLM THEODORE, publishing company executive; b. Detroit, Apr. 4, 1925; s. Fred Theodore and Lucille (Cayce) S.; m. Marion Philbin Guinan, Feb. 25, 1946; children: Geoffrey, Kevin, Jamie, David, Mary, Anne. Student, U. Richmond, Va., 1943-44; BEE, Ga. Inst. Tech., 1946; postgrad., U. Mich., 1946-49; DHumanities, Seattle U., 1994. With Gen. Motors Corp., 1949-62; with Boeing Co., Seattle, 1962-90, mgr. electronics ops., v.p., gen. mgr. turbine div., 1964-66; v.p., gen. mgr. Boeing Co. (747 Airplane program), 1966-69, v.p., gen. mgr. comml. airplane group, 1969-71, corp. sr. v.p. ops., 1971-72; pres. Boeing Co., 1972-85, vice chmn., 1985-90; CEO, Storytellers Ink Pub., Seattle, 1990—, also chmn. bd. dirs. Bd. dirs. Pro-Air Inc.; trustee The Conf. Bd., 1988—. Candidate for U.S. Ho. of Reps., Detroit, 1952; trustee, chmn. Seattle Art Mus.; nat. bd. dirs. Smithsonian Assocs. With USNR, 1943-46. Named Industrialist of Year, 1967; recipient Educator's Golden Key award, 1970, Elmer A. Sperry award, 1982, AIEE award, Ga. Inst. Tech. award, Sec. Dept. Health and Human Services, Silver Beaver award Boy Scouts Am., 1989, Literary Lions award, 1995; named to Engring. Hall of Fame. Mem. Nat. Alliance Businessmen, Phi Gamma Delta.

STAMPER, NORMAN H. protective services official; BS, MS in Criminal Justice Adminstrn., San Diego State U.; PhD in Leadership and Human Behavior, U.S. Internat. U. Chief of police Seattle Police Dept., 1994—. Exec. dir. Mayor Pete Wilson's Crime Control Commn.; apptd. (by U.S. Atty. Gen. and Sec. Health and Human Svcs.) Adv. Coun. Violence Against Women; mem. adv. panel on Excessive Force by Police, Police Exec. Rsch. Forum, Major Cities Chiefs; mem. steering com. Seattle Equal Justice Coalition; co-chair Ptnr's. in Pub. Edn's. Urban Scholar's Program; mem. bd. dirs. Leadership Tomorrow; trustee Ctr. for Ethical Leadership. Author: Removing Managerial Barriers to Effective Police Leadership, 1992; tchnical adv. Municipal Police Administration, 1992. Named to Alumni Hall of Fame Boys and Girls Club of Am.; recipient Katharine M. Bullitt award for Leadership Ptnrs. in Pub. Edn. Mem. Internat. Assn. Chiefs of Police. Office: Police Dept 1001 Public Safety Bldg 610 3rd Ave Seattle WA 98104-1824

STAMPER, ROBERT LEWIS, ophthalmologist, educator; b. N.Y.C., July 27, 1939; s. Louis and Ethel (Rabinowitz) S.; m. Naomi T. Belson, June 23, 1963; children: Juliet, Marjorie, Alison. BA, Cornell U., 1957-61; MD, SUNY-Downstate, 1965. Diplomate Am. Bd. Ophthalmology (assoc. examiner 1976-92, bd. dirs. 1992-99). Intern Mt. Sinai Hosp., N.Y.C., 1965-66; resident in ophthalmology Washington U.-Barnes Hosp., St. Louis, 1968-71; Nat. Eye Inst.-NIH fellow dept. ophthalmology Washington U., St. Louis, 1971-72, from instr. ophthalmology to asst. prof. dept. ophthalmology, 1971-72; asst. prof. dept. ophthalmology Pacific Presbyn. Med. Ctr., San Francisco, 1972-76, assoc. prof. ophthalmology, 1976-87; chmn. dept. ophthalmology Calif. Pacific Med. Ctr. (formerly Pacific Presbyn. Med. Ctr.), San Francisco, 1987-96; vice-chmn. dept./prof. clin. ophthalmology, dir. glaucoma U. Calif., San Franciso, 1999—. Asst. opthalmologist Barnes Hosp., St. Louis, 1971-72, Harkness Hosp., San Francisco, 1973-74; dir. ophthalmic photography and fluorescin angiography, dept. ophthalmology Washington U., St. Louis, 1969-72; dir. resident tng. Pacific Presbyn. Med. Ctr., 1972-89, dir. glaucoma svc., vice-chmn. dept. ophthalmology, 1974-87; chief ophthalmology svc. Highland Hosp., Oakland, Calif., 1974-76; clin. instr. dept. ophthalmology U. Calif., San Francisco, 1974-77, prof. clin. ophthalmology, 1998—; clin. asst. prof. ophthalmology U. Calif., Berkeley, 1974-78, asst. clin. prof. ophthalmology, 1978-85; sr. rsch. assoc. Smith-Kettlewell Inst. Visual Scis., San Francisco, 1972-89; project co-dir. ophthalmic curriculum for med. students Nat. Libr. Medicine, 1973-75; commr. Joint Commn. on Allied Health Pers. in Ophthalmology, 1975-87, bd. dirs., 1978-88, sec., 1980, v.p., 1982-83, pres., 1984-85; provisional asst. chief dept. ophthalmology Mt. Zion Hosp., San Francisco, 1976-87, assoc. chief dept. ophthalmology, 1982-86; ophthalmic cons. Ft. Ord, Calif., 1976—, Oakland Naval Hosp., 1978-83; instr. Stanford (Calif.) U., 1977—; glaucoma cons. U. Calif., Davis, 1978-84; vis. lectr. dept. ophthalmology Hadassah Hebrew U. Med. Ctr., Jerusalem, 1978, Oxford (Eng.) U. Eye Hosp., 1986; ind. med. examiner State of Calif., 1979—; mem. appeals hearing panel Accreditation Coun. for Grad. Med. Edn., 1986-93, mem. residency rev. com. for ophthalmology, 1993-98; mem. provisional courtesy staff Peralta Hosp., Oakland, 1988-92; mem. ophthalmic devices adv. panel USFDA, 1989-92; presenter, lectr. in field. Editor Ophthalmology Clinics of North Am., 1988—; mem. editl. adv. com. Ophthalmology, 1982-89, mem. editl. bd., 1983-94; sr. author: Becker and Shaffer's Diagnosis and Management of the Glaucomas, 7th edit., 1999; contbr. articles to profl. jours. Chmn. bd. Agy. for Jewish Edn., Oakland, 1986-89; bd. dirs. Jewish Fedn. Greater East Bay, Oakland, 1992-94; bd. dirs. Found. for Glaucoma Rsch.; mem. glaucoma adv. com. Nat. Soc. to Prevent Blindness, 1981—; mem. Am. Diabetes Assn. Surgeon USPHS, 1966-68. Recipient Nat. Soc. for Performance and Instrn. award for self-instrnl. material in ophthalmology, 1975, Honor award Am. Acad. Ophthalmology, 1982, Sr. Honor award, 1992, Statesmanship award Joint Commn. on Allied Health Pers. in Ophthalmology, 1989, Troutman Master Tchr. in Ophthalmology award, 2000; N.Y. State Regents scholar, 1961, N.Y. State scholar in medicine, 1965; Blalock student fellow UCLA Sch. Medicine, 1961, Fight for Sight student fellow dept. ophthalmology N.Y. Hosp. and Cornell Med. Ctr., 1962, 63, 64. Fellow Am. Acad. Ophthalmology and Otolaryngology (rep. to joint commn. on allied health pers., faculty home study course sect. X, chmn. sect. VIII 1983-85, bd. councilors, editl. adv. com. Opthalmology jour. 1982-89, editl. bd. Ophthalmology jour. 1983-94, and many others), ACS; mem. AMA (Physician's Recognition award 1989), Am. Ophthalmologic Soc., Assn. for Rsch. in Vision and Ophthalmology, Calif. Med. Assn. (asst. sec. sect. ophthalmology, chmn., sci. bd. rep. adv. panel on ophthalmology 1985-91), Nat. Soc. Prevent Blindness (mem. glaucoma adv. com. 1981—, bd. dirs. 1986—), No. Calif. Soc. Prevent Blindness, Calif. Assn. Ophthalmology, Pan Am. Ophthal. (bd. dirs. 1992-2000), Soc., N.Y. Acad. Scis., Las Vegas Ophthal. Soc. (hon.), Am. Glaucoma Soc. (v.p. 1997-99, pres. 1999-2000), Glaucoma Rsch. Found. (bd. dirs.). Office: Dept Opht UCSF Med Ctr 8 Kirkham St San Francisco CA 94143-0001 E-mail: stamper@itsa.ucsf.edu

STANCILL, JAMES MCNEILL, finance educator, consultant; b. Orange, N.J., July 30, 1932; s. James Sr. and Anne Jeanne (Sauter) S.; m. Catherine Jackson, Sept. 25, 1954; children: Martha A., Mary C., Christine E. AB, George Washington U., 1954, MBA, 1957; PhD in Fin. and Econs., U. Pa., 1965. Buyer Melpar Inc., Falls Church, Va., 1954-59; instr., adminstrv. officer U. Pa., Phila., 1959-64; prof. fin. U. So. Calif., L.A., 1964—. Prin. Stancill & Assocs., Pasadena, Calif., 1964—; chmn. S.W. Products Co., 1991-97. Author: Management of Working Capital, 1970, Entrepreneurial Finance: Financial Management for Developing Firms; contbr. numerous articles to Harvard Bus. Rev., 1977—. Avocations: genealogy, sailing. Office: U So Calif Marshall Sch Bus Los Angeles CA 90089-0001

STANCZAK, STEPHEN PHILLIP, environmental services administrator, lawyer; b. Waukegan, Ill., June 19, 1957; BS magna cum laude, W.Va. U., 1979; JD magna cum laude, U. Ill., 1982. Bar: Ill. 1982, U.S. Dist. Ct. (no. dist.) Ill. 1984. Counsel Amoco Corp., 1982-86; assoc. legal counsel Evang. Health Sys., 1986-87; corp. counsel Waste Mgmt. Inc., 1987-90; v.p., sec., assoc. gen. counsel Wheelabrator Techs., Inc., 1990-95; v.p. legal affairs, co. sec. Waste Mgmt. Internat. Plc, 1995-98; exec. v.p., gen. counsel, sec. U.S. Filter Corp., Palm Desert, Calif., 1999—. Mem. ABA, Internat. Bar Assn., U.K. Inst. Co. Secs., Am. Corp. Counsel Assn., Am. Soc. Corp. Secs., Ill. State Bar Assn. Office: US Filter Corp 40-004 Cook St Palm Desert CA 92211

STANEK, ALAN EDWARD, music educator, performer, administrator, retired; b. Longmont, Colo., July 3, 1939; s. Edward Thomas Stanke and Mary Rose (Hicks) Stanek MacDougall; m. Janette Elizabeth Swanson, Aug. 23, 1963; children: Michael Alan, Karen Leigh. B in Music Edn., U. Colo., 1961; MusM, Eastman Sch. Music, 1965; MusD, U. Mich., 1974. Dir. instrumental music Ainsworth Pub. Sch., Nebr., 1961-64, Cozad Pub. Sch., 1965-67; asst. prof. music Hastings Coll., 1967-76; prof., chmn. music dept. Idaho State U., Pocatello, 1976-2001, ret., 2001. Contbr., editor, reviewer profl. jours. including Clarinet, Idaho Music Notes, Nebr. Music Educator. Mem. Music Educators Nat. Conf., Idaho Music Educators Assn. (chmn. higher edn. 1978-86, 97-98, pres. 1988-90, chair state solo contest 1990-92), Internat. Clarinet Assn. (sec. 1978-84, v.p. 1986-88, pres. 1996-98), Coll. Music Soc., Nat. Assn. Coll. Wind and Percussion Instrs. (chmn. Idaho 1978-88), Nat. Assn. Schs. Music (sec. N.W. region 1979-82, vis. evaluator 1990—, chair N.W. region 1991-94), Rotary (pres. Gate City chpt. 1994-95). Office: Idaho State U Dept Music PO Box 8099 Pocatello ID 83209-0001 E-mail: stanalan@isu.edu

STANFILL, DENNIS CAROTHERS, business executive; b. Centerville, Tenn., Apr. 1, 1927; s. Sam Broome and Hattie (Carothers) S.; m. Therese Olivieri, June 29, 1951; children: Francesca, Sara, Dennis Carothers. BS, U.S. Naval Acad., 1949; MA (Rhodes scholar), Oxford U., 1953; LHD (hon.), U. S.C. Corporate finance specialist Lehman Bros., N.Y.C., 1959-65; v.p. finance Times Mirror Co., Los Angeles, 1965-69; exec. v.p. 20th Century-Fox Film Corp., 1969-71, pres., 1971, chmn. bd., chief exec. officer, 1971-81; pres. Stanfill, Bowen & Co., 1981-90; chmn. bd. dirs., chief exec. officer AME, Inc., 1990-91; co-chmn., co-CEO Metro-Goldwyn-Mayer, Inc., 1992-93; sr. advisor Credit Lyonnais, 1993-95; pres. Dennis Stanfill Co., 1995—. Trustee Calif. Inst. Tech.; bd. dirs. Weingart Found. Served to lt. USN, 1949-59; politico-mil. policy div. Office Chief Naval Ops., 1956-59.

STANFORD, JACK ARTHUR, biological station administrator; b. Delta, Colo., Feb. 18, 1947; s. LeRoy and Wilma (Tucker) S.; children: Jake, Chriss. BS in Fisheries Sci., Colo. State U., 1969, MS in Limnology, 1971; PhD in Limnology, U. Utah, 1975. Fisheries biologist Alaska-Fish and Game, Dillingham, 1968-69; rsch. biologist and limnologist instr. U. Mont., Missoula, 1973-74, dir. Flathead Lake Biol. Sta. Polson, 1980—, research prof. zoology Missoula, 1983-86, Jessie M. Bierman prof. Mont., 1986—; prof. N. Tex. State U., Denton, 1974-81. Panelist div. biotic system NSF, Washington, 1985—; chmn. Coun. of Aquatic Scis., 1998—. Editor: Ecology of Regulated Streams, 1979, Groundwater Ecology, 1994; editor Regulated Rivers: Rsch. and Mgmt., 1985-99, Ecol. Applications, 1996—; contbr. over 100 articles to profl. jours. Advisor Nature Conservancy, Boulder, Colo., 1982—. Named Bierman Prof. Ecology U. Mont., 1986—; grantee EPA, U.S. Army, U.S. Bur. Reclamation, NSF, U.S. Nat. Park Svc.; disting. scholar U. Mont., 1997. Mem. Mont. Acad. Aci., Am. Soc. Limnology and Oceanography, Ecol. Soc. Am. (pub. affairs com., 1984—), N.Am. Benthological Soc. (exec. com. 1979, 1988-89, pres. 1997), AAAS. Avocation: fly fishing, skiing. Office: U Mont Flathead Lake Biol Sta 311 Bio Station Ln Polson MT 59860-9659 E-mail: stanford@selway.umt.edu

STANFORD, JAMES M. oil company executive; BSc in Mining Engring., Loyola Coll., Montreal, 1958; BSc in Petroleum Engring., U. Alta., Can., 1960; LLD (hon.), U. Alberta, 2000, Concordia U., Montreal, 2000. Various engring. and mgmt. positions Mobil Oil Canada Ltd., 1959-78; gen. mgr. conventional prodn. Petro-Canada, Calgary, Alta., 1978-80, v.p., sr. v.p. prodn., 1980-82, pres., COO, 1990-92, pres., CEO, dir. Alta., 1993-2000, chmn., 2000. Past gov. bd. Can. Assn. Petroleum Producers; past dir. Coun. for Can. Unity; bd. dirs. Fortis, Inc., Inco Ltd., NOVA Chems., OMERS Resources; bd. govs. Moore Corp. Mem. Alta. Performing Arts Stblzn. Bd., chair awards com.; mem. Mt. Royal Coll. Found., Calgary; past bd. dirs. Govs. Club, U. Alta.; chmn. Found. for Sustainable Devel. Tech. in Can. Mem. Assn. Profl. Engrs., Geologists of Alta. Office: Petro-Canada Ctr West Tower 150-6th Ave SW Ste 3000 Calgary AB Canada T2P 3Y7

STANFORD, JANET LEE, physician, epidemiologist; RN, Grady Meml Hosp., Atlanta, 1974; BS, Ga. State U., 1980; MPH, Emory U., 1982; PhD, John Hopkins U., 1985. Various to asst. prof. dept. epidemiology Sch. of Pub. Health and Cmty. Medicine/U. Wash., Seattle, 1986-92; assoc. prof. Sch. Pub. Health and Cmty. Medicine U. Wash., Seattle, 1992-98, prof. epidemiology Sch. Pub. Health and Cmty. Medicine, 1999—; assoc. mem. program in epidemiology Divsn. Pub. Health Scis. Fred Hutchinson Cancer Rsch. Ctr., Seattle, 1991-96, co-investigator Cancer Surveillance System, 1993-96, co-prin. investigator Tracking Resource Ctr., 1995-96; dir. Utah State Cancer Registry/U. Utah, Salt Lake City, 1996-97; prof. Divn. Pub. Health Scis./Huntsman Cancer Inst. U. Utah, Salt Lake City, 1996-97; mem. program in epidemiology/Divsn. Pub. Health Scis. Fred Hutchinson Cancer Rsch. Ctr., Seattle, 1996—, head program in prostate cancer rsch., 1997—, affil. mem. cancer prevention rsch. program, 1999—. Rschr. and investigator in field of hormonal and environ. exposures that may alter cancer risk, and how such risks may be modified by genetic predisposition. Editor: Am. Jour. Epidemiology, 1999—, assoc. editor 1991-96; editl. bd.: Human Genome Epidemiology Network, 1999—; editl. positions: Am. Jour. Pub. Health, Annals of Epidemiology, Cancer, Cancer Causes and Control, Cancer Epidemiology, Biomarkers and Prevention, Human Molecular Genetics, others; contbr. numerous articles to profl. jours. and publs. Granteee HHS, 1982-83, NIH, 1983-85; fellowships Nat. Cancer Inst., NIH, HHS, 1985-86; recipient Preventive Oncology Acad. awards Nat. Cancer Inst., NIH, HHS, 1988-93. Mem. AHA, Soc. Epidemiologic Rsch., APHA, Assn. of Wash. State Epidemiologists, Sigma Theta Tau, others. Office: Fred Hutchinson Cancer Rsch Ctr PO Box 19024 1100 Fairview Ave N MW 814 Seattle WA 98109-1024

STANFORD, JOSEPH BARNEY, medical educator, physician; b. July 9, 1961; s. Kathleen Barnett; children: Matthew Joseph, Jesse Barnett, Hyrum Porter, Caleb Dean, Thomas Barnett. BA magna cum laude, Mankato State U., 1984; MD, U. Minn., 1988. Diplomate Am. Bd. Family Practice. Resident family and cmty. medicine U. Mo.-Columbia, 1988-91, chief resident family and cmty. medicine, 1990-91, academic fellow, clinical instr. dept. family and cmty. medicine, 1991-93; asst. prof. dept. family and preventive medicine U. Utah, Salt Lake City, 1993—. Part time staff physician Cherchez La Femme Birth Svcs. Ltd., Columbia, Mo., 1991-93; med. cons. U. Utah BirthCare HealthCare, 1994—; physician N.E. Family Health Ctr., Salt Lake Regional Med. Ctr., U. Utah Hosp., Primary Children's Med. Ctr., 1993; invited observer Pontifical Acad. Scis. Working Group on Natural Fertility Regulation, Vatican, Italy, 1994. Contbr to prof. jours. Mem. Soc. Tchrs. of Family Medicine (mem. group family centered perinatal care 1990—), Am. Acad. Family Physicians, Am. Acad. Natural Family Planning (chairperson sci. and rsch. com. 1993—), Am. Holistic Med. Assn., Am. Soc. Clinical Hypnosis, Collegium Aesculapium, North Am. Primary Care Rsch. Group, Alpha Omega Alpha, Phi Kappa Phi. Avocations: hiking, camping, reading, writing, skiing. Office: U Utah Dept Family Preventive Med 50 N Medical Dr Salt Lake City UT 84132-0001

STANG, BARRY, state legislator; b. Missoula, Mont., Dec. 5, 1950; BA in Acctg., Carroll Coll. Retail grocer; mem. Mont. State Senate, 1993—. Mem. Mineral County Tax Appeal Bd., 1984-85; chmn. Mineral County Housing Authority. Democrat. Home: Box 277 2 Mountain Hwy 125 S Saint Regis MT 59866

STANG, PETER JOHN, organic chemist; b. Nürnberg, Germany, Nov. 17, 1941; came to U.S., 1956; s. John Stang and Margaret Stang Pollman; m. Christine Schirmer, 1969; children: Antonia, Alexandra. BS, DePaul U., Chicago, 1963; Ph. D., U. California, Berkeley, 1966; hon. degr., Moscow State Lomonossov U., 1992, Russian Academy of Sciences, 1992. Instr. Princeton (N.J.) U., 1967-68; from asst. to assoc. prof. U. Utah, Salt Lake City, 1969-79, prof., 1979-92, Disting. prof. chemistry, 1992—. Co-author: Organic Spectroscopy, 1971; author: (with others) Vinyl Cations, 1979; editor: (with F. Diederich) Modern Acetylene Chemistry, 1995, Metal Catalyzed Cross Coupling Reactions, 1998, (with Z. Rappaport) Dicoordinated Carbocations, 1997; editor-in-chief Jour. Organic Chemsitry, 2000-

01; contbr. numerous articles to sci. publs. Humboldt-Forschungspreis, 1977; JSPS Fellowship, 1985; Fulbright-Hays Sr. Scholarship, 1988. Fellow AAAS; mem. NAS, Am. Chem. Soc. (assoc. editor Jour. Am. Chem. Soc. 1982-99). Office: U Utah Dept Chemistry 315 South 1400 East Salt Lake City UT 84112-0850 E-mail: stang@chemistry.utah.edu

STANGELAND, ROGER EARL, retail chain store executive; b. Chgo., Oct. 4, 1929; s. Earl and Mae E. (Shaw) S.; m. Lilah Fisher, Dec. 27, 1951; children: Brett, Cyndi Stangeland Meili, Brad. Student, St. Johns Mil. Acad., 1943-47, Carleton Coll., 1947-48; B.S., U. Ill., 1949-51. With Coast to Coast Stores, Mpls., 1960-78, pres., 1972-77; sr. v.p., exec. v.p. Household Merchandising, Chgo., 1978-84; chief exec. officer, chmn. bd. Vons Grocery Co., Los Angeles, 1984-85; past CEO The Vons Cos., Inc., Arcadia, Calif., chmn., 1986—, now chmn. emeritus. Chmn. Wauconda (Ill.) Bd. Edn., 1957-60, Hopkins (Minn.) Bd. Edn., 1968-74; bd. fellows Claremont (Calif.) U. Ctr. and Grad. Sch., 1986; bd. dirs. L.A. area Boy Scouts Am.; trustee Hugh O'Brian Youth Found.; mem. CEO bd. advisors U. So. Calif. Sch. Bus. Adminstrn.; trustee St. John's Mil. Acad; bd. visitors Peter F. Drucker Grad. Mgmt. Ctr. Mem. Am. Inst. Wine and Food (bd. dirs.), Food Mktg. Inst. (chmn. bd. dirs.), Food Employers Coun. (exec. com., bd. dirs.), Mchts. & Mfrs. Assn. (bd. dirs.), L.A. Area C. of C. (bd. dirs.), Jonathan Club (L.A.), Calif. Club. Home: 842 Oxford Rd San Marino CA 91108-1214 Office: Vons Grocery Co 618 Michillinda Ave Arcadia CA 91007-6300

STANISLAO, JOSEPH, consulting engineer, educator; b. Manchester, Conn., Nov. 21, 1928; s. Eduardo and Rose (Zaccaro) S.; m. Bettie Chloe Carter, Sept. 6, 1960. BS, Tex. Tech. U., 1957; MS, Pa. State U., 1959; Eng.ScD, Columbia U., 1970. Registered profl. engr., Mass., Mont. Asst. engr. Naval Ordnance Research, University Park, Pa., 1958-59; asst. prof. N.C. State U., Raleigh, 1959-61; dir. research Darlington Fabrics Corp., Pawtucket, R.I., 1961-62; from asst. prof. to prof. U. R.I., Kingston, 1962-71; prof., chmn. dept. Cleve. State U., 1971-75; prof., dean N.D. State U., Fargo, 1975-94, acting v.p. agrl. affairs, 1983-85, asst. to pres., 1983—, dir. Engring. Computer Ctr., 1984—, prof. emeritus indsl. engring. and mgmt., 1994—; pres. XOX Corp., 1984-90; chmn. bd., chief exec. officer ATSCO, 1989-94, chief engr., 1993—; prof. emeritus N.D. State U., 1994. Adj. prof. Mont. State U., 1994—, dir. indsl. and mgmt. engring. program, 1996—, mfg. rsch., sponsored by Nat. Sci. Found. 1997—; v.p., co-owner, bd. dirs. D.T.&J., Inc., Fargo, N.D., 1999—; v.p. engring. Roll-A-Ramp and Rolla-A-Latter, 2000—; cons. to healthcare sys., 1999—. Contbr. chpts. to books, articles to profl. jours.; patentee pump apparatus, pump fluid housing; patents pending roll-a-ramp and roll-a-latter. Served to sgt. USMC, 1948-51. Recipient Sigma Xi award, 1968; Order of the Iron Ring award N.D. State U., 1972, Econ. Devel. award, 1991; USAF recognition award, 1979, ROTC appreciation award, 1982 Mem. Am. Inst. Indsl. Engrs. (sr.; v.p. 1964-65), ASME, Am. Soc. Engring. Edn. (campus coord. 1979-81), Acad. Indsl. Engrs. Tex. Tech U., Lions, Elks, Am. Legion, Phi Kappa Phi, Tau Beta Pi (advisor 1978-79). Roman Catholic. Home: 8 Park Plaza Dr Bozeman MT 59715-9343

STANLEY, CLIFFORD L. career officer; b. Washington, Mar. 31, 1947; m. Rosalyn Hill; 1 child, Angela. Grad., S.C. State U., 1969; MS, Johns Hopkins U., 1977; student, Amphibious Warfare Sch., 1978, Naval War Coll., 1983, USMC Command Staff Coll., 1984, Nat. War Coll., 1988. Commd. 2d. lt. USMC, 1969, advanced through grades to brig. gen., 1994; various assignments Co. M, 3d. Bn., 8th. Marines; commdg. officer Hdqs. Co., 4th. Marines; exec. officer 1st. Bn., 6th. Marines; commdg. officer 1st. Marine Regt.; psychology leadership instr. U.S. Naval Acad.; exec. officer USMC Inst.; parade commdr. Marine Barracks, Washington; various assignments USMC, East Asia; depot insp., comdr. 1st. Recruit Tng. Bn., Parris Island; special asst. dir. of FBI Washington; fleet marine officer 2d. Fleet, USS Mt. Whitney, LCC-20, Norfolk, Va.; asst. dep. chief staff Manpower Res. Affairs Hdqs. USMC, Washington, dir pub. affairs, 1996-2000, comdg. gen., 2000. Decorated Legion of Merit. Office: USMC Air Ground Combat Ctr Twentynine Palms CA 92278

STANLEY, DONALD RUSSELL, engineering executive; DSc in Environ. Engring., Harvard U., 1953; DSc (hon.), U. Alta., 1988. Chmn. bd. (hon.) Stanley Tech. Group, Inc. (now Stantec Inc.), Edmonton, Alta., Can. Mem. expert adv. panel on environ. health WHO. Contbr. numerous articles to profl. jours. Recipient L.C. Charlesworth award Assn. Profl. Engrs., Geologists and Geophysicists of Alta., 1977, Frank Spragins award, 1982; Carson F. Morrison award Canadian Cons. Engr., 1984, Julian C. Smith award Engring. Inst. Can., 1986, Beubien award Assn. Cons. Engrs. Can., 1996, Albert E. Berry medal Can. Soc. Civil Engring. and ASCE, 1997. Fellow ASCE; mem. Am. Acad. Environ. Engrs. (diplomate), Can. Acad. Engring. Office: STANTECH Inc 10160 112th St Edmonton AB Canada T5K 2L6 E-mail: lhickling@stantec.com

STANLEY, PETER WILLIAM, academic administrator; b. Bronxville, N.Y., Feb. 17, 1940; s. Arnold and Mildred Jeanette (Pattison) S.; m. Mary-Jane Cullen Cosgrove, Sept. 2, 1978; 1 dau., Laura. B.A. magna cum laude, Harvard U., 1962, M.A., 1964, Ph.D., 1970; LHD (hon.), Occidental Coll., 1994. Asst. prof. history U. Ill., Chgo., 1970-72, Harvard U., 1972-78, lectr. history, 1978-79; dean of coll. Carleton Coll., Northfield, Minn., 1979-84; program officer in charge edn. and culture program Ford Found., 1984-87, dir. edn. and culture program, 1987-91; pres. Pomona Coll., Claremont, Calif., 1991—. Lectr. Fgn. Service Inst., Arlington, Va., 1977-89. Author: A Nation in the Making: The Philippines and the United States, 1974; co-author: Sentimental Imperialists: The American Experience in East Asia, 1981; editor, contbr.: Reappraising an Empire: New Perspectives on Philippine-American History, 1984; contbr. numerous articles to scholastic jours., 1966— . Trustee The Coll. Bd., 1991-99, vice chair, 1993-94, chair, 1994-96, Barnard Coll., 2000—; dir. The James Irvine Found., 1997—, The Hitachi Found., 1993—, 2000—, Assn. Am. Colls. and Univs., 1995—, vice-chair, 1998-99, chair, 1999—; bd. fellows Claremont Grad. U. and Claremont U. Ctr., 1991—; active humanities and scis. coun. Stanford U., 1986—; nat. adv. coun. Nat. Fgn. Lang. Ctr., 1992—; mem. exec. com. Consortium Financing Higher Edn., 1992-95; bd. dirs. Nat. Assn. Latino Elected Ofcls. Edn. Fund, Commn. on Internat. Edn., Am. Coun. Edn., 1992-95; mem. pres.' coun. divsn. III NCAA, 2000—. Fellow Charles Warren Ctr. for Studies in Am. History-Harvard U., 1975-76; Frank Knox Meml. fellow Harvard U., 1962-63. Mem. Am. Hist. Assn., Assn. Asian Studies, Coun. on Fgn. Rels., Phi Beta Kappa Home: 345 N College Ave Claremont CA 91711-4408 Office: Pomona Coll Pres Office Claremont CA 91711-6301

STANSKY, PETER DAVID LYMAN, historian; b. N.Y.C., Jan. 18, 1932; s. Lyman and Ruth (Macow) S. B.A., Yale U., 1953, King's Coll., Cambridge (Eng.) U., 1955, M.A., 1959; Ph.D., Harvard U., 1961; D.L. (hon.), Wittenburg U., 1984. Teaching fellow history and lit. Harvard U., 1957-61, instr., then asst. prof. history, 1961-68; assoc. prof. history Stanford U., 1968-73, prof., 1973-74, Frances and Charles Field prof., 1974—, chmn. dept. history, 1975-78, 79-82, 89-90, assoc. dean humanities and scis., 1985-88. Chmn. publs. com. Conf. Brit. Studies, 1970-78; pres. Pacific Coast Conf. Brit. Studies, 1974-76, N. Am. Conf. Brit. Studies, 1983-85; vis. fellow Wesleyan Center Humanities, Middletown, Conn., 1972, All Soul's Coll., Oxford (Eng.) U., 1979, St. Catherine's Coll., Oxford (Eng.) U., 1983 Author: Ambitions and Strategies, 1964, England Since 1867, 1973, Gladstone, 1979, William Morris, 1983, Redesigning the World, 1985, On or About December 1910, 1996, Another Book That Never Was, 1998, From William Morris to Sergeant Pepper, 1999; co-author: Journey to the Frontier, 1966, The Unknown Orwell, 1972, Orwell: The Transformation, 1979, London's Burning, 1994. Guggenheim fellow, 1966-67, 73-74; Am. Council Learned Socs. fellow, 1978-79; NEH fellow, 1983, 98-99, Royal Hist. Soc. fellow Ctr. for Advanced Study Behavioral Scis., 1988-89 Fellow Am. Acad. Arts and Scis. (coun. 1994-98); mem. Am. Hist. Assn. (pres. Pacific Coast br. 1988-89), Conf. on Brit. Studies, Victorian Soc., William Morris Soc., AAUP, Century Assn. Home: 375 Pinehill Rd Hillsborough CA 94010-6612 Office: Stanford U Dept History Stanford CA 94305 E-mail: stansky@stanford.edu

STANTON, LEWIS HARRIS, Internet learning company executive; b. London, Apr. 2, 1954; came to U.S., 1980; s. Gerald and Carole (Harris) S.;divorced; children: Graham, Joshua. BS, U. Birmingham, Eng., 1976. CPA, Calif.; chartered acct., Eng. Sr. mgr. Arthur Andersen & Co., L.A., London, 1976-88; chief fin. officer Data Analysis Inc., L.A., 1988-96; CEO WorldSite Networks Inc., Beverly Hills, Calif., 1996-97; exec. v.p., COO, CFO MAI Sys. Corp., Irvine, 1997-99; exec. v.p., CFO Univ. Access, Inc., L.A., 1999—. Chmn. L.A. Youth non-profit orgn., 1997. Fellow Inst. Chartered Accts.; mem. AICPA, Calif. Soc. CPAs (chmn. mems. in industry com. 1990-94), Assn. Western Securities Mgmt. (pres. 1989). Avocations: tennis, visual arts. Office: Univ Access Inc 6255 Sunset Blvd Ste 801 Los Angeles CA 90028

STANTON, MICHAEL JOHN, newspaper editor; b. New Britain, Conn., Mar. 30, 1944; s. John Martin and Helen (McNally) S.; m. Barbara Ann Mucha, Aug. 27, 1966; 1 child, Sean A.B. in English, Holy Cross Coll., 1966. Reporter, editor Providence (R.I.) Jour., 1968-72; press sec. Gov. R.I., Providence, 1972-77; asst. news editor St. Louis Globe-Dem., 1977-81; news copy desk chief Detroit Free Press, 1981-83, exec. news editor, 1983-85, asst. to exec. editor, 1985-86; exec. news editor Seattle Times, 1986—. Office: The Seattle Times PO Box 70 Fairview Ave N & John St Seattle WA 98111

STANTON, WILLIAM JOHN, JR. marketing educator, author; b. Chgo., Dec. 15, 1919; s. William John and Winifred (McGann) S.; m. Imma Mair, Sept. 14, 1978; children by previous marriage: Kathleen Louise, William John III. BS, Ill. Inst. Tech., 1940; MBA, Northwestern U., 1941, PhD, 1948. Mgmt. trainee Sears Roebuck & Co., 1940-41; instr. U. Ala., 1941-44; auditor Olan Mills Portrait Studios, Chattanooga, 1944-46; asst. prof., asso. prof. U. Wash., 1948-55; prof. U. Colo., Boulder, 1955-90; prof. emeritus, 1990—; head mktg. dept. U. Colo., 1955-71, acting dean, 1963-64; assoc. dean U. Colo. (Sch. Bus.), 1964-67. Author: Economic Aspects of Recreation in Alaska, 1953; (with Rosann Spiro) Management of a Sales Force, 10th edit., 1999 (also Spanish and Portuguese transl.), (with others) Challenge of Business, 1975, (with M. Etzel and B. Walker) Marketing, 12th edit., 2001 (also Spanish, Portuguese and Indonesian transls.), (with M.S. Sommers and J.G. Barnes) Can. edit. Fundamentals of Marketing, 8th edit., 1998, (with K. Miller and R. Layton) Australian edit., 3d edit., 1994, (with R. Varaldo) Italian edit., 2d edit., 1990, (with others) South African edit., 1992; monographs on Alaska Tourist Industry, 1953-54; contbr. articles to profl. jours. Mem. Am. Mktg. Assn., Western Mktg. Assn., Beta Gamma Sigma. Roman Catholic. Home: 1445 Sierra Dr Boulder CO 80302-7846

STANWAY, PAUL WILLIAM, newspaper editor; b. Manchester, Eng., Apr. 22, 1950; arrived in Canada, 1976; s. William and Gladys (Wright) S.; m. Erina Danyluk, May 5, 1976; children: Scott, Nicole. Reporter Nottingham (Eng.) Post, 1969-72, Express and Star, Wolverhampton, Eng., 1972-76, Free Press, Winnipeg, Can., 1976-77; city editor Edmonton (Can.) Sun, 1978-80, news editor, 1980-81, mng. editor, 1981-84, assoc. editor, columnist, 1988-90; editor Calgary (Can.) Sun, 1988-90; European bur. chief Toronto Sun Pub., London, 1990-96; editor-in-chief Edmonton Sun/Sun Media Corp., 1992—. Avocations: skiing, golf, fishing, travel. Office: The Edmonton Sun Sun Media Corp 4990 92d Ave Ste 250 Edmonton AB Canada T6B 3A1

STANZLER, JORDAN, lawyer; AB, Harvard U., 1967; JD, U. Chgo., 1972; LLM in Taxation, NYU, 1987. Bar: Calif. 1972, R.I. 1975, N.Y. 1981. Asst. U.S. atty. So. Dist. N.Y., 1982-88, chief tax unit, 1987-88; ptnr. Anderson Kill & Olick, San Francisco, 1988-99, Stanzler, Funderburk & Castellone, San Francisco, 1999—[00fe]. Lectr. ins. coverage matters. Author: (with Anderson and Masters) Insurance Coverage Litigation, 1997; contbr. articles to profl. jours. Office: Stanzler Funderburk & Castellone 180 Montgomery St Ste 1700 San Francisco CA 94104

STAPLETON, COREY, financial planner; b. Seattle, Sept. 17, 1967; BS, U.S. Naval Acad., 1992; MA, Temple U., 1995. Commd. officer USN, 1986, advanced through grades, 1997; fin. planner Prudential Ind. Fin. Svcs., 1997—. Mem. Midland Empire Pachyderm Club, 1998—; campaign aide Bob Dole for Pres. Campaign, 1996; campaign mgr. Norm Mills, Mont. State House Dist. 19, 1998; chair Yellowstone County Young Reps., 1999-2000. Mem. Am. Legion, Billings C. of C., Rotary. Office: 3614 Crater Lake Billings MT 59102 E-mail: stapletonct@aol.com

STAPRANS, ARMAND, electronics executive; b. Riga, Latvia, Feb. 28, 1931; s. Theodore and Elvira (Ulmanis) S.; m. Vija Spalvins, Sept. 25, 1955; children: Silvija, Armin, Erik. Student, Willamette U., 1949-52; BSEE, U. Calif., Berkeley, 1954, MSEE, 1955, PhDEE, 1959. Rsch. asst. dept. elec. engring. U. Calif., 1955-57; engr. microwave tube div. Varian Assocs., Palo Alto, Calif., 1957-60, engring. mgr., 1960-68, ops. mgr., 1978-78, 86-89, chief engr., 1978-86, gen. mgr. coupled cavity tube divsn., 1989-92, v.p., 1990-95; gen. mgr. microwave power tube products, 1992-95; pres. microwave power tube products divsn. Comms. and Power Inds., Palo Alto, Calif., 1995-98; mgmt. cons., 1999—. Contbr. articles to profl. jours., chpt. to book; patentee microwave tubes field. Fellow IEEE (electron device adminstrv. com. 1983-88). Home: 445 Knoll Dr Los Altos CA 94024-4732 Office: Comm & Power Inds M S B 100 Microwave Power Tube Prod Divsn PO Box 50750 Palo Alto CA 94303-0665 E-mail: AStaprans@aol.com

STARK, FORTNEY HILLMAN (PETE STARK), congressman; b. Milw., Nov. 11, 1931; s. Fortney Hillman Sr. and Dorothy M. (Mueller) S.; children: Jeffrey Peter, Beatrice Ann, Thekla Brumder, Sarah Gallun, Fortney Hillman Stark III; m. Deborah Roderick. BS, MIT; MBA, U. Calif. Teaching asst. MIT, Cambridge, 1953-54; prin. Skaife & Co., Berkeley, Calif., 1957-61; founder Beacon Savs. & Loan Assn., Antioch, 1961; pres., founder Security Nat. Bank, Walnut Creek, 1963-72; mem. U.S. Congress from 13th (formerly 9th) Calif. dist., 1973—; mem. ways and means com., formerly chmn., now ranking minority mem. health subcom.; mem.joint econ. com. Bd. dirs. ACLU, 1971, Common Cause, 1971, Starr King Sch.; del. Dem. State Cen. Com.; trustee Calif. Dem. Coun. Capt. USAF, 1955-57. Mem. Delta Kappa Epsilon. Office: Ho of Reps 239 Cannon Ho Office Bldg Washington DC 20515-0001*

STARK, JACK LEE, academic administrator, director; b. Urbana, Ind., Sept. 26, 1934; s. Lynn C. and Helen (Haley) S.; m. Jil Carolyn Harris, June 14, 1958; children: Janet, Jeffrey, Jennifer, Jonathan. BA, Claremont McKenna Coll., 1957; hon. degree, Redlands U., LDH, 1973. Asst. to pres. Claremont (Calif.) McKenna Coll., 1961-70, pres., 1970—. Active Pomona Valley Cmty. Hosp.; bd. dirs. Thacher Sch., Ojai, Calif. Capt. USMCR, 1957-60. Mem. Assn. Ind. Calif. Colls. and Univs. (chmn.), Ind. Colls. So. Calif. (bd. dirs.), Western Coll. Assn. (bd. dirs.). Club: California (Los Angeles) Home: 1679 Tulane Rd Claremont CA 91711-3426 Office: Claremont McKenna Coll Office of Pres 500 E 9th St Claremont CA 91711-5903

STARK, NELLIE MAY, forest ecology educator; b. Norwich, Conn., Nov. 20, 1933; d. Theodore Benjamin and Dorothy Josephine (Pendleton) Beetham; m. Oscar Elder Stark, Oct. 1962 (dec.). BA, Conn. Coll., 1956; AM, Duke U., 1958, PhD, 1962. Botanist Exptl. Sta., U.S. Forest Svc., Old Strawberry, Calif., 1958-66; botanist, ecologist Desert Rsch. Inst., Reno, 1966-72; prof. forest ecology Sch. Forestry, U. Mont., Missoula, 1972-92; pvt. cons. Philomath, Oreg. Pres. Camas Analytical Lab., Inc., Missoula, 1987-92. Author: Will Your Family Survive the 21st Century, 1997, Memories of Wren, Oregon, 1998; contbr. articles to profl. jours. Named Disting. Dau. Norwich, Conn., 1985; recipient Conn. award Conn. Coll., 1986, 54 grants. Mem. Ecol. Soc. Am. (chair ethics com. 1974, 76), Soc. Am. Foresters (taskforce 1987-88).

STARKS, JOHN LEVELL, professional basketball player; b. Tulsa, Aug. 10, 1965; m. Jacqueline Starks; children: John Jr., chelsea. Student, Okla. State U., 1988. Guard Golden State Warriors, 1988-89, Continental Basketball Assn./Cedar Rapids Silver Bullets, 1989-90, World Bakestball League/Memphis Rockers, 1990, New York Knicks, 1990-98. Active boys Brotherhood Republic, N.Y.C.; founder John Starks Found., Tulsa. Honoree in downtown parade on John Starks Day, tulsa, 1994; winner NBA Sixth Man award, 1996-97; named 1993 NBA All Defensive Second Team; participant in 1994 NBA All-Star Game. Avocations: tennis, jazz. Office: Golden State Warriors 1221 Broadway Fl 20 Oakland CA 94612-1837

STARR, CHARLES, state legislator, contractor, farmer; b. Eastland, Tex., Oct. 1932; m. Kathy Starr. BS in Agrl. Edn., U. Idaho; MS in Agrl. Bus. Mgmt., U. Calif., Davis. Mem. Oreg. Legislature, Salem, 1998—, mem. bus. and consumer affairs com., mem. pub. affairs com., mem. rev. com., chair rules and election com. Mem. Groner Elem. Sch. Bd., Hillsboro Union H.S. Bd. Republican. Home: 8330 SW River Rd Hillsboro OR 97123-9131 Office: S 312 State Capitol Salem OR 97310

STARR, KEVIN, librarian, educator; BA, U. San Francisco, 1962; MA, Harvard U., 1965, PhD, 1969; MLS, U. Calif., Berkeley, 1974; postgrad., Ch. Div. Sch. Pacific, Berkeley, 1983-84. From asst. to assoc. prof. Am. lit. Harvard U., Cambridge, Mass., 1969-74; city libr. San Francisco, 1973-76; prin. Kevin Starr Assocs., San Francisco, 1983-85; prof. comm. arts U. San Francisco, 1981-89; prof. Sch. Planning and Devel. U. So. Calif., 1989—; state libr. Calif., 1994—. Allston Burr sr. tutor Eliot House Harvard U., Cambridge, 1970-73; cons. Beyl and Boyd, Inc., San Francisco, 1979-83; sr. cons. Hill and Knowlton USA, San Francisco, 1983-84; vis. assoc. prof. English U. Calif., Berkely, 1974, vis. lectr. polit. sci., 1976, lectr. librarianship, 1978; adj. prof. humanities San Francisco State U., 1975-76; Regent's lectr. polit. sci. U. Calif., Riverside, 1977; adj. prof. English Santa Clara (Calif.) U., 1977-78; vis. prof. history U. Calif., Davis, 1985-86; vis. scholar, media fellow Hoover Inst., 1986-88; vis. fellow Ctr. Humanistic Studies, Claremont McKenna Coll., 1987; faculty master Embassy Residential Coll., 1990-94. Sr. editor New West Mag., 1977; vatican corr. Hearst Newspapers, Rome, 1978; columnist Examiner, San Francisco, 1977-83; contbng. editor L.A. Times, 1994—; contbr. articles to profl. jours., chpts. to books. Exec. aide to mayor San Francisco, 1973; bd. trustees Am. Issues Forum, 1975-76, Calif. Hist. Soc., 1992—; co-chmn. sister city com., San Francisco and Sydney, Australia, 1981-86; advisor Jr. League San Francisco, 1982-84; canidate San Francisco Bd. Suprs., 1984; councilor Am. Antiquarian Soc., 1996—; mem. Calif. Coun. Humanities, 1996—; regent Cathedral St. Mary Assumption, San Francisco, 1996—. Lt. German Army, 1962-64. Office: Calif State Lib PO Box 942837 Sacramento CA 94237-0001

STARR, ROSS MARC, economist, educator; b. Oak Ridge, Nov. 14, 1945; s. Chauncey and Doris E. S.; m. Susan S. Strauss, July 2, 1967; children: Daniel, Diana. BS, Stanford U., 1966, PhD, 1972. Cons. Rand Corp., summers 1966, 67, Western Mgmt. Sci. Inst., Grad. Sch. Mgmt., UCLA, summers 1967, 71; Cowles Found. staff rsch. economist Yale U., New Haven, 1970, faculty, 1970-74, assoc. prof. econs., 1974, U. Calif., Davis, 1975-76, prof. econs., 1976-80, San Diego, 1980—, chmn. dept., 1987-90. Vis. lectr. London Sch. Econs., 1973-74, Peoples U. China, Beijing, 1987; vis. scholar U. Calif., Berkeley, 1978-80, vis. prof., 1997. Author: General Equilibrium Theory: An Introduction, 1997; co-editor: Essays in Honor of Kenneth J. Arrow, 1986: v.1, Social Choice and Public Decision Making, v.2, Equilibrium Analysis, v.3, Uncertainty, Information and Communication; editor: Gen. Equilibrium Models of Monetary Economies, 1989; contbr. articles to profl. jours. NDEA fellow, 1966-69, Yale jr. faculty fellow, 1973-74, Guggenheim fellow, 1978-79; NSF grant, 1979-81, 83-85. Office: U Calif San Diego Dept Econs 0508 9500 Gilman Dr La Jolla CA 92093-0508 E-mail: rstarr@ucsd.edu

STARSHAK, JAMES L. lawyer; b. Chgo., Feb. 3, 1945; s. Norbert Phillip and Enda (Reiter) S.; m. Susanne M. Smith, Oct. 25, 1969; children: Lesle M., Phillip E. BBA, U. Notre Dame, 1966, JD, 1969. Bar: Ill. 1969, Hawaii 1972, U.S. Dist. Ct. (no. dist.) Ill., U.S. Tax Ct., U.S. Supreme Ct. Atty. estate tax IRS, Chgo., 1969-71, Honolulu, 1971-77; ptnr. Steiner & Starshak, Honolulu, 1971-79; assoc. Conahan & Conahan, Honolulu, 1979-86; ptnr. Carlsmith, Ball et al, Honolulu, 1986—. Office: Carlsmith Ball Pacific Tower 22d Fl 1001 Bishop St Honolulu HI 96813-3429

STASACK, EDWARD ARMEN, artist; b. Chgo., Oct. 1, 1929; s. Clifford Clement and Elizabeth Frances (Mallek) S.; m. Mary Louise Walters, June 20, 1953 (div. 1972); children: Caren Marie, Jennifer Elizabeth, John Armen, Michael Clifford; m. Diane Miura Hirsch, June 26, 1993. BFA with high honors, U. Ill., Urbana, 1955, MFA, 1956. Instr. in art U. Hawaii, 1956-61, prof. art, chmn. dept. art, 1969-72, program chmn. in printmaking, 1975-83, prof. emeritus, 1988; affiliate Downtown Gallery, N.Y.C., 1960-70. Author: (with J. Halley Cox) Hawaiian Petroglyphs, 1970, (with Georgia Lee) Petroglyphs of Kaho'olawe, 1993, Ka'upulehu Petroglyphs, 1994, Spirit of Place, Petroglyphs of Hawaii, 1999, (with Diane Stasack) Rock Art of Hawaii Volcanoes National Park, Nine Reports, 1995-2001; one-man shows include Honolulu Acad. Arts, 1961, 66, 69, 76, 87, U.S. embassies Istanbul and Izmir, Turkey, 1976, Am. Cultural Ctr., Bucharest, Romania, 1976, Cleve. Inst. Art, 1976, Hilo (Hawaii) Coll. Gallery, 1976, Amfac Plaza Gallery, 1978, Ryan Gallery, 1981, Art Loft, Honolulu, 1983, Commons Gallery, U. Hawaii, 1996, Hawaii Volcano Nat. Park Art Ctr., 1996; group shows include Carnegie Inst., Pitts., 1964, Krakow (Poland) Biennial, 1966, 68, Smithsonian Instn., Washington, 1967, Mexico City Mus. Modern Art, 1968, Leicester Gallery, London, 1965, Art Mus. Manila, The Philippines, 1982, 2d Internat. Biennial Print Exhibit Republic of China, 1986, Yuma Art Ctr., 1990; represented in permanent collections Mus. Modern Art, N.Y.C., Met. Mus. Art, N.Y.C., Chgo. Art Inst., Bklyn. Mus., Honolulu Acad. Arts, Hawaii State Found. Culture and the Arts, Libr. of Congress, Phila. Mus. Art, Boston Pub. Libr. Served with U.S. Army, 1952-54. Recipient numerous prizes, including; Boston Printmakers Mems. prize, 1967; Juror's awards Honolulu Printmakers, 1957, 58, 59, 62, 63, 66, 67, 68, 74, 77, 87; Soc. Am. Graphic Artists prizes, 1956, 57, 61, 62, 63, 68, 73, 78, 79, 80, 91; Tiffany Found. fellow, 1958, 62; Rockefeller Found. grantee, 1959, Hawaii Cmty. Found. grantee. 1997, 98, 99, 00; MacDowell Colony fellow, 1971, 75; Hawaii State and U.S. Bicentennial Commns. fellow, 1975 Mem. Soc. Am. Graphic Artists, Australian Rock Art Rsch. Assn., Rock Art Assn. Hawaii (emeritus pres.), Am. Rock Art Rsch. Assn., Soc. Hawaiian Archaeology, Sharlot Hall Mus., Smoki Mus. Office: 1878 Paradise Ln Prescott AZ 86305-5282

STASHOWER, ARTHUR L. lawyer; b. Cleve., Apr. 12, 1930; s. Joseph G. and Tillie (Merlin) S.; m. Joy Schary, Sept. 1, 1957 (div. 1982); children: Keren, Saul, David; m. Barbara Hayden, Jan. 17, 1985. AB, U. Mich., 1951, JD with distinction, 1953. Bar: Ohio 1953, Mich. 1953, Calif. 1957, U.S. Dist. Ct. (mid. dist.) Calif. 1957, U.S. Ct. Appeals (9th cir.) 1962.

Assoc. Kaplan Livingston Goodwin & Berkowitz, Beverly Hills, Calif., 1957-64; exec. United Artists Corp., L.A., 1964-65, Artists Agy. Corp., L.A., 1965-67; assoc. Greenberg & Glusker, Beverly Hills, 1967-68; ptnr. Swerdlow Glikbarg & Shimer, Beverly Hills, 1968-71, Sklar Coben & Stashower, L.A., 1971-84; of counsel Shea & Gould, L.A., 1985-88; ptnr. Chrystie & Berle, L.A., 1988-92, of counsel, 1993-97, Kenoff & Machtinger, L.A., 1997—. Arbitrator Hughes Aircraft, E.A.S.T. Mem. Anti-Defamation League, 1961-79, exec. com. 1967-73; mem. Assn. Alternative Pub. Schs., L.A., 1973-79. Lt. USCGR, 1953-57. Mem. ABA, Am. Arbitration Assn., L.A. Bar Assn., State Bar Assn. Calif., Beverly Hills Bar Assn., L.A. Copyright Soc. (trustee 1986-90), Fed. Mediation and Conciliation Svc. Democrat. Jewish. Avocations: jogging. Office: Ste 1020 1901 Avenue Of The Stars Los Angeles CA 90067-4609

STATLER, IRVING CARL, aerospace engineer; b. Buffalo, Nov. 23, 1923; s. Samuel William and Sarah (Strauss) S.; m. Renee Roll, Aug. 23, 1953; children: William Scott, Thomas Stuart B.S. in Aero. Engring., B.S. in Engring. Math., U. Mich., 1945; Ph.D., Calif. Inst. Tech., 1956. Research engr. flight research dept. Cornell Aero. Lab., Inc., Buffalo, 1946-53, prin. engr. flight research dept., 1956-57, asst. head aero-mechanics dept., 1957-63, head applied mechanics dept., 1963-70, sr. staff scientist aeroscis. div., 1970-71; research scientist U.S. Army Air Mobility Research and Devel. Lab., Moffett Field, Calif., 1971-73, dir. Aeromechanics Lab., 1973-85, dir. AGARD, 1985-88; sr. staff scientist NASA Ames Rsch. Ctr., 1988-92, chief Human Factors Rsch. Divsn., 1992—. Research scientist research analysis group Jet Propulsion Lab., Pasadena, Calif., 1953-55; chmn. flight mechanics panel adv. group aerospace research and devel. NATO, 1974-76; lectr. U. Buffalo, Millard-Fillmore Coll., Buffalo, 1957-58 Served with USAAF, 1945-46 Fellow AIAA (Internat. Cooperation in Space Sci. medal 1992), AAAS, German Aerospace Soc., Royal Aero Soc.; mem. Am. Helicoptor Soc., Sigma Xi. Home: 1362 Cuernavaca Circulo Mountain View CA 94040-3571 Office: NASA Ames Rsch Ctr MS 262-7 Moffett Field CA 94035 E-mail: istatler@mail.arc.nasa.gov

STAUBUS, GEORGE JOSEPH, accounting educator; b. Brunswick, Mo., Apr. 26, 1926; s. George Washington and Florence Lidwina (Pittman) S.; m. Sarah Mayer, Apr. 11, 1949; children: Lindsay, Martin, Paul, Janette. B.S., U. Mo., 1947; M.B.A., U. Chgo., 1949, Ph.D., 1954. C.P.A., Ill. Instr. U. Buffalo, 1947-49, U. Chgo., 1950-52; asst. prof. then prof. acctg. U. Calif.-Berkeley, from 1952, now Michael N. Chetkovich prof. emeritus. Vis. prof. NYU, 1965, London Bus. Sch., 1966-67, U. Kans., 1969-70; Erskine lectr. U. Canterbury, New Zealand, 1972, 91. Author: A Theory of Accounting to Investors, 1961, Activity Costing and Input-Output Accounting, 1971, Making Accounting Decisions, 1977, An Accounting Concept of Revenue, 1980, Activity Costing for Decisions, 1988, Economic Influences on the Development of Accounting in Firms, 1996, The Decision-Usefulness Theory of Accounting: A Limited History, 2000. Served with USN, 1944-46. Recipient Disting. prof. Calif. Soc. C.P.A.s, 1981 Fellow Acctg. Researchers Internat. Assn. (treas. 1981-83); mem. Am. Acctg. Assn. (disting. internat. lectr. 1982), Am. Inst. C.P.A.s, Fin. Execs. Inst. Office: UC Berkeley Haas Sch Bus Berkeley CA 94720-0001

STAVIG, MARK LUTHER, English language educator; b. Northfield, Minn., Jan. 20, 1935; s. Lawrence Melvin and Cora (Hjertaas) S.; m. Donna Mae Ring, July 3, 1957; children— Anne Ragnhild, Thomas Edward, Rolf Lawrence B.A., Augustana Coll., 1956, Oxford U., 1958, M.A., 1962; Ph.D., Princeton U., 1961. Instr. to asst. prof. English U. Wis., Madison, 1961-68; from assoc. prof. to prof. English Colo. Coll., Colorado Springs, 1968—. Author: John Ford and the Traditional Moral Order, 1968, The Forms of Things Unknown: Renaissance Metaphor in Romeo and Juliet and A Midsummer Night's Dream, 1995; editor: Ford, 'Tis Pity She's a Whore, 1966. Fellow Danforth Found., 1956-61, Woodrow Wilson Found., 1956-57; Fulbright scholar Oxford U., 1956-58 Mem. MLA, Shakespeare Assn. Am. Democrat Home: 1409 Wood Ave Colorado Springs CO 80907-7348 Office: Colo Coll Dept English Colorado Springs CO 80903

STEAD, JERRE L. investment company executive; b. Maquoketa, Iowa, Jan. 8, 1943; s. H. Victor and Anna Catherine (Grindrod) S.; m. Mary Joy Kloppenburg, Dec. 26, 1961; children: Joel A., Jay A. BBA, U. Iowa, 1965; grad. advanced mgmt. program, Harvard U., 1982. Mgr. regional sales Honeywell Corp., Phila., 1971-73, dir. prodn. Mpls., 1974-75, dir. distbn., 1975-76, v.p. fin. and adminstrn., Brussels, 1979-82; v.p., gen. mgr. Honeywell-Phillips Med. Electronics, Brussels, 1981-82, Honeywell Corp., Mpls., 1982-85, v.p., group exec., 1986; pres., COO Sq. D Co., Palatine, Ill., 1987-88, pres., CEO, chmn. bd., 1989-91, also bd. dirs.; chmn., CEO Global Info. Solutions AT&T, N.Y.C., 1991-95; CEO Legent Corp., Vienna, 1995-96; chmn., CEO Ingram Micro, Inc., Santa Ana, Calif., 1996-2000; chmn. Holland Am. Investment Corp., 2000—. Bd. dirs. Eljer Industries, Plano, Tex., Ameritech, Chgo., USG, Chgo., TJ Internat., Inc. Mem. Pres.' coun. Am. Lung Assn., N.Y.C., 1986—, The Wash. Ctr. Nat. Campaign Com.; bus. adv. com. N.C. A&T U.; trustee Coe Coll., Cedar Rapids, Iowa, 1987; mem. coun. on competitiveness Ill. Bus. Roundtable; bd. visitors U. Iowa, Iowa City. Mem. Nat. Elec. Mfrs. Assn. (bd. govs. 1984—), Nat. Assn. Elec. Distbrs. (edn. com.), Chgo. Com., Elec. Mfrs. Club. Republican. Methodist. Office: Holland Am Investment Corp PO Box 25125 565 Fifth Ave New York NY 10017

STEADMAN, JOHN MARCELLUS, III, English educator; b. Spartanburg, S.C., Nov. 25, 1918; s. John Marcellus and Medora Rice (Rembert) S. AB, Emory U., 1940, MA, 1941, DHL (hon.), 1976; MA (T.W. Hunt scholar), Princeton U., 1948, PhD, 1949; DHL (hon.), St. Bonaventure U., 1998. Instr. English Ga. Inst. Tech., 1941-42; asst. prof. U. N.C., 1949-51; ind. study and rsch. in English lit., 1953-61; from rsch. assoc.to sr. rsch. assoc. Henry E. Huntington Libr., San Marino, Calif., 1962—; mem. faculty U. Calif., Riverside, 1966—, prof. English, 1967—, faculty rsch. lectr., 1977, prof. emeritus, 1989—. Vis. disting. prof. City U. N.Y., fall, 1974 Author numerous books including Disembodied Laughter: Troilus and the Apotheosis Tradition, 1972, The Lamb and The Elephant: Ideal Imitation and the Context of Renaissance Allegory, 1974, Epic and Tragic Structure in Paradise Lost, 1976, Nature into Myth: Medieval and Renaissance Moral Symbols, 1979, Milton's Biblical and Classical Imagery, 1984, The Hill and the Labyrinth: Discourse and Certitude in Milton and His Near-Contemporaries, 1984, The Wall of Paradise: Essays on Milton's Poetics, 1985, Milton and the Paradoxes of Renaissance Heroism, 1987, Redefining a Period Style: "Renaissance," "Mannerist," and "Baroque" in Literature, 1990, Ryoanji Temple and Other Poems, 1993, Moral Fiction in Milton and Spenser, 1995, Reconnaissances: Poems, 1995, Winter Harvest, A Retrospective, 1996, In Earnest or Game: A Seriocomic Medley. Verses Early or Late, 1998, Siege of Contraries: Rumors of Wars Real or Metaphorical, Stories and Sketches, 1998; co-editor latest being A Milton Ency., vols. I-IX, 1978-83; editor: latest being Huntington Libr. Quar., 1962-81; mem. numerous editl. and advisory bds.; contbr. articles to profl. jours. Served to capt. USAAF, 1942-46; capt. AUS, 1951-52. Grantee Huntington Libr., 1961-62; Procter fellow Princeton U., 1949, Guggenheim fellow, 1979. Mem. Milton Soc. Am. (pres. 1973, honored scholar 1976), So. Calif. Renaissance Conf., Phi Beta Kappa, Chi Phi, Fine Arts Club. Democrat. Home: 250 S Oak Knoll Ave Apt 109 Pasadena CA 91101-2995 Office: Henry E Huntington Libr San Marino CA 91108

STEBBINS, ROBERT ALAN, sociology educator; b. Rhinelander, Wis., June 22, 1938; s. William Nelson and Dorothy May (Guy) S.; m. Karin Yvonne Olson, Jan. 11, 1964; children: Paul, Lisa, Christi. B.A., Macalester Coll., 1961; M.A., U. Minn., 1962, Ph.D., 1964. Assoc. prof. Presbyterian Coll., Clinton, S.C., 1964-65; assoc. prof.to prof. Meml. U. Nfld., St. John's, Can., 1965-73; prof. U. Tex.-Arlington, 1973-76; prof. sociology U. Calgary, Alta., Can., 1976-99, faculty prof. social scis. Can., 2000—, dept. head Can., 1976-82; head dept. sociology and anthropology Meml. U. Nfld., 1968-71. Author: Commitment to Deviance, 1971, The Disorderly Classroom: Its Physical and Temporal Conditions, 1974, Teachers and Meaning, 1975, Amateurs, 1979, The Magician, 1984, Sociology: The Study of Society, 2d edit., 1990, Canadian Football: The View from the Helmet, 1987, Deviance: Tolerable Differences, 1988, The Laugh-Makers: Stand-Up Comedy as Art, Business, and Life-Style, 1990, Amateurs, Professionals and Serious Leisure, 1992; co-editor: Fieldwork Experience, 1980, The Sociology of Deviance, 1982, Experiencing Fieldwork, 1991, Career, Culture, and Social Psychology in a Variety Art, 1993, Predicaments: Moral Difficulty in Everyday Life, 1993, The Franco-Calgarians: French Language, Leisure and Linguistic Lifestyle in an Anglophone City, 1994, The Connoisseur's New Orleans, 1995, The Barbershop Singer: Inside the Social World of a Musical Hobby, 1996, Tolerable Differences: Living with Deviance, 2d edit., 1996; After Work: The Search for an Optimal Leisure Lifestyle, 1998, The Urban Francophone Volunteer: Searching for Personal Meaning and Community Growth in a Linguistic Minority, 1998, The French Enigma: Survival and Development of Canada's Francophone Societies, 2000, Exploratory Research in the Social Sciences, 2001, New Directions in the Theory and Research of Serions Leisure, 2001. Pres. St. John's Orch., 1967-68; mem. Dallas Civic Symphony, 1973-76, Orch. Soc. of Calgary, 1978-97. Can. Coun. Sabbatical Leave fellow, 1972-72, Calgary Inst. for Humanities fellow, 1987-88, Killam resident fellow, 1990; NEH summer stipend, 1976; Acad. Leisure Scis. fellow, 1996—, Royal Soc. Can. fellow, 1999—. Mem. Leisure Studies Assn., Can. Sociology and Anthropology Assn. (pres. 1988-89), Internat. Sociol. Assn., Assn. for Can. Studies, World Leisure and Recreation Assn. (bd. dirs. 1997—), Social Sci. Fedn. Can. (pres. 1991-92), Can. Assn. for Leisure Studies (v.p. 1993-96). Home: 144 Edgemont Estates Dr NW Calgary AB Canada T3A 2M3 Office: U Calgary Dept Sociology 2500 University Dr NW Calgary AB Canada T2N 1N4

STECK, WARREN FRANKLIN, retired chemical company executive, biochemist; b. Regina, Sask., Can., May 10, 1939; m. 1963; 2 children. B in Eng., McGill U., 1960; PhD in Organic Chemistry, U. Sask., 1964. Rsch. assoc. Rsch. Inst. Okla. U., 1963-64; asst. rsch. officer Nat. Rsch. Coun. Can., 1964-70, assoc. rsch. officer, 1970-76, sr. rsch. officer, 1976-80, asst. dir., 1980-81, assoc. dir., 1982-83, dir. Plant Biotech. Inst., 1983-90, dir. gen. Plant Biotech Inst., 1991-94; asst. pres. Fytokem Inc., Saskatoon, Sask., 1995-97, v.p. tech., 1997—. Mem. Phytochem. Soc. N.Am., Soc. Cosmetic Chemists. Achievements include rsch. in insect sex attractants and pheromones, chem. ecology. Office: Fytokem Inc 101-110 Research Dr Saskatoon SK Canada S7N 3R3

STECKEL, RICHARD J. radiologist, academic administrator; b. Scranton, Pa., Apr. 17, 1936; s. Morris Leo and Lucille (Yellin) S.; m. Julie Raskin, June 16, 1960; children: Jan Marie, David Matthew. BS magna cum laude, Harvard U., 1957, MD cum laude, 1961. Diplomate Am. Bd. Radiology. Intern UCLA Hosp., 1961-62; resident in radiology Mass. Gen. Hosp., Boston, 1962-65; clin./rsch. assoc. Nat. Cancer Inst., 1965-67; faculty UCLA Med. Sch., 1967—, prof. radiol. scis. and radiation oncology, 1974-94; chmn. dept. radiol. scis. UCLA Med. Ctr., 1994-2000, prof. emeritus, 2000—; pres. Assn. Am. Cancer Insts., 1981. Dir. Jonsson Comprehensive Cancer Ctr., 1974-94. Author/editor 3 books; contbr. over 130 articles to profl. jours. Fellow Am. Coll. Radiology; mem. Radiol. Soc. N. Am., Am. Roentgen Ray Soc., Assn. Univ. Radiologists. Office: UCLA Med Ctr Dept Radiol Scis 10833 Le Conte Ave Los Angeles CA 90095-3075

STECKLER, CRAIG THEODORE, protective services official; b. Scottsfield, Ill., Feb. 3, 1944; s. Albert George and Mary Lorene (Johnston) S.; m. Karen Capellutto, Mar. 11, 1978; children: Theresa, Rachael, Suzanne, Mark. AA, Saddleback Coll., 1973; BA, Calif. State U., L.A., 1975; postgrad., U. Va., 1982, Peace Officer Standards & Tng., Pomona, Calif., 1986. Dist. mgr. Orange County Register, Santa Ana, Calif., 1962-68; police officer, sgt., then lt. City of San Clemente, 1968-80; police chief City of Piedmont, 1980-86; dep. police chief City of Fremont, 1986-92, chief of police, 1992—. Instr., Cypress (Calif.) Coll., 1975-77, Los Mondos Coll., Pittsberg, calif., 1982-83. Mem. Am. Mgmt. Assn., Calif. Peace Officers Assn., Calif. Police Chiefs Assn. (bd. dirs.), Command Coll. Grads. (bd. dirs.), Rotary. Republican. Roman Catholic. Avocation: golf. Office: Fremont Police Dept 2000 Stevenson Blvd Fremont CA 94538-2336

STECKLER, PHYLLIS BETTY, publishing company executive; b. N.Y.C. d. Irwin H. and Bertha (Fellner) Schwartzbard; m. Stuart J. Steckler; children: Randall, Sharon Steckler-Slotky. BA, Hunter Coll.; MA, NYU. Editorial dir. R.R. Bowker Co., N.Y.C., Crowell Collier Macmillan Info. Pub. Co., N.Y.C., Holt Rinehart & Winston Info. Systems, N.Y.C.; pres., CEO Oryx Press, Scottsdale, Ariz., 1973-76, Phoenix, 1976-01, Zephyr Info., Inc., Phoenix, 2001—. Adj. prof. mktg. scholarly publs. Grad. History dept., Ariz. State U., Tempe; mem. president's corp. adv. coun. Hunter Coll.; mem. dean's coun. Coll. of Extended Edn., Ariz. State U., Phoenix. Past chmn. Info. Industry Assn.; past chair Ariz. Ctr. for the Book; past pres. Contemporary Forum of Phoenix Art Mus.; founding mem. Nat. Edn. Network, U.S. Dept. Edn.; past pres. Friends of the Librs., U.S.A.; mem. Ariz. Women's Forum. Recipient Women Who Make a Difference award The Internat. Women's Forum, 1995, Excellence in Pub. award Ariz. Book Pub. Assn., 1997, The Pub. History Program Ariz. State U. Founding Friend award, 2000; elected to Hunter Coll. Hall of Fame. Mem. ALA, Ariz. Libr. Assn., Univ. Club of Phoenix (pres.). Home and Office: 6446 N 28th St Phoenix AZ 85016-8946 E-mail: pbs@zephyrinfo.com

STEDMAN, DONALD HUGH, chemist, educator; BA, Cambridge U., 1964; MSc, U. East Anglia, 1965, PhD, 1967. Postdoctoral fellow Kans. State U., Manhattan, 1967-69; sr. rsch. scientist Ford Motor Co., Dearborn, Mich., 1969-71; from vis. lectr. to prof. U. Mich., Ann Arbor, 1971-83; Brainerd F. Phillipson prof. chemistry U. Denver, 1983—. Mem. AAAS, Am. Chem. Soc. (award for creative advances in environ. technology 1996), Air Waste Mgmt. Soc. (Frank A Chambers award 1996). Home: 2620 S Fillmore St Denver CO 80210-6213 Office: U Denver Dept Chemistry University Park Denver CO 80208-0001

STEED, ALLAN J. physical science research administrator; Dir. Space Dynamics Lab. Utah State U., Logan, Utah. Office: Utah State U Space Dynamics Lab Logan UT 84341-1942

STEEFEL, DAVID SIMON, lawyer; b. Mpls., June 27, 1951; s. Lawrence D. Jr. and Marion (Charlson) S.; m. Mary Ann Moody, May 24, 1981; children: Emily, Daniel, Katherine. BA, Carleton Coll., 1973; JD, U. Colo., 1978. Bar: Colo. 1978, U.S. Dist. Ct. Colo. 1978, U.S. Ct. Appeals (10th cir.) 1978. Assoc. Gorsuch, Kirgis, Denver, 1978-80, Holme Roberts & Owen, Denver, 1980-84, ptnr., 1984—. Instr. U. Colo. Law Sch., Boulder, 1978, 91. Home: 1300 Green Oaks Dr Littleton CO 80121-1331 Office: Holme Roberts & Owen 1700 Lincoln St Ste 4100 Denver CO 80203-4541 E-mail: steefed@hro.com

STEEL, JON, advertising executive; Vice chmn., strategic planning dir. Goodby Silverstein & Ptnrs., San Francisco. Office: Goodby Silverstein & Ptnrs 720 California St San Francisco CA 94108-2404

STEEL, RONALD LEWIS, writer, historian, educator; b. Morris, Ill., Mar. 25, 1931; BA magna cum laude, Northwestern U., 1953; MA, Harvard U., 1955. Vice consul U.S. Fgn. Service, 1957-58; editor Scholastic mag., N.Y.C., 1959-62; sr. assoc. Carnegie Endowment for Internat. Peace, 1982-83; fellow Woodrow Wilson Internat. Ctr. Scholars, 1984-85; prof. internat. relations U. So. Calif., Los Angeles, 1986—; fellow Wissenschaftskolleg zu Berlin, Federal Republic of Germany, 1988. Vis. fellow Yale U., 1971-73; vis. prof. U. Tex., 1977, 79, 80, 85, Wellesley Coll., 1978, Rutgers U., 1980, UCLA, 1981, Dartmouth Coll., 1983, Princeton U., 1984; Shapiro prof. internat. rels. George Washington U., 1995-97. Author books including: The End of Alliance: America and the Future of Europe, 1964, (with G. Kimble) Tropical Africa Today, 1966, Pax Americana, 1967, Imperialists and Other Heroes, 1971, Walter Lippmann and the American Century, 1980, Temptations of a Superpower, 1995, In Love With Night: The American Romance with Robert Kennedy, 2000; editor various publs. for H.W. Wilson Co., 1961-67; contbr. to N.Y. Rev. Books; contbg. editor New Republic. Served with U.S. Army, 1954-56. Recipient Sidney Hillman award, 1968, Washington Monthly book award, 1980, Los Angeles Tims book award for non-fiction, 1980, Nat. Book Critics Circle award, 1981, Bancroft prize Columbia U., 1981, Am. Book award for biography, 1982; Guggenheim fellow, 1973-74 Mem. Council on Fgn. Relations Office: U So Calif Sch Internat Rels Los Angeles CA 90089-0001

STEELE, BRUCE CARL, magazine editor; b. York, Pa., Sept. 9, 1959; s. William Melvin and Kaye Marilyn (Meyer) S.; m. Christopher Cornell Oakley, Feb. 14, 1987. BA, U. Ala., 1981; MFA, Columbia U., 1987. Staff editor Alexandria (La.) Daily Town Talk, 1982-85; sr. editor Cahners Pub., N.Y.C., 1987-92; mng. editor Out Mag., N.Y.C., 1992-95, exec. editor, 1995-97, entertainment editor, 1997-99; exec. editor The Advocate, L.A., 1999—. Office: The Advocate 6922 Hollywood Blvd Fl 10 Los Angeles CA 90028-6117

STEELE, CHARLES GLEN, retired accountant; b. Faulkton, S.D., July 24, 1925; s. Clifford D. and Emily O. (Hanson) S.; m. Shirley June Ferguson, Nov. 9, 1947; children: Richard Alan (dec.), Deborah Ann Steele Most. B.B.A., Golden Gate U., San Francisco, 1951, M.B.A., 1962. With Deloitte Haskins & Sells, 1951-86, partner, 1963-86, partner charge Chgo. office, 1973-76, partner charge personnel and adminstrn., 1976-78, chmn., chief exec. officer, 1978-86. Instr. evening program Golden Gate U., 1952-58. Served with USNR, 1943-48. Recipient Elijah Watts Sells Gold medal for highest grade in U.S. for C.P.A. exam., 1951 Mem. Am. Inst. C.P.A.s. Home and Office: 26349 Rio Ave Carmel CA 93923

STEELE, CHARLES RICHARD, biomedical and mechanical engineering educator; b. Royal, Iowa, Aug. 15, 1933; married, 1969; 4 children. BS, Tex. A&M U., 1956; PhD in Applied Mechanics, Stanford U., 1960; PhD (hon.), Zaporozhye State U., Ukraine, 1997. Engring. specialist aircraft structure Chance-Vought Aircraft, Dallas, 1959-60; rsch. scientist shell theory Lockheed Rsch. Lab., Palo Alto, 1960-66; assoc. prof. Stanford (Calif.) U., 1966-71, prof. applied mechanics, 1971—. Lectr. U. Calif., Berkeley, 1964-65; vis. prof. Swiss Fed. Inst. Technology, Zurich, 1971-72, U. Luleá, Sweden, 1982, Chung Kung U., Taiwan, 1985, U. Cape Town, South Africa, spring 1993, U. Trento, Italy, fall 1999; tech. dir. Shelltech Assoc. Editor-in-chief: Internat. Jour. Solids Structures, 1985—. Recipient NIH Claude Pepper award, 1988, Humboldt award, 1994; named Eminent Academician Ukrainian Acad., 1998. Fellow ASME (chmn. exec. com. applied mechanics divsn. 1983-84, Warner T. Koiter medal 1999), Am. Acad. Mechanics (pres. 1989-90); mem. AIAA, NAE, Acoustical Soc. Am. Achievements include research in asymptotic analysis in mechanics; thin shell theory; mechanics of the inner ear; noninvasive determination of bone stiffness; and morphology of plants. Office: Stanford U Divsn Mechanics & Computat Durand Bldg 355A Stanford CA 94305-4040

STEELE, CRAIG, construction executive; CEO, pres. Schuck & Sons Constrn. Co., Glendale, AZ, 1972—. Mem. Home Aid Ariz., Maricopa Workforce Connection. Office: Schuck & Sons Contruction Co 8205 N 67th Ave Glendale AZ 85302-5505

STEELE, CYNTHIA, literary critic, translator, educator; b. Colusa, Calif., Aug. 7, 1951; d. Ned and Lorraine (Heard) S. BA in English and Spanish, Calif. State U., Chico, 1973; MA in Spanish Lit., U. Calif., San Diego, 1979, PhD in Spanish Lit., 1980. Asst. prof. Spanish Ohio State U., Columbus, 1980-85, Columbia U., N.Y.C., 1985-86; from asst. prof. to assoc. prof. Spanish U. Wash., Seattle, 1986-96, prof. Spanish, Comparative Lit. and Internat. Studies, 1996—. Mem. joint com. Latin Am. studies Social Sci. Rsch. Coun.-Am. Coun. Learned Socs., N.Y.C., 1994-96; del. West Coast MLA, N.Y.C., 1996—; bd. dirs. Inst. de Lit. Iberoamericana, Pitts., 1996—. Translator: Underground River and Other Stories by Inés Arredondo, 1996; (with David Laur) City of Memory (José Emilio Pacheco), 1997. Advanced grantee Social Sci. Rsch. Coun., 1990-91; Royalty Rsch. grantee U. Wash. Grad. Sch., 1997—. Mem. Latin Am. Studies Assn. Democrat. Avocations: movies, travel in Latin America. Office: U Wash Dept Spanish & Portuguese Seattle WA 98195-0001

STEELE, DALE F. women's healthcare company executive; Co-founder, CFO, M.W. Steele Group, 1983-89, corp. sec., treas., 1994-96; owner, mgr. Dale Fitzmorris, 1989-94; co-founder, co-CEO, As We Change, LLC, 1995-98; v.p. catalog ops. Women First HealthCare, Inc., San Diego, 1998—. Office: Women First HealthCare Inc 12220 El Camino Real Ste 400 San Diego CA 92130-2091 Fax: 619-509-1353

STEELE, DAVID H. state legislator; m. Sharon Nauta; 7 children. BS in Math., Utah State U., 1971, MEd, 1978, postgrad., 1986, Calif. Poly, 1984. Cert. tchr. and adminstr., Utah. Dir. instructional tech., dir. adult and continuing edn. Davis Sch. Dist.; mem. Utah Senate, Dist. 21, Salt Lake City, 1986—; mem. transp. and pub. safety com., mem. edn. com.; co-chair exec. and natural resources appropriations. Mem. steering com. Edn. Commn. of the states; chair Edn. and Job Tng. Com.; co-chair Info. Tech. Commn. Utah. Republican. Office: 320 S 500 E Kaysville UT 84037-3307

STEELE, KAREN DORN, journalist; b. Portland, Oreg., Oct. 27, 1943; d. Ronald Gottche and Margaret Elizabeth (Cates) Moxness; m. Charles Stuart Dorn, Oct. 30, 1965 (div. Oct. 1982); children: Trilby Constance Elizabeth Dorn, Blythe Estella Dorn; m. Richard Donald Steele, July 4, 1983. BA, Stanford U., 1965; MA, U. Calif., Berkeley, 1967. Prodr. Sta. KSPS-TV, Spokane, Wash., 1970-72, dir. news and pub. affairs, 1972-82; reporter Spokesman-Rev., Spokane, 1982-87, environ./spl. projects reporter, 1987—. Contbr. articles to sci. publs. (Olive Br. award NYU Ctr. War, Peace & The Media 1989). Bd. dirs. Women Helping Women, Spokane, 1994; trustee St. George's Sch., Spokane, 1988-92. Mid-career fellow Stanford Knight Fellowship Program, 1986-87, Arms Control fellow Ctr. for Internat. Security and Arms Control, Stanford U., 1986-87; Japan Travel grantee Japan Press Found., Tokyo, 1987, rsch. grantee John D. and Catherine T. MacArthur Found., 1992; recipient Gerald Loeb award Anderson Sch. Mgmt. UCLA, 1995, George Polk award L.I. U., 1995, William Stokes award U. Mo., 1988, Nat. Headliner award Wash. State Bar Assn., 2000; inductee State Hall of Journalistic Achievement, Wash. State U., Pullman, 1995. Unitarian. Office: Spokesman Rev PO Box 2160 999 W Riverside Ave Spokane WA 99201-1098 E-mail: karend@spokesman.com

STEELE, ROBERT EDWIN, orthopedic surgeon; b. Kansas City, Mo., Jan. 8, 1937; s. Robert Edwin and Margaret Jane (Levens) S.; m. Emily Wells Stephens, May 9, 1964; children: Edward Stephen, Thomas McKewon, Linda Katherine. AB, U. Mo., 1959; MD cum laude, Harvard U., 1963. Diplomate Am. Bd. Orthopedic Surgery; cert. Am. Acad. Orthopedic Surgeons, Assn. Arthritic Hip and Knee Surgery. Intern Mass. Gen. Hosp., Boston, 1963-64; resident in orthopedics Harvard U., 1966-71; instr. in orthopedic surgery Harvard Med. Sch., Boston, 1971; mem. med. staff Good Samaritan Hosp., Corvallis, Oreg., 1971—. Bd. dirs. Good Samaritan Hosp., 1984-88, pres. med. staff, 1985, chmn. peer rev. com., 1994. Author: Studies on Osteonecrusis, 1979. Lt. USNR, 1964-66, Vietnam. Recipient Kappa Delta award for Outstanding Orthopedic Rsch., Am. Acad. Orthopedic Surgeons, 1978. Mem. Corvallis Orthopedic Surgeons (pres. 1990). Achievements include performance of total knee replacement. Avocations: camping, cycling, hiking, skiing, white water boating. Office: Speciality Physicians & Surgeons Corvallis 3640 NW Samaritan Dr Corvallis OR 97330-3784

STEELE, SHELBY, writer, educator; b. Chgo., 1946; s. Shelby Sr. and Ruth S. Grad., Coe Loll., 1968; M in Sociology, So. Ill. U., 1971; PhD in English, U. Utah, 1974. Prof. dept English Calif. State U., San Jose; rsch. fellow Hoover Instn., Stanford, Calif. Author: The Content of Our Character: A New Vision of Race in America, 1991 (Nat. Book Critics Circle award 1991), A Dream Deferred: The Second Betrayal of Black Freedom in America, 1998; contbr. essays to profl. jours. Office: Hoover Inst Pub Affairs Stanford Univ Stanford CA 94305-6010

STEELE, VICTORIA LEE, librarian; b. L.A., Feb. 24, 1952; d. John Wilms and Marjorie (Lee) Erpelding; m. Timothy Reid, Jan. 14, 1979. BA, UCLA, 1974, MLS, 1981; MA, U. So. Calif., 1993, PhD, 2000. Libr. Belt Libr. of Vinciana UCLA, 1981-82, head history and spl. collections Biomed. Libr., 1983-86, dir. devel. librs., 1986-88; head spl. collections Young Rsch. Libr., 2000—; head spl. collections U. So. Calif., L.A., 1988-2000. Fundraising cons.; mem. adv. bd. KUSC Radio, 1997-2000. Author: Becoming a Fundraiser, 1992, 2d edit., 2000; prodr. film: Every time I See a Patient..., 1994; contbr. articles to profl. publs. Mem. adv. bd. Fulbright Program for So. Calif., 1995—, Mus. Found. Fashion Inst. Design and Merchandising, 2000—, Archives of Am. Art, 2000—; mem. adv. coun. Annenberg Sch. for Comm. U. So. Calif., 1994-2000; founder L.A. Preservation Network; vol. Save Outdoor Sculpture, 1995—; bd. dirs. Heritage Preservation. U. Calif. rsch. grantee, 1979, U. So. Calif. rsch. grantee, 1995; Fulbright fellow (U.K.), 1995, fellow L.A. Inst. for Humanities, 2000—. Mem. ALA (3M/JMRT award 1982, G.K. Hall award 1995), Calif. Hist. Soc. (bd. dirs. 2000—). Office: UCLA Young Rsch Libr Dept Spl Collections Box 951575 Los Angeles CA 90095-1575

STEEN, PAUL JOSEPH, retired broadcasting executive; b. Williston, N.D., July 4, 1932; s. Ernest B. and Inez (Ingebrigtson) S.; m. Judith Smith; children— Michael M., Melanie. BA, Pacific Luth. U., 1954; MS, Syracuse U., 1957. Producer, dir. Sta. KNTV, San Jose, Calif., 1957-58, Sta. KVIE, Sacramento, 1958-60; asst. prof. telecommunications Pacific Luth. U., Tacoma, 1960-67; dir. ops. Sta. KPBS San Diego State U., 1967-74; gen. mgr., 1974-93; prof. telecommunications and film, 1974-93; dir. univ. telecommunications. Co-chmn. Office of New Tech. Initiatives. Dir. (tel. program) Troubled Waters (winner Nat. Ednl. TV award of excellence 1970). With AUS. Named Danforth Assoc. Mem. Pacific Mountain Network (bd. dirs., chmn., bd. of govs. award 1993), NATAS, Assn. Calif. Pub. TV Stas. (pres.), Pi Kappa Delta. Home: 6068 Caminito De La Taza San Diego CA 92120-5323 E-mail: psteen@mail.sdsu.edu

STEER, REGINALD DAVID, lawyer; b. N.Y.C., July 16, 1945; s. Joseph D. and Rozica (Yusim) S.; m. Marianne Spizzy, July 22, 1983; children: Derek B., Trevor A. BA, U. Minn., 1966, JD, 1969. Bar: Minn. 1969, Calif. 1973, U.S. Dist. Ct. (no., ea. and cen. dists.) Calif., U.S. Ct. Mil. Appeals 1969, U.S. Ct. Appeals (9th cir.), U.S. Ct. Appeals (11th cir.), U.S. Supreme Ct. 1981, U.S. Ct. Internat. Trade, 1994. Assoc. Pillsbury, Madison & Sutro, San Francisco, 1973-79, ptnr., 1979-2000, Skjerven Morrill MacPherson, LLP, San Francisco, 2000—. Mem. exec. com., 1997-98; lectr. Calif. Continuing Edn. of Bar, San Francisco, 1981, Petroleum Attys. Meeting, Washington, 1996. Served to capt. U.S. Army, 1969-73. Fellow Am. Coll. Trial Lawyers; mem. ABA (antitrust and litigation sects.). Avocations: piano, tennis, photography. Office: Skjerven Morrill 3 Embarcadero Ctr 28th Fl San Francisco CA 94111 E-mail: rsteer@skjerven.com

STEERS, GEORGE W. lawyer; b. N.Y.C., Jan. 29, 1941; BA, Yale U., 1963; LLB cum laude, Columbia U., 1966. Bar: Wash. 1970. Law clk. U.S. Ct. Appeals (2d cir.), 1966-67; prin. Stoel Rives, LLP, Seattle, 1974—. Mem. ABA, Wash. State Bar Assn., Seattle-King County Bar Assn. Office: Stoel Rives LLP One Union Sq 600 University St Ste 3600 Seattle WA 98101-4109

STEFFAN, WALLACE ALLAN, entomologist, educator, museum director; b. St. Paul, Aug. 10, 1934; m. Sylvia Behler, July 16, 1966; 1 child, Sharon. BS, U. Calif., Berkeley, 1961, PhD, 1965. Entomologist dept. entomology Bishop Mus., Honolulu, 1964-85, head diptera sect., 1966-85, asst. chmn., 1979-85; dir. Idaho Mus. Natural History, Idaho State U., Pocatello, 1985-89, U. Alaska Mus., 1989-92; prof. biology U. Alaska, Fairbanks, 1989-92; exec. dir. Gt. Valley Mus. Natural History, 1992-94, Sun Cities Mus. Art, 1995-97, Burpee Mus. Natural History, Rockford, Ill., 1997-00, West Valley Art Mus., 2000—. Mem. grad. affiliate faculty dept. entomology, U. Hawaii, 1969-85; reviewer NSF, 1976-94; mem. affiliate faculty biology, Idaho State U., 1986-89. Acting editor Jour. Med. Entomology, 1966; assoc. editor Pacific Insects, 1980-85. Bd. dirs. Idaho State U. Fed. Credit Union, 1986-89; mem. adv. coun. Moesto Conv. and Visitors Bur., 1992-95; mem. Ft. Hall Replica Commn., 1986-89; judge Hawaii State Sci. and Engring. Fair, 1966-85, chief judge sr. display divsn., 1982, 83, 84; advisor to bd. Fairbanks Conv. and Visitors Bur., 1989-91; mem. vestry St. Christopher's Episcopal Ch., 1974-76, St. Matthew's Episcopal Ch., Fairbanks, 1990-91; pres. Alaska Visitors Assn., Fairbanks, 1991; advisor Fairbanks Conv. and Visitors Bur. Bd., 1989-91; bd. dirs. Kamehameha Fed. Credit Union, 1975-77, chmn., mem. supervisory com., 1980-84. With USAF, 1954-57. Grantee NIH, 1962, 63, 67-74, 76-81, 83-85, U.S. Army Med. Rsch. and Devel. Command, 1964-67, 73-74, NSF, 1968-76, 83-89, City and County of Honolulu, 1977, U.S. Dept. Interior, 1980, 81. Mem. Entomol. Soc. Am. (standing com. on systematics resources 1983-87), Pacific Coast Entomol. Soc., Soc. Systematic Zoology, Hawaiian Entomol. Soc. (pres. 1974, chmn. coms. 1966-85, editor procs. 1966), Hawaiian Acad. (councillor 1976-78), Sigma Xi (pres. San Joaquin chpt. 1994-95), Northwest Passage Immigrants and Ingenuity (pres. exec. com. 1998-00, v.p.), Ill. Assn. Museums (bd. dirs. 1998-00), Assn. Midwest Mus. (chair local arrangements com.), N.W. Valley C. of C. (bd. dirs. 2001—). Office: West Valley Art Mus 17420 N Ave of Arts Surprise AZ 85374

STEFFEN, THOMAS LEE, former state supreme court justice, lawyer; b. Tremonton, Utah, July 9, 1930; s. Conrad Richard and Jewel (McGuire) S.; m. LaVona Ericksen, Mar. 20, 1953; children— Elizabeth, Catherine, Conrad, John, Jennifer Student, U. So. Calif., 1955-56; BS, U. Utah, 1957; JD with honors, George Washington U., 1964; LLM, U. Va., 1988. Bar: Nev. 1965, U.S. Dist. Ct. Nev. 1965, U.S. Tax Ct. 1966, U.S. Ct. Appeals 1967, U.S. Supreme Ct. 1977. Contracts negotiator U.S. Bur. Naval Weapons, Washington, 1961-64; private practice Las Vegas, 1965-82; justice Supreme Ct. Nev., Carson City, 1982-94, chief justice, 1995-97, ret., 1997, chmn. code of jud. conduct study com., 1991; of counsel Hutchison & Steffen, Las Vegas, also Provo, Utah, 1997—. Vice chmn. Nev. State Jud. Edn. Coun., 1983-84; chmn. Nev. State-Fed. Jud. Coun., 1986-91, mem., 1986-93. Mem. editorial staff George Washington U. Law Rev., 1963-64; contbr. articles to legal jours. Bd. dirs. So. Nev. chpt. NCCJ, 1974-75; mem. exec. bd. Boulder Dam Area coun. Boy Scouts Am., 1979-83; bd. visitors Brigham Young U., 1985-89. Recipient merit citation Utah State U., 1983 Mem. Nev. Bar Assn. (former chmn. So. Nev. med.-legal screening panel), Nev. Trial Lawyers Assn. (former dir.) Republican. Mem. LDS Ch. Avocations: reading, spectator sports. Office: Lakes Business Park 8831 W Sahara Ave Las Vegas NV 89117-5865 also: 481 E Normandy Dr Provo UT 84604-5963 E-mail: Tlsrcjnset@aol.com

STEFFENSEN, DWIGHT A. medical products and data processing services executive; b. Fresno, Calif., 1943; BA, Stanford U., 1965. Corp. contr. Synergex Corp. (merged with Bergen Brunswig Corp. 1985), Orange, Calif., 1969-72, chief fin. officer, v.p., 1972-80, chief oper. officer, chief fin. officer, exec. v.p., treas., 1980-83, pres., chief exec. officer, 1983-85, exec. v.p., 1985—; pres. Drug Service Inc., 1975-80; pres., coo, dir. Bergen Brunswig Corp.; chmn. & CEO Merisel, Inc., El Segundo, Calif., 1996—. Office: Merisel Inc 200 Continental Blvd El Segundo CA 90245-4510

STEFFEY, EUGENE PAUL, veterinary medicine educator; b. Reading, Pa., Oct. 27, 1942; s. Paul E. and Mary M. (Balthaser) S.; children: Michele A., Bret E., Michael R., Brian T. Student, Muhlenberg Coll., 1960-63; D in Vet. Medicine, U. Pa., 1967; PhD, U. Calif., Davis, 1973. Diplomate Am. Coll. Vet. Anesthesiologists (pres. 1980). NIH spl. research fellow U. Calif., San Francisco, 1973, asst. prof. Davis, 1974-77, assoc. prof., 1977-80, prof. vet. medicine, 1980—, also chmn. dept. vet. surgery, 1980-93. Mem. scientific reviewers Am. Jour. Vet. Research, Schaumburg, Ill., 1984-87. Contbr. more than 150 articles to profl. jours. Mem. AVMA, Am. Coll. Vet. Anesthesiologists, Am. Physiol. Soc., Am. Soc. Pharmacology Exptl. Therapeutics, Am. Soc. Anesthesiologists, Assn. Vet. Anaesthetists, Calif. Soc. Anesthesiologists, European Coll. Vet. Anesthesia, Internat. Anesthesia Rsch. Soc., Pa. Vet. Med. Assn., Royal Coll. Vet. Surgeons (hon. assoc.), Sigma Xi, Phi Zeta. Office: U Calif Dept Surg Radiol Scis School of Vet Medicine Davis CA 95616

STEGEMEIER, RICHARD JOSEPH, oil company executive; b. Alton, Ill., Apr. 1, 1928; s. George Henry and Rose Ann (Smola) S.; m. Marjorie Ann Spess, Feb. 9, 1952; children: Richard Michael, David Scott, Laura Ann, Martha Louise. BS in Petroleum Engring., U. Mo., Rolla, 1950, cert. petroleum engr. (hon.), 1981; MS in Petroleum Engring., Tex. A&M U., 1951; D of Engring. (hon.), U. Mo., Rolla, 1990. Registered profl. engr., Calif. Various nat. and internat. mgmt. positions with Unocal Corp. (formerly Union Oil Co.), L.A., 1951—, pres. sci. and tech. div., 1979-80, sr. v.p. corp. devel., 1980-85, pres., COO, 1985-88, CEO, also chmn. bd. dirs., 1988-94, bd. dirs., 1988—. Bd. dirs. First Interstate Bancorp, Found. Health Corp., Halliburton Co., Northrop Corp., Outboard Marine Corp. Patentee in field. Bd. dirs. Calif. Econ. Devel. Corp.; bd. govs. Town Hall of Calif., The Music Ctr. of L.A. County; bd. overseers Exec. Coun. on Fgn. Diplomats, Huntington Libr.; chmn. L.A. World Affairs Coun., 1990-94; pres. World Affairs Coun. of Orange County, 1980-82; chmn. Brea (Calif.) Blue Ribbon Com., 1979-80 ; trustee Com. for Econ. Devel., U. So. Calif., Harvey Mudd Coll., Loyola Marymount U.; mem. adv. bds. Northwestern U. Kellogg Grad. Sch. of Mgmt.; bd. vis. UCLA Anderson Grad. Sch. of Mgmt., U. Mo., Rolla; mem. adv. bd. Calif. State U., Fullerton, adv. coun., Long Beach; bd. dirs. YMCA of L.A., L.A. Philharm. Assn., John Tracy Clinic; chmn. L.A. area coun. Boy Scouts of Am., Calif. C. of C. chmn., 1994; gen. campaign chmn. United Way of Greater L.A., 1990-91; trustee and immediate past pres. Hugh O'Brian Youth Found., 1993-94, L.A. Archdiocese Edn. Found. Recipient Merit award Orange County Engring. Coun., 1980, Outstanding Engr. Merit award Inst. Advancement Engring., 1981, Disting. Achievement medal Tex. A&M U., Hugh O'Brian Youth Found. Albert Schweitzer Leadership award, 1990, Human Rels. award Am. Jewish Com., 1990. Mem. AIChE (Disting. Career award So. Calif. sect. 1989), NAM (bd. dirs.), Nat. Acad. Engring., Am. Petroleum Inst. (bd. dirs.), Soc. Petroleum Engrs. (lectr. 1978), Nat. Petroleum Coun., 25 Yr. Club Petroleum Industry (past pres.), Calif. Bus. Roundtable, Calif. Coun. on Sci. and Tech., Calif. Club. Republican. Roman Catholic. Office: Unical 76 Corporation 376 Valencia Ave Brea CA 92823-6345

STEGNER, JOE, state legislator; Mem. Idaho Senate, Dist. 6, Boise, 1998—. Vice chair health and welfare com., mem. commerce and human resources and local govt. and tax. coms. Republican. Office: State Capitol PO Box 83720 Boise ID 83720-3720

STEIN, BENJAMIN J. television personality, writer, lawyer, economist; b. Washington, Nov. 25, 1944; s. Herbert and Mildred (Fishman) S.; m. Alexandra Denman, June 22, 1968. BA, Columbia U., 1966; LLB, Yale U., 1970. Bar: Conn. Trial lawyer FTC, Washington, 1970-72; speech writer The White House, Washington, 1973-74; columnist The Wall St. Jour., N.Y.C., 1974-76; writer, commentator, columnist The Los Angeles Herald-Examiner, 1978-87; currently TV personality Win Ben Stein's Money Comedy Ctrl., 1996—, host Turn Ben Stein On, 1999—. Fin. cons. LAACO, Inc., Los Angeles; contbg. editor The Am. Spectator, 1980—; law tchr. Pepperdine, Malibu, 1992—. Author: On The Brink. 1977, Moneypower, 1980, Financial Passages, 1986; author numerous articles on leveraged buy-outs and other fin. frauds for Barrons, 1984—. Recipient Emmy award for Best Game Show Host, 1999. Mem. Writers Guild Am., Screen Actors' Guild, Am. Fedn. TV and Radio Actors. Republican. Jewish. Clubs: Los Angeles Athletic, Calif. Yacht. Office: 8787 Shoreham Dr West Hollywood CA 90069-2231

STEIN, BEVERLY, county official; BA, U. Calif., Berkeley, 1970; JD, U. Wis., 1976. Chair Bd. County Commrs., Portland, Oreg., 1993—. Office: Portland Bldg 1120 SW 5th Ave Rm 1515 Portland OR 97204-1912

STEIN, GREG, legislative staff member; b. Calif. BA in Polit. Sci., U. Calif., San Diego, 1992. Assoc. software quality engr. Sci. Applications Internat. Corp., San Diego, 1988-89; asst. mgr. publs. U. Calif. San Diego Mac's Place Computing Ctr., 1989-92; acad. intern, asst. caseworker U.S. Rep. Bill Lowery, San Diego, 1992; sys. mgr., legis. asst. U.S. Rep. Jay Dickey, Washington, 1993-94; dir. field ops. Brian Bilbray for Congress Com., San Diego, 1994, campaign mgr., 1998; sr. legis. asst. U.S. Rep. Brian P. Bilbray, Washington, 1995-97, dist. dir. San Diego, 1998—. Longboard luau com. U. Calif. San Diego Cancer Ctr., 1997-99; mem. CEO roundtable, subcom. on immigration U. Calif. San Diego CONNECT, 1998; mem. 12th and 13th Ann. Celebri-T Auction com. San Diego Youth and Cmty. Svcs., chmn. assoc. bd. dirs. 1999; mem. Golden Fleece and Golden Watchdog awards com. San Diego County Taxpayers Assn., 1999; bd. mem. Rep. Assocs. San Diego County. Mem. U. Calif. San Diego Alumni Assn., Lincoln Club San Diego County, Order of Omega, Phi Kappa Theta (former nat. sec., bd. mem., chpt. pres., founder). Avocations: softball, sailing, running, surfing. Office: 1011 Camino Del Rio S Ste 330 San Diego CA 92108-3534 E-mail: greg.stein@mail.house.gov

STEIN, KARL N. plastic and reconstructive surgeon; b. Phila., July 1, 1940; m. Sandra Diane Segal; children: Laura, Leigh. BA in Chemistry, Temple U., 1962, MD, 1966. Diplomate Am. Bd. Plastic Surgery. Intern U. Pa. Grad. Hosp., 1966-67; resident in surgery Abington Meml. Hosp., 1967-68, SUNY Up-State Med. Ctr., 1970-71, instr. in surgery, 1970—; resident in plastic surgery Hosp. Albert Einstein Coll. Medicine, Bronx Mcpl. Hosp. Ctr., 1971-74, asst. instr. plastic surgery and hand surgery, 1974; pvt. practice in plastic surgery, 1974—. Surgeon Sherman Oaks (Calif.) Burn Ctr., 1975—; cons. L.A. Dept. Water and Power; med. legal expert for burns and plastic surgery. Author (patent) Treatment of Tar Burns, 1980. Capt. USAF, 1969-71. Fellow Am. Coll. Surgeons; mem. AMA, Am. Soc. Plastic and Reconstructive Surgeons, Am. Burn Assn., Am. Assn. Hand Surgery, Am. Soc. Aesthetic Plastic Surgery, Calif. Soc. Plastic Surgeons, Calif. Med. Assn., L.A. Soc. Plastic Surgeons, L.A. County Med. Assn. Office: PO Box 220340 Newhall CA 91322-0340

STEIN, MICHAEL A. pharmaceutical executive; CFO Marriott Internat., Inc., Washington; v.p., CFO ICOS Corp., Bothell, Wash., 2001—. Office: ICOS Corp 22021 20th Ave SE Bothell WA 98021

STEINBERG, CHARLES ALLAN, electronics manufacturing company executive; b. Bklyn., June 7, 1934; s. Joseph and Rose (Graff) S.; m. Helen Greene, June 16, 1956; children— Ruth, Steven, Bruce. B.S.E.E., CCNY, 1955; M.S.E.E., M.I.T., 1958. Mem. tech. staff Bell Telephone Labs., Whippany, N.J., 1955; research and teaching asst. MIT, 1955-58; engring. sect. mgr. Airborne Instruments Lab. div. Eaton Corp., Deer Park, N.Y., 1958-63; exec. v.p. Ampex Corp., Redwood City, Calif., 1963-86, pres., chief exec. officer, 1986-88; pres. broadcast and profl. co. Sony Corp. Am., Montvale, N.J., 1988-99, sr. advisor San Jose, Calif., 1999—. Contbr. numerous articles on med. electronics and diagnosis, info. systems to profl. jours.; patentee computer techniques in medicine. Bd. dirs. Santa Clara County (Calif.) United Fund, 1969-71. Mem. IEEE, CCNY Alumni Assn., M.I.T. Alumni Assn., Sigma Xi, Tau Beta Pi, Eta Kappa Nu. Office: Sony Electronics 3300 Zanker Rd San Jose CA 95134-1901

STEINBERG, DANIEL, preventive medicine physician, educator; b. Windsor, Ont., Can., July 21, 1922; came to U.S., 1922; s. Maxwell Robert and Bess (Krupp) S.; m. Sara Murdock, Nov. 30, 1946 (dec. July 1986); children: Jonathan Henry, Ann Ballard, David Ethan; m. Mary Ellen Stratthaus, Aug. 11, 1991; 1 stepchild: Katrin Seifert. B.S. with highest distinction, Wayne State U., 1941, M.D. with highest distinction, 1944; Ph.D. with distinction (fellow Am. Cancer Soc. 1950-51), Harvard U., 1951; M.D. (hon.), U. Gothenburg, 1991. Intern Boston City Hosp., 1944-45; physician Detroit Receiving Hosp., 1945-46; instr. physiology Boston U. Sch. Medicine, 1947-48; joined USPHS, 1951, med. dir., 1959; research staff lab. cellular physiology and metabolism Nat. Heart Inst., 1951-53, chief sect. metabolism, 1956-61, chief of lab. metabolism, 1962-68; lectr. grad. program NIH, 1955, mem. sci. adv. com. ednl. activities, 1955-61, com. chmn., 1955-60; mem. metabolism study sect. USPHS, 1959-61; chmn. heart and lung research rev. com. B Nat. Heart, Lung and Blood Inst., 1977-79; vis. scientist Carlsberg Labs., Copenhagen, 1952-53, Nat. Inst. Med. Research, London, 1960-61, Rockefeller U., 1981; pres. Lipid Research Inc., 1961-64, adv. bd., 1964-73; prof. medicine Sch. Medicine, U. Calif., San Diego, 1968—. Former editor Jour. Lipid Research; mem. editorial bd. Jour Clin. Investigation, 1969-74, Jour. Biol. Chemistry, 1980-84, Arteriosclerosis, 1980— ; exec. editor Analytical Biochemistry, 1978-80; contbr. articles to profl. jours. Bd. dirs. Found. Advanced Edn. in Scis., 1959-68, pres., 1956-62, 65-67. Served to capt. M.C. AUS, World War II. Mem. Nat. Acad. Scis., AAAS, Am. Acad. Arts and Scis., Am. Heart Assn. (mem. exec. com. coun. on arteriosclerosis 1960-63, 65-73, chmn. coun. arteriosclerosis 1967-69), Fedn. Am. Scientists (exec. com. 1957-58), Am. Soc. Biol. Chemists, Am. Soc. Clin. Investigation, Assn. Am. Physicians, Am. Fedn. Clin. Rsch., Inst. Medicine, European Atherosclerosis Discussion Group, Alpha Omega Alpha. Home: 7742 Whitefield Pl La Jolla CA 92037-3810 Office: U Calif San Diego Dept Medicine 9500 Gilman Dr La Jolla CA 92093-0682 E-mail: dsteinberg@ucsd.edu, dsteinb1@san.rr.com

STEINBERG, WARREN LINNINGTON, school principal; b. N.Y.C., Jan. 20, 1924; s. John M. and Gertrude (Vogel) S.; m. Beatrice Ruth Blass, June 29, 1947; children: Leigh William, James Robert, Donald Kenneth. Student, U. So. Calif., 1943-44; BA, UCLA, 1949, MEd, 1951, EdD, 1962. Tchr., counselor, coach Jordan H.S., Watts, L.A., 1951-57; tchr., athletic coord. Hamilton H.S., L.A., 1957-62; boys' vice prin. Univ. H.S., L.A., 1962-67, Crenshaw H.S., L.A., 1967-68; cons. Ctr. for Planned Change, L.A. City Sch., 1968-69; instr. edn. UCLA, 1965-71; boys' vice prin. LeConte Jr. J.S., L.A., 1969-71, sch. prin., 1971-77; adminstrv. cons. on integration L.A. Unified Sch. Dist., 1977-81, adminstr. student-to-student interaction program, 1981-82; prin. Gage Jr. H.S., 1982-83, Fairfax H.S., 1983-90. Pres. Athletic Coords. Assn., L.A. Unified Sch. Dist., 1959-60; v.p. P-3 Enterprises, Inc., Port Washington, N.Y., 1967-77, Century City (Calif.) Enterprises, 1966-88. Contbr. articles on race rels., youth behavior to profl. jours. and newspapers. V.p. B'nai B'rith Anti-Defamation League, 1968-70; mem. adv. com. L.A. City Commn. on Human Rels., 1966-71, 72-76, commr., 1976—, pres., 1978-87, also chmn. edn. com.; mem. human rels. commn. L.A. Unified Sch. Dist., 1999—, mem. citizens adv. com. for student integration, 1976-79; mem. del. assembly Cmty. Rels. Conf. So. Calif., 1975-91; chmn. So. Calif. Drug Abuse Edn. Month com., 1970; bd. dirs. DAWN, The Seedling, 1993-95, Project ECHO—Entrepreneurial Concepts, Hands-On, 1996—; mem., chmn. case conf. human rels. West L.A. Coordinating Coun. With USMCR, 1943-46. Recipient Beverly Hills B'nai B'rith Presdl. award, 1965, Pres.'s award Cmty. Rels. Conf. So. Calif., 1990, Lifetime Achievement award L.A. City Human Rels. Commn., 1996, award L.A. Unified Sch. Dist. Bd. Edn., 1997, commendation L.A. City Coun., 1968, 88. Mem. Beverly-Fairfax C. of C. (bd. dirs. 1986-88), Lions (bd. dirs. 1960-62), Kiwanis. Home: 2737 Dunleer Pl Los Angeles CA 90064-4303

STEINBOCK, JOHN THOMAS, bishop; b. L.A., July 16, 1937; Student, L.A. Diocesan sems. Ordained priest Roman Cath. Ch., 1963. Aux. bishop Diocese of Orange, Calif., 1984-87; bishop Diocese of Santa Rosa, 1987-91; titular bishop of Midila, 1984; bishop Diocese of Fresno, Calif., 1991—. Office: Diocese of Fresno 1550 N Fresno St Fresno CA 93703-3711 Fax: 559-488-7464

STEINER, HERBERT MAX, physics educator; b. Goeppingen, Germany, Dec. 8, 1927; came to U.S., 1939, naturalized, 1944; s. Albert and Martha (Epstein) S. B.S., U. Calif., Berkeley, 1951, Ph.D., 1956. Physicist Lawrence Berkeley Lab., Berkeley, Calif., 1956—; mem. faculty U. Calif., Berkeley, 1958—, prof. physics, 1966-2000, prof. emeritus, 2000—, William H. McAdams prof. physics, chmn. dept., 1992-95; vis. scientist European Center Nuclear Research, 1960-61, 64, 68-69, 82-83, Max Planck Inst. Physics and Astrophysics, Munich, 1976-77; vis. prof. Japanese Soc. Promotion Sci., 1978. Vis. prof. physics U. Paris, 1989-90; vis. scientist Deutsches Electron Synchrotron Lab., 1995-96. Author articles in field. Served with AUS, 1946-47. Recipient Sr. Am. Scientist award Alexander von Humboldt Found., 1976-77; Guggenheim fellow, 1960-61 Fellow Am. Phys. Soc. Office: U Calif Berkeley Dept Physics 7300 Berkeley CA 94720-0001

STEINER, KENNETH DONALD, bishop; b. David City, Nebr., Nov. 25, 1936; s. Lawrence Nicholas and Florine Marie (Pieters) S. B.A., Mt. Angel Sem., 1958; M.Div., St. Thomas Sem., 1962. Ordained priest Roman Catholic Ch., 1962, bishop, 1978; asso. pastor various parishes Portland and Coos Bay, Oreg., 1962-72; pastor Coquille Ch., Myrtle Point, Powers, 1972-76, St. Francis Ch., Roy, 1976-77; aux. bishop Diocese of Portland, 1977—; pastor St. Mary's Ch., Corvallis, 1986—. Adminstr. Archdiocese Portland, 1995-96. Democrat. Office: Saint Marys Cath Ch 501 NW 25th St Corvallis OR 97330-5415

STEINER, RICHARD RUSSELL, textile & apparel company executive; b. Chgo., Feb. 26, 1923; s. Frank Gardner and Ruth (Cowie) S.; m. Colleen M. Kearns, Dec. 6, 1949; children— Robert C., Kevin K., Sheila M. B.A., Dartmouth Coll., 1948. With Steiner Corp., Salt Lake City, 1948—, divisonal dir., v.p., 1951-59, pres., 1959-2000, chmn., 2000—. Dir. Am. Uniform Co. Served with USAAF, 1942-46. Decorated D.F.C. Mem. Phi Beta Kappa. Clubs: Alta, Salt Lake Country. Office: 505 E South Temple Salt Lake City UT 84102-1004

STEINER, SAMUEL J. judge; BA, U. Wash., 1949, JD, 1951. Bar: Wash. Pvt. practice, Seattle, 1954-78; bankruptcy judge for western Wash., Seattle, 1978—. With U.S. Army, 1951-54; mem. USAR, 1954-78. Office: US Bankruptcy Ct 315 Park Place Bldg 1200 6th Ave Ste 315 Seattle WA 98101-3130

STEINFELD, RAY, JR. food products executive; b. Portland, Oreg., Nov. 21, 1946; s. Ray and June Catherine (Cox) S.; children: Erik, Blair. Student, Wheaton Coll., 1964-66, Drew U., 1967; BS in Polit. Sci., Lewis and Clark Coll., 1968. Sales rep. Continental Can Co., L.A., 1969-72; co-chmn. bd., CEO, Steinfeld's Products Co., Portland, Oreg., 1972—. Chmn. Oreg. Mus. Sci. in Industry, 1992-94. Treas., bd. dirs. Portland Recycling Team, 1973—; pres. exec. bd. Stop Oreg. Litter and Vandalism, 1973-92, pres., 1976; chmn., exec. com. Oreg. Landmark of Quality, 1985-87, Oreg. Ballet Theatre, 1994—, bd. dirs., 1995—, v.p. devel., 1997—, pres., 1998—; pres. exec. com. William Temple House, 1985-91; vestry mem. Trinity Episcopal Ch., 1987-90; chmn. Oregn. Strategic Plan Agrl. Dept., 1988, World Trade Week, Portland, 1989; mem. Gov. Robert's Task Force, Salem, Oreg., 1991-92; bd. dirs. Oreg. Enterprise Forum, 1992-96, chmn., 1995; bd. dirs. Portland Advocates for Student Arts, 1999—. Mem. Pickle Packers Internat. (mem. mdse. com.), Portland C. of C. (bd. dirs. 1995-99). Democrat. Episcopalian. Avocations: tennis, golf, bridge. Office: 10001 N Rivergate Blvd Portland OR 97203-6526

STEINHARDT, HENRY, photographer; b. N.Y.C., Nov. 15, 1920; s. Maxwell and Ruth (Davis) S.; m. Elizabeth Smith, 1946 (dec. 1955); children: Elizabeth, Maxwell; m. Helene Fleck, Feb. 1, 1958; 1 child, Henry III. AB, Harvard U., 1942, MArch, 1949. Registered architect. Office mgr. R.H. Cutting, Architect, N.Y.C., 1951-53; ptnr., architect Steinhardt & Thompson, Architects, N.Y.C., 1953-61; architect The Cerny Assocs., St. Paul, 1961-63, John Graham & Co., Seattle, 1963-67, Morse/Kirk, Seattle, 1967-68, N.G. Jacobson & Assocs., Seattle, 1968-69; pvt. practice Mercer Island, Wash., 1969-75; architect USN, Bremerton, 1975-78; fine art photographer Mercer Island, 1979—. Prin. works exhibited at Washington, Seattle and Andover, Mass.; contbr. articles to fgn. archtl. jours. 1st lt. U.S. Army, 1943-46; capt. USAF, 1950-52. Recipient Design award Progressive Architecture, 1959, Archtl. award Fifth Ave. Assn., 1960. Fellow AIA. Democrat. Home and Office: 7825 SE 63rd Pl Mercer Island WA 98040-4813

STEINMAN, JOHN FRANCIS, psychiatrist; b. N.Y.C., May 5, 1916; s. David Barnard and Irene Stella (Hoffman) S.; m. Helen G. Meyer (div. 1963); children: James, Judith, Jill; m. Roxane Bear (div. 1972); m. Ellen M. Sears, Nov. 16, 1985. AB with hons., Columbia U., 1936, MD, 1940. Diplomate Am. Bd. Psychiatry and Neurology. Intern Strong Meml. Hosp., Rochester, N.Y. and Cin. Gen. Hosp., 1940-43; resident psychiatry Nebr. Psychiat. Inst., 1948, 58, R.I. Med. Ctr., 1961; psychiatrist, dir. Lincoln (Nebr.) and Lancaster County Child Guidance Ctr., 1948-61; instr. pediatrics, psychiatry and neurology U. Nebr., Lincoln, 1951-52; postdoctoral fellow in psychiatry Yale U., New Haven, 1962-64; psychiatrist U. Conn., Storrs, 1964-69, Community Mental Health Services, San Francisco, 1971-79; pvt. practice psychiatry San Francisco, 1979—. Delgate, chmn. Nebr. health com. White House Conf. Children and Youth, Washington, 1960. Served to capt. M.C., AUS, 1943-46, PTO. Mem. Am. Psychiat. Assn. (life), Am. Orthopsychiat. Assn., N.Y. Acad. Scis., Phi Beta Kappa. Home and Office: 164 Otsego Ave San Francisco CA 94112-2536 E-mail: steinman334@gateway.net

STEINMAN, LISA MALINOWSKI, English literature educator, writer; b. Willimantic, Conn., Apr. 8, 1950; d. Zenon Stanislaus and Shirley Belle Malinowski; m. James A. Steinman, Apr. 1968 (div. 1980); m. James L. Shugrue, July 23, 1984. BA, Cornell U., 1971, MFA, 1973, PhD, 1976. Asst. prof. English Reed Coll., Portland, Oreg., 1976-82, assoc. prof., 1982-90, prof., 1990—, Kenan prof. English lit. and humanities, 1993—. Cons. NEH, Washington, 1984-85. Author: Lost Poems, 1976, Made in America, 1987, All That Comes to Light, 1989, A Book of Other Days, 1992, Ordinary Songs, 1996, Masters of Repetition, 1998; editor Hubbub Mag., 1983—; editl. bd. Williams Rev., 1991—, Stevens Jour., 1994—; contbr. articles to profl. jours. Fellow Danforth Found., 1971-75, NEH, 1983, 96, Oreg. Arts Commn., 1983, Nat. Endowment for Arts, 1984; Rockefeller Found. scholar, 1987-88; recipient Pablo Neruda award, 1987, Oreg. Inst. Lit. Arts award, 1993. Mem. MLA, Poets and Writers, PEN (N.W. chpt., co-founder, officer 1989-93). Home: 5344 SE 38th Ave Portland OR 97202-4208 Office: Reed Coll Dept English 3203 SE Woodstock Blvd Portland OR 97202-8138 E-mail: lisasteinman@reed.edu

STEINMANN, JOHN COLBURN, architect; b. Monroe, Wis., Oct. 24, 1941; s. John Wilbur and Irene Marie (Steil) S.; m. Susan Koslosky, Aug. 12, 1978 (div. July 1989). BArch, U. Ill., 1964; postgrad., Ill. Inst. Tech., 1970-71. Registered architect, Wash., Oreg., Calif., N.Mex., Ariz., Utah, Alaska, Wis., Ill. Project designer C.F. Murphy Assocs., Chgo., 1968-71, Steinmann Architects, Monticello, Wis., 1971-73; design chief, chief project architect State of Alaska, Juneau, 1973-78; project designer Mithun Assos., architects, Bellevue, Wash., 1978-80; owner, prin. John C. Steinmann Assos., Architect, Kirkland, 1980-94; supr. head facilities sect. divsn. fin. Dept. Edn. State of Alaska, Juneau, 1994-96; docs. mgr. Loschky Marquardt and Nesholm, Architects, Seattle, 1996-98; project mgr. Dept. Gen. Adminstrn. Divsn. Engring. and Archtl. Svsc., State of Wash., Olympia, 1998-99; project mgr. URS Architects, Seattle, 2000—. Bd. dirs. Storytell Internat.; lectr. Ill. Inst. Tech., 1971-72. Prin. works include Grant Park Music Bowl, Chgo., 1971, Menomonee Falls (Wis.) Med. Clinic, 1972, Hidden Valley Office Bldg., Bellevue, 1978, Kezner Office Bldg., Bellevue, 1979, The Pines at Sunriver, Oreg., 1980, also Phase II, 1984, Phase III, 1986, The Pines at Sunriver Lodge Bldg., 1986, 2d and Lenora highrise, Seattle, 1981, Bob Hope Cardiovascular Rsch. Inst. lab animal facility, Seattle, 1982, Wash. Ct., Bellevue, 1982, Anchorage Bus. Park, 1982, Garden Townhouses, Anchorage, 1983, Vacation Internationale, Ltd. Corp. Hdqrs., Bellevue, 1983, Vallarta Torres III, Puerto Vallarta, Mex., 1987, Torres Mazatlan (Mex.) II, 1988, Canterwood Townhouses, Gig Harbor Wash., 1988, Inn at Ceres (Calif.), 1989, Woodard Creek Inn, Olympia, Wash., 1989, Northgate Corp. Ctr., Seattle, 1990, Icicle Creek Hotel and Restaurant, Leavenworth, Wash., 1990, Bellingham (Wash.), Market Pl., 1990, Boeing Hot Gas Test Facility, Renton, Wash., 1991, Boeing Longacres Customer Svc. Tng. Ctr. Support Facilities, Renton, 1992, Boeing Comml. Airplane Group Hdqrs., Renton, 1996, U. Wash./Cascade C.C., Bothell, 1999, Wash. State U., Pullman, Wash., Sea-Tac Airport Comm. Control Ctr., Seattle, 2000, McCarty, Internet Cafe and Residence Hall Renovation, U. Wash., Seattle, 2001, K'ima Med. Ctr. Dental Clinic, Hoopa, Calif.; also pvt. residences. Served to 1st lt. C.E., USAR, 1964-66, Vietnam. Decorated Bronze Star. Mem. AIA, Am. Mgmt. Assn., Nat. Coun. Archtl. Registration Bds., U. Wash. Yacht Club, Columbia Athletic Club, Alpha Rho Chi. Republican. Roman Catholic. Address: 4316 106th Pl NE Kirkland WA 98033-7919

STEINMETZ, SEYMOUR, pediatrician; b. Czechoslovakia, Oct. 6, 1934; s. Nathan and Gisela S. BA, Yeshiva U., N.Y.C., 1956; MD, Albert Einstein Coll. Medicine, Bronx, N.Y., 1960. Diplomate Am. Bd. Pediatrics. Intern UCLA Hosp., L.A., 1960-61, resident in pediat., 1961-62; chief resident in pediat. Montefiore Hosp., Bronx, N.Y., 1964-65; fellow in child psychiatry Jacobi Hosp., Bronx, 1965-66; pvt. practice, Gt. Neck, 1966-74; pvt. practice Fremont (Calif.) Pediatric Med. Group, 1974—, pres., 1984—. With USAF, 1962-64. With M.C., USAF, 1962-64. Fellow Am. Acad. Pediatrics. Office: Fremont Pediatric Med Group 3755 Beacon Ave Fremont CA 94538-1411

STELCK, CHARLES RICHARD, geology educator; b. Edmonton, Alta., Can., May 20, 1917; s. Robert Ferdinand and Florella Maud (Stanbury) S.; m. Frances Gertrude McDowell, Apr. 24, 1945; children— David, Brian, Leland, John (dec.) B.Sc., U. Alta., 1937, M.Sc., 1941; Ph.D., Stanford U., 1951. Registered profl. geologist, Alta. Field geologist B.C. Dept. Mines, Victoria, Can., 1939-41; field geologist Canol Project, Norman Wells, N.W.T., Can., 1941-43, Imperial Oil Co., Calgary, Alta., 1943-49; from lectr. to prof. emeritus geology U. Alta., Edmonton, 1946—. Contbr. numerous articles principally on biostratigraphy of Cretaceous to sci. publs. Decorated officer Order of Can.; recipient Disting. Educator award Am. Assn. Petroleum Geologists, 2001. Fellow Royal Soc. Can.; mem. Assn. Profl. Engrs., Geologists and Geophysicists Alta. (Centennial award 1979), Geol. Assn. Can. (Logan medal 1982), Geol. Soc. Am., Can. Soc. Petroleum Geologists (Douglas medal 1994), Order of Can. (officer 1997). Conservative Office: U Alta Dept Earth & Atmospheric Scis Edmonton AB Canada T6G 2E3

STELL, WILLIAM KENYON, neuroscientist, educator; b. Syracuse, N.Y., Apr. 21, 1939; arrived in Can., 1980; dual citizenship with Can., 1991; s. Henry Kenyon and Edith Doris (Lawson) S.; m. Judith Longbotham, June 27, 1974 (div. 1996); children: Jennifer Susan, Sarah Ruth; m. Kathie L. Roller, Oct. 26, 1996. B.A. in Zoology with high honors, Swarthmore Coll., 1961; Ph.D. in Anatomy, U. Chgo., 1966, M.D. with honors (E. Gellhorn prize 1967), 1967. Staff fellow, then sr. staff fellow Nat. Inst. Neurol. Diseases and Stroke, NIH, 1967-72; asso. prof., then prof. ophthalmology and anatomy UCLA Med. Sch., 1972-80; assoc. dir. Jules Stein Eye Inst., UCLA, 1978-80; prof. anatomy U. Calgary (Can.) Faculty Medicine, 1980—, head dept., 1980-85, prof. surgery and ophthalmology, 1992—. Dir. Lions Sight Ctr., Calgary, 1980-99; guest rschr. in physiology Lab. Physiologie Nerveuse, Ctr. Nat. de la Recherche Scientifique, Gif-sur-Yvette, France, 1985-86; vis. fellow Vision Scis. Ctr. Rsch. Sch. Biol. Scis. Australian Nat. U., Canberra, 1996. Served with USPHS, 1967-69. Grantee USPHS, Med. Rsch. Coun. Can., Alta. Heritage Found. Med. Rsch., Natural Scis. and Engring. Rsch. Coun. Can., NATO, Human Frontier Sci. Program, Canadian Inst. Health Rsch.; William and Mary Greve Internat. Research Scholar, 1979-80. Mem. Assn. Rsch. in Vision and Ophthalmology, Soc. Neurosci. Office: U Calgary 3330 Hospital Dr NW Calgary AB Canada T2N 4N1 E-mail: wstell@ucalgary.ca, wstell@hotmail.com

STELLWAGEN, ROBERT HARWOOD, biochemistry educator; b. Joliet, Ill., Jan. 6, 1941; s. Harwood John and Alma Dorothy (Handorf) S.; m. Joanne Kovacs, June 15, 1963; children: Robert Harwood, Alise Anne. AB, Harvard U., 1963; PhD, U. Calif.-Berkeley, 1968. Staff fellow NIH, Bethesda, Md., 1968-69; postdoctoral scholar U. Calif.-San Francisco, 1969-70; asst. prof. biochemistry U. So. Calif., L.A., 1970-74, assoc. prof., 1974-80, prof., 1980—, chmn. dept., 1981-86, vice chmn. dept., 1993—. Vis. scientist Nat. Inst. for Med. Research, Mill Hill, Eng., 1979 Contbr. articles to profl. jours. Recipient Henderson prize Harvard U., 1963; NSF fellow, 1963-67; NIH grantee, 1971-84 Mem. AAAS, Am. Soc. Biochemistry and Molecular Biology, Sierra Club, Phi Beta Kappa. Democrat. Office: U So Calif 2011 Zonal Ave Los Angeles CA 90033-1034 E-mail: stellwag@hsc.usc.edu

STELMAR, WAYNE J. chief financial officer home building company; m. Lisa Stelmar; children: Danielle, Katy, Brian. BA in Bus. Adminstrn., Ca. (Northridge) State U. CPA, lic. corp. broker, Ca. Sr. mgr. EY Kenneth Leventhal Real Estate Group, L.A.; mgr. Grant Thorton, L.A.; contr. Watt Industries, Inc., Santa Monica, 1988-90, CFO, 1990-94, 1994-98, WL Homes, Inc., 1998—. Mem. Am. Inst. CPA, Ca. Soc. CPA. Office: WL Homes Inc 19600 Fairchild Ste 150 Irvine CA 92612-2516

STEMMER, EDWARD ALAN, surgeon, educator; b. Cin., Jan. 20, 1930; s. Edward Purcell and Helen Marie (Smith) S.; m. Lois Jean Moss, May 1, 1954; children: Susan Helen, Linda Diane, Paul Frederick, Nancy Joan, Carol Jean. BA, U. Chgo., 1949, MD, 1953. Diplomate Am. Bd. Surgery, Am. Bd. Thoracic Surgery. Resident in surgery U. Chgo., 1953-60; chief resident in surgery Stanford U., Palo Alto, Calif., 1960-62, instr. surgery, 1962-64; asst. prof. surgery U. Utah, Salt Lake City, 1964-65; from asst. prof. surgery to prof. surgery U. Calif., Irvine, 1966—. Acting chmn. surgery U. Calif., Irvine, 1978-80; chief surg. svc. VA Hosp., Long Beach, Calif., 1965—. Editor: Vascular Disease in the Elderly, 1997; contbr. articles to profl. jours., chpts. to books. Capt. USAF, 1955-57, maj. USAFR, 1957-72. Grantee NIH, Am. Heart Assn., 1962-72; recipient disting. svc. award Am. Heart Assn., 1971. Mem. Am. Assn. Thoracic Surgery, Assn. VA Surgeons (pres. 1979-80, disting. svc. award 1995), Am. Surg. Assn., Am. Coll. Surgeons (pres. So. Calif. chpt. 1974-75), L.A. Surg. Soc. (pres. 1986-87), Sigma Xi. Avocations: carpentry, gardening, electronics. Home: 136 College Park Dr Seal Beach CA 90740-2527 Office: VA Med Ctr 5901 E 7th St Long Beach CA 90822-5201 E-mail: edward.stemmer@med.va.gov

STENCHEVER, MORTON ALBERT, obstetrician/gynecologist, educator; b. Paterson, N.J., Jan. 25, 1931; s. Harold and Lena (Suresky) S.; m. Diane Bilsky, June 19, 1955; children: Michael A., Marc R., Douglas A. A.B., NYU, 1951; M.D., U. Buffalo, 1956. Diplomate Am. Bd. Ob-Gyn. (bd. dirs. 1988—, v.p. 1990-92, treas. 1992-96, chmn. 1996-98, mem. resident rev. com. 1993-97, chmn. divsn. urogynecology of reconstructive pelvic surgery). Intern Mt. Sinai Hosp., 1956-57; resident obstetrics and gynecology Columbia-Presbyn. Med. Center, N.Y.C., 1957-60; asst. prof., Oglebey research fellow Case-Western Res. U., Cleve., 1962-66, asso. prof. dept. reproductive biology, 1967-70, dir. Tissue Culture Lab., 1965-70, coordinator Phase II Med. Sch. program, 1969-70; prof., chmn. dept. obstetrics-gynecology U. Utah Med. Sch., Salt Lake City, 1970-77; prof. ob-gyn. U. Wash. Sch. Medicine, Seattle, 1977-98; prof. emeritus, 1998—; chmn. dept. U. Wash. Sch. Medicine, Seattle, 1977-96. Chmn. test com. for ob-gyn. Nat. Bd. Med. Examiners, 1979-82; cons. in urogynecology Fedn. Internat. for Gynecology and Obstetrics, 1998—. Author: Labor: Workbook in Obstetrics, 1968, 2d edit., 1993, Human Sexual Behavior: A Workbook in Reproductive Biology, 1970, Human Cytogenics: A Workbook in Reproductive Biology, 1973, Introductory Gynecology: A Workbook in Reproductive Biology, 1974; co-author: Comprehensive Gynecology, 1987, 4th edit., 2001, Caring for the Older Woman, 1991, 2d edit., 1996, Health Care for the Older Woman, 1996, Office Gynecology, 1992, 2d edit., 1996, Good Health, Good Sex After 40: A Woman's Guide, 1997; sr. editor: Atlas of Gynecology, 5 vols., 1997-99; assoc. editor Ob-Gyn., 1986—, Ob-Gyn. Survey; mem. editorial bd. Western Jour. Medicine; contbr. articles to profl. jours. Served to capt. USAF, 1960-62. Fellow Am. Coll. Obstetricians and Gynecologists (com. on residency edn. 1974-80, learning resource commn. 1980-86, vice chmn. 1982-83, chmn. prolog self-assessment program 1982-86, vice chair com. health care for the underserved women 1995-97), Am. Assn. Obstetricians and Gynecologists, Am. Gynecol. Soc., Am. Soc. Ob-Gyn., Pacific Coast Ob-Gyn. Soc.; mem. AAAS, AMA, Assn. Profs. Gynecology and Obstetrics (chmn. steering com. teaching methodis in ob-gyn. 1970-79, v.p. 1975-76, pres. 1983-84, v.p. Found. 1986-87, pres. Found. 1987-91), Pacific N.W. Ob-Gyn. Soc., Wash. State Med. Assn., Seattle Gynec. Soc. (v.p. 1981, pres.-elect 1982, pres. 1982-83), Pacific Coast Ob-Gyn. Soc., Am. Soc. Human Genetics, Ctrl. Assn. Ob-Gyn., Soc. Gynecologic Investigation, Wash. State Obstet. Soc., Tissue Culture Assn., N.Y. Acad. Sci., Utah Ob-Gyn. Soc., Utah Med. Assn., Teratology Soc., Am. Fertility Soc. Home: 8301 SE 83rd St Mercer Island WA 98040-5644 Office: Ob-Gyn 130 Knickerson St Ste 211 Seattle WA 98109

STENNETT, WILLIAM CLINTON (CLINT STENNETT), radio and television station executive, state legislator; b. Winona, Minn., Oct. 1, 1956; s. William Jessie and Carole Lee (Halsey) S. BA in Journalism, Idaho State U., 1979. Gen. mgr. Wood River Jour., Hailey, Idaho, 1979-85, pres., pub., 1985-87; pres. Sta. KSVT-TV, Ketchum, Sta. KSKI-FM, Sun Valley; mem. Idaho Ho. of Reps., Boise, 1990-94; mem., minority leader Idaho Senate, Dist. 21, Boise, 1996—. Recipient Gen. Excellence award Idaho Newspaper Assn., 1985, 86-87; named Legislator of the Yr. Idaho Soil Conservation Dists., 1994, Idaho Wildlife Found., 1996. Mem. Idaho Broadcasters (bd. dirs.), Ketchum Sun Valley C. of C. (bd. dirs. 1990-95), Rotary. Democrat.

STENZEL, WILLIAM A. consulting services executive; b. Cambridge, Mass., Jan. 21, 1923; s. Herman Rheinhold and Helen (Proskurniak) S.; m. Pallie Jean Bottorff, July 25, 1952; children: Jeffrey Rheinhold, Anne Virginia, Peter Deane, Christopher James. B.A. cum laude, Harvard U., 1944, M.B.A., 1948. Advt. mgr. Waltham Watch Co., Mass., 1948-54; v.p. Tracer Lab. Inc., Waltham, 1954-62; sr. v.p. Premier Indsl. Corp., Cleve., 1962-85, Mex. Info. and Cons. Svcs., Inc., 1985—; v.p. Edn. Techs. and Cons., Inc. Bd. dirs. Greater Cleve. chpt. ARC, 1983-86, bd. dirs., mem. exec. com. Orange City chpt., Calif.; fundraiser Cleve. Orch., 1977-81; trustee Mid Town Corridor, 1985-87, Dunham Tavern Mus., 1985-87; bd. dirs., mem. fin. devel. com. Orange City chpt. ARC; bd. dirs. Blood, tissue svcs. So. Calif. region ARC, 1992-95; pres. San Clemente Friends of the Libr., 1995-98; treas. Friends of the Libr. Found., Orange County, 1997-98. Fellow Rowfant Club, 1985—. Clubs: Harvard Bus. Sch., Rowfant (Cleve.). Home and Office: 124 Avenida Cota San Clemente CA 92672-3327 E-mail: stenzelwa@cs.com

STEPANEK, JOSEPH EDWARD, industrial development consultant; b. Ellinwood, Kans., Oct. 29, 1917; s. Joseph August and Leona Mae (Wilson) S.; m. Antoinette Farnham, June 10, 1942; children: Joseph F., James B., Antoinette L., Debra L. BSChemE, U. Colo., 1939; DEng in Chem. Engring., Yale U., 1942. Registered profl. engr., Colo. Engr. Stearns-Roger Mfg., Denver, 1939-45; from asst. to assoc. prof. U. Colo., Boulder, 1945-47; from cons. to dir. UN, various countries, 1947-73; cons. internat. indsl devel., U.S.-China bus. relations Boulder, 1973—. Bd. dirs. 12 corps., 1973—. Author 3 books on indsl. devel.; contbr. 50 articles to profl. jours. Exec. dir. Boulder Tomorrow, 1965-67. Recipient Yale Engring. award Yale Engring. Assn., 1957, Norlin award U. Colo. 1978, Annual award India League of Am., 1982. Mem. AAAS. Democrat. Unitarian. Avocation: ranching. Home: 1622 High St Boulder CO 80304-4224

STEPHENS, ALBERT LEE, JR. federal judge; b. L.A., Feb. 14, 1913; m. Barbara, Sept. 29, 1939; 2 children. AB, U. So. Calif., 1936, LLB, 1938. Bar: Calif. 1939, U.S. Dist. Ct. Nev. 1939. Pvt. practice, L.A., 1939-43, 46-59; judge Superior Ct., L.A., 1959-61; now sr. judge U.S. Dist. Ct. (ctrl. dist.) Calif. Mem. legal profession panel U. So. Calif. Law Sch., 1961-65; lectr. UCLA Law Sch., 1954-55; sponsor, chair Dist. Judges Seminar (9th cir.), 1964-66. Lt. USNR, 1943-46, WWII. Nominated for appt. in 1961 by Pres. Kennedy. Mem. ABA, Calif. Bar Assn., L.A. County Bar Assn., Am. Jud. Soc., Jud. Conf. U.s. (trial practice and technique com.), U.S. Dist. Judges Assn. 9th Cir., Maritime Law Assn., U.s. Lawyers Club L.A., Chancery Club (pres. 1959). Office: US Dist Ct 232 S June St Los Angeles CA 90004-1046

STEPHENS, BOB, electronic executive; Pres., CEO Adaptec, Inc., Milpitas, Calif. Office: Adaptec Inc 691 S Milpitas Blvd Milpitas CA 95035-5484

STEPHENS, DONALD R(ICHARDS), investor; b. San Francisco, June 28, 1938; s. Donald Lewis and Anona Marie (O'Leary) S.; m. Christina Brinkman, Sept. 11, 1971 (div. 1996); m. Patricia Hamilton, Oct. 21, 2000; children: Lane B., Justin H., Nicholas W., Adam H. BS, U. So. Calif., 1961; JD, Hastings Coll., 1969. Pres. Campodonico & Stephens, San Francisco, 1963-65; pres., owner Union Investment Co., San Francisco, 1966-69; assoc. Law Offices of Louis O. Kelso, 1969-72; pres. D.R. Stephens & Co., San Francisco, 1972—. Chmn., CEO Bank of San Francisco Co., 1978-91, also bd. dirs.; chmn. N.Am. Trust REIT, also bd. dirs.; bd. dirs. Charles Schwab Family of Funds Inc. Bd. dirs. Bay Area Coun.; trustee St. Francis Meml. Hosp., San Francisco, 1976-82; mem. policy adv. bd. U. Calif., 1985—. Mem. Urban Land Inst., World Bus. Coun., Bohemian Club, Reserve Palm Desert. Republican. Presbyterian. Avocations: tennis, golf. E-mail: drs1220@aol.com

STEPHENS, ELISA, art college president, lawyer; Pres. Acad. Art Coll., San Francisco, 1993—. Office: Acad Art Coll Office Pres 79 New Montgomery St 6th Fl San Francisco CA 94105-3410

STEPHENS, GEORGE EDWARD, JR. lawyer; b. Lawrence, Kans., Mar. 26, 1936; s. George Edward and Mary Helen (Houghton) S.; m. Gretel Geiser, Dec. 31, 1965; children: Thaddeus Geiser, Edward Houghton, Mary Schoentgen. Student, U. Colo., Boulder, 1954-57, U. Colo., Denver, 1957-59; LLB, Stanford U., 1962. Bar: Calif. 1963, U.S. Dist. Ct. (cen. dist.) Calif. 1963, U.S. Ct. Appeals (9th cir.) 1971. Law clk. to judge U.S. Dist. Ct., L.A., 1962-64; assoc. ptnr. Pollock & Palmer, L.A., 1964-69; ptnr. Gates, Morris, Merrill & Stephens, L.A., 1969-72, Paul, Hastings, Janofsky & Walker, L.A., 1972—. Mem. Coordinating Coun. on Lawyer Competence, Conf. Chief Justices, 1983-86; chmn. probate sect. L.A. County Bar Assn., 1979-80. Nat. chmn. Stanford (Calif.) U. Law Fund Quad Program, 1980-87; mem. bd. visitors Stanford Law Sch., 1982-85; founder mus. Contemporary Art, L.A., 1982; bd. dirs. Pacific Oaks Coll., 1990-94. Recipient Stanford Assocs. award, 1982. Fellow Am. Bar Found., Am. Coll. Trust and Estates Counsel, Internat. Acad. Probate and Trust Law, Fellows of Contemporary Art (bd. dirs. 1991-92); mem. ABA (chmn. standing com. specialization 1979-82, standing com. lawyer referral svcs., 1969-76, consortium delivery legal svcs. and the pub., 1979-82), Stanford Law Soc. (pres. L.A. 1972-73, chmn. 1998-99). Episcopalian. Clubs: Chancery (L.A.), Annandale Golf (Pasadena, Calif.), Valley Hunt (Pasadena). Office: Paul Hastings Janofsky & Walker 555 S Flower St 23d Fl Los Angeles CA 90071-2300

STEPHENS, MARTIN R. state official; b. Ogden, Utah, Mar. 26, 1954; m. Carole Stephens. BSin Bus. Administrn., Weber State U. Mayor Farr West City, Utah, 1986-88; house speaker State of Utah, 1999—. Coun. mem. Farr West City, 1984-85, vice chair Weber Area Coun. of Govts., 1986-87, chair, 1988, elected Utah rep. White House Conf. Small Bus., Washington, 1986, majority leader, 1993-94, chair legis. mgmt. com., judiciary standing com., govt. ops. standing com., retirement com., exec. appropriations com. (chair 1993-94), commerce and revenue appropriations com., 1999—. Recipient Roy B. Gibson Freedom of Information award Soc. Profl. Journalists, 1991. Office: Utah Legis 318 State Capitol Salt Lake City UT 84114 also: 3159 N Higley Rd Farr West UT 84404-9380

STEPHENS, MICHAEL DEAN, hospital administrator; b. Salt Lake City, May 1, 1942; married. B, Columbia U., 1966, MHA, 1970. Adminstrv. resident Mt. Sinai Med. Ctr., N.Y.C., 1969-70; asst. administr. Greenville (S.C.) Gen. Hosp., 1970-71, assoc. adminstr., 1971-72, adminstr., 1972-75; pres., ceo. Hoag Meml. Hosp.-Presbyn., Newport Beach, Calif., 1975—. Trustee Am. Hosp. Assn. Mem. Am. Coll. Healthcare Execs. Home: 900 Alder Pl Newport Beach CA 92660-4121 Office: Hoag Meml Hosp Presbyn 1 Hoag Blvd PO Box 6100 Newport Beach CA 92658-6100

STEPHENS, TOM, forest products company executive; b. Crossett, Ark. m. Alice Stephens. M.Indsl. Engring., U. Ark. Engr. Olinkraft, West Monroe, La., 1963; with Johns Manfille Corp., Denver, exec. v.p., CFO, pres., CEO, 1986-90, chmn. bd., pres., CEO, 1990-96; pres., CEO MacMillan Bloedel Ltd., Vancouver, B.C., 1997—. Bd. dirs. MacMillan Bloedel Ltd., Qwest Comms., The Putnam Funds, New Century Energies, TransCan. Pipelines Ltd. Mem. Canadian Pulp and Paper Assn., Bus. Coun. of B.C., B.C. Coun. of Forest Industries. Office: Macmillan Bloedel 925 W Georgia St Vancouver BC Canada V6C 3L2

STEPHENSON, ARTHUR EMMET, JR. corporate and investment company executive; b. Bastrop, La., Aug. 29, 1945; s. Arthur Emmet (dec.) and Edith Louise Stephenson; m. Toni Lyn Edwards, June 17, 1967; 1 child, Tessa. BS in Fin. magna cum laude, La. State U., 1967; MBA (Ralph Thomas Sayles fellow), Harvard U., 1969. Chartered fin. analyst. Adminstrv. aide to U.S. Sen. Russell Long of La., Washington, 1966; security analyst Fidelity Funds, Boston, 1968; chmn. bd., pres. Stephenson & Co., Denver, Stephenson Mcht. Banking Inc., Circle Corp.; sr. ptnr. Stephenson Ventures, Stephenson Properties; founder, chmn. Gen. Comm., Inc., Denver; founder, chmn. bd. dirs. StarTek, Inc. Bd. dirs. Danaher Corp.; co-founder Pub. Network, Inc.; founder, chmn. Charter Bank and Trust, chmn., 1980-91; mem. adv. bd. First Berkshire Fund, Capital Resources Ptnrs., L.P.; former pub. Law Enforcement Product News, Colo. Book, Pub. Safety Product News, 1990-98, Colo. Book, Denver mag., Denver Bus. mag. Mem. assocs. coun. Templeton Coll. at Oxford U., Eng.; nat. trustee Nat. Symphony Orch. at John F. Kennedy Ctr. for Performing Arts, 1995-98; mem. nat. steering com. Norman Rockwell Mus., Stockbridge, Mass.; past mem. Colo. small bus. coun.; del. White House Conf., 1980; bd. dirs. Ptnrs. in Excellence La. State U. Recipient Hall of Fame award Inc. mag., 1994, Albert Einstein Tech. medal, 1999; named to Hall of Distinction, La. State U. Coll. Bus. Adminstrn., 1998. Mem. Harvard U. Bus. Sch. Assn. (internat. pres. 1987-88), Chief Execs. Orgn., World Pres.'s Orgn., Colo. Investment Advisors Assn. (treas., bd. dirs. 1975-76), Fin. Analysts Fedn., Denver Soc. Security Analysts (bd. dirs. 1975-77), Colo. Press Assn., Colo. Harvard Bus. Sch. Club (pres. 1980-81, chmn. 1981-82), Thunderbird Country Club (Rancho Mirage, Calif.), Annabel's (London), Jonathan Club (L.A.), Denver Petroleum Club, Harvard Bus. Sch. Clubs (N.Y.C., So. Calif. and Boston), Harvard Clubs (N.Y. and Boston), Glenmoor Country Club, Omicron Delta Kappa, Phi Kappa Phi, Beta Gamma Sigma, Kappa Sigma, Delta Sigma Pi. Office: 100 Garfield St Denver CO 80206-5597

STEPHENSON, HERMAN HOWARD, retired banker; b. Wichita, Kans., July 15, 1929; s. Herman Horace and Edith May (Wayland) S.; m. Virginia Anne Ross, Dec. 24, 1950; children: Ross Wayland, Neal Bevan, Jann Edith. BA, U. Mich., 1950; JD with distinction, U. Mo., Kansas City, 1958, LLD (hon.), 1993. Bar: Kans. 1958. With City Nat. Bank, Kansas City, Mo., 1952-54, City Bond & Mortgage Co., Kansas City, 1954-59, Bank of Hawaii, Honolulu, 1959-94, CEO, 1989-94, ret. chmn., 1994-2000. Bd. dirs. Cancer Rsch. Ctr. Hawaii. Bd. dirs. Maunalani Found.; chmn., bd. dirs. Pacific Fleet Submarine Meml. Assn. With U.S. Army, 1950-52. Mem. Navy League of U.S., Pacific Forum/CSIS (bd. govs.), U.S.-Korea Bus. Coun., Eagle Bend C.C., Kappa Sigma, Pi Eta Sigma, Oahu Country Club, Waialae Country Club, Rotary.

STEPHENSON, HOWARD A. state legislator; b. Fillmore, Utah, Nov. 7, 1950; m. Julie Snow; 5 children. BS in Psychology and Aerospace Studies, MPA, Brigham Young U. Formerly taxpayer advocate, pub. adminstr.; mem. Utah Senate, Dist. 4, 1992—; mem. edn. com., revenue and taxation com. Utah State Senate, co-chair pub. edn. appropriations com. Active Boy Scouts Am.; mem. Gov.'s Coun. for People with Disabilities; mem. Legis. Coalition for People with Disabilities. Recipient Hero on the Hill award. Mem. Utah Taxpayers Assn. (pres.), Nat. Taxpayers Conf. (chmn.), U.S. C. of C., Am. Legis. Exch. Coun., Coun. State Govts. Republican. Home: 1038 E 13590 S Draper UT 84020-9790

STEPHENSON, LARRY KIRK, stategic planner, management, geography educator; b. Seattle, Sept. 22, 1944; s. Norman Eugene and Virginia Dare (Frost) S.; m. Margery Alsever, Aug. 15, 1992; children: Matthew Alan, Leah Anela. BS, Ariz. State U., 1966, MA, 1971; PhD, U. Cin., 1973. Manpower rsch. analyst Employment Security Commn. of Ariz., 1969-70; asst. prof. geography U. Hawaii, Hilo, 1973-76, assoc. prof., 1976-78, chmn. dept. geography, 1975-77; planner Ariz. Dept. Health Svcs., Phoenix, 1978-84; strategic planner City of Glendale, Ariz., 1984-92; pub. health analyst Gila River Indian Comty., 1992-98, econ. devel. planner, 1998—. Vis. lectr. dept. geography Ariz. State U., 1978, adj. assoc. prof., 1979—; vis. assoc. prof. dept. geography, area devel. and urban planning U. Ariz., 1978; mem. faculty U. Phoenix, 1979—; adj. prof. Golden Gate U., 1981—; ptnr. Urban Rsch. Assocs., Phoenix, 1981—; adj. prof. Coll. St. Francis, 1982—; mem. faculty Troy State U., 1990—. Author: Statistics for Health Managers, 1981; co-author: Student Study Guide and Instructor's Manual to accompany Geography: A Modern Synthesis, 4 edits., 1975-83; editor: Kohala keia: Collected Expressions of a Community, 1977; contbr. articles to profl. jours., chpts. to textbooks. Mem. Hawaii Island Health Planning Coun., 1974-78, Glendale Comty. Colls. Pres.'s Coun., 1986-92. With U.S. Army, 1966-68. NDEA fellow 1971-72. Mem. Am. Inst. Cert. Planners, Am Planning Assn., Assn. Am. Geographers, Ariz. Planning Assn. (pres. 1987—), S.W. Profl. Geog. Assn., Lambda Alpha. Unitarian. Home: 9825 S 30th Dr Laveen AZ 85339 Office: PO Box 97 Sacaton AZ 85247-0097 E-mail: Lstephe739@aol.com

STERLING, DONALD T. professional basketball team executive; b. Chgo. Lawyer L.A. (formerly San Diego) Clippers, Nat. Basketball Assn., owner, also chmn. bd. Office: c/o LA Clippers LA Meml Sports Arena 3939 S Figueroa St Los Angeles CA 90037-1200

STERMER, DUGALD ROBERT, designer, illustrator, writer, consultant; b. Los Angeles, Dec. 17, 1936; s. Robert Newton and Mary (Blue) S.; m. Jeanie Kortum; children: Dugald, Megan, Chris, Colin, Crystal. B.A., UCLA, 1960. Art dir., v.p. Ramparts mag., 1965-70; freelance designer, illustrator, writer, cons. San Francisco, 1970—; founder Pub. Interest Communications, San Francisco, 1974; chmn. illustration dept. Calif. Coll. Arts and Crafts, 1994—. Bd. dirs. Am. Inst. Graphic Arts, Illustration Partnership Am.; mem. San Francisco Art Commn., 1997—. Cons. editor: Communication Arts mag., 1974-90; designer: Oceans mag., 1976-82; editor: The Environment, 1972, Vanishing Creatures, 1980; author: The Art of Revolution, 1970, Vanishing Creatures, 1980, Vanishing Flora, 1994, Birds and Bees, 1994; designer 1984 Olympic medals; illustration exhbn. Calif. Acad. Scis., 1986; one-man show Jernigan Wicker Gallery, San Francisco, 1996. Mem. Grand Jury City and County San Francisco, 1989; bd. dirs. Delancey St. Found., 1990—. Recipient various medals, awards for design and illustration nat. and internat. competitions. Office: 600 The Embarcadero # 204 San Francisco CA 94107-2121

STERN, ARTHUR PAUL, electronics company executive; b. Budapest, Hungary, July 20, 1925; came to U.S., 1951; s. Leon and Bertha (Frankfurter) S.; m. Edith M. Samuel; children: Daniel, Claude, Jacqueline. Diploma in Elec. Engring., Swiss Fed. Inst. Tech., Zurich, 1948; MSEE, Syracuse U., 1955. Mgr. electronic devices and applications lab. GE, Syracuse, N.Y., 1957-61; dir. engring. Martin Marietta Corp., Balt., 1961-64; dir. ops. Bunker Ramo Corp., Canoga Park, Calif., 1964-66; v.p., gen. mgr. advanced products divsn. Magnavox, Torrance, 1966-79; pres. Magnavox Advanced Products and Systems Co., Torrance, 1980-90; vice chmn., bd. dirs. Magnavox Govt. and Indsl.Electronics Co., Ft. Wayne, Ind., 1987-90; pres. Ea. Beverly Hills Corp., 1991—. Pres. Calif.-Israel C. of C., 1994-98, chmn. bd. 1998-2000; mem. governing coun. Am.-Jewish Congress, 1997-98; bd. dirs. Jewish Coun. Pub. Affairs, 1996—, Progressive Jewish Alliance, 1999—; non-resident staff mem. MIT, 1956-59; instr. GE Bus. Mgmt., 1955-57. Author: Transistor Broadcast Receivers, 1954; co-author: Transistor Circuit Engineering, 1957, Handbook of Automation, Computation and Control, 1961; also articles; U.S., fgn. patentee in field. Chmn. engring. divsn. United Jewish Appeal, Syracuse, 1955-57; mem. adv. bd. dept. elec. engring. U. Calif., Santa Barbara, 1980-92; mem. Sch. Engring. Adv. and Devel. Coun. Calif. State U., Long Beach, 1985-90; bd. dirs. Bur. Jewish Edn., L.A., 1995—; vice-chmn. Jewish Cmty. Rels. Com. L.A., 1998—; chmn. bd. dirs. Calif. Humanitarian Found. for Holocaust Survivors, 2000—. Fellow AAAS, IEEE (pres. 1975, bd. dirs., officer 1970-77, guest editor spl. issue IEEE Trans. on Circuit Theory 1956, invited guest editor spl. issue Procs. IEEE on Integrated Electronics 1964, Centennial medal 1984, Millennium medal 2000, Haraden Pratt award 2001).

STERN, EDWARD ABRAHAM, physics educator; b. Detroit, Sept. 19, 1930; s. Jacob Munich and Rose (Kravitz) S.; m. Sylvia Rita Sidell, Oct. 30, 1955; children: Hilary, Shari, Miri. BS, Calif. Tech., 1951, PhD, 1955. Post-doctoral fellow Calif. Tech., Pasadena, 1955-57; asst. prof. U. Md., College Park, 1957-61, assoc. prof., 1961-64, prof., 1964-65, U. Wash., Seattle, 1965—. Contbr. over 200 articles to profl. jours.; editor; three books. Recipient B. Warren award Am. Crystallography Assn., 1979, Outstanding Achievement award Internat. XAFS Soc., 2000; named Guggenheim fellow, Cambridge, Eng., 1963-64, NSF Sr. Post-doctoral fellow, Haifa, Israel, 1970-71, Fulbright fellow, Jerusalem, Israel, 1985-86. Fellow AAAS, Am. Physical Soc. Achievements include patent for x-ray focusing device; development of x-ray absorption fine structure technique; research on surface plasmons, nonlinear reflection from surfaces, electronic properties of alloys, structural phase transition. Office: U Wash Dept Physics PO Box 351560 Seattle WA 98195-1560 E-mail: stern@phys.washington.edu

STERN, JUDITH SCHNEIDER, nutritionist, researcher, educator; b. Bklyn. d. Sidney and Lillian (Rosen) Schneider; m. Richard C. Stern; 1 child, Daniel Arthur. BS, Cornell U., 1964; MS, Harvard U. Sch. Pub. Health, 1966, ScD, 1970. Rsch. asst., dept. food sci. and nutrition MIT, Cambridge, 1964-65; rsch. assoc. dept. human behavior and metabolism The Rockefeller U., N.Y.C., 1969-72, asst. prof. dept. human behavior and metabolism, 1972-74; contbg editor Vogue Mag., Conde Nast Publs., N.Y.C., 1974; asst. prof. nutrition U. Calif., Davis, 1975-77, assoc. prof. dept. nutrition, 1977-82, dir. food intake lab. group, 1980—, prof. dept. nutrition, 1982—, prof. divsn. endocrinology, clin. nutrition & vasc. biology, 1988—; co-dir. Ctr. for Complimentary and Alternativ Med., 1995—. Mem. editl. bd. Internat. Jour. Obesity, 1976-85, Appetite, 1990, Obesity Rsch., 1993—, Nutrition Today, 1999—. Mem. nutrition adv. bd. Avocado Growers Calif., 1975-98; bd. sci. advisors Am. Coun. Sci. and Health, 1980—; mem. U.S. Dept. Agr. Dietary Guidelines Adv. Com., 1983-85; bd. advisors Inst. Behavioral Edn.; mem. obesity task force NIDDK, AAAS; mem. expert com. U.S. Pharmacopeia Bioavailability and Nutrient Absorption, 2000—; mem. adv. bd. USDA Nat. Agrl. Rsch. Ext., Edn. and Econs., 2000—. NIH tng. grant, 1970—. Mem. Am. Soc. Clin. Nutrition (pres. 1995-96), Am. Dietetic Assn., N.Am. Assn. for Study of Obesity (pres. 1992-93), Inst. Medicine NAS, Inst. Food Technologists, Am. Obesity Assn. (v.p. 1995—), Am. Soc. Nutrition Sci. (chair pub. info. com. 1992-94), Sigma Xi, Delta Omega. Office: U Calif Dept Nutrition 1 Shields Ave Davis CA 95616-5271 E-mail: jstern@ucdavis.edu, sternshome@aol.com

STERN, LEONARD BERNARD, television and motion picture production company executive; b. N.Y.C., Dec. 23, 1923; s. Max and Esther (Marton) S.; m. Gloria Jane Stroock, Aug. 12, 1956; children: Michael Stroock, Kate Jennifer. Student, NYU, 1944. Dir. TV, L.A., 1946-53; writer, dir., producer Jackie Gleason Show/Honeymooners, Sergeant Bilko, Steve Allen Show N.Y.C., 1953-60; founder Price-Stern-Sloan, L.A., 1959-64, v.p., 1964-69, dir., 1969-80; pres. Heyday Prodns., L.A., 1962-69, 75-97; v.p. Talent Assocs./Norton Simon, L.A. and N.Y.C., 1965-75; pres. Tallfellow Prodns., L.A., 1997—. Author: (with Roger Price) Mad Libs, 1958, What Not to Name the Baby, 1960, Dear Attila the Hun, 1985; (with Roger Price and Larry Sloan) The Baby Boomer Book of Names, 1985, (with Diane L. Robison) A Martian Wouldn't Say That, 1994; writer, dir.: (motion pictures) Just You and Me, Kid, 1979, Target, 1985, Missing Pieces, 1990; creator, writer, dir. 21 TV series, including Get Smart, McMillan and Wife and He and She, 1953-89; media editor Dialogue newsletter. Mem. adv. coun. Sch. of Arts, NYU; bd. dirs. Nat. Coun. for Families and TV, Inst. for Mental Health Initiatives. Recipient Peabody award U. Ga., Writers Guild award 1956, 66, Nat. Assn. TV Arts and Scis. award 1956, 66-67, Emmy award 1956, 1966. Mem. Writers Guild Am., Dirs. Guild Am., Caucus for Producers, Writers and Dirs. (co-chmn., Mem. of Yr award 1987, Disting. Svc. award 1987), Producers Guild Am. (pres.), Bd. Motion Picure and TV Fund Found. Office: Tallfellow Prodns 1180 S Beverly Dr Ste 320 Los Angeles CA 90035-1154

STERN, MITCHELL, broadcast executive; B, U. Pa., 1976; MBA, U. Chgo., 1978. With CBS TV Stas. Divsn., 1978-86, dir. planning and adminstrn. WCBS-TV, dir. planning and adminstrn. WBBM-TV Chgo., fin. analyst corp. office; v.p., CFO Fox TV Stas., L.A., 1986-90, v.p., sta. mgr. KTTV-Fox 11, 1990-92, sr. v.p., 1990-92, exec. v.p., COO, 1992-93, pres., COO, 1993-98, chmn., CEO, 1998—, Twentieth TV, L.A., 1998—. Office: Fox TV Stas Inc 205 E 67th St New York NY 10021

STERN, MORT(IMER) P(HILLIP), journalism and communications educator, academic administrator, consultant; b. New Haven, Feb. 20, 1926; s. Bernard and Louise Eleanor (Spiro) S.; m. Patricia Ruth Freeman, Jan. 10, 1946; children: Susan C., Margaret L. AB, U. Ark., 1947; MS, Columbia U., 1949; postgrad., Harvard U., 1954-55; PhD, U. Denver, 1969. Reporter S.W.-Am., Ft. Smith, Ark., 1946-47; night bur. mgr. UPI, Little Rock, 1947-48; reporter, polit. writer, state editor Ark. Gazette, Little Rock, 1949-51; reporter, rewrite man Denver Post, 1951-53, night city editor, 1953-54, asst. editor Rocky Mountain Empire sect., 1955-56, mng. editor, 1956-58, assoc. editor, 1958, editorial page editor, 1958-65, asst. to pub., 1965-70, editorial page editor, 1971-73; dean Sch. Pub. communication U. Ala., 1973-74; dean Sch. Journalism U. Colo., Boulder, 1974-77; lectr. journalism U. Denver, 1953-54, adj. prof., 1970, exec. dir. pub. affairs, 1977-78, exec. asst. to chancellor, 1978-84; prof., chmn. dept. journalism and mass communication U. No. Colo., Greeley, 1985-90; pres. P. Paty & Co., Georgetown, Colo., 1989—. Atwood prof. journalism U. Alaska, Anchorage, 1981-82. With USAAF, 1944-45. Elected to Georgetown, Colo. Bd. of Selectmen, Apr. 7, 1997-99. Nieman fellow Harvard U., 1954-55; named Disting. Alumnus dept. journalism U. Ark., 1999; inducted to Fulbright Coll. Alumni Acad. U. Ark., 1999. Mem. Georgetown Libr. Assn. (v.p. 1999—, bd. dirs.), Assn. for Edn. in Journalism, Phi Beta Kappa, Omicron Delta Kappa, Sigma Delta Chi. Baptist. Home: PO Box 549 Georgetown CO 80444-0549 E-mail: editor220@aol.com

STERN, RICHARD DAVID, investment company executive; b. New Rochelle, N.Y., Nov. 5, 1936; s. Leo and Grace Marjorie (Phillips) S.; m. Phyllis Marlene Edelstein, Nov. 20, 1966; children: Marjorie Anne, Andrew Howard. AB, Princeton U., 1958; MBA, Harvard U., 1962. CFA. 1st v.p. Newburger, Loeb & Co., N.Y.C., 1962-74, also bd. dirs., 1969-74; sr. investment officer Ctrl. Trust Co., Cin., 1974-76, owner bus. valuation cons. co., 1976-78; v.p. Gt. Western Bank & Trust Co. (now Wells Fargo Bank), Phoenix, 1978-84; pres. Stern, Ludke & Co. (now Stellar Capital Mgmt. LLC.), Phoenix, 1984—, mng. mem., 2000—. Co-author: Air Cushion Vehicles, 1962. Trustee endowment trust Phoenix Chamber Music Soc., 1982-91; v.p., 1986-90, bd. dirs., 1982-91, 93-94; pres. Cen. Ariz. chpt. Arthritis Found., 1982-84, chmn. planned giving com., 1986-91, mem. nat. planned giving com., 1987-89; chmn. endowments and trusts com. Temple Beth Israel, Phoenix, 1980-83; dir., investment com. Endowment Found., Temple Solel, Paradise Valley, 1990—; pres. Am. Jewish Com., Phoenix, 1983-84, bd. dirs., 1980-84, adv. bd., 1985—; bd. dirs. Asian Arts Coun., Phoenix Art Mus., 1987-93, v.p., 1989-90, pres., 1990-92; trustee Ariz. Theatre Co., 1990-97, mem. regional nominating com., 1995-97, chmn., 1995-96, asst. treas., 1996-97. Mem. Phoenix Soc. Fin. Analysts (chmn. profl. conduct com. 1980-83, membership com. 1990-91, bd. dirs.), Anti-Defamation League (bd. Ctrl. Ariz. chpt. 1986—, exec. bd. 1989—, chair nominating com. 1990-94, chair bd. devel. 1993-94, treas. 1994—, assoc. nat. commr. 1998—), Princeton Alumni Assn. No. Ariz. (alumni schs. com. 1992—), Univ. Club Phoenix (bd. dirs. 1990-92, fin. com. 1990-91), Harvard Bus. Sch. Club Ariz. (bd. dirs. 1991—, pres. 1993-95, treas. 1995—). Republican. Home: 7547 N Lakeside Ln Paradise Vly AZ 85253-2857 Office: 2200 E Camelback Rd Ste 130 Phoenix AZ 85016-3455 E-mail: rstern@stellarmgt.com

STERN, STANLEY, psychiatrist; b. N.Y.C., Apr. 5, 1933; s. Frank and Gussie S.; children: Marcus F., David S. BA cum laude, N.Y. U., 1953; MD, SUNY, 1957. Intern Ohio State U. Hosp., Columbus, 1957-58; resident in psychiatry Inst. Living, Hartford, Conn., 1958-60, Austen Riggs Ctr., Stockbridge, Mass., 1960-61; psychoanalytic tng. We. New Eng. Inst. for Psychoanalysis, New Haven, 1965-73; asst. clin. prof. psychiatry Yale U., New Haven, 1975-81; assoc. clin. prof. psychiatry U. Calif., San Diego, 1982-84; pvt. practice New Haven, 1965-82, La Jolla, Calif., 1982-84, Phoenix, 1984—. Mem. faculty San Diego Psychoanalytic Inst., 1980-84; pres. Ariz. Psychoanalytic Study Group, Phoenix, 1986-88, Phoenix Psychoanalytic Study Group, 1986-88; tng. and supervising analyst So. Calif. Psychoanalytic Inst., 1989; chmn. edn. com. Ariz. Psychoanalytic New Tng. Facility, 1990-91; lectr., presenter, participant seminars and confs. in field. Contbr. article to profl. jours. Trustee, Gesell Inst., New Haven, 1986-88, Ctr. for the Exceptional Patient, New Haven; bd. dirs. ACLU. Capt. USAF, 1961-63. Mem. Am. Coll. Psychoanalysts, Am. Psychoanalytic Assn. (cert.), Am. Psychiatric Assn., Am. Acad. Psychoanalysts, Irene Josselyn Group Advancement of Psychoanalysis, So. Calif. Psychoanalytic Inst. and Soc. (faculty), San Diego Psychoanalytic Inst., Council for the Advancement of Psychoanalysis (treas. 1972-73, pres.-elect 1973-74, pres. 1974-75, councillor 1975-80), Phi Beta Kappa, Beta Lambda Sigma, Psi Chi. Home and Office: 3104 E Camelback Rd # 601 Phoenix AZ 85016 Address: 4438 E Arlington Rd Phoenix AZ 85018-1262

STERN, WALTER EUGENE, neurosurgeon, educator; b. Portland, Oreg., Jan. 1, 1920; s. Walter Eugene and Ida May (McCoy) S.; m. Elizabeth Naffziger, May 24, 1946; children: Geoffrey Alexander, Howard Christian, Eugenia Louise, Walter Eugene III. AB cum laude, U. Calif., MD, 1943. Diplomate: Am. Bd. Neurol. Surg. (vice chmn. 1975-80). Surg. intern, asst. resident surgery and neurol. surgery U. Calif. Hosp., 1943-46, asst. resident neurol. surgery and neuropathology, 1948; clin. clk. Nat. Hosp. Paralyzed and Epileptic, London, Eng., 1948-49; Nat. Research fellow med. sci. Johns Hopkins, 1949-50; asst. resident, resident U. Calif. Service, 1951; NIH spl. fellow univ. lab. physiology Oxford U., 1961-62; clin. instr. U. Calif., 1951; asst. prof. neurosurgery UCLA, 1952-56, assoc. prof., 1956 59, prof., 1959 87, now emeritus, chief div. neurosurgery, 1952-85, chmn. dept. surgery, 1981-87. Cons. neurosurgery, Wadsworth VA Hosp. Former mem., chmn. editorial bd. Jour. Neurosurgery; contbr. articles to sci. jours., chpts. in books. Lt. to capt. M.C. AUS, 1946-48. Fellow ACS (sec.); mem. AMA, Am. Surg. Assn., Pacific Coast Surg. Assn., L.A. Surg. Soc. (pres. 1978), Am. Assn. Neurol. Surgeons (pres. 1979-80, Cushing medalist, 1992), James IV Assn. Surgeons, Western Neurosurg. Soc. (past pres.), Soc. Neurol. Surgeons (past pres., Disting. Svc. award 1999), Neurosurg. Soc. Am., Am. Neurol. Assn., Soc. Univ. Surgeons, Soc. Brit. Neurol. Surgeons (hon.), Phi Beta Kappa, Sigma Xi, Alpha Omega Alpha. Republican. Epsicopalian. Home: 435 Georgina Ave Santa Monica CA 90402-1909 Office: U Calif Sch Med PO Box 95-7039 Los Angeles CA 90095-7039

STERRETT, JAMES KELLEY, II, lawyer; b. St. Louis, Nov. 26, 1946; s. James Kelley and Anastasia Mary (Holzer) S.; 1 child, Brittany. AB, San Diego State U., 1968; JD, U. Calif., Berkeley, 1971; LLM, U. Pa., 1973. Bar: Calif. 1972, U.S. Dist. Ct. (so. dist.) Calif. 1972. From assoc. to ptnr. Gray, Cary, Ames & Frye, San Diego, 1972-83; ptnr. Lillick, McHose & Charles, San Diego, 1983-90, Pillsbury, Madison & Sutro, San Diego, 1991-96, Dostart Clapp Sterrett & Coveney, LLP, 1996-99; sole practice, 1999—. Contbr. articles to profl. jours. Bd. dirs. Holiday Bowl, San Diego, 1980—, Mus. Photog. Arts, San Diego, 1985-88, San Diego Internat. Sports Coun., 1980—, pres., 1990, chmn., 1992. Capt. USAFR, 1972. Fellow U. Pa. Ctr. Study Fin. Instns., 1971-72. Mem. ABA, Calif. Bar Assn., San Diego County Bar Assn. Republican. Episcopalian. Club: Fairbanks Ranch Country (Rancho Santa Fe) (bd. dirs. 1985-87). Avocations: golf, college football, hiking. Office: Ste 291 3525 Del Mar Heights Rd San Diego CA 92130

STERRETT, JAMES MELVILLE, accountant, business consultant; b. Chicago, Dec. 25, 1949; s. James McAnlis and Antoinette (Galligan) S.; m. Joyce Mieko Motoda, Sept. 1, 1989; 1 child, Victoria Hanako. BS in Acctg., Chaminade U., Honolulu, 1988; MBA, Chaminade U., 1991. CPA, Hawaii. Cons. Profitability Cons., Honolulu, 1985-87; pres. Sterrett Cons. Group, Honolulu, 1987-88; auditor Deloitte & Touche, Honolulu, 1988-90; acct., cons. pvt. practice, Honolulu, 1990—. Mem. Nat. Soc. Pub. Accts., Nat. Assn. Tax Practitioners, Hawaii Soc. CPA's, Delta Epsilon, Sigma. Office: 1314 S King St Ste 855 Honolulu HI 96814-1979

STETSON, PETER BRAILEY, astronomer; b. Middleboro, Mass., Aug. 30, 1952; s. George Robert and Estelle Marie (Ives) S.; m. Frances Eileen Bogucki, Aug. 5, 1979; children: Whitney Ann, Brailey Marie, Garrett Wilson, Leete Anthony. BA, MA, Wesleyan U., 1974; MS, Yale U., 1975, PhD, 1979. Postdoctoral astronomy dept. Yale U., New Haven, 1979-80; Carnegie fellow Mt. Wilson and Las Campanas Obs., Pasadena, Calif., 1980-83; rsch. assoc. Dominion Astrophys. Obs., Victoria, B.C., Can., 1983-84, asst. rsch. officer Can., 1984-86, assoc. rsch. officer Can., 1986-89, sr. rsch. officer Can., 1989—; adj. prof. U. Victoria, 1988—. Contbr. articles to Astrophysical Jour., Jour. of Royal Astron. Soc. Can., Annual Reviews of Astronomy and Astrophysics, Astron. Jour., Publ. Astron. Soc. of Pacific. Recipient R.M. Petrie prize lectr. Can. Astron. Soc., 1991, Gold medal Sci. Coun. B.C., 1994, Maria and Eric Muhlmann award Astron. Soc. Pacific, 2000. Office: Dominion Astrophys Obs 5071 W Saanich Rd Victoria BC Canada V8X 4M6 E-mail: peter.stetson@nrc.ca

STEVENS, BERTON LOUIS, JR. data processing manager; b. Chgo., Apr. 4, 1951; s. Berton Louis Sr. and Mary Cover (Kochavaris) S.; m. Janet Alene Madenberg, May 20, 1990. Student, Ill. Inst. Tech., Chgo., 1969-73. Systems and applications programmer Judge & Dolph, Ltd., Elk Grove Village, Ill., 1978-91, mgr. data processing, 1991-99; bus. sys. coord. Meml. Med. Ctr., Inc., 2000-2001, lead sys. analyst, 2001—. Instr. Adler

Planetarium and Astron. Mus., Chgo., 1980-86. Editor and author newsletter Bert's Bull., 1987-90; editor newsletter No. Lights, 1990-98. Recipient Regional award North Ctrl. Region Astron. League, 1989. Mem. Nat. Assn. Sys. Programmers, Internat. Occulation Timing Assn. (sec. 1975-78), Chgo. Computer Soc., Chgo. Astron. Soc. (pres. 1977, 80, 84), Racine Astron. Soc. (pres. 1979), Astron. League (exec. sec. 1993-95, webmaster 1995—), Astron. Soc. Las Cruces (pres, 2001). E-mail: bstevens@cybermesa.com, bstevens@mmole.org

STEVENS, CHARLES J. lawyer, former prosecutor; BA in English, Colgate U., 1979; JD, U. Calif., Berkeley, 1982. Assoc. Gibson, Dunn & Crutcher, L.A., 1982-84, ptnr. in charge Sacramento, 1987-93; asst. U.S. atty. Office U.S. Atty., L.A., 1984-87; U.S. atty. ea. dist. Calif. U.S. Dept. Justice, Sacramento, 1993-97; ptnr. Steven & O'Connell LLP, Sacramento, 1997—. Mem. com. for ea. dist. Civil Justice Reform Act com. for ea. dist., 1991—, lawyer rep. to 9th cir., 1999—; panel spkr. and lectr. in field. Contbr. articles to profl. jours. Master Anthony M. Kennedy Am. Inn. of Ct.; mem. FBA (chair program com. Sacramento chpt. 1992-93), State Bar Calif. (bd. editors Criminal Law News 1991-93) Office: 400 Capitol Mall Ste 1400 Sacramento CA 95814-4498

STEVENS, GEORGE RICHARD, business consultant, public policy commentator; b. Chgo., Sept. 6, 1932; s. George and Irene (Kaczmarek) S.; m. Jeanne E. Sowden, Aug. 2, 1957; children: Stacey, Samantha, Pamela. BS with honors, Northwestern U., 1954. CPA, Ill. With Arthur Andersen & Co., 1954-78, mng. ptnr. Belgium, 1957-71, ptnr. Chgo., 1971-78; pres. Daubert Industries, Oak Brook, Ill., 1978-80, G.R. Stevens Group, 1981—; founder, pres. Stevens Ctr. for Pub. Policy Studies, 1981—. Mem. Chgo. Com., 1979—; commr. Ill. Ednl. Facilities Authority, 1989—. Commr. Ill. State Scholarship Commn., 1981-87; vice chmn. Ill. Ind. Higher Edn. Loan Authority, 1982-88. Home and Office: 22615 N Las Lomas Ln Sun City West AZ 85375-2022

STEVENS, PAUL IRVING, manufacturing company executive; b. Lawrence, Kans., Mar. 22, 1915; s. Ira F. and Ida M. S.; m. Artie Faye Womack, Nov. 10, 1935; children: Richard Irving, Constance Irene. Student bus. adminstrn., Pasadena (Calif.) Coll., 1933-35. Indsl. engr. Consol. Aircraft Co., San Diego, 1940-49; founder, prin. stockholder, pres. United Machine Co., Ft. Worth, 1950-61; exec. v.p. Clary Corp., San Gabriel, Calif., 1962-65; pres., owner Stevens Corp., Ft. Worth, 1965-69; pres., chief exec. officer Waltham Industries, N.Y.C., 1969-71, Stevens Industries, La Jolla, Calif., 1972—, Campbell Industries, San Diego., 1976-79; chmn., pres. Stevens Air Systems, El Cajon, Calif., 1974-81; pres. Womack Motors, Inc., El Centro, 1982-90. Chmn. bd. dirs., CEO Stevens Graphics Corp., Ft. Worth, 1986-95; bd. dirs. Rancho Santa Fe Nat. Bank, Calif., 1982-85, chmn. 1985-95; chmn., CEO Stevens Internat., Inc., 1995—; bd. dirs. Rancho Santa Fe. Mem. Nat. Mgmt. Assn. (exec. com.), Presidents Assn., Civic Round Table, La Jolla Country Club, Colonial Country Club, Canyon Country Club, University Club, Ft. Worth Club, Shady Oaks Country Club. Republican. Methodist. Home: 2585 Calle Del Oro La Jolla CA 92037-2005 Office: PO Box 950 La Jolla CA 92038-0950

STEVENS, RON A. lawyer, public interest organization executive; b. Indpls., Sept. 4, 1945; s. Granville Thomas and Charlotte May (Wheeler) S.; m. Judy Rohde, June 15, 1968; children: Samuel Thomas, Alison Elizabeth. BA, Okla. State U.; JD with honors, Ill. Inst. Tech., 1976. Bar: Ill. 1976. Staff atty. Legal Assistance Found. Chgo., 1976-79; staff atty., dir. housing agenda Bus. and Profl. People for Pub. Interest, Chgo., 1979-81; chief housing divsn. Office of Cook County State's Atty., Chgo., 1981-82; campaign coord. north lakefront Washington for Mayor, Chgo., 1982-83; program officer The Joyce Found., Chgo., 1983-86; pres. Citizens for a Better Environment, Chgo., 1986-89; exec. dir. United Way Santa Fe County, 1989—. Adv. bd. state support ctr. on environ. hazards Nat. Ctr. for Policy Alternatives, Washington, 1987-89; chair Local Bd. EFSP, 1989—, Santa Fe Affordable Housing Roundtable, 1992-97; chair Exec. Leadership Coun. for Cmty. Schs, 1998—; bd. dirs. No. N.Mex. Grantmakers Assn., v.p., 1999, pres., 2000. Mem. bldg. code enforcement com. Mayor's Transition Team Housing Task Force, Chgo., 1983, steering com. Chgo. Ethics Project, 1986-88; founder, chmn. Progressive Chgo. Area Network, 1981-84; bd. dirs. Uptown Recycling Sta., Chgo., 1987-89; mem. South Ctrl. Regional Coun., United Way of Am., 1993-98. Mem. Chgo. Coun. Lawyers (chmn. housing com. 1978-81, bd. govs. 1981-83, bd. dirs. Fund for Justice, 1986-88), Chgo. Area Runners Assn. (founder, v.p. 1977-81). Home: 739 Gregory Ln Santa Fe NM 87501-4257 Office: United Way Santa Fe County PO Box 261 Santa Fe NM 87504-0261

STEVENS, STANLEY DAVID, local history researcher, retired librarian; b. San Francisco, Nov. 10, 1933; s. David Franklin and Ellen Myrtle (Wixson) S.; m. Carli Ann Lewis, Sept. 3, 1960; adopted children: Alexander Lewis, Nikolas Harriman, Brooke Cayton Stevens Rich. BA, San Jose State U., 1959. Conf. officer polit. and security com. 14th Gen. Assembly, UN, N.Y.C., 1959; map libr. U. Calif., Santa Cruz, 1965-93, ret., 1993, coord. Hihn-Younger Archive, Univ. Libr., 1994—. Mem. Cartographic Users Adv. Coun., 1976-86, chmn., 1982-86; presenter in field, 1971—; adj. prof. libr. sci. San Jose (Calif.) State U., 1989, 91. Author: Catalog of aerial photos by Fairchild Aerial Surveys, Inc. now in the collections of the Department of Geography, University of California at Los Angeles, 1982, Correspondence of Charles B. Younger Sr. and Charles B. Younger Jr., Santa Cruz, California Attorneys and Counsellors at Law, (vols. 1-15 of approx. 70 completed to date), 1996—, indexed edit. Santa Cruz County, California, 1997; editor, Santa Cruz County History Journal, 1994-96, 98; also 10 others related to Hihn-Younger Archive; prodn. editor: Index to Boulder Creek Mountain Echo, 1896-1916, 1999; contbr. over 100 articles and book revs. to profl. jours. Mem. adv. com. archaeol. program Cabrillo Coll., Aptos, Calif., 1985—; bd. dirs. Santa Cruz County Hist. Soc., 1985-94, chmn. publs. com., 1985-96, mem. programs adv. coun., 1994-95; mem. Santa Cruz Co. Orgn. for Progress and Euthenics, 1987—; bd. dirs. Friends of U. Calif.-Santa Cruz Libr., 1994-97; founding mem. Rschr. Anonymous, Santa Cruz, 1994—; mem. U. Calif.-Santa Cruz Emeriti Group, sec.-treas. 1996—; mem. collections adv. com. Santa Cruz City Mus. Natural History, 1995—. With U.S. Army, 1954-56. Recipient honors award geography and map div. for outstanding achievement in map librarianship Spl. Librs. Assn., 1981, cert. of commendation Santa Cruz Hist. Soc., 1986, appreciation cert. for svcs. Assn. Info. and Image Mgmt., 1989, Proclamation of Honor, Santa Cruz County Bd. Suprs., 1998; grantee Librs. Assn. U. Calif., 1981-82, rsch. grantee Office of Pres., U. Calif., 1985-86. Mem. ALA (publs. com. Map and Geography Round Table 1985-86, editl. bd. Meridian 1989-2000, honors award Map and Geography Round Table 1992), ACLU (chmn. bd. dirs. Santa Cruz County chpt. 1962-68, bd. dirs. no. Calif. br. 1973-76), Western Assn. Map Librs. (hon. life, founding pres. 1967-68, treas. 1968-89, editor Info. Bull. 1969-84, Exec. Com. award 1984, Stanley D. Stevens Hon. Map presented at 30th anniversary meeting 1997), Calif. Hist. Soc., Calif. Map Soc., Pajaro Valley Hist. Assn., Santa Cruz County Geneal. Soc., Capitola Hist. Soc., El Paso de Robles Hist. Soc. (life). Democrat. Avocations: researching local history, listening to jazz and classical music. Home: 231 13th Ave Santa Cruz CA 95062-4831 Office: U Calif Dean E McHenry Libr Santa Cruz CA 95064 E-mail: sstevens@library.ucsc.edu

STEVENS, THEODORE FULTON, senator; b. Indpls., Nov. 18, 1923; s. George A. and Gertrude (Chancellor) S.; m. Ann Mary Cherrington, Mar. 29, 1952 (dec. 1978); children— Susan B., Elizabeth H., Walter C., Theodore Fulton, Ben A.; m. Catherine Chandler, 1980; 1 dau.; Lily Irene. B.A., U. Calif. at Los Angeles, 1947, LL.B., Harvard U., 1950. Bar: Calif., Alaska, D.C., U.S. Supreme Ct. bars. Pvt. practice, Washington, 1950-52, Fairbanks, Alaska, 1953; U.S. atty. Dist. Alaska, 1953-56; legis. counsel, asst. to sec., solicitor Dept. Interior, 1956-60; pvt. practice law Anchorage, 1961-68; mem. Alaska Ho. of Reps., 1965-68, majority leader, speaker pro tem, 1967-68; senator for Alaska U.S. Senate, 1968—, asst. Rep. leader, 1977-85, ranking mem. Senate Appropriations Com. Served as 1st lt. USAAF, World War II. Mem. ABA, Alaska Bar Assn., Calif. Bar Assn., D.C. Bar Assn., Am. Legion, VFW. Lodges: Rotary, Pioneers of Alaska, Igloo #4. Home: PO Box 100879 Anchorage AK 99510-0879 Office: US Senate 522 Hart Senate Bldg Washington DC 20510-0001

STEVENS, VAL, state legislator; m. Keith Stevens; 2 children. Mem. Wash. Senate, Dist. 39, Olympia, 1996—; mem. senate agr. and rural econ. devel. com. Wash. Legislature, Olympia, Wash. state chair Am. Legis. Exch. Coun., mem. agr. and rural econ. devel. com., mem. human svcs. and corrections com., mem. natural resources, parks and recreation com., mem. child abuse investigation work group, mem. joint selection com. on DNA, mem. family policy coun., mem. civil justice task force subcom. on Y2K, mem. Gov.'s coun. on substance abuse. Mem. Northshore Christian Ch.; bd. dirs. 1991 Concerned Women for Am.; past mem. Gov.'s Task Force for Natural Death Act; charter mem. Better Govt. Bur.; mem. ad hoc bd. dirs. Naval Aux. Air Sta. Mus. Recipient 100 Percent Voting Record award Wash. State Farm Bur., gold medal Ind. Bus. Assn., Sentinel award Wash. State Law Enforcement Assn., 1996, Outstanding Support Vocat. Tech. Edn. award WAVA, 1996, Cornerstone award Assn. Wash. Bus., Outstanding Support award Wash. Retail Assn., 1996, Guardian of Small Bus. award Nat. Fedn. Ind. Bus., Pub. Safety award Snohomish County Law Enforcement, 1993. Mem. Christian Armed Svcs. Assn. Republican. Office: 105 Irving Newhouse Ofc Olympia WA 98504-0001

STEVENS, WENDELL CLAIRE, retired anesthesiology educator; b. Mason City, Iowa, June 28, 1931; s. Lloyd Leroy and Amy Luella (Hodson) S.; m. Lola C. Claycomb, July 27, 1958; children: Amy P., Eric C., Mitchell L. AA, Mason City Jr. Coll., 1951; MD, U. Iowa, 1956. Diplomate Am. Bd. Anesthesiology. Intern City Hosp., Cleve., 1956-57; resident in gen. surgery U. Iowa Hosp., Iowa City, 1957-58, 60-61, resident in anesthesia, 1961-63; assoc. in anesthesia U. Iowa Coll. Medicine, Iowa City, 1963, asst. prof. anesthesia dept., 1963-67; asst. prof. U. Calif. Sch. Medicine, San Francisco, 1967-72, assoc. prof., 1972-77, prof., 1977; prof., chmn. anesthesia dept. U. Iowa Coll. Medicine, Iowa City, 1978-82, Oreg. Health Scis. U., Portland, 1982-92, prof., 1992-96, prof. emeritus, 1996—. Contbr. papers and book chpts. to profl. publs. Lt. USNR, 1958-60. Recipient anesthesiology rsch. grant U. Calif., San Francisco NIH, 1969-78. Mem. Oreg. Soc. Anesthesiologists, Am. Soc. Anesthesiologists, Oreg. Med. Assn., AMA, Christian Med. Soc. Republican. Baptist. Avocations: church related activities. Office: Oreg Health Scis Ctr Dept Anesthesiology 3181 SW Sam Jackson Park Rd Portland OR 97201-3011

STEVENSON, DAVID JOHN, planetary scientist, educator; b. Wellington, New Zealand, Sept. 2, 1948; came to U.S., 1971; s. Ian McIvor and Gwenyth (Carroll) S. BSc, Victoria U., New Zealand, 1971; PhD, Cornell U., 1976. Rsch. fellow Australian Nat. U., Canberra, Australia, 1976-78; asst. prof. UCLA, L.A., 1978-80; assoc. prof. Calif. Inst. Tech., Pasadena, 1980-84, prof., 1984—, George van Osdol prof., 1995—. Chmn. divsn. geol. & planetary scis. Calif. Inst. Tech., 1989-94. Contbr. about 100 articles to profl. jours. Named Fulbright scholar, USA, 1971-76. Fellow Am. Geophysical Union (Harry H. Hess medal 1998), Royal Soc. London, 1993; mem. AAAS, Am. Astron. Soc. (Urey prize 1984). Office: Calif Inst Tech 1200 E California Blvd Pasadena CA 91125-0001 E-mail: djs@gps.caltech.edu

STEVENSON, JAMES RICHARD, radiologist, lawyer; b. Ft. Dodge, Iowa, May 30, 1937; s. Lester Lawrence and Esther Irene (Johnson) S.; m. Sara Jean Hayman, Sept. 4, 1958; children: Bradford Allen, Tiffany Ann, Jill Renee, Trevor Ashley. BS, U. N.Mex., 1959, JD, 1987; MD, U. Colo., 1963. Diplomate Am. Bd. Radiology, Am. Bd. Nuc. Medicine, Am. Bd. Legal Medicine, 1989: Bar: N.Mex. 1987, U.S. Dist. Ct. N.Mex. 1988. Intern U.S. Gen. Hosp., Tripler, Honolulu, 1963-64, resident radiology Brook, San Antonio, 1964-67; radiologist, ptnr. Van Atta Labs., Albuquerque, 1970-88, Radiology Assocs. of Albuquerque, 1988—, pres., 1994-96. Radiologist, ptnr. Civerolo, Hansen & Wolf, Albuquerque, 1988-89; adj. asst. prof. radiology U. N.Mex., 1970-71; pres. med. staff AT & SF Meml. Hosp., 1979-80, chief of staff, 1980-81, trustee, 1981-83. Author: District Attorney manual, 1987. Participant breast screening Am. Cancer Soc., Albuquerque, 1987-88; dir. profl. divsn. United Way, Albuquerque, 1975. Maj. U.S. Army, 1963-70, Vietnam; col. M.C. USAR, 1988—. Decorated Bronze Star; Allergy fellow, 1960; Med.-Legal Tort scholar, 1987. Fellow Am. Coll. Radiology (councilor 1980-86, mem. med. legal com. 1990-96), Am. Coll. Legal Medicine, Am. Coll. Nuc. Medicine, Am. Coll. Nuc. Physicians, Radiology Assn. Albuquerque; mem. AMA (Physicians' Recognition award 1969—), Am. Soc. Law & Medicine, Am. Arbitration Assn., Albuquerque Bar Assn., Soc. Nuc. Medicine (v.p. Rocky Mountain chpt. 1975-76), Am. Inst. Ultrasound in Medicine, N.Am. Radiol. Soc. (chmn. med. legal com. 1992-95), N.Mex. Radiol. Soc. (pres. 1978-79), N.Mex. Med. Soc. (chmn. grievance com.), Albuquerque-Bernalillo County Med. Soc. (scholar 1959), Nat. Assn. Health Lawyers, ABA (antitrust sect. 1986—), N.Mex. State Bar, Albuquerque Bar Assn., Sigma Chi, Albuquerque Country Club, Elks, Masons, Shriners. Republican. Methodist. Home: 3333 Santa Clara Ave SE Albuquerque NM 87106-1530 Office: Medical Arts Imaging Ctr A6 Med Arts Sq 801 Encino Pl NE Albuquerque NM 87102-2612

STEVENSON, KAREN, lawyer; b. Bay Shore, N.Y., 02 Oct. BA summa cum laude, UCLA, 1971; JD, U. Calif., 1970. Bar: Calif. 1980, U.S. Dist. Ct. (no. dist.) Calif. Law clk. Judge William W. Schwarzer U.S. Dist. Ct. (no. dist.) Calif., 1980-81; v.p., assoc. gen. counsel Transam. Corp., 1987-88, v.p. law, sec., 1989-90; v.p., gen. counsel Knight-Ridder, Inc., San Jose, Calif. Mem. jury instrns. com. U.S. Ct. Appeals (9th cir.), 1983-84. Assoc. editor Calif. Law Rev., 1978-79, articles editor, 1979-80. Regents fellow, 1978-79. Mem. State Bar Calif. (mem. corps. com. 1991-94, legis. liaison 1991-92, vice-chair 1992-93, chair 1993-94), Phi Beta Kappa, Pi Gamma Mu. Office: 50 W San Fernando St Ste 1500 San Jose CA 95113-2434

STEVENSON, THOMAS RAY, plastic surgeon; b. Kansas City, Mo., Jan. 22, 1946; s. John Adolph and Helen Ray (Clarke) S.; m. Judith Ann Hunter, Aug. 17, 1968; children: Anne Hunter, Andrew Thomas. BA, U. Kans., 1968, MD. Diplomate Am. Bd. Plastic and Reconstructive Surgery, Am. Bd. Surgery. Resident in gen. surgery U. Va., Charlottesville, 1972-78; resident in plastic surgery Emory U., Atlanta, 1980-82; asst. prof. surgery U. Mich., 1982-88, assoc. prof. surgery, 1988-89. Chief plastic surgery Ann Arbor VA Hosp., 1982—, U. Calif., Davis, 1989—. Served to maj. USAR, 1978-80. Fellow ACS; mem. Am. Soc. Plastic and Reconstructive Surgery. Office: UC Davis Divsn Plas Surg 4301 X St Ste 2430 Sacramento CA 95817-2214

STEWARD, OSWALD, neuroscience educator, researcher; b. Sept. 12, 1948; m. Kathy L. Pyle; children: Jessica, Oswald IV. BA in Psychology magna cum laude, U. Colo., 1970; PhD in Psychobiology, U. Calif., Irvine, 1974. Asst. prof. neurosurgery and physiology U. Va. Sch. Medicine, Charlottesville, 1974-79, assoc. prof., 1979-84, prof., 1984-86, acting chmn. neurosci. dept., 1986-88, chmn., 1998-99; dir. Reeve Irvine Rsch. Ctr. U. Calif., Irvine, Calif., 1999—. Author: Principles of Cellular, Molecular, and Developmental Neuroscience, 1989, Functional Neuroscience, 2000; contbr. over 200 articles and revs. to profl. publs. Predoctoral fellow NIMH, Bethesda, Md., 1971-74; rsch. career devel. grantee NIH, 1978-83, Jacob Javitts neurosci. grantee NIH, 1987-94. Mem. Soc. for Neurosci. (Va. chpts. com. 1985-87) Office: U Calif Irvine 1101 Gillespie Neurosci Rsch Facility Irvine CA 92697-4292

STEWART, DEBORAH CLAIRE, dean; b. Freeport, Ill., Sept. 14, 1951; Student, Monterey Peninsula Coll., 1969-71; BS in Zoology, U. Calif., Davis, 1973; MD, U. Calif., San Francisco, 1977. Diplomate Am. Bd. Peds. Intern Children's Hosp. L.A., 1977-78, resident in peds., 1978-79, fellow in adolescent medicine, 1979-81, attending physician emergency med. svcs., 1980-81; med. dir. comprehensive adolescent program dept. ob-gyn. Charles R. Drew Postgrad. Med. Sch., L.A., 1981-83; asst. prof. dept. ob-gyn. UCLA/Charles R. Drew Postgrad. Med. Sch., 1982-83; mem. ped. staff Children's Hosp. of Orange County, Orange, Calif., 1983-86, U. Calif. Irvine Med. Ctr., Orange, 1983-99; assoc. prof. ob-gyn., assoc. prof. medicine U. Calif., Irvine, 1983-99, dir. child sexual abuse program, 1983-99, assoc. prof. clin. peds., chief divsn. gen. peds., dir. adol, 1988-95, assoc. dean for med. student and resident affairs, 1992-99; med. dir. child protection ctr. Meml. Miller Children's Hosp., Long Beach, Calif., 1995-99; assoc. dean med. edn. program U. Calif.-San Francisco, Fresno, 1999—. Project dir. South Ctrl. L.A. Sexual Trauma Program, 1983; med. cons. L.A. Commn. on Assaults Against Women, 1982-84, Calif. Children's Svcs., 1980-85, Sexual Assault Protocol Office of Criminal Justice Planning, 1984-86, Sexual Assault Protocol L.A. County, 1984-86; med. dir. Child Abuse Svcs. Team County of Orange, 1987—; physician mem. Calif. State Atty. Gen.'s Investigative Pilot Projects Rsch. and Evaluation Adv. Panel; cons. County of Orange Coroner's Office, 1994-99. Contbr. articles to profl. jours.; presenter in field; reviewer: Ped. and Adolescent Gyn., 1988—, Jour. Adolescent Health Care, 1986—, Peds., 1988—, Am. Jour. Obs. and Gyn., 1991— Mem. med. adv. bd. Planned Parenthood, 1983-94. Fellow Am. Acad. Pediatrics (pres. Dist. IX Chpt. 4, 1995-97, sec. chpt. IV, chair chpt. IV com. on child abuse 1983—); mem. N.Am. Soc. Pediatric And Adolescent Gynecology (co-chair collaborative rsch. com. 1988—), Orange County Ped. Assn. Office: U Calif San Francisco-Fresno Med Edn Program 2615 E Clinton Ave Fresno CA 93703-2223 E-mail: deborah.stewart@ucsfresno.edu

STEWART, FRANK MAURICE, JR. federal agency administrator; b. Okalona, Miss., Apr. 1, 1939; s. Frank Maurice Stewart and Henryne Annette (Walker) Goode; m. Regina Diane Mosley, Dec. 26, 1964; children: Lisa Ann, Dana Joy. BA, Wesleyan U., 1961, MA in Teaching, diploma further study, Wesleyan U., 1963; postgrad., Am. U., 1982-84. Dir. urban edn. corps N.J. State Dept. Edn., Trenton, 1969-70; dir. urban teaching intern program Sch. Edn. Rutgers U., New Brunswick, N.J., 1970-71; staff asst. White House Conf. on Aging, Washington, 1971-73; chief program devel. U.S. Office of Equal Edn. Opportunity, Washington, 1973-74; chief policy analysis U.S. Adminstrn. on Aging, Washington, 1974-75; asst. exec. sec. U.S. HEW, Washington, 1975-77; dir. govt. programs U.S. Dept. Energy, Washington, 1977-80, dir. instnl. conservation programs, 1980-84, dir. state and local assistance programs, 1984-90, dep. asst. sec. for tech. and fin. assistance, 1990-93; acting asst. sec. for energy efficiency and renewable energy, 1993-94; mgr. Golden (Colo.) Field Office, U.S. Dept. Energy, 1994—. Bd. dirs. Renewable Energy for African Devel., 1992-94; mem. U.S. Presdl. Del. on Sustainable Energy Devel. to South Africa, 1995, U.S. Del. to African-African-Am. Summit, Dakar, Senegal, 1995; bd. advisors Internat. Sustainable Tech. Bus. Ctr. Bd. dirs. Urban League of Met. Denver. Recipient Svc. Recognition award Assn. Phys. Plant Adminstrs., Washington, 1982, Svc. Appreciation award Nat. Assn. State Energy Officials, Washington, 1987, Midwest Rsch. Inst., 1996; named Energy Exec. of Yr. Assn. Energy Engrs., Atlanta, 1988. Mem. Sr. Execs. Assn., Nat. Assn. of Black Environmentalists (bd. dirs.), Am. Assn. of Blacks in Energy (bd. dirs. Denver chpt.), Denver Fed. Exec. Bd. Episcopalian. Home: 202 S Madison St Denver CO 80209-3010 Office: US Dept Energy Field Office 1617 Cole Blvd Golden CO 80401-3305 E-mail: frank_stewart@nrel.gov

STEWART, HOMER JOSEPH, engineering educator; b. Elba, Mich., Aug. 15, 1915; s. Earl Arthur and Alta Fern (Stanley) S.; m. Frieda Klassen, June 15, 1940; children— Robert Joseph, Katherine Stanley, Barbara Ellen. Student, U. Dubuque, 1932-33; B in Aero. Engring., U. Minn., 1936; PhD, Calif. Inst. Tech., 1940. Faculty Jet Propulsion Lab. Calif. Inst. Tech., Pasadena, 1938—, prof. aeros., 1949-80, prof. emeritus, 1980—, chief research analysis sect., 1945-56, chief Liquid Propulsion Systems div., 1956-58, spl. asst. to dir., 1960-62, chief Advanced Studies Office, 1963-67, advanced studies adviser, 1967-76. Dir. Sargent Industries, Inc., 1964-79, Office Program Planning and Evaluation, NASA, 1958-60; mem. tech. adv. bd. Aerojet-Gen. Corp., 1956-58, 61-70; mem. tech. evaluation group guided missile com. Research and Devel. Bd., 1948-50, chmn., 1951; mem. sci. adv. bd. USAF, 1949-56, 1959-64; mem. sci. adv. com. Ballistics Research Lab., 1959-69, 73-77. Author: Kinematics and Dynamics of Fluid Flow, sect. VI Handbook of Meteorology, 1945; Contbr. articles to tech. jours. Recipient Outstanding Achievement award U. Minn., 1954, NASA Exceptional Service medal, 1970, I.B. Laskowitz award N.Y. Acad. Scis., 1985 Fellow AIAA; mem. Am. Meteorol. Soc., Internat. Acad. Astronautics, Sigma Xi, Tau Beta Pi. Home: 2393 Tanoble Dr Altadena CA 91001-2729 Office: Aerospace Dept Calif Inst Tech Pasadena CA 91125-0001

STEWART, ISAAC DANIEL, JR. retired state supreme court justice; b. Salt Lake City, Nov. 21, 1932; s. Isaac Daniel and Orabelle (Iverson) S.; m. Elizabeth Bryan, Sept. 10, 1959; children: Elizabeth Ann, Shannon. BA with high honors, U. Utah, 1959, JD with high honors, 1962. Bar: Utah 1962, U.S. Dist. Ct. Utah 1962, U.S. Ct. Appeals (10th cir.) 1962, U.S. Ct. Appeals (4th cir.) 1963, U.S. Ct. Appeals (9th cir.) 1964, U.S. Ct. Appeals (8th cir.) 1965, U.S. Supreme Ct. 1965. Atty. antitrust divsn. Dept. Justice, Washington, 1962-65; asst. prof., then assoc. prof. U. Utah Coll. Law, 1965-70; ptnr. Jones, Waldo, Holbrook & McDonough, Salt Lake City, 1970-79; assoc. justice Utah Supreme Ct., 1979-2000, assoc. chief justice, 1986-88, 94-98, assoc. justice, 1999-2000; ret., 2000. Lectr. in field; mem. Utah Bd. Oil, Gas and Mining, 1976-78, chmn., 1977-78; Utah rep. Interstate Oil Compact Commn., 1977-78, exec. com. 1978-79; mem. adv. com. rules of procedure Utah Supreme Ct., 1983-87; chmn. com. on bar-press guidelines Utah Bar; mem. U. Utah search com., 1968-70; legal advisor, 1966-68. Editor-in-chief Utah Law Rev.; contbr. articles to legal jours. Chmn. subcom. on legal rights and responsibilities of youth Utah Gov's Com. on Youth, 1972; pres. Salt Lake chpt. Coun. Fgn. Rels., 1982; mem. Salt Lake City C. of C., 1974-79, mem. govtl. modernization com., 1976-78; missionary for Mormon Ch. in Fed. Republic Germany, 1953-56; bd. dirs. U. Utah Alumni Assn., 1986-89 Recipient Alumnus of Yr. award U. Utah Coll. Law, 1989. Mem. ABA, Utah Bar Assn. (com. on law and poverty 1967-69, com. on specialization 1977-78, pub. rels. com. 1968-69, chmn. com. on antitrust law 1977-78, com. on civil procedure reform 1968, mem. exec. com. bd. of appellate judges 1990—, liaison to supreme and adv. coms. evidence & profl. conduct 1986—, Appellate Judge of Yr. 1986), Salt Lake County Bar Assn., Am. Judicature Soc., Order of Coif, Phi Beta Kappa, Phi Kappa Phi, Sigma Chi (Significant Sig award 1987).

STEWART, JANICE MAE, judge; b. Medford, Oreg., Feb. 13, 1951; d. Glenn Logan and Eathel Mae (Jones) S.; m. F. Gordon Allen III, Aug. 10, 1975; children: Benjamin Stewart, Rebecca Mae. AB in Econs., Stanford U., 1972; JD, U. Chgo., 1975. Bar: Ill. 1976, Oreg. 1977, U.S. Dist. Ct. Oreg. 1977, U.S. Ct. Appeals (9th cir.) 1978. Assoc. Winston & Strawn, Chgo., 1975-76, McEwen, Gisvold, Rankin & Stewart, Portland, Oreg., 1976-81, ptnr., 1981-93; U.S. magistrate judge Portland, 1993—. Mem. Multonomah County Profl. Responsbility Com., Portland, 1979-82, Oreg.

Profl. Responsibility Bd., 1982-85, Oreg. State Bar Practice and Procedure Com., 1985-88, Profl. Liability Fund Def. Panel, Portland, 1985-93, Multnomah County Jud. Selection Com., 1985-88, Oreg. State Bar Professionalism Com., 1989-91, Oreg. State Bar Fed. Practice and Procedure Com., 1996-99, Coun. Ct. Procedures, 1991-93, lawyer rep. 9th Cir. Jud. Conf., 1990-93, Multnomah County Professionalism Com., 1997-2000. Mem. ABA, Am. Arbitration Assn. (arbitrator 1990-93), Oreg. Bar Assn., Multnomah County Bar Assn. (dir. 1990-93), Phi Beta Kappa. Democrat. Office: 1027 US Courthouse 1000 SW 3rd Ave Portland OR 97204-2930

STEWART, JOHN WRAY BLACK, college dean; b. Coleraine, Northern Ireland, Jan. 16, 1936; s. John Wray and Margaret Reid (Black) S.; m. Felicity Ann Patricia Poole, Aug. 7, 1965; children: J.W. Matthew, Hannah Louise. BSc with honors, Queen's U., Belfast, Northern Ireland, 1958, B.Agr. with honors, 1959, PhD, 1963, DSc, 1988. Registered profl. agrologist. Sci. officer chem. rsch. div. Ministry of Agr., Belfast, 1959-64; asst. prof. soil sci. dept. U. Sask., Saskatoon, Can., 1966-71, assoc. prof. Can., 1971-76, prof. Can., 1976-81, dir. Sask. Inst. Pedology, 1981-89, dean Coll. Agr., 1989-99; prof. emeritus, dean emeritus, 1999—. Tech. expert, cons. FAO/IAEA, U.N.D.P., Vienna, Austria, 1971, 74-75; mem. program com. Can. Global Change, 1985-98; sec.-gen. Sci. Com. on Problems of Environment, Paris, 1988-92, pres., 1992-95, past pres., 1995-98, editor-in-chief, 1999—; cons. UNESCO, Paris, 1990; trustee Internat. Inst. Tropical Agr., Nigeria, 1991-97; chair sci. adv. com. Inter-Am. Inst. on Global Change Rsch., 1994—. Contbr. articles to profl. publs., chpts. to books. Fellow Can. Soc. Soil Sci., Berlin Inst. Advanced Study, Am. Soc. Agronomy, Soil Sci. Soc. Am., Agrl. Inst. Can.; mem. Brit. Soc. Soil Sci., Brazilian Soc. Soil Sci., Internat. Soc. Soil Sci. Avocations: squash, golf, tennis.

STEWART, KIRK T. public relations executive; b. 1951; BA in polit. sci., U. So. Calif., 1973; MA in public rels./journalism, 1976. Account exec. Burson-Marsteller, 1976-79; pub. affairs dir. Info. Svcs. Dir. TRW, 1979-81; group supr. Manning Selvage & Lee, 1981-82, v.p., 1982-83, exec. v.p., 1983-84; exec. v.p., mng. dir. Manning Selvage & Lee/L.A., Calif., 1984-89; pres. Manning, Selvage & Lee Inc., N.Y.C., 1989-91, pres., CEO, 1992; chmn., CEO Manning, Selvage & Lee, Inc., N.Y.C., 1993-97; v.p. corp. comms. Nike Inc., Beaverton, Oreg., 1997—. Office: Nike Inc 1 Bowerman Dr Beaverton OR 97005-6453

STEWART, LINDSAY D. lawyer; BA, JD, Willamette U. Bar: Oreg. 1973. Corp. counsel Nike Inc., Beaverton, Oreg., 1981-94, v.p. law and corp. affairs, 1994—. Office: Nike Inc 1 Bowerman Dr Beaverton OR 97005-0979

STEWART, LUCILLE MARIE, retirede special education coordinator; b. Pitts., Feb. 24, 2000; d. William H. and Edna (Hoffman) S. BEd, Duquesne U.; MEd, U. Pitts.; postgrad., Columbia U., U. Calif., Calif. State U. Cert. elem. and secondary tchr., spl. edn. tchr., supr., adminstr. Tchr. Lincoln (Ill.) State Sch., 1953; group leader Retarded Edn. Alliance, N.Y.C., 1954-58; tchr. mentally retarded Ramapo Ctrl. Sch. Dist., Spring Valley, N.Y., 1958-60, tchr. seriously emotionally disturbed, 1960-64, supr. presch. program for educationally disadvantaged, 1965-67; program dir. Pomona (N.Y.) Camp for Retarded, summers 1960-63; tchr. Stockton Sch., San Diego, 1964-65, Cathedral City (Calif.) Sch., 1967-78; program specialist edn. Palm Springs (Calif.) Unified Sch. Dist., 1978-95, prin. elem. summer schs., 1971 72; prin. tchr. Summer Extended Sch. for Spl. Students, summer 1979-99. Mem. exec. com. U. Calif. Extension area adv. com. Mem. NEA, AAUW, ASCD, Calif. Tchrs. Assn., Palm Springs Tchrs. Assn., Palm Springs Ednl. Leadership Assn., Calif. Assn. Program Specialists, Calif. Adminstrs. of Spl. Edn. (desert cmty. mental health childrens com.), Coun. Exceptional Children (adminstrn. divsn., early childhood-learning handicap divsns.), Am. Assn. Childhood Edn., Toastmistress Club, Alpha Kappa Alpha, Phi Delta Kappa, Delta Kappa Gamma.

STEWART, MARLENE METZGER, financial planning practitioner, insurance agent; b. Portland, Oreg., Nov. 1, 1937; d. Eddie Charles and Helen M. (Grant) Metzger; m. Robert W. Stewart, Aug. 1, 1964 (dec. Jan. 1967); m. Melvin N. McBurney, Feb. 14, 1985. BA, U. Oreg., 1959; MA, U. Tex., El Paso, 1971. Exec. dir. Summer 72 Youth Com. Office of Mayor, Portland, 1972; registered rep. Mut. Life Ins. Co. N.Y., Portland, 1973-76, Prudential Life Ins. Co., Portland, 1976-77; ptnr. N.W. Fin. Planning, Portland, 1977-79; pres. Horizons Unltd. Fin. Planning, Portland, 1979-86; prin. EMR Fin. Adv. Svcs., Inc., Portland, 1986-89; registered rep. KMS Fin. Svcs., Inc., Portland, 1979—; owner Stewart Fin. Group, 1991—. Mem.-at-large nat. bd. YMCA's, 1971-73; bd. dirs. Met. YMCA, Portland, 1971-75; bd. dirs. YWCA, Portland, 1989-92, treas., 1990-92, chmn. investment com.; chmn. planned giving com. Arthritis Found., 1984-86. Bill Bottler scholar Portland chpt. CLU and Chartered Fin. Cons., 1981. Mem. Fin. Planning Assn., Oreg. Soc. Inst. CFP's (treas. 1985-86, Internat. Assn. Fin. Planners (pres. Oreg. chpt. 1987-88), Nat. Assn. Ins. & Fin. Adv., Soc. of Fin. Svc. Profls. and Portland Chpt. (treas. Portland chpt. 1985-86), Fin. Planning Assn., Assocs. Good Samaritan (steering com., chmn. 1991-92), Rotary (past chmn. World Cmty. Svc. com. 1998-2000). Republican. Presbyterian. Avocations: swimming, traveling, reading, knitting, sewing. Office: 5901 SW Macadam Ave Ste 135 Portland OR 97201 E-mail: stewfg@aol.com

STEWART, MILTON ROY, lawyer; b. Clovis, N.Mex., Dec. 16, 1945; s. Virgil Maurice and E. Marie (Collins) S. BA, Ind. U., 1968, JD summa cum laude, 1971. Bar: Oreg. 1971, U.S. Ct. Appeals (9th cir.) 1971, U.S. Dist. Ct. (no. dist.) Oreg. 1971. Assoc. firm Davies, Biggs et al, Portland, Oreg., 1971-75; v.p., gen. counsel U.S. Datacorp, Portland, 1975-77; pvt. practice Portland, 1977-86; ptnr. Davis, Wright, Tremaine & predecessor firm, Portland, 1987—, mem. exec. com., past chmn. firmwide bus. group, 1990-98. Chmn. emeritus Oreg. chpt. Nat. Multisclerosis Soc., 1994—; mem. bd. dirs. Nat. Multiple Sclerosis Soc.; mem. bd. vis. Ind. U. Sch. Law. Capt. U.S. Army, 1968-78. State Farm Found. fellow, 1970; John H. Edwards fellow Ind. U. Found., 1971. Mem. Oreg. State Bar Assn., Multnomah Athletic Club, Astoria Golf and Country Club. Office: Davis Wright Tremaine 1300 SW 5th Ave Ste 2200 Portland OR 97201-5667 E-mail: miltstewart@dwt.com

STEWART, RICHARD A. mayor; Mayor City of Moreno Valley, Calif. Office: City Hall 14177 Frederick St Moreno Valley CA 92553-9014 E-mail: richards@moval.org

STEWART, RICHARD ALFRED, business executive; b. Hartford, Conn., Nov. 2, 1945; s. Charles Alfred and Theresa (Procopio) S. BS, Valley Coll., 1967. Account exec. Bank Printing Inc., Los Angeles, 1967-70; pres. Carpet Closet Inc., Los Angeles, 1970-73; western sales mgr. Josten's, Los Angeles, 1973-84; pres. Western Internat. Premiums, Los Angeles, 1984-87; dir. corp. sales Tiffany and Co., Beverly Hills, Calif., 1987-90, dir. major program sales, 1990-92, dir. regional sales N.Y.C., 1992-93, dir. major programs, 1992-93; v.p. sales mktg. and recognition divsn. Jostens, Memphis, 1993—; prin. The Stewart Group Sales & Mktg. Cons., 1994—. V.p. sales & mktg. Am. Gem Corp.; recognition cons. L.A. Olympic Com., 1983-84. Contbr. articles to profl. mags.; developer medals for 1984 summer Olympics. Chmn. bd. dirs. Athletes and Entertainers for Kids. Avocations: tennis, basketball, photography.

STEWART, ROBERT LEE, retired career officer, astronaut; b. Washington, Aug. 13, 1942; s. Lee Olin and Mildred Kathleen (Wann) S.; m. Mary Jane Murphy; children: Ragon Annette, Jennifer Lee. BS in Math., U. So. Miss., 1964; MS in Aerospace Engring., U. Tex., 1972; grad., U.S. Army Air Def. Sch., 1964, grad. advanced course, guided missile systems officers course, 1970. Commd. 2d lt. U.S. Army, 1964, advanced through grades to brig. gen., 1986, fire team leader armed helicopter platoon 101st Aviation Bn., instr. pilot Primary Helicopter Sch., 1967-69, bn. ops. officer, bn. exec. officer 309th Aviation Bn., Korea, 1972-73, exptl. test pilot Aviation Engring. Flight Activity Edwards AFB, Calif., 1974-78; astronaut candidate NASA, 1978, mission specialist Space Shuttle Mission 41-B, 1984; mission specialist STS-5IJ, 1985; dep. comdr. U.S. Army Strategic Def. Command, Huntsville, Ala., 1987-89; dir. of plans U.S. Space Command, 1989-92. Decorated D.S.M., (2) Legion of Merit, (4) DFC, (2) Purple Hearts, Bronze star, Def. Superior Svc. medal, others; recipient NASA Space Flight medal, 1984, 85, Fineburg Meml. award Am. Helicopter Soc., 1984, Herman Oberth award AIAA, 1990; named Army Aviator of Yr., 1984. Mem. Soc. Exptl. Test Pilots, Assn. U.S. Army, Army Aviation Assn. Am., Assn. Space Explorers. Avocations: photography, woodworking, skiing. Home and Office: 815 Sun Valley Dr Woodland Park CO 80863-7729

STEWART, ROSS, chemistry educator; b. Vancouver, B.C., Can., Mar. 16, 1924; s. David Methven and Jessie (Grant) S.; m. Greta Marie Morris, Sept. 7, 1946; children— Cameron, Ian B.A., U. B.C., 1946, M.A., 1948; Ph.D., U. Wash., 1954. Lectr. chemistry Royal Roads Coll., Victoria, B.C., 1949-52, asst. prof., 1952-54, assoc. prof., 1954-55; asst. prof. chemistry U. B.C., Vancouver, 1955-59, assoc. prof., 1959-62, prof., 1962-89, hon. prof., 1989—. Author: Oxidation Mechanisms, 1964, Investigation of Organic Reactions, 1966, The Proton: Applications to Organic Chemistry, 1985, (with J.D. Roberts & M.C. Caserio) Organic Chemistry, Methane to Macromolecules, 1970; contbr. numerous articles to profl. jours. Fellow Royal Soc. Can., Chem. Inst. Can.; mem. B.C. Thoroughbred Breeders Soc. (pres. 1972-74), Can. Thoroughbred Horse Soc. (v.p. 1974-75). Club: Point Grey Golf (Vancouver) Avocations: breeding and racing thoroughbred horses; golf; gardening. Home: 4855 Paton St Vancouver BC Canada V6L 2H9 Office: U BC Dept Chemistry Vancouver BC Canada V6T 1Z1

STEWART, THOMAS J. wholesale distribution executive; b. Mar. 28, 1945; CEO Svcs. Group Am., 1985—. Office: Svcs Group of Am 4025 Delridge Way SW Ste 500 Seattle WA 98106-1271

STICKEL, FREDERICK A. publisher; b. Weehawken, N.J., Nov. 18, 1921; s. Fred and Eva (Madigan) S.; m. Margaret A. Dunne, Dec. 4, 1943; children— Fred A., Patrick F., Daisy E., Geoffrey M., James E., Bridget A. Student, Georgetown U., 1939-42; BS, St. Peter's Coll., 1943. Advt. salesperson Jersey Observer daily, Hoboken, N.J., 1945-51; retail advt. salesperson Jersey Jour., Jersey City, 1951-55, advt. dir., 1955-66, publisher, 1966-67; gen. mgr. Oregonian Pub. Co., Portland, Oreg., 1967-72, pres., 1972-86, publisher, 1975—. Bd. regents U. Portland; mem. adv. bd. Portland State U.; bd. dirs. Portland Rose Festival Assn., United Way Oreg.; chmn. Portland Citizens Crime Commn.; mem. adv. bd. St. Vincent's Hosp. Capt. USMC, 1942-45. Mem. Assn. for Portland Progress (dir.), Portland C. of C. (dir.), Oreg. Newspaper Pubs. Assn. (past pres.), Pacific N.W. Newspaper Assn. (pres.), Am. Newspaper Pubs. Assn., University Club, Multnomah Athletic Waverley Country Club, Arlington Club, Rotary. Office: Oregonian Pub Co 1320 SW Broadway Portland OR 97201-3499

STICKEL, PATRICK FRANCIS, publishing executive, newspaper; b. Hoboken, N.J., Apr. 17, 1950; s. Fred A. and Margaret (Dunne) S.; m. Debra Isaak, May 10, 1986. Degree in bus. mgmt., U. Portland, 1975. With advt. dept. Jersey Jour., Jersey City, 1966-67; with Oregonian Pub. Co., Portland, 1967-68, 70-75, pressman, with retail advt. dept., 1975-77, with retail & circulation depts., 1980-86, adminstrv. asst., 1987-89, gen. mgr., 1990-94, pres., 1994—; project mgr. Times Picayune, New Orleans, 1986-87. Exec. com. Oreg. Forum, Portland. 1st lt. USMC, 1977-80. Mem. Pacific N.W. Newspapers Assn. (bd. dirs.), Waverley Country Club, Univ. Club, Multnomah Athletic Club. Avocation: golf. Office: Oregonian Pub Co 1320 SW Broadway Portland OR 97201-3499

STICKLES, BONNIE JEAN, nurse; b. Waukesha, Wis., Nov. 24, 1944; d. Donald William and Betty Jane S. BSN, U. Wis., 1967; MSN in Midwifery, Columbia U., 1974. Mem. nursing staff Grace Hosp., Detroit, 1970-73; mem. faculty and staff U. Minn. Sch. Nursing and Nurse-Midwifery Svc., Mpls., 1974-76; chief nurse-midwife, clin. instr. St. Paul-Ramsey Med. Ctr., 1976-84; midwifery supr. IHS/PHS Chinle Hosp., 1984-85; program mgr. maternal health sect. N.Mex. Dept. Health and Environ., 1985-90, Lovelance Med. Ctr., 1990-91, St. Vincent's Hosp., 1991-94, NMC Dialysis Divsn., 1994-95; blackjack dealer, 1995-97; with CNM Penitentiary, N.Mex., 1997—. Author articles in field; patentee tchg. model. Mem. FDA Anesthetics, Life Support Adv. com.; adv. bd. Childbirth Edn. Assn., 1980-85. With USNR, 1965-70. Decorated Letter of Commendation. Mem. Am. Coll. Nurse-Midwives (chmn. profl. affairs com. 1975-80), Nurses Assn. Am. Coll. Obstetricians and Gynecologists (charter), Aircraft Owners and Pilot Assn., Gt. Plains Perinatal Orgn., Alpha Tau Delta.

STICKNEY, ROBERT ROY, fisheries educator; b. Mpls., July 2, 1941; s. Roy E. and Helen Doris (Nelson) S.; m. LuVerne C. Whiteley, Dec. 29, 1961; children: Robert Roy, Marolan Margaret. BS, U. Nebr., 1967; MA, U. Mo., 1968; PhD, Fla. State U., 1971. Cert. fisheries scientist. Research assoc. Skidaway Inst. Oceanography, Savannah, Ga., 1971-73, asst. prof., 1973-75, Texas A&M U., College Station, 1975-78, assoc. prof., 1978-83, prof., 1983-84; prof. zoology, dir. Fisheries Research Lab., So. Ill. U., Carbondale, 1984-85; dir. Sch. of Fisheries U. Wash., Seattle, 1985-91, prof., 1985-96; dir. Sea Grant Coll. program Tex. A&M U., Bryan, 1996—. Chmn. S-168 com. So. Regional Coop. Research Project, 1981-84. Author: Principles of Warmwater Aquaculture, 1979, Estuarine Ecology of the Southeastern United States and Gulf of Mexico, 1984; editor: Culture of Non-Salmonid Freshwater Fishes, 1986, 92, Flagship: A History of Fisheries at the University of Washington, 1989; co-editor: Fisheries: Harvesting Life from Water, 1989, 2d edit. 95, Culture of Salmonid Fishes, 1992, Principles of Aquaculture, 1994, Fish Culture in the United States: A Historical Survey, 1996; editor, revs. in Fisheries Scis., Encylopedia of Aquaculture, 2000; contbr. articles to profl. jours. Served with USAF, 1959-63. Fellow Am. Inst. Fisheries Rsch. Biologists (past bd. dirs. Tex. div.); mem. Am. Fisheries Soc. (pres. fish culture sect. 1983-84, pres. fish edn. sect. 1990-91, Tex. Aquaculturist of Yr. 1979, editor Aquaculture book rev.), World Aquaculture Soc. (bd. dirs., pres. 1991-92, editor World Aquaculture mag.), Western Regional Aquaculture Consortium (chmn. bd. dirs. 1987), Sea Grant Assn. (pres.-elect, sec. 2001—). E-mail: rrstickney@aol.com, stickney@tamu.edu

STIEBER, TAMAR, journalist; b. Bklyn., Sept. 15, 1955; d. Alfred and Florence (Spector) S. Student, student, Rockland C.C., 1972-75, West London (Eng.) Coll., 1973-74; BA in Film cum laude, U. Calif., Berkeley, 1985, postgrad. in comparative lit., 1985-86; grad. police reserve academy-cum laude, Napa Valley Coll., 1988. Office mgr., confidential sec. AP, San Francisco, 1981-83; stringer Daily Californian, Berkeley, Calif., 1983-84; film rsch. teaching asst. U. California, Berkeley, 1984-86; libr. and rsch. asst. Pacific Film Archive, Berkeley, 1984-86; intern San Francisco Examiner, 1984; reporter Sonoma (Calif.) Index-Tribune, 1987-88, Vallejo (Calif.) Times-Herald, 1988-89, Albuquerque Journal, 1989-94, freelancer, 1994—. Recipient Pulitzer prize for specialized reporting, 1990, first place pub. svc. divsn. N.Mex. Press Assn., 1990, pub. svc. award Albuquerque Press Club, 1990; first place newswriting N.Mex. Press Assn., 1991; honorable mention Assn. Press Managing Editors, 1994. Mem. AAUW, Phi Beta Kappa. Home: PO Box 9835 Santa Fe NM 87504-9835

STIEHM, E. RICHARD, pediatrician, educator; b. Milw., Jan. 22, 1933; s. Reuben Harold and Marie Dueno S.; m. Judith Hicks, July 12, 1958; children: Jamie Elizabeth, Carrie Eleanor, Meredith Ellen. B.S., U. Wis., 1954, M.D., 1957. Diplomate: Am. Bd. Pediatrics, Am. Bd. Allergy and Clin. Immunology (bd. dirs. 1977-83), Am. Bd. Diagnostic Lab. Immunology. Intern Phila. Gen. Hosp., 1957-58; fellow in physiol. chemistry U. Wis., 1959-61; med. officer USNR, Johnsville, Pa., 1961-63; resident in pediat. Babies Hosp., N.Y.C., 1963-65; rsch. fellow in pediat. immunology U. Calif., San Francisco, 1965-68; asst. prof. pediat. U. Wis., 1968-69, assoc. prof., 1969-72, UCLA, 1972-78, prof., 1978-87, chief div. immunology, allergy and rheumatology, 1972—, assoc. dir. Ctr. for Interdisciplinary Rsch. in Immunologic Diseases, 1981-82, co-dir. Cystic Fibrosis Ctr., 1988—, vice chair acad. affairs dept. pediatrics, 1989—; vis. scientist metabolism br. Nat. Cancer Inst., Bethesda, Md., 1982-88. Vis. prof. Yale U., Mayo Clinic, U. Cin., Great Ormond St. Hosp., U.K.; bd. sci. dirs. Immune Deficiency Found., 1981—, Eczema Found., 1988—, Pediat. AIDS Found., 1989-99; task force on pediat. allergy NIH, 1977; mem. gen. clin. rsch. ctr. study sect. NIH, 1978-82, 84-88; adv. com. Hartford Fellowship, 1984-88; co-dir. L.A. Pediat. AIDS Consortium, 1988—; commr. HHS adv. commn. on childhood vaccines, 1988-90. Editor: Immunologic Disorders in Infants and Children, 1972, 80, 89, 96; Am. editor: Pediatric Research, 1984-89; assoc. editor: Pediatrics Update, 1978-85; mem. editorial bd. Pediatrics, 1972-78, Pediatrics in Rev., 1978-81, Jour. Allergy and Clin. Immunology, 1976-80, Jour. Clin. Immunology, 1985-89, Jour. Asthma Pediatric Allergy and Immunology, 1987-91, Am. Jour. Diseases of Children, 1987-97, Contemporary Pediatrics, 1991-96, Am. Jour. Clin. Nutrition, 1992-97; contbr. articles to profl. jours. Mem. HHS Commn. on Childhood Vaccines, 1988-90; mem. clin. rsch. adv. com. Nat. Found. March of Dimes, 1992—. Recipient Career Devel. award Nat. Inst. Allergy and Infectious Diseases, 1967-69, E. Mead Johnson award for Pediat. Rsch., 1974, Alumni Citation award U. Wis. Med. Sch., 1988, Lifetime Achievement award Immune Deficiency Found., 1995, Med. Sci. award UCLA Med. Alumni, 1999, Disting. Alumni award Babies and Children's Hosp. Alumni Assn., N.Y., 1999; Markle scholar, 1967-72. Mem. AAAS, Am. Assn. Immunologists, Western Soc. Pediatric Research (coun. 1977-80, pres. 1983, Ross Rsch. award 1971), Soc. Pediatric Research, Am. Pediatric Soc., Am. Acad. Allergy and Clin. Immunology, Am. Acad. Pediatrics (infectious diseases com. 1971-77), Am. Soc. Clin. Investigation, Clin. Immunology Soc., Alpha Delta Phi, Phi Beta Kappa, Alpha Omega Alpha. Office: UCLA Dept Peds Divsn Immunology 10833 Le Conte Ave Los Angeles CA 90095-3075 E-mail: estiehm@mednet.ucla.edu

STINI, WILLIAM ARTHUR, anthropologist, educator; b. Oshkosh, Wis., Oct. 9, 1930; s. Louis Alois and Clara (Larsen) S.; m. Mary Ruth Kalous, Feb. 11, 1950; children— Patricia Laraine, Paulette Ann, Suzanne Kay. BBA, U. Wis., 1960, MS, 1967, PhD, 1969. Planner cost acct. Kimberly-Clark Corp., Niagara Falls, N.Y., 1960-62; from asst. prof. to assoc. prof. Cornell U., Ithaca, 1968-73; assoc. prof. U. Kans., Lawrence, 1973-76; prof. anthropology U. Ariz., Tucson, 1976—, prof. family and cmty. medicine, 1978—; panelist anthropology program NSF, 1976-78; cons. NIH, 1974—. Mem. Ariz. Cancer Ctr., 1995—; adj. prof. Nutritional Scis., 1997—; head dept. anthropology U. Ariz., 1980-89, prof. public health, 1998—; panelist NRC/NSF Grad. Fellowship Program, 1991-95. Author: Ecology and Human Adaptation, 1975, Nature, Culture and Human History - A Biocultural Introduction to Anthropology (with Davydd J. Greenwood), 1977, Physiological and Morphological Adaptation and Evolution, 1979 (with Frank E. Poirier and Kathy B. Wreden) In Search of Ourselves: An Introduction to Physical Anthropology, 1990, 5th edit., 1994; field editor phys. anthropology The Am. Anthropologist, 1980-83; editor-in-chief Am. Jour. Phys. Anthropology, 1983-89; assoc. editor Nutrition and Cancer, 1981-95; cons. editor Collegium Antropologicum, 1985—. Mem. Gov.'s Adv. Council on Aging, State of Ariz., 1980-83. Nat. Inst. Dental Rsch. tng. grantee, 1964-68; Clark Found. grantee, Cornell U., 1973; Nat. Dairy Coun. grantee, 1985-88; Wenner-Gren Found. grantee, 1991—; fellow Linacre Coll., Oxford, 1985; vis. fellow U. London, 1991. Fellow AAAS (steering group sect. H 1987-91), Am. Anthrop. Assn., N.Y. Acad. Scis.; mem. Am. Assn. Phys. Anthropologists (exec. com. 1978-81, pres. 1989-91), Human Biology Assn. (exec. com. 1978-81), Soc. for Study Social Biology, Am. Soc. Nutritional Scis., Am. Soc. on Aging, Sigma Xi. Home: 6240 N Camino Miraval Tucson AZ 85718-3025 Office: U Ariz Dept Anthropology Tucson AZ 85721-0001

STINSON, ALAN L. insurance company executive; Exec. v.p., CFO Fidelity Nat. Fin., Inc., Santa Barbara, Calif., 1998—. Office: Fidelity Nat Fin Inc Ste 200 4050 Calle Real Santa Barbara CA 93110

STISKA, JOHN CHARLES, lawyer; b. Chgo., Feb. 14, 1942; s. Rudolph and Elsie Sophie (Nelson) S.; m. Janet Hazel Osuch, Aug. 8, 1964; children: Julie, Thomas, Michael, Matthew. BBA, U. Wis., 1965, JD, 1970. Bar: Wis. 1970, Calif. 1971. Assoc., ptnr. Luce, Forward, Hamilton & Scripps, San Diego, 1970-81; ptnr. Aylward, Kintz & Stiska, San Diego, 1981-86; pres., CEO Triton Group Ltd., La Jolla, Calif., 1986-87; ptnr. Brobeck, Phleger & Harrison, San Diego, 1987-90; pres., COO Intermark, Inc., La Jolla, Calif., 1990-92; pres., CEO Triton Group Ltd., 1993-94; chmn., CEO, 1994-96; sr. v.p. Qualcomm, Inc., San Diego, 1996-98; pres., ceo DC Acquisition Corp., San Diego, 1998; chair Comml. Bridge Capital LLC, La Jolla, Calif., 1998—. Of counsel Latham & Watkins, San Diego, 1998—. 1st lt. U.S. Army, 1965-67. Mem. ABA. San Diego County Bar Assn., Calif State Bar Assn. Lutheran. Home: 5307 Soledad Rancho Ct San Diego CA 92109-1535 Office: Latham & Watkins 701 B St San Diego CA 92101-8101

STITZINGER, JAMES FRANKLIN, religious studies educator, library director; b. Abington, Pa., July 27, 1950; s. James Franklin and Elizabeth (Kocher) S.; m. Deborah Lynn Benner, July 22, 1972; children: Rachael, James, David, Jonathan. BA, Northwestern Coll., Roseville, Minn., 1975; MDiv, Central Sem., 1975; ThM, Grace Theol. Sem., 1977; MLS, Drexel U., 1978; postgrad., Westminster Theol. Sem., 1991—. Acquisition libr. Grace Theol. Sem., Winona Lake, Ind., 1975-77; libr., prof. ch. history Calvary Bapt. Sem., Lansdale, Pa., 1977-87; dir. libr. svcs., assoc. prof. hist. theology The Master's Coll. and Sem., Sun Valley, Calif., 1987—; chief exec. officer Books for Libraries, Inc., North Hollywood, 1989—. Mem. Am. Theol. Libr. Assn., Am. Soc. Ch. History, Evang. Theol. Soc. Republican. Baptist. Office: The Masters Sem 13248 Roscoe Blvd Sun Valley CA 91352-3739

STIVERS, WILLIAM CHARLES, forest products company executive; b. Modesto, Calif., June 22, 1938; m. Karen L. Gaspar, Aug. 6, 1961; children: William, Gregory, Michael, Kristy, Kelly, John, Jeffrey. BA, Stanford, 1960; MBA, U. So. Calif., 1963; certificate, U. Wash., 1969; grad., Advanced Mgmt. Program, Harvard U., 1977. Asst. cashier, asst. v.p., v.p. First Interstate Bank, San Francisco and Los Angeles, 1962-70; finance mgr. treas. dept. Weyerhaeuser Co., Tacoma, 1970, asst. treas., 1971, treas., 1972—, v.p., 1980-91, sr. v.p., chief fin. officer, 1991—, exec. v.p., CFO, 1991—. Treas. Weyerhaeuser Real Estate Co., 1970; bd. dirs., exec. com. mem. FM Global, Johnson, R.I.;bd. dirs., chmn., pres. S&S Land and Cattle Co. Chmn. fin. mgmt. com. Am. Forest and Paper Assn. Mem. Financial Execs. Inst.

STOCK, DAVID EARL, mechanical engineering educator; b. Balt., Feb. 2, 1939; s. Walter E. and Minnie H. (Bauer) S.; m. Mary R. Wilford, Aug. 4, 1962; children: Joseph W., Katherine W. BS, Penn State U., 1961; MS, U. Conn., 1965; PhD, Oreg. State U., 1972. Test engr. Pratt & Whitney Aircraft, East Hartford, Conn., 1961-65; vol. Peace Corps, Ghana, 1965-68; prof. Wash. State U., Pullman, 1972—, chair faculty senate, 1997-98. Contbr. articles to profl. jours. Fellow ASME (chair multiphase flow com. 1988-90, Freeman scholar 1994, exec. com. fluid engring. divsn.). Office: Wash State U Sch Mech Materials Engr PO Box 642920 Pullman WA 99164-2920 E-mail: stock@wsu.edu

STOCK, PEGGY A(NN), college president, educator; b. Jan. 30, 1936; married; 5 children. BS in Psychology, St. Lawrence U., 1957; MA in Counseling, U. Ky., 1963, EdD, 1970. Lic. psychologist, Ohio. Instr., rsch. asst. dept. psychology and spl. edn. U. Ky., Lexington, 1958-59, 63-67, staff psychologist Med. Ctr., 1964-66; dir. edn. United Cerebral Palsy of the Bluegrass, Lexington, 1962-64; exec. dir. Community Council for Physically Handicapped and Mentally Retarded, Lexington, 1964-66; dir. clin. program No. Ky. Regional Cmty. Mental Health Ctr., Covington, 1969-71; pres. Midwest Inst. Tng. and Edn., Cin., 1971-75; assoc. prof., counseling psychologist Mont. State U., Bozeman, 1975-79, asst. dean Office of Student Affairs and Service, 1977-79; spl. asst. to pres. U. Hartford, Conn., 1979-80, assoc. prof. Coll. Edn., 1980-85, v.p. adminstrn., 1981-86; prof., pres. Colby-Sawyer Coll., New London, N.H., 1986-95; pres. Westminster Coll., Salt Lake City, 1995—. Panelist Nat. Inst. Edn., 1985; cons. and lectr. in field; mem. wild horse and burro adv. bd. Dept. Interior/Bur. Land Mgmt., 1997-2000; bd. dirs. BMW Bank of N.Am., Pacificorp, Fed. Res. Bank, Salt Lake City, 2001—; trustee St. Mark's Hosp., 2000—. Contbr. chpts. to books, articles to profl. jours. Mem. coun. N.H. Coll. and Univ.; nat. bd. dirs. Med. Coll. Pa.; mem. New London Bus. Adv. Bd.; active numerous other civic orgns.; bd. dirs. Utah Partnership for Edn. and Econ. Devel., 1996—; mem. adv. bd. Wells Fargo, 1996—; chair Utah selection com. for the Rhodes Scholarships, 1995—; mem. adv. com. Rowland Hall-St. Mark's Sch., 1999—; hon. bd. dirs. Big Bros./Big Sisters, 1999—; mem. program com. Coun. Ind. Colls., 1996-2000. Recipient Disting. Alumna award St. Lawrence U., 1989; grantee in field, most recent George I. Alden Trust, Helen Fuld Health Trust, Surdna, Cogswell, U.S. Dept. Edn., 1981-89, numerous others; fellow U. Ky., 1966-68, Am. Council Edn., 1979-80, United Jewish Com., 1981. Mem. Am. Coun. on Edn., Am. Assn. for Higher Edn., Advancement Women in Higher Edn., Nat. Assn. Ind. Colls. and Univs. (bd. dirs. 1998—), Am. Assn. Pres.'s Ind. Colls. and Univs. (bd. dirs. 1996—), Salt Lake Area C. of C. (bd. govs. 1996-99), Utah Info. Techs. Assn. (trustee 1998-99). Avocations: breeding Arabian horses, reading, fishing. Office: Westminster Coll 1840 S 1300 E Salt Lake City UT 84105-3617

STOCKARD, R. L. state legislator; b. Bloomfield; Student, U. Albuquerque. State police capt.; mem. N.Mex. Legislature, Santa Fe, 1996—, mem. jud. com., mem. pub. affairs com. Republican. Office: PO Box 1364 Bloomfield NM 87413-1364

STOCKTON, JOHN HOUSTON, professional basketball player; b. Spokane, Wash., Mar. 26, 1962; m. Nada Stepovich, Aug. 16, 1986; 1 child, John Houston. Grad., Gonzaga U., 1984. With Utah Jazz, Salt Lake City, 1984—. Mem. U.S. Olympic Basketball Team, 1992. Named to NBA All-Star team, 1989-94; holder NBA single season rec. most assists, 1991; NBA Assists leader, 1987-1992; NBA Steals leader, 1989, 92; named NBA All-Star Co-MVP, 1993, All-NBA First Team, 1994. Led NBA in most assists per game, 1988-93; led NBA with highest steals per game avg., 1989,1992; shares single-game playoff record for most assists, 24, 1988. Office: Utah Jazz 301 W South Temple Salt Lake City UT 84101-1216

STOCKWELL, ROBERT PAUL, linguist, educator; b. Oklahoma City, June 12, 1925; s. Benjamin P. and Anna (Cunningham) S.; m. Lucy Louisa Floyd, Aug. 29, 1946; 1 child, Paul Witten. B.A., U. Va., 1946, M.A., 1949, Ph.D., 1952. Instr. English, Oklahoma City U., 1946-48; mem. linguistics staff Sch. Langs., Fgn. Service Inst., State Dept., 1952-56; mem. faculty UCLA, 1956-94, prof. English, 1962-66, prof. linguistics, 1986-94, chmn. dept., 1966-73, 80-84, prof. emeritus, 1994—. Mem. com. lang. programs Am. Council Learned Socs., 1965-69 Author: (with J.D. Bowen) Patterns of Spanish Pronunciation, 1960, Sounds of English and Spanish, 1965, (with J. D. Bowen, J.W. Martin) The Grammatical Structures of English and Spanish, 1965, The Major Syntactic Structures of English, 1973, (with P.M. Schachter, B.H. Partee) Foundations of Syntactic Theory, 1977, Workbook in Syntactic Theory and Analysis, 1977, (with Donka Minkova) English Words: History and Structure, 2001; also numerous articles.; editor: (with R.S.K. Macaulay) Linguistic Change and Generative Theory, 1972, ; assoc. editor: Lang., 1973-79, Festschrift: Rhetorica, Phonologica, Syntactica: A Festchrift for Robert P. Stockwell, 1989. Served with USNR, 1943-45. Am. Council Learned Socs. fellow, 1963-64 Mem. Linguistic Soc. Am. (exec. com. 1965-68), Philol. Assn. Great Britain. Home: 4000 Hayvenhurst Ave Encino CA 91436-3850 Office: UCLA Linguistics Dept Los Angeles CA 90025 E-mail: stockwel@ucla.edu

STODDART, J. FRASER, chemistry educator; b. Edinburgh, Scotland, May 24, 1942; BSc, Edinburgh U., Scotland, 1964; PhD, Edinburgh U., 1966, DSc, 1980. Postgrad. student U. Edinburgh, Scotland, 1964-66, Queen's U., Kingston, Ontario, Canada, 1967-70; rsch. fellow U. Sheffield, England, 1970, lectr. in Chemistry, 1970-78; rschr. ICI Corp. Lab., Runcorn, England, 1978-81; reader in Chemistry U. Sheffield, England, 1981-90; prof. Org. Chem. U. Birmingham, England, 1990-97, head Sch. Chem., 1993-97; Winstein chair U. Calif., L.A., 1997—. Lectr. in supramolecular and macromolecular sci. Contbr. articles to profl. jours. including Chem. Rev., Jour. Am. Chem. Soc., Chem. Eur. Jour. Recipient Hope prize 1964, Carbohydrate Chemistry award 1978, RSC Perkin Divsn. Career award 1980, 81, 82, Internat. Izalt-Christensen award in macrocyclic chemistry, 1993, Chaire Bruylants award 1994, Arthur C. Cope Scholar award 1999; Leverhulme rsch. fellow, 1988-89. Fellow Royal Soc., German Acad. Natural Scis. E-mial. Office: UCLA Dept Chem & Biochem 405 Hilgard Ave Los Angeles CA 90095-9000 E-mail: stoddart@chem.ucla.edu

STOEBUCK, WILLIAM BREES, law educator; b. Wichita, Kans., Mar. 18, 1929; s. William Douglas and Donice Beth (Brees) S.; m. Mary Virginia Fields, Dec. 24, 1951; children: Elizabeth, Catherine, Caroline. BA, Wichita State U., 1951; MA, Ind. U., 1953; JD, U. Wash., 1959; SJD, Harvard U., 1973. Bar: Wash. 1959, U.S. Supreme Ct. 1967. Pvt. practice, Seattle, 1959-64; asst. prof. law U. Denver, 1964-67; assoc. prof. U. Wash., Seattle, 1967-70, prof., 1970-95, Judson Falknor prof., 1995—; of counsel Karr, Tuttle, Campbell, Seattle, 1988—. Author: Washington Real Estate: Property Law, 1995, Washington Real Estate: Transactions, 1995, Basic Property Law, 1989, Law of Property, 1984, 3d edit., 2000, Nontrespassory Takings, 1977, Contemporary Property, 1996; contbr. articles to profl. jours. Bd. dirs. Cascade Symphony Orch., 1978-83, Forest Park Libr., 1975-80. 1st lt. USAF, 1951-56. Mem. Am. Coll. Real Estate Lawyers, Am. Coll. Mortgage Attys., Wash. State Bar Assn., Assn. Am. Law Schs., Order of Coif, Seattle Yacht Club. Home: 3515 NE 158th Pl Lake Forest Park WA 98155-6649 Office: U Wash Law Sch 1100 NE Campus Pkwy Seattle WA 98105-6605 E-mail: stoebuck@u.washington.edu

STOFFLE, CARLA JOY, university library dean; b. Pueblo, Colo., June 19, 1943; d. Samuel Bernard and Virginia Irene (Berry) Hayden; m. Richard William Stoffle, June 12, 1964; children: Brent William, Kami Ann. AA, So. Colo. State Coll., Pueblo, 1963; BA, U. Colo., 1965; MLS, U. Ky., 1969; postgrad., U. Wis., 1980. Head govt. publ. dept. John G. Crabbe Library, Eastern Ky. U., Richmond, 1969-72; head. pub. services U. Wis.-Parkside Library, Kenosha, 1972-76, exec. asst. to chancellor, 1978, asst. chancellor edn. services, 1979-85; assoc. dir. U. Mich. Library, Ann Arbor, 1985-91, dep. dir., 1986-91; mem. adv. commn. Sch. Libr. Sci. U. Mich., Ann Arbor, 1986-92; dean librs. U. Ariz., Tucson, 1991—, acting dir. Sch. Info. Resources and Libr. Sci., 1999—. Vol. Peace Corps, Barbados, W.I., 1965-67; mem. adv. bd. Bowker Libr., N.Y., 1985-90; mem. bd. advisors U. Ariz. Press, 1995-2000; mem. adv. coun. OCLC Rsch. Librs., 1995-2000; bd. dirs. Assn. for Rsch. Librs., chair com. on stats. and measurement, 1999—, mem. steering com. scholarly pub. and acad. resource program, 1998; mem. editl. bd. Internet and Higher Edn., 1998-99; bd, dirs. Ctr. for Rsch. Librs., treas., 1999—, budget and fin. com., 1994; presenter in field. Co-author: Administration Government Documents Collection, 1974, Materials and Method for History Research, 1979, Materials and Methods for Political Science Research, 1979; assoc. editor Collection Building, 1986-91, editorial bd., 1986-95; mem. editl. bd. The Bottom Line, 1989-95; contbr. numerous articles to profl. jours. Recipient Most Outstanding Reference Quar. Article award Reference Svc. Press, 1986, Woman on the Move award Tucson Young Women's Christian Assn., 1992, Pres.'s award Ariz. Ednl. Media Assn., 1993, Student Honor Soc. Mortar Bd. award for Faculty Excellence, 1995; named Outstanding Alumnus, Coll. Libr. and Info. Sci., U. Ky., 1989, Libr. of Yr. Ariz. Libr. Assn., 2000. Mem. ALA (treas. 1988-92, exec. bd. dirs. 1985-92, councilor 1983-92, endowment trustee 2001—), Assn. Coll. Rsch. Librs. (pres. 1982-83, Bibliographic Instrn. Libr. of Yr. 1991, Acad. Rsch. Libr. of Yr. 1992). Office: U Arizona Main Libr 1510 E University Blvd Tucson AZ 85721-0005

STOLLER, CLAUDE, architect; b. N.Y.C., Dec. 2, 1921; s. Max and Esther (Zisblatt) S.; m. Anna Maria Oldenburg, June 5, 1946 (div. Oct. 1972); children: Jacob, Dorothea, Elizabeth; m. Rosemary Raymond Lax, Sept. 22, 1978. Student, Black Mountain Coll., N.C., 1942; M.Arch., Harvard U., 1949. Architect Architects Collaborative, Cambridge, Mass., after 1949, Shepley, Bulfinch, Richardson & Abbot, Boston, 1951; co-founder, partner firm Marquis & Stoller, San Francisco, 1956; pvt. practice architecture N.Y.C. and San Francisco, 1974-78; founder, partner Stoller/Partners, Berkeley, Calif., 1978, Stoller, Knoerr Archs., 1988-95. Mem. faculty Washington U., St. Louis, 1955-56, U. Calif., Berkeley, 1957-91, prof. arch., 1968-92, acting chmn. dept., 1965-66, chair grad. studies, 1984-91; mem. Berkeley Campus Design Rev. Bd., 1985-91, chmn., 1992-93; commr. Calif. Bd. Archtl. Examiners, 1980-90, mem. exam. com., 1985-88; mem. diocesan commn. arch. Episcopal Diocese Calif., 1961-98; vis. arch. Nat. Design Inst., Ahmedabad, India, 1963; planning commr. City of Mill Valley, 1961-66, Marin County Planning Commn., 1966-67; mem. pub. adv. panel archtl. svcs. GSA, 1969-71; citizens urban design adv. com. City of Oakland, Calif., 1968; vis. com. nat. archtl. accrediting bd. U. Minn. and U. Wis., Milw., 1971; coun. Harvard Grad. Sch. Design Assn., 1976-77; mem. design rev. com. The Sea Ranch, Calif., 1990—. Prin. works include St. Francis Sq. Coop. Apts., San Francisco, 1961, Pub. Housing for Elderly, San Francisco, 1974, Learning Resources Bldg, U. Calif., Santa Barbara, 1975, Menorah Park Housing for Elderly, San Francisco, 1979, San Jose State U. Student Housing Project, 1984, Delta Airlines Terminal, San Francisco Internat. Airport, 1988. Served with AUS, 1943-46. Recipient numerous awards including AIA Honor awards, 1963, 64, AIA Bay Region Honor award, 1974, Concrete Reinforced Steel Inst. award, 1976, AIA award, 1976, CADA Site I Solar Housing award Sacramento, Calif., 1980, State of Calif. Affordable Housing award, 1981, PG&E Suntherm award, 1981, San Francisco Housing Authority award, 1983, Orchid award City of Oakland, 1989, Citation for achievement and svc. U. Calif., Berkeley, 1991, Design award Berkeley Design Advocates. Fellow AIA. Home: 2816 Derby St Berkeley CA 94705-1325 Office: Claude Stoller FAIA Arch 1818 Harmon St Berkeley CA 94703-2472 E-mail: stoller@uclink.berkeley.edu

STOLLERY, ROBERT, construction company executive; b. Edmonton, Alta., Can., May 1, 1924; s. Willie Charles and Kate (Catlin) S.; m. Shirley Jean Hopper, June 11, 1947; children: Carol, Janet, Douglas. BSc English, U. Alta., 1949, LLD (hon.), 1985, Concordia U., Montreal, Que., 1986, St. Stevens Coll., , 1999. Field engr. Poole Constrn. Ltd., Edmonton, 1949-54, project mgr., 1954-64, v.p., 1964-69, pres., 1969-81; chmn. bd. PCL Constrn. Group Inc., Edmonton, 1979-93; chmn. PCL Constrn. HOldings, Edmonton, 1993—. Bd. dirs. Melcor Devels. Ltd., Edmonton, Alta. Chmn. Edmonton Community Found. Recipient Exec. of Yr. award Inst. Cert. Mgmt. Cons. of Alta., 1988, Can. Businessman of Yr. award U. Alta., 1993. Fellow Can. Acad. Engring.; mem. Assn. Profl. Engrs. (Frank Spragins Meml. award 1981), Engring. Inst. Can. (Julian C. Smith medal 1990), Conf. Bd. Can. (vice chmn. 1980-82), Constrn. Assn. Edmonton (pres. 1972, Claude Alston Meml. award), Can. Constrn. Assn. (v.p. 1970, Can. Businessman of the Yr. award 1993). Conservative. Mem. United Ch. of Canada. Club: Mayfair Golf and Country (Edmonton). Office: PCL Constrn Group Inc 5410 99 St Edmonton AB Canada T6E 3P4

STOLOV, WALTER CHARLES, physician, rehabilitation educator, physiatrist; b. N.Y.C., Jan. 6, 1928; s. Arthur and Rose F. (Gordon) S.; m. Anita Carvel Noodelman, Aug. 9, 1953; children: Nancy, Amy, Lynne. BS in Physics, CCNY, 1948; MA in Physics, U. Minn., 1951, MD, 1956. Diplomate Am. Bd. Phys. Med. and Rehab., Am. Bd. Electrodiagnostic Medicine. Physicist U.S. Naval Gun Factory, Nat. Bur. Stds., Washington, 1948-49; teaching and rsch. asst. U. Minn., Mpls., 1950-54; from instr. to assoc. prof. U. Wash., Seattle, 1960-70, prof., 1970-99, prof. emeritus, 1999—, also chmn., 1987-99, prof. emeritus, 1999—. Editl. bd. Archives Phys. Medicine and Rehab., 1967-78, Muscle and Nerve, 1983-89, 92-95; cons. Social Security Adminstrn., Seattle, 1975—; sec. Am. Bd. Electrodiagnostic Medicine, 1995—. Co-editor: Handbook of Severe Disability, 1981; contbr. articles to profl. jours. Surgeon USPHS, 1956-57. Recipient Townsend Harris medal CCNY, 1990. Fellow AAAS, Am. Heart Assn.; mem. Am. Acad. Phys. Medicine & Rehab. (Disting. Clinician award 1987), Am. Congress Rehab. Medicine (Essay award 1959), Assn. Acad. Physiatrists, Am. Assn. Electrodiagnostic Medicine (pres. 1987-88), Am. Spinal Cord Injury Assn. Avocations: dancing, singing. Office: U Wash Box 356490 1959 NE Pacific St Seattle WA 98195-0001

STOLPER, EDWARD MANIN, secondary education educator; b. Boston, Dec. 16, 1952; s. Saul James and Frances A. (Liberman) S.; m. Lauren Beth Adoff, June 3, 1973; children: Jennifer Ann, Daniel Aaron. AB, Harvard U., 1974; M Philosophy, U. Edinburgh, Scotland, 1976; PhD, Harvard U., 1979. Asst. prof. geology Calif. Inst. Tech., Pasadena, 1979-82, assoc. prof. geology, 1982-83, prof. geology, 1983-90, William E. Leonhard prof. geology, 1990—, chmn. divsn. geol. and planetary sci., 1994—. Marshall scholar Marshall Aid Commemoration Commn., 1974-76, recipient Newcomb Cleve. prize AAAS, 1984, F.W. Clarke medal Geochem. Soc., 1985, Arthur Holmes medal European Union Geosci., 1997; Geochemistry fellow The Geochem. Soc. and The European Assn. for Geochemistry, 1997. Fellow Meteoritical Soc. (Nininger Meteorite award 1976), Am. Geophys. Union (James B. Macelwane award 1986), Mineral Soc. Am., Am. Acad. Arts and Scis.; mem. NAS, Geol. Soc. Am., Sigma Xi. Office: Calif Inst Tech Div Geol Planetary Sci Pasadena CA 91125-0001

STONE, DONALD D. investment and sales executive; b. Chgo., June 25, 1924; s. Frank J. and Mary N. (Miller) Diamondstone; m. Catherine Mauro, Dec. 20, 1970; 1 child, Jeffrey. Student, U. Ill., 1942-43; BS, DePaul U., 1949. Pres. Poster Bros., Inc., Chgo., 1950-71, Revere Leather Goods, Inc., Chgo., 1953-71; owner Don Stone Enterprises, Chgo., 1954—; v.p. Horton & Hubbard Mfg. Co. Inc. div. Brown Group, Nashua, N.H., 1969-71, Neevel Mfg. Co., Kansas City, Mo., 1969-71. Mem. adv. bd. San Diego Opera; founder Don Diego Meml. Scholarship Fund; mem. bd. overseers U. Calif., San Diego, chancellor's assoc.; mem. exec. bd. Chgo. Area council Boy Scouts of Am. Served with U.S. Army, 1943-46. Clubs: Bryn Mawr Country (Lincolnwood, Ill.) (dir.), Carlton, La Jolla Beach and Tennis, La Jolla Country, Del Mar Thoroughbred. Home: 8240 Caminito Maritimo La Jolla CA 92037-2204

STONE, EDWARD CARROLL, physicist, educator; b. Knoxville, Iowa, Jan. 23, 1936; s. Edward Carroll and Ferne Elizabeth (Baber) S.; m. Alice Trabue Wickliffe, Aug. 4, 1962; children: Susan, Janet. AA, Burlington Jr. Coll., 1956; MS, U. Chgo., 1959, PhD, 1964; DSc (hon.), Washington U., Saint Louis, 1992, Harvard U., , 1992, U. Chgo., 1992; BA (hon.), UCLA, 1998. Rsch. fellow in physics Calif. Inst. Tech., Pasadena, 1964-66, sr. rsch. fellow, 1967, mem. faculty, 1967—, prof. physics, 1976-94, David Morrisroe prof. physics, 1994—, v.p. for astron. facilities, 1988-90, v.p., dir. Jet Propulsion Lab., 1991-2001; Voyager project scientist, 1972—. Cons. Office of Space Scis., NASA, 1969-85, mem. adv. com. outer planets, 1972-73; mem. NASA Solar Sys. Exploration Com., 1983; mem. com. on space astronomy and astrophysics Space Sci. Bd., 1979-82; mem. NASA high energy astrophysics mgmt. operating working group, 1976-84, NASA Cosmic Ray Program Working Group, 1980-82, Outer Planets Working Group, NASA Solar Sys. Exploration Com., 1981-82, Space Sci. Bd., NRC, 1982-85, NASA Univ. Rels. Study Group, 1983, steering group Space Sci. Bd. Study on Major Directions for Space Sci., 1995-2015, 1984-85; mem. exec. com. Com. on Space Rsch. Interdisciplinary Sci. Commn., 1982-86; mem. commn. on phys. scis., math. and resources NRC, 1986-89; mem. adv. com. NASA/Jet Propulsion Labs. vis. sr. scientist program, 1986-90; mem. com. on space policy NRC, 1988-89; chmn. adv. panel for The Astronomers, KCET, 1989—. Mem. editl. bd. Space Sci. Instrumentation, 1975-81, Space Sci. Rev., 1982-85, Astrophysics and Space Sci., 1982—, Sci. mag. Bd. dirs. W.M. Keck Found. Recipient medal for exceptional sci. achievement NASA, 1980, Disting. Svc. medal, 1981, 98, Disting. Pub. Svc. medal, 1985, Outstanding Leadership medal, 1986, 95, Am. Edn. award, 1981, Dryden award, 1983, Aviation Week and Space Tech. Aerospace Laureate, 1989, Sci. Man of Yr. award ARCS Found., 1991, Pres.'s Nat. medal of Sci., 1991, Am. Acad. Achievement Golden Plate award, 1992, COSPAR award for outstanding contbn. to space sci., 1992, LeRoy Randle Grumman medal, 1992, Disting Pub. Svc. award Aviation/Space Writers Assn., 1993, Internat. von Karman Wings award, 1996, Alumni award S.E. C.C., Burlington, Iowa, 1998, CEO of Yr. award ARC, 1998, Carl Sagan award Am. Astronautical Soc. and Planetary Soc., Allan D. Emil Meml. award Internat. Astronautical Fedn.; Asteroid named for Edward C. Stone, 1996; Sloan Found. fellow, 1971-73; inducted to Hall of Fame Aviation Week and Space Tech., 1997; awarded Von Karman Lectureship in Astronautics, 1999. Fellow AIAA (assoc., Space Sci. award 1984, Von Karman lectureship in astronautics 1999), AAAS (award 1993), Am. Phys. Soc. (chmn. cosmic physics divsn. 1979-80, exec. com. 1974-76), Am. Geophys. Union, Internat. Astron. Union; mem. NAS, Internat. Acad. Astronautics, Am. Astron. Soc. (divsn. planetary scis. com. 1981-84, Space Flight award 1997), Am. Assn. Physics Tchrs., Am. Philos. Soc. (Magellanic award 1992), Calif. Assn. Rsch. in Astronomy (bd. dirs., vice chmn. 1987-88, 91-94, 97—, chmn. 1988-91, 94-97), Astron. Soc. Pacific (hon.), Nat. Space Club (bd. govs., Sci. award 1990), Calif. Coun. Sci. and Tech. Office: Jet Propulsion Lab 4800 Oak Grove Dr 180-904 Pasadena CA 91109-8001

STONE, GEORGE, artist, art educator; BA, Calif. State U., Long Beach, 1972; MFA, R.I. Sch. Design, 1974. Instr. R.I. Sch. Design, Providence, 1972-74; instr. sculpture Portsmouth (R.I.) Abbey Sch., 1973-74, Wayne State U., Detroit, 1974-75; vis. lectr., sculpture dept. Ohio U., Athens, 1976-77; instr., found. dept. Otis/Parsons Sch. Design, L.A., 1982-83; vis. lectr., sculpture dept. UCLA, 1986; assoc. prof. fine arts Art Inst. So. Calif., Laguna Beach, 1989-93; assoc. prof. visual art U La Verne, Calif., 1994-2000. Vis. artist Calif. State U. Long Beach, 1986, Crossroads H.S. for Arts and Sci., Santa Monica, 1987, Claremont (Calif.) Grad. Sch., 1987, 88, U. Calif. Santa Barbara, 1989, Art Ctr. Coll. Design, Pasadena, Calif., 1991, Yale U., New Haven, 1992, Chatham Coll., Pitts., 1992, Calif. State U. San Francisco, 1993; commd. artist City of West Hollywood, 1986, City of L.A. Cmty. Redevel. Agy., 1987, Metro Art L.A. County Met. Transp. Auth., 1990-97, City of L.A. Cultural Affairs Dept., 1995-97. Solo exhbns. include Forsythe Bldg., Detroit, 1975, Cline Bldg., Athens, Ohio, 1976, Lake Hope, Athens, 1977, Otis/Parsons Gallery, 1981, East Gallery Claremont Grad. Sch., 1985, Calif. State U. Long Beach Art Mus., 1986, Meyers/Bloom Gallery, Santa Monica, Calif., 1988, 91, Laguna Art Mus., Costa Mesa, Calif., 1990, Capp St. Project, 1991, New Langton Arts, San Francisco, 1991, Ruth Bloom Gallery, Santa Monica, 1993, Pitts. Ctr. Arts, 1994; 2-person exhbns. L.A. Contemporary Exhbns., 1985, Claremont Grad. Sch. Gallery, 1988; group exhbns. include Lehigh U. Art Gallery, Bethlemen, Pa., 1975, Wayne State U., 1975, U. Calif. Santa Cruz, 1978, Vanguard Gallery, L.A., 1979, L.A. Inst. Contemporary Art, 1979, NYU Art Gallery, N.Y.C., 1980, Charles Kobler and Assoc. Architects, L.A., 1983, Design Ctr. L.A., 1984, Univ. Art Mus. Calif. State U. Long Beach, 1985, IDM Corp. and Pub. Corp. Arts, Long Beach, 1985, CRA, L.A., 1987, Newport Harbor Art Mus., Newport Beach, Calif., 1988, Meyers/Bloom Gallery, 1989, Galerie Antoine Candeau, Paris, 1990, Sezon Mus. Art, Tokyo and Osaka, Japan, 1991, Muckenthaler Cultural Ctr., Fullerton, Calif., 1991, Contemporary Arts Ctr., New Orleans, 1993, Next Thread Waxing Space, N.Y.C., 1993, Contemporary Arts Forum, Santa Barbara, 1996, Armand Hammer Mus. Art and Cultural Ctr., UCLA, 1997, others; subject numerous catalogs, publs., and revs., 1984—. Home: 1815 Laurel Canyon Blvd Los Angeles CA 90046-2028 Fax: 323-654-3012

STONE, HERBERT ALLEN, management consultant; b. Washington, Sept. 14, 1934; s. Joseph and Marion (Solomon) S.; m. Marjorie Nelke Sterling, June 14, 1964; children: Joanna, Lisa. BSc, U. Mass., 1955, MSc, 1958; PhD, U. Calif., Davis, 1962. Specialist Exptl. Sta. U. Calif., Davis, 1961-62; food scientist SRI, Menlo Park, Calif., 1962-67, dir. food and plant sci., 1967-74; pres. Tragon Corp., Redwood City, 1974—. Mem. adv. bd. U. Mass. Food Sci., 1992—, Calif. Poly. U. Food Sci. and Nutrition, 1996—. Author: Sensory Evaluation Practices, 1985, 2d edit., 1993; assoc. editor Jour. Food Sci., 1977-80, 2000-02; contbr. sci. and tech. articles to profl. jours.; patentee in field. Fellow Inst. Food Exec. Com. (pres. S.E. divsn. 1977-78, exec. com.), Inst. Food Sci. and Tech.; mem. AAAS, Inst. Food Technologists (nat. exec. com. 1994-97), Am. Soc. Enology, European Chemoreception Orgn., Ladera Oaks Club (Menlo Park, Calif.). Home: 990 San Mateo Dr Menlo Park CA 94025-5640 Office: Tragon Corp 365 Convention Way Redwood City CA 94063-1402 E-mail: hstone@tragon.com

STONE, HERMAN HULL, internist; b. Noble, Ill., Dec. 12, 1915; s. Roy Edson and Carrie (Michels) S.; m. Marie Carlson Christensen; children, Patricia Marie Soln, Richard Allen. BS, U. Ill., 1937, MD, 1941. Resident in internal medicine U.S. VA Hosp., Hines, Ill., 1946-49; chief of medicine VA Hosp., Oklahoma City, 1949-50; with Riverside (Calif.) Med. Clinic, 1950-91; dir. Med. Libr., 1991—; clin. prof. medicine Loma Linda (Calif.) U., 1963—. Founder, dir. Patients' Info. Libr., Riverside, 1991—; pres. citizens univ. com. U. Calif. Riverside, 1979-81; trustee Calif. Blue Shield. Served to maj. M.C., AUS, 1942-46. Recipient Outstanding award Nat. Soc. Fund Raising Execs., 1996. Fellow ACP (life); mem. L.A. Acad. Medicine (trustee), Rotary Club. Avocations: golf, books, travel. Office: Patients Info Libr 3660 Arlington Ave Riverside CA 92506-3912 E-mail: rmfpil@aol.com

STONE, JEFFREY KYLE, mycologist, educator; b. East Liverpool, Ohio, Mar. 13, 1954; s. Harry C. and Mary L. (Coleman) S.; m. Daphne Fisher Smith, Aug. 29, 1981; children: Laurel Rebecca, Eliot Kyle. BA in Biology, Antioch Coll., 1976; PhD in Biology (Mycology), U. Oreg., 1986. Grad. rsch. assoc. dept. biology U. Oreg., Eugene, 1979-82, 84, grad. tchg. fellow dept. biology, 1982-85, postdoct. rsch. assoc. dept. biology, 1986, vis. asst. prof. dept. biology, 1987; rsch. assoc. dept. botany and plant pathology Oreg. State U., Corvallis, 1987-90, 90-93, asst. prof. dept. botany and plant pathology, 1993—. Invited participant, spkr. foliar fungi in old-growth forests; participant 5th Internat. Mycological Congress, 1994; invited spkr., instr. Workshop on Fungi and Sustainable Forestry, Xiacui, Oaxaca, Mex., 1997; bd. dirs. N.W. Mycological Cons., 1997—; mem. panel Nat. Biol. Survey Nat. Mus. Natural History Biodiversity Inventory, 1995. Assoc. editor: Mycologia, 1995—; reviewer manuscripts: Canadian Jour. Botany, Canadian Jour. Microbiology, Canadian Jour. Forest Pathology, Sydowia, APS Press, Mycologia, numerous others; contbr. numerous articles to profl. jours. Grantee USDA Forest Svc., 1993-94, 94-95, 95-96, 97-98, 98—, USDA ARS Nursery Crops Rsch., 1995-96, OSU Swiss Needle Cast Coop., 1997-98, 98—, Oregon Filbert Commn., 1998—. Mem. AAAS, Am. Phytopathological Soc. (mem. phylloplane microbiology com. 1995, Lee Hutchins award 1998), Brit. Mycological Soc., Internat. Symbiosis Soc., Lat. Am. Mycological Assn. Mycological Soc. Am. (chair local arrangements annual meeting 1992, chmn. 1995-98, mem. endowment com. 1995-98, councillor ecology/pathology 1996-98, treas. 1998—), N.W. Scientific Assn., Sigma Xi. Achievements include research in ecology, distribution, biodiversity of fungi causing asymptomatic infections of plants (endophytes); pathology, ecology and taxonomy of foliar and stem fungi of woody hosts, particularly those on conifers; taxonomy of conidial fungi, ecology, distribution, and diversity of microfungi; systematics and evolutionary biology of inoperculate discomycetes, particularly those parasitic on plants; research in alternatives to chemical fumigaion for control of Fusarium diseases in conifer nurseries, fungal and parasitic infections of Douglas fir and European hazelnut. Home: 30567 Le Bleu Rd Eugene OR 97405-9216 Office: Oreg State U Bot & Plant Pathology Dept Cordley 2082 Corvallis OR 97331-2902 Fax: 541-737-3573. E-mail: stonej@bcc.orst.edu

STONE, LAWRENCE MAURICE, lawyer, educator; b. Malden, Mass., Mar. 25, 1931; s. Abraham Jacob and Pauline (Bernstein) S.; m. Anna Jane Clark, June 15, 1963; children: Abraham Dean, Ethan Goldthwaite, Katharine Elisheva. AB magna cum laude, Harvard U., 1953, JD magna cum laude, 1956. Bar: Mass. 1956, Calif. 1958. Rsch. asst. Am. Law Inst., Cambridge, Mass., 1956-57; assoc. Irell and Manella, L.A., 1957-61, ptnr., 1963, 79-96, of counsel, 1997—; internat. tax coordinator U.S. Treasury Dept., Washington, 1961-62, tax. legis. counsel, 1964-66; prof. law U. Calif., Berkeley, 1966-78. Vis. prof. law Yale U., New Haven, 1969, Hebrew U. Jerusalem, 1973-74, U. So. Calif., L.A., 1984; mem. adv. group to commr. IRS, Washington, 1973-74; mem. President's Adv. Commn. on Tax Ct. Appointments, Washington, 1976-80; tax advisory bd. Little Brown Co., 1994-96. Author: (with Doernberg) Federal Income Taxation of Corporations and Partnerships, (with Klein, Bankman and Bittker) Federal Income Taxation; bd. editors Harvard Law Rev., 1955-56. Fellow Am. Coll. Tax Counsel; mem. ABA, Am. Law Inst., Internat. Fiscal Inst., Am. Arbitration Assn., L.A. County Bar Assn. (recipient Dana Latham award 1995), Phi Beta Kappa. Office: Irell & Manella 1800 Avenue Of The Stars Los Angeles CA 90067-4276

STONE, OLIVER, screenwriter, director; b. N.Y.C., Sept. 15, 1946; s. Louis and Jacqueline (Goddet) S. Student, Yale U., 1965; BFA, NYU Film Sch., 1971. Tchr., Cholon, Vietnam, 1965-66; wiper U.S. Mcht. Marine, 1966; taxi driver N.Y.C., 1971. Screenwriter Midnight Express, 1978 (Acad. award for screeplay, Writers Guild Am. for screenplay); screenwriter, dir.: The Hand, 1981, (with John Milius) Conan, the Barbari an, 1982 (writer), Scarface, 1983, (writer with Michael Cimino) Year of the Dragon, 1985, (writer with David Lee Henry) 8 Million Ways to Die, 1985; dir., writer (with Richard Boyle) Salvador, 1986, Platoon, 1986 (Acad. award, Dirs. Guild award, British Acad. award); co-writer, dir.: Wall Street, 1987, Talk Radio, 1988, The Doors, 1991, Any Given Sunday; screenwriter, prodr., dir.: Born on the Fourth of July, 1989 (Acad. award 1990), Heaven & Earth, 1993; co-writer, prodr., dir.: JFK, 1991, Natural Born Killers, 1994, Nixon, 1995 (Acad. award nominee for best screenplay with Stephen J. Rivele and Christopher Wilkinson 1996); co-prodr. Reversal of Fortune, 1990; prodr.: South Central, 1992, Zebrahead, 1992, The New Age, 1993, The Joy Luck Club, 1993, (TV mini-series) Wild Palms, 1993; exec. prodr. Killer: A Journal of Murder, 1995, (HBO) Indictment: The McMartin Preschool, 1995 (Emmy award), Freeway, 1996, The People vs. Larry Flynt, 1996, Cold Around the Heart, 1996, Evita (writer), U-Turn, 1997. Served with inf. U.S. Army, 1967-68, Vietnam. Decorated Purple Heart with oak leaf cluster, Bronze Star. Mem. Writers Guild Am., Dirs. Guild Am., Acad. Motion Picture Arts and Scis.

STONE, PATRICK F. insurance company executive; Grad., Oreg. State U. Various positions in title ins. industry; pres. Fidelity Nat. Title Co., Portland, Oreg., 1989, exec. v.p. Fidelity Nat. Fin. Inc. Irvine, Calif., 1995—, pres., COO Fidelity Nat. Fin. Inc., 1995—. Trustee Portland Art Mus. Mem. Bldg. Materials Dealers Assn. Portland (bd. dirs.), Oreg. Land Title Assn., Am. Land Title Assn. Office: Fidelity Nat Fin Inc 4050 Calle Real Ste 200 Santa Barbara CA 93110

STONE, RICHARD JAMES, lawyer; b. Apr. 30, 1945; s. Milton M. and Ruth Jean (Manaster) S.; m. Lee Lawrence, Sept. 1, 1979; children: Robert Allyn, Katherine Jenney, Grant Lawrence. BA in Econs., U. Chgo., 1967; JD, UCLA, 1970. Bar: Calif. 1971, Oreg. 1994, D.C., 2000. Assoc. O'Melveny & Myers, L.A., 1971-77; dep. asst. gen. counsel U.S. Dept. Def., Washington, 1978-79; asst. to sec. U.S. Dept. Energy, Washington, 1979-80; counsel Sidley & Austin, L.A., 1981, ptnr., 1982-88; ptnr., head litigation dept. Milbank, Tweed, Hadley & McCloy, L.A., 1988-94; mng. ptnr. Zelle & Larson, LLP, L.A., 1994-97; counsel Ball Janik LLP, Portland, Oreg., 1998—. Gen. counsel and staff dir. Study of L.A. Civil Disturbance for Bd. Police Commrs., 1992; adj. prof. law Lewis and Clark Northwestern Sch. Law, 1998-99; lawyer rep. 9th Cir. Jud. Conf., 1998-99. Editor-in-chief: UCLA Law Rev., 1970. Mem. Pub. Sector Task Force, Calif., State Senate Select Com. on Long Range Policy Planning, 1985-86, U.S. del. Micronesian Polit. Status Negotiations, 1978-79; mem. adv. panel Coun. Energy Resource Tribes, 1981-85; mem. vestry St. Aidan's Episcopal Ch., 1990-93, 97-98, sr. warden, 1998; dir. Legal Aid Found. L.A., 1991-99, officer, 1994-98, pres., 1997-98; dir. Portland City United Soccer Club, 1999-2000. Recipient Amos Alonzo Stagg medal and Howell Murray Alumni medal U. Chgo., 1967; honoree Nat. Conf. Black Mayors, 1980; recipient spl. citation for outstanding performance Sec. Dept. Energy, 1981. Fellow Am. Bar Found.; mem. ABA, FBA, Calif. Bar Assn., Oreg. Bar Assn., L.A. County Bar Assn. (trustee 1986-88), Assn. Bus. Trial Lawyers, Multnomah County Bar Assn., Phi Gamma Delta. Home: 3675 NW Gordon St Portland OR 97210-1285 Office: Ball Janik LLP 101 SW Main St Portland OR 97204-3228 E-mail: rstone@bjllp.com

STONE, THOMAS EDWARD, defense contractor, retired career officer; b. Selfridge, Mich., Oct. 21, 1939; m. Lucy Lee, June 9, 1962. BS, U.S. Naval Acad., 1962; MS in Elec. Engring., Naval Postgrad. Sch., 1968; postgrad., Destroyer Dept. Head Sch., 1969. Advanced through grades to rear adm. USN, 1990, ops. officer USS Sampson, 1970; aide, flag sec. to commdr. Attack Carrier striking Force /CTF 77, 7th Fleet Vietnam, 1971-72; communications/ops. officer to comdr. in chief U.S. Naval Forces, Europe, 1972-75; exec. officer USS Mitscher, 1976-78; asst. chief of staff for communications, comdr. Naval Surface Force Atlantic, 1978-80; comdg. officer USS Preble, 1980-82; surface ops. officer, staff of comdr. Cruiser Destroyer Group 12, 1982-83; dir. Space, Command and Control Devel. Div. USN, 1984-85; comdr. U.S. Naval Communications Master Sta., Western Pacific, Guam, Marianas Island, 1985-87; comdr. Naval Telecommunications Command, 1988-90; dir. Naval Commns. info systems of Naval opers. staff, 1990-91; dir. communication programs Space & Naval Warfare Systems Command, 1991-93; v.p. Def. Contractor. Decorated Legion of Merit with three gold stars. Roman Catholic. Office: Am Sys Corp 3033 5th Ave Ste 105 San Diego CA 92103-5828 E-mail: thomas.stone@2asc.com

STONE, WILLIAM EDWARD, academic administrator, consultant; b. Peoria, Ill., Aug. 13, 1945; s. Dean Proctor and Katherine (Jamison) S.; m. Deborah Ann Duncan; children: Jennifer, Allison, Molly. AB, Stanford U., 1967, MBA, 1969. Asst. dean Stanford U., 1969-71, asst. to pres., 1971-77; exec. dir. Stanford Alumni Assn., 1977-90, pres., CEO, 1990-98; pres., dir. Stanford Alumni Assn. divsn. Stanford U., 1998-2001, Stanford Sierra Programs LLC, South Lake Tahoe, Calif., 1998-2001, Alpine Chalet, Inc., Alpine Meadows, 1987-2001; pres.-emeritus Stanford Alumni Assn. Stanford U., 2001—, cons. in ednl. advancement, 2001—. Dir. Coun. Alumni Assn. Execs., 1989-93, v.p., 1990-91, pres., 1991-92; trustee Coun. for Advancement and Support of Edn., 1988-91; bd. dirs. Univ. ProNet, Inc., chmn., 1990-92, sec. 1996-2000. Bd. dirs. North County YMCA, 1975-76; bd. dirs., chmn. nominating com. faculty club Stanford U., 1979-81; trustee Watkins Discretionary Fund, 1979-82; mem. community adv. bd. Resource Ctr. for Women. Recipient K.M. Cuthbertson award Stanford U., 1987, Tribute award Coun. for Advancement and Support of Edn., 1991. Mem. Stanford Hist. Soc., Stanford Assocs. Club: Stanford Faculty. Home: 1061 Cathcart Way Stanford CA 94305-1048 Office: Stanford Alumni Assn Frances C Arrillaga Alumni Ctr Stanford CA 94305-6105 E-mail: westone@stanford.edu

STONEBRAKER, MICHAEL R. electrical engineering & computer science educator; BS, Princeton U., 1965; MS, U. Mich., 1966, PhD, 1971. Asst. prof. U. Calif., Berkeley, 1971-76, assoc. prof., 1976-81, prof., 1981-99; ret., 1999. Vis. engr. Nat. Bur. Stds., 1972; founder, cons., mem. bd. dirs. Relational Tech., Inc., 1980—, v.p. engring., 1984; vis. prof. Pontifico Univ. Catholique, Rio de Janeiro, 1976, U. Calif., Santa Cruz, 1977-78, U. Grenoble, France, 1984-85; founder INGRES Corp. (now INGRES Products Divsn. of ASK Computer Sys.), Illustra Info. Sys., Inc.; spkr. in field. Contbr. articles to profl. jours. Mem. ACM (past chmn. spl. interest group on mgmt. of data, SIGMOD Innovations award 1992). Office: Informix Corp 4100 Bohannon Dr Menlo Park CA 94025

STONECIPHER, HARRY CURTIS, manufacturing company executive; b. Scott County, Tenn., May 1936; BS, Tenn. Poly. Inst., 1960. With GE, 1960-61, 62-86, Martin Aircraft Co., 1961-62; exec. v.p. Sundstrand Corp., 1987, pres., COO, 1987-88, pres., CEO, 1988-94, chmn., 1991-94, also past bd. dirs.; pres., CEO McDonnell-Douglas Corp., St. Louis, 1994-97, Boeing Co., Seattle, 1997—; pres., CEO, COO Boeing Corp., 1997—. Bd. dirs. Milacron, Inc. Recipient John R. Allison award, 1996, Rear Adm. John J. Bergen Leadership medal Navy League, 1996. Fellow Royal Aero. Soc. Office: Boeing Co Mail Stop 10-26 Seattle WA 98124-2207

STOORZA GILL, GAIL, corporate professional; b. Yoakum, Tex., Aug. 28, 1943; d. Roy Otto and Ruby Pauline (Ray) Blankenship; m. Larry Sttorza, Apr. 27, 1963 (div. 1968); m. Ian M. Gill, Apr. 24, 1981; 1 child, Alexandra Leigh. Student, N. Tex. State U., 1961-63, U. Tex., Arlington, 1963. Stewardess Cen. Airlines, Ft. Worth, 1963; advt. and acctg. exec. Phillips-Ramsey Advt., San Diego, 1963-68; dir. advt. Rancho Bernardo, San Diego, 1968-72; dir. corp. communications Avco Community Developers, San Diego, 1972-74; pres. Gail Stoorza Co., San Diego, 1974—, Stoorza, Ziegaus & Metzger, San Diego, 1974—; CEO Stoorza, Ziegaust, Metzger, Inc., 1993—; chmn. Stoorza/Smith, San Diego, 1984-85, Stoorza Internat., San Diego, 1984-85; CEO ADC Stoorza, San Diego, 1987—, Franklin Stoorza, San Diego, 1993—. Trustee San Diego Art Found.; bd. dirs. San Diego Found. for Performing Arts, San Diego Opera, Sunbelt Nursery Groups, Dallas. Names Small Bus. Person of Yr. Selest Com. on Small Bus., 1984, one of San Diego's Ten Outstanding Young Citizens San Diego Jaycees, 1979; recipient Woman of Achievement award Women in Communications Inc., 1985. Mem. Pubs. Soc. Am., Nat. Assn. Home Builders (residential mktg. com.), COMBO. Methodist. Clubs: Chancellors Assn. U. Calif. (San Diego), Pub. Relations, San Diego Press. Home: 711 Silvergate Ave San Diego CA 92106-2850 Office: Stoorza Ziegaus & Metzger 225 Broadway Fl 18 San Diego CA 92101-5005

STORER, MARYRUTH, law librarian; b. Portland, Oreg., July 26, 1953; d. Joseph William and Carol Virginia (Pearson) Storer; m. David Bruce Bailey, 1981; children: Sarah, Allison. BA in History, Portland State U., 1974; JD, U. Oreg., 1977; M in Law Librarianship, U. Wash., 1978. Bar: Oreg. 1978. Assoc. law libr. U. Tenn., Knoxville, 1978-79; law libr. O'Melveny & Myers, L.A., 1979-88; dir. Orange County Pub. Law Libr., Santa Ana, Calif., 1988—. Mem. Am. Assn. Law Librs. (exec. bd. 1999—), So. Calif. Assn. Law Librs. (pres. 1986-87), Coun. Calif. County Law Librs. (sec.-treas. 1990-94, pres. 1994-96), Arroyo Seco Libr. Network (chair 2000—). Democrat. Episcopalian. Office: Orange County Public Law Library 515 N Flower St Santa Ana CA 92703-2304

STOREY, NORMAN C. lawyer; b. Miami, Fla., Oct. 11, 1943; BA cum laude, Loyola U., L.A., 1965; JD, U. Ariz., 1968. Bar: Ariz. 1968. Law clk. to Hon. James A. Walsh U.S. Dist. Ct. Ariz.; ptnr. Squire, Sanders & Dempsey, Phoenix. Mem. State Bar Ariz., Am. Arbitration Assn. (panelist). Office: Squire Sanders & Dempsey 40 N Central Ave Ste 2700 Phoenix AZ 85004-4498

STOTLER, ALICEMARIE HUBER, judge; b. Alhambra, Calif., May 29, 1942; d. James R. and Loretta M. Huber; m. James Allen Stotler, Sept. 11, 1971. BA, U. So. Calif., 1964, JD, 1967. Bar: Calif. 1967, U.S. Dist. Ct. (no. dist.) Calif. 1967, U.S. Dist. Ct. (cen. dist.) Calif. 1973, U.S. Supreme Ct. 1976; cert. criminal law specialist. Dep. Orange County Dist. Attys. Office, 1967-73; mem. Stotler & Stotler, Santa Ana, Calif., 1973-76, 83-84; judge Orange County Mcpl. Ct., 1976-78, Orange County Superior Ct., 1978-83, U.S. Dist. Ct. (cen. dist.) Calif., L.A., 1984—. Assoc. dean Calif. Trial Judges Coll., 1982; lectr., panelist, numerous orgns.; standing com. on rules of practice and procedure U.S. Jud. Conf., 1991—, chair, 1993-98; mem. exec. com. 9th Cir. Jud. Conf., 1989-93, Fed. State Jud. Coun., 1989-98, jury com., 1990-92, planning com. for Nat. Conf. on Fed.-State Jud. Relationships, Orlando, 1991-92, planning com. for We. Regional Conf. on State-Fed. Jud. Relationships, Stevens, Wash., 1992-93; chair dist. ct. symposium and jury utilization Ctrl. Dist. Calif., 1985, chair atty. liaison, 1989-90, chair U.S. Constn. Bicentennial com., 1986-91, chair magistrate judge com., 1992-93; mem. State Adv. Group on Juvenile Justice and Delinquency Prevention, 1983-84, Bd. Legal Specializations Criminal Law Adv. Commn., 1983-84, victim/witness adv. com. Office Criminal Justice Planning, 1980-83, U. So. Calif. Bd. Councilors, 1993—; active team in tng. Leukemia Soc. Am., 1993, 95, 97, 2000; legion lex bd. dirs. U. So. Calif. Sch. Law Support Group, 1981-83. Winner Hale Moot Ct. Competition, State of Calif., 1967; named Judge of Yr., Orange County Trial Lawyers Assn., 1978, Most Outstanding Judge, Orange County Bus. Litigation Sect., 1990; recipient Franklin G. West award Orange County Bar Assn., 1985. Mem. ABA (jud. adminstrn. divsn. and litigation sect. 1984—, nat. conf. fed. trial judges com. on legis. affairs 1990-91), Am. Law Inst., Am. Judicature Soc., Fed. Judges Assn. (bd. dirs. 1989-92), Nat. Assn. Women Judges, U.S. Supreme Ct. Hist. Soc., Ninth Cir. Dist. Judges Assn., Calif. Supreme Ct. Hist. Soc., Orange County Bar Assn. (mem. numerous com.s, Franklin G. West award 1984), Calif. Judges Assn. (mem. com. on jud. coll. 1978-80, com. on civil law and procedure 1980-82, Dean's coll. curriculum commn. 1981), Calif. Judges Found. Office: Ronald Reagan Fed Bldg & Courthouse 411 W 4th St Santa Ana CA 92701-4500

STOTT, BRIAN, software company executive, consultant; b. Eccles, Eng., Aug. 5, 1941; came to U.S., 1983; s. Harold and Mary (Stephens) S.; m. Patricia Ann Farrar, Dec. 3, 1983. BSc, Manchester U., 1962, MSc, 1963, PhD, 1971. Asst. prof. Middle East Tech. U., Ankara, Turkey, 1965-68; lectr. Inst. Sci. and Tech., U. Manchester (Eng.), 1968-74; assoc. prof. U. Waterloo (Ont., Can.), 1974-76; cons. Electric Energy Rsch. Ctr. Brazil, Rio de Janeiro, 1976-83; prof. Ariz. State U., Tempe, 1983-84; chmn. Power Computer Applications Corp., Mesa, Ariz., 1984-2000. Cons. in field. Contbr. numerous articles to rsch. publs. Fellow IEEE (Millennium medal). Office: Stott Inc 36 E Bishop Dr Tempe AZ 85282 E-mail: brianstott@ieee.org

STOTT, PETER WALTER, forest products company executive; b. Spokane, Wash., May 26, 1944; s. Walter Joseph and Rellalee (Gray) S.; m. Julie L. Neupert, Oct. 12, 1996; 1 child, Preston. Student, Portland State U., 1962-63, 65-68, U. Americas, Mexico City, 1964-65. Founder, chmn. bd. dirs. Market Transport Ltd., Portland, Oreg., 1969—. Bd. dirs., pres., CEO, prin. Crown Pacific, Sunshine divsn. Portland Police Bur. (hon.), Liberty Northwest; assoc. mem. adv. bd. Pacific Crest Outward Bound Sch.; mem. pres.'s adv. bd. for athletics Portland State U.; trustee Lewis & Clark Coll.; mem. adv. bd. Cascade Pacific coun. Boy Scouts Am. With USAR, 1966-72. Mem. Nat. Football Found. and Hall of Fame, Oreg. Sports Hall of Fame (lifetime), Stop Oreg. Litter and Vandalism (founders' circle), Arlington Club, Mazamas Club, Multnomah Athletic Club, Portland Golf Club, The Racquet Club, Univ. Club, Waverly Country Club, Valley Club. Republican. Roman Catholic. Office: Crown Pacific 121 SW Morrison St Ste 1500 Portland OR 97204-3160

STOTTER, LAWRENCE HENRY, lawyer; b. Cleve., Sept. 24, 1929; s. Oscar and Bertha (Lieb) S.; m. Ruth Rapoport, June 30, 1957; children: Daniel, Jennifer, Steven. BBA, Ohio State U., 1956, LLB, 1958, JD, 1967. Bar: Calif. 1960, U.S. Supreme Ct. 1973, U.S. Tax Ct. 1976. Pvt. practice, San Francisco, 1963—; ptnr. Stotter and Coats, San Francisco, 1981-97; sole practitioner, 1997—; mem. faculty Nat. Judicial Coll.; mem. Calif. Family Law Adv. Commn., 1979-80. Editor in chief: Am. Bar Family Advocate mag, 1977-82; TV appearances on Phil Donahue Show, Good Morning America. Pres. Tamalpais Conservation Club, Marin County, Calif.; U.S. State Dept. del. Hague Conf. Pvt. Internat. Law, 1979-80; legal adv. White House Conf. on Families, 1980—. Served with AUS, 1950-53. Mem. ABA (past chmn. family law sect.), Am. Acad. Matrimonial Lawyers (past nat. v.p.), Calif. State Bar (past chmn. family law sect.), San Francisco Bar Assn. (past chmn. family law sect.), Calif. Trial Lawyers Assn. (past chmn. family law sect.) Home: 2244 Vistazo St E Tiburon CA 94920-1970 Office: 1255 Columbus Ave # 200 San Francisco CA 94133-1326 E-mail: lhstotter@aol.com

STOUGHTON, W. VICKERY, healthcare executive; b. Peoria, Ill., Mar. 1, 1946; s. Warner Vickery and Mary Olive (McNamara) S.; m. Anne Stoughton; children: Zachary Benjamin, Samantha. BS, St. Louis U., 1968; MBA, U. Chgo., 1973. Asst. dir. Boston Hosp. for Women, 1973-74, Peter Bent Brigham Hosp., Boston, 1975-77, dir., 1978-80; pres. The Toronto Hosp., Ont., Can.; asst. prof. U. Toronto, 1982-90, assoc. prof., 1991; vice chancellor health affairs, chief exec. officer Duke U. Hosp., Durham, N.C., 1991-92; pres. Smithkline Beecham Clin. Labs., Collegeville, Pa., 1992-95, Smithkline Beecham Diagnostic Systems, King of Prussia, 1996; chmn., CEO Careside, Culver City, Calif., 1996—; dir. Biomira, 1998—. Bd. dirs. Sun Life Assurance Co. Bd. dirs. Toronto Symphony, 1983-86, Toronto United Way, 1988-91. Served to capt. AUS, 1969-72. Fellow Am. Coll. Hosp. Adminstrs. Home: 8820 Lookout Mountain Ave Los Angeles CA 90046-1820 Office: Careside 6100 Bristol Pkwy Culver City CA 90230-6604

STOUT, DENNIS LEE, prosecutor; b. 1948; BA, U. Calif., Riverside, 1970; JD, U. LaVerne, Calif., 1977. Adminstrv. aide City of Fontana, Calif., 1972-73; planning technician City of Pomona, 1973; dep. dist. atty. San Bernardino County, 1977-94, dist. atty., 1995—. Mayor City of Rancho Cucamonga, Calif., 1986-94. Named Vet. of the Yr., San Bernardino County, 1989. Office: San Bernardino County Dist Atty 316 N Mountain View Ave San Bernardino CA 92401-1610

STOUT, ELIZABETH WEST, foundation administrator; b. San Francisco, Mar. 4, 1917; d. Claudius Wilson and Sarah (Henderson) West; m. Bruce Churchill McDonald, Mar. 19 1944 (dec. 1952); children: Douglas, Anne; m. Charles Holt Stout, Oct. 27, 1958 (dec. 1992); stepchildren: Richard, George (dec.), Martha Stout Gilweit. Student, U. Nev., 1934-37; grad., Imperial Valley Coll., 1990. Cashier, acct. N.Y. Underwriters, San Francisco, 1937-42; sec. supply and accounts USN, San Francisco, 1942-44. Contbr. articles to profl. jours. Mem. adv. bd. Anza-Borrego Desert, Natural History Assn., 1974-84; founder Stout Paleontology Lab., Borrego Springs, Calif., 1982; found. trustee Desert Rsch. Inst., Reno, 1989—; active Black Rock Desert Project, 1989, Washoe Med. Ctr. League, 1953—, St. Mary's Hosp. Guild, 1953—. Named Disting. Nevadan U. Nev., 1993. Mem. Anza-Borrego Desert Natural History Assn. (dir. emeritus 1984), Soc. Vertebrate Paleontology, De Anza Desert Country Club, Kappa Alpha Theta. Republican. Episcopalian. Avocations: travel, writing, reading, golf.

STOVER, MILES RONALD, manufacturing executive; b. Glendale, Calif., Dec. 23, 1948; s. Robert Miles and Alberta Mae (Walker) S.; m. Cynthia McNeil, Jan. 25, 1975; children: Christopher, Matthew. BS, U. So. Calif., 1974; MBA, Pepperdine U., 1979; D of Bus. Adminstrn., U.S. Internat. U., 1982. Cert. fraud examiner; cert. turnaround profl.; cert. profl. cons. V.p., gen. mgr., CFO Johnson Controls Inc., L.A., 1974-82; gen. mgr. MG Products Inc., San Diego, 1982-84; exec. v.p., gen. mgr. ICU Med. Inc., Mission Viejo, 1984-86; v.p., COO B.P. John Inc., Santa Ana, Calif., 1986-88; gen. mgr. MG Products Inc., San Diego, 1988-90; pres. Lucks Co., Kent, Wash., 1991-96, also bd. dirs.; pres. Turnaround Mgmt. Group, 1996—. Cons. Turnaround Mgmt. Assn., Tacoma, 1990; bd. dirs. Ansyr Tech., LaFarge & Egge, Inc. With USN, 1967-71. Recipient Gallantry Cross medal USN, 1971, Award for Productivity U.S. Senate, 1978. Mem. Inst. Mgmt. Cons. (cert. mgmt. cons.), Inst. Mgmt. Accts., Mensa. Republican. Methodist. Home: 3415 A St NW Gig Harbor WA 98335-7843

STOWELL, CHRISTOPHER R. dancer; b. N.Y.C., June 8, 1966; s. Kent and Francia (Russell) S. Student, Pacific N.W. Ballet Sch., 1979-84, Sch. Am. Ballet, 1984-85. Entered corps de ballet San Francisco Ballet, 1986, promoted to soloist, 1987, prin., 1990—. Guest artist Ballet Met, Ohio, Pacific N.W. Ballet, Seattle, and with Jean Charles Gil, Marseilles, France, Asami Maki Ballet, Tokyo. Created leading roles in Handel-A Celebration, Con Brio, The Sleeping Beauty, New Sleep, Connotations, Pulcinella, Meistens Mozart; other roles include Calcium Light Night, Rubies, The Sons of Horus, The Four Temperaments, Hearts, Tarantella, Flower Festival, La Fille Mal Garde, Haffner Symphony, Forgotten Land, The End, Agon, In the Middle Somewhat Elevated, Le Quattro Stagioni, Swan Lake, Job, Company B, Tchaikousky Pas de Deux, Maelstrom, Mercutio in

Romeo and Juliet, The Dance House, Stars and Stripes, Ballo Della Regina, Drink to me Only With Thine Eyes, Pacific; performed in Reykjavik Arts Festival, Iceland, 1990, San Francisco Ballet at the Paris Opera Garnier, 1994, Bolshoi Theatre, Moscow, 1998. Avocations: cooking, reading, camping. Office: San Francisco Ballet 455 Franklin St San Francisco CA 94102-4471

STOWELL, KENT, ballet director; b. Rexburg, Idaho, Aug. 8, 1939; s. Harold Bowman and Maxine (Hudson) S.; m. Francia Marie Russell, Nov. 19, 1965; children: Christopher, Darren, Ethan. Student, San Francisco Ballet Sch., Sch. Am. Ballet; Lead dancer San Francisco Ballet, 1957-62, N.Y.C. Ballet, 1962-68; ballet dir., ballet master Frankfurt (Fed. Republic Germany) Opera Ballet, 1973-77; artistic dir. Pacific N.W. Ballet, Seattle, 1977—; prof. dance Ind. U., Bloomington, 1969-70; bd. dirs. Sch. of Am. Ballet, Dance/USA, Washington, 1986—. Choreographer: Silver Lining, Cinderella, Carmina Burana, Coppelia, Time & Ebb, Faurè Requiem, Hail to the Conquering Hero, Firebird, Over the Waves, Nutcracker, The Tragedy of Romeo and Juliet, Delicate Balance, Swan Lake, Time and Ebb, Through Interior Worlds, Quaternary, Orpheus. Bd. dirs. Sch. of Am. Ballet, N.Y.C., 1981—; mem. Goodwill Games Arts Com., Seattle, 1987—; chmn. dance panel NEA, 1981-85. Grantee NEA, 1980, 85; fellow NEA, 1979. Recipient Arts Service award King County Arts Commn., 1985, Outstanding Contbn. to Pacific N.W. Ballet State of Was., 1987, Best Dance Co. award The Weekly Newspaper, Seattle, 1987, Gov. Arts award, 1988, Dance Mag. award, 1996. Office: Pacific NW Ballet 301 Mercer St Seattle WA 98109-4600

STOWELL, ROBERT EUGENE, pathologist, retired educator; b. Cashmere, Wash., Dec. 25, 1914; s. Eugene Francis and Mary (Wilson) S.; m. Eva Mae Chambers, Dec. 1, 1945; children: Susan Jane, Robert Eugene Jr. Student, Whitman Coll., 1932-33; BA, Stanford U., 1936, MD, 1941; PhD, Washington U., 1944. Fellow in cytology Wash. U. Sch. Medicine, St. Louis, 1940-42; rsch. fellow Barnard Free Skin and Cancer Hosp., St. Louis, 1940-42, rsch. assoc., 1942-48; asst. resident in pathology Barnes, McMillan, St. Louis Children's Hosps., St. Louis, 1942-43, resident in pathology, 1943-44, asst. pathologist, 1944-48; instr. in pathology Washington U. Sch. Medicine, St. Louis, 1943-45, asst. prof. 1945-48, assoc. prof., 1948; advanced med. fellow Inst. for Cell Rsch., Stockholm, 1946-47; chmn. dept. oncology U. Kansas Med. Ctr., Kansas City, Kans., 1948-51, prof. pathology and oncology, dir. cancer rsch., 1948-59, chmn., 1951-59; sci. dir. Armed Forces Inst. Pathology, Washington, 1959-67; chmn. dept. pathology Sch. of Medicine U. Calif., Davis, 1967-69, asst. dean Sch. Medicine, 1967-72, prof. pathology Sch. Medicine, 1967-82, prof. emeritus, 1982—; dir. div. pathology Sacramento (Calif.) Med. Ctr., 1967-69. Vis. prof. U. Md. Sch. Medicine, Balt., 1960-67; acting dir. Nat. Ctr. for Primate Biology, U. Calif., Davis, 1968-69, dir., 1969-71; cons. U.S. Atomic Energy commn., Los Alamos, N.Mex., 1949-54, NIH, 1949-74, Cancer Control Div. USPHS, 1949-59, others; mem. adv. med. bd. Leonard Wood Meml. found., Washington, 1965-67, numerous univs.; prin. investigator, chmn. Expert Panel on Assessment of the Practical risk to Human Health from Nitrilotriacetic Acid in Household Laundry Products, 1984-85. Contbr. 120 articles, 30 abstracts to jours. in field; editor 32 biomed. books, monographs and conf. reports, 1941-88; mem. editorial bd. Cancer Rsch., 1949-59, Lab. Investigation, 1952-71, editor, 1967-71. Recipient Meritorious Svc. award Dept. Army, 1963, Exceptional Civilian Svc. award Dept. Army, 1965, Disting. Svc. award U. Calif. Sch. Medicine, 1988, Robert E. Stowell ann. Med. Student award Outstanding Excellence in Pathology, 1981—; Robert E. Stowell ann. lectureship established U. Calif. Sch. Medicine, 1991 and Am. Registry of Pathology, Washington, 1991. Mem. AMA, Am. Registry of Pathology (bd. dirs. 1976-83, exec. com. 1976-82, v.p. 1976-78, pres. 1978-79, Disting. Svc. award 1995), Am. Assn. Cancer Rsch., Am. Assn. Pathologists (Gold-headed Cane award 1990), Am. Assn. Pathologists and Bacteriologists (councilor 1965-72, v.p. 1969-70, pres. 1970-71), Am. Soc. Clin. Pathologists, Am. Soc. Exptl. Pathology (councilor 1962-66, v.p. 1963-64, pres. 1964-65), Calif. Med. Soc., Calif. Soc. Pathologists, Binford-Dammin Soc. Infectious Disease Pathologists, Coll. Am. Pathologists, Histochem. Soc., Internat. Acad. Pathology (councilor 1954-61, pres.-elect 1958-59, pres. 1995-60, Disting. Svc. award 1970, Diamond Jubilee award 1981, Stowell-Orbison award established 1982—), Soc. Cryobiology (bd. govs. 1968-71), Soc. Exptl. Biology and Medicine, U.S. and Can. Acad. Pathology, Yolo County Med. Soc., Assn. Mil. Surgeons U.S. (sustaining membership award 1965), Univs. Associated for Rsch. and Edn. in Path. (bd. dirs. 1975-90, sec.-treas. 1978-82, hon. dir. 1990—), Sigma Xi, Alpha Omega Alpha. Office: U Calif Sch Medicine Dept Pathology Davis CA 95616

STRAATSMA, BRADLEY RALPH, ophthalmologist, educator; b. Grand Rapids, Mich., Dec. 29, 1927; s. Clarence Ralph and Lucretia Marie (Nicholson) S.; m. Ruth Campbell, June 16, 1951; children: Cary Ewing, Derek, Greer. Student, U. Mich., 1947; MD cum laude, Yale U., 1951; DSc (hon.), Columbia U., 1984. Diplomate Am. Bd. Ophthalmology (vice chmn. 1979, chmn. 1980). Intern New Haven Hosp., Yale U., 1951-52; resident in ophthalmology Columbia U., N.Y.C., 1955-58; spl. clin. trainee Nat. Inst. Neurol. Diseases and Blindness, Bethesda, Md., 1958-59; assoc. prof. surgery/ophthalmology UCLA Sch. Medicine, 1959-63, chief div. ophthalmology, dept. surgery, 1959-68, prof. surgery/ophthalmology, 1963-68, prof. ophthalmology, 1968—, dir. Jules Stein Eye Inst., 1964-94, chmn. dept. ophthalmology, 1968-94; ophthalmologist-in-chief UCLA Med. Ctr., 1968-94. Lectr. numerous univs. and profl. socs. 1971—; cons. to surgeon gen. USPHS, mem. Vision Research Tng. Com., Nat. Inst. Neurol. Diseases and Blindness, NIH, 1959-63, mem. neurol. and sensory disease program project com., 1964-68; chmn. Vision Research Program Planning Com., Nat. Adv. Eye Council, Nat. Eye Inst., NIH, 1973-75, 75-77, 85-89; mem. med. adv. bd. Internat. Eye Found., 1970-79; mem. adv. com. on basic clin. research Nat. Soc. to Prevent Blindness, 1971-87; mem. med. adv. com. Fight for Sight, 1960-83; bd. dirs. So. Calif. Soc. to Prevent Blindness, 1967-77, Ophthalmic Pub. Co., 1975-93, v.p. 1990-93, Pan-Am. Ophthalmol. Found., 1985-95; chmn. sci. adv. bd. Ctr. for Partially Sighted, 1984-87; mem. nat. adv. panel Found. for Eye Research, Inc., 1984-94; mem. cons. com. Palestra Oftalmologica Panamericana, 1976-81; coord. com. Nat. Eye Health Edn. Program, 1989; mem. sci. adv. bd. Rsch. to Prevent Blindness, Inc., 1993—; mem. Internat. Coun. Opthalmology, 1993—. Editor-in-chief Am. Jour. Ophthalmology, 1993—; mem. editorial bd. UCLA Forum in Med. Scis., 1974-82, Am. Jour. Ophthalmology, 1974-91, Am. Intra-Ocular Implant Soc. Jour., 1978-79, EYE-SAT Satellite-Relayed Profl. Edn. in Ophthalmology, 1982-86; mng. editor von Graefe's Archive for Clin. and Exptl. Ophthalmology, 1976-88; contbr. over 450 articles to med. jours. Trustee John Thomas Dye Sch., Los Angeles, 1967-72. Served to lt. USNR, 1952-54. Recipient William Warren Hoppin award N.Y. Acad. Medicine, 1956, Univ. Service award UCLA Alumni Assn., 1982, Miguel Aleman Found. medal, 1992, Benjamin Boyd Humanitarian award Pan Am. Assn. Ophthalmology, 1991, Lucian Howe medal, Am. Ophthalmological Soc., 1992, Internat. Gold Medal award 3rd Singapore Nat. Eye Ctr. Internat. Meeting and 11th Internat. Meeting on Cataract, Implant, Microsurgery and Refractive Keratoplasty, 1998. Fellow Royal Australian Coll. Ophthalmologists (hon.); mem. Academia Ophthalmologica Internationales (pres. 1998—), Am. Acad. Ophthalmology (bd. councillors 1981, Life Achievement award 1999), Found. of Am. Acad. Ophthalmology (trustee 1989, chmn. bd. trustees 1989-92), Am. Acad. Opthalmology and Otolaryngology (pres. 1977), Am. Soc. Cataract and Refractive Surgery, AMA (asst. sec. ophthalmology sect. 1962-63, sec. 1963-66, chmn. 1966-67, coun. 1970-74), Am. Ophthalmol. Soc. (coun. 1985-90, v.p. 1992, pres. 1993), Assn. Rsch. in Vision and Ophthalmology (Mildred Weisenfeld award 1991), Assn. U. Profs. of Ophthalmology (trustee 1969-75, pres.-elect 1973-74, pres. 1974-75), Assn. VA Ophthalmologists, Calif. Med. Assn. (mem. ophthalmology adv. panel 1972-94, chmn. 1974-79, sci. bd. 1973-79, ho. of dels. 1974, 77, 79), Chilean Soc. Ophthalmology (hon.), Columbian Soc. Ophthalmology (hon.), Glaucoma Soc. Internat. Congress of Ophthalmology (hon.), Heed Ophthalmic Found. (chmn., bd. dirs. 1990-98), Hellenic Ophthalmol. Soc. (hon.), Internat. Coun. Ophthalmology (bd. dirs. 1993—), Los Angeles County Med. Assn., Los Angeles Soc. Ophthalmology, The Macula Soc., Pan-Am. Assn. Ophthalmology (coun. 1972—, pres. elect 1985-87, pres. 1987-89), Peruvian Soc. Ophthalmology (hon.), Retina Soc., Barraquer Inst. Ophthalmology (pres. 1996—), The Jules Gonin Club, West Coast Retina Study Club. Republican. Presbyterian. Avocations: music, tennis, scuba diving. Home: 3031 Elvido Dr Los Angeles CA 90049-1107 Office: UCLA 100 Stein Plz Los Angeles CA 90095-7065

STRACK, STEPHEN NAYLOR, psychologist; b. Rome, Nov. 13, 1955; s. Ralph and Grace (Naylor) S.; m. Leni Ferrero. BA, U. Calif., Berkeley, 1978; PhD, U. Miami, Fla., 1983. Psychologist L.A. County Dept. Mental Health, 1984-85; staff psychologist VA Outpatient Clinic, L.A., 1985—, dir. tng., 1992-97. Clin. assoc. U. So. Calif., L.A., 1986-95; adj. prof. Calif. Sch. Profl. Psychology, L.A., 1989—; clin. prof. Fuller Grad. Sch. Psychology, Pasadena, Calif., 1986—. Author (test): Personality Adjective Check List, 1987; co-author (book): Differentiating Normal and Abnormal Personality, 1994, Death and the Quest for Meaning, 1997, Essentials of Million Inventories Assessment, 1999; cons. editor Jour. Personality Disorders, N.Y.C., 1992—, Omega, 1997—, Jour. Personality Assessment, 1999—. U.S. Dept. VA grantee, 1986-93, 96-2000. Fellow APA, Soc. for Personality Assessment; mem. Internat. Soc. for the Study of Personality Disorders, Calif. Psychol. Assn., European Assn. Psychol. Assessment, Soc. for Interpersonal Theory and Rsch., Soc. for Rsch. in Psychopathology, Western Psychol. Assn., Sigma Xi. Office: VA Outpatient Clinic 351 E Temple St Los Angeles CA 90012-3328 E-mail: snstrack@aol.com

STRAHAN, JULIA CELESTINE, electronics company executive; b. Indpls., Feb. 10, 1938; d. Edgar Paul Pauley and Pauline Barbara (Myers) Shawver; m. Norman Strahan, Oct. 2, 1962 (div. 1982); children: Daniel Keven, Natalie Kay. Grad. high sch., Indpls. With Bechtel Nev./Lockheed Martin Nev. Techs., Las Vegas, 1967—; sect. head EG&G Co., 1979-83, mgr. electronics dept., 1984—. Recipient award Am. Legion, 1952, Excellence award, 1986. Mem. NAFE, Am. Nuclear Soc. (models and mentors), Internat. Platform Assn. Home: 5222 Stacey Ave Las Vegas NV 89108-3078 Office: EG&G PO Box 1912 Las Vegas NV 89125-1912 E-mail: jeweljcs@aol.com

STRAIGHT, RICHARD COLEMAN, photobiologist, natural philosopher; b. Rivesville, W.Va., Sept. 8, 1937; BA, U. Utah, 1961, PhD in Molecular Biology, 1967. Asst. dir. radiation biology summer inst. U. Utah, 1961-63; supervisory chemist med. svc. VA Hosp., 1965—; dir. VA Venom Rsch. Lab., 1975—; adminstrv. officer rsch. svc. VA Ctr., 1980—; dir. Dixon laser inst. U. Utah, Salt Lake City, 1985-90; pres. Western Inst. for Biomed. Rsch., Salt Lake City, 1990—. Dir. Utah Ctr. for Photo Medicine, Salt Lake City, 1993—, assoc. chief of staff for rsch., 1997—. Assoc. editor Lasers in Surgery and Medicine, 1990-95, Jour. Biomed. Optics, 1998—. Mem. AAAS, Am. Chem. Soc., Am. Soc. Photobiology, Biophysics Soc., Am. Soc. for Laser Medicine and Surgery, Utah Life Sci. Industries Assn. (charter). Achievements include research in photodynamic action on biomonomers and biopolymers, tumor immunology, effect of antigens on mammary adenocarcinoma of C3H mice, biochemical changes in aging, venom toxicology, mechanism of action of photoactive drugs, optical imaging and spectroscopy. Office: VAMC U Utah Western Inst Biomed Rsch 500 Foothill Dr Salt Lake City UT 84148-0001

STRAIT, EDWARD J. research physicist; Prin. scientist Stability Physics Group Gen. Atomics, San Diego. Recipient Excellence in Plasma Physics Rsch. award Am. Phys. Soc., 1994. Office: General Atomics PO Box 85608 San Diego CA 92186-5608

STRALING, PHILLIP FRANCIS, bishop; b. San Bernardino, Calif., Apr. 25, 1933; s. Sylvester J. and Florence E. (Robinson) S. BA, U. San Diego, 1963; MS in Child and Family Counseling, San Diego State U., 1971. Ordained priest Roman Catholic Ch., 1959, consecrated bishop, 1978. Mem. faculty St. John Acad., El Cajon, Calif., 1959-60, St. Therese Acad., San Diego, 1960-63; chaplain Newman Club, San Diego State U., 1960-72; mem. faculty St. Francis Sem., San Diego, 1972-76; pastor Holy Rosary Parish, San Bernardino, 1976-78; bishop Diocese of San Bernardino, 1978-95; pub. Inland Cath. newspaper, 1979-95; chmn. com. on lay ministry U.S. Cath. Conf./Nat. Cath. Conf. Bishops, 1993—; bishop of Reno, Nev., 1995—. Bd. dirs. Calif. Assn. Cath. Campus Mins., 1960s; exec. sec. Diocesan Synod II, 1972-76; Episcopal vicar San Bernardino Deanery, 1976-78. Mem. Nat. Cath. Campus Ministries Assn. (bishop rep. 1992-98). Office: 290 S Arlington Ste 200 Reno NV 89501

STRAND, ROGER GORDON, federal judge; b. Peekskill, N.Y., Apr. 28, 1934; s. Ernest Gordon Strand and Lisabeth Laurine (Phin) Steinmetz; m. Joan Williams, Nov. 25, 1961. AB, Hamilton Coll., 1955; LLB, Cornell U., 1961; grad., Nat. Coll. State Trial Judges, 1968. Bar: Ariz. 1961, U.S. Dist. Ct. Ariz. 1961, U.S. Supreme Ct. 1980. Assoc. Fennemore, Craig, Allen & McClennen, Phoenix, 1961-67; judge Ariz. Superior Ct., Phoenix, 1967-85, U.S. Dist. Ct. Ariz., Phoenix, 1985—. Assoc. presiding judge Ariz. Superior Ct., 1971-85; lectr. Nat. Jud. Coll., Reno, 1978-87; mem. jud. conf. U.S. com. on automation and tech. Past pres. cen. Ariz. chpt. Arthritis Found. Lt. USN, 1955-61. Mem. ABA, Ariz. Bar Assn., Maricopa County Bar Assn., Nat. Conf. Fed. Trial Judges, Phi Delta Phi, Aircraft Owners and Pilots Assn. Lodge: Rotary. Avocations: computer applications, golf, fishing. Home: 5825 N 3rd Ave Phoenix AZ 85013-1537 Office: Sandra Day O'Connor US Courthouse SPC 57 401 W Washington Phoenix AZ 85003-2156

STRANDJORD, PAUL EDPHIL, physician, educator; b. Mpls., Apr. 5, 1931; s. Edphil Nels and RuBelle Pearl (Corneliusen) S.; m. Margaret Thomas, June 27, 1953; children: Thomas Paul, Scott Nels. BA, U. Minn., 1951, MA, 1952; MD, Stanford U., 1959. Intern U. Minn., Mpls., 1959-60, resident, 1960-63, dir. divsn. chemistry, dept. lab. medicine, 1963-69, assoc. dir. clin. labs. dept. lab. medicine, 1967-69; assoc. prof. lab. medicine U. Wash., 1969, prof., chmn. dept. lab. medicine, 1969—; prof. emeritus, 1994—. Cons. VA Hosps. Author: (with E.S. Benson) Multiple Laboratory Screening, 1969, (with G. Schmer) Coagulation-Current Research and Clinical Applications, 1973. Pres. U. Wash. Physicians. With USN, 1952-55. Recipient Borden award Stanford U., 1959, Watson award U. Minn., 1962, Gerald T. Evans award Acad. Clin. Lab. Physicians and Scientists, 1976; Paul E. Strandjord and Kathleen Clayson Endowed Ednl. Fund established U. Wash. Fellow Am. Soc. Clin. Pathologists; mem. AAAS, Acad. Clin. Lab. Physicians and Scientists (pres., Paul E. Strandjord Nat. Young Investigator Award program established), Am. Assn. Clin. Chemistry, Am. Chem. Soc., Am. Fedn. Clin. Research, Internat. Acad. Pathology, Assn. Pathology Chmn. Home: 9410 Lake Washington Blvd NE Bellevue WA 98004-5409 Office: U Wash Dept Lab Medicine # Sb-10 Seattle WA 98195-0001 E-mail: edphil@uwashington.edu Died June 29, 2001.

STRANDNESS, DONALD EUGENE, JR. surgeon; b. Bowman, N.D., Sept. 22, 1928; s. Donald Eugene and Merinda Clarine (Peterson) S.; m. Edith V., June 30, 1957; children: Erik Lee, Tracy Lynn, Jill Marie, Sandra Kay. BA, Pacific Lutheran U., 1950; MD, U. Wash., 1954; MD (hon.), Lund (Sweden) U., 1999. From instr. to prof. U. Wash., Seattle, 1962—. Chief div. vascular surgery U. Wash., 1975-95. Served to capt. USAF, 1957-59. Recipient disting. alumnus award Pacific Lutheran U., 1980, U. Wash. Sch. Medicine, 1997. Fellow Soc. for Vascular Surgery (pres. 1988), Am. Venous Forum (pres. 1998); mem. Am. Coll. Surgeons, Am. Surg. Assn. Republican. Lutheran. Avocations: tennis, reading. Office: U Wash Dept Surgery 1959 NE Pacific St Seattle WA 98195-0001 E-mail: destrand@u.washington.edu

STRATTON, GREGORY ALEXANDER, computer specialist, administrator, mayor; b. Glendale, Calif., July 31, 1946; s. William Jaspar and Rita Phyllis (Smith) S.; m. Yolanda Margot Soler, 1967 (div. 1974); 1 child, Tiffany Schwarzer; m. Edith Carter, Sept. 27, 1975; stepchildren: Paul Henkell, D'Lorah Henkell Wismar. Student, Harvey Mudd Coll., 1964-65; BS in Physics, UCLA, 1968; MBA, Calif. Luth. U., 1977. Elec. engr. Naval Ship Weapon System Engrng. Sta., Port Hueneme, Calif., 1968-73; sr. staff mem. Univac, Valencia, 1973-74; v.p. Digital Applications, Camarillo, 1974-75; cons. Grumman Aerospace, Point Mugu, 1975-76; F-14 software mgr. Pacific Missle Test Ctr., Pt. Mugu, 1976-84; software mgr. Teledyne Systems, Northridge, Calif., 1984-92, dir. engrng. software dept., 1992-93; dep. dir. software engring. Teledyne Electronic Systems, Northridge, 1993-94; software mgr. Litton Guidance and Controls, Woodland Hills, 1995-2001, Northrup/Grumman Navigation Sys., Woodland Hills, 2001—. Bd. dirs. Simi Valley Hosp. Mem. City Coun., City of Simi Valley, Calif., 1979-86, mayor, 1986-98; mem. Rep. County Cen. Com., Ventura County, 2000—; mem. Rep. State Cen. Com., Calif., 1990—; bd. dirs. Simi Valley Hosp., 1987-2001; pres. Simi Valley Cultural Arts Found., 1999—. Mem. Rotary (Paul Harris award Simi Sunrise chpt. 1989), Jaycees (pres. Simi Valley chpt. 1974-75, nat. bd. dirs. 1975-76, v.p. Calif. state 1976-77). Republican. Lutheran. Home: 254 Goldenwood Cir Simi Valley CA 93065-6771 Office: Northrup Grumman Navigation Sys 5500 Canoga Ave Woodland Hills CA 91367-6698 E-mail: gstratton@aol.com, stratton@littongcs.com

STRATTON, JIM, state agency administrator; B in Recreation and Parks Mgmt., Univ. Oreg.; MBA, Alaska Pacific U. V.p., program fin. dir. Alaska Conservation Found.; dir. State Alaska. Dept. Natural Resources, Parks & Outdoors Rec, Anchorage, 1995—. Office: State Alaska Dept Nat Resources Parks & Outdoor Rec 3601 C St Ste 1200 Anchorage AK 99503-5921

STRATTON, RICHARD JAMES, lawyer; b. Sandwich, Ill., May 17, 1946; s. James L. and Dorothy (Olson) S.; m. Michele Disario, June 13, 1970; children: Matthew A., Laura D. AB, Harvard U., 1968, JD, 1972; MS, London Sch. of Econs., 1969. Bar: Calif. 1972, U.S. Dist. Ct. (no. dist.) Calif. 1972, U.S. Ct. Appeals (9th cir.) 1972, U.S. Dist. Ct. (cen. dist.) Calif. 1978, U.S. Dist. Ct. (so. and ea. dists.) Calif. 1979, U.S. Supreme Ct. 1979. Assoc. Bronson, Bronson & McKinnon LLP, San Francisco, 1972-79, ptnr., 1980—. Early neutral evaluator, mediator U.S. Dist. Ct. Co-author: Real Property Litigation, 1994. Trustee San Francisco Day Sch., 1987-94; bd. dirs. Legal Aid Soc. of San Francisco, 1989—. Fellow Am. Bar Found.; mem. ABA, Bar Assn. of San Francisco (bd. dirs. 1988-90), Calif. Bar Assn., Def. Rsch. Inst. (chmn. subcom. real estate brokers and agts. 1986-87), No. Calif. Assn. Def. Counsel, No. Calif. Assn. Bus. Trial Lawyers, San Francisco Barristers Club (pres. 1980), City Club, Harvard Club (San Francisco). Office: Bronson Bronson & McKinnon LLP 505 Montgomery St San Francisco CA 94111-2514

STRAUS, DAVID A. architectural firm executive; b. Medford, Oreg., 1943; m. Sherry Straus; 2 children. BArch, U. Oreg., 1967. Registered architect, Oreg. Founding ptnr. Skelton, Straus & Seibert, Medford, 1989—. Mem. Oreg. Transp. Commn., Rogue Valley Area Commn. on Transp. Past bd. dirs. Medford YMCA, Rogue Valley Art Assn.; past pres. Medford Arts Commn., Arts Coun. So. Oreg.; coach Rogue Valley Soccer Assn.; leader Boy Scouts Am.; bd. dirs., past pres. Schneider Mus. Art SOSC. Ret. lt. USNR, Vietnam. Mem. AIA (past pres. So. Oreg. chpt.), Archtl. Found. Oreg. (bd. dirs.), Univ. Club Medford (past pres.), Oreg. Club So. Oreg. (past pres.), U. Oreg. Alumni Assn., Medford/Jackson County C. of C. (past bd. dirs., Mem. of Yr. 2000), Rotary. Office: Skelton Straus & Seibert Arch 26 Hawthorne St Medford OR 97504-7114

STRAUS, JOZEF, manufacturing company executive; b. 1946; Various rsch. and mgmt. positions in fiber optic tech. Bell-No. Rsch. Ltd. and No. Telecom Ltd.; bd. dirs. JDS FITEL, 1981, v.p. sales and mktg., 1990-93, CEO, pres., 1993-99; co-chmn., CEO JDS Uniphase Corp. (merged with JDS FITEL), San Jose, Calif., 2000—. Office: 163 Baypointe Pkwy San Jose CA 95134 Fax: 408-954-0760

STRAUSFELD, NICHOLAS JAMES, neurobiology and evolutionary biology researcher, educator; b. Claygate, England, Oct. 22, 1942; BSc in Zoology, Univ. Coll. London, 1965, PhD in Neurophysiology, 1968; Habilitation, U. Frankfurt, Germany, 1985. Prof. neurobiology, ecology, evolutionary biology, entomology, anatomy U. Ariz., Tucson, also adj. prof. art. Author: Atlas of an Insect Brain, 1976, Functional Neuroanatomy, 1983, Neuroanatomical Techniques, Insect Nervous System, 1980. John Simon Guggenheim fellow, 1994, MacArthur fellow, 1995. Office: U Arizona PO Box 210077 Tucson AZ 85721-0077 also: Gould Simpson Bldg Rm 415 Tucson AZ 85721-0001*

STRAUSS, HERBERT LEOPOLD, chemistry educator; b. Aachen, Germany, Mar. 26, 1936; came to U.S., 1940, naturalized, 1946; s. Charles and Joan (Goldschmidt) S.; m. Carolyn North Cooper, Apr. 24, 1960; children: Michael Abram, Rebecca Anne, Ethan Edward. A.B., Columbia U., 1957, M.A., 1958, Ph.D., 1960; postgrad, Oxford U., 1960-61. Mem. faculty U. Calif., Berkeley, 1961—, prof. chemistry, 1973—, vice chmn. dept. chemistry, 1975-81, 92-95, asst. dean. Coll. Chemistry, 1986-92, assoc. dean, 1995—. Vis. prof. Indian Inst. Tech., Kanpur, 1968-69, Fudan U., Shanghai, 1982, U. Tokyo, 1982, U. Paris du Nord, 1987; chmn. IUPAC Commn. I.1, 1994-99. Author: Quantum Mechanics, 1968; assoc. editor Ann. Rev. Phys. Chemistry, 1976-85, editor, 1985-2000. Recipient Bomen-Michaelson award Coblentz Soc., 1994, Ellis Lippincott award Optical Soc. Am., 1994; Alfred P. Sloan fellow, 1966-70. Fellow Am. Phys. Soc., AAAS; mem. Am. Chem. Soc., Sigma Xi, Phi Beta Kappa, Phi Lambda Upsilon. Achievements include research in elucidation of vibrational spectra associated with large amplitude molecular motion in gases, liquids and solids. Home: 2447 Prince St Berkeley CA 94705-2021 Office: U Calif Dept Chemistry Berkeley CA 94720-1420 E-mail: hls@cchem.berkeley.edu

STRAUSS, JOHN, public relations executive; b. N.Y.C., Apr. 2, 1913; s. Nathan and Bertha Dorothy (Heineman) S.; m. Renee Valensi, Oct. 15, 1947; children: Susan Strauss Koenig, John Jay. Grad., Phillips Exeter Acad., 1931; BA, Yale U., 1935. Securities analyst Mabon & Co., N.Y.C., 1935-41; sales rep. Warner Bros. Pictures, Buffalo, 1941-45; publicist Warner Bros. Studios, Burbank, Calif., 1945-46, Columbia Studios, Hollywood, 1946-48; founder, pres. Cleary, Strauss & Irwin, 1948-64; pres. McFadden, Strauss & Irwin, Inc., 1964-75, ICPR, L.A., 1975-80, Communifax, Inc., L.A., 1980—; retired, 1998. Trustee Oakwood Schs., 1967-70, Acad. TV Arts and Scis., 1967-70, Columbia Coll., L.A., 1979-83. Mem. Acad. Motion Picture Arts and Scis. Home and Office: 4205 Stansbury Ave Sherman Oaks CA 91423-4233

STRAUSS, JON CALVERT, academic administrator; b. Chgo., Jan. 17, 1940; s. Charles E. and Alice C. (Woods) S.; m. Joan Helen Bailey, Sept. 19, 1959 (div. 1985); children: Susan, Stephanie; m. Jean Anne Sacconaghi, June 14, 1985; children: Kristoffer, Jonathon. BSEE, U. Wis., 1959; MS in Physics, U. Pitts., 1962; PhD in E.E., Carnegie Inst. Tech., 1965;

LLD (hon.), U. Mass., 1996. Assoc. prof. computer sci., elec. engring. Carnegie Mellon U., Pitts., 1966-70; dir. computer ctr., prof. computer sci. Tech. U. Norway, Trondheim, Norway, 1970; vis. assoc. prof. elec. engring. U. Mich., Ann Arbor, 1971; assoc. prof. computer sci. Washington U., St. Louis, 1971-74, dir. computing facilities, 1971-73; dir. computing activities U. Pa., Phila., 1974-76, faculty master Stouffer Coll. House, 1978-80, prof. computer, info. scis., prof. decision sci. Wharton Sch., 1974-81, exec. dir. Univ. Budget, 1975-78, v.p. for budget, fin., 1978-81; prof. elec. engring. U. So. Calif., Los Angeles, 1981-85, sr. v.p. adminstrn., 1981-85; pres. Worcester Poly. Inst., Mass., 1985-94; v.p., chief fin. officer Howard Hughes Med. Inst., Chevy Chase, Md., 1994-97; pres. Harvey Mudd Coll., Claremont, Calif., 1997—. Cons. Electronics Assocs., Inc., 1965, IBM Corp., 1960-64, Westinghouse Elec. Corp., 1959-60; bd. dirs. Transamerica Income Fund, Variable Ins. Fund, United Educators Ins. Contbr. articles on computer systems and university mgmt. to profl. jours.; co-holder patent. Bd. dirs. Presbyn.-U. Pa. Med. Ctr., Phila., 1980-81, U. So. Calif. Kenneth Norris Jr. Cancer Hosp., L.A., 1981-85, Med. Ctr. of Ctrl. Mass., 1986-94, Worcester Acad., 1986-91, Mass. Biotech. Rsch. Inst., 1985-94. Mem. New. Eng. Assn. Schs. and Colls., Inc., Commn. on Instns. of Higher Edn., Nat. Collegiate Athletic Assn. (pres.'s commn. 1990-94). Avocations: rowing, running, sailing, swimming. Office: Harvey Mudd Coll 301 E 12th St Claremont CA 91711-5901

STREET, ROBERT A. research physicist; Sr. rsch. fellow Xerox Corp., Palo Alto, Calif. Recipient David Adler Lectureship award Am. Phys. Soc., 1992. Office: Palo Alto Rsch Ctr Xerox Corp 3333 Coyote Hill Rd Palo Alto CA 94304-1314 E-mail: street@parc.xerox.com

STREET, ROBERT LYNNWOOD, civil, mechanical and environmental engineer; b. Honolulu, Dec. 18, 1934; s. Evelyn Mansel and Dorothy Heather (Brook) S.; m. Norma Jeanette Ensminger, Feb. 6, 1959; children: Brian Clarke (dec.), Deborah Lynne, Kimberley Anne. Student, USN ROTC Program, 1952-57; M.S., Stanford U., 1957, Ph.D. (NSF grad. fellow 1960-62), 1963. Mem. faculty Sch. Engring. Stanford U., 1962—, prof. civil engring., assoc. chmn. dept. Sch. Engring., 1970-72, chmn. dept. Sch. Engring., 1972-80, 94-95, prof. fluid mechanics and applied math. Sch. Engring., 1972—, dir. environ. fluid mechanics lab. Sch. Engring., 1985-91, assoc. dean rsch. Sch. Engring., 1971-83, vice provost acad. computing and info. sys., 1983-85, vice provost, dean rsch. and acad. info. sys., 1985-87, v.p. for info. resources, 1987-90, acting provost, 1987, v.p. librs. and info. resources, 1990-92, vice provost, dean of librs. and info. resources, 1992-94, William Alden and Martha Campbell prof. Sch. Engring., 1997—. Vis. prof. U. Liverpool, Eng., 1970-71, Ctr. for Water Rsch., U. Western Australia, 1985; vis. prof. mech. engring. James Cook U., Australia, 1995; trustee Univ. Corp. Atmospheric Rsch., 1983-94, chmn. sci. programs evaluation com., 1981, treas. corp., 1985, vice chmn. bd., 1986, chmn. bd., 1987-91; bd. dirs., sec.-treas. UCAR Found., 1987-91; bd. govs. Rsch. Libr. Group, 1990-91; chmn. Com. Preservation Rsch. Libr. Materials, Assn. Rsch. Librs., 1993; mem. higher edn. adv. bds. computer corps., 1983-94; mem. basic energy sci. adv. com. U.S. Dept. Energy, 1993-96; bd. dirs. Stanford U. Bookstore, Inc., 1993-98. With C.E.C., USN, 1957-60. Sr. postdoctoral fellow Nat. Center Atmospheric Research, 1978-79; sr. Queen's fellow in marine sci., Australia, 1985; fellow N.E. Asia-U.S. Forum on Internat. Policy at Stanford U., 1985-89. Fellow AAAS; mem. ASCE (chmn. publs. com. hydraulics divsn. 1978-80, Walter Huber prize 1972), ASME (R.T. Knapp award 1986), Am. Geophys. Union, Oceanographic Soc., Am. Phys. Soc., Phi Beta Kappa, Sigma Xi, Tau Beta Pi. Office: Stanford U Environ Fluid Mechs Lab Dept Civil/Environ Engring Stanford CA 94305-4020 E-mail: street@ce.stanford.edu

STREETER, STEPHANIE ANNE, executive; b. Boston, Sept. 19, 1957; d. Andrew Geoffrey Galef and Suzanne Jane (Cohen) Sidy; m. Edward Stanley Streeter, Feb. 22, 1980. BA in Polit. Sci., Stanford U., 1979. Mgr. market analysis Xerox Small Bus. System, Sunnyvale, Calif., 1980-81; regional sales mgr. Xerox Office Products Divsn., Sunnyvale, 1981-83; product mgr. Decision Data Computer Corp., Horsham, Pa., 1983-85; sr. product mgr. Avery, Covina, Calif., 1985-88; bus. mgr. indexes Avery Dennison, Covina, 1988-89, bus. mgr. computer supplies, 1989-90, dir. mktg., 1990-91, v.p. gen. mgr. office lab. Diamond Bar, 1991-93, v.p., gen. mgr., 1993-99. Bd. dirs. LAPD Parker Found., L.A., 1994—, MArch of Dimes, So. Calif., 1991—; coach Girls Basketball AAU, Pacific Palisades, Calif., 1992—. Fellow Internat. Women's Forum. Democrat. Avocations: bicycling, skiing. Office: Avery Dennison 50 Pointe Dr Brea CA 92821-3699

STREISAND, BARBRA JOAN, singer, actress, director; b. Bklyn., Apr. 24, 1942; d. Emanuel and Diana (Rosen) S.; m. Elliott Gould, Mar. 1963 (div.); 1 son, Jason Emanuel; m. James Brolin, July 1, 1998. Grad. high sch., Bklyn.; student, Yeshiva of Bklyn. N.Y. theatre debut Another Evening with Harry Stoones, 1961; appeared in Broadway musicals I Can Get It for You Wholesale, 1962, Funny Girl, 1964-65; motion pictures include Funny Girl, 1968, Hello Dolly, 1969, On a Clear Day You Can See Forever, 1970, The Owl and the Pussy Cat, 1970, What's Up Doc?, 1972, Up the Sandbox, 1972, The Way We Were, 1973, For Pete's Sake, 1974, Funny Lady, 1975, The Main Event, 1979, All Night Long, 1981, Nuts, 1987; star, prodr. film A Star is Born, 1976; prodr., dir., star Yentl, 1983, The Prince of Tides, 1991, The Mirror Has Two Faces, 1996; exec. prodr.: (TV movie) Serving in Silence: The Margarethe Cammermeyer Story, 1995; TV spls. include My Name is Barbra, 1965 (5 Emmy awards), Color Me Barbra, 1966; actress, prodr., dir. The Mirror Has Two Faces, 1996; rec. artist on Columbia Records; Gold record albums include People, 1965, My Name is Barbra, 1965, Color Me Barbra, 1966, Barbra Streisand: A Happening in Central Park, 1968, Barbra Streisand: One Voice, Stoney End, 1971, Barbra Joan Streisand, 1972, The Way We Were, 1974, A Star is Born, 1976, Superman, 1977, The Stars Salute Israel at 30, 1978, Wet, 1979, (with Barry Gibb) Guilty, 1980, Emotion, 1984, The Broadway Album, 1986, Til I Loved You, 1989; other albums include: A Collection: Greatest Hits, 1989, Just for the Record, 1991, Back to Broadway, 1993, Concert at the Forum, 1993, The Concert Recorded Live at Madison Square Garden, 1994, The Concert Highlights, 1995, Higher Ground, 1997. Recipient Emmy award, CBS-TV spl. (My Name Is Barbra), 1964, Acad. award as best actress (Funny Girl), 1968, Golden Globe award (Funny Girl), 1969, co-recipient Acad. award for best song (Evergreen), 1976, Georgie award AGVA 1977, Grammy awards for best female pop vocalist, 1963, 64, 65, 77, 86, for best song writer (with Paul Williams), 1977, 2 Grammy nominations for Back to Broadway, 1994; Nat. Acad. of Recording Arts & Sciences Lifetime Achievement Award, 1994. Office: ICM c/o Jeff Berg 8942 Wilshire Blvd Beverly Hills CA 90211-1934

STREITWIESER, ANDREW, JR. chemistry educator; b. Buffalo, June 23, 1927; s. Andrew and Sophie Streitwieser; m. Mary Ann Good, Aug. 19, 1950 (dec. May 1965); children: David Roy, Susan Ann; m. Suzanne Cope Beier, July 29, 1967. A.B., Columbia U., 1949, M.A., 1950, Ph.D., 1952; postgrad. (AEC fellow), MIT, 1951-52. Faculty U. Calif., Berkeley, 1952-92, prof. chemistry, 1963-92, prof. emeritus, 1993—. Researcher on organic reaction mechanisms, application molecular orbital theory to organic chemistry, effect chem. structure on carbon acidities; cons. to industry, 1957— Author: Molecular Orbital Theory for Organic Chemists, 1961, Solvolytic Displacement Reactions, 1962, (with J.I. Brauman) Supplemental Tables of Molecular Orbital Calculations, 1965, (with C.A. Coulson) Dictionary of Pi Electron Calculations, 1965, (with P.H. Owens) Orbital and Electron Density Diagrams, 1973, (with C.H. Heathcock and E.M. Kosower) Introduction to Organic Chemistry, 4th edit., 1992, A Lifetime of Synergy with Theory and Experiment, 1996; also numerous articles; co-editor: Progress in Physical Organic Chemistry, 11 vols., 1963-74. Recipient Humboldt Found. Sr. Scientist award, 1976, Humboldt medal, 1979, Berkeley citation, 1993. Fellow AAAS; mem. NAS, Am. Chem. Soc. (Calif. sect. award 1964, award in Petroleum Chemistry 1967, Norris award in phys. organic chemistry 1982, Cope scholar award 1989), Am. Acad. Arts and Scis., Bavarian Acad. Scis. (corr.), Phi Beta Kappa, Sigma Xi. Office: U Calif Dept Chemistry Berkeley CA 94720-1460 E-mail: astreit@socrates.berkeley.edu

STREVER, KEVIN KIRK, lawyer; b. Denver, July 4, 1960; s. Merle A. and Donna Jo (Ritchie) S.; m. Lauri Jean Rask, Apr. 1, 1989. BS in Polit. Sci. cum laude, So. Oreg. State Coll., 1982; JD, U. Oreg., 1985. Bar: Oreg. 1985, U.S. Dist. Ct. Oreg. 1986, U.S. Ct. Appeals (9th cir.) 1986. Musician, 1977-84; legal clk. E.F. Hutton & Co., N.Y.C., 1984; atty. Barton & Strever P.C., Newport, Oreg., 1985—. Author (book chpt.) Recovering for Psychological Injuries, 1990, chpt. 4, Torst (Oreg. CLE 1992), "Torts Arising From Sexual Misconduct. Author (book chpt.) Recovering for Psychological Injuries, 1990. Mem. Oreg. State Bar (pres. 1997-98, bd. govs. 1995-98), Oreg. Criminal Def. Lawyers Assn., Assn. Trial Lawyers Am., Oreg. Trial Lawyers Assn. (Pres.'s club 1989—), Lincoln County Bar Assn. (pres. 1989). Avocations: retired professional guitarist, scuba diving, vacuum tube amplification, electronics. Home: 421 NW 13th St Newport OR 97365-2402 Office: Barton & Strever PC 214 SW Coast Hwy Newport OR 97365-4927

STRICK, JEREMY, curator; BA in History of Art with highest honors, U. Calif., Santa Cruz, 1977; postgrad., Harvard U. Asst. curator 20th Century art Nat. Gallery Art, Washington, 1986-89, assoc. curator 20th Century art, 1989-93, acting dept. dept. 20th Century art, 1992-93, curator Nat. Sculpture Garden project, 1989-93; curator modern art St. Louis Art Mus., 1993-96; Frances and Thomas Dittmer curator 20th Century painting and sculpture Art Inst. Chgo., 1996-99; dir. Mus. Contemporary Art, L.A., 1999—. Curator N.Y. Interpreted: Joseph Stella and Alfred Stieglitz, Nat. Gallery Art, 1987, Milton Avery, 1990, Mark Rothko: The Spirit Myth, 1990-95, asst. curator A Century of Modern Sculpture: The Patsy and Raymond Nasher Collection, 1987, co-curator Twentieth-Century Art: Selections for the Tenth Anniversary of the East Building, 1987; curator Brice Marden: A Painting, Drawings, Prints, St. Louis Art Mus., 1993, Currents 58: Susan Crile—The Fires of War, 1994, Louise Bourgeois: The Personages 1946-1954, 1995, Currents 60: Jerald Ieans, 1994, Masterworks from Stuttgar: The Romantic Age in German Art, 1995, Currents 66: Michael Byron, 1996, Currents 67: Leonardo Drew, 1996; curator The Sublime Is Now: The Early Work of Barnett Newman, Walker Art Ctr., Mpls., Pace Gallery, N.Y.C., 1994; curator In the Light of Italy: Corot and Early Open-Air Painting, Nat. Gallery Art, Bklyn. Mus., St. Louis Art Mus., 1996; lectr., symposia participant and organizer, 1980—; juror Showhegan awards, 1995. Contbg. author: Works by Antoine-Louis Barye in the Collection of the Fogg Art Museum, Vol. IV, 1982; contbr. articles to exhbn. catalogs, newspapers, mags., ency. Instnl. fellow Samuel H. Kress Found., Paris, 1983-85, fellow Mrs. Giles Whiting Found., 1985-86. Office: Mus Contemporary Art Dept 20th Century Painting 250 S Grand Ave Los Angeles CA 90012-3021

STRICKLAND, TOM, prosecutor; married; three children. Bachelor's degree, La. State U., 1974; JD, U. Tex., 1977. Chief policy adv. to Gov. Dick Lamm, 1982-84; sr. ptnr. Brownstein, Hyatt, Farber, and Strickland, 1999; U.S. atty. Colo. dist. U.S. Dept. Justice, 1999—. Dem. candidate U.S. Sen., 1996. Office: 1961 Stout St Ste 1200 Denver CO 80294-1200

STRICKLER, JEFFREY HAROLD, pediatrician; b. Mpls., Oct. 14, 1943; s. Jacob Harold and Helen Cecelia (Mitchell) S.; m. Karen Anne Stewart, June 18, 1966; children: Hans Stewart, Liesl Ann. BA, Carleton Coll., 1965; MD, U. Minn., 1969. Diplomate Am. Bd. Pediatrics. Resident in pediatrics Stanford (Calif.) U., 1969-73; pvt. practice Helena, Mont., 1975—; chief staff Shodair Children's Hosp., Helena, 1984-86. Dir. maternal-child health Lewis and Clark County, Helena, 1978-88; chief of staff St. Peters Hosp., Helena, 1994-96; bd.chmn. Helena Health Alliance, 1996-99. Mem. Mont. Gov.'s Task Force on Child Abuse, 1978-79; mem. steering com. Region VIII Child Abuse Prevention, Denver, 1979-82; bd. dirs. Helena Dist. 1 Sch. Bd., 1982-88, vice chmn., 1985-87. Maj. M.C., USAF, 1973-75. Fellow Am. Acad. Pediatrics (vice chmn. Mont. chpt. 1981-84, chmn. 1984-87, Wyeth award 1987, mem. nat. nominating com. 1987-90, chmn. 1989-90, coun. on govt. affairs 1990-96, future of pediatric edn. II 1996-2000); mem. Rotary (youth exchange chmn. dist. 539, 1984-88, pres. Helena 1988-89, polio plus chair dist. 5390 1996—). Avocations: skiing, hiking. Office: Helena Pediatric Clinic 1122 N Montana Ave Helena MT 59601-3513 E-mail: drjeff@mt.net

STRIMAS, JOHN HOWARD, allergist, immunologist, pediatrician; b. Washington, Dec. 19, 1942; MD, Albany Med. Coll., 1969. Diplomate Am. Bd. Allergy and Immunology, Am. Bd. Pediat. Intern in pediat. Nassau County Med. Ctr., East Meadow, 1970-71, resident in pediat., 1971-73; fellow in allergy and immunology LSU Med. Ctr., New Orleans, 1985-88; with Bapt. Hosp., Nashville, Centennial Med. Ctr., Nashville; owner/dir. North Idaho Allergy, Asthma & Immunology Ctr., Coeur D'Alene, Idaho; exec. com. mem., chmn. pediatric panel Kootenai Med. Ctr., Coeur D'Alene, 1995. Mem. Am. Acad. Allergy and Immunology, Am. Coll. Allergy and Immunology, Tenn. Med. Assn., Idaho Med. Assn. Office: North Idaho Allergy Asthma & Immunology Ctr 1200 W Ironwood Dr Ste 202 Coeur D Alene ID 83814-2660

STRINGER, WILLIAM JEREMY, university official; b. Oakland, Calif., Nov. 8, 1944; s. William Duane and Mildred May (Andrus) S.; m. Susan Lee Hildebrand; children: Shannon Lee, Kelly Erin, Courtney Elizabeth. BA in English, So. Meth. U., 1966; MA in English, U. Wis., 1968, PhD in Ednl. Adminstrn., 1973. Dir. men's housing Southwestern U., Georgetown, Tex., 1968-69; asst. dir. housing U. Wis., Madison, 1969-73; dir. residential life, assoc. dean student life, adj. prof. Pacific Luth., Tacoma, 1973-78; dir. residential life U. So. Calif., 1978-79, asst. v.p., 1979-84, asst. prof. higher and post-secondary edn., 1980-84; v.p. student life Seattle U., 1984-89, v.p. student devel., 1989-92, assoc. provost, 1989-95, assoc. prof. edn., 1990—, chair ednl. leadership, 1994—. Author: How to Survive as a Single Student, 1972, The Role of the Assistant in Higher Education, 1973. Bd. dirs. N.W. Area LUth. Social Svcs. of Wash. and Idaho, pres.-elect, 1989, pres., 1990-91; bd. dirs. Seattle Coalition Ednl. Equity. Danforth Found. grantee, 1976-77. Mem. AAUP, Assn. Higher Edn., Nat. Assn. Student Pers. Adminstrs. (bd. dirs. region V 1985—, mem. editl. bd. Jour. 1995—), Am. Coll. Pers. Assn., Phi Eta Sigma, Sigma Tau Delta, Phi Alpha Theta. Lutheran. Home: 4553 169th Ave SE Bellevue WA 98006-6505 Office: Seattle U Dept Edn Seattle WA 98122 E-mail: stringer@seattleu.edu

STRINGFELLOW, GERALD B. engineering educator; b. Salt Lake City, Apr. 26, 1942; s. Paul Bennion and Jean (Barton) S.; m. Barbara Farr, June 9, 1962; children: Anne, Heather, Michael. BS, U. Utah, 1964; PhD, Stanford U., 1968. Staff scientist Hewlett Pacakrd Labs., Palo Alto, Calif., 1967-70, group mgr., 1970-80; disting. prof. elec. engring., materials sci. U. Utah, Salt Lake City, 1980—; chmn., 1994-98; adj. prof. physics U. Utah, Salt Lake City, 1988—, dean Coll. of Engring., 1998—. Cons. Tex. Instruments, Dallas, 1995-97, AT&T-Bell Labs., Holmdel, N.J., 1986-90, Brit. Telecom., London, 1989-92; editor-in-chief Phase Diagrams for Ceramics, Vol. IX. Author: Organometallic Vapor Phase Epitaxy, 1989, 2d edit., 1999; editor: Metal Organic Vapor Phase Epitaxy, 1986, American Crystal Growth, 1987, Alloy Semiconductor Physics and Electronics, 1989, Phase Equilibria Diagrams-Semiconductors and Chalcogenides, 1991, High Brightness LEDs, 1997; prin. editor Jour. Crystal Growth; letters editor Jour. Electronic Materials, 1992-99; contbr. over 360 articles to profl. jours. Recipient U.S. Sr. Scientist award Alexander von Humboldt Soc., Bonn, Germany, 1979, Gov.'s Sci. Tech. medal State of Utah, 1997; guest fellow Royal Soc., London, 1990. Fellow IEEE, Japan Soc. Promotion of Sci.; mem. Am. Phys. Soc., Electronic Materials Com. (pres. 1985-87), Nat. Acad. Engring. Achievements include pioneering development of organometallic vapor phase epitaxy, development of theories of thermodynamic properties of alloy semiconductors; discovery of phenomenon of compositional latching in alloy semiconductor layers grown by epitaxial techniques. Office: U Utah Coll Engring 1495 E 100 S Salt Lake City UT 84112-1109 E-mail: stringfellow@coe.utah.edu

STRINGHAM, RENÉE, physician; b. Mpls., July 16, 1940; d. Clifford Leonard and Helen Pearl (Marcineak) Heinrich; children: Lars Eric, Leif Erik, Lance Devon. BS, St. Lawrence U., 1962; MD, U. Ky., 1972. Diplomate Am. Bd. Family Practice. Intern U. Fla., Gainesville, 1972-73; physician Lee County Coop. Clinic, Marianna, Ark., 1973-74; pvt. practice Coastal Health Practitioners, Lincoln City, Oreg., 1975-84; county med. officer Lincoln County Health Dept., Newport, 1986-90; pvt. practice, 1984-90; student health Miami U., Oxford, Ohio, 1991-93; pvt. practice Macadam Clin., Portland, 1994; cons. student health Willamette U., 1994-95; contract physician West Salem Clinic, 1995-97; med. dir. Capital Manor, 1997-99; locum tenens, 1999—. Trustee Coast Home Nursing, Lincoln County, 1984-86; expert witness EPA, 1980. Facilitator Exceptional Living, 1984-86. Fellow Am. Acad. Family Practice; mem. Lincoln County Med. Soc. (pres. 1984), Oreg. Med. Assn. Avocations: spontaneous music, folk dancing, sailing.

STRITTMATTER, PETER ALBERT, astronomer, educator; b. London, Eng., Sept. 12, 1939; came to U.S., 1970. s. Albert and Rosa S.; m. Janet Hubbard Parkhurst, Mar. 18, 1967; children— Catherine D., Robert P. B.A., Cambridge U., Eng., 1961, M.A., 1963, Ph.D., 1967. Staff scientist Inst. for Astronomy, Cambridge, Eng., 1967-70; staff scientist dept. physics U. Calif.-San Diego, La Jolla, 1970-71; assoc. prof. dept. astronomy U. Ariz., Tucson, 1971-74, prof. dept. astronomy, 1974—, Regent's prof., 1994—. Dir. Steward Observatory, Tucson, 1975— ; mem. staff Max Planck Inst. Radio-astronomy, Bonn, W. Germany, 1981— Contbr. articles to profl. jours. Recipient Sr. award Humboldt Found., 1979-80, Karl Schwarzschild medal, 1998. Fellow Royal Astron. Soc.; mem. Am. Astron. Soc., Astronomische Gesellschaft. Office: U Ariz Steward Obs Tucson AZ 85721-0001

STROBER, MYRA HOFFENBERG, education educator, consultant; b. N.Y.C., Mar. 28, 1941; d. Julius William Hoffenberg and Regina Scharer; m. Samuel Strober, June 23, 1963 (div. Dec. 1983); children: Jason M., Elizabeth A.; m. Jay M. Jackman, Oct. 21, 1990. BS in Indsl. Rels., Cornell U., 1962; MA in Econs., Tufts U., 1965; PhD in Econs., MIT, 1969. Lectr., asst. prof. dept. econs. U. Md., College Park, 1967-70; lectr. U. Calif., Berkeley, 1970-72; asst. prof. grad. sch. bus. Stanford (Calif.) U., 1972-86, assoc. prof. sch. edn., 1979-90, prof. edn., 1990—, assoc. dean acad. affairs, 1993-95, interim dean, 1994; program officer in higher edn. Atlantic Philanthropic Svcs., Ithaca, N.Y., 1998-2000. Organizer Stanford Bus. Conf. Women Mgmt., 1974; founding dir. ctr. rsch. women Stanford U., 1974-76, 79-84, dir. edn. policy inst., 1984-86, dean alumni coll., 1992, mem. policy and planning bd., 1992-93, chair program edn. adminstrn. and policy analysis, 1991-93, chair provost's com. recruitment and retention women faculty, 1992-93, chair faculty senate com. on coms., 1992-93; mem. adv. bd. State of Calif. Office Econ. Policy Planning and Rsch., 1978-80; mem. Coll. Bd. Com. Develop Advanced Placement Exam. Econs., 1987-88; faculty advisor Rutgers Women's Leadership Program, 1991-93. Author: (with others) Industrial Relations, 1972, 1990, Sex, Discrimination and the Division of Labor, 1975, Changing Roles of Men and Women, 1976, Women in the Labor Market, 1979, Educational Policy and Management: Sex Differentials, 1981, Women in the Workplace, 1982, Sex Segregation in the Workplace: Trends, Explanations, Remedies, 1984, The New Palgrave: A Dictionary of Economic Theory and Doctrine, 1987, Computer Chips and Paper Clips: Technology and Women's Employment, Vol. II, 1987, Gender in the Workplace, 1987, Challenge to Human Capital Theory: Implications for the HR Manager, American Economic Review, 1995, Rethinking Economics Through a Feminist Lens, Feminist Economics, 1995, Making and Correcting Errors in Economic Analyses: An Examination of Videotapes, (with Agnes M.K. Chan) the Road Winds Uphill All the Way: Gender, Work, and Family in the U.S. and Japan, 1999; editor (with Francine E. Gordon) Bringing Women Into Management, 1975, (with others) Women and Poverty, 1986, Industrial Relations, 1990, Challenges to Human Capitol Theory: Implications for HR Managers, 1995, (with Sanford M. Dornbusch) Feminism, Children and the New Families, 1988, Rethinking Economics Through a Feminist Lens, 1995, (with Agnes M.K. Chan) The Road Winds Uphill All The Way: Gender, Work and Family in the U.S. and Japan, 1999; mem. bd. editors Signs: Jour. Women Culture and Soc., 1975-89, assoc. editor, 1980-85; mem. bd. editors Sage Ann. Rev. Women and Work, 1984—; mem. editorial adv. bd. U.S.-Japan Women's Jour., 1991—; assoc. editor Jour. Econ. Edn., 1991—; contbr. chpt. to book, articles to profl. jours. Mem. rsch. adv. task force YWCA, 1989—; chair exec. bd. Stanford Hillel, 1990-92; bd. dirs. Resource Ctr. Women, Palo Alto, Calif., 1983-84; pres. bd. dirs. Kaider Found., Mountain View, Calif., 1990-96. Fellow Stanford U., 1975-77, Schiff House Resident fellow, 85-87. Mem. NOW (bd. dirs. legal def. and edn. fund 1993-98), Am. Econ. Assn. (mem. com. status of women in the profession 1972-75), Am. Ednl. Rsch. Assn., Indsl. Rels. Rsch. Assn., Internat. Assn. for Feminist Econs. (pres. 1997-97, assoc. editor Feminist Econs. 1994—). Office: Stanford U School Edn Stanford CA 94305 E-mail: myra.strober@stanford.edu

STROBER, SAMUEL, immunologist, educator; b. N.Y.C., May 8, 1940; s. Julius and Lee (Lander) S.; m. Linda Carol Higgins, July 6, 1991; children: William, Jesse; children from a previous marriage: Jason, Elizabeth. AB in Liberal Arts, Columbia U., 1961; MD magna cum laude, Harvard U., 1966. Intern Mass. Gen. Hosp., Boston, 1966-67; resident in internal medicine Stanford U. Hosp., Calif., 1970-71; rsch. fellow Peter Bent Brigham Hosp., Boston, 1962-63, 65-66, Oxford U., Eng., 1963-64; rsch. assoc. Lab. Cell Biology Nat. Cancer Inst. NIH, Bethesda, Md., 1967-70; instr. medicine Stanford U., 1971-72, asst. prof., 1972-78, assoc. prof. medicine, 1978-82, prof. medicine, 1982—, Diane Goldstone Meml. lectr., 1978-97, John Putnam Merrill Meml. lectr., chief div. immunology & rheumatology, 1978-97. Investigator Howard Hughes Med. Inst., Miami, Fla., 1976-81; bd. dirs. La Jolla Inst. for Allergy and Immunology; founder Dendreon, Inc. Assoc. editor: Jour. Immunology, 1981-84, Transplantation, 1981-85, 99—, Internat. Jour. Immunotherapy, 1985—, Transplant Immunology, 1992—, Biol. Bone Marrow Transplantation, 1999—; contbr. articles to profl. jours. Served with USPHS, 1967-70. Recipient Leon Reznick Meml. Rsch. prize Harvard U., 1966. Mem. Am. Assn. Immunology, Am. Soc. Clin. Investigation, Am. Coll. Rheumatology, Transplantation Soc. (councilor 1986-89), Am. Soc. Tranplantation Physicians, Western Soc. Medicine, Am. Assn. Physicians, Clin. Immunology Soc. (pres. 1996), Alpha Omega. Home: 405 Minoca Rd Portola Vally CA 94028-7740 Office: Stanford U Sch Medicine 300 Pasteur Dr Palo Alto CA 94304-2203

STROCK, CARL A. career officer; BCE, Va. Military Inst.; MCE, Miss. State U. Registered profl. engr., Mo. Commd. 2d. lt. U.S. Army, 1972, advanced through grades to brigadier gen.; various assignments Columbus AFB; sr. tactics instr. British Royal Sch. Military Engring.; cols. assignment officer, personnel staff officer Office of Dep. Chief Staff for Personnel Hdqs. Dept. Army; comdr., divsn. engr. Pacific Ocean Divsn. U.S. Army Corps. Engrs., Fort Shafter, Hawaii. Decorated Legion of Merit with one oak leaf cluster, Bronze Star with one oak leaf cluster, Meritorious Svc. medal with two oak leaf clusters, Southwest Asia Svc. medal with three battle stars.

STROCK, DAVID RANDOLPH, brokerage house executive; b. Salt Lake City, Jan. 31, 1944; s. Clarence Randolph and Francis (Hornibrook) S.; m. Phyllis A. Tingley, Dec. 13, 1945 (div. June 15, 1982); children: Sarah, Heidi. AA, San Mateo Coll., 1967; BS, San Jose State U., 1970. Investment exec. Paine Webber, San Jose, Calif., 1970-78, corp. trainer N.Y.C., 1978-79, rsch. coord., 1979-82, br. mgr. Northbrook, Ill., 1982-84, Palos Verdes, Calif., 1984-89, Napa, 1989-90, investment exec., 1990—. Contbr. articles to profl. jours. Mem. San Jose Jr. C. of C. (chmn. 1977, v.p. 1978), North Napa Rotary (past pres.), Moose. Republican. Avocations: reading, Indy car racing, formula one racing, biking, whitewater rafting. E-mail. Home: 3324 Homestead Ct Napa CA 94558-4275 Office: Paine Webber 703 Trancas St Napa CA 94558-3014 E-mail: David.Strock@PaineWebber.com

STROCK, HERBERT LEONARD, motion picture producer, director, editor, writer; b. Boston, Jan. 13, 1918; s. Maurice and Charlotte Ruth (Nesselroth) S.; m. Geraldine Polinger, Dec. 25, 1941; children: Leslie Carol, Genoa Ellen, Candice Dell. BA, U. So. Calif., 1941, MA, 1942. Asst. editor Metro-Goldwyn-Mayer, Culver City, Calif., 1941-42; prodr., dir. IMPPRO, Culver City, 1946-51; dir., film editor Hal Roach Studios, Culver City, 1951-53, Ivan Tors Prodns., Culver City, 1951-58; prodr., dir. ZIV Prodns., Hollywood, Calif., 1956-61; dir. Warner Bros., Burbank, 1958-63; ind. dir., pres. Herbert L. Strock Prodns., Hollywood, 1963—. Pres., chmn. bd. Hollywood World Films Inc., lectr. U. So. Calif. Producer, dir.: I Led Three Lives, Mr. District Attorney, Favorite Story, Corliss Archer, Science Fiction Theater, Highway Patrol, Dr. Christian, Man Called X, Harbor Command, 1954; dir. Battle Taxi; assoc. producer, dir.: Tom Swift series,(TV shows) Mann of Action, Red Light and Siren Sky King; Maverick, Alaskans, Colt 45, Bronco, Cheyenne, 77 Sunset Strip, Bonanza, Hans Brinker Spl., Decisions-Decisions, (feature pictures) Perfect World of Rodney Brewster, I Was a Teenage Frankenstein, Blood of Dracula, How to Make a Monster, Rider on a Dead Horse, Strike Me Deadly, Search the Wild Wind, Magnetic Monster, Riders to the Stars, Gog - Storm Over Tibet; editor, dir.: The Crawling Hand, One Hour of Hell; editorial supr. Shark; writer, dir. Brother on the Run; editor: So Evil My Sister, Chamber-Mades; co-producer Small Miracle; editor, dir. (documentary) They Search for Survival; supervising film editor Hunger Telethon; editor (spl.) The Making of America, co-writer, film editor Hurray for Betty Boop; dir., chief prodn. coordinator for Miss World, 1976; editor (documentary) UFO Journals, UFO Syndrome, Legends, all 1979, Neighborhood Watch; co-dir., film editor Witches Brew, 1979; writer, film editor (TV series) Flipper, 1981. Editor post prodn. services: China--Mao to Now, Eucatastrophe, Tibet, El Papa, Night Screams, King Kung Fu; dir., editor Deadly Presence; producer, writer, dir. (med. documentary) A New Lease on Life; editor Snooze You Lose, Olympic Legacy, Water You Can Trust, Distance, Fish Outta Water; dir., editor Gramma's Gold; co-editor Infinity, Peaceful Sabbath; producer, writer, dir. (fund raising documentary) Combined Federal Campaign; co-dir., editor Detour; editor (experimental film) This Old Man..., Sidewalk Motel. Served with U.S. Army, 1940-41. Mem. Acad. Motion Picture Arts and Scis., Dirs. Guild Am., Am. Cinema Editors (dir., bd. mem. 1984-85), Motion Picture Editors Guild, Delta Kappa Alpha (pres. 1941-65), Editors Guild. Democrat. Avocation: photography. E-mail: herbstrock@earthlink.net

STROCK, JAMES MARTIN, management consultant, author, negotiation expert; b. Austin, Tex., Aug. 19, 1956; s. James Martin Strock Sr. and Augusta (Tenney) Mullins. AB, Harvard U., 1977, JD, 1981; postgrad, New Coll. Oxford U., 1981-82. Bar: Colo. 1983. Tchg. asst. Harvard U., 1980-81; spl. cons. to majority leader U.S. Senate, Washington, 1982-83; spl. asst. to adminstr. EPA, Washington, 1983-85, asst. adminstr. for enforcement, 1989-91; spl. counsel U.S. Senate Com. on Environment and Pub. Works, Washington, 1985-86; environ. atty. Davis, Graham & Stubbs, Denver, 1986-88; acting dir., gen. counsel U.S. Office Pers. Mgmt., Washington, 1988-89; sec. for environ. protection State of Calif., Sacramento, 1991-97; prin. James Strock & Co., San Francisco, 1997—. Adj. prof. U. So. Calif., 1996-97, mem. adv. bd. T.R. Fund 1998—, Global Nature Fund 1998—; mem. Intergovtl. Policy Adv. Com., rep. U.S. Trade, 1991-97; mem. Calif. State Pers. Bd., 1998; guest prof. U. Konstanz, 1998. Author: Reagan on Leadership, 1998, Theodore Roosevelt on Leadership, 2001; contbr. articles to profl. jours.; moderator, producer Lay It On The Line, Sta. WDSU-TV, New Orleans, 1973-74. Bd. dirs. Youth Svc. Am., Washington, 1988-89, Environ. Law Inst., 1992-97, Rose Resnick Lighthouse, 1999—; chair Calif. United State Employees Campaign, 1996. Capt. JAGC USAR, 1987-96. Recipient Retsie Arco Future award, 1992, Ross Essay award ABA, 1985, Environ. Leadership award Calif. Environ. Bus. Coun., 1994, Fed. Republic Germany Friendship award, 1996; Environ. Soc. India fellow, 1997, commendation Calif. Dist. Attys. Assn., 1997; Charles Joseph Bonaparte scholar Harvard U., 1976, Rotary Internat. scholar, 1981-82. Mem. Coun. Fgn. Rels., Pacific Coun. on Internat. Policy, Commonwealth Club Calif., Am. Arbitration Assn., Phi Beta Kappa. Republican. Office: 400 Spear St Ste 107 San Francisco CA 94105-1691 E-mail: jmstrock@pacbell.net

STROHMEYER, JOHN, writer, former editor; b. Cascade, Wis., June 26, 1924; s. Louis A. and Anna Rose (Saladunas) S.; m. Nancy Jordan, Aug. 20, 1949; children: Mark, John, Sarah. Student, Moravian Coll., 1941-43; A.B., Muhlenberg Coll., 1947; M.A. in Journalism, Columbia, 1948; L.H.D. (hon.), Lehigh U., 1983. With Nazareth Item, 1940-41; night reporter Bethlehem (Pa.) Globe-Times, 1941-43, 45-47; investigative reporter Providence Jour.-Bull., 1949-56; editor Bethlehem Globe-Times, 1956-84, v.p., 1961-84, dir., 1963-84. African-Am. journalism tchr. in Nairobi, Freetown, 1964; Atwood prof. journalism U. Alaska Anchorage, 1987-88, writer-in-residence, 1989—; Clendinen Prof., U. S. Fla., 2001. Author: Crisis in Bethlehem: Big Steel's Struggle to Survive, 1986, Extreme Conditions: Big Oil and The Transformation of Alaska, 1993. Lt. (j.g.) USNR, 1943-45. Pulitzer Traveling fellow, 1948; Nieman fellow, 1952-53; recipient Comenius award Moravian Coll., 1971; Pulitzer prize for editorial writing, 1972; Alicia Patterson Found. fellow, 1984, 85. Mem. Am. Soc. Newspaper Editors, Pa. Soc. Newspaper Editors (pres. 1964-66), Anchorage Racquet Club. Home: 6633 Lunar Dr Anchorage AK 99504-4550 E-mail: jstroh@gci.net

STROMBERG, ROSS ERNEST, lawyer; b. Arcata, Calif., May 5, 1940; s. Noah Anders and Anne Laura (Noyes) S.; m. Toni Nicholas, Dec. 16, 1961; m. Margaret Telonicher, Oct. 3, 1965; children: Kristin, Matthew, Gretchen, Erik. BS, Humboldt State U., 1962; JD, U. Calif., Berkeley, 1965. Bar: Calif. 1966, U.S. Dist. Ct. (no. dist.) Calif. 1966, U.S. Ct. Appeals (9th cir.) 1966. Assoc. Hanson Bridgett, San Francisco, 1965-70, ptnr., 1970-85, Epstein Becker Stromberg & Green, San Francisco, 1985-90, Jones Day Reavis & Pogue, L.A., 1990—. Chmn. Jones Day's Healthcare Specialized Industry Practice; bd. dirs. Sutter Med Ctr., Santa Rosa. Author: Economic Joint Venturing, 1985, Acquisition and Enhancement of Physician Practices, 1988. Pres. East Bay AHEC, Oakland, Calif., 1984-87; bd. dirs. Am. Cancer Soc., Oakland, 1984-95; bd. dirs. Wildflowers Inst., San Francisco, Sutton Med. Ctr., Santa Rosa, 2001—; pres. Am. Acad. Hosp. Attys. of Am. Hosp. Assn., Chgo., 1978. Mem. Health Fin. Mgmt. Assn., Am. Health Lawyers Assn. Democrat. Office: Jones Day Reavis & Pogue 555 W 5th St Ste 4600 Los Angeles CA 90013-1025

STRONG, DAVID F. university administrator; b. Botwood, Nfld., Can., Feb. 26, 1944; m. Lynda Joan Marshall; children: Kimberley, Joanna. B.Sc., Meml. U. Nfld., 1965; M.Sc., Lehigh U., 1967; PhD, U. Edinburgh, 1970. NRC postgrad. scholar U. Edinburgh, Scotland, 1970-72; assoc. prof. teaching and rsch. Meml. U. Nfld., 1972-74, prof., acting dept. head, 1974-75, E.W.R. Steacie fellow, 1975-77, prof. dept. earth scis. univ. rsch., 1985-90, spl. adv. to pres., 1985-87, v.p. (acad.), 1987-90; W.F. James prof. pure and applied scis. St. Francis Xavier U., N.S., 1981-82; vres., vice-chancellor U. Victoria, B.C., Can., 1990-2000. Swiney lectr. U. Edinburgh, 1981; mem. rsch. coun. Can. Inst. Advanced Rsch., 1986—. Editor or co-editor several books; contbr. more than 200 papers to sci. lit. Recipient Atlantic Provinces Young Scientist award (Frazer medal), 1973; NRC Can. E.W.R. Steacie fellow, 1975-77; Fgn. Exch. fellow to Japan, 1976, France, 1976-77. Fellow Geol. Assn. Can. (Past Pres.'s medal 1980), Geol. Soc. Am., Royal Soc. Can.; mem. Can. Inst. Mining and Metallurgy (Disting. Svc. award 1979, Disting Llctrs. award 1983-84), Soc. Econ. Geologists. Home: 3115 Norfolk Rd Victoria BC Canada V8R 6H5

STRONG, JOHN OLIVER, plastic surgeon, educator; b. Montclair, N.J., Feb. 1, 1930; s. George Joseph and Olivia (LeBrun) S.; m. Helen Louise Vrooman, July 19, 1958 (dec. Mar. 1973); m. Deborah Sperberg, May 20, 1978; children: John Jr., Jean LeB., Andrew D. BS, Yale U., 1952; MD, U. Pa., 1957. Cert. paleontologist, Calif. Practice medicine specializing in plastic and reconstructive surgery, Santa Ana, Calif., 1964-97; asst. clin. prof. plastic and reconstructive surgery U. Calif., Irvine, 1970—. Chief of staff Western Med. Ctr., Santa Ana, 1996-97, interim chmn. bd., 1996-97, bd. dirs.; bd. dirs. United Western Med. Ctrs., Orange Health Found. Fellow ACS; mem. Calif. Med. Assn. (chmn. sci. adv. panel 1983-89), Calif. Soc. Plastic Surgeons (pres. 1991-92). Republican. Office: PO Box 94 Borrego Springs CA 92004-0094

STRONG, JOHN WILLIAM, lawyer, educator; b. Iowa City, Aug. 18, 1935; s. Frank Ransom and Gertrude Elizabeth (Way) S.; m. Margaret Waite Cleary, June 16, 1962; children— Frank Ransom, Benjamin Waite. B.A., Yale U., 1957; J.D., U. Ill., 1962; postgrad, U. N.C., 1966-67. Bar: Ill. 1963, Oreg. 1976. Assoc. firm LeForgee, Samuels, Miller, Schroeder & Jackson, Decatur, Ill., 1963-64; asst. prof. law U. Kans., 1964-66; assoc. prof. Duke U., 1966-69; prof. U. Oreg., 1969-75; legal counsel Oreg. Task Force on Med. Malpractice, 1976; prof. U. Nebr., 1977-84, dean, 1977-82, vice chancellor for acad. affairs, 1981-84; Rosenstiel Disting. prof. law U. Ariz., 1984-98, prof. emeritus, 1998—. Nat. sec.-treas. Order of the Coif, 1992-98; cons. Nat. Judicial Coll. Author: (with others) Handbook on Evidence, 5th edit., 1999. Served with U.S. Army, 1957-59. Mem. Ill. Bar Assn., Oreg. Bar Assn., ABA, Am. Law Inst., Phi Delta Phi. Independent. Congregationalist. Home: 3220 E 3rd St Tucson AZ 85716-4233 Office: U Ariz Coll Law Tucson AZ 85721-0001 E-mail: strong@nt.law.arizona.edu

STROOCK, THOMAS FRANK, oil and gas company executive; b. N.Y.C., Oct. 10, 1925; s. Samuel and Dorthy (Frank) S.; m. Marta Freyre de Andrade, June 19, 1949; children: Margaret, Sandra, Elizabeth, Anne. BA in Econs., Yale U., 1948; LLB (hon.), U. Wyo., 1995. Landman Stanolind Oil & Gas Co., Tulsa, 1948-52; pres. Stroock Leasing Corp., Casper, Wyo., 1952-89, Alpha Exploration, Inc., 1980-89; ptnr. Stroock, Rogers & Dymond, Casper, 1960-82; dir. First Wyo. Bank, Casper, 1967-89; mem. Wyo. Senate, 1969-89, chmn. appropriations com., 1983-89, co-chmn. joint appropriations com., 1983-89, mem. mgmt. and audit com., pres., 1988-89; mem. steering com. Edn. Commn. of States; amb. to Guatemala Govt. of U.S., 1989-93; pres. Alpha Devel. Corp., 1992—; prof. pub. diplomacy U. Wyo., Laramie, 1993—. Dir. Wyo. Med. Ctr., 1996—. Rep. precinct committeeman, 1960-68; pres. Natrona County Sch. Bd., 1969; pres. Wyo. State Sch. Bds. Assn., 1965-66; chmn. Casper Cmty. Recreation, 1955-60; chmn. Natrona County United Fund, 1963-64; chmn. Wyo. State Rep. Com., 1975-78, exec. com. 1954-60; del. Rep. Nat. Conv., 1956-76; regional coord. campaign George Bush for pres., 1979-80, 87-88; chmn. Western States Rep. Chmn. Assn., 1977-78; chmn. Wyo. Higher Edn. Commn., 1969-71; mem. Nat. Petroleum Coun., 1972-77; chmn. trustees Sierra Madre Found. for Geol. Rsch., New Haven; chmn. Wyo. Nat. Gas Pipline Authority, 1987-88; bd. dirs. Ucross Found., Denver; mem. Nat. Pub. Lands Adv. Coun., 1981-85; chmn. Wyo. Health Reform Commn., 1993-95; trustee Nature Conservancy, 1993—; chmn. Universidad del Valle Found., Guatemala City, 1995-2000. Sgt. USMC, 1943-46. Mem. Rocky Mountain Oil and Gas Assn., Petroleum Assn. Wyo., Kiwanis, Casper Country Club, Casper Petroleum Club, Yale Club N.Y. Republican. Unitarian. Home and Office: PO Box 2875 Casper WY 82602-2875

STROPE, MICHAEL LEE, protective services official; BS cum laude, Drury Coll., 1975; MS, Cen. Mo. State U., 1978. From police officer to police lt. Mo. Police Dept., Springfield, 1970-84; chief of police City of Stillwater, Okla., 1984-87, City of College Station, Tex., 1987-92, Peoria (Ariz.) Police Dept., 1992—. Instr. Ariz. State U., Phoenix, 1996—, Wayland U., Luke AFB, Ariz., 1993—; security-mgmt. cons. SSRS Properties, Inc., College Station, 1992; dept. chmn. criminal justice Blinn Coll., Brenham, Tex., 1992; project assessor Commn. on Accreditation for Law Enforcement Agencies, Inc., 1990; lectr. Okla. Mcpl. League, 1986; adj. faculty Columbia (Mo.) Coll., 1982-84, Drury Coll., Springfield, 1976-82; project dir. Mo. Police Dept., Springfield, 1979-81; adv. bd. chmn. Tex. A&M Engring. Ext. Svc. Police Acad., 1990-92. Contbr. articles to profl. jours. Criminal justice adv. com. Brazos Valley Cmty. Devel. Coun., 1987-92; exec. bd. dirs. Brazos Valley Coun. on Alcohol and Substance Abuse, 1987-91; dep. chmn. Brazos County Emergency Mgmt. Coun., 1987-92. Recipient Mayors award C. of C., 1996, Best of the West award Cmty. Svc., 1994, Cmty. Svc. award SAR, Tex., 1992, Spl. Recognition award Spl. Olympics, Okla., 1986, Outstanding Cmty. Svc. award Delta Tau Delta, 1985; named one of Outstanding Young Men of Am., 1982. Mem. Internat. Assn. Chiefs Police (tng. and edn. com. 1984-92, juvenile justice com. 1995—), FBI Nat. Acad. Assoc., Ariz. Police Chiefs Assn. Office: Peoria Police Dept 8343 W Monroe St Peoria AZ 85345-6559 Fax: 623-773-9015

STROTE, JOEL RICHARD, lawyer; b. N.Y.C., Apr. 19, 1939; s. Jack and Fortuna (Benezra) S.; children: Jared, Noah, Sebastian; m. Elisa Ballestas, Dec. 14, 1991. BA, U. Mich., 1960; JD, Northwestern U., 1963. Bar: N.Y. 1964, D.C. 1965, Calif. 1967, U.S. Dist. Ct. (cen. dist.) Calif. 1967, U.S. Supreme Ct. 1971. Assoc. Damman, Blank, Hirsh & Heming, N.Y.C., 1964-65, ICC, Washington, 1965-66, Capitol Records, Hollywood, Calif., 1966-67; ptnr. Strote & Whitehouse, Beverly Hills, 1967-89; of counsel Selvin, Weiner & Ruben, Beverly Hills, 1989-94; ptnr. with Cohen, Strote & Young, 1992-94; sole practice law, 1994—. Judge pro tem L.A. County Mcpl. Ct., 1973—; probation monitor Calif. State Bar Ct., L.A. 1985—; pres. Liberace Found., Las Vegas, Nev., 1987—; bd. chmn. Tuesday's Child, L.A., 1989-91. Mem. Thousand Oaks Arts Commn., 1997-99. Cpl. USMC, 1963-64. Mem. Calif. State Bar Assn., L.A. County Bar Assn., L.A. Copyright Soc., Beverly Hills Bar Assn., Assn. Internat. Entertainment Lawyers, Internat. Fedn. of Festival Orgns. Democrat. Jewish. Avocations: swimming, bicycling, hiking, opera, travel. Office: Strote and Levinson 21700 Oxnard St Ste 340 Woodland Hills CA 91367-7560 E-mail: Strote@attglobal.net

STROTHER, ALLEN, biochemical pharmacologist, researcher; b. Nolan County, Tex., Feb. 20, 1928; s. Henry Allen and Minnie Etta (Taylor) S.; m. Julia Ann Gutch, Feb. 7, 1957; children: Wesley Allen, Lori Ann. BS, Tex. Tech U., 1955; MS, U. Calif., 1957; PhD, Tex. A&M U., 1963. Rsch. asst. Tex. A&M, Coll. Sta., 1959-63; rsch. biochemist FDA, Washington, 1963-65; asst. prof. pharmacology Loma Linda (Calif.) U., 1965-70, assoc. prof., 1970-75, prof., 1975-95, retired, vol. faculty, 1995—, prof. emeritus Physiology and Pharmacology, 1997—. Cons. WHO, Geneva, 1982-86. Contbr. numerous articles to profl. jours.; chpt. to WHO Bull. Pilot CAP/USAF Search and Rescue San Bernardino, Calif., 1967-95; pilot examiner CAP Air Force Aux., Norton AFB, 1970-86. Named Investigator of Yr. Walter E. McPherson Soc., Loma Linda U., 1984, Basic Sci. Fellow of Yr., 1986, Outstanding Faculty Rschr. of Yr. award, 1997. Mem. Am. Soc. Pharmacology and Exptl. Therapeutics, Am. Chem. Soc., Xenobiotic Soc. Avocations: flying, golf. Home: 74448 Nevada Cir E Palm Desert CA 92260-2269 Office: Loma Linda U Sch Medicine Loma Linda CA 92354

STROUP, ELIZABETH FAYE, librarian; b. Tulsa, Mar. 25, 1939; d. Milton Earl and Lois (Buhl) S. BA in Philosophy, U. Wash., 1962, MLS, 1964. Intern Libr. of Congress, Washington, 1964-65; asst. dir. North Cen. Regional Libr., Wenatchee, Wash., 1966-69; reference specialist Congl. Reference div. Libr. of Congress, Washington, 1970-71, head nat. collections Div. for the Blind and Physically Handicapped, 1971-73, chief Congl. Reference div., 1973-78, dir. gen. reference, 1978-88; city libr., chief exec. officer Seattle Pub. Libr., 1988-96; exec. dir. Wash. Literacy, Seattle, 1996-99; reference coord. Timberland Regional Libr., Olympia, Wash., 1999—. Cons. U.S. Info. Svc., Indonesia, Feb. 1987. Mem. adv. bd. KCTS 9 Pub. TV, Seattle, 1988—; bd. visitors Sch. Librarianship, U. Wash., 1988—; bd. dirs. Wash. Literacy, 1988—. Mem. ALA (pres. reference and adult svcs. div. 1986-87, div. bd. 1985-88), Wash. Libr. Assn., D.C. Libr. Assn. (bd. dirs. 1975-76), City Club, Ranier Club. Avocations: gardening, mountain climbing, reading. Office: Wash Literacy 220 Nickerson St Seattle WA 98109-1622

STROUP, RICHARD LYNDELL, economics educator, writer; b. Sunnyside, Wash., Jan. 3, 1943; s. Edgar Ivan and Inez Louise (Kellet) S.; m. Sandra Lee Price, Sept. 13, 1962 (div. Sept. 1981); children— Michael, Craig; m. Jane Bartlett Steidemann Shaw, Jan. 1, 1985; 1 child, David. Student, MIT, 1961-62; B.A., M.A., U. Wash., 1966, Ph.D. in Econs., 1970. Asst. prof. econs. Mont. State U., Bozeman, 1969-74, assoc. prof. econs., 1974-78; dir. Office Policy Analysis, Dept. Interior, Washington, 1982-84; prof. econs. Mont. State U., 1978—, asst. dept. head, 2000—. Vis. assoc. prof. Fla. State U., Tallahassee, 1977-78; sr. assoc. Polit. Economy Research Ctr., Bozeman, 1980—/lectr. summer univ., U. Aix (France), 1985— Co-author: Natural Resources, 1983, Economics: Private and Public Choice, 9th edit., 2000, Basic Economics, 1993, What Everyone Should Know About Economics and Prosperity, 1993; editor: Cutting Green Tape, 2000; also articles, 1972—; mem. editorial bd. Regulation, 1993—. Dir. Gallatin Valley Cmty. Sch. Adj. scholar Cato Inst., 1993—. Mem. Am. Econ. Assn., Western Econ. Assn., So. Econ. Assn., Mont Pelerin Soc., Phila. Soc., Pub. Choice Soc., Assn. of Pvt. Enterprise Edn. (dir.). Episcopalian Home: 9 W Arnold St Bozeman MT 59715-6127 Office: PERC 502 N 19th Ave Ste 211 Bozeman MT 59718-3124 E-mail: rstroup@montana.edu

STROUP, STANLEY STEPHENSON, lawyer, educator; b. Los Angeles, Mar. 7, 1944; s. Francis Edwin and Marjory (Weimer) S.; m. Sylvia Douglass, June 15, 1968; children: Stacie, Stephen, Sarah. A.B., U. Ill., 1966; J.D., U. Mich., 1969. Bar: Ill. 1969, Calif. 1981, Minn. 1984. Atty. First Nat. Bank Chgo., 1969-78, asst. gen. counsel, 1978-80, v.p., 1980; sr. v.p., chief legal officer Bank of Calif., San Francisco, 1980-84; sr. v.p., gen. counsel Norwest Corp., Mpls., 1984-93, exec. v.p., gen. counsel, 1993-98, Wells Fargo & Co., San Francisco, 1998—. Mem. adj. faculty Coll. Law, William Mitchell Coll., St. Paul, 1985-98; mem. Regulatory Affairs Coun., Bank Adminstrn. Inst., 1996—. Bd. dirs. San Francisco Zool. Soc., 2000—, Legal Aid Soc. San Francisco, 1999—. Mem. ABA, Ill. Bar Assn., State Bar Calif., Minn. Bar Assn., Bar Assn. San Francisco (bd. dirs. 2000—), Fin. Svcs. Roundtable. Office: Wells Fargo & Co 633 Folsom St San Francisco CA 94107-3600 E-mail: stroupss@wellsfargo.com

STRUHL, STANLEY FREDERICK, real estate developer; b. Bklyn., Oct. 10, 1939; s. Isidore and Yvette (Miller) S.; BS with honors in Engring., UCLA, 1961, MBA in Data Processing, 1963; m. Patricia Joyce Wald, Feb. 26, 1966; children: Marc Howard, Lisa Lynn. Mem. tech. staff Hughes Aircraft Co., Fullerton, Calif., 1963-65; sr. asso. Planning Research Corp., Los Angeles, 1965-70; mgr. corporate info. systems Logicon, Inc., Torrance, Calif., 1970-73; mgr. operations analysis System Devel. Corp., Santa Monica, Calif., 1973-77; gen. partner TST Developers, Canyon Country, Calif., 1977-81; pres. Struhl Enterprises, Inc., Northridge, Calif., 1977-85; owner Struhl Properties, Northridge, 1979— . Mem. planning sub. com. 12th council dist., L.A., 1986-98. Lic. real estate broker, Calif. Mem. San Fernando Valley Bd. Realtors, Trail Dusters, Tau Beta Pi, Beta Gamma Sigma, Alpha Phi Omega. Home: 7309 Easthaven Ln West Hills CA 91307-1257

STRUTTON, LARRY D. newspaper executive; b. Colorado Springs, Colo., Sept. 12, 1940; s. Merril and Gladys (Sheldon) S.; m. Carolyn Ann Croak, Dec. 3, 1960; children— Gregory L., Kristen A.A. in Electronics Engring., Emily Griffith Electronics Sch., 1968; B.S. in Bus. Mgmt. and Systems Mgmt., Met. State Coll., 1971; diploma in Advanced Mgmt. Program, Harvard U., 1988. Printer Gazette Telegraph, Colorado Springs, Colo., 1961-64; prodn. dir. Rocky Mountain News, Denver, 1964-80, pres., 1990, pres. and CEO, 1991—; exec. v.p. ops. and advt. Detroit Free Press, 1981-83; v.p. ops. Los Angeles Times, 1983-85, exec. v.p. ops., 1986-90; now pub. Rocky Mountain News, Denver. Mem. adv. com. Rochester Inst. Tech., 1984—. Mem. Am. Newspaper Pubs. Assn. (chmn. 1987, chmn. TEC com. 1985-86), R&E Council (research and engring. council of the Graphic Arts Industry Inc.). Club: Lakeside Golf (Los Angeles). Home: 182 Morgan Pl Castle Rock CO 80104-9061 Office: Rocky Mountain News 400 W Colfax Ave Denver CO 80204-2694

STRUTZ, RICHARD, bank executive; b. 1951; Exec. v.p. Nat. Bancorp, 1992—, comml. lending chief, 1987-92, teller, br. mgr., 1970-87; pres. Nat. Bancorp of Alaska, Inc., 1993—. Office: National Bancorp of Alaska Inc PO Box 100600 Anchorage AK 99510-0600 Home: 310 W Northern Lights Blvd Anchorage AK 99503-3801

STRUTZEL, J(OD) C(HRISTOPHER), escrow company executive; b. L.A., Sept. 20, 1947; s. James Rudolph and Charlotte Elizabeth (Weiss) S.; m. Christine Melba Kemp, Dec. 28, 1969; children: Jason James, Jess Warren. BS in Bus. Mgmt., Calif. State U., Long Beach, 1970. Bellman Edgewater Hyatt House Hotel, Long Beach, 1970, night auditor, 1970-71; asst. mgr. Sands Resort Hotel, Palm Springs, Calif., 1971-72, gen. mgr., 1972-73; sales coordinator Bendix Home Systems, Santa Fe Springs, Calif., 1973-74; loan rep. J.E. Wells Fin. Co., L.A., 1974-75; v.p. Express Escrow Co., Huntington Beach, Calif., 1976-78, pres., chmn. bd., bd. dirs., 1978—. Pres., chmn. bd., bd. dirs. Elsinore (Calif.) Escrow, Inc., 1977-79; bd. dirs. Sorrell Devel., Redondo Beach, Calif.; expert witness on escrow, litigation and cons., 1982—; chmn. liability reduction com. Escrow Agts.

Fidelity Corp., 1983-84, legis. chmn., 1985 86, 87 90, 95 97, vice-chmn. bd., 1989-90, 94-95, treas., 1992-93; bd. dirs., sec. Discovery Escrow Co., 1989-94; drafted sections of Calif. Fin. Code, Health and Safety Code, Calif. Adminstrv. Code. Contbr. articles to trade publs. Bd. dirs. publicity chmn. Fountain Valley (Calif.) Youth Baseball, 1986-87; AD HOC com. on Escrow Regulations Dept. Housing and Cmty. Devel., 1980; escrow adv. com. Dept. Corps., 1990-93. Recipient J.E. Wells Meml. award, 1988. Mem. Escrow Agts. Fidelity Corp. (bd. dirs. 1983-90, 91-97), Escrow Inst. of Calif. (bd. dirs. 1991), Calif. Manufactured Housing Assn. (treas., bd. dirs. 1984-86), Calif. Manufactured Housing Inst. (bd. dirs. 1986—, treas. 1986-87, legis. chmn. 1993—, Polit. Action Com. Man of Yr. award 1988, Orange County chpt. Man of Yr. award 1988, Chmn.'s award 1997, Pres. award 1999). Republican. Avocations: golf, war games, athletic coaching. Office: Express Escrow Co 7812 Edinger Ave Ste 300 Huntington Beach CA 92647-3727

STRYER, LUBERT, biochemist, educator; b. Tientsin, China, Mar. 2, 1938; B.S. with honors, U. Chgo., 1957; M.D. magna cum laude, Harvard U., 1961; DS (hon.), U. Chgo., 1992. Helen Hay Whitney fellow Harvard U., also Med. Research Council Lab., 1961-63; from asst. prof. to assoc. prof. biochemistry Stanford U., 1963-69; prof. molecular biophysics and biochemistry Yale U., 1969-76; Winzer prof. neurobiology Stanford U. Sch. Medicine, 1976—, chmn. dept. structural biology, 1976-79; chmn. sci. adv. bd. Affymetrix, Inc., 1993—; chmn., chief sci. officer Senomyx, Inc., La Jolla, Calif., 1999-2001, chmn. sci. adv. bd., 2001—. Cons. NIH, NRC; pres., sci. dir. Affymax Rsch. Inst., Palo Alto, Calif., 1989-90; mem. sci. adv. bd. Jane Coffin Childs Fund, 1982-90, Rsch. to Prevent Blindness, 1984-93, Pew Scholars Profs. in Biomed. Scis.; chmn. sci. adv. bd. Affymetrix, Inc., 1993—. Mem. editorial bd.: Jour. Molecular Biology, 1968-72, Jour. Cell Biology, 1981—; assoc. editor: Annual Revs. Biophysics and Bioengineering, 1970-76. Trustee Helen Hay Whitney Found., 1997—, McKnight Endowment for the Neuroscis., 1999—. Recipient Am. Chem. Soc. award in biol. chemistry Eli Lilly & Co., 1970, Alcon award in vision Alcon Rsch. Inst., 1992. Fellow AAAS (Newcomb Cleveland prize 1992), Am. Acad. Arts and Scis.; mem. NAS, Am. Chem. Soc., Am. Soc. Biol. Chemists, Biophys. Soc., Phi Beta Kappa. Office: Stanford Sch Medicine Fairchild Ctr D221 Stanford CA 94305-5125

STUART, ANDREW MARK, mechanical engineering educator; PhD, Oxford U., 1987. Assoc. prof. mech. engring. Stanford (Calif.) U. Office: Stanford U Dept Mech Engring Durand Bldg Rm 257 Stanford CA 94305

STUART, DAVID EDWARD, anthropologist, writer, educator; b. Calhoun County, Ala., Jan. 9, 1945; s. Edward George and Avis Elsie (Densmore) S.; m. Cynthia K. Morgan, June 14, 1971. BA (Wesleyan Merit scholar 1965-66), W.Va. Wesleyan Coll., 1967; MA in Anthropology, U. N.Mex., 1970, PhD, 1972, postdoctoral student, 1975-76; LHD, W.Va Weslyan Coll., 2001. Rsch. assoc. Andean Center, Quito, Ecuador, 1970; continuing edn. instr. anthropology U. N.Mex., 1971-72, rsch. archeologist Office Contract Archeology, 1974, rsch. coord., 1974-77, asst. prof. anthropology, 1975-77, assoc. prof. anthropology, 1984-99, prof. anthropology, 1999—, asst. v.p. acad. affairs, 1987-95, assoc. v.p. acad. affairs, 1995-99; assoc. provost, 1999—; asst. prof. Eckerd Coll., St. Petersburg, Fla., 1972-74. Cons. archeologist right-of-way divsn. Pub. Svc. Co. N.Mex., Albuquerque, 1977-78; cons. anthropologist Bur. Indian Affairs, Albuquerque, 1978, Historic Preservation Bur. N.Mex., Santa Fe, 1978-81, Nat. Park Svcs., 1980, Albuquerque Mus., 1981; sr. rsch. assoc. Human Sys. Rsch., Inc., 1981-83, Quivira Rsch. Ctr., Albuquerque, 1984-86; bd. dirs. Table Ind. Scholar, 1979-83, pres., bd. dirs. Rio Grande Heritage Found., Albuquerque and Las Cruces, 1985-87; advisor Human Sys. Rsch., Ind., Tularosa, N.Mex., 1978-80, Albuquerque Commn. on Hist. Preservation, 1984-86. Co-author: Archeological Survey: 4 Corners to Ambrosia, N.Mex., 1976, A Proposed Project Design for the timber Management Archeological Surveys, 1978, Ethnoarcheological Investigations of Shepherding in the Pueblo of Laguna, 1983; author: Prehistoric New Mexico, 1981, 2d edit., 1984, 3rd edit., 1989, Glimpses of the Ancient Southwest, 1985, The Magic of Bandelier National Monument, 1989, Power and Efficiency in Eastern Anasazi Architecture, 1994, Anasazi America, 2000, others; columnist New Mexico's Heritage, 1983-87, others; editor: Archeological Reports, No. 1, 1975, No. 2, 1982. Grantee Eckerd Coll., 1973, Historic Preservation Bur., 1978-80; recipient Essayist award N.Mex. Humanities Coun., 1986. Mem. Am. Anthrop. Assn., N.Mex. Archeol. Coun., Albuquerque Archeol. Soc. (pres. 1986-88), Descs. Signers Declaration Independence, Sigma Xi, Phi Kappa Phi. Office: U NMex Dane Smith Hall Rm 220 Albuquerque NM 87131-0001 E-mail: dstuart@unm.edu

STUART, DAVID R. academic administrator; Asst. exec. dir. Faculty Assn. Calif. C.C.s, Sacramento, 1997—. Office: Faculty Assn Calif CCs 926 J St Ste 211 Sacramento CA 95814-2706

STUART, DOROTHY MAE, artist; b. Fresno, Calif., Jan. 8, 1933; d. Robert Wesley Williams and Maria Theresa (Gad) Tressler; m. Reginald Ross Stuart, May 18, 1952; children: Doris Lynne Stuart Willis, Darlene Mae Stuart Cavalletto, Sue Anne Stuart Peters. Student, Calif. State U., Fresno, 1951-52, Fresno City Coll., , 1962-64. Artist, art judge, presenter demonstrations at schs., fairs and art orgns., Calif., 1962—. Editor, art dir. Fresno High School Centennial 1889-1989, 1989; art advisor Portrait of Fresno, 1885-1985; contbg. artist Heritage Fresno, 1975; exhibited in group shows, including M.H. De Young Mus., San Francisco, 1971, Charles and Emma Frye Mus., Seattle, 1971, Calif. State U.-Fresno tour of China, 1974. Mem. adv. Ctrl. Calif. Women's Conf., 1989—, Patrons for Cultural Arts, Fresno, 1987-92, bd. dirs., 1991-92. Recipient 53 art awards, 1966-84; nominated Woman of the Yr., Bus./Profl. of Fresno, 1990. Mem. Soc. Western Artists (bd. dirs. 1968-74, v.p. 1968-70), Fresno Womens Trade Club (bd. dirs. 1986-93, pres. 1988-90), Fresno Art Mus., Fresno Met. Mus., Native Daus. Golden West Fresno. Republican. Avocations: world travel, photography, collecting art and dolls of different cultures. Home and Office: 326 S Linda Ln Fresno CA 93727-5737

STUART, KENNETH D. plant research administrator, microbiologist; b. Boston, 1940; married; 3 children. BA, Northeastern U., 1963; MA, Wesleyan U., 1965; PhD in Zoology, U. Iowa, 1969. Rsch. biochemist Nat. Inst. Med. Rsch., London, 1969-71, SUNY, Stony Brook, 1971-72; rsch. biologist U. San Francisco, 1972-76; dir. Seattle Biomed. Rsch. Inst., 1982—; affiliate prof. microbiology U. Wash., Seattle, 1984—. Fellow AAAS; mem. Am. Soc. Microbiology, Am. Soc. Parasitology, Am. Soc. Cell Biology, Am. Soc. Advancement Sci. Office: Seattle Biomed Rsch Inst 4 Nickerson St Seattle WA 98109-1651

STUBBERUD, ALLEN ROGER, electrical engineering educator; b. Glendive, Mont., Aug. 14, 1934; s. Oscar Adolph and Alice Marie (LeBlanc) S.; m. May B. Tragus, Nov. 19, 1961; children: Peter A., Stephen C. B.S. in Elec. Engring, U. Idaho, 1956; M.S. in Engring, UCLA, 1958, Ph.D., 1962. From asst. prof. to assoc. prof. engring. UCLA, 1962-69; prof. elec. engring. U. Calif., Irvine, 1969—, assoc. dean engring., 1972-78, dean engring., 1978-83, chair elec. and computer engring., 1993-98, interim dean engring., 1994-96; chief scientist U.S. Air Force, 1983-85. Dir. Elec. Communications and Systems Engring. divsn. NSF, 1987-88. Author: Analysis and Synthesis of Linear Time Variable Systems, 1964, (with others) Feedback and Control Systems, 2d edit., 1990, (with others) Digital Control System Design, 2d edit., 1994; contbr. articles to profl. jours. Recipient Exceptional Civilian Svc. medal USAF, 1985, 90, Meritorious Civilian Svc. medal, 1996. Fellow IEEE (Centennial medal 1984, Millennium medal 2000), AIAA, AAAS, NYAS; mem. INFORMS, Sigma Xi, Sigma Tau, Tau Beta Pi, Eta Kappa Nu. Office: U Calif Dept Ece Irvine CA 92697-0001 E-mail: arstubbe@uci.edu

STUBBLEFIELD, THOMAS MASON, agricultural economist, educator; b. Taxhoma, Okla., Apr. 16, 1922; s. Temple Roscoe and Martha Lacy (Acree) S.; BS, N.Mex. State Coll., 1948; MS, A. and M. Coll. Tex., 1951, PhD, 1956; postgrad. U. Ariz., 1954; m. Martha Lee Miller, Mar. 7, 1943; children: Ellen (Mrs. Richard Damron), Paula (Mrs. James T. Culbertson), Thommye (Mrs. Gary D. Zingsheim). Specialist cotton mktg. N.Mex. State Coll., 1948; extension economist, then asst. agrl. economist U. Ariz., Tucson, 1951-58, from assoc. prof. to prof., 1958-64, prof. and agrl. economist, 1964-83, emeritus prof., 1983—, acting asst. dir. agrl. expt. sta., 1966-68, asst. to dir. sta., 1973-74, chief party Brazil contract, 1968-70. Mem. Pima Council Aging, 1974-77, 80-90; chmn. adv. com. Ret. Sr. Vol. Program, Pima County, 1974-77, 80-90, mem. 1974—. Chmn. bd. Saguaro Home Found., 1980-85. With AUS, 1942-45. Author bulls. in field. Adv. bd. Unified Cmty., 1994—. Home: 810 W Calle Milu Tucson AZ 85706-3925

STUBBS, CHRISTOPHER W. physics educator; Asst. prof dept. physics U. Calif., Santa Barbara, 1991-94; prof. physics, astronomy U. Washington, Seattle, 1994—. Fellow David & Lucile Packard Found., 1994, Initiatives in Rsch. award NAS, 1996. Office: U Washington Dept Astronomy PO Box 351580 Seattle WA 98195-1580

STUDEBAKER, IRVING GLEN, mining engineering consultant; b. Ellensburg, Wash., July 22, 1931; s. Clement Glen and Ruth (Krause) S.; (widowed); children: Ruth, Betty, Raymond, Karl, Donna. BS in Geol. Engring., U. Ariz., 1957, MS in Geology, 1959, PhD in Geol. Engring., 1977. Registered profl. engr., Wash., Nev., Ariz., Colo., Mont. Geophys. engr. Mobil, 1959-61; civil engr. City of Yakima, Wash., 1964-66; instr. Yakima Valley Coll., 1962-67; sr. rsch. geologist Roan Selection Trust, Kalulushi, Zambia, 1967-72; sr. mining engr. Occidental Oil Shale, Grand Junction, Colo., 1974-81; prof. Mont. Coll. Mining Sch., Butte, 1982-96; prof. emeritus, 1996—. Cons. in field. Sgt. U.S. Army, 1951-54, Korea. Mem. N.W. Mining Assn., Geol. Soc. Am., Soc. for Mining and Metall. Engring., Soc. Econ. Geologists, Sigma Xi (pres. Mont. tech. chpt. 1990-91). Avocations: golf, travel. Home and Office: 34222 1st Pl S Apt C Federal Way WA 98003-6537

STULL, MIKE, personal care industry executive; CFO Optiva Corp., Bellevue, Wash. Office: Optiva Corp PO Box 5000 Snoqualmie WA 98065-5000

STUMP, BOB, congressman; b. Phoenix, Apr. 4, 1927; s. Jesse Patrick and Floy Bethany (Fields) S.; children: Karen, Bob, Bruce. B.S. in Agronomy, Ariz. State U., 1951. Mem. Ariz. State Ho. of Reps., 1957-67, Ariz. State Senate, 1967-76, pres., 1975-76; mem. U.S. Congress from 3d Ariz. dist., Washington, 1977—; vice chmn. nat. security com.; chmn. vets. affairs com. With USN, 1943-46. Mem. Am. Legion, Ariz. Farm Bur. Republican. Seventh-day Adventist. Office: Ho of Reps 211 Canon HOB Washington DC 20515-0001 also: 230 N 1st Ave Ste 5001 Phoenix AZ 85025-0012*

STUMPF, BERNHARD JOSEF, physicist; b. Neustadt der Weinstrasse, Rhineland, Germany, Sept. 21, 1948; came to U.S., 1981; s. Josef and Katharina (Cervinka) S. Diploma physics, Saarland U., Saarbrucken, West Germany, 1975, Dr.rer.nat., 1981. Rsch. asst. physics dept. Saarland U., Saarbrucken, 1976-81; rsch. assoc. Joint Inst. Lab. Astrophysics, U. Colo., Boulder, 1981-84; instr. physics, physics dept. NYU, N.Y.C., 1984-86, asst. rsch. scientist Atomic Beams Lab., 1984-85, assoc. rsch. scientist Atomic Beams Lab., 1985-86; vis. assoc. prof. physics dept. U. Windsor (Ont., Can.), 1986-88; assoc. prof. physics dept. U. Idaho, Moscow, 1988—. Chmn. Conf. on Atomic and Molecular Collisions in Excited States, Moscow, 1990. Contbr. articles to profl. jours. German Sci. Found. postdoctoral fellow U. Colo., 1981-83. Mem. AAUP, German Phys. Soc., Am. Phys. Soc., Am. Chem. Soc., Optical Soc. Am. Home: 825 W C St Moscow ID 83843-2108 Office: U Idaho Dept Physics Moscow ID 83844-0903 E-mail: bjstumpf@uidaho.edu

STUMPF, PAUL KARL, biochemistry educator emeritus; b. N.Y.C., Feb. 23, 1919; s. Karl and Annette (Schreyer) S.; m. Ruth Rodenbeck, June 1947; children: Ann Carol, Kathryn Lee, Margaret Ruth, David Karl, Richard Frederic. AB, Harvard Coll., 1941; PhD, Columbia U., 1945. Instr. pub. health U. Mich., Ann Arbor, 1946-48; faculty U. Calif., Berkeley, 1948-58, prof., 1956-58, Davis, 1958-84, prof. emeritus, 1984—. Chief scientist Competitive Rsch. Grants Office USDA, Washington, 1988-91; cons. Palm Oil Rsch. Inst., Kuala Lumpur, Malaysia, 1982-92; mem. sci. adv. bd. Calgene, Inc., Davis, 1990-93; mem. sci. adv. panel Md. Biotech. Inst., 1990-92; Inaugural lectr. Tan Sri Dato'Seri B. Bek-Nielsen Found., Kuala Lumpur, 1996. Co-author: Outlines of Enzyme Chemistry, 1955, Outlines of Biochemistry, 5th edit., 1987; co-editor-in-chief Biochemistry of Plants, 1980; exec. editor Archives of Biochemistry/Biophysics, 1965-88; contbr. over 250 articles to profl. jours. Planning commn. City of Davis, 1966-68. Guggenheim fellow, 1962, 69; recipient Lipid Chemistry award Am. Oil Chemists Soc., 1974, Sr. Scientist award Alexander von Humboldt Found., 1976, Superior Svc. Group award USDA, 1992, Award of Excellence, Calif. Aggie Alumni Found., 1996. Fellow AAAS; mem. NAS, Royal Danish Acad. Scis., Am. Soc. Plant Physiologists (pres. 1979-80, chmn. bd. trustees 1986-90, Stephen Hales award 1974, Charles Reid Barnes Life Membership award 1992). Avocation: golf. Home: 764 Elmwood Dr Davis CA 95616-3517 Office: U Calif Molecular & Cellular Biology Davis CA 95616 E-mail: pkstumpf@ucdavis.edu

STUPPI, CRAIG, lawyer; b. San Francisco, Mar. 4, 1946; BA with honors, U. Calif., Santa Barbara, 1968; JD, Stanford U., 1971. Bar: Calif. 1972, U.S. Dist. Ct. (no., ctrl. and ea. dists.) Calif. 1972, U.S. Ct. Appeals (9th cir.) 1972, U.S. Supreme Ct. 1975. Ptnr. Bronson, Bronson & McKinnon LLP, San Francisco, 1992—. Mem. Am. Bankruptcy Inst., State Bar Calif., Bar Assn. San Francisco, Bar Area Bankruptcy Forum. Office: Bronson Bronson McKinnon 505 Montgomery St Ste 1 San Francisco CA 94111-2514

STURGEN, WINSTON, photographer, printmaker, artist; b. Harrisburg, Pa., Aug. 27, 1938; s. George Winston and Gladys Erma (Lenker) S.; m. Nancy Kathryn Otto, Jan. 23, 1959 (div. 1981); 1 child, Bruce Eugene Sturgen; m. Jessica Sheldon, Mar. 15, 1988 (div. Mar. 1999). BS in Forestry, Pa. State U., 1960; postgrad., U. N.H., 1961-62; M of Forestry, Pa. State U., 1964; postgrad., U. Oreg., 1966-68. Cert. profl. photographer. Devel. engr. Weyerhaeuser Co., Longview, Wash., 1964-66; mgr. Wickes Lumber Co., Elkhorn, Wis., 1968-70; dir. ops. Wickes Wanderland, Inc., Delavan, 1970-72; owner, mgr. Sturgen's Cleaners, Delavan, 1972-80, Images by Sturgen, Delavan, 1980-84. Instr. photography continuing edn. dept. Western N.Mex. U., 1988-90; juror numerous orgns., 1982—. One-man shows include Artesia (N.Mex.) Mus. and Art Ctr., 1992, Delavan Art Mus., 1984, Donnell Libr., N.Y.C., 1992; exhibited in group shows at Carlsbad (N.Mex.) Mus., 1992, Sister Kenny Inst., 1992, (3rd Pl.), 93 (1st Pl.), 94, Deming Ctr. for the Arts, N.Mex., 1991, Shellfish Collection, Silver City, N.Mex., 1989, 90, 91-95, Thompson Gallery, U. N.Mex., 1989, Profl. Photographers Assn. of N.Mex., 1985, 86, 87, 88 (awards), Union Gallery, U. N.Mex., 1987, Gallery Sigala, Taos, N.Mex., 1986, World Trade Ctr., N.Y.C., 1992, 93, 94, Internat. Exposition of Photography, 1983, 84, 85, 87, Beyond Photography Touring Exhibit, 1991-92, An Am. Collection Touring Exhibit, San Francisco, Washington, Brussels, Tokyo, 1993-95, Sapporo (Japan) Internat. Print Biennial, 1993, Very Spl. Arts/N.Mex. Touring Exhibit, 1993-94, Ctr. Contemporary Art, St. Louis, 1994 (purchase award), Internat. Photography Mus., Oklahoma City, 1999, Internat. Art & Soul, L.A., 1999, numerous others; donation of all personal work Southwestern Regional Med. Ctr., N.Mex., 1996; pub. poetry, numerous articles in field; work reviewed in various publs. Founder, chmn. Winter Arts Festival, Silver City, N.Mex., 1988-90; com. mem. Taos Fall Arts Festival, 1985; com. chair Oktoberfest, Delavan, 1976-80; invitee Renaissance Weekend, Washington, 1997. Residency grant Wurlitzer Found., 1987, 89. Mem. Very Spl. Artists N.Mex., Very Spl. Artists Washington. Avocations: painting, printmaking, photography, disabled artists advocacy.

STURGULEWSKI, ARLISS, state legislator, director; b. Blaine, Wash., Sept. 27, 1927; BA, U. Wash.; LLD (hon.), U. Alaska, Anchorage, 1993. Mem. Assembly Municipality of Anchorage; interim exec. dir. Alaska Sci. and Tech. Found., 1995. Vice chmn. New Capital Site Planning Commn., mem. Capital Site Selection Com.; chmn. Greater Anchorage Area Planning and Zoning Commn.; mem. Alaska State Senate, 1978-93; Rep. nominee Office Gov. Alaska, 1986, 90. Home: 2957 Sheldon Jackson St Anchorage AK 99508-4469 Office: 3201 C St Ste 405 Anchorage AK 99503-3967

STURROCK, PETER ANDREW, space science and astrophysics educator; b. South Stifford, Essex, England, Mar. 20, 1924; came to U.S., 1955; s. Albert Edward and Mabel Minnie (Payne) S.; m. Marilyn Fern Stenson, June 29, 1963; children: Deirdre, Colin; 1 child from previous marriage, Myra. BA, Cambridge (Eng.) U., 1945, MA, 1948, PhD, 1951. Scientist Telecommunications Rsch. Establishment, Malvern, Eng., 1943-46, Nat. Bur. Standards, Washington, 1949-50, Ecole Normale Superieure, Paris, 1950-51, Atomic Energy Rsch. Establishment, Harwell, 1951-53; fellow St. John's Coll., Cambridge U., 1952-55; rsch. assoc. Stanford (Calif.) U., 1955-61, prof. applied physics, dept. physics, 1961-98, dir. for plasma rsch., 1964-74, 80-83; dep. dir. Ctr. for Space Sci. and Astrophysics, 1983-92, dir., 1992-98. Author: Static and Dynamic Electron Optics, 1955, Plasma Physics, 1993, The UFO Enigma, 1999; editor: Plasma Astrophysics, 1967, Solar Flares, 1980, Physics of the Sun, vols. I, II, III, 1986. Recipient Gravity prize Gravity Found., 1967, Hale prize Am. Astron. Soc., 1986, Henryk Arctowski medal NAS, 1990, Space Sci. award AIAA, 1992; European Ctr. for Nuclear Rsch. fellow, 1957-58. Fellow AAAS, Royal Astron. Soc., Am. Phys. Soc.; mem. Internat. Astron. Union, Internat. Acad. Astronautics, Soc. for Sci. Exploration (pres. 1982-2001). Office: Stanford U Dept Physics Varian Bldg Rm 302G Stanford CA 94305 E-mail: sturrock@flare.stanford.edu

STYNE, DENNIS MICHAEL, physician, educator; b. Chgo., July 31, 1947; s. Irving and Bernice (Coopersmith) S.; m. Donna Petre, Sept. 5, 1971; children: Rachel, Jonathan, Juliana, Aaron. BS, Northwestern U., 1969, MD, 1971. Diplomate Am. Bd. Pediats. Intern in pediatrics U. Calif., San Diego, 1971-72, resident in pediatrics, 1972-73, Yale U., New Haven, 1973-74; fellow in pediatric endocrinology U. Calif., San Francisco, 1974-77, asst. prof. pediatrics, 1977-83, assoc. prof. Davis, 1983-90, prof., 1990—, chair pediatrics, 1989-97; now prof., sect. chief pediatric endocrinology U. Calif. Davis Med. Ctr., Sacramento. Author numerous book chpts., contbr. articles to profl. jours. Mem. Endocrine Soc., Soc. Pediat. Rsch., Am. Pediat. Soc., Am. Acad. Pediats., Lawson Wilkins Soc. for Pediat. Endocrinology, Western Assn. of Physicians. Avocations: sailing, music. Office: UC Davis Med Ctr Dept Pediat 2516 Stockton Blvd Fl 3 Sacramento CA 95817-2208

SU, JUDY YA HWA LIN, pharmacologist; b. Hsinchu, Taiwan, Nov. 20, 1938; came to U.S., 1962; d. Ferng Nian and Chiu-Chin (Cheng) Lin; m. Michael W. Su; 1 child, Marvin. BS, Nat. Taiwan U., 1961; MS, U. Kans., 1964; PhD, U. Wash., 1968. Asst. prof. dept. biology U. Ala., Huntsville, 1972-73; rsch. assoc. dept. anesthesiology U. Wash., Seattle, 1976-77, acting asst. prof. dept. anesthesia, 1977-78, rsch. asst. prof., 1978-81, rsch. assoc. prof., 1981-89, rsch. prof., 1989—. Mem. surg. anesthesiology & trauma study sect. NIH, 1987-91; vis. scientist Max-Planck Inst. Med. Rsch., Heidelberg, West Germany, 1982-83; vis. prof. dept. anesthesiology Mayo Clinic, Rochester, Minn., Med. Coll. Wis., 1988; editorial bd. cons. Jour. Molecular & Cellular Cardiology, London, 1987—, European Jour. Physiology, Berlin, Germany, Muscle & Nerve, Kyoto, Japan, 1989—, Anesthesiology, Phila., 1987—, Molecular Pharmacology, 1988—, Jour. Biol. Chemistry, 1989—, Am. Jour. Physiology, 1990—; mem. rsch. study com. Am. Heart Assn., 1992-95. Contbr. articles to profl. jours. Grantee Wash. Heart Assn., 1976-77, 1985-87, Pharm. Mfrs. Assn. Found., Inc., 1977, Lilly Rsch. Labs, 1986-88, Anaquest, 1987—, NIH, 1978—; recipient Rsch. Career Devel. award NIH, 1982-87; rsch. fellowship San Diego Heart Assn., 1970-72, Max-Planck Inst., 1982-83. Mem. AAAS, Biophys. Soc., Am. Soc. for Pharmacology and Exptl. Therapeutics, Am. Physiol. Soc., Am. Soc. Anesthesiologists. Home: 13110 NE 33rd St Bellevue WA 98005-1318 Office: U Wash Dept Anesthesiology PO Box 356540 Seattle WA 98195-6540

SUAZO, PETE, state legislator; b. Salt Lake City, June 5, 1951; m. Alicia Suazo; 4 children. BA in Criminology and Corrections, MS in Econs., U. Utah. Bus. cons.; mem. Utah Ho. of Reps., 1992-96, Utah Senate, Dist. 2, Salt Lake City, 1996—; mem. judiciary com., edn. com.; mem. exec. office, criminal justice and legis. appropriations. Active Girl Scouts U.S., Boy Scouts Am. Mem. NAACP (life), Footprinters Internat., Utah Falconers and Raptors Assn., Utah Hispanic C. of C., Utah Amateur Boxing Fedn. Democrat. Recipient Youth Svc. award Salt Lake Area Gang Project, 1992, Caesar Chavez Peace and Justice award, Dr. Martin Luther King Freedom award, 1994; named to Outstanding Young Men of Am., 1983. Home: 1307 Garnette St Salt Lake City UT 84116-1626

SUBACH, JAMES ALAN, information systems company executive, consultant; b. Lawrence, Mass., Mar. 24, 1948; s. Anthony John and Bernice Ruth (Pekarski) S. m. Marilyn Butler, Feb. 16, 1980. BS with distinction, U. Maine, 1970; MS, U. Ariz., 1975, PhD, 1979. Vis. scientist NASA Johnson Space Ctr., Houston, 1977-79; rsch. assoc. Baylor Coll. Medicine, Houston, 1977-79; pres. Subach Ventures, Inc., San Antonio, 1980-84, JAS & Assocs., Inc., Phoenix, 1984—, C.I.O. Inc., 1987-90; v.p. PTIMS, Inc., Phoenix, 1992-96; faculty assoc. Ariz. State U., Tempe, 1992-93; v.p. Multipoint Tax Systems, Scottsdale, Ariz., 1996-97; chief info. officer Multipoint Nat. Property Tax Info., Scottsdale, 1997-98. Co-founder Bridge Alliance LLC, Phoenix, 1998. Assoc. editor Jour. Applied Photog. Engring., 1973-78; author software Gen. Acctg. System, 1987; bus. computing columnist, 1987. Pres. Forest Trails Homeowners Assn., Phoenix, 1987-88. Mem. Phoenix C. of C. (Pres.'s Roundtable, Technology Roundtable), Toastmasters (treas. Phoenix chpt. 1984), Ariz. Progress Users Group (pres. 1997), Tau Beta Pi, Sigma Pi Sigma. Republican. Avocations: public speaking, cross-country skiing, photography, golf. Office: JAS & Assoc Inc 13236 N 7th St # 4-276 Phoenix AZ 85022-5343 E-mail: dr.jim.subach@worldnet.att.net

SUBER, ROBIN HALL, former medical and surgical nurse; b. Bethlehem, Pa., Mar. 14, 1952; d. Arthur Albert and Sarah Virginia (Smith) Hall; m. David A. Suber, July 28, 1979; 1 child, Benjamin A. BSN, Ohio State U., 1974. RN, Ariz., Ohio. Formerly staff nurse Desert Samaritan Hosp., Mesa, Ariz. Lt. USN, 1974-80. Mem. ANA, Sigma Theta Tau.

SUBRAMANYA, SHIVA, aerospace systems engineer; b. Hole-Narasipur, India, Apr. 8, 1933; s. S.T. Srikantaiah and S. Gundamma; m. Lee. S. Silva, Mar. 3, 1967; children: Paul Kailas, Kevin Shankar. BSc, Mysore U., Bangalore, India, 1956; MSc, Karnatak U., Dharwar, India, 1962; post-grad., Clark U., 1963; MBA, Calif. State U., Dominguez Hills, 1973; D in Bus. Adminstrn., PhD in Bus. Adminstrn., Nova Southeastern U., 1986. Sr. scientific officer AEC, Bombay, India, 1961-63; chief engr. TEI, Newport, R.I., 1964-67; prin. engr. Gen. Dynamics Corp., San Diego, 1967-73; asst. project mgr. def. and systems group TRW, Colorado Springs, Colo., 1973-87, asst. project mgr. space and def. group Redondo Beach, Calif., 1987-98; cons. aerospace industry Cerritos, 1998—. Cons. Contbr. over 150 articles to profl. jours. V.p. VHP of Am., Berlin, Conn., 1984-88; pres. IPF of Am., Redondo Beach, 1981-88; appointed by Pres. of India to Atomic Energy Commn., India. Winner of dozens of awards and commendations from U.S. Dept. of Defense and the Aerospace Industry. Mem. Armed Forces Comm. and Electronics Assn. (v.p.-elect Rocky Mountain chpt. 1986—, Meritorious Svc. award 1985, Merit medal 1990), Am. Acad. Mgmt. Hindu. Avocation: social service. Home and Office: 12546 Inglenook Ln Cerritos CA 90703-7837

SUCKIEL, ELLEN KAPPY, philosophy educator; b. June 15, 1943; d. Jack and Lilyan Kappy; m. Joseph Suckiel, June 22, 1973 A.B., Douglass Coll., 1965; M.A. in Philosophy, U. Wis., 1969, Ph.D. in Philosophy, 1972. Lectr. philosophy U. Wis., Madison, 1969-71; asst. prof. philosophy Fla. State U., Tallahassee, 1972-73, U. Calif., Santa Cruz, 1973-80, assoc. prof., 1980-95, prof., 1995—, provost Kresge Coll., 1983-89. Author: The Pragmatic Philosophy of William James, 1982, Heaven's Champion: William James's Philosophy of Religion, 1996, also articles, book introductions and chpts. Mem. Am. Philos. Assn., Soc. for Advancement Am. Philosophy Office: U Calif Cowell Coll Santa Cruz CA 95064

SUE, MICHAEL ALVIN, allergist; b. L.A., Apr. 15, 1956; MD, U. Chgo., 1980. Diplomate Am. Bd. Internal Medicine, Am. Bd. Allergy and Immunology. Intern, resident and fellow West Los Angeles VA Med. Ctr., L.A., 1980-86; allergist Kaiser Permanente, Panorama City, Calif., 1986—. Fellow Am. Coll. Allergy, Asthma, and Immunology; mem. Am. Acad. Allergy, Asthma, and Immunology. Office: Kaiser Permanente 13652 Cantara St Panorama City CA 91402-5497

SUEDFELD, PETER, psychologist, educator; b. Budapest, Hungary, Aug. 30, 1935; emigrated to U.S., 1948, naturalized, 1952; s. Leslie John and Jolan (Eichenbaum) Field; m. Gabrielle Debra Guterman, June 11, 1961 (div. 1980); children: Michael Thomas, Joanne Ruth, David Lee; m. Phyllis Jean Johnson, Oct. 19, 1991. Student, U. Philippines, 1956-57; B.A., Queens Coll., 1960; M.A., Princeton U., 1962, Ph.D., 1963. Research assoc. Princeton U.; lectr. Trenton State Coll., 1963-64; vis. asst. prof. psychology U. Ill., 1964-65; asst. prof. psychology Univ. Coll. Rutgers U., 1965-67, assoc. prof., 1967-71, prof., 1971-72, chmn. dept., 1967-72; prof. psychology U. B.C., Vancouver, 1972-2001, head dept., 1972-84, dean faculty grad. studies, 1984-90, disting. scholar-in-residence, P. Wall Inst. Adv. Studies, 2000, dean and prof. emeritus, 2001—. Disting. vis. scholar Ohio State U., 2000—; cons. in field; chmn. Can. Antarctic Rsch. Program, 1994-98. Author: Restricted Environmental Stimulation: Research and Clinical Applications, 1980; editor: Attitude Change: The Competing Views, 1971, Personality Theory and Information Processing, 1971, The Behavioral Basis of Design, 1976, Psychology and Torture, 1990, Restricted Environmental Stimulation: Theoretical and Empirical Developments in Flotation REST, 1990, Psychology and Social Policy, 1991, Light from the Ashes, 2001; editor Jour. Applied Social Psychology, 1975-82 ;assoc. editor Environment and Behavior, 1992—; contbr. articles to profl. jours. Served with U.S. Army, 1955-58. Recipient Antarctica svc. medal, 1994, Donald O. Hebb award, 1996, Zachor award, 2000, Harold D. Lasswell award, 2001; grantee NIMH, 1970-72, Can. Coun., 1973—, Soc. Sci. Rsch. Coun. Can., 1973—, Nat. Rsch. Coun. Can., 1973-90, NIH, 1980-84. Fellow Royal Soc. Can., Can. Psychol. Assn. (pres. 1998-99), APA, Am. Psychol. Soc., Acad. Behavioral Medicine Resch., Soc. Behavioral Medicine, N.Y. Acad. Scis.; mem. Internat. Soc. Polit. Psychol. (v.p. 1999-2001), Soc. Exptl. Social Psychology, Phi Beta Kappa, Sigma Xi. Office: U BC Dept Psychology Vancouver BC Canada V6T 1Z4

SUGARMAN, MICHAEL, physician, rheumatologist; b. Galveston, Tex., May 26, 1945; s. Harold and Amelia Sugarman; m. Hilda Roberta Krug, Aug. 26, 1967; children: Jason, Steven. BS, U. Calif., Berkeley, 1966; MD, U. Calif., San Francisco, 1970. Diplomate Am. Coll. Physicians, Am. Coll. Rheumatology. Rheumatologist Fullerton (Calif.) Internal Medicine Ctr., Fullerton, Calif., 1976-94. Pres. St. Jude Heritage Med. Group, 1996—. Bd. trustees St. Jude Hosp. Fellow Am. Coll. Rheumatology, Orange County Rheumatism Soc.; mem. AMA, Orange County Med. Assn. Office: St Jude Heritage Med Group 433 W Bastanchury Rd Fullerton CA 92835-3404

SUGARMAN, MYRON GEORGE, lawyer; b. San Francisco, Nov. 7, 1942; s. Irving Carden and Jane Hortense (Weingarten) S.; m. Cheryl Ann Struble, June 8, 1968 (div. 1993); children: Andrew, Amy, Adam; m. Cynthia Wilson Woods, Apr. 16, 1994. BS, U. Calif., Berkeley, 1964, JD, 1967. Assoc. Cooley Godward LLP, San Francisco, 1972-77, ptnr., 1977—. Served to capt. U.S. Army, 1968-71. Fellow Am. Coll. Trust and Estate Counsel, Am. Coll. Tax Counsel, Am. Bar Found.; mem. U. Calif. Alumni Assn. (bd. dirs. 1985-88), San Francisco Tax Club (pres. 1990), San Francisco Grid Club, Order of Coif, Phi Beta Kappa, Beta Gamma Sigma. Avocations: skiing, tennis. Office: Cooley Godward LLP 1 Maritime Plz San Francisco CA 94111-3404

SUH, DAE-SOOK, political science educator; b. Hoeryong, Korea, Nov. 22, 1931; came to U.S., 1952; s. Chang-Hee and Chong-Hee (Paek) S.; m. Yun-Ok Park, Oct. 29, 1960; children: Maurice, Kevin. BA, Tex. Christian U., 1956; MA, Ind. U., 1958; PhD, Columbia U., 1964. Asst. prof. U. Houston, 1965-67, assoc. prof., 1968-71; prof. polit. sci., dir. Ctr. for Korean Studies, U. Hawaii, Honolulu, 1972-95, Korea Found. prof. policy studies, 1994-99; George L. Paik prof. Yonsei U., 1972—. Author: The Korean Communist Movement, 1967, Documents of Korean Communism, 1970, Korean Communism, 1980, Kim Il Sung, 1988, Kim Il Sung and Kim Jong Il, 1996. Mem. Conv. Ctr. Authority, Honolulu, 1989-94. Grantee Social Sci. Rsch. Coun.-Am. Coun. Learned Socs., 1963, East-/West Ctr., Columbia U., 1971, The Wilson Ctr. for Scholars, 1985, Fulbright, 1988. Mem. Am. Polit. Sci. Assn. (life), Assn. for Asian Studies. Avocations: tennis, golf. Home: 7122 Niumalu Loop Honolulu HI 96825-1635 Office: U Hawaii Manoa Dept Political Sci 2424 Maile Way Honolulu HI 96822-2223 E-mail: daesook@hawaii.edu

SUINN, RICHARD MICHAEL, psychologist; b. Honolulu, May 8, 1933; s. Maurice and Edith (Wong) S.; m. Grace D. Toy, July 26, 1958; children: Susan, Randall, Staci, Bradley. Student, U. Hawaii, 1951-53; B.A. summa cum laude, Ohio State U., 1955; MA in Clin. Psychology, Stanford U., 1957, PhD in Clin. Psychology, 1959; PhD (hon.), Calif. Sch. Profl. Psychology, 1999. Lic. psychologist, Colo.; diplomate Am. Bd. Profl. Psychology. Counselor Stanford (Calif.) U., 1958-59, rsch. assoc. Med. Sch., 1964-66; asst. prof. psychology Whitman Coll., Walla Walla, Wash., 1959-64; assoc. prof. U. Hawaii, Honolulu, 1966-68; prof. Colo. State U., Ft. Collins, 1968-99, head dept. psychology, 1972-93, emeritus prof., 2000—. Cons. in field; psychologist U.S. Ski Teams, 1976, Olympic Games, U.S. Women's Track and Field, 1980 Olympic Games, U.S. Ski Jumping Team, 1988, U.S. Shooting Team, 1994; mem. sports psychology adv. com. U.S. Olympic Com., 1983-89; reviewer NIMH, 1977-80, 94-98. Author: The Predictive Validity of Projective Measures, 1969, Fundamentals of Behavior Pathology, 1970, The Innovative Psychological Therapies, 1975, The Innovative Medical-Psychiatric Therapies, 1976, Psychology in Sport: Methods and Applications, 1980, Fundamentals of Abnormal Psychology, 1984, 88, Seven Steps to Peak Performance, 1986, Anxiety Management Training, 1990; editorial bd.: Jour. Cons. and Clin. Psychology, 1973-86, Jour. Counseling Psychology, 1974-91, Behavior Therapy, 1977-80, Behavior Modification, 1977-78, Jour. Behavioral Medicine, 1978-83, Behavior Counseling Quar., 1979-83, Jour. Sports Psychology, 1980-91, Clin. Psychology: Science and Practice, 1994-97, Professional Psychology, 1994-97; author: tests Math. Anxiety Rating Scale, Suinn Test Anxiety Behavior Scale, Suinn-Lew Asian Self-identity Acculturation Scale. Mem. City Council, Ft. Collins, 1975-79, mayor, 1978-79; mem. Gov.'s Mental Health Adv. Council, 1983, Colo. Bd. Psychologist Examiners, 1983-86. Recipient cert. merit U.S. Ski Team, 1976, APA Career Contbn. to Edn. award, 1995; NIMH grantee, 1963-64; Office Edn. grantee, 1970-71. Fellow APA (chmn. bd. ethnic minority affairs 1982-83, chmn. edn. and tng. bd. 1986-87, policy and planning bd. 1987-89, publs. bd. 1993-97, bd. dirs. 1990-93, pres.-elect 1998, pres. 1999), Behavior Therapy and Rsch. Soc. (charter); mem. Am. Psychol. Found. (trustee 2000—), Assn. for Advancement Psychology (trustee 1983-86), Assn. for Advancement Behavior Therapy (sec.-treas. 1986-89, pres. 1992-93), Asian Am. Psychol. Assn. (bd. dirs. 1983-88), Am. Bd. Behavior Therapy (bd. dirs. 1987—), Phi Beta Kappa, Sigma Xi. Home: 808 Cheyenne Dr Fort Collins CO 80525-1560 Office: Colo State U Dept Psychology Fort Collins CO 80523-0001

SUISSA, DAVID, advertising executive; Exec. creative dir., chmn. bd. Suissa Miller Advt., L.A. Office: Suissa Miller Advt 11601 Wilshire Blvd Fl 16 Los Angeles CA 90025-1770

SUITER, THOMAS, advertising executive; Attended, San Diego State U., Art Ctr. Coll. Design, Pasadena, Calif. Creative dir., creative svcs. dir. Apple Computer; creative dir. Landor Assocs.; chief creative dir. CKS Partners, Cupertino, Calif.; chief creative officer US Web CKS, March First Inc., 2000—. Office: 410 Townsend St San Francisco CA 94107-1537

SUJANSKY, EVA BORSKA, pediatrician, geneticist, educator; b. Bratislava, Slovak Republic, Feb. 14, 1936; d. Stefan and Terezia (Kaiserova) Borsky; m. Eduard Sujansky, Apr. 2, 1960 (dec. Sept. 1979); children: Paul, Walter. MD, Comenius U., Bratislava, Czechoslovakia, 1959. Diplomate Am. Bd. Pediats., Am. Bd. Med. Genetics. Resident in pediats. U. Iowa, Iowa City, 1969-71; fellow in human genetics Mt. Sinai Sch. Medicine, N.Y.C., 1971-73; clin. geneticist Beth Israel Hosp., N.Y.C., 1973-74; dir. clin. genetics Sch. Medicine, U. Colo., Denver, 1974-90, assoc. prof. pediats., biochemistry, biophysics and genetics, 1981—; co-dir. divsn. genetic svcs. The Children's Hosp., U. Colo., Denver, 1990—. Contbr. articles to profl. jours. Fellow Am. Acad. Pediats., Am. Soc. Human Genetics, Am. Coll. Med. Genetics (founding fellow). Avocations: fine arts, reading, travel. Office: U Colo Med Ctr 1056 E 19th Ave Denver CO 80218-1007

SUKO, LONNY RAY, judge; b. Spokane, Wash., Oct. 12, 1943; s. Ray R. and Leila B. (Snyder) S.; m. Marcia A. Michaelsen, Aug. 26, 1967; children: Jolynn R., David M. BA, Wash. State U., 1965; JD, U. Idaho, 1968. Bar: Wash. 1968, U.S. Dist. Ct. (ea. dist.) Wash. 1969, U.S. Dist. Ct. (we. dist.) Wash. 1978, U.S. Ct. Appeals (9th cir.) 1978. Law clk. U.S. Dist. Ct. Ea. Dist. Wash., 1968-69; assoc. Lyon, Beaulaurier & Aaron, Yakima, Wash., 1969-72; ptnr. Lyon, Beaulaurier, Weigand, Suko & Gustafson, Yakima, 1972-91, Lyon, Weigand, Suko & Gustafson, P.S., 1991-95; U.S. magistrate judge, Yakima, 1971-91, 95—. Mem. Phi Beta Kappa, Phi Kappa Phi. Office: PO Box 2726 Yakima WA 98907-2726

SUKOV, RICHARD JOEL, radiologist; b. Mpls., Nov. 13, 1944; s. Marvin and Annette Sukov; Susan Judith Grossman, Aug. 11, 1968; children: Stacy Faye, Jessica Erin. BA, BS, U. Minn., 1967, MD, 1970; student, U. Calif.-Berkeley, 1962-64. Diplomate Am. Bd. Radiology; lic. physician Minn., Calif. Intern pediatrics U. Minn., Mpls., 1970-71; resident radiology UCLA Ctr. for Health Sci., 1973-76; fellow in ultrasound and computed tomography UCLA, 1976-77; staff radiologist Centinela Hosp. Med. Ctr., Inglewood, Calif., 1977-85, Daniel Freeman Meml. Hosp., Inglewood, 1977—, dir. radiology, 1988-90. Med. dir. dept. radiology Daniel Freeman Meml. Hosp., 1998—; asst. clin. prof. radiology UCLA Ctr. for Health Scis., 1977-83; adv. bd. Aerobics and Fitness Assn. Am., 1983—. Contbr. articles to profl. jours. Vol. Venice Family Clinic, 1985—. Lt. comdr. USPHS, 1970-72. U. Minn. fellow, 1964-65, 66, 70. Mem. Soc. Radiologists in Ultrasound (charter), Minn. Med. Alumni Assn., L.A. County Med. Assn., Calif. Med. Assn. Radiol. Soc. N.Am., L.A. Radiol. Soc. (continuing edn. com. 1990—, mgmt. com. 1996—, chmn., sec. 1997-98, treas. 1998—, pres.-elect 1999-2000, pres. 2000—), L.A. Ultrasound Soc., Am. Coll. Radiology (alt. councilor 2001—). Avocations: bicycling, skiing. Office: Ingelwood Radiology 323 N Prairie Ave Ste 160 Inglewood CA 90301-4503

SULICH, VASSILI, artistic director; b. Island of Brac, Yugoslavia, Dec. 29, 1929; came to U.S., 1964; s. Thomas and Vjekoslava (Orlandini) Sulic. From co. mem. to Dancer Etoile various dancing cos., Paris, 1952-64; prin. dancer Broadway prodn. Follies Bergere, N.Y.C., 1964, prin. dancer, ballet master Las Vegas prodn., 1964-72; ind. choreographer Europe and U.S., 1964—; founder, artistic dir. Nev. Dance Theatre, Las Vegas, 1972-97, cons., advisor, 1997-98. Choreographer: Suite Lyrique, Oedipe roi, Idomeneo with Luciano Pavarotti; creator, choreographer numerous dance works including Mantodea, Walls in the Horizon, Cinderella; prin. dancer: La Dryade, L'Echelle, Combat, Cyrano de Bergerac, Lovers of Teruel; performer (TV show) Geraldine starring Geraldine Chaplin. Named Outstanding Individual Artist Gov. of Nev., 1981, Disting. Nevadan U. Nev. Bd. Regents, 1987. Office: Nev Theater Ballet 1555 E Flamingo Rd Las Vegas NV 89119-5258

SULLIVAN, CHARLES, university dean, educator, author; b. Boston, May 27, 1933; s. Charles Thomas and Marion Veronica (Donahue) S.; divorced; children: Charles Fulford, John Driscoll, Catherine Page; m. Shirley Ross Davis, Sept. 6, 1997. BA in English, Swarthmore Coll., 1955; MA, NYU, 1968, PhD in Social Psychology, 1973; MPA, Pa. State U., 1978. Predoctoral fellow NYU, 1964-68; postdoctoral fellow Ednl. Testing Svc., Princeton, N.J., 1973-74; asst. prof. psychology Ursinus Coll., Collegeville, Pa., 1973-78; mgmt. cons., 1978-86; adj. prof. Pa. State U., Radnor, Pa., 1978-80; prof., head dept. pub. adminstrn., dir. student svcs. Southeastern U., Washington, 1986-89; asst. dean Grad. Sch. Arts and Scis. Georgetown U., Washington, 1989-92, assoc. dean Grad. Sch. Arts and Scis., 1992-97, professorial lectr., dept. psychology, 1994-95; exec. dir. Doylestown Found., Doylestown, Pa., 1958-73; assoc. dean, prof. Coll. Profl. Studies U. San Francisco, 1997-98. Adj. prof. social and behavioral scis. U. Md., 1984-96; lectr., spkr. on lit. and art Cooper-Hewitt Mus., N.Y.C., Nat. Soc. Arts and Letters, Washington, Martin Luther King Jr. Libr., Washington, Met. Mus. Art, N.Y.C., Smithsonian Instn., Washington, Children's Book Fair, N.Y.C., Nat. Mus. Women in Arts, Lombardi Cancer Rsch. Ctr., Georgetown U., Arts Club of Washington, Phillips Collection, Corcoran Gallery of Art, U. San Francisco Multicultural Lit. Program, Nat. Mus. Am. History, New Coll. of Calif., others. Author: Alphabet Animals, 1991, The Lover in Winter, 1991, Numbers at Play, 1992, Circus, 1992, Cowboys, 1993, A Woman of A Certain Age, 1994, Out of Love, 1996, American Folk, 1998, In a Certain Place, 1999; editor: America in Poetry, 1988, 2d edit., 1992, 3d edit., 1996, Imaginary Gardens, 1989, Ireland in Poetry, 1990, Children of Promise, 1991, 2d edit., 2001, Loving, 1992, American Beauties, 1993, Here Is My Kingdom, 1994, Fathers and Children, 1995, Imaginary Animals, 1996. Trustee Folger Poetry Bd., 1988-92; Nat. Soc. Arts and Letters, 1992-94, Am. Acad. Liberal Edn., 1995—, San Francisco Art Inst., 2000—; pres. Am. Found. Arts, 1995—; mem. collectors com. Nat. Gallery Art, Washington, 1998—; mem. Dir.'s Cir., San Francisco Mus. Modern Art, 1998—. Recipient Best Books for Young Adults award Young Adult Libr. Svcs. Assn., 1992, 98, Best Books for Teens award N.Y. Pub. Libr., 1992, 93. Mem. Am. Poetry Soc., Acad. Am. Poets, Cosmos Club, The Family. E-mail: artsfound@earthlink.net

SULLIVAN, EDWARD JOSEPH, lawyer, educator; b. Bklyn., Apr. 24, 1945; s. Edward Joseph and Bridget (Duffy) S.; m. Patte Hancock, Aug. 7, 1982; children: Amy Brase, Molly Elsasser, Mary Christine. BA, St. John's U., 1966; JD, Willamette U., 1969; MA, cert. Urban Studies, Portland State U., 1974; LLM, Univ. Coll., London, 1978; diploma in law, Univ. Coll., Oxford, 1984; MA, U. Durham, 1999. Bar: Oreg. 1969, D.C. 1978, U.S. Dist. Ct. Oreg. 1970, U.S. Ct. Appeals (9th cir.) 1970, U.S. Supreme Ct. 1972. Counsel Washington County, Hillsboro, Oreg., 1969-75; legal counsel Gov. of Oreg., Salem, 1975-77; ptnr. O'Donnell, Sullivan & Ramis, Portland, Oreg., 1978-84, Sullivan, Josselson, Roberts, Johnson & Kloos, Portland, Salem and Eugene, 1984-86, Mitchell, Lang & Smith, Portland, 1986-90, Preston Gates & Ellis, Portland, 1990—. Bd. dirs., pres. Oreg. Law Inst. Contbr. numerous articles to profl. jours. Chmn. Capitol Planning Commn., Salem, 1975-77, 78-81. Mem. ABA (local govt. sect., com. on planning and zoning, adminstrv. law sect.) Oreg. State Bar Assn., D.C. Bar Assn., Am. Judicature Soc., Am. Polit. Sci. Assn. Democrat. Roman Catholic. Office: Preston Gates & Ellis 222 SW Columbia Ste 1400 Portland OR 97201-6632

SULLIVAN, G. CRAIG, household products executive; b. 1940; BS, Boston Coll., 1964. With Procter & Gamble Co., 1964-69, Am. Express Co., 1969-70; regional sales mgr. Clorox Co., Oakland, Calif., 1971-76, v.p. mktg., 1976-78, mgr. food svc. sales devel., mgr. bus. devel., 1978-79, gen. mgr. food svc. products divsn., 1979-81, v.p. food svc. products divsn., 1981, v.p. household products, 1981-89, group v.p. household products, 1989-92, chmn. bd., pres., CEO, 1992-99, chmn. bd., CEO, 1999—. Office: The Clorox Co 1221 Broadway Oakland CA 94612-1888

SULLIVAN, GEORGE MURRAY, transportation consultant, former mayor; b. Portland, Oreg., Mar. 31, 1922; s. Harvey Patrick and Viola (Murray) S.; m. Margaret Eagan, Dec. 30, 1947; children: Timothy M., Harvey P. (dec. July 1996), Daniel A., Kevin Shane, Colleen Marie, George Murray, Michael J., Shannon Margaret, Casey Eagan. Student pub. schs.; D.P.A. (hon.), U. Alaska, 1981. Line driver Alaska Freight Lines, Inc., Valdez-Fairbanks, 1942-44; U.S. dep. marshal Alaska Dist., Nenana, 1946-52; mgr. Alaska Freight Lines, 1952-56; Alaska gen. mgr. Consol. Freightways Corp. of Del., Anchorage, 1956-67; mayor of Anchorage, 1967-82; exec. mgr. Alaska Bus. Council, 1968; sr. cons. to pres. Western Air Lines Inc., 1982-87; former legis. liaison for Gov. of Alaska; now cons. Past mem. Nat. Adv. Com. on Oceans and Atmosphere, Joint Fed.-State Land Use Planning Commn.; past chmn. 4-state region 10 adv. com. OEO; mem. Fairbanks City Council, 1955-59, Anchorage City Council, 1965-67, Greater Anchorage Borough Assembly, 1965-67, Alaska Ho. of Reps., 1964-65. Trustee U. Alaska Found.; chmn. Anchorage Conv. and Visitors Bur.; bd. dirs. Western council Boy Scouts Am., 1958-59. Served with U.S. Army, 1944-46. Mem. Nat. Def. Transp. Assn. (life mem., pres. 1962-63), Nat. League Cities (dir.), Pioneers of Alaska, Alaska Mcpl. League (past pres.), Anchorage C. of C. (exec. com. 1963-65, treas. 1965-66, dir.), Alaska Carriers Assn. (exec. com.), Alaska Transp. Conf. (chmn.), U.S. Conf. Mayors (exec. com.), VFW (comdr. Alaska 1952) Club: Elks. Home and Office: George M Sullivan Co 1345 W 12th Ave Anchorage AK 99501-4252

SULLIVAN, JAMES N. retired oil industry executive; b. San Francisco, 1937; Student, U. Notre Dame, 1959. Formerly v.p. Chevron Corp., until 1988, vice chmn., dir., 1988-2000; ret., 2000. Office: Chevron Corp 575 Market St San Francisco CA 94105-2856

SULLIVAN, KATHLEEN MARIE, law educator; BA, Cornell U., 1976, Oxford (Eng.) U., 1978; JD, Harvard U., 1981. Law clk. Hon. James L. Oakes U.S. Ct. Appeals (2d cir.), 1981-82; pvt. practice, 1982-84; asst. prof. Harvard U., Cambridge, Mass., 1984-89, prof., 1989-93, Stanford (Calif.) U., 1993—, Paradise fellow, 1995-96, Stanley Morrison prof., 1996—, dean, Richard E. Lang prof., 1999—. Vis. prov. U. So. Calif. Law Ctr., 1991, Stanford U., 1992; lectr., commentator on constnl. law. Co-editor: (with Gerald Gunther) Constitutional Law, 13th edit., 1997. Named one of 50 Top Women Lawyers Nat. Law Jour., 1998; recipient John Bingham Hurlbut award for excellence in tchg. Stanford U., 1996. Fellow Am. Acad. Arts and Scis. Office: Stanford U Law Sch Bldg Lawsh 559 Nathan Abbott Way Stanford CA 94305-8610

SULLIVAN, MICHAEL EVAN, investment and management company executive; b. Phila., Dec. 30, 1940; s. Albert and Ruth (Liebert) S. BS, N.Mex. State U., 1966, MA, 1967; BS, U. Tex., 1969; MBA, U. Houston, 1974; MS, U. So. Calif., 1976, MPA, 1977, PhD in Adminstrn., 1983; BS in Acctg., U. La Verne, 1981. Sr. adminstrv. and tech. analyst Houston Lighting & Power Co., 1969-74; electronics engr. U.S. Govt., Point Mugu, Calif., 1974-77; mem. tech. staff Hughes Aircraft Co., El Segundo, 1977-78; staff program adminstr. Ventura divsn. Northrop Corp., Newbury Park, 1978-79; divsn. head engring. Navastrogru, Point Mugu, 1979-82; br. head, divsn. head spl. programs head operational sys. Pacific Missile Test Ctr., Calif., 1983-90, head tech. devel. office, head capability devel., 1993-98; far west regional coord., exec. com., exec. bd. Fed. Lab. Consortium, 1998—. CNO, dir. rsch., devel. and acquisiiton The Pentagon, Washington, 1987-88, dir. rsch. devel. test and evaluation and tech., 1990-93; pres., chmn. bd. Diversified Mgmt. Sys., Inc., Camarillo, Calif., 1978—. Author: The Management of Research, Develoopment, Test and Evaluation Orgainzations; Organization Behavior Characteristics of Supervisors-Public versus Private Sectors; Self-Actualization in RDT & E Organizations: Self-Actualization in a Health Care Agency; others. V.p., bd. dirs. Ventura County Master Chorale and Opera Assn.; bd. dirs. So. Calif. Assn. of Pub. Adminstrn. (also mem. fin. com., programs com., student aid com., exec. bd., exec. com. fed. lab. consortium). Served with U.S. Army, 1958-62. Ednl. Rsch. Info. Clearing House fellow, 1965-67, Ednl. Rsch. Tng. Program fellow N.Mex. State U., 1967. Mem. IEEE, Am. Math. Soc., Math. Assn. Am., Am. Statis. Assn., IEEE Engring. Mgmt. Soc., Am. Soc. Pub. Adminstrn., So. Calif. Assn. Pub. Adminstrn. (bd. dirs., various coms.), Assn. Fedn. Tech. Transfer Execs., Fed. Mgrs. Assn., Am. Assn. Individual Investors, Mcpl. Mgmt. Assts. So. Calif., Acad. Polit. Sci., Internat. Soc. for the Sys. Scis., Assn. MBA Execs., Tech. Transfer Soc., Internat. Fedn. for Sys. Rsch., Phi Kappa Phi, Pi Gama Mu. Home: PO Box 273 Port Hueneme CA 93044-0273 Office: PO Box 447 Camarillo CA 93011-0447

SULLIVAN, PETER MEREDITH, lawyer; b. Santa Monica, Calif., Nov. 9, 1952; s. Charles H. and Mary Jane (Menzel) S.; m. Mary T. Krueger, May 25, 1978. AB, Columbia Coll., 1974; JD, Fordham U., 1977. Assoc. atty. Kaye, Scholer, N.Y., 1977-81, Gibson Dunn & Crutcher, L.A., CA, 1981-86, litigation, antitrust ptnr., 1986—. Contbr. articles to profl. jours. Mem. ABA, N.Y. State Bar Assn., Calif. State Bar Assn. Episcopalian. Office: Gibson Dunn & Crutcher 333 S Grand Ave Ste 50 Los Angeles CA 90071-1504 also: 200 Park Ave New York NY 10166-0005

SULLIVAN, ROBERT EDWARD, lawyer; b. San Francisco, May 18, 1936; s. Edward C. S. and Mary Jane (Sullivan) S.; m. Maureen Lois Miles, June 14, 1958 (dec. 1972); children: Teresa Ann, Andrew Edward, Edward Braddock. BS, U. San Francisco, 1958; LLB, U. Calif-Berkeley, 1961. Bar: Calif. 1962. Assoc. Pillsbury, Madison & Sutro, San Francisco, 1963-70, ptnr., 1971—. Lectr. bus. law Calif. Continuing Edn. Bar and Practicing Law Inst.; v.p., treas., dir. MPC Ins., Ltd., 1986-93. Contbr. articles to profl. jours. Bd. dirs., exec. com. mem., sec. San Francisco Opera Assn., 1993—. 1st lt. U.S. Army, 1961-63. Mem. ABA, State Bar Calif. (com. corps. 1979-82, chmn. 1981-82, mem. exec. com. bus. law sect. 1982-85, vice chmn. 1983-84, chmn. 1984-85, advisor 1985-86, mem. partnership com. 1990-92, chmn. ltd. liability co. drafting com. 1992-93), San Francisco Bar Assn., Bankers Club San Francisco (bd. dirs., sec., treas.). Democrat. Roman Catholic. Office: Pillsbury Winthrop LLP 50 Fremont St San Francisco CA 94105-2228

SULLIVAN, STUART FRANCIS, anesthesiologist, educator; b. Buffalo, July 15, 1928; s. Charles S. and Kathryn (Duggan) S.; m. Dorothy Elizabeth Faytol, Apr. 18, 1959; children: John, Irene, Paul, Kathryn. BS, Canisius Coll., 1950; MD, SUNY, Syracuse, 1955. Diplomate Am. Bd. Anesthesiology. Intern Ohio State Univ. Hosp., Columbus, 1955-56; resident Columbia Presbyn. Med. Ctr., 1958-60; instr. anesthesiology Columbia U. Coll. Physicians and Surgeons, N.Y.C., 1961-62, assoc., 1962-64, asst. prof., 1964-69, assoc. prof., 1969-73; prof. dept. anesthesiology UCLA, 1973-91, vice chair anesthesiology, 1974-77, exec. vice chair, 1977-90, acting chmn., 1983-84, 87-88, 90-91, prof. emeritus, 1991—. Capt. M.C., USAR, 1956-58. Fellow NIH, 1960-61; recipient research career devel. award NIH, 1966-69. Mem. Assn. Univ. Anesthetists, Am. Physiol. Soc., Am. Soc. Anesthesiologists. Home: 101 Foxtail Dr Santa Monica CA 90402-2047 Office: UCLA Sch Medicine Dept Anesthesiology Los Angeles CA 90095-0001

SULLIVAN, WILLIAM FRANCIS, lawyer; b. San Francisco, May 6, 1952; s. Francis Michael and Jane Frances (Walsh) S.; children: Matthew, Meghan, Kathleen; m. Kait Sullivan. AB, U. Calif., Berkeley, 1974; JD, UCLA, 1977. Bar: Calif. 1977, U.S. Dist. Ct. (no. dist.) Calif. 1977, U.S. Ct. Appeals (9th cir.) 1977, U.S. Dist. Ct. (ea. dist.) Calif. 1978, U.S. Ct. Appeals (D.C. cir.) 1979, U.S. Ct. Appeals (fed. cir.) 1985, U.S. Dist. Ct. (so. dist.) Calif. 1986, U.S. Dist. Ct. (cen. dist.) Calif. 1990, U.S. Supreme Ct. 1986. Assoc. Chickering & Gregory, San Francisco and Washington, 1977-81, Brobeck, Phleger & Harrison, San Diego and San Francisco, 1981-84, ptnr., 1984—, mng. ptnr. San Diego, 1992-96, firmwide mng. ptnr., 1996-98. Panelist Calif. Continuing Edn. Bar; instr. Fed. Practice Program, U.S. No. Dist., chair Litigation sect., 1992, U.S. Dist. Ct. (no. dist.) Calif., 1980; instr. Coll. of Advocacy, Hastings Law Sch.; adv. bd. AMICUS Info. Svcs. Mem. ABA, Assn. Bus. Trial Lawyers (bd. govs. San Diego chpt. 1993-95), Calif. Bar Assn. (litigation sect.), San Francisco Bar Assn., San Diego Bar Assn., Barristers Club San Francisco (bd. dirs. 1984-86, pres. 1985), Calif. Young Lawyers Assn. (bd. dirs. 1986-89, sec. 1987-99, 1st v.p. 1988-89). Democrat. Roman Catholic. Office: Brobeck Phleger & Harrison 12390 El Camino Real San Diego CA 92130-2081 E-mail: wsullivan@BroBeck.com

SULLIVANT, BRYAN STERLING, state legislator; b. Rochester, Minn., June 13, 1955; m. Melissa Sullivant; 1 child. BA, Westminster Coll., 1978; MBA, U. Phoenix. Energy conservation engr. Johnson Controls; mem. Colo. State Ho. of Reps. Dist. 62, Denver, 1995-98, Colo. State Senate, Denver, 1999—. Vice chmn. bus. affairs and labor com., mem. local govt. com. Former mem. CAP; former v.p. Plins Met. Dist., Summit Sch. Dist.; pres. Denver Young Reps.; sec. Denver Rep. Com.; mem. Denver Bd. Edn., 1992-94. Mem. Assn. Energy Engrs., Profl. Skl Instr. Am., Lincoln Club Colo. (v.p.), Rotary. Republican. Presbyterian. Office: Colo State Senate State Capitol 200 E Colfax Ave Ste 332 Denver CO 80203-1716 also: PO Box 2387 Dillon CO 80435-2387 Fax: 970-453-4954. E-mail: bsulliva@sni.net

SULLOWAY, FRANK JONES, psychologist, historian; b. Concord, N.H., Feb. 2, 1947; s. Alvah Woodbury and Alison (Green) S.; 1 child, Ryan. AB summa cum laude, Harvard U., 1969, AM in History of Sci., 1971, PhD History of Sci., 1978. Jr. fellow Harvard U. Soc. Fellows, 1974-77; mem. Sch. Social Sci. Inst. for Advanced Study, Princeton, N.J., 1977-78; rsch. fellow Miller Inst. for Basic Rsch. in Sci., U. Calif., Berkeley, 1978-80, MIT, Cambridge, 1980-81, vis. scholar, 1989-98; postdoctoral fellow Harvard U., Cambridge, 1981-82, vis. scholar, 1984-89; rsch. fellow Univ. Coll., London, 1982-84; Vernon prof. biography Dartmouth Coll., Hanover, N.H., 1986; vis. Miller rsch. prof. U. Calif., Berkeley, 1999—, vis. prof., 2000—. Author: Freud, Biologist of the Mind, 1979 (Pfizer award History Sci. Soc. 1980), Born to Rebel, 1996; contbr. numerous articles on Charles Darwin, Sigmund Freud, and personality devel. to profl. jours. Fellow NEH, 1980-81, NSF, 1981-82, John Simon Guggenheim Meml. Found., 1982-83, MacArthur Found., 1984-89, Dibner Inst., MIT, 1993-94, Ctr. for Advanced Study in Behavioral Scis., Stanford, Calif., 1998-99, recipient Randi award Skeptics Soc., 1997, Golden Plate award Am. Acad. Achievement, 1997. Fellow AAAS (mem. electorate nominating com. sect. L 1988-91, 94-97), Linnean Soc. London; mem. Am. Psychol. Soc., Human Behavior and Evolution Soc., History of Sci. Soc. (fin. com. 1987-92, com. on devel. 1988-92). Home: 1709 Shattuck Ave Apt 205 Berkeley CA 94709-1753 Office: U Calif Dept Psychology IPSR 4125 Tolman Hall Berkeley CA 94720-1603 E-mail: sulloway@uclink.berkeley.edu

SULPIZIO, RICHARD, communications company executive; BA in Liberal Arts, Calif. State U., L.A.; M in Systems Mgmt., U. So. Calif. Various positions including v.p. and gen. mgr. Unisys Corp.; from v.p. info. systems to sr. v.p. Qualcomm Inc., San Diego, 1991, chief operating officer, 1992-94, 95-98, pres. Omnitrac divsn., 1994-95, pres., chief operating officer, 1998—. Office: Qualcomm Inc 5775 Morehouse Dr San Diego CA 92121-1714

SULZBACH, CHRISTI ROCOVICH, lawyer; b. L.A. BA, U. So. Calif., 1976; JD, Loyola U., 1979. Bar: Calif., 1980. Various to assoc. gen. counsel Tenet Healthcare Corp., Santa Barbara, 1983-99, exec. v.p., gen. counsel Calif., 1999—. Bd. dirs. Nat. Health Found., L.A. Mem. State Bar of Calif., ABA (exec. v.p., gen. counsel), FBA (bd. dirs. L.A. chpt.), Fedn. Am. Health Sys. (bd. dirs.). Office: Tenet Healthcare Corp Corporate Office 3820 State St Santa Barbara CA 93105-3112 E-mail: christi.sulzbach@tenethealth.com

SUMMERS, CAROL, artist; b. Kingston, N.Y., Dec. 26, 1925; s. Ivan Franklin and Theresa (Jones) S.; m. Elaine Smithers, Oct. 2, 1954 (div. Aug. 1967); 1 son, Kyle; m. Joan Ward, May 6, 1974. BA, Bard Coll., 1951, DFA (hon.), 1974. Tchr. Hunter Coll., Sch. Visual Arts, Haystack Mountain Sch. Crafts, Bklyn. Mus. Art Sch., Pratt Graphic Art Ctr., Cheltenham Twp. Art Ctr., Valley Stream Community Art Ctr., U. Pa., Columbia Coll., U. Calif., Santa Cruz, San Francisco Art Inst., U. Utah, Logan, Art Study Abroad, Paris, Casa de Espiritus Alegres Marfil, Mex., USIS workshop tour, India, 1974, 79; folk art and textiles tour leader to Rajasthan, India, winters 1995-2001. Represented in permanent collections at, Mus. Modern Art, Bklyn. Mus., N.Y. Pub. Libr., Libr. of Congress, Nat. Gallery, Victoria and Albert Mus., London, Bibliotheque Nationale, Paris, Kinstmuseum, Basil, Lugan (Switzerland) Art Mus. Grenchen (Switzerland) Art Mus., Malmo (Sweden) Mus., Los Angeles County Mus., Phila. Mus., Balt. Mus., Seattle Mus., Boston Mus., Art Inst. Chgo., Am. embassies in Russia, Can., India, Thailand, Fed. Republic Germany and Eng.; traveling exhibit, Mus. Modern Art, 1964-66; retrospective exhbn. Brooklyn Mus., 1977, Nassau County Mus. Art, 1990, Belles Artes, San Miquel de Allende, Mex., 1992, Miami U. Art Mus., Oxford, Ohio, 1995, Egon Schiele Centrum Česky Krumlov, Czech Republic, 1997-98; 50-yr. retrospective at Mus. Art and History, Santa Cruz, 1999, Woodstock (N.Y.) Artists Assn., 1999, San Francisco Mus. Modern Art Rental Gallery, 2000. Served with USMCR, 1944-48, PTO. Named Artist of Yr., Santa Cruz County Arts Commn., 2001; Louis Comfort Tiffany Found. fellow, 1955, 60, John Simon Guggenheim Found. fellow, 1959, Fulbright fellow, Italy, 1961; Italian govt. study grantee, 1954-55, Coun. for Internat. Exch. Scholars rsch. grantee, India, 1993-94. Mem. NAD, Calif. Soc. Printmakers. Address: 2817 Smith Grade Santa Cruz CA 95060-9764

SUMMERS, CATHLEEN ANN, film producer; b. Chgo. d. Cecil Paul and Elizabeth Ann S.; m. Patrick Timothy Crowley. BA, U. So. Calif., 1973. Film editor, comml. producer, dir.'s asst. Roman Polanski, Rome, 1972; story editor Albert S. Ruddy Prodns. Paramount Pictures, L.A., 1973-74; exec. asst. Columbia Pictures, Burbank, Calif., 1974, story editor, 1974-76; devel. exec., v.p., producer Martin Ransohoff Prodns. Columbia Pictures, 1976; sr. v.p. Tri-Star Pictures, Century City, Calif., 1984-87; motion picture producer Cathleen Summers Prodns., L.A., 1989—. Motion picture producer, ptnr. Summers-Kouf Prodns., Burbank, 1986-87; motion picture producer Cathleen Summers Prodns., L.A., 1987, Summers-Quaid Prodns., Century City, Culver City, Calif., 1988—. Producer: (motion picture) Stakeout, 1987, DOA, 1991, Vital Signs, 1990, Mystery Date, 1991, Dogfight, 1991, The Sandlot, 1993, Stakeout II, 1993. Co-founder Diane Thomas Scholarship-UCLA, 1988—; bd. dirs. L.A. chpt. Nat. Parkinson's Found. Mem. Am. Film Inst. (pres. 3d Decade Coun. 1995, 96, 97).

SUMMERS, ROBERT P. career military officer; BS in Maths., USAF Acad., Colorado Springs, 1973; MS in Physics, Air Force Inst. Technology, Wright-Patterson AFB, 1978. Commd. USAF, advanced through grades to brigadier gen., 1998; crew mem., evaluator 341st Strategic Missile Wing, Malmstrom AFB, Mont., 1974-76; asst. prof. physics USAF Acad., 1978-82; chief ICBM deployment br., asst. sr. office matters HQ Strategic Air Command, Offutt AFB, Nebr., 1983-87; comdr. 564th Support Group, dep. comdr. 341st combat support Malmstrom AFB, 1987-89; arms control officer, chief personnel divsn. HQ U.S. European Command, Patch Barracks, Germany, 1989-91; asst. dir. nuclear ops. Def. Nuclear Agy., Alexandria, Va., 1992-95; comdr. 321st Missile Group, Grand Forks AFB, N.D., 1995-96; comdr. 90th space wing F.E. Warren AFB, Wyo., 1996-97; dep. dir. ops. HQ Air Force Space Command, Peterson AFB, Colo., 1997-98; vice comdr. Sacramento Air Logistics Ctr, McClellan AFB, Calif., 1998—.

SUMNER, DANIEL ALAN, economist, educator; b. Fairfield, Calif., Dec. 5, 1950; BS in Agrl. Mgmt., Calif. State Poly. U., 1971; MA in Econs., Mich. State U., 1973, U. Chgo., 1977, PhD, 1978. Post-doctoral fellow, labor and population group, econ. dept., Rand Corp., Santa Monica, Calif., 1977-78; asst. prof. N.C. State U., Raleigh, 1978-83, assoc. prof., 1983-87, prof., 1987-92; resident fellow Resources for the Future, Washington, 1986-87; sr. economist Pres.'s Council of Econ. Advisers, 1987-88; dep. asst. sec. for econs. USDA, 1990-91, asst. sec. for econs., 1992-93; Frank H. Buck Jr. prof. dept. agrl. econs. U. Calif., Davis, 1993—. Dir. U. Calif. Agrl. Issues Ctr., 1997—; chair Internat. Agrl. Trade Rsch. Consortium, 1997-99. Author and editor books and monographs; contbr. chpts. to books, articles in profl. jours. Named Alumnus of Yr., Calif. State Poly. U., 1991; recipient Quality of Rsch. Contbn. award Am. Agrl. Econ. Assn., 1996, Policy Contbrn., 1995, fellow, 1999. Mem. Am. Econ. Assn., Econometric Soc., Am. Agrl. Econs. Assn., Internat. Assn. Agrl. Economists. Office: U Calif Davis Dept Agrl Econ Davis CA 95616 E-mail: dasumner@ucdavis.edu

SUMNER, GORDON, JR. retired military officer; b. Albuquerque, July 23, 1924; s. Gordon and Esstella (Berry) S.; m. Frances Fernandes, May, 1991; children: Ward T., Holly Rose. AS, N.Mex. Mil. Inst., 1943; BA, La. State U., 1955; MA, U. Md., 1963. Commd. 2d. lt. U.S. Army, 1944, advanced through grades to lt. gen., 1975, ret., 1978; founder, chmn. Cypress Internat., 1978-96; chmn. La Mancha Co., Inc., 1981-89, Sumner Assoc. Cons. U.S. Depts. State and Def; amabassador at large for Latin Am.; spl. advisor U.S. Dept. State; nat. security advisor Pres.' Bi-Partisan Commn. Cen. Am.; cons. Los Alamos Nat. Lab. Contbr. articles to profl. jours. Decorated D.S.M., Silver Star, Legion of Merit with three oak leaf clusters, Disting. Flying Cross with 13 oak leaf clusters, Bronze Star, Army Commendation medal with oak leaf cluster, Purple Heart. Mem. Phi Kappa Phi, Pi Sigma Alpha. Office: La Mancha Co 100 Cienega St Ste D Santa Fe NM 87501-2003

SUNDBORG, FATHER STEPHEN V. academic administrator; s. George and Mary Sundborg. Ordained Jesuit, 1974. Tchr. religion and Latin Gonzaga Prep. Sch., Spokane, Wash., Jesuit High, Portland, Oreg.; tchr. theology Seattle U.; rector Seattle U. Jewish Cmty., 1986-90; provincial Oreg. Province, 1990-97; pres. Seattle U., 1997—. Office: Seattle U 900 Broadway Seattle WA 98122-4340

SUNDEL, HARVEY H. marketing research analyst, consultant; b. Bronx, N.Y., July 24, 1944; s. Louis and Pauline (Brotman) S. BBA, St. Mary's U., San Antonio, 1969, MBA, 1970; PhD, St. Louis U., 1974. Asst. dir. research Lone Star Brewery, San Antonio, 1970-71; cons. Tri-Mark, Inc., San Antonio, 1972-73; asst. prof. mktg. Lewis and Clark Coll., Godfrey, Ill., 1973-74, Met. State Coll., Denver, 1974-77, chmn., prof. mktg., 1977-86; pres. Sundel Rsch., Inc., Denver, 1976—. Cons. Frederick Ross Co., Denver, 1979-84, U.S. West Direct, Denver, 1986—, Monsanto Chems. Co., St. Louis, 1985-97, Mountain Bell, Denver, 1979-88, U.S. West Comm., Denver, 1988—, AT&T, 1986-91, Melco Industries, 1987-90, Norwest Banks, 1990-94, PACE Membership Warehouse, 1992-93, U.S. Meat Export Fedn., 1992—, G.D. Searle, 1996-98, Nextel Comms., 1996-2000, Solutia, 1997—, Ethyl Corp., 2000—, Watlow Electric Mfg. Co., 2000—; expert witness in legal cases. Contbr. papers and proceedings to profl. jours. Com. mem. Mile High United Way, Denver, 1975-80, Allied Jewish Fedn. Cmty. Rels. Action Com., 1995—, Hewlett Packard, 1998—, Agilent Techs., 1999—, Encore Media, 2000—. Jewish. Avocation: handball. Home: 1616 Glen Bar Dr Lakewood CO 80215-3014 Office: Sundel Rsch Inc 1150 Delaware St Denver CO 80204-3608 E-mail: sundel@rmi.net

SUNDGREN, DONALD E. construction executive; BS, La. State U. V.p. exec. dir. Dillingham Constrn,. Holdings, Inc., Pleasanton, Calif., 1996-97; pres., CEO Dillingham Construction Corp., Pleasanton, 1997—. Office: Dillingham Construction Corp 5960 Inglewood Dr Pleasanton CA 94588

SUNDT, HARRY WILSON, construction company executive; b. Woodbury, N.J., July 5, 1932; s. Thoralf Mauritz and Elinor (Stout) S.; m. Dorothy Van Gilder, June 26, 1954; children: Thomas D., Perri Lee Sundt Touche, Gerald W. BS in Bus. Adminstrn., U. Ariz., 1954, postgrad., 1957-59. Salesman ins. VanGilder Agys., Denver, 1956-57; apprentice carpenter M.M. Sundt Constrn. Co., Tucson, 1957-58, estimator, 1958-59, adminstrv. asst. Vandenberg AFB, 1959-62, sr. estimator Tucson, 1962-64, div. mgr., 1964-65, exec. v.p., gen. mgr., 1965-75, pres., chmn., 1975-79; chmn. Sundt Corp., Tucson, 1980-83, chmn., chief exec. officer, 1983-98; ret., 1999. Bd. dirs. Tucson Electric Power Co., Nations Energy Co., Schuff Steel Co. Pres. Tucson Airport Authority, 1982; bd. dirs. U. Ariz. Found. 1981. 1st lt. U.S. Army, 1954-56. Recipient Disting. Citizen award U. Ariz., 1982, Centennial Medallion award, 1989, Founders award Tucson C. of C., 2000. Mem. Tucson Country Club. Republican. Episcopalian. Avocation: tennis. Home: 6002 E San Leandro Tucson AZ 85715-3014

SUNG, KUO-LI PAUL, bioengineering educator; MA in Biology, Coll. William and Mary, 1975; MS in Physiology, Columbia U., 1977; PhD in Physiology, Rutgers-Columbia U., 1982; PhD in Bioengring. (hon.), Chongqing U., China, 1993. Rsch. asst. dept. biology Coll. Willam and Mary, 1972-74; lectr. divsn. of circulatory physiology and biophysics dept. of physiology and cellular biophysics, Coll. Physicians and Surgeons Columbia U., 1986, 87; lectr. Inst. Biomedical Sci. Academia Sinica, 1987; assoc. rsch sci. dept. physiology and cellular biophysics Coll. Physicians and Surgeons, Columbia U., 1982-88; organizer and instr. Cell Biophysics Workshop Academia Sinica and Nat. Sci. Coun., Taiwan, China, 1987; assoc. rsch. bioengineer III, lectr. dept. applied mechanics and engring. scis.-bioengineering U Calif.-San Diego, La Jolla, 1988-92, assoc. prof. of orthopaedic dept., Sch. Medicine, 1992-95, assoc. prof. orthopaedics and bioengring. depts., 1992-96; prof. U. Calif.-San Diego, La Jolla, 1996—; lectr. bioengineering ctr. Chongqing U., China, 1993. Full mem. cancer ctr. U. Calif., San Diego, 1991, Inst. for Biomedical Engring., 1991—; organizer Cellular Adhesion: Signaling and Molecular Regulation Am. Physiol. Soc., 1994, main speaker Cell Biophysics Workshop Academia Sinica and Nat. Sci. Coun., China, 1987, Cellular Adhesion Workshop, West China of Med. Scis., China, 1993; hon. prof. Chongqing U., China, 1992, West China U. Med. Sci., 1992, Sch. Medicine Shanghai Med. U. China, 1996. Author various publs. Recipient New Investigator Rsch. award NIH, 1984-87, Best Jour. Paper award ASME, 1989, Chancellor award U. Calif., San Diego, 1988-89, The Whitaker Found. award, 1990, Melville medal ASME, 1990, Lamport award Biomedical Engring. Soc., 1992; Dr. Yat-Sen Sun Fellow Taiwan, China, 1967; Walter Russell Scholar, 1980-82. Mem. AAAS, Am. Physiol. Soc., N.Am. Soc. of Biorheology, Internat. Soc. of Biorheology, Biomedical Engring. Soc., Microcirculatory Soc., Sigma Xi. Achievements include research in influence of tumor suppressor genes on tumor cell metastasis, biophysical properties and molecular organization of cell membranes, healing mechanism of human ligament cells, adhesion between osteoblast and biomaterials, biophysical properties of blood cells and endothelial cells in inflammatory reponse, energy balance and molecular mechanisms of cell-cell interactions in immune response, intracellular ions, intracellular transmition and cell activation. Office: U Calif San Diego Bioengring Orthop 0412 9500 Gilman Dr La Jolla CA 92093 Fax: 619-534-6896. E-mail: klpsung@bioeng.ucsd.edu

SUPPES, PATRICK, statistics, education, philosophy and psychology educator; b. Tulsa, Mar. 17, 1922; s. George Biddle and Ann (Costello) S.; m. Joan Farmer, Apr. 16, 1946 (div. 1970); children: Patricia, Deborah, John Biddle; m. Joan Sieber, Mar. 29, 1970 (div. 1973); m. Christine Johnson, May 26, 1979; children: Alexandra Christine, Michael Patrick. BS, U. Chgo., 1943; PhD (Wendell T. Bush fellow), Columbia U., 1950; LLD, U. Nijmegen, Netherlands, 1979; Dr. honoris causa, U. Rene Descartes, Paris, 1982, U. Regensburg, Germany, 1999, U. Bologna, Italy, 1999. Instr., Stanford U., 1950-52, asst. prof., 1952-55, assoc. prof., 1955-59, prof. philosophy, statistics, edn. and psychology, 1959-92, prof. emeritus. Founder, chief exec. officer Computer Curriculum Corp., 1967-90. Author: Introduction to Logic, 1957, Axiomatic Set Theory, 1960, Sets and Numbers, books 1-6, 1966, Studies in the Methodology and Foundations of Science, 1969, A Probabilistic Theory of Causality, 1970, Logique du Probable, 1981, Probabilistic Metaphysics, 1984, Estudios de Filosofía y Metodologí de la Ciencia, 1988, Language for Humans and Robots, 1991, Models and Methods in the Philosophy of Science, 1993; (with Davidson and Siegel) Decision Making, 1957, (with Richard C. Atkinson) Markov Learning Models for Multiperson Interactions, 1960, (with Shirley Hill) First Course in Mathematical Logic, 1964, (with Edward J. Crothers) Experiments on Second-Language Learning, 1967, (with Max Jerman and Dow Brian) Computer-assisted Instruction, 1965-66, Stanford Arithmetic Program, 1968, (with D. Krantz, R.D. Luce and A. Tversky) Foundations of Measurement, Vol. 1, 1971, (with M. Morningstar) Computer-Assisted Instruction at Stanford, 1966-68, 1972, (with B. Searle and J. Friend) The Radio Mathematics Project: Nicaragua, 1974-75, 1976 (with D. Krantz, R.D. Luce and A. Tversky) Foundations of Measurement, Vol. 2, 1989, Vol. 3, 1990, (with Colleen Crangle) Language and Learning for Robots, 1994, (with Mario Zanotti) Foundations of Probability with Applications, 1996. Served to capt. USAAF, 1942-46. Recipient Nicholas Murray Butler Silver medal Columbia, 1965, Disting. Sci. Contbr. award Am. Psychol. Assn., 1972, Tchrs. Coll. medal for disting. service, 1978, Nat. medal Sci. NSF, 1990; Center for Advanced Study Behavioral Scis. fellow, 1955-56; NSF fellow, 1957-58 Fellow AAAS, Am. Psychol. Assn., Am. Acad. Arts and Scis., Assn. Computing Machinery; mem. NAS, Math. Assn. Am., Psychometric Soc., Am. Philos. Assn., Am. Philos. Soc., Assn. Symbolic Logic, Am. Math Soc., Académie Internationale de Philosophie des Scis. (titular), Nat. Acad. Edn. (pres. 1973-77), Am. Psychol. Assn., Internat. Inst. Philosophy, Finnish Acad. Sci. and Letters, Internat. Union History and Philosophy of Sci. (div. logic, methodology and philosophy of sci., pres. 1975-79), Am. Ednl. Research Assn. (pres. 1973-74), Croatian Acad. Scis. (corr.), Russian Acad. Edn. (fgn.), Norwegian Acad. Sci. and Letters (fgn.), European Acad. Scis. and Arts, Chilean Acad. Scis., Sigma Xi.

SUSAKI, JOHN, construction executive; Controller Shapell Industries, Beverly Hills, Calif., 1994—. Office: Shapell Industries 8383 Wilshire Blvd Ste 700 Beverly Hills CA 90211-2472

SUSCHITZKY, PETER, cinematographer; Cinematographer The Skouras Agy., 1987—. Cinematographer: (films) It Happened Here, 1962, Privilege, 1967, A Midsummer Night's Dream, 1968, Charlie Bubbles, 1968, Leo the Last, 1970, Melody/Swalk, 1971, The Pied Piper, 1972, Henry VIII and His Six Wives, 1972, That'll Be the Day, 1974, All Creatures Great and Small, 1975, Lisztomania, 1975, The Rocky Horror Picture Show, 1976, Valentino, 1977, The Empire Strikes Back, 1980, Krull, 1983, Falling in Love, 1984, Dead Ringers, 1988, Where the Heart Is, 1990, Naked Lunch, 1992, The Public Eye, 1992, The Vanishing, 1993, M. Butterfly, 1993, Immortal Beloved, 1994, Crash, 1996, Mars Attacks!, 1996, eXistenZ, 1998, The Man in the Iron Mask, 1998, The Empire Strikes Back - Spl. Edition, 1999, Star Wars Trilogy- Spl. Edition, 1999, The Red Planet, 1999. Office: The Skouras Agy 631 Wilshire Blvd Ste 2C Santa Monica CA 90401-1513

SUSSKIND, CHARLES, engineering educator, writer, publishing executive; b. Prague, Czech Republic; came to U.S., 1945, naturalized, 1946; s. Bruno Bronislav and Gertruda (Seger) S.; m. Teresa Gabriel, May 1, 1945; children: Pamela Susskind Pettler, Peter Gabriel, Amanda Frances. Student, City U., London, 1939-40; BS, Calif. Inst. Tech., 1948; M in Engring., Yale U., 1949, PhD, 1951. Rsch. asst. Yale U., 1949-51; rsch. assoc. Stanford U., 1951-55, lectr., asst. dir. microwave lab., 1953-55; faculty U. Calif., Berkeley, 1955—, prof., 1964-91, prof. emeritus, 1991—; asst. dean U. Calif. Coll. Engring., 1964-68; statewide adminstr. U. Calif., 1969-74. Vis. prof. U. London, 1961-62, U. Geneva, Switzerland, 1968-69; cons. EPA Sci. Adv. Bd., 1982-92; bd. dirs. San Francisco Press, Inc. Author: (with M. Chodorow) Fundamentals of Microwave Electronics, 1964; (with L. Schell) Exporting Technical Education, 1968, Understanding Technology, 1973, 74, 85 (transl. into Dutch, French, Italian, Korean, Spanish, Indian edit. in English), Twenty-Five Engineers and Inventors, 1976; (with F. Kurylo) Ferdinand Braun, 1981; (with M.E. Rowbottom) Electricity and Medicine: History of their Interaction, 1984, Janáček and Brod, 1985, Heinrich Hertz: A Short Life, 1995; editor: (with M. Hertz) Heinrich Hertz: Memoirs, Letters, Diaries, bilingual edit., 1977; editor-in-chief Ency. Electronics, 1962. With USAAF, 1942-45. Named to Hon. Order Ky. Cols. Fellow IEEE; mem. AAAS, Histor of Sci. Soc., Soc. for History of Tech., Instn. Elec. Engrs. (London), Sigma Xi (pres. Berkeley chpt. 1972-73), Tau Beta Pi. Office: U Calif Coll Engring Berkeley CA 94720-0001

SUSSKIND, LEONARD, physicist, educator; BS, CCNY, 1962; PhD, Cornell U., 1965. NSF postdoc. fellow Cornell U., Ithaca, N.Y., 1965-66; from asst. to prof. Physics Belfer Grad. Sch. Sci. Yeshiva U., N.Y.C., 1966-79; prof. Physics Stanford U., Stanford, Calif., 1979—. Visiting prof. Physics U. Tel Aviv 1971-72. Recipient Pregel award 1975, J.J. Sakurai prize 1997; Loeb lectr. Harvard U. 1976. Mem. AAAS, Nat. Acad. Sci. Office: Dept Physics Stanford U Varian Bldg Rm 108 Stanford CA 94305-4060

SUSSKIND, TERESA GABRIEL, publishing executive; b. Watford, Eng., Aug. 15, 1921; came to U.S., 1945; d. Aaron and Betty (Fox) Gabriel; m. Charles Susskind, May 1, 1945; children: Pamela Pettler, Peter Gabriel, Amanda. Ed., U. London, 1938-40. Profl. libr. Calif. Inst. Tech., Pasadena, 1946-48, Yale U., New Haven, 1948-51, Stanford (Calif.) U., 1951-52, SRI Internat., Menlo Park, Calif., 1953; founder, pres. San Francisco Press, Inc., 1959—. Active in cultural affairs; bd. govs. San Francisco Symphony, 1986-89. With Women's Royal Naval Svc., 1943-45. With Women's Royal Naval Svc., 1943-45. Mem. Town and Gown Club (Berkeley, Calif.; pres. 1984-85). Office: PO Box 426800 San Francisco CA 94142-6800

SUSSMAN, WENDY RODRIGUEZ, artist, educator; b. N.Y.C., June 3, 1949; BA, Empire State Coll., 1978; MFA, Bklyn. Coll., 1980. Lectr. Touro Coll., N.Y.C., 1985-86, Pratt Inst., Bklyn., 1987-89; asst. prof. U. Calif., Berkeley, 1989-96, assoc. prof., 1996—. One-woman shows include Bowery Gallery, N.Y.C., 1982, 87, John Bergruen Gallery, San Francisco, 1992, D.P. Fong Gallery, San Jose, Calif., 1994, Platt Gallery U. Judaism, L.A., 1995, Jan Baum Gallery, L.A., 1996, The Jewish Mus., San Francisco, 1996; group shows include Bowery Gallery, 1980-88, Munson-Williams-Proctor Inst. Mus. Art, 1982, Reading (Pa.) Pub. Mus. and Art Gallery, 1983, Queens Mus., N.Y.C., 1983, Colby Coll. Mus. Art, Waterville, Maine, 1983, Butler Inst. Am. Art, Youngstown, Ohio, 1983, Bklyn. Coll., 1983, Am. Acad. Inst. Arts and Letters, N.Y.C., 1984, Am. Acad. in Rome, 1987, John Berggruen Gallery, San Francisco, 1992, San Francisco Arts Commn. Gallery, 1992, 94, D.P. Fong Gallery, 1994, Boulder Mus. Art, 1995, Gallery Paule Anglin, San Francisco, 1996, 98, Jan Baum Gallery, L.A., 1996, U. Calif. San Diego Art Gallery, 1997. Rome Prize fellow in painting Am. Acad. in Rome, 1986-87, Visual Arts fellow NEA, 1989, Guggenheim fellow, 1998; Pollock-Krasner grantee Pollock-Krasner Found., 1988; recipient Max and Sophie Adler award Jewish Mus., Judah Magners Mus., 1996. Office: U Calif Berkeley Dept Art Berkeley CA 94720-0001

SUTCLIFFE, ERIC, lawyer; b. Calif., Jan. 10, 1909; s. Thomas and Annie (Beare) S.; m. Joan Basché, Aug. 7, 1937; children: Victoria, Marcia, Thomas; m. Marie C. Paige, Nov. 1, 1975. AB, U. Calif., Berkeley, 1929, LLB, 1932. Bar: Calif. 1932. Mem. firm Orrick, Herrington & Sutcliffe, San Francisco, 1943-85, mng. ptnr., 1947-78. Trustee, treas., v.p. San Francisco Law Libr., 1974-88; founding fellow The Oakland Mus. of Calif.; bd. dirs. Merritt Peralta Found., 1988; past bd. dirs. Hong Kong Bank of Calif., Friends of U. Calif. Bot. Garden, sec. Fellow Am. Bar Found (life); mem. ABA (chmn state regulation securities com. 1960-65), San Francisco Bar Assn. (chmn. corp. law com., 1964-65), San Francisco C. of C. (past treas., dir.), State Bar Calif., Pacific Union Club, Bohemian Club, Phi Gamma Delta, Phi Delta Phi, Order of Coif. Home: 260 King Ave Oakland CA 94610-1231 Office: Old Fed Reserve Bank Bldg 400 Sansome St San Francisco CA 94111-3304

SUTHERLAND, DOUGLASS B. former mayor, tent and awning company executive; b. Helena, Mont., May 2, 1937; s. Chris and Marie Sutherland; m. Grace Sutherland, Sept. 5, 1986; children: Karen, Scott. B.A., Central Wash. U., 1959. Program specialist Boeing Co., Tacoma, 1960-71; owner, pres. Tacoma Tent & Awning, Inc., 1971-86; sec., pres., 1986-98; county exec. Pierce County, Wash. Bd. dirs. Tacoma-Pierce County Bd. Health, Tacoma-Pierce County Employment and Tng. Consortium; mayor City of Tacoma, 1982-89; pres. Puget Sound Regional Coun.; chair Urban County Caucus, Wash. Assn. of Counties. Mem. Assn. Wash. Cities, Tacoma-Pierce County C. of C. Republican. Lodge: Rotary Avocation: sailing. Office: Pierce County Exec 930 Tacoma Ave S Rm 737 Tacoma WA 98402-2100 E-mail: dsuther@co.pierce.wa.us

SUTHERLAND, IVAN E. computer scientist; b. Hastings, Nebr., May 16, 1938; Bachelor's, Carnegie Inst. Tech., 1959; master's, Calif. Inst. Tech., 1960; PhD in Elec. Engring., MIT, 1963. Dir. office info. processing techniques Advance Rsch. Projects Agy., 1964-66; assoc. prof. elec. engring. Harvard U., 1966-68; prof. elec. engring. U. Utah, Salt Lake City, 1968—73; co-founder Evans & Sutherland, 1968; chmn. dept. computer sci. Calif. Inst. Tech., 1976—80; established Sutherland, Sproull, and Assocs., 1980; fellow Sun Microsystems Inc., Palo Alto, Calif. Recipient A.M. Turing award Assn. Computer Machinery, 1988, John von Neumann medal, 1988, Smithsonian Price Waterhouse Info. Tech. Leadership award for Lifetime Achievement. Mem. NAE, NAS. Achievements include pioneer in computer graphics; inventor of computer program, known as Sketchpad, and head-mounted three-dimensional display, an integral part of many virtual reality systems. Office: Sun Microsystems Inc 901 San Antonio Rd Palo Alto CA 94303

SUTHERLAND, MICHAEL CRUISE, librarian; b. Morgantown, W.Va., Aug. 29, 1938; s. Charles Fish and Mildred (Haymond) S. BA in English, San Fernando Valley State U., 1967, postgrad., 1968-69, UCLA, 1967, MLS, 1970. Office asst., clk. Lindsay & Hall, L.A., 1959-60; libr. asst. I, bindery clk. Biomed. Libr. UCLA, 1961-65; jr. adminstrv. asst. Dept. Pub. Works City of L.A., 1967; intermediate clk. typist San Fernando Valley State U., Northridge, Calif., 1967-69; libr. I, tchg. asst. Grad. Sch. Libr. and Info. Sci. UCLA, 1970; spl. collections libr. Occidental Coll., L.A., 1970—. Attendee numerous workshops and seminars; organizer Western Books Exhbn. at various librs. throughout the Western U.S., 1992, 96; judging organizer, 1993. Author numerous exhbn. catalog booklets; author: (with others) Encyclopedia of Library and Information Sciences, 1979, Western Books Exhibition Catalog, 1986, Striking Research Gold: Distinguished Collections in California Independent Academic Libraries, 1988; contbr. articles to profl. jours. Active Neighborhood Watch, AIDS Quilt Program. Mem. Rounce and Coffin Club (sec., treas.), Robinson Jeffers Assn., Tor House Found., Zamorano Club, Book Club Calif. Office: Occidental Coll Mary Clapp Libr 1600 Campus Rd Los Angeles CA 90041-3314 E-mail: bun@oxy.edu

SUTTER, DARRYL JOHN, professional hockey coach; Player Chgo. Blackhawks, 1980-86, asst. coach, 1987-88, assoc. coach, 1991-92, head coach, 1992-95, cons., 1995-97; head coach San Jose Sharks, 1997—. Office: San Jose Sharks 525 W Santa Clara St San Jose CA 95113-1500

SUTTER, JOSEPH F. aeronautical engineer, consultant, retired aircraft company executive; b. Seattle, Mar. 21, 1921; m. Nancy Ann French, June 14, 1943 B.A., U. Wash., 1943. Various engring. positions Boeing Comml. Airplane Co., Seattle, 1946-65, dir. engring. for Boeing 747, 1965-71, v.p., gen. mgr. 747 div., 1971-74, v.p. program ops., 1974-76, v.p. ops. and product devel., 1976-81, exec. v.p., 1981-86, cons., 1986-87, 1987—. Chmn. aerospace safety adv. panel NASA, 1986; mem. Challenger Accident Commn., 1986. Served to lt. j.g. USN, 1943-45 Recipient Master Design award Product Engring. mag., 1965, Franklin W. Kolk Air Transp. Progress award Soc. Aero. Aerospace Coun., 1980, Elmer A. Sperry award, 1980, Nuts & Bolts award Transport Assn., 1983, Nat. Medal Tech., U.S. Pres. Reagan, 1985, Sir Kingsford Smith award Royal Aero. Soc. in Sydney, 1980, Wright Bros. Meml. Trophy, 1986, Alumnus Summa Laude Dignatus award U. Wash., 2001; Joseph F. Sutter professorship established in his honor at U. Wash., Boeing Co., 1992. Fellow Royal Aero Soc. (hon.), AIAA (Daniel Guggenheim award 1990); mem. Internat. Fedn. Airworthiness (pres. 1989). Address: Boeing 7755 E Marginal Way S Seattle WA 98108-4002

SUTTER, MORLEY CARMAN, medical scientist; b. Redvers, Sask., Can., May 18, 1933; s. Christian Benjamin and Amelia (Duke) S.; m. Virginia Frances Mary Laidlaw, June 29, 1957; children— Gregory Robert, F. Michelle, Brent Morley. M.D., B.Sc., U. Man., 1957, Ph.D., 1963. Intern Winnipeg (Man.) Gen. Hosp., 1956-57, resident, 1958-59; teaching fellow pharmacology U. Man., 1959-63; supr. Downing Coll., Cambridge U., 1963-65; asst. prof. pharmacology U. Toronto, 1965-66, U. B.C., 1966-68, asso. prof., 1968-71, prof., 1971-98, retired prof. emeritus, 1998—, head dept. pharmacology, 1971-87. Former mem. staff Vancouver (B.C.) Hosp. & Health Sci. Ctr., St. Paul's Hosp.; mem. Minister of Health's Adv. Com. on Drugs, Province of B.C., 1971-87. Contbr. articles to sci. jours. Recipient Gov. Gen. medal, 1950; Med. Research Council of Can. fellow, 1959-63; Wellcome Found. Travelling fellow, 1963; Imperial Chem. Industries fellow, 1963-65; Med. Research Council scholar, 1966-71 Mem. British Pharmacol. Soc., Am. Soc. Pharmacology and Exptl. Therapeutics. Office: U BC Faculty Medicine Therapeutics 2176 Health Scis Mall Dept Pharmacology Vancouver BC Canada V6T 1Z3 E-mail: mcsutter@interchange.ubc.ca

SUTTLES, VIRGINIA GRANT, advertising executive; b. Urbana, Ill., June 13, 1931; d. William Henry and Lenora (Fitzsimmons) Grant; m. John Henry Suttles, Sept. 24, 1977 (dec. July 1996); step-children: Linda, Peggy, Pamela Suttles Diaz, Randall. Grad. pub. schs., Mahomet, Ill. Media estimator and Procter & Gamble budget control Tatham-Laird, Inc., Chgo., 1955-60; media planner, supr. Tracy-Locke Co., Inc., Dallas and Denver, 1961-68; media dir., account exec. Lorie-Lotito, Inc., 1968-72; v.p., media dir. Sam Lusky Assocs., Inc., Denver, 1972-86; ind. media buyer, 1984-89; mktg. asst. mktg. dept. Del E. Webb Communities, Inc., Sun City West, Ariz., 1985-88, with telemktg. dept., 1989-90, homeonwer coord., 1993-97; mktg. coord. asst./media buyer Del Webb Corp., Phoenix, 1990-93. Lectr. sr. journalism class U. Colo., Boulder, 1975-80; condr. class in media sems. Denver Advt. Fedn., 1974, 77; Colo. State U. panelist Broadcast Day, 1978, High Sch. Inst., 1979, 80, 81, 82, 83. Founder Del E. Webb Meml. Hosp. Found.; patron founder Tree of Life Nat. Kidney Found. Colo.-Rockies Snow Mountain YMCA Ranch, Winter Park, Colo., Sun Health Found. Sun Cities, Ariz. State U. Found. Sundome Performing Arts Ctr. Mem. Denver Advt. Fedn. (bd. dirs. 1973-75, program chmn. 1974-76, 80-82, exec. bd., v.p. ops. 1980-81, chmn. Alfie awards com. 1980-81, Advt. Profl. of Yr. 1981-82), Denver Advt. Golf Assn. (v.p. 1976-77, pres. 1977-78), Colo. Broadcasters Assn., Sun City West Bowling Assn. (bd. dirs. 1987-88), Am. Legion Aux. (historian, pub. chmn. 1998-2000, sec. 1999—), VFW Aux. (life), Air Force Sgt.'s Assn. Aux. (life mem. Sun Health aux.), Sun City Art Mus. Women's League (treas. 1999-2000). Republican. Congregationalist. Home: 20002 N Greenview Dr Sun City West AZ 85375-5579

SUTTON, DANA FERRIN, classics educator; b. White Plains, N.Y., Oct. 10, 1942; s. Joseph Guy Jr. and Eleanor Sutton; m. Kathryn A. Sinkovich, Aug. 16, 1975. BA, The New Sch. for Social Rsch., N.Y.C., 1965; MA, U. Wis., 1966, PhD, 1970. Lectr. Herbert Lehman Coll., CUNY, 1969-72; postdoctoral rsch. Darwin Coll., Cambridge, Eng., 1972-74, U. Auckland, New Zealand, 1974-75; asst. prof. U. Ill., Urbana, 1975-79; prof. U. Calif., Irvine, 1979—, dept. chair., 1986-94. Author: The Greek Satyr Play, 1975, numerous other books and monographs; editor: William Gager: The Complete Works, 1994, The Complete Works of Thomas Watson (1556-1592), 1995, The Complete Latin Poetry of Walter Savage Landor, 1999; contbr. articles to profl. jours. John Guggenheim fellow, 1975-76. Mem. Am. Philol. Assn., Calif. Classical Assn. Office: U Calif Dept Classics 120 Hob Ii Irvine CA 92697-0001 E-mail: DanaS645632@aol.com

SUTTON, JOHN PAUL, lawyer; b. Youngstown, Ohio, July 24, 1934; m. Jane Williamson, Aug. 20, 1958; children— Julia, Susan, Elizabeth. B.A., U. Va., 1956; J.D., George Washington U., 1963. Bar: Calif. 1965. Patent examiner U.S. Patent Office, Washington, 1956, 59-62; law clk. U.S. Ct. Customs and Patent Appeals, Washington, 1962-64; assoc. Flehr, Hohbach, Test, Albritton & Herbert, San Francisco, 1964-68; ptnr. Limbach, Limbach & Sutton, San Francisco, 1969-91; spl. counsel Heller, Ehrman, White & McAuliffe, San Francisco, 1992-95; of counsel Medlin & Carroll, San Francisco, 1995, Bryan, Hinshaw & Barnet, San Francisco, 1996-99; sole practice, 2000—. Adj. instr. Practicing Law Inst., 1968-69; continuing edn. program Calif. State Bar, 1972, 75, U. Calif. Law Sch., Berkeley, 1975, 84. Contbr. articles to legal jours. Served with USNR, 1956-59. Mem. Calif. Patent Law Assn. (pres. 1975), San Francisco Patent Law Assn. (pres. 1976), State Bar Calif. (exec. com. patent sect. 1975-77), Am. Chem. Soc. Democrat. Episcopalian. Home and Office: 2421 Pierce St San Francisco CA 94115-1131

SUTTON, L. PAUL, criminal justice educator; b. Munich, Aug. 16, 1948; s. William L. Sutton and Paulette Mikkelson. BS in Polit. Sci. and History, U. Kans., 1970; MA in Criminal Justice, SUNY, Albany, 1971, PhD in Criminal Justice, 1975. Asst. prof. sociology U. N.Mex., Albuquerque, 1976-78; rsch. assoc. Hindelang Criminal Justice Rsch. Ctr., Albany, N.Y., 1974-76; prof. criminal justice San Diego State U., 1981—; sr. rsch. assoc. Nat. Ctr. for State Cts., Williamsburg, Va., 1978-81. Ind. filmmaker, N.Mex., Calif., 1982-92; cons. State of Calif. Dept. of Corrections, 1997-98; commr. cmty.-based punishment planning com., San Diego, 1996-97; bd. dirs. Nat. Forum on Criminal Justice, Springfield, Ill., 1980-81; expert witness on sentencing reform Nat. Acad. Scis., Washington, 1981. Producer documentary film Doing Time: Ten Years Later, 1991, Doing Time, 1979; co-author: The Search Warrant Process, 1984, Sentencing by Mathematics, 1982. Grantee Calif. State Dept. Corrections, 1997, NEH, 1979. Mem. AAUP, Am. Soc. Criminology,Acad. Criminal Justice Scis., Western Soc. Criminology, Phi Beta Kappa. Avocations: filmmaking, sailing, jogging. Office: San Diego State U Dept Criminal Justice San Diego CA 92182-4505 E-mail: psutton@mail.sdsu.edu

SUTTON, THOMAS C. insurance company executive; b. Atlanta, June 2, 1942; m. Marilyn Sutton; children: Stephen, Paul, Matthew, Meagan. BS in Math. and Physics, U. Toronto, 1965; postgrad., Harvard U., 1982. With Pacific Mut. Life Ins. Co., Newport Beach, Calif., 1963—, actuarial asst., 1966-69, successively asst. actuary, assoc. actuary, asst. v.p., 2d v.p., v.p. individual ins., 1969-80, successively v.p. individual fin., sr. v.p. corp. devel., exec. v.p. individual ins., 1980-87, pres., from 1987; now chmn. bd., CEO Pacific Life Corp., Newport Beach; also bd. dirs. Pacific Mut. Life Ins. Co., Newport Beach. Mem. affiliates adv. bd. U. Calif. Irvine Grad. Sch. Mgmt. Trustee South Coast Repertory; bd. dirs. Ind. Colls. So. Calif. Fellow Soc. of Actuaries (mem. numerous coms.); mem. Am. Acad. Actuaries (com. on dividend prins. and practices, 1978), Pacific States Actuarial Club, L.A. Actuarial Club (sec. 1974-75, pres. 1978-79). Office: Pacific Mut Life Ins Co 700 Newport Center Dr Newport Beach CA 92660-6307

SUWYN, MARK A. building products executive; b. Denver, Aug. 8, 1942; BS in Chemistry, Hope Coll., Holland, Mich., 1964; PhD in Inorganic Chemistry, Wash. State U., 1967. From R&D to gen. mgmt. positions DuPont Co., 1967-91, [illegible] v.p. Internat. Paper, Purchase, N.Y., 1992-95; CEO Louisianna Pacific Corp., Portland, 1995—. Office: Louisianna Pacific Corp 111 SW 5th Ave Portland OR 97204-3604

SUZUKI, BOB H. university president; Formerly v.p. acad. affairs Calif. State Univ., Northridge; pres. Calif. State Poly. Univ., Pomona, 1991—. Office: Calif State Polytech U Office of Pres 3801 W Temple Ave Pomona CA 91768-2557

SUZUKI, DAVID TAKAYOSHI, geneticist, science broadcaster; b. Vancouver, B.C., Can., Mar. 24, 1936; s. Kaoru Carr and Setsu (Nakamura) S.; m. Joane Setsuko Sunahara, Aug. 20, 1958 (div. 1965); children— Tamiko Lynda, Troy Takashi, Laura Miya; m. Tara Elizabeth Cullis, Dec. 10, 1972; children— Severn Setsu, Sarika Freda BA cum laude, Amherst Coll., Mass., 1958; PhD, U. Chgo., 1961; LLD (hon.), U. P.E.I., 1974, Queen's U., Ont., 1987; DSc (hon.), Acadia U., N.S., 1979, McMaster U., Ont., 1987, U. Windsor, 1979, Trent U., 1981, Lakehead U., 1986; DHL (hon.), Gov.'s State U., Ill., 1986. Research assoc. Oak Ridge Nat. Lab., 1961-62; asst. prof. U. Alta., Edmonton, Can., 1961-63; asst. prof. dept. zoology U. B.C., Vancouver, 1963-65, assoc. prof., 1965-69, prof., 1969—. Vis. prof. UCLA, 1966, U. Calif.-Berkeley, 1969, 1976-77, U. Utah, Salt Lake City, 1971-72, U. P.R., 1972, U. Toronto, 1978 Host TV programs Suzuki on Sci., CBC, Vancouver, 1971-72, Sci. Mag., Toronto, 1974-79, Quirks & Quarks, Vancouver, 1974-79, Nature of Things, Toronto, 1979—; host series on sci. TV programs Interface, 1974-75, Just Ask, Inc., 1980, Night Video, 1984, Futurescan, 1984; radio program Discovery, 1983— ; author: (textbook) Introduction to Genetic Analysis, 1976, David Suzuki Looks at Plants, 1985, David Susuki Looks at Insects, 1986, David Susuki Looks at Senses, 1986, Egg-Carton Zoo, 1986, Sciencescape: The Nature of Canada, 1986, British Columbia: Frontier for Ideas, 1986, From Pebbles to Computers, 1986; contbr. articles to profl. and popular publs. and mags. Bd. dirs. B.C. Civil Liberties Assn., 1973, Can. Civil Liberties Assn., 1982— Decorated officer Order of Can.; recipient W.R. Steacie Meml. award Nat. Research Council Can., 1969-72; Sci. and Engring. medal Sci. Council B.C., 1981; UN Environ. Programme medal, 1985; grantee Can. Nat. Research Council, AEC, Nat. Cancer Inst. Can., NIH also others; recipient UNESCO Kalinga prize, 1986, Royal Bank award, 1986. Mem. Alliance of Can. TV and Radio Artists (award 1986), Genetic Soc. Am., Sci. Council Can. Mem. New Democratic Party Avocations: scuba diving, fishing, skiing. Address: 2211 W 4th Ave # 210 Vancouver BC Canada V6K 4S2

SVEE, GARY DUANE, newspaper editor, writer, journalist; b. Billings, Mont., Nov. 11, 1943; s. Sigvart Oluf and Beatrice Evelyn (Lund) S.; m. C. Diane Schmidt, June 26, 1966; children— Darren Kirk, Nathan Jared B.A., U. Mont., 1967. Unit mgr. Midland Bank, Billings, Mont., 1967-69; reporter Billings Gazette, 1969-76, opinion editor, 1982—; pub. Bridger (Mont.) Bonanza, 1976-77; feature editor Missoulian, Missoula, Mont., 1977-81. Author: Spirit Wolf, 1987, Incident at Pishkin Creek, 1989, Sanctuary, 1990 (Best Western novel Western Writers Am. 1990), Single Tree. Vestryman St. Luke's Meml. Bd., Billings, 1989, Salvation Army, Missoula, 1980-82; vestryman Holy Spirit Parish, Missoula, 1980-82. Served to lt. USAR, 1966-72 Recipient Business Writing award U. Mo., 1974, Minority Affairs Reporting award N.W. region Sigma Delta Chi, 1980 Mem. Kiwanis (bd. dirs. Billings club 1988-89, 2d v.p. 1989, pres. 1990, 91-92), Theta Chi. Episcopalian. Avocations: fishing, golf, writing, sculpting, reading. Home: 474 Indian Trl Billings MT 59105-2706 Office: Billings Gazette PO Box 36300 Billings MT 59107-6300

SVENDSEN, ARTHUR E. construction executive; Chair, CEO Std. Pacific Corp., Costa Mesa, Calif., 1965—. Office: 1565 W McCartha Blvd Costa Mesa CA 92626

SVET, DON J. federal judge; Bar: N.Mex. Magistrate judge for N.Mex., U.S. Magistrate Ct., Albuquerque, 1994—. Address: US Magistrate 333 Lomas Blvd NW # 670 Albuquerque NM 87102-2276

SVORINICH, RUDY, JR. councilman; b. San Pedro, Calif. m. Deann Svorinich. BA, Calif. State U. Chief dep. to assemblyman Gerald N. Felando; city councilman dist. 15 City of L.A., 1991—; owner Indsl. Paint Co., Wilmington. Chmn. coun. adminstrn. svc. com., vice chmn. energy and natural resources com., mem. transp. com. L.A. City Coun. Mem. San Pedro Pirate and Banning Pilot Booster Clubs, Harbor City/Harbor Gateway Club, San Pedro and Wilmington C. of C., Dalmation Am. Club San Pedro (past pres.), Elks, Masons. Office: City Hall 200 N Main St Ste 507 Los Angeles CA 90012-4103

SWAIM, MICHAEL E. mayor; BA, UCLA, 1967, MA, 1968, JD, 1971. Lawyer Simon, McKinsey & Miller, 1971-78; pvt. practice, 1978—; mayor City of Salem, Oreg., 1997—. Office: City Hall 555 Libert St Rm 220 Salem OR 97301 E-mail: mswaim@open.org

SWALIN, RICHARD ARTHUR, scientist, company executive; b. Mpls., Mar. 18, 1929; s. Arthur and Mae (Hurley) S.; m. Helen Marguerite Van Wagenen, June 28, 1952; children: Karen, Kent, Kristin. B.S. with distinction, U. Minn., 1951, Ph.D., 1954. Rsch. assoc. GE, 1954-56; mem. faculty U. Minn., Mpls., 1956-77, prof., head Sch. Mineral and Metall Engring., 1962-68, assoc. dean Inst. Tech., 1968-71, dean Inst. Tech., 1971-77; acting dir. Space Sci. Center, 1965; v.p. tech. Eltra Corp., N.Y.C., 1977-80; v.p. R & D Allied-Signal Corp., Morristown, N.J., 1980-84; dean Coll. Engring. and Mines U. Ariz., Tucson, 1984-87, prof., 1984-94; pres. Ariz. Tech. Devel. Corp., Tucson, 1987; prof. emeritus U. Ariz., Tucson, 1995—. Guest scientist Max Planck Inst. für Phys. Chemie, Göttingen, Fed. Republic Germany, 1963, Lawrence Radiation Lab., Livermore, Calif., 1967; cons. to govt. and industry; bd. dirs. emeritus Medtronic Corp., BMC Industries; corp. adv. bd. AMP Inc., 1990-93. Author: Thermodynamics of Solids, 2d edit, 1972; Contbr. articles to profl. jours. Dir. div. indsl. coop. U. Ariz. Found., 1985-86; trustee Midwest Research Inst., 1975-78, Sci. Mus. Minn., 1973-77, Nat. Tech. U., 1983-90. Recipient Disting. Teaching award Inst. Tech., U. Minn., 1967, Leadership award U. Minn. Alumni, 1993; NATO sr. fellow in sci., 1971. Mem. Sigma Xi, Tau Beta Pi, Phi Delta Theta, Gamma Alpha. Home: PO Box 65454 Port Ludlow WA 98365-0454 Office: 4705 N Via De La Granja Tucson AZ 85718-7404 E-mail: rswalin@yahoo.com

SWAN, KENNETH CARL, surgeon; b. Kansas City, Mo., Jan. 1, 1912; s. Carl E. and Blanche (Peters) S.; m. Virginia Grone, Feb. 5, 1938; children: Steven Carl, Kenneth, Susan. A.B., U. Oreg., 1933, M.D., 1936. Diplomate: Am. Bd. Ophthalmology (chmn. 1960-61). Intern U. Wis., 1936-37; resident in ophthalmology State U. Iowa, 1937-40; practice medicine specializing in ophthalmology Portland, Oreg., 1945—; staff Good Samaritan Hosp.; asst. prof. ophthalmology State U. Iowa, Iowa City, 1941-44; asso. prof. U. Oreg. Med. Sch., Portland, 1944-45, prof. and head dept. ophthalmology, 1945-78. Chmn. sensory diseases study sect. NIH; mem. adv. council Nat. Eye Inst.; also adv. council Nat. Inst. Neurol. Diseases and Blindness. Contbr. articles on ophthalmic subjects to med. publs. Recipient Proctor Rsch. medal, 1953, Disting. Svc. award U. Oreg., 1963, Meritorious Achievement award U. Oreg. Med. Sch., 1968, Howe Ophthalmology medal, 1977, Aubrey Watzek Pioneer award Lewis and Clark Coll., 1979, Disting. Alumnus award Oreg. Health Scis. U. Alumni Assn., 1988, Disting. Svc. award, 1988, Mentor award Oreg. Health Scis. Found., 1996; named Oreg. Scientist of Yr. Oreg. Mus. Sci. and Industry, 1959. Mem. Assn. Research in Ophthalmology, Am. Acad. Ophthalmology (v.p. 1978, historian), Soc. Exptl. Biology and Medicine, AAAS, AMA, Pan. Ophthal. Soc. (Howe medal for distinguished service 1977), Oreg. Med. Soc., Sigma Xi, Sigma Chi (Significant Sig award 1977) Home: 4645 SW Fairview Blvd Portland OR 97221-2624 Office: Oreg Health Scis U Ophthalmology Dept Portland OR 97201

SWANN, ERIC JERROD, professional football player; b. Pinehurst, N.C., Aug. 16, 1970; Student, Wake Tech. Coll. Defensive tackle Ariz. Cardinals, Phoenix, 1991—. Selected to Pro Bowl, 1995. Office: Arizona Cardinals PO Box 888 Phoenix AZ 85001-0888

SWANSON, CHARLES ANDREW, mathematics educator; b. Bellingham, Wash., July 11, 1929; s. Clarence Otto and Esther (Hougen) S.; m. Carolyn Marie Dennis, Aug. 5, 1957; children— Laird Randall, Denise Claire. BA, U. B.C., 1951, MA, 1953; PhD, Cal. Inst. Tech., 1957. Prof. U. B.C., Vancouver, 1957-94, prof. emeritus math., 1994—. Author: An Introduction to Differential Calculus, 1962, Comparison and Oscillation Theory of Linear Differential Equations, 1968; Contbr. articles to tech., profl. jours. Office: U BC Dept Math Vancouver BC Canada V6T 1Z2

SWANSON, DALE CHARLES, small business owner, industrial engineer; b. Burbank, Calif., Jan. 2, 1927; s. Richard Nathaniel and Nell (Kerlee) S.; m. Doris Christine Rasmussen, May 20, 1951; children: Marilyn, Robert, Nancy. BS in Indsl. Engring., Mont. State U., 1950. Engr. Bonneville Power Adminstrn., Portland, Oreg., 1950-54; indsl. engr. Kaiser Aluminum, Spokane, Wash., 1954-59; pres. Pyrotek Inc., Spokane, 1959—. Inventor filter molten aluminum. Bd. dirs. Spokane Valley C. of C., 1970. Mem. Hayden Lake Country Club (bd. dirs.). Avocations: golf, tennis, fishing. Home: E # 23D Spokane WA 99216 Office: Pyrotek Inc 9503 E Montgomery Ave Spokane WA 99206-4115

SWANSON, DONALD ALAN, geologist; b. Tacoma, July 25, 1938; s. Leonard Walter and Edith Christine (Bowers) S.; m. Barbara Joan White, May 25, 1974. BS in Geology, Wash. State U., 1960; PhD in Geology, Johns Hopkins U., 1964. Geologist U.S. Geol. Survey, Menlo Park, Calif., 1965-68, 71-80, Hawaii National Park, 1968-71, sr. geologist Cascades Volcano Obs. Vancouver, Wash., 1980-90, rsch. scientist-in-charge, 1986-89, sr. geologist Seattle, 1990-96; assoc. dir. Volcano Systems Ctr. U. Wash., 1993-96; scientist-in-charge Hawaiian Volcano Obs., 1997—. Affiliate prof. U. Wash., 1992—; cons. U.S. Dept. Energy, Richland, Wash., 1979-83; volcanologist New Zealand Geol. Survey, Taupo, 1984; advisor Colombian Volcano Obs., Manizales, 1986. Assoc. editor Jour. Volcanology and Geothermal Rsch., 1976—, Jour. Geophys. Rsch., 1992-94; editor Bull. of Volcanology, 1985-90, exec. editor, 1995-99; contbr. numerous articles to profl. jours. Recipient Superior Service award U.S. Geol. Survey, 1980, Meritorious Service award U.S. Dept. Interior, 1985; postdoctoral fellow NATO, 1964-65. Fellow Geol. Soc. Am., Am. Geophys. Union, AAAS; mem. Sigma Xi. Avocation: hiking. Home: 417 Linaka St Hilo HI 96720-5927 Office: US Geol Survey Hawaiian Volcano Obs PO Box 51 Hawaii National Park HI 96718-0051 E-mail: donswan@usgs.gov

SWANSON, ERIK CHRISTIAN, museum director; b. Breckenridge, Colo., June 17, 1940; s. Glen Leonard and Eveitte Leona (Snell) S.; m. Elizabeth Jane Thompson, Aug. 22, 1976; children: Johannah Elizabeth, Nils Christian. Student, Royal U., Lund, Sweden, 1960-64; BA in History, German Lang., tchg. cert., U. No. Colo. Curator South Pk. City Mus., Fairplay, Colo., 1974-89; dir. Alma (Colo.) Fire House Mus., 1976-82; exec. dir. Cripple Creek (Colo.) Dist. Mus., 1988—. Chief of police Alma, Colo., 1977-80. With U.S. Army, 1966-68. Mem. Odd Fellows (past grand South Park Lodge # 10, Fairplay, Colo.), Masons (sr. warden Cripple Creek chpt. 1995), Elks. Republican. Home: PO Box 27 Alma CO 80420-0027 Office: Cripple Creek Dist Mus PO Box 1210 Cripple Creek CO 80813-1210

SWANSON, JANESE, entrepreneur, technology company executive; one child, Jackie. BA, San Diego State U., 1981; EdD, U. San Francisco, 1995. Tchr., San Diego, 1981; model; flight attendant; product mgr. Broderbund Software, 1988-92; prin., owner Kid One for Fun, Inc., 1992-95, Girl Tech., San Rafael, Calif., 1995-2000. Adv. com. Lemelson Ctr., 1998-99. Office: eDames c/o Dominican Univ San Rafael CA 94903 Fax: 415-472-3777. E-mail: grltec@aol.com, girltech@girltech.com

SWANSON, KENNETH J. museum administrator; Adminstr. Idaho State Hist. Mus., Boise. Office: Idaho State Hist Mus 610 Julia Davis Dr Boise ID 83702-7677

SWANSON, KURT, metal fabricating company executive; CFO Tang Industries Inc., Las Vegas. Office: Tang Industries Inc 3773 Howard Hughes PkwySte 350N Las Vegas NV 89109

SWANSON, PAUL RUBERT, minister; b. Bakersfield, Calif., May 13, 1943; s. Roland Hilding and Myrtle Isabelle (Magnuson) S.; m. Mary Elizabeth Greene, June 18, 1967; children: Kristen Ann, Karlynn Marie, Jonathan Paul. BA, Pacific Luth. U., 1966; MDiv, Luth. Sch. Theology, 1970. Ordained minister, Luth. Ch. Pastor 1st Luth. Ch., Anaconda, Mont., 1970-76, King of Kings Luth. Ch., Milwaukie, Oreg., 1976-84; asst. to bishop Pacific N.W. Synod-Luth. Ch. in Am., Portland, 1984-87; bishop Oreg. Synod-Evang. Luth. Ch. Am., Portland, 1987—. Bd. dirs. Legacy Health System, Portland. Regent Pacific Luth. U., Tacoma, 1987—; bd. dirs. Emanuel Hosp., Portland, 1987; chmn. bd. dirs. Hearthstone, Inc., Anaconda, 1973-76; bd. dirs. Ecumenical Ministries Oreg., Portland, 1984—. Recipient Disting. Svc. award Pacific Luth. U., 1993. Avocation: golf.

SWANSON, PHILLIP DEAN, neurologist; b. Seattle, Oct. 1, 1932; s. William Dean and Kathryn C. (Peterson) S.; m. Sheila N. Joardar, Apr. 20, 1957; children: Stephen, Jennifer, Kathryn, Rebecca, Sara. B.S., Yale U., 1954; student, U. Heidelberg, 1952-53; M.D., Johns Hopkins U., 1958; Ph.D. in Biochemistry, U. London, 1964. Intern Harvard med. svc. Boston City Hosp., 1958-59; resident in neurology Johns Hopkins Hosp., Balt. City Hosp., 1959-62; asst. prof. U. Wash. Sch. Medicine, Seattle, 1964-68, assoc. prof., 1968-73, prof., 1973—, head divsn. neurology, 1967-95. Mem. med. adv. bd. Puget Sound chpt. Nat. Multiple Sclerosis Soc., 1967-97, chmn., 1970-74; mem. com. to combat Huntington's Disease Nat. Sci. Council, 1975-84. Author: (with others) Introduction to Clinical Neurology, 1976; editor: Signs and Symptoms in Neurology, 1984; contbr. articles to profl. jours. NIH spl. fellow, 1962-64; NIH grantee. Fellow Am. Acad. Neurology; mem. Am. Neurol. Assn., Assn. Univ. Profs. Neurology (pres. 1975-76), Am. Heart Assn., Am. Soc. Neurochemistry, Internat. Soc. Neurochemistry, Biochem. Soc. (London), Am. Soc. Clin. Investigation (emeritus) Home: 6537 29th Ave NE Seattle WA 98115-7234 Office: U Wash Sch Medicine Dept Neurology PO Box 356465 Seattle WA 98195-6465 E-mail: swansonp@u.washington.edu

SWANSON, RICHARD WILLIAM, retired statistician; b. Rockford, Ill., July 26, 1934; s. Richard and Erma Marie (Herman) S.; m. Laura Yoko Arai, Dec. 30, 1970. BS, Iowa State U., 1958, MS, 1964. Ops. analyst Stanford Rsch. Inst., Monterey, Calif., 1958-62; statistician ARINC Rsch. Corp., Washington, 1964-65; sr. scientist Booz-Allen Applied Rsch., Vietnam, 1965-67, L.A., 1967-68; sr. ops. analyst Control Data Corp., Honolulu, 1968-70; mgmt. cons., Honolulu, 1970-73; exec. v.p. SEQUEL Corp., Honolulu, 1973-75; bus. cons. Hawaii Dept. Planning and Econ. Devel., Honolulu, 1975-77, tax rsch. and planning officer Dept. Taxation, 1977-82; ops. rsch. analyst U.S. Govt., 1982-89; shipyard statisician U.S. Govt., 1989-97; ret., 1997. Served with AUS, 1954-56. Mem. Hawaiian Acad. Sci., Sigma Xi. Home: 583 Kamoku St Apt 3505 Honolulu HI 96826-5241

SWANSON, ROBERT H. JR. consumer products company executive; With Nat. Semiconductor; founder Linear Tech. Corp., Milpitas, Calif., 1981, chmn., CEO, 1999—. Office: Linear Tech Corp 1630 Mccarthy Blvd Milpitas CA 95035-7417

SWANSON, ROBERT KILLEN, management consultant; b. Deadwood, S.D., Aug. 11, 1932; s. Robert Claude and Marie Elizabeth (Kersten) S.; m. Nancy Anne Oyaas, July 19, 1958; children: Cathryn Lynn, Robert Stuart, Bart Killen. BA, U. S.D., 1954; postgrad., U. Melbourne, Australia, 1955. With Gen. Mills, Inc., Mpls., 1955-58, 71-79, v.p., 1971-73, group v.p., 1973-77, exec. v.p., 1977-79; with Marathon Oil Co., Findlay, Ohio, 1958-60; sr. v.p., dir. Needham, Harper & Steers, Inc., Chgo., 1961-69; joint mng. dir. S. H. Benson (Holdings) Ltd., Eng., 1969-71; pres., chief operating officer Greyhound Corp., Phoenix, 1980; chmn., chief exec. officer Del E. Webb Corp., Phoenix, 1981-87; chmn. RKS Inc., Phoenix, 1987—. Bd. dirs. Am. S.W. Concepts Inc., ST Internat., Ltd. 2d lt. U.S. Army, 1955. Fulbright scholar, 1954-55; Woodrow Wilson scholar. Mem. U.K. Dirs. Inst., U.S. Internat. Scholars Assn., English Speaking Union, Phoenix Country Club. Episcopalian. Office: RKS Inc 5600 N Palo Cristi Rd Scottsdale AZ 85253-7543

SWARTZ, JAMES R. chemical engineer, educator; B in Chem. Engring., S.D. Sch. Mines and Tech.; DSci, MIT, 1978. Rsch. scientist Eli Lilly & Co., Indpls., Genentech, Inc., San Francisco, dir. dept. fermentation rsch. and process devel. Mem. NAE, Am. Chem. Soc. Office: Dept Chem Engring Stanford U Keck 185 Palo Alto CA 94301 E-mail: swartz@chemeng.stanford.edu

SWATT, STEPHEN BENTON, communications executive, consultant; b. L.A., June 26, 1944; s. Maurice I. and Lucille E. (Sternberger) S.; m. Susan Ruth Edelstein, Sept. 7, 1968; 1 child, Jeffrey Michael. BSBA, U. Calif., 1966, M in Journalism, 1967. Writer San Francisco Examiner, 1967; reporter United Press Internat., L.A., 1968-69; producer news Sta. KCRA-TV, Sacramento, 1969-70, reporter news, 1970-79, chief polit. and capitol corres., 1979-92; mng. ptnr. NCG Porter Novelli, Sacramento, 1992—. Adj. prof., guest lectr. Calif. State U., Sacramento. Contbr. articles to profl. jours. With USCG, 1966. Recipient No. Calif. Emmy NATAS, 1976-77, Pub. Svc. award Calif. State Bar, 1977, Exceptional Achievement Coun. advancement and Support of Edn., 1976, Nat. Health Journalism award Am. Chiropractic Assn., 1978. Mem. Soc. Profl. Journalists (8 awards), Capitol Corres. Assn., U. Calif. Alumni Assn., Sacramento Press Club. Avocations: hiking, jogging, fishing. Office: Nelson Comms Group 1029 J St Ste 400 Sacramento CA 95814-2878 E-mail: sswatt@ncgpn.com

SWAYZE, PATRICK, actor, dancer; b. Houston, Aug. 18, 1954; s. Patsy Swayze. Student, Harkness Sch., Joffrey Ballet Sch. Dancer (Broadway) Goodtime Charley, Grease; film appearances include (debut) Skatetown, U.S.A., 1979, The Outsiders, 1983, Uncommon Valor, 1983, Red Dawn, 1984, Grandview U.S.A., 1984, Youngblood, 1986, Dirty Dancing, 1987, Steel Dawn, 1987, Tiger Warsaw, 1988, Road House, 1989, Next of Kin, 1989, Ghost, 1989, Point Break, 1991, City of Joy, 1992, Father Hood, 1993, Tall Tale, 1994, To Wong Foo, Thanks for Everything, Julie Newmar, 1995, Three Wishes, 1995, Letters From a Killer, 1997, Vanished, 1998, Black Dog, 1998, Letters from a Killer, 1998, Without a Word, 1999, The Winddrinker, 2000, Wakin' Up In Reno, 2000, (tv series) Hollywood Squares, 1998. Recipient Golden Apple award. Office: William Morris 151 S El Camino Dr Beverly Hills CA 90212-2775

SWECKER, DAN, state legislator; m. Debby Swecker; children: Jenny, Joel, Devin, Amy. BA in Coop. Edn., Evergreen State Coll. Owner, operator Swecker Salmon Farm, Inc.; mem. Wash. Senate, Dist. 20, Olympia, 1995—; chair Senate Rep. Caucus Policy com. Wash. Senate, Olympia, 1999—, asst. majority whip, 1997-98; mem. agr. and rural econ. devel. com.; mem. edn. com.; mem. environ. quality and water resources com.; mem. transp. com.; mem. family policy coun.; mem. joint task force on land use and econ. devel. Mem. Wash. Water Policy Alliance, 1994, Water Rights Fee Task Force, 1993, Wash. Coun. for the Prevention of Child Abuse and Neglect. With U.S. Army, Vietnam. Decorated Bronze Star, Purple Heart; recipient 100 Percent Voting Record Wash. Water Policy Alliance, 1994. Mem. Wash. Fish Growers Assn. (exec. dir.), Nature Conservancy (trustee Wash. chpt.). Republican. Office: 103 Irving Newhouse Ofc Olympia WA 98504-0001

SWEENEY, ANNE M. cable television company executive; b. Nov. 4, 1957; BA, Coll. of New Rochelle, N.Y., 1979; EdM, Harvard U., 1980. With Nickelodeon/Nick at Nite, 1981-93, sr. v.p. program enterprises; chmn., CEO Fx Networks, N.Y.C., 1993-96; exec. v.p., pres. Disney/ABC Cable Networks, Burbank, 1996—. Bd. trustees Coll. of New Rochelle, Harvard U. Ptnrs. Coun.; hon. chair Cable Positive; bd. dirs. Walter Kaitz Found. Mem. Nat. Acad. Cable Programming (bd. dirs.), Women in Cable (founding mem.) N.Y. Women in Cable (Exec. of Yr. 1994), Am. Women in Radio and TV (Star award 1995), Am. Advt. Fedn. (inducted in Hall of Achievement). Office: Disney Channel 3800 W Alameda Ave Fl 5 Burbank CA 91505-4300

SWEENEY, DAVID BRIAN, lawyer; b. Seattle, June 23, 1941; s. Hubert Lee and Ann Louise (Harmon) S.; m. Janice Kay Goins, June 18, 1983; children: Stuart, Jennifer, Ann, Katharine. BA Magna cum laude, Yale U., 1963; LLB, Harvard U., 1967. Bar: Wash. 1968, U.S. Dist. Ct. (we. dist.) Wash. 1968, U.S. Ct. Appeals (9th cir.) 1968. Assoc. Roberts, Shefelman, Lawrence, Gay and Moch, Seattle, 1968-75; ptnr. Roberts, Shefelman, Lawrence, Gay & Moch (then Robert & Shefelman, then Foster, Pepper & Shefelman), 1976—. Mem. Seattle-King County Bar Assn., Wash. State Bar Assn., ABA, Estate Planning Council of Seattle. Republican. Presbyterian. Clubs: College, Harbor. Home: 17506 SE 46th St Bellevue WA 98006-6527 Office: Foster Pepper & Shefelman 1111 3rd Ave Fl 34 Seattle WA 98101-3292 E-mail: sweed@foster.com

SWEET, HARVEY, theatrical set designer, lighting designer; b. Detroit, Oct. 27, 1943; s. Sam and Rose Sweet; m. Susan Perrett, Mar. 16, 1964 (div. Mar. 1975); children: Deborah Anne, Rebecca Lynn, Jason Aaron; m. Patricia Ravn, Sept. 9, 1978 (div. July 1987). BS, Ea. Mich. U., 1965; MS, U. Wis., 1967, PhD, 1974. Instr. U. N.D., Grand Forks, 1967-69; asst. prof. Boise (Idaho) State Coll., 1972-73; instr. U. Wis., Madison, 1973-74; prof. of theater arts U. No. Iowa, Cedar Falls, 1974-89; dir. lighting Landmark Entertainment Group, L.A. and Tokyo, 1989-91; cons. Advanced Tech., Tokyo, 1991; tech. writer Walt Disney Imagineering, Glendale, Calif., 1992; project mgr., sr. designer, sr. estimator, tech. writer Tru Roll, Inc., Glendale, 1993-99; project mgr. estimator tech. sales LVH Entertainment Sys., Oxnard, 1999—. Owner, operator Sweet Studios Theatrical Equipment, Cedar Falls, 1981-89; dir. theater tech. and design U. No. Iowa, 1974-87. Author: Graphics for the Performing Arts, 1982, Handbook of Scenery, Properties and Lighting I and II, 1988, 2nd edit., 1995, The Complete Book of Drawing for the Theatre, 1995; scenic designer Summer Repretory Theatre, 1988, Timberlake Playhouse, 1988-89; lighting designer, scenic designer, tech. dir. various coll. theatrical prodns., 1964-89; themed lighting designer Sanrio Puroland, Tokyo, 1989, exec. dir. lighting, 1990. Mem. U.S. Inst. for Theatre Tech. (vice commr. 1979-81, commr. 1981-87, mem. graphic stds. bd. 1979-86, evaluation commn. 1983-88, mem. publs. com. 1986-89, bd. dirs. 1989). Avocations: travel, cooking. Office: LVH Entertainment Sys 300 Irving Dr Oxnard CA 93030 E-mail: cre8tivguy@aol.com

SWEITZER, MICHAEL COOK, healthcare product executive; b. Cin., July 29, 1961; s. Charles Samuel and Louise (Cook) S. BS in Biomedical Engring., Rensselaer Poly. Inst., 1983, M in Engring., 1985. Product specialist Siemens Med. Sys., Iselin, N.J., 1985-89, tech. mgr, 1989-90, nat. sales mgr., 1993-94, product mgr., 1994-96, cons., 1996-98, product specialist San Francisco, 1990-92; product mgr. Toshiba Am. Med. Sys., S. San Francisco, 1992-93. Contbr. chpt. to MRI Guide for Technologists, 1994. Mem. Am. Healthcare Radiology Adminstrs., Inst. for Indsl. Engrs. Office: Varian Med Sys Inc MS E 263 3100 Hansen Way Palo Alto CA 94304-1129

SWENKA, ARTHUR JOHN, retired food products executive; b. Lone Tree, Iowa, Oct. 21, 1937; s. Samuel Joseph and Verdis Mary (Weed) S.; m. Elizabeth Simms, July 1956 (div. 1976); children: Lee Arthur, Timothy John; m. Dixie Jo Meade, Feb. 1982. Gen. equivalency diploma, U.S. Army, 1957. Truck driver U.S. Mail, Oelwein, Iowa, 1958-59, Stiles Supermarket, Oelwein, 1959-60; salesman Hoxie Inst. Wholesale Co., Waterloo, Iowa, 1960-68, slaes mgr., 1968-69, br. mgr., 1969-70, Waterloo and Mason City, 1970-72, Nobel Inc., Albuquerque, 1972-81; pres. Nobel/Sysco Food Svcs. Co., Albuquerque, 1981-84, Denver, 1985-95; sr. v.p. ops. Sysco Corp., Houston, 1995—. Mem. Dirs. Coun., Houston, 1985—. Treas., bd. dirs. Albuquerque Conv. and Visitors Bur., 1975-80; v.p., bd. dirs. Albuquerque Internat. Balloon Festival, 1975-82; bd. dirs. New Day Home for Runaway Children, Albuquerque, 1980-89, Found. St. Joseph's Hosp., Kodak Internat. Balloon Fiesta, Albuquerque. Republican. Roman Catholic. Avocation: hot air ballooning. Home: 30 Twin Peaks Dr Estancia NM 87016-9732

SWENSON, KATHLEEN SUSAN, music and art educator; b. Reno, Oct. 23, 1938; d. Harold Ruthaford McNeil and Hollyce Margaret (Scruggs) McNeil Biggs; m. James Michael Phalan, 1956 (div. 1974); children: David Michael, Jeanine Louise Phalan Lawrence, Gregory Sean; m. Gerald Allen Swensen, Nov. 1976 (div. 1987); stepchildren: Craig Allen, Sarah Ann, Eric Sander. Student, U. Nev., Reno, 1956-58, Foothill Coll., , 1966-68; AA, West Valley Coll.; BA, U. Calif., Santa Cruz, 1983. Concert pianist, Nev.,Calif, 1950-64; pvt. piano instr. various locations, 1963—; pvt. art instr. various locations, 1970—; pvt. astrology instr. various locations, 1973—; founder, pres. AAM Triple Arts, Aptos, Calif., 1974—; founder, owner Aptos (Calif.) Acad. Music, 1991—. Producer, instr. art instrn. videos, music instrn. films, books. Mem. Soc Western Artists, Calif. Piano Tchrs. Assn., Los Gatos Art Assn. (pres. 1985-86), Saratoga Contemporary Artists (v.p. 1984-85), Nat. League Am. Pen Women (honorarian 1985), Soroptomists, Phi Beta Kappa. Republican. Episcopalian. Home and Office: Aptos Acad Music 3000 Wisteria Way Aptos CA 95003-3318 E-mail: Aamtriplearts@aol.com, aptsacademymusic@aol.com

SWENSON, RICHARD ALLEN, business owner, animal trainer; b. Willmar, Minn., Dec. 1, 1950; s. LeRoy Oswald Boe and Delores G. (Malghist) S.; children: Kristen, Richard Andrew, Kevin. Author: Secrets of Long Distance Sled Dog Racing. Treas. Pride, Alaska, 1993—. Recipient 1st pl. Iditarod, 1977, 79, 80, 81, 91 among others. Office: Denali Sled Dog Tours PO Box 86 Denali Park AK 99755-0086

SWERDLOFF, RONALD S. medical educator, researcher; b. Pomona, Calif., Feb. 18, 1938; s. Julius Lewis and Eva (Kelman) S.; m. Christina Wang; children: Jonathan Nicolai, Peter Loren, Paul Im, Michael Im. BS, U. Calif., 1959, MD, 1962. Diplomate Am. Bd. Internal Medicine, Am. Bd. Endocrinology. Intern U. Wash., Seattle, 1962-63, resident, 1963-64; rsch. assoc. NIH, Bethesda, Md., 1964-66; resident UCLA Sch. Medicine, 1966-67; rsch. fellow Harbor-UCLA Med. Ctr., Torrance, Calif., 1967-69, asst. prof., 1969-72, assoc. prof. divsn. Endocrinology, 1972-78, chief divsn. Endocrinology, 1973—, prof., 1978—, assoc. chair dept. medicine, 1997—; dir. UCLA Population Rsch. Ctr., Torrance, 1986-92, Mellon Found. Ctr. in Reproductive Medicine, 1997—. Dir. WHO Collaborating Ctr. Reprodn., Torrance; cons. WHO Geneva, 1982-90, NIH, Bethesda, 1982—, UN Fertility Planning Assn., Geneva, 1983—, Am. Bd. Internal Medicine, Phila., 1989—; inaugural lectr. Australian Soc. Reproductive Biology, Perth, 1990; mem. tech. adv. com. Contraceptive R&D Agy. (CONRAD, AID), 1992—. Editor 3 books; contbr. 100 chpts. to books, 250 articles to profl. jours. Bd. dirs., vice chair Harbor-UCLA Rsch. and Edn. Inst. Fellow Am. Coll. Physicians; mem. Am. Soc. Andrology (Serono award 1986, pres. 1992-93), Am. Assn. Physicians, Am. Soc. Clin. Rsch. (pres. western sect. 1972-73), Pacific Coast Fertility (Squibb award, Outstanding rsch. award 1976, 84, Wyeth award 1984, pres. 1984), Endocrinology Soc., We. Soc. Clin. Rsch. (pres. 1983-84, Mayo Soley award 2000). Office: Harbor UCLA Med Ctr Divsn Endocrinology 1000 W Carson St Torrance CA 90502-2004 E-mail: swerdloff@gcrc.humc.edu

SWETTE, BRIAN T. online computer executive; BA in Econ., Az. State U. Mgr. Procter & Gamble; exec. v.p./chief mktg. officer Pepsi-Cola, 1981-01. Office: EBay Inc 2145 Hamilton Ave San Jose CA 95125

SWIFT, RICHARD G(ENE), composer, educator; b. Middlepoint, Ohio, Sept. 24, 1927; s. Lisle Russell and Josephine (Ladd) S.; m. Dorothy Zackrisson, Feb. 10, 1951; children: Jeremy, John, Joel. MA, U. Chgo., 1956. Assoc. prof. music U. Calif., Davis, 1956-67, prof., 1967-91, prof. emeritus, 1991—, chmn. dept., 1963-71. Vis. prof. Princeton U., 1977; faculty research lectr. U. Calif., 1983-84. Composer: A Coronal, 1954, String Quartet I, 1956, II, 1958, III, 1964, Sonata for Clarinet and Piano, 1957, Sonata for Solo Violin, 1958, Eve, 1959, Stravaganza III for Clarinet, Violin and Piano, 1960, Concerto for Piano and Chamber Ensemble, 1961, Extravaganza for Orchestra, 1962, Domains, I, II, III, 1963, Bucolics, 1964, Concerto for Violin and Chamber Ensemble, 1967, Music for A While, 1969, Thanatopsis, 1971, Prime, 1973, Quartet IV, 1973, Specimen Days, 1976, Mein blaues Klavier, 1979, Concerto II for piano and chamber ensemble, 1980, Quartet V, 1982, Things of August, 1985, Roses Only, 1991, In Arcadia, 1994, Stravaganza XI, 1995, Getting Back In, 1997, Stravaganza XII, 1998, Stravaganza XIII, 1999, Stravaganza XIV, 2001, Stanzas, 2001; cons. editor 19th Century Music. Served with AUS, 1950-52. Recipient award Rockefeller Found., 1956, 68; award Fromm Found.; Composers String Quartet award, 1973; award Nat. Endowment for Arts, 1976; Inst. award Am. Acad. and Inst. Arts and Letters, 1978; Disting. Teaching award U. Calif., 1980 Fellow Inst. Creative Arts; mem. Am. Music Ctr., ASCAP, Am. Musicological Soc., Soc. for Music Theory, The Soc. of Composers. Home: 568 S Campus Way Davis CA 95616-3523

SWIFT, WILLIAM CHARLES, professional baseball player, Olympic athlete; b. Portland, Maine, Oct. 27, 1961; Student, Maine. Mem. U.S. Olympic Baseball Team, 1984; with Seattle Mariners, 1984-91; pitcher San Francisco Giants, 1991-94, Colo. Rockies, 1994-97; baseball player Balt. Orioles, Baltimore, MD, 1997; Baseball player Seattle Mariners, Seattle, 1998. Achievements include being the Nat. League Earned Run Average leader, 1992. Office: Seattle Mariners PO Box 4100 83 King Street Seattle WA 98104

SWIG, ROSELYNE CHROMAN, community consultant; b. Chgo., June 8, 1930; m. Richard Swig, Feb. 5, 1950 (dec.); children— Richard, Jr., Susan, Marjorie, Carol. Student, U. Calif.-Berkeley, UCLA; MFA (hon.), DHL (hon.), San Francisco Art Inst., 1988. Founder, pres. Roselyne C. Swig Artsource, San Francisco, 1977-94; apptd. by Pres. Clinton as dir. Art in Embassies Program U.S. Dept. of State, 1994-97; founder, pres. Comcon Internat., 1998—. Founder Ptnrs. Ending Domestic Abuse, San Francisco. Trustee San Francisco Mus. Modern Art, U. Art Mus., Berkeley, Calif.; ex officio bd. mem. Jewish Mus. San Francisco; bd. dirs., former treas. Am. Jewish Joint Distbn. Com.; vice chair fine art adv. panel Fed. Res.,

Washington; past trustee Mills Coll., Oakland, Calif.; past past pres., bd. dirs. Jewish Cmty. Fedn. San Francisco, the Peninsula, Marin and Sonoma Counties; past commr. San Francisco Pub. Libr.; past bd. dirs. San Francisco Opera, Am. Coun. for Arts, KQED Broadcasting Sys.; past. pres. Calif. State Summer Sch. Arts, past chair bd. trustees San Francisco Art Inst.; past pres. San Francisco Arts Commn.; past nat. v.p. Am./Israel Pub. Affairs Com.; past trustee United Jewish Appeal; past chair bd. trustees Univ. Art Mus. Mem. Women's Forum West (bd. dirs.), Internat. Women's Forum. Avocations: skiing, boating, tennis, fishing.

SWIHART, H. GREGG, real estate company executive; b. San Francisco, Sept. 25, 1938; s. Lawson Benjamin and Violet Mary (Watters) S.; m. Ilse Paula Rambacher, Dec. 24, 1958; children: Tatjana Etta, Brett Marc, Natascha Theda. BA, U. Ariz., 1958; postgrad., Heidelberg (Germany) U., 1961-65, Harvard U., 1959-60; MA, Boston U., 1961; postgrad., Freiburg (Germany) U., 1961-65. Cert. property mgr. Stockbroker Walston & Co., Tucson, 1966-71; with Solot Co., Tucson, 1971-74; pres. Cienega Properties, Inc., property mgmt. and investment, Tucson, 1975-77, GT Realty Assocs., Ltd., Tucson, 1977—. Me.m Tucson Com. Fgn. Rels., 1973—; pres. Forum for Greater Outdoors, 1977-79; bd. dirs. Tucson Mus. Art, 1968-74, pres., 1969-70; pres. and trustee, Canelo Hills Sch., 1977-79. Mem. Tucson Bd. Realtors, Inst. Real Estate Mgmt. (pres. Tucson-So. Ariz. chpt. 1982, mem. nat. governing coun. 1985-87), Inst. Real Estate Mgmt. (governing coun. 1985-87, Property Mgr. of Yr. award So. Ariz. chpt. 1988), Realtors Nat. Mktg. Inst., Harvard Club (pres. 1973-74), Active 20-30 Club (pres. 1973-74), Downtown Tucson Club. Home: Tunnel Springs Ranch PO Box 555 Sonoita AZ 85637-0555 Office: 5643 E Broadway Blvd Tucson AZ 85711

SWIHART, JAMES W., JR. diplomat; b. Washington, July 25, 1946; s. James Wilbur and Ruth (Inge) S.; m. Ellen Jane Cendo Mar. 30, 1968; children: Jennifer Anne, Christopher John; m. Kimberly Ann Mack, May 12, 2001. BA, Columbia Coll., 1968. Vice consul Am. Embassy, Belize, Brit. Honduras, 1970-72, 2nd sec., polit. officer Belgrade, Yugoslavia, 1972-74; ops. officer ops. ctr. Dept. State, Washington, 1974-75, country officer for Italy and the Vatican, 1975-78, polit./mil. officer for U.S. Mission Berlin, 1978-82, officer C.S.C.E. Bur. European Affairs, 1982-83, officer for Fed. Republic of Germany, 1983-84; consul gen., prin. officer U.S. Consulate Gen., Zagreb, Yugoslavia, 1984-1988; mem. sr. seminar Dept. State, Washington, 1988-89, dir. Bur. for Ea. European and Yugoslavia Affairs, 1989-1991; min. counselor, deputy chief of mission Am. Embassy, Vienna, Austria, 1991-94, Chargé d'Affaires ad interim Austria, 1993, amb. to Lithuania Vilnius, 1994-97; sr. fellow Inst. for Strategic Studies/Nat. Def. U., Washington, 1997-99; polit. advisor U.S. Space Command, Colorado Springs, Colo., 1999—. Avocations: piano, harpsichord, jogging, classical music appreciation. Home: 8445 Sutterfield Dr Colorado Springs CO 80920 Office: US Space Command Peterson AFB 250 S Peterson Blvd Ste 116 Colorado Springs CO 80914-3285

SWINDELLS, WILLIAM, JR. lumber and paper company executive; b. Oakland, CA, 1930; married B.S., Stanford U., 1953. With Willamette Industries, Inc., Portland, Oreg., 1953—, sr. v.p. prodn., mktg. bldg. materials, until 1978, exec. v.p., 1978-80, pres. forest products div., 1980-82, pres., chief exec. officer, 1982-96, also dir., chmn., 1984-97; chmn., CEO Willamette Industry, Portland, 1997, chmn. bd., 1997—. Dir. Oreg. Bank, Portland Office: Willamette Industries 1300 SW 5th Ave Ste 3800 Portland OR 97201-5671

SWING, WILLIAM EDWIN, bishop; b. Huntington, W.Va., Aug. 26, 1936; s. William Lee and Elsie Bell (Holliday) S.; M. Mary Willis Taylor, Oct. 7, 1961; children— Alice Marshall, William Edwin B.A., Kenyon Coll., Ohio, 1954-58; D.Div. (hon.), Kenyon Coll., 1980; M.A., Va. Theol. Sem., 1958-61, D.Div., 1980. Ordained priest Episcopal Ch. Asst. St. Matthews Ch., Wheeling, W.Va., 1961-63, vicar Chester, 1963-69, St. Thomas Ch., Weirton, 1963-69; rector St. Columba's Episcopal Ch., Washington, 1969-79; bishop Episcopal Ch. Calif., San Francisco, 1980—. Chmn. bd. Ch. Div. Sch. of the Pacific, 1983-84; founder, chmn. Episcopal Found. for Drama, 1976— . Republican. Home: 2006 Lyon St San Francisco CA 94115-1610 Office: Episcopal Ch Diocesan Office 1055 Taylor St San Francisco CA 94108-2209

SWOFFORD, ROBERT LEE, newspaper editor, journalist; b. Berryville, Ark., Aug. 22, 1949; s. Andrew Madison and Verna Mae (England) S.; m. Karen King, Jan. 24, 1969 (div. 1977); children: Teri, Toby; m. Sandra Dunn, 1978 (div. 1979); m. B. Joanna Rongren, Feb. 14, 1981; 1 child, Tyler. AA, Coll. of the Sequoias, 1969; student, Calif. State U., 1969-71. Photographer, reporter, news editor The Advance-Register, Tulare, Calif., 1965-78; city editor The Record Searchlight, Redding, 1978-81; suburban editor, Neighbors editor The Sacramento Bee, 1981-86; assoc. metro. editor, cmty. editor The Orange County Register, Santa Ana, Calif., 1986-89; exec. news editor The Press Democrat, Santa Rosa, 1989-90, mng. editor, 1990—. Recipient Pulitzer prize for news photography Press Dem., 1997. Mem. Am. Soc. Newspaper Editors, Assoc. Press Mng. Editors, Calif. Soc. of Newspaper Editors (bd. dirs.). Office: The Press Democrat 427 Mendocino Ave Santa Rosa CA 95401-6385

SWYSGOOD, CHARLES, state legislator; b. Ohio, Mar. 30, 1939; m. Dorothy Swysgood. Student, Wooster (Ohio) Schs. Ptnr. in trucking firm; farmer, businessman; mem. Mont. Ho. of Reps., 1987-92, Mont. State Senate, 1987—, chair fin. and claims com., vice chair legis. admin. com., vice chair jt. appropriations subcom. on health/human svcs., mem. joint appropriations subcom. on long-range planning, mem. fish and game com. Mem. Vocat. Edn. Adv. Coun.; former trustee Sch. Bd. Served with USAF. Mem. NRA (life). Republican. Home: 506 S Atlantic St Dillon MT 59725-2723

SYDANSK, ROBERT DUNN, chemist, petroleum engineer; b. 1943; BS in Chemistry, U. Colo., 1967. With Petroleum Tech. Rsch. Ctr. Marathon Oil Co., Littleton, Colo., 1967—, now sr. tech. cons. Cons. and lectr. in field. Tech. editor publs. Soc. Petroleum Engrs.; contbr. some 30 articles to profl. jours.; 56 patents in chem. improved oil recovery processes. Mem. Am. Chem. Soc. (award in indsl. chemistry 1997), Soc. Petroleum Engrs. (Henry Mattson Tech. Achievement award 1993, Disting. Lectr. 1997). Office: Marrathon Oil Co Petroleum Tech Ctr PO Box 269 Littleton CO 80160-0269

SYME, SHERMAN LEONARD, epidemiology educator; b. Dauphin, Man., Can., July 4, 1932; came to U.S., 1950; s. Robert and Rose (Bay) S.; m. Marilyn Elaine Egenes, July 28, 1932; children: Karen, David, Janet. BA, UCLA, 1953, MA, 1955; PhD, Yale U., 1957. Commd. USPHS, Washington, 1957-68, advanced through grades to chief Tng. Sta. San Francisco, 1962-68, sociologist Washington, 1957-60; exec. sec. NIH, Bethesda, Md., 1960-62; prof. emeritus epidemiology U. Calif., Berkeley, 1968—. Chmn. Dept. Epidemiology, U. Calif., 1975-80; vis. prof. Teikyo U., Tokyo, 1977, York (Eng.) U., 1975, St. Thomas Sch. Medicine, London, 1980, U. London, 1989; expert adv. panels WHO, Geneva, 1975—. Co-editor Social Stress and Heart Disease, 1967, Social Support and Health, 1985; contbr. 115 articles to profl. jours. Fellow Am. Heart Assn., Soc. Epidemiol. Research; mem. Inst. Medicine, Am. Epidemiol. Soc. Office: U Calif Sch Pub Health Pub Health Biology & Epidemiology 577 University Hall Berkeley CA 94720-1191

SYMES, LAWRENCE RICHARD, computer science educator, university dean; b. Ottawa, Ont., Can., Aug. 3, 1942; s. Oliver Lawrence and Maybell Melita Blanche (Gilliard) S.; m. Evelyn Jean Hewett, Apr. 3, 1964; children: Calvin Richard, Michelle Louise, Erin Kathleen. BA, U. Sask., Saskatoon, Can., 1963, postgrad. in math., 1964; MS, Purdue U., 1966, Phd, 1969. Asst. prof. Purdue U., West Lafayette, Ind., 1969-70; assoc. prof. computer sci. U. Regina, Sask., Can., 1970-74, prof. Can., 1974—, dir. computer ctr. Can., 1970-75, head dept. computer sci. Can., 1972-81, dean of sci. Can., 1982-92, dean grad. studies, assoc. rsch. v.p. Can., 1997-99, dir. info. svcs. Can., 1999—. Dir. tng. Software Tech. Ctr., 1993-94; exec. dir. postsecondary svcs. br. Saskatchewan Edn. Tng. and Employment Govt. of Saskatchewan, 1994-95, exec. dir. multimedia learning, 1995-96; invited lectr. Xian Jiaotong U., 1983, Shandong Acad. Sci., People's Republic of China, 1987 Contbr. articles to profl. jours. Bd. dirs. Hosp. System Study Group, Saskatoon, 1978-94, chmn. bd., 1980-83; dir. SSTA Computer Svcs., Regina, 1972-89; mem. adv. coun. Can./Sask. Advanced Tech. Agreement, 1985-87; mem. Sask. Agrl. Rsch. Found. Bd., 1987-88; mem. steering com. IBM/Sask. Agreement, 1990-92. Can. Fed. Govt. grantee, 1977-84. Mem. Assn. Computing Machinery, Can. Info. Processing (pres. 1979-80, accreditation com. 1988-94), IEEE Computer Soc., Sask. ADA Assn. (bd. dirs. 1990-93), Sask. Tech. Ctr. (bd. dirs. 1993-98), Sask. Comm. Network (bd. dirs. 1996—, chmn. 1998—, Provl. Action Com. on the Economy 1998-2000). Office: U Regina U Regina Info Svcs 3737 Wasaona Pkwy Regina SK Canada S4S 0A2

SYMMES, DANIEL LESLIE, technology executive, producer, director; b. Los Angeles, June 26, 1949; s. Louis Leslie and Mary (Warkentine) S. Student, Columbia Coll., Hollywood, Calif., 1970-71. Co-founder Stereovision Internat., Inc., North Hollywood, Calif., 1971; cons. Dimension 3e, Beverly Hills, 1975-87; pres., chmn. Spatial Techs. Inc., 3D Video Corp., Hollywood, 1987-95; pres., CEO Dimension 3, Beverly Hills, 1995—. Responsible for comml. 3D TV in U.S. and abroad; known worldwide as Mr. 3D. Author: Amazing 3-D; contbr. numerous articles to profl. jours.; dir. photography local 659 IATSE; patentee 3-D TV; inventor 1st reflex widescreen 3D filming system. Mem. SMPTE. Avocations: photography, expert scuba photography.

SYMONS, JAMES MARTIN, theater and dance educator; b. Jacksonville, Ill., May 7, 1937; s. James and Pauline (Barton) S.; m. Judith White, Nov. 14, 1959; children: Tracy, Kelly, Carrie. BA, Ill. Coll., 1959; MA, So. Ill. U., 1964; PhD, Cornell U., 1970. Asst. prof. Yankton (S.D.) Coll., 1964-67; assoc. prof. Coll. St. Catherine, St. Paul, 1970-74, SUNY, Albany, 1974-77; prof., chair Trinity U., San Antonio, 1977-84; prof., chair theatre and dance dept. U. Colo., Boulder, 1984-99, prof., 1999—, Pres.'s Tchg. scholar, 2000—. Actor Off-Broadway, N.Y.C., 1959, Mo. Repertory Theatre, Kansas City, 1984; dir., actor Colo. Shakespeare Festival, Boulder, 1985—, producing artistic dir., 1994-95; leader People-to-People Del. of Theater Educators, USSR and Czechoslovakia, 1991. Author: Meyerhold's Theatre of the Grotesque, 1971 (Freedley Meml. award Theatre Libr. Assn. 1971); contbr. articles to scholarly jours. Lt. (j.g.) USN, 1960-63. Mem. Assn. for Theatre in Higher Edn. (pres. 1989-91), Assn. for Communication Adminstrn. (pres. 1990). Democrat. Methodist. E-mial. Office: U Colo Dept Theatre & Dance Cb 261 Boulder CO 80309-0001 E-mail: james.symons@colorado.edu

SYMONS, ROBERT SPENCER, electronic engineer; b. San Francisco, July 3, 1925; s. Spencer W. and Avesia (Atkins) S.; m. Alice Faye Smith, Dec. 21, 1960; children: Julia Ann, Robert Spencer Jr. BS, Stanford U., 1946, MS, 1948. Engr. Eitel-McCullough, Inc., San Bruno, Calif., 1947, Heinz & Kaufman, South San Francisco, 1948, Pacific Electronics Co., Los Gatos, Calif., 1949; sr. engring. mgr. Varian Assocs., Palo Alto, 1950-83; tech. dir. CTO Litton Sys., Inc., San Carlos, 1983—. Patentee in field. 1st lt. AUS, 1950-53. Recipient Charles B. Thornton award for Advanced Tech. Achievement, 1991, 99. Fellow IEEE (assoc. editor Transactions on Electron Devices jour. 1980-83); mem. Commonwealth of Calif. Club, Phi Beta Kappa, Tau Beta Pi. Home: 290 Surrey Pl Los Altos CA 94022-2180 Office: Litton Industries 960 Industrial Rd San Carlos CA 94070-4194

SZABLYA, HELEN MARY, writer, language professional, lecturer; b. Budapest, Hungary, Sept. 6, 1934; came to U.S., 1963; d. Louis and Helen (Bartha) Kovacs; m. John Francis Szablya, June 12, 1951; children: Helen, Janos, Louis, Stephen, Alexandra, Rita, Dominique-Mary. Diploma in Sales, Mktg., U.B.C., 1962; BA in Fgn. Lang., Lit., Wash. State U., 1976. Freelance writer, translator, 1967—; columnist Cath. News, Trinidad, W.I., 1980-91; adult educator TELOS Bellevue (Wash.) C.C., 1987-89; adult educator Pullman-Spokane (Wash.) C.C., 1976-80; faculty Christian Writers' Conf., Seattle, 1983-88, Pacific N.W. Writers' Conf., Seattle, Tacoma, 1987—; hon. consul for Wash., Oreg., Idaho Republic of Hungary, 1993—. Lectr. Washington Commn. for Humanities, 1987-89. Author: (with others) Hungary Remembered, 1986 (Guardian of Liberty award, 1986, George Washington Honor medal, Freedoms Found. award 1988), 56-os Cserkèszcsapat, 1986, (with others) The Fall of the Red Star, 1996 (Hungarian translation 1999, 1st prize Wash. Press Assn., 1st prize Nat. Fedn. Press Women); pub., editor Hungary Internat. newsletter, 1990-93; columnist Hungarian Bus. Weekly, 1994-95; translator: Emlèkezünk, 1986, Mind Twisters, 1987. Recipient Nat. 1st place editl. Nat. Fedn. Press Women, 1987, Senator Tom Martin Meml. award Pacific N.W. Writers Conf., 1979; grantee Hungarian Am. Assn. Wash., 1986, Wash. Com. for Humanities, 1986; named Cmty. Woman of Yr., Am. Bus. Women Assn., 1990. Mem. AAUW, Wash. Press Assn. (pres. 1987-88, 1st and 2nd place awards, several editorial and profile awards 1983, 87, 89, 90, 91, 92, 96, Communicator of Achievement award 1987), Nat. Fedn. Press Women (Affiliate Pres.' award 1988, bd. dirs. edn. fund N.W. quadrant, mem. 21st century planning com.), Authors Guild, Am. Translators Assn., Arpad Acad. (Gold medal 1987), Nat. Writers Club, Internat. P.E.N. Club, Sigma Delta Chi (editl. award 1989). Avocations: children, reading, dancing, swimming, traveling. Home and Office: PO Box 578 Kirkland WA 98083-0578

SZABO, PETER JOHN, investment company executive, financial planner, mining engineer, lawyer; b. Bklyn., Nov. 22, 1946; s. Paul Simon and Marita Ellen (Coughlin) S.; m. Dorothy Anne Steward, Nov. 14, 1970; children: Peter, David, John Paul Steward. BS in Mining Engring., Columbia U., 1968; LLB, LaSalle Law Sch., 1975; MS in Fin. Planning, Coll. Fin. PLanning, 1994. registered profl. engr., CFP. Mining engr. Halecrest Co., Mt. Hope, N.J., 1973-74; mgr. solid fuels & minerals Ford, Bacon & Davis, N.Y.C., 1974-75; asst. v.p. Mfrs. Hanover Trust Co., N.Y.C., 1975-77, Irving Trust Co., N.Y.C., 1977; v.p. Republic Nat. Bank of Dallas, 1977-80; mgr. bus. devel. AMOCO Minerals, Denver, 1980-84; investment broker B.J. Leonard, Denver, 1984-85; investment exec. Wedbush Nobel Cook, Denver, 1985; regional sr. v.p. Alliance Fund Distbrs., N.Y.C., 1985-92, sr. v.p., 1992—. Mining engr. U.S. Bur. Mines, Dallas, 1971-72, IRS, Washington, 1972-73. Treas. Columbia Sch. Engring., 1968—. Lt. USMC, 1969-71, Vietnam, capt. Res. Mem. VFW (post sr. vice comdr. 1993-94, post comdr. 1994-95, all state team post comdrs. 1995, 16th dist. jr. vice comdr. 1995—, 16th dist. sr. vice comdr. 1996—, nat. aide-de-camp 1995-96), Mil. Order of the Cootie (sr. vice comdr. 1994-95). Republican. Roman Catholic. Avocations: sailing, golf, tennis, jogging, scripophily. Home and Office: Alliance Fund Distbrs 810 Oxford Way Benicia CA 94510-3646

SZEFLER, STANLEY JAMES, pediatrics and pharmacology educator; b. Buffalo, Aug. 24, 1948; s. Stanley and Bernice Laura (Platt) S.; m. Christine M. Drezek, Dec. 26, 1970; children: David, Paul. BS, SUNY, Buffalo, 1971, MD, 1975. Resident pediatrics Children's Hosp. Buffalo, 1975-77; postdoctoral fellow in clin. pharmacology and allergy immunology SUNY, Buffalo, 1977-79, asst. prof. pediatrics and pharmacology, 1979-82; assoc. prof. pediatrics and pharmacology U. Colo., Denver, 1982-90, prof. pediatrics, pharmacology, 1990—. Dir. clin. pharmacology Children's Hosp., Buffalo, 1979-82, Nat. Jewish Ctr. for Immunology and Respiratory Medicine, Denver, 1982—. Contbr. articles to profl. jours. Mem. steering com. asthma camp for children Am. Lung Assn., Denver, 1987-96. Maj. USAR, 1979-88. NIH grantee, 1980-84, 90—, FDA grantee, Denver, 1988-91. Fellow Am. Acad. Allergy, Asthma and Immunology (chmn. asthma, rhinitis and respiratory disease interest sect. 1995-97), Am.Acad. Pediats. (liaison mem. com. drugs). Avocations: baseball, soccer. Office: Nat Jewish Med & Rsch Ctr Dept Pediat 1400 Jackson St Denver CO 80206-2761

SZEGO, CLARA MARIAN, cell biologist, educator; b. Budapest, Hungary, Mar. 23, 1916; came to U.S., 1921, naturalized, 1927; d. Paul S. and Helen (Elek) S.; m. Sidney Roberts, Sept. 14, 1943. A.B., Hunter Coll., 1937; M.S. (Garvan fellow), U. Minn., 1939, Ph.D., 1942. Instr. physiology U. Minn., 1942-43; Minn. Cancer Research Inst. fellow, 1943-44; rsch. assoc. OSRD, Nat. Bur. Standards, 1944-45, Worcester Found. Exptl. Biology, 1945-47; rsch. instr. physiol. chemistry Yale U. Sch. Medicine, 1947-48; mem. faculty UCLA, 1948—, prof. biology, 1960—. Guggenheim fellow, 1956; named Woman of Year in Sci. Los Angeles Times, 1957-58; named to Hunter Coll. Hall of Fame, 1987. Fellow AAAS; mem. Am. Physiol. Soc., Am. Soc. Cell Biology, Endocrine Soc. (CIBA award 1953), Soc. for Endocrinology (Gt. Britain), Biochem. Soc. (Gt. Britain), Internat. Soc. Rsch. Reprodn., Phi Beta Kappa (pres. UCLA chpt. 1973-74), Sigma Xi (pres. UCLA chpt. 1976-77). Achievements include rsch. and numerous publs. on steroid protein interactions, mechanisms of hormone action and lysosome participation in normal cell function. Home: 1371 Marinette Rd Pacific Palisades CA 90272-2627 Office: U Calif Dept Molecular Cell & Devel Biology Los Angeles CA 90095-1606 E-mail: cmszego@ucla.edu

SZKODY, PAULA, astronomy educator, researcher; b. Detroit, July 17, 1948; d. Julian and Pauline (Wolski) S.; m. Donald E. Brownlee, Mar. 19, 1976; children: Allison, Carson. BS in Astrophysics, Mich. State U., 1970; MS in Astronomy, U. Wash., 1972, PhD in Astronomy, 1975. Rsch. asst. Observatoire de Geneve, 1969, Kitt Peak Nat. Obs., 1970; rsch., teaching asst. U. Wash., Seattle, 1970-75, rsch. assoc., lectr., 1975-82, sr. rsch. assoc., 1982-83, rsch. assoc. prof., 1983-91, rsch. prof., 1991-93, prof., 1993—. Part-time mem. faculty Seattle U., 1974-75, 82, Bellevue Coll., 1975-77; vis. scientist Kitt Peak Nat. Obs., 1976; vis. instr. UCLA, 1977, adj. asst. prof., 1980, 81; vis. asst. prof. U. Hawaii, 1978; vis. assoc. prof. Calif. Inst. Tech., 1978-79, 80, mem. XTE users com., 1996-99; mem. users com. Internat. Ultraviolet Explorer, 1983-85, 93-97; mem. A.J. Cannon adv. com. AAUW, 1986-91, chmn. 1988-90; mem. mgmt. ops. working group on Ultraviolet/Visual/Relativity, NASA, 1988-91. Contbr. numerous articles to profl. jours. Recipient Annie J. Cannon award, 1978. Fellow AAAS (mem. nominating com. 1990-93, chairperson 1993, mem.-at-large 1995-99); mem. Am. Assn. Variable Star Observers, Am. Astron. Soc. (councilor 1996-99), Internat. Astron. Union; mem. commn. 42 organizing com. 1991-97, v.p. 1997-00, pres. 2000—), Astron. Soc. Pacific (bd. dirs. 1988-92), Phi Beta Kappa. Office: U Wash Dept Astronomy PO Box 351580 Seattle WA 98195-1580 E-mail: szkody@astro.washington.edu

SZWARC, MICHAEL, polymer scientist; b. Poland, June 9, 1909; came to U.S., 1952; s. Maier and Regina (Prager) S.; m. Marja Frenkel, Aug. 6, 1933; children: Raphael, Myra, Rina. Ch.E., Warsaw Poly. Inst., Poland, 1932; PhD in Organic Chemistry, Hebrew U., Jerusalem, 1945; PhD in Phys. Chemistry, Manchester (Eng.) U., 1947, DSc (hon.), 1949; D (hon.), U. Leuven, Belgium, 1974; D.Sc. (hon), Uppsala U., Sweden, 1975, Louis Pasteur U., Strasbourg, France, 1978. Rschr. Hebrew U., Jerusalem, 1935-45, Manchester U., Eng., 1946-52, univ. fellow, lectr. phys. chemistry Eng., 1949-52; mem. faculty SUNY-Syracuse Coll. Environ. Scis., 1952-79; disting. prof. chemistry SUNY-Syracuse Coll. Forestry, 1964-80, dir. polymer ctr., 1966-80, prof. emeritus, 1980—. Baker lectr. Cornell U., 1970; Noble vis. prof. Uppsala U., 1968-72. Author: Carbanions, Living Polymers and Electron Transfer Processes, 1968, Ionic Polymerization and Living Polymers, 1993; editor: Ions and Ion Pairs in Organic Chemistry, Vol. I, 1972, Vol. II, 1974, Ionic Polymerization Fundamentals, 1996. Recipient Polymer Chemistry award Am. Chem. Soc., 1970, Herman Mark award, 1989; Gold medal Internat. Soc. Plastics Engrs., 1972, Benjamin Franklin Soc., 1978, Kyoto prize for advanced tech., 1991. Fellow Royal Soc. (London); mem. Polish Acad. Scis. (fgn.), Soc. Polymer Sci. (Japan). Office: U So Calif Hydrocarbon Rsch Inst Los Angeles CA 90089-0001

TABACHNICK, NORMAN DONALD, psychiatrist, educator; b. Toronto, Ont., Can., Feb. 21, 1927; BS, U. Ill., 1947, MD, 1949; PhD in Psychoanalysis, So. Calif. Psychoanalytic Inst., 1977. Diplomate Am. Bd. Med. Examiners, Am. Bd. Psychiatry and Neurology. Intern Michael Reese Hosp., 1949-50; resident in psychiatry U.S. VA Hosp., Bedford, Mass., 1950-51, U.S. AFB, Biloxi, Miss., 1951-52, L.A. County Gen. Hosp., 1953-54; staff psychiatrist Sepulveda VA Hosp., 1976-78; pvt. practice L.A.; mem. staff Resthaven Sanitarium, U. So. Calif. Med. Ctr., L.A. County, Westwood Hosp., Edgemont Hosp., Cedars-Sinai Med. Ctr.; mem. staff Neuropsychiatric Inst. UCLA; clin. prof. psychiatry U. So. Calif., L.A., 1970-75, UCLA, 1975—. Hon. mem. med. staf. Resthaven Cmty. Med. Health Ctr., 1973; guest lectr. Cedars-Sinai Med. Ctr., 1985; mem. adv. bd. divsn. psychoanalysis Nassau County Med. Ctr.; mem. faculty Calif. Sch. Profl. Psychology, L.A. Ctr. Group Psychotherapy, Grad. Ctr. Child Devel. and Psychotherapy; cons. L.A. County Coroner's Office, 1963-70, Bur. Vocat. Rehab., Jewish Family Svc., profl. adv. bd. Resthaven Sanitarium, Marianne Frostig Sch. Ednl. Therapy, W. Valley Ctr. Edl. Therapy. Author: Accident or Suicide?, 1973; mem. edtl. bd. Jour. Acad. Psychoanalysis, book rev. editor, 1978; mem. edtl. bd. Internat. Jour. Psycho-analytic Psychotherapy, 1979-83; reviewer Am. Jour. Psychiatry, 1983—, Jour. Neuropsychiatry and Clin. Neuro Scis., 1988-90; contbr. articles to profl. jours.; cons. (film) Suicide Prevention: The Physician's Role, 1967, Highlights of the 1964 American Psychiatric Association; cons., participant The Thin Edge--Guilt., 1975. Assoc. chief psychiatrist L.A. Suicide Prevention Ctr., 1968-76, prin. investigator; mem. adv. com. Walter Briehl Human Rights Found., 1984; v.p., bd. dirs. Suicide Prevention Ctr., Inc.; bd. dirs. Inst. Suicide Prevention, L.A., 1996, chmn. funding a crisis line com., 1997; bd. dirs. We. div. Am. Found. Suicide Prevention, 1998—. Rsch. grantee Founds. Fund Rsch. Psychiatry, 1963, NIMH, 1970. Fellow Am. Psychiatric Assn. (life), Am. Acad. Psychoanalysis (pres. 1974, chmn. nominating com. 1975, trustee, chmn. com. on rsch., mem. edtl. bd. The Acad., presdl. citation 1975); mem. Internat. Psychoanalytic Assn., Internat. Assn. Suicide Prevention, Am. Psychoanalytic Assn. (cert. 1977, mem. com. liason with AAAS 1977-80), Am. Assn. Suicidology, (founder, mem. edtl. bd. Life-Threatening Behavior, cert. recognition 1996) Inst. Contemporary Psychoanalysis (founding mem., trustee 1990-93), So. Calif. Psychoanalytic Inst. (pres., tng. and supervising analyst, mem. selection rsch. clin. assocs. com.), So. Calif. Psychoanalytic Soc. (dir. rsch. divsn. 1970-81, chief investigator 1976 88, chmn. com. rsch. award stds. 1979, pres.-elect 1980, 86, pres. 1981, 87-90), Med. Rsch. Assn. So. Calif., So. Calif. Psychiat. Soc. (mem. consultation and violence panel), L.A. County Med. Assn. Office: 505 N Bonhill Rd Los Angeles CA 90049-2325 E-mail: ndtmd@aol.com

TABRISKY, JOSEPH, radiologist, educator; b. Boston, June 23, 1931; s. [illegible] laude, Tufts U., 1956; m. Phyllis Eleanor Page, Apr. 23, 1955; children: Joseph Page, Elizabeth Ann, William Page. Flexible intern U. Ill. Hosp., 1956-57; resident in radiology Fitzsimons Army Hosp., 1958-60; instr, radiology Tufts U. Med. Sch., 1964-65; cons. radiologist Swedish Med. Center, Denver, 1966-68; chief radiologist Kaiser Found. Hosp., Harbor City, Calif., 1968-72; mem. faculty UCLA Med. Sch., 1972— , prof. radiol. scis., 1975-92, prof emeritus, 1993—, vice chmn. dept., 1976-92 , exec. policy com. radiol. scis.; chmn. radiology dept. Harbor-UCLA Med. Ctr., 1975-92 , pres. faculty soc., 1979-80, exec. dir. MR/CT Imaging Ctr., bd. dirs. Rsch. Ednl. Inst., Harbor Collegium/UCLA Found.; chief exec. officer Vascular Biometrics Inc.; steering com. Harvard U., 1952; cons. L.A. County Dept. Pub. Health; chmn. L.A. County Radiol. Standards Com., 1979. Mem. Harvard-Radcliffe Schs. Com.; chmn., bd. dirs., treas., Harbor-UCLA Med. Found.; chmn. UCLA Coun. for Ednl. Devel. Maj. M.C., U.S. Army, 1957-63. Recipient Silver Knight award Nat. Mgmt. Assn., 1992. Diplomate Am. Bd. Radiology. Fellow Am. Coll. Radiology, Univ. Radcom Assn. (chief exec. officer 1987-89); mem. Radiol. Soc. N. Am., Calif. Med. Assn., Calif. Radiol. Soc., L.A. Med. Assn., L.A. Radiol. Soc., Alpha Omega Alpha. Contbr. articles to med. jours. Office: 1000 W Carson St Torrance CA 90502-2004

TAFOYA, ARTHUR N. bishop; b. Alameda, N.Mex., Mar. 2, 1933; s. Nicholas and Rosita Tafoya. Ed., St. Thomas Sem., Denver, Conception (Mo.) Sem. Ordained priest Roman Cath. Ch., 1962. Asst. pastor Holy Rosary Parish, Albuquerque, 1962-65; pastor Northern N.Mex., from 1965, San Jose Parish, Albuquerque; rector Immaculate Heart of Mary Sem., Santa Fe; ordained bishop of Pueblo Colo., 1980—. Office: Diocese of Pueblo 1001 N Grand Ave Pueblo CO 81003-2915

TAFT, DAVID DAKIN, chemical executive; b. Cleve., Mar. 27, 1938; s. Kingsley A. and Louise D. T.; m. Sararose Leonard, July 8, 1961; children: Amy Rose, Kingsley Leonard, Elisabeth. AB, Kenyon Coll., 1960; PhD in Chemistry, Mich. State U., 1963. Sr. rsch. chemist Archer-Daniels Midland, 1964-67; mgr. polymer rsch. Ashland Chem., 1967-72; dir. comml. devel. Gen. Mills Chems., 1972-74; v.p., dir. R&D, Henkel Corp., 1973-78, group v.p. consumer and splty. products, 1978-81, exec. v.p. chem. products div., dir., 1981-82; gen. mgr. materials div. Raychem Corp., Menlo Park, Calif., 1983-84; gen. mgr. Telecom group, 1983-86; v.p. Raychem Corp., 1984-93, v.p. manufacuturing, 1986-93; COO Landec Corp., Menlo Park, Calif., 1993—. Author: Fundamentals of Powder Coatings; bd. editors Research Mgmt. Jour.; patentee in field. Trustee Mpls. Soc. Fine Arts, 1981-83, Kenyon Coll., 1990—; vice chmn. Mem. Comml. Devel. Assn., Indsl. Research Inst., Am. Chem. Soc., Kenyon Alumni Assn. (pres. 1978), Circus Club. Republican. Office: Landec Corp 3603 Haven Ave Menlo Park CA 94025-1010 E-mail: dtaft@landec.com

TAGOMORI, HOWARD H. protective services official; Chief of police, Maui, Hawaii; U.S. marshall Honolulu, 1999—. Office: US Marshall 300 Ala Moana Blvd Rm C101 Honolulu HI 96850-0101

TAKAKURA, TAMIO, bank official; BS, Kobe U., Japan; MBA, U. Ill. Various mgmt. positions Sanwa Bank Calif., Golden State Sanwa Bank, Bus. Credit Corp, San Francisco/L.A./Chgo., 1968-88; sr. mgr. Sanwa Bank, Ltd. Internat. Divsn., Japan, 1988-91; sr. exec. v.p., CEO Sanwa Bank Calif., 1991-96, pres., CEO, 1996—. Office: Sanwa Bank Calif 601 S Figueroa St Los Angeles CA 90017

TAKASUGI, PATRICK A. state agency administrator; m. Suzanne Takasugi; children: Taylor, Cole, Paige. BA in Polit. Sci., Albertson Coll. of Idaho, 1971. Dir./sec. Idaho State Dept. Agr., 1996—. Served to capt. U.S. Army. Recipient Outstanding Young Farmer and Rancher award Idaho Farm Bur., 1979, Young Farmer of Idaho award Idaho Jaycees, 1981, Outstanding Svc. award Idaho Crop Improvement Assn., 1991, Disting. Alumni Svc. award Albertson Coll. Idaho, 1996; named to Idaho Co-op Hall of Fame, 2000. Mem. Idaho Farm Bur. Fedn. (v.p.), Idaho Farm Bur. (bd. dirs.), Canyon County Farm Bur. (pres.), Western Assn. State Dirs. Agr. (v.p., pres., sec.-treas.), Nat. Assn. State Dirs. Agr. (bd. dirs.), Idaho Crop Improvement Assn. (pres.), N.W. Alfalfa Seed Growers Assn. (pres.), Idaho Alfalfa Seed Growers Assn. (pres.). Office: Idaho Dept Agr PO Box 790 Boise ID 83701-0790

TAKASUGI, ROBERT MITSUHIRO, federal judge; b. Tacoma, Sept. 12, 1930; s. Hidesaburo and Kayo (Otsuki) T.; m. Dorothy O. Takasugi; children: Jon Robert, Lesli Mari. BS, UCLA, 1953; LLB, JD, U. So. Calif., 1959. Bar: Calif. bar 1960. Practiced law, Los Angeles, 1960-73; judge East Los Angeles Municipal Ct., 1973-75, adminstrv. judge, 1974, presiding judge, 1975; judge Superior Ct., County of Los Angeles, 1975-76; U.S. dist. judge U.S. Dist. Ct. (cen. dist.) Calif., 1976—. Nat. legal counsel Japanese Am. Citizens League; guest lectr. law seminars Harvard U. Law Sch. Careers Symposium; commencement spkr.; mem. Legion Lex U. So. Calif. Law Ctr.; mem. Civil Justice Reform Act and Alt. Dispute Resolution Com., mem. Adv. Com. on Codes of Conduct of the Jud. Conf. of the U.S., 1987-92, Code of Conduct of Judges. Mem. editorial bd. U. So. Calif. Law Rev., 1959; contbr. articles to profl. jours. Calif. adv. com. Western Regional Office, U.S. Commn. on Civil Rights, 1983-85; chmn. blue ribbon com. for selection of chancellor L.A. C.C. With U.S. Army, 1953-55. Harry J. Bauer scholar, 1959; recipient U.S. Mil. Man of Yr. award for Far East Theater U.S. Army, 1954, Jud. Excellence award Criminal Cts. Bar Assn., cert. of merit Japanese-Am. Bar Assn., Lifetime Achievement award, 2000, Disting. Svc. award Asian Pacific Ctr. and Pacific Clinics, 1994, Freedom award Sertoma, 1995, Pub. Svc. award Asian Pacific Am. Legal Ctr. So. Calif., 1995, Trailblazer award So. Calif. region NAPABA, 1995, Spl. award Mex.-Am. Bar Assn., 1996, Spirit of Excellence award ABA, 1998, Pub. Svc. award Japanese Am. Citizens League, 1999; named Judge of Yr. Century City Bar Assn., 1995. Mem. U. So. Calif. Law Alumni Assn. (dir.). Office: US Dist Ct 312 N Spring St Los Angeles CA 90012-4701

TAKIS, STEPHANIE, state senator; Ret.; Dem. rep. dist. 36 Colo. Ho. of Reps., 1996-2000; Dem. senator dist. 25 Colo. State Senate, 2000—. Mem. bus. affairs and labor and fin. coms. Colo. Ho. of Reps.; mem. govt., vets. and mil. rels. and transp. and legis. audit coms. Colo. State Senate, vice chmn. bus., labor and fin. com. Office: 1927 Ironton Aurora CO 80010 also: Colo State Senate State Capitol 200 E Colfax Rm 307 Denver CO 80203 E-mail: stakis@sni.net

TAKUMI, ROY MITSUO, state legislator; b. Honolulu, Oct. 13, 1952; m. Wanda A. Kutaka; children: Aisha, Jaron. BA, Friends World Coll., 1991; MPA, U. Hawaii, 1993. Cmty. organizer, Osaka, Japan, 1977-83; program dir. Am. Friends Svc. Com., Honolulu, 1984-90; polit. dir. Hawaii State AFL-CIO, Honolulu, 1990-92, comms. dir., 1992—. Rep. Ho. of Reps., Honolulu, 1992—. Office: State Ho Reps State Capitol Honolulu HI 96813 E-mail: reptakumi@capitol.hawaii.gov

TALBERT, MELVIN GEORGE, bishop; b. Clinton, La., June 14, 1934; s. Nettles and Florence (George) T.; m. Marilyn Magee; 1 child, Evangeline. BA, So. U., 1959; MDiv, Interdenominational Theol. Ctr., Gammon Theol. Sem., Atlanta, 1962; DD hon., Huston Tillotson Coll., Austin, 1972; LLD (hon.), U. Puget Sound, Tacoma, 1987. Ordained deacon, Meth. Ch., 1960 , elder, 1962, elected to episcopacy, United Meth. Ch., 1980. Pastor Boyd Chapel, Jefferson City, Tenn., 1960-61, Rising Sun, Sunrise, 1960-61, St. John's Ch., L.A., 1961-62, Wesley Ch., L.A., 1962-64, Hamilton Ch., L.A., 1964-67; mem. staff So. Calif.-Ariz. Conf. United Meth. Ch., L.A., 1967-68, dist. supr. Long Beach dist., 1968-73; gen. sec. Gen. Bd. Discipleship, Nashville, 1973-80; resident bishop Seattle area Pacific N.W. conf. United Meth. Ch., 1980-88, sec. coun. bishops, 1988—96, bishop San Francisco area, 1988—2000; mem. exec. com. World Meth. Coun., 1976-81, 84—; mem. governing bd. Nat. Coun. Chs., 1980—; v.p., chmn. funding com. Gen. Commn. on Religion and Race, 1980-84, pres., 1984-88; chmn. Missional Priority Coordinating com. Gen. Coun. Ministries, 1980-84; mem. Gen. Commn. on Christian Unity and Interreligious Concerns, 1984—96, African Ch. Growth and Devel. Com., 1981-84; pres. Nat. Coun. of Churches in Christ in U.S.A., 1996—97. Mem. steering com. Student Non-Violent Coordinating com. Atlanta U. Ctr., 1960-61; trustee Gammon Theol. Sem., Atlanta, 1976— , U. Puget Sound, Tacoma, 1980-88 , Sch. Theology at Claremont, Calif., 1981-88, Pacific Sch. Religion, 1988—; bd. dirs. Glide Found., 1988—; ecumenical officer Coun. of Bishops, 2000-. Recipient award of merit for outstanding svc. in Christian edn. Gen. Bd. Edn., 1971; recipient Spl. achievement award Nat. Assn. Black Bus. Women, 1971; Nat. Meth. scholar, 1960; Crusade scholar, 1961 Mem. Theta Phi Democrat. Home: 108 Rausch Dr Brentwood TN 37027

TALBOT, STEPHEN HENDERSON, television producer, writer; b. Hollywood, Calif., Feb. 28, 1949; s. Lyle and Margaret (Epple) T.; m. Pippa Gordon; children: Dashiell, Caitlin. BA, Wesleyan U., 1970. Asst. to pres., lectr. Am. studies SUNY, Old Westbury, 1970-73; reporter Internews, Berkeley, Calif., 1973-79; producer, reporter KQED-TV, San Francisco, 1980-89; producer, writer Frontline (PBS), San Francisco, 1992—. Appeared in Leave It To Beaver as Gilbert, 1958-63, also Twilight Zone, Perry Mason, Lassie, others; prodr., co-writer for Frontline: The Best Campaign Money Can Buy (Columbia U. Dupont award), 1992, Rush Limbaugh's America, 1995, The Long March of Newt Gingrich, 1996, Justice for Sale, 1999 (Gold medal Houston Internat. Film Festival 2000); writer, co-prodr.: (PBS-TV) Beryl Markham, 1986, Ken Kesey, 1987, Carlos Fuentes, 1989, Maxine Hong Kingston, 1990, John Dos Passos, 1994, Frontline: Spying on Saddam, 1999; prodr., writer: (documentary) The Case of Dashiell Hammett, 1982 (Peabody award, Edgar Allan Poe award), 1968: The Year That Shaped a Generation, 1998, Frontline: The Battle Over School Choice, 2000; co-prodr., reporter: (documentary) Broken Arrow, 1980 (George Peabody & George Polk award), others; contbr. articles to mags. including Salon and Washington Post Mag. Recipient Thomas Storke Internat. Journalism award World Affairs Coun. No. Calif., San Francisco, 1983, 86, Golden Gate award San Francisco Film Festival, 1986, 89, Emmy award NATAS, 1980-83, 87-88, 90-91. Mem. Writer's Guild Am. West, Am. Fedn. TV and Radio Artists. Office: Ctr Investigative Reporting 131 Steuart St Ste 600 San Francisco CA 94105-1238 E-mail: talbot1@mindspring.com

TALBOTT, JOHN, mayor; m. Claudia Field; 2 children. BA in Soc. Sci., Coll. Great Falls, 1976; MA in Polit. Sci., Ctrl. Mich. U., 1978. Enlisted USAF, advanced through grades to col., ret., 1982, served in various assignments including Joint Svc. Commands, past comdr. commn. squadron Mont.; with Jet Propulsion Lab, to 1989; mayor City of Spokane, Washington. Active cmty. devel. and politics, Spokane, 1989—. Office: Office of Mayor City Hall 5th Fl 808 W Spokane Falls Blvd Spokane WA 99201-3333

TALIAFERRO, ROBERT See BROOKE, TAL

TALKE, FRANK EBERHARD, education educator; b. Dresden, Germany, Sept. 10, 1939; came to U.S., 1965; s. Artur and Louise T.; m. Kathryn Ann Talke; children: Stefan, Kristen, Kurt. Diploma Engring., U. Stuttgart, Germany, 1965; MS, U. Calif., Berkeley, 1966, PhD, 1968. Mgr. IBM, San Jose, Calif., 1969-86; prof. U. Calif. San Diego, 1986—, chair AMES dept., 1993-95. Vis. prof. U. Calif. Berkeley, 1984. Author numerous tech. papers; patentee in field. Mem. ASME, IEEE (chair local sect. 1990-92), Nat. Acad. Engring. Office: U Calif San Diego 9500 Gilman Dr La Jolla CA 92093-5004

TALLMAN, RICHARD C. federal judge, lawyer; b. Oakland, Calif., Mar. 3, 1953; s. Kenneth A. and Jean M. (Kemppe) T.; m. Cynthia Ostolaza, Nov. 14, 1981. BSC, U. Santa Clara, 1975; JD, Northwestern U., 1978. Bar: Calif. 1978, Wash. 1979, U.S. Dist. Ct. (no. dist.) Calif. 1979, U.S. Dist. Ct. (we. dist.) Wash. 1979, U.S. Ct. Appeals (9th cir.) 1979, U.S. Dist. Ct. Hawaii 1986, U.S. Supreme Ct. 1997, U.S. Dist. Ct. (ea. dist.) Wash. 1998. Law clk to Hon. Morrell E. Sharp U.S. Dist. Ct. (we. dist.) Wash., Seattle, 1978-79; trial atty. U.S. Dept. Justice, Washington, 1979-80; asst. U.S. atty. (we. dist.) Wash., Seattle, 1980-83; ptnr. Schweppe, Krug & Tausend, PS, Seattle, 1983-89; mem. Bogle & Gates, PLLC, Seattle, 1990-99; ptnr. Tallman & Severin, LLP, Seattle, 1999-2000; apptd. U.S. cir. judge U.S. Ct. Appeals (9th cir.), 2000—. Chmn. western dist. Wash. Lawyer Reps. to Ninth Cir. Jud. Conf., 1996-97. Instr. Nat. Park Svc. Seasonal Ranger Acad., Everett and Mt. Vernon, Wash., 1983-93; chmn. Edmonds C.C. Found., Lynnwood, Wash., 1990-92; gen. counsel Seattle-King County Crime Stoppers, 1987-99; mem. exec. bd. Chief Seattle coun. Boy Scouts Am., 1997—. Mem. ABA, FBA (trustee 1992-93, v.p. 1994, pres. 1995), Seattle-King County Bar Assn., Rainier Club, Wash. Athletic Club. Avocations: hunting, hiking, fishing. Office: Park Place Bldg 1200 Sixth Avenue 21st FL Seattle WA 98101-3123

TALMADGE, PHILIP ALBERT, state supreme court justice, former state senator; b. Seattle, Apr. 23, 1952; s. Judson H., Jr. and Jeanne C. T.; m. Darlene L. Nelson, Sept. 6, 1970; children: Adam, Matthew, Jessica, Jonathan, Annemarie. BA magna cum laude, Yale U., 1973; JD, U. Wash., 1976. Bar: Wash. 1976. Assoc. Karr Tuttle Campbell, 1976-89; pres. Talmadge & Cutler, P.S., 1989-95; senator State of Wash., 1979-94; justice Supreme Ct. Wash., 1995-2001. Chair Senate Judiciary Com., 1981, 83-87, Senate Health and Human Svcs. Com., 1992-95, Wash. Senate, 1978-94, ways and means com., children and family svc. com., edn. com. Fellow Am. Assn. Appellate Lawyers; mem. King County Bar Assn., Wash. State Bar Assn.. Author: The Nixon Doctrine and the Reaction of Three Asian Nations, 1973; editor Law Rev., U. Washl., 1975-76; contbr. articles to profl. jours.

TALMAGE, DAVID WILSON, microbiology and medical educator, physician, former university administrator; b. Kwangju, Korea, Sept. 15, 1919; s. John Van Neste and Eliza (Emerson) T.; m. LaVeryn Marie Hunicke, June 23, 1944; children: Janet, Marilyn, David, Mark, Carol. Student, Maryville (Tenn.) Coll., 1937-38; BS, Davidson (N.C.) Coll., 1941; MD, Washington U., St. Louis, 1944. Intern Ga. Baptist Hosp., 1944-45; resident medicine Barnes Hosp., St. Louis, 1948-50, fellow medicine, 1950-51; asst. prof. pathology U. Pitts., 1951-52; asst. prof., then assoc. prof. medicine U. Chgo., 1952-59; prof. medicine U. Colo., 1959—, prof. microbiology, 1960-86, disting. prof., 1986—, chmn. dept., 1963-65, assoc. dean, 1966-68, dean, 1969-71; dir. Webb-Waring Lung Inst., 1973-83, assoc. dean for research, 1983-86. Mem. nat. council Nat. Inst. Allergy and Infectious Diseases, NIH, 1963-66, 73-77 Author: (with John Cann) Chemistry of Immunity in Health and Disease; editor: Jour. Allergy, 1963-67, (with M. Samter) Immunological Diseases. Served with M.C. AUS, 1945-48. Markle scholar, 1955-60 Mem. NAS, Inst. Medicine, Am. Acad. Allergy (pres.), Am. Assn. Immunologists (pres.), Phi Beta Kappa, Alpha Omega Alpha. Fax: 303-388-6955. E-mail: davidtal@juno.com

TAM, ROD, state legislator; b. Honolulu, Oct. 3, 1953; s. Robert H.C. and Patsy Y.T. (Young) T.; m. Lynnette Tam, two children. BBA, U. Hawaii, 1977. Mem. Hawaii Ho. of Reps., Honolulu, 1982-94, Hawaii Senate, Dist. 13, Honolulu, 1994—; bus. agent Hawaii State Org. Police Ofcrs.; research analyst Hawaii Transportation Assoc.; admin. specialist Research Corp. U. Hawaii; budget analyst State Senate Ways & Means Com. Chmn. Neighborhood Bd., Honolulu, 1979-82; v.p. Chinese Physical Culture Assoc.; Kalihi-Liliha-Nuuanu-Palama Community Network. Named to Three Outstanding Young Persons o1 1983, Hawaii Jaycees, 1983; recipient Freedom award Sertoma Club, 1984, Librs. award for Leadership and Support, Librs. Assn. Hawaii, 1987. Democrat. Roman Catholic. Office: Hawaii State Capitol 415 S Beretania St Rm 220 Honolulu HI 96813-2407

TAMBS, LEWIS ARTHUR, diplomat, historian, educator; b. San Diego, July 7, 1927; s. Fred B. and Marguerite Johanna (Tambs) Jones; m. Phyllis Ann Greer, 1982; children: Kari, Kristin, Jennifer, Heidi, Greer, Michael, Alexa. B.S., U. Calif.-Berkeley, Berkeley, 1953; M.A., U. Calif.-Santa Barbara, 1962, Ph.D., 1967. Plant engr. Standard Brands, San Francisco, 1953-54; pipeline engr. Creole Petroleum Co., Caracas, Maracaibo, Venezuela, 1954-57; gen. mgr. Cacyp, Maracaibo, 1957-59; instr. Creighton U., 1965-67, asst. prof., 1967-69; prof. history Ariz. State U., Tempe, 1969-82, 87—, dir. Center Latin Am. Studies, 1972-76; cons. Nat. Security Council, 1982-83; U.S. ambassador to Colombia, 1983-85; U.S. ambassador to Costa Rica, 1985-87. Author: East European and Soviet Economic Affairs, 1975, Historiography, Method and History Teaching, 1975, (with others) Hitler's Spanish Legion, 1979; editor: United States Policy Toward Latin America, 1976, Inter-American Policy for the 80's; co-editor: Santa Fe IV, 2000; co-author periodical guides; contbr. articles to profl. jours. Bd. dirs. Ariz.-Mex. Commn., 1974-82, Coun. Inter-Am. Security, 1979-90. With U.S. Army, 1945-47, 50-51. Faculty grantee Ariz. State U., 1970, 71, 74, 78, 79. Roman Catholic. Office: Ariz State U Dept History Tempe AZ 85287-2501

TAMKE, GEORGE WILLIAM, printing/copying company executive; b. Beacon, N.Y., May 16, 1947; s. George William and Josephine Edna (Carbone) T.; m. Christine Barbara MacLeod, June 28, 1969; children: Kara Lee, Shannon. BSChemE, Vanderbilt U., 1969; MS in Mgmt. Sci., Stanford U., 1979. With IBM, N.Y., Fla., Calif., Ga., Minn., 1969-86, dir. orgn. planning and sec. to corp. mgmt. com. N.Y., 1981-82, v.p. mfg. Communication Products div., 1982-83, v.p. display products Communication Products div., 1983-84, asst. group exec. Info Systems, Products Group, 1984-86; pres. Cullinet Software, Inc., Westwood, Mass., 1986-87, chief ops. officer, 1987-88; exec. v.p. Emerson Electric Co., St. Louis, 1989—; CEO Kinkos, 2001—. CEO Astec (BSR) Plc, Hong Kong, 1989—. Contbr. articles to profl. jours. Avocations: tennis, golf. Home: 9915 Litzsinger Rd Saint Louis MO 63124-1129 Office: Kinkos 255 West Stanely Ave Ventura CA 93002

TAMKIN, CURTIS SLOANE, real estate development company executive; b. Boston, Sept. 21, 1936; s. Hayward and Etta (Goldfarb) T.; m. Priscilla Martin, Oct. 18, 1975; 1 child, Curtis Sloane. BA in Econs., Stanford U., 1958. V.p., treas., dir. Hayward Tamkin & Co., Inc., mortgage bankers, L.A., 1963-70; mng. ptnr. Property Devel. Co., L.A., 1970-82; pres. The Tamkin Co., 1982—. Mem. bd. govs. Music Ctr. L.A., 1974-98; pres. L.A. Master Chorale Assn., 1974-78; mem. vis. com. Stanford U. Librs., 1982-86; bd. dirs. L.A. Philharm. Assn., 1985—. Lt. (j.g.) USNR, 1960-63. Mem. Mem. Founders League L.A. Music Ctr. (pres. 1988-98, chmn. emeritus 1998), L.a. Jr. C. of c.. (dir. 1968-69), Pacific Coun. Internat. Policy, Burlingame Country. Home: 1230 Stone Canyon Rd Los Angeles CA 90077-2920 Office: 9460 Wilshire Blvd Beverly Hills CA 90212-2732

TAMKIN, S. JEROME, business executive, consultant; b. L.A., Apr. 19, 1926; s. William W. and Thelma (Brandel) T.; m. Judith Deborah, Mar. 23, 1963; children: Windy Lynn, Gary William, Sherry Dawn. B.S., U. So. Calif., 1950; M.A., Fremont Coll., 1951, Ph.D., 1952; LL.D., St. Andrews U., London, 1954. Mem. rsch. staff chemistry dept. U. Calif. at Los Angeles, 1943; rsch. chemist, analyst supr. synthetic rubber div. U.S. Rubber Co., 1943-44; pres., gen. mgr. Majicolor, Inc., Los Angeles, 1947-49; rsch. engr. Coll. Engring., U. So. Calif., 1946-48; gen. mgr. Pan Pacific Oil Co., Long Beach, Calif., 1948-55; plant mgr. indsl. sales and mfg., 1953-55; v.p., sales mgr. Wilco Co., Los Angeles, 1948-55, v.p. charge indsl. sales and mfg., 1953-55; v.p., sales mgr. Unit Chem. Corp., Los Angeles, 1955-56; pres. Phillips Mfg. Co. (merger Instl. Food Equipment Corp.), Los Angeles, 1957-62, Waste King Corp. (subs. Instl. Food Equipment Corp.), 1962-67; also dir.; v.p., dir. Dyna Mfg. Co., Los Angeles, 1962-68; pres., dir. Profl. Rsch. Inc., Los Angeles, 1965-73; exec. v.p. Am. Med. Internat., Inc., Beverly Hills, Calif., 1966-71, dir., 1966-89; sec., dir. Rodger Young, Inc., L.A., 1971-77; pres., chmn. bd. TGT Petroleum Corp., Wichita, 1972—; pres., dir. Tamkin Cons. Corp., 1978—; owner, operator Tamkin Securities Co., 1979-86; vice chair bd., dir. Integrated Voice Solutions Inc., Chattanooga, 1991-96; bd. dirs. CAPP Care Inc., Newport Beach, Calif., 1991-99. Tech. cons. Daylin Inc., Beverly Hills, 1973-75; bd. dirs. Healthcare Decisions, Inc., Newport Beach, Calif., 1996-99. Contbr. articles to profl. jours.; patentee electronic gas detector, circuits for automatic control hazardous vapors. Cmty. warden W. Adams-Baldwin Hills Cmty. CD, 1950—52; bd. govs. West Los Angeles County coun. Boy Scouts Am., Technion-Israel Inst. of Tech., 2001—; dep. sheriff L.A. County, 1949; bd. dir. Sunair Home Asthmatic Chilren; city commr. L.A. Bd. Environ. Quality, 1972—73; bd. dir. Recovery Found., Fund for Higher Edn.; mem. exec. com. adv. coun. crime prevention L.A. Police, 1985—; trustee, bd. visitors U. Calif.-Irvine Coll. Medicine, 1989—; bd.. visitors UCLA Sch. Medicine, 1990—; trustee Scripps Found. for Medicine and Sci., 1996—; bd. dir. U. of Judaism, 1999—, UCLA Brain Mapping Found., 1999—. Officer USNR, 1944—46. Mem. AIM, Am. Mgmt. Assn., Inst. Aero. Scis., Am. Soc. Naval Engrs., Soc. Am. Mil. Engrs., Am. Chem. Soc., IEEE, Soc. Motion Picture and TV Engrs., Am. Inst. Chem. Engrs., Soc. Advancement Mgmt., U.S. Naval Inst., Calif. Scholarship Fedn. (life), Nat. Eagle Scout Assn., Sunrise Country Club, The Springs Country Club, Malibu Riding and Tennis Club, Alpha Eta Rho. Office: 2100 Sawtelle Blvd Ste 201 Los Angeles CA 90025-6264

TAN, ENG MENG, immunologist, biomedical scientist; b. Seremban, Malaysia, Aug. 26, 1926; came to U.S., 1950; s. Ming Kee and Chooi Eng (Ang) T.; m. Liselotte Filippi, June 30, 1962; children: Philip, Peter. BA, Johns Hopkins U., 1952, MD, 1956. Intern Duke U., Durham, N.C., 1956-57; resident, fellow Case-We. Res. U., Cleve., 1957-62; rsch. assoc. Rockefeller U., N.Y.C., Calif., 1962-65; asst. prof. Washington U. Sch. Medicine, St. Louis, 1965-67; assoc. mem. Scripps Rsch. Inst., LaJolla, 1967-77; prof. U. Colo. Sch. Medicine, Denver, 1977-82; dir. Autoimmune Disease Ctr., LaJolla, Md., 1982—. Chmn. allergy & immunology rsch. com. NIH, Bethesda, Md., 1982-84; mem. nat. arthritis adv. bd. HHS, Washington, 1981-85. Contbr. chpts. in books, articles to profl. jours. Named to Nat. Lupus Hall Fame, 1984; recipient U.S. Sr. Scientist award Humboldt Found., Germany, 1986, award Ciba-Giegy-Internet League Against Rheumatism, 1989, Carol Nachman award Wiesbaden, Germany, 1989, Lee Howley Sr. award Arthritis Found., 1989, Paul Klemperer award and medal N.Y. Acad. Medicine, 1993, City Medicine award, Durham, N.C., 1996, Hon. prof. Shanghai 2d Med. U., Disting. Med. Alumnus award Duke U., 2000. Fellow AAAS; mem. Am. Coll. Rheumatology (pres. 1984-85, chmn. Blue Ribbon com. Future Acad. Rheumatology 1997-98, Disting. Investigator award 1991, Gold medal award 1998), Assn. Am. Physicians, Am. Soc. Clin. Investigation, Western Assn. Physicians (v.p. 1980-81), Am. Assn. Immunologists, Brazilian Soc. Rheumatology (hon.), Australian Ryeumatism Assn. (hon.), Brit. Soc. Rheumatology (hon.), Mex. Nat. Acad. Medicine (hon.). Achievements include research on antibodies and antigens in cancer and in autoimmune diseases, systemic lupus erythematosus, scleroderma, Sjogren's syndrome, myositis and mixed connective tissue disease; relationship of autoantibodies to pathogenesis. Home: 8303 Sugarman Dr La Jolla CA 92037-2224 Office: Scripps Rsch Inst 10550 N Torrey Pines Rd La Jolla CA 92037-1000 E-mail: emtan@scripps.edu

TAN, WILLIAM LEW, lawyer; b. West Hollywood, Calif., July 25, 1949; s. James Tan Lew and Choon Guey Louie; m. Shelly Mieko Ushio. BA, U. Pa., 1971; JD, U. Calif. Hastings Coll. Law, San Francisco, 1974. Bar: Calif. 1975, U.S. Dist. Ct. (cen. dist.) Calif. 1975, U.S. Ct. Appeals (9th cir.) 1975, U.S. Supreme Ct. 1979. Assoc. Hiram W. Kwan, Los Angeles, 1974-79; ptnr. Mock & Tan, Los Angeles, 1979-80; sole practice Los Angeles, 1980-81; ptnr. Tan & Sakiyama, L.A., 1981-86, 88—, Tan & Sakiyama, P.C., L.A., 1986-88. Bd. dirs. Am. Bus. Network, L.A.; pres., bd. dirs. Asian Rsch. Cons., L.A., 1983-85; mem. adv. bd. Cathay Bank, 1990-91; bd. dirs. Asian Pacific Am. Legal Ctr. Co-founder Asian Pacific Am. Roundtable, L.A., 1981; chmn. bd. dirs. Leadership Edn. for Asian-Pacifics, L.A., 1984-87; alt. del. Dem. Nat. Conv., San Francisco, 1984; mem. Calif. State Bd. Pharmacy, Sacramento, 1984-92, v.p., 1988-91, pres., 1991-92; mem. L.A. City and County Crime Crisis Task Force, 1981, L.A. Asian Pacific Heritage Week Com., 1980-85, Asian Pacific Women's Network, L.A., 1981, L.A. City Atty.'s Blue Ribbon Com. of Advisors, 1981, cmty. adv. bd. to Mayor of L.A., 1984, allocations vol. liaison team health and therapy divsn. United Way, L.A., 1986, mem. nominating com. bd. dirs. 1994-99; bd. dirs. Chinatown Svc. Ctr., L.A., 1983; conf. advisor U.S.-Asia, L.A., 1981-83; mem. L.A. city atty. Housing Adv. Com.; mem. Pacific Bell Consumer Product Adv. Panel, 1986-90; vice chair cmty. adv. bd. Sta. KCET-TV, PBA, 1993-94; mem. adv. commn. State of Calif. Com. on State Procurement Practices, 1989-90; mem. L.A. City Attys. Citizens' Task Force on Pvt. Club Discrimination, 1989-90; mem. Calif. Med. Summit, 1993; mem. Mayor's Commn. Children, Youth and Families, 1993-96; mem. pub. access subcom. Mayor's Spl. adv. Com. on Tech. Implementation, 1994-96; bd. dirs. Asian Pacific Am. Legal Ctr., 1993—, vice chair, 1999—. Named one of Outstanding Young Men of Am., 1979. Mem. Calif. State Bar Assn. (vice chmn. com. ethnic minority rels. 1983-85, chmn. pub. affairs com. 1981-82, mem. others), L.A. County Bar Assn. (trustee 1984-86, vice chair human rights com. 1980-82, mem. numerous coms.), So. Calif. Chinese Lawyers Assn. (pres. 1980-81, chmn. 1987-88, mem. various coms.), Minority Bar Assn. (chmn. 1981-82, sec. 1980-81, chmn. adv. bd. 1982-83), Asian Pacific Bar of Calif., Nat. Asian Pacific Am. Bar, Japanese Am. Bar Assn., Bench and Bar Media Coun., Consumer Attys. of Calif., Soc. Intercultural Edn. (conf. coord., advisor panelist tng. and rsch. com. 1983). Avocations: gourmet cooking, bicycling, swimming, tennis, water color painting. Office: 201 S Figueroa St Ste 390 Los Angeles CA 90012-2543 E-mail: wltlaw@aol.com

TANAKA, JOE SUEO, state legislator; b. Lahaina Maui, Hawaii, Sept. 15, 1941; m. Barbara Tanaka; children: Joanne, Aimee. AA, Golden West Coll.; BA in Econs. and Bus. Adminstrn., U. Hawaii, Hilo. Mem. Hawaii Senate, 1992-, asst. majority leader, 1992-93, mem. various coms., 1992-96, chair tourism and recreation com., 1993-96, vice chair transp. com., 1994, vice chair transp. & govt. affairs com., 1995-96; mem. Maui County Council, 1986-92. Mem. County Bd. Water Supply, Hawaii Criminal Justice Commn., Mayor's Com. for Betterment of Youth; mem. PTSA and band boosters Lihikai Sch.; mem. adv. bd. Family Cmty. Leadership; bd. dirs. Maui Econ. Opportunity, Inc., Maui Visitors Bur., Maui Econ. Bus. Devel.; chmn. econ. devel. and water devel. County Coun., 1986-88, chmn. econ. devel. and agr., 1988-90, chmn. human svcs., pks. and housing com., 1990-92. With U.S. Army, Vietnam. Democrat. Office: Hawaii State Capitol 415 S Beretania St Rm 223 Honolulu HI 96813-2407

TANAKA, KOUICHI ROBERT, hematologist, educator; b. Fresno, Calif., Dec. 15, 1926; s. Kenjiro and Teru (Arai) T.; m. Grace Mutsuko Sakaguchi, Oct. 23, 1965; children— Anne M., Nancy K., David K. B.S., Wayne State U., 1949, M.D., 1952. Intern Los Angeles County Gen. Hosp., 1952-53; resident, fellow Detroit Receiving Hosp., 1953-57; instr. Sch. Medicine, UCLA, 1957-59, asst. prof. medicine, 1959-61, assoc. prof. medicine, 1961-68, prof., 1968-97, prof. emeritus, 1998—; chief divsn. hematology Harbor-UCLA Med. Ctr., Torrance, 1961-97, chief hematology, 1998-2000. Served with AUS, 1946-48. Master ACP (gov. so. Calif. region I 1993-97); mem. Am. Fedn. Med. Rsch., Western Soc. Clin. Investigation, L.A. Soc. Internal Medicine (pres. 1971), Am. Soc. Hematology, Internat. Soc. Hematology, Western Assn. Physicians, Am. Soc. Clin. Investigation, Assn. Am. Physicians, Sigma Xi, Alpha Omega Alpha. Achievements include research on red cell metabolism. Home: 4 Cayuse Ln Rancho Palos Verdes CA 90275-5172 Office: Harbor UCLA Med Ctr Box 400 Torrance CA 90502-2059

TANAKA, RICHARD KOICHI, JR. architect, planner; b. San Jose, Calif., Oct. 16, 1931; s. Richard Inoru and Mae Yoshiko (Koga) T.; m. Barbara Hisako Kumagai, Oct. 7, 1961; children: Craig, Todd, Sandra, Trent. BArch, U. Mich., 1954; M in Urban Planning, Calif. State U., San Jose, 1978. Exec. v.p. Steinberg Group, San Jose, L.A., 1954—. Chair, bd. dirs. Happi House Restaurants, Inc., 1972—. Author: American on Trial, 1988. Dir. Human Rels. Com., San Jose, 1969-73; dir., pres. Bicentennial Com., San Jose, 1974-77; bd. dirs. Santa Clara County Sch. Bd. Assn., 1980—; pres. Internment of Local Japanese Ams., San Jose, 1984—; past pres., trustee East Side H.S. Dist., San Jose, 1971-92, Japanese Am. Citizens League, San Jose; mem. bd. govs. Boy Scouts Am., San Jose, 1978—, NCCJ, San Jose, 1976—; past pres. Tapestry and Talent, 1976-80; trustee San Jose/Evergreen C.C., 1992—, pres., 1993-94, 97-98; bd. dirs. Calif. C.C. Trustees, 1993—, pres., 1997-98. Mem. AIA, Am. Planning Inst., Constrn. Specification Inst., Rotary. Avocations: golf, painting. Home: 14811 Whipple Ct San Jose CA 95127-2570 Office: 60 Pierce Ave San Jose CA 95110-2819 E-mail: rktanaka@msn.com

TANCREDO, THOMAS G. congressman; b. North Denver, Colo., Dec. 20, 1945; m. Jackie Tancredo; 2 children. BA, U. No. Colo., 1968. Mem. Colo. State Ho. Reps., 1977-81; regional rep. U.S. Dept. Edn., 1981-93; mem. U.S. Congress from 6th Colo. dist., 1999—; mem. edn. and workforce, internat. rels., and resources coms. Office: US Ho Reps 418 Cannon Ho Office Bldgce Bldg Washington DC 20515-2701 also: 5601 S Broadway Ste 370 Littleton CO 80121-8079*

TANENBAUM, BASIL SAMUEL, engineering educator; b. Providence, Dec. 1, 1934; s. Harry Milton and Rena Ada (Herr) T.; m. Carol Binder, Aug. 26, 1956; children: Laurie, Stephen, David. BS summa cum laude, Brown U., 1956; MS, Yale U., 1957, PhD in Physics, 1960. Staff physicist Raytheon Co., Waltham, Mass., 1960-63; prof. engring. Case Western Res. U., Cleve., 1963-75; dean of faculty Harvey Mudd Coll., Claremont, Calif., 1975-93, prof. engring., 1975—, Norman F. Sprague, Jr. prof. of life scis., 1996—. Vis. scientist Cornell U., Arecibo (P.R.) Obs., 1968-69; vis. assoc. prof. Northwestern U., Evanston, Ill., 1970; vis. scholar U. Calif. Irvine Beckman Laser Inst., 1993-94, 98, 2000—; mem. sci. adv. com. Nat. Astronomy and Ionosphere Ctr., 1972-77, Calif. Poly. Inst., Pomona, 1976-87; mem. engring. and sci. adv. com. Calif. State U., Fullerton, 1976-87; mem. nat. adv. com. Rowan Coll., Glassboro, N.J., 1993-2000, chmn. curriculum subcom.; mem. Eisenhower adv. com. Calif. Postsecondary Edn. Com., 1993-97; dir. Minority Engrs. Indsl. Opportunity Program, 1973-75; dir. summer sci. program Thacher Sch., Ojai, Calif., 1977-82; mem. Pres.'s Adv. Coun., Olin Coll. Engring., Needham, Mass., 2001—; cons. various corps., univ. labs., govt. agys. Author: Plasma Physics, 1967. Trustee Western U. Health Scis., Pomona, Calif., 1997—. Woods Hole Oceanog. Inst. fellow, 1959; NSF fellow Yale U., 1956-60; sr. Sterling fellow Yale U., 1959; recipient Case Western Res. U. Wittke tchg. award, 1974, Henry T. Mudd prize Harvey Mudd Coll., 1996. Mem. AAAS, Am. Phys. Soc., Am. Soc. for Engring. Edn., IEEE, AAUP, Sigma Xi (rsch. award 1969) Home: 611 W Delaware Dr Claremont CA 91711-3458 Office: Harvey Mudd Coll 301 E 12th St Claremont CA 91711-5901 E-mail: sam_tanenbaum@hmc.edu

TANG, MAN-CHUNG, engineer, administrator; b. Xiao Qing, China, Feb. 22, 1938; came to U.S., 1968; s. Yu-Fung and Jing Tse Tang; m. Yee-Yun Fung, Aug. 26, 1966; children: Chin-Chung, Chin-Ning. BSc, Chu-Hai Coll., Hong Kong, 1959; MS, Tech. U. Darmstadt, Germany, 1964, PhD, 1965; DLitt (hon.), Chu-Hai U., Hong Kong, 1997. Registered profl. engr., N.Y., Mass., Fla., Ill., Wash., others. Bridge engr. GHH, Germany, 1965-68; sr. engr. Severud & Assocs., N.Y.C., 1968-70; v.p., chief engr. Dyckerhoff & Widmann, N.Y.C., 1970-78; pres. DRC Cons. Inc., N.Y.C., 1978—; chmn. bd. T.Y. Lin Internat., San Francisco, 1995—. Contbr. more than 100 articles to profl. jours. Recipient Leadership award Am. Segmental Bridge Inst., 1991, Roebling Life Achievement award Internat. Bridge Conf., 1998. Mem. ASCE (hon., named N.Y. Civil Engr. of Yr. 1989, Roebling award 1999), Nat. Acad. Engring. (life), Chinese Acad. Engring. (life mem.). Achievements include pioneer work in design and construction of cable-stayed and segmental bridges. Office: TY Lin Internat 825 Battery St San Francisco CA 94111-1528 E-mail: mtang@tylin.com

TANIGUCHI, BRIAN T. state senator; b. Honolulu, Nov. 7, 1951; m. Janice Taniguchi; children: Karli, Daniel. BA, U. Hawaii, 1973, JD, 1978. Law clk. to Judge Hiroshi Kato State Cir. Ct., Hawaii; pvt. practice atty.; legal counsel Internat. Savs. and Loan; Dem. rep. dist. 11 Hawaii Ho. of Reps., 1980-94; Dem. senator dist. 11 Hawaii State Senate, 1994—. Rsch. aide Gov. John Burns; bd. dirs. Koga Engring.; project coord. Hawaii Housing Authority; mem. health and human svcs., transp., mil. affairs, govt. ops. econ. devel. and tech. coms. Hawaii State Senate, chair ways and means com. Mem. Lyon Arboretum Coun.; advisor Waimanalo Residents Housing Devel.; adv. Ota Camp Residents Assn.; program coord. Waipahu Youth Project. E-mail: Sen.Taniguchi. Office: Hawaii State Senate Hawaii State Capitol Rm 210 415 S Beretania St Honolulu HI 96813 Fax: 808 586-6461

TANK, MAN-CHUNG, civil engineer; PhD in Engring., Tech. U., Darmstadt. Chmn. bd., tech. dir. T.Y. Lin Internat., San Francisco, 1995—. Mem. ASCE (Outstanding Civil Engring. Achievement award), NSPE (Outstanding Engring. Achievement award), Nat. Acad. Engring., Am. Concrete Inst., Prestressed Concrete Inst., Assn. Rational Environ. Alternatives, Internat. Assn. Bridge & Structural Engring. Office: T Y Lin Internat 825 Battery St San Francisco CA 94111-1528

TANNER, DEE BOSHARD, retired lawyer; b. Provo, Utah, Jan. 16, 1913; s. Myron Clark and Marie (Boshard) T.; m. Jane Barwick, Dec. 26, 1936 (div. Aug. 1962); children: Barry, Diane McDowell; m. Reeta Walker, Dec. 6, 1981. BA, U. Utah, 1935; LLB, Pacific Coast U., 1940; postgrad., Harvard U., 1936, Loyola U., L.A., 1937. Bar: Calif. 1943, U.S. Dist. Ct. (so. dist.) Calif. 1944, U.S. Ct. Appeals (9th cir.) 1947, ICC 1964, U.S. Dist. Ct. (ea. dist.) Calif. 1969, U.S. Supreme Ct. 1971. Assoc. Spray, Davis & Gould, L.A., 1943-44; pvt. practice L.A., 1944; assoc. Tanner and Sievers, L.A., 1944-47, Tanner and Thornton, L.A., 1947-54, Tanner, Hanson, Meyers, L.A., 1954-64; ptnr. Tanner and Van Dyke, L.A., 1964-65, Gallagher and Tanner, L.A., 1965-70; pvt. practice Pasadena, Calif., 1970-95; retired, 1995. Mem. L.A. Bar Assn., World Affairs Assn., Harvard Law Sch. Assn., Lawyers' Club L.A. Home and Office: 1720 Lombardy Rd Pasadena CA 91106-4127 E-mail: rpltd@aol.com

TANNER, DOUGLAS ALAN, lawyer; b. Palo Alto, Calif., Aug. 30, 1953; s. Bernard R. and Caroline (Orris) T.; m. Carol Scilacci, May 28, 1977; children: Lauren Elizabeth, Wynn Ann, Leigh Caroline. AB in History, Stanford U., 1974, MBA, JD, Stanford U., 1978. Bar: Calif. 1978, U.S. Dist. Ct. (no. dist.) Calif. 1978, U.S. Ct. Appeals (9th cir.) 1979, N.Y. 1987. Law clk. to judge U.S. Ct. Appeals (9th cir.), San Francisco, 1978-79; assoc. Orrick, Herrington & Sutcliffe, San Francisco, 1979-83, ptnr. San Jose, Calif., 1984-86, N.Y.C., 1986-89, Milbank, Tweed, Hadley & McCloy, L.A., 1989-92, Hong Kong, 1992-2001, Palo Alto, Calif., 2001—. Mem. San Francisco Barristers (chmn. corps. com. 1981-82), Order of Coif, Phi Beta Kappa. Republican. Episcopalian. Office: Milbank Tweed Hadley & McCloy LLP 630 Hansen Way 2nd Fl Palo Alto CA 94306 E-mail: dtanner@milbank.com

TANNER, GLORIA TRAVIS, state legislator; b. Atlanta, July 16, 1935; d. Marcellus and Blanche Arnold Travis; m. Theodore Ralph Tanner, 1955 (dec.); children: Terrance Ralph, Tanvis Renee, Tracey Lynne. BA, Met. State Coll., 1974; MUA, U. Colo., 1976. Office mgr. Great Western Mfg. Co., Denver, 1965-67; writer Rage mag., 1969-70; reporter, feature writer Denver Weekly News, 1970-75; dir. East Denver Cmty. Office, 1974—; also real estate agt.; mem. Colo. Ho. of Reps., 1985-94; mem. from dist. 33 Colo. Senate, 1994—. Minority caucus chairwoman; mem. appropriations, bus. affairs, labor coms. Dist. capt. Denver Dem. Com., Colo., 1973-75; chairwoman Senatorial Dist. 3 Dem. Com., 1974-82; adminstrv. aide Colo. State Senator Regis Groff, Denver, 1974-82; alt. del. Dem. Nat. Conv., 1976, del., 1980; commr. Colo. Status of Women, 1977—; chairwoman Colo. Black Women for Polit. Action, 1977—; exec. asst. to Lt. Gov., 1978-79; mem. adv. bd. United Negro Coll. Fund, Colo. State Treas. Served USAF, 1952-55. Recipient Outstanding Cmty. Leadership award Scott's Meth. Ch., 1974, Tribute to Black Women award, 1980; named Woman of Yr., Colo. Black Women Caucus, 1974. Mem. Colo. Black Media Assn. (pub. dir. 1972—), Reginas' Civic Club (founder, first pres. 1959—, Outstanding Woman of Yr. 1975), Nat. Assn. Real Estate Brokers. Roman Catholic. Democrat. Home: 2841 Colorado Blvd Denver CO 80207-3015 Office: State Senate 200 E Colfax Ave Ste 274 Denver CO 80203-1716

TANNER, JOHN DOUGLAS, JR. history educator, writer; b. Quantico, Va., Oct. 2, 1943; s. John Douglas and Dorothy Lucille (Walker) T.; m. Jo Ann Boyd, Jan. 1964 (div. Aug. 1966); 1 child, Lorena Desiree; m. Laurel Jean Selfridge, Dec. 19, 1967 (div. Oct. 1987); children: John DouglasIII, Stephen Douglas, Elizabeth Jane; m. Karen H. Olson, Apr. 16, 1988. BA, Pomona Coll., 1966; MA, Claremont Grad. U., 1968; postgrad., U. Calif., Riverside, 1976, 84-86, U. Calif., San Diego, 1984-87, U. Pacific, , 1993. Cert. tchr., Calif. Asst. swimming, water polo coach Pomona Coll., 1966-69; rsch. asst. history dept. Claremont Grad. U., 1967-69; prof. history Palomar Coll., San Marcos, Calif., 1969—, pres. faculty, 1970-71, v.p. faculty senate, 1971-72. Author: Olaf Swenson and his Siberian Imports jour., 1978 (Dog Writers Assn. Am. Best Series award 1979), Campaign for Los Angeles, 1846-47, 69; co-editor: Don Juan Forster, 1970, Alaskan Trails, Siberian Dogs, 1998; contbr. articles to profl. jours. Mem. citizens com. Fallbrook (Calif.) San. Dist., 1980; merit badge counselor Boy Scouts Am., 1975-85; Martin County Hist. Soc., Morgan County Hist. Soc., Fallbrook Hist. Soc., San Diego Opera Guild, San Diego Classical Music Soc., Opera Pacific Guild. Chautauqua fellow NSF, 1979. Mem. Nat. Assn. for Outlaw and Lawman History, Inc., Western Outlaw-Lawman History Assn. (adv. bd.), Custer Battlefield Hist. and Mus. Assn. (life), Western Writers Am., Old Trail Drivers Assn. Tex., The Westerners, Siberian Husky Assn. Am. (bd. dirs. 1974-78, 1st v.p. 1978-79), So. Calif. Siberian Husky Assn. (pres. 1972-79), U.S. Shooting Team (Inner Circle), Sons of the Rep. of Tex., Western History Assn. Republican. Episcopalian. Avocations: collecting S.W. Indian art, backpacking, wine making, writing, opera. Home: 2308 Willow Glen Rd Fallbrook CA 92028-8605 Office: Palomar Coll 1140 W Mission Rd San Marcos CA 92069-1415

TANNER, R. MARSHALL, lawyer; b. Santa Monica, Calif., Dec. 4, 1946; s. Stanley Robert and Kathryn (Lau) Tanner; m. Colleen Bonner, Sept. 3, 1969; children: David, Brent, Julie, Glenn, Scott, Holly. BA, Brigham Young U., 1970; JD, UCLA, 1977. Ptnr. Lawler, Felix & Hall, L.A., 1977-86, Pettit & Martin, Newport Beach, Calif., 1986-95, Sheppard, Mullin, Richter & Hampton, 1995—. Lt. USNR, 1970-74. Mem. Calif. State Bar Assn., Orange County Bar Assn. Mem. LDS Ch. Office: Sheppard Mullin Richter & Hampton 650 Town Center Dr Fl 4 Costa Mesa CA 92626-1993 E-mail: mtanner@smrh.com

TAO, CHIA-LIN PAO, humanities educator; b. Soochow, Kiangsu, China, July 7, 1939; came to U.S., 1961; d. Tsung-han and Hoi-chin Pao; m. Jing-shen Tao, Aug. 22, 1964; children: Rosalind, Jeanne, Sandy. BA, Nat. Taiwan U., Taipei, 1961; MA, Ind. U., 1963, PhD, 1971. Assoc. prof. Nat. Taiwan U., Taipei, 1969-76, 78-79; vis. assoc. prof. dept. East ASian studies U. Ariz., Tucson, 1976-78, 79-85, assoc. prof., 1989-2000, prof., 2000—. V.p. Hist. Soc. for 20th Century China in N.Am., 1992-93, pres., 1993-94. Editor, author: Studies in Chinese Women's History, 4 vols., 1979-95. Mem. Tucson-Taichung Sister-City Com., Tucson, 1984—; sec. Ariz. Asian Am. Assn., 1989, dir., 1989-93. Rsch. grantee Nat. Sci. Coun., Taipei, 1971-72, 73-74, Harvard-Yenching Inst., Cambridge, Mass., 1972-74, Pacific Cultural Found., Taipei, 1984-85. Mem. Assn. for Asian Studies (pres. Western conf. 1994), Tucson Chinese Am. Profl. Soc. (pres. 1996), Tucson Chinese Assn. (bd. dirs. 1996-98). Democrat. Office: U Ariz Dept E Asian Studies Tucson AZ 85721-0001 E-mail: cpaotao@u.arizona.edu

TAPPER, DAVID, pediatric surgeon; b. Balt., Aug. 26, 1945; s. Herman A. and Sylvia Phyllis (Golomb) T.; m. Susan Irene Wagner, June 25, 1968; children: JoEllen, Erica, Jacalyn, Aaron. BS, U. Md., College Park, 1966; MD, U. Md., Balt., 1970. Intern and resident in surgery U. Calif. San Francisco Med. Ctr., 1970-73; pediatric surg. rsch. fellow Boston Children's Hosp., 1973-75; sr. and chief surg. resident U. Calif., San Francisco, 1975-77; sr. and chief pediatric surg. fellow Children's Hosp., Boston, 1977-79; asst. prof. surgery Harvard Med. Sch., Boston, 1979-83; surgeon-in-chief Children's Hosp. Med. Ctr., Seattle, 1983—; prof. surgery and pediatrics U. Wash., Seattle, 1983—, vice-chmn. dept. surgery, 1986—. Exec. com. Am. Bd. Surgery, Phila., 1996-98, chmn. surg. forum, 1998-2000. Maj. USAR, 1971-82. Fellow ACS; mem. Am. Surg Assn., Am. Pediatric Surgery Assn. (bd. govs. 1993-96, pres. 2001), Soc. Univ. Surgeons, Pacific Coast Surg. Soc. (councilor N.W. region 1999—), Halsted Surg. Soc., Seattle Surg. Soc. (pres. 1999). Jewish. Office: Childrens Hosp Med Ctr 4800 Sand Point Way NE Seattle WA 98105-3901 E-mail: dtappe@chmc.org

TAPPER, JOAN JUDITH, magazine editor; b. Chgo., June 12, 1947; d. Samuel Jack and Anna (Swoiskin) T.; m. Steven Richard Siegel, Oct. 15, 1971. BA, U. Chgo., 1968; MA, Harvard U., 1969. Editor manuscripts Chelsea House, N.Y.C., 1969-71, Scribners, N.Y.C., 1971; editor books Nat. Acad. Scis., Washington, 1972-73; assoc. editor Praeger Pubs., Washington, 1973-74; editor New Rep. Books, Washington, 1974-79; mng. editor spl. pubs. Nat. Geog. Soc., Washington, 1979-83; editor Nat. Geog. Traveler, Washington, 1984-88; editor-in-chief Islands, internat. mag., Santa Barbara, Calif., 1989—; editl. dir. Islands Pub. Co., Santa Barbara, 1996—. Recipient Pacific Asia Travel Assn. Journalist of the Yr. award, 1995. Mem. Am. Soc. Mag. Editors, Soc. Am. Travel Writers (editors' coun.), Channel City Club. Democrat. Jewish. Avocations: travel, reading, tennis. Home: 603 Island View Dr Santa Barbara CA 93109-1508 Address: 6309 Carpinteria Ave Carpinteria CA 93013-2901

TARANTINO, QUENTIN, film director, screenwriter; b. Knoxville, Tenn., Mar. 27, 1963; s. Tony and Connie T. Screenwriter, dir., actor: Reservoir Dogs, 1992, Pulp Fiction, 1994 (Palme d'Or,Cannes Internat. Film Festival, 1994, Academy award best original screenplay 1994); screenwriter: True Romance, 1993; story: Natural Born Killers, 1994; producer: Killing Zoe, 1994; film appearances include Sleep With Me, 1994, Destiny Turns On the Radio, 1995; TV appearances include The Golden Girls, All-American Girl; actor: Desperado, 1995, Girl 6, 1996, From Dusk Till Dawn, 1996, Full Tilt Boogie, 1997; producer: Red Rain, 1995, Four Rooms, 1995, From Dusk Till Dawn, 1996, Curdled, 1996; dir., writer, prodr. Jackie Brown, 1997; dir. (TV series) ER, 1994; writer, dir. 40 Lashes, 2000. Address: 6201 W Sunset Blvd Ste 35 Los Angeles CA 90028-8704 also: WMA 151 S El Camino Dr Beverly Hills CA 90212-2704

TARAVELLA, ROSIE, actress, writer; b. Mt. Morris, N.Y., July 8, 1962; d. Charles James and Carrie (Sardinia) T.; m. Michael Anthony Valerio, May 27, 1994. BA in Dramatic Arts, San Diego State U., 1985. Entertainment dir., staff trainer Johnny Rockets, Inc., L.A., 1986-98; staff writer, voice talent The Rick Dees Weekly Top 40, L.A., 1990-93; freelance writer, voice talent The Premiere Comedy Radio Network, L.A., 1992-98; actress L.A., 1992—; writer L.A. Times Calendar Live! Website, 1999—. Theatrical prodr., cons. The Tamarind Theater, L.A., 1993-94. Author (plays) Rose's Bowl-O-Rama, 1992, The Wives, 1994, Pa's Funeral, 1995; (with Diane Kelber) Blue Grass, 1999; screenwriter: Carlo's Wake, 1997; actress (commls.) AT&T, Dial, Radio Shack and others, 1992—, (TV) Who's the Boss, Ellen, Full House, Married with Children, The Client, Almost Perfect, Brooklyn South, Sinatra, Norma Jean and Marilyn, George and Leo, Roswell; actress, co-writer (film) Carlo's Wake, 1999. Pres. Boards and Boards Prodns., North Hollywood, Calif., 1994-98. Recipient Am.'s Best Sitcom Writing Competition award, 1999. Mem. Mus. TV and Radio, KCRW-Nat. Pub. Radio, Am. Soc. Prevention Cruelty Animals, Nat. Geog. Soc. Democrat. Roman Catholic. Avocations: cooking, genealogy, Internet, film and TV history. Office: Broads and Boards 12828 Victory Blvd Ste 334 North Hollywood CA 91606-3013

TARBI, WILLIAM RHEINLANDER, secondary education educator, curriculum consultant, educational technology researcher; b. San Bernardino, Calif., Feb. 23, 1949; s. William Metro and Sue (Rheinlander) T.; m. Jenny Workman, Apr. 10, 1980 (div. 1985); m. Michele Hastings, July 4, 1990; children: Amy, Melissa. AA, Santa Barbara City Coll., 1969; BA in History, U. Calif., Santa Barbara, 1976; MA, U. Redlands, 1992. Cert. secondary edn. social studies tchr., Calif. Reporter AP, Santa Barbara, Calif., 1976-80, UPI, Seattle, 1980-85, Golden West Radio Network, Seattle, 1980-85; tchr. Redlands (Calif.) Unified Sch. Dist., 1988—. Cons. IMCOM, Redlands, 1985—. Mrm. E Clampus Vitus, Phi Delta Kappa. Avocations: painting, photography, writing, gardening, fencing.

TARDIO, THOMAS A. public relations executive; V.p. strategic planning and other positions Columbia Pictures Industries, 1979-88; CFO, v.p. adminstrn. Rogers & Cowan, Inc., L.A., 1988-89, exec. v.p. entertainment sect., 1989-91, pres., CEO, 1991-95, co-chmn., mng. dir., 1996—; mng. dir. Shandwick Convergence, L.A., 1997—; pres. Shandwick, United States, L.A., 1998—. Mem. IBM mobile computing mktg. adv. bd. Mem. So. Calif. chmn. U.S. Olympic Com.; mem. bd. visitors adv. bd. Loyola Law Sch. Mem. Pub. Rels. Soc. Am., Nat. Acad. Recording Arts and Scis., Pub. Communicators L.A. Office: Rogers & Cowan Inc 1888 Century Park E Ste 500 Los Angeles CA 90067-1709

TARN, NATHANIEL, poet, translator, educator; b. Paris, June 30, 1928; s. Marcel and Yvonne (Suchar) T.; children : Andrea, Marc. BA with honors, Cambridge (Eng.) U., 1948, MA, 1952; postgrad., U. Sorbonne, U. Paris, 1949-51; MA, U. Chgo., 1952, PhD, 1957; postgrad., London Sch. Econs., 1953-58. Anthropologist, Guatemala, Burma, Alaska, and other locations, 1952—; prof. comparative lit. Rutgers U., 1970-85, prof. emeritus modern poetry, comparative lit, anthropology, 1985. Vis. prof.

SUNY, Buffalo and Princeton, 1969-70. Author: Old Savage/Young City, 1964, Where Babylon Ends, 1968, The Beautiful Contradictions, 1969, October, 1969, A Nowhere for Vallejo, 1971, Lyrics for the Bride of God: Section: The Artemision, 1972, The Persephones, 1974, Lyrics for the Bride of God, 1975, The House of Leaves, 1976, Birdscapes, with Seaside, 1978, The Desert Mothers, 1985, At the Western Gates, 1985, Palenque, 1986, Seeing America First, 1989, Flying the Body, 1993, Multitude of One, 1995, Views from the Weaving Mountain: Selected Essays in Poetics and Anthropology, 1991, Scandals in the House of Birds: Shamans & Priests on Lake Atitlan, 1997, The Architextures, 2000, Three Letters From The City: The St. Petersburg Poems 1968-1998, 2000, Selected Poems 1950-2000, 2001; co-author: (with Janet Rodney) The Forest, 1978, Atitlan/Alashka, 1979, The Ground of Our Great Admiration of Nature, 1978; contbg. author: Penguin Modern Poets No. Seven: Richard Murphy, Jon Silkin, Nathaniel Tarn, 1965, A.P.E.N. Anthology of Contemporary Poetry, 1966, The Penguin Book of Modern Verse Translation, 1966, Poems Addressed to Hugh MacDiarmid, 1967, Music and Sweet Poetry: A Verse Anthology, 1968, Frontier of Going: Anthology of Space Poetry, 1969, Shaking the Pumpkin, 1972, America: A Prophecy, 1973, Open Poetry, 1973, Active Anthology, 1974, Symposium of the Whole, 1983, Random House Book of Twentieth Century French Poetry, 1983, Beneath a Single Moon: Buddhism in American Poetry, 1991, American Poetry since 1950: Innovators and Outsiders, 1993; translator: The Heights of Macchu Picchu (Pablo Neruda), 1966, Stelae (Victor Segalen), 1969, Zapotec Struggles, 1993; editor, co-translator: Con Cuba: An Anthology of Cuban Poetry of the Last Sixty Years, 1969, Selected Poems (Pablo Neruda), 1970; editor Cape Edits. and founder-dir. Cape Goliard Press, J. Cape Ltd., 1967-69. Recipient Guinness prize for poetry, 1963. Office: PO Box 8187 Santa Fe NM 87504-8187

TARNO, VERAL, state legislator; b. Nashville, Apr. 10, 1937; Student, Mt. San Antonio Jr. Coll., 1957, Southwestern C.C., 1972, FBI's Nat. Acad., 1976. Dep sheriff L.A. County, 1959-71, Coos County, Oreg., 1971-82, sheriff, 1982-93; mem. Oreg. Legislature, Salem, 1992—, mem. jud. com., mem. stream restoration and species recovery com., chair water and land use com., mem. subcom. on natural resources. Mem. State Inter-Agy. Hazard Comm. Coun., State All Terrain Vehicle Allotment Com. Mem. Oreg. State Sheriff's Assn., Rotary (past pres. Myrtle Point chpt.). Republican. Home: 310 E 1st St Coquille OR 97423-1806 Office: S-214 State Capitol Salem OR 97310-0001

TARNOFF, PETER, former federal agency administrator, business consultant; b. N.Y.C., Apr. 19, 1937; s. Norman Tarnoff and Henrietta (Goldfarb) Laing; m. Daniele Oudinot, Jan. 13, 1962 (div. Oct. 1981); children: Nicholas, Alexander; m. Mathea Falco, Dec. 24, 1981; 1 child, Benjamin. Student, U. Paris, 1956-57, postgrad., 60-61; BA, Colgate U., 1958; postgrad., U. Chgo., 1958-60. Joined Fgn. Svc., Dept. State, 1961; spl. asst. to amb. Am. Embassy, Bonn, Fed. Republic Germany, 1969; trainee Nat. Sch. Adminstrn., Paris, 1970; prin. officer Am. Consulate Gen., Lyon, France, 1971-73; dep. chief of mission Am. Embassy, Luxembourg, 1973-75; dir. Office Rsch. and Analysis for Western Europe Dept. State, Washington, 1975-76, exec. sec. Dept. State, 1977-81, fgn. affairs fellow San Francisco, 1981-82; exec. dir. World Affairs Coun. No. Calif., San Francisco, 1983-86; pres., dir. Coun. on Fgn. Rels., N.Y.C., 1986-93; under sec. state for polit. affairs Dept. State, Washington, 1993-97; pres. Internat. Adv. Corp., San Francisco, 1997—. Office: Internat Adv Corp 2028 Green St San Francisco CA 94123-4813 E-mail: iacmail@aol.com

TARR, GREGORY L. health and medical products company executive; With Alpha Beta Co., McKesson Corp., 1986-99, v.p., mgr. distbn. ctr., v.p. sales and ops. Everett, until 1997, sr. v.p. customer ops. group western region, 1997—; pres., CEO, URM Stores, Inc., Spokane, Wash., 1999—. Office: URM Stores Inc 7511 N Freya St Spokane WA 99217-8043

TARR, RALPH WILLIAM, lawyer, former federal government official; b. Bakersfield, Calif., Sept. 29, 1948; BA, Dartmouth Coll., 1970; MPA, Calif. State U., 1973; JD, U. Calif., Hastings, 1976. Extern to assoc. justice Calif. Supreme Ct., 1976; rsch. atty. to presiding justice Ct. Appeal (5th dist.) Calif., 1976-77; assoc. Baker, Manock & Jensen, Fresno, Calif., 1977-81, dir., mem. exec. com., 1981-82; mem. adminstrv. com. Fed. Register, Washington, 1982-85; dep. asst. atty. gen. U.S. Dept. Justice, Washington, 1982-84, acting asst. atty. gen., 1984-85; solicitor U.S. Dept. Interior, Washington, 1985-89, counselor, 1989-90; pvt. practice L.A., 1990—. Home: 24011 Alder Pl Calabasas CA 91302-2394 Office: Andrews & Kurth LLP 601 S Figueroa St Ste 1725 Los Angeles CA 90017-5747

TARTER, CURTIS BRUCE, physicist, science administrator; b. Louisville, Sept. 26, 1939; s. Curtis B. and Marian Turner (Cundiff) T.; m. Jill Cornell, June 6, 1964 (div. 1975); 1 child, Shana Lee; m. Marcia Cyrog Linn, Sept. 6, 1987. BS, MIT, 1961; PhD, Cornell U., 1967. Tchg. asst. Cornell U., Ithaca, N.Y., 1961-63, rsch. asst., 1964-67; physicist Lawrence Radiation Lab., Livermore, Calif., summers 1962, 63; staff mem. theoretical physics divsn. U. Calif., Lawrence Livermore Nat. Lab., 1967-69, group leader macroscopic properties of matter, 1969-71, assoc. divsn. leader, 1971-74, group leader opacities, 1972-78, divsn. leader, 1974-84; dep. assoc. dir. for physics Lawrence Livermore Nat. Lab., 1984-88, assoc. dir. for physics, 1988-94, dep. dir., 1994; dir., 1994—. Sr. scientist Applied Rsch. Labs. Aeronutronic divsn. Philco-Ford Corp.; cons. Hertz Found., 1970—, field com. study on astronomy in the 80's, NRC, 1980; mem. Army Sci. Bd., Washington, 1989-96; adj. prof. dept. applied sci., U. Calif., Davis, 1999; mem. Calif. Coun. on Sci. and Tech., 1996—, Pacific Coun. on Internat. Policy, 1998, lab. opers. bd. DOE, 1998—, Nuclear Energy Rsch. Adv. Bd., 1999—, Coun. Fgn. Rels., 1999—. Contbr. numerous articles to profl. jours. Recipient Roosevelts Gold Medal award for sci. Fellow Am. Phys. Soc.; mem. AAAS, Am. Astron. Soc., Internat. Astron. Union. Republican. Avocations: golf, squash, bridge. Home: 676 Old Jonas Hill Rd Lafayette CA 94549-5214 Office: Lawrence Livermore Nat Lab PO Box 808 Livermore CA 94551-0808 E-mail: tarter1@llnl.gov

TARTER, MICHAEL ERNEST, biostatistician, educator; b. Bronx, N.Y., Dec. 20, 1938; s. William Tarter and Frieda Browdy; m. Orna Benzenburg, Aug. 30, 1975; children: Douglas, Robin. BA in Math., UCLA, 1959, MA in Math., 1961, PhD in Biostats., 1963. Asst. prof. U. Mich., Ann Arbor, 1964-66, assoc. prof., 1967, U. Calif., Irvine, 1968-70, Berkeley, 1970-76, prof., 1977—. Author books and articles; editor: Jour. Am. Statis. Assn. (screening editor for applications 1971-80). Fellow Am. Statis. Assn. (chmn. com. resources biometrics sect. 1981—, editorial bds. computational stats. and data analysis 1983-86, biometrics 1976-84, stats. 1977-97). Office: U Calif Sch Pub Health Dept Biomed Environ Health Scis 140 Warren Hall Berkeley CA 94720-7360 E-mail: Tarter@uclink@Berkeley.edu

TASH, BILL, state senator; b. Dillon, Mont., Aug. 21, 1932; m. Marlene Tash. Student, Western Mont. Coll., Mont. State U. Rancher; Rep. rep. dist. 34 Mont. Ho. of Reps., 1992-2000; Rep. senator dist. 17 Mont. State Senate, 2000—. Mem. state adminstrn. com. Mont. State Senate, chair natural resources. With USN. Office: 240 Vista Dr Dillon MT 59725-3100 also: Mont State Senate Capitol Station Helena MT 59620

TASH, GRAHAM ANDREW, JR. automobile retail company executive; b. Seattle, Dec. 18, 1956; s. Graham Andrew and Charlotte Eleanor (Hawes) Tash; m. Julie Thompson Titus, Aug. 8, 1981; children: Jacqueline E., Katherine J., Graham A. III. BA, U. Puget Sound, 1979. Dist. mgr. Kenworth Truck Co., Atlanta, 1984-86; ops. mgr. Titus-Will Ford/Toyota, Tacoma, 1987-90, gen. mgr., 1991-94, pres., 1994—, bd. dirs. Bd. dirs. Titus-Will Ent. Bd. dirs. Christian Brotherhood Acad., Tacoma, 1996—; mem. activities coun. Tacoma Art Mus., 1993, 94, 95. Recipient Chairman's award Ford Motor Co., 1986, 87, 92, Pres.'s award Toyota Motor Sales USA, 1991, 92, 94, 95, 96. Mem. Tacoma C. of C. (bd. dirs. 1996—), Tacoma Country and Golf Club, Wash. Athletic Club, Tacoma Lawn Tennis Club. Republican. Episcopalian. Avocations: snow skiing, boating, hunting, golf. Office: Titus-Will Ford Toyota Sales Inc 3606 S Sprague Ave Tacoma WA 98409-7444

TASH, MARTIN ELIAS, publishing company executive; b. N.Y.C., Jan. 24, 1941; s. David and Esther (Milch) T.; m. Arlene Sue Klein, June 23, 1962; children: Nathan, Faye, Jill. B.B.A., Baruch Sch. City Coll. N.Y., 1962. C.P.A. Staff accountant S.D. Leidesdorf & Co. (C.P.A.'s), N.Y.C., 1962-66; v.p. fin., dir. LMC Data Inc., N.Y.C., 1966-71; with Plenum Pub. Corp., N.Y.C., 1971-98, chmn bd., pres., 1977-98; chmn. bd., pres., CEO Gradco Systems, Inc., 1990—. Office: Gradco Systems Inc 3753 Howard Hughes Pkwy Ste 200 Las Vegas NV 89109-0952

TASHIMA, ATSUSHI WALLACE, federal judge; b. Santa Maria, Calif., June 24, 1934; s. Yasutaro and Aya (Sasaki) T.; m. Nora Kiyo Inadomi, Jan. 27, 1957; children: Catherine Y., Christopher I., Jonathan I. AB in Polit. Sci., UCLA, 1958; LLB, Harvard U., 1961. Bar: Calif. 1962. Dep. atty. gen. State of Calif., 1962-67; atty. Spreckels Sugar divsn. Amstar Corp., 1968-72, v.p., gen. atty., 1972-77; ptnr. Morrison & Foerster, L.A., 1977-80; judge U.S. Dist. Ct. (ctrl. dist.) Calif., L.A., 1980-96, U.S. Ct. Appeals (9th cir.), Pasadena, Calif., 1996—. Mem. Calif. Com. Bar Examiners, 1978-80 With USMC, 1953-55. Mem. ABA, State Bar Calif., Los Angeles County Bar Assn. Democrat. Office: US Ct Appeals PO Box 91510 125 S Grand Ave Pasadena CA 91105-1652*

TATA, GIOVANNI, publishing executive; b. Taranto, Italy, Apr. 26, 1954; came to U.S., 1974, naturalized, 1982; s. Vito and Angela (Colucci) T.; m. Brenda Susan Smith, Feb. 14, 1978; children: Elizabeth Ariana, Katherine Allison, Margaret Anne, Michael Anthony, Hanna Amelia. BS cum laude, Brigham Young U., 1977, MA, 1980; grad. cert. area studies, U. Utah, 1980, PhD, 1986; postgrad., U. Turin, Italy, 1980-81. Archaeologist Utah State Hist. Soc., Salt Lake City, 1979; instr. dept. langs. U. Utah, Salt Lake City, 1983-85; Mediterranean specialist Soc. Early Hist. Archaeology, Provo, Utah, 1978-91; rsch. fellow Direzione Gen. Cooperazione Sci. Culturale e Technica, Rome, 1980-81; mus. curator Pioneer Trail State Park, Salt Lake City, 1982-83; instr. dept. art Brigham Young U., Provo, 1982-84, dir. creative works, 1996—; rsch. curator Utah Mus. Fine Arts, Salt Lake City, 1985-87; pres. Mus. Info. Sys., 1987-93, Transoft Internat., Inc., 1988—. Chmn. 35th Ann. Symposium on the Archaeology of the Scriptures, 1986, Taras Devel. Corp., 1994-97, MuseuMedia, Inc., 1995—. Patentee method and system for computerized learning, response, and evaluation. Mem. Utah State Hist. Soc. Brigham Young U. scholar. Mem. Am. Assn. Mus., Internat. Coun. Mus. Republican. Mem. Ch. Jesus Christ of Latter-day Saints. Home: PO Box 2194 Provo UT 84603-2194 Office: Transoft Internat 3325 N University Ave Ste 300 Provo UT 84604-7412 E-mail: tata@lexint.com

TATARSKII, VALERIAN IL'ICH, physics researcher; b. Kharkov, USSR, Oct. 13, 1929; s. Il'ya A. and Elizabeth A. (Lapis) T.; m. Maia S. Granovskaia, Dec. 22, 1955; 1 child, Viatcheslav V. MS, Moscow State U., 1952; PhD, Acoustical Inst. Acad. Scis., 1957; DSc, Gorky State U., 1962. Scientific rschr. Geophys. Inst. Acad. Sci. USSR, Moscow, 1953-56, Inst. Atmospheric Physics, Acad. Sci. USSR, Moscow, 1956-59, sr. scientific rschr., 1959-78, head lab., 1978-90; head dept. Lebedev. Phys. Inst. Acad. Sci., Moscow, 1990-91; sr. rsch. assoc. U. Colo. Coop. Inst. for Rsch. in Environ. Sci., Boulder, 1991—, NOAA/ERL. Environ. Tech. Lab., Boulder. Author: Wave Propagation in a Turbulent Medium, 1961, 67, The Effect of the Turbulent Atmosphere on Wave Propagation, 1971, Principles of Statistical Radiophysics, 1989; contbr. articles to profl. jours. Recipient of Max Born award, 1994, Optical Soc. of Am., USSR State prize, 1990. Fellow Optical Soc. Am. (Max Born award 1994), Inst. of Physics; mem. Russian Acad. Sci., U.S.A. Nat. Acad. Engring., N.Y. Acad. Sci. Avocations: classical music, kayaking. Office: NOAA ERL ETL 325 Broadway St Boulder CO 80305-3337 E-mail: vtatarskii@hotmail.com

TATE, JOHN WILLIAM, food products executive; BA in Econs., U. Tex., 1972. Various fin. and gen. mgmt. positions Dole Food Co. Inc., Westlake Village, Calif.; CFO fresh vegetables divsn. Dole Food Co., 1993-96, CFO Dole Europe, CFO Westlake Village, Calif., 1998—. With USAF, 1973-79. Office: Dole Food Co Inc PO Box 5132 Westlake Village CA 91359

TATE, PENFIELD, state senator; b. Phila., 19 May; m. Valencia Tate. BA, Colo. State U., 1978; JD, Antioch U., 1981. Atty. FTC, 1981-84, 1984—; Dem. rep. dist. 8 Colo. Ho. of Reps., 1996-2000; Dem. senator dist. 33 Colo. State Senate, 2000—. Mem. bus. affairs and labor and fin. coms. Colo. Ho. of Reps.; mem. joint budget com. Colo. State Senate, vice chmn. appropriations com. Mem. bd. dirs. Metro State Coll. Found., Colo. Housing and Fin. Authority; adminstr. asst. to Mayor of Denver, 1990-91; exec. dir. Colo. Dept. Adminstrn., 1993-94; 2d vice chair Colo. Dem. Party, 1995-97. Mem. Denver Metro C. of C. (bd. dirs.). Office: 2875 Albion St Denver CO 80207 also: Colo State Senate 200 E Colfax Rm 263 Denver CO 80203 E-mail: ptate@csn.net, ptate@sni.net

TATTINI, EUGENE L. career officer; BSc in Indsl. Mgmt., U. Ill., 1965; MBA, Okla. City U., 1978. Commd. 2d. lt. USAF, 1965, advanced through grades to lt. gen., 1999; exec. officer Wheelus Air Base, Libya, 1965-68; missile combat crew dep. comdr. Grand Forks AFB, N.D., 1968-69; aide to vice comdr. March AFB, Calif., 1969-72; various assignments Tinker AFB, Okla., 1972-75; dir. logistics Kwang Ju Air Base, South Korea, 1975-76; various assignments Space Defense Sys. Program Office Space Divsn., L.A. Air Force Station, 1977-81, 91-95, comdr., 1998—; acquisition logistics policy staff officer The Pentagon, Washington, 1981-84; dir. plans and programs Andrews AFB, Md., 1985-88; various assignments Wright-Patterson AFB, Ohio, 1988-91, 95; comdr. Sacramento (Calif.) Air Logistics Ctr., McClellan AFB, 1995-98. Decorated D.S.M., Legion of Merit with oak leaf cluster, Meritorious Svc. medal with three oak leaf clusters, Air Force Organizational Excellence award with three oak leaf clusters, Nat. Defense Svc. medal with svc. star, Air Force Overseas Ribbon-short, Air Force Overseas Ribbon-long, Air Force Longevity Svc. Award Ribbon with seven oak leaf clusters.

TATUM, JACKIE, former parks and recreation manager, municipal official; b. Kansas City, Mo., June 11, 1932; 2 children. BS in Phys. Edn., U. So. Calif. Tchr., Calif. With Ctrl. Recreation Ctr. Parks and Recreation Ctr. City of L.A., 1955; recreation dir. various recreation ctrs.; prin. recreation supr.; asst. gen. mgr. Valley Region, 1989-92; gen. mgr., 1992-98; cons. City of L.A., Dept. Recreation and Parks, 1998—. Chair nat. exec. com., creator, developer Wonderful Outdoor World (WOW); presenter in field. Contbr. articles to profl. jours.; appearances in tv, radio shows. Recipient Ticket to Life award Inner City Games; named Woman of the Yr. World Ops. Internat., 1976, City Employee of Yr. All City Employees Benefits Svc. Assn., 1992., One of Ten Most Powerful Black Women in L.A. Mem. Nat. Recreation and Parks Assn. (Disting. Svc. award 1997, tchr. Pacific Mktg. and Revenue Sources Mgmt. Sch.), Chi Kappa Rho (v.p., pres., past pres. Helen I. Pontius Nat. award of merit). Office: City of Los Angeles Recreation 200 N Main St Rm 1330 Los Angeles CA 90012-4110

TAU, LEONARD, communications company executive; Chmn. bd. dirs. Century Comms. Corp., 1989-90, CEO, chmn., 1990-91, CFO, 1991-97; dir., chmn. bd. dirs. Electric Lightwave, Vancouver, Wash., 1994—. Office: Electric Lightwave Inc 4400 NE 77th Ave Vancouver WA 98662

TAUBE, HENRY, chemistry educator; b. Sask., Can., Nov. 30, 1915; came to U.S., 1937, naturalized, 1942; s. Samuel and Albertina (Tiledetski) T.; m. Mary Alice Wesche, Nov. 27, 1952; children: Linda, Marianna, Heinrich, Karl. BS, U. Sask., 1935, MS, 1937, LLD, 1973; PhD, U. Calif., 1940; PhD (hon.), Hebrew U. of Jerusalem, 1979; DSc (hon.), U. Chgo., 1983, Poly. Inst., N.Y., 1984, SUNY, , 1985, U. Guelph, 1987; DSc honoris causa, Seton Hall U., 1988, Lajos Kossuth U. of Debrecen, Hungary, 1988; DSc, Northwestern U., 1990; hon. degree, U. Athens, 1993. Instr. U. Calif., 1940-41; instr., asst. prof. Cornell U., 1941-46; faculty U. Chgo., 1946-62, prof., 1952-62, chmn. dept. chemistry, 1955-59; prof. chemistry Stanford U., 1962-90; prof. emeritus chemistry Stanford U., 1990—; Marguerite Blake Wilbur prof. Stanford U., 1976, chmn. dept., 1971-74. Baker lectr. Cornell U., 1965 Hon. mem. Hungarian Acad., Scis., 1988. Guggenheim fellow, 1949, 55; recipient Harrison Howe award, 1961, Chandler medal Columbia U., 1964, F. P. Dwyer medal U. NSW, Australia, 1973, Nat. medal of Sci., 1976, 77, Allied Chem. award for Excellence in Grad. Tchg. and Innovative Sci., 1979, Nobel prize in Chemistry, 1983, Bailar medal U. Ill., 1983, Robert A. Welch Found. award in Chemistry, 1983, Disting. Achievement award Internat. Precious Metals Inst., 1986, Brazilian Order of Sci. Merit award, 1994, Hon. fellowship Royal Soc. Can., 1997. Fellow Royal Soc. Chemistry (hon.), Indian Chem. Soc. (hon.); mem. NAS (award in chem. scis. 1983), Am. Acad. Arts and Scis., Am. Chem. Soc. (Kirkwood award New Haven sect. 1965, award for nuclear applications in chemistry 1955, Nichols medal N.Y. sect. 1971, Willard Gibbs medal Chgo. sect. 1971, Disting. Svc. in Advancement Inorganic Chemistry award 1967, T.W. Richards medal NE sect. 1980, Monsanto Co. award in inorganic chemistry 1981, Linus Pauling award Puget Sound sect. 1981, Priestley medal 1985, Oesper award Cin. sect. 1986, G.M. Kosolapoff award Auburn sect. 1990), Royal Physiographical Soc. of Lund (fgn. mem.), Am. Philos. Soc., Finnish Acad. Sci. and Letters, Royal Danish Acad. Scis. and Letters, Coll. Chemists of Catalonia and Beleares (hon.), Can. Soc. Chemistry (hon.), Hungarian Acad. Scis. (hon. mem.), Royal Soc. (fgn. mem.), Brazilian Acad. Scis. (corr.), Engring. Acad. Japan (fgn. assoc.), Australian Acad. Scis. (corr.), Chem. Soc. Japan (hon. mem. 1993), Phi Beta Kappa, Sigma Xi, Phi Lambda Upsilon (hon.) Office: Stanford U Dept Chemistry Stanford CA 94305-5080 E-mail: cdpiercy@stanford.edu

TAUER, PAUL E. mayor, educator; b. 1935; m. Katherine Eldredge, Sept. 1, 1956; children: Paul E. Jr., Edward, Roch, Eugene, Kathryn, Tammie, Andrew, Timothy. BA in Historyand Edn., Regis Coll., 1961; MA in Edn. Adminstrn., U. No. Colo., 1964. Tchr. Denver Pub. Schs., 1961-92; ret., 1992. Mayor City of Aurora, Colo., 1987—, mem. Aurora City Coun., 1979-1987; mem. Adams County Coordinating Com., Gov.'s Met. Transp. Roundtable; active Aurora airport coms. Mem. N.O.I.S.E. Office: Office of Mayor 1470 S Havana St Aurora CO 80012-4014 E-mail: ptauer@ci.aurora.co.us

TAUSCHER, ELLEN O. congresswoman; b. Newark, 1951; m. William Y. Tauscher; 1 child, Katherine. BS in early Childhood Edn., Seton Hall U., 1974. With Bache Securities, N.Y.C., N.Y. Stock Exchange; dir. Tauscher Found.; mem. U.S. Congree from 10th Calif. dist., 1997—; mem. house armed svcs. com., house transp. com. U.S. Ho. Reps. Founder The ChildCare Registry; bd. regents Seton Hall U.; co-chair Delaine Eastin's State Supt. Pub. Instrn. Campaign, 1994; transp. and infrastructure com., surface transp. and water resources and environ. Author: The ChildCare Sourcebook, 1996. Active The Coalition, New Dem. Coalition, Bipartisan Freshman Campaign Fin. Reform Task Force, House Cancer Awareness Working Group, Congl. Caucus on the Arts; vice-chair Calif. Dem. Del.*

TAUSSIG, LYNN MAX, healthcare administrator, pulmonologist, pediatrician, educator; b. Milw., July 19, 1942; m. Lisa Peter; children: Heather, Jennifer. AB cum laude, Harvard U., 1964; MD, Washington U., St. Louis, 1968. Diplomate Am. Bd. Pediat., Nat. Bd. Med. Examiners, Am. Bd. Pediat. Pulmonary. Rsch. asst. dept. neuroanatomy Marquette U., Milw., 1965; intern in pediat. St. Louis Children's Hosp., 1968-69; resident in pediat. U. Colo. Med. Ctr., Denver, 1969-70; clin. assoc. pediat. metabolism br. Nat. Inst. Arthritis, Metabolism, and Digestive Diseases, NIH, Bethesda, Md., 1970-72; pulmonary fellow Montreal (Que., Can.) Children's Hosp., 1972-74; asst. prof. pediat. Ariz. Health Scis. Ctr., Tucson, 1974-77, cystic fibrosis ctr. dir., 1974-85, assoc. chief pulmonary function labs., 1974-85, dir. pulmonary sect., 1974-85, asst. dir. divsn. respiratory scis., 1976-92, assoc. prof. pediat., 1977-81, assoc. head dept. pediat., 1979-84, prof., 1981-93, head dept. pediat., 1985-93, dir. Steele Meml. Children's Rsch. Ctr., 1986-93; prof. pediats. U. Colo. Health Scis. Ctr., Denver, 1993—; pres., CEO Nat. Jewish Med. and Rsch. Ctr., Denver, 1993—. Frank Stevenson vis. prof. U. Con., 1977, 82; Robert Chinnock Meml. lectr. Loma Linda U., Calif., 1983; Jour. Pediats. vis. prof. U. Chgo., 1984; Brennenman lectr. L.A. Pediat. Soc., 1988, 94; Danis Meml. lectr. St. Louis U., 1989; Talamo Meml. lectr. Johns Hopkins U., Balt., 1989; Anna Zager vis. lectr. in pediats. Technion U., Haifa, Israel, 1990; Sir Clavering Fison vis. prof. Inst. Child Health, U. London, 1992; Benjamin Meaker vis. prof. U. Bristol, Eng., 1992; Ben Kagan vis. lectr. Cedars-Sinai Hosp., L.A., 1993. Mem. editl. bd. Chest, 1983-88, Am. Rev. Respiratory Diseases, 1983-89; contbr. articles to profl. jours. Trustee Congregation Anshei Israel, 1978-80; bd. dirs. Jewish Cmty. Ctr., 1982-90, sec., 1984-86, v.p., 1987-89; mem. allocations com. Jewish Fedn. So. Ariz., 1985, 88, Allied Jewish Fedn. Denver, 1996—; bd. dirs. Colo. Biomed. Venture Ctr., 1994—, Congregation Rodef Shalom, 1996—; active Martin Luther King Jr. Minority Scholarship Program, 1994—, Colo. Concern, 1995—. Cystic Fibrosis Found. Clin. fellow, 1972-74, Sr. Internat. fellow Fogarty Internat. Ctr., 1980-81; Young Investigator Pulmonary Rsch. grantee Nat. Heart and Lung Inst., 1974-76, and numerous other med. grants; Pfizer Labs. Med. scholar, 1966; recipient Lange Med. Book award, 1966 Mem. Am. Acad. Pediat. (mem. exec. com. sect. on diseases of chest 1978-80, mem. ad hoc com. for pediat. pulmonary bds., sect. on diseases of chest 1978-85), Am. Pediat. Soc., Am. Thoracic Soc. (mem. com. to advise pres. 1975-76, sec. sci. assembly for pediats. 1975-77, mem. respiratory care com. 1976-78, mem. nominating com. 1977, 84-85, chmn. prograom com. 1979-81, mem. ann. meeting com. 1979-81, mem. rsch. rev. com. 1981-82, chmn. publs. policy com. 1988-89, 90-92, mem. exec. com. 1989-90, sec.-treas. 1989-90, active many other coms.), Am. Coll. Chest Physicians (mem. steering group for com. on cardiopulmonary diseases in children 1977-79), Ariz. Pediat. Soc., Ariz. Lung Assn., Pima County Pediat. Soc., Soc. Pediat. Rsch. (founder Lung Club 1985), Western Soc. Pediat. Rsch. (mem. nominating com. 1979-80, elected to coun. 1994—), Rotary, Harvard Club of So. Ariz. (schs. com. 1982-93, sec.-treas. 1989-93), Harvard Club of Colo., Alpha Omega Alpha. Office: Nat Jewish Med & Rsch Ctr 1400 Jackson St Denver CO 80206-2761

TAVARES, TONY, professional hockey and baseball leagues executive; b. Fall River, Mass., Oct. 17, 1949; m. Elizabeth Tavares; children: Sheila, Kristen, Mark. BS in Acctg., Roger Williams Coll. Comptroller, acting dir. Providence Civic Ctr.; with Centrum, Worcester, Mass., New Haven Vets. Meml. Coliseum, Nassau Vets. Meml. Coliseum, Uniondale, N.Y., Spectacor Mgmt. Group, pres., CEO; cons. Walt Disney Co.; pres. Anaheim Sports Inc., Anaheim, Calif., 1993—; chmn., gov. Mighty Ducks of Anaheim, 1993—; pres. Anaheim Angels, 1996—. Mem. Internat. Assn. Auditorium Mgrs. Office: Mighty Ducks of Anaheim PO Box 61077 2695 E Katella Ave Anaheim CA 92803-6177

TAVERNA, RODNEY ELWARD, financial services company executive; b. Springfield, Ill., Aug. 8, 1947; s. Jerome Thomas and Virginia (Holcomb) T.; m. Cheryl Ann Walters, Sept. 4, 1968 (div. 1983); children: Lara Lyn, Melinda Marie, Ryan Thomas; m. Caroline Whiffen, Apr. 1985. BA, U. Mo., 1969; MBA in Fin., Nat. U., 1988. Commd. 2d lt., supply officer USMC, 1969, advanced through grades to maj., 1979; supply officer Central Svcs. Agy., Danang, Vietnam, 1970-71, Marine Air Control Squadron, Futenma, Okinawa, 1977-78; logistics officer Hdqrs. Marine Corps Recruit Depot, Paris Island, S.C., 1972-75; support officer Marine Barracks, Treasure Island, San Francisco, 1975-77; regimental supply officer 1st Marine Divsn., Camp Pendleton, Calif., 1978-79, asst divsn. supply officer, 1985-88; brigade supply officer 1st Marine Brigade, Kaneohe Bay, Hawaii, 1980-82; exec. officer 1st Maintenance Bn., Camp Pendleton, 1982-85; asst div. supply officer 1st Marine Div., 1985-88; pres. Freedom Fin. Group, 1991—; br. mgr. WMA Securities, Inc., 1994-97; sr. field dir. Premier Fin. Am., 1997-2000. Owner, mgr. Opportunities Unltd., Oceanside, Calif., 1985-91; cons. Incentive Leasing Corp., San Diego, 1985-86, The Profit Ctr., Santa Ana, Calif., 1991; founding mgr. Meditrend Internat., San Diego, 1987-88; founding dir. Am. 3-D Corp., Henderson, Nev., 1990-91. Republican. Avocations: computers, snow skiing, racquetball, scuba diving. Home and Office: 1632 Avenida Andante Oceanside CA 92056-6905 E-mail: FreedomFinancial@home.com

TAYLOR, ALLAN ROSS, linguist, educator; b. Palisade, Colo., Dec. 24, 1931; s. Athel Ross and Marjorie Verle (Walters) T.; m. Mary Callas, Sept. 8, 1958; children: Artemisia, Anthony, Peter, Anna, Yoana. AB, U. Colo., Boulder, 1953; PhD (Woodrow Wilson fellow, Fulbright fellow, NDEA fellow), U. Calif., Berkeley, 1969. Teaching asst., lectr. U. Calif., Berkeley, 1958-63; instr. U. Colo., 1964-65, asst. prof., 1965-70, assoc. prof., 1970-77, prof., 1977-93, prof. emeritus, 1993—, also past chmn. dept. linguistics, dept. French and Italian. Cons. bilingual edn. for Native Ams. Active Dem. Party and in environ. issues. With U.S. Army, 1954-57. NEH grantee, 1972-76, 80-82, 87-90, 89-93. Mem. Linguistic Soc. Am., Am. Anthrop. Assn. Home: 787 17th St Boulder CO 80302-7601 Office: U Colo Dept Linguistics PO Box 295 Boulder CO 80309-0295 E-mail: allan.taylor@colorado.edu

TAYLOR, BARRY E. lawyer; b. Mineola, N.Y., Mar. 14, 1948; BA magna cum laude, U. Va., 1970, JD, 1975. Bar: Calif. 1975. With Wilson, Sonsini, Goodrich & Rosati P.C., Palo Alto, Calif. Mem. ABA, State Bar Calif., Order Coif, Phi Beta Kappa. Office: Wilson Sonsini Goodrich & Rosati PC 650 Page Mill Rd Palo Alto CA 94304-1050

TAYLOR, BARRY LLEWELLYN, microbiologist, educator; b. Sydney, Australia, May 7, 1937; came to U.S., 1967; s. Fredrick Llewelyn and Vera Lavina (Clarke) T.; m. Desmyrna Ruth Tolhurst, Jan. 4, 1961; children: Lyndon, Nerida, Darrin. BA, Avondale Coll., Cooranbong, New South Wales, 1959; BSc with honors, U. New South Wales, Sydney, 1966; PhD, Case Western Res. U., 1973; postgrad., U. Calif., Berkeley, 1973-75. Vis. postdoctoral fellow Australian Nat. U., Canberra, 1975-76; asst. prof. biochemistry Loma Linda (Calif.) U., 1976-78, assoc. prof. biochemistry, 1978-83, prof. biochemistry, 1983—, prof., chmn. dept. microbiology and molecular genetics, 1988-2000, interim dir. Ctr. for Molecular Biology, 1989-94, 96-98, v.p. for rsch. affairs, 2000—. Contbr. articles to profl. publs. Rsch. grantee Am. Heart Assn., 1978-85, NIH, 1981—. Mem. Am. Soc. Microbiology, Am. Soc. Biochemistry and Molecular Biology. Office: Loma Linda U VP Rsch Affairs Loma Linda CA 92350-0001

TAYLOR, CARSON WILLIAM, electrical engineer; b. Superior, Wis., May 24, 1942; s. William Stanley and Elizabeth Marie (Christophersen) T.; m. Gudrun Renate Leistner, Dec. 28, 1966; 1 child, Natasha Marie. BSEE, U. Wis., 1965; M in Engring., Rensselaer Poly. Inst., 1969. Elec. engr. U.S. Bur. Reclamation, Billings, Mont., 1967-68, Bonneville Power Adminstrn., Portland, Oreg., 1969-89, prin. engr., 1989—. Prin. Carson Taylor Seminars, Portland, 1986—. Author: Power System Voltage Stability, 1994; contbr. papers to profl. publs.; patentee in field. Lt. U.S. Army, 1965-67. Lt. U.S. Army, 1965-67. Fellow IEEE (chmn. subcom. 1982—); mem. Conférence Internationale des Grands Réseaux Électriques a Haute Tension (CIGRE, disting. mem.), Eta Kappa Nu. Lutheran. Avocations: fishing, hunting, woodworking, reading, computers. Office: Bonneville Power Adminstrn PO Box 491 Vancouver WA 98666-0491

TAYLOR, DAVID GEORGE, retired banker; b. Charlevoix, Mich., July 29, 1929; s. Frank Flagg and Bessie (Strayer) T.; m. Robyne T. McCarthy, July 28, 1990; children from previous marriage: David, Amy, Jeanine. BS, Denison U., 1951; MBA, Northwestern U., 1953. With Continental Ill. Nat. Bank and Trust Co. Chicago, 1958-86, asst. cashier, 1961-64, 2d v.p., 1964-66, v.p., 1966-72, sr. v.p., 1972-74, exec. v.p., 1974-80, exec. v.p., treas., 1980-83, vice chmn., 1983-84, chmn., chief exec. officer, 1984; vice chmn. Irving Trust Co., N.Y.C., 1986-89; group exec. Chem. Bank, N.Y.C., 1989-94, ret., 1994. Mem. Dealer Bank Assn. Com. on Glass-Steagall Reform, 1985-86. Bd. dirs. Evanston Hosp., Glenbrook Hosp.; trustee Art Inst. Chgo., 1981-86; advisor J.L. Kellogg Grad. Sch. Mgmt., Northwestern U., 1984—; bd. dirs. CNA Income Shares. Served to lt. USN, 1953-56. Mem. Pub. Securities Assn. (bd. dirs. 1977-78, chmn. 1977, treas. 1978), Govt. and Fed. Agys. Securities Com. (chmn. bd. dirs. 1982-83), Assn. Res. City Bankers (asset/liability com/govt. relations com. 1983—). Republican. Presbyterian.

TAYLOR, FRANCIS MICHAEL, auditor, municipal official; b. Munich, Germany, 1960; came to the U.S., 1961; BS, Va. Tech., 1982. CPA, Va.; Cert. internal auditor. Pub. acct., Roanoke, Va., 1982-84; controller ARC Roanoke, Inc., Roanoke, 1984-87; audit supr. City of Roanoke, 1987-94; city auditor City of Stockton (Calif.), 1994—. Mem. AICPAs, Nat. Assn. Local Govt. Auditors (pres.-elect), Calif. Soc. CPAs, Inst. Internal Auditors, Govt. Fin. Officers Assn., Info. Sys. Audit and Control Assn. Office: 425 N El Dorado St Stockton CA 95202-1951

TAYLOR, GARY L. federal judge; b. 1938; AB, UCLA, 1960, JD, 1963. Assoc. Wenke, Taylor, Evans & Ikola, 1965-86; judge Orange County Superior Ct., 1986-90, U.S. Dist. Ct. (ctrl. dist.) Calif., Santa Ana, 1990—. With U.S. Army, 1964-66. Mem. Am. Coll. Trial Lawyers, State Bar Calif., Orange County Bar Assn. (bd. dirs. 1980-82, founder, chmn. bus. litigation com., Disting. Svc. award 1983). Office: US Dist Cts 411 W 4th St Santa Ana CA 92701-4500

TAYLOR, GEORGE FREDERICK, newspaper publisher, editor; b. Portland, Oreg., Feb. 28, 1928; s. George Noble and Ida Louise (Dixon) T.; m. Georga Bray, Oct. 6, 1951; children—Amelia Ruth, Ross Noble. BS, U. Oreg., 1950. Reporter Astoria (Oreg.) Budget, 1950-52, Portland Oregonian, 1952-54; copy reader Wall St. Jour., 1955-57, reporter, 1957-59, Detroit Bur. chief, 1959-64, Washington corr., 1964-68, asst. mng. editor, 1968-69, mng. editor N.Y.C., 1970-77, exec. editor, 1977-86; pub. North Bend (Oreg.) News, 1981-86, Prime Time, 1987—, Coquille Valley Sentinel, 1989-2000. Lt. USAF, 1955-57. Mem. Oregon Newspaper Publishers Assn. (bd. dirs. 1997-2000). E-mail: Ftaylor@harborside.com

TAYLOR, GUY WATSON, symphonic conductor; b. Anniston, Ala., Dec. 25, 1919; s. Stokely Brackston and Ola Mae (Shaw) T.; m. Renee Lifton, Oct. 19, 1947; children: Eric Anthony, Ellen Jane. Diploma, Birmingham Conservatory of Music, 1941, Juilliard Sch. Music, 1948; pvt. studies and workshops with, Dimitri Mitropoulos, 1941-42, L'Ecole Monteux, 1949, Eugene Ormandy, 1953, George Szell, 1956. Conductor Springfield (Ohio) Symphony Orch., 1948-51; conductor Nashville Symphony Orch., 1951-59, Phoenix Symphony Orch., 1959-69; Conductor Fresno Philharmonic Orch., 1969-84. Guest conductor, U.S., Gt. Britain, Philippines, P.R., Can. and Mexico City; musical commentator Springfield News & Sun, 1948-51, Ariz. Republic, 1959-61, Fresno Bee, 1970-76 Has appeared on, BBC Radio, CBS-TV. Served with AUS, 1942-45. Recipient Conductor Recognition award Am. Symphony Orch. League, 1960, Alice M. Ditson Orch. award, 1961, citation for adventuresome programming of contemporary music ASCAP, 1977 Mem. Am. Symphony Orch. League, Phi Mu Alpha Sinfonia. E-mail: gtrtnedwa@webtv.net

TAYLOR, HOWARD S. chemistry and physics educator, research physicist; b. N.Y.C., Sept. 17, 1935; m. 1959; 3 children. BA, Columbia U., 1956; PhD in Chem. Physics, U. Calif., Berkeley, 1959. NSF post-doctoral fellow in chemistry Free U. Brussels, 1959-61; from asst. prof. to prof. chemistry U. So. Calif., L.A., 1961—, Humboldt prof., 1974, prof. physics, 1975—. Cons. Jet Propulsion Lab. Calif. Inst. Tech., 1960—, Lawrence Livermore Nat. Lab., Los Alamos Sci. Lab.; guest prof. U. Amsterdam, U. Paris-Sud, Freiberg U. Recipient Max-Planck-Forschungs-prize Physics, Maths., Atstronomy, 1992. Fellow Am. Phys. Soc.; mem. Am. Chem. Soc. Achievements includes research in atomic and molecular physics, lasers, dynamics, spectroscopy, chaotic phenomena, signal processing in chemistry and physics. Office: USC Dept Chemistry University Park Los Angeles CA 90007 E-mail: taylor@chem4.usc.edu

TAYLOR, HUGH PETTINGILL, JR. geologist, educator; b. Holbrook, Ariz., Dec. 27, 1932; s. Hugh Pettingill and Genevieve (Fillerup) T.; m. Candis E. Hoffman, 1982. B.S., Calif. Inst. Tech., 1954; A.M., Harvard U., 1955; Ph.D., Calif. Inst. Tech., 1959. Asst. prof. geochemistry Pa. State U., 1960-62; mem. faculty div. geol. and planetary scis. Calif. Inst. Tech., 1962—, now prof. geology, Robert P. Sharp prof., 1981. Crosby vis. prof. M.I.T., 1978; vis. prof. Stanford U., 1981; William Smith lectr. Geol. Soc. London, 1976; Hofmann lectr. Harvard U., 1980; Cloos lectr. Johns Hopkins U., 1986; with U.S. Geol. Survey, Saudi Arabia, 1980-81 Author: The Oxygen Isotope Geochemistry of Igneous Rocks, 1968, Stable Isotopes in High Temperature Geological Processes, 1986, Stable Isotope Geochemistry, 1991; assoc. editor Bull. Geol. Soc. Am, 1969-71, Geochimica Cosmochimica Acta, 1971-76; editor Chem. Geology, 1985-91. Recipient Day medal Geol. Soc. Am., Urey medal European Assn. Geochem., 1995. Fellow NAS, Soc. Econ. Geol., Geol. Soc. Am., Am. Geophys. Union, Mineral. Soc. Am. (councillor), Am. Acad. Arts and Scis.; mem. Geochem. Soc. (councillor). Republican.

TAYLOR, JACK, state senator; b. Chgo., Nov. 22, 1935; m. Geneva Taylor. BS, Iowa State U. Businessman; Rep. rep. dist. 56 Colo. Ho. of Reps., 1992-2000; Rep. senator dist. 8 Colo. State Senate, 2000—. Mem. agr., livestock and natural resources coms. Colo. Ho. of Reps., chair bus. affairs and labor, vice chair legis. audit; mem. bus. affairs and labor and fin. and legis. audit coms. Colo. State Senate. Mem. bd. dirs. Irrigation Water Co.; former mem. Steamboat Springs Home Rule Charter Commn.; mem. Naval ROTC; chmn. Routt County Reps., 1989-92; mem. dist. bd. West Steamboat Water and Sanitation; past pres. Steamboat Springs Kiwanis Club. With USN. Mem. Steamboat Springs Chamber/Resort Assn. (former bd. dirs.). Office: PO Box 772867 Steamboat Springs CO 80477 also: Colo State Senate State Capitol 200 E Colfax Rm 274 Denver CO 80203

TAYLOR, JAMES L. naval officer; Grad., U.S. Naval Acad., 1965; M in Computer Systems, Naval Post Grad. Sch., Monterey, Calif., 1977, M in Mech. Engring., 1979. Commd. ensign USN, 1965, advanced through grades to rear adm., 1996; various assignments to dep. dir. for shipyard mgmt. Naval Sea Systems Command Hdqtrs., 1989-90; dir. Supportability, Maintenance and Modernization Divsn. Chief of Naval Opers., 1994-96; fleet maintenance officer, dep. chief of staff U.S. Pacific Fleet, 1996-99; sr. v.p., group mgr. Sci. Applications Internat. Corp., 1999—. Decorated Legion of Merit, Meritorious Svc. medal, Disting. Svc. medal. E-mail: james_taylor@amsec.com

TAYLOR, JAMES WALTER, business and management educator; b. St. Cloud, Minn., Feb. 15, 1933; s. James T. and Nina C. Taylor; m. Joanne Syktte, Feb. 3, 1956; children: Theodore James, Samuel Bennett, Christopher John. BBA, U. Minn., 1957; MBA, NYU, 1960; DBA, U. So. Calif., 1975. Mgr. research div. Atlantic Refining, Phila., 1960-65; dir. new product devel. Hunt-Wesson Foods, Fullerton, Calif., 1965-72; prof. mktg. Calif. State U., Fullerton, 1972-95; mng. dir. Innovative Mgmt. Devel. Co., Laguna Beach, Calif., 1975—. Cons. Smithkline Beecham Corp., Tokyo, Govt. of Portugal, Lisbon, Austrade, Govt. of Australia, Hagenfeldt-Affarerna AB, Stockholm. Author: Profitable New Product Strategies, 1984, How to Create a Winning Business Plan, 1986, Competitive Marketing Strategies, 1986, The 101 Best Performing Companies in America, 1987, The Complete Manual for Developing Winning Strategic Plans, 1988, Every Manager's Survival Guide, 1989, Developing Winning Strategic Plans, 1990, How to Develop Successful Advertising Plans, 1993, Marketing Planning: A Step by Step Guide, 1997, The Marketing Strategy and Planning Workbook, 2000. Fulbright scholar Ministry of Industry, Lisbon, Portugal, 1986-87, U. We. Sydney, Australia, 1989-90; recipient Merit award Calif. State U., 1986-90. Mem. The Planning Forum, Am. Mktg. Assn., Strategic Mgmt. Assn., Assn. for Consumer Rsch., Acad. Mktg. Sci. Home: 3190 Mountain View Dr Laguna Beach CA 92651-2056 E-mail: drjwtaylor@surfcity.net

TAYLOR, JOHN BRIAN, economist, educator; b. Yonkers, N.Y., Dec. 8, 1946; s. John Joseph and Lorraine (Crowley) T.; m. Raye Allyn Price, Dec. 30, 1972; children: Jennifer Lynn, John Andrew. AB in Econs. summa cum laude, Princeton U., 1968; PhD, Stanford U., 1973. Asst. prof. econs. Columbia U., N.Y.C., 1973-77, assoc. prof., 1977-79, prof., 1979-80; prof. econs. and pub. affairs Princeton U., 1980-84; prof. econs. Stanford U., 1984—, dir. Ctr. for Econ. Policy Rsch., 1994-97, dir. Introductory Econs. Ctr., 1997-2001; under sec. for internat. affairs U.S. Treasury, Washington, 2001—. Vis. prof. econs., Yale U., 1980; sr. staff economist Pres.'s coun. Econ. Advisers, 1976—77, mem., 1989—91; econometric cons. Townsend-Greenspan and Co., NY, 1978—81; rsch. adv. Fed. Res. Bank, Phila., 1981—84; rsch. assoc. Nat. Bur. Econ. Rshc., 1980—; rsch. economist Bank of Japan, Tokyo, 1987, hon. adv., 1994—2001; panel of econ. advisers Congl. Budget Office, 1995—2001. Author: (non-fiction) Macroeconomics, 1986, Macroeconomic Policy in the World Economy, 1993, Economics, 1995, Unemployment, Inflation, and Monetary Policy, 1998, Monetary Policy Rules, 1999, Handbook of Macroeconomics, 2000; co-editor: Am. Econ. Rev., 1985—89; editor (assoc.): Econometrica, 1981—85, (jour.) Jour. Econ. Dynamics and Control, 1978—85, Jour. Monetary Econs., 1978—83, Jour. Econ. Perspectives, 1997—2001;contbr. articles to profl. jours. NSF grantee, 1979-81, 81-83, 83-86, 86-89, 92-95; Guggenheim Found. fellow, 1983-84; sr. fellow Hoover Instn., 1996—. Fellow Econometric Soc., Am. Acad. of Arts and Sci.; mem. Am. Econ. Assn. (exec. com. 1991-94, v.p. 2000-01). Office: US Dept Treasury 1500 Pennsylvania Ave NW Washington DC 20220

TAYLOR, JOHN JOSEPH, nuclear engineer, researcher; b. Hackensack, N.J., Feb. 27, 1922; s. John J.D. and Johanna F. (Thibideau) T.; m. Lorraine Crowley, Feb. 5, 1943; children: John B., Nancy M., Susan M. BA, St. John's U., Jamaica, NY, 1942, St. John's U., Jamaica, N.Y., 1942; DSc (hon.), 1975; MS, U. Notre Dame, 1947. Mathematician Bendix Aviation Corp., Teterboro, N.J., 1946-47; engr. Kellex Corp., N.Y.C., 1947-50; v.p. water reactor div. Westinghouse Electric Corp., Pitts., 1950-81; v.p. nuclear power Electric Power Rsch. Inst., Palo Alto, Calif., 1981-95; energy cons., 1995—. Mem. adv. com. Oak Ridge (Tenn.) Nat. Lab., 1973-83, Brookhaven Nat. Lab., Upton, N.Y., 1986-92, Inst. for Nuclear Power Ops., 1988-95; mem. adv. com. Argonne (Ill.), Nat. Lab., 1980-86, bd. dirs.; cons. Office Tech. Assessment, Washington, 1975-93; mem. internat. adv. group IAEA, Vienna, Austria, 1992-95; mem. nuclear rsch. rev. com. NRC, 1995-97; mem. U.S.-Russian Commn. on Weapons Plutonium Disposition, 1996—, Nat. Acad. Bd. Radioactive Waste Mgmt., 1998—, DOE Nuclear Energy Rsch. Adv. Bd., 1998—. Co-author: Reactor Shielding Manual, 1953, Naval Reactor Physics Manual, 1956, Nuclear Power, Policy and Prospects, 1987, Management and Disposition of Excess Weapons Plutonium; contbr. articles to profl. jours. Bd. regents St. Mary's Coll., Moraga, Calif. Lt. (j.g.) USN, 1942-45. Recipient Order of Merit, Westinghouse Electric Corp., 1957, George Westinghouse Gold medal ASME, 1990. Fellow AAAS, Am. Phys. Soc., Am. Nuclear Soc. (bd. dirs. Walter Zinn award 1993); mem. NAE, Nat. Acad. Engring., Cosmos Club (Washington). Republican. Roman Catholic. Home: 15 Oliver Ct Menlo Park CA 94025-6685 Office: Electric Power Rsch Inst PO Box 10412 3412 Hillview Ave Palo Alto CA 94304-1344

TAYLOR, KENDRICK JAY, microbiologist; b. Manhattan, Mont., Mar. 17, 1914; s. William Henry and Rose (Carney) T.; m. Hazel Marguerite Griffith, July 28, 1945; children: Stanley, Paul (dec.), Richard. BS, Mont. State U., 1938; postgrad. (fellow), U. Wash., 1938-41, U. Calif., Berkeley, 1952, Drama Studio of London, , 1985. Rsch. microbiologist Cutter Labs., Berkeley, Calif., 1945-74; microbiologist Berkeley Biologicals, 1975-86. Committeeman Mount Diablo coun. Boy Scouts Am., 1955, dist. vice-chmn., 1960-61, dist. chmn., 1962-65, cubmaster, 1957, scoutmaster, 1966; active Contact Ministries, 1977-80; bd. dirs. Santa Clara Cmty. Players, 1980-84; vol. instr. ESL, 1979-80; vol. ARC Blood Ctr., 1985-96, VA Hosp., 1986-96, San Jose; life mem. PTA; census taker, 1980; mem. Berkely Jr. C. of C., 1946-49. With AUS, 1941-46, lt. col. Res., ret. Recipient Scout's Wood badge Boy Scouts Am., 1962, Golden Diploma Mont. State U., 1988, Silver Diploma, 1998. Mem. Am. Soc. Microbiology (chmn. local com. 1953, v.p. No. Calif. br. 1963-65, pres. 1965-67), Sons and Daus. Mont. Pioneers, Mont. State U. Alumni Assn., Mont. Hist. Soc., Gallatin County Hist. Soc., Headwaters-Heritage Hist. Soc., Am. Legion (post 89), PTA Calif. (life). Presbyterian (trustee 1951-53, elder 1954—). Home: 550 S 13th St San Jose CA 95112-2361

TAYLOR, LEIGH HERBERT, college dean; b. Chgo., Oct. 23, 1941; s. Herbert and Leona Taylor; m. Nancy E. Young; children: Jennifer, Jeremiah. BA, U. Tulsa, 1964, JD, 1966; LLM, NYU, 1969. Bar: Okla. 1966, Ill. 1976. Trial atty. Civil Rights div. Dept. Justice, Washington, 1966-68; prof. DePaul U. Coll. Law, Chgo., 1969-77, asst. dean, 1972-73, assoc. dean, 1973-77; dean Coll. Law, Ohio No. U., Ada, 1977-78, Sch. Law Southwestern U., L.A., 1978—. Mem. adv. bd. 1st Woman's Bank of L.A., 1981-85; dir. Law Sch. Admissions Svcs., Inc., 1982-86; chmn. audit com. Law Sch. Admissions Coun., 1989-91, trustee, 1991-98, chair-elect, 1994-95, chair, 1995-97; mem. bd. trustees Coun. on Legal Edn. Opportunity, 1993-96, NALP Found., 1999-2003. Editor-in-chief Tulsa Law Jour., 1966; author: Strategies for Law-Focused Education, 1977; (with others) Law in a New Land, 1972; mem. editorial bd. Family Law Quarterly, 1977-78. Bd. dirs. Criminal Def. Consortium Cook County (Ill.), Inc., 1975-77, L.A. Press Club Found., NALP Found., 1999—. With AUS, 1959. Fellow Am. Bar Found.; mem. ABA (accreditation com. 1991-95), Law in Am. Soc. Found., Ill. Bar Assn., Chgo. Bar Assn. (rec. sec.), L.A. County Bar Assn., Okla. Bar Assn. Office: Southwestern U Sch Law Office of Dean 675 S Westmoreland Ave Los Angeles CA 90005-3905 E-mail: ltaylor@swlaw.edu

TAYLOR, LESLIE GEORGE, mining and financial company executive; b. London, Oct. 8, 1922; came to U.S., 1925; s. Charles Henry and Florence Louisa (Renouf) T.; m. Monique S. Schuster, May, 1964 (div. 1974); children: Leslie G. Anthony II, Sandra J. Mira, Linda S. Marshall; m. Wendy Ann Ward, July 4, 1979. BBA, U. Buffalo, 1952. Asst. to pres. Kelsey Co., 1952-60; pres. Aluminum Industries and Glen Alden Co., Cin. and N.Y.C., 1960-63; pres., chmn. bd. dirs. DC Internat. (and European subs.), Denver, 1963-68; prin. Taylor Energy Enterprises, Denver, 1968—, Taylor Mining Enterprises, Denver, 1968—, Leslie G. Taylor and Co., Denver, 1968—. Del. Internat. Astronautical Soc., Stockholm, 1968, London, 69, Speditur Conv., 1976; bd. dir. Merendon Mining Internat., Calgary, Alta, Agri Health Internat., Agaro Internat., Inc.; sr. adv. Voice Mobility, Inc., Richmond, BC, Canada. Mem. USCG Aux. Mem. Soc. Automotive Engrs., Shriners, Masons, Scottish Rites. Republican. Episcopalian. Fax: 541-956-9699

TAYLOR, MIKE A. state legislator; b. Lewistown, Mont., June 12, 1941; m. Janna Taylor. Grad., Wilmington (Ohio) H.S. In bus. and agr.; mem. Mont. Senate, Dist. 37, Helena, 1996—; vice chair fish and game com.; vice chair jt. appropriations subcom. gen. govt. and transp.; mem. fin./claims com., natural resources com., rules com. Mem. Elks, Rotary. Republican. Home: PO Box 152 Proctor MT 59929-0152

TAYLOR, MINNA, lawyer; b. Washington, Jan. 25, 1947; d. Morris P. and Anne (Williams) Glushien; m. Charles Ellett Taylor, June 22, 1969; 1 child, Amy Caroline. BA, SUNY, Stony Brook, 1969; MA, SUNY, 1973; JD, U. So. Calif., 1977. Bar: Calif. 1977, U.S. Dist. Ct. (cen. dist.) Calif. 1978. Extern to presiding justice Calif. Supreme Ct., 1977; field atty. NLRB, L.A., 1977-82; dir. employee rels., legal svcs. Paramount Pictures Corp., L.A., 1982-85, v.p. employee rels. legal svcs., 1985-89; dir. bus. and legal affairs Wilshire Ct. Prodns., L.A., 1989-91; sr. counsel Fox Broadcasting Co., L.A., 1991-92, v.p. legal affairs, 1992-97, sr. v.p. legal affairs, 1997—. Editor notes and articles: U. So. Calif. Law Rev., 1976-77. Mentor MOSTE, L.A., 1986-87, 88-89; pres. Beverly Hills chpt. ACLU, L.A., 1985. Fellow ABA, Calif. State Bar (mem. copyright subcom. 1994-95), L.A. County Bar Assn.; mem. Beverly Hills Bar Assn., L.A. Bead Soc. (membership sec. 1992-94, mem. bd. dirs. 1994-95), Order of Coif. Office: Fox Broadcasting Co 10201 W Pico Blvd Los Angeles CA 90064-2606

TAYLOR, PALMER W. pharmacology educator; m. Susan Serota; three children. BS in Pharmacy, U. Wis., 1960, PhD in Phys. Pharmacy, 1964. Rsch. assoc. pharmacology-toxicology assoc. program Lab. Chem. Pharmacology, 1965-68; NIH fellow molecular pharmacology unit Med. Rsch. Coun., Cambridge, Eng., 1968-70; NIH fellow Max Planck Inst. for Phys. Chemistry, Gottingen, Germany, 1970; asst. prof. divsn. pharmacology dept. medicine U. Calif., San Diego, 1971-74, assoc. prof. divsn. pharmacology dept. medicine, 1974-78, prof. divsn. pharmacology dept. medicine, 1978-87, head divsn. pharmacology dept. medicine, 1979-87, prof., chair dept. pharmacology, 1987—, Sandra & Monroe Trout endowed chair pharmacology, 1994—. Mem. pharmacology study sect. NIH, 1974-78; mem. study sect. on chemotherapeutic agts. Multiple Sclerosis Soc., 1974-86; co-chmn. conf. on membrane receptors and diseases NIH-NIGMS, Bethesda, Md., 1978; participant Nat. Acad. Scis. Pharmacology Symposium, 1979; co-chair ASPET Symposium on Application of Molecular Pharmacology to Therapeutic Considerations, 1980; mem. pharmacol. scis. rev. com. NIH, 1980-85; vis. fellow Darwin Coll., U. Cambridge, 1980-81; Sterling Drug Co. vis. prof. U. Mich., 1985, U. Oreg., 1990; nat. adv. coun. mem. Nat. Inst. Gen. Med. Scis., 1988-92; vice chair, chair Gordon Conf. on Molecular Pharmacology, 1987-89; Krantz Meml. lectr. U. Md., 1989; Harold C. Hodge lectr. U. Rochester Med. Ctr., 1992; vis. prof., lectr. series Coll. de France, 1999, Tyler lectr. series Purdue U.; bd. trustees Gordon Rsch. Confs., 1999—. Co-editor: (with W.B. Pratt) Principles of Drug Action, 3d edit., 1990, (with A.G. Gilman, T.W. Rall and A.S. Nies) Godoman and Gilman's Pharmacological Basis of Therapeutics, 8th edit., 1990; assoc. editor Molecular Pharmacology, 1971-75; mem. editl. bd. Jour. Biol. Chemistry, 1981-86, 92-98, Molecular Pharmacology, 1983—, Trends in Pharmacol. Scis., 1983-90, Jour. Molecular Medicine, 1992-98, Pharm. News, 1997—; cons. editor Jour. Clin. Investigation, 1992-98; contbr. articles to profl. jours. Recipient Borden award, Phi Lambda Upsilon award in pharm. chemistry; Fogarty fellow U. Cambridge,

1980-81. Mem. NAS-Inst. Medicine, Internat. Union Pharmacology (del. 1995—), Am. Soc. for Clin. Investigation (hon.), Am. Soc. for Pharmacology and Exptl. Therapeutics (councillor 1987-90, pres.-elect 1994-95, pres. 1995-96), Am. Soc. for Biochemistry and Molecular Biology, Am. Assn. for Med. Sch. Pharmacology, Fedn. Exptl. Biologists (bd. mem. 1995-99). Office: Dept Pharmacology Basic Sci Bldg 9500 Gilman Dr La Jolla CA 92093-0636 E-mail: pwtaylor@ucsd.edu

TAYLOR, REESE HALE, JR. lawyer, former government administrator; b. Los Angeles, May 6, 1928; s. Reese Hale and Kathryn (Emery) T.; m. Lucille Langdon, Dec. 29, 1948 (div. 1959); children: Reese Hale (dec.), Stuart Langdon, Anne Kathryn, Lucille Emery; m. Jolene Yerby, June 30, 1972. B.A. with distinction, Stanford U., 1949; LL.B., Cornell U., 1952. Bar: Calif. 1954, Nev. 1966. Assoc. Gibson, Dunn & Crutcher, Los Angeles, 1952-58; pvt. practice Los Angeles, 1958-65; assoc. Wiener, Goldwater & Galatz, Las Vegas, Nev., 1966-67; chmn. Nev. Pub. Service Commn., Carson City, 1967-71; ptnr. Laxalt, Berry & Allison, Carson City, 1971-78, Allison, Brunetti, MacKenzie & Taylor, Carson City, 1978-81; chmn. ICC, Washington, 1981-85; ptnr. Heron, Burchette, Ruckert & Rothwell, Washington, 1986-90, Taylor & Morell, Washington and Long Beach, Calif., 1990-91, Taylor, Morell & Gitomer, Washington and Long Beach, 1992-94; of counsel Keesal, Young & Logan, Long Beach, 1994—. Vice chmn. Nev. Tax Commn., Carson City, 1967-69; mem. Nev. Gov.'s Cabinet, Carson City, 1967-70, Carson City Bd. Equalization, 1979-81, chmn., 1979-80; bd. dirs. U.S. Rail Assn., Washington, 1981-85 Del. Republican Nat. Conv., Kansas City, Mo., 1976, mem. platform com., 1976, alt. del., Detroit, 1980; mem. Rep. Nat. Com., 1980-81. Mem. ABA, Am. Judicature Soc., Order of Coif, Phi Gamma Delta, Phi Delta Phi. Episcopalian. Office: Keesal Young & Logan Union Bank Bldg PO Box 1730 Long Beach CA 90801-1730

TAYLOR, RICHARD EDWARD, physicist, educator; b. Medicine Hat, Alta., Can., Nov. 2, 1929; came to U.S., 1952; s. Clarence Richard and Delia Alena (Brunsdale) T.; m. Rita Jean Bonneau, Aug. 25, 1951; 1 child, Norman Edward. BS, U. Alta., 1950, MS, 1952; PhD, Stanford U., 1962; Docteur honoris causa, U. Paris-Sud, 1980; DSc, U. Alta., 1991; LLD (hon.), U. Calgary, Alta., 1993; DSc (hon.), U. Lethbridge, Alta., 1993, U. Victoria, B.C., Can., 1994; D honoris causa, U. Blaise Pascal, 1997; DSc honoris causa, Carleton U., Ottawa, Ont., 1999; DSc (hon.), U. Liverpool, U.K., 1999, Queen's U., Kingston, Ont., 2000. Boursier Lab. de l'Accelerateur Lineaire, Orsay, France, 1958-61; physicist Lawrence Berkeley Lab., Berkeley, Calif., 1961-62; staff mem. Stanford (Calif.) Linear Accelerator Ctr., 1962-68, assoc. dir., 1982-86, prof., 1968—. Fellow Guggenheim Found., 1971-72, von Humboldt Found., 1982; recipient Nobel prize in physics, 1990. Fellow AAAS, Am. Acad. Arts and Scis., Am. Phys. Soc. (W.K.H. Panofsky prize div. particles and fields 1989), Royal Soc. Can., Royal Soc. London; mem. Can. Assn. Physicists, Nat. Acad. Scis. (fgn. assoc.). Office: Stanford Linear Accelerator Ctr M/S 96 2575 Sand Hill Rd Menlo Park CA 94025-7015 E-mail: retaylor@slac.stanford.edu

TAYLOR, ROBERT BROWN, medical educator; b. Elmira, N.Y., May 31, 1936; s. Olaf C. Taylor and Elizabeth (Place) Brown; m. Anita Dopico; children: Diana Taylor Root, Sharon Taylor Oliverio. Student, Bucknell U., 1954-57; MD, Temple U., 1961. Diplomate Am. Bd. Family Practice. Gen. practice medicine, New Paltz, N.Y., 1964-78; faculty physician Sch. Medicine Wake Forest U., Winston-Salem, N.C., 1978-84; prof. dept. family medicine Oreg. Health Scis. U. Sch. Medicine, Portland, 1984—, chmn., 1984-98. Mem. comprehensive part II com. Nat. Bd. Med. Examiners, Phila., 1986-91. Author: Common Problems in Office Practice, 1972, The Practical Art of Medicine, 1974; editor: Family Medicine: Principles and Practice, 1978, 5th edit., 1998, Health Promotion: Principles and Clinical Applications, 1982, Difficult Diagnosis, 1985, Difficult Medical Management, 1991, Difficult Diagnosis II, 1992, Fundamentals of Family Medicine, 1996, Fundamentals of Family Medicine, 1998, Manual of Family Practice, 1997, Taylor's Review of Family Medicine, 1998, Manual of Ten-Minute Diagnosis, 2000; contbg. editor Physicians Mgmt. Mag., 1972-99; editl. bd. The Family Practice Rsch. Jour., 1980-90, The Female Patient, 1984—, Am. Family Physician, 1990-98, Jour. of Family Practice, 1990-93, Med. Tribune, 1993-99. Served as surgeon USPHS, 1961-64. Fellow Am. Acad. Family Physicians (sci. program com., Thomas Johnson award), Am. Coll. Preventive Medicine; mem. Soc. Tchrs. Family Medicine (bd. dirs., cert. of excellence), Assn. Am. Med. Colls., Am. Assn. for Study Headache, World Orgn. Family Physicians (chmn. sci. program com.), City Club, Multnomah Athletic Club, Phi Beta Kappa, Alpha Omega Alpha.. Home: 1414 SW 3rd Ave Apt 2904 Portland OR 97201-6629 Office: Oreg Health Scis U Sch Medicine Mail Code FP 3181 SW Sam Jackson Park Rd Portland OR 97201-3011 E-mail: taylorr@ohsu.edu

TAYLOR, ROBERT P. lawyer; b. Douglas, Ariz., May 6, 1939; s. Paul Burton and Mary Ruth (Hart) T.; m. Sybil Ann Cappelletti, May 30, 1963 (div. Apr. 1974); children: David Scott, Nicole; m. Anne Dale Kaiser, Sept. 21, 1991. BSEE, U. Ariz., 1961; JD, Georgetown U., 1969. Bar: U.S. Ct. Appeals (9th circ.) 1969, U.S. Ct. Appeals (1st, 2d, 3d, 6th, and Fed. circs.), U.S. Supreme Ct., 1975. Elec. engr. Motorola Corp., Phoenix, 1961, Bell & Howell, Pasadena, Calif., 1964-65; examiner U.S. Patent Office, Washington, 1966-69; atty. Pillsbury Madison & Sutro, San Francisco, 1969-96, Howrey, Simon, Arnold & White, LLP, Menlo Park, Calif., 1996—. Mem. adv. commn. Patent Law Reform, Washington, 1990-92; mem. adv. bd. Litigation Risk Analysis, Palo Alto, Calif., 1985—. Contbr. articles to profl. jours. Dir. Ind. Colls. of No. Calif., San Francisco, 1982-96, officer, 1988-96. Fellow Am. Coll. Trial Lawyers; mem. ABA (chair sect. antitrust 1991-92), Am. Law Inst. Avocations: bicycling, cooking, hiking. Office: Howrey Simon Arnold & White LLP 301 Ravenswood Ave Menlo Park CA 94025-3434

TAYLOR, ROBIN L. state legislator, lawyer; b. Sedro Woolley, Wash., Feb. 5, 1943; m. Kaye Marie Taylor; children: Robin, Tracy Lynn. BA, U. Wash., 1965; MA, Oreg. Coll. Edn., 1966; JD, Willamette U., 1969. Mem. Alaska Senate, Dist. A, Juneau, 1992—; chair adminstrv. regulation rev. com. Alaska Senate, chair judiciary com., vice-chair resources com. Pres. Alaska Judges Conf., 1981-82. Mem. Borough Assembly/City Coun., Ketchikan, 1973-76; vice mayor City of Ketchikan, 1974-75; dist. ct. judge, Alaska, 1977-82; pres. Pacific Conf., 1995-96; chmn. Western Legis. Forestry Task Force, 1996. Mem. NRA, Am. Judicature Soc. (nat. bd. dirs. 1980-83), Alaska Bar Assn., Pioneers of Alaska, Ketchikan Masons Lodge, Wrangell Elks Lodge, Petersburg Moose Lodge. Republican. Avocations: fishing, hunting, golf, gardening. Office: State Capitol 120 4th St Rm 30 Juneau AK 99801-1142 also: PO Box 1441 Wrangell AK 99929-1441 also: 50 Front St Ste 203 Ketchikan AK 99901-6439 Fax: 907-465-3922/907-874-3470/907-225-0713. E-mail: senatorrobintaylor@legis.state.ak.us

TAYLOR, RUTH ANNE, lawyer; b. Honolulu, Feb. 18, 1961; d. Gerald Lou and Charlotte Anne (Nelson) Allison; m. Thomas Scott Taylor, Dec. 28, 1985; children: Kyle Thomas, Kelly Gerald, Kory Scott. BA in Journalism, U. So. Calif., 1984; JD, N.Y. Law Sch., 1987. Bar: Calif. 1987, U.S. Dist. Ct. (so. dist.) Calif., U.S. Ct. Appeals (9th cir.). Assoc. Carlsmith, Wichman, Case Mukai & Ichiki, L.A., L.A., 1987-89, Christensen, White, Miller, Fink & Jacobs, L.A., 1989-93; assoc. gen. counsel Warner Bros. Records, Inc., 1993-98, v.p. legal and bus. affairs, 1998—. Mem. Los Angeles County Bar Assn., Beverly Hills Bar Assn. Republican. Avocations: scuba diving, skiing, photography, cooking.

TAYLOR, STEVEN BRUCE, agriculture company executive; b. Salinas, Calif., Dec. 29, 1954; s. Edward Horton and Joanne (Church) T.; m. Kathryn Hagler, Dec. 17, 1978; children: Meghan Jean, Kyle Hagler, Christian Steven. BA, U. Calif., Berkeley, 1978; MBA, Harvard U., 1985. Pres. Fresh Concepts, San Marino, Calif., 1985-87; mktg. staff Bruce Church, Inc., Salinas, 1987-91; pres. Fresh Express Retail Mktg., Salinas, 1991-93, Fresh Internat., Salinas, 1991-93; CEO, chmn. Fresh Express Fresh Foods (formerly Fresh Internat.), Salinas, 1993—. V.p. Salinas Valley Lettuce Co-op, Salinas, 1990—; bd. dirs. Produce for Better Health, Del., 1991—. Bd. Elders First Presbyn. Ch., Salinas, 1989-92, personnel com. 1989-94, bldg. com. 1990—; founding mem. Lincoln Club of Monterey County, Salinas, 1990. Avocations: basketball, skiing, soccer coach, bible study, board games. Home: 515 Santa Paula Dr Salinas CA 93901-1517 Office: Fresh Express Fresh Foods 1020 Merrill St Salinas CA 93901-4409

TAYLOR, TONY S. research scientist; Dir. exptl. sci. divsn. Gen. Atomics, San Diego. Recipient Excellence in Plasma Physics Rsch. award Am. Phys. Soc., 1994. Office: General Atomics PO Box 85608 San Diego CA 92186-5608

TAYLOR, WENDY, magazine editor; Editor PC Computing, San Francisco. Office: Smart Business 50 Beale St Fl 13 San Francisco CA 94105-1813

TAYLOR, WILLIAM AL, state supreme court justice; b. Lusk, Wyo., Nov. 2, 1928; m. Jane Y.; 3 children. BA, U. Wyo., 1951, LLD, 1959. Bar: Wyo. 1959. Teacher, Lusk, 1950-51,54-55; pvt. practice Lusk, 1959-78; city atty. Town of Lusk, 1962-74; atty. Niobrara County, Wyo., 1964-77; judge Wyo. Dist. Ct. (8th dist.), Cheyenne, 1980-93; justice Wyoming Supreme Ct., 1993—, chief justice, 1996-98. Exec. dir. Wyo. State Bar, 1977-80. Staff sgt. U.S. Army, 1951-53. Mem. Wyo. State Bar (Civil Rules com.), Wyo. Judicial Conf. (chmn. 1984-85),Tenth Cir. Bar Assn., Nat. Trial Judges, Am. Legion, Sigma Alpha Epsilon. Office: State Wyo Supreme Ct Supreme Ct Bldg Cheyenne WY 82002-0001

TAYLOR, WILLIAM JAMES (ZAK TAYLOR), lawyer; b. Milw., Jan. 26, 1948; s. William Elmer and Elizabeth Emily (Lupinski) T.; m. Marlou Belyea, Sept. 20, 1975; children: Danielle Belyea, James Zachary Belyea. BA in Econs., Yale U., 1970; JD, Harvard U., 1976. Bar: Calif. 1976, U.S. Dist. Ct. (cen. dist.) Calif. 1976, U.S. Dist. Ct. (no. dist.) Calif. 1977, U.S. Ct. Appeals (9th cir.) 1977, U.S. Dist. Ct. (ea. dist.) Calif. 1980, U.S. Supreme Ct. 1980, U.S. Tax Ct. 1988. Law clk. to hon. Shirley M. Hufstedler U.S. Ct. Appeals (9th cir.), L.A., 1976-77; assoc. Broebeck, Phleger & Harrison, San Francisco, 1977-83; ptnr. Broebeck, Phleger and Harrison, San Francisco, 1983-95; shareholder Taylor & Jenkins, P.C., Oakland, Calif., 1995-96, Chilvers & Taylor, P.C., Oakland, 1996-99; of counsel Brobeck, Phleger & Harrison, LLP, San Francisco, 2000—. Bd. dirs. Berkeley (Calif.) Law Found., 1988-91, Legal Svcs. for Children (recipient Jean Waldman Child Advocacy award, San Francisco 1988), 1983-89; co-chmn. Attys. Task Force for Children, San Francisco, 1983-89. Editor-in-chief Harvard Civil Rights, Civil Liberties Law Rev., 1976; bd. editors No. Dist. Calif. Digest, 1978-83; co-author: California Antitrust Law, 1991; contbg. editor: Calif. Bus. Law Reporter, 1995-96, Antitrust Law Developments, 1997. With U.S. Army, 1970-73. Mem. ABA, Bar Assn. San Francisco (bd. dirs. 1986-87, chair antitrust sect. 1987, chair fed. cts. sect. 1995-97), Am. Bus. Trial Lawyers Assn., Nat. Health Lawyers Assn., Calif. Soc. Healthcare Attorneys, Barristers of San Francisco (bd. dirs. 1980-82, v.p. 1982-83). Democrat. Office: Brobeck Phleger & Harrison LLP 1 Market Spear Tower San Francisco CA 94105-1420 E-mail: wtaylor@brobeck.com, wta9786011@cs.com

TCHAIKOVSKY, LESLIE J. judge; b. 1943; BA, Calif. State Univ., Hayward, 1967; JD, Univ. of Calif., Berkeley, 1976. Law clk. to Hon. John Mowbray Nev. Supreme Ct., 1976-77; with Dinkelspiel, Steefel, Leavitt & Weiss, 1977-80, Gordon, Peitzman & Lopes, 1981, Dinkelspiel, Donovan & Reder, 1981-88; bankruptcy judge U.S. Bankruptcy Ct. (Calif. no. dist.), 9th circuit, Oakland, 1988—. Office: US Courthouse 1300 Clay St Oakland CA 94612-1425

TEAGUE, ROBERT COLE, physician; b. Waxahachie, Tex., June 13, 1930; s. Isaac Lawson and Frances (Cole) T.; m. Virginia M. Teague, Nov. 11, 1960; children: Patrick, Michael. BA in Chemistry, Baylor U., Waco, Tex., 1951; MD, U. Tex., Galveston, 1955. Diplomate Am. Bd. Family Practice. Intern McLaren Hosp., Flint, Mich., 1955-56; med. officer USNR, 1956-58; physician family practice LaJolla, Calif., 1958-63, Phoenix, 1963—. Med. dir. Vis. Nurse Svc., Phoenix; chmn. Family Practice Humana Hosp., 1984-86, past chmn.; chmn. Family Practice Good Samaritan Hosp., 1990-91. Fellow Am. Acad. Family Physicians (charter); mem. Ariz. Acad. Family Physicians (past pres. 1988). Republican. Episcopalian. Avocations: golf, travel. Office: 1550 E Maryland Ave Phoenix AZ 85014-1448

TEBEDO, MARYANNE, state legislator; b. Denver, Oct. 30, 1936; m. Don Tebedo; children: Kevin, Ronald, Linda, Thomas, Christine. Mem. Colo. Ho. of Reps., Denver, 1982-88, Colo. Senate, Denver, 1988-. Profl. parliamentarian. Republican. Office: Colorado State Senate State Capitol Bldg 200 E Colfax Ave Ste 346 Denver CO 80203-1716

TECK, RONALD JAY, state legislator; b. Pueblo, Colo., Sept. 22, 1947; s. John Alan Teck and Chloie Beatrice (Barnett) Morris; m. Beverly Merline Smith Kanda, Sept. 9, 1978 (div. 1987); m. Patricia Kay Artz, Nov. 6, 1989; children: Michael Alan, John Franklin. BA in Chemistry, U. Colo., 1970. Chemist Nat. Ctr. Atmosphere Rsch., Boulder, Colo., 1970-74; cons. Dames & Moore, Park Ridge, Ill., 1974-75, Ambient Analysis Inc., Boulder, 1975; sales rep. Sargent-Welch Scientific, Denver, 1975-77; program analyst Bendix Field Engring., Grand Junction, Colo., 1977-83; realtor Gale & Co., others, Grand Junction, 1983-92; assesor Mesa County Govt., Grand Junction, 1992-98; mem. Colo. Senate, Dist. 7, Denver, 1998—. Contbr. articles to profl. jours. Mem. legis. com. Grand Junction Bd. of Realtos, 1988-92, pres. 1986-87. Named Realtor of Yr. Grand Junction Bd. of Realtors, 1988-92. Mem. Colo. Assessors Assn., Grand Junction C. of C. (govtl. affairs). Republican. Avocations: camping, cooking. Address: State Capitol 200 E Colfax Ave Ste 346 Denver CO 80203-1716

TEDFORD, CHARLES FRANKLIN, biophysicist; b. Lawton, Okla., June 26, 1928; s. Charles E. and Loula B. (Waters) T.; m. Julie Reme Sauret, Sept. 15, 1951; children: Gary Franklin, Mark Charles, Philip John. BS with distinction in Chemistry, S.W. Tex. State U., 1950, MS, 1954; postgrad. in radiobiology Reed Coll., 1957, in biophysics U. Calif., Berkeley, 1961-63. Enlisted USN, 1945-47, commd. ensign, 1950, advanced through grades to capt., 1968; biochemist U.S. Naval Hosp., San Diego, 1953-54, U.S. Naval Biol. Lab., Oakland, Calif., 1954-56; sr. instr., radiation safety officer Nuclear, Biol. and Chem. Warfare Def. Sch., Treasure Island, Calif., 1956-61; asst. chief nuclear medicine div. Navy Med. Sch., Bethesda, Md., 1963-66; adminstrv. program mgr. radiation safety br. Bur. Medicine and Surgery, Washington, 1966-72; dir. radiation safety and health physics program Navy Regional Med. Center, San Diego, 1972-74; mgr. Navy Regional Med. Clinic, Seattle, 1974-78, ret., 1978; dir. radiation health unit Ga. Dept. Human Resources, Atlanta, 1978-79; dir. Ariz. Radiation Regulatory Agy., Tempe, 1979-91; chief, Radiological Health Prog., Juneau, Alaska, 1991-93, ret. 1993; cons. 1993—. elected chmn. Conf. Radiation Program Dirs., 1987; named Ariz. Southwestern Low Level Radioactive Waste Compact Commr., 1990. Recipient Ariz. Adminstr. of Yr. award Ariz. Adminstrs. Assn., 1988; decorated Legion of Merit, Meritorious Service medal. Mem. Health Physics Soc., Am. Nuclear Soc. Contbr. articles on radiation safety to profl. publs.

TEEGUARDEN, DENNIS EARL, forest economist, educator; b. Gary, Ind., Aug. 21, 1931; s. Gary Leon and Mary Dessa (Purciful) T.; m. Sally Annette Gleason, Dec. 23, 1954; children— Jason Earl, Julie Annette, Justin Gary. B.S. in Forestry with honors, Mich. Tech. U., Houghton, 1953; M.Forestry, U. Calif., Berkeley, 1958, Ph.D. in Agrl. Econs. (Bidwell research fellow 1962-63), 1964. Rsch. aid U.S. Forest Service, 1957; asst. rsch. specialist U. Calif., Berkeley, 1958-63, mem. faculty, 1963-91, prof. forestry econs. Sch. Forestry, 1963-91, S.J. Hall prof. forest econs., 1989-91, prof. emeritus, 1991—, chmn. dept. forestry and resource mgmt., 1978-86, acting dir. forest products lab., 1987-88, assoc. dean for acad. affairs, 1990-92, assoc. dean rsch. and extension, 1992-93. Mem. Calif. Commn. on Agr. and Higher Edn., 1993-95, com. scientists Dept. Agr., 1977-80; cons. in field; mem. adv. bd. U. Calif. Forest Products Lab., 1994-98; mem. adv. coun. Alberta Heritage Found. for Sci. and Engring. Rsch., 2001—. Co-author: Forest Resource Management: Decision-Making Principles and Cases, 1979; contbr. articles to profl. jours. Trustee Mich. Tech. Fund, Mich. Tech. U., Houghton, 1994—. Lt. USNR, 1953-57, Korea. Recipient Outstanding Alumnus award Mich. Tech. U., 1993, Berkeley citation U. Calif., Berkeley, 1994; grantee U.S. Forest Svc., Bur. Land Mgmt.; named to Honor Acad. Sch. Forestry and Wood Products, Mich. Tech. U., 1995. Fellow Soc. Am. Foresters; mem. Western Forest Economists, Calif. Water Fowl Assn. Home: 4732 Westwood Ct Richmond CA 94803-2441 Office: U Calif Coll Natural Resources Berkeley CA 94720-0001

TEEL, JOYCE RALEY, supermarket and drugstore retail executive; b. 1930; Dir. Raley's, West Sacramento, 1950—; co-chmn. bd. dirs. Raley's, Bel Air Markets, Food Source, Nob Hill Foods, No. Calif., Nev., NMex., 1991—. Dir. non-profit Food for Families. Office: Raleys & Belaire 500 W Capitol Ave West Sacramento CA 95605-2696

TEEL, MICHAEL J. supermarket chain executive; b. May 15, 1951; s. James and Joyce (Raley) T.; m. Tina Teel. Degree in Bus. Adminstrn., Whittier Coll., 1974. Various positions Raley's, West Sacramento, Calif., 1974-83, leadership trainee, 1988-93, asst. to pres. and CEO, 1993-95; COO Raley's Inc., West Sacramento, 1995, pres., 1996, pres., CEO, 1996—; prin. food industry-related advtg. agy., 1983-88; pres. Raley's & Bel Air, West Sacremento. Past chmn., com. mem. Sacramento Cmty. Leaders' Prayer Breakfast; vice chmn. bd. dirs. Families First; mem. Sacrament Host Com. Mem. Sacramento Met. C. of C. (bd. dirs.). Office: Raleys Inc 500 W Capitol Ave West Sacramento CA 95605 Fax: 916-444-3733

TEELE, CYNTHIA LOMBARD, lawyer; b. Boston, Oct. 11, 1961; d. John Hughes and Patricia Jeanne (Linder) T. AB in Urban Studies magna cum laude, Brown U., 1983; JD, U. Va., 1986. Bar: Calif. 1986. Assoc. Lillick McHose & Charles, L.A., 1986-87, Wyman Bautzer Kuchel & Silbert, L.A., 1987-91; sr. atty. Paramount Pictures Corp.-TV Divsn., Hollywood, Calif., 1991-92, dir., legal, 1992-94, v.p., legal, 1994—. Home: 3644 Berryman Ave Los Angeles CA 90066-3306

TEERLINK, J(OSEPH) LELAND, real estate developer; b. Salt Lake City, July 16, 1935; s. Nicholas John and Mary Luella (Love) T.; m. Leslie Dowdle, Nov. 5, 1975; children: Steven, David, Andrew, Suzanne, Benjamin. Student, U. Utah, 1953-55. Sales rep. Eastman Kodak Co., Salt Lake City, 1960-69; founder Graphic Systems, Inc., Salt Lake City, 1969-82, pres., 1969-79, chmn. bd., 1979-82; founder Graphic Ink Co., Salt Lake City, 1973, pres., 1975-79, chmn. bd., 1979-82; founder G.S.I. Leasing Co., Salt Lake City, 1975, pres., 1975-82; chmn. bd. Graphic Sys. Holding Co., Inc., Salt Lake City, 1978-82; dir. leasing and acquisitions Terra Industries, Inc., real estate developers, 1982-86, ptnr., 1986—. Bd. dirs. ARC, Salt Lake City, 1979-82; co-founder, dir. Hope Living Ctr. Found. for Mothers and Children, 1993-99; vice consulate of the Netherlands for Utah, 1977-92; mem. active corps of execs., SBA, 1979-83; mem. adv. bd. House of Hope Mothers and Children Utah Alcoholism Found., 1992-94. Recipient Masters award Salt Lake Bd. Realtors, 1993; named Small Businessman of the Yr. for Utah, SBA, 1978. Mem. Graphic Arts Equipment and Supply Dealers of Am. (dir. 1978-82), Printing Industry of Am., Nat. Assn. Indsl. and Office Parks (pres. Utah chpt. 1986-87), Nat. Fedn. Ind. Businessman, Million Dollar Club (life). Republican. Mormon. Home: 2984 Thackeray Pl Salt Lake City UT 84108-2517 Office: 6925 Union Park Ctr Midvale UT 84047-4135 E-mail: receptionist@terrautah.com

TEES, RICHARD CHISHOLM, psychology educator, researcher; b. Montreal, Que., Can., Oct. 31, 1940; s. Ralph Charles and Helen Winnifred (Chisholm) T.; m. Kathleen F. Coleman, Sept. 1, 1962; children: Susan M., Carolyn V. B.A., McGill U., 1961; Ph.D., U. Chgo., 1965. Asst. prof. U. B.C., Vancouver, 1965-67, assoc. prof., 1969-75, prof. psychology, 1975—, head dept. psychology, 1984-94, 99—. Rsch. prof. U. Sussex, Brighton, Eng., 1972-73, 77-78; chmn. grant selection panel Nat. Scis. and Engring. Rsch. Coun. Can., Ottawa, 1993-96, B.C. Health Care Rsch. Found., Vancouver, 1984-87; chmn. studentship com. Med. Rsch. Coun., Ottawa, 1985-92; chmn. Can. Coun. Dept. Psyc., 1987-93. Author: (with Kolb) Cerebral Cortex of the Rat, 1990; mem. editorial bd. Can. Jour. Exptl. Psychology, 1975-84, 87—; contbr. articles to profl. jours., chpts. to books. Research fellow Killam Found., 1972-73, 77-78; research fellow Can. Council, 1972-73 Fellow APA, Am. Psychol. Soc., Can. Psychol. Assn.; mem. Soc. for Neurosci., Psychonomic Soc., Can. Soc. Brain, Behaviour, and Cognitive Sci. (pres. 1997-98), U. B.C. Senate. Home: 1856 Acadia Rd Vancouver BC Canada V6T 1R3 Office: U BC Dept Psychology Vancouver BC Canada V6T 1Z4 E-mail: rtees@cortex.psych.ubc.ca

TEETS, JOHN WILLIAM, retired diversified company executive; b. Elgin, Ill., Sept. 15, 1933; s. John William and Maudie Teets; m. Nancy Kerchenfaut, June 25, 1965; children: Jerri, Valerie Sue, Heidi Jayne, Suzanne. Student, U. Ill.; LLD (hon.), Trinity Coll., 1982; DBA in Foodsvc. Mgmt. (hon.), Johnson and Wales U., 1991; D in Comml. Sci. (hon.), Western Internat. U., 1992. Pres., ptnr. Winter Garden Restaurant, Inc., Carpenterville, Ill., 1957-63; v.p. Greyhound Food Mgmt. Co.; pres. Post Houses, Inc., and Horne's Enterprises, Chgo., 1964-68; pres., chief operating officer John R. Thompson Co., Chgo., 1968-71; pres., corp. v.p. pub. restaurant divsn. Canteen Corp., Chgo., 1971-75; divsn. pres. Jacques Restaurant Group, 1975; exec. v.p., CEO Bonanza Internat. Co., Dallas, 1975; group v.p. food svcs., pres. Greyhound Food Mgmt., Inc. (now named Restaura), Phoenix, 1975; vice chmn. The Greyhound Corp., Phoenix, 1980; chmn., CEO Greyhound Corp. (now The Dial Corp), Phoenix, 1981-96; chmn., pres., CEO The Dial Corp, Phoenix, 1996-97; chmn., CEO JW Teets Enterprises LLC, Phoenix; chmn. The FINOVA Group, Inc., Scottsdale, AZ, 2001; ret., 2001. Vice chmn. Pres.' Conf. on Foodservice Industry. Recipient Silver Plate award, Golden Plate award Internat. Foodsvc. Mgrs. Assn., 1980, Bus. Leadership award Harvard Bus. Sch. Club Ariz., 1985, Order of the Crown, Kingdom of Belgium, 1990, Ellis Island medal of honor Nat. Ethnic Coalition of Orgns. Found., 1995; named Top Bus. Spkr. of Yr., Forbes Mag., 1990, Capt. of Achievement, Acad. of Achievement, 1992, CEO of Yr., Leaders Mag., 1986. Mem. Nat. Inst. Foodsvc. Industry (trustee), Am. Mgmt. Assn., Christian Businessmen's Assn. (chmn. steering com. 1977). Office: JW Teets Enterprises LLC 1850 N Central Ave Phoenix AZ 85077-0001

TEICHROB, CAROL, Canadian provincial official; b. Sask., Can., Aug. 27, 1939; d. J. Delbert and Elizabeth (Spenst) Sproxton; m. Donald P. Teichrob, Mar. 1, 1958; children: Lori, Sharon, James. Sr. matriculation, Notre Dame Convent, Morinville, Alta., Can. Cert. profl. ct. reporter, exec. mem. Can. and Saskatchewan Fedns. Agriculture, 1976-81; chmn. Can. Turkey Mktg. Agy., 1980-81, Plains Poultry Wynyard, Sask., 1981-88; founding ptnr. Primrose Books, Saskatoon, 1988—. Reeve, Rural Muncipality of Corman Park, Saskatoon, 1981-91; active U. Sask. Senate, 1981-86; mem. legis. assembly N.D.P. Caucus, 1991-98; appointed to cabinet as Min. of Edn., 1991-93, Min. of Mcpl. Affairs, Culture, and Housing, 1995—, responsible for Sasktel, 1995-97. Recipient Golden Wheel award Sask. Rotary, 1990; named Woman of Yr. in Bus., Sask. YWCA, 1981, Woman of Yr., 1982. Mem. Saskatoon C. of C. Office: Min Mcpl Govt Aff Culture House Legis Bldg Rm 307 Regina SK Canada S4S 0B3

TELLEM, SUSAN MARY, public relations executive; b. N.Y.C, May 23, 1945; d. John F. and Rita C. (Lietz) Cain; m. Marshall R.B.. Thompson; children: Tori, John, Daniel. BS, Mt. St. Mary's Coll., L.A., 1967. Cert. pub. health nurse; RN. Pres. Tellem Pub. Rels. Agy., Marina del Rey, Calif., 1977-80, Rowland Grody Tellem, L.A., 1980-90; chmn. The Rowland Co., L.A., 1990—; pres., CEO Tellem, Inc., L.A., 1992-93. Instr. UCLA Extension, 1983-97; adj. prof. Pepperdine U., 1999—; speaker numerous seminars and confs. on pub. rels. Editor: Sports Medicine for the '80's, Sports Medicine Digest, 1982-84. Bd. dirs. Marymount High Sch., 1984-87, pres., 1984-86; bd. dirs. L.A. Police Dept. Booster Assn., 1984-87; mem. Cath. Press Coun.; mem. pres.'s coun. Mus. Sci. and Industry. Mem. Am. Soc. Hosp. Mktg. and Pub. Rels., Healthcare Mktg. and Pub. Rels. Assn., Pub. Rels. Soc. Am. (bd. dirs. 1994—), L.A. Counselors, PETA, Am. Lung Assn. (chair comm. com. L.A. chpt.) Soc. for Prevention of Cruelty to Animals (chair PetSet), Sports Club (L.A.). Roman Catholic. Avocations: reading, tennis, aerobic dance. Office: 23852 Pacific Coast Hwy # 928 Malibu CA 90265-4879 Fax: 310-589-6101

TELLER, EDWARD, physicist; b. Budapest, Hungary, Jan. 15, 1908; naturalized, 1941; s. Max and Ilona (Deutch) T.; m. Augusta Harkanyi, Feb. 26, 1934; children: Paul, Susan Wendy. Student, Inst. Tech., Karlsruhe, Germany, 1926-28, U. Munich, , 1928; Ph.D., U. Leipzig, Germany, 1930; D.Sc. (hon.), Yale U., 1954, U. Alaska, 1959, Fordham U., 1960, George Washington U., 1960, U. So. Calif., 1960, St. Louis U., 1960, Rochester Inst. Tech., 1962, PMC Colls., 1963, U. Detroit, 1964, Clemson U., 1966, Clarkson Coll., 1969; LL.D., Boston Coll., 1961, Seattle U., 1961, U. Cin., 1962, U. Pitts., 1963, Pepperdine U., 1974, U. Md. at Heidelberg, 1977; D.Sc., L.H.D., Mt. Mary Coll., 1964; Ph.D., Tel Aviv U., 1972; D.Natural Sci., DeLaSalle U., Manila, 1981; D. Med. Sci. (n.c.), Med. U. S.C., 1983. Research assoc., Leipzig, 1929-31, Goettingen, Germany, 1931-33; Rockefeller fellow Copenhagen, 1934; lectr. U. London, 1934-35; prof. physics George Washington U., Washington, 1935-41, Columbia, 1941-42; physicist U. Chgo., 1942-43, Manhattan Engr. Dist., 1942-46, Los Alamos Sci. Lab., 1943-46; prof. physics U. Chgo., 1946-52, U. Calif., 1953-60, prof. physics-at-large, 1960-70, Univ. prof., 1970-75, Univ. prof. emeritus, chmn. dept. applied sci., 1963-66; asst. dir. Los Alamos Sci. Lab., 1949-52; cons. Livermore br. U. Calif. Radiation Lab., 1952-53; asso. dir. Lawrence Livermore Lab., U. Calif., 1954-58, 60-75; dir. Lawrence Livermore Radiation Lab., U. Calif., 1958-60; now dir. emeritus, cons. Lawrence Livermore Nat. Lab., U. Calif., Manhattan Dist. of Columbia, 1942-46; also Metall. and Lab. of Argonne Nat. Lab., U. Chgo., 1942-43, 46-52, and Los Alamos, N.Mex., 1943-46, Radiation Lab., Livermore, Calif., 1952-75; sr. research fellow Hoover Instn. War, Revolution and Peace, Stanford U., 1975—. Mem. sci. adv. bd. USAF; bd. dirs. Assn. to the Unite the Democracies; past mem. gen. adv. com. AEC; former mem. Pres.'s Fgn. Intelligence Adv. Nat. Space Coun. Bd. Author: (with Francis Owen Rice) The Structure of Matter, 1949, (with A.L. Latter) Our Nuclear Future, 1958, (with Allen Brown) The Legacy of Hiroshima, 1962, The Reluctant Revolutionary, 1964, (with G.W. Johnson, W.K. Talley, G.H. Higgins) The Constructive Uses of Nuclear Explosives, 1968, (with Segre, Kaplan and Schiff) Great Men of Physics, 1969, The Miracle of Freedom, 1972, Energy: A Plan for Action, 1975, Nuclear Energy in the Developing World, 1977, Energy from Heaven and The Earth, 1979, The Pursuit of Simplicity, 1980, Better a Shield than a Sword, 1987, Conversations on the Dark Secrets of Physics, 1991. Past bd. dirs. Def. Intelligence Sch., Naval War Coll.; bd. dirs. Fed. Union, Hertz Found., Am. Friends of Tel Aviv U.; sponsor Atlantic Union, Atlantic Council U.S., Univ. Ctrs. for Rational Alternatives; mem. Com. to Unite Am., Inc.; bd. govs. Am. Acad. Achievement. Recipient Joseph Priestley Meml. award Dickinson Coll., 1957, Harrison medal Am. Ordnance Assn., 1955; Albert Einstein award, 1958; Gen. Donovan Meml. award, 1959; Midwest Research Inst. award, 1960; Research Inst. Am. Living History award, 1960; Golden Plate award Am. Acad. Achievement, 1961; Gold medal Am. Acad. Achievement, 1982; Thomas E. White and Enrico Fermi awards, 1962; Robins award of Am., 1963; Leslie R. Groves Gold medal, 1974; Harvey prize in sci. and tech. Technion Inst., 1975; Semmelweiss medal, 1977; Albert Einstein award Technion Inst., 1977; Henry T. Heald award Ill. Inst. Tech., 1978; Gold medal Am. Coll. Nuclear Medicine, 1980; A.C. Eringen award, 1980; named ARCS Man of Yr., 1980, Disting. Scientist, Nat. Sci. Devel. Bd., 1981; Paul Harris award Rotary Found., 1980; Disting. Scientist Phil-Am. Acad. Sci. and Engring., 1981; Lloyd Freeman Hunt Citizenship award, 1982; Nat. medal of Sci., 1983; Joseph Handleman prize, 1983, Sylvanus Thayer Medal, 1986; Shelby Cullom Davis award Ethics & Pub. Policy Assn., 1988; Presdl. Citizen medal Pres. Reagan, 1989; Ettore Majorana Erice Scienza Per La Pace award, 1990; Order of Banner with Rubies of the Republic of Hungary, 1990. Fellow Am. Nuclear Soc., Am. Phys. Soc., Am. Acad. Arts and Scis., Hungarian Acad. Scis. (hon.); mem. Nat. Acad. Scis., Am. Geophys. Union, Soc. Engring. Scis., Internat. Platform Assn. Achievements include research on chem., molecular and nuclear physics, quantum mechanics, thermonuclear reactions, applications of nuclear energy, astrophysics, spectroscopy of polyatomic molecules, theory of atomic nuclei. Office: Stanford U 434 Galvez Mall Hoover Inst Stanford CA 94305-6010 also: PO Box 808 Livermore CA 94551-0808 E-mail: smith44@llnl.gov

TELLEZ, CORA, healthcare company executive; BA, Mills Coll.; MPA, Calif. State U. Various exec. positions to v.p., regional mgr. Hawaii Region Kaiser Found. Health Plan, 1978-94; sr. v.p., regional CEO Blue Shield, Calif., 1994-97; pres., chairwoman Prudential Health Care Plan of Calif., Inc., 1997-98; pres. CEO Health Net Foundation Health Systems, Inc., 1998—. Bd. mem. Golden State Bancorp Ince., Inst. Med. Quality, Calif. Assn. Health Plans, Holy Names Coll., Asian Cmty. Mental Health Svcs., Inst. for the Future. Mem. Phi Beta Kappa. Office: Health Net 21600 Oxnard St Ste 2000 Woodland Hills CA 91367-4969

TELLIER, RICHARD DAVIS, management educator; b. Darby, Pa., Feb. 18, 1942; s. Joseph Campbell and Jane Grace (Davis) T.; m. Susan Gammon, June 10, 1974; children: John-Jo and Tiekka (twins). BSEE, Drexel U., 1967; MBA, Fla. State U., 1971, DBA, 1973. Elec. engr. Philco-Ford Corp., Phila., 1960-67; aerospace sys. engr. GE, Cape Canaveral, Fla., 1967-70; lectr. Fla. State U., Tallahassee, 1970-73; prof. mgmt. Calif. State U., Fresno, 1973-2000, chmn. dept. mgmt. and mktg., 1979-84, assoc. dean Sch. Bus., 1984-85, asst. dean, 1990-92, assoc. provost acad. resources, 1995-99, prof. emeritus, 2000—. Cons. ops. mgmt., market rsch. orgnl. behavior. Author: Operations Management: Fundamental Concepts and Methods, 1978, Production and Operations Management Test Bank, 1990 ; contbr. articles to profl. jours. Grantee 1975; recipient Meritorious Performance award, 1987, 88, 90. Mem. Ops. Research Soc. Am., Phi Kappa Phi. Home: 8294 N Academy Ave Clovis CA 93611-9454 Office: Calif State U Shaw and Maple Ave Fresno CA 93740-0001 E-mail: rickt@csufresno.edu

TEMBREULL, MICHAEL A. automotive executive; Gen. mgr. PACCAR, Inc., 1985—, sr. v.p., 1990-92, exec. v.p., 1992-95, dir., 1994—. Office: PACCAR Inc Paccar Bldg 777 106th Ave NE PO Box 1518 Bellevue WA 98009

TEMES, GABOR CHARLES, electrical engineering educator; b. Budapest, Hungary, Oct. 14, 1929; s. Erno and Rozsa (Angyal) Wohl-Temes; m. Ibi Kutasi-Temes, Feb. 6, 1954; children: Roy Thomas, Carla Andrea. Dipl.Ing., Tech. U. Budapest, 1952, DSc (hon.), 1991; Dipl. Phys., Eotvos U., Budapest, 1954; Ph.D., U. Ottawa, Ont., Can., 1961. Asst. prof. Tech. U. Budapest, 1952-56; project engr. Measurement Engring. Ltd., 1956-59; dept. head No. Electric Co. Ltd., 1959-64; group leader Stanford Linear Accelerator Center, 1964-66; corp. cons. Ampex Corp., 1966-69; prof. elec. engring. UCLA, 1969-90, chmn. dept., 1975-80; dept. head Oreg. State U., Corvallis, 1990—. Cons. Xerox Corp., ANT GmbH Author: (with others) Introduction to Circuit Synthesis and Design, 1977, Analog MOS Integrated Circuits for Signal Processing, 1986; assoc. editor: (with others) Jour. Franklin Inst, 1971-82; co-editor, contbg. author: (with others) Modern Filter Theory and Design, 1973, Oversampling Delta-Sigma Data Converters, 1991. Recipient Western Electric Fund award Am. Soc. Engring. Edn., 1982, Humboldt Sr. Rsch. award, 1991; NSF grantee, 1970— Fellow IEEE (life, editor Transactions on Circuit Theory 1969-71 Best Paper award 1969, 81, 85, Centennial medal 1984, Edn. award 1987, Tech. Achievement award 1989, Grad. Tchg. award 1998, Millenium medal 2000, CAS Golden Jubilee medal 2000). Home: 7100 NW Grandview Dr Corvallis OR 97330-2708 Office: Oreg State U Dept Elec Engring Corvallis OR 97331 E-mail: temes@ece.orst.edu

TEMKO, ALLAN BERNARD, writer; b. N.Y.C., Feb. 4, 1924; s. Emanuel and Betty (Alderman) T.; m. Elizabeth Ostroff, July 1, 1950 (dec. Aug. 1996); children: Susannah, Alexander. AB, Columbia U., 1947; postgrad, U. Calif., Berkeley, 1949-51, Sorbonne, , 1948-49, 51-52. Lectr. Sorbonne, 1953-54, Ecole des Arts et Metiers, Paris, 1954-55; asst. prof. journalism U. Calif., Berkeley, 1956-62, lectr. in city planning and social scis., 1966-70, lectr. Grad. Sch. Journalism, 1991; lectr. art Stanford U., 1981, 82; architecture critic San Francisco Chronicle, 1961-93, art editor, 1979-82. Archtl. planning cons.; chmn. Yosemite Falls Design Workshop, 1992; Pulitzer Prize juror, 1991-92; architecture advisor Roman Cath. Cathedral, Oakland, Calif., 2000—. Author: Notre Dame of Paris, 1955, Eero Saarinen, 1962, No Way To Build a Ballpark and Other Irreverent Essays on Architecture, 1993; contbr. articles to U.S. and fgn. mags. and newspapers; West Coast editor, Archtl. Forum, 1959-62. Served with USNR, 1943-46. Recipient Gold medal Commonwealth Club Calif., 1956, Silver medal, 1994, Journalism award AIA, 1961, Silver Spur award San Francisco Planning and Urban Renewal Assn., 1985, AIA Inst. Honor award, 1991, Nathaniel A. Owings award AIA Calif. Coun., 1995, 1st prize in archtl. criticism Mfrs. Hanover/Art World, 1986, Critic's award Mfrs. Hanover/Art World, 1987, Profl. Achievement award Soc. Profl. Journalists, 1988, Pulitzer Prize for criticism, 1990; grantee Rockefeller Found., 1962-63, 20th Century Fund, 1963-66, NEA, 1988, Graham Found., 1990; Guggenheim fellow, 1956-57. Home: 1015 Fresno Ave Berkeley CA 94707-2517

TEMPELIS, CONSTANTINE HARRY, immunologist, educator; b. Superior, Wis., Aug. 27, 1927; s. Harry and Thelma Marie (Hoff) T.; m. Nancy Louise Foster, Aug. 27, 1955; children: William H., Daniel S. BS, U. Wis.-Superior, 1950; MS, U. Wis.-Madison, 1953, PhD, 1955. Project assoc. immunology U. Wis., Madison, 1955-57; instr. immunology U. W.Va., Morgantown, 1957-58; asst. rsch. immunologist U. Calif., Berkeley, 1958-66, assoc. prof. immunology, 1966-72, prof., 1972-95, prof. emeritus, 1995—, prof. grad. sch., 1996—. Vis. scientist Wellcome Rsch. Labs., Beckenham, Kent, Eng., 1977-78, U. Innsbruck, Austria, 1985, 90, 91; cons. in field. Contbr. articles to profl. jours. Served with USNR, 1945-46. Recipient Rsch. Career Devel. award, 1965-70; Fogarty sr. internat. fellow NIH, 1977-78 Mem. AAAS, Am. Assn. Immunologists, Fedn. Am. Soc. Exptl. Biology, Sigma Xi. E-mial. Office: U Calif Sch Pub Health Berkeley CA 94720-0001 E-mail: chtemp@uclink4.berkeley.edu

TEMPLE, JOHN R. publishing executive; Mng. editor Rocky Mountain News, Denver. Office: Rocky Mountain News 400 W Colfax Ave Denver CO 80204-2694

TEMPLE, THOMAS C. oil company executive; V.p. supply and distbn. U.S. Oil & Refining Co., L.A., 1981-86, pres., CEO Tacoma, 1984—; exec. v.p. MacMillan Ring-Free Oil Co. Inc., N.Y.C., 1986—. Office: US Oil & Refining Co 3001 E Marshall Ave Tacoma WA 98421-3116

TENNENBAUM, MICHAEL ERNEST, private investor; b. St. Petersburg, Fla., Sept. 17, 1935; s. Reubin and Frieda (Miller) T.; m. Suzanne Stockfisch; children by previous marriage— Mark Stephen, Andrew Richard. BS, Ga. Inst. Tech., 1958; MBA with honors, Harvard U., 1962. Assoc. Burnham & Co., N.Y.C., 1962-64, Bear, Stearns & Co., N.Y.C., 1964-69, sr. mng. dir., 1969-96, vice chmn. investment banking div., 1988-93; chmn. bd. dirs. Tech. Park, Atlanta, 1978-81; mng. mem. Tennenbaum & Co., LLC, L.A., 1996—. Bd. dirs. TelePacific Corp., Pemco Aviation Group (chmn.), Party City Corp; bd. visitors UCLA Sch. Medicine, 2000—; bd. dirs. L.A. World Affairs Coun., 1997—. Bd. govs., nat. bd. trustees Boys and Girls Clubs Am.; mem. nat. adv. bd. Ga. Inst. Tech., 1971-77; mem. vis. com. Harvard U. Sch. Bus., Cambridge, Mass., 1986-92, bd. assocs., 1992—; bd. trustees Ga. Inst. Tech. Found., Inc., Atlanta, 1988-96; bd. dirs. Joffrey Ballet, 1990-92, chmn. exec. com., 1991-92; bd. dirs. Music Ctr. L.A. County Unified Fund Cabinet, 1990-91; chmn. L.A. Mayor's Spl. Adv. Com. on Fiscal Adminstrn., 1993-94; commr. Calif. Intercity HighSpeed Ground Transp. Commn.; chmn. Calif. High Speed Rail Authority, 1998-2001. Mem. L.A. World Affairs Coun. (dir. 1997—). Home: 118 Malibu Colony Rd Malibu CA 90265-4642 Office: Tennenbaum & Co LLC 11100 Santa Monica Blvd Ste 210 Los Angeles CA 90025-3335 Fax: 310-566-1010

TENNENT, VALENTINE LESLIE, accountant; b. Apia, Western Samoa, Apr. 5, 1919; came to U.S., 1922; s. Hugh Cowper and Madge Grace (Cook) T.; m. Jeanne Marie Elder, Dec. 10, 1941; children: Madeline Jeanne Walls, Hugh Cowper II, Michael Waller, Val Leslie, Paul Anthony. Student, U. Calif., Berkeley, 1938-40. CPA, Hawaii, La. Mgr. Tennent & Greaney, CPAs, Hilo, Hawaii, 1945-50; ptnr. Cameron, Tennent & Dunn, CPAs, Honolulu, 1950-56, KPMG LLP, Honolulu, 1956-79, cons., 1979-84. Ind. rschr. pub. fin. and banking, polit. economy, moral philosophy, San Diego, 1984-2000. Founding trustee, pres., treas. Tennent Art Found., Honolulu, 1955-77; trustee, treas. Watumull Found., Honolulu, 1963-90; bd. dirs. Iolani Sch., Inst. for Human Svcs., Honolulu, Lyman Mus., Hilo. Capt. USAF, 1941-45. Recipient Bishop's Cross for disting. svc. Protestant Episcopal Ch., Dist. Hawaii, 1965, G.J. Watumull award for disting. achievement Watumull Found., Honolulu, 1982. Mem. AICPA (governing coun. 1961-64), Hawaii Soc. CPAs (pres. 1960). Episcopalian. Avocations: swimming, fine arts, music, literature. Home and Office: 700 Front St Unit# 1607 San Diego CA 92101-6063

TENNYSON, PETER JOSEPH, lawyer; b. Winona, Minn., Mar. 18, 1946; s. Richard Harvey and Sylvia Josephine (Jadrich) T.; m. Mary Eileen Fay, Jan. 3, 1970; children: Mark Christian, Rachel Christine, Matthew Patrick, Erica Ruth/ BA, Purdue U., 1968; JD, U. Va., 1975. Bar: Calif. Assoc. atty. O'Melveny & Myers, L.A., 1975-82; v.p., gen. counsel Cannon Mills Co., Kannapolis, N.C., 1982-84; ptnr. Stradling, Yocca, Newport Beach, Calif., 1984-89, Jones, Day, Reavis & Pogue, Irvine, 1990-95, Paul, Hastings, Janofsky & Walker, Costa Mesa, 1995—. Mem. Calif. Commn. on Future of Legal Profession and State Bar, 1994; lectr. in field. Mem. adv. com. St. Joseph Hosp., Orange, Calif., 1987-93; bd. dirs. Lincoln Club Orange County, 1991-93, South Coast Symphony, 1989-92. Capt. U.S. Army, 1968-72. Mem. Orange County Bar Assn., Performing Arts Bus. Alliance South Coast Repertory Silver Circle. Roman Catholic. Avocations: downhill skiing, swimming. Home: 2621 Circle Dr Newport Beach CA 92663-5616 Office: Paul Hastings Janofsky & Walker LLP 695 Town Center Dr Fl 17 Costa Mesa CA 92626-1924 E-mail: petertennyson@paulhastings.com

TERADA, ALICE MASAE, retired elementary school teacher, writer; b. Hilo, Hawaii, Nov. 13, 1928; d. David Matsuo and Mitsuko (Sekido) Marutani; m. Harry T. Terada, Aug. 25, 1951; children: Suzanne T. Henderson, Keith Y., Lance S. Diploma, Queen's Hosp. Sch. Nursing, 1950; BS, We. Res. U., 1953; MEd, U. Hawaii, 1971. Cert. tchr., Hawaii. Registered nurse County Meml. Hosp., Hilo, Hawaii, 1950-51, U. Hosps., Cleve., 1952-53; lang. arts tchr. Dept. Edn., Honolulu, 1967-68; reading tchr. Reading Ctr., Honolulu, 1968-82; ret. Author: Under the Starfruit Tree, 1989, The Magic Crocodile, 1994. Mem. AAUW, Internat. Reading Assn., Zonta Club Internat., Zonta Club Honolulu (bd. dirs. 1996-97). Avocations: art, art history, porcelain antiques, yoga, swimming.

TERESI, JOSEPH, publishing executive; b. Mpls., Mar. 13, 1941; s. Cliff I.A. and Helen Ione (Leslie) T.; divorced; 1 child, Nicholas. CEO Jammer Cycle Products Inc., Burbank, Calif., 1968-80, Paisano Pubs. Inc., Agoura Hills, 1970-98, chmn. bd., 1998—. Promoter motorcycle events; prodr. Easyriders Video mag.; owner Teresi Dyno Drags. Pub. (mags.) Easyriders, 1971—, In the Wind, 1974—, Biker Lifestyle, 1986—, Tattoo, 1986—, Am. Rodder, 1987, Womens Enterprise, 1987-89, Eagles Eye, 1989—, Tattoo Flash, 1993—, Tattoo Savage, 1993—, VQ, 1994—, Early-Riders, 1994-96, Quick Throttle, 1995-99, Roadware, 1995—, Tailgate, 2000, Tattoo Industry, 2000. Achievements include holding the world speed record for motorcycles set at 322 miles per hour, 1990. Avocations: motorcycles, race cars, boats, marlin fishing, skiing. Office: Paisano Pubs Inc PO Box 3000 Agoura Hills CA 91376-3000

TER KEURS, HENK E. D. J. cardiologist, educator; b. Delft, The Netherlands, Aug. 27, 1942; married; 3 children. Degree, Huygens Lyceum, Voorburg, The Netherlands, 1960; MD, State Univ. Leiden, The Netherlands, 1966, PhD cum laude, 1970, Splty. Cert. Med. Physiology, 1980, Splty. Cert. Cardiology, 1983. Cert. cardiology specialist, Can., 1988. Rsch. asst. dept. physiology State Univ. Leiden, 1963-66, docent dept. physiology, 1966-73, sr. rsch. assoc dept. cardiology, 1973-84; med. scientist Alta. (Can.) Heritage Found., 1984—; prof. medicine and med. physiology U. Calgary, Alta., 1984—, Merck Frosst chair in cardiovascular rsch., 1994—. Established investigator dept. cardiology Netherlands Heart Found., State U. Leiden, 1976-81; rsch. fellow Midhurst Med. Rsch. Inst., U.K., 1979-85; chmn. sci. rev. com. Heart and Stroke Found. Can., 1992-94; mem. cardiovascular A com. Med. Rsch. Coun. Can., 1990-93; mem. cardiovascular study sect. NIH, 1991—; vis. scholar dept. anesthesiology U. Wash., 1976-77; guest lectr. dept. physiology U. Surinam, 1972-75; adj. prof. pharm. Columbia U., N.Y. Assoc. editor: Can. Jour. Physiology and Pharmacology, 1989—, editorial referee, 1984—; editorial referee Pflugers Archive Jour. Gen. Physiology, 1977—, Jour. Gen. Physiology, 1977—, Jour. Cellular Molecular Cardiology, 1984—, Jour. Neurosci. Methodology, 1984—, Biophys. Jour., 1985—, Circulatory Rsch., 1989—; contbr. articles, abstracts to Cardiovascular Rsch., Brain Rsch., Jour. Physiology, Circulation, Biophysics Jour., others. Sec./treas. Einthoven Found., 1983-84, adv. coun., 1989—; fellow Coun. Circulation Am. Heart Assn., 1986. Recipient AKZO Medicine prize Dutch Sci. Soc., 1980. Fellow Royal Coll. Physicians and Surgeons Can.; mem. Am. Biophys. Soc., Dutch Fedn. Physiology, Can. Cardiovascular Soc., Physiolog. Soc. U.K. (fgn.). Office: U Calgary Cardiovascular Rsch 3330 Hospital Dr NW Calgary AB Canada T2N 4N1 E-mail: kerkeurs@ucalgary.ca

TERR, LENORE CAGEN, psychiatrist, writer; b. N.Y.C., Mar. 27, 1936; d. Samuel Lawrence and Esther (Hirsh) Cagen; m. Abba I. Terr; children: David, Julia. AB magna cum laude, Case Western Res. U., 1957; MD with honors, U. Mich., 1961. Diplomate Am. Bd. Psychiatry and Neurology, Am. Bd. Child and Adolescent Psychiatry. Intern U. Mich. Med. Ctr., Ann Arbor, 1961-62; resident Neuropsychiat. Inst. U. Mich., Ann Arbor, 1962-64, fellow Children's Psychiat. Hosp., 1964-66; from instr. to asst. prof. Case Western Res. U. Med. Sch., Cleve., 1966-71; pvt. practice Terr Med. Corp., San Francisco, 1971—; from asst. clin. prof. to clin. prof. psychiatry Sch. Medicine U. Calif., San Francisco, 1971—. Lectr. law, psychiatry U. Calif., Berkeley, 1971-90, Davis, 1974-88. Author: Too Scared to Cry, 1990, Unchained Memories, 1994, Beyond Love and Work, 1999; contbr. articles to profl. jours. Rockefeller Found. scholar-in-residence, Italy, 1981, 88; project grantee Rosenberg Found., 1977, 80-81, William T. Grant Found., 1986-87; recipient Career Tchr. award NIMH, 1967-69, Child Advocacy award, APA, 1994. Fellow Am. Psychiat. Assn. (Child Psychiatry Rsch. award 1984, Clin. Rsch. award 1987), Am. Coll. Psychiatrists (program chair 1991-92, Bowis award 1993), Am. Acad. Child and Adolescent Psychiatry (coun. 1984-87); mem. Phi Beta Kappa, Alpha Omega Alpha. Avocations: piano, walking, travel, gardening. Office: Terr Med Corp 450 Sutter St Rm 2534 San Francisco CA 94108-4204

TERRAS, AUDREY ANNE, mathematics educator; b. Washington, Sept. 10, 1942; d. Stephen Decatur and Maude Mae (Murphy) Bowdoin. BS with high honors in Math., U. Md., 1964; MA, Yale U., 1966, PhD, 1970. Instr. U. Ill., Urbana, 1968-70; asst. prof. U. P.R., Mayaguez, 1970-71, Bklyn. Coll., CUNY, 1971-72; asst. prof. math. U. Calif.-San Diego, La Jolla, 1972-76, assoc. prof., 1976-83, prof., 1983—. Prin. investigator NSF, 1974-88; vis. positions U. Aachen, Germany, 1998, Tsuda Coll., Tokyo, 1999, MIT, fall 1977, 83, U. Bonn (W.Ger.), spring 1977, Inst. Mittag-Leffler, Stockholm, winter, 1978, Inst. Advanced Study, spring 1984, Math. Scis. Rsch. Inst., Berkeley, Calif., winter 1992, spring 1995, CRM, U. Montreal, 1999, others; dir. West Coast Number Theory Conf., U. Calif.-San Diego, 1976, AMS joint summer rsch. conf., 1984; lectr. in field. Author: Harmonic Analysis on Symmetric Spaces and Applications, Vol. I, 1985, Vol. II, 1988, Fourier Analysis on Finite Groups and Applications, 1999; contbr. chpts. to books and articles to profl. jours. Woodrow Wilson fellow, 1964, NSF fellow, 1964-68, NSF grantee Summer Inst. in Number Theory, Ann Arbor, Mich., 1973. Fellow AAAS (nominating com. math. sect. project 2061); mem. Am. Math. Soc. (com. employment and ednl. policy, com. on coms., coun., trans. editor, com. for the yr. 2000, western sect. program com., assoc. editor book revs. Bull., assoc. editor Notices), Math. Assn. Am. (program com. for nat. meeting 1988-90, chair joint com. Am. Math. Soc. and Math. Assn. Am. 1991), Soc. Indsl. and Applied Math., Assn. for Women in Math. [illegible], Assn. for Women in Sci. Achievements include research in harmonic analysis on symmetric spaces and number theory. Office: U Calif San Diego Dept Math La Jolla CA 92093-0112

TERREL, RONALD LEE, civil engineer, business executive, educator; b. Klamath Falls, Oreg., Sept. 2, 1936; s. Theodore Thomas and Ruth Margaret (Fausset) T.; m. Susan Laura Harrower, Feb. 28, 1959 (div. July 1981); children: Douglas Scott, Nancy Dawn, Janet Lynn; m. 2d Alice Marie Blanchard, July 23, 1981. B.S.C.E., Purdue U., 1960, M.S., 1961; Ph.D., U. Calif.-Berkeley, 1967. Estimator J.H. Pomeroy & Co., San Francisco, 1955; lab. asst. Purdue U., 1956-60; asst. field geologist Bear Creek Mining Co., Mpls., 1957-58; materials engr. U.S. Bur. Reclamation, Denver, 1960-64; project engr. J.H. Pomeroy & Co., Antigua, B.W.I. and, Calif., 1964-65; research asst. U. Calif.-Berkeley, 1965-67; asst. prof. civil engr. U. Wash., Seattle, 1967-70, assoc. prof., 1970-75, prof., 1975-85, prof. emeritus, 1985—, head Transp. Constrn. and Geometronics divsn., 1976-79; prof., sr. researcher Oreg. State U., 1989-94; pres. Pavement Systems Inc., 1970-82; exec. v.p. Seattle Engring. Internat., Inc., 1979-81; pres. Terrel Assocs., Inc., 1981-85; owner Terrel Research, 1986—; v.p. Pavement Technologies Inc., 1985-86; chmn., CEO RL Techs. Ltd., 1996—. Bd. dirs., v.p. Hydrogenesis, Inc.; cons. in field. Patentee in field. Co-founder, dir. Wash. State Transp. Ctr., 1981-84. Nominated Constrn. Man of Yr. Engring. News-Record, 1972; Purdue Alumni scholar, 1959-60; Ford fellow, 1965-67 Mem. ASTM, ASCE, Tranps. Rsch. Bd., Assn. Asphalt Paving Technologists (bd. dirs. 1979-83, Emmons award 1983, 95, award of merit 1990), Triaxial Inst. (chmn. 1971-73), Can. Tech. Asphalt Assn., Internat. Soc. for Asphalt Pavements (founding mem. 1987), Sigma Xi, Tau Beta Pi, Chi Epsilon, Sigma Gamma Epsilon. Office: 9703 241st Pl SW Edmonds WA 98020-6512 E-mail: rterrel@u.washington.edu

TERRELL, JAMES (NELSON JAMES TERRELL), physicist; b. Houston, Aug. 15, 1923; s. Nelson James Sr. and Gladys Delphine (Stevens) T.; m. Elizabeth Anne Pearson, June 9, 1945; children— Anne (dec.), Barbara, Jean B.A., Rice U., 1944, M.A., 1947, Ph.D., 1950. Research asst. Rice U., Houston, 1950; asst. prof. physics Western Res. U., Cleve., 1950-51; mem. staff Los Alamos Nat. Lab., U. Calif., 1951-89, assoc., 1989-94; affiliate, 1994—. Producer (computer generated movie) The X-Ray Sky, 1969-76; contbr. articles to profl. jours. and encys. Served to 1st lt. AUS, 1944-46 Graham Baker scholar Rice U., 1943-44; fellow Rice U., 1946-48, AEC, 1948-50 Fellow Am. Phys. Soc., AAAS; mem. Am. Astron. Soc., Internat. Astron. Union, Phi Beta Kappa, Sigma Xi Achievements include research in relativity, quasars, x-ray and gamma ray astronomy, nuclear physics, lasers. Home: 85 Obsidian Loop Los Alamos NM 87544-2528 Office: Los Alamos Nat Lab Mail Stop D436 Los Alamos NM 87545-0001

TERRELL, W(ILLIAM) GLENN, university president emeritus; b. Tallahassee, May 24, 1920; s. William Glenn and Esther (Collins) T.; m. Gail Strandberg Terrell; children by previous marriage: Francine Elizabeth, William Glenn III. BA, Davidson Coll., 1942, LLD (hon.), 1969; MS, Fla. State U., 1948; PhD, State U. Iowa, 1952; LLD (hon.), Gonzaga U., 1984, Seattle U., 1985. Instr., then asst. prof. Fla. State U., Tallahassee, 1948-55; asst. prof., then assoc. prof., chmn. dept. psychology U. Colo., Boulder, 1955-59, acting dean Coll Arts and Scis., 1963-65; prof. psychology, dean Coll. Liberal Arts and Scis., U. Ill. at Chgo. Circle, 1963-65, dean faculties, 1965-67; pres. Wash. State U., Pullman, 1967-85, pres. emeritus, 1985—. Pres. Nat. Assn. State Univs. and Land-Grant Colls., 1977-78; cons. The Pacific Inst., Seattle, 1987—. Contbr. articles to profl. jours. Served to capt. inf. U.S. Army, 1942-46, ETO. Recipient Disting. Alumnus award U. Iowa, 1985; Disting. Grad. Dept. Psychology, U. Iowa, 1996. Fellow APA, Soc. Rsch. in Child Devel.; mem. AAAS, Sigma Xi, Phi Kappa Phi. Avocations: golf, reading, travel. Home: 2438 36th Ave W Seattle WA 98199-3704 Office: The Pacific Inst 1709 Harbor Ave SW Seattle WA 98126-2073 E-mail: gterrell@pac-inst.com

TERRILL, KAREN STAPLETON, retired medical planning consultant; b. Milw., Mar. 21, 1939; d. Thomas John and Olive Patrea (Thorbjornsen) Stapleton; m. Max Kurt Winkler, Dec. 18, 1965 (dec. June 1976); m. Richard Terrill, Jan. 23, 1991 (dec. May 1991). BS in Nursing, U. Mich., 1961; MBA, U. Nev., 1974. RN, Calif. Project nurse Langley Porter N.P.I., San Francisco, 1962-64; asst. dir. nursing Milw. County Mental Health Ctr., 1964-66; instr. Fond du Lac (Wis.) Sch. Dist., 1966-67; sch. nurse Inglewood (Calif.) Sch. Dist., 1968-69; instr. nursing U. Nev., Reno, 1969-74; health planner manpower State of Nev. Comp B. Agy., Carson City, 1974-75; planning analyst St. Mary's Hosp., Reno, 1974-76; sr. system analyst U. Calif., San Francisco, 1976-79; med. planning cons. Stone Marraccini & Patterson, San Francisco, 1979-93. Mem. citizen's adv. group City of Richmond, Calif., 1987-88; founding dir. of B.O.A.T. non-profit corp. to promote ferry transit on San Francisco Bay. Mountain State Regional Planning Commn. grantee, 1973-74. Home: 1308 Mallard Dr Richmond CA 94801-4113 E-mail: ktturkish@aol.com

TERRITO, MARY C. health facility administrator, oncologist; BS in Biology, Wayne State U., 1965, MD, 1968. Intern/resident in internal medicine Parkland Hosp., Dallas, 1971-73; fellow in hematology/oncology Harbor-U. Calif., L.A., 1973-74, UCLA, 1974-75; rsch. assoc. Wadsworth VA Hosp., L.A., 1975-81; asst. prof. dept. medicine UCLA, 1975-81, assoc. prof., 1981-96, prof., 1996—, dir. bone marrow transplant program Ctr. Health Scis., 1981—. Contbr. articles to profl. jours. Office: UCLA Bone Marrow Transplantation Program Ctr 42-121 CHS 10833 Le Conte Ave Los Angeles CA 90095-3075

TERRY, RICHARD FRANK, data transcriber; b. Ogden, Utah, July 19, 1949; s. Frank Nebeker and Gertrude Angeline (Berghout) T. BA, Weber State Coll., 1979. Data transcriber IRS, Marriott, Utah, 1976—. Mem. Ch. of Jesus Christ of Latter Day Saints. Avocation: reading the Spanish Bible.

TERRY, ROBERT DAVIS, neuropathologist, educator; b. Hartford, Conn., Jan. 13, 1924; m. Patricia Ann Blech, June 27, 1952; 1 son, Nicolas Saul. AB, Williams Coll., 1946, DSc (hon.), 1991; MD, Albany (N.Y.) Med. Coll., 1950. Diplomate: Am. Bd. Pathology, Am. Bd. Neuropathology. Postdoctoral tng. St. Francis Hosp., Hartford, 1950, Bellevue Hosp., N.Y.C., 1951, Montefiore Hosp., N.Y.C., 1952-53, 54-55, Inst. Recherches sur le Cancer, Paris, France, 1953-54, sr. postdoctoral fellow, 1965-66; asst. pathologist Montefiore Hosp., 1955-59; assoc. prof. dept. pathology Einstein Coll. Medicine, Bronx, N.Y., 1959-64, prof., 1964-84, acting chmn. dept. pathology, 1969-70, chmn., 1970-84; prof. depts. neuroscis. and pathology U. Calif.-San Diego, 1984-94, prof. emeritus, 1994—. Mem. study sect. pathology NIH, 1964-68; study sects. Nat. Multiple Sclerosis Soc., 1964-72, 74-78; mem. bd. sci. counselors Nat. Inst. Neurol. and Communicative Disorders and Stroke, NIH, 1976-80, chmn., 1977-80; mem. nat. sci. coun. Huntington's Disease Assn., 1978-81; mem. med. and sci. adv. bd. Alzheimer Assn., 1978-88; mem. sci. adv. bd. Max Planck Inst., Martinsried, 1990-96. Mem. editorial adv. bd. Jour. Neuropathology and Exptl. Neurology, 1963-83, 85-88, Lab. Investigation, 1967-77, Revue Neurologique, 1977-87, Annals of Neurology, 1978-82, Ultrastructural Pathology, 1978-86, Am. Jour. Pathology, 1985-89. Served with AUS, 1943-46, ETO. Recipient Potamkin prize for Alzheimer Rsch., 1988, Met. Life Found. award, 1991. Fellow AAAS, Am. Acad. Arts and Sci.; mem. Am. Assn. Neuropathologists (pres. 1969-70, Meritorious Contbn. award 1989), N.Y. Path. Soc. (v.p. 1969-70, pres. 1971-73), Am. Assn. Pathologists, Am. Neurol. Assn., Am. Acad. Neurologists. Achievements include research and publications on Alzheimer's disease and Tay Sachs disease. E-mail: rterry.ucsd.edu. Office: U Calif San Diego Dept Neuroscis La Jolla CA 92093

TERRY, ROGER, pathologist, consultant; b. Waterville, N.Y., May 8, 1917; s. Orrin and Mary Isabelle (Kennedy) T.; m. Eleanor Virginia Wallace, Dec. 13, 1942; children: Robin, Orrin. AB magna cum laude, Colgate U., 1939; MD, U. Rochester, 1944. Cert. anatomic pathologist. Intern then resident Strong Meml. Hosp., Rochester, N.Y., 1944-51; asst. prof. U. Rochester Sch. Medicine, 1951-56, assoc. prof., 1956-61, prof. pathology, 1961-69, U. So. Calif. Sch. Medicine, Los Angeles, 1969-82; pathologist San Gabriel (Calif.) Valley Med. Ctr., 1982—. Exec. dir. Calif. Tumor Tissue Registry, Los Angeles, 1969-84. Contbr. articles to profl. jours. Served to capt. USAF, 1954-56. Fellow Am. Soc. Clin. Pathologists, Coll. Am. Pathologists; mem. AMA, Internat. Acad. Pathology (councilor 1973-76), Am. Soc. Investigative Pathology, L.A. Soc. Pathologists, Am. Soc. Cytopathology, Internat. Soc. Dermatopathology, Phi Beta Kappa, Sigma Xi, Alpha Omega Alpha. Republican. Episcopalian. Avocations: ballroom dancing, snorkeling, tandem bike riding. Home: 2841 Shakespeare Dr San Marino CA 91108-2230 Office: San Gabriel Valley Med Ctr 438 W Las Tunas Dr San Gabriel CA 91776-1216 Fax: 626-457-3201

TESH, JOHN, television talk show host, musician; b. Garden City, N.Y., 1953; s. John and Mildred Tesh; m. Connie Sellecca, Apr. 4, 1992; children: Gib, Prima. Co-host Entertainment Tonight, 1986-96; host One-On-One with John Tesh, 1991; co-host John and Leeza from Hollywood, 1993. Television appearances include: The U.S. Open Tennis Championship, 1985, Macy's Thanksgiving Day Parade, 1987, Wimbledon, 1991, TV film Hollyrock-a-Bye Baby, 1993, The Olympic Games, Barcelona, 1992, Atlanta, 1996, Star Trek, 1987; film appearances include Shocker, 1989, Soapdish, 1991, Love Affair, 1996; albums include Tour de France, 1988, The Early Years, 1990, Ironman, 1992, The Games, 1992, Monterey Nights, 1993, A Romantic Christmas, 1993, Wintersong, Sax by the Fire, Sax on the Beach, John Tesh Live at Red Rocks, Discovery, Avalon, A Family Christmas, 1995, Music in the Key of Love, 1995, Choirs of Christmas, 1996, Holiday Collection, 1996, Victory: The Sports Collection, 1997, Sax All Night, 1997, Grand Passion, 1998, One World, 1999; composers theme music Bobby's World, 1990, The Knife and Gun Club, 1990, One on One, 1991, NFL Live, NCA in NBC Theme, 1993. Recipient 4 Emmy awards for composing, 2 Emmy awards for reporting. Office: Garden City Music Teshmedia Group 13245 Riverside Dr # 305 Sherman Oaks CA 91423

TESTER, JON, state legislator; m. Sharla Tester. In agr. and bus.; mem. Mont. Senate, Dist. 45, Helena, 1998—; mem. state adminstrn. com., bills and jour. com., conf. com.; mem. joint select com. on jobs and income; mem. agr., livestock and irrigation com., local govt. com. Democrat. Home: RR 1 Box 709 Big Sandy MT 59520-9708 E-mail: Tester@3Rivers.net

TEVRIZIAN, DICKRAN M., JR. federal judge; b. Los Angeles, Aug. 4, 1940; s. Dickran and Rose Tevrizian; m. Geraldine Tevrizian, Aug. 22, 1964; children: Allyson Tracy, Leslie Sara. BS, U. So. Calif., 1962, JD, 1965. Tax acct. Arthur Andersen and Co., Los Angeles, 1965-66; atty., ptnr. Kirtland and Packard, Los Angeles, 1966-72; judge Los Angeles Mcpl. Ct., Los Angeles, 1972-78, State of Calif. Superior Ct., Los Angeles, 1978-82; ptnr. Manatt, Phelps, Rothenberg & Tunney, Los Angeles, 1982-85, Lewis, D'Amato, Brisbois & Bisgaard, Los Angeles, 1985-86; judge U.S. Dist. Ct., Los Angeles, 1986—. Adv. dir. sch. pub. policy U. Calif., L.A. Adv. dir. UCLA Sch. Pub. Policy. Named Trial Judge of the Yr., Calif. Trial Lawyers Assn., 1987, L.A. County Bar Assn., 1994-95; recipient Peter the Great Gold Medal of Honor Russian Acad. Natural Scis., 1998, Ellis Island Medal of Honor award, 1999. Mem. Calif. Trial Lawyer's Assn. (trial judge of yr. 1987), L.A. County Bar Assn. (trial judge of yr. 1994-95), Malibu Bar Assn. (fed. ct. trial judge of yr. 1998). Office: US Dist Ct Royal Federal Bldg 255 E Temple St Los Angeles CA 90012-3332

TEXTOR, ROBERT BAYARD, cultural anthropology writer, consultant, educator; b. Cloquet, Minn., Mar. 13, 1923; s. Clinton Kenney and Lillian (Nickles) T.; divorced; children: Alexander Robertson, Marisa Elizabeth. Student, Lafayette Coll., 1940-41, Antioch Coll., 1941-43; B.A. in Asian Studies, U. Mich., 1945; Ph.D. in Cultural Anthropology, Cornell U., 1960. Civil info. and edn. officer Mil. Govt., Kyoto-Wakayama, Japan, 1946-48; rsch. fellow anthropology and S.E. Asia studies Yale U., 1959-60, assoc., 1960-61; rsch. fellow in stats. Harvard U., 1962-64; assoc. prof. edn. and anthropology Stanford U., 1964-68, prof. edn. and anthropology, 1968-86, prof. anthropology, 1986-90, prof. anthropology emeritus, 1990—; courtesy prof. internat. studies U. Oreg., 1991—. Vis. prof. U. Saar, Saarbrücken, Germany, 1984-85; cons. Motorola, Inc., 1991—, Ministry of Planning, Kuwait, 1999; mem. S.E. Asia Coun., 1974-77; cons. cultural anthropology to govt. agys., 1957-58, 61-62. Author: Roster of the Gods: An Ethnography of The Supernatural in a Thai Village, 6 vols., 1973, Austria 2005: Projected Sociocultural Effects of the Microelectronic Revolution, 1983, Anticipatory Anthropology, 1985, (with Sippanondha Ketudat) The Middle Path for the Future of Thailand, 1990, (with others) Uncompromising Integrity: Motorola's Global Challenge, 1998; assoc. editor Jour. Conflict Resolution, 1965-70; mem. editorial bd. Human Orgn., 1966-71, Jour. Cultural Futures, 1979-87; adv. editor Behavior Sci. Rsch., 1974-86. Bd. dirs. Vols. in Asia, Stanford, Calif., 1968-73; mem. Metro Portland Future Vision Commn., 1993-95; mem. Portland, Oreg., Organizing Com. for Lewis and Clark Bicentennial, 1996-97. Served with U.S. Army, 1943-46. Fellow Rockefeller Found., 1951-52, fgn. area tng. fellow Ford Found., Thailand 1955-58, Carnegie fellow, 1958-59, Fulbright West Europe rsch. fellow, 1984-85, East-West Ctr. fellow, 1988-90; NSF grantee, Thailand, U.S., 1969-73, Volkswagen Found. grantee, Thailand and Germany, 1984. Fellow Am. Anthrop. Assn. (life), Soc. Applied Anthropology; mem. Siam Soc. (life), Assn. Asian Studies (life), Council on Anthropology and Edn. (pres. 1974-75), AAUP (pres. Stanford chpt. 1975-76), Phi Kappa Phi. E-mail: robertbtextor@home.com

THACHER, CARTER POMEROY, diversified manufacturing company executive; b. 1926; With Wilbur-Ellis Co., San Francisco, 1960—, v.p., 1963-67, pres., from 1967, vice chmn., 1989—, also bd. dirs. Office: Wilbur-Ellis Co 345 California St Fl 27 San Francisco CA 94104-2644

THAL, LEON JOEL, neuroscientist; b. N.Y.C., June 17, 1944; s. Bernard and Esther (Beller) T.; m. Donna Jean Norbo, June 25, 1967. MD, Downstate Med. Ctr., N.Y.C., 1969. Diplomate Am. Bd. Psychiatry and Neurology. Instr., asst. prof., assoc. prof. neurology Albert Einstein Coll. Medicine, Bronx, N.Y., 1975-85; assoc. prof. neuroscis. U. Calif. San Diego, 1985-89; prof. neuroscis. U. Calif., San Diego, 1989—, chmn. dept. neuroscis., 1993—. Editor: Cognitive Disorders, 1992; contbr. chpts. in books and articles to profl. jours. Lt. comdr. USPHS, 1970-72. Office: U Calif San Diego Dept Neuroscience 9500 Gilman Dr La Jolla CA 92093-5004

THALL, RICHARD VINCENT, school system administrator; b. San Francisco, Sept. 12, 1940; s. Albert Vincent and Alice Stella (O'Brien) T.; m. Ellyn Marie Wisherop, June 15, 1963; children: Kristen Ellyn, Richard Vincent Jr. AA, City Coll. San Francisco, 1961; BA, San Francisco State Coll., 1964; MA, San Francisco State U., 1971. Cert. elem. tchr., Calif.; cert. secondary tchr., Calif.; cert. community coll. tchr., Calif. Tchr. biology San Francisco Unified Sch. Dist., 1965-66, Mt. Diablo Unified Sch. Dist., Concord, Calif., 1966-79, program dir. water environ. studies program, 1979—. Ranger/naturalist State of Calif., Brannan Island, 1973-78; naturalist Adventure Internat., Oakland, Calif., 1979-81; lectr. Princess Cruise Lines, 1982—, Sea Goddess, 1986—, Sun Lines, 1987, Sitmar Lines, 1989, Royal Caribbean Internat., 1989—; lectr. naturalist Posh Talks, Inc., 1982—; spkr. commencements U. Calif., Berkeley, 1989. Author: Ecological Sampling of the Sacramento-San Joaquin Delta, 1976; Water Environment Studies Program, 1986; co-author: Project MER Laboratory Manual, 1982. Mem. Contra Costa County (Calif.) Natural Resources Commn., 1975-78, vice-chmn., 1977-78; active Save Mt. Diablo, Concord, 1969-76, v.p., 1974-75; mem. citizens com. Assn. Bay Area Govt. Water Quality, 1979-82, vice-chmn., 1980-82; active John Marsh Home Restoration Com., Martinez, Calif., 1977-78; troop com. chmn. Boy Scouts Am., Concord, 1984-86, asst. scoutmaster, 1985-87. Recipient Recognition and Excellence cert. Assn. Calif. Sch. Adminstrs., 1984, Wood Badge award Boy Scouts Am., 1986; grantee State Calif., 1982, 84, San Francisco Estuary Project, 1992, EPA, 1992, Shell Oil Co., 1993. Mem. AAAS, Nat. Assn. Biology Tchrs., Nat., Audubon Soc., Am. Mus. Natural Hist., Nat. Geog. Soc., Smithsonian Instn. (assoc.). Republican. Roman Catholic. Avocations: skiing, jogging, reading, hiking, photography. Home: 1712 Lindenwood Dr Concord CA 94521-1109 Office: Mt Diablo Unified Sch Dist 1936 Carlotta Dr Concord CA 94519-1358 E-mail: rothall@aol.com

THARP, FRED C., JR. federal judge, lawyer; BS, Hardin-Simmons U., 1958; JD, U.N.Mex., 1967. Bar: N.Mex. 1967. Ins. claims adjuster, claims mgr. Gen. Adjustment Bur., Clovis, 1958-64; law clk. to Hon. Joe Wood N.Mex. Ct. Appeals, 1967-68; pvt. practice Clovis, N.Mex., 1968—; part-time magistrate judge for N.Mex. U.S. Magistrate Ct., Clovis. Mem. staff U. N.Mex. Natural Resources Jour., 1966-67. Office: 716 Mitchell St Clovis NM 88101-6568

THARP, RICHARD, athletic director; b. Mar. 10, 1948; m. Melinda Siebert; children: Travis, Taylor, Tucker. BA, DePauw U., 1970; JD, U. Colo., 1973. Asst. univ. coun. Colo. U., 1973-76, v.p., univ. coun., 1989-95; ptnr. Martin and Mehaffy, 1984-89. Former bd. dirs. Boulder Cmty. Hosp. Found., 1986-90, dir. Lifecare Internat., 1985—. Recipient British Blue, 1969. Mem. Colo. Bar Assn., Alumni C-Club (hon.). Office: Univ Colorado Box 368 UCB Boulder CO 80309-0368

THARP, ROLAND GEORGE, psychology, education educator; b. Galveston, Tex., June 6, 1930; s. Oswald Roland and Berma Lucille (Keefer) T.; m. Stephanie Dalton; children: Donald Martin, Thomas Roland, David Michael, Julie. Student, Middlebury Coll., 1956, 60; BA cum laude, U. Houston, 1957; MA, U. Mich., 1958, PhD, 1961. Cert. Am. Bd. Examiners in Profl. Psychology. Reporter Tex. City Sun, 1946-47; mgr. Tharp Lumber Co., LaMarque, Tex., 1949-54; intern VA Hosp., Menlo Park, Calif., 1960; asst. prof. U. Ariz., Tucson, 1961-65, assoc. prof., 1965-68; prof., dir. clin. studies, dir. multicultural ctr. for higher edn. U. Hawaii, Honolulu, 1968-87; provost and v.p. for acad. affairs U.S. Internat. U., San Diego, 1987-89; prof. edn., psychology U. Calif., Santa Cruz, 1990—; dir. Nat. Rsch. Ctr. for Diversity, 1995—. Dir. Ctr. for Rsch. on Edn., Diversity and Excellence, 1996—; prin. investigator Kamehameha Early Edn. Program, Honolulu, 1969-89; field selection officer Peace Corps, Washington, 1965-67. Author: (poetry) Highland Station, 1978; co-author: Behavior Modification in the Natural Environment, 1969, Self-Directed Behavior, 1980, Rousing Minds to Life, 1988, Teaching Transformed, 2000; writer, producer, dir. film Scenes from the Life, 1981 (Purchase prize The Contemporary Mus. 1981). Mem. Bd. Psychologist Examiners, Ariz., 1964-67; pres. Hawaii Literary Arts Coun., Honolulu, 1982. Robert Frost fellow Middlebury Coll., 1960; recipient Am. Film Mag. award for filmmaking Hawaii Internat. Film Festival, 1990, Grawemeyer award edn., 1993. Mem. Am. Ednl. Rsch. Assn., Am. Anthropol. Assn. Episcopalian. Avocations: tennis, painting. Office: U Calif CREDE 1156 High St Santa Cruz CA 95064-1077

THAYER, MICHAEL J. secondary education educator; Tchr. Las Cruces (N.Mex.) Mid. Sch., 1972-94, Las Cruces H.S., 1994—. Named N.Mex. Tchr. of Yr., 1992. Office: Las Cruces HS 1755 El Paseo St Las Cruces NM 88001-6011

THEEUWES, FELIX, physical chemist; b. Duffel, Belgium, May 25, 1937; Licentiaat physics, Cath. U. Louvain, 1961, DSc in Physics, 1966. Tchr. St. Vincent Sch., Westerlo, Belgium, 1961-64; rsch. fellow CERN, Geneva, 1964-66; rsch. assoc. chemistry U. Kans., 1966-68, asst. prof., 1968-70; rsch. scientist pharm. chemistry Alza Corp., Palo Alto, Calif., 1970-74, prin. scientist, 1974—, v.p. product R & D, 1980-82, v.p.rsch., chief scientist, 1982-94, pres. Tech. Inst., chief scientist, 1994-95, pres. R&D, chief scientist, 1995-97, pres. new ventures, chief scientist, 1997—; chmn. chief sci. office Durect Corp., Cupertino, 2000—. Louis Busse lectr. dept. pharmacology U. Wis., 1981. Named Inventor of Yr., Peninsula Patent Law Assn., 1980. Fellow Am. Assn. Pharm. Scientists (award for advancement of indsl. pharmacy 1983); mem. AAAS, Controlled Release Soc., Acad. Pharm. Sci. Achievements include research in osmosis, diffusion, solid state physics, cryogenics, high pressure, thermodynamics, pharmacology, pharmacokinetics, calorimetry. Office: Alza Corp PO Box 10950 950 Page Mill Rd Palo Alto CA 94304-1080 also: Durect Corp 10240 Bubbrode Cupertino CA 95014-4166

THELANDER, BEVERLY, oil company executive; BS, MBA in Fin., UCLA. Variuos fin. positions ARCO, 1981-98, v.p. comm. pub. affairs & investor rels., 1998—. Office: ARCO 333 S Hope St Los Angeles CA 90071-1406

THEOFANOUS, THEO G. engineering educator, consultant; b. Athens, Greece, May 21, 1942; s. George T. and Smaro (Voudouris) T.; m. Danae P. Kembe, May 15, 1969; children: George, Lydia. BS in Chem. Engring., Nat. Tech. U., Athens, Greece, 1965; PhD in Chem. Engring., U. Minn., 1969; D in Laaperanta (hon.), U. Finland, 1999. Instr. in chem. engring. U. Minn., Mpls., 1968-69; asst. prof. chem. engring. Purdue U., West Lafayette, Ind., 1969-73, assoc. prof. chem. engring., 1973-74, assoc. prof. nuc. engring., 1974-76, prof. nuc. engring., 1976-85; prof. chem. and nuc. engring. U. Calif., Santa Barbara, 1985—, dir. Ctr. for Risk Studies and Safety, 1985—, prof. mech. and environ. engring., 1994—. V.p. Fauske, Grolmes, Henry & Theofanous, Ltd., Hinsdale, Ill., 1979-81; pres. Theofanous & Co., Inc., Santa Barbara, 1981—; cons. in field. Recipient Ernest Orlando Lawrence Meml. award U.S. Dept. of Energy, 1996. Fellow Am. Nuc. Soc.; mem. AIChE, AAAS, NAE. Achievements include finding the mechanism that caused the Sevesco accident; invented a methodology for risk assessment and mgmt. of high-consequence hazzards; contbr. in risk analyses of nuc. reactors and in mitigating the consequence of severe accidents. Office: U Calif Dept Chem Engring Santa Barbara CA 93106-5080 E-mail: theo@theo.ucsb.edu

THERRIAULT, GENE, state senator; b. Fairbanks, Alaska, Jan. 31, 1960; m. Jo Therriault; children: Justin, Jordyn. AA in Computer Info. Systems, BBA, U. Alaska, 1983. Ptnr. Hector's Welding Inc., T.H.E. Co.; Rep. senator dist. Q Alaska State Senate, 1992—. Mem. St. Nicholas Parish. Office: Alaska State Senate State Capitol Rm 121 Juneau AK 99801-1182 also: 119 N Cushman St Ste 226 Fairbanks AK 99701 Fax: 907 465 3884; 907 488 4271. E-mail: Senator_Gene_Therriault@legis.state.ak.us

THEWALT, MICHAEL L. W. physics educator; b. Karlsruhe, Germany, Dec. 5, 1949; married; 1 child. BS, McMaster U., Can., 1972; MS, U. B.C., Can., 1975; PhD in Physics, U. B.C., 1977. Rsch. fellow T.J. Watson Rsch. Ctr. IBM, Yorktown Heights, N.Y., 1978-80; prof. physics Simon Fraser U., Burnaby, Can., 1980—. Recipient Rutherford Meml. medal in physics Royal Soc. Can., 1994. Fellow Am. Phys. Soc., Royal Soc. Can.; mem. Can. Assn. Physicists, Materials Rsch. Soc., IEEE. Office: Simon Fraser U Physics Dept Burnaby BC Canada V5A 1S6

THIBAUDEAU, PATRICIA, state legislator; BA, Whitman Coll.; MSW, Smith Coll. Mem. Wash. Senate, Dist. 43, Olympia, 1995—; chair legis. and long term care com. Wash. Legislature, Olympia, 1999, Dem. caucus vice chair, 1997, Dem. asst. whip, 1994, mem. jud. com., mem. ways and means com. Mem. King's County Women's Polit. Caucus; mem. adv. com. Youth Care Bd.; mem. Wash. Ceasefire. Recipient award N.W. Women's Law Ctr., Bailey Boushay Citizen's award Youth Care Outstanding Cmty. Advocate, 1995, Cert. Recognition Wash. Alliance for Mentally Ill. Mem. AAUW. Democrat. Office: 414 John Cherberg Bldg Olympia WA 98504-0001

THIEBAUT, WILLIAM, state legislator, lawyer; b. Santa Fe, Dec. 11, 1947; m. Mary Ann Thiebaut. BA, U. N.Mex.; JD, Oklahoma City U. Bar: Colo. Mem. Colo. Ho. of Reps., Denver, 1986-93, Colo. Senate, Dist. 3, Denver, 1993—; asst. minority leader. Mem. appropriations com., edn. com., judiciary com., transp. com., joint legis. coun. Mem. Colo. Gov.'s Task Force on Govtl. Immunity, on Deinstitutionalization Mentally Ill, on Worker's Compensatoin Premium Rate Increases, Criminal Justice Comm.; mem. adv. com. Colo. 4-H Youth; chmn. labor-mgmt. com. Pueblo (Colo.) Depot Activity Assistance Program. Mem. Colo. Bar Assn., Pueblo County Bar Assn., Eagles. Democrat. Office: Colo State Senate State Capitol 200 E Colfax Ave Ste 274 Denver CO 80203-1716 also: PO Box 262 Pueblo CO 81002-0262 Fax: 719-544-8899

THIEL, PHILIP, design educator; b. Bklyn., Dec. 20, 1920; s. Philip and Alma Theone (Meyer) T.; m. Midori Kono, 1955; children: Philip Kenji, Nancy Tamiko, Susan Akiko, Peter Akira (dec.). BSc, Webb Inst. Naval Architecture, 1943; MSc, U. Mich., 1948; BArch, MIT, 1952. Registered arch., Wash. Instr. naval architecture MIT, Cambridge, 1949-50; instr. U. Calif., Berkeley, 1954-56, asst. prof., 1956-60; assoc. prof. U. Wash., Seattle, 1961-66, prof. visual design and experiential notation, 1966-91; guest prof. Tokyo Inst. Tech., 1976-78; vis. prof. Sapporo (Japan) Sch. of Arts, 1992-98. Lectr., U.S., Can. Japan, Norway, Denmark, Sweden, Eng., Austria, Switzerland, Peru, Bolivia, Korea; cons. FAO, Rome, 1952; co-founder Environment and Behavior, 1969; founder Ctr. for Experiential Notation, Seattle, 1981. Author: Freehand Drawing, 1965, Visual Awareness and Design, 1981, People, Paths and Purposes, 1997; patentee in field. Soc. Naval Architects and Marine Engrs. scholar, 1947; Rehmann scholar AIA, 1960; NIMH grantee, 1967, Nat. Endowment for Arts, 1969, Graham Found., 1995. Mem. Soc. Naval Architects and Marine Engrs. (assoc.), Phi Beta Kappa, Sigma Xi.

THIEMENS, MARK H. chemistry educator; b. St. Louis, Jan. 6, 1950; BS, U. Miami, 1972; MS, Old Dominion U., 1974; postgrad., Fla. Inst. Technology, 1974-75; PhD, U. Chgo., 1980. Grad. rsch. asst. dept. oceanography Old Dominion U., Norfolk, Va., 1972-74; grad. rsch. asst. dept. physics Fla. Inst. Technology, Melbourne, 1974-75; participant trace element aerosol rsch. program Fla. State U., Tallahassee, 1975-76; researcher dept. atmospheric chemistry Brookhaven Nat. Labs., Upton, N.Y., 1976-77; rsch. assoc. Enrico Fermi Inst. U. Chgo., 1977-80; vis. prof. dept. chemistry U. Calif., San Diego, La Jolla, 1980-81, asst. prof. step II dept. chemistry, 1981-83, asst. prof. step IV dept. chemistry, 1983-85, assoc. prof. step I dept. chemistry, 1985-87, assoc. prof. dept. chemistry step II, 1987-88, assoc. prof. step III dept. chemistry, 1988-89, prof. step I dept. chemistry, 1989-91, prof. step II dept. chemistry, 1991-93, prof. step III dept. chemistry, 1993-95, prof. step VII dept. chemistry, 1996-2000, prof. step IX dept. chemistry, 2000—, chair dept. chemistry, 1996-99, dean divsn. phys. sci., 1999—. Dir. Cr. Environ Rsch. and Tng. U. Calif., San Diego, 1996—, mem. Ctr. Astrophysicis and Space Sci., 1980—, Scripps Inst. Oceanography, 1996—; mem. workshop panel Origins of Solar Sys. NASA, 1989, mem. panel cosmochemistry divsn. group b isotope geochemistry, 1996—, cosmochemistry rev. panel Johnson Space Ctr., 1997; organizer, convenor 1997 Informal Symposium on Kinetic and Photochemical Processes in the Atmosphere, 1997. Contbr. numerous articles to profl. jours. Alexander von Humboldt fellow Inst. Phys. Chemistry U. Göttingen (Germany), 1990-91, 93; Camille and Henry Dreyfus tchg. scholar, 1983-88; recipient Ernest Orlando Lawrence Meml. award U.S. Dept. of Energy, 1998. Fellow Meteoritical Soc. Achievements include development of analytical capability to measure stable isotope variations at ultra-high precision in sulfur, oxygen, carbon and nitrogen to use in development of experimental programs in varying research fields including atmospheric chemistry, physical chemistry of gas phase photochemical eractions, electrical plasmas, early solar system history, and gas-solid conversion mechanisms; development of the ability to measure sulfur isotopic in meteoritic and lunr material to a precision greater than an order-of-magnitude over previous laboratory determination to determine the nature of pre-solar sulfur chemistry, cosmic-ray-spallation, and nucleosynthetic inputs; development of rocket borne atmospheric sampling and analysis. Office: U Calif Chem & Biochem Dept Urey Hall 9500 Gilman Dr La Jolla CA 92093-5004 E-mail: mht@checfs2.ucsd.edu

THIGPEN, STEPHEN P. horticulture products company executive; b. 1956; BS in Plant and Soil summa cum laude, U. Mass.; PhD in Plant Physiology, U. Calif., Davis. Joined Weyerhauser Co., 1981, gen. mgr. Vacaville nursery, 1985; pres., CEO Hines Horticulture, INc., Irvine, Calif., 1995—, chmn. bd., 2000—. Bd. dirs. Coun. for a Green Environment. Office: Hines Horticulture Inc 12621 Jeffrey Rd Irvine CA 92620 Office Fax: 949-786-0968

THIRY, KENT J. health facility administrator; BA in Polit. Sci., Stanford U., 1978; MBA with honors, Harvard U., 1983. Sr. cons. Andersen Consulting, 1978-81; ptnr. Bain & Co.; pres., COO Vivra, Inc., San Francisco, 1991-92, pres., CEO, 1992-97; CEO, chmn. bd. dirs. Total Renal Care, Inc., Torrance, Calif., 1999—. Bd. dirs. Oxford Healthcare, Vol. Ctr. San Mateo County. Mem. Phi Beta Kappa. Office: Total Renal Care Inc 21250 Hawthorne Blvd Torrance CA 90503

THISTLETHWAITE, DAVID RICHARD, architect; b. Burlington, Iowa, Aug. 24, 1947; s. Robert and Nona (Binder) T.; m. Carol Anne Armstrong, Aug. 22, 1970. BArch, Iowa State U., 1971. Registered arch., Calif., Minn.; registered Nat. Coun. Archtl. Registration Bds.; cert. Health Care arch., Am. Coll. Healthcare Archs., 2000. Designer Morrison Architects, St. Paul, 1971-73, Times Architects, Mpls., 1973-74; project architect Bentz/Thompson Assocs., Mpls., 1974-77; project mgr. Setter Leach Lindstrom, Mpls., 1977-78; project architect Wurster Bernardi Emmons, San Francisco, 1978-79, Strotz & Assocs., Tiburon, Calif., 1979-81, Hood Miller Assoc., San Francisco, 1981-84; prin., ptnr. R S T Architects, San Francisco, 1984-88; prin. Thistlethwaite Archtl. Group, San Francisco, 1988—. Contbr. articles to profl. jours. Mem. AIA (nat. profl. devel. com. 1983-86, treas. San Francisco chpt. 1985-86, chmn. Calif. coun. health facilities com. 1994-96, chmn. design com. Acad. Architecture for Health, 1994-96, mem. Calif. coun. ins. bd. trustees 1988-2000, mem. Calif. coun. legis. com. 1996-98), Am. Soc. Healthcare Engring., Design Profls. Safety Assn. (bd. dirs.). Office: 230 Powell St San Francisco CA 94102-2206 E-mail: dthistlethwaite@tagarchitects.com

THOM, RICHARD DAVID, retired aerospace executive; b. St. Louis, Oct. 4, 1944; s. Reginald James and Vlasta (Koukl) T.; m. Linda Marie Hunt, Sept. 9, 1967; children: Elizabeth Marie, Robert James. BS in Physics, U. Mo., Rolla, 1967; MSEE, UCLA, 1971. Co-op engr. McDonnell Aircraft Corp., St. Louis, 1962-67; head advanced tech. group IR systems dept., aerospace group Hughes Aircraft Co., Culver City, Calif., 1967-72; mem. tech. staff Santa Barbara Rsch. Ctr., Hughes Aircraft Co., Goleta, 1972-76, asst. mgr. R&D Lab., 1976-80, mgr. advanced applications, 1980-83, chief engr., 1984-86, chief scientist, 1986-90, dir. tech., 1990-95; tech. program exec. Hughes Aircraft Co., Goleta, 1995-98; asst. mgr. Raytheon Santa Barbara Rsch. Ctr., Goleta, 1998-99; ret. Contbr. articles to profl. jours.; patentee in field. Recipient Hughes Group Patent award for pioneering contbns. in infrared detector tech., 1990. Mem. IEEE, Tau Beta Pi, Sigma Pi Sigma, Delta Sigma Phi. Republican. Avocations: freelance travel writing and photography, specializing in railway travel around the world. Home: 38 Fawn Run Pl PO Box 326 Coupeville WA 98239-0326 E-mail: Richthommail@aol.com

THOMAS, BRIAN CHESTER, state legislator, engineer; b. Tacoma, May 19, 1939; s. Ralph R. and Katheryne (Chester) T.; m. Judith Lynn Adams, Feb. 20, 1965; children: Jeffrey, Kyle, Cheryl. BS in Engring., Oreg. State U., 1961; postgrad., U. Wash., 1968-70; MBA, Pacific Luth. U., 1979. Civil engr. U.S. Coast Guard, Seattle, 1962-63, ops. officer Astoria, Oreg., 1964-65; sr. sales engr. Puget Sound Power & Light Co., Bellevue, Wash., 1965-70, mgr. market rsch., 1971-80, rsch. adminstr., 1981-89, prin. engr., rsch. dir., 1989-97; mem. Wash. Ho. of Reps., Olympia, 1993-2001, mem. forecast coun., 1996-2001, mem. joint select com. on edn. restructuring, 1995-2001, chmn. fin. com., 1995-2001, chmn. Sch. Constrn. Task Force, 1998-99, energy, utilities coms., 1999-2001, mem. Edn. Com., 1999-2001. Chair EEI Rsch. Mgmt. Com., Washington, 1988-89, EPRI Renewable Com., Palo Alto, Calif., 1989-90; adv. bd. Nat. Renewable Energy Lab., Golden, Colo., 1990-93; mem. adv. bd. sch. elec. engring. Oreg. State U., Corvallis, 1991-97; dep. dir. region 10 U.S. Dept. Transp. Emergency Orgn., Seattle, 1989-93. Bd. dirs. Issaquah (Wash.), Sch. Dist., 1989-93, pres. 1992; trustee Mcpl. League of King County, 2000-01; v.p. Friendship Force of Seattle, 2001, pres.-elect 2001. Capt. USCGR, 1961-84. Mem. Preston Aboretum (dir., pres.), Issaquah Rotary (pres. 1982-83), Phi Sigma Kappa. Republican. Home: 14715 182nd Pl SE Renton WA 98059-8028 Office: Wash Ho Reps PO Box 40610 Olympia WA 98504-0610 E-mail: brianthomas@prodigy.net

THOMAS, CHARLES ALLEN, JR. molecular biologist, educator; b. Dayton, Ohio, July 7, 1927; s. Charles Allen and Margaret Stoddard (Talbott) T.; m. Margaret M. Gay, July 7, 1951; children: Linda Carrick, Stephen Gay. AB, Princeton (N.J.) U., 1950; PhD, Harvard U., 1954. Rsch. scientist Eli Lilly Co., Indpls., 1954-55; NCR fellow U. Mich., Ann Arbor, 1955-57; prof. biophysics Johns Hopkins U., Balt., 1957-67; prof. biol. chemistry Med. Sch. Harvard U., Boston, 1967-78; chmn. dept. cellular biology Scripps Clinic & Rsch. Found., La Jolla, Calif., 1978-81; pres., dir. Helicon Found., San Diego, 1981—; founder, CEO The Syntro Corp., San Diego, 1981-82; founder, CEO, now dir. of R&D Pantox Corp., San Diego, 1989—. Mem. genetics study sect. NIH, 1968-72; mem. rsch. grants com. Am. Cancer Soc., 1972-76, 79-85. Mem. editorial bd. Virology, 1967-73, Jour. Molecular Biology, 1968-72, BioPhysics Jour., 1965-68, Chromosoma, 1969-79, Analytic Biochemistry, 1970-79, Biochim Biophys. ACTA, 1973-79, Plasmid, 1977—. With USNR, 1945-46. NRC fellow, 1965-66. Mem. AAAS, Am. Acad. Arts and Scis., Am. Fedn. Biol. Chemists, Genetics Soc. Am., Am. Chem. Soc. Achievements include rsch. in genetic and structural orgn. of chromosomes and devel. of a practical assessment of ind. antioxidant def. system by analytical biochemistry. Home: 1640 El Paso Real La Jolla CA 92037-6304 Office: Pantox Labs 4622 Santa Fe St San Diego CA 92109-1601

THOMAS, CLAUDEWELL SIDNEY, psychiatry educator; b. N.Y.C., Oct. 5, 1932; s. Humphrey Sidney and Frances Elizabeth (Collins) T.; m. Carolyn Pauline Rozansky, Sept. 6, 1958; children: Jeffrey Evan, Julie-Anne Elizabeth, Jessica Edith. BA, Columbia U., 1952; MD, SUNY, Downstate Med. Ctr., 1956; MPH, Yale U., 1964. Diplomate Nat. Bd. Med. Examiners, Am. Bd. Psychiatry, Am. Bd. Forensic Medicine, Am. Bd. Psychological Splties. From instr. to assoc. prof. Yale U., New Haven, 1963-68, dir. Yale tng. program in social community psychiatry, 1967-70; dir. div. mental health service programs NIMH, Washington, 1970-73; chmn. dept. psychiatry U.M.D.N.J., Newark, 1973-83; prof. dept. psychiatry Drew Med. Sch., 1983—, chmn. dept. psychiatry, 1983-93; prof. dept. psychiatry UCLA, 1983-94, vice chmn. dept. psychiatry, 1983-93, prof. emeritus dept. psychiatry, 1994—; med. dir. Tokanui Hosp., TeAwamutu, N.Z., 1996. Cons. A.K. Rice Inst., Washington, 1978-80, SAMSA/PHS Cons., 1991—; mem. L.A. County Superior Ct. Psych. Panel, 1991-97. Author: (with B. Bergen) Issues and Problems in Social Psychiatry, 1966; editor (with R. Bryce LaPorte) Alienation in Contemporary Society, 1976, (with J. Lindenthal) Psychiatry and Mental Health Science Handbook; mem. editorial bd. Internat. Jour. Mental Health, Adminstrn. In Mental Health. Bd. dirs. Bay Area Found., 1987—. Served to capt. USAF, 1959-61. Fellow APHA, Am. Psychoanalytic Assn. (hon.), Am. Psychiat. Assn. (life), Royal Soc. Health, N.Y. Acad. Sci., N.Y. Acad. Medicine; mem. Am. Sociol. Assn., Am. Coll. Mental Health Adminstrs., Am. Coll. Forensic Examiners, Am. Coll. Psychiatrists, Sigma Xi. Avocations: tennis, racquetball, violin, piano. Home and Office: 30676 Palos Verdes Dr E Palos Verdes Peninsula CA 90275-6354 E-mail: cysid32@ucla.edu

THOMAS, CRAIG, senator; b. Cody, Wyo., Feb. 17, 1933; s. Craig E. and Marge Oweta (Lynn) T.; m. Susan Roberts; children: Peter, Paul, Patrick, Alexis. BS, U. Wyo., 1955. V.p. Wyo. Farm Bur., Laramie, 1959-66; with Am. Farm Bur., 1966-75; gen. mgr. Wyo. Rural Elec. Assn., 1975-89; mem. Wyo. Ho. of Reps., 1984-89; rep. from Wyo. U.S. Ho. of Reps., Washington, 1989-94; senator from Wyo. U.S. Senate, Washington, 1995—. Mem. energy and natural resources com., environment and pub. works com., fgn. rels. com., Indian affairs com. Former chmn. Natrona County (Wyo.) Rep. Com.; state rep. Natrona County Dist.; del. Rep. Nat. Conv., 1980. Capt. USMC. Mem. Am. Soc. Trade Execs., Masons. Methodist. Office: US Senate 109 Hart Senate Office Bldg Washington DC 20510-0001*

THOMAS, DANIEL FOLEY, financial services company executive; b. Washington, Aug. 24, 1950; s. Richard Kenneth and Margaret (Foley) T.; m. Barbara Jane Clark, June 30, 1973; 1 child, Alison Clark. BS in Acctg., Mt. St. Mary's Coll., 1972. CPA, Va. Auditor Deloitte, Haskins and Sells, Washington, 1972-74; various fin. positions Communications Satellite Corp., Washington, 1974-78, asst. treas., 1984-85, treas., 1986-87, controller, 1987-89, Comsat Telesystems, Washington, 1978-79; mgr. acctg. and taxes Satellite Bus. Systems, McLean, Va., 1979-81, treas., 1981-84; v.p. fin. Comsat Tech. Products, Inc., Washington, 1985-86, Comsat Video Enterprises, Inc., Washington, 1989-90; exec. v.p. Leasetec Corp., Boulder, Colo., 1990—. Mem. AICPA, Va. Jaycees (life), Great Falls Jaycees (pres. 1978). Roman Catholic. Avocations: running, golf. Home: 1299 S Teal Ct Boulder CO 80303-1480 Office: Leasetec Corp 1000 S Mccaslin Blvd Superior CO 80027-9456 E-mail: blthom@aol.com

THOMAS, DAVID ALBERT, law educator, director; b. L.A., Feb. 4, 1944; s. Albert Rees and Betty Lou (Adams) T.; m. Paula Rasmussen, Aug. 7, 1967; children: Rebecca, David R., John H., Matthew A., Susannah, Amanda, Christina, Erin. BA, Brigham Young U., 1967; JD, Duke U., 1972; MLS, Brigham Young U., 1977. Jud. clk. U.S. Dist. Ct. Utah, Salt Lake City, 1972-73; pvt. practice Salt Lake City, 1973-74; asst. prof. Law Sch. Brigham Young U., Provo, Utah, 1974-76, assoc. prof. Law Sch., 1976-79, prof. Law Sch., 1979—, dir. law libr. Law Sch., 1974-90. Accreditation site insp. ABA, Chgo., 1978—. Author: Utah Civil Procedure, 1980, (with others) A Practical Guide to Disputes Between Adjoining Landowners, 1989, Utah Civil Practice, 1992, (with others) Thomas and Backman on Utah Real Property Law, 1999; prin. author, editor-in-chief: Thompson on Real Property, Thomas Edition, 15 vols., 1994; contbr. articles to profl. jours. With U.S. Army, 1969-71, Vietnam. Mem. ABA (chair real property probate & trust sect. legis. com. 1990-98, real property divsn. adv. bd. 1998—). Home: 907 Rivertree Dr Oceanside CA 92054-7014 Office: Brigham Young U Law Sch Provo UT 84602

THOMAS, DAVID G. advertising executive; b. Ogden, Utah, Oct. 15, 1950; s. Glenn and Norma (Beard) T.; m. Kathleen Lynn Alford, Aug. 27, 1969; children: Troy, Matthew, Brett. BS, Weber State Coll., 1977; MS, Brigham Young U., 1980. Musician, Utah, 1968-77; tchr., counselor Sandridge Jr. High Sch., Roy, 1977-81; writer, producer Salt Lake City, 1981-82; chmn. Thomas/Phillips/Clawson Advt., Salt Lake City, 1982-86; exec. v.p., mng. dir. Cole & Weber Advt., Inc., Salt Lake City, 1986—; pres. Publicis, Salt Lake City. Councilman, asst. mayor, Plain City, Utah, 1972-78; scout master Boy Scouts Am., Farmington, Utah, 1977-85. Recipient Clio finalist award, 198-86, IBA awards (7) Hollywood Broadcasters, N.Y. Film and Video Gold awards N.Y. Film Soc., 1987. Mem. Utah Advt. Fedn. (43 Gold awards 1981-87), AAAA. Democrat. Mormon. Avocations: skiing, water skiing, camping. Home: 2073 Kingston Rd Farmington UT 84025-4107 Office: Publicis 110 Social Mall Ave Salt Lake City UT 84111

THOMAS, DAVID SNOW, plastic surgeon; b. Chgo., Feb. 7, 1951; s. Allan Perry and Verna Bea (Snow) T.; m. Becky Williams Thomas, Aug. 25, 1973; children: Nathan David, Abigail, Elizabeth. BA, U. Utah, 1974, MD, 1978. Diplomate Am. Bd. Plastic Surgery, Am. Bd. Surgery. Resident surgery UCLA, 1978-83, resident plastic surgery, 1983-85, fellow craniofacial surgery, 1985; pvt. practice Salt Lake City, 1986—; chief plastic surgery Primary Childrens Med. Ctr., Salt Lake City, 1988-90, LDS Hosp., 1993-99. Clin. asst. prof. U. Utah Plastic Surgeons, Salt Lake City, 1986-89, assoc. prof. surgery, 1990-93, clin. assoc. prof., 1993—. Bd. Dirs. AMICUS, Salt Lake City, Utah, 1990-92. Fellow Am Coll. Surgeons; mem. Am. Soc. Plastic & Reconstructive Surgery, Am. Soc. Maxillofacial Surgery, Am. Cleft Palate Craniofacial Assn., Am. Soc. Aesthetic Plastic Surgery, Interplast (pres. Salt Lake City, 1992—, bd. dirs. Palo Alto, Calif., 1992—), The Country Club (Salt Lake City). Office: 370 9th Ave Ste 200 Salt Lake City UT 84103-3185

THOMAS, EDWARD DONNALL, physician, researcher; b. Mart, Tex., Mar. 15, 1920; married; 3 children. BA, U. Tex., 1941, MA, 1943; MD, Harvard U., 1946; MD (hon.), U. Cagliari, Sardinia, 1981, U. Verona, Italy, 1991, U. Parma, 1992, U. Barcelona, Spain, 1994, U. Warsaw, Poland, 1996, U. Jagiellonski, Cracow, Poland, 1996. Lic. physician Mass., N.Y., Wash.; diplomate Am. Bd. Internal Medicine. Intern in medicine Peter Bent Brigham Hosp., Boston, 1946-47, rsch. fellow hematology, 1947-48; NRC postdoctoral fellow in medicine dept. biology MIT, Cambridge, 1950-51; chief med. resident, sr. asst. resident Peter Bent Brigham Hosp., 1951-53, hematologist, 1953-55; instr. medicine Harvard Med. Sch., Boston, 1953-55; rsch. assoc. Cancer Rsch. Found. Children's Med. Ctr., Boston, 1953-55; physician-in-chief Mary Imogene Bassett Hosp., Cooperstown, N.Y., 1955-63; assoc. clin. prof. medicine Coll. Physicians and Surgeons Columbia U., N.Y.C., 1955-63; attending physician U. Wash. Hosp., Seattle, 1963-90; prof. medicine Sch. Medicine U. Wash., Seattle, 1963-90, head divsn. oncology Sch. Medicine, 1963-85, prof. emeritus medicine Sch. Medicine, 1990—; dir. med. oncology Fred Hutchinson Cancer Rsch. Ctr., Seattle, 1974-89, assoc. dir. clin. rsch. programs, 1982-89, mem., 1974—. Mem. hematology study sect. NIH, 1965-69; mem. bd. trustees and med. sci. adv. com. Leukemia Soc. Am., Inc., 1969-73; mem. clin. cancer investigation review com. Nat. Cancer Inst., 1970-74; 1st ann. Eugene C. Eppinger lectr. Peter Bent Brigham Hosp. and Harvard Med. Sch., 1974; Lilly lectr. Royal Coll. Physicians, London, 1977; Stratton lectr. Internation Soc. Hematology, 1982; Paul Aggeler lectr. U. Calif., San Francisco, 1982; 65th Mellon lectr. U. Pitts. Sch. Medicine, 1984; Stanley Wright Meml. lectr. Western Soc. Pediatric Rsch., 1985; Adolfo Ferrata lectr. Italian Soc. Hematology, Verona, Italy, 1991. Mem. editl. bd. Blood, 1962-75, 77-82, Transplantation, 1970-76, Proc. of Soc. for Exptl. Biology and Medicine, 1974-81, Leukemia Rsch., 1977-87, Hematological Oncology, 1982-87, Jour. Clin. Immunology, 1982-87, Am. Jour. Hematology, 1985—, Bone Marrow Transplantation, 1986—. With U.S. Army, 1948-50. Recipient A. Ross McIntyre award U. Nebr. Med. Ctr., 1975, Philip Levine award Am. Soc. Clin. Pathologists, 1979, Disting. Svc. in Basic Rsch. award Am. Cancer Soc., 1980, Kettering prize Gen. Motors Cancer Rsch. Found., 1981, Spl. Keynote Address award Am. Soc. Therapeutic Radiologists, 1981, Robert Roesler de Villiers award Leukemia Soc. Am., 1983, Karl Landsteiner Meml. award Am. Assn. Blood Banks, 1987, Terry Fox award Can., 1990, Internat. award Gairdner Found., 1990, N.Am. Med. Assn. Hong Kong prize, 1990, Nobel prize in medicine, 1990, Presdl. medal of sci. NSF, 1990, Mem. NAS, Am. Assn. Cancer Rsch., Am. Assn. Physicians (Kober medal 1992), Am. Fedn. Clin. Rsch., Am. Soc. Clin. Oncology (David A. Karnoksky Meml. lectr. 1983), Am. Soc. Clin. Investigation, Am. Soc. Hematology (pres. 1987-88, Henry M. Stratton lectr. 1975), Internat. Soc. Exptl. Hematology, Internat. Soc. Hematology, Academie Royale de Medicine de Belgique (corresponding mem.), Swedish Soc. Hematology (hon.), Swiss Soc. Hematology, Royal Coll. Physicians and Surgeons Can. (hon.), Western Assn. Physicians, Soc. Exptl. Biology and Medicine, Transplantation Soc., Nat. Acad. Medicine Mexico (hon.). Office: Fred Hutchinson Cancer Ctr 1100 Fairview Ave N D5-100 PO Box 19024 Seattle WA 98109-1024

THOMAS, EUGENE C. lawyer; b. Idaho Falls, Idaho, Feb. 8, 1931; s. C.E. Thomas; m. Jody Raber; children: Michael E., Stephen R. A.B., Columbia U., 1952, J.D., 1954, LLD (hon.) Univ. Idaho, 1986, LLD (hon.), Coll. of Idaho, 1987. Bar: Idaho, 1954, U.S. Dist. Ct. Idaho 1957, US Ct. Appeals (9th cir.) 1958, U.S. Supreme Ct. 1970. Pros. atty. Ada County, Boise, Idaho, 1955-57; founding ptnr. Moffatt, Thomas, Barrett, Rock & Fields, Boise, 19578—; bd. dirs. Shore Lodge, Inc., McCall, Idaho, Nelson-Ball Paper Products, Inc., Longview, Wash., Peregrine Industries, Inc., Boise. Bd. editors ABA Jour., 1980-87. Bd. dirs. St. Luke's Regional Med. Ctr. and Mountain States Tumor Inst., Boise, 1963— , pres., chmn. bd. 1972-79; trustee Coll. of Idaho, 1980—, mem. exec. com., 1982—; trustee Associated Taxpayers of Idaho, 1983—, chmn., 1988-90. trustee Boise Futures Found., 1973—, bd. dirs., 1981—, bd. dirs. Univ./Community Health Scis. Assn., 1981—; chmn. Mayor's Select Com. on Downtown Devel., 1982-83. Named Exec. of Yr., Boise chpt. Nat. Secs. Assn., 1978, John Price lectr. 1987 ann. conf. Nat. Coll. Dist. Attys.; recipient disting. svc. award Idaho Pros. Attys., 1985, disting. svc. award Chgo. Vol. Legal Svc. Found., 1986. Fellow Internat. Acad. Trial Lawyers, Am. Bar Found. (trustee 1980-82, 86-87), Am. Law Inst.; mem. ABA (ho. of dels. 1971— , chmn. ho. of dels. 1980-82, bd. govs. 1980-82, pres. 1986-87, chmn. spl. com. on internat. affairs 1987-88), Idaho State Bar (pres. 1971-72, disting. lawyer award 1980, 86), Def. Research Inst. (state chmn. Pacific region 1978—), Idaho Assn. Def. Counsel (trustee 1966-69, pres. 1967-68), Internat. Assn. Ins. Counsel, Am. Bd. Trial Advocates, Fourth Dist. Bar Assn. (pres. 1962-63), Internat. Bar Assn. (chmn. biennial conf., governing coun. 1985-86), Conference of Pres. Union Internat. des Avocats (pres.), Nat. Conf. Bar Pres. (trustee 1974-76), Law Soc. Eng. and Wales (hon.), La Barra Mexicana (hon.), New Zealand Law Soc. (hon.), Can. Bar Assn. (hon.), Integrated Bar of the Philippines (hon.), Rocky Mountain Oil and Gas Assn. (chmn. Idaho legal com. 1978—). Clubs: Arid (dir. 1977-79), Hillcrest Country (bd. dirs. 1969-72) (Boise). Office: Moffatt Thomas Barrett Rock & Fields PO Box 829 Boise ID 83701-0829

THOMAS, FRANK JOSEPH, retired nuclear engineer; b. Pocatello, Idaho, Apr. 15, 1930; s. Emil C. and Jean (Jones) T.; m. Carol Jones, Feb. 4, 1949; children: Dale, Wayne, Keith. BSEE, U. Idaho, 1952; MS, U. Calif., Berkeley, 1957. Registered profl. mech. engr., Calif. Engr. Sandia Corp., Albuquerque, 1952-56; mgr. engring. div. Aerojet Gen., San Ramon, Calif., 1957-64; dir. nuclear program Office Sec. Defense, Washington, 1964-67; sr. scientist Rand Corp., Santa Monica, Calif., 1967-71; chmn. Pacific-Sierra Rsch. Corp., L.A., 1971-98, ret., 1998. Lectr. U. Calif., Berkeley, 1956-58; chmn. treaty evaluation panel Def. Advanced Rsch. Projects Agy., Washington, 1969-71; clear sky panel USAF, Washington,

1967-73. Author: Evasive Foreign Nuclear Testing, 1971, Blackjack Strategy, 1961; contbr. articles to profl. jours. including Nature, Physics Letters. Recipient Master Design award Product Engring. Mag., 1963. Mem. AAAS, Am. Inst. Aeronautics and Astro. Achievements include development and operation of the first closed-cycle gas turbine power plant in the U.S.

THOMAS, FRED, state legislator; b. Stevensville, Mont., June 27, 1958; m. Suzzie Thomas. BS, Mont. State U., 1981. Cert. ins. counselor. Ins. agt.; mem. Mont. Ho. of Reps., 1985-92, Mont. Senate, Dist. 31, Helena, 1996—; vice chair labor and employment rels. com.; vice chair pub. health, welfare and safety com.; mem. bus. and industry com., conf. com., rules com.; mem. select com. on Constl. amendments. Bd. dirs. Stevensville Cmty. Found. Mem. Profl. Inst. Agts. Mont. (past pres., Agt. of Yr.), Mont. C. of C., Bitterroot C. of C. (bd. dirs. 1994—), Civic Club Stevensville (pres. 1982-83). Republican. Home: 3566 Holly Ln Stevensville MT 59870-6634 E-mail: fthomas@bitterroot.net

THOMAS, GARETH, metallurgy educator; b. Maesteg, U.K., Aug. 9, 1932; came to U.S., 1960, naturalized, 1977; s. David Bassett and Edith May (Gregory) T.; 1 child, Julian Guy David. B.Sc., U. Wales, 1952; Ph.D., Cambridge U., 1955, Sc.D., 1969; DCs (hon.), Lehigh U., 1996. I.C.I. fellow Cambridge U., 1956-59; asst. prof. U. Calif., Berkeley, 1960-63, asso. prof., 1963-67, prof. metallurgy, 1967—, assoc. dean grad. div., 1968-69, asst. chancellor, acting vice chancellor for acad. affairs, 1969-72; founder, sci. dir. Nat. Ctr. Electron Microscopy, 1982-93. Cons. to industry. Author: Transmission Electron Microscopy of Metals, 1962, Electron Microscopy and Strength of Crystals, 1963, (with O. Johari) Stereographic Projection and Applications, 1969, Transmission Electron Microscopy of Materials, 1980; manual dir. Acta Met. Inc., 1998—; contbr. articles to profl. jours.; patentee in field. Recipient Curtis McGraw Rsch. award Am. Soc. Engring. Edn., 1966, E.O. Lawrence award Dept. Energy, 1978, I-R 100 award R & D mag., 1987, Henry Clifton Sorby award Internat. Metallographic Soc., 1987, Albert Sauveur Achievement award, 1991; Guggenheim fellow, 1972. Fellow Am. Soc. Metals (Bradley Stoughton Young Tchrs. award 1965, Grossman Publ. award 1966), Am. Inst. Mining, Metall. and Petroleum Engrs.; mem. Electron Microscopy Soc. Am. (prize 1965, pres. 1976), Am. Phys. Soc., Nat. Acad. Scis., Nat. Acad. Engring., Brit. Inst. Metals (Rosenheim medal 1977), Internat. Fedn. Electron Microscopy Socs. (pres. 1986-90), Brit. Iron and Steel Inst. Club: Marylebone Cricket (Eng.). Office: U Calif Dept Materials Sci & Engring 561 Evans Hall Berkeley CA 94720-1775

THOMAS, GARY EDWARD, science educator, researcher; b. Lookout, W.V., Oct. 25, 1934; s. Garland Eugene Thomas and Dorothy Mae (Fish) Johnson; m. Susan Jude Cherup, Jan. 20, 1963; 1 child, Jennifer Ann. BS, N.Mex. State U., 1957; PhD, U. Pitts., 1963. Rsch. assoc. Svc. d'Aeronomie du CNRS, Paris, France, 1962-63; staff scientist Aerospace Corp., El Segundo, Calif., 1965-67; prof. U. Colo., Boulder, 1967—. Sec. Internat. Comm. on Meteorology of the Upper Atmosphere, 1988-95; disting. vis. prof. U. Adelaide, Australia, 1995. Contbr. more than 100 articles to profl. jours. 1st lt. Signal Corps U.S. Army, 1963-65. Recipient Award Rsch. Excellence U. Colo., 1994; fellowship U. Colo., 1974-75. Mem. Am. Geophysical Union (assoc. editor 1992-95). Office: U Colo Cb 392 Boulder CO 80309-0001

THOMAS, HAYWARD, manufacturing company executive; b. Los Angeles, Aug. 9, 1921; s. Charles Sparks and Julia (Hayward) T.; m. Phyllis Mary Wilson, July 1, 1943; children: H. David, Steven T. BS, U. Calif., Berkeley, 1943. Registered profl. engr. Staff engr. Joshua Hendy Corp., Los Angeles, 1946-50; prodn. mgr. Byron Jackson Co., Los Angeles, 1950-55; mgr. mfg. Frigidaire div. Gen. Motors Corp., Dayton, Ohio, 1955-70; group v.p. White Motor Corp., Cleve., 1971-73; sr. v.p. Broan Mfg. Co., Hartford, Wis., 1973-85; pres. Jensen Industries, Los Angeles, 1985-87; retired, 1987. Served to lt. USNR, 1943-46. Mem. Soc. Mfg. Engrs. (chmn. mfg. mgmt. council 1984-86). Republican. Episcopalian. Avocations: tennis, fishing. Home: 1320 Granvia Altamira Palos Verdes Peninsula CA 90274-2006

THOMAS, JACK WARD, wildlife biologist; b. Ft. Worth, Sept. 7, 1934; s. Scranton Boulware and Lillian Louise (List) T.; m. Farrar Margaret Schindler, June 29, 1957 (dec. Feb. 1994); children: Britt Ward, Scranton Gregory; m. Kathleen Connelly, Feb. 11, 1997. BS, Tex. A&M U., 1957; MS, W.Va. U., 1969; PhD, U. Mass., 1972; PhD (hon.), Lewis & Clark Coll., 1994, Lakehead U., 2001. Biologist Tex. Game & Fish Commn., Sonora, 1957-60; rsch. biologist Tex. Parks & Wildlife Dept., hlano, 1962-67; wildlife rsch. biologist, forestry sci. lab., Northeastern Forest Exptl. Sta. U.S. Forest Svc., Morgantown, W.Va., 1967-71; project dir. environ. forestry rsch. Pinchot Inst. Environ. Forestry, 1971-73; project leader range & wildlife habitat rsch. Pacific Northwest Forest Exptl. Sta. U.S. Forest Svc., LaGrande, Oreg., 1973-93; chief U.S. Dept. Agr.- Forest Svc., Washington, 1993-96; Boone & Crockett prof. wildlife conservation U. Mont., Missoula, 1996—. Author, editor: Wildlife Habitats in Managed Forests, 1979 (award The Wildlife Soc. 1980), Elk of North America, 1984 (award The Wildlife Soc. 1985); contbr. numerous articles to profl. jours. Served to lt. USAF, 1957, USNR. Recipient Conservation award Gulf Oil Corp., 1983, Earle A. Childs award Childs Found., 1984, Disting. Svc. award USDA, Disting. Citizen's award, E. Oreg. State Coll., Nat Wildlife Fedn. award for Sci., 1990, Disting. Achievement award Soc. for Cons. Biology, 1990, Giraffe award The Giraffe Project, 1990, Scientist of Yr. award Oreg. Acad. Sci., 1990, Disting. Svc. award Soc. Conservation Biology, 1991, Sci. Conservation award Nat. Wildlife Fedn., 1991, Chuck Yeager award Nat. Fish and Wildlife Found., 1992, Conservationist of Yr. award Oreg. Rivers Coun., 1992, Chief's Tech. Transfer award USDA, 1992, Tech. Transfer award Fed. Lab. Consortium, 1993. Fellow Soc. Am. Foresters; mem. The Wildlife Soc. (cert., hon., pres. 1977-78, Oreg. Chpt. award 1980, Arthur Einarsen award 1981, spl. svcs. award 1984, Aldo Leopold Meml. medal 1991, group achievement award 1990), Am. Ornithologists Union, Am. Soc. Mammalogists, W.Va. U. Alumni Assn., U. Mass.-Amherst Alumni Assn., Lions, Elks. Avocations: hunting, fishing, white-water rafting, shooting, carpentry. Office: U Mont Sch Forestry Missoula MT 59812-0001

THOMAS, JIM, former professional basketball team executive; Mng. gen. ptnr. Sacramento Kings.

THOMAS, JOHN D., JR. career officer; b. Plymouth, Pa. BA in History, Wilkes Coll.; MA in Internat. Rels., U. So. Calif.; grad., disting. grad. in Field Artillery, Officer's Candidate Sch., Ft. Sill, Okla. Enlisted U.S. Army, commd. 2d lt., advanced through grades to maj. gen., early assignments include command and staff positions, co. comdr. Germany, exec. officer 1st Army Security Aviation Co., svc. in intelligence and electronic warfare staff positions Korea, comdr. 3d Mil. Intelligence bn. Korea; dep. chief for Intelligence, Spl. Tech. Ops. Divsn. The Jt. Staff, Washington; comdr 111th Mil. Intelligence brigade U.S. Army, Ft. Huachuca, Ariz.; dep. comdg. gen., asst. comdr. U.S. Army Intelligence Ctr., Ft. Huachuca; assoc. dep. dir. ops., Mil. Support Nat. Security Agy.; dep. chief Ctrl. Security Svc.; comdr. U.S. Army Intelligence Security Command, U.S. Mil. Intelligence Corps, Ft. Huachuca, 1998—. Decorated Legion of Merit with oak leaf cluster, Meritorious Svc. Medal with oak leaf cluster, Jt. Svc. Commendation medal, Def. Disting. Svc. medal, Def. Superior Svc. medal, others. Achievements include being a master army aviator. E-mail: John.thomas@hua.army.mil

THOMAS, JOHN RICHARD, retired chemist; b. Anchorage, Aug. 26, 1921; s. John R. and Mildred (Woods) T.; m. Beatrice Ann Davidson, Dec. 7, 1944; children: Jonnie Sue Jacobs, Richard G. B.S., U. Calif., Berkeley, 1943, Ph.D., 1947. With U.S. AEC, 1949-51; rsch. chemist Chevron Rsch. Co., Richmond, Calif., 1948-49, sr. rsch. assoc., 1951-60, sr. rsch. scientist, 1961-67, pres., also bd. dirs., 1970-86; v.p. petroleum rsch. Chevron Corp., 1984-86, ret., 1986; mgr. R&D Ortho div. Chevron Chem. Co., Richmond, 1967-68; asst. sec. Standard Oil Co., Calif., 1968-70. Contbr. articles to profl. jours.; patentee in field. Mem. Am. Chem. Soc. Republican. Home: 847 Mcellen Way Lafayette CA 94549-5134 Office: Chevron Rsch Co 576 Standard Ave Richmond CA 94801-2016

THOMAS, JOSEPH FLESHMAN, retired architect; b. Oak Hill, W.Va., Mar. 23, 1915; s. Robert Russel and Effie (Fleshman) T.; m. Margaret Ruth Lively, Feb. 28, 1939 (dec.); children: Anita Carol, Joseph Stephen; m. Dorothy Francene Root, Apr. 29, 1967 (div.); m. Bonnie Abbott Buckley, June 15, 1991 (dec.). Student, Duke, 1931-32; B.Arch., Carnegie-Mellon U., 1938. Practice architecture various firms, W. Va., Va., Tenn., Calif., 1938-49; staff architect Calif. Div. Architecture, Los Angeles, 1949-52; prin. Joseph F. Thomas, architect, Pasadena, Calif., 1952-53; pres. Neptune & Thomas (architects-engrs.), Pasadena and San Diego, 1953-78. Mem. Pasadena Planning Commn., 1956-64, chmn., 1963-64; pres. Citizens Coun. for Planning, Pasadena, 1966-67; mem. steering com. Pasadena NOW, 1970-74; mem. Pasadena Design Com., 1979-86; mem. adv. bd. Calif. Office Architecture and Constrn., 1970-72; mem. archtl. adv. com. Calif. State U. System, 1981-84; mem. adv. coun. Sch. Environ. Design Calif. Poly. Inst., 1983—; mem. outreach for architecture com. Carnegie Mellon U., 1989-95, pres.'s devel. com., 1991-95. Prin. works include Meth. Hosp., Arcadia, Calif., Foothill Presbyn. Hosp., Glendora, Calif., master plans and bldgs., Citrus Coll., Azusa, Calif., Riverside (Calif.) Coll., Westmont Coll., Monticeto, Calif., Northrop Inst. Tech., Inglewood, Calif, Indian Valley Coll., Marin County, Calif., Pepperdine U., Malibu, Calif., UCLA, U. Calif., San Diego, Long Beach (Calif.) State U., Calif. Inst. Tech., Pasadena, Calif., other coll. bldgs. Pacific Telephone Co., Pasadena, L.A. County Superior Ct. Bldg., U.S. Naval Hosp., San Diego. Trustee Almansor Edn. Ctr., 1986-92; bd. dirs., co-founder Syncor Internat., 1973-83; founding dir. Bank of Pasadena, 1962-65. Lt. (j.g.) USNR, 1943-46. Recipient Service award City of Pasadena, 1964; Disting. Service award Calif. Dept. Gen. Services, 1972; Gold Crown award Pasadena Arts Council, 1981 Fellow AIA (4 awards honor, 13 awards merit 1957-78, dir. Calif. coun. 1966-68, exec. com. 1974-77, pres. Pasadena chpt. 1967, chmn. Calif. sch. facilities com. 1970-72, mem. nat. jud. bd. 1973-74, nat. dir. 1974-77, treas. 1977-79, exec. com., planning com., chmn. finance com.); mem. Breakfast Forum (chmn. 1983), Annandale Golf Club, Pi Kappa Alpha. Republican. Methodist. Home: 330 San Miguel Rd Pasadena CA 91105-1446

THOMAS, KAREN P. composer, conductor; b. Seattle, Sept. 17, 1957; BA in Composition, Cornish Inst., 1979; MusM in Composition and Conducting, U. Wash., 1985. Condr. The Contemporary Group, 1981-85; condr., music dir. Wash. Composers Forum, 1984-86; artistic dir., condr. Seattle Pro Musica, 1987—. Conducting debut Seattle, 1987; composer: Four Delineations of Curtmantle for Trombone or Cello, 1982, Metamorphoses on a Machaut Kyrie for Strong Orch. or Quartet, 1983, Cowboy Songs for Voice and Piano, 1985, There Must Be a Lone Range for Soprano and Chamber Ensemble, 1987, Brass Quintet, 1987, Four Lewis Carroll Songs for Choir, 1989, (music/dance/theater) Boxiana, 1990, Elementi for Clarinet and Percussion, 1991, (one-act children's opera) Coyote's Tail, 1991, Clarion Dances for Brass Ensemble, 1993, Roundup for Sax Quartet, 1993, Three Medieval Lyrics for Choir, 1992, Sopravvento for Wind Quartet and Percussion, 1994, When Night Came for Clarinet and Chamber Orch. or Clarinet and Piano, 1994, Over the City for Choir, 1995, also numerous others. Recipient Composers Forum award N.W. Chamber Orch., 1984, King County Arts Commn., 1987, 90, Artist Trust, 1988, 93, 96, Seattle Arts Commn., 1988, 91, 93, New Langton Arts, 1988, Delius Festival, 1993, Melodious Accord award 1993; fellow Wash. State Arts Commn., 1991; Charles E. Ives scholar AAAI. Mem. Am. Choral Dirs. Assn., Broadcast Music, Am. Music Ctr., Internat. Alliance for Women in Music, Soc. Composers, Chorus Am., Conductors Guild. Office: 4426 1st Ave NW Seattle WA 98107-4306 E-mail: kpthomas1@aol.com

THOMAS, LES, real estate development executive; Pres. So. Calif. divsn. Shea Homes, Walnut, Calif., 1996—. Office: J F Shea Homes Inc PO Box 489 Walnut CA 91788-0489

THOMAS, LISA, food service executive; Co-founder Kali's Sweets and Savories (now Clif Bar, Inc.), 1986—, CEO Calif., 1996—. Office: Clif Bar Inc 1610 5th St Berkeley CA 94710-1715

THOMAS, LOWELL, JR. writer, lecturer, former lieutenant governor, former state senator; b. London, Oct. 6, 1923; s. Lowell Jackson and Frances (Ryan) T.; m. Mary Taylor Pryor, May 20, 1950; children: Anne Frazier, David Lowell. Student, Taft Sch., 1942; BA, Dartmouth Coll., 1948; postgrad., Princeton Sch. Pub. and Internat. Affairs, 1952. Asst. cameraman Fox Movietone News, S.Am., 1939, Bradford Washburn Alaskan mountaineering expdn., 1940; illustrated lecturer, 1946—; asst. economist, photographer with Max Weston Thornburg, Turkey, 1947, Iran, 1948; film prodn. Iran, 1949; Tibet expdn. with Lowell Thomas, Sr., 1949; field work Cinerama, S.Am., Africa, Asia, 1951-52; travels by small airplane with wife, writing and filming Europe, Africa, Middle East, 1954-55; mem. Rockwell Polar Flight, first flight around the world over both poles, Nov., 1965; mem. Alaska State Senate, 1967-74; lt. gov. State of Alaska, 1974-79; owner Talkeetna Air Taxi, Inc., air contract carrier, Anchorage, 1980-94. Producer series of films Flight to Adventure, NBC-TV, 1956; producer, writer TV series High Adventure, 1957-59; producer documentary film Adaq, King of Alaskan Seas, 1960; producer two films on Alaska, 1962, 63, film on U. Alaska, 1964, South Pacific travel documentary, 1965, film on Arctic oil exploration, Atlantic-Richfield Co., 1969. Author: Out of this World, A Journey to Tibet, 1950, (with Mrs. Lowell Thomas, Jr.) Our Flight to Adventure, 1956, The Silent War in Tibet, 1959, The Dalai Lama, 1961, The Trail of Ninety-Eight, 1962, (with Lowell Thomas Sr.) More Great True Adventures, 1963, Famous First Flights that Changed History, 1968. Past pres. Western Alaska coun. Boys Scouts Am.; bd. dirs. Anchorage unit Salvation Army, Alaska Conservation Found. 1st lt. USAAF, 1943-45. Mem. Nat. Parks and Conservation Assn. (bd. dirs.), Alaska C. of C., Aircraft Owners and Pilots Assn. Clubs: Explorers, Marco Polo, Dutch Treat (N.Y.C.); Rotary, (Anchorage), Press (Anchorage); Dartmouth Outing; American Alpine Address: 10800 Hideaway Lake Dr Anchorage AK 99516-1145

THOMAS, PAUL EMERY, mathematics educator; b. Phoenix, Feb. 15, 1927; m. Jean Chan, 1958; children: Jenny, Valerie. BA, Oberlin Coll., 1950, Oxford U., Eng., 1952; PhD in Math, Princeton U., 1955. Rsch. instr. Columbia U., 1955-56; asst. prof. math. U. Calif., Berkeley, 1956-60, assoc. prof., 1960-63, prof., 1963-91, prof. emeritus, 1991—; prof. Miller Inst. Basic Rsch. in Sci., 1966-67, mem. exec. com., 1983-89; exec. dir. Miller Inst. Basic Research in Sci., 1987-89; dep. dir. Math. Scis. Rsch. Inst., 1987-90. Vis. prof. Princeton U., fall 1971, mem. adv. coun. dept. math., 1987-99. Served with USNR, 1945-46. NSF fellow Princeton U., 1955, U. Calif., 1958-59; Guggenheim Meml. Found. fellow, 1961; Rhodes scholar Oxford U., 1950-53. Mem. Am. Math. Soc. (trustee 1980-84, chmn. bd. trustees 1983) Office: U Calif Evans Hall Mathematics Dept Hl Berkeley CA 94720-0001

THOMAS, RICHARD VAN, state supreme court justice; b. Superior, Wyo., Oct. 11, 1932; s. John W. and Gertrude (McCloskey) T.; m. Lesley Arlene Ekman, June 23, 1956; children: Tara Lynn, Richard Ross, Laura Lee, Sidney Marie. B.S. in Bus. Adminstrn. with honors, U. Wyo., 1954, LL.B. with honors, 1956; LL.M., NYU, 1961. Bar: Wyo. 1956, U.S. Ct. Appeals (10th cir.) 1960, U.S. Ct. Mil. Appeals 1960, U.S. Supreme Ct. 1960. Law clk. to judge U.S. Ct. Appeals (10th Circuit), Cheyenne, 1960-63; asso. firm Hirst & Applegate, Cheyenne, 1963-64; partner firm Hirst, Applegate & Thomas, Cheyenne, 1964-69; U.S. atty. Dist. Wyo., Cheyenne, 1969-74; justice Wyo. Supreme Ct., Cheyenne, 1974—, chief justice, 1985-86. Pres. Laramie County United Way, 1972, trustee, 1973-74, chmn. admissions and allocations com., 1968-69, chmn. exec. com., 1973, chmn. combined fed. campaign, 1974; bd. dirs. Goodwill Industries Wyo., Inc., 1974-77; exec. com. Cheyenne Crusade for Christ, 1974; v.p., exec. com. Wyo. Billy Graham Crusade, 1987; bd. dirs. Cheyenne Youth for Christ, 1978-81; chancellor Episcopal Diocese of Wyo., 1972— , lay dep. gen. conv., 1973— , chmn. search evaluation nomination com., 1976-77, lay reader, 1969— ; bd. dirs. Community Action of Laramie County, 1977-82; chmn. Cheyenne dist. Boy Scouts Am., 1977-78, mem. nat. council, 1982-84, mem. Longs Peak council, 1977— , v.p. dist. ops., v.p. membership relationships, 1979-81, pres., 1981-83; mem. North Cen. Region Exec. Bd., 1986—, pres. Old West Trails Area, 1988—; chmn. Laramie County Health Planning Com., 1980-84. Served with JAGC USAF, 1957-60. Named Boss of Year, Indian Paintbrush chpt. Nat. Secs. Assn., 1974; Civil Servant of Year, Cheyenne Assn. Govt. Employees, 1973; Vol. of Yr., Cheyenne Office, Youth Alternatives, 1979; recipient St. George Episcopal award, 1982, Silver Beaver award Boy Scouts Am., 1985. Mem. Am., Laramie County bar assns., Wyo. State Bar, Phi Kappa Phi, Phi Alpha Delta, Omicron Delta Kappa, Sigma Nu. Clubs: Kiwanis (Cheyenne) (program com. 1969-70, dir. 1970-72, chmn. key club com. 1973-76, disting. pres. 1980-81), Masons (Cheyenne) (33 deg., past master); Shriners; Nat. Sojourners (Cheyenne). Office: Wyo Supreme Ct Supreme Ct Bldg 2301 Capitol Ave Cheyenne WY 82002-0001

THOMAS, SIDNEY R. federal judge; b. Bozeman, Mont., Aug. 14, 1953; m. Martha Sheehy. BA in Speech-Comm., Mont. State U., 1975, JD cum laude, 1978; D (hon.), Rocky Mountain Coll., 1998. Bar: Mont. 1978, U.S. Dist. Ct. Mont. 1978, U.S. Ct. Appeals (9th cir.) 1980, U.S. Dist. Ct. (9th cir.) 1980, U.S. Ct. Fed. Claims 1986, U.S. Supreme Ct. 1994. Shareholder Moulton, Bellimgham, Longo and Mather, P.C., Billings, 1978-96; judge U.S. Ct. Appeals 9th Cir., Billings, 1996—. Adj. instr. Rocky Mountain Coll., Billings, 1982-95. Contbr. articles to profl. jours. Recipient Gov.'s award for pub. svc., 1978, Outstanding Faculty award Rocky Mountain Coll., 1988. Mem. ABA, State Bar Mont., Yellowstone County Bar Assn. Office: US Ct Appeals Ninth Circuit PO Box 31478 Billings MT 59107-1478*

THOMAS, THOMAS DARRAH, chemistry educator; b. Glen Ridge, N.J., Apr. 8, 1932; s. Woodlief and Jean (Darrah) T.; m. Barbara Joan Rassweiler, Sept. 8, 1956; children: David, Steven, Kathleen, Susan. BS, Haverford Coll., 1954; PhD, U. Calif., Berkeley, 1957. Instr. chemistry U. Calif., Berkeley, 1957-58, asst. prof., 1958-59; rsch. assoc. Brookhaven Nat. Lab., Upton, N.Y., 1959-61; asst. prof. Princeton (N.J.) U., 1961-66, assoc. prof., 1966-71; prof. Oreg. State U., Corvallis, 1971-89, disting. prof., 1989-97, chmn. dept. chemistry, 1981-84, dir. Ctr. Advanced Materials Rsch., 1986-91, Disting. prof. emeritus, 1997—. Cons. Los Alamos (N.Mex.) Sci. Lab., 1965. Contbr. articles to profl. jours. Fellow Alfred P. Sloan Found., 1966-68, Guggenheim Found., 1969, U. Liverpool, Eng., 1984-85. Fellow AAAS, Am. Phys. Soc.; mem. Am. Chem. Soc., Sigma Xi, Phi Beta Kappa. Home: 1470 NW Greenwood Pl Corvallis OR 97330-1827 Office: Oreg State U Dept Chemistry 153 Gilbert Hall Corvallis OR 97331-8546 E-mail: thomast@chem.orst.edu

THOMAS, TIMOTHY R. lawyer; b. Olney, Ill. B in Fin., JD, U. Ill. With Judge Advocate Gen.'s Corps USN, San Diego; atty. corp. law dept. Unocal, El Segundo, Calif., 1974-76, assoc. counsel, 1976-90, dep. counsel, 1990-93, gen. counsel 76 Products Co., 1993—. Mem. Calif. Bar Assn., L.A. County Bar Assn. Office: 2141 Rosecrans Ave Ste 4000 El Segundo CA 90245

THOMAS, WILLIAM GERAINT, museum administrator; b. Columbo, Sri Lanka, June 27, 1931; came to U.S., 1941; s. Cecil James and Iris Katharine (Evans) T.; m. Maria Alcalde, Jan. 2, 1976; 1 child, Laura. BA, U. Calif., Berkeley, 1952. Reporter, editor San Francisco Chronicle, 1952-64; asst. to mayor City of San Francisco, 1964-66; chief cons. majority caucus Calif. State Assembly, Sacramento, 1966-68; adminstrv. asst. U.S. Congressman Phillip Burton, Washington, 1968-70; cons. interior com. U.S. Ho. of Reps., Washington, 1970-72; ptnr. Thomas & Iovino, San Francisco, 1972-78; asst. regional dir. Nat. Park Svc., San Francisco, 1978-89; supt. San Francisco Maritime NHP, 1989—. Mem. Nat. Dem. Club; bd. dirs. Nat. Libery Ship Meml., 1978-80. Sgt. U.S. Army, 1952-54, Korea. Mem. Nat. Maritime Mus. Assn., Nat. Maritime Hist. Soc., Press Club of San Francisco (pres. 1973-74, Best News Story 1963). Episcopalian. Avocation: sailing. Office: San Francisco Maritime Bldg E Ft Mason San Francisco CA 94123

THOMAS, WILLIAM MARSHALL, congressman; b. Wallace, Idaho, Dec. 6, 1941; s. Virgil and Gertrude Thomas; m. Sharon Lynn Hamilton, Jan. 1968; children: Christopher, Amelia. B.A., San Francisco State U., 1963, M.A., 1965. Mem. faculty dept. Am. govt. Bakersfield (Calif.) Coll., 1965-74, prof., 1965-74; mem. Calif. State Assembly, 1974-78, U.S. Congress from 21st Calif. dist., 1979—; chmn. ways and means com., 2001—; chmn. Com. on House Oversight, 1995-2001. Mem. del. to Soviet Union, by Am. Council Young Polit. Leaders, 1977; chmn. Kern County Republican Central Com., 1972-74; mem. Calif. Rep. Com., 1972-80; del. Republican Party Nat. Conv., 1980, 84, 88; mem. Rep. Leader's Task Force on Health Care Reform. Office: House Reps 2208 Rayburn Ho Office Bldg Washington DC 20515-0001*

THOMASCH, ROGER PAUL, lawyer; b. N.Y.C., Nov. 7, 1942; s. Gordon J. and Margaret (Molloy) T.; children: Laura Leigh, Paul Butler. BA, Coll. William and Mary, 1964; LLB, Duke U., 1967. Bar: Conn. 1967, Colo. 1974. Assoc. atty. Cummings & Lockwood, Stamford, Conn., 1967-70; trial atty. U.S. Dept. Justice, Washington, 1970-73; ptnr. Roath & Brega, Denver, 1975-87; mng. ptnr. Denver office of Ballard, Spahr, Andrews & Ingersoll LLP, 1987—. Vis. assoc. prof. of law Drake U. Sch. Law, Des Moines, 1973-74; frequent lectr. in field, U.S. and Can.; adj. faculty mem. U. Denver Coll. Law, 1976-80. Recipient Leland Forrest Outstanding Prof. award, Drake U. Sch. Law, 1973. Fellow Am. Coll. of Trial Lawyers, Colo. Bar Found.; mem. ABA, Colo. Bar Assn., Denver Country Club, Univ. Club. Office: Ballard Spahr Andrews & Ingersoll LLP 1225 17th St Ste 2300 Denver CO 80202-5535 E-mail: Thomasch@BallardSpahr.com

THOMASHOW, LINDA SUZANNE, microbiologist; b. Norwood, Mass. d. John Michael and E. Jean (Cole) Ravinski. BS, U. Mass., 1968; PhD, UCLA, 1979. Asst. prof. Wash. State U., Pullman, 1983-84; rsch. geneticist USDA Agrl. Rsch. Svc., Pullman, 1985—. Adj. prof. dept. plant pathology Wash. State U. Editorial bd. Applied & Environ. Microbiology, Washington, 1990—; contbr. articles to profl. jours. Mem. Am. Soc. Microbiology, Am. Phytopathol. Soc. (Ruth Allen award 1997), Internat. Soc. for Molecular Plant-Microbe Interactions. Achievements include research in production of antibiotics by beneficial bacteria that live in association with the roots of plants, structure, function and regulation of genes involved in antibiotic synthesis by bacteria, the ecological significance of antibiotic production in natural environments. Office: Wash State Univ PO Box 646430 Dept Plant Pathology Pullman WA 99164-6430

THOMASON, SCOTT, automobile executive; b. 1953; BS, U of Oregon, Portland. Prin. Thomason Toyota, Gladstone; pres. Dee A. Thomason Ford Co., Gladstone, 1974—, Thomason Nissan Inc., Gladstone, 1990—, Heritage Auto Ctr. Inc., Kirkland, Wash., 1991—, Thomason Auto Group, Portland, Oreg. Office: Thomason Auto Group PO Box 276 Gladstone OR 97027-0276

THOMPSON, ANNE KATHLEEN, entertainment journalist; b. N.Y.C., Aug. 10, 1954; d. Charles Torrington Thompson and Eleanor Josephine (Callahan) Dekins; m. David Christopher Chute, Oct. 23, 1983; 1 child, Nora Thompson Chute. BA in Cinema Studies, NYU, 1976. Assoc. editor Film Comment, N.Y.C., 1981-82; West Coast editor Film Comment Mag., N.Y.C., 1982-96; publicity dir. Twentieth Century Fox Pictures, 1983-85; columnist Risky Bus., L.A. Weekly, L.A. Times Syndicate, 1985-93, Inside Film, 1988-90; U.S. editor Empire Mag., London, 1989-91; sr. writer Entertainment Weekly, 1993-96; west coast editor Premier Mag., 1996—. Account exec. P/M/K Pub. Rels., N.Y.C., 1979-81; publicist United Artists, N.Y.C., 1976-79; asst. mgr. Bleecker St. Cinema, N.Y.C., 1975-76. Unit publicist Terms of Endearment, The Adventures of Buckaroo Banzai, 1983; contbr. Entertainment Weekly, 1991—, (weekly variety) 7 Days mag., 1990, N.Y. Times, 1992—. Mem. Nat. Writer's Union, Women in Film. Office: Premiere 1990 S Bundy Dr Ste 250 Los Angeles CA 90025-5244

THOMPSON, ANTHONY WAYNE, metallurgist, educator, consultant; b. Burbank, Calif., Mar. 6, 1940; s. William Lyman and Mary Adelaide (Nisbet) T.; m. Mary Ruth Cummings, Aug. 24, 1963; children: Campbell Lyman, Michael Anthony. BS, Stanford U., 1962; MS, U. Wash., 1965; PhD, MIT, 1970. Research engr. Jet Propulsion Lab., Pasadena, Calif., 1962-63; mem. tech. staff Sandia Labs., Livermore, 1970-73, Rockwell Sci. Ctr., Thousand Oaks, 1973-77; assoc. prof. Carnegie Mellon U., Pitts., 1977-79, prof., 1980-94, dept. head, 1987-90; staff scientist Lawrence Berkeley Lab., Berkeley, Calif., 1994-99; rsch. engr. U. Calif., Berkeley, 1995—. Vis. scientist U. Cambridge, Eng., 1983, Risø, Denmark, 1987, U. Calif., 1991; cons. Sandia Labs., 1977—, GE, 1988—. Editor: Work Hardening, 1976, Metall. Transactions, 1983-88; co-editor: Hydrogen in Metals, 1974, Hydrogen Conf. Proc., 1976, 81, 89, 94; mem. editl. bd. Internat. Metals Revs., 1980-88; contbr. articles to profl. jours. Overseas fellow Churchill Coll. Cambridge U., 1982 Fellow Am. Soc. Metals; mem. AAAS, AIME, Sigma Xi Democrat. Clubs: Sierra, Nat. Model R.R. Assn. Home: 2942 Linden Ave Berkeley CA 94705-2328 Office: Lawrence Berkeley Lab Material Sci Divsn Berkeley CA 94720-0001

THOMPSON, BETTY JANE, small business owner; b. Ladysmith, Wis., Nov. 18, 1923; d. Edward Thomas and Mayme Selma (Kratwell) Potter; m. Frederick Sturdee Thompson, Apr. 19, 1945 (div. Apr. 1973); children: Denise Alana, Kent Marshall; m. J.R. Critchfield, Feb. 14, 1977 (div. 1989). Student, Jamestown (N.D.) Coll., 1946-47, U. Calif., Long Beach, 1964-69; AA, Orange Coast Coll., 1976; postgrad., Monterey Peninsula Coll., 1979-80; SBA Cert., Hartnell Coll., 1982. Cert. fashion cons. Owner, mgr., buyer Goodview (Minn.) Food Mart, 1947-50; dist. mgr. Beauty Counselor of Minn., Winona County, 1951-61; Boy Scout liaison J.C. Penney Co., Newport Beach, Calif., 1969-72; dept. mgr. and buyer boyswear At Ease, Newport Beach, 1972-77; mgr. Top Notch Boys Wear, Carmel, Calif., 1977-83, buyer, 1984-88; owner, mgr. Top Notch Watch, Sun City, Ariz., 1989-95; editor H&R Block, 1995-98. V.p., chmn. Don Loper Fashion Show, 1967, pres., 1968, bd. dirs., 1969. Co-editor Aux. Antics mag., 1965. Vol. fundraising leadership Family Svc. Assn., Orange County, Calif., 1962-68, other orgns.; chmn. publicity, study group, Sunday sch. tchr., Congl. Ch., Winona, Minn., 1956-58, fellowship pres., Santa Ana, Calif., 1963-65; pres. Goodview Civic Club, 1948; active Wells Fargo and Co. Bank Silver Bullets, Sr. Citizens of the Sun Cities, Phoenix, 1998—; counselor AARP Tax Aide, 1997—; moderator Congrl. Christian Fellowship, 1999-2001; sec. Tont Ct. Condominium, 1998—. Recipient Athena award Panhellenic Assn. Orange City, Calif., 1968, El Camino Real Dist. Svc. award Orange Empire coun. Boy Scouts Am., Baden-Powell award, Outstanding Leadership award, El Camino Real Dist., Calif., 1972. Ringling North award, 1949; named Outstanding Svc. Vol. Family Svc. Assn., 1969. Mem. Carmel Bus. Assn. Avocations: travel, photography, ballroom dance, bicycling, skiing. Home and Office: 10048 W Hawthorn Dr Sun City AZ 85351-2829 E-mail: tbjtonto@aol.com

THOMPSON, C. MICHAEL, congressman; b. St. Helena, Calif., Jan. 24, 1951; s. Charles Thompson and Beverly (Forni) Powell; m. Janet Thompson, Mar. 8, 1982; children: Christopher, Jon. MA, Chico State U. Owner, maintenance supr. Beringer Winery; mem. Calif. State Senate, 1990-99, U.S. Congress from 1st Calif. dist., 1999—; mem. armed svcs. com., agr. com. Former chair select com. on Calif.'s Wine Industry; former chair Calif. Senate budget com.; former vice chair Calif. Senate natural resources com. Staff sgt. U.S. Army, Vietnam. Decorated Purple Heart. Named Freshman Legislator of the Yr. Calif. Sch. Bds. Assn., 1990, Legislatorof the Yr. Calif. Abortion Rights Action League, Legislator of the Yr. Calif. Assn. Persons with Handicaps, Legislator of the Yr. Police Officers Rsch. Assn. Calif., Legislator of the Yr. Disabled in State Svc., 1994, Senator of the Yr. Calif. Assn. Homes and Svcs. for Aging, 1995; Recipient Disting. Svc. award Calif. State Assn. Counties, Disting. Svc. award Calif. Assn. Hosps., Legis. Leadership award Calif. Assn. Health Svcs. Home, 1994, Disting. Svc. award Aids Project L.A., 1995, Outstanding Senator award Planned Parenthood Affiliates Calif., 1996, Outstanding Senator of the Yr. award Calif. Sch. Bds. Assn., 1996, Outstanding Senator of the Yr. award Calif. Profl. Firefighters, 1996 Democrat. Roman Catholic. Office: 119 Cannon House Office Bldg Washington DC 20515-0001*

THOMPSON, CAROLINE WARNER, film director, screenwriter; b. Washington, Apr. 23, 1956; d. Thomas Carlton Jr. and Bettie Marshall (Warner) T.; m. Alfred Henry Bromell, Aug. 28, 1982 (div. 1985). BA summa cum laude, Amherst Coll., 1978. Film dir., screenwriter William Morris Agy., Inc., Beverly Hills, Calif. Author: First Born, 1983; screenwriter: (films) Edward Scissorhands, 1990, The Addams Family, 1991, Homeward Bound: The Incredible Journey, 1993, The Secret Garden, 1993, Tim Burton's The Nightmare Before Christmas, 1993; screenwriter, dir.: Black Beauty, 1994, Buddy, 1997. Mem. Phi Beta Kappa. Avocation: horseback riding. Office: William Morris Agency Inc 151 S El Camino Dr Beverly Hills CA 90212-2775

THOMPSON, CHARLOTTE ELLIS, pediatrician, educator, author; d. Robert and Ann Ellis; divorced; children: Jennifer Ann, Geoffrey Graeme. BA, Stanford U., 1950, MD, 1954. Diplomate Am. Bd. Pediat. Intern Children's Hosp., San Francisco, 1953-54; resident UCLA, 1960-61, L.A. Children's Hosp., 1962-63; pvt. practice La Jolla, Calif., 1963-75; dir. Muscle Disease Clinic, Univ. Hosp.-U. Calif. Sch. Medicine, San Diego, 1969-80, asst. clin. prof. pediat., 1969—; dir. Ctr. for Handicapped Children and Teenagers, San Francisco, 1981—. Cons. U.S. Naval Hosp., San Diego, 1970-91; dep. dir. Santa Clara County Child Health and Disability, Santa Clara, Calif., 1974-75; dir. Ctr. for Multiple Handicaps, Oakland, Calif., 1976-81; co-dir. Muscle Clinic Children's Hosp., San Diego, 1963-69; dir. muscle program U. Rochester, 1957-60. Author: Raising a Handicapped Child: A Helpful Guide for Parents of the [illegible], 1980, [illegible] edit., 1991, rev., expanded edit., 2000, Allein leben: Ein umfassendes Handbuch für Frauen, 1993, Making Wise Choices: A Guide for Women, 1993, Raising a Child with a Neuromuscular Disorder, 1999, Raising A Handicapped Child, 1999; contbr. articles to med. jours., including Clin. Pediat., New Eng. Jour. Medicine, Neurology, Jour. Family Practice, Mothering, Jour. Pediatric Orthopedics, Pediatrician, Am. Baby, Pediatric News, also chpts. to books. Mem. Calif. Children's Svc. Com., 1977—. Fellow Am. Acad. Pediat. Avocations: tennis, ice skating, opera. Office: Ctr for Handicapped Children and Teenagers 2000 Van Ness Ave Ste 307 San Francisco CA 94109-3020 E-mail: cetmd@earthlink.net

THOMPSON, CRAIG DEAN, sports association executive; b. Estherville, Iowa, Aug. 1, 1956; s. Maurice Ray and Dorothy Jean (Ross) T.; m. Carla Kaye Nealy, July 30, 1983; children: Theodore Edgar, Emma Beth. BA, U. Minn., 1978. Asst. sports info. dir. Kans. State U., Manhattan, 1978-80; dir. pub. rels. and promotions Kansas City Kings, Mo., 1980-83; dir. of comms. Metro Conf., Atlanta, 1983-87; commr. Am. South Conf., New Orleans, 1987-91, Sun Belt Conf., New Orleans, 1991-98, Mountain West Conf., Colorado Springs, Colo., 1998—. Mem. 1993 NCAA Final Four Exec. Planning Com., New Orleans. Mem. Collegiate Commrs. Assn. (past v.p.). Republican. Presbyterian. Avocation: coin collecting.

THOMPSON, CRAIG SNOVER, corporate communications executive; b. Bklyn., May 24, 1932; s. Craig F. and Edith (Williams) T.; m. Masae Sugizaki, Feb. 21, 1957; children: Lee Anne, Jane Laura. Grad., Valley Forge Mil. Acad., 1951; B.A., Johns Hopkins U., 1954. Newspaper and radio reporter Easton (Pa.) Express, 1954-55, 57-59, Wall St. Jour., 1959-60; account exec. Moore, Meldrum & Assocs., 1960; mgr. pub. relations Cen. Nat. Bank of Cleve., 1961-62; account exec. Edward Howard & Co., Cleve., 1962-67, v.p., 1967-69, sr. v.p., 1969-71; dir. pub. relations White Motor Corp., Cleve., 1971-76; v.p. pub. relations No. Telecom Inc., Nashville, 1976-77, White Motor Corp., Farmington Hills, Mich., 1977-80, v.p. corp. communications, 1980-81; dir. exec. communications Rockwell Internat. Corp., Pitts., 1981-86, El Segundo, Calif., 1986-91, Seal Beach, 1992-97, sr. communications exec., 1997; pres. Craig S. Thompson. Inc., 1997—. Bd. dirs. Shaker Lakes Regional Nature Center, 1970-73. Served to 1st lt., inf. U.S. Army, 1955-57. Mem. Pub. Rels. Soc. Am. (accredited), Alumni Assn. Valley Forge Mil. Acad. (bd. dirs. 1988-94).

THOMPSON, DAVID A. electrical engineer; BS in Elec. Engring., Carnegie Inst. Tech., 1962, MS in Elec. Engring., 1963, PhD in Elec. Engring., 1966. Dir. advanced magnetic rec. lab. IBM Almaden Rsch. Ctr., San Jose, Calif. Recipient Inventor of Yr. award N.Y. State Patent, Trademark and Copyright Law ssn., Inc., 1993; named to Silicon Valley Engring. Hall of Fame, 1996. Fellow IEEE (Cledo Brunetti award 1992); mem. NAE. Achievements include pioneering work in miniature magnetic devices for data storage and design and development of thin film magnetic head technology for use in high-density data storage. Office: Advanced Magnetic Rec Lab IBM Almaden Rsch Ctr 650 Harry Rd San Jose CA 95120-6099

THOMPSON, DAVID C. electronics manufacturing company executive; b. 1930; Pres., CEO Stephens Engring. Assocs., Inc., SEA Inc.; prin. fin. and acctg. officer Datamarine Internat., Inc., 1995-97, sec., treas., 1996—, pres., CEO Wash., 1997—. Office: 7030 220th SW Mountlake Terrace WA 98045

THOMPSON, DAVID RENWICK, federal judge; b. 1930; BS in Bus., U. So. Calif., 1952, LLB, 1955. Pvt. practice law with Thompson & Thompson (and predecessor firms), 1957-85; judge U.S. Ct. Appeals (9th cir.), 1985-98, sr. judge, 1998—. Served with USN, 1955-57. Mem. ABA, San Diego County Bar Assn., Am. Bd. Trial Lawyers (sec. San Diego chpt. 1983, v.p. 1984, pres. 1985). Office: US Ct Appeals 940 Front StRm 2193 San Diego CA 92101-8919*

THOMPSON, GEORGE ALBERT, geophysics educator; b. Swissvale, Pa., June 5, 1919; s. George Albert Sr. and Maude Alice (Harkness) T.; m. Anita Kimmell, July 20, 1944; children: Albert J., Dan A., David C. BS, Pa. State U., 1941; MS, MIT, 1942; PhD, Stanford U., 1949. Geologist, geophysicist U.S. Geol. Survey, Menlo Park, Calif., 1942-49; asst. prof. Stanford (Calif.) U., 1949-55, assoc. prof., 1955-60, prof. geophysics, 1960—, chmn. geophysics dept., 1967-86, chmn. geology dept., 1979-82, Otto N. Miller prof. earth scis., 1980-89, dean sch. earth scis., 1987-89. Part-time geologist U.S. Geol. Survey, Menlo Park, 1949-76; cons. adv. com. on reactor safeguards Nuclear Regulation Commn., Washington, 1974-94; mem. bd. earth sci. NRC, 1986-88, vice chmn. Yucca Mountain Hydrology-tectonics panel NRC, 1990-92; mem. exec. com. Inc. Rsch. Inst. for Seismology, Washington, 1990-92; mem. sr. external events rev. com. Lawrence Livermore Nat. Lab., 1989-93; mem. Coun. on Continental Sci. Drilling, 1990-94; cons. Los Alamos Nat. Lab. on volcano-tectonic processes, 1993-96, S.W. Rsch. Inst., 1993; chair com. to review sci. issues NRC, Ward Valley, Calif., 1994-95; mem. panel on probabalistic volcanic hazard analysis Geomatrix Cons., Inc., 1995-96. Author over 100 research papers. With USNR, 1944-46. Recipient G.K. Gilbert award in seismic geology, 1964, John Wesley Powell award U.S. Geol. Survey, 1999; NSF postdoctoral fellow, 1956-57; Guggenheim Found. fellow, 1963-64 Fellow AAAS, Geol. Soc. Am. (coun. mem. 1983-86, George P. Woollard award 1983, v.p. 1995, pres. 1996), Am. Geophys. Union; mem. NAS, Seismol. Soc. Am., Soc. Exploration Geophysicists. Avocation: forestry. Home: 421 Adobe Pl Palo Alto CA 94306-4501 Office: Stanford U Geophysics Dept Stanford CA 94305-2215 E-mail: thompson@pangea.stanford.edu

THOMPSON, GORDON, JR. federal judge; b. San Diego, Dec. 28, 1929; s. Gordon and Garnet (Meese) T.; m. Jean Peters, Mar. 17, 1951; children— John M., Peter Renwick, Gordon III. Grad., U. So. Calif., 1951, Southwestern U. Sch. Law, Los Angeles, 1956. Bar: Calif. 1956. With Dist. Atty.'s Office, County of San Diego, 1957-60; partner firm Thompson & Thompson, San Diego, 1960-70; U.S. dist. judge So. Dist. Calif., San Diego, 1970—, chief judge, 1984-91, sr. judge, 1994—. Mem. ABA, Am. Bd. Trial Advocates, San Diego County Bar Assn. (v.p. 1970), San Diego Yacht Club, Delta Chi. Office: US Dist Ct 940 Front St San Diego CA 92101-8994

THOMPSON, HERBERT ERNEST, tool and die company executive; b. Jamaica, N.Y., Sept. 8, 1923; s. Walter and Louise (Joly) T.; m. Patricia Elaine Osborn, Aug. 2, 1968; children: Robert Steven, Debra Lynn. Student, Stevens Inst. Tech., 1949-51. Foreman Conner Tool Co., 1961-62, Eason & Waller GrindingCorp., 1962-63; owner Endco Machined Products, 1966-67, Thompson Enterprises, 1974—. Pres. Method Machined Products, Phoenix, 1967; pres., owner Quality Tool, Inc., 1967-96. Served to capt. USAAF, 1942-46. Decorated DFC, Air medal with cluster. Home: 14009 N 42nd Ave Phoenix AZ 85053-5306

THOMPSON, J. KEN, gas, oil industry executive; Mgr., v.p. Arco Exploration Prodn. Tech., Plano, Tex. Office: ARCO Alaska Inc PO Box 100360 Anchorage AK 99510-0360

THOMPSON, JACK EDWARD, mining company executive; b. Central City, Nebr., Nov. 17, 1924; s. Ray Elbert and Bessie Fay (Davis) T.; m. Maria del Carmen Larrea, May 8, 1948; children: Jack Edward, Ray Anthony, Robert Davis. Student, Northwestern U., 1942-43, Colo. Sch. Mines, 1943-45, D of Engring. (hon.), 1993. V.p. Cía. Química Comercial de Cuba S.A., 1946-60, Cía. de Fomento Químico S.A., 1946-60; with Newmont Mining Corp., N.Y.C., 1960-86, asst. to pres., 1964-67, v.p., 1967-71, dir., 1969-86, exec. v.p., 1971-74, pres., 1974-85, vice chmn., 1985-86, cons., 1986-90. Chmn. bd. trustees Minerals Industry Ednl. Found.; mem. Pres.'s Coun. Colo. Sch. Mines. Recipient Distinguished Achievement medal Colo. Sch. Mines, 1974 Mem. AIME, Mining and Metall. Soc. Am., Mining Found. of S.W. (past pres., bd. govs.), Tucson Country Club. E-mail: rayonera@aol.com

THOMPSON, JEFFREY L. automotive parts manfacturing executive; V.p./gen. mgr., COO Edelbrock Corp., Torrance, Calif., 1988—, dir., 1994—. Office: Edelbrock Corp 2700 California St Torrance CA 90503

THOMPSON, JILL LYNETTE LONG, federal agency administrator, former congresswoman; b. Warsaw, July 15, 1952; BS, Valparaiso U., 1974; MBA, Ind. U., 1978, PhD, 1984. Mgmt. cons. campbell and Pryor, 1985-86; mem. 101st-103rd Congresses from 4th Ind. dist., 1989-95; mem. agrl. com.; mem. vets. affairs com.; under sec. for rural development USDA, 1995—. Asst. instr., lectr. Indiana U., Bloomington; adj. prof. Indiana U.-Purdue U. Ft. Wayne,; asst. prof. Valparaiso U. Councilwoman City of Valparaiso, Ind., 1984; chair Congrl. Rural Congress. Democrat. Methodist. Office: FSA State Office 101 SW Main St Stee 1300 Portland OR 97204-3221

THOMPSON, JOHN, museum director; Gen. mgr. Copper King Mus., Butte, Mont., 1990—. Office: Copper King Mansion 219 W Granite St Butte MT 59701-9235

THOMPSON, JOHN WILLIAM, international management consultant; b. Hurricane, Utah, Oct. 14, 1945; s. Thomas Thurman and Lula (Brinkerhoff) T.; m. Pamela Ruth Williams, Sept. 14, 1991. BSEE, Utah State U., 1969, MBA, 1972; PhD, U. Oreg., 1978. Rsch. asst. Utah State U., Logan, Utah, 1967-69, tching. asst., 1971-72; elec. engr. Collins Radio, Newport Beach, Calif., 1969-72; tching. fellow U. Oreg., Eugene, 1972-78; tng. dir. Lifespring Inc., San Rafael, Calif., 1978-80; pres., CEO Human Factors Inc., San Rafael, 1980—; chmn. bd. Acumen Internat., San Rafael, 1985—. Author: The Human Factor: An Inquiry into Communication and Consciousness, 1983, Leadership in the 21st Century in New Traditions in Business, 1992, The Renaissance of Learning in Learning Organizations: Developing Cultures for Tomorrow's Workplace, 1994, The Human Factor, 1996; author of software based management assessment programs, system theory based management development courses, 1980-92. Rockefeller Found. grantee, 1971. Avocations: sailing, breeding Koi, gardening, bicycling, scuba diving. Office: Human Factors Inc 4000 Civic Center Dr Ste 500 San Rafael CA 94903-4177

THOMPSON, JOSEPH STANTON, career officer; m. Sandra Kay Kirby; children: Sarah, Joshua, Annah. BSc, U. Mo., 1970, B in Journalism, 1974. Enlisted USN, 1970, advanced through grades to rear adm.; stationed on USS Kilauea, 1970-72; recalled to active duty Operations Desert Shield/Desert Storm, 1990; exec. dir. Lafayette County Mo. Office Farm Svc. Agy. U.S. Dept. Agrl., 1972—; various assignments Inshore Undersea Warfare Group One, San Diego; comdr. Inshore Undersea Warfare Group Two, 1992-95; dep. comdr. Hdqs. Staff Naval Reserve Readiness Command Region Ten, New Orleans, 1995-96, U.S. Coast Guard Maritime Defense Command Seven, Miami, Fla., 1996—. Decorated Legion of Merit, Meritorious Svc. medal with two gold stars.

THOMPSON, JUDITH KASTRUP, nursing researcher; b. Marstal, Denmark, Oct. 1, 1933; came to the U.S., 1951; d. Edward Kastrup and Anna Hansa (Knudsen) Pedersen; m. Richard Frederick Thompson, May 22, 1960; children: Kathryn Marr, Elizabeth Kastrup, Virginia St. Claire. BS, RN, U. Oreg., 1958, MSN, 1963. RN, Calif., Oreg. Staff nurse U. Oreg. Med. Sch., Eugene, 1957-58, Portland, 1958-61, head staff nurse, 1960-61; instr. psychiat. nursing U. Oreg. Sch. Nursing, Portland, 1963-64; rsch. asst. U. Oreg. Med. Sch., Portland, 1964-65, U. Calif., Irvine, 1971-72; rsch. assoc. Stanford (Calif.) U., 1982-87; rsch. asst. Harvard U., Cambridge, Mass., 1973-74; rsch. assoc. U. So. Calif., L.A., 1987—. Contbg. author: Behavioral Control and Role of Sensory Biofeedback, 1976; contbr. articles to profl. jours. Treas. LWV, Newport Beach, Calif., 1970-74; scout leader Girl Scouts Am., Newport Beach, 1970-78. Named Citizen of Yr. State of Oreg., 1966. Mem. Soc. for Neurosci., Am. Psychol. Soc. (charter), ANA, Oreg. Nurses Assn. Republican. Lutheran. Avocations: art collecting, travel, tennis. Home: 28 Sky Sail Dr Corona Del Mar CA 92625-1436 Office: U So Calif University Park Los Angeles CA 90089-0001 E-mail: judith@neuro.usc.edu

THOMPSON, LARRY ANGELO, producer, lawyer, personal manager; b. Clarksdale, Miss., Aug. 1, 1944; s. Angelo and Anne (Tuminello) T.; m. Kelly Ann LeBlanc, 1999. BBA, U. Miss., 1966, JD, 1968. Bar: Miss. 1968, Calif. 1970. In-house counsel Capitol Records, Hollywood, Calif., 1969-71; sr. ptnr. in entertainment law Thompson, Shankman and Bond, Beverly Hills, 1971-77; pres. Larry A. Thompson Orgn., Inc., 1977—. Co-owner New World Pictures, 1983-85; lectr. entertainment bus. UCLA, U. So. Calif., Southwestern U. Law Sch. Author: How to Make a Record Deal and Have Your Songs Recorded, 1975, Prime Time Crime, 1982; producer (TV) Jim Nabors Show, 1977 (Emmy nominee), Mickey Spillane's Margin for Murder, 1981, Bring 'Em Back Alive, 1982, Mickey Spillane's Murder Me, Murder You, 1982, The Other Lover, 1985, Convicted, 1986, Intimate Encounters, 1986, The Woman He Loved, 1988 (Emmy nominee, Golden Globe nominee), Original Sin, 1989, Class Cruise, 1989, Little White Lies, 1989, Lucy and Desi: Before The Laughter, 1990 (Emmy nominee), Broken Promises, 1993, Separated By Murder, 1994, Face of Evil, 1996, Replacing Dad, 1998, The Beat Goes On: The Sonny and Cher Story, 1999 (Emmy nominee), Murder in the Mirror, 2000; (motion pictures) Crimes of Passion, 1984, Fraternity Vacation, 1985, Quiet Cool, 1987, My Demon Lover, 1987, Breaking the Rules, 1992. Co-chmn. Rep. Nat. Entertainment Com.; apptd. by Gov. of Calif. to Calif. Entertainment Commn.; mem. Inauguration of Thompson Ctr. for Fine Arts in Clarksdale, 1986. Served with JAGC, U.S. Army, 1966-72. Recipient Show Bus. Atty. of Yr. award Capitol Records, 1971, Vision award, 1993; named Showman of Yr., U.S. TV Fan Assn., 1997. Mem. ABA, Miss. Bar Assn., Calif. Bar Assn., Inter-Am. Bar Assn., Hon. Order Ky. Cols., Am. Film Inst., Nat. Acad. Rec. Arts and Scis., Acad. TV Arts and Scis. Republican. Roman Catholic. Home: 9451 Hidden Valley Pl Beverly Hills CA 90210-1310 Office: Larry A Thompson Orgn 9663 Santa Monica Blvd Ste 801 Beverly Hills CA 90210-4303

THOMPSON, LEONARD RUSSELL, pediatrician; b. Columbus, Ohio, Sept. 29, 1934; s. Oliver Bernard and Christina (Nichols) T.; m. Candice Elizabeth Brisken, Dec. 6, 1980; children: Ryan, Deron, Hillary, Jon, Christina, Lisa. BA, Ohio State U., 1956, MD, 1960. Diplomat Am. Bd. Pediatrics. Intern Fitzsimmons Gen. Hosp., Denver, 1960-61, resident, 1961-63; chief pediatrics Ireland Army Hosp., Ft. Knox, Ky., 1965-66; chmn. dept. pediatrics Fresno (Calif.) Med. Group, 1966-80; pediatrician pvt. practice, Fresno, 1990—; clinical prof. pediatrics UCSF, Fresno, 1990—. Pres. med. staff Valley Children's Hosp., Fresno, 1992. Maj. U.S. Army, 1960-66. Fellow Am. Acad. Pediatrics. Office: 1187 E Herndon Ave # 104 Fresno CA 93720-3114 E-mail: lrthompson1@att.net

THOMPSON, LOHREN MATTHEW, oil company executive; b. Sutherland, Nebr., Jan. 21, 1926; s. John M. and Anna (Eklund) T.; children: Terence M., Sheila M., Clark M. Ed., U. Denver. Spl. rep. Standard Oil Co., Omaha, 1948-56; sales mgr. Frontier REF. Co., 1956-67, v.p. mktg., 1967-68; mgr. mktg. U.S. region Husky Oil Co., Denver, 1968-72; v.p.

Westar Stas., Inc., Denver, 1967-70; chmn. bd. Colo. Petroleum, Denver, 1971—. Served with USAAF, 1944-46 Mem. Colo. Petroleum Council, Am. Petroleum Inst., Am. Legion Lutheran. Clubs: Denver Petroleum, Denver Oilman's, Lodge: Lions. Home: 2410 Spruce Ave Estes Park CO 80517-7146 Office: Colo Petroleum 4080 Globeville Rd Denver CO 80216-4906

THOMPSON, MARK LEE, art educator, sculptor; b. Ft. Sill, Okla., 1950; s. James B. and Beverly J. T. Student, Va. Polytech Inst., 1968-70; BA in Art, U. Calif., Berkeley, 1972, MA in Sculpture, 1973. Lectr. conceptual design San Francisco State U., 1988-89, lectr. sculpture, 1991-93; adj. prof. sculpture Calif. Coll. Arts and Crafts, 1993—. Vis. lectr. U. Coll. London, 1990; grad. workshop San Francisco State U., 1992, U. Colo., Boulder, 1994, Chgo. Sch. Art Inst. Chgo., 1995, Stanford U., 1995, So. Ill. U., Carbondale, 1995; presenter in field. Exhibits include Va. Polytech. Inst., Blacksburg, 1969, U. Calif., Berkeley, 1973, San Francisco Civic Ctr. Plz., 1975, San Francisco Art Commn. Gallery, 1986, Headlands Ctr. for Arts, Fort Barry, Calif., 1987, Headlands Ctr. Arts, 1987, Steirischer Herbst '87, 1987, Intersection for Arts, 1989, Artpark, 1989, Kunstlerhaus Bethanien, Ressource Kunst, 1989, New Langton Arts, 1989, Palo Alto (Calif.) Cultural Ctr., 1990, Whitechapel Art Gallery, London, 1990, M.H. de Young Meml. Mus., Ctr. Arts, Yerba Buena Gardens, Exploratorium, Haus am Waldsee, 1990, Edge 90, 1990, Hartnell Coll., Salinas, Calif., 1993, M.H. de Young Meml. Mus., San Francisco, 1995, Oliver Art Ctr. Calif. Coll. Arts and Crafts, 1995, Boulder Mus. Contemporary Art, 1996, Pro Arts Gallery, 1997, Gallery Paule Anglim, 2001, Yerba Buena Ctr. Arts, 1999, mus. Contemporary Art, 1998-99, others; contbr. articles to profl. jours. Recipient Visual Artists award Flintridge Found., 1997-1998, Wattis Artists-in-Residence award Yuerba Buena Ctr. Arts, 1999; project grantee fund U.S. Artists Internat. Festivals Rockefeller Found. U.S. Info. Agy. Nat. Endowment Arts, 1989, project grantee, Inc., Art Matters, N.Y., 1989, Visual Arts fellowship grantee Nat. Endowment Arts, 1989, AVA 11 Artist fellowship grantee Awards in Visual Arts, 1991-92, New Genre Artists fellowship grantee Calif. Arts Coun., 1992; U.S.-Japan Creative Artist Exch. fellow Nat. Endowment Arts/Japan-U.S. Friendship Commn., 1990, Creative Artist sculpture fellow Cultural Arts, City of Oakland, Calif., 1994, Civitella Ranieri Ctr. fellow, Umbertide, Italy, 2001—. Office: Calif Coll Arts & Crafts 5212 Broadway Oakland CA 94618-1426

THOMPSON, PAUL HAROLD, university president; b. Ogden, Utah, Nov. 28, 1938; s. Harold Merwin and Elda (Skeen) T.; m. Carolyn Lee Nelson, Mar. 9, 1961; children: Loralyn, Kristyn, Shannyn, Robbyn, Daylyn, Nathan. BS, U. Utah, 1964; MBA, Harvard U., 1966, D Bus. Adminstrn., 1969. Rsch. assoc. Harvard U., Cambridge, Mass., 1966-69, asst. prof., 1969-73; assoc. prof. bus. Brigham Young U., Provo, Utah, 1973-78, prof., 1978-84, asst. dean, 1978-81, dean, 1984-89, v.p., 1989-90; pres. Weber State U., Ogden, 1990—. Cons. Goodyear, Hughes Aircraft, Portland GE, Esso Resources Ltd., GE. Co-author: Organization and People: Readings, Cases, and Exercises in Organizational Behavior, 1976, Novations: Strategies for Career Management, 1986; also articles. Named Outstanding Prof. of Yr., Brigham Young U., 1981; Baker scholar Harvard U., 1966. Mem. Am. Assn. State Colls. and Univs. (com. 1991—), Ogden C. of C. (exec. com. 1990—), Rotary (program com. Ogden 1991—, Harris fellow 1992—), Phi Beta Kappa. Office: Weber State U Presidents Office 3750 Harrison Blvd Ogden UT 84408-0001

THOMPSON, PAUL N. college president; m. Doriann Thompson; 3 children. BA in Math., Gustavus Adolphus Coll., St. Peter, Minn.; AM, PhD in Higher Edn. Adminstrn., U. Ill. Pres. Olney Ctrl. Coll. of Ill. Ea. C.C., 1975-77; v.p. for instructional svcs. Joliet (Ill.) Jr. Coll., 1977-81; pres. Bellevue (Wash.) C.C., 1981-88, William Rainey Harper Coll., Palatine, Ill., 1988 98, Aims C.C., Greeley, Colo., 1998 . Speaker in field. Author 2 math. textbooks; contbr. articles to profl. jours. Bd. dirs. Northwest 2001. Recipient Disting. Alumni citation Gustavus Adolphus Coll. Mem. Am. Assn. Cmty. Colls. (bd. dirs.), C.C. Pres.' Coun. (past pres.), Rotary club of Arlington Hts., N.W. Suburban Assn. of Commerce and Industry. Avocations: travel, music and art, reading, golf, skiing. Office: Aims Cmty Coll PO Box 69 Greeley CO 80632-0069

THOMPSON, PETER LAYARD HAILEY, SR. landscape and golf course architect; b. Modesto, Calif., Apr. 26, 1939; BS in East Asian Studies, U. Oreg., 1962, B in Landscape Architecture, M in Urban Planning, U. Oreg., 1971; postgrad., U. Calif., Berkeley, 1975, Nat. U. Registered landscape arch., Calif., Oreg., Wash., Nev. With Oreg. Planning Commn., Lane County, 1965-70, commr. Eugene, 1981-83; sr. assoc. Ruff, Cameron, Lacoss, Eugene, 1971-75; prin. Peter L. H. Thompson & Assocs., Eugene, 1975-83, John H. Midby & Assocs., Las Vegas, Nev., 1983-86, Thompson-Wihlborg, Ltd., Corte Madera, Calif., 1982-89, Thompson Planning Group (now Thompson Golf Planning), Ltd., San Rafael, 1989—. With Oreg. Planning Commn., commr., 1981-83, Novato, Calif. Planning Commn., commr. 1989-93, pres. 1989-93; spkr. Oreg. Home Builders Conf., 1980, Pacific Coast Builders Conf., 1984, Tacoma Country Club Pro-Pres. Tournament, 1991, Madrona Links Men's Golf Club, 1991, Twin Lakes Country Club Pro-Pres. Tournament, 1992, Golf Expo, Palm Springs, Calif., 1993, 95, Golf Expo, Nashville, 1993, Golf Expo, Monterey, Calif., 1994, others. Contbr. articles to mags. Mem. citizen's adv. bd. City of Eugene, Oreg., City of Las Vegas. Mem. USGA, Am. Soc. Landscape Archs., Am. Assn. Planners, Nat. Golf Found., Urban Land Inst., Rotary Internat. Office: Thompson Golf Planning Ltd 1510 Grant Ave Ste 305 Novato CA 94945-3146

THOMPSON, RAYMOND HARRIS, retired anthropologist, educator; b. Portland, Me., May 10, 1924; s. Raymond and Eloise (MacIntyre) T.; m. Molly Kendall, Sept. 9, 1948; children: Margaret Kelsey Luchetta, Mary Frances. B.S., Tufts U., 1947; A.M., Harvard U., 1950, Ph.D., 1955. Fellow div. hist. research Carnegie Instn., Washington, 1950-52; asst. prof. anthropology, curator Mus. Anthropology, U. Ky., 1952-56; faculty U. Ariz., 1956-97, prof. anthropology, 1964—, Riecker Disting. prof., 1980-97, head dept., 1964-80; emeritus, 1997; dir. Ariz. State Mus., 1964-97; emeritus, 1997. Mem. adv. panel program in anthropology NSF, 1963-64, mem. mus. collections program, 1983-85; mem. NSF grad. fellowship panel Nat. Acad. Scis.-NRC, 1964-66; mem. research in nursing in patient care rev. com. USPHS, 1967-69; com. on social sci. commn. edn. in agr. and natural resources Nat. Acad. Scis., 1968-69; mem. anthropology com. examiners Grad. Record Exam., 1967-70, chmn., 1969-70; mem. com. recovery archaeol. remains, 1972-77, chmn., 1973-77; collaborator Nat. Park Service, 1972-76; mem. Ariz. Hist. Adv. Commn., 1966-97, chmn., 1971-74, chmn. hist. sites rev. com., 1971-83; chmn. Ariz. Humanities Council, 1973-77, mem., 1979-85; adv. bd. Ariz. Hist. Recors, 1976-84; mem. research review panel for archaeology NEH, 1976-77, mem. rev. panel for museums, 1978, Ariz. Archaeology Adv. Commn., 1985-97; cons. task force on archaeology Adv. Council on Historic Preservation, 1978. Author: Modern Yucatecan Maya Pottery Making, 1958; editor: Migrations in New World Culture History, 1958, When is a Kiva, 1990; mem. editl. bd. Science, 1972-77. Trustee Mus. No. Ariz., 1969-84, 86-90; bd. dirs. Tucson Art Mus., 1974-77; cons. Nat. Mus. Act Coun., 1984-86. Served with USNR, 1944-45, PTO. Recipient Pub. Svc. award Dept. Interior, 1990. Fellow AAAS (chmn. sect. H 1977-78), Tree-Ring Soc., Am. Anthrop. Assn. (Disting. Svc. award 1980); mem. Soc. Am. Archaeology (editor 1958-62, exec. com. 1963-64, pres. 1976-77, disting. svc. award 1998), Am. Soc. Conservation Archaeology (Conservation award 1980), Seminario de Cultura Maya, Am. Assn. Museums (accreditation vis. com. 1972, 82-90, cons. mus. assessment program 1983-89, repatriation task force 1987, steering com. mus. data collection program 1988-93), Internat. Coun. Museums (assoc.), Coun. Mus. Anthropology (dir. 1978-79, pres. 1980-83), Assn. Sci. Mus. Dirs. (sec.-treas. 1978-80), Ariz. Acad. Sci., Ariz. Archaeol. and Hist. Soc. (Byron Cummings award 1993), Mus. Assn. Ariz. (pres. 1983, 84), Phi Beta Kappa, Sigma Xi. Office: Univ Ariz Ariz State Museum Tucson AZ 85721-0001

THOMPSON, RICHARD, financial executive; Bachelor's degree, Western Wash. U., 1965; JD, U. Wash., 1968. Pvt. law practice, Snohomish, Wash., 1968-76; atty., then adminstr. city govt., 1976-80; city mgr. city govt. Puyalla, 1981-84; chief of staff Gov. Booth Gardner, 1987-88; sec. Dept. Social and Health Svcs., 1989-92; chair Western Wash. Growth Mgmt. Bd., 1992-93; pres. United Way King County, Seattle, 1993-96; dir. Office of Fin. Mgmt., Olympia, Wash., 1997-99; dir. govt. rels. U. Wash. Office Govt. Rels., Seattle, 1999—. Recipient Citizenship award Comty. of Color of State of Wash., 1991. Mem. Nat. Assn. State Budgeters, Wash. Bar Assn. Office: U Wash Office Govt Rels PO Box 531278 Seattle WA 98195-0001

THOMPSON, RICHARD DICKSON, lawyer; b. Lexington, Ky., Aug. 14, 1955; s. Lawrence Sidney and Algernon Smith (Dickson) T.; m. Bobbi Dale Magidoff, Aug. 3, 1980; children: Anne Katherine, Harrison Asher. AB, Harvard U., 1977; JD, Stanford U., 1980. Bar: Calif. 1980, U.S. Dist. Ct. (so. dist.) Calif. 1980. Assoc. Rosenfeld Meyer & Susman, Beverly Hills, Calif., 1980-83, Silverberg Rosen Leon & Behr, L.A., 1983-86, ptnr., 1986-89; assoc., then ptnr. Silverberg Katz Thompson & Braun, L.A., 1989-95. Bd. trustees L.A. Copyright Soc. Mem. Order of the Coif, Phi beta Kappa. Office: Brodia Group 221 Main St Fl 16 San Francisco CA 94105-1936

THOMPSON, RICHARD FREDERICK, psychologist, neuroscientist, educator; b. Portland, Oreg., 1930; s. Frederick Albert and Margaret St. Clair (Marr) T.; m. Judith K. Pedersen, May 22, 1960; children: Kathryn M., Elizabeth K., Virginia St. C. B.A., Reed Coll., 1952; M.S., U. Wis., 1953, Ph.D., 1956. Asst. prof. med. psychology Med. Sch. U. Oreg., Portland, 1959-63, assoc. prof., 1963-65, prof., 1965-67; prof. psychobiology U. Calif., Irvine, 1967-73, 75-80; prof. psychology Harvard U., Cambridge, Mass., 1973-74, Lashley chair prof., 1973; prof. psychology, Bing prof. human biology Stanford U., Palo Alto, Calif., 1980-87; Keck prof. psychology and biol. scis. U. So. Calif., L.A., 1987—, dir. neuroscience program, 1989—. Author: Foundations of Physiological Psychology, 1967, (with others) Psychology, 1971, Introduction to Physiological Psychology, 1975; Psychology editor (with others), W.H. Freeman & Co. publs., chief editor, Behavioral Neurosci., 1983—; editor: Jour. Comparative and Physiol. Psychology, 1981-83; regional editor: (with others) Physiology and Behavior; contbr. (with others) articles to profl. jours. Fellow AAAS, APA (Disting. Sci. Contbn. award 1974, governing coun. 1974—), Soc. Neurosci. (councilor 1972-76); mem. NAS, Am. Acad. Arts and Scis., Internat. Brain Rsch. Orgn., Am. Philos. Soc., Psychonomic Soc. (gov. 1972-77, chmn. 1976), Am. Psychol. Soc. (pres. 1994-96), Western Psychol. Assn. (pres. 1994-95), Soc. Exptl. Psychology (Warren medal). Office: Univ of So Calif Neuroscis Program HNB 122 Univ Park Los Angeles CA 90007

THOMPSON, RUFUS E. lawyer; b. Lubbock, Tex., Aug. 15, 1943; s. Glenn Wesley and Naomi Elvina T.; m. Sandra Jean Lemons, Aug. 8, 1965; children— Michael Glenn, Mark Gregory, Matthew Wesley. B.B.A., U. Tex., Austin, 1965, J.D., 1968. Bar: Tex. bar 1968, N.Mex. bar 1969. Assoc. firm Atwood & Malone, Roswell, N.Mex., 1968-71; ptnr. firm Atwood, Malone, Mann & Cooter, Roswell, 1971-78, U.S. Atty. Dist. N.Mex., Albuquerque, 1978-81; now ptnr. firm Modrall, Sperling, Roehl, Harris & Sisk, Albuquerque, 1981—. Mem. Nat. Conf. Commrs. on Uniform State Laws, 1975-79; chmn. N.Mex. Supreme Ct. Com. on Rules of Evidence, 1972-94; U.S. Atty. for N.Mex. Com., 1978-82; mem. U.S. Atty. Gen.'s Adv. Com., 1980—, chmn., 1981. Mem. N.Mex. Democratic Party Central Com., 1972-78; mem. N.Mex. State Senate, 1973-78; mem. Gov's. Commn. on Prevention of Organized Crime, 1985-89. Mem. Am. Bar Assn. (exec. council young lawyers sect. 1972), N.Mex. Bar Assn. (chmn. young lawyers sect. 1970) Baptist. Office: PO Box 2168 Albuquerque NM 87103-2168 also: Modrall Sperling Roehl Harris & Sisk 500 4th St NW Albuquerque NM 87102-5324

THOMPSON, TERENCE WILLIAM, lawyer; b. Moberly, Mo., July 3, 1952; s. Donald Gene and Carolyn (Stringer) T.; m. Caryn Elizabeth Hildebrand, Aug. 30, 1975; children: Cory Elizabeth, Christopher William, Tyler Madison. BA in Govt. with honors and high distinction, U. Ariz., 1974; JD, Harvard U., 1977. Bar: Ariz. 1977, U.S. Dist. Ct. Ariz. 1977, U.S. Tax Ct. 1979. Assoc. Brown & Bain P.A., Phoenix, 1977-83, ptnr., 1983-92, Gallagher and Kennedy, P.A., Phoenix, 1992—. Legis. aide Rep. Richard Burgess, Ariz. Ho. of Reps., 1974; mem. bus. adv. bd. Citibank Ariz. (formerly Great Western Bank & Trust, Phoenix), 1985-86. Mem. staff Harvard Law Record, 1974-75; rsch. editor Harvard Internat. Law Jour. ,1976; lead author, editor-in-chief: Arizona Corporate Practice, 1996; contbr. articles to profl. jours. Mem. Phoenix Mayor's Youth Adv. Bd. 1968-70, Phoenix Internat.; active 20-30 Club, 1978-81, sec. 1978-80, Valley Leadership, Phoenix, 1983-84, citizens task force future financing needs City of Phoenix, 1985-86; exec. coun. Boys and Girls Clubs of Met. Phoenix, 1990-2000, sr. coun. 2000—; bd. dirs. Phoenix Bach Choir, 1992-94; deacon Shepherd of Hills Congl. Ch., Phoenix, 1984-85; pres. Maricopa County Young Dems., 1982-83, Ariz. Young Dems., 1983-84, sec. 1981-82, v.p. 1982-83; exec. dir. Young Dems. Am., 1985, exec. com. 1983-85; others. Fellow Ariz. Bar Found.; mem. State Bar Ariz. (vice chmn. internt. law sect. 1978, sec. securities law sect. 1990-91, vice chmn. sect. 1991-92, chmn.-elect 1992-93, chmn. 1993-94, exec. coun. 1988-96, sec. bus. law sect. 1992-93, vice chmn. 1993-94, chmn. 1994-95, exec. coun. 1996-98), Nat. Assn. Bond Lawyers, Nat. Health Lawyers, Greater Phoenix Black C. of C. (bd. dirs. 1999-2001), Blue Key, Phi Beta Kappa, Phi Kappa Phi, Phi Eta Sigma. Home: 202 W Lawrence Rd Phoenix AZ 85013-1226 Office: Gallagher & Kennedy PA 2575 E Camelback Rd Phoenix AZ 85016-9225

THOMPSON, WILLIAM BENBOW, JR. obstetrician/gynecologist, educator; b. Detroit, July 26, 1923; s. William Benbow and Ruth Wood (Locke) T.; m. Constance Carter, July 30, 1947 (div. Feb. 1958); 1 child, William Benbow IV; m. Jane Gilliland, Mar. 12, 1958; children: Reese Ellison, Belinda Day. AB, U. So. Calif., 1947, MD, 1951. Diplomate Am. Bd. Ob-Gyn. Resident Gallinger Mun. Hosp., Washington, 1952-53, George Washington U. Hosp., Washington, 1953-55; asst. ob-gyn. La. State U., 1955-56; asst. clin. prof. UCLA, 1957-64; assoc. prof. U. Calif.-Irvine Sch. Med., Orange, 1964-92, dir. gynecology, 1977-92, prof. emeritus, 1993—, vice chmn. ob-gyn., 1978-89. Assoc. dean U. Calif.-Irvine Coll. Med., Irvine, 1969-73. Inventor: Thompson Retractor, 1976; Thompson Manipulator, 1977. Bd. dirs. Monarch Bay Assn. Laguna Niguel, Calif. 1969-77, Monarch Summitt II A ssn. 1981-83. With U.S. Army, 1942-44, PTO. Fellow ACS, Am. Coll. Ob-Gyn. (life), L.A. Ob-Gyn. Soc. (life); mem. Orange County Gynecology and Obstetrics Soc. (hon.), Capistrano Bay Yacht Club (commodore 1975), Internat. Order Blue Gavel, Dana West Yacht Club. Avocation: boating. Office: UCI Med Ctr OB/GYN 101 The City Dr S Orange CA 92868-3201 E-mail: Benbow1923@aol.com

THOMSEN, CARL, electronics company executive; b. 1945; BSBA, Valparaiso U.; MBA, U. Mich. CPA. Former controller Audio-Video Systems Divsn. Ampex; former sr. v.p., chief fin. officer Measurex Corp.; chief fin. officer, sr. v.p., sec. DMC Stratex Networks, Inc., San Jose, Calif., 1995—. Mem. Fin. Exec. Inst., Calif. Soc. CPAs. E-mail: www.dmcwave-.com. Office: DMC Stratex Networks Inc 170 Rose Orchard Way San Jose CA 95134-1396

THOMSON, JAMES ALAN, research company executive; b. Boston, Jan. 21, 1945; s. James Alan and Mary Elizabeth (Pluff) T.; m. Darlene Thomson; children: Kristen Ann, David Alan. BS, U. N.H., 1967; MS, Purdue U., 1970, PhD, 1972, DSc (hon.), 1992; LLD (hon.), Pepperdine U., 1996. Research fellow U. Wis., Madison, 1972-74; systems analyst Office Sec. Def., U.S. Dept. Def., Washington, 1974-77; staff mem. Nat. Security Council, White House, Washington, 1977-81; v.p. RAND, Santa Monica, Calif., 1981-89, pres., chief exec. officer, 1989—; chmn. bd. Entrust Techs, Inc., 2000—. Bd. dirs. L.A. World Affairs Coun., AK Steel Holding Corp., Tex. Biotech. Corp. Contbr. articles to profl. jours. and chpts. to books. Mem. Internat. Inst. for Strategic Studies (coun. 1985-99), Coun. Fgn. Rels. Office: RAND 1700 Main St Santa Monica CA 90401-3297 E-mail: thomson@rand.org

THONG, TRAN, biomedical company executive; b. Saigon, Vietnam, Dec. 8, 1951; came to U.S., 1969, naturalized, 1980. s. Vy and Vinh-Thi (Nguyen) T.; m. Thuy Thi-Bich Nguyen, Jan.12, 1978. BSEE, Ill. Inst. Tech., 1972; MS in Engring., Princeton U., 1974, PhD, 1975. Rsch. scientist Western Geophys., Houston, 1975-76; computer devel. engr. GE Co., Syracuse, N.Y., 1976-79; dir. electronic system lab. Tektronix, Inc., Beaverton, Oreg., 1980-90; v.p. engring., and digital signal processing gen. mgr. Tektronix Fed. Systems Inc., Beaverton, 1990-93; v.p. systems design and devel. Micro Systems Engring., Inc., Lake Oswego, 1993—; prin. N.W. Signal Processing, Inc. Adj. asst. prof. Syracuse U., 1979-81, Oreg. State U., Corvallis, 1980-83, U. Portland, Oreg., 1981-83; adj. prof. Oreg. Grad. Ctr., Beaverton, 1984—; mem. adv. bd. Biomed. Engring. Inst., U. Erlangen, Germany, 1996—. Author numerous sci papers and U. S. patents. Bd. dirs. S.E. Asia Scholarship Fund, 1994—, Fellow IEEE (com. chmn. 1982-88, assoc. editor Trans. 1979-81, gen. chmn, 1989, exec. v.p. circuits and sys. 1989); mem. Vietnamese Assn. for Computing Engring. Tech. and Sci. (founding mem., chmn. 1994-95, past pres, 1995-96, pres. 1998-99), Sigma Xi, Eta Kappa Nu, Tau Beta Pi. Republican. Office: Micro Sys Engring 6024 Jean Rd Lake Oswego OR 97035-5308

THOR, LINDA MARIA, college president; b. L.A., Feb. 21, 1950; d. Karl Gustav and Mildred Dorrine (Hofius) T.; m. Robert Paul Huntsinger, Nov. 22, 1974; children: Erik, Marie. BA, Pepperdine U., 1971, EdD, 1986; MPA, Calif. State U., Los Angeles, 1980. Dir. pub. info. Pepperdine U., Los Angeles, 1971-73; pub. info. officer L.A. C.C. Dist., 1974-75, dir. comm., 1975-81, dir. edn. svcs., 1981-82, dir. high tech., 1982-83, sr. dir. occupl. and tech. edn., 1983-86; pres. West Los Angeles Coll., Culver City, Calif., 1986-90, Rio Salado C.C., Phoenix, 1990—. Editor: Curriculum Design and Development for Effective Learning, 1973; author: (with others) Effective Media Relations, 1982, Performance Contracting, 1987; contbr. articles to profl. jours. Bd. dirs. Coun. for Adult and Experiential Learning, 1990—, Tech. Exch. Ctr., 1986-99, Grtr. Phoenix Econ. Coun., 1994-99; active Am. Assn. C.C. Commn. Acad. and Student Devel., 1995-97, Continuous Quality Improvement Network for Cmty. Colls., 1991—, Am. Coun. Edn. Commn. on Leadership Devel., 1995-98; mem. Ariz. Gov.'s Adv. Coun. on Quality, 1992-96; pres. Ariz. Cmty. Coll. Pres.'s Coun., 1995-96. Recipient Delores award Pepperdine U., 1986, Alumni Medal of Honor, 1987, Outstanding Achievement award Women's Bus. Network, 1989; named Woman of the Yr., Culver City Bus. and Profl. Women, 1988. Office: 2323 W 14th St Tempe AZ 85281-6950

THORBURN, LISA A. acoustical consulting company executive; BS in Scientific & Tech. Comm., Mich. Tech. U. With Sisters of St. Dominic, Anshen & Allen, IWERKS Entertainment, Don Dommer Assocs., STUDIOS Architecture, Harveys Resort Hotel/Casino, South Lake Tahoe, Helsing Group, Brava, Inc.; prin. designer Thorburn Assocs., Castro Valley, Calif. Contbr. tech. articles to profl. jours. Mem. AIA, NAFE, Soc. Tech. Comm., Soc. Mktg. Profl. Svcs., Constrn. Specifications Inst. Office: 2867 Grove Way Castro Valley CA 94546-6709

THORNBURG, RON, newspaper editor; BA in Polit. Sci., Purdue U., 1971. Reporter Jour. and Courier, Lafayette, Ind., 1972-73; mng. editor The Evening Times, Melbourne, Fla., 1973-75; met. editor, asst. news editor, copy editor, bur. chief Today, Melbourne, 1975-78, mng. editor, 1978-80; exec. editor News Press, Fort Myers, Fla., 1980-86; news exec. Comty. Newspapers, Gannet Co., Inc., Rosslyn, Va., 1986-88; editor Burlington (Vt.) Free Press, 1988-94; mng. editor Standard Examiner, Ogden, Utah, 1994—. E-mial. Office: Standard Examiner 332 S Ward Ave PO Box 12790 Ogden UT 84412-2790 E-mail: rthornburg@standard.net

THORNE, DAVID W. lawyer; b. Walla Walla, Wash., Aug. 9, 1945; BA, Wash. State U., 1967; MBA, U. Wash., 1969, JD, 1974. Bar: Wash. 1974. Mem. Davis Wright Tremaine LLP, Seattle. Mem. ABA, Am. Coll. Real Estate Lawyers, Am. Coll. Mortgage Attys., Am. Land Title Assn. Lender Counsel Group, Wash. State Bar Assn. (past mem. exec. com. real property, probate and trust sect., past chmn. 1991-92), Pacific Real Estate Inst. (past pres. 1994, founding trustee 1989-96), Phi Delta Phi. Office: Davis Wright Tremaine LLP 2600 Century Sq 1501 4th Ave Ste 2600 Seattle WA 98101-1688

THORNE, JERROLD L. state legislator; b. Idaho Falls, May 1, 1929; m. Lois Thorne; children: Mark, Jon. BS in Edn., Brigham Young U., 1951. Mem. Idaho Senate, Dist. 12, Boise, 1984—. Chair local govt. and tax. com., mem. fin. and transp. coms. With USNR, 1948-55. Recipient Silver Beaver award, Boy Scouts Am. Mem. PTA, C. of C. (past pres.), Rotary (pres. 1977-78, Paul Harris fellow). Republican. Office: State Capitol PO Box 83720 Boise ID 83720-3720

THORNE, KIP STEPHEN, physicist, educator; b. Logan, Utah, June 1, 1940; s. David Wynne and Alison (Comish) T.; m. Linda Jeanne Peterson, Sept. 12, 1960 (div. 1977); children: Kares Anne, Bret Carter; m. Carolee Joyce Winstein, July 7, 1984. B.S. in Physics, Calif. Inst. Tech., 1962; A.M. in Physics (Woodrow Wilson fellow, Danforth Found. fellow), Princeton U., 1963, Ph.D. in Physics (Danforth Found. fellow, NSF fellow), 1965, postgrad. (NSF postdoctoral fellow), 1965-66; D.Sc. (hon.), Ill. Coll., 1979; Dr.h.c., Moscow U., 1981; D.Sc. (hon.), Utah State U., 2000, U. Glasgow, 2001. Research fellow Calif. Inst. Tech., 1966-67, assoc. prof. theoretical physics, 1967-70, prof., 1970—, William R. Kenan, Jr. prof., 1981-91, Feynman prof. theoretical physics, 1991—. Fulbright lectr., France, 1966; vis. assoc. prof. U. Chgo., 1968; vis. prof. Moscow U., 1969, 75, 78, 82, 83, 86, 88, 90, 98; vis. sr. rsch. assoc. Cornell U., 1977, A.D. White prof.-at-large, 1968-92; adj. prof. U. Utah, 1971-98; mem. Internat. Com. on Gen. Relativity and Gravitation, 1971-80, 92-01, Com. on U.S.-USSR Coop. in Physics, 1978-79, Space Sci. Bd., NASA, 1980-83; co-founder, chair steering com. LIGO, 1984-87. Co-author: Gravitation Theory and Gravitational Collapse, 1965, Gravitation, 1973, Black Holes: The Membrane Paradigm, 1986, Black Holes and Time Warps: Einstein's Outrageous Legacy, 1994. Alfred P. Sloan Found. Rsch. fellow, 1966-68; John Simon Guggenheim fellow, 1967; recipient Sci. Writing award in physics and astronomy Am. Inst. Physics, 1969, 94, P.A.M. Dirac Meml. lectureship Cambridge U., 1995, Karl Schwarzschild medal Astron. Soc. Germany, 1996, J. Robert Oppenheimer Meml. lectureship U. Calif., 1999, Charles Darwin Meml. Lectureship Royal Astron. Soc., 2000, Arthur Holly

Compton Meml. lectureship Washington U., 2001, Herzberg Meml. Lectureship Can. Assn. Physicists, 2001. Fellow Am. Phys. Soc. (Julius Edgar Lilienfeld prize 1996, chair tropical group in gravity 1997-98); mem. Am. Philosophical Soc., Nat. Acad. Scis., Am. Acad. Arts and Scis., Am. Astron. Soc., Internat. Astron. Union, AAAS, Russian Acad. Scis., Sigma Xi, Tau Beta Pi. Office: California Inst Tech 130-33 Theoretical Astrophysics 1200 E California Blvd Pasadena CA 91106

THORNE, MIKE, state agency administrator; Exec. dir. Port of Portland, Oreg. Office: Port of Portland Office Exec Dir PO Box 3529 Portland OR 97208

THORNE, RICHARD MANSERGH, physicist; b. Birmingham, Eng., July 25, 1942; s. Robert George and Dorothy Lena (Goodchild) T.; children: Peter Baring, Michael Thomas, Thomas Mansergh. BSc, Birmingham U., 1963; PhD, MIT, 1968. Grad. asst. M.I.T., 1963-68; asst. prof. dept. atmospheric scis. UCLA, 1968-71, asso. prof., 1971-75, prof., 1975—, chmn. dept., 1976-79. Vis. fellow St. Edmund's Coll., Cambridge (Eng.) U., 1986-87, 92; cons. NATO Adv. Group for Aerospace R&D, 1973, Jet Propulsion Lab., Aerospace Corp. Contbr. articles to profl. jours. Recipient numerous grants NSF, NASA, NATO, Jet Propulsion Lab.; Fulbright scholar, 1963-70; fellow Royal Norwegian Coun. for Sci. and Indsl. Rsch., 1973, sr. vis. fellow U. Sussex, 1979-80, rsch. fellow Royal Soc. London, 1986-87. Fellow Am. Geophys. Union; mem. Internat. Union Radio Scis. Home: 10390 Caribou Ln Los Angeles CA 90077-2809 Office: UCLA Dept Atmospheric Scis Los Angeles CA 90095-0001

THORNLEY, ANTHONY S. telecommunications company executive; BS in Chemistry, U. Manchester, Eng. With Coopers and Lybrand; corp. contr. Nortel Ltd., various mgmt. positions; v.p. fin., CFO Qualcomm Inc., San Diego, 1994-96, sr. v.p., 1996-97, exec. v.p., CFO, 1997—. Fellow Inst. of Chartered Accts. in Eng. and Wales. Office: Qual Comm Inc 5775 Morehouse Dr San Diego CA 92121

THORNTON, CHARLES VICTOR, lawyer; b. Takoma Park, Md., July 18, 1942; s. Charles Victor and Margaret Louise (Wiggins) T.; m. Suzanne Thorne, May 16, 1970; children: Christopher, Matthew, Joshua, Jeremy. AB, Cornell U., 1964; JD, U. Mich., 1967. Bar: Calif. 1969, U.S. Dist. Ct. (cen. dist.) Calif. 1969. Instr. U. Pa. Law Sch., Phila., 1967-68; assoc. Paul, Hastings, Janofsky & Walker, L.A., 1968-74, ptnr., 1975—, mng. ptnr. L.A. office, 1992-96, mng. partner San Francisco office, 1997-2000. Contbr. articles to publs. Pres. Info. and Referral Fedn. Los Angeles County, 1988-95; mem. exec. com. Los Angeles County United Way, 1988-92. Named Bd. Vol. of Yr. United Way, 1986. Mem. Calif. Club, Los Angeles Country Club, San Francisco YMCA (bd. dirs. 1998—). Avocations: running, golf. Office: Paul Hastings Janofsky & Walker 345 California St San Francisco CA 94104-2606 E-mail: charlesthornton@paulhastings.com

THORNTON, D. WHITNEY, II, lawyer; b. Miami, Fla., Oct. 17, 1946; s. Dade Whitney and Hilda (Bryan) T.; m. Jane Collis, Nov. 27, 1971; children: Bryan Whitney, Elizabeth Jane, Virginia Anne. BA, Washington and Lee U., 1968, JD cum laude, 1970. Bar: Va. 1970, D.C. 1976, U.S. Ct. Appeals (4th cir.) 1978, U.S. Supreme Ct. 1980, Calif. 1987, U.S. Ct. Appeals (9th cir.) 1987. Atty. Naval Air Sys. Command, Dept. Navy, Washington, 1970-73; asst. counsel to comptr. Dept. Navy, 1973-74, asst. to gen. counsel, 1974-76; assoc. Sullivan & Beauregard, Washington, 1976-77, ptnr., 1977-81, Bowman, Conner, Touhey & Thornton, Washington, 1981-83; pres. Continental Maritime Industries, Inc., San Francisco, 1983-87; ptnr. Dempsey, Bastianelli, Brown & Touhey, San Francisco, 1987-91, Seyfarth Shaw, San Francisco, 1992—. Contbr. articles to profl. jours. Mem. ABA (pub. contract law sect., chmn. suspension and debarment com. 1977), FBA (vice chmn. govt. contracts coun., Disting. Svc. award 1981), Washington Golf and Country Club (Arlington, Va.), Blackhawk Country Club (Danville, Calif.). Republican. Methodist. Office: Seyfarth Shaw 101 California St Ste 2900 San Francisco CA 94111-5858 E-mail: wthornton@sf.seyfarth.com

THORNTON, J. DUKE, lawyer; b. Murray, Ky., July 11, 1944; s. Arthur Lee and Ruth Maxine (Billings) T.; m. Carol Caceres, Dec. 26, 1966 (dec.); children: Jennifer, Carey. BBA, U. N.Mex., Albuquerque, 1966, JD, 1969. Bar: N.Mex. 1969, U.S. Ct. Appeals (10th cir.) 1969, N.Y. 1985, U.S. Supreme Ct. 1992. With Butt, Thornton & Baehr, P.C., Albuquerque, 1971—, now chmn. bd. Legal counsel N.Mex. Jaycees, 1972; clk. N.Mex. Supreme Ct., Santa Fe, 1969; mem. com. N.Mex. Uniform Jury Instructions, 1987-88. Author: Trial Handbook for New Mexico Lawyers, 1992. Bd. dirs. N.Mex. Bd. of Dentistry, Santa Fe, 1987-88; commr. N.Mex. Racing Commn., Albuquerque, 1988-95. Mem. ABA, Assn. Coll. and Univ. Counsel, Internat. Assn. Ins. Counsel, Am. Bd. Trial Advs., Albuquerque Bar Assn. (bd. dirs. 1978-79), Nat. Collegiate Athletic Assn. (agt.). Avocation: pilot. Office: Butt Thornton & Baehr PC PO Box 3170 Albuquerque NM 87190-3170

THORNTON, JOHN S., IV, retired bishop; Bishop Diocese of Idaho, Boise, 1990-98; ret. Home: Episcopal Diocese of Idaho Box 936 1304 E Bannock Boise ID 83712

THORP, EDWARD OAKLEY, investment management company executive; b. Chgo., Aug. 14, 1932; s. Oakley Glenn and Josephine (Gebert) T.; m. Vivian Sinetar, Jan. 28, 1956; children: Raun, Karen, Jeffrey. BA in Physics, UCLA, 1953, MA, 1955, PhD in Math., 1958. C.L.E. Moore instr. MIT, Cambridge, Mass., 1959-61; asst. prof. N.Mex. State U., 1961-63, assoc. prof. math., 1963-65, U. Calif., Irvine, 1965-67, prof. math., 1967-77, prof. fin., 1977-82, regents lectr., 1992-93. Vis. prof. UCLA, 1991; chmn. Oakley Sutton Mgmt. Corp., Newport Beach, Calif., 1972-91; mng. gen. ptnr. Princeton/Newport Ptnrs., Newport Beach, 1969-91, OSM Ptnrs., MIDAS Advisors, Newport Beach, 1986-89; gen. ptnr. Edward O. Thorp & Assocs., L.P., Newport Beach, 1989—, Ridgeline Ptnrs., Newport Beach, 1994—; portfolio mgr., cons. Glenwood Investment Corp., Chgo., 1992-94; prin., cons. Grosvenor Capital Mgmt., Chgo., 1992-93; pres. Noesis Corp., 1994—. Author: Beat the Dealer: A Winning Strategy for the Game of Twenty-One, 1962, rev. edit., 1966, Elementary Probability, 1966, The Mathematics of Gambling, 1984; co-author: Beat The Market, 1967, The Gambling Times Guide to Blackjack, 1984; columnist Gambling Times, 1979-84, Wilmott 2001— Grantee NSF, 1954-55, 62-64, Air Force Office Sci. Rsch., 1964-73. Fellow NSF, Inst. Math. Stats.; mem. Phi Beta Kappa, Sigma Xi. Avocations: astronomy, distance running. Office: Edward O Thorp & Assocs LP 610 Newport Center Dr Ste 1240 Newport Beach CA 92660-6436

THORPE, DOUGLAS L. lawyer; b. Wahoo, Nebr., Jan. 25, 1937; BSCE, U. Nebr., 1959; JD cum laude, So. Meth. U., 1968. Bar: Calif. 1969. Mem. Perkins Coie, L.A., 1988—. Bd. dirs. Pub. Counsel, 1980-83. Mem. ABA (antitrust law sect., corp., banking and bus. law sect., litigation sect., econs. of law practice sect.), State Bar Calif., L.A. County Bar Assn. (del. to State Bar Conf. of Dels. 1981, 1983-84, exec. com. antitrust law sect. 1981-83), Century City Bar Assn. (bd. govs. 1982-85), Order of the Coif, Barristers, Phi Delta Phi, Sigma Tau, Tau Beta Pi, Chi Epsilon. Office: Perkins Coie 26th St Fl 6 1620 South Tower Santa Monica CA 90404

THORSEN, JAMES HUGH, retired aviation director, airport manager, retired; b. Evanston, Ill., Feb. 5, 1943; s. Chester A. and Mary Jane (Currie) T.; m. Nancy Dain, May 30, 1980. BA, Ripon Coll., 1965. FAA cert. comml. pilot, flight instr. airplanes and instruments. Bd. dirs. Internat. Northwest Aviation Coun. Pres. Thorsen Aviation Cons. Recipient Region Safety award FAA N.W. Mountain. Mem. Am. Assn. Airport Execs. (past pres. N.W. chpt., Disting. Svc. award 1999), Mensa, Idaho Falls W. Rotary Club, Quiet Birdmen, Sigma Alpha Epsilon. Home: 334 Westmorland Dr Idaho Falls ID 83402-4607

THORSEN, NANCY DAIN, real estate broker; b. Edwardsville, Ill., June 23, 1944; d. Clifford Earl and Suzanne Eleanor (Kribs) Dain; m. David Massie, 1968 (div. 1975); 1 child, Suzanne Dain Massie; m. James Hugh Thorsen, May 30, 1980. BSc in Mktg., So. Ill. U., 1968, MSc in Bus. Edn., 1975; grad., Realtor Inst., Idaho, 1983. Cert. resdl. and investment specialist, fin. instr.; designated real estate instr. State of Idaho; accredited buyer rep. Personnel officer J.H. Little & Co. Ltd., London, 1969-72; instr. in bus. edn. Spl. Sch. Dist. St. Louis, 1974-77; mgr. mktg./ops. Isis Foods, Inc., St. Louis, 1978-80; asst. mgr. store Stix, Baer & Fuller, St. Louis, 1980; assoc. broker Century 21 Sayer Realty, Inc., Idaho Falls, Idaho, 1981-88, RE/MAX Homestead Realty, 1989—. Spkr. RE/MAX Internat. Conv., 1990, 94, RE/MAX Stars Cruise, 1993, RE/MAX Pacific N.W. Conv., 1994, Century 21, Austral-Asia, 1995, women's seminar Clemson U., 1996, 98; real estate fin. instr. State of Idaho Real Estate Commn., 1994; founder Nancy Thorsen Seminars, 1995. Bd. dirs. Idaho Vol., Boise, 1981-84, Idaho Falls Symphony, 1982; pres. Friends of Idaho Falls Libr., 1981-83; chmn. Idaho Falls Mayor's Com. for Vol. Coordination, 1981-84; power leader Power Program, 1995; mem. Mtn. River Valley Red Cross, chair capital campaign, cmty. gifts chair ARC. Recipient Idaho Gov.'s award, 1982, cert. appreciation City of Idaho Falls/Mayor Campbell, 1982, 87, Civitan Disting. Pres. award, 1990, Bus. Women of the Yr. award C. of C., 1998; named to Two Million Dollar Club, 1987, 88, Four Million Dollar Club, 1989, 90, Top Investment Sales Person for Eastern Idaho, 1985, Realtor of Yr. Idaho Falls Bd. Realtors, 1990, Outstanding Realtors Active in Politics, Mem. of Yr. Idaho Assn. Realtors, 1991, Women of Yr. Am. Biog. Inst., 1991, Profiles of Top Prodrs. award Real Estate Edn. Assn., Above the Crowd award 1997; named Western Region Power Leader, Darryl Davis Seminars. Mem. Nat. Spkrs. Assn., Idaho Falls Bd. Realtors (chmn. Orientation 1982-83, chmn. edn. 1983, chmn. legis. com. 1989, 95—, chmn. program com. 1990, 91), Idaho Assn. Realtors (pres. Million Dollar Club 1988—, edn. com. 1990-93), Women's Coun. Realtors, Am. Bus. Women's Assn., So. Ill. U. Alumni Assn., Idaho Falls C. of C. (Bus. Woman of the Yr.-Professions, 1997), newcomers Club, Civitan (pres. Idaho Falls chpt. 1988-89, Civitan of Yr. 1986, 97, Outstanding Pres. award 1990, Hall of Fame 1998), Real Estate Educators Assn. Office: RE/MAX Homestead Inc 1301 E 17th St Ste 1 Idaho Falls ID 83404-6273 E-mail: thorsen@srv.net

THORSON, LEE A. lawyer; b. Seattle, Nov. 10, 1949; s. Theodore Arthur and Irene Mary (Dakers) T.; m. Elizabeth Clayton Hay, June 7, 1975; children: Kirk Hunter, Alex Peter. BA, U. Wash., 1971; JD, U. Pacific, Sacramento, 1975; LLM Taxation, Boston U., 1976. Atty. Dahlgren & Dauenhauer P.S., Seattle, 1976-79, Lane Powell Spears Lubersky, Seattle, 1980-93; shareholder Birmingham Thorson & Barnett, P.C., 1993—; affiliate prof. U. Wash. Grad. Program in Taxation, 1995—. Mem. ABA (health law forum), Internat. Found. Employee Benefits, Employee Benefits and Health Law coms., Wash. State Bar Assn. Avocations: bicycling, skiing. Office: Birmingham Thorson Barnett 601 Union St Ste 3315 Seattle WA 98101-4018 E-mail: lthorson@btbpc.com

THOULESS, DAVID JAMES, physicist, educator; b. Bearsden, Scotland, Sept. 21, 1934; came to U.S., 1979; U.S. citizen, 1994; s. Robert Henry and Priscilla (Gorton) T.; m. Margaret Elizabeth Scrase, July 26, 1958; children: Michael, Christopher, Helen. BA, U. Cambridge, Eng., 1955, ScD, 1986; PhD, Cornell U., 1958. Physicist Lawrence Berkeley Lab., Calif., 1958-59; rsch. fellow U. Birmingham, Eng., 1959-61, prof. math. physics Eng., 1965-78; lectr., fellow Churchill Coll. U. Cambridge, Eng., 1961-65; prof. physics Queen's U., Kingston, Ont., Can., 1978; prof. applied sci. Yale U., New Haven, 1979-80; prof. physics U. Wash., Seattle, 1980—. Author: Quantum Mechanics of Many Body Systems, 2d edit., 1972, Topological Quantum Numbers in Nonrelativistic Physics, 1998. Recipient Maxwell medal Inst. Physics, 1973, Holweck prize Soc. Francaise de Physique-Inst. Physics, 1980, Fritz London award for Low temperature physics, Fritz London Meml. Fund, 1984, Wolf prize in physics, 1990, Paul Dirac medal Inst. Physics, 1993, Lars Onsager prize Am. Phys. Soc., 2000; Edwin Uehling disting. scholar U. Wash., 1988-98. Fellow Royal Soc., Am. Acad. Arts and Scis., Nat. Acad. Sci. Office: U Wash PO Box 351560 Seattle WA 98195-1560 E-mail: Thouless@phys.washington.edu

THRASHER, JACK DWAYNE, toxicologist, researcher, consultant; b. Nashville, Aug. 13, 1936; s. Harold A. and Margaret E. (Bolin) T.; m. Diane L. Walton, June 29, 1963; children: Traci L., Kristen I. BS, Longbeach State U., 1959; PhD, UCLA, 1964. Asst. prof. U. of Colo. Sch. of Medicine, Denver, 1964-66, UCLA Sch. of Medicine, L.A., 1966-72; application specialist Millipore Corp., Bedford, Mass., 1973-75; cons. Thrasher and Assocs., L.A., 1975-92, Alto, N.Mex., 1992-96; mem. faculty E. N. Mex. U., Ruidoso, 1992-97; mentor Columbia Pacific U., San Rafael, Calif., 1992-96. Bd. dirs., chmn. Internat. Inst. Rsch. for Chem. Hypersensitivity, Alto, N. Mex., 1991-94; advisor Chem. Impact Project Mill Valley, Calif., 1993—. Author: (books) Cellular and Molecular Renewal in the Mammalian Body, 1971, The Poisoning of our Homes and Work Places, 1990; editor-in-chief Informed Consent, 1993-94. Grantee: USPHS, NIH, 1966-69. Avocations: golf, fishing, wood working. Home and Office: Sam-1 Trust PO Box 874 110 Raven Court Alto NM 88312 E-mail: sam-1trust@zianet.com

THRONER, GUY CHARLES, JR. engineering executive, scientist, engineer, inventor, consultant; b. Mpls., Sept. 14, 1919; s. Guy Charles and Marie (Zechar) T.; m. Jean Holt, Dec. 5, 1943; children— Richard, Carol Anne, Steven BA, Oberlin Coll., 1943; postgrad., UCLA, 1960, 61. Registered profl. engr., Calif. Br. head Naval Weapon Ctr., China Lake, Calif., 1946-53; mgr. ordnance div., mgr. weapon systems div. Aerojet Gen. Corp., Azusa, 1953-64; v.p., div. mgr. FMC Corp., San Jose, 1964-74; research dir. Vacu Blast Corp., Belmont, 1976-78; v.p., devel. mfg. Dahlman, Inc., Braham, Minn., 1978-79; mgr. ordnance systems & tech. Battelle Meml. Inst., Columbus, Ohio, 1979-85; pres. Guy C. Throner & Assocs., tech. and mgmt. cons., 1985—. Dir. Omron Corp. Am., Chgo., 1976-77 Inventor, patentee indls., med. and mil. systems design Served as officer USNR, World War II Recipient Am. Order St. Barbara medal U.S. Army Arty, 1983, IR-100 award Indsl. Research Mag., Chgo., 1971, Congl. Commendation, 1985, Commendation, State of Ohio Ho. of Reps., 1995, also various commendations Mem. AIAA, Am. Def. Preparedness Assn. (Bronze medal 1974, Simon Silver medal 1985), Lake Wildwood Country Club, Sigma Xi. Republican. Avocations: astronomy, photography, golf. Home and Office: 17992 Jayhawk Dr Penn Valley CA 95946-9205 E-mail: guytlww@nccn.net

THUESON, DAVID OREL, pharmaceutical executive, researcher, educator, writer; b. Twin Falls, Idaho, May 9, 1947; s. Orel Grover and Shirley Jean (Archer) T.; m. Sherrie Linn Lowe, June 14, 1969; children: Sean, Kirsten, Eric, Ryan, Todd. BS, Brigham Young U., 1971; PhD, U. Utah, 1976; Postdoctoral fellow U. Tex. Med. Br., Galveston, 1976-77, [illegible] prof., 1977-82; sr. rsch. assoc. Parke-Davis Pharms., Ann Arbor, Mich., 1982-88; dir. pharmacology Immunetech Pharms., San Diego, 1988-90; dir. immunopharmacology Tanabe Rsch. Labs., San Diego, 1990-92; v.p. discovery Cosmederm Techs., San Diego, 1992-97. Contbr. articles to profl. jours.; patentee in field. Scout leader Boy Scouts Am., Mich., Tex. and Calif., 1979—. NIH grantee, 1978-81. Mem. Am. Acad. Allergy and Clin. Immunology, Am. Assn. Immunologists, Am. Thoracic Soc. Republican. Mormon. Avocations: water skiing, tennis, scuba diving. Home: 1356 Winchester Ave Mckinleyville CA 95519-8801 Office: 2330 Central Ave Ste 3 Mckinleyville CA 95519-3696 E-mail: thueson@reninet.com

THURSTON, GEORGE R. lumber company executive; b. 1942; BS, Northwestern U., 1965, MBA, 1966. With Cummins Engine Co., 1966-78; exec. v.p. fin. and treas. North Pacific Lumber Co., Portland, 1987—. Office: North Pacific Lumber Co PO Box 3915 Portland OR 97280-3915

THURSTON, MORRIS ASHCROFT, lawyer; b. Logan, Utah, May 25, 1943; s. Morris Alma and Barbara (Ashcroft) T.; m. Dawna Lyn Parrett, Sept. 10, 1966; children: Morris III, David, Ashley, Tyson. BA, Brigham Young U., 1967; JD, Harvard U., 1970. Bar: Calif. 1971, U.S. Dist. Ct. (cen. dist.) Calif. 1971, U.S. Supreme Ct. 1978. Assoc. Latham & Watkins, L.A., 1970-77, ptnr. Costa Mesa, Calif., 1978—. Jud. arbitrator Orange County Superior Ct., Calif., 1980—. Mem. Calif. Bar Assn., Orange County Bar Assn., Assn. Bus. Trial Lawyers. Republican. Mormon. Avocations: family history, writing, basketball. Home: 9752 Crestview Cir Orange CA 92861-1313 Office: Latham & Watkins 650 Town Center Dr Ste 2000 Costa Mesa CA 92626-7135

THURSTON, WILLIAM PAUL, mathematician; b. Washington, Oct. 30, 1946; s. Paul Ambrose and Margaret (Martt) T.; m. Karen T. Barris, Dec. 10, 1993; children: Hannah, Nathaniel, Dylan, Emily. Mem. Inst. Advanced Study, Princeton, N.J., 1972-73; asst. prof. Sloan fellow MIT, Cambridge, 1973-74; prof. math. Princeton (N.J.) U., 1974-91, U. Calif., Berkeley, 1991-96, dir. Math. Sci. Rsch. Inst., 1992-96, prof. math Davis, 1996—. Recipient Waterman award NSF, Fields Medal IMU, 1982. Fellow Nat. Acad. Scis., Am. Acad. Sci.; mem. Am. Math. Soc. Democrat. Office: Dept Mathematics UC Davis 1 Shields Ave Davis CA 95616-5270 E-mail: wpt@math.ucdavis.edu

THURSTON, WILLIAM RICHARDSON, oil and gas industry executive, geologist; b. New Haven, Sept. 20, 1920; s. Edward S. and Florence (Holbrooke) T.; m. Ruth A. Nelson, Apr. 30, 1944 (div. 1966); children: Karin R., Amy R., Ruth A.; m. Beatrice Furnas, Sept. 11, 1971; children: Mark P., Stephen P., Douglas P., Jennifer P. AB in Geol. Sci. with honors, Harvard U., 1942. Field geologist Sun Oil Co., Corpus Christi, Tex., 1946-47, asst. to div. geologist Dallas, 1947-50; chief geologist The Kimbark Co., Denver, 1952-59; head exploration dept. Kimbark Exploration Co., Denver, 1959-66; co-owner Kimbark Exploration Ltd., Denver, 1966-67, Kimbark Assocs., Denver, 1967-76, Hardscrabble Assocs., Denver, 1976-80; pres. Weaselskin Corp., Durango, Colo., 1980—. Bd. dirs. Denver Bot. Gardens, 1972-99, Crow Canyon Ctr. for Archaeology, Cortez, Colo., 1980-92. Comdr. USNR, World War II, Korea. Decorated D.F.C. with 2 gold stars, air medal with 10 gold stars. Mem. Am. Assn. Petroleum Geologists, Denver Assn. Petroleum Landmen, Rocky Mountain Assn. Petroleum Geologists, Four Corners Geol. Soc. Republican. Avocations: photography, gardening, reading. Office: Weaselskin Corp 12995 Highway 550 Durango CO 81303-6674

THYDEN, JAMES ESKEL, diplomat, educator, lecturer; b. L.A., Apr. 10, 1939; s. Eskel A. and Mildred Aileene (Rock) T.; m. Patricia Irene Kelsey, Dec. 15, 1959; children: Teresa Lynn, Janice Kay, James Blaine. BA in Biology, Pepperdine U., 1961; MA in Scandinavian Area Studies, U. Wash., 1992. Cert. secondary tchr., Calif., Wash. Tchr. Gompers Jr. High Sch., L.A., 1962-64; fgn. svc. officer U.S. Dept. State, Washington, 1964-90; rschr. U. Wash., Seattle, 1992-93; exec. dir. Seattle chpt. UN Assn., 1993-96. Travel lectr. Cunard Lines' Royal Viking Sun, 1995, and Royal Caribbean's Splendour of the Seas, 1997. Editor govt. report, ann. human rights reports, 1983-86; author, editor in-house govt. reports, documents. Dir. Office of Human Rights, 1983-86; counselor Embassy for Polit. Affairs, Am. Embassy, Oslo, Norway, 1986-90. Named Outstanding Young Man Am., 1969, Alumnus of Yr., Pepperdine U., 1984. Mem. Am. Fgn. Svc. Assn., World Affairs Coun. Seattle. Avocations: travel, reading, gardening. Home: 5631 153rd Pl SW Edmonds WA 98026-4239 E-mail: jethyden@aol.com

THYRET, RUSS, recording industry executive; Sales person L.A. WEA Br.; singles sales mgr. Warner Bros. Records Inc., 1971-73, sales mgr., 1973-75, v.p. sales dept., 1975-76, v.p. promotion, 1976-81, sr. v.p. mktg. dept., 1981-83, sr. v.p. mktg. and promotion, 1983, vice chmn., chmn., CEO, 1995—. Office: Warner Bros Records 3300 Warner Blvd Burbank CA 91505-4694

TIANO, ANTHONY STEVEN, television producer, book publishing executive; b. Santa Fe, Mar. 27, 1941; s. Joseph A. and Marian (Adlesperger) T.; m. Kathleen O'Brien, Dec. 29, 1972; children: Mark A., A. Steven. BA, U. N.Mex., 1969, MA, 1971; LittD (hon.), Calif. Sch. Profl. Psychology, 1985. Dir. programming Sta. KNME-TV U. N.Mex., Albuquerque, 1968-72; sta. mgr. Sta. WHA-TV U. Wis., Madison, 1972-76; exec. dir. Sta. KETC-TV, St. Louis, 1976-78; pres., CEO KQED, Inc., San Francisco, 1978-93; chmn., CEO Santa Fe Ventures, Inc., San Francisco, 1993—. Vice-chair bd. dirs. Calif. Sch. Profl. Psychology, San Francisco, 1985-90. Mem. Nat. Assn. Pub. TV Stas. (vice chair bd. dirs. 1986). Office: Santa Fe Ventures 751 Bryant St San Francisco CA 94107-1014

TIBBITTS, J. BRETT, lawyer, food products executive; b. L.A., June 29, 1955; AB magna cum laude, UCLA, 1977, MBA, JD, UCLA, 1982. Bar: Calif. 1982. V.p., corp. gen. counsel, corp. sec. Dole Food Co., Inc., Westlake Village, Calif. Mem. ABA, Phi Beta Kappa, Pi Gamma Mu, Pi Sigma Alpha, Omicron Delta Epsilon. Office: Dole Food Co Inc 31365 Oak Crest Dr Westlake Vlg CA 91361-4633

TIBSHRAENY, JAY, mayor; b. Chandler, Ariz. m. Karen Tibshraeny; 1 child, Lauren. BS in Acctg., Ariz. State U. Owner property mgmt. firm, Chandler; citrus grower Chandler; mem. Chandler City Coun., 1986—; elected vice mayor City of Chandler, 1990—, elected mayor, 1994—. Chmn. Regional Pub. Transp. Authority, City of Chandler; mem. Maricopa Assn. Govts. Regional Coun., Greater Phoenix Econ. Coun., Ariz. Mcpl. Water Users Assn., Ariz. League of Cities and Towns Resolutions Com., Williams Air Force Redevel. Partnership, Nat. League of Cities Transp. and Comm. Com. Mem. Chandler Friends of the Libr.; adv. bd. Chandler-Gilbert Assn. for Retarded Citizens, Child Crisis Ctr., Chandler; mem. City Coun. Pub. Safety com., Chandler Pub. Safety Retirement Sys. Bd., Chandler Vol. Firemen Pension bd. Mem. Chandler Hist. Soc., Chandler C. of C. (bd. dirs.). Office: Office of Mayor Mail Stop 603 PO Box 4008 Chandler AZ 85244-4008

TICKNOR, CAROLYN M. computer company executive; BA in Psychology, U. Redlands, Calif.; MA in Indsl. Psychology, San Francisco State U.; MBA, Stanford U. From programming, ops. mgr. to pres., CEO Hewlett-Packard Co., Palo Alto, Calif., 1977-94, pres., CEO laser jet imaging sys., 1994—. Office: Hewlett Packard Co 300 Hanover St Palo Alto CA 94304

TIEDEMAN, DAVID VALENTINE, education educator; b. Americus, [illegible] Marjorie I(da) Denman, Sept. 26, 1942 (div. Jan. 2, 1973); children— David Michael, Jeffrey Denman; m. Anna Louise Miller, Jan. 6, 1973. AB, Union Coll., Schenectady, 1941; AM, U. Rochester, 1943; EdM, Harvard,

1948, EdD, 1949. Staff mem. NRC com. selection and tng. aircraft pilots U. Rochester, 1941-43; staff mem. test constrn. dept. Coll. Entrance Exam. Bd., 1943-44; assoc. head statistics div. Manhattan Project, 1944-46; Milton teaching fellow, instr. edn. Harvard Grad. Sch. Edn., 1946-48, Sheldon travelling fellow, 1948-49, instr. edn., 1949-51, asst. prof. edn., 1951-52, from lectr. edn. to prof., 1952-71, assoc. dir., research assoc. Center for Research in Careers, 1963-66, also chmn. exec. com., info. system for vocat. decisions, 1966-69; prin. research scientist Palo Alto office Am. Insts. for Research, 1971-73; prof. edn. No. Ill. U., DeKalb, 1973-80; dir. ERIC Clearinghouse in Career Edn., 1973-76; coordinator Office Vocat., Tech., and Career Edn., 1978-80; prof. career and higher edn. U. So. Calif., Los Angeles, 1981-84, prof. emeritus, 1984—; exec. dir. Nat. Inst. Advancement of Career Edn., 1981-84; pres. Internat. Coll., 1985-86; v.p. Lifecareer Found., 1985—; provost William Lyon U., 1988-91; faculty Walden U., 1992—. Mem. Adv. Council on Guidance Dept. Edn. Commonwealth Mass., 1957-63; chmn. commn. on tests Coll. Entrance Exam. Bd., 1967-70; mem. advisory screening com. in edn. Council Internat. Exchange of Scholars, 1975-79, chmn., 1978-79 Co-author 8 books.; editorial assoc.: Jour. Counseling Psychology, 1957-63, Personnel and Guidance Jour., 1960-63, Character Potential: A Record of Research, 1977-82, Jour. Career Edn., 1979-85; contbr. articles to profl. jours., chpts. to books. Bd. dirs. Mass. Com. Children and Youth, 1961-63. Fellow Ctr. for Advanced Study in Behavioral Scis.; spl. fellow NIMH, 1963-64 Fellow Am. Psychol. Soc., APA (prs. divsn. counseling psychology 1965-66); mem. ACA, Nat. Career Devel. Assn. (pres. 1965-66, Eminent Career award 1979), Nat. Coun. Measurement in Edn. (pres. 1962-63), Phi Beta Kappa, Sigma Xi, Phi Delta Kappa, Phi Kappa Phi. Fax: 760-724-0083. E-mail: annamt1@home.com

TIEDJE, TOM, physics and astronomy educator; BASc in Engring. Sci., U. Toronto, Can., 1973; MSc in Physics, U. B.C., Can., 1975, PhD in Physics, 1977. Registered profl. engr., B.C. With corp. rsch. lab. Exxon Rsch. and Engring. Co., N.J., 1977-87; prof. dept. physics and astronomy U. B.C., 1987—, prof. dept. elec. and computer engring., 1987—, dir. Advanced Materials and Process Engring. Lab., 1994-97. Contbr. articles to profl. jours. Recipient Herzberg medal Can. Assn. Physicists, 1989, Killam Rsch. prize, 1993, B.C. Sci. Coun. Gold medal, 1994; NSERC Steacie fellow, 1990-92. Fellow Am. Phys. Soc. Achievements include research on the growth of semiconductor heterostructures by molecular beam epitaxy, real time optical growth monitoring of surface morphology and kinetic roughening of semiconductor surfaces, distributed feedback laser fabrication for analog signal transmission, scanning probe microscopy for structural characterization and nanolithography. Office: Dept Physics and Astronomy 6224 Agricultural Rd Vancouver BC Canada V6T 1Z1 Fax: 604-822-6339. E-mail: tiedje@physics.ubc.ca

TIEN, CHANG-LIN, mechanical engineer, educator; b. Wuhan, China; came to U.S., 1956; m. Di-Hwa Tien; children: Norman, Phyllis, Christine. Bachelor's, Nat. Taiwan U.; master's, U. Louisville, 1957; MA, PhD, Princeton U., 1959; numerous doctoral degrees (hon.), univs. in U.S. and abroad. With faculty mech. engring. U. Calif., Berkeley, 1959-88, 90—, prof. mech. engring., A. Martin Berlin Chair prof. mech. engring., vice chancellor rsch., 1983-85, exec. vice chancellor, UCI disting. prof. Irvine, 1988-90, univ. prof. emeritus, NEC disting. prof. engring. Berkeley. Chmn. Chief Exec.'s Commn. on Innovation and Tech., Hong Kong, 1980; mem. U.S. Nat. Sci. Bd., U.S. Nat. Commn. on Math. and Sci. Tchg. for 21st Century; sr. advisor to numerous high-tech venture funds and cos.; co-chair Nat. Commn. on Asia in schs.; bd. dirs. Wells Fargo Bank, Kaiser Permanente, Shanghai Comml. Bank. Author one book; editor numerous vols.; editor three internat. jours.; contbr. numerous articles to profl. jours. Active cmty. rels. activities and ednl. reform programs. Named mega oil tanker named in his honor Chang-Lin Tien, 2000; recipient Max Jakob Meml. award, 1981, steroid named in his honor Tien Chang-Lin Star, Internat. Astron. Union, 1999. Fellow AAAS; mem. NAE, Pacific Coun. on Internat. Policy, Coun. Fgn. Rels., Asia Found. (chmn.), San Francisco Bay Area Econ. Forum (chmn.). Achievements include research in microscale heat transfer, effects of short length scales, short time scales, and the material microstructure on thermophysical phenomena, thermal radiation. Office: Dept Mech Engring U Calif 6101 Etcheverry Hall Berkeley CA 94720-1740 Fax: 510-643-3887. E-mail: nancie@me.berkeley.edu

TIERNEY, JACK, consumer products company executive; Contr. Dial Corp., Scottsdale, Ariz., CFO, 2000—. Office: The Dial Corp 15501 N Dial Blvd Scottsdale AZ 85260-1619

TIETZ, NORBERT WOLFGANG, clinical chemistry educator, administrator; b. Stettin, Germany, Nov. 13, 1926; s. Joseph and Anna (Kozalla) T.; m. Gertrud Kraft, Oct. 17, 1959; children— Margaret, Kurt, Annette, Michael Student, Tuebingen, Germany, 1945-46; D.Sc., Tech. U., Stuttgart, W.Ger., 1950. Chmn. dept. chemistry Reid Meml. Hosp., Richmond, Ind., 1956-59; prof., dir. clin. chemistry Mt. Sinai Med. Ctr. and Chgo. Med. Sch., Chgo., 1959-76, U. Ky. Med. Ctr., Lexington, 1976-96; prof. pathology U. Calif., San Diego, 1996—. Research fellow and asst. U. Munich, W.Ger., 1951-54; research fellow dept. pathology U. Chgo. and St. Luke's Hosp., Chgo., 1955-56, Rockford Meml. Hosp., Ill., 1954-55; cons. Ill. Dept. Pub. Health, 1967-76, VA Hosp., Hines, Ill., 1974-76; prof. biochemistry and pathology Rush Med. Coll., Chgo., 1975-76; vol. cons. VA Hosp., Lexington, 1976-96; cons. Dept. VA Med. Ctr., San Diego, 1997—. Editor: Fundamentals of Clinical Chemistry, 1970, 76, 87, Clinical Guide to Laboratory Tests, 1983, 90, 95, Textbook of Clinical Chemistry, 1986, A Study Guide to Clinical Chemistry, 1987, Applied Laboratory Medicine, 1992; assoc. editor: Dictionary and Encyclopedia of Laboratory Medicine and Technology, 1983; contbr. numerous articles to profl. jours. Recipient A. Dubin award Nat. Acad. Clin. Biochemistry, 1995, Disting. Internat. Svc. award Internat. Fedn. Clin. Chemistry, 1996. Fellow Acad. Clin. Lab. Physicians and Scientists, Am. Inst. Chemists; mem. Am. Assn. Clin. Chemistry (clin. chemist award 1971, award for outstanding efforts in edn. and tng. 1976, Disting. Alumnus award 1977, Steuben Bowl award 1978, Bernard F. Gerulat award N.J. chpt. 1988, award for Outstanding Contbns. to Clin. Chemistry 1989, Donald D. Van Slyke award N.Y. Met. chpt. 1989), AAAS, Am. Chem. Soc., Am. Soc. Clin. Pathologists, Man. Soc. Clin. Chemists (ann. Lectureship award 1987), Sigma Xi. Roman Catholic. Home: 7472 Caminito Rialto La Jolla CA 92037-3957 Office: U Calif Dept Pathology 9500 Gilman Dr La Jolla CA 92093-0612 E-mail: ntietz@ucsd.edu

TIFFANY, JOSEPH RAYMOND, II, lawyer; b. Dayton, Ohio, Feb. 5, 1949; s. Forrest Fraser and Margaret Watson (Clark) T.; m. Terri Robbins, Dec. 1, 1984. AB magna cum laude, Harvard U., 1971; MS in Internat. Relations, London Sch. Econs., 1972; JD, U. Calif., Berkeley, 1975. Bar: U.S. Dist. Ct. (no. dist.) 1975, U.S. Dist. Ct. (ea. dist.) 1977, U.S. Ct. Appeals (9th cir.) 1982. Assoc. Pillsbury, Madison & Sutro, San Francisco, 1975-82, ptnr., 1983-2001, Pillsbury Winthrop LLP, San Francisco, 2001—. Mem. ABA (antitrust, intellectual property, litigation sects.), Calif. Bar Assn., Harvard Club. Office: Pillsbury Winthrop LLP 2550 Hanover St Palo Alto CA 94304-1115 E-mail: jtiffany@pillsburywinthrop.com

TIFFANY, SANDRA L. state legislator; b. Spokane, Wash., June 30, 1949; m. Ross M. Tonkens; 1 child, Courtney. Student, U. Calif. Mem. Nev. Assembly, 1993—. Mem. Nev. Rep. State Ctrl. com., Clark County Rep. Ctrl. com.; mem. adv. bd. Boys and Girls Club of Henderson; bd. dirs. Desert Rsch. Inst. Mem. Nat. Assn. Women Bus. Owners, Nat. Conf. State Legislatures, Nat. Orgn. Women Legislators, Am. Legis. Exchange coun., Nat. Rep. Leadership Assn., Exec. Devel. Assn., Henderson C. of C. (mktg. and tourism com., issues com.), Nev. Rep. Women's Club, Green Valley Cmty. Assn., Variety Club. Home: 2156 Sun Swept Way Henderson NV 89014-4273 Office: Nev Assembly State Capitol Carson City NV 89710-0001

TIFFT, WILLIAM GRANT, astronomer, educator; b. Derby, Conn., Apr. 5, 1932; s. William Charles and Marguerite Howe (Hubbell) T.; m. Carol Ruth Nordquist, June 1, 1957 (div. July 1964); children: Jennifer, William John; m. Janet Ann Lindner Homewood, June 2, 1965; 1 child, Amy, stepchildren: Patricia, Susan, Hollis. AB, Harvard Coll., 1954; PhD, Calif. Inst. Tech., 1958. Nat. sci. postdoctoral Australian Nat. U., Canberra, 1958-60; rsch. assoc. Vanderbilt U., Nashville, 1960-61; astronomer Lowell Obs., Flagstaff, Ariz., 1961-64; assoc. prof. U. Ariz., Tucson, 1964-73, prof., 1973—. Joint author: Revised New General Catalog, 1973; joint editor: Modern Mathematical Models of Time and Their Applications to Physics and Cosmology, 1997; contbr. over 100 articles to profl. jours. NSF Predoctoral fellow, 1954-58, NSF Postdoctoral fellow, 1958-60; grantee NASA, NSF, ONR, Rsch. Corp. Fellow Am. Astron. Soc.; mem. Internat. Astron. Union. Achievements include discovery of redshift quantization and correlations relating to it, including variability; first to detect voids in mapping of large scale supercluster structure; investigations of three-dimensional time in cosmology and particle physics. Office: U Arizona Dept Astronomy Tucson AZ 85721-0001 E-mail: wtifft@as.arizona.edu

TIGHE, JAMES C. publishing executive; b. Edmonton, Alta., Can., Sept. 30, 1950; s. James Donald and Ellen Grant (Drever) T.; m. Barbara C. Teske, Dec. 2, 1972; children: Teresa M., Jason M. Grad. high sch., Edmonton. Area supr. Edmonton Jour., 1969-73; circulation mgr. Thomson Newspapers, Western Can., 1973-79; dir. circulation Edmonton sun, 1979-81, gen. mgr., 1981-82, UP Can., Toronto, Ont., 1982-84; pub. Calgary (Alta.) Sun, 1984-88; gen. mgr. Toronto Sun, 1988-89, pub., 1991-94, v.p. corp. planning, 1994-95; pres. Island Pub. Ltd., Can., 1995—. Office: Island Pub Ltd 1824 Store St Victoria BC Canada VAT 4R4

TIGHT, DEXTER CORWIN, lawyer; b. San Francisco, Sept. 14, 1924; s. Dexter Junkins and Marie (Corwin) T.; m. Elizabeth Callander, Apr. 20, 1951; children: Dexter C. Jr., Kathyryn Marie Loken, Steven M., David C. AB, Denison U., 1948; JD, Yale U., 1951. Bar: Calif. 1951. Assoc. Pillsbury, Madison & Sutro, San Francisco, 1953-60; gen. atty. W.P. Fuller & Co., San Francisco, 1960-61; gen. counsel Schlage Lock Co., San Francisco, 1961-77; dir. govt. affairs Crown Zellerbach Corp., San Francisco, 1977-78; sr. v.p., internat. and gen. counsel The Gap Inc., San Bruno, Calif., 1978-90; cons. in field, 1990-99; gen. coun. The Nature Co., 1990-96. Bd. dirs. Shaw-Clayton Plastics, San Rafael, Calif., Granite Rock Co., Watsonville, Calif., Internat. Diplomacy Coun, Boys and Girls Club of the Peninsula; mem. World Affairs Coun.; chmn. That Man May See, San Francisco, 1997, 98. Trustee Denison U., 1978-99, chmn. capital fund dr., 1988-94; trustee Calvary Presbyn. Ch., 1968, 73, elder, 1969-90; elder Valley Presbyn. Ch., 1992—; vol. Internat. Exec. Svc. Corps. 1st lt. U.S. Army, 1943-45, 51-52. Mem. ABA, Calif. Bar Assn., San Francisco Bar Assn. (chmn. various coms.), Commonwealth Club Calif. (past bd. dirs., exec. com.), Menlo Country Club, Bohemian Club (San Francisco), Guardsman Club (1st v.p. 1961), Phi Beta Kappa. Republican. Presbyterian. Avocations: horseback riding, fishing, tennis, golf, photography. Home: 170 Wildwood Way Redwood City CA 94062-2352

TILDEN, WESLEY RODERICK, writer, retired computer programmer; b. Saint Joseph, Mo., Jan. 19, 1922; s. Harry William and Grace Alida (Kinnaman) T.; m. Lorraine Henrietta Frederick, June 20, 1948 (dec. Mar. 1999). Grad., Navy Supply Corps Sch., 1945; BS, UCLA, 1948; BA, Park Coll., Mo., 1990. Purchasing agent Vortox Co., Claremont, Calif., 1951-61; lang. lab. dir. Mount San Antonio Coll., Walnut, 1962-65, computer programmer, operator General Dynamics, Pomona, 1967-70; ret., 1970. Author: (book) Scota, The Egyptian Princess, 1994, Merit-Sekhet: Foster Mother of Moses?, 1996; photographer, textbooks, mags., newspaper, catalogs. Historian Claremont Sister City Assn., 1963-66. Lt. USNR, 1942-46 PTO. Recipient with Lorraine Tilden People to People award Reader's Digest Found., 1963-64, 1964-65; named Hon. Citizen Guanajuato, Mexico, 1963. Mem. Soc. Mayflower Descendants, Scottish Clans, UCLA Alumni Assn., Park Coll. Alumni Assn., Univ. Club of Claremont, The Scituate (Mass.) Hist. Soc. Republican. Avocations: history, genealogy, photography, gardening. Home: 351 Oakdale Dr Claremont CA 91711-5039

TILLINGHAST, CHARLES CARPENTER, III, marketing company executive; b. N.Y.C., Nov. 16, 1936; s. Charles Carpenter, Jr. and Lisette (Micoleau) T.; m. Cynthia Branch, Sept. 28, 1974; children by previous marriage: Avery D., Charles W., David C. B.S. in Mech. Engring, Lehigh U., 1958; M.B.A., Harvard U., 1963. Asst. to dir. devel. Lehigh U., Bethlehem, Pa., 1958-61; adminstrv. asst. Boise Cascade Corp., Portland, Oreg., 1963, asst. to v.p. Boise, Idaho, 1964-65, gen. mgr. office supply div., 1965-67, gen. mgr. paper distbn. div., 1966, v.p. bus. products, 1967-69, sr. v.p. housing group, 1969-71, sr. v.p., 1971-73; pres. CRM div. Ziff-Davis Pub. Co., Inc., Del Mar, Calif., 1971-75; pres., treas. Value Communications, Inc., La Jolla, 1975-76; pres. Oak Tree Publs., Inc., San Diego, 1976-81, Advanced Mktg. Services Inc., San Diego, 1982-94, chmn., 1994—. Served to 2d lt. AUS, 1959. Home: 1762 Nautilus St La Jolla CA 92037-6413 Office: Advanced Mktg Svcs Inc 5880 Oberlin Dr Ste 400 San Diego CA 92121-4794

TILSON, DANIEL, elementary education educator; Tchr. Eastwood Elem. Sch., Roseburg, Oreg., 1985—. Recipient Excellence in Sci. Tchg. award, 1990, Milken Nat. Edn. award, 1992, State Tchr. of Yr. elem. award Oreg., 1992; Christa McAuliffe fellow, 1988. Office: Eastwood Elem Sch 2550 SE Waldon Ave Roseburg OR 97470-3805 E-mail: dtilson@roseburg.k12.or.us

TILSON THOMAS, MICHAEL, symphony conductor; b. L.A., 1944; s. Ted and Roberta T. Studies with, Ingolf Dahl, U. So. Calif., others; student conducting, Berkshire Music Festival, Tanglewood, Mass.; student conducting (Koussevitsky prize 1968); LL.D., Hamilton Coll.; L.H.D. (hon.), D'Youville Coll., 1976. Asst. condr. Boston Symphony Orch., 1969, assoc. condr., 1970-72, prin. guest condr., 1972-74; also Berkshire Music Festival, summer 1970, 74; music dir., condr. Buffalo Philharmonic Orch., 1971-79; music dir., prin. condr. Great Woods Ctr. for Performing Arts, 1985-88; prin. condr. London Symphony Orch., 1988-95; artistic dir. New World Symphony, Fla., 1988—; prin. guest condr. London Symphony Orch., 1995—; music dir. San Francisco Symphony, 1995—. Condr., dir., N.Y. Philharmonic Young People's Concerts, CBS-TV, 1971-77; vis. condr. numerous orchs., U.S., Europe, Japan; chief condr. Ojai Festival, 1967, dir., 1972-77; opera debut, Cin., 1975; condr.: Am. premiere Lulu (Alban Berg), Santa Fe Opera, summer 1979; prin. guest condr., L.A. Philharm., 1981-85, Am. premiere Desert Music (Steve Reich), 1984; prin. condr. Gershwin festival London Symphony Orch., Barbican Ctr., 1987; composer: Grace (A Song for Leonard Bernstein), 1988, Street Song (for Empire Brass Quintet), 1988, From the Diary of Anne Frank (for orchestra and narrator Audrey Hepburn and New World Symphony), 1990; commd. by UNICEF for Concerts for Life's European premiere, 1991; recording artist Sony Classical/CBS Masterworks, 1973—; co-artistic dir. Pacific Music Festival, 1990—, with Leonard Bernstein 1st ann. Pacific Music Festival, Sapporo, Japan, 1990; co-artistic dir. 2d ann. Pacific Music festival, 1991, Salzburg Festival, 1991; conducted Mozart Requiem. Named Musician of Year, Musical Am. 1970; recipient Koussevitsky prize, 1968, Grammy award for Carmina Burana with Cleve. Orch., 1976, for Gershwin Live with Los Angeles Philharm., 1983, Grammy nomination, Best Classical Album - Debussy: Le Martyre de Saint Sebastien (with the London Symphony Orchestra), 1994. Office: 888 7th Ave Fl 37 New York NY 10106-3799 also: San Francisco Symphony Davies Symphony Hall 201 Van Ness Ave San Francisco CA 94102-4595

TILTON, DAVID LLOYD, savings and loan association executive; b. Santa Barbara, Calif., Sept. 21, 1926; s. Lloyd Irving and Grace (Hart) T.; m. Mary Caroline Knudtson, June 6, 1953; children: Peter, Jennifer, Michael, Catharine. AB, Stanford U., 1949, MBA, 1951. With Santa Barbara Savs. & Loan Assn., 1951-90, pres., 1965-84; now pres. Fin. Corp., Santa Barbara. Trustee, chmn. Calif. Real Estate Investment Trust, 1988. Served with USNR, World War II. Mem. Calif. Savs. and Loan League (dir. 1980), Delta Chi. Home: 630 Oak Grove Dr Santa Barbara CA 93108-1402 Office: Fin Corp Santa Barbara 1187 Coast Village Rd Ste 1-322 Santa Barbara CA 93108-2761 E-mail: dtilton@earthlink.net

TILTON, GEORGE ROBERT, geochemistry educator; b. Danville, Ill., June 3, 1923; s. Edgar Josiah and Caroline Lenore (Burkmeyer) T.; m. Elizabeth Jane Foster, Feb. 7, 1948; children— Linda Ruth, Helen Elizabeth, Elaine Lee, David Foster, John Robert Student, Blackburn Coll., 1940-42; B.S., U. Ill., 1947; Ph.D., U. Chgo., 1951; D.Sc. (hon.), Swiss Fed. Inst. Tech., Zurich, 1984. Phys. chemist Carnegie Instn., Washington, 1951-65; prof. geochemistry U. Calif.-Santa Barbara, 1965-91, emeritus, 1991—, chmn. dept. geol. scis., 1973-77. Guest prof. Swiss Fed. Inst., Zurich, 1971-72; prin. investigator NSF research grant, 1965— ; mem. earth scis. panel NSF, 1966-69, 82-85 Assoc. editor Jour. Geophys. Research, 1962-65, Geochimica et Cosmochimica Acta, 1973— ; contbr. articles to profl. jours. Served with AUS, 1942-45 Decorated Purple Heart; recipient Sr. Scientist award Alexander von Humboldt Found., 1989. Fellow AAAS, Am. Geophys. Union, Geol. Soc. Am.; mem. Nat. Acad. Scis., Geochem. Soc. (pres. 1981), Sigma Xi. Episcopalian Home: 2661 Tallant Rd Apt 512 Santa Barbara CA 93105-4807 Office: U Calif Dept Geol Scis Santa Barbara CA 93106

TILTON, JOHN ELVIN, mineral economics educator; b. Brownsville, Pa., Sept. 16, 1939; s. John Elvin Sr. and Margaret Julia (Renn) T.; m. Elizabeth Martha Meier, June 18, 1966; children: Margaret Ann, John Christian. AB, Princeton U., 1961; PhD in Econs., Yale U., 1965. Staff analyst Office of Sec. of Def., Washington, 1965-67; rsch. assoc. Brookings Inst., Washington, 1967-70; asst. prof. econs. U. Md., College Park, 1970-72; assoc. prof. mineral econs. Pa. State U., University Park, 1972-75, prof., 1975-85; Coulter prof. Colo. Sch. Mines, Golden, 1985—, dir. Divsn. Econs. and Bus., 1987-98. Officer econ. affairs commodities divsn. UN Conf. on Trade and Devel., Geneva, 1977; leader rsch. Internat. Inst. Applied Systems Analysis, Laxenburg, Austria, 1982-84; joint dir. mineral econs. and policy Program of Resources for Future, Colo. Sch. Mines, Washington, 1982-86; vice chmn. bd. mineral and energy resources NRC, Washington, 1980-83, mem. nat. materials adv. bd., 1987-89; vis. prof. Pontifica Cath. U., Santiago, Chile, 1998-99. Author: International Diffusion of Technology, 1971, The Future of Nonfuel Minerals, 1977; editor: Material Substitution, 1983, World Metal Demand, 1990, Mineral Wealth and Economic Development, 1992, View from the Helm, 1995; co-editor: Economics of Mineral Exploration, 1987, Competitiveness in Metals, 1992. Capt. U.S. Army, 1965-67. Fulbright scholar Ecole Nat. Supérieure des Mines de Paris, 1992. Mem. Am. Econ. Assn., Am. Inst. Mining Metall. and Petroleum Engrs. (Mineral Econs. award 1985), Mineral Econs. and Mgmt. Soc. (pres. 1993-94), Mining and Metall. Soc. Am. Avocations: skiing, hiking. Office: Colo Sch Mines Divsn Econs & Bus Golden CO 80401 E-mail: jtilton@mines.edu

TIMLIN, ROBERT J. judge; b. 1932; BA cum laude, Georgetown U., 1954, JD, 1959, LLM, 1964. Atty. Douglas, Obear and Campbell, 1960-61, Law Offices of A.L. Wheeler, 1961, with criminal divsn. U.S. Dept. Justice, 1961-64; atty. U.S. Atty. Office (ctrl. dist.) Calif., 1964-66, Hennigan, Ryneal and Butterwick, 1966-67; city atty. City of Corona, Calif., 1967-70; prin. Law Office of Robert J. Timlin, 1970-71, 75-76; ptnr. Hunt, Palladino and Timlin, 1971-74, Timlin and Coffin, 1974-75; judge Mcpl. Ct., Riverside, Calif., 1976-80, Calif. Superior Ct., Riverside, 1980-90; assoc. justice Calif. Ct. Appeals, 1990-94; judge U.S. Dist. Ct. (ctrl. dist.) Calif., L.A., 1994—. Part-time U.S. Magistrate judge Ctrl. Dist. Calif., 1970-74. Served U.S. Army, 1955-57. Mem. ABA, Calif. Judges Assn., Phi Alpha Delta. Office: US Dist Ct Central District of Calif Eastern Divsn 3470 12th St Riverside CA 92501

TIMMER, BARBARA, United States Senate official, lawyer; b. Holland, Mich., Dec. 13, 1946; d. John Norman and Barbara Dee (Folensbee) T. BA, Hope Coll., Holland, Mich., 1969; JD, U. Mich., 1975. Bar: Mich. 1975, U.S. Supreme Ct., 1995. Assoc. McCrosky, Libner, VanLeuven, Muskegon, Mich., 1975-78; apptd. to Mich. Women Commn. by Gov., 1976-79; staff counsel subcom. commerce, consumer & monetary affairs Ho. Govt. Ops. Com., U.S. Ho. of Reps., 1979-82, 85-86; exec. v.p. NOW, 1982-84; legis. asst. to Rep. Geraldine Ferraro, 1984; atty. Office Gen. Counsel Fed. Home Loan Bank Bd., 1986-89; gen. counsel Com. on Banking, Fin. and Urban affairs U.S. Ho. of Reps., Washington, 1989-92; asst. gen. counsel, dir. govt. affairs ITT Corp., Washington, 1992-96; ptnr. Alliance Capitol, Washington, 1994—; sr. v.p., dir. govt. rels. Home Savs. of Am., Irwindale, Calif., 1996-99; ptnr. Manatt, Phelps & Phillips, Washington, 1999—; gen. counsel MyPrimeTime, Inc., San Francisco, 2000-01; asst. sec. U.S. Senate, 2001—. Editor: Compliance With Lobbying Laws and Gift Rule Guide, 1996. Recipient Affordable Housing award Nat. Assn. Real Estate Brokers, 1990, Acad. of Women Achievers, YWCA, 1993. Mem. ABA (bus. law sect., electronic fin. svcs. subcom.), FBA (chair, exec. coun. banking law com., Exchequer Club, bd. dirs. Women in Housing and Fin., 1992-94, gen. counsel 1994-98), Supreme Ct. Bar Assn., Supreme Ct. Hist. Soc., Mich. Bar Assn., Bar of Dist. Columbia. Episcopalian. Address: PO Box 21777 Washington DC 20009-9777 E-mail: btimmerdc@earthlink.net

TIMMERHAUS, KLAUS DIETER, chemical engineering educator; b. Mpls., Sept. 10, 1924; s. Paul P. and Elsa L. (Bever) T.; m. Jean L. Mevis, Aug. 3, 1952; 1 dau., Carol Jane. BS in Chem. Engring, U. Ill., 1948, MS, 1949, PhD, 1951. Registered profl. engr., Colo. Process design engr. Calif. Rsch. Corp., Richmond, 1952-53; extension lectr. U. Calif., Berkeley, 1952; mem. faculty U. Colo., Boulder, 1953-95, prof. chem. engring., 1961-95, asso. dean engring., 1963-86, dir. engring. rsch. ctr. coll. engring., 1963-86, chmn. aerospace dept., 1979-80, chmn. chem. engring. dept., 1986-89, Patten Chair Disting. prof., 1986-89, presdl. teaching scholar, 1989—. Chem. engr. cryogenics lab. Nat. Bur. Standards, Boulder, summers 1955,57,59,61; lectr. U. Calif. at L.A., 1961-62; sect. head engring. div. NSF, 1972-73; cons. in field. Bd. dirs. Colo. Engring. Expt. Sta., Inc., Engring. Measurements Co., both Boulder Editor: Advances in Cryogenic Engineering, vols. 1-25, 1954-80; co-editor: Internat. Cryogenic Monograph Series, 1965— . Served with USNR, 1944-46. Recipient Disting. Svc. award Dept. Commerce, 1957, Samuel C. Collins award for outstanding contbns. to cyrogenic tech., 1967, Meritorious Svc. award Cryogenic Engring. Conf., 1987, Disting. Pub. Svc. award NSF, 1984; named CASE Colo. Prof. of Yr., 1993, Disting. Lectr., L-T Fan, 2001. Fellow AAAS (v.p. 1985, pres. 1986, Southwestern and Rocky Mountain divsn. Pres.'s award 1989), Internat. Inst. Refrigeration (v.p. 1979-87, pres. 1987-95, U.S. nat. commn. 1983—, pres. 1983-86, W.T. Pentzer award 1989), AIChE (v.p. 1975, pres. 1976, Alpha Chi Sigma award for chem. engring. rsch., 1968, Founders award 1978, Eminent Chem. Engr. award 1983, W.K. Lewis award 1987, F.J. Van Antwerpen award 1991, Inst. Lecture award 1995), Am. Soc. for Engring. Edn. (bd. dirs. 1986-88, George Westinghouse award 1968, 3M Chem. Engring. divsn. award 1980, Engring. Rsch. Coun.

award 1990, Delos Svc. award 1991); mem. NAE, Am. Astron. Soc., Austrian Acad. Sci., Cryogenic Engring. Conf. (chmn. 1956-67, bd. dirs.), Internat. Cryocooler Conf. (bd. dirs. 1980—), Soc. Automotive Engrs. (Ralph Teetor award 1991), Sigma Xi (v.p. 1986-87, pres. 1987-88, bd. dirs. 1981-89), Verein Deitscher ingenieure, Cryogenic Soc. Am., Sigma Tau, Tau Beta Pi, Phi Lambda Upsilon. Home: 905 Brooklawn Dr Boulder CO 80303-2708 E-mail: klaus.timmerhaus@colorado.edu

TIMMRECK, THOMAS C. health sciences and health administration educator; b. Montpelier, Idaho, June 15, 1946; s. Archie Carl and Janone (Jensen) T.; m. Ellen Prusse, Jan. 27, 1971; children: Chad Thomas, Benjamin Brian, Julie Anne. AA, Ricks Coll., 1968; BS, Brigham Young U., 1971; MEd, Oreg. State U., 1972; MA, No. Ariz. U., 1981; PhD, U. Utah, 1976. Program dir. Cache County Aging Program, Logan, Utah, 1972-73; asst. prof. div. health edn. Tex. Tech U., Lubbock, 1976-77; asst. prof. dept. health care adminstrn. Idaho State U., Pocatello, 1977-78; dept. chair, asst. prof. health services program No. Ariz. U., Flagstaff, 1978-84; cons., dir. grants Beth Israel Hosp., Denver, 1985; prof. dept. health scis. and human ecology, coordinator grad. studies, coordinator health adminstrn. and planning Calif. State U., San Bernardino, 1985—; pres. Health Care Mgmt. Assocs., 1985—. Presenter at nat. confs.; dept. chair health and wellness dept., faculty Loretto Heights Coll., Denver; adj. faculty Dept. Mgmt. U. Denver, Dept. Mgmt. and Health Adminstrn. U. Colo., Denver, dept. bus. adminstrn. U. Redlands (Calif.), U. So. Calif., L.A., Chapman U. Author: Dictionary of Health Services Management, rev. 2d edit., 1987, Health Services Cyclopedic Dictionary, 3d edit., An Introduction to Epidemiology, 1994, 2d edit., 1998, Planning and Program Development and Evaluation: A Handbook for Health Promotion, Aging, and Health Services, 1995; mem. editl. bd. Jour. Health Values, 1986—, Basic Epidemiological Methods and Biostats., Dictionary of Epidemiology and Public Health, 1996; contbr. numerous articles on health care adminstrn., behavioral health, gerontology and health edn. to profl. jours. Chmn., bd. dirs. Inland Counties Health System Agy.; mem. strategic planning com. chmn. Vis. Nurses Assn. of Inland Counties; bd. dirs. health svc. orgns. With U.S. Army, 1966-72, Vietnam. Mem. Assn. Advancement of Health Edn., Am. Acad. Mgmt., Assn. Univ. Programs in Health Care Adminstrn., Healthcare Forum. Republican. Mormon. Office: Calif State U Dept Health Scis & Human Ecology San Bernardino CA 92407

TIMMS, EUGENE DALE, wholesale business owner, state senator; b. Burns, Oreg., May 15, 1932; s. Morgan Oscar and Dorothy Vera (Payne) T.; m. Edna May Evans, Aug. 24, 1953; children: Tobi Eugene, Trina Maria. BA, Willamette U., 1954; grad. studies, U. Wash. Mem. Oreg. Senate, Salem, 1982-; st. republican leader, 1992-94. Sen. State of Oreg., 1982, 84, 88, 92; pres. Harney City C. of C.; bd. trustees Assoc. Oreg. Industries; chmn. Parks & Recreation Dist. Bd.; mem. Harney City Hosp. Bd. Mem. SBA, Jaycees (state v.p.), Elk Lodge, Masonic Lodge, Al Kader Harney City Shrine Club. Presbyterian. Avocations: fishing, hunting, reading, going to the movies, sports. Home: 1049 N Court Ave Burns OR 97720-1016 Address: Oreg Senate S-219 State Capitol Salem OR 97310-0001

TIMMS, MICHELE, professional basketball player; b. Australia, June 28, 1965; Guard Australia's Women's Nat. Basketball League - Bulleen Boomers, 1984-85, Nunawading Spectres, 1985, Lotus Munchen, Germany, 1989-90, Perth Breakers, Australia, 1991-92, Basket Firenze, Italy, 1993-94, Sydney Flames, Australia, 1995, WTV Wuppertal, Germany, 1995-96, Phoenix Mercury, 1997—. Named WNBL Player of Yr., 1995, 96. Avocations: tennis, golf. Office: Phoenix Mercury 201 E Jefferson St Phoenix AZ 85004-2412

TIMPE, RONALD E. insurance company executive; Grad., Lewis & Clark Coll.; grad. advanced mgmt. program, Harvard U. CLU. With Standard Ins. Co., Portland, Oreg., 1968—, asst. actuary, asst. v.p., actuary, v.p. group pensions, sr. v.p. group ins. and corp. fin. svcs., pres., 1993—, chmn., pres., CEO, also bd. dirs. Bd. dirs. Oreg. Bus. Coun., Oreg. Health Scis. Found., Oreg. Ind. Coll. Found., Oreg. Symphony. Fellow Soc. of Actuaries; mem. Portland Met. C. of C. (past chmn.), Alexis de Tocqueville Soc. (co-chmn. United Way). Office: StanCorp Fin Group Inc 1100 SW 6th Ave Portland OR 97204

TINDALL, ROBERT EMMETT, lawyer, educator; b. N.Y.C., Jan. 2, 1934; s. Robert E. and Alice (McGonigle) T.; children: Robert Emmett IV, Elizabeth. BS in Marine Engring., SUNY, 1955; postgrad., Georgetown U. Law Sch., 1960-61; LLB, U. Ariz., 1963; LLM, NYU, 1967; PhD, City U., London, 1975. Bar: Ariz. 1963. Mgmt. trainee GE, Schenectady, N.Y., Lynn, Mass., Glens Falls, N.Y., 1955-56, 58-60; law clk. Haight, Gardner, Poor and Havens, N.Y.C., 1961; prin., mem. Robert Emmett Tindall & Assocs., Tucson, 1963—; assoc. prof. mgmt. U. Ariz., Tucson, 1969—. Vis. prof. Grad. Sch. of Law, Soochow U., China, 1972, Grad. Bus. Ctr., London, 1974, NYU, 1991—; dir. MBA program U. Ariz., Tucson, 1975-81, dir. entrepreneurship program, 1984-86; investment cons. Kingdom of Saudi Arabia, 1981—; lectr. USIA, Eng., India, Mid. East, 1974; lectr. bus. orgn. and regulatory laws Southwestern Legal Found., Acad. Am. and Internat. Law, 1976-80. Actor cmty. theatres, Schenectady, 1955-56, Harrisburg, Pa., 1957-58, Tucson, 1961-71; appeared in films Rage, 1971, Showdown at OK Corral, 1971, Lost Horizon, 1972; appeared in TV programs Gunsmoke, 1972, Petrocelli, 1974; author: Multinational Enterprises, 1975; contbr. articles on domestic and internat. bus. to profl. jours. Served to lt. USN, 1956-58. Fellow Ford Found., 1965-67; grantee Asia Found., 1972-73. Mem. Strategic Mgmt. Soc., State Bar of Ariz., Acad. Internat. Bus., Screen Actors Guild, Honourable Soc. of Mid. Temple (London), Phi Delta Phi, Beta Gamma Sigma, Assn. Corp. Growth, Royal Overseas League (London). Home: PO Box 42196 Tucson AZ 85733-2196 Office: Coll Bus & Public Adminstrn U Ariz Dept Mgmt & Policy Tucson AZ 85721-0001

TING, ALBERT CHIA, bioengineering researcher; b. Hong Kong, Sept. 7, 1950; came to U.S., 1957; s. William Su and Katherine Sung (Bao) T.; m. Shirley Roung Wang, July 30, 1988. BA, UCLA, 1973; MS, Calif. State U., L.A., 1975, Calif. Inst. Tech., , 1977; PhD, U. Calif., San Diego, 1983. Rsch. asst. Calif. Inst. Tech., Pasadena, 1975-77, U. Calif., San Diego, 1982-83; sr. staff engr. R&D Am. Med. Optics, Irvine, Calif., 1983-86; project engr., rsch. Allergan Med. Optics, Irvine, 1987-89, sr. project engr., rsch., 1989-92, sr. project engr., engring., 1993-94; bioengr. cons. Pharmacia Iovision, Inc., Irvine, 1995-97; sr. engr. D & E, 1997, sr. engr., project mgr., 1998-99; rsch. and devel. mgr., surg. Bausch & Lomb, Irvine, 1999—; R & D mgr. Visiogen, Inc., Irvine, 2001—. Inventor med. and optical devices, recipient patent awards 1988, 89, 91, 92, 93, 95; contbr. articles to sci. jours. Mem. AAAS, Biomed. Engring. Soc., Assn. for Rsch. in Vision and Ophthalmology, Biomed. Optics Soc. Office: Visiogen Inc 4 Jenner St # 180 Irvine CA 92618

TINGLE, AUBREY JAMES, pediatric immunologist, research administrator; b. St. Paul, Can., June 28, 1943; s. Cyril Nisbet Tingle and Margaret Lucy (Fraser) Tarbuck; m. Valerie Jean Anderson, Nov. 2, 1968; children: Heather Lynn, Brian James. MD, U. Alta., Edmonton, 1967; PhD, McGill U., Montreal, Que., Can., 1974. Asst. prof. dept. pediatrics U. B.C., Vancouver, Can., 1974-79, head div. immunology dept. pediatrics Can., 1974-86, assoc. prof. Can., 1979-86, prof. Can., 1986—, prof. dept. pathology Can., 1986—; dir. rsch. B.C. Rsch. Inst. for Children's and Women's Health, Vancouver, 1992-2001; asst. dean rsch. Faculty of Medicine, U. B.C., Vancouver, 1992-2001; v.p. rsch. & edn. Children's & Women's Health Ctr B.C., Vancouver, 1997-2001; pres., CEO Michael Smith Found. for Health Rsch., Vancouver, 2001—. Fellow Royal Coll. Physicians and Surgeons Can., Soc. Pediatric Research, Am. Acad. Pediatrics; mem. Western Soc. Pediatric Research. Office: Michael Smith Found 1285 W Broadway Vancouver BC Canada V6H 3X8 E-mail: atingle@msfhr.org

TINGLE, JAMES O'MALLEY, retired lawyer; b. N.Y.C., June 12, 1928; s. Thomas Jefferson and Mercedes (O'Malley) T. B.S., U. Mont., 1950, B.A., LL.B., U. Mont., 1952; LL.M., U. Mich., 1953, S.J.D., 1958. Bar: Calif. 1959, Mont. 1952, N.Y. 1961. Asst. prof. law U. Mont., Missoula, 1955-56; atty. Shell Oil Co., N.Y.C., 1957-62; assoc. Pillsbury, Madison & Sutro, San Francisco, 1962-68, ptnr., 1969-2000. Author: The Stockholder's Remedy of Corporate Dissolution, 1959; editor: State Antitrust Laws, 1974. Served to 1st lt. USAF, 1953-55. William W. Cook fellow U. Mich. Mem. Mont. Bar Assn., Calif. Bar Assn., ABA Democrat.

TINGLEY, WALTER WATSON, computer systems manager; b. Portland, Maine, July 24, 1946; s. Edward Allen Tingley and Ruth Annie (Howard) Tuttle; m. Elizabeth A. Fletcher, May 1970 (div. 1975); m. Carol S. Gadoury, Dec. 1998. BS, U. Md., 1974. Programmer analyst U.S. Ry. Assn., Washington, 1974-80, Digital Equipment Corp., Maynard, Mass., 1980-81, Interactive Mgmt. Sys., Belmont, 1981; sys. designer Martin Marietta Data Sys., Greenbelt, Md., 1982-84; mgr. computer ops. Genex, Rockville, 1984; sys. mgr. Applied Rsch. Corp., Landover, 1985; programmer analyst Input/Output Computer Svcs., Washington, 1986-87, Lockheed Engring. and Scis., Las Vegas, Nev., 1987-91, Los Alamos (N.Mex.) Nat. Lab., 1992-96, Miller Internat., Denver, 1997-99, Ferrell Ventures, Denver, 1999—. Author tech. book revs., software revs. With USAF, 1964-68. Mem. Computer Soc. of IEEE, Assn. Computing Machinery. Avocations: skiing, hiking, swimming. Home: 8271 Johnson Ct Arvada CO 80005-2155

TINKER, MARK CHRISTIAN, producer, director; b. Stamford, Conn., Jan. 16, 1951; s. Grant Almerin Tinker and Ruth Prince Byerly Fricke; m. Kristin Harmon, Apr. 16, 1988; 1 child, James. BS, Syracuse U., 1973. Producer, dir., writer TV series: The White Shadow, 1978-81, St. Elsewhere, 1982-88 (Emmy, Peabody award, Peoples Choice award); dir. TV Movie: Babe Ruth, 1991, Bonanza: Under Attack, 1995; producer, dir. TV series: Civil Wars, 1991—; dir. episode TV series: ER (Going Home), 1994; dir. TV series: NYPD Blue, 1993—. Mem. Nat. Acad. TV Arts and Scis.

TINNIN, THOMAS PECK, real estate professional; b. Albuquerque, May 15, 1948; s. Robert Priest and Frances (Ferree) T.; m. Jamie Tinnin Garrett, Dec. 12, 1986; children: Megan Ashley, Courtney Nicole, Robert Garrett. Student, U. Md., 1969-72; BA, U. N.Mex., 1973. Ins. agt. Occidental Life of Calif., Albuquerque, 1972—; gen. agt. Transamerica-Occidental Life, Albuquerque, 1978-93; pres. Tinnin Investments, Albuquerque, 1978—, Tinnin Enterprises, Albuquerque, 1978—, Tinnin Real Estate & Devel., Albuquerque, 1989—. Mem. N.Mex. State Bd. Fin., Santa Fe., 1985-87, 90—, sec. 1990-96; del. White House Conf. on Small Bus., Washington, 1986; bd. dirs. Albuquerque Econ. Devel., 1987-88. Bd. dirs. Albuquerque Conv. and Visitor's Bureau, 1982-84, St. Joseph's Hosp, Better Bus. Bur., 1983, Albuquerque, 1984-86, N.Mex. Jr. Livestock Found., pres. 1988, Presbyn. Heart Inst., 1989-91, N.Mex. First Confs., 1992, mem. exec. com., 1997—, chmn., 1999; chmn. Manzano Dist. Boy Scouts Am., 1981-82; chmn. Manzano Dist. Finance, 1983; del. White House Conf. Small Bus., 1986; trustee N.Mex. Performing Arts Coun., 1989-90; chmn. N.Mex. State Fair, 1997—; bd. mem. Mus. Natural History, 1997—; mem. Gov.'s Bus. Execs. for Edn., 1998—. Mem. NALU, N.Mex. Life Leaders Assn., Nat. Assn. Real Estate Appraisers, Albuquerqye Armed Forces Adv. Assn., Albuquerque C. of C. (bd. dirs. 1978-84, chmn. ambassador's com. 1983), N.Mex. Life Underwriters Assn., Albuquerque Country Club. Republican. Presbyterian. Avocations: hunting, fishing, skiing, water skiing. Home: 2303 Candelaria Rd NW Albuquerque NM 87107-3055

TIPTON, GARY LEE, retired services company executive; b. Salem, Oreg., July 3, 1941; s. James Rains and Dorothy Velma (Dierks) T. BS, Oreg. Coll. Edn., 1964. Credit rep. Standard Oil Co. Calif., Portland, Oreg., 1964-67; credit mgr. Uniroyal Inc., Dallas, 1967-68; ptnr., mgr. bus. Tipton Barbers, Portland, 1968-94; ret., 1994. Mem. Rep. Nat. Com., 1980—, Sen. Howard Baker's Presdl. Steering Com., 1980; dep. dir. gen. Internat. Biog. Ctr., Cambridge, Eng., 1987—; mem. U.S. Congl. adv. bd. Am. Security Coun., 1984-93; mem. steering com. Coun. on Fgn. Rels. Portland Com., 1983-84, chmn. 1984-86, mem. exec. com., 1988-90, bd. dirs., 1990-91. Recipient World Culture prize Accademia Italia, 1984, Presdl. Achievement award, 1982, cert. Disting. Contbn. Sunset High Sch. Dad's Club, 1972, 73, Cert. of Perfection award Tualatin Valley Fire and Rescue Dist., 1994. Fellow Internat. Biog. Assn. (life, Key award 1983, U.K.); mem. Sunset Mchts. Assn. (co-founder, treas. 1974-79, pres. 1982-83), Internat. Platform Assn., Smithsonian Assocs., UN Assn. (steering com. UN day 1985), World Affairs Coun. of Oreg., City Club of Portland.

TIPTON, HARRY BASIL, JR. state legislator, physician; b. Salida, Colo., Mar. 14, 1927; s. Harry Basil Sr. and Nina Belle (Hailey) T.; m. Dorothy Joan Alexander, Sept. 16, 1950; children: Leslie Louise, Harry Basil III, Robert Alexander. BA, U. Colo., 1950, MD, 1953. Diplomate Am. Bd. Family Practice. Postgrad. med. tng. Good Samaritan Hosp., Phoenix., Ariz., Maricopa County Hosp., Phoenix; ptnr., dir. Lander (Wyo.) Med. Clinic, 1954—; mem. Wyo. Ho. Reps., Cheyenne, 1981—, chmn. judiciary com., 1986-98, speaker pro tem, 1999-2001, mem. appropriations com., 2001—. Cons. Indian Health Svc., Ft. Washakie, Wyo., 1968—; dir NOWCAP Family Planning, Worland, Wyo., 1975-90. Mem., pres. Fremont County Sch. Dist. # 1, Lander, 1958-78. With USMC, 1945-46, capt. USNR Med. Corps, 1950-87. Recipient Dr. Nathon Davis award, AMA, 1999; named Capt. Med. Corps. USNR, 1974. Fellow Am. Coll. Ob.-Gyn., Am. Assn. Family Practice (charter); mem. Wyo. Med. Soc. (Physician of Yr. 1989), Rotary (pres. 1960-61), Elks. Republican. Avocations: fishing, skiing, bird hunting, military history. Office: Lander Med Clin PC 745 Buena Vista Dr Lander WY 82520-3431

TIRRELL, DAVID A. research scientist, educator; b. Jan. 10, 1953; BS in Chemistry, MIT, 1974; MS in Polymer Sci. and Engring., U. Mass., 1976, PhD in Polymer Sci. and Engring., 1978. Rsch. assoc. Kyoto U., 1978; asst. prof. chemistry Carnegie-Mellon U., 1978-82, assoc. prof. chemistry, 1982-84; assoc. prof. polymer sci. and engring. U. Mass., 1984-87, prof. polymer sci. and engring., 1987-92, Barrett prof. polymer and sci. and engring., 1992-98; Ross McCollum-William H. Corcoran prof. Calif. Inst. Tech., 1998—, chair chemistry divsn. & chem. engring., 1999—. Adj. prof. chemistry U. Mass., 1991; dir. NSF materials rsch. lab., 1991-94, dir. NSF material rsch. sci. and engring. ctr., 1994—; mem. molecular and cellular biology faculty, 1990—; vis. prog. chemistry U. Queensland, Australia, 1987, Inst. Charles Sadron, Strasbourg, 1991; mem. materials rsch. adv. com. NSF, 1988-91; chmn. com. on synthetic hierarchical structures Nat. Rsch. Coun., 1990-94, mem panel on biomolecular materials, 1991—, mem. naval rsch. lab. polymers in biosystems, Oxnard, 1994; co-chmn. grad. polymer rsch. conf. State Coll., Pa., 1994; program com. IUPAC Macromolecular Symposium, 1994; chmn. Gordon Rsch. Conf. on Chemistry of Supramolecules and Assemblies, 1995. Editor Jour. of Polymer Sci., 1988—; assoc. editor New Polymeric Materials, 1986-87; editl. bd. Indsl. and Engring. Chemistry, Product Rsch. and Devel., 1983-86, Jour. of Bioactive and Compatible Polymers, 1986—, Biomaterials, 1986—, New Polymeric Materials, 1987—, Jour. of Macromolecular Sci.-Chemistry, 1990—, Progress in Polymer Sic., 1992—, Macromolecular Reports, 1992, Materials Sci. and Engring., 1993—, Chem. and Engring. News, 1995—; contbr. articles to profl. jours. Univ. fellow, 1974-77, Alfred P. Sloan Rsch. fellow, 1982-84, Rotschild fellow Institut Curie, 1995-97; recipient Presdl. Young Investigator award, 1984-89, Fulbright Sr. scholar award, 1987, Harrison Howe award Am. Chem. Soc., 1996. Mem. AAAS, Am. Chem. Soc., N.Y. Acad. Scis., Materials Rsch. Soc., Sigma Xi, Phi Lambda Upsilon. Office: Calif InstTech Divsn Chemistry 225 Spalding Pasadena CA 91125-0001*

TIRRELL, JOHN ALBERT, organization executive, consultant; b. Boston, Feb. 11, 1934; s. George Howard and Helen Sarah (Hitchings) T.; m. Helga Ruth Eisenhauer, Jan. 29, 1966; children: Steffanie Ruth, Sabina Lisette, Monica Susanne. BA in Psychology, The King's Coll., Briarcliff Manor, N.Y., 1961; MEd, U. Ariz., 1975. Various positions for several orgns., 1962-68; analyst instrnl.-ednl. systems GE, Daytona Beach, Fla., 1969-72; dir. curriculum and program devel. Brookdale C.C., Lincroft, N.J., 1972; dir. learning and faculty resources Pima C.C., Tucson, 1972-76; dir. human resources planning and devel. Miami divsn. Cyprus Copper Co., Claypool, Ariz., 1976-79; exec. dir. Calvary Missionary Fellowship, Tucson, 1983-85; interim pastor Sagauro Evang. Ch., Tucson, 1985-86; pastor Midvale Evangelical Ch., Tucson, 1986-87; founder, pres. The Jethro Consultancy, Birmingham, Mich., 1979—; v.p. mgmt. svc. AA Gage, Ferndale, 1987-88; pastor Desert Hills Bapt. Ch., Tucson, 1993-95. Mem. adv. bd. UIM Internat., Flagstaff, Ariz., 1983-92, mem. fin. com., 1983-94, sec. support svcs. field bd., 1993—, sec. pers. com., 1997—, sec., 1998—, also bd. dirs., 1993—; assoc. faculty mem. Gila Pueblo Campus Ea. Ariz. Coll., Globe, 1978; adj. prof. Montclair State Coll., Upper Montclair, N.J., 1972; chmn. mgmt. and pers. com. Wildwood Ranch, Inc., Howell, Mich., 1989-92; interim pres., v.p. programs, v.p. devel. Detroit Rescue Mission Ministries, 1990-92; v.p. corp. planning, tng., productivity George Instrument Co., Royal Oak; mem. mgmt., comm., sociology Tucson Campus U. Phoenix, 1997—, area chair for social scis., 2001—; adj. faculty mem. psychology Pima County C.C., 1999—. Contbr. articles to profl. jours. Mem. Ariz. Coun. for Econ. Conversion, 1992-94; mem. facilities task force Grace Evang. Free Ch., Birmingham, 1989-90, chmn. bylaws revision com., 1989-90, chmn. property devel. com., 1990-92; interim pastor Desert Hills Bapt. Ch., Tucson, 1992-93; elder 1st Evang. Free Ch., Tucson, 1979-81, 86-87, 97, supt. Sunday sch., 1981-84, supr. adult Sunday sch., 1992-93, chmn. gen. bd., elder bd., 1979-82, short-term missions coord., missions bd., 1992-93; bd. dirs. S.W. Border dist. Evang. Free Ch. Am., 1996—, mem. comm. com., 1996—, chmn. comm. com., 1998-99; bd. dirs. Clearing House of Operational Resources for Christian Orgns., Royal Oak, Mich., 1991; bd. dirs. Shadow Roc Homeowners Assn., 1996-98, treas., 1997; v.p. parent-tchr. fellowship Palo Verde Christian Sch., Tucson, 1980-81. Staff sgt. USAF, 1952-56. Mem. ASTD (treas., Old Pueblo chpt. 1982, bd. dirs.-at-large 1983, Human Resources Devel. award Valley of the Sun chpt. 1977), Birmingham-Bloomfield C. of C. (mem. profl. devel. edn. com. 1987-91, mem. pub. rels. mktg. com. 1989), King's Coll. Alumni Assn. (class gov. 1988-95). Republican. Avocations: photography, Bible teaching. Home and Office: 1205 E Deer Canyon Rd Tucson AZ 85718-1069 Fax: (253) 681-8198. E-mail: jack.tirrell@att.net

TIRRELL, MATTHEW, chemical engineering, materials science educator; b. Phillipsburg, N.J., Sept. 5, 1950; s. Matthew Vincent Tirrell Jr. and Loraine (Wier) Gonsky; m. Pamela LaVigne, Aug. 1993. BS, Northwestern U., 1973; PhD, U. Mass., 1977. Mem. coop. edn. program Cin. Milacron Chem. Inc., 1970-72; tchg. and rsch. asst. U. Mass., Amherst, 1973-77; asst. prof. U. Minn., Mpls., 1977-81, assoc. prof., 1981-85, prof. chem. engring. and materials sci., 1985—, Shell disting. prof. chem. engring., 1986-91, acting head, 1992-93, Earl E. Bakken prof. biomed. engring., 1993-98, head chem. engring. and materials sci., 1995-99; dir. Biomed. Engring. Inst., 1995-98; prof., dean coll. of engring. U. Calif., Santa Barbara, 1999—. Author: Modeling of Polymerization Processes, 1995. Recipient Charles M.A. Stine award, 1996; Guggenheim fellow, 1986. Mem. NAE, AIChE (editor jour. 1991—, Profl. Progress award 1994, Allan P. Colburn award 1985), Am. Chem. Soc., Am. Phys. Soc. (John H. Dillon medal 1987), Materials Rsch. Soc. Avocations: gourmet cooking, movies, distance running. Office: U Calif Coll Engring Santa Barbara CA 93106

TITLE, GAIL MIGDAL, lawyer; b. Waldenberg, Germany, May 31, 1946; AB, Wellesley Coll., 1967; JD, U. Calif., Berkeley, 1970. Bar: Calif. 1971. Mng. ptnr. Katten Muchin Zavis (formerly Katten Muchin & Zavis), Beverly Hills. Adj. prof. law Loyola U., 1976-96; trustee Ctr. for Law in the Pub. Interest. Mem. ABA (litigation sect., forum com. entertainment), Assn. Bus. Trial Lawyers, State Bar Calif. (standing com. pub. interest law 1976—), L.A. County Bar Assn. (del. conf. dels. 1974-76, 88-89), Beverly Hills Bar Assn., L.A. Copyright Soc. (trustee), Office: Katten Muchin Zavis 1999 Ave Of Stars Ste 1400 Los Angeles CA 90067-6115

TITLEY, SPENCER ROWE, geology educator; b. Denver, Sept. 27, 1928; m. Clara Helen Ruxton, May 1951; children: Ronald, Jane, Jennifer. Geol. Engr., Colo. Sch. Mines, 1951; PhD in Geology, U. Ariz., 1958. Ops. geologist N.J. Zinc Co., Gilman, Colo., 1951, 53-55; instr. U. Ariz., Tucson, 1955-58; regional geologist S.W. N.J. Zinc Co., 1958-60; from asst. to full prof. geology U. Ariz., 1960—. Panel mem. NSF, Divsn. Biol., Math. and Geophysical Scis. and Engring., 1978-81; sec. Soc. Econ. Geologists Found., 1972-83; mem. Apollo Field Geology Investigation Team, U.S. Geol. Survey, 1969-72; pres. Ariz. Geol. Soc., 1973-74. Mem. editl. bd. Econ. Geology, 1970-75, Ore Geology Reviews, 1984—; editor 5 books; contbr. over 85 articles to profl. jours. With U.S. Army Corps Engrs., 1951-53, Korea. Recipient Disting. Achievement medal Colo. Sch. Mines, 1975, Excellence in Tchg. award Burlington No. Found., 1985, Creative Tchg. award U. Ariz. Found., 1986, D.C. Jackling award Soc. Mining, Mettalurgy and Exploration of AIME, 1997; Fulbright Sr. lectr. Fed. U. Para'Brazil, 1986, Phoebe Apperson Hearst Disting. lectr. U. Calif., Berkeley, 1988. Fellow Geol. Soc. Am., Soc. Econ. Geologists (councilor 1980-83, Thayer Lindsley lectr. 1985, Disting. lectr. 1995, Penrose medal 1996), Mineral. Soc. Am., Australasian Inst. Mining and Metallurgy; mem. Soc. Applied Geology. Home: 6920 E Taos Pl Tucson AZ 85715-3343 Office: Univ Ariz Dept Geosciences Simpson Bldg Tucson AZ 85721-0001

TITUS, ALICE CESTANDINA (DINA TITUS), state legislator; b. Thomasville, Ga., May 23, 1950; m. Thomas Clayton Wright. AB, Coll. William and Mary, 1970; MA, U. Ga., 1973; PhD, Fla. State U., 1976. Prof. polit. sci. U. Nev., Las Vegas, 1977—; mem. from dist. 7 Nev. Senate, 1989—, minority fl. leader, 1993—, mem. Legislative commn., 1991—. Chmn. Nev. Humanities Com., 1984-86; mem. Eldorado Basin adv. group to Colo. River Commn.; active Gov. Commn. Bicentennial of U.S. Constn.; former mem. Gov. Commn. on Aging. Author: Bombs in the Backyard: Atomic Testing and American Politics, 1986, Battle Born: Federal-State Relations in Nevada during the 20th Century, 1989. Mem. Western Polit. Sci. Assn., Clark County Women's Dem. Club, Amer. Pen Women, Aquavision, PEO. Greek Orthodox. Home: 1637 Travois Cir Las Vegas NV 89119-6283 Office: Nev Senate 401 S Carson St Rm 114F Carson City NV 89701-4747

TJIAN, ROBERT TSE NAN, biochemistry educator, biology researcher, virology researcher; b. Hong Kong, Sept. 22, 1949; naturalized Brit. citizen. m. 1976. BA, U. Calif., Berkeley, 1971; PhD in Molecular Biology, Harvard U., 1976. Staff investigator molecular virology Cold Spring Harbor Lab., 1976-79, Robertson fellow, 1978; prof. biochemistry U. Calif., Berkeley, 1979—, prof. molecular and cell biology. Named Passano Found. laureate; recipient Lewis S. Rosentiel award for disting. work in basic med. rsch. Brandeis U., 1995. Mem. NAS (Molecular Biology award 1991). Achievements include research in oncogenic viruses and their interctions with the host cell; control of gene expression; simian virus 40; a small DNA containing oncogenic virus, tumor antigen, its structure and function. Office: U Calif Molecular and Cell Biology Dept 401 Barker Hall Berkeley CA 94720-0001*

TOBIAS, ANITA, publishing executive; V.p. U.S. syndication L.A. Times Syndicate, 1998—. Office: Los Angeles Times Syndicate Times Mirror Sq 145 S Spring St Fl 10 Los Angeles CA 90012-3601

TOBIN, ALLAN JOSHUA, biologist; b. Manchester, N.H., Aug. 22, 1942; s. Maurice and Eve (Alter) T.; m. Elaine Munsey, Apr. 7, 1968 (div.); children: David, Adam; m. Janet Ruth Hadda, Mar. 22, 1981. BS, MIT, 1963; PhD, Harvard U., 1969. Asst. prof. biology Harvard U., Cambridge, Mass., 1971-75, UCLA, 1975-81, assoc. prof. biology, 1981-86, prof. biology, 1986—, chair interdepartmental program for neurosci., 1989-95, dir. Brain Rsch. Inst., 1995—, Eleanor Leslie Chair in neuroscience, 1996—. Sci. dir. Hereditary Disease Found., Santa Monica, Calif., 1979—, mem. sci. adv. bd., 1979—; vis. scientist Laboratoire de Neurobiologie Moleculaire, Inst. Pasteur, Paris, 1982; cons. Curriculum Resources Group, Inst. for Svs. to Edn., Ednl. Devel. Ct., Newton, Mass.; centennial speaker Nat. Student Rsch. Forum, U. Tex. Med. Br., 1991. Named Research fellow Dept. Biology MIT, 1970-71, Vis. Research fellow Dept. Biophysics Weizmann Inst. Science, 1969-70, Mary Jennifer Selznick fellow Hereditary Disease Found., 1978, fellow Com. to Combat Huntington's Disease, 1973-75, Postdoctoral fellow U.S. Pub. Health Service; recipient Javits Neuroscience Investigator award Nat. Inst. Neurological Disorders, 1993, Nat. Med. Rsch. award Nat. Health Coun., 1993, David Gillespie Meml. Lectureship Med. Coll. Pa. and Hahnemann U., Phila., 1996, Excellence award Text and Acad. Authors Assn., 1999, 2000; named to Manchester (N.H.) Ctrl. H.S. Hall of Fame, 1998-00. Mem. AAAS, Soc. for Neurosci., NIH (mem. Neurology C. study sect. 1985-89), NINDS (chair stategic planning group neurodegenerative disease 1998—), Molecular Biology Inst., Soc. for Devel. Biology, Am. Soc. Neurochemistry. Office: UCLA Brain Rsch Inst 2506 Gonda Neurosci Genetics Ctr PO Box 951761 Los Angeles CA 90095-1761 E-mail: atobin@mednet.ucla.edu

TOBIN, GARY ALLAN, cultural and community organization educator; b. St. Louis, July 26, 1949; PhD in City and Regional Planning, U. Calif., Berkeley. Pres. Inst. for Jewish and Cmty. Rsch., San Francisco; dir. Abramson Program in Jewish Policy Rsch. Ctr. for Policy Options, U. Judaism, L.A.; former dir. Cohen Ctr. for Modern Jewish Studies Brandeis U., Waltham, Mass. Rsch. on synagogue affiliation, antisemitism, racial and ethnic diversity, Jewish orgn. planning and philanthropy in Jewish Cmty. and Jewish Family Founds. Author: Jewish Perceptions of Antisemitism, Church and Synagogue Affiliation, Opening the Gates: How Proactive Conversion Can Revitalize the Jewish Community, Rabbis Talk About Intermarriage. Office: Inst Jewish & Cmty Rsch 3198 Fulton St San Francisco CA 94118

TOBIN, JAMES MICHAEL, lawyer; b. Santa Monica, Calif., Sept. 27, 1948; s. James Joseph and Glada Marie (Meisner) T.; m. Kathleen Marie Espy, Sept. 14, 1985. BA with honors, U. Calif., Riverside, 1970; JD, Georgetown U., 1974. Bar: Calif. 1974, Mich. 1987. From atty. to gen. atty. So. Pacific Co., San Francisco, 1975-82; v.p. regulatory affairs So. Pacific Communications Co., Washington, 1982-83; v.p., gen. counsel Lexitel Corp., Washington, 1983-85; v.p., gen. counsel, sec. ALC Communications Corp., Birmingham, Mich., 1985-87, sr. v.p., gen. counsel, sec., 1987-88; of counsel Morrison & Foerster, San Francisco, 1988-90, ptnr., 1990—. Mem. ABA, Calif. Bar Assn., Mich. Bar Assn., Fed. Communications Bar Assn. Republican. Unitarian. Avocations: carpentry, travel. Home: 3134 Baker St San Francisco CA 94123-1805 Office: Morrison & Foerster 425 Market St Ste 3100 San Francisco CA 94105-2482 E-mail: jtobin@mofo.com

TOBIN, VINCENT MICHAEL, professional football coach, former sports team executive; b. Burlington Junction, Mo., Sept. 29, 1943; BE, U. Mo., 1965, M in Guidance and Counseling, 1966. Def. ends coach Missouri, 1967-70, def. coord., 1971-76, Brit. Columbia Lions CFL, 1977-82, Phila./Balt. Stars USFL, 1983-85, Chgo. Bears NFL, 1986-92, Indpls. Colts NFL, 1994-95; head coach Ariz. Cardinals, 1996—. Office: Arizona Cardinals PO Box 888 Phoenix AZ 85001-0888

TOBIN, WILLIAM JOSEPH, newspaper editor; b. Joplin, Mo., July 28, 1927; s. John J. and Lucy T. (Shoppach) T.; m. Marjorie Stuhldreher, Apr. 26, 1952; children: Michael Gerard, David Joseph, James Patrick. BJ, Butler U., 1948. Staff writer AP, Indpls., 1947-52, news feature writer N.Y.C., 1952-54, regional membership exec. Louisville, 1954-56, corr. Juneau, Alaska, 1956-60, asst. chief bur. Balt., 1960-61, Helena, Mont., 1961-63; mng. editor Anchorage Times, 1963-73, assoc. editor, 1973-85, gen. mgr., 1974-85, v.p., editor-in-chief, 1985-89, editor editl. page, 1990, asst. pub., 1991; sr. editor Voice of the Times, 1991—. Mem. devel. com. Anchorage Winter Olympics, 1984-91, bd. dirs. Anchorage organizing com., 1985-91; bd. dirs. Alaska Coun. Econ. Edn., 1978-84, Boys Clubs Alaska, 1979-83, Anchotage Symphony Orch., 1986-87, Blue Cross Wash. and Alaska, 1987—, chmn., 1990-91; chmn. Premera Corp., 1994-99; mem. adv. bd. Providence Hosp., Anchorage, 1974-91, chmn., 1980-85. Sgt. U.S. Army, 1950-52. Mem. Alaska AP Mems. Assn. (pres. 1964), Anchorage C. of C. (bd. dirs. 1969-74, pres. 1972-73), Alaska World Affairs Coun. (pres. 1967-68), Alaska Press Club (pres. 1968-69), Commonwealth North Club (Anchorage). Home: 2130 Lord Baranof Dr Anchorage AK 99517-1257 Office: Anchorage Times PO Box 100040 Anchorage AK 99510-0040

TOBIS, JEROME SANFORD, physician; b. Syracuse, N.Y., July 23, 1915; s. David George and Anna (Feinberg) T.; m. Hazel Weisbard, Sept. 18, 1938; children: David, Heather, Jonathan. B.S., CCNY, 1936; M.D., Chgo. Med. Sch., 1943. Diplomate: Am. Bd. Phys. Medicine and Rehab. Intern Knickerbocker Hosp., 1943-44; resident Bronx VA Hosp., 1946-48; med. dir. state fever therapy unit USPHS, Brookhaven, Miss., 1944-46; practice medicine N.Y.C., 1948-70; prof. dir. dept. phys. medicine and rehab. N.Y. Med. Coll., Flower and Fifth Av. Hosps., 1948-61; prof. rehab. medicine Albert Einstein Coll. of Medicine, 1963-70; chief div. rehab. medicine Montefiore Hosp., 1961-70; dir. vis. physician Met., Bird S. Coler hosps., 1952-61; prof., chmn. dept. phys. medicine and rehab. Calif. Coll. Medicine, U. Calif. at Irvine, 1970-82, prof., dir. program in geriatric medicine and gerontology, 1980-86; mem. adv. com. Acad. Geriatric Resource program, 1984-86, 95—. Mem. expert med. com. Am. Rehab. Found., 1961-70; cons. Dept. Health, N.Y.C., Long Beach VA Hosp., 1970—, Fairview State Devel. Ctr., 1976—; mem. adv. coun. phys. medicine and rehab. for appeals com. Calif. Med. Assn., 1971-74, adv. com. U. Calif. Acad. Geriatric Resource Program, 1995—; NIH Internat. Fogarty fellow, hon. lectr., dept. geriatric medicine U. Birmingham, 1979-80; chair ethics com. U. Calif.-Irvine Med. Ctr., 1986—; mem. rev. panel musculoskeletal diseases NIH, 1996; rsch. prof. dept. phys. medicine & rehab. U. Calif., Irvine, 1986—, chair med. ethics com., 1986—; mem. Ctr. Health Policy Rsch. U. Calif., Davis, 1996—. Mem. editorial bd.: Heart and Lung, 1973-76, Geriatrics, 1975-80, Archives of Phys. Medicine and Rehab, 1958-73. Named Physician of the Year, 1957; recipient Distinguished Alumnus award Chgo. Med. Sch., 1972, Acad. award Nat. Inst. on Aging, 1981-86; named hon. faculty mem. Calif. Zeta chpt. Alpha Omega Alpha, 1981; Leavitt Meml. lectureship Baylor Coll. Medicine, 1983, Griffith Meml. lectureship Am. Geriatric Soc., 1984; Australian Coll. Rehabilitation Medicine, 1984; Jerome S. Tobis Ann. Conf. on Geriatric Medicine established in his name, U. Calif. at Irvine, 1986. Fellow ACP, Am. Coll. Cardiology; mem. AMA (mem. residency rev. com. Coun. Med. Edn. 1973), AAAS, Am. Acad. Cerebral Palsy, Am. Acad. Phys. Medicine and Rehab. (Disting. Clinician award 1993), Am. Congress Rehab. Medicine (pres. 1962), Calif. Coun. Gerontology and Geriatrics (bd. dirs. 1980-86, pres. 1985), N.Y. Acad. Medicine, N.Y. Acad. Sci., Orange County Med. Soc., Assn. U. Calif. Irvine (chair emeritae/i 1996-97). Home: 1115 Goldenrod Ave Corona Del Mar CA 92625-1508 Office: U Calif Dept Phys Medicine & Rehab Irvine CA 92668 E-mail: jstobis@uci.edu

TOBISMAN, STUART PAUL, lawyer; b. Detroit, June 5, 1942; s. Nathan and Beverly (Porvin) T.; m. Karen Sue Tobisman, Aug. 8, 1965; children: Cynthia Elaine, Neal Jay. BA, UCLA, 1966; JD, U. Calif., Berkeley, 1969. Bar: Calif. 1969. Assoc. O'Melveny & Myers, L.A., 1969-77, ptnr., 1977—. Dir. Burton G. Bettingen Corp. Contbr. articles to profl. jours. Trustee L.A. County Bar Assn., 1983-84. With USN, 1961-63. Fellow Am. Coll. Trust and Estate Counsel; mem. Phi Beta Kappa, Order of Coif. Office: O'Melveny & Myers LLP 1999 Avenue Of The Stars Los Angeles CA 90067-6035

TODARO, GEORGE JOSEPH, pathologist, researcher; b. N.Y.C., July 1, 1937; s. George J. and Antoinette (Piccinni) T.; m. Jane Lehv, Aug. 12, 1962; children: Wendy C., Thomas M., Anthony A. BS, Swarthmore Coll., 1958; MD, NYU, 1963. Intern NYU Sch. Medicine, N.Y.C., 1963-64, fellow in pathology, 1964-65, asst. prof. pathology, 1965-67; staff assoc. Viral Carcinogenesis br. Nat. Cancer Inst., Bethesda, Md., 1967-70, head molecular biology sect., 1969-70; chief Viral Carcinogenesis br. Nat. Cancer Inst. (Lab. Viral Carcinogenesis), 1970-83; sci. dir., pres. Oncogen, Seattle, 1987-90; sr. v.p. exploratory biomed. rsch. Bristol-Myers Squibb Pharm. Rsch. Inst., 1990; pres., CEO Sytokine Networks, Inc., Seattle, 1998—; now prof. pathobiology U. Wash., Seattle. Adj. prof. pathology U. Wash., Seattle, 1983—, past chmn. dept. pathobiology; sr. v.p., sci. dir. Pathogenesis Corp., Seattle, 1992-95; mem. Fred Hutchin son Cancer Rsch. Ctr., Seattle, 1991-93. Editor: Cancer Research, 1973-86, Archives of Virology, 1976— , Jour. Biol. Chemistry, 1979— ; contbr. articles to profl. jours. Served as med. officer USPHS, 1967-69. Recipient Borden Undergrad. Research award, 1963, USPHS Career Devel. award, 1967, HEW Superior Service award, 1971, Gustav Stern award for virology, 1972, Parke-Davis award in exptl. pathology, 1975; Walter Hubert lectr. Brit. Cancer Soc., 1977 Mem. Nat. Acad. Scis., Am. Soc. Microbiology, Am. Assn. Cancer Research, Soc. Exptl. Biology and Medicine, Am. Soc. Biol. Chemists, Am. Soc. Clin. Investigation. Home: 1940 15th Ave E Seattle WA 98112-2829

TODD, HAROLD WADE, retired association executive, retired air force officer; b. Chgo., Jan. 17, 1938; s. Harold Wade and Jeanne (Fayal) T.; m. Wendy Yvonne Kendrick, July 12, 1981; children by previous marriage: Hellen J. Wilson, Kenneth J., Stephen D., Joseph M., Michelle M. Adams, Mark A.; stepchildren: Jamie Y. White, James K. Mills, Timothy S. Emerson. BS, U.S. Air Force Acad., 1959; grad., Nat. War Coll., 1975. Commd. 2d lt. U.S. Air Force, 1959, advanced through grades to maj. gen., 1982; aide to comdr. (2d Air Force (SAC)), Barksdale AFB, La., 1970-71; exec. aide to comdr.-in-chief U.S. Air Forces Europe, Germany, 1971-74; spl. asst. chief of staff USAF, 1975-76; chief Concept Devel. Divsn., 1976-77; chief Readiness and NATO Staff Group, Hdqrs. USAF, 1977-78; exec. asst. to chmn. Joint Chiefs Staff Washington, 1978-80; comdr. 25th region N. Am. Aerospace Def. Command McChord AFB, Wash., 1980-82; chief staff 4th Allied Tactical Air Force Heidelberg, 1982-85; commandant Air War Coll., 1985-89; vice comdr. Air U., 1985-89, ret., 1989; ind. cons. Colorado Springs, Colo., 1989-95; pres., CEO, Nat. Stroke Assn., Englewood, 1995-00. Founder, pres. Bossier City (La.) chpt. Nat. Assn. for Children with Learning Disabilities, 1970-71. Decorated Def. DSM, Air Force DSM (2), Legion of Merit (2), DFC, Air medal (8), Air Force Commendation medal. Mem. Air Force Assn., USAF Acad. Assn. Grads., Nat. War Coll. Alumni Assn. Home: 1250 Big Valley Dr Colorado Springs CO 80919-1015

TODD, HARRY WILLIAMS, aircraft propulsion system company executive; b. Oak Park, Ill., 1922; BSME, U. So. Calif., 1947, BSIE, 1948, MBA, 1950. With Rockwell Internat., Pitts., 1947-76, former v.p. ops.; pres., chmn., chief exec. officer, bd. dirs. The L.E. Myers Co., Pitts., 1976-80; with Rohr Industries, Inc., Chula Vista, Calif., 1980-90, chief operating officer, 1980-82, pres., chief exec. officer, chmn., 1982-90, retired, 1990, Chula Vista; mng. ptnr. Carlise Enterprises, 1990-97; mng. dir. Carlisle Ent., Calif., 1990—. Bd. dirs. Rohr Industries, Pacific Scientific, Helmerich & Payne, Garrett Aviation Svcs. Trustee Scripps Clinic and Rsch. Found. With U.S. Army, 1944-46. Office: Carlisle Enterprises 7777 Fay Ave Ste 200 La Jolla CA 92037-4390

TODD, JOHN, mathematician, educator; b. Carnacally, Ireland, May 16, 1911; came to U.S., 1947, naturalized, 1953; s. William Robert and Catherine (Stewart) T.; m. Olga Taussky, Sept. 29, 1938. B.S., Queen's U., Belfast, Ireland, 1931; research student, St. John's Coll., Cambridge (Eng.) U., 1931-33. Lectr. Queen's U., 1933-37, King's Coll., London, 1937-49; chief computation lab., then chief numerical analysis Nat. Bur. Standards, 1947-57; prof. math. Calif. Inst. Tech., 1957—; Fulbright prof. Vienna, Austria, 1965. Author, editor books on numerical analysis and tables; editor in chief: Numerische Mathematik, 1959—; assoc. editor Aequationes Mathematicae, 1967-85, 89-95, Jour. Approximation Theory, 1967-93. Mem. Am. Math. Soc., Soc. Indsl. and Applied Math., Math. Assn. Am. (gov. 1980-83) Office: Calif Inst Technology Mathematics 253 # 37 Pasadena CA 91125-3700 Fax: (626) 585-1728

TODD, JOHN J. computer company executive; BA, Longwood Coll.; MBA, Coll. William and Mary, 1960. CFO Boston Market, 1996-97, Allied Signal Aftermarket-Aerospace, Allied Signal Engines, Phoenix; sr. v.p., CFO Gateway, Inc., San Diego, 1998—. Held several exec. positions in fin., strategic planning, bus. devel. PepsiCo. Bd. dirs. Sharp HealtCare, Nat. Alzheimer's Assn., San Diego Internat. Sports Coun. Office: Gateway Inc San Diego CA 92121

TODD, KATHLEEN GAIL, physician; b. Portland, Oreg., Aug. 31, 1951; d. Horace Edward and Lois Marie (Messing) T.; m. Andrew Richard Embick, March 31, 1980; children: Elizabeth Todd Embick, Margaret Todd Embick. BA, Pomona Coll., 1972; MD, Washington U., St. Louis, 1976. Diplomate Am. Bd. Family Practice. Resident U. Wash. Affiliated Hosps., Seattle, 1976-79; pvt. practice Valdez (Alaska) Med. Clinic, 1980—; chief of staff Valdez Community Hosp., 1986—. Mem. AMA, AAFP, Am. Acad. Family Practice, Alaska State Med. Assn. (counselor-at-large 1986-87). Democrat. Episcopalian. Avocations: skiing, kayaking, camping, music. Office: Valdez Med Clinic PO Box 1829 Valdez AK 99686-1829

TODD, KENNETH S., JR. parasitologist, educator; b. Three Forks, Mont., Aug. 25, 1936; s. Kenneth S. and Anna Louise (Seeman) T. BS, Mont. State U., 1962, MS, 1964; PhD, Utah State U., 1967. Asst. prof. U. Ill., Urbana, 1967-71, assoc. prof., 1971-76, prof. vet. parasitology, 1976-94, chmn. div. parasitology, 1983-90, asst. head vet. pathobiology, 1984-87, prof. vet. programs in agr., 1984-94, acting head vet. pathobiology, 1987-90, head, 1990-94; prof. emeritus, 1994. Affiliate scientist Ill. State Natural History Survey, 1987-94; adj. prof. microbiology Mont. State U., 1994—. Served with USAF, 1954-58. NSF grad. fellow, 1966-67 Mem. AVMA, Am. Assn. Vet. Parasitologists, Am. Micros. Soc., Am. Soc. Parasitologists, Am. Soc. Tropical Medicine and Hygiene, Helminthologic Soc. Washington, Midwest Conf. Parasitologists, Wildlife Disease Assn., Soc. Protozoologists, Mont. Acad. Scis., Rocky Mountain Conf. Parasitologists, World Assn. for Advancement of Vet. Parasitology. Office: Mont State U Dept Microbiology Bozeman MT 59715 E-mail: umbkt@gemini.oscs.montana.edu

TOEWS, DARYL, state senator; b. Glasgow, Mont., May 24, 1949; m. Jean Toews. Student, Tabor Coll., Mont. State U. Farmer, realtor; mem. Mont. State Senate, 1992—, chair edn. and cultural resources com., vice chair jt. appropriation subcom. edn./cultural resources, mem. fin. and claims com., mem. hwys. and transp. com. Trustee Sch. Bd., 9 yrs. Mem. Valley County Devel. Coun. and C. of C. Republican. Home: HC 66 Box 34 Lustre MT 59225-9703

TOFFEL, ALVIN EUGENE, corporate executive, business and governmental consultant; b. Los Angeles, July 14, 1935; s. Harry and Estelle Charlotte Toffel; m. Neile McQueen; children: Stephanie, Elizabeth, Michelle; stepchildren: Terry (dec.), Chad. B.A., UCLA, 1957. Dir. mgmt. systems and organizational planning Rockwell Internat., 1963-69; Exec. Office for the Pres. White House, Washington, 1969-70; nat. chmn., campaign dir. McCloskey for Pres., 1971-72; polit. cons., 1971—. Cons. personal bus. and govt. Norton Simon and Norton Simon, Inc., Los Angeles, 1972-80; pres. Norton Simon Found., Pasadena, Calif., 1977-80; cons. exec. asst. to pres. Twentieth Century Fox Film Corp., 1980; bd. dirs. Geometrics, Inc.; pres. So. Shellfish Inc., Atlantic Internat. Ins. Ltd., Toffel Thoroughbred Racing; lectr. mgmt. UCLA, Stanford U. Pres. Norton Simon Mus. Art, Pasadena; vice chmn. U.S. Pension Svcs., Inc. With SAC USAF, 1958-63. Recipient White House Interchange Exec. Outstanding Achievement, 1971; recipient Achievement Am. Advtg. Council, 1972 Mem. Ky. Cols., Presdl. Interchange Execs. Assn., Assn. Old Crows Achievements include developing standard U.S. govt. program performance measurement system, aerospace engrng. techniques of program mgmt., aerospace manuals. Home and Office: 2323 Bowmont Dr Beverly Hills CA 90210-1808

TOFTNESS, CECIL GILLMAN, lawyer, consultant; b. Glasgow, Mont., Sept. 13, 1920; s. Anton Bernt and Nettie (Pedersen) T.; m. Chloe Catherine Vincent, Sept. 8, 1951. AA, San Diego Jr. Coll., 1943; student, Purdue U., Northwestern U.; BS, UCLA, 1947; JD cum laude, Southwestern U., 1953. Bar: Calif. 1954, U.S. Dist. Ct. (so. dist.) Calif. 1954, U.S. Tax Ct. 1974, U.S. Supreme Ct. 1979. Pvt. rpactice, palos Verdes Estates, Calif., 1954—. Chmn. bd., pres., bd. dirs. Fishermen & Mchts. Bank, San Pedro, Calif., 1963-67; v.p., bd. dirs. Palos Verdes Estates Bd. Realtors, 1964-65; participant Soc. Expdn. through the Northwest Passaage. Chmn. capital campaign fund Richstone Charity, Hawthorne, Calif., 1983; commencement spkr. Glasgow H.S., 1981. Served to lt. (j.g.) USN, 1938-46, ETO, PTO, commdg. officer USS Ptarmigan, 1941-45. Decorated Bronze Star; mem. Physicians for Prevention of Nuclear War which received Nobel Peace prize, 1987; named Man of Yr., Glasgow, 1984. Mem. South Bay Bar Assn., Southwestern Law Sch. Alumni Assn. (class rep. 1980—), Themis Soc.-Southwestern Law Sch., Schumacher Founders Cir.-Southwestern Law Sch. (charter), Kiwanis (sec.-treas. 1955-83, v.p., pres., bd. dirs.), Masons, KT. Democrat. Lutheran. Home: 2229 Via Acalones Palos Verdes Peninsula CA 90274-1646 Office: 2516 Via Tejon Palos Verdes Estates CA 90274-6802 E-mail: cgtoftness@aol.com

TOKUMARU, ROBERTA, principal; Prin. Aikahi Elem. Sch., 1984— Recipient DOE Elem. Sch. Recognition award, 1989-90. Office: Aikahi Elem Sch 281 Ilihau St Kailua HI 96734-1698

TOLANEY, MURLI, environmental engineering executive; b. Aug. 1, 1941; BS in Civil Engring., MS in Environ. Engring., U. Kans. Jr. engr. Coun. Sci. and Indsl. Resources, New Delhi, 1963-66; project engr. L.A. County Sanitary Dist., 1966-70; with Montgomery Watson Assn., Pasadena, Calif., 1970—, chmn., CEO. Office: Montgomery Watson Ams 300 N Lake Ave Ste 1200 Pasadena CA 91101-4184

TOLBERT, MARGARET A. geochemistry educator; Prof. dept. chemistry U. Colo., Boulder. Recipient James B. Macelwane Young Investigator medal Am. Geophys. Union, 1993. Office: U Colo Dept Chemistry PO Box 215 Boulder CO 80309-0215

TOLER, PENNY, former professional basketball player, sports team executive; b. Mar. 24, 1966; B of Psychology, Long Beach State U., 1989. Guard, Montecchio, Italy, 1989-91, Pescara, Italy, 1991-94, Sporting Flash, Greece, 1994-96, Ramat HaSharon, Israel, 1996-97, Los Angeles Sparks, (WNBA), 1997-99; gen. mgr. L.A. Sparks, 1999—. Named All-Am & Co-Player of Yr./Big West, 1988, 89. Avocations: table tennis, tennis, craps. Office: LA Sparks Great Western Forum 3900 W Manchester Blvd Inglewood CA 90305-2200

TOLIVER, LEE, mechanical engineer; b. Wildhorse, Okla., Oct. 3, 1921; s. Clinton Leslie and Mary (O'Neall) T.; m. Barbara Anne O'Reilly, Jan. 24, 1942 (dec. Jan. 1999); children: Margaret Anne, Michael Edward. BSME, U. Okla., 1942. Registered profl. engr., Ohio. Engr. Douglas Aircraft Co., Santa Monica, Calif., 1942, Oklahoma City, 1942-44, Los Alamos (N.Mex.) Sci. Lab., 1946; instr. mech. engring. Ohio State U., Columbus, 1946-47; engr. Sandia Nat. Labs., Albuquerque, 1947-82; instr. computer sci. and math. U. N.Mex., Valencia County, 1982-84; number theory researcher Belen, N.Mex., 1982—. Author: (computer manuals with G. Carli, AF. Schkade) Experience with an Intelligent Remote Batch Terminal, 1972; (with C.R. Borgman, T.I. Ristine) Transmitting Data from PDP-10 to Precision Graphics, 1973, Data Transmission-PDP-10/Sykes/Precision Graphics, 1975; Relations Between Prime and Relatively Prime Integers, 1998. With Manhattan Project (Atomic Bomb) U.S. Army, 1944-46. Mem. Math. Assn. Am., Am. Math. Soc. Achievements include devel. of 44 computer programs with manuals. Home: 206 Howell St Belen NM 87002-6225

TOLLENAERE, LAWRENCE ROBERT, retired industrial products company executive; b. Berwyn, Ill., Nov. 19, 1922; s. Cyrille and Modesta (Van Damme) T.; m. Mary Elizabeth Hansen, Aug. 14, 1948; children: Elizabeth, Homer, Stephanie, Caswell, Mary Jennifer. BS in Engring., Iowa State U., 1944, MS in Engring., 1949; MBA, U. So. Calif., 1969; LLD (hon.), Claremont Grad. Sch., 1977. Specification engr. Aluminum Co. Am., Vernon, Calif., 1946-47; asst. prof. indsl. engring. Iowa State U., Ames, 1947-50; sales rep. Am. Pipe and Constrn. Co. (now AMERON), South Gate, Calif., 1950-53, spl. rep. S.Am., 1952-54, 2nd v.p., mgr. Columbian divsn. S.Am., 1955-57, divsn. v.p., mgr. Calif., 1957-63, v.p. concrete pipe ops., 1963-65, pres. corp. hdqrs., 1965-67; pres., CEO Ameron Inc., Monterey Park, 1967-89, CEO, pres. Pasadena, 1989-93, chmn. bd. dirs., 1989-94, ret., 1994. Trustee The Huntington Library, Art Gallery and Bot. Gardens; emeritus mem. bd. fellows Claremont U. Ctr.; bd. gov.'s Iowa State U. Found. Mem. Newcomen Soc. N.Am., Calif. C. of C. (bd. dirs. 1977-92), Calif. Club (past pres.), Jonathan Club, Bohemian Club, San Francisco Club, Commanderie de Bordeaux Club, L.A. Confrerie des Chevaliers du Tastevin Club, Twilight Club, Lincoln Club, Beavers Club (past pres., hon. dir.), Valley of Montecito Club, Alpha Tau Omega. Republican. Avocations: fishing, hunting, equestrian, philately. Home: 1400 Milan Ave South Pasadena CA 91030-3930 Office: 750 E Green St Ste 301 Pasadena CA 91101-2134

TOMAN, MARY ANN, federal official; b. Pasadena, Calif., Mar. 31, 1954; d. John James and Mary Ann Zajec T.; m. Milton Allen Miller, Sept. 10, 1988; 1 child, Mary Ann III. BA with honors, Stanford U., 1976; MBA, Harvard U., 1981. Mgmt. cons. Bain and Co., Boston, 1976-77; brand mgr. Procter & Gamble Co., Cin., 1977-79; summer assoc. E.F. Hutton, N.Y.C., 1980; head corp. planning The Burton Group, PLC, London, 1981-84; pres., founder Glendair Ltd., London, 1984-86; pres. London Cons. Group, London, Beverly Hills, Calif., 1987-88; mem. U.S. Presdl. Transition Team, Bus. and Fin., 1988-89; dep. asst. sec. commerce, automotive affairs, consumer goods U.S. Dept. Commerce, Washington, 1989-93; commr., chmn. L.A. Indsl. Devel. Authority, 1993-95; dep. treas. State of Calif., Sacramento, 1995-99. Bd. dirs. U.S. Coun. of Devel. Fin. Agencies, 1994-97. Founder, chair Stanford U. Fundraising, London, 1983-88; chair Reps. Abroad Absentee Voter Registration, London, 1983-88; bd. dirs. Harvard Bus. Sch. Assn., London, 1984-87; vol. Bush-Quayle Campaign, 1988; trustee Bath Coll., Eng., 1988—; apptd. by Gov. Wilson to State of Calif. Econ. Devel. Adv. Coun., 1994—, Jobs Tng. Coordinating Coun., 1998—; first vice chmn. Rep. Party L.A. County, 1996-99; chmn. Republican Party Los Angeles County, 1999—; mem. exec. bd. Coun. Calif. County Chairmen, 1999—; mem. U.S. Presdl. Transition Team, 2000-2001. Named Calif. Mother of Yr., 1997. Mem. Stanford Club U.K. (pres. 1983-88), Harvard Club N.Y., Harvard Club Washington, Nat. Assn. of Urban Rep. County Chmn. (chmn.). Roman Catholic. Home: 604 N Elm Dr Beverly Hills CA 90210-3421 Office: PO Box 71483 Los Angeles CA 90071-0483

TOMASH, ERWIN, retired computer equipment company executive; b. St. Paul, Nov. 17, 1921; s. Noah and Milka (Ehrlich) T.; m. Adelle Ruben, July 31, 1943; children: Judith Sarada Tomash Diffenbaugh, Barbara Ann Tomash Bussa. B.S., U. Minn., 1943; M.S., U. Md., 1950. Instr. elec. engring. U. Minn., 1946; assoc. dir. computer devel. Univac div. Remington Rand Corp., St. Paul, 1947-51; dir. West Coast ops. Univac div. Sperry Rand Corp., L.A., 1953-55; pres. Telemeter Magnetics, Inc., L.A., 1956-60; v.p. Ampex Corp., L.A., 1961; founder, pres. Dataproducts Corp., L.A., 1962-71, chmn. bd., 1971-80, chmn. exec. com., 1980-89; chmn. bd., dir.. Newport Corp., Irvine, Calif., 1982-94. Founder, trustee, dir. Charles Babbage Found., U. Minn.; dir. and nat. gov. Coro Found., L.A. Served to capt. Signal Corps AUS, 1943-46. Decorated Bronze Star; recipient Outstanding Grad. award U. Minn., 1983. Mem. IEEE (sr., computer entrepreneur award 1988), Am. Soc. for Technion, History of Sci. Soc., Soc. for History of Tech., Assn. Internationale du Bibliophile. Home: 110 S Rockingham Ave Los Angeles CA 90049-2514 E-mail: etomash@ieee.org

TOMASI, DONALD CHARLES, architect; b. Sacramento, Oct. 24, 1956; s. Thomas M. and Anita (Migliavacca) T.; m. Loretta Elaine Goveia, Feb. 1, 1986; children: Jeffrey, Genna, Michael. AB in Architecture with honors, U. Calif., Berkeley, 1979; MArch, U. Wash., 1982. Registered architect, Calif. Project mgr. Robert Wells and Assocs., Seattle, 1982-84, Milbrandt Architects, Seattle, 1984, T.M. Tomasi Architects, Santa Rosa, Calif., 1984-86; prin. Tomasi Architects, Santa Rosa, 1986-93, TLCD Architecture, Santa Rosa, 1993—. Grad. Leadership Santa Rosa, 1992; mem. design rev. com. Sonoma County, 1988-90; chmn. Santa Rosa Design Rev. Bd., 1990-97. Recipient Honor award Coalition for Adequate Sch. Housing, 1991, 93, 96, 99, Merit award, 1991. Mem. AIA (chpt. bd. dirs. 1990-91, 98, v.p. 1999, pres. 2000, Merit award 1986). Avocations: snow skiing, wine, travel.

TOMASSON, HELGI, dancer, choreographer, dance company executive; b. Reykjavik, Iceland, 1942; m. Marlene Rizzo, 1965; children: Kristinn, Erik. Student, Sigridur Arman, Erik Bidsted, Vera Volkova, Sch. Am. Ballet, Tivoli Pantomime Theatre, Copenhagen. With Joffrey Ballet, 1961-64; prin. dancer Harkness Ballet, 1964-70, N.Y.C. Ballet, 1970-85; artistic dir. San Francisco Ballet, 1985—, also dir. Debut with Tivoli Pantomime Theatre, 1958; created roles in A Season of Hell, 1967, Stages and Reflections, 1968, La Favorita, 1969, The Goldberg Variations, 1971, Symphony in Three Movements, 1972, Coppélia, 1974, Dybbuk Variations, 1974, Chansons Madecasses, 1975, Introduction and Allegro, 1975, Union Jack, 1976, Vienna Waltzes, 1977; choreographer Theme and Variations, Polonaise, Op. 65, 1982, Ballet d'Isoline, 1983, Menuetto (for N.Y.C. Ballet) 1984, Beads of Memory, 1985, Swan Lake, 1988, Handel-a Celebration, 1989, Sleeping Beauty, 1990, Romeo and Juliet, 1994, others. Decorated Knight Order of Falcon (Iceland), 1974, Comdr. Order of Falcon, 1990; recipient Silver medal Internat. Moscow Ballet Competition, 1969, Golden Plate award Am. Acad. Achievement, 1992, Dance Mag. award, 1992. Office: c/o San Francisco Ballet 455 Franklin St San Francisco CA 94102-4438

TOMBRELLO, THOMAS ANTHONY, JR. physics educator, consultant; b. Austin, Tex., Sept. 20, 1936; s. Thomas Anthony and Jeanette Lilian (Marcuse) T.; m. Esther Ann Hall, May 30, 1957 (div. Jan. 1976); children: Christopher Thomas, Susan Elaine, Karen Elizabeth; m. Stephanie Carhart Merton, Jan. 15, 1977; 1 stepchild, Kerstin Arusha. BA in Physics, Rice U., 1958, MA, 1960, PhD, 1961; Doctoral Degree (hon.), Uppsala (Sweden) U., 1997. Rsch. fellow in physics Calif. Inst. Tech., Pasadena, 1961-62, 64-65, asst. prof. physics, 1965-67, assoc. prof., 1967-71, prof., 1971—, William R. Kenan Jr. prof., 1997—, tech. assessment officer, 1996—, chair divsn. physics, math. and astronomy, 1998—; asst. prof. Yale U., New Haven, 1963. Cons. in field; disting. vis. prof. U. Calif.-Davis, 1984; v.p., dir. rsch. Schlumberger-Doll Rsch., Ridgefield, Conn., 1987-89; mem. U.S. V.P.'s Space Policy Adv. Bd., 1992; mem. sci. adv. bd. Ctr. of Nanoscale Sci. and Technology, Rice U., 1995—; bd. dirs. Schlumberger Tech. Corp., Schlumberger Found. Assoc. editor Nuc. Physics, 1971-91, Applications Nuc. Physics, 1980—, Radiation Effects, 1985-88, Nuc. Instruments and Methods B, 1993—. Recipient Alexander von Humboldt award von Humboldt Stiftung, U. Frankfurt, Germany, 1984-85; named Disting. Alumnus, Rice U., 1998; NSF fellow Calif. Inst. Tech., 1961-62, A.P. Sloan fellow, 1971-73. Fellow Am. Phys. Soc.; mem. AAAS, Materials Rsch. Soc., Phi Beta Kappa, Sigma Xi, Delta Phi Alpha. Democrat. Avocations: reading, jogging. Office: Calif Inst Tech Dept Physics Mail Code 200 36 Pasadena CA 91125-0001

TOMJACK, T.J. wholesale distribution executive; b. Aug. 25, 1942; BBA, U. Notre Dame, 1964. With Peat Marwick Mitchell & Co., 1964-71, Potlatch Corp., 1971-85; exec. v.p. sales North Pacific Lumber Co., Portland, Oreg., 1971-85, exec. v.p., COO, 1987, pres., 1988—, chmn., CEO, 1989—. Office: North Pacific Group Inc 815 NE Davis Portland OR 97208-3915

TOMLINSON, WARREN LEON, lawyer; b. Denver, Apr. 2, 1930; s. Leslie Aultimer and Esther (Hasler) T.; m. Lois Elaine Retallack, Aug. 8, 1953 (div. 1987); children: Stephanie Lynn, Brett Louis; m. Linda Jane Beville, May 17, 1989. BA, U. Denver, 1951; JD, NYU, 1954. Bar: Colo. 1954, U.S. Dist. Ct. Colo., U.S. Ct. Appeals (10th cir.) 1958, U.S. Supreme Ct.. 1960. Assoc. Holland & Hart, Denver, 1958-63, ptnr., 1963-95, mediator, arbitrator, 1995—. Contbr. numerous articles to profl. jours. Lt. U.S. Army, 1954-58. Fellow Coll. Labor and Employment Lawyers; mem. ABA (chmn. law practice mgmt. sect. 1988-89, charter fellow Coll. of Law Practice Mgmt. 1994). Republican. Episcopalian. Avocations: skiing, white-water rafting. Home: 5017 Main Gore Dr S Apt 4 Vail CO 81657-5426 Office: Holland & Hart 555 17th St Ste 2900 Denver CO 80202-3979 E-mail: wltvail@aol.com

TOMLINSON, WILLIAM M. lawyer; b. Paris, France, Sept. 2, 1948; BA, Princeton U., 1970; JD, U. Oreg., 1974. Bar: Oreg. 1974, Wash. 1986. Atty. Lindsay, Hart, Neil & Weigler, Portland, Oreg. Mem. ABA (mem. torts and ins. practice sect.), Oreg. State Bar, Oreg. Assn. Def. Counsel, Wash. State Bar Assn., Multnomah County Bar Assn. Office: Lindsay Hart Neil & Weigler 1300 SW 5th Ave Ste 3400 Portland OR 97201-5640

TOMLINSON-KEASEY, CAROL ANN, university administrator; b. Washington, Oct. 15, 1942; d. Robert Bruce and Geraldine (Howe) Tomlinson; m. Charles Blake Keasey, June 13, 1964; children: Kai Linson, Amber Lynn. BS, Pa. State U., 1964; MS, Iowa State U., 1966; PhD, U. Calif., Berkeley, 1970. Lic. psychologist, Calif. Asst. prof. psychology Trenton (N.J.) State Coll., 1969-70, Rutgers U., New Brunswick, N.J., 1970-72; prof. U. Nebr., Lincoln, 1972-77, U. Calif., Riverside, 1977-92, acting dean Coll. Humanities and Social Scis., 1986-88, chmn. dept. psychology, 1989-92, vice provost for academic planning and pers. Davis, 1992-97, vice provost for academic initiatives, 1997-99, chancellor, 1999—. Author: Child's Eye View, 1980, Child Development, 1985; also numerous chpts. to books; articles to profl. jours. Recipient Disting. Tchr. award U. Calif., 1986. Mem. APA, Soc. Rsch. in Child Devel., Riverside Aquatics Assn. (pres.). Office: 1170 W Olive Ave Ste I Merced CA 95348-1959

TOMPKINS, RONALD K. surgeon; b. Malta, Ohio, Oct. 14, 1934; s. Kenneth Steidley and Mildred Lillian (Loomis) T.; m. Suzanne Colbert, June 9, 1956; children: Gregory Alan, Teresa Susan, Geoffrey Stuart. BA, Ohio U., 1956; MD, Johns Hopkins U., 1960; MS, Ohio State U., 1968; DSc (hon.), U. Bordeaux, 1995. Diplomate: Am. Bd. Surgery. Intern in surgery Ohio State U., 1960-61, resident in surgery, 1964-68, adminstrv. chief resident in surgery, 1968-69, NIH trainee in acad. surgery, instr. physiol. chemistry, 1966-69; asst. prof. surgery UCLA, 1969-73, asso. prof., 1973-79, prof., 1979-2001; prof. emeritus, 2001—; chmn. basic surg. tng. program UCLA, 1970-79, asst. dean student affairs, 1979-82, chief div. gen. surgery, 1982-88, chief gastrointestinal surgery, 1986-97, assoc. dean, 1988-91, dir. surg. edn., 1996—. Cons. VA Hosps. Editor-in-chief World Jour. Surgery, 1993— With M.C. USAF, 1961-64. NIH grantee, 1968-70; John A. Hartford Found. grantee, 1970-79; Royal Soc. Medicine Eng. travelling fellow, 1976-77 Fellow ACS; mem. Am. Surg. Assn., Am. Gastroenterol. Assn., Am. Fedn. Clin. Rsch. Am. Inst. Nutrition, AMA, Assn. Acad. Surgery, Pacific Coast Surg. Assn. (recorder 1986-91, pres. 1995), Soc. Clin. Surgery, Soc. Surgery Alimentary Tract (sec. 1982-85, pres.-elect 1985, pres. 1986, chmn. bd. trustees 1987), Soc. Univ. Surgeons, Societe Internationale de Chirurgie (U.S. chpt. sec. 1990-94, pres. 1996-98), Internat. Biliary Assn. (pres. 1979-81), Bay Surg. Soc., L.A. Surg. Soc. (pres. 1981), ACS (So. Calif. chpt. pres. 1987), Robert M. Zollinger/Ohio State U. Surg. Soc. (pres. 1988-90), Longmire Surg. Soc. (pres. 1997-99), Phi Beta Kappa, Sigma Xi, Alpha Omega Alpha, Delta Tau Delta. Republican. Achievements include research numerous publs. in gastrointestinal surgery and gastrointestinal metabolism and biochemistry. Office: U Calif Dept of Surgery Los Angeles CA 90024

TOMPKINS, SUSIE, apparel company executive, creative director; children: Quincey, Summer. Design cons. Esprit de Corp, San Francisco. Office: Esprit de Corps Internat 3 Embarcadero Ctr Ste 2290 San Francisco CA 94111-4045 also: 1370 Broadway Fl 16 New York NY 10018-7302

TOMS, JUSTINE WILLIS, educational organization executive; b. Evanston, Ill., Oct. 16, 1942; d. Robert Jacques and Ruth (Herzfeld) W.; m. Donald Carroll Welch, Nov. 1962 (div. 1969); 1 child, Robert Gregory Welch; m. Michael Anthony Toms, Dec. 16, 1972. BS, Auburn U., 1967. Elem. sch. tchr. Sylacauga (Ala.) Sch. System, 1966-69; exec. dir. New Dimensions Radio, Ukiah, Calif., 1973—. Seminar leader in field. Co-author: True Work: Doing What You Love and Loving What You Do, 1998; editor (quar. jour.) New Dimensions Jour., 1987—. Democrat. Buddhist. Avocations: horseback riding, drumming.

TONELLO-STUART, ENRICA MARIA, political economist; b. Monza, Italy; d. Alessandro P. and Maddalena M. (Marangoni) Tonello; m. Albert E. Smith; m. Charles L. Stuart. BA in Internat. Affairs, Econs., U. Colo., 1961; MA, Claremont Grad. Sch., 1966, PhD, 1971. Sales mgr. Met. Life Ins. Co., 1974-79; pres., CEO, ETS R&D, Inc., Palos Verdes Peninsula, Calif., 1977—. Dean internat. studies program Union U., L.A. and Tokyo; lectr. internat. affairs and mktg. UCLA Ext., Union U. Pub., editor Tomorrow Outline Jour., 1963—, The Monitor, 1988; pub. World Regionalism-An Ecological Analysis, 1971, A Proposal for the Reorganization of the United Nations, 1966, The Persuasion Technocracy, Its Forms, Techniques and Potentials, 1966, The Role of the Multinationals in the Emerging Globalism, 1978; developed the theory of social ecology and econsociometry. Organizer 1st family assistance program Langley FB Tractical Air Command, 1956-58. Recipient vol. svc. award VA, 1956-58, ARC svc. award, 1950-58. Mem. Corp. Planners Assn. (treas. 1974-79), Investigative Reporters and Editors, World Future Soc. (pres. 1974-75), Asian Bus. League, Soc. Environ. Journalists, Chinese Am. Assn. (life), Japan Am. Assn., L.A. World Trade Ctr., Palos Verdes C. of C. (legis. com.), L.A. Press Club (bd. dirs.), Zonta (chmn. internat. com. South Bay), Pi Sigma Alpha. Avocations: writing, collecting old books and maps, community service, travel.

TONG, SIU WING, computer programmer; b. Hong Kong, May 20, 1950; came to U.S., 1968; BA, U. Calif., Berkeley, 1972; PhD, Harvard U., 1979; MS, U. Lowell, 1984. Rsch. assoc. Brookhaven Nat. Lab., Upton, N.Y., 1979-83; software engr. Honeywell Info. Systems, Billerica, Mass., 1984-85; sr. programmer, analyst Hui Computer Cons., Berkeley, Calif., 1985-88; sr. v.p. devel., chief fin. officer Surgicenter Info. Systems, Inc., Orinda, 1989-94; sr. sys. specialist Info. Sys. Divsn. Contra Costa County Health Svcs., Martinez, 1995-97, info. tech. supr. Info. Sys. Divsn., 1997—. Vol. tchr. Boston Chinatown Saturday Adult Edn. Program of Tufts Med. Sch., 1977-79. Muscular Dystrophy Assn. fellow, 1980-82. Mem. AAAS, IEEE, Assn. Computing Machinery, N.Y. Acad. Scis. Home: 17 Beaconsfield Ct Orinda CA 94563-4203 Office: Contra Costa County Health Svcs 595 Center Ave Ste 210 Martinez CA 94553-4634 E-mail: swtong@hsd.co.contra-costa.ca.us

TONJES, MARIAN JEANNETTE BENTON, education educator; b. Rockville Center, N.Y., Feb. 16, 1929; d. Millard Warren and Felicia E. (Tyler) Benton; m. Charles F. Tonjes (div. 1965); children: Jeffrey Charles, Kenneth Warren. BA, U. N.Mex., 1951, cert., 1966, MA, 1969; EdD, U. Miami, 1975. Dir. recreation Stuyvesant Town Housing Project, N.Y.C., 1951-53; tchr. music., phys. edn. Sunset Mesa Day Sch., Albuquerque, 1953-54; tchr. remedial reading Zia Elem. Sch., Albuquerque, 1965-67; tchr. secondary devel. reading Rio Grande High Sch., Albuquerque, 1967-69; rsch. asst. reading Southwestern Coop. Ednl. Lab., Albuquerque, 1969-71; assoc. dir., vis. instr. Fla. Ctr. Tchr. Tng. Materials U. Miami, 1971-72; asst. prof. U.S. Internat. U., San Diego, 1972-75; prof. edn. Western Wash. U., Bellingham, 1975-94, prof. emerita, 1994—; dir. summer study at Oriel Coll. Oxford (Eng.) U., 1979-94. Adj. prof. U. N.Mex., Albuquerque, 1995—, reading supr. Manzanita Ctr., 1968; vis. prof. adult edn. Palomar (Calif.) Jr. Coll., 1974; vis. prof. U. Guam, Mangilao, 1989-90; spkr., cons. in field; invited guest Russian Reading Assn., Moscow, 1992. Author: (with Miles V. Zintz) Teaching Reading/Thinking Study Skills in Content Classroom, 3rd edit., Secondary Reading, Writing and Learning, 1991, (with Roy Wolpow and Miles Zintz) Integrated Content Literacy, 1999. Trustee The White Mountain Sch., 2000—; tour assoc. In the Footsteps of Dickens, England, 2001. Tng. Tchr. Trainers grantee, 1975; NDEA fellow Okla. State U., 1969. Mem.: Internat. Soc. Rwy. Travelers, Albuquerque Tennis Club, Delta Delta Delta, Am. Reading Forum (chmn. bd. dirs. 1983—85), Internat. Reading Assn. (mem. travel, interchange and study tours com. 1984—86, mem. non-print media and reading com. 1980—83, workshop dir. S.W. regional confs. 1982, mem. com. internat. devel. N.Am. 1991—96, Outstanding Tchr. Educator 1988—), UK Reading Assn. (spkr. 1977—93, spkr. Edinburgh 1991, spkr. Malmo 1993, spkr. Budapest 1995), European Conf. in Reading (spkr. Berlin 1989), European Coun. Internat. Schs. (The Hague, spkr. 1993), Am. Reading Forum, World Congress in Reading Buenos Aires (spkr. 1994), PEO (past chpt. pres.), Nat. Coun. Tchrs. English, Internat. Reading Assn. Avocations: miniatures, tennis, bridge, art, travel.

TONN, ELVERNE MERYL, pediatric dentist, dental benefits consultant, forensic odontologist; b. Stockton, Calif., Dec. 10, 1929; s. Emanuel M. and Lorna Darlene (Bryant) T.; m. Ann G. Richardson, Oct. 28, 1951; children: James Edward, Susan Elaine Tonn. AA, La Sierra U., Riverside, Calif., 1949; DDS, U. So. Calif., 1955; BS, Regents Coll., U. State N.Y., 1984. Lic. dentist; diplomate Am. Bd. Forensic Dentistry, Am. Bd. Quality Assurance and Utilization Rev. Physicians; cert. dental benefits cons. Pediatric dentist, assoc. Walker Dental Group, Long Beach, Calif., 1957-59, Children's Dental Clinic, Sunnyvale, 1959-61; pediatric dentist in pvt. practice Mountain View, 1961-72; pediatric dentist, ptrn. Pediatric Dentistry Assocs., Los Altos, 1972-83; pediatric dentist, ptnr. Valley Oak Dental Group, Manteca, 1987—; from clin. instr. to assoc. prof. U. Pacific, San Francisco, 1964-84; assoc. prof. U. Calif., San Francisco, 1984-86. ; pediatric dental cons. Delta Dental Plan, San Francisco, 1985—; chief dental staff El Camino Hosp., Mountain View, 1964-65, 84-85; lectr. in field. Weekly columnist Manteca Bull., 1987-92; producer 2 teaching videos, 1986; contbr. articles to profl. jours. Lectr. to elem. students on dental health Manteca Unified Sch. Dist., 1982—; dental health screener Elem. Schs., San Joaquin County Pub. Health, 1989-92; dental cons. Interplast program Stanford U. Sch. Medicine. Capt. U.S. Army, 1955-57. Fellow Am. Coll. Dentists, Internat. Coll. Dentists, Am. Acad. Pediatric Dentistry, Royal Soc. Health (Eng.), Acad. of Dentistry for Handicapped, Pierre Fauchard Acad., Acad. Dental Materials, Am. Soc. Dentistry for Children; mem. ADA, Internat. Assn. Pediatric Dentistry, Internat. Assn. Dental Rsch., Am. Acad. Forensic Scis., Am. Soc. Forensic Odontology, Fedn. Dentaire Internationale, Am. Assn. Dental Cons., Calif. Dental Assn., Calif. Soc. Dentistry for Children (pres. 1968), Calif. Soc. Pediatric Dentists, N.Y. Acad. Scis., Calif. Acad. Sci., Rotary Internat., Nat. Assn. for Healthcare Quality, Am. Coll. Med. Quality. Republican. Avocations: photography, travel, medieval history. Home: 374 Laurelwood Cir Manteca CA 95336-7122 Office: Valley Oak Dental Group Inc 1507 W Yosemite Ave Manteca CA 95337-5182 Fax: 209-823-7836. E-mail: emtonn@aol.com

TONSETH, RALPH G. airport executive; Dir. aviation San Jose (Calif.) Airport, 1990—. Office: San Jose Airport 1732 N 1st St Ste 600 San Jose CA 95112-4544

TOOKEY, ROBERT CLARENCE, consulting actuary; b. Santa Monica, Calif., Mar. 21, 1925; s. Clarence Hall and Minerva Maconachie (Anderson) T.; m. Marcia Louise Hickman, Sept. 15, 1956; children: John Hall, Jennifer Louise, Thomas Anderson. BS, Calif. Inst. Tech., 1945; MS, U. Mich., 1947. With Prudential Ins. Co. Am., Newark, 1947-49; assoc. actuary in group Pacific Mut. Life Ins. Co., L.A., 1949-55; asst. v.p. in charge reins. sales and svc. for 17 western states Lincoln Nat. Life Ins. Co., Ft. Wayne, Ind., 1955-61; dir. actuarial svcs. Peat, Marwick, Mitchell & Co., Chgo., 1961-63; mng. prin. So. Calif. office Milliman & Robertson, cons. actuaries, Pasadena, 1963-76; pres. Robert Tookey Assocs., Inc., 1977—. Committeeman troop 501 Boy Scouts Am., 1969-72. Served to lt. (j.g.) USNR, 1943-45, 51-52. Fellow Soc. Actuaries, Conf. Consulting Actuaries; mem. Am. Acad. Actuaries, Pacific Ins. Conf., Rotary Club (Pasadena), Union League Club (Chgo.). Home and Office: PO Box 646 La Canada CA 91012-0646

TOOLE, KENNETH R., JR. state senator; b. Missoula, Mont., June 18, 1955; m. Nancy Toole; 3 children. BA, U. Mont., 1981. Program dir. Rural Employment Opportunities; investigator Mont. Human Rights Commn.; personnel dir. Mont. Office Pub. Interest; co-dir. Mont. Human Rights Network, 1996-2000; Dem. senator dist. 27 Mont. State Senate, 2000—. Mem. Mont. Adv. Com. to U.S. Commn. on Civil Rights. Caucus chair N.W. Energy Coalition; bd. dirs. No. Plains Resource Coun., Plan Helena, Renewable N.W.; chair Local Ctrl. Com. Dems.; west chair rep. Mont. State Dem. Bd. Office: PO Box 1462 Helena MT 59624 E-mail: samt@mcn.net

TOOLEY, CHARLES FREDERICK, communications executive, consultant; b. Seattle, Sept. 29, 1947; s. Creath Athol and Catherine Ella (Wainman) T.; m. Valerie Adele Gose, Mar. 7, 1981 (dec. Feb. 1991); children: Paige Arlene Chytka, Marni Higdon Tooley; m. Joan Marie Stapleton, Feb. 21, 1998. BA, Lynchburg Coll., 1968. Producer, stage mgr., tech. dir. various theatre cos. and performing arts orgns., 1965-74; field underwriter N.Y. Life Ins. Co., Billings, Mont., 1974-77; market adminstr. Mountain Bell Telephone Co., Butte and Billings, 1978-83; pres. BCC Inc., Billings, 1983—. Dir. Mont. Elec. and Gas Alliance, 2000—. Mem. Mont. Arts Coun., 1982-92, Mont. Cultural Advocacy, 1982-92; Christian Chs. in Mont., 1983—, divsn. of overseas ministries Christian Ch. Disciples of Christ, 1997—; elder Ctrl. Christian Ch., Billings, 1983—; precinct committeeman Dem. party, Billings, 1976—; del. Dem. Nat. Conv., 1980; mem. Mont. Dem. Exec. Bd., 1982-87; mem. adv. bd. Salvation Army, Billings, 1984—; Dem. candidate Mont. Ho. of Reps., 1986; mem. Billings City Coun., 1988-94, mayor pro tem, 1992-94; mayor City of Billings, 1996—; mem. Common Global Ministries, 1997—; chair U.S. Com. Mayors on Resource Conservation and Population, 1999—. Sgt. U.S. Army, 1969-72, Vietnam. Recipient communication and leadership award Toastmasters Internat., 1999. Mem. Masons, Shriners, Elks. Mem. Disciples of Christ. Avocations: theatre productions.

TOPP, ALPHONSO AXEL, JR. environmental scientist, consultant; b. Indpls., Oct. 15, 1920; s. Alphonso Axel and Emilia (Karlsson) T.; m. Mary Catherine Virtue, July 7, 1942; children: Karen, Susan, Linda, Sylvia, Peter, Astrid, Heidi, Eric, Megan, Katrina. BS in Chem. Engring., Purdue U., 1942; MS, UCLA, 1948. Commd. 2d lt. U.S. Army, 1942, advanced through grades to col., 1966, ret., 1970; environ. protection scientist radiation protection sect. State of N. Mex., Santa Fe, 1970-78, program mgr. licensing and registration sect., 1978-81, chief radiation protection bur., 1981-83, cons., 1984—. Decorated Legion of Merit, Bronze Star with 2 oak leaf clusters, U.S. Army. Mem. Rotary, Triangle, Sigma Xi. Republican. Presbyterian. Home and Office: 1200 Calle Cordoniz Los Osos CA 93402-4428 E-mail: alphons188@aol.com

TORBET, LAURA, writer, artist, photographer, graphic designer; b. Paterson, N.J., Aug. 23, 1942; d. Earl Buchanan and Ruth Claire (Ehlers) Robbins; m. Bruce J. Torbet, Sept. 9, 1967 (div. 1971); m. Peter H. Morrison, June 19, 1983 (dec. Nov. 1988); m. Salam Habibi, Aug. 23, 1995 (div. 2000). BA, BFA, Ohio Wesleyan U., 1964. Mng. editor Suburban Life mag., East Orange, N.J., 1964-65; asst. pub. rels. dir. United Funds N.J., Newark, 1965-67; art dir. Alitalia Airlines, N.Y.C., 1967-69; propr. Laura Torbet Studio, N.Y.C., 1969-84. Author: Macrame You Can Wear, 1972, Clothing Liberation, 1973, Leathercraft You Can Wear, 1975, The T-Shirt Book, 1976, The Complete Book of Skateboarding, 1976, How To Do Everything with Markers, 1977; (with Doug McLaggan) Squash: How to Play, How to Win, 1977, The Complete Book of Mopeds, 1978; (with Luree Nicholson) How to Fight Fair With Your Kids...and Win!, 1980; editor: Helena Rubenstein's Book of the Sun, 1979, The Encyclopedia of Crafts, 1980; (with George Bach) A Time for Caring, 1983, The Inner

Enemy, 1983; (with Hap Hatton) Helpful Hints for Hard Times, 1982, The Virgin Homeowners Handbook, 1984, Helpful Hints for Better Living, 1984; (with James Braly) Dr. Braly's Optimum Health Program, 1985; (with Bernard Gittelson) Intangible Evidence, 1987; (as writer for Harville Hendrix) Keeping the Love Your Find, 1992, The Couples Companion, 1994, The Personal Companion, 1996, (as writer for Peter Lambrou and George Pratt) Instant Emotional Healing, 1999; editor, ghostwriter, co-author books. Pres., bd. dirs. The Living/Dying Project. Mem. Boss Ladies. Home and Office: 1111 Butterfield Rd San Anselmo CA 94960-1181 E-mail: lulutorbet@aol.com

TORGERSON, JOHN, state senator; b. Iowa City, Oct. 21, 1947; m. Marjorie Torgerson; children: Leila, Jolene, Marissa. Gen. edn. diploma, 1966. Mem. Kenai Peninsula Borough Assembly; Rep. senator dist. D Alaska State Senate, 1994—. Former pres. Alaska Mcpl. League, Kenai Peninsula Caucus. Founding bd. dirs., past pres. Peninsula Winter Games; mem., past pres. Kenai Eagles; mem. Kasilof Eagles, Pioneers of Alaska. With U.S. Army. Mem. Nat. Assn. Devel. Orgns., VFW (life), Seward Am. Legion, Soldotna Elks, Soldotna C. of C. (past pres.), Ala. C. of C. (former bd. dirs.). Avocations: hiking, goldpanning. Office: Alaska State Senate State Capitol Rm 427 Juneau AK 99801-1182 also: Ste 101B 35477 Kenai Spur Hwy Kenai AK 99669 Fax: 907 465-4779; 907 260-3044. E-mail: Senator_John_Torgerson@legis.state.ak.us

TORGESON, JOHN, state senator; b. Iowa City, Oct. 21, 1947; m. Marjorie Torgeson; children: Leila, Jolene, Marissa. Grad. H.S. Mem. Alaska State Senate, co-chair fin. com., mem. senate judiciary com., mem. legis. coun., mem. select com. on legis. ethics. Former mem. Kenai Peninsula Borough Assembly; former pres. Alaska Mcpl. League and Kenai Peninsula Caucus; western states rep. Nat. Assn. Devel. Orgn.; founding bd. mem., past pres. Peninsula Winter Games. With U.S. Army. Mem. Soldotna C. of C. (past pres.), Kenai Eagles (past pres.), Soldotna Elks, Kasilof Eagles, Am. Legion (seward), Pioneers of Alaska, VFW (life). Republican. Avocations: hiking, goldpanning. Office: State Capitol 120 4th St Rm 30 Juneau AK 99801-1142 Fax: 907-465-3922

TORGOW, EUGENE N. electrical engineer; b. Bronx, N.Y., Nov. 26, 1925; s. Frank and Blanche Anita (Revzin) T.; m. Cynthia Silver, Mar. 19, 1950; children: Joan, Martha, Ellen. BSEE, Cooper Union, 1946; MSEE, Poly. Inst. Bklyn., 1949; Engr. in E.E., Poly. Inst. N.Y., 1980; postgrad., UCLA, 1983. Rsch. assoc., sect. leader Microwave Rsch. Inst., Poly. Inst. Bklyn., 1947-51, 53-60, instr., 1954-59; mgr. microwave lab. A.B. Dumont Labs, East Patterson, N.J., 1951-53; chief engr., mgr. microwave products Dorne & Magolin, Inc., Westbury, L.I., N.Y., 1960-64; chief engr., dir. rsch., dir. mktg. Rantec divsn. Emerson Electric, Calabasas, Calif., 1964-68; with Missle Sys. Group, Hughes Aircraft Co., Canoga Park, 1968-85, assoc. labs. mgr., 1981-85. Cons. various electronics firms, N.Y.C., 1956-59; cons., 1986—; cons. Exec. Svc. Corps of So. Calif., 1996—; pres. Cons. Adv. Coun., 1999-2000; lectr. Calif. State U., Northridge, 1986 91. Contbr. articles to profl. jours.; patentee in field. Mem. Fair Housing Coun., San Fernando Valley, L.A., 1967—; mem. L.A. County Mus. Assn., 1976—; bd. trustees Amiotropic Lateral Sclerosis Assn. So. Calif., 1999—. Served with USAAF, 1946-47. Recipient Engr. '85 Merit award San Fernando Valley Engrs. Coun., 1985. Fellow IEEE, Inst. for Advancement Engring.; mem. WINCON (bd. dirs. 1984-89, chmn. bd. dirs. 1988-89), Microwave Theory and Techniques Soc. of IEEE (pres. 1966, mem. adminstrn. com. 1962-72, Svc. award 1978), Accreditation Bd. Engring. and Tech. (mem. engring. accreditation com. 1994-99) Hughes Mgmt. Club (edn. chmn. 1979-80), Sigma Xi. Democrat. Office: 9531 Donna Ave Northridge CA 91324-1816

TORLAKSON, TOM A. state senator; b. Daly City, Calif., July 19, 1949; m. Diana Torlakson; children: Tiffany, Tamara. BA, U. Calif., Berkeley, 1971, Tchg. Cert., 1972, MA, 1977. Tchr., coach, 1973-83; landscaper, 1977; with Kosich Ins. Co., 1989—; Dem. rep. dist. 11 Calif. Ho. of Reps., 1996-2000; Dem. senator dist. 7 Calif. State Senate, 2000—. Mem. budget and local govt. coms. Calif. Ho. of Reps., chair select com. on jobs-housing balance and transp. Mem. Delta Kiwanis, 1975—; dir. Holiday Run and Walk Against Drugs, 1976—; past pres. Many Hands Recycling Ctr., Mt. Diable Regional Group, Sierra Club, 1966—; mem. Planning and Conservation League, Save San Francisco Assn., Sierra Club, 1966—; mem. Antioch City Coun., 1978-80; mem. bd. suprs. Contra Costa County, 1980-96; co-chair Local Govt. Caucus, 1997—; mem. SMART Growth Caucus, 1999—. With Merchant Marines, 1967-69. Mem. NAACP (life), Pitts. C. of C., Antioch C. of C., Concord C. of C. Office: 815 Estudillo St Martinez CA 94553 also: Calif State Senate PO Box 942849 State Capitol Rm 2003 Sacramento CA 94249-0010 E-mail: tom@tomtorlakson.com, Assemblymember.Torlakson@assembly.ca.gov

TORME, MARGARET ANNE, public relations executive, communications consultant; b. Indpls., Apr. 5, 1943; d. Ira G. and Margaret Joy (Wright) Barker; children: Karen Anne, Leah Vanessa. Student, Coll. San Mateo, 1961-65. Pub. rels. mgr. Hoefer, Dieterich & Brown (now Chiat-Day), San Francisco, 1964-73; v.p., co-founder, creative dir. Lowry & Ptnrs., San Francisco, 1975-83; pres., founder Torme & Co., San Francisco, 1983—. Cons. in communications. Mem. Coun. Pub. Rels. Firms, San Francisco C. of C. (Outstanding Achievement award for Women Entrepreneurs 1987), Jr. League (adv. bd.), Pub. Rels. Orgn. Internat. (v.p., dir.). Office: 545 Sansome St San Francisco CA 94111-2908

TORNESE, JUDITH M. financial institution executive; b. Pitts., Aug. 26, 1942; d. Ilario and Rose Mary Tornese; m. Jerry E. Winters. Student, U. Pitts., Golden Gate U. CPCU. Various positions Transam Corp., San Francisco, 1971-81; dir. risk mgmt. TransAm. Corp., San Francisco, 1981-87; dir. X.L. Ins. Co., 1987-92; v.p. risk mgmt. TransAm. Corp., San Francisco, 1987—; dir., chair devel. com. St. Vincent de Paul Soc., 1994—. Dir. San Francisco Suicide Prevention, 1984-90; mem. Earthquake Ins. and Recovery Fin. Com. of Seismic Safety Commn., 1988-91. Named Risk Mgr. of Yr. Bus. Ins. Mag., 1992. Mem. Risk and Ins. Mgmt. Soc. (soc. dir. 1981—, chair nominating com. 1987-92, strategic planning com., 1996—), Mfr.'s Alliance Productivity and Innovation (risk mgmt. coun. 1981-85). Office: Transam Corp 600 Montgomery St San Francisco CA 94111-2702

TORRES, ART, state legislator; b. L.A. children: Joaquin, Danielle. AA, East L.A. C.C.; BA, U. Calif., Santa Cruz; JD, U. Calif. John F. Kennedy teaching fellow Harvard U.; senator State of Calif., L.A. Chmn. Senate Com. Ins., Claims and Corps., Assembly Health Com., Senate Toxics and Pub. Safety Mgmt. Com., Select Com. Pacific Rim, Senate Spl. Rask Force on New L.A.; founder Calif. EPA; sr. mem. Senate Edn. Com.; author 1992 Immigrant Workforce Preparation Act; mem. Nat. Conf. State Legislatures Coalition on Immigration, Senate Appropriations Com., Senate Energy and Pub. Utilities Com., Senate Govtl. Orgn. Com., Senate Judiciary Com., Senate Natural Resources Com., Senate Transp. Com., chmn. California Dem. Party. Mem. Coun. Fgn. Rels., N.Y., Nat. Commn. Internat. Migration and Econ. Devel.; participant IVth Nobel Prizewinners Meeting Nova Spes Internat. Found., Vatican, Rome, 1989—. Recipient Legislator of Yr. award Calif. Orgn. Policy and Sheriffs, 1990, Outstanding Legislator of Yr. award Calif. Sch. Bd. Assn., 1990, Outstanding Alumnus award U. Calif. Santa Cruz, Dreamer award Boys and Girls Club Am., 1990, Achievement award Latin Am. Law Enforcement Assn., 1992. Office: 911 20th St Sacramento CA 95814-3115

TORRES, ESTEBAN EDWARD, former congressman, business executive; b. Miami, Ariz., Jan. 27, 1930; s. Esteban Torres and Rena Baron (Gomez) T.; m. Arcy Sanchez, Jan. 22, 1955; children: Carmen D'Arcy, Rena Denise, Camille Bianca, Selina Andre, Esteban Adrian. Student, East Los Angeles Coll., 1960, Calif. State U., Los Angeles, 1963, U. Md., , 1965, Am. U., 1966; PhD (hon.), Nat. U., 1987. Chief steward United Auto Workers, local 230, 1954-63, dir. polit. com., 1963; organizer, internat. rep. United Auto Workers (local 230), Washington, 1964; asst. dir. Internat. Affairs Dept., 1975-77; dir. Inter-Am. Bureau for Latin Am., Caribbean, 1965-67; exec. dir. E. Los Angeles Community Union (TELACU), 1967-74; U.S. ambassador to UNESCO, Paris, 1977-79; chmn. Geneva Grp., 1977-78; chmn. U.S. del. Gen. Conf., 1978; spl. asst. to pres. U.S., dir. White House Office Hispanic Affairs, 1979-81; mem. 98th-103rd Congresses from 34th Dist. Calif., 1983-98; mem. appropriations com., subcom. fgn. ops., subcom. transp. Campaign coordinator Jerry Brown for Gov., 1974; Hispanic coordinator Los Angeles County campaign Jimmy Carter for Pres., 1976; mem. Sec. of State Adv. Group, 1979-81; v.p. Nat. Congress Community Econ. Devel., 1973-74; pres. Congress Mex.-Am. Unity, 1970-71, Los Angeles Plaza de la Raza Cultural Center, 1974; dir. Nat. Com. on Citizens Broadcasting, 1977; cons. U.S. Congress office of tech. assessment, 1976-77; del to U.S. Congress European Parliament meetings, 1984; ofcl. congl. observer Geneva Arms Control Talks; chmn. Congl. Hispanic Caucus, 1987; speaker Wrights Del. to USSR, 1987; Dem. dep. Whip, 1990; chmn. Nat. Latino Media Coun. Contbr. numerous articles to profl. jours. Co-chmn. Nat. Hispanic Dems., 1988—; chmn. Japan-Hispanic Inst. Inc.; bd. visitors Sch. Architecture U. Calif. at Los Angeles, 1971-73; bd. dirs. Los Angeles County Econ. Devel. Com., 1972-75, Internat. Devel. Conf., 1976-78; chmn. Congrl. Hispanic Caucus, 1985-86; pres. Plaza de la Raza Cultural Ctr., 1972-73; trustee Am. Coll. Paris, 1977-79. Served in AUS, 1949-53, ETO. Recipient Congrl. award Nat. Leadership award 1997. Mem. Americans for Dem. Action (exec. bd. 1975-77), VFW Post 6315, Pico Rivera, Calif., Am. Legion, Smithsonian Inst. (regent 1997—), S.W. Voter Inst., Calif. Transp. Commn. Address: 908 E Lucille Ave West Covina CA 91790-5221*

TORRES, RALPH CHON, minister; b. San José, Calif., Oct. 18, 1948; s. Chon Poncé and Dora (Grijalva) T.; m. Pamela Ellen Hansen, Mar. 6, 1971; children: Chon, Brita, Samuel, Sarah. BTh, L.I.F.E. Bible Coll., L.A., 1970. Ordained to ministry Internat. Ch. of the Foursquare Gospel, 1981. Missionary asst. Internat. Ch. of Foursquare Gospel, Mexicali, Mex., 1970, youth pastor Redondo Beach, Calif., 1971-72, Pueblo, Colo., 1972-74; sr. pastor Internat. Ch. of Foursquare Gospel., Pasadena, Calif., 1984—; youth pastor Ch. on the Way, Van Nuys, 1975-84. Asst., dir. children's camps, Jr. and Sr. High camps for So. Calif. Dist. Foursquare Chs., 1978—; tchr. L.I.F.E. Bible Coll., L.A., 1979-86; bd. dirs. Holy Ghost Repair Svc., Hollywood, Calif., Centrum of Hollywood, Christians in Govt., L.A., Camp Cedar Crest, Running Springs, Calif.; bd. dirs., speaker Mainstream Inc., Tacoma, 1978-83. Composer: Kids of the Kingdom, 1976. Mem. Prop. 98 Sch. Report Card Com., Pasadena, 1989-90; adv. com. Marshall Fundamental Sch., Pasadena, 1989-90, Pasadena Unified Sch. Dist., 1990—. Recipient commendation for svc. Mayor of Pasadena, 1990. Office: Pasadena Foursquare Ch 174 Harkness Ave Pasadena CA 91106-2007

TORRES-GIL, FERNANDO M. federal official, academic administrator; b. Salinas, Calif., June 24, 1948; BA in Polit. Sci., San Jose State U., 1970; MSW, Brandeis U., 1972, PhD, 1976. Spl. asst. to sec. Dept. Health, Edn. and Welfare, Washington, 1978 79, Dept. Health and Human Svcs., Washington, 1979-80, asst. sec. for aging, 1993—; prof. gerontology and pub. adminstrn. U. So. Calif., 1981-91, assoc. dir. Nat. Resource Ctr. on Minority Aging Populations, 1988-92, prof. social welfare, 1991-93; assoc. dean Sch. Pub. Policy and Soc. Rsch. UCLA. Staff dir. Select Com. on Aging, U.S. Ho. of Reps., Washington, 1985-87. Contbr. articles to profl. jours. White House fellow, 1978-79. Mem. Am. Soc. Aging (pres. 1989-92). Office: UCLA Sch Pub Plicy & Social Rsch Box 951656 3250 Public Policy Blvd Los Angeles CA 90095-1656

TORREY, ELLA KING, academic administrator; Graduate, Yale U., U. Miss. Program officer for culture The Pew Charitable Trusts, 1995; founder, dir. Pew Fellowships in the Arts, 1985-91, 1985-91; pres. San Francisco Art Inst., 1995—. Founder, pres. Grantmakers in the Arts; panelist NEA, NEH; mem. Mayor's Cultural Adv. Coun. City of Phila.; art adv. com., adv. com. Art in City Hall; cons., adv. in field; curator Ctr. Study So. Culture, Miss., Whitney Mus., N.Y.C., Harvard Theater Collection, Cambridge, Mass., others; mem. profl. coms. Coun. on Founds. Bd. dirs. nat. Campaign Freedom of Expression. Office: San Francisco Art Inst President's Office 800 Chestnut St San Francisco CA 94133-2206

TORREY, JAMES D. mayor, communications executive, consultant; b. Drayton, N.D., July 16, 1940; s. Howard J. Torrey and Gertrude (Carpenter) Steenson; m. Katherine Joann Kowal, Sept. 2, 1958; children: Tamara, Timonthy (dec.), Teresa, Todd. Student, U. Oreg., 1959-61. Mgr. Waldport (Oreg.) Food Market, 1959-67; dist. mgr. Obie Outdoor Advt., Aberdeen, Wash., 1967-68; dir. sales Obie Media Corp., Eugene, Oreg., 1968-71, exec. v.p., 1971-78, pres., CEO, 1980-88, Total Comm., Inc., Eugene, 1989-91; N.W. area market mgr. 3M Nat. Advt., Eugene, 1978-80; dir. mktg. State Accident Ins. Fund, Salem, 1988-89. Mem. exec. com. affiliate bd. Mut. Broadcasting, 1981-87. Pres. Waldport City Coun., 1962-67; coach Eugene Kidsports, 1968-92, Am. Softball Assn. Girls Softball Team, 1988; mem. adv. com. 4 J Sch. Dist., 1988-90; bd. dirs. Lane County United Way, 1983-86, dir., 1992, Lane County Goodwill Industries, 1989-90; mem. Eugene City Budget Com., 1992-94, Eugene City Coun., 1994-97; mayor City of Eugene, Oreg., 1997—. Named JCI senator, Oreg. State Jaycees, 1966, Citizen of Yr., City of Waldport, 1967, Outstanding Vol., City of Eugene, 1991. Mem. Oreg. Outdoor Advt. Assn. (pres. 1971-80), Oreg. Assn. Broadcasters (dir. 1984-87), Eugene C. of C. (bd. dirs., pres. 1991-92), Eugene Rotary (dir., pres. 1984, Paul Harris fellow 1985). Republican. Roman Catholic. Avocation: youth coaching. Office: Mayor's Office 777 Pearl St Ste 105 Eugene OR 97401-2720

TOSTI, DONALD THOMAS, psychologist, consultant; b. Kansas City, Mo., Dec. 6, 1935; s. Joseph T. Tosti and Elizabeth M. (Parsons) Tosti Addison; m. Carol J. Curless, Jan. 31, 1957 (dec. 1980); children: Rene, Alicia, Roxanna, Brett, Tabitha, Todd Marcus; m. Annette Brewer, Dec. 29, 1989. BSEE, U. N.Mex., 1957, MS in Psychology, 1962, PhD in Psychology, 1967. Chief editor Tchg. Machines, Inc., Albuquerque, 1960-64; divsn. mgr. Westinghouse Learning Corp., Albuquerque, 1964-70; founder, sr. v.p. Ind. Learning Sys., San Raphael, Calif., 1970-74, pres., 1974-76; chmn. bd. Omega Performance, San Francisco, 1976-77; pres. Operants, Inc., San Rafael, 1978-81; v.p. Forum Corp., San Rafael, 1981-83; mng. ptnr. Vanguard Cons. Group, San Francisco, 1983—. Author: Basic Electricity, Advanced Algebra, Fundamentals of Calculus, TMI Programmed Mathematics Series, 1960-63, Behavior Technology, 1970, A Guide to Child Development, Tactics of Communication, 1973; co-author: Learning Is Getting Easier, 1973, Indtroductory Psychology, 1981, Usibility Factors in Hardware and Software Design, 1982, Comparative Usibility, 1983, Performance Based Management, Positive Leadership, 1986, Strategic Alliances, 1990, The Professional Manager, 1995, Power and Governance, 1996, Global Fluency, 1999, Organizational Alignment, 2000, Internal Branding, 2000, Principles of Performance Consulting, 2001. Mem. APA, Internat. Soc. for Performance Improvement (v.p. rsch. 1983-85, treas. 1997-99, Outstanding Mem. award 1984, Life Membership award 1984, Outstanding product award 1974). Home: 41 Marinita Ave San Rafael CA 94901-3443

TOTTEN, GEORGE OAKLEY, III, political science educator; b. Washington, July 21, 1922; s. George Oakley Totten Jr. and Vicken (von Post) Börjesson Totten Barrois; m. Astrid Maria Anderson, June 26, 1948 (dec. Apr. 26, 1975); children: Vicken Yuriko, Linnea Catherine; m. Lilia Huiying Li, July 1, 1976; 1 child, Blanche Maluk Lemes. Cert., U. Mich., 1943; AB, Columbia U., 1946, AM, 1949; MA, Yale U., 1950, PhD, 1954; docentur i japanologi, U. Stockholm, 1977. Lectr. Columbia U., N.Y.C., 1954-55; asst. prof. MIT, Cambridge, 1958-59, Boston U., 1959-61; assoc. prof. U. R.I., Kingston, 1961-64; assoc. prof. polit. sci. U. So. Calif., L.A., 1965-68, prof., 1968-92, chmn. dept., 1980-86, prof. emeritus, 1992—. Dir., founder Calif. Pvt. Univs. and Colls. Yr.-in-Japan program Weseda U., 1967-73; dir. East Asian Studies Ctr., 1974-77; 1st dir. USC-UCLA Joint East Asian Studies Ctr., 1976-77; sr. affiliated scholar Ctr. for Multiethnic and Transnat. Studies, 1993-98; chair USC Korea Project, 1998—; vis. prof. U. Stockholm, 1977-79, 1st dir. Ctr. Pacific Asia Studies, 1985-89, sr. counselor bd. dirs., 1989—; hon. pres. Huaxiu Pvt. Sch., Anyang City, Henan Province, China, 1999—. Author: Social Democratic Movement in Prewar Japan, 1966, Chinese edit., 1987, Korean edit., 1997; co-author: Socialist Parties in Postwar Japan, 1966, Japan and the New Ocean Regime, 1984, Japan in the World, the World in Japan, Fifty Years of Japanese Studies at Michigan, 2001; editor: Helen Snow's Song of Ariran, 1973, Korean edit., 1991, Chinese edit., 1993, Kim Dae-jung's A New Beginning, 1996, Lee Hee-ho's (Mrs. Kim Dae-jung's) Praying for Tomorrow: Letters to My Husband in Prison, 1999; author, co-editor: Developing Nations: Quest for a Model, 1970, Japanese edit., 1975, China's Economic Reform: Administering the Introduction of the Market Mechanism, 1992, Community in Crisis: The Korean American Community After the Los Angeles Civil Unrest of April 1992, 1994; co-translator: Ch'ien Mu's Traditional Government in Imperial China, 1982, 1st paperback edit.; contbr. The Politics of Divided Nations, 1991, Chinese edit., 1995, Japanese edit., 1997; editl. bd. Acta Koreana, 1997—. Mem. U.S.-China People's Friendship Assn., Washington, 1974—, World Feds., 1962—; mem. Com. on U.S.-China Relations, N.Y.C., 1975—; chmn. L.A.-Pusan Sister City Assn., L.A., 1976-77; bd. dirs. L.A.-Guangzhou Sister City Assn., 1990—; mem. nat. adv. com. Japan Am. Student Conf., 1984—, Assn. Korean Polit. Studies in N.Am., 1992—, v.p. 1996-98; bd. dirs. Assn. for the Study of Korean Culture and Identity, Korea, 1999-2000; mem. coun. China Soc. for People's Friendship Studies, Beijing, 1991—. 1st lt. AUS, 1942-46, PTO. Recipient Plaque for program on Korean studies Consulate Gen. of Republic of Korea, 1975, Disting. Emeritus award U. So. Calif., 1996; Social Sci. Rsch. Coun. fellow, 1952-53; Ford Found. grantee, 1955-58, NSF grantee, 1979-81, Korea Found. grantee, 1993, Rebuild L.A. grantee, 1993, Philippine Liberation medal, 1994. Mem. Assn. Asian Studies, Am. Polit. Sci. Assn., Asia Soc., Internat. Polit. Sci. Assn., Internat. Studies Assn., Japanese Polit. Sci. Assn., Japanese-Am. Soc. Calif. (bd. dirs. 1990-94), European Assn. Japanese Studies, U. So. Calif. Faculty Ctr., Phi Beta Delta (founding mem. Beta Kappa chpt. 1993—). Episcopalian. Home: 5129 Village Green Los Angeles CA 90016-5205 Office: USC Korea Project Dept Polit Sci VKC 327 Los Angeles CA 90089-0044 E-mail: totten@usc.edu

TOUFF, MICHAEL, lawyer; Officer, law firm Holmes & Starr, Ireland, Stapleton, Pryor & Pascoe, P.C., 1992-94; v.p., gen. counsel Richmond Amer Homes, 1994—, sr. v.p., gen. counsel, 1999—. Office: Richmond Amer Homes 3600 S Yosemite St Ste 900 Denver CO 80237-1812

TOULMIN, STEPHEN EDELSTON, humanities educator, educator; b. London, Mar. 25, 1922; BA in Math. and Physics, King's Coll., Cambridge, Eng., 1942; PhD, King's Coll., 1948; D Tech. (hon.), Royal Inst. Tech., Stockholm, 1991. Lectr. in philosophy of sci. Oxford U., Eng., 1949-55; prof., chmn. dept. of philosophy U. Leeds, Yorkshire, Eng., 1955-59; dir. unit for history of ideas Nuffield Found., London, 1960-65; prof. history of ideas and philosophy Brandeis U., Waltham, Mass., 1965-69; prof. philosophy Mich. State U., East Lansing, 1969-72; prof. humanities U. Calif., Santa Cruz, 1972-73; prof. com. social thought U. Chgo., 1973-86; Avalon prof. humanities Northwestern U., Evanston, Ill., 1986-92, Avalon prof. emeritus, 1992—; Henry R. Luce prof.Ctr. Multiethnic and Transnational Studies U. So. Calif., L.A., 1993-2001. Vis. prof. U. Melbourne, Australia, 1954-55, Stanford U., 1959, Columbia U., N.Y.C., 1960, Hebrew U., Jerusalem, 1964, U. South Fla., 1972, Dartmouth Coll., 1979, SUNY, Plattsburgh, 1980, Colo. Coll., 1980, 82, MacMaster U., 1983, Harvard Project Physics Grad. Sch. Edn., Harvard U., 1965; counselor Smithsonian Inst., Washington, 1967-77; cons., staff mem. Nat. Commn. Protection Human Subjects Biomed. Behavioral Rsch., 1975-78; sr. vis. scholar, fellow Inst. Soc. Ethics and Life Scis., Hastings-on-Hudson, N.Y., 1981-2001; regent's lectr. U. Calif. Med. Sch., Davis, 1985; Mary Flexner lectr. Bryn Mawr Coll., 1977; Reyerson lectr. U. Chgo., 1979, John Nuveen lectr., 1980; Tate-Wilson lectr. So. Meth. U., 1980; Or Emet lectr. Osgoode Hall Law Sch., 1981; McDermott lectr. U. Dallas, 1985; lectr. Sigma Xi, 1965-66, Phi Beta Kappa, 1978-79, Phi Beta Kappa-AAAS, 1984, Thomas Jefferson lectr. NEH, Washington, 1997; Tanner lectr. Clare Hall, Cambridge U., 1998; guest prof. social and human scis. Wolfgang Goethe Universitat, Frankfurt, Germany, 1987; vis. fellow Internationales Forschungszentrum Kulturwissenschaften (IFK), Vienna, 1995. Author: The Place of Reason in Ethics, 1949, The Philosophy of Science: an Introduction, 1953, The Uses of Argument, 1958, Foresight and Understanding, 1961, Human Understanding, vol. 1, 1972, Knowing and Acting, 1976, The Return to Cosmology, 1982, Cosmopolis, 1989; (with J. Goodfield) The Fabric of the Heavens, 1961, The Architecture of Matter, 1963, The Discovery of Time, 1965; (with A. Janik) Wittgenstein's Vienna, 1973; (with R. Rieke and A. Janik) An Introduction to Reasoning, 1978; (with A. Jonsen) The Abuse of Casuistry, 1987; (with B. Gustavsen) Beyond Theory, 1996, Return to Reason, 2001; contbr. numerous sci. articles to profl. jours. Recipient Honor Cross 1st class (Austria), 1991; Getty Ctr. for History of Art and Humanities scholar, 1985-86, First Book of the Year prize Am. Soc. Social Philosophy, 1992; Ctr. for Psychosocial Studies fellow, 1974-76. Fellow Am. Acad. Arts and Scis. Office: U So Calif Cmts Gfs 306 Los Angeles CA 90089-1694

TOURTELLOTTE, WALLACE WILLIAM, neurologist, educator; b. Great Falls, Mont., Sept. 13, 1924; s. Nathaniel Mills and Frances Victoria (Charlton) T.; m. Jean Esther Toncray, Feb. 14, 1953; children: Wallace William, George Mills, James Millard, Warren Gerard. PhB, BS, U. Chgo., 1945, PhD, 1948, MD, 1951. Intern Strong Meml. Hosp. U. Rochester (N.Y.) Sch. Medicine and Dentistry, 1951-52; resident in neurology U. Mich. Med. Ctr., Ann Arbor, 1954-57, asst. prof. neurology, 1957-59, assoc. prof., 1959-66, prof., 1966-71; prof. dept. neurology UCLA, 1971—, vice chmn. dept. neurology, 1971-98, emeritus vice chmn. dept. neurology, 1998; chief neurology svcs. VA Wadsworth, West Los Angeles, Calif., 1971-99, emeritus, 1991-99, emeritus dir. tng. program, 1991—, staff neurologist, neuroscientist, 1991—. Vis. assoc. prof. Washington U., St. Louis, 1963-64; hon. mem. med. adv. bd. Nat. Multiple Sclerosis Soc., 1968—, 1994—, So. Calif. Multiple Sclerosis Socs., 1972—; dir. Multiple Sclerosis Rsch. and Treatment Ctr., Human Brain and Spinal Fluid Resource Ctr., 1971—. Co-editor (with Cedric Raines, Henry McFarland): Multiple Sclerosis, Clinical and Pathogenetic Basis, 1997; mem. editorial bd. Jour. Neurol. Sci., Revue Neurologica, Italian Jour. Neurol. Sci., Multiple Sclerosis Jour.; dedicated The Wallace W. Tourtellotte Clin. and Neurosci. Libr., 1999; called the 13th most quoted neurologist in USA, 1999. Lt. (j.g.) M.C., USNR, 1952-54. Recipient Disting. Alumni Service award U. Chgo., 1982. Fellow Am. Acad. Neurology (S. Weir Mitchell Neurology Reseach award 1959); mem. Am. Assn. Univ. Neurol. Prof. (emeritus), Am. Neurol. Assn. (counselor 1982—, v.p. 1992), World Fedn. Neurology (founding mem.), Am. Assn. Neuropathologists, Internat. Soc. Neurochemsitry (founding mem.), Am. Soc. Pharmacology and Exptl. Therapeutics, Am. Soc. Neurochemistry (founding mem.), Soc. Neurosci.,

Confrerie de la Chaine des Rotisseur, Argentier du Baillage de Los Angeles (vice chancellier, comdr.), Ordre Mondial des Gourmets Degustateurs Etats-Unis Chevalier, Pasadena Wine and Food Soc., Physician Wine & Food Soc., Soc. Med. Friends of Wine, Sigma Xi. Republican. Presbyterian. Home: 1140 Tellem Dr Pacific Palisades CA 90272-2244 Fax: 310-454-7650. E-mail: wtourtel@ucla.edu

TOWE, A. RUTH, museum director; b. Circle, Mont., Mar. 4, 1938; d. David and Anna Marie (Pedersen) James; m. Thomas E. Towe, Aug. 21, 1960; children: James Thomas, Kristofer Edward. BA, U. Mont., 1960, MA, 1970; postgrad., Am. U., 1964. Bookkeeper, copywriter Sta. KGVO, Missoula, Mont., 1960-61; grad. asst. Sch. of Journalism U. Mont., Missoula, 1961-62; editorial asst. Phi Gamma Delta mag., Washington, 1964; reporter The Chelsea (Mich.) Standard, 1965-66; dir. Mont. Nat. Bank, Plentywood, 1966-73; bookkeeper, legal sec. Thomas E. Towe, Atty. of Law, Billings, Mont., 1967-68; dir. Mont. Nat. Bank, Browning, 1972-73; mus. exec. dir. The Moss Mansion Mus., Billings, 1988—. Bd. dirs. Billings Depot, Inc., sec., 1999—. Mem. Mont. Coun. of Family Rels. & Devel., 1970; pres. Mont. Assn. of Symphony Orchs., 1987-88; sheriff Yellowstone Corral of Westerners, Billings, 1993; pres. Yellowstone Hist. Soc., 1998-2000; vice-chmn. Yellowstone Dem. Ctrl. Com., Billings, 1983-84; mem. Billings Friends Mtg., 1986—. Mem. AAUW, PEO, Mont. Assn. Female Execs., Mus. Assn. Mont. (pres. 1990-92, bd. dirs. 1989-96), Jr. League, Theta Sigma Phi (hon.). Avocation: gardening. E-mail: mossmansion.com;. Office: The Moss Mus 914 Division St Billings MT 59101-1921 E-mail: tomt@mcn.net

TOWE, THOMAS EDWARD, lawyer; b. Cherokee, Iowa, June 25, 1937; s. Edward and Florence (Tow) T.; m. Ruth James, Aug. 21, 1960; children: James Thomas, Kristofer Edward. Student, U. Paris, 1956; BA, Earlham Coll., 1959; LLB, U. Mont., 1962; LLM, Georgetown U., 1965. Ptnr. Towe, Ball, Enright, Mackey & Sommerfeld, Billings, Mont., 1967—; legislator Mont. House of Rep., Billings, 1971-75, Mont. State Senate, Billings, 1975-87, 91-94. Served on various coms. Mont. Senate, 1975-87, 91-94. Contbr. articles to law revs. Mem. Alternatives, Inc., Halfway House, Billing, 1977-99, pres., 1985-86; mem. adv. com. Mont. Crime Control Bd., 1973-78, Youth Justice Coun., 1981-83; mem. State Dem. Exec. Com., 1969-73; candidate for Congress, 1976; bd. dirs. Mont. Consumer Affairs Coun., Regl. Cmty. Svcs. for the Devel. Disabled, 1975-77, Rimrock Guidance Found., 1975-80, Vols. of Am., Billings, 1984-89, Youth Dynamics Inc., 1989-96, Zoo Mont., 1985-2001, Inst. for Peace Studies, 1993—, Mont. State Parks Assn., 1993—. Capt. U.S. Army, 1962-65. Named as one of 100 Most Influential Montanans in 20th Century, Missoulian newspaper. Mem. Mont. Bar Assn., Yellowstone County Bar Assn., Am. Hereford Assn., Billings C. of C. Mem. Soc. of Friends. Avocation: outdoor recreation. Home: 2739 Gregory Dr S Billings MT 59102-0509 Office: 2525 6th Ave N Billings MT 59101-1358 E-mail: tomt@mcn.net

TOWERS, KEVIN, baseball team executive; b. Medford, Oreg., Nov. 11, 1961; m. Kelley Owens, Dec. 1996. Student, Brigham Young U. Pitcher San Diego Padres farm sys., 1982-88; area scout San Diego Padres, Tex., La., 1989-91; pitching coach San Diego Single-A affiliate, Spokane, Wash., 1989-90; regional cross-checker, then nat. cross-checker Pitts. Pirates, 1992-93; scouting dir. San Diego Padres, 1993-96, sr. v.p., gen. mgr., 1995—. Achievement: San Diego Padres won the National League Pennant in 1998. Office: c/o San Diego Padres PO Box 2000 San Diego CA 92112-2000

TOWERY, JAMES E. lawyer; b. Los Alamos, N.Mex., July 12, 1948; s. Lawson E. and Irma (Van Apeldorn) T.; m. Kathryn K. Meier, July 20, 1991; 1 child, Mark J. BA, Princeton U., 1973; JD, Emory U., 1976. Assoc. Morgan Beauzay Hammer, San Jose, Calif., 1977-79; ptnr. Morgan & Towery, San Jose, 1979-89; assoc. Hoge Fenton Jones & Appel, San Jose, 1989-90, ptnr., 1990—. Chmn. bd. trustees Alexian Bros. Hosp., San Jose, Calif., 1995-98. Mem. ABA (ho. of dels. 1989-98, standing com. client protection 1996—, chair 1998-00), State Bar Calif. (v.p. and chair discipline com. 1994-95, bd. govs. 1992-96, pres. 1995-96, presiding arbitrator, fee arbitration program 1990-92), Santa Clara County Bar Assn. (counsel 1984-85, treas. 1987, pres. 1989). Office: Hoge Fenton Jones 60 S Market St San Jose CA 95113-2351

TOWNE, DAVID L. zoological park administrator; b. Winslow, Wash., Dec. 1, 1931; BA, U. Wash., 1958. Supt. Dept. Parks and Recreation, Seattle, 1972-77; v.p. Earl Combs, Inc., Bellevue, Wash., 1982-84; dir. Woodland Park Zool. Gardens, Seattle, 1984-2000. Fellow Am. Zoos and Aquariums; mem. N. Am. Giant Panda Plan (pres.), Am. Assn. Zoos and Aquariums (past pres.), Woodland Park Zool. Soc. (pres., CEO). Office: Woodland Park Zoological Gardens 5500 Phinney Ave N Seattle WA 98103-5865 E-mail: clave.towne@zoo.org

TOWNE, ROBERT, screenwriter; b. 1936; m. Luisa Towne; 2 children. Student, Pomona Coll. Screenwriter Creative Artists Agy., Beverly Hills, Calif. Screenplays include The Last Woman on Earth, 1960 (also actor), The Tomb of Ligeia, 1965, Villa Rides, 1968, The Last Detail, 1973 (Acad. award nomination for best original screenplay), Chinatown, 1974 (Acad. award best original screenplay), (with Warren Beatty) Shampoo, 1975 (Acad. award best original screenplay nomination), (with Paul Schrader) The Yazuka, 1975, (also prodr., dir.) Personal Best, 1982, (with Michael Austin) Greystoke, 1984, (also dir.) Tequila Sunrise, 1988, The Two Jakes, 1990, Days of Thunder, 1990, The Firm (with David Rayfiel and David Rabe), 1992, Mission Impossible (with David Koepp), 1996, Without Limits (with Kenneth Moore), 1998 (also dir.), Mission Impossible 2, 1999. Office: Creative Artists Agy 9830 Wilshire Blvd Beverly Hills CA 90212-1825

TOWNES, CHARLES HARD, physics educator; b. Greenville, S.C., July 28, 1915; s. Henry Keith and Ellen Sumter (Hard) T.; m. Frances H. Brown, May 4, 1941; children: Linda Lewis, Ellen Screven, Carla Keith, Holly Robinson. B.A., B.S., Furman U., 1935; M.A., Duke U., 1937; Ph.D., Calif. Inst. Tech., 1939. Mem. tech. staff Bell Telephone Lab., 1939-47; assoc. prof. physics Columbia U., 1948-50, prof. physics, 1950-61; exec. dir. Columbia Radiation Lab., 1950-52, chmn. physics dept., 1952-55; provost and prof. physics MIT, 1961-66, Inst. prof., 1966-67; v.p., dir. research Inst. Def. Analyses, Washington, 1959-61; prof. physics U. Calif., Berkeley, 1967-86, 94, prof. physics emeritus, 1986-94, prof. grad. sch., 1994—. Guggenheim fellow, 1955-56; Fulbright lectr. U. Paris, 1955-56, U. Tokyo, 1956; dir. Enrico Fermi Internat. Sch. Physics, 1963; Richtmeyer lectr. Am. Phys. Soc., 1959; Scott lectr. U. Cambridge, 1963; Centennial lectr. U. Toronto, 1967; Lincoln lectr., 1972-73, Halley lectr., 1976, Krishnan lectr., 1992, Nishina lectr., 1992; Weinberg lectr. Oak Ridge (Tenn.) Nat. Lab., 1997, Rajiv Gandhi lectr., 1997, Henry Norris Russell lectr. Am. Astron. Soc., 1998; dir. Gen. Motors Corp., 1973-86, Perkin-Elmer Corp., 1966-85; mem. Pres.'s Sci. Adv. Com., 1966-69, vice chmn., 1967-69; chmn. sci. and tech. adv. com. for manned space flight NASA, 1964-70; mem. Pres.'s Com. on Sci. and Tech., 1976; rschr. on nuclear and molecular structure, quantum electronics, interstellar molecules, radio and infrared astrophysics. Author: (with A.L. Schawlow) Microwave Spectroscopy, 1955, Making Waves, 1996, How the Laser Happened. Adventures of a Scientist, 1999 (best book on sci. 1999 Am. Inst. Physics); author, co-editor: Quantum Electronics, 1960, Quantum Electronics and Coherent Light, 1964; editorial bd. Rev. Sci. Instruments, 1950-52, Phys. Rev., 1951-53, Jour. Molecular Spectroscopy, 1957-60, Procs. Nat. Acad. Scis., 1978-84, Can. Jour. Physics, 1995—; contbr. articles to sci. publs.; patentee masers and lasers. Trustee Calif. Inst. Tech., Carnegie Instn. of Washington, Grad. Theol. Union, Calif. Acad. Scis.; mem. corp. Woods Hole Oceanographic Instn. Decorated officier Légion d'Honneur (France); recipient numerous hon. degrees and awards including Nobel prize for physics, 1964; Stuart Ballantine medal Franklin Inst., 1959, 62; Thomas Young medal and prize Inst. Physics and Phys. Soc., Eng., 1963; Disting. Public Service medal NASA, 1969; Wilhelm Exner award Austria, 1970; Niels Bohr Internat. Gold medal, 1979; Nat. Sci. medal, 1982, Berkeley citation U. Calif., 1986; Common Wealth award, 1993, ADION medal Obs. Nice, 1995; Mendel award Villanova U; Frank Annunzio award Christopher Columbus Fellowship Found., 1999; Rabindranath Tagore Birth Centenary plaque Asiatic Soc., 1999; named to Nat. Inventors Hall of Fame, 1976, Engrng. and Sci. Hall of Fame, 1983. Fellow IEEE (life, Medal of Honor 1967), Am. Phys. Soc. (pres. 1967, Plyler prize 1977), Optical Soc. Am. (hon., Mees medal 1968, Frederick Ives medal 1996), Indian Nat. Sci. Acad., Calif. Acad. Scis.; mem. NAS (coun. 1968-72, 78-81, chmn. space sci. bd. 1970-73, Comstock award 1959, Carty medal 1962), Am. Philos. Soc., Am. Astron. Soc., Am. Acad. Arts and Scis., Royal Soc. (fgn. mem.), Russian Acad. Scis. (fgn. mem., Lomonosov medal 2000), Pontifical Acad. Scis., Max-Planck Inst. for Physics and Astrophysics (fgn. mem.), N.Y. Acad. Scis. (hon. life); elected to NAE 1998 (founders award 2000). Office: U Calif Dept Physics 366 Leconte # 7200 Berkeley CA 94720-0001 E-mail: cht@sunspot.ssl.berkeley.edu

TOWNES, JOHN W., III, career officer; Grad., U.S. Naval Acad., 1972; MS in Nat. Security and Strategic Study, Naval War Coll./Armed Forces, Staff Coll.; postgrad., Harvard U. Commd. ensign USN, 1972, advanced through ranks to rear adm.; various assignments to exec. asst. to chief Naval Personnel and dep. chief Naval Opers., Manpower and Personnel, Washington; comdr. Navy Region Hawaii, Naval Surface Group, Cruiser Destroyer Group 8. Office: Comcrudesgru 8 Unit 60009 FPO AE 09506-4704

TOWNSEND, RANDOLPH J. state legislator; b. L.A., Jan. 24, 1947; m. Robyne Townsend. Student, San Francisco State U.; BS, MEd, U. Nev. Advt. exec.; mem. Nev. Senate, Washoe Dist. 4, Carson City, 1982—. Adj. faculty U. Nev., Reno. Mem. adv. bd. Com. to Aid Abused Women; mem. Nev. Bus. Week, Inc.; active Teen View, Inc.; chair Coalition for Affordable Energy, 1980—; mem. Nat. Coun. Sr. Citizens; chair Washoe Assn. Retarded Citizens; mem. spl. programs adv. bd. U. Nev., Reno; mem. Am. Legis. Exch. Coun. Mem. Pi Delta Phi. Republican. Home: PO Box 20923 Reno NV 89515-0923

TRABITZ, EUGENE LEONARD, aerospace company executive; b. Cleve., Aug. 13, 1937; s. Emanuel and Anna (Berman) T.; m. Caryl Lee Rine, Dec. 22, 1963 (div. Aug. 1981); children: Claire Marie, Honey Caryl; m. Kathryn Lynn Bates, Sept. 24, 1983; 1 stepchild, Paul Francis Rager. BA, Ohio State U., 1965. Enlisted USAF, 1954, advanced through grades to maj.; served as crew commdr. 91st Stragetic Missile Div., Minot, S.D., 1968-70; intelligence officer Fgn. Tech. Div., Dayton, Ohio, 1970-73; dir. external affairs Aero Systems Div., Dayton, 1973-75; program mgr. Air Force Armament Div., Valparaiso, Fla., 1975-80; dir. ship ops. Air Force Ea. Test Range, Satellite Beach, 1980-83; dep. program mgr. Air Force Satellite Text Ctr., Sunnyvale, Calif., 1983-84; ret., 1984; sr. staff engr. Ultrasystems Inc., 1984-86; pres. TAWD Systems Inc., Palo Alto, Calif., 1986-92, Am. Telenetics Co., San Mateo, 1992—. Cons. Space Applications Corp., Sunnyvale, 1986-87, Litton Computer Svcs., Mountain View, Calif., 1987-91, Battelle Meml. Inst. Columbus, 1993—. V.p. Bd. County Mental Health Clinic, Ft. Walton Beach, Fla., 1973-75. Decorated Bronze Star. Mem. DAV (life), World Affairs Coun., U.S. Space Found. (charter), Air Force Assn. (life), Assn. Old Crows, Nat. Sojourners, Commonwealth Club Calif., Masons (32 degree). Avocations: golf, tennis, racketball, sailing, bridge. Home: 425 Anchor Rd Apt 317 San Mateo CA 94404-1058

TRACY, ROBERT (EDWARD), English language educator, poetry translator; b. Woburn, Mass., Nov. 23, 1928; s. Hubert William and Vera Mary (Hurley) T.; m. Rebecca Garrison, Aug. 26, 1956; children: Jessica Janes, Hugh Garrison, Dominick O'Donovan. AB in Greek with honors, Boston Coll., 1950; MA, Harvard U., 1954, PhD, 1960. Teaching fellow Harvard U., Cambridge, Mass., 1954-58; instr. Carleton Coll., Northfield, Minn., 1958-60; from asst. prof. English, to assoc. prof., then prof. U. Calif., Berkeley, 1960-89, prof. English and Celtic Studies, 1989—, assoc. dir. Dickens Project, 1994-95. Vis. prof., Bruern fellow in Am. studies U. Leeds, Eng., 1965-66; vis. prof., Leverhulme fellow Trinity Coll., Dublin, 1971-72; vis. Kathryn W. Davis prof. slavic studies Wellesley (Mass.) Coll., 1979; Charles Mills Gayley lectr. U. Calif., Berkeley, 1989-90; vis. prof. Anglo-Irish lit. Trinity Coll., 1995-96. Author: Trollope's Later Novels, 1978, The Unappeasable Host: Studies in Irish Identities, 1998; translator (poems by Osip Mandelstam): Stone, 1981, 2d edit., 1991; editor J.M Synge's The Aran Islands, 1962, The Way We Live Now (Anthony Trollope), 1974, The Macdermots of Ballycloran (Anthony Trollope), 1989, Nina Balatka and Linda Tressel (Anthony Trollope), 1991, In A Glass Darkly (Sheridan Le Fanu) 1993, Rhapsody in Stephen's Green (Flann O'Brien), 1994; adv. editor The Recorder, 1985—, LIT (Lit., Interpretation, Theory), 1989—; contbr. articles and revs. to numerous jours. including Shakespeare Quarterly, So. Rev., Nineteenth-Century Fiction, Irish Univ. Rev., Eire-Ireland, Irish Literary Supplement, others; poetry translations in New Orleans Rev., Poetry, N.Y. Rev. of Books, Ploughshares, others. Appointed mem. cultural panel San Francisco-Cork Sister City Com. Fulbright travel grantee, 1965-66; recipient humanities research fellowships U. Calif., Berkeley, 1962, 69, 78, 81, 86 , 92; Guggenheim fellow, 1981-82. Mem. MLA, Philol. Assn. Pacific Coast, Am. Conf. for Irish Studies, Internat. Assn. for Study of Irish Lit. Avocation: exploring western Ireland and no. Calif. Office: U Calif Dept English Berkeley CA 94720-0001

TRAFTON, STEPHEN J. bank executive; b. Mt. Vernon, Wash., Sept. 17, 1946; m. Diane Trafton; children: John, Roland. BS in Zoology, Wash. State U., 1968. V.p., mgr. dept. money market Seattle-First Nat. Bank, 1968-79; v.p., mgr. bank consulting group Donaldson Lufkin Jennrette, N.Y.C., 1980; exec. v.p., treas. Gibraltar Savings Bank, L.A., 1980-84; banking cons., 1984-86; v.p., treas. Hibernia Bank, San Francisco, 1986-88; sr. v.p., treas. Goldome Bank, Buffalo, 1988-90; sr. exec. v.p., CFO Glenfed Inc., 1990-91, vice chmn., CFO, 1991—, pres., 1992—; sr. exec. v.p., CFO Glendale Fed. Bank, 1990-91, vice chmn., CFO, 1991, pres., COO, 1991-92, chmn. bd., pres., CEO, 1992-99, COO, also bd. dirs.; exec. v.p. Golden State Bancorp, 1999—. Mem. Phi Eta Sigma. Office: Golden State Bancorp Inc 135 Main St San Francisco CA 94105

TRAN, KHANH T. insurance company executive; CFO, Pacific Life Ins. Co., Newport Beach, Calif. Office: Pacific Life Ins Co PO Box 9000 Newport Beach CA 92658-9030

TRAPP, GERALD BERNARD, retired journalist; b. St. Paul, May 7, 1932; s. Bernard Edward and Lauretta (Mueller) T.; m. Bente Joan Moe, Jan. 29, 1954; children— Eric Gerald, Lise Joan, Alex Harold. B.A., Macalester Coll., St. Paul, 1954. Editor Mankato (Minn.) Free Press, 1954-57; with AP, 1957-80, nat. broadcast exec. charge sales East of Miss., 1966-68, gen. broadcast news editor, 1968-79, dep. dir. broadcast services, 1979-80, liaison broadcast networks, 1968-80; v.p., gen. mgr. Intermountain Network, Salt Lake City, 1980-87; v.p., dir. mktg. Travel Motivation, Inc., Salt Lake City, 1987-88; ops./program mgr. Mountain Cable Network, Inc., Salt Lake City, 1988-89; sr. v.p. Travel Motivation, Inc., Salt Lake City, 1990-92; mktg. specialist Morris Travel, 1992-95, pricing analyst, 1995-97. Bd. dirs. Westminster Coll. Found. Mem. Radio TV News Dir. Assn., Oratorio Soc. Utah (bd. dirs.), Pro Musica, Sigma Delta Chi. Mem. United Ch. Christ. Home: 785 Three Fountains Cir Apt 17 Salt Lake City UT 84107-5063 Office: 240 Morris Ave Salt Lake City UT 84115-3223

TRAPP, LANSFORD E. air force officer; m. Nancy Trapp; 1 child, Bethany. BSEE, S.D. State U., 1969; posgrad., Squadron Officer Sch., Maxwell AFB, Ala., 1974; MPA, Pepperdine U., 1976; postgrad., Armed Forces Staff Coll., Norfolk, Va., 1981, Nat. War Coll., Washington, 1988, MIT, , 1993, Syracuse U., 1997, Johns Hopkins U., 1997. Commd. 2d lt. USAF, 1969, advanced through grades to lt. gen., 1997, OV-10A forward air contr., 22nd Tactical Air Control Vietnam, 1970-71, OV-10A instr. pilot 549th Tactical Air Control Tng. Squadron Hurlburt Field, Fla., 1971-74, A-7D fighter pilot, 74th Tactical Fighter Squadron England AFB, La., 1974-77, fighter assignment officer, dep. chief fighter Randolph AFB, Tex., 1977-80, F-4E and F-16A fighter pilot, ops. officer 10th Tactical Hahn AB, West Germany, 1981-83, chief std. and evaluation divsn. 50th Tactical Command West Germany, 1983, ops. officer, comdr. 313th Tactical Fighter Squadron West Germany, 1983-85, tactical force programmer, directorate programs Hdqrs. Washington, 1985-86, exec. officer, dep. chief of staff programs and resources, 1986-87, comdr. 832nd Combat Support Group Luke AFB, Ariz., 1988, comdr. 24th Composite Wing Howard AFB, Panama, 1989-90, chief Gen. Officer Group Hdqrs. Washington, 1990-91, mil. asst. sec. Air Force, Hdqs., 1991-93, comdr. 355th Wing Davis-Monthan AFB, Ariz., 1993—94, comdr. 366th Wing Mountain Home AFB, Ohio, 1994—95, dep. dir. to leg. liaison office of sec. Washington, 1995—97, comdr. 12th Air Force and U.S. Southern Command Air Forces Davis-Monthan AFB, Ariz., 1997—99; vice comdr. hdqrs. Pacific Air Forces, Hickam AFB, Hawaii, 1999—; vice comdr. FAF. Decorated Legion of Merit with two oak leaf clusters, Disting. Flying Cross with oak leaf cluster, Purple Heart, Disting. Svc. medal, Meritorious Svc. medal with two oak leaf clusters, air medal with eight oak leaf clusters, Air Force commendation medal with oak leaf cluster, Presdl. unit citation with oak leaf cluster, Rep. of Vietnam Campaign medal with four svc. stars, Rep. of Vietnam Gallantry Cross with Palm. Office: 25 E St Ste G214 Hickam AFB HI 96853-5400

TRASK, ROBERT RILEY CHAUNCEY, author, lecturer, foundation executive; b. Albuquerque, Jan. 2, 1939; s. Edward Almon Trask and Florence Jane (White) Jones; m. Katie Lucille Bitters (div. 1981); m. Mary Jo Chiarottino, Dec. 1, 1984; 1 child, Chauncey Anne. Student pub. schs., San Diego. Lic. master sea capt. Entertainer, singer, comedian, 1964--; founder, pres. Nat. Health & Safety Svcs., San Francisco, l968-7l, ARAS Found., Issaquah, Wash., 1978—; capt., dive master San Diego Dive Charters, 1972-75; sr. capt., dive master Pacific Sport Diving Corp., Long Beach, Calif., 1975-77; lectr., bus. cons., 1978—. Cons., tng. developer Nissan, Gen. Dynamics, AT&T, religious orgns., also other corps., 1978--. Author: (manual) Tulip, 1971, Living Free, 1982, God's Phone Number, 1987, (video program for adolescents) Breaking Free, also seminar manuals. Mem. SAG. Avocations: fishing, boating, diving, exploring, gardening. Office: ARAS Found PMB # 93 3020 Issaquah Pine Lake Rd SE Sammamish WA 98075

TRAUGOTT, ELIZABETH CLOSS, linguistics educator, researcher; b. Bristol, Eng., Apr. 9, 1939; d. August and Hannah M.M. (Priebsch) Closs; m. John L. Traugott, Sept. 26, 1967; 1 dau., Isabel. BA in English, Oxford U., Eng., 1960; PhD in English lang., U. Calif., Berkeley, 1964. Asst. prof. English U. Calif., Berkeley, 1964-70; lectr. U. East Africa, Tanzania, 1965-66, U. York, Eng., 1966-67; lectr., then assoc. prof. linguistics and English Stanford U., Calif., 1970-77, prof., 1977—, chmn. linguistics dept., 1980-85, vice provost, dean grad. studies, 1985-91, mem. grad. record examinations bd., 1989-93, mem. test of English as a fgn. lang. bd., 1989-91, chmn. test of English as a fgn. lang. bd., 1991-92, 2000—. Mem. higher edn. funding coun. Eng. Assessment Panel, 1996, 2001. Author: A History of English Syntax, 1972, (with Mary Pratt) Linguistics for Students of Literature, 1980, (with Paul Hopper) Grammaticalization, 1993; editor: (with ter Meulen, Reilly, Ferguson) On Conditionals, 1986, (with Heine) Approaches to Grammaticalization, 2 vols., 1991, series co-editor: Topics in English Linguistics; contbr. numerous articles to profl. jours. Am. Coun. Learned Socs. fellow, 1975-76, Guggenheim fellow, 1983-84, Ctr. Advanced Study of Behavioral Scis. fellow, 1983-84. Fellow AAAS; mem. MLA, AAUP, AAUW, Linguistics Soc. Am. (pres. 1987, sec.-treas. 1994-98), Internat. Soc. Hist. Linguistic (pres. 1979-81), Internat. Pragmatics Assn. (bd. dirs. 2000—). Office: Stanford Univ Dept Linguistics Bldg 460 Stanford CA 94305-2150

TRAUTMAN, WILLIAM ELLSWORTH, lawyer; b. San Francisco, Nov. 27, 1940; s. Gerald H. and Doris Joy (Tucker) T.; m. Dorothy Williamson, June 17, 1962; children: Darcey, Torey. AB, U. Calif., Berkeley, 1962, LLB, 1965. Bar: Calif. U.S. Supreme Ct., Calif. Dist. Ct., U.S. Ct. Appeals (9th and fed. cirs.). Assoc. Chickering & Gregory, San Francisco, 1965-71, ptnr., 1972-81, Brobeck, Phleger & Harrison, San Francisco, 1981—, mng. ptnr., 1992-96, litigation dept. chair, 1984-91. Pres. Oakland (Calif.) Mus. Assn., 1981-83; mem. profl. ethics com. State Bar Calif., 1974-77. Fellow Am. Coll. Trial Lawyers; mem. Legal Aid Soc. (bd. dirs. 1982-93, pres. 1985-88), Bar Assn. San Francisco (bd. dirs. 1972-73), Calif. Barristers (bd. dirs., v.p.), Barrister's Club of San Francisco (v.p. 1973), Boalt Hall Alumni Assn. (bd. dirs. 1993-99, pres. 1997-98), U. Calif.-Berkeley Found. (bd. trustees 1998—). Office: Brobeck Phleger & Harrison 1 Market St San Francisco CA 94105-1420 E-mail: wtrautman@brobeck.com

TRAVERS, JUDITH LYNNETTE, human resources executive; b. Buffalo, Feb. 25, 1950; d. Harold Elwin and Dorothy (Helsel) Howes; m. David Jon Travers, Oct. 21, 1972; 1 child, Heather Lynne. BA in Psychology, Barrington Coll., 1972; cert. in paralegal course, St. Mary's Coll., Moraga, Calif., 1983; postgrad., Southland U., 1982-84. Exec. sec. Sherman C. Weeks, P.A., Derry, N.H., 1973-75; legal asst. Mason-McDuffie Co., Berkeley, Calif., 1975-82; paralegal asst. Blum, Kay, Merkle & Kauftheil, Oakland, 1982-83; CEO, bd. dirs. Dela Pers. Svcs. Inc., Concord, 1983—; pres. All Ages Sitters Agy., Concord, 1986-95; CEO, bd. dirs. Guardian Security Agy., Concord, Calif., 1992—. Sec., bd. dirs. Per Diem Staffing Systems, Inc., Securicorp. Vocalist record album The Loved Ones, 1978. Vol. local Congl. campaign, 1980, Circle of Friends, Children's Hosp. No. Calif., Oakland, 1987—; mem. Alameda County Sheriff's Mounted Posse, 1989, Contra Costa Child Abuse Prevention Coun., 1989; employer adv. coun. Ctrl. Contra Costa County, 1993—. Mem. NAFE, Am. Assn. Respiratory Therapy, Soc. for Human Resource Mgmt., Am. Mgmt. Assn., Gospel Music Assn., Palomino Horse Breeders Am., DAR, Barrington Oratorio Soc., Commonwealth Club Calif., Nat. Trust Hist. Preservation, Alpha Theta Sigma. Republican. Baptist. Avocations: boating, horses. Home: 3900 Brown Rd Oakley CA 94561-2664 Office: Delta Pers Svcs Inc 1820 Galindo St Ste 3 Concord CA 94520-2447

TRAVERS, PAUL, company executive; With Strand Hotels Ltd., Grand Met. Group; fin. dir. Europe Inter-Continental Hotels and Resorts, fin. dir. Forum Hotels, v.p. fin. Middle East and Africa, sr. v.p., group fin. contr., sr. v.p. property mgmt.; CFO REZsolutions, Inc., until 1999; pres. REZsolutions Hospitality Group. Office: REZsolutions Inc 7500 N Dreamy Draw Dr Ste 120 Phoenix AZ 85020-4668

TRAVIS, VANCE KENNETH, petroleum business executive; b. Coriander, Sask., Can., Jan. 30, 1926; s. Roy Hazen and Etta Orilla (Anderson) T.; m. Louise Mary, Nov. 30, 1948 (div. 1979); children: Stuart, Shirley, Gordon, Donald, Marian; m. Mildred Elaine, June 29, 1979; stepchildren: Susan, Nancy, Gordon, Sandra, Karen. Chmn. bd. Turbo Resources Ltd., 1970-83, Challenger Internat., 1977-83, Bankeno Mines Ltd., 1977-83, [illegible] Mgmt. Inc., Mpls., 1984-86, Triad Internat. Inc., 1985—; dir. Health Resource Mgmt. Ltd., Edmonton, 1990-97. Bd. dirs. Vencap Equities Alta. Ltd., Edmonton, 1981-86, L.K. Resources Ltd., Calgary, 1973-84. Mem.

Young. Pres.'s Orgn., Calgary, 1964-76, World Pres. Orgn. Recipient Presdl. pin Jr. Achievement, 1963, Best Pitcher award Petroleum Fastball League, 1955. Clubs: Calgary Petroleum, Ranchmen's. Office: Triad Internat Inc 3030 Sunridge Way NE Ste 21 Calgary AB Canada T1Y 7K4 also: Med Tech Corp 100 Med Tech Plz 6005-11 St SE Calgary AB Canada T2H 2Z3 E-mail: mtravis@cadvision.com

TRAVOUS, KENNETH E. state agency administrator; Exec. dir. Ariz. State Parks Bd., Phoenix. Office: Ariz State Parks Bd 1300 W Washington St Phoenix AZ 85007-2929

TRAYNOR, JOHN MICHAEL, lawyer; b. Oakland, Calif., Oct. 25, 1934; s. Roger J. and Madeleine (Lackmann) T.; m. Shirley Williams, Feb. 11, 1956; children: Kathleen Traynor Millard, Elizabeth Traynor Fowler, Thomas. BA, U. Calif., Berkeley, 1955; JD, Harvard U., 1960. Bar: Calif. 1961, U.S. Supreme Ct. 1966. Dep. atty. gen. State of Calif., San Francisco, 1961-63; spl. counsel Calif. Senate Com. on Local Govt., Sacramento, 1963; assoc. firm Cooley Godward, LLP, San Francisco, 1963-69, ptnr., 1969—. Adviser 3d Restatement of Unfair Competition, 1988-95, 3d Restatement of Torts; Products Liability, 1992-97, Apportionment, 1994-99, 1988 Revs. 2d Restatement of Conflict of Laws, 3rd Restatement of Restitution and Unjust Punishment, 1997-2000; lectr. U. Calif. Boalt Hall Sch. Law, Berkeley, 1982-89, 1996-98; chmn. EarthJustice Legal Def. Fund (formerly Sierra Club Legal Defense Fund), 1989-91, pres. 1991-92, trustee, 1974-96. Mem. bd. overseers Inst. for Civil Justice The RAND Corp., 1991-97; bd. dirs. Environ. Law Inst., 1991-97, 00—, Sierra Legal Def. Fund (Can.), 1990-96. Served to 1st lt. USMC, 1955-57. Fellow AAAS, Am. Bar Found. (life); mem. Am. Law Inst. (coun. 1985—, pres. 2000—), Bar Assn. San Francisco (pres. 1973). Home: 3131 Eton Ave Berkeley CA 94705-2713 Office: Cooley Godward LLP 1 Maritime Plz Ste 2000 San Francisco CA 94111-3510 E-mail: traynormt@cooley.com

TREADWAY-DILLMON, LINDA LEE, athletic trainer, actress, stuntwoman; b. Woodbury, N.J., June 4, 1950; d. Leo Elmer and Ona Lee (Wyckoff) Treadway; m. Randall Kenneth Dillmon, June 19, 1982. BS in Health, Phys. Edn. & Recreation, West Chester State Coll., 1972, MS in Health and Phys. Edn., 1975; postgrad., Ctrl. Mich. U., 1978; Police Officer Stds. Tng. cert. complaint dispatcher, Goldenwest Coll., 1982. Cert. in safety edn. West Chester State Coll.; cert. EMT, Am. Acad. Orthopaedic Surgeons. Grad. asst., instr., asst. athletic trainer West Chester (Pa.) State Coll., 1972-76; asst. prof., program dir., asst. athletic trainer Ctrl. Mich. U., Mt. Pleasant, 1976-80; police dispatcher City of Westminster, Calif., 1980-89; oncology unit sec. Children's Hosp. Orange County, Orange, 1989-96; control clk. food & beverage Marriott Hotel, Anaheim, 1996—. Stuntwoman, actress United Stunt Artists, SAG, L.A., 1982—; dancer Disneyland, Anaheim, Calif., 1988—; contbr. articles to profl. jours. Athletic trainer U.S. Olympic Women's Track and Field Trials, Frederick, Md., 1972, AAU Jr. World Wrestling Championships, Mt. Pleasant, Mich., 1977, Mich. Spl. Olympics, Mt. Pleasant, 1977, 78, 79. Recipient bronze and gold Spirit of Disneyland Resort awards, 1997; named Outstanding Phys. Educator, Delta Psi Kappa, Ctrl. Mich. U., 1980, Outstanding Young Woman of Am., 1984; named to Disneyland Entertainment Hall of Fame, 1995. Mem. SAG, Nat. Athletic Trainers Assn. (cert., women and athletic tng. ad hoc com. 1974-75, placement com. 1974-79, program dirs. coun. 1976-80, ethics com. 1977-80, visitation team 1978-80, 25 Yr. award 1997), U.S. Field Hockey Assn. (player), Pacific S.W. Field Hockey Assn. (player, Nat. Champion 1980, 81, 82), L.A. Field Hockey Assn. (player), Swing Shift Dance Team (dancer). Presbyterian. Avocations: flying, piano, athletics, stitchery, travel. Home: 18073 Scanlan Ct Fountain Valley CA 92708-5865

TREAS, JUDITH KAY, sociology educator; b. Phoenix, Jan. 2, 1947; d. John Joseph and Hope Catherine (Thomas) Jennings; m. Benjamin C. Treas II, May 14, 1969; children: Stella, Evan. BA, Pitzer Coll., Claremont, Calif., 1969; MA, UCLA, 1972, PhD, 1976. Instr. U. So. Calif., L.A., 1974-75, asst. prof., 1975-81, assoc. prof., 1981-87, dept. chair, 1984-89, prof., 1987-89, U. Calif., Irvine, 1989, dept. chair, 1989-94. Bd. overseers Gen. Social Survey, 1986-88; cons. social sci. and population study sect. NIH, 1989-92. Contbr. articles to profl. jours. Trustee Pitzer Coll., 1977-79. Recipient Rsch. award NSF, 1978-81, 84-91, NIH, 1979-81; Univ. scholar U. So. Calif., 1982-83. Fellow Gerontological Assn. Am.; mem. Golden Key (hon.), Am. Sociol. Assn., Population Assn. Am. Office: U Calif Dept Sociology Irvine CA 92697-0001

TREAT, JOHN ELTING, management consultant; b. Evanston, Ill., June 20, 1946; s. Carlin Alexander and Marjorie Ann (Mayland) T.; adopted s. Howard Elting Jr.; m. Barbara Laflin, May 27, 1984; children: Charles, Luli, Tyler, Tucker, Wayland. BA, Princeton U., 1967; MA, Johns Hopkins U., 1969. Legis. asst. U.S. Senate, 1966; assoc. ops. officer Office of Sec., U.S. Dept. State, 1971-73; research coordinator Presdl.-Congressional Commn. on Orgn. of Govt. for Conduct of Fgn. Policy, Washington, 1973-74; dir. research trade U.S. Fed. Energy Adminstrn., Washington, 1974-78; dep. asst. sec. U.S. Dept. Energy, Washington, 1979-80; staff mem. Nat. Security Council, 1980-81; sr. v.p. N.Y. Merc. Exchange, N.Y.C., 1981-82, pres., 1982-84; ptnr. Bear Stearns & Co., Los Angeles, 1984-85; exec. pub. Petroleum Intelligence Weekly, N.Y.C., 1985-87; pres. Regent Internat., Washington and The Hague, 1987-89; v.p., ptnr. Booz, Allen & Hamilton, Inc., San Francisco, 1989—. Chmn. spl. gifts Am. Cancer Soc., 1983; chmn. bd. dirs. Mirror Repertory Co., 1987-90; trustee, mem. exec. com., chmn. corp. rels. com. No. Calif. World Affairs Coun.; mem. San Francisco Fgn. Rels. com.; bd. trustees Am. U. of Cairo. With USNR, 1969-71. Decorated AF Commendation medal; Ford Found. European Area Travel grantee, 1972; Woodrow Wilson fellow, 1967; McConnell fellow, 1966 Mem. Coun. Fgn. Rels., Internat. Assn. for Energy Econs. Democrat. Unitarian. Clubs: Colonial (Princeton, N.J.), St. Francis Yacht Club, Bankers (San Francisco). Home: 1149 Manor Dr Sonoma CA 95476 E-mail: treat_john@bah.com

TREECE, JAMES LYLE, lawyer; b. Colorado Springs, Colo., Feb. 6, 1925; s. Lee Oren and Ruth Ida (Smith) T.; m. Ruth Julie Treece, Aug. 7, 1949 Idiv. 1984); children: James (dec.), Karen Pelletier, Teryl Wait, Jamilyn Smyser, Carol Crowder. Student, Colo. State U., 1943, Colo. U., 1943, U.S. Naval Acad., 1944-46; BS, Mesa Coll., 1946; JD, U. Colo., 1950; postgrad., U. N.C., 1976-77. Bar: Colo. 1952, U.S. Dist. Ct. Colo. 1952, U.S. Ct. Appeals (10th cir.) 1952, U.S. Supreme Ct. 1967. Assoc. Yegge, Hall, Treece & Evans and predecessors, 1951-59, ptnr., 1959-69; U.S. atty. Colo., 1969-77; pres. Treece & Bahr and predecessor firms, Littleton, 1977-91; mcpl. judge, 1967-68; mem. faculty Nat. Trial Advocacy Inst., 1973-76, Law-Sci. Acad., 1964. Chmn. Colo. Dept. Pub. Welfare, 1963-68; chmn. Colo. Dept. Social Svcs., 1968-69; mem. Littleton Bd. Edn., 1977-81. Served with USNR, 1944-46. Recipient awards Colo. Assn. Sch. Bds., 1981, IRS, 1977, FBI, 1977, DEA, 1977, Fed. Exec. Bd., 1977. Mem. Fed. Bar Assn. (pres. Colo. 1975, award 1975), Colo. Bar Assn. (bd. govs.), Denver Bar Assn. (v.p., trustee). Republican. Episcopalian. Home: 12651 N Pebble Beach Dr Sun City AZ 85351-3327 E-mail: jltreece@juno.com

TREIGER, IRWIN LOUIS, lawyer; b. Seattle, Sept. 10, 1934; s. Sam S. and Rose (Steinberg) T.; m. Betty Lou Friedlander, Aug. 18, 1957; children: Louis H., Karen I., Kenneth B. BA, U. Wash., 1955, JD, 1957; LLM in Taxation, NYU, 1958. Bar: Wash. 1958, D.C. 1982, U.S. Dist. Ct. (we. dist.) Wash., U.S. Ct. Appeals (9th cir.), U.S. Supreme Ct. Assoc. Bogle & Gates, Seattle, 1958-63, ptnr., 1964-99, chmn., 1986-94; ptnr. Dorsey & Whitney LLP, Seattle, 1999—. Pres. Jewish Fedn. Greater Seattle, 1993-95; chmn. Mayor's Symphony Panel, 1986, Corp. Coun. for the Arts, 1987-88; pres. Seattle Symphony Found., 1986—; trustee, co-chmn. Cornish Coll. of the Arts, 1990-96; trustee The Seattle Found., 1992—, vice chair, 1999—; trustee Samis Found., 1989—; chmn. King County Baseball Pk. Commn., 1995. Fellow Am. Coll. Tax Counsel; mem. ABA (chmn. taxation sect. 1988-89, sect. del. 1990-96, bd. govs. 2000—), Wash. State Bar Assn. (chmn. taxation sect. 1975, co-chmn. nat. conf. lawyers and accts. 1997-2000), Greater Seattle C. of C. (chmn. 1993-94), Seattle Rotary (trustee 1998-2000), Seattle Rotary Svc. Found. (v.p. 1995-96, pres. 1996-97). Jewish. Office: Dorsey & Whitney LLP 1420 5th Ave Ste 3400 Seattle WA 98101-4010 E-mail: treiger.irwin@dorseylaw.com

TREISTER, GEORGE MARVIN, lawyer; b. Oxnard, Calif., Sept. 5, 1923; s. Isadore Harry and Augusta Lee (Bloom) T.; m. Jane Goldberg, Jan. 24, 1946; children: Laura, Neil, Adam, Dana. B.S., UCLA, 1943; LL.B., Yale U., 1949. Bar: Calif. 1950. Law clk. to chief justice Calif. Supreme Ct., 1949-50; law clk. to Assoc. Justice Hugo L. Black U. S. Supreme Ct., 1950-51; asst. U.S. atty. So. Dist. Calif., 1951-53; dep. atty. gen. Calif., 1953; practiced in Los Angeles, 1953—; mem. Stutman, Treister and Glatt, 1953—; instr. U. So. Calif. Law Sch., 1954-98, Stanford U. Law Sch., 1977-81. Mem., former vice chmn. Nat. Bankruptcy Conf.; former mem. adv. com. on bankruptcy rules Jud. Conf. U.S. Contbr. articles to profl. jours. Served with USNR, 1943-46. Mem. Am. Law Inst., Am. Judicature Soc. Home: 1201 Neil Creek Rd Ashland OR 97520-9778 Office: 3699 Wilshire Blvd Los Angeles CA 90010-2719

TREMBLAY, WILLIAM ANDREW, English language educator; b. Southbridge, Mass., June 9, 1940; s. Arthur Achille and Irene (Fontaine) T.; m. Cynthia Ann Crooks, Sept. 28, 1962; children: William Crooks, Benjamin Philip, John Fontaine. BA, Clark U., 1962, MA, 1969; MFA in Poetry, U. Mass., 1972. English tchr. Southbridge (Mass.) High Sch., 1962-63, Sutton (Mass.) High Sch., 1963-65, Tantasqua Regional High Sch., Sturbridge, Mass., 1965-67; asst. prof. Leicester (Mass.) Jr. Coll., 1967-70; teaching asst. U. Mass., Amherst, 1970-72; instr. Springfield (Mass.) Coll., 1972-73; prof. English Colo. State U., Fort Collins, 1973—, dir. MFA program in creative writing. Fulbright-Hays lectureship, Lisbon, Portugal, 1979, NEH summer program, 1981; mem. program dirs. coun. Associated Writing Programs, 1984-86. Author: The June Rise: The Apocryphal Letters of Antoine Janis, 1994, (poetry) Rainstorm Over the Alphabet, 2001, Duhamel: Ideas of Order in Little Canada, 1986, Second Sun: New and Selected Poems, 1985, Home Front, 1978, The Anarchist Heart, 1977, Crying in the Cheap Seats, 1971; editor-in-chief: Colo. Rev., 1983-91. Summer writing fellow Corp. of Yaddo, 1989, Creative Writing fellow Nat. Endowment for Arts, 1985; recipient Pushcart prize Pushcart Prize Anthology, 1987. Mem. Puerto del Sol (bd. advisors). Home: 3412 Lancaster Dr Fort Collins CO 80525-2817 Office: Colo State U Dept English Fort Collins CO 80523-0001

TRENBERTH, KEVIN EDWARD, atmospheric scientist; b. Christchurch, New Zealand, Nov. 8, 1944; came to U.S., 1977; s. Edward Maurice and Ngaira Ivy (Eyre) T.; m. Gail Neville Thompson, Mar. 21, 1970; children: Annika Gail, Angela Dawn. BSc with honors, U. Canterbury, Christchurch, 1966; ScD, MIT, 1972. Meteorologist New Zealand Meteorol. Service, Wellington, 1966-76, supt. dynamic meteorology, 1976-77; assoc. prof. meteorology U. Ill., Urbana, 1977-82, prof., 1982-84; scientist Nat. Ctr. Atmospheric Research, Boulder, Colo., 1984-86, sr. scientist, 1986—, leader empirical studies group, 1987, head sect. climate analysis, 1987—; dep. dir. climate and global dynamics divsn. Nat. Ctr. Atmospheric Rsch., Boulder, 1991-95. Mem. joint sci. com. for world climate rsch. programme, com. climate changes and the ocean Tropical Oceans Global Atmosphere Program Sci. Steering Group, 1990-94; mem. Climate Variability and Predictability Sci. Steering Group, 1995—, co-chair, 1996-99; mem. joint sci. com. World Climate Rsch. Program, 1999—. Editor: Climate System Modeling, 1992, Earth Interactions, 1996-98; contbr. Intergovernmental Panel on Climate Change, 1990, 92, lead author, 1995, 2001; contbr. articles to profl. jours. Grantee NSF, NOAA, NASA. Fellow Am. Meteorol. Soc. (editor sci. jour. 1981-86, com. chmn. 1985-87, Editor's award 1989, Jule G. Charney award 2000), AAAS (coun. del. sect. atmosphere and hydrosphere sci. 1993-97), Royal Soc. New Zealand (hon.); mem. NAS (earth scis. com. 1982-85, tropical oceans global atmosphere adv. panel 1984-87, polar rsch. bd. 1986-90, climate rsch. com. 1987-90, global oceans atmosphere land sys. panel 1994-98, panel on reconciling temperature observations, 1999-2000, com. on global change rsch. 1999—), Meterol. Soc. New Zealand. Home: 1445 Landis Ct Boulder CO 80303-1122 Office: Nat Ctr Atmospheric Rsch PO Box 3000 Boulder CO 80307-3000 E-mail: trenbert@ucar.edu

TRESHIE, R. DAVID, former newspaper publishing executive; Publ. The Orange County Register, Santa Ana, Calif., ret., 1999. Office: The Orange County Register 625 N Grand Ave Santa Ana CA 92701-4347

TREVINO, MARIO H. protective services official; b. Bellingham, Wash., July 27, 1952; AAS, Shoreline C.C.; BA in Pub. Adminstrn. summa cum laude, Seattle U., 1986. Firefighter Seattle Fire Dept., 1973-96, bat. chief, capt. fire investigations, chief emergency med. svcs., dep. chief support svcs.; fire chief Las Vegas Fire Dept., 1996—. Mem. Met. Fire Chiefs, Internat. Assn. Fire Chiefs, Western Fire Chiefs, Nev. Fire Chiefs, So. Nev. Fire Chiefs. Office: Las Vegas Fire Svcs Dept 500 N Casino Center Blvd Las Vegas NV 89101-2944

TREVITHICK, RONALD JAMES, underwriter; b. Portland, Oreg., Sept. 13, 1944; s. Clifford Vincent and Amy Lois (Turner) T.; m. Delberta Russell, Sept. 11, 1965; children: Pamela, Carmen, Marla, Sheryl. BBA, U. Wash., 1966. CLU, CPA, ChFC, accredited estate planner. Mem. audit staff Ernst & Ernst, Anchorage, 1966, 68-70; pvt. practice acctg. Fairbanks, Alaska, 1970-73; with Touche Ross & Co., Anchorage, 1973-78, audit ptnr., 1976-78. Exec. v.p., treas., bd. dirs. Veco Internat., Inc., 1978-82; pres., bd. dirs. Petroleum Contractors Ltd., 1980-82; bd. dirs. P.S. Contractors A/S, Norcon, Inc., OFC of Alaska, Inc., V.E. Systems Svcs., Inc., Veco Turbo Svcs., Inc., Veco Drilling Inc., Vemar, Inc., 1978-82; with Coopers & Lybrand, Anchorage, 1982-85; field underwriter, registered rep. New York Life Ins., 1985-2000, Princor, 2000—, Prin. Fin. Group, 2000—; instr. acctg. U. Alaska, 1971-72; lectr. acctg. and taxation The Am. Coll., 1972, 97, instr. adv. sales Life Underwriters Tng. Coun., 1988-89; bd. dirs. Ahtna Devel. Corp., 1985-86. Divsn. chmn. United Way, 1975-76, YMCA, 1979; bd. dirs., fin. chmn. Anchorage Arts Coun., 1975-78, Am. Diabetes Assn., Alaska affiliate, 1985-91, chmn. bd. 1988-89, chmn. hon. bd. 1992-96, Am. Heart Assn., Alaska affiliate, 1986-87, Anchorage dist. com., 1994-96, treas. 1996-98, Alaska State Youth Soccer Assn.; mem. Anchorage Estate Planning Coun., 1996-2000, treas., 1998-99, sec. 1999-2000. With U.S. Army, 1967-68. Mem. Fin. Execs. Inst. (pres. Alaska chpt. 1981-83), Soc. Fin. Svcs. Profs. (v.p. Alaska chpt. 1993-94, pres. 1994-96), Alaska Assn. Life Underwriters (sec., treas. 1987-90), Alaska Goldstrikers Soccer Club (pres. 1992-93, youth coach 1985-95, Ina K tournament dir. 1992-98), Petroleum Club (treas. 1996-2000), Beta Alpha Psi. Home: 4421 Huffman Rd Anchorage AK 99516-2211 Office: 1600 A St Ste 110 Anchorage AK 99501-5146 E-mail: ron4berta@aol.com

TRICOLES, GUS PETER, electromagnetic engineer, physicist, consultant; b. San Francisco, Oct. 18, 1931; s. Constantine Peter and Eugenia (Elias) T.; m. Beverly Mildred Ralsky, Dec. 20, 1953 (dec. Dec. 1974); children: Rosanne, Robin; m. Aileen Irma Aronson, Apr. 1, 1980 (div. June 1980). BA in Physics, UCLA, 1955; MS in Applied Math., San Diego State U., 1958; MS in Applied Physics, U. Calif., San Diego, 1962, PhD in Applied Physics, 1971. Engr. Convair divsn. Gen. Dynamics, San Diego, 1955-59, engr. Electronics divsn., 1962-75, engring. mgr. Electronics divsn., 1975-89, sr. engring. staff specialist, 1989-95, Tracor, 1995-99; engr. Smyth Rsch. Assn., San Diego, 1959-61; rsch. asst. Scripps Instn. Oceanography, La Jolla, Calif., 1961-62; sr. engring. staff specialist G.D.E. Systems, Inc., San Diego, 1992—, BAE Sys., 1999—. Engring. staff specialist B&M Sys., 2000; cons. Ga. Inst. Tech., Atlanta, 1972, 79-80, Transco Industries, L.A., 1973, Aero Geo Industries, San Antonio, 1980-82, Vantage Assocs., San Diego, 1988; rsch. reviewer NRC, NAS, Boulder, Colo., 1986-88. Author: (with others) Radome Engineering Handbook, 1970, Antenna Handbook, 1988; contbr. articles to profl. jours.; 19 patents in field. With USN, 1952-53. Fellow IEEE (antenna standards com. 1980—, advancement com. 1988), Optical Soc. Am. (local sect. v.p. 1966); mem. N.Y. Acad. Scis., Am. Geophys. Union. Avocations: woodworking, photography. Home: 4633 Euclid Ave San Diego CA 92115-3226 Office: BAE Sys PO Box 509009 San Diego CA 92127

TRIEWEILER, TERRY NICHOLAS, state supreme court justice; b. Dubuque, Iowa, Mar. 21, 1948; s. George Nicholas and Anne Marie (Oastern) T.; m. Carol M. Jacobson, Aug. 11, 1972; children: Kathryn Anne, Christina Marie, Anna Theresa. BA, Drake U., 1970, JD, 1972. Bar: Iowa 1973, Wash. 1973, U.S. Dist. Ct. (so. dist.) Iowa 1973, U.S. Dist. Ct. (we. dist.) Wash. 1973, Mont. 1975, U.S. Dist. Ct. Mont. 1977. Staff atty. Polk County Legal Services, Des Moines, 1973; assoc. Hullin, Roberts, Mines, Fite & Riveland, Seattle, 1973-75, Morrison & Hedman, Whitefish, Mont., 1975-77; sole practice, Whitefish; justice Mont. Supreme Ct., Helena, 1991—; lectr. U. Mont. Law Sch., 1981—; mem. com. to amend civil proc. rules Mont. Supreme Ct., Helena, 1984, commn. to draft pattern jury instrns., 1985; mem. Gov.'s Adv. Com. on Amendment to Work Compensation Act, adv. com. Mont. Work Compensation Ct. Mem. ABA, Mont. Bar Assn. (pres. 1986-87), Wash. Bar Assn., Iowa Bar Assn., Assn. Trial Lawyers Am., Mont. Trial Lawyers Assn. (dir., pres.). Democrat. Roman Catholic. Home: 1079 Woodbridge Dr Helena MT 59601-5477 Office: Mont Supreme Ct PO Box 203001 Justice Bldg Rm 410 215 N Sanders St Helena MT 59601-4522

TRIGIANO, LUCIEN LEWIS, physician; b. Easton, Pa., Feb. 9, 1926; s. Nicholas and Angeline (Lewis) T.; children: Lynn Anita, Glenn Larry, Robert Nicholas. Student, Tex. Christian U., 1944-45, Ohio U., 1943-44, 46-47, Milligan Coll., 1944, Northwestern U., 1945, Temple U., 1948-52. Diplomate Am. Bd. Phys. Medicine & Rehab. Intern Meml. Hosp., Johnstown, Pa., 1952-53; resident Lee Hosp., Johnstown, 1953-54; gen. practice Johnstown, 1953-59; med. dir. Pa. Rehab. Ctr., Johnstown, 1959-62, chief phys. medicine & rehab., 1964-70; fellow phys. medicine & rehab. N.Y. Inst. Phys. Medicine & Rehab., 1964-70; dir. rehab. medicine Lee Hosp., 1964-71, Ralph K. Davies Med. Ctr., San Francisco, 1973-75, St. Joseph's Hosp., San Francisco, 1975-78, St. Francis Meml. Hosp., San Francisco, 1978-83, Rehab. Ctr. Nev., Las Vegas, 1998—. Asst. prof. phys. medicine and rehab. Temple U. Sch. Medicine; founder Disability Alert. Served with USNR, 1944-46. Mem. AMA, Am. Coll. Physicians, Pa. Med. Soc., San Francisco County Med. Soc., Am. Acad. Phys. Medicine & Rehab., Am. Congress Phys. Medicine, Calif. Acad. Phys. Medicine, Nat. Rehab. Assn., Babcock Surg. Soc. Home and Office: 1421 Casa Del Rey Ct Las Vegas NV 89117-1538 E-mail: lltmdmd@aol.com

TRILLING, GEORGE HENRY, physicist, educator; b. Bialystok, Poland, Sept. 18, 1930; came to U.S., 1941; s. Max and Eugenie (Walfisz) T.; m. Madeleine Alice Monic, June 26, 1955; children: Stephen, Yvonne, David. BS, Calif. Inst. Tech., Pasadena, 1951, PhD, 1955. Research fellow Calif. Inst. Tech., Pasadena, 1955-56; Fulbright post-doctoral fellow Ecole Polytechnique, Paris, 1956-57; asst. to assoc. prof. U. Mich., Ann Arbor, 1957-60; assoc. to prof. dept. physics U. Calif., Berkeley, 1960-94, prof. emeritus, 1994—. Fellow Am. Phys. Soc., Am. Acad. Arts and Scis.; mem. NAS. Achievements include: research in high energy physics. Office: Lawrence Berkeley Nat Lab Berkeley CA 94720-0001

TRIMBLE, PHILLIP RICHARD, law educator; b. Springfield, Ohio, Nov. 12, 1937; s. Melvin R. and Dorothy (Lang) T.; m. Stephanie Gardner, July 20, 1963 (div. 1977); children: John, William. BA, Ohio U., 1958; MA, Tufts U., 1959; JD, Harvard U., 1963. Bar: NY 1964. Legal writing instr. U. Calif., Berkeley, 1963-64; assoc. Cravath, Swaine & Moore, N.Y.C., 1964-70; staff mem. fgn. rels. com. U.S. Senate, Washington, 1971-72; asst. legal adviser Dept. State, Washington, 1973-78; counsel to the mayor N.Y.C., 1978; dep. mayor N.Y.C., 1979; U.S. ambassador Nepal, 1980-81; prof. law UCLA, 1981—, vice provost internat. studies, 1999—. Mem. exec. com. Asia Soc. So. Calif. Ctr., L.A., 1981-94; vis. prof. law Stanford U., 1988-89, U. Mich., 1995-96; U.S. panelist under U.S.-Can. Free Trade Agreement, NAFTA; cons. ACDA, 1989-92. Mem. bd. editors Am. Jour. Internat. Law, 1993-98. Fellow Explorers Club; mem. Am. Soc. Internat. Law, Am. Alpine Club (bd. dirs. 1978-87). Democrat. Avocation: mountaineering. Office: UCLA Bunche Hall 405 Hilgard Ave Los Angeles CA 90095-9000

TRIMBLE, STANLEY WAYNE, hydrology and geography educator; b. Columbia, Tenn., Dec. 8, 1940; s. Stanley Drake and Clara Faye (Smith) T.; m. Alice Erle Gunn, Aug. 16, 1964; children: Alicia Anne, Jennifer Lusanne. BS, U. North Ala., 1964; MA, U. Ga., 1970, PhD, 1973. Asst. prof. hydrology and geography U. Wis., Milw., 1972-75; from assoc. prof. to prof. UCLA, 1975—. Vis. asst. prof. U. Chgo., 1978, vis. assoc. prof., 1981, vis. prof. environ. geography, 1990—, vis. prof. U. Durham (Eng.), 1998; vis. lectr. U. London, 1985; hydrologist U.S. Geol. Survey, 1974-84; vis. prof. U. Vienna, 1994, 99; Frost lectr. Brit. Geomorphological Rsch. Group, Durham, Eng., 1994; vis. rsch. lectr. Oxford U., 1995; Fulbright scholar in U.K., 1995; vis. fellow Keble Coll., Oxford U., 1995, Hatfield Coll. U. Durham, 1998. Author: Culturally Accelerated Sedimentation on the Middle Georgia Piedmont, 1971, Man-Induced Erosion on the Southern Piedmont, 1700-1970, 1974, Soil Conservation and the Reduction, 1982, Sediment Characteristics of Tennessee Streams, 1984; joint editor-in-chief: Catena, 1995—; contbr. articles to profl. jours. Served to 1st lt. U.S. Army, 1963-65. Grantee U.S. Geol. Survey, Washington, 1974-79, Wis. Dept. Natural Resources, Madison, 1978, 82, 93, 94, 95, NSF, Washington, 1976, Agrl. Rsch. Svc. of USDA, Washington, 1972, Nat. Geographic Soc., 1993. Mem. NAS-NRC (com. on watershed mgmt. 1996-98), Assn. Am. Geographers, Am. Geophys. Union, Soil Conservation Soc. Am., Brit. Geomorphol. Rsch. Group, Sigma Xi. Republican. Avocations: historic houses, documentation and restoration. Office: UCLA Dept Geography 405 Hilgard Ave Los Angeles CA 90095-9000 E-mail: trimble@geog.ucla.edu

TRIPLETT, ARLENE ANN, management consultant; b. Portland, Oreg., Jan. 21, 1942; d. Vincent Michael and Lorraine Catherine (Starr) Jakovich; m. William Karrol Triplett, Jan. 27, 1962; children: Stephen Michael, Patricia Ann. BABA, U. Calif., Berkeley, 1963. Budgets and reports analyst Cutter Labs., Berkeley, 1963-66; controller Citizens for Reagan, 1975-76; dir. adminstrn. Republican. Nat. Com., 1977-80; asst. sec. Dept. Commerce, Washington, 1981-83; assoc. dir. mgmt. Office Mgmt. and Budget, Exec. Office of Pres., Washington, 1983-85; prin. assoc. McManis Assocs., Inc., 1985-87, v.p., 1987-89, sr. v.p., 1989-93; from v.p. to exec. v.p. Am. Tours Internat., Inc., L.A., 1993-97; prin. McManis Assoc., Manhattan Beach, Calif., 1997-98, IBM, Manhattan Beach, 1999—. Roman Catholic. Office: IBM 228 18th St Manhattan Beach CA 90266-4651

TRIPPENSEE, GARY ALAN, aerospace executive, retired; b. Jefferson City, Mo., May 23, 1940; s. Walter Anton and Juanita (Schneider) T.; m. Concha Elvira Perez, Aug. 18, 1981; children: Jena, Darin. BSME, U. Mo., Rolla, 1962; AA in Bus., Antelope Valley Coll., Lancaster, Calif., 1974. Lic. airframe and powerplant mechanic, FAA; single/multi-engine comml. aircraft lic. land & sea, Inst.; cert. flight instr., instrument. Aircraft flight test engr. McDonnell Douglas, St. Louis, 1965-79; project mgr.

NASA/Dryden Flight Rsch. Ctr., Edwards, Calif., 1979—, project mgr. F14, 1983-84, project mgr. F15, 1984-85, project mgr. X-29, 1985-91, project mgr. X-31, 1991-92, internat. test. orgn. dir. X-31, 1993-95, project mgr. X-33, 1996-2000, project mgr. X-37, 2000-01, ret., 2001. Capt. U.S. Army C.E., 1962-65, Vietnam. Recipient Laurels award for aeronautics/propulsion Aviation Week & Space Tech., 1990, 93, Outstanding Alumni award U. Mo.-Rolla, 2000. Mem. EAA, Acad. Mech. Engrs. Avocations: flying, fishing, R/C models. Home: 357 Airport Dr Grove OK 74344

TRISKA, JAN FRANCIS, retired political science educator; b. Prague, Czechoslovakia, Jan. 26, 1922; came to U.S., 1948, naturalized, 1955; s. Jan and Bozena (Kubiznak) T.; m. Carmel Lena Burastero, Aug. 26, 1951; children: Mark Lawrence, John William. JUD, Charles U., Prague, 1948; LLM, Yale U., 1950, JSD, 1952; PhD, Harvard U., 1957. Co-dir. Soviet treaties Hoover Instn., Stanford, Calif., 1956-58; lectr. dept. polit. sci. U. Calif., Berkeley, 1957-58; asst. prof. Cornell U., Ithaca, N.Y., 1958-60; assoc. prof. Stanford U., Calif., 1960-65, prof. polit. sci., 1965-89, assoc. chmn. dept., 1965-66, 68-69, 71-72, 74-75, prof. emeritus, 1990—. Cons. Inst. State and Law, Czech Acad. Scis., Prague, 1995—. Co-author: (with Slusser) The Theory, Law and Policy of Soviet Treaties, 1962; (with Finley) Soviet Foreign Policy, 1968; (with Cocks) Political Development and Political Change in Eastern Europe, 1977; (with Ike, North) The World of Superpowers, 1981, (with Gati) Blue Collar Workers in Eastern Europe, 1981, Dominant Powers and Subordinate States, 1986, The Great War's Forgotten Front, 1998 (Czech, German, Slovene & Italian edits.); mem. editl. bd. East European Quar. Comparative Politics, Internat. Jour. Sociology, Jour. Comparative Politics, Studies in Comparative Communism, Soviet Statutes and Decisions, Documents in Communist Affairs. Recipient Rsch. award Ford Found., 1963-68, Josef Hlavka Commemorative medal Czechoslovak Acad. Scis., 1992, M.A. Comenius 1592-1992 Meml. medal Czechoslovak Pedagogical Mus., Prague, 1991; fellow NSF, 1971-72, Sen. Fulbright fellow, 1973-74, Woodrow Wilson fellow Internat. Ctr. for Scholars, 1980-81. Mem. Am. Polit. Sci. Assn. (sec. pres. conf. on communist studies 1970-76), Assn. Advancement Slavic Studies (bd. dirs. 1975-83), Am. Soc. Internat. Law (exec. coun. 1964-67), Czechoslovak Soc. Arts and Scis. (pres. 1978-80, 90-92), Inst. for Human Scis. Vienna (acting for Commn. European Communities, Brussels, com. experts on transformation of nat. higher edn. and rsch. system in Ctrl. Europe, Brussels 1991—), Fly Fishers Club (Palo Alto, Calif.). Democrat. Home: 720 Vine St Menlo Park CA 94025-6154 Office: Stanford U Dept Polit Sci Stanford CA 94305 E-mail: triska@stanford.edu

TROIDL, RICHARD JOHN, banker; b. Buffalo, July 2, 1944; s. Henry Albert and Lola Julian (Davern) T.; m. Diane Budney, Nov. 20, 1982; children: Nicholas, Holly. AAS, SUNY, Buffalo, 1973. Sr. v.p. Empire Am. Fed. Savs. Bank, Buffalo, 1969-93; pres. Express Svcs. of Am., Inc., Las Vegas, Nev., 1993—. With U.S. Army, 1965-71. Office: Express Svcs Am Inc 6120 W Tropicana Ave Ste A16 Las Vegas NV 89103-4697

TRONCOSO, JOSE GERARDO, protective services official; b. Juarez-Chin, Mex., Dec. 26, 1952; MA in Pub. Adminstrn., LaSalle U., 1991. Cert. Peace Officer Standards-Tng., Nev. Police officer N. Las Vegas Police Dept., 1974-97; U.S. marshall U.S. Marshall Svc., 1997—. Tchr. Clark Co. traffic sch., City Las. Vegas traffic sch./DUI instr. Mem. Nat. Safety Council., Hispanics in Politics. Mem. N. Las Vegas Police Officers Assn. (chmn. bd. dirs.), Nev. Conf. Police and Sheriffs, Lation Peace Officers Assn., Latin C. of C., Internat. Union Police Assocs., Internat. Assn. Chiefs of Police. Office: PO Box 16039 300 Las Vegas Blvd S Las Vegas NV 89101-5833

TROST, BARRY MARTIN, chemist, educator; b. Phila., June 13, 1941; s. Joseph and Esther T.; m. Susan Paula Shapiro, Nov. 25, 1967; children: Aaron David, Carey Daniel. BA cum laude, U. Pa., 1962; PhD, MIT, 1965; D (hon.), U. Claude Bernard, Lyons, France, 1994, Technion, Israel, 1997. Mem. faculty U. Wis., Madison, 1965—, prof., chemistry, 1969—, Evan P. and Marion Helfaer prof. chemistry, from 1976, Vilas rsch. prof. chemistry; prof. chemistry Stanford U., 1987—, Tamaki prof. humanities and scis., 1990, chmn. dept., 1996—. Cons. Merck, Sharp & Dohme, E.I. duPont de Nemours.; Chem. Soc. centenary lectr., 1982 Author: Problems in Spectroscopy, 1967, Sulfur Ylides, 1975; editor-in-chief Comprehensive Organic Synthesis, 1991—, ChemTracts/Organic Chemistry, 1993—; editor: Structure and Reactivity Concepts in Organic Chemistry series, 1972—; assoc. editor Jour. Am. Chem. Soc., 1974-80; mem. editl. bd. Organic Reactions Series, 1971—, Chemistry A European Jour., 1995—, Sci. of Synthesis, Houben-Weyl Methods of Molecular Transformations, 1995—; contbr. numerous articles to profl. jours. Recipient Dreyfus Found. Tech.-Scholar award, 1970, 77, Creative Work in Synthetic Organic Chemistry award, 1981, Baekland medal, 1981, Alexander von Humboldt award, 1984, Guenther award, 1990, Janssen prize, 1990, Roger Adams award Am. Chem. Soc. 1995, Presdl. Green Univ. Challenge award, 1998, Nichols medal, 2000; named Chem. Pioneer, Am. Inst. Chemists, 1983; NSF fellow, 1963-65, Sloan Found. fellow, 1967-69, Am. Swiss Found. fellow, 1975—, Zencca fellow, 1997; Cope scholar, 1989. Mem. AAAS, Am. Chem. Soc. (award in pure chemistry 1977, Roger Adams award 1995, Herbert C. Brown award for creative rsch. in synthetic methods 1999), Nat. Acad. Scis., Am. Acad. Arts and Scis., Chem. Soc. London. Office: Stanford U Dept Chemistry Stanford CA 94305

TROTT, STEPHEN SPANGLER, federal judge, musician; b. Glen Ridge, N.J., Dec. 12, 1939; s. David Herman and Virginia (Spangler) T.; children: Christina, Shelley; m. Carol C. BA, Wesleyan U., 1962; LLB, Harvard U., 1965; LLD (hon.), Santa Clara U., 1992. Bar: Calif. 1966, U.S. Dist. Ct. (cen. dist.) Calif. 1966, U.S. Ct. Appeals (9th cir.) 1983, U.S. Supreme Ct. 1984. Guitarist, mem. The Highwaymen, 1958—; dep. dist. atty. Los Angeles County Dist. Atty.'s Office, Los Angeles, 1966-75, chief dep. dist. atty., 1975-79; U.S. dist. atty. Central Dist. Calif., Los Angeles, 1981-83; asst. atty. gen. criminal div. Dept. Justice, Washington, 1983-86; mem. faculty Nat. Coll. Dist. Attys., Houston, 1973—; chmn. central dist. Calif. Law Enforcement Coordinating Com., Houston, 1981-83; coordinator Los Angeles-Nev. Drug Enforcement Task Force, 1982-83; assoc. atty. gen. Justice Dept., Washington, 1986-88; chmn. U.S. Interpol, 1986-88; judge U.S. Ct. of Appeals 9th Cir., Boise, Idaho, 1988—. Trustee Wesleyan U., 1984-87; bd. dirs., pres. Children's Home Soc., Idaho, 1990—; pres., bd. dirs. Boise Philharm. Assn., 1995—, v.p., 1997-99, pres., 1999—. Recipient Gold record as singer-guitarist for Michael Row the Boat Ashore, 1961, Disting. Faculty award Nat. Coll. Dist. Attys., 1977 Mem. Am. Coll. Trial Lawyers, Wilderness Fly Fishers Club (pres. 1975-77), Brentwood Racing Pigeon Club (pres. 1977-82), Idaho Racing Pigeon Assn., Magic Castle, Internat. Brotherhood Magicians, Idaho Classic Guitar Soc. (founder, pres. 1989—). Republican. Office: US Ct Appeals 9th Cir 667 US Courthouse 550 W Fort St Boise ID 83724-0101

TROTTER, F(REDERICK) THOMAS, retired academic administrator; b. L.A., Apr. 17, 1926; s. Fred B. and Hazel (Thomas) T.; m. Gania Demaree, June 27, 1953; children— Ruth Elizabeth, Paula Anne (dec.), Tania, Mary. AB, Occidental Coll., 1950, DD, 1968; STB, Boston U., 1953, PhD, 1958; LHD, Ill. Wesleyan U., 1974, Cornell Coll., 1985, Westmar Coll., 1987; LLD, U. Pacific, 1978, Wesleyan Coll., 1981; EdD, Columbia Coll., 1984; LittD, Alaska Pacific U., 1987. Exec. sec. Boston U. Student Christian Assn., 1951-54; ordained elder Calif.-Pacific, Methodist Ch., 1953; pastor Montclair (Calif.) Meth. Ch., 1956-59; lectr. So. Calif. Sch. Theology at Claremont, 1957-59, instr., 1959-60, asst. prof., 1960-63, assoc. prof., 1963-66, prof., 1966, dean, 1961; prof. religion and arts, dean Sch. Theology Claremont, 1961-73; mem. Bd. Higher Edn. and Ministry, United Meth. Ch., 1972-73, gen. sec., 1973-87; pres. Alaska Pacific U., Anchorage, 1988-95; ret., 1995. Dir. Inst. for Antiquity and Christianity at Claremont. Author: Jesus and the Historian, 1968, Loving God with One's Mind, 1987, God Is with Us, 1997, Politics, Morality, and Higher Education, 1997, weekly column local newspapers; editor-at-large: Christian Century, 1969-84. Trustee Dillard U. Served with USAAF, 1944-46. Kent fellow Soc. for Values in Higher Edn., 1954; Dempster fellow Meth. Ch., 1954 Mem. Rotary Internat. (Anchorage Downtown), Commonwealth North. Home: 75-136 Kiowa Dr Indian Wells CA 92210

TROUNSTINE, PHILIP JOHN, communications consultant; b. Cin., July 30, 1949; s. Henry P. and Amy May (Joseph) Trounstine; children: Jessica, David; m. Deborah Williams, May 1, 1993; children: Amy, Ryan, Patrick Wilkes. Student, U. Vt., 1967-68, Stanford U., 1968-70; BA in Journalism, San Jose State U., 1975. Graphic artist Eric Printing, San Jose, Calif., 1972-75; reporter Indpls. Star, Ind., 1975-78, San Jose Mercury News, Calif., 1978-83, editl. writer, 1983-86, polit. editor, 1986-99; ednl. cons. Teen Recovery Strategies, 1995-99; comms. dir. Gov. Gray Davis, Calif., 1999-2001, comm. cons., 2001—. Co-author: Movers & Shakers: The Study of Community Power, 1981. Creator, writer SPJ Gridiron Show, San Jose, 1981-91. Pulliam fellow, 1975, Duke U., 1991, J.S. Knight Stanford U., 1993-94. Mem. Soc. Profl. Journalists (mem. nat. ethics com. 1993-96). Jewish. Avocations: golf, fishing. Home: 620 Middlefield Dr Aptos CA 95003 E-mail: phil@trounstine.com

TROUSDALE, STEPHEN RICHARD, newspaper editor; b. L.A., May 29, 1963; s. Richard Gardner Trousdale and Geraldine Barbara Wisdom. AB, Stanford U., 1985. News editor L.A. Daily Commerce, 1986-87; edit. page editor L.A. Daily Jour., 1987-89, mng. editor, 1989-96; bus. editor Copley L.A. Newspapers, 1996-97; dep. bus. editor Contra Costa Newspapers, 1997-2000, bus. editor, 2000—. Mem. Soc. Profl. Journalists (past pres. L.A. chpt.), AP Mng. Editors, Calif. Soc. Newspaper Editors, Soc. Am. Bus. Editors and Writers. Avocations: skiing, karate. Home: 1820 Virginia St Apt B Berkeley CA 94703-1345 Office: Contra Costa Newspapers 2640 Shadelands Dr Walnut Creek CA 94598-2513 E-mail: strousdale@cctimes.com

TROUT, LINDA COPPLE, state supreme court chief justice; b. Tokyo, Sept. 1, 1951; BA, U. Idaho, 1973, JD, 1977; LLD (hon.), Albertson Coll. Idaho, 1999. Bar: Idaho 1977. Judge magistrate divsn. Idaho Dist. Ct. (2d jud. divsn.), 1983-90, dist. judge, 1991-92, acting trial ct. adminstr., 1987-91; justice Idaho Supreme Ct., 1992—, chief justice, 1997—. Instr. coll. law U. Idaho, 1983, 88. Mem. Idaho State Bar Assn., Clearwater Bar Assn. (pres. 1980-81).

TROW, CLIFFORD W. state legislator; b. Topeka, July 27, 1929; m. Jo Anne J. Trow. BA, Kansas Wesleyan U., 1951; MA, U. Colo., 1958, PhD, 1966. Prof. history Oreg. State U., 1965-97; mem. Oreg. Legislature, Salem, 1974—, vice chair gen. govt. com., mem. ways and means com., mem. subcom. on edn., mem. subcom. on gen. govt. Mem. Oreg. Dem. Leadership Fund, 1998, Oreg. Sen. Dem. Com., 1996, Dem. Party, 1996-98, Early Intervention Coun., 1991, Emergency Bd., 1985-91, High Desert Mus., Oreg. Pub. Broadcasting; chair Benton County Dem. Ctrl. Com., 1972-74; mem. United Ch. of Christ. Mem. LWV, Oreg. Hist. Soc., Common Cause, Triad Club (Oreg. State U.), Lions (Corvallis), Beaver Club. Democrat. United Ch. of Christ. Office: S-319 State Capitol Salem OR 97310-0001

TROWBRIDGE, THOMAS, JR. mortgage banking company executive; b. Troy, N.Y., June 28, 1938; s. of Thomas and Elberta (Wood) T.; m. Delinda Bryan, July 3, 1965; children: Elisabeth Tacy, Wendy Bryan. BA, Yale U., 1960; MBA, Harvard U., 1965. V.p. James W. Rouse & Co., Balt., 1965-66, Washington, 1966-68, San Francisco, 1968-73, 76-78; pres. Rouse Investing Co., Columbia, Md., 1973-76, Trowbridge, Kieselhorst & Co., San Francisco, 1978-97, CEO, chmn., 1997-2000; ret., 2000. Bd. dirs. Columbia Assn., 1975-76; trustee, treas. The Head-Royce Sch., Oakland, Calif., 1980-84; trustee, pres. Gen. Alumni Assn. Phillips Exeter Acad., 1984-90. Lt. USNR, 1960-63. Mem. Urban Land Inst., Calif. Mortgage Bankers Assn. (bd. dirs. 1991-98, pres. 1996-97), Mortgage Bankers Assn. Am. (bd. govs. 1993-2000), Olympic Club, Pacific Union Club, Lambda Alpha Internat. Republican. Presbyterian. Avocation: golf. Home: 4 Ridge Ln Orinda CA 94563-1318

TROY, FREDERIC ARTHUR, II, medical biochemistry educator; b. Evanston, Ill., Feb. 16, 1937; s. Charles McGregor and Virginia Lane (Minto) T.; m. Linda Ann Price, Mar. 23, 1959; children: Karen M., Janet R. BS, Washington U., St. Louis, 1961; PhD, Purdue U., 1966; postdoctoral, Johns Hopkins U., 1968. Asst. prof. U. Calif. Sch. Medicine, Davis, 1968-74, assoc. prof., 1974-80, prof., 1980—, chmn., 1991-94; vis. prof. Karolinska Inst. Med. Sch., Stockholm, 1976-77. Cons. NIH, Bethesda, Md., 1974—, NSF, Washington, 1975—, Damon Runyon Cancer Found., N.Y.C., 1980-81, VA, Washington, 1984-88, U.S. Army Breast Cancer Study Sect., 1999—. Mem. editl. bd. Jour. Biol. Chem., 1988—, Glycobiol., 1990—; contbr. articles to profl. jours. Recipient Research Cancer Devel. award Nat. Cancer Inst., 1975-80; Eleanor Roosevelt Internat. Cancer fellow Am. Cancer Soc., 1976-77. Mem. AAAS, Am. Soc. Biol. Chemistry and Molecular Biology, Am. Assn. Cancer Rsch., Am. Chem. Soc., Am. Soc. Virologists, Biochemistry Soc., Biophysics Soc., Am. Fedn. for Clin. Rsch., N.Y. Acad. Scis., Soc. for Glycobiol. (pres. 1991-92), Am. Med. and Grad. Sch. Dept. Biochem. (pres.-elect 1995—), Sigma Xi. Office: U Calif Sch Medicine Davis CA 95616

TROY, JOSEPH FREED, lawyer; b. Wilkes-Barre, Pa., Aug. 16, 1938; s. Sergei and Shirley Jean T.; m. Brigitta Ann Balos, June 9, 1962; children: Darcy Kendall, Austin Remy. BA, Yale U., 1960; LLB, Harvard U., 1963. Bar: Calif. 1964, D.C. 1979. Assoc. Hindin, McKittrick & Marsh, Beverly Hills, Calif., 1964-68, ptnr., 1968-70; pres. Troy & Gould, Los Angeles, 1970—; lectr. Calif. Continuing Edn. of Bar, 1972-80, 94; dir. Amerigon Inc., 1993-96, Movie Gallery, Inc., 1994—, Digital Video Systems, Inc., 1996-98, Argoquest, Inc., 2000-2001. Author: Let's Go: A Student Guide to Europe, 1962, Accountability of Corporate Management, 1979; co-author: Protecting Corporate Officers and Directors from Liability, 1994, Advising and Defending Corporate Directors and Officers, 1998. Pres. L.A. Chamber Orch. Soc., 1968-75, chmn. bd. dirs., 1975-78, vice chmn. bd. dirs., 1978-81; bd. dirs. L.A. Opera, 1972-2001, mem. exec. com., 1987-99; hon. consul of Tunisia, L.A., 1984-88; chmn. Internat. Festival Soc.; bd. dirs. Brentwood Pk. Property Owners Assn., 1988-2001. Reid Hall fellow U. Paris, 1958 Mem. ABA, Calif. State Bar Assn. (chmn. task force on complex litigation 1997-99), D.C. Bar Assn., L.A. County Bar Assn. (chmn. bus. and corp. law sect. 1977-78), French Am. C. of C. U.S. (exec. v.p. 1983-85), French Am. C. of C. L.A. (chmn. 1982-84), Wine and Food Soc. So. Calif. Inc. (bd. dirs.), Beach Club, Calif. Club. Office: 1801 Century Park E Ste 1600 Los Angeles CA 90067-2318 E-mail: jftroy@troygould.com

TROY, NANCY J. art history educator; BA magna cum laude with honors in art, Wesleyan U., 1974; MA, Yale U., 1976, PhD, 1979. Gallery asst. Waddington Galleries, London, 1973; rsch. asst. Soc. Anonyme Collection, Yale U., New Haven, 1975, tchg. asst. history of art dept., 1975-76; asst. prof. dept. history of art Johns Hopkins U., Balt., 1979-83; asst. prof. dept. art history Northwestern U., Evanston, Ill., 1983-85, assoc. prof., 1985-92, prof., 1992-93, chmn. dept., 1990-92; vis. prof. UCLA, 1994; vis. prof. art history U. So. Calif., L.A., 1994-95, prof., 1995—, chmn. dept., 1997—. Scholar-in-residence Getty Rsch. Inst. for History Art and Humanities, L.A., 1993-96, organizer Work in Progress lecture series, 1993-98; series co-editor Histories, Culturs, Contexts, Reaktion Book, London; curatorial coord., spl. cons. to Ilya Bolotowsky Retrospective, Solomon R. Guggenheim Mus., N.Y.C., summers 1972-74; asst. to curator French paintings Nat. Gallery Art, Washington, summer 1975, bd. advisors Ctr. for Advanced Study in VisualArts, 1999-2002; guest curator Yale U. Art Gallery, 1979; mem. fine arts accessions com. and com. on collections Balt. Mus. Art, 1979-82; cons. De Stijl: 1917-1931, Visions of Utopia exhbn. Walker Art Ctr., Mpls., Washington, The Netherlands, 1982; cons. amplifying art program Art Inst. Chgo., 1984-85; mem. vis. com. Harvard U. Art Mus., Cambridge, Mass., 1992-98; lectr., chmn., moderator numerous symposia, 1980—; numerous invited lectures, 1975—, including U. Brighton, Eng., U. London, Middlexex U., London, Royal Coll. Art, London, U. Toronto, Mt. Holyoke Coll., Barnard Coll., Columbia U., Newcomb Coll., Tulane U., Los Angeles County Mus. Art, Art Inst. Chgo., Terra Mus. Am. Art, Chgo., N.C. Mus. Art, Raleigh, McGill U., Montreal, Vassar Coll; mus. projects peer rev. panelist NEH, 1991; peer reviewer Woodrow Wilson Ctr., Washington, 1994, 96; external reviewer dept. art history U. Mich., 1987; bd. dirs. Nat. Com. for History Art, 1998—; peer reviewer for promotion and tenure Boston U., Lake Forest Coll., Middlesex U., Occidental Coll., U. Mo., Columbia, U. Va., 1996-98. Author: The De Stijl Environment, 1983, Modernism and the Decorative Arts in France: Art Nouveau to Le Corbusier, 1991, (exhbn. catalog) Mondrian and Neo-Plasticism in America, 1979; editor: (with Eve Blau) Architecture and Cubism, 1997; mem. editl. bd. Art Bull., 1993—; contbr. articles and book revs. to profl. jours., including Decorative Arts Soc. Jour., Design Issues, Art Bull., October, Archithese, Arts mag., Portfolio, Design Book Rev., chpts. to books. Mem. Md. Coun. on Arts, 1981-82; trustee Wesleyan U., 1994-97. Recipient Disting. Alumna award Wesleyan U., 1991, postdoctoral tchg. award Lilly Endowment, 1985; Fulbright-Hays grantee, The Netherlands, 1977-78, travel grantee Kress Found., summer 1976, spring 1977, grantee Am. Coun. Learned Soc., summers 1981, 91, 98-99; grantee Graham Found. for Advanced Studies in Fine Arts, 1982, publ. grantee, 1989; grantee NEH, 1982-83, Am. Philos. Soc., 1986, Inst. for Advanced Study Sch. Hist. Studies, 1987, Getty Rsch. Inst. for History Art and Humanities, 1989-90, Zumberge Faculty Rsch. and Innovation Fund, U. So. Calif., 1998-99, Guggenheim Found., 1998-99; AT&T rsch. fellow Northwestern U., 1992-93. Mem. Coll. Art Assn. Am. (nominating com. 1990, bd. dirs. 1992-97, ann. meeting local host com. L.A. 1998-99), Soc. Archtl. Historian (sec. Chgo. chpt. 1984-85, peer reviewer Jour. 1996). Office: U So Calif Dept Art History University Park 104 Watt MC 0293 Los Angeles CA 90089-0001

TRUCKER, ALBERT, plastic surgeon; b. St. Joseph, Mich., Aug. 5, 1924; s. Albert and Louise (Goebel) T. BA, Johns Hopkins U., 1951; MD, U. Md., 1956. Diplomate Am. Bd. Plastic Surgery. Intern in gen. surgery U. Calif., San Francisco, 1956-59; resident in plastic surgery Mayo Clinic, Rochester, Minn., 1959-62; pvt. practice Santa Rosa, Calif., 1962—. Mem. Am. Soc. Plastic Surgery, Calif. Soc. Plastic Surgery. Office: 200 Montgomery Dr Santa Rosa CA 95404-6633

TRUE, JEAN DURLAND, entrepreneur, oil company executive; b. Nov. 27, 1915; d. Clyde Earl and Harriet Louise (Brayton) Durland; m. Henry Alfonso True Jr., Mar. 20, 1938; children: Tamma Jean (Mrs. Donald G. Hatten), Henry Alfonso III, Diemer Durland, David Lanmon. Student, Mont. State U., 1935-36. Ptnr. True Drilling LLC, Casper, Wyo., 1951—, True Oil Co., Casper, 1951-94, Eighty-Eight Oil LLC, 1955-94, True Geothermal Energy Co., 1980—, True Ranches, 1981-94. Officer, dir. White Stallion Ranch, Inc., Tucson, Smokey Oil Co., Casper. Mem. steering com. YMCA, Casper, 1954-55, bd. dirs., 1956-68; mem. bd. dirs. Gottsche Rehab. Ctr., Thermopolis, Wyo., 1966-93, mem. exec. bd., 1966-93, v.p., 1983-90; mem. adv. bd. for adult edn. U. Wyo., 1966-68; mem. Ft. Casper Commn., Casper, 1973-79; bd. dirs. Mus. of Rockies, Bozeman, Mont., 1983-87, mem. Nat. Adv. Bd., 1997-2000; bd. dirs. Nicolaysen Art Mus., 1988-93, Nat. Cowboy Hall of Fame and Western Heritage Ctr., 1997—; mem. Nat. Fedn. Rep. Women's Clubs; dep. Rep. nat. conv., 1972; trustee Trooper Found., 1995—. Mem. Casper Area C. of C., Alpha Gamma Delta, Casper Country Club, Petroleum Club. Episcopalian. Office: PO Box 2360 Casper WY 82602-2360

TRUEBA, FERNANDO, film director and producer, screenwriter; b. Madrid, Jan. 18, 1955; s. Maximo Rodriguez and Palmira Trueba; m. Cristina Huete, Oct. 8, 1982; 1 child, Jonas-Groucho. Film critic El Pais, newspaper, Madrid, 1976-79; editor, dir. Casablanca, film mag., Madrid, 1981-83; film dir., prodr., screenwriter Creative Artists Agy., Beverly Hills, Calif. Dir., screenwriter Opera Prima, 1980 (Silver Hugo award Chgo. Film Festival 1980), Mientras el Cuerpo Aguante, 1982, Sal Gorda, 1983, Se Infiel y No Mires con Quien, 1985, El Año de Las Luces, 1986 (Silver Bear award Berlin Film Festival 1987), The Mad Monkey, 1989, Belle époque, 1992 (Academy Award, Best Foreign Language Film, 1993), Two Much, 1996; producer, screenwriter A Contratiempo, 1981, De Tripas Corazon, 1984, La Mujer de tu Vida, 1988-89; producer Lulu de Noche, 1985, El Juego Mas Divertido, 1987, Earth Magicians, 1989—, Amo tu cama rica, 1991, Alas de mariposa, 1991 (Concha of Gold award San Sebastian Film Festival 1991), Sublet, 1992, La Buena Vida, 1996; dir. La Nina de Tos Ojos, 1998, also dir. short films. Mem. Acad. Motion Pictures Spain (pres. 1988). Home: Bueso Pineda 29 28043 Madrid Spain Office: CAA c/o Emanuel Nunez 9830 Wilshire Blvd Beverly Hills CA 90212-1804

TRUEBLOOD, HARRY ALBERT, JR. oil company executive; b. Wichita Falls, Tex., Aug. 28, 1925; s. Harry A. and Marguerite (Barnhart) T.; m. Lucile Bernard, Jan. 22, 1953; children: Katherine T. Astin, John B. Student, Tex. A&M Coll., 1942-43; BS in Petroleum Engring., U. Tex., 1948. Petroleum engr. Cal. Co., 1948-51; chief engr. McDermott & Barnhart Co., Colo., Tex., 1951-52; cons. petroleum and geol. engr. Denver, 1952-55; pres. Colo. Western Exploration Inc., Denver, 1955-58, Consol. Oil and Gas., Inc., 1958-88, chmn. bd., chief exec. officer, 1969-88, Princeville Devel. Corp., 1979-87, pres., 1984-86; chmn. bd., chief exec. officer Columbus Energy Corp., 1983-2000; pres., mng. mem. HAT Resources LLC, 2001—. Chmn. bd., CEO, Princeville Airways, Inc., 1979-87; chmn. bd. dirs., pres. CEC Resources, Ltd., 1984-99; bd. dirs. Carbon Energy Corp., 2000—. With USNR, 1944-46, ensign, 1949-55. Mem. Soc. Petroleum Engrs., Am. Petroleum Inst., World Pres. Orgn., Chief Execs. Orgn. (bd. dirs.), Ind. Petroleum Assn. Am. (exec. com.), Natural Gas Supply Assn. (exec. com.), Denver Petroleum Club, Cherry Hills Country Club, Univ. Club, One Hundred Club. Roman Catholic. Home: 2800 S University Blvd Apt 82 Denver CO 80210-6056 Office: Columbus Energy Corp 1660 Lincoln St Ste 2400 Denver CO 80264-2401

TRUJILLO, SOLOMON D. telecommunications executive; m. Corine Trujillo; 3 children. BS, MBA, U. Wyo. With US West, Denver, 1974-92, pres., CEO mktg. resources, 1992-95, pres., CEO, 1995-97; CEO Graviton, Inc., San Diego, 1997—. Bd. dirs. Dayton Hudson Corp., Bank of Am., World Econ. Forum; mem. Nat. Security Telecom. Coun.; advisor U.S. govt. on trade policy as appointee Investment and Svcs. Policy Adv. Com., Office of the Pres. Bd. trustees Aspen Inst., chair ann. seminar on Hispanic Ams. and the Bus. Cmty.; bd. dirs. Tomás Rivera Policy Inst.; mem. corp. bd. advisors Nat. Coun. of La Raza; bd. fellows Claremont Grad. U.; chmn. bd. trustees Ctr. for the New West, Denver. Named one of 100 Most Influential Latinos in the Nation by Hispanic Bus. Mag.; recipient Cmty. Svc. award NCCJ, Disting. Svc. award Colo. Civil Rights Commn., Corp. Advocate of the Yr. award U.S. Hispanic C. of C. Office: Graviton Inc Ste 200 11025 N Torrey Pines Rd La Jolla CA 92037

TRUJILLO, THOMAS P. state agency administrator; b. Los Alamos, N.Mex. BA in Jour. and Mass Comm., N. Mex. State Univ. Coord. Keep Am. Beautiful County Park and Recreation Dept., Los Alamos, N.Mex.; dir. park and recreation City of Santa Fe, 1992-95; dir. State N.Mex., State Parks Divsn., Santa Fe, 1995—. Bd. dris. N. Mex. Clean and Beautiful Program; mem. N. Mex. Recreation Parks Assn. (past pres.), Tri-area Econ. Devel. Com. Recipient numerous awards in mktg. and advt. Mem. Los Alamos C. of C. Office: State NMex Parks Divsn PO Box 1147 2040 S Pacheco St Santa Fe NM 87505-5472 Fax: 505-827-1376

TRULY, RICHARD H. academic administrator, former federal agency administrator, former astronaut; b. Fayette, Miss., Nov. 12, 1937; s. James B. Truly; m. Colleen Hanner; children: Richard Michael, Daniel Bennett, Lee Margaret. B.Aero. Engring., Ga. Inst. Tech., 1959. Commd. ensign U.S. Navy, 1959; advanced through grades to vice adm.; assigned Fighter Squadron 33; served in U.S.S. Intrepid; served in U.S.S. Enterprise; astronaut Manned Orbiting Lab. Program USAF, 1965-69, NASA, from 1969, comdr. Columbia Flight 2, 1981, Challenger Flight 3, 1983; dir. Space Shuttle program, 1986-89; adminstr. NASA, 1989-92; v.p., dir. Georgia Tech Rsch. Inst., Atlanta; dir. Nat. Renewable Energy Lab., Golden, Colo. Recipient Robert H. Goddard Astronautics award AIAA, 1990. Mem. NAE. Office: Nat Renewable Energy Lab 1617 Cole Blvd Golden CO 80401-3305

TRUMAN, JAMES, magazine editor; Newspaper reporter, London; Am. editor, columnist The Face, N.Y.C.; featured editor Vogue Mag., 1988-90; editor-in-chief Details Mag., 1990-94; editl. dir. Archtl. Digest (Conde Nast Pubs.)., 1994—. Contbr. articles to The Village Voice, The London Sunday Times, HG, others. Office: 6300 Wilshire Blvd Los Angeles CA 90048-5204

TRUNDLE, W(INFIELD) SCOTT, publishing executive newspaper; b. Maryville, Tenn., Mar. 24, 1939; s. Winfield Scott and Alice (Smith) T.; m. Elizabeth Latshaw, Oct. 14, 1989; children: Stephen, Allison. BA, Vanderbilt U., 1961, JD, 1967. Bar: Tenn. 1967. Spl. agt. U.S. Secret Service, 1963-66; asso. to partner firm Hunter, Smith, Davis & Norris, Kingsport, Tenn., 1967-72; pub. Kingsport (Tenn.) Times-News, 1972-78; pres. Greensboro (N.C.) Daily News, 1978-80; exec. v.p. Jefferson Pilot Publs., Inc., Greensboro and Clearwater, Fla., 1980-82; v.p., bus. mgr. Tampa Tribune (Fla.), 1982-91; sr. v.p. Hillsborough C.C., 1991-93; publisher Ogden (Utah) Standard Examiner, 1993—. Assoc. prof. East Tenn. State U., 1973-77; bd. dirs., pres. Ogden Indsl. Devel. Corp.; bd. dirs. Weber Econ. Devel. Corp.; treas., bd. dirs. Utah Def. Alliance. Trustee, chmn. Eccles Dinosaur Park and Mus. Found.; chmn. Weber County Legacy Trust. Mem. Tenn. Bar Assn., Weber Ogden C. of C. (bd. dirs.). Methodist. Home: 1580 Maule Dr Ogden UT 84403-0413 Office: Ogden Publ Corp PO Box 12790 Ogden UT 84412-2790 E-mail: strundle@aol.com

TRUSCIO, JAMES, JR. banker; b. Bronx, N.Y., June 19, 1942; s. James and Louise Marie (Jones) T.; m. Patricia Ann Stanulla, Oct. 16, 1971 (div. 1977); m. Felicie Dorothy Varin, Sept. 22, 1979; children: Robert Stephen, Christine Marie. Grad. high sch., Bronx, N.Y., 1961. Ops. officer, asst. sec. Mfrs. Hanover Trust Co., N.Y.C., 1961-89; asst. treas., compliance officer The Trust Co. of N.J., Ridgefield, 1989-90; asst. mgr. Natureworks N.Mex. Mus. Natural History, Albuquerque, 1992—. Author books of poetry: Feelings Within, 1978, First, Last and Always, 1978. Vice chmn. cable com. Rio Rancho, N.Mex. Republican. Roman Catholic. Avocations: pen and ink drawings, writing, computer graphics, fishing, photography. Office: JT Enterprises 77 Parkside Rd SE Rio Rancho NM 87124-3984

TRUSSELL, R(OBERT) RHODES, environmental engineer; b. National City, Calif. s. Robert L. and Margaret (Kessing) T.; m. Elizabeth Shane, Nov. 26, 1969; children: Robert Shane, Charles Bryan. BSCE, U. Calif., Berkeley, 1966, MS, 1967, PhD, 1972. With Montgomery Watson Inc. (formerly Mongomery Cons. Engrs.), Pasadena, Calif., 1972—, v.p., 1977, sr. v.p., 1986, dir. applied tech., 1988-92, sr. v.p., dir. corp. devel., 1992—. Mem. com. on water treatment chems. Nat. Acad. Sci., 1980-82, mem. com. 3d part cert., 1982-83, com. on irrigation-induced water quality problems, 1986-88, indirect potable reuse, 1996-98, chmn. com. on drinking water contaminants, 1998—, Am. Water Work Commn. on mixing of water treatment chems., 1988-90; mem. U.S./German rsch. com. on corrosion of water sys., 1984-85, U.S./Dutch rsch. com. on organics in water, 1982-83, U.S./USSR rsch. com. on water treatment, 1985-88, U.S./E.C. Com. Corrosion in Water, 1992-94; mem. Water Sci. and Tech. Bd., 1998—. Mem. jt. editl. bd. Standards Methods for Examination of Water and Wastewater, 1980-89; mem. editl. adv. bd. Environ. and Sci. and Tech., 1977-83; mng. editl. bd. Environ. Sci. and Tech., 2001—; contbr. articles to profl. publs. Mem. AIChE, AEEP, Acad. Environ. Engring. (Kappe lectr. 1999), Nat. Acad. Engrs., Water Works Assn. (editl. adv. bd. jour. 1987-94, EPA SAB com. on drinking water 1988-91, 94—, cons. radon disinfectant by-products, 1993, cons. on disinfection and disinfection by-products 1994, ad hoc sci. adv. com. on arsenic 1995-96), Bd. Sci. Couns. Com. on AS, 1997, Internat. Water Supply Assn. (U.S. rep. to standing com. on water quality and treatment 1990-94, chmn. com. disinfection and mem. sci. and tech. coun. 1994—), Water Environ. Fedn., Internat. Water Quality Assn., Am. Chem. Soc., Nat. Assn. Corrosion Engrs., Sigma Xi. Office: Montgomery Watson 300 N Lake Ave Ste 1200 Pasadena CA 91101-4184

TRYGSTAD, LAWRENCE BENSON, lawyer; b. Holton, Mich., Mar. 22, 1937; BA, U. Mich., 1959; JD, U. So. Calif., 1967. Bar: Calif. 1968, U.S. Supreme Ct. 1974. Legal counsel Calif. Tchrs. Assn., United Tchrs. L.A., L.A., 1968-71; ptnr. Trygstad & Odell, L.A., 1971-80; pres. Trygstad Law Corp., L.A., 1980—. Instr., tchr. negotiation U. Calif.-Northridge; panelist TV shows Law and the Teacher. Bd. dirs. George Washington Carver Found., L.A. Mem. ABA, Calif. Bar Assn., L.A. County Bar Assn., Calif. Trial Lawyers Assn., L.A. Trial Lawyers Assn., Nat. Orgn. Lawyers for Edn. Assns., Am. Trial Lawyers Assn., Phi Alpha Delta. Home: 4209 Aleman Dr Tarzana CA 91356-5405 Office: 1880 Century Park E Ste 404 Los Angeles CA 90067-1609

TSANG, DAVID D. computer company executive; Chmn., CEO, pres. Oak Tech, Sunnyvale, Calif., also bd. dirs. Office: Oak Tech 139 Kifer Ct Sunnyvale CA 94086-5160

TSCHERNISCH, SERGEI P. academic administrator; BA, San Francisco State U.; MFA in Theatre, Stanford U.; student, San Francisco Actors' Workshop, Stanford Repertory Theatre. Founding mem. Calif. Inst. of Arts, 1969, mem. faculty, assoc. dean Sch. Theatre, dir., 1969-80; prof. dept. theatre U. Md., College Park, 1980-82; dir. divsn. performing and visual arts Northeastern U., Boston, 1982-92; dean Coll. of Comm. and Fine Arts Loyola Marymount U., L.A., 1992-94; pres. Cornish Coll. of Arts, Seattle, 1994—. Advisor NEA; mem. com. USIA; cons. to many festivals. Office: Cornish Coll Arts 710 E Roy St Seattle WA 98102-4604

TSIEN, RICHARD WINYU, biology educator; b. Tating, Kweichow, People's Republic China, Mar. 3, 1945; s. Hsue-Chu and Yi-Ying (Li) T.; m. Julia Shiang Aug. 29, 1971; children: Sara Shiang-Ming, Gregory Shiang-An, Alexa Tsien-Shiang. BS, MIT, 1965, MS, 1966; DPhil, Oxford U., Eng., 1970. Rsch. student Eaton Peabody Lab. Auditory, Physiology, Mass. Eye and Ear Infirmary, 1966; asst. prof. dept. physiology, Yale U. Sch. Medicine, New Haven, 1970-74, assoc. prof., 1974-79, prof., 1979-88; George D. Smith prof. molecular and cellular physiology Stanford (Calif.) U., 1988—, chmn. dept., 1988-94. Established investigator Am. Heart Assn., 1974-79. Author: Electric Current Flow in Excitable Cells, 1975. Recipient Otsuka award Internat. Soc. Heart Rsch., 1985; Rhodes Scholar, 1966; Weir Rsch. fellow, 1966-70 Univ. Coll., Oxford, 1966-70, lecturing fellow Balliol Coll., Oxford, 1969-70 Mem. Soc. Gen. Physiologists (pres. 1988), Biophys. Soc. (Kenneth S. Cole award 1985), Soc. for Neurosci. Democrat. Home: 866 Tolman Dr Palo Alto CA 94305-1026 Office: Stanford U Dept Molecular & Cellular Physiology 300 Pasteur Dr Palo Alto CA 94304-2203

TSIEN, ROGER YONCHIEN, chemist, cell biologist; b. N.Y.C., Feb. 1, 1952; s. Hsue Chu and Yi Ying (Li) T.; m. Wendy M. Globe, July 30, 1982. AB summa cum laude in Chemistry and Physics, Harvard Coll., 1972; PhD in Physiology, U. Cambridge, 1977; D (hon.), Katholieke U., Leuven, Belgium, 1995. Rsch. asst. U. Cambridge, Eng., 1975-78; asst. prof. Dept. Physiology-Anatomy U. Calif., Berkeley, 1981-85, assoc. prof., 1985-87, prof., 1987-89, prof. pharmacology, chemistry and biochemistry San Diego, 1989—; co-found. Aurora Bioscis. Corp., 1994. T.Y. Shen vis. prof. Medicinal Chem., MIT, 1991. Contbr. chpts. to books, articles to profl. jours. Recipient Lamport prize N.Y. Acad. Scis., 1986, Javits Neurosci. Investigator award Nat. Inst. Neurol. Disorders and Stroke, 1989—, Young Scientist award Passano Found., 1991, W. Alden Spencer Neurobiology award Columbia U., 1991, Bowditch lectureship Am. Physiol. Soc., 1992, Gairdner Found. Internat. award, 1995, Doctorate honoris causa, Katholieke Universiteit Leuven, Belgium, 1995; Artois-Baillet-Latour Health prize (Belgium), 1995, Basic Rsch. prize Am. Heart Assn., 1995, Faculty Rsch. lectureship U. Calif., San Diego, 1997, Faculty Rsch. Lectureship, Univ. Calif., San Diego, Acad. Senate, 1997, EG&G Wallac award for Innovation in High Throughput Screening Soc. for Biomolecular Screening, 1998; Comyns Berkeley Rsch. fellow Gonville & Caius Coll., 1977-81; Marshall scholar British Govt., 1972-75, Searle scholar, 1983-86. Mem. AAAS (Amer. Acad. Arts and Scis.), NAS (Natl. Acad. of Scis.), Inst. Medicine, Phi Beta Kappa. Achievements development and extensive biological application of molecules to measure and/or manipulate intracellular calcium, sodium, and hydrogen ions, cyclic adenosine-3', 5'-monophosphate, nitric oxide, inositol phosphates, membrane potential, protein trafficking, protein-protein interaction, and gene expression; developed biochemistry and redesign of green fluorescent protein; elucidation fo signal transduction mechanisms in calcium oscillations and synaptic plasticity; inventor new methods for microscopic imaging and pharmaceutical high-throughput screening. Office: U Calif San Diego Dept Pharmacology Bldg CM-W 9500 Gilman Dr La Jolla CA 92093-5004 E-mail: rtsien@ucsd.edu

TSOSIE, LEONARD, state legislator, lawyer; b. 1958; BS, JD, U. N.Mex. Pvt. practice, Crown Point; mem. N.Mex. Senate, Dist. 22, Santa Fe, 1992—; mem. fin. com. N.Mex. Senate, mem. jud. com. Democrat. Office: PO Box 1003 Crownpoint NM 87313

TU, JOHN, engineering executive; b. 1941; With Motorola Co., Wiesbaden, Germany, 1966-74; pres. Tu Devel., L.A., 1975-82, Camintonn Corp., Santa Ana, Calif., 1982-85; v.p., gen. mgr. AST Rsch., Irvine, 1985-87; pres. Newgen Systems Corp., Fountain Valley, 1987—; CEO, pres. Kingston Tech., Fountain Valley, 1988—. Office: Kingston Tech Co 17600 Newhope St Fountain Valley CA 92708-4220

TUAZON, JESUS OCAMPO, electrical engineer, educator, consultant; b. Manila, Jan. 2, 1940; came to U.S., 1963; s. Filomeno and Patrocino (Ocampo) T.; m. Norma Mamangun, Oct. 12, 1963; children: Maria, Noel, Norman, Mary, Michelle. BSEE, Mapua Inst., Manila, 1962; MSEE, Iowa State U., 1965, PhD, 1969. Elec. prof. Calif. State U., Fullerton, Calif., 1969—; scientist Jet Propulsion Lab., Pasadena, 1984—. Computer cons. Hughes Aircraft, Fullerton, 1977, Gen. Dynamic, Pomona, Calif., 1983, U.S. Naval Weapon Sta., Seal Beach, Calif., 1978-83. Author of papers for profl. confs. Mem. IEEE, Am. Assn. Engring Educators. Democrat. Roman Catholic. Avocations: jogging, swimming, chess. Home: 816 S Verona St Anaheim CA 92804-4035 Office: Calif State Univ 800 N State College Blvd Fullerton CA 92831-3547 also: Jet Propulsion Lab 4800 Oak Grove Dr Pasadena CA 91109-8001

TUCKER, GARY JAY, physician, educator; b. Cleve., Mar. 6, 1934; s. Isadore Martin and Blanche Hanna (Luftig) T.; m. Sharon Ruth Pobby, June 10, 1956; children: Adam, Clare. AB, Oberlin Coll., 1956; MD, Case Western Res. U., 1960; postdoctoral fellow, Yale U., 1961-64; MA (hon.), Dartmouth Coll., 1977. Diplomate Am. Bd. Psychiatry and Neurology. Asst. prof. psychiatry Sch. Medicine Yale U., New Haven, 1967-70, assoc. prof. psychiatry, 1970-71; with Dartmouth Med. Sch., Hanover, N.H., 1971-85, prof. psychiatry, 1974-85, chmn. dept., 1978-85; chmn. psychiatry and behavioral scis. Sch. Med. U. Wash., Seattle, 1985-98; prof. psychiatry U. Wash., Seattle, 1985—. Bd. dirs. Am. Bd. Psychiatry and Neurology. Co-author: Rational Hospital Psychiatry, 1974, Behavioral Neurology, 1985; contbr. articles to profl. jours. Lt. Commdr. USN, 1964-67. Fellow Am. Psychiat. Assn.; mem. W. Coast Coll. Biol. Psychiatry, Sigma Xi, Alpha Omega Alpha. Democrat. Jewish. Avocations: photography, motorcycles. Office: U Washington Dept Psychiatry PO Box 356560 Seattle WA 98195-6560

TUCKER, SHIRLEY LOIS COTTER, botany educator, researcher; b. St. Paul, Apr. 4, 1927; d. Ralph U. and Myra C. (Knutson) Cotter; m. Kenneth W. Tucker, Aug. 22, 1953. BA, U. Minn., 1949, MS, 1951; PhD, U. Calif., Davis, 1956. Asst. prof. botany La. State U., Baton Rouge, 1967-71, assoc. prof., 1971-76, prof., 1976-82, Boyd prof., 1982-95, prof. emerita, 1995—. Adj. prof. dept. biology U. Calif., Santa Barbara, 1995—. Co-editor: Aspects of Floral Development, 1988, Advances in Legume Systematics, Vol. 6, 1994; contbr. numerous articles on plant devel. to profl. jours. Recipient, Outstanding Alumni Achievement award U. Minn., 1999; fellow Linnean Soc., London, 1975—, Fulbright fellow Eng., 1952-53. Mem. Bot. Soc. Am. (v.p. 1979, program chmn. 1975-78, pres.-elect 1986-87, pres. 1987-88, Merit award 1989), Am. Bryological and Lichenological Soc., Brit. Lichenological Soc., Am. Inst. Biol. Scis., Am. Soc. Plant Taxonomists (pres.-elect 1994-95, pres. 1995-96), Phi Beta Kappa, Sigma Xi. Home: 3987 Primavera Rd Santa Barbara CA 93110-1467 Office: U Calif Dept Biology EEMB Santa Barbara CA 93106 E-mail: tucker@lifesci.ucsb.edu

TUELL, JACK MARVIN, retired bishop; b. Tacoma, Nov. 14, 1923; s. Frank Harry and Anne Helen (Bertelson) T.; m. Marjorie Ida Beadles, June 17, 1946; children— Jacqueline, Cynthia, James. B.S., U. Wash., 1947, LL.B., 1948; S.T.B., Boston U., 1955; M.A., U. Puget Sound, 1961, DHS, 1990; D.D., Pacific Sch. Religion, 1966; LLD, Alaska Pacific U., 1980. Bar: Wash. 1948; ordained to ministry Meth. Ch., 1955. Practice law with firm Holte & Tuell, Edmonds, Wash., 1948-50; pastor Grace Meth. Ch., Everett, Wash., 1950-52, South Tewksbury Meth. Ch., Tewksbury, Mass., 1952-55, Lakewood Meth. Ch., Tacoma, 1955-61; dist. supt. Puget Sound dist. Meth. Ch., Everett, 1961-67; pastor 1st United Meth. Ch., Vancouver, Wash., 1967-72; bishop United Meth. Ch., Portland, Oreg., 1972-80, Calif.-Pacific Conf., United Meth. Ch., L.A., 1980-92; interim sr. pastor First United Meth. Ch., Boise, Idaho, 1995. Mem. gen. conf. United Meth. Ch., 1964, 66, 68, 70, 72; pres. coun. of Bishops United Meth. Ch., 1989-90. Author: The Organization of the United Methodist Church, 1970, 8th edit. 1997. Pres. Tacoma U.S.O., 1959-61, Vancouver YMCA, 1968; v.p. Ft. Vancouver Seamens Cnt., 1969-72; vice chmn. Vancouver Human Rels. Commn., 1970-72; pres. Oreg. Coun. Alcohol Problems, 1972-76; trustee U. Puget Sound, 1961-73, Vancouver Meml. Hosp., 1967-72, Alaska Meth. U., Anchorage, 1972-80, Willamette U., Salem, Oreg., 1972-80, Willamette View Manor, Portland, 1972-80, Rogue Valley Manor, Medford, Oreg., 1972-76, Sch. Theology at Claremont, Calif., 1980-92, Methodist Hosp., Arcadia, Calif., 1983-92; pres. nat. div. bd. global ministries United Meth. Ch., 1972-76, pres. ecumenical and interreligious concerns div., 1976-80, Commn. on Christian Unity and intereligious concerns, 1980-84, Gen. Bd. of Pensions,1984-92, Calif. Coun. Alcohol Problems, 1985-88. Jacob Sleeper fellow, 1955 Home and Office: 816 S 216th St # 637 Des Moines WA 98198-6331

TUETING, SARAH, professional hockey player; b. Winnetka, Ill., Apr. 26, 1976; Degree in neurobiology, Dartmouth Coll. Goal keeper U.S. Nat. Women's Hockey Team, 1996—. Recipient ice hockey Gold medal Olympic Games, Nagano, Japan, 1998. Avocations: soccer, tennis, playing piano and cello. Office: c/o USA Hockey 1775 Bob Johnson Dr Colorado Springs CO 80906

TUKEY, HAROLD BRADFORD, JR. horticulture educator; b. Geneva, May 29, 1934; s. Harold Bradford and Ruth (Schweigert) T.; m. Helen Dunbar Parker, June 25, 1955; children: Ruth Thurbon, Carol Tukey Schwartz, Harold Bradford. BS, Mich. State U., 1955, MS, 1956, PhD, 1958. Research asst. South Haven Expt. Sta., Mich., 1955; AEC grad. research asst. Mich. State U., 1955-58; NSF fellow Calif. Inst. Tech, 1958-59; asst. prof. dept. floriculture and ornamental horticulture Cornell U., Ithaca, N.Y., 1959-64, assoc. prof., 1964-70, prof., 1970-80; prof. urban horticulture U. Wash., Seattle, 1980-97, prof. emeritus, 1997—, dir. Arboreta, 1980-92, dir. Ctr. Urban Horticulture, 1980-92. Cons. Internat. Bonsai mag., Electric Power Rsch. Inst., P.R. Nuclear Ctr., 1965-66; mem. adv. com. Seattle-U. Wash. Arboretum and Bot. Garden, 1980-92, vice chmn., 1982, chmn., 1986-87; vis. scholar U. Nebr., 1982, 98; vis. prof. U. Calif., Davis, 1973; lectr. U. Western Sydney-Hawkesburg U. Melbourne, Victoria Coll. Agrl. and Horticulture, 1995, Massey U., 1996; Hill prof. U. Minn., 1996; mem. various coms. Nat. Acad. Scis.-NRC; bd. dirs. Arbor Fund Bloedel Res., 1980-92, pres., 1983-84. Mem. editorial bd. Jour. Environ. Horticulture, Arboretum Bull. Mem. nat. adv. com. USDA, 1990—; pres. Ithaca PTA; troop advisor Boy Scouts Am., Ithaca. Lt. U.S. Army, 1958. Recipient B.Y. Morrison award USDA, 1987; NSF fellow, 1958-59; named to Lansing (Mich.) Sports Hall of Fame, 1987; grantee NSF, 1962, 75, Bot. Soc. Am., 1964; hon. dr. Portuguese Soc. Hort., 1985. Fellow Am. Soc. Hort. Sci. (dir. 1970-71); mem. Internat. Soc. Hort. Sci. (U.S. del. to coun. 1971-90, chmn. commn. for amateur horticulture 1974-83, exec. com. 1974-90, v.p. 1978-82, pres. 1982-86, past pres. 1986-90, chmn. comm. Urban Horticulture 1990-94, hon. mem. 1994), Wash. State Nursery and Landscape Assn. (hon. mem. 1995), Internat. Plant Propagators Soc. (hon., ea. region dir. 1969-71, v.p. 1972, pres. 1973, internat. pres. 1976), Am. Hort. Soc. (dir. 1972-81, exec. com. 1974-81, v.p. 1978-80, citation of merit 1981), Royal Hort. Soc. (London) (v.p. hon. 1993—), Bot. Soc. Am., N.W. Horticulture Soc. (dir. 1980-92), Arboretum Found. (dir. 1980-92), Rotary, Sigma Xi, Alpha Zeta, Phi Kappa Phi, Pi Alpha Xi, Xi Sigma Pi. Presbyterian. Home: 3300 E St Andrews Way Seattle WA 98112-3750 Office: U Wash Ctr Urban Horticulture PO Box 354115 Seattle WA 98195-4115 E-mail: tukeyhb@email.msn.com

TULLY, HERBERT BULLARD, chemical manufacturing executive; b. Glen Ridge, N.J., Sept. 3, 1943; s. Richard Golfe and Marie Foster (Towne) T.; m. Nancy Dee Zook, Dec. 22, 1967; children: Kimberly, Christine, Gregory. BS, U. Calif., Berkeley, 1967. Mem. fin. mgmt. staff Gen. Electric Co., San Jose, Calif., 1967-70, mem. corp. audit staff Schenectady, N.J., 1970-73, mgr. acct. dept. San Leandro, Calif., 1973-75; mgr. audit dept. Am. Express Co., Fireman's Fund, San Francisco, 1975-77; asst. controller Fireman's Fund Ins. Co., San Francisco, 1977-81; controller Wilbur-Ellis Co., San Francisco, 1981-86, asst. treas., 1986-89, treas., 1989—, CEO, pres. Bd. dirs. Overseas Cos., San Francisco. Home: 7 Spring Rd PO Box 1735 Ross CA 94957-1735 Office: Wilbur Ellis 345 California Street Flr 27 San Francisco CA 94104

TULLY, SUSAN BALSLEY, pediatrician, educator; b. San Francisco, July 12, 1941; d. Gerard E. Balsley Sr. and Norma Lilla (Hand) Carey; m. William P. Tully, June 19, 1965; children: Michael William, Stephen Gerard. BA in Premed. Studies, UCLA, 1963, MD, 1966. Diplomate Am. Bd. Pediatrics, Am. Bd. Pediatric Emergency Medicine. Intern L.A. County-U. So. Calif. Med. Ctr., 1966-67, jr. resident pediatrics, 1967-68; staff pediatrician, part-time Permanente Med. Group, Oakland, Calif., 1968; sr. resident pediatrics Kaiser Found. Hosp., Oakland, 1968-69, Bernalillo County Med. Ctr., Albuquerque, 1969-70, chief resident pediatric outpatient dept., 1970; instr. pediatrics, asst. dir. outpatient dept. U. N.Mex. Sch. Medicine, 1971-72; asst. prof. pediatrics, dir. (ambulatory pediatrics) U. Calif., Irvine, 1972-76, asst. prof. clin. pediatrics, vice chair med. edn., 1977-79; staff pediatrician Ross-Loos Med. Group, Buena Park, Calif., 1976-77; assoc. prof. clin. pediatrics and emergency medicine U. So. Calif. Sch. Medicine, 1979-86; dir. pediatric emergency dept. L.A. County/U. So. Calif. Med. Ctr., 1979-87; prof. clin. pediatrics and emergency medicine U. So. Calif. Sch. Medicine, 1986-89; dir. ambulatory pediatrics L.A. County/U. So. Calif. Med. Ctr., 1987-89, L.A. County-Olive View/UCLA Med. Ctr., 1989—; clin. prof. pediatrics UCLA, 1989-93, prof. clin. pediats., 1993-97; prof. emeritus, 1997—; dir. ambulatory pediatrics Olive View-UCLA Med. Ctr., 1989-96, chief pediatrics, 1996-97; vice chair pediat. UCLA, 1996-97. Pediatric toxicology cons. L.A. County Regional Poison Control Ctr. Med. Adv. Bd., 1981-97; clin. faculty rep. UCLA Sch. Medicine, 1992-93; pediatric liaison dept. emergency medicine Olive View/UCLA Med. Ctr., 1989-96, dir. lead poisoning clinic, 1993-99; mem. quality assurance com. Los Angeles County Cmty. Health Plan, 1986-89; mem. survey team pediatric emergency svcs. L.A. Pediatric Soc., 1984-86; mem. adv. bd. preventive health project univ. affiliated program Children's Hosp. L.A., 1981-83; active numerous coms. Author: (with K.E. Zenk) Pediatric Nurse Practitioner Formulary, 1979; (book chpt. with W.A. Wingert) Pediatric Emergency Medicine: Concepts and Clinical Practice, 1992, 2d edit., 1997; (with others) Educational Guidelines for Ambulatory/General Pediatrics Fellowship Training, 1992, Physician's Resource Guide for Water Safety Education, 1994; reviewer Pediatrics, 1985-89; editl. cons. Advanced Pediatric Life Support Course and Manual, 1988-89, Archives of Pediatrics and Adolescent Medicine, 1996—; dept. editor Pediatric Pearls Jour. Am. Acad. Physician Assts., 1989-94; tech. cons., reviewer Healthlink TV Am. Acad. Pediatrics, 1991; reviewer Pediatric Emergency Care, 1992—; question writer sub-bd. pediatric emergency medicine Am. Bd. Pediatrics, 1993-98; assoc. editor: Curriculum for the Training of General Pediatricians, 1996; cons. to lay media NBC Nightly News, Woman's Day, Sesame Street Parents, Parenting, Los Angeles Times; author numerous abstracts; contbr. articles to profl. jours. Cons. spl. edn. programs Orange County Bd. Edn., 1972-79; mem. Orange County Health Planning Coun., 1973-79; co-chairperson Orange County Child Health and Disability Prevention Program Bd., 1975-76; mem. Orange County Child Abuse Consultation Team, 1977-79; mem. project adv. bd. Family Focussed "Buckle Up" Project, Safety Belt Safe, U.S.A., 1989— Fellow Am. Acad. Pediatrics (life, active numerous sects. and coms., active Calif. chpt.); mem. APHA, Ambulatory Pediatric Assn., L.A. Pediatric Soc. (life). Democrat. Avocations: art needlework, reading. Office: Olive View UCLA Med Ctr Pediatrics 3A108 14445 Olive View Dr Sylmar CA 91342-1437 E-mail: SBTully@aol.com

TULSKY, FREDRIC NEAL, journalist; b. Chgo., Sept. 30, 1950; s. George and Helen (Mailick) T.; m. Kim Rennard, June 20, 1971; children: Eric George, Elizabeth Rose. B.J., U. Mo., 1972; J.D. cum laude, Temple U., Phila., 1984. Bar: Pa. 1984. Reporter Saginaw News, Mich., 1973-74, Port Huron Times Herald, 1974-75, Jackson Clarion-Ledger, Miss., 1975-78, Los Angeles Herald Examiner, 1978-79, Phila. Inquirer, 1979-93; mng. editor Ctr. for Investigative Reporting, San Francisco, 1993-94, exec. dir., 1994; reporter L.A. Times, 1995—. Adj. prof. urban studies U. Pa., 1990-93. Recipient nat. awards including Robert F. Kennedy Found. award, 1979, Heywood Broun award Newspaper Guild, 1978, Disting. Svc.

medal Sigma Delta Chi, 1978, 97, Pub. Svc. award AP Mng. Editors, 1978, Silver Gavel award ABA, 1979, 87, Pulitzer prize for investigative reporting, 1987, Pub. Svc. award Nat. Headliners Club, 1987, Investigative Reporters and editors medal, 1997; Nieman fellow Harvard U., 1989, Alicia Patterson fellow, 1998. Mem. Investigative Reporters and Editors (pres. 1988-91, chair 1991-93), Kappa Tau Alpha. Office: LA Times Times Mirror Sq Los Angeles CA 90053 E-mail: rick.tulsky@latimes.com

TUNE, BRUCE MALCOLM, pediatrics educator, renal toxicologist; b. N.Y.C., Aug. 26, 1939; s. Buford M. and Sylvia T.; m. Nancy Carter Doolittle, Sept. 13, 1969; children: Sara E., Steven M. AB, Stanford U., 1963, MD, 1965. Diplomate Am. Bd. Pediatrics, Am. Bd. Pediatric Nephrology, Nat. Bd. Med. Examiners. Intern in medicine and pediatrics Strong Meml. Hosp., Rochester, N.Y., 1965-66; rsch. assoc. Lab. Kidney and Electrolyte Metabolism, Nat. Heart Inst., NIH, Bethesda, Md., 1967-69, clin. assoc., 1968-69; resident in pediatrics Stanford (Calif.) U. Sch. Medicine, 1966-67, chief resident, 1969-70, fellow in pediatric renal and metabolic disease, 1970-71, asst. prof. pediat., 1971-77, assoc. prof., 1977-83, prof., 1983—, acting chmn. dept., 1991-93, dir. pediatric nephrology, 1971-97, prof. pediatrics divsn. pediatric nephrology, 1998—. Attending physician, chief pediatric renal svcs. Stanford U. Hosp., Palo Alto, Calif., 1971-96, Children's Hosp. at Stanford, Palo Alto, 1971-91; cons. physician Santa Clara Valley Med. Ctr., San Jose, Calif., 1973—; attending physician, chief pediatric renal svcs. Lucile Salter Packard Children's Hosp. at Stanford, 1991-98, acting chief pediatric medicine, 1991-93, attending physician, 1997; mem. rev. panel internat. study kidney diseases in children NIH, N.Y.C., 1973, 74, polycystic kidney disease study group, Albuquerque, 1984; mem. spl. study sect. on genetics and kidney maturation, Bethesd, Md., 1992; cons. Lilly Rsch. Labs., Indpls., 1980, Merck Sharp and Dohme Labs., Rahway, N.J., 1980, Bristol Labs., Syracuse, N.Y., 1982, ICI Pharms., Cheshire, Eng., 1992, Gilead Scis., Foster City, Calif., 1993, Zeneca Pharms., Mereside, Eng., 1994—; organizing mem., chmn. session on antibiotics NIH and EPA Conf. on Nephrotoxicity of Drugs and Environ. Toxicants, Pinehurst, N.C., 1981; co-dir. Coop. Study Therapy of Steroid-Resistant Focal Glomerulosclerosis in Children, 1988—; mem. rsch. grant rev. panel Ont. (Can.) Ministry Health, 1992—, Wellcome Trust, London, 1994—; reviewer bd. environ. studies and toxicology NRC, 1994. Mem. editl. bd. Am. Jour. Kidney Diseases, 1981-94; guest editor Contemporary Issues in Nephrology, 1984, Jour. Am. Soc. Nephrology, 1991; contbr. articles to med. jours. Grantee NIH, 1974-77, 79-83, 85-89, 90-95. Mem. Am. Soc. Nephrology, Internat. Soc. Nephrology, Am. Soc. Pediatric Nephrology (coun. 1978-82, rsch. subcom. 1993—), Internat. Pediatric Nephrology Assn., Western Soc. for Pediatric Rsch., Soc. for Pediatric Rsch., Am. Pediatric Nephrology Soc., Am. Heart Assn. (coun. on kidney diseases, grantee 1985-88, 89-92), Am. Soc. for Pharmacology and Exptl. Therapeutics, Phi Beta Kappa, Alpha Omega Alpha. Office: Stanford U Sch Medicine Dept Pediatrics 300 Pasteur Dr Rm G306 Palo Alto CA 94304-2203

TUNE, JAMES FULCHER, lawyer; b. Danville, Va., May 13, 1942; s. William Orrin and Susan Agnes (Fulcher) T.; m. Katherine Del Mickey, Aug. 2, 1969; children: Katherine Winslow, Jeffrey Bricker. BA, U. Va., 1964; MA, Stanford U., 1970, JD, 1974. Bar: Wash. 1974, U.S. Dist. Ct. (we. dist.) Wash. 1974. Assoc. Bogle & Gates, Seattle, 1974-79, ptnr., 1980-99, head comml./banking dept., 1985-93, mng. ptnr., 1986-93, chmn., 1994-99; ptnr. Dorsey & Whitney LLP, Seattle, 1999-2001, Stoel Rives LLP, Seattle, 2001—. Bd. dirs. BIEC Internat. Inc., Vancouver, Wash., BHP Steel Ams. Inc., Long Beach, Calif., Keynetics Inc., Boise, Idaho, Nichirei U.S.A., Inc., Seattle, Tengu Co., Santa Fe Springs, Calif.; chmn. Seattle-King City Econ. Devel. Coun., 1992. Chmn. Seattle Repertory Theatre, 1995; vice chmn. Corp. Coun. for the Arts, 2001. Lt. USN, 1964-69, Vietnam. Woodrow Wilson fellow, 1964, Danforth Found. fellow, 1964. Mem. ABA, Wash. State Bar Assn. (lectr. CLE 1976, 78, 84, 99), Seattle C. of C. (vice chmn. City Budget Task Force 1980-82), Ranier Club, Seattle Tennis Club, Phi Beta Kappa. Presbyterian. Office: Stoel Rives LLP 600 University St Ste 3600 Seattle WA 98101-3197 E-mail: jftune@stoel.com

TUNG, PRABHAS, plastic surgeon; b. Ubol, Thailand, Apr. 3, 1944; s. Sathee and Seng (Ngium) T.; m. Patarin C. Sinjin; children: Tony, Tommy. MD, Mahidol U., Bangkok, 1968. Diplomate Am. Bd. Plastic Surgery. Plastic surgeon pvt. practice, Flint, Mich., 1980-82, Sacramento, 1982—. Office: 2801 K St Ste 200 Sacramento CA 95816-5118

TUPA, RON, state senator; b. Harbor Beach, Mich., Aug. 25, 1966; BA in Philosophy, U. Tex., 1989; Tchg. Cert. in Secondary Edn., U. Colo., 1994; grad., Darden Sch. Polit. Leadership, 1996. Dockworker, 1991-94; tchr. social studies, 1994—; Dem. rep. dist. 14 Colo. Ho. of Reps., 1994-2000; Dem. senator dist. 18 Colo. State Senate, 2000—. Mem. state, vets. and mil. affairs coms. Colo. Ho. of Reps.; mem. edn. and legis. audit coms. Colo. State Senate, vice chmn. vets. and mil. affairs and transp. coms. Mem. Dem. Party Com., 1992-95; mem. Boulder County Exec. Com., 1992-96; pres. Colo. Young Dems., 1993-95. Mem. U. Colo. Alumni Assn., U. Tex., TX-Exes Alumni Assn. Office: 3455 Table Mesa Dr # A-108 Boulder CO 80305 also: Colo State Senate State Capitol 200 E Colfax Rm 271 Denver CO 80203 E-mail: tuparep14@aol.com, rtupa@sni.net

TURBIN, RICHARD, lawyer; b. N.Y.C., Dec. 25, 1944; s. William and Ruth (Fiedler) T.; m. Rai Saint Chu-Turbin, June 12, 1976; children: Laurel Mei, Derek Andrew. BA magna cum laude, Cornell U., 1966; JD, Harvard U., 1969. Bar: Hawaii 1971, U.S. Dist. Ct. Hawaii 1971. Asst. atty. gen., Western Samoa, Apia, 1969-70; dep. pub. defender Pub. Defender's Office, Honolulu, 1970-74; dir. Legal Aid Soc. Hawaii, Kaneohe, 1974-75; sr. atty., pres. Law Offices Richard Turbin, Honolulu, 1975—. Legal counsel Hawaii Crime Commn., 1980-81. Co-author: Pacific; author: Medical Malpractice, Handling Emergency Medical Cases, 1991; editor Harvard Civil Rights-Civil Liberties Law Rev., 1969. Legal counsel Dem. Party, Honolulu County, 1981-82; elected Neighborhood Bd., 1985, elected chair, 1990-97; bd. dirs. Hawaii chpt. ACLU, 1974-78, East-West Ctr. grantee, 1971, 72. Mem. ATLA, ABA (chair internat. torts and ins. law and practice com., mem. governing coun., chair tort and ins. practice sect. 1999-2000, chair-elect 1998-99), Hawaii Bar Assn., Hawaii Trial Lawyers Assn. (bd. govs.), Hawaii Jaycees (legal counsel 1981-82), Chinese Jaycees Honolulu (legal counsel 1980-81), Honolulu Tennis League (undefeated player 1983), Hawaii Harlequin Rugby Club (sec., legal counsel 1978-82), Pacific Club, Outrigger Canoe Club. Jewish. Home: 4817 Kahala Ave Honolulu HI 96816-5231

TURCOTTE, GLENN W. electrical products company executive; b. 1941; With Katy Industries, Inc., Englewood, Colo., 1981—, exec. v.p., 1993—, dir., 1995—, COO, 1998—, COO, exec. v.p., dir., 2000—; pres., CEO Glit, Inc., Wrens, Ga., Microtron Abrasives, Pineville, N.C., Moldan Corp., Pineville; chmn. bd. Duckback Products, Chico, Calif. Office: Katy Industries Inc 6300 S Syracuse Way #300 Englewood CO 80111-6723 Fax: (303) 290-9344

TURK, AUSTIN THEODORE, sociology educator; b. Gainesville, Ga., May 28, 1934; s. Hollis Theodore and Ruth (Vandiver) T.; m. Janet Stuart Irving, Oct. 4, 1957 (div. 1977); children: Catherine, Jennifer; m. Ruth-Ellen Marie Grimes, July 27, 1985. BA cum laude, U. Ga., 1956; MA, U. Ky., 1959; PhD, U. Wis., 1962. Acting instr. sociology U. Wis., Madison, 1961-62; from instr. to prof. sociology Ind. U., Bloomington, 1962-74; prof. U. Toronto, Can., 1974-88, U. Calif., Riverside, 1988—, chmn. dept. sociology, 1989-94; interim dir. Robert B. Presley Ctr. for Crime and Justice Studies, 1994-95. Author: Criminality and Legal Order, 1969, Political Criminality, 1982; gen. editor crime and justice series SUNY Press, Albany, 1990—; contbr. articles to jours. in field. Mem. Calif. Mus. Photography, 1988—, Citizens Univ. Com., 1990—. Recipient Paul Tappan award Western Soc. Criminology, 1989. Fellow Am. Soc. Criminology (pres. 1984-85); mem. Am. Sociol. Assn. (chair criminology sect. 1975-76), Law and Soc. Assn. (trustee 1982-85), Acad. Criminal Justice Scis. Democrat. Avocations: gardening, reading, swimming, tennis. Office: Dept Sociology U Calif Riverside Riverside CA 92521-0001 E-mail: austin.turk@ucr.edu

TURLINGTON, CHRISTY, model; b. Walnut Creek, Calif., Jan. 2, 1969; d. Dwain and Elizabeth T. With Ford Models, Inc., 1985; model Calvin Klein, 1986; face of Calvin Klein's Eternity Fragrance, 1988—; with Maybelline Cosmetics, 1992; rep. (abroad) Ford Models, Paris. Beauty spread with Vogue, 1987; has worked with Herb Ritts, Patrick Demarchelier, Steven Meisel; has worked for Anne Klein, Michael Kors, Chanel, Perry Ellis; appeared in George Michael's "Freedom" video. Office: United Talent Agy 9560 Wilshire Blvd Ste 500 Beverly Hills CA 90212-2427 also: 344 E 59th St New York NY 10022-1513

TURNAGE, JEAN ALLEN, retired state supreme court chief justice; b. St. Ignatius, Mont., Mar. 10, 1926; JD, Mont. State U., 1951; D Laws and Letters (non.), U. Mont., 1995. Bar: Mont. 1951, U.S. Supreme Ct. 1963. Formerly ptnr. Turnage, McNeil & Mercer, Polson, Mont.; formerly Mont. State senator from 13th Dist.; pres. Mont. State Senate, 1981-83; chief justice Supreme Ct. Mont., 1985-2001. Mem. Mont. State Bar Assn., Nat. Conf. Chief Justices (past pres.), Nat. Ctr. State Courts (past chair). Office: Turnage O'Neill & Mercer PO Box 460 Polson MT 59860

TURNBAUGH, ROY CARROLL, archivist; b. Peoria, Ill., Oct. 16, 1945; s. Roy Carroll and Zora (Alexander) T.; m. Donna Marie Chase, Mar. 28, 1970; children: Andrew, Peter. BA, Aurora Coll., 1969; AM, U. Ill., 1973, PhD, 1977. Asst. prof. U. Ill., Urbana, 1977-78; archivist Ill. State Archives, Springfield, 1978-85; dir. Oreg. State Archives, Salem, 1985—. Mem. Nat. Hist. Publs. and Records Comm., 2000—. Mem. Nat. Assn. Govt. Archives Records Adminstrs. (pres. 1998-2000), Soc. Am. Archivists (C.F.W. Coker prize 1984, Fellows Posner prize 1999). Office: Oreg State Archives 800 Summer St NE Salem OR 97310-1347 E-mail: roy.c.turnbaugh@state.or.us

TURNER, ANDREW L. healthcare management company executive; BA, Ohio State Univ. Adminstr skilled nursing facility, Springfield, Ohio, 1970-75; mgr. regional nursing home chain; sr. v.p. ops. Hillhaven Corp.; co-founder Horizon Healthcare Corp., 1986-89; founder Sun Healthcare Group, Albuquerque, 1989, now chmn., CEO. Office: Sun Healthcare Group Inc 101 Sun Ave NE Albuquerque NM 87109-4373

TURNER, BONESE COLLINS, artist, educator; b. Abilene, Kans. d. Paul Edwin and Ruby (Seybold) Collins; m. Glenn E. Turner; 1 child, Craig Collins. BS in Edn., MEd, U. Idaho; MA, Calif. State U., Northridge, 1974. Instr. art L.A. Pierce Coll., Woodland Hills, Calif., 1964—. Prof. art Calif. State U., Northridge, 1986-89; art instr. L.A. Valley Coll., Van Nuys, 1987-89, Moorpark (Calif.) Coll., 1988-98, Arrowmont Coll. Arts & Crafts, Gatlinburg, Tenn., 1995-96; advisor Coll. Art and Arch. U. Idaho, 1988—; juror for art exhbns. including Nat. Watercolor Soc., 1980, 91, San Diego Art Inst., Brand Nat. Watermedia Exhbn., 1980, 96-97, prin. gallery Orlando Gallery, Tarzana, Calif. Represented in permanant collections Smithsonian Inst., Olympic Arts Festival, L.A.; one-woman shows include Angel's Gate Gallery, San Pedro, Calif., 1989, Art Store Gallery, Studio City, Calif., 1988, L.A. Pierce Coll. Gallery, 1988, Brand Art Gallery, Glendale, Calif., 1988, 93, 2000, Coos (Oreg.) Art Mus., 1988, U. Nev., 1987, Orlando Gallery, Sherman Oaks, Calif., 1993, 98, Brand Libr., Glendale, Calif., 2000, Burbank (Calif.) Creative Arts Ctr., 2000; prin. works in pub. collections The Smithsonian Inst., Hartung Performing Arts Ctr., Moscow, Idaho, Home Savs. and Loan, San Bernardino Sun Telegram Newspapers, Oreg. Coun. for the Arts, Newport, Oreg. Pub. Librs., Brand Libr., Glendale, Lincoln (Nebr.) Indsl. Tile Corp. Recipient Springfield (Mo.) Art Mus. award, 1989, 1st prize Brand XXVIII, 1998, Glendale, Calif., 1998, Butler Art Inst. award, 1989, Nat. award Acrylic Painters Assn. Eng. and U.S.A., 1996. Mem. Nat. Acrylic Painters Assn. of Eng. (award 1996), Nat. Mortar Bd. Soc., Nat. Watercolor Soc. (life, past pres., Purchase prize 1979), Watercolor U.S.A. Honor Soc. (award), Watercolor West. Avocations: bicycling, music, singing.

TURNER, CRAIG, journalist; b. Pasadena, Calif., May 24, 1949; s. Donald Leslie and Dorothy A. (Kupseck) T.; m. Ellen Bevier, Oct. 10, 1973 (div. Dec. 1983); m. Joyce Huyett, Sept. 10, 1988. BS in Journalism, San Jose State U., 1971. Reporter L.A. Times, Orange County, Calif., 1971-79, asst. city editor San Diego, 1979-83, asst. met. editor L.A., 1983-89, met. editor, 1989-93, fgn. corr. Toronto, Ont., 1994-95; bur. chief UN, 1997-99; editor Nat. Edition, L.A. Times, 1999—. Co-recipient Pulitzer Prize for journalism, 1993, George Polk award Long Island U., 1993, Korn Ferry award, 1998. Mem. Soc. Profl. Journalists. Episcopalian. Avocations: outdoor activities, travel, theatre. Office: Los Angeles Times 202 W 1st St Los Angeles CA 90012 E-mail: craig.turner@latimes.com

TURNER, ELLEN, marketing professional; MBA. Sr. v.p. mktg./sales Kinkos, Ventura, Calif. Office: Kinkos Inc PO Box 8000 Ventura CA 93002-8000

TURNER, FLORENCE FRANCES, ceramist; b. Detroit, Mar. 9, 1926; d. Paul Pokrywka and Catherine Gagal; m. Dwight Robert Turner, Oct. 23, 1948; children: Thomas Michael, Nancy Louise, Richard Scott, Garry Robert. Student, Oakland C.C., Royal Oak, Mich., 1975-85, U. Ariz., Yuma, 1985, U. Las Vegas, , 1989—. Pres., founder Nev. Clay Guild, Henderson, 1990-94, mem. adv. bd., 1994-2000, v.p., 2000—. Workshop leader Greenfield Village, Dearborn, Mich., 1977-78, Plymouth (Mich.) Hist. Soc., 1979, Las Vegas Sch. System, 1989-90, Detroit Met. area, 1977-85. Bd. dirs. Las Vegas Art Mus., 1987-91; corr. sec. So. Nev. Creative Art Ctr., Las Vegas, 1990-94. Mem.: So. Nev. Rock Art Enthusiasts, Las Vegas Gem Club, Nev. Camera Club, Phi Kappa Phi. Avocations: photography, collecting gems, travel. Office: Nev Clay Guild PO Box 50004 Henderson NV 89016-0004

TURNER, HENRY BROWN, finance executive; b. N.Y.C., Sept. 3, 1936; s. Henry Brown III and Gertrude (Adams) T.; m. Sarah Jean Thomas, June 7, 1958 (div.); children: Laura Eleanor, Steven Bristow, Nancy Carolyn. A.B., Duke U., 1958; M.B.A., Harvard U., 1962. Controller Fin. Corp. of Ariz., Phoenix, 1962-64; treas., dir. corporate planning Star-Kist Foods, Terminal Island, Calif., 1964-67; dir., 1st v.p. Mitchum, Jones & Templeton, Los Angeles, 1967-73; asst. sec. Dept. Commerce, Washington, 1973-74; v.p. fin. N-Ren Corp., Cin., 1975-76; v.p. Oppenheimer & Co., N.Y.C., 1976-78; exec. v.p., mng. dir. corporate fin. Shearson Hayden Stone Inc., N.Y.C., 1978-79; sr. mng. dir. Ardshiel Inc., 1980-81, pres., 1981-93, chmn. emeritus, 1994—. Vis. lectr. U. Va. Sch. of Bus.; bd. dirs. MacDonald & Co., Pembrook Mgmt., Inc., Golden State Vitners, Inc., Cellu-Tissue Corp., Wrangler Stewart Ranch, Cave Creek, Ariz. Sponsor Jr. Achievement, 1964-67. Served to lt. USNR, 1958-60. Coll. Men's Club scholar Westfield, N.J., 1954-55 Mem. Fed. Govt. Accountants Assn. (hon.), Duke Washington Club, Omicron Delta Kappa.

TURNER, LILLIAN ERNA, retired nurse; b. Coalmont, Colo., Apr. 22, 1918; d. Harvey Oliver and Erna Lena (Wackwitz) T. BS, Colo. State U., 1940, Columbia U., 1945; cert. physician asst., U. Utah, 1978, Commd. 2d lt. Nurse Corps, U.S. Army, 1945; advanced through grades to lt. comdr. USPHS, 1964; 1st lt. U.S. Army, 1945-46; U.S. Pub. Health Svc., 1964-69; dean of women U. Alaska, Fairbanks, 1948-50; head nurse Group Health Hosp., Seattle, 1950-53; adviser to chief nurse Hosp. Am. Samoa, Pago Pago, 1954-60; head nurse Meml. Hosp., Twin Falls, Idaho, 1960-61; shift supr. Hosp. Lago Oil and Transport, Siero Colorado, Aruba, 1961-63; nurse adv. Province Hosp., Danang, South Vietnam, 1964-69, Cho Quan Hosp., South Vietnam, 1970-72; chief nurse, advisor Truk Hosp., Moen, Ea. Caroline Islands, 1972-74; nurse advisor Children's Med. Relief Internat., South Vietnam, 1975; physician's asst. U. Utah, 1976-78, Wagon Circle Med. Clinic, Rawlins, Wyo., 1978-89, Energy Basin Clinic Carbon County Meml. Hosp., Hanna, 1989-96; ret., 1996. Named Nat. Humanitarian Physician Asst. of Yr., 1993, Wyo. Physician Asst. of Yr., 1992, Disting. Alumnus of Yr., Columbia U.-Presbyn. Hosp., N.Y.C., 1997. Mem. VFW (life), Wyo. Acad. Physician Assts. (bd. dirs. 1982-83), Am. Acad. Physician Assts., Nat. Assn. Physician Assts. Avocations: reading, wood carving, sewing, hiking, beach combing, watching Denver Bronco football. Home: PO Box 337 Hanna WY 82327-0337

TURNER, MARSHALL C., JR. investment manager, consultant; b. Santa Monica, Calif., 1941; s. Marshall C. and Winifred H. T.; m. Ann, 1965; children: Erin, Benjamin, Brian. BSME, Stanford U., 1964, MS in Product Design, 1965; MBA with distinction, Harvard U., 1970. Indsl. designer Mattel Toy Co., Hawthorne, Calif., 1965; rsch. engr. GM Def. Rsch. Lab., Santa Barbara, 1965-66; med. engr. NIH, Bethesda, Md., 1966-68; White House fellow Washington, 1970-71; asst. to dep. adminstr. EPA, Washington, 1971-73; venture analyst Crocker Assocs., L.P., San Francisco, 1973-75; v.p. fin., COO Sierra R.R., 1973-75; pres., CEO Liquid Crystal Tech., Inc., San Leandro, Calif., 1975-80, chmn. bd. dirs., 1975-82; gen. ptnr. Taylor & Turner Assocs., Ltd., San Francisco, 1981-98; investment mgr. Turner Venture Assocs., San Francisco, 1998—. Bd. dirs. DuPont Photomasks, Inc., Austin, Tex., Alliance Tech. Fund, N.Y., vari ous privately held cos.; chmn. bd. dirs. Corp. Pub. Broadcasting, Washington, 1990-92; chmn. bd. dirs. KQED, Inc., San Francisco, 1985-87, acting CEO, 1993. Contbr. articles to profl. jours. Trustee Reed Union Sch. dist., Tiburon, Calif., 1977-81, chmn., 1979-81; bd. dirs. George Lucas Ednl. Found., San Rafael, Calif., 1992—, PBS, Alexandria, Va., 1993-99, PBS Enterprises, Inc., 1992-2000; trustee Mus. TV and Radio, N.Y.C., 1991-92. Lt. USPHS, 1966-68; adv. bd. Nat. Mus. Natural History, Washington, 1997—. Recipient Creative design award Machinery Inst., 1965. Avocations: fly fishing, theatrical set design. Office: Turner Venture Assocs Penthouse 10 220 Montgomery St San Francisco CA 94104-3402

TURNER, RALPH HERBERT, sociologist, educator; b. Effingham, Ill., Dec. 15, 1919; s. Herbert Turner and Hilda Pearl (Bohn) T.; m. Christine Elizabeth Hanks, Nov. 2, 1943; children: Lowell Ralph, Cheryl Christine. B.A., U So. Calif., 1941, M.A., 1942; postgrad., U. Wis., 1942-43; Ph.D., U. Chgo., 1948. Rsch. assoc. Am. Coun. Race Relations, 1947-48; faculty UCLA, 1948—, prof. sociology and anthropology, 1959-90, prof. emeritus, 1990—, chmn. dept. sociology, 1963-68; chmn. Acad. Senate U. Calif. System, 1983-84. Vis. summer prof. U. Wash., 1960 , U. Hawaii, 1962; vis. scholar Australian Nat. U., 1972; vis. prof. U. Ga., 1975, Ben Gurion U., Israel, 1983; vis. fellow Nuffield Coll. Oxford U., 1980; disting. vis. prof. Am. U., Cairo, Egypt, 1983; adj. prof. China Acad. Social Scis., Beijing, People's Republic China, 1986. Author: (with L. Killian) Collective Behavior, 1957, 2d edit., 1972, 3d edit., 1987, The Social Context of Ambition, 1964, Robert Park on Social Control and Collective Behavior, 1967, Family Interaction, 1970, Earthquake Prediction and Public Policy, 1975, (with J. Nigg, D. Paz, B. Young) Community Response to Earthquake Threat in So. Calif., 1980, (with J. Nigg and D. Paz) Waiting for Disaster, 1986; editl. cons., 1959-62; editor: Sociometry, 1962-64; acting editor: Ann. Rev. of Sociology, 1977-78; assoc. editor, 1978-79, editor, 1980-86; adv. editor: Am. Jour. Sociology, 1954-56, Sociology and Social Rsch., 1961-74; editl. staff: Am. Sociol. Rev., 1955-56; assoc. editor: Social Problems, 1959-62, 67-69; cons. editor: Sociol. Inquiry, 1968-73, Western Sociol. Rev., 1975-79; mem. editl. bd. Mass Emergencies, 1975-79, Internat. Jour. Crit. Sociology, 1974-76, Symbolic Interaction, 1977-90, 95—, Mobilization, 1996—. Mem. behavioral scis. study sect. NIH, 1961-66, chmn., 1963-64; dir.-at-large Social Sci. Rsch. Coun., 1965-66; chmn. panel on pub. policy implications of earthquake predictions Nat. Acad. Scis., 1974-75, also mem. earthquake study del. to Peoples Republic of China, 1976; mem. policy adv. bd. So. Calif. Earthquake Preparedness program, 1987-92, mem. com. social edn. and action L.A. Presbytery, 1954-56. Served to lt. (j.g.) USNR, 1943-46. Recipient Faculty prize Coll. Letters and Scis. UCLA, 1985; Faculty Rsch. fellow Social Sci. Rsch. Coun., 1953-56; Sr. Fulbright scholar U.K., 1956-57; Guggenheim fellow, U.K., 1964-65; Faculty Rsch. lectr. UCLA, 1987, UCLA Emeritus of Yr., 1997. Mem. AAAS (exch. del. to China 1988), AAUP, Am. Sociol. Assn. (coun. 1959-64, chmn. social psychology sect. 1960-61, pres. 1968-69, chmn. sect. theoretical sociology 1973-74, chmn. collective behavior and social movements sect. 1983-84, Cooley-Mead award 1987), Pacific Sociol. Assn. (pres. 1957), Internat. Sociol. Assn. (coun. 1974-82, v.p. 1978-82), Soc. Study Social Problems (exec. com. 1962-63), Soc. for Study Symbolic Interaction (pres. 1982-83, Charles Horton Cooley award 1978, George Herbert Mead award 1990), Sociol. Rsch. Assn. (pres. 1989-90), Am. Coun. of Learned Soc. (exec. com. of coun. 1990-93), UCLA Emeriti Assn. (coun. , pres. 1992-93), U. of Calif. Emeriti Assns. (pres. 1992-93, chair-elect 1996-97, chair 1997-98). Home: 1126 Chautauqua Blvd Pacific Palisades CA 90272-3808 Office: UCLA 405 Hilgard Ave Los Angeles CA 90095-9000

TURNER, ROBERT ELWOOD, physicist; b. Covington, Ky., Dec. 8, 1937; s. Elwood Fletcher and Margaret Belle (Gunn) T. BS in Physics, U. Cin., 1959, MS in Physics, 1960; MA in Physics, Columbia U., 1963; PhD in Physics, Washington U., St. Louis, 1970. Research physicist U. Mich., Ann Arbor, 1970-73, Environ. Research Inst. Mich., Ann Arbor, 1973-77; sr. scientist Sci. Applications Internat. Corp., Monterey, Calif., 1977—. Rsch. assoc. Inst. for Space Studies, NASA, N.Y.C., 1962, Washington U., 1964-69; astronomer McDonnell Planetarium, St. Louis, 1965-68; lectr. U. Mich., 1971-77; Gordon Conf. lectr., 1980. Contbr. articles to profl. jours. and books. Rep. precinct leader, Ann Arbor, 1972. Laws fellow, 1959; recipient Group Achievement award NASA, 1976. Mem. AAAS, Am. Assn. Physics Tchrs., Monterey Inst. Rsch. in Astronomy, N.Y. Acad. Scis., Math. Assn. Am., Toastmasters (ednl. v.p. Dayton 1986, pres. 1987, sec. 1989, treas. 1991), Sigma Xi (programs co-chair Air Force chpt. 1988-89). Methodist. Club: Toastmasters (ednl. v.p. Dayton 1986, pres. 1987, sec. 1989). Avocations: swimming, tennis, ice skating, hiking. Home: 930 Casanova Ave Apt 40 Monterey CA 93940-6821 Office: Sci Applications Internat 550 Camino El Estero Ste 205 Monterey CA 93940-3231

TURNER, ROSS JAMES, investment corporation executive; b. Winnipeg, Man., Can., May 1, 1930; permanent U.S. resident, 1980; s. James Valentine and Gretta H. (Ross) T.; children: Ralph, Rick, Tracy. , U. Man. Extension, 1951, Banff Sch. Advanced Mgmt., 1956. Chmn./pres., CEO Genstar Corp., San Francisco, 1976-86, also bd. dirs.; chmn. Genstar Investment Corp., San Francisco, 1987—. Bd. dirs. Rio Algom Ltd., Blue Shield of Calif., U. Man. Found. USA. Fellow Soc. Mgmt. Accts. Can.; mem. Toronto Club, Pacific Union Club, Rancho Santa Fe Golf Club, Peninsula Golf and Country Club. Office: Genstar Investment Corp 555 California St Ste 4850 San Francisco CA 94104-1700 E-mail: dcordell@gencap.com

TURNER, TOM, writer, editor; b. Oakland, Calif., 1942; m. Mary Jorgensen; children: Bret and Kathryn (twins). BA in Polit. Sci., U. Calif., 1965. Vol. Peace Corps, Turkey, 1965-67; grant analyst Head Start, 1968; editor adminstry. asst. Sierra Club, 1968-69; various positions including exec. dir. Friends of the Earth, 1969-86, also editor Not Man Apart; staff writer, dir. publs., sr. editor Earthjustice, 1986—. Author: Wild By Law: the Sierra Club Legal Defense Fund and the Places It Has Saved, 1990, Sierra

Club: 100 Years of Protecting Nature, 1991; contbr. to The Ency. of the Environment, 1994, also chpts. to books; contbr. articles to Sierra, Defenders, Wilderness, San Francisco Chronicle, San Francisco Examiner, L.A. Times, Oakland Tribune,Washington Post, Mother Earth News, Outside, others. Office: Earthjustice 180 Montgomery St Ste 1400 San Francisco CA 94104-4236 E-mail: tturner@earthjustice.org

TURNER, WALLACE L. reporter; b. Titusville, Fla., Mar. 15, 1921; s. Clyde H. and Ina B. (Wallace) T.; m. Pearl Burk, June 12, 1943; children: Kathleen Turner, Elizabeth Turner Everett. B.J., U. Mo., 1943; postgrad. (Nieman fellow), Harvard U., 1958-59. Reporter Springfield (Mo.) Daily News, 1943, Portland Oregonian, 1943-59; news dir. Sta. KPTV, Portland, 1959-61; asst. sec. HEW, Washington, 1961-62; reporter N.Y. Times, San Francisco, 1962—, bur. chief, 1970-85, Seattle bur. chief, 1985-88. Author: Gamblers Money, 1965, The Morman Establishment, 1967. Recipient Heywood Broun award for reporting, 1952, 56; Pulitzer Prize for reporting, 1957 Office: Box 99269 Magnolia Sta Seattle WA 98199-4260

TURNER, WILLIAM WEYAND, writer; b. Buffalo, Apr. 14, 1927; s. William Peter and Magdalen (Weyand) T.; m. Margaret Peiffer, Sept. 12, 1964; children: Mark Peter, Lori Ann. BS, Canisius Coll., 1949. Spl. agt. in various field offices FBI, 1951-61; free-lance writer Calif., 1963—; sr. editor Ramparts Mag., San Francisco, 1967—. Investigator and cons. Nat. Wiretap Commn., 1975; U.S. del. J.F.K. Internat. Seminar, Rio de Janeiro, 1995. Author: The Police Establishment, 1968, Invisible Witness: The Use and Abuse of the New Technology of Crime Investigation, 1968, Hoover's F.B.I.: The Men and the Myth, 1970, Power on the Right, 1971, (with Warren Hinckle and Eliot Asinof) The Ten Second Jailbreak, 1973, (with John Christian) The Assassination of Robert F. Kennedy, 1978, (with Warren Hinckle) The Fish is Red: The Story of the Secret War Against Castro, 1981, updated, expanded, retitled as Deadly Secrets: The CIA-Mafia War Against Castro and the Assassination of JFK, 1992, Rearview Mirror: Looking Back at the FBI, the CIA and Other Tails, 2001; contbg. author: Investigating the FBI, 1973; contbr. articles to popular mags. Dem. candidate for U.S. Congress, 1968. Served with USN, 1945-46. Mem. Authors Guild, Internat. Platform Assn., Press Club of San Francisco. Roman Catholic. Avocation: tennis. Home and Office: 163 Mark Twain Ave San Rafael CA 94903-2820

TURNLUND, JUDITH RAE, nutritionist; b. St. Paul, Sept. 28, 1936; d. Victor Emanuel and Vida Mae (Priddy) Hanson; m. Richard Wayne Turnlund, Nov. 9, 1957; children: Michael Wayne, Mark Richard, Todd Hanson. BS in Chemistry and Psychology, Gustavus Adolphus Coll., 1958; PhD in Nutrition, U. Calif., Berkeley, 1978. Registered dietitian. Postdoctoral fellow U. Calif., Berkeley, 1978-80, lectr., 1984-92, adj. assoc. prof., 1989-97; rsch. nutrition scientist Western Regional Rsch. Ctr./Western Human Nutrition Ctr., USDA, San Francisco, Albany, and Davis, Calif., 1980—; rsch. leader Western Human Nutrition Ctr. USDA, San Francisco, 1993-96; adj. prof. U. Calif., Davis, 2000—. Vis. asst. prof. Am. U. Beirut, Lebanon, 1979, 80. Editor: Stable Isotopes in Nutrition, 1984; contbr. articles to profl. jours. Recipient Cert. of Merit, USDA/ARS, 1984, 93, 98, Disting. Alumni citation Gustavus Adolphus Coll., 1988, Am. Inst. Nutrition's Lederle award in Human Nutrition, 1996; USDA grantee, 1982-90, Nat. Dairy Coun. grantee, 1986. Mem. Am. Inst. Nutrition, Am. Soc. Clin. Nutrition, Am. Dietetic Assn. Home: 2276 Great Hwy San Francisco CA 94116-1555 Office: U Calif USDA/ARS Western Human Nutrition Rsch One Shields Ave Davis CA 95616 E-mail: jturnlun@whnrc.usda.gov

TURNOVSKY, STEPHEN JOHN, economics educator; b. Wellington, New Zealand, Apr. 5, 1941; came to U.S., 1981; s. Frederick and Liselotte Felicitas (Wodak) T.; m. Michelle Henriette Louise Roos, Jan. 21, 1967; children: Geoffrey George, Jacqueline Liselotte. BA, Victoria U., Wellington, 1962, MA with honors, 1963; PhD, Harvard U., 1968. Asst. prof. econs. U. Pa., Phila., 1968-71; assoc. prof. U. Toronto, Ont., Can., 1971-72; prof. Australian Nat. U., Canberra, 1972-82; IBE disting. prof. econs. U. Ill., Champaign, 1982-87; prof. econs. U. Wash., Seattle, 1987—, chmn. dept., 1990-95; Castor prof., 1993—. Rsch. assoc. Nat. Bur. Econ. Rsch., Cambridge, Mass., 1983-93. Author: Macroeconomic Analysis and Stabilization Policy, 1977, International Macroeconomic Stabilization Policy, 1990, Methods of Macroeconomic Dynamics, 1995, 2d edit., 2000, International Macroeconomic Dynamics, 1997; mem. editl. bd. several jours.; contbr. articles to profl. jours. Fellow Econometric Soc., Acad. Social Scis. in Australia; mem. Soc. Econ. Dynamics and Control (pres. 1982-84, editor Jour. Econ. Dynamics and Control 1981-87, 95—). Avocations: skiing, hiking, music. Home: 6053 NE Kelden Pl Seattle WA 98105-2045 Office: Dept Econs U Wash Box 353330 Seattle WA 98195-3330 E-mail: sturn@u.washington.edu

TURPIN, DAVID HOWARD, biologist, educator; b. Duncan, B.C., Can., July 14, 1956; s. George Howard and Marilyn Elizabeth (Jones) T.; m. S. Laurene Clark, Oct. 4, 1985; children: Chantal, Joshua. BSc in Biology, U. B.C., 1977, PhD in Botany, Oceanography, 1980. Post-doctoral rsch. fellow Natural Sci. & Engring. Coun., 1980-81; rsch. assoc. Simon Fraser U., 1980; v.p. Sigma Resource Cons., Vancouver, B.C., 1980-81; from asst. prof. to assoc. prof. Queen's U., Kingston, Ont., Can., 1981-90, prof. biology, 1990-91, dean arts & sci., 1993-95, vice prin. acad., 1995-2000; prof., head botany U. B.C., 1991-93; pres., vice-chancellor U. Victoria, B.C., 2000—. Invited speaker profl. meetings, univs. worldwide, pres. and vic-chancellor, U. Victoria, England, 2000. Co-editor: Plant Physiology, Biochemistry and Molecular Biology, 1990, 2nd edit., 1996; mem. editl. bd. Jour. Phycology, 1992-96, Plant Physiology, 1988-92, Plant Cell and Environ., 1994—, Jour. Exptl. Botany, 1995—; contbr. chpts. to books; author numerous articles, conf. procs. V.p. Great Lakes Tomorrow, 1986-90; mem. program com. Great Lakes Course-Ont. Sci. Ctr., 1988; Kingston City rep. Cataraqui Regional Conservation Authority, 1984-86. Recipient Excellence in Teaching Alumni award Queen's U., 1989, Outstanding Alumni award U. B.C., 1990, Darbaker prize in phycology Am. Bot. Assn., 1991; Natural Sci. and Engring. Rsch. Can. E.W.R. Stacie Meml. fellow, 1989-90; Capt. T.S. Byrne Meml. scholar U. B.C., 1980; postgrad. scholar Natural Scis. and Engring. Rsch. Coun., 1979-81, Edith Ashton Meml. scholar U. B.C., 1979, Nat. Rsch. Coun. scholar, 1978-79; Natural Scis. and Engring. Rsch. Coun. grantee, 1982—. Fellow Royal Soc. Can.; mem. Phycological Soc. Am., Am. Soc. Limnology and Oceanography, Can. Soc. Plant Physiologists (C.D. Nelson award 1989), Am. Soc. Plant Physiologists (cert. recognition 1992) Office: Off of the Pres - U Victoria Business & Economic Bldg Rm 454 Victoria BC Canada V8W 2Y2

TURRENTINE, HOWARD BOYD, federal judge; b. Escondido, Calif., Jan. 22, 1914; s. Howard and Veda Lillian (Maxfield) T.; m. Virginia Jacobsen, May 13, 1965 (dec.); children: Howard Robert, Terry Beverly; m. Marlene Lipsey, Nov. 1, 1991. AB, San Diego State Coll., 1936; LLB, U. So. Calif., 1939. Bar: Calif. 1939. Practiced in, San Diego, 1939-68; judge Superior Ct. County of San Diego, 1968-70, U.S. Dist. Ct. (so. dist.) Calif., Calif., sr. judge, 1970—. Served with USNR, 1941-45. Mem. ABA, Fed. Bar Assn., Am. Judicature Soc. Office: US Dist Ct 940 Front St San Diego CA 92101-8994

TUTASHINDA, KWELI (BRIAN P. ALTHEIMER), chiropractic physician, educator; b. Wynne, Ark., May 14, 1956; s. Joe Porché and Lura Ella (Darden) Altheimer; divorced; 1 child, Chinyere R.; m. Leonor Quiñonez, June 13, 1987; children Xihuanel, Rukiya, Jomoké. BA in Philosophy summa cum laude, U. Ark., 1978; D of Chiropractic cum laude, Life Chiropractic Coll. West, San Lorenzo, Calif., 1989. Tchr. English Oakland (Calif.) Pub. Schs., 1984-86; tchr. spl. programs U. Calif., Berkeley, 1984-92, 94-95, 98-00; instr. phys. diagnosis and chiropractic tech. Life Chiropractic Coll. West, San Lorenzo, Calif., 1989-99; pvt. practice Berkeley, 1989—; owner Imhotep Chiropractic & Wellness Clinic; dir. Imhotep Wellness Workshops & Seminars. Editor, pub. Foresight Mag., 1982-84; author, pub. Toward a Holistic Worldview, 1985, Therapeutic Exercises for the Spine, 1999; contbr. articles to Chiropractic History. Recipient 1st degree Black Belt Tae Kwon Do, 1976. Mem. Assn. Chiropractic History, Somatics Soc. Mem. Sufi Order of the West, Naqshbandi Sufi Order. Islam. Avocations: yoga, martial arts, writing, reading, jogging. Office: 3358 Adeline St Berkeley CA 94703-2737 E-mail: tutateam@awol

TUTHILL, WALTER WARREN, financial executive, business consultant; b. Madison, N.J., Nov. 28, 1941; s. Walter Warren and Elizabeth Emma (Kniskern) T.; m. Barbara Ann Stephens, Apr. 22, 1967. BSBA, U. N.C., 1964. CPA, Calif., N.Y., N.J., N.C.; cert. info systems auditor, cert. internal auditor. Sr. mgr. Price Waterhouse, N.Y.C., 1964-77; dir. internal audit Carter Hawley Hale Stores Inc., L.A., 1977-82, gen. auditor, 1982-85, v.p., 1985-93; sr. v.p. retail control Broadway Stores, Inc., L.A., 1993-96; v.p. retail control Federated Dept. Stores, Inc., L.A., 1996-97; coo Gelfand, Rennert & Feldman, (divsn. of PricewaterhouseCoopers LLP), L.A., 1997-2001; ptnr. Wong, Holland, LLP, CPAs, Woodland Hills, Calif., 2001—. Lectr. in field. Contbr. articles to profl. jours. Pres. Twin W Rescue Squad, Princeton Junction, N.J., 1976-77. Mem. AICPA, N.Y. Soc. CPAs, Am. Acctg. Assn., Nat. Retail Mchts. Assn. (chmn. bd. internal audit group 1982-84, bd. dirs.), EDP Auditors Assn. Avocations: international travel, computers, classical music, photography. E-mail: wtuthill@ wongholland-.com. Office: Wong Holland LLP CPA 4919 Topanga Canyon Blvd Woodland Hills CA 91364-3113

TUTOR, RONALD N. construction company executive; b. Oct. 13, 1940; BS in Finance, U. So. Calif., 1963. Pres., CEO Tutor-Saliba Corp.; COO, also dir. Perini Corp., Framingham, Mass. Bd. dirs. Southdown Corp.; mem. adv. com. U. So. Calif. Sch. Engring. Recipient L.A. Conservancy Preservation award, 1994, Greater L.A. African-Am. C. of C. Contractor of yr. award, 1994, U.S. Army C.E. L.A. Dist. Contractor of Yr. award, 1994, NCCJ Real Estate and Constrn. Industry Humanitarian award, 1992. Mem. Am. Concrete Inst.

TUTTLE, RICK, city controller; b. New Haven, Jan. 5, 1940; s. Frederick Burton and Mary Emily; m. Muff Singer; 1 child, Sarah Emily Tuttle Singer. BA with honors and distinction, Wesleyan U., 1962; MA, UCLA, 1964, PhD, 1975. From asst. dean of students to student affairs officer UCLA, 1971-85; contr. City of L.A., 1985—. Civil rights worker, Ga. and Miss., 1963; co-chmn. Calif. Young Citizens Robert F. Kennedy, 1968; pres. Calif. Fedn. Young Dems., 1969-71; trustee L.A. Community Coll., 1977-85, pres. 1982-83; bd. dirs. univ. rel. conf. UCLA. Recipient Svc. award, UCLA Alumni Internship Assn., 1988, Equal Justice in Govt. award, NAACP Legal Def. and Edn. Fund, L.A., 1986, Disting. Pub. Svc. award Anti Defamation League, L.A., 1991, Pub. Svc. award UCLA Alumni Assn., 1994, Disting. Leadership award Local Govt. Assn. Govt. Accts., 1996. Mem. Govt. Fin. Officers Assn., L.A. Bus. Coun. (life). Democrat. Office: City of Los Angeles Office Contr Rm 1200 200 N Main St Ofc Contr Los Angeles CA 90012-4110

TWIFORD, JIM, state legislator; b. Wheaton, Wy., Nov. 17, 1942; m. Jenne Lee Twiford. Pres. senate Wy. Ho. of Reps. Roman Catholic. Office: 33 Fairway Dr Douglas WY 82633-9515 Fax: 307-358-3515. E-mail: jimjenne@aol.com

TWIGG, NANCY L. nursing association administrator; Exec. dir. State of N.Mex. Bd. Nursing, Albuquerque. Office: State NMex Bd Nursing 4206 Louisiana Blvd NE Ste A Albuquerque NM 87109-1841

TWIGGS, JERRY T. state legislator; b. Blackfoot, Idaho, Mar. 25, 1933; m. Sandra Twiggs; children: Jerry D., Quinn D., Cindy, Ted, Thane. Farmer; in agribus.; ret.; elected senator, dist. 31 Idaho Senate, Boise, 1984—. Senate pres. pro tempore; mem. state affairs com. Republican. Office: State Capitol PO Box 83720 Boise ID 83720-3720

TWIGG-SMITH, THURSTON, newspaper publisher; b. Honolulu, Aug. 17, 1921; s. William and Margaret Carter (Thurston) Twigg-S.; m. Bessie Bell, June 9, 1942 (div. Feb. 1983); children: Elizabeth, Thurston, William, Margaret, Evelyn; m. Laila Roster, Feb. 22, 1983 (div. Dec. 1994); m. Sharon Smith, Feb. 28, 1996. B.Engring., Yale U., 1942. With Honolulu Advertiser, 1946-2000, mng. editor, 1954-60, asst. bus. mgr., 1960-61, pub., 1961-86; pres., dir., chief exec. officer Honolulu Advertiser, Inc., 1962-93, chmn., 1993-2000. Chmn., dir., CEO Persis Corp.; bd. dirs. Atalanta/Sosnoff Capital Corp., N.Y. Trustee Honolulu Acad. Arts, The Contemporary Mus., Hawaii, The Skowhegan Sch., Maine, Yale Art Gallery, New Haven. Maj. AUS, 1942-46. Mem. Waialae Country Club, Pacific Club, Oahu Country Club, Outrigger Canoe Club. Office: Persis Corp 2447 Makiki Heights Dr Honolulu HI 96822-2547 E-mail: ttwigg@persiscorp.com

TWINING, CHARLES HAILE, ambassador; b. Balt., Nov. 1, 1940; s. Charles Haile and Martha R. (Caples) T.; m. Irene Verann Metz, May 30, 1972; children: Daniel, Steven. BA, U. Va., 1962; MA, Johns Hopkins U., 1964; postgrad., Cornell U., 1977-78. Joined Fgn. Svc., Dept. State, Washington, 1964; with Am. Embassy, Tananarive, 1964-66, Cords Dalat, Vietnam, 1966-68; desk officer Ivory Coast, Upper Volta, Nigeria; with Dept. of State, Washington, 1970-72, Am. Embassy, Abidjan, 1972-74, Bangkok, 1975-77; dep. office dir. for Australia and New Zealand Dept. of State, Washington, 1978-80, with East Asian pers., 1980-82; former charge d'affaires Am. Embassy, Cotonou, 1982-83; former prin. officer Am. Con Gen, Douala, 1983-85; former dep. chief of mission Am. Embassy, Ouagadougou, Burkina Faso, 1985-88; former dir. Office of Vietnam, Laos and Cambodia Dept. State, Washington, 1988-91; spl. rep., amb. to Cambodia Phnom Penh, 1991-95; amb. to Cameroon and Equatorial Guinea Dept. State, Yaounde, 1996-98; fgn. policy advisor USCINCPAC. Contbr.: Cambodia: 1975-78, 1990. Office: Fgn Policy Advisor HQ USCINCPAC PO Box 64028 Camp H M Smith HI 96861-4028

TWISS, ROBERT MANNING, prosecutor; b. Worcester, Mass., Aug. 2, 1948; s. Robert Sullivan Jr. and Marion (Manning) T.; m. Joan Marie Callahan, Aug. 4, 1979. BA, U. Mass., 1970; JD, U. San Francisco, 1975; MA in Criminal Justice, Wichita State U., 1979; LLM, Georgetown U., 1981. Bar: Mass. 1976, Calif., 1988, U.S. Ct. Appeals Armed Forces 1976, U.S. Dist. Ct. Mass. 1976, U.S. Ct. Appeals (1st cir.) 1976, U.S. Ct. Appeals (5th cir.) 1986, U.S. Ct. Appeals (9th cir.) 1988, U.S. Dist. Ct. (ea. and cen. dist.) Calif. 1989. Atty. office chief counsel IRS, Washington, 1980-86; trial atty. criminal div. U.S. Dept. Justice, Washington, 1986-87, asst. U.S. atty. Sacramento, 1987-93, 94—, chief organized crime and narcotics, 1991-92, 1st asst. U.S. atty., 1992-93, U.S. atty., 1993, exec. assst. U.S. atty., 1994. Contbr. articles to profl. jours. Capt. JAGC, U.S. Army, 1976-80 Named to McAuliffe Honor Soc. U. San Francisco, 1975; recipient Markham award Office Chief Counsel IRS, Washington, 1985. Avocation: athletics. Office: Office US Atty 501 I St 10th Fl Sacramento CA 95814-7306

TYKESON, DONALD ERWIN, broadcast executive; b. Portland, Oreg., Apr. 11, 1927; s. O. Ansel and Hillie Martha (Haveman) T.; m. Rilda Margaret Steigleder, July 1, 1950; children: Ellen, Amy, Eric. BS, U. Oreg., 1951. V.p., dir. Liberty Comm., Inc., Eugene, Oreg., 1963-67, pres., CEO, dir., 1967-83; mng. ptnr. Tykeson/Assocs. Enterprises, 1983—; chmn. bd. Bend Cable Comm., LLC, 1983—, Telecomm Svcs., 1988—, Ctrl. Oreg. Cable Advt., LLC, 1992—, Bend Cable Data Svcs. LLC, 1998—. Pres. Tykeson Found., 1995—. Bd. dirs. Nat. Multiple Sclerosis Soc., 1987—, Nat. Coalition Rsch. in Neurol. and Communicative Disorders, 1984-89, Sacred Heart Med. Ctr. Found., 1995—; chmn. Nat. Coalition Rsch. pub. and govt. info. com., 1986-89, C-SPAN, 1980-89; mem. bus. adv. coun. U. Oreg. Coll. Bus. Adminstrn., 1973—, steering com. 1997—, dean search com., 1998-99; trustee U. Oreg. Found., 1996—; vice-chmn. we. area Nat. Multiple Sclerosis Soc., 1983—, dir., mem. rsch. and med. programs com., 1986-99; trustee Eugene Art Found., 1980-85, Oreg. Health Scis. U. Found., 1988-91, investment com., 1992-95, neurosci. com., 1999—; mem. Oreg. Investment Coun. State of Oreg., vice-chmn., 1988-92. Mem. Nat. Assn. Broadcasters, Nat. Cable TV Assn. (dir. 1976-83), Chief Execs. Orgn., Vintage Club (bd. dirs. 1996-99, chmn. fin. com., treas. 1996-99, pres. Custom Lot Assn. 1992-97), Country Club Eugene (dir. 1975-77, sec. 1976, v.p. 1977), Multnomah Athletic Club, Arlington Club, Rotary, Alexis de Tocquevill Soc. Home: 447 Spyglass Dr Eugene OR 97401-2091 Office: Tykeson Assocs Enterprises PO Box 70006 Eugene OR 97401-0101

TYLER, DARLENE JASMER, retired dietitian; b. Watford City, N.D., Jan. 26, 1939; d. Edwin Arthur and Leola Irene (Walker) Jasmer; m. Richard G. Tyler, Aut. 26, 1977 (dec.); children: Ronald, Eric, Scott. BS, Oreg. State U., 1961. Registered dietitian. Clin. dietitian Salem (Oreg.) Hosp., 1965-73; sales supr. Sysco Northwest, Tigard, Oreg., 1975-77; clin. dietitian Physicians & Surgeons Hosp., Portland, 1977-79; food svc. dir. Meridian Park Hosp., Tualatin, 1979-2000; ret., 2000. Mem. Am. Soc. Hosp. Food Svc. Adminstrs., Am. Dietetic Assn., Oreg. Dietetic Assn., Portland Dietetic Assn. Episcopalian. Home: 4314 Botticelli Lake Oswego OR 97035 E-mail: darlenejtyler@aol.com

TYLER, GAIL MADELEINE, nurse; b. Dhahran, Saudi Arabia, Nov. 21, 1953; (parents Am. citizens); d. Louis Rogers and Nona Jean (Henderson) T.; m. Alan J. Moore, Sept. 29, 1990; 1 child, Sean James. AS, Front Range C.C., Westminster, Colo., 1979; BSN, U. Wyo., 1989. RN, Colo. Ward sec. Valley View Hosp., Thornton, Colo., 1975-79; nurse Scott and White Hosp., Temple, Tex., 1979-83, Meml. Hosp. Laramie County, Cheyenne, Who., 1983-89; dir. DePaul Home Health, 1989-91; field staff nurse Poudre Valley Hosp. Home Care/Poudre Care Connection, 1991-98, Rehab. and Vis. Nurses Assn., Fort Collins, Colo., 1999—. Mem., parish nurse Rocky Mountain Health Ministry. Avocations: collecting internat. dolls, sewing, reading, travel.

TYLER, GEORGE LEONARD, electrical engineering educator; b. Bartow, Fla., Oct. 18, 1940; s. George Leonard and Mable Leona (Bethea) T.; m. Joanne Lynne Phelps, Nov. 17, 1977; children: Virginia L., Matthew L. BEE, Ga. Inst. Tech., 1963; MS, Stanford U., 1964, PhD in Elec. Engring., 1967. Engr. Lockheed Aircraft Corp., Marietta, Ga., 1963; rsch. assoc. Ctr. for Radar Astronomy, Stanford (Calif.) U., 1967-69, rsch. engr., 1969-72, sr. rsch. assoc., 1972-74, rsch. prof. elec. engring., 1974-90, prof., 1990—, dir. Space, Telecom. and Radiosci. Lab., 1993-98. Cons. SRI-Internat., NASA, Jet Propulsion Lab., also other orgns., 1972—; mem. com. on planetary exploration of space sci. bd. NAS, 1983-87, mem. naval studies bd. panel on advanced radar tech., 1990-91. Contbr. over 200 articles to sci. jours., chpts. to books. Recipient Medal for Exceptional Sci. Achievement, NASA, 1977, 81, 86, Pub. Svc. medal, 1992; fellow NSF, 1964-66. Fellow IEEE; mem. Am. Geophys. Union, Am. Astron. Soc., Internat. Astron. Union, Internat. Radio Sci. Union, Electromagnetics Acad., Phi Kappa Phi, Tau Beta Pi. Achievements include co-discovery of Crab Nebula pulsar, first high-resolution measurement of the directional spectrum of the sea, development and application of occultation technique for outer planets, measurement of Titan's atmosphere. Office: Stanford U Ctr Radar Astronomy Dept Elec Engring Stanford CA 94305 9515

TYLER, RICHARD, fashion designer; b. Sunshine, Australia, Sept. 22, 1950; m. Doris Taylor (div.); 1 child, Sheridan; m. Lisa Trafficante, 1989; 1 child, Edward Charles. Prin. Zippity-doo-dah, Melbourne, Australia, 1968-80, Tyler-Trafficante, L.A., 1988—; design dir. Anne Klein Collection, N.Y.C., 1993-94, 99; fashion dir. owner Tyler Trafficante, Inc., 1999—. Designer Richard Tyler Couture introduced for Women, 1989, Richard Tyler Collection debut for Men, April 1997, Richard Tyler Shoes for Women, 1996, Richard Tyler Collection for Women, 1997, Richard Tyler Shoes for Men, 1997. Recipient New Fashion Talent Perry Ellis award Coun. Fashion Designers Am., 1993, Womenswear Designer of Yr. award, 1994, Perry Ellis award for new fashion talent in menswear, 1995.

TYNDALL, GAYE LYNN, secondary education educator; b. Reno, Apr. 21, 1953; d. Chris H. and Ellen (Hutchinson) Gansberg; m. Dave Tyndall, Mar. 17, 1973; children: Jody, Dave. BS, U. Nev., Reno, 1987, postgrad. Cert. secondary tchr. Tchr. math, sci. Douglas High Sch., Minden, Nev., 1987—. Treas. Nev. Sci. Project, Reno, 1990—; presenter Reading and Writing in the Math Classroom Internat. Reading Assn., Nat. Sci. Tchrs., Assn., 1990-92. Recipient Nev. State Tchr. of Yr. award Nev. Bd. Edn., 1993. Mem. Nat. Coun. Tchrs. Math., Calif. Math Coun. Avocations: momming, rodeo, family activities. Office: Douglas High Sch PO Box 1888 Minden NV 89423-1888

TYNER, NEAL EDWARD, retired insurance company executive; b. Grand Island, Nebr., Jan. 30, 1930; s. Edward Raymond and Lydia Dorothea (Kruse) T.; children: Karen Tyner Redrow, Morgan. BBA, U. Nebr., 1956. Jr. analyst Bankers Life Nebr., Lincoln, 1956-62, asst. v.p. securities, 1962-67, v.p. securities, treas., 1967-69, fin. v.p., treas., 1970-72, sr. v.p. fin., treas., 1972-83, pres., chief exec. officer, 1983-87, chmn., pres., chief exec. officer, 1987-88, chmn., CEO, 1988-95. Bd. dirs. Union Bank & Trust Co., Union Bank of Ariz., N.A.; chmn. emeritus Ameritas Life Ins. Corp. Trustee U. Nebr. Found., Lincoln Found.; bd. govs. Nebr. Wesleyan U. Capt. USMC, 1950-54, Korea. Fellow CFAs; mem. Omaha/Lincoln Soc. Fin. Analysts, Paradise Valley Country Club. Lutheran. Avocations: tennis, computers. Office: 8225 N Golf Dr Scottsdale AZ 85253-2716

TYRRELL, D. LORNE J. university dean; Dean U. Alta. Faculty Medicine and Dentistry, Edmonton, Can., 1994—, now dean Can. Office: U Alta Fac Med & Dentistry 2J2 00 WMC Edmonton AB Canada T6G 2R7

TYSON, DAVID T. university president; Pres. U. Portland, Oreg. Office: U Portland Office Pres 5000 N Willamette Blvd Portland OR 97203-5743

TYSON, LAURA D'ANDREA, dean, economist, educator; b. Bayonne, N.J., June 28, 1947; BA, Smith Coll., 1969; PhD, MIT, 1974. Prof. econ. and bus. adminstrn. U. Calif., Berkeley, 1978-98, BankAmerica dean Haas Sch. Bus., 1998—; chmn. Pres.'s Coun. Econ. Advisors, Washington, 1993-95; nat. econ. advisor to Pres. U.S. Nat. Econ. Coun., Washington, 1995-96. Editor: (with John Zysman) American Industry in International Competition, 1983, (with Ellen Comisso) Power, Purpose and Collective Choice: Economic Strategy in Socialist States, 1986, (with William Dickens and John Zysman) The Dynamics of Trade and Employment, 1988, (with Chalmers Johnson and John Zysman) Politics and Productivity: The Real Story of How Japan Works, 1989, Who's Bashing Whom? Trade Conflict in High Technology Industries, 1992. Office: Haas Sch Bus 545 Student Srvs # 1900 Berkeley CA 94720-0001

UDALL, CALVIN HUNT, lawyer; b. St. Johns, Ariz., Oct. 23, 1923; s. Grover C. and Dora (Sherwood) U.; m. Doris Fuss, Dec. 11, 1943; children: Fredric, Margaret Udall Moses, Julie (Mrs. Blair M. Nash), Lucinda Udall Romney, Tina Udall Rodriguez. LL.B., U. Ariz., 1948. Bar: Ariz. 1948. Ptnr. Fennemore Craig, 1953—. Ariz. spl. counsel Arizona v. California, 1954-62; mem. Coun. on Legal Edn. Opportunity, 1983-93. Mem. cast, Phoenix Mus. Theatre, 1959-65. Fellow Am. Coll. Trial

Lawyers, Am. Bar Found. (bd. dirs. 1986-89, fellows chmn. 1988-89), Ariz. Bar Found. (Disting. Svc. award 1993); mem. ABA (ho. dels. 1962-92, bd. govs. 1981-84, exec. com. 1983-84, chmn. task force on minorities 1984-86), Maricopa County Bar Assn. (pres. 1957, Disting. Pub. Svc. award 1986), State Bar Ariz. (bd. govs. 1960-65), Ariz. Law Coll. Assn. (bd. dirs. 1967-80, pres. 1978-79, U. Ariz. Disting. Citizen award 1984, bd. visitors 1991—). Office: Fennemore Craig 3003 N Central Ave Ste 2600 Phoenix AZ 85012-2913

UDALL, MARK, congressman; b. Tucson, July 18, 1950; m. Maggie Fox; children: Jed, Tess. B.Am. Civilization, Williams Coll., 1972. Course dir., educator Colo. Outward Bound Sch., 1975-85, exec. dir., 1985-95; mem. dist. 13 Colo. Ho. of Reps., 1997-99; mem. U.S. Congress from 2d Colo. dist., Washington, 1999—; Dem. dep. regional whip for western U.S.; mem. resources com., small bus. com., sci. com. Democrat. Avocation: mountain climbing. Office: US Ho Reps 502 Cannon Ho Office Bldg Washington DC 20515-0001 also: 1333 W 120th Ave Ste 210 Denver CO 80234-2710*

UDALL, THOMAS (TOM UDALL), congressman; b. Tucson, May 18, 1948; s. Stewart and Lee Udall; m. Jill Z. Cooper; 1 child, Amanda Cooper. BA, Prescott Coll., 1970; LLB, Cambridge U., Eng., 1975; JD, U. N.Mex., 1977. Law clk. to Hon. Oliver Seth U.S. Ct. Appeals (10th cir.), Santa Fe, 1977-78; asst. U.S. atty. U.S. Atty.'s Office, 1978-81; pvt. practice Santa Fe, 1981-83; chief counsel N.Mex. Health & Environ. Dept., 1983-84; ptnr. Miller, Stratvert, Togerson & Schlenker, P.A., Albuquerque, 1985-90; atty. gen. State of N.Mex., 1991-98; mem. 106th Congress from NM 3rd dist., 1999—, mem. small bus. com., mem. resources com., mem. vets.' affairs com. Past pres. Rio Chama Preservation Trust; mem. N.Mex. Environ. Improvement Bd., 1986—87; bd. dirs. La Compania de Teatro de Albuquerque, Santa Fe Chamber Music Festival, Law Fund. Mem. Nat. Assn. Attys. Gen. (pres. 1996), Kiwanis. Democrat. Office: US Ho Reps 502 Cannon HOB Washington DC 20515-0001 E-mail: tom.udall@mail.house.gov

UDLAND, DUANE S. protective services official; b. Minot, N.D., Apr. 15, 1950; m. Judi Udland; 1 child, Eric. Grad., Spokane Police Acad., 1973; BA in Sociology, Ea. Washington State Coll., 1973; grad., FBI Nat. Acad., 1987. From law enforcement officer to detective Spokane (Wash.) County Sheriffs Office, 1972-78; from patrol officer to sgt. Soldotna (Alaska) Police Dept., 1978-82, chief, 1982-88; dep. chief Anchorage (Alaska) Police Dept., 1988-97, chief, 1997—. Bd. dirs. Alaska Native Justice Ctr.; past chmn. Cen. Peninsula 911 Bd.; mem. Govs. Juvenile Justice Conf. on Youth and Justice; criminal justice adv. bd. State of Alaska; we. states working group FBIs Criminal Justice Info. Sys.; dept. rep. Police Minority Rels. Task Force. Mem. FBI Nat. Acad. Assn., Internat. Assn. Chiefs of Police, Alaska Assn. Chiefs of Police, Alaska Peace Officers Assn., Anchorage C. of C. (crime com.). Home: 1743 W 15th Ave Anchorage AK 99501-4911 Office: Anchorage Police Dept 4501 S Bragaw St Anchorage AK 99507-1500

UDVAR-HAZY, STEVEN F. leasing company financial executive; b. Budapest, Hungary, Feb. 23, 1946; came to U.S., 1958. m. Christine L. Henneman, June 7, 1980; 3 children. BA, UCLA, 1968; HHD (hon.), U. Utah (Dixie Coll.), 1990. Cert. airline transp. jet pilot. Pres. Internat. Lease Fin. Corp., Beverly Hills, Calif., 1973—. Bd. dirs. Sky West Inc., St. George, Utah. Mem. Wings Club (Achievement to Aviation award 1989). Office: Internat Lease Fin Corp Ste 3900 1999 Avenue Of The Stars Los Angeles CA 90067-6032

UDWADIA, FIRDAUS ERACH, engineering educator, consultant; b. Bombay, Aug. 28, 1947; came to U.S., 1968. s. Erach Rustam and Perin P. (Lentin) U.; m. Farida Gagrat, Jan. 6, 1977; children: Shanaira, Zubin. BS, Indian Inst. Tech., Bombay, 1968; MS, Calif. Inst. Tech., 1969, PhD, 1972; MBA, U. So. Calif., 1985. Mem. faculty Calif. Inst. Tech., Pasadena, 1972-74; asst. prof. engring. U. So. Calif., Los Angeles, 1974-77, assoc. prof. mech., civil, and aerospace engring. and bus. adminstrn., 1977-83, prof. mech. engring., civil engring. and bus. adminstrn., 1983-86, prof. engring, bus. adminstrn., maths., 1986—, prof. engring., bus. adminstrn., math., 1999—; also bd. dirs. Structural Identification Computing Facility, U. So. Calif. Cons. Jet Propulsion Lab., Pasadena, 1978—, Argonne Nat. Lab., 1982-83, Air Force Rocket Lab., Edwards AFB. Calif., 1984—; vis. prof. applied mechanics and mech. engring. Calif. Inst. Tech., Pasadena, 1993. Editor (assoc.): (jour.) Applied Math. and Computation, Jour. Optimization Theory and Applications, Jour. Franklin Inst., Jour. Differential Equations and Dynamical Sys., Nonlinear Studies, Jour. Math. Analysis and Applications, Jour. Math. Problems in Engring.; editor: Jour. of Aerospace Engring.; author: (book) Analytical Dynamics, A New Approach, 1996; mem. adv. bd.: jour. Jour. Tech. Forecasting and Social Change; editor: Advances in Dynamics and Control, 1999;contbr. articles to profl. jours. Bd. dirs. Crisis Mgmt. Ctr., U. So. Calif. NSF grantee, 1976—; recipient Golden Poet award, 1990. Mem. AIAA, ASCE, Am. Acad. Mechanics, Soc. Indsl. and Applied Math., Seismological Soc. Am., Sigma Xi (Earthquake Engring. Research Inst., 1971, 74, 84). Avocations: writing poetry, piano, chess. Home: 2100 S Santa Anita Ave Arcadia CA 91006-4611 Office: U So Calif 430K Olin Hall University Park Los Angeles CA 90007 E-mail: fudwadia@usc.edu

UEBERROTH, JOHN A. air transportation executive; b. Phila., 1944; Student, U. Calif., Berkeley, U. So. Calif. Formerly pres. Ask Mr. Foster Travel, Encino, Calif.; formerly v.p. TCU Travel Corp.; formerly pres., COO 1st Travel Corp., Van Nuys, Calif.; with Carlson Travel Group, Mpls., 1983-89, Contrarian Group Inc., Newport Beach, Calif., 1989—; chmn. bd., CEO Hawaiian Airlines, Inc., 1990—, also bd. dirs. Office: Ambassadors International Inc Dwight D Eisenhower Bldg 110 S Ferrall St Spokane WA 99202 also: First Travel Corp 7833 Haskell Ave Van Nuys CA 91406-1908 also: Carlson Cos Inc 12755 Highway 55 Minneapolis MN 55441-3837

UEBERROTH, PETER VICTOR, former baseball commissioner; b. Evanston, Ill., Sept. 2, 1937; s. Victor and Laura (Larson) U.; m. Virginia Nicolaus, Sept. 1959; children— Vicky, Heidi, Keri, Joe B.S. in Bus., San Jose State Coll., 1959. Ops. mgr. then v.p. Trans Internat., 1959-62; founder, chmn. Transp. Cons. Internat., 1963-79; pres., mng. dir. Los Angeles Olympic Organizing Com., 1979-84; commr., chief exec. officer of major league baseball N.Y.C., 1984-89; co-chmn. Doubletree Hotels Corp., Phoenix, 1993—. Former chmn. Ask Mr. Foster Travel Service; chmn. Colony Hotels, Intercontinental Tours, Inc., First Travel Corp; mem. bd. dirs. California Angels. Author: Made in America, 1985 Named Man of Yr., Time mag. and Sporting News, 1984; recipient Scopus award Am. Friends of Hebrew U., Jerusalem, 1985 Office: Ambassadors International Inc 110 S. Ferrall St Spokane WA 99202

UFIMTSEV, PYOTR YAKOVLEVICH, physicist, electrical engineer, educator; b. Ust'-Charyshskaya Pristan', Altai Region, Russia, July 8, 1931; s. Yakov Fedorovich and Vasilisa Vasil'evna (Toropchina) U.; m. Tatiana Vladimirovna Sinelschikova; children: Galina, Ivan, Vladimir. Grad., Odessa State U., USSR, 1954; PhD, Cen. Rsch. Inst. of Radio Industry, Moscow, 1959; DSc, St. Petersburg State U., Russia, 1970. Engr., sr. engr., sr. scientist Cen. Rsch. Inst. of Radio Industry, Moscow, Russia, 1954-73; sr. scientist Inst. Radio Engring. & Electronics Acad. Scis., Moscow, Russia, 1973-90; vis. prof., adj. prof. UCLA, 1990—; prin. engr. Northrop Grumman Corp., 1993—2001. Mem. Sci. Bd. of Radio Waves, Acad. Scis., Moscow, 1960-90. Author: Method of Edge Waves in the Physical Theory of Diffraction, 1962; contbr. articles to profl. jours. Recipient USSR State Prize, Moscow, 1990, Leroy Randle Grumman medal for outstanding sci. achievement, N.Y.C., 1991, 20th Century Achievement medal, Cambridge, 1996, Hall of Fame medal, Cambridge, 1996. Fellow IEEE; assoc. fellow AIAA; mem. Electromagnetics Acad. (U.S.), A.S. Popov Sci. Tech. Soc. Radio Engring., Electronics & Telecommunication (Russia). Achievements include origination of the Physical Theory of Diffraction, used for design of American stealth aircrafts and ships; for radar-cross-section calculation, and antenna design. Office: UCLA Dept Elec Engring 405 Hilgard Ave Los Angeles CA 90095-9000

UHDE, LARRY JACKSON, joint apprentice administrator; b. Marshalltown, Iowa, June 2, 1939; s. Harold Clarence and Rexine Elizabeth (Clemens) U.; m. Linda-Lee Betty Best, Nov. 19, 1960; children: Mark Harold, Brian Raymon. Student, Sacramento City Coll., 1966, Am. River Coll., Sacramento, 1975. Equipment supr. Granite Constrn., Sacramento, 1962-69; truck driver Iowa Wholesale, Marshalltown, Iowa, 1969-70; mgr. Reedy & Essex, Inc., Sacramento, 1970-71; dispatcher Operating Engrs. Local Union 3, Sacramento, 1971-73; tng. coord. Operating Engrs. Joint Apprenticeship Com., Sacramento, 1973-83, apprenticeship div. mgr., 1983-87, adminstr., 1987-95; ret., 1995; instr. asst. advanced transp. tech. Sacremento City Coll., 1996—. Chmn. First Women in Apprenticeship Seminar, 1972, Calif. Apprentice Coun., 1992, chair Blue Ribbon com.; com. mem. Sacramento Gen. Joint Apprenticeship Com., 1973-74; rep. Sacramento Sierra's Bldg. and Constrn. Trades Coun., 1973-75; com. mem. Valley Area Constrn. Opportunity Program, 1974-77; commr. State of Calif. Dept. Indsl. Rels., Calif. Apprenticeship Coun., chmn. 1992; mem. Apprenticeship Adv. Com. Internat. Union Oper. Engrs. Contr: Options; contbr. articles to trade papers. Mgr., v.p. Little League, 1971-75; co-chmn. Fall Festival St. Roberts Ch., 1973-75; v.p. Navy League Youth Program, 1978-81; instr. ARC, 1978-87; counselor United Way 1980—; bd. mem. County CETA Bd., 1981-82; coun. mem. Calif. Balance of State Pvt. Industry Coun., 1982-83, Sacramento Pvt. Industry Coun., 1982-83; coord. Alcholic Recovery Program, 1984-87. With USN, 1956-60. Inducted into Calif. Apprenticeship Hall of Fame, 1996. Mem. Western Apprenticeship Coords. Assn. (statewide dir. 1987—), U.S. Aprenticeship Assn., Sacramento Valley Apprenticeship Tng. Coords. Assn. (rep.), Rancho Murieta County, U.S. Golf Assn., Bing Maloney Golf Club. Democrat. Roman Catholic. Avocations: golf, archery, bowling, hunting, camping, dancing.

UHLENHUTH, EBERHARD HENRY, psychiatrist, educator; b. Balt., Sept. 15, 1927; s. Eduard Carl Adolph and Elisabeth (Baier) U.; m. Helen Virginia Lyman, June 20, 1952; children: Kim Lyman, Karen Jane, Eric Rolf. BS in Chemistry, Yale U., 1947; MD, Johns Hopkins U., 1951. Intern Harborview Hosp., Seattle, 1951-52; resident in psychiatry Johns Hopkins Hosp., Balt., 1952-56, asst. psychiatrist in charge outpatient dept., 1956-61, psychiatrist in charge, 1961-62; chief adult psychiatry clinic U. Chgo. Hosps. Clinics, 1968-76; instr. psychiatry Johns Hopkins U., 1956-59, asst. prof., 1959-67, assoc. prof., 1967-68, U. Chgo., 1968-73, prof., 1973-85, acting chmn., 1983-85; prof. psychiatry U. N.Mex., Albuquerque, 1985-97, prof. emeritus, 19976, vice chmn. for edn., 1991-94. Cons. in field; mem. clin. psychopharmacology rsch. rev. com. NIMH, 1968-72, treatment devel. and assessment rev. com., 1987; mem. psychopharmacology adv. com. FDA, 1974-78; mem. adv. group to Treatment of Depression Collaborative Rsch. Program, NIMH, 1978-92; study rev. com. Xanax Discontinuation Program, The UpJohn Co., 1988-92, Nat. Adv. Coun. on Drug Abuse, NIDA, 1989-92, Coop. Studies Evaluation Com., VA, 1989-92. Mem. editl. bd. Jour. Affective Disorders, 1978—, Psychiatry Rsch., 1979-96, Behavioral Medicine, 1982—, Neuropsychopharmacology, 1992-94, Exptl. and Clin. Psychopharmacology, 1992-99, Anxiety, 1993—; contbr. articles to profl. jours. Recipient Research Career Devel. award USPHS, 1962-68, Research Scientist award, 1976-81 Fellow Am. Coll. Neuropsychopharmacology (pres. 1986), Am. Psychiat. Assn., Am. Psychopath. Assn.; mem. Balt.-Washington Soc. for Psychoanalysis, Collegium Internat. Neuro-Psychopharmacologicum, Psychiat. Rsch. Soc. Office: U NMex Dept Psychiatry 2400 Tucker NE Albuquerque NM 87131-5326 E-mail: uhli@unm.edu

UKROPINA, JAMES R. lawyer; b. Fresno, Calif., Sept. 10, 1937; s. Robert J. and Persida (Angelich) U.; m. Priscilla Lois Brandenburg, June 16, 1962. A.B., Stanford U., 1959, M.B.A., 1961; LL.B., U. So. Calif., 1965. Bar: Calif. 1966. Assoc. firm O'Melveny & Myers, Los Angeles, 1965-72, ptnr., 1972—80, 1992—2000, of counsel, 2001—; exec. v.p., gen. counsel Santa Fe Internat. Corp., Alhambra, Calif., 1980-84, dir., 1981-86; exec. v.p., gen. counsel Pacific Enterprises, Los Angeles, 1984-86, pres. and dir., 1986-89, chmn. bd. and chief exec. officer, 1989-91. Bd. dirs. Lockheed Martin Corp., Pacific Life Ins. Co., Trust Co. of the West, Ctrl. Natural Resources., Indymac Bancorp, Keck Found. Editor in chief So. Calif. Law Rev, 1964-65. Trustee Stanford U., 1991-2000 Mem. ABA, Calif. Bar Assn., Los Angeles County Bar Assn., Annandale Golf Club, Calif. Club, Beta Theta Pi. Office: O'Melveny & Myers 400 S Hope St Los Angeles CA 90071-2899

ULIN, SAMUEL ALEXANDER, computer systems developer; b. Nov. 8, 1955; s. Webster Beattie Ulin and Ann (Fletcher) Rainier; m. Lida Ohan, May 30, 1992. Student, U. Del., 1973-78. Systems design cons. Alpha Ro Inc., Wilmington, Del., 1982-83, Command Computer Svcs., N.Y.C., 1983-84; systems designer DBS Films, Inc., Malvern, Pa., 1984-86; dir. engring. Flight Safety Inc., ISD, Malvern, 1986-87, Irving, Tex., 1987-89; sr. system designer Litigation Scis., Culver City, Calif., 1989-96; v.p. engring. IDEA, Inc., Seattle, 1996—. Designer software for interactive tng. on aircraft sys., 1983, one of first interactive ct. evidence presentation systems used in fed. ct., 1987. Avocations: electronics, stamp and coin collecting, winter sports. Home: 12500 Lithuania Dr Granada Hills CA 91344 Office: Luminent Inc 20550 Nordhoff St Chatsworth CA 91311 E-mail: sulin@trialpro.com

ULLAS, YVONNE L. primary school educator; AA, Yakima Valley C.C., 1979; BA in Edn., 1981; postgrad., Ctrl. Wash. U., 1991, Antioch U., 1992; MEd, Heritage Coll., 1995. Parent educator Yakima Sch. Dist., 1975-79; camp dir. Yakima Parks and Recreation, 1979-86; tchr. St. Joseph's Grade Sch., Yakima, 1981-86, Naches Primary Sch., 1988—. Commr. Gov.'s commn. on Early Learning, 1998-2000; bd. dirs. Gov.'s Profl. Educator Standards bd. Named Wash. State Tchr. of Yr., 1998, Tchr. of Month KAPP TV, 1993, US West Washington State Outstanding Tchr., 1994; grantee Share 105 Tech., 1997. Mem. NEA, Wash. Edn. Assn., Naches Edn. Assn. (dist. del.), Naches Edn. Assn. (bldg. rep.), Yakima Valley C.C. Alumni Assn., Ctrl. Washington U. Alumni Assn., Heritage Coll. Alumni Assn., Retired Tchrs. Assn., N.W. Regional Ednl. Lab., Nat. State Tchr. of Yr. Assn., Parent, Tchr., Student Assn. Office: Naches Valley Primary Sch 2700 Old Naches Hwy Yakima WA 98908-8900

ULLMAN, JEFFREY DAVID, computer science educator; b. N.Y.C., Nov. 22, 1942; s. Seymour and Nedra L. (Hart) U.; m. Holly E., Nov. 19, 1967; children: Peter, Scott, Jonathan. B.S., Columbia U., 1963; Ph.D., Princeton U., 1966; Ph.D. hon., U. Brussels, 1975, U. Paris-Dauphine, 1992. Mem. tech. staff Bell Labs., Murray Hill, N.J., 1966-69, cons., 1969-89; prof. elec. engring., computer sci. Princeton U., 1969-79; prof. computer sci. Stanford (Calif.) U., 1979—, chmn. dep., 1990-94, Stanford W. Ascherman prof. computer sci., 1994—. Mem. computer sci. adv. panel NSF, 1974-77, mem. info., robotics and intelligent sys. adv. panel, 1986-88; mem. exam. com. for computer sci. grad. record exam. Ednl. Testing Svc., 1978-86; chmn. doctoral rating com. for computer sci. N.Y. State Regents, 1989-93, 98-99; bd. dirs. Junglee Corp., 1996-98, [illegible] 2000—, Enosys Markets, 2000—; mem. tech. adv. bd. Google.com, 1998—, Viquity, 1999—, ccrewards.com., 1999—, Surromed, 1999—, Whizbang Labs, 1999—, Quiq, 1999—; adv. bd. World Wide Web Consortium, 1998-99. Author: Principles of Database and Knowledge-Base Systems, 1988, 89, (2 vols.), (with A.V. Aho and J.E. Hopcroft) Data Structures and Algorithms, 1983, (with A.V. Aho, R. Sethi) Compilers: Principles, Techniques and Tools, 1986, (with A.V. Aho) Foundations of Computer Science, 1992, Elements of ML Programming, 1994, 98, (with J. Widom) A First Course in Database Systems, 1997, (with H. Garcia-Molina and J. Widom) Database Design and Implementation, 1999. Guggenheim fellow, 1989. Fellow Assn. Computing Machinery (coun. 1978-80, Spl. Interest Group on Mgmt. of Data Contbns. award 1996, Karl Karlstrom award 1998, Knuth prize 2000); mem. NAE, Spl. Interest Group on Automata and Computability Theory (sec.-treas. 1973-77), Spl. Interest Group on Mgmt. Data (vice chn. 1983-95), Computing Rsch. Assn. (bd. dirs. 1994-2000). Home: 1023 Cathcart Way Palo Alto CA 94305-1048 Office: Stanford U Dept Computer Sci 411 Gates Hall 4A-Wing Stanford CA 94305-9040 E-mail: Ullman@cs.stamford.edu

ULLMAN, MYRON EDWARD, III, retail executive; b. Youngstown, Ohio, Nov. 26, 1946; s. Myron Edward Jr. and June (Cunningham) U.; m. Cathy Emmons, June 20, 1969; children: Myron Cayce, Denver Tryan, Peter Brynt, Benjamin Kyrk, Kathryn Kwynn, Madylin Ming Yan. BS in Indsl. Mgmt., U. Cin., 1969; postgrad. Inst. Ednl. Mgmt., Harvard U., 1977. Internat. account mgr. IBM Corp., Cin., 1969-76; v.p. bus. affairs U. Cin., 1976-81; White House fellow The White House, Washington, 1981-82; exec. v.p. Sanger Harris div. Federated Stores, Dallas, 1982-86; mgr. dir., chief oper. officer Wharf Holdings Ltd., Hong Kong, 1986-88; chmn., CEO, dir. R.H. Macy & Co. Inc., N.Y.C., 1988-95; dir. Federated Dept. Stores, Inc.; chmn., CEO DFS Group Ltd., San Francisco, 1995-98, group chmn., 1999-2000; also bd. dirs.; dir. gen., group mng. dir., dir. LVMH, Louis Vuitton Moet Hennessy, Paris, 1999—. Mng. dir. Lane Crawford Ltd., Hong Kong, 1986-88; bd. advisors Gt. Traditions Corp., Cin.; dep. chmn. Omni Hotels, Hampton, N.H., 1988; vice chmn. bd. dirs. Mercy Ships Internat. Internat. v.p. U. Cin. Alumni Assn., 1980—; bd. dirs. Nat. Multiple Sclerosis Soc., N.Y.C.; bd. dirs. Brunswick Sch., Greenwich, Conn., U. Cin. Found., Lincoln Ctr. Devel., Deafness Rsch. Found., 1997—, U. Calif. Med. Ctr. Found., San Francisco, 1998—. Mem. White House Fellow Alumni Assn., Econ. Club N.Y.C. (bd. dirs., exec. com.), Nat. Retail Fedn. (vice chmn., bd. dirs., exec. com. 1993—), Delta Tau Delta (treas. 1967-68). Republican. Office: DFS Group Ltd 575 Market St San Francisco CA 94105-2823 also: LVMH 30 Ave Hoche 75008 Paris France E-mail: mike.ullman@lvmh.sf.com

ULLMAN, TRACEY, actress, singer; b. Slough, Eng., Dec. 30, 1959; m. Allan McKeown, 1984; children: Mabel Ellen, John Albert Victor. Student, Itaia Conti Stage Sch., London. Appeared in plays Gigi, Elvis, Grease, The Rocky Horror Show, Four in a Million, 1981 (London Theatre Critics award), The Taming of the Shrew, 1990, The Big Love, (one-woman stage show) 1991; films include The Young Visitors, 1984, Give My Regards to Broad Street, 1984, Plenty, 1985, Jumpin' Jack Flash, 1986, I Love You To Death, 1990, Household Saints, 1993, I'll Do Anything, 1994, Bullets over Broadway, 1994, Ready to Wear (Prêt-à-Porter), 1994, Everybody Says I Love You, 1996; Brit. TV shows include Three of a Kind, A Kick Up the Eighties, Girls on Top; actress TV series: The Tracey Ullman Show, from 1987-90 (Emmy award Best Performance, Outstanding Writing, 1990, Golden Globe award Best Actress, 1987), Tracey Takes On, 1996— (four Emmys including Outstanding Music, Comedy and Variety Show 1997, Cable Ace award for best comedy variety series 1996); album You Broke My Heart in Seventeen Places (Gold album). Recipient Brit. Acad. award, 1983, Am. Comedy award, 1988, 90, 91, Emmy award for Best Performance in a Variety/Music Series for "Tracey Ullman Takes on New York", 1994. Office: IFA Talent Agy 8730 W Sunset Blvd Ste 490 Los Angeles CA 90069-2248

ULMER, FRANCES ANN, lieutenant governor; b. Madison, Wis., Feb. 1, 1947; m. Bill Council; children: Amy, Louis. BA in Econs. and Polit. Sci., U. Wis.; JD with honors, Wis. Sch. Law. Polit. advisor Gov. Jay Hammond, Alaska, 1975-81; former mayor City of Juneau; mem. Alaska Ho. of Reps., 1986-94, minority leader, 1992-94; lt. gov. State of Alaska, 1995—. Home: 1700 Angus Way Juneau AK 99801-1411 Office: Office Lt Gov PO Box 110015 Juneau AK 99811-0015 E-mail: lt_governor@gov.state.ak.us

ULRICH, PETER HENRY, banker; b. Munich, Germany, Nov. 24, 1922; s. Hans George and Hella (Muschweck) U.; m. Carol A. Peek, Oct. 21, 1944; children: Carol Jean Hewes, Patricia Diane (Mrs. Damon Eberhart), Peter James. Student, Northwestern U., 1941-42, U. Iowa, 1943, Sch. Mortgage Banking, 1954-56. Lic. real estate broker, cert. mortgage banker; cert. rev. appraiser; cert. mortgage underwriter. Escrow officer Security Title Ins. Co., Riverside, Calif., 1946-53; asst. cashier Citizens Nat. Trust & Savs., Riverside, 1953-57; v.p. Security First Nat. Bank, Riverside, 1957-63; sr. v.p. Bank of Calif. (N.A.), Los Angeles, 1963-72; pres. Ban Cal Mortgage Co., 1972-74, Ban Cal Tri-State Mortgage Co., 1974-75; cons., 1975-76; pres., dir. Beneficial Standard Mortgage Co., 1976-88; real estate cons., 1988—. Instr. real estate and bus. San Bernardino Valley Coll., Riverside City Coll., Pasadena City Coll. Pres. Residential Rsch. Com. So. Calif., 1965, Riverside Opera Assn., 1956-59, Riverside Symphony Soc., 1959-61; trustee Idyllwild Arts Found., 1957—, pres., 1970-73, sec., 1986-87; mem. adv. bd. Salvation Army, 1959—, vice chmn., 1971-74, chmn., 1975; chmn. Harbor Light Com., 1965-68; convocator Calif. Luth. U., 1976-80, 81-83, regent, 1981-90; bd. dirs. Guild Opera Co., v.p., 1991-99; bd. dirs. Lark Ellen Lions Charities, pres., 1987-90, 94—; treas. Opera Buffs, 1983—; mem. Arcadia Beautiful Commn., 1989-95, vice chair, 1991-92, chmn., 1992-93; trustee Calif. Luth. Edn. Found., 1989—; bd. dirs. Arcadia Tournament Roses Assn., v.p. 1997, bd. dirs. Am. Heart Assn. Foothill divsn. chair, 1997-99; mem. Arcadia City Coun., 1995-96; trustee Arcadia Pub. Libr., 1997—, chair, 1999; bd. dirs. South Pasadena-Arcadia Adult Reading Ctrs., 1998—, v.p. 2000. Served with AUS, 1943-46. Recipient Resolution of Commendation Riverside City Council, 1963; Resolution of Appreciation Los Angeles City Council, 1968, 1973, Arcadia Vol. of Yr., 1997. Mem. Nat. Mortgage Bankers Assn. (chmn. Life Ins. Co. com. 1986-87), Calif. Mortgage Bankers Assn. (sec. 1965, dir. 1972-75, Disting. Svc. award 1997), So. Calif. Mortgage Bankers Assn. (dir. 1975, 80-81, v.p. 1982, pres. 1983), Indland Empire Mortgage Bankers Assn. (pres. 1962, hon. dir.), Assn. Corp. Real Estate Execs. (sec. 1967-71, pres. 1974-75), Lambda Alpha. Lutheran. Home: 447 Fairview Ave Unit 2 Arcadia CA 91007-6877 Office: 37 E Huntington Dr Arcadia CA 91006-3210 E-mail: pulrich@sprintmail.com

ULRICH, THEODORE ALBERT, lawyer; b. Spokane, Wash., Jan. 1, 1943; s. Herbert Roy and Martha (Hoffman) Ulrich; m. Nancy Allison, May 30, 1966; children: Donald Wayne, Frederick Albert. BS cum laude, U.S. Mcht. Marine Acad., 1965; JD cum laude, Fordham U., 1970; LLM, NYU, 1974. Bar: N.Y. 1971, U.S. Ct. Appeals (2nd cir.) 1971, U.S. Supreme Ct. 1974, U.S. Ct. Claims 1977, U.S. Customs Ct. 1978, U.S. Ct. Internat. Trade 1981, U.S. Ct. Appeals (5th cir.) 1988, U.S. Ct. Appeals (D.C. cir.) 1992, Colo. 1993, U.S. Ct. Appeals (10 cir.) 1994. Mng. clk. U.S. Dept. Justice, N.Y.C., 1968-69, law clk. to federal dist. judge, 1969-70; assoc. Cadwalader, Wickersham & Taft, N.Y.C., 1970-80, ptnr., 1980-94, Popham, Haik, Schnobrich & Kaufman, Ltd., Denver, 1994-96; sole practice law Denver, 1996—. Co-author: Encyclopedia of International Commercial Litigation, 1991, Arbitration of Construction Contracts, V, 1991; contbg. author: Marine Engineering Economics and Cost Analysis, 1995; author, editor Fordham Law Rev., 1969. Leader Boy Scouts Am., Nassau County, N.Y., 1984-94, Denver, 1994—. Capt. USCGR, 1965-86. [illegible] Internat. Law, Soc. Naval Architects and Marine Engrs., U.S. Naval Inst., Am. Arbitration Assn. Home and Office: 4300 E 6th Ave Denver CO 80220-4940

UNDERWOOD, PAUL LESTER, cardiologist; b. Knoxville, Tenn., Mar. 23, 1960; MD, Mayo Med. Sch., 1984. Diplomate Am. Bd. Cardiovascular Disease. Intern Henry Ford Hosp., Detroit, 1984-85; resident in internal medicine Mayo Grad. Sch. Medicine, Rochester, Minn., 1985-87; fellow in cardiology Cleve. Clinic, 1990-93; fellow in interventional cardiology Iowa Heart Ctr., Des Moines, 1993; dir. emergency medicine, dir. ICU St. Croix Hosp., U.S. V.I., 1987-90; staff Advanced Cardiac Specialists, Phoenix, 1994—. Mem. AMA, Nat. Med. Assn., Assn. Black Cardiologists, Am. Coll. Cardiology, Am. Heart Assn., Soc. for Cardiac Angiography and Interventions. Office: Phoenix Heart Ctr 525 N 18th St Ste 301 Phoenix AZ 85006 E-mail: phoenixheart@earthlink.net

UNDERWOOD, ROBERT ANACLETUS, congressman, university official; b. Tamuning, Guam, July 13, 1948; m. Lorraine Aguilar; 5 children. BA with honors in History, Calif. State U., 1969, MA in History, 1971; cert. edn. adminstrn., U. Guam, 1976; DEd, U. So. Calif., 1987. Loader, sorter United Parcel Svc., L.A., 1966-72; tchr. George Washington High Sch., 1972-74; asst. prin. for bus. and student pers. George Washington H.S., 1974-76; asst. and acting prin. Inarajan Jr. H.S., 1976; instr., dir. bilingual bicultural tng. program U. Guam, 1976-81, asst. prof., 1981-83, dir. bilingual edn. assistance for Micronesia project, 1983-88, dean Coll. Edn., 1988-90, acad. v.p., 1990—; mem. del. 103d-107th Congress from Guam, Washington, 1993—. Mem. House resources com., armed svcs.; chmn. Asian Pacific Caucus 106th Congress; part-time curriculum writer Guam Bilingual Edn. Project, 1973-76; chmn. Chamorro Lang. Commn., 1979-90. Named Citizen of Yr., Nat. Assn. Bilingual Edn., 1996, Alumnus of Yr. Calif. State U., 1999. Roman Catholic. Office: US Ho Reps 2418 Rayburn Ho Office Bldg Washington DC 20515-0001 E-mail: guamtodc@mail.house.gov

UNDERWOOD, RONALD BRIAN, director, producer; b. Glendale, Calif., Nov. 6, 1953; s. Laurence Joseph and Ella Julia (Green) U.; m. Sandra Joyce Archer, June 8, 1974; children: Larissa, Lana, Lauren. BA in Cinema, U. So. Calif., 1974. Freelance dir. TV and films, 1975—. Dir. (films) Deer in the Works, 1980, The Mouse and the Motorcycle, 1986, Runaway Ralph, 1988, Tremors, 1990, City Slickers, 1991, Heart and Souls, 1993, Speechless, 1994, Mighty Joe Young, 1998. Recipient Peabody award, 1986; Am. Film Inst. fellow, 1975. Office: United Talent Agy 9560 Wilshire Blvd Fl 5 Beverly Hills CA 90212-2400

UNDERWOOD, VERNON O., JR. grocery stores executive; b. 1940; With Young's Market Co., L.A., pres., 1976-97, chmn. bd., 1989—, also CEO, 1997, chmn. bd. Office: Young's Market Co 2164 N Batavia St Orange CA 92865-3109

UNGER, RICHARD WATSON, history educator; b. Huntington, W.Va., Dec. 23, 1942; s. Abraham I. and Marion Patterson (Simons) U.; 1 child, Emily Patterson. BA, Haverford Coll., Pa., 1963; AM, U. Chgo., 1965; MA, Yale U., 1967, MPhil, 1969, PhD, 1971. Prof. dept. history U. B.C., Vancouver, Can., 1969—. Author: Dutch Shipbuilding Before 1800, 1978; The Ship in the Medieval Economy, 600-1600, 1980; The Art of Medieval Technology: The Image of Noah the Shipbuilder, 1991, Ships and Shipping in the North Sea and Atlantic, 1400-1600, 1997, A History of Brewing in Holland, 900-1900, Economy, Technology and the State, 2001; editor: Cogs, Caravels and Galleons, 1994; co-editor Studies in Medieval and Renaissance History, 1978-95; contbr. articles to profl. jours. Trustee Vancouver Maritime Mus., 1979-83, 97-98. Mem. Medieval Assn. Pacific (pres. 1994-96), Econ. History Soc., Soc. Nautical Rsch., Soc. Hist. Tech. Office: U BC Dept History 1297-1873 East Mall Vancouver BC Canada V6T 1Z1 E-mail: richard.unger@ubc.ca

UNIS, RICHARD L. judge; b. Portland, Oreg., June 11, 1928; BS, JD, U. Oreg. Bar: Oreg. 1954, U.S. Dist. Ct. Oreg. 1957, U.S. Ct. Appeals (9th cir.) 1960, U.S. Supreme Ct. 1965. Judge Portland Mcpl. Ct., 1968-71, Multnomah County Dist. Ct., 1972-76, presiding judge, 1972-74; former judge Oreg. Cir. Ct. 4th Judicial Dist., 1977-90; former sr. dep. city atty. City of Portland; assoc. justice Oreg. Supreme Ct., Portland, 1990-96; spl. master U.S. Dist. Ct. House, Portland, 1996—. Adj. prof. of local govt. law and evidence Lewis & Clark Coll. Northwestern Sch. Law, 1969-76, 77-96; spl. master supr. La.-Pacific Inner-Seal Siding nationwide class action litig.; faculty mem. The Nat. Judicial Coll., 1971-2000; former faculty mem. Am. Acad. Judicial Edn. Author: Procedure and Instructions in Traffic Court Cases, 1970, 101 Questions and Answers on Preliminary Hearings, 1974. Bd. dirs. Oreg. Free from Drug Abuse; mem. Oreg. Adv. Com. on Evidence Law Revision, chmn. subcom., 1974-79. Maj. USAFR, JAGC, ret. Recipient Meritorius Svc. award U. Oregon sch. Law, 1988; named Legal Citizen of Yr. Oreg. Law Related Edn., 1987; inducted into The Nat. Judicial Coll. Hall of Honor, 1988. Mem. Am. Judicature Soc. (bd. dirs. 1975, Herbert Harley Nat. award 1999), Am. Judges Assn., Multnomah Bar Found., Oregon Judicial Conf. (chmn. Oreg. Judicial Coll. 1973-80, legis. com. 1976—, exec. com. of judicial edn. com., judicial conduct com.), N.Am. Judges Assn. (tenure, selection and compensation judges com.), Dist. Ct. Judges of Oreg. (v.p., chmn. edn. com.), Nat. Conf. Spl. Ct. Judges (exec. com.), Oreg. State Bar (judicial adminstrn. com., sec. local govt. com., com. on continuing certification, uniform jury instrn. com., exec. com. criminal law sect., trial practice sect. standards and certification com., past chmn., among others), Oreg. Trial Lawyers Assn. (named Judge of Yr. 1984). Office: US Dist Ct House 1000 SW 3rd Ave Portland OR 97204-2930

UNRUH, WILLIAM G. physics educator, researcher; b. Winnipeg, Man., Can., Aug. 28, 1945; m. Patricia Truman, Apr. 19, 1974; 1 child, Daniel B. BSc (hon.), U. Man., Winnipeg, 1967; MA, Princeton U., 1969, PhD, 1971. Postdoctoral fellow NRC Can., London, Eng., 1971-72; Miller fellow U. Calif., Berkeley, 1973-74; asst. prof. McMaster U., Hamilton, Ont., Can., 1974-76; asst. prof. to prof. physics U. B.C., Vancouver, Can., 1976—; rsch. fellow Can. Inst. Advanced Rsch., Toronto, Ont., 1986—, dir. Cosmology Program, 1986-96. Contbr. tech. papers to profl. publs. Rutherford Meml. fellow Royal Soc. Can., 1971; Alfred P. Sloan rsch. fellow U. B.C., 1978-80; Steacie fellow Nat. Sci. and Eng. Rsch. Coun., 1984-86; Japan Soc. Promotion Sci. sr. fellow Japan, 1986; recipient Rutherford medal Royal Soc. Can., 19982, Hertzberg medal Can. Assn. Physicists, 1983, Steacie medal, 1984, Medal of Achievement, 1995; recipient Gold medal B.C. Sci. Coun., 1991, Killam prize in Nat. Sci., 1996, medal in Math. &Theoretical Physics CAP/CRM, 1996; Rutherford lectr. Royal Soc. Can. to Royal Soc. London, 1985. Fellow Royal Soc. Can., Am. Phys. Soc. Office: Univ BC Dept Physics & Astron 6224 Agricultural Rd Vancouver BC Canada V6T 1Z1

UNTERMAN, THOMAS, venture capitalist, lawyer; b. Newport, R.I., Oct. 23, 1944; s. Martin D. and Ruth (Marcus) U.; m. Janet M. Mead, Sept. 27, 1980; children: Rebecca, Amy. AB, Princeton U., 1966; JD, U. Chgo., 1969. Bar: Calif. 1970. Assoc. Orrick, Herrington & Sutcliffe, San Francisco, 1969-75, ptnr., 1975-86, Morrison & Foerster, San Francisco, 1986-92; sr. v.p., gen. counsel The Times Mirror Co., L.A., 1992-95, sr. v.p., CFO, 1995—, exec. v.p., CFO, 1998-99; mng. ptnr. Rustic Canyon Ventures, Santa Monica, Calif., 2000—. Dir. The Tribune Co. Ticketmaster Online-Citysearch. Democrat. Jewish. Office: Rustic Canyon Ventures 2425 Olympic Blvd Ste 6050W Santa Monica CA 90404-4030

UPSON, DONALD V. financial executive, retired; b. Hutchinson, Kans., Feb. 8, 1934; s. William Ernest and Luella Beatrice (Hutchison) U.; m. Janis Carol Anderson, Sept. 16, 1956; children: Mark Steven, Brent William. B.S., Kans. State U., 1956. C.P.A. With Peat, Marwick, Mitchell & Co., 1956, 60-81, ptnr., 1974-81; exec. v.p., dir. internal audit Del E. Webb Corp., Phoenix, 1981-85; mgr. info. systems Tiernay Turbines Inc., Phoenix, 1986; chief fin. officer Schomac Corp., Tucson, 1986-88; adminstr. U. Ariz., Tucson, 1988-90; pres., chief exec. officer Ariz. Commerce Bank, Tucson, 1990-91; chief fin. officer O'Connor, Cavanagh, Anderson, Westover, Killingsworth & Beshears, P.A., Phoenix, 1991-94; fin. cons., 1995-97; ret., 1997. Pres. Community Orgn. for Drug Abuse, Alcohol and Mental Health Services, Inc., 1977-78; bd. dis. Phoenix council Boy Scouts Am., elder Presbyterian Ch. Served to lt. USAF, 1956-59. Mem. Am. Inst. C.P.A.s, Ariz. Soc. C.P.A.s, Beta Theta Pi (pres. 1955-56) Republican. Home and Office: 1313 E Sheena Dr Phoenix AZ 85022-4485 E-mail: DVUPSON@aol.com

URENA-ALEXIADES, JOSE LUIS, electrical engineer; b. Madrid, Spain, Sept. 5, 1949; s. Jose L. and Maria (Alexiades Christodulakis) Urena y Pon. MSEE, U. Madrid, Spain, 1976; MS in Computer Science, UCLA, 1978. Rsch. asst. UCLA, 1978; systems analyst Honeywell Info. Systems, L.A., 1978-80; mem. tech. staff Jet Propulsion Lab., Pasadena, Calif., 1980-91; exec. dir. Empresa Nacional de Innovacion S.A., L.A., 1991-96; sr. technologist Boeing Satellite Sys., L.A., 1996—. Contbr. various articles to profl. jours. Two times recipient NASA Group Achievement award. Mem. IEEE, IEEE Computer Soc., IEEE Communications Soc., Assn. for Computer Machinery, World Federalist Assn., Spanish Profl. Am. Inc. Roman Catholic. Avocations: active photographer, Master's swimming. Home: 904 Dickson St Marina Dl Rey CA 90292-5513 Office: Hughes Space & Comm Mail Stop S50 x366 1700 E Imperial Hwy Los Angeles CA 90059-2559

URIOSTE, FRANK J. film editor; Cert. Am. Cinema Editors. Film editor The Mirisch Agy., L.A. Films include Whatever Happened to Aunt Alice, The Grissom Gang, Boys in Company C, Fast Break, Loving Couples, Jazz Singer, The Entity, Trenchcoat, Amityville 3-D, Conan II, The Destroyer, Red Sonja, The Hitcher, Robocop (Acad. award nomination), Total Recall, Basic Instinct, Cliffhanger, Tombstone, Terminal Velocity, Cutthroat Island, Executive Decision, Conspiracy Theory, (co-editor) Midway, Hoosiers, Die Hard (Acad. award nomination); prodr.; Beach House, 1995. Office: c/o Lawrence Mirisch The Mirisch Agency 10100 Santa Monica Blvd Ste 700 Los Angeles CA 90067-4100 also: 1610 Highland Ave Glendale CA 91202-1260

URIS, PATRICIA FIRME, health science association administrator; b. Muskegon, Mich. BSN, U. Colo., 1974, MS in Psychiatric/Mental Health Nursing, 1978, PhD in Nursing, 1993. Staff nurse Colo. Mental Health Inst., Denver, 1984-76; on-call staff Bethesda PsycHealth Sys., Denver, 1977; clin. specialist Pk. E. Comprehensive Cmty. Mental Health Ctr., Denver, 1978; asst. exec. dir. Colo. Nurses Assn., Denver, 1979-80; project co-dir. Western Interstate Commn. Higher Edn., Boulder, Colo., 1980-85; project dir. Western Inst. Nursing/Western Soc. Rsch. Nursing, Boulder, 1987-90, assoc. dir., 1987-90, spl. cons., 1990-94; program devel., mgmt. cons. Arvada, Colo., 1994-95; asst. prof. U. Colo. Health Scis. Ctr., Denver, 1995-99; program adminstr. Bd. Nursing Colo. Dept. Regulatory Agys., Denver, 1999—. Guest lectr. U. Colo. Health Scis. Ctr., 1979-82, 80-83, 94-97, Metro. State Coll., 1979-82; cons. U. Alaska, 1982, Wyo. Dept. Health and Social Svcs., 1982, Utah Dept. Health, 1982; reviewer Appleton-Century-Crofts Pub. Co., 1985, Colo. Dept. Health and Environment, 1996, 97, Nat. Assn. Sch. Nurses, Inc., 1997, HHS, 1997, 98, 99. Cons. Rocky Mountain Ctr. Healthcare Ethics; mem. clin. adv. bd. ONEDAY/The Family AIDS Project, Denver; mem. stds. based edn. com. Arvada W. Sch. Improvement Leadership Team, Jefferson County, Colo. Recipient NIH stipend, 1976-78; Calloway scholar U. Colo. Health Scis. Ctr. Mem. ANA, Am. Psychiatric Nurses Assn., Assn. Child and Adolescent Psychiatric Nurses, Soc. Edn. and Rsch. Psychiatric-Mental Health Nursing, Nat. Assn. Sch. Nurses, Colo. Nurses Assn. (ANA del. 1982, 84, mem. commn. social and legis. concerns 1981-85, chair 1981-83, Virginia S. Paulson award 1981), Colo. Mental Health Assn. (pro bono vol.), Sigma Theta Tau (chpt. bd. dirs. 1993-96, mem. rsch. com. 1995-99, chmn. 1995-96, Henrietta Loughran scholar 1993).

URQUHART, JOHN, medical researcher, educator; b. Pitts., Apr. 24, 1934; s. John and Wilma Nelda (Martin) U.; m. Joan Cooley, Dec. 28, 1957; children: Elizabeth Urquhart Vdovjak, John Christopher (dec. 1965), Robert Malcolm, Thomas Jubal. BA with honors, Rice U., 1955; MD with honors, Harvard U., 1959; D (honoris causa), U. Utrecht, 1997. Lic. physician, Calif. Walter B. Cannon fellow in physiology Harvard Med. Sch., Boston, 1956; Josiah Macy, Jr. fellow, 1956-58, 59-61; intern in surgery Mass. Gen. Hosp., 1959-60; asst. resident, 1960-61; investigator Nat. Heart Inst., NIH, Bethesda, Md., 1961-63; asst. prof. physiology U. Pitts. Sch. Medicine, 1963-66; assoc. prof., 1966-68; prof., 1968-70; prof. biomed. engring. U. So. Calif., L.A., 1970-71; prin. scientist ALZA Corp., Palo Alto, Calif., 1970-86; dir. biol. scis., 1971-74; pres. rsch. divsn., 1974-78; dir., 1976-78; chief scientist, 1978-82; sr. v.p., 1978-85. Co-founder APREX Corp., Fremont, Calif., pres., 1986-88, dir., 1986-95, chmn., 1988-91, chief scientist, 1988-95; co-founder, chief scientist AARDEX Ltd., Zug, Switzerland, 1995—; vis. prof. pharmacology U. Limburg Sch. Medicine (now Maastricht U.), Maastricht, The Netherlands, 1984-85, vis. prof. pharmaco-epidemiology, 1986-91; prof. pharmaco-epidemiology, 1992—; adj. prof. biopharm. scis. U. Calif.-San Francisco, 1984—; mem. dir.'s adv. com. NIH, 1986-88; Boerhaave lectr. U. Leiden, The Netherlands, 1991, 94, 95, 97. Co-author: Risk Watch, 1984; contbr. numerous articles to sci. jours.; patentee therapeutic systems for controlled drug delivery and regimen compliance monitoring (43). Trustee Kettering U. (formerly GMI Engring. and Mgmt. Inst.), Flint, Mich., 1983—; bd. dirs. Inveresk Clin. Rsch., Ltd., Edinburgh, Scotland, Net Force, Inc., San Francisco. Served with USPHS, 1961-63. NIH grantee, 1963-70; Bowditch lectr. Am. Physiol. Soc., 1969. Fellow Royal Coll. Physicians of Edinburgh, AAAS; mem. Biomed. Engring. Soc. (pres. 1976), Boyleston Med. Soc., Internat. Soc. Pharmaco-epidemiology, Am. Soc. Clinical Pharmacology and Therapeutics, Soc. for Clinical Trials, Endocrine Soc., Saturday Morning Club Palo Alto, Am. Physiol. Soc., Soc. Risk Analysis, Calif. Acad. Medicine. Home and Office: 975 Hamilton Ave Palo Alto CA 94301-2213 E-mail: urquhart@ix.netcom.com

USHIJIMA, JOHN TAKEJI, state legislator, lawyer; b. Hilo, Hawaii, Mar. 13, 1924; s. Buhachi and Sano (Nitahara) U.; m. Margaret Kunishige, June 6, 1954. B.A., Grinnell Coll., 1950; J.D., George Washington U., 1952. Bar: Hawaii, 1953. Ptnr. Pence & Ushijima, Hilo, 1953-61, Ushijima & Nakamoto, Hilo, 1961-69; mem. Hawaii Senate, 1959—, pres. pro tem, 1974—. Bd. dirs. Cyanotech Corp., Woodinville, Wash. Bd. dirs. Waiakea Settlement YMCA. With AUS, 1943-46, ETO. Mem. Am. Bar Assn., Phi Delta Phi. Democrat. Home: 114 Melani St Hilo HI 96720-2766 Office: 192 Kapiolani St Hilo HI 96720-2687

USUI, LESLIE RAYMOND, retired clothing executive; b. Wahiawa, Hawaii, Feb. 2, 1946; s. Raymond Isao and Joyce Mitsuyo (Muramoto) U.; m. Annie On Nor Hom, Oct. 23, 1980; 1 child, Atisha. BA in Zool., U. Hawaii, 1969, MA in Edn., 1972. Cert. tchr., Hawaii. Flight steward United Airlines, Honolulu, 1970; spl. tutor Dept. Edn., 1971-73; v.p. Satyuga, Inc., Honolulu, 1974-80, pres., 1980-97; also bd. dirs.; ret., 1997. Cons. Hawaii Fashion Guild, 1978-79. Composer: Song to Chenrayzee, Song to Karmapa. Co-founder, bd. dirs. Kagyu Thegchen Ling Meditation Ctr., 1974—, pres., 1997-99; bd. dirs. Maitreya Inst., 1983-86, Palpung Found., 1984—; mem. U.S. Senatorial Bus. Adv. Bd., Washington, 1988; charter mem. Citizens Against Govt. Waste, 1988—, Citizens for Sound Economy, 1987-91, Nat. Tax Limitation Com., 1988-89. Mem. Am. Biog. Inst. (life, bd. govs. 1990), Internat. Biog. Centre (life), World Inst. Achievement (life), Cousteau Soc., Nature Conservancy, Waikiki Aquarium. Republican. Buddhist. Avocations: oriental gardening, music. Home: PO Box 161257 Honolulu HI 96816-0926 Office: Satyuga Inc PO Box 161257 Honolulu HI 96816-0926

UTHOFF, MICHAEL, dancer, choreographer, artistic director; b. Santiago, Chile, Nov. 5, 1943; came to U.S., 1962; s. Ernst and Lola (Botka) U.; m. dau., Michelle. Grad. biology, high sch., Chile; dance tng. with Juilliard Sch., 1962-65, Martha Graham, 1962-63, Joffrey Ballet, 1965-68, Sch. Am. Ballet, 1962-64; Laureate in Humanities, St. Joseph Coll., Hartford, Conn. Leading dancer Jose Limon Dance Co., 1964-65, City Center Joffrey Ballet, 1965-68, N.Y.C. Opera, 1968-69; leading dancer, asst. dir. First Chamber Dance Co. N.Y., from 1969; artistic dir. Hartford Ballet Co., 1972-92, Ballet Ariz., 1992—. Mem. faculty Juilliard Sch. Music, N.Y.C., from 1969; guest artist, tchr. Princeton Ballet Soc.; prof. dance SUNY, Purchase, 1972-74; instr. dance and drama movement, Yale U.; works premiered by Compania Nacional de Danzas, Mexico City, 1989; guest choreographer Shanghai Ballet, Republic of China, 1986; led Hartford Ballet on 3-week 11-city tour of Peoples Republic of China by invitation of Shanghai Internat. Culture Assn., 1988, 5-week 9-country tour Latin Am., 1991. Choreographer, dancer-actor film Seafall, 1968; opera prodns. Aida and La Cenerentola, Honolulu, 1972, Conn. Opera Romeo et Juliette, 1989, Pitts. Opera Aida, 1988; choreographer Quartet, City Center Joffrey Ballet, 1968, The Pleasure of Merely Circulating, Juilliard Sch. Music, 1969, Windsong, Reflections, Dusk, Promenade, First Chamber Dance Co., 1969-70, Mozart's Idomeneo for Caramoor Music Festival, 1970, Concerto Grosso for Ballet Clasico 70 of Mexico, also restaged Dusk, 1972, Aves Mirabiles, 1973, Danza a Quattro, 1973, Marosszek Dances, 1973, Duo, 1974, Pastorale, 1974, Brahms Variations, 1974, Autumalal, 1975, Mir Ken Geharget Veren, 1976, Tom Dula, 1976, Unstill Life, 1977, Songs of a Wayfarer, 1977, Ask Not..., 1977, White Mountains Suite, 1978, Bach Cantata, 1978, The Nutcracker, 1979, Romeo and Juliet, 1981, Cachivaches, 1981, Reflections on the Water, 1981, Weeping Willow, 1982, Carmencita Variations, 1982, Hansel and Gretel, 1983, Coppelia, 1986, Speak Easy, 1986, New England Triptych, 1986, Los Copihues, 1988, Petrouchka, 1988, RFD #1, 1989, Classical Symphoniette, 1990, Alice in Wonderland, 1991, Nocturnes, 1991, Sinfonia Danzante, 1991; Nat. Endowment Arts commns. for choreography: Primavera, Minn. Dance Theatre, 1975, Panvezitos, Greater Houston Civic Ballet, 1976, Sonata, The Prodigal Son, Hartford Ballet, 1977, 79. Recipient award for best choreography for Murmurs of the Stream, Chilean Nat. Press, 1983, Critic's Circle Best of Yr. in Arts award, Chile, 1984, Milagno en la Alameda award for Chilean Nat. Women, 1995; grantee various founds. Office: Ballet Ariz 3645 E Indian School Rd Phoenix AZ 85018-5126

UTTAL, WILLIAM R(EICHENSTEIN), psychology and engineering educator, research scientist; b. Mineola, N.Y., Mar. 24, 1931; s. Joseph and Claire (Reichenstein) U.; m. Michiye Nishimura, Dec. 20, 1954; children: Taneil, Lynet, Lisa. Student, Miami U. Oxford, Ohio, 1947-48; B.S. in Physics, U. Cin., 1951; Ph.D. in Exptl. Psychology and Biophysics, Ohio State U., 1957. Staff Psychologist, mgr. behavioral sci. group IBM Research Center, Yorktown Heights, N.Y., 1957-63; assoc. prof. U. Mich., Ann Arbor, 1963-68, prof. psychology, 1968-86, research scientist, 1963-86, prof. emeritus, 1986—; grad. affiliate faculty dept. psychology U. Hawaii, 1986-88; research scientist Naval Ocean Systems Ctr.-Hawaii Lab., Kailua, 1985-88; prof., chmn. dept. psychology Ariz. State U., Tempe, 1988-92, prof. dept. indsl. engring., 1992—, affiliated prof., Dept. of Computer Sci. and Engring., 1993-98, prof. emeritus, 1999— Vis. prof. Kyoto (Japan) Prefectural Med. U., 1965-66, Sensory Sci. Lab., U. Hawaii, 1968, 73, U. Western Australia, 1970-71, U. Hawaii, 1978-79, 80-81, U. Auckland, 1996, U. Freiburg, 1997, U. Sydney, 1999; pres. Nat. Conf. on On-Line Uses Computers in Psychology, 1974. Author: Real Time Computers: Techniques and Applications in the Psychological Sciences, 1968, Generative Computer Assisted Instruction in Analytic Geometry, 1972, The Psychobiology of Sensory Coding, 1973, Cellular Neurophysiology and Integration: An Interpretive Introductin, 1975, An Autocorrelation Theory of Visual Form Detection, 1975, The Psychobiology of Mind, 1978, A Taxonomy of Visual Processes, 1981, Visual Form Detection in Three Dimensional Space, 1983, Principles of Psychobiology, 1983, The Detection of Nonplanar Surfaces in Visual Space, 1985, The Perception of Dotted Forms, 1987, On Seeing Forms, 1988, The Swimmer: A Computational Model of a Perceptual Motor System, 1992, Toward a New Behaviorism: The Case Against Perceptual Reductionism, 1998, A Computational Model of Vision: The Role of Combination, 1999, The War Between Mentalism and Behaviorism, 2000, The New Phrenology: Limits on the Localization of Cognitive Processes in the Brain, 2001; also numerous articles; editor: Readings in Sensory Coding, 1972; assoc. editor Behavioral Research Method and Instrn., 1968-90, Computing: Archives for Electronic Computing, 1963-75, Jour. Exptl. Psychology; Perception and Performance, 1974-79; cons. editor Jour. Exptl. Psychology: Applied, 1994—. Patentee in field. Served to 2d lt. USAF, 1951-53. USPHS spl. postdoctoral fellow, 1965-66; NIMH research scientist award, 1971-76 Fellow AAAS, Am. Psychol. Soc. (charter), Soc. Exptl. Psychologists (chmn. 1994-95); mem. Psychonomics Soc. Office: Ariz State U Dept Indsl Engring Tempe AZ 85287-1104 E-mail: aowru@asu.edu

UTTER, ROBERT FRENCH, retired state supreme court justice; b. Seattle, June 19, 1930; s. John and Besse (French) U.; m. Elizabeth J. Stevenson, Dec. 28, 1953; children: Kimberly, Kirk, John. BS, U. Wash., 1952; LLB, 1954. Bar: Wash. 1954. Pros. atty., King County, Wash., 1955-57; individual practice law Seattle, 1957-59; ct. commr. King County Superior Ct., 1959-64, judge, 1964-69, Wash. State Ct. Appeals, 1969-71, Wash. State Supreme Ct., 1971-95, chief justice, 1979-81; ret., 1995; lectr. Ctrl. and Eastern European Legal Inst., Prague, Czech Republic, 2000, 01, dean faculty Czech Republic, 2001—. Lectr. in field, leader comparative law tour People's Republic of China, 1986, 87, 88, 91, USSR, 1989, Republic of South Africa, 1997, Ukraine, Hungarian and Czech Republic, 1998; adj. prof. constl. law U. Puget Sound, 1987, 88, 89, 90, 91, 92, 93, 94; cons. CEELI, 1991, 93—, USIA, 1992; visitor to Kazakhstan, Kyrgystan Judiciary, 1993, 94, 95, 96, Outer Mangolia, 1997; lectr. to Albanian Judiciary, 1994, 95, 2000, to Georgian Judiciary, 1999. Editor books on real property and appellate practice. Pres., founder Big Brother Assn., Seattle, 1955-67; pres., founder Job Therapy Inc., 1963-71; mem. exec. com. Conf. of Chief Justices, 1979-80, 81-86; pres. Thurston County Big Bros./Big Sisters, 1984; lectr. Soviet Acad. Moscow, 1991; USIA visitor to comment on jud. system, Latvia, 1992, Kazakstan, 1993-94; trustee Linfield Coll. Named Alumnus of Yr., Linfield Coll., 1973, Disting. Jud. Scholar, U. Ind., 1987, Judge of Yr., Wash. State Trial Lawyers, 1989, Outstanding Judge, Wash. State Bar Assn., 1990, Outstanding Judge, Seattle-King County Bar Assn., 1992, Conder-Faulkner lectr. U. Wash. Sch. Law, 1995, Disting. Alumnus Sch. Law U. Wash., 1995; recipient Henry Jackson Disting. Pub. Svc. award Nat. Wash. Sch. Law, 2000. Fellow Chartered Inst. Arbitrators; mem. ABA (commentator on proposed constns. of Albania, Bulgaria, Romania, Russia, Lithuania, Azerbaijan, Uzbekistan, Byelarus, Kazakhstan and Ukraine), Am. Judicature Soc. (sec. 1987—, chmn. bd. dirs., mem. exec. com., Herbert Harley award 1983, Justice award 1998), Order of Coif. Baptist.

UTZ, SARAH WINIFRED, nursing educator; b. San Diego; d. Frederick R. and Margaret M. (Gibbons) U.; BS, U. Portland, 1943, EdM, 1958; MS, UCLA, 1970; PhD, U. So. Calif., 1979. Clin. instr. Providence Sch. Nursing, Portland, Oreg., 1946-50, edn. dir., 1950-62; edn. dir. Sacred Heart Sch. Nursing, Eugene, Oreg., 1963-67; asst. prof. nursing Calif. State U., L.A., 1969-74, assoc. prof., 1974-81, prof., 1981—, assoc. chmn. dept.

nursing, 1982—; cons. in nursing curriculum, 1978—; healthcare cons., 1991—; past chmn. ednl. adminstrs., cons., tchrs. sect. Oreg. Nurses Assn., past pres. Oreg. State Bd. Nursing; mem. rsch. program Western Interstate Commn. on Higher Edn. in Nursing; chmn. liaison com. nursing edn. Articulation Coun. Calif. Author articles and lab manuals. Served with Nurse Corps, USN, 1944-46. HEW grantee, 1970-74, Kellogg Found. grantee, 1974-76, USDHHS grantee, 1987—; R.N., Calif., Oreg. Mem. Am. Nurses Assn., Calif. Nurses Assn. (edn. commr. region 6 1987—, chair edn. interest group region 6 , 1987—), Am. Ednl. Rsch. Assn., AAUP, Phi Delta Kappa, Sigma Theta Tau. Formerly editor Oreg. Nurse; reviewer Western Jour. Nursing Rsch. Home: 1409 Midvale Ave Los Angeles CA 90024-5454 Office: 5151 State University Dr Los Angeles CA 90032-4226

UYEHARA, CATHERINE FAY TAKAKO (YAMAUCHI), physiologist, educator, pharmacologist; b. Honolulu, Dec. 20, 1959; d. Thomas Takashi and Eiko (Haraguchi) Uyehara; m. Alan Hisao Yamauchi, Feb. 17, 1990. BS, Yale U., 1981; PhD in Physiology, U. Hawaii, Honolulu, 1987. Postdoctoral fellow SmithKline Beecham Pharms., King of Prussia, Pa., 1987-89; mem. grad. faculty in pediatrics U. Hawaii John Burns Sch. Medicine, Honolulu, 1991—; rsch. pharmacologist Kapiolani Med. Ctr. for Women and Children, Honolulu, 1990-91. Statis. cons. Tripler Army Med. Ctr., Honolulu, 1984-87, 89—, chief rsch. pharmacology , 1991—, dir. collaborative rsch. program, 1995—; mem. grad. faculty in pharmacology U. Hawaii John A. Burns Sch. Medicine, 1993—; grad. faculty Interdisciplinary Biomed. Sci. program, 1995-98, Cell and Molecular Biology program, 1998—, mem. grad. faculty in physiology, 1999—. Contbr. articles to profl. jours. Mem. Am. Fedn. for Med. Rsch., Am. Physiol. Soc., Soc. Uniformed Endocrinologists, Endocrine Soc., We. Soc. Pediatric Rsch., N.Y. Acad. Scis., Hawaiian Acad. Sci., Sigma Xi. Democrat. Mem. Christian Ch. Avocations: swimming, diving, crafts, horticulture, music. Office: Dept Clin Investigation 1 Jarrett White Rd Bldg 40 Tripler Army Medical Center HI 96859

UYEMOTO, JERRY KAZUMITSU, plant pathologist, educator; b. Fresno, Calif., May 27, 1939; married, 1965; 1 child. BS in Agronomy, U. Calif., Davis, 1962, MS in Plant Pathology, 1964, PhD in Plant Pathology, 1968. Lab. tech. U. Calif., Davis, 1964-66; from asst. to assoc. prof. virology N.Y. State Agrl. Expt. Sta., Cornell U., 1968-77; prof. Kansas State U., Manhattan, 1977-81; sr. staff scientist Advanced Genetic Scis., 1982-84; vis. scientist U. Calif., Davis, 1984-86, rsch. plant pathology, USDA Agrl. Rsch. Svc., 1986—. Recipient Lee M. Hutchins award Am. Phytopath. Soc., 1993. Mem. Assn. Applied Biologists, Am. Phytopath Soc.. Achievements include research on a variety of crop plants; research contributions were also made on virus diseases of pome, stone fruit, and annual crop plants; ELISA protocols tested and/or established for serological indexing of ilarviruses in all Prunus tree sources used for scion buds and seeds. Office: UC Davis Dept Plant Path USDA ARS Davis CA 95616

VACANO, JOST, cinematographer; Cinematographer The Skouras Agy., Santa Monica, Calif., 1977—. Cinematographer: (films) Soldier of Orange, 1977, Spetters, 1980, Das Boot, 1981, The Neverending Story, 1984, 52 Pick-up, 1986, Robocop, 1987, Rocket Gibraltar, 1988, Total Recall, 1990, Untamed Heart, 1993, Showgirls, 1995, Starship Troopers, 1997, The Hollow Man, 1999. Office: The Skouras Agy 631 Wilshire Blvd Ste 2C Santa Monica CA 90401-1513

VACQUIER, VICTOR DIMITRI, biology educator; b. Pitts., July 20, 1940; s. Victor and Vera (Vinogradoff) V.; m. Judith Ellen Payne, July 1, 1973; children: Paul Andre, Marc Christian. AB, San Diego State U., 1963; PhD, U. Calif., Berkeley, 1968. Rsch. asst. U. Calif., Berkeley, 1963-68; rschr. Internat. Lab. Genetics & Biophys., Naples, Italy, 1968-69, Hopkins Marine Sta., Stanford U., Pacific Grove, Calif., 1970-71; asst. rsch. biologist Scripps Inst. Oceanography, U. Calif., La Jolla, 1971-73, assoc. prof. biology, 1978-80, prof., 1980—. Asst. prof. zoology U. Calif.-Davis, 1973-75, assoc. prof., 1975-78. Assoc. editor Gamete Rsch., 1980—, Devel. Biology, 1983—. Mem. Am. Soc. Cell Biology, Soc. Devel. Biology, Internat. Soc. Devel. Biology. Office: U Calif Scripps Instn Oceanography Marine Biology Rsch Divsn La Jolla CA 92093-0202

VAIL, CHARLES DANIEL, veterinarian, consultant; b. Denver, June 11, 1936; s. Allan Paden and Katherine Marie (Phillips) V.; m. Jean Williams Ebsen, June 15, 1963; children: Ellen Marie, David Elston. BS, Colorado A&M, 1958; DVM, Colo. State U., 1960. Asst. veterinarian Colo. Racing Commn., Littleton, 1958-60; equine practitioner Littleton Large Animal Clinic, 1960-86; track veterinarian Centennial Race Track, Littleton, 1962-63. Editor in chief Equine Practice, 1986-2000; contbr. articles to profl. jours. Mem. selection com. Outstanding Biology Tchr. award Colo., 1978-80, 88—, Arapahoe Fair Assn., Littleton, 1965-84, gallery disting. grads. Colo. State U. Coll. Vet. Medicine, 1989; chmn. Littleton Rotary Western Heritage Art Fair; bd. dirs. Animal Assistance Found. Denver, 1991—, v.p., 1995-96, pres., 1996-97; bd. dirs. Western Vet. Conf., 1997-2000, v.p., 2001; bd. dirs. Friends Littleton Pub. Libr./Mus., 2000—, Rocky Mountain Stroke Assn.; active Colo. State U. Alumni Found., 1997—, pres.-elect, 2000. Recipient Honor Alumni award Coll. Vet. Medicine, Colo. State U., 1991. Mem. AVMA (publs. com. 1981-87), Am. Assn. Equine Practitioners (pres. 1985), Colo. Vet. Medicine Assn. (pres. 1980, Veterinarian of Yr. award 1987), Denver Area Vet. Medicine Soc. (pres. 1975), Arapahoe Town and Gown Soc. (v.p. 1999, pres. 2000), Nottingham Club, Rotary (pres. Littleton 1992-93), Sigma Alpha Epsilon, Omicron Delta Kappa. Home: 5921 S Cherrywood Cir Littleton CO 80121-2465 Office: Littleton Large Animal Clinic PC 8025 S Santa Fe Dr Littleton CO 80120-4305 Office Fax: 303-794-9466

VALADEZ, RAMON, state senator; BSEE, U. Ariz., 1989. Exec. mgmt. intern Pima County; asst. to U.S. Senator Dennis DeConcini, 1989-91; So. Ariz. campaign coord. Pastor for Congress Campaign; asst. to U.S. Rep. Ed Pastor; So. Ariz. campaign coord. Eddie Basha for Gov. Campaign, 1994; spl. asst. to supr. Eckstrom; Dem. Senator dist. 10 Arizona State Senate , 1996—. Mem. State Adv. Task Force for Runaway and Homeless Youth; mem. ways and means, govt. ops., human svcs. coms. Ariz. Ho. of Reps.; bd. dirs. Open Inn, Project YES, U. Ariz. Hispanic Alumni. Hispanic task force co-chair United Way Tucson/Pima County Cmty. Profile; former mem. Ariz. Hispanic Cmty. Forum, League of United Latin Am. Citizens, Labor Coun. for Latin Am. Advancement; precinct committeeman; advisor Univ. Dems.; Southside campaign coord. Martin Luther King, Jr.-Victory Together Campaign, 1992. Recipient Outstanding Precinct Committeeman award State Dem. Party, 1994, award Labor Coun. Latin Am. Advancement, award Pueblo Gardens Neighborhood Assn., award FBI, award Pio Decimo Ctr., award City of Tucson, award John Valenzuela Ctr., award City of South Tucson, award Tucson AIDS Project, award League of United Latin Am. Citiznes, award Tucson Juneteenth Com. Mem. Am. Fedn. State, County and Mcpl. Employees (local 449), Legis. Dist. 10 Dem. Club. Office: Arizona State Senate Capitol Complex Office 331 1700 W Washington Phoenix AZ 85007 E-mail: rvaladez@azleg.state.az.us

VALDEZ, TROY, business executive; b. Mar. 13, 1938; CEO Tranex Inc., Colorado Springs, Colo., 1986—. Office: 2350 Executive Cir Colorado Springs CO 80906-4138

VALENTINE, DEAN, broadcast executive; Pres. Walt Disney TV/Touchstone TV, pres., CEO United Paramount Network, L.A., 1997—. Office: United Paramount Network 11800 Wilshire Blvd Los Angeles CA 90025-6602

VALENTINE, JAMES WILLIAM, paleobiology educator, writer; b. Los Angeles, Nov. 10, 1926; s. Adelbert Cuthbert and Isabel (Davis) V.; m. Grace Evelyn Whysner, Dec. 21, 1957 (div. 1972); children— Anita, Ian; m. Cathryn Alice Campbell, Sept. 10, 1978 (div. 1986); 1 child, Geoffrey; m. Diane Mondragon, Mar. 16, 1987. BA, Phillips U., 1951; MA, UCLA, 1954, PhD, 1958. From asst. prof. to assoc. prof. U. Mo., Columbia, 1958-64; from assoc. prof. to prof. U. Calif., Davis, 1964-77, prof. geol. scis. Santa Barbara, 1977-90, prof. integrative biology Berkeley, 1990-93, emeritus, 1993—. Author: Evolutionary Paleoecology of the Marine Biosphere, 1973; editor: Phanerozoic Diversity, 1985; co-author: Evolution, 1977, Evolving, 1979; also numerous articles, 1954— Served with USNR, 1944-46; PTO Fulbright research scholar, Australia, 1962-63; Guggenheim fellow Yale U., Oxford U., Eng., 1968-69; Rockefeller Found. scholar in residence, Bellagio, Italy, summer 1974; grantee NSF, NASA Fellow AAAS, Am. Acad. Arts and Scis., Geol. Soc. Am.; mem. NAS, Paleontol. Soc. (pres. 1974-75, medal 1996). Avocation: collecting works of Charles Darwin. Home: 1351 Glendale Ave Berkeley CA 94708-2025 Office: U Calif Dept Integrative Biology Berkeley CA 94720-0001 E-mail: jwvsossi@socrates.berkeley.edu

VALENTINE, JOHN LESTER, state legislator, lawyer; b. Fullerton, Calif., Apr. 26, 1949; s. Robert Lester and Pauline C. (Glood) V.; m. Karen Marie Thorpe, June 1, 1972; children: John Robert, Jeremy Reid, Staci Marie, Jeffrey Mark., David Emerson, Patricia Ann. BS in Acctg. and Econs., Brigham Young U., 1973, JD, 1976. Bar: Utah 1976, U.S. Dist. Ct. Utah, U.S. Ct. Appeals (10th cir.), U.S. Tax Ct.; CPA. Atty. Howard, Lewis & Petersen, Provo, Utah, 1976—; mem. Utah Ho. Reps., 1988-98, Utah Senate, Dist. 14, Salt Lake City, 1999—. Instr. probate and estates Utah Valley State Coll.; instr. fin. planning., adj. prof. law Brigham Young U.; chmn. revenue and taxation com. Utah Senate, 1999-2000, vice chmn. exec. appropriations com., judiciary com., pub. edn. subcom.; mem. exec offices, cts., corrections and legis. appropriations subcom., Utah Ho. of Reps., 1988-90, capital facilities subcom., 1988-90, retirement com., 1988-90, judiciary com., 1988-92, strategic planning steering com., 1988-90, interim appropriations com., 1988-94, tax. review commn., 1989-98, ethics com., 1990-92, human svcs. and health appropriations subcom., 1990-92, revenue and taxation com., 1988-98, vice chmn. 1990-92; vice chmn. exec. appropriations., 1990-92; chmn. exec. appropriations com., 1992-94, chmn. rules com., 1994-96, higher edn. appropriations com. 1994-96, asst. majority whip, 1996-98; apptd. to state senate, 1998, elected, 2000, majority whip, 2000—. Mem. adv. bd. Internat. Sr. Games, 1988—; active Blue Ribbon Task Force on Local Govt. Funding, Utah League Cities and Towns, 1990-94, Criminal Sentencing Guidelines Task Force, Utah Judicial Coun., 1990-92, Access to Health Care Task Force, 1990-92, Utah County Sheriff Search and Rescue, Orem Met. Water Bd., Alpine Sch. Dist. Boundary Line Com., 1986-90, Boy Scouts Am.; bd. regents Legis. Adv. Com. UVCC.; mem. exec. bd. Utah Nat. Parks Coun.; mem. adv. coun. Orchard Elem. Sch., Mountainlands Com. an Aging; bd. trustees Utah Opera Co.; judge nat. and local competitions Moot Ct.; voting dist. chmn.; state, county del.; lt. incident command sys. Utah County Sheriff. Recipient Silver Beaver award Boy Scouts Am., Taxpayer Advocate award Utah Taxpayer Assn. Mem. ABA (tax sect.), Utah State Bar, CPA Com., Tax Sect. Specialization Com., Bicentennial Com. Republican. Mormon. Avocation: mountain climbing. Office: Howard Lewis & Petersen 120 E 300 N Provo UT 84606-2907

VALENTINE, MARK CONRAD, dermatologist; b. Parkersburg, W.Va., Sept. 26, 1948; s. Sestel and Margaret Elaine (Sabolo) V.; m. Elizabeth Michelle Monezis, Apr. 21, 1975; children: Perry Martin, Owen Mark. BA, W.Va. U., 1970; MD, Johns Hopkins U., 1974. Intern, resident U. Hosps. Cleve., 1974-76, resident, 1976-79; dermatologist pvt. practice, Everett, Wash., 1979—. Clin. assoc. prof. U. Wash., Seattle, 1979—; active med. staff Providence Gen. Med. Ctr., Everett, 1979—. Editl. bd. Jour. of Am. Acad. Dermatology, 1998—. Bd. dirs., sec. City Libr. Bd., Mukilteo, Wash., 1994-99; bd. dirs., v.p. Everett Symphony Bd., 1982-85, 2001—; bd. dirs. Book Arts Guild, Seattle, 1988-90. Nat. Merit scholar, 1966. Mem. AMA, Am. Acad. Dermatology (adv. coun. 1983-86), Wash. State Dermatological Assn. (pres.-elect 1996, pres. 1996-97), Seattle Dermatology Soc. (pres. 1985-86), Rotary (Everett), Phi Beta Kappa. Avocations: book collecting, book binding, guitar, piano. Office: 3327 Colby Ave Everett WA 98201-6403 E-mail: mark1105@aol.com

VALENTINE, WILLIAM EDSON, architect; b. Winston-Salem, N.C., Sept. 3, 1937; s. Howard Leon and Sally (Cunningham) V.; m. Jane Dorward, Aug. 13, 1939; children: Anne, Karen, William. BArch, N.C. State U., 1960; MArch, Harvard U., 1962. Co-chmn. Hellmuth, Obata & Kassabaum Inc., San Francisco, 1962—. Chmn. Hellmuth, Obata & Kassabaum Design Bd., also bd. dirs. Served to 1st lt. U.S. Army, 1960-61. Fellow AIA. Club: Harvard. Office: Hellmuth Obata Kassabaum Inc 71 Stevenson St Ste 2200 San Francisco CA 94105-2979

VALERIO BARRAD, CATHERINE M. lawyer; BA, U. Calif., San Diego, 1982; MBA, UCLA, 1984; JD magna cum laude, Northwestern U., 1993. Ba: Calif. 1993, U.S. Ct. Appeals (9th cir.) 1994. Law clk. to Hon. Douglas H. Ginsburg, U.S. Dt. Appeals for D.C. Circuit, Washington, 1993-94; assoc. Sidley & Austin, L.A., 1994—. Contbg. author: Federal Appellate Practice Guide, Ninth Circuit, 1994; articles editor Northwestern U. Law Rev., 1992-93; contbr. articles to legal publs. Mem. Order of Coif. Office: Sidley & Austin 555 W 5th St Los Angeles CA 90013-1010 Fax: 213-896-6688. E-mail: cbarrad@sidley.com

VALLEE, ROY, electronics company executive; Field salesman, sys. bus. mgr., gen. sales mgr. Avnet, Inc., Great Neck, N.Y., from 1977, regional dir., v.p., until 1989, pres. Hamilton/Avnet Computer, 1989-90, sr. v.p., dir. worldwide electronics ops., 1990-91, vice chmn., pres., COO, 1991-98, chmn., CEO Phoenix, 1998—, also mem. bd. dirs. Office: Avnet Inc 2211 S 47th St Phoenix AZ 85034-6403

VALLERGA, BERNARD A. engineering administrator; BS, U. Calif. Berkeley, 1943, MS, 1948. Materials testing engr. Hershey Inspection Bur., Oakland, Calif., 1946-48; asst. prof. civil engring. U. Calif. Berkeley, 1948-53; mng. engr. Pacific Coast Divsn. Asphalt Inst., San Francisco, 1953-60; v.p. prodn. devel. & mktg. GBO Divsn. Witco Chem. Co., L.A., 1960-64; pres. & CEO Material Rsch. & Devel., Inc., Oakland, 1964-72; v.p., mng. prin. Woodward-Clyde Consults, San Francisco-Oakland, 1968-76; pres. B.A. Vallerga, Inc. Consulting Civil Engring., Oakland, 1977—. Chmn. Triaxial Inst. Structural Design Pavements, 1950-52; bd. dirs. Woodward-Clyde Consultants, 1980-82; mem. bd. dirs., v.p. Asphalt Inst., 1962-64; v.p. Design Divsn., Am. Road Builders Assn., 1968-70; chmn. bd. dirs. Woodward Envicon, 1969-72, Subcom. Asphalt Durability, Transp. Rsch. Bd., 1980—; gen. cons. Off Energy Related Inventions, Bur. Stds., Dept. Com., 1980—. Fellow ASCE (mem. Airfield Pavement Com. 1972-79); mem. ASTM (Provost Hubbard award 1989), Internat. Soc. Asphalt Pavements, Assn. Asphalt Paving Technologists (mem. bd. dirs. 1960-62, Recognition award 1988), Nat. Acad. Engring., Sigma Xi. Office: Nichols Vallerga & Assocs 1970 Broadway Ste 630 Oakland CA 94612-2218

VALLES, JUDITH, mayor, former academic administrator; b. San Bernardino, Calif., Dec. 14, 1933; d. Gonzalo and Jovita (Lopez-Torices) V.; m. Chad Bradbury, Sept. 30, 1956 (dec. Sept. 1969); children: Edith Renella, Nohemi Renella, Chad; m. Harry Carl Smith, Oct. 13, 1985. BA in English, Redlands (Calif.) U., 1956; MA in [illegible] Riverside, 1966; doctorate (hon.), U. Redlands, 2000. Instr. Spanish San Bernardino (Calif.) Valley Coll., 1963-84, head dept. fgn. lang., 1971-76, chair div. humanities, 1976-81, dean extended day, 1981-83, adminstrv. dean acad. affairs, 1983-87, exec. v.p. acad. and student affairs, 1987-88; pres. Golden West Coll., Huntington Beach, Calif., 1988—; mayor San Bernardino, 1998—. Mem. adv. com. Police Officers Standards and Tng. Commn., Scaramento, 1991—. Author fgn. lang. annals and sociol. abstracts. Speaker statewide edn. and community orgns., 1988—; bd. dirs. exec. coun. and chief exec. officers Calif. Community Colls., 1990—. Named One of Outstanding Women Orange County YWCA, 1990, Citizen of Achievement LWV, 1989, Woman of Distinction Bus. Press, 1998, Influential Latina of the Yr. Hispanic Lifestyle, 1998, State of Calif. Woman of the Yr., 1999, Humanitarian Yr. Cath. charities, 1999, Citizen Yr. Boy Scouts Am., 1999, Empire Woman Yr. State Assembly, 1999; inducted into Hall of Fame, San Bernardino Valley Coll. Mem. Women's Roundtable Orange County, Conf. and Visitors Bur., C. of C. (Vanguard), Kiwanis, Charter 100. Avocations: opera, theater, reading, running. Office: Conf Mayors 300 N D St San Bernardino CA 92418-0001

VALLONE, JOHN CHARLES, motion picture production designer; b. Phila., June 23, 1953; s. Louis Phillip and Laura Anne (Gagilione) V.; divorced; children: Gabriella, Lilli. BFA, NYU, 1975. Pres., owner Archtl. Dreams, Plate City, Utah, 1997—, Against the Wind Prodns. Ltd., La Jolla, Vallone Design Group, La Jolla, VDG Aircraft Co. Ltd., La Jolla. Prodn. designer: (feature films) Southern Comfort, 1981, 48 Hours, 1982, Brainstorm, 1983, Streets of Fire, 1984, Brewster's Millions, 1985, Commando, 1985, Predator, 1987, Red Heat, 1988, The Adventures of Ford Fairlane, 1990, Die Hard 2, 1990, Rambling Rose, 1991, Cliffhanger, 1993, Bad Boys, 1995, 3 Wishes, 1995, (TV pilots) Private Eye, 1987, Sweet Justice, 1994, (TV movies) Shannon's Deal, 1989, Angel City, 1990, (TV series) Cover Me, 1999-2000; art dir.: (film) Star Trek: The Motion Picture, 1979 (Academy award nomination best art direction 1979). Mem. AOPA, SMPTVAD, Acad. Motion Picture Arts and Scis. (Best Art Direction award nomination 1981). Republican. Avocations: restoration of wooden yacht, pilot, sailing, woodworking, skiing.

VAN ALFEN, NEAL K. plant pathologist; b. Ogden, Utah, July 17, 1943; s. Gerrit Johan and Marguerite (Noorda) Van A. BS, Brigham Young U., 1968, MS, 1969; PhD, U. Calif., Davis, 1972. Asst. plant pathologist Conn. Agr. Exp. Sta., New Haven, 1972-75; asst. prof. biology Utah State U., Logan, 1975-78, extension plant pathologist, 1975-78, assoc. prof. of biology, 1978-82, prof. of biology and molecular biology/biochem., 1982-90; prof. and head/dept. of plant pathology/microbiology Tex. A&M U., College Station, Tex., 1990-99; dean agrl. and environ. scis. U. Calif., Davis, 1999—. Fellow AAAS, Am. Phytopathol. Soc.; mem. Am. Phytopathol. Soc. (councilor-at-large 1994-97, v.p., pres. 1997-2000), Am. Soc. for Microbiology. Office: U Calif-Davis Coll Agrl and Environ Scis 1 Shields Ave Davis CA 95616-5270 E-mail: nkvanalfen@ucdavis.edu

VAN ARSDALE, DICK, professional basketball team executive; b. Indpls., Feb. 22, 1943; m. Barbara V.; children: Jill, Jason. AB in economics, Indiana U., 1965. Player New York Knicks (Nat. Basketball Assn.), N.Y.C., 1965-68; with Phoenix Suns, Phoenix, 1968-77, color commentator, TV broadcasts, from 1977, interim mgr., 1987, v.p., player personnel, dir. player personnel. Named "Mr. Basketball" of Indiana during high school, NCAA All-American, Indiana U. Office: c/o Phoenix Suns 201 E Jefferson St Phoenix AZ 85004-2412

VAN ATTA, DAVID MURRAY, lawyer; b. Berkeley, Calif., Oct. 20, 1944; s. Chester Murray and Rosalind (Eisenstein) Van A.; m. Jo Ann Masaoka; 1 child, Lauren Rachel. BA, U. Calif., Berkeley, 1966; JD, U. Calif., Hastings, 1969. Bar: Calif. 1970. Asst. gen. counsel Boise Cascade Corp., Palo Alto, Calif., 1970-73; ptnr. Miller, Starr & Regalia, San Francisco, 1973-87, Graham & James, San Francisco, 1987-93, Hanna & Van Atta, Palo Alto, 1993—. Instr. Golden Gate U., San Francisco, 1984-85; U. Calif., Berkeley, 1976-84. Author: (with Hanna) California Common Interest Developments Law and Practice, 1999. Mem. ABA, Am. Coll. Real Estate Lawyers (bd. govs.), Calif. Bar Assn. (vice chmn. exec. com. real property law sect. 1982-85, chmn. condominium and subdivsn. com. real property law sect. 1981-83), Cmty. Assn. Inst., Urban Land Inst., Anglo-Am. Real Property Inst., Rotary Club Palo Alto, Lambda Alpha Internat. Soc. Avocations: skiing, tennis, painting. Office: Hanna & Van Atta 525 University Ave Ste 705 Palo Alto CA 94301-1921

VAN CAMP, BRIAN RALPH, judge; b. Halstead, Kans., Aug. 23, 1940; s. Ralph A. and Mary Margaret (Bragg) Van C.; m. Diane D. Miller, 1992; children: Megan M., Laurie E. AB, U. Calif., Berkeley, 1962, LLB, 1965. Bar: Calif. 1966. Dep. atty. gen., State Calif., 1965-67; agy. atty. Redevel. Agy., City of Sacramento, 1967-70; asst./acting sec. Bus. and Trans. Agy., State of Calif., 1970-71; commr. of corps. State of Calif., Sacramento, 1971-74; partner firm Diepenbrock, Wulff, Plant & Hannegan, Sacramento, 1975-77, Van Camp & Johnson, Sacramento, 1978-90; sr. ptnr. Downey, Brand, Seymour & Rohwer, 1990-97; judge Superior Ct., Sacramento County, 1997—. Lectr. Continuing Edn. Bar, Practicing Law Inst., Calif. CPA Soc. Contbr. articles to profl. jours. Mem. Rep. State Ctrl. Com. Calif., 1974-78; pres. Sacramento Area Commerce and Trade Orgn., 1986-87; mem. electoral coll. Presdl. Elector for State of Calif., 1976; mem. Calif. Health Facilities Fin. Authority, 1985-89; mem. Capital Area Devel. Authority, 1989-97, chmn., 1990-97; mem. Calif. Jud. Coun. Task Force on Quality of Justice, 1998-99; bd. dirs. Sacramento Symphony Assn., 1973-85, 92-94, Sacramento Symphony Found., 1993—, Sacramento Valley Venture Capital Forum, 1986-90, League to Save Lake Tahoe, 1988-95, Valley Vision, Inc., 1993-97; elder Fremont Presbyn. Ch., 1967—. Recipient Sumner-Mering Meml. award Sacramento U. of Calif. Alumni Assn., 1962, Thos. Jefferson award Am. Inst. Pub. Svc., 1994, Excellence in Achievement award Calif. Alumni Assn., 1997; named Outstanding Young Man of Yr., Sacramento Jaycees, 1970, Internat. Young Man of Yr., Active 20-30 Club Internat., 1973. Mem. Boalt Hall Alumni Assn. (bd. dirs. 1991-94), Lincoln Club Sacramento Valley (bd. dirs., pres. 1984-86), U. Calif Men's Club (pres. 1968), Sutter Club, Kanadhar Ski Club, Rotary Club Sacramento (pres. 1993-94, Paul Harris Fellow award 1995), Comstock Club (pres. 1976-77). Republican. Presbyterian. Office: 720 9th St Sacramento CA 95814-1302 E-mail: Vancamp@saccourt.com

VAN DAM, HEIMAN, psychoanalyst; b. Leiden, The Netherlands; s. Machiel and Rika (Knorringa) van D.; m. Barbara C. Strona, Oct. 6, 1945; children: Machiel, Claire Ilena, Rika Rosemary. AB, U. So. Calif., 1942, MD, 1945. Fellowship child psychiatry Pasadena (Calif.) Child Guidance Clinic, 1950; gen. practice psychiatry and psychoanalysis L.A., 1951—; instr. L.A. Psychoanalytic Inst., 1959—, co-chmn. com. on child psychoanalysis, 1960-67, tng. and supervising psychoanalyst, 1972—; supr. child and adolescent psychoanalysis So. Calif. Psychoanalytic Inst., 1986—. Cons. Reiss Davis Child Study Center, 1955-76, Neighborhood Youth Assn., Los Angeles, 1964-69; asso. clin. prof. psychiatry and pediats. UCLA Sch. Medicine, 1960-96, clin. prof. psychiatry and pediats., 1996—; vis. supr. child psychoanalysis San Francisco Psychoanalytic Inst., 1969-79, Denver Psychoanalytic Inst., 1972-74; mem. adv. bd. Western State U. Coll. Law, Fullerton, Calif., 1965-83. Corr. editor Arbeits Hefte Kinderanalyse, 1985— ; contbr. articles to profl. jours. Trustee, mem. edn. com. Center for Early Edn., 1964-92, v.p., 1978-79; bd. dirs. Child Devel. and Psychotherapy Tng. Program, Los Angeles, 1975-80, pres., 1975-77; bd. [illegible] clinic Jewish Family Service, Los Angeles, 1978-86; bd. dirs. Lake Arrowhead Crest Estates, 1990-99. Served to capt. M.C. AUS, 1946-48. Mem. Am. Psychoanalytic Assn. (com. on ethics 1977-80), Assn. Child

Psychoanalysis (councillor 1966-69, sec. 1972-74, mem. nominating com. 1978-84, membership com. 1988—, Marianne Kris lectr. 1995), Internat. Assn. Infant Psychiatry (co-chmn. program com. 1980-83), Internat. Soc. Adolescent Psychiatry (sci. adv. com. 1988—), Phi Beta Kappa. Office: 10436 Santa Monica Blvd Los Angeles CA 90025-5079

VANDAMENT, WILLIAM EUGENE, retired academic administrator; b. Hannibal, Mo., Sept. 6, 1931; s. Alva E. and Ruth Alice (Mahood) V.; m. Margery Vandament, Feb. 2, 1952; children: Jane Louise, Lisa Ann. BA, Quincy Coll., 1952; MS, So. Ill. U., 1953; MS in Psychology, U. Mass., 1963, PhD, 1964; LittD, No. Mich. U., 1997. Psychologist Bacon Clinic, Racine, Wis., 1954-61; NDEA fellow U. Mass., Amherst, 1961-64; asst. prof. SUNY, Binghamton, 1964-69, univ. examiner and dir. instl. research, 1969-73, asst. v.p. planning, instl. research, 1972-76; exec. asst. to pres., dir. budget and resources Ohio State U., Columbus, 1976-79, v.p. fin. and planning, 1979-81; sr. v.p. adminstrn. NYU, N.Y.C., 1981-83; provost, vice chancellor acad. affairs Calif. State U. System, Long Beach, 1983-87; Trustees prof. Calif. State U., Fullerton, 1987-92; pres. No. Mich. U., 1991-97, ret., 1997. Contbr. articles to psychol. jours. and books on higher edn. Office: 2662 E 20th St Apt 310 Signal Hill CA 90804-5616 E-mail: vandament@aol.com

VAN DE KAMP, JOHN KALAR, lawyer; b. Pasadena, Calif., Feb. 7, 1936; s. Harry and Georgie (Kalar) Van de K.; m. Andrea Fisher, Mar. 11, 1978; 1 child, Diana. BA, Dartmouth Coll., 1956; JD, Stanford U., 1959. Bar: Calif. 1960. Asst. U.S. atty., L.A., 1960-66; U.S. atty. L.A., 1966-67; dep. dir. Exec. Office for U.S. Attys., Washington, 1967-68, dir., 1968-69; spl. asst. Pres.'s Commn. on Campus Unrest, 1970; fed. pub. defender L.A., 1971-75; dist. atty. Los Angeles County, 1975-83; atty. gen. State of Calif., 1983-91; ptnr. Dewey Ballantine, L.A., 1991-96, of counsel, 1996—; pres. Thoroughbred Owners, Calif., 1996—. Bd. dirs. United Airlines. Mem. Calif. Dist. Attys. Assn. (pres. 1975-83), Nat. Dist. Attys. Assn. (v.p. 1975-83), Peace Officers Assn. L.A. County (past pres.), Nat. Assn. Attys. Gen. (exec. com. 1983-91), Conf. Western Attys. Gen. (pres. 1986). Office: Dewey Ballantine LLP 333 So Grand Ave Ste 2600 Los Angeles CA 90071-1530

VANDENBERG, EDWIN JAMES, chemist, educator; b. Hawthorne, N.J., Sept. 13, 1918; s. Albert J. Alida C. (Westerhoff) V.; m. Mildred Elizabeth Wright, Sept. 9, 1950; children: David James, Jean Elizabeth. ME with distinction, Stevens Inst. Tech., 1939, Dr.Engring. (hon.), 1965. Rsch. chemist Hercules Inc. Rsch. Ctr., Wilmington, Del., 1939-44; asst. shift supr. Sunflower Ordnance Works, Kans., 1944-45; rsch. chemist Rsch. Ctr., Wilmington, 1945-57, sr. rsch. chemist, 1958-64, rsch. assoc., 1965-77, sr. rsch. assoc., 1978-82. Adj. prof. chemistry Ariz. State U., Tempe, 1983-91, rsch. prof. chemistry, 1992—; chmn. Gordon Rsch. Conf. on Polymers, 1978. Author: Polyethers, 1975; Coordination Polymerization, 1983; Contemporary Topics in Polymer Science V, 1984, Catalysis in Polymer Synthesis, 1992; patentee in field; adv. bd. Jour. Polymer Sci. 1967-93, Macromolecules, 1979-81. Recipient Indsl. Rsch. 100 award, 1965, Internat. award Soc. Plastics Engrs., 1994. Mem. Am. Chem. Soc. (councillor Del. sect. 1974-81, chmn. 1976, chmn. divsn. polychemistry 1979, coord. insl. sponsors 1982—, Del. sect. award 1965, 79, Polymer Chemistry award 1981, Exceptional Svc. award 1983, 95, Applied Polymer Sci. award 1991, Charles Goodyear medal 1991, Herman F. Mark award 1992). Home: 16223 E Inca Ave Fountain Hls AZ 85268-4518 Office: Ariz State U Dept Chemistry and Biochemistry Tempe AZ 85287-1604 E-mail: ejv5809@imap2.asu.edu

VANDENBERG, PETER RAY, magazine publisher; b. Geneva, Sept. 8, 1939; s. Don George and Isabel (Frank) V.; m. Kathryn Stock, June 1973 (div. Apr. 1977). BBA, Miami U., 1962. Creative adminstr. E.F. McDonald Incentive Co., Dayton, Ohio, 1966-73; mfrs.' rep. Denver, 1974-75; mgr. Homestake Condominiums, Vail, Colo., 1975-76; desk clk. Vail Run Resort, 1976-77; sales rep. Colo. West Advt., Vail, 1977-79, pres., 1980-83, Colo. West Publ., Vail, 1983—, casa-sol.com Mexican Vacation Rentals, Puerto Vallarta, Mexico, 1999—. With U.S. Army, 1963-66. Mem. Sigma Chi. Avocations: sports, music, reading.

VAN DEN BERGHE, PIERRE LOUIS, sociologist, anthropologist; b. Lubumbashi, Congo, Jan. 30, 1933; s. Louis and Denise (Caullery) van den B.; m. Irmgard C. Niehuis, Jan. 21, 1956; children— Eric, Oliver, Marc. B.A., Stanford U., 1952, M.A., 1953; Ph.D., Harvard U., 1960. Asst. prof. sociology Wesleyan U., Middletown, Conn., 1962-63; asso. prof. sociology SUNY, Buffalo, 1963-65; prof. sociology and anthropology U. Wash., Seattle, 1965-98, prof. emeritus, 1998—. Vis. prof. U. Natal, South Africa, 1960-61, Sorbonne, Paris, 1962, U. Nairobi, Kenya, 1967-68, U. Ibadan, Nigeria, 1968-69, U. Haifa, Israel, 1976, U. New South Wales, Australia, 1982, U. Strasbourg, France, 1985, U. Tuebingen, Fed. Republic Germany, 1986, Tel Aviv U., 1988, U. Cape Town, South Africa, 1989; fellow Advanced Study in Behavioral Scis., Stanford, Calif., 1984-85 Author: 22 books including South Africa, A Study in Conflict, 1965, Race and Racism, 1967, Academic Gamesmanship, 1970, Man in Society, 1978, Human Family Systems, 1979, The Ethnic Phenomenon, 1981, Stranger in Their Midst, 1989, State Violence and Ethnicity, 1990, The Quest for the Other, 1994. Served with M.C. U.S. Army, 1954-56. Mem. Am. Sociol. Assn., Am. Anthrop. Assn., Sociol. Research Assn., Human Behavior and Evolution Soc. Home: 2006 19th Ave E Seattle WA 98112-2902 Office: U Wash Dept Sociology 353340 Seattle WA 98195-0001 E-mail: plvdb@u.washington.edu

VAN-DEN-NOORT, STANLEY, neurologist, educator; b. Lynn, Mass., Sept. 8, 1930; s. Judokus and Hazel G. (Van Blarcom) van den N.; m. June Le Clere, Apr. 17, 1954; children: Susanne, Eric, Peter, Katherine, Elizabeth. A.B., Dartmouth, 1951; M.D., Harvard, 1954. Intern then resident Boston City Hosp., 1954-56, resident neurology, 1958-60; research fellow neurochemistry Harvard, 1960-62; instr. medicine Case Western Res. U., Cleve., 1962-66, asst. prof., 1966-69, assoc. prof., 1969-70; prof. neurology U. Calif., Irvine, 1970—, chair dept. neurology, 1970-72, 86-98, assoc. dean Coll. Medicine, 1972-73, dean, 1973-85. Mem. cons. staff U. Calif., Irvine Med. Center; mem. Long Beach (Calif.) Meml. Hosp., Long Beach VA Hosp.; mem. com. of revision U.S. Pharmacopoeial Conv., 1990-95. Mem. med. adv. bds., Nat. Multiple Scierosis Soc./Myasthenia Gravis, 1971—, Orange County chpt. Nat. Multiple Sclerosis Soc., 1971—, Orange County Health Planning Coun., 1971-85, Nat. Com. Rsch. in Neurol. Disease, 1982-87. Lt. M.C. USNR, 1956-58. Fellow ACP, Am. Acad. Neurol.; mem. AAUP, AMA, Am. Neurol. Assn., Nat. Multiple Sclerosis Soc. (chief med. officer 1997), Orange County Med. Assn., Calif. Med. Assn., Am. Heart Assn. Home: 17592 Orange Tree Ln Tustin CA 92780-2353 Office: U Calif Dept Neurology 100 Irvine Hall Irvine CA 92697-4275 E-mail: svandenn@uci.edu

VANDERET, ROBERT CHARLES, lawyer; b. Bklyn., Apr. 12, 1947; s. James Gustav and Bernadette Cecelia (Heaney) V.; m. Sharon Kay Brewster, Oct 3, 1970; children: Erin Anne Brewster, Aidan McKenzie Brewster. AB, UCLA, 1969; JD, Stanford U., 1973. Bar: Calif. 1973, U.S. Dist. Ct. (cen. and so. dists.) Calif. 1974, U.S. Ct. Appeals (9th cir.) 1976, N.Y. 1978, U.S. Supreme Ct. 1978, U.S. Dist. Ct. (no. dist.) Calif. 1980, U.S. Dist. Ct. (ea. dist.) Calif. 1981, U.S. Dist. Ct. (so. dist.) N.Y. 1997. Extern law clk. to Justice Tobriner Calif. Supreme Ct., 1972-73; assoc. O'Melveny & Myers, Los Angeles, 1973-80, ptnr., 1980—. Transition aide Chief Justice Rose Bird, Calif. Supreme Ct., 1976. Del. Dem. Nat. Conv., 1968; bd. dirs. Legal Aid Found. L.A., 1978-90, Constn. Rights Found., 1990, Inner City Law Ctr., 1994—; trustee Lawyers Commn. for Civil Rights Under Law, 1993—; vice chancellor Episcopal Diocese of L.A. Mem. ABA (chair media law and defamation torts com. 1991-92), Calif. State Bar (chair, com. on adminstrn. of justice 1996-97), L.A. Bar Assn. (pro bono coun. chair 1993-95). Democrat. Home: 834 Greentree Rd Pacific Palisades CA 90272-3911 Office: O'Melveny & Myers 400 S Hope St Los Angeles CA 90071-2899

VANDERHOEF, LARRY NEIL, academic administrator; b. Perham, Minn., Mar. 20, 1941; s. Wilmar James and Ida Lucille (Wothe) V.; m. Rosalie Suzanne Slifka, Aug. 31, 1963; children: Susan Marie, Jonathan Lee. B.S., U. Wis., Milw., 1964, M.S., 1965; Ph.D., Purdue U., 1969. Postdoctorate U. Wis., Madison, 1969-70, research assoc., summers 1970-72; asst. prof. biology U. Ill., Urbana, 1970-74, assoc. prof., 1974-77, prof., 1977-80, head dept. plant biology, 1977-80; provost Agrl. and Life Scis., U. Md., College Park, 1980-84; exec. vice chancellor U. Calif., Davis, 1984-91, exec. vice chancellor, provost, 1991-94; chancellor, 1994—. Vis. investigator Carnegie Inst., 1976-77, Edinburgh (Scotland) U., 1978; cons. in field. NRC postdoctoral fellow, 1969-70, Eisenhower fellow, 1987; Dimond travel grantee, 1975, NSF grantee, 1972, 74, 76, 77, 78, 79, NATO grantee, 1980 Mem. AAAS, Am. Soc. Plant Physiology (bd. editors Plant Physiology 1977-82, trustee, mem. exec. com., treas. 1982-88, chmn. bd. trustees 1994-97), Nat. Assn. State Univ. and Land Grant Colls. (exec. com. 2000—). Home: 16 College Park Davis CA 95616-3607 Office: U Calif Davis Office Chancellor Davis CA 95616

VAN DERVEER, TARA, university athletic coach; b. Niagara Falls, N.Y., June 26, 1953; Grad., Indiana U., 1975. Coach women's basketball Stanford U. Cardinals, 1985—, U.S. Nat. Women's Team, 1995-96. Coach gold medalist Women's Olympic Team, 1996. Achievements include champions NCAA Divsn. 1 A, 1990, 92. Office: Stanford U Womens Basketball Dept Athletics Stanford CA 94305

VAN DEVENDER, J. PACE, physical scientist, management consultant; b. Jackson, Miss., Sept. 12, 1947; m. Nancy Jane Manning, 1971; 3 children. BA in Physics, Vanderbilt U., 1969; MA in Physics, Dartmouth Coll., 1971; PhD in Physics, U. London, 1974. Physicist diagnostics devel. Lawrence Livermore Lab., 1969; mem. tech. staff pulsed power rsch. and devel. Sandia Nat. Labs., 1974-78, divsn. supr. pulsed power rsch. divsn., 1978-82, dept. mgr. fusion rsch., 1982-84, dir. pulsed power scis., 1984-93, dir. corp. comm., 1993, dir. Nat. Indsl. Alliances Ctr., 1993-95; pres. Prosperity Inst., 1995-98; dir. strategic scis. ctr. Scandia Nat. Labs., Albuquerque, 1998—; Chief info. officer Sandia Nat. Labs., 1998—. Mem. bd. trust Vanderbilt U., 1969-73. With U.S. Army, 1969-71. Recipient Ernest Orlando Lawrence Meml. award U.S. Dept. Energy, 1991; named one of 100 Most Promising Scientists Under 40, Sci. Digest, 1984; Marshal scholar U. London, 1971-74. Fellow Am. Phys. Soc.; Phi Beta Kappa, Omicron Delta Kappa, Sigma Xi. Office: Scandia Nat Labs MS 0630 PO Box 5800 Albuquerque NM 87185-0100

VAN DRESER, MERTON LAWRENCE, ceramic engineer; b. Des Moines, June 5, 1929; s. Joseph Jerome and Victoria (Love) Van D.; m. Evelyn Lenore Manny, July 12, 1952; children: Peter, Jennifer Sue. BS in Ceramic Engring., Iowa State U., 1951. Tech. supt. Owens-Corning Fiberglas Corp., Kansas City, Mo., 1954-57; rsch. engr. Kaiser Aluminum & Chem. Corp., Milpitas, Calif., 1957-60, rsch. sect. head, 1960-63, lab. mgr., 1963-65, assoc. dir. rsch., 1965-69, dir. refractories rsch. Pleasanton, 1969-72, dir. non-metallic materials rsch., 1972-83, v.p., dir. rsch. Indsl. Chem. div. and Harshaw/Filtrol Partnership, 1983-85, dir. bus. devel. Pleasanton, 1985-88, cons., 1988—. Mem. adv. bd. dept. ceramic engring. U. Ill., 1974-78; chmn. tech. adv. com. Refractories Inst., 1980-84; mem. nat. materials adv. bd. Nat. Acad. Sci.; mem. Indsl. Rsch. Inst. Contbr. articles to sci. jours.; patentee in field. Sustaining membership chmn. local dist. Boy Scouts Am., 1980; pres. PTA, 1967-68; vol. exec. Pakistan Internat. Exec. Svc. Corps, 1990-91. Aviator C.E., U.S. Army, 1951-54. Recipient Profl. Achievement citation Iowa State U., 1978; named to Lambda Chi Alpha hall of fame, 1996. Fellow Am. Ceramic Soc. (v.p. 1973-74); mem. ASTM (hon.; com.), Brit. Ceramic Soc., Nat. Inst. Ceramic Engrs., Keramos (pres. 1976-78, herald 1980-84, Greaves Walker Roll of Honor award), Metall. Soc., AIME. Lodges: Rotary (Paul Harris fellow, pres.-elect Pleasanton Club 2001), Masons. Avocation: comml. pilot. E-mail: m_evandreser@msn.com

VAN DYCK, WENDY, dancer; b. Tokyo; Student, San Francisco Ballet Sch. With San Francisco Ballet, 1979—, prin. dancer, 1987-96, instr., tchr., 1996; assoc. dir. Lawrence Pech Dance, San Francisco, 1996—. Performances include Forgotten Land, The Sons of Horus, The Wanderer Fantasy, Romeo and Juliet, The Sleeping Beauty, Swan Lake, Concerto in d: Poulenc, Handel-a Celebration, Menuetto, Intimate Voices, Hamlet and Ophelia pas de deux, Connotations, Sunset, Rodin, In the Night, The Dream: pas de deux, La Sylphide, Beauty and the Beast, Variations de Ballet, Nutcracker, The Comfort Zone, Dreams of Harmony, Rodeo, Duo Concertant, Who Cares; performed at Reykjavik Arts Festival, Iceland, 1990, The 88th Conf. of the Internat. Olympic Com., L.A., 1984, with Kozlov and Co. Concord Pavilion; guest artist performing role Swan Lake (Act II), San Antonio Ballet, 1985, Giselle, Shreveport Met. Ballet, 1994; featured in the TV broadcast of Suite by Smuin. Office: San Francisco Ballet 455 Franklin St San Francisco CA 94102-4471

VAN DYKE, CRAIG, psychiatrist, director; b. Detroit, Oct. 4, 1941; married; two children. BS, U. Wash., 1963, MD, 1967. Asst. prof. psychiatry Yale U., New Haven, 1974-78; from assoc. to prof. psychiatry U. Calif., San Francisco, 1979-86, prof., chmn. dept. psychiatry, 1994—. Mem. Am. Psychosom. Soc., Internat. Coll. Psychosom. Medicine, Soc. Neurosci., Internat. Neuropsychol. Soc. Office: U Cal San Francisco Langley Porter Psychiatric Inst 401 Parnassus Ave San Francisco CA 94143-9911 E-mail: cvd@lppi.ucsf.edu

VAN DYKE, JERRY, actor, comedian; b. Danville, Ill., July 27, 1931; Stand-up comedian for years, performing in Las Vegas, Atlantic City, other major showrooms; TV work includes (series) The Judy Garland Show, My Mother The Car, 1964, Coach, ABC-TV, 1990-97 (Emmy nomination, Supporting Actor - Comedy Series, 1994), You Wish, 1997, Teen Angel, 1997, (TV movies) To Grandmother's House We Go, 1992, (voice) Annabelle's Wish, 1997, Merry Christmas George Bailey, 1997; film work includes The Courtship of Eddie's Father, Palm Springs Weekend. With USAF, 1952-54. Office: Sutton Barth Vennari 145 S Fairfax Ave Ste 310 Los Angeles CA 90036-2173

VAN DYKE, MILTON DENMAN, aeronautical engineering educator; b. Chgo., Aug. 1, 1922; s. James Richard and Ruth (Barr) Van D.; m. Sylvia Jean Agard Adams, June 16, 1962; children: Russell B., Eric J., Nina A., Brooke A. and Byron J. and Christopher M. (triplets). BS, Harvard U., 1943; MS, Calif. Inst. Tech., 1947, PhD, 1949. Research engr. NACA, 1943-46, 50-54, 55-58; vis. prof. U. Paris, France, 1958- 59; prof. aero. Stanford, 1959—; prof. emeritus, 1992—. Pres. Parabolic Press. Author: Perturbation Methods in Fluid Mechanics, 1964, An Album of Fluid Motion, 1982; editor: Ann. Rev. Fluid Mechanics, 1969-99. Trustee Soc. For Promotion of Sci. and Scholarship, Inc. Served with USNR, 1944-46. Guggenheim and Fulbright fellow, 1954-55 Mem. Am. Acad. Arts and Scis., Nat. Acad. Engring., Am. Phys. Soc., Phi Beta Kappa, Sigma Xi, Sierra Club. Office: Stanford U Div Mechs & Computation Stanford CA 94305-4040

VAN EMBURGH, JOANNE, lawyer; b. Palmyra, N.J., Nov. 18, 1953; d. Earl Henry and Clare (Kemmerle) Van E.; m. Samuel Michael Surloff, July 6, 1993. BA summa cum laude, Catholic U., 1975; JD cum laude, Harvard Law Sch., 1978. Bar: Calif. 1978. Assoc. atty. Agnew Miller & Carlson, L.A., 1978-82; ptnr. Sachs & Phelps, L.A., 1982-91, Heller, Ehrman, White & McAuliffe, L.A., 1991-93; mng. council Toyota Motor Sales, USA, Inc., Torrance, 1993—, asst. gen. coun., 2000—. Mem. ABA. Avocations: reading, cooking, sports. Office: Toyota Motor Sales USA Inc 19001 S Western Ave Torrance CA 90501-1106

VAN EXEL, NICKEY MAXWELL, professional basketball player; b. Kenosha, Wis., Nov. 27, 1971; s. Nickey Maxwell and Joyce Van Exel; 1 child, Nickey Maxwell III. Attended, Trinity Valley C.C., 1989-91, U. Cin., 1993. Profl. basketball player L.A. Lakers, 1993-98; guard Denver Nuggets, 1998-. Named to NBA All-Rookie 2d team, 1994. Office: Denver Nuggets 1000 Chopper Cir Denver CO 80204-5809

VANG, TIMOTHY TENG, religious organization administrator; b. Xieng Khouang, Laos, May 10, 1956; came to U.S., 1976; s. Nao Chai and Mai (Yang) V.; m. Chee Yang, Jan. 1, 1974 (dec. June 1975); m. Lydia Joua Xiong, July 7, 1979; children: Jennifer P., Nathan K., Victor C., Richard M., Tiffany P. BS in Missions, Cin. Bible Coll., 1984; MDiv in Ch. Ministries, Can. Theol. Sem., Regina, Sask., 1991; DMin in Ch. Leadership, Fuller Theol. Sem., Pasadena, Calif., 1999. Ordained to ministry Ch. of Christ, 1984, Christian and Missionary Alliance, 1986. Machine operator Pellet Co., Green Bay, Wis., 1977-78; mental health worker Inst. Human Design, Oshkosh, 1978-80; ch. planter Ch. of Christ, Eau Claire, 1984-86; pastor Boulder (Colo.) Hmong Alliance Ch., 1986-87; dir. Christian edn. Hmong dist. Christian and Missionary Alliance, Brighton, Colo., 1986-87, dist. supt., 1991-96; sr. pastor Sacramento Hmong Alliance, 1997—. Mem. bd. mgrs. Christian and Missionary Alliance, 1994-97; trustee Crown Coll., 1992-96. Organizer Fox Valley Lao/Hmong Assn., Appleton, Wis., 1979. Lt. U.S./Hmong Allied Army, 1971-75. Avocations: reading, writing, walking. Office: Sacramento Hmong Alliance Ch 9131 Locust St Elk Grove CA 95624-2017 E-mail: drtmvang@cs.com

VAN GORDER, CHRIS, medical executive; MS in Health Adminstrn., U. So. Calif., 1984, MS in Pub. Adminstrn., 1986. Chief of health care opers., exec. v.p. Scripps Health System, 1999—; pres., CEO Scripps Health, 2000—. Office: 4275 Campus Point Ct San Diego CA 92121-1513

VAN GUNDY, SEYMOUR DEAN, nematologist, plant pathologist, educator; b. Feb. 24, 1931; s. Robert C. and Margaret (Holloway) Van G.; m. Wilma C. Fanning, June 12, 1954; children: Sue Ann, Richard L. BA, Bowling Green State U., 1953; PhD, U. Wis., 1957. Asst. nematologist U. Calif., Riverside, 1957-63, assoc. prof., 1963-68, prof. nematology and plant pathology, 1968-73, assoc. dean rsch., 1968-70, vice chancellor rsch., 1970-72, chmn. dept. nematology, 1972-84; prof. nematology and plant pathology, assoc. dean rsch. Coll. Natural and Agrl. Scis., 1985-88, acting dean, 1986, interim dean, 1988-90, dean, 1990-93, emeritus dean, prof., 1993—. Former mem. editl. bd. Rev. de Nematologie, Jour. Nematology and Plant Disease; contbr. numerous articles to profl. jours. NSF fellow, Australia, 1965-66; grantee Rockefeller Found., Cancer Rsch., NSF, USDA. Fellow AAAS, Am. Phytopathol. Soc., Soc. Nematologists (editor-in-chief 1968-72, v.p. 1972-73, pres. 1973-74, hon. mem. 1997). Home: 1188 Pastern Rd Riverside CA 92506-5619 Office: U Calif Dept Nematology Riverside CA 92521-0001 E-mail: seymour.vangundy@ucr.edu

VAN HOESEN, BETH MARIE, artist, printmaker; b. Boise, Idaho, June 27, 1926; d. Enderse G. and Freda Marie (Soulen) Van H.; m. Mark Adams, Sept. 12, 1953. Student, Escuela Esmaralda, Mexico City, 1945, San Francisco Art Inst., , 1946, 47, 51, 52, Fontainbleau (France) Ecole des Arts, Acad. Julian and Acad., 5Grande Chaumier, Paris, 1948-51; B.A., Stanford U., 1948; postgrad., San Francisco State U., 1957-58. One-Woman shows include, De Young Mus., San Francisco, 1959, Achenbach Found., Calif. Palace Legion of Honor, San Francisco, 1961, 74, Santa Barbara (Calif.) Mus., 1963, 74, 76, Oakland (Calif.) Mus., 1980, John Berggruen Gallery, San Francisco, 1981, 83, 85, 88, 91; traveling exhibit Am. Mus. Assn., 1983-85; group shows include, Calif. State Fair, Sacramento, 1951 (award), Library of Congress, Washington, 1956, 57, San Francisco Mus. Modern Art, 70 (award), Boston Mus. Fine Arts, 1959, 60, 62, Pa. Acad. Fine Arts, Phila., 1959, 61, 63, 65, Achenbach Found., 1961 (award), Bklyn. Mus., 1962, 66, 68, 77, Continuing Am. Graphics, Osaka, Japan, 1970, Hawaii Nat. Print. Exhbn., Honolulu, 1980 (award), Oakland Mus., 1975 (award); represented in permanent collections, including, Achenbach Found., San Francisco, Fine Arts Mus., Bklyn. Mus., Mus. Modern Art, N.Y.C., Oakland Mus., San Francisco Mus. Modern Art, Victoria and Albert Mus., (London), Chgo. Art Inst., Cin. Mus., Portland (Oreg.) Art Mus. (Recipient award of Honor, San Francisco Art Commn. 1981); author: Collection of Wonderful Things, 1972, Beth Van Hoesen Creatures, 1987, Beth Van Hoesen: Works on Paper, 1995, Beth Van Hoesen Teddy Bears, 2000. Mem. Calif. Soc. Printmakers (award 1993), San Francisco Women Artists. Office: c/o John Berggruen 228 Grant Ave Fl 3D San Francisco CA 94108-4612

VAN HOLDE, KENSAL EDWARD, biochemistry educator; b. Eau Claire, Wis., May 14, 1928; s. Leonard John and Nettie (Hart) Van H.; m. Barbara Jean Watson, Apr. 11, 1950; children: Patricia, Mary, Stephen, David. B.S., U. Wis., 1949, Ph.D., 1952. Research chemist E.I. du Pont de Nemours & Co., 1952-55; research assoc. U. Wis., 1955-56; asst. prof. U. Wis. at Milw., 1956-57; mem. faculty U. Ill., Urbana, 1957-67; prof. dept. biochemistry and biophysics Oreg. State U., Corvallis, 1967; Am. Cancer Soc. rsch. prof., 1977-93; disting. prof., 1988-93; disting. prof. emeritus, 1993—; instr.-in-charge physiology course Marine Biol. Lab., Woods Hole, Mass., 1977-80; mem. research staff Centre des Recherches sur les Macromolecules, Strasbourg, France, 1964-65; mem. study sect. USPHS, 1966-69, 91—; staff Weizmann Inst., Israel, 1981, Lab. Léon Bnillouin, Saclay, France, 1989-90. Author: Physical Biochemistry, 1971, Chromatin, 1988; (with C. Mathews) Biochemistry, 1989, 2nd edit., 1995; editor: Biochmica Biophysica Acta, 1966-68; mem. editl. bd. jours. Biol. Chemistry, 1968-75, 81-87, 91-92, assoc. editor, 1992—, Biochemistry, 1973-76, 82-89; contbr. profl. jours. Trustee Marine Biol. Lab., Woods Hole, 1979-82, 84-92. NSF sr. postdoctoral fellow, 1964-65; Guggenheim fellow, 1973-74; European Molecular Biology Orgn. fellow, 1975; Humbolt fellow, 2000-01. Fellow AAAS; mem. NAS, Am. Soc. Biochemistry and Molecular Biology, Biophys. Soc., Am. Acad. Arts and Scis. Home: 229 NW 32nd St Corvallis OR 97330-5020 Office: Oreg State U Dept Biochemistry Corvallis OR 97331 E-mail: vanholdk@ucs.orst.edu

VAN HOOMISSEN, GEORGE ALBERT, state supreme court justice; b. Portland, Oreg., Mar. 7, 1930; s. Fred J. and Helen F. (Flanagan) Van H.; m. Ruth Madeleine Niedermeyer, June 4, 1960; children: Geroge T., Ruth Anne, Madeleine, Matthew. BBA, U. Portland, 1951; JD, Georgetown U., 1955, LLM in Labor Law, 1957; LLM in Jud. Adminstrn., U. Va., 1986. Bar: D.C. 1955, Oreg. 1956, Tex. 1971, U.S. Dist. Ct. Oreg. 1956, U.S. Ct. Mil. Appeals 1955, U.S. Ct. Customs and Patent Appeals 1955, U.S. Ct. Claims 1955, U.S. Ct. Appeals (9th cir.) 1956, U.S. Ct. Appeals (D.C. cir.) 1955, U.S. Supreme Ct. 1960. Law clk. for Chief Justice Harold J. Warner Oreg. Supreme Ct., 1955-56; Keigwin teaching fellow Georgetown Law Sch., 1956-57; dep. dist. atty. Multnomah County, Portland, 1957-59; pvt. practice Portland, 1959-62; dist. atty. Multnomah County, 1962-71; dean nat. coll. dist. attys., prof. law U. Houston, 1971-73; judge Cir. Ct., Portland, 1973-81, Oreg. Ct. Appeals, Salem, 1981-88; assoc. justice Oreg. Supreme Ct., Salem, 1988—. Adj. prof. Northwestern Sch. Law, Portland, Willamette U. Sch. Law, Portland State U.; mem. faculty Am. Acad. Judicial Edn., Nat. Judicial Coll.; Keigwin Teaching fellow Georgetown U.

Law Sch. Mem. Oreg. Ho. of Reps., Salem, 1959-62, chmn. house jud. com. With USMC, 1951-53; col. USMCR (ret.). Recipient Disting. Alumnus award U. Portland, 1972. Master Owen M. Panner Am. Inn of Ct.; mem. ABA, Oreg. State Bar, Tex. Bar Assn., Oreg. Law Inst. (bd. dirs.), Arlington Club, Multnomah Athletic Club, Univ. Club. Roman Catholic. E-mial. Office: Oreg Supreme Ct 2105 SW Elm St Portland OR 97201 E-mail: gavanhoomissen@qwest.net

VAN HORN, O. FRANK, retired counselor, consultant; b. Grand Junction, Colo., Apr. 16, 1926; s. Oertel F. and Alta Maude (Lynch) Van H.; m. Dixie Jeanne MacGregor, Feb. 1, 1947 (dec. Nov. 1994); m. Evelyn Anne Carroll, Mar. 22,1998; children: Evelyn, Dorothy. AA, Mesa Coll., 1961; BA, Western State Colo., 1963; MEd, Oreg. State U., 1969. Counselor, mgr. State of Oreg.-Employment, Portland and St. Helens, 1964-88; pvt. practice counselor and cons. St. Helens, 1988-96. Chair Task Force on Aging, Columbia County, 1977-79; advisor Western Interstate Commn. on Higher Edn., Portland, 1971, Concentrated Employment and Tng., St. Helens, 1977, County Planning Bd., Columbia County, Oreg., 1977-80, City Planning Bd., St. Helens, 1978, Youth Employment Coun., St. Helens, 1978, Task Force on Disadvantaged Youth, St. Helens, 1980; counselor Career Mgmt. Specialists Internat.; instr. Portland C.C. Mem. ACA, Oreg. Counseling Assn., Internat. Assn. Pers. in Employment Svc. (Outstanding Achievement award 1975), Nat. Employment Counselors Assn. Democrat. Home: 1364 Mesa Ave Grand Junction CO 81501-7632

VAN HORNE, JAMES CARTER, economist, educator; b. South Bend, Ind., Aug. 6, 1935; s. Ralph and Helen (McCarter) Van H.; m. Mary A. Roth, Aug. 27, 1960; children: Drew, Stuart, Stephen. AB, De Pauw U., 1957, DSc (hon.), 1986; MBA, Northwestern U., 1961, PhD, 1964. Comml. lending rep. Continental Ill. Nat. Bank, Chgo., 1958-62; prof. fin. Stanford U. Grad. Sch. Bus., 1965-75, A.P. Giannini prof. fin., 1976—, assoc. dean, 1973-75, 76-80; dep. asst. sec. Dept. Treasury, 1975-76. Bd. dirs. United Calif. Bank, BB&K Internat. Fund, BB&K Fund Group, EFTC Corp.; chmn. Montgomery St. Income Securities; commr. workers compensation Rate Making Study Commn., State of Calif., 1990-92. Author: Function and Analysis of Capital Market Rates, 1970, Financial Market Rates and Flows, 2001; co-author: Fundamentals of Financial Management, 2001; assoc. editor Jour. fin. and Quantitative Analysis, 1969-85, Jour. Fin., 1971-73, Jour. Fixed Income, 1990—. Mem. bd. trustees DePauw U., 1989-96. With AUS, 1957. Mem. Am. Fin. Assn. (past pres., dir.), Western Fin. Assn. (past pres., dir.), Fin. Mgmt. Assn. Home: 2000 Webster St Palo Alto CA 94301-4049 Office: Stanford U Grad Sch Bus Stanford CA 94305

VAN HORNE, R. RICHARD, oil company executive; b. Milw., June 7, 1931; s. Ralph Rupert and Edna (Benson) Van H.; m. Elizabeth Whitaker Dixon, July 3, 1954; children— Ann Van Horne Arms, R. Ross, Margaret Van Horne Shuya B.B.A., U. Wis., 1953. Various positions Anaconda Am. Brass Co., Milw. and Kenosha, Wis., 1955-72, pres., chief exec. officer Waterbury, Conn., 1972-74, Anaconda Aluminum Co., Louisville, 1974-82; sr. v.p. pub. affairs Atlantic Richfield Co., Los Angeles, 1982-85. Bd. visitors Sch. Bus., U. Wis., Madison; mem. U. Wis. Found.; trustee Louisville Cmty. Found. 1st lt. U.S. Army, 1953-55 Sr. fellow Bellarmine Coll. Mem. Mchts. and Mfrs. Assn. (bd. dirs. 1983-85), Am. Petroleum Inst., Nat. Planning Assn. (com. on new Am. realities 1982-84), Bascom Hill Soc., Minocqua Country Club, Sara Bay Country Club. Republican. Episcopalian. Avocations: golf; reading; gardening. Home: Unit 261 3040 Grand Bay Blvd Longboat Key FL 34228-4401 Office: Atlantic Richfield Co 515 S Flower St Ste 3700 Los Angeles CA 90071-2201

VAN HORSSEN, CHARLES ARDEN, manufacturing executive; b. Mpls., June 28, 1944; s. Arden Darrel and Margaret E. (Ellingsen) V H.; m. Mary Katherine Van Kempen, Sept. 11, 1967 (div. 1975); children: Lisa, Jackie; m. Mary Ann Pashuta, Aug. 11, 1983; children: Vanessa, Garrett. BSEE, U. Minn., 1966. Design engr. Sperry Univac, Mpls., 1966-68, sr. project engr. Salt Lake City, 1975-80; systems engr. EMR Computer, Mpls., 1968-75; pres. A&B Industries Inc., Phoenix, 1980—, Axian Tech Inc., Phoenix. Patentee in field. Mem. Ariz. Tooling and Machining Assn. (bd. dirs., v.p. 1987-89, pres. 1989-91). Republican. Episcopalian. Office: Axian Tech Inc 21622 N 14th Ave Phoenix AZ 85027-2841 E-mail: van@darkmill.com

VANHOWE, WILLIAM REMI, lawyer; b. Denver, June 25, 1948; s. Joseph L. and Mildred VanHowe; m. Gemma VanHowe, Feb. 7, 1971; 3 children. BS, Colo. State U., 1970; JD, U. Idaho, 1976. Bar: Idaho 1976, U.S. Dist. Ct. Idaho 1976, U.S. Dist. Ct. (ea. dist.) Wis. 1998, U.S. Ct. Appeals (9th cir.) 1983. Law clk. to judge U.S. Dist. Ct. Idaho, Boise, 1976-78; assoc. Quane, Smith, Howard & Hull, Boise, 1978-81, Langroise, Sullivan & Smylie, Boise, 1981-83; asst. U.S. atty. U.S. Dept. of Justice, Boise, 1983-87; U.S. atty. Dist. of Idaho, 1984-85; assoc. gen. counsel Boise Cascade Corp., 1987—. Served with U.S. Army, 1970-72 Mem. ABA, Fed. Bar Assn., Idaho Bar Assn., Idaho Assn. Def. Counsel, Def. Rsch. Inst., Am. Judicature Soc. Republican Avocations: skiing, fishing, golf. Office: Boise Cascade Corp PO Box 50 Boise ID 83728-0050

VAN KIRK, JOHN ELLSWORTH, retired cardiologist; b. Dayton, Ohio, Jan. 13, 1942; s. Herman Corwin and Dorothy Louise (Shafer) Van K.; m. Patricia L. Davis, June 19, 1966 (div. Dec. 1982); 1 child, Linnea Gray. BA cum laude, DePauw U., Greencastle, Ind., 1963; BS, Northwestern U., Chgo., 1964, MD with distinction, 1967. Diplomate Am. Bd. Internal Medicine, Am. Bd. Internal Medicine subspecialty in cardiovasc. disease; cert. Nat. Bd. Med. Examiners. Intern Evanston (Ill.) Hosp., 1967-68; staff assoc. Nat. Inst. of Allergy & Infectious Diseases., Bethesda, Md., 1968-70; resident internal medicine U. Mich. Med. Ctr., Ann Arbor, 1970-72, fellow in cardiology, 1972-74, instr. internal medicine, 1973-74; staff cardiologist Mills Meml. Hosp., San Mateo, Calif., 1974—, vice-chief medicine, 1977-78, dir. critical care, 1978-96, critical care utilizaton rev., 1988-99, dir. pacemaker clinic, 1976-99; staff cardiologist Mills-Peninsula Hosp., Burlingame, 1996-99; ret., 1999. Dir. transitional care, 1996-99; mem. courtesy staff Sequoia Hosp., 1984—, ret., 1999. Contbr. rsch. articles to profl. jours. Recipient 1st prize in landscaping Residential Estates, State of Calif., 1977. Fellow Am. Coll. Cardiology; mem. AMA (Physician's Recognition award 1968, 72, 75, 77, 80, 82, 85, 87, 89, 93, 97, 2000), Calif. Med. Assn., San Mateo County Med. Soc., Am. Heart Assn., San Mateo County Heart Assn. (bd. dirs. 1975-78, mem. Bay area rsch. com. 1975-76, mem. edn. com. 1975-77, pres.-elect 1976-77, pres. 1977-79), Alpha Omega Alpha. Republican. Mem. United Brethren Ch. Avocations: gardening, computer science, tennis, woodworking, electronics, ham radio. Home: 235 Amherst Ave San Mateo CA 94402-2201 E-mail: John-VanKirk@msn.com

VAN LINT, VICTOR ANTON JACOBUS, physicist; b. Samarinda, Indonesia, May 10, 1928; came to U.S., 1937; s. Victor J. and Margaret (DeJager) Van L.; m. M. June Woolhouse, June 10, 1950; children: Lawrence, Kenneth, Linda, Karen. BS, Calif. Inst. Tech., Pasadena, 1950, PhD, 1954. Instr. Princeton (N.J.) U., 1954-55; staff mem. Gen. Atomic, San Diego, 1957-74; physics cons. San Diego, 1974-75; staff mem. Mission Research Corp., San Diego, 1975-82, 83-91; cons., 1991—; spl. asst. to dep. dir. sci. and tech. Def. Nuclear Agy., Washington, 1982-83. Author, editor: Radiation Effects in Electronic Materials, 1976; contbr. articles to profl. jours. Served with U.S. Army, 1955-57. Recipient Pub. Service award NASA, 1981. Fellow IEEE. Republican. Mem. United Ch. of Christ. Home and Office: 1032 Skylark Dr La Jolla CA 92037-7733

VANLUVANEE, DONALD ROBERT, electronics executive; b. Neosho, Mo., July 3, 1944; s. Harry Earl and Joyce Elizabeth (Skillen) VanLuvanee; m. Lynne Marie Hodge; children: Kenneth Richard, Daryl Robert. BSEE, Rensselaer Poly. Inst., 1966, MEEE, 1972. Sr. engr., br. mgr. Tex. Instruments, Dallas, 1972-80; v.p. product design, research and devel. Syntex Dental Products, Valley Forge, Pa., 1980-82; v.p. research and devel. Kulicke and Soffa Industries, Inc., Willow Grove, 1982, v.p. domestic ops., 1982-84, pres., chief operating officer, 1984—, also bd. dirs. Contbr. articles to profl. jours.; patentee in field. Varsity coach Methacton Ice Hockey Assn., Eagleville, Pa.; head coach, exec. v.p. Colonials of Valley Forge Ice Hockey Assn. Mem. Nat. Assn. Corp. Dirs., Am. Mgmt. Assn., IEEE. Avocations: fishing, model aircraft, folk guitar and banjo, ice hockey. Office: ELECTRO SCIENTIFIC INDUSTRIES, INC 13900 NW SCIENCE PARK DR. PORTLAND OR 97229-5497

VAN MAERSSEN, OTTO L. aerospace engineer, consulting firm executive; b. Amsterdam, The Netherlands, Mar. 2, 1919; came to U.S., 1946; s. Adolph L. and Maria Wilhelmina (Edelmann) Van M.; m. Hortensia Maria Velasquez, Jan. 7, 1956; children: Maria, Patricia, Veronica, Otto, Robert. BS in Chem. Engring., U. Mo., Rolla, 1949. Registered profl. engr., Tex., Mo. Petroleum engr. Mobil Oil, Caracas, Venezuela, 1949-51; sr. reservoir engr. Gulf Oil, Ft. Worth and San Tome, Venezuela, 1952-59; acting dept. mgr. Sedco of Argentina, Comodoro Rivadavia, 1960-61; export planning engr. LTV Aerospace and Def., Dallas, 1962-69, R & D adminstr. ground transp. div., 1970-74, engr. specialist new bus. programs, 1975-80; mgr. cost and estimating San Francisco and Alaska, 1981-84; owner OLVM Cons. Engrs., Walnut Creek, Calif., 1984—. Cons. LTV Aerospace and Def., Dallas, 1984—. Served with Brit. Army. Intelligence, 1945, Germany. Mem. Soc. Petroleum Engrs. (Legion of Honor), Toastmasters (sec.-treas. Dallas chpt. 1963-64), Pennywise Club (treas. Dallas chpt. 1964-67). Democrat. Roman Catholic. Avocations: travel, photography. Home and Office: OLVM Cons Engrs 1649 Arbutus Dr Walnut Creek CA 94595-1705 E-mail: ottovm@home.com

VAN MASON, RAYMOND, dancer, choreographer; Prin. dancer Ballet West, Salt Lake City; ballet master, choreographer Ballet Pacifica, Irvine, Calif., 1999—. Dance performances include Swan Lake, Gisells, Sleeping Beauty, Romeo & Juliet, Anna Karenina, The Nutcracker, Carmina Burana, White Mourning, Ophelia; choreographer: Requiem: A Liturgical Ballet, 1990, A Pilgrimage: A Liturgical Ballet, 1992, Lady Guinevere, Chameleon, Carmina Burana, Symphony # 7, 1992, others. Office: Ballet Pacifica 1824 Kaiser Ave Irvine CA 92614-5708

VAN MOLS, BRIAN, publishing executive; b. L.A., July 1, 1931; s. Pierre Matthias and Frieda Carthyll (MacArthur) M.; m. Barbara Jane Rose, Oct. 1, 1953 (dec. 1968); children— Cynthia Lee, Matthew Howard, Brian; m. Nancy Joan Martell, June 11, 1977; children— Thomas Bentley, Cynthia Bentley, Kristi A.B. in English, Miami U., Oxford, Ohio, 1953. Media supr. McCann-Erickson Inc., 1955-58; salesman Kelly Smith Co., 1959; with sales Million Market Newspaper Inc., 1959-63; sales mgr. Autoproducts Mag., 1964; sr. salesman True Mag., 1965-68, Look Mag., 1969-70; regional advt. dir. Petersen Pub. Co., Los Angeles, 1971-74; pub. Motor Trend, 1982-84; nat. automotive mktg. mgr. Playboy Enterprises, Inc., N.Y.C., 1984-85, nat. sales mgr., 1985—; western advt. dir. Playboy mag., 1985-86; assoc. pub., advt. dir. Cycle World CBS, Inc., Newport Beach, Calif., 1974-81, pub., 1981; v.p., advt. dir. Four Wheeler Mag., Canoga Pk., 1986-88; v.p., dir. advt. western div. Gen. Media, Inc., 1988-91; v.p., dir. new bus. devel. Paisano Pub., Inc., Agoura Hills, Calif., 1991-92; dir. mktg. Crown Publs., 1993-94; exec. v.p. Voice Mktg. Inc., Thousand Oaks, Calif., 1994, DMR The Reis Co., Tustin, 1995-96; COO Mesa Exhaust Products, Inc., Costa Mesa, 1996-97. Mktg. dir. McMullen Argus Pub., Inc., Anaheim, Calif., 1998-2001. Served with U.S. Army, 1953-55 Mem. Los Angeles Advt. Club, Adcraft Club Detroit, Advt. Sportsmen of N.Y. Republican. Episcopalian Home: 57 St Andrews Cir Durango CO 81301 E-mail: evanmols@frontier.net

VANNIX, C(ECIL) ROBERT, programmer, systems analyst; b. Glendale, Calif., June 14, 1953; s. Cecil H. Jr. and Gloria Jenny (Zappia) V.; married, 1980; children: Robert Jeremy, Leslie Ann. AS in Plant Mgmt., BS in Indsl. Arts, Loma Linda U., 1977; AS in Info. Systems, Ventura City Coll., 1985. Instr. indsl. arts Duarte (Calif.) High Sch., 1977-79, Oxnard (Calif.) High Sch., 1979-81; computer cons. Litton Data Comand Systems, Agoura, Calif., 1976-81, sr. engr. instr., 1981-85; computer cons. McLaughlin Research Corp., Camarillo, 1976-77, sr. program analyst, 1985-88, Computer Software Analysts, Camarillo, 1988-90; sr. systems analyst, mgr. S/W systems devel. V.C. Systems, 1990—. Recipient Spl. Achievement award One Way Singers, Glendale, 1975. Mem. Apple PI Computer Club, Litton Computer Club (pres. 1975-76). Republican. Adventist. Avocations: woodworking, automotives, photography, skiing. Home and Office: 2580 Rose Ln Camarillo CA 93012-5125 E-mail: bvannix@vcsystems.com

VAN SCHOONENBERG, ROBERT G. lawyer; b. Madison, Wis., Aug. 18, 1946; s. John W. and Ione (Henning) Schoonenberg. BA, Marquette U., 1968; MBA, U. Wis., 1972; JD, U. Mich., 1974. Bar: Calif. 1975, Fla. 1976. Atty. Gulf Oil Corp., Pitts., 1974-81; exec. v.p., gen. counsel, sec. Avery Dennison Corp., Pasadena, Calif., 1981—. Judge pro tem Pasadena Mcpl. Ct., 1987-89. Dir., v.p. fin. adminstrn. Am. Cancer Soc., San Gabriel Vally Unit, 1987—; v.p., treas., dir., v.p. investments Pasadena Symphony Assn.; bd. dirs. Pasadena Recreation and Parks Found., 1983-84; mem. Pasadena Citizens Task Force on Crime Control, 1983-84; dir. Boy Scouts, San Gabriel Valley Coun., dir. public coun.; bd. dirs. Verugo Hills Hosp. Found.; trustee Southwestern U. Sch. Law. Mem. ABA, Am. Corp. Counsel Assn. (bd. dirs.), Am. Soc. Corp. Secs. (bd. dirs., pres. Southern Calif. chpt.), L.A. County Bar Assn. (past chair, corp. law dept. sect.), Corp. Counsel Inst. (bd. govs.), Jonathon Club, Flint Canyon Tennis Club, The Calif. Club, Wis. Union. Clubs: Athletic (Pasadena); Wis. Union. Office: Avery Dennison Corp 150 N Orange Grove Blvd Pasadena CA 91103-3534

VAN SICKLE, FREDERICK L. federal judge; b. 1943; m. Jane Bloomquist. BS, U. Wis., 1965; JD, U. Wash., 1968. Ptnr. Clark & Van Sickle, 1970-75; prosecuting atty. Douglas County, Waterville, Wash., 1971-75; judge State of Wash. Superior Ct., Grant and Douglas counties, 1975-79, Chelan and Douglas Counties, 1979-91, U.S. Dist. Ct. (ea. dist.) Wash., Spokane, 1991—. Co-chair rural ct. com. Nat. Conf. State Trial Judges, 1987-91. 1st lt. U.S. Army, 1968-70. Mem. ABA (nat. conf. fed. judges jud. adminstrn.), Am. Adjudicature Soc., Wash. State Bar Assn., Masons (pres. Badger mountain lodge 1982-83), Scottish Rite, Spokane Rotary, Shriners. Office: US Dist Cts US Courthouse PO Box 2209 920 W Riverside Ave Rm 914 Spokane WA 99201-1010

VANSICKLE, SHARON DEE, public relations executive; b. Portland, Oreg., Nov. 10, 1955; BA in Mktg. and Journalism, U. Portland, 1976, postgrad., 1977-79. Reporter Willamette Week, Portland, 1976-77; dir. pub. rels. Tektronix, Portland, 1977-83; prin. pub. rels. KVD Pub. Rels., Portland, 1983-98; CEO KVO Pub. Rslc., Portland, 1999—. Chmn. Pinnacle Worldwide, bd. dirs. pub. rels. coun. Vice chair Portland Met. Area Reg. Arts and Culture Coun.; bd. dirs. CPRF, The Oreg. Entrepreneur's Forum, Dean's Coun. on Arts & Sci., U. Portland. Mem. Pub. Rels. Soc. Am. (pres. Portland chpt. 1994-95, chair-elect N. Pac. dist., mem. counsilor's acad., bd mem. and chair tech. com. 1999 Spring conf.). Office: KVO Pub Rels 200 SW Market St Ste 1400 Portland OR 97201-5741

VAN VALKENBURG, EDGAR WALTER, lawyer; b. Seattle, Jan. 8, 1953; s. Edgar Walter and Margaret Catherine (McKenna) Van V.; m. Turid L. Owren, Sept. 29, 1990; children: Ingrid Catherine, Andrew Owren. BA, U. Wash., 1975; JD summa cum laude, Willamette Coll. of Law, 1978; LLM, Columbia U., 1984. Bar: Oreg. 1978, U.S. Dist. Ct. Oreg. 1979, U.S. Ct. Appeals (9th cir.) 1980. Law clk. to assoc. justice Oreg. Supreme Ct., Salem, 1978-79; assoc. Stoel, Rives, Boley, Fraser & Wyse, Portland, Oreg., 1979-82, 84-86; ptnr. Stoel Rives LLP, Portland, 1986—; instr. Columbia U., N.Y.C., 1982-84. Bd. dirs. Portland Oregon Sports Authority. Editor-in-chief: Williamette Law Jour. 1977-78. Bd. dirs., chmn. Multnomah County Legal Aid, 1997-98; bd. dirs. Oreg. Legal Aid, 1998—. Mem. ACLU (pres. Oreg. chpt. 1991-93), Oreg. State Bar (chmn. antitrust sect. 1989-90, mem. Ho. of Dels. 1996-98). Office: Stoel Rives LLP 900 SW 5th Ave Ste 2300 Portland OR 97204-1229 E-mail: wvanvalkenburg@stoel.com

VAN WEELDEN, THOMAS H. waste industry company executive; b. 1955; With Waste Mgmt.; co-owner hauling co. and 3 landfills, nr. Chgo.; exec. v.p. Allied Waste Industries, Inc., Houston, 1997-97, pres., COO Phoenix, 1992-97, CEO, pres. Scottsdale, Ariz., 1997—, chmn., 1998—, also bd. dirs. Bd. dirs. Reid Plastics, Inc. Office: Allied Waste Industries Inc Ste 100 15880 N Greenway Hayden Loop Scottsdale AZ 85260-1649

VARAIYA, PRAVIN P. electrical engineer; Mem. tech. staff Bell Labs., 1962-63; instr. MIT, Fed. U. Rio de Janeiro; prof. econ. U. Calif., Berkeley, 1975-92, James Fife prof. elec. engring. and computer scis., Nortel Networks disting. prof. elec. engring./computer sci. Dir. Calif. PATH. Mem. editl. bd. Transp. Rsch. Part C, Discrete Event Dynamical Sys: Theory and Applications, Jour. Econ. Dynamics and Control, (Birkhauser series) Progress in Sys. and Control Theory; contbr. numerous articles to profl. jours. Guggenheim fellow; Miller Rsch. prof. Fellow IEEE. Office: Dept Elec Engring U Calif 271M Cory Hall Berkeley CA 94720 Fax: 510-642-6330. E-mail: varaiya@eecs.berkeley.edu

VARANASI, USHA, environmental scientist; b. Bassien, Burma; BSc, U. Bombay, 1961; MS, Calif. Inst. Technology, 1964; PhD in Chemistry, U. Wash., 1968. Rsch. assoc. lipid biochemistry Oceanic Inst., Oahu, Hawaii, 1969-71; assoc. rsch. prof. Seattle U., Oahu, 1971-74; supr. rsch. chemist and task mgr. NOAA/NMFS Northwest Fisheries Sci. Ctr., 1975-87, dir. Environ. Conservation Divsn., 1987-93; rsch. prof. chemistry Seattle U., 1975—; sci dir. NOAA/NMFS N.W. Fisheries Sci. Ctr., 1994—. Vis. scientist Pioneer Rsch. Unit, NOAA/NMFS Northwest Fisheries Sci. Ctr., nat. Marine Fisheries Svc., nat. oceanic & Atmospheric Adminstrn., Wash., 1969-72; from affil. assoc. to affil. prof. chem. U. Wash., 1984—. Recipient Gold medal U.S. Dept. Commerce, 1993, Presdl. Meritorious Exec. Rank award, 2000. Mem. AAAS. Office: Northwest Fisheries Sci Ctr 2725 Montlake Blvd E Seattle WA 98112-2097

VARAT, JONATHAN D. dean, law educator; b. 1945; BA, U. Pa., Phila., 1967, JD, 1972. Law clk. to judge Walter Mansfield U.S. Ct. Appeals (2d cir.), N.Y.C., 1972-73; law clk. to justice Byron White U.S. Supreme Ct., Washington, 1973-74; assoc. O'Melveny & Myers, Los Angeles, 1974-76; acting prof. UCLA, 1976-81, prof., 1981—, assoc. dean, 1982-83, 91-92; dean UCLA Sch. Law, 1998—. Office: UCLA Sch Law 405 Hilgard Ave Los Angeles CA 90095-9000

VARELA, VICKI, state official; b. Aurora, Colo. m. Brett J. DelPorto: 2 children. Student, U. Colo., 1976; BA in English, Brigham Young U., 1978. Reporter Associated Press, Denver, Cheyenne, N.Y.C., 1978-79, Deseret News, Salt Lake City, 1979-83, edn. editor, 1983-86; asst. commr. higher edn. for pub. affairs Utah Higher Education Commn., Salt Lake City, 1986-92; dep. chief of staff to gov. State of Utah, Salt Lake City, 1992—. Exec. dir. Olympics Referendum Campaign, Salt Lake City, 1989. Vol. worker with Republican Inst. to train political candidates and campaign mgrs. in developing democracies (helped conduct seminar in Veronezh, Russia, 1995); mem. comty adv. com. First Presbyn. Ch. Restoration/ Preservation Project; active in European Comty. Visitors' Program, 1996; studied in Germany, Spain, Brussels and Great Britain. Office: Office Gov 210 State Capitol Salt Lake City UT 84114

VARGA, JEANNE-MARIE, women's healthcare company executive; BS in Med. Tech., Towson State U.; MA in Mgmt. and Supervision, Ctrl. Mich. U. Sr. sci. reviewer Ctr. for Devices and Radiol. Health, FDA, 1980-83; mgr. U.S. regulatory affairs Sorin Biomedica S.P.A., 1983-87; dir. quality assurance and regulatory affairs Baxter Diagnostics, Inc., 1987-92; v.p. worldwide regulatory and quality Sanofi Diagnostics Pasteur, Inc., 1992-98; v.p. regulatory affairs and quality sys. Women First HealthCare, Inc., San Diego, 1998—. Office: Women First HealthCare Inc 12220 El Camino Real Ste 400 San Diego CA 92130-2091 Fax: 619-509-1353

VARGAS, DIANA LISA, television station executive; BA in Mass Media, Hunter Coll., 1983. Acct. exec. Sta. KTTV, L.A., 1988-90, sales, 1990-91, local sales mgr., 1991-94, v.p. gen. sales mgr., 1994-97, v.p. gen. mgr., 1997—. Office: Sta KTTV 1999 S Bundy Dr Los Angeles CA 90025-5203

VARGO, RICHARD JOSEPH, accounting educator, writer; BS, Marietta Coll., 1963; MBA, Ohio U., 1965; PhD, U. Wash., 1969. CPA, Calif. Asst. prof. acctg. Sch. Bus. Adminstrn. U. So. Calif., 1968-71; assoc. prof. acctg., chair dept. acctg. Sch. Bus. Adminstrn. Coll. William and Mary, 1971-73; assoc. prof. Coll. Bus. Adminstrn. U. Tex., Arlington, 1973-74, assoc. dean for grad. studies Coll. Bus. Adminstrn., 1974-76, prof. acctg. Coll. Bus. Adminstrn., 1976-81; prof. acctg. Eberhardt Sch. Bus. U. of Pacific, 1981—. Adj. prof. Family Practice and Cmty. Medicine, U. Tex. Southwestern Med. Sch., Dallas, 1977-81; adj. prof. acctg. McGeorge Sch. Law, U. of Pacific, 1982-93; spkr. in field. Author: Effective Church Accounting, 1989; co-author: (with Paul Dierks) Readings in Governmental and Nonprofit Accounting, 1982, (with Lanny Solomon and Larry Walther) Principles of Accounting, 1983, 5th edit., 1996, (with Lanny Solomon and Larry Walther) Financial Accounting, 1985, 4th edit., 1996; contbr. articles to profl. jours. Recipient grant U. Tex. Sys. Organized Rsch. Funds, 1973-74, 75-76, grant U. of Pacific and Kosciuszko Found., 1987, grant Kemper Found., 1989, grant U.S. Dept. Edn. and Rockefeller Bros. Found., 1991. Mem. Beta Alpha Psi (pres. Ohio U. chpt. 1964-65), Beta Gamma Sigma, Phi Kappa Phi. Office: Univ Pacific Eberhardt School Bus Weber Hall Rm 201-13 Stockton CA 95211-0001

VARIAN, HAL RONALD, economics educator; b. Wooster, Ohio, Mar. 18, 1947; s. Max Ronald and Elaine Catherine (Shultzman) V.; m. Carol Johnston, Nov. 1986. S.B., MIT, 1969; M.A., Ph.D. (NSF fellow), U. Calif.-Berkeley, 1973. Asst. prof. econs. MIT, 1973-77; prof. U. Mich., 1977-95, prof. fin., 1983-95, Reuben Kempf prof. econs., 1984-95; prof. sch. bus., dean sch. info. mgmt. and sys. U. Calif., Berkeley, 1995—, Class of 1944 prof., 1996—. Siena chair in econs., U. Siena, Italy, 1990. Author: Microeconomic Analysis, 1978, Intermediate Microeconomics, 1987, Information Rules, 1998; co-editor Am. Econ. Rev., 1987-90. Guggenheim fellow, 1979-80; Fulbright scholar, 1990 Fellow AAAS, Econometric Soc.; mem. Am. Econ. Soc. Home: 1198 Estates Dr Lafayette CA 94549-2749 Office: U Calif Sims 102 South Hl Berkeley CA 94720-0001

VARKER, BRUCE, real estate development executive; CFO Shea Homes, Walnut, Calif., 1998—. Office: J F Shea Co Inc PO Box 489 Walnut CA 91788-0489

VARLEY, HERBERT PAUL, Japanese language and cultural history educator; b. Paterson, N.J., Feb. 8, 1931; s. Herbert Paul and Katharine L. (Norcross) V.; m. Betty Jane Geiskopf, Dec. 24, 1960 B.S., Lehigh U., 1952; M.A., Columbia U., 1961, Ph.D., 1964; DHL (hon.), Lehigh U., 1988. Asst. prof. U. Hawaii, Honolulu, 1964-65; asst. prof. dept. East Asian Langs. and Cultures Columbia U., N.Y.C., 1965-69, assoc. prof., 1969-75, prof., 1975-94, prof. emeritus Japanese history, 1994—, chmn. dept. East Asian Langs. and Cultures, 1983-89. Sen Soshitsu XV prof. Japanese Cultural History U. Hawaii, spring 1991-93, 94—. Author: The Onin War, 1967, The Samurai, 1970, Imperial Restoration in Medieval Japan, 1971, Japanese Culture, 1973, 4th edit., 2000, A Chronicle of Gods and Sovereigns, 1980, Tea in Japan: Essays on the History of Chanoyu, 1989, Warriors of Japan, As Portrayed in the War Tales, 1994. Bd. govs. Japanese Cultural Ctr. of Hawaii. Served with U.S. Army, 1952-54, Japan Recipient Imperial Decoration Govt. Japan, Order of Rising Sun, Gold Rays With Rosette Mem. Assn. Asian Studies, Japan Soc., Soc. Am. Magicians (pres. local chpt. 1983-84) Avocations: sleight of hand magic; piano. Home: 38 S Judd St Apt 15B Honolulu HI 96817-2609 Office: U Hawaii History Dept Sakamaki Hall A 203 2530 Dole St Honolulu HI 96822-2303 E-mail: pvarley@hawaii.edu

VARNER, CARLTON A. lawyer; b. Creston, Iowa, July 14, 1947; BA, U. Iowa, 1969; JD magna cum laude, U. Minn., 1972. Bar: Calif. 1972. Mng. ptnr. Sheppard Mullin Richter & Hampton, L.A., 1991-98. Author: The Microsoft Case, Exclusionary Innovation, 1998, California Antitrust Law, 1999; co-author: Antitrust Law Developments, 4th edit., 1998. Mem. ABA, L.A. County Bar Assn. (chmn. antitrust sect. 1993-94). Office: Sheppard Mullin Richter & Hampton LLP 333 S Hope St Fl 48 Los Angeles CA 90071-1406 Fax: 213-620-1398. E-mail: cvarner@smrh.com

VARSHAVSKY, ALEXANDER JACOB, molecular biologist; b. Moscow, Nov. 8, 1946; came to U.S., 1977; s. Jacob M. and Mary B. (Zeitlin) V.; m. Vera Bingham, Aug. 30, 1990; children: Roman, Anna, Victoria. BS in Chemistry, Moscow State U., 1970; PhD in Biochemistry, Inst. of Molecular Biology, Moscow, 1973. Asst. prof. dept. biology MIT, Cambridge, 1977-80, assoc. prof., 1980-86, prof., 1986-92; Smits prof. cell biology Calif. Inst. Tech., Pasadena, 1992—. Author more than 150 articles in the field of genetics and biochemistry; holder 14 patents. Recipient Novartis-Drew award Novartis, 1998, Merit award NIH, 1998, Gairdner Internat. award, 1999, Shubitz prize U. Chgo., 2000, Hoppe-Seyler award (Germany), 2000, Sloan prize GM Cancer Rsch. Found., 2000, Lasker award, 2000, Merck award Am. Soc. Biochemistry and Molecular Biology, 2001, Pasarow Found. award, 2001, Wolf prize Wolf Found., 2001, Horowitz prize Columbia U., 2001. Mem. AAAS, NAS, Am. Acad. Microbiology, Am. Philos. Soc. Achievements include discoveries in the fields of DNA replication, chromosome structure, ubiquitin system, and intracellular protein turnover. Office: Calif Inst Tech Divsn Biology Pasadena CA 91125-0001

VASCHE, MARK, newspaper editor; Exec. editor Modesto (Calif.) Bee, 1997—. Office: Modesto Bee PO Box 5256 Modesto CA 95352-5256

VASCONCELLOS, JOHN, state legislator; b. San Jose, Calif., May 11, 1932; s. John and Teresa (Jacobs) V. BS, Santa Clara U., 1954, LLB, 1959. Bar: Calif. 1960. Assoc. Ruffo & Chadwick, San Jose, 1959; travel sec. Gov. Pat Brown, Sacramento, 1960; mem. Calif. State Legislature, Sacramento, 1966-96, chmn. ways and means com., 1980-96; mem. CA State Senate, 1996—. Chmn. Assembly Dem. Econ. Prosperity Team, Sacramento, 1992—. Author: A Liberating Vision, 1979; developer program Toward a Healthier State. Founder Calif. Task Force to Promote Self Esteem and Personal and Social Responsibility, 1987; mem. Strategic Action Agenda--Toward a Calif./Japan Partnership, 1993. 1st lt. U.S. Army, 1954-56. Named Legislator of the Decade, Calif. C.C. Faculty Assn., 1980, Hi-Tech Legislator of Yr., Am. Electronics Assn., 1983, more than 100 other awards. Avocations: racquetball, reading. Office: CA State Senate State Capitol Rm 4074 San Jose CA 95113

VASEY, WILLIAM JOSEPH, state legislator, college program director; b. Saratoga, Wyo., Jan. 13, 1939; s. George Oliver and Marjorie Elizabeth (Munz) V.; m. Judith Lesley Bakken, Aug. 21, 1968; children: Susan, Michael, Richard. BS, Valley City State Coll., 1969; MEd, U. Wyo., 1984. Tchr. Zeeland (N.D.) Pub. Schs., 1968-69; salesman 3M Co., Bismark, N.D., 1969-70; tchr. Saratoga Pub. Schs., 1970-73; supr. Peter Kiewit Sons, Sheridan, Wyo., 1973-83; Kellogg Grant coord. Carbon County Libr., Rawlins, 1984-89; dir. Carbon County Higher Edn. Ctr., Rawlins, 1989—; mem. Wyo. Senate, Dist. 11, Cheyenne, 1998-. State rep. Wyo. State Legislature, Cheyenne, 1989—. Bd. dirs. Spl. Olympics, Casper, Wyo., 1992—, COVE Family Violence Protection, Rawlins, 1991—, devel. disabilities workshop ARK Industries, Laramie, 1989—; mem. Rawlins City Coun., 1988-89; trustee Carbon County Meml. Hosp., Rawlins, 1985-89, Sch. Dist. 2, Saratoga, 1980-84. Mem. Wyo. Assn. Continuing, Community and Adult Edn. (Disting. Svc. award 1993). Democrat. Avocations: golf, reading, hiking. Office: Carbon County Higher Edn Ctr 1717 Loch Ness Dr Rawlins WY 82301-4238

VAUGHN, JAMES ENGLISH, JR. neurobiologist; b. Kansas City, Mo., Sept. 17, 1939; s. James and Sue Katherine (Vaughn); m. Christine Singleton, June 18, 1961; children: Stephanie, Stacey. BA, Westminster Coll., 1961; PhD, UCLA, 1965. Postdoctoral rsch. fellow in brain rsch. U. Edinburgh, Scotland, 1965-66; asst. prof. Boston U. Sch. Medicine, 1966-70; head sect. molecular neuromorphology Beckman Rsch. Inst., City of Hope, Duarte, Calif., 1970—, pres. rsch. staff, 1986, chmn. divsn. neurosci., 1987—2001. Editor (assoc. editor): (Jour.) Jour. Neurocytology, 1978—86;contbr. articles to profl. jours.; mem. editl. bd. (Jour.) Synapse, 1986—, reviewer for Jour. Comparative Neurology, 1974—, Brain Research, 1976—. Fellow Neurosci. Rsch. Program, 1969; grantee rsch. grantee, NIH, 1969—, NSF, 1983—87. Office: City of Hope Beckman Rsch Inst 1450 Duarte Rd Duarte CA 91010-3011

VAUGHN, JOHN VERNON, banker, industrialist; b. Grand Junction, Colo., June 24, 1909; s. John S. and Alice Ann (Baylis) V.; m. Dorothy May Pickrell, Oct. 12, 1934; children: Dorothy (Mrs. Richard H. Stone), John Spencer. AB, UCLA, 1932; LLD (hon.), Pepperdine U., 1974. Br. mgr. Nat. Lead Co., 1932-37; sales mgr. Sillers Paint & Varnish Co., 1937-46, pres., gen. mgr., dir., 1946-58; pres., chmn. Dartell Labs., Inc., 1959-70; vice chmn. bd. Crocker Nat. Bank and Crocker Nat. Corp., San Francisco, 1970-75, dir., 1969-85; hon. dir. Crocker Nat. Bank. Cons. Coopers & Lybrand, 1975-85; chmn. bd. Recon Optical, Inc., 1979-90; bd. dirs. Trust Svcs. Am., Forest Lawn Corp., Am. Security & Fidelity Corp.; IT Group Corp. Chmn. San Marino Recreation Commn., 1956-58, La. Better Bus. Bur., 1959-61, Invest-in-Am., 1970-73; chmn. citizen's adv. Council Pub. Transp., 1965-67; commr. Los Angeles Coliseum Commn., 1971-74; trustee Calif. Mus. Found., 1968-79; bd. dirs. Orthopaedic Hosp., 1965-87, pres., 1974-78, chmn. bd., 1978-79; bd. dirs. YMCA, Los Angeles, 1965-77, Central City Assn., So. Calif. Visitors Council, 1970-76, NCCJ, Calif. Museum Sci. and Industry, United Way of Los Angeles, Am. Heart Assn.; mem. Los Angeles Adv. Bd., Friends of Claremont Coll., 1973-78, Los Angeles Beautiful, 1972-74; regent U. Calif., 1958-59; hon. trustee UCLA Found., 1967—, Forest Lawn Meml. Park, 1968—, Claremont Men's Coll., 1970-71, Pepperdine U., 1972-99, life regent, 1999—; regent, mem. bd. visitors Grad. Sch. Bus. Adminstrn. UCLA, 1971-85; mem. Chancellor's Assocs., Calif. State Univs. and Colls. mem. Assistance League, So. Calif. Adv. Bd., 1974—. Recipient Disting. Svc. award UCLA, 1965, Outstanding Community Svc. award UCLA, , 1970, Alumnus of Yr. UCLA award, 1971; Brotherhood award NCCJ, 1971; Los Angeles Jaycees award of merit, 1972; Most Disting. Citizen Los Angeles Realty Bd., 1972; other honors. Mem. Los Angeles Area C. of C. (bd. dirs. 1961, pres. 1969, chmn. 1970), World Affairs Coun. (chpt. v.p., treas. 1970-85, hon. dir. 1985—), Iranian-Am. Chamber Industry and Commerce (pres. 1971-79), Paint, Varnish and Lacquer Assn. (past nat. v.p., past chpt. pres.), Town Hall Calif. (dir. 1973-75), Young Pres.'s Orgn., Jonathan Club (pres. 1964), Los Angeles Country Club (bd. dirs. 1979-85), California Club, San Gabriel Country Club (bd. dirs. 1964-68), Valley Hunt Club, Pasadena Athletic Club, Internat. Order St. Hubertus, Masons, Beta Theta Pi (pres. 1960). Republican. Presbyterian. Avocations: fishing, hunting, golf. Home and Office: 454 S Orange Grove Blvd Pasadena CA 91105-1707

VAUGHN, KATHY, municipal official; Pres. bd. commrs. Pub. Utility Dist., Everett, Wash. Home: PO Box 1107 Everett WA 98206-1107 Office: Office Bd Commrs Pub Utility Dist 2320 California St Everett WA 98201-3750

VAUGHN, MO (MAURICE SAMUEL VAUGHN), professional baseball player; b. Norwalk, Conn., Dec. 15, 1967; Student, Seton Hall U., 1987-89. Infielder Boston Red Sox, 1989-98, Anaheim (Calif.) Angels, 1998—. Active cmty. svc. with youth groups, Boston. Named MVP Baseball Writers' Assn., 1995; named to Sporting News Silver SLugger team, 1995, Am. League All-Star Team, 1995. Office: c/o Anaheim Angels 2000 Gene Autry Way Anaheim CA 92806-6100

VAUGHN, WILLIAM WEAVER, lawyer; b. Los Angeles, Aug. 29, 1930; s. William Weaver and Josephine (Sweigert) V.; m. Claire Louise M'Closkey, June 2, 1962; children: Robert, Gregory, Elizabeth, Anthony, Christina, James. BA, Stanford U., 1952; LLB, UCLA, 1955. Bar: Calif. 1956. With O'Melveny & Myers, L.A., 1955-56, 57—, ptnr., 1964-96, of counsel, 1996—. Served with U.S. Army, 1956-57. Recipient Learned Hand award Am. Jewish Com., 1991, Joseph A. Ball award for outstanding advocacy Brennan Ctr. for Justice, 1998. Fellow Am. Coll. Trial Lawyers (bd. regents 1992-95); mem. L.A. County Bar Assn. (trustee 1976-78, 80-82), L.A. County Bar Found. (bd. dirs. 1991-95), Assn. Bus. Trial Lawyers (bd. govs. 1980-82), Order of Coif, Calif. Club, Chancery Club I(pres. 1997-98). Office: O'Melveny & Myers 400 S Hope St Los Angeles CA 90071-2899

VAZ, KATHERINE ANNE, English language educator, writer; b. Castro Valley, Calif., Aug. 26, 1955; d. August Mark and Elizabeth (Sullivan) Vaz; m. Michael Trudeau, May 1, 1994. BA, U. Calif., Santa Barbara, 1977; MFA, U. Calif., Irvine, 1991. Assoc. prof. English U. Calif., Davis, 1995-99. Keynote or featured spkr. at Libr. of Congress (1997), literary confs. at U. of the Azores, U. Calif. Berkeley, U. Mass., Dartmouth U., Rutgers U. Author: (novel) Saudade, 1994, Mariana (6 langs.), 1997, (short stories) Fado & Other Stories, 1997 (winner 1997 Drue Heinz Lit. prize). Recipient grant fellowship Nat. Endowment for the Arts, 1993, Davis Humanities Inst., U. Calif. Davis, 1998-99. Mem. Authors Guild, Pen/Am., Portuguese-Am. Leadership Coun. of the U.S., U.S. Presidential Delegation to Expo 98/World's Fair, Lisbon, Portugal. Democrat. Roman Catholic.

VAZIRI, NOSRATOLA DABIR, internist, nephrologist, educator; b. Tehran, Iran, Oct. 13, 1939; came to U.S., 1969, naturalized, 1977; s. Abbas and Tahera Vaziri. MD, Tehran U., 1966. Diplomate Am. Bd. Internal Medicine, Am. Bd. Nephrology; cert. hypertension specialist Am. Soc. Hypertension. Intern Cook County Hosp., Chgo., 1969-70; resident Berkshire Med. Ctr., Pittsfield, Mass., 1970-71, Wadsworth VA Med. Ctr., L.A., 1971-72, UCLA Med. Ctr., 1972-74; prof. medicine U. Calif.-Irvine, 1979—, prof. physiology and biophysics, 2001—, chief nephrology and hypertension divsn., 1977—, dir. hemodialysis unit, 1977-94, vice chmn. dept. medicine, 1982-94, chmn. dept. medicine, 1994-98, chair faculty Coll. Medicine, 1998 . : Sr. assoc. editor Jour. Spinal Cord Medicine; mem. editl. bd. Am. Jour. Nephrology, Nephron, ASAIO Jour., Advances in Renal Replacement Therapies, Internat. Jour. Artificial Organs, Spinal Cord Medicine; contbr. numerous articles to med. jours. Mem. sci. adv. coun. Nat. Kidney Found., 1977—. Recipient Golden Apple award, 1977; named Outstanding Tchr. U. Calif., Irvine, 1975, 78, 79, 80, 82, Lauds and Laurels award for faculty achievement, 1999. Master ACP; mem. Am. Soc. Nephrology, Am. Physiol. Soc., Am. Paraplegia Soc. (pres. 1992-94), Western Assn. Physicians, Coun. Highblood Pressure Rsch., Assn. Profs. Medicine, Alpha Omega Alpha. Home: 66 Balboa Cv Newport Beach CA 92663-3226 Office: U Calif Irvine Med Ctr Div Nephrology Dept Medicine 101 The City Dr Orange CA 92868-3201 E-mail: ndvaziri@uci.edu

VAZQUEZ, MARTHA ALICIA, judge; b. Santa Barbara, Calif., Feb. 21, 1953; d. Remigio and Consuelo (Mendez) V.; m. Frank Mathew, Aug. 7, 1976; children: Cristina Vazquez Matthew, Nicholas Vazquez Matthew, Nathan Vazquez Matthew. BA in Govt., U. Notre Dame, 1975, JD, 1978. Bar: N.Mex. 1979, U.S. Dist. Ct. (we. dist.) N.Mex. 1979. Atty. Pub. Defender's Office, Santa Fe, 1979-81; ptnr. Jones, Snead, Wertheim, Rodriguez & Wentworth, Santa Fe, 1981-93; judge U.S. District Ct. N.Mex., Santa Fe, 1993—. Chmn. City Santa Fe Grievance Bd. Mem. N.Mex. Bar Assn. (fee arbitration com., chmn. trial practice sect. 1984-85, mem. task force on minority involvement in bar activities), Santa Fe Bar Assn. (jud. liasion com.), Nat. Assn. Criminal Def. Lawyers, Assn. Trial Lawyers Am., N.Mex. Trial Lawyers Assn. Democrat. Roman Catholic. Office: US Courthouse PO Box 2710 Santa Fe NM 87504-2710

VEBLEN, JOHN ELVIDGE, lawyer; b. Seattle, Feb. 14, 1944; AB magna cum laude, Harvard U., 1965; BA, MA with first class honors, Oxford U., Eng., 1967; JD, Yale U., 1971. Bar: Wash. 1971, N.Y. 1973. Law clerk U.S. Ct. Appeals (9th cir.), 1971-72; prin. Stoel Rives LLP, Seattle, 1972—. Mem. ABA, Wash. State Bar Assn., Seattle-King County Bar Assn., Phi Beta Kappa. Office: Stoel Rives LLP One Union Sq 600 University St Ste 3600 Seattle WA 98101-4109

VECCHIO, TONY, zoological park administrator; BS, Pa. State U., State College, 1977; MS, U. S.C., 1985. Curator Atlanta Zoo, 1986-87; dir. Roger Williams Park Zoo, Providence, 1989-98, Oreg. Zoo, Portland, 1998—. Office: Oreg Zoo 4001 SW Canyon Rd Portland OR 97221-2705

VEDROS, NEYLAN ANTHONY, microbiologist, educator; b. New Orleans, Oct. 6, 1929; s. Phillip John and Solange Agnes (Melancon) V.; m. Elizabeth Corbett, Apr. 9, 1955; children: Sally Ann, Philippa Jane. B.S. in Chemistry, La. State U., 1951, M.S. in Microbiology, 1957; Ph.D., U. Colo., 1960. Postdoctoral fellow Nat. Inst. Allergy and Infectious Diseases, U. Oreg., Portland, 1960-62; microbiologist Naval Med. Research Inst., Bethesda, Md., 1962-66; research microbiologist Naval Biosci. Lab., Oakland, Calif., 1966-67; assoc. prof. med. microbiology and immunology U. Calif., Berkeley, 1967-72, prof., 1972-91, prof. emeritus, 1991—. Dir. Naval Biosci. Lab., 1968-81; mem. expert panel on bacteriology WHO, 1972-91. Bd. trustees Alameda (Calif.) Library, 1973-78. Served to comdr. M.S.C. USNR, 1952-55, 62-67. Mem. Am. Assn. Immunologists, Am. Soc. Microbiology, Internat. Assn. Human and Animal Mycology, Internat. Assn. Microbiol. Sci., Internat. Assn. Aquatic Animal Medicine, Assn. Mil. Surgeons. Home: 209 Almond Way Healdsburg CA 95448 Office: U Calif 239 Warren Hall Berkeley CA 94725 E-mail: nvedros@earthlink.net

VEGA, GREGORY A. prosecutor; b. East Chicago, Ind. BS in Acctg., Ind. U., 1975; JD, Valparaiso U., 1980. Honors program trial atty. Office of Chief Counsel IRS, Chgo.; with U.S. Atty.'s Office for No. Dist. of Ind., 1983-87; asst. U.S. atty. in maj. frauds and econ. crimes unit U.S. Atty.'s Office, San Diego, 1987; U.S. atty. so. dist. Calif. U.S. Dept. Justice, 1999—. Instr. Atty. Gen.'s Advocacy Inst., Nat. Inst. Trial Advocacy. Mem. Hispanic Nat. Bar Assn. (past pres. 1997-98), State Bar Calif. (chmn. criminal law adv. commn. 1992-93, bd. legal specialization 1993-96), San Diego County Bar Assn. (jud. evaluation com. 1993), San Diego La Raza Lawyers Assn. (past bd. dirs.). Office: 880 Front St Ste 6293 San Diego CA 92101-8807

VEGA, J. WILLIAM, aerospace engineering executive, consultant; b. Elizabeth, N.J., Jan. 30, 1931; s. John Charles and Margaret (Walker) V.; m. Carolyn Louise Burt, June 7, 1957 (div. 1976); children: Lynn Vega Membreño, Lore Vega Hynes, Susan; m. Pauline Anne Garner, Apr. 27, 1983. BSE, Princeton U., 1952, postgrad., 1955-56; MS, U.S. Internat. U., 1973. Sr. engr. Reaction Motors, Inc., Denville, N.J., 1956-58, Convair div. Gen. Dynamics, San Diego, 1958, project engr., sr. project engr., asst. chief engr., 1970-75, dir. advanced programs, 1975-83, v.p. advanced programs, 1983-88, v.p. rsch. and engring., 1988-90; cons. aerospace mgmt., 1991—. Past pres. bd. dirs. Durango (Colo.) Art Ctr.; pres. bd. dirs. Durango Cmty. Access TV; bd. dirs. Cmty. Found. of S.W. Colo.; bd. pres. Durango Cmty. Access TV. Lt. USN, 1952-55. Recipient Outstanding Vol. Fundraiser award State Colo., 1999. Fellow AIAA (assoc.); mem. Phi Beta Kappa. Avocations: skiing, boating, hiking, camping.

VEIGEL, JON MICHAEL, science administrator; b. Mankato, Minn., Nov. 10, 1938; s. Walter Thomas and Thelma Geraldine (Lein) V.; m. Carol June Bradley, Aug. 10, 1962. BS, U. Washington, 1960; PhD, UCLA, 1965. Program mgr., congl. sci. fellow Office of Tech. Assessment, U.S. Congress, Washington, 1974-75; div. mgr. Calif. Energy Commn., Sacramento, 1975-78; asst. dir. Solar Energy Rsch. Inst., Golden, Colo., 1978-81; pres. Alt. Energy Corp., Rsch. Triangle Park, N.C., 1981-88, Oak Ridge (Tenn.) Associated Univs., 1988-96. Bd. dirs. Am. Coun. Energy Efficient Economy, Washington, Pacific Internat. Ctr. for High Tech. Rsch., Honolulu; cons. Sunhunner Assocs., LLC, 1996—. Contbr. articles to jours. Trustee Maryville Coll., 1990-96, Mendeleyev U., Moscow, Russia. 1st lt. USAF, 1965-68. Mem. AAAS (past mem. com. on sci. and engring. pub. policy, past chair). Avocations: photography. Office: SunRunner Assocs LLC 16259 W Spring Canyon Way Surprise AZ 85374-4961 E-mail: Jonmv@Earthlink.net

VEINOTT, ARTHUR FALES, JR. university educator; b. Boston, Oct. 12, 1934; m. 1960; children: Elisabeth, Michael; m. 1988. BS, BA, Lehigh U., 1956; D Eng Sc, Columbia U., 1960. From asst. prof. to assoc. prof. indusl. engring. Stanford (Calif.) U., 1962-67, prof. ops. rsch., 1967—, chmn. dept. indsl. engring., 1975-85, prof. mgmt. sci. engring., 1999—. Cons. Rand Corp., 1965, IBM Rsch. Ctr., 1968-69, 89-90; vis. prof. Yale U., 1972-73. Editor Jour. Math. Ops. Rsch., 1974-80. 1st lt. USAF, 1960-62 Guggenheim fellow 1978-79. Fellow Inst. Math. Stats.; mem. Nat. Acad. Engring., Inst. Mgmt. Sci., Ops. Rsch. Soc. Am. Achievements include development of lattice programming, qualitative theory of optimization for predicting the direction of change of optimal decisions resulting from alteration of problem parameters; structure and computation of optimal policies for supply chains and dynamic programs. Office: Stanford U Dept Mgmt Sci Engring Terman 415 Stanford CA 94305-4026

VENEGAS, ARTURO, JR. protective services official; b. San Nicolas de Ibarra, Jalisco, Mexico, Dec. 22, 1948; m. Anna Marie Venegas; children: Angela, Adriana, Anthony, Andrew. BA, U. San Francisco, 1978; MS in Mgmt., Calif. Poly., Pomona, 1991. Police officer Fresno (Calif.) Police Dept., 1970-75, police specialist, 1975-79, sgt., field supr., 1979, 80-85, lt., 1985-90, lt., acting divsn. comdr. adminstrv. svcs., 1990-92, dep. chief police investigations divsn., 1992-93; chief program devel., program mgr. State Office Criminal Justice Planning, Sacramento, 1979 80; chief police Sacramento Police Dept., 1993—. Mem. Calif. Atty. Gen.'s Policy Coun. on Violence Prevention; bd. dirs. Safety Ctr.; mem. exec. bd. Sacramento Safe Sts.; mem. adv. bd. Cath. Social Svcs. With U.S. Army, 1966-68. Mem. Internat. Assn. Chiefs of Police, Calif. Assn. Chiefs of Police, Calif. Peace Officers Assn. (chair law and legis. com.), Police Exec. Rsch. Forum, Ctrl. Sierra Police Chiefs Assn., FBI Nat. Acad. Assocs., Latino Peace Officers Assn., Hispanic-Am. Command Officers Assn., Am. Legion, Footprinters Internat., KC. Office: Police Dept Hall Justice 900 8th St Sacramento CA 95814-2506

VENNING, ROBERT STANLEY, lawyer; b. Boise, Idaho, July 24, 1943; s. William Lucas and Corey Elizabeth (Brown) V.; m. Sandra Macdonald, May 9, 1966 (div. 1976); 1 child, Rachel Elizabeth; m. Laura Siegel, Mar. 24, 1979; 1 child, Daniel Rockhill Siegel. AB, Harvard U., 1965; MA, U. Chgo., 1966; LLB, Yale U., 1970. Bar: Calif., U.S. Dist. Ct. (no. dist.) Calif., 1971, U.S. Dist. Ct. (cen. dist.) Calif. 1973, U.S. Ct. Appeals (9th cir.) 1977, U.S. Supreme Ct. 1977, U.S. Ct. Appeals (fed. cir.) 1986, U.S. Ct. Appeals (D.C. cir.) 1987. Assoc. Heller Ehrman White & McAuliffe, San Francisco, 1970-73, 73-76, ptnr., 1977—, mem. exec. com., 1991-94. Vis. lectr. U. Wash., Seattle, 1973, Boalt Hall Sch. Law, U. Calif., Berkeley, 1982-85, 89, Sch. Bus., Stanford U., 1986-87. Editor Yale Law Jour., 1969-70. Early neutral evaluator U.S. Dist. Ct. (no. dist.) Calif., 1987—; mem. Natural Resources Def. Coun. Fellow Am. Bar Found. (life); mem. ABA, San Francisco Bar Assn. (past chair judiciary com.), CPR Inst. for Dispute Resolution, Olympic Club. Office: Heller White & McAuliffe 333 Bush St San Francisco CA 94104-2806

VERANT, WILLIAM J. state agency administrator; b. Washington, Dec. 19, 1941; m. Donna M. Verant; children: Bill Jr., Sharon. BSBA, Am. U. Various sr. mgmt. positions various comml. banks, savs. and loan and mortgage banks, Washington, Calif., N.Mex.; dir. fin. instns. divsn., regulation and licensing dept. State of N.Mex., Santa Fe, 1995—, acting dir. securities divsn. Acting dir. securities divsn. State of N.Mex. Avocation: restoring old cars. Office: State NMex PO Box 25101 725 Saint Michaels Dr Santa Fe NM 87504-7605

VERCAUTEREN, RICHARD FRANK, career officer; b. Manchester, N.H., Feb. 9, 1945; s. Louis P. and Janet (Beliveau) V.; m. Gail Anne Settoon, June 3, 1972. BA in Sociology, Providence Coll., 1967; MA in Bus. Mgmt., George Washington U., 1980; MA in Internat. Studies, Georgetown U., 1996. Commd. 2d lt. USMC, 1967, advanced through grades to brig. gen., 1993; platoon comdr. 2d bn., 9th Marines, Vietnam, 1968; comdg. officer Rifle Co., Hawaii, 1971-73; mil. observer UN, Egypt, Israel, Lebanon, 1976-78; comdg. officer Spl. Task Force, S.Am., 1982; aide de camp Marine Forces Atlantic, Norfolk, Va., 1983-84; bn. comdr. 3d bn., 2nd Marines, Camp Lejeune, N.C., 1985-87; regional comdr. Embassy Guards SubSahara Africa, Nairobi, Africa, 1987-90; dep. dir. plans Hdqs., USMC, Washington, 1990-92, dir. plans, 1990-92; comdg. officer 2nd Marine Regiment, Camp Lejeune, 1992-93; comdg. gen. 1st Marine Exped Brigade, Honolulu, 1993-95; dir. stragety and plans Hdqr. USMC, 1995—. Mem. exec. bd. Capitol dist. Boy Scouts Am., Washington, 1991-92; sr. counselor Seminar XXII, MIT, Washington, 1995-96; bd. dirs. Girl Scouts U.S. Decorated Silver Star medal, Legion of Merit, Distinguished Svc. Medal; recipient Holland M. Smith award Navy League, 1982; MIT Ctr. Internat. Tech. Studies fellow in fgn. politics, 1991, fellow in nat. security studies Harvard U., 1995. Mem. Navy League (bd. dirs.), Army-Navy Club (Washington), Oahu Country Club (Honolulu), Plaza Club, Rotary. Avocations: running, golfing, skiing, history, travel. Office: Lockheed Martin IMS PO Box 240579 Honolulu HI 96824-0579

VERHEY, JOSEPH WILLIAM, psychiatrist, educator; b. Oakland, Calif., Sept. 28, 1928; s. Joseph Bernard and Anne (Hanken) V.; BS summa cum laude, Seattle U., 1954; MD, U. Wash., 1958; m. Darlene Helen Seiler, July 21, 1956. Intern, King County Hosp., Seattle, 1958-59; resident Payne Whitney Psychiatric Clinic, N.Y. Hosp., Cornell Med. Center, N.Y.C., 1959-62, U. Wash. Hosp., Seattle, 1962-63; pvt. practice, Seattle, 1963-78; mem. staff U. Providence Hosp., 1963-78, Fairfax Hosp., 1963-78, VA Med. Center, Tacoma, 1978-83, chief inpatient psychiatry sect., 1983—; clin. instr. psychiatry U. Wash. Med. Sch., 1963-68, clin. asst. prof. psychiatry, 1968-82, clin. assoc. prof., 1982—; cons. psychiatry U.S. Dept. Def., Wash. State Bur. Juvenile Rehab.; examiner Am. Bd. Psychiatry and Neurology. Diplomate Am. Bd. Psychiatry and Neurology. Fellow N. Pacific Soc. Psychiatry and Neurology, Am. Psychiat. Assn.; mem. AMA, Am. Fedn. Clin. Rsch., World Fedn. Mental Health, Soc. Mil. Surgeons of U.S., Wash. Athletic Club, Swedish Club (life). Home: 1100 University St Seattle WA 98101-2848 Office: Va Med Ctr Tacoma WA 98493-0001

VERKAMP, JOHN, lawyer, state legislator; b. Grand Canyon, Ariz., July 31, 1940; s. Jack and Mary (O'Leary) V.; m. Linda L. Meline, Sept. 14, 1965; children— Melanie, Jay, Gregory. B.S. in Bus. Adminstrn., U. Ariz., 1962, J.D., 1965. Bar: Ariz. 1965, U.S. Ct. Mil. Appeals 1965, U.S. Supreme Ct. 1973. Dep. county atty. Coconino County, Flagstaff, Ariz., 1970-71, county atty., 1981-92; assoc. Mangum, Wall & Stoops, Flagstaff, 1972-74; ptnr. Verkamp & Verkamp, Flagstaff, 1974-80; assoc. Morgan, Wall, Stoops & Warden, 1993—; mem. governing bd. Ariz. Pros. Attys. Adv. Council, Phoenix, 1981-92, chmn. 1985—. Chmn. Coconino County Republican Com., Flagstaff, 1974-76, Coconino County Legal Aid, 1976-78; vice chmn. Cath. Social Services, 1982-83. Served as capt. JAGC, U.S. Army, 1965-70, Europe. Mem. Nat. Dist. Attys. Assn., Ariz. County Attys. and Sheriffs Assn. (pres. 1985-86), Ariz. Alliance Police Chiefs, Sheriffs and County Attys. (Ariz. County Atty. of Yr. 1985, 87), Ariz. Assn. Counties (pres. 1989), Flagstaff C. of C., Am. Legion. Home: 2620 N Fremont Blvd Flagstaff AZ 86001-1021 Office: Ariz Ho Reps 2620 N Fremont Blvd Flagstaff AZ 86001-1021

VERMA, INDER M. biochemist; b. Sangrur, Punjab, India, Nov. 28, 1947; MSc, Lucknow U., India, 1966; PhD in Biochemistry, Weizmann Inst. Sci., Rehovot, Israel, 1971. From asst. prof. to assoc. prof. Salk Inst., 1974-83; sr. mem. Molecular Biology & Virology Lab, 1983-85; prof. Molecular Biology, 1985-95; prof. Lab. Genetics Salk Inst., 1995—. Fellow Jane Coffin Childs Meml. Fund, 1970-73; Reverend Soloman B. Caulker Meml. fellow, 1967-70; adj. assoc. prof. U. Calif. San Diego, 1979-83, adj. prof. Biology, 1983—; mem. Virology Study Sec., 1981-85. Recipient medal Outstanding Scientist N. Am. Scientists of Indian Origin, 1985-86; merit award NIH, 1987, outstanding investigator award, 1988; bd. trustees Salk Inst., 1989-91 & 94—; mem. acad. coun., 1989—; vchmn. Fac. and Acad. coun., 1989-90 & 94-95; chmn., 1991-92 & 96-97; prof. Molecular Biology, Am. Cancer Soc., 1990; lectr. Purdue U., 1991, Sch. Med. Vanderbilt U., 1992, TATA Meml. Hosp., Bombay, India, 1992, U. Chgo., 1992, Queenstown, New Zealand, 1993, N.Y.U., 1993, Bar-Ilan U., Ramat Gan, Israel, and others. Mem. Nat. Acad. Sci., Am. Cancer Soc. Office: Salk Inst Biol Studies 10010 N Torrey Pines Rd La Jolla CA 92037-1099

VERMEIJ, GEERAT JACOBUS, marine biologist, educator; b. Sappemeer, Groningen, The Netherlands, Sept. 28, 1946; s. J.L. V.; m. Edith Zipser, 1972; 1 child. AB in Biology, Princeton U., 1968; MA in Philosophy, Yale U., 1970, PhD in Biology & Geology, 1971. Zoology instr. U. Md., 1971-72, asst. prof., 1972-74, assoc. prof., 1974-80, prof., 1980-88; prof. dept. geology U. Calif., Davis, 1989—. Author: Biogeography and Adaptation: Patterns of Marine Life, 1978, Evolution and Escalation: An Ecological History of Life, 1987, A Natural History of Shells, 1993. Recipient Guggenheim fellowship, 1975-76, fellowship MacArthur Found., 1992—, Daniel Giraud Elliot Medal, NAS, 2000. Fellow AAAS, Calif. Acad. Scis. Office: U Calif Dept Geology Davis CA 95616

VERNON, JACK ALLEN, otolaryngology educator, laboratory administrator; b. Kingsport, Tenn., Apr. 6, 1922; s. John Allen and Mary Jane (Peters) Vernon Hefley; m. Betty Jane Dubon, Dec. 12, 1946 (div. 1972); children: Stephen Mark, Victoria Lynn; m. Mary Benson Meikle, Jan. 2, 1973 B.A. in Psychology, U.Va., 1948, M.A. in Psychology, 1950, Ph.D. in Psychology, 1952. Instr. psychology Princeton U., N.J., 1952-54, asst. prof., 1954-60, assoc. prof., 1960-64, prof., 1964-66; prof. otolaryngology Oreg. Health Sci. U., Portland, 1966—, also dir. Oreg. Hearing Rsch. Ctr. Author: Inside the Black Room, 1963; editor: Tinnitus, Q&A's, Tinnitus, Treatments and Relief, Mechanisms of Tinnitus; inventor in field. Adv. Office Civil Defense, Washington, 1961-62. Served to 2d lt. USAAF, 1943-44 Recipient Guest of Honor award 1st Internat. Tinnitus Seminar, 1979, Opticon Focus on People award, 2001. Mem. Assn. Rsch. in Otolaryngology (pres. 1973-74), Am. Acad. Ophthalmology and Otolaryngology, Rotary. Democrat. Avocations: woodworking, sailing, skiing, reading. Office: Oreg Hearing Rsch Ctr 3181 SW Sam Jackson Park Rd Portland OR 97201-3011

VERNON, L. SKIP, state legislator, lawyer; b. Inglewood, Calif., Oct. 12, 1956; BS, N.Mex. State U.; JD, U. N.Mex. Pvt. practice; mem. N.Mex. Legislature, Santa Fe, 1984—, mem. conservation com., mem. Indian and cultural affairs com., minority whip. Republican. Office: PO Box 3827 Albuquerque NM 87190-3827

VERNON, TIMOTHY, artistic director; Artistic director Pacific Opera, Victoria, Can. Office: 1316B Govt St Victoria BC Canada V8W 1Y8

VERRONE, PATRIC MILLER, lawyer, writer; b. Glendale, N.Y.C., Sept. 29, 1959; s. Pat and Edna (Miller) V.; m. Margaret Maiya Williams, 1989; children: Patric Carroll Williams, Marianne Emma Williams, Theodore Henry Williams. BA, Harvard U., 1981; JD, Boston Coll., 1984. Bar: Fla. 1984, Calif. 1988, U.S. Dist. Ct. (mid. dist.) Fla. 1984, U.S. Dist. Ct. (ctrl. dist.) Calif. 1995, U.S. Ct. Appeals (9th cir.) 1995. Assoc. Allen, Knudsen, Swartz, DeBoest, Rhoads & Edwards, Ft. Myers, Fla., 1984-86; writer The Tonight Show, Burbank, Calif., 1987-90. Adj. prof. Loyola Law Sch., L.A., 1998-2000. Dir., producer, writer The Civil War--The Lost Episode, 1991; writer The Larry Sanders Show, 1992-94, The Critic, 1993-95; producer, writer The Simpsons, 1994-95, Muppets Tonight!, 1995-97 (Emmy award Best Children's Program 1998), Pinky and the Brain, 1998, Futurama, 1998— (Environ. Media award 2000); editor Harvard Lampoon, 1978-84, Boston Coll. Law Rev., 1983-84, Fla. Bar Jour., 1987-88, L.A. Lawyer, 1994—; issue editor: Ann. Entertainment Law Issue, 1995-2001; contbr. articles to profl. jours. including Elysian Fields Quar., Baseball and the American Legal Mind, White's Guide to Collecting Figures, Frank Sinatra: The Man, The Music, The Legend. Bd. dirs. Calif. Confcdn. of Arts, 1994-98, Mus. Contemporary Art, 1994 95. Mem. ABA (vice-chair arts, entertainment and sports law com. 1995-96), Calif. Bar, Calif. Lawyers for Arts, L.A. County Bar Assn. (sec. barristers exec. com., chair artists and the law com., steering com. homeless shelter project, intellectual property and entertainment law sect., state appelate jud. evaluation com., legis. activity com.), Fla. Bar Assn., Writers Guild Am. West (exec. com. animation writers caucus, bd. dirs., membership com., fin. com., legis. support com., 2001 contract negotiating com.), Harvard Club Lee County (v.p. 1985-86), Harvard Club So. Calif. Republican. Roman Catholic. Avocation: baseball. Home and Office: PO Box 1428 Pacific Palisades CA 90272-1428

VERSCH, ESTHER MARIE, artist; b. Santa Monica, Calif., May 27, 1927; d. Claro Contreras Santellanes and Juana Hernandez; m. Chester Ray Fraelich, Nov. 14, 1943 (div. Nov. 1964); children: Joe Fraelich, Diane Fraelich Foster Preston; m. Terry Lee Versch, June 21, 1969; stepchildren: Fred, Roman, Joseph, Terry Jr., Michael. Student, East L.A. Coll., Pasadena City Coll. Lic. vocat. nurse. Nurse pvt. dr.'s office, L.A., 1968-69, U. So. Calif. Med. Ctr., L.A., 1963-68; artist Altadena, Calif., 1972—. Artist: (front cover) Library Services L.A., 1983, Christmas card for Western Greeting Inc., (back cover) Moccasin Tracks, 1984-85; one woman shows include Republic Fed. Savings, Altadena, Calif., Pasadena Pub. Libr., Whites Art Store and Gallery, La Canada, Calif., 1979, Windmill Gallery, 1985; group exhibitions: Women Artists of the West Internat. Exhibition and Sale, Cody Western and Wildlife Classyc, 1979, Nat. Cowgirl Hall of Fame, Hereford, Tex., 1978, Beauty for the Beast Benefit, 1980, Ducks Unltd. Invitational Art Show, Taylor, Mich., 1986-87, Lawrence (Kans.) Indian Art Show, Mus. Anthropology, 1989-90, Snake River Showcase, Lewiston, Idaho, 1992, Women Artists of the West, 1992, 98, 99, Death Valley 49's Invitational Art Show, 1994-2000, 2001, George Ohr Cultural Arts and Cultural Ctr., Biloxi, Miss., 1998, Western and Wildlife Invitational Art Show, Estes Park, Colo., 2000; collections: Johnson Humrick House Mus., Coshocton, Ohio, and other private collections; illustrator back cover Moccasin Tracks, 1984-85. Vol. nurses aide City View Hosp., L.A., 1960-63; vol. Arroyo Rep., Pasadena, Calif., St. Luke Hosp., Pasadena, 1990-94, flu immunization ARC, 1977-78. Recipient Gold medal for watercolor San Gabriel Fine Arts, 1979, Best of Show award for watercolor Am. Indian and Western, 1990, Hon. mention San Gabriel Fine Arts, 1990, 3rd Place Watercolor Women Artists of the West Saddle Back Art Gallery, 1982. Mem. Women Artists of the West (emeritus mem., treas., asst. sec., editor West Wind, membership chmn.). Republican. Roman Catholic. Avocations: walking, gardening, sewing. E-mail: everschart@newsguy.com

VER STEEG, DONNA LORRAINE FRANK, nurse, sociologist, educator; b. Minot, N.D., Sept. 23, 1929; d. John Jonas and Pearl H. (Denlinger) Frank; m. Richard W. Ver Steeg, Nov. 22, 1950; children: Juliana, Anne, Richard B. BSN, Stanford, 1951; MSN, U. Calif., San Francisco, 1967; MA in Sociology, UCLA, 1969, PhD in Sociology, 1973. Clin. instr. U. N.D. Sch. Nursing, 1962-63; USPHS nurse rsch. fellow UCLA, 1969-72; spl. cons., adv. com. on physicians' assts. and nurse practitioner progs. Calif. State Bd. Med. Examiners, 1972-73; asst. prof. UCLA Sch. Nursing, 1973-79, assoc. prof., 1979-94, asst. dean, 1979-81, chmn. primary ambulatory care, 1976-87, assoc. dean, 1983-86, prof. emeritus, chair primary care, 1994-96, prof. emeritus, 1996—. Co-prin. investigator PRIMEX Project, Family Nurse Practitioners, UCLA Ext., 1974-76; assoc. cons. Calif. Postsecondary Edn. Commn., 1975-76; spl. cons. Calif. Dept. Consumer Affairs, 1978; accredited visitor Western Assn. Schs. and Colls., 1985; mem. Calif. State Legis. Health Policy Forum, 1980-81; mem. nurse practitioner adv. com. Calif. Bd. RNs, 1995-97; mem. Edn. Industry Interface, Info. Devel. Mktg. Sub Coms., 1995-99, recruitment, 1999—; archivist Calif. Strategic Planning Com. Nursing/Colleagues in Caring Project, 1995—. Contbr. chpts. to profl. books and articles to profl. jours. Recipient Leadership award Calif. Area Health Edn. Ctr. Sys., 1989, Commendation award Calif. State Assembly, 1994; named Outstanding Faculty Mem., UCLA Sch. Nursing, 1982. Fellow Am. Acad. Nursing; mem. AAAS, AAUW, ANA (pres. elect Calif. 1977-79, pres. Calif. 1979-81), ANA© (interim chair Calif. 1995-96), Nat. League Nursing, Calif. League Nursing, N.Am. Nursing Diagnosis Assn., Am. Assn. History Nursing, Stanford Nurses Club, Sigma Theta Tau (Alpha Eta chpt. Leadership award Gamma Tau chpt. 1994), Sigma Xi. Home: 708 Swarthmore Ave Pacific Palisades CA 90272-4353 Office: UCLA Sch Nursing Box 956917 Los Angeles CA 90095-6917

VESTAL, JOSEPHINE BURNET, lawyer; b. Iowa City, June 13, 1949; d. Allen Delker and Dorothy (Walker) V. Student, Williams Coll., 1970; BA, Mt. Holyoke Coll., 1971; JD, U. Wash., 1974. Bar: Wash. 1974, U.S. Dist. Ct. (we. dist.) Wash. 1974, U.S. Ct. Appeals (9th cir.) 1984, U.S. Ct. Appeals (D.C. cir.) 1984, U.S. Dist. Ct. (ea. dist.) Wash. 1993. Ptnr. Selinker, Vestal, Klockars & Andersen, Seattle, 1974-80; assoc. Williams, Kastner & Gibbs, Seattle, 1981-87; mem. Williams, Kastner & Gibbs, PLLC, Seattle, 1988—. Mem. ABA (labor and employment sect.), Def. Rsch. Inst. (labor and employment sect.), Wash. State Bar Assn., King County Bar Assn. Office: Williams Kastner & Gibbs PO Box 21926 Seattle WA 98111-3926 E-mail: jvestal@wkg.com

VICKREY, HERTA MILLER, microbiologist; b. San Gregorio, Calif. d. John George and Hertha Lucy Miller; m. William David Vickrey; children: Ellean H., Carlene L. Smith, Corrine A. Pochop, Arlene A.; m. Robert James Fitzgibbon, Dec. 28, 1979. BA, San Jose State U., 1957; MA, U. Calif., Berkeley, 1963, PhD in Bacteriology and Immunology, 1970. Cert. immunologist, pub. health microbiologist, clin. lab. scientist. Pub. health microbiologist Viral & Rickettsial Diseases Lab., Calif. State Dept. Pub. Health, Berkeley, 1958-60, 61-62, Berkeley, 1964; postgrad. rsch. bacteriologist dept. bacteriology U. Calif., Berkeley, 1963-64; bacteriologist Children's Hosp. Med. Ctr. No. Calif., Oakland, 1958-70; asst. prof. U. Victoria, B.C., Can., 1970-72; rsch. assoc. rsch. dept. Wayne County Gen. Hosp., Wayne, Mich., 1972-83; lab. supr. med. rsch. and edn. U. Mich., Ann Arbor, 1977-83; pub. health lab. dir. Shasta County Pub. Health Svcs., Redding, Calif., 1983-84; sr. pub. health microbiologist Tulare County Pub. Health Lab., Tulare, 1984—, tech. supr. Visalia, 1992-93, med. technologist Tulare, 1994-96, clin. lab. scientist, 1996—. Vis. scientist MIT, Cambridge, 1982; organizer, lectr. mycology workshop Tulare County Health Dept. Lab., Visalia, 1988; USPHS trainee U. Calif., Berkeley, 1965, 66. Author: Isolation and Identification of Mycotic Agents, 1987-88; contbr. articles to profl. jours. Fundraiser Battered Women's Shelter, Redding, 1983, Real Opportunities for Youth, Visalia, 1985, 86, Open Gate Ministries, Dinuba, Visalia, 1987-94, 97-99. Fellow NIH, 1966-69, Dr. E.E. Dowdle rsch. fellow, U. Calif., 1969-70; grantee U. Victoria, 1970-72, Med. Rsch. and Edn. and Med. Adminstrn., U. Mich., 1973-83. Mem. No. Calif. Assn. Pub. Health Microbiologists, Calif. Scholarship Soc., Am. Soc. Clin. Pathologists (assoc.), Phi Beta Kappa, Delta Omega, Phi Kappa Phi, Beta Beta Beta. Avocations: biking, hiking, swimming. Home: 3505 W Campus Dr Apt 5 Visalia CA 93277-1869 Office: Tulare County Pub Health Lab 1062 S K St Tulare CA 93274-6421

VICTOR, ROBERT EUGENE, real estate corporation executive, lawyer; b. N.Y.C., Dec. 17, 1929; s. Louis and Rebecca (Teitelbaum) V.; m. Dorothy Saffir, Oct. 14, 1951; children— Priscilla Saffir Victor Faubel, Pandora Saffir. LL.B., St. John's U., 1953, J.D., 1968. Bar: N.Y. bar 1953, Calif. bar 1965. With firm Szold and Brandwen, N.Y.C., 1953-54; atty. Dept. Army, Phila., 1955-56; with Hughes Aircraft Co., Culver City, Calif., 1956-62; v.p., gen. counsel Packard Bell Electronics Corp., Los Angeles, 1962-70; sr. v.p., gen. counsel Cordon Internat. Corp., Los Angeles, 1970-78; also dir.; gen. counsel Am. Harp Soc., 1969-85; pres. Vanowen Realty Corp., 1978-93, also dir. Mem. Los Angeles County Bar Assn. Club: Masons. Office: 722 Walden Dr Beverly Hills CA 90210-3125

VICTORINO, LOUIS D. lawyer; b. Lemoore, Calif., May 27, 1945; s. Louis and Mayme (Garcia) V.; m. Kathleen Gilman Berl, June 7, 1975. BA, Stanford U., 1967; JD, UCLA, 1970. Assoc./ptnr. Pettit & Martin, San Francisco, L.A., 1970-84; ptnr. Seyfarth, Shaw, Fairweather & Geraldson, L.A., 1984-88, Pillsbury & Madison, L.A., 1988-93, Fried, Frank, Harris, Shriver & Jacobson, L.A., 1993—. Adv. bd. Govt. Contractor, Washington, 1990—; legal advisor Commn. Govt. Procurement, 1971. Co-author: Proving & Pricing Construction Claims, 1990, Government Contractor Briefing Papers Collection, 1987-95. Mem. ABA (pub. contract law sect., reg. pres. 1975, editl. bd. Pub. Contract Law Jour. 1992-95), Fed. Bar Assn. (reg. v.p.), Ct. Fed. Claims Bar Assn., Bd. Contract Appeals Bar Assn. Office: Fried Frank Harris Shrive & Jacobson 725 S Figueroa St Ste 1200 Los Angeles CA 90017-5443

VIDALE, JOHN EMILIO, geologist; b. Phila., Mar. 15, 1959; s. Guido Levi and Rosemary (Jacobson) V.; 1 child, Laura. BS, Yale U., 1981; PhD, Calif. Inst. Tech., 1986. Scientist U. Calif., Santa Cruz, 1987-90, U.S. Geol. Survey, Menlo Park, Calif., 1991-95; assoc. prof. UCLA, 1995-99, prof., 1999—. Editor Bulletin Seismology Soc. Am., 1988-93; contbr. articles to profl. jours. Gilbert fellow U.S. Geol. survey, 1994-95; Co-Recipient James B. Macelwane YoungInvestigator medal Am. Geophysical Union, 1994 Fellow Am. Geophys. Union (Macelwane medal 1994). Home: 10421 Colina Way Los Angeles CA 90077-2041 Office: UCLA Dept Earth & Space Sci PO Box 951567 Los Angeles CA 90095-1567

VIDOVICH, MARK A. paper products executive; CEO Day Runner, Inc., Irvine, Calif., 1986-2000, chmn. bd. dirs., 2000—. Office: Day Runner Inc 15295 Alton Pky Irvine CA 92618

VIGIL, DANIEL AGUSTIN, academic administrator; b. Denver, Feb. 13, 1947; s. Agustin and Rachel (Naranjo) V.; m. Claudia Cartier. BA in History, U. Colo., Denver, 1978, JD, 1982. Bar: Colo. 1982, U.S. Dist. Ct. Colo. 1983. Project mgr. Mathematics Policy Rsch., Denver, 1978; law clk. Denver Dist. Ct., 1982-83; ptnr. Vigil and Bley, Denver, 1983-85; asst. dean sch. law U. Colo., Boulder, 1983-89, assoc. dean sch. law, 1989—. Apptd. by chief justice of Colo. Supreme Ct. to serve on Colo. Supreme Ct. Ad Hoc Com. on miniority participation in legal profession, 1988-94; adj. prof. U. Colo. Sch. Law; mem. Gov. Colo. Lottery Commn., 1990-97; mem. Colo. Supreme Ct. Hearing Bd., 1998—. Editor (newsletter) Class Action, 1987-88; co-editor (ethics com. column) Colo. Lawyer, 1995-97. Bd. dirs. Legal Aid Soc. Met. Denver, 1986-99, chmn. bd. dirs., 1998-99; past v.p. Colo. Minority Scholarhip Consortium, pres. 1990-91; mem. Task Force on Community Race Rels., Boulder, 1989-94; past mem. jud. nomination rev. com. U.S. Senator Tim Wirth; chmn. bd. dirs. Colo. Legal Svcs., 2000-. Mem. Colo. Bar Assn. (mem. legal edn. and admissions com. 1989-94, chmn. 1989-91, bd. govs. 1991, 97—), Hispanic Nat. Bar Assn. (chmn. scholarship com. 1990-95), Colo Hispanic Bar Assn. (bd. dirs. 1985-89, pres. 1990), Denver Bar Assn. (joint com. on minorities in the legal profession), Boulder County Bar Assn. (ex-officio mem., trustee), Phi Delta Phi (faculty sponsor). Roman Catholic. Avocations: skiing, cosmology. Home: 828 3d Ave PO Box 518 Lyons CO 80540-0518 Office: U Colo Sch Law PO Box 401 Boulder CO 80303 E-mail: Daniel.Vigil@colorado.edu

VIGIL, JEFFREY L. infant and child products manufacturing executive; b. 1954; BS in Acctg., U. Wyo., 1976. Sr. auditor Arthur Andersen & Co., 1976; internal auditor Guaranty Bank and Trust Co., 1979; v.p., treas., contr. Sunnyside Mines, Inc., 1989-90; v.p. fin. Energy Fuels Corp., 1980; v.p. acquisitions Northwestern Growth Corp., Huron, S.D., 1993; v.p. fin. and adminstrn., treas., sec. Koala Corp., Denver, 1996—. Mem. AICP. Office: Unit D 11600 E 53d Ave Denver CO 80239-2312 E-mail: ir@koalabear.com

VIGIL-GIRON, REBECCA, state official; b. Taos, N.Mex., Sept. 4, 1954; d. Felix W. and Cecilia (Santistevan) Vigil; m. Rick Giron; 1 child, Andrew R. AA in Elem. Edn., N.Mex. Highlands U., 1978, BA in French, 1991. Sec., project monitor, customer svc. rep. Pub. Svc. Co. N.Mex., 1978-86; sec. of state N.Mex., 1987-90, 98—; exec. dir. N.Mex. Commn. Status of Women, 1991; electoral observer UN, Angola, Africa, 1992, Internat. Found. Electoral Sys., Dominican Republic, 1994, Equatorial Guinea, Africa, 1996, Washington, 1996. Participant AMPART, Mex., 1991. Dem. nominee U.S. Ho. Reps., 1990. Named among 100 MOst Influential Hispanics in Nation, Hispanic Bus. Mag., 1990; recipient Trio Achievers award S.W. Assn. Student Assistance Programs, 1993, Gov.'s award Outstanding N.Mex. Women, 1994. Mem. Albuquerque Hispano C. of C. (membership rep., sr. sales mktg. rep., corp. rels. coord.) Office: Sec State 325 Don Gaspar Ste 300 Santa Fe NM 87503-0001

VILARDI, AGNES FRANCINE, real estate broker; b. Monson, Mass., Sept. 29, 1918; d. Paul and Adelina (Mastroianni) Vetti; m. Frank S. Vilardi, Dec. 2, 1939; children: Valerie, Paul. Cert. of Dental assisting, Pasadena Jr. Coll., 1954. Lic. real estate broker. Real estate broker, owner Vilardi Realty, Yorba Linda, Calif. Cons. in property mgmt. Mem. Am. Dental Asst. Assn., North Orange County Bd. Realtors (sec./treas. 1972), Yorba Linda Country Club, Desert Princess Country Club. Home and Office: 18982 Villa Ter Yorba Linda CA 92886-2610

VILLABLANCA, JAIME ROLANDO, medical neuroscientist, educator; b. Chillàn, Chile, Feb. 29, 1929; came to U.S., 1971; naturalized, 1985; s. Ernesto and Teresa (Hernàndez) V.; m. Guillermina Nieto, Dec. 3, 1955; children: Amparo C., Jaime G., Pablo J., Francis X., Claudio I. Bachelor in Biology, Nat. Inst. Chile, 1946; licentiate medicine, U. Chile, 1953, MD, 1954. Cert. neurophysiology. Rockefeller Found. postdoctoral fellow in physiology John Hopkins and Harvard Med. Schs., 1959-61; Fogarty internat. rsch. fellow in anatomy UCLA, 1966-68, assoc. research anatomist and psychiatrist, 1971-72; assoc. prof. psychiatry and biobehavioral scis. UCLA Sch. Medicine, 1972-76; prof. psychiatry and biobehavioral scis. UCLA, 1976—, prof. neurobiology, 1977—. Mem. faculty U. Chile Sch. Medicine, 1954-71, prof. exptl. medicine, 1970-71; vis. prof. neurobiology Cath. U. Chile Sch. Medicine, 1974; cons. in field. Author numerous rsch. papers, book chpts., abstracts; chief regional editor Developmental Brain Dysfunction, 1988-99. Decorated Order Francisco de Miranda (Venezuela); recipient Premio Reina Sofia, Madrid, 1990, Fgn. Scientist Traveling grant Tokyo (Japan) Met. Govt., 1995; fellow Rockefeller Found., 1959-61, Fogarty Internat. Rsch. fellow NIH, 1966-68; grantee USAF Office Sci. Rsch., 1962-65, Found. Fund Rsch. Psychiatry, 1969-72, USPHS-Nat. Inst. Child Human Devel., 1972-96, USPHS-Nat. Inst. Drug Abuse, 1981-85, USPHS-Nat. Inst. Neurol. Disorders and Stroke, 1988-92. Mem. AAAS, AAUP, Am. Assn. Anatomists, Mental Retardation Rsch. Ctr., Brain Rsch. Inst., Internat. Brain Rsch. Orgn., Am. Physiol. Soc., Soc. for Neurosci., Assn. Venezolana Padres de Niños Excepcionales, Sci. Coun. Internat. Inst. Rsch. and Advice in Mental Deficiency (Madrid), Soc. Child and Adolescent Psychiatry and Neurology (Chile) (hon.), Sigma Xi. Home: 200 Surfview Dr Pacific Palisades CA 90272-2911 Office: UCLA Dept Psychiatry & Biobehavioral Scis Los Angeles CA 90024-1759 E-mail: jvillablanca@mednet.ucla.edu

VILLARAIGOSA, ANTONIO R. state official; m. Corina; chilren: Marisela, Prisila, Antonio Jr., Natilia Fe. Mem. assembly State of Calif., 1995, Dem. whip and mem. appropriations and budget coms., majority leader, 1997; speaker Calif. State Assembly, 1998-2000. Mem. Greater Eastside Voter Registration and Edn. Project, Jobs with Peace, LAUSD Mex. Am. Edn. Commn., L.A. Ctr. for Law and Justice. Office: Calif Assembly PO Box 942849 Sacramento CA 94249-0001 also: 1910 W Sunset Blvd Ste 500 Los Angeles CA 90026-3291

VILLAVECES, JAMES WALTER, allergist, immunologist; b. San Luis Obispo, Calif., Nov. 4, 1933; s. Robert and Solita (Combariza) V. BA, UCLA, 1955; MD, U. Calif. Med. Sch., 1960. Cert. Am. Bd. Allergy and Immunology. Intern Sawtelle VA Hosp., L.A., 1960-61; preceptorship in adult allergy L.A. County Hosp., Los Angeles, 1964-66; fellow in allergy White Meml. CCM, L.A., 1966-67; chief allergy divsn. Ventura (Calif.)

Med. Ctr., 1969-87; practice medicine specializing in allergy-immunology Ventura, 1984—. Cons. Bio-Dynamics Co., Ventura, 1975-80, Norwich-Eaton and Pharmacia and 3M, Ventura, 1980-85; founder botanical weed allergy walks, 1970; producer Ventura County cities street-tree guide for asthma patients; pharmacy and therapeutics com. Wellpoint (Blue Cross Calif.) Inc., 1995-99, former cons. and lectr. in field. Writer, prodr., editor films; contbr. articles on biology of pollens and molds of Ventura County to profl. jours.; patentee in field. Bd. dirs. Am. Lung Assn., Ventura, 1969-85, pres., 1974, advisor air pollution control com., 1971-74; judge Ventura Sci. Fair, 1970-85. Recipient Commendation, County Bd. Suprs., Ventura, 1974. Fellow Am. Acad. Allergy, Am. Coll. Allergists; mem. Calif. Soc. Allergy-Immunology, Calif. Med. Assn., Ventura County med. Assn., Gold Coast Tri-County Allergy Soc. (pres. 1987), CAL Club (hon.), Ventura County Sports Hall of Fame (mem. founding bd.), Mensa. Republican. Avocations: writing, photography, lecturing, pistol target shooting, fishing. Home: 928 High Point Dr Ventura CA 93003-1415 Office: Dudley Profl Ctr 4080 Loma Vista Rd Ste M Ventura CA 93003-1811 E-mail: jvillavece@aol.com

VINCENT, DAVID RIDGELY, management consulting executive; b. Detroit, Aug. 9, 1941; s. Charles Ridgely and Charlotte Jane (McCarroll) V.; m. Margaret Helen Anderson, Aug. 25, 1962 (div. 1973); children: Sandra Lee, Cheryl Ann; m. Judith Ann Gomez, July 2, 1978; 1 child, Amber; stepchildren: Michael Jr., Jesse Joseph Flores (dec.). BS, BA, Calif. State U., Sacramento, 1964; MBA, Calif. State U., Hayward, 1971; PhD, Somerset U., 1991. Cert. profl. cons. to mgmt., 1994. Sr. ops. analyst Aerojet Gen. Corp., Sacramento, 1960-66; contr. Hexcel Corp., Dublin, 1966-70; mng. dir. Memorex, Vienna, Austria, 1970-74; sales mgr. Ampex World Ops., Friebourg, Switzerland, 1974-76; dir. product mgmt. NCR, Sunnyvale, Calif., 1976-79; v.p. Boole & Babbage Inc., Sunnyvale, 1979-85; gen. mgr. Inst. Info. Mgmt., Sunnyvale Calif., Calif., 1979-85; pres., CEO The Info. Group, Inc., Santa Clara, 1985—. Author: Perspectives in Information Management, Information Economics, 1983, Handbook of Information Resource Management, 1987, The Information-Based Corporation: stakeholder economics and the technology investment, 1990, Reengineering Fundamentals: Business Processes and the Global Economy, 1994-96; contbr. monographs and papers to profl. jours. U.S. Soccer Fedn. soccer referee emeritus. Mem.: Nat. Alliance Bus. Economists (chair bus. devel. com.), Am. Electronics Assn., Soc. Competitive Intelligence Profls., World Future Soc., Product Devel. and Mgmt. Assn., Assn. Fin. Profls., Nat. Investor Rels. Inst. Home: 2803 Kalliam Dr Santa Clara CA 95051-6838 Office: The Info Group Inc 4675 Stevens Creek Blvd Ste 100 Santa Clara CA 95051-6763

VINCENT, EDWARD, state legislator; b. Steubenville, Ohio, 1934; Student, State U. Iowa; BA in Corrections and Social Welfare, Calif. State U. With L.A. County Probation Dept. Mcpl. and Superior Cts.; mayor City of Inglewood, Calif., 1982-96; mem. Calif. Ho. of Reps. from 51st dist., Sacramento, 1996-2000, Calif. Senate from 25th dist., Sacramento, 2001—. Bd. dirs. Inglewood Neighbors, Inglewood Neighborhood Housing Svcs., Inc.; mem. Urban League, New Frontier Dem. Club, Inglewood Dem. Club, Morningside High Sch. PTA, Monroe Jr. High Sch. PTA, Kew-Bennett PTA; pres. Morningside High Sch. Dad's Club. With U.A. Army, 1957-1959. Mem. NAACP, Calif. Probation Parole Corrections Assn., Black Probation Officers Assn., Calif. Narcotic Officers Assn., Mexican-Am. Corrections Assn., S.W, Horeseman, Assn., Imperial Village Blck Club, Inglewood Block Club (chmn. human affairs). Office: 1 W Manchester Blvd Ste 601 Inglewood CA 90301-1750

VINCENT, STEVE, environmental engineer; b. 1951; BS in Oceanography, U. Wash., 1974. With Weyerhaeuser, Tacoma, 1974-85, Columbia Analytical Svc., Kelso, Wash., 1986—, now pres. Office: Columbia Analytical Svc 1317 S 13th Ave Kelso WA 98626-2845

VINCENT, VERNE SAINT, protective services official; Chief police Aurora (Colo.) Police Dept., 1995—. Office: Aurora Police Dept 15001 E Alameda Dr Aurora CO 80012-1546

VINCENTI, SHELDON ARNOLD, law educator, lawyer; b. Ogden, Utah, Sept. 4, 1938; s. Arnold Joseph and Mae (Burch) V.; children: Matthew Lewis, Amanda Jo. AB, Harvard U., 1960, JD, 1963. Bar: Utah 1963. Sole practice law, Ogden, 1966-67; ptnr. Lowe and Vincenti, Ogden, 1968-70; legis. asst. to U.S. Rep. Gunn McKay, Washington, 1971-72, adminstrv. asst., 1973; prof., assoc. dean U. of Idaho Coll. of Law, Moscow, Idaho, 1973-83, dean, prof. law, 1983-95, prof. law, 1995—. Home: 2480 W Twin Rd Moscow ID 83843-9114 Office: U Idaho Coll Law 6th & Rayburn St Moscow ID 83843

VINCENTI, WALTER GUIDO, aeronautical engineer, emeritus educator; b. Balt., Apr. 20, 1917; s. Guido A. and Agnes (Nicolini) V.; m. Joyce H. Weaver, Sept. 6, 1947; children— Margaret Anna, Marc Guido. AB, Stanford U., 1938, Aero. Engr., 1940. Aero. research scientist NACA, 1940-57; prof. aero. and astronautics and history of tech. Stanford U., 1957-83, prof. emeritus, 1983—. Cons to industry, 1957— ; mem. adv. panel engrng. sec. NSF, 1960-63 Author: (with Charles H. Kruger, Jr.) Introduction to Physical Gas Dynamics, 1965, (with Nathan Rosenberg) The Britannia Bridge, 1978, What Engineers Know and How They Know It, 1990; also papers.; co-editor (with Milton Van Dyke) Annual Review of Fluid Mechanics, 1970-76. Served with USN, 1945-46. Recipient Gold medal Pi Tau Sigma, 1948, Engr.-Historian award ASME, 1997; Rockefeller Pub. Service award, 1956; Guggenheim fellow, 1963 Fellow AIAA; mem. Internat. Acad. Astronautics (corr.), Soc. History Tech. (Usher prize 1984, Leonardo da Vinci medal 1998), Nat. Acad. Engrng., Newcomen Soc., Phi Beta Kappa, Sigma Xi, Tau Beta Pi. Home: 13200 E Sunset Dr Los Altos CA 94022-3427 Office: Stanford U Stanford CA 94305 E-mail: sts@leland.stanford.edu

VINE, NAOMI, museum administrator; b. Seattle; MA and PhD, U. Chgo., 1976; postgrad., Emory U., 1991—. Dir. of edn. Mus. of Contemporary Art, Chgo., 1980-86; chief curator Dayton (Ohio) Art Inst., 1986-88; assoc. dir. High Mus. of Art, Atlanta, 1988; chief exec. ofr., pres. Orange County Mus. of Art, Newport Beach, Calif. Address: Orange Cty Museum of Art 850 San Clemente Dr Newport Beach CA 92660

VINSON, WILLIAM THEODORE, lawyer, diversified corporation executive; BS, USAF Acad., 1965; JD, UCLA, 1969. Bar: Calif. 1970. Judge advocate USAF, 1970-74; trial counsel Phillips Petroleum, San Mateo, Calif., 1974-75; atty. Lockheed Corp., Westlake Village, 1975-90, v.p. & sec., 1990-92, v.p., gen. couns., 92-95; v.p., chief counsel Lockheed Martin Corp., Westlake Village, 1995-98; cons. Lockheed Corp., Westlake Village, 1998; dir. Entex Govt. Svcs., Inc., 2001—. Bd. dirs. Entex Govt. Svcs., Inc. Bd. dirs. Westminster Free Clinic, 2001—. Office: 5560 E Napoleon Ave Oak Park CA 91377-4746

VIOLA, BILL, artist, writer; b. N.Y.C., Jan. 25, 1951; s. William John and Wynne Viola; m. Kira Perov; children: Blake, Andrei. BFA, Syracuse U., 1973, DFA, 1995, Sch. Art Inst. Chgo., 1997, Calif. Coll. Arts & Crafts, Oakland, 1998, Mass. Coll. Art, , 1999, Calif. Inst. of the Arts, Valencia, 2000, U. Sunderland, Eng., 2000. Tech. dir. Art/Tapes/22 Video Studio, Florence, Italy, 1974-76; artist-in-residence Sta. WNET, N.Y.C., 1976-83, Sony Corp., Atsugi Labs., Japan, 1980-81, San Diego Zoo, 1984; instr. Calif. Inst. of Arts, Valencia, 1983; represented by Anthony d'Offay Gallery, London, James Cohan Gallery, N.Y.C. Solo exhbns. include The Kitchen Ctr., N.Y., 1974, Everson Mus. Art, Syracuse, N.Y., 1975, Mus. Modern Art, N.Y.C., 1979, 87, Whitney Mus. Art, N.Y.C., 1982, Musee d'Art Moderne, Paris, 1983, Mus. Contemporary Art, L.A., 1985, Fukui Prefectural Mus. Art, Fukui City, Japan, 1989, Staditsche Kunsthalle Düsseldorf, 1992, Moderna Musee, Stockholm, 1993, Museo Nacional Centro de Arte Reina Sofia, Madrid, 1993, Musee Cantonal des Beaux-Arts, Lausanne, Switzerland, 1993, Whitechapel Art Gallery, London, 1993, Tel Aviv Mus. Art, 1994, Musée d'Art Contemporain, Montreal, 1993, Centro Cultural/Banco de Brazil, Rio de Janeiro, 1994, 46th Venice Biennale, 1995, Festival d'Automne Paris, 1996, Bill Viola: A 25 Year Survey Exhbn., Whitney Mus. Am. Art, N.Y., travels to Whitney Mus. Am. Art, 1997, L.A. County Mus. Am. Art, 1998, Stedelijk Mus., Amsterdam, 1998, Mus. Pur Moderne Kunst and Shirnkunstalle Dominkankloister, Germany, 1999, San Francisco Mus. Modern Art, 1999, Art Inst. Chgo., 1999-2000, 2KM, Karlsruhe, Germany, 2000, James Cohan Gallery, N.Y., 2000, Anthony d'Offay Gallery, London, 2001; group exhbns. include De Saisset Art Gallery and Mus., Santa Clara, Calif., 1972, Whitney Mus. Am. Art, 1975-87, 89, 93, Stedelijk Mus., Amsterdam, 1984, Carnegie Mus. Art, Pitts., 1988, Kölnischer Kunstverein, Cologne, Germany, 1989, Israel Mus., Jerusalem, 1990, Musée Nat. d'Art Moderne, Ctr. Georges Pompidou, Paris, 1990, Martin Gropius Bau, Berlin, 1991, Mus. Moderne Kunst, Frankfurt, Germany, 1991, Royal Acad., London, 1993, Denver Art Mus., Columbus (Ohio) Art Mus., 1994, Anthony d'Offay Gallery, London, 1995, Mus. Modern Art, N.Y.C., 1995, Tate Gallery, London, 1995, Albright-Knox Art Gallery, 1996, Fabric Workshop, Phila., 1997, MOMA, N.Y., 1999, La Beauté, Found Cartier, 2000, Tate Modern, London, 2000, Nat. Gallery, London, 2000; spl. screening film: Dèserts, Vienna, Austria, 1994, WhiteCahpel Art Gallery, London, 2001, 49th Venice Biennale, 2001, Perth Festival, Australia, 2001, Commune di Ferrara, Italy, 2001, Musse d'Art Contemporian de Montreal, Canada, 2001; commns. include The Stopping mind, Mus. Moderne Kunst, Frankfurt, 1991, Nantes Triptych, Dèlegation aux Arts Plastiques, Nantes, France, 1992, Slowly Turning Narrative, Isnt. Contemporary Art, Phila., Va. Mus. Fine Art, Richmond, 1992, Tiny Deaths, Biennale d'Art Contemporain de Lyon, France, 1993, Dèserts, Konzerthause, Vienna, 1994, 3e Biennale d'Art contemporaire de Lyon, Musèe d'art contemporain, Lyon, France, 1995, Helaba Main Tower, Frankfurt, Germany, 2000, Gotesborgs Musiken, Sweden, 2001, Deserts, Konzerthaus, Vienna, 2001, Deserts, Carnigie Hall, New York, 2001, Deserts, Royal Festival Hall, London, 2001, Deserts, IRCAM, Centre Pomidou Main Hall, Paris, 2001, others; composer: (album) David Tudor-Rainforest IV, 1981; (video) Chott el-Djerid, Anthem, 1983, Hatsu-Yume, 1981, The Reflecting Pool, 1977-79, The Space Between the Teeth, 1976, Bill Viola: Selected Works, 1986, I Do Not Know What It Is I Am Like, 1986, The Passing, 1991, The City of Man, 1989, Mantes Triptych, 1992, Slowley Turning Narritive, 1992, Tiny Deaths, 1993, The Greetings, 1995, The Crossing, 1996, The Quintet of Remembrance, 2000, The Quintet of the Unseen, 2000, The Quintet of the Astonished, The Qyuintet of the Silent, 2000, Surrender, 2001, Catherine's Room, 2001, Five Angles for the Millenium, 2001. Japan/U.S. Creative Arts fellow NEA, 1980, Rockefeller Found. Video Artist fellow, 1982, Visual Artist fellow NEA, 1983-89, Guggenheim Meml. Found. fellow, 1985, Intercultural Film/Video fellow Rockefeller Found., 1991; recipient Jury prize U.S. Film and Video Festival, 1982, Grand prize, 1983, Jury prize Video Culture/Can., 1983, Grand prize for video art, 1984, First prize for video art Athens (Ohio) Film/Video Festival, 1984, Maya Deren award Am. Film Inst., 1987, First prize Festival Internat. d'Art Video et des Nouvelles Images Electroniques de Locarno, 1987, John D. and Catherine T. MacArthur Found. award, 1989, Skowhegan medal, 1993, First prize Festival Internat. de Video, Cidade de Vigo, Spain, 1993, Medienkunstpreis, Siemens Kulturprogramm and Zentrum fur Kunst und Medientechnologie, Germany, 1993; scholar-in-residence The Getty Rsch. Inst. for History of Art and Humanities, L.A., 1998. Office: 282 Granada Ave Long Beach CA 90803 E-mail: info@billviola.com

VIOLETTE, GLENN PHILLIP, transportation engineer; b. Hartford, Conn., Nov. 15, 1950; s. Reginald Joseph and Marielle Theresa (Bernier) B.; m. Susan Linda Begam, May 15, 1988. BSCE, Colo. State U., 1982. Registered profl. engr., Colo. Engring. aide Colo. State Hwy. Dept., Glenwood Springs, Colo., 1974-79, hwy. engr., 1980-82, Loveland, 1979-80, project engr. Glenwood Canyon, 1983-97; resident engr. Colo. State Dept. Transp., Craig, 1998—. Guest speaker in field. Contbg. editor, author, photographer publs. in field. Recipient scholarship Fed. Hwy Adminstrn., 1978. Mem. ASCE, Amnesty Internat., Nat. Rifle Assn., Siera Club, Audubon Soc., Nature Conservancy, World Wildlife Fund, Cousteau Soc., Chi Epsilon. Office: Colo Dept Transp 270 Ranney St Craig CO 81625-2840 E-mail: glenn.violette@dot.state.co.us

VITERBI, ANDREW JAMES, electrical engineering and computer science educator, business executive; b. Bergamo, Italy, Mar. 9, 1935; came to U.S., 1939, naturalized, 1945; s. Achille and Maria (Luria) V.; m. Erna Finci, June 15, 1958; children: Audrey, Alan, Alexander. SB, SM, MIT, 1957; PhD, U. So. Calif., 1962; DEng (honoris causa), U. Waterloo, 1990; DTelecom Engring., U. Rome, 1997. Research group supr. C.I.T. Jet Propulsion Lab., 1957-63; mem. faculty Sch. Engring. and Applied Sci., UCLA, 1963-73, assoc. prof., 1965-69, prof., 1969-73; exec. v.p. Linkabit Corp., 1973-82; pres. M/A-Com Linkabit, Inc., 1982-84; chief scientist, sr. v.p. M/A-Com. Inc., 1985; prof. elec. engring. and computer sci. U. Calif., San Diego, 1985-94; vice chmn. Qualcomm Inc., 1985—. Chmn. U.S. Commn. C, URSI, 1982-85; vis. com. dept. elec. engring. and computer sci. MIT, 1984— Author: Principles of Coherent Communication, 1966, CDMA: Principles of Spread Spectrum Communications, 1995, (with J. K. Omura) Principles of Digital Communication and Coding, 1979; bd. editors: Information and Control, 1967, Transactions on Info. Theory, 1972-75. Recipient award for valuable contbns. to telemetry, space electonics and telemetry group IRE, 1962, best original paper award Nat. Electronics Conf., 1963, outstanding papers award, info. theory group IEEE, 1968, Christopher Columbus Internat. Comms. award, 1975, Aerospace Comm. award AIAA, 1980, Outstanding Engring. Grad. award U. So. Calif., 1986; co-recipient NEC Corp. C and C Found. award, 1992, S.O. Rice award, 1994, Edward Rhein Found. award, 1994; Marconi Internat. fellow, 1990. Fellow IEEE (Alexander Graham Bell medal 1984, Shannon lectr. internat. symposium on info. theory 1991); mem. NAE, NAS. Office: Qualcomm Inc 10185 Mckellar Ct San Diego CA 92121-4233

VIVIAN, LINDA BRADT, sales and public relations executive; b. Elmira, N.Y., Nov. 22, 1945; d. Lorenz Claude and Muriel (Dolan) Bradt; m. Robert W. Vivian, Apr. 5, 1968 (div. Sept. 1977). Student, Andrews U., 1963-66. Adminstrv. asst. Star-Gazette, Elmira, 1966-68; editor Guide, staff writer Palm Springs (Calif.) Life mag., 1970-75; dir. sales and mktg. Palm Springs Aerial Tramway, 1975-97; domestic tourism mgr. Palm Springs Desert Resorts, Rancho Mirage, Calif., 1998—. Sec. Hospitality and Bus. Industry Coun. Palm Springs Desert Resorts, 1989-91, 1997, vice-chmn. 1991-94, chmn., 1994-95. Mem. Hotel Sales and Mktg. Assn. (allied nominating chmn. Palm Springs chpt. 1986-88), Am. Soc. Assn. Execs., Travel Industry Assn., Hospitality Industry and Bus. Coun. of Palm Springs Resorts (sec. 1989-91, vice-chmn. 1991-94, chmn. 1994-95), Nat. Tour Assn. (co-chair Team Calif. promotions com. 1993-97, ambs. subcom. 2000), Calif. Travel Industry Assn., Desert Gay Tourism Guild, Palm Springs C. of C. (bd. dirs. 1984-85). Republican. Avocations: golf, reading. Office: Palm Springs Deserts Resorts CVA 69-930 Hwy 111 # 201 Rancho Mirage CA 92270 E-mail: lvivian@palmspringsusa.com

VIZARD, MICHAEL, periodical editor; Editor PC Week, Computerworld, Digital Review; editor news InfoWorld, 1995-97, v.p. news, 1997, editor-in-chief. Office: InfoWorld Pub 155 Bovet Rd Ste 800 San Mateo CA 94402-3150

VLASAK, WALTER RAYMOND, state official, human resource manager; b. Hartsgrove, Ohio, Aug. 31, 1938; s. Raymond Frank and Ethel (Chilan) V.; m. Julia Andrews, Feb. 25, 1966; children: Marc Andrew, Tanya Ethel. BSBA, Kent State U., 1963; MA, U. Akron, 1975. Commd. 2d lt. U.S. Army, 1963; platoon leader, anti-tank platoon leader and battalion adjutant 82d Airborne Div., 1963-65; combat duty Viet Nam, 1965-66, 68-69; exec. officer, co. comdr. and hdqrs. commandant of the cadre and troops U.S. Army Sch. Europe, Oberammergau, Fed. Republic Germany, 1966-68; asst. prof. Mil. Sci. Kent (Ohio) State U., 1970-74; infantry battalion exec. officer 9th Infantry Div., Ft. Lewis, Wash., 1976-77, orgnl. effectiveness cons. to commanding gen., 1977-79, brigade exec. officer, 1980-82; orgnl. effectiveness cons. to commanding gen. 8th U.S. Army, U.S. Forces, Korea, 1979-80; advanced through ranks to lt. col. U.S. Army, 1980, ret., 1984; pres. Comsult, Inc., Tacoma, 1984—; mgr. employee devel. tng. dept. social and health svcs. State of Wash., Tacoma, 1985—. Decorated Legion of Merit, Bronze Star with V device and two oak leaf clusters, Air medal, Purple Heart, Vietnamese Cross of Gallantry with Silver Star. Mem. Am. Soc. for Tng. and Devel., Assn. U.S. Army (bd. dirs. Tacoma 1984—). Avocations: hiking, camping, fishing. Home: 10602 Hill Terrace Rd SW Tacoma WA 98498-4337 Office: State Wash Dept Social & Health Svcs 8425 27th St W Tacoma WA 98466-2722 E-mail: wrvlasak@qwest.net

VOELLGER, GARY A. retired career officer; B in Indsl. rels. Pers. mgmt., San Jose State U., 1967; grad., Squadron Officer Sch., 1971; M in psychology, Peperdine U., 1976; grad., Air Command Staff Coll., Maxwell AFB, 1979, Air War Coll., 1987; cert. in Joint Flag Officer War Fighting, Maxwell AFB, 1997; cert.in sr. mgrs. govt. seminar, Harvard U., 1997. Commd. 2d. lt. USAF, 1967, advanced through grades to maj. gen., 1996; pers. officer 379th Combat Support Grp., Wurtsmith AFB, Mich., 1967-69; undergrad. navigator trng. Mather AFB, Calif., 1969-69; weapons syss. officer 46th Tactical Fighter Squadron, MacDill AFB, Fla., 1970-70, 91st Tactical Fighter Squadron, Royal Air Force Bentwaters, Eng., 1970-72; undergrad. pilot trng. Loredo AFB, Tex., 1972-72; F-111 transition trng. Nellis AFB, Nev., 1973-73; F-111 pilot 428th Tactical Fighter Squadron, Takhli Royal AFB, Thailand, 1973-74; F-111 instr. pilot, flight comdr., standardization and evaluation flight examiner 523rd Tactical Fighter Squadron, 27th Tactical Fighter Wing, Cannon AFB, N.Mex., 1974-79; air ops. staff officer, politico-mil. affairs officer, asst. dep. dir. Joint Nat. Security Coun. Matters Hdqs. USAF, Washington, 1980-84; comdr. 55th Tactical Fighter Squadron, Royal Air Force, Upper Heyford, Eng., 1984-87; asst. dep. comdr. ops. 20th Tactical Fighter Wing, Royal Air force, Eng.; dep. comdr. ops. 4450th Tactical Group, Nellis AFB, Nev., 1988-89, vice comdr., 1989-90; comdr. 552nd Air Control Wing, Tinker AFB, Okla., 1990-92, Coll. Aerospace Doctrine, Rsch. and Edn., Air U., Maxwell AFB, Ala., 1992-93, 43rd Air Refueling Wing, Malmstrom AFB, Mont., 1993-94, 92nd Air Refueling Wing, Fairchild AFB, Wash., 1994-95, 437th Airlift Wing, Charleston AFB, S.C., 1995-96; dir. ops. Hdqs. Air Mobility Command, Scott AFB, Ill., 1996-98; NATO force comdr. Hdqs. NATO Airborne Early Warning Force, Mons, Belgium, 1998-2000; ret. Decorated D.D.S.M., Legion of Merit with oak leaf Cluster, Bronze Star medal, Meritorious Svc. medal with two oak leaf clusters, Air medal with oak leaf cluster, Armed Forces Expeditionary medal, Rep. Vietnam Gallantry Cross with Palm. Office: NAEWF/CC Bldg 101 Rm K-123 2704 Brookstone Ct Las Vegas NV 89117

VOELZ, DAVID GEORGE, electrical engineer; b. Idaho Falls, Idaho, Feb. 24, 1959; s. George Leo and Emily Jane (Neunast) V.; m. Judi Rae Gore, Aug. 12, 1983. MSEE, U. Ill., 1983, PhD in Elec. Engring., 1987. Rsch. asst. U. Ill., Urbana, 1981-86; electronics engr. Phillips Lab. (formally USAF Weapons Lab.), Kirtland AFB, N.Mex., 1986—. Contbr. articles to Jour. of Geophysical Rsch., Applied Optics, and Optics Letters. Boy scout master Boy Scouts Am., Albuquerque, 1988-90. Recipient, Engineering Excellence award Optical Society of Am., 1995. Fellow Soc. of Photo-Optical Instrumentation Engrs.; mem. IEEE, Optical Soc. Am. Republican. Lutheran. Home: 5232 Camino Sandia NE Albuquerque NM 87111-5769 Office: AFRL/DEBS Kirtland AFB NM 87117

VOGEL, ROBERT LEE, college administrator, clergyman; b. Phillipsburg, Kans., Sept. 27, 1934; s. Howard and Marie V.; m. Sally M. Johnson, June 3, 1956; children— Susan, Kirk B.A., Wartburg Coll., 1956; B.D., M.Div., Wartburg Theol. Sem., 1960, D.D. (hon.), 1976. Ordained to ministry Am. Lutheran Ch., 1960. Organizing pastor Faith Luth. Ch., Golden, Colo., 1960-65; regional dir. div. youth activity Am. Luth. Ch., Chgo., 1965-67, dir. parish resources, div. youth activity Mpls., 1967-69; sr. pastor Our Savior's Luth. Ch., Denver, 1969-73; exec. asst. to pres. Am. Luth. Ch., Mpls., 1973-80; pres. Wartburg Coll., Waverly, Iowa, 1980-98; interim pres. Grand View Coll., 1999. V.p. Internat. Luther League, Am. Luth. Ch., 1953-58, pres., 1958-60; ofcl. observer Luth. World Fedn. Assembly, 1957; mem. com. on laity Am. Luth. Ch., 1964-67. Mem. nominating com., theol. edn. coord. com. Evang. Luth. Ch. Am., 1996—. Recipient Alumni citation Wartburg Coll., 1978 Mem. Coun. Ind. Colls., Iowa Assn. Ind. Colls. and Univs. (chmn. bd. 1987-88), Luth. Ednl. Conf. N. Am. (pres. 1988-89), Nat. Assn. Ind. Colls. and Univs. (commn. mem.). Home and Office: 900 Saint Paul St Denver CO 80206-3940

VOGELSBERG, ROSS TIMM, education educator, researcher; b. Bryn Mawr, Pa., Feb. 23, 1945; s. Robert Wilhelm Vogelsberg and Jean Byram (Fishburn) Blanchard. BS, Colo. State U., 1968; MS, Utah State U., 1974; PhD, U. Ill., 1979. Part-time assoc. Gateways Inc., Ft. Collins, Colo., 1968; master resource tchr. Utah State U., Logan, 1972-74, assoc. dir. project, 1974-77; rsch. assoc. U. Ill., Urbana, 1977-79; project dir., asst. prof. U. Vt., Burlington, 1979-85; project dir., assoc. prof. Temple U., Phila., 1985-94; exec. dir., prof. Rural Inst. Disabilities U. Mont., Missoula, 1995—. Contbr. numerous articles to profl. jours. and chpts. in books. With U.S. Army, 1969-71, ETO. Named one of Outstanding Young Men of Am., U.S. Jaycees, 1982; recipient Svc. award United Cerebral Palsy Pa., 1986. Mem. Assn. for Spl. Edn. Tech., Am. Ednl. Rsch. Assn., Assn. for Persons Analysis, Assn. for Persons with Severe Handicaps, Nat. Soc. for Performance and Instruction, Assn. for the Advancement of Behavior Therapy, Coun. for Exceptional Children, Am. Asns. on Mental Deficiency. Office: U Mont Rural Inst 634 Eddy Ave Missoula MT 59812-0001

VOGT, ERICH WOLFGANG, physicist, academic administrator; b. Steinbach, Man., Can., Nov. 12, 1929; s. Peter Andrew and Susanna (Reimer) V.; m. Barbara Mary Greenfield, Aug. 27, 1952; children: Edith Susan, Elizabeth Mary, David Eric, Jonathan Michael, Robert Jeremy. BS, U. Man., 1951, MS, 1952; PhD, Princeton U., 1955; DSc (hon.), U. Man., 1982, Queen's U., 1984; LLD (hon.), U. Regina, 1986; DSc (hon.), Carleton U., 1988, U. B.C., 1999; LLD (hon.), Simon Fraser U., 1996. Rsch. officer Chalk River (Ont.) Nuclear Labs., 1956-65; prof. physics U. B.C., Vancouver, 1965-95, prof. emeritus, 1995—, assoc. dir. TRIUMF Project, 1968-73, dir. TRIUMF Project, 1981-94, v.p. univ., 1975-81; chmn. Sci. Council B.C., 1978-80. Co-editor: Advances in Nuclear Physics, 1968—; Contbr. articles to profl. jours. Decorated officer Order of Can.; recipient Centennial medal of Can., 1967 Fellow Royal Soc. Can., Am. Phys. Soc.; mem. Can. Assn. Physicists (past pres., gold medal for achievement in physics 1988). Office: Triumf 4004 Wesbrook Mall Vancouver BC Canada V6T 2A3

VOGT, ROCHUS EUGEN, physicist, educator; b. Neckarelz, Germany, Dec. 21, 1929; came to U.S., 1953; s. Heinrich and Paula (Schaefer) V.; m. Micheline Alice Yvonne Bauduin, Sept. 6, 1958; children: Michele, Nicole. Student, U. Karlsruhe, Germany, 1950-52, U. Heidelberg, 1952-53; SM, U. Chgo., 1957, PhD, 1961. Asst. prof. physics Calif. Inst. Tech., Pasadena, 1962-65, assoc. prof., 1965-70, prof., 1970—, R. Stanton Avery disting.

svc. prof., 1982—, chmn. faculty, 1975-77, chief scientist Jet Propulsion Lab., 1977-78, chmn. div. physics, math. and astronomy, 1978-83, acting dir. Owens Valley Radio Obs., 1980-81, v.p. and provost, 1983-87. Vis. prof. physics MIT, 1988-94; dir. Caltech/MIT Laser Interferometer Gravitational Wave Observatory Project, 1987-94. Author: Cosmic Rays (in World Book Ency.), 1978, (with R.B. Leighton) Exercises in Introductory Physics, 1969; contbr. articles to profl. jours. Fulbright fellow, 1953-54; recipient Exceptional Sci. Achievement medal NASA, 1981, Profl. Achievement award U. Chgo. Alumni Assn., 1981. Fellow AAAS, A. Phys. Soc. Achievements include research in astrophysics and gravitation. Office: Calif Inst Tech Dept Physics 103-33 Pasadena CA 91125-0001 E-mail: vogt@caltech.edu

VOHS, JAMES ARTHUR, health care program executive; b. Idaho Falls, Idaho, Sept. 26, 1928; s. John Dale and Cliff Lucille (Packer) V.; m. Janice Hughes, Sept. 19, 1953 (dec. Oct. 1999); children: Lorraine, Carol, Nancy, Sharla. B.A., U. Calif., Berkeley, 1952; postgrad., Harvard Sch. Bus., 1966. Employed by various Kaiser affiliated orgns., 1952-92; chmn., pres., CEO Kaiser Found. Hosps. and Kaiser Found. Health Plan, INc., Oakland, Calif., 1975-92, chmn. emeritus; chmn. bd. dirs. Holy Names Coll., 1981-92; chmn. Marcus Foster Inst., 1981—. Chmn. Fed. Res. Bank San Francisco, 1991-94. Bd. dirs. Oakland-Alameda County Coliseum Complex, 1986-96, Bay Area Coun., 1985-94, chmn., 1991-92; mem. Oakland Bd. Port Commrs., 1993-96. With AUS, 1946-48. Mem. NAS, Inst. Medicine.

VOJTA, PAUL ALAN, mathematics educator; b. Mpls., Sept. 30, 1957; s. Francis J. and Margaret L. V. B in Math., U. Minn., 1978; MA, Harvard U., 1980, PhD, 1983. Instr. Yale U., New Haven, 1983-86; fellow Math. Scis. Rsch. Inst., Berkeley, Calif., 1986-87, Miller Inst. for Basic Rsch., Berkeley, 1987-89; assoc. prof. U. Calif., Berkeley, 1989-92, prof., 1992—. Mem. Inst. for Advanced Study, Princeton, 1989-90, 96-97. Author: Diophantine Approximations and Value Distribution Theory, 1987. Recipient perfect score Internat. Math. Olympiad, 1975. Mem. Am. Math. Soc. (Frank Nelson Cole Number Theory prize 1992), Math. Assn. Am., Phi Beta Kappa, Tau Beta Pi. Avocations: computer, skiing. Office: Univ Calif Dept Math 970 Evans Hall # 3840 Berkeley CA 94720-3840

VOLBERDING, PAUL ARTHUR, academic physician; b. Rochester, Minn., Sept. 26, 1949; s. Walter A. and Eldora M. (Prescher) V.; m. Juline Christofferson, June 15, 1971 (div. June 1976); m. Mary M. Cooke, June 6, 1980; children: Alexander, Benjamin, Emily. AB, U. Chgo., 1971; MD, U. Minn., 1975. Resident in internal medicine U. Utah, Salt Lake City, 1975-78; fellow in oncology U. Calif., San Francisco, 1978-81; dir. med. oncology San Francisco Gen. Hosp., 1981—, dir. AIDS program, 1983—; dir. Ctr. for AIDS Rsch. U. Calif., San Francisco, 1988—, prof. medicine, 1990—. Bd. dirs. Dignity Ptnrs. Inc., 1996—. Editor: Medical Management in AIDS, 1986; editor Jour. of AIDS, 1990—. Fellow ACP, AAAS; mem. Internat. AIDS Soc. (founder, chmn. bd.). Office: U Calif San Francisco San Francisco AIDS Program 995 Potrero Ave San Francisco CA 94110-2859

VOLGY, THOMAS JOHN, political science educator, organization official; b. Budapest, Hungary, Mar. 19, 1946; BA magna cum laude, Oakland U., 1967; MA, U. Minn., 1969, PhD, 1972. Prof. polit. sci. U. Ariz., Tucson; dir. U. Teaching Ctr.; mayor City of Tucson, 1987-91. Exec. dir. Internat. Studies Assn., 1995—; chmn. telecom. com. U. Conf. Mayors, 1988—; Dem. nominee for congress, 1998; cons. H.S. curriculum project Ind. U. Co-author: The Forgotten Americans, 1992; editor: Exploring Relationships Between Mass Media and Political Culture: The Impact of Television and Music on American Society, 1976; contbr. articles to profl. jours.; producer two TV documentaries for PBS. Mem. Nat. Women's Polit. Caucus Conv., 1983, U.S. Senate Fin. Com., 1985, U.S. Ho. of Reps. Telecomm. Com., 1988—, Polit. Sci. Adminstrn. Com., 1986, Gov.'s Task Force on Women and Poverty, 1986, United Way, 1985-87; bd. dirs. Honors Program, 1981—, U. Teaching Ctr., 1988—, Tucson Urban League, 1981, Ododo Theatre, 1984, So. Ariz. Mental Health Care Ctr., 1987, Nat. Fedn. Local Cable TV Programmers; chmn. Internat. Rels. Caucus, 1981, 86—, Transp. and Telecommunications Com. Nat. League Cities, 1986, 88-91. NDEA scholar, 1964-76; NDEA fellow, 1967-70; recipient Oasis award for oustanding prodn. of local affairs TV programming; named Outstanding Young Am., 1981, Outstanding Naturalized Citizen of Yr., 1980; faculty research grantee U. Ariz., 1972-75, 77-78. Mem. Pima Assn. Govts., Nat. Fedn. Local Cable Programmers. Democrat. Jewish. Office: U Ariz Polit Dept Sci Tucson AZ 85721-0001

VOLLRATH, FREDERICK E. career officer; BBA in Mgmt., U. Miami; MA in Pers. Mgmt./Adminstrn., Cen. Mich. U.; grad., U.S. Army Command/Gen. Staff, U.S. Army War Coll. Commd. 2d lt. U.S. Army, 1963, advanced through grades to lt. gen., 1996, ret., 1998, chief pers. mgmt. sect., mil. pers. divsn. Off. Adj. Gen. Vietnam, 1967-68; chief pers. svcs. divsn., then dep. adjutant gen. 4th Adjutant Gen. Co., 4th Infantry Divsn., Ft. Carson, Colo., 1972-74; adjutant gen., dep. chief of staff 4th Infantry Divsn. Ft. Carson, 1977-80; dir. pers. svc. support, enlisted pers. mgmt. 1st pers. cmd. U.S. Army Europe and 7th Army, Germany, 1981-84, dep. comdr. 1st pers. command, 1986-88; comdg. gen. U.S. Army Pers. Info. Sys. Command, Alexandria, Va., 1988; dir. mil. pers. mgmt. Office of Dep. Chief of Staff Pers. U.S. Army, Washington, 1995-96, dep. chief of staff for pers., 1996-98; corp. v.p. human resources Computer Sci. Corp., El Segundo, Calif. Decorated Meritorious Svc. medal with 4 oak leaf clusters. Office: Computer Sci Corp 2100 El Grand Ave El Segundo CA 90245

VOLMAN, DAVID HERSCHEL, chemistry educator; b. Los Angeles, July 10, 1916; s. Carl Herman and Blanche (Taylor) V.; m. Ruth Clare Jackson, Sept. 15, 1944; children: Thomas Peter, Susan Frances, Daniel Henry. B.A., UCLA, 1937; M.S., 1938; Ph.D. (Standard Oil Co. fellow), Stanford U., 1940. Mem. faculty U. Calif.-Davis, 1940-41, 46—, prof. chemistry, 1956-87, emeritus prof. chemistry, 1987—, chmn. dept., 1974-81, chmn. Acad. Senate, 1971-72; research chemist OSRD, 1941-46; research fellow Harvard U., 1949-50. Vis. prof. U. Wash. 1958 Editor: Advances in Photochemistry, 1983-98; mem. editorial bd. Jour. Photochemistry and Photobiology, 1972-98; contbr. articles to profl. jours. Grantee Research Corp. Am.; Grantee NIH; Grantee U.S. Army Research Office; Grantee NSF; Guggenheim fellow, 1949-50 Mem. Am. Chem. Soc., AAUP, Inter-Am. Photochem. Soc., Assn. Harvard Chemists, Sigma Xi. Office: U Calif Davis Dept Chemistry 1 Shields Ave Davis CA 95616

VOLPE, PETER ANTHONY, surgeon; b. Columbus, Ohio, Dec. 17, 1936; s. Peter Anthony and Jeanette Katherine (Volz) V.; m. Suzanne Stephens, Sept. 5, 1959 (div. 1977); children: John David, Michael Charles; m. Kathleen Ann Townsend, Mar. 28, 1978 (div. 1999); 1 child, Mark Christopher; m. Theresa Ann Morse, Aug. 27, 2000. BA cum laude, Ohio State U., 1958, MD summa cum laude, 1961. Diplomate Am. Bd. Surgery, Am. Bd. Colon and Rectal Surgery (pres. 1988). Pvt. practice, San Francisco, 1969—; sr. ptnr. Volpe, Chui, Abel, Yee, Sternberg, San Francisco, 1987—; clin. prof. surgery U. Calif., San Francisco, 1995—. Asst. clin. prof. surgery U. Calif., San Francisco, 1972-95, clin. prof., 1995—; chmn. dept. surgery St. Mary's Hosp. and Med. Ctr., San Francisco, 1978-90. Contbr. articles to profl. jours. Lt. USN, 1962-64. Fellow ACS (bd. govs. 1988-94), Am. Soc. Colon and Rectal Surgeons (treas. 1985-89, pres. 1990); mem. San Francisco Surg. Soc., San Francisco Med. Soc. Republican. Roman Catholic. Office: Volpe Chiu Abel and Yee Sternberg 3838 California St San Francisco CA 94118-1522

VOLPERT, RICHARD SIDNEY, lawyer; b. Cambridge, Mass., Feb. 16, 1935; s. Samuel Abbot and Julia (Fogel) V.; m. Marcia Flaster, June 11, 1958; children: Barry, Sandy, Linda, Nancy. B.A., Amherst Coll., 1956; LL.B. (Stone scholar), Columbia U., 1959. Bar: Calif. bar 1960. Atty. firm O'Melveny & Myers, Los Angeles, 1959-86, ptnr. L.A., 1967-86, Skadden, Arps, Slate, Meagher & Flom, L.A., 1986-95, Munger, Tolles & Olson, L.A., 1995—. Pub. Jewish Jour. of Los Angeles, 1985-87 . Editor, chmn.: Los Angeles Bar Jour, 1965, 66, 67, Calif. State Bar Jour, 1972-73. Chmn. community relations com. Jewish Fedn.-Council Los Angeles, 1977-80; bd. dirs. Jewish Fedn.-Council Greater Los Angeles, 1976-99, v.p., 1978-81; pres. Los Angeles County Natural History Mus. Found., 1978-84, trustee, 1974—, chair bd. dirs., 1992-97, pres., bd. govs., 1997—; chmn. bd. councilors U. So. Calif. Law Center, 1979-85; vice chmn. Nat. Jewish Community Relations Adv. Council, 1981-84, mem. exec. com., 1978-85; bd. dirs. U. Judaism, 1973-89, bd. govs., 1973-89; bd. dirs. Valley Beth Shalom, Encino, Calif., 1964-88; mem. capital program major gifts com. Amherst Coll., 1978-86; bd. dirs., mem. exec. com. Los Angeles Wholesale Produce Market Devel. Corp., 1978-95, v.p., 1981-93, pres. 1993-96; mem. exec. bd. Los Angeles chpt. Am. Jewish Com., 1967—, pres., 1999—; vice-chmn. Los Angeles County Econ. Devel. Council, 1978-81; bd. dirs. Jewish Community Found., 1981—, Brandeis-Bardin Inst., 1995-2000; mem. Pacific S.W. regional bd. Anti Defamation League B'nai B'rith, 1964—. Named Man of Year, 1978 Fellow Am. Bar Found.; mem. Los Angeles County Bar Assn. (trustee 1968-70, chmn. real property sect. 1974-75), Los Angeles County Bar Found. (trustee 1977-80, 96-99), Calif. Bar Assn. (com. on adminstrn. justice 1973-76), Am. Coll. Real Estate Lawyers (bd. govs. 1996-99), Anglo-Am. Real Property Inst. (treas. 1995-98), Amherst Club of So. Calif. (dir. 1968-85, pres. 1972-73), City Club (L.A.). Jewish. Home: 16055 Royal Oak Rd Encino CA 91436-3913 Office: Munger Tolles & Olson 355 S Grand Ave 35th Fl Los Angeles CA 90071-1560 E-mail: volpertrs@mto.com

VON BARGEN, SALLY, stock image photography company executive; BA in Psychology, U. Calif., Santa Cruz; MEd, Seattle U. Circulation dir. CommTek Comm.; founding v.p. sales and mktg. Netlink; cons. Gen. Instruments, Citicorp, Fingerhut and Viacom; advisor and orgnl. cons. to CEO and pres. Photo Disc, founding mem. mgmt. team, co-pres.; pres. Getty One, Seattle. Mem. Satellite Broadcasting Assn. (nat. bd. dirs.). Office: Getty Images Inc 701 N 34th St Ste 400 Seattle WA 98103-3415

VON BRANDENSTEIN, PATRIZIA, production designer; Prodn. designer The Mirisch Agy., L.A., 1978—. Prodn. designer films including Heartland, 1979, Breaking Away, 1979, Ragtime, 1981 (Academy Award nomination best art direction 1981), Silkwood, 1983, Amadeus, 1984 (Academy Award best art direction 1984), A Chorus Line, 1985, The Money Pit, 1986, No Mercy, 1987, The Untouchables, 1987 (Academy Award nomination best art direction 1987), Working Girl, 1988, The Lemon Sisters, 1990, Postcards From the Edge, 1990, Billy Bathgate, 1992, Sneakers, 1992, Leap of Faith, 1993, Six Degrees of Separation, 1993, The Quick and the Dead, 1995, Just Cause, 1995, The People vs. Larry Flynt, 1996, A Simple Plan, 1998, Man on the Moon, 1999, Shaft, 2000; costume designer films including Between the Lines, 1977, Saturday Night Fever, 1977, A Little Sex, 1982.

VONDER HAAR, THOMAS H. meteorology educator; b. Quincy, Ill., Dec. 28, 1942; m. Dee M. Clark, 1980; children: Kim, Kurt, Nicholas, Krista, Matthew. BS, St. Louis U., 1963; MS, U. Wis., 1964, PhD in Meteorology, 1968. Assoc. scientist meteorology Space Sci. & Engring. Ctr. U. Wis., Madison, 1968-70; assoc. prof. meteorology Colo. State U., Ft. Collins, 1970-77, prof. atmospheric sci., 1977—, univ. disting. prof., 1994, head dept. atmospheric sci., 1974-84, acting dean Coll. Engring., 1981-82. Cons. U.S. Army, ITT Aerospace, Sci. and Tech. Corp., World Meteor Orgn. UN, Ball Aerospace Corp., 1969—. Mem. Am. Meteorol. Soc., Sigma Xi. Office: Coop Inst Rsch in Atmosphere Colo State U 515 S Howes St Fort Collins CO 80523-1375

VON DER HEYDT, JAMES ARNOLD, federal judge; b. Miles City, Mont., July 15, 1919; s. Harry Karl and Alice S. (Arnold) von der H.; m. Verna E. Johnson, May 21, 1952. BA, Albion (Mich.) Coll., 1942; JD, Northwestern, 1951. Bar: Alaska 1951. Pvt. practice, Nome, 1953-59; judge superior ct. Juneau, Alaska, 1959-66; from judge to sr. judge U.S. Dist. Ct. Alaska, 1966—; U.S. commr. Nome, 1951—; U.S. atty. div. 2 Dist. Alaska, 1951-53; mem. Alaska Ho. of Reps., 1957-59. Author: Mother Sawtooth's Nome, 1990, Alaska, The Short and Long of It, 2000. Pres. Anchorage Fine Arts Mus. Assn. Recipient Disting. Alumni award Albion Coll., 1995. Mem. Alaska Bar Assn. (mem. bd. govs. 1955-59, pres. 1959-60), Am. Judicature Soc., Masons (32d degree), Shriners, Phi Delta Phi, Sigma Nu. Club: Mason (32 deg.), Shriner. Avocation: researching Arctic bird life, creative writing. Office: US Dist Ct 222 W 7th Ave Box 40 Anchorage AK 99513-7564

VON HIPPEL, PETER HANS, chemistry educator, molecular biology researcher; b. Goettingen, Germany, Mar. 13, 1931; came to U.S., 1937, naturalized, 1942; s. Arthur Robert and Dagmar (franck) von H.; m. Josephine Baron Raskind, June 20, 1954; children: David F., James A., Benjamin J. B.S., MIT, 1952, M.S., 1953, Ph.D., 1955. Phys. biochemist Naval Med. Research Inst., Bethesda, Md., 1956-59; from asst. prof. to assoc. prof. biochemistry Med. Sch. Dartmouth Coll., 1959-67; prof. chemistry, mem. Inst. Molecular Biology U. Oreg., 1967-79, dir. Inst. Molecular Biology, 1969-80, chmn. dept. chemistry, 1980-87; rsch. prof. chemistry Am. Cancer Soc., 1989—. Chmn. biopolymers Gordon Conf., 1968; mem. trustees vis. com. biology dept. MIT, 1973-76; mem. bd. sci. counsellors Nat. Inst. Arthritis, Metabolic and Digestive Diseases, NIH, 1974-78, mem. coun. Nat. Inst. Gen. Med. Scis., 1982-86, mem. dir.'s adv. com., 1987-92; mem. sci. and tech. ctrs. adv. com. NSF, 1987-89; bd. dirs. Fedn. Am. Socs. for Exptl. Biology, 1994-98; mem. NIH-CSR panel on boundaries for sci. rev., 1998—. Mem. editl. bd. Jour. Biol. Chemistry, 1967-73, 76-82, Biochem. Biophys. Acta, 1965-70, Physiol. Revs., 1972-77, Biochemistry, 1977-80, Trends in Biochem. Soc., 1987—, Protein Sci., 1990-95; editor Jour. Molecular Biology, 1986-94; contbr. articles to profl. jours., chpts. to books. Lt. M.S.C. USNR, 1956-59. Recipient Merck award Am. Soc. Biochem. and Molecular Biology, 2000; NSF predoctoral fellow, 1953-55; NIH postdoctoral fellow, 1955-56; NIH sr. fellow, 1959-67; Guggenheim fellow, 1973-74 Fellow Am. Acad. Arts and Scis.; mem. AAAS, Am. Chem. Soc., Am. Soc. Biol. Chemists, Biophys. Soc. (mem. coun. 1970-73, pres. 1973-74), Nat. Acad. Scis., Fedn. Biochem. and Molecular Biology, Am. Scientists, Sigma Xi. Home: 1900 Crest Dr Eugene OR 97405-1753

VON KALINOWSKI, JULIAN ONESIME, lawyer; b. St. Louis, May 19, 1916; s. Walter E. and Maybelle (Michaud) von K.; m. Penelope Jayne Dyer, June 29, 1980; children by previous marriage: Julian Onesime, Wendy Jean von Kalinowski. BA, Miss. Coll., 1937; JD with honors, U. Va., 1940. Bar: Va. 1940, Calif. 1946. Assoc. Gibson, Dunn and Crutcher, L.A., 1946-52, ptnr., 1953-85, mem. exec. com., 1962-82, adv. ptnr., 1985—; CEO, chmn. Litigation Scis., Inc., Culver City, Calif., 1991-94, chmn. emeritus Torrance, 1994-96, Dispute Dyamics, Inc., Torrance, 1996-2000. Instr. Columbia Law Sch., Parker Sch. Fgn. and Comparative Law, summer 1981; instr. antitrust law So. Meth. Sch. of Law, summer 1982-84, bd. visitors, 1982-85; v.p., bd. dirs., dir. W.M. Keck Found.; mem. faculty Practising Law Inst., 1971, 76, 78, 79, 80; instr. in spl. course on antitrust litigation Columbia U. Law Sch., N.Y.C., 1981; mem. lawyers dels. com. to 9th Cir. Jud. Conf., 1953-67; UN expert Mission to People's Republic China, 1982. Contbr. articles to legal jours.; author: Antitrust Laws and Trade Regulation, 1969, desk edit., 1981; gen. editor: World Law of Competition, 1978, Antitrust Counseling and Litigation Techniques, 1984; gen. editor emeritus Antitrust Report. With USN, 1941-46, capt. Res. ret. Fellow Am. Bar Found., Am. Coll. Trial Lawyers (chmn. complex litigation com. 1984-87); mem. ABA (ho. of dels. 1970, chmn. antitrust law sect. 1972-73), State Bar Calif. (Anti-Trust Lawyer of Yr. award 2000), L.A. Bar Assn., U. Va. Law Sch. Alumni Assn., Calif. Club, L.A. Country Club, La Jolla Beach and Tennis Club, Phi Kappa Psi, Phi Alpha Delta. Republican. Episcopalian. Home: 12320 Ridge Cir Los Angeles CA 90049-1151 E-mail: JOvonK@aol.com

VON STUDNITZ, GILBERT ALFRED, state official; b. Hamburg, Germany, Nov. 24, 1950; came to U.S., 1954. s. Helfrid and Rosemarie Sofie (Kreiten) von S.; m. Erica Lynn Hoot, May 26, 1990. BA, Calif. State U., L.A., 1972. Adminstrv. hearing officer State of Calif., Montebello, 1987-91, mgr. III driver control policy unit Dept. Motor Vehicles Sacramento, 1991-93; ops. mgr. Driver Safety Review, 1993-95; contract mgr. State Dept. Health Svcs., 1995-97; staff mgr. licensing ops. policy Dept. Motor Vehicles, Sacramento, 1997-2000; Welcare-to-Work regional mgr. State Health and Human Svcs. Agy., Sacramento, 2000—. Author: Aristocracy in America, 1989; editor publs. on German nobility in U.S., 1986—. Active L.A. Conservancy, West Adams Heritage Assn., dir., 1989-91. Fellow: Entente Cordiale for Chivalric and Heraldic Traditions, Am. Soc. for Chivalric Rsch. (hon.); mem.: Assn. German Nobility in N.Am. (pres. 1985—), Benicia Hist. Soc., Intertel, Orders and Medals Soc. Am., Mensa, Sierra Club, Phi Sigma Kappa (v.p. chpt. 1978), Calif. State mgrs. Assn., Nat. Assn. Managed Care Regulators, Driver Improvement Assn. Calif. (v.p. 1992—96, dir. media rels. 1996—). Roman Catholic. Avocations: genealogical research, collecting. Home: 1101 W 2nd St Benicia CA 94510-3125

VOORHEES, JAMES DAYTON, JR. lawyer; b. Haverford, Pa., Nov. 14, 1917; s. James Dayton Voorhees and Elsa Denison Jameson; m. Mary Margaret Fuller, Sept. 5, 1942 (dec. Apr. 1991); children: J. Dayton III, Susan F. Voorhees-Maxfield, Jane Voorhees Kiss. BA, Yale U., 1940; JD, Harvard U., 1943. Bar: N.H. 1947, Colo. 1948, U.S. Dist. Ct. Colo. 1948, U.S. Ct. Appeals (10th cir.) 1949, U.S. Ct. Appeals (5th cir.) 1956, U.S. Supreme Ct. 1960. Assoc. Johnson & Robertson, Denver, 1947-50; atty. Conoco Inc., Denver, 1950-56; ptnr. Moran, Reidy & Voorhees, Denver, 1956-78, Kutak, Rock & Huie, Denver, 1978-80; ptnr., counsel Davis, Graham & Stubbs, Denver, 1980—. Bd. dirs. Japex (U.S.) Corp., Houston. Mem. Denver Bd. Edn., 1965-71, pres. 1967-69. Lt. comdr. USNR, 1941-46, ATO, PTO. Mem. ABA, Colo. Bar Assn., Denver Bar Assn., Denver Country Club, University Club. Republican. Avocation: golf.

VOORHEES, JOHN LLOYD, columnist; b. DeWitt, Iowa, Aug. 30, 1925; s. Lloyd William and Elsie Irene (Bousselot) V. BA in History, U. Iowa, 1951; BA in Journalism, U. Wash., 1953. Tchr. Oelwein (Iowa) High Sch., 1951-52; columnist Seattle Post-Intelligencer, 1953-71; columnist, critic Seattle Times, 1971-98. With U.S. Army, 1946-48. Democrat.

VOSBECK, ROBERT RANDALL, architect; b. Mankato, Minn., May 18, 1930; s. William Frederick and Gladys (Anderson) V.; m. Phoebe Macklin, June 21, 1953; children: Gretchen, Randy, Heidi, Macklin. BArch, U. Minn., 1954. Various archtl. positions, 1956-62; ptnr. Vosbeck-Vosbeck & Assocs., Alexandria, Va., 1962-66, VVKR Partnership, Alexandria, 1966-79; exec. v.p. VVKR Inc., 1979-82, pres., 1982-88; prin. Vosbeck/DMJM, Washington and Alexandria, Va., 1989-94; v.p. DMJM Arch. and Engring., 1990-94; pvt. practice archtl. cons., 1994—. Mem. Nat. Capital Planning Commn., 1976-81, U.S./USSR Joint Group on Bldg. Design and Constrn., 1974-79; mem. Nat. Park System Adv. Bd., 1984-88. Archtl. works include Pub. Safety Ctr., Alexandria, Va., 1987, Yorktown (Va.) Visitors Ctr, 1976, Frank Reeves Mcpl. Office Bldg., Washington, 1986, Fed. Bldg., Norfolk, Va., 1979, Jeff Davis Assocs. Office Complex, Arlington, Va., 1991, Westminster Continued Care Retirment Community, Lake Ridge, Va., 1993. Pres. Alexandria Jaycees, 1960-61; v.p. Va. Jaycees, 1962-63; pres. Alexandria Ch. of Com., 1974-75. Engring. officer USMC, 1954-56. Recipient Plaque of Honor Fedn. Colegios Architects (Republic of Mexico) Alumni Achievement award U. Minn. Coll. Arch., 2001; named Outstanding Young Man in Va., 1963, Acadamecian, Internt. Acad. Architecture, hon. fellow Royal Archtl. Inst. Can., Soc. Architects of Mexico; recipient hon. fellowship Colegios Architects Spain, Union Bulgarian Architects. Fellow AIA (bd. dirs. 1976-78, v.p. 1979-80, pres. 1981), Internat. Union Architects (coun. 1981-87), Nat. Trust Hist. Preservation. Presbyterian. Home and Office: 770 Potato Patch Dr Unit A Vail CO 81657-4462 E-mail: vosbeckr@cs.com

VOTH, ALDEN H. political science educator; b. Goessel, Kans., May 4, 1926; s. John F. and Helena (Hildebrandt) V.; m. Norma E. Jost, Aug. 18, 1956; children: Susan, Thomas. BA, Bethel Coll., 1950; MS in Econs., Iowa State U., Ames, 1953; PhD in Internat. Rels., U. Chgo., 1959. Assoc. prof. polit. sci. Upland (Calif.) Coll., 1960-63; prof. polit. sci. San Jose (Calif.) State U., 1963-65, 67-91, prof. emeritus, 1991—. Vis. prof. polit. sci. Am. U. in Cairo, 1965-67. Author: Moscow Abandons Israel, 1980, (with others) The Kissinger Legacy, 1984. Trustee Pomona (Calif.) Valley Am. Assn. UN, 1963; participant China Ednl. Exch., 1996. Am. U. in Cairo Rsch. grantee, 1966; Nat. Coun. on U.S.-Arab Rels. fellow, 1990—. Home: 1385 Kimberly Dr San Jose CA 95118-1426 Office: San Jose State U One Washington Sq San Jose CA 95192 E-mail: ahvoth@aol.com

VREDEVOE, DONNA LOU, research immunologist, microbiologist, educator; b. Ann Arbor, Mich., Jan. 11, 1938; d. Lawrence E. and Verna (Brower) V.; m. John Porter, Aug. 22, 1962; 1 child, Verna. BA in Bacteriology, UCLA, 1959, PhD in Microbiology, 1963. USPHS postdoctoral fellow Stanford U., 1963-64; instr. bacteriology UCLA, 1963, postgrad.rsch. immunologist dept. surgery Ctr. Health Scis., 1964-65, asst. research immunologist dept. surgery Center Health Scis., 1964-67; asst. prof. Sch. Nursing, Center Health Scis., 1967-70, asso. prof., 1970-76, prof., 1976—, asso. dean Sch. Nursing, 1976-78, acting assoc. dean Sch. Nursing., 1985-86, asst. dir. space planning Cancer Center, 1976-78, dir. space planning, 1978-90, cons. to lab. nuclear medicine and radiation biology, 1967-80; acting dean Sch. Nursing Center Health Scis., 1995-96. Chair UCLA Acad. Senate, 1999-2000; vice chancellor acad. personnel UCLA, 2001—. Contbr. articles to profl. publs. Postdoctoral fellow USPHS, 1963-64; Mabel Wilson Richards scholar UCLA, 1960-61; research grantee Am. Cancer Soc., Calif. Inst. Cancer Research, Calif. div. Am. Cancer Soc., USPHS, Am. Nurses Found., Cancer Research Coordinating Com. U. Calif., Dept. Energy, UCLA. Mem Am. Soc. Microbiology, Am. Assn. Immunologists, Am. Assn. Cancer Research, Nat. League Nursing (2d v.p. 1979-81), Sigma Xi, Alpha Gamma Sigma, Sigma Theta Tau (nat. hon. mem.) Office: UCLA Sch Nursing Los Angeles CA 90095-0001

VROLYK, JOHN R. computer systems company executive; BA in Philosophy, Calif. State U., Northridge; postgrad. in computer sci., Stanford U. Found., pres., CEO Arete (Arix) Sys. Corp.; v.p., gen. mgr. DDS Workgroup and Impact Group Xerox Corp.; sr. v.p. computer sys. bus. unit Silicon Graphics, Inc., Mountain View, Calif., sr. v.p. product group. Office: Silicon Graphics Inc 1600 Amphitheatre Pkwy Mountain View CA 94043-1351

VUCANOVICH, BARBARA FARRELL, former congresswoman; b. Fort Dix, N.J., June 22, 1921; d. Thomas F. and Ynez (White) Farrell; m. Ken Dillon, Mar. 8, 1950 (dec. 1964); children: Patty Dillon Cafferata, Mike, Ken, Tom, Susan Dillon Anderson; m. George Vucanovich, June 19, 1965 (dec. Dec. 1998). Student, Manhattanville Coll. of Sacred Heart, 1938-39. Owner, operator Welcome Aboard Travel, Reno, 1968-74; Nev.

rep. for Senator Paul Laxalt, 1974-82; mem. 98th-104th Congresses from 2d Nev. dist., 1983-96; chmn. appropriations subcom. on military construction; Rep. natl. committeewoman Nev. Rep. Party, 1996-2000. Pres. Nev. Fedn. Republican Women, Reno, 1955-56; former pres. St. Mary's Hosp. Guild, Lawyer's Wives. Roman Catholic. Club: Hidden Valley Country (Reno).*

WACHBRIT, JILL BARRETT, accountant, tax specialist; b. Ventura, Calif., May 27, 1955; d. Preston Everett Barrett and Lois JoAnne (Fondersmith) Batchelder; m. Michael Ian Wachbrit, June 21, 1981; children: Michelle, Tracy. AA, Santa Monica City Coll., 1975; BS, Calif. State U., Northridge, 1979; M in Bus. Taxation, U. So. Calif., 1985. CPA. Supervising sr. tax acct. Peat, Marwick, Mitchell & Co., Century City, Calif., 1979-82; sr. tax analyst Avery Internat., Pasadena, 1982-83; tax mgr., asst. v.p. First Interstate Leasing, Pasadena, 1983-88; v.p. Security Pacific Corp., L.A., 1988-92; tax mgr., acct. El Camino Resources Ltd., Woodland Hills, Calif., 1992-95; tax mgr. Herbalife Internat. of Am., Century City, 1995-97; sr. tax mgr. PMC, Inc., Sun Valley, 1997—. Republican. Jewish. Avocations: reading, travel, collecting. E-mail: jillw@pmcglobalinc.com

WACHS, MARTIN, urban planning educator, author, consultant; b. N.Y.C., June 8, 1941; s. Robert and Doris (Margolis) W.; m. Helen Pollner, Aug. 18, 1963; children: Faye Linda, Steven Brett. BCE, CUNY, 1963; MS, Northwestern U., 1965, PhD, 1967. Asst. prof. U. Ill., Chgo., 1967-69, Northwestern U., Evanston, Ill., 1969-71; assoc. prof. urban planning UCLA, 1971-76, prof., 1976-96; dir. U. Calif. Transp. Ctr., 1996-99; prof. civil and environ. engrng. and city/regional planning U. Calif., Berkeley, 1996—, dir. Inst. Transp. Studies, 1999—. Vis. disting. prof. Rutgers U., New Brunswick, N.J., 1983-84; mem. exec. com. Transp. Rsch. Bd., 1995—, chmn., 2000; vis fellow Oxford (Eng.) U., 1976-77. Author: Transportation for the Elderly: Changing Lifestyles, Changing Needs, 1979, Transportation Planning on Trial, 1996, also numerous articles; editor: Ethics in Planning, 1984, The Car and the City, 1992. Mem. steering com. L.A. Parking Mgmt. Study, 1976-78; bd. dirs. L.A. Commuter computer, 1978-94, mem. Calif. Commn. on Transp. Investment, 1995. Served to capt. Ordnance Corps, U.S. Army, 1967-69. Recipient Pike Johnson award Transp. Rsch. Bd., 1976, Disting. Tchg. award UCLA Alumni Assn., 1986, Disting. Planning Educator award Calif. Planners Found., 1986; Guggenheim fellow, 1977; Rockefeller Found. humanities fellow, 1980. Fellow Am. Coun. Edn.; mem. ASCE, Am. Planning Assn., Am. Inst. Cert. Planners, Inst. Transp. Engrs. Jewish. Home: 1106 Grizzly Peak Blvd Berkeley CA 94708-1704 Office: U Calif Berkeley Inst Transp Studies 109 Mclaughlin Hall Berkeley CA 94720-1720 E-mail: mwachs@uclink4.berkeley.edu

WACHTEL, ALBERT, writer, educator; b. N.Y.C., Dec. 20, 1939; s. Jacob and Sarah Rose (Kaplansky) W.; m. Sydelle Farber, Mar. 9, 1958; children: Sally Rose, Seth Laurence, Stephanie Allyson, Synthia Laura, Jonathan Benjamin, Jessica Eden, Jacob Ethan. BA, CUNY, 1960; PhD, SUNY, Buffalo, 1968. Instr. SUNY, Buffalo, 1963-66, asst. to dean, 1966-68; asst. prof. U. Calif., Santa Barbara, 1968-74; prof. English, creative writing Pitzer Coll., The Claremont (Calif.) Colls., 1974—. Playwright: Paying the Piper, 1968, Prince Hal, 1995; co-editor Modernism: Challenges and Perspectives, 1986; author: The Cracked Looking Glass: James Joyce and the Nightmare of History, 1992; contbr. stories, creative essays to lit. jours., newspapers, and mags. NDEA fellow, 1960-63, fellow Creative Arts Inst., U. Calif., Berkeley, 1970, NEH Summer Inst., Dartmouth Coll., 1987; Danforth Found. assoc., 1978, NEH Seminar, Cornell U., 1998. Jewish. Office: Pitzer Coll Claremont Colls Claremont CA 91711-6101 E-mail: awachtel@pitzer.edu

WADDELL, THEODORE, painter; b. Billings, Mont., Oct. 6, 1941; Student, Bklyn. Mus. Art Sch., 1962; BS, Ea. Mont. Coll., 1966; MFA, Wayne State U., 1968. One-man shows include U. Calif., San Diego, 1984, Cheney Cowles Meml. Mus., Spokane, Wash., 1985, The New West, Colorado Springs, 1986, Bernice Stein Baum Gallery, N.Y., 1992; exhibited in group shows 38th Corcoran Biennial, Corcoran Gallery, Washington, 1983; represented in permanent collections Ea. Mont. Coll., Yellowstone Art Ctr., Billings, Sheldon Meml. Art Gallery, U. Nebr., Lincoln, City of Great Falls, Mont., Dallas Mus. Art, San Jose (Calif.) Mus. Office: c/o Stremmel Gallery 1400 S Virginia St Reno NV 89502-2806

WADDINGHAM, JOHN ALFRED, artist, journalist; b. London, Eng., July 9, 1915; came to U.S., 1927, naturalized, 1943; s. Charles Alfred and Mary Elizabeth (Coles) W.; m. Joan Lee Larson, May 3, 1952; children: Mary Kathryn, Thomas Richard. Student, Coronado (Calif.) Sch. Fine Arts, 1953-54, Portland Art Mus., 1940-65, U. Portland, 1946-47; pupil, Rex Brandt, Eliot Ohara, George Post. Promotion art dir. Oreg. Jour., Portland, 1946-59; with The Oregonian, Portland, 1959-81, editl. art dir., 1959-81; tchr. watercolor Oreg. Soc. Artists, 1954-56; tchr. art Oreg. Sch. Arts and Crafts, 1981—, Portland C.C., Multnomah Athletic Club, Mittleman Jewish Cmty. Ctr. Represented by several galleries, Oreg. and Wash. One man shows include Art in the Gov.'s Office, Oreg. State Capitol, 1991 and more than 30 shows in the Northwest; rep. mus. rental collections, Portland Art Mus., Bush House, Salem, Ore., U. Oreg. Mus., Vincent Price collection, Ford Times collection, also Am. Watercolor Soc. Travelling Show; paintings included in Salmagundi Club, N.Y.C., UN Bldg., Watercolor, U.S.A. of Springfield, Mo., others; judge art events, 1946— , over 50 one-man shows; ofcl. artist, Kiwanis Internat. Conv., 1966; designed, dir. constrn. cast: concrete mural Genesis, St. Barnabas Episcopal Ch., Portland, 1960; spl. work drawings old Portland landmarks and houses; propr. John Waddingham Hand Prints, fine arts serigraphs and silk screen drawings, 1965—; featured artist: Am. Artist mag., Watercolor mag., Oreg. Painters, the First Hundred Years, (1859-1959), others. Artist mem. Portland Art Mus. With USAAF, 1942-46. Recipient gold medal Salone Internazionale dell' Umorismo, Italy, 1974, 76, 80; honored with a 45 yr. retrospective Assignment: The Artist as Journalist Oreg. Hist. Soc., 1991; winner Palme do Oro in three exhbns., Bordighera, Italy. Mem. Portland Art Dirs. Club (past pres.), N.W. Watercolor Soc., Am. Watercolor Soc. (hon. sustaining), Watercolor Soc. Oreg., Oreg. Soc. Artists (watercolor tchr.), Multnomah Athletic Club, Jewish Community Ctr., Univ. Oreg. Med. Sch., Art in the Mounts., Oreg. Old Time Fiddlers, Clan Macleay Bagpipe Band. Home: 955 SW Westwood Dr Portland OR 97201-2744

WADDINGTON, RAYMOND BRUCE, JR. English language educator; b. Santa Barbara, Calif., Sept. 27, 1935; s. Raymond Bruce and Marjorie Gladys (Waddell) W.; m. Linda Gayle Jones, Sept. 7, 1957 (div.); children: Raymond Bruce, Edward Jackson; m. Kathleen Martha Ward, Oct. 11, 1985 BA, Stanford U., 1957; PhD, Rice U., 1963; postdoctoral (Univ. fellow in Humanities), Johns Hopkins U., 1965-66. Instr. English U. Houston, 1961-62; instr. U. Kans., 1962-63, asst. prof., 1963-65; asst. prof. English lit. U. Wis., Madison, 1966-68, assoc. prof., 1968-74, prof., 1974-82; prof. English lit. U. Calif., Davis, 1982—. Author: The Mind's Empire, 1974; co-editor: The Rhetoric of Renaissance Poetry, 1974, The Age of Milton, 1980, The Expulsion of the Jews, 1994; mem. editl. bd. The Medal, 1991, Renaissance Quar., 2000; sr. editor: Sixteenth Century Jour.; editor: Garland Studies in the Renaissance. Huntington Library fellow, 1967, 75; Inst. Research in Humanities fellow, 1971-72; Guggenheim fellow, 1972-73; NEH fellow, 1977, 83; Newberry Library fellow, 1978; Am. Philos. Soc. grantee, 1965 Mem. Renaissance Soc. Am., Milton Soc. Am., Am. Numismatic Soc., 16th Century Studies Conf. (pres. 1985), Brit. Art Medal Soc., Logos Club. Home: 39 Pershing Ave Woodland CA 95695-2845 Office: U Calif Dept English Davis CA 95616 E-mail: rbwaddington@ucdavis.edu

WADDOUPS, MICHAEL G. state legislator; b. Idaho Falls, Idahp, June 12, 1948; m. Anna Kay Waddoups. AD in Acctg., Ricks Coll.; BS in Bus. Mgmt., Brigham Young U. Grad. Inst. Real Estate Mgmt.; cert. property mgr. Property mgr.; mem. Utah Ho. of Reps., 1988-96, majority whip, 1995-96; mem. Utah Senate, Dist. 6, 1996—; chair transp. and pub. safety com. Utah State Senate, 1999—, mem. revenue and taxation com., rules com., co-chair exec. office, criminal justice/legis. appropriation. Scouting Commr., State of Utah; mem. Multi-state Hwy. Transp. Agreement. Mem. Inst. Real Estate Mgmt., Apt. Assn. Utah (bd. dirs.). Republican. Office: 2005 W 5620 S Taylorsville UT 84118-1485

WADE, BILL, airport executive; Gen. mgr. Met. Oakland (Calif.) Internat. Airport, 1994—. Office: Met Oakland Intl Airport 1 Airport Dr Box 45 Oakland CA 94621-1430

WADE, BOOKER, television executive; b. Memphis, 1952; BA in Polit. Sci., Calif. State U., 1964; JD, Stanford U., 1974. Pvt. practice, 1974-92; gen. mgr. KMTP Minority TV Project, San Francisco, 1992—. Office: KMTP 1504 Bryant St San Francisco CA 94103-4808

WADE, KAREN, federal agency administrator; b. Cortez, Colo. m. John W. Wade (div.). Student, U. Colo., 1960-62; B.Bus., Ft. Lewis Coll., 1962-64; postgrad., U. No. Ariz., 1973, U. Tenn., Knoxville, 1977. So. region trail coord. Appalachian Trail Project Nat. Park Svc., 1978-83; mgmt. asst. Shenandoah Nat. Park, Va., 1983-85; supt. Ft. McHenry Nat. Monument and Historic Shrine Hampton Nat. Hist. Park, Balt., 1985-87; supt. Guadalupe Mountains Nat. Park, Tex., 1987-90, Wrangell-St. Elias Nat. Park and Preserve, Alaska, 1990-94, Great Smoky Mountains Nat. Park, Gatlinburg, Tenn., 1994—, dir., 1999—. Office: Dir Intermountain Reg Nat Park Svc PO Box 25287 Denver CO 80225-0287 also: 12795 Alameda Pky Denver CO 80228 E-mail: karen_wade@nps.gov

WADLOW, JOAN KRUEGER, academic administrator; b. LeMars, Iowa, Aug. 21, 1932; d. R. John and Norma I. (IhLe) Krueger; m. Richard R. Wadlow, July 27, 1958; children: Dawn, Kit. BA, U. Nebr., Lincoln, 1953; M.A. (Seacrest Journalism fellow 1953-54), Fletcher Sch. Law and Diplomacy, 1956; PhD (Rotary fellow 1956-57), U. Nebr., Lincoln, 1963; cert., Grad. Inst. Internat. Studies, Geneva, 1957. Mem. faculty U. Nebr., Lincoln, 1966-79, prof. polit. scis., 1964-79, assoc. dean Coll. Arts and Scis., 1972-79; prof. polit. scis., dean Coll. Arts and Scis., U. Wyo., Laramie, 1979-84, v.p. acad. affairs, 1984-86; prof. polit. sci., provost U. Okla., Norman, 1986-91; chancellor U. Alaska, Fairbanks, 1991-99. Cons. on fed. grants; bd. dirs. Alaska Sea Life Center, Key Bank Alaska; mem. Commn. Colls. N.W. Assn.; pres. Lan Constrn., Inc., 1999—. Author articles in field. Bd. dirs. Nat. Merit Scholarship Corp., 1988-97, Lincoln United Way, 1976-77, Bryan Hosp., Lincoln, 1978-79, Washington Ctr., 1986-99, Key Bank of Alaska, AlaskaSeaLife Ctr.; v.p., exec. commr. North Cen. Assn., pres., 1991; univ. pres. mission to Isreal, 1998; pres. adv. bd. Lincoln YWCA, 1970-71; mem. def. adv. com. Women in the Svcs., 1987-89; mem. community adv. bd. Alaska Airlines; mem. Univ. Pres.'s Mission to Israel, 1998. Recipient Mortar Board Teaching award, 1976, Disting. Teaching award U. Nebr., Lincoln, 1979, Rotary Internat. Alumni Scholar Achievement award, 1998; fellow Conf. Coop. Man, Lund, Sweden, 1956 Mem. NCAA (divsn. II pres. coun. 1997-99), Internat. Studies Assn. (co-editor Internat. Studies Notes 1978-91), Nat. Assn. State Univs. and Land-Grant Colls. (exec. com. coun. acad. affairs 1989-91, chair internat. affairs counsel 1996-97), Western Assn. Africanists (pres. 1980-82), Assn. Western Univs. (pres. 1993), Coun. Colls. Arts and Scis. (pres. 1983-84), Greater Fairbanks C. of C., Gamma Phi Beta. Republican. Congregationalist. E-mail: wadlow.oregon.vos.edu. Address: Chancellor Emerita PO Box 246 Oceanside OR 97134-0246

WADSWORTH, HAROLD WAYNE, lawyer; b. Logan, Utah, Oct. 12, 1930; s. Harold Maughan and Nellie Grace (Grosjean) W.; m. Laila Anita Ingebritsen, Dec. 27, 1957; children: Warren, Kenneth, Jeffrey, Theresa, Erik. BS, Utah State U., 1952; JD with honor, George Washington U., 1959. Bar: D.C. 1959, Utah 1961, U.S. Dist. Ct. Utah 1961, U.S. Ct. Appeals (10th cir.) 1962, U.S. Ct. Appeals (9th cir.) 1978, U.S. Supreme Ct. 1972. Spl. agt. FBI, Atlanta and Macon, 1959-60; assoc. atty., ptnr. Hanson, Wadsworth & Russon, Salt Lake City, 1961-77; ptnr. Watkiss & Campbell, Salt Lake City, 1978-89, Watkiss & Saperstein, Salt Lake City, 1990-91, Ballard, Spahr, Andrews & Ingersoll, Salt Lake City, 1992-95, Jones Waldo Hollbrook & McDonough, Salt Lake City, 1996-98; solo practice atty. Salt Lake City, 1998—. 1st lt. U.S. Army, 1952-54. Republican. Mem. LDS Ch. Avocations: horsemanship, hunting, fishing, opera, Shakespeare. Office: 1338 Foothill Dr Ste 274 Salt Lake City UT 84108-2321

WAFER, THOMAS J., JR. newspaper publisher; Pub. The Daily Breeze, Torrance, Calif., 1993—. Office: 5215 Torrance Blvd Torrance CA 90503-4009

WAGGENER, MELISSA, public relations executive; b. 1954; With Tektronix Inc., Beaverton, Oreg., 1975-80, Regis McKenna, Portland, 1980-83, Waggener Edstrom, Inc., 1983—, now pres. and CEO. Office: Waggener Edstrom Inc 3 Centerpointe Dr Ste 300 Lake Oswego OR 97035-8663

WAGGONER, JAMES CLYDE, lawyer; b. Nashville, May 7, 1946; s. Charles Franklin and Alpha (Noah) W.; m. Diane Dusenbery, Aug. 17, 1968; children: Benjamin, Elizabeth. BA, Reed Coll., 1968; JD, U. Oreg., 1974. Bar: Oreg. 1974, U.S. Dist. Ct. Oreg. 1975, U.S. Ct. Appeals (9th cir.) 1980, U.S. Tax Ct. 1979, U.S. Supreme Ct. 1979. Clerk to presiding justice Oreg. Supreme Ct., Salem, 1974-75; assoc. Martin, Bischoff & Templeton, Portland, Oreg., 1975-78, ptnr., 1978-82, Waggoner, Farleigh, Wada, Georgeff & Witt, Portland, 1982-89, Davis Wright Tremaine, Portland, 1990—. Contbr. articles to profl. jours. Fulbright scholar U. London, 1968-69. Mem. ABA, Oreg. Bar Assn., Multnomah Bar Assn., Reed Coll. Alumni Assn. (v.p. 1988, pres. 1989, bd. mgmt.) Alzheimers Assn. of Columbia-Willamette (v.p. 1992, pres. 1993), Order Coif, Phi Beta Kappa. Democrat. Avocations: wood turning, calligraphy. Office: Davis Wright Tremaine 1300 SW 5th Ave Ste 2300 Portland OR 97201-5682

WAGIE, DAVID A. career military officer; BS in Engring. Scis., USAF Acad., Colorado Springs, 1972; MS, Stanford U., 1973, U. So. Calif., 1977; PhD, Purdue U., 1984. Commd. 2d lt. USAF, 1972, advanced through grades to brigadier gen., 1998; pilot 310th Air Refueling Squadron, Plattsburgh AFB, N.Y., 1974-79; instr. USAF Academy, 1979-81; EC-135 rsch. pilot, dir. test ops. 4952d Test Squadron, Wright-Patterson AFB, Ohio, 1984-85; EC-135 rsch. pilot, dep. chief Aircraft & Avionics Divsn. 4950th Test Wing, Wright-Patterson AFB, 1985-86; assoc. prof. Air Command and Staff Coll., 1986-87, USAF Academy, 1987-92, prof., dep. commandant mil. instrn., T-43 pilot, 1992-94, dir. Ctr. Character Devel., T-41 pilot, 1994-96, vice dean faculty, T-41 instr. pilot, 1996-98, dean faculty, T-41 instr. pilot, 1998—.

WAGMEN, LEE H. real estate executive; Degree Wharton Sch. Bus., U. Pa.; degree, U. Pa. Law Sch. Ptnr. Bryan Cave Law Firm, St. Louis; chmn. Hycel Properties Co.; pres., CEO, TrizecHahn Devel. Corp., San Diego. Office: TrizecHahn Ctrs 4350 La Jolla Village Dr San Diego CA 92122-1243

WAGNER, CARRUTH JOHN, physician; b. Omaha, Sept. 4, 1916; s. Emil Conrad and Mabel May (Knapp) W. A.B., Omaha U., 1938; B.Sc., U. Nebr., 1938, M.D., 1941, D.Sc., 1966. Diplomate: Am. Bd. Sugery, Am. Bd. Orthopaedic Surgery. Intern U.S. Marine Hosp., Seattle, 1941-42; resident gen. surgery and orthopaedic surgery USPHS hosps., Shriners Hosp., Phila., 1943-46; med. dir. USPHS, 1952-62; chief orthopaedic service USPHS Hosp., San Francisco, 1946-51, S.I., N.Y., 1951-55, health mblzn., 1959-62; asst. surgeon gen. dep. chief div. hosps. UPHS, 1957-59; chief div. USPHS, 1962-65, USPHS (Indian Health), 1962-65; dir. Bur. Health Services, 1965-68; Washington rep. AMA, 1968-72; health services cons., 1972-79; dept. health services State of Calif., 1979—. Contbr. articles to med. jours. Served with USCGR, World War II. Recipient Pfizer award, 1962; Meritorious award Am. Acad. Gen. Practice, 1965; Disting. Svc. medal, 1968, Calif. Dept. Health Svcs. Pub. Health Recognition award, 1995. Fellow A.C.S. (bd. govs.), Am. Soc. Surgery Hand, Am. Assn. Surgery Trauma, Am. Geriatrics Soc., Am. Acad. Orthopaedic Surgeons; mem. Nat. Assn. Sanitarians, Am. Pub. Health Assn. Sanitarians, Am. Pub. Health Assn., Washington Orthopaedic Club, Am. Legion, Alpha Omega Alpha. Lutheran. Club: Mason (Shriner). Home: 6234 Silverton Way Carmichael CA 95608-0757 Office: PO Box 638 Carmichael CA 95609-0638

WAGNER, CHRISTIAN NIKOLAUS JOHANN, materials engineering educator; b. Saarbrucken-Dudweiler, Germany, Mar. 6, 1927; came to U.S., 1959, naturalized, 1969; s. Christian Jakob and Regina (Bungert) W.; m. Rosemarie Anna Mayer, Apr. 5, 1952; children— Thomas Martin, Karla Regine, Petra Susanne. Student, U. Poitiers, France, 1948-49; Licence es Sci., U. Saar, Ger., 1951, Diplom-Ingenieur, 1954, Dr.rer.nat., 1957. Research asst. Inst. fur Metallforschung, Saarbrucken, 1953-54; vis. fellow M.I.T., 1955-56; research asso. Inst. fur Metallforschung, 1957-58; teaching, research asst. U. Saarbrucken, 1959; asst. prof. Yale U., New Haven, 1959-62, assoc. prof., 1962-70; prof. dept. materials engrng. UCLA, 1970-91, prof. emeritus, 1991—, chmn. dept., 1974-79, asst. dean undergrad. studies Sch. Engrng. and Applied Sci., 1982-85, acting chmn., 1990-91. Vis. prof. Tech. U., Berlin, 1969, U. Saarbrücken, 1979-80 Contbr. articles to profl. jours. Recipient U.S. Sci. Humboldt award U. Saarbrucken, 1989-90, 92. Fellow Am. Soc. Metals Internat.; mem. Am. Crystallographic Assn., Minerals, Metals and Materials Soc. Home: 37621 Golden Pebble Ave Palm Desert CA 92211-1430 Office: UCLA 6532 Boelter Hl Los Angeles CA 90095-0001 E-mail: cnjw@ix.netcom.com

WAGNER, DARRYL WILLIAM, lawyer; b. Dixon, Ill., Jan. 14, 1943; s. Earl L. and Lois Mae W.; m. Susan A. Aldrich; children: Peter Alan, Nicholas William. BA, Northwestern U., 1965, JD, 1968. Bar: Ill. 1968, U.S. Dist. Ct. (no. dist.) Ill. 1969, U.S. Ct. Appeals (7th cir.) 1971, Calif. 1982. Sr. counsel Sidley Austin Brown & Wood, Chgo., 1969—. Dir. Housing Options for People to Excell, Inc., 1992-94, 96—. Co-author: Illinois Municipal Law: Subdivisions and Subdivisions in Controls, 1978, 81. Mem. ABA, Internat. Assn. Attys. and Execs. in Corp. Real Estate, Ill. State Bar Assn., Chgo. Bar Assn. Presbyn. Home: 526 A San Ysdidro Rd Santa Barbara CA 93108 Office: Sidley Austin Brown & Wood 555 W 5th St Ste 4000 Los Angeles CA 90013-3000 E-mail: dwagner@sidley.com, wwagneresq@springmail.com

WAGNER, DAVID JAMES, lawyer; b. Cleve., Feb. 7, 1946; m. Martha Wilson, June 22, 1979; 1 child, Diana Jane. BS, USAF Acad., 1969; JD, Georgetown U., 1973. Bar: Colo. 1973, U.S. Supreme Ct. 1975, U.S. Dist. Ct. of Colo. 1973, U.S. Tax Ct. 1974. Asst. assoc. gen. counsel Presdl. Clemency Bd., Washington, 1974-75; sec., gen. counsel Cablecomm-Gen. Inc., Denver, 1975-77; adj. prof. law Metro. State Coll., Denver, 1975-80; atty., mng. prin. Wagner & Waller, P.C., Denver, 1977-84; chmn. bd. GILA Comm., Inc., Denver, 1987; pvt. practice David Wagner & Assocs., P.C., Englewood, Colo., 1984—. Dir. Colo. Sch. of Mines Found., 1999. Editor Am. Criminal Law Rev., Georgetown U. Law Sch., 1972-73. Trustee Kent Denver Sch., Cherry Hills Village, Colo., 1990-96, treas., 1992, pres., 1992-96; treas., dir. Denver Chamber Orch., 1979-81; dir. Leadership Denver Assn., 1978-80; trustee Colo. Sch. Mines, 1999. Capt. USAF, 1973-75. Republican. Episcopalian. Office: David Wagner & Assocs PC Penthouse 8400 E Prentice Ave Ph Englewood CO 80111-2927

WAGNER, JOHN LEO, lawyer, former magistrate judge; b. Ithaca, N.Y., Mar. 12, 1954; s. Paul Francis and Doris Elizabeth (Hoffschneider) W.; m. Marilyn Modin, June 18, 1987. Student, U. Nebr., 1973-74; BA, U. Okla., 1976, JD, 1979. Bar: Okla. 1980, Calif. 1999, U.S. Dist. Ct. (we. dist.) Okla. 1980, U.S. Dist. Ct. (no. and ea. dists.) Okla. 1981, U.S. Dist. Ct. (mid. dist.) Calif. 2000, U.S. Ct. Appeals (10th cir.) 1982. Assoc. Franklin, Harmon & Satterfield Inc., Oklahoma City, 1980-82; ptnr. Franklin, Harmon & Satterfield, Inc., Oklahoma City, 1982; assoc. Kornfeld, Franklin & Phillips, Oklahoma City, 1982-85, ptnr., 1985; magistrate judge U.S. Dist. Ct. No. Dist. Okla., Tulsa, 1985-97; dir. Irell & Manella LLP Alt. Dispute Resolution Ctr., Newport Beach, Calif., 1997—. Pres. U. Okla. Coll. Law Assn., 1991-92. Fellow Am. Coll. Civil Trial Mediators, ABA, Internat. Acad. Mediators; mem. Fed. Magistrate Judge's Assn. (dir. 10th cir. 1987-89), 10th Cir. Edn. Com., Okla. Bar Assn., Council Oak Am. Inn of Cts. (pres. 1992-93), Jud. Conf. U.S. (com. ct. adminstrn. and case mgmt. 1992-97), CPR-Georgetown Commn. Ethics and Standards in ADR. Republican. Office: Irell & Manella LLP Alt Dispute Resolution Ctr 840 Newport Center Dr Ste 450 Newport Beach CA 92660-6321 E-mail: jwagner@irell.com, usmag1@home.com

WAGNER, JUDITH BUCK, investment firm executive; b. Altoona, Pa., Sept. 25, 1943; d. Harry Bud and Mary Elizabeth (Rhodes) B.; m. Joseph E. Wagner, Mar. 15, 1980; 1 child, Elizabeth. BA in History, U. Wash., 1965; grad., N.Y. Inst. Fin., 1968. Registered Am. Stock Exch., N.Y. Stock Exch., investment advisor. Security analyst Morgan, olmstead, Kennedy & Gardner, L.A., 1968-71, Boettcher & Co., Denver, 1972-75; pres. Wagner Investment Mgmt., Denver, 1975—. Chmn. The Women's Bank, N.A., Denver, 1977-94, organizational group pres., 1975-77; chmn. Equitable Bankshares Colo., Inc., Denver, 1980-94; pres. Equitable Bank of Littleton, Colo., 1985; lectr. Denver U., Metro State, 1975-80. Author: Woman and Money series Colo. Woman Mag., 1976, moderator "Catch 2' Sta. KWGN-TV, 1978-79. Pres. Bit Sisters Colo., Denver, 1977-82, bd. dirs., 1972-83; bd. fellows U. Denver, 1985-90; bd. dirs. Red Cross, 1980, Assn. Children's Hosp., 1985, Colo. Health Facilities Authority, 1978-84, Jr. League Cmty. ADv. Com., 1979-82, Bros. Redevel., Inc., 1979-80; mem. agy. rels. com. Mile High United Way, 1978-81, chmn. United Way Venture Way, 1978-81, chmn. United Way Venture Grant com., 1980-81; bd. dirs. Downtown Dener, Inc., 1988-95; bd. dirs., v.p., treas. The Women's Found. Colo., 1987-91; treas., trustee, v.p., Graland Country Day Sch., 1990-97, pres., 1994-97; trustee Denver Rotary Found., 1990-95; trustee Hunt Alternatives Fund, 1992-97, The Colo. Trust, 1998—. Recipient Making It award Cosmopolitan Mag., 1977, Women on the Go award, Savvy Mag., 1983, Minouri Yasoui award, 1986, Salute Spl. Honoree award, Big Sisters, 1987; named one of the Outstanding Young Women Am., 1979; recipient Woman Who Makes A Difference award Internat. Women's Forum, 1987. Fellow Assn. Investment Mgmt. & Rsch.; mem. Women's Forum Colo. (pres. 1979), Women's Found. Colo., Inc (bd. dirs. 1986-91), Denver Soc. Security Analysts (bd. dirs. 1976-83, v.p. 1980-81, pres. 1981-82), Colo. Investment Advisors assn., Rotary (treas. Denver chpt. found., pres. 1993-94), Leadership Denver (Outstanding Alumna award 1987), Pi Beta Phi (pres. U. Wash. chpt. 1964-65). Office: Wagner Investment Mgmt Inc Ste 240 3200 Cherry Creek South Dr Denver CO 80209-3245

WAGNER, NORMAN ERNEST, corporate education executive; b. Edenwold, Sask., Can., Mar. 29, 1935; s. Robert Eric and Gertrude Margaret (Brandt) W.; m. Catherine Hack, May 16, 1957; children: Marjorie Dianne, Richard Roger, Janet Marie. BA, MDiv, U. Sask., 1958; MA, U. Toronto, 1960, PhD in Near Eastern Studies, 1965; LLD, Wilfrid Laurier U., 1984. Asst. prof. Near Eastern studies Wilfrid Laurier U., Waterloo, Ont., 1962-65, assoc. prof., 1965-69, prof., 1970-78, dean grad. studies and rsch., 1974-78; pres. U. Calgary, Alta., Can., 1978-88; chmn. bd. Alta. Natural Gas Co., Ltd., 1988—; pres. emeritus U. Calgary, Can., 1988-95; chmn. Knowledge at Work Found., 1995—. Bd. dirs., chmn. Terry Fox Humanitarian Award Program; pres. The Corp. Higher Edn. Forum, 1996-2000; chmn. Knowledge Navigators Internat. Inc. Author: From Chaos to Wisdom: A Framework for Understanding, 1998, (with others) The Moyer Site: A Prehistoric Village in Waterloo County, 1974. Mem. Adv. Coun. on Adjustment, OCO '88, Alta. Heritage Found. for Med. Rsch., Nat. Adv. Bd. Sci. and Tech., Internat. Trade Adv. Com. Decorated officer Order of Can. Mem. Can. Soc. Bibl. Studies. Lutheran. Home: 1320 720 13th Ave SW Calgary AB Canada T2R 1M5 Office: The Corp Higher Edn Forum 440 1010 8th Ave SW Calgary AB Canada T2P 1J2 E-mail: newal1@aol.com

WAGNER, PATRICIA HAMM, lawyer; b. Gastonia, N.C., Feb. 1, 1936; d. Luther Boyd and Mildred Ruth (Wheeler) Hamm; married; children: David Marion, Michael Marion, Laura Marion. AB summa cum laude, Wittenberg U., 1958; JD with distinction, Duke U., 1974. Bar: N.C. 1974, Wash. 1984. Asst. univ. counsel Duke U., Durham, N.C., 1974-75, assoc. univ. counsel health affairs, 1977-80; atty. N.C. Meml. Hosp., 1975-77; assoc. N.C. Atty. Gen. Office, 1975-77, Powe, Porter & Alphin, Durham, 1980-81, prin., 1981-83; assoc. Williams, Kastner & Gibbs, 1984-86, Wickwire, Goldmark & Schorr, 1986-88; spl. counsel Heller, Ehrman, White & McAuliffe, 1988-90, ptnr., 1990—. Arbitrator Am. Arbitration Assn., 1978—; arbitrator, pro tem judge King County Superior Ct., 1986—; tchr. in field. Mem. bd. vis. Law Sch. Duke U., 1992-98; bd. dirs. Seattle Edn. Ctr., 1990-91, Metroctr. YMCA, 1991-94, Cmty. Psychiat. Clinic, Seattle, 1984-86; bd. dirs., sec.-treas. N.C. Found. Alternative Health Programs, Inc., 1982-84; bd. dirs., sec.-treas. N.C. Ctr. Pub. Policy Rsch., 1976-83, vice-chmn., 1977-80; mem. task force on commitment law N.C. Dept. Human Resources, 1978; active Def. Rsch. Inst. 1982-84; bd. dirs. Law Fund, 1992—, v.p., 1993-97, pres., 2000-01; mem. ADR Roundtable, 1996-2001. Fellow Am. Bar Found.; mem. ABA (mem. ho. dels. Seattle-King County Bar Assn. 1991-94, mem. litigation sect.), Am. Soc. Hosp. Attys., Am. Law Inst., Wash. State Bar Assn. (mem. domestic rels. task force 1991-93), Seattle-King Bar Assn. (mem. bd. trustees 1990-93, sec. bd. 1989-90, chair judiciary and cts. com. 1987-89, mem. King County Superior Ct. delay reduction task force 1987-89, mem. gender bias com. 1990-94, chair 1990-91), Wash. Def. Trial Lawyers (chmn. ct. rules and procedures com. 1987, co-editor newsletter 1985-86), Wash. State Soc. Hosp. Attys., Wash. Women Lawyers (treas. 1986, 87). Office: Heller Ehrman White & McAuliffe Ste 6100 701 5th Ave Seattle WA 98104-7098 E-mail: pwagner@hewm.com

WAGNER, RICHARD, athletics consultant, former baseball team executive; b. Central City, Nebr., Oct. 19, 1927; s. John Howard and Esther Marie (Wolken) W.; m. Gloria Jean Larsen, May 10, 1950; children—Randolph G., Cynthia Kaye. Student, pub. schs., Central City. Gen. mgr. Lincoln (Nebr.) Baseball Club, 1955-58; mgr. Pershing Mcpl. Auditorium, Lincoln, 1958-61; exec. staff Ice Capades, Inc., Hollywood, Calif., 1961-63; gen. mgr. Sta. KSAL, Salina, Kans., 1963-65; dir. promotion and sales St. Louis Nat. Baseball Club, 1965-66; gen. mgr. Forum, Inglewood, Calif., 1966-67; asst. to exec. v.p. Cin. Reds, 1967-70, asst. to pres., 1970-74, v.p. adminstrn., 1975, exec. v.p., 1975-78, gen. mgr., 1977-83, pres., 1978-83, Houston Astros Baseball Club, 1985-87; spl. asst. Office of Baseball Commr., 1988-93; asst. to chmn. Major League Exec. Coun., 1993-94. Pres. RGW Enterprises, Inc., Phoenix, 1978-97. Served with USNR, 1945-47, 50-52. Named Exec. of Yr., Minor League Baseball, Sporting News, 1958. Republican. Methodist.

WAGNER, WILLIAM GERARD, university dean, physicist, consultant, information scientist, investment manager; b. St. Cloud, Minn., Aug. 22, 1936; s. Gerard C. and Mary V. (Cloone) W.; m. Janet Agatha Rowe, Jan. 30, 1968 (div. 1978); children: Mary, Robert, David, Anne; m. Christiane LeGuen, Feb. 21, 1985 (div. 1989); m. Yvonne Naomi Moussette, Dec. 4, 1995. B.S., Calif. Inst. Tech., 1958, Ph.D. (NSF fellow, Howard Hughes fellow), 1962. Cons. Rand Corp., Santa Monica, Calif., 1960-65; sr. staff physicist Hughes Research Lab., Malibu, 1960-69; lectr. physics Calif. Inst. Tech., Pasadena, 1963-65; asst. prof. physics U. Calif. at Irvine, 1965-66; assoc. prof. physics and elec. engring. U. So. Calif., L.A., 1966-69, prof. depts. physics and elec. engring., 1969—, dean div. natural scis. and math. Coll. Letters, Arts and Scis., 1973-87, dean interdisciplinary studies and developmental activities, 1987-89, spl. asst. automated record services, 1975-81; founder program in neural, informational & behavioral scis., 1982—. Chmn. bd. Malibu Securities Corp., L.A., 1971—; cons. Janus Mgmt. Corp., L.A., 1970-71, Croesus Capital Corp., L.A., 1971-74, Fin. Horizons Inc., Beverly Hills, Calif., 1971—; allied mem. Pacific Stock Exch., 1974-82; fin. and computer cons. Hollywood Reporter, 1979-81; mem. adv. coun. for emerging engring. techs. NSF, 1987-89. Contbr. articles on physics to sci. publs. Richard Chase Tolman postdoctoral fellow, 1962-65 Mem. Am. Phys. Soc., Nat. Assn. Security Dealers, Sigma Xi. Home: 2828 Patricia Ave Los Angeles CA 90064-4425 Office: U So Calif Hedco Neurosci Bldg Los Angeles CA 90089-0001

WAGONER, DAVID EVERETT, lawyer; b. Pottstown, Pa., May 16, 1928; s. Claude Brower and Mary Kathryn (Groff) W.; children: Paul R., Colin H., Elon D., Peter B., Dana F.; m. Jean Morton Saunders; children: Constance A., Jennifer L., Melissa J. BA, Yale U., 1950; LLB, U. Pa., 1953. Bar: D.C. 1953, Pa. 1953, Wash. 1953. Law clk. U.S. Ct. Appeals (3d cir.), Pa., 1955-56; law clk. U.S. Supreme Ct., Washington, 1956-57; ptnr. Perkins & Coie, Seattle, 1957-96. Panel mem. of arbitration forum worldwide including People's Republic of China, B.C. Internat. Comml. Arbitration Ctr., Hong Kong Internat. Arbitration Centre, Asian/Pacific Ctr. for Resolution of Internat. Bus. Disputes and the Ctr. for Internat. Dispute Resolution for Asian/Pacific Region. Mem. sch. com. Mcpl. League Seattle and King County, 1958— , chmn., 1962-65; mem. Seattle schs. citizens coms. on equal ednl. opportunity and adult vocat. edn., 1963-64; mem. Nat. Com. Support Pub. Schs.; mem. adv. com. on community colls., to 1965, legislature interim com. on edn., 1964-65; mem. community coll. adv. com. to state supt. pub. instrn., 1965; chmn. edn. com. Forward Thrust, 1968; mem. Univ. Congl. Ch. Council Seattle, 1968-70; bd. dirs. Met. YMCA Seattle, 1968; bd. dirs. Seattle Pub. Schs., 1965-73, v.p., 1966-67, 72-73, pres., 1968, 73; trustee Evergreen State Coll. Found., chmn. 1986-87, capitol campaign planning chmn.; trustee Pacific NW Ballet, v.p. 1986. Served to 1st lt. M.C., AUS, 1953-55 Fellow Am. Coll. Trial Lawyers (mem. ethics com., legal ethics com.), Chartered Inst. Arbitrators, Singapore Inst. Arbitrators; mem. ABA (chmn. standing com. fed. jud. imprisonment, chmn. appellate advocacy com., mem. commn. on separation of powers and jud. independence), Wash. State Bar Assn., Seattle-King County Bar Assn., Acad. Experts, Swiss Arbitration Assn., Comml. Bar Assn. London, Nat. Sch. Bds. Assn. (bd. dirs., chmn. coun. Big City bds. [illegible] Phi. Home: 4215 E Blaine St Seattle WA 98112-3229 Office: Internat Arbitration Chambers US BankCtr 1420 5th Ave Fl 22 Seattle WA 98101-4087

WAGONER, DAVID RUSSELL, writer, educator; b. Massillon, Ohio, June 5, 1926; s. Walter Siffert and Ruth (Banyard) W.; m. Patricia Lee Parrott, July 8, 1961 (div. June 1982); m. Robin Heather Seyfried, July 24, 1982; children: Alexandra Dawn, Adrienne Campbell. B.A. in English, Pa. State U., 1947; M.A. in English, Ind. U., 1949. Instr. English DePauw U., 1949-50; instr. Pa. State U., 1950-53; asst. prof. U. Wash., 1954-57, assoc. prof., 1958-66, prof., 1966-2000, prof. emeritus, 2000—. Elliston lectr. U. Cin., 1968; editor Poetry NW, 1966— ; poetry editor Princeton U. Press, 1977-81, Mo. Press, 1983— Author: (poetry books) Dry Sun, Dry Wind, 1953, A Place to Stand, 1958, The Nesting Ground, 1963, Staying Alive, 1966, New and Selected Poems, 1969, Working Against Time, 1970, Riverbed, 1972, Sleeping in the Woods, 1974, Collected Poems, 1976, Who Shall Be the Sun?, 1978, In Broken Country, 1979, Landfall, 1981, First Light, 1983, Through the Forest, 1987, Walt Whitman Bathing, 1996, Traveling Light: Collected and New Poems, 1999; (novels) The Man in the Middle, 1954, Money, Money, Money, 1955, Rock, 1958, The Escape Artist (also film 1982), 1965, Baby, Come on Inside, 1968, Where is My Wandering Boy Tonight?, 1970, The Road to Many a Wonder, 1974, Tracker, 1975, Whole Hog, 1976, The Hanging Garden, 1980; editor: Straw for the Fire: From the Notebooks of Theodore Roethke, 1943-63, 1972. Recipient Morton Dauwen Zabel prize Poetry mag., 1967, Blumenthal-Leviton-Blonder prize, 1974, 2 Fels prizes Coordinating Coun. Lit. Mags., 1975, Tietjens prize, 1977, English-Speaking Union prize, 1980, Sherwood Anderson award, 1980, Ruth Lilly Poetry prize, 1991, Levinson prize, 1994; Union League Prize, 1987, Pacific N.W. Booksellers award, 2000; Guggenheim fellow, 1956, Ford fellow, 1964, Nat. Inst. Arts and Letters grantee, 1967, Nat. Endowment for Arts grantee, 1969 Mem. Acad. Am. Poets (chancellor 1978—), Soc. Am. Magicians, Nat. Assn. Blackfeet Indians (asso.) Home: 5416 154th Pl SW Edmonds WA 98026-4348 Office: U Wash PO Box 354330 Seattle WA 98195-4330 E-mail: renogawd@aol.com

WAGONER, ROBERT VERNON, astrophysicist, educator; b. Teaneck, N.J., Aug. 6, 1938; s. Robert Vernon and Marie Theresa (Clifford) W.; m. Lynne Ray Moses, Sept. 2, 1963 (div. Feb. 1986); children: Alexa Frances, Shannon Stephanie; m. Stephanie Brewster, June 27, 1987. BME, Cornell U., 1961; MS, Stanford U., 1962, PhD, 1965. Rsch. fellow in physics Calif. Inst. Tech., 1965-68, Sherman Fairchild Disting. scholar, 1976; asst. prof. astronomy Cornell U., 1968-71, assoc. prof., 1971-73; assoc. prof. physics Stanford U., 1973-77, prof., 1977—. George Ellery Hale disting. vis. prof. U. Chgo., 1978; mem. Com. on Space Astronomy and Astrophysics, 1979-82, theory study panel Space Sci. Bd., 1980-82, physics survey com. NRC, 1983-84; grant selection com. NSERC (Can.), 1990-93; active Laser Interferometer Gravitational-Wave Obs. Sci. Collaboration. Contbr. articles on theoretical astrophysics and gravitation to profl. jours., mags.; co-author Cosmic Horizons, 1982; patentee in field. Sloan Found. rsch. fellow, 1969-71; Guggenheim Meml. fellow, 1979; grantee NSF, 1973-90, 2000—, NASA, 1982-99. Fellow Am. Phys. Soc.; mem. Am. Astron. Soc., Internat. Astron. Union, Tau Beta Pi, Phi Kappa Phi Office: Stanford U Dept Physics Stanford CA 94305-4060 E-mail: wagoner@stanford.edu

WAGONFELD, JAMES B. gastroenterologist; b. Bronx, N.Y., Jan. 30, 1946; m. Judith Wagonfeld; children: Temira Lital, Ariella Lirit. BA, NYU, 1966; MD, U. Health Scis., Chgo., 1970. Diplomate Nat. Bd. Med. Examiners, Am. Bd. Internal Medicine, Am. Bd. Internal Med. subsplt. gastroenterology cert.; lic. M.D. Ill., Oreg., Wash. Med. intern Duke U. Med. Ctr., Durham, N.C., 1970-71; jr. asst. resident in medicine U. Chgo. Hosps. and Clinics, 1971-72, sr. asst. resident in medicine, 1972-73, NIH fellow in gastroenterology, 1973-75, instr. medicine, 1975-76; asst. prof. medicine U. Oreg. Health Scis. Ctr., Portland, 1976-78; attending physician Portland VA Hosp., 1976-78; pvt. practice Digestive Disease Consultants, Inc. P.S., Tacoma; dir. gastrointestinal study unit Allenmore Hosp., Tacoma, 1979-93, Tacoma Gen. Hosp., 1987—; co-dir. gastrointestinal diagnostic nit St. Joseph Hosp. and Health Care Ctr., 1988-90. Cons. FDA panel on rev. of vitamins, minerals, and hematinic drug products, 1974-75. Contbr. articles to profl. jours. Physician Benita Juarez Clinic, Chgo., 1971-73, Cardiac Rehab. Program Tacoma-Pierce County Family YMCA, 1980-84; advisor Portlan dAssn. for Childbirth Edn., 1976-78, RESOLVE, An Advocacy Orgn. for Infertile Couples, 1976-78, Colon Cancer Screening in Sr. Citizens, Multinomah County Pub. Health Dept. and Southwest Wash. Health Dist., 1977-78; scientific advisor Shaw Meml. Lecture series, Oreg. Med. Assn., 1977-78; bd. med. advisors Pacific Northwest Soc. of Gastrointestinal Assts., 1982; trustee Charles Wright Acad., 1984-87, chmn. devel. com., 1985-87, chmn. edn. fund, 1985-86. Recipient NIH rsch. award, 1975-76. Fellow ACP, Am. Coll. Gastroenterology; mem. AMA, Am. Gastroenterologic Assn., Am. Soc. for Gastrointestinal Endoscopy, Pacific Northwest Endoscopy Soc., The Wilderness Med. Soc., Wash. State Med. Assn., Med. Soc. Pierce County, Alpha Omega Alpha. Office: Digestive Disease Cons 1901 S Union Ave Ste B-4006 Tacoma WA 98405-1898

WAHL, ARTHUR CHARLES, retired chemistry educator; b. Des Moines, Sept. 8, 1917; s. Arthur C. and Mabel (Mussetter) W.; m. Mary Elizabeth McCauley, Dec. 1, 1943; 1 child, Nancy Wahl Miegel. BS, Iowa State Coll., 1939; PhD, U. Calif., Berkeley, 1942. Group leader Los Alamos (N.Mex.) Nat. Lab., 1943-46; assoc. prof. chemistry Washington U., St. Louis, 1946-53, Farr prof. of radiochemistry, 1953-83, prof. emeritus, 1983—. Cons. Los Alamos Nat. Lab., 1950—. Author, editor: Radioactivity Applied to Chemistry, 1951; contbr. articles to profl. jours. NSF fellow, 1967; recipient Sr. Vis. Scientist Humboldt award Humboldt Found., 1977. Mem. Am. Chem. Soc. Office: Los Alamos Nat Lab Ms # 514 Los Alamos NM 87545-0001 E-mail: awahl@lanl.gov

WAHLKE, JOHN CHARLES, political science educator; b. Cin., Oct. 29, 1917; s. Albert B.C. and Clara J. (Ernst) W.; m. Virginia Joan Higgins, Dec. 1, 1943; children: Janet Parmely, Dale. A.B., Harvard U., 1939, M.A., 1947, Ph.D., 1952. Instr., asst. prof. polit. sci. Amherst (Mass.) Coll., 1949-53; assoc. prof. polit. sci. Vanderbilt U., Nashville, 1953-63; prof. polit. sci. SUNY, Buffalo, 1963-66, U. Iowa, 1966-71, SUNY, Stony Brook, 1971-72, U. Iowa, Iowa City, 1972-79, U. Ariz., Tucson, 1979-87, prof. emeritus, 1988—, retired. Author: (with others) The Legislative System, 1962, Government and Politics, 1966, The Politics of Representation, 1978; co-author: Introduction to Political Science—Reason, Reflection, and Analysis, 1997 Served to capt., F.A. AUS, 1942-46. Decorated Air medal with 2 oak leaf clusters, ETO Ribbon, 6 Battle Stars. Mem. AAAS, Am. Polit. Sci. Assn. (past pres.), Internat. Polit. Sci. Assn., So. Polit. Sci. Assn., Midwest Polit. Sci. Assn. (past pres.), Western Polit. Sci. Assn., Southwestern Polit. Sci. Assn., Assn. Politics and the Life Scis. (Founders award 1997), Internat. Soc. of Polit. Psychology. Home: 5462 N Entrada Catorce Tucson AZ 85718-4851 Office: U Ariz Social Sci Bldg Rm 315 Dept Polit Sci Tucson AZ 85721 E-mail: wahlke@email.arizona.edu

WAINWRIGHT, DAVID STANLEY, intellectual property professional; b. New Haven, May 23, 1955; s. Stanley Dunstan and Lillian (Karelitz) W.;m. Catherine Demetra Kefalas, Aug. 11, 1984; children: Maxwell Stanley Hector, Eric George Alexander. BSc with 1st class honors in Physics, Dalhousie U., Halifax, N.S., 1976; MSc in Physics, U. B.C., Vancouver, 1979. Registered patent agt., U.S., Can. Model plant supr., scientist, technician Moli Energy Ltd., Maple Ridge, B.C., Can., 1978-84, project leader cell devel. Can., 1984-88, cell devel. mgr. Can., 1988-90, Moli Energy (1990) Ltd., Maple Ridge, 1990-92, mgr. intellectual property, 1992-98; patent agt. Ballard Power Sys., Burnaby, B.C., Canada, 1998—. Contbr. articles to profl. jours. Mem. Patent and Trademark Inst. Can. Home: 2585 W 1st Ave Vancouver BC Canada V6K 1G8 Office: Ballard Power Sys Inc 9000 Glenlyon Pky Burnaby BC Canada V5J 5J9 E-mail: davwai@ballard.com

WAITE, RIC, cinematographer; b. Sheboygan, Wis., July 10, 1933; s. Howard Pierce and Bertha Ann (Pippert) W.; m. Judy Lescher, Apr. 24, 1965; children: Richard R., Burgandy B. Student, U. Colo. Cinematographer: (films) Other Side of the Mountain Part II, 1978, Defiance, 1980, The Long Riders, 1980, Tex, 1982, 48 Hrs., 1982, The Border, 1982, Class, 1983, Footloose, 1984, Red Dawn, 1984, Volunteers, 1985, Summer Rental, 1985, Brewster's Millions, 1985, Cobra, 1986, Adventures in Babysitting, 1987, Great Outdoors, 1989, Marked for Death, 1990, Price of Our Blood, 1990, Out for Justice, 1991, Rapid Fire, 1992, On Deadly Ground, 1994, Truth or Consequences, N.Mex., 1997; (TV) Nakia, 1974, The November Plan, 1976, Nero Wolfe, 1977, Tail Gunner Joe, 1977, The Initiation of Sarah, 1978, And Baby Makes Six, 1979, Revenge of the Stepford Wives, 1980, Baby Comes Home, 1980, Dempsey, 1983, Police Story: Burnout, 1988, Scam, 1993, Last Light, 1993, Andersonville, 1996, Money Plays, 1997, Last Stand at Saber River, 1997, Hope, 1997. 1st lt. USAF, 1951-56. Recipient Emmy award, 1976. Mem. Am. Soc. Cinematographers. Avocations: sailing, flying. Home: 517 Mitchell Bay Rd Friday Harbor WA 98250-8568 Office: 1216 Roulac Ln Friday Harbor WA 98250-9572 also: Prime Artists Derren Sugar 7650 Topanga Canyon Blvd Warner Center CA 91304 E-mail: ricwaite@aol.com

WAITS, THOMAS ALAN, composer, actor, singer; b. Pomona, Calif., Dec. 7, 1949; s. Frank W. and Alma (Johnson) McMurray; m. Kathleen Patricia Brennan, Aug. 10, 1980; children: Kellesimone Wylder, Casey Xavier, Sullivan Blake. Composer 16 albums including Closing Time, 1973, The Heart of Saturday Nite, 1974, Nighthawks at the Diner, 1975, Small Change, 1976, Foreign Affairs, 1978, Blue Valentine, 1979, Heart Attack and Vine, 1980, One From the Heart, 1981, Swordfishtrombones, 1983, Rain Dogs, 1985, Anthology, 1985, Frank's Wild Years, 1987, Big Time, 1988, Bone Machine, 1992, Night on Earth, 1992, The Black Rider, 1993, Beautiful Maladies, 1998, Mule Variations, 1999 (Grammy Award, 1999); composer (film scores) One from the Heart, 1983, Streetwise, 1985, Night on Earth, 1991; co-author music and songs (with Kathleen Brennan) for Night on Earth, 1991, End of Violence, 1997, Bunny, 1999, Dead Man Walking, film American Heart; composer songs and music for The Black Rider opera, Hamburg, Germany, 1990; composer songs and music, writer (with Kathleen Brennan) Alice in Wonderland opera, Hamburg, 1992, oprea Woyzeck, Copenhagen, 2000; actor (musical) Frank's Wild Years, 1986, (stage play) Demon Wine, 1989; appeared in films Paradise Alley, 1978, The Outsiders, 1983, Rumble Fish, 1983, The Cotton Club, 1984, Down by Law, 1986, Ironweed, 1987, Candy Mountain, 1987, Big Time, 1988, Cold Feet, 1989, The Bearskin, 1991, Queen's Logic, 1991, At Play in the Fields of the Lord, 1991, Bram Stoker's Dracula, 1992, Short Cuts, 1993, Mystery Men, 1999. Recipient Acad. Award nomination Best Song Score for One from the Heart, 1983; Grammy award for best alternative album Bone Machine, 1992, Grammy award for Mule Variations as best contemporary folk music, 2000, Dramalogue award for actor Demon Wine, Danish Theater award for Woyzeck as best musical, 2001. Mem. ASCAP (Founders award for career achievement in songwriting 2001), Musicians Union Local 47, SAG, AFTRA, Motion Picture Acad. Office: care Howard Grossman 10960 Wilshire Blvd Ste 2150 Los Angeles CA 90024-3807

WAITT, TED W. computer company executive; CEO Gateway, San Diego, former chmn., pres., chmn., CEO, chmn. Office: Gateway 4545 Towne Centre Ct San Diego CA 92121-1900

WAITZKIN, HOWARD BRUCE, internist, sociologist, educator; b. Akron, Ohio, Sept. 6, 1945; s. Edward and Dorothy (Lederman) W.; m. Stephany Borges, Mar. 13, 1983 (div.); 1 stepchild, Daren; 1 child, Sofia. BA summa cum laude, Harvard U., 1966, MA, 1969, MD, PhD, 1972. Diplomate Am. Bd. Internal Medicine, Am. Bd. Geriatric Medicine. Resident in medicine Stanford (Calif.) U. Med. Ctr., 1972-75, Robert Wood Johnson clin. scholar depts. sociology-medicine, 1973-75; sr. resident in medicine Mass. Gen. Hosp., Boston, 1977-78; assoc. prof. sociology, clin. asst. prof. medicine U. Vt., Burlington, 1975-77; vis. assoc. prof. health and med. scis. U. Calif., Berkeley, 1978-82, clin. asst. prof. medicine San Francisco, 1978-82; internist La Clínica de la Raza, Oakland, Calif., 1978-82; prof. medicine and social scis. U. Calif., Irvine, 1982-96, chief div. gen. internal medicine and primary care, 1982-90; med. dir. U. Calif.-Irvine-North Orange County Community Clinic, Anaheim, 1982-90; prof. medicine and sociology, Latin Am. studies U. N.Mex., Albuquerque, 1997—. Regional rep., nat. sec. bd. dirs. Physicians for Nat. Health Program, Cambridge, Mass., 1989-91; cons. documentary Health Care Across the Border, Nat. Pub. TV, N.Y.C., 1989-90, documentary on U.S. health care system Nat. TV Austria, 1991; cons. BBC, 1992, Pew Health Professions Commn., 1992-94, Assn. Am. Med. Colls., 1992-93, Robert Wood Johnson Found., 1992, Rsch. and Tng. Group in Social Medicine, Santiago, Chile, 1990—, Eisenhower Rural Health Ctrs., Idyllwild, Calif., 1995-96; lectr. med. sociology U. Amsterdam, The Netherlands, 1977; vis. prof. Northwestern U., 1994, U. Ill., Chgo., 1994, U. Wash., 1996, U. N.Mex., 1996, U. Ky., 1996, U. Guadalajara, 1997, Simon Fraser U., 1997, U. Campinas, Brazil, 1999, Cornell Med. Coll., 1999; mem. expert panel on comm. with elderly patients Nat. Inst. Aging, 1997; prin. investigator U.S. Agy. for Healthcare, Rsch. and Quality, NIMH, 2001. Co-author: The Exploitation of Illness in Capitalist Society, 1974; author: The Second Sickness: Contradictions of Capitalist Health Care, 1983, paperback edit., 1986, revised edit., 2000, The Politics of Medical Encounters: How Patients and Doctors Deal with Social Problems, 1991, paperback edit., 1993, At the Front Lines of Medicine: How the Health Care System Alienates Doctors and Mistreats patients...and Waht We Can Do About It, 2001; mem. editl. bd. Internat. Jour. Health Svcs., Social Problems, Western Jour. Medicine, Cambio y Salud (Chile), Investigacion en Salud (Mex.). Cons. on health policy Jesse Jackson Presdl. Campaign, 1988; bd. dirs., mem. com. on litigation Orange County Pub. Law Ctr., 1990-96. Fellow in ind. study & rsch. NEH, 1984-85, Fulbright fellow, 1983, 88-90, 93-94, sr. fellow NIA, 1989-91, Fogarty Internat. Ctr., NIH, 1994-98. Fellow ACP, Am. Acad. Physician and Patient; mem. APHA, Am. Sociol. Assn. (nat. coun.-at-large med. sociology sect. 1989-92, coord. resolution process concerning nat. health program 1990-91, Leo G. Reeder award for disting. career in medicine and social scis. 1997), Soc. Gen. Internal Medicine, Phi Beta Kappa. Avocations: music, athletics, gardening, mountain hiking. Office: U NMex Sch Medicine Divsn Cmty Med 2400 Tucker NE Albuquerque NM 87131-0001 E-mail: waitzkin@unm.edu

WAKATSUKI, LYNN Y. commissioner; Commr. fin. instns. divsn. fin. instns. Dept. Commerce and Consumer Affairs, Honolulu, 1995—. Office: Dept Commerce Consumer Affairs Divsn Fin Instns PO Box 2054 Honolulu HI 96805

WAKE, DAVID BURTON, biology educator; b. Webster, S.D., June 8, 1936; s. Thomas B. and Ina H. (Solem) W.; m. Marvalee Hendricks, June 23, 1962; 1 child, Thomas Andrew BA, Pacific Luth. U., 1958; MS, U. So. Calif., 1960, PhD, 1964. Instr. anatomy and biology U. Chgo., 1964-66, asst. prof. anatomy and biology, 1966-69; assoc. prof. zoology U. Calif., Berkeley, 1969-72, prof., 1972-89, prof. integrative biology, 1989—, John and Margaret Gompertz prof., 1991-97. Dir. Mus. Vertebrate Zoology U. Calif., Berkeley, 1971-98; curator Herpetology Mus. Vertebrate Zoology, U. Calif., 1969—. Author: Biology, 1979; co-editor: Functional Vertebrate Morphology, 1985, Complex Organismal Functions: Integration and Evolution in the Vertebrates, 1989. Recipient Quantrell Teaching award U. Chgo., 1967, Outstanding Alumnus award Pacific Luth. U., 1979, Joseph Grinnell medal Mus. Vertebrate Zoology, 1998, Henry S. Fitch award Am. Soc. Ichthyologists and Herpetologists, 1999; grantee NSF, 1965—; Guggenheim fellow, 1982. Fellow AAAS, Am. Acad. Arts and Scis.; mem. NAS, NRC (bd. biology 1986-92), Am. Philos. Soc., Internat. Union for Conservation of Nature and Natural Resources (chair task force on declining amphibian populations 1990-92), Am. Soc. Zoologists (pres. 1992), Am. Soc. Naturalists (pres. 1989), Am. Soc. Ichthyologists and Herpetologists (bd. govs.), Soc. Study Evolution (pres. 1983, editor 1979-81), Soc. Systematic Biology (coun. 1980-84), Herpetologist's League (Disting. Herpetologist 1984). Home: 999 Middlefield Rd Berkeley CA 94708-1509 E-mail: wakelab@uclink4.berkeley.edu

WAKE, MARVALEE HENDRICKS, biology educator; b. Orange, Calif., July 31, 1939; d. Marvin Carlton and Velvalee (Borter) H.; m. David B. Wake, June 23, 1962; 1 child, Thomas A. BA, U. So. Calif., 1961, MS, 1964, PhD, 1968. Teaching asst./instr. U. Ill., Chgo., 1964-68, asst. prof., 1968-69; lectr. U. Calif., Berkeley, 1969-73, asst. prof., 1973-76, assoc. prof., 1976-80, prof. zoology, 1980-89, chmn. dept. zoology, 1985-89, chmn. dept. integrative biology, 1989-91, 99—, assoc. dean Coll. Letters and Sci., 1975-78, prof. integrative biology, 1989—, Chancellor's prof., 1997-2000. Mem. NAS/NRC Bd. on Sustainable Devel., 1995-99, NSF Bio Adv. Commn., 1997—. Editor, co-editor: Hyman's Comparative Vertebrate Anatomy, 1979, The Origin and Evolution of Larval Forms, 1999; co-author: Biology, 1978; contbr. articles to profl. jours. NSF grantee, 1978—; Guggenheim fellow, 1988-89. Fellow AAAS (chair Biology Sect. G 1998), Calif. Acad. Sci. (trustee 1992-98, hon. trustee 1998—); mem. Am. Soc. Ichthyologists and Herpetologists (pres. 1984, bd. govs. 1978—), Soc. Integrative Comparative Biol. (pres. 2001—), Internat. Union Biol. Scis. (U.S. nat. com. 1986—, chair 1992-95, pres. 2000—, World Congress of Herpetology (sec. gen. 1994-97). Office: U Calif Dept Integrative Biology Berkeley CA 94720-0001

WAKEMAN, FREDERIC EVANS , JR. historian, educator; b. Kansas City, Kans., Dec. 12, 1937; s. Frederic Evans and Margaret Ruth (Keyes) W.; divorced; children: Frederic Evans III, Matthew Clark, Sarah Elizabeth. BA, Harvard Coll., 1959; postgrad., Institut d'Etudes Politiques, U. Paris, 1959-60; MA, U. Calif., Berkeley, 1962, PhD, 1965. Asst. prof. history U. Calif., Berkeley, 1965-67, assoc. prof., 1968-70, prof., 1970-89, Haas prof. Asian Studies, 1989—, dir. Ctr. Chinese Studies, 1972-79; humanities research prof., vis. scholar Corpus Christi Coll., U. Cambridge, Eng., 1976-77, Beijing U., 1980-81, 85. Acad. adviser U.S. Ednl. Del. for Study in China; chmn. Joint Com. Chinese Studies Am. Coun. Learned Socs./Social Sci. Rsch. Coun.; sr. adviser Beijing office NAS; pres. Social Sci. Rsch. Coun., 1986-89, chmn. com. on scholarly comm. with China, 1995-2000; dir. Inst. East Asian Studies, Berkeley, 1990-2001; vis. prof. U. Heidelberg, Germany, 2000. Author: Strangers at the Gate, 1966, History and Will, 1973, The Fall of Imperial China, 1975, Conflict and Control in Late Imperial China, 1976, Ming and Qing Historical Studies in the People's Republic of China, 1981, The Great Enterprise, 1986, Shanghai Sojourners, 1992, Policing Shanghai, 1995, Shanghai Badlands, 1996, China's Quest for Modernization, 1997, Reappraising Republican China, 2000. Harvard Nat. scholar, 1955-59; Tower fellow, 1959-60; Fgn. Area fellow, 1963-65; Am. Coun. Learned Socs. fellow, 1967-68; Guggenheim fellow, 1973-74; NRC fellow, 1985. Mem. Am. Acad. Arts and Scis., Coun. on Fgn. Rels., Am. Hist. Assn. (pres.), Am. Philos. Soc. Home: 501 Delancey St Apt 409 San Francisco CA 94107-1432 Office: U Calif Inst East Asian Studies Berkeley CA 94720-0001 E-mail: jingcha@socrates.berkeley.edu

WALCH, PETER SANBORN, museum director, publisher; b. Portland, Maine, Oct. 10, 1940; s. J. Weston and Ruth Dyer (Sanborn) W.; m. Margaret S. Segal, June 29, 1962 (div. 1983); children: Maximilian F.S., Abigail M.; m. Linda P. Tyler, Aug. 3, 1990. BA, Swarthmore Coll., 1962; MFA, Princeton U., 1964, PhD, 1968. Asst. prof. fine arts Pomona Coll., Claremont, Calif., 1966-68, Vassar Coll., Poughkeepsie, N.Y., 1968-69, Yale U., New Haven, 1969-71; assoc. prof. U. N.Mex., Albuquerque, 1971-85, dir. Art Mus., 1985—. Chmn., bd. dirs. J. Weston Walch, Pub., Portland, 1990—. Author: (exhbn. catalog) French Eighteenth-Century Oil Sketches, 1980, French Oil Sketches and the Academic Tradition, 1994; editor N.Mex. Studies in the Fine Arts jour., 1978-86. Mem. Contemporary Art Soc., Cogawesco Club. Home: 1520 Columbia Dr NE Albuquerque NM 87106-2635 Office: Univ NMex Art Mus Fine Arts Ctr Albuquerque NM 87131-0001

WALCHER, ALAN ERNEST, lawyer; b. Chgo., Oct. 2, 1949; s. Chester R. and Dorothy E. (Kullgren) W.; m. Penny Marie Walcher; children: Dustin Alan, Michael Alan, Christopher Ray; 1 stepchild, Ronald Edwin Culver. BS, U. Utah, 1971, cert. in internat. rels., 1971, JD, 1974. Bar: Utah 1974, U.S. Dist. Ct. Utah 1974, U.S. Ct. Appeals (10th cir.) 1977, Calif. 1979, U.S. Dist. Ct. (cen. dist.) Calif. 1979, U.S. Ct. Appeals (9th cir.) 1983, U.S. Dist. Ct. (ea., no., and so. dists.) Calif. 1994. Sole practice, Salt Lake City, 1974-79; ptnr. Costello & Walcher, L.A., 1979-85, Walcher & Scheuer, 1985-88, Ford & Harrison, 1988-91, Epstein Becker & Green, 1991—; judge pro tem Los Angeles Mcpl. Ct., 1986-91; dir. Citronia, Inc., Los Angeles, 1979-81. Trial counsel Utah chpt. Common Cause, Salt Lake City, 1978-79. Robert Mukai scholar U. Utah, 1971. Mem. Soc. Bar and Gavel (v.p. 1975-77), ABA, Fed. Bar Assn., Los Angeles County Bar Assn., Century City Bar Assn., Assn. Bus. Trial Lawyers, Phi Delta Phi, Owl and Key. Club: Woodland Hills Country (Los Angeles). Home: 17933 Sunburst St Northridge CA 91325-2848 Office: Epstein Becker & Green 1875 Century Park E Ste 500 Los Angeles CA 90067-2506

WALDEN, GREG, congressman; b. The Dalles, Oreg., Jan. 10, 1957; m. Mylene Walden; 1 child. BS in Journalism, U. Oreg., 1981. Owner Columbia Gorge Broadcasters, Inc., The Dalles, 1986—; mem. Oreg. Ho. of Reps., 1989-95, house majority leader, 1991-93; mem. Oreg. Senate, 1995-97, asst. majority leader, 1995-97; press sec., chief of staff Congressman Denny Smith, Washington, 1981-86; mem. U.S. Congress from 2d Oreg. dist., Washington, 1999—, mem. com. on energy and commerce, com. on resources. Dir. Columbia Bancorp. Bd. dirs., exec. com. Assoc. Oreg. Industries; bd. dirs. Oreg. Health Scis. Found.; former dir. Hood River Meml. Hosp. Named Outstanding Young Oregonian, Oreg. Jaycees, 1991, Legislator of the Yr., Nat. Rep. Legislators Assn., 1993. Mem. Hood River C. of C., Nat. Fedn. Ind. Bus., Elks, Rotary. Republican. Office: US Ho Reps 1404 Longworth HOB Washington DC 20515 also: 843 E Main St Ste 400 Medford OR 97504-7137 E-mail: greg.walden@mail.house.gov

WALDMAN, ANNE LESLEY, poet, performer, editor, publisher, educational administrator; b. Millville, N.J., Apr. 2, 1945; d. John Marvin and Frances (Le Fevre) W.; m. Reed Eyre Bye; 1 son, Ambrose. B.A., Bennington Coll., 1966. Dir. The Poetry Project, St. Marks Ch. In-the-Bowery, N.Y.C., 1968-78; dir. Jack Kerouac Sch. of Disembodied Poetics at Naropa Inst., Boulder, Colo., 1974—. Adj. faculty Inst. Am. Indian Arts, Santa Fe; bd. dirs. Com. for Internat. Poetry, Eye and Ear Theatre, N.Y.C.; poet-in-residence with Bob Dylan's Rolling Thunder Rev.; dir. Naropa Study Abroad in Bali, Indonesia, 1998; guest dir. Schule fur Dichtung, Vienna, 1999. Author: (poetry) On the Wing, 1968, O My Life, 1969, Baby Breakdown, 1970, Giant Night, 1970, No Hassles, 1971, Life Notes, 1973, Fast Speaking Woman, 1975, Journals and Dreams, 1976, Shaman, 1977, Countries, 1980, Cabin, 1981, First Baby Poems, 1982, Makeup on Empty Space, 1983, Invention, 1986, Skin Meat Bones, 1986, The Romance Thing, 1987, Blue Mosque, 1988, Helping the Dreamer: New and Selected Poems, 1989, Not a Male Pseudonym, 1990, Lokapala, 1991, Troubairitz, 1993, Iovis: All is Full of Jove, 1993, Kill or Cure, 1994, Iovis II, 1997; editor: Nice To See You: Homage to Ted Berrigan, 1991, The Beat Book, 1996, (anthologies) The World Anthology, 1969, Another World, 1972, Talking Poetics From Naropa Institute vol. 1, 1978, vol. 2, 1979, Out of This World, 1991, (with Andrew Schelling) Disembodied Poetics: Annals of the Jack Kerovac School, 1994, (with Anselm Hollo and Jack Collom) Polemics; translator (with Andrew Schelling) Sons & Daughters of the Buddha, 1996; publisher: anthologies Angel Hair Books, N.Y.C., Full Ct. Press, N.Y.C.; recordings: The Dial-a-Poem Poets Disconnected, Anne Waldman/John Giorno, Fast Speaking Woman, The Nova Convention, Big Ego, Uh-oh Plutonium!, 1982, Crack in My World, 1986, Assorted Singles, 1990; performance videos include Eyes in All Heads, 1990, Live at Naropa, 1991, Battle of the Bards, 1991; featured on nat. pub. radio show All Things Considered, also featured in the poetry documentary Poetry In Motion. Dir. summer writing program Naropa; organizer Surrealist, Objectivist, Feminist, Pan Am. Ecology, Performance Confs., and The Robert Creeley Symposium. Recipient Dylan Thomas Meml. award New Sch., N.Y.C., 1967, Blue Ribbon Am. Film Festival, Nat. Literary Anthology award, 1970; named Heavyweight Champion Poet, 1989, 90; Cultural Artists Program grantee, 1976-77; NEA grantee, 1979-80; recipient Shelley Meml. award, 1996. Mem. PEN Club, Amnesty Internat. Office: c/o Naropa Inst 2130 Arapahoe Ave Boulder CO 80302-6602

WALDO, JAMES CHANDLER, lawyer; b. Seattle, Oct. 23, 1948; s. Burton Chandler and Margaret (Hoar) W.; m. Sharon B. Barber; children: Sara K., William K., John J. Grad., Whitman Coll., 1970; JD, Willamette U., 1974. Bar: Wash. 1974, U.S. Ct. Appeals (9th cir.) 1976. Exec. asst. Dept. of Labor, Washington, 1974-76; asst. U.S. atty. Justice Dept., Seattle, 1976-79; of counsel ESTEP & LI, Seattle, 1979-80; prin. Gordon, Thomas, Honeywell, Malanca, Peterson & Daheim, P.L.L.C., Seattle, 1981—. Chmn. N.W. Renewable Resources Ctr., Seattle, 1984-97, Wash. State Energy Strategy Com., 1991-93; spl. counsel on Water for Gov., 2001—. Trustee Western Wash. U., Bellingham, 1981-93. Recipient Outstanding Alumnus of Yr. Whitman Coll., 1994, Dir.'s award Wash. Dept. Fisheries, 1986, Pres.'s award Assn. Wash. Bus., 1988, Outstanding Citizen award Western Assn. Fish & Wildlife Agys., 1987. Republican. Office: Gordon Thomas Honeywell Malanca Peterson & Daheim PLLC PO Box 1157 Tacoma WA 98401-1157 Address: PO Box 1157 Tacoma WA 98401-1157

WALEN, JOANNE MICHELE, secondary education educator, consultant; b. Reno, July 8, 1942; d. John Baptista and Helen Hattie (Laakonen) Pollastro; m. Wallace Donald Walen, Feb. 20, 1961; children: Lisa M. Mays, Kevin M. Walen. BA, U. Nev., Reno, 1965, MA, 1974. Cert. secondary sch. tchr., curriculum supr., Nev. Tchr. Washoe County Sch. Dist., Reno, 1965-85, English program coord., 1985-95; dir. WCSD Shakespeare in the Schs., Reno, 1985-95; cons. Shakespeare Express, Reno, 1995—, McDougal Littell, 1998—. Head reader, trainer Nev. State Dept. Edn., Carson City, 1980—; co-dir. Lit. Inst. U. Nev., Reno, 1986-90; essay reader ETS, Princeton, N.J., 1990-94; cons. IBEU, Rio de Janiero, Brazil, 1996, 98; cons. in field. Sr. editor (book) Secondary Writing Guide, 1995; author: (booklet) Handbook for Writing Traits, 1993; contbr. articles to profl. jours. Founder, dir. Shakespeare Performance Festival, Reno, 1986-95; co-dir. Washoe K-16 Coun. Lang. Consortium, Reno, 1995-96. Recipient Humanities award Nev. Humanities Com. State of Nev., 1991; grantee Summer Seminar NEH, Stratford Upon Avon, UK, 1994. Mem. NEA, Nat. Coun. Tchrs. of English (liaison officer 1994—, chair CEE commn 1996-98, chair writing awards adv. com. 1999-2002), No. Nev. Writing Project, Alpha Delta Kappa (pres. 1982-84). Lutheran. Avocations: reading, theater, travel. Home: 11500 Pickens Dr Reno NV 89511-9445 E-mail: shaxpur@aol.com

WALENDOWSKI, GEORGE JERRY, accounting and business educator; b. Han-Minden, Germany, Mar. 25, 1947; came to U.S., 1949; s. Stefan (dec.) and Eugenia (Lewandowska) W. AA, L.A. City Coll., 1968; BS, Calif. State U., L.A., 1970, MBA, 1972; cert. completion, Inst. Mgmt. Accts., 2000—. Cert. community coll. instr. acctg. and mgmt., Calif. Acct. Unocal (formerly Union Oil Co. Calif.), L.A., 1972-76, data control supr., 1976-78, acctg. analyst, 1978-79; sr. fin. analyst Hughes Aircraft Co., El Segundo, Calif., 1979-83, fin. planning specialist, 1983-84, program controls specialist, 1984-86, bus. mgmt. specialist, 1986-92, bus. analyst, 1993-95. Adj. instr. bus. math. L.A. City Coll., 1976-80, adj. instr. acctg., 1980-97, 99—, substitute instr. acctg., 1998, mem. acctg. adv. com., 1984, 87, 89, 99; adj. instr. acctg. and bus. Pasadena City Coll., 1996—; reviewer conf. papers Western Acad. Mgmt., 1996, 97, Inst. Behavior and Applied Mgmt., 1997, So. Mgmt. Assn., 1999. Contbr. articles to profl. jours. Mem. commn. Rep. Pres. Task Force, 1986. Recipient Medal of Merit, Rep. Presdl. Task Force, 1984, cert. of merit, named registered life mem. commn., 1986, named Honor Roll life mem., 1989; recipient Vice-Presdl. Cert. of Commendation, Rep. Nat. Hall of Honor, 1992, Rep. Congl. cert. of Appreciation, 1993, Rep. Congl. Order of Freedom award Nat. Rep. Congl. Com., 1995, Recognition award L.A. chpt. Strategic Leadership Forum, 1983. Mem. Acad. Mgmt. (reviewer social issues in mgmt. divsn. 1991, mgmt. edn. and devel. divsn. program rev. com. 1998, 99), Inst. Mgmt. Accts. (author's cir. L.A. chpt. 1980, Robert Half author's trophy 1980, cert. of appreciation 1980, 83), Am. Acctg. Assn. (competitive manuscript com. 1997-98, reviewer tchg. curr. sect. 1998), Nat. Bus. Edn. Assn., Fin. Mgmt. Assn., Soc. Advancement Mgmt. (selection com. mem. Internat. Conf. 2000, editl. bd. Advanced Mgmt. Jour. 1999—), Eastern Fin. Assn. (program com. 2000), U.S. Chess Fedn., Beta Gamma Sigma, Delta Pi Epsilon. Republican. Roman Catholic. Home: 426 N Citrus Ave Los Angeles CA 90036-2632 Office: Pasadena City Coll Bus Edn 1570 E Colorado Blvd Pasadena CA 91106-2003 E-mail: geowalen@msn.com

WALKER, BURTON LEITH, psychotherapist, engineering writer; b. Mt. Morris Twp., Mich., Oct. 23, 1927; s. Dalton Hugh and Muriel Joyce (Black) W.; m. Norva Jean Throcman, June 28, 1949; children: Paul, Cynthia Halverson, Mark; m. Carol Jean D'Andrea, July 31, 1981. AA, Alan Hancock Coll., 1971; BA, Chapman Coll., 1974, MA, 1975. Cert. psychology tchr.; lic. psychotherapist, hypnotherapist, Calif. Contract estimator Ryan Aeronautics, San Diego, 1949-59; logistics rep. GD/A, San Diego, 1960-62; sys. engr. cons. fgn. svc. Ralph M. Parsons, L.A., 1962-68; lead engring. writer, sr. analyst Fed. Electric, Vandenberg AFB, Calif., 1969-86; psychotherapist Family Guidance Svc. Santa Ynez; Access, Vandenberg Village, 1978—; clin. dir. Valley Cmty. Counseling, Los Olivos, 1999—. Part-time prof. Allan Hancock Coll., Santa Maria, Calif., 1974-92, ret.; small bus. owner 1974-86. Active Santa Ynez Valley Presbyn. Ch. Mem. Am. Assn. Christian Counselors, Nat. Mgmt. Assn. (Outstanding Svc. award 1982), Calif. Assn. Marriage and Family Therapists, Assn. for Advancement Ret. People. Republican. Home: 3149 E Highway 246 Santa Ynez CA 93460-9634

WALKER, CARLENE M. state legislator; BS, Brigham Young U., 1969. Supr. coding & data entry the Wirthlin Group, 1982-86; cons. D.K. Shifflet & Assocs., 1987-88; ptnr., mgr. Covecrest Properties, 1978-99; dir. adminstrn. Energy Lock, Inc., 1992-99; tech. recruiter Manpower Tech., 1999-2000; mem. Utah State Senate, Salt Lake City, 2001—. Cons. Wash. Times Newspaper, 1987-88. Bd., chair fundraising com. Granite Edn. Found., 1989-90. Office: 4085 E Prospector Dr Salt Lake City UT 84121*

WALKER, DOUGLAS, computer developement company executive; Graduate, Vanderbilt U., 1976. With Western Data Corp., Seattle, 1976-80, Walker, Richer & Quinn, Inc., Seattle, 1980—, now pres., 1989—, CEO. Office: Walker Richer & Quinn Inc 1500 Dexter Ave N Seattle WA 98109-3032

WALKER, ELJANA M. DU VALL, civic worker; b. France, Jan. 18, 1924; came to U.S., 1948; naturalized, 1954; m. John S. Walker, Jr., Dec. 31, 1947; children: John, Peter, Barbara. Pres. Loyola Sch. PTA, 1959-59; bd. dirs. Santa Claus Shop, 1959-73; treas. Archdiocese Denver Catholic Women, 1962-64; rep. Cath. Parent-Tchr. League, 1962-65; pres. Aux. Denver Gen. Hosp., 1966-69; precinct committeewoman Arapahoe County Women's Com., 1973-74; mem. re-election com. Arapahoe County Rep. Party, 1973-78, Reagan election com., 1980. Block worker Arapahoe County March of Dimes, Heart Assn., Hemophilia Drive, Muscular Dystrophy and Multiple Sclerosis Drive, 1979-81, cen. city asst. Guild Debutante Charities, Inc. Recipient Dist. Svc. award Am.-by-choice, 1966; nmaed to Honor Roll, ARC, 1971. Mem. Cherry Hills Symphony, Lyric Opera Guild, Alliance Franciase (life mem.), ARC, Civic Ballet Guild (life mem.), Needlework Guild Am. (v.p. 1980-82), Kidney Found. (life), Denver Art Mus., U. Denver Art and Conservation Assns. (chmn. 1980-82), U. Denver Women's Lib. Assn., Chancellors Soc., Passage Inc., Friends of the Fine Arts Found. (life), Children's Diabetes Found. (life), Littleton Pub. Sch. Pioneers, Union (Chgo.), Denver Athletic, 26 (Denver), Welcome to Colo. Internat. Roman Catholic. Address: 2301 Green Oaks Dr Littleton CO 80121

WALKER, FRANCIS JOSEPH, lawyer; b. Aug. 5, 1922; s. John McSweeney and Sarah Veronica (Meechan) W.; m. Julia Corinne O'Brien, Jan. 27, 1951; children: Vincent Paul, Monica Irene Hylton, Jill Marie Nudell, John Michael, Michael Joseph, Thomas More. BA, St. Martin's Coll., 1947; JD, U. Wash., 1950. Bar: Wash. Asst. atty. gen. State of Wash., 1950-51; pvt. practice Olympia, Wash., 1951—. Gen. counsel Wash. Cath. Conf., 1967-76. Lt. (j.g.) USNR, 1943-46; PTO. Home and Office: 2723 Hillside Dr SE Olympia WA 98501-3460 E-mail: FJWalker@QWest.net

WALKER, FRANKLIN CURTIS, federal agency administrator; b. Sept. 10, 1945; s. Howard and Edna Walker; m. Judy Provins, May 29, 1967; children: Mark, Kathy, Phillip. BS in Biology, N.Mex. State U., 1967. Park ranger White Sands Nat. Monument Nat. Park Svc., 1970-72, park ranger Jefferson Nat. Expansion Meml., 1972-73, park ranger Gulf Islands Nat. Seashore, 1973-77, naturalist south dist. Yellowstone Nat. Park, 1977-80, chief of interpretation Carlsbad Caverns Nat. Park, 1980-85, park supt. Ft. Clatsop Nat. Meml., 1985-90, supt. Nez Perce Nat. Hist. Park Mont., 1990-98, supt. Saguaro Nat. Park Tucson, 1998—. 1st lt. U.S. Army, 1967-69. Home: 10311 E Camino Quince Tucson AZ 85748-6806 Office: Saguaro Nat Park 3693 S Old Spanish Trl Tucson AZ 85730-5601

WALKER, GORDON ARTHUR HUNTER, astronomy educator; b. Kinghorn, Scotland, Jan. 30, 1936; came to Can., 1962; s. Frederic Thomas and Mary T. (Hunter) W.; m. Sigrid Helene, Apr. 21, 1962; children—Nicholas Ian, Eric G.T. B.S. with honors, Edinburgh U., Scotland, 1958; Ph.D., Cambridge U., Eng., 1962. Postdoctoral fellow Can. Nat. Research Council, Victoria, B.C., 1962-64; research scientist II Dept. Energy, Mines and Resources, Victoria, 1964-69; assoc. prof. dept. geophysics and astronomy U. B.C., Vancouver, 1969-74, prof., 1974—, dir. Inst. Astronomy and Space Sci., 1972-76. Mem. Can. Astron. Soc. (pres. 1980-82) Office: U BC Dept Geophys/Astron 6224 Agricultural Rd Vancouver BC Canada V6T 1Z1

WALKER, HENRY GILBERT, health care executive, consultant; b. Gowanda, N.Y., Feb. 16, 1947; s. Henry George and Grace Dayton (Moore) W.; m. Elaine Ruth Darbee, July 18, 1970 (div. Dec. 1979); 1 child, Matthew Case; m. Patricia Ann Andrade, May 14, 1983; children: Michael David, Christopher John. B.S. in Indsl. Engring., Cornell U., 1969; M.B.A., U. Chgo., 1975. Evening adminstr. Rush-Presbyn. St.-Luke's Med. Ctr., Chgo., 1973-75; mgmt. cons. Booz, Allen & Hamilton, Chgo., 1975-79; regional adminstr., v.p. S.W. Community Health Service, Albuquerque, 1979-83, adminstr., v.p., 1983-86, v.p., 1986—; exec. v.p. Presbyn. Healthcare Services, Albuquerque, 1986-92; pres., CEO Tucson Med. Ctr., 1992—. Campaign mgr. United Fund, Newport, R.I., 1971, 72; bd. dirs. Park Dist., Elmhurst, Ill., 1978, 79; mem. Dist. III Community Action Com., Albuquerque, 1985; div. chmn. United Way of Albuquerque., 1985, 88. Recipient Hosp. Survey award U. Chgo., 1975, Bachmeyer award U. Chgo., 1975, Outstanding Midshipman award Cornell U., 1969; named one of Emerging Healthcare Leaders, Hosp. Forum Mag., 1985, 86, Healthcares Up and Comers, Modern Healthcare Mag., 1987. Mem. Am. Coll. Healthcare Execs., Healthcare Fin. Mgmt. Assn., Am. Hosp. Assn., N.Mex. Hosp. Assn. (chmn. bd. dirs. 1983-85, treas. 1991—), Healthcare Forum (bd. dirs., chmn. elect). Democrat. Presbyterian Avocations: reading; hiking; skiing; tennis.

WALKER, HILL M. educator; Recipient Rsch. award Coun. for Exceptional Children, 1993. Office: U Oregon Ctr Ctr Human Devel 901 E 18th Ave Eugene OR 97403-1354

WALKER, JAMES BRADLEY, academic institution administrator; b. N.Y.C., Apr. 10, 1948; s. James Bradley and Mary Jane (Thayer) W.; m. Virginia Lynn, Apr. 11, 1969; children: Carol Renee, Laura Jane. BS, Calif. Poly. State U., 1975. Comptroller Albuquerque Western Industries, 1975-78; CFO U. N.Mex. Hosp., Albuquerque, 1978-84, Univ. Hosp., Portland, Oreg., 1984-97; v.p. fin. and adminstrn. Oreg. Health Scis. U., Portland, 1992—, exec. v.p., 1998—. Sgt. USAF, 1969-72. Avocations: golfing, travel. Office: Oreg Health Scis U Hosp 3181 SW Sam Jackson Park Rd Portland OR 97201-3011

WALKER, JOHN P. pharmaceutical executive; Pres., CEO Arris Pharm. Corp., South San Francisco; chmn. & CEO Axys Pharms Inc., San Francisco. Office: Axys Pharm Inc 180 Kimball Way South San Francisco CA 94080-6218

WALKER, JOHN SUMPTER , JR. lawyer; b. Richmond, Ark., Oct. 13, 1921; s. John Sumpter and Martha (Wilson) W.; m. Eljana M. duVall, Dec. 31, 1947; children: John Stephen, Barbara Monika Ann, Peter Mark Gregory. BA , Tulane U., 1942; MS, U. Denver, 1952, JD, 1960; diploma, Nat. Def. U., 1981. Bar: Colo. 1960, U.S. Dist. Ct. Colo. 1960, U.S. Supreme Ct. 1968, U.S. Ct. Appeals (10th cir.) 1960, U.S. Tax Ct. 1981. With Denver & Rio Grande Western R.R. Co., 1951-61, gen. solicitor, 1961-89; pres. Denver Union Terminal Rlwy. Co. Apptd. gen. counsel Moffat Tunnel Commn., 1991; life mem. Children's Diabetes Fund. With U.S. Army, 1942-46. Decorated Bronze Star. Mem.: Colo. Bar Assn., Arapahoe County Bar Assn., Alliance Francaise (life), Order of St. Ives, U. Denver Chancellor's Soc., Cath. Lawyers Guild. Republican. Roman Catholic.

WALKER, LARRY KENNETH ROBERT, professional baseball player; b. Maple Ridge, B.C., Dec. 1, 1966; Grad. high sch., B.C., Can. With Montreal Expos, 1989-94; outfielder Colo. Rockies, 1995—. Named "The Sporting News" Nat. League All-Star Team, 1992, "The Sporting News" NAt. League Silver Slugger Team, 1992; recipient Gold Glove as outfielder, 1992-93. Office: Colo Rockies Coors Field 2001 Blake St Denver CO 80205-2008

WALKER, LORENZO GILES, surgeon, educator; b. Phila., June 29, 1957; s. Manuel Lorenzo and Romaine Yvonne (Smith) W.; m. Yvonne Ruiz; children: Zachary Giles, Benjamin Lee. BA cum laude, U. Pa., 1978; MD, Harvard U., 1982. Diplomate Am. Bd. Orthopaedic Surgery, Nat. Bd. Med. Examiners; lic. surgeon, Mass., Calif.; cert. added qualification hand surgery, 1993. Intern in surgery New England Deaconess-Harvard Surg. Svc., Boston, 1982-83, asst. resident in surgery, 1983-84; resident in orthopaedic surgery Harvard U., Boston, 1985-88; fellow in hand surgery UCLA Med. Sch., 1988-89, asst. clin. prof. orthopaedic surgery, 1988—, attending physician dept. orthopedics Hand Clinic, 1996-98; ptnr. Ventura (Calif.) Orthopaedic Hand and Sports Med. Group, 1994-98; solo practice hand surgery, 1998—. Staff physician St. John's Plasant Valley Hosp., Camarillo, Calif., St. John's Regional Med. Ctr., Oxnard, Calif., Cmty. Meml. Hosp., Ventura, Calif.; attending physician, cons. Sepulveda, Calif. VA Hosp.; presenter in field. Cons. reviewer Clin. Orthopaedics and related Rsch., 1990-92; contbr. numerous articles to profl. jours. Vol. Spl. Olympics, Ventura, 1994-96, Direct Relief Internat., Santa Barbara, Calif.,

1994-96, Ventura County Rescue Mission, 1994-98. Recipient Cert. of Appreciation, Am. Heart Assn., 1994; UCLA faculty fellow, 1988-89. Mem. Am. Soc. for Surgery of the Hand, Am. Assn. for Hand Surgery, AMA, Calif. Med. Assn., Calif. Orthopaedic Assn., Calif. Ringside Physician, Ventura County Med. Soc., Internat. Soc. Aquatic Medicine, Western Orthopaedic Assn., Orthopaedic Overseas, UCLA Hand Club, Arthroscopy Assn. N.Am., Alpha Epsilon Delta, Onyx Honor Soc., Philomathean Soc. Avocations: photography, scuba diving, sports memorabilia, fishing, travel. Home: 3041 Shadow Mesa Cir Thousand Oaks CA 91360-1061

WALKER, OLENE S. lieutenant governor; b. Ogden, Utah, Nov. 15, 1930; d. Thomas Ole and Nina Hadley (Smith) W.; m. J. Myron Walker, 1957; children: Stephen Brett, David Walden, Bryan Jesse, Lori, Mylene, Nina, Thomas Myron. BA, Brigham Young U., 1954; MA, Stanford U., 1954; PhD, U. Utah, 1986; HHD (hon.), Weber State U., 1997. V.p. Country Crisp Foods, 1969-92; mem. Utah Ho. of Reps. Dist. 24; lt. gov. State of Utah, 1993—. Mem. Salt Lake Edn. Found. bd. dirs. 1983-90; dir. community econ. devel.; mem. Ballet West, Sch. Vol., United Way, Commn. on Youth, Girls Village, Salt Lake Conv. and Tourism Bd.; mem. adv. coun. Weber State U. Mem. Nat. Assn. Secs. of State (Western chmn., nat. lt. gov.'s conf., pres. 1997-98). Mormon. Office: Lt Gov 210 State Capitol Building Salt Lake City UT 84114-1202

WALKER, RALPH CLIFFORD, lawyer; b. Bradenton, Fla., Apr. 30, 1938; s. Julius Clifford and Dorothy (Hefner) W.; m. Katherine Marie Christensen, Oct. 10, 1971; children: Laura Elizabeth, Mark Clifford, Tyler Lanier. BA cum laude, Vanderbilt U., 1959; LLB, U. Calif., Berkeley, 1965. Bar: Calif. Ptnr. Orrick Herrington & Sutcliffe, San Francisco, 1965—. Town councilman Town of Ross, Calif., 1970-72.Lt. (j.g.) USN, 1959-62. Mem. ABA, State Bar Calif., San Francisco Bar Assn., University Club (San Francisco, dir. 1986-88, counsel 1983—), Meadow Club (Fairfax, Calif.), Order of Coif. Republican. Presbyterian. Avocations: golf, wine, youth sports. Office: Orrick Herrington & Sutcliffe 400 Sansome St San Francisco CA 94111-3143

WALKER, RANDALL H. air transportation executive; b. Boulder City, Nev. m. Terry Walker; 6 children. BS in Acctg. magna cum laude, Brigham Young U. Budget analyst Clark County (Nev.) Mgr.'s Office; bus. mgr. Las Vegas Met. Police Dept.; dep. city mgr. City of Las Vegas; Las Vegas rep. to Nev. State Legislature; asst. county mgr. Clark County, dir. dept. fin.; dep. dir. Clark County Dept. Aviation, now dir. Office: c/o McCarran Internat Airport PO Box 11005 Las Vegas NV 89111-1005

WALKER, RAYMOND FRANCIS, business and financial consulting company executive; b. Medicine Lake, Mont., Nov. 9, 1914; s. Dennis Owen and Rose (Long) W.; m. Patricia K. Blakey, May 15, 1951; children: Richard A., Mark D., Maxie R. Forest, Victoria L. Le Huray, Suzanne J. Walker, Tracy A. Grad. pub. schs.; student, Edison Vocat. Sch., 1935-39. Truck mgr. Pacific Food Products, Seattle, 1939-42; machinist Todd Shipyard, Seattle, 1943-45; owner Delbridge Auto Sales, Seattle, 1945-48; pres. Pacific Coast Acceptance Corp., 1949-60; v.p. West Coast Mortgage, Seattle, 1960-67, United Equities Corp., Seattle, 1965-69; pres. Income Mgmt. Corp., Seattle, 1970-90; v.p. Internat. Mint and Foundry, Redmond, Wash., 1983-87; pvt. practice bus. and fin. cons. Sequim, 1987—. Cons. Life Ins. Co. Am., Bellevue, Wash., 1982-87, Consumer Loan Svc., Lynwood Wash., 1980-92; dir., cons., v.p. fin. Am. Campgrounds, Bellevue, 1971-79; cons., bd. dirs. Straits Forest Products, Inc. , Port Angeles, Wash.; dir., cons. Synergy Techs., Inc., Sequim, 1990-97, co-founder, dir. Sequim Tech., Inc., 1994-97. Mem. Nat. Assn. Security Dealers. Methodist. Lodge: Elks. Home: 3347 W Sequim Bay Rd Sequim WA 98382-8430 E-mail: raypatricekw@prodigy.net

WALKER, RAYMOND JOHN, physicist; b. L.A., Oct. 26, 1942; s. Raymond Osmund and Marie Dorothy (Peterman) W. BS, San Diego State U., 1964; MS, UCLA, 1969, PhD, 1973. Rsch. assoc. U. Minn., Mpls., 1973-77; rsch. geophysicist Inst. Geophysics and Planetary Physics UCLA, 1977—, prof. in residence Inst. Physics and Planetary Geophysics and Dept. Earth and Space Sci., 1999—. Mgr. planetary plasma interactions node project scientist NASA Planetary Data System; mem. numerous coms. on space physics and the mgmt. of space physics data NRC and NASA. Contbr. articles to profl. jours. Mem. AAAS, Am. Geophys. Union (chair info. tech. com. 1990-92, Edward A. Flinn III award 1996), Am. Astron. Soc. (div. Planetary Sci.). Achievements include research in magnetospheric physics, in planetary magnetospheres, in global magnetohydrodynamic simulation of solar wind-magnetosphere interaction, in data management, in magnetic field modeling. Home: 11053 Tennessee Ave Los Angeles CA 90064-1936 Office: UCLA IGPP 405 Hilgard Ave Los Angeles CA 90095-1567 E-mail: rwalker@igpp.ucla.edu

WALKER, RICHARD K. lawyer; b. Knoxville, Tenn., Oct. 21, 1948; BA with honors, U. Kans., 1970, JD, 1975; student, U. Bonn, Germany; grad. student, U Tübingen, Germany. Bar: Ariz. 1975, D.C. 1977, U.S. Supreme Ct. 1977. Asst. prof. law U. S.C., 1977-81, assoc. prof. law, 1981-82; ptnr. Bishop, Cook, Purcell & Reynolds, Washington, 1981-90, Winston & Strawn, Washington, 1990-93; dir. Streich Lang, Phoenix, 1993-2000; ptnr. Quarles & Brady Streich Lang, Phoenix, 2000—. Bd. trustees Ariz. Theatre Co., 1995-2001; bd. dirs. Phoenix Cmty. Alliance, 2001—. Fulbright Direct Exchange scholar. Mem. ABA, Labor and Employment Law Sec. (mem. equal employment opportunity law com. and devel. of the law under the NLRA com., 1979—), Litigation Sec. (mem. class actions and derivitive suits com. and trial pratice com., 1998—, mem. employment rels. and labor law com., 1979—), Ariz. Assn. Def. Counsel (bd. dirs. 1997-2000), Phoenix Cmty. Alliance (bd. dirs. 2001—). Office: Quarles & Brady Streich Lang Renaissance One 2 N Central Ave Phoenix AZ 85004-2345 E-mail: rwalker@quarles.com

WALKER, ROBERT HARRIS, historian, writer, editor; b. Cin., Mar. 15, 1924; m. Grace Burtt; children: Amy, Rachel, Matthew. BS, Northwestern U., 1945; MA, Columbia U., 1950; PhD, U. Pa., 1955. Edn. specialist U.S. Mil. Govt., Japan, 1946-47; instr. Carnegie Inst. Tech., 1950-51, U. Pa., 1953-54; asst. prof., dir. Am. studies U. Wyo., 1955-59; asso. prof. George Washington U., 1959-63, prof. Am. civilization, 1963-94, dir. Am. studies program, 1959-66, 68-70. First dir. edn. and pub. programs NEH, 1966-68; fellow Woodrow Wilson Internat. Ctr., 1972-73, Rockefeller Rsch. Ctr., 1979, Hoover Instn., Huntington Libr., 1980; specialist grants to Japan, Germany, Thailand, Iran, Greece, Israel, Brazil, China, People's Republic of Korea, Hong Kong, 1964-91; Fulbright lectr., Australia, New Zealand, Philippines, 1971, Sweden, France, West Germany, Norway, all 1987; Am. Coun. Learned Socs. alt. del. UNESCO Gen. Info. Program, 1978—; co-founder Algonquin Books, 1982. Author: Poet and Gilded Age, 1963, Life in the Age of Enterprise, 1967, American Society, 1981, 2d edit., 1995, Reform in America (nominated for Pulitzer prize in history), 1985, (with R.H. Gabriel) Course of American Democratic Thought, 3d edit., 1986, Cincinnati and the Big Red Machine, 1988, Everyday Life in Victorian America, 1994; editor, compiler: American Studies in the U.S., 1958, American Studies Abroad, 1975, Reform Spirit in America, 1976, 85, American Studies: Topics and Sources, 1976, Frieds of Raoul Wallenberg, 1987-1997, 1998; editor: Am. Quar., 1953-54; sr. editor: Am. Studies Internat., 1970-80, Am. studies series for Greenwood Press, 1972—, over 100 vols. Founding mem. Japan-U.S. Friendship Commn., 1977-80; founding pres. Friends of Raoul Wallenberg Found., 1987-99. With USNR, 1943-46, 50. Mem. Am. Studies Assn. (nat. pres. 1970-71), Cosmos Club, Phi Beta Kappa. Office: 4006 County Road 115 Glenwood Springs CO 81601-9020

WALKER, ROGER GEOFFREY, geology educator, consultant; b. London, Mar. 26, 1939; s. Reginald Noel and Edith Annie (Wells) W.; m. Gay Parsons, Sept. 18, 1965; children: David John, Susan Elizabeth. BA, Oxford U., Eng., 1961, DPhil in Geology, 1964. Prof. emeritus McMaster U., Hamilton, Ont., Can., 1998—; NATO postdoctoral fellow in geology Johns Hopkins U., Balt., 1964-66; from asst. to assoc. prof. McMaster U., Hamilton, Ont., Can., 1966-73, prof. geology Can., 1973-98; vis. scientist Denver Rsch. Ctr., Marathon Oil Co., Littleton, Colo., 1973-74, Amoco Can. Petrol Co., Calgary, Alta., Can., 1982; vis. fellow Australian Nat. U., Canberra, 1981. Tchr. 80 profl. short courses on various aspects of oil exploration in clastic reservoirs, Can., U.S., Brazil, Australia, Japan, Italy, Venezuela, Norway; mem. grant selection com. earth scis. sect. Nat. Scis. and Engring. Rsch. Coun. Can., 1981-84; Judd A. & Cynthia S. Oualline Centennial lectr. U. Tex., Austin, 1986; vis. prof. Fed. U. Ouro Preto, Brazil, 1987, 89, 90, 91, Fed. U. Rio Grande do Sul, Brazil, 1992; adj. prof. U. Regina, 1997—; pres. Roger Walker Cons., Inc., 1997—. Editor: Facies Models, 1979, 3d edit., 1992; contbr. over 140 articles to profl. jours. Recipient operating and strategic grants Nat. Scis. and Engring. Rsch. Coun. Can., 1966—. Fellow Royal Soc. Can.; mem. Geol. Assn. Can. (assoc. editor 1977-80, Past President's medal 1975, Disting. Svc. award 1994, Logan medal 1999), Can. Soc. Petroleum Geologists (Link award 1983, R.J.W. Douglas Meml. medal 1990), Am. Assn. Petroleum Geologists (Disting. lectr. 1979-80, disting. educator award 1999), Soc. Econ. Paleontologists and Mineralogists (pres. eastern sect. 1975-76, coun. for mineralogy 1979-80, hon. mem. 1991, assoc. editor 1970-78), Soc. Sedimentary Geology (Francis J. Pettijohn medal 1997), Can. Assn. Univ. Tchrs., Internat. Assn. Sedimentologists. Achievements include research in sedimentary facies analysis, sedimentology of turbidites, quantitative basin analysis, sedimentology of Western Canadian Cretaceous clastic wedge. Avocations: skiing, classical music, photography, model railroading. Home and Office: Roger Walker Cons 83 Scimitar View NW Calgary AB Canada T3L 2B4 E-mail: walkerrg@cadvsion.com

WALKER, TIMOTHY BLAKE, lawyer, educator; b. Utica, N.Y., May 21, 1940; s. Harold Blake and Mary Alice (Corder) W.; m. Sandra Blake; children: Kimberlee Corder, Tyler Blake, Kelley Loren. AB magna cum laude, Princeton U., 1962; JD magna cum laude, U. Denver, 1967, MA in Sociology, 1969. Bar: Colo. 1968, Calif. 1969, Ind. 1971. Asst. prof. law U. Pacific, 1968-69; vis. assoc. prof. U. Toledo, 1969-70; assoc. prof. Indpls. Law Sch., Ind. U., 1970-71, U. Denver, 1971-75, prof., 1975-99; prof. emeritus, 1999—; dir. adminstrn. of justice program U. Denver, 1971-78; pvt. practice Denver, 1972-79; of counsel Robert T. Hinds, Jr. & Assocs. PC, Littleton, Colo., 1980-85; ptnr., of counsel Cox, Mustain-Wood, Walker & Schumacher, Littleton, 1985—. Cons., lectr. in field; rsch. on lay representation in adminstrv. agys., Colo., 1975-76. Contbr. articles to profl. jours.; editor: Denver Law Jour., 1966-67; editor-in-chief: Family Law Quar., 1983-92. Mem. Ind. Child Support Commn., 1970-71; pres. Shawnee (Colo.) Water Consumers Assn., 1975-84, 93-95; del. Colo. Rep. Conv., 1978. Colo. Bar Assn. grant, 1975-76. Fellow: Am. Sociol. Assn., Am. Acad. Matrimonial Lawyers, Internat. Acad. Matrimonial Lawyers, Am. Bar Found.; mem.: ABA (vice chmn. child custody subcom., sec. Family Law sect. 1992—93, vice chmn., sec. 1993—94, chmn. elect family law sect. 1994—95, chmn. 1995—96, chmn. child custody task force 2000—, alimony, maintenance and support com. 2000—, family sect. del. ho. of dels. 2000—), Calif. Bar Assn., Colo. Bar Assn., Ind. Bar Assn., Colo Trial Lawyers Assn. Presbyterian. Home: 7329 Rochester Ct Castle Rock CO 80104-9281 Office: 1900 Olive St Denver CO 80220-1857 also: 6601 S University Blvd Littleton CO 80121-2913

WALKER, VAUGHN R. federal judge; b. Watseka, Ill., Feb. 27, 1944; s. Vaughn Rosenworth and Catharine (Miles) W. AB, U. Mich., 1966; JD, Stanford U., 1970. Intern economist SEC, Washington, 1966, 68; law clk. to the Hon. Robert J. Kelleher U.S. Dist. Ct. Calif., L.A., 1971-72; assoc. atty. Pillsbury Madison & Sutro, San Francisco, 1972-77, ptnr., 1978-90; judge U.S. Dist. Ct. (no. dist.) Calif., San Francisco, 1990—. Mem. Calif. Law Revision Commn., Palo Alto, 1986-89; bd. advisors Law and Econs. Ctr., George Mason U., 1999—. Dir. Jr. Achievement of Bay Area, San Francisco, 1979-83, St. Francis Found., San Francisco, 1991-97, 98—. Woodrow Wilson Found. fellow U. Calif., Berkeley, 1966-67. Fellow Am. Bar Found.; mem. ABA (jud. rep., antitrust sect. 1991-95), Lawyers' Club of San Francisco (pres. 1985-86), Assn. Bus. Trial Lawyers (dir. 1996-98), Am. Law Inst., Am. Saddlebred Horse Assn., San Francisco Mus. Modern Art, Bohemian Club, Olympic Club, Pacific-Union Club. Office: US Dist Ct 450 Golden Gate Ave San Francisco CA 94102-3482

WALKER, WALTER FREDERICK, professional basketball team executive; b. Bradford, Pa., July 18, 1954; m. Linda Walker. Diploma, U. Va.; MBA, Stanford U., 1987; BA, U. Va., 1976. Chartered Fin. Analyst. Player Portland (Oreg.) Trail Blazers, 1976-77, Seattle SuperSonics, 1977-82, pres., gen. mgr., 1994—; player Houston Rockets, 1982-84; with Goldman Sachs and Co., San Francisco, 1987-94; prin. Walker Capital, Inc., San Francisco, 1994. Mem. USA gold medal World Univ. Games basketball team, 1973; broadcaster basketball Raycom Network, 1989-94; cons. Seattle SuperSonics, 1994. Bd. dirs. Red Hook Ale Brewery; bd. dirs. Advanced Digital Info. Corp., Drexler Tech. Corp. Named 1st team Acad. All-Am. U. Va.; named to Pa. State Sports Hall of Fame. Nat. trustee Boys and Girls Clubs of Am. Office: Seattle SuperSonics 351 Elliott Ave W Seattle WA 98119-4101

WALKER, WILLIAM TIDD, JR. investment banker; b. Detroit, Sept. 5, 1931; s. William Tidd and Irene (Rhode) W.; m. Patricia Louise Frazier, Sept. 10, 1953; children— Donna Louise, Carol Ann, Sally Lynn, Alyssa Jane. Student, Stanford, 1950. Stockbroker William R. Staats & Co., Los Angeles, 1952-57, sales mgr., 1957-58, syndicate partner, 1958-65; sr. v.p. Glore Forgan, William R. Staats Inc., N.Y.C., 1965-68; partner, exec. com. Lester, Ryons & Co., Los Angeles, 1968; exec. v.p. Bateman Eichler, Hill Richards Inc., Los Angeles, 1969-85. Pres., CEO, WTW Inc.; chmn., CEO Walker Assocs., bd. dirs. Sensory Sci. Corp., Elevision, Inc., Aviation Distbrs., Inc., Supralife Internat., Stone Mountain Data Ctrs. Inc., Desert Health Products Inc.; adv. mem. Am. Stock Exch., 1981—. With USAF, 1949-52. Mem. Securities Industry Assn. (dir. nat. syndicate com., chmn. Calif. Dist. 10), Pacific Coast Stock Exch. (bd. govs. 1971-72), Investment Bankers Assn. (nat. pub. rels. com. 1966—), Bond Club L.A. (pres. 1973), Calif. Yacht Club, Newport Harbor Yacht Club. Office: Walker Assocs PO Box 10684 Beverly Hills CA 90213-3684

WALKUP, ROBERT E. mayor; b. Ames, Iowa, Nov. 14, 1936; m. Beth Walkup; 3 children; 2 stepchildren. BS in Indsl. Engring., Iowa State U. Exec. Rockwell Internat., Fairchild Republic; sr. exec. Hughes Aircraft Co.; mayor Tucson, 1999—. Chmn. Greater Tucson Econ. Coun.; founder, first chmn. Ariz. Space Commn.; vol. Tucson Cmty. Food Bank; co-founder Pima-Santa Cruz County Sch.-to-Work Program; co-founder El Centro Cultural de las Americas. Capt. U.S. Army. Republican. Avocations: playing guitar, sketching, studying astronomy, restoring antique cars and motorcycles. Office: City Hall 255 W Alameda St Tucson AZ 85701-1362 Fax: 520-791-5348

WALL, DONALD ARTHUR, lawyer; b. Lafayette, Ind., Mar. 17, 1946; s. Dwight Arthur and Myra Virginia (Peavey) W.; m. Cheryn Lynn Heinen, Aug. 29, 1970; children: Sarah Lynn, Michael Donald. BA, Butler U., 1968; JD, Northwestern U., 1971. Bar: Ohio 1971, U.S. Dist. Ct. (no. dist.) Ohio 1973, U.S. Supreme Ct. 1980, Ariz. 1982, U.S. Dist. Ct. (no. dist.) W.Va. 1982, U.S. Ct. Appeals (6th cir.) 1982, U.S. Dist. Ct. Ariz. 1983, U.S. Ct. Appeals (9th and 10th cirs.) 1984, U.S. Ct. Appeals (3rd cir.) 1988. Assoc. Squire, Sanders & Dempsey, Cleve., 1971-80, ptnr., 1980-82, Phoenix, 1983—. Spkr. at profl. meetings; program moderator. Contbr. articles to profl. jours. Trustee Ch. of the Saviour Day Ctr., Cleveland Heights, 1979-82; mem. adminstrv. bd. Ch. of Saviour, Cleveland Heights, 1980-83; fin. com. Paradise Valley (Ariz.) United Meth. Ch., 1986-87; bd. dirs., divsn. commr. North Scottsdale (Ariz.) Little League, 1983-92; bd. dirs. Epilepsy Found. N.E. Ohio, 1976-82, pres., 1981-82; bd. dirs. N.E. Cmty. Basketball Assn., 1993-99; bd. visitors U. Ariz. Law Sch., 1996—; bd. mgrs. Scottsdale-Paradise Valley YMCA, 1999—. Mem. ABA (torts and ins. practice and litigation sect., past chmn. r.r. law com., litigation sect.), Def. Rsch. Inst., Ariz. Bar Assn. (labor and trial practice sects.), Maricopa County Bar Assn., Ariz. Assn. Def. Counsel. Methodist. Office: Squire Sanders & Dempsey LLP 40 N Central Ave Ste 2700 Phoenix AZ 85004-4498 E-mail: dwall@ssd.com

WALL, JAMES EDWARD, telecommunications, petroleum and pharmaceutical executive; b. Santa Barbara, Calif., Nov. 24, 1947; s. Charles Caswell II and Lydia (Sinn) W.; m. Judith Ann Hochman, Aug. 1, 1976. AA, Bakersfield Coll., 1967; BS, Calif. State U., Los Angeles, 1969; MBA, UCLA, 1970; D of Profl. Studies (ABD), Pace U., 1985; PMD, Harvard U. Sch. Bus., 1987. CPA, Calif. Agt. IRS, Los Angeles, 1971-74, agt. service office internat. ops. Washington, 1974-76; mgr. fin. forecasts Am. Ultramar, Ltd., Mt. Kisco, N.Y., 1976-80, treas., 1980-85, v.p., treas., 1985-91; exec. dir. fin. and adminstrn. Ultramar Exploration, London, 1991; v.p., treas. Ultramar Corp., Greenwich, Conn., 1992-94; v.p., corp. treas. ICN Pharms., Costa Mesa, Calif., 1994-95; treas. AirTouch Comms., Inc., San Francisco, 1995-97, treas., controller, 1997-99; CFO Metricom, Inc., San Jose, Calif., 1999—. Chief fin. officer Enstar Corp., Indonesia; mem. bd. mgmt. Unimar Co., 1985-91. Recipient award in acctg. UCLA, 1972, award in gen. bus. mgmt., 1973 Mem. AICPA, Fin. Execs. Inst. (pres. San Francisco chpt. 2000—), UCLA Grad. Sch. Alumni Assn., Harvard U. Bus. Sch. Alumni Assn. Office: Metricom Inc 333 W Julian St San Jose CA 95110-2335

WALL, LLOYD L. geological engineer; b. Jerome, Idaho, Feb. 2, 1936; s. Lloyd and Ola (Buck) W.; m. Myrna Bradshaw, Aug. 25, 1954; children: Jeffrey B., Julie, Neil S., Charlene, Gail, Matthew W., Suzzane, Michael L., Connie. AS in Chemistry, Coll. Eastern Utah, 1956; BS in Geology, Brigham Young U., 1958. Pres., owner Cons. Geologist, Salt Lake City and Brigham City, 1958—; plant mgr. Thiokol, Brigham City, Utah, 1958-66; mgr. ops. Sealcraft, Salt Lake City, 1966-68; mgr. programs Eaton-Kenway, Bountiful, Utah, 1968-76; pres., owner HydraPak, Inc., Salt Lake City, 1976-86; pres. Kolt Mining Co., Salt Lake City, 1979—; owner Lloyd L. Wall & Assocs., Salt Lake City, 1986—. Author: Seal Technology, 1993; developer largest rocket motor vacuum casting system in free world, only high pressure water reclamation system for solid propellant rocket motors in free world, only acceptable seal mfg. process for NASA Space Shuttle rocket motor. Vol. tchr. Alta Acad., Salt Lake City, 1983—. Served as sgt. N.G., 1954-62. Mem. Geol. Soc. Am., Utah Geol. Assn. Republican. Mormon. Avocations: hunting, fishing, mountain climbing, photography, flying. Home: 2180 Claybourne Ave Salt Lake City UT 84109-1727 Office: 2180 E Claybourne Ave Salt Lake City UT 84109

WALL, M. DANNY, financial services company executive; BArch, N.D. State U., 1963. Exec. dir. Urban Renewal Agy., Fargo, N.D., 1964-71, Salt Lake City Redevel. Agy., 1971-75; dir. legis. Office U.S. Senator Jake Garn, Washington, 1975-78; minority staff dir. Senate Com. for Banking, Housing and Urban Affairs, Washington, 1979-80, staff dir., 1980-86, Rep. staff dir., 1987; chmn. Fed. Home Loan Bank Bd./Fed. Home Loan Mortgage Corp., Washington, 1987-89; dir. Office Thrift Supervision (formerly Fed. Home Loan Bank Bd.), 1989-90; fin. svcs. cons., 1990—; sr. v.p. Dougherty Funding LLC, 1997—. Bd. dirs. Escrow Bank USA. E-mail: dwall@dfg-companies.com

WALLACE, HELEN MARGARET, physician, educator; b. Hoosick Falls, N.Y., Feb. 18, 1913; d. Jonas and Ray (Schweizer) W. AB, Wellesley Coll., 1933; MD, Columbia U., 1937; MPH cum laude, Harvard U., 1943. Diplomate Am. Bd. Pediatrics, Am. Bd. Preventive Medicine. Intern Bellevue Hosp., N.Y.C., 1938-40; child hygiene physician Conn. Health Dept., 1941-42; successively jr. health officer, health officer, chief maternity and new born div., dir. bur. for handicapped children N.Y.C. Health Dept., 1943-55; prof., dir. dept. pub. health N.Y. Med. Coll., 1955-56; prof. maternal and child health U. Minn. Sch. Pub. Health, 1956-59; chief prof. tng. U.S. Children's Bur., 1959-60, chief child health studies, 1961-62; prof. maternal and child health U. Calif. Sch. Pub. Health, Berkeley, 1962-80, 99; prof., head divsn. maternal and child health Sch. Pub. Health San Diego State U., 1980—; Univ. Research lectr. San Diego State U., 1985—. Cons. WHO numerous locations, including Uganda, The Philippines, Turkey, India, Geneva, Iran, Burma, Sri Lanka, East Africa, Australia, Indonesia, China, Taiwan, 1961—, traveling fellow, 1989—; cons. Hahnemann U., Phila., 1993, Ford Found., Colombia, 1971; UN cons. to Health Bur., Beijing, China, 1987; fellow Aiiku Inst. on Maternal and Child Health, Tokyo, and NIH Inst. Child Health and Human Devel., 1994; dir. Family Planning Project, Zimbabwe, 1984-87; vis. prof. U. Calif., Berkeley, 1999, 00, prof. emeritus, 2000—; mem. adv. com., faculty APHA Com. on Continuing Edn. Author, editor 15 textbooks; sr. editor: Health & Social Reform For Families for the 21st Century, 1998, Health & Welfare Reform for Families in the 21st Century, 1998, Health and Welfare for Families in the 21st Century, 1999 (award Am. Coll. Nurseing, Am. Jour. Nursing); editor Health and Welfare Reform; contbr. 335 articles to profl. jours. Mem. coun. on Disabled Children to Media, 1991; dir. San Diego County Infant Mortality Study, 1989—, San Diego Study of Prenatal Care, 1991. Recipient Alumnae Achievement award Wellesley Coll., 1982, U. Minn. award, 1985; Ford Found. study grantee, 1986, 87, 88; fellow World Rehab. Fund, India, 1991-92, Fulbright Found., 1992—, NIH Inst. Child Health and Human Devel., 1994, Aiiku Inst. of Maternal-Child Health, Tokyo, 1994. Fellow APHA (officer sect., chmn. com. on internat. maternal and child health, mem. faculty and adv. com. maternal and child health program 2000, Martha May Eliot award 1978), Am. Acad. Pediatrics (Job Smith award 1980, award 1989); mem. AMA, Assn. Tchrs. Maternal and Child Health, Am. Acad. Cerebral Palsy, Ambulatory Pediatric Assn., Am. Sch. Preventive Medicine. Home: 850 State St San Diego CA 92101-6046

WALLACE, J. CLIFFORD, federal judge; b. San Diego, Dec. 11, 1928; s. John Franklin and Lillie Isabel (Overing) W.; m. Virginia Lee Schlosser, 1957 (dec.); m. Elaine J. Barnes, Apr. 8, 1996 (dec.); m. Dixie Jenee Robison Zenger, Apr. 2, 2001. B.A., San Diego State U., 1952; LL.B., U. Calif., Berkeley, 1955. Bar: Calif. 1955. With firm Gray, Cary, Ames & Frye, San Diego, 1955-70; judge U.S. Dist. Ct. for So. Dist. Calif., 1970-72, U.S. Ct. Appeals for 9th Circuit, San Diego, 1972-96, sr. circuit judge, 1996—. Contrbr. articles to profl. jours. Served with USN, 1946-49. Mem. Am. Bd. Trial Advocates, Inst. Jud. Adminstrn. Mem. LDS Ch. (stake pres. San Diego East 1962-67, regional rep. 1967-74, 77-79). Office: US Ct Appeals 9th Cir 940 Front St Ste 4192 San Diego CA 92101-8918

WALLACE, JULIA DIANE, newspaper editor; b. Davenport, Iowa, Dec. 3, 1956; d. Franklin Sherwood and Eleanor Ruth (Pope) W.; m. Doniver Dean Campbell, Aug. 23, 1986; children: Emmaline Livingston Campbell, Eden Jennifer Campbell. BS in Journalism, Northwestern U., 1978. Reporter Norfolk (Va.) Ledger-Star, 1978-80, Dallas Times Herald, 1980-82; reporter, editor News sect. USA Today, Arlington, Va., 1982-89, mng. editor spl. projects, 1989-92; mng. editor Chgo. Sun-Times, 1992-1996; exec. editor Statesman Jour., 1996, mng. editor Arizona Republic, Phoenix. Mem. Am. Soc. Newspaper Editors. Office: Arizona Republic PO Box 1950 Phoenix AZ 85001-1950

WALLACE, MATTHEW WALKER, retired entrepreneur; b. Salt Lake City, Jan. 7, 1924; s. John McChrystal and Glenn (Walker) W.; m. Constance Cone, June 22, 1954 (dec. May 1980); children: Matthew, Anne; m. Susan Struggles, July 11, 1981. BA, Stanford U., 1947; MCP, MIT, 1950. Prin. planner Boston City Planning Bd., 1950-53; v.p. Nat. Planning and Rsch., Inc., Boston, 1953-55; pres. Wallace-McConaughy Corp., Salt Lake City, 1955-69, Ariz. Ranch & Metals Co., Scottsdale, 1969-84, Idaho TV Corp., Channel 6, ABC, Boise, 1976-78; chmn. Wallace Assocs., Inc., Salt Lake City, 1969-98. Dir. 1st Interstate Bank, Salt Lake City, 1956-90, dir. Arnold Machinery Co., 1988—, dir. Roosevelt Hot Springs Corp., 1978—; mem. adv. bd. Mountain Bell Telephone Co., Salt Lake City, 1975-85. Pres. Downtown Planning Assn., Salt Lake City, 1970; chmn. Utah State Arts Coun., Salt Lake City, 1977; chmn. hon. bd. Planned Parenthood; mem. Humanities and Scis. Coun., Stanford U., also mem. athletics bd., mem. alumni assn. exec. bd., bd. vis. sch. law; mem. nat. adv. bd. Coll. Bus., U. Utah; lifetime dir. Utah Symphony Orch.; chmn. arts, adv. coun. and Capital Campaign Westminster Coll. Lt. (j.g.) USN, 1944-46, PTO. Recipient Contbn. award Downtown Planning Assn,. 1977, Gov.'s award in the Arts, 1991, Utah Nat. Guard Minuteman award, 1994. Mem. Am. Inst. Cert. Planners (charter), Am. Arts Alliance (bd. dirs. 1991), Alta Club (dir.), Cottonwood Club (pres. 1959-63), Salt Lake Country Club (dir.), Desert Island Golf and Country Club (Rancho Mirage, Calif.), Flat Rock Club (Island Park., Idaho pres. 1994-98), Phi Kappa Phi (hon., life). Home: 2510 Walker Ln Salt Lake City UT 84117-7729

WALLACE, RUSSELL JOHN, physicist; Rsch. scientist Lawrence Livermore Nat. Lab. Recipient Excellence in Plasma Physics award Am. Phys. Soc., 1995. Office: Lawrence Livermore Nat Lab PO Box 808 Livermore CA 94551-0808

WALLACE, TERRY CHARLES, SR. retired technical administrator, researcher; b. Phoenix, May 18, 1933; s. Terry Milton Wallace and Fair June (Hartman) Wallace Timberlake; m. Yvonne Jeannette Owens, May 21, 1955; children: Terry Charles, Randall James, Timothy Alan, Sheryl Lynn, Janice Marie. BS, Ariz. State U., 1955; PhD, Iowa State U., 1958. Staff Los Alamos Nat. Lab., 1958-71, dep. group leader, 1971-80, group leader, 1980-83, assoc. divsn. leader, 1983-89, tech. program coord., 1989-91, ret., 1991. Sr. tech. adv. SAIC, Inc., 1994-95; ptnr. Stonewall Enterprises, Los Alamos, 1966-71. Contbr. chpts., articles to profl. jours.; patentee in field. Fundraiser Los Alamos County Republican Party, N.Mex., 1983-84. Served to 1st lt. Chem. Corps, U.S. Army, 1959-61. Mem. Am. Chem. Soc., AAAS, Lab. Retiree Group, Inc. (Los Alamos, treas., bd. dirs. 1995-98), Los Alamos Ret. and Sr. Orgn. (pres., bd. dirs. 1999-2001), Mil. Order World Wars (MG Franklin E. Miles chpt. adj. treas. 1997-2001). Methodist. Home and Office: 1913 Spruce St Los Alamos NM 87544-3041

WALLACH, LESLIE ROTHAUS, architect; b. Pitts., Feb. 4, 1944; s. Albert and Sara F. (Rothaus) W.; m. Susan Rose Berger, June 15, 1969; 1 child, Aaron. BS in Mining Engring., U. Ariz., 1967, BArch, 1974. Registered architect, Ariz.; registered contractor, Ariz. Prin. Line and Space LLC, Tucson, 1978—. Mem. awards jury Sunset mag., 1997, Ariz. Homes of Yr., 1997, L.A. AIA; keynote spkr. various confs.; chair Coll. of Arch. Design Coun., U. Ariz., 1998. Representative projects include Ariz. Sonora Desert Mus. Restaurant Complex, Tucson, Elgin Elem. Sch., Ariz., Hillel Student Ctr. U. Ariz., Tucson, Boyce Thompson Southwestern Arborteum Vis. Ctr., Superior, Ariz., San Pedro Riparian Ctr., Sierra Vista, Ariz., Nat. Hist. Trails Ctr., Casper, Wyo., 1996, Nat. Law Ctr. for Inter-Am. Free Trade, Vis. Ctr. and Arborteum, Flagstaff, Ariz., 2001; contbr. Sunset Mag., Architecture Mag. and Fine Homebuilding; pub.: Space and Society (Italy), Hinge (Hong Kong), Wallpaper (London); exhibited at U. Ariz., AIA Nat. Conv., Washington. Bd. dirs Tucson Regional Plan, Inc.; pres. Civitas Sonoran (The Environ. Design Coun. of the U. of Ariz. Coll. of Arch.). Recipient Roy P. Drachman Design award, 1982, 85, 93, 2001, Electric League Ariz. Design award, 1987, 88, Gov. Solar Energy award, 1989, Desert Living awards citation, 1991, Ariz. Architect's medal, 1989, Disting. Alumni award U. Ariz., 1998, also 35 additional design awards, including 4 received in 1995. Fellow AIA (Ariz. Honor award 1989, 92, 96, AIA/ACSA Nat. Design award 1991, Western Mountain region Design award 1992, 96, CA AIA/Phoenix Homes and Gardens Home of the Yr. Honor award 1992, 96, Western Region Silver medal 1996); mem. SAC AIA (past pres., Design award 1985, 88, 90), Mountain Region AIA (named Firm of Yr. 1999). Office: Line and Space 627 E Speedway Blvd Tucson AZ 85705-7433 E-mail: studio627@lineandspace.com

WALLACH, PATRICIA, mayor, retired; b. Chgo. m. Ed Wallach; 3 children. Grad., Pasadena City Coll. Mem. city coun. City of El Monte, Calif., 1990-92, mayor, 1992-99; ret., 1997. Ret. tchr.'s aide Mountain View Sch. Dist. Past trustee El Monte Union High Sch. Dist., L.A. County High Sch. for the Arts; chief amb. of goodwill Zamora, Michoacan, Mex., Marcq-en-Baroeul, France, Yung Kang, Hsiang, Republic of China, Min-hang, Peoples Republic of China; mem. L.A. County Libr. Commn.; chairperson of bd. Cmty. Redevel. Agy.; mem. bd. El Monte Cmty. Access TV Corp.; mem. PTA, Little League Assns.; v.p. exec. bd., treas. Foothill Transit. Mem. League of Calif. Cities, San Gabriel Valley Coun. of Govts., Independent Cities Assn., U.S./Mex. Sister Cities Assn., Sister Cities Internat., Women of the Moose, El Monte Women's Club.

WALLACH, STEPHEN JOSEPH, cardiologist; b. Bklyn., Dec. 16, 1942; s. Frank and Sylvia B. (Meisel) W.; m. Vicki Wallach, June 30, 1968; children: Jonathan, Rachel. BS, L.I. U. Pharmach, 1965; MD, U. Okla., 1969. Intern Emory Affiliated, Atlanta, 1960-70, med. resident, 1970-71; gen. med. officer USN, 1971-74; med. resident USN Naval Res. Med. Ctr., Phila., 1974-75, fellow cardiology, 1975-76, mem. staff interstat medicine, 1976-77; asst. prof. John Burns Sch. Medicine, Honolulu, 1977-78; pvt. practice cardiology Queens Med. Ctr., Honolulu, 1978—, chief dept. medicine, 1993-2000, dir. utilization mgmt., dir. inhospital svcs., 1998. Clin. assoc. prof. medicine John A. Burns Sch. Medicine, 1998. Bd. dirs. Am. Heart Assn., Honolulu, 1980-86, pres. Honolulu chpg., 1994-95. Ltd. comdr. USNR, 1971. Fellow Am. Coll. Cardiology; mem. Honolulu County Med. Assn. (pres. 1990-91), Hawaii Med. Assn. (pres. 1991-92), Hawaii Soc. Internal Medicine (pres. 1996—). Jewish. Avocations: movies, hiking, music. Office: Queens Med Ctr 1301 Punchbowl St Ste 206 Honolulu HI 96813-2413

WALLACK, RINA EVELYN, lawyer; b. Pitts.; d. Erwin Norman and Gloria A. (Schacher). AD in Nursing, Delta Coll., 1973; BS cum laude in Psychology, Eastern Mich. U., 1980; JD cum laude, Wayne State U., 1983. Registered nurse Mich.; bar: Calif. 1983. Psychiat. head nurse Ypsilanti (Mich.) State Hosp., 1973-77, instr., nursing educator, 1977-80; teaching asst. contracts Wayne State U., Detroit, 1981-83; legal asst. Wayne County Prosecutor's Office, 1982-83; atty. NLRB, L.A., 1983-86, dir. employee rels. legal svcs. Paramount Pictures Corp., L.A., 1986-89, v.p., 1989-98, v.p., sr. counsel, 1998—. Contbr. articles to profl. jours. Instr. ARC, Mich., 1978-80. Recipient Am. Jurisprudence Book award, 1983. Mem. ABA, L.A. County Bar Assn., Am. Trial Lawyers Assn., Mich. Bar Assn., Calif. Bar Assn., Order of Coif. Avocations: shooting, movies, dancing, reading, photography.

WALLER, PETER WILLIAM, public affairs executive; b. Kewanee, Ill., Oct. 1, 1926; s. Ellis Julian and Barodel (Gould) W.; m. Anne-Marie Appelius van Hoboken, Nov. 10, 1950; children: Catherine, Hans. BA with hons., Princeton U., 1949; MA with hons., San Jose State U., 1978. Bur. chief Fairchild Publs., San Francisco, 1953-55; freelance writer Mountain View, Calif., 1956-57; pub. relations coord. Lockheed Missiles and Space, Sunnyvale, 1957-64; info. mgr. for 1st missions to Jupiter, Saturn, Venus NASA Ames Rsch. Ctr., Mountain View, 1964-83, mgr. pub. info., 1983-95; cons. NASA-Ames Galileo, Lunar Prospector, 1996-97; prodr. space films PacPAW Assoc., 1998—. Speechwriter for pres. Lockheed Missiles and Space, 1960-64. Producer (documentary) Jupiter Odyssey, 1974 (Golden Eagle, 1974); producer, writer NASA Aero. program, 1984; contbr. articles to profl. jours, encyclopedias. Cons. on preservation of Lake Tahoe, Calif. Resources Agy., Sacramento, 1984. Mem. No. Calif. Sci. Writers Assn., Sierra Club. Democrat. Congregationalist. Avocations: skiing, travel, architecture, construction, hiking. Home: 3655 La Calle Ct Palo Alto CA 94306-2619

WALLER, STEPHEN, air transportation executive; b. 1949; Student, New Zealand U., 1970-74. Courier, country mgr., european mktg. mgr. DHL Airways, Inc., London, 1975-80, Tehran, Iran, 1975-80, v.p. field svcs. Redwood City, Calif., 1980-93, sr. v.p. Network Trans. divsn., 1994—. Office: DHL Worldwide 333 Twin Dolphin Dr Redwood City CA 94065-1496

WALLERSTEIN, GEORGE, astronomer, educator; b. N.Y.C., Jan. 13, 1930; s. Leo Wallerstein; m. Julie Haynes Lutz, 1998. BA, Brown U., 1951; MS, Calif. Inst. Tech., Pasadena, 1954; PhD, Calif. Inst. Tech., 1958. Postdoc. rschr. Calif. Inst. Tech., Pasadena, 1957-58; from instr. to assoc. prof. U. Calif., Berkeley, 1958-65; prof. astronomy U. Wash., Seattle, 1965—. Contbr. articles to Astron. Jour., Astrophys. Jour., Sci. Bd. trustees Brown U., Providence, R.I., 1975-80. Lt. U.S. Navy, 1951-53, Korea. Fellow Royal Astron. Soc.; mem. Astron. Soc. Pacific, Am. Astron. Soc. Avocations: mountaineering, skiing, softball. Office: Astronomy Dept 351580 U Wash Seattle WA 98195-0001

WALLIS, ERIC G. lawyer; b. Astoria, N.Y., Jan. 8, 1950; AB magna cum laude, U. Pacific, 1972; JD, U. Calif., Hasting Coll. of Law, 1975. Bar: Calif. 1975. Mem. Crosby, Heafey, Roach & May PC, Oakland, Calif., 1982—. Editl. assoc. Hastings Law Jour., 1974-75. Mem. ABA (sect. litigation), State Bar Calif., Alameda County Bar Assn. Office: Crosby Heafey Roach & May PC 1999 Harrison St Fl 26 Oakland CA 94612-3520 E-mail: ewallis@chnm.com

WALLOCK, TERRENCE J. lawyer; JD, UCLA, 1970. Bar: Calif. 1971. V.p., gen. counsel Denny's Inc.; sr. v.p., sec., gen. counsel Vons Cos., Arcadia, Calif., 1990—; now sr. v.p., sec., gen. counsel Ralphs Grocery Co., L.A., 1990-98, ret., 1998. Office: Ralphs Grocery Co PO Box 54143 Los Angeles CA 90054-0143

WALLSTRÖM, WESLEY DONALD, bank executive; b. Turlock, Calif., Oct. 4, 1929; s. Emil Reinhold and Edith Katherine (Lindberg) W.; m. Marilyn Irene Hallmark, May 12, 1951; children: Marc Gordon, Wendy Diane. Student, Modesto (Calif.) Jr. Coll., 1955-64; cert. Pacific Coast Banking Sch., U. Wash., 1974. Bookkeeper, teller First Nat. Bank, Turlock, 1947-50; v.p. Gordon Hallmark Inc., Turlock, 1950-53; asst. cashier United Calif. Bank, Turlock, 1953-68, regional v.p. Fresno, 1968-72, v.p., mgr. Turlock, 1972-76; founding pres., dir. Golden Valley Bank, Turlock, 1976-84; pres. Wallström & Co., Turlock, 1985—. Campaign chmn. United Crusade, Turlock, 1971; chmn., founding dir. Covenant Village Retirement Home, Turlock, 1973-94, treas. Covenant Retirement Cmtys. West; founding pres. Turlock Regional Arts Coun., 1974, dir., 1975-76. Served with U.S. N.G., 1948-56. Mem. Nat. Soc. Accts. for Coops., Ind. Bankers No. Calif., Am. Bankers Assn., U.S. Sailing Assn., No. Calif. Golf Assn., Turlock C. of C. (dir. 1973-75), Stanislaus Sailing Soc. (commodore 1980-81), Pacific Inter-Club Yacht Assn. (bd. dirs. 1994—, commodore), Turlock Golf and Country Club (pres. 1975-76, v.p. 17, dir. 1977, 93), Stockton Sailing Club, Grindstone Joe Assn., Recreational Boaters Calif. (dir. 1998), Masons, Rotary. Republican. Mem. Covenant Ch. Home: 1720 Hammond Dr Turlock CA 95382-2850 Office: Wallstrom & Co 2925 Niagra St Turlock CA 95382-1056

WALP, ROBERT M. communications carrier and internet/cable provider-executive; b. Charlottesville, Va., 1927; Degree, Calif. Inst. Tech., 1951, degree, 1953. Vice chmn. Gen. Commn., Inc., Anchorage. Office: Gen Comm Inc 2550 Denali St Ste 1000 Anchorage AK 99503-2736 Fax: (907) 265-5676

WALSH, BILL, former professional football coach; b. Los Angeles, Nov. 30, 1931; Student, San Mateo Jr. Coll.; BA, San Jose State U., 1954, MA in Edn., 1959. Asst. coach Monterey Peninsula Coll., 1955, San Jose State U., 1956; head coach Washington Union High Sch., Fremont, Calif., 1957-59; asst. coach U. Calif., Berkeley, 1960-62, Stanford U., 1963-65, Oakland Raiders, Am. Football League, 1966-67, Cin. Bengals, 1968-75, San Diego Chargers, Nat. Football League, 1976; head coach Stanford U., 1977-78; head coach, gen. mgr. San Francisco 49ers, NFL, 1979-89, exec. v.p., 1989; broadcaster NBC Sports, 1989-91; head coach Stanford U., 1992-95; cons. San Francisco Forty Niners, 1996-99, v.p., gen. mgr., 1999—. Named NFL Coach of Yr., Sporting News, 1981; coached Stanford U. winning team Sun Bowl, 1977, Bluebonnet Bowl, 1978, Blockbuster Bowl, 1993, San Francisco 49ers to Super Bowl championships, 1981, 84, 88; elected to Pro Football Hall of Fame, 1993. Office: San Francisco 49ers 4949 Centennial Blvd Santa Clara CA 95054-1229

WALSH, DANIEL FRANCIS, bishop; b. San Francisco, Oct. 2, 1937; Grad., St. Joseph Sem., St. Patrick Sem., Catholic U. Am. Ordained priest, Roman Catholic Ch., 1963. Ordained titular bishop of Tigia, 1981; aux. bishop of San Francisco, 1981-87; bishop of Reno-Las Vegas, 1987—. Office: Diocese Reno-Las Vegas Office Bishop PO Box 18316 Las Vegas NV 89114-8316

WALSH, DENNY JAY, reporter; b. Omaha, Nov. 23, 1935; s. Gerald Jerome and Muriel (Morton) W.; m. Peggy Marie Moore, Feb. 12, 1966; children by previous marriage— Catherine Camille, Colleen Cecile; 1 son, Sean Joseph. B.J., U. Mo., 1962. Staff writer St. Louis Globe-Democrat, 1961-68; asst. editor Life mag., N.Y.C., 1968-70, assoc. editor, 1970-73; reporter N.Y. Times, 1973-74, Sacramento Bee, 1974—. Served with USMC, 1954-58. Recipient Con Lee Kelliher award St. Louis chpt. Sigma Delta Chi, 1962; award Am. Polit. Sci. Assn., 1963; award Sigma Delta Chi, 1968; Pulitzer prize spl. local reporting, 1969; 1st prize San Francisco Press Club, 1977 Office: Sacramento Bee 21st & Q Sts Sacramento CA 95813 E-mail: dwalsh@sacbee.com

WALSH, DON, marine consultant, executive; b. Berkeley, Calif., Nov. 2, 1931; s. J. Don and Marguerite Grace (Van Auker) W.; m. Joan A. Betzmer, Aug. 18, 1962; children— Kelly Drennan, Elizabeth McDonough BS, U.S. Naval Acad., 1954; MS, Tex. A&M U., 1967, PhD, 1968; MA, San Diego State U., 1968. Commd. ensign USN, 1954, advanced through grades to capt., 1974, officer-in-charge Bathyscaph Trieste, 1959-62, comdr. in USS Bashaw, 1968-69; dir. Inst. Marine and Coastal Studies, prof. ocean engring. U. So. Calif., L.A., 1975-83; pres., CEO Internat. Maritime, Inc., L.A., 1976—; mng. dir. Deep Ocean Engring., Inc., 1990—, also bd. dirs. Dir. Ctr. for Marine Transp. Studies, U. So. Calif., 1980-83, Coastal Resources Ctr., 1990-94; trustee USN Mus. Found., 1989—; mem. Nat. Adv. Com. on Oceans and Atmosphere, 1979-85; bd. govs. Calif. Maritime Acad., 1985-95; pres. Parker Diving, 1989-94. Editor, contbr.: Law of the Sea: Issues in Ocean Resource Management, 1977, Energy and Resources Development of Continental Margins, 1980, Energy and Sea Power: Challenge for the Decade, 1981, Waste Disposal in the Oceans: Minimizing Impact, Maximizing Benefits, 1983; editor Jour. Marine Tech. Soc., 1975-80; mem. editorial bd. U.S. Naval Inst., 1974-75. Bd. dirs. Charles and Anne Lindbergh Found., 1996—. Decorated Legion of Merit (2); Woodrow Wilson Internat. Ctr. for Scholars fellow, 1973-74. Fellow Marine Tech. Soc., Acad. Underwater Arts and Scis., Explorers Club (hon. life, bd. dirs. 1994-2000, Explorers Medal, 2001), Royal Geog. Soc. (Eng.); mem. AAAS, Soc. Naval Archs. and Marine Engrs., Am. Soc. Naval Engrs., Navy League, Navy Inst., Adventurers Club (hon. life), Am. Geog. Soc. (hon. life), Nat. Acad. Engring. Home and Office: Internat Maritime Inc 14758 Sitkum Ln 14758 Sitkum Ln Myrtle Point OR 97458-9726 E-mail: imiwalsh@worldnet.att.net

WALSH, EDWARD JOSEPH, toiletries and food company executive; b. Mt. Vernon, N.Y., Mar. 18, 1932; s. Edward Aloysius and Charlotte Cecilia (Borup) W.; m. Patricia Ann Farrell, Sept. 16, 1961; children: Edward Joseph, Megan Simpson, John, Robert. BBA, Iona Coll., 1953; MBA, NYU, 1958. Sales rep. M & R Dietetic Labs., Columbus, Ohio, 1955-60; with Armour & Co., 1961-71, Greyhound Corp., 1971-87; v.p. toiletries div. Armour Dial Co., Phoenix, 1973-74, exec. v.p., 1975-77; pres. Armour Internat. Co., Phoenix, 1978-84, The Dial Corp. (formerly Armour-Dial Co.), Phoenix, 1984-87, chief exec. officer, 1984-87; pres., chief exec. officer Purex Corp., 1985; chmn., chief exec. officer The Sparta Group Ltd., Scottsdale, Ariz., 1988—. Bd. dirs. Guest Supply Inc., New Brunswick, N.J., WD-40 Co., San Diego, Nortrust Ariz. Holding Corp., Phoenix, No. Trust Bank of Ariz., N.A., Inc., Gum Tech. Internat., Phoenix. Trustee Scottsdale Meml. Health Found., 1995-98; pres. Mt. Vernon Fire Dept. Mems. Assn., 1960-61. Served with U.S. Army, 1953-55, Germany. Mem. Am. Mgmt. Assn., Nat. Meat Canner Assn. (pres. 1971-72), Cosmetic, Toiletries and Fragrance Assn. (bd. dirs. 1985—), Nat. Food Processors Assn. (bd. dirs.). Republican. Roman Catholic. Office: The Sparta Group Ltd 6623 N Scottsdale Rd Scottsdale AZ 85250-4421

WALSH, GARY L. consumer products company executive; b. 1942; Sr. mgmt. Sara Lee Corp. and Sysco Foods, 1966-77; CEO Miller Cascade Foodsvc. of Am., 1977-1990; chmn., pres., CEO, Core-Mark Internat., Inc., South San Francisco, 1990-98; chmn. bd. Core-Mark, San Francisco, 1998—. Office: Core Mark Internat Inc 395 Oyster Point Blvd Ste 415 South San Francisco CA 94080-1932 also: Core Mark Interrlated Cos 311 Reed Cir Corona CA 92879-1349

WALSH, JOHN, museum director; b. Mason City, Wash., Dec. 9, 1937; s. John J. and Eleanor (Wilson) W.; m. Virginia Alys Galston, Feb. 17, 1962; children: Peter Wilson, Anne Galston, Frederick Matthiessen. B.A., Yale U., 1961; postgrad., U. Leyden, Netherlands, 1965-66; MA, Columbia U., 1965, PhD, 1971; LHD (hon.), Wheaton Coll., 2000. Lectr., rsch. asst. Frick Collection, N.Y.C., 1966-68; assoc. higher edn. Met. Mus. Art, N.Y.C., 1968-71, assoc. curator European paintings, 1970-72, curator dept. European paintings, 1972-74, vice-chmn., 1974-75; adj. asso. prof. art history Columbia U., N.Y.C., 1969-72, adj. prof., 1972-75; prof. art history Barnard Coll., Columbia U., N.Y.C., 1975-77; Mrs. Russell W. Baker curator paintings Mus. Fine Arts, Boston, 1977-83; dir. J. Paul Getty Mus., Malibu, Calif., 1983-2000, dir. emeritus, 2000—. Vis. prof. fine arts Harvard U., 1979; mem. governing bd. Yale U. Art Gallery, 1975—, Smithsonian Coun., 1990—. Contbr. articles to profl. jours. Mem. Dem. County Com., N.Y.C., 1968-71; mem. vis. com. Fogg Mus., Harvard U., 1982-87; bd. fellows Claremont U. Ctr. and Grad. Sch., 1988-2000. With USNR, 1957-63. Fulbright grad. fellow The Netherlands, 1965-66 Mem. Am. Acad. Arts and Scis., Coll. Art Assn., Am. Assn. Mus., Archaeol. Inst. Am., Am. Antiquarian Soc., Assn. Art Mus. Dirs. (trustee 1986-90, pres. 1989-90), Century Assn. N.Y.C. Office: J Paul Getty Mus 1200 Getty Center Dr Ste 1000 Los Angeles CA 90049-1687

WALSH, KENNETH ANDREW, biochemist; b. Sherbrooke, Que., Can., Aug. 7, 1931; s. George Stanley and Dorothy Maud (Sangster) W.; m. Deirdre Anne Clarke, Aug. 22, 1953; children: Andrew, Michael, Erin. BSc in Agr., McGill U., 1951; MS, Purdue U., 1953; PhD, U. Toronto, 1959. Postdoctoral fellow U. Wash., Seattle, 1959-62, from asst. prof. to assoc. prof. Biochemistry, 1962-69, prof. Biochemistry, 1969—, chair, 1990-2000. Author (book) Methods in Protein Sequence Analysis, 1986. Mem. The Protein Soc. (sec.-treas. 1987-90), Am. So. Biochemistry/Molecular Biology. Office: U Wash Box 357350 Seattle WA 98195-7350

WALSH, THOMAS A. production designer; Prodn. designer Doug Apatow Agy., Culver City, Calif., 1980—. Prodn. designer: (IMAX films) Flyers, 1980, Speed, 1984, The Discoverers, 1993, (TV movies) Miss Lonely Hearts, 1981, A Gathering of Old Men, 1986 (Emmy award nomination outstanding art direction 1987), Eugene O'Neill, 1986, War Story: Vietnam, 1988, Without Warning: The James Brady Story, 1990 (Emmy award nomination outstanding art direction 1991), Blindspot, 1992, In Search of Dr. Seuss, 1994, (documentaries) John Huston, 1988, MGM: When the Lion Roars, 1992 (Emmy award outstanding art direction 1993), (feature films) The Handmaid's Tale, 1990, Prayer of the Rollerboys, 1990. Office: Doug Apatow Agency 12049 W Jefferson Blvd #200 Culver City CA 90230-6219

WALSH, WILLIAM DESMOND, investor; b. N.Y.C., Aug. 4, 1930; s. William J. and Catherine Grace (Desmond) W.; m. Mary Jane Gordon, Apr. 5, 1951; children: Deborah, Caroline, Michael, Suzanne, Tara Jane, Peter. BA, Fordham U., 1951; JD, Harvard U., 1955. Bar: N.Y. State bar 1955. Asst. U.S. atty. So. dist. N.Y., N.Y.C., 1955-58; counsel N.Y. Commn. Investigation, N.Y.C., 1958-61; mgmt. cons. McKinsey & Co., N.Y.C., 1961-67; sr. v.p. Arcata Corp., Menlo Park, Calif., 1967-82; chmn. Sequoia Assocs. LLC, 1982—; pres., chief exec. officer Atacra Liquidating Trust, 1982-88. Chmn. bd. dirs. Consol. Freightways Corp., Vancouver, Wash., Clayton Group, Inc., Tampa, Fla., Newell Indsl. Corp., Roanoke, Va., Neuroscis. Inst./Scripps; bd. dirs. URS Corp., San Francisco, UNOVA, Woodland Hills, Calif., Crown Vantage, Cin., Ohio, Ameriscape, Inc., North Salem, N.Y., Bemiss Jason Corp., Newark, Calif., Am. Ireland Fund. Mem. Harvard Law Sch., co-chair dean's adv. bd.; trustee Fordham ; mem. bd. overseers Hoover Inst. Mem. N.Y. State Bar Assn., Harvard Club (N.Y.C. and San Francisco), Fordham Club No. Calif., Knights of Malta (amb. to Bolivia). Home: 279 Park Ln Atherton CA 94027-5448 Office: Bldg 2 3000 Sand Hill Rd Ste 140 Menlo Park CA 94025-7113

WALSHAW, L. SCOTT, commissioner; BA in Art History, BA in Econ., Calif. State U.; MBA, U. Nev. Sr. examiner Nev. Fin. Instns., Carson City, Nev.; asst. nat. bank examiner Office the Comptr. the Currency, Carson City; commr. Fin. Instns., Carson City, 1983—. Past chmn. Am. Coun. State Savs. Supr.; past. chmn., trustee Inst. Supr. Edn.; past mem. state liaison com. Fed. Fin. Instns. Examination Coun. Office: State Nev Fin Instns Divsn 406 E 2nd St Ste 3 Carson City NV 89701-4758

WALSTON, RODERICK EUGENE, state government official; b. Gooding, Idaho, Dec. 15, 1935; s. Loren R. and Iva M. (Boyer) W.; m. Margaret D. Grandey; children: Gregory Scott W., Valerie Lynne W. A.A., Boise Jr. Coll., 1956; B.A. cum laude, Columbia Coll., 1958; LL.B. scholar, Stanford U., 1961. Bar: Calif. 1961, U.S. Supreme Ct. 1973. Law clk to judge U.S. Ct. Appeals 9th Cir., 1961-62; dep. atty. gen State of Calif., San Francisco, 1963-91, head natural resources sect, 1969-91, chief asst. atty. gen. pub. rights div., 1991-99; spl. dep counsel Kings County, Calif., 1975-76; gen. counsel Metropolitan Water Dist. So. Calif., 2000—. Mem. environ. and natural resources adv. coun. Stanford (Calif.) Law Sch. Contbr. articles to profl. jours.; bd. editors: Stanford Law Rev., 1959-61, Western Natural Resources Litigation Digest, Calif. Water Law and Policy Reporter; spl. editor Jour. of the West. Co-chmn. Idaho campaign against Right-to-Work initiative, 1958; Calif. rep. Western States Water Coun., 1986—; environ. and natural resources adv. coun., Stanford Law Sch. Nat. Essay Contest winner Nat. Assn. Internat. Rels. Clubs, 1956, Stanford Law

Rev. prize, 1961; recipient Best Brief award Nat. Assn. Attys. Gen., 1997; Astor Found. scholar, 1956-58. Mem. ABA (chmn. water resources com. 1988-90, vice chmn. and conf. chmn. 1985-88, 90—), Contra Costa County Bar Assn., U.S. Supreme Ct., Hist. Soc., Federalist Soc., World Affairs Coun. No. Calif. Office: Metro Water Dist 700 N Alameda St Los Angeles CA 90012

WALT, MARTIN, physicist, consulting educator; b. West Plains, Mo., June 1, 1926; s. Martin and Dorothy (Mantz) W.; m. Mary Estelle Thompson, Aug. 16, 1950; children: Susan Mary, Stephen Martin, Anne Elizabeth, Patricia Ruth. B.S., Calif. Inst. Tech., 1950; M.S., U. Wis., 1951, Ph.D., 1953. Staff mem. Los Alamos Sci. Lab., 1953-56; research scientist, mgr. physics Lockheed Missiles and Space Co., Palo Alto (Calif.) Rsch. Lab., 1956-71, dir. phys. scis., 1971-86, dir. research, 1986-93; cons. prof. Stanford U., 1986—. Mem. adv. com. NRC, NASA, Dept. Def., U. Calif. Lawrence Berkeley Lab. Author 2 books; contbr. articles to sci. jours. Served with USNR, 1944-46. Wis. Research Found. fellow, 1950-51; AEC fellow, 1951-53 Fellow Am. Geophys. Union, Am. Phys. Soc.; mem. Am. Inst. Physics (bd. govs.), Fremont Hills Country Club. Home: 12650 Viscaino Ct Los Altos CA 94022-2517 Office: Stanford U Starlab Packard 352 Stanford CA 94305 E-mail: walt@nova.stanford.edu

WALTERBOS, RENÉ ANTONIUS, astronomer; BA in Astronomy, Physics, U. Leiden, 1979, MS in Astronomy, Physics cum laude, 1982, PhD in Astronomy, 1986. Postdoc. rschr. Inst. Advanced Study, Princeton, N.J., 1986-87, U. Calif., Berkeley, 1987-90; asst. prof. astronomy N.Mex. State U., Las Cruces, 1991-96, head dept., assoc. prof. astronomy, 1996—. Vis. asst. prof. dept. physics U. Calif., Davis, 1989-90. Hubble fellow Space Telescope Sci. Inst., 1990-91; Cottrell scholar Rsch. Corp., 1994. Mem. Internat. Astron. Union, Am. Astron. Soc., Netherlands Astron. Soc., Astron. Soc. Pacific. Achievements include research in structure and evolution of galaxies, properties of the diffuse interstellar medium in galaxies, interaction of massive stars with the interstellar medium in galaxies. Office: New Mex State U Dept Astronomy PO Box 30001 Las Cruces NM 88003-8001

WALTERS, DANIEL RAYMOND, political columnist; b. Hutchinson, Kans., Oct. 10, 1943; s. Howard Duke and Glenna Lucille (Hesse) W.; m. Doris K. Winter, June 16, 1995; children: Danielle, Staci. Mng. editor Hanford (Calif.) Sentinel, 1966-69, Herald News, Klamath Falls, Oreg., 1969-71, Times-Standard, Eureka, Calif., 1971-73; polit. writer and columnist Sacramento (Calif.) Union, 1973-84; polit. columnist, state editor Capitol Bur., Sacramento Bee, 1984—. Author: The New California: Facing the 21st Century, 1986; founding editor Calif. Polit. Almanac, 1989. Office: The Sacramento Bee Capitol Bur 925 L St Ste 1404 Sacramento CA 95814-3704

WALTERS, JESSE RAYMOND, JR. state supreme court justice; b. Rexburg, Idaho, Dec. 26, 1938; s. Jesse Raymond and Thelma Rachael (Hodgson) W.; m. Harriet Payne, May 11, 1959; children: Craig T., Robyn, J. Scott. Student, Ricks Coll., 1957-58; BA in Polit. Sci., U. Idaho, 1961, JD, 1963; postgrad., U. Washington, 1962; LLM, U. Va., 1990. Bar: Idaho 1963; U.S. Dist. Ct. Idaho 1964, U.S. Ct. Appeals (9th cir.) 1970. Law clk. to chief justice Idaho Supreme Ct., 1963-64; solo practice Boise, Idaho, 1964-77; atty. Idaho senate, Boise, 1965; dist. judge 4th Jud. Dist., Idaho, 1977-82, adminstrv. dist. judge, 1981-82; chief judge Idaho Ct. Appeals, Boise, 1982-97. Chmn. magistrate's commn. 4th jud. dist.; chmn. Supreme Ct. mem. services; chmn. Criminal Pattern Jury Instrn. Com.; mem. Civil Pattern Jury Instrn. Com. Republican committeeman Boise, 1975-77; mem. Ada County Rep. Ctrl. Com., 1975-77. Mem. Idaho Bar Assn. (bankruptcy com.), Idaho Adminstrv. Judges Assn., ABA, Am. Judicature Soc. (dir.), Assn. Trial Lawyers Am., Idaho Trial Layers Assn., Coun. Chief Judges Ct. Appeals (pres. 1994-95), Boise Estate Planning Coun., Jaycees (nat. dir. 1969-70, pres. Boise chpt. 1966-67), Lions, Elks, Eagles. Mormon. Office: Supreme Ct Idaho PO Box 83720 Boise ID 83720-3720

WALTERS, PAUL, protective services official; b. Reading, Eng., 1945; (parents Am. citizens); m. Linda Koskewich; children: Gary, Michael. AA, Orange Coast Coll., 1972; BA in Criminal Justice, Calif. State U., Fullerton, 1986; MPA, U. So. Calif., 1992; JD, Am. Coll. of law, 1977; grad., Calif. Command Coll., 1986, Police Exec. Rsch. Forum, Sr. Mgmt. Inst., Harvard U. From patrol officer to capt. City of Santa Ana (Calif.) Police Dept., 1971-88, chief of police, 1988—. Sgt. USAF. Recipient Appreciation cert. Orange County Bar Assn., 1990, Commendation cert. Orange County Human Rels. Commn., 1990, Orange County Cmty. Policing award, 1994. Mem. Orange County Chiefs of Police and Sheriff's Assn. (mem. exec. com., past pres.). Office: Santa Ana Police Dept M-97 PO Box 1981 Santa Ana CA 92702-1981

WALTERS, RITA, councilwoman; b. Chgo., Aug. 14, 1930; children: David, Susan, Philip. BA, Shaw U., Raleigh, N.C., 1975; MBA, UCLA, 1984. Tchr. adult divsn. L.A. Sch. Dist., 1975-79; instr. Ednl. Founds. Dept. Calif. State U., L.A., 1981; pres. L.A. Bd. Edn., 1985-88; city councilwoman L.A., 1991—. Chair Arts Health and Humanities Com., Public Works, Budget & Fin. Office: City Hall Rm 508 200 N Main St Los Angeles CA 90012-4110

WALZ, KENT, publishing executive; Editor Albuquerque Jour. Office: Albuquerque Jour Pub Co PO Drawer J 7777 Jefferson St NE Albuquerque NM 87103

WAN, RONG-YU, metallurgist; b. China, Jan. 12, 1932; s. Zheng-Lin and Juan-Ying Yan Wan; m. KeZhong Wang, June 1, 1957; 1 child, Joseph J. BS in Chem. Engring., Chiao Tung U., Shanghai, China, 1952; PhD in Metallurgy and Metall. Engring., U. Utah, 1984. Metallurgy engr. engring. and design Inst. for Nonferrous Metall. Industries, Beijing, 1953-79; supervising chief Beijing Mining and Metall. Rsch. Inst., Beijing, 1958-79; rsch. assoc., asst. rsch. prof. U. Utah, 1980-87; sr. metallurgist Newmont Exploration Ltd., Metall. Svc., Salt Lake City, 1987-91, mgr. metall. rsch., 1992—. Adj. prof. metallurgy dept. U. Utah, 1987—. Contbr. articles to profl. jours. Recipient numerous awards from Chinese Govt., Ministry Metall. Industries, 1955-79. Mem. Minerals, Metals and Materials Soc. (vice chmn. aqueous processes com., vice chmn. precious metals com., honors and awards com., Extractive Metallurgy Tech. award 1989), Soc. for Mining, Metallurgy and Exploration, Mining Metall. Soc. Am. Achievements include 4 patents for new technologies of gold metallurgy, refractory gold ores treatment; research and development in innovative technologies and processes for gold recovery, gold recovery using noncyanide lixiviants, pressure oxidatioln of sulfide minerals fundamental and applications; technical contributions in the areas of nonferrouis extractive metallurgy and mineral processing. Office: Newmont Exploration Ltd Ste 210 417 Wakara Way Salt Lake City UT 84108 Fax: 801-583-8923

WANG, CHARLES PING, engineering executive; b. Shanghai, Republic of China, Apr. 25, 1937; came to U.S., 1962; s. Kuan-Ying and Ping-Lu (Ming) W.; m. Lily L. Lee, June 29, 1963. BS, Taiwan U., Republic of China, 1959; MS, Tsinghua U., Singchu, Republic of China, 1961; PhD, Calif. Inst. Tech., 1967. Mem. tech. staff Bellcomm, Washington, 1967-69; research engr. U. San Diego, 1969-74; sr. scientist Aerspace Corp., Los Angeles, 1976-86; pres. Optodyne, Inc., Compton, Calif., 1986—. Adj. prof. U. Calif., San Diego, 1979-90; pres. Chinese-Am. Engr. and Scientists Assn. So. Calif., Los Angeles, 1979-81; program chmn. Internation Conf. of Lasers, Shanghai, 1979-80; organizer and session chmn. Lasers Conf., Los Angeles, 1981-84, program chmn., Las Vegas, 1985. Editor in chief Series in Laser Tech., 1983-91; contbr. articles to profl. jours.; inventor discharge excimer laser. Calif. Inst. Tech. scholar, 1965. Fellow Am. Optical Soc., AIAA (assoc., jour. editor 1981-83). Office: Optodyne Inc 1180 W Mahalo Pl Compton CA 90220-5443 E-mail: optodyne@aol.com

WANG, CHEN CHI, electronics company, real estate, finance company, investment services, and international trade executive; b. Taipei, Taiwan, Aug. 10, 1932; came to U.S., 1959, naturalized, 1970; s. Chin-Ting and Chen-Kim Wang; m. Victoria Rebisoff, Mar. 5, 1965; children: Katherine Kim, Gregory Chen, John Christopher, Michael Edward. BA in Econs., Nat. Taiwan U., 1955; BSEE, San Jose State U., 1965; MBA, U. Calif., Berkeley, 1961. With IBM Corp., San Jose, Calif., 1965-72; founder, CEO Electronics Internat. Co., Santa Clara, 1968-72, owner, gen. mgr., 1972-81; reorganized as EIC Group, 1981-2000; chmn. bd., CEO EIC Investment Corp., 1982—; dir. Systek Electronics Corp., Santa Clara, 1970-73; founder, sr. ptnr. Wang Enterprises (name changed to Chen Kim Enterprises 1982), Santa Clara, 1974-75, Hanson & Wang Devel. Co., Woodside, Calif., 1977-85; chmn. bd. Golden Alpha Enterprises, San Mateo, 1979-99; mng. ptnr. Woodside Acres-Las Pulgas Estate, Woodside, 1980-85; founder, sr. ptnr. DeVine & Wang, Oakland, Calif., 1977-83, Van Heal & Wang, West Village, 1981-82; founder, chmn. bd. EIC Fin. Corp. (now EIC Investment Corp.), Redwood City, 1985-90; chmn. bd. Maritek Corp., Corpus Christi, Tex., 1988-89; chmn. EIC Internat. Trade Corp., Lancaster, Calif., 1989-90, EIC Capital Corp., Redwood City, 1990-91. Mng. mem. Sixtieth West, LLC, 1997—, Land Investment Co. Calif., LLC, 1998—, Aceh Capital, LLC, 1998—. Author: Monetary and Banking System of Taiwan, 1955, The Small Car Market in the U.S., 1961. Served to 2d lt., Nationalist Chinese Army, 1955-56. Mem. Internat. Platform Assn., Tau Beta Pi. Mem. Christian Ch. Home: 195 Brookwood Rd Woodside CA 94062-2302 Office: EIC Group Head Office Bldg 2055-2075 Woodside Rd Redwood City CA 94061-3355

WANG, DAVID N.K. chemical company executive; PhD in Material Science, U. California-Berkeley. Rschr. Bell Labs., Murray Hill, N.J., 1980; mgr. Worldwide Bus. Ops.; 0; sr. v.p. Applied Materials, Inc., Santa Clara, Calif., 1998—. Office: Applied Materials Inc 3050 Bowers Ave Santa Clara CA 95054-3201

WANG, HUAI-LIANG WILLIAM, mechanical engineer; b. Hsinchu, Taiwan, Republic of China, Apr. 4, 1959; came to U.S., 1984; s. Feng-Chi and Hu-Mei (Chou) W.; m. Wen-Pei Chen, June 28, 1986; children: James, Edward. BSME, Tatung Inst. of Tech., Taipei, Taiwan, 1981; MSME, Okla. State U., 1985. Asst. engr. Teco Electric and Machinery Corp., Taipei, Taiwan, 1984; electro-mech. engr. Microsci. Internat. Corp., Sunnyvale, Calif., 1987-89; engr. Lockheed Engring. and Scis. Co., Houston, 1989-91, sr. engr., 1991-92; mgr. mech. engring. Orbiter Tech. Co., Fremont, Calif., 1992; sr. engr. Avatar Sys. Corp., Milpitas, 1993, Quantum Corp., Milpitas, 1994-2000; sr. opto-mech. engr. Phaethon Comms., Fremont, Calif., 2000-01; sr. mech. engr. Paracer Inc., Santa Clara, 2001—. Mem. IEEE, ASME. Office: Paracer 3303 Octavius Dr Ste 100 Santa Clara CA 95054 E-mail: williamwang@yahoo.com, william@paracer.com

WANG, JAW-KAI, agricultural engineering educator; b. Nanjing, Jiangsu, People's Republic of China, Mar. 4, 1932; came to U.S., 1955; s. Shuling and Hsi-Ying (Lo) W.; m. Kwang Mei Chow, Sept. 7, 1957 (div. Oct. 1989); children: Angela C.C., Dora C.C., Lawrence C.Y.; m. Bichuan Li, Sept. 25, 1999. BS, Nat. Taiwan U., 1953; MS in Agrl. Engring., Mich. State U., 1956, PhD, 1958. Registered profl. engr., Hawaii. Faculty agrl. engring. dept. U. Hawaii, Honolulu, 1959-93, assoc. prof., chmn. dept. agrl. engring., 1964-68, prof., chmn. dept. agrl. engring., 1968-75, dir. Aquaculture Program, 1990-96; prof. biosystems engring. dept. U. Hawaii-Manoa, Honolulu, 1994—; spl. asst., Internat. Rsch. Dept., Office of Internat. Cooperation and Devel. U.S. Dept. Agr., 1988; pres. Aquaculture Tech., Inc., 1990—. Co-dir. internat. sci. and edn. coun. USDA; vis. assoc. dir. internat. programs and studies office Nat. Assn. State Univs. and Land-Grant Colls., 1979; vis. prof. Nat. Taiwan U., 1964-65, U. Calif., Davis, 1980; cons. U.S. Army Civilian Adminstrn., Ryukus, Okinawa, 1965, Internat. Rice Rsch. Inst., The Philippines, 1971, Pacific Concrete and Rock Co. Ltd., 1974, AID, 1974, Universe Tankships, Del., 1980-81, World Bank, 1981, 82, ABA Internat., 1981-85, Internat. Found. for Agrl. Devel./World Bank, 1981, Rockefeller Found., 1980, Orizaba, Inc., 1983, Agrisys./FAO, 1983, Info. Processing Assocs., 1984, County of Maui, 1984, 85, Dept. of State, 1985, Alexander and Baldwin, 1986; mem. expert panel on agrl. mechanization FAO/UN, 1984-90; sr. fellow East-West Ctr. Food Inst., 1973-74; dir. Info. Sys. and Svcs. Internat., Inc., 1986-90. Author: Irrigated Rice Production Systems, 1980; editor: Taro-A Review of Colocasia Esculenta and its Potentials, 1983; mem. editl. bd. Aquacultural Engring., 1982—. Recipient Exemplary State Employee award State of Hawaii, 1986, State of Hawaii Disting. Svc. award Office of Gov., 1990. Fellow Am. Soc. Agrl. Engrs. (chmn. Hawaii sect. 1962-63, chmn. grad. instrn. com. 1971-73, various coms., Engr. of Yr. 1976, Tech. Paper award 1978, Kishida Internat. award 1991), Am. Inst. Med. and Biol. Engring.; mem. Nat. Acad. Engring., Aquaculture Engring. Soc. (pres. 1993-95), Sigma Xi, Gamma Sigma Delta (pres. Hawaii chpt. 1974-75), Pi Mu Epsilon. Office: U Hawaii MBBE Dept 1955 East West Rd Honolulu HI 96822

WANG, SHIH-HO, electrical engineer, educator; b. Kiangsu, China, June 29, 1944; came to U.S., 1968; s. C.C. Wang and Man Shih. BEE, Nat. Taiwan U., Taipei, 1967; MEE, U. Calif., Berkeley, 1970, PhD in Elec. Engring., 1971. Asst. prof. elec. engring. U. Colo., Colo. Springs, 1973-76, Boulder, 1976-77; asst. prof. electrical engring. U. Md., College Park, 1977-78, assoc. prof., 1978-84; prof. U. Calif., Davis, 1984—. Cons. Lawrence Livermore (Calif.) Nat. Lab., 1986—; scientific officer Office Naval Research, Arlington, Va., 1983-84. Assoc. editor Internat. Jour. Robotics and Automation, 1986—. Served to 2d lt. China Air Force, Taiwan, 1967-68. Mem. IEEE (hon. mention award control systems soc. 1975). Office: Univ Calif Dept Elec Computer Engring Davis CA 95616 E-mail: wang@ece.ucdavis.edu

WANG, STANLEY, electronics executive; b. 1943; MBA, Temple U. Mgr. Philco-Ford, Sunnyvale, Calif., 1964-71; materials mgr., mktg. rep. Intersil Corp., Cupertino, 1971-73; with Pantronix Corp., San Jose, 1974—, pres. Office: Pantronix Corp 2710 Lakeview Ct Fremont CA 94538-6534

WANG, SUSAN S. manufacturing company executive; BA in Acctg., U. Tex.; MBA, U. Conn. CPA, Calif. With Price Waterhouse & Co., N.Y.C.; various fin. and acctg. mgmt. positions Xerox Corp., Westvaco Corp.; dir. fin. Solectron Corp., Milpitas, Calif., 1984, v.p. fin., CFO, 1986, sr. v.p., 1990—, also bd. dirs. Mem. adv. bd. YWCA, Santa Clara County; chairperson Fin. Exec. Rsch. Found. Recipient Top Women in Industry award YWCA; named one of San Francisco Bay Area's most powerful corp. women. Mem. AICPA, N.Y. State Soc. CPA, Fin. Execs. Inst. Office: Solectron Corp 777 Gibraltar Dr Milpitas CA 95035-6328

WANG, WILLIAM KAI-SHENG, law educator; b. N.Y.C., Feb. 28, 1946; s. Yuan-Chao and Julia Ying-Ru (Li) W.; m. Kwan Kwan Tan, July 29, 1972; 1 child, Karen You-Chuan. BA, Amherst Coll., 1967; JD, Yale U., 1971. Bar: Calif. 1972. Asst. to mng. partner Gruss & Co., N.Y.C., 1971-72; asst. prof. law U. San Diego, 1972-74, asso. prof., 1974-77, prof., 1977-81, Hastings Coll. Law, U. Calif., San Francisco, 1981—. Vis. prof. law U. Calif., Davis, 1975-76, Hastings Coll. Law, U. Calif., 1980, U. Calif., L.A., 1990; Reuschlein vis. prof. law Villanova U., 1999; vis. prof. Bklyn. Law Sch., fall 2000; cons. to White House Domestic Policy Staff, Washington, 1979; participant, trustee, chair investment policy oversight group Law Sch. Admissions Coun.; mem. steering com. Legal Svcs. for Entrepreneurs. Co-author: Insider Trading, 1996, supplement, 2001; contbr. articles to newspapers, mags., scholarly jours. Mem. State Bar Calif., Am. Law Inst., Assn. of Am. Law Schs. (mem., then chair com. on audit and assn. investment policy 1995-98). Home: 455 39th Ave San Francisco CA 94121-1507 Office: U Calif Hastings Coll Law 200 McAllister St San Francisco CA 94102-4707 E-mail: wangw@uchastings.edu

WANG, WILLIAM SHI-YUAN, linguistics educator; b. Shanghai, China, Aug. 14, 1933; came to U.S., 1948, naturalized, 1960; s. Harper and Lily W.; children: Eugene, Yulun, Yumei, Yusi. A.B., Columbia U., 1955; M.A., U. Mich., 1956, Ph.D., 1960. Assoc. prof., chmn. dept. linguistics Ohio State U., Columbus, 1963-65; prof. linguistics U. Calif., Berkeley, 1966—, dir. Project on Linguistic Analysis, 1966—; prof. grad. sch., 1994—. Fellow Center Advanced Studies in Behavioral Scis., 1969-70, 83-84; sr. Fulbright lectr. in, Sweden, 1972, India, 1979 Author: Explorations in Language, 1991; editor: The Lexicon in Phonological Change, 1977, Human Communication, 1982, Language Writing and the Computer, 1986; co-editor: Individual Differences in Language Ability and Language Behavior, 1979; assoc. editor Language, 1967-73; founding editor Jour. Chinese Linguistics, 1973— ; contbr. numerous articles to profl. jours. Guggenheim Found. fellow, 1978-79 Mem. Linguistic Soc. Am., Acoustical Soc. Am., Academia Sinica, Internat. Assn. Chinese Linguistics (pres. 1992-93). Office: U Calif 2222 Piedmont Ave Berkeley CA 94720-2170

WANGER, OLIVER WINSTON, federal judge; b. L.A., Nov. 27, 1940; m. Lorrie A. Reinhart; children: Guy A., Christopher L., Andrew G., W. Derek, Oliver Winston II. Student, Colo. Sch. Mines, 1958-60; BS, U. So. Calif., 1963; LLB, U. Calif., Berkeley, 1966. Bar: Calif. 1967, U.S. Dist. Ct. (ea. dist.) Calif. 1969, U.S. Tax Ct. 1969, U.S. Dist. Ct. (cen. dist.) Calif. 1975, U.S. Dist. Ct. (so. dist.) Calif. 1977, U.S. Dist. Ct. (no. dist.) Calif. 1989, U.S. Ct. Appeals (9th cir.) 1989. Dep. dist. atty. Fresno (Calif.) County Dist. Atty., 1967-69; ptnr. Gallagher, Baker & Manock, Fresno, 1969-74; sr. ptnr. McCormick, Barstow, Sheppard, Wayte & Carruth, Fresno, 1974-91; judge U.S. Dist. Ct. (ea. dist.) Calif., Fresno, 1991—. Adj. prof. law Humphreys Coll. Law, Fresno, 1968-70. Fellow Am. Coll. Trial Lawyers, Internat. Acad. Trial Lawyers; mem. Am. Bd. Trial Advs. (pres. San Joaquin Valley chpt. 1987-89, nat. bd. dirs. 1989-91), Am. Bd. Profl. Liability Attys. (founder, diplomate), Calif. State Bar (mem. exec. com. litigation sect. 1989-92, mem. com. on fed. cts. 1989-90), San Joaquin Valley Am. Inn of Ct. (pres. 1992-93), Beta Gamma Sigma. Office: US Dist Ct 5104 US Courthouse 1130 O St Fresno CA 93721-2201

WANGSGARD, CHRIS PRINCE, lawyer; b. Ogden, Utah, July 16, 1941; s. Scott Maughn and Elizabeth (Prince) W.; m. Erica Gwilliam, June 25, 1979; children: Kirk, Sten, Dane. BS, U.S. Military Acad., 1963; JD, U. Utah, 1972. Bar: Utah 1972, U.S. Dist. Ct. (Utah) 1972, U.S. Ct. Appeals (10th cir.) 1972. Commd. 2d lt. U.S. Army, 1963, advanced through grades to capt., resigned, 1969; atty. Van Cott, Bagley, Cornwall & McCarthy, Salt Lake City, 1972-91, ptnr., 1977-91, Parsons Behle & Latimer, Salt Lake City, 1991—. Adj. prof. Coll. of Law U. of Utah, 1983-87. Mem. Am. Inns of Ct. (Master of the Bench). Office: Parsons Behle & Latimer 201 S Main St Ste 1800 Salt Lake City UT 84111-2218

WANLASS, DENNIS L. manufacturing executive; b. Salt Lake City, Jan. 14, 1949; s. Robert Hancock and Virginia Lee (Swofford) W.; m. Karen Sue Peterson, Nov. 9, 1966; children: Stacey Lee, Stephanie Ann, Dennis Robert, Lindsey Carol, Julie Ann. BS in Acctg., U. Utah, 1970. CPA. Sr. supr. Peat Marwick Mitchell, Salt Lake City, 1970-75; corp. controller Eastman Christensen Co., Salt Lake City, 1975-88; controller Geneva Steel, Vineyard, Utah, 1988-89, v.p., chief fin. officer, 1989—. Bd. dirs., exec. com. Jr. Achievement, Salt Lake City, 1990-91. Office: 10 S Geneva Rd Vineyard UT 84058

WARA, DIANE, dean; BS in Biology, Standord U., 1964; MD, U. Calif., Irvine, 1969. Intern in peds. Harbor Gen. Hosp., Torrance, Calif., 1969-70; resident in peds. U. Calif., San Francisco, 1970-72; fellow immunology divsn. dept. peds. USPHS, 1974-75; asst. prof. peds. U. Calif., San Francisco, 1975-79, assoc. prof. peds., 1979-84, prof. peds., 1984—, chief divsn. ped. immunology/rheumatology, program dir. ped., 1985—, assoc. dean for minority and women's affairs sch. med., 1991—. Mem. NIH study sect. on immunological scis., 1985-87, chair, 1987-89; vice chair universitywide task force on AIDS, 1989-92; vice chair ped. core com. AIDS Clinical Trials Group, 1991-92, chair ped. core com., 1992-94; mem. AIDS rsch. adv. com. NIH, 1990-95; mem. AIDS program adv. com. NIAID, 1990-94; mem. GCRC study sect., 1993-97, chair study sect., 1996-97. Contbr. articles to profl. jours. Recipient Eleanor Roosevelt award Am. Cancer Soc., 1983, Rsch. Career Devel. award Nat. Inst. of Child Health and Human Devel., 1978-83. Mem. NAS (elected to Inst. Medicine 1998), Am. Ped. Soc., Am. Rheumatism Assn., Am. Assn. Immunology, Am. Soc. for Clin. Investigation, Soc. for Ped. Rsch., Western Soc. for Ped. Rsch. (sec.-treas. 1979-83, pres. 1990-91). Office: U Calif Childrens Med Ctr 505 Parnassus Ave # M-601 San Francisco CA 94122-2722

WARD, CHESTER LAWRENCE, physician, retired county health official, retired military officer; b. Woodland, Yolo, Calif., June 8, 1932; s. Benjamin Briggs and Nora Elizabeth (Cash) W.; m. Sally Diane McCloud, Dec. 10, 1960; children: Katharine, Lynda. BA, U. Calif., Santa Barbara, 1955; MD, U. So. Calif., 1962; MPH, U. Calif., Berkeley, 1966; grad., Indsl. Coll. Armed Forces, 1978. Commd. 2d lt., inf. U.S. Army, 1954; advanced through grades to brig. gen., 1980; surgeon 5th Spl. Forces, Ft. Bragg, N.C. and Vietnam, 1963-64; chief aviation medicine, preventive medicine and aeromed. consultation service Ft. Rucker, Ala., 1967-68; surgeon Aviation Brigade and USA Vietnam Aviation Medicine Cons., 1968-69; flight surgeon Office of U.S. Army Surgeon Gen., 1970-71; physician The White House, Washington, 1971-75, 76; dir. environ. quality research U.S. Army Med. Research and Devel. Commd., 1975-76; comdr. Womack Community Hosp.; surgeon XVIII Airborne Corps, Ft. Bragg, N.C., 1978-80; comdr. William Beaumont Army Med. Center, El Paso, Tex., 1980-82; med. dir. Union Oil Co., Schaumburg, Ill., 1982-83, dir. domestic medicine Los Angeles, 1983-84; exec. dir. continuing med. edn. and clin. prof. emergency medicine U. So. Calif. Sch. Medicine, Los Angeles, 1984-85; dir., health officer Dept. Health, Butte County, Calif., 1985-95; cons., contractor, pvt. med. practice, 1996—. Apptd. by Gov. Wilson Calif. Commn. Emergency Med. Svcs., past commr.; elected trustee, pres. Oroville Union H.S. Dist., 1998—. Decorated D.S.M., Legion of Merit (2), Bronze Star, Air medal (5). Fellow Am. Coll. Preventive Medicine (past regent), Aerospace Med. Assn., Butte-Glenn County Med. Soc. (past pres.), Calif. Med. Assn. (past del.), No. Calif. Emergency Med. Svcs. (dir.), Ret. Officers Assn. (past chpt. pres.). Home: 4 Lemon Hill Ct Oroville CA 95966-3700 Office: Enloe Outpatient Ctr 888 Lakeside Vlg Commons Chico CA 95928-3979

WARD, DAVID SCHAD, screenwriter, film director; b. Providence, Oct. 24, 1947; s. Robert McCollum and Miriam (Schad) W.; children: Joaquin Atwood, Sylvana Soto. B.A., Pomona Coll., 1967; M.F.A., UCLA, 1970. Scriptwriter: films include Steelyard Blues, 1971, The Sting, 1973 (Acad award best original screenplay 1973), The Milagro Beanfield War, 1988, (with Nora Ephron and Jeff Arch) Sleepless in Seattle, 1993 (Academy award nominee Best Original Screenplay 1993), (with John Eskow, Ted

Elliott and Terry Rossio) The Mask of Zorro; writer, dir. films include Cannery Row, 1981, Major League, 1989, King Ralph, 1991, The Program, 1993, Major League II, 1995, Down Periscope, 1996. Mem. Dirs. Guild Am., Acad. Motion Picture Arts and Scis. Office: c/o CAA Ken Stovitz 9830 Wilshire Blvd Beverly Hills CA 90212-1804

WARD, DORIS M. county official; BA in Govt., MS in Edn., Ind. U.; MA in Counseling, San Francisco State U.; PhD in Edn., U. Calif., Berkeley. Tchr. Indpls. Pub. Schs., 1959-67, team leader, supr. tchg. interns, 1967-68; adviser, counselor San Francisco STEP program, 1969-70; coord. curriculum San Mateo County Office of Edn., Redwood City, Calif., 1968-89; mem. bd. govs. San Francisco C.C., 1973-79; mem. bd. suprs. City and County San Francisco, 1980-92, pres. bd. suprs., 1991-92, assessor, recorder, 1992—, elected assessor-recorder, 1996. Adj. assoc. prof. Sch. Edn. Calif. State U., 1969-70, 72-73; advisor to External Masters Degree Program, U. San Francisco, 1972-76; chief cons. Calif. Assembly on regional govt., 1989-92. Contbr. articles to ednl. and polit. jours. Bd. dirs. Nat. Dem. County Officials 1987—, pres. 1994—; mem. Dem. Nat. Com., 1992—, del. 1984, 88, 92, 96 convs. Named Woman of Yr., Zeta Phi Beta, 1984; recipient Disting. Alumni award San Francisco State U., 1993, Disting. Comty. award, U. San Francisco, 1994, Spl. Merit award Sun Reporter Newspaper and numerous other awards for comty. svc. by activist orgns; grantee: NDEA, 1967, 68, Ind. State U., Terre Haute, Ind., Lilly Found., 1967, Rockefeller Found., U. Calif., Berkeley, 1974. Mem. Bay Area Assessors Assn. (sec. 1994, v.p. 95, pres. 96), Calif. Assessors' Assn. (mem. legis. com. 1993, exec. com. 95), Nat. Assn. Counties (bd. dirs. 1989-91, chair human svcs. and edn., 1991-92), Nat. Assn. Black County Officials (bd. dirs. 1987—, regional dir. 1987—), Nat. League of Cities (bd. dirs. 1991-92, vice chair and steering com. Fed. Adminstrn. Intergovtl. Rels. 1990-91), Nat. Black Caucus of Local Elected Officials (bd. dirs. 1987-95), Pi Sigma Alpha, Pi Lambda Theta. Office: City County San Francisco Assessor Recorder Office Rm 190 1 Dr Carlton B Goodlett Pl San Francisco CA 94102-4603

WARD, JERRY, state legislator, real estate executive; b. Anchorage, July 19, 1948; m. Margaret Ward; children: Katheleen Bloodgood, Kirsten Deacon, Jeri Ann. Real estate businessman; mem. Alaska Ho. of Reps., 1982-96, Alaska Senate, Dist. E, Juneau, 1996—; chair state affairs com., chair transp. com. Alaska Senate, mem. cmty. and regional affairs com. Past mem. Mcpl. Health Commn.; commr. Mcpl. Transp., Mcpl. Vet. Affairs; rural affairs coord. Dept. Corrections; legis. aide. Decorated Vietnam Svc. medal. Mem. VFW, Am. Legion. Republican. Avocations: fishing, hunting, boating. Office: State Capitol 120 4th St Rm 423 Juneau AK 99801-1142 Fax: 907-465-3766. E-mail: senatorjerryward@legis.state.ak.us

WARD, JOHN J. bishop; b. Los Angeles, 1920; Student, St. John's Sem., Camarillo, Calif., Catholic U. Am. Ordained priest, Roman Catholic Ch., 1946. Apptd. titular bishop of Bria, aux. bishop Diocese of Los Angels Roman Cath. Ch., 1963—, vicar gen., 1963—. Office: Archdiocese LA 3424 Wilshire Blvd Los Angeles CA 90010-2241

WARD, JOHN ROBERT, physician, educator; b. Salt Lake City, Nov. 23, 1923; s. John I. and Clara (Elzi) W.; m. Norma Harris, Nov. 5, 1948; children: John Harris, Pamela Lyn, Robert Scott, James Alan. BS, U. Utah, 1944, MD, 1946; MPH, U. Calif., Berkeley, 1967; Masters, Am. Coll. of Rheumatology, 1990. Diplomate Am. Bd. Internal Medicine. Intern Salt Lake County Gen. Hosp., 1947-48, asst. resident, 1949-50, resident physician internal medicine, 1950-51, asst. physician, 1957-58, assoc. physician, 1958-69, clin. fellow medicine Harvard U., Boston, 1955-57, instr. medicine U. Utah Med. Sch., Salt Lake City, 1954-58, asst. prof., 1958-63, assoc. prof., 1963, prof., 1966-93, chmn. dept. preventive medicine, 1966-70, emeritus prof. internal medicine, 1993—, chief div. rheumatology, 1957-88; prof. internal medicine emeritus U. Utah. Med. Sch., Salt Lake City, 1994—; attending physician internal medicine Salt Lake City VA Hosp., 1957-70. Nora Eccles Harrison prof. medicine, Am. Coll. Rheumatology Served as capt. M.C. AUS, 1951-53. Master Am. Coll. Rheumatology; fellow ACP; mem. Am. Coll. Rheumatology (Disting. rheumatologist award 1994), Utah State Med. Assn. (hon. pres. 1994-95), U. Utah Sch. Medicine Alumni Assn. (Disting. Alumnus 1996). Home: 1249 E 3770 S Salt Lake City UT 84106-2446 Office: U Utah Health Scis Ctr 50 N Medical Dr Salt Lake City UT 84132-0001

WARD, LESLIE ALLYSON, journalist, editor; b. L.A., June 3, 1946; d. Harold Gordon and Marilyn Lucille (Dahlstead) W.; m. Robert L. Biggs, 1971 (div. 1977); m. Colman Robert Andrews, May 26, 1979 (div. 1988). AA, Coll. San Mateo, 1966; BA, UCLA, 1968, MJ, 1971. Reporter, researcher L.A. Bur. Life mag., 1971-72; reporter, news asst. L.A. bur. N.Y. Times, 1973-76; sr. editor New West mag., L.A., 1976-78, 79-80; L.A. bur. chief US mag., 1978-79; Sunday style editor L.A. Herald Examiner, 1981-82, editor-in-chief Sunday mags., 1982-83, Olympics editor, 1984, sports editor, 1985-86, sr. writer, 1986; sr. editor L.A. Times Mag., 1988-90; travel editor L.A. Times, 1990—. Democrat. Office: LA Times Times Mirror Sq Los Angeles CA 90053

WARD, MILTON HAWKINS, former mining company executive; b. Bessemer, Ala., Aug. 1, 1932; s. William Howard and Mae Ivy (Smith) W.; m. Sylvia Adele Randle, June 30, 1951; children: Jeffrey Randle, Lisa Adele. BS in Mining Engring., U. Ala., 1955, MS in Engring., 1981; MBA, U. N.Mex., 1974; DEng (hon.), Colo. Sch. of Mines, 1994; PhD, U. London, 1995. Registered profl. engr., Tex., Ala. Supr., engr. San Manuel (Ariz.) Copper Corp., 1955-60; gen. supt. of mines Kerr-McGee Corp., Oklahoma City, 1960-66; gen. mgr. Homestake Mining Co., Grants, 1966-70; v.p. ops. Ranchers Exploration & Devel. Corp., Albuquerque, 1970-74; pres., COO Freeport-McMoRan, Inc., New Orleans, 1974-92, also bd. dirs.; chmn., pres. CEO Cyprus Amax Minerals Co., Englewood, Colo., 1992-99; dir. Kinross Gold (formerly Amax Gold Inc.), 1993-99. Bd. dirs. Mineral Info. Inst., Inc., Internat. Copper Assn.; mem. Geoscience and Environment Ctr's. adv. bd. Sandia Nat. Labs., 1998—. Bd. trustees Western Regional Coun.; bd. dirs. Smithsonian Nat. Mus. Natural History, Nat. Mining Hall of Fame and Mus.; disting. engring. fellow U. Ala., mem. Pres.'s cabinet. Recipient Daniel C. Jackling award and Saunders gold medal Soc. Mining, Metallurgy and Exploration, 1992; inductee Am. Mining Hall of Fame, State of Ala. Engring. Hall of Fame, 1996; Honoree of Yr. Achievement Rewards Coll. Scientists, 1998-99. Fellow Inst. Mining and Metallurgy (London); mem. NAE, AIME (former sect. chmn., Disting. Mem. award), Am. Mining Congress, Nat. Mining Assn. (dir.), Am. Australian Assn., Mining and Metall. Soc. Am. (pres., exec. com.), Can. Inst. Mining and Metall., Nat. Rsch. Coun. (com. on earth and scis.), NAM (natural resources com.), Internat. Copper Assn. (bd. dirs.), Copper Club, Met. Club (Washington), Met. Club (Englewood), Las Campanas Country Club (Santa Fe, N.M.), Ventana Canyon Country Club (Tucson, Ariz.). Republican. Presbyterian. Office: Cyprus Amax Minerals Co Kinross Gold Corp 40 King St W 57th Fl Toronto ON 85004-3012 Canada M5H 3Y2

WARD, RICHARD, computer company executive; B in Aero. Engring., St. Louis U. Customer svc. rep. Hamilton Electro Sales Avnet, Inc., L.A., 1969-72, br. mgr. Balt. office, 1972-75, regional mgr. mid-Atlantic region, 1975-77, area dir. ea. U.S., v.p., pres. desktop and sys. bus. units, exec. v.p. Avnet Computer, corp. sr. v.p. parent co., group pres. Avnet Computer Mktg. Group, 1994—. With USN. Office: Corp Hdqs 3011 S 52d St Tempe AZ 85282

WARD, ROB, company executive; Pres. Westcor Ptnrs., Phoenix, 1989—. Office: 11411 N Tatum Blvd Phoenix AZ 85028-2305

WARD, WILLIAM E. career officer; b. Balt. BA in Polit. Sci., Morgan State U., 1971; M in Polit. Sci., Pa. State U., 1979; grad., Command and Gen. Staff Coll., Army War Coll. Commd. 2d lt. U.S. Army, advanced through grades to maj. gen.; various assignments U.S. and overseas; asst. prof. dept. social scis. U.S. Mil. Acad.; logistics staff officer 210th Field Arty. Group, Herzo Base, Germany, 1983-85; from cmty. exec. officer to exec. officer 3d Inf. Divsn., Aschaffenburg, Germany, 1985; European/NATO plans officer Army Hdqrs., Washington; comdr. 5th bn. 9th Inf. Rgt., 1988-92, 2d Commando Brigade 10th Mt. Divsn., 1992; exec. officer to vice chief of staff of Army Army Hdqrs., Washington; dep. dir. ops. Nat. Mil. Command Ctr., 1995-96; asst. divsn. comdr. for support 82d Airborne Divsn., 1996-98; U.S. def. rep., chief Office Mil. Coop., Egypt; comdr. 25th Inf. Divsn. U.S. Army Pacific, Fort Shaffer, Hawaii. Decorated Def. Superior Svc. medal with oak leaf cluster, Legion of Merit with 2 oak leaf clusters, Def. Meritorious Svc. medal, Meritorious Svc. medal with 6 oak leaf clusters, Presdl. Order of Merit (Arab Rep. of Egypt).

WARDLAW, KIM A.M. federal judge; b. San Francisco, July 2, 1954; m. William M. Wardlaw Sr., Sept. 8, 1984. Student, Santa Clara U., 1972-73, Foothill C.C., Los Altos Hills, Calif., 1973-74; AB in Comm. summa cum laude, UCLA, 1976, JD with honors, 1979. Bar: Calif., U.S. Dist. Ct. (cen. dist.) Calif. 1979, U.S. Dist. Ct. (so. dist.) Calif. 1982, U.S. Dist. Ct. Nev. 1985, U.S. Dist. Ct. (no. dist.) Calif. 1992, U.S. Dist. Ct Mont. 1993, U.S. Dist. Ct. Minn. 1994, U.S. Dist. Ct. (no. dist.) Ala. 1994, U.S. Dist. Ct. (so. dist.) Miss. 1995, U.S. Supreme Ct. Law clk. U.S. Dist. Ct. Cen. Dist. Calif., 1979-80; assoc. O'Melveny and Myers, 1980-87, ptnr., 1987-95; circ. judge U.S. Dist. Ct. Calif., L.A., 1995-98; cir. judge U.S. Ct. Appeals (9th cir.), 1998—. Presdl. transition team Dept. Justice, Washington, 1993; mayoral transition Team City of L.A., 1995—; bd. govs., vice-chair UCLA Ctr. for Comm. Policy, 1994—; cons. in field. Co-author: The Encyclopedia of the American Constitution, 1986; contbr. articles to profl. jours. Pres. Women Lawyers Pub. Action Grant Found., 1986-87; del. Dem. Nat. Conv., 1992; founding mem. L.A. Chamber Orchestra, 1992—; active Legal Def. and Edn. Fund, Calif. Leadership Coun., 1993—, Blue Ribbon of L.A. Music Ctr., 1993—. Named one of Most Prominent Bus. Attys. in L.A. County, L.A. Bus. Jour., 1995; recipient Buddy award NOW, 1995. Mem. ABA, NOW, Mex.-Am. Bar Assn. L.A. County, Calif. Women Lawyers, Women Lawyers Assn. L.A., L.A. County Bar Assn. (trustee 1993-94), Assn. Bus. Trial Lawyers (gov. 1988—), Orgn. Women Execs., Downtown Women Ptnrs, Chancery Club, Breakfast Club, Hollywood Womens Polit. Com., City Club Bunker Hill, Phi Beta Kappa. Office: US Dist Ct 9th Cir 125 S Grand Ave Rm 400 Pasadena CA 91109*

WARDLOW, BILL, record industry consultant, entertainer; b. Columbus, Ohio, Jan. 2, 1921; s. Clayton Jesse and Angeline Naomi (Peckham) W. B.B.A., Ohio State U., 1942; cert., Am. Mgmt. Assn., N.Y.C., 1964. Vice pres. Capitol Records, Los Angeles, 1947-56; gen. mgr. Columbia Record Club, N.Y.C., 1957-61; exec. v.p. Hammond Industries, N.Y.C., 1961-64; assoc. pub. Billboard Mag., N.Y.C., 1964-83; pres. Bill Wardlow & Assocs., Los Angeles, 1983—; ptnr. Dealmakers Connection, Inc., Los Angeles, 1983—; cons. to disco industry, worldwide, 1974-83. Author: (preface) This Business of Disco, 1976, (biography) Against All Odds, 1999; TV appearances include 60 Minutes, Merv Griffin Show, Mike Douglas Show, Ted Turner Network, Good Morning America. Named Father of Disco, Rec. Industry Am., 1976; reipient numerous Gold and Platinum records, 1974-83 Mem. Regines Club (N.Y.C. and Paris). Episcopalian. Home and Office: 2212 Laurel Canyon Blvd Los Angeles CA 90046-1503

WARD-STEINMAN, DAVID, composer, music educator, pianist; b. Alexandria, La., Nov. 6, 1936; s. Irving Steinman and Daisy Leila (Ward) W.-S.; m. Susan Diana Lucas, Dec. 28, 1956 (div. 1993); children: Jenna, Matthew; m. Patrice Dawn Madura, May 28, 2001. MusB cum laude, Fla. State U., 1957; MusM, U. Ill., 1958, DMA, 1961; studies with Nadia Boulanger, Paris, 1958-59; postdoctoral vis. fellow, Princeton U., 1970. Grad. instr. U. Ill., 1957-58; mem. faculty San Diego State U., 1961—, prof. music, 1968—, dir. comprehensive musicianship program, 1972—, composer in residence, 1961—, univ. research lectr., 1986-87. Mem. summer faculty Eastman Sch. Music Workshop, 1969; Ford Found. composer in residence Tampa Bay (Fla.) Area, 1970-72, Brevard Music Ctr., N.C., summer 1986; acad. cons. U. North Sumatra (Indonesia), 1982; concert and lecture tour U.S. Info. Agy., Indonesia, 1982; mem. faculty Coll. Music Soc. Nat. Inst. for Music in Gen. Studies, U. Colo., 1983, 84, Calif. State Summer Sch. for the Arts, Loyola Marymount U., 1988; master tchr. in residence Atlantic Ctr. for the Arts, New Smyrna Beach, Fla., summer 1996; vis. artist in residence Victorian Ctr. for the Arts, Melbourne, Australia, summer 1997. Composer: Symphony, 1959, Prelude & Toccata for orch., 1962, Concerto No. 2 for chamber orch., 1962, ballet Western Orpheus, 1964, Cello Concerto, 1966, These Three ballet, 1966, The Tale of Issoumbochi chamber opera, 1968, Rituals for Dancers and Musicians, 1971, Antares, 1971, Arcturus, 1972, The Tracker, 1976, Brancusi's Brass Beds, 1977; oratorio Song of Moses, 1964; Jazz Tangents, 1967, Childs Play, 1968; 3-act opera Tamar, 1977; Golden Apples, 1981; choral suite Of Wind and Water, 1982; Christmas cantata And In These Times, 1982; Moiré for piano and chamber ensemble, 1983, And Waken Green, song cycle on poems by Douglas Worth, 1983, Olympics Overture for orchestra, 1984, Children's Corner Revisited, song cycle, 1984, Summer Suite for oboe and piano, 1984, Quintessence for double quintet and percussion, 1985, Chroma concerto for multiple keyboards, percussion and chamber orch., 1985, Winging It for chamber orchestra, 1986, Elegy for Astronauts, for orchestra, 1986, What's Left for piano, 1987, Gemini for 2 guitars, 1988, Intersections II: Borobudur, Under Capricorn, 1989, Voices from the Gallery, 1990, Cinnabar for viola and piano, 1991, Seasons Fantastic for chorus and harp, 1992, Cinnabar Concerto for Viola and Chamber Orchestra, 1993, Night Winds Quintet # 2 for woodwinds, 1993, Double Concerto for Two Violins and Orchestra, 1995, Prisms and Reflections (3rd Piano Sonata), 1996, Millenium Fanfare for Symph. Orch., 2000, Millenium Dances for Symph. Orch., 2001; recs. include Fragments from Sappho, 1969; Duo for cello and piano, 1974, Childs Play for bassoon and piano, 1974, The Tracker, 1989, Brancusi's Brass Beds, 1984, concert suite from Western Orpheus, 1987, Sonata for Piano Fortified, 1987, Moiré, 1987, 3 Songs for Clarinet and Piano, 1987, Concerto #2 for Chamber Orchestra, 1990, Prisms and Reflections, 1999, Cinnabar, 1999, Sonata for Piano Fortified, 1999, Night Winds, 1999, Borobudur, 1999, Cello Concerto, 2000, Cinnabar Concerto, 2000, Chroma Concerto, 2000, Millenium Dances, 2001; commd. by Chgo. Symphony, Joffrey Ballet, San Diego Symphony, numerous others; author: (with Susan L. Ward-Steinman) Comparative Anthology of Musical Forms, 2 vols, 1976, Toward a Comparative Structural Theory of the Arts, 1989. Recipient Joseph H. Bearns prize in Music Columbia U., 1961, SAI Am. Music award, 1962, Dohnanyi award Fla. State U., 1965, ann. BMI awards, 1970—, Broadcast Music prize, 1954, 55, 60, 61; named Outstanding Prof., Calif. State Univs. and Colls., 1968, Outstanding Alumnus of Yr., Fla. State U., 1976; Fulbright sr. scholar La Trobe U. and Victorian Coll. Arts, Victorian Arts Ctr., Melbourne, Australia, 1989-90. Mem. Coll. Music Soc. (nat. bd. for composition 1991-93), Broadcast Music, Inc., Soc. of Composers, inc., Nat. Assn. of Composers U.S.A., Golden State Flying Club. Presbyterian. Office: San Diego State U Dept Music San Diego CA 92182 E-mail: dwardste@mail.sdsu.edu

WARE, JAMES W. federal judge; b. 1946; BA, Calif. Luth. U., 1969; JD, Stanford U., 1972. Assoc. Blase, Valentine & Klein, Palo Alto, Calif., 1972-77, ptnr., 1977; judge Santa Clara County Superior Ct., U.S. Dist. Ct. (no. dist.) Calif., 1990—. Pro bono East Palo Alto Law Project. Active Am. Leadership Forum; mem. bd. visitors Stanford Law Sch.; active Martin Luther King Papers Project. 2nd lt. USAR, 1969-86. Office: US Dist Cts 280 S 1st St Rm 4150 San Jose CA 95113-3002

WARE, WILLIS HOWARD, computer scientist; b. Atlantic City, Aug. 31, 1920; s. Willis and Ethel (Rosswork) W.; m. Floy Hoffer, Oct. 10, 1943; children— Deborah Susanne Ware Pinson, David Willis, Alison Floy Ware Manoli. BSEE, U. Pa., 1941; MSEE, MIT, 1942; PhD in Elec. Engring, Princeton U., 1951. Research engr. Hazeltine Electronics Corp., Little Neck, N.Y., 1942-46; mem. research staff Inst. Advanced Study, Princeton, N.J., 1946-51, North Am. Aviation, Downey, Calif., 1951-52; mem. corp. research staff, research engr. Rand Corp., Santa Monica, 1952—. Adj. prof. UCLA Extension Service, 1955-68; first chmn. Am. Fedn. Info. Processing Socs., 1961, 62; chmn. HEW sec.'s Adv. Com. on Automated Personal Data Systems, 1971-73; mem. Privacy Protection Study Commn., 1975-77, vice chmn., 1975-77; mem. numerous other adv. groups, spl. coms. for fed. govt., 1959— Author: Digital Computer Technology and Design, vols. I and II, 1963. Recipient Computers Scis. Man of Yr. award Data Processing Mgmt. Assn., 1975, Exceptional Civilian Svc. medal USAF, 1979, Disting. Svc. award Am. Fedn. Info. Processing Socs., 1986, Nat. Computer Sys. Security award Nat. Computer Sys. Lab./Nat. Computer Security Ctr., 1989, Computer Pioneer award IEEE Computer Soc., 1993, Pioneer award Electronic Frontier Found., 1995, Kristain Beckman award Internat. Fedn. Info. Processing, 1999; named one of Fed. 100 of 1994, Fed. Computer Week. Fellow IEEE (Centennial medal 1984), AAAS, Assn. for Computing Machinery; mem. NAE, AIAA, Sigma Xi, Eta Kappa Nu, Pi Mu Epsilon, Tau Beta Pi. Office: The Rand Corp 1700 Main St Santa Monica CA 90406-3297 E-mail: willis@rand.org

WAREHAM, JOHN L. electronics executive; B in Pharmacy, Creighton U.; MBA, U. Wash. With SmithKline Beecham Corp., Phila., 1968-84, pres. Norden Labs., 1979-84; v.p. diagnostics sys. group Beckman Coulter Inc., Fullerton, Calif., 1984—, pres., COO, 1993-98, pres., CEO, chmn. bd., 1998—. Office: Beckman Coulter Inc 4300 N Harbor Blvd Fullerton CA 92834-3100

WARK, ROBERT RODGER, curator; b. Edmonton, Can., Oct. 7, 1924; came to U.S., 1948, naturalized, 1970; s. Joseph Henry and Louise (Rodger) W. BA, U. Alta., 1944, MA, 1946, LLD (hon.), 1986; AM, Harvard, 1949, PhD, 1952. Instr. art Harvard U., 1952-54; instr. history art Yale U., 1954-56; curator art Henry E. Huntington Library and Art Gallery, San Marino, Calif., 1956-90. Lectr. art Calif. Inst. Tech., 1960-91, UCLA, 1966-80. Author: Sculpture in the Huntington Collection, 1959, French Decorative Art in the Huntington Collection, 1961, Rowlandson's Drawings for a Tour in a Post Chaise, 1963, Rowlandson's Drawings for the English Dance of Death, 1966, Isaac Cruikshank's Drawings for Drolls, 1968, Early British Drawings in the Huntington Collection 1600-1750, 1969, Drawings by John Flaxman, 1970, Ten British Pictures 1740-1840, 1971, Meet the Ladies: Personalities in Huntington Portraits, 1972, Drawings from the Turner Shakespeare, 1973, Drawings by Thomas Rowlandson in the Huntington Collection, 1975, British Silver in the Huntington Collection, 1978; editor: Sir Joshua Reynolds: Discourses on Art, 1959. Served with RCAF, 1944-45; Served with RCNVR, 1945. Mem. Coll. Art Assn. Home: 1330 Lombardy Rd Pasadena CA 91106-4120 Office: Huntington Libr 1151 Oxford Rd San Marino CA 91108-1299

WARMER, RICHARD CRAIG, lawyer; b. Los Angeles, Aug. 12, 1936; s. George A. and Marian L. (Paine) W.; children: Craig McEchron, Alexander Richard. AB, Occidental Coll., 1958; MA, Tufts U., 1959; LLB, NYU, 1962. Bar: Calif. 1963, D.C. 1976. Assoc. O'Melveny & Myers, LLP, Los Angeles, 1962-69, ptnr., 1970-75, mng. ptnr. Washington, 1976-92, mem. mgmt. com., 1986-92, with San Francisco, 1994—. Speaker in field. Contbr. articles to profl. jours. Trustee Law Ctr. Found. NYU, 1981-94; dir. Headland Ctr. for Arts, San Francisco Jazz Orgn. Mem. ABA, D.C. Bar, State Bar Calif., Order of Coif, Phi Beta Kappa, Cosmos Club. Home: 2224 Green St San Francisco CA 94123-4710 Office: O'Melveny & Myers LLP Embarcadero Ctr W 275 Battery St San Francisco CA 94111-3305 E-mail: rwarmer@omm.com

WARNATH, MAXINE AMMER, organizational psychologist, mediator; b. N.Y.C., Dec. 3, 1928; d. Philip and Jeanette Ammer; m. Charles Frederick Warnath, Aug. 20, 1952; children: Stephen Charles, Cindy Ruth. BA, Bklyn. Coll., 1949; MA, Columbia U., 1951, EdD, 1982. Lic. lic. psychologist Oreg. Various profl. positions Hunter Coll., U. Minn., U. Nebr., U. Oreg., 1951-62; asst. prof. psychology Oreg. Coll. Edn., Monmouth, 1962-77; assoc. prof. psychology, chmn. dept. psychology & spl. edn. Western Oreg. U., Monmouth, 1978-83, prof., 1983-96, prof. emeritus, 1996—. Dir. organizational psychology program, 1983—96; pres. Profl. Perspective Internat., Salem, Oreg., 1987—; cons., dir. Orgn. R&D , Salem, Oreg., 1983—87; seminar leader Endeavors for Excellence program. Author: (novels) Power Dynamism, 1987. Mem.: APA (com. pre-coll. psychology 1970—74), Am. Psychol. Soc., N.Y. Acad. Scis., Oreg. Acad. Sci., Oreg. Psychol. Assn. (pres. 1980—81, pres.-elect 1979—80, legis. liaison 1977—78), Western Psychol. Assn. Office: Profl Perspectives Internat PO Box 2265 Salem OR 97308-2265 E-mail: warnatm@wou.edu

WARNER, DENNIS ALLAN, psychology educator; b. Idaho Falls, Idaho, Apr. 27, 1940; s. Perry and Marcia E. (Finlayson) W.; m. Charyl Ann DeHart, Dec. 12, 1962; children: Lisa Rae, Sara Michelle, David Perry, Matthew Arie. BS, Brigham Young U., 1964; MS with honors, U. Oreg., 1966, PhD, 1968. Asst. prof. edn. Wash. State U., Pullman, 1968-72, assoc. prof. edn., 1972-78, prof. edn., 1978-85, dir. tchr. edn., 1983-85, prof., chmn. ednl. counseling psychology, 1985-93, interim dir. Partnership Ctr., 1993-94, prof. edn. leadership and counseling psychology Pulman, 1994—, assoc. dean Coll. Edn., 1999—. Vis. asst. prof. psychology U. Idaho, Moscow, 1971. Author: Interpreting and Improving Student Test Performance, 1982; contbr. articles to profl. jours. Postdoctoral research assoc. U. Kans., 1976-77. Fellow APA; mem. Delta Kappa. Mem. LDS Ch. Home: 645 SW Mies St Pullman WA 99163-2057 Office: Wash State Univ Dept Ednl & Counsel Psych Cleveland Hl Rm 160B Pullman WA 99164-0001 E-mail: dawarner@wsu.edu

WARNER, HAROLD CLAY, JR. banker, investment management executive; b. Knoxville, Tenn., Feb. 24, 1939; s. Harold Clay and Mary Frances (Waters) W.; m. Patricia Alice Rethorst, Sept. 1, 1961; children— Martha Lee, Carol Frances. B.S. in Econs, U. Tenn., 1961, Ph.D., 1965. Asst. to pres. First Fed. Savs., Savannah, Ga., 1965-67; v.p. and economist No. Trust Co., Chgo., 1967-73; sr. v.p. and chief economist Crocker Nat. Bank, San Francisco, 1974-79, sr. v.p. liability mgmt., 1979-82; exec. v.p., dir. fixed income mgmt. BA Investment Mgmt. Corp., 1982-84, dir., pres., chief operating officer, 1984-86; dir., pres. Montgomery St. Income Securities, Inc., 1984-86; sr. v.p. Bank of Am., San Francisco, 1982-86; chmn. BA Investment Mgmt. Internat., Ltd., 1985-86; pres. Arthur D. Gimbel, Inc., San Mateo, Calif., 1986-87; exec. v.p., chief investment officer Riggs Nat. Bank Washington, 1987-88; chmn. Riggs Investment Mgmt. Corp., 1988-89; sr. v.p., chief economist Bank of Calif., San Francisco, 1989-93; pres., chief investment officer MERUS Capital Mgmt., San Francisco, 1989-93; pres. Govett Asset Mgmt. Co., 1993-95, Govett Fin. Svcs. Ltd., 1993-95; pres., COO Fisher Investments, Inc., Woodside, Calif., 1996; pres. Warner Fiduciary Counsel, LLC, San Francisco, 1997; sr. v.p. Mellon Pvt. Asset Mgmt., San Francisco, 1998—. Lectr. dept.

econs. U. Tenn., 1962-63, Grad. Sch. Bus., Loyola U., Chgo., 1969-73; lectr. Pacific Coast Banking Sch., U. Wash., 1978-79. Bd. trustees Children's Hosp., Oakland, Calif. NDEA fellow, 1961-64 Mem. Burlingame Country Club, Phi Gamma Delta, Phi Eta Sigma, Beta Gamma Sigma, Omicron Delta Kappa, Phi Kappa Phi. Home: PO Box 2449 Yountville CA 94599-2449 Office: 1 Embarcadero Ctr Ste 2200 San Francisco CA 94111-3711 E-mail: warnerfc@msn.com, warner.hc@mellon.com

WARNER, HOMER R. physiologist, educator; b. Salt Lake City, Apr. 18, 1922; married, 1946; 6 children. BA, U. Utah, 1946, MD, 1949; PhD in Physiology, U. Minn., 1953; Doctorate (hon.), Brigham Young U., 1971, U. Linkoping, Sweden, 1990. Intern Parkland Hosp., Dallas, 1949-50; resident in medicine U. Minn. Hosp., 1950-51; fellow Mayo Clinic, 1951-52, U. Minn., 1952-53; rsch. instr. dept. internal medicine U. Utah, Salt Lake City, 1953-54, asst. rsch. prof. dept. physiology, 1957-64, prof., chmn. dept. biophysiology and bioengring., 1964-73, rsch. prof. dept. surgery, 1966-83, spl. asst. info. mgmt. to v.p. health sci., 1983-93, prof., chmn. dept. medicine informatics, 1973-96, dir., chmn. computer health sci., 1993-96, prof. emeritus, 1996—. Dir. cardiovasc. lab. Latter-Day Sts. Hosp., 1954-70; mem. adv. com. computers NIH, 1961-63, chmn. computer rsch. study sect., 1963-66; vis. prof. U. Hawaii, 1968, U. So. Calif., 1972; mem. Biomed. Libr. Rev. Com., Nat. Libr. Medicine, 1982-86, chmn. grant rev. study sect., 1985-86. Recipient James E. Talmage Sci. Achievement award, 1968. Mem. Inst. Medicine-NAS (sr.), Am. Physiol. Soc., Am. Coll. Med. Informatics (pres. 1989). Office: U Utah Sch Medicine Dept Med Informatics Ab193 Med Ctr Salt Lake City UT 84132-0001

WARNER, JOHN D. aerospace company executive; b. Glendale, Calif., Jan. 4, 1940; Student, Drury Coll.; bachelor's, master's, PhD in Aero. Engring., U. Mich. Engr. supersonic transport program The Boeing Co., 1968—, engr. Boeing Comml. Airplanes Group, mgr. NASA terminal configured flight-test activity Va., 1974, chief tech. Boeing Comml. Airplanes Group, dir. devel. new digital auto pilot and navigation sys., 1980-82, mgr. airplane sys. design B-2 program, 1982-85, chief engr., 1985-87, advanced program mgr., 1987, v.p. engring. Boeing Comml. Airplanes Group, 1989-91, v.p. computing, 1991, pres. Boeing computer svcs., 1993-95, pres. Boeing info. and support svcs., 1995-97, sr. v.p., chief adminstrv. officer, 1997—; Boeing Sloan fellow Grad. Sch. Bus. Stanford U., 1976. Active various cmty. orgns.; bd. dirs. Pacific Sci. Ctr., Seattle Alliance Edn., Seattle Found., United Way Endowement Bd., Partnership for Learning, Corp. Coun. Arts, Washington Transp. Alliance. Fellow AIA, Royal Aero. Soc.; mem. NAE. Office: The Boeing Co 7755 E Marginal Way S Seattle WA 98108

WARNER, JOHN HILLIARD, JR. technical services, military and commercial systems and software company executive; b. Santa Monica, Calif., Mar. 2, 1941; s. John Hilliard and Irene Anne (Oliva) W.; m. Helga Magdalena Farrington, Sept. 4, 1961; children: Tania Renee, James Michael. BS in Engring. with honors, UCLA, 1963, MS in Engring., 1965, PhD in Engring., 1967. Mem. staff Marquardt Corp., Van Nuys, Calif., 1963; mem. faculty West Coast U., Los Angeles, 1969-72; mem. staff TRW Systems Group, Redondo Beach, Calif., 1967-70, sect. mgr., 1970-73; mem. staff Sci. Applications Internat. Corp., San Diego, 1973-75, asst. v.p., 1975-77, v.p., 1977-80, corp. v.p., 1980-81, sr. v.p., 1981-87, sector v.p., 1987-89; exec. v.p. Sci. Applications Internat Corp., San Diego, 1989-96, bd. dirs., 1988—; corp. exec. v.p. Sci. Applications Internat. Corp., San Diego, 1996—. Cons. Rand Corp., Santa Monica, 1964-66; bd. dirs. AMSEC LLC, OnlineSuppliers.com. Contbr. articles to profl. jours. Trustee Scripps Health, 2001—; bd. dirs. Corp. Dirs. Forum, 2001—. AEC fellow, 1963, 66, NSF fellow, 1964, 65. Mem. AIAA, Healthcare Info. and Mgmt. Sys. Soc., Assn. U.S. Army, Air Force Assn. Am. Def. Preparedness Assn., Am. Security Coun., Armed Forces Communications and Electronics Assn., Navy League U.S., La Jolla Chamber Music Soc. (bd. dirs. 1990-97, adv. bd. 1998—), San Diego C. of C. (bd. dirs. 2000—), Calif. C. of C. (bd. dirs. 2000—), Calif. Bus. Roundtable, Sigma Nu, Tau Beta Pi. Methodist. Avocations: bicycling, fishing, music. Office: SAIC 10260 Campus Point Dr San Diego CA 92121-1522

WARNER, PAUL M. prosecutor; BA, Brigham Young U., 1973, JD, 1976, MPA, 1984. With Utah Atty. Gen.'s Office, 1991-98; U.S. atty. Utah dist. U.S. Dept. Justice, 1998—. Office: 185 S St Ste 400 Salt Lake City UT 84103-4139

WARNER, VINCENT W. bishop; Bishop Diocese of Olympia, Seattle, 1990—. Office: Diocese of Olympia PO Box 12126 1551 10th Ave E Seattle WA 98102-4298

WARNKING, REINHARD JOHANNES, medical device company executive; M Electronics, U. RWTH, Achen, Germany, 1979. Apprentice Stadtwerke Bremerhaven, Germany, 1966-69, rsch. asst. Helmholtz-Inst. for Biomed. Engring., 1979-80; in charge tech. documentation Kranzbuhler Medizin Elektronik, Solingen, Germany, 1981-84, mgr. R & D Germany, 1983-84; mgr. advanced devel., then program mgr. ADR Ultrasound, Phoenix, 1984-85; tech. dir. with powr of atty. Squibb Med. Sys., Solingen, 1985-86, gen. mgr., then v.p. internat., 1986-89; founder Warnking Medizintechnik GmbH (acquired by Dornier Medizin), Solingen, 1989-90; dept. head with power of atty., orgnizer ultrasound divsn. Dornier Medizintechnik GmbH, Solingen, 1990, head ultrasound divsn. Germering, Germany, 1990-93; pres., CEO Acoustic Imaging Techs. Corp., Phoenix, 1991-83; pres., COO, EndoSonics Corp., Rancho Cordova, Calif., 1993-95, CEO, 1995—. Contbr. articles to sci. jours.; patentee for automatical optimization of image uniformity of ultrasound imaging sys., lithotripter comprizing a coupling detector. Res. officer German Army, 1972-73. Office: EndoSonics Corp 2870 Kilgore Rd Rancho Cordova CA 95670-6133

WARNOCK, JOHN EDWARD, computer company executive; b. Salt Lake City, Oct. 6, 1940; BS in Math. and Philosophy, U. Utah, 1961, MS in Math., 1964, PhD in Elec. Engring. and Computer Sci., 1969. With Evans & Sutherland Computer Corp., Computer Scis. Corp., IBM; prin. scientist Xerox Palo Alto Rsch. Ctr., Calif., 1978-81; co-founder, chmn., CEO Adobe Sys., Inc., San Jose, Calif., 1982—. Bd. dirs. Netscape Comm. Corp., Red Brick Sys., Evans & Sutherland Computer Corp. Patentee in field; contbr. articles to profl. jours. and industry mags.; spkr. in field. Chmn. Tech Mus. Innovation; mem. entrepreneurial bd. adv. com. Am. Film Inst. Recipient Computer Achievement award Assn. for Computing Machinery SIGGRAPH, 1989, Tech. Excellence award Nat. Graphics Assn., 1989, ACM Software Sys. award, 1989, Lifetime Achievement award for tech. excellence, PC Mag., 1989, J. Anderson Disting. Achievement award, 1991, Disting. Alumnus award U. Utah, 1995, Cary award Rochester Inst. Tech., 1995; named Entrepreneur of Yr. Ernst & Young, Merril Lynch, Inc., 1991. Mem. NAE. Office: Adobe Sys Inc 345 Park Ave San Jose CA 95110-2704

WARREN, CHRISTOPHER CHARLES, electronics executive; b. Helena, Mont., July 27, 1949; s. William Louis and Myrtle Estelle (Moren) W.; m. Danette Marie Geordge, Apr. 21, 1972; 1 child, Jeffrey Scott. Grad. high sch., Helena, 1967. Electrician Supreme Electronics, Helena, 1972-81; v.p., svc. technician Capital Music Inc., Helena, 1981—. State exec. Amusement & Music Operators Assn. Coun. of Affiliated States, Chgo., 1990-92. Sgt. USAF, 1968-72, Vietnam. Mem. Internat. Flipper Pinball Assn. (sec./treas. 1991-92, pres. 1993-94), Mont. Coin Machine Operators Assn. (pres. 1989-91, 97-99, treas. 2000), Mont. Coin Machine Operators State 8-Ball (chmn.), Valley Nat. 8 Ball Assn. (charter), Amusement and Music Operators Assn. (bd. dirs. 1992-95, v.p. 1995-2000, sec. 2000—), Ducks Unltd., Ea gles, Moose, Rocky Mountain Elk Found. Avocations: photography, restoring old cars and trucks, hunting, fishing. Home: 8473 Green Meadow Dr Helena MT 59602-8312 Office: Capital Music Inc PO Box 5416 Helena MT 59604-5416

WARREN, DAVID HARDY, psychology educator; b. Chelsea, Mass., July 28, 1943; s. Roland Leslie and Margaret (Hodges) W.; m. Katherine V. Warren; children: Michael Jonathan Warren, Gabriel Kristopher Coy. A.B. in Psychology, Yale U., 1965; Ph.D. in Child Devel, U. Minn., 1969. Prof. psychology U. Calif., Riverside, 1969—, dean Coll. Humanities and Social Scis., 1977-85, dir. Univ. honors program, 1989-92, chair dept. psychology, 1992-94, exec. vice chancellor, 1994—. Author: Blindness and Early Childhood Development, 1977, 84, Blindness and Children: An Individual Differences Approach, 1994; contbr. articles to profl. jours. Mem. Psychonomic Soc., AAAS. Office: U Calif Office Exec Vice Chancellor Riverside CA 92521-0001

WARREN, DIANE, song writer; Owner Real Songs, L.A. Author over 75 top ten pop songs including How Do I Live, I Don't Want to Miss a Thing, If You Asked Me To, Don't Turn Around, Set The Night To Music, I'll Still Love You More, Because You Loved Me, Rhythm of the Night, many others. Office: Realsongs 6363 W Sunset Blvd Fl 8 Hollywood CA 90028-7330

WARREN, JAMES RONALD, retired museum director, writer, columnist; b. Goldendale, Wash., May 25, 1925; stepson H.S. W.; m. Gwen Davis, June 25, 1949; children: Gail, Jeffrey. B.A., Wash. State U., 1949; M.A., U. Wash., 1953, Ph.D., 1963. Adminstrv. v.p. Seattle Community Coll., 1965-69; pres. Edmonds Community Coll., Lynnwood, Wash., 1969-79; dir. Mus. of History and Industry, Seattle, 1979-89. Lectr. in field. Author history books; columnist Seattle Post Intelligencer, 1979-92, Seattle Times, 1992-96. Served with U.S. Army, 1943-45, ETO, prisoner-of-war, Germany. Mem. VFW, Am. Ex-POW Assn., 42d (Rainbow) Div. Vets., Rotary, also others. Home and Office: 3235 99th Ave NE Bellevue WA 98004-1803

WARREN, KATHERINE VIRGINIA, art gallery director; b. Balt., Aug. 10, 1948; d. Joseph Melvin and Hilda Virginia (Thiele) Heim; m. David Hardy Warren; 1 child, Gabriel Kristopher Coy; 1 stepchild, Michael Jonathan Warren. BA, U. Calif., Riverside, 1976, MA, 1980. Asst. curator Calif. Mus. Photography, Riverside, 1979-80, acting dir., 1980-81, asst. dir., curator of edn., 1981-84; dir. univ. art gallery U. Calif., Riverside, 1980—. Bd. dirs. Riverside Arts Found., 1980-89, chmn. bd., 1986-88. Marius De Brabant fellow U. Calif., 1977-79. Mem. Am. Assn. Mus., Western Mus. Conf. Office: Sweeney Art Gallery U Calif Riv Side Riverside CA 92521-0001

WARREN, LARRY MICHAEL, clergyman; b. Bonne Terre, Mo., Nov. 25, 1946; s. Orson Wesley and Ruth Margaret (Stine) W.; m. Bonnie Jean Monk Chandler, Apr. 9, 1983; children: Samantha Chandler, John, Abigail Chandler, Anne, Meredith. BA cum laude, Lincoln U., 1969; MDiv with honors, St. Paul Sch. Theology, Kansas City, Mo., 1976; D of Ministry, San Francisco Theol. Sem., 1987. Ordained elder United Meth. Ch., 1978. Pastor Cainsville (Mo.) United Meth. Ch., 1975-76, Lakelands Parish, Rathdrum, Idaho, 1976-78; assoc. pastor Audubon Park United Meth. Ch., Spokane, Wash., 1978-83; pastor Faith United Meth. Ch., Everett, 1983-90, Tacoma First United Meth. Ch., 1990-95; co-pastor Renton First United Meth. Ch., 1995—. Adviser Kairos Prison Ministry Wash., Monroe, 1984-92; conf. rep. grad. bd. St. Paul Sch. Theology, Kansas City, 1984, 94-96. Contbr. to col. Dialogue Everett Herald, 1984-88. Adviser DeMolay, Spokane, 1979-81; team mem. Night-Walk, inner-city ministry, Spokane, 1979-82; coord. Ch. Relief Overseas Project Hunger Walk, Spokane and Everett, 1981, 85; vol. chaplain Gen. Hosp. Everett, 1983-90; trustee Deaconess Children's Svcs., Everett, 1983-88. Recipient Legion of Honor DeMolay Internat., 1982. Mem. Fellowship of Reconciliation, North Snohomish County Assn. Chs. (v.p. 1985-89), Pacific N.W. Ann. Conf. Bd. Global Ministries (sec. 1988-92, pres. 1993-97), Renton Ecumenical Assn. Chs. (pres. 1996-98). Democrat. Avocations: reading, traveling, stamps and coins, woodworking. Home: 121 Monterey Pl NE Renton WA 98056-4032 Office: Renton First United Meth Ch 2201 NE 4th St Renton WA 98056-4073 E-mail: revlmw@aol.com

WARREN, RICHARD WAYNE, obstetrician/gynecologist; b. Puxico, Mo., Nov. 26, 1935; s. Martin R. and Sarah E. (Crump) W.; m. Rosalie J. Franzoia, Aug. 16, 1959; children: Lani Marie, Richard W., Paul D. BA, U. Calif., Berkeley, 1957; MD, Stanford U., 1961. Diplomate Am. Bd. Ob-Gyn. Intern Oakland (Calif.) Naval Hosp., 1961-62; resident on ob-gyn. Stanford (Calif.) Med. Ctr., 1964-67; pvt. practice specializing in ob-gyn. Mountain View, Calif., 1967—. Mem. staff Stanford Hosp., El Camino Hosp.; pres. Warren Medical Corp.; assoc. clin. prof. ob-gyn Stanford Sch. Medicine. Contbr. articles to profl. jours. With USN, 1961-64. Fellow Am. Coll. Ob-Gyn.; mem. AMA, Am. Fertility Soc., Am. Assn. Gynecologic Laparoscopists, Calif. Med. Assn., San Francisco Gynecol. soc., Peninsula Gynecol. Soc., Assn. Profs. Gynecology and Obstetrics, Royal Soc. Medicine, Shufelt Gynecol. Soc. Santa Clara Valley. Home: 102 Atherton Ave Menlo Park CA 94027-4021 Office: 2500 Hospital Dr Mountain View CA 94040-4106

WARRICK, BROOKE, marketing executive; MS in Psychology, San Francisco State U. Past mktg. dir. VALS program Stanford Rsch. Inst.; pres. Am. Lives, San Francisco, 1989—. Internat. spkr. in field; condr. tng. sessions. various orgns. Author: The Builder's Guide to Moveup Buyers; prodr. (video) An American Portrait. Office: Am Lives Inc 6114 Lasalle Ave Ste 590 Oakland CA 94611-1825

WARRICK, SHERIDAN, magazine editor; Former editor Pacific Discovery/Calif. Acad. Scis., San Francisco; exec. editor food and nutrition Time Inc.'s Health, San Francisco, 1987—. Author: (book) The Natural History of the UC Santa Cruz Campus, 1983. Office: Time Incs Health 2 Embarcadero Ctr Ste 600 San Francisco CA 94111-3827

WASHBURN, JON, artistic director; Founder, condr., artistic dir. Vancouver (B.C., Can.) Chamber Choir, 1971—; condr., artistic dir., exec. dir. Phoenix (Ariz.) Bach Choir, 1992-98. Tchg. resident U. Cin., 1999, Ind. U., 2000, City U. Rio de Janeiro, 2000; guest condr. CBC Vancouver Orch., Masterpiece Ensemble, Phoenix Chamber Orch., Calgary, Edmonton, Nova Scotia, Phoenix and Vancouver Symphony Orchs.; guest condr. Santa Fe Desert Chorale, Estonian Philharmonic Chamber Choir, L.A. Master Chorale, Taipei Philharmonic Chorus, 2000; assoc. composer Can. Music Ctr.; mem. artistic juries Can. Coun.; mem. adv. coun. Internat. Music Festivals in U.S.; tchr. in field. Composer, arranger Rossetti Songs, The Star, A Stephen Foster Medley, Chinese Melodies, Rise!Shine!, Noel Sing We; co-author God's Lamb; gen. choral editor Jaymar Music Ltd. Co-recipient Music award Vancouver Awards; recipient Govt. of Can. Celebration 88 cert. of merit, Queen Elizabeth's Silver Jubilee medal, Louis Botto award Chorus Am., 2000, Disting. Svc. award Assn. Can. Choral Condrs., Margaret Hillis award for choral excellence, 1998. Mem. Chorus Am. (bd. dirs.). Office: Vancouver Chamber Choir 186 W 18th Ave Vancouver BC Canada V5Y 2A5 E-mail: info@vancouverchamberchoir.com

WASHINGTON, A. EUGENE, medical educator; b. Houston, 1950; MD, U. Calif., San Francisco, 1976. Diplomate Am. Bd. Ob-Gyn., Am. Bd. Gen. Preventive Medicine. Intern USPHS, Staten Island, N.Y., 1976-77; resident Preventive Medicine Harvard U., 1977-79; resident Ob-Gyn. Stanford U., 1986-89; fellow Health Policy Inst. Health PS/U. Calif., San Francisco, 1983-86; prof. Ob-Gyn., Preventive Medicine U. Calif., San Francisco, prof. chair., obstetrics, gynecology, 1989—. Mem. AAAS, APHA, Soc. for Epidemiol. Rsch. Office: U Calif San Francisco PO Box 0132 San Francisco CA 94143-0001

WASHINGTON, DENNIS, construction executive; CEO Washington Corp., Missoula, Mont. Office: Washington Corp 101 International Way Missoula MT 59808-1549

WASHINGTON, DENNIS R. contracting company executive; Chmn., pres., CEO Morrison-Knudsen, 1999—. Office: Morrison-Knudsen Morrison Knudsen Plz Boise ID 83712

WASHINGTON, JAMES WINSTON, JR. artist, sculptor; b. Gloster, Miss., Nov. 10, 1909; s. James and Lizie (Howard) W.; m. Janie R. Miller, Mar. 29, 1943. Student, Nat. Landscape Inst., 1944-47; D.F.A., Center Urban-Black Studies, 1975. Tchr. summer class N.W. Theol. Union Seattle U., 1988. One man shows U.S.O. Gallery, Little Rock, 1943, Foster-White Gallery, Seattle, 1974, 78, 80, 83, 89 (also at Bellevue Art Mus., 89), Charles and Emma Frye Art Mus., Seattle, 1980, 95, Mus. History and Industry, Seattle, 1981; exhibited in group shows Willard Gallery, N.Y.C., 1960-64, Feingarten Galleries, San Francisco, 1958-59, Grosvenor Gallery, London, Eng., 1964, Lee Nordness Gallery, N.Y.C, 1962 Woodside Gallery, Seattle, 1962-65, Foster-White Gallery, Seattle, 1974, 76, 89, 92, Smithsonian Instn., 1974, San Diego, 1977, others; retrospective exhbn. Bellevue Art Mus., Washington, 1989; represented in permanent collections Seattle, San Francisco, Oakland art museums, Seattle First Nat. Bank, Seattle Pub. Libr. YWCA, Seattle, Meany Jr. H.S., Seattle World's Fair, Expo 70 Osaka, Japan, Whitney Mus. Am. Art, N.Y.C.; commd. sculpture: Bird With Covey, Wash. State Capitol Mus., Olympia, 1983, Obelisk with Phoenix and Esoteric Symbols of Nature in granite, Sheraton Hotel Seattle, 1982, Life Surrounding the Astral Alter, In Matrix, owner T.M. Rosenblume, Charles Z. Smith & Assocs., Seattle, 1986, The Oracle of Truth (6 1/2 ton sculpture) Mt. Zion Bapt. Ch., Seattle, 1987, commd. sculptures King County Arts Commn., 1989, Bailey Gatzent Elem. Sch., Seattle, 1991, Twin Eaglets of the Cosmic Cycle (Quincy Jones), 1993, Fountain of Triumph (Bangasser Assocs. Inc.), 1992-93, Seattle, 1993-94, 94-95, Child in Matrix, 1995, Blunt Tail Owl, 1996, Bunny Rabbit and Robbin, 1996; author book of poetry Poems of Life, 1997 (Internat. Hall of Fame Nat. Soc. Poets). Passover leader Mt. Zion Baptist Ch., Seattle, 1974-87; founder James W. Washington, Jr. and Mrs. Janie Rogella Washington Found. Recipient Spl. Commendation award for many contbns. to artistic heritage of state Gov., 1973, plaque City of Seattle, 1973, plaque Benefit Guild, Inc., 1973, arts service award King County Arts Commn., 1984, cert. of recognition Gov. of Wash., 1984, Editor's Choice award Outstanding Achievement in Poetry Nat. Libr. Poetry, 1993; named to Wash. State Centennial Hall of Honor, Wash. State Hist. Soc., 1984; home and studio designated historic landmark (city and state), 1991; Dr. James W. Washington Jr. and Mrs. Janie Rosella Washington Found. established, 1997. Mem. Internat. Platform Assn., Internat. Soc. Poets (life, awards 1993), Profl. Artists Phila., Masons (33d degree). Home: 1816 26th Ave Seattle WA 98122-3110

WASHINGTON, MAURICE E. state legislator; b. Albuquerque, July 25, 1956; s. Willy Edward and Marion (Moore) W.; m. Donna Marie Bartee, Mar. 3, 1978; children: Michelle Denise, Jason Maurice, Angelise Marie, Dennis Bartee. BS, U. Nev., Reno. Journeyman electrician IBEW Local 401, Nev., 1978-84; owner D&M Enterprises, Reno, 1984-86; sales rep. Sierra Office Concepts, Reno, 1986-90, Reno-Gazette Jour., 1990-94; pastor/founder Ctr. of Hope, Sparks, Nev., 1989—; mem. Nev. Senate, Washoe Dist. 2, Carson City, 1994—; mem. standing com. judiciary, human resources Nev. Senate, 1995—, vice chmn. transp. com., 1995—, asst. majority whip, 1997—. Adjutant State Bishops Cabinet, Cogic, Nev., 1993; bd. dirs. Safe Harbor Ministries, Sparks, Nev., 1995; mem. steering com. Grace Project, Reno, 1994. Contbr. articles to profl. jours. Mem. Reno Citizens Policy Planning Adv. Commn., 1988; mem. platform com. Washoe County Rep. Ctrl. Com., Reno, 1994; chmn. Nat. Panel on Welfare Reform, 1996. Recipient Outstanding Svc. award Families of Murder Victims and Stop DUI, 1995. Mem. Am. Coun. Young Polit. Leaders (delegation to Israel 1996), Nat. Black Rep. Roundtable (Fredrick Douglass award 1996), Rotary Internat. Office: Nev Senate 401 S Carson St Rm 239 Carson City NV 89701-4747 Address: PO Box 1166 Sparks NV 89432-1166

WASHINGTON, WARREN MORTON, meteorologist; b. Portland, Oreg., Aug. 28, 1936; s. Edwin and Dorothy Grace (Morton) W.; m. LaRae Herring, July 30, 1959 (div. Aug. 1975); children: Teri, Kim, Marc (dec.), Tracy; m. Jona Ann, July 3, 1978 (dec. Jan. 1987); m. Mary Elizabeth Washington, Apr., 1995. B.S. in Physics, Ore. State U., 1958, M.S. in Meteorology, 1960; Ph.D. in Meteorology, Pa. State U., 1964. Dir. of climate and global dynamics div. Nat. Center Atmospheric Research, Boulder, Colo., 1978-95; affiliate prof. meteorology oceanography U. Mich. at Ann Arbor, 1968-71; mem. Nat. Adv. Com. for Oceans and Atmospheres, 1978-84. Mem. sec. of energy adv. bd. U.S. Dept. Energy, 1990-93. Contbr. articles to meteorol. jours. Mem. Boulder Human Relations Commn., 1969-71; mem. Gov.'s Sci. Adv. Com., 1975-78. Recipient Disting. Alumni award Oreg. State U., 1991, E.B. Lemon Disting. Alumni award Pa. State U., 1991, Le Verrier medal Soc. Meteorol. France, 1995, Bonfils-Stanton Found. award, 2000; inductee NAS portrait collection African Am. in Sci., Engring., and Medicine, 1997; named Sigma Xi Disting. lectr., 1998-99. Fellow AAAS (bd. dirs.), Am. Meteorol. Soc. (pres. 1994, Anderson award 2000); mem. Am. Geog. Union, Nat. Sci. Bd. (1994—). Home: 725 Pinehurst Ct Louisville CO 80027-3285 Office: PO Box 3000 Boulder CO 80307-3000

WASSERBURG, GERALD JOSEPH, geology and geophysics educator; b. New Brunswick, N.J., Mar. 25, 1927; s. Charles and Sarah (Levine) W.; m. Naomi Z. Orlick, Dec. 21, 1951; children: Charles David, Daniel Morris. Student, Rutgers U.; BS in Physics, U. Chgo., 1951, MSc in Geology, 1952, PhD, 1954, DSc (hon.), 1992; Dr. Hon. Causa, Brussels U., 1985, U. Paris, 1986; DSc (hon.), Ariz. State U., 1987; Dr. (hon.), U. Rennes, 1998; DSc (hon.), U. Turin (Italy), 2000. Research assoc. Inst. Nuclear Studies, U. Chgo., 1954-55; asst. prof. Calif. Inst. Tech., Pasadena, 1955-59, assoc. prof., 1959-62, prof. geology and geophysics, 1962-82, John D. MacArthur prof. geology and geophysics, 1982—. Served on Juneau Ice Field Rsch. Project, 1950; cons. Argonne Nat. Lab., Lamont, Ill., 1952-55; former mem. U.S. Nat. Com. for Geochem., com. for Planetary Exploration Study, NRC, adv. coun. Petroleum Rsch. Fund, Am. Chem. Soc.; me. lunar sample analysis planning team (LSAPT) manned Spacecraft Ctr., NASA, Houston, 1968-71, chmn., 1970; lunar sample rev. bd., 1970-72; mem. Facilities Working Group LSAPT, Johnson Space Ctr., 1972-82; mem. sci. working panel for Apollo missions, Johnson Space Ctr., 1971-73; advisor NASA, 1968-88, phys. scis. com., 1971-75, mem. lunar base steering com., 1984; chmn. com. for planetary and lunar exploration, mem. space sci. bd. NAS, 1975-78; chmn. divsn. Geol. and Planetary Scis., Calif. Inst. Tech., 1987-89; vis. prof. U. Kiel, Fed. Republic of Germany, 1960, Harvard U., 1962, U. Bern, Switzerland, 1966, Swiss Fed. Tech. Inst., 1967, Max Planck Inst., Mainz and Heidelberg, Fed. Republic of Germany, 1985; invited lectr., Vinton Hayes Sr. fellow Harvard U., 1980, Jaeger-Hales lectr. Australian Nat. U., 1980, Harold Jeffreys lectr. Royal Astron. Soc., 1981, Ernst Cloos lectr. Johns Hopkins U., 1984, H.L. Welsh Disting. lectr. U. Toronto, Can., 1986, Danz lectr. U. Washington, 1989,

Goldschmidt Centennial lectr. Norwegian Acad. Sci. and Letters, 1989, Lindsay lectr. Goddard Space Flight Ctr., 1996; plenary spkr. 125th Anniversary Geol. Soc. Sweden, 1996; 60th Anniversary Symposium spkr. Hebrew U., Jerusalem, 1985, 75th Anniversary Symposium spkr., 2000. Served with U.S. Army, 1944-46. Decorated Combat Inf. badge. Recipient Group Achievement award NASA, 1969, Exceptional Sci. Achievement award NASA, 1970, Disting. Pub. Svc. medal NASA, 1973, J.F. Kemp medal Columbia U., 1973, Profl. Achievement award U. Chgo. Alumni Assn., 1978, Goldschmidt medal Geochem. Soc., 1978, Disting. Pub. Svc. medal with cluster NASA, 1978, Wollaston medal Geol. Soc. London, 1985, Sr. Scientist award Alexander von Humboldt-Stiftung, 1985, Crafoord prize Royal Swedish Acad. Scis., 1986, Holmes medal, 1987, Regents fellow Smithsonian Inst., Gold medal Royal Astron. Soc., 1991; named Hon. Fgn. fellow European Union Geoscis., 1983. Fellow Am. Acad. Arts and Scis., Geol. Soc. London (hon.), Am. Geophys. Union (planetology sect., Harry H. Hess medal 1985), Geol. Soc. Am. (life, Arthur L. Day medal 1970), Meteoritical Soc. (pres. 1987-88, Leonard medal 1975), Geochemical Society and the European Assn. for Geochemistry, 1996; mem. Nat. Acad. Scis. (Arthur L. Day prize and lectureship 1981, J. Lawrence Smith medal 1985), Norwegian Acad. Sci. and Letters, Am. Phil. Soc. Achievements include research in geochemistry and geophysics and the application of the methods of chemical physics to problems in the earth scis. Major researches have been the determination of the time scales of nucleosynthesis, connections between the interstellar medium and solar material, the time of the formation of the solar system, the chronology and evolution of the earth, moon and meteorites, the establishment of dating methods using long-lived natural radio-activities, the study of geologic and cosmic processes using nuclear and isotopic effects as a tracer in nature, the origin of natural gases, and the application of thermodynamic methods to geologic systems. Office: Calif Inst Tech Divsn Geol & Planetary Scis Pasadena CA 91125-2500 E-mail: isotopes@gps.caltech.edu

WASSERMAN, ANTHONY IRA, software company executive, educator; b. Bronx, N.Y., Mar. 1, 1945; s. Joseph K. and Frances (Hirsch) W.; m. Susan Gail Cohen, June 11, 1966; children: Mark, Michelle. AB in Math. and Physics, U. Calif., Berkeley, 1966; MS in Computer Sci., U. Wis., 1967, PhD in Computer Sci., 1970. Prof. med. info. sci. U. Calif., San Francisco, 1973-88; pres., CEO Interactive Devel. Environments, Inc., San Francisco, 1983-93, also chmn. bd. dirs.; pres. Software Methods and Tools, San Francisco, 1997—. Lectr. computer sci. U. Calif., Berkeley, 1971-86, vis. prof., 1996. Editor: Software Development Environments, 1981, Software Design Techniques, 4th edit., 1983, others; contbr. articles to prol. jours. Recipient Silver Core award Internat. Fedn. Info. Processing, 1986. Fellow IEEE, Assn. Computing Machinery (editor-in-chief ACM Computing Surveys 1983-86, Disting. Svc. award 1995). Democrat. Avocations: running, photography. E-mail: twasserman@mindspring.com

WASSERMAN, BARRY L(EE), architect; b. Cambridge, Mass., May 25, 1935; s. Theodore and Adelaide (Levin) W.; m. Wilma Louise Greenfield, June 21, 1957 (div. 1971); children: Tim Andrew, Andrew Glenn; m. Judith Ella Michalowski, Apr. 22, 1979. B.A., Harvard U., 1957, M. Arch., 1960. Registered architect, Calif. Assoc. John S. Bolles Assocs., San Francisco, 1960-69; prin. Wasserman-Herman Assocs., San Francisco, 1969-72; prin., dir. Office Lawrence Halprin U Assocs., San Francisco, 1972-76; dep. state architect State of Calif., Sacramento, 1976-78, state architect, 1978-83; prof. dept. architecture, dir. Inst. Environ. Design, Sch. Environ. Design Calif. State Poly. U., Pomona, 1983-87, chair dept. architecture, Coll. Environ. Design, 1988-96, prof. emeritus, 1997—; cons. architecture, Sacramento, 1983—; program advisor Fla. A&M U., Tallahassee, 1981-83. Architect Wasserman House, San Rafael, Calif., 1963 (AIA-Sunset Mag. award of Merit 1965-66), Anna Waden Library, San Francisco, 1969 (AIA award of Merit 1970), Capitol Area Plan, Sacramento, 1977 (Central Valley chpt. AIA Honor award 1979), co-author: Ethics and the Practice of Architecture, 2000. Recipient Awards citation Progressive Architecture 26th awards Program, 1979, Octavius Morgan award Calif. Architects Bd., 2000. Fellow AIA chmn. architecture in govt. com. (1979) Democrat. Jewish. Home: 6456 Fordham Way Sacramento CA 95831-2218 E-mail: blw2@mindspring.com

WASSERMAN, LEW R. film, recording and publishing company executive; b. Cleve., Mar. 15, 1913; m. Edith T. Beckerman, July 5, 1936; 1 dau., Lynne Kay. D (hon.), Brandeis U., NYU. Nat. dir. advt. and publicity Music Corp. Am., 1936-38, v.p., 1938-39, became v.p. charge motion picture div., 1940; now chmn., chief exec. officer, dir., mem. exec. com. MCA, Inc., also chmn. bd., chief exec. officer, dir. subsidiary corps.; now chmn. emeritus. Chmn. emeritus Assn. Motion Picture and TV Producers. Trustee John F. Kennedy Libr., John F. Kennedy Ctr. Performing Arts, Jules Stein Eye Inst., Carter Presdl. Ctr., Lyndon Baines Johnson Found.; pres. Hollywood Canteen Found.; chmn. Rsch. to Prevent Blindness Found.; hon. chmn. bd. Ctr. Theatre Group L.A. Music Ctr.; bd. dirs. Amateur Athletic Found. of L.A. (chmn. fin. com.), L.A. Music Ctr. Found.; bd. gov.'s Ronald Reagan Presdl. Found. Recipient Jean Hersholt Humanitarian award Acad. Motion Picture Arts and Scis., 1973. Democrat. Office: Universal City Studios Inc 100 Universal City Plz Universal City CA 91608-1085

WASSERMAN, STEPHEN IRA, physician, educator; b. Los Angeles, Dec. 17, 1942; m. Linda Morgan; children: Matthew, Zachary. BA, Stanford U., 1964; MD, UCLA, 1968. Diplomate Am. Bd. Internal Medicine, Am. Bd. Allergy and Immunology. Intern, resident Peter B. Brigham Hosp., Boston, 1968-70; fellow in allergy, immunology Robert B. Brigham Hosp., Boston, 1972-75; asst. prof. medicine Harvard U., Boston, 1975-79, assoc. prof., 1979, U. Calif.-San Diego, La Jolla, 1979-85, prof., 1985—, chief allergy tng. program Sch. Medicine, 1979-85, chief allergy div. Sch. Medicine, 1985-93, acting chmn. dept. medicine, 1986-88, chmn. dept. medicine, 1988-2000, Helen M. Ranney prof., 1992—. Co-dir. allergy sect. Robert B. and Peter B. Brigham Hosps., 1977-79; dir. Am. Bd. Allergy and Immunology; dir. Am. Bd. Internal Medicine., chair, 1999-2000. Contbr. articles to profl. jours. Served to lt. comdr. USPHS, 1970-72, San Francisco. Fellow Am. Acad. Allergy and Immunology (pres. 1997-98); mem. Am. Soc. Clin. Investigation, Assn. Am. Physicians, Am. Assn. Immunologists, Collegium Internationale Allergologicum, Phi Beta Kappa, Alpha Omega Alpha. Office: U Calif San Diego Stein Clin Rsch Bldg Rm 244 9500 Gilman Dr MC 0637 San Diego CA 92093-0637

WASSERMAN, STEVE, editor; b. Vancouver, Wash., Aug. 3, 1952; s. Abraham and Ann (Dragoon) W.; m. Michelle Krisel, Mar. 7, 1982; children: Claire, Paul, Isaac. AB in Criminology, U. Calif., Berkeley, 1974. Asst. editor City Mag. of San Francisco, 1975-76; dep. editor opinion sect. Los Angeles Times, 1977-83; editor in chief New Republic Books The New Republic, N.Y.C., 1984-87; pub. Hill and Wang div. Farrar, Straus and Giroux Inc., N.Y.C., 1987-90; The Noonday Press div. Farrar, Straus and Giroux Inc., N.Y.C., 1987-90; editorial dir. Times Books divsn. Random House, N.Y.C., 1990-96; editor L.A. Times Book Rev., 1996—; founder L.A. Inst. Humanities, 1998—. Cons. editor The Threepenny Rev., Berkeley, Calif., 1980-86, Tikkun, Oakland, Calif., 1986-90; founder, co-dir. L.A. Inst. for the Humanities, 1998—; Donald and Doris Fischer lectr. Grad. Sch. of Journalism U. Calif. Berkeley, 1999; instr., master profl. writing program U. So. Calif., 2000. Contbr. articles and revs. to mags. and newspapers. Mem. PEN Office: LA Times 202 W 1st St Los Angeles CA 90012-4105

WASSERMAN, WILLIAM PHILLIP, lawyer; b. Los Angeles, Sept. 13, 1945; s. Al and Ceil (Diamond) W.; married; children: Sam, George. BA, U. Calif., Berkeley, 1967; JD, U. Calif., 1970. Bar: Calif. 1971, U.S. Tax Ct. 1971. Ptnr. Ernst & Young LLP, Los Angeles, 1970—. Lectr. in field.; participant in numerous programs, confs., and workshops in field in field. Mem. Editorial adv. bd.: Real Estate Taxation: A Practitioner's Guide, 1984—, Federal Tax Annual: Real Estate, 1982; contbr. numerous articles to profl. jours. Mem. ABA (nat. chmn Tax Sect. com. on real estate problems 1985-87), State Bar Calif., Los Angeles County Bar Assn., Calif. Bd. Legal Specialization (cert. taxation law specialist). Office: Ernst & Young LLP 725 S Figueroa St Los Angeles CA 90017-5524

WASTERLAIN, CLAUDE GUY, neurologist; b. Courcelles, Belgium, Apr. 15, 1935; s. Desire and Simone (De Taeye) W.; m. Anne Marguerite Thomsin, Feb. 28, 1967; 1 child, Jean Michel. Cand. Sci., U. Liege, 1957, MD, 1961; LS in Molecular Biology, U. Brussels, 1969. Resident Cornell U. Med. Coll., N.Y.C., 1964-67, instr. neurology, 1969-70, asst. prof., 1970-75, assoc. prof., 1975-76, UCLA Sch. Medicine, 1976-79, prof., 1979—, vice chair dept. neurology, 1976—; chief neurology svc. VA Med. Ctr., Sepulveda, Calif., 1976—; cons. neurologist Olive View Med. Ctr., Sylmar, 1976—. Attending neurologist UCLA Ctr. Health Scis., 1976—; chief neurology Greater L.A. VA Health Care System, 1998—. Author, editor: Status Epilepticus, 1984, Neonatal Seizures, 1990, Molecular Neurobiology and Epilepsy, 1992, Progressive Nature of Epileptogenesis, 1996; contbr. articles to med. jours. William Evans fellow, U. Auckland, New Zealand, 1984; recipient N.Y. Neurol. Soc. Young Investigator award, 1965, Rsch. Career Devel. award NIH, 1973-76, Worldwide AES award, 1992, Golden Hammer Teaching award, 1996. Fellow Am. Acad. Neurology; mem. Am. Neurol. Assn., Am. Soc. Neurochemsitry (coun. mem. 1991-97), Internat. Neurochemistry, Am. Epilepsy Soc., Royal Soc. Medicine . Avocations: tennis, skiing, jazz, theatre. Office: West LA VA Med Ctr 11301 Wilshire Blvd West Los Angeles CA 90073 Fax: 818-895-5801

WATANABE, CORINNE KAORU AMEMIYA, judge, state official, lawyer; b. Wahiawa, Hawaii, Aug. 1, 1950; d. Keiji and Setsuko Amemiya; m. Edwin Tsugio Watanabe, Mar. 8, 1975; children: Traciann Keiko, Brad Natsuo, Lance Yoneo. BA, U. Hawaii, 1971; JD, Baylor U., 1974. Bar: Hawaii 1974. Dep. atty. gen. State of Hawaii, Honolulu, 1974-84, 1st dep. atty. gen., 1984-85, 87-92, atty. gen., 1985-87; assoc. judge Hawaii Intermediate Ct. Appeals, Honolulu, 1992—. Mem. ABA, Hawaii Bar Assn. Democrat. Office: Hawaii Intermediate Ct Appeals 426 Queen St 2d Fl Honolulu HI 96813

WATANABE, MAMORU, former university dean, physician, researcher; b. Vancouver, B.C., Can., Mar. 15, 1933; s. Takazo and Nao (Suginobu) W.; m. Marie Katie Bryndzak, June 1, 1974; 1 child, David. M.D., McGill U., 1957, Ph.D., 1963. Intern Royal Victoria Hosp., Montreal, 1957-58, resident in medicine, 1958-63; prof. medicine U. Alta., Edmonton, 1967-74; head internal medicine U. Calgary, Alta., 1974-76, assoc. dean edn., 1976-80, assoc. dean research, 1980-81, acting dean medicine, 1981-82, dean faculty medicine, 1982-92. Med. staff Foothills Hosp., Calgary, 1974— Fellow Royal Coll. Physicians and Surgeons (Can.); mem. Endocrine Soc., Can. soc. Clin. Investigation, Can. Soc. Endocrinology and Metabolism, Can. Hypertension Soc. Home: 162 Pumpridge Place SW Calgary AB Canada T2V 5E6 Office: U Calgary 3330 Hospital Dr NW Calgary AB Canada T2N 1N4 E-mail: watanabe@ucalgary.ca

WATERMAN, MICHAEL SPENCER, mathematics educator, biology educator; b. Coquille, Oreg., 1942; s. Ray S. and Bessie E. Waterman; m. Vicki Lynn Buss, Aug. 14, 1962 (div. Mar. 1977); 1 child, Tracey Lynn B.S., Oreg. State U., 1964, M.S., 1966; M.A., Mich. State U., 1968, Ph.D., 1969. Assoc. prof. Idaho State U., Pocatello, 1969-75; mem. staff Los Alamos Nat. Lab., 1975-82, cons., 1982—; USC Assocs. Endowed Chair U. So. Calif., L.A., prof. math. and biology, 1982—, U. So. Calif. Assocs. Endowed Chair, 1991—. Vis. prof. math. U. Hawaii, Honolulu, 1979-80; vis. prof. structural biology U. Calif.-San Francisco, 1982; vis. prof. Mt. Sinai Med. Sch., N.Y.C., 1988; 150th anniversary vis. prof. Chalmers U.; Aisenstadt chair U. Montreal, 2001. Author: Introduction to Computational Biology, 1995; editor: Mathematical Methods for DNA Sequences, Calculating the Secrets of Life, 1995, Genetic Mapping and DNA Sequencing, 1996, Mathematical Support for Molecular Biology, 1999; assoc. editor Bull. Math. Biology; mem. editl. bd. Jour. Advances in Applied Math. Jour., Annals of Combinatories, Methodology and Computing in Applied Probability, Genomics, Soc. for Indsl. and Applied Math. Jour. Applied Math.; editor-in-chief: Jour. Computational Biology; contbr. numerous articles on math. stats., biology to profl. jours. Grantee NSF, 1971, 72, 75, 88—, Los Alamos Nat. Lab, 1976, 81, Sys. Devel. Found., 1982-87, NIH, 1986-99, Sloan Found., 1990-91; Guggenheim Found. fellow, 1995. Fellow AAAS, Am. Acad. Arts and Scis., Celera Genomics, Inst. Math. Stats.; mem. NAS, Am. Statis. Assn., Soc. Math. Biology, Soc. Indsl. and Applied Math. Office: U So Calif Dept Math Los Angeles CA 90007

WATERMAN, MIGNON REDFIELD, public relations executive, state legislator; b. Billings, Mont., Oct. 13, 1944; d. Zell Ashley and Mable Erma (Young) Redfield; m. Ronald Fredrick Waterman, Sept. 11, 1965; children: Briar, Kyle. Student, U. Mont., 1963-66. Lobbyist Mont. Assn. Chs., Helena, 1986-90; mem. Mont. Senate, Dist. 26, Helena, 1990—; with pub. rels. dept. Mont. Coun. Tchrs. Math., Helena, 1991-96. Mem. edn., pub. welfare and instns. sub-com. fin. and claims commn. Mont. Senate, rev. oversight com., 1995—, post-secondary policy & budget com., 1995—. Sch. trustee Helena (Mont.) Sch. Dist. 1, 1978-90; bd. dirs. Mont. Hunger Coalition, 1985—; pres. Mont. Sch. Bds. Assn., 1989-90; active Mont. Alliance for Mentally Ill (Mon Ami award 1991). Recipient Marvin Heintz award Mont. Sch. Bds. Assn., 1987, Friends of Edn. award Mont. Assn. Elem. and Middle Sch. Prins., 1989, Child Advocacy award Mont. PTA, 1991, award Mont. Alliance for Mentally Ill, 1991, Outstanding Adv. award Nat. Easter Seals Soc., 1997, Pres.'s award Mont. Assn. Rehab., 1997. Mem. Mont. Sch. Bds. Assn. (Marvin Heintz award 1988, pres.1989-90), Mont. Elem. Sch. Prins., Mont. Parent, Teacher, Student Assn. (child advocacy award 1991). Democrat. Methodist. Home and Office: 530 Hazelgreen Ct Helena MT 59601-5410 Office: Mt State Senate State Capitol Helena MT 59620

WATERS, CHARLES R., JR. executive editor; married; 3 children. BA in Liberal Arts, U. Ariz. Editor-pub. Mohave Valley News, Bullhead City, Ariz., 1969-73; editor, pub. The Courier, Prescott, 1973-84; profl.-in-residence (vis. asst. prof.) U. Kans., 1984-85; asst. city editor, then night/weekend editor metro-state St. Petersburg (Fla.) Times, 1985-86; asst. mng. editor Reno Gazette-Jour., 1986-87, mng. editor, 1987-89, exec. editor, 1989-90; asst. features editor L.A. Times, 1990-97; exec. editor L.A Times Mag., 1997-98, Fresno Bee, 1998—. Keynote spkr. Nat. Writers Workshop nat. conf., Salt Lake City, 1994; writing and editing cons. Dayton (Ohio) Daily News, 1992; law and media seminar panelist Ford Found., 1980. Trustee William Allen White Found., U. Kans., 1991—; dir. Salvation Army, 1974-84, pres. Prescott adv. bd., 1982, bd. dirs. Reno adv. bd., 1988-90, dir. Fresno adv. bd., 1998—. Nev. State Press Asn. (dir., v.p. 1989-90), Ariz. Press Club (dir., v.p. 1982-84). Office: Fresno Bee 1626 E St Fresno CA 93786-0002

WATERS, LAUGHLIN EDWARD, federal judge; b. L.A., Aug. 16, 1914; s. Frank J. and Ida (Bauman) W.; m. Voula Davanis, Aug. 22, 1953; children: Laughlin Edward, Maura Kathleen, Deirdre Mary, Megan Ann, Eileen Brigid. A.B., UCLA, 1939; J.D., U. So. Calif., 1946. Bar: Calif. 1946. Dep. atty. gen. Calif., Los Angeles, 1946-47; individual practice law Los Angeles, 1947-53; sr. ptnr. Nossaman, Waters, Krueger & Marsh, 1961-76; U.S. atty. So. Dist. Calif., 1953-61; judge U.S. Dist. Ct. (cen. dist.) Calif., 1976—, now sr. judge. Cons. U.S. Dept. State in London, 1970; mem. U.S. Del. to Conf. Environ. Problems in Prague, 1971, White House Conf. on Aging, 1970-71; sr. dist. judge rep. Jud. Coun.; judge Atty Gen.'s Adv. Inst. Mem. Calif. Legislature, 1946-53; vice chmn. Rep. State Ctrl. Com., 1950-51, chmn., 1952-53; bd. dirs. Legal Aid Found., 1954-60; past pres. Cath. Big Brothers. Served as capt. U.S. Army, 1942-46. Decorated Bronze Star with oak leaf cluster, Purple Heart with oak leaf cluster, Combat Inf. badge. Fellow Am. Bar Found., Am. Coll. Trial Lawyers; mem. ABA (chmn. com. on housing and urban devel. 1977-79), Fed. Bar Assn. (founder, past pres.), L.A. County Bar Assn., Am. Judicature Soc., Assn. Bus. Trial Lawyers, U. So. Calif., UCLA Law Assn., Am. Legion , U. So. Calif. Legion Lex, Order Blue Shield, Town Hall, Polish Order Merit Cross with Swords, Hon. Citizen of Chambois, Trun, France, 10th Polish Dragoons (hon.), Soc. Friendly Sons St. Patrick (past pres., Medallion of Merit award), Knights of Malta, Anchor Club, Calif. Club, L.A. Club (past pres.). Roman Catholic. Office: US Dist Ct 255 E Temple St Los Angeles CA 90012-3332

WATERS, MAXINE, congresswoman; b. St. Louis, Aug. 15, 1938; d. Remus and Velma (Moore) Carr; m. Sidney Williams, July 23, 1977; children: Edward, Karen. Grad. in sociology, Calif. State U., L.A.; hon. doctorates, Spelman Coll., N.C. Agrl. &, Tech. State U., Morgan State U. Former tchr. Head Start. Mem. Calif. Assembly from dist. 48, 1976-91, Dem. caucus chair, 1984; mem. U.S.Congress from 35th Calif. dist., 1991—; mem. Banking, Fin., Urban Affairs com., Ho. subcom. on banking, capitol subcom. on banking, employment and tng. subcom. on vets., veterans affairs com., banking and fin. svcs. com., ranking house subcom. on gen. oversight and investigations; chair Congl. Black Caucus. Mem. Dem. Nat. Com., Dem. Congrl. Campaign com.; del. Dem. Nat. Conv., 1972, 76, 80, 84, 88, 92, mem. rules com. 1984; mem. Nat. Adv. Com. for Women, 1978—; bd. dirs. TransAfrica Found., Nat. Women's Polit. Caucus, Ctr. Nat. Policy, Clara Elizabeth Jackson Carter Found. Spellman Coll., Nat. Minority AIDS Project, Women for a Meaningful Summit, Nat. Coun. Negro Women, Black Women's Agenda; founder Black Women's Forum. Office: US Ho Reps 2344 Rayburn HOB Washington DC 20515-0001*

WATKINS, CHARLES REYNOLDS, medical equipment company executive; b. San Diego, Oct. 28, 1951; s. Charles R. and Edith A. (Muff) W.; children: Charles Devin, Gregory Michael, Joshua Tomas. BS, Lewis and Clark Coll., 1974; postgrad., U. Portland, 1976. Internat. salesman Hyster Co., Portland, Oreg., 1975-80, Hinds Internat. Corp., Portland, 1980-83; mgr. internat. sales Wade Mfg. Co., Tualatin, Oreg., 1983-84; regional sales mgr. U.S. Surg., Inc., Norwalk, Conn., 1984-86; nat. sales mgr. NeuroCom Internat., Inc., Clackamas, Oreg., 1986-87; pres. Wave Form Systems, Inc., Portland, 1987-98; pres., dir. Wave Form Mfg., Inc., Portland, 1998—; prin. Wave Form Lithotripsy LLC, Portland, 1998—; pres. Wave Form Mfg., Inc., 1998—. Bd. dirs. Portland World Affairs Coun., 1980. Mem. Am. Soc. Laser Medicine and Surgery, Am. Assn. Gynecol. Laparoscopists, Ind. Med. Distbrs. Assn., Portland City Club. Republican. Avocations: flying, photography, travel. Office: Wave Form Sys Inc PO Box 3195 Portland OR 97208-3195

WATKINS, DEAN ALLEN, electronics executive, educator; b. Omaha, Oct. 23, 1922; s. Ernest E. and Pauline (Simpson) W.; m. Bessie Ena Hansen, June 28, 1944; children— Clark Lynn, Alan Scott, Eric Ross. B.S., Iowa State Coll., 1944; M.S., Calif. Inst. Tech., 1947; Ph.D., Stanford, 1951. Engr. Collins Radio Co., 1947-48; mem. staff Los Alamos Lab., 1948-49; tech. staff Hughes Research Labs., 1951-53; asso. prof. elec. engring. Stanford, 1953 56; prof., dir. Electron Devices Lab., 1956-64, lectr. elec. engring., 1964-70; co-founder, pres., chief exec. officer, dir. Watkins Johnson Co., Palo Alto, Calif., 1957-67, chmn., chief exec. officer, dir., 1967-80, chmn., dir., 1980-2000. Cons. Dept. Def., 1956-66; mem. White House Sci. Coun., 1988-89. Patentee in field; contbr. articles to profl. jours. Legis. chmn., dir. San Meteo County Sch. Bds. Assn., 1959-69; gov. San Francisco Bay Area Coun., 1966-75; Rep. precinct capt. Portola Valley, 1964; vice chmn. San Mateo County Fin. Com., 1967-69; mem. Calif. Rep. Ctrl. Com., 1964-68; trustee Stanford, 1966-69; regent U. Calif., 1969-96, chmn., 1972-74; mem. governing bd. Sequoia Union H.S. Dist., 1964-68, chmn., 1967-68; mem. governing bd. Portola Valley Sch. Dist., 1958-66; mem. bd. overseers Hoover Instn. on War, Revolution and Peace, Stanford, 1969—, chmn., 1971-73, 85-86; adv. policy commn. Santa Clara County Jr. Achievement; trustee Nat. Security Indsl. Assn., 1965-78. Served from pvt. to 1st lt. C.E., O.R.C. AUS, 1943-46. Fellow IEEE (7th region Achievement award 1957, Frederik Philips award 1981), AAAS; mem. Am. Phys. Soc., Am. Mgmt. Assn., Western Electronic Mfrs. Assn. (chmn. San Francisco coun. 1967, v.p., dir.), Calif. C. of C. (dir. 1965-92, treas. 1978, pres. 1981), Nat. Acad. Engring., Mounted Patrol San Mateo County (spl. dep. sheriff 1960-70), San Mateo County Horseman's Assn., San Benito County Farm Bur., Calif. Cattlemen's Assn., Delta Upsilon. Clubs: Palo Alto (Palo Alto), University (Palo Alto); Shack Riders (San Mateo County); Commonwealth (San Francisco); Rancheros Visitadores.

WATKINS, JOHN FRANCIS, management consultant; b. Alhambra, Calif., May 21, 1925; s. Edward F. and Louise (Ward) W.; divorced; children— Stephen, Katherine, John Francis, William. BSCE, U. Tex., Austin, 1947. With Earle M. Jorgensen Co., Lynwood, Calif., 1947-90, sr. v.p. adminstrn., 1978-90, ret.; owner John F. Watkins Assocs., Pasadena, 1990—. Bd. dirs. Boys Republic, Chino Hills, Calif., 1970—, pres., 1977-80; bd. dirs. St. Luke Hosp., Pasadena, 1979-86, chmn. bd., 1982-86; pres. bd. Poly. Sch., Pasadena, 1978-80, Holy Family Sch., 1994—; bd. dirs. Econ. Literacy Coun. Calif., 1980-87, Pasadena Hist. Mus., 1990-99; adv. bd. mem. Serra H.S., Verbum Dei H.S., Dolores Mission Sch., 1996—; pres. coun. Coll. Sci. and Engring./Loyola Marymount U.; posse sheriff Huntington Westerners; adv. bd. Bishop Mora Salesian H.S., 1994—; mem. Edn. Found. Archdiocese L.A., 1995—; St. Gabriel pastoral region bd. dirs. Cath. Charities, 1994—. Mem. U.S. Navy League (nat. bd. dirs. 1989—, pres. Pasadena coun. 1992-93), Calif. Club, Annandale Golf Club, Serra Club (pres. 1995-97), Valley Club (San Marino, Calif.). Republican. Roman Catholic. Home and Office: 410 California Ter Pasadena CA 91105-2419 E-mail: jwatkins@dacorworld.com

WATKINS, JOHN GOODRICH, psychologist, educator; b. Salmon, Idaho, Mar. 17, 1913; s. John Thomas and Ethel (Goodrich) W.; m. Evelyn Elizabeth Browne, Aug. 21, 1932; m. Doris Wade Tomlinson, June 8, 1946; m. Helen Verner Huth, Dec. 28, 1971; children: John Dean, Jonette Alison, Richard Douglas, Gregory Keith, Rodney Philip, Karen Stroobants, Marvin R. Huth. Student, Coll. Idaho, 1929-30, 31-32; BS, U. Idaho, 1933, MS, 1936; PhD, Columbia U., 1941. Instr. high sch., Idaho, 1933-39; faculty Ithaca Coll., 1940-41, Auburn U., 1941-43; assoc. prof. Wash. State U., 1946-49; chief clin. psychologist U.S. Army Welch Hosp., 1945-46; clin. psychologist VA Hosp., American Lake, Wash., 1949-50; chief clin. psychologist VA Mental Hygiene Clinic, Chgo., 1950-53, VA Hosp., Portland, Oreg., 1953-64; prof. psychology U. Mont., Missoula, 1964-84, prof. emeritus, 1984—, dir. clin. tng., 1964-80. Lectr. numerous univs.; clin. asso. U. Oreg. Med. Sch., 1957; pres. Am. Bd. Examiners in Psychol. Hypnosis, 1960-62 Author: Objective Measurement of Instrumental Performance, 1942, Hypnotherapy of War Neuroses, 1949, General Psychotherapy, 1960, The Therapeutic Self, 1978, (with others) We, The Divided Self, 1982, Hypnotherapeutic Techniques, 1987, Hypnoanalytic Techniques, 1992, Ego States: Theory and Therapy, 1997; contbr. articles to profl. jours. Mem. Internat. Soc. Clin. and Exptl. Hypnosis (co-founder, pres. 1965-67, recipient awards 1960-65), Soc. Clin. and Exptl. Hypnosis (pres. 1969-71, Morton Prince award), Am. Psychol. Assn. (pres. divsn. 30 1975-76, recipient award 1993), Sigma Xi, Phi Delta Kappa. Home and Office: 413 Evans Ave Missoula MT 59801-5827

WATKINS, STEPHEN EDWARD, accountant, newspaper executive; b. Oklahoma City, Sept. 1, 1922; s. Ralph Bushnell and Jane (Howell) W.; m. Suzanne Fowler, Aug. 16, 1976; children— Elizabeth Ann Watkins Racicot, Stephen Edward. B.B.A., U. N.Mex., 1944. C.P.A., N.Mex. With Peat, Marwick, Mitchell & Co., 1944-67; pres. The New Mexican daily newspaper, Santa Fe, 1967-78, 90—; pvt. practice pub. acctg. Santa Fe, 1978—. Vestryman Ch. of Holy Faith; trustee St. Vincent Hosp., 1979-85, Orchestra Santa Fe, 1976-82, Hist. Santa Fe Found. (pres. 1990). Mem. AICPA, Sons of Am. Revolution, Rotary. Home: 1325 Don Gaspar Ave Santa Fe NM 87505-4627 Office: 223 E Palace Ave Santa Fe NM 87501-1947

WATKINS, WILLIAM D. technology company executive; BS in Polit. Sci., U. Tex. Exec. Domain Tech., 1990-96; sr. v.p. Conner Peripherals, 1996-98; COO, exec. v.p. Seagate Technology, Inc., Milpitas, Calif., 1998—. Office: Seagate Tech Inc 155 S Milpitas Blvd Milpitas CA 95035

WATSON, DIANE EDITH, congresswoman; b. L.A., Nov. 12, 1933; d. William Allen Louis and Dorothy Elizabeth (O'Neal) Watson. AA, L.A. City Coll., 1954; BA, UCLA, 1956; MS, Calif. State U., L.A.; PhD, Claremont Grad. Sch., 1987. Tchr., sch. psychologist L.A. Unified Sch. Dist., 1960-69, 73-74; assoc. prof. Calif. State U., L.A., 1969-71; health occupations specialist Bur. Indsl. Edn., Calif. Dept. Edn., 1971-73; mem. L.A. Unified Sch. Bd., 1975-78, Calif. Senate from dist. 26, 1978-98, chairperson health and human svcs. com.; U.S. amb. to Micronesia Dept. of State, 1999-2001; mem. U.S. Congress from 32d Calif. dist., 2001—; mem. govt. reform com. and internat. rels. com. Legis. Black Caucus, mem. edn. com., budget and fiscal rev. com., criminal procedure com., housing and land use com.; del. Calif. Democratic Party; mem. exec. com. Nat. Conf. State Legislators; amb. to the Federated States of Micronesia, 1999. Author: Health Occupations Instructional Units-Secondary Schools, 1975, Planning Guide for Health Occupations, 1975; co-author: Introduction to Health Care, 1976. Del. Dem. Nat. Conv., 1980. Recipient Mary Church Terrell award, 1976, Brotherhood Crusade award, 1981, Black Woman of Achievement award NAACP Legal Def. Fund, 1988; named Alumnus of Yr., UCLA, 1980, 82. Mem. Calif. Assn. Sch. Psychologists, L.A. Urban League, Calif. Tchrs. Assn., Calif. Commn. on Status Women. Roman Catholic. Office: US Ho Reps 2413 Rayburn Ho Office Bldg Washington DC 20515 Fax: 691-320-2186*

WATSON, DON, auto parts company executive; CFO, sr. v.p., treas. CSK Auto Corp., Phoenix. Office: OSK Auto Corp 645 E Missouri Ave Ste 400 Phoenix AZ 85012

WATSON, GEORGE W. energy company executive; BSEE, MBA in Fin. Mktg., Queen's U.; grad. advanced mgmt. program, Harvard U., 1988. With Can. Imperial Bank of Commerce, Toronto; asst. gen. mgr. worldwide, oil and gas divsn. Calgary, 1981; dir. fin. Dome Petroleum, v.p. fin.; v.p., treas. Amoco Can.; pres., CEO Intensity Resources, 1988-90; chief fin. officer TransCanada, 1990-93, pres., 1993-99, CEO, 1994-99; ptnr. Northridge Can. Inc., 1999—. Bd. dirs. Badger Daylighting Inc., Geodyne Energy Ltd., Cdn 88 Energy Inc; exec. chmn. Vertical Builder.com Inc. Bd. dirs. Queen's U.

WATSON, JOHN S. oil company executive; Mgr. credit card, products, investor relations Chevron, 1980; pres. Chevron Canada, Ltd.; dir. Caltex Corp.; v.p. strategic planning Chevron Corp., v.p. fin., CFO, 2000—. Office: Chevron Corp 575 Market St San Francisco CA 94105

WATSON, KENNETH MARSHALL, physics educator; b. Des Moines, Sept. 7, 1921; s. Louis Erwin and Irene Nellie (Marshall) W.; m. Elaine Carol Miller, Mar. 30, 1946; children: Ronald M., Mark Louis. BS, Iowa State U., 1943; PhD, U. Iowa, 1948; ScD (hon.), U. Ind., 1976. Rsch. engr. Naval Rsch. Lab., Washington, 1943-46; staff Inst. Advanced Study Princeton (N.J.) U., 1948-49; rsch. fellow Lawrence Berkeley (Calif.) Lab., 1949-52, staff, 1957-81; asst. prof. physics U. Ind., Bloomington, 1952-54; assoc. prof. physics U. Wis., Madison, 1954-57; prof. physics U. Calif., Berkeley, 1957-81, prof. oceanography, dir. marine physics lab. San Diego, 1981-93. Cons. Sci. Application Corp.; mem. U.S. Pres.'s Sci. Adv. Com. Panels, 1962-71; adviser Nat. Security Coun., 1972-75; mem. JASON Adv. Panel; sci. adv. bd. George C. Marshall Inst., 1989—. Author: (with M.L. Goldberger) Collision Theory, 1964; (with J. Welch and J. Bond) Atomic Theory of Gas Dynamics, 1966; (with J. Nutall) Topics in Several Particle Dynamics, 1970; (with Flatté, Munk, Dashen) Sound Transmission Through a Fluctuating Ocean, 1979. Mem. Nat. Acad. Scis. Home: Unit 2008 8515 Costa Verde Blvd San Diego CA 92122-1150 Office: U Calif Marine Physics Lab La Jolla CA 92093 E-mail: kmw@mpl.ucsd.edu

WATSON, NOEL G. construction executive; b. 1936; BSChemE, U. N.D., 1958; postgrad., Colo. Sch. Mines, 1958-60. With Jacobs Engring., 1960-62, AMAX Inc., 1962-65; pres., COO Jacobs Engring. Group Inc., Pasadena, Calif., 1965-92, pres., CEO, 1992—. Office: Jacobs Engring Group 1111 S Arroyo Pkwy Pasadena CA 91105

WATSON, ROBERT A. finance and insurance company executive; Various positions Montgomery Ward fin. opers. GE Capital Corp., 1968, gen. mgr. retail fin. svcs., head Montgomery Ward fin. opers.; pres., CEO Transam. Comml. Fin. Corp. Transam. Corp., 1990—. Office: TransAmerica Corp 600 Montgomery St Ste 2300 San Francisco CA 94111-2770

WATT, KENNETH EDMUND FERGUSON, zoology educator; b. Toronto, July 13, 1929; s. William Black Ferguson Watt and Irene Eleanor (Hubbard) Dodd; m. Genevieve Bernice Bendig, Oct. 28, 1955; children: Tanis Jocelyn, Tara Alexis. BA with honor, U. Toronto, 1951; PhD in Zoology, U. Chgo., 1954; LLD, Simon Fraser U., 1970. Biometrician Rsch. div. Dept. Lands and Forests, Ont., Canada, 1954-57; sr. biometrician Can. Dept. Agr., Ottawa, 1957-60; head, statis. rsch. and svcs. Canadian Dept. Forestry, Ottawa, 1960-63; from assoc. prof. to prof. Dept. Zoology, U. Calif., Davis, 1963-93. Author: Ecology and Resource Management, 1968, Principles of Environmental Sciences, 1973, Understanding the Environment, 1982, Taming the Future, 1991; editor-in-chief: Human Ecology, The Encyclopedia Legacy of H.G. Wells, 2000. Recipient Gold medal Entomol. Soc., 1969. Achievements include development of new approach to forecasting future based on exhaustive statistic testing of nonlinear math. equations to long runs of historical data; discovery that change through time in real world systems violates Markov principles. Home: 2916 Quail St Davis CA 95616-5711 Office: U Calif Dept Evolution & Ecology Davis CA 95616

WATTENBERG, DAVE, state legislator, rancher; b. Walden, Colo., Apr. 4, 1940; Student, Iowa State U., 1958-60. Rancher, Walden; mem. Colo. State Ho. of Reps., Denver, 1982-84, Colo. State Senate, Denver, 1984—. Chmn. agrl., natural resources and energy com., mem. bus. affairs and labor com., joint legal svcs. com.; bd. dirs. North Park State Bank. Mem. North Park Edn. Edn.; co-chmn. Colo. Gov.'s Roundtable on Hwys. and Transp. Mem. Nat. Cattleman's Assn., Colo. Cattlemen's Assn. Republican. Office: Colo State Senate State Capitol 200 E Colfax Ave Ste 346 Denver CO 80203-1716 also: PO Box 797 Walden CO 80480-0797

WATTERS, RICHARD JAMES, professional football player; b. Harrisburg, Pa., Apr. 7, 1969; Degree in design, U. Notre Dame. With San Francisco 49'ers, 1991-94; running back Phila. Eagles, 1995-98, Seattle Seahawks, 1998—. Selected to Pro Bowl, 1992-94. Achievements include member San Francisco 49'ers Super Bowl XXIX Champions, 1994, holds NFL postseason single game for most points (30), most touchdowns (5), Jan. 15, 1994 vs N.Y. Giants. Office: Seattle Seahawks 11220 NE 53d St Kirkland WA 98033

WATTERSON, SCOTT, home fitness equipment manufacturer; Chmn., CEO ICON Health & Fitness, Inc., Logan, Utah. Office: ICON Health & Fitness Inc 1500 S 1000 W Logan UT 84321-8206

WATTS, DAVID H. construction company executive; b. Newark, 1938; Grad., Cornell U., 1960. Pres., CEO Granite Constrn. Inc., Watsonville, Calif.; chmn. Granite Contrn. Inc., Watsonville, 1999—. Office: Granite Constrn Inc 585 W Beach St Watsonville CA 95076-5125

WATTS, MARVIN LEE, minerals company executive, chemist, educator; b. Portales, N.Mex., Apr. 6, 1932; s. William Ellis and Jewel Reata (Holder) W.; m. Mary Myrtle Kiber, July 25, 1952; children: Marvin Lee, Mark Dwight, Wesley Lyle. BS in Chemistry and Math., Ea. N.Mex. U., 1959, MS in Chemistry, 1960; postgrad., U. Okla., 1966, U. Kans., 1967. Analytical chemistr Dow Chem. Co., Midland, Mich., 1960-62; instr. chemistry N.Mex. Mil. Inst., Roswell, 1962-65, asst. prof., 1965-67; chief chemist AMAX Chem. Corp., Carlsbad, N.Mex., 1967-78, gen. surface supt., 1978-84; pres. N.Mex. Salt and Minerals Corp., 1984—. Chem. cons. Western Woils Lab., Roswell, 1962-67; instr. chemistry N.Mex. State U., Carlsbad, 1967—; owner, operator cattle ranch, Carlsbad and Loving, N.Mex., 1969—; bd. dirs. Mountain States Mut. Casualty Co., 1981; gen. mgr. Eddy Potash, Inc., 1987—, v.p., gen. mgr., 1987-95; cons. Potash Industry, 1995—. Pres. Carlsbad Dept. Devel., 1996. N.Mex. BLM Resoource Adv. Coun., 1994; chmn. Eddy County Land USF Commn., Eddy County Labor Rels. Bd.; dir. Soil Donservation Svc.; mem. Roswell dist. adv. bd. Bur. Land Mgmt.; bd. dirs. Southeastern N.Mex. Regional Sci. Fair, 1996; mem. adv. bd. Roswell dist. Bur. Land Mgmt.; mem. Eddy County Fair Bd., 1976—, chmn., 1978, 82; mem. pub. sch. reform com.; chmn. higher edn. reform com.; mem. sponsor of N.Mex. pub. Sch. Reform Act; bd. dirs. Carlsbad Found., 1979-82; adv. bd. N.Mex. State U. at Carlsbad, 1976-80; vice chmn. bd. Guadalupe Med. Ctr.; bd. dirs. N.Mex. Legis, 1984-89; mem. Rep. State Exec. com., 1972—; Rep. chmn. Eddy County (N.MEx.), 1970-74, 78-82, dirs. Conquistador coun. Boy Scouts Am., Regional Environ. Ednl. Rsch. and Improvement Orgn. With Mil. Police Corps, AUS, 1953-55, Germany. Recipient Albert K. Mitchell award as outstanding Rep. in N.Mex., 1976; hon. state farmer N.Mex. Future Farmers Am.; hon. mem. 4-H. Fellow N.Mex. Acad. Sci.; mem. Am. Chem. Soc. (chmn. subsect.), Western States Pub. Lands Coalition, Carlsbad C. of C. (dir. 1979-83), N.Mex. Mining Assn. (dir.), AIME (chmn. Carlsbad potash sect. 1975), Carlsbad Mental Health Assn. (pres. 1994—), N.Mex. Inst. Mining and Tech. (adv. bd. mining dept.), Am. Angus Assn., Am. Quarter Horse Assn., N.Mex. Cattle Growers Assn. (bd. dirs. 1989—), Carlsbad Farm and Ranch Assn., Nat. Cattlemen's Assn., Kiwanis (Disting. lt. gov.). Baptist. Home: PO Box 56 Carlsbad NM 88221-0056 Office: PO Box 101 Carlsbad NM 88221-5603

WATTS, OLIVER EDWARD, engineering consultancy company executive; b. Hayden, Colo., Sept. 22, 1939; s. Oliver Easton and Vera Irene (Hockett) W.; m. Charla Ann French, Aug. 12, 1962; children: Erik Sean, Oliver Eron, Sherilyn. BS, Colo. State U., 1962. Registered profl. engr., Colo., Calif.; profl. hand surveyor, Colo. Crew chief Colo. State U. Rsch. Found., Ft. Collins, 1962; with Calif. Dept. Water Resources, Gustine and Castaic, 1964-70; land and water engr. CF&I Steel Corp., Pueblo, Colo., 1970-71; engring. dir. United Western Engrs., Colorado Springs., 1971-76; ptnr. United Planning and Engring Co., Colorado Springs, 1976-79; owner Oliver E. Watts, Cons. Engr., Colorado Springs, 1979—. Dir. edn. local Ch. of Christ, 1969-71, deacon, 1977-87, elder, 1987-96. 1st lt. C.E., AUS, 1962-64. Recipient Individual Achievement award Colo. State U. Coll. Engring., 1981 Fellow ASCE (v.p. Colorado Springs br. 1975, pres. 1978); mem. NSPE (pres. Pike's Peak chpt. 1975, sec. Colo. sect. 1976, v.p. 1977, pres. 1978-79, Young Engr. award 1976, Pres.'s award 1979), Cons. Engrs. Coun. Colo. (bd. dirs. 1981-83), Am. Cons. Engrs. Coun., Profl. Land Surveyors Colo., Colo. Engrs. Coun. (del. 1980—), Colo. State U. Alumni Assn. (v.p., dir. Pike's Peak chpt. 1972-76), Lancers, Lambda Chi Alpha. Home: 7195 Dark Horse Pl Colorado Springs CO 80919-1442 Office: 614 Elkton Dr Colorado Springs CO 80907-3514 E-mail: owatts8167@aol.com, OllieWatts@aol.com

WAUGH, RICHARD B., JR. aircraft company executive, lawyer; b. Cleve., Sept. 1, 1943; s. Richard B. Waugh. BS, Ohio State U., 1965, JD, 1968. Bar: Ohio, Calif. CPA. Asst. prof. econs. and bus. adminstrn. Waynesburg (Ohio) Coll.; sr. tax acct. Price Waterhouse & Co.; sr. tax counsel western region Rockwell Internat. Corp.; corp. dir. tax adminstrn. Northrop Grumman Corp., L.A., from 1978, corp. v.p. taxes, risk mgmt. and bus. analysis, until 1993, corp. v.p., CFO, 1993—. Mem. ABA, AICPA, Calif. Bar Assn., Ohio Bar Assn., Tax Execs. Inst., Fin. Execs. Inst., Leading Chief Fin. Officers. Office: Northrop Grumman Corp 1840 Century Park E Los Angeles CA 90067-2101

WAY, E(DWARD) LEONG, pharmacologist, toxicologist, educator; b. Watsonville, Calif., July 10, 1916; s. Leong Man and Lai Har (Shew) W.; m. Madeline Li, Aug. 11, 1944; children: Eric, Linette. BS, U. Calif., Berkeley, 1938, MS, 1940; PhD, U. Calif., San Francisco, 1942. Pharm. chemist Merck & Co., Rahway, N.J., 1942; instr. pharmacology George Washington U., 1943-46, asst. prof., 1946-48; asst. prof. pharmacology U. Calif., San Francisco, 1949-52, assoc. prof., 1952-57, prof., 1957-87, prof. emeritus, 1987—, chmn. dept. pharmacology, 1973-78. USPHS spl. rsch. fellow U. Berne, Switzerland, 1955-56, China Med. Bd.; rsch. fellow, vis. prof. U. Hong Kong, 1962-63; Sterling Sullivan disting. vis. prof. Martin Luther King U., 1982; hon. prof. pharmacology and neurosci. Guangzhou Med. Coll., 1987; mem. adv. com. Pharm. Mfrs. Assn. Found., 1968-98; mem. coun. Am. Bur. for Med. Advancement in China, 1982; bd. dirs. Li Found., 1970—, pres., 1985-98, bd. dirs. Haight Ashbury Free Clinics, 1986-93; Tsumura prof. neuropsychopharmacology med. sch. Gunma U., Maebashi, Japan, 1989-90; sr. staff fellow Nat. Inst. on Drug Abuse, 1990-91; researcher on drug metabolism, analgetics, devel. pharmacology, drug tolerance, drug dependence and Chinese materia medica. Editor: New Concepts in Pain, 1967, (with others) Fundamentals of Drug Metabolism and Drug Disposition, 1971, Endogenous and Exogenous Opiate Agonists and Antagonists, 1979; mem. editl. bd. Clin. Pharmacology, Therapeutics, 1975-87, Drug, Alcohol Dependence, 1976-87, Progress in Neuro-Psychopharmacology, 1977-91, Research Communications in Chem. Pathology and Pharmacology, 1978-91, Alcohol and Drug Dependence, 1986-91, Asian Pacific Jour. Pharm., 1985—, Jour. Chinese Medicine, 1993—; contbr. numerous articles and revs. to profl. publs. Recipient Faculty Rsch. Lectr. award U. Calif., San Francisco, 1974, San Francisco Chinese Hosp. award, 1976, Cultural citation and Gold medal Ministry of Edn., Republic of China, 1978, Nathan B. Eddy award Coll. on Problems in Drug Dependence, 1979, Chancellor's award for pub. svc. U. Calif., 1986, Disting. Alumnus award U. Calif., San Francisco, 1990, Asian Pacific Am. Systemwide Alliance award, 1993, Lifetime Achievement aard Chinese Hist. Soc., 2001. Fellow Am. Coll. Neuropsychopharmacology (life, emeritus), Am. Coll. Clin. Pharmacology (hon.), Coll. on Problems of Drug Dependence (exec. com. 1978-92, chmn. bd. dirs. 1978-82); mem. AAAS, Am. Soc. Pharmacology, Exptl. Therapeutics (bd. editors 1957-65, pres. 1976-77, Torald Sollman award 1992), Fedn. Am. Socs. Exptl. Biology (exec. bd. 1975-79, pres. 1977-78), Am. Pharm. Assn. (life, Rsch. Achievement award 1962), AMA, Soc. Aid and Rehab. Drug Addicts (Hong Kong, life), Western Pharmacology Soc. (pres. 1963-64), Japanese Pharm. Soc. (hon.), Coun. Sci. Soc. Pres.' (exec. com. 1979-84, treas. 1980-84), Chinese Pharmacology Soc. (hon.), Academia Sinica (academician). Office: U Calif Dept Cellular and Molecular Pharmacology 1210 S San Francisco CA 94143-0001

WAY, JACOB EDSON, III, museum director; b. Chgo., May 18, 1947; s. Jacob Edson Jr. and Amelia (Evans) W.; m. Jean Ellwood Chappell, Sept. 6, 1969; children: Sarah Chappell Quiroga, Rebecca Stoddard, Jacob Edson IV. BA, Beloit Coll., 1968; MA, U. Toronto, 1971, PhD, 1978. Instr. Beloit (Wis.) Coll., 1972-73, asst. prof., 1973-80, assoc. prof., 1980-85; dir. Logan Mus. Anthropology, Beloit, 1980-85, Wheelwright Mus. Am. Indian, Santa Fe, 1985-89; interim dir. N.Mex. Mus. Natural History, Albuquerque, 1990-91; exec. dir. Space Ctr. Internat. Space Hall of Fame, Alamogorgo, N.Mex., 1991-94; dir. N.Mex. Farm and Ranch Heritage Mus., 1994-99; cultural affairs officer State of N.Mex., Santa Fe, 1997—. Evaluator Nat. Park Service, Denver, 1986. Contbr. articles to profl. jours. Mem. Nuke Watch, Beloit, 1983-84; cultural affairs officer State of N.Mex., 1997—. Research grants Wis. Humanities Com., 1984, NSF, 1981; grantee Cullister Found., 1978-84; fellow U. Toronto, 1971. Mem. Am. Assn. Mus., Am. Assn. Phys. Anthropology, Can. Assn. for Phys. Anthropology, N.Mex. Assn. Mus. (pres. 1994-96), Soc. Am. Archaeology, Wis. Fedn. Mus. (adv. bd. 1982-85). Mem. Soc. Friends. Avocations: camping, skiing, fishing, reading, horseback riding. Office: Office Cultural Affairs 228 E Palace Ave Santa Fe NM 87501-2000

WAYBURN, EDGAR, internist, environmentalist; b. Macon, Ga., Sept. 17, 1906; s. Emanuel and Marian (Voorsanger) W.; m. Cornelia Elliott, Sept. 12, 1947; children: Cynthia, William, Diana, Laurie. AB magna cum laude, U. Ga., 1926; MD cum laude, Harvard U., 1930. Hosp. tng. Columbia-Presbyn. Hosp., N.Y.C., 1931-33; assoc. clin. prof. Stanford (Calif.) U., 1933-65, U. Calif., San Francisco, 1960-76; practice medicine specializing in internal medicine San Francisco, 1933-1985; mem. staff Pacific Presbyn. Med. Ctr., San Francisco, 1959-86, chief endocrine clinic, 1959-72, vice chief staff, 1961-63, hon. staff, 1986—. Editor: Man Medicine and Ecology, 1970; contbr. articles to profl. and environ. jours. Mem. Sec. of Interior's Adv. Bd. on Nat. Park System, 1979-83, mem. world commn. on protected areas Internat. Union for Conservation Nature and Natural Resources; leader nat. campaigns Alaska Nat. Interest Lands Conservation Act; trustee Pacific Presbyn. Med. Ctr., 1978-86; bd. dirs. Garden Sullivan Hosp., 1965-80; chmn. People For a Golden Gate Nat. Recreation Area, 1971—; mem. citizens' adv. commn. Golden Gate Nat. Recreation Area, San Francisco, 1974—, leader nat. campaigns, 1955-90; prin. citizen advocate Redwood Nat. Park, 1968, 78; dir. The Antarctica Project; mem. adv. bd. Pacific Forest Trust; hon. chmn. Tuolomne River Preservation Trust; prin. adv. Enlargement of Mt. Tamalpais State Pk.; leader campaign to establish Golden Gate Nat. Recreation Area, 1972. Maj. USAF, 1942-46. Recipient Douglas award Nat. Pks. and Conservation Assn., 1987, Leopold award Calif. Nature Conservancy, 1988, Fred Packard award Internat. Union Conservation Nature, 1994, Laureate of Global 500 Roll of Honour award U.N. Environment Programme, 1994, 1st Conservation award Ecotrust, 1994, Albert Schweitzer prize, 1995, Presdl. Medal of Freedom, 1999. Fellow ACP; mem. AMA, Am. Soc. Internal Medicine, Calif. Med. Assn. (del. 1958-83, Recognition award 1986, Leadership and Quality awards 1986), San Francisco Med. Soc. (pres. 1965, Resolution of Congratulations 1986), Sierra Club (pres. 1961-64, 67-69, John Muir award 1972, hon. pres. 1993), Sierra Club Found. (dir. 1960-87, pres. 1971-78, hon. pres. 1998—), Fedn. Western Outdoor Clubs (pres. 1953-55). Avocations: exploration, hiking. Home: 1450 Post St Apt 1008 San Francisco CA 94109

WAYBURN, PEGGY (CORNELIA ELLIOTT WAYBURN), writer, editor; b. N.Y.C., Sept. 2, 1917; d. Thomas Ketchin and Cornelia (Ligon) E.; m. Edgar Wayburn Sept. 12, 1947; children: Cynthia, William, Diana, Laurie. BA cum laude, Barnard, 1942. Copywriter Vogue Mag., N.Y.C., 1943-45, J. Walter Thompson, San Francisco, 1945-47; self employed freelance writer, San Francisco, 1948—. Author: Adventuring in the San Francisco Bay Area, Adventuring in Alaska; (prize-winning audio visual series) Circle of Life; contbr. articles to mags. and profl. jours. Bd. advisors Am. Youth Hostels; past trustee Sierra Club Found. Recipient Annual award Calif. Conservation Assn., 1966. Mem. Sierra Club (hon. v.p., Spl. Svc. award 1967, Women's award 1989), Phi Beta Kappa. Avocations: traveling, hiking, river-running. Home: 1450 Post St Apt 1008 San Francisco CA 94109

WAYLAND, NEWTON HART, conductor; b. Santa Barbara, Calif., Nov. 5, 1940; s. L.C. Newton and Helen Bertha (Hart) W.; m. Judith Anne Curtis, July 3, 1969 (div. 1986). MusB, New Eng. Conservatory Music, 1964, MusM, 1966. Host, composer, performer Sta. WGBH-TV, Boston, 1963-82; pianist, harpsichordist Boston Symphony Orch., 1964-71; music dir. Charles Playhouse, 1965-67; pianist, guest condr., arranger Boston Pops Orch., 1971-74; resident Pops condr. Midwest Pops Orch., South Bend, Ind., 1979-91, Oakland Symphony Orch., Calif., 1980-85, Houston Symphony Orch., 1986-93; prin. Pops condr. Denver Symphony Orch., 1987-89, Vancouver (B.C.) Symphony Orch., 1993—. Guest condr. numerous orchs. U.S. and Canada, 1977—. Recs. include: Music for Zoom (PBS Emmy-winning TV show), 1971-78, Music for Nova (award-winning PBS-TV show), 1972-78, America Swings, 1987, Gershwin Plays Gershwin, 1987, Pop Go the Beatles, 1987, Classical Jukebox, 1988, Stompin' at the Savoy, 1988, Sophisticated Ladies, 1988, A Touch of Fiedler, 1989, Prime Time, 1989; arranger, performer: Jazz Loves Bach, 1968, Fiedler in Rags, 1974; arranger, condr.: Berlin to Broadway with Kurt Weill, 1972; condr. Oedipus Tex (Grammy award 1991); arranger, composer, performer (songs A&M Records) Come On and Zoom, Zoom Tunes. Recipient highest honors New Eng. Conservatory Music, 1974, Chadwick Disting. Achievement medal New Eng. Conservatory Music, 1966. Avocations: hiking, history, theatre. Home and Office: 2970 Hidden Valley Ln Santa Barbara CA 93108-1619

WAYMAN, ROBERT PAUL, computer company executive; b. Chgo., July 5, 1945; s. Lowell Roger and Dorothy Emma (Francke) W.; m. Susan O. Humphrey; children: Jennifer, Allison, Grant, Kirsten, Clayton. BS in Sci. Engring., Northwestern U., 1967, MBA, 1969. Cost acct. Hewlett-Packard Co., Loveland, Calif., 1969-71, mgr. cost accounts, 1971-73, div. controller, 1973-76; instrument group controller Palo Alto, 1976-83; corp. controller Palo Alto, 1983-84; CFO Palo Alto, 1984—. Mem. Fin. Execs. Inst., Council Fin. Execs., Private Sector Coun., dir. Hewlett-Packard, CNF Transportation Sybase. Office: Hewlett-Packard Co 3000 Hanover St Palo Alto CA 94304-1181

WAYMOUTH, ROBERT, chemistry educator; Prof. dept. chemistry Stanford (Calif.) U. Recipient Arthur C. Cope Scholar award Am. Chem. Soc., 1995, Alan T. Waterman award NSF, 1996. Office: Stanford U Dept Chem S G Mudd Bldg Rm 191 Stanford CA 94305-1928

WAYNE, KYRA PETROVSKAYA, writer; b. Crimea, USSR, Dec. 31, 1918; came to U.S., 1948, naturalized, 1951; d. Prince Vasily Sergeyevich and Baroness Zinaida Fedorovna (Fon-Haffenberg) Obolensky; m. George J. Wayne, Apr. 21, 1961; 1 child, Ronald George. BA, Leningrad Inst. Theatre Arts, 1939, MA, 1940. Actress, concert singer, USSR, 1939-46; actress U.S., 1948-59; enrichment lectr. Royal Viking Line cruises, Alaska-Can., Greek Islands-Black Sea, Russia/Europe, 1978-79, 81-82, 83-84, 86-8, 88. Author: Kyra, 1959, Kyra's Secrets of Russian Cooking, 1960, 93, The Quest for the Golden Fleece, 1962, Shurik, 1971, 92, The Awakening, 1972, The Witches of Barguzin, 1975, Max, The Dog That

Refused to Die, 1979 (Best Fiction award Dog Writers Assn. Am. 1980), Rekindle the Dreams, 1979, Quest For Empire, 1986, Li'l Ol' Charlie, 1989, Quest For Bigfoot, 1996, Pepper's Ordeal, 2000. Founder, pres. Clean Air Program, L.A. County, 1971-72; mem. women's coun. KCET-Ednl. TV, Monterey County Symphony Guild, 1989-91, Monterey Bay Aquarium, Monterey Peninsula Mus. Art, Friends of La Mirada, Fresno Art Mus., Fresno Met. Mus., Valley Children's Hosp. Served to lt. Russian Army, 1941-43. Decorated Red Star, numerous other decorations USSR; recipient award Crusade for Freedom, 1955-56; award L.A. County, 1972, Merit award Am. Lung Assn. L.A. County, 1988, Award of Merit The Congress of Russian Ams., 1999. Mem. PEN, Soc. Children's Book Writers, Authors Guild, UCLA Med. Faculty Wives (pres. 1970-71, dir. 1971-75) UCLA affiliates (life), L.A. Lung Assn. (life), Friends of the Lung Assn. (pres. 1988), Carmel Music Soc. (bd. dirs. 1992-94), Idyllwild Sch. Music, Art and Theatre Assn. (trustee 1987), Los Angelenos Club (life), Fresno Philharmonic, Club 25. Home: 561 E Mariners Cir Fresno CA 93720-0848

WAYNE, MARVIN ALAN, emergency medicine physician; b. Detroit, Dec. 11, 1943; s. Jack I. and Marian M. (Berk) W.; m. Joan A. Tobin, Dec. 30, 1971; children: Michelle, Dana. MD, U. Mich., 1968. Diplomate Am. Bd. Emergency Medicine. Fellow St. Bartholomew's Hosp., London, 1968, Virginia Mason Hosp., Seattle, 1973-74; resident in surgery U. Colo. Med. Ctr., Denver, 1968-71; pvt. practice Bellingham, Wash., 1974—; staff emergency dept. St. Joseph's Hosp. (merger St. Joseph's Hosp. and St. Luke's Hosp.), Bellingham, 1974—, vice chmn. dept. emergency medicine, 1980-83, chmn., 1984-86; med. dir. Emergency Med. Svcs., Bellingham, 1975—; assoc. clin. prof. sch. medicine U. Wash., Seattle, 1986—; asst. clin. prof. Yale U. Sch. of Medicine, New Haven. Vice chmn. emergency med. svcs. com. State of Wash., 1982-83, chmn., 1983-86; med. dir. Med-Flight Helicopter, 1980—, Inst. for Pre-Hosp. Medicine, 1980—; pres. Whatcom County Emergency Med. Svcs. Coun., 1979; med. advisor Mt. Baker Ski Patrol; spkr. nat. and internat. edn. programs; founder, owner Dr. Cookie Inc., Edmonds, Wash., 1985—. Contbr. articles to med. jours. Bd. dirs. YMCA, Bellingham, 1980-84. Maj. M.C., U.S. Army, 1971-73, Vietnam. Recipient Outstanding Achievement award Whatcom County Emergency Med. Svcs. Coun., 1980, Outstanding Ednl. Achievement award Abbott Labs., 1982, Outstanding Advanced Life Support System award State of Wash., 1983, Emergency Med. Svc. rsch. award Wash. Assn. Emergency Med. Technicians and Paramedics, 1983. Fellow Am. Coll. Emergency Physicians (bd. dirs. Wash. chpt. 1977-84, pres. 1978, sci. meetings com. 1984, Outstanding Ednl. Achievement award 1982), Royal Soc. Medicine (Eng.); mem. Wash. State Med. Soc. (emergency med. svc. adv. com. 1978-), Whatcom County Med. Soc., Univ. Assn. for Emergency Medicine, Soc. Critical Care Medicine, Am. Trauma Soc. (founding), Nat. Assn. Emergency Med. Svc. Physicians, Am. Soc. Automotive Medicine, Nat. Assn. Emergency Med. Technicians. Avocations: sailing, windsurfing, skiing, baking. Office: Emergency Med Svcs 1800 Broadway Bellingham WA 98225-3133

WAYTE, ALAN (PAUL WAYTE), lawyer; b. Huntington Park, Calif., Dec. 30, 1936; s. Paul Henry and Helen Lucille (McCarthy) W.; m. Beverly A. Bruen, Feb. 19, 1959 (div. 1972); children: David Alan, Lawrence Andrew, Marcia Louise; m. Nancy Kelly Wayte, July 5, 1975. AB, Stanford U., 1958, JD, 1960. Bar: Calif. 1961, U.S. Dist. Ct. (so. dist.) Calif. 1961, U.S. Supreme Ct. 1984. Ptnr. Adams, Duque & Hazeltine, Los Angeles, 1966-85, Dewey Ballantine, Los Angeles, 1985—. Mem. L.A. County Bar Assn. (chmn. real property sect. 1981-82), Am. Coll. Real Estate Lawyers (bd. govs. 1989—, pres. 1994), Am. Coll. Mortgage Attys., Anglo-Am. Real Property Inst. (bd. govs. 1989-91), L.A. Philharm. Assn. (exec. com. bd. dirs. 1973—), Chancery Club, Calif. Club (L.A.), Valley Hunt Club (Pasadena). Home: 1745 Orlando Rd Pasadena CA 91106-4131 Office: Dewey Ballantine 333 S Hope St Los Angeles CA 90071-1406 E-mail: awayte@deweyballantine.com

WAZZAN, A(HMED) R(ASSEM) FRANK, engineering educator, dean; b. Lattakia, Syria, Oct. 17, 1935; married, 1959; 3 children. BS, U. Calif., Berkeley, 1959, MS, 1961, PhD in Engring. Sci., 1963. From asst. prof. to assoc. prof. engring. UCLA, 1962-69, prof. engring. and applied sci., 1974—, assoc. dean Henry Samueli Sch. Engring. and Applied Sci., 1981-86, dean Henry Samueli Sch. Engring. and Applied Sci., 1986—. Cons. McDonnell Douglas Corp., 1962-71, Lawrence Radiation Lab., 1965-67, Westinghouse Electric Corp., 1974-76, N.Am. Aviation, 1975-78, Rand Corp., 1975—; Honeywell Corp., 1976-78; vis. scholar Electricité de France, Paris, Office of Commr. Atomic Energy, Saclay, France, 1973-79. Reviewer Applied Mech. Rev., 1971-87. Guggenheim fellow, 1966. Fellow Am. Nuclear Soc. Achievements include research in modeling of fuel elements for fast breeder reactor, stability and transition of laminar flows, thermodynamics of solids and of dense gases, and thermal hydraulics of pressurized water reactors. Office: UCLA Henry Samueli Sch Engring Sci Box 951600 7400 Boelter Hall Los Angeles CA 90095-1600

WEAR, BYRON, councilman; Coun. mem. 2nd dist. City of San Diego. Office: 202 C St San Diego CA 92101-4806

WEATHERLEY-WHITE, ROY CHRISTOPHER ANTHONY, surgeon, consultant; b. Peshawar, India, Dec. 1, 1931; S. Roy and Elfreda (Milward) Boehm, m. Dorian Jeanne Freeman Weatherley-White, Dec. 27, 1961; children: Carl Christopher, Matthew Richard, Larissa Chantal. MA, Cambridge U., 1953; MD, Harvard U., 1958. Surgeon Biomedical Cons., Denver, 1970—; pres. Plastic Surgery Group, Denver, 1992-97. Chmn. Plastic Surgery Rsch. Coun., 1975-76; pres. Rocky Mountain Assn. Plastic Surgeons, 1973-74; v.p. Am. Cleft Palate Assn. Author: Plastic Surgeru of the Female Breast, 1982; contbr. over 45 articles to profl. jours. Cons. Colo. Biomedical Venture Ctr., Denver, 1993—; chmn. bd. trustees Colo. Venture Ctrs., 1999—; bd. chairperson Operation Smile, Colo., 2000—. Recipient Rsch. award Am. Soc. Plastic Surgery, 1962, 64. Mem. Harvard Club of N.Y., Oxford-Cambridge Club, Denver Country Club, Denver Athletic Club. Episcopalian. Avocations: flying, skiing, scuba diving, archaeology. Home: 2101 E Hawthorne Pl Denver CO 80206-4116 Office: Biomedical Cons Inc 100 S Humboldt St Denver CO 80209-2516

WEATHERUP, ROY GARFIELD, lawyer; b. Annapolis, Md., Apr. 20, 1947; s. Robert Alexander and Kathryn Crites (Hesser) W.; m. Wendy Gaines, Sept. 10, 1977; children: Jennifer, Christine. AB in Polit. Sci., Stanford U., 1968, JD, 1972. Bar: Calif. 1972, U.S. Dist. Ct. 1973, U.S. Ct. Appeals (9th cir.) 1975, U.S. Supreme Ct. 1980. Assoc. Haight, Brown & Bonesteel, Santa Monica, Santa Ana, L.A., 1972-78, ptnr., 1979—. Judge Moot Ct. UCLA, Loyola U., Pepperdine U.; arbitrator Am. Arbitration Assn.; mem. com. Book Approved Jury Instrns. L.A. Superior Ct. Mem. ABA, Calif. Acad. Appellate Lawyers, Los Angeles County Bar Assn., Town Hall Calif. Republican. Methodist. Home: 17260 Rayen St Northridge CA 91325-2919 Office: Haight Brown & Bonesteel Ste 800 6080 Center Dr Los Angeles CA 90045 E-mail: weatherup@hbblaw.com

WEAVER, DELBERT ALLEN, lawyer; b. Shoshone, Idaho, May 28, 1931; s. Arlo Irving and Kate Rosamond (McCarter) W.; m. Jeanne Carol Alford, June 1959; children: Tobin Elizabeth, Michael Andrew, Matthew Stewart, Edward Malcolm. BA, U. Oreg., 1953, LLB, 1956. Bar: Oreg. 1956, U.S. Dist. Ct. Oreg. 1956, U.S. Ct. Appeals (9th cir.) 1968. Ptnr. Weaver & Oram, Eugene, Oreg., 1956-59; dep. atty. City of Portland, 1959-68; assoc. Winfree, Latourette, Murphy, et al., Portland, 1968-71; stockbroker Dupont Glore Forgan, Portland, 1971-73; securities examiner corp. div. State of Oreg., Salem, 1973-75, dep. commr. corp. div., 1975-80; pvt. practice Portland, 1980-87; counsel Schwabe, Williamson & Wyatt, Portland, 1987-90, sr. ptnr., 1991-96; pvt. practice Portland, 1996-2000; counsel Dunn, Carney, Portland, 2000—. Office: Ste 1500 851 SW 6th Ave Portland OR 97204-1001

WEAVER, HOWARD C. newspaper executive; b. Anchorage, Oct. 15, 1950; s. Howard Gilbert and Lurlene Eloise (Gamble) W.; m. Alice Laprele Gauchay, July 16, 1970 (div. 1974); m. Barbara Lynn Hodgin, Sept. 16, 1978. BA Johns Hopkins U., 1972, MPhil Cambridge U., 1993. Reporter, staff writer Anchorage Daily News, 1972—76, columnist, 1979—80, mng. editor, 1980—83, editor, 1983—95; editor, owner Alaska Advocate, 1976—79; asst. to pres. McClatchy Newspapers, 1995—97, editor of editl. pages, 1997—2001; v.p. news The McClatchy Co., 2001—. Internat. co-chair Northern News Svc., 1989—94; disting. lectr. journalism U. Alaska, Fairbanks, 1991. Recipient Pulitzer prize juror, 1988—89, , 1994—95, Pulitzer prize, 1976, , 1989, Headliner award, Press Club of Atlantic City, 1976, 1989, Gold medal, Investigative Reporters and Editors, 1989, Pub. Svc. award, AP Mng. Editor's Assn., 1976, 1989. Mem.: Alaska Press Club (bd. dirs. 1972—84), Upper Yukon River Press Club (pres. 1972), Sigma Delta Chi, Am. Soc. Newspaper Editors, Investigative Reporters and Editors. Avocations: ice hockey, foreign travel, opera .

WEAVER, MAX KIMBALL, social worker, consultant; b. Price, Utah, Apr. 4, 1941; s. Max Dickson and Ruth (Kimball) W.; m. Janet Hofheins, Sept. 13, 1963; children: Kim, Cleve, Chris, Wendy, Michael, Amyanne, Heather. Student, So. Utah State Coll., 1959-60; BS, Brigham Young U., 1965; MSW, U. Utah, 1967. Lic. clin. social worker and marriage counselor, Utah. Cons. Utah State Tng. Sch. (now Devel. Ctr.), American Fork, 1966; dir. Dept. Pub. Welfare, Cedar City, Utah, 1967-70; social worker Latter Day St. Social Services, Cedar City, 1970-75; with Mental Retardation Devel. Disabled Adult Services Dept. Social Services, Cedar City, 1975—. Cons. nursing homes, Utah, 1974-95; tchr. So. Utah State Coll., Cedar City, 1972, 77; home health social worker, 1993—. Contbr. articles to mags. Pres. Am. Little League Baseball, 1977-84, 86, Cedar High Booster Club, 1984-95; chmn. Rep. Precinct #1, 1984; v.p. Big League Baseball, 1986-95. Recipient Silver Beaver award, 1996. Mem. Nat. Assn. Social Work (nominating com., licensing com.), Am. Pub. Welfare Assn., Utah Pub. Employees Assn. Mormon. Lodge: Rotary. Avocations: reading, sports, scouting, gardening. Home: 157 Rountree Dr Cedar City UT 84720-3532 Office: Dept Human Svcs 106 N 100 E Cedar City UT 84720-2608

WEAVER, MICHAEL JAMES, lawyer; b. Bakersfield, Calif., Feb. 11, 1946; s. Kenneth James and Elsa Hope (Rogers) W.; m. Valerie Scott, Sept. 2, 1966; children: Christopher James, Brett Michael, Karen Ashley. AB, Calif. State U., Long Beach, 1968; JD magna cum laude, U. San Diego, 1973. Bar: Calif., 1973, U.S. Dist. Ct. (so. dist.) Calif. 1973, U.S. Ct. Appeals (9th cir.) 1975, U.S. Supreme Ct. 1977. Law clk. to chief judge U.S. Dist. Ct. (so. dist.) Calif., San Diego, 1973-75; assoc. Luce, Forward, Hamilton & Scripps, San Diego, 1975-80, ptnr., 1980-86, Sheppard, Mullin, Richter & Hampton, San Diego, 1986-99, Latham & Watkins, San Diego, 1999—. Judge pro tem San Diego Superior Ct.; master of the Bench of the Inn, Am. Inns of Ct., Louis M. Welch chpt.; lectr. Inn of Ct., San Diego, 1981—, Continuing Edn. of Bar, Calif., 1983—, Workshop for Judges U.S. Ct. Appeals (9th cir.), 1990; mem. task force on establishment of bus. cts. sys. Jud. Coun. Calif., 1996-97. Editor-in-chief: San Diego Law Rev., 1973; contbr. articles to profl. jours. Bd. dirs., pres. San Diego Kidney Found., 1985-90; bd. dirs. San Diego Aerospace Mus., 1985-97; trustee La Jolla (Calif.) Playhouse, 1990-91. lt. USNR, 1968-74. Fellow Am. Coll. Trial Lawyers; mem. San Diego Assn. Bus. Trial Lawyers (founding mem., bd. govs.), San Diego Def. Lawyers Assn. (dir.), Am. Arbitration Assn., 9th Cir. Jud. Conf. (del. 1987-90), Calif. Supreme Ct. Hist. Assn. (bd. dirs. 1998—), Safari Club Internat. (San Diego chpt.), San Diego Sportsmen's Club, Coronado Yacht Club. Republican. Presbyterian. Avocations: reading, family activities, flying, skiing. Office: Latham & Watkins 701 B St Ste 2100 San Diego CA 92101-8197 E-mail: mike.weaver@lw.com

WEAVER, WILLIAM SCHILDECKER, electric power industry executive; b. Pitts., Jan. 15, 1944; s. Charles Henry and Louise (Schildecker) W.; m. Janet Kae Jones, Mar. 7, 1981. BA, Hamilton Coll., 1965; JD, U. Mich., 1968. Bar: Wash. 1968. Assoc. Perkins Coie, Seattle, 1968-74, ptnr., 1975-91; exec. v.p., CFO Puget Sound Power & Light Co., Bellevue, Wash., 1991-97; vice chmn., chmn. unregulated subsidiaries Puget Sound Energy, 1997—, pres., COO, 1997, pres., CEO, 1998—, also bd. dirs. Bd. dirs. Hydro Electric Devel. Co., Bellevue, Connex T, Inc., Seattle, Edison Electric Inst. Bd. dirs. Wash. Rsch. Coun., Seattle, 1991-97, chmn., 1995-97; trustee Seattle Repertory Theatre, 1992-95, 99-2000, chmn., 2000—, Corp. Coun. Arts, 1995—, Pacific Sci. Ctr., 1997—. Mem. ABA, Wash. State Bar Assn., Wash. Bus. Round Table, Cmty. Devel. Round Table, Seattle Yacht Club, Rainier Club. Office: Puget Sound Energy PO Box 97034-obc- Bellevue WA 98009

WEBB, CARL B. bank officer; BA, W. Tex. State U., 1972; attended, Tex. Tech. U., Masters Bus.; grad., Southern Methodist U., 1981. Corp. banking divn. InterFirst Bank, Dallas; v.p., dir. Gerald Ford's First United Bank Group, 1983; pres., COO First Nat. Bank, Lubbock, Tex., 1983-88, First Gibraltar Bank, 1988-93, First Nationwide Bank, 1994-97, Ca. Federal Bank, 1997—. Office: Golden State Bancorp 135 Main St San Francisco CA 94105-1812

WEBB, EUGENE, English language educator; b. Santa Monica, Calif., Nov. 10, 1938; m. Marilyn Teruko Domoto, June 4, 1964. BA, U. Calif., L.A., 1960; MA, Columbia U., 1962, PhD, 1965. Asst. prof. Simon Fraser U., 1965-66, U. Wash., Seattle, 1966-70, assoc. prof., 1970-75, prof. comparative lit. and comparative religion, 1975-2000, prof. emeritus internat. studies, 2001—. Author: Samuel Beckett: A Study of His Novels, 1970, The Plays of Samuel Beckett, 1972, The Dark Dove: The Sacred and Secular in Modern Literature, 1975, Eric Voegelin: Philosopher of History, 1981, Philosophers of Consciousness: Polanyi, Lonergan, Voegelin, Ricoeur, Girard, Kierkegaard, 1988, The Self Between: From Freud to the New Social Psychology of France, 1993. Active Colloquium on Violence and Religion. Mem. Phi Beta Kappa. Episcopalian. Home: 6911 57th Ave NE Seattle WA 98115-7834 Office: U Wash Jackson Sch Internat Studies PO Box 353650 Seattle WA 98195-3650

WEBB, H. LAWRENCE, real estate executive; m. Janet Hadley; children: Laura, Emily. Pres. Calif. divsn. John Laing Homes; CEO, WL Homes LLC (merger John Laing Homes and Watt Homes), Irvine, Calif., 1996—. Bd. dirs. Orange County Housing Authority, Interval House. Mem. Nat. Assn. Home Builders (bd. trustees Nat. Sales and Mktg. Coun., inducted into Legends of Mktg. Hall of Fame). Office: WL Homes LLC 19600 Fairchild Ste 120 Irvine CA 92612-2509

WEBB, WELLINGTON E. mayor; b. Chgo., Feb. 17, 1941; BA in Edn., Colo. State Coll., 1964; MA in Edn., U. No. Colo., 1970. Tchr., 1964-76; elected Colo. Ho. of Reps., 1972, 74, 76; regional dir. HEW, 1977-81; gov.'s cabinet, 1981-87; elected auditor City of Denver, 1987-91, mayor, 1991—. Pres. U.S. Conf. of Mayors, 1993—, Nat. Conf. Black Mayors, 2000—. Office: Office Mayor City & County Bldg Rm 350 1437 Bannock St Denver CO 80202-5337

WEBBER, CHRIS, III (MAYCE EDWARD CHRISTOPHER WEBBER), professional basketball player; b. Detroit, Mar. 1, 1973; s. Mayce and Doris Webber. Student, U. Mich., 1991-93. Drafted Orlando (Fla.) Magic, 1993; forward Golden State Warriors, San Francisco, 1993-94, Washington Bullets, 1994-98, Sacramento Kings, 1998-. Founder Timeout Found. Drafted 1st round Orlando Magic, 1993; named Nat. H.S. Player of Yr., 1990-91, Mr. Basketball State of Mich., 1991, Coca-Cola Classic NBA Player of Yr., 1994, Brut Bullets Player of Yr., 1994-95, NBA All-Rookie 1st Team, 1994. Avocations: collecting signed historical documents of prominent African-Americans. Office: Sacremento Kings One Sports Parkway Sacramento CA 95834

WEBBER, WILLIAM ALEXANDER, university administrator, physician; b. Nfld., Can., Apr. 8, 1934; s. William Grant and Hester Mary (Constable) W.; m. Marilyn Joan Robson, May 17, 1958; children— Susan Joyce, Eric Michael, George David. MD, U. B.C., Can., Vancouver, , 1958; LLD, U. B.C., 2000. Intern Vancouver Gen. Hosp., 1958-59; fellow Cornell U. Med. Coll., N.Y.C., 1959-61; asst. prof. medicine U. B.C., 1961-66, assoc. prof., 1966-69, prof., 1969—, dean faculty medicine, 1977-90, assoc. v.p. acad., 1990-96. Mem. B.C. Med. Assn., Can. Assn. Anatomists, Am. Assn. Anatomists. Achievements include research on renal structure and function. Home: 2478 Crown St Vancouver BC Canada V6R 3V8 Office: U BC 2177 Westbrook Mall Vancouver BC Canada V6T 1Z3 E-mail: webber@interchange.ubc.ca

WEBER, CHARLES L. electrical engineering educator; b. Dayton, Ohio, Dec. 2, 1937; BSEE, U. Dayton, 1958; MSEE, U. So. Calif., 1960; PhD, UCLA, 1964. Tech. staff Hughes Aircraft Co., Calif., 1958-62; from asst. prof. to prof. elec. engring. U. So. Calif., 1964—. Fellow IEEE. Office: U So Calif Comm Scis Inst Dept Elec Engring Sys Los Angeles CA 90089-2565

WEBER, EUGEN, historian, educator, writer; b. Bucharest, Romania, Apr. 24, 1925; came to U.S., 1955; s. Emanuel and Sonia (Garrett) W.; m. Jacqueline Brument-Roth, June 12, 1950. Student, Inst. d'études politiques, Paris, 1948-49, 51-52; M.A., Emmanuel Coll., Cambridge U., 1954, M.Litt., 1956. History supr. Emmanuel Coll., 1953-54; lectr. U. Alta., 1954-55; asst. prof. U. Iowa, 1955-56; asst. prof. history UCLA, 1956, assoc. prof., 1959-63, prof., 1963—, Joan Palevsky prof. modern European history, 1984—, chmn. dept., 1965-68; dir. study center U. Calif., France, 1968-70; dean social scis. UCLA, 1976-77, dean Coll. Letters and Scis., 1977-82. Frum Meml. lectr. Toronto U., 1999; Ford faculty lectr. Stanford U., 1965; Patten lectr. Ind. U., 1981; vis. prof. Collège de France, Paris, 1983; dir. d'ètudes Ecole des hautes ètudes, Paris, 1984-85; Christian Gauss lectr., Princeton U., 1990. Author: Nationalist Revival in France, 1959, The Western Tradition, 1959, Paths to the Present, 1960, Action Française, 1962, Satan Franc-Maçon, 1964, Varieties of Fascism, 1964; (with H. Rogger) The European Right, 1965, A Modern History of Europe, 1970, Europe Since 1715, 1972, Peasants into Frenchmen, 1976 (Commonwealth prize Calif. 1977), La Fin des Terroirs, 1983 (Prix de la Société des gens de lettres 1984), France Fin-de-siècle, 1986 (Commonwealth prize Calif. 1987), The Western Tradition (WGBH/PBS TV series), 1989, My France, 1990, Movements, Currents, Trends, 1991, The Hollow Years, 1994, La France des années trente (Prix littèraire Etats-Unis/France, 1995, Prix Maurice Baumont 1995, Prix de Jeux Floraux 1997), 1995, Apocalypses, 1999; adv. editor Jour. Contemporary History, 1966—, French History, 1985—, French Cultural Studies, 1990—, Am. Scholar, 1992-98, Nuova Storia Contemporanea, 1999—. Served as capt. inf. Brit. Army, 1943-47. Recipient Luckman Disting. Teaching award UCLA Alumnae Assn., 1992; decorated Ordre Nat. des Palmes Academiques, France; Fulbright fellow, 1952, 82-83; research fellow Am. Philos. Soc., 1959, Social Sci. Research Council, 1959-61, Am. Council Learned Socs., 1962; Guggenheim fellow, 1963-64; NEH sr. fellow, 1973-74, 82-83. Fellow Netherlands Inst. Advanced Studies, Assn. française de science politique, Am. Acad. Arts and Scis., Am. Philos. Soc.; mem. Am. Hist. Assn. (scholary distinction award 1999), Soc. d'histoire moderne, Soc. French Hist. Studies, Phi Beta Kappa (hon., Ralph Waldo Emerson prize 1977, senator 1988-2000). Office: UCLA Dept History Los Angeles CA 90095-0001

WEBER, FRANCIS JOSEPH, archivist, museum director; b. Jan. 22, 1933; s. Frank J. and Katherine E. (Thompson) W. Student, L.A. Coll., 1953, St. Johns Coll., 1955, St. Johns Seminary, 1959, Cath. U. Am., 1962, Am. U., Washington. Ordained priest Roman Cath. Ch., 1959. Archivist Archdiocese L.A., 1962—; prof. history Queen Angels Sem., 1962-72; chaplain St. Catherine Mil. Sch., 1972-75; pastor San Buenaventura Mission, 1975-81; dir. Borromeo Guild, 1984-87; archivist Hist. Mus. Archival Ctr., Mission Hills, Calif. Dir. San Fernando Mission, 1981—. Editor The Tidings, 1990, Hoja Volante, 1984-95, Miniature Book Soc. Newsletter, 1995-97; contbr. articles to profl. jours. Pres. Zamorano Club, 1991-93; sheriff L.A. Corral Westerners, 1995; hist. rev. commn. Diocese of Monterey. Decorated Grand Cross Isabel la Catolica, 1993, Knighthood of The Holy Sepulchre; recipient Commendation award El Pueblo do L.A. State Historic Park, 1970, L.A. County Bd. Supr., 1972, L.A. City Coun., 1981, L.A. County Bd. Supr., 1992, Merit award Rounce and Coffin Club, 1969, 71, 75, 77, 79-80, 84-86, 88, 92-95, Archivist Excellence award Calif. Heritage Preservation Commn., 1995. Fellow Calif. Hist. Soc. (Merit award 1972, 83), Hist. Soc. So. Calif. (bd. dirs.); mem. Assn. Cath. Diocesan Archivists (pres. 1996-97), Santa Barbara Mission Archves (bd. dirs.), Assn. Cath. Diocesan Archives (bd. dirs.). Democrat. Roman Catholic. Office: Hist Mus Archival Ctr 15151 San Fernando Mission Blv Mission Hills CA 91345-1109

WEBER, FRED J. retired state supreme court justice; b. Deer Lodge, Mont., Oct. 6, 1919; s. Victor N. and Dorothy A. (Roberts) W.; m. Phyllis M. Schell, June 2, 1951; children: Anna Marie, Donald J., Mark W., Paul V. B.A., U. Mont., 1943, J.D., 1947. Bar: Mont. 1947. Atty. Kuhr & Weber, Havre, Mont., 1947-55, Weber, Bosch & Kuhr, and successors, 1956-80; justice Supreme Ct. Mont., Helena, 1981-95. Served to capt. inf. U.S. Army, 1943-46. Fellow Am. Bar Found., Am. Coll. Probate Counsel; mem. ABA, Am. Judicature Soc.

WEBER, FREDRIC G. former broadcast executive; Student, U. Mich., Babson Coll.; JD, Mich. State U. Bar: Mich., Fla. CEO and gen. mgr. Sta. KFYI-AM, Phoenix, 1985—, Sta. KKFR-FM, Phoenix, 1985-98; ret., 1998. Bd. dir. Valley Commerce Bank, The U.S. Selective Svc. Sys. for Ariz., The Arthritis Found., Ariz. Govs. Film and TV Adv. Mem. One Hundred Club Phoenix. Office: KFYI Radio 631 N 1st Ave Phoenix AZ 85003-1514

WEBER, LAVERN JOHN, marine science administrator, educator; b. Isabel, S.D., June 7, 1933; s. Jacob and Irene Rose (Bock) W.; m. Shirley Jean Carlson, June 19, 1959 (div. 1992); children: Timothy L., Peter J., Pamela C., Elizabeth T.; m. Patricia Rae Lewis, Oct. 17, 1992. AAS, Everett Jr. Coll., 1956; BA, Pacific Luth. U., 1958; MS, U. Wash., 1962, PhD, 1964. Instr. U. Wash., Seattle, 1964-67, asst. prof., 1967-69, acting state toxicologist, 1968-69; assoc. prof. Oreg. State U., Corvallis, 1969-75, prof., 1976—, asst. dean grad. sch., 1974-77; dir. Hatfield Marine Sci. Ctr. Oregon State U., Newport, 1977—, supt. Coastal Oreg. Marine Exptl. Sta., 1989-98, assoc. dean Coll. Agrl. Sci., 1998—. Pres., trustee Newport Pub. Libr., 1991-92, Yaquina Bay Econ. Found., Newport, 1991-92; chmn. Oreg. Coast Aquarium, 1983-95. Recipient Pres. award Newport Rotary, 1984-85. Mem. South Slough Mgmt. Commn., Am. Soc. Pharm. and Exptl. Therapy, West Pharm. Soc., Soc. Toxicology, Soc. Exptl. Biol. Med. (n.w.

divsn., pres. 1978, 82, 87) , Pacific N.W. Assn. Toxicologists (chair 1985-86, coun. 1991-93), Nat. Assn. Marine Lab. (pres.-elect 1998-99), Western Assn. Marine Lab. (pres. 1993). Avocations: woodworking, reading, walking, scuba, gardening. Office: Oregon State Univ Hatfield Marine Sci Ctr 2030 SE Marine Science Dr Newport OR 97365-5229

WEBER, STEPHEN LEWIS, university president; b. Boston, Mar. 17, 1942; s. Lewis F. and Catherine (Warns) W.; m. Susan M. Keim, June 27, 1965; children: Richard, Matthew. BA, Bowling Green State U., 1964; postgrad., U. Colo., 1964-66; PhD, U. Notre Dame, 1969; EdD (hon.), Capital Normal U., China, 1993. Asst. prof. philosophy U. Maine, Orono, 1969-75, assoc. prof., 1975-79, asst. to pres., 1976-79; dean arts and scis. Fairfield (Conn.) U., 1979-84; v.p. acad. affairs St. Cloud (Minn.) State U., 1984-88; pres. SUNY Oswego, 1988-95; interim provost SUNY, Albany, 1995-96; pres. San Diego State U., 1996—. Participant Harvard Inst. Ednl. Mgmt., Cambridge, Mass., 1985. Contbr. numerous articles on philosophy and acad. adminstrn. to profl. jours. Mentor Am. Coun. Edn. Fellowship Program, Am. Coun. on Edn., Commn. on Internat. Edn. and Commn. on Govtl. Rels.; bd. govs. The Peres Ctr. for Peace, San Diego Found.; bd. dirs. San Diego Regional Econ. Devel. Corp.; mem. internat. adv. bd. Found. for the Children of the Californias. Named Outstanding Humanities Tchr., U. Maine, 1975; Rsch. fellow U. Notre Dame, 1968-69. Mem. Am. Philos. Assn., Am. Assn. Higher Edn. Democrat. Avocations: art, woodworking, swimming, boating. Office: San Diego State Univ Office Pres 5500 Campanile Dr San Diego CA 92182-8000 E-mail: presidents.office@sdsu.edu

WEBER, STEPHEN VANCE, physics researcher, astrophysicist; b. Wooster, Ohio, Oct. 31, 1951; s. Dale Sarge and Lucy June (Smith) W.; m. Marie Christensen, June 21, 1980; children: Erik, Kristina. AB in Physics, Princeton U., 1973; MA in Astronomy, U. Calif., Berkeley, 1974, PhD, 1978. Rsch. fellow Calif. Inst. Tech., Pasadena, 1978-80; asst. prof. Dartmouth Coll., Hanover, N.H., 1980-82; rsch. scientist, physicist Lawrence Livermore Nat. Lab., Livermore, Calif., 1982—. Contbr. articles to profl. jours. Mem. Am. Astronomical Soc., Am. Physical Soc. (excellence in plasma physics award 1995). Achievements include investigations of Rayleigh-Taylor instability and implosions in inertial confinement fusion. Office: Lawrence Livermore Nat Lab MS L16 PO Box 808 Livermore CA 94551-0808 E-mail: svweber@llnl.gov

WEBSTER, MICHAEL ANDERSON, experimental psychologist; b. Atlanta, Mar. 24, 1958; s. John Calvin and Evelyn Gayle (Cox) W.; m. Shernaaz Michael Irani, Aug. 6, 1983; children: Anjali Dianne, Menka Linda. Exch. student, Am. U., Cairo, 1978-79; BA in Psychology, U. Calif., San Diego, 1981; MA in Psychology, U. Calif., Berkeley, 1985, PhD in Psychology, 1988. Postdoctoral fellow dept. exptl. psychology U. Cambridge, Eng., 1988-94; assoc. prof. dept. psychology U. Nev., Reno, 1994—. Contbr. articles to profl. jours. NATO fellow NSF, Cambridge U., 1988. Fellow Nat. Eye Inst. (First award 1994); mem. We. Psychol. Assn. (Outstanding Rsch. award 1998), Rocky Mountain Psychol. Assn., Exptl. Psychology Soc. (Eng.), Assn. for Rsch. in Vision and Ophthalmology, Optical Soc. Am. Achievements include research in psychophysical studies of human color vision. Office: Univ Nevada Dept Psychology Reno NV 89557-0001

WEBSTER, PETER JOHN, meteorology educator; b. Cheshire, U.K., May 30, 1942; s. James Robert and Olive W.; children: Benjamin, David. BS, Royal Melbourne Inst. Technol., Australia, 1965; PhD, MIT, 1971. Meteorologist Commn. Bur. Meteorology, 1961-67; postdoctoral fellow UCLA, 1972-73; asst. prof. U. Wash., Seattle, 1973-77; rsch. scientist CSIRO, Melbourne, Australia, 1977-83; adj. prof. Monash U., Melbourne, Australia, 1979-83; prof. Penn State U., University Pk., 1983-91; dir. program in atmospheric and oceanic scis. U. Colo., Boulder, 1991—. Chmn. TOGA Sci. Steering Group, 1986-90, TOGA COARE panel, 1989-95; co-chmn. TOGA COARE Sci. Working Group, 1988-95. Recipient Wilson Rsch. award Penn State U., 1989, Jule G. Charney award Am. Meterol. Soc., 1990, Creativity award NSF, 1990, Alexander von Humboldt Found. award, 1991. Fellow Am. Meteorol. Soc. Office: Univ Colo Prog Atmos & Ocean Scis PO Box 311 Boulder CO 80309-0311

WEBSTER, RONALD B. lawyer; b. Cle Elum, Wash., June 11, 1942; s. Burnette O. and Lucille (Beck) W.; m. M. Gail Skinner, June 26, 1971; children: Noel, Michelle. BA, U. Wash., 1964; JD, Gonzaga U., 1969. Bar: Wash., U.S. Dist. Ct. (ea. and we. dists.) Wash., U.S. Ct. Appeals (9th cir.). Dep. pros. atty. Cowlitz County, Kelso, Wash., 1970-73; ptnr. Hickman, Webster, Ensley & Carpenter, Colfax, 1973-90, Hickman, Webster & Moulton, 1990-92, Hickman & Webster, P.S., 1992-95. Mem. Whitman County Bd. Mental Health, Pullman, Wash., 1973-83; chmn. civil svc. commn. Whitman County Sheriffs Office, Colfax, 1973—; pres. Colfax and Cmty. Fund, 1973-74; pres. Whitman Cmty. Concerts, 1990-93; mem. ch. coun. Peace Luth. Ch., 1996-98; chmn. bd. dirs. Whitman County Libr., 1997—, chmn. bd. trustees, 1998—. Named Rotarian of Yr., 1998, Paul Harris fellow, 1998. Mem. Whitman County Bar Assn. (pres. 1981-82), Wash. State Bar Assn. (inter profl. com. 1986-89—, disciplinary com. 1986-97). Club: Colfax Golf and Country. Lodge: Rotary (pres. Colfax club 1983-84). Home: 1801 N Oak St Colfax WA 99111-9705 Office: Hickman Webster Tracy PLLC 302 N Mill St Colfax WA 99111-1865

WEBSTER, WILLIAM C. engineering educator; PhD in Naval Arch., U. Calif., Berkeley, 1966. With U. Calif., Berkeley, 1969—, prof., vice provost academic planning and facilities. Contbr. numerous articles to profl. jours. Fellow SNAME (Humboldt fellow, Davidson medal); mem. NAE. Achievements include research in non-linear coupled motions of offshore structures, operations research, shallow water fluid mechanics, steep water waves, wave energy. Office: Office of the Chancellor 222 California Hall MC 1500 Univ of Calif Berkeley CA 94720-1500 E-mail: wwebster@socrates.berkeley.edu

WEBSTER, WILLIAM G., JR. army officer; b. Baton Rouge, July 3, 1951; BS, U.S. Mil. Acad., 1974. Commd. 2d lt. U.S. Army, 1974, advanced through grades to brig. gen., comdr. 3d bn., 77th armor in 4th inf. divsn., 1991-93; sr. armor observer contr. Cobra Team Nat. Tng. Ctr., Ft. Irwin, Calif., 1993-94; comdr. 1st brigade, 1st cavalry divsn. Ft. Hood, 1995-97; asst .divsn. comdr. 3d Inf. Divsn., Ft. Stewart, Ga., 1997-98; comdr. Ft. Irwin and Nat. Tng. Ctr., 1998—. Decorated Legion of Merit with 2 oak leaf clusters, numerous others. Office: Nat Tng Ctr & Ft Irwin PO Box 105001 Fort Irwin CA 92310-5001

WECHSLER, MARY HEYRMAN, lawyer; b. Green Bay, Wis., Jan. 8, 1948; d. Donald Hubert and Helen (Polcyn) Heyrman; m. Roger Wechsler, Aug. 1971 (div. 1977); 1 child, Risa Heyrman; m. David Jay Sellinger, Aug. 15, 1981; 1 stepchild, Kirk Benjamin; 1 child, Michael Paul. Student, U. Chgo., 1966-67, 68-69; BA, U. Wash., 1971; JD cum laude, U. Puget Sound, 1979. Bar: Wash. 1979. Assoc. Law Offices Ann Johnson, Seattle, 1979-81; ptnr. Johnson, Wechsler, Thompson, Seattle, 1981-83; pvt. practice Seattle, 1984-87; ptnr. Mussehl, Rosenberg et al, Seattle, 1987-88, Wechsler, Becker, Erickson, Ross, Roubik & Edwards, Seattle, 1988—. [illegible] Bar of Ct. Com., 1996-2001, bd. dirs. U. Wash. Law Sch. Child Advocacy Clinic, 1996-99; mem. Walsh Commn. on Jud. Selection, 1995-96; mem. Wash. State commn. on domestic rels., 1996-97, 99-2001; chair edn. com. Access to Justice Bd., 1996-99, pub. trust and confidence com., 2000-2001; presenter in field. Author: Family Law in Washington, 1987, rev. edit., 1988, Marriage and Separation, Divorce and Your Rights, 1994; contbr. articles to legal publs. Mem. Wash. State Ethics Adv. Com., 1992-95; bd. dirs. Seattle LWV, 1991-92. Fellow Am. Acad. Matrimonial Lawyers (sec.-treas. Wash. state chpt. 1996, profl. com. nat. 1996-97, v.p. 1997-98, pres. 1999-2000, nat. arbitration com. 1999-2000, nat. interdisciplinary com. 1999-2000, nat. admissions procedure com. 2000-01); mem. ABA (chmn. membership Wash. state 1987-88), Wash. State Bar Assn. (exec. com. family law sect. 1985-91, chair 1988-89, ct. improvement com. 1998-2000, legs. com. 1991-96, Outstanding Atty. of Yr. family law sect. 1988, comms. com. 1997-98, disciplinary hearing officer 1998—), Wash. Women Lawyers, King County Bar Assn. (legis. com. 1985-2000, vice-chair 1990-91, chair family law sect. 1986-87, chair domestic violence com. 1986-87, trustee 1988-90, policy planning com. 1991-92, 2d v.p. 1992-93, 1st v.p. 1993-94, pres. 1994-95, long-range planning com. 1998-99, awards com. 1997-99, Outstanding Atty. award 1999), Nat. Conf. of Bar Pres. (commn. com. 1994-95, long range planning com. 1998-99), King County Bar Found. (trustee 1997-2000), Am. Judicature Soc. (v.p. Washington chpt. 2000-2001). Office: Wechsler Becker Erickson Ross Roubik & Edwards 701 5th Ave Seattle WA 98104-7097

WEDDIG, FRANK O. state legislator; b. West Bend, Wis., Nov. 1, 1944; m. Patricia Weddig. Student, Bethany Coll., Waukesha Vocat. Sch., C.C. Denver. Comml. constrn. electrician, Aurora, Colo.; mem. Colo. State Senate, Denver, 1994-2001, Colo. State Ho. Reps., 2001—, mem. logal govt. com., vets. and mil. affairs. com. Mem. local govt. com., state, vets. and mil. affairs com. Mem. Aurora City Coun., 1981-94, mayor pro tem, 1986-87; bd. dirs. Met. Waste Water Reclamation Dist.; past mem. Aurora Planning and Zoning Commn. With USAF, 1962-66. Mem. NOW, Dem. Leadership Coun., Am. Legion, Common Cause. Democrat. Office: Colo State Ho Reps State Capitol 200 E Colfax Rm 271 Denver CO 80203 also: 15818 E 8th Cir Aurora CO 80011-7304 Fax: 303-360-0462. E-mail: fweddig@eazy.net

WEDEPOHL, LEONHARD MARTIN, electrical engineering educator; b. Pretoria, Republic of South Africa, Jan. 26, 1933; s. Martin Willie and Liselotte B.M. (Franz) W.; m. Sylvia A.L. St. Jean; children: Martin, Graham. B.Sc. (Eng.), Rand U., 1953; Ph.D., U. Manchester, Eng., 1957. Registered profl. engr., B.C. Planning engr. Escom, Johannesburg, Republic of South Africa, 1957-61; mgr. L.M. Erricson, Pretoria, Republic of South Africa, 1961-62; sect. leader Reyrolle, Newcastle, Eng., 1962-64; prof., head dept. Manchester U., 1964-74; dean engring. U. Manitoba, Winnipeg, Can., 1974-79; dean applied sci. U. B.C., Vancouver, Can., 1979-85, prof. elec. engring. Can., 1985-97, prof. emeritus Can., 1998—, dean applied sci. emeritus Can., 1998—. Mem. Sci. Rsch. Coun., London, 1968-74; dir. Manitoba Hydro, Winnipeg, 1975-79, B.C. Hydro, Vancouver, 1980-84, B.C. Sci. Coun., 1982-84; cons. Horizon Robotics, Saskatoon, 1986; chmn. implementation team Sci. Place, Can., 1985; cons. CEPEL, Rio de Janeiro; adv. Manitoba High Voltage D.C. Rsch. Ctr.; tech. advisor RTDS Techs., Inc., Winnipeg, 1994—; head protection devel. Rolls Royce Indsl. Power Group, 1995-96. Contbr. articles to sci. jours.; patentee in field Named Hon. Citizen City of Winnipeg, 1979 Fellow Instn. Elec. Engrs. (premium 1967), Engring. Inst. Can.; mem. Assn. Profl. Engrs. B.C. Avocations: music, cross-country skiing, hiking. Office: 1511 Chardonnay Pl Westbank BC Canada V4T 2P9 E-mail: wedepohl@home.com

WEEKER, ELLIS, emergency physician; b. New Orleans, June 7, 1944; s. Harry and Marion W.; m. Gail Otis, July 3, 1982; children: Michael, Lisa, Elizabeth, Matthew. BS, Tulane U., 1966; MD, La. State U., 1970. Diplomate Am. Bd. Emergency Medicine. Intern Kaiser Found. Hosp., Oakland, 1970-71, resident in internal medicine, 1972-73, Highland Gen. Hosp., Oakland, 1972-73, assoc. chief emergency svcs., 1973-75; staff physician Calif. Emergency Physicians Med. Group, Oakland, 1975—, also bd. dirs.; med. dir. capitation svcs. Calif. Emergency Physicians/Medamerica, 1994—. Med. dir. Calif. Emergency Physicians Med. Group, Oakland, 1976-95, regional med. dir., 1978—, chmn. bd. dirs., 1979-87; mem. staff Good Samaritan Hosp., San Jose, Calif., 1975—, chmn. emergency dept., 1977-82. Commnr. Emergency Med. Care Commn., Santa Clara County, Calif., 1990-92. Mem. Am. Heart Assn. (chmn. bd. Santa Clara chpt. 1991-92, pres. 1988-89, nat. affiliate faculty ACLS 1982-91). Republican. Roman Catholic. Avocations: music, skiing, sailing. Office: Calif Emergency Physicians Med Group 588 Blossom Hill Rd San Jose CA 95123-3212

WEEKS, GERALD, psychology educator; b. Morehead City, N.C., Nov. 20, 1948; s. Marion G. and Ada (Willis) W.; m. Kathleen Glass, Sept. 2, 1972. BA in Philosophy and Psychology, East Carolina U., 1971, MA in Gen. Psychology, 1973; PhD in Clin. Psychology, Ga. State U., 1979. Diplomate Am. Bd. Profl. Psychology (pres. 1987-88, bd. dirs. 1982-87), Am. Bd. Family Psychology, Am. Bd. Sexology; cert. marital and family therapist; lic. practicing psychologist, N.C., Pa.; registered Health Care Providers in Psychology. Intern in family therapy Harlem Valley Psychiatric Ctr., Wingdale, N.Y., 1978-79; assoc. prof. psychology U. N.C., Wilmington, 1979-85; dir. tng. Penn Coun. for Relationships, 1985—; clin. asst. prof. psychology Sch. Medicine U. Pa., Phila., 1985-87, clin. assoc. prof., 1988-98; chair, prof. dept. counseling U. Nev.-Las Vegas, 1999—. Pvt. practice Carolina Ob-gyn Ctr., Wilmington, 1980-85. Author: Promoting Change Through Paradoxical Therapy, 1985, Treating Couples: The Intersystem Model of the Marriage Council of Philadelphia, 1989, Promoting Change through Paradoxical Therapy, 1991, (with L. L'Abate) Paradoxical Psychotherapy: Theory and Practice with Individuals, Couples, and Families, 1982, (with R. Sauber, L. L'Abate) Family Therapy: Basic Concepts and Terms, 1985, (with L. Hof) Integrating Sex and Marital Therapy: A Clinicians Guide, 1987, (with S. Treat) Couples in Treatment, 1992, rev. edit., 2001, Integrative Solutions: Treating Common Problems in Couple's Therapy, 1995, (with Nancy Gambescia) Erectile Dysfunction, 2000, (with Rita DeMaria and Larry Hof) Focused Genograms: Intergenerational Assessment of Individuals, Couples and Families, 1999; mem. editl. bd. Am. Jour. Family Therapy, Am. Jour. Family Psychology; contbr. articles to profl. jours. Fellow Am. Assn. Marital and Family Therapy (clin. mem., nat. adv. bd., approved supr.); mem. APA, Acad. Family Psychology, Interpersonal and Social Skills Assn. (founding mem.), Acad. Psychologists in Marital, Sex, and Family Therapy. Office: U Nev PO Box 453007 4505 S Maryland Pkwy Las Vegas NV 89154-9900 E-mail: gweeks@nevada.edu

WEEKS, JOHN ROBERT, geographer, sociology educator; b. Sacramento, June 1, 1944; s. Robert Louis and Thelma Hope (Evans) W.; m. Deanna Jean Hosea, May 16, 1965; children: John Robert, Gregory, Jennifer. AB, U. Calif., Berkeley, 1966, MA, 1969, PhD, 1972. Asst. prof. sociology Mich. State U., East Lansing, 1971-74, San Diego State U., 1974-78, assoc. prof., 1978-81, prof., 1981-92, prof. geography, 1992—, chmn. dept., 1978-85; adminstrv. dir. Internat. Population Ctr., 1985—; clin. prof. family & preventive medicine U. Calif. Sch. Medicine, San Diego, 1998—. Vis. rsch. demographer U. Calif., Berkeley, 1972; cons. Allied Home Health Assn., 1978-80, Area Agy. on Aging, San Diego, 1979-81, Los Angeles Regional Family Planning Coun., 1986—, East County Econ. Devel. Coun., 1986—. Author: Teenage Marriages, 1976, Population, 8th edit., 2002, Aging, 1984, Demography of Islamic Nations, 1988, High Fertility Among Indochinese Refugees, 1989, Demographic Dynamics of the U.S.-Mex. Border, 1992. Grantee USPHS, 1983-84, 87-88, 88-89, 90—, U.S. Adminstrn. on Aging, 1979-80, U.S. Bur. of Census, 1988-89, Andrew W. Mellon Found., 1998-2001, NSF, 2001—; trainee USPHS, 1967-71 Mem. Population Assn. Am., Am. Sociol. Assn., Internat. Union for Sci. Study Population, Am. Assn. Geographers. Democrat. Office: San Diego State U Dept Geography San Diego CA 92182 E-mail: john.weeks@sdsu.edu

WEEKS, WILFORD FRANK, retired geophysics educator, glaciologist; b. Champaign, Ill., Jan. 8, 1929; married; 2 children. BS, U. Ill., 1951, MS, 1953; PhD in Geology, U. Chgo., 1956. Geologist mineral deposits br. U.S. Geol. Survey, 1952-55; glaciologist USAF Cambridge Research Ctr., 1955-57; asst. prof. Washington U., St. Louis, 1957-62; adj. prof. earth scis. Dartmouth Coll., Hanover, N.H., 1962-85; glaciologist Cold Regions Rsch. and Engring. Lab., Hanover, 1962-89; chief scientist Alaska Synthetic Aperture Radar Facility, Fairbanks, 1986-93; prof. geophysics Geophys. Inst. U. Alaska, Fairbanks, 1986-96. Cons. in field, 1996—; vis. prof. Inst. Low Temperature Sci. Hokkaido U., Sapporo, Japan, 1973; chair Arctic marine sci. USN Postgrad. Sch., Monterey, Calif., 1978-79; mem. earth sys. sci. com. NASA, Washington, 1984-87; advisor U.S. Arctic Rsch. Commn., divsn. polar programs NSF, Washington, 1987-88; chmn. NAS Com. on Cooperation with Russia in Ice Mechanics, 1991-92; mem. environ. task force MEDEA Cons. Group, 1992—. Capt. USAF, 1955-57. Recipient Emil Usibelli Prize for Rsch., 1996, U. Ill. Dept. Geology Alumni Achievment award, 1999. Fellow Arctic Inst. N.Am., Am. Geophys. Union; mem. NAE, Internat. Glaciological Soc. (v.p. 1969-72, pres. 1973-75, Seligman Crystal award 1989), Am. Polar Soc. (hon.). Avocations: skiing, diving, contrabassist. Home and Office: 6533 SW 34th Ave Portland OR 97201-1077 E-mail: w-f-weeks@excite.com

WEESE, BRUCE ERIC, pharmaceutical sales executive; b. Chewelah, Wash., Mar. 22, 1942; s. Harry M. and Roberta B. (Carman) W.; m. Elaine M. Smith, June 18, 1962 (div. July 1972); children: Sandra G., Michael D.; m. Vera B. Reed, Mar. 22, 1975; stepchildren: Kevin E. Bayron, Kelly M. Bayron. BA in Edn., Ea. Wash. State U., Cheney, 1964; MBA, Pepperdine U., 1981. Tchr. Grant Joint Union High Sch. Dist., Sacramento, 1964-70; pharm. sales McNeil Labs., San Jose, Calif., 1970-77, Adria Labs., San Francisco, 1977-83, Serono Labs., San Francisco, 1983-84, Boehringer Ingelheim, Santa Rosa, Calif., 1984-91, mgr. govt. affairs (lobbyist) for western states, 1991-97, area mgr. managed care, 1997-98; pharm. sales rep. Olympia, Wash., 2000—. Bd. dirs. Russian River Health Ctr., Guerneville, Calif., 1994-95, 98—, Redwood Empire br. Am. Lung Assn., 1998—. Mem. United Anglers, Sequoia Paddlers, Santa Rosa Sailing Club, Sierra Club. Democrat. Avocations: kayaking, sailing, fishing. Home and Office: 4013 Grove Rd NW Olympia WA 98502-3766

WEGGE, LEON LOUIS FRANÇOIS, retired economics educator; b. Breendonk, Antwerp, Belgium, June 9, 1933; came to U.S., 1959; s. Petrus Maria and Alberta (De Maeyer) W.; m. Beate Maria Teipel, Nov. 22, 1962; children: Simone, Robert, Elizabeth. B in Thomistical Philosophy, Cath. U. Louvain, Belgium, 1957, Licentiate in Econ. Sci., 1958; PhD in Indsl. Econs., MIT, 1963. Assoc. lectr. U. New S. Wales, Kensington, Australia, 1963-66; prof. econs. U. Calif., Davis, 1966-94, retired, 1994—. Vis. prof. U. Bonn, Fed. Republic Germany, 1980-81. Assoc. editor Jour. Internat. Econs., 1971-84; contbr. articles to profl. jours. Rsch. fellow Ctr. for Ops. Rsch. and Econometrics, 1972-73, fellow The Netherlands Inst. for Advanced Study, 1987-88. Mem. Econometric Soc., Am. Statistical Assn. Roman Catholic. Home: 26320 County Rd # 98 Davis CA 95616

WEH, ALLEN EDWARD, airline executive; b. Salem, Oreg., Nov. 17, 1942; s. Edward and Harriet Ann (Hicklin) W.; m. Rebecca Ann Roberton, July 5, 1968; children: Deborah Susan, Ashley Elizabeth, Brian Roberton. BS, U. N.Mex., 1966, MA, 1973. Asst. to chief adminstrv. officer Bank N.Mex., Albuquerque, 1973; pres. N.Mex. Airways, Inc., Albuquerque, 1974; dep. dir. N.Mex. Indochina Refugee Program, Santa Fe, 1975-76; dir. pub. affairs UNC Mining & Milling Co., Albuquerque, 1977-79; pres., CEO, CSI Aviation Svcs., Inc., Albuquerque, 1979—. Mem. steering com. Colin McMillan for lt. gov., Albuquerque, 1982; bd. dirs. N.Mex. Symphony Orgh., Albuquerque Conv. and Visitors Bur., 1982; mem. Albuquerque Police Adv. Bd., 1977-78; co-chmn. fin. com. Rep. Heather Wilson (Rep.-N.Mex.) Re-Election Campaign, 1999—; mem. state fin. com. G.W. Bush for Pres.; co-chmn. N.Mex. Victory, 2000; mem. nat. adv. bd. U. N.Mex. Anderson Sch. Bus.; elected del. GOP Nat. Conv., 2000. Capt. USMC, 1966-71, Vietnam; col. USMCR, 1971-97, Col. USMC, 1990-91, Persian Gulf, 1992-93, Somalia. Decorated Silver Star, Legion of Merit, Bronze Star with V device, Purple Heart with two gold stars, Meritorious Svc. medal with gold star, Air medal. Mem. Marine Corps Res. Officers Assn. (life, bd. dirs. 1973, 86), Res. Officers Assn. U.S. (life), SCV (life), Mil. Order Stars and Bars (life), SAR, N.Mex. Retail Assn. (chmn. 1999-2000). Republican. Episcopalian. Home: 6722 Rio Grande Blvd NW Albuquerque NM 87107-6330 Office: CSI Aviation Svcs Inc 3700 Rio Grande Blvd NW Albuquerque NM 87107-2876

WEIDER, JOSEPH, wholesale distribution executive; Chmn. bd., treas. Weider Health and Fitness, Woodland Hills, Calif., 1970—. Mem. chmn. bd. Weider Health and Fitness, Great Am. Foods. Office: Mens Fitness 21100 Erwin St Woodland Hills CA 91367-3712

WEIDNER, MARK, environmental research executive; b. 1952; MS in Analytical Chemistry, Purdue U., 1976. With Mich. State U., East Lansing, 1976-78; instr. Finnigan Corp., San Jose, Calif., 1978-80; sr. chemist Metro Lab., Seattle, 1980-85; now pres., treas. Analytical Resources, Inc., Seattle, 1985—. Office: Analytical Resources Inc 333 9th Ave N Seattle WA 98109-5187

WEIERMILLER, KATHY, publishing executive; V.p., CFO Orange County Register, Santa Ana, Calif. Office: The Orange County Register 625 N Grand Ave Santa Ana CA 92701-4347

WEIGAND, WILLIAM KEITH, bishop; b. Bend, Oreg., May 23, 1937; Ed., Mt. Angel Sem., St. Benedict, Oreg., St. Edward's Sem. and St. Thomas Sem., Kenmore, Wash. Bishop Diocese Salt Lake City, 1980-93, Diocese Sacramento, 1993—. Ordained priest Roman Cath. Ch., 1963. Office: Diocese Sacramento 2110 Broadway Sacramento CA 95818-2518

WEIGHT, DOUG, professional hockey player; b. Warren, Mich., Jan. 21, 1971; Student, Lake Superior State Coll., Mich. Center N.Y. Rangers, 1990-93; traded Edmonton Oilers, 1993, center, 1993—. Named to CCHA All-Rookie team, 1989-90, NCAA All-Am. West 2d team, 1990-91, CHA All-Star 1st team, 1990-91; selected for NHL All-Star Game, 1996. Office: Edmonton Oilers 11230 110th St 2d Fl Edmonton AB Canada T5G 3G8

WEIGLE, WILLIAM OLIVER, immunologist, educator; b. Monaca, Pa., Apr. 28, 1927; s. Oliver James and Caroline Ellen (Alsing) W.; m. Kathryn May Lotz, Sept. 4, 1948 (div. 1980); children: William James, Cynthia Kay; m. Carole G. Romball, Sept. 24, 1983. B.S., U. Pitts., 1950, M.S., 1951, Ph.D., 1956. Research assoc. pathology U. Pitts., 1955-58, asst. prof. immunochemistry, 1959-61; assoc. div. exptl. pathology Scripps Rsch. Inst., La Jolla, Calif., 1961-62, assoc. mem. div., 1962-63, mem. dept. exptl. pathology, 1963-74, mem. dept. immunopathology, 1974-82, chmn. dept. immunopathology, 1980-82, mem., vice chmn. dept. immunology, 1982-85, mem. dept. immunology, 1982-97, chmn. dept. immunology, 1985-87, prof. dept. immunology, 1997-98, prof. emeritus, 1998—. Adj. prof. biology U. Calif., San Diego; McLaughlin vis. prof. U. Tex., 1977; mem. adv. bd. Immunetech Pharm., San Diego, 1988-93; cons. in field. Author: Natural and Acquired Immunologic Unresponsiveness, 1967; assoc. editor: Clin. and Exptl. Immunology, 1972-79; Jour. Exptl. Medicine, 1974-84; Immunochemistry 1964-71; Procs. Soc. Exptl. Biology and Medicine, 1967-72; Jour. Immunology, 1967-71; Infection and Immunity, 1969-86, Aging: Immunology and Infectious Disease, 1987-96; sect. editor: Jour. Immunology, 1971-75; editorial bd.: Contemporary Topics in Immunobiology, 1971-93; Cellular Immunology, 1984-96; contbr. articles to profl. jours. Emeritus Coun. of the Trustees, Lovelace Inst., Albuquerque, 1996—. Pub. Health Research fellow, Nat. Inst. Neurol. Diseases and Blindness, 1956-59; NIH sr. research fellow, 1959-61, Research Career award, 1962. Mem. Am. Assn. Immunologists, Am. Soc. Exptl. Pathology (Parke Davis award 1967), Am. Soc. Microbiology, N.Y. Acad. Scis., Am. Assn. Pathologists, Soc. Exptl. Biology and Medicine. Home: 688 Via De La Valle Solana Beach CA 92075-2461 Office: Scripps Rsch Inst Dept Immunology IMM9 10550 N Torrey Pines Rd La Jolla CA 92037-1000 E-mail: weigle@scripps.edu

WEIGNER, BRENT JAMES, secondary education educator; b. Pratt, Kans., Aug. 19, 1949; s. Doyle Dean and Elizabeth (Hanger) W.; m. Sue Ellen Weber Hume, Mar. 30, 1985; children: Russell John Hume, Scott William Hume. BA, U. No. Colo., 1972; MEd, U. Wyo., 1977, PhD, 1984. Cert. Nat. Bd. for Profl. Tchg. Stds. Cert. Counselor, coach Olympia Sport Village, Upson, Wyo., summer 1968; dir. youth sports F.E. Warren AFB, Cheyenne, summers 1973, 74; instr. geography Laramie County Community Coll., Cheyenne, 1974-75; tchr. social sci. McCormick Jr. High Sch., Cheyenne, 1975—, Laramie County Sch. Dist. 1, Cheyenne, 1975—; head social studies dept. McCormick Jr. High Sch., 1987-99, 2001—; curriculum adv. coun. chmn. Laramie County Sch. Dist. No. 1, 1988-89. 'ectr. ednl. methods U. Wyo., 1989, mem. clin. faculty, 1992-94; nat. chmn. Jr. Olympic cross-country com. AAU, Indpls., 1980-81; pres. Wyo. Athletic Congress, 1981-87; tchr. cons. Nat. Geog. Soc. Geography Inst., summer 1991; bd. dirs. Shadow Mountain Lodge, Aspen, Colo., 1992-93, United Med. Ctr. of Wyo. Found., 1995—; South Pole marathon cons. Adventure Network Internat., 2001—. Fgn. exch. student U. Munich, 1971-72; head coach Cheyenne Track Club, 1976—, pres., 1980; race dir. Wyo. Marathon, 1978—; deacon 1st Christian Ch., Cheyenne, 1987-90, elder, 1991-93; rep. candidate gen. election Wyo. Legis., 1991; bd. dirs. Cheyenne Boys and Girls Club, 1999—. Named Wyoming State bd. edn. Disting. Educator, Wyo. U.S. West Outstanding Tchr., 1989, Wyo. Coun. for the Social Studies K-8 Tchr. of Yr., 1994-95, Jr. High Coach of Yr., Wyo. Coaches Assn., 1996, Vol. of Yr., office Youth Alternatives, 2000; fellow Taft Found., 1976, Earthwatch-Hearst fellow, Punta Allen, Mex., summer 1987, Christa McAuliffe fellow, 1991-92, Wyo. Christa Mcauliffe Fellowship Selection Com., 1994, 95, 01; Fulbright grantee, Israel, summer 1984; Fulbright scholar Ghana and Senegal, 1990; People-to-People Internat. Ambassador to Vietnam, 1993; recipient Masons of Wyo. Disting. Tchr. award 1994. Mem. ASCD, NEA, Nat. Network for Ednl. Renewal, Nat. Coun. Social Studies, Nat. Coun. Geog. Edn., Dominican Rep. Nat. Coun. for Geog. Edn. (Cram scholarship 1992), Wyo. Geog. Alliance (steering com., Amazon Workshop Fellowship 1998), Cheyenne Tchrs. Edn. Assn. (govtl. rels. com., instrn. and profl. devel. com.), U. No. Colo. Alumni Assn., Cheyenne C. of C., Wyo. Heritage Soc., Wyo. Edn. Assn. (World Book Ency. classroom rsch. project cons. 1976—, accountability task force 1989-90), Fulbright Alumni Assn. (life), U. Wyo. Alumni Assn. (life), Cheyenne Sunrise, Lions (bd. dirs. Cheyenne 1987, pres. 1995-96, 1st v.p. 1993-94, Melvin Jones Fellowship, 1995), Phi Delta Kappa (life, bd. dirs. Cheyenne 1989—, v.p., edn. award for rsch. 1990, pres. 1992-93, ednl. found. rep. 1993-94, area 4-D coord. 1994-95, Gerald Read Internat. Seminar scholar 1994; mem. outstanding doctoral dissertation com. 1994, 96), Phi Delta Kappa (Ed. award for Svc. 2000). Achievements include world record holder as first person in the world to run ultramarathon races on all seven continents; cons. Adventure Network Internat. South Pole Marathon, 2001—. Home: 402 W 31st St Cheyenne WY 82001-2527 Office: McCormick Jr HS 6000 Education Dr Cheyenne WY 82009-3991 E-mail: RunWyo26point2@compuserve.com

WEIHAUPT, JOHN GEORGE, geosciences educator, scientist, university administrator; b. La Crosse, Wis., Mar. 5, 1930; s. John George and Gladys Mae (Ash) W.; m. Audrey Mae Reis, Jan. 28, 1961. Student, St. Norbert Coll., De Pere, Wis., 1948-49; BS, U. Wis., 1952, MS, 1953, U. Wis.-Milw., 1971; PhD, U. Wis., 1973. Exploration geologist Am. Smelting & Refining Co., Nfld., 1953, Anaconda Co., Chile, S.Am., 1956-57; seismologist United Geophys. Corp., 1958; geophysicist Arctic Inst. N.Am., Antarctica, 1958-60, Geophys. and Polar Research Center, U. Wis., Antarctica, 1960-63; dir. participating Coll. and Univ. program, chmn. dept. phys. and biol. sci. U.S. Armed Forces Inst., Dept. Def., 1963-73; assoc. dean for acad. affairs Sch. Sci., Ind. U.-Purdue U., Indpls., 1973-78, prof. geology, 1973-78; asst. dean (Grad. Sch., prof. geoscis. Purdue U.), 1975-78; prof. geology, assoc. acad. v.p., dean grad. studies and research, v.p. Univ. Research Found., San Jose (Calif.) State U., 1978-82; vice chancellor for acad. affairs U. Colo., Denver, 1982-86, prof. geoscis., 1987—. Sci. cons., mem. sci. adv. bd. Holt Reinhart and Winston, Inc., 1967—; sci. editor, cons. McGraw-Hill Co., 1966—; hon. lectr. U. Wis., 1963-73; geol. cons., 1968—; editorial cons. John Wiley & Sons, 1968; editorial adv. bd. Dushkin Pub. Group, 1971— Author: Exploration of the Oceans: An Introduction to Oceanography; mem. editorial bd. Internat. Jour. Interdisciplinary Cycle Research, Leiden; co-discoverer USARP Mountain Range (Arctic Inst. Mountain Range), in Victoria Land, Antarctica, 1960; discoverer Wilkes Land Meteorite Crater, Antarctic. Mem. Capital Community Citizens Assn.; mem. Madison Transp. Study Com., Found. for Internat. Energy Research and Tng.; U.S. com. for UN Univ.; mem. sci. council Internat. Center for Interdisciplinary Cycle Research; mem. Internat. Awareness and Leadership Council; mem. governing bd. Moss Landing Marine Labs.; bd. dirs. San Jose State U. Found. Served as 1st lt. AUS, 1953-55, Korea. Mt. Weihaupt in Antarctica named for him, 1966; recipient Madisonian medal for outstanding community service, 1973; Outstanding Cote Meml. award, 1974; Antarctic medal, 1968 Fellow Geol. Soc. Am., Explorers Club; mem. Antarctican Soc., Nat. Sci. Tchrs. Assn., Am. Geophys. Union, Internat. Council Corr. Edu., Soc. Am. Mil. Engrs., Wis. Alumni Assn., Soc. Study Biol. Rhythms, Internat. Soc. for Chronobiology, Marine Tech. Soc., AAAS, Univ. Indsl. Adv. Council, Am. Council on Edn., Expdn. Polaire France (hon.), Found. for Study Cycles, Assn. Am. Geographers, Nat. Council Univ. Research Adminstrs., Soc. Research Adminstrs., Man-Environ. Communication Center, Internat. Union Geol. Scis., Internat. Geog. Union, Internat. Soc. Study Time, Community Council Pub. TV, Internat. Platform Assn., Ind., Midwest assns. grad. schs., Western Assn. Grad. Schs., Council Grad. Schs. in U.S., Wis. Alumni Assn. of San Francisco, Kiwanis, Carmel Racquet Club (Rinconada), The Ridge at Hiwan (Evergreen, Colo., pres. 1991-93). Achievements include discovery of the Wilkes Land Anomaly and of the USARP Mt. Range in Victoria Land, both in Antarctica; also credited with revision of the discovery date of Antarctic continent by 3 centuries. Home: 23906 Currant Dr Golden CO 80401-9243 Office: U Colo Campus Box 172 PO Box 173364 Denver CO 80217-3364

WEIHRICH, HEINZ, management educator; b. Fed. Republic of Germany; came to U.S., 1959; s. Paul and Anna Weihrich; m. Ursula Weihrich, Aug. 3, 1963. BS, UCLA, 1966, MBA, 1967, PhD, 1973; Dr. (hon.), San Martin de Porres U., Peru, 2000. Assoc. Grad. Sch. Mgmt. UCLA, 1968-73; from asst. to assoc. prof. Ariz. State U., Tempe, 1973-80; prof. global mgmt. and behavioral sci. U. San Francisco, 1980—. Mem. faculty China Europe Bus. Sch., Shanghai, Grad. Sch. Bus. Adminstrn., Switzeland; global mgmt. cons. in field. Author: (with Harold Koontz and Cyril O'Donnell) Management, 7th edit., 1980, Japanese, Chinese and Indonesian edits., 8th edit., 1984, Singapore edit., 1985, Indonesian edit., 1986, Philippines edit., Bengali edit., 1989, Taiwan edit., 1985 (with Harold Koontz) 9th edit., 1988, Singapore edit., 1988, Chinese edit., 1989, Spanish edit., 1990, best-seller Spanish speaking world, Korean edit., 1988, 90, Pengurusan (Malaysian) edit., 1991, Czech edit., 1993. Hungarian edit., 1992, Management: A Global Perspective, 10th edit. (with Harold Koontz), 1993, Spanish edit., 1993, best-seller Spanish speaking world, Chinese, 1998, Singapore edit., 1993, Korean edit., 1996, Croatian edit., 1995, 11th edit., 1998, Administração Fundamentos da Teoriae da Cienca, Primeiro Volume 1986, Administração Organização Planejamento e Controle, Segundo Volume, 1987, Administração Recursos Humanos: Desenvolvimento de Administradores, Terceiro Volume, 1987, (with Harold Koontz and Cyril O'Donnell) Management: A Book of Readings, 5th edit., 1980, (with George Odiorne and Jack Mendleson) Executive Skills: A Management by Objectives Approach, 1980, (with Harold Koontz) Measuring Managers--A Double-Barreled Approach, 1981, (with Harold Koontz and Cyril O'Donnell) Essentials of Management, 3d edit. 1982, Taiwan, Philippines, Chinese and India edits., 4th edit., 1986, Singapore edit., 1986, 5th edit., 1990, (with Harold Koontz) Manajamen, Jilid 1, Indonesian edit., 1987, Manajamen, Jilid 2, 1986, Elementos de Administracion, 3d edit., 1983, 4th edit. 1988, Management Excellence--Productivity through MBO, 1985, Singapore edit. 1986, Japanese edit., 1990, Greek edit., Produttivita con L' Italian edit. 1987, Administracion, 1985, Management Basiswissen, German edit., 1986, Excelencia Administrativa (Mex.), Spanish edit., 1987, Chinese edit., 1997, (with Harold Koontz and Cyril O'Donnell) Adminstracion Moderna, Tomo 1, 1986, (with Harold Koontz) Management: A Global Perspective, internat. edit., 1993, Administración: Una Perspectiva Global, 1994, Korean edit., 1993, 96, Croatian edit., 1996, Czech edit., 1993, 96; editor: (with Jack Mendleson) Management: An MBO Approach, 1978; contbr. numerous articles and papers to profl. jours. Grantee Am. Mgmt. Assn., 1970. Fellow Internat. Acad. Mgmt., mem. Acad. Mgmt., Assn. Mgmt. Excellence (trustee 1985-87), Assn. Bus. Simulation Exptl. Learning, Acad. Internat. Bus., Beta Gamma Sigma, Sigma Iota Epsilon. Roman Catholic. Office: U San Francisco 2130 Fulton St San Francisco CA 94117-1080

WEIL, ANDREW THOMAS, physician, educator; b. Phila., June 8, 1942; s. Daniel Pythias and Jenny (Silverstein) W. BA, Harvard U., 1964, MD, 1968. Intern Mt. Zion Hosp. Med. Ctr., San Francisco, 1968-69; assoc. Harvard Bot. Mus., Cambridge, Mass., 1971-84; fellow Inst. Current World Affairs, N.Y.C., 1971-75; lectr. U. Ariz., Tucson, 1983—, dir. program in integrative medicine, clin. prof. medicine, 1996—. Founder Nat. Integrative Medicine Coun., Tucson, 1995—. Author: Natural Mind, 1972, Marriage of the Sun and Moon, 1980, Chocolate to Morphine, 1983, Health and Healing, 1984, Natural Health, Natural Medicine, 1990, Spontaneous Healing, 1995, 8 Weeks to Optimum Health, 1997, Eating Well for Optimum Health, 2000, (newsletter) Self-Healing, (website) Ask Dr. Weil. Served to lt. USPHS, 1969-70. Fellow Linnean Soc. London; mem. Am. Acad. Achievement, Sigma Xi. Democrat. Buddhist. Avocations: gardening, backpacking. Home: 6700 S X9 Ranch Rd Vail AZ 85641-6202 Office: Ariz Health Scis Ctr PO Box 245153 Tucson AZ 85724-5153 E-mail: mnhardin@ix.netcom.com

WEIL, JOHN DAVID, financial executive; b. Chgo., Sept. 28, 1947; s. Leslie Joseph and Carlyne (Strauss) W.; m. Marcie Bornfriend, July 4, 1981; children: Jessica Lauren, Michael Brandon, Samantha Leigh. BS in Econs., U. Ill., 1969; MBA in Fin., Northwestern U., 1971. Asst. to chmn. bd. Stanwood Industries, Lake Forest, Ill., 1971-74; pres. Kent Paper Co., Ridgewood, N.Y., 1974-81; pres., CEO Am. Envelope Co., Chgo., 1982-94; operating affiliate McCown De Leeuw & Co., 1995—; dir. Dimac Holdings, 1998—. Pres., CEO U.S.A. Internat. Data Response Corp., Scottsdale, Ariz., 1998-99; CFO DIMAC Holdings, 1999-2001. Mem. Envelope Mfrs. Am. (bd. dirs. 1986-94), Northmoor Country Club, Ancala Country Club. Office: 8655 E Via De Ventura Ste G207 Scottsdale AZ 85258-3359

WEIL, LEONARD, banker; b. 1922; married With U.S. Dept. State, Vienna, Austria, 1946; with Union Bank, Los Angeles, 1946-62; pres., CEO Mfrs. Bank, Los Angeles, 1962-86, pres. emeritus, 1986—. Adj. asst. prof. fin. Anderson Grad. Sch. Mgmt., UCLA. Trustee UCLA Found.; bd. visitors UCLA Grad. Sch. Mgmt.; past pres. Town Hall; bd. dirs. Braille Inst. Served with U.S. Army, 1943-45 Mem. Calif. Bankers Assn. (bd. dirs., past pres.), Am. Mgmt. Assn., Am. Econs. Assn., Am. Bankers Assn. (past dir.). Office: 233 Wilshire Blvd Fl 6 Santa Monica CA 90401-1205

WEIL, LOUIS ARTHUR, III (CHIP), retired newspaper publishing executive; b. Grand Rapids, Mich., Mar. 14, 1941; s. Louis Arthur, Jr. and Kathryn (Halligan) W.; m. Mary Elizabeth Buckingham, Sept. 7, 1963 (div. June 1977); children: Scott Arthur, Christopher Davison, Timothy Buckingham; m. Daryl Hopkins Goss, Jan. 26, 1980. B.A. in English, Ind. U., 1963; DHL (hon.), Mercy Coll., Grand Valley State U. Various positions Times Herald, Port Huron, Mich., 1966-68; personnel dir., pub. Journal and Courier, Lafayette, Ind., 1968-73; gen. mgr., pub. Gannett Westchester Rockland Newspapers, White Plains, N.Y., 1973-74, pres., gen. mgr., 1974-77, pres., pub., 1977-79; v.p. devel. Gannett Co., Inc., N.Y.C., 1979-83, sr. v.p. planning and devel., 1982-86; chmn., pub. Gannett Westchester Rockland Newspapers, White Plains, 1984-86; pres. The Detroit News, 1986-89, pub., 1987-89; U.S. pub. Time Mag., 1989-91; pub., chief exec. officer, exec. v.p. Ariz. Republic, Phoenix Gazette, Ariz. Bus. Gazette, 1991-96; chmn., pres., CEO Central Newspapers, Inc., Phoenix, 1996-2000. Bd. dirs. Ctrl. Newspapers, Inc., Prudential. Trustee, mem. adv. bd. Ariz. Cancer Ctr. at U. Ariz., Am. Grad. Sch. Internat. Mgmt.; bd. dirs. Ariz. Cmty. Found., Heard Mus.; campaign chmn. Valley of the Sun United Way, 1992; past chmn. Greater Phoenix Leadership; past pres. bd. trustees Phoenix Art Mus. With USN. Office: 5112 N 40th St Ste 101 Phoenix AZ 85018

WEIL, MAX HARRY, physician, medical educator, medical scientist; b. Baden, Switzerland, Feb. 9, 1927; came to U.S., 1937, naturalized, 1944; s. Marcel and Gretl (Winter) W.; m. Marianne Judith Posner, Apr. 1955; children: Susan Margot, Carol Juliet. AB, U. Mich., 1948; MD, SUNY, N.Y.C., 1952; PhD, U. Minn., 1957. Diplomate Am. Bd. Internal Medicine and Critical Care Medicine, Nat. Bd. Med. Examiners. Intern in internal medicine U. Cin. Med. Ctr., 1952-53; resident U. Minn. Hosps., Heart Hosp., VA Hosp., Mpls., 1953-55; rsch. fellow U. Minn., Mpls., 1955-56; sr. fellow Nat. Heart Inst., Mayo Clinic, Rochester, Minn., 1956-57; chief cardiology City of Hope Med. Ctr., Duarte, Calif., 1957-59; asst. clin. prof. U. So. Calif. Sch. Medicine, L.A., 1957-59, asst. prof., 1959-63, assoc. prof., 1963-71, prof., 1971-81; chmn. L.A. Com. on Emergency Med. Svcs., 1968-73; prof., chmn. dept. medicine, chief divsn. cargiology Chgo. Med. Sch., Finch U. Health Scis., North Chicago, Ill., 1981-91, disting. univ. prof., 1992-94, disting. univ. prof. emeritus, 1994—, Finch U. Health Scis., North Chgo., 1994—. Adj. prof. medicine Northwestern U. Med. Sch., Chgo., 1992—; prof. clin. med. bioengring. U. So. Calif., L.A., 1972-91, adj. prof. medicine, 1981-94, clin. prof. anesthesiology, 1995—, rsch. prof. surgeyr, 1996—; disting. univ. prof. Inst. Critical Care Medicine, Palm Springs, Calif., 1995—. Sect. editor Archives Internal Medicine, 1983-86, JAMA, 1969-72; guest editor Am. Jour. Cardiology, 1982, Critical Care Medicine, 1985; mem. editl. bd. Am. Jour. Medicine, 1971-79, Chest, 1980-95, Jour. Circulatory Shock, 1979-92, Clin. Engring. Newsletter, 1980—, Methods of Info. in Medicine, 1977-91, Jour. Clin. Illness, 1986—, Clin. Intensive Care, 1989—; mem. editl. adv. bd. Emergency Medicine, 1978—, Issues in Health Care Tech., 1983-86; assoc. editor Critical Care Medicine, 1973-74, mem. editl. bd., 1973-91, 94-96, sr. editor, 1997; editor-in-chief Acute Care, 1983-90; contbr. over 1000 articles to profl. jours.; patentee in field. Pres. Temple Brotherhood, Wilshire Blvd. Temple, L.A., 1967-68; bd. dirs. Hollywood Presbyn. Med. Ctr., 1976-81, L.A. chpt. Met. Am. Heart Assn., 1962-67, Chgo. chpt. Met. Am. Heart Assn., 1982-88. With U.S. Army, 1946-47. Recipient prize in internal medicine SUNY, 1952, Alumni medallion SUNY, 1970; Disting. Svc. award Soc. Critical Care Medicine, 1984; numerous rsch. grants, 1959—; named Disting. Alumni Lectr., 1967, Oscar Schwindetzky Meml. Lectr. Internat. Anesthesia Rsch. Soc., 1978; recipient Lawrence R. Medoff award Chgo. Med. Sch., 1987, Morris L. Parker Rsch. award, 1989, Mission of Mercy award Israeli Nat. Emergency Svcs., 2001; Lilly scholar, 1988-89. Master ACP; fellow Am. Coll. Cardiology (chmn. emergency cardiac care com. 1974-81); master, fellow Am. Coll. Chest Physicians (coun. clin. cardiology, coun. critical care medicine), Am. Coll. Clin. Pharmacology, Am. Coll. Critical Care Medicine (Disting. Investigator award 1990, 96, A.S. Laerdal Achievement award 2000, Lifetime Achievement award 2001), Am. Heart Assn. (coun. circulation, coun. basic sci., coun. cardiopulmonary and critical care, coun. clin. cardiology, Dickinson W. Richards Meml. lectureship 1998, Emergency Cardiac Care Lifetime Achievement award 2000), N.Y. Acad. Sci., Chgo. Soc. Internal Medicine; mem. AMA (sect. editor jour. 1969-72), IEEE, L.A. County Med. Assn., Am. Physiol. Soc. Am. Soc. Pharmacology and Exptl. Therapeutics, Am. Soc. Echocardiography, Am. Soc. Nephrology, Am. Trauma Soc. (founding mem.), Assn. Computing Machinery, Assn. Am. Med. Colls., Ctrl. Soc. Clin. Rsch., Chgo. Cardiol. Group (sec.-treas. 1986-88, chmn. 1988-90), Chgo. Soc. Internal Medicine, Lake County Heart Assn. (bd. govs. 1983-86), Intensive Care Soc. U.K., L.A. Soc. Internal Medicine, Soc. Exptl. Biology and Medicine, Western Soc. Clin. Rsch., Fedn. Am. Socs. Exptl. Biology, Am. Soc. Parenteral and Enteral Nutrition, Nat. Acad. Practice (disting. practitioner), Skull and Dagger, Sigma Xi, Alpha Omega Alpha. Jewish. Avocations: swimming, tennis, photography, philosophy-economics. Office: Inst Critical Care Medicine 1695 N Sunrise Way Bldg 3 Palm Springs CA 92262-5309 E-mail: weilm@aol.com

WEILL, HANS, medical educator; b. Berlin, Aug. 31, 1933; came to U.S., 1939; s. Kurt and Gerda (Philipp) W.; m. Kathleen Burton, Apr. 3, 1958; children: Judith, Leslie, David. B.S., Tulane U., 1955, M.D., 1958. Diplomate: Am. Bd. Internal Medicine. Intern Mt. Sinai Hosp., N.Y.C., 1958-59; resident Tulane Med. Unit, Charity Hosp. La., New Orleans, 1959-60, chief resident, 1961-62, sr. vis. physician, 1972—; NIH research fellow dept. medicine and pulmonary lab. Sch. Medicine Tulane U., New Orleans, 1960-61, instr. medicine, 1962-64, asst. prof. medicine, 1964-67, assoc. prof., 1967-71, prof. medicine, 1971—, Schlieder Found. prof. pulmonary medicine, 1985-97; chief Environ. Medicine sect. Tulane Med. Center, 1980-96; dir. univ. Ctr. for Bioenviron. Rsch., 1989-93; dir. interdisciplinary research group in occupational lung diseases Nat. Heart, Lung and Blood Inst., 1972-92, mem. nat. adv. council, 1986-90, chmn. pulmonary disease adv. com., 1982-84; active staff Tulane Med. Center Hosp., 1976—; program dir. Nat. Inst. for Environ. Health Sci., 1992-96. Cons. pulmonary diseases Touro Infirmary, New Orleans, 1962—; cons. NIH, Nat. Inst. Occupational Safety and Health, Occupational Safety and Health Adminstrn., USN, NAS, EPA; lectr., participant workshops and confs. profl. groups in U.S., France, Can., U.K.; dir. Nat. Inst. Environ. Health Scis Superfund. Basic Rsch. Program, 1992-96. Mem. editorial bd. Am. Rev. of Respiratory Disease, 1980-85, CHEST, 1987-91; editor Respiratory Diseases Digest, 1981; guest editor Byssinosis conf. supplement, CHEST, 1981. Fellow Am. Acad. Allergy, Royal Soc. Medicine, ACP; mem. Am. Thoracic Soc. (pres. 1976), Am. Lung Assn. (bd. dirs. 1975-78), New Orleans Acad. Internal Medicine (sec., treas. 1973-75), Am. Coll. Chest Physicians (gov. for La. 1970-75), Am. Fedn. Clin. Research, So. Soc. Clin. Investigation, N.Y. Acad. Scis., Brit. Thoracic Assn., Internat. Epidemiol. Assn., Am. Heart Assn. (task force on environment and cardiovascular system 1978), Brit. Thoracic Soc., Phi Beta Kappa, Alpha Omega Alpha. Home and Office: 755 Hearthstone Dr Basalt CO 81621-8205

WEIMER, ROBERT JAY, geology educator, energy consultant, civic leader; b. Glendo, Wyo., Sept. 4, 1926; s. John L. and Helen (Mowrey) W.; m. Ruth Carol Adams, Sept. 12, 1948; children: Robert Thomas, Loren Edward (dec.), Paul Christner, Carl Scott. BA, U Wyo., 1948, MA, 1949; PhD, Stanford U., 1953. Registered profl. engr., Colo. Geologist Union Oil Co. Calif., 1949-54; cons. geologist U.S. and fgn. petroleum exploration, 1954—; prof. geology Colo. Sch. Mines, 1957-83, prof. emeritus, 1983—, Getty prof. geology, 1978-83; vis. prof. U. Colo., 1961, U. Calgary, Can., 1970, Inst. Tech., Bandung, Indonesia, 1975. Fulbright lectr. U. Adelaide, South Australia, 1967; disting. lectr. and continuing edn. lectr. Am. Assn. Petroleum Geologists, Soc. Expl. Geophysicists, ednl. cons. to petroleum cos., 1964—; mem. energy rsch. adv. bd. Dept. Energy, 1985-90, Bd. on Mineral and Energy Resources, Nat. Rsch. Coun., 1988. Editor: Guide to Geology of Colorado, 1960, Symposium on Cretaceous Rocks of Colorado and Adjacent Area, 1959, Denver Earthquakes, 1968, Fossil Fuel Exploration, 1974, Studies in Colorado Field Geology, 1976, Petroleum System, Denver Basin, 1996. Trustee Colo. Sch. Mines Research Found., 1967-70; pres. Rockland Found., 1982-83; bd. dirs. Foothills Art Ctr., 1997—. With USNR, 1944-46. Recipient Disting. Alumnus award U. Wyo., 1982, Mines medal Colo. Sch. Mines, 1984, Brown medal, 1990, Parker medal Am. Inst. Profl. Geologists, 1986, Exemplary Alumni award U. Wyo., 1994. Fellow Geol. Soc. Am. (chmn. Rocky Mountain sect. 1966-67), AAAS; mem. Am. Assn. Petroleum Geologists (hon. pres. 1992, Sidney Powers medal 1983, Dist. Educator award 1996), Soc. Econ. Paleontologists and Mineralogists (hon., sec.-treas. 1966-67, v.p. 1971, pres. 1972, Twenhofel medal 1995), Colo. Sci. Soc. (hon., pres. 1981), Rocky Mountain Assn. Geologists (hon., pres. 1969, found. bd. 1976-86, Scientist of Yr. 1982), Wyo. Geol. Assn. (hon.), Colo. Sch. Mines Alumni Assn. (hon., Coolbaugh award 1996), Am. Geol. Inst. Found. (sec., treas. 1984-88), Geol. Soc. Am. Found., Nat. Acad. Engring. (ch. sec. 11 1999, ISEM Hedberg award 2001), Northwoodside Inc. Conservancy Found. (v.p. 1995-96, pres. 1997—), Mt. Vernon Country Club (Golden, bd. dirs. 1956-59, 81-84, pres. 1983-84). Home: RR 3 25853 Mt Vernon Rd Golden CO 80401-9699 E-mail: rweimer@mines.edu

WEINBERG, D. MARK, health insurance company executive; b. Aug. 4, 1952; s. Melvin Weinberg; m. Allyson Weinberg; children: Amanda, Sarah, Tiffany, Sean. BS in Elec. Engring., U. Mo., 1975. Gen. mgr. CTX Products div. Pet, Inc., St. Louis, 1975-81; prin. Touche-Ross and Co., Chgo., 1981-87; exec. v.p. Blue Cross of Calif., Thousand Oaks, 1987-92, Wellpoint Health Networks, Woodland Hills, 1992—. Pres. UNICARE Bus., 1995—. Contbr. articles to profl. jours. Mem. exec. bd. United Way; pres. Sr. Alliance, Inc.; vice-chmn. Calif. Ins. Mktg. Svc., Inc. Mem. Conejo Valley C. of C. (bd. dirs.). Address: Wellpoint 4553 La Tienda Rd Thousand Oaks CA 91362-3800

WEINBERG, JOHN LEE, federal judge; b. Chgo., Apr. 24, 1941; s. Louis Jr. and Jane Kitz (Goldstein) W.; m. Sarah Kibbee, July 6, 1963; children: Ruth, Leo. BA, Swarthmore Coll., 1962; JD, U. Chgo., 1965. Bar: Ill. 1966, Wash. 1967, U.S. Dist. Ct. (we. dist.) Wash. 1967, U.S. Ct. Appeals (9th cir.) 1967. Law clk. to Hon. Henry L. Burman Ill. Appellate Ct., Chgo., 1965-66; law clk. to Hon. Walter V. Schaefer Ill. Supreme Ct., Chgo., 1966; law clk. to Hon. William T. Beeks U.S. Dist. Ct. Wash., Seattle, 1967-68; atty. Perkins Coie Law Firm, Seattle, 1968-73; magistrate judge U.S. Dist. Ct.; U.S. Magistrate judge Seattle, 1973—. Author: Federal Bail and Detention Handbook, 1988. Mem. ABA, Am. Judicature Soc., Wash. State Bar Assn., Seattle-King County Bar Assn., Fed. Magistrate Judges Assn. (nat. pres. 1982-83). Avocations: sports and physical fitness activities, bridge. Office: US Magistrate Judge 304 US Courthouse 1010 5th Ave Seattle WA 98104-1195

WEINBERG, LAWRENCE, professional basketball team owner; Owner, formerly pres. Portland Trail Blazers, Nat. Basketball Assn., Oreg.; now pres. emeritus Portland Trail Blazers. Office: c/o Portland Trail Blazers One Ctr Ct Ste 200 Portland OR 97227

WEINBERG, LEONARD BURTON, political scientist; b. N.Y.C., Nov. 10, 1939; s. Max R. and Rose (Levin) W.; m. Ellen Bach, Aug. 23, 1966 (div.); 1 son, David; m. Sinikka Palomaki, June 4, 1986. B.A., Syracuse U., 1961, Ph.D., 1967; M.A., U. Chgo., 1963. Instr. polit. sci. U. Wis., Milw., 1966-67; asst. prof. polit. sci. U. Nev., Reno, 1967-71, assoc. prof., 1971-78, prof., 1978—, chmn. dept., 1979-82. Vis. prof. U. Florence, Italy,

1992. Author: Comparing Public Policies, 1977, After Mussolini, 1979, The Rise and Fall of Italian Terrorism, 1987, Introduction to Political Terrorism, 1989; editor: Political Parties and Terrorist Groups, 1992, Revival of Right-Wing Extremism in the 1990s, 1996; co-editor: Encounters with the Radical Right, 1992, The Transformation of Italian Communism, 1994, Revival of Right-Wing Extremism in the 1990s, 1997, The Emergence of a Euro-American Radical, 1998. Recipient Fulbright Rsch. award, 1984; Italian Govt. Borsa di Studio, 1965-66; Fulbright grantee, 1965-66, Harry F. Guggenheim grantee, 1995-96. Mem. Am. Polit. Sci. Assn., Internat. Polit. Sci. Assn. (political sociology com.), Conf. Group on Italian Politics of Am. Polit. Sci. Assn., Phi Kappa Phi. Jewish. Office: U Nev Dept Polit Sci Reno NV 89557-0001 E-mail: WeirBrl@unr.nevada.edu

WEINBERG, WILLIAM HENRY, chemical engineer, chemical physicist, educator; b. Columbia, S.C., Dec. 5, 1944; s. Ulrich Vivian and Ruth Ann (Duncan) W. BS, U. S.C., 1966; PhD in Chem. Engring, U. Calif., Berkeley, 1970; NATO postdoctoral fellow in phys. chemistry, Cambridge U., Eng., 1971. Asst. prof. chem. engring. Calif. Inst. Tech., 1972-74, assoc. prof., 1974-77, prof. chem. engring. and chem. physics, 1977-89, Chevron disting. prof. chem. engring. and chem. physics, 1981-86; prof. chem. engring. and chemistry U. Calif., Santa Barbara, 1989—, assoc. dean Coll. Engring., 1992-96; chief tech. officer Symyx Techs., Santa Clara, Calif., 1996—. Vis. prof. chemistry Harvard U., 1980, U. Pitts., 1987-88, Oxford U., 1991; Alexander von Humboldt Found. fellow U. Munich, 1982; cons. E.I. DuPont Co. Author: (with Van Hove and Chan) Low-Energy Electron Diffraction, 1986; editor 4 books in field; mem. editl. bd. Jour. Applications Surface Sci., 1977-85, Handbook Surfaces and Interfaces, 1978-80, Surface Sci. Reports, 1980—, gen. editor, 1992—, Applied Surface Sci., 1985—, Langmuir, 1990-96, Surface Sci., 1992—, Jour. Combinatorial Chemistry, 1998—; contbr. articles to profl. jours., chpts. to books. Recipient Giuseppe Parravano award Mich. Catalysis Soc., 1989, Disting. Teaching award Coll. of Engring., U. Calif. Santa Barbara, 1995; fellow NSF, 1966-69, Alfred P. Sloan Found., 1976-78, Camille and Henry Dreyfus Found., 1976-81. Fellow AAAS, Am. Phys. Soc. (Nottingham prize 1972), Am. Vacuum Soc.; mem. AIChE (Colburn award 1981), Am. Chem. Soc. (LaMer award 1973, Kendall award 1991, Arthur W. Adamson award 1995), N.Am. Catalysis Soc., Nat. Acad. Engring., Phi Beta Kappa. Office: Symyx Technologies 3100 Central Expy Santa Clara CA 95051-0801 E-mail: hweinberg@symyx.com

WEINER, LESLIE PHILIP, neurology educator, researcher; b. Bklyn., Mar. 17, 1936; s. Paul Larry and Sarah (Paris) W.; m. Judith Marilyn Hoffman, Dec. 26, 1959; children: Patrice, Allison, Matthew, Jonathan. BA, Wilkes Coll., 1957; MD, U. Cin., 1961. Diplomate Am. Bd. Psychiatry and Neurology. Intern in medicine SUNY, Syracuse, 1961-62; resident in neurology Johns Hopkins Hosp., Balt., 1962-65, fellow, 1967-69; resident Balt. City Hosp., 1962-63; fellow in virology Slow Virus Lab., Nat. Inst. Neurol and Communicative Disorders-Stroke, NIH, Balt., 1969; asst. prof. neurology Johns Hopkins U., 1969-72, assoc. prof., 1972-75; prof. neurology and microbiology U. So. Calif. Sch. Medicine, L.A., 1975—, chmn. dept. neurology, 1979—, Richard Angus Grant Sr. chair in neurology, 1987—. Chief neurologist U. So. Calif. Univ. Hosp., 1991-96, mem. bd. govs.; chief neurologist L.A. county-U. So. Calif. Med. Ctr., 1979-94,; chmn. U. So. Calif. Gen. Clin. Res. Ctr., 1994-95; bd. dirs. John Douglas French Found., L.A., 1987-2000; mem. neurosci. tng. study sect. NIH, 1990-93; chmn., mem. sci. adv. bd. Hereditary Disease Found., 1992—, chmn., 1994-96, programs rsch. adv. com., 2000—. Contbr. over 120 articles on neurology, immunology and virology to med. jours., chpts. to books; assoc. editor: Neurobase, 1994-95, Neuronet; mem. editl. bd. Infectious and Geographic Neurol., 1994—; assoc. editor: Neurobase. Bd. dirs. Starbright Found., L.A., 1991. Capt. M.C., U.S. Army, 1965-67. Grantee NIH, 1999-2003, Kenneth Norris Found., 1995—, Conrad Hilton Found., 1995-97, McDonald Found., Oxnard Found., Gogan Found., Heron Found., Nat. Multiple Sclerosis Soc., 2000—. Fellow Am. Acad. Neurology; mem. AAAS, Am. Health Assistance Found., Am. Neurology Assn., Soc. Neurosci., Johns Hopkins U. Soc. Scholars, L.A. Acad. Medicine, Assn. Univ. Profs. Neurology, Alpha Omega Alpha. Democrat. Jewish. Avocations: collecting books, concerts, plays. Home: 625 S Rimpau Blvd Los Angeles CA 90005-3842 Office: U So Calif Keck Sch Med 1975 Zonal Ave KAM 410 Los Angeles CA 90033-1039 Fax: 323-442-3015. E-mail: lweiner@hsc.usc.edu

WEINER, PETER H. lawyer; b. N.Y.C., July 10, 1944; BA, Harvard U., 1966; MSc, London Sch. Econs., 1967; LLB, Yale U., 1970. Bar: Calif. 1971. Ptnr. Paul, Hastings, Janofsky & Walker LLP, San Francisco, 1997—. Mem. Phi Beta Kappa. Office: Paul Hastings Janofsky & Walker LLP 345 California St Fl 29 San Francisco CA 94104-2642

WEINGARTEN, SAUL MYER, lawyer; b. Los Angeles, Dec. 19, 1921; s. Louis and Lillian Dorothy (Alter) W.; m. Miriam Ellen Moore, Jan. 21, 1949; children: David, Steven, Lawrence, Bruce. AA, Antelope Valley Coll., 1940; AB, UCLA, 1942; cert., Cornell U., 1943; JD, U. Southern Calif., 1949. Bar: Calif. 1950, U.S. Supreme Ct., 1960. Prin. Saul M. Weingarten Assocs., Seaside, Calif., 1954—. Atty. City of Gonzales, Calif., 1954-74, City of Seaside, 1955-70; gen. counsel Redevel. Agy., Seaside, 1955-76, Security Nat. Bank, Monterey, Calif., 1968-74; bd. dirs., exec. com. Frontier Bank, Cheyenne, Wyo., 1984-99; pres. Quaestor, Inc., 1991-98. Author: Practice Compendium, 1950; contbr. articles to profl. jours. Del. Internat. Union of Local Authorities, Brussels, Belgium, 1963, 73; candidate state legislature Dem. Com., Monterey County, 1958; counsel Monterey Peninsula Mus. of Art, Inc., 1972-80; gen. counsel Monterey County Symphony Assn., Carmel, Calif., 1974-98, Mountain Plains Edn. Project, Glasgow, Mont., 1975-81; chmn. fund raising ARC, Monterey, 1964; chmn., bd. dirs. fund raising United Way, Monterey, 1962-63; pres., bd. dirs. Alliance on Aging, Monterey, 1968-82; bd. dirs. Family Svc. Agy., Monterey, 1958-66, Monterey County Cultural Coun., 1986-94, Clark Found., 1982—; dir., mem. exec. com. Monterey Bay Performing Arts Ctr., 1990. Served to commdr. USN, 1942-46, 50-54, Korea. Grad. fellow Coro Found., 1949-50. Mem. Calif. Bar Assn., Monterey County Bar Assn., Monterey County Trial Lawyers Assn., Rotary (pres. 1970-71, 82-83), Commonwealth Club, Meadowbrook Club. Jewish. Avocations: travel. Home: 4135 Crest Rd Pebble Beach CA 93953-3008 Office: Ste D 1123 Fremont Blvd Seaside CA 93955-5759 E-mail: lsm147@juno.com

WEINHARDT, J. W. computer company executive; Chmn. bd. dirs., CEO SJW Corp., San Jose, Calif. Office: SJW Corp 374 W Santa Clara St San Jose CA 95113-1502

WEINMAN, GLENN ALAN, lawyer; b. N.Y.C., Dec. 9, 1955; s. Seymour and Iris Rhoda (Bergman) W. BA in Polit. Sci., UCLA, 1978; JD, U. So. Calif., 1981. Bar: Calif. 1981. Assoc. counsel Mitsui Mfrs. Bank, L.A., 1981-83; assoc. McKenna, Conner & Cuneo, L.A., 1983-85, Stroock, Stroock & Lavan, L.A., 1985-87; sr. counsel Buchalter, Nemer, Fields & Younger, L.A., 1987-91; ptnr. Keck, Mahin & Cate, L.A., 1991-93; sr. v.p., gen. counsel Western Internat. Media Corp., L.A., 1993-96; v.p. gen. counsel and human resources, sec. Guess?, Inc., L.A., 1996-2000; also bd. dirs.; chief adminstrv. officer Competitive Knowledge, Inc., 2000; v.p., gen. counsel, sec. Luminent, Inc., Chatsworth, Calif., 2000-01; exec. v.p., COO InsoVery Svcs. Group, Woodland Hills, 2001—. Bd. dirs. Guess? Retail Inc., Guess? Licensing, Inc., Guess.com., Inc. Mem. ABA (corp. banking and bus. law sect., com. on savs. instns., com. on banking law corp. counsel sect.), Calif. Bar Assn. (bus. law sect., com. fin. instns. 1989-91, com. consumer svcs. 1991-94), L.A. County Bar Assn. (corp. legal depts. sect., bus. and corps. law sect., subcom. on fin. instns.), Calif. Fashion Assn. (exec. bd. 1997-2000), , Am. Apparel Mfrs. Assn. (govt. rels. com. 1997-2000), Legion Lex, U. So. Calif. Law Alumni Assn., Phi Alpha Delta. Avocation: tennis. Office: 20550 Nordhoff St Chatsworth CA 91311 E-mail: gaweinman@aol.com

WEINSHIENK, ZITA LEESON, federal judge; b. St. Paul, Apr. 3, 1933; d. Louis and Ada (Dubov) Leeson; m. Hubert Troy Weinshienk, July 8, 1956 (dec. 1983); children: Edith Blair, Kay Anne, Darcy Jill; m. James N. Schaffner, Nov. 15, 1986. Student, U. Colo., 1952-53; BA magna cum laude, U. Ariz., 1955; JD cum laude, Harvard U., 1958; Fulbright grantee, U. Copenhagen, Denmark, 1959; LHD (hon.), Loretto Heights Coll., 1985; LLD (hon.), U. Denver, 1990. Bar: Colo. 1959. Probation counselor, legal adviser, referee Denver Juvenile Ct., 1959-64; judge Denver Mcpl. Ct., 1964-65, Denver County Ct., 1965-71, Denver Dist. Ct., 1972-79; judge, then sr. judge U.S. Dist. Ct. Colo., Denver, 1979—. Precinct committeewoman Denver Democratic Com., 1963-64; bd. dirs. Crime Stoppers. Named one of 100 Women in Touch with Our Time Harper's Bazaar Mag., 1971, Woman of Yr., Denver Bus. and Profl. Women, 1969; recipient Women Helping Women award Soroptimist Internat. of Denver, 1983, Hanna G. Solomon award Nat. Coun. Jewish Women, Denver, 1986. Fellow Colo. Bar Found., Am. Bar Found.; mem. ABA, Denver Bar Assn., Colo. Bar Assn., Nat. Conf. Fed. Trial Judges (exec. com., past chair), Dist. Judges' Assn. of 10th Cir. (past pres.), Colo. Women's Bar Assn., Fed. Judges Assn., Denver Crime Stoppers Inc. (bd.dirs.), Devner LWV, Women's Forum Colo., Harvard Law Sch. Assn., Phi Beta Kappa, Phi Kappa Phi, Order of Coif (hon. Colo. chpt.). Office: US Dist Ct US Courthouse Rm C-418 1929 Stout St Denver CO 80294-1929

WEINSTEIN, GERALD D. dermatology educator; b. N.Y.C., Oct. 13, 1936; m. Marcia Z. Weinstein; children: Jeff, Jon, Debbie. BA, U. Pa., 1957, MD, 1961. Diplomate Am. Bd. Dermatology. Intern Los Angeles County Gen. Hosp., 1961-62; clin. assoc. dermatology br. Nat. Cancer Instn. NIH, Bethesda, Md., 1962-64; resident dept. dermatology U. Miami, Fla., 1964-65; asst. prof. Dept. Dermatology U. Miami, 1966-71, assoc. prof., 1971-74, prof., 1975-79; prof., chmn. dept. dermatology U. Calif., Irvine, 1979—, acting dean Coll. Medicine, 1985-87. Attending staff VA Med. Ctr., Long Beach, Calif., 1979—, UCI Med. Ctr., Orange, Calif., 1979—, St. Joseph Hosp., Orange, 1980—. Contbr. articles to profl. jours., chpts. to books. Recipient Lifetime Achievement award Nat. Psoriasis Found., 1994; co-recipient award for psoriasis rsch. Taub Internat. Meml., 1971; NIH spl. postdoctoral fellow, 1965-67. Mem. Am. Acad. Dermatology (chmn. task force on psoriasis 1986—, bd. dirs. 1984-88). Office: U Calif Irvine Coll Medicine Dept Dermatology C340 Med Scis Bldg 1 Irvine CA 92697-0001

WEINSTEIN, IRWIN MARSHALL, internist, hematologist; b. Denver, Mar. 5, 1926; m. Judith Braun, 1951. Student, Dartmouth Coll., 1943-44, Williams Coll., 1944-45; MD, U. Colo., Denver, 1949. Diplomate Am. Bd. Internal Medicine (assoc. bd. govs. hematology subcom.). Intern Montefiore Hosp., N.Y.C., 1949-50, jr. asst. resident in medicine, 1950-51; sr. asst. resident in medicine U. Chgo., 1951-52, resident in medicine, 1952-53, instr. in medicine, 1953-54, asst. prof. medicine, 1954-55; vis. assoc. prof. medicine U. Calif. Center for Health Scis., L.A., 1955-56, assoc. clin. prof., 1957-60, clin. prof., 1970—; hon. prof., 1996—; sect. chief in medicine, hematology sect. Wadsworth Gen. Hosp., VA Center, L.A., 1956-59; pvt. practice medicine specializing in hematology and internal medicine Los Angeles, 1959—; mem. staff Cedars-Sinai Med. Center, L.A., 1959—; chief of med. staff Cedars-Sinai Med. Ctr., 1972-74, bd. govs., 1974—. Mem. staff U. Calif. Ctr. Health Scis., Wadsworth Gen. Hosp., VA Ctr.; vis. prof. Hadassah Med. Ctr., Jerusalem, 1967; adv. for health affairs to Hon. Alan Cranston, 1971-92; mem. com. on space biology and medicine Space Sci. Bd.; active UCLA Comprehensive Cancer Ctr. Contbr. articles to profl. publs.; editor: (with Ernest Beutler) Mechanisms of Anemia, 1962. Recipient Pioneer in Medicine award Cedars-Sinai Med. Ctr., 1997. Master ACP (gov. So. Calif. Region I 1989-93); fellow Israel Med. Assn. (hon.); mem. AAAS, Am. Fedn. Clin. Rsch., Am. Soc. Hematology (exec. com. 1974-78, chmn. com. on practice 1978-87, mem. council 1974-78), Am. Soc. Internal Medicine, Assn. Am. Med. Colls., Internat. Soc. Hematology, Internat. Soc. Internal Medicine, L.A. Acad. Medicine, L.A. Soc. Nuclear Medicine, Inst. of Medicine NAS, N.Y. Acad. Sci., Reticulo-Endothelial Soc., Royal Soc. Medicine, Western Soc. Clin. Rsch., Alpha Omega Alpha. Office: 8635 W 3rd St Ste 665 Los Angeles CA 90048-6109

WEINSTEIN, MARTA, packaging services company executive; Founder iLogistix (formerly Logistix), Fremont, Calif., 1984—, co-chair, 1998—. Office: iLogistix 48301 Lakeview Blvd Fremont CA 94538-6533

WEINSTEIN, RONALD S. pathologist, educator; b. Schenectady, N.Y., Nov. 20, 1938; s. H. Edward and Shirley (Diamond) W.; m. Mary Dominica Corabi, July 12, 1964; children: Katherine Eiliesh, John Benjamin. B.S., Union Coll., Schenectady, 1960; M.D., Tufts U., 1965. Diplomate: Am. Bd. Pathology; 1972. Chemist Marine Biol. Lab., Woods Hole, Mass., 1960-62; intern Mass. Gen. Hosp., Boston, 1965-66, clin. and research fellow, 1965-70, resident in pathology, 1966-70; dir. Mixter Lab., 1966-70; vice chmn. pathology Aerospace Med. Research Labs., Dayton, Ohio, 1970-72; asso. prof. pathology Tufts U., 1972-75; Harriet Blair Borland prof., chmn. dept. pathology Rush Med. Coll. and Rush-Presbyn.-St. Luke's Med. Center, Chgo., 1975-90; prof., head dept. pathology U. Ariz. and U. Med. Ctr., Tucson, 1990—; dir. Ariz. Telemedicine Program, Tucson, 1996—. Teaching fellow Harvard Med. Sch., 1966-70; dir. Central Pathology Lab., Nat. Bladder Cancer Group, 1983-89, mem. editorial bd. Pathology, 1991—, J. Urologic Pathology, 1992—. Mem. editorial bd. Ultrastructural Pathology, 1979—, Human Pathology, 1980—, assoc. editor, 1983-92, mem. editorial bd. Lab. Investigation, 1983—; assoc. editor Advances in Pathology, 1985-91, editor, 1991—; contbr.: articles profl. jours. Served as maj. USAF, 1970-72. Ford Found. fellow, 1959; Congressional intern, 1959; USPHS fellow, 1965-68 Mem. AMa, Am. Soc. Cell Biology, Internat. Acad. pathology (councilor 1980-82, internat. councilor 1982-84), U.S. and Can. Acad. Pathology (pres. 1988-89), Assn. Pathol. (chmn., sec.-treas. 1989-90, v.p. 1998—), Chgo. Pathol. Soc. (pres. 1979-80), Internat. Soc. Urologic Pathology (pres.-elect 1992-94, pres. 1995-96), Internat. Coun. Soc. Pathology (v.p. 1992-98, pres. 1998—). Office: U Ariz Dept Pathology 1501 N Campbell Ave Tucson AZ 85724-0001

WEINSTOCK, HAROLD, lawyer; b. Stamford, Conn., Nov. 30, 1925; s. Elias and Sarah (Singer) W.; m. Barbara Lans, Aug. 27, 1950; children—Nathaniel, Michael, Philip. B.S. magna cum laude, N.Y. U., 1947; J.D., Harvard, 1950. Bar: Conn. bar 1950, Ill. bar 1950, Calif. bar 1958. Atty. SEC, Washington, 1950-52, IRS, 1952-56; tax atty. Hunt Foods & Industries, Inc., Los Angeles, 1956-58; pvt. practice Beverly Hills, Calif., 1958-71, Los Angeles, 1971—; mem. Weinstock, Manion, Reisman, Shore & Neumann (and predecessor firms), 1958—. Lectr. extension div., estate planning courses U. Calif. at Los Angeles, 1959— ; estate planning and taxation courses Calif. Continuing Edn. of the Bar, 1960— . [illegible] Planning An Estate, 4th edit., 1995; contbr. articles to profl. publs. Nat. trustee Union Am. Hebrew Congregations, 1976-79; bd. trustees Jewish Cmty. Found., L.A.; adv. bd. Estate Planning Inst. UCLA Law Sch., 1979-92, NYU Inst. on Fed. Taxation, 1986-95. Mem. ABA, Calif. Bar Assn., Beverly Hills Bar Assn. (chmn. probate and trusts com. 1967-68), Los Angeles Bar Assn., Beverly Hills Estate Planning Council (pres. 1968-69), Estate Counselors Forum of Los Angeles (pres. 1963-64) Jewish (pres. temple 1974-76). Office: Weinstock Manion 1875 Century Park E Fl 15 Los Angeles CA 90067-2501

WEIR, ALEXANDER, JR. utility consultant, inventor; b. Crossett, Ark., Dec. 19, 1922; s. Alexander and Mary Eloise (Field) W.; m. Florence Forschner, Dec. 28, 1946; children: Alexander III, Carol Jean, Bruce Richard BSChemE, U. Ark., 1943; MChemE, Poly Inst. Bklyn., 1946; PhD, U. Mich., 1954; cert., U. So. Calif. Grad. Sch. Bus. Adminstrn., 1968. Chem. engr. Am. Cyanamid Co., Stamford Rsch. Labs., 1943-47; with U. Mich., 1948-58; rsch. assoc., project supr. Engring. Rsch. Inst., U. Mich., 1948-57; lectr. chem. and metall. engring. dept. U. Mich., 1954-56, asst. prof., 1956-58; cons. Ramo-Woolridge Corp., L.A., 1956-57; mem. tech. staff, sect. head, asst. mgr. Ramo-Wooldridge Corp., L.A., 1957-60, incharge Atlas Missile Captive test program, 1956-60; tech. adv. to pres. Northrop Corp., Beverly Hills, Calif., 1960-70; prin. scientist for air quality So. Calif. Edison Co., L.A., 1970-76, mgr. chem. sys. R & D, 1976-86, chief rsch. scientist, 1986-88; utility cons. Playa Del Rey, Calif., 1988—. Rep. Am. Rocket Soc. to Detroit Nuc. Coun., 1954-57; chmn. session on chem. reactions Nuc. Sci. and Engring. Congress, Cleve., 1955; U.S. del. AGARD (NATO) Combustion Colloquium, Liege, Belgium, 1955; Western U.S. rep. task force on environ. R & D goals Electric Rsch. Coun., 1971; electric utility advisor Electric Power Rsch. Inst., 1974-78, 84-87; industry advisor dept. chemistry and biochemistry Calif. State U., L.A., 1981-88. Author: Two and Three Dimensional Flow of Air through Square-Edged Sonic Orifices, 1954; (with R.B. Morrison and T.C. Anderson) Notes on Combustion, 1955, also tech. papers; inventor acid rain prevention device used in 5 states. Sea scout leader, Greenwich, Conn., 1944-48, Marina del Rey, Calif., 1965-70; bd. govs., past pres. Civic Union Playa del Rey, chmn. sch., police and fire, nominating, civil def., army liaison coms.; mem. Senate, Westchester YMCA, chmn. Dads sponsoring com., active fundraising; chmn. nominating com. Paseo del Rey Sch. PTA, 1961; mem. L.A. Mayors Cmty. Adv. Com.; asst. chmn. advancement com., merit badge dean Cantinella dist. L.A. Area coun. Boy Scouts Am. Recipient Nat. Rsch. Coun. Flue Gas Desulfurization Industrials Scale Reliability award NAS, 1975, Power Environ. Achievement award EPA, 1980, Excellence in Sulfur Dioxide Control award EPA, 1985. Mem. AIChE, Am. Geophys. Union, Navy League U.S. (v.p. Palos Verdes Peninsula coun. 1961-62), N.Y. Acad. Scis., Sci. Rsch. Soc. Am., Am. Chem. Soc., U.S. Power Squadron (hon. capt. of fleet 1997), St. Andrew Soc. So. Calif., Clan Macnachtan Assn., Clan Buchanan Soc. Am., Clan Farquharson Assn., Betty Washington Lewis Soc. of Children of Am. Revolution (past pres.), Ark. Soc. of Children of Am. Revolution (past pres.), Santa Monica Yacht Club (lifetime hon. cannoneer), Sigma Xi, Phi Kappa Phi, Phi Lambda Upsilon, Alpha Chi Sigma, Lambda Chi Alpha. Office: 8229 Billowvista Dr Playa Del Rey CA 90293-7807

WEISEL, THOMAS W. investment company executive; Sr. ptnr., CEO Montgomery Securities, San Francisco; chmn., founder, CEO Thomas Weisel Ptnrs., San Francisco, 1998—. Office: Thomas Weisel Ptnrs 1 Montgomery St San Francisco CA 94104

WEISENBURGER, THEODORE MAURICE, retired judge, poet, educator, writer; b. Tuttle, N.D., May 12, 1930; s. John and Emily (Rosenau) W.; children: Sam, Jennifer, Emily, Todd, Daniel, Dwight, Holly, Michael, Paul, Peter; m. Maylyne Chu, Sept. 19, 1985; 1 child, Irene. BA, U. N.D., 1952, LLB, 1956, JD, 1969; BFT, Am. Grad Sch. Internat. Mgmt., Phoenix, 1957. Bar: N.D. 1963, U.S. Dist. Ct. N.D. 1963. County judge, tchr. Bensen County, Minnewaukan, N.D., 1968-75, Walsh County, Grafton, 1975-87; trial judge Devils Lake Sioux, Ft. Totten, 1968-84, Turtle Mountain Chippewa, Belcourt, 1974-87; U.S. magistrate U.S. Dist. Ct., Minnewaukan, 1972-75; Justice of the Peace pro tem Maricopa County, Ariz., 1988-92; instr. Rio Salado C.C., 1992—. Tchr. in Ethiopia, 1958-59. Author: Poetry and Other Poems, 1991. 1st lt. U.S. Army, 1952-54. Recipient Humanitarian award U.S. Cath. Conf., 1978, 82, Right to Know award Sigma Delta Chi, 1980, Spirit of Am. award U.S. Conf. Bishops, 1982. Home: 4353 E Libby St Phoenix AZ 85032-1732 E-mail: tmw@qwest.net

WEISER, PAUL DAVID, manufacturing company executive; b. N.Y.C., May 30, 1936; s. Irving Julius and Rose (Peckerman) W.; m. Paula Lee Block, June 19, 1960; children: Amy Helen, Deborah Susan. B.S. in Metallurgy, M.I.T., 1959; LL.B. (editor law rev.), U. Calif., Berkeley, 1963. Bar: Calif. 1963. Assoc. firm Mitchell, Silberberg & Knupp, Los Angeles, 1963-68; sec., gen. counsel Hitachi Koki Imaging Solutions, Inc. (formerly Dataproducts Corp.), 1968—, sr. v.p., sec. Calif.; chmn. adv. com. shareholder communications SEC, 1981. Contbr. articles legal publns. Served with USAR, 1959-60. Mem. Am. Bar Assn., Am. Soc. Corp. Secs. Jewish. Office: 1757 Tapo Canyon Rd Simi Valley CA 93063-3391

WEISER, TIMOTHY L. athletic director; b. Gt. Bend, Kans., Jan. 30, 1958; 3. Susan Conway; children: Rudy, Melanie. BS in Psychology, Emporia (Kans.) State U., 1981, MS in Counseling, 1982. Admissions counselor Emporia State U., 1982-83; asst. to dir. athletics Wichita (Kans.) State U., 1983-85, asst. dir. athletics, 1985-87, assoc. dir., 1987-88; dir. athletics Austin Peay State U., 1988-93, Ea. Mich. U., 1993-98, Colo. State U., Ft. Collins, 1998—. Office: Colo State U Colo State Athletics Fort Collins CO 80523-0001

WEISGERBER, JOHN SYLVESTER, provincial legislator; b. Barrhead, Alta., Can., June 12, 1940; s. Sylvester Weisgerber and Eva (Kilshaw) Harrison; m. Judith Muriel Janke, June 30, 1961; children: Joanne, Pamela. BBA, N. Alta. Inst. Tech., 1962. Owner Carland Ltd., 1975-81; econ. devel. commr. Peace River-Liard Regional Dist., Dawson Creek, 1982-84; sales mgr. Timberline Pontiac Buick GMC Ltd., Dawson Creek, 1984-86; mem. legis. assembly Govt. of B.C. (Can.), Victoria, 1986—, parliamentary sec. to atty. gen., 1987-88, min. of state for Nechako and N.E., 1988-89, min. native affairs, 1989-91. Chmn. Cabinet Com. on Native Affairs, Victoria, 1988-90; mem. Cabinet Com. on Sustainable Devel., Victoria, 1988-90; mem. Select Standing Com. of Forests and Lands, Victoria, 1988-90; mem. Select Standing Com. on Agr. and Fisheries, Victoria, 1988-90; interim leader B.C. Social Credit Party, 1992-93; leader Reform Party of B.C., 1995-97; ind. mem. legis. assembly, 1997—. Bd. dirs., pres. Dawson Creek and Dist. Fall Fair, 1980-86. Mem. Rotary (past pres.), Mile O Riding Club (bd. dirs., pres. 1976-81). Avocations: hunting, fishing, downhill skiing. Office: Parliament Bldgs Rm 144 Victoria BC Canada V8V 1X4

WEISS, CARL, aerospace company executive; b. Bklyn., Dcc. 6, 1938; s. Morris Harold and Sonia B. (Botwinick) W.; m. Judith Fellner, Jan. 27, 1963; children: Daniel Oren, Jonathan Michael. BBA, CUNY, 1961, MBA, 1968; postgrad., Harvard U., Boston, 1971. CPA, N.Y. Acct. Joseph Warren & Co., N.Y.C., 1965-68; asst. contr. Fisher Radio Corp., L.I., N.Y., 1968-69; sr. v.p. Deutsch Relays, Inc., East Northport, 1969-83; owner, exec. v.p. Logical Solutions, Inc., Melville, 1983-92; owner, pres., COO [illegible] 1992—. Bd. dirs. Deutsch Dagan, Inc. With U.S. Army, 1961-67. Mem. AICPA (future issues com. 1985-88); N.Y. Soc. CPA. Office: G & H Tech Inc 750 W Ventura Blvd Camarillo CA 93010-8382

WEISS, ERIC R. direct response programming executive; Exec. v.p. Westwood One, Inc.; vice chmn. Premiere Radio Networks; vice chmn., CEO BuyItNow.com.; vice chmn. COO, pres. E4L, Inc., Encion, Calif., 1998—. Bd. dirs. Nat. Media Corp., Phila. Office: 15821 Ventura Blvd Encino CA 91436

WEISS, JULIE, costume designer; Costume designer: (stage) The Elephant Man, 1979 (Tony award nomination best costume design 1979); (films) I'm Dancing as Fast as I Can, 1982, Independence Day, 1983, Second Thoughts, 1983, Spacehunter: Adventures in the Forbidden Zone, 1983, Testament, 1983, The Mean Season, 1985, Creator, 1985, F/X, 1986, Cherry 2000, 1987, Masters of the Universe, 1987, The Whales of August, 1987, 1969, 1988, Tequila Sunrise, 1988, Steel Magnolias, 1989, Wicked Stepmother, 1989, The Freshman, 1990, Married to It, 1991, Honeymoon in Vegas, 1992, House of Cards, 1993, Searching for Bobby Fischer, 1993, Naked in New York, 1993, It Could Happen to You, 1994, 12 Monkeys, 1995 (Acad. award nominee for best costume design 1996), Marvin's Room, 1996, The Edge, 1997, Touch, 1997, A Simple Plan, 1998, Finding Graceland, 1998, Fear and Loathing in Las Vegas, 1998, Isn't She Great, 1999, American Beauty, 1999; (TV movies) The Gangster Chronicles, 1981, The Elephant Man, 1982 (Emmy award nominee for best costume design 1982), Little Gloria...Happy at Last, 1982 (Emmy award nominee for best costume design 1983), The Dollmaker, 1984 (Emmy award for best costume design 1984), Do You Remember Love?, 1985, Evergreen, 1985 (Emmy award nominee for best costume design 1985), Conspiracy of Love, 1987, A Woman of Independant Means, 1994 (Emmy award for best costume design), Love She Sought, 1990, The Portrait, 1993. Office: c/o Costume Designers Guild 13949 Ventura Blvd Ste 309 Sherman Oaks CA 91423-3570

WEISS, MARTIN HARVEY, neurosurgeon, educator; b. Newark , Feb. 2, 1939; s. Max and Rae W.; m. R. Debora Rosenthal, Aug. 20, 1961; children: Brad, Jessica, Elisabeth. AB magna cum laude, Dartmouth Coll., 1960, BMS, 1961; MD, Cornell U., 1963. Diplomate Am. Bd. Neurol. Surgery (bd. dirs. 1983-89, vice chmn. 1987-88, chmn. 1988-89). Intern Univ. Hosps., Cleve., 1963-64, resident in neurosurgery, 1966-70; sr. instr. to asst. prof. neurosurgery Case Western Res. U., 1970-73; asso. prof. neurosurgery U. So. Calif., 1973-76, prof., 1976-78, prof., chmn. dept., 1978—, Martin H. Weiss chair in neurol. surgery, 1997—. Chmn. neurology B study sect. NIH; mem. residency rev. com. for neurosurgery Accreditation Commn. for Grad. Med. Edn., 1989—, vice chmn., 1991-93, chmn., 1993-95, mem. appeals coun. in neurosurgery, 1995—; Courville lectr. Loma Linda U. Sch. Medicine, 1989; Edgar Kahn vis. prof. U. Mich., 1987; W. James Gardner lectr. Cleve. Clinic, 1993; Edwin Boldrey vis. prof. U. Calif., San Francisco, 1994; hon. guest San Francisco Neurol. Soc., 1994, Australian Neurosurg. Soc., 1996; Aurthur Ward vis. prof. U. Wash., 1988; John Raff vis. prof. U. Oreg., 1995; Afrox traveling prof. South African Congress Neurol. Surgeons, 1989; Loyal Davis lectr. Northwestern U., 1990; vis. prof. U. Melbourne, 1996, U. Sydney, 1996; Wagner lectr. U. Medicine and Dentistry N.J., 1997. Author: Pituitary Diseases, 1980; editor-in-chief Clin. Neurosurgery, 1980-83; assoc. editor Bull. L.A. Neurol. Socs., 1976-81, Jour. Clin. Neurosci., 1981—; mem. editl. bd. Neurosurgery, 1979-84, Neurol. Rsch., 1980—, Jour. Neurosurgery, 1987—, chmn., 1995—, assoc. editor, 1996—. Served to capt. USAR, 1964-66. Spl. fellow in neurosurgery NIH, 1969-70; recipient Jamieson medal Australasian Neurosurg. Soc., 1996. Mem. ACS (adv. coun. neurosurgery 1985-88), Soc. Neurol. Surgeons (v.p. 1999, pres.-elect 2000—, pres. 2001-02), Neurosurg. Soc. Am., Am. Acad. Neurol. Surgery (exec. com. 1988-89, v.p. 1992-93), Rsch. Soc. Neurol. Surgeons, Am. Assn. Neurol. Surgeons (bd. dirs. 1988-91, sec. 1994-97, pres.-elect 1998-99, pres. 1999-2000, past pres. 2000-2001), Congress Neurol. Surgeons (v.p. 1982-83), Western Neurosurg. Soc., Neurosurg. Forum, So. Calif. Neurosurg. Soc. (pres. 1983-84), Phi Beta Kappa, Alpha Omega Alpha. Home: 357 Georgian Rd La Canada-Flintridge CA 91011-3520 Office: 1200 N State St Los Angeles CA 90033-1029 E-mail: weiss@hsc.usc.edu

WEISS, MAX TIBOR, retired aerospace company executive; b. Hajduananas, Hungary, Dec. 29, 1922; came to U.S., 1929, naturalized, 1936; s. Samuel and Anna (Hornstein) W.; m. Melitta Newman, June 28, 1953; children: Samuel Harvey, Herschel William, David Nathaniel, Deborah Beth. BEE, CCNY, 1943; MS, MIT, 1947, PhD, 1950. Rsch. assoc. MIT, 1946-50; mem. tech. staff Bell Tel. Labs., Holmdel, N.J., 1950-59; assoc. head applied physics lab. Hughes Aircraft Co., Culver City, Calif., 1959-60; dir. electronics rsch. lab. The Aerospace Corp., L.A., 1961-63, gen. mgr. labs. div., 1963-67, gen. mgr. electronics and optics div., 1968-78, v.p., gen. mgr. lab. ops., 1978-81, v.p. engring. group, 1981-86; v.p. tech. and electronics system group Northrop Corp., L.A., 1986-91, v.p., gen. mgr. electronics systems div. Hawthorne, Calif., 1991-94; corp. v.p., dep. gen. mgr. electronics/systems integration Northrop Grumman Corp., Bethpage, N.Y., 1994-96, corp. v.p., 1996. Asst. mgr. engring. ops. TRW Systems, Redondo Beach, Calif., 1967-68; mem. sci. adv. bd. USAF; bd. dirs. Concorde Solutions, Inc., Concord, Calif. Contbr. articles to physics and electronics jours.; patentee in electronics and communications. With USNR, 1944-45. Fellow Am. Phys. Soc., IEEE (Centennial medal, 1983, Fredrik Philips award, 1993), AIAA, AAAS; mem. NAE, Sigma Xi. E-mail: maxweiss@mediaone.net

WEISS, NOEL S. epidemiologist; b. Chgo., Mar. 10, 1943; s. Sidney and Dorothy (Bloom) W.; m. Chu Chen, Oct. 12, 1980; children: Jessica, Jeremy. BA, Stanford U., 1965, MD, 1967; MPH, Harvard U., 1969, DrPH, 1971. Epidemiologist Nat. Ctr. for Health Stats., Rockville, Md., 1971-73; prof. U. Washington, Seattle, 1973—; epidemiologist Fred Hutchinson Cancer Rsch. Ctr., Seattle. Author: Clinical Epidemiology: The Study of the Outcome of Illness, 1996. Recipient Rsch. Career Devel. award Nat. Cancer Inst., 1975, Outstanding Investigator award Nat. Cancer Inst., 1985. Mem. Inst. of Medicine, Soc. for Epidemiol. Rsch., Am. Epidemiol. Soc. Democrat. Office: U Wash Sch Pub Health & Cmty Med Dept Epidemiology Box 357236 Seattle WA 98195-7236

WEISS, ROBERT MICHAEL, dermatologist; b. N.Y.C. s. Leonard Seymour and Edith Rose (Levine) W.; 1 child, Michael Louis. Ba, U. Pa., 1970; MD, SUNY, Buffalo, 1974. Diplomate Am. Bd. Dermatology. Intern in internal medicine SUNY, Buffalo, 1974-75, resident in internal medicine, 1975-76, resident in dermatology, 1976-79; pvt. practice in dermatology Las Vegas, Nev., 1979—. Fellow Am. Acad. Derrmatology; mem. AMA. Office: Robert M Weiss MD 2300 S Rancho Dr Ste 106 Las Vegas NV 89102-4507

WEISS, ROBERT STEPHEN, medical manufacturing company financial executive; b. Oct. 25, 1946; s. Stephen John and Anna Blanche (Lescinski) W.; m. Marilyn Annette Chesick, Oct. 29, 1970; children: Christopher Robert, Kim Marie, Douglas Paul. BS in Acctg. cum laude, U. Scranton, 1968. CPA, N.Y. Supr. KPMG (formerly Peat, Marwick, Mitchell & Co.), N.Y.C., 1971-76; asst. corp. contr. Cooper Labs., Inc., Parsippany, N.J., 1977-78; group contr. Coopen Vision, Inc., 1980; v.p., corp. contr. Cooper Labs., Palo Alto, Calif., 1981-83, The Cooper Cos., Inc. (formerly CooperVision, Inc.), Palo Alto, 1984-89; v.p., treas., CFO The Cooper Cos., Inc., Pleasanton, 1989—, sr. v.p., 1992-95, exec. v.p. fin., 1995—. Bd. dirs. The Cooper Cos., Inc., Pleasanton, Calif. With U.S. Army, 1969-70. Decorated Bronze Star with oak leaf cluster, Army Commendation medal. Mem. AICPA, N.Y. State Soc. CPAs. Home: 1775 Spumante Pl Pleasanton CA 94566-6478 Office: The Cooper Companies Inc Ste 590 6140 Stoneridge Mall Rd Pleasanton CA 94588 E-mail: rweiss@cooperco.com

WEISS, WALTER STANLEY, lawyer; b. Newark, Mar. 12, 1929; s. Jack and Mollie (Orkin) W.; m. Misty M. Moore; children from previous marriage: Jack Stephen, Andrew Scott. A.B., Rutgers U., 1949, J.D., 1952. Bar: D.C. 1952, N.J. 1956, Calif. 1961. Trial atty. IRS, Phila., Los Angeles, 1957-62; asst. U.S. atty., chief tax div. Los Angeles, 1962-63; ptnr. firm Goodson & Hannam, Los Angeles, 1963-67; mng. ptnr. firm Long & Levit, Los Angeles, 1967-79; ptnr. firm Greenberg & Glusker, Los Angeles, 1979-81, Rosenfeld, Meyer and Susman, Beverly Hills, Calif., 1981-93; prin. Law Office of Walter S. Weiss, L.A., 1993—. Judge pro tem L.A. and Santa Monica (Calif.) Mcpl. Cts., 1994—. Contbr. articles to legal jours. Served to capt. JAGC USAF, 1953-56. Named Arbitrator Nat. Assn. Securities Dealers, 1974 Fellow Am. Coll. Trial Lawyers; mem. ABA, Los Angeles County Bar Assn., Beverly Hills Bar Assn. Home: 12349 Ridge Cir Los Angeles CA 90049-1183 Office: 12400 Wilshire Blvd Ste 1300 Los Angeles CA 90025-1055 E-mail: wsweiss@aol.com

WEISSBRODT, ARTHUR S. federal judge; BA, Pa. State U., 1966; JD, Columbia U., 1969. Law clk. to Hon. Edward J. Dimock U.S. Dist. Ct. (so. dist.) N.Y.; apptd. bankruptcy judge no. dist. U.S. Dist. Ct. Calif., 1989. Office: 280 S 1st St Rm 3035 San Jose CA 95113-3010

WEISSENBUEHLER, WAYNE, former bishop, pastor; Bishop of Rocky Mountain Evang. Luth. Ch. in Am., Denver, 1993; pastor Bethany Luth. Ch., Englewood, Colo., 1993—. Office: Bethany Luth Ch 4500 E Hampton Englewood CO 80110

WEISSMAN, EUGENE YEHUDA, chemical engineer; b. Bucharest, Romania, Sept. 23, 1931; came to U.S., 1958; s. Alfred A. and Paula D. (Braunstein) W.; children: Ian A., Michael L. BS, Israel Inst. Tech., 1953; MS, U. Mich., 1959; PhD in chem. engr., Case Western Reserve U., 1963; MBA, U. Chgo., 1972. Registered profl. engr. Mgr. Israel Atomic Energy Comm., 1953-58; process engr. Hercules Powder Co., 1960-61; sr. engr. Gen. Electric Co., 1963-65, mgr. R&D, 1965-68; head rsch. dept. Johnson Controls, 1968-73; dir. rsch. B.A.S.F. Corp., 1973-91; dir. technology transfer Nat. Ctr. for Mfg. Scis., 1991-92; exec. dir. Ctr. for Process Analytical Chemistry U. Wash., 1992-94; pres. Weissman Assocs., Seattle, 1994-98, prin., 1998—. Adv. coun. Coll. Engring. U. Akron; mem. editorial and tech. adv. bd. PI Quality; adj. prof. dept. mgmt. in sci. and tech. Oreg. Grad. Inst. Sci. and Tech., 1996—. Contbr. articles to profl. jours.; patentee in field. Fellow USPHS, 1959, 62. Mem. AAAS, AIChE (dir. heat transfer and energy conversion divsn.), NRC (co. rep.), Catalysis Soc. New Eng. (dir.), Electrochem. Soc., Nat. Membership Com., Am. Soc. for Quality Control, Indsl. Rsch. Inst. (bd. dirs., chmn. bd. editors, chmn. nominating com., univ. rels. com., advanced study groups com., fin. com.), Am. Chem Soc. (corp. assocs. com.), Nat. Coun. Advancement Rsch. (conf. com.), Coun. Chem. Rsch. (Univ. Ind. interaction com.), Tech. Transfer Soc., Inst. Mgmt. Cons., Product Devel. and Mgmt. Assn., Am. Translators Assn. N.W. Translators and Interpreters Soc., Mich. Materials Processing Inst. (bd. dirs.), Internat. Forum Process Analytical Chemistry (sci. bd.). Home and Office: 4119 NE 142nd St Seattle WA 98125-3841 E-mail: eweissman@att.net

WEISSMAN, IRVING L. medical scientist; b. Great Falls, Mont., Oct. 21, 1939; married, 1961; 4 children. BS, Mont. State Coll., 1960, DSc (hon.), 1992; MD, Stanford U., 1965. NIH fellow dept. radiology Stanford U., 1965-67, rsch. assoc., 1967-68, from asst. prof. to assoc. prof. dept. pathology, 1969-81, prof. pathology Sch. Medicine, 1981—, prof. devel. biology, 1989—; prof. pathology & developmental biology Stanford U. Sch. Medicine. James McGinnis Meml. lectr. Duke U., 1982; George Feigen Meml. lectr. Stanford U., 1987; Albert Coons Meml. lectr. Harvard U., 1987; Jame Stahlman lectr. Vanderbilt U., 1987, R. E. Smith lectr. U. Tex. Sys. Cancer Ctr., 1988; Chauncey D. Leake lectr. U. Calif., 1989; Harvey lectr. Rockefeller U., 1989; Rose Litman lectr., 1990; sr. Dernham fellow, Calif. divsn. Am. Cancer Soc., 1969-73; mem. immunobiology study sect. NIH, 1976-80; mem. sci. rev. bd. Howard Hughes Med. Inst., 1986—; mem. sci. adv. com. Irvington House Inst., 1987—; co-founder Systemix, Inc., 1988, bd. dirs., 1988—; Karel & Avice Beekhuis prof. cancer biology, 1987; 5th Ann. vis. prof. cancer biology U. Tex. Health Sci. Ctr., 1987; disting. lectr. Western Soc. Clin. Investment, 1990; chmn. U.S.-Japan Immunology Bd., 1992-94; chmn. sci. adv. com. of McLaughlin Rsch. Inst., 1992—, trustee, 1992—; bd. govs. Project Inform, 1995—. Recipient Pasarow award, 1989, Faculty Rsch. award Nat. Am. Cancer Soc., 1974-78, Mont. Conservationist of Yr. Mont. Land Reliance, 1994; named One of Top 100 Alumni Mont. State U., 1993; Josiah Macy Found. scholar, 1974-75. Fellow AAAS; mem. NAS (steering com. NIOM AIDS panel 1985-86), Am. Acad. Arts and Scis., Am. Assn. Immunologists (pres. 1994-95), Am. Assn. Univ. Pathologists, Am. Assn. Pathologists, Am. Soc. Microbiology, Am. Assn. Cancer Rsch., Inst. Immunology. Office: Stanford U Sch Medicine B257 Beckman Ctr Stanford CA 94305-5323

WEISWASSER, STEPHEN, electronics manufacturing executive; BA, Wayne State U.; postgrad., Johns Hopkins U.; JD magna cum laude, Harvard U. Ptnr. Wilmer, Cutler & Pickering; sr. v.p. Capital Cities/ABC, Inc.; pres., CEO Americast, 1995-98; ptnr. Covington & Burling, Washington, 1998-99; exec. v.p., gen. counsel Gemstar Internat. Group Ltd., Pasadena, Calif., 1999—, also bd. dirs. Woodrow Wilson Nat. fellow Johns Hopkins U. Office: Gemstar Internat Group Ltd Ste 800 135 N Los Roldes Ave Pasadena CA 91101 Office Fax: 626-792-0257

WEISWASSER, STEPHEN ANTHONY, lawyer, broadcast executive; b. Detroit, Nov. 21, 1940; s. Avery and Eleanor (Sherman) W.; m. July 3, 1962 (div. 1985); children: Jonathan, Gayle; m. Andrea Timko, Apr. 19, 1986; children: Anne, Emily. BA, Wayne State U., 1962; student, Johns Hopkins U., 1962-63; JD, Harvard U., 1966. Bar: D.C. 1967, U.S. Supreme Ct. 1970. Law clk. to chief judge U.S. Ct. Appeals, Washington, 1966-67; assoc. Wilmer, Cutler and Pickering, Washington, 1967-74, ptnr., 1974-86; sr. v.p., gen. counsel Capital Cities/ABC, Inc., N.Y.C., 1986-91, sr. v.p., exec. v.p. ABC-TV network group, 1991, sr. v.p., exec. v.p. ABC News, 1991-93, sr. v.p., 1993; sr. v.p., pres. Multimedia Group, N.Y.C., 1993-95; pres., CEO Americast, L.A., 1995-98; ptnr. Covington & Burling, Washington, 1998-99; exec. v.p., gen. counsel Gemstar Internat. Group, Ltd., Pasadena, Calif., 1999—. Bd. dirs. Ctr. Comm.; pres. Internat. Radio and TV Soc. Found., Inc., 1995-97. Trustee Woodrow Wilson Found., 1994—, Greater Washington Ednl. TV Assn., 1999—; bd. dirs. Kennedy Ctr. Electronic Prodns., Inc., 1998—, The Fanfare Classical Music Channel, 1999. Mem. ABA, Fed. Comm. Bar Assn. Jewish. Home: 2718 32nd St NW Washington DC 20008-2712 Office: Gemstar Internat Group Ltd 135 N Los Robles Ave Ste 800 Pasadena CA 91101

WEITHORN, STANLEY STEPHEN, lawyer; b. N.Y.C., Aug. 28, 1924; s. Louis W. and Florence O. (Mandel) W.; m. Corinne J. Breslow, Dec. 26, 1949 (dec. 1987); children: Lois Ann, Michael J.; m. Muriel Casper, Sept. 9, 1990; 1 stepchild, Corey Casper. BSBA, Hofstra U., Hempstead, N.Y., 1947; JD, NYU, 1954, LLM in Taxation, 1956. Bar: N.Y. 1955. Assoc. firm Olwine, Connelly, Chase O'Donnell & Weyher, N.Y.C., 1956-61; ptnr. firm Lewis, McDonald & Varian, N.Y.C., 1961-62; pvt. practice N.Y.C., 1962-63, 67-68; ptnr. firm Wormser, Koch, Keily & Alessandroni, N.Y.C., 1963-66; sr. ptnr. firm Baer, Marks & Upham (successor to Upham, Meeker & Weithorn), N.Y.C., 1968-88, Epstein, Becker & Green, N.Y.C., 1988-89; sr. counsel Reid & Priest, N.Y.C., 1989-94, Morrison & Foerster, Palo Alto, Calif., 1994—. Spl. prof. law Hofstra U., 1974-78; adj. prof. law U. Miami, Fla., 1975-79; mem. adv. com. U. Miami Law Ctr. Ann. Inst. Estate Planning, 1974-80; coordinator fed. budget and tax policy course nat. policy studies program New Sch. Social Rsch., N.Y.C., 1975; mem. fund raising mgmt. adv. com. Grad. Sch. Mgmt. and Urban professions, New Sch. for Social Rsch., N.Y.C., 1977-84; mem. adv. com. N.Y. U. Inst. on Fed. Taxation, 1980-90; program chmn. Practicing Law Inst. confs., N.Y.C., 1962-78, N.Y. Law Jour. confs., 1980, NYU Inst. on Fed. Taxation confs., 1955-88; tax cons. Pres's Coun. on Environ. Quality, 1970; lectr. fed. taxation to univ. insts., non-profit org. confs., profl. bus. meetings. Author: Penalty Taxes on Accumulated Earnings and Personal Holding Companies, 1963, Tax Techniques for Foundations and Other Exempt Organizations, 7 vols, 1964, The Accumulated Earnings Tax, 1966; Contbg. editor, mem. adv. bd.: Tax Mgmt, 1959-68; feature columnist: Nat. Law Jour, 1978-79; Contbr. articles to profl. jours. Co-chmn. Port Washington-Manhasset (N.Y.) unit New Dem. Coalition, 1968-69; tax adviser nat. finance com. McGovern for Pres., 1971-72, mem. N.Y. fin. com., 1971-72; bd. dirs., exec. com. Equal Employment Coun. Inc., N.Y.C., 1968-71; bd. dirs., sec. New Priorities Edn. Fund, 1969-70; bd. dirs., exec. com., sec., co-chmn. Fund for New Priorities in Am., 1969—; bd. dirs., treas. Cow Bay Manpower Devel. Corp., Port Washington, 1969-71; bd. dirs., chmn. exec. com., pres. L.I. (N.Y.) Pub. Affairs Coun., 1973-78; bd. dirs., pres. Mental Health Assn. Nassau County, N.Y., 1980-85, Herman and Amelia Ehrmann Found., 1977—; bd. dirs. Jewish Family and Children's Svcs., San Francisco, 1994—; mem. legacy com. United Cerebral Palsy, N.Y.C., 1975-90; bd. dirs. Community Action for Legal Svcs., 1976-78, Frederick and Amelia Schimper Found., 1977—, Florence Weithorn Warner Found., N.Y.C., 1967-72, N.Y. Fedn. Reform Synagogues, 1973-78, Nat. Coalition for Children's Justice, 1980-90, N.Y. Fedn. Reform Synagogues, 1973-78, Am. Inst. for Philanthropic Studies, L.A. and N.Y.C., 1981-92, Nat. Health Council, 1984-92, Laurent and Alberta Gerschel Found., 1986—, Interns for Peace, 1985—, Am.-Israeli Civil Liberties Coalition, 1987—, Inst. Am. Values, 1987-91, Fund for Human Dignity, 1989-90, Found. Fund, 1986—, L.I. Community Found., 1989-93, Cancer Prevention Rsch. Inst., 1989—, Green Seal, 1989-92; mem. Emergency Task Force on Juvenile Delinquency Prevention, 1976-79; mem. adv. panel N.Y. chpt. Am. Jewish Com., 1978-80; mem. com. on deferred giving Fedn. Jewish Philanthropies N.Y., 1978-86; mem. legal and tax panel United Jewish Appeal/Fedn. Jewish Philanthropies, N.Y., 1986—; nat. chair Planned Giving Program, Am. Assocs. Ben-Gurion U. Negev, 1992—, mem. exec. com. N.W. region; mem. com. tax policy Nat. Assembly Vol. Health, Social Welfare Orgns. Inc., N.Y.C., 1961-73; mem. com. bequests and legacies Nat. Jewish Hosp., Denver, 1965-78; mem. estate planning com. ARC of Greater N.Y., 1970—; mem. leadership coun. United Jewish Appeal, N.Y.C., 1966-70; mem. adv. com., project on ch., state and taxation NCCJ, 1980-85; mem. legacy adv. coun. Am. Jewish Congress, N.Y.C., 1968-72; mem. Internat. Coun. on Environ. Law, 1982—; mem. Pres.'s adv. com. ACLU Found., 1983—; chmn. Uptown Tax Discussion Group, 1957-69, Exempt Orgns. Discussion Group, 1973-79, Fresh Meadows Civic Assn., 1961-63; mem. legal activities policy bd. Tax Analysts, 1974—. Served with AUS, 1943-46, ETO. Recipient Allard K. Lowenstein Meml. award Am. Jewish Congress, 1988; honoree Mental Health Assn. Nassau County, N.Y., 1991. Fellow Am. Coll. Tax Counsel; mem. ABA (chmn. subcom. exempt orgns. 1965-69, subcom. charitable contbns. 1971-75), Am. Soc. Technion-Israel Inst. Tech. (bd. dirs. N.W. region 1992—), N.Y. State Bar Assn. (exec. com. 1967-69), Assn. of Bar of City of N.Y., Internat. Acad. Estate and Trust Law (exec. coun. 1974-78, 90—), Univ. Club, Knickerbocker Yacht Club (bd. dirs. 1986-88). Jewish (trustee synagogue 1970-74). Home: 150 Central Park S # 1610 New York NY 10019-1566 Office: Morrison & Foerster 755 Page Mill Rd Palo Alto CA 94304-1018

WEITKAMP, WILLIAM GEORGE, retired nuclear physicist; b. Fremont, Nebr., June 22, 1934; s. Alvin Herman and Georgia Ann (Fuhrmeister) W.; m. Audrey Ann Jensen, June 2, 1956; children— Erick, Jay, Gretchen, Laurie. BA, St. Olaf Coll., 1956; MS, U. Wis., 1961, PhD, 1965. Rsch. asst. prof. U. Wash., Seattle, 1965-67; asst. prof. U. Pitts., 1967-68; tech. dir., rsch. prof. Nuclear Physics Lab., U. Wash., Seattle, 1968-95; ret., 1995; rsch. prof. emeritus, 1995—. With USAF, 1956-59. Acad. guest Eidgenossische Technische Hochschule Zurich, Switzerland, 1974-75. E-mial. Home: 2019 E Louisa St Seattle WA 98112-2207 Office: Univ Wash Nuc Physics Lab Gl 10 Seattle WA 98195-0001 E-mail: weitkamp@u.washington.edu

WEITZEL, JOHN QUINN, bishop; b. Chgo., May 10, 1928; s. Carl Joseph and Patricia (Quinn) W. BA, Maryknoll (N.Y.) Sem., 1951, M of Religious Edn., 1953; PMD, Harvard U. Ordained priest Roman Cath. Ch., 1955. With ednl. devel. Cath. Fgn. Mission Soc. of Am., Maryknoll, 1955-63, nat. dir. vocations for Maryknoll, dir. devel. dept. and info. services, 1963-72, mem. gen. council, 1972-78; asst. parish priest Cath. Ch., Western Samoa, 1979-81, pastor, vicar gen. Western Samoa, 1981-86; consecrated bishop, 1986; bishop Cath. Ch., Am. Samoa, 1986—. Office: Diocese Samoa-Pago Pago PO Box 3594 Pago Pago AS 96799-3594

WEITZEN, JEFFREY, computer manufacturing company executive; b. Perth Amboy, N.J., Apr. 15, 1956; BA in Econs., Wesleyan U.; MBA, U. Chgo. Various positions AT&T, 1980-98, exec. v.p. bus. markets divsn., until 1998; pres. Gateway, Inc., San Diego, 1998—, CEO, 2000—, also bd. dirs. Bd. dirs. San Diego Zool. Soc. Mem. U.S. C. of C. (bd. dirs.). Office: Gateway Inc 4545 Towne Centre Ct San Diego CA 92121-1900

WEITZMAN, WILLIAM, communications executive; b. 1939; Pres., CEO Electro Rent Corp., Van Nuys, Calif. Office: Electro Rent Corp 6060 Sepulveda Blvd Van Nuys CA 91411-2501

WELBORN, R. MICHAEL, bank executive; Chmn., CEO Citibank Ariz., CEO, 1996—. Active Greater Phoenix Econ. Coun., Valley of the Sun United Way, Ariz. Bankers Assn. Recipient Torch of Liberty Humanitarian of the Yr. award Anti-Defamation League, 1996. Office: Bank One Ctr 201 N Central Ave Phoenix AZ 85073-0073 Fax: 602-221-4840

WELCH, CAROL MAE, lawyer; b. Oct. 23, 1947; d. Leonard John and LaVerna Helen (Ang) Nyberg; m. Donald Peter Welch, Nov. 23, 1968 (dec. Sept. 1976). BA in Spanish, Wheaton Coll., 1968; JD, U. Denver, 1976. Bar: Colo. 1977, U.S. Dist. Ct. Colo. 1977, U.S. Ct. Appeals (10th cir.) 1977, U.S. Supreme Ct. 1981. Tchr. State Hosp., Dixon, Ill., 1969, Polo Cmty. Schs., 1969-70; registrar Sch. Nursing Hosp. of U. Pa., Phila., 1970; assoc. Hall & Evans, Denver, 1977-81, ptnr., 1981-92, spec. counsel, 1993-94; mem. Miller & Welch, L.L.C., Denver, 1995—. Mem. Colo. Supreme Ct. Jury Inst., Denver, 1982—; vice chmn. com. on conduct U.S. Dist. Ct., Denver, 1982-83, chmn., 1983-84; lectr. in field. Past pres. Family Tree, Inc. Named to Order St. Ives, U. Denver Coll. Law, 1977. Mem. ABA, Am. Coll. Trial Lawyers (state com.), Internat. Soc. Barristers, Internat. Assn. Def. Counsel, Am. Bd. Trial Advs. (treas. Colo. chpt. 1991-92, pres. 1992-93), Colo. Def. Lawyers Assn. (treas. 1982-83, v.p. 1983-84, pres. 1984-85), Denver Bar Assn., Colo. Bar Assn. (mem. litigation sect. coun. 1987-90), Colo. Bar Found. (trustee 1992—, pres. 1995-97), Def. Rsch. Inst. (chmn. Colo. chpt. 1987-90, regional v.p. 1990-93, bd. dirs. 1993-96), William E. Doyle Inn, The Hundred Club. Office: Miller & Welch LLC 730 17th St Ste 925 Denver CO 80202-3598

WELCH, DOMINIC, publishing executive; Pres., pub. The Salt Lake Tribune, Salt Lake City. Office: 400 Tribune Bldg Salt Lake City UT 84111

WELCH, LLOYD RICHARD, electrical engineering educator, communications consultant; b. Detroit, Sept. 28, 1927; s. Richard C. and Helen (Felt) W.; m. Irene Althea Main, Sept. 12, 1953; children: Pamela Irene Towery, Melinda Ann Bryant, Diana Lia Worthington. BS in Math., U. Ill., 1951; PhD in Math., Calif. Inst. Tech., 1958. Mathematician NASA-Jet Propulsion Lab., Pasadena, Calif., 1956-59; staff mathematician Inst. Def. Analyses, Princeton, N.J., 1959-65; prof. elec. engring. U. So. Calif., L.A.,

1965-99, prof. emeritus, 1999—. Cons. in field of elec. comms. Contbr. articles to profl. jours. Served with USN, 1945-49, 51-52 Fellow IEEE; mem. Nat. Acad. Engring., Am. Math. Soc., Math. Assn. Am., Soc. for Indsl. and Applied Math., Phi Beta Kappa, Sigma Xi, Phi Kappa Phi, Pi Mu Epsilon, Eta Kappa Nu Office: U So Calif Elec Engring Bldg 500A Los Angeles CA 90089-0001 E-mail: lloydwelch@earthlink.net

WELCH, RICHARD LEROY, personal improvement company executive; b. Lincoln, Nebr., Oct. 15, 1939; s. Raymond Nathanial and Helen Lila (Ludwig) W.; m. Donna Lee Gysegem, Nov. 3, 1991; children: Terri L. Flowerday, Julie A. Kuhl; 1 stepchild, Shannon Panzo. Student, U. Nebr.; PhD (hon.), Devonshire U., Eng., 2000. Agt. Gurantee Mut. Life, Lincoln, Nebr., 1960-61; agt., mgr. Mut. of Omaha, 1962-68; gen. agt. Loyal Protective Life, Omaha, 1969-70; mgr. Mut. Benefit Life, Dallas, 1971-73; br. mgr. Great West Life, San Jose, Calif., 1973-74; pres. Internat. Speedreading Inst., Phoenix, 1975-80; CEO, founder Educom, Inc./Subliminal Dynamics, Dynamic Brain Mgmt., Aurora, Colo., 1980—. Mem. adv. bd. Great West Life, San Jose, 1973; pres. bd. dirs. Internat. Speedreading Inst., Phoenix, 1975-80, Subliminal Dynamics, Inc., San Jose, 1980-93, Educom, Inc., Aurora, 1993—; scientist, spkr., author, educator in field. Author: Brain Management, 1996. Inductee Lincoln H.S. Athletic Hall of Fame, 2000. Mem. Shriners, Masons (32d degree). Democrat. Avocations: sports, music, travel. Office: Educom Inc DBA Subliminal Dynamics 19744 E Union Dr Aurora CO 80015-3486 Fax: (303) 627-2870. E-mail: subdyn@subdyn.com

WELCH, S(TEPHEN) ANTHONY, university administrator, Islamic studies and arts educator; b. Phila., Apr. 29, 1942; s. Arnold DeMerritt and Mary Scott Welch; m. Hyesoon Kim; children: Nicholas, Bronwen, Emily. Student, U. Munich, Free U. of Berlin; BA in German Lit. with honors, Swarthmore Coll., 1965; MA, Harvard U., 1967, PhD History of Art and Architecture, 1972. Lectr. dept. history in art U. Victoria, B.C., 1971-72, asst. prof., 1972-75, assoc. prof., 1975-80, prof., 1980—, assoc. dean, 1982-85, Dean of Faculty of Fine Arts, 1985-98, exec. dir. office of internat. affairs. Vis. prof. U. Minn., U. Wash., U. Chgo.; specialist in Iranian painting, Mughal painting in India, Islamic calligraphy and Sultanate architecture in medieval India. Author: Shah 'Abbas and the Arts of Isfahan, 1973, Artists for the Shah, 1976, Collection of Islamic Art, Prince Sadruddin Aga Khan, 4 Vols., 1972-78, Calligraphy in the Arts of the Muslim World, 1979, Arts of the Islamic Book, 1982, Treasures of Islam, 1985; contbr. articles to scholarly and profl. jours. Office: Office Internat Affairs Univ Victoria Victoria BC Canada V8W 2Y2 E-mail: world@oia.uvic.ca

WELK, RICHARD ANDREW, plastic surgeon; b. Aug. 9, 1956; BS, U. Mich., 1977, MD, 1981. Diplomate Am. Bd. Surgery, Am. Bd. Plastic Surgery. Resident gen. surgery, Grand Rapids, Mich., 1981-86; resident plastic surgery U. Calif., Irvine, 1986-88; plastic surgeon pvt. practice, Kirkland, Wash., 1988-91, Polyclinic, Seattle, 1991—. Mem. Am. Soc. Plastic & Reconstructive Surgery, Am. Soc. Aesthetic Plastic Surgery, Wash. State Med. Assn., Wash. Soc. Plastic Surgeons (pres. 1995-96). Office: Polyclinic 1145 Broadway Seattle WA 98122-4299

WELLBORN, CHARLES IVEY, science and technology business consultant; b. Houston, Dec. 9, 1941; s. Fred W. and Emily R. (Gladu) W.; m. JD McCausland, Aug. 14, 1965; children: Westly O., Kerry S. BA in Econs., U. N.Mex., 1963, JD, 1966; LLM, NYU, 1972. Bar: N.Mex. 1963, U.S. Dist. Ct. N.Mex. 1966. Assoc. Neal & Matkins, Carlsbad, N.Mex., 1966-68, Robinson & Stevens, Albuquerque, 1969-71; ptnr. Schlenker, Parker, Payne & Wellborn, Albuquerque, 1971-76, Parker & Wellborn, Albuquerque, 1976-82, Modrall, Sperling, Roehl, Harris & Sisk, Albuquerque, 1982-95; pres., CEO Sci. & Tech. Corp. at U. N.Mex., Albuquerque, 1995-2000; pres. Wellborn Strategies LLC, Albuquerque, 2000—. Contbr. articles to law revs. Bd. dirs. N.Mex. Symphony Orch., 1988-91, U. N.Mex. Anderson Schs. Mgmt. Found., 1989-94, N.Mex. First, 1989-93, 2000—, Accion N.Mex., 1995-97; vice chair U. N.Mex. Found., Inc., 1990-95; mem. Gov.'s Bus. Adv. Coun., 1989—, SBA Fin. Svcs. Adv., N.Mex., 1989; mem. venture capital mgmt. adv. com. N.Mex. State Investment Coun., 1991-98; mem. Econ. Forum, 1986—, chmn., 1995-96; chmn. Roots and Wings Found., 1989-93; v.p. N.Mex. Dem. Bus. Coun., 1992-96; mem. Gov.'s Prayer Breakfast Com., 1991—, chair, 2000—. Sgt. USAF, 1968-69, Korea. Fellow Am. Bar Found.; mem. ABA (ho. of dels. 1984-91), Albuquerque Bar Assn. (pres. 1977-78), N.Mex. Bar Found. (pres. 1980-82), State Bar N.Mex. (pres. 1982-83). Democrat. Roman Catholic. Office: Wellborn Strategis LLC 3819 La Hacienda Dr NE Albuquerque NM 87110-6115

WELLER, DEBRA ANNE, elementary educator; b. New Orleans, Feb. 4, 1954; d. James Garretson and Elizabeth Gene (Blakely) Hyatt; m. Bruce Weller, June 15, 1974; children: Jenny, Todd. AA in Art, St. Petersburg Jr. Coll., 1974; BA in Art Edn., Glassboro State Coll., 1983; MS in Curriculum and Instrn., Nat. U., 1991. Cert. tchr. Profl. storyteller, Mission Viejo, Calif., 1980—; tchr. Capistrano Unified Sch. Dist., San Juan Capistrano, 1989—; elem. tchg. asst. prin. Bathgate Elem., 1998—, stds. curriculum specialist. Edn. dir. South Coast Storytellers Guild, Costa Mesa, Calif., 1990—; workshop presenter Orange County Dept. Edn., Costa Mesa, 1991—, Imagination Celebration, Irvine, Calif., 1993—; bd. mem. Calif. Kindergarten Assn. Author: (pamphlets) Image-U-Telling Clubs, 1995, Storytelling, the Cornerstone of Literacy, also articles. Sec. Mission Viejo Cultural Com., 1995—. Cultural Arts grantee Dana Point (Calif.) Cultural Commn., 1993. Mem. NEA, Nat. Storytelling Network (Pacific region liaison), Calif. Tchrs. Assn., Calif. Kindergarten Assn. (bd. dirs.). Mormon. Avocations: calligraphy, composing, playing banjo, dulcimer and guitar.

WELLER, DIETER M. botanist, researcher; Rsch. scientist IBM Almaden Rsch. Ctr., San Jose, Calif. Recipient Ruth Allen award Am. Phytopathol. Soc., 1997. Office: IBM Almaden Rsch Ctr MSK11-D1 650 Harry Rd San Jose CA 95120-6099 E-mail: dieter@almaden.ibm.com

WELLER, GUNTER ERNST, geophysics educator; b. Haifa, June 14, 1934; came to U.S., 1968; s. Erich and Nella (Lange) W.; m. Sigrid Beilharz, Apr. 11, 1963; children: Yvette, Kara, Britta. BS, U. Melbourne, Australia, 1962, MS, 1964, PhD, 1968. Meteorologist Bur. Meteorology, Melbourne, 1959-61; glaciologist Australian Antarctic Exps., 1964-67; from asst. prof. to assoc. prof. geophysics Geophys. Inst., U. Alaska, Fairbanks, 1968-72, prof., 1973-98, dep. dir., 1984-86, 90-98; prof. emeritus Geophys. Inst., U. Ala., Fairbanks, 1998—; project dir. NASA-UAF Alaska SAR Facility, Fairbanks, 1983-93. Program mgr. NSF, Washington, 1972-74; pres. Internat. Commn. Polar Meteorology, 1980-83; chmn. polar rsch. bd. NAS, 1985-90, Global Change Steering Com. Sci. com. on Antarctic Rsch., 1988-92; chmn. Global Change Working Group Internat. Arctic Sci. Com., 1990-97; dir. Ctr. for Global Change and Arctic Sys. Rsch., U. Alaska, 1990—; dir. Coop. Inst. Arctic Rsch., 1994—; exec. dir. Arctic Climate Impact Assessment, Arctic Coun., 2000—. Contbr. numerous articles to profl. jours. Recipient Polar medal Govt. Australia, 1969; Mt. Weller named in his honor by Govt. Australia, Antarctica; Weller Bank named in his honor by U.S. Govt., Arctic. Fellow AAAS (exec. sec. arctic divsn. 1982-93), Arctic Inst. N.Am.; mem. Internat. Glaciological Soc., Am. Meteorol. Soc. (chmn. polar meteorology com. 1980-83), Am. Geophys. Union. Home: PO Box 81024 Fairbanks AK 99708-1024 Office: U Alaska Coop Inst Arctic Rsch Fairbanks AK 99775-7740 E-mail: gunter@gi.alaska.edu

WELLES, JOHN GALT, retired museum director; b. Orange, N.J., Aug. 24, 1925; s. Paul and Elizabeth Ash (Galt) W.; m. Barbara Lee Chrisman, Sept. 15, 1951; children: Virginia Chrisman, Deborah Galt, Barton Jeffery, Holly Page. BE, Yale U., 1946; MBA, U. Pa., 1949; LHD (hon.), U. Denver, 1994. Test engr. Gen. Electric Co., Lynn, Mass., 1947; labor rels. staff New Departure divsn. Gen. Motors Corp., Bristol, Conn., 1949-51; mem. staff Mountain States Employers Coun., Denver, 1952-55; head indsl. econs. divsn. U. Denver Rsch. Inst., 1956-74; v.p. planning and devel. Colo. Sch. Mines, Golden, 1974-83; regional adminstr. EPA, Denver, 1983-87; exec. dir. Denver Mus. Natural History, 1987-94, exec. dir. emeritus, 1994—. Contbr. articles to profl. jours., newspapers. Sr. cons. Secretariat, UN Conf. Human Environment, Geneva, 1971-72; cons. Bus. Internat., S.A., Geneva, 1972; trustee Tax Free Fund of Colo., N.Y., 1987-2000, Denver Pub. Libr. Friends Found., 1996—; mem. Rocky Mountain regional adv. bd. Inst. Internat. Edn., 1996—; exec. com. Denver Com. on Fgn. Rels., 1987—; bd. dirs. Gulf of Maine Found., 1995—; chmn. Colo. Front Range Project, Denver, 1979-80. Recipient Disting. Svc. award Denver Regional Coun. Govts., 1980, Barnes award EPA, 1987. Mem. AAAS, Am. Assn. Mus. (ethics commn. 1991-94, v.p. 1992-95), Denver Exec. Club (pres. 1967-68), World Future Soc., Univ. Club (Denver), Tau Beta Pi, Blue Key. Republican. Episcopalian. E-mail: jgwbcw@aol.com

WELLINGTON, WILLIAM GEORGE, entomologist, ecologist, educator; b. Vancouver, B.C., Can., Aug. 16, 1920; s. George and Lilly (Rae) W.; m. Margret Ellen Reiss, Sept. 22, 1959; children: Katherine Jean, Stephen Ross. B.A., U. B.C., 1941; M.A., U. Toronto, 1945, Ph.D., 1947. Meteorol. officer Can. Meteorol. Service, Toronto, 1942-45; research entomologist Can. Dept. Agr., Sault Ste. Marie, Ont., 1946-51; head bioclimatology sect. Can. Dept. Forestry, Sault Ste. Marie, Ont., Victoria, B.C., 1951-67, prin. scientist Victoria, 1964-68; prof. ecology U. Toronto, 1968-70; dir. Inst. Animal Resource Ecology, U. B.C., Vancouver, 1973-79, prof. plant sci. and resource ecology, 1970-86, hon. prof. dept. plant sci., 1986—, prof. emeritus, 1986—; Killam sr. research fellow U. B.C., 1980-81. Inaugural lectr. C.E. Atwood Meml. Seminar Series, Dept. Zoology, U. Toronto, 1993; vis. prof. N.C. State U., 1972, 75, 81, San Diego State U., 1975, Laval U., 1981, U. Calgary, 1983, Simon Fraser U., 1987. Contbr. articles to profl. jours. Named Prof. of Yr., Faculty Agrl. Sci., U. B.C., 1986 Fellow Entomol. Soc. Can. (pres. 1976-78, Gold medal 1968), Royal Soc. Can., Explorers Club; mem. Am. Meteorol. Soc. (award 1969), Entomol. Soc. Am. (C. J. Woodworth award 1979), Japanese Soc. Population Ecology, Entomol. Soc. Ont. Anglican. Club: Am. Philatelic Soc. Home: 2350 130A St Surrey BC Canada V4A 8Y5 Office: U BC ARE and Dept Plant Sci Vancouver BC Canada V6T 1W5

WELLIVER, CHARLES HAROLD, hospital administrator; b. Wichita, Kans., Feb. 14, 1945; married. BA, Wichita State U., 1972; MHA, U. Mo., 1974. Asst. dir. St. Luke's Hosp., Kansas City, 1974-79, assoc. dir., 1979-80; adminstr. Spelman Meml. Hosp., Smithville, Mo., 1980-82; sr. adminstr., COO Good Samaritan Med. Ctr., Phoenix, 1982-86, v.p., CEO, 1989—, Thunderbird Samaritan Hosp., Glendale, Ariz., 1986-89; exec. vice-chmn., COO Good Samaritan Med. Ctr., Glendale. Office: Good Samaritan Regional Med Ctr 1441 N 12th St Phoenix AZ 85006-2837

WELLS, ANNIE, photographer; b. 1954; B in Sci. Writing, U. Calif., Santa Cruz; past postgrad., San Francisco State U. Past photographer Herald Jour., Logan, Utah, Greeley (Colo.) Tribune, Associated Press, San Francisco; photographer Press Dem., Santa Rosa, Calif., 1989-97, L.A. Times, 1997—. Represented in permanent collections Nat. Mus. Women Arts, Washington. Recipient Pulitzer prize spot news photography, 1997. Office: LA Times 202 West First St Los Angeles CA 90012 E-mail: annie.wells@latimes.com

WELLS, CHRISTOPHER BRIAN, lawyer; b. Belleville, Ill., Jan. 23, 1948; s. Frederick Meyers and Ethel Pauline (Morris) W.; m. Gaynelle Vansandt, June 6, 1970; 1 child, Deva Marie. BA in Econs., U. Kans., BS in Bus., 1970, JD, 1973. Enforcement atty. SEC, Seattle, 1977-82; ptnr. Lane, Powell, Spears , Lubersky, LLP, Seattle, 1982—. Capt. U.S. Army, 1973-77. Mem. ABA, Wash. State Bar Assn., King County Trial Lawyers Assn., Wash. Soc. CPA's., Kans. Bar Assn., Securities Industry Assn. (legal and compliance divsn.). Democrat. Office: Lane Powell Spears Lubersky LLP 1420 5th Ave Ste 4100 Seattle WA 98101-2338 E-mail: wellsc@lanepowell.com

WELLS, JACK MOORE, state legislator; b. Neihart, Mont., Sept. 13, 1937; m. Mary Gay Wells; 4 children, 4 stepchildren. AB, Dartmouth Coll., 1959, MS, 1960. Cert. comml. pilot. Elec. engr. N.Y. Telephone Co., 1959-60; commd. 2d lt. USAF, 1960, advanced through grades to col., ret., 1990; mem. Mont. Ho. of Reps., 1995-98, Mont. Senate, Dist. 14, Helena, 1998—; mem. state adminstrn. com., fish and game com. Mont. State Senate, mem. edn. and cultural resources com. Active Gallatin Valley Presbyn. Ch. Mem. NRA, AARP, Mont. Pilots Assn., Mont. Landlords Assn., Exptl. Aircraft Assn., Nat. Fedn. Ind. Bus., Ret. Officers Assn., Pachyderm Cub, Bozeman Elks Club. Republican. Presbyterian. Home: 150 Coulee Dr Bozeman MT 59718-7717 E-mail: jmgwells@imt.net

WELLS, KENNETH B. medical educator; Prof. psychiatry & biobehavioral scis. UCLA Sch. Medicine, L.A. Address: 1700 Main St Santa Monica CA 90401-3208

WELSH, MARY MCANAW, family mediator, educator; b. Cameron, Mo., Dec. 7, 1920; d. Francis Louis and Mary Matilda (Moore) McAnaw; m. Alvin F. Welsh, Feb. 10, 1944 (dec.); children: Mary Celia, Clinton F., M. Ann. AB, U. Kans., 1942; MA, Seton Hall U., 1960; EdD, Columbia U., 1971. Reporter Hutchinson (Kans.) News Herald, 1942-43; house editor Worthington Pump & Machine Corp., Harrison, N.J., 1943-44; tchr., housemaster, coord. Summit (N.J.) Pub. Schs., 1960-68; prof. family studies N.Mex. State U., Las Cruces, 1972-85; adj. faculty dept. family practice Tex. Tech Regional Acad. Health Ctr., El Paso, 1978-82, Family Mediation Practicce, Las Cruces, 1986—. Author: A Good Family is Hard to Found, 1972, Parent, Child and Sex, 1970; contbr. articles to profl. jours.; writer, presenter home econs. and family study series KRWG-TV, 1974; moderator TV series The Changing Family in N.Mex./LWV, 1976. Mem. AAUW (pres. N.Mex. 1981-83), N.Mex. Coun. Women's Orgn. (founder, chmn. 1982-83), Delta Kappa Gamma, Kappa Alpha Theta. Democrat. Roman Catholic. Home and Office: 1975 Avenida Antigua Las Cruces NM 88005

WELSOME, EILEEN, journalist; b. N.Y.C., Mar. 12, 1951; d. Richard H. and Jane M. (Garity) W.; m. James R. Martin, Aug. 3, 1983. BJ with honors, U. Tex., 1980. Reporter Beaumont (Tex.) Enterprise, 1980-82, San Antonio Light, 1982-83, San Antonio Express-News, 1983-86, Albuquerque Tribune, 1987-94, Westword Newspaper, Denver, 2000-01. Author: The Plutonium Files, 1999. Recipient Clarion award, 1989, News Reporting award Nat. Headliners, 1989, John Hancock award, 1991, Mng. Editors Pub. Svc. award AP, 1991, 94, Roy Howard award 1994, James Aronson award, 1994, Gold Medal award Investigative Reporters and Editors, 1994, Sigma Delta Chi award, 1994, Investigative Reporting award Nat. Headliners, 1994, Selden Ring award, 1994, Heywood Broun award, 1994, George Polk award, 1994, Sidney Hillman Found. award, 1994, Pulitzer Prize for nat. reporting, 1994, PEN/Martha Albrand award for first nonfiction, 2000, PEN/[illegible] award for book nonfiction PEN, 2000, John S. Knight fellow Stanford U., 1991-92. Emai. E-mail: ewelsome@aol.com

WELTER, WILLIAM MICHAEL, marketing and advertising executive; b. Evanston, Ill., Nov. 18, 1946; s. Roy Michael and Frances (DeShields) W.; m. Pamela Bassett, June 11, 1971; children: Barclay, Robert Michael. BS, Mo. Valley Coll., 1966. Account exec. Leo Burnett Co., Inc., Chgo., 1966-74; v.p., account supr. Needham Harper Worldwide, Chgo., 1974-80; v.p. mktg. Wendy's Internat., Inc., Dublin, 1981, sr. v.p. mktg., 1981-84, exec. v.p., 1984-87; owner, chief exec. officer Haunty & Welter Advt. Agy., Worthington, 1987-91; sr. exec. v.p. mktg. Rax Restaurants Inc., Dublin, 1992; exec. v.p. mktg. Metromedia Steakhouses, Inc., Dayton, 1992-93; sr. v.p. mktg. Metromedia Co., Dayton, 1993-95; exec. v.p., chief mktg. officer Heartland Foods Inc., Dublin, 1995-96; exec. v.p. brand mgmt. Late Nite Magic, Inc., Las Vegas, Nev., 1996—; pres., CEO W.M. Welter & Assocs., Las Vegas, 1996—; pres. Wings West LLC, Las Vegas, 2000—, Buffalo Wild Wings, Inc., Las Vegas, 2001—. Founder Santa's Silent Helpers, Columbus, Ohio, 1985 Mem. Advt. Fedn. Las Vegas, Scioto Country Club, Red Rock Country Club, T.P.C. Golf Club. Avocations: golf, fishing. Home: 1517 Angelberry St Las Vegas NV 89117-1372 Office: 8084 W Sahara Las Vegas NV 89117 Fax: 702 360-8379. E-mail: wmw1@compuserve.com

WELTY, JOHN DONALD, academic administrator; b. Amboy, Ill., Aug. 24, 1944; s. John Donald and Doris (Donnelly) W.; m. Sharon Welty; children: Anne, Elisabeth, Bryan, Darren, Heather. B.S., Western Ill. U., 1965; M.A., Mich. State U., 1967; Ed.D., Ind. U., 1974. Asst. v.p. for student affairs SW State U., Marshall, Minn., 1973-74; dir. residences SUNY-Albany, 1974-77, assoc. dean for student affairs, 1977-80; v.p. for student and univ. affairs Indiana U. of Pa., 1980-84, pres., 1984-91, Calif. State U., Fresno, 1991—. Lectr. in field; chair Am. Humanics. Contbr. articles to profl. jours. Recipient Chancellor's award SUNY, 1977, Chief Exec. Leadership award Coun. for Advancement and Support of Edn., 1999, John Templeton Found. award for leadership in student character devel., 1999. Mem. Fresno Bus. Coun., Fresno Econ. Devel. Commn., Sunnyside Country Club. Roman Catholic. Lodge: Rotary Office: Calif State U 5241 S Maple Ave Fresno CA 93725-9739

WEMPLE, JAMES ROBERT, psychotherapist; b. Hardin, Mont., May 31, 1943; s. Charles Clifford and Lillian Louise (Smith) W.; m. Sarah Ann House, May 7, 1983; children: Brian Matthew, Laura Ashley, Kerri Ann, Jaime Marie, Kevin James. BA, U. Mont., 1966, MA, 1970, postgrad., 1970-71; PhD, Wash. State U., 1979. Diplomate Am. Acad. Pain Mgmt. Tchr., coach Custer County High Sch., Miles City, Mont., 1966-67; sch. psychologist Missoula, 1970-71; grad. asst. U. Mont., Missoula, 1970-71; dir. counseling Medicine Hat (Alberta) Coll., Canada, 1971-73; counselor Lethbridge (Alberta) C.C., 1973-76; head resident Wash. State U., Pullman, 1976-79; mental health specialist Missoula Rehab., 1979-82; clin. mental health counselor Missoula, 1982—. With U.S. Army, 1960-69, Korea. Fellow Am. Bd. Med. Psychotherapists; mem. Am. Psychol. Assn., Soc. for Clin. and Exptl. Hypnosis, Am. Soc. for Clin. Hypnosis, Internat. Soc. for Hypnosis, Nat. Acad. Cert. Clin. Mental Health Counselors, Soc. for Personality Assessment, AACD, Phi Kappa Phi. Avocations: fishing, hunting. Home: 2410 Clydesdale Ln Missoula MT 59804-9297 Office: 255 W Front St # B Missoula MT 59802-4301

WENDER, PAUL ANTHONY, chemistry educator; BS, Wilkes Coll., 1969; PhD, Yale U., 1973; PhD (hon.), Wilkes U., 1993. Asst. prof., assoc. prof. Harvard U., 1974-81; prof. chemistry Stanford U., 1981—; Bergstrom prof. chemistry, 1994—. Cons. Eli Lilly & Co., 1980—, lectr. Am. Chem. Soc.. Recipient ICI Am. Chem. award Stuart Pharm., merit award NIH, Pfizer rsch. award, 1995. Fellow AAAS; mem. Am. Chem. Soc. (Arthur C. Cope Sholan award 1990, Guenther award, award for creative work in synthetic organic chemistry 1998). Office: Stanford U Mudd Bldg Rm 390 Mail Code 5080 Stanford CA 94305

WENDLING, LOUISE, wholesale distribution executive; Sr. v.p., gen. mgr. ea. Can. region Costco Wholesale, Issaquah, Wash. Office: Costco Wholesale 999 Lake Dr Ste 200 Issaquah WA 98027-5367

WENDT, RICHARD L. manufacturing executive; b. 1931; From mgr. of frame factory to mgr. ops. Caradco; CEO Jeld-Wen Inc., Klamath Falls, Oreg., 1960—. Address: Jeld Wen Inc PO Box 1329 Klamath Falls OR 97601-0268 Office: Jen Weld Inc 3250 Lakeport Blvd Klamath Falls OR 97601

WENDT, STEVEN WILLIAM, business educator; b. Rockford, Ill., Sept. 18, 1948; s. Roy W. Wendt and Betty Lou (Phillips) Wendt Oser. AAS, Clark County Community Coll., North Las Vegas, Nev., 1982; BS, U. Nev., 1985, MBA, 1987. Cert. vocat. adult educator, Nev. Electronics tech. engr. Rockford Automation, Inc., 1972-74; owner, operator S.W. Ltd., Rockford, 1972-76, S.W. Enterprises, Henderson, Nev., 1977—; instr. electronics Nev. Gaming Sch., Las Vegas, 1977-83; gen. mgr., corp. sec. treas. Customs by Peter Schell, Las Vegas, 1977-83; field engr. Bell & Howell Mailmobile Ops. div., Zeeland, Mich., 1982-90; instr. bus. U. Nev., Las Vegas, 1985-2000; dir. Wing Fong & Family Microcomputer Labs. Coll. Bus. and Econs. U. Nev., 1990-97. Sr. arbitrator Better Bus. Bur., Las Vegas, 1982—; bus. cons. Small Bus. Devel. Ctr., Las Vegas, 1985—; incorporator, v.p. Info. Sys., Warren, Mich., 1990-91; fin. officer, gen. ptnr. Obsidian Pub. Press, Henderson, Nev., 1991-96; mem. faculty senate U. Nev., 1993-96; bd. dirs. Gem Crafters Inc., Warren; CAD/CAM dir. Casino Displays, Las Vegas, 2000—. Author: Intro to Microcomputers, For Future PC Experts, 1992. Treas. U. Nev. Grad. Student Assn, 1986-87. Served with USN, 1967-71. Recipient Cert. Appreciation UNICEF, 1984. Mem. IEEE, Computer Soc., Assn. Info. Systems, Fin. Mgmt. Assn. (Nat. Honor Soc. 1985), Strategic Gaming Soc., U. Nev. Computer User Group (exec. com., chair stds. com.), U. Nev. Alumni Assn., Am. Legion, VFW (life), Phi Lambda Alpha. Avocations: geology, numismatics, philatelitics. Home: 1325 Chestnut St Henderson NV 89015-4208 Office: U Nev 4505 S Maryland Pkwy Las Vegas NV 89154-4208 E-mail: swwendt@usa.net

WENTWORTH, THEODORE SUMNER, lawyer; b. Bklyn., July 18, 1938; s. Theodore Sumner and Alice Ruth (Wortmann) W.; m. Sharon Linelle Arkush, 1965 (dec. 1987); children: Christina Linn, Kathrun Allison; m. Diana Webb von Welanetz, 1989; 1 stepchild, Lexi von Welanetz. AA, Am. River Coll., 1958; JD, U. Calif., Hastings, 1962. Bar: Calif. 1963, U.S. Dist. Ct. (no. and ctrl. dists.) Calif., U.S. Ct. Appeals (9th cir.), U.S. Supreme Ct.; cert. trial specialist; diplomate Nat. Bd. Trial Advocacy; assoc. Am. Bd. Trial Advocates. Assoc. Adams, Hunt & Martin, Santa Ana, Calif., 1963-66; ptnr. Hunt, Liljestrom & Wentworth, Santa Ana, 1967-77; pres. Solabs Corp.; chmn. bd., exec. v.p. Plant Warehouse, Inc., Hawaii, 1974-82; prin. Law Offices of Wentworth, Paoli & Purdy, Newport Beach & Temecula, Calif.; judge pro tem Superior Ct. Attys. Panel Harbor Mcpl. Ct. Owner Eagles Ridge Ranch, Temecula, 1977—. Author: Build a Better Spouse Trap, 2001. Pres., bd. dirs. Santa Ana-Tustin Cmty. Chest, 1972; v.p., trustee South Orange County United Way, 1973-75; pres. Orange County Fedn. Funds, 1972-73; bd. dirs. Orange County Mental Health Assn. Mem. ABA, Am. Bd. Trial Advocates (assoc.), State Bar Calif., Orange County Bar Assn. (dir. 1972-76), Am. Trial Lawyers Assn., Calif. Trial Lawyers Assn. (bd. govs. 1968-70), Orange County Trial Lawyers Assn. (pres. 1967-68), Lawyer-Pilots Bar Assn., Aircraft Owners and Pilots Assn., Bahia Corinthian Yacht Club, Pacific Club, Newport. Achievements include research in vedic princ., natural law, quantum physics and mechanics. Office: 4631 Teller Ave Ste 100 Newport Beach CA 92660-8105 also: 41530 Enterprise Cir S Temecula CA 92590-4816 E-mail: ocrawfirm@aol.com

WERB, ZENA, cell biologist, educator; BSc in Biochemistry, U. Toronto, 1966; PhD in Cell Biology, Rockefeller U., 1971. Postdoctoral fellow in protein chemistry Strangeways Rsch. Lab., Cambridge, Eng., 1971-73, rsch. scientist Eng., 1973-75; vis. asst. prof. medicine Dartmouth Med. Sch., Hanover, N.H., 1975-76; asst. prof. radiobiology and radiology U. Calif., San Francisco, 1976-80, asst. prof. anatomy, 1979-80, asst. prof. anatomy and radiology, 1980-83, prof. anatomy, 1983—. Vis. prof. Sir William Dunn Sch. Pathology, U. Oxford, Eng., 1985-86. Mem. editl. bd. Jour. Cell Biology, 1982-85, Am. Jour. Physiology, 1982-87, Neoplasia, 1999—, Jour. Cell Scis., 1999—; adv. editor Jour. Exptl. medicine, 1985—; bd. reviewing editors Sci., 1990—; assoc. editor Matrix Biology, 1999—; contbr. numerous articles to profl. jours. U Recipient Excellence in Sci. award Am. Soc. Exptl. Biology, Women's Excellence in Scis. award Fdn. Am. Socs. Exptl. Biology, 1996; U. Toronto scholar, 1963-66; John Simon Gugenheim Found. fellow, 1985-86, other grants and awards. Mem. AAAS, ASCB, ASIP, ASBMB, ISMB. Office: U Calif Dept Anatomy HSW 1320 513 Parnassus Ave San Francisco CA 94143-0001

WERDEGAR, KATHRYN MICKLE, state supreme court justice; b. San Francisco; d. Benjamin Christie and Kathryn Marie (Clark) Mickle; m. David Werdegar; children: Maurice Clark, Matthew Mickle. Student, Wellesley Coll., 1954-55; AB with honors, U. Calif., Berkeley, 1957; JD with highest distinction, George Washington U., 1962; JD, U. Calif., Berkeley, 1990. Bar: Calif. 1964, U.S. Dist. Ct. (no. dist.) Calif. 1964, U.S. Ct. Appeals (9th cir.) 1964, Calif. Supreme Ct. 1964. Legal asst. civil rights divsn. U.S. Dept. Justice, Washington, 1962-63; cons. Calif. Study Commn. on Mental Retardation, 1963-64; assoc. U. Calif. Ctr. for Study of Law and Soc., Berkeley, 1965-67; spl. cons. State Dept. Mental Hygiene, 1967-68; cons. Calif. Coll. Trial Judges, 1968-71; atty., head criminal divsn. Calif. Continuing Edn. of Bar, 1971-78; assoc. dean acad. and student affairs, assoc. prof. Sch. Law, U. San Francisco, 1978-81; sr. staff atty. Calif. 1st Dist. Ct. Appeal, 1981-85, Calif. Supreme Ct., 1985-91; assoc. justice Calif. 1st Dist. Ct. Appeal, 1991-94, Calif. Supreme Ct., San Francisco, 1994—. Regents' lectr. U. Calif., Berkeley, 2000. Author: Benchbook: Misdemeanor Procedure, 1971, Misdemeanor Procedure Benchbook, 1975, 83; contbr. California Continuing Education of the Bar books; editor: California Criminal Law Practice series, 1972, California Uninsured Motorist Practice, 1973, I California Civil Procedure Before Trial, 1977. Recipient Charles Glover award George Washington U., 1962, J. William Fulbright award for disting. pub. svc. George Washington U. Law Sch. Alumni Assn., 1996, excellence in achievement award, Calif. Alumni Assn., 1996, Roger J. Traynor Appellate Justice of Yr. award, 1996, Justice of Yr. award Consumer Attys. of Calif., 1998, also 5 Am. Jurisprudence awards, 1960-62. Mem. Nat. Assn. Women Judges, Am. Law Inst., Calif. Judges Assn., Nev./Calif. Women Judges Assn., Order of the Coif. Office: Calif Supreme Court 350 McAllister St San Francisco CA 94102-4783

WERNER, DAVID A. paper company executive; BS, MBA, U. So. Calif. CPA. With Peat, Marwick, Mitchell & Co., 1974-78; various mgmt. positions Lear Siegler's Telecomms. divsns./subsidiaries, Anaheim, Calif., 1978-86, v.p. fin. and adminstrn., 1986-90; v.p., CFO Microdot Components Group, 1990-94; exec. v.p., dir. Kaynar Technologies Inc. (formerly Microdot Components), Orange, Calif., 1994-99; exec. v.p., CFO Day Runner, Irvine, 1999—. Office: Day Runner Inc 15295 Alton Pkwy Irvine CA 92618

WERNER, GLORIA S. librarian; b. Seattle, Dec. 12, 1940; d. Irving L. and Eva H. Stolzoff; m. Newton Davis Werner, June 30, 1963; 1 son, Adam Davis. BA, Oberlin Coll., 1961; ML, U. Wash., 1962; postgrad. UCLA, 1962-63. Reference librarian UCLA Biomed Library, 1963-64, asst. head pub. services dept., 1964-66, head pub. services dept., head reference div., 1966-72, asst. biomed. librarian public services, 1972-77, asso. biomed. librarian, 1977-78, biomed. librarian, assoc. univ. librarian, dir. Pacific S.W. regional Med. Library Service, 1979-83; asst. dean library services UCLA Sch. Medicine, 1980-83; assoc. univ. librarian for tech. services, 1983-89, dir. libraries, acting univ. librarian, 1989-90, univ. librarian, 1990—; adj. lectr. UCLA Grad. Sch. Library and Info. Sci., 1977-83. Editor, Bull. Med. Library Assn., 1979-82, asso. editor, 1974-79; mem. editorial bd. Ann. Stats. Med. Sch. Libraries U.S. and Can., 1980-83; mem. accrediting commn. Western Assn. Schs. and Colls., N.W. Assn. Schs. and Colls. Mem. ALA, Assn. Rsch. Librs. (bd. dirs. 1993-98, v.p./pres.-elect 1995-96, pres. 1996-97, past pres. 1997-98). Office: UCLA Rsch Libr Adminstrv Office 405 Hilgard Ave Los Angeles CA 90095-9000

WERNER, TOM, television producer, professional baseball team executive; m. Jill Werner; 3 children, Teddy, Carolyn, Amanda. BA, Harvard Univ., 1971. With ABC Television, Inc., 1972-82; co-owner Carsey-Werner Co., Studio City, Calif., 1982—; chmn. San Diego Padres, 1991-94. Mem. bd. dirs.: Old Globe Theatre; Sharp Hospital. Co-exec. producer TV series: Oh, Madeline, 1983, 3rd Rock from the Sun, 1996, Cosby, 1996; exec. producer: The Cosby Show, (Emmy awd. Outstanding Comedy Series-1985), 1984-92, A Different World, 1987-93, Roseanne, 1988—, Chicken Soup, 1989-90, Grand, 1990, Davis Rules, 1991, You Bet Your Life, 1992-93, Frannie's Turn, 1992, Cybill, 1995, Townies, 1996, Damon, 1998. Office: Carsey Werner Prodns 4024 Radford Ave Bldg 3 Studio City CA 91604-2101

WERNER, WILLIAM ARNO, architect; b. San Francisco, Dec. 11, 1937; s. William Arno and Sophie (Menutis) W.; m. Wendy Rolston Wilson, Feb. 3, 1963 (div. Jan. 1983); 1 child, Christa Nichol. BA with honors, Yale U., 1959, BArch, 1962, MArch, 1963. Drafter Serge Chermayeff, Paul Rudolph and Charles Brewer, New Haven, 1961-63; project designer Johnson, Poole & Storm, San Francisco, 1963-64, Leo S. Wou & Assocs., Honolulu, 1965-66, v.p. of design, 1971-72; project architect John Tatom Assocs., Honolulu, 1965-66; sr. designer Skidmore, Owings & Merrill, San Francisco, 1968-71, assoc./project architect, 1972-76; prin. W.A. Werner Assocs., San Francisco, 1976-80; ptnr. Werner & Sullivan, San Francisco, 1980—. Mem. planning commn. City of Sausalito, Calif.; bd. govs. Yale U., New Haven; visitorship in architecture U. Auckland Found., New Zealand, 1994. Prin. works include Alameda Mcpl. Credit Union, Lane Pub. Co., Menlo Park, Calif., Pacific Data Images, Mountain View, Calif., Saga Corp., Menlo Park, Tiffany & Co., Union Square, San Francisco, Somerset Collection, Troy, Mich., Touche Ross & Co., Oakland, U.S. Post Office, San Francisco, (renovations) Fed. Express Co., San Francisco, KD's Grog N' Grocery, San Francisco, Jessie Street. Substation, San Francisco, Lakeside Tower Health Ctr./Mt. Zion Hosp., Qantas Bldg, San Francisco, Women's Care, San Francisco, Moon Residence, Dillon Beach, Calif., Shenkar Residence, San Francisco, Tacker Residence, Denver, Lasky Residence, San Francisco, Starring Residence, San Francisco, Whitehead Residence, Monte Rio, Calif., various laboratories, theatres and rsch. facilities, urban design. Recipient Progressive Architecture Design award Jessie St. Substation, 1980, DuPont Co. Design award Touche Ross & Co., 1983, award of Excellence Woodwork Inst. of Calif., 1989, USPS/NEA Nat. Honor award for Design Excellence, 1990, Tucker Design Excellence award Bldg. Stone Inst., Tiffany & Co., 1992. Mem. AIA (San Francisco chpt.), Found. for San Francisco's Architectural Heritage (hon.). Home: 213 Richardson St Sausalito CA 94965-2422 Office: Werner & Sullivan 207 Powell St Ste 800 San Francisco CA 94102-2209

WERNER-JACOBSEN, EMMY ELISABETH, developmental psychologist; b. Eltville, Germany, May 26, 1929; came to U.S., 1952, naturalized, 1962; d. Peter Josef and Liesel (Kunz) W. B.S., Johannes Gutenberg U., Germany, 1950; M.A., U. Nebr., 1952, Ph.D., 1955; postgrad., U. Calif., Berkeley, 1953-54. Research asso. Inst. Child Welfare, U. Minn., 1956-59; vis. scientist NIH, 1959-62; asst. prof. to prof. human devel., rsch. child psychologist U. Calif., Davis, 1962-94, rsch. prof., 1995—. Sr. author: The Children of Kauai, 1971, Kauai's Children Come of Age, 1977; author: Cross-Cultural Child Development: A View from the Planet Earth, 1979, Vulnerable, but Invincible, 1982, 3d edit., 1998, Child Care: Kith, Kin and Hired Hands, 1984, Overcoming the Odds, 1992, Pioneer Children on the Journey West, 1995, Reluctant Witnesses: Children's Voices From the Civil War, 1998, Through the Eyes of Innocents: Children Witness World War II, 2000, Unschuldige Zeugen, 2001, Journeys From Childhood to Mid Life: Risk, Resilience and Recovery, 2001; contbr. articles to profl. jours. Fellow Am. Psychol. Soc., German Acad. Social Pediats. (hon.), Soc. for Rsch. in Child Devel.

WERNICK, SANDRA MARGOT, advertising and public relations executive; b. Tampa, Sept. 13, 1944; d. Nathan and Sylvia (Bienstock) Rothstein. BA in English, U. Fla., 1966. Tchr. English Miami Beach (Fla.) Sr. High Sch., 1967; adminstrv. asst. pub. rels. Bozell & Jacobs, Inc., N.Y.C., 1968-69; asst. to dir. pub. rels. Waldorf-Astoria, N.Y.C., 1969-70; dir. advt. and pub. rels. Hyatt on Union Square, San Francisco, 1974-82; pres. Wernick Mktg. Group, San Francisco, 1982—; exec. dir. Sales and Mktg. Execs. of the Bay Area, 1995-2000; mng. ptnr. The Stanford Group, 1998-99. Bd. dirs. Nat. Kidney Assn., San Francisco, 1985-87; advisor Swords to Plowshares, San Francisco, 1988-89; mem. mktg. com. to bd. Boy Scouts of Greater East Bay, 1995-2000. Recipient Award of Merit, San Francisco Advt. and Cable Car Awards, 1979, Award of Excellence, San Francisco Art Dirs. 1978, Disting. Mktg. award Sales and Mktg. Internat., 1997, awards Am. Hotel and Motel Assn., 1981, 1982, awards of excellence San Francisco Publicity Club, 1990, 1994, 1995, 1996, 97. Mem. NAFE, Women in Comms. (bd. dirs. 1987-89), Am. Women in Radio and TV (bd. dirs. 1989-90), Pub. Rels. Soc. Am., San Francisco Publicity Club (pres. 1989), Variety Club, Profl. Bus. Women's Assn., Calif. Pacific Med. Ctr. (aux. 1988-95). Democrat. Jewish. Home: 1690 Broadway San Francisco CA 94109-2417 Office: Wernick Mktg Group 417 Montgomery St Ste 410 San Francisco CA 94104-1111 E-mail: prgal3@aol.com, wmgteam@aol.com

WERTHEIM, ROBERT HALLEY, national security consultant; b. Carlsbad, N.Mex., Nov. 9, 1922; s. Joseph and Emma (Vorenberg) W.; m. Barbara Louise Selig, Dec. 26, 1946; children: Joseph Howard, David Andrew. Student, N.Mex. Mil. Inst., 1940-42; B.S., U.S. Naval Acad., 1945; M.S. in Physics, M.I.T., 1954; postgrad., Harvard U., 1969. Commd. ensign U.S. Navy, 1945, advanced through grades to rear adm., 1972; assigned Spl. Projects Office, Washington, 1956-61, Naval Ordnance Test Sta., China Lake, 1961-62, Office Sec. Def., Washington, 1962-65; head Missile br. Strategic Systems Project Office, Washington, 1965-67, dep. tech. dir., 1967-68, tech. dir., 1968-77, dir., 1977-80; sr. v.p. Lockheed Corp., 1981-88; cons. nat. def., 1988—. Emeritus mem. Draper Lab., Inc.; mem. U. Calif. Pres. Adv. Coun.; mem. sci. adv. group Dept. Def., Dept. Energy, U.S. Strategic Command; mem. nat. security adv. Lawrence Livermore Nat. Lab. Decorated D.S.M. with cluster, Legion of Merit, Navy Commendation medal, Joint Svc. Commendation medal; recipient Rear Adm. William S. Parsons award Navy League U.S., 1971, Chmn. Joint Chiefs of Staff Disting. Pub. Svc. award, 1996, Sec. of Def. medal for outstanding pub. svc., 1996. Fellow AIAA, Calif. Coun. Sci. Tech.; mem. Am. Soc. Naval Engrs. (hon. mem., Gold medal 1972), Nat. Acad. Engring., U.S. Naval Inst., Bernardo Heights Country Club, Masons, Sigma Xi, Tau Beta Pi. Home: 17705 Devereux Rd San Diego CA 92128-2084 Office: Sci Applications Internat Corp 1200 Prospect St La Jolla CA 92037-3608

WERTHEIMER, ROBERT E. paper company executive; b. 1928; married. BSME, U. Wash., 1950; MBA, Harvard U., 1952. With Longview (Wash.) Fibre Co., 1952—, package engr., 1955-59, asst. mgr. container ops., 1959-60, asst. mgr. container sales, 1960-63, v.p. container sales West, 1963-75, v.p. prodn., 1975, group v.p. containers, now exec. v.p., dir., 1956—. Office: Longview Fibre Co 120 Montgomery St Ste 2200 San Francisco CA 94104-4325

WESBURY, STUART ARNOLD, JR. health administration and policy educator; b. Phila., Dec. 13, 1933; s. Stuart Arnold and Jennie (Glazewska) W.; m. June Carol Davis, Feb. 23, 1957; children: Brian, Brent, Bruce, Bradford. BS, Temple U., 1955; MHA, U. Mich., 1960; PhD, U. Fla., 1972. Capt. health svcs. officer USPHS, 1955, served as adminstrv. officer, hosp. and clinic pharmacist, resigned, 1958; adminstrv. asst. Del. Hosp., 1960-61; asst. adminstr. Bronson Meth. Hosp., 1961-66; assoc. dir., asst. prof. U. Fla. Tchg. Hosp., 1966-67, dir., assoc. prof., 1967-69; v.p. Computer Mgmt. Corp., Gainesville, Fla., 1969-72; dir., prof. grad. studies in health svcs. mgmt. U. Mo., Columbia, 1972-78; pres. Am. Coll. Healthcare Execs., Chgo., 1979-91; sr. v.p. TriBrook Group, Inc., Westmont, Ill., 1992-94; prof. Sch. of Health Adminstrn. and Policy Ariz. State U., Tempe, 1994-2000, dir., exec. edn. programs Coll. Bus., 1996-2000, prof. emeritus, 2000—. Vice chmn. bd. trustees, bd. dirs. Blood Sys., Inc., Scottsdale, Ariz. Co-author: Why We Spend Too Much on Health Care; contbr. articles to profl. jours. Bd. dirs. Health Task, Inc., Atlanta, Boys Clubs, Gainesville, Heartland Inst.; chmn. bd. dirs. Mid-Am. chpt. ARC, 1988-91, DuPage County Dist., 1984-87; active Boy Scouts Am.; chmn. adminstrv. bd. Meth. Ch.; trustee Nat. Blood Found.; Rep. Congl. candidate Dist. 13, Ill. Fellow Am. Coll. Health Care Adminstrs. (hon.), Am. Coll. Healthcare Execs. (Silver Medal award 1991); mem. APHA, Am. Hosp. Assn., Hosp. Mgmt. Sys. Soc., Assn. Univ. Programs in Health Adminstrn. (chmn. 1977-78), Am. Assn. Healthcare Cons. (hon.), Rotary (past pres.). Home and Office: 6711 E Camelback Rd Unit 25 Scottsdale AZ 85251-2064 Fax: 480-990-7334. E-mail: stu.wesbury@asu.edu

WESCOTT, WILLIAM BURNHAM, oral maxillofacial pathologist, educator; b. Pendleton, Oreg., Nov. 10, 1922; s. Merton Girard and Josephine (Creasey) W.; m. Barbara L., Dec. 31, 1944 (dec. June 12, 1969); children: William Douglas, Diane Elizabeth; m. Gloria Greer-Collins, Aug. 28, 1989. DMD, U. Oreg., Portland, 1951, MS, 1962. Asst. prof. to assoc. dean admin. U. Oreg. Dental Sch., Portland, 1953-72; co-dir. oral disease rsch. VA, Houston, 1972-75, dir. dental edn. ctr. L.A., 1980-85; acting dir. Reg. Med. Edn. Ctr., Birmingham, Ala., 1978-80; chief dental svc. Dept. of Veteran's Affairs, San Francisco, 1985-94; clin. prof. U. Calif., San Francisco, 1994—; cons. Northern System of Clinics Dept. Vets. Affairs, 1994—. Dental surgeon, Oreg. Air N.G., Portland, 1954-68; cons. Madigan Army Med. Ctr., Ft. Lewis, W. Va., 1971-74, VA Med. Ctrs., No. Calif., 1985—, prof. pathology Duke U. Med. Sch., 1977-79. Contbr. 80 articles to profl. jours. and several chpts. to profl. books; 4 chtps. to books. Dist. chmn. Boys Scouts Am., Portland, 1965-67; bd. dirs. Am. Cancer Soc., Portland, 1964-67; comdr. Veterans Foreign Wars Post 5731, Gridley, Calif., 1994-95, comdr., 1996-98; chmn. Mil. Vets Ct. of Honor Meml., No. Calif., 1997—. With Oreg. N.G., 1938-40; with U.S. Army, 1940-42; lt. col. USAF, 1942-68. Decorated DFC with oak leaf cluster, USAF, Oreg. N.G. Merit Svc. Medal, Portland, Fedn. des Anciens Combattants Français medal, 1944. Fellow Am. Acad. Oral and Maxillofacial Pathology, Omicron Kappa Upsilon, Sigma Xi. Avocations: woodworking, fishing. Home: 437 Justeson Ave Gridley CA 95948-9434 Office: U Calif Sch of Dentistry S 512 San Francisco 3rd & Parnassus San Francisco CA 94143-0424 E-mail: globil@manznet.com

WESLING, DONALD TRUMAN, English literature educator; b. Buffalo, May 6, 1939; s. Truman Albert and Helene Marie (Bullinger) W.; m. Judith Elaine Dulinawka, July 28, 1961; children: Benjamin, Molly, Natasha. BA, Harvard U., 1960, PhD, 1965; BA, Cambridge U., Eng., 1962. Asst. prof. U. Calif. at San Diego, La Jolla, 1965-67, assoc. prof., 1970-80, prof., 1981—. Lectr. U. Essex, Colchester, Eng., 1967-70. Author: Wordsworth and Landscape, 1970, Chances of Rhyme, 1981, The New Poetries, 1985, The Scissors of Meter, 1996, (with T. Slawek) Literary Voice, 1995. Mem. Amnesty Internat. Home: 4968 Foothill Blvd San Diego CA 92109 Office: U Calif Lit # 0410 La Jolla CA 92093

WESSELLS, NORMAN KEITH, biologist, educator, university administrator; b. Jersey City, May 11, 1932; s. Norman Wesley and Grace Mahan Wessells; m. Catherine Pyne Briggs; children: Christopher, Stephen, Philip, Colin, Elizabeth. B.S., Yale U., 1954, Ph.D., 1960. Asst. prof. biology Stanford (Calif.) U., 1962-65, asso. prof., 1965-70, prof., 1971—, chmn. biol. sci., 1972-78; acting dir. Hopkins Marine Sta., 1972-75, asso. dean humanities and scis., 1977-81, dean, 1981-88; prof. biology, provost, v.p. acad. affairs U. Oreg., Eugene, 1988—. Author: (with F. Wilt) Methods in Developmental Biology, 1965, Vertebrates: Adaptations, 1970, Vertebrates: A Laboratory Text, 1976, 81, Tissue Interactions and Development, 1977, Vertebrates; Adaptations; Vertebrates: Physiology, 1979, (with S. Subtelny) The Cell Surface, 1980, (with J. Hopson) Biology, 1988, (with Hopson) Essentials of Biology, 1990. Served with USNR, 1954-56. Am. Cancer Soc. postdoctoral fellow, 1960-62; Am. Cancer Soc. scholar cancer research, 1966-69; Guggenheim fellow, 1976-77 Mem. Soc. Devel. Biology (pres. 1979-80), Am. Soc. Zoologist. Office: U Oreg Office Provost Johnson Hall Eugene OR 97403

WESSLER, MELVIN DEAN, farmer, rancher; b. Dodge City, Kans., Feb. 11, 1932; s. Oscar Lewis and Clara (Reiss) W.; m. Laura Ethel Arbuthnot, Aug. 23, 1951; children: Monty Dean, Charla Cay, Virgil Lewis. Grad. high sch. Farmer, rancher, Springfield, Colo., 1950—. Dir., sec. bd. Springfield Co-op. Sales Co., 1964-80, pres. bd., 1980— . Pres., Arkansas Valley Co-op. Council, SE Colo. Area, 1965-87, Colo. Co-op. Council, 1969-72, v.p. 1974, sec. 1980-86; community com. chmn. Baca County, Agr. Stablzn. and Conservation Svc., Springfield, 1961-73, 79—, vice chmn. Baca County Com., 1980-90; mem. spl. com. on grain mktg. Far-Mar-Co. Mem. adv. bd. Denver Bapt. Bible Coll., 1984-89; chmn. bd. dirs. Springfield Cemetery Bd., 1985—; apptd. spl. com. Farmland Industries spl. project Tomorrow, 1987—. Recipient The Colo. Cooperator award Colo. Coop. Coun., 1990. Mem. Colo. Cattlemen's Assn., Colo. Wheat Growers Assn., Southeast Farm Bus. Assn. (bd. dirs. 1991-95), Big Rock Grange (treas. 1964-76, master 1976-82), Southwest Kans. Farm Bus. Assn. (dir. 1996—, pres. 1999-2001). Address: 18363 County Road Pp Springfield CO 81073

WESSLING, ROBERT BRUCE, lawyer; b. Chgo., Oct. 8, 1937; s. Robert Euans and Marguerite (Rickert) W.; m. Judith Ann Hanson, Aug. 26, 1961; children: Katherine, Jennifer, Carolyn. BA, DePauw U., 1959; JD, U. Mich., 1962. Bar: U.S. Dist. Ct. (cen. dist.) Calif. 1963, U.S. Ct. Appeals (9th cir.) 1965. Assoc. Latham & Watkins, L.A., 1962-70, ptnr., 1970-94, of counsel, 1995—. Bd. govs. Fin. Lawyers Conf., Los Angeles, 1974-2000. Mem. World Affairs Coun., L.A., Town Hall, L.A.; trustee DePauw U. Mem. ABA, Los Angeles Bar Assn., Phi Beta Kappa, Phi Delta Phi, Phi Eta Sigma, Order of Coif. Democrat. Methodist. Avocations: tennis, travel. Office: 633 W 5th St Ste 4000 Los Angeles CA 90071-2005 E-mail: bbwessling@aol.com

WEST, EDWARD ALAN, graphics communications executive; b. L.A., Dec. 25, 1928; s. Albert Reginald and Gladys Delia (White) W.; m. Sonya Lea Smith, Jan. 2, 1983; children: Troy A., Tamara L.; stepchildren: Debra, Chris, Donna. AA, Fullerton Coll., 1966; student, Cerrotos Coll., 1957, UCLA, 1966-67. Circulation mgr. Huntington Park (Calif.) Signal Newspaper, 1946-52; newspaper web pressman Long Beach (Calif.) Press Telegram, 1955-62; gravure web pressman Gravure West, Los Angeles, 1966-67; sales engr. Halm Jet Press, Glen Head, N.Y., 1968-70; salesman Polychrome Corp., Glen Head, 1970-74; supr. reprographics Fluor Engring & Construction, Irvine, Calif., 1974-81; dir. reprographics Fluor Arabia, Dhahran, Saudi Arabia, 1981-85, Press Telegram, Long Beach, 1986-97; with Suburban LA Newspaper Group, 1998—. Printing advisor Saddleback C.C., Mission Viejo, Calif., 1979, 80. Author: How to Paste up For Graphic Reproduction, 1967. Sgt. USMC, 1952-55, Korea. Decorated Korean War Svc. medal with 3 battle stars, Combat Action ribbon, Good Conduct medal, UN Svc. medal, Navy commendation medal, Nat. Def. Svc. medal. Mem.: VFW (life), Am. Legion, Shriners (pres. South Coast club 1991, editor blue and gold unit Legion of Honor El Bekal Temple 1989—92, comdr. Legion of Honor (life) 1992, Shriner of Yr. award 1994), Western Shrine Assn. (emeritus) (comdr. 1996—97), Masons (50-yr. mem.), Internat. High Twelve 500 (Capistrano pres. 1995, Capistrano pres. 1996), Royal Order of Jesters Ct. 161, Order of Quetzalcoatl, KT, In-Plant Printing Assn. (cert. graphics comm. mgr. 1977, editor newsletter 1977, pres.Orange County chpt. 1979—80, Internat. Man of Yr. award 1980), Internat. Assn. Legions of Honor (emeritus), 1st Marine Divsn. Assn. (life). Presbyterian. Home: 198 Monarch Bay Dr Dana Point CA 92629-3437 Office: Suburban LA Newspaper Group 1210 N Azusa Canyon Rd West Covina CA 91790-1003

WEST, JAMES E. state legislator; Student, U. Nev., Reno, Spokane C.C., Spokane Falls C.C.; BA, Gonzaga U. Former police officer, dep. sheriff; mem. Wash. Senate, Dist. 6, Olympia, 1983—; senate Rep. leader Wash. Senate, Olympia, 1999—; mem. labor, commerce and fin. instns. com., rules com.; mem. small bus. improvement coun.; mem. state horse racing commn.; chair caseload forecast coun., mem. legis. com. econ. devel.; mem. K-20 ednl. network bd. Inst. Pub. Policy. Bd. dirs. Morning Star Boys Ranch. With U.S. Army, 82d Airborne Divsn. Recipient Outstanding Young Citizen of Spokane award Jaycees, 1982. Mem. Rotary Club. Republican. Office: PO Box 40406 302 Legislative Bldg Olympia WA 98504 E-mail: west_ja@leg.wa.gov

WEST, JERRY ALAN, professional basketball team executive; b. Chelyan, W.Va., May 28, 1938; s. Howard Stewart and Cecil Sue (Creasey) W.; m. Martha Jane Kane, May, 1960 (div. 1977); children: David, Michael, Mark; m. Karen Christine Bua, May 28, 1978; 1 son, Ryan. BS, W.Va. Coll.; LHD (hon.), W.Va. Wesleyan Coll. Mem. Los Angeles Lakers, Nat. Basketball Assn., 1960-74, coach, 1976-79, spl. cons., 1979-82, gen. mgr., 1982-94; exec. v.p. basketball operations L. A. Lakers, 1994—; mem. first team Nat. Basketball Assn. All-Star Team, 1962-67, 70-73, mem. second team, 1968, 69. Mem. NBA champion L.A. Lakers, 1972. Author: (with William Libby) Mr. Clutch: The Jerry West Story, 1969. Capt. U.S. Olympic Basketball Team, 1960; named Most Valuable Player NBA Playoff, 1969, All-Star Game Most Valuable Player, 1972; named to Naismith Meml. Basketball Hall of Fame, 1979, NBA Hall of Fame, 1980; mem. NBA 35th Anniversity All-Time Team, 1980; named NBA Exec. of Yr. Sporting News, 1994-95.

WEST, JOHN BURNARD, physiologist, physician, educator; b. Adelaide, Australia, Dec. 27, 1928; came to U.S., 1969; s. Esmond Frank and Meta Pauline (Spehr) W.; m. Penelope Hall Banks, Oct. 28, 1967; children: Robert Burnard, Joanna Ruth. MB, BChir, Adelaide U., 1951, MD, 1958, DSc, 1980; PhD, London U., 1960; PhD (hon.), U. Barcelona, Spain, 1987. Resident Royal Adelaide Hosp., 1952, Hammersmith Hosp., London, 1953-55; physiologist Sir Edmund Hillary's Himalayan Expdn., 1960-61; dir. respiratory research group Postgrad. Med. Sch., London, 1962-67, reader medicine, 1968; prof. medicine and physiology U. Calif., San Diego, 1969—. Wiltshire lectr., London, 1971, Schwidetzky lectr., 1975, Fleischner lectr., 1977, Robertson lectr. Adelaide U., 1978, McClement lectr. NYU, 1996; leader Am. Med. Rsch. Expdn. to Mt. Everest, 1981; U.S. organizer China-U.S. Conf. on respiratory failure, Nanjing, 1986; mem. life scis. adv. com. NASA, 1985-88, task force sci. uses of space sta., 1984-87, aerospace med. adv. com., 1988-89, chmn. sci. verification com.

Spacelab SLS-1, 1983-92; prin. investigator Spacelabs SLS 1, 2, LMS, Neurolab, 1983—; co-investigator European Spacelabs, D2, Euromir, 1987—; mem. commn. on respiratory physiol. Internat. Union Physiol. Scis., 1985—; mem. commn. on clin. physiol., 1991—, mem. commn. gravitation physiol., 1986—; mem. study sect. NIH, chmn., 1973-75; Doris J.w. Escher lectr. Montefiore Med. Ctr., N.Y., 2001. Author: Ventilation/Blood Flow and Gas Exchange, 1965, Respiratory Physiology-The Essentials, 1974, Translations in Respiratory Physiology, 1975, Pulmonary Pathophysiology-The Essentials, 1977, Translations in Respiratory Physiology, 1977, Bioengineering Aspects of the Lung, 1977, Regional Differences in the Lung, 1977, Pulmonary Gas Exchange (2 vols.), 1980, High Altitude Physiology, 1981, High Altitude and Man, 1984, Everest-The Testing Place, 1985, Best and Taylor's Physiological Basis of Medical Practice, 1985, 91, Study Guide for Best and Taylor, 1985, High Altitude Medicine and Physiology, 1989, The Lung: Scientific Foundations, 1991, 2d edit., 1997, Lung Injury, 1992, Respiratory Physiology: People and Ideas, 1996, High Life: A History of High Altitude Physiology and Medicine, 1998. Recipient Ernest Jung prize for medicine, Hamburg, 1977; Presdl. citation Am. Coll. Chest Physicians, 1977; Reynolds prize for history Am. Physiol. Soc., 1987; I.J. Flance lectr. Washington U., 1978; G.C. Griffith lectr. Am. Heart Assn., 1978; scholar Macy Found., 1974; Kaiser teaching award 1980; W.A. Smith lectr. Med. Coll. S.C., 1982, S. Kronheim lectr. Undersea Med. Soc., 1984, D.W. Richards lectr. Am. Heart Assn., 1980, E.M. Papper lectr. Columbia U., 1981, I.S. Ravdin lectr. ACS, 1982, Burns Amberson lectr. Am. Thoracic Soc., 1984, Harry G. Armstrong lectr. Aerospace Med. Assn., 1984, Annual Space Life Scis. lectr. Federation Associated Socs. of Exptl. Biology, 1991, Hermann Rahn lectr. SUNY Buffalo, 1992, Menkes lectr. Johns Hopkins, 1992; Jeffries Med. Rsch. award AIAA, 1992; Macalllum lectr. U. Toronto, Can., 1989, Macleod lectr. Southampton U., U.K., 1990, Bulatto lectr. U. Philippines, Manila, 1990, Mohaideen lectr. L.I. Coll., Bklyn., 1992, Bullard lectr. Uniformed Svcs. U., Bethesda, Md., 1993, Raven lectr. Am. Coll. Sports Medicine, Dallas, 1995, Waksman lectr. N.J. Thoracic Soc., 1998, James Hardy lectr. Yale U., 1998, Gillian Hanson lectr. Intensive Care Soc., London, 1998, George Dock lectr. Huntington Hist. Soc., Pasadena, 1999; Simon Rodbard lectr. Am. Coll. Chest Physicians, Chgo., 1999; James V. Warren Med. Humanities lectr., Ohio State U., 2000; Doris J.W. Escher lectr. Montefiore Med. Ctr., N.Y.C., 2001; external examiner Nat. U. Singapore, 1995; founder, editor-in-chief High Altitude Medicine and Biology, 2000—. Fellow Royal Coll. Physicians (London), Royal Australasian Coll. Physicians, Royal Geog. Soc. (London), AAAS (med. sci. nominating com. 1987-93, coun. del. sect. med. scis.), Am. Inst. for Med. and Biol. Engring. (founder fellow 1992), Internat. Soc. for Mountain Medicine (pres. 1991-94); mem. NAS (com. space biology and medicine 1986-90, subcom. on space biology 1984-85, com. advanced space tech. 1992-94, panel on small spacecraft tech. 1994), Nat. Bd. Med. Examiners (physiology test com. 1973-76), Am. Physiol. Soc. (pres. 1984-85, coun. 1981-86, chmn. sct. on history of physiology 1984-92, hist. pubs. adv. com., Ray Daggs award 1998), Am. Acad. Arts and Scis., Am. Soc. Clin. Investigation, Physiol. Soc. Gt. Britain, Am. Thoracic Soc., Assn. Am. Physicians, Am. Acad. Arts and Scis., Western Assn. Physicians, Russian Acad. Sci. (elected fgn. mem.), Explorers Club, Fleischner Soc. (pres. 1985), Harveian Soc. (London), Royal Instn. Gt. Britain, Royal Soc. Medicine (London), Hurlingham Club (London), La Jolla Beach & Tennis Club. Home: 9626 Blackgold Rd La Jolla CA 92037-1110 Office: U Calif San Diego Sch Medicine 0623 Dept Medicine La Jolla CA 92093

WEST, MARJORIE EDITH, former elementary education educator; b. Lawrence, Kans., Aug. 18, 1940; d. Merwin Hales and Helen Aletha (Fellows) Wilson Polzin; m. Hammond Dean Watkins, Feb. 17, 1968 (div. 1971); 1 child, Michele Dawn; m. Merlin Avery West, Apr. 2, 1975 (div. 1984). BA in Elem. Edn., U. No. Colo., 1962, MA in Reading, 1970; postgrad., La. State U., 1981-82, U. New Orleans, 1981-82. Cert. tchr., Colo. Tchr. Sch. Dist. 11, Colorado Springs, Colo., 1962-64, Nat. Def. Overseas Teaching Program, Wiesbaden, Fed. Republic Germany, 1964-65, Alaska On-Base Schs., Fairbanks, 1965-66, Great Bend (Kans.) Sch. Dist., 1966-67, Killeen (Tex.) Sch. Dist., 1967-68, Jefferson County Schs., Lakewood, Colo., 1969-99; ret., 1999. Recipient Alumni Trail Blazer award U. No. Colo., 1988; named Colo. Tchr. of Yr., 1994, finalist Nat. Tchr. of Yr., 1994; inductee into Nat. Tchrs.' Hall of Fame, 1995. Mem. NAFE, AAUW, NEA, PTA (by-laws com. 1989-90, hon. life mem.), Colo. Edn. Assn. (del. to assembly 1985-90), Jefferson County Edn. Assn. (spl. svcs. com. 1989-90), Internat. Reading Assn., Phi Delta Kappa, Pi Lambda Theta, Epsilon Sigma Alpha (edn. chair 1989-90, chair ways and means com. 1990-91, publicity chair 1991-93). Democrat. Avocations: football, travel, golf, reading. Home: 10810 W Exposition Ave Lakewood CO 80226-3818

WEST, NATALIE ELSA, lawyer; b. Greenwich, Conn., Mar. 11, 1947; AB, Smith Coll., 1968; JD, U. Calif., Berkeley, 1973. Bar: Calif. 1974. Counsel Calif. Fair Polit. Practices Commn., Sacramento, 1975-79; city atty. City of Berkeley, Calif., 1980-85, City of Novato, 1985-92, City of Brentwood, 1994-99; gen. counsel Livermore-Amador Valley Water Mgmt. Agy., 1996—; shareholder McDonough, Holland & Allen, Oakland, Calif., 1991—. Lectr. law U. Calif., Berkeley, 2000—. Pres. city attys. dept. League of Calif. Cities, 1986-87, bd. dirs., 1995-97. Mem. State Bar Calif., Alameda County Bar Assn. Office: McDonough Holland & Allen 1999 Harrison St Ste 1300 Oakland CA 94612-3582

WEST, RICHARD VINCENT, art museum director; b. Prague, Czechoslovakia, Nov. 26, 1934; came to U.S., 1938, naturalized, 1947; s. Jan Josef and Katherine Frieda (Mayer) Vyslouzil; 1 child, Jessica Katherine Student, UCLA, 1952-55, Music Acad. of the West, 1958-60; BA with highest honors, U. Calif., Santa Barbara, 1961; postgrad., Akademie der Bildenden Kuenste, Vienna, 1961-62, Hochschule fur Musik und darstellende Kuenste, 1961-62; MA, U. Calif., Berkeley, 1965. Curatorial intern Cleve. Art Mus., 1965-66, Albright-Knox Art Gallery, Buffalo, 1966-67; curator Mus. Art Bowdoin Coll., Brunswick, Maine, 1967-69, dir., 1969-72, Crocker Art Mus., Sacramento, 1973-82, Santa Barbara Mus. Art, 1983-91; pres. Artmuse Assocs., Benicia, 1991-92; dir. Newport (R.I.) Art Mus., 1992-94, Frye Art Mus., Seattle, 1995—. Mem. Joint Yugoslav-Am. Excavations at Sirmium, 1971; bd. dirs. Sacramento Regional Art Coun., 1973-77; bd. overseers Strawbery Banke, 1993-99. Author: Painters of the Section d'Or, 1967, Language of the Print, 1968; The Walker Art Building Murals, 1972, Munich and American Realism in the 19th Cen., 1978, An Enkindled Eye: The Paintings of Rockwell Kent, 1985, Standing in the Tempest: Painters of the Hungarian Avant-Garde, 1991, America in Art, 1991, A Significant Story: American Painting and Decorative Arts from the Karolik Collection, 1993; editor: Contemporary American Marine Art, 1997, Circle of Lyon: 7 French Painters of Reality, 1998, Children of the Yellow Kid: The Evolution of the American Comic Strip, 1998, Carlo Maria Mariani: The Mysterious Enchantment of Beauty, 1999, This Tranquil Land: Hudson River Paintings from the Herson Collection, 2000, Winold Reiss: Native American Portraits, 2000, Graham Nickson: Dual Natures, 2000, Representing LA: Pictorial Currents in Southern California Art, 2001; exhbn. catalogues, also various revs. and articles. Founding mem. New England Community Mus. Consortium; active USCG Aux., 1989—. Served with USN, 1956-57. Ford Found. fellow, 1965-67; Smithsonian fellow, 1971 Mem. Assn. Art Mus. Dirs., Am. Assn. Mus., Coll. Art Assn., Internat. Coun. Mus., Western Assn. Art Mus. (pres. 1975-78), Calif. Assn. Mus. (bd. dirs. 1980-82, v.p. 1986-91), Newport Reading Rm., Rotary, Rainier Club. Office: Frye Art Mus 704 Terry Ave Seattle WA 98104-2019

WEST, STEPHEN ALLAN, lawyer; b. Salt Lake City, Mar. 23, 1935; s. Allan Morrell and Ferne (Page) W.; m. Martha Sears, Mar. 21, 1960; children: Stephen Allan, Jr., Page, Adam. JD, U. Utah, 1961, BS in Philosophy, 1962. Law clk. to judge U.S. Dist. Ct., Utah, 1961-62; assoc. Marr, Wilkins & Cannon, Salt Lake City, 1962-65, ptnr., 1965-67; atty. Jennings, Strouss, Salmon & Trask, Washington, 1967-68, Marriott Corp., Washington, 1968-71, asst. gen. counsel, 1971-74, v.p. and assoc. gen. counsel, 1974-87, v.p. and dep. gen. counsel, 1987-93; sr. v.p., gen. counsel Marriott Internat., Inc., Washington, 1993-94; pres. Tex. San Antonio mission Ch. of Jesus Christ of Latter-day Saints, 1995-98, Gen. Authority, 1998—. Mem. exec. bd. Interfaith Conf. Met. Washington, 1989-93, vice chmn., 1992-93; mem. exec. bd. Christa McAuliffe Inst. Task Force of Nat. Found. for Improvement Edn. Mem. ABA (exec. coun. young lawyers sect. 1964-65), Utah Bar Assn. (exec. com. young lawyers sect. 1962-67), D.C. Bar Assn., Utah Profl. Rels. Com., U. Utah Alumni Assn. (Disting. Alumni award 1971), Skull and Bones, Owl and Key, Phi Delta Phi, Sigma Chi. Office: Ch Jesus Christ Latter-day Saints 47 E South Temple Salt Lake City UT 84150-1700 Home: 1117 Fox Farm Rd Logan UT 84321-4807

WEST, TONY, former state official; b. Phoenix, Oct. 29, 1937; m. Margaret O'Malley, 1962; 3 children: William A., III, John Patrick, Stephen Michael. BS, Ariz. State Univ., 1961. Formerly pres., chief exec. officer Shenendoah Ranches; Ariz. state rep., 1973-82; former Ariz. state senator, dist. 18; Ariz. state treas., 1998; corp. commr. Ariz. Corp. Commn., Phoenix, 1999. Mem. Ariz. Club (formerly pres.), Ariz. Found. for Handicapped (pres.), John C. Lincoln Hosp. Found. Republican. Office: Ariz Corp Commn 1200 W Washington St Phoenix AZ 85007-2927

WESTCOTT, BRIAN JOHN, manufacturing executive; b. Rexford, N.Y., June 19, 1957; s. John Campbell and Norma (Cornell) W.; m. Andrea Belrose, Apr. 23, 1988; children: Sarah Katharine, Paul Brian. BS, Lehigh U., 1979; MS, Stanford U., 1980, PhD, 1987. Engr. Combustion Engring., Windsor, Conn., 1980-81; rsch. engr. Gen. Electric Corp. Rsch., Niskayuna, N.Y., 1981-83; rsch. fellow Stanford (Calif.) Grad. Sch. Bus., 1987-88; mgr. Gen. Electric Corp. Mgmt., Bridgeport, Conn., 1988-89; prin. A.T. Kearney Tech. Inc., Redwood City, Calif., 1989—; chief exec. officer Westt, Inc., Menlo Park, 1990—; CEO e Innovate, 1999—. Author: (with others) Paradox and Transformation, 1988; contbr. articles to profl. jours.; inventor, patentee in field. Mem. Menlo Park Vitality Task Force, 1993-94. Recipient Tech 500 award Westt, Inc., 1996, 97, 98, Inc. 500 award, 1997, Silicon Valley Tech fast 50 award, 1997, 98; postdoctoral rsch. fellow Stanford U. Grad. Sch. Bus., 1987, 88; rsch. fellow Electric Power Rsch., Stanford, 1983-87. Mem. ASME. Avocations: sports, politics. Office: Westt Inc 1090 Obrien Dr Menlo Park CA 94025-1409

WESTER, JOHN CHARLES, bishop; b. San Francisco, 1950; B of Philosophy, St. Joseph's Coll., Mt. View, Calif.; Master's degree, St. Patrick's Coll.; M Applied Spirituality, U. San Francisco; M Pastoral Counseling, Holy Names Coll. Ordained priest Roman Cath. Ch., 1976. Tchr. Marin Cath. H.S., 1979-82, dir. campus ministry, 1982-84, pres., 1984-86; assoc. pastor St. Raphael Parish, San Rafael, Calif., 1976-79; asst. supt. schs. Marin Cath. H.S., 1979; pastor St. Stephen Parish, San Francisco, 1993-97; vicar for clergy Archdiocese of San Francisco, 1997-98, consecrated aux. bishop, 1998—. Office: 445 Church St San Francisco CA 94114-1720

WESTER, KEITH ALBERT, film and television recording engineer, real estate developer; b. Seattle, Feb. 21, 1940; s. Albert John and Evelyn Grayce (Nettell) W., m. Judith Elizabeth Jones, 1968 (div. Mar. 1974); 1 child, Wendy Elizabeth; m. Joan Marie Bursler, Feb. 2001. AA, Am. River Coll., Sacramento, 1959; BA, Calif. State U., L.A., 1962; MA, UCLA, 1965. Lic. multi-engine rated pilot. Prodn. asst. Sta. KCRA-TV, Sacramento, 1956; announcer Sta. KSFM, Sacramento, 1960; film editor, sound rec. technician Urie & Assocs., Hollywood, Calif., 1963-66; co-owner Steckler-Wester Film Prodns., Hollywood, 1966-70; owner Profl. Sound Recorders, Studio City, Calif., 1970—, Aerocharter, Studio City, 1974—, Wester Devel., Sun Valley, Coeur d'Alene, Idaho, 1989—, also Studio City, 1989—; majority stockholder Channel 58 TV, Coeur d'Alene/Spokane, 1993-99. Prodn. sound mixer: (films) Carolina, 2001, Orange County, 2001, Princess Diaries, 2000, The Perfect Storm, 1999 (acad. award co-nominee for best sound 2001), Never Been Kissed, 1999, Runaway Bride, 1999, Armageddon, 1998 (Acad. award co-nominee 1999), Mouse Hunt, 1997, Air Force One, 1997 (Acad. award co-nominee for best sound 1998), Shadow Conspiracy, 1996, G.I. Jane, 1997, The Rock, 1996 (Acad. award co-nominee for best sound, 1997), Waterworld, 1995 (Acad. award co-nominee for best sound 1996), The Shadow, 1994, Wayne's World II, 1993, Coneheads, 1993, Body of Evidence, 1992, Indecent Proposal, 1992, School Ties, 1991, Frankie and Johnny, 1991, Another You, 1991, Thelma and Louise, 1990, Shattered, 1990, Desperate Hours, 1989, Joe vs. the Volcano, 1989, Black Rain, 1989 (Acad. award co-nominee 1990), Sea of Love, 1988, Real Men, 1985, Mask, 1984, Thief of Hearts, 1983, Young Doctors in Love, 1982, First Monday in October, 1981. Mem. NATAS (Emmy award An Early Frost 1986, Emmy nominations in 1982, 84, 85, 87), SAG, Acad. Motion Picture Arts and Scis., Brit. Acad. Film and TV Arts (award nomination for The Rock 1997, The Perfect Storm 2001), Cinema Audio Soc. (sec. 1985-91, Sound award 1987), Soc. Motion Picture and TV Engrs., Internat. Sound Technicians, Local 695, Assn. Film Craftsmen (sec. 1967-73, treas. 1973-76), Aircraft Owners and Pilots Assn. (Confederate Air Force col.), Am. Radio Relay League (K6DGN). Home: 4146 Bellingham Ave Studio City CA 91604-1601 Office: Profl Sound Recorders 6324 Variel Ave Ste 308 Woodland Hills CA 91367

WESTERFIELD, PUTNEY, management consulting executive; b. New Haven, Feb. 9, 1930; s. Ray Bert and Mary Beatrice (Putney) W.; m. Anne Montgomery, Apr. 17, 1954; children: Bradford, Geoffrey, Clare. Grad., Choate Sch., 1942-47; B.A., Yale, 1951. Co-founder, v.p. Careers, Inc., N.Y.C., 1950-52; mgr. S.E. Asia Swen Publs., Inc., Manila, Philippines, 1952; mem. joint adv. commn. Korea, 1953-54; polit. officer Am. embassy, Saigon, Vietnam, 1955-57; asst. to pub. Time mag., N.Y.C., 1957-59, asst. circulation dir., 1959-61, circulation dir., 1961-66, asst. pub., 1966-68, Life mag., N.Y.C., 1968; pub. Fortune mag., N.Y.C., 1969-73; pres. Chase World Info. Corp., N.Y.C., 1973-75; v.p. Boyden Assocs. Internat., San Francisco, 1976-80, sr. v.p., western mgr., 1980-84, pres., chief exec. officer N.Y.C. and San Francisco, 1984-90, mng. dir., 1990—. Chmn. bd. dirs. Upside Media Inc. Bd. dirs. Urban League, N.Y.C., 1969-71, Children's Village, 1968-71, Mediterranean Sch. Found., 1969-71, Nat. Boys Club, 1970-73, U.S. -S. Africa Leaders Exch. Program, 1971—, Bus. Coun. for Internat. Understanding, 1974-76, Yale-China Assn., 1975-78, East Meets West Found., 1991—; trustee Choate Sch., Wallingford, Conn., 1967-76, Westover Sch., Middlebury, Conn., 1975-79, Watch Hill Chapel Soc., 1963-77, Assn. Yale Alumni, 1972-75, 80-83. Mem. Burlingame Country Club, Pacific Union Club, Bohemian Club. Home and Office: 10 Greenview Ln Hillsborough CA 94010-6424 E-mail: putneyw@pacbell.net

WESTERFIELD, RANDOLPH W. university dean, business educator; B.A., M.A., PhD, UCLA. Asst. prof. fin. The Wharton Sch., U. Pa., Phila., 1968-73, assoc. prof. fin., 1973-81, sr. rsch. assoc., Rodney L. White Ctr. Fin. Rsch., 1977-88, prof. fin., 1981-88, chair fin. dept., 1986-88; Charles B. Thornton prof. fin., bus. econs. chair U. So. Calif. Sch. Bus. Adminstrn., L.A., 1988-93; dean, Robert R. Dockson chair in bus. adminstrn. Marshall Sch. Bus., U. So. Calif., L.A., 1993—. Vis. prof. fin. Claremont (Calif.) Grad. Sch., 1983, Stanford U., Palo Alto, Calif., 1981-82, U. Nova de Lisboa, Portugal, 1984; [illegible] Continental Bank, Phila., 1979-88; mem. pension rsch. coun., The Wharton Sch., 1979-88; mem. editl. adv. bd. John Wiley & Sons (Asia) Pte Ltd., 1996; mem. authors adv. coun., Times Mirror-Irwin Co., 1987-97; chmn. Consortium for Grad. Study in Mgmt., 1997; past cons. AT&T, Mobil Oil, UN, U.S. Depts. Labor and Justice. C-author: (with Stephen A. Ross and Bradford Jordan) Fundamentals of Corporate Finance, 1992, 93, 95, 97 (including South African, Can., Australian, Chinese, Dutch and Spanish edits.), Essentials of Corporate Finance, 1996, (with Stephen A. Ross and Jeffrey Jaffe) Corporate Finance, 1988, 90, 93, 96 (including Can., Australian and internat. edits.); author monographs; contbr. chpts. to books, numerous articles to profl. jours. and conf. procs.; assoc. editor Fin. Rev., 1985-92. Mem. Nat. Assn. Corp. Bds. (mem. bd. L.A. chpt. 1996). Office: Marshall Sch Bus Adminstrn U So Calif Hoffman Hall 800 701 Exposition Blvd Los Angeles CA 90089-0001 Fax: (213) 740-5432. E-mail: rwesterfield@marshall.usc.edu

WESTFALL, DAVID PATRICK, academic administrator, educator; b. Harrisville, W.Va., June 9, 1942; s. Creed Simpson and Cecilia Rita (McKay) W.; m. Shirley Anne Spencer, June 27, 1965; children: Timothy David, Alison. AB, Brown U., 1964; MS, W.Va. U., 1966, PhD, 1968. Demonstrator in pharmacology Oxford (Eng.) U., 1968-70; asst. prof. W.Va. U., Morgantown, 1970-73, assoc. prof., 1973-77, prof., 1977-82; prof., chair Sch. Medicine U. Nev., Reno, 1982-97, v.p. acad. affairs, 1997—. Author chpts. in books; contbr. articles to profl. jours. Mem. Am. Soc. Pharmacology & Exptl. Therapeutics, Western Pharm. Soc. (cons.), Sigma Xi. Avocations: skiing, golf. Office: U Nev Dept Of Pharmacology Reno NV 84537

WESTHEIMER, DAVID KAPLAN, novelist; b. Houston, Apr. 11, 1917; s. Adolf and Esther (Kaplan) W.; m. Doris Gertrude Rothstein, Oct. 9, 1945; children: Fred, Eric. B.A., Rice Inst., Houston, 1937. Successively asst. amusement editor, radio editor, mag. editor, TV editor Houston Post, 1939-41, 45-46, 50, 53-60, columnist, 1984-88. Author: Summer on the Water, 1948, The Magic Fallacy, 1950, Watching Out for Dulie, 1960, Von Ryan's Express, 1964, My Sweet Charlie, 1965, Song of the Young Sentry, 1968, Lighter Than a Feather, 1971, Over the Edge, 1972, Going Public, 1973, Tha Avila Gold, 1974, The Olmec Head, 1974, Rider on the Wind, 1979, Von Ryan's Return, 1980, The Great Wounded Bird, and other poems, 2000, (with John Sherlock) The Amindra Gamble, 1982, Sitting It Out, 1992, Death Is Lighter Than a Feather, 1995, (with Karen Westheimer) LoneStar Zodiac, 1995, (play) My Sweet Charlie, 1966, (TV films) Trouble Comes to Town, 1972, A Killer Among Us, 1990. Served to capt. USAAF, 1941-45, ETO; served to capt. USAF, 1950-53; lt. col. USAF; ret. Decorated Air medal, D.F.C. Mem. ACLU, NAACP, Writer's Guild Am. West. Author's Guild, Ret. Officers Assn., Calif. Writers Club. Democrat. Avocation: reading. Home and Office: 11722 Darlington Ave Apt 2 Los Angeles CA 90049-5525 E-mail: dwestheime@aol.com

WESTON, JANE SARA, plastic surgeon, educator; b. Oceanside, N.Y., May 21, 1952; m. Jan K. Horn; children: Jonathan Spencer Horn, Jennifer Danielle Horn. MD, Stanford U., 1975-79. Diplomate Am. Bd. Plastic Surgery. Resident gen. surgery Sch. Medicine Stanford (Calif.) U., 1979-82, resident plastic surgery Sch. Medicine, 1982-83; fellow craniofacial surgery Hopital des Enfants Malades, Paris, 1983-84; plastic surgeon Kaiser Permanente Med. Group, San Jose, Calif., 1985-90; pvt. practice Palo Alto, 1990—. Mem. faculty Stanford U. Med. Sch., 1994-95. Active Leadership Palo Alto, 1993. Fellow ACS; mem. Am. Soc. Plastic and Reconstructive Surgeons (chair women plastic surgeons com. 1993-96, chair ethics com. 1998-99). Avocation: harp. Office: 750 Welch Rd Ste 321 Palo Alto CA 94304-1510

WESTON, JOHN FREDERICK, business educator, consultant; b. Ft. Wayne, Ind., Feb. 6, 1916; s. David Thomas and Bertha (Schwartz) W.; children: Kenneth F., Byron L., Ellen J. B.A., U. Chgo., 1937, M.B.A., 1943, Ph.D., 1948. Instr. U. Chgo. Sch. Bus., 1940-42, asst. prof., 1947-48; prof. The Anderson Sch. UCLA, 1949—, Cordner prof. The Anderson Sch., 1981-94, prof. emeritus recalled The Anderson Sch., 1986—, dir. rsch. program in competition and bus. policy, 1969—, dir. Ctr. for Managerial Econs. and Pub. Policy, 1983-86. Econ. cons. to pres. Am. Bankers Assn., 1945-46; disting. lecture series U. Okla., 1967, U. Utah, 1972, Miss. State U., 1972, Miami State U., 1975. Author: Scope and Methodology of Finance, 1966, International Managerial Finance, 1972, Impact of Large Firms on U.S. Economy, 1973, Financial Theory and Corporate Policy, 1979, 2d edit., 1983, 3d edit., 1988, Mergers, Restructuring and Corporate Control, 1990, Takeovers, Restructuring and Corporate Governance, 3d edit., 2000, Managerial Finance, 9th edit, 1992; assoc. editor: Jour. of Finance, 1948-55; mem. editorial bd., 1957-59; editorial bd. Bus. Econs., Jour. Fin. Rsch., Managerial and Decision Econs.; manuscript referee Am. Econ. Rev., Rev. of Econs. and Statistics, Engring. Economist, Bus. Econs., Fin. Mgmt. Bd. dirs. Bunker Hill Fund. Served with Ordnance Dept. AUS, 1943-45. Recipient Abramson Scroll award Bus. Econs., 1989-94; McKinsey Found. grantee, 1965-68; GE grantee, 1967; Ford Found. Faculty Rsch. fellow, 1961-62. Fellow Nat. Assn. Bus. Economists; mem. Am. Finance Assn. (pres. 1966, adv. bd. 1967-71), Am. Econ. Assn., Western Econ. Assn. (pres. 1962), Econometric Soc., Am. Statis. Assn., Royal Econ. Soc., Fin. Analysts Soc., Fin. Mgmt. Assn. (pres. 1979-80) Home: 258 Tavistock Ave Los Angeles CA 90049-3229 Office: UCLA 258 Tavistock Ave Los Angeles CA 90049-3229

WESTON, WILLIAM LEE, dermatologist; b. Grand Rapids, Minn., Aug. 13, 1938; s. Eugene and Edith Kathryn (Lee) W.; m. Janet J. Atkinson, June 9, 1964; children: Elizabeth Carol, William Kemp. AB, Whitman Coll., 1960; B in Med. Sci., U. S.D., 1963; MD, U. Colo., 1965. Resident in pediatrics U. Calif., San Francisco, 1967-68; intern, then resident in pediatrics U. Colo., Denver, 1965-67, resident in dermatology, 1970-72, asst. prof. dermatology and pediatrics, 1972-76, prof., 1976—, chmn. dept. dermatology, 1976—. Author: Practical Pediatric Dermatology, 1979, rev. edit., 1985, Color Textbook of Pediatric Dermatology, 1991, rev. edit., 1996; editor-in-chief Current Problems in Dermatology, 1988-93. With AUS, 1968-70. Mem. Soc. Pediatric Dermatology (founder, sec.-treas. 1975-80, pres. 1984-85), Colo. Dermatol. Soc. (pres.), Soc. Investigative Dermatology (bd. dirs.), Am. Acad. Dermatology (bd. dirs.). Methodist. Home: 8550 E Ponderosa Dr Parker CO 80138-8233 Office: 4200 E 9th Ave Denver CO 80220-3706

WESTPHAL, JAMES ADOLPH, planetary science educator; b. Dubuque, Iowa, June 13, 1930; s. Henry Ludwig and Nancy Kathryn (Wise) W.; m. Lois Jean, Apr. 17, 1956 (div. 1966); 1 child, Andrew Johnathan; m. Barbara Jean Webster, Nov. 2, 1967. BS, U. Tulsa, 1954. Team leader Sinclair Rsch. Labs., Tulsa, 1955-61; sr. engr. Calif. Inst. Tech., Pasadena, 1961-66, sr. rsch. fellow, 1966-71, assoc. prof., 1971-76, prof., 1976-98, prof. emeritus, 1998—; dir. Palomar Obs., Pasadena, 1994-97, Prin. investigator Hubble space telescope NASA, Calif. Inst. Tech., Pasadena, 1977—. Fellow MacArthur Found., 1991; recipient Space Science award Am. Inst. Aeronautics and Astronautics, 1995. Mem. Am. Astron. Soc. Office: Calif Inst Tech Ms 150 21 Pasadena CA 91125-0001 E-mail: jaw@caltech.edu

WESTPHAL, PAUL, professional basketball coach; b. Torrance, Calif., Nov. 30, 1950; m. Cindy Westphal; children: Victoria, Michael Paul. Degree in phys. edn., U. So. Calif., 1972. Player Boston Celtics, 1972-75, Phoenix Suns, 1975-80, 83-84, Seattle Supersonics, 1980-81, N.Y. Knicks, 1981-83; coach S.W. Coll., Phoenix, 1985-86, Grand Canyon Coll., 1986-88; asst. coach. Phoenix Suns, 1988-92, head coach, 1992—. Named All-Star 5 times, Comeback Player of Yr.; uniform number retired by Suns, 1989. Office: Seattle Supersonics 351 Elliott Ave W Seattle WA 98119-4101

WESTWOOD, JAMES NICHOLSON, lawyer; b. Portland, Oreg., Dec. 3, 1944; s. Frederick Alton and Catherine (Nicholson) W.; m. Janet Sue Butler, Feb. 23, 1980; children: Laura, David. BA, Portland State U., 1967; JD, Columbia U., 1974. Bar: Oreg. 1974, U.S. Dist. Ct. Oreg. 1974, U.S. Ct. Appeals (9th cir.) 1978, U.S. Supreme Ct. 1981, U.S. Ct. Appeals (fed. cir.) 1984, U.S. Ct. Appeals (D.C. cir.) 1997. Assoc. Miller, Anderson, Nash, Yerke & Wiener, Portland, 1974-76, 78-81; asst. to pres. Portland State U., 1976-78; ptnr. Miller, Nash, Wiener, Hager & Carlsen, Portland, 1981-99, Stoel Rives LLP, Portland, 1999—. Recipient Disting. Svc. award Portland State U. Found., 1984, Outstanding Alumni award Portland State U., 1992. Mem. ABA (chmn. forest resources com. 1987-89), Oreg. Bar Assn. (chmn. appellate practice sect. 1996-97), Am. Acad. Appellate Lawyers, Univ. Club (bd. govs. 1994), City Club (pres. 1991-92), Park Blocks Found. (pres. 1999—). Republican. Unitarian. Home: 3121 NE Thompson St Portland OR 97212-4908 Office: Stoel Rivers LLP 900 SW 5th Ave Ste 2600 Portland OR 97204-1268 E-mail: jnwestwood@stoel.com

WESTWOOD, MELVIN NEIL, horticulturist, pomologist; b. Hiawatha, Utah, Mar. 25, 1923; s. Neil and Ida (Blake) W.; m. Wanda Mae Shields, Oct. 12, 1946; children: Rose Dawn, Nancy Gwen, Robert Melvin, Kathryn Mae. Student, U. Utah, 1948-50; BS in Pomology, Utah State U., 1952; PhD in Pomology, Wash. State U., 1956. Field botanist Utah State U., Logan, 1951-52, supt. Howell Field Sta., 1952-53; rsch. asst. State Coll. Wash., 1953-55; rsch. horticulturist Agrl. Rsch. Svc. USDA, Wenatchee, Wash., 1955-60; assoc. prof. Oreg. State U., Corvallis, 1960-67, prof., 1967-80, prof. emeritus, 1986—; rsch. dir. Nat. Clonal Germplasm Repository, Corvallis, 1980-83, nat. tech. advisor, 1984-86. Author: Deciduous Fruit and Nut Production, 1976, Temperate-Zone Pomology: Physiology and Culture, 1978, 3d edit., 1993, Contract Military Air Transport: From the Ground Up, 1995, Pear Varieties and Species, 1996; author: (with others) Cherry Nutrition, 1966, Pear Rootstocks, 1987, Management and Utilization of Plant Germplasm, 1988, Maintenance and Storage: Clonal Germplasm, 1989, Genetic Resources of Malus, 1991; contbr. articles to profl. jours. With U.S. Air Transport Command, 1943-45, USAAF, 1946-47. Grantee NSF, 1966; recipient Hartman Cup award Oreg. Hort. Soc., 1989, Earl Price Excellence in Rsch. award Oreg. State U., 1983. Fellow Am. Soc. Hort. Sci. (bd. dirs. 1974-75, chmn. com. environ. quality 1971, adv. coun. 1974-79, mem. pomology sect. 1967-74, publs. com. 1971-74, pres. Western region 1974, Joseph Harvey Gourley award for Pomology 1958, 77, Stark award for Pomology 1969, 77, Outstanding Rschr. award 1986); mem. AAAS, Am. Soc. Plant Physiologists, Am. Pomological Soc. (mem. adv. bd. 1970-75, mem. exec. bd. 1980-84, Paul Howe Shepard award 1968, 82, Wilder medal 1980), UN Assn. USA, Ams. United for Separation of Ch. and State, Amnesty Internat., Phi Kappa Phi, Gamma Sigma Delta. Baptist. Achievements include patent for Autumn Blaze ornamental pear; research on Pyrus (pear), Malus (apple) and Prunus (plum, cherry, peach) and on the physiology of rootstock genera. Office: Oreg State U Dept Horticulture Corvallis OR 97331

WETEKAM, DONALD J. career officer; BS, USAF Academy, Colorado Springs, 1973; M in Engring. Adminstrn., U. Utah, 1978. Commd. 2d lt. USAF, 1973, advanced through grades to brigadier gen., 1999; officer in charge 4th Munitions Maintenance Squadron, Seymour Johnson AFB, N.C., 1974-75, 635th Munitions Maintenance Squadron, U-Tapao Royal Thai Naval, Airfield, Thailand, 1975-76; munitions svc. officer, officer in charge 388th Tactical Fighter Wing, Hill AFB, Utah, 1976-79; officer in charge 313th Aircraft Maintenance Unit, Hahn Air Base, Germany, 1981-84; maintenance staff officer HQ Tactical Air Command, Langley AFB, Va., 1984-86; comdr. 56th Equipment Maintenance Squadron, MacDill AFB, Fla., 1986-89; F-15 and standard avionics logistics program mgr. HQ USAF, Pentagon, 1989-93; comdr. 49th Logistics Group, Holloman AFB, N.M., 1994-95; dir. aircraft mgmt. directorate Oklahoma City Air Logistics Ctr., Tinker AFB, 1995-97, vice comdr., 1997-98; dir. logistics HQ Pacific Air Forces, Hickam AFB, Hawaii, 1998—.

WETTACK, F. SHELDON, academic administrator; AB, San Jose State U., 1960, MA, 1962; PhD, U. Tex., Austin, 1967. From asst. prof. to prof. Hope Coll., Holland, Mich., 1967-82, dean nat. and social scis., 1974-82; dean faculty arts and scis. U. Richmond, 1982-89; pres. Wabash Coll., Crawfordsville, Ind., 1989-93; v.p., dean of faculty Harvey Mudd Coll., Claremont, Calif., 1993—. Office: Harvey Mudd Coll 301 E 12th St Claremont CA 91711-5901 E-mail: sheldon_wettack@hmc.edu

WETTAW, JOHN, state legislator, chemistry educator; b. St. Louis, Apr. 17, 1939; BA in Chemistry, So. Ill. U.; PhD in Phys. Chemistry, Mich. State U. NSF post-doctoral rschr. Tex. A&M U.; prof. No. Ariz. U.; mem. Ariz. Ho. of Reps., 1972-92, Ariz. State Senate, 1992—, mem. appropriations com., vice-chmn. judiciary com., chmn. commerce, agr. and natural resources com., chmn. appropriations subcom. on health and welfare, mem. banking, ins. and elections com., mem. joint com. on capital rev., mem. joint legis. budget com., pres. pro tempore. Mem. adv. bd. Grand Canyon Boy Scout Coun. Mem. Kiwanis, No. Ariz. U. Booster Club. Republican. Presbyterian. Office: State Capitol Bldg 1700 W Washington St # 302 Phoenix AZ 85007-2812 also: 1824 Spencer Cir Flagstaff AZ 86004-7301 E-mail: jwettaw@azleg.state.az.us

WETTERAU, MARK S. food products/distributor executive; BA, Westminster Coll. Pres., CEO Golden State Foods. Office: Golden State Foods Ste 1100 18301 Von Karman Ave Irvine CA 92612

WETZEL, JODI (JOY LYNN WETZEL), history and women's studies educator; b. Salt Lake City, Apr. 5, 1943; d. Richard Coulam and Margaret Elaine (Openshaw) Wood; m. David Nevin Wetzel, June 12, 1967; children: Meredith (dec.), Richard Rawlins. BA in English, U. Utah, 1965, MA in English, 1967; PhD in Am. Studies, U. Minn., 1977. Instr. Am. studies and family social sci. U. Minn., 1973-77, asst. prof. Am. studies and women's studies, 1977-79, asst. to dir. Minn. Women's Ctr., 1973-75, asst. dir., 1975-79; dir. Women's Resource Ctrs. U. Denver, 1980-84, mem. adj. faculty history, 1981-84, dir. Am. studies program, dir. Women's Inst., 1983-84; dir. Women in Curriculum U. Maine, 1985-86, mem. coop. faculty sociology, social work and human devel., 1986; dir. Inst. Women's Studies and Svcs. Met. State Coll. Denver, 1986—, assoc. prof. history, 1986-89, prof. history, 1990—. Speaker, presenter, cons. in field; vis. prof. Am. studies U. Colo., 1985. Co-author: Women's Studies: Thinking Women, 1993; co-editor: Readings Toward Composition, 2d edit., 1969; contbr. articles to profl. publs. Del. at-large Nat. Women's Meeting, Houston, 1977; bd. dirs. Rocky Mountain Women's Inst., 1981-84; treas. Colo. Women's Agenda, 1987-91. U. Utah Dept. English fellow, 1967; U. Minn. fellow, 1978-79; grantee NEH, 1973, NSF, 1981-83, Carnegie Corp., 1988; named to Outstanding Young Women of Am., 1979. Mem. Am. Hist. Assn., Nat. Assn. Women in Edn. (Hilda A. Davis Ednl. Leadership award 1996, Sr. Scholar 1996), Am. Assn. for Higher Edn., Am. Studies Assn., Nat. Women's Studies Assn., Golden Key Nat. Honor Soc. (hon.), Alpha Lambda Delta, Phi Kappa Phi. Office: Met State Coll Den Campus Box 36 PO Box 173362 Denver CO 80217-3362

WEXLER, ROBERT, university administrator; Pres. U. of Judaism, L.A. Office: U Judaism 15600 Mulholland Dr Los Angeles CA 90077-1599

WEYAND, FREDERICK CARLTON, retired career officer; b. Arbuckle, Calif., Sept. 15, 1916; s. Frederick C. W. and Velma Semans (Weyand); m. Lora Arline Langhart, Sept. 20, 1940; children: Carolyn Ann, Robert Carlton, Nancy Diane. A.B., U. Calif.-Berkeley, 1939; LL.D. (hon), U. Akron, 1975. Officer U.S. Army, advanced to gen. chief of staff, 1940-76; sr. v.p. First Hawaiian Bank, Honolulu, 1976-82; trustee Estate of S.M. Damon, Honolulu, 1982—. Bd. dirs. First Hawaiian, Inc., Ltd., First Hawaiian Bank, First Hawaiian Credit Corp. Chmn. ARC, Honolulu, 1982, Hawaiian Open golf Tourney, 1981-82. Decorated D.S.C. U.S. Army, 1967, D.S.M. Army (3), Dept. Def. (1), 1966-76, other U.S. and fgn. mil. decorations. Mem. Am. Def. Preparedness Assn., Assn. U.S. Army, U.S. Strategic Inst. (v.p. 1976—), USAF Assn. Lutheran. Clubs: Waialae Country. Lodge: Masons. Home: 2121 Ala Wai Blvd Ph 1 Honolulu HI 96815-2272 Office: SM Damon Estate 999 Bishop St Fl 28 Honolulu HI 96813-4423

WEYERHAEUSER, GEORGE H., JR. paper manufacturing company executive; B in Philosophy/Maths., Yale U., 1976; MS, MIT, 1986. Tech. forester, contract logger adminstr., sawmill supr. Weyerhaeuser Co., Dierks, Ark., 1978-80, v.p., mill mgr. Containerboard Valliant, Okla., 1981-90, v.p. mfg. pulp & paper bus. Federal Way, 1990-93, pres., CEO Can. divsn., 1993-98, sr. v.p. technology, 1999—. Office: Weyerhaeuser Co PO Box 2999 Tacoma WA 98477-2999

WHALEN, JEROME DEMARIS, lawyer; b. Portland, Oreg., Feb. 9, 1943; s. William F. and Rose (Demaris) W. BA, U. Wash., 1965; JD, Harvard U., 1969. Bar: Wash. 1969. Assoc. Foster Pepper & Shefelman, Seattle, 1969-74, ptnr., 1974-91, mng. ptnr., 1982-85; ptnr. Whalen, Firestone, Landsman, Fleming & Dixon, Seattle, 1991—. Adj. prof. corps. Law Sch., U. Puget Sound, Tacoma, 1976-77; instr. securities regulation Law Sch., U. Wash., Seattle, 1979; bd. dirs. Wright Runstad & Co., Seattle. Author: Commercial Ground Leases, 1988, 2d edit., 2001. Mem. Port of Seattle Ctrl. Waterfront Devel. Panel, 1988-90; trustee Corp. Coun. for Arts, Seattle, 1989-98; trustee Pratt Fine Arts Ctr., Seattle, 1989-94, 2000—, pres., 1991-93, Seattle Internat. Music Festival, 1992-97. Mem. Wash. State Bar Assn. (chmn. corp. bus. and banking law sect. 1980-81), Phi Beta Kappa. Office: Whalen Firestone Landsman Fleming & Dixon 1191 2nd Ave Ste 2150 Seattle WA 98101-2968

WHALEN, JOHN SYDNEY, management consultant; b. Moncton, N.B., Can., Sept. 26, 1934; s. Harry Edward and Sarah Maude (Bourgeois) W.; m. Margaret Joan Carruthers, May 3, 1958; children: Bradley Graham, Elizabeth Ann. Grad., Can. Inst. Chartered Accts., 1959. Chartered acct. Coopers & Lybrand (formerly McDonald, Currie & Co.), St. John, N.B., 1954-63; with Kaiser Services, Oakland, Calif., 1963-75, telecommunications mgr., 1966-69, asst. controller, 1969-70, controller, 1970-74; mgr. corp. acctg. Kaiser Industries Corp., Oakland, 1975; controller Kaiser Engrs., Inc., Oakland, 1975-76, v.p. fin. and adminstrn., 1976-82; mgmt. cons., owner Whalen & Assocs., Inc., Alamo, Calif., 1983—. Pres. Round Hill Holdings, Inc., 1993-99. Mem. Commonwealth Club. Club: Round Hill Golf and Country; Commonwealth. Home: 2216 Nelda Way Alamo CA 94507-2004 Office: 3195 Danville Blvd Ste 4 Alamo CA 94507-1920 E-mail: sydwhalen@aol.com

WHALEN, LUCILLE, retired academic administrator; b. Los Angeles, July 26, 1925; d. Edward Cleveland and Mary Lucille (Perrault) W. B.A. in English, Immaculate Heart Coll., Los Angeles, 1949; M.S.L.S., Catholic U. Am., 1955; D.L.S., Columbia U., 1965. Tchr. elem. and secondary parochial schs., Los Angeles, Long Beach, Calif., 1945-52; high sch. librarian Conaty Meml. High Sch., Los Angeles, 1950-52; reference/serials librarian, instr. in library sci. Immaculate Heart Coll., 1955-58; dean Immaculate Heart Coll. (Sch. Library Sci.), 1958-60, 65-70; assoc. dean, prof. SUNY, Albany, 1971-78, 84-87, prof. Sch. Info. Sci. and Policy, 1979-87; dean grad. programs, libr. Immaculate Heart Coll. Ctr., Los Angeles, 1987-90; ret. libr. (part-time) Glendale Community Coll., 1990—. Dir. U.S. Office Edn. Instn. Author, editor: (with others) Reference Services in Archives, 1986. author: Human Rights: A Reference Handbook, 1989. Mem. ACLU, Common Cause, Amnesty Internat. Democrat. Roman Catholic. Home: 320 S Gramercy Pl Apt 101 Los Angeles CA 90020-4542 Office: Glendale CC 1500 N Verdugo Rd Glendale CA 91208-2809

WHALEN, PHILIP GLENN, poet, novelist; b. Portland, Oreg., Oct. 20, 1923; s. Glenn Henry and Phyllis Bush W. B.A., Reed Coll., 1951. Ordained Zen Buddhist priest, 1973. Head monk Dharma Sangha, Santa Fe, 1984-87; abbot Hartford St. Zen Ctr., San Francisco, 1991-96. Lectr., tchr., 1955—. Author: poetry Three Satires, 1951, Self-Portrait, From Another Direction, 1959, Like I Say, 1960, Memoirs of an Inter-Glacial Age, 1960, Every Day, 1965, Highgrade, 1966, On Bear's Head, 1969, Severance Pay, 1971, Scenes of Life at the Capitol, 1971, The Kindness of Strangers, 1975, Enough Said, 1980, Heavy Breathing, 1983, Canoeing Up Cabarga Creek, 1996; novels You Didn't Even Try, 1967, Imaginary Speeches for a Brazen Head, 1972; interviews Off the Wall, 1978; prose text The Diamond Noodle, 1980; juvenile The Invention of the Letter, 1967; Recipient Poet's Found. award 1962, V.K. Ratcliff award 1964; By & Large, tape cassette reading his own poems, 1987. Served with USAAF, 1943-46. Am. Acad. Arts and Letters grantee-in-aid, 1965, 91, Morton Dauwen Zabel award for Poetry, 1986, Fund for Poetry award, 1987, 91; Com. on Poetry grantee, 1968, 70, 71. Office: 57 Hartford St San Francisco CA 94114-2013

WHALEN, THOMAS EARL, psychology educator; b. Toledo, June 26, 1938; s. T. Mylo and Alice E. (Tallman) W.; m. Carolyn Margaret Lapham, Dec. 24, 1960; children: Jennifer Susan, Holly Elizabeth. BA, UCLA, 1960; MA, San Diego State U., 1967; PhD, U. Conn., 1970. Cert. secondary tchr., Calif. Secondary tchr. San Diego City Schs., 1964-68; rsch. assoc. Southwest Regional Lab., Inglewood, Calif., 1969; prof. Calif. State U., Hayward, 1970—, chair ednl. psychology dept., 1977-79, assoc. dean sch. edn., 1987-89, 95-96, prof. emeritus, 1997. Rsch. con. Evaluation Assocs., San Sanfrancisco Bay Area Schs., 1971-88, Lawrence Livermore (Calif.) Nat. Lab., 1982-83. Author: (text book) Ten Steps to Behavioral Research, 1989; contbr. articles to profl. jours. Lt. USN, 1960-63. U.S. Office of Edn. fellow U. Conn., 1968-70, post doctoral scholar Am. Edn. Rsch. Assn., U. Iowa, 1972. Mem. Am. Ednl. Rsch. Assn., APA, Calif. Ednl. Rsch. Assn. (bd. dirs. 1982-84), Bay Area Coun. on Measurement and Evaluation in Edn. (pres. 1976-77), United Profs. of Calif. (exec. bd. Calif. State U. Hayward 1975-76). Avocations: golf, travel, gardening. Home: 325 Conway Dr Danville CA 94526-5511 Office: Calif State U 25800 Carlos Bee Blvd Hayward CA 94542-3001

WHALEY, ROBERT HAMILTON, judge; m. Lucinda schilling; 1 child. BA, Princeton U., 1965; JD, Emory U., 1968. Litigator land and natural resources divsn. Dept. Justice, 1969-71; asst. U.S. atty. U.S. Dist. Wash. (ea. dist.), 1971-72; assoc. Winston & Cashatt, Spokane, Wash., 1972-76, ptnr., 1976—; judge Spokane County Superior Ct., 1992-95, U.S. Dist. Ct. (ea. dist.) Wash., Spokane, 1995—. Office: US Dist Ct Ea Dist Wash PO Box 283 920 Riverside Ave W Spokane WA 99210

WHALIN, W. TERRY, writer, editor; b. Huntington, W.Va., Aug. 12, 1953; s. Wallace Eugene and Rose Terry (Estill) W.; children: Jonathan David, Timothy Benjamin; m. Christine Elizabeth Johnson, May 3, 1995. BA, Ind. U., 1975; cert., Multnomah Sch. of Bible, 1977; MA, U. Tex., Arlington, 1984. Linguist Wycliffe Bible Translators, Huntington Beach, Calif., 1975-85, mng. editor In Other Words, 1985-93; assoc. editor Decision mag. Billy Graham Evangelistic Assn., Mpls., 1993-94; CEO, pres. Whalin & Assocs., Colorado Springs, Colo., 1994—. Instr. Inst. of Children's Lit., 1997—. Author: When I Grow Up, 1992, Never Too Busy, 1993, A Strange Place to Sing, 1994, Chuck Colson, 1994, Today's Heroes Series, 1994, The Brave But Gentle Shepherd, 1996, Samuel Morris, Heroes of the Faith series, 1997, Sojourner Truth Heroes of the Faith Series, 1997, Luis Palau, Men of Faith Series, 1996, Billy Sunday, Young Reader's Christian Libr., 1996, John Perkins, 1996, Today's Heroes Series, 1996, Luis Palau, Young Reader's Christian Libr., 1998, Pocket Prayer Companion series: Prayers for My Son, Prayers for My Daughter, Prayers for My Wife, Prayers for My Husband, 1999, Lighthouse Psalms, 1999, Love Psalms, 1999, Billy Graham, Men of Faith Series, 2000; co-author: One Bright Shining Path, 1993, Ayacucho Para Cristo, 1995, Bottom-Line Faith, Ten Characteristics of Committed Christians, 1995, Let the Walls Fall Down, 1996, The World at Your Door, 1997, Better Men on the Path to Purity, 1998, The Book of Prayers: A Man's Guide to Reaching God, 1998, Sharing God with Others, 1998, Lessons from the Pit, 1999, Money for Life, 1999; ghostwriter (books): Seeking Christ, 1994, Freedom From Addiction, 1996, Pathway to His Prescence, 2000; contbr. articles to profl. publs. and mags. Treas. Evangelical Press Assn., Earlysville, Va., 1992-94. Mem. Evangelical Press Assn., Am. Soc. Journalists and Authors, Soc. Children's Book Writers and Ilustrators. Republican. Office: 445 E Cheyenne Mtn Blvd #C-368 Colorado Springs CO 80906-4570

WHAM, DOROTHY STONECIPHER, state legislator; b. Centralia, Ill., Jan. 5, 1925; d. Ernest Joseph and Vera Thelma (Shafer) Stonecipher; m. Robert S. Wham, Jan. 26, 1947; children: Nancy S. Wham Mitchell, Jeanne Wham Ryan, Robert S. II. BA, MacMurray Coll., 1946; MA, U. Ill., 1949; D of Pub. Adminstrn. (hon.), MacMurray Coll., 1992. Counsellor Student Counselling Bur. U. Ill., Urbana, 1946-49; state dir. ACTION program, Colo./Wyo. U.S. Govt., Denver, 1972-82; mem. Colo. Ho. of Reps., 1986-87, Colo. Senate, 1987-2000, chair jud. com., 1988-2000. With capital devel. com., health, environ., welfare, instns., legal svcs. Mem. Civil Rights Commn. Denver, 1972-80; bd. dirs. Denver Com. on Mental Health, 1985-88, Denver Symphony, 1985-88. Mem. APA, AAUW, LWV, Colo. Mental Health Assn. (bd. dirs. 1986-88), Civitan. Republican. Avocations: travel, furniture refinishing. Home: 2790 S High St Denver CO 80210-6352

WHANGER, PHILIP DANIEL, biochemistry educator and researcher, nutrition educator; b. Lewisburg, W.Va., Aug. 30, 1936; married, 1964; 2 children. BS, Berry Coll., 1959; MS, W.Va. U., 1961; PhD in Nutrition, N.C. State U., 1965. From asst. to assoc. prof. Oreg. State U., Corvallis, 1966-78, prof. nutrition & biochemistry, 1978—. Rsch. assoc. biochemistry Mich. State U., 1965-66; mem. assoc. staff Harvard Med. Sch., 1972-73; vis. scientist Gen. Acad. Exch. Svc., U. Tubingen, 1986, Commonwealth Sci. & Industry Rsch. Orgn., Wembley, Western Australia, Acad. Preventive Medicine, Beijing, 1988. Rsch. fellow NIH, 1966-67, Spl. fellow, 1972; Internat. fellow NSF, 1980-81; Rsch. grantee Oreg. State U., 1968—. Mem. Am. Inst. Nutrition, Am. Soc. Animal Sci., Internat. Bioinorg Scientists, Soc. Environ. Geochemistry and Health. Achievements include research in altered metabolic pathways under selenium deficiency, relationships of vitamin E and selenium in myopathies, biochemical properties of selenium and cadmium metallo-proteins, metabolic pathways for incorporation of selenium into proteins, selenium and gluthathione peroxidise in human blood fractions, selenium deficiencies in primates, selenium intake on human blood and urine fractions. Office: Oreg State U Dept Agrl Chemistry Corvallis OR 97331

WHEATLEY, MELVIN ERNEST, JR. retired bishop; b. Lewisville, Pa., May 7, 1915; s. Melvin Ernest and Gertrude Elizabeth (Mitchell) W.; m. Lucile Elizabeth Maris, June 15, 1939; children: Paul Melvin, James Maris, John Sherwood (dec.). AB magna cum laude, Am. U., 1936, DD, 1958; BD summa cum laude, Drew U., 1939; DD, U. of Pacific, 1948. Ordained to ministry Meth. Ch., 1939. Pastor area Meth. ch., Lincoln, Del., 1939-41; assoc. pastor First Meth. Ch., Fresno, Calif., 1941-43; pastor Centenary Meth. Ch., Modesto, 1943-46, Cen. Meth. Ch., Stockton, 1946-54, Westwood Meth. Ch., L.A., 1954-72, bishop Denver Area, 1972-84; ret., 1984. Instr. philosophy Modesto Jr. Coll., 1944; summer session instr. Hebrew-Christian heritage U. of Pacific; instr. Homiletics U. So. Calif., So. Calif. Sch. Theology, Clarement; lectr. St. Luke's Lectures, Houston, 1966; mem. Bd. of Ch. and Soc., Commn. on Status and Role of Women, United Meth. Ch., 1976-84; condr. European Christian Heritage tour, 1961, Alaska and Hawaii Missions, 1952, 54. Author: Going His Way, 1957, Our Man and the Church, 1968, The Power of Worship, 1970, Family Ministries Manual, 1970, Christmas Is for Celebrating, 1977; contbr. articles to profl. jours. Chmn. Community Rels. Conf. So. Calif., 1966-69; pres. So. Calif.-Ariz. Conf. Bd. Edn., 1960-68; hon. trustee Iliff Sch. Theology; hon. dir., active mem. Parents and Friends of Lesbians and Gays, 1980—. Recipient Disting. Alumnus award Am. U., 1979, Ball award Meth. Fedn. Social Action, 1984, Prophetic Leadership award The Consultation on Homosexuality, Tolerance and Roman Cath. Theology, 1985, Human Rights award Universal Fellowship of Met. Community Congregations, 1985, award for social justice Calif.-Pacific Meth. Fedn. for Social Action, 2000, Lifetime Achievement award Denver Parents, Families and Friends of Lesbians and Gays, 2000. Home: 859 Ronda Mendoza Unit A Laguna Hills CA 92653-5940 E-mail: lmwheatley@webtv.net

WHEELER, DENNIS EARL, mining company executive, lawyer; b. Wallace, Idaho, Dec. 17, 1942; s. Earl L. and Virginia (Rice) W.; m. Jacquline Rae, May 16, 1971; children: Michelle, Maura, Wendy, Brad. BS in Bus., U. Idaho, 1965, JD, 1967. Bar: Idaho 1967. Ptnr. Hull, Hull & Wheeler, Wallace, 1967-78; sr. v.p., gen. counsel Coeur d'Alene (Idaho) Mines Corp., 1978-80, pres., 1980-86, CEO, 1986—, chmn., 1992—. Bd. dirs. Sierra Pacific Resources; vice chmn., dir. Ctr. for Democracy; dir. World Gold Coun., Geneva, 1994—. Pres. Idaho Bd. Edn., 1984-87; founder Jobs Plus, Coeur d'Alene, 1987—; bd. dirs. Ctr. for Democracy, Washington, 1992—, Children's Village, Coeur d'Alene, 1994—, Wildlife Habitat Enhancement Coun., Silver Spring, Md., 1992—, Idaho chpt. Nature Conservancy, Sun Valley, Idaho, 1992—; mem. exec. bd. Boy Scouts Am., Coeur d'Alene, 1994—,=. Recipient Environ. Conservation Disting. Svc. award Soc. for Mining, Metallurgy and Exploration, 1993. Mem. ABA, Idaho Bar Assn., Silver Inst. (pres. 1992-94), Am. Mining Congress (chmn. western bd. govs. 1993—), Elks, Sigma Chi (Significant Sig award 1992). Avocations: fishing, skiing, boating. Office: Coeur D'Alene Mines Corp PO Box 1 Coeur D Alene ID 83816-0316

WHEELER, DOLORES, food products executive; married. Pres., CEO Gossner Foods, Logan, Utah. Bd. dir. Bus. and Econ. Delvel., Logan, Utah. Office: Gossner Foods 1051 N 1000 W Logan UT 84321-6852 Fax: 435-752-3147

WHEELER, JOHN HARVEY, political scientist, writer; b. Waco, Tex., Oct. 17, 1918; m. Norene Burleigh; children: David Carroll, John Harvey III, Mark Jefferson. B.A., Ind. U., 1946, M.A., 1947; Ph.D., Harvard U., 1950. Instr. dept. govt., asst. dir. Summer Sch., Harvard U., 1950; asst. prof. Johns Hopkins U., 1950-54; assoc. prof. Washington and Lee U., 1954-56, prof. polit. sci., 1956-60; fellow in residence Ctr. for Study Dem. Instns., 1960-69; program dir., 1970-75; chmn., pres. Inst. Higher Studies, Carpinteria, Calif., 1975—. Martha Boaz rsch. prof. in acad. info. systems U. So. Calif. Libr. Systems, 1986—, Martha Boaz disting. rsch. prof., 1987—; cons. Fund for Republic, 1958-61; adj. prof. New Sch., 1986—, ISIM, 1989—; founder, bd. dirs. The Virtual Acad., 1987; mem. faculty Western Behavioral Scis. Inst., 1990—; mem. BESTnet, Nat. Rsch. and Edn. Network; pres. C-Mode Inst., 1992—; bd. dirs. Silicon Beach Comm. Author: The Conservative Crisis, 1958, (with Eugene Burdick) Fail-Safe, 1962, repub., 1999 (film 1962, TV re-make 2000), Democracy in a Revolutionary Era, 1968, The Politics of Revolution, 1971, The Virtual Library, 1987, The Virtual Society, 1988, 2d edit., 1992; editor, contbg. author: Beyond Punitive Society, 1973, Structure of Ancient Wisdom, 1983, Bioalgebra of Judgment, 1986, Fundamental Structures Human Reflexion, 1990; editor: (with George Boas) Lattimore, The Scholar, 1953; co-founder, joint chief editor: (with James Danielli) Jour. Social and Biol.

Structures, 1973-95; joint editor Goethe's Science, 1986; developed computer-mediated "Freshman Academy", 1993; contbr. articles on constitutionalism and Francis Bacon to profl. jours. Served with AUS, 1941-46. Office: Inst Higher Studies PO Box 704 Carpinteria CA 93014-0704 E-mail: verulan@mindspring.com

WHEELER, JOHN OLIVER, geologist; b. Mussoorie, India, Dec. 19, 1924; s. Edward Oliver and Dorothea Sophie (Danielsen) W.; m. Nora Jean Hughes, May 17, 1952; children: Kathleen Anna Wheeler Hunter, Jennifer Margaret Wheeler Crompton. B.A.Sc. in Geol. Engring, U. B.C., 1947; Ph.D. in Geology, Columbia U., 1956; D.Sc. (hon.), U. B.C., 2000. Geologist Geol. Survey Can., Ottawa, Ont., 1951-61, Vancouver, B.C., 1961-65, rsch. scientist, 1965-70, rsch. mgr., 1970—, chief regional and econ. geology div., 1970-73, dep. dir. gen., 1973-79; rsch. scientist Geol. Survey Can. (Cordilleran div.), 1979-90, rsch. scientist emeritus, 1990—. Gen. editor: Geology of Canada, 8 vols., 1989-98; compiler of regional geol. maps of we. Can., Can. and no. N.Am. and Greenland; contbr. articles to profl. jours. Recipient Queen's Silver Jubilee medal, 1977, Can. 125 medal, 1994, Earth Sci. Sector and Dept. awards Nat. Resources Can., 1996, Spl. award of B.C.-Yukon Chamber of Mines for outstanding contbn. to Can. Cordilleran geology, 2000. Fellow Royal Soc. Can., Geol. Assn. Can. (pres. 1970-71, Logan medal 1983, Disting. fellow 1996), Geol. Soc. Am. (councillor 1971-74), Can. Geosci. Council (pres. 1981); mem. Can. Inst. Mining and Metallurgy., Can. Geol. Found. (pres. 1974-79) Anglican. Clubs: Can. Alpine, Am. Alpine. Office: Geol Survey Can 101-605 Robson St Vancouver BC Canada V6B 5J3

WHEELER, LARRY RICHARD, accountant; b. Greybull, Wyo., Nov. 30, 1940; s. Richard F. and Olive B. (Fredrickson) W.; m. Patricia C. Marturano, Dec. 3, 1977; children: Anthony, Richard, Teresa, Kara. BS, U. Wyo., 1965. CPA, Colo. Staff acct. H. Greger CPA, Ft. Collins, Colo., 1965-66; sr. acct. Lester, Wickham & Draney, Colorado Springs, 1966-67; acct., contr., treas. J.D. Adams Co., Colorado Springs, 1967-74; ptnr. Wheeler Pierce & Hurd, Inc., Colorado Springs, 1974-80; gen. mgr., v.p. Schneebeck's, Inc., Colorado Springs, 1980-81; prin. L.R. Wheeler & Co., PC, Colorado Springs, 1981-94; pres. Wheeler & Gilmartin Assocs., PC, Colorado Springs, 1994-95, L.R. Wheeler & Co., PC, Colorado Springs, 1995—. Dir. Schneebeck's Industries, Williams Printing, Inc., Colorado Springs Small Bus. Devel. Ctr. Active U.S. Taekwondo Union; bd. dirs. Domestic Violence Prevention Ctr. Paul Stock Found. grant, 1962. Mem. AICPA, Colo. Soc. CPA's, Nat. Assn. Cert. Valuation Analysts. Office: 317 E San Rafael St Colorado Springs CO 80903-2405

WHEELER, MALCOLM EDWARD, lawyer, law educator; b. Berkeley, Calif., Nov. 29, 1944; s. Malcolm Ross and Frances Dolores (Kane) W.; m. Donna Marie Stambaugh, July 25, 1981; children: Jessica Ross, M. Connor. SB, MIT, 1966; JD, Stanford U., 1969. Bar: Calif. 1970, Colo. 1992, U.S. Dist. Ct (cen. dist.) Calif. 1970, U.S. Ct. Appeals (9th cir.) 1970, U.S. Ct. Appeals (10th cir.) 1973, U.S. Dist. Ct. (no., so., ea. and cen. dists.) Calif. 1975, U.S. Ct. Appeals (11th cir.) 1987, U.S. Ct. Appeals (D.C. cir.) 1987, U.S. Supreme Ct. 1976, U.S. Ct. Appeals (3d cir.) 1989, (4th cir.) 1992, (8th cir.) 1993, (5th cir.) 1995, (Fed. cir.) 1998. Assoc. Howard, Prim, Smith, Rice & Downs, San Francisco, 1969-71; assoc. prof. law U. Kans., Lawrence, 1971-74; assoc. Hughes Hubbard & Reed, Los Angeles, 1974-77, ptnr., 1977-81, 83-85, cons., 1981-83; ptnr. Skadden, Arps, Slate, Meagher & Flom, Los Angeles, 1985-91; dir. Parcel, Mauro, Hultin & Spaanstra P.C., Denver, 1991-98, Wheeler Trigg & Kennedy, P.C., Denver, 1998—. Vis. prof. U. Iowa, 1978, prof., 1979; prof. U. Kans., Lawrence, 1981-83; chief counsel U.S. Senate Select Com. to Study Law Enforcement Undercover Activities, Washington, 1982-83. Mem. editorial bd. Jour. Products Liability, 1984—; bd. editors Fed. Litigation Guide Reporter, 1986—; contbr. articles to profl. jours. Mem. ABA, Calif. Bar Assn., Colo. Bar Assn., Am. Law Inst. Home: 100 Humboldt St Denver CO 80218-3932

WHEELER, RALPH I. (MOON), state legislator, pharmacist; b. American Falls, Idaho, Aug. 10, 1932; s. Ralph Merrill and Monne Mary (Zemo) W.; m. Patricia J. Howard (dec.); children: Vickie D., Michael M., Jodi L.; m. Ann F. Reed, June 19, 1965; children: Clark R., Ryan M. BS, Idaho State U., 1954. Registered pharmacist. Owner Rockland Pharmacy, 1960-88, part-time staff, 1988-90; mem. Idaho Senate, Dist. 35, Boise, 1994—; commissioner Power County, 1982-94; mem. Idaho Ho. of Reps., 1973-76; mayor American Falls, Idaho, 1965-72; city councilman American Falls, 1957-1965. Pres. Assn. Idaho Cities, Boise, 1971-72, Idaho State Pharmaceutical Assn., 1979-80. Pres. Lion's Club, American Falls, 1962; rep. State Legis. Boise, Idaho, 1972-76; county commr. Power County, American Falls, 1982-94; senator State of Idaho, 1994—, vice chair local govt. and taxation com. Named Pharmacist of Yr., Idaho Pharmaceutical Assn., 1972. Mem. Legislative Chair, Idaho Assoc. of Counties, 1987-90; pres., Idaho Pharmacy Assoc., 1970, pres., Assoc. Idaho Cities, 1971-72, Chamber of Commerce, Lion's Club. Republican. Roman Catholic. Avocations: fly fishing, fly tying, rafting, current events. Home: 659 Gifford Ave American Falls ID 83211-1315 Office: State Capitol PO Box 83720 Boise ID 83720-3720

WHEELER, RAYMOND LOUIS, lawyer; b. Ft. Sill, Okla., Feb. 10, 1945; s. Raymond Louis and Dorothy Marie (Hutcherson) W.; m. Priscilla Wheeler, July 1, 1966 (div. 1982); children: Jennifer, Hilary; m. Cynthia Lee Jackson, July 14, 1984 (div. 1994); children: Matthew Raymond, Madeline Elizabeth; m. Freddie Kay Park, June 10, 1995. BA, U. Tex., 1967; JD, Harvard U., 1970. Bar: Calif. 1972, U.S. Dist. Ct. (no., cen., ea. dists.) Calif., U.S. Ct. Appeals (9th cir.), U.S. Supreme Ct. Law clk. to hon. Irving L. Goldberg U.S. Ct. Appeals 5th cir., 1970-71; assoc. Morrison & Foerster, San Francisco, 1971-76, ptnr., 1976-90, Palo Alto, Calif., 1990—. Chmn. labor and employment law dept. Morrison & Foerster, San Francisco, 1984-88, 92—; lectr. labor and EEO law. Exec. editor Harvard Law Rev., 1969-70; editor in chief The Developing Labor Law; mem. nat. adv. bd. Indsl. Rels. Law Jour., 1980—; contbr. articles to law jours. Fellow Coll. Labor and Employment Lawyers; mem. ABA (chmn. com. on law devel. under labor rels. act 1990-93, coun. mem. sect. labor and employment 1994—). Republican. Office: Morrison & Foerster 755 Page Mill Rd Palo Alto CA 94304-1018 E-mail: rwheeler@mofo.com

WHEELER, STEPHEN FREDERICK, legal administration; BA in Polit. Sci., Mt. Union Coll., Alliance, Ohio, 1968; MS in Adminstrn. of Justice, Am. U., 1974. Probation officer 19th Dist. Juvenile and Domestic Rels. Ct. Prince William County, Manassas, Va., 1972-75; ct. systems planner Office of Jud. Planning Ky. Jud. Coun., Frankfort, 1975-76; co-dir. Ky. pretrial svcs. Adminstrv. Office of Cts. Ky. Ct. of Justice, Frankfort, 1976-81; ct. adminstr. Jud. Dist. 27A, Gastonia, N.C., 1982-87, Colorado Springs (Colo.) Mcpl. Ct., 1987—. Ct. systems cons. Nat. Criminal Justice Collaborative, Sea Island, Ga., 1981-85. Office: City of Colorado Springs Mcpl Ct PO Box 2169 Colorado Springs CO 80901-2169 E-mail: swheeler@ci.colospgs.co.us

WHEELER, STEVEN M. lawyer; b. Evanston, Ill., Jan. 5, 1949; AB, Pricneton U., 1971; JD with distinction, Cornell U., 1974. Bar: Ariz. 1974. Mem. Snell & Wilmer, Phoenix, ptnr., 1980—. Mng. editor Cornell Law Review, 1973-74; contbr. articles to profl. jours. Mem. ABA, Order Coif, Phi Kappa Phi. Office: Snell & Wilmer 1 Arizona Ctr Phoenix AZ 85004-0001

WHEELER, WILLIAM ROY, technical advisor; b. Sept. 24, 1923; Sr. tech. advisor KLA-TENCOR, Milpitas, Calif., 1976—. Recipient Albert Nerken award Am. Vacuum Soc., 1996. Office: KLA-TENCOR 1 Technology Dr Milpitas CA 95035-7916

WHEELON, ALBERT DEWELL, physicist; b. Moline, Ill., Jan. 18, 1929; s. Orville Albert and Alice Geltz (Dewell) W.; m. Nancy Helen Hermanson, Feb. 28, 1953 (dec. May 1980); children: Elizabeth Anne, Cynthia Helen; m. Cicely J. Evans, Feb. 4, 1984. B.Sc., Stanford U., 1949; Ph.D., Mass. Inst. Tech., 1952. Teaching fellow, then rsch. assoc. physics MIT, Boston, 1949-52; with Douglas Aircraft Co., 1952-53, Ramo-Wooldridge Corp., 1953-62; dep. dir. sci. and tech. CIA, Washington, 1962-66; with Hughes Aircraft Co., L.A., 1966-88, chmn., chief exec. officer, 1987-88. Vis. prof. MIT, 1989; mem. Def. Sci. Bd., 1968-76; mem. Pres.'s Fgn. Intelligence, 1983-88; mem. Presdl. Commn. on Space Shuttle Challenger Accident, 1986; trustee Aerospace Corp., 1990-93, Calif. Inst. Tech., Rand Corp., 1993-2001. Author Electromagnetic Scintillation: Vol. 1 and 2, 2001; contbr. 30 papers on radiowave propagation and guidance systems. Recipient R.V. Jones Intelligence award, 1994. Fellow IEEE, AIAA (Von Karman medal 1986, Goddard Astronautics award 1997), Am. Phys. Soc.; mem. NAE, Sigma Chi. Episcopalian. Independent. Address: 181 Sheffield Dr Montecito CA 93108-2242

WHELAN, JOHN WILLIAM, lawyer, law educator, consultant; b. Cleve., Apr. 23, 1922; s. Walter Edmund and Stacia Miriam W.; m. Maryrose Shields, May 29, 1947; children: Moira Ann Whelan Dykstra, Thomas M. AB, John Carroll U., 1943; JD, Georgetown U., 1948. Assoc. prof. law Columbus U., Washington, 1948-50; asst. prof. law U. Va., Charlottesville, 1955-56; asso. prof. law U. Wis., Madison, 1956-59; prof. law Georgetown U., Washington, 1959-67, U. Calif., Davis, 1967-75, Hastings Coll. Law U. Calif., San Francisco, 1975-91; prof. emeritus Hasting Coll. Law U. Calif., San Francisco, 1991—. Vis. prof. Nihon U. Coll. Law, Tokyo, summer 1989; cons. to atty. gen. Trust Ty. Pacific Islands, 1976-78; mem. atomic energy com. Bd. Contract Appeals, 1965-73; hearing examiner Medi-Cal Fiscal Intermediary Contract, 1979-82; adminstrn. law judge constrn. contracts Trust Ter. Pacific Island, 1984-86; cons. on govt. contracts to Polish govt., 1992. Author: (with R.S. Pasley) Federal Government Contracts, 1975; (with K.H. York) Insurance, 1983, 2d edit., 1988, Federal Government Contracts, 1985, Supplement, 1989, Understanding Government Contracts, 1994; (with K.H. York, Leo Martinez) Insurance, 4th edit., 2001; editor: Yearbook of Procurement Articles, 1965-90; mem. editl. bd. Pub. Procurement Law Rev. (U.K. pub.), 1991—; contbr. articles to profl. jours. Served with inf. AUS, 1943-45; served with J.A.G., 1950-55, Decorated Bronze Star; Ford Found. grantee, 1958-59, 63-64, summer 1970 Mem. ABA, Fed. Bar Assn., D.C. Bar Assn., Nat. Contract Mgmt. Assn., Bds. of Contract Bar Assn., Fed. Cir. Bar Assn. Home: 306 Bristol Pl Mill Valley CA 94941-4005 Office: U Calif Hastings Coll Law 200 Mcallister St San Francisco CA 94102-4707

WHETTEN, JOHN D. food products executive; b. Chgo., June 8, 1940; s. Lester and Kate (Allred) W.; m. Becky Pearse; children: Carma, Rebecca, Mary Coza. BS, Brigham Young U., 1965; MBA, U. Calif., Berkeley, 1967. Advt. and mktg. mgr. The Clorox Corp., Oakland, Calif., 1967-79; pres., CEO Challenge Dairy Products, Inc., Dublin, 1982—; CEO DairyAmerica, Inc., Dublin, 1995-98. U.S. rep. Internat. Dairy Mktg. and Promotion Ann. Meeting, 1996. Co-chair U.S. Butter Task Force, 1990-97; bd. dirs. U.S. Diry Export Coun., 1995-98, Epidermolysis Bullosa Med. Rsch. Found., 1991—; mem. nat. steering com. Brigham Young U. Sch. Mgmt., 1992-95. Mem. Am. Butter Inst. (bd. dirs. 1982—, v.p. 1995-99, pres. 1999—, Pres.'s Disting. Svc. award 1991), Am. Dairy Products Inst. (bd. dirs. 1982-98, hon. life dir. 1999—), Dairy Export Incentive Program Coalition (pres. 1994—), Dairy Mktg. Coop. Fedn. (pres. 1992—), Barbecue Industry Assn. (dir. 1974-79, pres. 1977-78), Western Assn. Milk Mktg. Coop. (bd. dirs. 1992—, sec. 1994—). Office: Challenge Dairy Products Inc 11875 Dublin Blvd Ste B230 Dublin CA 94568-2818 E-mail: john@challengedairy.com

WHETTEN, JOHN THEODORE, geologist, researcher; b. Willimantic, Conn., Mar. 16, 1935; s. Nathan Laselle and Theora Lucille (Johnson) W.; m. Carol Annette Jacobsen, July 14, 1960; children— Andrea, Krista, Michelle. AB with high honors, Princeton U., 1957, PhD, 1962; MS, U. Calif., Berkeley, 1959. Mem. faculty U. Wash., Seattle, 1963-81, research instr. oceanography, 1963-64, asst. prof., 1964-68, assoc. prof., 1968-72, prof. geol. scis. and oceanography, 1972-81, chmn. dept. geol. scis., 1969-74; assoc. dean Grad. Sch., 1968-69; geologist U.S. Geol. Survey, Seattle, 1975-80; asst. div. leader geoscis. div. Los Alamos Nat. Lab., 1980-81, dep. div. leader earth and space scis. div., 1981-84, div. leader earth and space scis. div., 1984-86, assoc. dir. energy and tech., 1986-92, assoc. dir. quality, policy and performance, 1992-93; lab. affiliate, 1994—; cons. in nat. lab. partnerships and tech. transfer Motorola Corp., 1994-97; sr. cons. Motorola U., 1998-2001, Motorola Labs, 2001—. Mem. adv. com. Pacific N.W. Nat.. Lab., 1999—. Contbr. articles to profl. jours. Fulbright fellow, 1962-63 Home and Office: 381 Kings Point Rd Lopez Island WA 98261-8223 E-mail: john.whetten@motorola.com

WHINNERY, JOHN ROY, electrical engineering educator; b. Read, Colo., July 26, 1916; s. Ralph V. and Edith Mable (Bent) W.; m. Patricia Barry, Sept. 17, 1944; children— Carol Joanne, Catherine, Barbara. B.S. in Elec. Engring, U. Calif. at Berkeley, 1937, Ph.D., 1948. With GE, 1937-46; part-time lectr. Union Coll., Schenectady, 1945-46; asso. prof. elec. engring. U. Calif., Berkeley, 1946-52, prof., vice chmn. div. elec. engring., 1952-56, chmn., 1956-59, dean Coll. Engring., 1959-63, prof. elec. engring., 1963-80, Univ. prof. Coll. Engring., 1980—. Vis. mem. tech. staff. Bell Telephone Labs., 1963-64; research sci. electron tubes Hughes Aircraft Co., Culver City, 1951-52; disting. lectr. IEEE Microwave Theory and Technique Soc., 1989-92. Author: (with Simon Ramo) Fields and Waves in Modern Radio, 1944, 3d edit. (with Ramo and Van Duzar), 1994, (with D.O. Pederson and J.J. Studer) Introduction to Electronic Systems, Circuits and Devices; also tech. articles. Chmn. Commn. Engring. Edn., 1966-68; mem. sci. and tech. com. Manned Space Flight, NASA, 1963-69; mem. Pres.'s Com. on Nat. Sci. Medal, 1970-73, 79-80; standing com. controlled thermonuclear research AEC, 1970-73. Recipient Lamme medal Am. Soc. Engring. Edn., 1975, Centennial medal, 1993, Engring. Alumni award U. Calif.-Berkeley, 1980, Nat. Medal of Sci. NSF, 1992; named to Hall of Fame Modesto High Sch. (Calif.), 1983, ASEE Hall of Fame, 1993.; Guggenheim fellow, 1959. Fellow IRE (bd. dirs. 1956-59), IEEE (life, bd. dirs. 1969-71, sec. 1971, Edn. medal 1967, Centennial medal 1984, Medal of Honor 1985), Optical Soc. Am., Am. Acad. Arts and Scis.; mem. NAS, NAE (Founders award 1986), IEEE Microwave Theory and Techniques Soc. (Microwave Career award 1977, Okawa prize in info. and telecomm. 1997), Phi Beta Kappa, Sigma Xi, Tau Beta Pi, Eta Kappa Nu (eminent mem.). Congregationalist. Home: 1804 Wales Dr Walnut Creek CA 94595-2472 Office: U Calif Dept Elect Engring Berkeley CA 94720-1770

WHINSTON, ARTHUR LEWIS, lawyer; b. N.Y.C., Feb. 5, 1925; s. Charles Nathaniel and Charlotte (Nalen) W.; m. Melicent Ames Kingsbury, Mar. 19, 1949; children: Ann Kingsbury, James Pierce, Melicent Ames, Louise Ellen, Patricia Kingsbury. B.C.E., Cornell U., 1945; M.S.E., Princeton U., 1947; J.D., N.Y. U., 1957. Bar: N.Y. 1957, Oreg. 1964, U.S. Supreme Ct 1966, U.S. Patent Office 1958, U.S. Ct. Appeals (fed. cir.) 1959; registered profl. engr., N.Y., Oreg. Engr. Chas. N. & Selig Whinston, N.Y.C., 1947-50; lectr. Coll. City N.Y., 1950-51; structures engr. Republic Aviation Corp., Farmingdale, N.Y., 1951-57; practice in N.Y.C., 1957-64, Portland, Oreg., 1964—; patent lawyer Arthur, Dry & Kalish, 1957-64; partner Klarquist, Sparkman, Campbell, Leigh & Whinston, 1964—; chmn. Oreg. Bar com. on patent, trademark and copyright law, 1968-69, 77-78, mem. com. unauthorized practice law, 1970-73, chmn., 1972-73, com. on [illegible]ility, 1977-78. Served to ensign USNR, 1943-46. Recipient Fuertes medal Cornell U. Sch. Civil Engring., 1945 Mem. ABA, Oreg. Bar Assn., N.Y. Bar Assn., Multnomah County Bar Assn., Am. Intellectual Property Law Assn., N.Y. Intellectual Property Law Assn., Oreg. Patent Law Assn. (pres. 1977-78), Profl. Engrs. Oreg. (past state legis. chmn.), Sigma Xi, Chi Epsilon, Phi Kappa Phi. Republican. Unitarian. Club: Multnomah Athletic. Home: 3824 SW 50th Ave Portland OR 97221-2112 Office: One World Trade Ctr Ste 1600 Portland OR 97204

WHISENHUNT, DONALD WAYNE, history educator; b. Meadow, Tex., May 16, 1938; s. William Alexander Whisenhunt and Beulah (Johnson) King; m. Betsy Ann Baker, Aug. 27, 1960; children: Donald Wayne Jr., William Benton. BA, McMurry Coll., 1960; MA, Tex. Tech U., 1962, PhD, 1966. Tchr. Elida (N.Mex.) High Sch., 1961-63; from asst. to assoc. prof. history Murray (Ky.) State U., 1966-69; assoc. prof., chmn. dept. Thiel Coll., Greenville, Pa., 1969-73; Dean Sch. Liberal Arts and Scis., Ea. N.Mex. U., Portales, 1973-77; v.p. acad. affairs U. Tex., Tyler, 1977-83; v.p., provost Wayne (Nebr.) State Coll., 1983-91, interim pres., 1985; prof. history, chmn. dept. Western Wash. U., Bellingham, 1991—. Fulbright lectr. Peoples Republic of China, 1995. Author: Environment and American Experience, 1974, Depression in the Southwest, 1979, Chronological History of Texas, Vol. 1, 1982, Vol.2, 1987, Texas: Sesquicentennial Celebration, 1984; editor: Encyclopedia USA, 1988—, Poetry of the People: Poems to the President, 1929-1945, 1996, Tent Show: Arthur Names and His Famous Players, 2000, It Seems to Me: Selected Letters of Eleanor Roosevelt, 2001. Democrat. Methodist. Office: Western Wash U Dept History Bellingham WA 98225

WHISLER, JAMES STEVEN, lawyer, mining and manufacturing executive; b. Centerville, Iowa, Nov. 23, 1954; s. James Thomas and Betty Lou (Clark) W.; m. Ardyce Dawn Christensen, Jan. 20, 1979; children: James Kyle, Kristen Elyse. BS, U. Colo., Boulder, 1975; JD, U. Denver, 1978; MS, Colo. Sch. Mines, Golden, 1984, DSc (hon.), 2001; AMP, Harvard Bus. Sch., 1998; DEng (hon.), Colo. Sch. Mines, Golden, 2001. Bar: Colo. 1978; CPA, Ariz. Assoc. gen. counsel, sec. Western Nuclear, Inc., Denver, 1979-81; exploration counsel Phelps Dodge Corp., N.Y.C., 1981-85, legal and adminstrv. mgr. Phoenix, 1985-87, v.p., gen. counsel, 1987-88, sr. v.p., gen. counsel, 1988-91; pres. Phelps Dodge Mining Co., 1991-98; pres., COO Phelps Dodge Corp., Phoenix, 1997-99, chmn., pres., CEO, 2000—. Bd. dirs. Phelps Dodge Corp., Burlington No. Santa Fe Corp., So. Peru Copper Corp., Am. West Holdings Corp., Copper Devel. Assn., Internat. Copper Assn., Nat. Mining Assn.; mem. Bus. Roundtable. Trustee Heard Mus., Phoenix, 1989-94, Rocky Mountain Mineral Law Found., 1989-92; mem. Dean's Coun. of 100, Ariz. State U., 1992—; mem. nat. bd. advs. Coll. Bus. and Pub. Adminstrn., U. Ariz., 1992-97; bd. dirs. Met. Phoenix YMCA, 1989-92, Copper Bowl Found., Tucson, 1990-91, Ariz. Town Hall, 1991-96, Greater Phoenix Leadership, 1999-2001, We. Regional Coun., 1991-99, Mont. Tech. Found., 1996-2000. Mem. AICPA, AIME, Soc. Mining Engrs., Colo. Bar Assn., Phoenix Country Club, Sky Club, Mining and Metallurgical Soc. of Am. Office: Phelps Dodge Corp 2600 N Central Ave Phoenix AZ 85004-3050

WHITE, BETTY, actress, comedienne; b. Oak Park, Ill., Jan. 17, 1922; m. Allen Ludden, 1963 (dec.). Student pub. schs., Beverly Hills, Calif. Appearances on radio shows This Is Your FBI, Blondie, The Great Gildersleeve; actress: (TV series) including Hollywood on Television, The Betty White Show, 1954-58, Life With Elizabeth, 1953-55, A Date With The Angels, 1957-58, The Pet Set, 1971, Mary Tyler Moore Show, 1974-77, The Betty White Show, 1977, The Golden Girls, 1985-92 (Emmy award for best actress 1986), The Golden Palace, 1992-93, Maybe This Time, 1995—, The Story of Santa Claus, 1996, A Weekend in the Country, 1996; (TV miniseries) The Best Place to be, 1979, The Gossip Columnist, 1980, (films) Advise and Consent, 1962, Dennis the Menace 2, 1998, Hard Rain, 1998 ; guest appearances on other programs; summer stock appearances Guys and Dolls, Take Me Along, The King and I, Who Was That Lady?, Critic's Choice, Bells are Ringing. Recipient Emmy award NATAS, 1975, 76, 86; L.A. Area Emmy award, 1952. Mem. AFTRA, Am. Humane Assn., Greater L.A. Zoo Assn. (dir.). Office: c/o William Morris Agy Betty Fanning 151 S El Camino Dr Beverly Hills CA 90212-2704

WHITE, BEVERLY JANE, cytogeneticist; b. Seattle, Oct. 9, 1938; Grad., U. Wash., 1959, MD, 1963. Diplomate Nat. Bd. Med. Examiners, Am. Bd. Pediatrics, Am. Bd. Med. Genetics; lic physician and surgeon, Wash., N.J., Calif. Rsch. trainee dept. anatomy Sch. Medicine U. Wash., Seattle, 1960-62, pediatric resident dept. pediatrics, 1967-69; rotating intern Phila. Gen. Hosp., 1963-64; rsch. fellow med. ob-gyn. unit Cardiovascular Rsch. Inst. U. Calif. Med. Ctr., San Francisco, 1964-65; staff fellow lab. biomed. scis. Nat. Inst. Child Health and Human Devel. NIH, Bethesda, Md., 1965-67, sr. staff fellow, attending physician lab. exptl. pathology Nat. Inst. Arthritis, Metabolism and Digestive Diseases, 1969-74, acting chief sect. cytogenetics, 1975-76, rsch. med. officer, attending physician sect. cytogenetics lab. cellular biology and genetics, 1974-86, dir. cytogenetics unit, interinstitute med. genetics program clin. ctr., 1987-95; dir. cytogenetics Corning Clin. Labs., Teterboro, N.J., 1995-96; assoc. med. dir. cytogenetics Nichols Inst.-Quest Diagnostics, San Juan Capistrano, Calif., 1996-97, med. dir. cytogenetics, 1998-2000, med. dir. genetics, 2000—. Vis. scientist dept. pediat. divsn. genetics U. Wash. Sch. Medicine, 1983-84; intramural cons. NIH, 1975-95; cons. to assoc. editor Jour. Nat. Cancer Inst., 1976; cons. dept. ob-gyn. Naval Hosp., Bethesda, 1988-89; lectr., presenter in field. Recipient Mosby Book award, 1963, Women of Excellence award U. Wash. and Seattle Profl. chpt. Women in Comm., 1959, Reuben award Am. Soc. for Study Sterility, 1963. Fellow Am. Coll. Med. Genetics (founding), Am. Acad. Pediatrics; mem. AMA. Am. Soc. Human Genetics, Assn. Genetic Technologists (program com. 1989). Home: One St Maxime Laguna Niguel CA 92677 Office: Nichols Inst Quest Diagnostics Inc Dept Cytogenetics San Juan Capistrano CA 92690-6130 E-mail: bjwsur@aol.com

WHITE, BONNIE YVONNE, management consultant, retired educator; b. Long Beach, Calif., Sept. 4, 1940; d. William Albert and Helen Iris (Harbaugh) W. BS, Brigham Young U., 1962, MS, 1965, EdD in Ednl. Adminstrn., 1976; postgrad., Harvard U., 1987. Tchr. Wilson High Sch., Long Beach, Calif., 1962-63; grad. asst. Brigham Young U., Provo, Utah, 1963-65; instr., dir. West Valley Coll., Saratoga, Calif., 1965-76; instr., evening adminstr. Mission Coll., Santa Clara, 1976-80; dean gen. edn. Mendocino Coll., Ukiah, 1980-85; dean instrn. Porterville (Calif.) Coll., 1985-89, dean adminstrv. svc., 1989-93. Rsch. assoc. SAGE Rsch. Internat., Orem, Utah, 1975-99. Mem. AAUW, Faculty Assn. Calif., Cmty. Colls., Calif., Coun. Fine Arts Deans, Assn. Calif. C.C. Adminstrs., Assn. Calif. C.C. Adminstrs. Liberal Arts, Zonta (intern), Soroptimists (intern). Republican. Mem. LDS Ch.

WHITE, BRITTAN ROMEO, manufacturing company executive; b. N.Y.C., Feb. 13, 1936; s. Brittan R. and Matilda H. (Baumann) W.; m. Esther D. Friederich, Aug. 25, 1958 (dec. May 1981); children: Cynthia E., Brittan R. VII; m. Peggy A. Lee, Aug. 30, 1990. BSChemE, Drexel U., 1958; MBA, Lehigh U., 1967; JD, Loyola U., Los Angeles, 1974; MA, Pepperdine U., 1985. Bar: Calif., U.S. Dist. Ct. Calif.; registered profl. engr., Calif. Process engr. Air Reduction Co., Bound Brook, N.J., 1958-64; area supr. J.T. Baker Chem. Co., Phillipsburg, 1964-66; asst. plant mgr. Gamma Chem. Co., Great Meadows, 1966-69; plant mgr. Maquite Corp., Elizabeth, 1969-70; purchasing mgr. Atlantic Richfield Co., Los Angeles, 1970-79; dir. mfg. Imperial Oil, Los Angeles, 1979-82; mgr. chem. mgmt. program Hughes Aircraft Co., Los Angeles, 1982-94; pres. The Crawford Group, 1994—. Bd. dirs. Diversified Resource Devel. Inc., Los Angeles, 1979—; seminar moderator and speaker Energy Conservation Seminars 1979-83. Editor Rottweiler Rev., 1979-81; chief award judge Chem. Processing mag., 1976, 78, 80; contbr. articles to profl. jours. Vice chmn. Bd. Zoning and Adjustment, Flemington, N.J., 1970-72; pres. bd. dirs.

Homeowners' Assn., Palm Springs, Calif., 1983-90, Prescott, Ariz., 1997—; vice chmn. State Legis. Com., 1998—; mem. indsl. adv. com. sci., tech. and globalization program Embry-Riddle Aeronaut. U., 1998—. Capt. C.E., U.S. Army, 1958-60, res., 1960-68. Mem. ABA, Am. Inst. Chem. Engrs., Am. Chem. Soc., Mensa, Psi Chi. Republican. Lodge: Elks. Avocations: antiques, show dogs, psychology. Home: 1091 Pine Country Ct Prescott AZ 86303-6403 Office: The Crawford Group PO Box 3020 Prescott AZ 86302-3020 E-mail: bpwhite@msn.com

WHITE, DEVON MARKES, professional baseball player; b. Kingston, Jamaica, Dec. 29, 1962; With Calif. Angels, 1981-90, Toronto Blue Jays, 1990-95, Florida Marlins, Miami, 1996—; outfielder Los Angeles Dodgers, 1998-. Player Am. League All Star Team, 1989, 93. Recipient Gold Glove award, 1988-89, 91-94; named Am. League leader put outs by outfielder, 1987, 91-92. Office: Los Angeles Dodgers 1000 Elysian Park Ave Los Angeles CA 90012-1199

WHITE, DON WILLIAM, rancher, minister; b. Santa Rita, N.Mex., June 27, 1942; s. Thomas Melvin and Barbara (Smith) W.; m. Jacqueline Diane Bufkin, June 12, 1965; children: Don William Jr., David Wayne. BBA, Western N.Mex. U., 1974, MBA, 1977. Field acct. Stearns Roger Corp., Denver, 1967-70; controller, adminstrv. mgr. USNR Mining and Minerals Inc., Silver City, N.Mex., 1970-72; devel. specialist County of Grant, Silver City, 1973-77; divisional controller Molycorp. Inc., Taos, N.Mex., 1977-78; mgr. project adminstrn. Kennecott Minerals Co., Hurley, 1978-83; sr. v.p. Sunwest Bank Grant County, Silver City, 1983-84, exec. v.p., 1984-85, pres., chief exec. officer, 1985-97; rancher Deming, 1997—; pastor Berean New Bapt. Ch. Bd. dirs. Bank of Grant County. Bd. dirs. Sunwest Bank of Grant County, Silver City/Grant County Econ. Devel., 1983—; councilman Town of Silver City, 1977; chmn. Dems. for Senator Pete Domenici, 1986; pres. Gila Regional Med. Found., 1989-92; pres. SWNM Econ. Devel. Corp., 1984-2000; trustee Indian Hills Bapt. Ch., 1988-89; chmn. State of N.Mex. Small Bus. Adv. Coun.; vice chmn. vocat. edn. adv. com. Western N.Mex. U., 1989; mem. Silver Schs.-Sch./Bus. Partnership Coun. Named Outstanding Vol., Silver City/Grant County Econ. Devel., 1987, 94, FFA, 1985, Western N.Mex. U. Outstanding Alumni, 1998. Mem. Am. Bankers Assn., N.Mex. Bankers Assn., Bank Adminstrn. Inst., Assn. Commerce and Industry (bd. dirs. 1988-91), N.Mex. Mining Assn. (assoc.), Rotary (past pres., dist. gov. rep.). Avocations: snow skiing, water skiing, hunting, fishing, golf. Office: 12025 Dwyer Rd NW Deming NM 88031

WHITE, DOUGLAS JAMES, JR. lawyer; b. N.Y.C., Mar. 20, 1934; s. Douglas James and Margaret (Stillman) W.; m. Denise Beale, May 28, 1960; children: Brian Douglas, James Roderick. BA, U. Oreg., 1955; LLB, Willamette U., 1958. Bar: Oreg. 1958. Law clk. to assoc. justice Oreg. Supreme Ct., Salem, 1958-59; assoc. Schwabe, Williamson & Wyatt (formerly known as Mautz, Souther, Spaulding, Kinsey & Williamson), Portland, Oreg., 1959-69; shareholder, gen. ptnr. Schwabe, Williamson & Wyatt, P.C. (formerly known as Schwabe, Williamson, Wyatt, Moore & Roberts), Portland, 1969-79, sr. ptnr., 1979-93; shareholder, 1994-98; of counsel, 1999—. Bd. dirs. Portland Iron Works and Affiliates. Trustee Jesuit H.S., Beaverton, 1991-94; bd. dirs. St. Vincent de Paul Child Devel. Ctr., Portland, 1979-90, Portland Coun., Soc. St. Vincent de Paul, 1989-92, Portland House of Umoja, 1995—; bd. dirs., officer Maryville Nursing Home, Beaverton, 1993-99, St. Vincent de Paul Conf. of St. Thomas More, Portland, 1966—; active Saturday Acad. Beaverton, 1982—. Mem. ABA, Oreg. State Bar Assn. (real estate and land use sect. exec. com. 1984-85), Multnomah Athletic Club (Portland), Flyfisher Club of Oreg. Republican. Roman Catholic. Avocations: fly-fishing, cross-country skiing, bridge, hiking. Home: 6725 SW Preslynn Dr Portland OR 97225-2668 Office: Schwabe Williamson & Wyatt 1211 SW 5th Ave Ste 1700 Portland OR 97204-3713

WHITE, DOUGLAS RICHIE, anthropology educator; b. Mpls., Mar. 13, 1942; s. Asher Abbott and Margaret McQuestin (Richie) W.; m. Jayne Chamberlain (div. Feb. 1971); m. Lilyan Amdur Brudner, Mar. 21, 1971; 1 child, Scott Douglas. BA, U. Minn., 1964, MA, 1967, PhD, 1969. Asst. prof. U. Pitts., 1967-72, assoc. prof., 1972-76, U. Calif., Irvine, 1976-79, prof., 1979—. Dep. dir. Lang. Attitudes Rsch. Project, Dublin, Ireland, 1971-73; vis. prof. U. Tex., Austin, 1974-75, Ecole des Hautes Etudes en Science Sociales, Paris, 1999-2001, Institut Nat. d'Etudes Démographique, 2000; chmn. Linkages: World Devel. Res. Coun., Md., 1986—, pres. 1986-90. Co-editor: Research Methods in Social Networks, 1989, Anthropology of Urban Environments, 1972, Kinship, Networks and Exchange, 1998; founder, gen. editor World Cultures Jour., 1985-90; author sci. software packages; contbr. articles to profl. jours. Fellow Ctr. for Advanced Studies, Western Behavioral Sci. Inst., La Jolla, Calif., 1981-84; recipient Sr. Scientist award Alexander von Humboldt Stiftung, Bonn, Germany, 1989-91, Bourse de Haute Niveau award Ministry of Rsch. and Tech., Paris, 1992. Mem. Social Sci. Computing Assn. (pres. elect 1991, pres. 1992), Santa Fe Inst. (mem. working groups 1999, 2000, 2001). Democrat. Home: 8633 Via Mallorca Unit C La Jolla CA 92037-2599 Office: U Calif School Social Sci Irvine CA 92697-0001

WHITE, EDWARD ALLEN, electronics company executive; b. Jan. 1, 1928; s. Joseph and Bessie (Allen) W.; m. Joan Dixon, Dec. 22, 1949 (div. Aug. 1978); children: Dixon Richard, Leslie Ann; m. Nancy Rhoads, Oct. 6, 1979. BS, Tufts U., 1947. Vice chmn. White Electronic Designs Corp., Phoenix, 1951—. Vice chmn. White Technology Inc., Phoenix, 1980-86; pres. Ariz. Digital Corp., Phoenix, 1975-91; chmn., CEO AHI, Inc., Ft. Wayne, Ind., 1970-88; pres. EBH Corp., Ft. Wayne, 1994—, Interactive Digital Corp., Phoenix, 1992—; mem. World Pres's. Orgn., Washington D.C., 1978—. Patentee in field. Bd. dirs. Gov.'s Coun. Children, Youth and Families, Phoenix, 1982-84, Planned Parenthood Fedn. Am., 1984-88; pres., bd. dirs. Planned Parenthood Ctrl. and No. Ariz., 1984-88; trustee Internat. House, N.Y.C., 1973-75, Tufts U., 1973-83. Recipient Horatio Alger award, 1962. Mem. Paradise Valley Country Club, Tau Beta Pi. Home: 5786 N Echo Canyon Cir Phoenix AZ 85018-1242 Office: White Electronic Designs Corp 3601 E University Dr Phoenix AZ 85034-7254 E-mail: ewhite@whiteedc.com

WHITE, GARY RICHARD, electrical engineer, plant operator; b. Detroit, Nov. 15, 1962; s. Thomas Richard and Davene (Reynolds) W. BSEE, Wayne State U., 1986. Electronics engr. U.S. Army Info. Sys. Engring. Command, Ft. Belvoir, Va., 1987-88, Ft. Shafter, Hawaii, 1988-92; elec. worker U.S. Navy Pub. Works Ctr., Pearl Harbor, 1992-96, plant operator helper, 1996—. Mem. IEEE, NRA, NSPE, Assn. Computing Machinery, Am. Assn. Individual Investors, Am. Mgmt. Assn. Avocations: weightlifting, hiking, hardware and software, rock concerts, movies. Office: PO Box 19055 Honolulu HI 96817-8055

WHITE, JAMES EDWARD, geophysicist, educator; b. Cherokee, Tex., May 10, 1918; s. William Cleburne and Willie (Carter) W.; m. Courtenay Brumby, Feb. 1, 1941; children: Rebecca White Vanderslice, Peter McDuffie, Margaret Marie White Jamleson, Courtenay White Forte. BA, U. Tex., 1940, MA, 1946; PhD, MIT, 1949. Dir. Underwater Sound Lab., MIT, Cambridge, 1941-45; scientist Def. Research Lab., Austin, Tex., 1945-46; research assoc. MIT, 1946-49; group leader, field research lab. Mobil Oil Co., Dallas, 1949-55; mgr. physics dept. Denver Research Center, Marathon Oil Co., 1955-69; v.p. Globe Universal Scis., Midland, Tex., 1969-71; adj. prof. dept. geophysics Colo. Sch. Mines, Golden, 1972-73, C.H. Green prof., 1976-87, prof. emeritus, 1986—; L.A. Nelson prof. U. Tex., El Paso, 1973-76. Esso vis. prof. U. Sydney, Australia, 1975; vis. prof. MIT, 1982, U. Tex.-Austin, 1985, Macquarie U., Sydney, 1988; del. U.S.-USSR geophysics exch. Dept. State, 1965; mem. bd. Am. Geol. Inst., 1972; mem. space applications bd. NAE, 1972-77; NAS exch. scientist US-USSR, Zagreb, Yugoslavia, 1973-74; del. conf. on oil exploration China Geophys. Soc.-Soc. Exploration Geophysicists, 1981; cons. world bank Chinese U. Devel. Project II, 1987. Author: Seismic Waves: Radiation, Transmission, Attenuation, 1965, Underground Sound: Application of Seismic Waves, 1983, (with R.L. Sengbush) Production Seismology, 1987, Seismic Wave Propagation: Collected Works of J.E. White, 2000; editor: Vertical Seismic Profiling (E.I. Galperin), 1974; contbr. articles to profl. jours.; patentee in field. Recipient Halliburton award, 1987, Kapitsa Gold medal Russian Acad. Natural Scis., 1996. Fellow Acoustical Soc. Am.; mem. NAE, Soc. Exploration Geophysicists (hon., Maurice Ewing medal 1986), Cosmos Club, Sigma Xi. Unitarian. Office: Colo Sch Mines Dept Geophysics Golden CO 80401

WHITE, LORAY BETTY, TV talk show host, writer, producer, singer, actress, director; b. Houston, Nov. 27, 1934; d. Harold White and Joyce Mae (Jenkins) Mills; m. Sammy Davis Jr., 1957 (div. 1958); 1 child, Deborah R. DeHart. Student, UCLA, 1948-50, 90-91, Nichiren Shoshu Acad., 1988-92; AA in Bus., Sayer Bus. Sch., 1970; study div. mem. dept. L.A., Soka U., Japan, 1970-86. Editor, entertainment writer L.A. Community New, 1970-81; exec. sec. guest rels. KNBC Prodns., Burbank, Calif., 1969-75; security specialist Xerox X10 Think Tank, L.A., 1975-80; exec. asst. Ralph Powell & Assocs., L.A., 1980-82; pres., owner, producer LBW & Assocs. Pub. Rels., L.A., 1980—; owner, producer, writer, host TV prodn. co. Pub. Pub. Rels., L.A., 1987—. Dir., producer L.B.W. Prodn. "Yesterday, Today, Tomorrow, L.A., 1981—; with CBS news dept./Bogey's Corner, The Vol. Brigade Corps, KCBS News, 1999. Actor: (films) Ten Commandments, 1956; singer: (films) The Jazz Review, 1960—65, (Broadway plays) Joy Ride, —. Vol. ARC, 1995, L.B.W. & Assocs., Ltd. Ann. Prodn. of Mother and Daughter of the Yr. Tribute, 1999, L.B.W. & Assocs., United Peace and Cultural Exch. Dinner and Awards Show, 1999; mem. Habitat for Humanity Internat, Nat. Com. Preserve Soc. Sec. and Medicare, 1998-99, Nat. Black Network Assn., AARP, So. Calif. Com. Sr. Citizens, re-elect Scott Wildmen Rep. campaign; mem. Com. to Reelect Ted McConkey to Burbank City Coun., 1999; bd. dirs. Chabmlee Found. of Calif., 1998-99; exec. prodr. The Fifth L.B.W. and Assocs. Internat. Ann. Achievement Awards Show, 1999. The Sixth L.B.W. and Assocs. Internat. Ann. Achievement Awards Show, 2000. Recipient Cert. of Honor, ARC, 1984, Internat. Orgn. Soka Gakkai Internat. of Japan, Cmty. Vols. of Am. award, 1994, Mother and Daughter of Yr. Tribune, 2000-01, 6th Internat. Achievement award L.B.W. and Assoc.; named Performer of Yr. Cardella Demillo, 1976-77. Mem. ARC (planning, mktg., prodn. event com. 1995), UCLA Alumni Assn., Lupus Found. Am. (So. Calif. chpt.), Nat. Fedn. Blind, Myohoji-Hokkeko Internat., Libr. of Congress Assocs. (charter). Buddhist. Avocations: singing, acting, TV writing and producing. E-mail: lbwbootsie@aol.com

WHITE, PATRICIA DENISE, dean, law educator; b. Syracuse, N.Y., July 8, 1949; d. Theodore C. and Kathleen (Cowles) Denise; m. Nicholas P. White, Feb. 20, 1971 (div. 1997); children: Olivia Lawrence, Alexander Cowles. BA, U. Mich., 1971, MA, JD, 1974. Bar: D.C. 1975, Mich. 1988, Utah 1995. Assoc. Steptoe & Johnson, Washington, 1975-76; vis. asst. prof. Coll. of Law U. Toledo, 1976-77; assoc. Caplin & Drysdale, Washington, 1977-79; asst. prof. Law Ctr. Georgetown U., 1979-84, assoc. prof. Law Ctr., 1985-88; vis. prof. Law Sch. U. Mich., Ann Arbor, 1988-94; prof. U. Utah, Salt Lake City, 1994-98; counsel Parson, Behle and Latimer, Salt Lake City, 1995-98; dean, prof. Ariz. State U. Coll. Law, 1999—. Counsel Bodman, Longley and Dahling, Detroit, Ann Arbor, 1990-95. Contbr. articles to profl. jours. Office: Ariz State U Coll Law McAllister & Orange Sts PO Box 877906 Tempe AZ 85287-7906

WHITE, RAYMOND LESLIE, geneticist; b. Orlando, Fla., Oct. 23, 1943; s. Lawrence and Marjorie White; m. Joan Palmer Distin, June 1, 1968; children: Juliette, Jeremy. BS in Microbiology, U. Oreg., 1965; PhD in Microbiology, MIT, 1971; postdoctoral studies, Stanford. Rsch. assoc., instr. MIT, Cambridge, 1971-72; postdoctoral fellow Sch. Medicine Stanford (Calif.) U., 1972-75; asst. prof. Dept. Microbiology U. Mass. Sch. Medicine, Worcester, 1975-78, assoc. prof. Dept. Microbiology, 1978-80; investigator Howard Hughes Med. Inst. U. Utah Med. Ctr., 1980-94; assoc. prof. Dept. Cellular, Viral and Molecular Biology U. Utah Sch. Medicine, 1980-84, co-chmn. Dept. Human Genetics, 1984-94, prof. Dept. Oncological Scis., 1985—; prof. Dept. of Human Genetics U. Utah Sch. of Medicine, 1985—; chmn. Dept. Oncological Scis. U. Utah Sch. Medicine, 1994—, dir. Huntsman Cancer Inst., 1994—; chief sci. officer DNA Scis., Inc., 2000—. Adv. coun. Nat. Deafness and Other Comm. Disorders, 1989-91, ad hoc mem. NIH Gen. Med. Sci. Inst. Coun., 1984, mem. NIH study sect., 1979-83. Consulting editor Jour. Clin. Investigation; subject area editor Genomics, 1987-90; contbr. articles to profl. jours. Woodrow Wilson fellow, 1965-66, NIH grad. fellow, 1966-71, Jane Coffins Childs Found. fellow, 1971-75; Nat. Cancer Inst. Cancer Ctr. Support grantee, 1995—, U.S. Army Med. Rsch. grantee, 1994—; recipient Sword Hope award Am. Cancer Soc., 1995, Lewis S. Rosenstiel award Disting. Work Basic Med. Scis., Brandeis U., 1992, Nat. Med. Rsch. award Nat. Health Coun., 1991, Friedrich von Recklinghausen award Nat. Neurofibromatosis Found., 1990, Charles S. Mott prize Gen. Motors Cancer Rsch. Found., 1990. Mem. NAS, Am. Soc. Human Genetics (Allen Cancer Rsch. award 1989, assoc. editor Cancer Rsch.), Utah Acad. Scis. Achievements include the development of a new technology for mapping and ultimately identifying human genes causing disease and the discovery of fundamental genes and genetic mechanisms important in the inherited and cellular pathways to cancer. Avocations: sailing, biking, rafting, fishing, hiking. Office: DNA Scis Inc 6540 Kaiser Dr Fremont CA 94555-3613

WHITE, RICHARD CLARENCE, lawyer; b. Sioux City, Iowa, Oct. 31, 1933; m. Beverly Frances Fitzpatrick, Feb. 22, 1955; children— Anne, Richard, William, Christopher. B.A.; LL.B., Stanford U., 1962. Bar: Calif. 1963, U.S. Supreme Ct. 1970, N.Y. 1983. Assoc. O'Melveny & Myers, L.A., 1962-70, ptnr., 1970-94; lectr. in field. Bd. dirs. Equal Employment Adv. Coun., Washington, 1976-80, 83, Performing Arts Ctr. of Orange County 1983-86. Capt. USMC, 1954-59. Fellow Coll. Labor and Employment Lawyers (founding, bd. govs.); mem. ABA (co-chmn. com. on practice and procedure labor and employment law sect. 1977-80, mem. equal opportunity law com. 1980-85, co-chmn. com. on insts. and meetings 1985-87, coun. 1987-97).

WHITE, RICHARD MANNING, electrical engineering educator; b. Denver, Apr. 25, 1930; s. Rolland Manning and Freeda Blanche (Behny) W.; m. Chissie Lee Chamberlain, Feb. 1, 1964 (div. 1975); children: Rolland Kenneth, William Brendan. AB, Harvard U., 1951, AM, 1952, PhD in Applied Physics, 1956. Rsch. assoc. Harvard U., Cambridge, Mass., 1956; mem. tech. staff GE Microwave Lab., Palo Alto, Calif., 1956-63; prof. elec. engring. U. Calif., Berkeley, 1963—, Chancellor's prof., 1996-99. Chmn. Grad. Group on Sci. and Math. Edn., U. Calif. at Berkeley, 1981-85; co-dir. Berkeley Sensor and Actuator Ctr., 1986—, Co-author: Solar Cells: From Basics to Advanced Systems, Microsensors, 1991, Electrical Engineering Uncovered, 1997, Acoustic Wave Sensors, 1997; editor ElectroTechnology Rev.; patentee in field. Guggenheim fellow, 1968. Fellow AAAS, IEEE (Cledo Brunetto award 1986, Achievement award 1988, Disting. lectr. 1989, Cady award 2000); mem. Nat. Acad. Engring., Acoustical Soc. Am., Am. Phys. Soc., Phi Beta Kappa, Sigma Xi. Avocations: photography, hiking, skiing, running, music. Office: U Calif Sensor & Actuator Ctr Eecs Dept Ctr Berkeley CA 94720-0001

WHITE, RICK, lawyer, former congressman; b. Nov. 6, 1953; BA in Govt. and French, Dartmouth Coll., 1975; postgrad., Pantheon-Sorbonne; JD, Georgetown U., 1980. Mem. 104th to 105th Congresses from 1st Wash. dist., 1995-98; mem. house commerce com.; ptnr. Perkins Coie LLP, Seattle, 1999—. Founder Congl. Internet Caucus. Founder Books for Kids. Republican. Office: Perkins Coie LLP 1201 3d Ave Ste 4800 Seattle WA 98101-3099

WHITE, ROBERT C. air transportation executive; b. 1943; Student, Wake Forest U., 1961-65. With Procter & Gamble, Columbus, Ohio, 1971-73; asst. dir. Shreveport (La.) Airport Authority, 1973-75; airport mgr. Gainesville (Fla.) Regional Airport, 1975-78; dep. dir. aviation Jacksonville (Fla.) Port Authority, 1978-80; exec. dir. Peninsula Airport Commn., Newport News, Va., 1980-82; dir./cons. Lockheed Air Terminal, Burbank, Calif., 1982—; exec. dir. Reno Tahoe Internat. Airport, 1988—. With USN, 1966-71. Office: Reno Tahoe Internat Airport PO Box 12490 Reno NV 89510-2490

WHITE, ROBERT JOEL, lawyer; b. Chgo., Nov. 1, 1946; s. Melvin and Margaret (Hoffman) W.; m. Gail Janet Edenson, June 29, 1969 (div. Dec. 1982); m. Penelope K. Bloch, Dec. 22, 1985. BS in Accountancy, U. Ill., 1968; JD, U. Mich., 1972. Bar: Calif. 1972, N.Y. 1985, U.S. Dist. Ct. (cen., ea., so. dists.) Calif. 1972, U.S. Ct. Appeals (9th cir.) 1978, U.S. Ct. Appeals (5th cir.) 1983, U.S. Ct. Appeals (6th cir.) 1984, U.S. Supreme Ct. 1977. Staff auditor Haskin & Sells, Chgo., 1968-69; assoc. O'Melveny & Myers, L.A., 1972-79, ptnr., 1980-2001, chair reorgn. and restructuring dept., 1986—; CEO O'Melvey Cons. LLC, 2001—. Vis. lectr. U. Mich. Law Sch., Ann Arbor, 1986; lectr. Profl. Edn. Sys., Inc., Dallas, 1987, L.A., 1987, 89, Phoenix, 1990, Practicing Law Inst., San Francisco and N.Y.C., 1989-93, Southwestern Legal Found., Dalalas, 1991, UCLA Bankruptcy Inst., 1993, UCLA, 1993; mem. L.A. Productivity Commn., 1993-96. Contbr. articles to profl. jours. Active Constl. Rights Found., 1980—; active Am. Cancer Soc., 1989—, mem. L.A. bd. dirs., 1995—; mem. Nat. Bankruptcy Conf., exec. com., 1999—. Fellow Am. Coll. Brankruptcy; mem. ABA (litigation sect., mem. comml. law and bankruptcy com. 1972—), L.A. County Bar Assn. (comml. law and bankruptcy sect., chmn. fed. cts. com. 1981-82, exec. com. 1982—), Assn. Bus. Trial Lawyers (bd. govs. 1983-85), Fin. Lawyers Conf. (bd. govs. 1986—, pres. 1990-91), Am. Bankruptcy Inst. Avocations: skiing, running, U.S. history. Office: O'Melveny & Myers 400 S Hope St Los Angeles CA 90071-2899

WHITE, ROBERT LEE, electrical engineer, educator; b. Plainfield, N.J., Feb. 14, 1927; s. Claude and Ruby Hemsworth Emerson (Levick) W.; m. Phyllis Lillian Arlt, June 14, 1952; children: Lauren A., Kimberly A., Christopher L., Matthew P. BA in Physics, Columbia U., 1949, MA, 1951, PhD, 1954. Assoc. head atomic physics dept. Hughes Rsch. Labs., Malibu, Calif., 1954-61; head magnetics dept. Gen. Tel. and Electronics Rsch. Lab., Palo Alto, 1961-63; prof. elec. engring., materials sci. and engring. Stanford U., Palo Alto, 1963, chmn. elec. engring. dept., 1981-86, William E. Ayer prof. elec. engring., 1985-88; exec. dir. The Exploratorium, San Francisco, 1987-89; dir. Inst. for Electronics in Medicine, 1973-87, Stanford Ctr. for Rsch. on Info. Storage Materials, 1991—. Initial ltd. ptnr. Mayfield Fund, Mayfield II and Alpha II Fund, Rainbow Co-Investment Ptnrs., Halo Ptnrs.; vis. prof. Tokyo U., 1975; cons. in field. Author: (with K.A. Wickersheim) Magnetism and Magnetic Materials, 1965, Basic Quantum Mechanics, 1967; Contbr. numerous articles to profl. jours. With USN, 1945-46. Fellow Guggenheim Oxford U., 1969-70, Canton Hosp., Swiss Fed. Inst. Tech., Zurich, 1977-78, Christensen fellow Oxford U., 1986, IEEE Magnetics Soc. Disting. lectr., 1998; Sony sabbatical chair, 1994. Fellow Am. Phys. Soc., IEEE; mem. Sigma Xi, Phi Beta Kappa. Home: 450 El Escarpado Stanford CA 94305-8431 Office: Stanford U Dept Material Sci Engr Stanford CA 94305 E-mail: white@ee.stanford.edu

WHITE, ROBERT MILTON, lawyer; b. Tachikawa AFB, Japan, Oct. 10, 1948; came to U.S., 1948; s. Triggs Reeves and Josephine (Fowler) W. BA, U. N.Mex., 1970; JD, U. Houston, 1973. Bar: N.Mex. 1973, U.S. Dist. Ct. 1973, U.S. Ct. Appeals (10th cir.) 1996, U.S. Supreme Ct. 1996. Ptnr. Levy, White, Ferguson and Grady, Albuquerque, 1973-80, Lastrapes and White, Albuquerque, 1980-83; deputy dir. Dept. of Corrections City of Albuquerque, 1983-86; asst. city atty. City of Albuquerque, 1986-92; pvt. practice Albuquerque, 1992-93; city atty. City of Albuquerque. Bd. dirs. Quote-Unquote, Inc., 1984-89, New Art Connections, 1990—, Internat. Mcpl. Lawyers Assn., 1998—; mem. Hogares, Inc., 1983—, pres., 1990-92; mem. Med. Review Commn. State Bar of N.Mex., 1987. Mem. Albuquerque City Coun., 1979-83, pres. 1983, Nat. League of Cities, Wilmington, Del. (steering com. on transp. and communications), 1981-83, Arthritis Found. 1983-85. Mem. Internat. Mcpl. Lawyers Assn. (bd. dirs. 1998—), State Bar N.Mex. (prof. devel. com. 1994-96, task force on minorities in the bar 1997), N.Mex. Mcpl. Attys. (pres. 1994-95), Order of Barons, Phi Delta Phi. Democrat. Home: 1508 Princeton Dr SE Albuquerque NM 87106-3025 Office: PO Box 1293 Albuquerque NM 87103-1293

WHITE, ROBERT STEPHEN, physics educator; b. Ellsworth, Kans., Dec. 28, 1920; s. Byron F. and Sebina (Leighty) W.; m. Freda Marie Bridgewater, Aug. 30, 1942; children: Nancy Lynn, Margaret Diane, John Stephen, David Bruce. AB, Southwestern Coll., 1942, DSc hon., 1971; MS, U. Ill., 1943; PhD, U. Calif., Berkeley, 1951. Physicist Lawrence Radiation Lab., Berkeley, Livermore, Calif., 1948-61; head dept. particles and fields Space Physics Lab. Aerospace Corp., El Segundo, 1962-67; physics prof. U. Calif., Riverside, 1967-92, dir. Inst. Geophysics and Planetary Physics, 1967-92, chmn. dept. physics, 1970-73, prof. emeritus physics dept., rsch. physicist, 1992—. Lectr. U. Calif., Berkeley, 1953-54, 57-59. Author: Space Physics, 1970, Why Science?, 1998; contbr. articles to profl. jours. Officer USNR, 1944-46. Sr. Postdoctoral fellow NSF, 1961-62; grantee NASA, NSF, USAF, numerous others. Fellow AAAS, Am. Phys. Soc. (exec. com. 1972-74); mem. AAUP, Am. Geophys. Union, Am. Astron. Soc. Home: 5225 Austin Rd Santa Barbara CA 93111-2905 E-mail: swhite146@home.com

WHITE, STANLEY ARCHIBALD, research electrical engineer; b. Providence, Sept. 25, 1931; s. Clarence Archibald White and Lou Ella (Givens) Arford; m. Edda María Castaño-Benítez, June 6, 1956; children: Dianne, Stanley Jr., Paul, John. BSEE, Purdue U., 1957, MSEE, 1959, PhD, 1965. Registered profl. engr., Ind., Calif. Engr. Rockwell Internat., Anaheim, Calif., 1959-68, mgr., 1968-84, sr. scientist, 1984-90; pres. Signal Processing and Controls Engring. Corp., 1990-99; ind. cons., 2000—. Adj. prof. elec. engring. U. Calif., 1984-97; cons. and lectr. in field; bd. dirs. Asilomar Signals, Systems and Computers Conf. Corp. Contbr. chpts. to books; articles to profl. jours.; patentee in field. With USAF, 1951-55. N.Am. Aviation Sci. Engring. fellow, 1963-65; recipient Disting. Lectr. award Nat. Electronics Conf., Chgo., 1973, Engr. of Yr. award Orange County (Calif.) Engring. Coun., 1984, Engr. of Yr. award Rockwell Internat., 1985, Leonardo da Vinci Medallion, 1986, Sci. Achievement award, 1987, Disting. Engring. Alumnus award Purdue U., 1988, Meritorious Inventor's award Rockwell Internat. Corp., 1989, Outstanding Elec. Engr. award Purdue U., 1992, Boeing N. Am. Aviation Top Inventor award, 1998. Fellow AAAS (life), AIAA, IEEE (life, Centennial medalist Millenium medalist, chair of ICASSP and ISCAS, Signal Processing Soc. disting. lect. and founding chmn. L.A. coun. chpt., Circuits and Sys. Soc. Tech. Achievement award 1996, Golden Jubilee medal 1999), Inst. for Advancement Engring., N.Y. Acad. Scis. (life); mem. VFW (life), Air Force Assn. (life), Am. Legion (life), Sigma Xi (life, founding pres. Orange County chpt., pres. 1988-2000), Eta Kappa Nu (disting. fellow, internat. dir. emeritus), Tau Beta Pi. Avocation: choral music. Home: 433 E Avenida Cordoba San Clemente CA 92672-2350 E-mail: stan.white@ieee.org

WHITE, STEPHEN HALLEY, biophysicist, educator; b. Wewoka, Okla., May 14, 1940; s. James Halley and Gertrude June (Wyatt) W.; m. Buff Ertl, Aug. 20, 1961 (div. 1982); children: Saill, Shell, Storn, Sharr, Skye, Sunde; m. Jackie Marie Dooley, Apr. 14, 1984. BS in Physics, U. Colo., 1963; MS in Physics, U. Wash., 1965, PhD in Physiology and Biophysics, 1969. USPHS postdoctoral fellow biochemistry U. Va., Charlottesville, 1971-72; asst. prof. physiology and biophysics U. Calif., Irvine, 1972-75, assoc. prof. physiology and biophysics, 1975-78, prof. physiology and biophysics, 1978—, vice chmn. physiology and biophysics, 1974-75, chmn. physiology and biophysics, 1977-89. Guest biophysicist Brookhaven Nat. Lab., Upton, L.I., N.Y., 1977-99. Contbr. numerous articles to profl. jours. Served to capt. USAR, 1969-71. Recipient Research Career Devel. award USPHS, 1975-80, Kaiser-Permanente Tchg. award, 1975, 92; grantee NIH, 1971—, NSF, 1971—. Mem. NSF (adv. panel for molecular biology 1982-85, mem. nat. steering com. advanced neutron source 1992-95), Internat. Union Pure and Applied Biophysics (U.S. nat. com. 1997—, chmn. 2000—), Fedn. Am. Soc. for Exptl. Biology (bd. mem. 1998—), Biophys. Soc. (chmn. membrane biophysics subgroup 1977-78, acting sec., treas. 1979-80, coun. 1981-84, exec. bd. 1981-83, program chmn. 1985, ann. meeting sec. 1987-95, pres. 1996-97, Disting. Svc. award 1999), Am. Physiol. Soc. (editl. bd. 1981-93, membership com. 1985-86, publ. com. 1987-91), Assn. Chmn. Depts. Physiology (rep. to coun. acad. scos. 1981-82, councilor 1982-83, pres. 1986-87), Soc. Gen. Physiologists (treas. 1985-88, The Protein Soc. (electronic pub. coord. 1993—). Avocations: skiing, cooking, travel. Office: U Calif Dept Physiology & Biophysics Med Sci I-D346 Irvine CA 92697-4560

WHITE, TERRENCE HAROLD, academic administrator, sociologist; b. Ottawa, Ont., Canada, Mar. 31, 1943; s. William Harold and Shirley Margaret (Ballantine) W.; m. Susan Elizabeth Hornaday; children: Christine Susan, Julie Pamela. Ph.D., U. Toronto, 1972. Head dept. sociology and anthropology U. Windsor, Ont., Can., 1973-75; prof., chmn. dept. sociology U. Alta., Edmonton, 1975-80, dean faculty of arts, 1980-88; pres. T.H. White Orgn. Research Services Ltd., Edmonton, 1975—, Brock U., St. Catharines, Ont., 1988-96, U. Calgary, Alta., 1996—; dir. Labatt's Brewing Alta., Edmonton, 1981-88. Author: Power or Pawns: Boards of Directors, 1978, Human Resource Management, 1979; editor: Introduction to Work Science, 1981, QWL in Canada: Case Studies, 1983. Bd. dirs. Progressive Conservative Assn., Edmonton South, 1976-81, 1st v.p., 1981-85, pres., 1985-87; bd. dirs. Tri-Bach Festival Found., Edmonton, 1981-88, Alta. Ballet Co., 1985-88, Edmonton Conv. and Tourism Authority, Arch Enterprises, 1984-88, Niagara Symphony Soc., YMCA, St. Catharines, 1988-92; chair United Way Campaign St. Catharines, 1992, Fox Found., 1990-96, Canada Summer Games 2001 Bid Com.; bd. dirs. Edmonton Symphony Soc., v.p., 1986-88; bd. govs. U. Alta., 1984-88, Brock U., 1988-96, Ridley Coll., 1990—, Alberta Heritage Found. for Med. Rsch.; mem. Calgary R&D Authority, 1997; divsn. chair Calgary United Way Campaign, Calgary Econ. Devel. Authority, 1997—. Recipient Can. 125 Commemorative medal, Govt. of Can. Mem. Calgary Petroleum Club, Ranchmen's Club, Rotary (pres. Edmonton South 1981-82), Delta Tau Kappa, Alpha Kappa Delta Home: Box 68028 28 Crowfoot Terr NW Calgary AB Canada T3G 3N8 Office: U Calgary 2500 University Dr NW Calgary AB Canada T2N 1N4

WHITE, TIMOTHY, newspaper publisher; Publ. Times Union; publisher Hearst's San Francisco Examiner, San Francisco, 1999-2000. Office: 5 Clarendon Ave San Francisco CA 94114-2101 E-mail: twhite@sfna.com

WHITEHEAD, IAN, insurance company executive; CEO, pres. London PCF Lf & Annuity Co., Sacramento, now vice chmn., sec. London. Office: London PCF Lf & Annuity Co 1755 Creekside Oaks Dr Sacramento CA 95833-3637

WHITESELL, JOHN EDWIN, motion picture company executive; b. DuBois, Pa., Feb. 23, 1938; s. Guy Roosevelt and Grace Ethlyn (Brisbin) W.; m. Amy H. Jacobs, June 12, 1960; 1 child, Scott Howard; m. Martha Kathlyn Hall, Sept. 3, 1975; m. Phyllis Doyle, May 8, 1993. B.A., Pa. State U., 1962. Asst. mgr. non-theatrical div. Columbia Pictures Corp., N.Y.C., 1963-66; with Warner Bros., Inc., 1966—, nat. sales mgr. non-theatrical div. Calif., 1968-75, v.p., 1975-76; v.p. internat. sales adminstrn. Warner Bros. Internat. TV Distbn., 1976-2001, cons., 2001—. Bd. dirs. Mastermedia Internat. Inc.; past bd. dirs. Found. Entertainment Programming in Higher Edn.; mem. self-study com. Nat. Entertainment Conf., 1974-75. Served with USNR, 1956-58. Recipient Alumni Fellow award Pa. State U., 2001, Outstanding Alumnus award Pa. State U. DuBois Campus, 1995, Founders award Nat. Entertainment Conf., 1975. Mem. Nat. Audio-Visual Assn. (motion picture coun. 1973-76, exec. com. film coun. 1969-76, ednl. materials producers coun. 1970-76), Acad. TV Arts and Scis., Nat. Assn. Media Educators (adv. com. 1973-76)

WHITESIDE, CAROL GORDON, foundation executive; b. Chgo., Dec. 15, 1942; d. Paul George and Helen Louise (Barre) G.; m. John Gregory Whiteside, Aug. 15, 1964; children: Brian Paul, Derek James. BA, U. Calif., Davis, 1964. Pers. mgr. Emporium Capwell Co., Santa Rosa, 1964-67; pers. asst. Levi Strauss & Co., San Francisco, 1967-69; project leader Interdatum, San Francisco, 1983-88; with City Coun. Modesto, 1983-87; mayor City of Modesto, 1987-91; asst. sec. for intergovtl. rels. The Resources Agy., State of Calif., Sacramento, 1991-93; dir. intergovtl. affairs Gov.'s Office, Sacramento, 1993-97; pres. Great Valley Ctr., Modesto, Calif., 1997—. Trustee Modesto City Schs., 1979-83; nat. pres. Rep. Mayors and Local Ofcls., 1990. Named Outstanding Woman of Yr. Women's Commn., Stanislaus County, Calif., 1988, Woman of Yr., 27th Assembly Dist., 1991; Toll fellow Coun. of State Govts., 1996. Republican. Lutheran. Office: Great Valley Ctr 911 13th St Modesto CA 95354-0903 E-mail: carol@greatvalley.org

WHITESIDE, NEAL, mechanical engineer; BSME, U. Alberta, Canada, 1992; MA, U. British Columbia, 1994. Engr. asst. Western Gas Mktg., 1989; fluid dynamic rsch. asst. Nova Husky Rsch. Corp, 1990; mech. engr. student Novacorp Internat. Cons.Inc., 1991; design engr. Kerr Wood Leidal Assocs. Ltd, 1994—. Recipient T.C. Keefer medal Can. Soc. for Civil Engring., 1996. Office: Kerr Wood Leidel Assocs Ltd 139 W 16th St North Vancouver BC Canada V7M 1T3

WHITE-THOMSON, IAN LEONARD, opera company administrator; b. Halstead, Eng., May 3, 1936; came to U.S., 1969; s. Walter Norman and Leonore (Turney) W-T.; m. Barbara Montgomery, Nov. 24, 1971. B.A. with 1st class honors, New Coll., Oxford U., 1960, M.A., 1969. Mgmt. trainee Borax Consol. Ltd., London, 1960-61, asst. to sales mgr., 1961-64, asst. to sales dir., 1964; comml. dir. Hardman & Holden Ltd., Manchester, Eng., 1965-67, joint mng. dir., 1967-69; v.p. mktg. dept. U.S. Borax Inc., Los Angeles, 1969-73, exec. v.p. mktg., 1973-88, pres., 1988-98, also dir., chmn., 1996-99; group exec. Pa. Glass Sand Corp., Ottawa Silica Co., U.S. Silica Co., 1985-87; exec. dir. L.A. Opera, 2000—. Bd. dirs. Canpotex Ltd., chmn. bd., 1974-76. Bd. dirs. L.A. Opera. Served with Brit. Army, 1954-56. Named Mfr. of Yr., Calif. Mfrs. Assn., 1997. Mem. Can. Potash Prodrs. Assn. (v.p. 1976-77, dir. 1972-77), Chem. Industry Coun. of Calif. (bd. dirs. 1982-85, chmn. 1984), Am. Mining Congress (bd. dirs. 1989), RTZ Borax and Minerals (bd. dirs. 1992, chief exec. 1995-99), Kerr-McGee Corp. (bd. dirs. 1999—), Calif. Club, Valley Hunt Club. Home: 851 Lyndon St South Pasadena CA 91030-3712

WHITFIELD, ROY A. pharmaceutical executive; b. Crewe, England; BS in math.with first class honors, Oxford U.; MBA with distinction, Stanford U. Cons. Boston Consulting Group; various positions Technicon Instrument Corp. (formerly CooperBiomedical, Inc.), 1984-89; pres. Ideon Corp. subs. Invitron Corp., 1989-91; CEO IncyteGenomics (formerly Incyte Pharms., Inc.), Palo Alto, Calif., 1993—, dir., 1991—, pres., 1991-97, treas., 1991-95; dir. Aurora Bioscis. Corp. Office: Incyte Genomics Inc 3160 Porter Dr Palo Alto CA 94304-1212 Fax: 650-855-0555

WHITFORD, JOSEPH PETER, lawyer; b. N.Y.C., Apr. 30, 1950; BA, Union Coll., 1972; JD, Syracuse U., 1975; LLM in Taxation, George Washington U., 1978. Bar: N.Y. 1976, D.C. 1977, Wash. 1979. Staff atty. divsn. corp. fin. SEC, Washington, 1975-78; assoc. Foster Pepper & Shefelman, Seattle, 1978-83, mem., 1983—. Chmn. bd. dirs. MIT Forum on the Northwest, 1992-93. Office: Foster Pepper & Shefelman PLLC 1111 3rd Ave Ste 3400 Seattle WA 98101-3299

WHITHAM, GERALD BERESFORD, mathematics educator; b. Halifax, Eng., Dec. 13, 1927; came to U.S., 1956; s. Harry and Elizabeth (Howarth) W.; m. Nancy Lord, Sept. 1, 1951; children— Ruth H., Michael G., Susan C. BS, Manchester U., Eng., 1948, MS, 1949, PhD, 1953. Lectr. Manchester U., 1953-56; assoc. prof. NYU, N.Y.C., 1956-59; prof. math. MIT, Cambridge, 1959-62; prof. aeros. and math. Calif. Inst. Tech., Pasadena, 1962-67, prof. applied math., 1967-83, Charles Lee Powell prof. applied math., 1983-98, emeritus, 1998—. Author: Linear and Nonlinear Waves, 1974; also research papers on applied math. and fluid dynamics. Recipient Wiener prize in applied math., 1980 Fellow Royal Soc., Am. Acad. Arts and Scis. Home: 1689 E Altadena Dr Altadena CA 91001-1855 Office: Calif Inst Tech Applied Math 217-50 Pasadena CA 91125-0001 E-mail: Sheila@acm.caltech.edu

WHITING, ALLEN SUESS, political science educator, writer, consultant; b. Perth Amboy, N.J., Oct. 27, 1926; s. Leo Robert and Viola Allen (Suess) W.; m. Alice Marie Conroy, May 29, 1950; children: Deborah Jean, David Neal, Jeffrey Michael, Jennifer Hollister. B.A., Cornell U., 1948; M.A., cert. Russian Inst., Columbia U., 1950, Ph.D., 1952. Instr. polit. sci. Northwestern U., 1951-53; asst. prof. Mich. State U., East Lansing, 1955-57; social scientist The Rand Corp., Santa Monica, Calif., 1957-61; dir. Office Research and Analysis Far East U.S. Dept. State, Washington, 1962-66; dep. consul gen. Am. Consulate Gen., Hong Kong, 1966-68; prof. polit. sci. U. Mich., Ann Arbor, 1968-82; prof. U. Ariz., Tucson, 1982-93, Regents prof., 1993—, dir. Ctr. for East Asian Studies, 1982-93; cons. U.S. Dept. State, 1968-88; dir. Nat. Com. on U.S.-China Relations, N.Y.C., 1977-94; assoc. The China Council, 1978-88; pres. So. Ariz. China Coun., Tucson, 1983-95. Fellow Woodrow Wilson Ctr., Washington, 1995-96. Author: Soviet Policies in China: 1917-1924, 1954, China Crosses the Yalu, 1968, Chinese Calculus of Deterrence, 1975, Siberian Development and East Asia, 1981, China Eyes Japan, 1989, others; contbr. articles to profl. jours.; spl. commentator McNeill-Lehrer Program; CBS and NBC Spls. on China. Served with U.S. Army, 1945. Social Sci. Rsch. Coun. fellow, 1950, 74-75; Ford Found. fellow, 1953-55; Rockefeller Found. fellow, 1978; Woodrow Wilson Ctr. fellow, 1995-96. Mem. Assn. Asian Studies. Home: 973 Highway Contract 34 Klamath Falls OR 97601-9140 Office: U Ariz Dept Polit Sci Tucson AZ 85721-0001

WHITLEY, DAVID SCOTT, archaeologist; b. Williams AFB, Ariz., Mar. 5, 1953; s. Edgar Duer and Yvonne Roca (Wightman) W.; m. Tamara Katherine Koteles, Feb. 13, 1987; 1 child, Carmen. AB Anthro and Geography magna cum laude, U. Calif., 1976, MA in Geography, 1979, PhD in Anthropology, 1982. Soc. Profl. Archeology. Chief archeologist Inst. Archeology UCLA, L.A., 1983-87; rsch. fellow Archeology Dept. U. Witwatersrand, Johannesburg, 1987-89; pres. W&S Cons., Simi Valley, Calif., 1989—. U.S. rep. internat. com. rock art Internat. Coun. Monuments and Sites, 1992—, exec. com., 1997-99, mem. coun. dirs., 1997—. Author: A Guide to Rock Art Sites: Southern California and Southern Nevada, 1996, L'Art des chamanes: art rupestre en Californie, 1997, Handbook of Rock Art Research, 2001; editor: archeological monographs; contbr. articles to profl. jours. Prehistoric Archeologist, State of Calif. Hist. Resources Commn., 1986-87; mem. rsch. adv. com. Chauvet Cave, France, 1996—. Recipient post doctoral fellowship, Assn. for Field Archeology, 1983, tech. specialist grant, U.S. AID, 1986, Thomas F. King award for excellence in cultural resource mgmr. Soc. for Calif. Archaeology, 2001. Fellow Am. Anthrop. Assn.; mem. Soc. Am. Archeology, SAR, Sons of the Indian Wars, Mayflower Soc. Home: 447 3d St Fillmore CA 93015-1413 Office: W&S Consultants 2422 Stinson St Simi Valley CA 93065

WHITMAN, MARGARET, C, internet executive; BA in Econ., Princeton U.; MBA, Harvard U. Brand asst. Procter & Gamble; v.p. Bain & Co.; sr. v.p. mktg. consumer products divsn. Walt Disney Co.; exec. v.p. Keds divsn. Stride Rite Corp., pres. Stride Rite divsn.; pres., CEO, Florists Transworld Delivery; gen. mgr. presch. divsn. Hasbro Inc.; pres., CEO Ebay, San Jose, Calif. Office: Ebay 2125 Hamilton Ave San Jose CA 95125-5905

WHITMORE, BRUCE G. lawyer; BA, Tufts U., 1966; JD, Harvard U., 1969. Bar: N.Y. 1970, Calif. 1973, Pa. 1979. Gen. atty. ARCO Transp. Co., 1985-86; assoc. gen. counsel corp. fin. ARCO, 1986-90; v.p., gen. counsel ARCO Chem. Co., 1990-94; sr. v.p., gen. counsel, corp. sec. Atlantic Richfield Co., L.A., 1995-2000. Mem. ABA.

WHITNEY, DAVID See MALICK, TERRENCE

WHITSELL, HELEN JO, lumber executive; b. Portland, Oreg., July 20, 1938; d. Joseph William and Helen (Cornwell) Copeland; m. William A. Whitsell, Sept. 2, 1960; 2 children. BA, U. So. Calif., 1960. With Copeland Lumber Yard Inc., Portland, 1960—, pres., chief exec. officer, 1973-84, chmn., chief exec. officer, 1984—. Office: Copeland Lumber Yards Inc 901 NE Glisan St Portland OR 97232-2784

WHITSITT, ROBERT JAMES, professional basketball team executive; b. Madison, Wis., Jan. 10, 1956; s. Raymond Earl and Dolores June (Smith) W.; m. Jan Leslie Sundberg; children: Lillian Ashley, Sean James. BS, U. Wis., Stevens Point, 1977; MA, Ohio State U., 1978. Intern Indiana Pacers, Inpls., 1978, bus. tickets mgr., 1979, dir. bus. affairs and promotions, 1980, asst. gen. mgr., 1981-82; v.p. mktg. Kansas City (Mo.) Kings, 1982-84, v.p., asst. gen. mgr., 1984-85, Sacramento Kings, 1985-86; pres. Seattle Supersonics, 1986-97, Portland Trail Blazers, 1997—. Mem. Nat. Basketball Assn. (alternate gov., mem. competition and rules com.). Republican. Lutheran. Lodge: Rotary. Avocations: skiing, jogging, reading, music. Office: Portland Trailblazers 1 Center Ct Ste 200 Portland OR 97227-2103

WHITTEN, CHARLES ALEXANDER, JR. physics educator; b. Harrisburg, Pa., Jan. 20, 1940; s. Charles Alexander and Helen (Shoop) W.; m. Joan Emann, Nov. 20, 1965; 1 son, Charles Alexander III. B.S. summa cum laude, Yale U., 1961; Ph.D. in Physics, Princeton U., 1966. Research asso. A.W. Wright Nuclear Structure Lab., Yale U., 1966-68; asst. prof. physics UCLA, 1968-74, assoc. prof., 1974-80, prof., 1980—, vice chmn. physics dept., 1982-86. Vis. scientist Centre d'Etudes Nucléaires de Saclay Moyenne Energie, 1980-81, 86-87. Contbr. articles to profl. jours. Mem. Am. Phys. Soc., Sigma Pi Sigma, Phi Beta Kappa. Home: 9844 Vicar St Los Angeles CA 90034-2719 E-mail: whitten@physics.ucla.edu

WHITTEN, DAVID GEORGE, chemistry educator; b. Washington, Jan. 25, 1938; s. David Guy and Miriam Deland (Price) W.; m. Jo Wright, July 9, 1960; children: Jenifer Marie, Guy David. A.B., Johns Hopkins U., 1959; M.A., John Hopkins U., 1961, Ph.D., 1963. Asst. prof. chemistry U. N.C., Chapel Hill, 1966-70, assoc. prof., 1970-73, prof., 1973-80, M.A. Smith prof., 1980-83; C.E. Kenneth Mees prof. U. Rochester, N.Y., 1983-97, chair dept. chemistry, 1988-91, 95-97, dir. Ctr. for Photoinduced Charge Transfer, 1989-95; mem. tech. staff Los Alamos Nat. Lab., 1997-2000; co-founder, chief tech. officer QTL Biosystems, LLC, 2000—; prof. chemistry and biochemistry Ariz. State U., 2000—. Mem. adv. com. for chemistry NSF; cons. Eastman Kodak Co.; Rochester, N.Y. Editor-in-chief, Langmuir, 1998—. Alfred P. Sloan fellow, 1970; John van Geuns fellow, 1973; recipient special U.S. scientist award Alexander von Humboldt Found., 1975; Japan Soc. for Promotion of Sci. fellow, 1982 Mem. AAAS, Am. Chem. Soc. (award in colloid and surface chemistry 1992), Internat. Union of Pure and Applied Chemistry (commn. on photochemistry), Interam. Photochem. Soc. (award 1998). Democrat. Home: 811D W Manhattan Ave Santa Fe NM 87501-3786 Office: QTL Biosys LLC 2778 Agua Fria St Bldg C Santa Fe NM 87507 E-mail: whitten@qthbio.com

WHITWORTH, A. LIN, state legislator; b. Inkom, Idaho, Dec. 28, 1933; m. Carol Whitworth; 7 children. Farmer; railroad conductor; mem. Idaho Senate, Dist. 33, Boise, 1994—. Ranking Dem., health and welfare, resources and environment, trasp., and joint legis. coms., mem. oversight com. Bannock county chair, legis. rep., United Transp. Union. Mem. United Transp. Union (local 265), Elks. Democrat. Mormon. Office: State Capitol PO Box 83720 Boise ID 83720-3720

WHORTON, M. DONALD, occupational and environmental health physician, epidemiologist; b. Las Vegas, N.Mex., Jan. 25, 1943; s. R.H. and Rachel (Siegal) W.; m. Diana L. Obrinsky, Apr. 9, 1972; children: Matthew Richard, Laura Elizabeth, Julie Hannah. Student, U.S. Naval Acad., 1961-62; B of Biology, N.Mex. Highlands U., 1964; MD, U. N.Mex., 1968; MPH, Johns Hopkins U., 1973. Intern Boston City Hosp., 1968-69; resident in pathology U. N.Mex., Albuquerque, 1969-71; instr., resident in medicine Balt. City Hosp., 1972-74; instr. Johns Hopkins U., Balt.; assoc. dir. divsn. emergency medicine Balt. City Hosps., 1974-75; clin. asst. prof. divsn. ambulatory and cmty. medicine U. Calif. Sch. Medicine, San Francisco, 1975-77; lectr. U. Calif. Sch. Pub. Health, San Francisco, 1975-79; med. dir. labor occup. health program Inst. Indsl. Rels., Ctr. for Labor Rsch. and Edn., 1975-79, assoc. clin. prof. occup. medicine, 1979-87; prin. Environ. Health Assocs., Inc., Oakland, 1978-88; v.p. ENSR Health Scis., 1988-94; pvt. practice Alameda, Calif., 1994-2001; with WorkCare, 2001—. Chmn. adv. com. for hazard evaluation service and info. system Indsl. Relations Dept. State of Calif., 1979-84; cons. in field; chmn., statewide adv. com. U. Calif. Ctrs. on occupational and environmental health, 1996—. Contbr. articles to profl. jours. Recipient Upjohn Achievement award, 1968; Robert Wood Johnson Found. clin. scholar, 1972-74 Fellow Am. Coll. Epidemiology, Am. Coll. Occupational and Environ. Medicine; mem. Am. Pub. Health Assn., Soc. for Occupational and Environ. Health, Calif. Med. Assn. (adv. panel on occupational and environmental medicine), Inst. Medicine, Nat. Acad. Sci., Alpha Omega Alpha. Office: 1320 Harbor Bay Pkwy # 115 Alameda CA 94502-6556 E-mail: dwhorton@workcare.com, whobren@lmi.net

WHYBROW, PETER CHARLES, psychiatrist, educator, author; b. Hertfordshire, Eng., June 13, 1939; U.S. citizenship, 1975; s. Charles Ernest and Doris Beatrice (Abbott) W.; children: Katherine, Helen. Student, Univ. Coll., London, 1956-59; MB BS, Univ. Coll., 1962; diploma psychol. medicine, Conjoint Bd., London, 1968; MA (hon.), Dartmouth Coll., 1974, U. Pa., 1984. House officer endocrinology Univ. Coll. Hosp., 1962, sr. house physician psychiatry, 1963-64; house surgeon St. Helier Hosp., Surrey, Eng., 1963; house officer pediatrics Prince of Wales Hosp., London, 1964; resident psychiatry U. N.C. Hosp., 1965-67, instr., research fellow, 1967-68; mem. sci. staff neuropsychiat. research unit Charshalton, Surrey, 1968-69; dir. residency tng. psychiatry Dartmouth Med. Sch., Hanover, N.H., 1969-71, prof. psychiatry, 1970-78, chmn. dept., 1970-78, exec. dean, 1980-83; prof., chmn. dept. psychiatry U. Pa., Phila., 1984-96, Ruth Meltzer prof. psychiatry, 1992; psychiatrist-in-chief Hosp. U. Pa., 1984-96; prof. psychiatry and biobehavioral scis., chmn. dept. psychiatry Sch. Medicine UCLA, 1996—, dir. Neuropsychiatric Inst., 1996—, physician-in-chief Neuropsychiatric Hosp., 1996-99, Judson Braun Prof. of Psychiatry, 1999—. Dir. psychiatry Dartmouth Hitchcock Affiliated Hosp., 1970-78; vis. scientist NIMH, 1978-79; cons. VA, 1970—, NIMH, 1972— ; chmn. test com. Nat. Bd. Med. Examiners, 1977-84; researcher psychoendrocrinology. Author: Mood Disorders: Toward a New Psychobiology, 1984, The Hibernation Response, 1988, A Mood Apart, 1997; editor: Psychosomatic Medicine, 1977; mem. editl. bd. Cmty. Psychiatry, Psychiat. Times, Directions in Psychiatry, Neuropsychopharmacology, Depression; contbr. articles to profl. jours. Recipient Anclote Manor award psychiat. rsch. U. N.C., 1967, Sr. Investigator award nat. Alliance for Rsch. into Schizophrenia and Depression, 1989; Josiah Macy Jr. Found. scholar, 1978-79; fellow Cen. for Advanced Studies in Behavioral Sci., Stanford, 1993-94; recipient Lifetime Investigator award NDMDA, 1996; decorated Knight of Merit, Sovereign Order of St. John of Jerusalem, 1993. Fellow AAAS, Am. Psychiat. Assn., Royal Coll. Psychiatrist (founding mem.), Am. Coll. Psychiatrists, Ctr. Advanced Study of Behavioral Scis. (hon.), Soc. Psychosomatic Rsch. London (hon.); mem. Am. Assn. Chmn. Depts. Psychiatry (pres. 1977-78), Royal Soc. Medicine, Am. Psychopath Assn., Am. Coll. Neuropsychopharmacology, Soc. Biol. Psychiatry, N.Y. Acad. Scis., Soc. Neurosci., Sigma Xi, Alpha Omega Alpha. Office: UCLA Sch Medicine Neuropsychiat Rsch Inst 760 Westwood Plz Los Angeles CA 90095-8353

WHYTE, RONALD M. federal judge; b. 1942; BA in Math., Wesleyan U., 1964; JD, U. So. Calif., 1967. Bar: Calif. 1967, U.S. Dist. Ct. (no. dist.) Calif. 1967, U.S. Dist. Ct. (cen. dist.) Calif. 1968, U.S. Ct. Appeals (9th cir.) 1986. Assoc. Hoge, Fenton Jones & Appel, Inc., San Jose, Calif., 1971-77, mem., 1977-89; judge Superior Ct. State of Calif., 1989-92, U.S. Dist. Ct. (no. dist.) Calif., San Jose, 1992—. Judge pro-tempore Superior Ct. Calif., 1977-89; lectr. Calif. Continuing Edn. of Bar, Rutter Group, Santa Clara Bar Assn., State Bar Calif.; legal counsel Santa CLara County Bar Assn., 1986-89; mem. county select com. Criminal Conflicts Program, 1988. Bd. trustees Santa Clara County Bar Assn., 1978-79, 84-85. Lt. Judge Advocate Gen.'s Corps, USNR, 1968-71. Recipient Judge of Yr. award Santa Clara County Trial Lawyers Assn., 1992, Am. Jurisprudence award. Mem. Calif. Judges Assn., Assn. Bus. Trial Lawyers (bd. govs. 1991-93), Santa Clara Inn of Ct. (exec. com. 1993—), San Francisco Bay area Intellectual Property Inn of Ct. (exec. com. 1994—). Office: US Courthouse 280 S 1st St Rm 2112 San Jose CA 95113-3002

WIATT, JAMES ANTHONY, theatrical agency executive; b. L.A., Oct. 18, 1946; s. Norman and Catherine (Sonners) W.; m. Randle Laine. BA, U. So. Calif., 1969. Campaign coord. Tunney for Senate, L.A., 1969-71; adminstrv. asst. Senator John V. Tunney, L.A., 1972-75; agt. FCA, L.A., 1976-78; lit. agt. Internat. Creative Mgmt., L.A., 1978-81, motion picture agt., 1981-83, head of motion picture dept., 1983-85, pres., COO, from 1985, co-chmn., co-CEO Beverly Hills, Calif., to 1999; pres., co-CEO William Morris Agy., Beverly Hills, 1999—. Office: William Morris Agy 151 S El Camino Dr Beverly Hills CA 90212-2775

WICK, PHILIP, wholesale distribution executive; CEO Les Schwab Tire Ctrs., Prineville, Oreg. Office: PO Box 667 Prineville OR 97754-0667

WICKES, GEORGE, English literature educator, writer; b. Antwerp, Belgium, Jan. 6, 1923; came to U.S., 1923; s. Francis Cogswell and Germaine (Attout) W.; m. Louise Westling, Nov. 8, 1975; children by previous marriage: Gregory, Geoffrey, Madeleine (dec.), Thomas, Jonathan. BA, U. Toronto, Ont., Can., 1944; MA, Columbia U., 1949; PhD, U. Calif., Berkeley, 1954. Asst. sec. Belgian Am. Ednl. Found., N.Y.C., 1947-49; exec. dir. U.S. Ednl. Found. in Belgium, 1952-54; instr. Duke U., Durham, N.C., 1954-57; from asst. prof. to prof. Harvey Mudd Coll. and Claremont Grad. Sch., Calif., 1957-70; prof. English and comparative lit. U. Oreg., Eugene, 1970—, dir. comparative lit., 1974-77, head English dept., 1976-83. Lectr. USIS, Europe, 1969, Africa, 1978, 79; vis. prof. U. Rouen, France, 1970, U. Tübingen, Germany, 1981, U. Heidelberg, Germany, 1996. Editor: Lawrence Durrell and Henry Miller Correspondence, 1963, Henry Miller, Letters to Emil, 1989, Henry Miller and James Laughlin: Selected Letters, 1995; Author: Henry Miller, 1966, Americans in Paris, 1969, The Amazon of Letters, 1976: translator: The Memoirs of Frederic Mistral, 1986. Served with U.S. Army, 1943-46. Fulbright lectr. France, 1962-63, 66, 78; sr. fellow Ctr. for Twentieth Century Studies, U. Wis.-Milw., Milwaukee, 1971, Creative Writing fellow Nat. Endowment Arts, 1973, Camargo fellow, 1991. Mem. PEN. Office: U Oreg English Dept Eugene OR 97403

WICKHAM, DIANNE, nursing administrator; b. Dillon, Mont., Feb. 26, 1952; d. William Byron Wickham and Margaret Dewalt (Lovell) Starkweather. ADN, No. Mont. Coll., 1974; BSN, Mont. State U., 1978, MSN, 1980. RN, Mont. Clin. dir. St. Patrick Hosp., Missoula, Mont., 1980-81; asst. prof. Lewis Clark State Coll., Lewiston, Idaho, 1981-83, Mont. State U., Bozeman, Mont., 1983-86; home health nurse West Mont. Home Health, Helena, 1986-87, dir. clin. svcs., 1987-90; critical care nurse St. James Hosp., Butte, Mont., 1986-87; exec. dir. Mont. State Bd. of Nursing, Helena, 1990—. Mem. long term care com. Gov. Task Force on Aging, Helene, Mont., 1993-95, mem. task force to devel. investigator tng. Nat. Com. of State Bds. Nursing, Chgo., 1993—, mem. adj. faculty Mont. State U., Bozeman, 1993—, cons. in field, 1994—. Judge Soroptomists scholarship award, 1993, JC Penneys Golden Rule award, Helena, 1995. Recipient State award for excellence Am. Acad. Nurses Practitioners, 1994. Office: Mont State Bd Nursing 111 N Jackson St Helena MT 59601-4140

WICKIZER, MARY ALICE See BURGESS, MARY ALICE

WICKLAND, J. AL, JR. petroleum product executive, real estate executive; CEO Wickland, to 1995, chmn. emeritus, 1995—. Office: Wickland Corp 3600 American River Dr Ste 145 Sacramento CA 95864-5997 also: PO Box 13648 Sacramento CA 95853-4648

WIDAMAN, GREGORY ALAN, financial executive, accountant; b. St. Louis, Oct. 4, 1955; s. Raymond Paul Sr. and Louise Agnes (Urschler) W. BS in Bus. and Econs. cum laude, Trinity U., 1978. CPA, Tex. Sr. auditor Arthur Andersen LLP, Houston, 1978-82; sr. cons. Price Waterhouse, Houston, 1983-85; fin. advisor to segment pres. Teledyne, Inc., Century City, Calif., 1985-95; sr. mgr. ops. planning for consumer products ABC Broadcasting/TV The Walt Disney Co., Burbank, 1995-97; v.p. internal audit and spl. projects Hilton Hotels Corp., Beverly Hills, 1997—. Cons. Arthur Andersen LLP, Price Waterhouse, Teledyne, Walt Disney Co., Hilton Hotels Corp. Mem. AICPAs, Calif. Soc. CPAs, Christian Bus. Mens com. of U.S.A., World Affairs Coun., MIT/Calif. Tech. Enterprise Forum. Republican. Avocations: white water rafting, water and snow skiing, camping, business, chess. Home: 1416 S Barrington Ave No 4 Los Angeles CA 90025-2363 Office: Hilton Hotels Corp World Hdqrs 9336 Civic Center Dr Beverly Hills CA 90210-3604

WIDYOLAR, SHEILA GAYLE, dermatologist; b. Vancouver, B.C., Can., June 11, 1939; d. Walter Herbert and Olive Louise (O'Neal) Roberts; Kithi K. Widyolar, 1960 (div. 1979); 1 child, Keith. BS, Loma Linda U., 1962; MD, Howard U., 1972. Resident U. Calif., Irvine, 1973-76; dermatologist pvt. practice, Laguna Hills, Calif., 1976—. Clin. instr. U. Calif. Sch. Medicine, 1978-86. Chmn. bd. dirs. Opera Pacific, Costa Mesa, Calif., 1996-97. Fellow Am. Acad. Dermatology, Am. Soc. Dermatophthology; mem. AMA, Calif. Med. Assn., Dermatological Soc. Orange County (pres. 1983), Alpha Omega Alpha. Avocations: music, travel. Office: Ste 403 23911 Calle de Mag Dalena Laguna Hills CA 92653

WIEBE, LEONARD IRVING, radiopharmacist, educator; b. Swift Current, Sask., Can., Oct. 14, 1941; s. Cornelius C. and Margaret (Teichroeb) W.; m. Grace E. McIntyre, Sept. 5, 1964; children: Glenis, Kirsten, Megan BSP, U. Sask., 1963, MS, 1966; PhD, U. Sydney, Australia, 1970. Pharmacist Swift Current Union Hosp., 1963-64; sessional lectr. U. Sask., Can., 1965-66; asst. prof. U. Alta., Can., 1970-73, assoc. prof. Can., 1973-78, prof. Can., 1978—, dir. Slowpoke Reactor Facility Can., 1975-89, 2001—, asst. dean rsch. Can., 1984-87, assoc. dean Can., 1990-99; prof. dept. exptl. oncology, 1999—; sessional lectr. U. Sydney, Australia, 1973; pres. Internat. Bionucleonics Cons. Lts., 1991-97; dir. BMH, Australian Nuclear Sci. Tech. Orgn., 1990, Noujaim Inst. Pharm. Oncology, 1994-2000. Rsch. assoc. Cross Cancer Inst., Edmonton, 1978—, Med. Rsch. Coun. Can.; vis. prof. Royal P.A. Hosp., Sydney, 1983-84, Searle vis. profl., 1986; MRC vis. prof., Toronto, 1987; PMAC vis. prof., 1988; McCalla prof. U. Alta, 1993-94; radiopharmacy cons. Australian Atomic Energy Commn., Sydney, 1983-84; mem. MRC standing com. on sci. and rsch., 1995-98; hon. liason prof. Peoples U. Bangladesh. Editor: Liquid Scintillation: Science and Technology, 1976, Advances in Scintillation Counting, 1983; guest editor Jour. of Radioanalytical Chemistry, 1981; editor Internat. Jour. Applied Radiation Instrumentation Sect. A, 1988-90; regional editor Internat. Jour. Nuclear Biology and Medicine, 1992-95; mem. editl. bd. Jour. Pharmacy & Pharm. Sci., Jour. Applied Radiation Isotopes, 1995—. Recipient Janssen-Ortho Rsch. award, 1998; Commonwealth Univs. Exchange grantee, 1966; Alexander von Humboldt fellow, 1976-79, 82. Mem. Pharm. Bd. of New South Wales, Sask. Pharm. Assn., Soc. Nuclear Medicine, Assn. Faculties of Pharmacy of Can. (McNeil Rsch. award 1988), Can. Radiation Protection Assn., Can. Assn. Radiopharm. Scientists, Am. Pharm. Assn., Am. Assn. Pharm. Sci., Australian Nuclear Sci. Tech. Orgn. (dir., biomedicine and health 1990), Internat. Assn. Radiopharmacy (exec. sec. 1991-95), Can. Assn. Pharm. Scis. (founding), Univ. Club (Edmonton) (pres. 1985). Mem. Mennonite Ch.

WIEDEN, DAN G. advertising executive; b. 1945; With Georgia-Pacific Corp., Portland, Oreg., 1967-72; free-lance writer, 1972-78; with McCann-Erickson, Portland, 1978-80, William Cain, Portland, 1980-82; pres. Wieden & Kennedy, Portland, 1982—. Office: Wieden & Kennedy Inc 224 NW 13th Ave Portland OR 97209-2953

WIEDERRICK, ROBERT, museum director; Pres. Lemhi County Hist. Mus., Salmon, Idaho. Office: Lemhi County Hist Mus 210 Main St Salmon ID 83467-4111

WIEDOW, CARL PAUL, electromechanical and geophysical instruments company executive; b. Pasadena, Calif., Dec. 3, 1907; s. Carl and Clara Minna (Matthes) W.; m. Mary Maletia Foulks, 1935 (div. Jan. 1946); m. Mary Louise Montesano, Nov. 27, 1947. A.B. in Math., Occidental Coll., 1933; M.S. in Physics, Calif. Inst. Tech., 1945, M.S. in Elec. Engring., 1946; Ph.D. in Elec. Engring., Oreg. State U., 1956. Registered profl. engr., Calif. Assoc. prof. electronics U.S. Naval Postgrad. Sch., Monterey, Calif., 1956-59; design specialist Gen. Dynamics Astronautics, San Diego, 1955-61, Ryan Aerospace div., San Diego, 1961-62; prof., head dept. physics Calif. Western U., San Diego, 1962-66; staff engr. Marine Advisors, La Jolla, Calif., 1966-67; chief of research Humphrey Inc., San Diego, 1967—; cons. engr. Elgin Nat. Watch Co., West Coast Micronics div., 1959-60, Gen. Dynamics Astronautics, San Diego, 1963-64, Havens Industries, San Diego, 1962-64, Solar, San Diego, 1964-66, Anka Industries, Chula Vista, Calif., 1979—. Counselor, judge Sci. Fair, San Diego, 1962—; acad. asst. NSF, 1966-68. Mem. AAUP, Optical Soc. San Diego, Soc. Wireless Pioneers, Quarter Century Wireless Assn., Old Time Communicators, Sigma Xi, Sigma Tau, Sigma Pi Sigma, Pi Mu Epsilon.

WIEMAN, CARL E. physics educator; b. Corvallis, Oreg., Mar. 26, 1951; m. Sarah Gilbert. BS, MIT, 1973; PhD, Stanford U., 1977; DS (hon.), U. Chgo., 1997. Asst. rsch. physicist dept. physics U. Mich., Ann Arbor, 1977-79, asst. prof. physics, 1979-84; assoc. prof. physics U. Colo., Boulder, 1984-87, prof., 1987-97, disting. rsch. prof., 1997—; fellow Joint Inst. for Lab. Astrophysics, Boulder, 1985—. Loeb lectr. Harvard U., 1990-91; Rosenthal Meml. lectr. Yale U., Columbia U., 1988; Cherwell-Simon Meml. lectr. Oxford U., 1999; Phi Beta Kappa vis. scholar, 1999—. Recipient Ernest Orlando Lawrence Mem. award U.S. Dept. Energy, 1993, Einstein medal for laser sci. Soc. Optical and Quantum Electronics, 1995, Fritz London prize for low temperature physics, 1996, Newcomb Cleveland prize AAAS, 1996, King Faisal Internat. prize for Sci., 1997, Sci. award Bonfils Stanton Found., 1998, Lorentz medal Netherlands Royal Acad. Sci., 1998, Franklin medal for physics Franklin Inst., 2000; Frew fellow Australia Acad. Sci., 1998. Fellow Am. Phys. Soc. (Davisson-Germer prize 1994, Schawlow prize in laser sci. 1998); mem. NAS, Optical Soc. Am. (R.W. Wood prize 1999), Am. Assn. Physics Tchrs. (Richtmyer lectr. award), Am. Acad. Arts and Sci. First acheivement of Bose-Einstein condensation, 1995. Office: U Colo PO Box 390 Boulder CO 80309-0390

WIEMER, ROBERT ERNEST, film and television producer, writer, director; b. Highland Park, Mich., Jan. 30, 1938; s. Carl Ernest and Marion (Israelian) W.; m. Rhea Dale McGeath, June 14, 1958; children: Robert Marshall, Rhea Whitney. BA, Ohio Wesleyan U., 1959. Ind. producer, 1956-60; dir. documentary ops. WCBS-TV, N.Y.C., 1964-67; ind. producer of television, theatrical and bus. films N.Y.C., 1967-72; exec. producer motion pictures and TV, ITT, N.Y.C., 1973-84, pres. subs. Blue Marble Co., Inc., Telemontage, Inc., Alphaventure Music, Inc., Betaventure Music, Inc., 1973-84; founder, chmn., chief exec. officer Tigerfilm, Inc., 1984—; chmn., bd. dirs. Golden Tiger Pictures, Hollywood, Calif., 1988—; pres, CEO Tuxedo Pictures Corp., Hollywood, 1993—. Bd. dirs., v.p. prodn. Las Vegas Internat. Film Festival; v.p. prodn. Cinevegas. Writer, prodr., dir.: (feature films) My Seventeenth Summer, Witch's Sister, Do Me a Favor, Anna to the Infinite Power, Somewhere, Tomorrow, Night Train to Kathmandu; exec. prodr.: (children's TV series) Big Blue Marble (Emmy and Peabody awards); dir. (TV episodes) New York Undercover, seaQuest DSV, Star Trek: The Next Generation, Deep Space Nine, The Adventures of Superboy; composer (country-western ballad) Tell Me What To Do. Capt. USAF, 1960-64. Recipient CINE award, 1974, 76, 77, 79, 81, Emmy award, 1978. Mem. NATAS, ASCAP, Info. Film Producers Assn. (Outstanding Producer award), Nat. Assn. TV Programming Execs., Am. Women in Radio and TV, N.J. Broadcasters Assn., Dirs. Guild Am., v.p., bd. mem. CineVegas The Las Vegas Internat. Film Festival. Office: Golden Tiger Pictures 3896 Ruskin St Las Vegas NV 89147-1097

WIENER, JON, history educator; b. St. Paul, May 16, 1944; s. Daniel N. and Gladys (Aronsohn) Spratt. BA, Princeton U., 1966; PhD, Harvard U., 1971. Acting asst. prof. UCLA, 1973-74; asst. prof. history U. Calif.-Irvine, 1974-83, prof., 1984—. Vis. prof. U. Calif.-Santa Cruz, 1973; plaintiff Freedom of Info. Lawsuit against FBI for John Lennon Files, 1983—. Author: Social Origins of the New South, 1979; Come Together: John Lennon in His Time, 1984, Professors, Politics, and Pop, 1991, Gimme Some Truth: The John Lennon FBI File, 2000; contbg. editor The Nation mag.; contbr. articles to profl. jours. including The New Republic and New York Times Book Rev. Rockefeller Found. fellow, 1979, Am. Coun. Learned Socs.- Ford Found. fellow, 1985. Mem. Am. Hist. Assn., Nat. Book Critics Circle, Orgn. Am. Historians, Nat. Writers' Union, Liberty Hill Found. (bd. dirs.). Office: U Calif Dept History Irvine CA 92697-3275 E-mail: wiener@uci.edu

WIENER, VALERIE, state senator, communications consultant, positioning strategist, author; b. Las Vegas, Nev., Oct. 30, 1948; d. Louis Isaac Wiener and Tui Ava Knight. BJ, U. Mo., 1971, MA, 1972, U. Ill., Springfield, 1974; postgrad., McGeorge Sch. Law, 1976-79. Producer Checkpoint Sta. KOMU-TV, Columbia, Mo., 1972-73; v.p., owner Broadcast Assocs., Inc., Las Vegas, 1972-86; pub. affairs dir. First Ill. Cable TV, Springfield, 1973-74; editor Ill. State Register, Springfield, 1973 74; prodr. and talent Nevada Realities Sta. KLVX-TV, Las Vegas, 1974-75; account exec. Sta. KBMI (now KFMS), Las Vegas, 1975-79; nat. traffic dir. six radio stas., Las Vegas, Albuquerque and El Paso, Tex., 1979-80; exec. v.p., gen. mgr. Stas. KXKS and KKJY, Albuquerque, 1980-81; exec. adminstr. Stas. KSET AM/FM, KVEG, KFMS and KKJY, 1981-83; press sec. U.S. Congressman Harry Reid, Washington, 1983-87; adminstrv. asst Friends for Harry Reid, Nev., 1986; press sec. U.S. Senator Harry Reid, Washington, 1987-88; owner Wiener Comm. Group, Las Vegas, 1988—; mem. Nev. Senate, Dist. 3 Clark County, 1996—; Senate Dem. Whip, 2001; owner PowerMark Pub., 1998—. Author: Power Communications: Positioning Yourself for High Visibility (Fortune Book Club main selection 1994, Money Book Club selection 1995), Gang Free: Friendship Choices for Today's Youth, 1995, 2d edit., 1996, The Nesting Syndrome: Grown Children Living at Home, 1997, Winning the War Against Youth Gangs, 1999, Power Positioning: Advancing Yourself as The Expert, 2000, Power Master Handbook Series, 2000; contbg. writer The Pacesetter, ASAE's Comm. News. Sponsor Futures for Children, Las Vegas, Albuquerque, El Paso, 1979-83; mem. El Paso Exec. Women's Coun., 1981-83; mem. VIP bd. Easter Seals, El Paso, 1982; media chmn. Gov.'s Coun. Small Bus., 1989-93; mem. Gov.'s Commn. on Aging, 1997—, Clark Coun. Sch. Dist. and Bus. Cmty. PAYBAC Spkrs. and Partnership Programs, 1989—, chair legis. com. on juv. justice, 1999-2000; chair Commn. on Sch. Safety of Juv. Violence, 1999-2000; various state and nat. legis. commns. and coms.; med. dir. 1990 Conf. on Women, Gov. of Nev.; media chmn. Congl. Awards Coun., 1989-93; vice-chmn. Gov.'s Commn. on Postsecondary Edn., 1992-96; bd. dirs. BBB So. Nev., 1994—. Named Outstanding Vol., United Way, El Paso, 1983, SBA Nev. Small Bus. Media Adv. of Yr., 1992; Woman of Achievement in Media award, 1992, Outstanding Achievement award Nat. Fedn. Press Women, 1991, Disting. Leader award Nat. Assn. for Cmty. Leadership, 1993, Outstanding Women Advocate for Edn. award Va. Commonwealth U., 2000, Disting. Sr. Athlete in Nev., 2000, over 140 other comm. awards; received gold medal Nev. Sr. Olympics in Fitness and Weightlifting, 1998, 99, 2000, Internat. Cmty. Svc. award Internat. New Thought Alliance, 2001. Mem. Nat. Assn. of Women Bus. Owners (media chmn., nat. rep. So. Nev. 1990-91, Nev. Adv. of Yr. award 1992), Nev. Press Women, Nat. Spkrs. Assn., Small Pubs. Assn. N.Am., Dem. Press Secs. Assn., El Paso Assn. Radio Stas., U.S. Senate Staff Club, Las Vegas C. of C. (Circle of Excellence award 1993), Soc. Profl. Journalists. Democrat. Avocations: reading, writing, fitness and weightlifting training and competition, pub. speaking, community involvement. Office: 1500 Foremaster Ln Ste 2 Las Vegas NV 89101-1150

WIENS, ARTHUR NICHOLAI, psychology educator; b. McPherson, Kans., Sept. 7, 1926; s. Jacob T. and Helen E. (Kroeker) W.; m. Ruth Helen Avery, June 11, 1949; children: Barbara, Bradley, Donald. B.A., U. Kans., 1948, M.A., 1952; Ph.D., U. Portland, 1956. Diplomate: Am. Bd. Examiners Profl. Psychology. Clin. psychologist Topeka State Hosp., 1949-53; sr. psychologist outpatient dept. Oreg. State Hosp., Salem, 1954-58, chief psychologist, 1958-61, dir. clin. psychology internship program, 1958-61; clin. instr. U. Oreg. Med. Sch., Portland, 1958-61, asst. prof., 1961-65, assoc. prof., 1965-66, prof. med. psychology, 1966—; clin. assoc. prof. psychology U. Portland, 1959-61. Field assessment officer Peace Corps, 1965; cons. psychologist Portland Center for Hearing and Speech, 1964-67, Dammasch State Hosp., 1967-69, Raleigh Hills Hosp., 1968-84, Oreg. Vocat. Rehab. Div., 1973-2001, mem. state adv. com., 1976-93; cons. William Temple Rehab. House, Episcopal Laymen's Mission Soc., 1968-88; chmn. State Oreg. Bd. Social Protection, 1971-84, State Oreg. Bd. Psychologist Examiners, 1974-77; v.p. bd. dirs. Raleigh Hills Research Found., 1974-80 Contbr. articles to profl. jours. Fellow AAAS, APA (chmn. com. on vis. psychologist program 1972-76, chmn. accreditation com. 1978, mem. task force edn. and credentialing 1979-84); mem. Am. Assn. State Psychology Bds. (pres. 1978-79), Nat. Register Health Svc. Providers in Psychology (bd. dirs. 1985-92), Profl. Exam. Svc. (bd. dirs. 1982-88, 90-96, chmn. 1986-88), Sigma Xi. Home: 74 Condolea Way Lake Oswego OR 97035-1010 Office: Oreg Health Scis U Portland OR 97201 E-mail: wiensa@ohsu.edu

WIENS, BEVERLY JO, educator; b. Oildale, Calif., Oct. 2, 1947; d. Ernest and Irene Josephine (Klassen) Bartel; m. Gary D. Wiens, Aug. 19, 1967; children: Nicole Marie Wiens Cook, Katie Lyn Wiens. BA, San Jose State U., 1969, MA, 1971, Santa Clara U., 1992. Lic. counselor, Calif. Tchr. West Valley Coll., Saratoga, Calif., 1971-76, San Jose (Calif.) City Coll., 1974-75, San Jose State U., 1978; marriage, family therapist Coalition of Counseling Centers, Los Gatos, Calif., 1982-86; assoc. prof. San Jose Bible Coll., 1982-87; prof., dept. chair, counseling psychology San Jose Christian Coll., 1988—. Lectr. in field. Mem. Am. Assn. Christian Counselors, Am. Counseling Assn., Assn. Religious Value in Counseling, Assn. Counselor Training, Supervision, Calif. Assn. Marital Family Therapists. Republican. Mem. Mennonite Brethren. Office: San Jose Christian Coll 790 S 12th St San Jose CA 95112-2304 E-mail: bwiens@sjchristian.edu

WIESLER, JAMES BALLARD, retired banker; b. San Diego, July 25, 1927; s. Harry J. and Della B. (Ballard) W.; m. Mary Jane Hall, Oct. 3, 1953; children: Tom, Ann, Larry. B.S., U. Colo., 1949; postgrad., Stonier Sch. Banking, Rutgers U., 1962, Advanced Mgmt. Program, Harvard U., 1973. With Bank of Am., NT & SA, 1949-87; v.p., mgr. main office San Jose, Calif., 1964-69; regional v.p. Cen. Coast adminstrn. San Jose, 1969-74; sr. v.p., head No. European Area office Frankfurt, Fed. Republic of Germany, 1974-78; exec. v.p., head Asia div. Tokyo, 1978-81; exec. v.p., head N.Am. div. Los Angeles, 1981-82; vice chmn., head retail banking San Francisco, 1982-87; ret., 1987. Bd. dirs. Visa USA, Visa Internat., Sci. Applications Internat. Corp.; bd. dirs., chmn. Bank Adminstrn. Inst., 1986-87. Pres. Santa Clara County United Fund, 1969, 70, San Jose C. of C., 1968; fin. chmn. Santa Clara County Reps., 1967-74; bd. dirs. San Diego Armed Svcs., YMCA, Sidney Kimmell Cancer Ctr.; trustee, chmn. bd. dirs. Sharp Meml. Hosp.; hon. consul-gen. for Japan, 1990-95. With USN, 1945-46. Mem. San Diego Hosp. Assn. (bd. dirs., treas.), San Diego Zool. Soc., Greater San Diego C. of C. (pres., CEO 1998-99), Bohemian Club, DeAnza Country Club, San Diego Yacht Club. Presbyterian. Home: 605 San Fernando St San Diego CA 92106-3312 Office: Bank Am Nat Trust & Savs 450 B St San Diego CA 92101-8001

WIESNER, CAROL A. financial services company executive; BS in Bus. Adminstrn., Pa. State U., 1960. CPA, Calif. Sr. auditor Price Waterhouse & Co., 1960-67; various positions Litton Industries, Inc., Woodland Hills, Calif., 1967-88, v.p., treas., 1988-94, v.p., controller, 1994—. Mem. AICPA, Calif. Soc. CPA. Office: 21240 Burbank Blvd Woodland Hills CA 91367-6675

WIEST, WILLIAM MARVIN, education educator, psychologist; b. Loveland, Colo., May 8, 1933; s. William Walter and Katherine Elizabeth (Buxman) W.; m. Thelma Lee Bartel, Aug. 18, 1955; children: William Albert, Suzanne Kay, Cynthia May. BA in Psychology summa cum laude, Tabor Coll., 1955; MA, U. Kans., 1957; PhD, U. Calif., Berkeley, 1962. Rsch. asst. psychol. ecology U. Kans., 1955-57; rsch. asst. measurement cooperative behavior in dyads U. Calif., Berkeley, 1958-59; from asst. to assoc. prof. Reed Coll., Portland, Oreg., 1961-74, prof., 1974-95, prof. emeritus, 1995—. Adj. investigator Ctr. Health Rsch., Portland, 1985—; project coord. WHO, Geneva, 1976-84; fgn. travel leader Assiniboine Travel, Winnipeg, Man., Can., 1990-91, Willamette Internat. Travel, Portland, 1993-95; lectr. Fgn. Travel Club, Portland, 1990, 94; vis. scientist Oceanic Inst., Waimanalo, Hawaii, 1967-68; chmn. dept. psychology Reed Coll., Portland, 1973-75, 86; social sci. adv. com. Population Resource Ctr., N.Y.C., 1978—; vis. investigator Health Svcs. Rsch. Ctr., Portland, 1975-76, cons. 1976-80; com. protection human subjects Kaiser Permanente Med. Care Program, Portland, 1978-81, cons. WHO, 1980-81, U.S. Dept. Energy, 1980-83; mem. panel population study sect. HHS. Consulting editor Population and Environment, 1981—; jour. referee Health Psychology, Jour. Social Biology, Jour. Personality and Social Psychology, Memory and Cognition; contbr. articles to profl. jours. Sloan Found. Faculty Rsch. fellow, 1972-73, NSF fellow, 1975-76, USPSH fellow U. Calif., 1957-58, Woodrow Wilson Found. fellow U. Calif., 1960-61. Mem. AAAS, APHA, Am. Hist. Soc. Germans from Russia (conv. spkr. 1991, 97), Germans from Russia Heritage Soc., Am. Psychol. Assn., Population Assn. Am., Phi Beta Kappa, Sigma Xi. Home: 5009 SE 46th Ave Portland OR 97206-5048 Office: Reed Coll Dept Psych SE Woodstock Blvd Portland OR 97202

WIGAN, GARETH, film company executive; Co-vice chair Columbia Tristar Motion Picture Group. Office: Columbia TriStar Motion Picture Group 10202 Washington Blvd Culver City CA 90232-3119

WIGGS, EUGENE OVERBEY, ophthalmologist, educator; b. Louisville, Apr. 27, 1928; s. Eugene Overbey and Marie Helen (Martin) W.; children: Susan, Christopher, Karen, Mark. AB, Johns Hopkins U., 1950; MD, Duke U., 1955. Intern Denver Gen. Hosp., 1955-56; resident in ophthalmology Wilmer Inst. Johns Hopkins Hosp., 1956-59; ophthalmic plastic fellow Byron Smith, MD, N.Y.C., 1969; pvt. practice specializing in oculoplastic surgery Denver, 1961—. Clin. prof. U. Colo. Med. Ctr.; lectr. ophthalmic plastic surgery various med. ctrs. Contbr. articles to med. jours. With USNR, 1959-61. Mem. AMA, Denver Med. Soc., Colo. Med. Soc., Am. Soc. Ophthalmic Plastic and Reconstructive Surgery, Am. Acad. Ophthalmology (svc. award 1982), Colo. Ophthalmology Soc. Republican. Roman Catholic. Office: 2005 Franklin St Denver CO 80205-5401

WIGHTMAN, THOMAS VALENTINE, rancher, researcher; b. Sacramento, Oct. 7, 1921; s. Thomas Valentine and Pearl Mae (Cutbirth) W.; m. Lan Do Wightman. Student, U. Calif., Berkeley, 1945-46; B of Animal Husbandry, U. Calif., Davis, 1949; student, Cal. Poly. Inst., 1949-50. Jr. aircraft mechanic SAD (War Dept.), Sacramento, 1940-42; rancher Wightman Ranch, Elk Grove, 1950-59; machinest Craig Ship-Bldg. Co., Long Beach, 1959-70; rancher Wightman Ranch, Austin, Nev., 1970-88; dir. Wightman Found., Sacramento, 1988—. Dir. med. rsch. Staff sgt. U.S. Army, 1942-45. Recipient scholarship U.S. Fed. Govt., 1945-50. Fellow NRA, VFW, U. Calif. Alumni Assn., U. Calif. Davis Alumni Assn., Bowles Hall Assn.; mem. Confederate Air Force, The Oxford Club. Republican. Avocations: antique automobiles and aircraft. Home and Office: Wightman Found 2130 51st St Apt 129 Sacramento CA 95817-1507

WIGMORE, JOHN GRANT, lawyer; b. L.A., Mar. 14, 1928; s. George Theodore and Mary (Grant) W.; m. Dina Burnaby, July 27, 1968 (dec. 1994); children: Alexander Trueblood, Adam Trueblood, John G. Jr., Mary. BS in Geology, Stanford U., 1949; JD, UCLA, 1958. Geologist Western Geophys., Calif., Colo., Mo., 1953-55; assoc. Lawler, Felix & Hall, L.A., 1958-62, ptnr., 1963-86, Pillsbury, Madison & Sutro, L.A., 1986-90; ret. Lectr. in field. Contbr. articles to profl. jours. Trustee L.A. County Mus.

Natural History, 1970—; participant various local & state election campaigns, 1965-80. Officer USN, 1950-53. Fellow Am. Coll. Trial Lawyers, Am. Bar Found.; mem. ABA (chair litigation com. antitrust sect. 1970-74), Calif. State Bar (L.A. County bar del. 1965-75), L.A. County Bar Assn. (exec. com. trial sect. 1965-68), L.A. County Bus. Trial Lawyers (exec. com. 1984-87), Barristers (exec. com. 1960-65). Home: 870 Neptune Ave Encinitas CA 92024-2062

WIKSTROM, FRANCIS M. lawyer; b. Missoula, Mont., Aug. 20, 1949; BS, Weber State Univ., 1971; JD, Yale U., 1974. Bar: Utah 1974, U.S. Supreme Ct. 1980. Asst. U.S. atty. U.S. Dist. Ct. Utah, 1979-80, U.S. atty., 1981; mem. Parsons Behle & Latimer, Salt Lake City. Mem. Utah State Bar Commn.; former chmn. Utah Judicial Conduct Commn.; chmn. adv. com. on rules civil procedure Utah Supreme Ct.; mem. 10th Cir. Adv. Com. Fellow Am. Bar Found., Am. Coll. Trial Lawyers; mem. ABA, Salt Lake County Bar Assn. (pres. 1993-94), Am. Inns Ct. II (master bench). Office: Parsons Behle & Latimer PO Box 45898 One Utah Ctr 201 S Main St Ste 1800 Salt Lake City UT 84111-2218

WILBUR, BRAYTON, JR. distribution company executive; b. San Francisco, Oct. 2, 1935; s. Brayton and Matilda (Baker) W.; m. Judith Flood, June 29, 1963; children: Jennifer, Edward, Claire, Michael. B.A., Yale U., 1957; M.B.A., Stanford U., 1961. With Arthur Young & Co., San Francisco, 1962-63; v.p. Wilbur-Ellis Co., San Francisco, 1963-74, exec. v.p., 1974-89, also dir.; dir. Chronicle Pub. Co., San Francisco, 1983-89; pres., CEO Wilbur-Ellis Co., San Francisco, 1989-99, chmn., 2000—. Bd. dir. Safeway Stores, 1977-86. Pres. San Francisco Symphony, 1980-87; v.p. Sponsors for Performing Arts Ctr., San Francisco, 1975—; trustee Fine Art Mus. of San Francisco, 1978-81, Asia Found., 1972—, chmn. 1990—. Served with USAR, 1958-63. Mem. Council on Fgn. Relations, Bohemian Club, Pacific Union Club, Cypress Point Club, Burlingame Country Club. Republican. Home: 821 Irwin Dr Burlingame CA 94010-6327 Office: Wilbur Ellis Co 345 California St Fl 27 San Francisco CA 94104-2644

WILBUR, COLBURN SLOAN, foundation trustee, former executive; b. Palo Alto, Calif., Jan. 20, 1935; s. Blake Colburn and Mary (Sloan) W.; m. Maria Grace Verburg, Sept. 1, 1961; children: Marguerite Louise, Anne Noelle. BA in Polit. Sci., Stanford U., 1956, MBA, 1960. Asst. cashier United Calif. Bank, San Francisco, 1960-65; v.p. Standata, San Francisco, 1965-68; adminstrv. mgr. Tab Products, San Francisco, 1968-69; exec. dir. Sierra Club Found., San Francisco, 1969-76, David and Lucile Packard Found., Los Altos, Calif., 1976—. Bd. dirs. Colo. Coll., Colorado Springs; sr. fellow Coun. on Founds., Washington. Bd. dirs. Philanthropic Ventures Found.; former bd. dirs., mem. adv bd. Global Fund Women, Palo Alto, Calif.; past bd. dirs. Big Bros. San Francisco, Calif. Confederation Arts, Peninsula Grantmakers, Women's Fund Santa Clara; former bd. dirs., pres. Big Bros. Peninsula, North Fork Assn., Peninsula Conservation Ctr.; past bd. dirs., chmn. No. Calif. Grantmakers; bd. dirs., mem. adv. bd. Sierra Club Found., Stanford Theater Found., Palo Alto, U. San Francisco/Inst. Nonprofit Orgn. Mgmt. With U.S. Army, 1957-58. Mem. Commonwealth Club (bd. advisors). Office: David & Lucile Packard Found 300 2nd St Los Altos CA 94022-3694 E-mail: c.wilbur@packfound.org

WILCOX, DAVID CORNELL, ballet company director; b. L.A., May 7, 1951; s. Robert Carlos and Eileen Germaine (Babcock) W.; m. Tami Hirabayashi, Nov. 8, 1989; 1 child, Nicole Marie. Soloist Heidelberg (Germany) Ballet, 1971-72, Nuremberg (Germany) Ballet, 1973-74, Berlin (Germany) Ballet, 1975-78; founder, dir. L.A. Classical Ballet (founded as Long Beach Ballet), Long Beach, Calif., 1981—. Dir. Ballet Arts Ctr., Long Beach, 1981—; asst. prof. Calif. State U., Long Beach, 1984-88; guest faculty Columbia (S.C.) City Ballet, 1991-92. Choreographer various ballets. Mem. Royal Acad. Dancing (assoc.), Dance USA. Avocations: flying, skiing, computer programming. Home: 2630 Faust Ave Long Beach CA 90815-1336 Office: LA Classical Ballet 1122 E Wardlow Rd Long Beach CA 90807-4726

WILCOX, RONALD BRUCE, biochemistry educator, researcher; b. Seattle, Sept. 23, 1934; s. Howard Bruce and Edna Jane (McKeown) W.; m. Susan Lenore Folkenberg, May 15, 1937; children: Deanna Marie, Lisa Suzanne. B.S., Pacific Union Coll., 1957; Ph.D., U. Utah, 1962. Research fellow Harvard Med. Sch., Boston, 1962-65; asst. prof. Loma Linda U., Calif., 1965-70, assoc. prof., 1970-73, prof., 1973—, chmn. dept. biochemistry, 1973-83. Mem. gen. plan rev. com. City of Loma Linda, 1981-92; bd. dirs. East Valley United Way, 1990-97. Fellow Danforth Found., St. Louis, 1957; fellow Bank Am. Giannini Found. San Francisco, 1965 Mem. Am. Thyroid Assn., Endocrine Soc. Democrat. Seventh-day Adventist. Home: 25516 Lomas Verdes St Loma Linda CA 92354-2417 Office: Loma Linda U Dept Biochemistry Loma Linda CA 92350-0001 E-mail: bwilcox@som.llu.edu

WILD, NELSON HOPKINS, lawyer; b. Milw., July 16, 1933; s. Henry Goetseels and Virginia Douglas (Weller) W.; m. Joan Ruth Miles, Apr. 12, 1969; children: Mark, Eric. A.B., Princeton U., 1955; LL.B., U. Wis., 1961. Bar: Wis. 1962, Calif. 1967; cert. specialist in probate, estate planning and trust law State Bar of Calif. Research assoc. Wis. Legis. Council, Madison, 1955-56; assoc. Whyte, Hirschboeck, Minahan, Harding & Harland, Milw., 1961-67, Thelen, Marin, Johnson & Bridges, San Francisco, 1967-70; sole practice law San Francisco, 1970—. Mem. State Bar Calif. Client Trust Fund Commn., 1983, mem. exec. com. conf. dels., 1985-88. Contbr. articles to legal jours. Bd. dirs. Neighborhood Legal Assistance Found., San Francisco, 1974-85, chmn. bd., 1978-81. Served with USAF, 1956-58. Mem. ABA, Calif. Bar Assn., San Francisco Bar Assn., Am. Bar Found., Lawyers of San Francisco Club (gov. 1975, treas. 1981, v.p. 1982, pres.-elect 1983, pres. 1984), Calif. Tennis Club (bd. dirs. 1995-97, pres. 1997). Office: 332 Pine St Ste 710 San Francisco CA 94104-3230

WILDE, THOMAS ANDREW, state legislator, home remodeler, writer; b. Mpls., Feb. 11, 1956; m. Melinda Wilde. BA, U. Minn. Mem. Oreg. Legislature, Salem, 1996—, vice chair agr. and natural resources com., mem. pub. affairs com., vice chair rev. com., mem. water and land use com., mem. subcom. on natural resources. Democrat. Office: 3826 N Longview Ave Portland OR 97227-1024 E-mail: wilde.sen@state.or.us

WILDER, JAMES D. geology and mining administrator; b. Wheelersburg, Ohio, June 25, 1935; s. Theodore Roosevelt and Gladys (Crabtree) W.; children: Jaymie Deanna, Julie Lynne. Graduated high sch., Wheelersburg. Lic. real estate agt., Ohio. Real estate agt., Portsmouth, Ohio; mgr. comml. pilots, fixed base operator Scioto County Airport; mgr. and part owner sporting goods store, Portsmouth; cons. geologist Paradise, Calif., 1973-81; pres. Mining Cons., Inc., Paradise, 1981-84; dir. geology and devel. Para-Butte Mining, Inc., Paradise, 1984-88, pres., 1988-90, pres., chief exec. officer, 1990—. Served with U.S. Army, 1956-57. Avocations: hunting, fishing, camping. Home and Office: Para Butte Mining Inc PO Box 564 Paradise CA 95967-0564

WILENSKY, HAROLD L. political science and industrial relations educator; b. New Rochelle, N.Y., Mar. 3, 1923; s. Joseph and Mary Jane (Wainsten) W.; children: Stephen David, Michael Alan, Daniel Lewis Student, Goddard Coll., 1940-42; AB, Antioch Coll., 1947; MA, U. Chgo., 1949, PhD, 1955. Asst. prof. sociology U. Chgo., 1951-53, asst. prof. indsl. relations, 1953-54; asst. prof. sociology U. Mich., Ann Arbor, 1954-57, assoc. prof., 1957-61, prof., 1961-62, U. Calif., Berkeley, 1963-82, prof. polit. sci., 1982—, research sociologist Inst. Indsl. Relations, 1963—, project dir. Inst. Internat. Studies, 1970-90; project dir. Ctr. for German and European Studies, Berkeley, 1994-96, Inst. Govtl. Studies, 1996—. Mem. research career awards com. Nat. Inst. Mental Health, 1964-67; cons. in field Author: Industrial Relations: A Guide to Reading and Research, 1954, Intellectuals in Labor Unions: Organizational Pressures on Professional Roles, 1956, Organizational Intelligence: Knowledge and Policy in Government and Industry, 1967, The Welfare State and Equality: Structural and Ideological Roots of Public Expenditures, 1975, The New Corporatism, Centralization, and the Welfare State, 1976, (with C.N. Lebeaux) Industrial Society and Social Welfare, 1965, (with others) Comparative Social Policy, 1985, (with L. Turner) Democratic Corporatism and Policy Linkages, 1987; editor: (with C. Arensberg and others) Research in Industrial Human Relations, 1957, (with P.F. Lazarsfeld and W. H. Sewell) The Uses of Sociology, 1967; contbr. articles to profl. jours. Recipient aux. award Social Sci. Rsch. Coun., 1962, Book award McKinsey Found., 1967; fellow Ctr. for Advanced Study in Behavioral Scis., 1956-57, 62-63, German Marshall Fund, 1978-79; Harry A. Millis rsch. awardee U. Chgo., 1950-51. Fellow AAAS; mem. AAUP, Internat. Sociol. Assn., Internat. Polit. Sci. Assn., Indsl. Relations Research Assn. (exec. com. 1965-68), Soc. for Study Social Problems (chmn. editorial com.), Am. Polit. Sci. Assn., Am. Sociol. Assn. (exec. council 1969-72, chmn. com. on info. tech. and privacy 1970-72), Council European Studies (steering com. 1980-83). Democrat. Jewish Avocations: music, trumpet, skiing. Office: U Calif Dept Polit Sci 210 Barrows Hall Berkeley CA 94720-1902 E-mail: hwilensk@socrates.berkeley.edu

WILES, DAVID MCKEEN, chemist; b. Springhill, N.S., Can., Dec. 28, 1932; s. Roy McKeen and Olwen Gertrude (Jones) W.; m. Valerie Joan Rowlands, June 8, 1957; children: Gordon Stuart, Sandra Lorraine. B.Sc. with honors, McMaster U., 1954, M.Sc., 1955; Ph.D. in Chemistry, McGill U., 1957. Research officer chemistry div. Nat. Research Council of Can., Ottawa, 1959-66, head textile chemistry sect. chemistry div., 1966-75, dir. chemistry div., 1975-90; pres. Plastichem Cons., Victoria, B.C., Can., 1990—. Bd. dirs. MLB Industries, Malahat Sys. Corp.; chmn. Can. High Polymer Forum, 1967-69; v.p. N.Am. Chem. Congress, Mexico City, 1975 Contbr. articles to profl. jours.; mem. editl. adv. bd. numerous profl. jours.; patentee in field. Can. Ramsay Meml. fellow, 1957-59 Fellow Chem. Inst. Can. (chmn. bd. dirs. 1972-74, pres. 1975-76, Dunlop Lectr. award 1981), Royal Soc. Chem. London, Royal Soc. Can.; mem. Am. Chem. Soc. (Polymer Chem. div.). Home and Office: 3965 Juan Fuca Terr Victoria BC Canada V8N 5W9 E-mail: dmwiles@telus.net

WILETS, LAWRENCE, physics educator; b. Oconomowoc, Wis., Jan. 4, 1927; s. Edward and Sophia (Finger) W.; m. Dulcy Elaine Margoles, Dec. 21, 1947; children: Ileen Sue, Edward E., James D.; m. Vivian C. Wolf, Feb. 8, 1976. BS, U. Wis., 1948; MA, Princeton, 1950, PhD, 1952. Research asso. Project Matterhorn, Princeton, N.J., 1951-53, U. Calif. Radiation Lab., Livermore, 1953; NSF postdoctoral fellow Inst. Theoretical Physics, Copenhagen, Denmark, 1953-55; staff mem. Los Alamos Sci. Lab., 1955-58; mem. Inst. Advanced Study, Princeton, 1957-58; mem. faculty U. Wash., Seattle, 1958—, prof. physics, 1962-95, prof. emeritus, 1995—. Cons. to pvt. and govt. labs.; vis. prof. Princeton, 1969, Calif. Inst. Tech., 1971 Author: Theories of Nuclear Fission, 1964, Nontopological Solitons, 1989; contbr. over 180 articles to profl. jours. Del. Dem. Nat. Conv., 1968. NSF sr. fellow Weizmann Inst. Sci., Rehovot, Israel, 1961-62; Nordita prof. and Guggenheim fellow Lund (Sweden) U., also Weizmann Inst., 1976—; Sir Thomas Lyle rsch. fellow U. Melbourne, Australia, 1989; recipient Alexander von Humboldt sr. U.S. scientist award, 1983 Fellow Am. Phys. Soc., AAAS; mem. Fedn. Am. Scientists, AAUP (pres. chpt. 1969-70, 73-75, pres. state conf. 1975-76), Phi Beta Kappa (chpt. pres. 1996-97), Sigma Xi. Club: Explorers. Achievements include research on theory of nuclear structure and reactions, nuclear fission, atomic structure, atomic collisions, many body problems, subnuclear structure and elementary particles. Office: U Wash Dept Physics PO Box 351560 Seattle WA 98195-1560 E-mail: wilets@u.washington.edu

WILEY, MICHAEL E. gas and oil executive; BS in Petroleum Engring., U. Tulsa; MBA, U. Dallas. Various engring. and operational positions ARCO Gas and Oil Co., various locations, 1972, sr. v.p., pres., exec. v.p., 1997—; pres. Vastar, 1993-94, CEO, 1994-96, chmn. bd. dirs. Office: Atlantic Richfield Co 333 S Hope St Los Angeles CA 90071-2256

WILFERT, CATHERINE M. medical association administrator, medical educator; Asst. prof. pediatrics Duke U., 1969-80, prof. pediatrics and microbiology, chief pediatric infectious diseases, 1980-98, prof. emeritus; sci. dir. Elizabeth Glaser Pediat. AIDS Found., Santa Monica, Calif. Mem. Inst. Medicine. Office: Elizabeth Glaser Pediatric AIDS Found 2950 31st St Ste 125 Santa Monica CA 90405-3092

WILHELM, ROBERT OSCAR, lawyer, civil engineer, developer; b. Balt., July 7, 1918; s. Clarence Oscar and Agnes Virginia (Grimm) W.; m. Grace Sanborn Luckie, Apr. 4, 1959. BSCE, Ga. Tech. Inst., 1947, MSIM, 1948; JD, Stanford U., 1951. Bar: Calif. 1952, U.S. Supreme Ct. Mem. Wilhelm, Thompson, Wentholt and Gibbs, Redwood City, Calif., 1952—; gen. cousnel Bay Counties Gen. Contractors; pvt. practice civil engring., Redwood City, 1952. Pres. Bay Counties Builders Escrow, Inc., 1972-88. Author: The Manual of Procedures for the Construction Industry, 1971, Manual of Procedures and Form Book for Construction Industry, 9th edit., 1995, Construction Law for Contractors, Architects and Engineers; columnist Law and You in Daily Pacific Builder, 1955—. With C.E., AUS, 1942-46. Named to Wisdom Hall of Fame, 1999. Mem. Bay Counties Civil Engrs. (pres. 1957), Peninsula Builders Exch. (pres. 1958-71, dir.), Calif. State Builders Exch. (treas. 1971), Del Mesa Carmel Cmty. Assn. (bd. dirs. 1997-99), Masons, Odd Fellows, Eagles, Elks. Home: 134 Del Mesa Carmel Carmel CA 93923-7950 Office: 702 Marshall St Ste 510 Redwood City CA 94063-1826

WILKEN, CLAUDIA, judge; b. Mpls., Aug. 17, 1949; BA with honors, Stanford U., 1971; JD, U. Calif., Berkeley, 1975. Bar: Calif. 1975, U.S. Dist. Ct. (no. dist.) Calif. 1975, U.S. Ct. Appeals (9th cir.) 1976, U.S. Supreme Ct. 1981. Asst. fed. pub. defender U.S. Dist. Ct. (no. dist.) Calif., San Francisco, 1975-78, U.S. magistrate judge, 1983-93, dist. judge, 1993—; ptnr. Wilken & Leverett, Berkeley, Calif., 1978-84. Adj. prof. U. Calif., Berkeley, 1978-84; prof. New Coll. Sch. Law, 1980-85; mem. jud. br. com. Jud. Conf. U.S.; past mem. edn. com. Fed. Jud. Ctr.; chair 9th cir. Magistrates Conf., 1987-88. Mem. ABA (mem. jud. adminstrn. divsn.), Alameda County Bar Assn. (judge's membership), Nat. Assn. Women Judges, Order of Coif, Phi Beta Kappa. Office: US Dist Ct No Dist 1301 Clay St # 2 Oakland CA 94612-5217

WILKEN, GARY R. state legislator; b. Tacoma, Jan. 24, 1946; m. Susan Wilken; children: Matthew, Allison, Karen, Bob. BS, Oreg. State U., 1968, MBA, 1970. Mem. Alaska Senate, Dist. O, Juneau, 1996—; mem. fin. com., mem. health, edn. and social svcs. com.; mem. state affairs com., mem. legis. budget and audit com. Active Fairbanks Youth Sports Bd., 1981—, Fairbanks Pub. Utility Bd., 1983-95, Alaska Coun. on Econ. Edn., 1984-96, MAPCO Alaska-Citizens Adv. Bd., 1986-96, Alaska Crippled Children Bd., 1989-95, USAF Civilian Adv. Bd., 1994—, chair Cmty. Activity Ctr. Task Force, 1985-89; pres. Lathrop High Basketball Boosters, 1987-89, 93-96, Fairbanks Youth Sports Found., 1988—; chair Meth. Ch. Pastor Parish Rels. Com., 1994-95. Recipeint Cmty. Svc. award News Miner, 1990; named UAF Bus. Leader of the Yr., 1995; inductee Oreg. State U. Sports Hall of Fame, 1993. Mem. Rotary Fairbanks (pres. 1987, Rotarian of Yr. 1990), Fairbanks C. of C. (chmn. 1992). Republican. Avocations: family activities, hunting, flying, cyberspace, the future. Office: State Capitol 120 4th St Rm 514 Juneau AK 99801-1142 E-mail: senatorgarywilken@legis.state.ak.us

WILKENING, LAUREL LYNN, academic administrator, planetary scientist; b. Richland, Wash., Nov. 23, 1944; d. Marvin Hubert and Ruby Alma Wilkening; m. Godfrey Theodore Sill, May 18, 1974 BA, Reed Coll., Portland, Oreg., 1966; PhD, U. Calif., San Diego, 1970; DSc (hon.), U. Ariz., 1996. From asst. prof. to assoc. prof. U. Ariz., Tucson, 1973-80, dir. Lunar and Planetary Lab., head planetary scis., 1981-83, vice provost, prof. planetary scis., 1983-85, v.p. rsch., dean Grad. Coll., 1985-88; divsn. scientist NASA Hdqrs., Washington, 1980; prof. geol scis., adj. prof. astronomy, provost U. Washington, Seattle, 1988-93; prof. earth system sci., chancellor U. Calif., Irvine, 1993-98. Dir. Rsch. Corp., 1991—, Seagate Tech., Inc., 1993-2000, Empire Ranch Found., 1998—; vice chmn. Nat. Commn. on Space, Washington, 1984-86, Adv. Com. on the Future of U.S. Space Program, 1990-91; chair Space Policy Adv. Bd., Nat. Space Coun., 1991-92; co-chmn. primitive bodies mission study team NASA/European Space Agy., 1984-85; chmn. com. rendezvous sci. working group NASA, 1983-85; mem. panel on internat. cooperation and competition in space Congl. Office Tech. Assessment, 1982-83; trustee NASULGC, 1994-97, UCAR, 1988-89, 97-98, Reed Coll., 1992—. Editor: Comets, 1982. U. Calif. Regents fellow, 1966-67; NASA trainee, 1967-70. Fellow Meteoritical Soc. (councilor 1976-80), Am. Assn. Advanced Sci.; mem. Am. Astron. Soc. (chmn. div. planetary scis. 1984-85), Am. Geophys. Union, AAAS, Planetary Soc. (dir. 1994-2000, v.p. 1997-2000), Phi Beta Kappa. Democrat. Avocations: gardening, camping, swimming.

WILKERSON, LUANN, dean; BA magna cum laude, Baylor U., 1969; MA in English, U. Tex., 1972; EdD, U. Mass., 1977. Tchg. asst. dept. English U. Tex., Austin, 1970-72; tchr. grade 8 lang. arts Quabbin Regional H.S., Barre, Mass., 1974-75; rsch. asst. Clinic to Improve Univ. Tchg. U. Mass., Amherst, 1974-76, staff assoc., 1976-77; dir. tchg. and media resource ctr., asst. prof. speech and theatre Murray (Ky.) State U., 1977-80; acting dir., coord. faculty devel. office ednl. devel. and resources Coll. Osteopathic Medicine Ohio U., Athens, 1980-81; assoc. dir. office curricular affairs, asst. prof. family medicine Med. Coll. Wis., Milw., 1981-83; ednl. specialist ednl. devel. unit Michael Reese Hosp. and Med. Ctr., Chgo., 1983-84; dir. faculty devel. office ednl. devel. Harvard Med. Sch., Boston, 1984-91, lectr. in med. edn., 1988-91; dir. Ctr. for Ednl. Devel. and Rsch. UCLA Sch. Medicine, 1992-99, asst. dean med. edn., 1992-94, assoc. prof. medicine, 1992-95, prof. medicine, 1996—, assoc. dean med. edn., 1995-97, sr. assoc. dean med. edn., 1998—. Mem. editl. bd. Advances in Health Scis. Edn., 1995—; assoc. editor: Acad. Medicine, 1994; reviewer: Acad. Medicine, 1989—, Tchg. and Learning in Medicine, 1990—, Jour. Gen. Internal Medicine, 1988—, Am. Ednl. Rsch. Assn., 1987—, Rsch. Med.Edn. Ann. Conf., 1988—; contbr. articles to profl. jours. and chpts. to books; lectr. in field. Recipient Clinician Tchr. award Calif. Regional Soc. Gen. Internal Medicine, 1995, Excellence in Edn. award UCLA Sch. Medicine, 1998. Mem. Am. Assn. Med. Colls. (mem. rsch. med. edn. com. 1990-93, western chair group on ednl. affairs 1995-97, co-dir. fellowship in med. edn. rsch. 1995-97, convenor spl. interest group on faculty devel. 1997-98, chair group on ednl. affairs 1997—), Am. Ednl. Rsch. Assn., Profl. and Orgnl. Devel. Network (mem. nat. core com. 1977-80, 84-86, exec. dir. 1984-85), Phi Beta Kappa. Office: UCLA Sch Medicine Ctr Ednl Devel & Rsch PO Box 951722 Los Angeles CA 90095-1722 E-mail: lawiker@ucla.edu

WILKIE, DONALD WALTER, biologist, aquarium museum director; b. Vancouver, B.C., Can., June 20, 1931; s. Otway James Henry and Jessie Margaret (McLeod) W.; m. Patricia Ann Archer, May 18, 1980; children: Linda, Douglas, Susanne. B.A., U. B.C., 1960, M.Sc., 1966. Curator Vancouver Pub. Aquarium, 1961-63, Phila. Aquarama, 1963-65; exec. dir. aquarium-mus. Scripps Instn. Oceanography, La Jolla, Calif., 1965-93, exec. dir. emeritus, 1993—. Cons. aquarium design, rschg. exhibit content; sci. writer and editor naturalist-marine edn. programs. Author books on aquaria and marine ednl. materials; contbr. numerous articles to profl. jours. Bd. mem. Miramar Trip & Skeet Club. Mem. Am. Soc. Ichthyologists and Herpetologists, San Diego Zool. Soc., Home: 4548 Cather Ave San Diego CA 92122-2632 Office: U Calif San Diego Scripps Instn Oceanography Libr 9500 Gilman Dr La Jolla CA 92093-5004 E-mail: dwilkie@ussd.edu, donaqua27@aol.com

WILKINS, BURLEIGH TAYLOR, philosophy educator; b. Bridgetown, Va., July 1, 1932; s. Burleigh and Helen Marie (Taylor) W.; children: Brita Taylor, Carla Cowgill, Burleigh William. BA summa cum laude, Duke U., 1952; MA, Harvard U., 1954, Princeton U., 1963, PhD, 1965. Instr. MIT, Cambridge, 1957-60, Princeton U., 1960-61, 63; asst. prof. Rice U., Houston, 1965-66, assoc. prof., 1966-67, U. Calif., Santa Barbara, 1967-68, prof., 1968—. Author: Carl Becker, 1961, The Problem of Burke's Political Philosophy, 1967, Hegel's Philosophy of History, 1974, Has History Any Meaning?, 1978, Terrorism and Collective Responsibility, 1992. Mem. Phi Beta Kappa. Office: U Calif Dept Philosophy Santa Barbara CA 93106

WILKINS, CAROLINE HANKE, consumer agency administrator, political worker; b. Corpus Christi, Tex., May 12, 1937; d. Louis Allen and Jean Guckian Hanke; m. B. Hughel Wilkins, 1957; 1 child, Brian Hughel. Student, Tex. Coll. Arts and Industries, 1956-57, Tex. Tech. U., 1957-58; BA, U. Tex., 1961; MA magna cum laude, U. Ams., 1964. Instr. history Oreg. State U., 1967-68; adminstr. Consumer Svcs. divsn. State of Oreg., 1977-80, Wilkins Assocs., 1980—. Mem. PFMC Salmon Adv. subpanel, 1982-86. Author: (with B. H. Wilkins) Implications of the U.S.-Mexican Water Treaty for Interregional Water Transfer, 1968. Dem. precinct committeewoman, Benton County, Oreg., 1964-90; publicity chmn. Benton County Gen. Election, 1964; chmn. Get-Out-the-Vote Com., Benton County, 1966; vice chmn. Benton County Dem. Ctrl. Com., 1966-70; vice chmn. 1st Congl. Dist., Oreg., 1966-68, chmn., 1969-74; mem. exec. com. Western States Dem. Conf., 1970-72; vice chmn. Dem. Nat. Com., 1972-77, mem. arrangements com., 1972, 76, mem. Dem. Charter Commn., 1973-74; mem. Dem. Nat. Com., 1972-77, 85-89, mem. size and composition com., 1987-89, rules com., 1988; mem. Oreg. Govt. Ethics Commn., 1974-76; del., mem. rules com. Dem. Nat. Conv., 1988; 1st v.p. Nat. Fedn. Dem. Women, 1983-85, pres., 1985-87, parliamentarian, 1993-95, 99— ; mem. Kerr Libr. bd. Oreg. State U., 1989-95, pres., 1994-95; mem. Corvallis-Benton County Libr. Found., 1991—, sec., 1993, v.p., 1994, pres., 1995, mission and goals com. chair 2000—; bd. dirs. Oreg. chpt. U.S. Lighthouse Soc., pres., 1997-98; bd. dirs. Oreg. State U.-Corvallis Symphony, 1998—, v.p. 1999-2000, resources com.; pres. Oreg. Fedn. Dem. Women, 1997—. Named Outstanding Mem., Nat. Fedn. Dem. Women, 1992, Woman of Achievement, Oreg. State U. Women's Ctr., 1998. Mem. Nat. Assn. Consumer Agy. Adminstrs., Soc. Consumer Affairs Profls., Oreg. State U. Folk Club (pres. faculty wives 1989-90, scholarship chair, 2000—), Zonta Internat. (vice area bd. dirs. dist. 8 1992-94, area dir., bd. dist. 8 1994-96, by laws and resolutions chair 1997-98, internat. rels. coord. dist. 8, 2000). Office: 3311 NW Roosevelt Dr Corvallis OR 97330-1169

WILKINS, MICHAEL JON, state supreme court justice; b. Murray, Utah, May 13, 1948; s. Jack L. and Mary June (Phillips) W.; m. Diane W. Wilkins, Nov. 9, 1967; children: Jennifer, Stephanie, Bradley J. BS, U. Utah, 1975, JD, 1976; LLM, U. Va., 2001. Bar: Utah 1977, U.S. Dist. Ct. Utah 1977, U.S. Ct. Appeals (10th cir.) 1987, U.S. Supreme Ct. 1986. Mng. ptnr. Wilkins, Oritt & Headman, Salt Lake City, 1989-94; judge Utah Ct. Appeals, 1994-00; justice Utah Supreme Ct, 2000—, mem. jud. coun., 2000—. Mem. Gov.'s Adv. Com. on Corp., Salt Lake City, 1989-94; mem.

Utah Supreme Ct. Complex Steering Com., 1993-94; mem. Judiciary Standing Com. on Tech., 1995-2000, chmn., 1995-2000; mem. Legis. Compensation Commn., 1994-95. Trustee Utah Law Related Edn. Project, Inc., Salt Lake City, 1991-95, chmn., 1992-94. 1st lt. U.S. Army, 1968-72. Mem. LDS Ch. Office: Utah Supreme Ct 450 S State St PO Box 140210 Salt Lake City UT 84114-0210

WILKINSON, ALAN HERBERT, nephrologist, medical educator; b. Johannesburg, So. Africa, July 11, 1948; came to U.S., 1985; s. Raymond C. and Nonie (Levick) W.; m. Angelika A. E. Adami, Dec. 22, 1973; one child: Rebecca Kate Adami. BS in Physiology, Biochem., Philosophy, U. Witwatersrand, So. Africa, 1969, BS with honors in Biochemistry, 1970, MB, BCh, 1975; cert. health care mgmt., U. Calif., Irvine, 1998. Fellow Royal Coll. Physicians (U.K.), specialist in clin. hypertension. Visiting assoc. Dept. Internal Medicine U. Iowa, Iowa City, 1987-88; assoc. prof. of medicine UCLA Sch. Med., L.A., 1988-95, prof. med., 1995—; dir. clin. nephrology UCLA Dept. Med., L.A., 1988-93, dir. kidney and pancreas transplantation, 1993—. Bd. dirs. UCLA Ctr. Health Schs., 1994-97. Contbr. articles to profl. jours. Mem. Nat. Kidney Fdn. Steering Comm., U.S. Transplant Games, L.A., 1992. Recipient Exceptional Svc. award, Nat. Kidney Fdn, S.C., 1992. Fellow Nat. Kidney Rsch.; mem. Am. Soc. Transplant Physicians, Internat. Nephrology Soc., Am. Soc. Nephrology. Avocations: ornithology, gardening. Office: UCLA Dept Med 200 Medical Plz Box 951693 Los Angeles CA 90095-1693

WILKNISS, PETER E. foundation administrator, researcher; b. Berlin, Sept. 28, 1934; U.S. citizen. s. Fritz and Else (Stueber) W.; m. Edith P. Koester, May 25, 1963; children: Peter F., Sandra M. MS in Chemistry, Tech. U., Munich, Ger., 1958, PhD in Radio and Nuclear Chemistry, 1961. Rsch. chemist, radiological protection officer U.S. Naval Ordnance Sta., 1961-64, head nuclear chemistry branch, 1964-66; rsch. oceanographer U.S. Naval Rsch. Lab., 1966-70, head chemical oceanography branch, 1970-75; mgr. Nat. Ctr. Atmospheric Rsch. Program NSF, Washington, 1975-76, mgr. Internat. Phase of Ocean Drilling/Ocean Sediment Coring Program, 1976-80, mgr. Ocean Drilling Project Team, AAEO Directorate, 1980, dir. divsn. Ocean Drilling Programs, 1980-81, sr. sci. assoc. Office of Dir., 1981-82, dep. asst. dir. Sci, Tech., Internat. Affairs Directorate, 1982-84, dir. divsn. Polar Programs, 1984-93, sr. sci. assoc. Geoscis. Directorate, 1993-96; pres. Polar Kybernetes Internat. LLC, Fairbanks, Alaska, 1997—, Transnat. Arctic and Antarctic Inst., Fairbanks, 1997—. Liaison mem. NRC, NAS, Marine Bd., 1978-81, Polar Rsch. Bd., 1984-93; mem. atmospheric chemistry and radioactivity com. Am. Meteorological Soc., 1975-78; mem. interagy. com. atmospheric scis., 1975-76, space station adv. com., NASA, 1988-93. Ontbr. over 60 articles to sci., tech. jours., USN reports; over 100 formal presentations nat., internat. sci. confs., symposia, meetings; participant 16 nat., internat. workshops. Resdl. citation AIA, 1993; Wilkniss mountain Antarctic named in his honor Sec. Interior, U.S. Bd. Geographic Names, 1992. Mem. AAAS, Am. Geophys. Union, Assn. for Machine Translation in the Americas, Am. Polar Soc., Antarctican Soc. Episcopalian. Avocations: soccer, swimming, skiing. Office: Polar Kybernetes Internat 1305 W 7th Ave Anchorage AK 99501-3210 E-mail: pwilkniss@aol.com

WILKS, LEWIS O. telecommunications company executive; BS in Pub. Rels. and Computer Sci., Ctrl. Mo. State U. With Wang Labs., MCI Corp.; pres. GET Comms.; pres. bus. markets Qwest Commns. Internat., Denver, pres. Internet and Multimedia Markets. Bd. dirs. Qwest Cyber Solutions, Slingshot Networks, Salus Media Corp. Vice chmn. Spl. Olympics Colo.; co-chmn. Colo. Commn. Sci. and Tech. Office: Internet's Multimedia Markets Quest Comms Internat 1801 California St Denver CO 80202

WILLARD, H(ARRISON) ROBERT, electrical engineer; b. Seattle, May 31, 1933; s. Harrison Eugene and Florence Linea (Chelquist) W. BSEE, U. Wash., 1955, MSEE, 1957, PhD, 1971. Lic. profl. engr., Wash. Staff assoc. Boeing Sci. Rsch. Labs., Seattle, 1959-64; rsch. assoc. U. Wash., 1968-72, sr. engr., rsch. prof. applied physics lab., 1972-81; sr. engr. Boeing Aerospace Co., Seattle, 1981-84; dir. instrumentation and engring. MetriCor Inc. (formerly Tech. Dynamics, Inc.), Woodinville, Wash., 1984-92; sr. engr. B.E. Meyers & Co., Inc., Woodinville, 1992—. Contbr. articles to profl. jours.; patentee in field. With AUS, 1957-59. Mem. IEEE, Am. Geophys. Union, Phi Beta Kappa, Sigma Xi, Tau Beta Pi. Office: 17525 NE 67th Ct Redmond WA 98052-4939

WILLARD-JONES, DONNA C. lawyer; b. Calgary, Alberta, Can., Jan. 19, 1944; m. Douglas E. Jones. BA with honors, U. B.C., 1965, student, 1965-66; JD, U. Oreg., 1970. Bar: Ala. 1970, U.S. Dist. Ct. Ala. 1970, U.S. Ct. Appeals (9th cir.) 1971, U.S. Customs Ct. 1972, U.S. Tax Ct. 1975, U.S. Supreme Ct. 1981. Assoc. Boyko & Walton, 1970-71, Walton & Willard, 1971-73; ptnr. Gruenberg & Willard, 1974, Gruenberg, Willard & Smith, 1974-75, Richmond, Willoughby & Willard, 1976-81, Willoughby & Willard, 1981-89; pvt. practice Anchorage, 1990—. Chmn. fed. adv. group Implementation of Civil Justice Reform Act of 1990, 1991-92; lawyer rep. 9th Cir. Jud. Conf., 1979-80; mem. spl. com. on contempt Ala. Supreme Ct., 1991-92; chmn. Bankruptcy Judge Merit Screening com., 1979; mem. Am. Judicature Soc., 1973-92, Am. Trial Lawyers Assn., 1981-92; bd. dirs. Ala. Legal Svcs. Corp., 1979-80; spkr. in field. Mem. U. B.C. Law Rev.; assoc. editor Oreg. Law Rev.; copy editor Ala. Bar Rag, 1979-84, contbg. editor, 1979-92; annual reviser Probate Counsel, 1972-88. Mem. Anchorage Port Commn., 1987-93, chmn., 1990-93; chmn. Ala. State Officers Compensation Commn., 1986-92; mem. Anchorage Transp. Commn., 1983-87, chmn., 1986-87; vice-chmn. Ala. Code Revision Commn., 1976-78; bd. trustees Ala. Indian Arts, Inc., 1970-92; mem. Chilkat Dancer Ala., 1965—. Fellow Am. Bar Found. (life); mem. ABA (ho. dels. 1980-84, 86—, bd. govs. 1992—, sec. 1996—), Nat. Conf. Bar Pres. (exec. coun. 1985-88), Nat. Conf. Bar Founds. (bd. trustees 1983-90), Am. Arbitration Assn., We. States Bar Conf. (pres. 1983-84), Ala. Bar Assn. (Bd. Govs. Disting. Svc. award 1991, bd. govs. 1977-80, numerous coms.), Presbyterian. Office: 124 E 7th Ave Anchorage AK 99501-3608 also: Am Bar Assn 750 N Lake Shore Dr Chicago IL 60611-4403 Fax: 907-278-0449

WILLEM, KAREN J. business software company financial executive; BA in Biology, Bucknell U.; MBA in Fin., U. Pitts. V.p., corp. contr. Network Gen., v.p. worldwide sales ops.; exec. v.p. fin. and ops., CFO, Brio Tech., Palo Alto, Calif. Office: Brio Tech 3460 W Bayshore Rd Palo Alto CA 94303-4227

WILLERDING, MARGARET FRANCES, mathematician, educator; b. St. Louis, Apr. 26, 1919; d. Herman J. and Mildred F. (Icenhower) W. A.B., Harris Tchrs. Coll., 1940; M.A., St. Louis U., 1943, Ph.D., 1947. Tchr. (Pub. Schs.), St. Louis, 1940-46; instr. math. Washington U., St. Louis, 1947-48; asst. prof. Harris Tchrs. Coll., St. Louis, 1948-56; mem. faculty San Diego State Coll., 1956—, asso. prof., 1959-65, prof. math., 1966-76, prof. emeritus, 1976—. Author: Intermediate Algebra, 1969, Elementary Mathematics, 1971, College Algebra, 1971, College Algebra and Trigonometry, 1971, Arithmetic, 1968, Probability: The Science of Chance, 1969, Mathematics Around the Clock, 1969, Mathematical Concepts, 1967, From Fingers to Computers, 1969, Probability Primer, 1968, Mathematics: The Alphabet of Science, 1972, 74, 77, A First Course in College Mathematics, 1973, 77, 80, Mathematics Worktext, 1973, 77, Business and Consumer Mathematics for College Students, 1976, The Numbers Game, 1977. Mem. Nat. Council Tchrs. Math., Assn. Tchrs. Sci. and Math., Am. Math. Soc., Math. Assn. Am., Greater San Diego Math. Council (dir. 1963-65), Sigma Xi, Pi Mu Epsilon. Home: 10241 Vivera Dr La Mesa CA 91941-4370 Office: San Diego State Coll Dept Math San Diego CA 92085

WILLERT, SISTER ST. JOAN, health care corporation executive; b. Wheeling, W.Va., June 13, 1924; d. Arthur Edgar and Viola (Fitzsimmons) W. BA, Mt. St. Mary's Coll., 1946; human relations cert., Loyola U., L.A., 1951; MS, Mt. St. Mary's Coll., 1953; health care adminstrn., St. Louis U., 1975. Cert. health care adminstrn., elem. sch. adminstrn., secondary sch. adminstrn. Elem. sch. tchr. Diocese of San Francisco, L.A., and Fresno, 1945-54; elem. sch. prin. several cities, 1954-65; secondary sch. prin. Queen of the Valley Acad., Fresno, Calif., 1965-67, Salpointe Catholic High Sch., Tucson, 1967-70; regional superior Sisters of St. Joseph, L.A., 1970-74, Washington, 1974-77; with health care adminstrn. Daniel Freeman Hosp., Inglewood, Calif., 1977-79; pres., chief exec. officer Health Care Corp. Ariz., Tucson, 1979—. Bd. dirs. Freeman Health Ventures, St. John of God, L.A.; bd. sec. Downtown Devel. Corp., Tucson, 1986—; bd. pres. Our Lady of Lourdes Health Ctr., Pasco, Wash., 1975-81, 85—; bd. chairperson Health Care Corp., St. Louis, 1986—. Contbr. articles to MSMC, 1966, Health Progress, 1982. Chairperson state campaign Arizonans to Protect Quality Health Svc., Phoenix, Tucson, 1984-85. Named for Outstanding Svc. to Community Una Noche Plateada, Tucson, 1982; honoree Tucson Diocesan Found. Mem. Ariz. Hosp. Assn. (bd. dirs. 1979—, sec. 1988, chairperson-elect 1989-90, Salisbury Leadership award 1985), Cath. Health Assn. (bylaws com. 1985-86, nominating com. 1984-85), Health Care Corp. Sisters of St. Joseph (chairperson 1985—). Democrat. Roman Catholic. Avocations: reading, tennis, writing. Office: Carondelet St Marys Hosp 1601 W Saint Marys Rd Tucson AZ 85745-2623

WILLES, MARK HINCKLEY, media industry executive; b. Salt Lake City, July 16, 1941; s. Joseph Simmons and Ruth (Hinckley) W.; m. Laura Fayone, June 7, 1961; children: Wendy Anne, Susan Kay, Keith Mark, Stephen Joseph, Matthew Bryant. AB, Columbia Coll., 1963, PhD, 1967. Staff banking and currency com. Ho. of Reps., Washington, 1966-67; asst. prof. fin. Wharton Sch. U. Pa., Phila., 1967-69; economist Fed. Res. Bank, Phila., 1967, sr. economist, 1969-70, dir. rsch., 1970-71, v.p., dir. rsch., 1971, 1st v.p., 1971-77; pres. Fed. Res. Bank of Mpls., 1977-80; exec. v.p., chief fin. officer Gen. Mills, Inc., Mpls., 1980-85, pres., COO, 1985-92, vice-chmn., 1992-95; chmn., pres., CEO Times Mirror Co., L.A., 1995-2000; pub. L.A. Times, 1997-99. Pres. Hawaii Honolulu Mission Ch. of LDS, 2001. E-mail: mark. Office: Hawaii Honolulu Mission Ch of LDS 1500 S Beretania St #410 Honolulu HI 96826 E-mail: willes@byu.edu

WILLETTE, DONALD CORLISS, pastor; b. Lemmon, S.D., June 26, 1941; s. Corliss Noah Willette and Marion Alice (Egland) Allen. BA, St. Mary's Coll./Sem., 1963; MDiv, St. Thomas Sem., Denver, 1984. ordained Roman Catholic priest. Owner, operator Edel Haus Restaurant, Estes Park, Colo., 1975-77; owner, real estate broker Better Homes Gardens, Estes Park, 1977-84; assoc. pastor St. Thomas More, Englewood, Colo., 1984-87, St. Jude Ch., Lakewood, 1987-88; pastor St. Theresa Ch., Frederick, 1988-91, St. Louis Ch., Louisville, 1991—. Founding bd. dirs. Mary's Dream Ltd., Frederick, 1989-92, Migrant Outreach Ministry, Longmont, Colo., 1991-95; tour leader Holy Land Pilgrimages, Jerusalem, 1984-94. With USAF, 1967-73, advanced through grades to col. USAFR, Colo. NG. Mem. Am. Legion (chaplain 1977—), K. of C. (chaplain 1984—), VFW, Elks (chaplain 1979-96, 96—). Avocations: salt water sailing, Holy Land pilgrimage leader. Office: St Louis Ch 902 Grant Ave Louisville CO 80027-1916

WILLHITE, CALVIN CAMPBELL, toxicologist; b. Salt Lake City, Apr. 27, 1952; s. Jed Butler and Carol (Campbell) W. BS, Utah State U., 1974, MS, 1977; PhD, Dartmouth Coll., 1980. Toxicologist USDA, Berkeley, Calif., 1980-85, State of Calif., Berkeley, 1985—. Adj. assoc. prof. toxicol. Utah State U., 1984-94; mem. data safety rev. bds. Johns Hopkins Sch. Medicine, 1996; mem. Calif./OSHA Gen. Industry Safety Order PEL Adv. Bd., 1994, 96; mem. com. toxicology NAS, 1998—; mem. com. validation alternative methods Nat. Toxicology Program, 2000, rev. bd. Ctr. Evaluation Risk Human Reproduction, 2001. Mem. editl. bd. Toxicology and Applied Pharmacology, 1989—; editor N.Y. Acad. Scis., 1993, Toxicology, 1996—, Jour. Toxicol. Environ. Health (B), 1996—, Toxicology Letters, 1998—, Reproductive Toxicol., 2001—; contbr. articles on birth defects to profl. jours. Mem. WHO IARC Cancer Prevention Work Group, 1999; commr. City of Novato, Calif., 2000—. Nat. Inst. Child Health and Human Devel. grantee, 1985-92, March of Dimes Birth Defects Found. grantee, 1987-91, Hoffmann LaRoche grantee, 1992-94. Mem. NIH (Health Promotion/Disease Prevention Study sect. 1998), NSF (mem. health effects adv. bd. 1986—), Am. Conf. Govt. Indsl. Hygienists (mem. threshold limit values com. 1989-99), Soc. Toxicology (program com. 1995-99, Frank R. Blood award 1986), Teratology Soc. Democrat. Mem. United Ch. of Christ. Home: 10 Altamira Ct Novato CA 94949 6154 Office: State Calif 700 Heinz Ave Berkeley CA 94710-2721 E-mail: calvinwillhite@hotmail.com

WILLIAMS, A. CODY, councilman; b. Phoenix, Mar. 5, 1960; m. Jeri Williams; children: Alanna, Alan Travis, Cody Jerard. Student, U. Okla.; MBA, Ariz. State U.; postgrad., Harvard U. Diverse workforce specialist and affirmative action officer Intel; v.p., affirmative action officer Security Pac Bank; pres. Alms & Hosanna Consulting Firm; councilman dist. 8 Phoenix City Coun., 1994—. Chmn. econ. and downtown subcom., mem. housing and neighborhoods subcom., mem. family and youth subcom. and transportation subcom. Office: Phoenix City Coun 200 W Washington St Fl 11 Phoenix AZ 85003-1611 E-mail: cwilliams@ci.phoenix.AZ.US

WILLIAMS, AENEAS DEMETRIUS, professional football player; b. New Orleans, Jan. 29, 1968; Degree in acctg., So. Univ. La., 1990. Cornerback Ariz. Cardinals, Phoenix, 1991. Selected to Pro Bowl, 1994-96; tied for NFL lead in interceptions (9), 1994. Office: c/o Ariz Cardinals PO Box 888 Phoenix AZ 85001-0888

WILLIAMS, ARTHUR COZAD, broadcasting executive; b. Forty Fort, Pa., Feb. 12, 1926; s. John Bedford and Emily Irene (Poyck) W.; m. Ann Cale Bragan, Oct. 1, 1955; children: Emily Williams Van Hoorickx, Douglas, Craig. Student, Wilkes U., 1943-44; B.A. cum laude, U. So. Calif., 1949. With Kaiser Aluminum, 1949, Sta. KPMC, 1950-51; v.p., mgr. KFBK and KFBK-FM Radio Stas., Sacramento, 1951-80; with public relations dept. Sacramento Bee, McClatchy Newspapers, 1981-86. Dir.-treas. Norkal Opportunities, Inc.; pres. Sacramento Bee Credit Union. Served with AUS, 1944-46. Mem. Sigma Delta Chi. Clubs: Rotary, Sutter, Valley Hi Country, Masons, Shriners. Home: 1209 Nevis Ct Sacramento CA 95822-2532 Office: 1125 Brownwyk Dr Sacramento CA 95822-1028 E-mail: artcwilliams@earthlink.net

WILLIAMS, BARRY LAWSON, real estate executive; b. N.Y.C., July 21, 1944; s. Otis Lenzy and Ilza Louise (Berry) W.; m. Adrienne Maria Foster, May 24, 1977; children: Barry C., Jaime, Andrew. AB, Harvard U., 1966, JD, MBA, Harvard U., 1971. Bar: Calif. 1975. Sr. cons. McKinsey & Co., San Francisco, 1971-78; mng. prin. Bechtel Investments Inc., San Francisco, 1979-87; pres. Williams Pacific Ventures Inc., Redwood City, Calif., 1987—. Ptnr. WDG-Ventures, CAC, Redwood City, 1987—; pres. C.N. Flagg Inc., Meriden, Conn., 1988—; bd. dirs. Am. Pres. Co., Oakland, Calif., 1984—, Northwestern Life Ins. Co., Milw., 1987—; chmn. bd. Pacific Presbyn. Med. Ctr., San Francisco, 1980—. Republican. Episcopalian. Avocation: tennis. Office: Williams Pacific Ventures Inc 1200 Bayhill Dr Ste 300 San Bruno CA 94066-3006

WILLIAMS, CARLTON L. communications executive; Pres., CEO Karlkani Infinity Inc., L.A., 1989—. Office: Karlkani Infinity Inc 500 Molino St Ste 215 Los Angeles CA 90013-2268

WILLIAMS, (JOHN) CHRISTOPHER (RICHARD), bishop; b. Sale, Cheshire, Eng., May 22, 1936; arrived in Can., 1960; s. Frank Harold and Ceridwen Roberts (Hughes) W.; m. Rona Macrae Aitken, Mar. 18, 1964; children: Andrew David, Judith Ann. BA in Commerce, Manchester U., Eng., 1958; diploma in theology, Cranmer Hall, Durham, Eng., 1960; DD, Emmanuel St. Chad Coll., Saskatoon, Can., 1997, Wycliffe Coll., Toronto, 2000. Ordained deacon Anglican Ch. of Can., 1960, priest, 1962. Missionary in charge Anglican Ch. Can., Sugluk, Que., Can., 1961-72, Cape Dorset, N.W.T., Can., 1972-75, Baker Lake, 1975-78, archdeacon of the Keewatim, 1975-87, rector Holy Trinity N.W.T., 1978-87; bishop suffagan Diocese of the Arctic, Can., 1987-90, diocesan bishop Can., 1990—. Trustee Can. Churchman, Anglican Ch. Can., 1976-82, mem. nat. exec. com., 1976-79, 92-95. Coord., trans. into Eskimo Inukkitut New Testament, 1992 Avocations: reading, skiing, swimming.

WILLIAMS, CLEVELAND, municipal or county official; BA in Psychology, M in Pub. Adminstrn., San Jose U. Recreation supr. City of San Jose, Calif., 1965-68; asst. to city mgr. City of Seaside, 1971-82; mgr. recreation svcs. Oakland (Calif.) Office Parks and Recreation, 1982-86; supt. parks and recreation Portland (Oreg.) Bur. Parks/Recreation, 1986-90; asst. dir. parks and recreation, dir. Oakland Office Parks and Recreation, 1990-96; dir. parks, recreation and cmty. svcs. City of Santa Ana, Calif., 1996—. Home: 3650 S Bear St Apt H Santa Ana CA 92704-7284 Office: Santa Ana Recreation & Cmty Svcs PO Box 1988 M23 888 W Santa Ana Blvd # 200 Santa Ana CA 92702 Fax: 714-571-4235

WILLIAMS, DAVID MICHAEL, manufacturing executive; b. Bklyn., Feb. 25, 1936; s. Robert Irving and Patricia Margaret (Flanagan) W.; m. Carol Bultmann, Nov. 13, 1965; children: Mark, Jennifer. Cert., NYU, Ctr. for Safety Engring., Manhattan, N.Y., 1960. Mgr. various mfrs., 1956-79; pres. D.M. Williams, Inc., Livermore, Calif., 1979—. Cons. various mfrs., 1979—. Candidate for Gov., Calif., 1990; candidate for Congress, Calif., 1986, 88, 89, 92, 94, 96, 98; active Rep. Ctrl. Com., Calif., 1987-88. Cole grantee NYU, 1960. Mem. Inst. Packaging Profls. (bd. dirs. no. Calif. chpt., 1982-85, chmn. 1985-86), ASTM, Mensa (founder interest group 1983-86). Roman Catholic. Avocation: politics. Office: 1560 Kingsport Ave Livermore CA 94550-6149

WILLIAMS, DAVID WELFORD, federal judge; b. Atlanta, Mar. 20, 1910; s. William W. and Maude (Lee) W.; m. Ouida Maie White, June 11, 1939; children: David Welford, Vaughn Charles. A.A., Los Angeles Jr. Coll., 1932; A.B., UCLA, 1934; LL.B., U. So. Calif., 1937. Bar: Calif. 1937. Practiced in, Los Angeles, 1937-55; judge Mcpl. Ct., Los Angeles, 1956-62, Superior Ct., Los Angeles, 1962-69, U.S. Dist. Ct. (cen. dist.) Calif., Los Angeles, 1969—, now sr. judge; judge Los Angeles County Grand Jury, 1965. Recipient Russwurm award Nat. Assn. Newspapers, 1958; Profl. Achievement award UCLA Alumni Assn., 1966 Office: US Dist Ct 312 N Spring St Ste 1621 Los Angeles CA 90012-4718

WILLIAMS, DELWYN CHARLES, telephone company executive; b. Idaho Falls, Idaho, Apr. 27, 1936; s. Charles H. and Vonda (Wood) W.; m. Marlene Grace Nordland, Feb. 29, 1964; children— Stephen, Kirstin, Nicole. B.S. in Bus., U. Idaho, 1959. C.P.A., Calif. Accountant Peat, Marwick, Mitchell & Co. (C.P.A.s), San Francisco, 1960-65; treas. Dohrmann Instruments Co., Mountain View, Calif., 1965-68; with Continental Telephone Co. of Calif., Bakersfield, 1968-84, controller, 1969-70, v.p., treas., 1970-77, v.p., gen. mgr., 1977-79, pres., 1977-84, also dir.; pres. J.H. Evans, Inc., and subs., 1984-95, CEO, 1995—, Via Wireless LLC, 1996—. Home: 10052 Oak Branch Cir Carmel CA 93923-8000 Office: 4918 Taylor Ct Turlock CA 95382-9579

WILLIAMS, DONALD CLYDE, lawyer; b. Oxnard, Calif., Oct. 12, 1939; s. Leslie Allen and Elizabeth Esther (Orton) W.; m. Miriam Arline, Oct. 5, 1966; children Erin K., Nikki Dawn. B.A. in Gen. Bus, Fresno State Coll., 1963; J.D., Willamette U., 1967. Bar: Oreg. 1967. Practice in, Grants Pass, 1967-70; ptnr. Myrick, Seagraves, Williams & Nealy, 1968-70, Carlsmith, Ball, Wichman, Murray & Ichiki, 1977—; asst. atty. gen. Am. Samoa, 1970-71, atty. gen., 1971-75; assoc. justice High Ct. Trust Ter. of Pacific Islands, 1975-77. Served with USCGR, 1958-59. Mem. ABA, Calif. Bar Assn., Oreg. Bar Assn., Am. Samoa Bar Assn., Guam Bar Assn., Hawaii Bar Assn., Commonwealth No. Mariana Islands Bar Assn., Fed. States of Micronesia Bar Assn., Guam C. of C. Office: Carlsmith Ball 444 S Flower St Fl 9 Los Angeles CA 90071-2901 E-mail: dwilliams@carlsmith.com

WILLIAMS, DUSTON, electronics company executive; BS in Acctg., Bentley Coll., 1980; MBA, U. So. Calif., 1989. Cert. Mgmt. Acct. With Calcomp; from mgr. corp. planning to v.p. fin. personal storage Western Digital Corp., Irvine, Calif., 1986-94, v.p., treas., 1994-96, sr. v.p. corp. officer, 1996-2000; CFO Enterprise Networking Sys., Inc., Redwood City, 2000—. Bd. dirs. Orange County chpt. ARC. Office: Enterprise Networking Sys Inc Western Digital Corp 70 Convention Way Redwood City CA 94062

WILLIAMS, EMMA, management executive; b. Cleveland, Ark., Feb. 8, 1928; d. James and Frazier (Byers) Wallace; m. Augusta Griggs, Mar. 20, 1954 (dec.); children: Judy A., Terri V.; m. John Williams. Grad. H.S., Chgo. Pres., CEO Burlington No. Inc., Inglewood, Calif., 1986—. Republican. Avocations: reading, gardening, housekeeping. Office: Burlington No Corp 2nd Fl 2650 Lou Menk Dr Fort Worth TX 76131-2830 E-mail: judygr7@aol.com

WILLIAMS, FORMAN ARTHUR, engineering science educator, combustion theorist; b. New Brunswick, N.J., Jan. 12, 1934; s. Forman J. and Alice (Pooley) W.; m. Elsie Vivian Kara, June 15, 1955 (div. 1978); children: F. Gary, Glen A., Nancy L., Susan D., Michael S., Michelle K.; m. Elizabeth Acevedo, Aug. 19, 1978. BSE, Princeton U., 1955; PhD, Calif. Inst. Tech., 1958. Asst. prof. Harvard U., Cambridge, Mass., 1958-64; prof. U. Calif.-San Diego, 1964-81; Robert H. Goddard prof. Princeton U., N.J., 1981-88; prof. dept. applied mechs. and engring. scis. U. Calif., San Diego, 1988—, predsidential chair in Energy and Combustion Rsch, 1994—. Author: Combustion Theory, 1965, 2d edit., 1985; contbr. articles to profl. jours. Fellow NSF, 1962; fellow Guggenheim Found., 1970; recipient U.S. Sr. Scientist award Alexander von Humboldt Found., 1982, Silver medal Combustion Inst., 1978, Bernard Lewis Gold medal Combustion Inst., 1990, Pendray Aerospace Literature award Am. Inst. of Aeronautics and Astronautics, 1993 Fellow AIAA ; mem. Am. Phys. Soc., Combustion Inst., Soc. for Indsl. and Applied Math., Nat. Acad. Engring., Nat. Acad. Engring Mex. (fgn. corr. mem.), Sigma Xi. Home: 8258 Caminito Maritimo La Jolla CA 92037-2204 Office: U Calif San Diego Ctr Energy Rsch 9500 Gilman Dr La Jolla CA 92093-5004 E-mail: faw@mae.ucsd.edu

WILLIAMS, HAROLD MARVIN, foundation official, former government official, former university dean, former corporate executive; b. Phila., Jan. 5, 1928; s. Louis W. and Sophie (Fox) W.; m. Nancy Englander; children: Ralph A., Susan J., Derek M. AB, UCLA, 1946; postgrad. in law, U. So. Calif., 1955-59; DHL (hon.), Johns Hopkins U., 1987, Occidental Coll., 1997, Calif. State U., 1998. Bar: Calif. 1950. Pvt. practice, L.A., 1950, 53-55; with Hunt Food and Industries Inc., L.A., 1955-68, v.p., 1958-60, exec. v.p., 1960-68, pres., 1968; gen. mgr. Hunt-Wesson Foods, 1964-66, pres., 1966-68; chmn. fin. com. Norton Simon, 1968-70; prof. mgmt. UCLA, 1970-77; chmn. SEC, Washington, 1977-81; pres., CEO J. Paul Getty Trust, 1981-98, pres. emeritus; of counsel Skadden Arps et al, 1998—. Bd. dirs. Times-Mirror Corp., SunAmerica, Calif. Endowment,

Pub. Policy Inst.; pres., dir. Special Investments and Securities Inc., 1961-66. Mem. Commn. Econ. Devel. State Calif., 1973-77; energy coordinator City of L.A., 1973-74; pub. mem. Nat. Advt. Review Bd., 1971-75; co-chmn. Pub. Commn. L.A. County Govt.; mem. Coun. Fgn. Rels., Com. Econ. Devel.; regent U. Calif., 1983-94; commn. to rev. Master Plan for Higher Edn., State of Calif., 1985-87; co-chair Calif. Citizens Commn. Higher Edn.; trustee Nat. Humanities Ctr., 1987-93; dir. Ethics Resource Ctr.; mem. Pres.' Com. on Arts and Humanities; mem. Commn. on the Acad. Presidency. Served as 1st Lt. AUS, 1950-53. Mem. State Bar Calif. Office: J Paul Getty Trust 1200 Getty Center Dr Ste 1100 Los Angeles CA 90049-1668

WILLIAMS, HARRY EDWARD, management consultant, management consultant, consultant; b. Oak Park, Ill., July 20, 1925; s. Harry E. and Mary E.; m. Jean Horner; 1 child, Jeanne. Student, West Coast U., Los Angeles, 1958-60; BS in Engring., Calif. Coast Coll., Santa Ana, 1975; MA, Calif. Coast Coll., 1975; PhD, Golden State U., Los Angeles, 1981. Registered profl. engr., Calif. Mgr. Parker Aircraft Co., Los Angeles, 1958-60, Leach Corp., Los Angeles, 1968-69, Litton, Data Systems, Van Nuys, Calif., 1969-72; dir. Electronic Memories, Hawthorne, 1972-78, Magnavox Co., Torrance, 1978-80; v.p. Stacoswitch Inc., Costa Mesa, 1981-87; mgmt. cons., Westminster, 1987—. Cons. in field. Contbr. articles to profl. jours. With USAF, 1943-46. Recipient Mgr. of the Yr. award Soc. for Advancement of Mgmt., 1984, Phil Carroll award for outstanding contbns. in field of ops. mgmt., 1985, Profl. Mgr. citation, 1984. Fellow Internat. Acad. Edn. Republican. Methodist. Avocation: target shooting. E-mail: nanpop@juno.com

WILLIAMS, HIBBARD EARL, medical educator, physician; b. Utica, N.Y., Sept. 28, 1932; s. Hibbard G. and Beatrice M. W.; m. Sharon Towne, Sept. 3, 1982; children: Robin, Hans. AB, Cornell U., 1954, MD, 1958. Diplomate Am. Bd. Internal Medicine. Intern Mass. Gen. Hosp., Boston, 1958-59, resident in medicine, 1959-60, 62-64, asst. physician, 1964-65; clin. assoc. Nat. Inst. Arthritis and Metabolic Diseases, NIH, Bethesda, MD, 1960-62; instr. medicine Harvard U., Boston, 1964-65; asst. prof. medicine U. Calif., San Francisco, 1965-68, assoc. prof., 1968-72, prof., 1972-78, chief divsn. med. genetics, 1968-70, vice chmn. dept. medicine, 1970-78; prof., chmn. dept. medicine Cornell U. Med. Coll., N.Y.C., 1978-80; physician-in-chief N.Y. Hosp.-Cornell Med. Ctr., N.Y.C., 1978-80; dean Sch. Medicine U. Calif., Davis, 1980-92, prof. internal medicine, 1980-2000; prof. emeritus, 2000—. Mem. program project com. NIH, Nat. Inst. Arthritis and Metabolic Diseases, 1971-73 Editor med. staff confs. Calif. Medicine, 1966-70; mem. editl. bd. Clin. Rsch., 1968-71, Am. Jour. Medicine, 1978-88; cons. editor Medicine, 1978-86; assoc. editor Metabolism, 1970-80; mem. adv. bd. physiology in medicine New Eng. Jour. Medicine, 1970-75; contbr. articles to med. jours. With USPHS, 1960-62. Recipient Career Devel. award USPHS, 1968; recipient award for excellence in teaching Kaiser Found., 1970, Disting. Faculty award U. Calif. Alumni-Faculty Assn., 1978; John and Mary R. Markle scholar in medicine, 1968 Fellow ACP; mem. AAAS, Am. Fedn. Clin. Rsch., Am. Soc. Clin. Investigation (sec.-treas. 1974-77), Assn. Am. Physicians, Assn. Am. Med. Colls. (adminstrv. bd., coun. deans 1989-92, exec. coun. 1990-92), Calif. Acad. Medicine (pres. 1984), San Francisco Diabetes Assn. (bd. dirs. 1971-72), Western Assn. Physicians (v.p. 1977-78), Western Soc. Clin. Rsch., Calif. Med. Assn. (chmn. coun. sci. affairs 1990-95, bd. dirs. 1990-95), Calif. Med. Assn. Found. (chmn. bd. dirs. 1997-99), Gianinni Found. (sci. adv. bd. 1990-2000—), St. Francis Yacht Club, Alpha Omega Alph. Office: U Calif Sch Medicine TB150 Davis CA 95616

WILLIAMS, HOWARD RUSSELL, lawyer, educator; b. Evansville, Ind., Sept. 26, 1915; s. Clyde Alfred and Grace (Preston) W.; m. Virginia Merle Thompson, Nov. 3, 1942 (dec. Dec. 2000); 1 son, Frederick S.T. AB, Washington U., St. Louis, 1937; LLB, Columbia U., 1940. Bar: N.Y. 1941. With firm Root, Clark, Buckner & Ballantine, N.Y.C., 1940-41; prof. law, asst. dean U. Tex. Law Sch., Austin, 1946-51; prof. law Columbia U. Law Sch., N.Y.C., 1951-63; Dwight prof. Columbia Law Sch., 1959-63; prof. law Stanford U., 1963-85, Stella W. and Ira S. Lillick prof., 1968-82, prof. emeritus, 1982, Robert E. Paradise prof. natural resources, 1983-85, prof. emeritus, 1985—. Oil and gas cons. President's Materials Policy Commn., 1951; mem. Calif. Law Revision Commn., 1971-79, vice chmn., 1976-77, chmn., 1978-79 Author or co-author: Cases on Property, 1954, Cases on Oil and Gas, 1956, 5th edit., 1987, Decedents' Estates and Trusts, 1968, Future Interests, 1970, Oil and Gas Law, 8 vols., 1959-64 (with ann. supplements/rev. 1964-95), abridged edit., 1973, Manual of Oil and Gas Terms, 1957, 11th edit., 2000. Bd. regents Berkeley Bapt. Divinity Sch., 1966-67; trustee Rocky Mountain Mineral Law Found., 1964-66, 68-85. With U.S. Army, 1941-46. Recipient Clyde O. Martz Tchg. award Rocky Mountain Mineral Law Found., 1994. Mem. Phi Beta Kappa. Democrat. Home: 360 Everett Ave Apt 4B Palo Alto CA 94301-1422 Office: Stanford U Sch Law Nathan Abbott Way Stanford CA 94305

WILLIAMS, HOWARD WALTER, aerospace engineer, executive; b. Evansville, Ind., Oct. 18, 1937; s. Walter Charles and Marie Louise (Bollinger) W.; m. Phyllis Ann Scofield, May 4, 1956 (div. Sept. 1970); m. Marilee Sharon Mulvane, Oct. 30, 1970; children: Deborah, Steven, Kevin, Glenn, Lori, Michele. AA, Pasadena City Coll., 1956; BSME, Calif. State U., Los Angeles, 1967; BSBA, U. San Francisco, 1978; PhD in Comml. Sci. (hon.), London Inst. Applied Rsch., 1992. Turbojet, rocket engr. Aerojet-Gen. Corp., Azusa, Calif., 1956-59, infrared sensor engr., 1959-60, rocket, torpedo engr., 1960-66, power, propulsion mgr. propulsion divsn. Sacramento, 1967-73, high speed ship systems mgr., 1974-78, combustion, power mgr., rocket engine and energy mktg. mgr., 1979-89, dir. strategic planning, 1989-94; strategic analyst, program mgr. Pratt & Whitney Space Propulsion, San Jose, Calif., 1995—. Author: (with others) Heat Exchangers, 1980, Industrial Heat Exchangers, 1985, History of Liquid Rocket Engine Development in the U.S., 1992, Aerojet: The Creative Company, 1997; co-inventor Closed Cycle Power System, 1969. Recipient Energy Innovation award U.S. Dept. Energy, 1985. Mem. AIAA (sr., Best Paper 1966), Am. Soc. Metals (organizing dir. indsl. heat exch. confs. 1985). Avocations: bicycling, grandchildren.

WILLIAMS, J. D. state controller; b. Malad, Idaho; m. Rosemary Zaugg; 4 daus. MPA, Brigham Young U.; JD, Am. Univ. Bar: Idaho, D.C., several fed. cts.; cert. govt. fin. mgr. Apptd. law clk. D.C. Ct. Appeals; dep. Idaho Atty. Gen. Boise; lawyer Preston, Idaho; mayor City of Preston; appt. auditor State of Idaho, Boise, 1989-94, elected controller, 1994—. Mem. Info. Tech. Res. Coun., Idaho. Past mem. Idaho Law Enforcement Planning Commn., past chmn. Idaho Youth Commn.; past chmn. Preston Sch. Dist. Excellence in Edn. com.; past mem. Idaho Water Resource Bd. Named Fin. Mgr. of Yr., Idaho. Nat. Assn. State Comptrollers (past pres.), Nat. Assn. State Auditors, Comptrollers and Treasurers (sec. exec. com., Pres.'s award for outstanding svc. in fin. mgmt. to U.S.), Nat. Electronic Commerce Coordinating Coun. (chmn.). Office: Office State Contr State Capital Boise ID 83720-0001

WILLIAMS, J. STANLEY, state senator; Rep. rep. dist. 31 Idaho Ho. of Reps., 1998-2000; Rep. senator dist. 31 Idaho State Senate, 2000—. Mem. agrl. affairs, edn., commerce/human resources coms. Idaho Ho. of Reps. Office: 1286 W 200 S Pingree ID 83262 Fax: 208 684-9211

WILLIAMS, J. VERNON, lawyer; b. Honolulu, Apr. 26, 1921; s. Urban and W. Amelia (Olson) W.; m. Malvina H. Hitchcock, Oct. 4, 1947 (dec. May 1970); children— Carl H., Karin, Frances E., Scott S.; m. Mary McLellan, Sept. 6, 1980. Student, Phillips Andover Acad., 1937-39; B.A. cum laude, Amherst Coll., 1943; LL.B., Yale, 1948. Bar: Wash. 1948. Assoc. Riddell, Riddell & Hemphill, 1948-50, ptnr., 1950-95; sr. prin. emeritus Riddell Williams, P.S., Seattle, 1996—. Sec., dir. Airborne Freight Corp., 1968-79, gen. counsel, 1968-96. Chmn. March of Dimes, Seattle, 1954-55; Mem. Mayor's City Charter Rev. Com., 1968-69; chmn. Seattle Bd. Park Commrs., 1966-68; co-chmn. parks and open space com. Forward Thrust, 1966-69; dir. bd. and commrs. br. Nat. Recreation and Parks Assn., 1968-69; chmn. Gov.'s adv. com. Social and Health Services, 1972-75; Bd. dirs. Seattle Met. YMCA, 1965— , pres., 1976-79; trustee Lakeside Sch., 1971-79; mem. alumni council Phillps Andover Acad., 1970-73, Yale Law Sch., 1969-77; chancellor St. Mark's Cathedral, Seattle, 1964-2000. Served with USAAF, 1943-45. Mem. Univ. Club, Seattle Tennis Club, Birnam Wood Golf Club. Home: 1100 38th Ave E Seattle WA 98112-4434 Office: 4500 1001 4th Ave Plz Seattle WA 98154-1065

WILLIAMS, JAMES E. food products manufacturing company executive; married. With Golden State foods Corp., 1961—, chief exec. officer Calif., 1978-1999. Office: Golden State Foods Corp 18301 Von Karman Ave Ste 1100 Irvine CA 92612-0133

WILLIAMS, JAMES FRANKLIN, II, university dean, librarian; b. Montgomery, Ala., Jan. 22, 1944; s. James Franklin and Anne (Wester) W.; m. Madeline McClellan, Jan. 1966 (div. May 1988); 1 child, Madeline Marie; m. Nancy Allen, Aug. 1989; 1 child, Audrey Grace. BA, Morehouse Coll., 1966; MLS, Atlanta U., 1967. Reference libr. Wayne State U. Sci. Libr., Detroit, 1968-69; document delivery libr. Wayne State U. Med. Libr., Detroit, 1969-70, head of reference, 1971-72, dir. med. libr. and regional med. libr. network, 1972-81, regional dir., 1975-82; assoc. dir. of librs. Wayne State U., 1981-88; dean librs. U. Colo., Boulder, 1988—. Bd. regents Nat. Libr. Medicine, Bethesda, Md., 1978-81; bd. dirs. Denver Art Mus., 1997—, pres. 1999—; bd. dirs. Ctr. Rsch. Librs., 1998—; pres. Big Twelve Plus Libr. Consortium, 2000. Mem. editl. bd. ACRL Publications in Librarianship, College and Research Libraries; contbr. articles to profl. jours., chpts. to books; book editor and author. Bd. dirs. Educom, 1997-98, Boulder Cmty. Hosp., 2000—. Subject of feature interview in centennial issue Am. Librs. jour., 1976. Mem. ALA (Visionary Leader award 1988), Coll. and Rsch. Librs. (editl. bd.), Assn. Rsch. Librs. (bd. dirs. 1994-96), Boulder C. of C. (bd. dirs.). Avocations: cycling, travel, fishing. Office: U Colo Office Dean Librs PO Box 184 Boulder CO 80309-0184

WILLIAMS, JASON, professional basketball player; b. Nov. 18, 1975; Student, U. Fla. Guard Sacramento Kings NBA, 1999—. Named Schick All-Rookie First Team, 1998-99. Office: c/o Sacramento Kings One Sports Pkwy Sacramento CA 95834

WILLIAMS, JOHN JAMES, JR. architect; b. Denver, July 13, 1949; s. John James and Virginia Lee (Thompson) W.; m. Mary Serene Morck, July 29, 1972. BArch, U. Colo., 1974. Registered architect, Colo., Calif., Idaho, Va., Utah, Nev., N.Mex., Wyo., Ohio, Nebr. Project architect Gensler Assoc. Architects, Denver, 1976, Heinzman Assoc. Architects, Boulder, Colo., 1977, EZTH Architects, Boulder, 1978-79; prin. Knudson/Williams PC, Boulder, 1980-82, Faber, Williams & Brown, Boulder, 1982-86, John Williams & Assocs., Denver, 1986-97; John Williams Architecture P.C., 1997—. Panel chmn. U. Colo. World Affairs Conf.; vis. faculty U. Colo. Sch. Architecture and Planning, Coll. Environ. Design, 1986-91; mem. dean's adv. bd. Coll. Arch. and Planning, 2000—. Author (with others) State of Colorado architect licensing law, 1986. Commr. Downtown Boulder Mall Commn., 1985-88; bd. dirs. U. Colo. Fairway Club, 1986-88; mem. Gov's. Natural Hazard Mitigation Coun., State of Colo., 1990. Recipient Teaching Honorarium, U. Colo. Coll. Architecture and Planning, 1977, 78, 79, 80, 88, Excellence in Design and Planning award City of Boulder, 1981, 82, Citation for Excellenc, WOOD Inc., 1982, 93, Disting. Profl. Svc. award Coll. Environ. Design U. Colo., 1988, James Sudler Svc. award AIA, Denver, 1998. Mem. AIA (sec. 1988, bd. dirs. Colo. North chpt. 1985-86, chair Colo. govtl. affairs com. 1995-98, Design award 1993, pres. 1990, sec. Colo. chpt. 1988, ednl. fund Fisher I traveling scholar 1988, state design conf. chair 1991, North chpt. Design award 1993, treas. Denver chpt. 1998, v.p. 1999, pres. edn. Colo. chpt. 2001), Architects and Planners of Boulder (v.p. 1982), Nat. Coun. Architect Registration Bd., Nat. Golf Found. (sponsor), Kappa Sigma (chpt. pres. 1970). Avocations: golf, polit. history, fitness and health. Home: 1031 Turnberry Cir Louisville CO 80027-9594 Office: John Williams Architecture PC 3012 Huron St Ste 200 Denver CO 80202-1032

WILLIAMS, J(OHN) TILMAN, insurance executive, real estate broker, city official; b. Detroit, Feb. 26, 1925; s. Aubrey and Martha (Lou) W.; m. Sally Jane Robinson, Aug. 22, 1947; children: Leslie Ann, Martha Lou. B.S. in Agr, Mich. State U., 1951. Pres. Satellite Ins. Brokerage, Garden Grove, Calif., 1959—. Pres. Satellite Real Estate, Satellite Mortgage & Loan Co. Mayor Garden Grove, 1976-78, re-elected, 1987, mem. coun., 1980-92, apptd. vice mayor, 1989—; mem. Ad Hoc Com. on Property Tax to Limit Govt. Spending with Spirit of 13 Initiative; elected to Orange County Dem. Cen. Com., 68th Assembly Dist., 1996; past pres. Garden Grove High Sch. Band Boosters; trustee Garden Grove Unified Sch. Dist., 2000—. With USAAF, World War II, PTO. Mem. Bd. Realtors, Ind. Ins. Agts. Assn., Orange County Esperanto Assn. (pres. 1985—), Am. Legion, VFW. Democrat. Methodist. Clubs: Toastmasters (Anaheim, Calif.); Fifty-Plus Sr. Citizens of Garden Grove (pres. 1986—). Lodges: Lions, Elks. Home: 11241 Chapman Ave Garden Grove CA 92840-3301 Office: 12311 Harbor Blvd Garden Grove CA 92840-3809

WILLIAMS, JOHN TOWNER, composer, conductor; b. Flushing, N.Y., Feb. 8, 1932; Student, UCLA; pvt. studies with Mario Castelnuovo-Tedesco, Los Angeles; student, Juilliard Sch.; pvt. studies with, Madame Rosina Lhevinne, N.Y.C.; hon. degree, Berklee Coll. Music, Boston, Northeastern U., Tufts U., U. So. Calif., Boston U., New Eng. Conservatory Music, Providence Coll.; others. Condr. Boston Pops Orch., 1980-98; retired; condr., composer Gorfaine & Schwartz, Sherman Oaks, Calif. Works include: composer (film scores) I Passed for White, 1960, Because They're Young, 1960, The Secret Ways, 1961, Bachelor Flat, 1962, Diamond Head, 1962, Gidget Goes to Rome, 1963, The Killers, 1964, John Goldfarb, Please Come Home, 1964, None But the Brave, 1965, How to Steal a Million, 1966, The Rare Breed, 1966, Not With My Wife, You Don't, 1966, The Plainsman, 1966, Penelope, 1966, A Guide for the Married Man, 1967, Valley of the Dolls, 1967 (Acad. award nominee), Fitzwilly, 1968, Sergeant Ryker, 1968, The Reivers, 1969 (Acad. award nominee), Daddy's Gone A-Hunting, 1969, Goodbye, Mr. Chips, 1969 (Acad. award nominee), The Story of A Woman, 1970, Fiddler on the Roof, 1971 (Acad. award for musical adaptation 1971), The Cowboys, 1972, The Poseidon Adventure, 1972 (Acad. award nominee), Images, 1972 (Acad. award nominee), Pete 'n' Tillie, 1972, The Paper Chase, 1973, The Long Goodbye, 1973, The Man Who Loved Cat Dancing, 1973, Cinderella Liberty, 1973 (Acad. award nominee), Tom Sawyer, 1973 (Acad. award nominee), Sugarland Express, 1974, Earthquake, 1974, The Towering Inferno, 1974 (Acad. award nominee), Conrack, 1974, Jaws, 1975 (Acad. award 1976, Grammy award, Golden Globe award), The Eiger Sanction, 1976, Family Plot, 1976, Midway, 1976, The Missouri Breaks, 1976, Raggedy Ann and Andy, 1977, Black Sunday, 1977, Star Wars, 1977 (Acad. award, 3 Grammy awards, Golden Globe award), Close Encounters of the Third Kind, 1977 (2 Grammy awards, Acad. award nominee), The Fury, 1978, Jaws II, 1978, Superman, 1978 (2 Grammy awards), Meteor, 1979, Quintet, 1979, Dracula, 1979, "1941", 1979, The Empire Strikes Back, 1980 (2 Grammy awards, Acad. award nominee), Raiders of the Lost Ark, 1981 (Grammy award, Acad. award nominee), Heartbeeps, 1981, E.T., 1982 (Acad. award for best original score, 3 Grammy awards, Golden Globe award), Monsignor, 1982, Yes, Giorgio, 1982 (Acad. award nominee), Superman III, 1983, Return of the Jedi, 1983 (Acad. award nominee), Indiana Jones and the Temple of Doom, 1984 (Acad. award nominee), The River, 1984 (Acad. award nominee), Space Camp, 1986, Emma's War, 1986, The Witches of Eastwick, 1987 (Acad. award nominee), Empire of the Sun, 1987 (Acad. award nominee), Jaws: The Revenge, 1987, Superman IV: The Quest for Peace, 1987, The Secret of My Success, 1987, The Accidental Tourist, 1988 (Acad. award nominee, Indiana Jones and the Last Crusade, 1989 (Acad. award nominee), Always, 1989, Born On The Fourth of July, 1989 (Acad. award nominee), Stanley and Iris, 1990, Presumed Innocent, 1990, Home Alone, 1990 (Acad. award nominee), Hook, 1991 (Acad. award nominee), JFK, 1991 (Acad. award nominee), Far and Away, 1992, Home Alone II, 1992, Jurassic Park, 1993, Schindler's List, 1993 (Acad. award for best original score 1993), Sabrina, 1995 (Acad. award nominee for best original score 1996, Nixon, 1995 (Acad. award nominee for best dramatic score 1996); composer music for songs including: (from Sabrina, lyrics by Alan and Marilyn Bergman) Moonlight, 1995 (Acad. award nominee for best original song 1996); composer: (TV programs) Heidi, 1969 (Emmy award), Jane Eyre, 1971 (Emmy award), others; composer numerous concert pieces and symphonies including Jubilee 350 Fanfare for the Boston Pops, 1980, theme to the 1984 Summer Olympic Games, Liberty Fanfare, 1987; recorded numerous albums with Boston Pops Orch. including Pops in Space, That's Entertainment (Pops on Broadway), Pops on the March, Pops Around the World (Digital Overtures), Aisle Seat, Pops Out of This World, Boston Pops on Stage, America, the Dream Goes On; collaborator: (with Jessye Norman) With A Song in My Heart, Swing, Swing, Swing, Unforgettable; guest condr. major orchs. including London Symphony Orch., Cleve. Orch., Phila. Orch., Toronto Orch., Montreal Orch. Served with USAF. Recipient several gold and platinum records Rec. Industry Assn. Am. Office: Gorfaine & Schwartz c/o Michael Gorfaine 13245 Riverside Dr Ste 450 Sherman Oaks CA 91423-2172

WILLIAMS, JOUSTON L. service industry executive; Pres., CEO Pacific Network Supply Inc., San Jose, Calif., 1987—. Office: Pacific Network Supply Inc 2320 Kruse Dr San Jose CA 95131-1231

WILLIAMS, JUDI, communications executive; children: Wayne, two daughters. Founder Telect, Liberty Lake, Wash., 1982—. Office: Telect 2111 N Molter Rd Liberty Lake WA 99019

WILLIAMS, JULIE FORD, mutual fund officer; b. Long Beach, Calif., Aug. 7, 1948; d. Julious Hunter and Bessie May (Wood) Ford; m. Walter Edward Williams, Oct. 20, 1984; 1 child, Andrew Ford BA in Econs., Occidental Coll., 1970. Legal sec. Kadison, Pfaelzer, Woodard, Quinn & Rossi, L.A., 1970-71, 74-77; legal sec. Fried, Frank, Harris, Shriver & Jacobson, N.Y.C., 1971-72, Pallot, Poppell, Goodman & Shapo, Miami, Fla., 1973-74; adminstrv. asst. Capital Research-Mgmt., Los Angeles, 1978-82; corp. officer Cash Mgmt. Trust Am., 1982—, Bond Fund Am., 1982—, Tax-Exempt Bond Fund Am., 1982—, AMCAP Fund, 1984-98, 2000—, Am. Funds Income Series, 1985—, Am. Funds Tax-Exempt Series II, 1986—, Capital World Bond Fund, 1987—, Am. High-Income Trust, 1987—, Intermediate Bond Fund Am., 1987—, Tax-Exempt Money Fund Am., 1989—, U.S. Treasury Money Fund Am., 1991—, Fundamental Investors, 1992-2000, Ltd. Term Tax-Exempt Bond Fund Am., 1993—, Am. High-Income Mcpl. Bond Fund, 1994—; v.p. fund bus. mgmt. group Capital Rsch. Mgmt., 1986—; sec. Growth Fund of Am., 1998-2000; Am. Mutual Fund, 2000—. Pres. Alumni Bd. Govs. Occidental Coll., 1997-98; bd. trustees Occidental Coll., 1999—. Democrat. Episcopalian. Office: Capital Rsch & Mgmt Co 333 S Hope St Ste 5000 Los Angeles CA 90071-1452

WILLIAMS, KATHLEEN, advertising executive; Pres., CEO Williams Worldwide, Santa Monica, Calif., 1987—. Office: Williams Worldwide Inc 3130 Wilshire Blvd Fl 4 Santa Monica CA 90403-2358

WILLIAMS, KEITH ROY, museum director; b. Sunnyside, Wash., Sept. 5, 1958; s. Charles N. Williams and Ruth Arlene (Plank) Hicks; m. Nancy Maxson, 1980 (div. 1984); m. Deanna Lynn Murphy, Oct. 26, 1987; children: Steven, Jeremy. AA in Gen. Studies, Columbia Basin C.C., Pasco, Wash., 1979; BA in Anthropology, Wash. State U., 1981, MA in History/Pub. History, 1984, PhD in History, 1991. Interpretive ranger Nez Perce Nat. Hist. Pk. Nat. Pk. Svc., 1984, historian Alaska regional office, 1986; dir. Wenatchee Valley Mus. and Cultural Ctr., Wenatchee, 1987—. Cons. Office Archaeology and Hist. Preservation, 1985, Batelle N.W. DOSE Reconstruction Project, Hanford, 1987, 88; instr. Wenatchee Valley C.C., 1988, 93—; Wash. state adviser Smithsonian Instn. exhibit Barn Again, 2000-01; field assessor and surveyor Am. ASsn. Musuems Mus. Assessment program, 1996—; spkr. in field. Author: (video, booklet) The People and The Plow, 1987; contbr. articles to profl. jours. Active Wash. State Heritage Coun., Olympia, 1988-90, Wash. Centennial Com., Wenatchee, 1989; mem. design com. Wenatchee Downtown Assn., 1993-96; bd. dirs. Wash. Friends Humanities, Seattle, 1990—, Wenatchee Centennial Com., 1992, Wash. Consortium for the Humanities, 2001—. Grantee Assn. Humanities Idaho, Wash. Commn. Humanities, various other founds. Mem. Wash. Mus. Assn. (bd. dirs. 1988-90, 94-96), Kiwanis (bd. dirs. 1998-99). Avocations: boating, gardening, hunting, camping, reading. E-mial. Office: Wenatchee Valley Mus and Cultural Ctr 127 S Mission St Wenatchee WA 98801-3039 E-mail: kwilliams@cityofwenatchee.com

WILLIAMS, KENNETH SCOTT, entertainment company executive; b. Tulsa, Okla., Dec. 31, 1955; s. David Vorhees Williams and Mary Louise (Newell) Rose; m. Jann Catherine Wolfe, May 20, 1989; children: Catherine Eloise, Michael Holbrook. BA, Harvard Coll., 1978; MS, Columbia U., 1985. Bank officer Chase Manhattan Bank, N.Y.C., 1978-82; asst. treas. Columbia Pictures Entertainment, N.Y.C., 1982-84, v.p., treas., 1984-89, sr. v.p. fin. and adminstrn. Burbank, Calif., 1990-91; sr. v.p. corp. ops. Sony Pictures Entertainment, Culver City, 1991-95, exec. v.p., 1995-96; pres. Digital Studio divsn. Sony Pictures Entertainment, 1996-2000; pres., CEO Stan Lee Media, Inc., Encino, Calif., 2000—. Mem. Blue Hill Troupe, N.Y.C., 1979—; past pres., bd. dirs. L.A. Conservancy; bd. govs. L.A. Music Ctr.; former chmn. Entertainment Tech. Ctr., U. So. Calif.; trustee the Buckley Sch., U. Calif. Riverside; mem. adv. com. UCLA Extension Sch.; mem. pres.'s adv. bd. Santa Monica Jr. Coll., Acad. Entertainment and Tech. Mem. N.Y. Soc. Securities Analysts, Fin. Execs. Inst., Harvard Club. So. Calif. (bd. dirs.), Beta Gamma Sigma. Home: 457 Cuesta Way Los Angeles CA 90077-3434 Office: Stan Lee Media Inc PO Box 116 Van Nuys CA 91408 E-mail: kenneth_s_williams@hotmail.com

WILLIAMS, LEONA RAE, lingerie shop owner, consultant; b. Fairfield, Nebr., July 1, 1928; d. Melton M. and Helga D. (Sorensen) Brown; m. Eugene F. Williams, June 6, 1946; 1 child, Dennis D. Grad. high sch., Fairfield. Owner Alice Rae Apparel Shop, Tucson, 1953-96, second location, 1967-96, Green Valley, Ariz., 1976-93, Sun City, 1979-96; ret., 1996; owner Boutique on Wheels, 2001—, prin., 2001—. Cons. in field. Sponsor Distributive Edn. Program, 1978-82; coord. fashion shows Am. Cancer Soc., Tucson, 1987, 88, 89. Mem. Exec. Women's Internat. Assn. (chpt. pres. 1994), Mchts. Assn. (pres. 1987-89), Soroptomists, C. of C. Better Bus. Bur. Republican. Baptist. E-mail: leonagene@msn.com

WILLIAMS, LEWIS T. (RUSTY WILLIAMS), education educator; Pres. Chiron R&D, 1994—, chief scientific officer, 1999; adj. prof. medicine U. Calif., San Francisco. E-mail: rusty_williams@cc.chiron.com

WILLIAMS, LOWELL CRAIG, lawyer, employee relations executive; b. Tehachapi, Calif., Dec. 3, 1947; s. Lyndon Williams and Gertrude (White) Sievert; m. Marsha Mendelssohn; children: John S., Jeffrey A. Bescheinigungeschichte, Georg August U., Germany, 1968; BA, U. Calif., Santa Barbara, 1969; JD, Columbia U., 1972. Bar: N.Y. 1973, U.S. Ct. Appeals (2nd cir.) 1974, U.S. Supreme Ct. 1974. Assoc. Sullivan & Cromwell, N.Y.C., 1972-75; sr. v.p. Elf Aquitaine, Inc., N.Y.C., 1976-95; v.p. Compagnie des Machines Bull, N.Y.C., 1995—, exec. v.p. group human resources, 1998-99; exec. dir. Exult Inc., N.Y.C., 1999—. Past pres. Scarsdale Synagogue. Mem. Internat. Bar Assn., German Law Assn. (dir.). Office: Exult Inc 4 Park Plz Ste 1000 Irvine CA 92614-2552 E-mail: lowell.williams@exult.net

WILLIAMS, MARION LESTER, government official; b. Abilene, Tex., Dec. 1, 1933; s. Martin Lester and Eddie Faye (Wilson) W.; m. Johnnie Dell Ellinger, Dec. 14, 1957; children: Tammy Dawn Cole, Pamela DeAnn Ritterbush. BS, Tex. A&M U., 1956; MS, U. N.Mex., 1967; PhD, Okla. State U., 1971. Test engr. Sandia Nat. Labs., Albuquerque, 1959-61; weapons sys. engr. Naval Weapons Evaluation Facility, Albuquerque, 1961-66; ops. rsch. analyst Joint Chiefs of Staff/Joint Task Force II, Albuquerque, 1966-68; chief reliability div. Field Command DNA, Albuquerque, 1969-71; prin. scientist SHAPE Tech. Ctr., The Hague, Netherlands, 1971-74; chief tech. advisor HQ AF Test & Evaluation Ctr., Albuquerque, 1974-81; chief scientist HQ AF Operational Test & Evaluation Ctr., Albuquerque, 1981-89, tech. dir., 1989—. Vis. adv. com. Okla. State U., Stillwater, 1988—; adv. com. U. N.Mex., Albuquerque, 1985—. Editor T&E Tech. Jour., 1987—; contbr. articles to profl. jours. Sci. advisor N.Mex. Sci. & Tech. Oversigh Com., Albuquerque, 1988; bd. advisors U. N.Mex. Cancer Ctr., 1987—; bd. dirs. Contact Albuquerque, 1986-87. 1st lt. USAF 1956-59. Recipient Presdl. Rank award, 1987, 92. Fellow Mil. Ops. Rsch. Soc. (pres. 1982-83, bd. dirs. 1976-81, Wanner award 1991), Internat. Test & Evaluation Ctr. (bd. dirs. 1984-86, 88-90, v.p. 1990, pres. 1992-93), Ops. Rsch. Soc. Am., Tau Beta Pi, Phi Eta Sigma, Alpha Pi Mu, Sigma Tau, Kappa Mu Epsilon. Democrat. Baptist. Avocations: skiing, computers. Home: 1416 Stagecoach Ln SE Albuquerque NM 87123-4429 Office: HQ AF Operational Test Ctr Kirtland AFB Albuquerque NM 87117-0001 E-mail: williams505@flash.net

WILLIAMS, MATT (MATTHEW DERRICK WILLIAMS), professional baseball player; b. Bishop, Calif., Nov. 28, 1965; Student, U. Nev., Las Vegas. With San Francisco Giants, 1987-96, Cleveland Indians, 1997, Ariz. Diamondbacks, 1997—. Player Nat. League All-Star Team, 1990, 94. Recipient Gold Glove award, 1991, 93, 94, Silver Slugger award, 1990, 93-94; named to Sporting News Nat. League All-Star team, 1990, 93-94, Coll. All-Am. team Sporting News, 1986; Nat. League RBI Leader, 1990. Office: Arizona Diamondbacks Bank One Ballpark 401 E Jefferson St Phoenix AZ 85004-2438

WILLIAMS, MICHAEL ANTHONY, lawyer; b. Mandan, N.D., Sept. 14, 1932; s. Melvin Douglas and Lucille Ann (Gavin) W.; m. Marjorie Ann Harrer, Aug. 25, 1962 (div. 1989); children: Ann Margaret, Douglas Raymond, David Michael; m. Dorothy Ruth Hand, 1989. B.A., Coll. of St. Thomas, 1954; LL.B., Harvard U., 1959. Bar: Colo. 1959, N.D. 1959, U.S. Dist. Ct. Colo. 1959, U.S. Ct. Appeals (10th cir.) 1959, U.S. Supreme Ct. 1967. Assoc. Sherman & Howard and predecessor Dawson, Nagel, Sherman & Howard, Denver, 1959-65, ptnr., 1965-91; pres. Williams, Youle & Koenigs, P.C., Denver, 1991—. Served as 1st lt. USAF, 1955-57. Mem. Am. Coll. Trial Lawyers, Am. Bd. Trial Advs., Colo. Bar Found., Am. Law Inst., ABA, Colo. Bar Assn., Denver Bar Assn., Arapahoe County Bar Assn. Office: Williams Youle & Koenigs PC 950 17th St Ste 2450 Denver CO 80202-2811

WILLIAMS, MIKEL HOWARD, magistrate judge; b. Lewiston, Idaho, Jan. 2, 1946; m. Lorette Biaggne Williams; children: Dayna, Holly. BA, U. Idaho, LLB, 1969. Bar: Idaho 1969, U.S. Dist. Ct. Idaho 1969, U.S. Ct. Appeals (9th cir.) 1974, U S. Ct. Mil. Appeals 1969, U.S. Supreme Ct. 1969. Asst. U.S. atty. Dist. of Idaho, 1973-77; ptnr. Collins, Manley & Williams, 1977-84; magistrate judge U.S. Dist. Ct., Boise, 1984—. Author in field. Served to lt. col. JAGC, U.S. Army, 1969-93. Rocky Mountain Mineral Law Found. scholar, 1967. Mem. Idaho State Bar. Office: US Dist Ct 550 W Fort St Msc 039 Boise ID 83724-0001

WILLIAMS, PAT, former congressman; b. Helena, Mont., Oct. 30, 1937; m. Carol Griffith, 1965; children: Griff, Erin, Whitney. Student, U. Mont., 1956-57, William Jewell U.; BA, U. Denver, 1961; postgrad., Western Mont. Coll.; LLD (hon.), Carroll Coll., Montana Coll. of Mineral Sci. and Tech. Mem. Mont. Ho. of Reps., 1967, 69; exec. dir. Hubert Humphrey Presdl. campaign, Mont., 1968; exec. asst. to U.S. Rep. John Melcher, 1969-71; mem. Gov.'s Employment and Tng. Council, 1972-78, Mont. Legis. Reapportionment Commn., 1973; co-chmn. Jimmy Carter Presdl. campaign, Mont., 1976; mem. 96th-102nd Congresses from 1st Mont. dist., 1979-96; sr. fellow W. U. Mont., Missoula, 1996—. Ranking mem. postsecondary edn. subcom. Coordinator Mont. Family Edn. Program, 1971-78. Served with U.S. Army, 1960-61; Served with Army N.G., 1962-69. Mem. Mont. Fedn. Tchrs. Democrat. Lodge: Elks. Home: 3533 Lincoln Hills Pt Missoula MT 59802-3381 Office: U Montana O Connor Ctr Rocky Mtn W Milw Sta 2nd Fl Missoula MT 59812-0001*

WILLIAMS, PATRICIA C. federal judge; Apptd. bankruptcy judge ea. dist. U.S. Dist. Ct. Wash., 1997. Office: 904 W Riverside Ave Ste 304 Spokane WA 99201-1011 Fax: 509-454-5636

WILLIAMS, PAUL HAMILTON, composer, singer; b. Omaha, Sept. 19, 1940; s. Paul Hamilton and Bertha Mae (Burnside) W.; m. Hilda Keenan Wynn, Apr. 16, 1993. Grad. high sch. Assoc. A & M Records, 1970—; pres. Hobbitron Enterprises, 1973—. Songwriter: (with Roger Nichols) Out in the Country, 1969, Talk it Over in the Morning, 1970, We've Only Just Begun, 1970, (with Craig Doerge) Cried Like A Baby, 1970, (with Jack S. Conrad) Family of Man, 1971, Rainy Days and Mondays, 1971, An Old Fashioned Love Song, 1972, Family of Man, 1972, Let Me Be the One, 1972, (with John Williams) You're So Nice to Be Around, 1973 (Acad. award nomination best song), The Hell of It, 1974, (with Barbara Streisand) Evergreen, 1976 (Acad. award best song, 1976, Golden Globe award 1977, Grammy award 1977), (with Michael Colombier) Wings, 1977, (with Charles Fox) My Fair Share, 1977, (with Kenny Ascher) The Rainbow Connection, 1979; film appearances include The Loved One, 1964, The Chase, 1966, Planet of the Apes, 1967, Watermelon Man, 1970, The Phantom of the Paradise, 1974 (also score 1974, Acad. award nomination best score 1974), Smokey and the Bandit, 1977, The Cheap Detective, 1978, The Muppet Movie, 1979, Stone Cold Dead, 1980, Smokey and the Bandit II, 1980, Smokey and the Bandit III, 1983, The Chill Factor, 1990, The Doors, 1991, A Million to Juan, 1994, Headless Body in Topless Bar, 1995; wrote songs for: The Getaway, 1972, (with John Williams) The Man Who Loved Cat Dancing, 1972, (with Williams) Cinderella Liberty, 1973, (with John Barry) The Day of The Locust, 1975; wrote scores for: (with Ascher) A Star is Born, 1976 (Golden Globe award best score 1976), Bugsy Malone, 1976, One on One, 1977, The End, 1978, (with Ascher) The Muppet Movie, 1979, Agatha, 1979, (with Jerry Goldsmith) The Secret of Nihm, 1982, Ishtar, 1987, The Muppet Christmas Carol, 1992; TV scores include (series) The McLean Stevenson Show, 1976-77, (with Charles Fox) The Love Boat, 1977-86, Sugar Time!, 1977-78, It Takes Two, 1982-83, (movies) No Place to Run, 1972, Emmet Otter's Jug Band Christmas, 1980; numerous TV appearances including 4 NBC Midnight spls; co-host on: numerous TV appearances including Mike Douglas show; actor, voice (TV series) Batman: Gotham Knights, 1997; other TV appearances including, Merv Griffin, Jonathan Winters, others; albums include Simeday Man: Just An Old-Fashioned Love Song, 1971, Life Goes On, 1972, A Little Bit of Love, 1974, Here Comes Inspiration, 1974, Ordinary Fools, 1975, Classics, 1977, A Little on the Windy Side, 1979, Crazy For Loving You, 1981. Co-recipient Best Songwriter Grammy award, 1977. Mem. ASCAP, Nat. Acad. Rec. Arts and Scis. (trustee) Office: 11601 Wilshire Blvd # 2350 Los Angeles CA 90025 also: Tugboat Prodns 4508 Noeline Ave Encino CA 91436-3336 also: Robert Light Agy 6404 Wilshire Blvd Ste 900 Los Angeles CA 90048-5511

WILLIAMS, QUENTIN CHRISTOPHER, geophysicist, educator; b. Wilmington, Del., Jan. 1, 1964; s. Ferd Elton and Anne Katherine W.; m. Elise Barbara Knittle, Dec. 19, 1987; children: Byron Frederick, Alanna Katherine, Lynette Barbara, Benjamin Ferd. AB, Princeton U., 1983; PhD, U. Calif., Berkeley, 1988. Rsch. geophysicist Inst. of Tectonics, U. Calif., Santa Cruz, 1988-91; asst. prof. dept. earth sci. U. Calif., Santa Cruz, 1991-95, assoc. prof. dept. earth sci., 1995-99, prof. dept. earth sci., 1999—. Contbr. articles to profl. jours. Presdl. Faculty fellow, 1993-98. Fellow Am. Geophys. Union (Macelwane medal 2000), Mineral. Soc. Am. (award 2000); mem. Am. Phys. Soc. Office: U Calif Santa Cruz Dept Earth Sciences Santa Cruz CA 95064 E-mail: qwilliams@emerald.ucsc.edu

WILLIAMS, QUINN PATRICK, lawyer; b. Evergreen Park, Ill., May 6, 1949; s. William Albert and Jeanne Marie (Quinlan) W.; m. Ingrid E. Haas; children: Michael Ryan, Mark Reed, Kelly Elizabeth. BBA, U. Wis., 1972; JD, U. Ariz., 1974. Bar: Ariz. 1975, N.Y. 1984, U.S. Dist. Ct. Ariz. 1976. V.p., sec., gen. counsel Combined Comm. Corp., Phoenix, 1975-80; sr. v.p. legal and adminstrn. Swensen's Inc., Phoenix, 1980-86; of counsel Winston & Strawn, Phoenix, 1985-87, ptnr., 1987-89, Snell & Wilmer, Phoenix, 1989—. Chmn. Ariz. Tech. Incubator, 1993-94, Ariz. Venture Capital Conf., 1993, 94; co-chmn. Gov.'s Small Bus. Advocate Exec. Coun., 1993—; chair, bd. dirs. Greater Phoenix Econ. Coun., 1996—, Scottsdale Partnership; vice chair Gov. Regulatory Coun., 1995-97; sec. GSPED High Tech. Cluster, 1993—. Served with USAR, 1967-73. Mem. ABA, State Bar Ariz., Maricopa County Bar Assn., N.Y. Bar Assn., Internat. Franchise Assn., Scottsdale C. of C. (bd. dirs.), Paradise Valley Country Club, Scottsdale Charros. Republican. Roman Catholic. Home: 6201 E Horseshoe Rd Paradise Valley AZ 85253 Office: Snell & Wilmer One Arizona Ctr Phoenix AZ 85004 E-mail: qwilliams@msn.com

WILLIAMS, RALPH CHESTER, JR. physician, educator; b. Washington, Feb. 17, 1928; s. Ralph Chester and Annie (Perry) W.; m. Mary Elizabeth Adams, June 23, 1951; children— Cathy, Frederick, John (dec.), Michael, Ann. AB with distinction, Cornell U., 1950, MD, 1954; MD (hon.), U. Lund, Sweden, 1991. Diplomate Am. Bd. Internal Medicine. Intern Mass. Gen. Hosp., Boston, 1954-55, asst. resident in internal medicine, 1955-56; resident in internal medicine N.Y. Hosp., 1956-57; chief resident Mass. Gen. Hosp., Boston, 1959-60; guest investigator Rockefeller Inst., N.Y.C., 1961-63; physician in internal medicine and rheumatology, 1963—; assoc. prof. U. Minn., Mpls., 1963-68, prof., 1968-69; prof., chmn. dept. medicine U. N.Mex., Albuquerque, 1969-88; Schott prof. rheumatology and medicine U. Fla., Gainesville, 1988-98; with rheumatology dept. U. N.Mex. Sch. Medicine, Albuquerque, 1998, emeritus prof. medicine, 1998—. Diplomate Am. Bd. Internal Medicine. Assoc. editor: Jour. Lab. and Clin. Medicine, 1966-69; mem. editl. bd.: Arthritis and Rheumatism, 1968—; contbr. articles to profl. jours. Capt. USAF, 1957-59. Master Am. Coll. Rheumatology; fellow ACP; mem. Am. Assn. Immunology, Assn. Am. Physicians, Am. Fedn. Clin. Rsch., Am. Soc. Clin. Investigation, Ctrl. Soc. Clin. Rsch., Western Soc. Clin. Investigators, Phi Beta Kappa, Alpha Omega Alpha. Achievements include rsch. in immunologic processes and connective tissue diseases. Home: 624 E Alameda St Apt 13 Santa Fe NM 87501-2293 E-mail: coolypa@dellnet.com

WILLIAMS, RICHARD THOMAS, lawyer; b. Evergreen Park, Ill., Jan. 14, 1945; s. Raymond Theodore and Elizabeth Dorothy (Williams) W. AB with honors, Stanford U., 1967, MBA, JD, Stanford U., 1972. Bar: Calif. 1972, U.S. Supreme Ct. 1977. Assoc.,then ptnr. Kadison Pfaelzer Woodard Quinn & Rossi, L.A., 1972-87; ptnr. Whitman & Ransom, 1987-93, Whitman, Breed, Abbott & Morgan, L.A., 1993-2000, Holland & Knight, LLP, L.A., 2000—. Contbg. editor Oil and Gas Analyst, 1978-84. Mem. ABA, L.A. County Bar Assn. Office: Holland & Knight LLP 633 W 5th St Los Angeles CA 90071-2005

WILLIAMS, ROBERT MARTIN, economist, consultant; b. N.Y.C., May 4, 1913; s. Joseph Tuttle and Mary Adeline (Johnson) W.; m. Vera Jean Bobsene, July 31, 1956; 1 son, Kenneth Martin. B.A., Pomona Coll., 1934; M.A., UCLA, 1942; Ph.D., Harvard U., 1950. Teaching fellow physics Dartmouth Coll., 1935-36; mgmt. trainee Western Electric Co., Inc., Los Angeles, 1936-40; lectr. UCLA, 1947-51, asst. prof., 1951-56, assoc. prof., 1956-63, prof. bus. econs. and statis. Grad. Sch. Mgmt., 1963-83, prof. emeritus, 1983—, vice chmn. dept. mgmt., 1961-67, dir. bus. forecasting project, 1952-81, consulting, 1981—; dir. Imperial Corp. Am., 1975-86, emeritus dir., 1986—; dir. Am. Savs. and Loan Assn. Kans., 1982-86, Silver State Savs. and Loan Assn. Colo., 1982-86; mem. exec. com., dir. Imperial Savs. and Loan Assn. Calif., 1978-82. Econ. cons. Fed. Res. Bank Kansas City, Lockheed Aircraft Corp., others, also state and fed. agys. Editor, contbr. The UCLA Business Forecast for the Nation and California, 1961-88; contbr. numerous articles on bus. forecasting and regional econ. devel. Served to lt. comdr. USNR, 1942-46. Resources for Future, Inc. Research grantee, 1962; NSF grantee, 1965 Mem. Am. Econ. Assn., Am. Statis. Assn., Nat. Assn. Bus. Economists, World Future Soc., Centre for Internat. Rsch. on Econ. Tendency Surveys, Ostomy Assn. L.A. (exec. v.p. 1989—). Home: 750 Enchanted Way Pacific Palisades CA 90272-2818 Office: UCLA John E Anderson Grad Sch Mgmt Bus Forecasting Project Los Angeles CA 90095-0001

WILLIAMS, ROBERT STONE, protective services official; b. Mathews, Va., Jan. 22, 1952; s. Charles H. and Anne (Stone) W.; m. Danielle Williams, July 1987. AAS, Rowan Tech. Inst., 1972; BS in Fire Protection and Safety Engring, Okla. State U., 1975, MBA, 1976. Adminstrv. specialist Oklahoma City Fire Dept., 1977-79; dep. fire chief Clovis Fire Dept., N.Mex., 1979-82; fire chief Billings Fire Dept., Mont., 1982-88, City of Spokane, Wash., 1988—. Mem. Wash. State Bldg. Code Coun., 1989-94; bd. dirs. Salvation Army, Billings, 1984-85, Am. Heart Internat. Fire Code Inst., 1993-94, 94-95, mem., 1990—. Named Fireperson Yr. Billings Downtown Exchange Club, 1988. Mem. Western Fire Chiefs Assn. (1st v.p. 1984-85, pres. 1985-86), Internat. Assn. Fire Chiefs, Nat. Fire protection Assn., Curry County Jaycees (v.p. 1981-82, Jaycee of Yr. 1982), Billings Jaycees (bd. dirs. 1983-87, v.p. cmty. devel. 1985, Outstanding Jaycee 1983, Disting. Svc. award 1985), Mont. Jaycees (treas. 1986-87, speak-up program mgr. 1986-87, Outstanding Young Montanan award 1985-86). Roman Catholic. Office: Spokane Fire Dept W 44 Riverside Ave Spokane WA 99201-0114

WILLIAMS, ROBERTA GAY, pediatric cardiologist, educator; b. Rocky Mount, N.C., Oct. 23, 1941; BS, Duke U., 1963; MD, U. N.C., 1968. Diplomate Am. Bd. Pediats. (mem. com. ofcl. examiners 1985—, bd. dirs. and rep. sub-bd. chmn. com. 1992—, mem. exec. com. 1993—), Am. Bd. Pediat. Cardiology (chmn. 1991-92, cons. 1993). Med.-pediat. intern N.C. Meml. Hosp., Chapel Hill, 1968-69; pediat. resident Columbia Presbyn. Med. Ctr., N.Y., 1969-70; fellow in cardiology Children's Hosp. Med. Ctr., Boston, 1970-73, from asst. in cardiology to assoc. in cardiology, 1973-75, sr. assoc. in cardiology, 1976-82; from instr. pediats. to asst. prof. pediats. Harvard Med. Sch.-Children's Hosp., Boston, 1973-82; assoc. prof. pediats. UCLA Med. Ctr., 1982-86, chief divsn. pediat. cardiology, 1982-95, prof. pediats., 1986-95; chmn. pediat. U. N.C. Sch. Medicine, Chapel Hill, 1995-2000, U. So. Calif., L.A., 2000—; v.p. pediat. and acad. affairs Children's Hosp. L.A., 2000—. Attending physician Cardiac Med. Svcs., Children's Hosp. Med. Ctr., Boston, 1974, cardiology cons. Cardiothoracic Surgery Svc., 1974, med. dir. Cardiovasc. Surgery ICU, 1974-79, dir. Cardiac Graphic Lab. and Cost Ctr., 1977-82, mem. com. neonatal ICU, 1978-79, v.p. med. staff, 1980-81; guest lectr., invited spkr., seminar leader in field; cons. FDA, 1998—; chmn. pediatric cardiac svcs. subcom. N.Y. State Cardiac Adv. Com., 1996—; mem. adv. com. Nat. Heart, Lung and Blood Inst., 1999—. Mem. editl. bd.: Pediat. Cardiology, 1979, Circulation, 1983-91, Am. Jour. Cardiology, 1984-91, Jour. Applied Cardiology, 1985, Clin. Cardiology, 1988, Internat. Jour. Cardiology, 1992-95, Archives of Pediats. and Adolescent Medicine, 1994—; editl. cons. Jour. of Am. Coll. of Cardiology, 1992-94. Mem. exec. coun. cardiovasc. disease in the young Am. Heart Assn., 1979-85, mem. subcom. congenital cardiac defects, 1980-82, subcom. nominating com., 1982-83; mem. Am. Heart Assn.-Greater L.A. affiliate, 1983—, exec. com. and rsch. com., 1984—, judge young investigator competition, 1984, mem. program com., 1986-90, v.p. med.-exec. com., 1991-92, pres.-elect, 1992-93, and numerous other coms.. Fellow Am. Coll. Cardiology (allied health profls. com. 1984-87, mem. physician workforce adv. com. 1988-94, mem. manpower adv. com. 1988—, mem. extramural continuing edn. com. Heart House 1990—, co-chmn. Bethesda conf. 1993, gov. So. Calif. chpt. 1994—, pres. Calif. chpt. 1994—, govt. rels. com., 1998—, trustee 2001—), Am. Acad. Pediats. (sec. exec. com. sect. on cardiology 1985-87, mem. com. on fetus and newborn 1985-88, mem. exec. com. sect. on cardiology 1985—, chmn. program com. 1988-89, mem. subcom. Am. Heart Assn. task force on assessment of diagnosis and therapeutic cardiovascular procedures 1989, chairperson sec. cardiology 1989, mem. mem. coun. on sects. mgmt. com. 1995—); mem. Soc. for Pediat. Rsch., Am. Pediat. Soc. (dept. chair 1995, exec. com. 1997), Am. Soc. Echocardiography (mem. exec. com. 1975-78, com. on guidelines for technician tng. 1975-78, bd. dirs. 1976-80, treas. exec. coun. com. 1981-83, steering com. Future of Pediatric Edn. Task Force, 1996-99), chmn. Future of Pediatric Subspeciality Workgroup, 1996-99). Avocations: photography, hiking. Office: U So Calif Dept Pediat Childrens Hosp LA MS 71 4050 Sunset Blvd Los Angeles CA 90027 E-mail: rwilliams@chla.usc.edu

WILLIAMS, ROGER STEWART, physician; b. San Diego, Feb. 15, 1941; s. Manley Samuel and Ethelyn Mae W.; children: Roger S., Karen E., David G., Sarah E. MD cum laude, Emory U., 1966. Diplomate Am. Bd. Psychiatry and Neurology. Intern, Grady Hosp., Atlanta, 1966-67. Med. resident Emory U., Atlanta, 1966-68; resident neurology Mass. Gen. Hosp., Boston, 1970-73, assoc. neurologist, 1973-87; assoc. prof. neurology Harvard Med. Sch., Boston, 1977-87; neurologist Billings (Mont.) Clinic, 1987-97; adj. prof. Mont. State U., Bozeman. Contbr. articles to profl. jours. Served to lt. comdr. USN, 1968-70. Kennedy fellow Kennedy Found., Washington, 1973-75; NIMH grantee, Bethesda, Md., 1979-87. Fellow Am. Acad. Neurology; mem. AMA, Mont. Med. Assn., Alpha Omega Alpha.

WILLIAMS, RONALD DEAN, minister, religious organization administrator; b. Decatur, Ill., Oct. 23, 1940; s. Henry Lawrence and Ella Loudica Williams; m. Carole Jeanette Lane, June 16, 1962; children: Scott Allan, Mark Lawrence, Derek James. BTh, LIFE Bible Coll., L.A., 1965; DD, Internat. Ch. Foursquare Gospel, L.A., 1992. Ordained to ministry Internat. Ch. Foursquare Gospel, 1966. Pastor Foursquare Gospel Ch., Surrey, B.C., Can., 1965-69, missionary Hong Kong, 1969-85; prof. LIFE Bible Coll., 1985-95; mng. editor Foursquare World ADVANCE, 1993—; comm. officer Internat. Ch. of Foursquare Gospel, 1988-2000. Bd. dirs. Foursquare Gospel Ch.; pres. exec. bd. Internat. Pentecostal Press Assn., Oklahoma City, 1990-98; comm. officer Pentecostal/Charismatic Chs. North Am., Memphis, 1994—; coord. E. Coun. Foursquare Miss., 1979-82. Editor: The Vine and The Branches, 1992; mng. editor Foursquare World ADVANCE mag., 1985. Coord. 19th Pentecostal World Conf., 2001. With USAF, 1958-61. Avocations: writing, golf, reading, music. Office: Internat Ch Foursquare Gospel 1910 W Sunset Blvd Ste 200 Los Angeles CA 90026-3295

WILLIAMS, RONALD OSCAR, systems engineer; b. Denver, May 10, 1940; s. Oscar H. and Evelyn (Johnson) W. BS in Applied Math. Coll. Engring., U. Colo., 1964; postgrad., U. Colo., U. Denver, George Washington U. Computer programmer Apollo Sys. dept. Missile and Space div. Gen. Electric Co., Kennedy Space Ctr., Fla., 1965-67, Manned Spacecraft Ctr., Houston, 1967-68; computer programmer U. Colo., Boulder, 1968-73; computer programmer analyst Def. Sys. divsn. Sys. Devel. Corp. for NORAD, Colo. Springs, 1974-75; engr. def. sys. and command-and-info. sys. Martin Marietta Aerospace, Denver, 1976-80; sys. engr. space and comm. group, def. info. sys. divsn. Hughes Aircraft Co., Aurora, Colo., 1980-89; rsch. analyst Math. Rsch. Ctr., Littleton, 1990—, dir., sr. rsch. mathematician, 1996—. Vol. fireman Clear Lake City (Tex.) Fire Dept., 1968; officer Boulder Emergency Squad, 1969-76, rescue squadman, 1969-76, liaison to cadets, 1971, pers. officer, 1971-76, exec. bd., 1971-76, award of merit, 1971, 72, emergency med. technician, 1973—; spl. police officer Boulder Police Dept., 1970-75; spl. dep. sheriff Boulder County Sheriff's Dept., 1970-71; mem. nat. adv. bd. Am. Security Coun., 1979-91, Coalition of Peace Through Strength, 1979-91. Served with USMCR, 1958-66. Decorated Organized Res. medal. Mem. AAAS, AIAA (sr.), Math. Assn. Am., Am. Math Soc., Soc. Indsl. and Applied Math., Math. Study Unit of Am. Topical Assn., Armed Forces Comm. and Electronics Assn., Assn. Old Crows, Nat. Def. Indsl. Assn., Marine Corps Assn., Air Force Assn., U.S. Naval Inst., Nat. Geog. Soc., Smithsonian Inst., Nat. Space Soc., Soc. Amateur Radio Astronomers, Met. Opera Guild, Colo. Hist. Soc., Hist. Denver Inc., Historic Boulder Inc., Hawaiian Hist Soc., Denver Bot. Gardens, Denver Mus. Nature and Sci., Denver Zool. Found. Inc., Mensa. Lutheran.

WILLIAMS, SPENCER MORTIMER, federal judge; b. Reading, Mass., Feb. 24, 1922; s. Theodore Ryder and Anabel (Hutchison) W.; m. Kathryn Bramlage, Aug. 20, 1943; children: Carol Marcia (Mrs. James B. Garvey), Peter, Spencer, Clark, Janice, Diane (Mrs. Sean Quinn). AB, UCLA, 1943; postgrad., Hastings Coll. Law, 1946; JD, U. Calif., Berkeley, 1948. Bar: Calif. 1949, U.S. Supreme Ct. 1952. Assoc. Beresford & Adams, San Jose, Calif., 1949, Rankin, O'Neal, Center, Luckhardt, Bonney, Marlais & Lund, San Jose, Evans, Jackson & Kennedy, Sacramento; county counsel Santa Clara County, 1955-67; adminstr. Calif. Health and Welfare Agy., Sacramento, 1967-69; judge U.S. Dist. Ct. (no. dist.) Calif., San Francisco, from 1971, now sr. judge. County exec. pro tem, Santa Clara County; adminstr. Calif. Youth and Adult Corrections Agy., Sacramento; sec. Calif. Human Relations Agy., Sacramento, 1967-70 Chmn. San Jose Christmas Seals Drive, 1953, San Jose Muscular Dystrophy Drive, 1953, 54; team capt. fund raising drive San Jose YMCA, 1960; co-chmn. indsl. sect. fund raising drive Alexian Bros. Hosp., San Jose, 1964; team capt. fund raising drive San Jose Hosp.; mem. com. on youth and govt. YMCA, 1967-68; Candidate for Calif. Assembly, 1954, Calif. Atty. Gen., 1966, 70; Bd. dirs. San Jose Better Bus. Bur., 1955-66, Boys City Boys' Club, San Jose, 1965-67; pres. trustees Santa Clara County Law Library, 1955-66. Served with USNR, 1943-46; to lt. comdr. JAG Corps USNR, 1950-52, PTO. Named San Jose Man of Year, 1954 Mem. ABA, Calif. Bar Assn. (vice chmn. com. on publicly employed attys. 1962-63), Santa Clara County Bar Assn., Sacramento Bar Assn., Internat. Assn. Trial Judges (pres. 1995-96), Calif. Dist. Attys. Assn. (pres. 1963-64), Nat. Assn. County Civil Attys. (pres. 1963-64), 9th Cir. Dist. Judges Assn. (pres. 1981-83), Fed. Judges Assn. (pres. 1982-87), Kiwanis, Theta Delta Chi. Office: US Dist Ct 280 S 1st St Rm 5150 San Jose CA 95113-3002

WILLIAMS, STEPHEN, anthropologist, educator; b. Mpls., Aug. 28, 1926; s. Clyde Garfield and Lois (Simmons) W.; m. Eunice Ford, Jan. 6, 1962; children: Stephen John, Timothy. BA, Yale U., 1949, PhD, 1954; MA, U. Mich., 1950; MA (hon.), Harvard, 1962. Asst. anthropology dept. Peabody Mus., Yale U., 1950-52; mem. faculty Harvard U., Cambridge, Mass., 1958—, prof. anthropology, 1967-72, Peabody prof., 1972-93, prof. emeritus, 1993—, chmn. dept., 1967-69; rsch. fellow Peabody Mus., Harvard U., Cambridge, 1954-57, mem. staff, 1954—, dir. mus., 1967-77. Curator N.Am. Archaeology, 1962-93, hon. curator 1993—; dir. rsch. of Peabody Mus.'s Lower Miss. Survey, 1958-93. Author books and articles on N.Am. archaeology, "Fantastic" archaeology and the history of Am. archaeology. Home: 1017 Foothills Trail Santa Fe NM 87505-4537 Office: PO Box 22354 Santa Fe NM 87502-2354 E-mail: williamsstephen@msn.com

WILLIAMS, THEODORE EARLE, retired industrial distribution company executive; b. Cleve., May 9, 1920; s. Stanley S. and Blanche (Albaum) W.; m. Rita Cohen, Aug. 28, 1952; children: Lezlie, Richard Atlas, Shelley, William Atlas, Wayne, Marsha, Patti Blake, Jeff Blake. Student, Wayne U., 1937-38; BS in Engring, postgrad. in bus. adminstrn, U. Mich., 1942. Pres. Wayne Products Co., Detroit, 1942-43, L.A., 1947-49; pres. Williams Metal Products Co., Inglewood, Calif., 1950-69; chmn. bd. Bell Industries, L.A., 1970-2000; ret., 2000. Instr. U. Mich., 1942 Patentee in field. Served to 1st lt. AUS, 1943-46. Recipient Humanitarian award City of L.A., 1977. Democrat. Home: 435 N Layton Way Los Angeles CA 90049-2022

WILLIAMS, WILLIAM ARNOLD, agronomy educator; b. Johnson City, N.Y., Aug. 2, 1922; s. William Truesdall and Nellie Viola (Tompkins) W.; m. Madeline Patricia Moore, Nov. 27, 1943; children— David, Kathleen, Andrew B.S., Cornell U., 1947, M.S., 1948, Ph.D., 1951. Prof. emeritus U. Calif., Davis, 1993—. Editor agr. sect. McGraw-Hill Ency. Sci. & Tech.; contbr. articles to profl. jours. Mem. Nat. Alliance for Mentally Ill. Served to lt. U.S. Army, 1943-46 Grantee NSF, 1965-82, Kellogg Found., 1963-67; Fulbright scholar, Australia, 1960, Rockefeller Found. scholar, Costa Rica, 1966 Fellow AAAS, Am. Soc. Agronomy, Crop Sci. Soc. Am.; mem. Soil Sci. Soc. Am., Soc. Range Mgmt., Am. Statis. Assn., Assn. for Tropical Biology, Fedn. Am. Scientists. Democrat Home: 1515 Shasta Dr Davis CA 95616-3337 Office: U Calif Dept Agronomy & Range One Shields Ave Davis CA 95616-8515

WILLIAMS, WILLIAM COREY, theology educator, consultant; b. Wilkes-Barre, Pa., July 12, 1937; s. Edward Douglas and Elizabeth Irene (Schooley) W.; m. Alma Simmenroth Williams, June 27, 1959; 1 child, Linda. Diploma in Ministerial Studies, NE Bible Inst., 1962; BA in Bibl. Studies, Cen. Bible Coll., 1963, MA in Religion, 1964; MA in Hebrew and Near Ea. Studies, NYU, 1966, PhD in Hebrew Lang. and Lit., 1975; postgrad., Hebrew U., 1977-78, Inst. Holyland Studies, 1986. Ref. libr. Hebraic section Libr. of Congress, Washington, 1967-69; prof. Old Testament So. Calif. Coll./Vanguard U., Costa Mesa, 1969—; adj. prof. Old Testament Melodyland Sch. Theology, Anaheim, Calif., 1975-77; vis. prof. Old Testament Fuller Theol. Sem., Pasadena, 1978-81, 84, Asian Theol. Ctr. for Evangelism and Missions, Singapore and Sabah, E. Malaysia, 1985, Continental Bible Coll., Saint Pieters-Leeuw, Belgium, 1985, 2000-01, Mattersey Bible Coll., Eng., 1985, Inst. Holy Land Studies, Jerusalem, 1986, Regent U., 1994. Transl. cons. and reviser New Am. Std. Bible, 1969-94; transl. cons. The New Internat. Version, 1975-76, New Century Version, 1991, The New Living Translation, 1992-95, New Internat. Version, Reader's Version, 1993-94; transl. cons. and editor Internat. Children's Version, 1985-86. Author: (books, tapes) Hebrew I: A Study Guide, 1986, Hebrew II: A Study Guide, 1986; contbr. articles to International Standard Bible Encyclopedia, New International Dictionary of Old Testment Theology and Evangelical Dictionary of Biblical Theology; contbr. articles to profl. jours.; contbr. notes to Spirit Filled Life Study Bible. Nat. Def. Fgn. Lang. fellow NYU, 1964-67; Alumni scholar N.E. Bible Inst., 1960-61; NEH fellow, summer 1992; recipient Disting. Educator's award Assemblies of God, 1997. Mem. Soc. Bibl. Lit., Evang. Theol. Soc. (exec. office 1974-77), Inst. Bibl. Rsch., The Lockman Found. (hon. mem. bd. dirs. 1992-94, mem. editl. bd. 1974-94). Home: 1817 Peninsula Pl Costa Mesa CA 92627-4591 Office: So Calif Coll 55 Fair Dr Costa Mesa CA 92626-6520

WILLIAMSON, ALAN BACHER, English literature educator, poet, writer; b. Chgo., Jan. 24, 1944; s. George and Jehanne (Bacher) W.; m. Anne Winters, Oct. 12, 1968 (div. Feb. 1988); 1 child, Elizabeth Kilner. BA, Haverford Coll., 1964; MA, Harvard U., 1965, PhD, 1969. Asst. prof. U. Va., Charlottesville, 1969-75; Briggs-Copeland lectr. Harvard U., Cambridge, Mass., 1977-80; Fannie Hurst lectr. Brandeis U., Waltham, 1980-82; prof. English, U. Calif., Davis, 1982—. Poetry panelist Nat. Endowment for Arts, 1989. Author: (criticism) Pity the Monsters, 1974, Introspection and Contemporary Poetry, 1984, Eloquence and Mere Life, 1994, Almost a Girl, 2001, (poetry) Presence, 1983, The Muse of Distance, 1988, Love and the Soul, 1995, Res Publica, 1998. Poetry fellow Nat. Endowment for Arts, 1973; Guggenheim fellow, 1991. Mem. MLA (exec. com. div. on poetry 1987-91). Democrat. Zen Buddhist. Office: U Calif Dept English Davis CA 95616 E-mail: abwilliamson@ucdavis.edu

WILLIAMSON, CHARLES R. energy company executive; PhD in Geology, U. Tex., Austin, 1978. Rsch. assoc. Sci. and Tech. Divsn. Unocal Corp., Brea, Calif., 1977-83, chief exploration geologist U.K., 1983-86; exploration mgr., dir. Unocal Netherlands, The Hague, 1986-89; v.p. exploration Unocal Thailand, Bangkok, 1989-92; v.p. Energy Resources Divsn. Unocal, 1992-94, v.p. planning and info. svcs., 1994-95, v.p. corp. planning and econs., 1995-96, group v.p. internat. energy opers., 1996-97, group v.p. Asia Opers., 1997-99; exec. v.p. internat. energy ops. Unocal Corp., El Segundo, Calif., 1999—; also bd. dirs. Unocal. Mem. adv. bd. earth scis. dept. Stanford U. Mem. Am. Soc. Petroleum Geologists, Soc. Econ. Paleontologists and Mineralogists, Soc. Petroleum Engrs., Internat. Assn. Sedimentologists. Office: Unocal Corp 2141 Rosecrans Ave Ste 4000 El Segundo CA 90245-4746

WILLIAMSON, CORLISS, professional basketball player; b. Russellville, Ark., Dec. 4, 1973; Student, U. Ark., 1992-95. Forward Sacramento Kings. Office: c/o Sacramento Kings 1 Sports Pkwy Sacramento CA 95834-2300

WILLIAMSON, JACK (JOHN STEWART), writer; b. Bisbee, Ariz., Apr. 29, 1908; s. Asa Lee and Lucy Betty (Hunt) W.; m. Blanche Slaten Harp, Aug. 15, 1947 (dec. Jan. 1985); stepchildren: Keign Harp (dec.), Adele Harp Lovorn. BA, MA, Eastern N.Mex. U., 1957, LHD (hon.), 1981; PhD, U. Colo., 1964. Prof. English Eastern N.Mex. U., Portales, 1960-77, prof. emeritus, 1977—. Author numerous sci. fiction books including The Legion of Space, 1947, Darker Than You Think, 1948, The Humanoids, 1949, The Green Girl, 1950, The Cometeers, 1950, One Against the Legion, 1950, Seetee Scock, 1950, Seetee Ship, 1950, Dragon's Island, 1951, The Legion of Time, 1952, (with Frederik Phhl) Star Bridge, 1955, Dome Around America, 1955, The Trial of Terra, 1962, Golden Blood, 1964, The Reign of Wizardry, 1965, Bright New Universe, 1967, Trapped in Space, 1968, The Pandora Effect, 1969, People Machines, 1971, The Moon Children, 1972, H.G. Wells: Critic of Progress, 1973, Teaching SF, 1975, The Early Williamson, 1975, The Power of Blackness, 1976, The Best of Jack Williamson, 1978, Brother to Demons, Brother To Gods, 1979, Teaching Science Fiction: Education for Tomorrow, 1980, The [illegible] Humanoid Touch, 1980, Manseed, 1982, The Queen of a Legion, 1983, Wonder's Child: My Life in Science Fiction, 1984 (Hugo award 1985), Lifeburst, 1984, Firechild, 1986, Mazeway, 1990, Undersea Quest, 1954, Undersea Fleet, 1955, Undersea City, 1956, The Reefs of Sapce, 1964, Starchild, 1965, Rogue Star, 1969, The Farthest Star, 1975, Wall Around a Star, 1983, Land's End, 1988, Mazeway, 1990. (with Frederik Phol) The Singers Of Time, 1991, Beachhead, 1992, Demon Moon, 1994, The Black Sun, 1996, The Fortress of Utopia, 1998, The Silicon Dagger, 1999, The Stone from the Green Star, 1999, Terraforming Earth, 2001; (with Miles J. Breuer) The Birth of an New Republic, 1981. Served as staff sgt. USAAF, 1942-45. Mem. Sci. Fiction Writers Am. (pres. 1978-80, Grand Master Nebula award 1976), Sci. Fiction Research Assn. (Pilgrim award 1968), World Sci. Fiction, Planetary Soc. Avocations: travel, astronomy, photography. Home: PO Box 761 Portales NM 88130-0761 Office: Ea NMex U Golden Libr Portales NM 88130 E-mail: Jack.Williamson@enmu.edu

WILLIAMSON, KEVIN, writer, producer, director; b. New Bern, N.C., Mar. 14, 1965; Exec. prodr. (TV series) Wasteland, 1999, Dawson's Creek, 1998; prodr. Scream 3, 1999; exec. prodr., writer Scream 2, 1997; writer The Faculty, 1998, I Know What You Did Last Summer, 1997, Scream, 1996 (Saturn award Acad. of Sci. Fiction, Horror and Fantasy Films); writer, dir. Teaching Mrs. Tingle, 1999; writer, co-exec. prodr. Halloween H20: Twenty Years Later, 1998; actor Dirty Money, 1994, (TV) Another World, 1990. Office: Geibelson Young & Co c/o Melody Young c/o Melody Young 16501 Ventura Blvd 304 Encino CA 91436

WILLIAMSON, LAIRD, stage director, actor; b. Chgo., Dec. 13, 1937; s. Walter B. and Florence M. (Hemwell) W. BS in Speech, Northwestern U., 1960; MFA in Drama, U. Tex., 1965. Dir. Am. Conservatory Theatre, San Francisco, 1974-2000; stage dir. A Christmas Carol, 1976-81, The Matchmaker (tour of Soviet Union), 1976, A Month in the Country, 1978, The Visit, 1979, Pantagleize, 1980, Sunday in the Park, 1986, End of the World, 1988, Imaginary Invalid, 1990, Machinal, 1997, Long Day's Journey, 1999; dir. Oreg. Shakespearean Festival, Ashland, 1972-2000, Western Opera Theatre, San Francisco, 1976-77, Theater Fest, Santa Maria, Calif., 1971-84, Denver Theater Ctr., 1981-2000, Bklyn. Acad. Music, 1981, Seattle Repertory Theatre, 1990, Old Globe Theatre, San Diego, 1977, 92, 94, 97; artistic dir. Theater Fest, Solvang, Calif., 1981-83, Intiman Theatre, 1986, 88, Berkeley Shakespeare Festival, 1990, Guthrie Theatre, 1991, 93, The Shakespeare Theatre, Washington, 1995, 96, 98; actor in Othello, 1973, Twelfth Night, 1974, Cyrano, 1974, Enrico IV, 1977, Judas, 1978, Hamlet, 1979, The Bacchae, 1981, Hamlet, 2000, Shrew, 2000. Mem. Soc. Stage Dirs. Actors Equity Assn., Screen Actors Guild.

WILLIAMSON, OLIVER EATON, economics and law educator; b. Superior, Wis., Sept. 27, 1932; s. Scott Gilbert and Lucille S. (Dunn) W.; m. Dolores Jean Celeni, Sept. 28, 1957; children: Scott, Tamara, Karen, Oliver, Dean. SB, MIT, 1955; MBA, Stanford U., 1960; PhD, Carnegie-Mellon U., 1963; PhD (hon.), Norwegian Sch. Econs. and Bus. Adminstrn., 1986; PhD in Econ. Sci. (hon.), Hochschule St. Gallen, Switzerland, 1987, Groningen U., , 1989, Turku Sch. Econs. & Bus. Admin, St. Petersburg, Russia, 1996, HEC, Paris, 1997, Copenhagen Bus. Sch., , 2000, U. Chile, 2000. Project. engr. U.S. Govt., 1955-58; asst. prof. econs. U. Calif., Berkeley, 1963-65; assoc. prof. U. Pa., Phila., 1965-68, prof., 1968-83, Charles and William L. Day prof. econs. and social sci., 1977-83; Gordon B. Tweedy prof. econs. law and orgn. Yale U., 1983-88; Transam. prof. of bus., econs. and law U. Calif., Berkeley, 1988-94, Edgar F. Kaiser prof. bus. adminstrn., prof. econs. and law, 1994—. Spl. econ. asst. to asst. atty. gen. for antitrust Dept. Justice, 1966-67; dir. Ctr. for Study Orgnl. Innovation, U. Pa., 1976-83; Edgar F. Kaiser prof. bus., econs. and law U. Calif., Berkeley, 1988—; cons. in field. Author: The Economics of Discretionary Behavior, 1964, Corporate Control and Business Behavior, 1970, Markets and Hierarchies, 1975, The Economic Institutions of Capitalism, 1985, Economic Organization, 1986, Antitrust Economics, 1987, The Mechanisms of Governance, 1996; assoc. editor Bell. Jour. Econs., 1973-74, editor, 1975-82; co-editor Jour. Law, Econs. and Orgn., 1983—. Fellow Ctr. for Advanced Study in Behavioral Scis., 1977-78; Guggenheim fellow, 1977-78; Fulbright scholar, 1999; Am. Acad. Arts and Scis. fellow, 1983; recipient Alexander Henderson award Carnegie-Mellon U., 1962, Alexander von Humboldt Rsch. prize, 1987, Irwin award Acad. of Mgmt., 1988, John von Newmann prize, 1999. Fellow Econometric Soc., Am. Acad. Polit. and Social Sci.; mem. NAS, Internat. Soc. for New Instnl. Econs. (pres. 1999-2001), Am. Econ. Assn. (v.p. 2000—), Am. Law and Econs. Assn. (pres. 1997-98), Western Econ. Assn. (pres. 1999-2000). Office: U Calif Dept Econs Berkeley CA 94720-0001

WILLIS, CLIFFORD LEON, geologist; b. Chanute, Kans., Feb. 20, 1913; s. Arthur Edward and Flossie Duckworth (Fouts) W.; m. Serreta Margaret Thiel, Aug. 21, 1947 (dec.); 1 child, David Gerard. BS in Mining Engring., U. Kans., 1939; PhD, U. Wash., 1950. Geophysicist The Carter Oil Co. (Exxon), Tulsa, 1939-42; instr. U. Wash., Seattle, 1946-50, asst. prof., 1950-54; cons. geologist Harza Engring. Co., Chgo., 1952-54, 80-82, chief geologist, 1954-57, assoc. and chief geologist, 1957-67, v.p., chief geologist, 1967-80; pvt. practice cons. geologist Tucson, 1982—. Cons. on major dam projects in Iran, Iraq, Pakistan, Greece, Turkey, Ethiopia, Argentina, Venezuela, Colombia, Honduras, El Salvador, Iceland, U.S. Lt. USCG, 1942-46. Recipient Haworth Disting. Alumnus award U. Kans., 1963. Fellow Geol. Soc. Am., Geol. Soc. London; mem. Am. Assn. Petroleum Geologists, Soc. Mining, Metallurgy and Exploration Inc., Assn. Engring. Geologists, Sigma Xi, Tau Beta Pi, Sigma Tau, Theta Tau. Republican. Roman Catholic. Avocations: travel, reading. Home: 4795 E Quail Creek Dr Tucson AZ 85718-2630

WILLIS, FRANK ROY, history educator; b. Prescot, Lancashire, Eng., July 25, 1930; s. Harry and Gladys Reid (Birchall) W.; children from previous marriage, Jane, Clare, Geoffrey. BA, Cambridge (Eng.) U., 1952, cert. in edn., 1955, diploma in devel. econs., 1974; PhD, Stanford U., 1959. Instr. Stanford (Calif.) U., 1959-60; from instr. to assoc. prof. history U. Wash., Seattle, 1960-64; assoc. prof. then prof. U. Calif., Davis, 1964—. Author: The French in Germany, 1962, France, Germany and the New Europe, 1945-1967, 1968, Europe in the Global Age, 1968, Italy Chooses Europe, 1971, Western Civilization: An Urban Perspective, 1973, World Civilizations, 1982, The French Paradox, 1982, Western Civilization: A Brief Introduction, 1987. Fellow Rockefeller Found., Paris, 1962-63, Guggenheim Found., 1966-67, Social Scis. Research Council, Cambridge, 1973-74. Avocation: travel. Office: U Calif Dept History Davis CA 95616

WILLIS, JUDY ANN, lawyer; b. Hartford, Conn., July 7, 1949; d. Durward Joseph and Angeline Raphael (Riccardo) W. BA, Cen. Conn. State U., 1971; postgrad., U. Conn. Law Sch., 1976-77; JD, Boston Coll., 1979. Bar: Mass. 1979, U.S. Dist. Ct. Mass. 1980, Calif. 1990. Sr. atty. H.P. Hood Inc., Charleston, Mass., 1979-83; v.p. law Parker Bros., Beverly, 1983-89; sr. v.p. bus. affairs Mattel, Inc., El Segundo, Calif., 1989—. Bd. dirs. Children Affected by AIDS Found. Office: Mattel Inc M1-0920 333 Continental Blvd El Segundo CA 90245-5012 E-mail: judy.willis@Mattel.com

WILLIS, SELENE LOWE, electrical engineer, software consultant; b. Birmingham, Ala., Mar. 4, 1958; d. Lewis Russell and Bernice (Wilson) Lowe; m. André Maurice Willis, June 12, 1987. BSEE, Tuskegee U., 1980; postgrad., UCLA, 1993-94, 99—, U. So. Calif., 1996. Component engr. Hughes Aircraft Corp., El Segundo, Calif., 1980-82; reliability and lead engr. Aero Jet Electro Sys. Corp., Azusa, 1982-84; sr. component engr. Rockwell Internat. Corp., Anaheim, 1984, Gen. Data Comm. Corp., Danbury, Conn., 1984-85; design engr. Lockheed Missile & Space Co., Sunnyvale, Calif., 1985-86; property mgr. Penmar Mgmt. Co., L.A., 1987-88; aircraft mechanic McDonnell Douglas Corp., Long Beach, 1989-93; Unix sys. adminstrn. Santa Cruz Ops., 1994; bus. ops. mgr., cons. New Start, Santa Monica, Calif., 1995; software developer Nat. Advancement Corp., 1996; entrepreneur Datatronics, 1996—; exec. v.p., owner L.A. Network Engr. Jet Propulsion Lab., L.A., 1996-2000; software engr., network engr., application engr., lead engr. Jet Propulsion Lab, Pasadena, Calif., 1996-2000, project mgr., 1999-2000, lead UNIX engr. L.A., 1998-2000; mgmt. sys. engr. Tech. Jet Propulsion Lab., Pasadena, 1998-2000, project element mgr., 1999—; cons., sr. project mgr. Amgen, Thousand Oaks, Calif., 1999-2000, sr. sys. engr., 2000—. Cons., software designer Kern & Wooley, attys., Westwood, Calif., 1995; software developer Nat. Advancement Corp., Santa Ana, Calif., 1995—. Vol. Mercy Hosp. and Children's Hosp., Birmingham, 1972-74; mrm. L.A. Gospel Messengers, 1982-84, West Angeles Ch. of God and Christ, L.A., 1990; cons., mgr. bus. ops. New Start/Santa Monica (Calif.) Bay Area Drug Abuse Coun., 1995; vol. Pres. Clinton's Going-To-Coll. Program through UCLA, 1997—; chair UCLA Transfer Coll. Scholarship Program, 1998. Scholar Bell Labs., 1976-80, UCLA, 1994, Gem award, UTA, 1999, Outstanding Group award, JPL, 1999. Mem. IEEE, ASME, Aerospace and Aircraft Engrs., So. Calif. Profl. Engring. Assn., Tuskegee U. Alumni Assn., UCLA Alumni Assn. (scholarship and adv. com.), Eta Kappa Nu. Mem. Christian Ch. Avocations: piano, computers, softball, real estate. E-mail: s_willis@socal.rr.com

WILLISCROFT-BARCUS, BEVERLY RUTH, lawyer; b. Conrad, Mont., Feb. 24, 1945; d. Paul A. and Gladys L. (Buck) W.; m. Kent J. Barcus, Oct. 1984. BA in Music, So. Calif. Coll., 1967; JD, John F. Kennedy U., 1977. Bar: Calif., 1977. Elem. tchr., Sunnyvale, Calif., 1968-72; legal sec., legal asst. various law firms Bay Area, 1972-77; assoc. Neil D. Reid, Inc., San Francisco, 1977-79; sole practice Concord, Calif., 1979—. Exam. grader Calif. Bar, 1979—; real estate broker, 1980-88; tchr. real estate King Coll., Concord, 1979-80; lectr. in field; judge pro-tem Mcpl. Ct., 1981-93. Co-author: Adoption Law in California, Adoption Practice, Procedure and Pitfalls in California. Bd. dirs. Contra Costa Musical Theatre, Inc., 1978-82, v.p. adminstrn., 1980-81, v.p. prodn., 1981-82; mem. community devel. adv. com. City of Concord, 1981-83, vice chmn.,, 1982-83, mem. status of women com., 1980-81, mem. redevel. adv. com., 1984-86, planning commnr. 1986-92, chmn., 1990; mem. exec. bd. Mt. Diablo coun. Boy Scouts Am., 1981-85; bd. dirs. Pregnancy Ctrs. Contra Costa County, 1991—, chmn., 1993—. Mem. Concord C. of C. (bd. dirs., chmn. govt. affairs com. 1981-83, v.p. 1985-87, pres. 1988-89, Bus. Person of Yr. 1986), Calif. State Bar (chmn. adoptions subcom. north, 1994), Contra Costa County Bar Assn., Todos Santos Bus. and Profl. Women (co-founder, pres. 1983-84, pub. rels. chmn. 1982-83, Woman of Achievement 1980, 81), Soroptimists (fin. sec. 1980-81). Office: PO Box 981 Pittsburg CA 94565-0098 E-mail: Beverlywb@msn.com

WILLISON, BRUCE GRAY, banker; b. Riverside, Calif., Oct. 16, 1948; s. Walter G. and Dorothy (Phillips) W.; m. Gretchen A. Illig; children: Patrick, Bruce G., Kristen, Jeffery, Geoffrey, Lea. B.A. in econs., UCLA, 1970; M.B.A., U. So. Calif., 1973. With Bank of Am., Los Angeles, 1973-79; dir. mktg. First Interstate Bancorp, Los Angeles, 1981; sr. v.p. corp. banking group First Interstate Bank, L.A., 1982, mgr. trust divsn., 1983, exec. v.p. world banking group Los Angeles, 1983-85; pres., chief exec. officer First Interstate Bank Ltd., 1985-86; chmn., chief exec. officer First Interstate Bank Oreg., Portland, 1986-91; chmn., pres., chief exec. officer First Interstate Bank of Calif., L.A., 1991-99; dean U. Calif. Anderson Sch. Bus., L.A., 1999—. Served to lt. USN, 1970-72. Office: The Anderson Sch Mgmt/UCLA 110 Westward Plz Box 951481 Los Angeles CA 90075-1481

WILLNER, ALAN ELI, electrical engineer, educator; b. Bklyn., Nov. 16, 1962; s. Gerald and Sondra (Bernstein) W.; m. Michelle Frida Green, June 25, 1991. BA, Yeshiva U., 1982; MS, Columbia U., 1984, PhD, 1988. Summer tech. staff David Sarnoff Rsch. Ctr., Princeton, N.J., 1983, 84; grad. rsch. asst. dept. elec. engring. Columbia U., N.Y.C., 1984-88; postdoctoral mem. tech. staff AT&T Bell Labs., Holmdel, N.J., 1988-90; mem. tech. staff Bell Communications Rsch., Red Bank, 1990-91; assoc. prof. U. So. Calif., L.A., 1992—, assoc. dir. Ctr. Photonic Tech., 1994—. Head del. Harvard Model UN Yeshiva U., 1982; instr. Columbia U., 1987; rev. panel mem. NSF, Washington, 1992, 93, 94; invited optical comm. workshop NSF, Washington, 1994, chair panel on optical info. and comm., 1994. Author 1 book; contbr. articles to IEEE Photonics Tech. Letters, Jour Lightwave Tech., Jour. Optical Engring., Jour. Electrochem. Soc., Electronics Letters, Applied Physics Letters, Applied Optics; assoc. editor Jour. Lighwave Tech., guest editor; editor-in-chief IeEE Jour. Selected Topics in Quantum Electronics. Mem. faculty adv. bd. U. So. Calif. Hillel Orgn., 1992. Grantee NSF, Advanced Rsch. Projects Agy., Packard Found., Powell Found., Ballistic Missile Def. Orgn.; fellow Semiconductor Rsch. Corp., 1986, NATO/NSF, 1985, Sci. and Engring. fellow David and Lucile Packard Found., 1993, presdl. faculty fellow NSF, 1994, Sr. Scholar fellow Fulbright Found., 1997; recipient Armstrong Found. prize Columbia U., 1984, young investigator award NSF, 1992. Fellow Optical Soc. Am. (vice chair optical comm. group, symposium organizer ann. mtg. 1992, 95, panel organizer ann. mtg., 1993, 95, program com. for conf. on optical fiber commn. 1996, 97); mem. IEEE (sr. mem.), IEEE Lasers and Electro-Optics Soc. (v.p. tech. affairs, mem. optical comm. tech. com., bd. govs., chmn. optical commn. tech. com., chmn. optical comm. subcom. ann. mtg. 1994, mem. optical networks tech. com.), Soc. Photo-Instrumentation Eng ring. (program chair telecomm. engring. photonics west 1995, chmn. conf. on emerging technologies for all-optical networks, photonics west, 1995, program com. for Conf. on Optical Fiber Comm., 1996, conf. program com. components for WDM), Sigma Xi. Achievements include patents for localized photochemical etching of multilayered semiconductor body, optical star coupler utilizing fiber amplifier technology, and one-to-many simultaneous optical WDM 2-dim. plane interconnections. Home: 9326 Sawyer St Los Angeles CA 90035-4102 Office: U So Calif Dept Elec Engring Eeb 538 Los Angeles CA 90089-0001

WILLOUGHBY, JAMES RUSSELL, artist, writer; b. Toronto, Ohio, Apr. 22, 1928; s. Russell Lee and Edna Gertrude (McKeown) W.; m. Dorothy M. Ponder, Sept. 12, 1952 (div. 1958); children: Jim Jr., David; m. Susan N. Boettjer, Nov. 28, 1980. AA, Pasadena City Coll., 1951; postgrad., Art Ctr. Sch. Mem. staff Chrysler Corp., Maywood, Calif., 1951-57; adminstrv. asst., tech. artist Ramo-Wooldridge, El Segundo, 1957-59; adminstr. asst. Space Tech. Labs., El Segundo, 1959-61; intelligence analyst Aerospace Corp., El Segundo, 1961-65; freelancer Calif., 1965-72, Filmation Studios, Reseda, 1972-82, various orgns., 1982—. Storyboard designer Hanna-Barbera, Disney Studios, 1987-90. Author, illustrator: Cowboy Country Cartoons, 1988, Birds of the Southwest, 1997, Do You Pray, Duke?, 1999; co-author, illustrator: Cowboy Cartoon Cookbook, 1990, Cactus County, 1992, Sharlot Hall Coloring Book, 1994, Cowboy Cartoons: Quick on the Draw, 1996, A Dude's Guide to the West, 1996; illustrator: Arizona Humoresque, 1992, Cowpies Ain't No Dish You Take To The County Fair, 1997; editl. cartoonist Prescott Daily Courier. Recipient Disting. Alumnus award Toronto (Ohio) H.S., 1999. Mem. Nat. Cartoonist Soc., Westerners Internat., Prescott Corral. Avocations: hiking. Home: 1407 Sierra Vista Dr Prescott AZ 86303-4545

WILLOUGHBY, STEPHEN SCHUYLER, mathematics educator; b. Madison, Wis., Sept. 27, 1932; s. Alfred and Elizabeth Frances (Cassell) W.; m. Helen Sali Shapiro, Aug. 29, 1954; children: Wendy Valentine (Mrs. Peter Gallen), Todd Alan. AB (scholar), Harvard U., 1953, AM in Teaching, 1955; EdD (Clifford [illegible] Newton (Mass.) Pub. Schs., 1954-57, Greenwich (Conn.) Pub. Schs., 1957-59; instr. U. Wis., Madison, 1960-61, asst. prof. math. edn. and math., 1961-65; prof. math. edn. and math. NYU, 1965-87, dir. math. edn. dept.,

1967-83, chmn. math., sci. and stats. edn. dept., 1970-80, 86-87, chmn. Univ. Faculty Council, 1981-82; prof. math. U. Ariz., Tucson, 1987—. Mem. nat. bd. advisor Sq. One TV, 1983-94, U.S. Commn. on Math. Instrn., 1984-95, chmn., 1991-95; math. adv. com. Nat. Tchr. Exam. Successor (Praxis), 1989-94; edn. panel New Am. Schs. Devel. Corp., 1991-97; U.S. Nat. rep. Internat. Commn. on Math. Instrn., 1991-95. Author: Contemporary Teaching of Secondary School Mathematics, 1967, Probability and Statistics, 1968, Teaching Mathematics: What Is Basic, 1981, Mathematics Education for a Changing World, 1990, Real Math, 1981, 85, 87, 91, Math: Explorations and Applications, 1998, College Mathematics Through Applications, 1999; contbr. articles to profl. jours. and encys., chpts. to yearbooks and anthologies. Recipient Leadership in Math. Edn. Lifetime Achievement medal, 1995. Mem. Nat. Coun. Tchrs. Math. (dir. 1968-71, pres. 1982-84), Coun. Sci. Soc. Pres. (chmn. 1988). Home: 5435 E Gleneagles Dr Tucson AZ 85718-1805 Office: U Ariz Dept Math Tucson AZ 85721-0001

WILLRICH, MASON, energy industry executive; b. L.A., 1933; m. Patricia Rowe, June 11, 1960 (dec. July 1996); m. Wendy Webster, Aug. 30, 1997; children: Christopher, Stephen, Michael, Katharine. BA magna cum laude, Yale U., 1954; JD, U. Calif., Berkeley, 1960. Atty. Pillsbury Madison and Sutro, San Francisco, 1960-62; asst. gen. coun. U.S. Arms Control and Disarmament Agy., 1962-65; assoc. prof. law U. Va., 1965-68, prof. law, 1968-75, John Stennis prof. law, 1975-79; dir. internat. rels. Rockefeller Found., N.Y.C., 1976-79; v.p. Pacific Gas & Electric, San Francisco, 1979-84, sr. v.p., 1984-88, exec. v.p., 1988-89; CEO, pres. PG&E Enterprises, San Francisco, 1989-94; exec. Pacific Gas and Electric Co., San Francisco, 1979-94; chmn. EnergyWorks, 1995-98; prin. Nth Power Technologies, Inc., 1996-99, spl. ltd. ptnr., 1999—. Author: Non-Proliferation Treaty, 1969, Global Politics of Nuclear Energy, 1971, (with T.B. Taylor) Nuclear Theft, 1974, Energy and World Politics, 1975, Administration of Energy Shortages, 1976, (with R.K. Lester) Radioactive Waste Management and Regulation, 1977. Trustee, past chmn. World Affairs Coun. No. Calif.; trustee, past chmn. Midland Sch.; dir. Evergreen Solar, Inc., Winrock Internat., Atlantic Coun. Guggenheim Meml. fellow, 1973. Mem. Phi Beta Kappa, Order of Coif. Office: 38 Dudley Ct Piedmont CA 94611-3442 E-mail: willrichm@aol.com

WILLS, J. ROBERT, academic administrator, drama educator, writer; b. Akron, Ohio, May 5, 1940; s. J. Robert and Helen Elizabeth (Lapham) W.; m. Barbara T. Salisbury, Aug. 4, 1984 (dec. 1998). BA, Coll. of Wooster, 1962; MA, U. Ill., 1963; PhD, Case-Western Res. U., 1971; cert. in arts adminstrn, Harvard U., 1976. Instr. to asst. prof., dir. theatre Wittenberg U., Springfield, Ohio, 1963-72; assoc. prof., dir. grad. studies, chmn. dept. theatre U. Ky., Lexington, 1972-77, prof. theatre, dean Coll. Fine Arts, 1977-81; prof. drama, dean Coll. Fine Arts U. Tex., Austin, 1981-89, Effie Marie Cain Regents chair in Fine Arts, 1986-89; provost, prof. theatre Pacific Luth. U., Tacoma, 1989-94; prof. theatre, dean coll. fine arts Ariz. State U., Tempe, 1994—. Cons. colls., univs., arts orgns., govt. agencies Author: The Director in a Changing Theatre, 1976, Directing in the Theatre: A Casebook, 1980, rev. edit., 1994; dir. 92 plays; contbr. articles to profl. jours. Bd. dirs. various art orgns., Ky., Tex., Wash., Ariz. Recipient grants public and pvt. agencies. Mem. Nat. Assn. State Univs. and Land-Grant Colls.(chmn. commn. on arts 1981-83), Coun. Fine Arts Deans (exec. com. 1984-89, sec./treas. 1986-89), Univ. and Coll. Theatre Assn. (pres. 1981-82), Assn. for Communication Adminstrn. (pres. 1986-87), Ky. Theatre Assn. (pres. 1976). Office: Ariz State U Coll Fine Arts Tempe AZ 85287-2101 E-mail: bob.wills@asu.edu

WILLS, JOHN ELLIOT, JR. history educator, writer; b. Urbana, Ill., Aug. 8, 1936; s. John Elliot and George Anne (Hicks) W.; m. Carolin Connell, July 19, 1958; children: Catherine, Christopher John, Jeffrey David, Joanne, Lucinda. BA in Philosophy, U. Ill., 1956; MA in East Asian Studies, Harvard U., 1960, PhD in History and Far Ea. Langs., 1967. History instr. Stanford (Calif.) U., 1964-65, U. So. Calif., L.A., 1965-67, asst. prof., 1967-72, assoc. prof., 1972-84, prof., 1984—, acting chair East Asian Langs. and Cultures, 1987-89; dir. East Asian Studies Ctr. USC-UCLA Joint East Asian Studies Ctr., L.A., 1990-94. Rsch. abroad in The Netherlands, Taiwan, China, Japan, Macao, Philippines, Indonesia, India, Italy, Spain, Portugal, Eng. Author: Pepper, Guns, and Parleys: The Dutch East India Company and China, 1662-1681, 1974, Embassies and Illusions: Dutch and Portuguese Envoys to K'ang-hsi, 1666-1687, 1984, Mountain of Fame: Portraits in Chinese History, 1994, 1688: A Global History, 2001; co-editor: (with Jonathan D. Spence) From Ming to Ch'ing: Conquest, Region, and Continuity in Seventeenth-Century China, 1979; contbr. articles to profl. jours. Grantee Nat. Acad. Scis., 1985, Am. Coun. Learned Soc., 1979-80; Younger Humanist fellow NEH, 1972-73. Mem. Assn. for Asian Studies, Am. Hist. Assn., Phi Beta Kappa, Phi Kappa Phi (recognition award 1986, 95). Avocation: travel. Office: U So Calif Dept History Los Angeles CA 90089-0034 E-mail: jwills@usc.edu

WILLS, RICHARD H. electronics manufacturing executive; B in Computer Sys., Linfield Coll.; MBA, U. Oreg. Various positions Tektronix, Inc., Beaverton, Oreg., 1979-91, head TDS line, 1991-93, worldwide dir. mktg., 1993-94, v.p., gen. mgr. design svc. and test bus. unit, 1995-97, pres. European ops., 1997-99, pres. measurement bus., 1999-2000, pres., CEO, 2000—, also bd. dirs. With USAF. Office: Tektronix Inc 14200 SW Karl Braun Dr Beaverton OR 97077

WILLSON, JOHN MICHAEL, retired mining company executive; b. Sheffield, England, Feb. 21, 1940; s. Jack Desmond and Cicely Rosamond (Long Price) W.; m. Susan Mary Partridge, Aug. 26, 1942; children: Marcus J., Carolyn A. BSc in Mining Engring. with honors, Imperial Coll., London, 1962, MSc in Mining Engring., 1985. With Cominco Ltd., 1966-74, v.p. No. Group B.C., Can., 1981-84; pres. Garaventa (Canada) Ltd., Vancouver, 1974-81; pres., CEO Western Can. Steel Ltd., Vancouver, 1985-88, Pegasus Gold Inc., Spokane, Wash., 1989-92, Placer Dome, Inc., Vancouver, B.C., Can., 1993-2000; ret., 2000. Bd. dirs. Nexen Inc., Finning Internat. Ltd. Pres. N.W.T. Chamber Mines, Yellowknife, Can., 1982-84; chmn. bd. dirs. Western States Pub. Lands Coalition, Pueblo, Colo., 1990-91; bd. dirs. World Gold Coun. Mem. AIME, Can. Inst. Mining and Metallurgy, Inst. Mining and Metallurgy (London), Assn. Profl. Engrs. and Geologists N.W.T., N.W. Mining Assn. (bd. dirs. Corp. Leadership award 1991), World Gold Coun. (chmn. 1999-2001). Avocations: cycling, tennis, squash, sailing, skiing. Home: 4722 Drummond Dr Vancouver BC Canada V6T 1B4 Fax: 604-228-9664

WILLSON, PRENTISS, JR. lawyer; b. Durham, N.C., Sept. 20, 1943; s. Prentiss and Lucille (Giles) W. AB, Occidental Coll., 1965; JD, Harvard U., 1968. Bar: Calif. 1969, U.S. Dist. Ct. (no. dist.) Calif. 1971, U.S. Ct. Appeals (9th cir.) 1971, U.S. Tax Ct. 1971, U.S. Supreme Ct. 1975. Instr. law Miles Coll., Birmingham, Ala., 1968-70; ptnr. Morrison & Foerster, San Francisco, 1970-98, Ernst & Young, Walnut Creek, Calif., 1998—. Prof. Golden Gate U., 1971-84; lectr. Stanford U. Sch. Law, 1985-88. Contbr. articles to profl. jours. Mem. ABA, Calif. Bar Assn. Democrat. Office: Ernst & Young 1331 N California Blvd Walnut Creek CA 94596 E-mail: prentiss.willson@ey.com

WILNER, PAUL ANDREW, journalist; b. N.Y.C., Feb. 12, 1950; s. Norman and Sylvia (Rubenstein) W.; m. Alyson Paula Bromberg, June 3, 1980; children: Anne Charlotte, Daniel Joseph. Student, U. Calif., Berkeley, 1968; BA, CUNY, 1976. Copy clk. N.Y. Times, 1976-80; reporter L.A. Herald Examiner, 1980-85; mng. editor Hollywood Reporter, L.A., 1985-87; asst. mng. editor features San Francisco Examiner, 1987—. Sr. instr. U. So. Calif., L.A., 1983-85. Author: (poetry) Serious Business, The Paris Rev., 1977. Office: SF Examiner Mag 110 5th St San Francisco CA 94103-2972

WILSKEY, MIKE, marketing professional; b. Seattle; B in Journalism, U. Oreg., 1978. Adv. mgr. Nike, 1984, product line mgr. for cross-tng., internat. advertising mgr., 1990-92, dir. mktg. Asia-Pacific hdqrs., 1993-96, dir. global brand mktg., 1997-98, v.p., dir. global brand mktg., 1998—. Advt. mgr. Gresham Outlook, Valley Observer, 1978-79; mktg. mgr. Oreg. Bus. mag., 1979-80. Office: Nike Inc One Bowerman Dr Beaverton OR 97005

WILSON, ARCHIE FREDRIC, medical educator; b. L.A., May 7, 1931; s. Louis H. and Ruth (Kert) W.; m. Tamar Braverman, Feb. 11, 1937; children: Lee A., Daniel B. BA, UCLA, 1953, PhD, 1967; MD, U. Calif., San Francisco, 1957. Intern L.A. County Gen. Hosp., 1957-58; resident U. Calif., San Francisco, 1958-61; fellow in chest disease dept. medicine UCLA, 1966-67, asst. prof., 1967-70, U. Calif., Irvine, 1970-73, assoc. prof., 1973-79, prof., 1979—. Editor: Pulmonary Function Test: Interpretation, 1986; contbr. articles to profl. jours. Bd. mem. Am. Lung Assn., Orange County, 1970-90, Am. Heart Assn., Calif., 1990—. Capt. USMC, 1961-63. Mem. Am. Fedn. Clin. Rsch., Western Soc. Clin. Investigation. Office: U Calif 101 The City Dr S Orange CA 92868-3201

WILSON, BETH A. college official; BA, Calif. State Coll., Sonoma; MBA, Nat. U. Asst. dir. Am. Bus. Coll., 1976-81; scholarship adminstr. Nat. U., 1982-84; v.p. br. ops. Nat. Coll., 1990-91; from exec. dir. bus. sch., group mgr. to v.p. adminstrn. United Edn. and Sofware, 1984-90; exec. dir. Capital Hill campus, then area ops. mgr. Nat. Edn. Ctrs., Inc., 1991-95; ops. dir., regional ops. dir. Corinthian Schs., Inc., Santa Ana, Calif., 1995-97, regional ops. dir. coll. region of Rhodes Colls. divsn., 1997-98, v.p. ops. parent co., 1998—. Office: Corinthian Colls Inc 6 Hutton Centre Dr Ste 400 Santa Ana CA 92707-5764

WILSON, BILL, state senator; b. Great Falls, Mont., Mar. 28, 1961; m. Robin Wilson. Student, U. Mont., Coll. of Great Falls. Locomotive engr. Burlington No. R.R.; pres. United Transp. Union, 1986-89; mem. Mont. State Senate, 1992—, mem. bills. and jour. com., state adminstrn. com., conf. com, mem. labor and employment rels. com., natural resources com., mem. select com. on Constl. amendments, vice chair labor com., 1993-95. Bd. dirs. Heisey Youth Ctr.; mem. Mont. Boating Adv. Coun. Recipient Gov.'s medal of Valor, 1997. Democrat. Home: 1305 2d Ave N Great Falls MT 59401-3265 E-mail: bwl305@worldnet.att.net

WILSON, CHARLES B. neurosurgeon, educator; b. Neosho, Mo., Aug. 31, 1929; married; 3 children. BS, Tulane U., 1951, MD, 1954. Resident pathologist Tulane U., 1955-56, instr. neurosurgery, 1960-61; resident Ochsner Clinic, 1956-60; instr. La. State U., 1961-63; from asst. prof. to prof. U. Ky., 1963-68; prof. neurosurgery U. Calif., San Francisco, 1968—. Mem. Am. Assn. Neurol. Surgery, Soc. Neurol. Surgery. Achievements include research in brain and pituitary tumors. Office: U Calif U 125 Sch Medicine Box 0350 San Francisco CA 94143

WILSON, DAVID EUGENE, former magistrate judge, lawyer; b. Columbia, S.C., Jan. 12, 1940; s. David W. and Emma (Moseley) W.; m. Nancy Ireland, Sept. 5, 1964; children: Amy R., Cara S. BA, U. S.C., 1963, JD, 1966; MA, Boston U., 1971. Bar: Vt. 1972, D.C. 1973, Wash. 1980, U.S. Dist. Ct. Vt. 1972, U.S. Dist. Ct. (we. dist.) Wash. 1976. Asst. atty. gen. State of Vt., Montpelier, 1972-73; asst. U.S. atty. U.S. Dist. Ct. D.C., Washington, 1973-76, U.S. Dist. Ct. (we. dist.) Wash., Seattle, 1976-89, U.S. atty., 1989, asst. U.S. atty., chief criminal div., 1989-92; U.S. magistrate judge Seattle, 1992-2000; ptnr. McKay-Chadwell, 2000—. Mem. faculty Atty. Gen.'s Advocacy Inst., Washington, 1979—, Nat. Inst. Trial Advocacy, Seattle, 1987—. Capt. U.S. Army, 1966-71, col. USAR. Recipient Disting. Community Svc. award B'nai Brith, 1987. Fellow Am. Coll. Trial Lawyers; mem. Fed. Bar Assn., Wash. State Bar, Seattle-King County Bar. Avocations: hunting, fishing, skiing, books. Office: McKay Chadwell PLLC 7201 Bank of Am Tower 701 5th Ave Seattle WA 98104

WILSON, EDWARD LAWRENCE, civil engineering educator, structural engineering consultant; b. Ferndale, Calif., Sept. 5, 1931; s. James Charles and Josephine (Christen) W.; m. Barbara Diane Farrington, July 24, 1960; children— Michael Edward, Teresa Diane A.A., Sacramento City Coll., 1952; B.S., U. Calif.-Berkeley, 1954, M.S., 1958, D.Eng., 1962. Bridge engr. State of Calif., Sacramento, 1953-64; research engr. Aerojet Gen. Corp., Sacramento, 1963-65; from asst. prof. to assoc. prof. U. Calif.-Berkeley, 1965-72, prof. computational methods for structural analysis, 1972-99, prof. emeritus, 1999—; pres. Structural Analysis Programs, Inc., El Cerrito, Calif., 1980—. Dir. BCDC, San Francisco Author numerous papers, reports. Served with U.S. Army, 1955-56; Korea Recipient E.E. Howard award ASCE, 1995. Mem. ASCE, Structural Engring. Assn. No. Calif., Nat. Acad. Engring. Home: 1050 Leneve Pl El Cerrito CA 94530-2750 Office: U Calif 583 Davis Hl Berkeley CA 94720-0001

WILSON, GAYLE ANN, civic worker; b. Phoenix, Nov. 24, 1942; d. Clarence Arthur and Charlotte Evelyn (Davison) Edlund; m. Theodore William Graham, Sept. 14, 1963 (div. May 1983); children: Todd Chandler, Philip Edlund; m. Pete Wilson, May 29, 1983. BA, Stanford U., 1965; postgrad., U. San Diego, 1982. First lady State of Calif., Sacramento, 1991-99; bd. directors ARCO, Los Angeles, CA, 1999—. Adv. for early childhood health and improved math. and sci. edn.; bd. dirs. Ctr. for Excellence in Edn., McLean, Va., 1985—, also former chmn.; mem. Jr. League San Diego, 1968—, also past pres.; bd. dirs. Calif. Inst. Tech., Pasadena, 1995—, Children's Inst. Internat., Phoenix House; former spokesperson Access for Infants and Mothers (AIM), Calif. Breast Cancer Initiative, Never Shake a Baby Campaign, Partnership for Responsible Parenting; mem. Calif. Sesquicentennial Commn.; hon. chmn. Calif. Sci. Fair, Calif. 4-H Found., Calif. Perinatal Outreach-BabyCal, Calif. Commn. on Improving Life Through Svc., Keep Calif. Beautiful; hon. co-chmn. Calif. Mentor Initiative; mem. adv. coun. Ct. Apptd. Spl. Advs.; mem. adv. coun. computers in schs. program Detweiler Found.; hon. chmn. bd. dirs. Leland Stanford Mansion Restoration Found.; founding mem. Achievement Rewards for Coll. Scientists; mem. San Diego Park and Recreation Commn., 1980-83; regent Children's Hosp. L.A. Found., 1998—; bd. dirs. Center Theatre Group, L.A., 1998—, ARCO. Recipient Guardian Angel award L.A. ChildShare, 1995, lifetime achievemecnt award Jr. League L.A., 1996. Mem. Phi Beta Kappa. Republican. Avocations: lyric writing, singing, performing, watercolors. Office: 2132 Century Park Ln Apt 301 Los Angeles CA 90067-3320

WILSON, GRAHAM MCGREGOR, energy company executive; b. Kilwinning, Scotland, Aug. 2, 1944; s. Peter and Jessie (Scott) W.; m. Josee Perrault; children: Stefanie, Richard, Patrick. BS, McGill U., Montreal, Que., Can., 1967; MBA, U. Western Ont., London, Can., 1969. Investment analyst Greenshields Inc., 1969-72; asst. treas. Genstar, 1972-74; various fin. positions, v.p. fin. MacMillan Bloedel Ltd., Vancouver, B.C., Can., 1974-83; v.p. fin. and adminstrn. Petro-Can. Inc., Calgary, Alta., 1983-88; exec. v.p., CFO Westcoast Energy Inc., Vancouver, 1988—. Bd. dirs. Foothills Pipe Lines Ltd., Calgary, Enlogiso, Inc., Toronto, Westcoast Gas Svcs., Calgary, Centra Gas Inc., Toronto, Ont., Centra Gas Alta., Inc., Leduc Centra Gas B.C. Inc., Victoria, Itron Inc., Spokane, Wash., Union Gas Ltd., Chatham, Ont., Union Energy Inc., Toronto, Westcoast Energy Internat. Inc., Lake Superior Power Inc., Westcoast Capital Corp., Engage Energy. Avocations: squash, golf. Office: Westcoast Energy Inc 1333 W Georgia St Vancouver BC Canada V6E 3K9

WILSON, HEATHER ANN, congresswoman; b. Keene, N.H., Dec. 30, 1960; d. George Douglas Wilson and Martha Lou Wilson-Kernozicky. BS, USAF Acad., 1982; M. Philosophy, Oxford U., 1984, PhD, 1985. U.S. mission NATO, Brussels, 1987-89, Nat. Security Coun., Washington, 1989-91; pres. Keystone Internat., Inc., Albuquerque, 1991-95; cabinet sec. N.Mex. Dept. Children, Youth and Families, Santa Fe, 1995-98; mem. U.S. Congress from 1st N.Mex. Dist., Washington, 1998—; mem. armes svcs. com., energy and commerce com. Adj. prof. U. N.Mex.; mem. Def. Adv. Com. on Women in the Svcs. Contbr. articles to profl. jours. Capt. USAF, 1982-89. Rhodes scholar, 1982. Republican. Avocations: parenting, hiking, skiing. Office: 318 Cannon House Office Blg Washington DC 20515*

WILSON, HUGH STEVEN, lawyer; b. Paducah, Ky., Nov. 27, 1947; s. Hugh Gipson and Rebekah (Dunn) W.; m. Clare Maloney, Apr. 28, 1973; children: Morgan Elizabeth, Zachary Hunter, Samuel Gipson. BS, Ind. U., 1968; JD, U. Chgo., 1971; LLM, Harvard U., 1972. Bar: Calif. 1972, U.S. Dist. Ct. (cen. dist.) Calif. 1972, U.S. Dist. Ct. (so. dist.) Calif. 1973, U.S. Ct. Appeals (9th cir.) 1975, U.S. Dist. Ct. (no. dist.) Calif. 1977, U.S. Supreme Ct. 1978, U.S. Dist. Ct. (ea. dist.) 1980. Assoc. Latham & Watkins, L.A., 1972-78, ptnr., 1978—. Recipient Jerome N. Frank prize U. Chgo. Law Sch., 1971. Mem. Calif. Club, Coronado Yacht Club, Order of Coif. Republican. Avocations: lit., zoology. E-mail: steve.wilson@lw.com

WILSON, IAN ANDREW, molecular biology educator; b. Perth, Scotland, Mar. 22, 1949; BS in Biochemistry, U. Edinburgh, Scotland, 1971; DPhil in Molecular Biology, Oxford U., Eng., 1976. Tutor and tchg. asst. in biochemistry Harvard U., 1978-82, rsch. assoc. biochemistry and molecular biology, 1980-82; asst. mem. dept. immunology Scripps Rsch. Inst., LaJolla, Calif., 1982-83, asst. mem. dept. molecular biology, 1983-84, assoc. mem. dept. molecular biology, 1984-90, chmn. structure and chem. affinity group, 1987—, prof., lectr. molecular & cell biology/structure and chem., 1988—, prof. molecular biology, 1991—, prof. Skaggs Inst. Chem. Biology, 1996—. Contbr. articles to profl. jours. Recipient Newcomv-Cleve. prize, 1996-97. Mem. Brit. Biophys. Soc., Am. Soc. Virologists, Am. Assn. Pathologists, Am. Crystallographic Assn., Brit. Soc. Immunologists, Protein Soc., Am. Chem. Soc. Office: Scripps Rsch Inst BCC206 Dept Molecular Biol 10550 N Torrey Pines Rd La Jolla CA 92037-1000

WILSON, JAMES RIGG, aircraft manufacturing company executive; b. 1941; BA, Coll. Wooster, 1963; MBA, Harvard U., 1965. V.p. Textron, Providence, 1967-76; with Fairchild Industries Inc., Chantilly, Va., 1977-80, 82-87, chief fin. officer, 1977—, v.p., 1977-80, sr. v.p., 1982-85, exec. v.p., 1985—; chief fin. officer, sr. v.p. Wickes Cos., San Diego, 1980-82; exec. v.p., CFO Thiokol Corp., Ogden, Utah, 1989-93, pres., CEO, 1993—; Pres.Chrmn,& CEO Cordant Technologies Inc, Salt Lk City, UT. Office: Cordant Technologies Inc 15 W South Temple Ste 1600 Salt Lake City UT 84101-1532

WILSON, JOHN B. clothing company executive; BS in Chem. Engring., Rensselaer Polytechnic Inst.; MBA, Harvard U. Former v.p. Bain & Co.; former sr. v.p. corp. planning Northwest Airlines; exec. v.p., fin. and strategy, CFO Staples, Inc., 1992-96, exec. v.p., chief administrv. officer The Gap, Inc., San Francisco, 1996-98, exec. v.p., COO, 1998—. Office: The Gap Inc 1 Harrison St San Francisco CA 94105-1602

WILSON, JOHN FRANCIS, religious studies educator, archaeologist; b. Springfield, Mo., Nov. 4, 1937; s. Frederick Marion and Jessie Ferrell (Latimer) W.; m. L. Claudette Faulk, June 9, 1961; children: Laura, Amy, Emily. BA, Harding U., Searcy, Ark., 1959; MA, Harding U., Memphis, 1961; PhD, U. Iowa, 1967. Dir. Christian Student Ctr., Springfield, 1959-73; prof. religious studies S.W. Mo. State U., Springfield, 1961-83; prof. of religion, dean Seaver Coll. Arts, Letters and Scis. Pepperdine U., Malibu, Calif., 1983-98; dir. Inst. for the Study of Religion and Archaeology, 1998—. Author: Religion: A Preface, 1982, 2d edit., 1989; co-author: Discovering the Bible, 1986, Excavations at Capernaum, 1989; contbr. articles, revs. to profl. publs. Mem. Archaeol. Inst. Am., Am. Schs. of Oriental Rsch., Soc. Bib. Lit., Am. Numismatic Soc., Palestine Exploration Soc. Mem. Ch. of Christ. Office: Pepperdine U Seaver Coll 24255 Pacific Coast Hwy Malibu CA 90263-0002 E-mail: jwilson@pepperdine.edu

WILSON, JOHN JAMES, federal judge; b. Boston, Dec. 23, 1927; s. John J. and Margaret (Thomas) W.; m. Joan Ellen Bostwick, Sept. 1, 1951 (div. Sept. 1975); children: Jeffrey, John, Julie; m. Elizabeth Brower, Dec. 4, 1975; 1 child, Stephane. AB, Tufts U., 1951; LLB, Stanford U., 1954. Bar: Calif. 1954, Mass. 1954, Oreg. 1982, U.S. Dist. Ct. (no., cen., ea. and so. dists.) Calif., U.S. Dist. Ct. Oreg. Asst. U.S. atty., L.A., 1958-60; ptnr. Hill, Farrer & Burrill, L.A., 1960-85; bankruptcy judge U.S. Dist. Ct. Calif., San Bernardino, 1985-88, Santa Ana, Calif., 1989-99; ret., 1999. Lt. (j.g.) USN, 1945-50. Seventh Day Adventist. Office: 507 Calle Amigo San Clemente CA 92673-3000 E-mail: j.dub@home.com

WILSON, JOHN PASLEY, law educator; b. Newark, Apr. 7, 1933; s. Richard Henry and Susan Agnes (Pasley) W.; m. Elizabeth Ann Reed, Sept. 10, 1955 (div.); children: David Cables, John Pasley, Cicely Reed. AB, Princeton U., 1955; LLB, Harvard U., 1962. Bar: N.J. 1962, Mass. 1963, U.S. Dist. Ct. N.J. 1962, U.S. Dist. Ct. Mass. 1963. Budget examiner Exec. Office of Pres., Bur. of the Budget, Washington, 1955-56; assoc. Riker, Danzig, Scherer & Brown, Newark, 1962-63; asst. dean Harvard U. Law Sch., Cambridge, Mass., 1963-67; assoc. dean Boston U. Law Sch., 1968-82; dean Golden Gate U. Sch. Law, San Francisco, 1982-88, prof., 1988—. Vis. prof. dept. health policy and mgmt. Harvard U., 1988; cons. Nat. Commn. for the Protection of Human Subjects of Biomed. and Behavioral Rsch.; mem. Mass. Gov.'s Commn. on Civil and Legal Rights of Developmentally Disabled; former chmn. adv. com. Ctr for Cmty. Legal Edn., San Francisco. Author: The Rights of Adolescents in the Mental Health System; contbr. chpts. to books, articles to profl. jours. Bd. dirs. Greater Boston Legal Svcs., Chewonki Found.; mem. Health Facilities Appeals Bd., Commonwealth of Mass.; assoc. mem. Dem. Town Com., Concord; chmn. Bd. Assessors, Concord; bd. overseers Boston Hosp. for Women, past chmn. med. affairs com.; past mem. instl. rev. bd. Calif. Pacific Hosp., San Francisco. Served to lt. (j.g.) USNR, 1956-59. NIMH grantee, 1973. Mem. Nat. Assn. Securities Dealers (arbitrator). Office: Golden Gate U Sch Law 536 Mission St San Francisco CA 94105-2967 E-mail: jwilson@ggu.edu, jwlsn@earthlink.net

WILSON, JOHNNY LEE, group publisher; b. Santa Maria, Calif., Oct. 20, 1950; s. John Henry and Bobbie Lou (Henson) W.; m. Susan Lynne Leavelle, Aug. 28, 1970 (div. 1998); children: Jennifer Lynne, Jonathan Lee; m. Wai Lam Chu, May 21, 1999; children: William Chu, Talyn Chu. BA, Calif. Bapt. Coll., Riverside, 1972; MDiv, Golden Gate Bapt. Seminary, Mill Valley, Calif., 1975; ThM, So. Bapt. Theol. Seminary, Louisville, 1978, PhD, 1981. Pastor Rollingwood Bapt. Ch., San Pablo, Calif., 1974-75, Temple Bapt. Ch., Sacramento, 1975-77, Hermosa-Redondo Beach (Calif.) Ministries, 1981-82, Immanuel. Bapt. Ch., La Puente, Calif., 1982-86; asst. editor Computer Gaming World, Anaheim, 1986-89, editor, 1989-93, editor-in-chief San Francisco, 1993-99; group pub. Wizards of the Coast, Renton, Wash., 1999—; pres. and prof. of Old Testament Calif. Korean Bapt. Seminary, Walnut, 1990-93. Adj. prof. O.T. studies So. Calif. Ctr., Garden Grove, Calif., 1981-86; mem. com. Software Pub. Assn. Ratings Group, Washington, 1994; mem. adv. coun. Recreation Software Adv. Coun., 1995; bd. govs. Acad. Interactive Arts and Scis., 1995; bd. dirs. Turbine Entertainment. Author: The Sim City Planning Commission Handbook, 1990, The Sim Earth Bible, 1991; co-author: The Mercer Dictionary of Bible, 1990, Sid Meier's Civilization: Rome on 640K A Day, 1992, Civilization: Call to Power Official Strategy Guide, 1999, Civilization: Call to Power 2 Strategy Guide, 2000. Named to Outstanding Young Men of Am., Jaycees, Ala., 1977, Best Software Reviewer, Software Pubs. Assn., Washington, 1990. Mem. Sci. Fiction and Fantasy Writers Am. (assoc.). Avocations: drama, miniatures gaming, writing. Home: 4664 144th Pl SE Bellevue WA 98006-3158 Office: Wizards of the Coast 1801 Lind Ave SW Renton WA 98055-4068 E-mail: jlwilson@wizards.com

WILSON, LERRY, public relations executive; Pres. Wilson McHenry Co, San Mateo, Calif., 1989—. Office: Wilson McHenry Co 393 Vintage Park Dr Ste 140 Foster City CA 94404-1172

WILSON, LESLIE, biochemist, cell biologist, biology educator; b. Boston, June 29, 1941; s. Samuel Paul Wilson and Lee (Melnicker) Kamerling; m. Carla Helena Van Wingerden, Sept. 9, 1989; children from previous marriage: Sebastian A. Michael, Naomi Beth. BS, Mass. Coll. Pharmacy and Allied Health Scis., 1963; PhD, Tufts U., 1967; postdoctoral study, U. Calif. at Berkeley, 1967-69; doctorate honoris causa, U. de la Méditerranée, Marseille, France, 1998. Asst. prof. dept. pharmacology Stanford U. Sch. Medicine, 1969-74; assoc. prof. dept. biol. scis. U. Calif., Santa Barbara, 1975-78, prof. biochemistry, 1979—, chmn. dept. biol. scis., 1987-91, head divsn. molecular, cellular, devel. biol., 1992-93. Sci. adv. panel mem. cell and devel. biology Am. Cancer Soc., Atlanta, 1984-88; cons. Eli Lilly & Co., Indpls., 1980—, Tularik Corp., San Francisco, Amgen Corp., Thousand Oaks, Calif.; scientific adv. bd. Myco Genetics Panphytica, Inc., 1997-99, co-organizer Internat. Colloquium on the Cytoskeleton and human dis., Marseille, France, 2001. Editor: (book series) Methods in Cell Biology, 1987—; assoc. editor Biochemistry; contbr. numerous rsch. papers to profl. publs. Bd. dirs. Cancer Found. Santa Barbara. Rsch. grantee NIH, 1970—, Am. Cancer Soc., 1986-97, Lilly Rsch. Labs., 1990—, Phone-Poulenc-Rover, France, 1998—. Mem. AAAS, Am. Soc. Cell Biology (chmn. sci. program 1977), Am. Soc. Biol. Chemistry and Molecular Biology, Am. Soc. Pharmacology and Exptl. Therapeutics, Am. Chem. Soc. Democrat. Office: U Calif Dept Molecular Cellular & Devel Biology Santa Barbara CA 93106 E-mail: wilson@lifesci.wcsb.edu

WILSON, MATTHEW FREDERICK, newspaper editor; b. San Francisco, May 10, 1956; s. Kenneth E. and Verna Lee (Hunter) W. BA in Philosophy, U. Calif., Berkeley, 1978. Copy person San Francisco Chronicle, summers 1975, 76, 77, copy editor, 1978-82, editorial systems coord., 1982-84; budget analyst San Francisco Newspaper Agy., 1984085; asst. news editor San Francisco Chronicle, 1985-87, asst. to exec. editor, 1987-88, mng. editor, 1988-95, exec. editor, 1995—. Mem. Am. Soc. Newspaper Editors, AP Mng. Editors, Calif. Soc. Newspaper Editors. Office: San Francisco Chronicle 901 Mission St San Francisco CA 94103-2905

WILSON, MIRIAM GEISENDORFER, retired physician, educator; b. Yakima, Wash., Dec. 3, 1922; d. Emil and Frances Geisendorfer; m. Howard G. Wilson, June 21, 1947; children— Claire, Paula, Geoffrey, Nicola, Marla. B.S., U. Wash., Seattle, 1944, M.S., 1945; M.D., U. Calif., San Francisco, 1950. Mem. faculty U. So. Calif. Sch. Medicine, L.A., 1965—, prof. pediatrics, 1969—. Office: U So Calif Med Ctr 1129 N State St Rm 1g24 Los Angeles CA 90033-1044

WILSON, MYRON ROBERT, JR. retired psychiatrist; b. Helena, Mont., Sept. 21, 1932; s. Myron Robert Sr. and Constance Ernestine (Bultman) W. BA, Stanford U., 1954, MD, 1957. Diplomate Am. Bd. Psychiatry and Neurology. Dir. adolescent psychiatry Mayo Clinc, Rochester, Minn., 1965-71; pres. and psychiatrist in chief Wilson Ctr., Faribault, 1971-86; ret., 1986; chmn. Wilson Ctr., 1986-90; ret., 1990. Assoc. clin. prof. psychiatry UCLA, 1985-99. Contbr. articles to profl. jours. Chmn., CEO C.B. Wilson Found., L.A., 1972—; mem. bd. dirs. Pasadena Symphony Orchestra Assn., Calif., 1987; vestryman, treas. St. Thomas' Parish, L.A., 1993-96. Lt. comdr., 1958-60. Fellow Mayo Grad. Sch. Medicine, Rochester, 1960-65. Fellow Am. Psychiat. Assn., Am. Soc. for Adolescent Psychiatry, Internat. Soc. for Adolescent Psychiatry (founder, treas. 1985-88, sec. 1985-88, treas. 1988-92); mem. Soc. Sigma Xi (Mayo Found. chpt.). Episcopalian. Office: Wilson Found 2565 Zorada Dr Los Angeles CA 90046-1747 E-mail: rwilso4488@aol.com

WILSON, NANCY LINDA, religious organization administrator; b. Mineola, N.Y., July 13, 1950; Grad., Allegheny Coll.; student, Boston U.; MDiv, SS, Cyril and Methodius Sem. Ordained to ministry Universal Fellowship of Met. Cmty. Chs. Dist. coord. N.E. dist. Universal Fellowship of Met. Cmty. Chs., clk. bd. of elders Fellowship hdqrs., 1979-86, sr. pastor Met. Comty. Ch., 1986—; vice-moderator UFMCC, L.A., 1993—. Bd. trustees Samaritan Inst. Religious Studies; founder, chief ecumenical officer Ecumenical Witness and Ministry; vice chair Progressive Religious Alliance. Author: Our Tribe: Queer Folks, God, Jesus and the Bible, 1995; co-author: Amazing Grace; prodr.: (brochure) Our Story Too. Rockefeller scholar. Office: Met Cmty Ch 8714 Santa Monica Blvd West Hollywood CA 90069-4508

WILSON, OWEN MEREDITH, JR. lawyer; b. Oakland, Calif., Dec. 22, 1939; s. O. Meredith and Marian Wilson; m. Sandra A. Wilson (div.); children: Ann, Melissa, Jennifer; m. Teddi Anne Wilson; children: Amanda, Lisa. Student, U. Utah, 1957-59; AB, Harvard U., 1961; LLB, U. Minn., 1965. Bar: Oreg. 1965, Wash. 1985. Ptnr. Lane Powell Spears Lubersky, Portland, Oreg., 1969—. Mem. mediation panel U.S. Dist. Ct., 1986—. Mem. bd. visitors Law Sch. U. Minn., 1990-96. Mem. ABA, Oreg. State Bar Assn., Wash. State Bar, Multnomah Bar Assn. Office: 601 SW 2nd Ave Ste 2100 Portland OR 97204-3158 E-mail: wilsonm@lanepowell.com

WILSON, PETE, former governor; b. Lake Forest, Ill., Aug. 23, 1933; s. James Boone and Margaret (Callaghan) W.; m. Betty Robertson (div.); m. Gayle Edlund, May 29, 1983 B.A. in English Lit., Yale U., 1955; J.D., U. Calif., Berkeley, 1962; LL.D., Grove City Coll., 1983, U. Calif., San Diego, 1983, U. San Diego, , 1984. Bar: Calif. 1962. Mem. Calif. Legislature, Sacramento, 1966-71; mayor City of San Diego, 1971-83; U.S. Senator from Calif., 1983-91; gov. State of Calif., 1991-98; mng. dir. Pacific Capital Group, Beverly Hills, Calif., 1999—. Trustee Conservation Found.; mem. exec. bd. San Diego County council Boy Scouts Am.; hon. trustee So. Calif. Council Soviet Jews; adv. mem. Urban Land Inst., 1985-86; founding dir. Retinitis Pigmentosa Internat.; hon. dir. Alzheimer's Family Ctr., Inc., 1985; hon. bd. dirs. Shakespeare-San Francisco, 1985 Recipient Golden Bulldog award, 1984, 85, 86, Guardian of Small Bus. award, 1984, Cuauhtemoc plaque for disting. svc. to farm workers in Calif., 1991, Julius award for outstanding pub. leadership U. So. Calif., 1992, award of appreciation Nat. Head Start, 1992; named Legislator of Yr., League Calif. Cities, 1985, Man of Yr. N.G. Assn. Calif., 1986, Man of Yr. citation U. Calif. Boalt Hall, 1986; ROTC scholar Yale U., 1951-55. Mem. Nat. Inst. Family Assn. (adv. bd.), Phi Delta Phi, Zeta Psi Republican. Episcopalian

WILSON, RICHARD ALLAN, landscape architect; b. Chgo., Feb. 5, 1927; s. Edgar Allan and Lois Helena (Hearn) W.; m. Lisabet Julie Horchler, May 31, 1958; children: Gary Allan, Carl Bruce. BS, U. Calif., Berkeley, 1952. Engring. draftsman Freeland Evanson & Christenson, San Diego, 1952-53; designer, estimator Blue Pacific Nursery & Landscape Co., San Diego, 1955-59; prin. Richard A. Wilson, FASLA and Assocs., San Diego, 1959—. Sec. Calif. Coun. Landscape Architects, 1982-85; expert witness for law firms, 1983—. Designer Phil Swing Meml. Fountain, 1967. Mem. landscape com. Clairemont Town Coun., San Diego, 1955. With U.S. Army, 1944-46, Korea. Recipient First Pl. award for landscape So. Calif. Expdn., Del Mar, 1963. Fellow Am. Soc. Landscape Architects (del. coun. 1982-85), Am. Inst. Landscape Architects (treas. 1970, 2d v.p. 1971). Republican. Home and Office: 2570 Tokalon Ct San Diego CA 92110-2232

WILSON, ROBIN SCOTT, university president, writer; b. Columbus, Ohio, Sept. 19, 1928; s. John Harold and Helen Louise (Walker) W.; m. Patricia Ann Van Kirk, Jan. 20, 1951; children: Kelpie, Leslie, Kari, Andrew. B.A., Ohio State U., 1950; M.A., U. Ill., 1951, Ph.D., 1959. Fgn. intelligence officer CIA, Washington, 1959-67; prof. English Clarion State Coll., (Pa.), 1967-70; assoc. dir. Com. Instnl. Cooperation, Evanston, Ill., 1970-77; assoc. provost instrn. Ohio State U., Columbus, 1977-80; univ. pres. Calif. State U., Chico, 1980-93, pres. emeritus, 1993—. Author: Those Who Can, 1973, Death By Degrees, 1995, Paragons, 1996; short stories, criticism, articles on edn. Lt. USN, 1953-57. Mem. AAAS, Phi Kappa Phi E-mail: wilson@redshift.com

WILSON, S. LIANE, bank executive; Sr. v.p. info. systems Wash. Mut. Inc., Seattle, exec. v.p. corp. comm., 1995-2000, vice-chmn., 2000—. Office: Wash Mut Inc 1201 3rd Ave # Wmt1500 Seattle WA 98101-3029

WILSON, STEPHEN VICTOR, federal judge; b. Hartford, Conn., Mar. 26, 1942; s. Harry and Rae (Ross) W. BA in Econs., Lehigh U., 1963; JD, Bklyn. Law Sch., 1967; LLM, George Washington U., 1973. Bar: N.Y. 1967, D.C. 1971, Calif. 1972, U.S. Ct. Appeals (9th cir.), U.S. Dist. Ct. (so., cen. and no. dists.) Calif. Trial atty. Tax divsn. U.S. Dept. Justice, 1968-71, asst. U.S. atty., 1971-77, chief spl. prosecutions, 1973-77; ptnr. Hochman, Salkin & Deroy, Beverly Hills, Calif., 1977—; judge U.S. Dist. Ct. (cen. dist.) Calif., L.A., 1985—. Adj. prof. law Loyola U. Law Sch., 1976-79; U.S. Dept. State rep. to govt. W.Ger. on 20th anniversary of Marshall Plan, 1967; del. jud. conf. U.S. Ct. Appeals (9th cir.), 1982-86. Co-editor Tax Crimes--Corporate Liability, BNA Tax Management Series, 1983; contbr. articles to profl. jours. Recipient Spl. Commendation award U.S. Dept. Justice, 1977. Mem. ABA, L.A. County Bar Assn., Beverly Hills Bar Assn. (chmn. criminal law com.), Fed. Bar Assn. Jewish. Home: 9100 Wilshire Blvd Beverly Hills CA 90212-3415 Office: US Courthouse 312 N Spring St Ste 217J Los Angeles CA 90012-4704

WILSON, SUE, state legislator; b. Albuquerque; BA, So. Meth. U. Mem. N.Mex. Senate, Dist. 19, Santa Fe, 1996—; mem. fin. com. N.Mex. Senate, mem. Indian and cultural affairs com. Republican. Home: 812 Sagebrush Ct SE Albuquerque NM 87123-4121

WILSON, THEODORE HENRY, retired electronics company executive, aerospace engineer; b. Eufaula, Okla., Apr. 23, 1940; s. Theodore V. and Maggie E. (Buie) W.; m. Barbara Ann Tassara, May 16, 1958 (div. 1982); children: Debbie Marie, Nita Leigh, Wilson Axten, Pamela Ann, Brenda Louise, Theodore Henry II, Thomas John, Margaret Mariana; m. Colleen Fagan, Jan. 1, 1983 (div. 1987); m. Karen L. Lerohl, Sept. 26, 1987 (div. 1997); m. Sandra Rivadeneira, Mar. 27, 1997. BSME, U. Calif., Berkeley, 1962; MSME, U. So. Calif., 1964, MBA, 1970, MSBA, 1971. Sr. rsch. engr. N.Am. Aviation Co. div. Rockwell Internat., Downey, Calif., 1962-65; propulsion analyst, supr. div. applied tech. TRW, Redondo Beach, 1965-67, mem. devel. staff systems group, 1967-71, sr. fin. analyst worldwide automotive dept. Cleve., 1971-72, contr. systems and energy group Redondo Beach, 1972-79, dir. fin. control equipment group Cleve., 1979-82, v.p. fin. control indsl. and energy group, 1982-85, mem. space and def. group Redondo Beach, 1985-93, ret., 1993. Lectr., mem. com. acctg. curriculum UCLA Extension, 1974-79. Mem. Fin. Execs. Inst. (com. govt. bus.), Machinery and Allied Products Inst. (govt. contracts coun.), Nat. Contract Mgmt. Assn. (bd. advisors), Aerospace Industries Assn. (procurement and fin. coun.), UCLA Chancellors Assocs., Tau Beta Pi, Beta Gamma Sigma, Pi Tau Sigma. Republican. Avocations: golf, bridge. Home: 3617 Via La Selva Palos Verdes Peninsula CA 90274-1115

WILSON, THOMAS, museum director; Dir. Mus. of N.Mex, Santa Fe. Office: Mus of NMex 107 W Palace Ave Santa Fe NM 87501-2014

WILSON, WARREN SAMUEL, clergyman, bishop; b. New Orleans, May 15, 1927; s. Charlie Price and Warnie (Heart) W.; m. Lillie Pearl Harvey, Mar. 31, 1949; 1 child, Barbara LaJoyce. BA, So. U., Baton Rouge, 1950; DDiv, Moody Coll., Chgo., 1952; DDiv (hon.), Trinity Hall Coll. and Sem., Springfield, Ill., 1975. Ordained to ministry Ch. of God in Christ, 1952, crowned bishop, apptd. state bishop, Calif., 1970. Min. St. Bernard St. Church of God in Christ, New Orleans, until 1960, Fresno (Calif.) Temple Ch. of God in Christ, 1960—. Served with USN, 1942-46, PTO. Mem. NAACP (life). Avocations: bass fishing, boating.

WILSON-MCKEE, MARIE, museum director; Dir. Wyo. State Mus., Cheyenne. Office: Wyo State Mus Barrett Bldg 2301 Central Ave Cheyenne WY 82001-3173

WILTON, PETER CAMPBELL, marketing educator; b. Adelaide, S.A., Australia, Jan. 28, 1951; came to U.S., 1975; s. Murray and Kathleen (Ratcliffe) W. B in Commerce with hons., U. New South Wales, Sydney, 1972; PhD in Mgmt., Purdue U., 1979. Product mgr. Colgate Palmolive, Sydney, 1973-75; mktg. prof., Hass Sch. of Bus. U. Calif., Berkeley, 1979-87, 92—; COO Myer Pacific Corp., Melbourne, Australia, 1987-90; sr. assoc. Melbourne U., 1990, Sir Donald Hibberd lectr., 1991. Vis. fellow Griffith U., Brisbane, Australia, 1982; vis. assoc. prof. Duke U., Durham, N.C., 1985-86; pres., dir. Applied Mktg. Analysis, Inc., Wilmington, Del., 1987—, Orbis Assocs., San Francisco, 1992—. Contbr. articles to profl. jours. Recipient Mktg. Rsch. Soc. Australia prize, 1973; Australian Govt. fellow, 1975-79; grantee NSF, 1981, 84. Mem. Assn. Pub. Opinion Rsch. (officer 1985), Am. Mktg. Assn. (officer 1982-84), Australian-Am. C. of C. (dir. 1993-95). Avocations: flying, sailing, music, travel. Office: Haas Sch of Bus UCAL Berkeley S 545 Haas Berkeley CA 94720-1900

WIMER, MARK G. healthcare management company executive; BS in Bacteriology, U. Idaho; M of Health Adminstrn., St. Louis (Mo.) U. Pres. skilled nursing facility subs. Sun Healthcare Group, Albuquerque, 1993-97, sr. v.p. inpatient svcs., pres. COO, 1997—. Office: Sun Healthcare Group Inc 101 Sun Ave NE Albuquerque NM 87109-4373

WINBLAD, ANN, investment company executive; BA in Math. and Bus. Adminstrn., MA in Internat. Econs. and Edn., Coll. St. Thomas. Programmer; co-founder Open Sys, Inc., 1976-83; strategic planning cons.; ptnr. Hummer Winblad Venture Ptnrs., San Francisco, 1989—. Co-author: Object-Oriented Software, 1990. Office: Hummer Winblad Venture Ptnrs 2 S Park St 2d Fl San Francisco CA 94107-1807

WINCHESTER, ED, protective services official; Chief of police, Fresno, Calif. Office: 2323 Mariposa St Fresno CA 93721-2202

WINDELS, SUE, state senator; b. Nampa, Idaho, July 11, 1946; m. Carl Windels; children: Derek, Daniel. BA, Ea. Wash. U., 1967, MA, 1973. Vol. Peace Corps, 1967-69; tchr., 1969—; Dem. rep. dist. 27 Colo. Ho. of Reps., 1998-2000; Dem. senator dist. 19 Colo. State Senate, 2000—. Mem. edn., state, vets. and mil. affairs and stat audit com. Colo. Ho. of Reps.; mem. edn., judiciary and capitol devel. coms. Colo. State Senate. Founder (legis. newsletter) Voter's Voice, 1996-98. Mem. Interfaith Alliance; legis. dir. Jefferson County PTA, 1996-98; dir. pub. policy Colo. PTA, 1997. Mem. AAUW. LWV, Kiwanis. Office: Colo State Senate State Capitol 200 E Colfax Rm 307 Denver CO 80203 also: 13925 W 73d Ave Arvada CO 80005 E-mail: windels@sni.net, suewindels@aol.com

WINDER, DAVID KENT, federal judge; b. Salt Lake City, June 8, 1932; s. Edwin Kent and Alma Eliza (Cannon) W.; m. Pamela Martin, June 24, 1955; children: Ann, Kay, James. BA, U. Utah, 1955; LLB, Stanford U., 1958. Bar: Utah 1958, Calif. 1958. Assoc. firm Clyde, Mecham & Pratt, Salt Lake City, 1958-66; law clk. to chief justice Utah Supreme Ct., 1958-59; dep. county atty. Salt Lake County, 1959-63, chief dep. dist. atty., 1965-66; asst. U.S. atty. Salt Lake City, 1963-65; partner firm Strong & Hanni, Salt Lake City, 1966-77; judge U.S. Dist. Ct., Salt Lake City, 1977-79, 1979-93, chief judge, 1993-97, sr. judge, 1997—. Examiner Utah Bar Examiners, 1975-79, chmn., 1977-79; mem. jud. resources com. Served with USAF, 1951-52. Mem. Am. Bd. Trial Advocates, Utah State Bar (Judge of Yr. award 1978), Salt Lake County Bar Assn., Calif. State Bar. Democrat. Office: US Dist Ct 110 US Courthouse 350 S Main St Salt Lake City UT 84101-2106

WINDER, ROBERT OWEN, mathematician, computer engineer, geophysicist; b. Boston, Oct. 9, 1934; s. Claude V. and Harriet O. W.; m. Kathleen C. Winder; children by previous marriage: Katherine, Amy. A.B., U. Chgo., 1954; B.S., U. Mich., 1956; M.S., Princeton U., 1958, Ph.D., 1962; MS, Ariz. State U., 2000. With RCA, 1957-78, group head N.J., 1969-75, dir. microprocessors, 1975-77, dir. systems, 1977-78; mgr. workstation devel. Exxon Enterprises, Inc., Princeton, 1978-85; v.p. Syntex Computer Systems Inc., Bordentown, N.J., 1985-88; mgr. product engring., Princeton Operation, Intel Corp., 1988-93; mgr. engring. ops. video products div., Intel, Chandler, Ariz., 1993-95. Vis. scholar dept. geol. scis., Ariz. State U., 2001—. Contbr. articles to profl. jours.; patentee in field. NSF fellow, 1956-57; Recipient David Sarnoff award RCA, 1975. Fellow IEEE. E-mail: winder@asu.edu

WINDERS, GLENDA, publishing executive; Editl. dir. Copley News Svc., San Diego, 1997—. Office: Copley News Svc PO Box 120190 San Diego CA 92112-0190

WINE, MARK PHILIP, lawyer; b. Iowa City, Jan. 6, 1949; s. Donald Arthur and Mary Lepha (Schneider) W.; children: Kathryn Bouquet, Nicholas Cox, Meredith Kathryn. AB, Princeton U., 1971; JD, U. Iowa, 1974. Bar: Iowa 1974, Minn. 1976, Calif. 1997, U.S. Dist. Ct. Minn. 1976, U.S. Ct. Appeals (8th cir.) 1976, U.S. Supreme Ct. 1984, U.S. Ct. Appeals (4th cir.) 1985, U.S. Ct. Appeals (7th and Fed. cirs.) 1992, U.S. Ct. Appeals (9th cir.) 1997, U.S. Dist. Ct. (so., no. and ctrl. dists.) Calif. 1997. Law clk. to judge U.S. Ct. Appeals (8th cir.), St. Louis, 1974-76; ptnr. Oppenheimer Wolff & Donnelly LLP, Mpls., 1976—. Mem. ABA, Internat. Assn. Def. Counsel (chair spl. com. on intellectual property), Princeton Club of Southern Calif., Calif. Bar Assn., L.A. Bar Assn. Democrat. Avocations: cooking, reading, biking, golf. Home: 2960 Neilson Way Unit 303 Santa Monica CA 90405-5373 Office: Oppenheimer Wolff & Donnelly LLP 2029 Century Park E Fl 38 Los Angeles CA 90067-2901 E-mail: mwine@oppenheimer.com

WINFIELD, ROY A. pharmaceutical company executive; CEO Incyte Pharms., Palo Alto, Calif. Office: Incyte Pharms 3160 Porter Dr Palo Alto CA 94304-1212

WINFREE, ARTHUR TAYLOR, biologist, educator; b. St. Petersburg, Fla., May 15, 1942; s. Charles Van and Dorothy Rose (Scheb) W.; m. Ji-Yun Yang, June 18, 1983; children: Rachael, Erik from previous marriage. B of Engring. Physics, Cornell U., 1965; PhD in Biology, Princeton U., 1970. Lic. pvt. pilot. Asst. prof. theoretical biology U. Chgo., 1969-72; assoc. prof. biology Purdue U., West Lafayette, Ind., 1972-79, prof., 1979-86; prof. ecology and evolutionary biology U. Ariz., Tucson, 1986-88, Regents' prof., 1989—. Pres., dir. rsch. Inst. Natural Philosophy, Inc., 1979-88; Aisenstadt chair applied math. U. Montreal, 2000. Author: The Geometry of Biological Time, 1980, 2d ed., 2001, When Time Breaks Down, 1986, The Timing of Biological Clocks, 1987. Recipient Career Devel. award NIH, 1973-78, The Einthoven award Einthoven Found. and Netherlands Royal Acad. Scis., 1989, Norbert Wiener prize Am. Math. Soc. and Soc. Ind. Applied Maths., 2000-2004; NSF grantee, 1966—; MacArthur fellow, 1984-89, John Simon Guggenheim Meml. fellow, 1982. Home: 1210 E Placita De Graciela Tucson AZ 85718-2834 Office: U Ariz Dept Ecology & Evol Biology 326 BSW Tucson AZ 85721-0001 E-mail: winfree@email.u.arizona.edu

WINGATE, C. KEITH, law educator; b. Darlington, S.C., May 12, 1953; s. Clarence L. and Lilly W.; m. Gloria Farley; stepchildren: Brenda, Marvin, Terry and Oliver Champion. BA in Polit. Sci., U. Ill., 1974, JD cum laude, 1978. Bar: Calif., 1978. Assoc. litigation dept. Morrison & Foerster, San Francisco, 1978-80; from asst. to assoc. prof. law U. Calif.-Hastings, San Francisco, 1980-86, prof., 1986—. Dir. Coun. Legal Edn. Opportunity Region I Inst., 1989; vis. prof. law Stanford Law Sch., fall 1990, 94, spring 1998; chair Minority Law Tchrs.' Conf. Com., 1990; mem. acad. assistance work group, 1991; trustee Law Sch. Admission Coun., 1997-2001. Author: (with David I. Levine and William R. Slomanson) Cases and Materials on California Civil Procedure, 1991, (with William R. Slomanson) California Civil Procedure in a Nutshell, 1992, (with Donald L. Doernberg) Federal Courts, Federalism and Separation of Powers, 1994, 2nd edit., 2000. Bd. dirs. Cmty. Housing Devel. Corp., North Richmond, 1990-99. Recipient 10 Outstanding Persons award U. Ill. Black Alumni Assn., 1980; Harno fellow U. Ill., Coll. of Law, 1976. Mem. Assn. Am. Law Schs. (chair sect. minority groups 1990, exec. com. mem. sect. civil proceedure 1991), Charles Houston Bar Assn., Phi Sigma Alpha. Office: U Calif Hastings Coll Law 200 Mcallister St San Francisco CA 94102-4707

WINKLEBY, MARILYN A. medical researcher; BA in Social Sci., Calif. State U., Sacramento, 1968, MA in. Clin. Psychology, 1974; MPH in Epidemiology/Biostat, U. Calif., Berkeley, 1983, PhD in Epidemiology, 1986. Project dir. cervical cancer screening study UCLA Sch. Pub. Health, 1974-77; co-prin. investigator Calif. Ctr. Sudden Infant Death Syndrome Risk Factor Study, Sch. Medicine, Dept. Cmty. Health U. Calif., Davis, 1977-81, co-investigator cmty. cardiovascular surveillance program, adj. lectr. Sch. Medicine, Dept. Cmty. Health, 1981-82, project coord. epidemiology unit, stress and hypertension study Dept. Epidemiology Berkeley, 1983-87, rsch. epidemiologist Dept. Behavioral and Devel. Pediat. San Francisco, 1986-91; sr. rsch. scientist/prin. investigator Stanford Ctr. Rsch. in Disease Prevention, Stanford U. Sch. of Medicine, Palo Alto, Calif., 1987—. Epidemiology coord. SIDS Info. and Counseling Project, Dept. Health, State of Calif., Berkeley, 1980-83; founder, dir. Stanford Med. Youth Sci. Program, 1988—; lectr. divsn. health rsch. and policy, dept.

medicine Stanford U., 1989—. Contbr. articles to profl. jours. Bd. dirs. Loaves and Fishes Family Kitchen, San Jose, Calif., 1988-92, Mountain View Cmty. Health Clinic, 1992-95. Fellow Am. Heart Assn. (coun. epidemiology 1989, Established Investigator award 1996). Office: Stanford Ctr Rsch in Disease Prevention 1000 Welch Rd Ste 302 Palo Alto CA 94304-1808

WINKLER, AGNIESZKA M. Internet executive; b. Rome, Feb. 22, 1946; came to U.S., 1953; naturalized, 1959; d. Wojciech A. and Halina Z. (Owsiany) W.; children from previous marriage: children: Renata G. Ritcheson, Dana C Wworakowski; m. Arthur K. Lund. BA, Coll. Holy Name, 1967; MA, San Jose State U., 1971; MBA, U. Santa Clara, 1981. Teaching asst. San Jose State U., 1968-70; cons. to ea. European bus. Palo Alto, Calif., 1970-72; pres./founder Commart Communications, Palo Alto, 1973-84; pres./founder, chmn. bd. Winkler Advt., Santa Clara, Calif., 1984—; chmn. bd. SuperCuts, Inc.; chmn., founder TeamToolz, 2000—. Bd. dirs. Reno Air, Lifeguard, Lifeguard Life Ins. Author: Warp Speed Branding, 1999. Trustee Santa Clara U., 1991—; trustee O'Connor Found., 1987-93, mem. exec. com., 1988—, mem. Capital Campaign steering com., 1989; mem. nat. adv. bd. Comprehensive Health Enhancement Support System, 1991—; mem. mgmt. west com. A.A.A.A. Agy., 1991—, vice chair no. Calif. coun., 1996—; project dir. Poland Free Enterprise Plan, 1989-92; mem. adv. bd. Normandy France Bus. Devel., 1989-92; mem. bd. regents Holy Names Coll., 1987—; bd. dirs. San Jose Mus. Art, 1987; mem. San Jose Symphony, Gold Baton, 1986; mem. nat. adv. com. Chess, 1991—; dir. Bay Area Coun., 1994—. Recipient CLIO award in Advt., Addy award and numerous others; named to 100 Best Women in Advt., Ad Age, 1988, Best Woman in Advt., AdWeek and McCall's Mag., 1993, one of 100 Best and Brightest Women in Mktg. & Advt., Nat. Assn. Women Bus. Owners, 1996. Mem. Family Svc. Assn. (trustee 1980-82), Am. Assn. Advt. Agys. (agy. mgmt. west com. 1991), Bus. Profl. Advt. Assn., Polish Am. Congress, San Jose Advt. Club, San Francisco Ad Club, Beta Gamma Sigma (hon.), Pi Gamma Mu, Pi Delta Phi (Lester-Tinneman award 1966, Bill Raskob Found. grantee 1965). Office: Team Toolz 301 Howard St San Francisco CA 94105-2252

WINKLER, HOWARD LESLIE, business, finance, government relations consultant; b. N.Y.C., Aug. 16, 1950; s. Martin and Magda (Stark) W.; m. Robin Lynn Richards, Sept. 12, 1976; 1 child, David Menachem. AA in Mktg., Los Angeles City Coll., 1973, AA in Bus. Data Processing, 1977, AA in Bus. Mgmt., 1981. Sr. cons. Fin. Cons. Inc., Los Angeles, 1972-81; asst. v.p. Merrill Lynch, Inc., Los Angeles, 1981-83; v.p. Drexel, Burnham, Lambert, Inc., Beverly Hills, Calif., 1983-84; pres. Howard Winkler Investments, Beverly Hills, 1984-90, Landmark Fin. Group, L.A., 1990-96. Ptnr. N.W.B. Assocs., L.A., 1988-91; chmn. bd. United Cmty. and Housing Devel. Corp., L.A., 1986-96; bd. mem./sec. United Housing & Cmty. Svcs. Corp., 1995-97; bd. dirs. Earth Products Internat., Inc., Kansas City, Kans., 1992, Fed. Home Loan Bank of San Francisco, 1991-93. Nat. polit. editor B'nai B'rith Messenger, 1986-95. Mem. Calif. Rep. Cent. Com., 1985-93; mem. L.A. County Rep. Cent. Com., 1985-92, chmn. 45th Assembly Dist., 1985-90; mem. Rep. Senatorial Inner Circle, 1986—, Rep. Presdl. Task Force, 1985— (Legion of Merit award 1992); mem. Rep. Eagles, 1988-92; Nat. Rep. Senatorial Com., 1986—, Golden Circle Calif., 1986-92, GOP Platform Planning Com. at Large del., 1992, 96; del. to GOP nat conv., Houston, 1992, San Diego, 1996; Calif. chmn. Jack Kemp for Pres., 1988, mem. nat. steering com. Bush-Quayle '88, 1987, nat. exec. com. Bush-Quayle '92, 1991; mil. adminstrv. supr. CID US Army, 1969-72, SE Asia; legis. and civic action Agudath Israel Calif., 1985—; mem. L.A. County Narcotics and Dangerous Drugs Commn., 1988—, L.A. County Drug Ct. Planning Com., 1996—; trustee, sec.-treas. Minority Health Professions Edn. Found., 1989-94; program chmn. Calif. Lincoln Clubs Polit. Action Com., 1987-88; state co-chmn. Pete Wilson for Gov. Campaign, 1989, John Seymour for Lt. Gov. Campaign, 1989-90; chpt. pres. Calif. Congress of Reps., 1989-93; chmn. Claude Parrish for Bd. of Equalization, 1989-90; founder, dir. Community Rsch. & Info. Ctr., 1986—; mem. fin. com. John Seymour for Senate '92, 1991. Decorated Legion of Merit; recipient Cmty. Svc. award Agudath Israel Calif., 1986, Pres.'s Cmty. Leadership award, 1986, Disting. Cmty. Svc. U.S. Senator Pete Wilson, 1986, Calif. Gov.'s Leadership award, 1986, Cmty. Svc. award U.S. Congresswoman Bobbi Fiedler, 1986, Resolution of Commendation Calif. State Assembly, 1986, Outstanding Cmty. Svc. Commendation Los Angeles County Bd. Suprs., 1986, 90, Outstanding Citizenship award City of Los Angeles, 1986, 90, 94, Cmty. Leadership award Iranian-Jewish Community L.A., 1990, 95, Resolution of Commendation, State of Calif., 1992, Cmty. Svc. Commendation, 1993, Rep. Senatorial Medal of Freedom award, Sentorial Inner Circle, 1994, Commendation L.A. County Bd. Suprs., 1994, 25 Yrs. of Excellent Svc. to the Cmty. award, 1996, Rep. Senatorial Medal of Freedom, 1999. Mem. Calif. Young Reps., Calif. Rep. Assembly, VFW, Jewish War Veterans. Jewish. Avocations: philanthropy, family time. Office: PO Box 480454 Los Angeles CA 90048-1454

WINKLER, LEE B. business consultant; b. Buffalo; s. Jack W. and Caroline (Marienthal) W.; 1 child, James; m. Maria Mal Verde. B.S. cum laude, NYU, 1945, M.S. cum laude, 1947. Pres. LBW, Inc. (formerly Winkler Assocs. Ltd.), N.Y.C., Beverly Hills, Calif., 1948—, Winkler Assocs. Ltd., Beverly Hills, Calif., and N.Y.C., 1958—; exec. dir. Global Bus. Mgmt. Inc., Beverly Hills, 1967—. V.p. Bayly Martin & Fay Inc., N.Y.C., 1965-68, John C. Paige & Co., N.Y.C., 1968-71; cons. Albert G. Ruben Co., Beverly Hills, 1971— Served with AUS, 1943-45. Decorated chevalier comdr. Order Holy Cross Jerusalem, also spl. exec. asst., charge d'affaires, 1970; chevalier comdr. Sovereign Order Cyprus, 1970 Mem. Nat. Acad. TV Arts and Scis., Nat. Acad. Recording Arts and Scis., Beverly Hills C. of C., Phi Beta Kappa, Beta Gamma Sigma, Mu Gamma Tau, Psi Chi Omega. Office: 15250 Ventura Blvd Sherman Oaks CA 91403-3201

WINMILL, B. LYNN, judge; m. Judy Jones; 4 children. BA, Idaho State U., 1974; JD, Harvard U., 1977. Atty. Holland and Hart, Denver, 1977-79, Hawley, Troxell, Ennis and Hawley, Pocatello, Idaho, 1984-87; judge Idaho Sixth Jud. Dist. Ct., Pocatello, 1987-95; chief judge U.S. Dist. Ct. Idaho, Boise. Office: US Dist Ct Idaho US Courthouse 550 W Fort St 6th Fl Boise ID 83724-0001 Fax: (208) 334-9209

WINN, C(OLMAN) BYRON, former mechanical engineering educator; b. Canton, Mo., Nov. 21, 1933; s. Colman Kersey and Kiula Elmeda (Ingold) W.; m. Donna Sue Taylor, Aug. 25, 1957; children: Byron, Derek, Julie. BS in Aeronautics, U. Ill., 1958; MS in Aeronautics, Stanford U., 1960, PhD, 1967. Engr. Lockheed Missiles & Space Co., Palo Alto, Calif., 1958-60, sr. engr., 1962-64; rsch. scientist Martin-Marietta, Denver, 1960-62; lectr. Santa Clara (Calif.) U., 1963-65; assoc. prof. Colo. State U., Ft. Collins, 1966-74, prof. mech. engring., 1974—, prof., head dept., 1982-95, assoc. dean, 1995—. Cons. Space Rsch. Corp., North Troy, Vt., 1969-73; pres. Solar Environ. Engring. Co., 1973-85. Author: Controls in Solar Energy Systems, 1982, Controls in Solar Energy Systems, 1993; assoc. editor Jour. Solar Energy Engring., 1982-89, Passive Solar Jour., 1987, Advances in Solar Energy, 1996—. Loaned exec. United Way, Ft. Collins, 1992. With U.S. Army, 1953-55. Named Disting. Alumnus U. Ill., 1984, J.E. Cermak Adv. award, 1986, EPPEC award Platte River Power Authority, 1992, ABELL Svc. award, 1997. Fellow ASME; mem. AIAA (Energy Systems award 1991), Internat. Solar Energy Soc. (bd. dirs. 1980-89), Am. Solar Energy Soc. (bd. dirs. 1979-86, solar action com. 1991-93), Tau Beta Pi. Achievements include development of controllers for solar energy systems; design and development of the reconfigurable passive evaluation analysis and test facility; founding of the Energy Analysis and Diagnostic Center, The Waste Minimization Assessment Center, The Industrial Assessment Center and Manufacturing Excellence Center at Colo. State U. Office: Colo State U Dept Mech Engring Fort Collins CO 80523-0001

WINN, H. RICHARD, surgeon; b. Chester, Pa., 1942; MD, U. Pa., 1968; BA, Princeton U., 1964. Diplomate Am Bd. Neurological Surgeons. Intern U. Hosp., Cleve., 1968-69, resident surgery, 1969-70; resident neurolog. surgery U. Hosp. Va., Charlottesville, 1970-74; neurol. surgeon U. Wash. Hosp., Seattle, 1983—; prof., chmn. neurol. surgery U. Wash., Seattle, 1983—. Dir. Am. Bd. Neurol. Surgery. Founding editor Neurosurgical Clinics of North America; mem. editl. bd. Jour. Neurosurgery, Am. Jour. Physiology, Am. Jour. Surgery. Fellow AAAS, ACS (gov.), Soc. Brit. Neurol. Surgeons (hon.); mem. AMA, Am. Assn. Neurol. Surgeons, Soc. Neurol. Surgeons, Congress of Neurol. Surgeons, Am. Bd. Neurol. Surgeons (vice chmn. 2000-01). Office: U Wash Dept Neurosurg 325 9th Ave # 359766 Seattle WA 98104-1834 Fax: 206-521-1881

WINN, STEVEN JAY, critic; b. Phila., Apr. 25, 1951; s. Willis Jay and Lois (Gengelbach) W.; m. Katharine Weber, Sept. 15, 1979 (div. Dec. 1985); m. Sally Ann Noble, July 22, 1989; 1 child, Phoebe Ann. BA, U. Pa., 1973; MA, U. Wash., 1975. Staff writer, editor Seattle Weekly, 1975-79; theater critic San Francisco Chronicle, 1980—. Co-author: Ted Bundy: The Killer Next Door, 1980, Great Performances: A Celebration, 1997; contbr. articles to various publs. Wallace Stegner fellow Stanford U., 1979-80. Office: San Francisco Chronicle 901 Mission St San Francisco CA 94103-2905

WINNER, KARIN E. newspaper editor; Editor San Diego Union-Tribune, 1995—. Office: Copley Press Inc 350 Camino De La Reina San Diego CA 92108-3003 E-mail: Karin.winner@uniontrib.com

WINNICK, GARY, fiber optics company executive; b. Roslyn, N.Y. married Karen; 3 children. Grad., C.W. Post Coll. Founder, chmn., CEO Pacific Capital Group, 1985—; chmn., founder Global Crossings Ltd., Beverly Hills, Calif., 1997—. Nat. adv. bd. Chase Manhattan Bank. Office: Global Crossings Ltd 360 N Crescent Dr Beverly Hills CA 90210-4802

WINNOWSKI, THADDEUS RICHARD (TED WINNOWSKI), bank executive; b. Albany, N.Y., Feb. 20, 1942; s. Thaddeus Walter and Harriet Frances (Witko) W.; m. Sheila Margaret Neary, June 15, 1968; children: Dona, Paul. BS in Econs., Siena Coll., 1963; postgrad., R.P.I., 1968-72. Adminstrv. v.p. Key Bank N.A., Albany, N.Y., 1978-80; pres. Key Bank L.I., Sayville, 1980-85; pres., CEO Key Bank Oreg., Woodburn, 1985-86, chmn., CEO Portland, 1986-95, chmn., 1995-97; exec. v.p., group exec. N.W. region Key Corp., Seattle, 1995-97, chmn., CEO, 1996-97; pres., CEO Centennial Bank, Eugene, Oreg., 1998—. Bd. dirs. Portland Opera, Blue Cross/Blue Shield Oreg.; bd. regents U. Portland. 1st lt. U.S. Army, 1964-66. Mem. Oreg. Bankers Assn., Portland Met. C. of C. (hon. bd. dirs., former chmn.). Roman Catholic.

WINSLEY, SHIRLEY J. state legislator, insurance agent; b. Fosston, Minn., June 9, 1934; d. Nordin Marvel Miller and Helga Christine Sorby; m. Gordon Perry Winsley, July 19, 1952; children: Alan, Nancy. ABS, Tacoma C.C., 1970; BA, Pacific Luth., 1971. Mem. legis. staff Wash. Senate, Olympia, 1971-75; appraiser Pierce County Assessor, Tacoma, 1971-75; mem. Wash. Ho. of Reps., Olympia, 1974, 77-92; exec. dir. Lakewood (Wash.) Chamber, 1975-76; mem. Wash. Senate, Dist. 28, Olympia, 1993—; ins. agent, family counselor New Tacoma Cemetary & Funeral Home, 1996—. Mem., Wash. St. Advisory Council Accrditation of Vocational-Technical Institutes, Wash. St. Historical Soc., Lakewood Sr. Ctr., LEAP. Republican. Lutheran. Home: 1109 Garden Cir Tacoma WA 98466-6218 Office: PO Box 40428 Olympia WA 98504-0428

WINSLOW, DAVID ALLEN, chaplain, retired naval officer; b. Dexter, Iowa, July 12, 1944; s. Franklin E. and Inez Maude (McPherson) W.; children: Frances, David. BA, So. Nazarene U., 1968; MDiv, Drew U., 1971, STM, 1973; cert. of achievement, Emergency Mgmt. Inst., FEMA, 1997. Ordained to ministry United Meth. Ch. Detroit Annual Conf., 1969; cert. FEMA instr. Clergyman, 1969—; assoc. minister All Sts. Episcopal. Ch., Millington, N.J., 1969-70; asst. minister Marble Collegiate Ch., N.Y.C., 1970-71; min. No. N.J. Conf. United Meth. Ch., 1971-75; joined chaplain corps USN, 1974, advanced through grades to lt. comdr., 1980, ret., 1995; with Oak Knoll Naval Med. Ctr., Oakland, Calif., 1993-95; disaster cons. Ch. World Svc., Cupertino, 1997—. NDMS/DMAT, CA-6, Contra/Costa County, Calif., 1997—. Author: The Utmost for the Highest, 1993, Epiphany: God Still Speaks, 1994, Be Thou My Vision, 1994, Evening Prayers At Sea, 1995, Wiseman Still Adore Him, 1995, God's Power At Work, 1996; (with Walsh) A Year of Promise: Meditations, 1995, editor: The Road to Bethlehem: Advent, 1993, Preparation for Resurrecton: Lent, 1994, God's Promise: Advent, 1994, The Way of the Cross: Lent, 1995; contbr. articles to profl. jours. Bd. dirs. disaster svcs. and family svcs. ARC, Santa Ana, Calif., 1988-91, Child Abuse Prevention Ctr., Orange, Calif., 1990-91; bd. dirs. Santa Clara County Coun. Chs., 1993-94, del., 1995-98; bd. dirs. Salvation Army Adult Rehab. Ctr. Adv. Coun., San Jose, Calif; bd. dirs. emergency svcs. Santa Clara Valley chpt. ARC, San Jose, 1995-98; bd. dirs. disaster svcs. Interfaith Svc., Inc., San Jose Internat. Airport. Fellow Am. Acad. Experts in Traumatic Stress (cert. expert); mem. ACA, USN League (hon.), Sunrise Exch. Club (chaplain 1989-91), Dick Richards Breakfast Club (chaplain 1988-91), Kiwanis, Masons (charter), Shriners, Scottish Rite. Avocations: golf, skiing, sailing.

WINSLOW, NORMAN ELDON, business executive; b. Oakland, Calif., Apr. 4, 1938; s. Merton Conrad and Roberta Eilene (Drennen) W.; m. Betty June Cady, Jan. 14, 1962 (div. Aug. 1971); 1 child, Todd Kenelm; m. Ilene Ruth Jackson, Feb. 3, 1979. BS, Fresno (Calif.) State U., 1959. Asst. mgr. Proctors Jewelers, Fresno, 1959-62; from agt. to dist. mgr. Allstate Ins. Co., Fresno, 1962-69; ins. agt. Fidelity Union Life Ins., Dallas, 1969-71; dist. and zone mgr. The Southland Corp., Dallas, 1971-78; owner Ser-Vis-Etc., Goleta, Calif., 1978—. Expert witness, cons. Am. Arbitration/Calif. Superior Cts. Pub./editor FranchiserviceNews; author: Hands in Your Pockets, 1992; contbr. numerous articles to profl. jours. With USAFNG, 1961-67. Mem. Nat. Coalition of Assn. of 7-11 Franchises (affiliate, mem. adv. bd. Glendale, Calif. chpt. 1984-90). Republican. Methodist. Avocations: gardening, photography, traveling, model railroading. Home: 1179 N Patterson Ave Santa Barbara CA 93117-1813 Office: Ser-Vis-Etc PO Box 8276 Goleta CA 93118-8276 E-mail: elru2379@aol.com, serv-vis-etc@aol.com

WINSLOW, PAUL DAVID, architect; b. Phoenix, June 12, 1941; s. Fred D. and Thelma E. (Ward) W.; m. Carole Lynn Walker, June 13, 1964; 1 child, Kirk David. BArch, Ariz. State U., 1964. Lic. architect, Ariz., Calif., Nev. Ptnr. The Orcutt/Winslow Partnership, Phoenix, 1972—. Speaker solar energy workshops, Phoenix, 1986-89; adj. prof. Ariz. State U., 1991; mem. faculty Advanced Mgmt. Inst., San Francisco; mem. profl. adv. coun. Ariz. State U. Coll. Architecture, Tempe, 1970—, bd. dirs. Architecture Found., 1972-76; mem. adv. com. City of Phoenix Bldg. Safety Bd., 1981; mem. adv. bd. Herberger Ctr.; pres. Ariz. State U. Coll. Architecture, Coun. for Design Excellence; bd. dirs. Ctrl. Ariz. Project Assn., Phoenix, 1971-74, Ariz. Ctr. for Law in the Pub. Interest, Phoenix, 1979-86, Phoenix Cmty. Alliance; chmn. Encanto Village Planning Com., Phoenix, 1981-86; chmn. Indian Sch. Citizens adv. com. Ind. Sch. Land Use Planning Team; lectr. on planning Ariz. State U., 1989, city of Presott, Phoenix and Tempe, 1988-89; active Coun. Ednl. Facilities Planners Internat. Mem. Steering Com. on Re-inventing Neighborhoods Project; chmn. Central and Roosevelt Coalition, 1998-99; chmn. City of Phoenix Neighborhood Initiative Area Steering Com., 1998-99; pres. bd. dirs. Harrington House Internat. Ctr. for Universal Design, 1998-99; pres. bd. dirs. Maryvale Edn. Mall, 1998-99; exec. com. Phoenix Cmty. Alliance. Fellow AIA (bd. dirs. ctrl. Ariz. chpt., also sec., treas., pres.); mem. Ariz. Soc. Architects (bd. dirs. 1970-71, 78-82), Bldg. Owners and Mgrs. Assn. Greater Phoenix (pres. 1989-90, 90-91), Boar Valley Forward Assn. (exec. com. 1994-99), Ariz. Club (Phoenix). Methodist. Home: 5941 E Edgemont Ave Scottdale AZ 85257 Office: The Orcutt/Winslow Partnership 1130 N 2nd St Phoenix AZ 85004-1896 E-mail: winslow.p@owp.com

WINSLOW, WALTER WILLIAM, psychiatrist, educator; b. Lacombe, Alta., Can., Nov. 23, 1925; came to U.S., 1959, naturalized, 1964; s. Floyd Raymond and Lily Evangeline (Palmer) W.; m. Barbara Ann Spiker; children: Colleen Denise, Dwight Walter, Barbara Jean, Wendi Jae. BS, La Sierra Coll., 1949; MD, Loma Linda U., 1952. Diplomate: Am. Bd. Psychiatry and Neurology. Intern Vancouver Gen. Hosp., 1952; psychiat. resident Provincial Mental Hosp., Essondale, B.C., 1957-59, Harding Hosp., Worthington, Ohio, 1959-60; instr. dept. psychiatry and indsl. medicine U. Cin., 1960-66, dept. preventive medicine, 1964-66; asst. prof. psychiatry U. N.Mex., Albuquerque, 1966-68, assoc. prof. psychiatry, 1969-74, prof., chmn. dept. psychiatry, 1974-91, dir. mental health programs, 1976-91; med. dir. Charter Hosp. of Albuquerque, 1991-95, Charter-Heights BHS, Albuquerque, 1995—. Assoc. prof. psychiatry Georgetown U., Washington, 1968-69; dir. bernalillo County Mental Health/Mental Retardation Ctr., 1970-78, 81-91. Contbr. articles to profl. jours. Recipient N.Mex. Gov.'s Commendation for 10 yrs. service in mental health, 1979 Fellow Am. Psychiat. Assn. (life, area VII rep. 1981-85, Assembly Speaker's award 1984), Am. Coll. of Psychiatrists, Am. Assn. Community Psychiatrists (hon.); mem. AMA, Am. Assn. Psychiatry and the Law, N.Mex. Psychiat. Assn. (pres. 1974-75) Republican. Office: 1625 Catron SE Albuquerque NM 87123-4255

WINSOR, DAVID JOHN, cost consultant; b. Duluth, Minn., May 27, 1947; s. Alphonse Joseph and Sylvia Mae (Petrich) W.; div. BA in Bus., U. Puget Sound, 1978; M of Mech. Engring., Pacific Western U., 1979. Jr. engr. J.P. Head Mech., Inc., Richland, Wash., 1965-67; estimator, project engr. Subs. of Howard S. Wright Co., Seattle, 1972-75; sr. estimator Massart Co., Seattle, 1975-76; project mgr. Univ. Mechanical, Portland, Oreg., 1976; cons. Kent, Wash., 1976-79; owner Leasair, Federal Way, 1978-83; pres., owner Expertise Engring. & Cons., Inc., Bellevue, 1979-82, 90-95; cons. Winsor & Co., Walnut Creek, Calif., 1983—; estimator IDC, Portland, Oreg., 1996-99; cons., 1999—. Cons. NASA, Mountain View, Calif., 1986, Lockheed Missile & Space, Sunnyvale, Calif., 1984-87, The Boeing Co., Seattle, 1979-82. Author: (with others) Current Construction Costs, 1987, 88, 89, Construction Materials Inventory Systems, 1973, 74, Construction Inflation Trends, 1975, 76, 77, 78, 79, 80, 81, Construction Claims and Prevention, 1981, 82. Served to sgt. USAF, 1967-71. Mem. Jaycees (state dir. 1972-73, state chmn. 1973-74). Republican. Roman Catholic. Avocations: flying, golf, car and gun collecting.

WINSTON, GEORGE, solo pianist, guitarist, harmonica player; b. Hart, Mich., 1949; Ind. musician, 1967—; founder Dancing Cat Productions, Santa Cruz, CA, 1983—. Eight solo piano albums, including Ballads and Blues, 1972, Autumn, 1980, Winter Into Spring, 1982, December, 1982, Summer, 1991, Forest, 1994, Linus & Lucy: The Music of Vince Guaraldi, 1996, Plains, 1999; audiobook soundtracks: (with Meryl Streep) The Velveteen Rabbit, 1985, Birth of the Constitution (Peanuts), 1988, (with Liv Ullmann) Sadako and the Thousand Paper Cranes, 1995; prodr. 30 albums of the masters of traditional Hawaiian slack key (finger style) guitar. Office: c/o Dancing Cat Prodns PO Box 639 Santa Cruz CA 95061-0639 E-mail: ml@dancingcat.com

WINTERMAN, CRAIG L. lawyer; b. Denver, Oct. 29, 1950; BS, U. Oreg., 1973; JD, Southwestern U., 1976. Bar: Calif. 1977, U.S. Dist. Ct. (cen. dist.) Calif. 1977, U.S. Dist. Ct. (so. and no. dists.) Calif. 1980, U.S. Ct. Appeals (9th cir.) 1980, U.S. Supreme Ct. 1980. Ptnr. Herzfeld & Rubin, L.A., 1986—. Mem. State Bar Calif., Assn. So. Calif. Def. Counsel, Assn. Advancement Auto. Medicine, U. Oreg. Alumni Assn. (pres. so. Calif. chpt. 1999-2001). Office: Herzfeld & Rubin 1925 Century Park E Ste 600 Los Angeles CA 90067-2783 E-mail: cwinterman@hrla.net

WINTERS, BARBARA JO, musician; b. Salt Lake City; d. Louis McClain and Gwendolyn (Bradley) W. AB cum laude, UCLA, 1960, postgrad., 1961, Yale, 1960. Mem. oboe sect. L.A. Philharm., 1961-94, prin. oboist, 1972-94; ret. Clinician oboe, English horn, Oboe d'amore. Recs. movie, TV sound tracks. Avocation: painting in oils and mixed media. Home: 3529 Coldwater Canyon Ave Studio City CA 91604-4060 Office: 135 N Grand Ave Los Angeles CA 90012-3013

WINTHROP, JOHN, wines and spirits company executive; b. Salt Lake City, Apr. 20, 1947; children: Grant Gordon, Clayton Hanford. AB cum laude, Yale U., 1969; JD magna cum laude, U. Tex., 1972. Bar: Calif. 1972. Law clk. 9th cir. U.S. Ct. Appeals, L.A., 1972-73; conseil juridique Coudert Freres, Paris, 1973-75; v.p. gen. counsel MacDonald Group, Ltd., L.A., 1976-82; pres., CEO MacDonald Mgmt. Corp. and MacDonald Group Ltd., L.A., 1982-86; pres., chief exec. officer MacDonald Corp. (gen. contractors), L.A., 1982-86; chmn., CEO Comstock Mgmt. Co., L.A., 1986—; pres., CEO Winthrop Investment Properties, Los Angeles, 1986—; CEO Veritas Imports, L.A., 1995—. Bd. dirs. Plus Prods., Tiger's Milk Prods., Irvine, Calif., 1977-80. Contbr. articles to profl. jours. Bd. dirs., sec. L.A. Sheriff's Dept. Found.; bd. dirs. L.A. Opera. Mem. Nat. Eagle Scout Assn. (life), French-Am. C. of C. (bd. dirs. 1982-87), Urban Land Inst., Yale Club N.Y., Calif. Club, The Beach Club, Elizabethan Club, Order of the Coif, Beta Theta Pi. Republican. Office: Veritas Imports Penthouse 9460 Wilshire Blvd Beverly Hills CA 90212-2720

WINTHROP, KENNETH RAY, insurance executive; b. N.Y.C., Dec. 29, 1950; s. Ralph and Lore (Bruck) W.; m. Sharon Swinnich, 1976 (div. 1978); m. Diane Louise Denney, June 27, 1981; children: Alyssa Louise, Matthew Lawrence, Andrew Lee. BA in English, SUNY, Buffalo, 1972. CLU. Agt. Northwestern Mut. Life Ins., Woodland Hills, Calif., 1975-78, Nat. Life of Vermont, L.A., 1978-93; mgr. Mass Mut., L.A., 1993-97, agt., 1997—. Referee Am. Youth Soccer Orgn., L.A., 1996—. Mem. Million Dollar Round Table (life). Avocations: racquetball, snow skiing, trout fishing, gardening. Home: 1404 5th St Manhattan Beach CA 90266-6338 Office: 4601 Wilshire Blvd Fl 3 Los Angeles CA 90010-3880 E-mail: kwinthrop@finsvcs.com

WINTHROP, LAWRENCE FREDRICK, lawyer; b. Apr. 18, 1952; s. Murray and Vauneta (Cardwell) W. BA with honors, Whittier Coll., 1974; JD magna cum laude, Calif. Western Sch., 1977. Bar: Ariz. 1977, Calif. 1977, U.S. Dist. Ct. Ariz. 1977, U.S. Dist. Ct. (so. dist.) Calif. 1981, U.S. Ct. Appeals (9th cir.) 1981, U.S. Dist. Ct. (cen. dist.) Calif. 1983, U.S. Supreme Ct. 1983. Assoc. Snell and Wilmer, Phoenix, 1977-83, ptnr., 1984-93, Doyle, Winthrop, P.C., Phoenix, 1993—. Judge pro tem Maricopa County Superior Ct., 1987-97, Ariz. Ct. Appeals, 1992—; lectr. Ariz. personal injury law and practice and state and local tax law Tax Exec. Inst., Nat. Bus. Inst., Profl. Edn. Systems, Inc., Ariz. Trial Lawyers Assn., Maricopa County Bar Assn.; bd. dirs. Valley of the Sun Sch., 1989-97, chmn., 1994-96; mem. Vol. Lawyers Program, Phoenix, 1980—. Editor-in-chief: Calif. Western Law Rev., 1976-77. Fellow Ariz. Bar Found., Maricopa Bar Found.; mem. ABA, Calif. Bar Assn., Ariz. Bar Assn. (mem. com. on exam. 1995—), Ariz. Tax Rsch. Assn. (bd. dirs. 1989-93),

Maricopa County Bar Assn., Ariz. Assn. Def. Counsel (bd. dirs., pres. 1988-89, chmn. med.-malpractice com. 1993-95), Aspen Valley Club, LaMancha Racquet Club. Republican. Methodist. Avocations: music, golf, tennis. Home: 6031 N 2nd St Phoenix AZ 85012-1210 Office: Doyle and Winthrop PC 3300 N Central Ave Ste 1600 Phoenix AZ 85012 E-mail: lwinthrop@doylewinthrop.com

WINTRODE, RALPH CHARLES, lawyer; b. Hollywood, Calif., Dec. 21, 1942; s. Ralph Osborne and Maureen (Kavanagh) W.; m. Leslie Ann O'Rourke, July 2, 1966 (div. Feb. 1994); children: R. Christopher, Patrick L., Ryan B. BS in Acctg., U. So. Calif., 1966, JD, 1967. Bar: Calif. 1967, N.Y. 1984, Japan 1989, Washington 1990. From assoc. to ptnr. to of counsel Gibson, Dunn & Crutcher, Tokyo, L.A., Newport Beach and Irvine, Calif., 1967—. Sec. Music Ctr. Los Angeles County, 1986-88; bd. dirs. Coro Found., L.A. County, 1986-87. Mem. Newport Harbor Club, Am. Club Tokyo. Avocations: sailboat racing, car racing, flying. Office: Gibson Dunn & Crutcher 4 Park Plz Ste 1400 Irvine CA 92614-8557 also: 333 S Grand Ave Ste 4400 Los Angeles CA 90071-1548

WINTROUB, BRUCE URICH, dermatologist, educator, researcher; b. Milw., Nov. 8, 1943; s. Ernest Bernard and Janet (Zien) W.; m. Marya Kraus, Jan. 20, 1973; children: Annie, Ben, Molly. BA, Amherst Coll., 1965; MD, Washington U., St. Louis, 1969. Diplomate Am. Bd. Internal Medicine, Am. Bd. Dermatology. Intern in medicine Peter Bent Brigham Hosp., Boston, 1969-70, jr. asst. resident in medicine, 1970-71, jr. assoc. in medicine, 1976-80, asst. then attending physician, 1976-81; resident in dermatology Harvard Med. Sch., Boston, 1974-76, instr., 1976-78, asst. prof., 1978-82; assoc. prof. dermatology Sch. Medicine, U. Calif., San Francisco, 1982-85, attending physician med. ctr., 1982—, prof., mem. exec. com. dept. dermatology, 1985-95, 2000—; chmn. exec. com. dept. dermatology U. Calif., San Francisco, 1985-95, 2000—; mem. dean's adv. com., governing bd. continuing med. edn., other coms. Sch. Medicine, U. Calif., San Francisco, 1986-95; exec. vice dean Sch. Medicine U. Calif., San Francisco, 1995-97; chief med. officer U. Calif.-San Francisco Stanford Health Care, San Francisco, 1997-99; assoc. dean sch. medicine U. Calif., San Francisco, 1990-95, 2000—, Stanford (Calif.) U., 1990—; dir. Dermatology Assocs., San Francisco, 1982-85. Cons. in dermatology Mass. Gen. Hosp., Boston, 1976-82, Beth Israel Hosp. and Children's Hosp. Med. Ctr., Boston, 1978-82, Parker Hill Med. Ctr., Boston, 1980-82; attending physician Robert B. Brigham Hosp. div. Brigham and Women's Hosp., Boston, 1980-81, assoc., 1980-82; chief dermatology svc. Brockton (Mass.) VA Med. Ctr., 1980-82; asst. chief dermatology VA Med. Ctr., San Francisco, 1982-85, mem. space com., 1984-85, dean's adv. com., 1985—, chmn. budget com., 1987—; clin. investigator Nat. Inst. Allergy, Metabolism and Digestive Disease, NIH, 1978; assoc. dean Sch. Medicine Stanford U., 1997—. Author: (with others) Biochemistry of the Acute Allergic Reactions, Fifth International Symposium, 1988; contbr. numerous articles, abstracts to profl. jours. NIH clin. fellow and grantee, 1967-69. Fellow Am. Acad. Dermatology (com. evaluations 1985—, coun. govt. liaison 1987—, congress on tech. plannning commn. 1988—, assoc. editor Dialogues in Dermatology jour. 1982-85, Stellwagon prize 1976); mem. Soc. Investigative Dermatology (chmn. pub. rels. com. 1987-88), Assn. Profs. Dermatology (chmn. program com. 1987—, bd. dirs.), Pacific Dermatol. Assn. (chmn. program com. 1987—), San Francisco Dermatol. Soc., Am. Fedn. Clin. Rsch. (chmn. dermatology program 1988-89), Am. Assn. Immunology, Dystrophic Epidermolysis Bullosa Rsch. Am. (bd. dirs. 1981), Internat. Soc. Dermatology, Internat. Soc. Cutaneous Pharmacology (founding mem.), Am. Soc. Clin. Investigation, Skin Pharmacology Soc., Calif. Med. Soc., San Francisco Med. Soc., Clin. Immunology Soc., Dermatology Found., (bd. dirs., exec. com.), AAAS, Am. Assn. Physicians, Calif. Acad. Medicine, Am. Dermatol. Assn., Sigma Xi, Alpha Omega Alpha. Avocation: golf. Office: Univ Calif Sch Medicine 513 Parnassus Ave Rm S224 San Francisco CA 94134-0410

WIPKE, W. TODD, chemistry educator; b. Dec. 16, 1940; BS, U. Mo., Columbia, 1962; PhD, U. Calif., Berkeley, 1965. Rsch. chemist Esso Rsch. and Engrng. Co., Baton Rouge, 1962; postdoctoral rsch. fellow Harvard U., 1967-69; asst. prof. Princeton U., 1969-75; assoc. prof. chemistry U. Calif., Santa Cruz, 1975-81, prof. chemistry, 1981—. Founder, cons. Molecular Design Ltd., San Leandro, Calif., 1978-91, Ciba-Geigy, Basle, Switzerland, 1978-82, BASF, Ludwigshafen, Fed. Republic Germany, 1974-78, Squibb, Princeton, N.J., 1976-81; adv. EPA, 1984—. Editor: Computer Representation and Manipulation of Chemical Information, 1973, Computer-Assisted Organic Synthesis, 1977; editor-in-chief: (jour.) Tetrahedron Computer Methodology, 1987-92; editor: Tetrahedron and Tetrahedron Letters, 1987-92; contbr. articles to profl. jours. Capt. U.S. Army, 1966-67. Recipient Eastman Kodak Rsch. award, 1964, Texaco Outstanding Rsch. award, 1962, Alexander von Humboldt Sr. Scientist award, 1987; Merck Career Devel. grantee, 1970; NIH fellow, 1964-65. Mem. NAS, Am. Chem. Soc. (assoc., Computers in Chemistry award 1987, St. Charles Found. Alumni award 1996), Assn. Computing Machinery, Chem. Soc., Am. Assn. Artificial Intelligence (charter), Chem. Structure Assn. (charter), Internat. Soc. Study Xenobiotics. Office: U Calif Dept Chemistry Santa Cruz CA 95064

WIRKKALA, JOHN LESTER, cable company executive; b. Wadena, Minn., Sept. 25, 1947; s. Ruben Richard and Virginia Grace (Plank) W.; m. Connie Lee Cardarelle (div.); children: Scott, Todd; m. Lynn Diane Braund, Feb. 14, 1984; children: Scott, Seth, Shawn. AS in Electronic Tech., Brown Inst., 1982. Acct. La Maur Inc., Mpls., 1969-72, regional sales mgr., 1976-78; controller Nat. Beauty Supply, Mpls., 1972-76; store mgr. Schaak Electronics, Mpls., 1980-82; divsn. mgr. Mktg. Link, Denver, 1982-85; owner, operator Computer Systems Cons., Aurora, Colo., 1985-87; v.p. sales and mktg. Mgmt. Info. Support, Lakewood, 1987-89; sales mgr. Foothills Software Inc., Littleton, 1989-93; ops. mgr. Data Packaging Corp., Denver, 1993-96; pres. Practical Bus. Concepts, Aurora, Colo., 1996; v.p. affiliate rels. Across Media Networks, Golden, 1996—. Contbr. articles to profl. jours. and mags.; speaker at seimnars and industry trade shows. With U.S. Army, 1966-69, Vietnam. Mem. VFW (quartermaster post # 6331 1993-94). Home and Office: 11211 Winona Ct Westminster CO 80031-7811 E-mail: jwirkkala@hotmail.com

WIRKLER, NORMAN EDWARD, architectural, engineering, construction management firm executive; b. Garnavillo, Iowa, Apr. 1, 1937; s. Herbert J. and Irene (Kregel) W.; m. Margaret Anne Gift, Oct. 16, 1959; children: Chris Edward, Scott Norman, Elizabeth Anne. BArch, Iowa State U., 1959. Designer The Durrant Group Inc., Dubuque, Iowa, 1959-64, assoc., 1964-67, prin., 1967-82, pres. Denver, 1982-98; chmn. of bd. The Durrant Group, Denver, 1998—; co-owner Wirkler Property Mgmt., Snowmass, Colo., 1993; pres. Foresite Capital Facilities Corp., Denver County, 1993—. Commr., mem. exec. com. Commn. on Accreditation on Corrections, 1985-91; archtl. cons. to Am. Correctional Assn. Standards Program; mem. Am. Correctional Assn. Standards Com., 1992-98; v.p. Garnavillo (Iowa) Bank Corp. Co-author: Design Guide for Secure Adult Correctional Facilities, 1983 Bd. dirs. United Way, Dubuque, 1984. Fellow AIA (pres. Iowa chpt. 1977; mem. nat. com. on arch. for justice 1974—, chmn. 1979; chmn. AIA Ins. Trust 1985-87, mem. Colo. chpt. 1987—); mem. ASTM (detention component standards com. 1982-84), Dubuque C. of C. (legis. com. 1978-83, chmn. 1979; v.p. 1984, exec. com. 1982-85), [illegible] of Denver Coun. Club. Republican. Avocations: flying, skiing, jogging, golf, hunting. Office: 3773 Cherry Creek North Dr Denver CO 80209-3804 E-mail: nwirkler@durrant.com

WIRT, MICHAEL JAMES, library director; b. Sault Ste. Marie, Mich., Mar. 21, 1947; s. Arthur James and Blanche Marian (Carruth) W.; m. Barbara Ann Hallesy, Aug. 12, 1972; 1 child, Brendan. BA, Mich. State U., 1969; MLS, U. Mich., 1971; postgrad., U. Wash., 1990. Cert. libr., Wash. Acting libr. U. Mich. Ctr. for Rsch. on Econ. Devel., Ann Arbor, 1971-72; instnl. svcs. libr. Spokane County (Wash.) Libr. Dist., 1972-76, asst. dir., 1976-79, acting dir., 1979, dir., 1980—. Mem. adv. com. Partnership for Rural Improvement, Spokane, 1982-85, Wash. State Libr. Planning and Devel. Com., 1984-85, Ea. Wash. U. Young Writers Project Adv. Bd., 1988-89; mem. issues selection com. Citizens League of Greater Spokane, 1991-93, City of Spokane Indian Trail Specific Plan Task force, 1992-95; mem. comm. com. United Way Spokane County, 1994, campaign chair local govt. divsn., 1996. Mem. Wash. Libr. Assn. (2d v.p. 1984-86, Merit award 1984, dir. 1989-91, legis. planning com., 1991—, pub. rels. com. 1993-2001, coord. comm. 1996-98, 2001 conf. local arrangements chair 1999-2001, Pres. award 1998), Wash. Libr. Network (rep. Computer Svc. Coun. 1983-86, v.p., treas. State Users Group 1986-87), Am. Libr. Assn. (Pub. Libr. Affiliates Network 1990-93, PLA Bus. Coun. 1990-94, chmn. 1991-94), Spokane Valley C. of C. (local govt. affairs com. 1987-2000, co-chair 1996-98, pub. policy com. 2000—), Spokane Area C. of C. (local govt. com. 1990-94, human svcs. com. 1990-92, chmn. 1991-92, govt. reorgn. task force 1995), Spokane Civic Theatre (bd. dirs. 1996—, v.p. 1997-98, sec. 1998-2000, v.p. 2000—), Momentum (local govt. strategy com. 1992-94), New Century (govt. collaboration com. 1997-98), Inland N.W. Coun. Librs. (bd. dirs. 1979—, chmn. 1997-98). Office: Spokane Ct Libr Dist 4322 N Argonne Rd Spokane WA 99212-1853 E-mail: mwirt@scld.lib.wa.us

WIRTA, RAYMOND E. real estate company executive; Grad., Calif. State U.; M in Internat. Mgmt., Golden Gate U. With Golden West Fin. Corp., Bank of Am., The Irvine Co.; CEO Koll Real Estate Svcs., 1994-97, CB Richard Ellis, El Segundo, Calif., 1999—. Office: CB Richard Ellis Svcs Inc 200 N Sepulveda Blvd El Segundo CA 90245-4380

WIRTHLIN, JOSEPH B. religious organization administrator; b. Salt Lake City, June 11, 1917; s. Joseph L. and Madeline (Bitner) W.; m. Elisa Young Rogers, May 26, 1941; 8 children. Degree in Bus. Adminstrn., U. Utah. Ordained apostle LDS Ch., 1986. Served a mission to Germany, Austria and Switzerland LDS Ch., 1930s, served in stake and ward aux. positions, counselor, bishop to mem. stake presidency, until 1971, 1st counselor Sunday Sch. Gen. Presidency, 1971-75, asst. to coun. of 12 apostles, 1975-76, gen. authority area supr. Europe area, 1975-78, mem. 1st Quorum of Seventy, 1976-86, exec. adminstr. to S.E. area U.S. and Caribbean Islands, 1978-82, mng. dir. Melchizedek Priesthood Com., Relief Soc. and Mil. Rels. Com., 1978-84, exec. adminstr. Brazil, 1982-84, pres. Europe area of ch., 1984-86, mem. presidency of 1st Quorum of Seventy, exec. dir. curriculum dept., editor ch. mags., 1986, apostle, 1986—, mem. missionary exec. coun., gen. welfare svcs. coms., 1986—. Office: LDS Ch Joseph Smith Meml Bldg 47 E North Temple Salt Lake City UT 84150-9704

WIRTHLIN, MILTON ROBERT, JR. periodontist; b. Little Rock, July 13, 1932; s. Milton Robert and Margaret Frances (Clark) W.; m. Joan Krieger, Aug. 1, 1954; children: Michael, Steven, Laurie, David, Aina. DDS, U. Calif., San Francisco, 1956, MS, 1968. Diplomate Am. Bd. Periodontology. Commd. ensign USN, 1955, advanced through grades to capt., 1976, retired, 1985; assoc. prof. U. Pacific, San Francisco, 1985-86; assoc. clin. prof. U. Calif., San Francisco, 1986-96, clin. prof., 1996—, dir. postgrad. periodontology, 1996-99, clin. prof. emeritus, 2000—. Contbr. articles to profl. jours. Asst. scoutmaster Boy Scouts Am., San Bruno, Calif., 1968, com. chmn. Explorer Post, San Francisco, 1981-83; bd. dirs. ARC, Chgo., 1976-81, chair social svc. com., San Francisco, 1981-83. Decorated Meritorious Svc. medal with 2 gold stars; recipient Gabbs prize U. Calif., 1956. Fellow Internat. Coll. Dentists; mem. Am. Dental Assn., Am. Acad. Perdioontology, Western Soc. Periodontology, Med-Dental Study Guild San Francisco (pres. 1993), Internat. Assn. Dental Rsch., Omicron Kappa Upsilon. Avocations: HO scale model railroading, fly tying, trout fishing, genealogy. Office: U Calif Med Ctr Sch Dentistry San Francisco CA 94143-0001

WISE, GEORGE EDWARD, lawyer; b. Chgo., Feb. 26, 1924; s. George E. and Helen L. (Gray) W.; m. Patricia E. Finn, Aug. 3, 1945; children: Erich, Peter, Abbe, Raoul, John. J.D., U. Chgo. Bar: Calif. 1949, U.S. Dist. Ct. (no. dist.) Calif. 1948, U.S. Ct. Appeals (9th cir.) 1948, U.S. Dist. Ct. (cen. dist.) 1950, U.S. Supreme CT. 1955. Law clk. Calif. Supreme Ct., 1948-49; sr. ptnr. Wise, Wiezorek, Timmons & Wise, Long Beach, 1949—; of counsel Wise Pearce Yocis & Smith, Long Beach. With USNR, 1943-45. Fellow Am. Coll. Trial Lawyers; mem. ABA, Los Angeles County Bar Assn., Long Beach Bar Assn. (pres. 1970, Atty. of Yr. 1990), Calif. State Bar. Home: 5401 E El Cedral St Long Beach CA 90815-4112 Office: Wise Pearce Yocis & Smith 249 E Ocean Blvd Ste 440 Long Beach CA 90802-4806

WISE, WOODROW WILSON, JR. retired small business owner; b. Alexandria, Va., Mar. 9, 1938; s. Woodrow Wilson Sr. and Helen (Peverill) W.; m. Barbara Jean Hatton, Oct. 6, 1956 (div. 1975); m. Sandra Kay Habitz, Dec. 17, 1983; children: Anthony P., Laura J. Gen. mgr. Alexandria (Va.) Amusement Corp., 1956-73; curator Harold Lloyd Estate, Beverly Hills, Calif., 1973-75; pres. Discount Video Tapes, Inc./Hollywood's Attic, Burbank, 1975-2000; ret., 2000. Office: Discount Video Tapes Inc PO Box 7122 833A N Hollywood Way Burbank CA 91505-2814

WISNIEWSKI, STEPHEN ADAM, professional football player; b. Rutland, Vt., Apr. 7, 1967; Student, Pa. State U. Offensive guard L.A. Raiders/Oakland Raiders, 1989—. Named All-Pro Team Guard by Sporting News, 1990-93, Coll. All-Am. Team, 1987, 88. Played in Pro Bowl, 1990-91, 93. Office: Oakland Raiders 1220 Harbor Bay Pkwy Alameda CA 94502-6570

WISTRICH, ANDREW J. federal judge; b. 1951; AB, U. Calif., Berkeley, 1972; JD, U. Chgo., 1976. Law clk. to Hon. Charles Clark U.S. Ct. Appeals (5th cir.), 1976-77; with McCutchen, Doyle, Brown & Enersen, San Francisco, 1978-83, Brown & Bain, Palo Alto, Calif., 1983-94; apptd. magistrate judge cen. dist. U.S. Dist. Ct. Calif., 1994. Office: 255 E Temple St Rm 6100 Los Angeles CA 90012-3332

WITHERS, HUBERT RODNEY, radiotherapist, radiobiologist, educator; b. Queensland, Australia, Sept. 21, 1932; came to the U.S., 1966; s. Hubert and Gertrude Ethel (Tremayne) W.; m. Janet Macfie, Oct. 9, 1959; 1 child, Genevieve. MB, BChir, U. Queensland, Brisbane, Australia, 1956; PhD, U. London, 1965, DSc, 1982. Bd. cert. Ednl. Coun. for Fgn. Med. Grads. Intern Royal Brisbane and Associated Hosps., 1957; resident in radiotherapy and pathology Queensland Radium Inst. and Royal Brisbane Hosp., 1958-63; Univ. Queensland Gaggin fellow Gray Lab., Mt. Vernon Hosp., Northwood, Middlesex, Eng., 1963-65, Royal Brisbane Hosp., 1966; radiotherapist Prince of Wales Hosp., Randwick, Sydney, Australia, 1966; vis. rsch. scientist lab. physiology Nat. Cancer Inst., Bethesda, Md., 1966-68; assoc. prof. radiotherapy sect. exptl. radiotherapy U. Tex. Sys. Cancer Ctr. M.D. Anderson Hosp. & Tumor Inst., Houston, 1968-71, prof. radiotherapy, chief sect. sect. exptl. radiotherapy, 1971-80; prof. dir. exptl. radiation oncology dept. radiation oncology UCLA, 1980-89, prof., vice-chair dir. exptl. radiation oncology dept. radiation oncology, 1991-94, Am. Cancer Soc. Clin. Rsch. prof. dept. radiation oncology, 1992—, interim dir. Jonsson Comprehensive Cancer Ctr., 1994-95, chmn. radiation oncology, 1994—. Assoc. grad. faculty U. Tex., Grad. Sch. Biomed. Scis, Houston, 1969-73, mem. grad. faculty, 1973-80; prof. dept. radiotherapy Med. Sch., U. Tex. Health Sci. Ctr., Houston, U. Tex. Med. Sch., Houston, 1975-80; prof., dir. Inst. Oncology, The Prince of Wales Hosp., U. NSW, Sydney, Australia, 1989-91; mem. com. mortality mil. pers. present-at-atmosphere tests of nuclear weapons Inst. Medicine, 1993-94; mem. radiation effects rsch. bd. NRC, 1993—; mem. com. neutron dose reporting Internat. Commn. Radiation Units and Measurements, 1982—, mem. report com. clin. dosimetry for neutrons, 1993—; mem. task force non-stochastic effects radiation Internat. Com. Radiation Protection, 1980-84, mem. com. 1, 1993—; mem. radiobiology com. Radiation Therapy Oncology Group, 1979—, mem. dose-time com., 1980-89, mem. gastroenterology com., 1982-89; mem. edn. bd. Royal Australian Coll. Radiology, 1989-91; mem. cancer rsch. coord. com. U. Calif., 1991-97, mem. standing curriculum com. UCLA biomed. physics grad. program, 1993—; cons. exptl. radiotherapy U. Tex. System Cancer Ctr., 1980—. Mem. Am. editl. bd.: Internat. Jour. Radiat. Oncol. Biol. Phys., 1982-89, 91—, internat. editl. bd., 1989-91; cons. editor: The European Jour. Cancer, 1990-95; editl. bd. dirs.: Endocurietherapy/Hyperthermia Oncology, 1991—, Radiation Oncology Investigations, 1992—; assoc. editor: Cancer Rsch., 1993-94, editl. bd. 1995-97. Mem. Kettering selection com. Gen. Motors Cancer Rsch. Found., 1988-89, chmn., 1989, awards assembly, 1990-94. Decorated officer Order of Australia, 1998; recipient Medicine prize Polish Acad. Sci., 1989, Second H.S. Kaplan Disting. Scientist award Internat. Assn. for Radiation Rsch., 1991, Gray medal Internat. Commn. Radiation Units, 1995, U.S. Dept. Energy Fermi award 1997, Am. Radium Soc. Janeway medal, 1994, Am. Soc. Therapeutic Radiology, Oncology Gold medal, 1991, Radiation Rsch. Soc. Failla award, 1988, Gold Medal Australasia Coll. Radiology, 1997, Kettering prize GM, 1998; named Gilbert H. Fletcher lectr. U. Tex. Sys. Cancer Ctr., 1989, Clifford Ash lectr. Ont. Cancer Inst., Princess Margaret Hosp., 1987, Erskine lectr. Radiol. Soc. N.Am., 1988, Ruvelson lectr. U. Minn., 1988, Milford Schultz lectr. Mass. Gen. Hosp., 1989, Del Regato Found. lectr. Hahnemann U., 1990, Bruce Cain Meml. lectr. New Zealand Soc. Oncology, 1990, others. Fellow Royal Australasian Coll. Radiologists (bd. cert., Gold medal 1997), Am. Coll. Radiology (bd. cert. therapeutic radiology, adv. com. patterns of care study 1988—, radiation oncology advisory group 1993-97, others), Am. Radium Soc. (mem. and credential c om. 1986-89, 93-94, treas. 1993-94, pres.-elect 1995-96, pres. 1996-97, others), Am. Soc. Therapeutic Radiology and Oncology (awards com. 1993, publs. com. 1993-97, vice-chair Publs. Commn., 1996-98, keynote address 1990); mem. Nat. Cancer Inst. (ad-hoc rev. coms. 1970—, radiation sudy sect. 1971-75, cons. U.S.-Japan Coop. Study high LET Radiotherapy 1975-77, cancer rsch. emphasis grant rev. com. 1976, clin. cancer ctr. rev. com. 1976-79, toxicology working group 1977-78, reviewer outstanding investigator grants 1984-93, bd. sci. counselors, 1986-88), Nat. Cancer Inst. Can. (adv. com. rsch. 1992-95), Pacific N.W. Radiol. Soc. (hon.), Tex. Radiol. Soc. (hon.), So. Calif. Radiation Oncology Soc. (sec., treas., 1992-94, pres. 1996-97), European Soc. Therapeutic Radiology and Oncology (hon.; Regaud lectr. 2000), Polish Oncology Soc. (hon.) Austrian Radiation Oncology Soc. (hon.), Phila. Roentgen Ray Soc. (hon.), Radiation Rsch. Soc. (pres. 1982-83, honors and awards com. 1984-88, ad hoc com. funds utilization 1987-89, adv. com. Radiation Rsch. Jour. 1988-96). Office: UCLA Med Ctr 10833 Le Conte Ave Los Angeles CA 90095-3075 E-mail: withers@radone.ucla.edu

WITHERS, STEPHEN GEORGE, chemistry educator; b. Eng., 1953; BS, Bristol U., 1974, PhD in Chemistry, 1977. Fellow dept. biochemistry U. Alta., 1977-79, asst. prof., 1979-82; from asst. prof. to assoc. prof. dept. chemistry U. B.C., Can., 1982-91, prof. dept. chemistry and biochemistry Can., 1991—; Khorana prof. biol. chemistry, 1997—. Recipient Corday Morgan medal Royal Soc. Chemistry U.K., 1990, Rutherford medal Royal Soc. Can., 1993, Killam Rsch. prize, 1996. Mem. Am. Chem. Soc., Canadian Soc. Chemistry (Merck award 1989), Canadian Biochem. Soc. Office: U BC Dept Chemistry Vancouver BC V6T 1Z1 Canada E-mail: withers@chem.ubc.ca

WITHERSPOON, SOPHIA, professional basketball player; b. July 6, 1969; BA in Recreation, U. Fla., 1991. Guard Nyon, Switzerland, 1991-92, Rouen, France, 1994-95, Ferencvarosi, Hungary, 1995-96, Alcamo, Italy, 1996-97, N.Y. Liberty, N.Y.C., 1997-99, Portland Fire, 1999—. Named Italian All-Star, 1996-97, WNBA Player of the Wk., 1997. Office: Portland Fire 1 Center Ct Ste 150 Portland OR 97227-2104

WITKIN, JOEL-PETER, photographer; b. Bklyn., Sept. 13, 1939; s. Max and Mary (Pellegrino) W.; 1 child, Kersen Ahanu. B.F.A., Cooper Union, 1974; M.F.A., U. N.Mex., 1986; student (fellow), Columbia U., 1973-74. Artist in residence Zerybthia Rome, Italy, summer 1996; represented by Pace/McGill (now named Pace Wilden-Stein MacGill), N.Y.C., Fraenkel Gallery, San Francisco, Galerie Baudoin Lebon, Paris; artist in residence Berlin, fall 1998, Paris, winter 1998. Lectr. Am. Acad. Rome, 1996, Camera Work, Berlin, El Escorial, Spain, 1998, Soc. Photographic Edn., 1999. Exhibited in Projects Studio One, N.Y.C., 1980, Galerie Texbraun, Paris, 1982, Baudoin Lebon, Paris, 1982, 86, 90, 97, 2000, Kansas Ctiy Art Inst., 1983, Stedelijk Mus., Amsterdam, 1983, Fraenkel Gallery, 1983-84, 87, 91, 93, 95, 97, Pace WildenStein MacGill Gallery, N.Y.C., 1983, 84, 87, 89, 91, 93, 95, 97, Pace WildenStein, L.A., 1998, San Francisco Mus. Modern Art, 1985, Bklyn. Mus., 1986, Galerie Baudoin Lebon, Paris, 1987, 89, 91, 95, 97, 2000, Centro de Arte Reina Sofia Mus., Madrid, 1988, Palais de Tokyo, Paris, 1989, Fahey/Klein Gallery, L.A., 1987, 89, 91, 97, 98, Mus. Modern Art, Haifa, Israel, 1991, Photo Picture Space Gallery, Osaka, Japan, 1993, Guggenheim Mus., N.Y.C., 1995, Interkamera, Prague, 1995, Il Castello de Rivoli Mus., Turin, 1995, Encontros de Fotografia, Colombia, Portugal, 1996, Rencontres de la Photographie, Arles, France, 1996, Taipei Photo Gallery, Taiwan, 1994, 96, 98, Mus. of Fine Arts, Santa Fe, 1998, Wildenstein Gallery, Tokyo, 1998, Sternburg Mus., Prague, 1999, Sternburg Mus., Prauge, 1999, Mesiac Fotographie, Slovakia, 1999, Hotel De Sully, Paris, 2000, Catherine Edelman Gallery, Chgo., 2000, Athens Sch. Fine Art, 2000, Ctr. Contemporary Art, Honolulu, 2000, Etherton Gallery, Tuscon, 2001; group shows: Mus. Modern Art, N.Y.C., 1959, San Francisco Mus. Moder Art, 1981, Whitney Biennial, 1985, Palais de Tokyo, Paris, 1986, La Phorographie Contemporaine en France, 1996, Foto Masson, Goteberg, Sweden, 1997, Hanlin Museum, So. Korea, 1997, Bogardenkapel, Bruges, 1998, Hayward Gallery, London, 1997, Strasborg Mus. d'Art Moderne et Contemporaine, 1998, The Ansel Adams Ctr., San Francisco, 1999, Camera Work, San Francisco, 1999, The Louvre, Paris, 2000, Museé Bourdelle, Paris, 2000, John Gibson Gallery, N.Y.C., 2000, The High Mus. Art, Ga., 2000, The Fotografie Forum, Frankfort, 2001; represented in permanent collections, Mus. Modern Art, N.Y.C., San Francisco Mus. Modern Art, 1980, Nat. Gallery Art, Washington, Victoria and Albert Mus., London, George Eastman House, N.Y., The Getty Collection, Moder Museet, Stockholm, Sweden, Whitney Mus., N.Y.C., The Guggenheim Mus., N.Y.C., Tokyo Met. Mus. Photography; subject of monographs: Joel-Peter Witkin, 1985, 88-89, 91, 93, 95-96, 98, 99, 2000, 01; editor: Masterpieces of Medical Photography, 1987, Harms Way, 1994; artist residency, Rome, 1996, Berlin, 1998, Paris, 1998, 2000. Served with U.S. Army, 1961-64. Decorated Commandeur des Arts et de Lettres (France), 2000, The Augustus Saint Gaudens medal The Cooper Union, 1996; recipient Disting. Alumni award The Cooper Union, 1986, Internat. Ctr. Photography award, 1988, award for N.Y. Times "The Plague Yr." Soc. Publ. Designers, 2000; Ford Found. grantee, 1977, 78, Nat. Endowment in Photography grantee, 1980, 81, 86, 92. Address: 1707 Five Points Rd SW Albuquerque NM 87105-3017

WITT, DAVID L. curator, writer; b. Kansas City, Mo., Nov. 3, 1951; s. Lloyd Vernon and Dean Witt. BS in Polit. Sci., Kans. State U., 1974; M Liberal Studies, U. Okla., 2000. Naturalist Naish Nature Ctr., Edwardsville, Kans., summers 1967-70; asst. curator Seton Mus., Cimarron, N.Mex., summers 1972-74; curatorial asst. Riley County Hist. Mus., Manhattan, Kans., 1973-74; mus. asst. Millicent Rogers Mus., Taos, N.Mex., 1976-77; curator The Gaspard House Mus., Taos, 1978-79, The Harwood Found., Taos, 1979—. Author: The Taos Artists, 1984, Taos Moderns: Art of the New, 1992 (Southwest Book award Border Regional Libr. Assn. 1993); co-author: Spirit Ascendant: The Art and Life of Patrociño Barela, 1996 (Southwest Book award Border Regional Libr. Assn. 1997); contbr. Taos Artists and Their Patrons, 1898-1950; contbr. articles to profl. jours. Organizer first N.Mex. Art History Conf., 1986; founder S.W. Art Hist. Coun., 1990. Mem. PEN, Am. Assn. Mus., N.Mex. Assn. Mus. (pres. 1986-88). Democrat. Home: PO Box 317 Taos NM 87571-0317 Office: 4081 NDCBU Taos NM 87571-6004 E-mail: dlw@laplaza.org

WITT, MELVIN SYLVAN, periodical editor, publisher; b. Stockton, Calif., Dec. 25, 1925; s. Arnold and Sarah (Peletz) W.; m. Dorothy Halling, June 17, 1949; children: Ann, Mallory. BS, U. Calif., Berkeley, 1948; JD, U. Calif., San Francisco, 1951. Bar: Calif. 1952. Trial atty. State Compensation Ins. Fund, L.A., 1954-57; appellate atty. Calif. Indsl. Accident Commn., San Francisco, 1957-60, trial referee, 1961-64; pvt. practice Berkeley, 1966-68; rsch. atty. Calif. Continuing Edn. of Bar, Berkeley, 1969-75; sec., dep. commr. Calif. Workers' Compensation Appeals Bd., San Francisco, 1964-66, chmn., 1975-80, Calif. Workers' Compensation Adv. Commn. to Calif. State Bar, 1974-75; founder, editor, pub. Calif. Workers' Compensation Reporter, Berkeley, 1973—. Adj. prof. law Golden Gate U. Law Sch., San Francisco, 1971—75, 1981, McGeorge Law Sch., U. of Pacific, Sacramento, 1973—75. Editor, co-author: California Workers' Compensation Practice, 2nd edit., 1973. With inf., U.S. Army, 1944-46, ETO. Named Pub. Ofcl. of Yr., Calif. Applicants' Attys. Assn., Sacramento, 1980; recipient commendation by resolution Calif. State Legislature, Sacramento, 1981; CAAA scholar, 1999. Mem. 78th Inf. Divsn. Vets. Assn. Democrat. Avocations: WWII history, travel. Bus. Office: Calif Workers Compensation Reporter PO Box 975 Berkeley CA 94701-0975 E-mail: editor@cwcr.com

WITTE, MARLYS HEARST, internist, educator; b. N.Y.C., 1934; MD, NYU Sch. Medicine, 1960. Intern N.C. Meml. Hosp., Chapel Hill, 1960-61; resident Bellevue Hosp. Ctr., N.Y.C., 1961-63; fellow NYU Hosp., St. Louis, 1965-69; instr. Washington U., St. Louis, 1965-69; prof. surgery U. Ariz., 1969—; attending internist Ariz. Health Sci. Ctr., Tucson, 1965-69, 69—. Mem. AAAS, AMA, Alpha Omega Alpha. Office: U Ariz Coll Medicine PO Box 245063 1501 N Campbell Ave Tucson AZ 85724-0001

WITTE, OWEN NEIL, microbiologist, molecular biologist, educator; b. Bklyn., May 17, 1949; BS, Cornell U., 1971; MD, Stanford U., 1976. Predoctoral fellow Stanford U. Med. Sch., Palo Alto, Calif., 1971-76, MIT Ctr. Cancer Rsch., Cambridge, Mass., 1976-80; asst. prof. UCLA Dept. Microbiology, Molecular Genetics, 1980-82, assoc. prof., 1982-86, prof., 1986—, pres.'s chair in devel. immunology, 1989—; investigator UCLA Howard Hughes Med. Inst., 1986—. Am. Cancer Soc. faculty scholar, 1982-87; recipient Faculty award UCLA, 1990, award in basic cancer rsch. Milken Family Med. Found., 1990, Richard and Hinda Rosenthal Found. award Am. Assn. Cancer Rsch., 1991, William Dameshek prize ASH, 1993; Outstanding Investigator grantee Nat. Cancer Inst. Fellow Am. Acad. Arts and Scis., Am. Acad. Microbiology; mem. NAS.

WITTE, PEGGY, metal products executive; m. Bill Witte. Chair, CEO, pres. Royal Oak Mines, Inc., Kirkland, Wash. Office: Royal Oak Mines Inc 501 Lakeview Dr Kirkland WA 98033

WITTER, DEAN, III, computer company executive; b. N.Y.C., May 27, 1947; s. Dean and Faith (Atkins) W.; m. Rebekah Ann Ferran, June 14, 1969; children: Allison C., Brooks A. BA, Harvard U., 1969; MBA, Stanford U., 1973. Lease underwriter Matrix Leasing Internat., San Francisco, 1973-74, U.S. Leasing Internat., San Francisco, 1974-76; lease mgr. Amdahl Corp., Sunnyvale, Calif., 1976-78, dir. leasing, 1978-81, controller U.S. ops., 1981-83, treas., 1983-89, v.p., 1985-89; Preemptive Techs., Inc., Emeryville, 1989-90; chief fin. officer Provista Corp., San Jose, 1990—. Bd. dirs. Zack Electronics, San Francisco. Trustee Dean Witter Found., San Francisco, 1981—, Sorensen Found., San Francisco, 1988—; bd. dirs. Mission Hospice Inc. of San Mateo County. Served with U.S. Army, 1969-71. Mem. Phi Beta Kappa. Republican. Office: Hello Direct Inc 5893 Rue Ferrari San Jose CA 95138

WITTMANN, OTTO, museum executive; b. Kansas City, Mo., Sept. 1, 1911; s. Otto and Beatrice Knox (Billingsley) W.; m. Margaret Carlisle Hill, June 9, 1945 (dec. July 1997); children: William Hill, John Carlisle. Student, Country Day Sch., Kansas City; AB, Harvard U., 1933; postgrad., 1937-38, postgrad. Carnegie scholar, summer 1937; LLD, U. Toledo; DFA, Hillsdale Coll., Bowling Green State U., U. Mich., Kenyon Coll., Skidmore Coll. Curator prints Nelson Gallery Art, Kansas City, 1933-37; instr. history of art Emerson Sch., Boston, 1937-38; curator Hyde Collection, Glens Falls, N.Y., 1938-41; instr. history of art Skidmore Coll., Saratoga Springs, 1938-41; asst. dir. Portland (Oreg.) Mus. Art, 1941; assoc. dir. Toledo Mus. Art, 1946-59, trustee, 1958—, dir., 1959-76, dir. emeritus, 1977—. V.p., cons., art advisor, 1977— ; trustee, cons. Los Angeles County Mus. Art, 1977-78; vice chmn., trustee, cons. J. Paul Getty Trust, 1977— ; organizer exhbns. art activities Am. museums USIA, 1953-55; editl. cons. Gazette des Beaux Arts; vice chmn. Nat. Collection Fine Arts Commn.; bd. dirs. Toledo Trust Co.; cons. Clark Art Inst., 1990—. Editl. chmn. Toledo Mus. Catalogue of European Paintings and Guide to Collections; writer numerous museum catalogues, profl. articles. Founding mem. Nat. Coun. Arts; mem. mus. panel NEH; chmn. adv. panel Nat. Found. Arts and Humanities; mem. art adv. panel IRS; mem. nat. arts accessions com. U.S. embassies; mem. U.S.-ICOM Nat. Com.; former sec. gen. com. pour Musées du Verre, ICOM; founding mem. Ohio Arts Coun.; sponsor Nat. Trust Sch., Attingham, Shropshire, Eng. Maj. AUS, USAAF, OSS, 1941-46. Decorated officer Legion of Honor, France, officer Order Orange Nassau, Netherlands, comdr. Arts and Letters France; comdr. Order of Merit Italy). Fellow Museums Assn. (Eng.); mem. Intermus. Conservation Assn. (pres. 1955-56, trustee), Harvard Soc. Contemporary Art (co-dir. 1931-33), Assn. Art Mus. Dirs. (pres. 1961-62, 71-72), Am. Assn. Museums (former v.p., Disting. Service to Mus. award 1987), Coll. Art Assn., Archeol. Inst. Am., Internat. Inst. for Conservation of Hist. and Artistic Works, Soc. Archtl. Historians, Verien der Freunde Antiker Kunst, Am. Soc. French Legion Honneur, Alliance Francaise de Toledo (trustee), Phi Kappa Phi. Episcopalian (vestryman). Clubs: Traveller's (London); Century Assn. (N.Y.C.); Toledo, Harvard (pres. 1956-57), Rotary (pres. 1963-64). Home: 300 Hot Springs Rd Apt 184 Montecito CA 93108-2068 Office: J Paul Getty Trust 1200 Getty Center Dr Ste 400 Los Angeles CA 90049-1681

WITTROCK, MERLIN CARL, educational psychologist; b. Twin Falls, Idaho, Jan. 3, 1931; s. Herman C. and Mary Ellen (Baumann) W.; m. Nancy McNulty, Apr. 3, 1953; children: Steven, Catherine, Rebecca. BS in Biology, U. Mo., Columbia, 1953, MS in Ednl. Psychology, 1956; PhD in Ednl. Psychology, U. Ill., Urbana, 1960. Prof. grad. sch. edn. UCLA, 1960—, founder Ctr. Study Evaluation, chmn. divsn. ednl. psychology, chmn. faculty, exec. com.; univ. com. on outstanding teaching. Dir. math. and humanities program, 1997; co-founder Urban Tchr. Edn. Program, 1996; co-dir. Imagination Project, 1998; fellow Ctr. for Advanced Study in Behavioral Scis., 1967-68; vis. prof. U. Wis., U. Ill., Ind. U., Monash U., Australia; bd. dirs. Far West Labs., San Francisco; chmn. com. on evaluation and assessment L.A. Unified Sch. Dist.; mem. nat. adv. panel for math. scis. NRC of NAS, 1988-89; chmn. nat. bd. Nat. Ctr. for Rsch. in Math. Scis. Edn., chmn. charges com. UCLA; adv. bd. Kauffman Found., Kansas City, Mo., 1995—; bd. dirs. Western Edn. Lab. for Edn. Rsch., Far West Lab. Author, editor: The Evaluation of Instruction, 1970, Changing Education, 1973, Learning and Instruction, 1977, The Human Brain, 1977, Danish transl., 1980, Spanish transl., 1982, The Brain and Psychology, 1980, Instructional Psychology: Education and Cognitive Processes of the Brain, Neuropsychological and Cognitive Processes of Reading, 1981, Handbook of Research on Teaching, 3d edit., 1986, The Future of Educational Psychology, 1989, Research in Learning and Teaching, 1990, Testing and Cognition, 1991, Generative Science Teaching, 1994, Problem-Solving Transfer, 1996, Taxonomy for Learning, Teaching and Assessing, 2001. Mentor Edn. Leadership Program. Capt. USAF, 1953-55. Recipient Thorndike award for outstanding psychol. rsch., 1987, Disting. Tchr. of Univ. award UCLA, 1990, Greenfield award for rsch. in learning UCLA Grad. Sch. Edn., 1988; Ford Found. grantee. Fellow AAAS, APA (pres. divsn. ednl. psychology 1984-85, assn. coun. 1988-91, award for Outstanding Svc. to Ednl. Psychology 1991, 93, Disting. Svc. award for svc. to sci. adv. coun.), Am. Psychol. Soc., (charter fellow), Am. Ednl. Rsch. Assn. (chmn. ann. conv., chmn. publs. 1980-83, assn. coun. 1986-89, bd. dirs. 1987-89, chmn. com. on ednl. TV 1989—, Outstanding Contbns. award 1986, Outstanding Svc. award 1989), Phi Delta Kappa. Office: UCLA 3339 Moore Hl Los Angeles CA 90095-0001

WITTRY, DAVID BERYLE, physicist, educator; b. Mason City, Iowa, Feb. 7, 1929; s. Herman Joseph and Edna Pearl (Filbey) W.; m. Mildred Elizabeth DuBois, July 1, 1955; children: James David, Robert Andrew, Kristopher Lee, Diane Marie, Linda Beryle. B.S., U. Wis., 1951; M.S., Calif. Inst. Tech., 1953, Ph.D., 1957. Research fellow Calif. Inst. Tech., Pasadena, 1957-59; asst. prof. U. So. Calif., Los Angeles, 1959-61, assoc. prof. dept. elec. engring., 1961-69, prof. dept. materials sci. and elec. engring., 1969-98, disting. prof. emeritus, 1998—. Cons. Hughes Semiconductors, 1958-59, Applied Research Labs., Inc., 1958-83, Exptl. Sta., E.I. du Pont de Nemours & Co., 1962-71, Gen. Telephone and Electronics Research Labs., 1966-72, Autonetics div. N. Am. Aviation, 1961-63, Electronics Research div. Rockwell Internat., 1976-81, Atlantic Richfield Co. Corp. Tech. Lab., 1981-87, Jet Propulsion Lab., 1985-88, Hitachi Instruments, 1989-90; vis. scientist Japan Soc. Promotion of Sci., U. Osaka Prefecture, 1974. Editor 3 proceedings of cons. Contbr. articles to profl. jours. Patentee in field. Recipient first award essays on gravity, Gravity Research Found., 1949, Disting. Scientist award phys. scis. Microscopy Soc. Am., 1995, Disting. Svc. citation U. Wis. Coll. Engring., 1996; Guggenheim fellow, 1967-68; Knapp scholar U. Wis., 1949-51. Mem. IEEE, Electron Microscopy Soc. Am. (dir. phys. scis. 1979-81, pres. 1983), Microbeam Analysis Soc. (sec. organizing com. 1966, exec. council 1970-72, pres. 1988, Presdl. award 1980, Birks award 1987, 89, hon. mem.), Am. Phys. Soc., Sigma Xi. Methodist. Office: U So Calif Dept Materials Sci Los Angeles CA 90089-0001

WITWORTH, CLARK L. sports team executive; CFO Larry H. Miller Group, Murray, Utah. Office: Larry H Miller Group 5650 S State St Murray UT 84107-6131

WOERNER, ROBERT LESTER, landscape architect; b. Rochester, N.Y., Jan. 31, 1925; s. William John and Loretta Bertha (Hettel) W.; m. Mary Jane Warn, May 12, 1952; children: Jane Marie, Anne Louise. B.S., SUNY Coll. Forestry, Syracuse, 1949. Cert. landscape architect, Wash., Idaho. Draftsman N.A., Rotunno Landscape Architects, Syracuse, 1947-49; landscape architect Park Dist., Plan Commn., Yakima, Wash., 1949-50; asst. supt. parks Spokane Park Dept., Spokane, 1950-56; dir. Denver Bot. Gardens, 1956-58; pvt. practice landscape architect Spokane, 1959-2000; chmn. bd. registration Landscape Architects State of Wash., 1976-78; pres. Council Landscape Archtl. Registration Bds., 1978-79. Mem. Zoning Bd. Adjustment, Spokane, 1983; mem. Urban Design Com., 1983; mem. Capitol Campus Design Adv. Com., 1982-94. Cpl. U.S. Army, 1943-45, ETO. Recipient Indsl. Landscaping Award Am. Assn. Nurserymen, Lincoln Bldg., Spokane, 1966; recipient Cert. of Merit Wash. Water Power, 1967, State Indsl. Landscaping award Wash State Nurserymen's Assn., Wash. Water Power, 1968 Fellow Am. Soc. Landscape Architects (pres. 1979-80, Disting. Svc. award 1976); mem. Kiwanis, Masons. Republican. Roman Catholic.

WOERTZ, PATRICIA A. petroleum industry executive; b. Mar. 1953; B in Acctg., Pa. State U. Acct. Ernst & Young, Pitts., 1974; with Gulf Oil Corp., Pitts., 1977-81, Houston, 1981-85; with debt. reduction process, merger of Gulf and Chevron, 1985-87; fin. mgr. Chevron Info. Tech. Co., 1989-91, strategic planning mgr., 1991-93; pres. Chevron Can. Ltd., Vancouver, B.C., 1993-96, Chevron Internat. Oil Co., 1996-98; v.p. logistics and trading Chevron Products Co., Chevron Corp., 1996-98; pres. Chevron Products Co., 1998—; v.p. Chevron Corp., 1998—. Bd. dirs. Dynegy Inc., Houston. Mem. Am. Petroleum Inst. (mem. downstream com.), Calif. C. of C. (bd. dirs.). Office: Chevron Corp 6001 Bollinger Canyon Rd San Ramon CA 94583-2398 also: Chevron Corp 575 Market St San Francisco CA 94105

WOGSLAND, JAMES WILLARD, retired heavy machinery manufacturing executive; b. Devils Lake, N.D., Apr. 17, 1931; s. Melvin LeRoy and Mable Bertina (Paulson) W.; m. Marlene Claudia Clark, June 1957; children: Karen Lynn, Steven James. BA in Econs., U. Minn., 1957. Various positions fin. dept. Caterpillar Tractor Co., Peoria, Ill., 1957-64, treas., 1976-81; mgr. fin. Caterpillar Overseas S.A., Geneva, 1965-70, sec.-treas., 1970-76; dir.-pres. Caterpillar Brasil S.A., São Paulo, 1981-87; exec. v.p. Caterpillar, Inc., Peoria, 1989-90, also bd. dirs., vice-chmn., 1990-95; bd. dirs. Ameren Corp., St. Louis, 1997—. Bd. dirs. Ameren Corp., St. Louis. Mem. adv. bd. St. Francis Hosp., Peoria, 1987-95; bd. dirs. Peoria Area Cmty. Found., 1986-92; trustee Eureka Coll., 1987-95; commr. Kootenai County Planning and Zoning Commn., 1997—. Sgt. USAF, 1951-55. Mem. Hayden Lake Golf and Country Club. Republican. Presbyterian. Home: 9675 Easy St Hayden Lake ID 83835-9526

WOHLGENANT, RICHARD GLEN, lawyer, director; b. Porterville, Calif., Dec. 2, 1930; s. Carl Ferdinand and Sara Alice (Moore) W.; m. Teresa Joan Bristow, Dec. 27, 1959; children: Mark Thomas, Tracy Patrice, Timothy James. B.A., U. Mont., Missoula, 1952; LL.B., Harvard U., Cambridge, Mass., 1957. Bar: Colo. 1957, U.S. Dist. Ct. Colo. 1957. Assoc. Holme Roberts & Owen LLP, Denver, 1957-62; ptnr./mem. Holme Roberts & Owen, Denver, 1962-99, of counsel, 2000—. Bd. dirs. Adopt-A-Sch., Denver, 1976-80, St. Joseph Found., Denver, 1990-93, Denver Com. Coun. Fgn. Rels., 1988-98, Japanese-Am. Soc. Colo., 1993-98, Rocky Mountain chpt. U.S. Mex. C. of C., 1993-00; bi-nat. bd. U.S./Mex. C. of C., 2000—; mem. Chamber of th Americas, 2001—; adv. bd. Human Med. Genetics Prgm., U. Colo. H.S.C., 2000—. Mem. ABA, Colo. Bar Assn., Denver Bar Assn., Am. Coll. Real Estate Lawyers, Univ. Club, Law Club, City Club. Republican. Roman Catholic. Home: 300 Ivy St Denver CO 80220-5855 Office: Holme Roberts & Owen LLP 1700 Lincoln St Denver CO 80203-4500

WOIKE, LYNNE ANN, computer scientist; b. Torrance, Calif., Oct. 20, 1960; d. Stephen J. and Virginia (Ursich) Shane; m. Thomas W. Woike, Feb. 13, 1988; 1 child, Karla. BSc in Computer Sci. cum laude, Calif. State U., Dominguez Hills, 1994. Computer cons. Unocal Oil Co., Wilmington, Calif., 1992-94; x-window/motif software developer Logican Inc., San Pedro, 1994-95; reticle engr. TRW, Inc., Redondo Beach, 1982-88, sr. mem. tech. staff product data mgmt. database adminstr., 1995-98, chmn. product data mgmt. change control bd., 1995—, staff engr., 1999-99, sr. Unix/NT system adminstr., 1999; tech. lead, subscriber database DIRECTV, Inc., El Segundo, Calif., 1999—. Mem. IEEE, IEEE Computer Sci., Assn. for Computing Machinery (chmn. student chpt. 1993-94), Calif. State U. Sci. Soc. (computer sci. rep. 1993-95). Office: DIRECTV Inc 200 N Sepulveda Blvd El Segundo CA 90245-4340 E-mail: woike@pacbell.net

WOJAHN, R. LORRAINE, state senator; b. Tacoma, Sept. 17, 1920; m. Gilbert M. Wojahn (dec.); children: Mark C., Gilbert M. Jr. (dec.). Mem. Wash. State Ho. of Reps., Olympia, 1969-76, Wash. State Senate, Olympia, 1977—. Pres. pro tempore; vice chmn. rules, health and human svcs. com.; mem. labor and commerce, ways and means coms. Bd. dirs. Allenmore Hosp.; trustee Consumer Credit Counseling Svcs., Inc., Tacoma-Pierce County; active, past pres. Eastside Boys and Girls Club, Tacoma-Pierce County; active Wash. State Hist. Soc. Democrat. Office: Wash Senate PO Box 40427 Olympia WA 98504-0427

WOJCICKI, STANLEY GEORGE, physicist, educator; b. Warsaw, Poland, Mar. 30, 1937; came to U.S., 1950; s. Franciszek and Janina (Kozlow) W.; m. Esther Denise Hochman, Nov. 17, 1961; children: Susan Diane, Janet Maia, Anne Elizabeth. A.B., Harvard U., 1957; Ph.D., U. Calif., Berkeley, 1962. Physicist Lawrence Radiation Lab., Berkeley, 1961-66; asst. prof. physics Stanford U., 1966-68, assoc. prof., 1968-74, prof., 1974—, chmn. dept., 1982-85, dep. dir. Superconducting Supercollider Central Design Group, 1984-89; chmn. Stanford Linear Accelerator Center Exptl. Program Adv. Com., 1979-81. Chmn. High Energy Physics Adv. Panel, 1990-96. Assoc. editor Phys. Rev. Letters for Exptl. High Energy Physics, 1978-80. Recipient Alexander von Humboldt Sr. Am. Scientist award, 1981; NSF fellow, 1964-65; Sloan Found. fellow, 1968-72; Guggenheim fellow, 1973-74 Fellow Am. Phys. Soc. Office: Stanford U Dept Physics Stanford CA 94305-4060

WOLANER, ROBIN PEGGY, internet and magazine publisher; b. Queens, N.Y., May 6, 1954; d. David H. and Harriet (Radlow) W.; m. Steven J. Castleman, 1992; children: Terry David, Bonnie Lee. BS in Indsl. and Labor Rels., Cornell U., 1975. Sr. editor Viva Mag., N.Y.C., 1975-76; editor Impact Mag., N.Y.C., 1976-77; circulation mgr. Runner's World Mag., Mountain View, Calif., 1977-79; cons. Ladd Assocs., San Francisco, 1979-80; gen. mgr. Mother Jones Mag., San Francisco, 1980-81, pub., 1981-85; founder, pub. Parenting Mag., San Francisco, 1985-91, pres., 1991-92; v.p. Time Pub. Ventures, 1990-96; pres., CEO Sunset Pub. Corp., 1992-95; exec. v.p. CNET, 1997—. Bd. dirs. Burnham Pacific Properties, Health Ctrl. Com., OnLine Ptnrs. Com. Jewish. Office: 150 Chestnut St San Francisco CA 94111 E-mail: robin2@cnet.com

WOLD, DAVID C. bishop; Bishop of Southwestern Wash. Evang. Luth. Ch. in Am., Tacoma, 1988—. Office: Synod of Southwestern Washington 420 121st St S Tacoma WA 98444-5218

WOLD, JOHN SCHILLER, geologist, former congressman; b. East Orange, N.J., Aug. 31, 1916; s. Peter Irving and Mary (Helff) W.; m. Jane Adele Pearson, Sept. 28, 1946; children: Peter Irving, Priscilla Adele, John Pearson. AB, St. Andrews U., Scotland and Union Coll., Schenectady, 1938; MS, Cornell U., 1939; LLD (hon.), U. Wyo., 1991. Dir. Fedn. Rocky Mountain States, 1966-68; v.p. Rocky Mountain Oil and Gas Assn., 1967, 68; mem. Wyo. Ho. of Reps., 1957-59; Wyo. Republican candidate for U.S. Senate, 1964, 70; mem. 91st Congress at large from, Wyo.; chmn., CEO Wold Trona Co., Inc.; pres., chmn. Wold Talc Co.; ret. Wold Nuclear Co., Wold Mineral Exploration Co., Casper, Wyo.; founding pres. Wyo. Heritage Soc.; founder Central Wyo. Ski Corp. Chmn. Wyo. Natural Gas Pipeline Authority, 1987-91; chmn. bd. Nuclear Exploration and Devel. Corp., Mineral Engring. Co. Contbr. articles to profl. jours. Chmn. Wyo. Rep. Com., 1960-64, Western State Rep. Chmns. Assn., 1963-64; mem. exec. com. Rep. Nat. Com., 1962-64; chmn. Wyo. Rep. State Fin. Com.; Active Little League Baseball, Boy Scouts Am., United Fund, YMCA, Boys Clubs Am.; former pres. bd. trustees Casper Coll.; trustee Union Coll. Served to lt. USNR, World War II. Named Wyo. Man of Yr. AP-UPI, 1968; Wyo. Mineral Man of Yr., 1979, Wyo. Heritage award, 1992, Wyo. Oil/Gas and Mineral Man of 20th Century, Am. Heritage Ctr. of U. Wyo., 1999; named Benefactor of Yr., Nat. Coun. for Resource Devel., 1993. Mem. Wyo. Geol. Assn. (hon. life, pres. 1956), Am. Assn. Petroleum Geologists, Ind. Petroleum Assn. Am., AAAS, Wyo. Mining Assn., Sigma Xi, Alpha Delta Phi. Episcopalian (past vestryman, warden). Home: 1231 W 30th St Casper WY 82601-5372 Office: Mineral Resource Ctr 139 W 2nd St Casper WY 82601-2473 E-mail: WOPI@Trib.com

WOLD, KIMBERLY G. legislative staff member; Grad., Brigham Young U. Pub. affairs program mgr. Phoenix Met. C. of C., 1982-86; asst. dist. dir. U.S. Congressman Jon Kyl, 1987-93, dist. dir., 1993-95; dep. campaign mgr. John Kyl Campaign for U.S. Senate, 1994; dep. state dir. U.S. Sen. John Kyl, 1995-98, state dir., 1998—. Bd. dirs. Drugs Don't Work in Ariz., Maricopa County Victim Compensation Bd.; mem. Gov.'s Commn. on Violence Against Women. Home: 2560 N Lindsay Rd Apt 46 Mesa AZ 85213-1521 Office: Office of Sen Jon Kyl 2200 E Camelback Rd Ste 120 Phoenix AZ 85016-3455

WOLDEGABRIEL, GIDAY, research geologist; b. Mai Misham/Adwa, Tigray, Ethiopia, Sept. 3, 1955; came to U.S., 1982; s. Giday WoldeGabriel and Mislal Mesfin; m. Almaz Berhane Tesfamichael, Jan. 15, 1994. BS in Geology with honors, Addis Ababa (Ethiopia) U., 1978, MS in Geology, 1980; PhD in Geology, Case Western Res. U., 1987. Lectr. geology Addis Ababa U., 1980-82; dir.'s postdoctoral fellow Los Alamos (N.Mex.) Nat. Lab., 1987-90, cons., 1990-92, mem. tech. staff, 1992—. Mem. Am. Geophysical Union. Avocations: running, camping, skiing, body building, swimming. Home: 45 Paige Cir Los Alamos NM 87544-3638 Office: Los Alamos Nat Lab Eees 1 Ms D462 Los Alamos NM 87545-0001 E-mail: wgiday@lanl.gov

WOLF, ALFRED, rabbi; b. Eberbach, Germany, Oct. 7, 1915; came to U.S., 1935, naturalized, 1941; s. Hermann and Regina (Levy) W.; m. Miriam Jean Office, June 16, 1940; children: David B., Judith C. (dec.), Dan L. BA, U. Cin., 1937; MHL, Hebrew Union Coll., 1941; DD, 1966; PhD, U. So. Calif., 1961; DHL, U. Judaism, 1987, Loyola Marymount U., 1990. Ordained rabbi, 1941. Rabbi Temple Emanuel, Dothan, Ala., 1941-46; S.E. regional dir. Union Am. Hebrew Congregations, 1944-46, Western regional dir., 1946-49; rabbi Wilshire Blvd. Temple Los Angeles, 1949-85, rabbi emeritus, 1985—; dir. Skirball Inst. on Am. Values of Am. Jewish Com., 1985-95; founding dir., 1996—. Lectr. U. So. Calif., 1955-69, Hebrew Union Coll., Jewish Inst. Religion, Calif., 1963-65, 74; lectr. religion Seven Seas div. Chapman Coll., 1967; adj. prof. theology Loyola U. Los Angeles, 1967-74; lectr. sociology Calif. State U., Los Angeles, 1977; co-chair First Nationwide Conf. for Cath. Jewish and Protestant seminiaries, Chgo., 1993. Author: (with Joseph Gaer) Our Jewish Heritage, 1957, (with Monsignor Royale M. Vadakin) Journey Of Discovery - A Resource Manual for Catholic-Jewish Dialogue, 1989; editor Teaching About World Religions: A Teacher's Supplement, 1991. Mem. camp commn. adminstrv. com. Camp Hess Kramer, 1951—; mem. L.A. Com. on Human Rels., 1956-72, mem. exec. bd., 1960—, chmn., 1964-66, hon. mem., 1972—; pres. Anytown U.S.A., 1964-66; mem. United Way Planning Coun. Bd., chmn., 1974-78; mem. youth adv. com. NCCJ, 1968-72, exec. bd., 1972-93; founding pres. Interreligious Coun. So. Calif., 1970-72; chmn. clergy adv. com. L.A. Sch. Dist., 1971-81; chmn. Nat. Workshop on Christian-Jewish Rels., 1978; bd. govs. Hebrew Union Coll., bd. alumni overseers, 1972—; mem. L.A. 2000 Com., 1986-89, The 2000 Partnership, 1989-95, Berlin Sister City Com., L.A., 1987-89; bd. dirs.

Jewish Fedn. Coun., 1978-85, bd. govs., 1985—; bd. dirs. Jewish Family Svc. L.A., sec., 1978-80. Recipient Samuel Kaminker award as Jewish educator of year Western Assn. Temple Educators, 1965, John Anson Ford Human Relations award County Commn. on Human Relations, 1972, 90, Harry Hollzer Meml. award Los Angeles Jewish Fedn. Council, 1978, Volpert Community Service award, 1986, Community Service award United Way of Los Angeles, 1980, Leadership award Los Angeles Bd. Edn., 1981, Service to Edn. award Associated Adminstrs. Los Angeles, 1983, Pub. Service award Jewish Chautauqua Soc., 1986, N.Am. Interfaith Leadership award Nat. Workshop for Christian-Jewish Rels., 1990, Lifetime Achievement award U. So. Calif., 1998. Mem. Bd. Rabbis So. Calif. (pres.), Am. Jewish Com. (exec. com. Los Angeles chpt., Max Bay Meml. award 1986), Central Conf. Am. Rabbis (exec. bd., mem. commn. on Jewish edn. 1970-72, treas. 1975-79, chmn. interreligious activities com. 1975-79, hon. mem. 1991—), Pacific Assn. Reform Rabbis (pres.), So. Calif. Assn. Liberal Rabbis (pres.), Synagogue Council Am. (mem. com. interreligious affairs), Alumni Assn. Hebrew Union Coll.-Jewish Inst. Religion, Town Hall, Los Angeles World Affairs Council, U. So. Calif. Alumni Assn. Home: 3389 Ley Dr Los Angeles CA 90027-1315 Office: Skirball Inst Am Values 635 S Harvard Blvd Ste 214 Los Angeles CA 90005-2501 E-mail: almirwolf@aol.com

WOLF, ARTHUR HENRY, museum administrator; b. New Rockford, N.D., June 18, 1953; s. Louis Irwin and Vivian Joyce (Grinde) W.; m. Holly M. Chaffee, Oct. 18, 1984. BA in Anthropology, U. Nebr., 1975; MA, U. Ariz., 1977. Lab. asst., acting curator anthropology U. Nebr. State Mus., Lincoln, 1973-75; rsch. asst. Ariz. State Mus., Tucson, 1975-77; curator of collections Sch. Am. Rsch., Santa Fe, 1977-79; dir. Millcent Rogers Mus., Taos, 1979-87, Nev. State Mus. and Hist. Soc., Las Vegas, 1988-92, Mus. of Rockies, Bozeman, Mont., 1992-96; pres. High Desert Mus., Bend, Oreg., 1996—. Speaker in field; cons. Pueblos of Zuni, Picuris, San Ildefonso and Taos. Contbr. articles and revs. to profl. jours. Trustee Kokopelli Archeol. Rsch. Fund, Bozeman, 1992-96; active Mont. Ambs. Recipient Young Alumnus award U. Nebr. Lincoln, 1990. Mem. Am. Assn. Mus. (bd. dirs. 1994—, vis. com. roster 1989—, vice chair 1996-97), Rotary, Assn. Sci. Mus. Dirs. Avocations: travel, reading, music. Home: 110 NW Wau St Bend OR 97701 Office: The High Desert Mus 59800 S Highway 97 Bend OR 97702-7963

WOLF, CHARLES, JR. economist, educator; b. N.Y.C., Aug. 1, 1924; s. Charles and Rosalie W.; m. Theresa van de Wint, Mar. 1, 1947; children: Charles Theodore, Timothy van de Wint. B.S., Harvard U., 1943, M.P.A., 1948, Ph.D. in Econs., 1949. Economist, fgn. service officer U.S. Dept. State, 1945-47, 49-53; mem. faculty Cornell U., 1953-54, U. Calif., Berkeley, 1954-55; sr. economist The Rand Corp., Santa Monica, Calif., 1955-67, head econs. dept., 1967-81; dean The Rand Grad. Sch., 1970-97, sr. econ. advisor, 1981—, corp. fellow in internat. econs., 1996—; sr. fellow Hoover Inst., 1988—. Bd. dirs. Capital Income Builder Fund, Capital World Growth Fund; lectr. econs. UCLA, 1960-72; mem. adv. bd. grad. ch. pub. policy Carnegie-Mellon U., 1992—; mem. adv. bd. ctr. internat. bus. and econ. rsch., UCLA Anderson Grad. Sch., 1996—. Author: The Costs and Benefits of the Soviet Empire, 1986, Markets or Governments: Choosing Between Imperfect Alternatives, 1988, 93, Linking Economic Policy and Foreign Policy, 1991, Long-Term Economic and Military Trends: The United States and Asia, 1994-2015, 1995, The Economic Pivot in a Political Context, 1997; co-author: Economic Openness: Many Facets, Many Metrics, 1999, Asian Economic Trends and Their Security Implications, 2000; bd. editors Korean Jour. of Def. Econs., 1995—; editl. adv. bd. Society, 1997—; contbr. articles to profl. jours. Mem. Assn. for Public Policy Analysis and Mgmt. (pres. 1980-81), Am. Econs. Assn., Econometric Soc., Coun. on Fgn. Rels., Internat. Inst. Strategic Studies London. Clubs: Cosmos (Washington); Riviera Tennis (Los Angeles); Harvard (N.Y.). Office: The Rand Grad Sch 1700 Main St Santa Monica CA 90401-3208

WOLF, CYNTHIA TRIBELHORN, librarian, library educator; b. Denver, Dec. 12, 1945; adopted d. John Baltazar and Margaret (Kern) Tribelhorn; m. H.Y. Rassam, Mar. 21, 1969 (div. Jan. 1988); children: Najma Christine, Yousuf John; adopted children: Leonard Joseph Lucero, Lakota E. Rassam-Lucero, McKinley William Osborn, Kevin Trey, Jackson Andrew Lee; m. Walter Larry Peck, June 21, 1965 (div. Feb. 1967). BA, Colo. State U., 1970; MLS, U. Denver, 1985. Cert. permanent profl. librarian, N.Mex. Elem. tchr. Sacred Heart Sch., Farmington, N.Mex., 1973-78; asst. prof. libr. sci. edn. U. N.Mex., Albuquerque, 1985-91, dir. libr. sci. edn. divsn., 1989-91; pres. Info. Acquisitions, Albuquerque, 1990-99; libr. dir. Southwestern Coll., Santa Fe, 1992-94; mem. youth resources Rio Grande Valley Libr. Sys., Albuquerque, 1994-95, adult reference svc., 1995-98; with Albuquerque Pub. Schs., 1998—; instr. U. N.Mex., 1998-99. Fine arts resource person for gifted edn. Farmington Pub. Schs., 1979-83; speaker Unofficial Mentorships and Market Rsch., 1992-98. Mem. Farmington Planning and Zoning Commn., 1980-81; bd. dirs. Farmington Mus. Assn., 1983-84; pres. Farmington Symphony League, 1978. Mem. ALA, N.Mex. Library Assn., LWV (bd. dirs. Farmington, 1972-74, 75, pres.). Avocations: mixed media graphics design, market research, creative approaches to personal journals, board game design.

WOLF, G. VAN VELSOR, JR. lawyer; b. Balt., Feb. 19, 1944; s. G. Van Velsor and Alice Roberts (Kimberly) W.; m. Ann Holmes Kavanagh, May 19, 1984; children: George Van Velsor III, Timothy Kavanagh (dec.), Christopher Kavanagh, Elisabeth Huxley. BA, Yale U., 1966; JD, Vanderbilt U., 1973. Bar: N.Y. 1974, U.S. Dist. Ct. (so. dist.) N.Y. 1974, U.S. Ct. Appeals (2d cir.) 1974, Ariz. 1982, U.S. Dist. Ct. Ariz. 1982, U.S. Ct. Appeals (9th cir.) 1982. Agrl. advisor U.S. Peace Corps., Tanzania and Kenya, 1966-70; assoc. Milbank, Tweed, Hadley & McCloy, N.Y.C., 1973-75; vis. lectr. law Airlangga U., Surabaya, Indonesia, 1975-76; editor-in-chief Environ. Law Reporter, Washington, 1976-81; assoc. Lewis & Roca, Phoenix, 1981-84, ptnr., 1984-91, Snell & Wilmer, Phoenix, 1991—. Vis. lectr. law U. Ariz., 1990, Vanderbilt U., 1991, U. Md., 1994, Ariz. State U., 1995; cons. Nat. Trust Hist. Preservation, Washington, 1981. Editor: Toxic Substances Control, 1980; editor in chief Environ. Law Reporter 1976-81; contbr. articles to profl. jours. Bd. dirs. Ariz. divsn. Am. Cancer Soc., 1985—96, sec., 1990—92, vice-chmn., 1992—94, chmn., 1994—96, bd. dirs. S.W. divsn., 1996—, chmn., 1996—98, nat. bd. dirs., 1999—; bd. dirs. Herberger Theatre Ctr., 1998—, sec., 2001—; bd. dirs. Phoenix Little Theatre, 1983—90, chmn., 1986—88. Recipient St. George medal Am. Cancer Soc., 1998. Mem. ABA (vice-chmn. SONREEL commn. state and regional environ. coop. 1995-98, co-chmn. 1998-2000, vice-chmn. environ. audits task force 1998-99, vice-chmn. SONREEL ann. meeting planning com. 1998-99), Assn. of Bar of City of N.Y., Ariz. State Bar Assn. (coun. environ. & nat. res. law sect. 1988-93, chmn. 1991-92, CLE com. 1992-98, chmn. 1997-98), Maricopa County Bar Assn., Ariz. Acad., Union Club N.Y.C., Univ. Club Phoenix, Phoenix Country Club. Office: Snell & Wilmer 1 Arizona Ctr Phoenix AZ 85004-0001 E-mail: vwolf@swlaw.com

WOLF, HANS, opera company director; b. Hamburg, Germany; grad., PhD, New Vienna Cons. of Music. Conductor Innsbruck (Austria) Symphony Orch., orchs. in Germany and Austria; music dir. Remington Records, Vienna, 1950-52, Livingston (N.J.) Audio Products, 1952-60; conductor Riverside (Calif.) Opera Co., 1961-69; assoc. conductor, chorus master Seattle Opera Assn., 1969-83; co-founder Tacoma Opera, 1981, artistic dir., conductor, 1981-95; with Cmty. Outreach Prodns., Seattle, 1974—. Office: Seattle Opera PO Box 9248 Seattle WA 98109-0248

WOLF, HANS ABRAHAM, retired pharmaceutical company executive; b. Frankfurt, Fed. Republic Germany, June 27, 1928; came to U.S., 1936, naturalized, 1944; s. Franz Benjamin and Ilse (Nathan) W.; m. Elizabeth J. Bassett, Aug. 2, 1958; children: Heidi Elizabeth, Rebecca Wolf Eckert, Deborah Wolf Streeter, Andrew Robert. AB magna cum laude, Harvard U., 1949, MBA, 1955; PhB, Oxford U., 1951. Math instr. Tutoring Sch., 1946-47; statis. research Nat. Bur. Econ. Research, N.Y.C., 1948-49; researcher Georgetown U., 1951-52; confidential aide Office Dir. Mut. Security, Washington, 1952; analyst Ford Motor div. Ford Motor Co., Dearborn, Mich., summer 1954; foreman prodn. M&C Nuclear Inc., Attleboro, Mass., 1955-57; asst. supt. prodn. Metals & Controls Corp., Attleboro, 1957-59, mgr. product dept., 1959-62, controller, 1962-67; asst. v.p., controller materials and services group Tex. Instruments Inc., Dallas, 1967-69, treas., v.p., 1969-75; v.p. fin., chief fin. officer Syntex Corp., Palo Alto, Calif., 1975-78, exec. v.p., 1978-86, vice chmn., chief adminstrv. officer, 1986-92, vice chmn., 1992-93, also bd. dirs., 1986-93. Bd. dirs. Tab Products Co., San Jose, Calif., chmn., 1995—; bd. dirs. Network Equipment Techs., Fremont, Calif., chmn., 1996—; bd. dirs. Satellite Dialysis Ctrs., Inc., Redwood City, Calif. Author: Motivation Research—A New Aid to Understanding Your Markets, 1955. Mem. Norton (Mass.) Sch. Bd., 1959-62, chmn., 1961-62; pres., bd. dirs. Urban League Greater Dallas, 1971-74; bd. dirs. Dallas Health Planning Coun., mem. community adv. com., 1973-75; bd. dirs., pres. Children's Health Coun. of the Mid Peninsula; cubmaster Boy Scouts Am., 1976-78; elder United Ch. Christ, 1970-73, vice chmn. gen. bd., 1970-71, moderator, 1978-80; trustee Pacific Sch. Religion, 1986-94, chmn., 1990-94; trustee World Affairs Coun. San Francisco, 1986-92, 94-97; dir. Tech Mus. San Jose, 1992-98. With USAF, 1952-53. Mem. Am. Mgmt. Assn. (planning council fin. div. 1970-76), Phi Beta Kappa. Office: Network Equipment Technologies Inc 6500 Paseo Padre Pkwy Fremont CA 94555

WOLF, HAROLD HERBERT, pharmacy educator; b. Quincy, Mass., Dec. 19, 1934; s. John I. and Bertha F. (Sussman) W.; m. Joan Z. Silverman, Aug. 11, 1957; children: Gary Jerome, David Neal. B.S., Mass. Coll. Pharmacy, 1956; Ph.D., U. Utah, 1961; LLD (hon.), U. Md., 1994. Asst. prof. pharmacology Coll. Pharmacy Ohio State U., 1961-64, assoc. prof., 1964-69, prof., 1969-76, Kimberly prof., 1975-76, chmn. div. pharmacology, 1973-76; dean Coll. of Pharmacy, U. Utah, Salt Lake City, 1976-89, prof. pharmacology, 1989—, dir. Anticonvulsant Drug Devel. Program, 1989—. Vis. prof. U. Sains Malaysia, 1973-74; mem. Nat. Joint Commn. on Prescription Drug Use, 1976-80; mem. NIH rev. com. Biomed. Rsch. Devel. Grant Program, 1978-79; external examiner U. Malaya, 1978, 92, 96, U. Sains Malaysia, 1980. Contbr. articles in field of central nervous system pharmacology and field of pharm. edn. Recipient Alumni Achievement award Mass. Coll. Pharmacy, 1978, Disting. Faculty award U. Utah, 1989, Rosenblatt prize, 1989, Disting. Alumnus award Coll. Pharmacy, U. Utah, 1991, Weaver prize, 2000. Fellow AAAS, Acad. Pharm. Scis.; mem. Am. Soc. Pharmacology and Exptl. Therapeutics, Am. Pharm. Assn. (task force on edn. 1982-84), Am. Assn. Colls. of Pharmacy (pres. 1977, Disting. Pharmacy Educator award 1988, scholar in residence 1989, chmn. commn. on implementing change in pharmacy edn. 1989-92, 95-96), Am. Soc. Hosp. Pharmacists (commn. on goals 1982-84), Am. Coun. on Pharm. Edn. (bd. dirs. 1985-88), Soc. Neurosci. Jewish. Home: 4467 Adonis Dr Salt Lake City UT 84124-3922 Office: Univ Utah Coll Pharmacy Salt Lake City UT 84112

WOLF, JACK KEIL, electrical engineer, educator; b. Newark, Mar. 14, 1935; s. Joseph and Rosaline Miriam (Keil) W.; m. Toby Katz, Sept. 10, 1955; children: Joseph Martin, Jay Steven, Sarah Keil. B.S., U. Pa., 1956; M.S.E., Princeton, 1957, M.A., 1958, Ph.D., 1960. With R.C.A., Princeton, N.J., 1959-60; asso. prof. N.Y. U., 1963-65; from asso. prof. to prof. elec. engrng. Poly. Inst. Bklyn., 1965-73; prof. dept. elec. and computer engrng. U. Mass., Amherst, 1973-85, chmn. dept., 1973-75; Stephen O. Rice prof. Ctr. Magnetic Rec. Research, dept. elec. engrng. and computer sci. U. Calif.-San Diego, La Jolla, 1985—. Mem. tech. staff Bell Telephone Labs., Murray Hill, N.J., 1968-69; prin. engr. Qualcomm Inc., San Diego, 1985. Editor for coding IEEE Transactions on Information Theory, 1969-72. Served with USAF, 1960-63. NSF sr. postdoctoral fellow, 1971-72; Guggenheim fellow, 1979-80 Fellow AAAS, IEEE (pres. info. theory group 1974, co-recipient info. theory group prize paper award 1975, co-recipient Comm. Soc. prize paper award 1993, Koji Kobayashi medal 1998, Claude Shannon lectr. 2001), Nat. Acad. Engring.; mem. Sigma Xi, Sigma Tau, Eta Kappa Nu, Pi Mu Epsilon, Tau Beta Pi. Achievements include research on information theory, communication theory, computer/communication networks, magnetic recording. Home: 8529 Prestwick Dr La Jolla CA 92037-2025 Office: U Calif San Diego 9500 Gilman Dr La Jolla CA 92093-5004

WOLF, JOSEPH ALBERT, mathematician, educator; b. Chgo., Oct. 18, 1936; s. Albert M. and Goldie (Wykoff) W. BS, U. Chgo., 1956, MS, 1957, PhD, 1959. Mem. Inst. for Advanced Study, Princeton, 1960-62, 65-66; asst. prof. U. Calif., Berkeley, 1962-64, assoc. prof., 1964-66, prof., 1966—, Miller research prof., 1972-73, 83-84; prof. honorario Universidad Nacional de Cordoba, Argentina, 1989. Vis. prof. Rutgers U., 1969-70, Hebrew U., Jerusalem, 1974-76, Tel Aviv U., 1974-76, Harvard U., 1979-80, 86 Author: Spaces of Constant Curvature, 1967, 72, 74, 77, 84, Unitary Representations on Partially Holomorphic Cohomology Spaces, 1974, Unitary Representations of Maximal Parabolic Subgroups of the Classical Groups, 1976, Classification and Fourier Inversion for Parabolic Subgroups with Square Integrable Nilradical, 1979; co-editor, author: Harmonic Analysis and Representations of Semisimple Lie Groups, 1980, The Penrose Transform and Analytic Cohomology in Representation Theory, 1993, Geometry and Representation Theory of Real and P-Adic Grps., 1997; editor Letters in Math. Physics, Jour. of Group Theory in Physics; contbr. articles to profl. jours. Alfred P. Sloan rsch. fellow, 1965-67, NSF fellow, 1959-62; recipient Médaille de l'Université de Liège, 1977, Humboldt prize, 1995. Mem. Am., Swiss Math. Socs. Office: U Calif Dept Math Berkeley CA 94720-0001 E-mail: jawolf@math.berkeley.edu

WOLF, PATRICIA B. museum director; Dir., exec. dir. Anchorage Mus. History and Art, 1989—. Office: Anchorage Mus History & Art 121 W 7th Ave Anchorage AK 99501-3611

WOLFE, AL, marketing and advertising consultant; b. Wyo., May 3, 1932; s. Clyde A. and Margaret V. (Joyce) W.; m. F. Carilouise, 1957 (div. 1994); m. Helen S., 1997; children: Kirk, Kelley, Alison. B.A. in Psychology, U. Wyo., 1958. Product mgr., merchandising mgr. Gen. Mills, Mpls., 1958-62; asst. mktg. dir., v.p., account supr. Compton Advt., Chgo. and N.Y.C., 1963-66; v.p., account supr., exec. v.p., gen. mgr. Wells Rich Greene, N.Y.C., 1967-76; exec. v.p., dir. N.W. Ayer ABH Internat., N.Y.C., 1976-81; mng. dir., pres., bd. dirs. DDB Needham Worldwide, Chgo., 1981-87, pres. U.S. Div., 1987-88; pres. Al Wolfe Assocs., Inc., Mktg. and Advt. Cons., Sedona, Ariz., 1989—. Bd. dirs. Clorox Co., Oakland, Calif. Bd. dirs. U. Wyo. Found., pres., 1993-94; past pres. bd. dirs. U. Wyo. Art Mus.; chmn. Sedona Med. Ctr. Found.; bd. dirs. Sedona Acad.; bd. dirs. Sedona Cultural Park. Recipient Disting. Alumnus award U. Wyo. 1981 Mem. Econ. Club (Chgo.), Sedona 30 Club. Home: 134 Back O Beyond Cir Sedona AZ 86336-6806 Office: Al Wolfe Assocs Inc PO Box 2367 Sedona AZ 86339-2367

WOLFE, CAMERON WITHGOT, JR. lawyer; b. Oakland, Calif., July 7, 1939; s. Cameron W. and Jean (Brown) W.; m. Frances Evelyn Bishopric, Sept. 2, 1964; children: Brent Everett, Julie Frances, Karen Jean. AB, U. Calif., Berkeley, 1961, JD, 1964. Bar: Calif. 1965, U.S. Dist. Ct. (no. dist.) Calif. 1965, U.S. Ct. Appeals (9th cir.) 1965, U.S. Tax Ct. 1966, U.S. Ct. Claims 1977, U.S. Ct. Appeals (3d cir.) 1980, U.S. Supreme Ct. 1986. Assoc., then ptnr. Orrick, Herrington & Sutcliffe, San Francisco, 1964—. Bd. dirs. Crowley Maritime Corp.; mem. steering com. Western Pension Conf. Pres. League To Save Lake Tahoe, 1979, 80; chmn. League To Save Lake Tahoe Charitable Truste, 1966-91, Piedmont Ednl. Fund Campaign, 1982-83; pres. Piedmont Ednl. Found., 1986-90; bd. dirs. Yosemite Fund, 1993—. With U.S. Army, 1957; with USAR, 1957-65. Mem. ABA (taxation com.), Calif. State Bar, San Francisco Bar Assn., San Francisco Tax Club (pres. 1997-98), Pacific Union Club, Claremont Country Club (Oakland, Calif.), Order of Coif, Phi Beta Kapa. Home: 59 Lakeview Ave Piedmont CA 94611-3514 Office: Orrick Herrington & Sutcliffe 400 Sansome St San Francisco CA 94111-3143

WOLFE, ROBERT A. aerospace executive; BS in Aerospace Engring., MS in Aerospace Engring., Ga. Inst. Tech. With McDonnell Douglas Corp.; sys. integration dir. for the Peacekeeper MIssile Martin Marietta, 1981-84; exec. v.p. govt. and space propulsion bus. Pratt & Whitney, 1990-93, sr. v.p. Ams., exec. v.p. Pratt & Whitney Group, 1994-97; pres. Pratt & Whitney Aircraft divsn. United Techs., 1994-97; pres. Aerojet GenCorp, Inc., Rancho-Cordova, Calif., 1997—, chmn., CEO, 1997—. With USN. Office: GenCorp Inc PO Box 537012 Sacramento CA

WOLFE, WILLIAM JEROME, librarian, English language educator; b. Chgo., Feb. 24, 1927; s. Fred Wiley and Helen Dorothea (Lovaas) W.; m. ViviAnn Lundin O'Connell, June 25, 1960 (div. 1962); 1 child, Lund. AB, U. Chgo., 1948; BA, Roosevelt U., Chgo., 1953; MEd, Chgo. State U., 1963; AA with high honors, Pima C.C., 1992; BA in Art magna cum laude, U. Ariz., 1994. Tchr. English John Marshall High Sch., Chgo., 1956-60; libr. Safford Jr. High Sch., Tucson, 1961-71, Santa Rita High Sch., Tucson, 1971-75, Tucson High Sch., 1975-87. Tutor Eastside Ctr., Literacy Vols. Tucson, 1988—, supr., 1993—. Co-founder Tucson Classic Guitar Soc., 1969-72; docent U. Ariz. Mus. Art, Tucson, 1989—; mem. adv. bd. U. Ariz. Sch. Music, 1995—; singer U. Ariz. Collegium Musicum, 1981-96, Lane Justus Chorale, 1996—; mem. U. Ariz. Scholarship Devel. Adv. Coun., 2000—. With U.S. Army, 1945-46, ETO. Recipient U. Ariz. Alumni Assn. Slonaker award, 2001. Mem. U. Ariz. Pres. Club, Assn. Literary Scholars and Critics, Tucson Guitar Soc. (treas. 2001—), Phi Kappa Phi. Mem. Ch. of Christ Scientist. Avocations: poetry writing, drawing, singing, piano, classical guitar. Home: 8460 E Rosewood St Tucson AZ 85710-1702 E-mail: wjwolfe@att.net

WOLFEN, WERNER F. lawyer; b. Berlin, May 15, 1930; came to U.S., 1939; s. Martin and Ruth Eva (Hamburger) W.; m. Mary Glasier, July 1, 1956; children: Richard, James, Lawrence (dec.). BS, U. Calif., Berkeley, 1950, JD, 1953. Bar: Calif. 1953. Assoc. Irell & Manella, L.A., 1953-57, ptnr., 1957-98, sr. ptnr. emeritus, 1999—; pres. Capri Investment Co. LLC, 1999—. Bd. dirs. BroadCom Corp., Rokenbok Toy Co., Vixel Corp., Sequal Tech. Corp. Bd. govs. UCLA Found., 1992—, L.A. Goal, 1994—, pres., 1994-99 Mem. ABA. Democrat. Jewish. Office: Capri Investment Co LLC 1800 Avenue of the Stars Los Angeles CA 90067-4212

WOLFF, BRIAN RICHARD, metal manufacturing company executive; b. L.A., Dec. 11, 1955; s. Arthur Richard and Dorothy Virginia (Johnson) W.; divorced; children: Ashley Rachael, Taryn Nicole. BSBA, Calif. State U., Chico, 1980; postgrad., U. Phoenix, 1990—. Registered counseling practitioner, Calif., 1996, guidance practitioner, Calif., 1996; ordained min. Progressive Universal Life Ch., 1996. Sales rep. Federated Metals Corp./ASARCO, Long Beach, Calif., 1980-82, dist. sales mgr., 1983-84; sales mgr. Copper Alloys Corp., Beverly Hills, 1982-83; dir. mktg. Federarted-Fry Metals/Cookson, Long Beach, Industry and Paramount, Calif., 1984-87; regional sales mgr. Colonial Metals Co., L.A., 1987-91; nat. sales mgr. Calif. Metal X/Metal Briquetting Co., L.A., 1991-93; sales engr. Ervin Industries, Inc., Ann Arbor, Mich., 1993-95. Tech. sales mgr. GSP Metals & Chems. Co., 1987-91; cons. sales Calif. Metal Exch., L.A., 1987-91, Atlas Pacific Inc., Bloomington, Calif., 1993—. Co-prodn. Issues, pub. comedy weekly TV show. Mem. citizens adv. com. on bus. Calif. Legis., 1983; ordained min. Universal Life, 1996. Mem. Non Ferrous Founders Soc., Am. Foundrymen Soc., Calif. Cast Metals Assn., Steel Structures Painting Coun., Am. Electroplaters Soc., Soc. Die Cast Engrs., NRA. Republican. Presbyterian. Avocations: scuba diving, tennis, freshwater fishing, trap shooting, hunting.

WOLFF, GEOFFREY ANSELL, novelist, critic, educator; b. L.A., Nov. 5, 1937; s. Arthur Saunders III and Rosemary (Loftus) W.; m. Priscilla Bradley Porter, Aug. 21, 1965; children: Nicholas Hinckley, Justin Porter. Grad., Choate Sch., 1955; student, Eastbourne (Eng.) Coll., 1955-56; BA summa cum laude, Princeton U., 1961; postgrad., Churchill Coll., Cambridge U., Eng., 1963-64. Lectr. in comparative lit. Robert Coll., Istanbul, Turkey, 1961-63; lectr. in Am. civilization Istanbul U., 1962-63; lectr. aesthetics Md. Inst. Coll. Art, 1965-69; vis. lectr. creative arts Princeton (N.J.) U., 1970-71, Ferris prof., 1980, 92; writer-in-residence Brandeis U., Waltham, Mass., 1982-95; prof. English and creative writing U. Calif., Irvine, 1995—. Lectr. English lit. Middlebury (Vt.) Coll., 1976, 78; vis. lectr. Columbia U., N.Y.C., 1979, Brown U., Providence, 1981, 88, Boston U., 1981; mem. policy panel in lit. NEA; book critic Esquire mag., 1979-81; founder Golden Horn lit. mag., 1972; vis. prof. Williams Coll., 1994; dir. program writing, prof. English U. Calif., Irvine, 1995—. Author: Bad Debts, 1969, The Sightseer, 1974, Black Sun, 1976, Inklings, 1978, The Duke of Deception, 1979, Providence, 1986; editor: Best American Essays, 1989, The Final Club, 1990, A Day at the Beach, 1992, The Age of Consent, 1995; book editor Washington Post, 1964-69, Newsweek mag., 1969-71, New Times mag., 1974-79; contbr. to mags. Recipient Award in Lit., Am. Acad. of Arts and Letters, 1994, R.I. Gov.'s Arts award, 1992; Woodrow Wilson fellow, 1961-62, 63-64, Fulbright fellow, 1963-64, Guggenheim fellow, 1972-73, 77-78, NEH sr. fellow, 1974-75, NEA fellow, 1979-80, 86-87, Am. Coun. Learned Socs. fellow, 1983-84, Lila Wallace Writing fellow, 1992. Mem. PEN, Princeton Club (N.Y.C.), Colonial CLub (Princeton), Dunes Club. Office: U Calif Program in Writing Dept English Irvine CA 92797-2650

WOLFF, HERBERT ERIC, banker, former army officer; b. Cologne, Germany, May 24, 1925; s. Hugo and Juanna Anna (Van Dam) W.; m. Alice (Billy) Rafael, Nov. 13, 1946 (dec. July, 1987); children: Karen (dec. Jan., 1992), Herbert E., Allen R. BA, Rutgers U., 1953; BS, U. Md., 1957; MA, George Washington U., 1962; grad., U.S. Army War Coll., 1962, Harvard U., 1979. Commd. 2nd lt. U.S. Army, 1945, advanced through grades to maj. gen.; served in Fed. Republic of Germany, Greece, Iran, Republic of Korea, Australia, New Guinea, The Phillipines, Japan and Socialist Republic of Vietnam; dep. dir. ops. NSA-CSS, Ft. Meade, Md., 1973-75; dep. corps. comdr. V. Corps U.S. Army, Frankfurt, Germany, 1975-77, comdr. gen. U.S. Army Western Command Hawaii, 1977-81; with First Hawaiian Bank, Honolulu, 1981-2000, sr. v.p., corp. sec., to 2000; hon. consul gen. (Datό) U.S. Pacific region Govt. of Malaysia, Honolulu, 1985—. Author: The Man on Horseback, 1962, The Tenth Principle of War, 1964, Public Support, 1964, The Military Instructor, 1968. Mem. exec. bd. Aloha coun. Boy Socuts Am.; bd. dirs. USO, Girl Scouts of U.S., Hawaii; v.p. Hawaii Com. Fgn. Rels.; past pres. Pacific Asian Affairs Coun.; pres. Hawaii Army Mus. Soc. Decorated Bronze Star with V and 3 oak leaf clusters U.S. Army, Air medal (24) U.S. Army, Joint Services commendation medal U.S. Army, Army Commendation medal U.S. Army, Purple Heart, Gallantry Cross with 2 palms, Gallantry Cross with palm and silver star Nat. Order 5th class S. Vietnam, Order Nat. Security Merit Choen-Su S. Korea, D.S.M. with oak leaf clusters (2), U.S. Army, Silver Star with oak leaf cluster U.S. Army, Legion of Merit with 3 oak leaf clusters U.S. Army,

D.F.C. U.S. Army, Combat Infantry Badge with two stars, master parachutist, Army aviator; named Citizen of Yr. Fed. Exec. Bd., 1987. Mem. 1st Inf. Divsn. Assn., 1st Cav. Divsn. Assn., Plaza Club (pres., bd. dirs.), Honolulu Country Club, Waialae Country Club, Rotary, Phi Kappa Phi. Office: First Hawaiian Center 999 Bishop St Honolulu HI 96813-0001 E-mail: generalherbwolff@aol.com

WOLFF, MANFRED ERNST, medicinal chemist, pharmaceutical company executive; b. Berlin, Feb. 14, 1930; came to U.S., 1933; s. Adolph Abraham and Kate (Fraenkel) W.; m. Helen S. Scandalis, Aug. 1, 1953 (div. 1971); children: Stephen Andrew, David James, Edward Allen; m. Susan E. Hurbert, Jan. 19, 1973 (div. 1975); m. A. Gloria Johnson, Dec. 25, 1982. BS, U. Calif. at Berkeley, 1951, MS, 1953, PhD, 1955. Registered U.S. patent agt. Rsch. fellow U. Va., 1955-57; sr. medicinal chemist Smith, Kline & French Labs., Phila., 1957-60; mem. faculty U. Calif., San Francisco, 1960-82, prof. medicinal chemistry, 1965-82, chmn. dept. pharm. chemistry, 1970-82; dir. discovery rsch. Allergan Labs, Irvine, Calif., 1982-84; v.p. discovery rsch. Allergan Pharms., Irvine, 1984-89; v.p. R & D Immunopharmaceutics Inc., San Diego, 1989-91, sr. v.p. R & D, 1991-95; pres. Intellepharm., Inc., Laguna Beach, Calif., 1997—. Adj. prof. medicinal chemistry U. So. Calif., 1982—; elected mem. U.S. Pharm. Conv. Com. of Revision, 1990—. Editor: Burger's Medicinal Chemistry and Drug Discovery, Vol. 1-5, 5th edit., 1995-97; asst. editor Jour. Medicinal Chemistry, 1968-71; mem. editl. bd. Medicinal Chemistry Rsch., 1991-95, PharmSci., 1999—; contbr. articles to profl. jours.; patentee in field. Fellow AAAS, Am Assn. Pharm. Scientists; mem. Am. Chem. Soc., Licensing Execs. Soc. Achievements include discovery of Alphagan and Lumigan medicines for glaucoma, Tazorac medicine for psoriasis, and Sitaxsentan medicine for congestive heart failure. E-mail: drwolff@aol.com

WOLFF, SHELDON, radiobiologist, educator; b. Peabody, Mass., Sept. 22, 1928; s. Henry Herman and Goldie (Lipchitz) W.; m. Frances Faye Farbstein, Oct. 23, 1954; children: Victor Charles, Roger Kenneth, Jessica Raye. B.S. magna cum laude, Tufts U., 1950; M.A., Harvard U., 1951, Ph.D., 1953. Teaching fellow Harvard U., 1951-52; sr. research staff biology div. Oak Ridge Nat. Lab., 1953-66; prof. cytogenetics and radiology U. Calif., San Francisco, 1966-94; prof. emeritus, 1994—; dir. Lab. Radiobiology and Environ. Health U. Calif., San Francisco, 1983-95; vice chmn., chief rsch. Radiation Effects Rsch. Found., Hiroshima, Japan, 1996-2000. Vis. prof. radiation biology U. Tenn., 1962, lectr., 1953-65; cons. several fed. sci. agys.; mem. health and environ. rsch. adv. com. U.S. Dept. Energy, 1986—, chmn., 1987-95; co-chmn. Joint NIH/Dept. Energy Subcom. on Human Genome, 1989-94. Editor: Chromosoma, 1983-97 ; assoc. editor: Cancer Research, 1983-97; Editorial bd.: Radiation Research, 1968-72, Photochemistry and Photobiology, 1962-72, Radiation Botany, 1964-86, Mutation Research, 1964-97, Caryologia, 1967-96, Radiation Effects, 1969-81, Genetics, 1972-85; Contbr. articles to sci. jours. Recipient E.O. Lawrence meml. award U.S. AEC, 1973, 1st ann. Belle award, 1998. Mem. Genetics Soc. Am., Radiation Rsch. Soc. (counselor for biology 1968-72, Failla lectr. 1992, medal 1992), Am. Soc. Cell Biology, Environmental Mutagen Soc. (coun. 1972-75, pres. 1980-81, award 1982), Internat. Assn. Environ. Mutagen Socs. (treas. 1978-85), Sigma Xi. Democrat. Home: 41 Eugene St Mill Valley CA 94941-1717 Office: U Calif Dept Radiology San Francisco CA 94143-0001

WOLFF, SIDNEY CARNE, astronomer, observatory administrator; b. Sioux City, Iowa, June 6, 1941; d. George Albert and Ethel (Smith) Carne; m. Richard J. Wolff, Aug. 29, 1962 BA, Carleton Coll., 1962, DSc (hon.), 1985; PhD, U. Calif., Berkeley, 1966. Postgrad. research fellow Lick Obs, Santa Cruz, Calif., 1969; asst. astronomer U. Hawaii, Honolulu, 1967-71, assoc. astronomer, 1971-76; astronomer, assoc. dir. Inst. Astronomy, Honolulu, 1976-83, acting dir., 1983-84; dir. Kitt Peak Nat. Obs., Tucson, 1984-87, Nat. Optical Astronomy Observatories, 1987-2001; dir. Gemini Project Gemini 8-Meter Telescopes Project, 1992-94; astronomer, project scientist Large Synoptic Survey Telescope, 2001—. Pres. SOAR Inc., 1999—. Author: The A-Type Stars--Problems and Perspectives, 1983, (with others) Exploration of the Universe, 1987, Realm of the Universe, 1988, Frontiers of Astronomy, 1990, Voyages Through the Universe, 1996, Voyages to the Planets, 1999, Voyages to the Stars and Galaxies, 1999; contbr. articles to profl. jours. Trustee Carleton Coll., 1989—. Rsch. fellow Lick Obs. Santa Cruz, Calif., 1967; recipient Nat. Meritorious Svc. award NSF, 1994. Fellow Royal Astronical Soc.; mem. Astron. Soc. Pacific (pres. 1984-86, bd. dirs. 1979-85), Am. Astron. Soc. (coun. 1983-86, pres.-elect 1991, pres. 1992-94). Office: Nat Optical Astronomy Obs PO Box 26732 950 N Cherry Ave Tucson AZ 85719-4933

WOLFF, TOBIAS (JONATHAN ANSELL WOLFF), writer; b. Birmingham, Ala., June 19, 1945; s. Arthur Saunders and Rosemary (Loftus) W.; m. Catherine Dolores Spohn, 1975, children: Michael, Patrick, Mary Elizabeth. BA, Oxford Univ., 1972, MA, 1975, Stanford Univ., 1978; LHD (hon.), Santa Clara Univ., 1996. Mem. faculty Stanford (Calif.) U., Goddard Coll., Plainfield, Vt., Ariz. State U., Tempe, Syracuse (N.Y.) U., Stanford (Calif.) U.; reporter Washington Post. Author: In the Garden of the North American Martyrs, 1981 (St. Lawrence award for fiction 1982), The Barracks Thief, 1984 (PEN/Faulkner award for fiction 1985), Back in the World, 1985, This Boy's Life: A Memoir, 1989 (L.A. Times Book prize 1989), In Pharaoh's Army: Memories of the Lost War, 1994 (Esquire-Volvo-Winterstone's award, Eng., 1994), The Night in Question, 1996; editor: Matters of Life and Death: New American Stories, 1983, The Stories of Anton Chekhov, 1987, Best American Short Stories, 1994, The Vintage Book of Contemporary American Stories, 1994. Recipient Wallace Stegner fellowship in creative writing, 1975-76; Nat. Endowment for the Arts fellowship in creative writing, 1978, 85; Mary Roberts Rinehart award, 1979; Ariz. Coun. on Arts and Humanities fellowship in creative writing, 1980, Guggenheim fellowship, 1982; Rea award, 1989; Whiting Writer's award, 1989, Lila-Wallace-Reader's Digest award, 1993, Lyndhurst Found. award, 1994, award of merit Am. Acad. Arts and Letters, 2001. Office: Stanford U Dept English Stanford CA 94305-2087

WOLFGANG, BONNIE ARLENE, musician, bassoonist; b. Caribou, Maine, Sept. 29, 1944; d. Ralph Edison and Arlene Alta (Obetz) W.; m. Eugene Alexander Pridonoff, July 3, 1965 (div. Sept. 1977); children: George Randall, Anton Alexander, Stephan Eugene. MusB, Curtis Inst. Music, Phila., 1967. Soloist Phila. Orch., 1966; soloist with various orchs. U.S., Cen. Am., 1966-75; prin. bassoonist Phoenix Symphony, 1976—, with Woodwind Quintet, 1986—. Home: 9448 N 106th St Scottsdale AZ 85258-6056

WOLFINGER, RAYMOND EDWIN, political science educator; b. San Francisco, June 29, 1931; s. Raymond Edwin and Hilda (Holm) W.; m. Barbara Kaye, Aug. 8, 1960; 1 son, Nicholas Holm. A.B., U. Calif.-Berkeley, 1951; M.A., U. Ill., 1955; Ph.D., Yale U., 1961. Asst. prof. polit. sci. Stanford (Calif.) U., Calif., 1961-66; assoc. prof. Stanford U., 1966-70, prof., 1970-71, U. Calif.-Berkeley, 1971—, Heller prof. polit. sci., 1995—. Dir. U. Calif. Data Archive and Tech. Assistance, 1980-92; chmn. bd. overseers Nat. Election Studies, Ann Arbor, Mich., 1982-86 Author: The Politics of Progress, 1974, (with others) Dynamics of American Politics, 1976, 80, (with Steven J. Rosenstone) Who Votes, 1980, (with others) The Myth of the Independent Voter, 1992; mem. editorial bd. Brit. Jour. Polit. Sci., 1980-84, Am. Polit. Sci. Rev., 1985-88. Bd. dirs. S.W. Voter Rsch. Inst., San Antonio, 1988-96, Consortium of Social Sci. Assns., 1987-93, pres. 1988-90. 1st lt. U.S. Army, 1951-53. Fellow Ctr. for Advanced Study in Behavioral Scis., 1960-61; Guggenheim fellow, 1965; Ford Found. faculty research fellow, 1970-71 Fellow Am. Acad. Arts and Scis. (chair Class III membership com. 1998-99); mem. Am. Polit. Sci. Assn. (sec. 1981-82), AAUP (council 1981-84), Western Polit. Sci. Assn. (v.p. 1988-89, pres. 1989-90). Democrat. Office: U Calif Dept Polit Sci Berkeley CA 94720-1950

WOLFLE, DAEL LEE, public affairs educator; b. Puyallup, Wash., Mar. 5, 1906; s. David H. and Elizabeth (Pauly) W.; m. Helen Morrill, Dec. 28, 1929 (dec. July 1988); children: Janet Helen (Mrs. Wilhelm G. Christophersen), Lee Morrill, John Morrill. B.S., U. Wash., 1927, M.S., 1928; postgrad., U. Chgo., summers 1929, 30; Ph.D., Ohio State U., 1931, D.Sc., 1957, Drexel U., 1956, Western Mich. U., 1960. Instr. psychology Ohio State U., 1929-32; prof. psychology U. Miss., 1932-36; examiner in biol. scis. U. Chgo., 1936-39, asst. prof. psychology, 1938-43, assoc. prof., 1943-45; on leave for war work with Signal Corps, 1941-43; with OSRD, 1944-45; exec. sec. Am. Psychol. Assn., 1946-50; dir. commn. on human resources and advanced tng. Assoc. Research Councils, 1950-54; exec. officer AAAS, 1954-70; editor Sci., 1955, pub., 1955-70; prof. pub. affairs U. Wash., Seattle, 1970-76, prof. emeritus, 1976—. Mem. sci. adv. bd. USAF, 1953-57; mem. def. sci. bd. Dept. Def., 1957-61; mem. adv. council on mental health NIMH, 1960-64; mem. nat. adv. health council USPHS, 1965-66; mem. commn. on human resources NRC, 1974-78; mem. adv. bd. Geophys. Inst., Fairbanks, Alaska., 1970-93, chmn. adv. bd., 1972-81 Author: Factor Analysis to 1940, 1941, Science and Public Policy 1959, The Uses of Talent, 1971, The Home of Science, 1972, Renewing a Scientific Society, 1989; editor: America's Resources of Specialized Talent, 1954. Trustee Russell Sage Found., 1961-78, Pacific Sci. Cent. Found., 1962-80, Biol. Scis. Curriculum Study, 1980-85; chmn. bd. J. McK. Cattell Fund, 1962-82. Named Alumnus Summa Laude Dignatus, U. Wash., 1979; named one of 100 Alumni of the Century, U. Wash., 1999. Mem. AAAS, (pres. Pacific divsn. 1991-92, exec. com. 1990—), AAUP, APA, Am. Acad. Arts and Scis. (exec. com. western sect. 1985-92), Sigma Xi. Home: University House 4400 Stone Way N Apt #433 Seattle WA 98103 Office: U Wash Box 353055 Grad Sch Pub Affairs Seattle WA 98195-3055

WOLFMAN, EARL FRANK, JR. surgeon, educator; b. Buffalo, Sept. 14, 1926; s. Earl Frank and Alfreda (Peterson) W.; m. Lois Jeannette Walker, Dec. 28, 1946; children— Nancy Jeannette, David Earl, Carol Anne. BS cum laude, Harvard U., 1946; MD cum laude, U. Mich., 1950. Diplomate Am. Bd. Surgery. Intern U. Mich., Ann Arbor, 1950-51, asst. resident in surgery, 1951-52, resident in surgery, 1954-55, from jr. clin. instr. surgery to assoc. prof., 1955-66, asst. to dean, 1960-61, asst. dean, 1961-64; practice medicine specializing in surgery, 1957—, Sacramento, 1966—; prof. surgery Sch. Medicine, U. Calif., Davis, 1966—, chmn. dept. surgery, 1966-78, assoc. dean, 1966-76, mem. staff, chief surg. svcs. Med. Ctr., 1966-78, chmn. div. surg. scis., 1966-78. Contbr. articles to profl. jours. Served to lt. M.C. USNR, 1952-54. Fellow ACS; mem. AMA (del. 1987-99), Ctrl. Surg. Soc., Western Surg. Soc., Sacramento Surg. Soc., Pacific Coast Surg. Soc., Calif. Acad. Medicine, Frederick A. Coller Surg. Soc., Soc. Surgery Alimentary Tract, Am. Assn. Endocrine Surgeons, Sacramento Med. Soc., Yolo Med. Soc., Calif. Med. Assn. (trustee 1991-2000), Am. Soc. Gen. Surgeons. Methodist. Home: 44770 N El Macero Dr El Macero CA 95618-1085 Office: U Calif Davis Sch Medicine Dept Surgery 2221 Stockton Blvd Fl 3 Sacramento CA 95817-2214 E-mail: efwolfman@ucdavis.edu

WOLFORD, RICHARD, food products executive; CEO Del Monte Foods, San Francisco, 1997—. Office: Del Monte Foods PO Box 193575 San Francisco CA 94119-3575

WOLFSON, MARK ALAN, investor, business educator; b. Chgo., Sept. 25, 1952; s. Jack and Maribelle (Simen) W.; m. Sheila Rae Aronesti, Aug. 3, 1975; children: Laura Rachel, Charles Michael. BS in Acctg. and Fin., U. Ill., 1973, M Acctg. Sci., 1974, PhD in Acctg., U. Tex., 1977. Asst. prof. acctg. Stanford (Calif.) U., 1977-81, assoc. prof., 1981-85, prof., 1985-87, Joseph McDonald prof., 1987-92, assoc. dean, 1990-93; Dean Witter prof. acctg. and fin., 1992-96; prof. acctg. and fin., 1996-2000; mng. ptnr. Oak Hill Capital Mgmt., 1998—; ptnr. Oak Hill Venture Ptnrs., 1999—; prin. Oak Hill Platinum Ptnrs., 2001—. Ford Found. vis. assoc. prof. U. Chgo., 1981-82; Thomas Henry Carroll vis. prof. Harvard U., Boston, 1988-89; cons. Fin. Acctg. Stds. Bd., Norwalk, Conn., 1985, 89-92; rsch. assoc. Nat. Bur. Econ. Rsch., Cambridge, Mass., 1988—; steering com. Stanford Inst. Econ. Policy Rsch., 1990-2000; task force Fed. Home Loan Bank Bd., 1989; v.p. Keystone Inc., 1995—; bd. dirs. Investment Tech. Group, Caribbean Restaurants, DaVinci I, eGain Comm., Fin. Engines, Inc., Oreck Corp.; bd. advisors FEP Capital, 230 Park Investors; gen. ptnr. P & PK Family Ltd. Partnership; cons. in field. Mem. numerous editl. bds. of finance, econs., and acctg. jours.; contbr. numerous articles to profl. jours. Recipient Pomerance prize Chgo. Bd. Options Exch., 1981, Disting. Tchg. award Stanford U., 1990, Notable Contbn. to Lit. award AICPA-Am. Acctg. Assn., 1990, 92, Wildman award, 1991; named Disting. Accountancy Alumnus, U. Ill., 1989. Jewish. Office: Oak Hill Capital 2775 Sand Hill Rd Ste 220 Menlo Park CA 94025-7019

WOLINSKY, LEO C. newspaper editor; BA in Journalism, U. So. Calif., 1972. Journalist, 1972—; staff writer L.A. Times, 1977-86, dep. chief Sacramento bur., 1987-89, city editor, 1990, Calif. polit. editor, 1991, metro editor, asst. mng. editor, 1994-97, mng. editor, 1997-99, exec. editor, 2000—. Office: Los Angeles Times Times Mirror Sq Los Angeles CA 90053

WOLK, BRUCE ALAN, law educator; b. Bklyn., Mar. 2, 1946; s. Morton and Gertrude W.; m. Lois Gloria Krepliak, June 22, 1968; children: Adam, Daniel. BS, Antioch Coll., 1968; MS, Stanford U., 1972; JD, Harvard U., 1975. Bar: D.C. 1975. Assoc. Hogan & Hartson, Washington, 1975-78; prof. U. Calif. Sch. Law, Davis, 1978—, acting dean, 1990-91, dean, 1993-98. Danforth Found. fellow, 1970-74, NSF fellow, 1970-72, Fulbright sr. research fellow, 1985-86. Mem. ABA, Am. Law Inst. Office: Univ Cal Davis Sch Law King Hall 400 Mrak Hall Dr Davis CA 95616-5201

WOLK, MARTIN, physicist, electronics engineer; b. Long Branch, N.J., Jan. 13, 1930; s. Michael and Tillie (Barron) W.; 1 child, Brett Martin. BS, George Washington U., 1957, MS, 1968; PhD, U. N.Mex., 1973. Physicist Naval Ordnance Lab., White Oak, Md., 1957-59, Nat. Oceanic and Atmospheric Adminstrn., Suitland, 1959-66; solid state physicist Night Vision Lab., Fort Belvoir, Va., 1967-69; rsch. asst. U. N.Mex., Albuquerque, 1969-73; electronics engr. Washington Navy Yard, 1976-83, TRW, Inc., Redondo Beach, Calif., 1983-84; physicist Metrology Engrng. Ctr., Pomona, 1984-85; electronics engr. Naval Aviation Depot North Island, San Diego, 1985—. Cons. Marine Corps Logistics Base, Barstow, Calif., 1985—, Naval Weapons Station, Fallbrook, Calif., 1987-89, Naval Weapons Support Ctr., Crane, Ind., 1989—. Contbr. articles to Jour. Quantitative Spectroscopy and Radiative Transfer, Monthly Weather Rev., Proceedings of SPIE, Procs. of EUROPTO. Cpl. 11th Airborne Div., 511 Parachute Infantry Reg., U.S. Army, 1946-49, Japan. Mem. IEEE, Soc. Photo-Optical Instrumentation Engrng., European Optical Soc., Sigma Pi Sigma, Sigma Tau. Achievements include development of first Tiros meteorological satellites; research on electron-beam for micro-circuit device fabrication; development of electro-optical calibration systems for the TOW missile system optical and night vision sights for the Marine Corps; development of visible and infrared spectral radiometric system utilizing a Fourier Transform Interferometer spectrometer and dual conjugate Cassegrainian optical telescopes for primary standards calibration of thermal radiation sources for the Navy. Home: 740 Eastshore Ter Unit 91 Chula Vista CA 91913-2421

WOLKOV, HARVEY BRIAN, radiation oncologist, researcher; b. Cleve., Feb. 8, 1953; s. Sidney and Norma (Levin) W.; m. Lauren Cronin, Jan. 9, 1993; 1 child, Nicole. BSc, Purdue U., 1975, MSc, 1977; MD, Medical Coll. Ohio, 1979. Diplomate Am. Bd. Radiology. Intern U. Calif., San Francisco, 1979-80; res. Stanford Med. Ctr., Stanford, Calif., 1980-83; rsch. asst. Stanford (Calif.) U., 1982; from asst. clin. prof. to assoc. clin. prof. U. Calif., Davis, 1983-97, assoc. clin. prof., 1997—; medical dir. Mercy Hosps., Sacramento, 1987-90; med. dir. Sutter Cancer Ctr. Dept. Radiation Oncology, Sacramento, 1990—. Co-prin. investigator Pediat. Oncology Group, Chgo., 1989—; adv. bd. Nat. Graves Disease Found., Jacksonville, Fla., 1993—; dir. Sutter Gamma Knife Ctr., 1997—; bd. dirs. Sutter Hosps. Found., Sacramento. Author: (with others) Intraoperative Radiation, 1989, Frontiers in Radiation, 1991, Textbook Radiation Oncology, 1998, Internat. Jour. Bd. Biol. Physics; contbr. 30 articles to profl. jours. Fellow Am. Cancer Soc., 1978, 1983, Am. Coll. Radiology, 1997; recipient Travel award Am. Soc. Therapeutic Radiology Oncology, Reston, Va., 1987. Mem. Am. Coll. Radiolgy (chmn. standards accreditation com. 1997—, councilor at large 1999, alt. councilor 2000—, mem. expert panels), Am. Cancer Soc. (reviewer 1990—), Assn. Residents Radiation Oncology (exec. com. 1997—), Council Affiliated Radiation Oncology Soc. (pres. 1999-2001), No. Calif. Radiation Oncology Soc. (pres. 1999—), Radiation Therapy Oncology Group (com. chair 1986-90, publication com. 1990—, mem. com. 1990—, lung and brain com. 1990—), Am. Soc. Therapeutic Radiology and Oncology (vice chair outcome rsch., fin. com., bd. dirs. 2000—), Calif. Radiation Oncology Soc. (pres.-elect 1999, pres. 2000-2001), Sulter Inst. for Medical Rsch., 1989— (chair rsch. com. 1996—). Jewish. Avocations: oil painting, sculpture, travel. Office: Sutter Cancer Ctr 2800 L St Ste 10 Sacramento CA 95816-5616 E-mail: hbwolkov@aol.com

WOLLENBERG, RICHARD PETER, paper manufacturing company executive; b. Juneau, Alaska, Aug. 1, 1915; s. Harry L. and Gertrude (Arnstein) W.; m. Leone Bonney, Dec. 22, 1940; children: Kenneth Roger, David Arthur, Keith Kermit, Richard Harry, Carol Lynne. BSME, U. Calif., Berkeley, 1936; MBA, Harvard U., 1938; grad., Army Indsl. Coll., 1941; D in Pub. Affairs (hon.), U. Puget Sound, 1977. Prodn. control Bethlehem Ship, Quincy, Mass., 1938-39; with Longview (Wash.) Fibre Co., 1939—, safety engr., asst. chief engr., chief engr., mgr. container operations, 1951-57, v.p., 1953-57, v.p. ops., 1957-60, exec. v.p., 1960-69, pres., 1969-78, pres., chief exec. officer, 1978-85, pres., chief exec. officer, chmn. bd., 1985—, also bd. dirs. Mem. Wash. State Council for Postsecondary Edn., 1969-79, chmn., 1970-73; mem. western adv. bd. Factory Mutual Ins Co. Bassoonist SW Washington Symphony. Trustee Reed Coll., Portland, 1962—, chmn. bd. 1982-90. Served to lt. col. USAAF, 1941-45. Recipient Alumni Achievement award Harvard U., 1994. Mem. NAM (bd. dirs. 1981-86), Pacific Coast Assn. Pulp and Paper Mfrs. (pres. 1981-92), Inst. Paper Sci. and Tech. (trustee), Wash. State Roundtable. Home: 1632 Kessler Blvd Longview WA 98632-3633 Office: Longview Fibre Co PO Box 606 Longview WA 98632-7391

WOLLERSHEIM, JANET PUCCINELLI, psychology educator; b. Anaconda, Mont., July 24, 1936; d. Nello J. and Inez Marie (Ungaretti) Puccinelli; m. David E. Wollersheim, Aug. 1, 1959 (div. June 1972); children: Danette Marie, Tod Neil; m. Daniel J. Smith, July 17, 1976. AB, Gonzaga U., 1958; MA, St. Louis U., 1960; PhD, U. Ill., 1968. Lic. psychologist, Mont. Asst. prof. psychology, asst. dir. testing/counseling ctr. U. Mo., 1968-71; prof. psychology U. Mont., Missoula, 1971—, dir. clin. psychology, 1980-87; chair Mont. Bd. Psychologists, 1977-78; cons. Mont. State Prison, 1971-85, Trapper Creek Job Corps, 1973—; pvt. practice Missoula, 1971—. Author numerous rsch. articles. Bd. dirs. Crisis Ctr., Missoula, 1972-73; mem. profl. adv. bd. Head Start, Missoula, 1972-79. Recipient Disting. scholar award U. Mont., 1991. Fellow Am. Psychol. Assn. (bd. dirs. div. clin. psychology 1990-92); mem. Rocky Mountain Psychol. Assn. (pres. 1983-84), Nat. Coun. Univ. Dirs. Clin. Psychology (bd. dirs. 1982-88). Home and Office: 105 Greenwood Ln Missoula MT 59803-2401 E-mail: jpwoller2000@yahoo.com

WOLPER, DAVID LLOYD, motion picture and television executive; b. N.Y.C., Jan. 11, 1928; s. Irving S. and Anna (Fass) W.; m. Margaret Dawn Richard, May 11, 1958 (div.); children: Mark, Michael, Leslie; m. Gloria Diane Hill, July 11, 1974. Student, Drake U., 1946, U. So. Calif., 1948. V.p., treas. Flamingo Films, TV sales co., 1948-50, v.p. West Coast Ops., 1954-58; chmn., pres. Wolper Prodns., L.A., 1958—. Cons., exec. producer Warner Bros., Inc., 1976—. TV prodns. include Race for Space, Making of the President 1960, 64, Biography series, Story of... series, The Yanks are Coming, Berlin: Kaiser to Khrushchev, December 7: Day of Infamy, The American Woman in the 20th Century, Hollywood and The Stars, March of Time Specials, The Rise and Fall of the Third Reich, The Legend of Marilyn Monroe, Four Days in November, Krebiozen and Cancer, National Geographic, Undersea World of Jacques Cousteau, China: Roots of Madness, The Journey of Robert F. Kennedy, Say Goodbye, George Plimpton, Appointment With Destiny, American Heritage, Smithsonian, They've Killed President Lincoln, Sandburg's Lincoln, Primal Man, The First Woman President, Chico and the Man, Get Christie Love, Welcome Back, Kotter!, Collison Course, Roots, Victory at Entebbe, Roots: The Next Generations, Moviola, The Thorn Birds, North and South Books I, II, III, Napoleon and Josephine, Alex Haley's Queen, Men Of The Dragon, Unwed Father, The Morning After; feature films include The Hellstrom Chronicle, Devil's Brigade, The Bridge at Remagen, If It's Tuesday, This Must Be Belgium, Willy Wonka and The Chocolate Factory, Visions of Eight, This is Elvis, Murder in the First, Surviving Picasso, L.A. Confidential; live spl. events include Opening and Closing Ceremonies 1984 Olympic Games, Liberty Weekend July 3-6, 1986. Trustee L.A. County Mus. Art, Am. Film Inst., L.A. Thoracic and Cardiovascular Found., Boys and Girls Clubs Am., U.S. Golf Assn. Found.; bd. dirs. Amateur Athletic Assn. L.A., L.A. Heart Inst., Acad. TV Arts and Scis. Found., So. Calif. Com. for Olympic Games, U. Soc. Calif. Cinema/TV Dept.; bd. govs. Cedars Sinai Med. Ctr.; com. mem. U.S. Olympic Team Benefit; mem. adv. com. Nat. Ctr. Jewish Film. Recipient award for documentaries San Francisco Internat. Film Festival, 1960, 7 Golden Globe awards, 5 George Foster Peabody awards, Disting. Service award U.S. Jr. C. of C.; 40 Emmy awards, 145 Emmy nominations Acad. TV Arts and Scis.; Monte Carlo Internat. Film Festival award, 1964, Cannes Film Festival Grand Prix for TV Programs, 1964; Oscar award, 11 Oscar nominations, Jean Hersholt Humanitarian award Acad. Motion Picture and TV Scis., medal of Chevalier The French Nat. Legion of Honor, 1990; named to TV Hall of Fame, 1988. Mem. Nat. Acad. TV Arts and Scis., Acad. Motion Picture Arts and Scis., Producers Guild Am., Caucus for Producers, Writers and Dirs. Office: c/o Warner Bros Inc 4000 Warner Blvd Burbank CA 91522-0001

WOLTIL, ROBERT D. healthcare management company executive; BS in Acctg. and Finance, U. South Fla. CPA, Fla. Various positions including pres., CEO pharmacy subs. Beverly Enterprises Inc., then CFO; CFO, sr. v.p. fin. svcs. Sun Healthcare Group Inc., Albuquerque, 1996—. Office: Sun Healthcare Group Inc 101 Sun Ave NE Albuquerque NM 87109-4373

WOLYNES, PETER GUY, chemistry researcher, educator; b. Chgo., Apr. 21, 1953; s. Peter and Evelyn Eleanor (Etter) W.; m. Jane Lee Fox, Nov. 26, 1976 (div. 1980); m. Kathleen Cull Bucher, Dec. 22, 1984; children: Margrethe Cull, Eve Cordelia, Julia Jean. AB with highest distinction, Ind. U., 1971; AM, Harvard U., 1972, PhD in Chem. Physics, 1976; DSc (hon.), Ind. U., 1988. Rsch. assoc. MIT, Cambridge, 1975-76; asst. prof., assoc. prof. Harvard U., Cambridge, 1976-80; vis. scientist Max Planck Inst. für Biophysikalische Chemie, Gottingen, Fed. Republic Germany, 1977; assoc. prof. chemistry U. Ill., Urbana, 1980-83, prof. chemistry, 1983-2000, prof.

physics, 1985-2000, prof. physics and biophysics, 1989-2000, mem. Ctr. for Advanced Study, 1989-2000; William H. and Janet LyCan prof. chemistry Ctr. for Advanced Study U. Ill., Urbana, 1993-96, Robert Eiszner prof., 1996-2000; prof. chemistry and biochemistry U. Calif., San Diego, 2000—, Francis H.C. Crick prof., 2001—. Vis. prof. Inst. for Molecular Sci., Okazaki, Japan, 1982, 87; vis. scientist Inst. for Theoretical Physics, Santa Barbara, Calif., 1987, Ecole normale Supérieure, Paris, 1992, Merski lectr. U. Nebr., 1986, Denkewalter lectr., Loyola U., 1986; Hinshelwood lectr. Oxford U., 1997, Harkins lectr., U. Chgo., 1997; FMC lectr. Princeton U., 1998. Contbr. numerous articles to profl. jours. Sloan fellow, 1981-83, J.S. Guggenheim fellow, 1986-87; Beckman assoc. Ctr. for Advanced Study, Urbana, 1984-85; Fogarty scholar NIH, 1994-98. Fellow AAAS, Am. Phys. Soc., Am. Acad. Arts and Scis.; mem. NAS, Am. Chem. Soc. (Pure Chemistry award 1986, Peter Debye award 2000), N.Y. Acad. Scis., Biophys. Soc., Phi Beta Kappa, Sigma Xi, Phi Lambda Upsilon (Fresenius award 1988), Sigma Pi Sigma, Alpha Chi Sigma. Home: 12737 Sandy Crest Ct San Diego CA 92130-2795 Office: U Calif San Diego Dept Chem and Biochemistry 9500 Gilman Dr La Jolla CA 92093-3617 E-mail: pwolynes@ucsd.edu

WOMACK, THOMAS HOUSTON, manufacturing company executive; b. Gallatin, Tenn., June 22, 1940; s. Thomas Houston and Jessie (Eckel) W.; Linda Walker Womack, July 20, 1963 (div. Dec. 1989); children: Britton Ryan, Kelley Elizabeth; m. Pamela Ann Reed, Apr. 20, 1991. BSME, Tenn. Tech. U., Cookeville, 1963. Project engr. U.S. Gypsum Co., Jacksonville, Fla., 1963-65; project mgr. Maxwell House Div. Gen. Foods Corp., Jacksonville, 1965-68, mfg. mgr. Hoboken, N.J., 1968-71, div. ops. planning mgr., 1971-73; industry sales mgr. J.R. Schneider Co., Tiburon, Calif., 1973-79; pres., CEO Womack Internat., Inc., Mare Island, 1979—; chmn., CEO Ceramic Microlight Technologies, Inc., Mare Island, 1995—; pres., CEO WestAmerica Engring. and Mfg. Co., 1997—. Holder 5 U.S. patents. Mem. Soc. Tribologists and Lubrication Engrs., Am. Filtration Soc., Soc. Mfg. Engrs., Am. Soc. Chem. Engrs. Avocations: skiing, vintage exotic sports cars. Office: Womack Internat Inc PO Box 2175 Vallejo CA 94592-0175 Fax: 707-562-1010

WONG, ALFRED YIU-FAI, physics educator; b. Macao, Portugal, Feb. 4, 1937; s. Ka Ku and Wai Fong (Mak) W.; m. Lydia Yun Li, June 19, 1965; children: Alan C., Christopher C. BA in Sci., U. Toronto, 1958, MA, 1959; MSc, U. Ill., 1961; PhD, Princeton U., 1963. Research assoc. Princeton U., 1962-64; asst. prof. physics UCLA, 1964-68, assoc. prof. physics, 1968-72, prof., 1972—. Cons. TRW Systems, Redondo Beach, Calif., 1965-79; bd. dirs. Hipas Observatory, Ark. Contbr. articles to profl. jours. A.P. Sloan fellow UCLA, 1966-67. Fellow Am. Phys. Soc. (Excellence in Plasma Physics award 1985), Sigma Xi, Sigma Pi Sigma. Baptist. Office: UCLA Dept Physics 405 Hilgard Ave Los Angeles CA 90095-9000

WONG, CARRIE, executive; BS in Cellular & Molecular Biology, U. Wash. Ptnr. Niehaus Ryan Wong, South San Francisco. Avocation: bug collecting. Office: 601 Gateway Blvd Ste 900 South San Francisco CA 94080-7006

WONG, CHI-HUEY, chemistry educator; b. Taiwan, Aug. 13, 1948; came to U.S., 1979; m. Yieng-Lii, Mar. 26, 1975; children: Heather, Andrew. BS in Biochemistry, Nat. Taiwan U., 1970, MS in Biochemistry, 1977; PhD in Chemistry, MIT, 1982. Asst. rsch. fellow Inst. Biol. Chemistry Acad. Sinica, Taipei, Taiwan, 1974-79; from asst. prof. to prof. chemistry Tex. A&M U., 1983-89; Ernest W. Hahn prof. chemistry Scripps Rsch. Inst., La Jolla, Calif., 1989—. Cons. Miles Labs., 1985-88, Dow Chem., 1985-90, G. D. Searle, 1988-90; sci. advisor Amylin, San Diego, 1989-92, Cytel, 1990-97, Osi Pharm., 1992-98, Combichem, Inc., 1994—, Madimox, Inc., 1996—, Advanced Medicine, Inc., 1997—, Kosan Biosci., 1997—; head lab. glycosci. frontier rsch. program Riken, Japan, 1991-99. Author: Enzymes in Synthetic Organic Chemistry, 1991; mem. editl. bd. Bicatalysis; contbr. over 320 articles to profl. jours.; patentee in field. Lt. Taiwan Army, 1970-71. Recipient Presdl. Young Investigator in Chemistry award NSF, Washington, 1986, Internat. Carbohydrate award Internat. Carbohydrate Assn., 1994; Searle scholar, 1985. Mem. Am. Acad. Arts and Scis., Am. Chem. Soc. (Arthur C. Cope Scholar Award, 1993, Claude Hudson award in carbohydrate chemistry 1999), Am. Soc. Biochemistry and Molecular Biology, N.Y. Acad. Sci. Office: Scripps Rsch Inst Dept Chemistry 10550 N Torrey Pines Rd La Jolla CA 92037-1000 E-mail: wong@scripps.edu

WONG, DAVID YUE, academic administrator, physics educator; b. Swatow, China, Apr. 16, 1934; came to U.S., 1953; s. Fan and Wen (Tsang) W.; m. Katherine Young, Sept. 3, 1960 (div. Mar. 1988); children: Amy, Eric; m. Elizabeth Lewis, Mar. 26, 1988 BA, Hardin Simmons U., 1954; PhD, U. Md., 1957. Theoretical physicist Lawrence Radiation Lab., U. Calif., Berkeley, 1958-59; asst. prof. physics U. Calif., San Diego, 1960-63, assoc. prof., 1963-67, prof., 1967—, chair dept. physics, 1977-80, provost Warren Coll., 1985-94. Alfred P. Sloan fellow, 1966-68 Mem. Am. Inst. Physics.

WONG, JAMES BOK, economist, engineer, technologist; b. Canton, China, Dec. 9, 1922; came to U.S., 1938, naturalized, 1962; s. Gen Ham and Chen (Yee) W.; m. Wai Ping Lim, Aug. 3, 1946, (dec.)children: John, Jane Doris, Julia Ann. BS in Agr., U. Md., 1949, BS in Chem. Engring., 1950; MS, U. Ill., 1951, PhD, 1954. Rsch. asst. U. Ill., Champaign-Urbana, 1950-53; chem. engr. Standard Oil of Ind., Whiting, 1953-55; process design engr., rsch. engr. Shell Devel. Co., Emeryville, Calif., 1955-61; sr. planning engr., prin. planning engr. Chem. Plastics Group, Dart Industries, Inc. (formerly Rexall Drug & Chem. Co.), L.A., 1961-66, supr. planning and econs., 1966-67, mgr. long range planning and econs., 1967, chief economist, 1967-72, dir. econs. and ops. analysis, 1972-78, dir. internat. techs., 1978-81; pres. James B. Wong Assocs., L.A., 1981—. Chmn. bd. dirs. United Pacific Bank, 1988—; tech. cons. various corps. Author: Jade Eagle, 2000; contbr. articles to profl. jours. Bd. dirs., pres. Chinese Am. Citizens Alliance Found.; mem. Asian Am. Edn. Commn., 1971-81. Served with USAAF, 1943-46. Recipient Los Angeles Outstanding Vol. Service award, 1977. Mem. Am. Inst. Chem. Engrs., Am. Chem. Soc., VFW (vice comdr. 1959), Commodores (named to exec. order 1982), Sigma Xi, Tau Beta Pi, Phi Kappa Phi, Pi Mu Epsilon, Phi Lambda Upsilon, Phi Eta Sigma. Home: 2460 Venus Dr Los Angeles CA 90046-1646

WONG, JOE, physical chemist; b. Hong Kong, Aug. 8, 1942; arrived in U.S., 1966; s. Po-lim and Mildred (Tam) W.; m. Mei-Ngan, Dec. 20, 1969; children: Glenn, Christina, Theresa. BSc, U. Tasmania, Australia, 1965, BSc with honors, 1966, DSc, 1986; PhD, Purdue U., 1970. Rsch. chemist Electrolytic Zinc of Australia, Tasmania, 1966; lectr. in phys. chemistry Royal Hobart Coll., Tasmania, 1966; rsch. chemist GE R&D Ctr., Schenectady, N.Y., 1970-86; sr. rsch. chemist Lawrence Livermore (Calif.) Nat. Lab., 1986—. Adj. prof. chemistry SUNY, Albany, 1981-86; cons. prof. Stanford Synchrotron Rad. Lab., 1993—. Author: Glass: Structure by Spectroscopy, 1976; contbr. articles to profl. jours.; 7 patents in field. Sr. fellowship Sci. and Tech. Agy., 1991; recipient Humboldt Rsch. award Humboldt Found., 1991, RD-100 awards, 1990, 91. Fellow Am. Inst. [illegible] Materials Rsch. Soc., Sigma Xi. Home: 871 El Cerro Blvd Danville CA 94526-2704 Office: Lawrence Livermore Nat Lab PO Box 808 Livermore CA 94551-0808

WONG, OTTO, epidemiologist; b. Canton, China, Nov. 14, 1947; came to U.S., 1967, naturalized, 1976; m. Betty Yeung, Feb. 14, 1970; children: Elaine, Jonathan. BS, U. Ariz., 1970; MS, Carnegie Mellon U., 1972, U. Pitts., 1973, ScD, 1975. Cert. epidemsiologist Am. Coll. Epidemiology, 1982. USPHS fellow U. Pitts., 1972-75; asst. prof. epidemiology Georgetown U. Med. Sch., 1975-78; mgr. epidemiology Equitable Environ. Health Inc., Rockville, Md., 1977-78; dir. epidemiology Tabershaw Occuopational Med. Assocs., Rockville, 1978-80; dir. occupational rsch. Biometric Rsch. Inst., Washington, 1980-81; exec. v.p., chief epidemiologist ENSR Health Scis., Alameda, Calif., 1981-90; chief epidemiologist, pres. Applied Health Scis., San Mateo, 1991—. Adj. prof. epidemiology and biostats. Tulane U. Med. Ctr., New Orleans; vis. prof. epidemiology and occupl. health Nat. Def. Med. Ctr., Taipei, Taiwan, Shanghai Med. U.; adj. prof. dept. cmty. & family medicine Chinese U. Hong Kong; cons. WHO, Nat. Cancer Inst., Nat. Inst. Occupl. Safety and Health, Occupl. Safety and Health Adminstrn., Nat. Heart, Lung and Blood Inst., Internat. Agy. for Rsch. on Cancer, U.S. EPA, Ford Motors Co., Gen. Electric, Mobil, Chevron, Union Carbide, Fairfax (Va.) Hosp., Agy. for Toxic Substances and Disease Registry, U. Ariz. scholar, 1967-68. Assoc. editor Annals Epidemiology; contbr. articles to profl. jours. Fellow Am. Coll. Epidemiology, Human Biology Council; mem. Am. Pub. Health Assn., Biometric Soc., Soc. Epidemiologic Rsch., Phi Beta Kappa, Pi Mu Epsilon. Republican. Office: Applied Health Scis PO Box 2078 181 2nd Ave Ste 628 San Mateo CA 94401-3812

WONG, SAMUEL, conductor; b. Hong Kong, Apr. 12, 1962; m. Hae-Young Ham, Oct. 27, 1991. AB, Harvard U., 1984, MD, 1988. Music dir. N.Y. Youth Symphony, N.Y.C., 1988-93, Ann Arbor (Mich.) Symphony, from 1992; asst. conductor N.Y. Philharm., N.Y.C., 1990-94; music dir. Honolulu Symphony, 1996—. Internat. guest conductor various orchs., in Montreal, Toronto, Vancouver, Seattle, Oreg., New Orleans, Hong Kong, Singapore, Brussels, Budapest, Israel, Mex., and New Zealand, Houston; guest conductor Japan Philharm., Tokyo, KBS Orch., Seoul. Operas conducted include The Barber of Seville, Madame Butterfly, La Bohème, Rigoletto. Office: Honolulu Symphony Orch Castle Cook Bldg 650 Iwilei Rd Ste 202 Honolulu HI 96817

WONG, WALLACE, medical supplies company executive, real estate investor; b. Honolulu, July 13, 1941; s. Jack Yung Hung and Theresa (Goo) W.; m. Amy Ju, June 17, 1963; children: Chris, Bradley, Jeffery. Student, UCLA, 1960-63. Chmn., pres. South Bay Coll., Hawthorne, Calif., 1965-86; chmn. Santa Barbara (Calif.) Bus. Coll., 1975—; gen. ptnr. W B Co., Redondo Beach, Calif., 1982—; CEO Cal Am. Med. Supplies, Rancho Santa Margarita, 1986-96, Cal Am. Exports, Inc., Rancho Santa Margarita, 1986-96, Pacific Am. Group, Rancho Santa Margarita, 1991-96; chmn., CEO Alpine, Inc., Rancho Santa Margarita, Calif., 1993-96; pres. Bayside Properties, Rancho Santa Margarita, 1993—, San Juan Capistrano, Calif., 1993—. Bd. dirs. Metrobank, L.A. FFF Enterprises; chmn. bd. 1st Ind. Fin. Group., San Juan Capistrano, 1994—; chmn. Affinity Fin. Corp., 1996—. Acting sec. of state State of Calif., Sacramento, 1982; founding mem. Opera Pacific, Orange County, Calif., 1985; mem. Hist. and Cultural Found., Orange County, 1986; v.p. Orange County Chinese Cultural Club, Orange County, 1985. Named for Spirit of Enterprise Resolution, Hist. & Cultural Found., Orange Country, 1987; recipient resolution City of Hawthorne, 1973. Mem. Westren Accred Schs. & Colls. (v.p. 1978-79), Magic Castle (life), Singapore Club. Avocations: travel, skiing. Office: Bayside Properties 24681 La Plz Ste 230 Dana Point CA 92629-2563 E-mail: WWong1025@aol.com

WONG, WALTER FOO, county official; b. San Francisco, Apr. 11, 1930; s. Harry Yee and Grace (Won) W. AA, Hartnell Coll., 1952; BS, U. Calif., Berkeley, 1955; MPH, U. Hawaii, 1968. Registered sanitarian, Calif. Sanitarian Stanislaus County Health Dept., Modesto, Calif., 1955-56, Monterey County Health Dept., Salinas, 1956-67, sr. sanitarian, 1968-69, supervising sanitarian, 1969-70, dir. environ. health, 1971—. Sec. Monterey County Solid Waste Mgmt. Com., 1976—, Monterey County Hazardous Waste Mgmt. Com., 1987—; coord. Monterey County Genetic Engring. Rev. Com., 1987—; mem. Monterey County Genetic Engring. Experiment Permit Rev. Panel, 1995; mem. Monterey County Hazardous Materials Response Task Force, 1988—; mem. tech. adv. com. Monterey Peninsula Water Mgmt. Dist., 1985—, Monterey Regional Water Pollution Control Agy., 1985—; chmn. task force Monterey Regional Wastewater Reclamation Study for Agr., EPA and State of Calif. Chmn. Salinas Bicentennial Internat. Day Celebration, 1974, Pollution Clean-up Com. of Fort Ord Task Force, 1992; mem. Calif. Base Closure Environ. adv. com., 1993. Recipient Community Svc. award Monterey County Med. Soc., 1998. Mem. Calif. Conf. Dirs. Environ. Health (pres. 1982-83), Assn. Environ. Health Adminstrs. (pres. 1982-83), Salinas C. of C. (Mem. of Yr. award 1971), U. Calif. Berkeley Alumni Assn., U. Hawaii Alumni Assn. (Disting. Alumni award 1992), Monterey County Hist. Soc. (pres. 1995-96), Ethnic Cultural Coun. (chmn. 1995). Republican. Presbyterian. Avocations: sports, music, outdoor recreation. Home: 234 Cherry Dr Salinas CA 93901-2807 Office: Monterey County Health Dept 1270 Natividad Rd Rm 301 Salinas CA 93906-3198

WONG-STAAL, FLOSSIE, geneticist, medical educator; BA, UCLA, 1968, PhD, 1972. Tchg. asst. UCLA, 1969-70, rsch. asst., 1970-72; post-doctoral fellow U. Calif., San Diego, 1972-73; Fogarty fellow Nat. Cancer Inst., Bethesda, Md., 1973-75, vis. assoc., 1975-76, cancer expert, 1976-78, sr. investigator, 1978-81, chief molecular genetics of hematopoietic cells sect., 1982-89; Florence Seeley Riford chair in AIDS rsch., prof. medicine U. Calif. San Diego, La Jolla, 1990—. Vis. prof. Inst. Gen. Pathology, First U. Rome, Italy, 1985. Mem. editl. bd. Gene Analysis Techniques, 1984—, Cancer Letters, 1984-94, Leukemia, 1987—, Cancer Rsch., 1987, AIDS Rsch. and Human Retroviruses (sect. editor), 1987—, DNA and Cell Biology (sect. editor), 1987—, Microbial Pathogenesis, 1987-90, AIDS: An Internat. Jour., 1987—, Internat. Jour. Acquired Immunodeficiency Syndrome, 1988—, Oncogene, 1988—, Jour. Virology, 1990—; contbr. articles to profl. jours. Recipient Outstanding Sci. award Chinese Med. and Health Assn., 1987, The Excellence 2000 award U.S. Pan Asian Am. C. of C. and the Orgn. of Chinese Am. Women, 1991. Mem. Am. Soc. for Virology (charter), Phi Beta Kappa. Office: U Calif San Diego Dept Med 0665 9500 Gilman Dr La Jolla CA 92093-5003

WOO, SHARON Y. healthcare organization executive; b. Honolulu; BA in Music and Math., Mills Coll.; secondary tchg. credential, San Francisco State U. Bd. dirs. Sutter Health Inc., Sacramemto. Trustee Gateway H.S., Golden Gate nat. Parks Assn., Multicultural Alliance, San francisco Ballet, numerous others; chmn. adv. coun. San Francisco Sch. Vols. Office: Sutter Health Inc One Capitol Mall Sacramento CA 95814

WOO, VERNON YING-TSAI, lawyer, real estate developer, judge; b. Honolulu, Aug. 7, 1942; s. William Shu-Bin and Hilda Woo; children: Christopher Shu-Bin, Lia Gay. BA, U. Hawaii, 1964, MA, 1966; JD, Harvard U., 1969. Pres. Woo Kessner Duca & Maki, Honolulu, 1972-87; pvt. practice law Honolulu, 1987—. Judge per diem Honolulu Dist. Family Ct., 1978-84, 95—. Bd. dirs. Boys and Girls Club of Honolulu,. 1985-95, pres., 1990-92. Mem. ABA, Hawaii Bar Assn., Honolulu Bd. Realtors. Home: 1221 Victoria St Apt 2403 Honolulu HI 96814-1454 Office: Harbor Ct 55 Merchant St Ste 1900 Honolulu HI 96813

WOOD, DAVID LEE, entomologist, educator; b. Jan. 8, 1931; BS, SUNY, Syracuse, 1952; PhD, U. Calif., Berkeley, 1960. Lic. forester Calif. Prof. entomology, emeritus dept. Environ. Sci. Policy, Mgmt. U. Calif., Berkeley, 1960—. Lectr., reviewer, cons. in field. Contbr. articles to profl. jours. Recipient Silver medal Swedish Coun. for Forestry and Agril. Rsch., 1983. Fellow Entomol. Soc. Can., Entomol. Soc. Am. (Founder's award 1986, Founder's award Western Forest Insect Work Conf. 1992); mem. AAAS, AIBS, Entomol. Soc. Am., Entomol. Soc. Can., Internat. Soc. Chem. Ecology (Silver medal 2001), Soc. Am. Foresters, Sigma Xi. Home: 26 Hardie Dr Moraga CA 94556-1134 Office: U Calif Divsn Insect Biology 201 Wellman Hall Berkeley CA 94720-3112 E-mail: bigwood@nature.berkeley.edu

WOOD, GEORGE H. investment executive; b. Kansas City, Mo., Sept. 7, 1946; s. George H. and Helen Lee (Hansen) W. BSBA, U. Mo., 1968, MBA, 1972. Chartered fin. analyst. Securities analyst Kansas City Life Ins. Co., 1972-75, asst. dir. securities, 1975-76; sr. trust officer Commerce Bank of Kansas City, N.A., 1976-79, v.p., fixed income and portfolio group mgr., 1979-80, v.p., mgr. investment dept., 1980-82, sr. v.p., 1982-88, chief investment officer, 1988-90; mng. dir. Merus Capital Mgmt., 1990-94; v.p. Pacivic Investment Mgmt. Co., 1994-97, sr. v.p., 1997-99, exec. v.p., 1999-2000; head acct. mgmt. Europe, exec. v.p., mng. dir. Allianz/Pimco Asset Mgmt. Co., 2000—. Bd. dirs. Harvest Techs. Inc. Past bd. dirs., pres. Young Audiences, Inc. With AUS, 1969-71. Mem. Inst. Chartered Fin. Analysts (past chmn. curriculum com.), Assn. Investment Mgmt. and Rsch., Fin. Analysts Fedn., San Francisco Soc. Fin. Analysts (bd. dirs.), U. Mo. Alumni Assn., Phi Delta Theta. Home: 840 Newport Center Dr Newport Beach CA 92660-6310 Office: Pacific Investment Mgmt Co 840 Newport Center Dr Ste 360 Newport Beach CA 92660-6392

WOOD, JAMES MICHAEL, lawyer; b. Oakland, Calif., Mar. 22, 1948; s. Donald James and Helen Winifred (Reimann) W.; children: Nathan, Sarah, Ruth, Alexandra; m. Cynthia Ahart Wood. BA, St. Mary's Coll., 1970; JD, U. San Francisco, 1973. Bar: Calif. 1973, U.S. Dist. Ct. (no., cen. and so. dists.) Calif. 1973. Rsch. atty. Alameda County Superior Ct., Oakland, 1973-76; ptnr. Crosby, Heafey, Roach & May, Oakland, 1976—. Mem. adv. com. Food Drug Law Inst., 1999—; presenter profl. confs. Contbr. articles to profl. jours. Chair alumni-faculty devel. fund St. Mary's Coll. Alumni Bd. Dirs., 1990-94. Mem. ABA (litigation sect., health law litigation com., litigation products liability com.), ATLA (assoc.), State Bar Calif., Calif. Trial Lawyers Assn. (assoc.), No. Calif. Assn. Def. Counsel, Alameda County Bar Assn., Def. Rsch. and Trial Lawyers Assn., Am. Acad. Hosp. Attys., Am. Soc. Pharmacy Law, Nat. Health Lawyers Assn., Drug Info. Assn., Food Drug Law Inst. Office: Crosby Heafey Roach & May 1999 Harrison St Ste 2200 Oakland CA 94612-3572 E-mail: jwood@chrm.com

WOOD, JEANNINE KAY, legislative staff member; b. Dalton, Nebr., Apr. 22, 1944; d. Grover L. and Elsie M. (Winkelman) Sanders; m. Charles S. Wood, Dec. 7, 1968; children: Craig C., Wendi L. Wood Armstrong. Exec. sec. Idaho Hosp. Assn., Boise, 1966-71; com. sec. Idaho State Senate, Boise, 1976-81, jour. clk., 1981-85, asst. to sec. of senate, 1985-91, sec. of senate, 1991-97; pvt. practice typing svc. Boise, 1979-86. Mem. Am. Soc. Legis. Clks. and Secs. Methodist. Home: 3505 S Linder Rd Meridian ID 83642-6837 Office: Idaho State Capitol PO Box 83720 Boise ID 83720-3720

WOOD, KENNETH ARTHUR, retired newspaper editor, writer; b. Hastings, Sussex, Eng., Feb. 25, 1926; came to U.S., 1965; s. Arthur Charles and Ellen Mary (Cox) W.; m. Hilda Muriel Harloe, Sept. 13, 1952. Educated in Eng. Editor Stamp Collector newspaper Van Dahl Publs., Albany, Oreg., 1968-80, editor emeritus, 1980—. Author (ency.) This Is Philately, 1982, (atlas) Where in the World, 1983, Basic Philately, 1984, Post Dates, 1985, Modern World, 1987; author several hundred articles and columns published in the U.K. and U.S.A., 1960—. Served with Brit. Army WW II. Recipient Disting. Philatelist award Northwest Fedn. Stamp Clubs, 1974, Phoenix award Ariz. State Philatelic Hall of Fame, 1979, Disting. Philatelist award Am. Topical Assn., 1979. Fellow Royal Philatelic Soc. (London); mem. Am. Philatelic Soc. (Luff award 1987, Hall of Fame Writers Unit, 1984). Avocations: philately, aviation history, modern history, gardening. Office: 2430 Tudor Way SE Albany OR 97321-5661

WOOD, LINDA MAY, librarian; b. Ft. Dodge, Iowa, Nov. 6, 1942; d. John Albert and Beth Ida (Riggs) Wiley; m. C. James Wood, Sept. 15, 1964 (div. Oct. 1984). BA, Portland State U., 1964; M in Librarianship, U. Wash., 1965. Reference libr. Multnomah county Libr., Portland, Oreg., 1965-67, br. libr., 1967-72, adminstrv. asst. to libr., 1972-73, asst. libr., asst. dir., 1973-77; asst. city libr. L.A. Pub. Libr., 1977-80; libr. dir. Riverside (Calif.) City and County Pub. Libr., 1980-91; county libr. Alameda County Libr., Fremont, Calif., 1991—. Adminstrv. coun. mem. Bay Area Libr. and Info. Svcs., Oakland, Calif., 1991—. Chair combined charities campaign County of Alameda, Oakland, Calif., 1992; bd. dirs. Inland AIDS project, Riverside, Calif., 1990-91; vol. United Way of Inland Valleys, Riverside, 1986-87, Bicentennial Competition on the Constitution, 36th Congl. Dist., Colton, Calif., 1988-90. Mem. ALA (CLA chpt. councilor 1992-95), Calif. Libr. Assn. (pres. 1985, exec. com., ALA chpt. councilor 1992-95), Calif. County Librs. Assn. (pres. 1984), League of Calif. Cities (cmty. svcs. policy com. 1985-90), OCLC Users Coun. (Pacific Network del. 1986-89). Democrat. Avocations: folk dancing, opera, reading. Office: Alameda County Libr 2450 Stevenson Blvd Fremont CA 94538-2326

WOOD, MARCUS ANDREW, lawyer; b. Mobile, Ala., Jan. 18, 1947; s. George Franklin and Helen Eugenia (Fletcher) W.; m. Sandra Lee Pellonari, July 25, 1971; children: Edward Alan, Melinda Janel. BA cum laude, Vanderbilt U., 1969; JD, Yale U., 1974. Bar: Oreg. 1974, U.S. Dist. Ct. Oreg. 1974, U.S. Ct. Appeals (9th cir.) 1982. Assoc., then ptnr. Rives, Bonihadi & Smith, Portland, Oreg., 1974-78; ptnr. Stoel Rives LLP and predecessor firms, Portland, 1974—. Pres., bd. dirs. Indochinese Refugee Ctr., Portland, 1980, Pacific Ballet Theatre, Portland, 1986-87; bd. dirs. Outside In, Portland, 1989—. Lt. USNR, 1969-71. Mem. ABA, Phi Beta Kappa. Home: 9300 NW Finzer Ct Portland OR 97229-8035 Office: Stoel Rives 900 SW 5th Ave Ste 2300 Portland OR 97204-1229

WOOD, NANCY ELIZABETH, psychologist, educator; d. Donald Sterret and Orne Louise (Erwin) W. B.S., Ohio U., 1943, M.A., 1947; Ph.D., Northwestern U., Evanston, Ill., 1952. Prof. Case-Western Res. U., Cleve., 1952-60; specialist, expert HEW, Washington, 1960-62; chief rsch. US-PHS, Washington, 1962-64; prof. U. So. Calif., L.A., 1965—. Learning disabilities cons., 1960-70; assoc. dir. Cleve. Hearing and Speech Ctr., 1952-60; dir. licensing program Brit. Nat. Trust, London. Author: Language Disorders, 1964, Language Development, 1970, Verbal Learning, 1975 (monograph) Auditory Disorders, 1978, Levity, 1980, Stoneskipping, 1989, Bird Cage, 1994, Out of Control, 1999. Pres. faculty senate U. So. Calif., 1987-88. Recipient Outstanding Faculty award Trojan Fourth Estate, 1982, Pres.' Svc. award U. So. Calif., 1992. Fellow APA (cert.), AAAS, Am. Speech and Hearing Assn. (legis. coun. 1965-68); mem. Internat. Assn. Scientists. Republican. Methodist. Office: U So Calif University Park Los Angeles CA 90089-0001

WOOD, ROBERT WARREN, lawyer; b. Des Moines, July 5, 1955; s. Merle Warren and Cecily Ann (Sherk) W.; m. Beatrice Wood, Aug. 4, 1979; 1 child, Bryce Mercedes. Student, U. Sheffield, Eng., 1975-76; AB, Humboldt State U., 1976; JD, U. Chgo., 1979. Bar: Ariz. 1979, Calif. 1980, Wyo. 2000, N.Y. 1989, D.C. 1993, Mont. 1998, U.S Tax Ct. 1980, Wyo.; Roll of Solicitors of Eng. and Wales, 1998. Assoc. Jennings, Strouss, Phoenix, 1979-80, McCutchen, Doyle, San Francisco, 1980-82, Broad, Khourie, San Francisco, 1982-85, Steefel, Levitt & Weiss, San Francisco, 1985-87, ptnr., 1987-91, Bancroft & McAlister, San Francisco, 1991-93; prin. Robert W. Wood, P.C., San Francisco, 1993—. Instr. in law U. Calif. San Francisco, 1981-82. Author: Taxation of Corporate Liquidations: A

Complete Planning Guide, 1987, 2nd edit., 1994, The Executive's Complete Guide to Business Taxes, 1989, Corporate Taxation: Complete Planning and Practice Guide, 1989, S Corporations, 1990, The Ultimate Tax Planning Guide for Growing Companies, 1991, Taxation of Damage Awards and Settlement Payments, 1991, 2nd edit., 1998, Tax Strategies in Hiring, Retaining and Terminating Employees, 1991, The Home Office Tax Guide, 1991; co-author: (with others) California Closely Held Corporations: Tax Planning and Practice Guide, 1987, Legal Guide to Independent Contractor Status, 3d edit., 2000; editor: California Small Businees Guide, 4 vols., 1998, Home Office Money & Tax Guide, 1992, Tax Aspects of Settlements and Judgements, 1993, 2d edit., 1998, cumulative supplement, 2000; editor-in-chief The M & A Tax Report; editor: Limited Liability Companies: Formation, Operation and Conversion, 1994, 2d edit., 2001, Limited Liability Partnerships: Formation, Operation and Taxation, 1996; mem. editl. bd. Real Estate Tax Digest, The Practical Accountant, Jour. Real Estate Taxation. Fellow Am. Coll. Tax Counsel; mem. Calif. Bd. Legal Specialization (cert. specialist taxation), Candian Bar Assn., Bohemian Club, Law Coun. Australia. Republican. Office: 477 Pacific Ave # 300 San Francisco CA 94133-4614

WOOD, STUART KEE, retired engineering manager; b. Dallas, Mar. 8, 1925; s. William Henry and Harriet (Kee) Wood; m. Loris V. Poock, May 17, 1951 (dec. June 1990); children: Linda S. Kuehl, Thomas N., Richard D.; m. Lois H. Morton, Nov. 25, 1994. BS in Aero. Engring., Tex. A&M U., 1949. Aircraft sheet metal worker USAF SAC, Kelly Field, San Antonio, 1942-45; structural design engr. B-52, 367-80, KC-135, 707 Airplanes Boeing, Seattle and Renton, Wash., 1949-55, thrust reverser design engr. 707 and 747 Airplanes Renton, 1955-66, supr. thrust reverser group 747 Airplane Everett, Wash., 1966-69; supr. rsch. basic engine noise 727 airplane FAA, NASA, 1969-74; supr. jetfoil propulsion Jetfoil Hydrofoil Boeing, Renton, 1974-75; supr. rsch. basic engine performance loss JT9D Pratt & Whitney, 1975-79; supr. propulsion systems 757 Airplane Boeing, Renton, 1979-90, supr., propulsion systems thrust reverser 737, 747, 757, 767 Kent, Wash., 1990-94, ret., 1994. Patentee in field. Recipient Ed Wells award AIAA, N.W. chpt., Bellevue, Wash., 1992. Republican. Presbyterian. Avocations: photography, computers, travel. Home: 3831 46th Ave SW Seattle WA 98116-3723 E-mail: stuwood@aol.com

WOOD, WILLIAM BARRY, III, biologist, educator; b. Balt., Feb. 19, 1938; s. William Barry, Jr. and Mary Lee (Hutchins) W.; m. Marie-Elisabeth Renate Hartisch, June 30, 1961; children: Oliver Hartisch, Christopher Barry. A.B., Harvard U., 1959; Ph.D., Stanford U., 1963. Asst. prof. biology Calif. Inst. Tech., Pasadena, 1965-68, assoc. prof., 1968-69, prof. biology, 1970-77; prof. molecular, cellular and developmental biology U. Colo., Boulder, 1977—, chmn. dept., 1978-83. Mem. panel for developmental biology NSF, 1970-72; physiol. chemistry study sect. NIH, 1974-78; mem. com. on sci. and public policy Nat. Acad. Scis., 1979-80; mem. NIH Cellular and Molecular Basis of Disease Rev. Com., 1984-88. Author: (with J. H. Wilson, R.M. Benbow, L.E. Hood) Biochemistry: A Problems Approach, 2d edit., 1981, (with L.E. Hood and J.H. Wilson) Molecular Biology of Eucaryotic Cells, 1975, (with L.E. Hood and I.L. Weissman) Immunology, 1978, (with L.E. Hood, I.L. Weissman and J.H. Wilson) Immunology, 2d edit., 1984, (with L.E. Hood and I.L. Weissman) Concepts in Immunology, 1978; editl. rev. bd. Science, 1984-92; mem. editl. bd. Cell, 1984-87, Developmental Biology, 1995—; contbr. articles to profl. jours. Recipient U.S. Steel Molecular Biology award, 1969; NIH Rsch. grantee, 1965—, Merit awardee, 1986-96; Guggenheim fellow, 1975-76. Fellow AAAS; mem. Nat. Acad. Scis., Am. Acad. Arts and Scis., Am. Soc. for Cell Biology, Genetics Soc. Am. Soc. for Developmental Biology, Soc. Nematology. Office: Dept MCD Biology Box 347 U Colorado Boulder CO 80309

WOOD, WILLIS BOWNE, JR. retired utility holding company executive; b. Kansas City, Mo., Sept. 15, 1934; s. Willis Bowne Sr. and Mina (Henderson) W.; m. Dixie Gravel, Aug. 31, 1955; children: Bradley, William, Josh. BS in Petroleum Engring., U. Tulsa, 1957; grad. advanced mgmt. program, Harvard U., 1983; JD (hon.), Pepperdine U., 1996. With So. Calif. Gas Co., L.A., 1960-74, from v.p. to sr. v.p., 1975-80, exec. v.p., 1983-84; pres., CEO Pacific Lighting Gas Supply Co., L.A., 1981-83; from sr. v.p. to chmn., pres., CEO, Pacific Enterprises, L.A., 1984-93, chmn., CEO, 1993-98; ret., 1998. Bd. dirs. Washington Mut., Seattle, Automobile Club Soc. Calif.; trustee U. So. Calif. Trustee, past vice-chmn. Harvey Mudd Coll., Claremont, Calif., 1984—; trustee emeritus, past chmn. Calif. Med. Ctr. Found., L.A., 1983-2000; trustee, past pres. S.W. Mus., L.A.; trustee John and Dora Haynes Found., 1998—; past bd. dirs. L.A. World Affairs Coun.; past dir., past chmn. bus. coun. for Sustainable Energy Future, 1994—; past dir. Pacific Coun. for Internat. Affairs. Recipient Disting. Alumni U. Tulsa, 1995; inductee U. Tulsa Engring. Hall of Fame, 2001. Mem. Soc. Petroleum Energy Engrs., Am. Gas Assn., Pacific Coast Gas Assn. (past bd. dirs.), Pacific Energy Assn., Calif. State C. of C. (past bd. dirs.), Am. Automobile Assn. (vice-chmn. 2001), Nat. Assn. of Mfrs. (past bd. dirs.), Hacienda Golf CLub, Ctr. Club, Calif. Club. Republican.

WOODALL, DAVID MONROE, research engineer, dean; b. Perryville, Ark., Aug. 2, 1945; m. Linda Carol Page, June 6, 1966; 1 child, Zachary Page. BA, Hendrix Coll., 1967; MS, Columbia U., 1968; PhD, Cornell U., 1976. Registered profl. engr., Idaho. Nuc. engr. Westinghouse Corp., Pitts., 1968-70; asst. prof. U. Rochester, N.Y., 1974-77, U. N.Mex., Albuquerque, 1977-79, assoc. prof., 1979-83, chair dept., 1980-83, prof., 1984-86; group physics mgr. Idaho Nat. Engring. Lab., Idaho Falls, 1986-92; assoc. dean, dir. rsch. U. Idaho, Moscow, 1992-99, acting dean, 1999; dean coll. sci., engring., math. U. Alaska, Fairbanks, 1999—; dir. Ctr. for Nanosensor Tech., 2001—. EAC commr. Accreditation Bd. Engring. Tech., 1990-95, bd. dirs.; cons. in field. Contbr. articles to profl. jours. Grantee NSF, DOE, AFOSR, Office Naval Rsch., DMEA, others. Mem. IEEE, Am. Nuc. Soc. (chpt. chair 1982-83), Am. Soc. Engring. Edn. (divsn. chair 1993, 95, bd. dirs. engring. rsch. coun.). Office: U Alaska Coll Sci Engring Math PO Box 755940 Fairbanks AK 99775-5940 E-mail: ffdmw1@uaf.edu

WOODARD, ALVA ABE, business consultant; b. Roy, N.Mex., June 28, 1928; s. Joseph Benjamin and Emma Lurania (Watkins) W.; m. Esther Josepha Kaufmann, Apr. 5, 1947 (div. Sept. 1991); children: Nannette, Gregory, Loreen, Arne, Mark, Kevin, Steven, Curtis, Marlee, Julie, Michelle; m. Margaret Adele Evenson, Oct. 1, 1994. Student, Kinman Bus. U., 1948-49, Whitworth Coll., 1956, Wash. State U., 1953-54. Sec.-treas., dir. Green Top Dairy Farms, Inc., Clarkston, Wash., 1948-52; v.p., treas., sec., dir. ASC Industries, Inc. (subs. Gifford-Hill and Co.), Spokane, 1952-75; dir. Guenther Irrigation, Inc., Pasco, 1966-71; mng. dir. Irrigation Rental, Inc., Pasco, 1968-75, Rain Chief Irrigation Co., Grand Island, Nebr., 1968-75; sec., dir. Keeling Supply Co., Little Rock, 1969-72; pres., dir. Renters, Inc., Salt Lake City, 1971-75, Woodard Western Corp., Spokane, 1976-86, Woodard Industries, Inc., Auburn, Wash., 1987-90; cons. Woodard Assocs., Spokane, 1985—. Pres., dir. TFI Industries, inc., Post Falls, Idaho, 1989-90; v.p., sec., treas., dir. Trans-Force, Inc., Post Falls, 1989-90, TFI Computer Scis., Inc., Post Falls, 1989-90. Newman Lake (Wash.) Rep. precinct committeeman, 1964-80; Spokane County del. Wash. Rep. Conv., 1968-80. Mem. Adminstrv. Mgmt. Soc. (bd. dirs. 1966-68), Optimists. Avocations: fishing, theater, golf, reading, dancing. Home and Office: 921 E 39th Ave Spokane WA 99203-3034

WOODARD, DOROTHY MARIE, insurance broker; b. Houston, Feb. 7, 1932; d. Gerald Edgar and Bessie Katherine (Crain) Floeck; student N.Mex. State U., 1950; m. Jack W. Woodard; June 19, 1950 (dec. May 1972); m. Norman W. Libby, July 19, 1982 (dec. Dec. 1991). Ptnr. Western Oil Co., Tucumcari, N.Mex., 1950—; owner, mgr. Woodard & Co., Las Cruces, N.Mex., 1959-67; agt., dist. mgr. United Nations Ins. Co., Denver, 1968-74; agt. Western Nat. Life Ins. Co., Amarillo, Tex., 1976—. Exec. dir. Tucumcari Indsl. Commn., 1979—; dir. Bravo Dome Study Com., 1979—; owner Libby Cattle Co., Libby Ranch Co.; regional bd. dirs. N.Mex., Eastern Plains Council Govts., 1979—. Mem. NAFE, Tucumcari C. of C., Mesa Country Club. Home: PO Box 823 Tucumcari NM 88401-0823

WOODBRIDGE, JOHN MARSHALL, architect, urban planner; b. N.Y.C., Jan. 26, 1929; s. Frederick James and Catherine (Baldwin) W.; m. Sally Byrne, Aug. 14, 1954; children: Lawrence F., Pamela B., Diana B.; m. Carolyn Kizer, Apr. 8, 1975. B.A. magna cum laude, Amherst Coll., 1951; M.F.A. in Architecture, Princeton U., 1956. Designer John Funk, architect, San Francisco, 1957-58; designer, asso. partner Skidmore, Owings & Merrill, San Francisco, 1959-73; staff dir. Pres.'s Adv. Council and Pres.'s Temporary Commn. on Pennsylvania Ave., Washington, 1963-65; exec. dir. Pennsylvania Ave. Devel. Corp., Washington, 1973-77. Lectr. architecture U. Calif., Berkeley; vis. prof. U. Oreg., Washington U., St. Louis. Co-author: Buildings of the Bay Area, 1960, A Guide to Architecture in San Francisco and Northern California, 1973, Architecture San Francisco, 1982, San Francisco Architecture, 1992. Recipient Fed. Design Achievement award Nat. Endowment for Arts, 1988; Fulbright scholar to France, 1951-52. Fellow AIA (emeritus); mem. Nat. Trust Historic Preservation, Soc. Archtl. Historians, Phi Beta Kappa. Democrat. Episcopalian. Home and Office: 19772 8th St E Sonoma CA 95476-3849

WOODBURY, LAEL JAY, theater educator; b. Fairview, Idaho, July 3, 1927; s. Raymond A. and Wanda (Dawson) W.; m. Margaret Lillian Swenson, Dec. 19, 1949; children: Carolyn Inez (Mrs. Donald Hancock), Shannon Margaret (Mrs. J. Michael Busenbark), Jordan Ray, Lexon Dan. BS, Utah State U., 1952; MA, Brigham Young U., 1953; PhD (Univ. fellow), U. Ill., 1954. Teaching asst. U. Ill., 1953; assoc. prof. Brigham Young U., 1954-61; guest prof. Colo. State Coll., 1962; asst. prof. Bowling Green State U., 1961-62; asso. prof. U. Iowa, 1962-65; producer Ledges Playhouse, Lansing, Mich., 1963-65; prof. speech and dramatics, chmn. dept. Brigham Young U., 1966-70, assoc. dean Coll. Fine Arts and Communications, 1969-73, dean Coll. Fine Arts and Communications, 1973-82. Vis. lectr. abroad; bd. dirs. Eagle Systems Internat.; bd. dir. workshop Fedn. for Asian Cultural Promotion, Republic of China; dir. European study tour. Author: Play Production Handbook, 1959, Mormon Arts, vol. 1, 1972, Mosaic Theatre, 1976, also articles, original dramas; profl. actor PBS and feature films. Chmn. gen. bd. drama com. Young Men's Mut. Improvement Assn., 1958-61; bd. dirs. Repertory Dance Theatre; bd. dirs., chmn. greater ctrl. Utah ARC; chmn. Utah Alliance for Arts Edn.; mem. adv. coun. Utah Arts Festival; missionary LDS Ch., N.Y.C., 1994. With USN, 1942-46. Recipient Creative Arts award Brigham Young U., 1971, Disting. Alumni award, 1975, Tchr. of Yr. award, 1988, Excellence in Rsch. award, 1992, Disting. Svc. award, 1992. Mem. Rocky Mountain Theatre Conf. (past pres.), Am. Theatre Assn. (chmn. nat. com. royalties 1972—, mem. fin. com. 1982—), NW Assn. Univs. and Colls. (accrediting officer), Am. Theatre Assn. (v.p. Univ. and Coll. Theatre Assn.), Theta Alpha Phi, Phi Kappa Phi. Home: 1303 Locust Ln Provo UT 84604-3651

WOODBURY, MARDA LIGGETT, librarian, writer; b. N.Y.C., Sept. 20, 1925; d. Walter W. and Edith E. (Fleischer) Liggett; m. Philip J. Evans, Sept. 1948 (div. 1950); 1 child, Mark W. Evans; m. Mark Lee Woodbury, 1956 (div. 1969); children: Brian, Heather. Student, Bklyn. Coll., 1942-44; BA in Chemistry and Polit. Sci., Bard Coll., 1946; BS in L.S., Columbia U., 1948; postgrad., U. Calif., Berkeley, 1955-56, 60-61, MJ, 1995. Cert. tchr. Libr. various spl., med. and pub. librs., San Francisco, 1946-60, Coll. Pk. High Sch., Mt. Diablo, Calif., 1962-67; elem. sch. libr. Oakland and Berkeley, 1967-69; libr. dir. Far West Lab. Ednl. Rsch. & Devel., San Francisco, 1969-73; libr., editor Gifted Resource Ctr., San Mateo, Calif., 1973-75; libr. cons. Rsch. Ventures, Berkeley, 1975—; libr. dir. Life Chiropractic Coll., San Lorenzo, 1980-95. Author: A Guide to Sources of Educational Information, 1976, 2d edit., 1982, Selecting Instructional Materials, 1978, Selecting Materials for Instruction, Vol. I: Issues and Policies, 1979, Vol. II: Media and the Curriculum, 1980, Vol. III: Subject Areas and Implementation, 1980, Childhood Information Resources, 1985 (Outstanding Ref. Work, Assn. Ref. Librs. 1985), Youth Information Resources, 1987, Stopping the Presses: The Murder of Walter W. Liggett, 1998; mem. editorial bd. Ref. Libr., 1980-95. Mem. Med. Libr. Assn. (editor Chiropractic Librs. 1990-92), Minn. Hist. Soc., Investigative Reporters and Editors. Home: 145 Monte Cresta Ave Apt 402 Oakland CA 94611-4809 E-mail: mardawoodbury@msn.com

WOODEN, JOHN ROBERT, former basketball coach; b. Martinsville, Ind., Oct. 14, 1910; s. Joshua Hugh and Roxie (Rothrock) W.; m. Nellie C. Riley, Aug. 8, 1932; children: Nancy Anne, James Hugh. B.S., Purdue U., 1932; M.S., Ind. State U., 1947. Athletic dir., basketball and baseball coach Ind. State Tchrs. Coll., 1946-48; head basketball coach UCLA, 1948-75. Lectr. to colls., coaches, business. Author: Practical Modern Basketball, 1966, They Call Me Coach, 1972; Contbr. articles to profl. jours. Served to lt. USNR, 1943-46. Named All-Am. basketball player Purdue U., 1930-32, Coll. Basketball Player of Yr., 1932, to All-Time All-Am. Team Helms Athletic Found., 1943, Nat. Basketball Hall of Fame, Springfield (Mass.) Coll., as player, 1960, as coach, 1970, Ind. State Baksetball Hall of Fame, 1962, Calif. Father of Yr., 1964, 75, Coach of Yr. U.S. Basketball Writers Assn., 1964, 67, 69, 70, 72, 73, Sportsman of Yr. Sports Illustrated, 1973, GTE Acad. All-Am., 1994; recipient Whitney Young award Urban League, 1973, 1st ann. Velvet Covered Brick award Layman's Leadership Inst., 1974, 1st ann. Dr. James Naismith Peachbasket award, 1974, medal of excellence Bellarmine Coll., 1985, Sportslike Pathfinder award to Hoosier with extraordinary svc. on behalf of Am. youth, 1993, GET All Am. Acad. Hall of Fame, 1994, 40 for the Age award Sports Illustrated, 1994, the 1st Frank G. Wells Disney award for role model to youth, 1995, Disting. Am. award Pres. Reagan, 1995, Svc. to Mankind award Lexington Theol. Sem., 1995, NCAA Theodore Roosevelt Sportsman award, 1995, Vince Lombardi award for excellence, 2000, Ind. Legend award, 2000; named Basketball Coach of the Century, 2000.

WOODHOUSE, GAY VANDERPOEL, state attorney general; b. Torrington, Wyo., Jan. 8, 1950; d. Wayne Gaylord and Sally (Rouse) Vanderpoel; m. Randy Woodhouse, Nov. 26, 1953; children: Dustin, Houston. BA with honors, U. Wyo., 1972, JD, 1977. Bar: Wyo. 1978, U.S. Dist. Ct. Wyo., U.S. Supreme Ct. Dir. student Legal Svcs., Laramie, Wyo., 1976-77; assoc. Donald Jones Law Offices, Torrington, 1977-78; asst. atty. gen. State of Wyo., Cheyenne, 1978-84, sr. asst. atty. gen., 1984-89, spl. U.S. atty., 1987-89, asst. U.S. atty., 1990-95, chief dept. atty. gen., 1995-98, atty. gen., 1998—. Chmn. bd. Pathfinder, 1987; bd. dirs. S.E. Wyo. Mental Health; chmn. Wyo. Tel. Consumer Panel, Casper, 1982-86; spl. projects cons. N.Am. Securities Adminstrs. Assn., 1987-89; advisor Cheyenne Halfway House, 1984-93; chmn. Wyo. Silent Witness Initiative Zero Domestic Violence by 2010, 1997; chmn. Wyo. Domestic Violence Elimination Coun., 1999-2001. Mem. Laramie County Bar Assn. Republican. Avocations: inline speed skating, stained glass. Office: 123 Capitol Bldg Cheyenne WY 82002-0001 E-mail: gwoodh@state.wy.us

WOODLAND, IRWIN FRANCIS, lawyer; b. New York, Sept. 2, 1922; s. John James and Mary (Hynes) W.; m. Sally Duffy, Sept. 23, 1954; children: Connie, J. Patrick, Stephen, Joseph, William, David, Duffy. BA, Columbia U., 1948; JD, Ohio State U., 1959. Bar: Calif. 1960, Wash., 1991, U.S. Dist. Ct. (cen. dist.) Calif. 1960, U.S. Dist. Ct. (no. dist.) Calif. 1962, U.S. Dist. Ct. (so. dist.) Calif. From assoc. to ptnr. Gibson, Dunn & Crutcher, L.A., 1959-88. Bd. dirs. Sunlaw Energy Corp., Vernon, Calif. With USAF, 1942-45, ETO. Mem. ABA, Calif. Bar Assn., L.A. Bar Assn., Wash. State Bar Assn., Phi Delta Phi, Jonathan Club. Roman Catholic. Address: Gibson Dunn & Crutcher 333 S Grand Ave Ste 4400 Los Angeles CA 90071-1548

WOODLEY, DAVID TIMOTHY, dermatology educator; b. Aug. 11, 1948; s. Raoul Ramos-Mimosa and Marian (Schlueter) W.; m. Christina Paschall Prentice, May 4, 1974; children; David Thatcher, Thomas Colgate, Peter paschall. AB, Washington U., St. Louis, 1968; MD, U. Mo., 1973. Diplomate Am. Bd. Internal Medicine, Am. Bd. Dermatology, Nat. Bd. Internal Medicine. Intern Beth Israel Med. Ctr., Mt. Sinai Sch. Medicine, N.Y. Hosp., Cornell U. Sch. Medicine, N.Y.C., 1973-74; resident in internal medicine U. Nebr., Omaha, 1974-76; resident in dermatology U. N.C., Chapel Hill, 1976-78; asst. prof. dermatology U. N.C., Chapel Hill, 1983-85, assoc. prof. dermatology, 1985-88; prof. medicine, co-chief divsn. dermatology Cornell U. Med. Ctr., N.Y.C., 1988-89; prof., vice chair dept. dermatology Stanford (Calif.) U., 1989-93; prof., chair dept. dermatology Northwestern U., Chgo., 1993-99; co-chief dermatology U. So. Calif. Sch. Medicine, L.A., 1999—. Research fellow U. Paris, 1978-80; expert NIH, Bethesda, Md., 1983-89; prof., assoc. chmn. dermatology Stanford U Sch. Medicine, 1989-93; chmn. dermatology Sch. Medicine Northwestern U., 1993-99; prof., co-chmn. dermatology U. So. Calif., 1999—; mem. study sect. NIH. Contbr. chpts. to books and articles in field to profl. jours. Mem. Potomac Albicore Fleet, Washington, 1982-83, Friends of the Art Sch., Chapel Hill, 1983—, Jungian Soc. Triangle Area, Chapel Hill, 1983—. Fellow Am. Acad. Dermatology; mem. ACS (assoc.), Dermatology Found., Am. Soc. for Clin. Rsch., Soc. Investigative Dermatology, Assn. Physician Poets, Am. Soc. for Clin. Investigation. Office: U So Calif Divsn Dermatology LAC & USC Med Ctr 8th Fl 1200 N State St Los Angeles CA 90033-1029 E-mail: dwoodley@hac.usc.edu

WOODRUFF, FAY, paleoceanographer, geological researcher; b. Boston, Jan. 23, 1944; d. Lorande Mitchell and Anne (Fay) W.; m. Alexander Whitehill Clowes, May 20, 1972 (div. Oct. 1974); m. Robert G. Douglas, Jan. 27, 1980; children: Ellen, Katerina. RN, Mass. Gen. Hosp. Sch. Nursing, Boston, 1966; BA, Boston U., 1971; MS, U. So. Calif., 1979. Rsch. assoc. U. So. Calif., L.A., 1978-81, rsch. faculty, 1981-96. Keynote spkr. 4th Internat. Symposium on Benthic Foraminifera, Sendai, Japan, 1990. Contbg. author: Geological Society of America Memoir, 1985; contbr. articles to profl. jours. Life mem. The Nature Conservancy, Washington, 1992; bd. dirs. Friends of Friendship Park, Inc., 1995-2001; co-founder, v.p. Resources Families Adopted Ea. European Children, Inc., L.A., 1996-2000. NSF grantee, 1986-94. Mem. Am. Geophys. Union, Geol. Soc. Am., Internat. Union Geol. Scis. (internat. commn. on stratigraphy, subcommn. on Neogene stratigraphy 1991-99), Soc. Woman Geographers (sec. So. Calif. chpt. 1990-96), Soc. Econ. Paleontologists and Mineralogists (sec., editor N.Am. Micropaleontology sect. 1988-90), Sigma Xi. Office: U So Calif Earth Scis Los Angeles CA 90089-0001

WOODRUFF, GENE LOWRY, nuclear engineer, university dean; b. Greenbrier, Ark., May 6, 1934; s. Clarence Oliver and Avie Erscilla (Lowry) W.; m. Marylou Munson, Jan. 29, 1961; children— Gregory John, David Reed B.S. with honors, U.S. Naval Acad., 1956; M.S. in Nuclear Engring., MIT, 1963, Ph.D. in Nuclear Engring., 1966. Registered profl. engr., Wash. Asst. prof. nuclear engring. U. Wash., Seattle, 1965-70, assoc. prof., 1970-76, prof., 1976-93, chmn. dept., 1981-84, dir. nuclear engring. labs., 1973-76, dean Grad. Sch., 1984-93, prof. chem. engring. environ. studies, 1989-98, dean emeritus, prof. emeritus, 1998—. Vice-chair, chair-elect Grad. Record Exam., 1991-92, chair, 1992-93; cons. to govt. and industry. Contbr. numerous articles to sci. and tech. jours. Served to lt. USN, 1956-60 Mem. Nat. Soc. Profl. Engrs. (Achievement award 1977), Am. Nuclear Soc. (Achievement award 1977, chmn. honors/awards com. 1981-84, nat. program com. 1971-75, exec. com. fusion div. 1976-80, vice chmn. edn. div. 1983-84, Arthur Holly Compton award 1986), Am. Soc. Engring. Edn., Assn. Grad. Schs. (v.p./pres.-elect 1990-91, pres. 1991-92). Democrat Home: 19081 11th Ave NW Shoreline WA 98177-2610 Office: U Wash Box 351750 Seattle WA 98195-1750 E-mail: woodruff@u.washington.edu

WOODRUFF, KAY HERRIN, pathologist, educator; b. Charlotte, N.C., Sept. 22, 1942; d. Herman Keith and Helen Thelma (Tucker) Herrin; m. John T. Lyman, May 3, 1980; children: Robert, Geoffry, Carolyn. BA in Chemistry, Duke U., 1964; MD, Emory U., 1968. Diplomate Am. Bd. Pathology (trustee 1993—, sec. 1998-2000, v.p. 2000-2001, pres. 2001—). Medicine and pediat. intern U. N.C., Chapel Hill, 1968-69, resident in anatomic pathology, 1969-70; chief resident in anatomic pathology, instr. U. Okla., Oklahoma City, 1970-71, fellow in electron microscopy-pulmonary pathology, instr., 1971-72; chief resident in clin. pathology U. Calif., San Francisco, 1972-74, asst. clin. prof. dept. anatomic pathology, 1974-91, assoc. clin. prof., 1991—; chief electron microscopy VA Hosp., San Francisco, 1974-75; pvt. practice, San Pablo, Calif., 1981—. Pres. med. staff Brookside Hosp., San Pablo, 1994, med. dir. Regional Cancer Ctr., 1995-98 ; assoc. pathologist Children's Hosp., San Francisco, 1979-81, St. Joseph's Hosp., San Francisco, 1977-79; cons. pathologist Lawrence Berkeley (Calif.) Lab., 1974-93; med. dir. Bay Area Tumor Inst. Tissue Network, San Pablo, 1989—; asst. clin. prof. pathology health and med. scis. program U. Calif., Berkeley and U. Calif., San Francisco Joint Med. Program, 1985-91, assoc. clin. prof., 1991—, others. Contbr. articles and abstracts to med. jours. Mem. exec. bd. Richmond (Calif.) Quits Smoking, 1986-90, Bay Area Tumor Inst., Oakland, Calif., 1987—; mem. exec. bd. Contra Costa unit Am. Cancer Soc., Walanut Creek, Calif., 1985-87, mem. profl. edn. com., 1985-90, mem. pub. edn. com., 1985-86, mem. task force on breast health Calif. div., 1992-93; mem. transfusion adv. com. Irwin Meml. Blood Bank, San Francisco, 1977-83; chmn. transfusion adv. com. Alameda Contra County Blood Bank, 1989-92; commr. Calif. Bd. Med. Quality Assurance, 1978-80; pres. Brookside Found., San Pablo, Calif., 1998-2000. Recipient young investigator award Am. Lung Assn., 1975-77; Outstanding Svc. awards Am. Cancer Soc., 1986, 87, Disting. Svc. award, 1988; Disting. Clin. Tchg. award U. Calif., San Francisco and Berkeley Joint Med. Program, 1987, Outstanding Tchg. award, 1988, Excellence in Basic Sci. Instrn. award, 1990, Excellence in Tchr. Clin. Scis. award, 1993; cert. of recognition Cmty. Svc. Richmond, 1989. Mem. AMA, Coll. Am. Pathologists (editl. bd. CAP Today 1986-90, bd. govs. 1990-96, chmn. coun. on practice mgmt. 1994, William Kuhn award for outstanding comm. 1996, Presdl. Medal of Honor 1995, 96), Am. Med. Women's Assn. (exec. bd. 1984-87, regional bd. govs. 1984-87), No. Calif. Women's Med. Assn. (pres. 1982-84), Calif. Soc. Pathologists (bd. dirs. 1988-90), No. Calif. Oncology Group, South Bay Pathology Soc. (pres. 1987), Am. Assn. Blood Banks, Calif. Med. Assn., Alameda-Contra Costa County Med. Soc., Am. Soc. Clin. Pathology, Calif. Pathology Soc. Avocation: classical piano. Office: Doctors Med Ctr 2000 Vale Rd San Pablo CA 94806-3808

WOODRUFF, NEIL PARKER, agricultural engineer; b. Clyde, Kans., July 25, 1919; s. Charles Scott and Myra (Christian) W.; m. Dorothy Adele Russ, June 15, 1952; children: Timothy C., Thomas S. B.S., Kans. State U., 1949, M.S., 1953; postgrad., Iowa State U., 1959. Agrl. engr. Agrl. Research Service, Dept. Agr., Manhattan, Kans., 1949-63, research leader, 1963-75; cons. engr. Manhattan, 1975-77; civil engr. Kans. Dept. Transp., Topeka, 1977-79; prof., mem. grad. faculty Kans. State U., civil engr.

facilities planning, 1979-84. Mem. sci. exchange team to, Soviet Union, 1974; with W/PT Cons., 1984—. Contbr. articles to tech. jours. and books. Fellow Am. Soc. Agrl. Engrs. (Hancor Soil Water Engring. award 1975); mem. Sigma Xi, Gamma Sigma Delta. Home and Office: 12906 W Blue Bonnet Dr Sun City West AZ 85375-2538

WOODRUFF, TRUMAN O(WEN), physicist, emeritus educator; b. Salt Lake City, May 26, 1925; s. Wilford Owen and Evelyn (Ballif) W.; m. Ambrosina Lydia Solaroli, Sept. 14, 1948 (dec. June 1991); m. Patricia O'Keefe Vincent, Sept. 23, 1995. AB, Harvard U., 1947; BA, Oxford (Eng.) U., 1950; PhD, Calif. Inst. Tech., 1955. Nat. scholar Harvard, 1942-44, 46-47, Sheldon traveling fellow, 1947-48; Rhodes scholar Oxford U., 1948-50; Dow Chem. Co. fellow, Howard Hughes fellow Calif. Inst. Tech., 1950-54; research asso. physics U. Ill., 1954-55; physicist Gen. Elec. Research Lab., 1955-62; prof. physics Mich. State U., 1962-85, prof. emeritus, 1985—, chmn. dept., 1972-75; sr. scientist research labs. Hughes Aircraft Co., Malibu, Calif., 1986-87; cons. in physics Los Angeles, 1987-91. Vis. prof. Scuola Normale Superiore, Pisa, Italy, 1982—. Contbr. articles to sci. jours. Served with USNR, 1944-46. Fulbright fellow U. Pisa, 1968-69 Fellow Am. Phys. Soc.; mem. Assn. Harvard Chemists, Phi Beta Kappa, Sigma Xi.

WOODS, GRANT, lawyer, former state attorney general; b. Elk City, Okla., May 19, 1954; m. Marlene Galán; children: Austin, Lauren, Cole, Dylan. BA, Occidental Coll., 1976; JD, Ariz. State U., 1979. Atty. gen., Ariz., 1990-99; ptnr. Goldstein, McGroder & Woods Ltd., Phoenix, 1999-2000; pvt. practice Phoenix, 2000—. Founder Mesa Boys and Girls Club. Mem. State Bar Ariz., Ariz. Trial Lawyers Assn. Office: 1700 N 7th St Phoenix AZ 85006-2230

WOODS, GURDON GRANT, sculptor; b. Savannah, Ga., Apr. 15, 1915; s. Frederick L. and Marion (Skinner) W. Student, Art Student's League N.Y.C., 1936-39, Bklyn. Mus. Sch., 1945-46; Ph.D. (hon.), Coll. San Francisco Art Inst., 1966. Exec. dir. San Francisco Art Inst., 1955-64; dir. Calif. Sch. Fine Arts, 1955-65; prof. Adlai E. Stevenson Coll., U. Calif. at Santa Cruz, 1966-74; dir. Otis Art Inst., Los Angeles, 1974-77; asst. dir. Los Angeles County Mus. Natural History, 1977-80; Sculptor mem. San Francisco Art Commn., 1954-56; mem. Santa Cruz County Art Commn., Regional Arts Council of Bay Area. Exhibited: N.A.D., 1948, 49, San Francisco Art Assn. anns., 1952-54, Denver Mus. Anns., 1952, 53, Whitney Mus. Ann., 1953, Sao Paulo Biennial, 1955, Bolles Gallery San Francisco, 1969, 70, 72, L.A. Mcpl. Gallery, 1977, San Jose Inst. Contemporary Art (Calif.), Washington Project for the Arts retrospective, 1968-85, Washington, 1985, Retrospective Art Mus. Santa Cruz County, Calif., 1987, d.p. Fong Gallery, 1993, 94, Michael Angelo Gallery, Santa Cruz, 1995; commns. include: cast concrete reliefs and steel fountain, IBM Ctr., San Jose, Calif., fountain, Paul Masson Winery, Saratoga, Calif., McGraw Hill Pubs. (now Birkenstock), Novato, Calif.; work in permanent collection Oakland (Calif.) Mus.; papers in Archives of Am. Art, Smithsonian Instn., Washington. Recipient citation N.Y.C., 1948; prize N.A.D., 1949; Chapelbrook Found. research grantee, 1965-66; Sequoia Fund grantee, 1967; Research grantee Creative Arts Inst., U. Calif., 1968; grantee Carnegie Corp., 1968-69 Mem. Artists Equity Assn (pres. No. Calif. chpt. 1950-52, nat. dir. 1952-55) Address: 125 Heather Terr Aptos CA 95003

WOODS, JAMES C. museum director; Dir. Herrett Ctr. Arts and Sci. and Faulkner Planetarium, Twin Falls, Idaho. Office: Coll Southern Idaho Herrett Ctr Arts & Sci 315 Falls Ave Twin Falls ID 83301-3367

WOODS, JAMES ROBERT, lawyer; b. San Francisco, Aug. 3, 1947; s. Robert H. and Grace (Snowhill) W.; m. Linda Stephens; children: Heather F., Adam Boyd. AB with honors, U. Calif., Berkeley, 1969; JD, U. Calif., Davis, 1972. Bar: Calif. 1972, N.Y. 1973, U.S. Dist. Ct. (so. & ea. dists.) N.Y. 1975, U.S. Ct. Appeals (2d cir.) 1975, U.S. Dist. Ct. (no. dist.) Calif. 1984. Ptnr. LeBoeuf, Lamb, Greene & MacRae L.L.P., San Francisco, 1983—. Co-author: California Insurance Law and Practice; contbr. articles to profl. jours. Office: LeBoeuf Lamb Greene & MacRae LLP 1 Embarcadero Ctr Ste 400 San Francisco CA 94111-3619

WOODS, JAMES STERRETT, toxicologist; b. Lewistown, Pa., Feb. 26, 1940; s. James Sterrett and Jane Smith (Parker) W.; m. Nancy Fugate, Dec. 20, 1969; 1 dau., Erin Elizabeth. AB, Princeton U., 1962; MS, U. Wash., 1968, PhD, 1970; MPH, U. N.C., 1978. Diplomate Am. Bd. Toxicology. Rsch. assoc. dept. pharmacology Yale U. Sch. Medicine, New Haven, 1970-72; staff fellow environ. toxicology. Nat. Inst. Environ. Health Scis. br. NIH, Research Triangle Park, N.C., 1972-75, head biochem. toxicology sect., 1975-77; sr. rsch. leader environ.-occupational health risk evaluation Battelle Ctrs. for Pub. Health Rsch. and Evaluation, Seattle, 1978—; rsch. prof. U. Wash., Seattle, 1979—. Pres. Am. Bd. Toxicology, 1997-98. Contbr. articles to profl. jours. With USN, 1962-66. Scholar USPHS, 1966-70; Fellow Am. Cancer Soc., 1970-72. Mem. AAAS, Am. Assn. Cancer Rsch., Am. Soc. Pharmacology and Exptl. Therapeutics, Pacific NW Assn. Toxicologists (founding pres.), Soc. Epidemiology Rsch., Sox. Toxicology, Am. Coll. of Epidemiology, Am. Bd. Toxicology (pres. 1997-98). Home: 4525 E Laurel Dr NE Seattle WA 98105-3838 Office: Battelle Research Ctr PO Box 5395 Seattle WA 98105-0395 E-mail: woods@battelle.org

WOODS, LAWRENCE MILTON, airline company executive; b. Manderson, Wyo., Apr. 14, 1932; s. Ben Ray and Katherine (Youngman) W.; m. Joan Frances Van Patten, June 10, 1952; 1 dau., Laurie. B.Sc. with honors, U. Wyo., 1953; M.A., N.Y. U., 1973, Ph.D., 1975; LL.D., Wagner Coll., 1973. Bar: Mont. 1957; C.P.A., Colo., Mont. Accountant firm Peat, Marwick, Mitchell & Co. (C.P.A.'s), Billings, Mont., 1953; supervisory auditor Army Audit Agy., Denver, 1954-56; accountant Mobil Producing Co., Billings, Mont., 1956-59; planning analyst Socony Mobil Oil Co., N.Y.C., 1959-63, planning mgr., 1963-65; v.p. North Am. div. Mobil Oil Corp., N.Y.C., 1966-67, gen. mgr. planning and econs., 1967-69, v.p., 1969-77, exec. v.p., 1977-85, also dir.; pres., chief exec. officer, dir. Centennial Airlines, Inc., 1985-87; pres., dir. Woshakie Travel Corp., 1988—, High Plains Pub. Co. Inc., 1988—. Bd. dirs. The Aid Assn. for Lutherans Mutual Funds. Author: Accounting for Capital, Construction and Maintenance Expenditures, 1967, The Wyoming Country Before Statehood, 1971, Sometimes the Books Froze, 1985, Moreton Frewen's Western Adventures, 1986, British Gentlemen in the Wild West, 1989; editor: Wyoming Biographies, 1991, Wyoming's Big Horn Basin, 1996, Agent R, 2000; co-author: Takeover, 1980; editor: Wyoming Biographies, 1991; contbr.: Accountants' Encyclopedia, 1962. Bd. dirs. U. Wyo. Research Corp. Served with AUS, 1953-55. Mem. ABA, Mont. Bar Assn., Am. Inst. CPA's, Chgo. Club. Republican. Lutheran. Office: High Plains Pub Co PO Box 1860 Worland WY 82401-1860

WOODS, NANCY FUGATE, dean, women's health nurse; BS, Wis. State U., 1968; MSN, U. Wash., 1969; PhD, U. N.C., 1978. Staff nurse Sacred Heart Hosp., Wis., 1968, Univ. Hosp., 1969-70, St. Francis Cabrini Hosp., 1970; nurse clinician Yale-New Haven Hosp., 1970-71; instr. nursing Duke U., Durham, N.C., 1971-72, from instr. to assoc. prof., 1972-78; assoc. prof. physiology U. Wash., Seattle, 1978-82, prof. physiology, 1982-84, chairperson dept. parent and child nursing, 1984-90, prof. dept. parent and child nursing, 1990—, dean Sch. Nursing, 1998—, dir. Ctr. Women's Health Rsch., U. Wash., Seattle, 1989—. Pres. scholar U. Calif., San Francisco, 1985-86. Contbr. articles to profl. jours. Fellow ANA, Am. Acad. Nursing, Inst. Medicare, N.A.S.; mem. AAUP, APHA, Am. Coll. Epidemiology, Soc. Menstrual Cycle Rsch. (v.p. 1981-82, pres. 1983-85), Soc. Advancement Women's Health Rsch. Office: U Wash Sch Nursing PO Box 357260 Seattle WA 98195-7260

WOODS, SANDRA KAY, real estate executive; b. Loveland, Colo., Oct. 11, 1944; d. Ivan H. and florence L. (Betz) Harris; m. Gary A. Woods, June 11, 1967; children: Stephanie Michelle, Michael Harris. BA, U. Colo., 1966, MA, 1967. Personnel mgmt. specialist CSC, Denver, 1967; asst. to regional dir. HEW, Denver, 1968-69; urban renewal rep. HUD, Denver, 1970-73, dir. program analysis, 1974-75, asst. regional dir. cmty. planning and devel., 1976-77, regional dir. fair housing, 1978-79; mgr. ea. facility project Adolph Coors Co., Golden, Colo., 1980, dir. real estate, 1981, v.p. chief environ. health and safety officer, 1982-96, v.p. strategic selling initiatives, 1996—; pres. Industries for Jefferson County, 1985; with Woods Properties LLP, Golden. Mem. Exec. Exch., The White House, 1980. Bd. dirs. Golden Local Devel. Corp., 1981-82; fundraising dir. Coll. Arts and Scis., U. Colo., boulder, 1982-89, U. Colo.found.; mem. exec. bd. NCCJ, Denver, 1982-94; v.p. women in bus. Inc., Denver, 1982-83; mem. steering com. 1984 Yr. for All Denver Women, 1983-84; mem. 10th dist. Denver br. Fed. Res. Bd., 1990-96, chmn. bd., 1995-96; bd. dirs. Nat. Jewish Hosp., 1994—; chmn. Greater Denver Corp., 1991—. Named one of Outstanding Young Women Am., U.S. Jaycees, 1974, 78, Fifty Women to Watch, Businessweek, 1987, 92, Woman of Achievement YWCA, 1988. Mem. Indsl. Devel. Resources Coun. (bd. dirs. 1986-89), Am. Mgmt. Assn., Denver C. of C. (bd. dirs. 1988-96, Disting. Young Exec. award 1974, mem. Leadership Denver, 1976-77), Colo. Women's Forum, Nat. Assn. Office and Indsl. Park Developers (sec. 1988, treas. 1989), Committee of 200 (v.p. 1994-95), Phi Beta Kappa, Pi Alpha Alpha, PEO Club (Loveland). Republican. Presbyterian. E-mail: Sandrawoods@uoli.com

WOODWARD, LESTER RAY, lawyer; b. Lincoln, Nebr., May 24, 1932; s. Wendell Smith and Mary Elizabeth (Theobald) W.; m. Marianne Martinson, Dec. 27, 1958; children: Victoria L. Woodward Eisele, Richard T., David M., Andrew E. BSBA, U. Nebr., 1953; LLB, Harvard U., 1957; LLD (hon.), Bethany Coll., 1974. Bar: Colo., 1957. Assoc. Davis, Graham & Stubbs, Denver, 1957-59, 60-62, ptnr., 1962—. Teaching fellow Sch. Law Harvard U., 1959-60. Bd. dirs. Bethany Coll., Lindsborg, Kans., 1966-74, 87-95, chmn., 1989-92; bd. dirs. Pub. Edn. Coalition, Denver, 1985-92, chmn., 1988-89; mem. Colo. Commn. Higher Edn., Denver, 1977-86, chmn., 1979-81; mem. bd. edn. Denver Pub. Schs., 1999—. Mem. ABA, Colo. Bar Assn., Am. Law Inst. Republican. Lutheran. Home: 680 Bellaire St Denver CO 80220-4935 Office: Davis Graham & Stubbs 1150 17th St Ste 500 Denver CO 80202-5682

WOODWARD, STEPHEN RICHARD, newspaper reporter; b. Fukuoka City, Japan, July 27, 1953; came to U.S., 1954; s. Leonard Edwin and Etsuko (Okumura) W.; m. Sandra Elizabeth Richardson, Dec. 31, 1979; children: Daniel Joseph, Elizabeth Etsuko. BA in English, Wright State U., 1975; MA in Journalism, U. Mo., 1979. Advt. coordinator Wright State U., Dayton, Ohio, 1976-77; reporter Kansas City (Mo.) Star, 1979-82; assoc. editor then editor Kansas City Bus. Jour., 1982-83; editor then gen. mgr. Portland (Oreg.) Bus. Jour., 1984-86; exec. bus. editor The Hartford (Conn.) Courant, 1986-87; editor San Francisco Bus. Times, 1987-88; bus. editor The Oregonian, Portland, 1989-93, reporter, 1993—. Recipient 1st Place Investigative Reporting award Assn. Area Bus. Publs., 1983, 1st Place Column Writing award Assn. Area Bus. Publs., 1985. Mem. Investigative Reporters and Editors Inc. Avocations: astronomy, chess, creative writing. Office: The Oregonian 1320 SW Broadway Portland OR 97201-3499

WOOLF, MICHAEL E. lawyer; b. Phoenix, Mar. 17, 1949; BS, Ariz. State U., 1971, JD cum laude, 1974. Bar: ariz. 1974. Ptnr. O'Connor, Cavanagh, Anderson, Killingsworth & Beshears, P.A., Phoenix, 1977-99, Mariscal Weeks McIntyre & Friedlander PA, Phoenix, 1999—. Mem. ABA, Maricopa County Bar Assn., State Bar Ariz. Office: Mariscal Weeks McIntyre & Friedlander PA 2901 N Central Ave Ste 200 Phoenix AZ 85012-2705

WOOLFENDEN, JAMES MANNING, nuclear medicine physician, educator; b. L.A., Nov. 8, 1942; BA with distinction, Stanford U., 1964; MD, U. Wash., 1968. Diplomate Am. Bd. Nuclear Medicine (chmn. credentials com. 1993-94, vice chmn. exams. com. 1993-95, chmn. exam. com. 1995-96, sec. 1994-96, chmn. 1996-97), Nat. Bd. Med. Examiners. Med. intern L.A. County-U. So. Calif. Med. Ctr., 1968-69; med. resident West L.A. VA Med. Ctr., 1969-70; nuclear medicine resident L.A. County-U. So. Calif. Med. Ctr., 1972-74; from asst. prof. radiology to assoc. prof. radiology U. Ariz., Tucson, 1974-84, prof. radiology, 1984—. Mem. med. staff Univ. Med. Ctr., Tucson, 1974—; cons. VA Med. Ctr., 1974—; cons. med. staff Tucson Med. Ctr., 1975—, Carondelet St. Joseph's Hosp., 1974-98, St. Mary's Hosp., Tucson, 1976-90; mem. Nat. Cancer Inst. site visit team NIH, 1976, mem. NHLB Inst. site visit team NIH, 1976, mem. diagnostic radiology study sect., 1993-97, chmn., 1995-97; mem. med. liaison officer network EPA, 1983—; cons.-tchg. med. staff Kino Comty. Hosp., 1984-94; med. officer Clin. Ctr., NIH, Bethesda, 1984-85; mem. Ariz. Cancer Ctr., U. Ariz., 1988—, sr. clin. scientist Univ. Heart Ctr., 1990—; Ariz. bd. regents U. Ariz. Presdl. Search Com., 1990-91; chmn. Ariz. Atomic Energy Commn., 1979-80, Ariz. Radiation Regulatory Hearing Bd., 1981—; bd. dirs. Calif. Radioactive Materials Mgmt. Forum, 1989—, chmn.-elect, 1993-94, chmn., 1994-95, Western Forum Edn. in Safe Disposal of Low-Level Radioactive Waste, 1990—, vice chmn., 1991-92, chmn., 1992-94. Manuscript reviewer: Noninvasive Med. Imaging, 1983-84, Jour. Nuclear Medicine, 1985—, Investigative Radiology, 1989-94, Archives of Internal Medicine, 1990—; contbr. book chpts.: Diagnostic Nuclear Medicine, 2d edit., 1988, Adjuvant Therapy of Cancer, 1977, Fundamentals of Nuclear Medicine, 1988, others; contbr. articles and book revs. to profl. publs. Mem. Am. Heart Assn. Coun. on Cardiovasc. Radiology. Maj. U.S. Army, 1970-72, Vietnam. Fellow Am. Coll. Nuclear Physicians (long range planning com. 1981-83, govt. affairs com. 1984-94, exec. com. 1987-91, sec. 1989-91, parliamentarian 1991-95, treas. 1996-98, mem. publs. com. 1993—, chmn. publs. com. 1993-94, pres.-elect 1998-99, pres. 1999-2000, and many others); mem. AMA (diagnostic and therapeutic tech. assessment reference panel 1982-98), Am. Nuclear Soc., Soc. Nuclear Medicine (com. on audit 1992—, bd. trustees 1992-96, ho. dels. 1996—, fin. com. 1996—, bd. dirs. 1997-99, bronze medal for sci. exhibit 1984, bd. dirs., sec.-treas. So. Calif. chpt. 1993-95, pres.-elect 1995-96, pres. 1996-99), Assn. Univ. Radiologists, Ariz. Med. Assn., Pima County Med. Soc., Radiol. Soc. N.Am. Office: Ariz Health Scis Ctr Nuc Medicine 1501 N Campbell Ave Tucson AZ 85724-5068

WOOLHISER, DAVID ARTHUR, hydrologist; b. LaCrosse, Wis., Jan. 21, 1932; s. Algie Duncan and Blanche Lenore (Jasperson) W.; m. Kathryn Brown, Apr. 21, 1957; children: Carl David, Curt Fredric, Lisa Kathryn. BS in Agriculture, BSCE, U. Wis., 1955, PhD, 1962; MS, U. Ariz., 1959. Instr. U. Ariz., Tucson, 1955-58; hydraulic engr. Agrl. Rsch. Svc. USDA, Madison, Wis., 1959-61, Columbia, Mo., 1961-63; asst. prof. Cornell U., Ithaca, N.Y., 1963-67; rsch. hydraulic engr. Agrl. Rsch. Svc., Ft. Collins, Colo., 1967-81, Tucson, 1981-91, collaborator, 1991-92; faculty affiliate Colo. State U., 1994—. Vis. scientist Inst. Hydrology, Wallingford, Eng., 1977-78; vis. prof. Imperial Coll., London, 1977-78; faculty affiliate Colo. State U., 1967-84; adj. prof. U. Ariz., 1981-92; vis. prof. Va. Poly. Inst. and State U., 1992; sr. rsch. sci. Colo. State U., 1993-94, faculty affiliate 1994—; vis. prof. U. Cordoba, Spain, 1993-94, 96. Contbr. articles to profl. jours. Recipient disting. svc. citation Coll. Engring. U. Wis., Madison, 1991, Feb. Lab. Consortium award for excellence in tech. transfer, 1998, Ray K. Linsky award Am. Inst. Hydrology, 2000. Fellow Am. Geophys. Union (Robert E. Horton award 1983); mem. NAE, ASCE (Hunter Rouse lectr. 1994, arid lands hydraulic engring. award 1988). Office: 1631 Barnwood Dr Fort Collins CO 80525-2069 E-mail: woolhiserd@aol.com

WOOLLATT, PAUL G. financial company executive; COO Downey Fin. Corp., Newport Beach, Calif., 1998—. Office: Downey Fin Corp 3501 Jamboree Rd Newport Beach CA 92660

WOOLLS, ESTHER BLANCHE, library science educator; b. Louisville, Mar. 30, 1935; d. Arthur William and Esther Lennie (Smith) Sutton; m. Donald Paul Woolls, Oct. 21, 1953 (div. Nov. 1982); 1 son, Arthur Paul AB in Fine Arts, Ind. U., 1958, MA in Libr. Sci., 1962, PhD in Libr. Sci., 1973. Elem. libr. Hammond Pub. Schs., Ind., 1958-65, libr. coord., 1965-67, Roswell Ind. Schs., N.Mex., 1967-70; prof. libr. sci. U. Pitts., 1973-97; prof., dir. Sch. Lib. and Info. Sci. San Jose (Calif.) State U., 1997—. Exec. dir. Beta Phi Mu, 1981-95. Author: The School Library Media Manager, 1995, 2d edit., 1999, So You're Going to Run a Library, 1995, Ideas for School Library Media Centers, 1996; co-author: Information Literacy, 1999; editor: Continuing Professional Education and IFLA: Past, Present, and a Vision for the Future, 1993, Delivering Lifelong Continuing Professional Education Across Space and Time, 2001. Fulbright scholar, 1995-96; recipient disting. svc. award Pa. Sch. Librs. Assn., 1993. Mem. ALA (mem. coun. 1985-89, 95—), Am. Assn. Sch. Librs. (bd. dirs. 1983-88, pres. 1993-94, disting. svc. award 1997), Pa. Learning Resources Assn. (pres. 1984-85), Internat. Assn. Sch. Librs. (pres. 1998-2001), Internat. Fedn. Libr. Assns. (mem. standing com. sch. librs. sect. 1991-99, sec. Continuing Profl. Edn. Round Table 2000—). Home: 201 S 4th St San Jose CA 95112-3600 Office: San Jose State U Sch Lib & Info Sci 1 Washington Sq San Jose CA 95192-0029

WOOLRIDGE, ORLANDO, former professional basketball coach, Olympic coach; Profl. player Chgo. Bulls, 1981, N.J. Nets, L.A. Lakers, 1988-90, Denver Nuggets, Detroit Pistons, Milw. Bucks, Phila. 76ers, 1993-94; asst. coach L.A. Sparks, 1997-98, head coach, 1998-99; asst. coach USA Women's Basketball, 1999—. Cons. L.A. Sparks. Coach various recreational league;s asst. girls coach Harvard-Westlake H.S., Studio City, Calif. Office: USA Basketball 5465 Mark Dabling Blvd Colorado Springs CO 80918

WOOLSEY, LYNN, congresswoman; b. Seattle, Nov. 3, 1937; BS, U. San Francisco, 1981. Mem. U.S. Congress from 6th Calif. dist., 1993—; mem. edn. and workforce com., sci. com. Mem. Petaluma City Coun., 1984-92 Democrat. Office: US Ho Reps 2263 Rayburn Ho Office Bldg Washington DC 20515-0506*

WOOLSEY, ROBERT EUGENE DONALD, mineral economics, mathematics and business administration educator; b. Fort Worth, Oct. 31, 1936; s. Eugene Ralph W. and Ruby Ruth (White) Binder Woolsey; m. Ronita Elaine Packer, Sept. 17, 1958; children: Wysandria W.W., Darrell E. B.A., U. Tex., 1959, M.A., 1967, Ph.D., 1969. Staff mem. Sandia Corp., Albuquerque, 1966-68; assoc. dir. Computer Center U. Tex., Austin, 1968-69; assoc. prof. math. Colo. Sch. Mines, Golden, 1969-72, prof. math., 1972-74, prof. mineral econs., 1974-79, prof., head dept., 1979-81, MAPCO Found. prof., 1981-84, prof., program dir. Ops. Rsch./Mgmt. Sci. program divsn. econs. & bus., 1988—. Vis. coll. Colo. Women's Coll., Denver, 1979-81; adj. prof. U. Waterloo, Ont., Can., 1972—, Instituto Technologico de Monterrey, Nuevo Leon, Mexico, 1974—, U. Witwatersrand, Johannesburg, S. Africa, 1984—; vis. prof. dept. engring. U.S. Mil. Acad., West Point, N.Y., 1986-87; prof. core faculty Walden U., 1990—; bd. dirs. Southland Energy Corp., Tulsa, New Tech. Devel. Co., Inc., Vancouver, B.C., Can. Author: Operations Research for Immediate Application, 1975, Applied Management Science, 1980; editor: Transactions of the Institute of Industrial Engineering, 1981-84, Production and Inventory Management, 1984— , Interfaces, 1975-82, Jour. Ops. Mgmt., 1986-87; contbr. articles to profl. jours. Pres. Rocky Mountain Fire Brigade, Inc., Golden, Colo., 1972-83. Served to capt. USAF, 1959-62. Named tchr. of yr. Standard Oil Ind., 1972,96, Hon. Col. 115 Engr. Regiment U.S. Army, 1987; recipient 1st Harold Larnder Meml. prize Can. Operational Rsch. Soc., 1986, Disting. Civilian Svc. medal U.S. Dept. Army, 1987, Comdrs. medal, 1991, Outstanding Civilian Svc. medal, 1995, award Inst. Ops. Rsch. and Mgmt. Sci., 1999. Fellow Am. Inst. Decision Sci. (v.p. 1981-83); mem. Inst. Mgmt. Scis. (council 1976-78, pres. 1986-87), Inst. Indsl. Engrs. (sr. mem., editor 1981-84), Ops. Rsch. Soc. Am. (editor 1975-82), Newcomen Soc. Republican. Episcopalian. Home: 401 S Russell Ave Lot 182 Douglas WY 82633-3114 Office: Colo Sch Mines Divsn Econs & Bus Golden CO 80401 E-mail: rwoolsey@mines.edu

WOOSLEY, ANNE I. cultural organization administrator; Dir. The Amerind Found., Inc., Dragoon, Ariz. Office: The Amerind Found Inc PO Box 400 2100 N Amerind Rd Dragoon AZ 85609

WOOSLEY, RAYMOND, pharmacology and medical educator; b. Ky., Oct. 2, 1942; m. Julianne Buchert. BS, Western Ky. U., 1964; PhD, U. Louisville, 1967; MD, U. Miami, 1973. Intern, resident Vanderbilt U. Hosp., Nashville, 1973-76; sr. pharmacologist, dir. rsch. Meyer (Glaxo) Labs., Ft. Lauderdale, Fla., 1968-71; instr. dept. medicine, pharmacology Vanderbilt U., Nashville, 1976-77, asst. prof., 1977-79, assoc. prof., 1979-84, assoc. dir. clin. rsch. ctr., 1981-88, prof., 1984-88; prof. pharmacology, medicine, chmn. dept. pharmacology Georgetown U. Sch. Medicine, Washington, 1988-2000; assoc. dean clin. rsch., 2001—; also chief divsn. clin. pharmacology Georgetown U. Sch. Medicine, Washington, 1988-94; dir. Inst. for Cardiovascular Scis., Washington, 1995-2000, Gen. Clin. Rsch. Ctr., Washington, 1999-2001; v.p. Ariz. Health Scis. Ctr., dean Sch. Medicine U. Ariz., 2001—. Researcher in field. Editor: Cardiovascular Pharmacology and Therapeutics, 1994; contbr. chpts. to books and articles to profl. jours. NIH Predoctoral fellow NIH, 1964-67, postdoctoral fellow U. Louisville, 1967-68, Vanderbilt U., 1976-77, Am. Coll. Clin. Pharmacology fellow, 1974; Ogden scholar Western Ky. U., 1960-64; recipient Career Devel. award in Clin. Pharmacology Pharm. Mfrs. Assn. Found., 1977-80. Fellow ACP, Am. Coll. Clin. Pharmacology; mem. Am. Heart Assn. (fellow coun. clin. cardiology 1985—), Am. Soc. Pharmacology and Exptl. Therapeutics (clin. pharmacology exec. com. 1981-92, Harry Gold award 2001), Am. Fedn. Clin. Rsch., Am. Soc. Clin. Pharmacology and Therapeutics (v.p. 1998-99, pres.1999, Rawls-Palmer award 1990), Am. Bd. Clin. Pharmacology, Assn. Med. Sch. Pharmacology (pres. 1996-98), Soc. for Women's Health Rsch. (bd. dirs. 1999—). Office: Ariz Health Sci Ctr 245018 AHSCCl 1501 N Campbell Ave # 2222 Tucson AZ 85724-5018 E-mail: WoosleyR@u.arizona.edu

WOOSTER, WARREN S(CRIVER), marine science educator; b. Westfield, Mass., Feb. 20, 1921; s. Harold Abbott and Violet (Scriver) W.; m. Clarissa Pickles, Sept. 13, 1948; children: Susan Wooster Allen, Daniel, Dana. Sc.B., Brown U., 1943; M.S., Calif. Inst. Tech., 1947; Ph.D., UCLA, 1953. From research asst. to prof. Scripps Instn. Oceanography, U. Calif., 1948-73; dir. UNESCO Office Oceanography, 1961-63; dean Rosenstiel Sch. Marine Atmospheric Sci., U. Miami, 1973-76; prof. marine studies and fisheries U. Wash., Seattle, 1976-91, prof. emeritus, 1992, dir. Inst. Marine Studies, 1979-82. Contbr. to books, profl. jours. Served with USNR, 1943-46. Fellow Am. Geophys. Union, Am. Meteorol. Soc.; mem. Sigma Xi. Office: U Wash Sch Marine Affairs 3707 Brooklyn Ave NE Seattle WA 98105-6715 E-mail: wooster@u.washington.edu

WOOTEN, CECIL AARON, religious organization administrator; b. Laurel, Miss., June 3, 1924; s. Cecil A. and Alice (Cox) W.; m. Helen Moss, Apr. 4, 1947; children: Michael, Margaret, Martin, Marsha, Mark. B.S. in Mech. Engring, U. Ala., 1949. With CBI Industries, 1941—, bd. dirs., 1965-83; mng. dir. CBI Constructors Ltd., London, 1957-62; mgr. (Houston sales dist.), 1962-64; v.p., mgr. corp. services Oak Brook, Ill., 1968-69; sr. v.p.-gen. sales mgr., 1969-78; sr. v.p. comml. devel. Chgo. Bridge & Iron Co. (subs. CBI Industries), 1978-79; sr. v.p. corp. adminstrn. CBI Industries, Oak Brook, 1980-83; dir. devel. Christian Family Services, Gainesville, Fla., 1983-86, Denver Ch. of Christ, 1986-88, Boston Ch. of Christ, 1988-92; pres. Internat. Chs. of Christ, Inc., L.A., 1994-99; chair Internat. Chs. Christ, L.A., 1999—. Bd. dirs. Oak Brook (Ill.) Bank. Former trustee Elmhurst (Ill.) Coll.; former bd. sponsors Good Samaritan Hosp., Downers Grove, Ill. Served to 1st lt. AUS, 1943-46. Mem. ASME, Nat. Soc. Profl. Engrs. Lodge: Rotary. Home: 1032 Lavender Ln La Canada CA 91011-2337 Office: Internat Chs of Christ 3530 Wilshire Blvd Ste 1750 Los Angeles CA 90010-2238

WOOTEN, FREDERICK (OLIVER), applied science educator; b. Linwood, Pa., May 16, 1928; s. Frederick Alexander and Martha Emma (Guild) W.; m. Jane Watson MacPherson, Aug. 30, 1952; children: Donald, Bartley. BS in Chemistry, MIT, 1950; PhD in Chemistry, U. Del., 1955. Sr. scientist Lawrence Livermore (Calif.) Lab., 1957-72; prof. applied sci. U. Calif., Davis, 1972-99, prof. emeritus, 1999—. Vis. prof. physics Drexel U., Phila., 1964, Chalmers Tech. H.S., Goteborg, Sweden, 1967-68, Heriot-Watt U., Edinburgh, Scotland, 1979, Trinity Coll., Dublin, Ireland, 1986, Mich. State U., East Lansing, 1993, Boston U., 1996; vis. scholar in math. U. Mass., Amherst, 1991; staff physicist All-Am. Engring. Co., Wilmington, Del., 1955-57; chmn. applied sci. U. Calif., Davis, 1973-93, chmn. designated emphasis in computational sci., 1989-2000; cons. in field. Author: Optical Properties of Solids, 1972. Mem. AAAS, Am. Phys. Soc., N.Y. Acad. Scis., Sigma Xi. Home: 2328 Alameda Diablo Diablo CA 94528 Office: U Calif Dept Applied Sci Davis CA 95616 E-mail: wooten@netvista.net

WORLEY, LLOYD DOUGLAS, English language educator; b. Lafayette, La., Sept. 11, 1946; s. Albert Stiles and Doris (Christy) W.; m. Maydean Ann Mouton, Apr. 4, 1966; children: Erin Shawn, Albert Stiles II. BA, U. SW La., 1968, MA, 1972; PhD, So. Ill. U., 1979. Ordained priest, Liberal Cath. Ch. Tchr. Lafayette H.S., 1969-74; vis. asst. prof. dept. English So. Ill. U., Carbondale, 1979-80; asst. prof. dept. English Pa. State U., DuBois, 1980-87; assoc. prof., assoc. dir. composition dept. English U. No. Colo., Greeley, 1987-88, prof. dept. English, 1988—. Acting dir. Writing Component Ctr. Basic Skills, So. Ill. U., 1980. Editor: Ruthven Literary Bull., 1988-92; contbr. book chpts., articles. Rector Parish of St. Albertus Magnus, sec-treas. Am. Province; provost Am. Clerical Synod Chpt.; Sovereign Grand Master, Order of Holy Sepulchre, 1982—. Decorated Knight Bachelor, 1996, Hereditary Knight of San Luigi, 1996, Knight Cmdr. Order of Merit St. Angilbert, 1993, Prelate Comdr. Order of Noble Companions of Swan, 1993, Grand Chamberlain, 1995, Knight Order of Guadalupe, 1995, Knight Comdr. Justice Sovereign Order St. John, Knight Grand Cross of Bear of Alabona, 1995, Knight Grand Cross Order St. Stanislaus, 1998, Knight Comp. Crown of Alabona, 1998, Knight Grand Cross Order St. John, 1998, Knight Grand Cross Order Sts. Constantine the Great and Helen, Grand Cross with Collar of Order of Noble Companion of Swan, 2000; created hereditary Baron, Royal and Serene House of Alabona-Ostrogojsk et de Garama, HRSH Prince William I, created Count Palatine of Maxalla, 1996, created Hereditary Duke of Maxalla, 2000. Fellow Philalethes Soc.; mem. ASCD, Internat. Assn. for Fantastic in Arts (divsn. head Am. Lit. 1987-93), Lord Ruthven Assembly (pres. 1988-94, founding pres. emeritus 1994), Conf. Coll. Composition and Commn., Nat. Coun. Tchrs. English, Am. Conf. Irish Studies, Sigma Tau Delta (bd. dirs. 1990-96, high plains regent various states 1992-96, 10-Yr. Outstanding Advisor award 1997), Masons (century lodge #190), Order of DeMolay (chevalier, cross of honor, legion of honor), Knights Holy Sepulchre (Sov. Grand Master), Rose Croix Martinist Order (pres. premier nat. coun.). Democrat. Office: 2146 35th Ave # 107 Greeley CO 80634-3910 Fax: 419-793-6884

WORTHAM, THOMAS RICHARD, English language educator; b. Liberal, Kans., Dec. 5, 1943; s. Tom and Ruth (Cavanaugh) W. AB, Marquette U., 1965; PhD, Ind. U., 1970. From asst. prof. to assoc. prof. UCLA, 1970-82, prof., 1982—, vice-chmn. and dir. undergrad. studies, 1993-97, chmn. dept., 1997—. Vis. prof. Am. lit. U. Warsaw, Poland, 1976-77; sr. rsch. fellow Am. Coun. of Learned Socs., 1983-84. Editor: James Russell Lowell's The Biglow Papers: A Critical Edition, 1977, Letters of W. D. Howells, vol. 4, 1892-1901, 1983, The Early Prose Writings of William Dean Howells, 1853-1861, 1990, William Dean Howells' My Mark Twain, 1996, Mark Twain's Chapters From My Autobiography, 1999; asst. editor Nineteenth-Century Fiction, 1971-75, mem. adv. bd., 1976-83, co-editor, 1983-86; co-editor Nineteenth-Century Literature, 1986-95, editor, 1995—; mem. editl. bd. The Collected Works of Ralph Waldo Emerson, 1996—, Am. Documentary Heritage Libr., 1999—. Regent's faculty fellow in the humanities U. Calif., 1971; travel grantee Nat. Endowment for the Humanities, 1985-86, 88-89; grants-in-aid of rsch. Am. Philos. Soc., 1976, 81. Mem. MLA Am. (Norman Foerster prize com. of Am. Lit. sect. 1973, chmn. Pacific coast region, com. on manuscript holdings of Am. Lit. sect. 1972-78, mem. Hubbell prize com. of Am. Lit. sect. 1989-91), Am. Studies Assn., Ralph Waldo Emerson Soc. (bd. dirs. 1992-95), Assn. for Document Editing, Internat. Assn. Univ. Profs. English, Soc. Textual Scholarship. Episcopalian. Avocations: breeding and training Arabian horses. Office: U Calif Dept English 405 Hilgard Ave Los Angeles CA 90095-1530 E-mail: wortham@humnet.ucla.edu

WORTHINGTON, BRUCE R. lawyer; Sr. v.p. and gen. counsel PG&E Corp, San Francisco, 1995—. Office: PG&E Corp Ste 2400 One Market Spear Tower San Francisco CA 94105

WOTT, JOHN ARTHUR, arboretum and botanical garden executive, horticulture educator; b. Fremont, Ohio, Apr. 10, 1939; s. Arthur Otto Louis and Esther Wilhelmina (Werth) W.; children: Christopher, Timothy, Holly. BS, Ohio State U., 1961; MS, Cornell U., 1966, PhD, 1968. Mem. staff Ohio State Coop. Extension Svc., Bowling Green, 1961-64; rsch. asst. Cornell U., Ithaca, N.Y., 1964-68; prof. Purdue U., West Lafayette, Ind., 1968-81; prof. Ctr. Urban Horticulture U. Wash., Seattle, 1981—; assoc. dir. Ctr. Urban Horticulture U. Wash., Seattle, 1990-93; dir. arboreta Washington Park Arboretum, Seattle, 1993—. Writer columns for Nursery Mgmt. Profession, Balls and Burlap, Am. Nurseryman, The Arboretum Found.; contbr. articles to profl. jours. and papers including Nursery Mgr. Profl., Balls and Burlap, Arboreteum Found. Bull., Am. Nurseryman. Mem. Am. Soc. Hort. Sci. (com. chmn. 1967-82), Am. Assn. Bot. Gardens and Arboreta, Internat. Plant Propagators Soc. (internat. pres. 1984, internat. sec.-treas. 1985—). Avocations: music, antiques. Office: Internat Plant 2300 Arboretum Dr E Seattle WA 98112-2300 E-mail: jwott@u.washington.edu

WOZNIAK, CURTIS S. electronics company executive; Various positions in mfg., mktg. and ops. Gen. Motors Corp.; prodn. engring. mgr. Hewlett-Packard Co.; v.p. Desktop Graphics devel. Sun Microsys. Computer Corp., v.p., gen. mgr. Ednl. Products divsn., v.p. engring., v.p. worldwide mktg.; pres., COO Xilinx Inc.; CEO Electroglas Inc., 1996—, also chmn., 1997—. Bd. dirs. SEMI/SEMATECH consortium, Mgmt. Inst. Office: Electroglas 6024 Silver Creek Valley Rd San Jose CA 95138-1011

WRIGHT, ANDREW, English literature educator; b. Columbus, Ohio, June 28, 1923; s. Francis Joseph and Katharine (Timberman) W.; m. Virginia Rosemary Banks, June 27, 1952; children: Matthew Leslie Francis, Emma Stanbery. A.B., Harvard U., 1947; M.A., Ohio State U., 1948, Ph.D., 1951. Prof. English lit. U. Calif., San Diego, 1963—, chmn. dept. lit., 1971-74; dir. U. Calif. Study Center, U.K. and Ireland, 1980-82. Vis. prof. U. Queensland, Australia, 1984, Colegio de la Frontera Norte, San Antonio del Mar, Baja, Calif., 1991-92. Author: Jane Austen's Novels: A Study In Structure, 1953, Joyce Cary: A Preface to His Novels, 1958, Henry Fielding: Mask and Feast, 1965, Blake's Job: A Commentary, 1972, Anthony Trollope: Dream and Art, 1983; Fictional Discourse and Historical Space, 1987; contbg. author numerous books, articles to profl. jours., numerous short stories to lit. mags.; editorial bd. Nineteenth Century Fiction, 1964-86. Bd. dirs. Calif. Coun. Humanities, 1983-87. Guggenheim fellow, 1960, 70; Fulbright Sr. Research fellow, 1960-61 Fellow Royal Soc. Lit.; mem. MLA, Jane Austen Soc., Athenaeum (London), Trollope Soc., Santayana Soc., Phi Beta Kappa. Home: 7227 Olivetas Ave La Jolla CA 92037-5335 Office: U Calif San Diego Dept Lit La Jolla CA 92093-0410 E-mail: ahwright@ucsd.edu

WRIGHT, BILL, state legislator; b. American Fork, Utah, Apr. 20, 1947; m. Kathy; 10 children. Student, Utah State U. Mem. Utah Ho. Reps., Salt Lake City, 1998-2000, Utah State Senate, Salt Lake City, 2001—. Mem. Farm Bur., Elberta Hunting Assn. (past pres.), Utah Dairy Herd Improvement Assn. (past pres.), Utah Holstein Assn. (past pres.). Office: PO Box 178 Elberta UT 84626 E-mail: bwright@le.state.ut.us*

WRIGHT, CATHIE, state legislator; b. Old Forge, Pa., May 18, 1929; 1 child, Victoria. AA in Acctg., Lackawanna Jr. Coll.; student, U. Scranton. Former mayor and city councilwoman City of Simi Valley; mem. Calif. State Assembly, 1980-92, Calif. State Senate, 1992—. Chair Simi Valley Cmty. Devel. Com., Simi Valley Drug Abuse Program; former mem. transp., adv. planning, criminal justice planning bd., animal control com. for Ventura County. Named Woman of Yr., Simi Valley C. of C., 1979, Am. Mothers' Legis. Mother of the Yr., 1985, Outstanding Woman of the Yr., Zonta-Santa Clarita Valley, 1986. Mem. VFW, Las Manitas Aux. Republican. Office: State Capitol Rm 5052 Sacramento CA 95814 also: 2345 Erringer Rd Ste 212 Simi Valley CA 93065-2204 E-mail: senator.wright@sen.ca.gov

WRIGHT, CHATT GRANDISON, academic administrator; b. San Mateo, Calif., Sept. 17, 1941; s. Virgil Tandy and Louise (Jeschien) W.; children from previous marriage: Stephen Brook, Jon David, Shelley Adams; m. Janice Teply, Nov. 28, 1993. Student, U. Calif., Berkeley, 1960-62; BA in Polit. Sci., U. Calif., Davis, 1964; MA in Econs., U. Hawaii, 1968. Instr. econs. U. Hawaii, Honolulu, 1968-70; mgr. corp. planning Telecheck Internat., Inc., Honolulu, 1969-70; economist State of Hawaii, Honolulu, 1970-71; adminstr. manpower City & County of Honolulu, 1971-72; bus. adminstr., dean. Hawaii Pacific U., Honolulu, 1972-74, v.p., 1974-76, pres., 1976—. Mem. City and County of Honolulu Manpower Area Planning Commn., 1976-82; mem. Mayor's Salary Commn. City of County of Honolulu, 1977-80; mem. Honolulu City Ethics Commn., 1978-84; mem. City and County of Honolulu Labor Market Adv. Coun., 1982-84; bd. dirs. Hawaii Econ. Devel. Corp., 1980-84; trustee Queen's Med. Ctr., Honolulu, 1986-92, Honolulu Armed Svcs. YMCA, 1984-86, Hawaii Maritime Ctr., 1990-92; chmn. bd. trustees Hist. Hawaii Found., 1995-96, trustee, 1990-96; mem. adv. bd. Cancer Rsch. Ctr. Hawaii, 1987; trustee St. Andrew's Priory Sch., 1994-98; bd. dirs. Hawaii Visitors Bur., 1995-97; bd. govs. Hawaii Coun. on Econ. Edn., 1998—; bd. dirs. Downtown Improvement Assn., 1988-96, Outrigger Duke Kahanamoku Found., 1996-98, Hawaii Opera Theatre, 1997-99; trustee Oceanic Inst., 1998—; mem. Hawaii Execs. Coun., 1996—, chmn. 1999; bd. govs. Hawaii Med. Libr., 1989-92; mem. adv. bd. Aloha coun. Boy Scouts Am., 1991—; trustee Molokai Gen. Hosp., 1991-92; mem. Pacific Asian Affairs Coun., 1998—; steering com. Asian Devel. Bank, 2000—. With USN, 1968-70. Recipient Pioneer award Pioneer Fed. Savs. Bank, 1982, Stephen J. Jackstadt award; named Sales Person of Yr., Sales and Mktg. Execs. of Honolulu, 1998; Paul Harris fellow Rotary, 1986. Mem. Am. Assn. Higher Edn., Assn. Governing Bds. Univs. and Colls., Japan-Am. Soc. Honolulu, Soc. Sci. Assn., Nat. Assn. Intercollegiate Athletics (vice chair NAIA coun. of pres. 1994, mem. 1985-98), Hawaii Joint Coun. Econ. Edn. (bd. dirs. 1982-88), Western Coll. Assn. (exec. com. 1989-92), Hawaii Assn. Ind. Colls. and Univs. (chmn. 1986), Outrigger Canoe Club, Pacific Club (Honolulu), Plaza Club (bd. govs. 1992-97), Waialae Country Club. Republican. Episcopalian. Avocations: hunting, fishing, reading, travel. Office: Hawaii Pacific U Office of Pres 1166 Fort Street Mall Honolulu HI 96813-2708 E-mail: president@hpu.edu

WRIGHT, DENNIS I. career officer; Diplomat Am. Bd. Pediatrics, Am. Bd. Neonatal-Perinatal Medicine. Commd. ensign USN, 1968, advanced through ranks to rear adm., 1997; intern/resident in pediatrics U. Miss. Med. Ctr., 1971; various assignments to fleet surgeon/U.S. Pacific Fleet U.S. Pacific Command, Camp H.M. Smith, Hawaii, 1997—. Assoc. prof. pediatrics USUHS. Decorated Legion of Merit, Meritorious Svc. medal with gold star in lieu of second award, Joint Svc. Commendation medal. Office: PO Box 64045 Camp H M Smith HI 96861-4045 E-mail: diwright@hq.pacom.mil

WRIGHT, DONALD FRANKLIN, retired newspaper executive; b. St. Paul, July 10, 1934; s. Floyd Franklin and Helen Marie (Hansen) W.; m. Sharon Kathleen Fisher, Dec. 30, 1960; children: John, Dana, Kara, Patrick. BME, U. Minn., 1957, MBA, 1958. With Mpls. Star & Tribune Co., 1958-77, research planning dir., then ops. dir., 1971-75, exec. editor, 1975-77; exec. v.p., gen. mgr. Newsday, Inc., L.I., 1977-78, pres., chief operating officer, 1978-81, L.A. Times, 1981-87; sr. v.p. Times Mirror Co., L.A., from 1988; pres., CEO L.A. Times; exec. v.p. Times Mirror Co., L.A., 1998-99; ret., 1999. Former vice chmn. bd. trustees Claremont Grad. Sch. and Univ. Ctr.; past chmn. L.A. Area coun. Boy Scouts Am., 1989-99, past pres. western region, mem. nat. exec. bd., past pres. area IV; dir. emeritus Assocs. Calif. Inst. Tech.; chmn. bd. dirs. U. Minn. Found.; past bd. dirs. United Way Long Island, Calif. Mem. Am. Newspaper Pubs. Assn. (past chmn. telecom. com. and prodn. mgmt. com.), U. Minn. Alumni Assn., Mpls. Club. Presbyterian.

WRIGHT, ERNEST MARSHALL, physiologist, consultant; b. Belfast, Ireland, June 8, 1940; came to U.S., 1965; BSc, U. London, 1961, DSc, 1978; PhD, U. Sheffield, Eng., 1964. Research fellow Harvard U., Boston, 1965-66; from asst. prof. to full prof. physiology UCLA Med. Sch., 1967—, chmn. dept. physiology, 1987—. Cons. NIH, Bethesda, Md., 1982—, Senator Jacob K. Javits neurosci. investigator, 1985. Office: UCLA Sch Med Dept Physiology 10833 Le Conte Ave Los Angeles CA 90095-3075

WRIGHT, EUGENE ALLEN, federal judge; b. Seattle, Feb. 23, 1913; s. Elias Allen and Mary (Bailey) W.; m. Esther Ruth Ladley, Mar. 19, 1938; children: Gerald Allen, Meredith Ann Wright Morton. AB, U. Wash., 1935, JD, 1937; LLD, U. Puget Sound, 1984. Bar: Wash. 1937. Assoc. Wright & Wright, Seattle, 1937-54; judge Superior Ct. King County, Wash., 1954-66; v.p., sr. trust officer Pacific Nat. Bank Seattle, 1966-69; sr. judge U.S. Ct. Appeals (9th cir.), Seattle, 1969—. Acting municipal judge, Seattle, 1948-52; mem. faculty Nat. Jud. Coll., 1964-72; lectr. Sch. Communications, U. Wash., 1965-66, U. Wash. Law Sch., 1952-74; lectr. appellate judges' seminars, 1973-76, Nat. Law Clks. Inst., La. State U., 1973; chmn. Wash. State Com. on Law and Justice, 1968-69; mem. com. on appellate rules Jud. Conf., 1978-85, mem. com. on courtroom photography, 1983-85, com. jud. ethics, 1984-92, com. Bicentennial of Constn., 1985-87. Author: (with others) The State Trial Judges Book, 1966; also articles; editor: Trial Judges Jour., 1963-66; contbr. articles to profl. jours. Chmn. bd. visitors U. Puget Sound Sch. Law, 1979-84; mem. bd. visitors U. Wash. Sch. Law, 1996; bd. dirs. Met. YMCA, Seattle, 1955-72; lay reader Episc Ch. Served to lt. col. USAR, 1941-46, col. Res., ret. Decorated Bronze Star, Combat Inf. badge; recipient Army Commendation medal, Disting. Service award U.S. Jr. C. of C., 1948, Disting. Service medal Am. Legion. Fellow Am. Bar Found.; mem. ABA (coun. div. jud. adminstrn. 1971-76), FBA (Disting. Jud. Svc. award 1984), Wash. Bar Assn. (award of merit 1983), Seattle-King County Bar Assn. (Spl. Disting. Svc. award 1984. William L. Dwyer Outstanding Jurist award 2001), Order of Coif, Wash. Athletic Club, Rainier Club, Masons (33 degree), Shriners, Delta Upsilon (Disting. Alumni Achievement award 1989), Phi Delta Phi. Office: US Ct Appeals 9th Cir 902 US Courthouse 1010 5th Ave Seattle WA 98104-1195

WRIGHT, FREDERICK HERMAN GREENE, II, computer systems engineer; b. Quincy, Mass., Feb. 23, 1952; s. Frederick Herman Greene and Dorothy Louise (Harrold) W. Student, MIT, 1968-69. Test and measurement technician The Foxboro (Mass.) Co., 1968; hardware and software designer MIT Project MAC, Cambridge, Mass., 1969, Info. Internat., Brookline, 1969, Stanford Artificial Intelligence Lab, Palo Alto, Calif., 1971-73, Systems Concepts, San Francisco, 1970, 73-74, San Francisco, 1976-90; hardware and software designer, then pres. Resource One, San Francisco, 1974-76; pvt. cons. San Rafael, Calif., 1991—. Computer cons. Langley-Porter Neuropsychiatric Inst., San Francisco, 1976. Membership chmn. Pacific Soaring Coun., San Francisco, 1983-85, bd. dirs., 1984-85; active Mayflower Cmty. Chorus, 1993—. Recipient Gold Soaring Badge Fed. Aeronautique Internat., 1983. Mem. Soaring Soc. Am., Aircraft Owners and Pilots Assn., Nat. Space Soc., Bay Area Soaring Assn. Avocations: soaring, flying, singing. Home and Office: 251 C St San Rafael CA 94901-4916

WRIGHT, GEARLD LEWIS, mayor, retired educator; b. Lyman, Wyo., Feb. 22, 1933; s. Alton and Ida Mabel (Jensen) W.; m. Lila Lynn Florence, July 16, 1953; children: Jeri Lynn, Alan Kay, Lori Marie, Daryl Wilmer, Merlin Craig, Craig Alton. diploma in secondary instr., diploma in provisional counseling, Brigham Young U., 1961. Educator Granite Sch. Dist., Salt Lake County, Utah, 1961-87, retired, 1987; mayor West Valley City, 1993—. Mem. exec. com. Coun. of Govts., Utah Econ. Devel. Corp. Utah, trustee; mem. Pub. Safety Com., Econ. Devel. Com., Utah League Cities, Towns Policy Com., Govs Task Force on Weapons, Nat. League Cities Transp. and Comms. Com., transp. and comms. com. Pres. Hunter Coun.; mem. Joh Short Feasibility Study Com.; rep. Salt Lake County Assn. Cmty. Couns.; past pres. Jackson Hole Home Owners Assn., Conf. Salt Lake Valley Mayors; active PTA, PTSA; parents adv. com. mem. Primary Children's Med. Ctr., spl. cons., organizer Family Living Seminar; sec., treas. Joseph Thompson Family Orgn.; past. chmn., com. mem. Westfest Internat. Festival. Recipient Dist. Merit award Westview Scouting Dist., West Valley, Utah, 1986. Mem. Wasatch Front Regional Coun. (bd. dirs.). Avocations: sports, history, religion, travel. Home: 5432 Janette Ave West Valley City UT 84120-4464 Office: West Valley City 3600 Constitution Blvd West Valley City UT 84119-3700

WRIGHT, JAMES W. entertainment company executive; b. Ind. BFA in Theatre, U. Ill., 1973. Production coord., asst. gen. dir. Lyric Opera of Kansas City, 1977-81; production mgr. Tulsa Opera, 1981-83; dir. production, gen. mgr. Anchorage Opera Co., 1983-88; pres., gen. dir. Opera Carolina, 1989-99; gen. dir. Vancouver Opera, 1999—. Bd. dirs. Opera Am., 1993—; cons. Orlando Opera, Winston-Salem Children's Theatre Bd., Union County N.C. Symphony, Triangle Opera Theatre, Internat. Black Writers, Western Piedmont Lyric Theatre. Contbr. to mags. Bd. dirs. KSKA-FM pub. radio, 1984-87, Ala. Arts Alliance, 1985-88, N.C. Assn. Arts Coun., 1992—; adv. com. Anchorage Performing Arts Ctr., 1986-88; panel mem. Ctrl. Opera Svc. Nat. Conf., 1989, Nat. Endowment for the Arts Advancement, 1987; peer adv. network mem. N.C. Assn. of the Arts Coun., 1991—, N.C. Assn. Arts. Coun. 1991—; v.p. , KSKA-FM pub. radio, 1985-87, N.C. Assn. Arts Coun., 1992—; selection com. mem. N.C. Gov. Bus. Awards, 1993; on site reporter Nat. Endowment for the Arts, 1993. Mem. Rotary. Avocations: cooking, reading, bird watching. Office: Vancouver Opera Assn 845 Canbie St Ste 500 Vancouver BC Canada V4B 429

WRIGHT, JOHN MACNAIR, JR. retired career officer; b. L.A., Apr. 14, 1916; s. John MacNair and Ella (Stradley) W.; m. Helene Tribit, June 28, 1940; children: John MacNair III, Richard Kenneth. B.S., U.S. Mil. Acad., 1940; grad., Airborne Sch., 1947, Strategic Intelligence Sch., 1948; advanced course, Inf. Sch., 1951, Command and Gen. Staff Coll., 1953; M.B.A., U. So. Calif., 1956; grad., Army Logistics Mgmt. Sch., 1957, Advanced Mgmt. Program, U. Pitts., 1959, Nat. War Coll., 1961, Army Aviation Sch., 1965; M.S. in Internat. Affairs, George Washington U., 1973. Enlisted U.S. Army, 1935, comd. 2d. lt., 1940, advanced through grades to lt. gen., 1970; comdr. Battery Wright Corregidor, P.I., 1942; with intelligence div. War Dept. Gen. Staff, 1946-48; mil. attache Am. embassy, Paraguay, 1948-50; bn. comdr. 508th Airborne Regtl. Combat Team, 1951-52; asst. chief of staff for pers. 7th Inf. Div., Korea, 1953, asst. chief staff logistics Korea, 1954; assigned office U.S. Army Chief of Staff, 1956-60; chief staff 8th Inf. Div., 1961-62; asst. chief staff plans and ops. 7th Corps, 1962-63; asst. chief staff plans and ops. 7th Army, 1963-64; asst. div. comdr. 11th Air Assault Div., 1964-65; asst. div. comdr. 1st Cav. Div. (Airmobile) Vietnam, 1965-66; assigned office asst. Chief Staff Force Devel., 1966-67; comdg. gen. U.S. Army Inf. Ctr., 1967-69; comdt. U.S. Army Inf. Sch., 1967-69; comdg. gen. 101st Airborne Div. (Airmobile), Vietnam, 1969-70; controller of the Army Washington, 1970-72; ret., 1973. Dir. R&D Boy Scouts Am., 1973, nat. dir. program, 1974-77, nat. dir. program support, 1977-78; nat. dir. exploring, 1978-81, mem. nat. exploring com., 1981—; pres. Chattahoochee (Ga.) coun. Boy Scouts Am., 1968-69, mem. exec. bd. region 5, 1967-69; mem. nat. coun., 1964-73; tech. adviser Vietnamese Boy Scout Assn., 1965-66; Regent for Life Nat. Eagle Scout Assn., 1988—; exploring chmn. five nations dist. Calif. Inland Empire Coun., 1992-96, mem.-at large 1996—. Prisoner of war of Japanese, 1942-45. Decorated D.S.M. with 2 oak leaf clusters, Silver Star with oak leaf cluster, Legion of Merit with oak leaf cluster, D.F.C., Bronze Star with oak leaf cluster, Air medal with 59 oak leaf clusters, Army Commendation medal, Prisoner of War medal, Purple Heart with oak leaf cluster, Combat Inf. badge, Master Parachutist, Sr. Army Aviator, numerous area and campaign ribbons, fgn. decorations; recipient Silver Beaver award Boy Scouts Am., 1961, Silver Antelope award, 1969, Distinguished Eagle Scout award, 1971, Disting. Svc. award Founders and Patriots Am., 1988, Freedoms Found. at Valley Forge Hon. medal, 1992; elected Army Aviation Hall of Fame, 1986. Mem. Am. Defenders Bataan and Corregidor, Am. Ex-Prisoners of War, Nat. Eagle Scout Assn. (regent for life), Hon. Order Ky. Cols., Assn. U.S. Army, Army Aviation Assn Am., (pres. 1974-76), 101st Airborne Divsn. Assn., 1st Cavalry Divsn. Assn., SAR (pres. Tex. Soc. 1987-88, pres. Inland Empire chpt. 1992-93, Silver Good Citizenship medal 1984, 87, Meritorious Svc. medal 1986, Patriot, Liberty and Gold Good Citizenship medals 1988), Ret. Officers Assn., West Point Soc., Mil. Order World Wars (Patrick Henry award 1986, 90, comdr. Dallas chpt. 1985-86, vice comdr. dept. ctrl. Calif. 1991-92, comdr. Inland Empire chpt. 1992-93), Nat. Gavel Soc., Nat. Order Founders and Patriots of Am. (sec.-gen. 1986-88, gov. gen. 1988-90, councillor gen. Calif. Soc. 1990-95), Soc. of the Cin., Soc. Descendants of Colonial Clergy, Flagon and Tchr. Soc., Soc. Colonial Wars (lt. gov. Calif. soc. 1992-93, gov. 1997-98), Sons of the Revolution in State of Calif. (pres. 1993-94), Soc. War of 1812 (dist. dep. pres. gen. 1991-93, v.p. Calif. soc. 1993-94, pres. 1994-95), Nat. Huguenot Soc., Soc. Sons and Daus. of Pilgrims, Order Ams. Armorial Ancestry, Soc. Descs. Founders of Hartford, Old Plymouth Colony Descs.,

Mil. Order of the Loyal Legion of the U.S., Mil. Order Fgn. Wars of the U.S. (pres. Calif. Soc. 1996-97), Mil. Order of Purple Heart, Hereditary Order of First Families of Mass., Order of Crown Charlemagne, Baronial Soc. Magna Charta, DFC Soc., Order of Daedalians, Mil. Order of Carabao, Masons, Shriners, Sojourner, Phi Kappa Phi, Beta Gamma Sigma, Alpha Kappa Psi. Home: 21227 George Brown Ave Riverside CA 92518-2881

WRIGHT, KENNETH BROOKS, lawyer; b. Whittier, Calif., June 5, 1934; s. Albert Harold and Marian (Schwey) W.; m. Sandra Beryl Smith, June 20, 1959; children: Margo Teresa, Daniel Brooks, John Waugh. B.A. cum laude, Pomona Coll., 1956; J.D., Stanford U., 1960. Bar: Calif. 1961, U.S. Supreme Ct. 1979. Assoc., then ptnr. Lawler, Felix & Hall, 1961-77; ptnr. Morgan, Lewis & Bockius, Los Angeles, 1978-99, counsel, 1999—. Teaching team leader Nat. Inst. Trial Advocacy, 1978-80; mem. governing com. Calif. Continuing Edn. of Bar, 1973-77, chmn., 1975-76; nat. panel arbitrators Am. Arbitration Assn., 1970—; lectr. ABA Sect. Litigation Nat. Inst., 1979-86; bd. dirs. L.A. Internat. Comml. Arbitration Ctr. Chmn. bd. editors: Am. Bar Jour, 1977-81. Pres. Pomona Coll. Alumni Assn., 1970-71; pres. parent tchr. coun. Campbell Hall Sch., 1973-74, bd. dirs., 1976—, vice chmn., 1994—; counsel Vol. League San Fernando Valley, 1979-81; chmn. sect. adminstrn. of justice Town Hall of Calif., 1970-71; sr. warden Episcopal Ch., 1973-74. Served with U.S. Army, 1956-57. Mem. ABA (dir. programs litigation sect. 1977-81, mem. coun. 1982-88, mem. standing com on comm. 1978-88, chmn. 1987-88, chmn. sect. book pub. com. 1986-89, pres. fellows young lawyers 1985-86, bd. dirs. 1980-89), Internat. Bar Assn., Assn. Bus. Trial Lawyers (chair com. alt. dispute resolution 1991-93, bd. dirs. 1993-96), Am. Law Inst., Am. Bar Found., Am. Bd. Trial Advs., State Bar Calif. (mem. gov. com. continuing edn. of the bar 1972-77, chmn. 1975-76), Conf. Barristers (exec. com. 1966-69, 1st v.p. 1969), L.A. County Bar Assn. (com. on judiciary 1981-83, chmn. continuing legal edn. adv. com. 1989-91, vice-chmn. continuing legal edn. com. 1991-93, bd. dirs. L.A. Lawyers 1989-94), L.A. County Bar Found. (bd. dirs., trustee 1993-99, mem. exec. com. internat. sect. 1996-99), U.S. Supreme Ct. Hist. Soc., Jonathan Club, Chancery Club, Phi Beta Kappa. Republican. Avocations: skiing, tennis. Home: 3610 Longridge Ave Sherman Oaks CA 91423-4918 Office: Morgan Lewis & Bockius 300 S Grand Ave Los Angeles CA 90071-3109

WRIGHT, MALCOLM STURTEVANT, nuclear facility manager, retired career officer; b. Orange, N.J., Sept. 2, 1941; s. Malcolm Everett and Margaret Sommer (Kohler) W.; m. Barbara Jean Larsen, June 5, 1963 (div. Aug., 1988); children: Tracy Ann, Karen Elizabeth; m. Lya Hanfri Baughman, Nov. 5, 1988; children: Zachary Seth, Sara Ann. BS in Engring., U.S. Naval Acad., 1963; MA in Polit. Sci., Villanova U., 1974. Commd. ensign USN, 1963, advanced through grades to capt., 1983, retired, 1993; dir. tactical tng. dept. US Naval Submarine Sch., Groton, Conn., 1982-84; commanding officer USS Alabama, Silverdale, Wash., 1984-87; planner polit.-mil. strategy Staff of Chmn. Joint Chiefs of Staff, Pentagon, Washington, 1987-90; comdr. Submarine Squadron Seventeen, Silverdale, Wash., 1990-92; chief of staff to comdr. Naval Base Seattle, 1992-93; mgr. waste and decontamination plant Westinghouse Hanford Co., Richland, Wash., 1993-96; mgr. 324/327 facility stabilization project Babcock and Wilcox Hanford Co., Richland, 1996-99; dir. 324 bldg. deactiviation project Fluor Hanford Co., Richland, 1999—. Tech. advisor Disney Studios, Burbank, Calif., 1994-95. Vol. ARC, East Orange, N.J., 1957-59. Decorated Legion of Merit, USN, 1982, 86, 92, 93, Meritorious Svc. medal 1984, Defense Superior Svc. medal, 1990. Mem. U.S. Naval Inst., U.S. Naval Submarine League, U.S. Naval Acad. Alumni Assn. Republican. Presbyterian Avocations; military history, civil war, Scottish culture, golf. Home: 3512 W 30th Ave Kennewick WA 99337-2500 Office: Flour Hanford Inc PO Box 1000 Richland WA 99352-1000

WRIGHT, MARY ROSE, parks and recreation director; b. Hartford, Conn., Jan. 12, 1949; d. J. William and Eileen J. (Walsh) Bigoness; m. Roy C. Gunter III, June 24, 1972 (div. Feb. 1988); m. Kenneth Ross Wright, Dec. 1, 1988. BA, Marquette U., 1970; MS, U. Mo., 1972. Prgram analyst State Calif. Dept. Health, Sacramento, 1972-76; tng. ctr. dir. State Calif. Dept. Parks and Recreation, Pacific Grove, 1976-81, visitor svcs. mgr. Monterey, 1981-83, Monterey dist. supr., 1983-92, dep. dir., 1992-93; Monterey dist. supt. Calif. Dept. Parks and Recreation, 1993-99, chief dep. dir., 1999—. Hist. preservation commr. City of Monterey, 1984-92. Bd. dirs. Big Sur Health Ctr., 1993—; bd. govs. Santa Lucia Conservancy, 1995-99. Office: Calif Dept Parks and Recreation Chief Dep Dir 1416 9th St Rm 1405 Sacramento CA 95814-5511

WRIGHT, ROSALIE MULLER, magazine and newspaper editor; b. Newark, June 20, 1942; d. Charles and Angela (Fortunata) Muller; m. Lynn Wright, Jan. 13, 1962; children: James Anthony Meador, Geoffrey Shepard. BA in English, Temple U., 1965. Mng. editor Suburban Life mag., Orange, N.J., 1960-62; assoc. editor Phila. mag., 1962-64, mng. editor, 1969-73; founding editor Womensports mag., San Mateo, Calif., 1973-75; editor scene sect. San Francisco Examiner, 1975-77; exec. editor New West mag., San Francisco and Beverly Hills, Calif., 1977-81; features and Sunday editor San Francisco Chronicle, 1981-87, asst. mng. editor features, 1987-96; v.p. and editor-in-chief Sunset Mag, Menlo Park, Calif., 1996—. Tchr. mag. writing U. Calif., Berkeley, 1975-76; participant pub. procedures course Stanford U., 1977-79; chmn. mag. judges at conf. Coun. Advancement and Support of Edn., 1980, judge, 1984. Contbr. numerous mag. articles, critiques, revs., Compton's Ency. Mem. Am. Assn. Sunday and Feature Editors (treas. 1984, sec. 1985, 1st v.p. 1986, pres. 1987, Hall of Fame 1999), Am. Newspaper Pubs. Assn. (pub. task force on minorities in newspaper bus. 1988-89, Chronicle minority recruiter 1987-94), Internat. Women's Forum, Women's Forum West (bd. dirs. 1993—, sec. 1994), Western Pub. Assn., Am. Soc. Mag. Editors. Office: Sunset Magazine 80 Willow Rd Menlo Park CA 94025-3691 E-mail: rwright@sunset.com

WRIGHTON, NICHOLAS C. research scientist; BA in Biochemistry, MA in Biochemistry, Oxford U.; PhD in Molecular Biology, Nat. Inst. Med. Rsch. Postdoct. researcher DNAX Rsch. Inst., Palo Alto, Calif.; rsch. scientist Affymax, Palo Alto. Recipient Newcomb Cleveland prize AAAS, 1996-97. Achievements include discovery (with others) of EPO mimetics. Office: Affymax Rsch Inst 4001 Miranda Ave Palo Alto CA 94304-1218

WU, DAVID, congressman; b. Taiwan, Apr. 8, 1955; came to U.S., 1961; m. Michelle Wu; children: Matthew, Sarah. BS, Stanford U., 1977; student, Harvard Med. Sch.; JD, Yale U., 1982. Ptnr. Cohen & Wu, 1988-98; mem. edn. and workforce com., sci. com. 106th Congress from 1st Oreg. dist., 1999—. Mem. Congl. Asian Pacific Caucus (vice chair), New Democrat Coalition Office: 510 Cannon House Office Bldg Washington DC 20515-0001 also: 620 NW Main Ste 606 Portland OR 97205

WU, JAMES CHEN-YUAN, aerospace engineering educator; b. Nanking, China, Oct. 5, 1931; came to U.S., 1953, naturalized, 1963; s. Chien Lieh and Cheng-Ling Wu; m. Mei-Ying Chang, Sept. 7, 1957; children—Alberta Yee-Hwa, Norbert Mao-Hwa. Student, Nat. Taiwan (Formosa) U., 1949-52; BS, Gonzaga U., 1954; postgrad., Columbia U., 1954; MS (univ. fellow), U. Ill., 1955, PhD, 1957. Engr. Wah Chang Corp., N.Y.C., 1954; researcher Mass. Inst. Tech. at Cambridge, 1957; asst. prof. Gonzaga U., Spokane, Wash., 1957-59; research specialist Douglas Aircraft Co., 1959-65, group leader, 1960-61, supr., 1961-62, br. chief, 1963-65; prof. aerospace engring. Ga. Inst. Tech., 1965-96; pres. Applied Aero, LLC, 1996—. Cons. N.Am. Aviation Co., Geophys. Tech. Corp., European Atomic Energy Commn., Ispra, Italy, European Atomic Energy Commn. (research center), U.S. Army Research Office, Durham, S.C. Contbr. articles to profl. jours. Chmn. bd. dirs. Chinese-Am. Inst. Recipient profl. achievement award Douglas Aricraft Co., 1963, Outstanding Tchrs. award Gonzaga U., 1959; Asso. fellow Am. Inst. Aeros. and Astronautics Mem. Am. Soc. Engring. Sci. (founding), Soc. Indsl. and Applied Math. (vice-chmn. Pacific N.W. 1958-59), Am. Astron. Soc. (sr.), Am. Phys. Soc., Nat. Assn. Chinese Ams. (pres. Atlanta chpt.), Sigma Xi, Tau Beta Pi, Sigma Alpha Nu. Office: Sch Aerospace Engring Georgia Inst Tech 48365 Avalon Heights Ter Fremont CA 94539-8005

WU, LI-PEI, banker; b. Changhwa, Taiwan, Sept. 9, 1934; came to U.S., 1968; m. Jenny S. Lai, Mar. 24, 1963; children: George T., Eugene Y. BA, Nat. Taiwan U., 1957; MBA, Kans. State U., Ft. Hays, 1969; Comml. Banking Exec. Program, Columbia U., 1974. Staff acct., asst. controller, asst. v.p., v.p. Nat. Bank Alaska, Anchorage, 1969-73, v.p. controller, 1973-76, sr. v.p. chief fin. officer, 1976-78; chmn. exec. com. Alaska Nat. Bank of the North, Anchorage, 1978-79, chief adminstrv. officer, 1979-80, pres., 1980-81; pres., chief exec. officer Gen. Bank & GBC Bancorp, Los Angeles, 1982-84, chmn., pres, chief exec. officer, 1984-98, chmn., CEO, 1998-2000, chmn., 2001—. Sr. advisor to Pres. Taiwan, 2000; dir. Pacific Coast Banking Sch., 1995-99; bd. advisors Asia Soc., 1998—; mem. Pacific Coun. on Internat. Policy, 1999; chmn. United Taiwanese Found. of So. Calif., 1998—. Founder, pres. Taiwanese Am. Polit. Action Com., 1992-93; pres. Taiwanese United Fund, 1990-92; founder, 1st pres. Nat. Taiwanese Am. Citizens League, 1989-91; mem. White House Pacific Rim Econ. Conf., 1995. Recipient Alumni Achievement award Fort Hays U., 1995, Entrepreneur of Yr. award Greater L.A. Ernst & Young, 1998. Office: Gen Bank 800 W 6th St Los Angeles CA 90017-2704 E-mail: lpw@generalbank.com

WUDL, FRED, chemistry educator; b. Cochabamba, Bolivia, Jan. 8, 1941; came to U.S., 1958; s. Robert and Bertha (Schorr) W.; m. Linda Raimondo, Sept. 2, 1967. BS, UCLA, 1964, PhD, 1967. Postdoctoral rsch. fellow Harvard U., 1967-68; asst. prof. dept. chemistry SUNY, Buffalo, 1968-72; mem. tech. staff AT&T Bell Labs., Murray Hill, N.J., 1972-82; prof. chemistry and materials U. Calif., Santa Barbara, 1982-97; Courtaulds prof. UCLA, 1997—. Recipient arthur C. Cope scholar award Am. Chem. Soc., 1993, Award for Chemistry of Materials, 1996, Natta medal Italian Chem. Soc., 1994, Wheland medal U. Chgo., 1994. Fellow AAAS. Office: UCLA Dept Chemistry Los Angeles CA 90095-1569

WULBERT, DANIEL ELIOT, mathematician, educator; b. Chgo., Dec. 17, 1941; s. Morris and Anna (Greenberg) W.; children: Kera, Noah. BA, Knox Coll., 1963; MA, U. Tex., Austin, 1964, PhD, 1966. Research assoc. U. Lund (Sweden), 1966-67; asst. prof. U. Wash., Seattle, 1967-73; prof. U. Calif.-San Diego, La Jolla, 1973—. Vis. prof. Northwestern U., Evanston, Ill., 1977. Contbr. articles in field. Office: U Calif San Diego Dept Math # 0112 La Jolla CA 92093 E-mail: dwulbert@ucsd.edu

WUNNICKE, BROOKE, lawyer; b. Dallas, May 9, 1918; d. Rudolph von Falkenstein and Lulu Lenore Brooke; m. James M. Wunnicke, Apr. 11, 1940; (dec. 1977); 1 child, Diane B. BA, Stanford U., 1939; JD, U. Colo., 1945. Bar: Wyo. 1946, U.S. Dist. Cty. Wyo. 1947, U.S. Supreme Ct. 1958, Colo. 1969, U.S. Dist. Ct. Colo. 1970. Pvt. practice law, 1946-56; ptnr. Williams & Wunnicke, Cheyenne, Wyo., 1956-69; of counsel Calkins, Kramer, Grimshaw & Harring, Denver, 1969-73; chief appellate dep. atty. Dist. Atty's Office, Denver, 1973-86; of counsel Hall & Evans L.L.C., Denver, 1986—. Adj. prof. law U. Denver Coll. of Law, 1978-97; lectr. Internat. Practicum Inst. Denver, 1978—. Author: Ethics Compliance for Business Lawyers, 1987; co-author: Standby Letters of Credit, 1989, Corporate Financial Risk Management, 1992, Legal Opinion Letters Formbook, 1994, (Supplement 2001), UCP 500 and Standby Letters of Credit-Special Report, 1994, Standby and Commercial Letters of Credit, 1996, 3d edit., 2000; columnist Letters of Credit Report; contbr. articles to profl. jours. Pres. Laramie County Bar Assn., Cheyenne, Wy., 1967-68; Dir. Cheyenne C. of C., Cheyenne, Wy., 1965-68. Recipient awards for Outstanding Svc., Colo. Dist. Attys. Coun., 1979, 82, 86, Disting. Alumni award U. Colo. Sch. of Law, 1986, 93, Lathrop Trailblazer award Colo. Women's Bar Assn., 1992, William Lee Knous award U. Colo., 1997, Eleanor P. Williams award disting. svc. to legal profession, 1997, Potter Lifetime Profl. Svc. award, 1999, Def. Rsch. Inst. Ann. Nat. award, 1999; named first Frank H. Ricketson Jr. Adj. Prof., U. Denver Coll. Law, 1997. Fellow Colo. Bar Found. (hon.); mem. ABA, Wyo. State Bar, Denver Bar Assn. (hon. life; trustee 1977-80), Colo. Bar Assn. (hon., life, Award of Merit 1999), Am. Arbitration Assn. (nat. panel, regional panel), William E. Doyle Inn of Ct. (hon.), Order of Coif, Phi Beta Kappa. Republican. Episcopalian. Avocations: reading, writing, teaching, lecturing. Office: Hall & Evans L L C 1200 17th St Ste 1700 Denver CO 80202-5817

WURTELE, MORTON GAITHER, meteorologist, educator; b. Harrodsburg, Ky., July 25, 1919; s. Edward Conrad and Emily Russell (Gaither) W.; m. Zivia Syrkin, Dec. 31, 1942; children— Eve Syrkin, Jonathan Syrkin. S.B., Harvard, 1940; M.A., UCLA, 1944, Ph.D., 1953. Asst. prof. meteorology Mass. Inst. Tech., Cambridge, 1953-58; asso. prof. meteorology U. Calif. at Los Angeles, 1958-64, prof., 1964—, chmn. dept., 1971-76. Vis. prof. U. Buenos Aires, 1962, U. Jerusalem, 1965; vis. scholar U. Calif.-Berkeley, 2000—. Prin. contbr.: Glossary of Meteorology; co-editor: Progress in Desert Research; contbr. articles to profl. jours. Trustee Univ. Corp. for Atmospheric Rsch.; pres., dir. Sage Resources, Inc. With USNR, 1940-41. Fulbright grantee, 1949-50, 65; NATO sr. fellow, 1961-62 Fellow Am. Meteorol. Soc.; mem. Am. Profs. for Peace in Middle East (nat. exec. 1974—), Royal Meteorol. Soc., Am. Geophys. Union, Phi Beta Kappa, Sigma Xi. Club: Harvard So. Calif. Home: 1317 Shattuck Ave Berkeley CA 94709-1414 Office: Hilgard Hall U Calif Berkeley CA 94720

WYANT, JAMES CLAIR, engineering company executive, educator; b. Morenci, Mich., July 31, 1943; s. Clair William and Idah May (Burroughs) W.; m. Louise Doherty, Nov. 20, 1971; 1 child, Clair Frederick. BS, Case Western Reserve, 1965; MS, U. Rochester, 1967, PhD, 1968. Engr. Itek Corp., Lexington, Mass., 1968-74; instr. Lowell (Mass.) Tech. Inst., 1969-74; prof. U. Ariz., Tucson, 1974—; pres. WYKO Corp., Tucson, 1984-97; dir. optical sci. ctr. U. Ariz., 1999—. Chmn. Gordon Conf. on Holography Plymouth (N.H.) State Coll., 1984; vis. prof. U. Rochester, N.Y., 1983. Editor: Applied Optics and Optical Engineering, vols. VII-X, 1979-80, 83, 87. Recipient of Joseph Fraunhofer-Robert M. Burley Prize, 1992, Optical Soc. Am. Mem. Optical Soc. Am. (bd. dirs. 1979-81, Joseph Fraunhofer award 1992), Soc. Photo-Optical Instrumentation Engring. (pres. 1986). Home: 1881 N King St Tucson AZ 85749-9367 Office: U Ariz Optical Scis Ctr Tucson AZ 85721-0001 E-mail: jcwyant@optics.arizona.edu

WYATT, BILL, government staff; b. Astoria, Oreg. Student, Willamette U., U. Oreg. Mem. Oreg. Legislature, 1975; dir. employee benefits and govt. rels. Oreg. State Employees Assn.; dir. intergovtl. affairs City of Portland; exec. dir. Assn. for Portland Progress; pres. Oreg. Bus. Coun.; chief of staff Gov. of Oreg., Salem, 1995—. Bd.dirs. Crabbe-Huson family mut. funds. Past chmn. bd. Urban League of Portland; bd. dirs. Oreg. Pub. Broadcasting. Mem. City Club of Portland (past bd. govs.). Office: Office of Gov State Capitol Bldg Rm 254 Salem OR 97310-0001

WYATT, EDITH ELIZABETH, elementary education educator; b. San Diego, Aug. 13, 1914; d. Jesse Wellington and Elizabeth (Fultz) Carne; m. Lee Ora Wyatt, Mar. 30, 1947 (dec. Jan. 1966); children: Glenn Stanley (dec.), David Allen. BA, San Diego State Coll., 1936. Elem. tchr. Nat. Sch. Dist., National City, Calif., 1938-76. Sec. San Diego County Parks Soc., 1986-96, sec.-treas., 1998—; librarian Congl. Ch. Women's Fellowship, Chula Vista, Calif., 1980—; active Boy Scouts Am, 1959—. Recipient Who award San Diego County Tchrs. Assn., 1968, Silver Fawn award Boy Scouts Am. Mem. AAUW (sec. 1978-80, pub. rels. 1985—), Calif. Ret. Tchrs. Assn. (scholarship com. 1985-90, 92-95, treas. South Shores divsn. # 60 1996—), Starlite Hiking Club (sec.-treas. 1979—). Avocation: hiking. Home: 165 E Millan St Chula Vista CA 91910-6255

WYATT, JAMES LUTHER, drapery hardware company executive; b. Williamsburg, Ky., May 13, 1924; s. Jesse Luther and Grace Edwina (Little) W.; m. Barbara Christman, Aug. 28, 1946; children— Linda Lou, William Charles Christman (dec.). B.S., U. Ky., 1947, M.S., 1948; Sc.D., Mass. Inst. Tech., 1952. Registered profl. engr., Ohio, Pa. Devel. engr. titanium div. Nat. Lead Co., Sayreville, N.J., 1948-50; tech. mgr., head, dept. metall. engring., mgr. new products Horizons, Inc., Cleve., 1953-57; cons., asso. Booz, Allen & Hamilton, N.Y.C., 1957-61; v.p. program devel. Armour Research Found., Chgo., 1961-63; v.p. new product devel. Joy Mfg. Co., Pitts., 1963-67; v.p. corp. devel. Nat. Gypsum Co., Buffalo, 1967-69, Max Factor & Co., Hollywood, Calif., 1969-71; pres. Wyatt & Co., 1971—, Jimbabs, Inc., 1983—, Ambassador Industries, Inc., Los Angeles, 1988—. U.S. del. 1st World Metall. Congress. Contbr. tech., mgmt. papers to profl. lit.; patentee in field. Mem. Pompano Beach Power Squadron, adminstr. officer, 1991, exec. officer, 1992, comdr., 1993; chmn. bd. trustees Meth. Ch., 1992, mem. fin. com., 1993, mem. adminstrv. bd.; chmn. bd. trustees 1st United Meth. Ch., Boca Raton; bd. dirs., v.p. Golden Harbour Homeowners Assn., 1997—. Lt. col. USAAF, 1942-46. Elected to U. Ky. Hall of Distinction, 2001. Mem. AIME, Am. Soc. Metals, Econ. Club (Chgo.), Execs. Club (Chgo.), Univ. Club (N.Y.C.), Calif. Yacht Club, Pompano Beach Power Squadron (comdr.), Sigma Phi Epsilon, Alpha Chi Sigma. Clubs: Econs. (Chgo.), Execs. (Chgo.); Univ. (N.Y.C.); Calif. Yacht. Home: 510 Golden Harbour Dr Boca Raton FL 33432-2942 Office: Bunker Hill Twr 800 W 1st St Apt 507 Los Angeles CA 90012-2413 E-mail: jim_wyatt@juno.com

WYATT, JOSEPH LUCIAN, JR. lawyer, writer; b. Chgo., Feb. 21, 1924; s. Joseph Lucian and Cecile Gertrude (Zadico) W.; m. Marjorie Kathryn Simmons, Apr. 9, 1954; children: Daniel, Linn, Jonathan. AB in English Lit. with honors, Northwestern U., 1947; LLB, Harvard U., 1949. Bar: Calif. 1950, U.S. Dist. Ct. (cen. dist.) Calif. 1950, U.S. Ct. Appeals (9th cir.) 1950, U.S. Tax Ct., U.S. Supreme Ct. 1965. Assoc. firm Brady, Nossaman & Walker, Los Angeles, 1950-58, ptnr. L.A., 1958-61; pvt. practice L.A., 1961-71; sr. mem. Cooper, Wyatt, Tepper & Plant, P.C., L.A., 1971-79; of counsel Beardsley, Hufstedler & Kemble, L.A., 1979-81; ptnr. Hufstedler & Kaus, L.A., 1981-95; sr. of counsel Morrison & Foerster, L.A., 1995—. Mem. faculty Pacific Coast Banking Sch., Seattle, 1963-92, Southwestern Grad. Sch. Banking, 1988-89; adviser Am. Law Inst., 1988—, Restatement, Trusts 3d, 1988—. Author: Trust Administration and Taxation, 4 vols., 1964—; editor: Trusts and Estates, 1962-74. Lectr. continuing legal edn. programs, Calif. and Tex.; trustee Pacific Oaks Coll. and Children's Sch., 1969-97; counsel, parliamentarian Calif. Democratic party and presdl. conv. dels., 1971—; mem. Calif. State Personnel Bd., 1961-71, v.p., 1963-65, pres., 1965-67; bd trustees Calif. Pub. Employees Retirement System, 1963-71. Served with USAAF, 1943-45. Fellow Am. Coll. of Trust and Estate Counsel; mem. ABA, Internat. Acad. Estate and Trust Law (treas. 1990-96), Am. Law Inst., Calif. State Bar Assn. (del. state conf. 1956, 62-67), L.A. Bar Assn. (trustee 1956). Democrat. Christian Scientist. Avocations: poetry, fishing. Home: 1119 Armada Dr Pasadena CA 91103-2805 E-mail: jwyatt@mofo.com, jwyatt@earthlink.net

WYDEN, RON, senator; b. Wichita, Kans., May 3, 1949; s. Peter and Edith W.; m. Laurie Oseran, Sept. 5, 1978; 1 child, Adam David Student, U. Santa Barbara, 1967-69; A.B. with distinction, Stanford U., 1971; J.D., U. Oreg., 1974. Campaign aide Senator Wayne Morse, 1972, 74; co-founder, co-dir. Oreg. Gray Panthers, 1974-80; dir. Oreg. Legal Services for Elderly, 1977-79; instr. gerontology U. Oreg., 1976, U. Portland, 1980, Portland State U., 1979; mem. 97th-104th Congresses from 3d Oreg. dist., Washington, 1981-96; senator from Oreg. U.S. Senate, 1996—, mem. aging com., mem. budget com., mem. commerce sci. and transp. com., mem. energy and natural resources com., mem. environ. and pub. works com. Recipient Service to Oreg. Consumers award Oreg. Consumers League, 1978, Citizen of Yr. award Oreg. Assn. Social Workers, 1979, Significant Service award Multnomah County Area Agy. on Aging, 1980; named Young Man of Yr. Oreg. Jr. C. of C., 1980 Mem. Am. Bar Assn., Iowa Bar Assn. Democrat. Jewish. Office: US Senate 516 Hart Senate Office Bldg Washington DC 20510-0001*

WYDICK, RICHARD CREWS, lawyer, educator; b. Pueblo, Colo., Nov. 1, 1937; s. Charles Richard and Alice Wydick; m. Judith Brandli James, 1961; children: William Bruce, Derrick Cameron. B.A., Williams Coll., 1959; LL.B., Stanford U., 1962. Bar: Calif. bar 1962. Asso. firm Brobeck, Phleger & Harrison, San Francisco, 1966-71; mem. faculty U. Calif. Law Sch., Davis, 1971—, prof. law, 1975—, dean, 1978-80. Author: Plain English for Lawyers, 4th edit., 1998. Served to capt. USAR, 1962-66. Office: Sch Law U Calif Davis CA 95616

WYLE, FREDERICK S. lawyer; b. Berlin, Germany, May 9, 1928; came to U.S., 1939, naturalized, 1944; s. Norbert and Malwina (Mauer) W.; m. Katinka Franz, June 29, 1969; children: Susan Kim, Christopher Anthony, Katherine Anne. B.A. magna cum laude, Harvard U., 1951, LL.B., 1954. Bar: Mass. 1954, Calif. 1955, N.Y. 1958. Teaching fellow Harvard Law Sch., 1954-55; law clk. U.S. Dist. Ct., No. Dist. Calif., 1955-57; assoc. firm Paul, Weiss, Rifkind, Wharton & Garrison, N.Y.C., 1957-58; pvt. practice San Francisco, 1958-62; spl. asst. def. rep. U.S. del. to NATO, Paris, 1962-63; mem. Policy Planning Council, Dept. State, Washington, 1963-65; dep. asst. sec. def. for European and NATO affairs Dept. Def., Washington, 1966-69; v.p. devel., gen. counsel Schroders, Inc., N.Y.C., 1969-71, atty., cons., 1971-72; chief exec. officer Saturday Rev. Industries, Inc., San Francisco, 1972-76; individual practice law San Francisco, 1976—. Internat. counsel to Fed. States Micronesia, 1974-82; cons. Rand Corp., Dept. of Def., Nuclear Regulatory Commn.; trustee in bankruptcy, receiver various corps since 1974. Contbr. to: Ency. Brit, 1972, also articles in profl. publs., newspapers. Trustee for U.S. Interest Bicycle Club Casino, 1996-99. Served with AUS, 1946-47. Mem. Internat. Inst. Strategic Studies, Phi Beta Kappa. Office: 3 Embarcadero Ctr Fl 7 San Francisco CA 94111-4065

WYLIE, RICHARD THORNTON, aerospace engineer; b. Long Beach, Calif., July 11, 1956; s. Howard Hance and Marcella Dart (Metcalf) W. BS, Calif. State Poly. U., Pomona, 1978; MS, U. Calif., Berkeley, 1979. Registered profl. engr., Calif. Engr. Aerocraft Heat Treating, Paramount, Calif., 1991-94, TRW, Inc., Redondo Beach, 1980-91, 94—. Vol. tutor TRW Bootstrap, 1981—. Mem. Mensa (scholarship chmn. Harbor area 1995—, editor Harbor area newsletter 1996-99). Avocation: Graphoanalysis. Home: 1005 Kornblum Ave Torrance CA 90503-5113

WYMAN, RICHARD VAUGHN, engineering educator, exploration company executive; b. Painesville, Ohio, Feb. 22, 1927; s. Vaughn Ely and Melinda (Ward) W.; m. Anne Fenton, Dec. 27, 1947; 1 son, William Fenton. BS, Case Western Res. U., 1948; MS, U. Mich., 1949; PhD, U. Ariz., 1974. Registered profl. engr., Nev., Ariz.; registered geologist, Ariz., Calif.; lic. water right surveyor, Nev. Geologist N.J. Zinc Co., 1949, 52-53, Cerro de Pasco Corp., 1950-52; chief geologist Western Gold & Uranium, Inc., St. George, Utah, 1953-55, gen. supt., 1955-57, v.p., 1957-59; pres. Intermountain Exploration Co., Boulder City, Nev., 1959-93; tunnel supt. Reynolds Electric & Engring. Co., 1961-63, mining [illegible] mgr. ops. Reynolds Electric and & Engring. Co., 1967-69; constrn. supt. engr. Sunshine Mining Co., 1963-65; lectr. U. Nev., Las Vegas, 1969-73, assoc. prof., 1973-80, dept. chmn., 1976-80, prof., 1980-92, prof. emeritus,

1992—, chmn. dept. civil and mech. engring., 1984-90, chmn. dept. civil and environ. engring., 1990-91. Mineral rep. Ariz. Strip Adv. Bd., 1976-80, U.S.B.L.M.; mem. peer rev. com. Nuclear Waste Site, Dept. Energy, Las Vegas, 1978-82; pres. Ariz. Juno Resources, Boulder City, 1980-87, v.p., 1990-97; pres. Wyman Engring. Cons., 1987—; cons. Corp. Andina de Fomento, Caracas, Venezuela, 1977-78; v.p. Comstock Gold, Inc., 1984-93; program evaluator Accreditation Bd. for Engring. and Tech., 1995—. Contbr. articles to profl. jours. Sec. Washington County Republican Party, Utah, 1958-60; del. Utah Rep. Conv., 1958-60; scoutmaster Boy Scouts Am., 1959-69; mem. citizens adv. com., tech. adv. com. Clark County Regional Flood Control Dist., 1998—. Served with USN, 1944-46. Recipient Order of Engr. award, 2000. Fellow ASCE (life; edn. divsn. 1990, local rep. nat. conv. Las Vegas), Soc. Econ. Geologists (life); mem. AIME/SME (life, chmn. So. Nev. sect. 1971-72, dir. 1968—, sec.-treas. 1974-92, chmn. Pacific S.W. Minerals Conf. 1972, gen. chmn. nat. conv. 1980, Disting. Mem. award 1989, Legion of Honor 1999), Assn. Engring. Geologists (dir. S.W. sect. 1989-91), Am. Inst. Minerals Appraisers, Am. Water Works Assn., Nev. Mining Assn. (assoc.), Assn. Ground Water Scientists and Engrs., Arctic Inst. N.Am. (life), Am. Soc. Engring. Edn., Soc. for History of Discoveries, Am. Philatelic Soc., SAR, Am. Legion, Kiwanis, Sigma Xi (pres. Las Vegas sect. 1986-91), Phi Kappa Phi (pres. U. Nev. Las Vegas chpt. 100 1982-83), Sigma Gamma Epsilon, Tau Beta Pi (hon.). Congregationalist. Home: 610 Bryant Ct Boulder City NV 89005-3017 Office: Wyman Engring PO Box 60473 Boulder City NV 89006-0473

WYNAR, BOHDAN STEPHEN, librarian, writer, editor; b. Lviv, Ukraine, Sept. 7, 1926; came to U.S., 1950, naturalized, 1957; s. John I. and Euphrosina (Doryk) W.; m. Olha Yarema, Nov. 23, 1992; children: Taras, Michael, Roxolana, Yarynka. Diplom-Volkswirt Econs., U. Munich, Germany, 1949, Ph.D., 1950; M.A., U. Denver, 1958. Methods analyst, statistician Tramco Corp., Cleve., 1951-53; freelance journalist Societ Econs., Cleve., 1954-56; adminstrv. asst. U. Denver Librs., 1958-59, head tech. svcs. div., 1959-62; assoc. prof. Sch. Librarianship, U. Denver, 1962-66; dir. div. libr. edn. State U. Coll., Geneseo, N.Y., 1966-67, dean Sch. Libr. Sci., prof., 1967-69; pres. Libraries Unlimited Inc., 1969—. Author: Soviet Light Industry, 1956, Economic Colonialism, 1958, Ukrainian Industry, 1964, Introduction to Bibliography and Reference Work, 4th edit, 1967, Introduction to Cataloging and Classification, 8th edit, 1992, Major Writings on Soviet Economy, 1966, Library Acquisitions, 2d edit, 1971, Research Methods in Library Science, 1971, Economic Thought in Kievan Rus', 1974; co-author: Comprehensive Bibliography of Cataloging and Classification, 2 vols., 1973, Ukraine: A Bibliographic Guide to English Language Publications, 1990, Independent Ukraine: A Bibliographic Guide to English Language Publications, 1989-99, 2000, Wynar's Introduction to Cataloging and Classification, 2000; editor Ukrainian Quar., 1953-58, Preliminary Checklist of Colorado Bibliography, 1963, Studies in Librarianship, 1963-66, Research Studies in Library Science, 1970— , Best Reference Books, 3d edit., 1985, 4th edit., 1992, Colorado Bibliography, 1980; gen. editor: American Reference Books Ann., 1969—; editor: ARBA Guide to Subject Encyclopedias and Dictionaries, 1985, ARBA Guide To Biographical Dictionaries, Reference Books in Paperback, An Annotated Guide, 2d edit., 1976, 3rd edit., 1991, Dictionary of Am. Library Biography, 1978, Ukraine-A Bibliographic Guide to English-Language Publications, 1990, 99, International Writings of Bohdan S. Wynar 1949-1992, 1993, Independent Ukraine, Bibliographic Guide, 2000, Recommended Reference Books for Medium-Sized and Small Libraries, 1981—; co-editor, contbr. Ency. Ukraine, 1955—; editor Library Sci. Ann., 1984-90, 98, Libr. Info. Sci. Annual 1984-90, 98—. Bd. dirs., mem. exec. bd. ZAREVO, Inc. Mem. ALA (pres. Ukrainian Congress com. br., Denver 1976), Colo. Library Assn., N.Y. Library Assn., Am. Assn. Advancement Slavic Studies (pres. Ukrainian Research Found. 1976-90), AAUP, Ukrainian Hist. Assn. (exec. bd.), Sevčenko Societe Scientifique (Paris), Ukrainian Acad. Arts and Scis. (N.Y.C.). Office: Librs Unltd Inc 6931 S Yosemite St Englewood CO 80112-1415 E-mail: BSW@lu.com

WYNN, STEPHEN A. hotel, entertainment facility executive; b. 1941; married. Pres., chief exec. officer Best Brands, Inc., 1969-72; chmn. bd. dirs., pres., CEO Mirage Resorts Inc. (formerly Golden Nugget Inc.), 1973—. Office: Mirage Resorts Inc 3400 Las Vegas Blvd S Las Vegas NV 89109-8923 also: G N L V 3260 Industrial Rd Las Vegas NV 89109-1132

WYNNE-EDWARDS, HUGH ROBERT, geologist, educator, entrepreneur; b. Montreal, Que., Can., Jan. 19, 1934; s. Vero Copner and Jeannie Campbell (Morris) W.-E.; married; children from previous marriages: Robin Alexander, Katherine Elizabeth, Renée Elizabeth Lortie, Krista Smyth, Jeannie Elizabeth, Alexander Vernon. B.Sc. with 1st class honors, U. Aberdeen, Scotland, 1955; M.A., Queen's U., 1957, Ph.D., 1959; D.Sc. (hon.), Meml. U., 1975. Registered profl. engr. B.C., 1995—. With Geol. Survey Can., 1958-59; lectr. Queen's U., Kingston, Ont., 1968-72, asst. prof., then assoc. prof., 1961-68, prof., head dept. geol. scis., 1968-72; prof., then Cominco prof., head dept. geol. scis. U. B.C., Vancouver, 1972-77; asst. sec. univ. br. Ministry of State for Sci. and Tech., Ottawa, 1977-79; sci. dir. Alcan Internat. Ltd., Montreal, 1979-80, v.p. R&D, chief sci. officer, 1980-89; CEO Moli Energy Ltd., Vancouver, 1989-90; pres. Terracy Inc., Vancouver, 1989—; sci. advisor Teck Corp., Vancouver, 1989-91; pres., CEO B.C. Rsch. Inc., Vancouver, 1993-97, exec. chmn., pres., 1997-2000. Chmn. Silvagen Inc., 1996-99; advisor Directorate Mining and Geology, Uttar Pradesh, India, 1964, Grenville project Que. Dept. Natural Resources, 1968-72; vis. prof. U. Aberdeen, 1965-66, U. Witwatersrand, Johannesburg, South Africa, 1972; UN cons., India, 1974, SCITEC, 1977-78; mem. sci. adv. com. CBC, 1980-84; mem. Sci. Coun. Can., 1983-89, Nat. Adv. Bd. on Sci. and Tech., 1987-90 indsl. liaison com. UN Ctr. for Sci. and Tech. in Devel., 1982-84; vice chmn. tech. adv. group Bus. Coun. for Sustainable Devel., Geneva, 1991; mem. Nat. Biotech. Adv. Coun., 1995-98; chmn. Neurosci. Can. Partnership, 1999—; pres. Silvagen Holdings Inc., 1999-2000; bd. dirs. Atomic Energy Can. Ltd., CTS Coldswitch Techs., Inc., Welichem Biotech Inc. Bd. dirs. Royal Victoria Hosp., Montreal, 1984-89. Decorated officer Order of Can., 1991; recipient Spendiarov prize 24th Internat. Geol. Congress, Montreal, 1972. Fellow Can. Acad. Engring., Royal Soc. Can.; mem. Can. Rsch. Mgmt. Assn. (vice chmn. 1982-84, chmn. 1984-85, assn. medal 1987), Univ. Club (Montreal). Mem. United Ch. Canada. Avocations: tennis, skiing, carpentry. Office: Terracy Inc 2030 27th St West Vancouver BC Canada V7V 4L4

WYSE, ROGER EARL, physiologist, department chairman; b. Wauseon, Ohio, Apr. 22, 1943; BS in Agr., Ohio State U., 1965; MS, Mich. State U., 1967, PhD in Crop Sci., 1969. Fellow Mich. State U., 1969-70; plant physiologist Agr. Rsch. Svc. USDA, 1970-86; dean of rsch. Cook Coll. Rutgers U., 1986-92; dean, dir. Coll. Agr. and Life Sci. U. Wis., Madison, 1992-98; mng. dir. Burrill & Co., San Francisco, 1998—. Recipient Arthur Flemming award, 1982. Fellow Am. Soc. Agronomy, Crop Sci. Soc. Am.; mem. AAAS, Am. Soc. Plant Physiol. Office: Burrill & Co 120 Montgomery St Ste 1370 San Francisco CA 94104-4316

WYSE, WILLIAM WALKER, lawyer, real estate executive; b. Spokane, Wash., July 20, 1919; s. James and Hattie (Walker) W.; m. Janet E. Oswalt, Jan. 30, 1944; children: Wendy L., Scott C., Duncan E. AB, U. Wash., 1941; JD, Harvard U., 1948. Bar: Oreg. 1948. Pvt. practice, Portland; ptnr. Stoel, Rives, Boley, Jones & Gray, 1953-88; pres. Wyse Investment Svcs., 1988—. Past dir. Treasureland Savs. and Loan Assn.; past trustee, sec. Pacific Realty Trust; past trustee Holladay Park Plaza; dir. Costa Pacifica Co., 1999-2000. Bd. dirs. Cmty. Child Guidance Clinic, 1951-57, pres., 1956-57; chmn. ctrl. budget com. United Fund, 1958-60; 1st v.p. United Good Neighbors; chmn. bd. dirs. Portland Sch. Bd., 1959-66; bd. dirs. Oreg. Symphony Soc., 1965-74, 93-99, pres., 1968-70; pres. Tri-County Cmty. Coun., 1970-71; bd. dirs. Portland Mental Health Assn.; bd. dirs., sec. Oreg. Parks Found., Loaves and Fishes Ctrs., Inc., 1997—. Mem. ABA, Oreg. Bar Assn., Multnomah County Bar Assn., Am. Coll. Real Estate Lawyers, Univ. Club, Arlington Club, Portland City Club (past gov.), Wauna Lake Club, Delta Upsilon. Republican. Presbyterian. Home: 3332 SW Fairmount Ln Portland OR 97201-1446 Office: 200 SW Market St Ste 345 Portland OR 97201-5753 E-mail: jwwyse@aol.com, lthomas@wyseinvestment.com

XIE, GANQUAN, mathematician, computational geophysical scientist, educator; b. Changsha, Hunan, People's Republic of China, July 2, 1943; s. Shuming Xie and Sumen Liu; m. Jianhua Li, Sept. 29, 1969; children: Feng, Lee. BCS, Hunan U., ChangSha City, 1966; PhD, SUNY, 1984; postdoctoral rsch., Courant Inst. Math., 1984-86. Asst. prof. Hunan Computer Research Inst., 1967-80; vice-chmn. Soc. Computational Math., Hunan, 1979-81; postdoctoral research Courant Inst. Math., N.Y.C., 1984—; prof., dir. Hunan Computer Rsch. Tech. Inst., 1987-88; staff scientist Lawrence Berkely Nat. Lab., 1991—. Chmn. Chinese Computational Math. Soc., 1986-88; vis. rscher SUNY, 1989; vis. prof. KSU, 1990. Mem. editorial com. Jour. Computational Math., Beijing, 1987-88; inventor in field; contbr. to profl. jours. Nat. Sci. Found. grantee, 1986-87, recipient Chinese Scientific prize, 1978. Mem. N.Y. Acad. Scis., Soc. Indsl. Applied Math., Soc. of Exploration Geophysicists, Am. Geophys. Union. Avocations: applied math., numerical inversse tomography of the seismic exploration and electromagnetic exploration. Home: 1413 Glendale Ave Berkeley CA 94708-2027 Office: Lawrence Berkeley Nat Lab Bldg 90 MS 90-1116 Earth Scis Divsn Berkeley CA 94720 E-mail: g_xie@ibl.gov

YABLONOVITCH, ELI, electrical engineering educator; b. Puch, Austria, Dec. 15, 1946; BSc, McGill U., 1967; AM, Harvard U., 1969, PhD in Applied Physics, 1972. Mem. tech. staff Bell Labs, 1972-74; asst. prof. applied physics Harvard U., 1974-76, assoc. prof., 1976-79; rsch. assoc., group head Exxon Rsch. Ctr., 1979-84; mem. tech. staff Bellcore, 1984-90, disting. mem. staff, 1990-93, dir. solid state physics, 1991-93; prof. elec. engring. UCLA, 1993—. A.P. Sloan fellow, 1978-79. Fellow Am. Physics Soc., Optical Soc. Am. (Adolph Lomb medal 1978, R.W. Wood prize 1996); mem. IEEE (sr.). Achievements include research solid cells, strained-semiconductor lasers, photonic band structure. Office: UCLA Dept Elec Engring 56 125B Engring Bldg IV Los Angeles CA 90095-0001

YACOUB, IGNATIUS I. university dean; b. Dwar Taha, Syria, Jan. 5, 1937; came to U.S. 1978; s. Immanuel and Martha (Kharma) Y.; m. Mary Haddad, Sept. 14, 1961; children— Hilda, Lena, Emile. A.B., Middle East Coll., Beirut, Lebanon, 1960; M.A., Pacific Union Coll., Angwin, Calif., 1964; Ph.D., Claremont Grad. Sch., Calif., 1976. Dean studies Middle East Coll., Beirut, Lebanon, 1967-73, 75-78; dir. dept. edn. Afro-Mideast div. Seventh-Day Adventist Ch., 1970-73, dir. dept. pub. affairs, 1975-78; prof., chmn. dept. bus. econs. Southwestern Union Coll., Keene, Tex., 1978-80; prof., chmn. dept. bus. and econs. Loma Linda U., Riverside, Calif., 1980-86, dean Sch. of Bus. and Mgmt., 1986-90; prof. mgmt., 1995—; dean Sch. Bus. and Mgmt., La Sierra U., Riverside, Calif., 1990-95; prof. adminstrn. and mgmt. Loma Linda (Calif.) U., 1995—. Bd. dirs. Riverside Nat. Bank; bd. advisors City Nat. Bank, 1997—. Mem. Exec. 2000 Coun. Riverside Cmty. Hosp. Found., 1991-95. Recipient Gov.'s Appreciation award, Lions Club, Lions Club award, Beirut, cert. Appreciation Exec. 2000 Coun., 1994, 95, Cert. of Appreciation Claremont Grad. Sch. Alumni Coun., 1996, Mentemoreles Univ. Mex., 1992, 94. Mem. Am. Mgmt. Assn., Acad. Mgmt., Soc. for Advancement Mgmt., Greater Riverside C. of C. (Svc. award 1995), Corona C. of C. Seventh-day Adventist Home: 2722 Litchfield Dr Riverside CA 92503-6213

YAFFE, BARBARA MARLENE, journalist; b. Montreal, Que., Can., Mar. 4, 1953; d. Allan and Anne (Freedman) Y.; m. Wilson E. Russell, Aug. 30, 1985. Student, McGill U., 1970-73; BA, U. Toronto, 1974; B in Journalism, Carleton U., 1974. Reporter Montreal Gazette, 1975-76, Toronto Globe and Mail, 1976-79, reporter, columnist N.S., 1979-81; TV bur. chief CBC-TV, St. Johns, Nfld., 1981-84, Edmonton, Alta., 1983; reporter Toronto Globe and Mail, St. John's, 1984-86; editor Sunday Express, St. John's, 1987-88, Vancouver Sun, 1988-93, columnist, 1993—. Recipient Gov. Gen.'s award Roland Michener Found., 1977. Jewish. Office: c/o Vancouver Sun 200 Granville St Vancouver BC Canada V6C 3N3 E-mail: byaffe@pacpress.southam.ca

YAFFE, JAMES, writer; b. Chgo., Mar. 31, 1927; s. Samuel and Florence (Scheinman) Y.; m. Elaine Gordon, Mar. 1, 1964; children: Deborah Ann, Rebecca Elizabeth, Gideon Daniel. Grad., Fieldston Sch., 1944; B.A. summa cum laude, Yale U., 1948. Prof. Colo. Coll., Colo. Springs, 1968—. Author: Poor Cousin Evelyn, 1951, The Good-for-Nothing, 1953, What's the Big Hurry?, 1954, Nothing But the Night, 1959, Mister Margolies, 1962, Nobody Does You Any Favors, 1966, The American Jews, 1968, The Voyage of the Franz Joseph, 1970, So Sue Me!, 1972, Saul and Morris, Worlds Apart, 1982, A Nice Murder for Mom, 1988, Mom Meets Her Maker, 1990, Mom Doth Murder Sleep, 1991, Mom Among the Liars, 1992, My Mother the Detective, 1997; play The Deadly Game, 1960, (with Jerome Weidman) Ivory Tower, 1967, Cliffhanger, 1985; also TV plays, stories, essays, revs. Served with USNR, 1945-46. Recipient Nat. Arts Found award, 1968 Mem. P.E.N., Authors League, Writers Guild of Am., Dramatists Guild, A.A.U.P., Mystery Writers of Am., Phi Beta Kappa. Jewish. Club: Elizabethan (Yale). Avocations: music, bridge, movies. Address: 1215 N Cascade Ave Colorado Springs CO 80903-2303 Office: Colo Coll Colorado Springs CO 80903

YAKI, MICHAEL J. municipal official; Mem. bd. suprs. City of San Francisco. Office: San Francisco Bd Suprs 401 Van Ness Ave Ste 308 San Francisco CA 94102-4522

YALAM, ARNOLD ROBERT, allergist, immunologist, consultant; b. N.Y.C., Apr. 1, 1940; s. Herman and Sylvia (Taber) Y.; m. Carol Ann Strocker, June 16, 1964; children: John, Matthew. AB, Johns Hopkins U., 1960; MD, U. Md., Balt., 1964. Diplomate Am. Bd. Internal Medicine, Am. Bd. Allergy and Immunology. Intern Jackson Meml. Hosp., Miami, Fla., 1964-65; resident in internal medicine SUNY Downstate Med. Ctr., Bklyn., 1965-67; fellow Scripps Clinic and Rsch. Found., La Jolla, Calif., 1967-68; cons. allergist and immunologist San Diego, 1970—. Maj. US Army, 1968-70. Fellow Am. Acad. Allergy and Immunoloy; mem. Am. Soc. Addiction Medicine (cert.), San Diego Allergy Soc. Office: 8929 University Center Ln San Diego CA 92122-1006

YALMAN, ANN, judge, lawyer; b. Boston, June 9, 1948; d. Richard George and Joan (Osterman) Y. BA, Antioch Coll., 1970; JD, NYU, 1973. Trial atty. Fla. Rural Legal Svcs., Immokalee, Fla., 1973-74; staff atty. EEO, Atlanta, 1974-76; pvt. practice Santa Fe, 1976—; probate judge Santa Fe County, 1999—. Part time U.S. magistrate, N. Mex., 1988-96. Commr. Met. Water Bd., Santa Fe, 1986-88. Mem. N.Mex. Bar Assn. (commr. Santa Fe chpt. 1983-86). Home: 441 Calle La Paz Santa Fe NM 87505-2821 Office: 304 Catron St Santa Fe NM 87501-1806

YAMAGUCHI, COLLEEN S. lawyer; BBA, U. Hawaii, 1982, MBA, 1985; JD, Georgetown U., 1986. Bar: Wash. 1986. Law firm, Seattle, from 1986; ptnr. Sidley & Austin, L.A., 1998—. Assoc. editor Tax Lawyer, 1995-86. Former mem. steering com. Women in Leadership, Wash. Mem. Exec. Devel. Inst., Japanese Am. C. of C. Office: Sidley & Austin 555 W 5th St Los Angeles CA 90013-1010 Fax: 213-896-6600. E-mail: cyamaguc@sidley.com

YAMAMOTO, IRWIN TORAKI, editor, publisher investment newsletter; b. Wailuku, Maui, Hawaii, Apr. 5, 1955; s. Torao and Yukie (Urata) Y. B in Bus. Adminstrn., Mktg., Chaminade U., 1977. Pres., editor, publisher The Yamamoto Forecast, Kahului, Hawaii, 1977—. Author: (book) Profit Making in the Stock Market, 1983; columnist The Hawaii Herald, 1978—. Named Top Market Timer, Top Gold Timer, Top Bond Timer, and to Timer Digest Honor Roll by Timer Digest, also honored by Select Info. Exchange and Rating the Stock Selectors. Avocations: exercise, music, reading, philosophy. Home and Office: PO Box 573 Kahului HI 96733-7073

YAMAMOTO, JOE, psychiatrist, educator; b. Los Angeles, Apr. 18, 1924; s. Zenzaburo and Tomie (Yamada) Y.; m. Maria Fujitomi, Sept. 5, 1947; children: Eric Robert, Andrew Jolyon. Student, Los Angeles City Coll., 1941-42, Hamline U., 1943-45; B.S., U. Minn., 1946, M.B., 1948, M.D., 1949. Asst. prof. dept. psychiatry, neurology, behavioral sci. U. Okla. Med. Center, 1955-58, asst. prof., 1958-60; assoc. prof. dept. psychiatry U. So. Calif. Sch. Medicine, Los Angeles, 1961-69, prof., 1969-77, co-dir. grad. edn. psychiatry, 1963-70; prof. UCLA, 1977-94, emeritus prof., 1994—; dir. Psychiat. Outpatient Clinic, Los Angeles County-U. So. Calif. Med. Center, 1958-77; dir. adult ambulatory care services UCLA Neuropsychiat. Inst., 1977-88, chief Lab. for Cross Cultural Studies. Contbr. articles in field to profl. jours. Served to capt., M.C. U.S. Army, 1953-55. Fellow Am. Psychiat. Assn. (life), Pacific Rim Coll. Psychiatrists, Am. Acad. Psychoanalysis (trustee, mem. exec. com., pres. 1978-79), Am. Coll. Psychiatrists, Am. Orthopsychiat. Assn. (pres.-elect 1993-94, pres. 1994-95, past pres.), Am. Assn. for Social Psychiatry (trustee 1981-84, v.p. 1984-86); mem. So. Calif. Psychoanalytic Inst. and Soc. (pres. 1972-73), Soc. for Study of Culture and Psychiatry, Group for Advancement Psychiatry (bd. dirs. 1992-94), Kappa Phi, Alpha Omega Alpha. Office: UCLA Neuro psychiat Inst 760 Westwood Plz Los Angeles CA 90095-8353

YAMAMOTO, KAORU, retired psychology and education educator; b. Tokyo, Mar. 28, 1932; came to U.S., 1959; s. Saburo and Hideko (Watanabe) Y.; m. Etsuko Hamazaki, Apr. 6, 1959 (div. 1986); m. Carol-Lynne Moore, Oct. 4, 1986; children: Keita Carey Moore, Kiyomi Lynne Moore. BS in Engring., U. Tokyo, 1953; MA, U. Minn., 1960, PhD, 1962. Engr. Toppan Printing Co., Tokyo, 1953; engr., rsch. chemist Japan Oxygen Co., Tokyo, 1954-57, 58-59; asst. prof. Kent (Ohio) State U., 1962-65; from asst. to assoc. prof. U. Iowa, Iowa City, 1965-68; prof. Pa. State U., University Park, 1968-72, Ariz. State U., Tempe, 1972-87, U. Colo., Denver, 1987-99, prof. emeritus, 1999—. Vis. prof. U. Minn., Mpls., 1974, Simon Fraser U., Burnaby, B.C., Can., 1984, U.Victoria, B.C., 1986, U. Wash., Seattle, 1987, Zhejiang Normal U., Jinhua, China, 1991; Fulbright lectr. U. Iceland, 1985. Author: The Child and His Image, 1972, Their World, Our World, 1993; author, editor 7 books, including Children and Stress, 2001; co-author: Beyond Words, 1988; editor Am. Ednl. Rsch. Jour., 1972-75, Ednl. Forum, 1984-92; contbr. chpts. to books and articles to profl. jours. Landsdowne scholar U. Victoria, 1985, Ctr. scholar Ctr. for Rsch. on Ethics and Values Azusa Pacific U., 1998-2000. Fellow APA; mem. Motus Humanus. Avocations: winter sports, travel, classical music, reading. Office: U Surrey Sch Performing Art CO CL Moore GU2 5XH Guildford Surrey England

YAMAMOTO, KEITH ROBERT, molecular biologist, educator; b. Des Moines, Feb. 4, 1946; BS, Iowa State U., 1968; PhD, Princeton U., 1973. Asst. prof. biochemistry U. Calif., San Francisco, 1976-79, assoc. prof., 1979-83, prof. biochemistry, 1983-93, dir. biochemistry and molecular biology program, 1988—, prof., chmn. cellular and molecular pharmacology, 1994—. Mem. genetic biology rev. panel NSF, Washington, 1984-87; chmn. molecular biology study sect. NIH, Bethesda, Mdf., 1987-90, mem. nat. adv. coun. for human genome rsch., 1990-91. Co-author: Gene Wars: Military Control over the New Genetic Technologies, 1988; co-editor: Transcriptional Regulation, 1992 ; assoc. editor Jour. Molecular Biology, 1988—, editor Molecular Biology of the Cell, 1991—. Mem. Com. for Responsible Genetics, Boston, 1989—; testifier hearings on biol. warfare com. on govtl. affairs U.S. Senate, Washington, 1989. Recipient Gregory Pincus medal Worchester Found. for Exptl. Biology, 1990; Dreyfus tchr.-scholar, 1982-86. Fellow Am. Acad. Arts and Scis.; mem. AAAS, NAS (panel on sci. responsibility and conduct of rsch. 1990-91), Protein Soc., Am. Soc. for Cell Biology (coun. 1991-92), Am. Soc. for Biochemistry and Molecular Biology (publs. com. 1990-93), Am. Soc. for Devel. Biology. Office: U Calif San Francisco Dept Cellular Molecular Phm 513 Parnassus Ave San Francisco CA 94143-0001

YAMAMOTO, MICHAEL TORU, journalist; b. San Francisco, July 9, 1960; s. Harry Naoto and Noriko (Yoshitomi) Y.; m. Marianne Chin, Oct. 9, 1993. BA Psychology, BA Journalism, San Francisco State U., 1981. Editor San Francisco State U. Phoenix, 1980; news editor Hayward (Calif.) Daily Rev., 1979-80, Long Beach (Calif.) Press-Telegram, 1981; nat. desk editor L.A. Times, 1981-85, night news editor, 1986-87, investigative projects editor, 1988; dep. city editor San Francisco Chronicle, 1989-92, exec. projects editor, 1993, city editor, 1993-95; mng. editor news CNET, San Francisco, 1996—. Adj. prof. Am. U., Washington, 1987, Calif. State U. at Northridge, Calif., 1984-85; vis. faculty mem. Am. Press Inst., Reston, Va., 1994, Poynter Inst. for Media Studies, St. Petersburg, Fla., 1995, San Francisco Unified Sch. Dist., 1994; fellow Coro Found., San Francisco, 1990-91. Recipient Dow Jones Newspaper Fund scholarship, Princeton, N.J., 1980. Mem. Asian Am. Journalism Assn., White House Corr. Assn., Soc. Profl. Journalists., World Affairs Coun. Office: CNET 150 Chestnut St San Francisco CA 94111-1004

YAMAMOTO, STANLY TOKIO, prosecutor; b. San Jose, Calif., July 22, 1948; s. George and Bettie (Nakamura) Y.; m. Yuri Honda, July 21, 1973; children: Miharu Lesley, Kiyomi Jill. BA, San Jose State U., 1971; JD, Santa Clara U. Sch. Law, 1978. Bar: Calif., 1980, U.S. Dist. Ct. (no. dist.) Calif., 1980, U.S. Dist. Ct. (ea. dist.) Calif., 1983, U.S. Dist. Ct. (ctrl. dist.) Calif., 1993, U.S. Supreme Ct., 1990. Adminstrv. asst. City of Sunnyvale, Calif., 1980-82, dep. city atty., 1982-84, asst. city atty., 1984-85, acting city atty., 1985-87; city atty. City of Modesto, 1987-92, City of Riverside, 1992—. Minorities-in-planning intern HUD, 1971-73; adv. Gov.'s Local Govt. Policy Com., 1993. With USAR, 1968-74. Nat. Urban fellow, 1978-79. Mem. League Calif. Cities, Internat. Mcpl. Lawyers. Office: Office of City Atty 3900 Main St Riverside CA 92522-0001

YAMARONE, CHARLES ANTHONY, JR. aerospace engineer, consultant; b. Bronxville, N.Y., Oct. 30, 1936; s. Charles Anthony and Mildred (La Manna) Y.; m. Catherine MacMullan, May 31, 1957; children: Charles Anthony III, Thomas, Stephen, Mark, James. BSEE, Manhattan Coll., 1958. Design engr. Gen. Precision Inc., Pleasantville, N.Y., 1958-62; engr. supr. Jet Propulsion Lab., Calif. Inst. Tech., Pasadena, 1962-69, sect. mgr., 1969-76, data processing mgr. Topex/Poseidon, 1976-80, project mgr., 1980-96, program mgr. Eart Sci. Flight Projects, 1996—. Recipient Astronautique medal Assn. Aeronautique et Astronautique de France, 1992, medal Ctr. Nat. d'Etudes Spatiales, 1994, Outstanding Leadership medal NASA, 1993. Mem. Am. Geophys. Union, Am. Inst. for Advancement of Science. Office: Jet Propulsion Lab Stop 254686 Topex Project Office 4800 Oak Grove Dr Pasadena CA 91109-8001

YAMASHITA, FRANCIS ISAMI, magistrate judge; b. Hilo, Hawaii, May 14, 1949; s. Yuji and Sadako (Hirayama) Y.; m. Alexa D. M. Fujise, Feb. 26, 1983. BA, Pacific U., 1971; JD, U. Chgo., 1974. Bar: Hawaii 1974. Law clk. 1st Cir. Ct., Hawaii, 1975-76; dep. pros. atty. City/County of Honolulu, 1976-79, 82-87; assoc. Ikazaki, Devens, Lo, Youth & Nakano, Honolulu, 1979-82; dist. judge State of Hawaii, Honolulu, 1987-92, U.S. magistrate judge, 1992—. Office: US Dist Ct Hawaii 300 Ala Moana Blvd Rm C209 Honolulu HI 96850-0209

YAMIN, JOHN, food service executive; b. Troy, N.Y., May 23, 1956; married; 1 child, Jessica. B in Psychology, Skidmore Coll. With Unity House, Troy, Saga; divsn. mgr. ARA Svcs., L.A.; COO, oper. ptnr. Louise's Trattoria, Inc., Torrance, Calif., 1989; v.p. retail Caravali Coffee; joined Starbucks, 1996; dir. Cafe Starbucks, Seattle. Avocations: weight lifting, fly fishing. Office: Cafe Starbucks 600 Pine St Seattle WA 98101-3700

YANCEY, GARY, electronics company executive; Pres., CEO Applied Signal Tech., Sunnyvale, Calif. Office: Applied Signal Tech 400 W California Ave Sunnyvale CA 94086-5151

YANG, HENRY T. university chancellor, educator; b. Chungking, China, Nov. 29, 1940; s. Chen Pei and Wei Gen Yang; m. Dilling Tsui, Sept. 2, 1966; children: Maria, Martha. BSCE, Nat. Taiwan U., 1962; MSCE, W.Va. U., 1965; PhD, Cornell U., 1968; D honoris causa, Purdue U., 1996. Structural engr. Gilbert Assocs., Reading, Pa., 1968-69; asst. prof. Sch. Aeros. and Astronautics, Purdue U., West Lafayette, Ind., 1969-72, assoc. prof., 1972-76, prof., 1976-94, Neil A. Armstrong Disting. prof., 1988-94, sch. head, 1979-84; dean engring. Purdue U., 1984-94; chancellor U. Calif., Santa Barbara, 1994—. Mem. sci. adv. bd. USAF, 1985-89; mem. aero. adv. com. NASA, 1985-89; mem. engring. adv. com. NSF, 1988-91; mem. mechanics bd. visitors ONR, 1990-93; mem. def. mfg. bd. DOD, 1988-89, def. sci. bd., 1989-91; mem. acad. adv. bd. Nat. Acad. Engring., 1991-94; mem. tech. adv. com. Pratt & Whitney, 1993-95; bd. dirs. Allied Signal, 1996-99; mem. Naval Rsch. Adv. Com., 1996-98. Recipient 12 Best Tchg. awards Purdue U., 1971-94, Outstanding Aerospace Engr. award Purdue U., 1999. Fellow AIAA, Am. Soc. Engring. Edn. (Centennial medal 1993, Benjamin Garver Lamme award 1998); mem. NAE, Academia Sinica. Office: U Calif Chancellors Office Santa Barbara CA 93106

YANG, HSIN-MING, immunologist; b. Taipei, Taiwan, Dec. 2, 1952; came to U.S., 1980; s. Sze Piao and Yun-Huan (Chang) Y.; m. Yeasing Yeh, June 28, 1980; children: Elaine, Albert. BS, Nat. Taiwan U., 1976, MS, 1983; PhD, U. Wash., 1985. Rsch. assoc. Tri-Svc. Gen. Hosp., Taipei, 1979-80; fellow Scripps Clinic and Rsch. Found., La Jolla, Calif., 1986-88, sr. rsch. assoc., 1988-90; asst. prof. U. Nebr. Med. Ctr., Omaha, 1990-91; sr. rsch. scientist Pacific Biotech, Inc., San Diego, 1991-95; mgr. Scantibodies Lab., Inc., Santee, Calif., 1995-99, dir., 1999-2000; staff scientist Wyntek Diagnostics, Inc., San Diego, 2000—, Genzyme Diagnostics, 01—. Lectr. Yun-Pei Coll. Med. Tech., Shinchiu, Taiwan, 1979-80. Contbr. articles to profl. jours., chpt. to book; inventor in field; patentee on analyte detection device including a hydrophobic barrier for improved fluid flow. Joseph Drown Found. fellow, 1986, Nat. Cancer Ctr. fellow, 1987-88. Mem. Am. Assn. for Cancer Rsch., Am. Assn. Clin. Chemistry, N.Y. Acad. Scis. Avocations: tennis, swimming, table tennis. Office: Scantibodies Lab Inc 9336 Abraham Way Santee CA 92071-2861

YANG, JERRY, online computer services executive; b. Taiwan; BS, MSEE, Stanford U. Co-creator online guide Yahoo!, Santa Clara, Calif., 1994—; co-founder Yahoo!, Inc., Santa Clara, 1995—, chief Yahoo, bd. dirs., 1996—. Office: Yahoo! Inc 3420 Central Expy Santa Clara CA 95051-0703

YANG, YANG, science educator; b. Kaohsiung, Taiwan, Nov. 7, 1958; came to U.S., 1985; s. Shun-Wen and Huang-Yin Yang; m. Danmei Lee, May 30, 1987; 1 child, Jonathan Lee Yang. BS in Physics, Nat. Cheng Kung U., 1982; MS in Physics, U. Mass., 1988, PhD in Physics, 1992. Rsch. asst. U. Mass., Lowell, 1989-91; rsch. assoc. U. Calif., Riverside, 1991-92; rsch. scientist UNIAX Corp., Santa Barbara, Calif., 1992-96; prof. UCLA, 1997—. Contbr. articles to profl. jours. Mem. Am. Phys. Soc., Material Rsch. Soc. Office: UCLA Dept Materials Sci Engring Los Angeles CA 90095-0001

YANKOVIC, (WEIRD) AL, singer, satirist; b. Oct. 23, 1959; BArch, Calif. Polytechnic State U. Songs include My Bologna, 1983, Eat It, 1984, I Lost on Jeopardy, 1984, Like a Surgeon, 1985, Yoda, 1985; albums include Weird Al Yankovic, 1983, Weird Al Yankovic in 3-D, 1984, Dare to Be Stupid (Grammy nomination), 1985, (with Wendy Carlos) Peter and the Wolf, 1988; films include UHF, 1989. Office: Close Personal Friends of Al PMB 4018 8033 W Sunset Blvd Los Angeles CA 90046-2427

YANOFSKY, CHARLES, biology educator; b. N.Y.C., Apr. 17, 1925; s. Frank and Jennie (Kopatz) Y.; m. Carol Cohen, June 19, 1949, (dec. Dec. 1990); children: Stephen David, Robert Howard, Martin Fred; m. Edna Crawford, Jan. 4, 1992. BS, CCNY, 1948; MS, Yale U., 1950, PhD, 1951, DSc (hon.), 1981, U. Chgo., 1980. Rsch. asst. Yale U., 1951-54; asst. prof. microbiology Western Res. U. Med. Sch., 1954-57; mem. faculty Stanford U., 1958—, prof. biology, 1961—, Herzstein prof. biology, 1966—. Career investigator Am. Heart Assn., 1969-95. Served with AUS, 1944-46. Recipient Lederle Med. Faculty award, 1957, Eli Lilly award bacteriology, 1959, U.S. Steel Co. award molecular biology, 1964, Howard Taylor Ricketts award U. Chgo., 1966, Albert and Mary Lasker award, 1971, Townsend Harris medal Coll. City N.Y., 1973, Louisa Gross Horwitz prize in biology and biochemistry Columbia U., 1976, V.D. Mattia award Roche Inst., 1982, medal Genetics Soc. Am., 1983, Internat. award Gairdner Found., 1985, named Passano Laureate, Passano Found., 1992; recipient William C. Rose award in biochemistry and molecular biology, 1997, Abbott Lifetime Achievement award Am. Soc. Microbiology, 1998. Mem. NAS (Selman A. Waksman award in microbiology 1972), Am. Acad. Arts and Scis., Genetics Soc. Am. (pres. 1969, Thomas Hunt Morgan medal 1990), Am. Soc. Biol. Chemists (pres. 1984), Royal Soc. (fgn. mem.), Japanese Biochem. Soc. (hon.) Home: 725 Mayfield Ave Stanford CA 94305-1016 Office: Stanford U Dept Of Biological Sci Stanford CA 94305

YANSOUNI, CYRIL J. computer company executive; BSEE, U. Louvian, Belgium; MSEE, Stanford U. Various tech. and mgmt. positions including v.p., gen. mgr. Hewlett-Packard Co., 1967-86; pres. Convergent Techs. (now Unisys Corp.), 1986-88; various sr. mgmt. positions including exec. v.p. Unisys Corp., 1988-91; CEO, chmn. Read-Rite, Milpitas, Calif., 1997-2000, chmn., 2000—. Dir. Informix Software, Inc., PeopleSoft, Inc., Raychem Corp., ActiveCard, Inc. Office: 345 Los Coches St Milpitas CA 95035-5428

YAPLE, HENRY MACK, library director; b. Vicksburg, Mich., May 30, 1940; s. Henry J. and Pauline B. (Spencer) Y.; m. Marilyn Lou Bales, Dec. 31, 1971; children: Sean H., Kendra S. BA in English with hons., Kalamazoo Coll., 1963; MA, U. Idaho, 1966; postgrad., U. d'Aix-Marseille, France, 1965-66, U. Toronto, , 1966-69; MLS, W. Mich. U., 1972. Order libr. Mich. State U., E. Lansing, 1972-74, humanities bibliographer, 1974-78; acquisitions libr. U. Wyo., Laramie, 1978-87; libr. dir. Whitman Coll., Walla Walla, Wash., 1987—. Mem. Wyo. Coun. for the Humanities, 1982-86. U. Toronto scholar, 1966-69; Rotary fellow, 1965, 66; U. Wyo. rsch. grantee, 1982, 86. Mem. ALA, Wyo. Libr. Assn. (pres. 1984-85), Nat. Ski Patrol System (sr. patroller 1978-95, nat. #6946 1988), Wash. Libr. Assn., Northwest Assn. of Pvt. Colls. and U. Librs. (pres. 1987-88, 94-95), Beta Phi Mu. Avocations: book collecting, skiing, kayaking. Home: 1889 Fern St Walla Walla WA 99362-9393 Office: Whitman Coll Penrose Libr 345 Boyer Ave Walla Walla WA 99362-2067 E-mail: yaple@whitman.edu

YAPP, JEFF, broadcast executive; Pres. Fox Video, L.A. Office: Hollywood Entertainment Corp d/b/a Hollywood Video 9275 SW Peyton Ln Wilsonville OR 97070

YARED, GABRIEL, composer; b. Lebanon, 1949; Composer, orchestrator, 1973—. Composer for Johnny Hallyday, Charles Aznavour, Gilbert Becaud, Mireille Mathieu, Sylvie Vartan, Tania Maria, Francoise Hardy, (filmography) Sauve Qui Peut La Vie, 1980, Malevil, 1980, L'Invitation au voyage, 1981, Interdit au moins de treize ans, 1982, La Lune dans le carniveau, 1983 (Gran Prix de la SACEM 1984), La Jave des ombres, 1983, La Scarlatine, 1983, Sarah, 1983, Les Petites guerres, 1983, Nemo, 1984, Hanna K, 1984 (Gran Prix de la SACEM 1984), La Diagonale du fou, 1984, Tir à vue, 1984, Le Téléphone sonne toujours deux fois, 1985, Adieu Bonaparte, 1985, Scout toujours, 1985, 37 2 le Matin (nominated aux Césars 1988, aux Victiores 1988), Gandahar contre les hommes machines, 1987, Beyond Therapy, 1987, Agent Trouble, 1987, Clean and Sober, 1988, Le Testament d'un poète juif assassiné, Les Saisons du plasir, 1988, L'Homme voilé, 1988, Une Nuit à l'Assemblée nationale, 1988, La Romana, 1988, Camille Claudel, 1988 (nominated aux Césars 1989, Victoire de la Musique 1989), Tennessee Nights, 1989, Romero, 1989, Tennessee Waltz, 1989, Les Mille et une nuits, 1989, Vincent and Theo, 1990, Vincent et Théo, 1990, Tatie Danielle, 1990, La Putain du roi, 1990, L'Amant, 1991 (Vitoire de la Musique 1992, César de la Musique 1993, nominated au Internat. Musical Visual award 1993), L'Arche et les déluges, 1991, IP5, 1991, Map of the Human Heart, 1992, Coeur de métisse, 1992 (nominated au Australian Film Inst. award 1993), La Fille de l'air, 1992, L'Instinct de l'ange (nominated au Midem award pour l'ensemble de son oeuvre 1993), Les Marmottes, 1993 (nominated aux Victoires 1994), Des Feux mal éteints, 1993, Profil bas, 1993 (nominated au Midem award pour l'ensemble de son oeuvre 1994), Wings of Courage, 1994, Noir comme le souvenir, 1995 (nominated aux Victoires de la Musique 1996), Hercule et Sherlock, 1996, English Patient, 1996 (Golden Globe award 1996, First Golden Satellite award 1997, Oscar 1997, British Acad. Arts and TV award 1997, Indie award 1997, Grammy awards 1998, Victoire de la Musique 1998, Grand Prix de la SACEM 1998, AA nomination 1996, Cmdr. des Arts et Lettres), Tonka, 1997, City of Angels, 1998 (Film and TV Music award 1998, nominated Golden Satellite award 1998, nominated Grammy awards 1998), Message in a Bottle, 1999.

YARINGTON, CHARLES THOMAS, JR. surgeon, administrator; b. Sayre, Pa., Apr. 26, 1934; s. C.T. and Florence (Hutchinson) Y.; m. Barbara Taylor Johnson, Sept. 28, 1963; children: Leslie Anne, Jennifer Lynne, Barbara Jane. AB, Princeton, 1956; MD, Hahnemann Med. Coll., 1960; grad., Army Command and Gen. Staff Coll., 1969, Air War Coll., 1973, Indsl. Coll. Armed Forces, 1974. Intern Rochester (N.Y.) Gen. Hosp., 1960-61; resident Dartmouth Hosp., 1961-62, U. Rochester Strong Meml. Hosp., 1962-65; instr. otolaryngology U. Rochester Sch. Medicine, 1962-65; asst. prof. surgery W.Va. U. Sch. Medicine, 1967-68; assoc. prof., chmn. dept. otorhinolarygology U. Nebr. Med. Center, 1968-69, prof., chmn. dept. otorhinolarygology, 1969-74; clin. prof. otolaryngology U. Wash., Seattle, 1974—; clin. prof. surgery Uniformed Services U. Health Scis., Bethesda, 1985—; chief otolaryngology Virginia Mason Med. Ctr., Seattle, 1978-88, 92-95, chief dept. surgery, 1988-91; surgeon Mason Clinic, Seattle, 1974-97. Cons. Surg. Gen. USAF, Hunter Group Med. Mgmt. Cons., 1996-98, Seattle Multispecialty Panel, 1998—; pres. Virginia Mason Rsch. Ctr., Seattle, 1983-85; trustee Mason Clinic, 1988-91; adv. coun. Nat. Inst. Neurol. Diseases, Communicative Diseases, Stroke of NIH, Bethesda, Md., 1986-90; bd. dirs. Virginia Mason Hosp., Mirginia Mason Med. Ctr., bd. govs., 1989-98. Author books and articles in field.; Mem. editorial bd. Aviation, Space, Environ. Med. Jour., Otol. Clinics of N. Am., Mil. Medicine, Otolaryngology-Head and Neck Surgery Trustee Seattle Opera Assn., 1983-89. Maj., M.C. AUS, 1965-67; brig. gen. USAF Res., to 1986. Decorated D.S.M., Legion of Merit; named Commdr. Venerable Order St. John (Gt. Britain), Companion with Star, Order Orthodox Hospit, Republic of Cypress; recipient Sir Henry Wellcome medal, 1984, Knight Grand Cross, Mil. and Hospitaller Order of St. Lazarus. Fellow ACS, Royal Soc. Medicine, Am. Acad. Otolaryngology (Barraquer Meml. award 1968, mem. standing com., bd. govs. 1982-88, Honor award 1974); mem. AMA, Am. Broncho-Esophagological Assn. (council, treas. 1982-86, pres. 1987-88), Am. Laryngol. Assn., Pacific Coast Soc. Ophthalmology and Otolaryngology (coun., pres. 1987-88), Soc. Med. Cons. to Armed Forces, Am. Soc. Head and Neck Surgery, N.W. Acad. Head and Neck Surgery (pres. 1984-86), Am. Soc. Otology, Rhinology and Laryngology (v.p. 1992-93, coun. 1997-2000), Res. Officers Assn. (past pres. Seattle chpt., nat. officer), Pan-Pacific Surg. Assn., Sons of Revolution (pres. Wash. 1985-87, Internat. Power Boat Assn. (comdr. 1999-2000), Seattle Yacht Club, Princeton Quadrangle Club, Broadmoor Golf Club, RAF Club (London), Cosmos CLub (Washington), Sigma Xi.

YARIV, AMNON, electrical engineering educator, scientist; b. Tel Aviv, Israel, Apr. 13, 1930; came to U.S., 1951, naturalized, 1964; s. Shraga and Henya (Davidson) Y.; m. Frances Pokras, Apr. 10, 1972; children: Elizabeth, Dana, Gabriela. B.S., U. Calif., Berkeley, 1954, M.S., 1956, Ph.D., 1958. Mem. tech. staff Bell Telephone Labs., 1959-63; dir. laser research Watkins-Johnson Co., 1963-64; mem. faculty Calif. Inst. Tech., 1964—, Martin Summerfield prof. applied physics, 1966—; chmn. bd. ORTEL Inc. Co-founder, bd. mem. Arroyo Optics, Inc. Author: Quantum Electronics, 1967, 75, 85, Introduction to Optical Electronics, 1971, 77, 89, Theory and Applications of Quantum Mechanics, Propagation of Light in Crystals. Served with Israeli Army, 1948-50. Recipient Pender award U. Pa., Harvey prize Technion, Israel, 1992. Fellow IEEE (Quantum Electronics award 1980), Am. Optical Soc. (Ives medal 1986, Esther Beller medal 1998), Am. Acad. Arts and Scis.; mem. NAS, NAE, Am. Phys. Soc. Office: 1201 E California Blvd Pasadena CA 91125-0001

YARNELL, MICHAEL ALLAN, lawyer; b. Chgo., Sept. 10, 1944; s. Howard Winfred and Mary Elizabeth (Card) Y.; m. Karen Alice Hockenyos, June 12, 1971 (div. Mar. 1994); children: Sarah Munro, Jacob Rainey; m. Kristina Louise Renshaw, July 17, 1996. BS, Ariz. State U., 1967; JD with honors, U. Ill., 1971. Bar: Ariz. 1971. Ptnr. Streich, Lang, Weeks & Cardon, Phoenix, 1971-91, also bd. dirs.; mem. Myers, Barnes & Jenkins, Phoenix, 1991; judge Maricopa County Superior Ct., Phoenix, 1991—. Author: Ins and Outs of Foreclosure, 1981, 11th edit., 2000; projects editor Law Rev. U. Ill. Law Forum, 1970; contbr. articles to profl. jours. Chairperson Phoenix Children's Theatre, 1987; vol. Habitat for Humanity, Adopt-a-Home sponsor; chmn. Legal Cmty. Builds, 1999. 1st lt. U.S. Army, 1971-72, Korea. Fellow Ariz. Bar Found.; mem. ABA, Am. Judicature Assn., Maricopa Bar Assn., State Bar Ariz. (Outstanding Contbn. to Continuing Legal Edn. award 1988, Com. on Profl. Conduct award 2000), Order of Coif, Lorna Lockwood Inn of Ct. (co-pres. 2000-2001), Phi Kappa Phi, Ariz. Yacht Club (vice comdr. 2000, comdr. 2001—). Republican. Avocations: computers, small boat sailing, white water rafting. Office: Maricopa County Superior Ct 101 W Jefferson St Phoenix AZ 85003-2206 E-mail: michael@yarnell.net

YASSIN, ROBERT ALAN, museum administrator, curator; b. Malden, Mass., May 22, 1941; s. Harold Benjamin and Florence Gertrude (Hoffman) Y.; m. Marilyn Kramer, June 9, 1963; children: Fredric Giles, Aaron David. BA (Rufus Choate scholar), Dartmouth Coll., 1962; postgrad., Boston U., 1962-63; M.A., U. Mich., 1965, postgrad. (Samuel H. Kress Found. fellow), 1968-70, Ph.D. candidate, 1970; postgrad (Ford Found. fellow), Yale U., 1966-68. Asst. to dir. Mus. Art U. Mich., 1965-66, asst. dir., 1970-72, asso. dir., 1972-73, acting dir., 1973, instr. dept. history of art, 1970-73; co-dir. Joint Program in Mus. Tng., 1970-73; chief curator Indpls. Mus. Art, 1973-75, 87-89, acting dir., 1975, dir., 1975-89; exec. dir. Tucson Mus. Art, 1990—. Adj. prof. Herron Sch. Art Ind. U./Purdue U., 1975-89. Contbr. to mus. publications. Mem. Ariz. Mus. Assn., Tucson Mus. Assn., Bd. Ctrl. Arts Collective. Mem. Am. Assn. Mus. (bd. dirs. Internat. Coun. Mus. 1986-89), Coll. Art Assn. Am., Tucson C. of C., Nat. Trust Historic Preservation, Western Mus. Assn., Ariz. Assn. Mus. Jewish. Home: 3900 N Calle Casita Tucson AZ 85718-7204 Office: Tucson Mus Art 140 N Main Ave Tucson AZ 85701-8290 E-mail: ryassin@tucarts.com

YATES, ALBERT CARL, academic administrator, chemistry educator; b. Memphis, Sept. 29, 1941; s. John Frank and Sadie L. (Shell) Y.; m. Ann Young; children: Steven, Stephanie, Aerin Alessandra, Sara Elizabeth. B.S., Memphis State U., 1965; Ph.D., Ind. U., 1968. Research assoc. U. So. Calif., Los Angeles, 1968-69; prof. chemistry Ind. U., Bloomington, 1969-74; v.p. research, grad. dean U. Cin., 1974-81; exec. v.p., provost, prof. chemistry Washington State U., Pullman, 1981-90; pres. Colo. State U., Fort Collins, 1990—; chancellor Colo. State U. System, Fort Collins, 1990—. Mem. grad. record exam. bd. Princeton (N.J.) U., 1977-81; undergrad. assessment program coun. Ednl. Testing Svc., 1977-81, NRC, 1975-82, Office Edn., HEW, 1978-80; mem. exec. coun. acad. affairs Nat. Assn. State Univs. and Land Grant Colls., 1983-87, Am. Coun. on Edn., 1983-87, nat adv. coun. gen. med. scis. NIH, 1987-90. Contbr. research articles to Jour. Chem. Physics; research articls to Phys. Rev.; research articles to Jour. Physics, Phys. Rev. Letters, Chem. Physics Letters. Served with USN, 1959-62. Recipient univ., state and nat. honors and awards Mem. AAAS, Am. Phys. Soc., Am. Chem. Soc., Sigma Xi, Phi Lambda Upsilon. Home: 1744 Hillside Dr Fort Collins CO 80524-1965 Office: Colo State U 102 Administration Bldg Fort Collins CO 80523-0100 E-mail: ayates@lamar.colostate.edu

YATES, DAVID JOHN C. chemist, researcher; b. Stoke-on-Trent, Staffordshire, Eng., Feb. 13, 1927; came to U.S., 1958; s. Eric John and Beatrice Victoria (Street) Y.; m. Natalie Chmelnitsky, June 22, 1983 B.S. with honors, U. Birmingham, U.K., 1949; Ph.D., U. Cambridge, Eng., 1955, Sc.D., 1968. Rsch. physicist Kodak Labs., Wealdstone, London, 1949-50; rsch. chemist Brit. Ceramic Rsch. Assn., Stoke-on-Trent, 1950-51; rsch. assoc. dept. colloid sci. U. Cambridge, 1951-58; lectr. Sch. Mines and dept. chemistry Columbia U., N.Y.C., 1958-60; sr. rsch. fellow Nat. Phys. Lab., Teddington, U.K., 1960-61; rsch. assoc. corp. labs. Exxon Rsch. and Engring., Annandale, N.J., 1961-86; rsch. prof. dept. of chem. engring. Lafayette Coll., Easton, Pa., 1986-87; rsch. prof. dept. materials sci. Rutgers U., Piscataway, N.J., 1987-88; cons. San Diego, 1988—. Contbr. over 70 articles to profl. jours., chpts. to books; 13 U.S. patents, numerous fgn. patents. Fellow Inst. of Physics (U.K.), Royal Soc. Chemistry (U.K.), N.Y. Catalysis Club (chmn. 1966-67). Club: N.Y. Catalysis (chmn. 1965-66) Avocations: photography, bicycling, gliding, travel, sports cars.

YATES, GARY L. marriage and family therapist; b. Washington, Aug. 16, 1944; s. Lewis Edward and Norma Jean (Andruss) Y.; m. Cynthia Ann Pagay, Aug. 16, 1974; children: David, Jonathan, Daniel, Matthew, Nathan. BA, Am. U., 1967; MA, U. No. Colo., 1978. Tchr. St. Anthony's, Kailua, Hawaii, 1970-74, Acad. of Pacific, Honolulu, 1974-79; adminstr. Dept. Pub. Health, San Bernardino, Calif., 1979-81, Charles Drew Sch. of Medicine, L.A., 1981-82; assoc. dir. Divsn. of Adolescent Medicine/Children's Hosp., L.A., 1982-92; sr. program officer Calif. Wellness Found., Woodland Hills, Calif., 1992-93, program dir., 1993-94, pres., CEO, 1995—. Asst. clin. prof. U. So. Calif., 1988—; mem. bd. dirs. Calif. Wellness Found. Contbr. articles to profl. jours.; contbg. author: Multi Agency System of Care, 1990. Mem. L.A. Roundtable for Children, 1988-92, United Way Task Force on AIDS, L.A., 1988-92, San Bernardino Comm. Coun., 1980-82; chmn. Hawaii Sch. Counseling Assn., Honolulu, 1978-79. S(sgt.) U.S. Army, 1968-70. Recipient NACO Achievement award Nat. Assn. U.S. Counties, 1980, 3rd Century award Hollywood Coord. Coun., 1989, Gov.'s Victim's Svc. award Gov. of Calif., 1990, Commendation award Calif. State Senate, 1992. Mem. Am. Assn. Humanistic Psychologists, Soc. for Adolescent Medicine, Calif. Assn. Marriage and Family Therapists, Am. Pub. Health Assn., Bd. of Dirs. Found. Consortium (chmn. 1995—). Democrat. Methodist. Avocations: reading, walking. Office: Calif Wellness Found 6320 Canoga Ave Ste 1700 Woodland Hills CA 91367-2565

YATES, KEITH LAMAR, retired insurance company executive; b. Bozeman, Mont., Oct. 29, 1927; s. Thomas Bryan and Altha (Norris) Y.; m. Dolores Hensel, Aug. 30, 1948; children: Thomas A., Molly Yates McIntosh, Richard A., Nancy Yates Sands, Penny Dannielle Yates, Pamela Yates Beeler. BA, Eastern Wash. U., 1953. Salesman Ancient Order United Workmen, Spokane, Wash., 1952-53, sales mgr., 1953-56, corp. sec., 1956-73, Neighbors of Woodcraft, Portland, Oreg., 1973-89, pres., 1989-92; ret., 1992. Author: Life of Willie Willey, 1966, The Fogarty Years, 1972, History of The Woodcraft Home, 1975, An Enduring Heritage, 1992; tuba player Beaverton Cmty. Band, 1987—, One More Time Around Again Marching Band, 1987—, Rose City Banjoliers, 1993—. Pres. Wash. State Christian Mens Fellowship, Seattle, 1965-67; pres. Met. Area Assn. Christian Chs., 1981-83; mem. regional bd. Christian Chs. Oreg., 1990-94. Command sgt.-maj., ret., 1987; served with USN, USAF, USANG, 1946-87. Mem. Wash. State Frat. Cong., (cert. Commendation 1969, sec. 1957-68, pres., mem. exec. bd., chmn. conv. program advt. com. 1960-73), Oreg. State Frat. Cong. (Outstanding Frat. 1975-76, Spl. Appreciation award 1984, Frat. Family of Yr. 1986, 98, sec. 1975-87, pres., mem. exec. bd. 1974—), Nat. Fraternal Congress Am. (conv. arrangement com. 1964, 90, publicity com. 1964, 65, 68, 90, credentials com. 1970, 77, 78, pres. press & pub. rels. sec. 1971-72, pub. rels. com. 1971-73, chmn. 1972, co-chmn. press and pub. rels. frat. seminar 1972, frat. monitor com. 1974-75, mem. com. 1975-76, family life com. 1978-80, constitution com. 1980, pres. state frat. congs. sec. 1981-82, historian 1987—), Washington County's Disting. Patriot, Portland Ins. Acctg. and Statis. Soc. Assn. Records Mgrs. and Adminstrs. (Oreg. chpt.), Portland C. of C., Wash. Ins. Coun., Wash. Claims Assn., Seattle Underwriting Assn. Home: 29860 SW Buckhaven Rd Hillsboro OR 97123-8821 E-mail: kayndee@email.msn.com

YATES, STEVEN A. artist, curator; b. Chgo., Nov. 14, 1949; s. Thomas A. and Phyllis E. (Wilson) Y.; m. Lynne A. Smith, Aug. 5, 1972; children: Kelsey Victoria, Mackenzie Phyllis. BFA, U. Nebr., 1972; MA, U. N.Mex., 1975, MFA, 1978. Curatorial asst. Sheldon Meml. Art Gallery, 1972-73, U. Art Mus., U. N.Mex., 1973-75; faculty dept. art Claremong (Calif.) Coll. and Pomona, 1976; part-time faculty U. N.Mex., Albuquerque, 1976-79, assoc. adj. prof. art and art history; curator prints, drawings and photographs Mus. of N.Mex., Santa Fe, 1980-84; curator of photography Mus. Fine Arts, 1985—. Vis. prof. 19th and 20th century photography Santa Fe Cmty. Coll., 1997—; frequent lectr. in contemporary and early modern history of photography internationally; guest artist Tamarind Inst., Albuquerque, 1988. One-man shows include Sheldon Meml. Art Gallery, Lincoln, Nebr., 1978, Gallery A-3, Moscow, 1996, Up and Down Gallery, Kharkov, Ukraine, 1997, U. Nebr., 1997, Mus. Photography, Riga, Latvia, 1998, Photographic Din-De-Siecle Self-Potrait, Andrew Smith Gallery, Sante Fe, 2000; group shows include San Francisco Mus. Modern Art, 1980, 81, 84, 86, 96, Cinema Ctr., Moscow, 1991, St. Petersburg, Russia, 1997, Photographic Icons: Film Form and Montage, A homage to Sergei Eisenstein adn Gustav Klucis, Latvia, 1998, Wmpires: Russia Past and Present, 1998; represented in permanent collections San Francisco Mus.

Modern Art, Sheldon Art Gallery, Mint Mus., Art Mus. U. N.Mex., Ctr. for Creative Photography, Tucson; editor: The Essential Landscape, The New Mexico Photographic Survey, 1985; guest editor spl. issue Contemporary Photography, 1987, El Palacio, 1987, Poetics of Space: A Critical Photographic Anthology, 1995, Betty Hahm: Photography or Maybe Not, 1995, numerous mus. catalogs and pubs. nationally and internationally. Ford Found. fellow, 1977, Nat. Endowment Arts fellow, 1980; recipient Vreeland award U. Nebr., 1972, Outstanding Alumni Achievement award U. Nebr., 1994; Sr. Fulbright Scholars award USSR, 1991, Russian Fedn., 1995.

YAU, STEPHEN SIK-SANG, computer science and engineering educator, computer scientist, researcher; b. Wusei, Kiangsu, China, Aug. 6, 1935; came to U.S., 1958, naturalized, 1968; s. Pen-Chi and Wen-Chum (Shum) Y.; m. Vickie Liu, June 14, 1964; children: Andrew, Philip. BS in Elec. Engring, Nat. Taiwan U., China, 1958; MS in Elec. Engring, U. Ill., Urbana, 1959, PhD, 1961. Asst. prof. elec. engring. Northwestern U., Evanston, Ill., 1961-64, assoc. prof., 1964-68, prof., 1968-88, prof. computer scis., 1970-88, Walter P. Murphy prof. Elec. Engring. and Computer Sci., 1986-88, also chmn. dept. computer scis., 1972-77, chmn. dept. elec. engring. and computer sci., 1977-88; prof. computer and info. sci., chmn. dept. U. Fla., Gainesville, 1988-94; prof. computer sci. and engr., chmn. Ariz. State U., 1994—. Conf. chmn. IEEE Computer Conf., Chgo., 1967; gen. chmn. Nat. Computer Conf., Chgo., 1974, First Internat. Computer Software and Applications Conf., Chgo., 1977; Trustee Na. Electronics Conf., Inc., 1965-68; chmn. organizing com. 11th World Computer Congress, Internat. Fedn. Info. Processing, San Francisco, 1989; gen. co-chmn. Internat. Symposium on Autonomous Decentralized Systems, Japan, 1993, gen. chmn., Phoenix, 1995; conf. co-chair 24 Annual Internat. Computer Software and Applications Conf., Taipei, 2000. Editor-in-chief Computer mag., 1981-84; assoc. editor Jour. Info. Scis., 1983—; editor IEEE Trans. on Software Engring., 1988-91; contbr. numerous articles on software engring., distributed and parallel processing systems, computer sci., elec. engring. and related fields to profl. publs.; patentee in field. Recipient Louis E. Levy medal Franklin Inst., 1963, Golden Plate award Am. Acad. of Achievement, 1964, The Silver Core award Internat. Fedn. Info. Processing, 1989, Spl. award, 1989. Fellow IEEE (mem. governing bd. Computer Soc. 1967-76, pres. 1974-75, dir. Inst. 1976-77, chmn. awards com., 1996-97; Richard E. Merwin award Computer Soc. 1981, Centennial medal 1984, Extraordinary Achievement 1985, Outstanding Contbn. award Computer Sci. Soc. 1985), AAAS, Franklin Inst.; mem. Assn. for Computing Machinery, Am. Fedn. Info.-Processing Socs. (mem. exec. com. 1974-76, 79-82, dir. 1972-82, chmn. awards com. 1979-82, v.p. 1982-84, pres. 1984-86; chmn. Nat. Computer Conf. Bd. 1982-83), Am. Soc. Engring. Edn., Sigma Xi, Tau Beta Pi, Eta Kappa Nu, Pi Mu Epsilon. Office: Ariz State U PO Box 875406 Tempe AZ 85287-5406

YEAGER, CAROLINE HALE, radiologist, consultant; b. Little Rock, Sept. 5, 1946; d. George Glenn and Crenor Burnelle (Hale) Y.; m. William Berg Singer, July 8, 1978; children: Adina Atkinson Singer, Sarah Rose Singer. BA, Ind. U., Bloomington, 1968; MD, Ind. U., Indpls., 1971. Diplomate Am. Bd. Radiology; med. lic. State of Calif. Intern Good Samaritan Hosp., Los Angeles, 1971-72; resident in radiology King Drew Med. Ctr. UCLA, Los Angeles, 1972-76; dir. radiology Hubert Humphrey Health Ctr., Los Angeles, 1976-77; asst. prof. radiology UCLA, Los Angeles, 1977-84, King Drew Med. Ctr. UCLA, Los Angeles, 1977-85, dir. ultrasound, 1977-84; ptnr. pvt. practice Beverly Breast Ctr., Beverly Hills, Calif., 1984-87; cons. Clarity Communications, Pasadena, 1981—; pvt. practice radiology Claude Humphrey Health Ctr., 1991-93; dir. sonograms and mammograms Rancho Los Amigos Med. Ctr., 1993-94. Trustee Assn. Teaching Physicians, L.A., 1976-81; cons. King Drew Med. Ctr., 1984, Gibraltar Savs., 1987, Cal Fed. Inc., 1986, Medical Faculty At Home Professions, 1989—, Mobil Diagnostics, 1991-92, Xerox Corp., 1990-91, Frozen Leopard, Inc., 1990-91. Author: (with others) Infectious Disease, 1978, Anatomy and Physiology for Medical Transcriptionists, 1992; contbr. articles to profl. jours. Trustee U. Synagogue, Los Angeles, 1975-79; mem. Friends of Pasadena Playhouse, 1987-90. Grantee for innovative tng. Nat. Fund for Med. Edn., 1980-81. Mem. Am. Inst. Ultrasound in Medicine, L.A. Radiology Soc. (ultrasound sect.), Nat. Soc. Performance and Instrn. (chmn. conf. Database 1991, publs. L.A. chpt. 1990, info. systems L.A. chpt. 1991, dir. adminstrn. L.A. chpt. 1992, Outstanding Achievement in Performance Improvement award L.A. chpt. 1990, bd. dirs. 1990-93, Pres. award for Outstanding Chpt. 1992, v.p. programs 1993), Stanford Profl. Women L.A. Jewish. Avocations: geneology, writing, humor. Home and Office: 3520 Yorkshire Rd Pasadena CA 91107-5440

YEAGER, KURT ERIC, research institute official; b. Cleve., Sept. 11, 1939; s. Joseph Ellsworth and Karolyn Kristine (Pedersen) Y.; m. Rosalie Ann McMillan, Feb. 5, 1960; children: Geoffrey, Phillip; m. Regina Ursula Querfurt, May 12, 1970; 1 dau., Victoria. BA in Chemistry, Kenyon Coll., 1961; postgrad., Ohio State U., 1961-62; MS in Physics, U. Calif., Davis, 1964. Tchg. asst. Ohio State U., 1961-62; officer, program mgr. Air Force Tech. Applications Ctr., Alexandria, Va., 1962-68; assoc. dept. dir. Mitre Corp., McLean, 1968-72; dir. energy rsch. and devel. planning EPA, Washington, 1972-74; dir. fossil power plants dept. Electric Power Rsch. Inst., Palo Alto, Calif., 1974-79, dir. coal combustion systems, 1979-83, v.p. coal combustion systems, 1983-88, v.p. generation and storage, 1988-96, pres., CEO, 1996—. Mem. commerce tech. adv. bd., Oak Ridge fossil energy adv. bd. Nat. Acad. Engring.; mem. exec. bd. Nat. Coal Council. Contbr. articles to profl. jours. Pres. No. Va. Youth Football Assn., 1973-74. Capt. USAF, 1962-68. Decorated Air Force Commendation medals (2); recipient Outstanding Svc. award EPA, 1974. Mem. ASME (Rsch. Policy Bd.), AAAS, Am. Chem. Soc., Palo Alto C. of C. Republican. Episcopalian. E-mail: KYeager@EPRI.com

YEARLEY, DOUGLAS CAIN, mining and manufacturing company executive; b. Oak Park, Ill., Jan. 7, 1936; s. Bernard Cain and Mary Kenny (Howard) Y.; m. Elizabeth Anne Dunbar, Feb. 8, 1958; children: Sandra, Douglas Jr., Peter, Andrew. BMetE, Cornell U., 1958; postgrad., Harvard U., 1968. Engr. welding Gen. Dynamics, Groton, Conn., 1958-60; devel. engrs. Phelps Dodge Copper Products, Elizabeth, N.J., 1960-68; mgr. ops. Phelps Dodge Internat. Co., N.Y.C., 1969-71; v.p. ops. Phelps Dodge Tube Co., L.A., 1971-73; exec. v.p. Phelps Dodge Cable and Wire Co., Yonkers, N.Y., 1973-75; pres. Phelps Dodge Brass Co., Lyndhurst, N.J., 1975-79, Phelps Dodge Sales Co., N.Y.C., 1979-84, v.p. mktg., 1981-82; sr. v.p. Phelps Dodge Corp., Phoenix, 1982-86, exec. v.p., 1987-89, chmn., CEO, 1989-2000, pres., 1991-97, chmn. emeritus, 2000—, also bd. dirs. Bd. dirs. USX Corp., Pitts., Lockheed Martin Corp., Bethesda, Md. Bd. dirs. Am. Grad. Sch. Internat. Mgmt., 1990-92, Phoenix Symphony, 1988-2000; chmn. Arts Coalition, 1989-90; trustee Phoenix Art Mus., 1994-96. Mem. Nat. Elec. Mfrs. Assn. (bd. dirs. 1983-92), Internat. Copper Assn. (bd. dirs. 1987-2000, chmn. 1990-97), Am. Mining Congress (vice chmn.), Nat. Mining Assn. (chmn. 1997-98), Copper Devel. Assn. (chmn. 1989-93, dir. 1989-92), Nat. Assn. Mfrs. (bd. dirs. 1988-94), Bus. Roundtable, Bus. Coun., Sky Club, Echo Lake Country Club, Blind Brook Country Club. Republican. Congregationalist. Avocations: tennis, golf, classical music. Office: Phelps Dodge Corp 2600 N Central Ave 15th Fl Phoenix AZ 85004-3089

YEATS, ROBERT SHEPPARD, geologist, educator; b. Miami, Fla., Mar. 30, 1931; s. Robert Sheppard and Carolyn Elizabeth (Rountree) Y.; m. Lillian Eugenia Bowie, Dec. 30, 1952 (dec. Apr. 1991); children: Robert Bowie, David Claude, Stephen Paul, Kenneth James, Sara Elizabeth; m. Angela M. Hayes, Jan. 7, 1993. B.A., U. Fla., 1952; M.S., U. Wash., 1956, PhD, 1958. Registered geologist, Oreg., Calif. Geologist, petroleum exploration and prodn. Shell Oil Co., Ventura and Los Angeles, Calif., 1958-67; Shell Devel. Co., Houston, 1967; assoc. prof. geology Ohio U., Athens, 1967-70, prof., 1970-77; prof. geology Oreg. State U., Corvallis, 1977-97, prof. oceanography, 1991-97, prof. emeritus, 1997—, chmn. dept., 1977-85; geologist U.S. Geol. Survey, 1968, 69, 75; Glomar Challenger scientist, 1971; co-chief scientist, 1973-74, 78; mem. Oreg. Bd. Geologist Examiners, 1981-83; chmn. Working Group 1 Internat. Lithosphere Program, 1987-90; mem. geophysics study com. NRC, 1987-94; chmn. task force group on paleoseismology Internat. Lithosphere Program, 1990-98; chmn. subcom. on Himalayan active faults Internat. Geol. Correlation Program, Project 206, 1984-92. Researcher on Cenozoic tectonics of So. Calif., Oreg., New Zealand and Himalaya; active faults of Calif. Transverse Ranges, deep-sea drilling in Ea. Pacific; vis. scientist N.Z. Geol. Survey, 1983-84, 99, Geol. Survey of Japan, 1992, Inst. de Phys. du Globe de Paris, 1993; sr. cons. Earth Conss. Internat., 1997—. Author: The Geology of Earthquakes, 1997, Living with Earthquakes in the Pacific Northwest, 1998, Living with Earthquakes in California-A Survivor's Guide, 2001. Mem. Ojai (Calif.) City Planning Commn., 1961-62, Ojai City Council, 1962-65. 1st lt. U.S. Army, 1952-54. Named Richard H. Jahns Disting. Lectr. in Engring. Geology, 1995; Ohio U. rsch. fellow, 1973-74; grantee NSF, U.S. Geol. Survey. Fellow AAAS, Geol. Soc. Am. (chmn. structural geology and tectonics divsn. 1984-85, Cordilleran sect. 1988-89, assoc. editor bull. 1987-89); mem. Am. Assn. Petroleum Geologists (Outstanding Educator award Pacific sect. 1991, Michel T. Halbouty human needs award 1998), Am. Geophys. Union, Seismol. Soc. Am., Oreg. Acad. Sci. Home: 1654 NW Crest Pl Corvallis OR 97330-1812 Office: Oreg State U Dept Geoscis Corvallis OR 97331-5506

YEE, ALFRED ALPHONSE, structural engineer, consultant; b. Honolulu, Aug. 5, 1925; s. Yun Sau and Kam Ngo (Lum) Y.; m. Janice Ching (div.); children: Lailan, Mark, Eric, Malcolm, Ian; m. Elizabeth Wong, June 24, 1975; children: Suling, Trevor, I'Ling. BSCE, Rose Hulman Inst. Tech., 1948, Dr. of Engring. (hon.), 1976; MEng in Structures, Yale U., 1949. Registered profl. engr., Hawaii, Calif., Guam, Tex., Minn., No. Marianas Islands. With civil engring. dept. Dept. Pub. Works, Terr. of Hawaii, Honolulu, 1949-51; structural engr. 14th Naval Dist., Pearl Harbor, Hawaii, 1951-54; pvt. practice structural engring. cons. Honolulu, 1954-55; structural engring. cons. Park & Yee Ltd., Honolulu, 1955-60; pres. Alfred A. Yee & Assocs. Inc., Honolulu, 1960-82; v.p., tech. adminstr. Alfred. A. Yee div. Leo A. Daly, Honolulu, 1982-89; pres. Applied Tech. Corp., Honolulu, 1984—. Patentee in concrete tech., land and sea structures; contbr. articles to profl. jours. Served with U.S. Army, 1946-47. Named Engr. of Yr., Hawaii Soc. Profl. Engrs., 1969, one of Men Who Made Marks in 1970, Honolulu, 1970. Mem. ASCE (hon.), NSPE, CASE, ACEC, NAE, Am. Concrete Inst. (hon.), Post-Tensioning Inst., Precast-Prestressed Concrete Inst. (PCI medal of honor award 1997), Prestressed Concrete Inst. (State of Art award 1991), Structural Engrs. Assn. Hawaii, Yale Sci. and Engring. Assn. (Martin P. Korn award 1965, Robert J. Lyman award 1984), Singapore Concrete Inst. Avocations: golfing, swimming. Office: 1441 Kapiolani Blvd Ste 810 Honolulu HI 96814-4457 E-mail: atc@lava.net

YEE, JIMMIE R. mayor; Mayor City of Sacramento, Calif. Office: City Hall 915 I St Rm 205 Sacramento CA 95814-2672 E-mail: jyee@cityofsacramento.org

YEE, KEITH PHILIP, accountant, finance company executive; b. Luton, Eng., Apr. 26, 1958; came to the U.S., 1985; m. Ginny Sung, Feb. 9, 1985; children: Ashley, Brittany. BA in Acctg. with honors, Exeter (Eng.) U., 1979. CPA, Calif. Audit sr. Ernst & Whinney, London, 1979-83, investigation supr. Hong Kong, 1983-85, audit mgr. Memphis, 1985-86; audit sr. mgr. Ernst & Young, San Francisco, 1986-91, internat. resident, 1991-93, audit sr. mgr., 1993-95, Price Waterhouse, San Jose, Calif., 1995-97, Adaptec, Milpitas, 1997-98, Synnex Info. Tech., Fremont, 1998-2000, Tripath Tech., Inc., Santa Clara, 2000—. Vice chmn. adv. coun. for svcs. to srs. Salvation Army, San Francisco, 1989. Grad. leadership San Francisco program San Francisco C. of C., 1990. Fellow Inst. Chartered Accts. in Eng. and Wales; mem. AICPA, Assn. Am. CPAs (mem. adv. bd. 1994-95), Calif. Soc. CPAs, Inst. for Internat. Edn. (student programs com. 1990-95), San Francisco C. of C. (internat. bus. devel. com. 1993-95), Asian Am. Mfrs. Assn., Churchill Club. Avocations: internat. travel, music, sports. Office: Tripath Tech Inc 3900 Freedom Cir Santa Clara CA 95054-1204 E-mail: keith@tripath.com

YEH, RAYMOND WEI-HWA, architect, educator; b. Shanghai, China, Feb. 25, 1942; came to U.S., 1958, naturalized, 1976; s. Herbert Hwan-Ching and Joyce Bo-Ding (Kwan) Y.; m. Hsiao-Yen Chen, Sept. 16, 1967; children— Bryant Po Yung, Clement Chung-Yung, Emily Su-Yung. B.A., U. Oreg., 1965, B.Arch., 1967; M.Arch., U. Minn., 1969. Cert. Nat. Coun. Archtl. Registration Bds.; registered architect, Tex., Okla., Calif., Hawaii. Draftsman, designer various archtl. firms, 1965-68; design architect Ellerbe Architects, St. Paul, 1968-70; v.p., dir. design Sorey, Hill, Binnicker, Oklahoma City, 1973-74; prin. architect Raymond W.H. Yeh & Assos., Norman, Okla., 1974-80; asst. prof. to prof. U. Okla., Norman, 1970-79; head dept. architecture, prof. Calif. Poly. State U., San Luis Obispo, 1979-83; dean Coll. Architecture U. Okla., Norman, 1983-92; prin. architect W.H. Raymond Yeh, Norman, 1983-93; dean sch. architecture U. Hawaii at Manoa, Honolulu, 1993—. Profl. adviser Neighborhood Conservation and Devel. Center, Oklahoma City, 1977 79 Works include: St. Thomas More U. Parish and Student Center, Norman, Summit Ridge Center Retirement Community, Harrah, Okla., (recipient Nat. Design award Guild Religious Architecture 1978). Nat. Endowment for Arts fellow, 1978-79 Fellow AIA (dir., pres. Okla. chpt. 1986, design awards, nat. com. chmn. 1989); mem. Calif. Coun. Archtl. Edn. (dir., pres. 1982-83), Okla. Found. for Architecture (founding chair bd. 1989-90), Asian Soc. Okla. (award of Excellence 1992), Asia Pacific Ctr. for Arch. (founding bd. dirs. 1996). Presbyterian. Office: U Hawaii Manoa Sch Architecture Honolulu HI 96822

YEH, WILLIAM WEN-GONG, civil engineering educator; b. Szechwan, China, Dec. 5, 1938; s. Kai-Ming and Der-Chao (Hu) Y.; m. Jennie Pao, Mar. 25, 1967; children: Michael, Bobby. B.S.C.E., Nat. Cheng-Kung U., Taiwan, 1961; M.S.C.E., N.Mex. State U., 1964; Ph.D. in Civil Engring., Stanford U., 1967. Acting asst. prof. Stanford U., 1967; asst. research engr. UCLA, 1967-69, asst. prof. civil engring., 1969-73, assoc. prof., 1973-77, prof., 1977—, chmn. dept., 1985-88. Cons. Office of Hydrology, UNESCO, Paris, 1974, Jet Propulsion Lab., Pasadena, Calif., 1975-78, U.S. Bur. Reclamation, Phoenix, 1977-81, Dept. Water and Power, São Paulo, Brazil, 1981—, Rockwell Internat., 1983-88, U.S. AID, 1987-91, Met. Water Dist. of So. Calif., 1989—. Contbr. numerous articles to scholarly jours. Recipient Disting. Faculty award UCLA Engring. Alumni Assn., 1975; recipient Engring. Found. Fellowship award United Engring. Trustees, 1981, Centennial Disting. Alum award N.Mex. State U., 1996, Warren A. Hall medal, U. Coun. Water Resources, 1999, numerous research grants including NSF, 1967—. Fellow Am. Geophys. Union (Robert E. Horton award 1989), ASCE (hon., editor Jour. Water Resources Planning and Mgmt. 1988-93, Julian Hinds award 1994); mem. Am. Water Resources Assn. Home: 822 Hanley Ave Los Angeles CA 90049-1914 Office: U Calif 5732 B BH 405 Hilgard Ave Los Angeles CA 90095-9000

YEN, SAMUEL S(HOW)-C(HIH), obstetrics and gynecology educator, reproductive endocrinologist; b. Beijing, Feb. 22, 1927; s. K.Y. and E.K. Yen; children: Carol Amanda, Dolores Amelia, Margaret Rae. BS, Cheeloo U., China, 1949; MD, U. Hong Kong, 1954, DSc, 1980. Diplomate Am. Bd. Ob-Gyn (bd. examiners 1973-78), Am. Bd. Reproductive Endocrinology (bd. examiners 1976-82). Intern Queen Mary Hosp., Hong Kong, 1954-55; resident Johns Hopkins U., Balt., 1956-60; assoc. prof. reproductive biology Case Western Res. U., Cleve., 1967-70; prof. ob-gyn U. Calif., San Diego, 1972-83, chmn. dept. reproductive medicine, 1972-83, prof. reproductive medicine, 1983—; dir. reproductive endocrinology U. Calif. Med. Ctr., San Diego, 1983-98, W.R. Persons chair, 1987. Assoc. dir. obstetrics Univ. Hosp., Cleve., 1968-70; DeGroof lectr., 1987; Van Campenhaut lectr. Can. Fertility and Andrology Soc., 1995. Editor: Reproductive Endocrinology Physiology, Pathophysiology and Clinical Management, 1978, 4th edit., 1999; mem. editorial bd. Endocrine Revs., 1984—. Recipient Axel Munthe Found. award, 1982, Simpson medal U. Edinburgh, Scotland, 1996; Oglebay fellow, 1968-69. Fellow Royal Coll. Ob-Gyn., Royal Coll. Obstetricians and Gynecologists (ad eundem, London); mem. NAS Inst. Medicine, Assn. Am. Physicians, Soc. for Gynecol. Investigation (pres. 1981, Disting. Scientist award 1992), Endocrine Soc. (Rorer Clin. Investigator award 1992). Office: U Calif San Diego Reproductive Medicine # 0633 La Jolla CA 92093

YEN, TEH FU, civil and environmental engineering educator; b. Kun-Ming, China, Jan. 9, 1927; came to U.S., 1949; s. Kwang Pu and Ren (Liu) Y.; m. Shiao-Ping Siao, May 30, 1959 BS, Cen. China U., 1947; MS, W.Va. U., 1953; PhD, Va. Poly. Inst. and State U., 1956; hon. doctoral degree, Pepperdine U., 1982, Internat. U. Dubna, Russia, 1996, All Russian Petroleum Exploration Inst., St. Petersburg, Russia, 1999. Sr. research chemist Good Yr. Tire & Rubber Co., Akron, 1955-59; fellow Mellon Inst., Pitts., 1959-65; sr. fellow Carnegie-Mellon U., Pitts., 1965-68; assoc. prof. Calif. State U., Los Angeles, 1968-69, U. So. Calif., 1969-80, prof. civil engring. and environ. engring., 1980—. Hon. prof. Shanghai U. Sci. and Tech., 1986, U. Petroleum, Beijing, 1987, Daqing Petroleum Inst., 1992; cons. Universal Oil Products, 1968-76, Chevron Oil Field Rsch. Co., 1968-75, Finnigan Corp., 1976-77, GE, 1977-80, United Techs., 1978-79, TRW Inc., 1982-83, Exxon, 1981-82, DuPont, 1985-88, Min. Petroleum, Beijing, 1982—, Biogas Rsch. Inst.-UN, Chengdu, 1991. Author numerous tech. books; contbr. articles to profl. jours. Recipient Disting. Svc. award Tau Beta Pi, 1974, Imperial Crown Gold medal, Iran, 1976, Achievement award Chinese Engring. and Sci. Assocs. So. Calif., 1977, award Phi Kappa Phi, 1982, Outstanding Contbn. honor Pi Epsilon Tau, 1984, Svc. award Republic of Honduras, 1989, award in Petroleum Chem. Am. Chem. Soc., 1994, Kapitsa Gold medal Russian Fedn., 1995. Fellow Royal Chem. Soc., Inst. Petroleum, Am. Inst. Chemists; mem. Am. Chem. Soc. (bd. dirs. 1993, councillor, founder and chmn. geochemistry divsn. 1979-81, Chinese Acad. Scis. (standing com.), Acad. Scis. Russian Fedn. (academician, fgn. mem.). Home: 2378 Morslay Rd Altadena CA 91001-2716 Office: U So Calif 3620 S Vermont Ave Rm 224A Los Angeles CA 90089-0082 E-mail: ttyen@mizdr.usc.edu

YEO, RON, architect; b. Los Angeles, June 17, 1933; s. Clayton Erik and Rose G. (Westman) Y.; m. Birgitta S. Bergkvist, Sept. 29, 1962; children: Erik Elov, Katarina Kristina. B.Arch., U. So. Calif., 1959. Draftsman Montierth & Strickland (Architects), Long Beach, Calif., 1958-61; designer Gosta Edberg S.A.R. Arkitekt, Stockholm, 1962; partner Strickland & Yeo, Architects, Garden Grove, Calif., 1962-63; pres. Ron Yeo, Architect, Inc., Corona del Mar, 1963—. Cons., lectr. in field. Archtl. works include Garden Grove Civic and Community Center, 1966, Hall Sculpture Studio, 1966, Garden Grove Cultural Center, 1978, Gem Theater, 1979, Festival Amphitheatre, 1983, Los Coyotes Paleontol. Interpretive Ctr., 1986, Calif. State U. Fullerton Alumni House, 1997, O'Neill Regioanl Pk. Nature Ctr., 1998, Upper Newport Bay Interpretive Ctr., 2000, Stough Canyon Nature Ctr., 2000. Mem. Orange County Planning Commn., 1972-73, 1975-76; chmn. Housing and Community Devel. Task Force, 1978, Orange County Fire Protection Planning Task Force, City of Newport Beach City Arts Commn., 1970-72; pres. Orange County Arts Alliance, 1980-81. Fellow AIA; mem. Constrn. Specifications Inst. Democrat. Office: Ron Yeo FAIA Architect Inc 500 Jasmine Ave Corona Del Mar CA 92625-2308

YEOMANS, DONALD KEITH, astronomer; b. Rochester, N.Y., May 3, 1942; s. George E. and Jessie (Sutherland) Y.; m. Laurie Robyn Ernst, June 20, 1970; children: Sarah, Keith. BA, Middlebury (Vt.) Coll., 1964; MS, U. Md., 1967, PhD, 1970. Supr. Computer Scis. Corp., Silver Spring, Md., 1973-76; sr. rsch. astronomer Jet Propulsion Lab., Pasadena, Calif., 1976-92, supr., 1993—. Discipline specialist Internat. Halley Watch, 1982-89; sci. investigator NASA Comet Mission, 1987-91, Near-Earth Asteroid Rendezvous Mission, 1994-2001, Multi-Comet Flyby Mission, 1997—, Comet Impact Mission, 1999—; project scientist for asteroid sample return mission, 1998—. Author: Comet Halley: Once in a Lifetime, 1985, The Distant Planets, 1989, Comets: A Chronological History of Observation, Science, Myth, and Folklore, 1991. Recipient Space Achievement award AIAA, 1985, Exceptional Svc. medal NASA, 1986, Achievement award Middlebury Coll. Alumni, 1987; named NASA/JPL Sr. Rsch. Scientist, 1993. Mem. Internat. Astron. Union, Am. Astron. Soc. Democrat. Presbyterian. Avocations: tennis, history of astronomy. Office: Jet Propulsion Lab #301-150 4800 Oak Grove Dr Pasadena CA 91109-8001 E-mail: donald.k.yeomans@jpl.nasa.gov

YESTADT, JAMES FRANCIS, music director, conductor; b. Harrisburg, Pa., Nov. 24, 1921; s. Frederic John and Emelie Josephine (Speer) Y.; m. Victoria Ann Turco; children: Gregory James, Frederic John II, James Francis Jr. MusB, Lebanon Valley Conservatory Music, Pa., 1947; MA in Music, Columbia U., 1952; postgrad., New Sch. Music, Pa.; cert. in performance, Lucerne (Switzerland) Conservatory, 1962. Assoc. music prof. Xavier U., New Orleans, 1947-58; music dir., condr. New Orleans Summer Pops, 1954-58; resident condr. New Orleans Philharm. Symphony Orch., 1960-63; condr., dir. Transylvania Symphony Orch., Brevard, N.C., 1963-66; music dir., condr. Mobile (Ala.) Symphony Orch., 1965-71; dir. orchestral studies U. So. Miss., Hattiesburg, 1971-76; music dir., condr. Baton Rouge Symphony Orch., 1976-82; dir. orchestral studies La. State U., Baton Rouge, 1976-88; music dir., condr. Sun Cities Symphony of the West Valley, Sun City, Ariz., 1988—. Dir., condr. Mobile Opera Co., 1966-82; guest condr. Jackson (Miss.) Symphony Orch., 1986, Zurich Radio Orch., Orquesta Sinfonica de castillia y Leon, Spain, New Orleans Opera, numerous festivals, U.S., Europe. Numerous TV appearances and radio shows Served with U.S. Army, 1942-46, ETO. Mem. Music Educators Nat. Conf. (Performance award 1984), Coll. Music Soc., Am. Symphony Orch. League. Office: Sun Cities Symphony Orch Assn 10451 W Palmeras Dr Ste 210 Sun City AZ 85373-2081

YGLESIAS, KENNETH DALE, college president; b. Tampa, Fla. s. Jose and Julia Yglesias; m. Donna Carmen Belli, Nov., 1977. BA, U. South Fla., 1969; MA, Western Carolina U., 1973; EdD, U. So. Calif., 1977. Cert. tchr., Calif., Fla. Tchr., coach pub. schs., Tampa, 1969-73; tchr., dept. chmn. Am. Sch. Madrid, 1973-76; fgn. svc. officer USIA, Washington and Tel Aviv, 1977-79; assoc. prof. Pepperdine U., L.A., 1979-83; prof., dir. El Camino Coll., Torrance, Calif., 1981-83; adminstrv. dean Coastline Coll., Fountain Valley, 1983-88; v.p. Coast C.C. Dist., Costa Mesa, 1988-95; pres. Golden West Coll., Huntington Beach, 1995—. Contbr. articles to profl. jours. Bd. dirs. C.C.'s for Internat. Devel., 1988-94, Orange County Marine Inst., Costa Mesa, 1990-93, United Way Orange County, Santa Ana, Calif., 1991-94. Mem. Am. Assn. for Higher Edn. (Hispanic caucus), Assn. Calif. C.C. Adminstrs., Phi Delta Kappa. Democrat. Roman Catholic. Avocations: basketball fan, walking. Office: Golden West Coll PO Box 2748 Huntington Beach CA 92647-0748

YGUADO, ALEX ROCCO, economics educator; b. Lackawanna, N.Y., Jan. 17, 1939; s. Manuel and Rose (Barrillio) Y.; m. Patricia Ann Rieker; children: Gary Alexander, Melissa Rose, Charissa Ann. BA, San Fernando State Coll., Northridge, 1968; MA, Calif. State U., Northridge, 1970; MS, U. So. Calif., 1972. Contractor, L.A., 1962-69; instr. Calif. Poly. State U., San Luis Obispo, 1969-70, U. So. Calif., L.A., 1970-74; prof. econs. L.A.

Mission Coll., San Fernando, Calif., 1975—, acad. senate pres., 1992-93, cluster chair profl. studies, 1993-2001, dean acad. affairs, 2001—. Cons. Community Service Orgn., Los Angeles, 1969-71. Author: Principles of Economics, 1978; contbr. chpts. in books. Served with U.S. Army, 1957-60. Recipient: Blue Ribbon landscape design City of Albuquerque, 1962, Cert. Appreciation Los Angeles Mission Coll., 1978; Fulbright scholar, 1986-87. Mem. Calif. Small Bus. Assn. Democrat. Roman Catholic. Clubs: Newman (Los Angeles), Sierra Retreat (Malibu, sponsor). Avocations: gardening, skiing, photography. Home: 25323 Oak Ridge Dr Santa Clarita CA 91350-3300 Office: LA Mission Coll 13356 Eldridge Ave Sylmar CA 91342-3200 E-mail: yguadoar@laccd.cc.ca.us

YIH, MAE DUNN, state legislator; b. Shanghai, China, May 24, 1928; d. Chung Woo and Fung Wen (Feng) Dunn; m. Stephen W.H. Yih, 1953; children: Donald, Daniel. BA, Barnard Coll., 1951; postgrad., Columbia U., 1951-52. Asst. to bursar Barnard Coll., N.Y.C., 1952-54; mem. Oreg. Ho. Reps. from 36th dist., 1977-83, Oreg. Senate from 19th dist., 1983—. Mem. Clover Ridge Elem. Sch. Bd., Albany, Oreg., 1969-78, Albany Union H.S. Bd., 1975-79; mem. Joint Legis. Ways and Means Com., Senate Transp. Com., 1999, Senate pres. pro-temore, 1993. Episcopalian Home: 34465 Yih Ln NE Albany OR 97321-9557 Office: Oreg Senate S 307 State Capitol Salem OR 97310-0001

YOCAM, DELBERT WAYNE, retired software products company executive; b. Long Beach, Calif., Dec. 24, 1943; s. Royal Delbert and Mary Rose (Gross) Y.; m. Janet McVeigh, June 13, 1965; children— Eric Wayne, Christian Jeremy, Elizabeth Janelle. BA in Bus. Adminstrn., Calif. State U.-Fullerton, 1966; MBA, Calif. State U., Long Beach, 1971. Mktg.-supply changeover coordinator Automotive Assembly div. Ford Motor Co., Dearborn, Mich., 1966-72; prodn. control mgr. Control Data Corp., Hawthorne, Calif., 1972-74; prodn. and material control mgr. Bourns Inc., Riverside, 1974-76; corp. material mgr. Computer Automation Inc., Irvine, 1976-78; prodn. planning mgr. central staff Cannon Electric div. ITT, World hdqrs., Santa Ana, 1978-79; exec. v.p., COO Apple Computer, Inc., Cupertino, 1979-91; pres., COO, dir. Textronix Inc., Wilsonville, Oreg., 1992-95; chmn., CEO Borland Internat., Inc./Inprise Corp., Scotts Valley, Calif., 1996-2000, ret., 2000. Mem. faculty Cypress Coll., Calif., 1972-79; bd. dirs. Adobe Sys Inc., San Jose, Calif., Xircom, Inc., Thousand Oaks, Calif., Softricity, Inc., Boston ; vice chmn. Tech. Ctr. Innovation, San Jose, Calif., 1989-90. Mem. Am. Electronics Assn. (nat. bd. dirs. 1988-89), Control Data Corp. Mgmt. Assn. (co-founder 1974), L.A. County Heart Assn. (active 1966). E-mail: yocam@aol.com

YOHALEM, HARRY MORTON, lawyer; b. Phila., Jan. 21, 1943; s. Morton Eugene and Florence (Mishnun) Y.; m. Martha Caroline Remy, June 9, 1967; children: Seth, Mark. BA with honors, U. Wis., 1965; JD cum laude, M in Internat. Affairs., Columbia U., 1969. Bar: N.Y. 1969, D.C. 1981, Calif. 1992, U.S. Supreme Ct. 1985. Assoc. Shearman & Sterling, N.Y.C., 1969-71; asst. counsel to gov. State of N.Y., Albany, 1971-73, counsel office planning svcs., 1973-75; asst. gen. counsel FEA, Washington, 1975-77; mem. staff White House Energy Policy and Planning Office, Washington, 1977; dep. gen. counsel for legal svcs. Dept. Energy, Washington, 1978-80, dep. under sec., 1980-81; ptnr. Rogers & Wells, Washington, 1981-91; gen. counsel Calif. Inst. Tech., Pasadena, 1991—. Editor comments Columbia Jour. Transnat. Law, 1967-68, rsch. editor, 1968-69. Prin. Coun. for Excellence in Govt., Washington, 1990—; pres. Opera Bel Canto, Washington, 1984-87; mem. Lawyers Com. for Arts, Washington, 1981-88; bd. visitors dept. English U. Wis., 1999—. Harlan Fiske Stone scholar Columbia U., 1967, 69. Mem. ABA, Calif. Bar Assn., D.C. Bar Assn. Athenaeum, Phi Kappa Phi, Columbia Club N.Y. Home: 702 E California Blvd Pasadena CA 91106 Office: Calif Inst Tech JPL 180-305 4800 Oak Grove Dr Pasadena CA 91109-8001 E-mail: harry.yohalem@caltech.edu

YOKOUCHI, KATHY, nursing administrator; Exec. officer Hawaii Bd. Nursing, Honolulu. Office: Hawaii Bd Nursing PO Box 3469 Honolulu HI 96801-3469

YORK, GARY ALAN, lawyer; b. Glendale, Calif., Aug. 29, 1943; m. Lois York, 1987; 1 child, Jonathan Alan. BA, Pomona Coll., 1965; LLB, Stanford U., 1968. Bar: Calif. 1969. Ptnr. Dewey Ballantine, L.A., 1985-95, Buchalter, Nemer, Fields & Younger, L.A., 1995-98, Le Boeuf, Lamb, Greene & MacRae, L.A., 1998—. Instr. law sch. UCLA, 1968-69. Bd. editors Stanford Law review, 1966-68. Mem. ABA (chmn. real estate fin. com., real property probate and trust sect. 1987-89, chmn. usury com. 1992-93), L.A. County Bar Assn. (chmn. real estate fin. sect. 1993-96, exec. com. 1995—), State Bar of Calif., Am. Coll. Real Estate Lawyers, Am. Coll. Mortgage Attys. Office: Le Boeuf Lamb Greene & MacRae 725 S Figueroa St Ste 3100 Los Angeles CA 90017-5436 E-mail: GYork@LLGm.com

YORK, HERBERT FRANK, physics educator, government official; b. Rochester, N.Y., Nov. 24, 1921; s. Herbert Frank and Nellie Elizabeth (Lang) Y.; m. Sybil Dunford, Sept. 28, 1947; children: David Winters, Rachel, Cynthia. AB, U. Rochester, 1942, MS, 1943; PhD, U. Calif., Berkeley, 1949; DSc (hon.), Case Inst. Tech., 1960; LL.D., U. San Diego, 1964, Claremont Grad. Sch., 1974. Physicist Radiation Lab., U. Calif., Berkeley, 1943-58, assoc. dir., 1954-58; asst. prof. physics dept. U. Calif., Berkeley, 1951-54, assoc. prof., 1954-59, prof., 1959-61; dir. Lawrence Radiation Lab., Livermore, 1952-58; chief scientist Advanced Rsch. Project Agy., U.S. Dept. Def., 1958; dir. advanced rsch. projects divsn. Inst. for Def. Analyses, 1958; dir. def. rsch. and engring. Office Sec. Def., 1958-61; chancellor U. Calif.-San Diego, 1961-64, 70-72, prof. physics, 1964—, chmn. dept. physics, 1968-69, dean grad. studies, 1969-70, dir. program on sci., tech. and pub. affairs, 1972-88; dir. Inst. Global Conflict and Cooperation, 1983-88, dir. emeritus, 1988—. Amb. Comprehensive Test Ban Negotiations, 1979-81; trustee Aerospace Corp., Inglewood, Calif., 1961-87; mem. Pres.'s Sci. Adv. Com., 1957-58, 64-68, vice chmn., 1965-67; trustee Inst. def. Analysis, 1963-96; gen. adv. com. ACDA, 1962-69; mem. Def. Sci. Bd. , 1977-81; spl. rep. of sec. def. at space arms control talks, 1978-79; mem. coun. nat. labs. Pres. U. Calif., 1991—; mem. task force future nat. labs. Sec. Emergy, 1994-95; cons. Stockholm Internat. Peach Rsch. Inst.; rschr. in application atomic energy to nat. def. problems of arms control and disarmament, elem. particles. Author: Race to Oblivion, 1970, Arms Control, 1973, The Advisors, 1976, Making Weapons, Talking Peace, 1987, Does Strategic Defense Breed Offense?, 1987, (with S. Lakoff) A Shield in the Sky, 1989, Arms and the Physicist, 1994; also numerous articles on arms or disarmament; bd. dirs. Bull. Atomic Scientists. Trustee Bishop's Sch., La Jolla, Calif., 1963-65. Recipient E.O. Lawrence award AEC, 1962, Vannevan Bush award, 2000, Clark Kerr award, 2000, Enrico Fermi award, 2000; Guggenheim fellow, 1972. Fellow AAAS, Am. Phys. Soc. (forum on physics and soc. award 1976, Leo Szilard award 1994), Am. Acad. Arts and Sci.; mem. Internat. Acad. Astronautics, Fedn. Am. Scientists (chmn. 1970-71, exec. com. 1969-76, 95-2000, pub. svc. award 1992), Pugwash Movement 1969—, Phi Beta Kappa, Sigma Xi. Home: 6110 Camino De La Costa La Jolla CA 92037-6520 Office: U Calif San Diego Mail Code 0518 La Jolla CA 92093 E-mail: hyork@ucsd.edu

YORK, JAMES ORISON, real estate executive; b. Brush, Colo., June 27, 1927; s. M. Orison and Marie L. (Kibble) Y.; m. Janice Marie Sjoberg, Aug. 1, 1959; children: Douglas James, Robert Orison. Student, U. Calif. at Berkeley, 1945-46; B.A. cum laude, U. Wash., 1949. Tchg. fellow U. [illegible] Blyth & Co. (real estate and venture capital), Seattle and N.Y.C., 1953-60, ptrn. Seattle, 1960-66, pres. San Francisco, 1966-71; pres., chief exec. officer R.H. Macy Properties, N.Y.C., also sr. v.p. planning and devel., dir. R.H. Macy & Co., Inc., 1971-88; chmn. James York Assocs. (real estate and venture capital), 1988—. Dir. emeritus UBP Properties, Inc.; chmn., N.Y.C. retail div. Am. Cancer Soc. Contbg. author: Shopping Towns-USA, 1960. Trustee ICSC Ednl. and Rsch. Found. With USNR, 1945-47. Recipient Disting. Alumnus award U. Wash., 1989. Fellow Phi Beta Kappa; mem. Am. Soc. Real Estate Counselors, Urban Land Inst., Internat. Real Estate Fedn., Internat. Council Shopping Centers, Lambda Alpha. Episcopalian. Clubs: Olympic (San Francisco); American Yacht (Rye, N.Y.); Corinthian Yacht (Seattle); Union League (N.Y.C.); Knights of Malta, Order St. John, Washington Athletic (Seattle), Royal Victoria (B.C.) Yacht. Home and Office: 4 Riverstone Laguna Niguel CA 92677-5309 also: Sunrise Country Club 6 Malaga Dr Rancho Mirage CA 92270-3820 E-mail: jysail@aol.com

YORK, THEODORE ROBERT, consulting company executive; b. Mitchel Field, N.Y., May 4, 1926; s. Theodore and Helen (Zierak) Y.; m. Clara Kiefer, Jan. 3, 1952; children: Theodore R. II, Sharon L., Scott K., Krista A. Miller. BS, U.S. Mil. Acad., 1950; MBA, George Washington U., 1964; MPA, Nat. U., 1984. Commd. 2d lt. USAF, 1950, advanced through grades to col., 1970, ret., 1974; pres. T. R. York Cons., Fairfax, Va., 1974-79, T. R. Cons., San Diego, 1979-85, ULTRAPLECS Intelligent Bldgs., Sandy, Utah, 1991—; dir. Software Productivity Consortium, Herndon, Va., 1985-90. Mem. Loudoun County Rep. Com., Leesburg, Va., 1990-91. Decorated DFC, Air medal (5), Meritorius Svc. medal, Joint Svcs. Commendation medal, Air Force Commendation medal (5). Mem. Internat. Facilities Mgmt. Assn., Intelligent Bldgs. Inst. (advisor), Instituto Mexicana Del Edificios Intelegente (hon.), Office Planners and Users Group, Shriners, Masons. Avocations: computers, electronics. Office: ULTRAPLECS Intelligent Bldg 12189 Bluff View Dr Sandy UT 84092-5922 E-mail: tedusma50@hotmail.com

YORN, RICK, talent agent; Ptnr. Artists Mgmt. Group, Beverly Hills, Calif. Office: Artists Management Group 9465 Wilshire Blvd Ste 212 Beverly Hills CA 90212-2610

YOUGA, TONY, winery executive; CFO E.&J. Gallo Winery, Modesto, Calif. Office: E&J Gallo Winery PO Box 1130 Modesto CA 95353-1130 E-mail: tony.youga@ejgallo.com

YOUMANS, JULIAN RAY, neurosurgeon, educator; b. Baxley, Ga., Jan. 2, 1928; s. John Edward and Jennie Lou (Milton) Y.; children— Reed Nesbit, John Edward, Julian Milton. B.S., Emory U., 1949, M.D., 1952; M.S., U. Mich., 1955, Ph.D., 1957. Diplomate: Am. Bd. Neurol. Surgery. Intern U. Mich. Hosp., Ann Arbor, 1952-53, resident in neurol. surgery, 1953-55, 56-58; fellow in neurology U. London, 1955-56; asst. prof. neurosurgery U. Miss., 1959-62, assoc. prof., 1962-63, Med. U. S.C., 1963-65, prof., 1965-67, chief div. neurosurgery, 1963-67; prof. U. Calif., Davis, 1967-91; prof. emeritus, 1991—; chmn. dept. neurosurgery U. Calif., 1967-82. Cons. USAF, U.S. VA, NRC. Editor: Neurological Surgery, 1973; contbr. articles to profl. jours. No. vice chmn. Republican State Central Com. of Calif., 1979-81. Served with U.S. Navy, 1944-46. Mem. ACS (bd. govs. 1972-78), Congress of Neurol. Surgeons (exec. com. 1967-70), Am. Acad. Neurology, Am. Assn. Neurol. Surgeons, Am. Assn. Surgery of Trauma, Pan-Pacific Surg. Assn., Western Neurosurg. Soc., Neurosurg. Soc. Am., Soc. Neurol. Surgeons, Soc. Univ. Neurosurgeons, N. Pacific Soc. Neurology and Psychiatry, Royal Soc. Medicine, Am. Trauma Soc., U.S. C. of C., Bohemian Club, Sutter Club, Capital Club of Sacramento, Rotary. Republican. Episcopalian.

YOUNG, BRYANT COLBY, football player; b. Chicago Heights, Ill., Jan. 27, 1972; Student, Notre Dame U. Defensive tackle San Francisco 49ers, 1994—. Named to Pro Bowl, 1996. Office: care San Francisco 49ers 4949 Centennial Blvd Santa Clara CA 95054-1229

YOUNG, BRYANT LLEWELLYN, lawyer, business executive; b. Rockford, Ill., Mar. 9, 1948; s. Llewellyn Anker and Florence Ruth Y. AB, Cornell U., 1970; JD, Stanford U., 1974. Bar: Calif. 1974, Nev. 1975, D.C. 1979. Law clk. U.S. Dist. Ct. (no. dist.) Calif., San Francisco, 1974-75; assoc. Dinkelspiel, Pelavin, Steefel & Levitt, San Francisco, 1975-77; White House fellow, spl. asst. to sec. HUD, Washington, 1977-78, spl. asst. to sec., 1978-79, acting dep. exec. asst. for ops. Office of Sec., 1979; from dep. gen. mgr. to acting gen. mgr. New Cmty. Devel. Corp., 1979-80; mgmt. cons. AVCO Corp., 1980; spl. asst. to chmn. bd., CEO U.S. Synthetic Fuels Corp., Washington, 1980-81, exec. dir., 1981; pres. Trident Mgmt. Corp., San Francisco, 1981-87; of counsel Pelavin, Norberg, Harlick & Beck, San Francisco, 1981-82, ptnr., 1982-87; mng. ptnr. bus. section Carroll, Burdick & McDonough, San Francisco, 1987-90; founding ptnr. Young, Vogl & Harlick, San Francisco, 1990-93, Young, Vogl, Harlick, Wilson & Simpson, LLP, San Francisco, 1993-99; pres. Young Enterprises, Inc., 1995—; mgr. SRY Industries LLC, 1997—, KML Hospitality Industries LLC, 1997—; ptnr. Young Vogl LLP, 1999—. Dir. The Whitman Inst. Pub. affairs com. San Francisco Aid Retarded Citizens, Inc., 1977; U.S. co-chmn. New Towns Working Group, U.S.-USSR Agreement on Cooperation in Field of Housing and Other Constrn., 1979-80; treas., bd. dirs. White House Fellows Found., 1980-84; prin. Coun. Excellence in Govt., Washington, 1986-94; adv. com. Nat. Multi-Housing Coun., 1987-92; mem. Ross Sch. Found., 1994-97, sec., 1995-97; bd. dirs. Marin AIDS Project, 1996-97, sec., 1997; trustee Ross Sch., 1997—. Mem. ABA (real property, trust and probate law sects. 1975-96), White House Fellows Assn. (chmn. ann. meeting 1979, del. China 1980), Marin County Sch. Bds. Assn., Am. Field Svc. Returnees Assn., Can.-Am. C. of C. No. Calif. (v.p., bd. dirs. 1992), Chile-Calif. Found. (exec. com., bd. dirs. 1993-96). Office: 425 California St Ste 2550 San Francisco CA 94104-2212 E-mail: bly@ebzlaw.net

YOUNG, C. CLIFTON, state supreme court justice; b. Nov. 7, 1922, Lovelock, Nev.; m. Jane Young. BA, U. Nev., 1943; LLB, Harvard U., 1949. Bar: Nev. 1949, U.S. Dist. Ct. Nev. 1950, U.S. Supreme Ct. 1955. Justice Nev. Supreme Ct., Carson City, 1985—, chief justice, 1989-90. Office: Nev Supreme Ct 201 S Carson St Carson City NV 89701-4702

YOUNG, DONALD ALLEN, writer, consultant; b. Columbus, Ohio, June 11, 1931; s. Clyde Allen and Helen Edith (Johnston) Y.; m. Rosemary Buchholz, Feb. 26, 1955 (div. Nov. 1976); children: Kent Allen, Kelly Ann; m. Marjorie Claire Shapiro, Aug. 20, 1977; stepchildren: Jo Alene, Andrea Lynn, Beth Ellen. Student, Ohio State U., 1949-51, Columbia Coll., 1952, North Cen. Coll., Naperville, Ill., 1956, Coll. DuPage, , 1978. Editor various newspapers, mags., Detroit, Chgo., Columbus, 1946-63, 1973-74, 1978-79; v.p. Frydenlund Assocs., Chgo., 1963; pub. relations mgr. info. systems divsn. Gen. Electric Co., Phoenix, 1963-70; publs. dir. Data Processing Mgmt. Assn., Park Ridge, Ill., 1970-72; pub. relations mgr. Addressograph-Multigraph Corp., Arlington Heights, 1975-76; acct. exec. John Ripley & Assocs., Glenview, 1977-78; editorial dir. Radiology/Nuclear Medicine mag., Des Plaines, 1979-81; pres. Young Byrum Inc., Hinsdale, 1982-83; writer, consultant Tucson, 1983—. Cons. in field; sports reporter, Copley newspapers, 1975-83; mem. adv. council Oakton C.C., 1970-75. Author: Principles of Automatic Data Processing, 1965, Data Processing, 1967, Rate Yourself as a Manager, 1985, Nobody Gets Rich Working for Somebody Else, 1987, 2d edit., 1993, Rate Your Executive Potential, 1988, If They Can...You Can, 1989, The Entrepreneurial Family, 1990, How to Export, 1990, Women in Balance, 1991, Sleep Disorders: America's Hidden Nightmare, 1992, Small Business Troubleshooter, 1994, Crime Wave: America Needs a New Get-Tough Policy, 1996, Popcorn Publications, 1996, Adventure Guide to Southern California, 1997, Romantic Weekends: America's Southwest, 1998, Adventure Guide to the Pacific Northwest, 1998, Momentum: How to Get It-How to Keep It, 1999, Don't Get Mad-Get Rich, 1999, Walking Places in Washington DC, 2000. Arbitrator Better Bus. Bur., Tucson, 1987-92; docent Ariz. Sonora Desert Mus., 1988-92, Tucson/Pima Arts Coun., 1993-94. With USAF, 1952-56. Recipient Jesse Neal award Assn. of Bus. Pub., 1959, 61, Silver Anvil award Pub. Rels. Soc. of Am., 1976. Mem. Publicity Club of Chgo. (pres. 1978-79). Soc. Southwestern Authors (pres. 1992), Glen Ellyn (Ill.) Jaycees (bd. dirs., SPOKE award 1959, Outstanding Jaycee 1960), Young Reps. Club (v.p. 1960). Avocations: photography, travel, hiking, fishing. Home: 4866 N Territory Loop Tucson AZ 85750-5948 E-mail: dyoung1030@aol.com

YOUNG, DONALD E. congressman; b. Meridian, Calif., June 9, 1933; m. Lula Fredson; children— Joni, Dawn. AA, Yuba Jr. Coll., 1952; BA ., Chico (Calif.) State Coll., 1958. Former educator, river boat capt.; mem. Fort Yukon City Council, 6 years, mayor, 4 years; mem. Alaska Ho. of Reps., 1966-70, Alaska Senate, 1970-73, U.S. Congress from Alaska, 1973—; now ranking mem. transp. & infrastructure com., chmn. resources com., steering com. With U.S. Army, 1955-57. Republican. Episcopalian. Office: US Ho Reps 2111 Rayburn House Ofc Bldg Washington DC 20515*

YOUNG, DOUGLAS REA, lawyer; b. L.A., July 21, 1948; s. James Douglas and Dorothy Belle (Rea) Y.; m. Terry Forrest, Jan. 19, 1974; 1 child, Megann Forrest. BA cum laude, Yale U., 1971; JD, U. Calif., Berkeley, 1976. Bar: Calif., 1976, U.S. Dist. Ct. (no. dist.) Calif. 1976, U.S. Ct. Appeals (6th and 9th cirs.) 1977, U.S. Dist. Ct. (ctrl. dist.) Calif. 1979, U.S. Dist. Ct. Hawaii, U.S. Dist. Ct. (so. dist.) Calif., U.S. Supreme Ct. 1982; cert. specialist in appellate law. Law clk. U.S. Dist. Ct. (no. dist.) Calif., San Francisco, 1976-77; assoc. Farella, Braun & Martel LLP, San Francisco, 1977-82, ptnr., 1983—. Spl. master U.S. Dist. Ct. (no. dist.) Calif., 1977-78, 88, 96, 2000; mem. Criminal Justice Act Def. Panel no. dist. Calif.; mem. faculty Calif. Continuing Edn. of Bar, Berkeley, 1982—, Nat. Inst. Trial Advocacy, Berkeley, 1984—, Practicing Law Inst., 1988—; adj. prof. Hastings Coll. Advocacy, 1985—; vis. lectr. law Boalt Hall/U. Calif., Berkeley, 1986; judge pro tem San Francisco Mcpl. Ct., 1984—, San Francisco Superior Ct., 1990—. Author: (with Purver and Davis) California Trial Handbook, ed edit., (with Hon. Richard Byrne, Purver and Davis), 3d edit., (with Purver, Davis and Kerper) The Trial Lawyers Book, (with Hon. Eugene Lynch, Taylor, Purver and Davis) California Negotiation and Settlement Handbook; contbr. articles to profl. jours. Bd. dirs. Berkeley Law Found., 1977-78, chmn., 1978-79; bd. dirs. San Francisco Legal Aid Soc., pres., 1993—; bd. dirs. Pub. Interest Clearinghouse, San Francisco, chmn., 1987—, treas., 1988—; chmn. Attys. Task Force for Children, Legal Svcs. for Children, 1987—; mem. State Bar Appellate Law Adv. Commn., 1994—. Recipient award of appreciation Berkeley Law Found., 1983. Fellow Am. Coll. Trial Lawyers; mem. ABA (Pro Bono Pub. award 1992), San Francisco Bar Assn. (founding chmn. litigation sect. 1988-89, award of appreciation 1989, bd. dirs. 1990-91, pres. 2001), Calif. Acad. Appellate Lawyers, McFetridge Am. Inn of Ct. (master), Lawyers Club San Francisco. Democrat. Office: Farella Braun & Martel 235 Montgomery St Ste 3000 San Francisco CA 94104-2902

YOUNG, ERNEST D. national historic site official; Park ranger, law enforcement officer, mus. curator Pu'ukahola Nat. Hist. Site, Kawaihae, Hawaii, also interpretive specialist, in charge Visitor Ctr. Office: PO Box 44340 Kamuela HI 96743

YOUNG, FRANK NOLAN, JR. commercial building contracting company executive; b. Tacoma, Wash., Feb. 26, 1941; s. Frank N. and Antoinette (Mahncke) Y.; m. Susan E. Bayley, Aug. 13, 1965; children— Sandra Susanne, Frank Nolan III. B.A. in Bus. and Fin., U. Wash., 1963. Vice pres. Strand Inc., Bellevue, Wash., 1966-73; chmn., treas., chief exec. officer, dir. Gall Landau Young Constrn. Co. Inc., Bellevue, 1973— ; v.p., sec., dir. Cascade Structures, Kirkland, Wash., 1972— . Mem. Assoc. Gen. Contractors (pres. Seattle 1985, trustee 1968— , nat. dir.). Republican. Episcopalian. Clubs: Lakes, TAS Ski Found. (pres. 1983-84), Overlake Golf and Country; Seattle Yacht (trustee, 1992-95). Lodges: Elks, Masons, Shriners, Royal Order Jesters (impresario 1983-89). Home: 2929 81st Pl SE Unit P Mercer Island WA 98040-3044 Office: Gall Landau Young PO Box 6728 Bellevue WA 98008-0728

YOUNG, GLADYS, business owner; m. H. Timothy Kuhn; 3 children. Pres. Young Pontiac Cadillac Dealership, Escondido, Calif. Dir. Downtown Escondido Redevel., Palomar Coll. Pres.'s Assn.; contbr. St. Clare's Home, The North County Interfaith Crisis Ctr., Palomar Pomerado Hosp. Health Found., EYE Counseling and Crisis Ctr., Calif. Ctr. Arts. Recipient Quality Dealer award Time Mag., 1996. Mem. New Car Dealers Assn. (San Diego county chpt. award), Escondido Auto Park Assn. (pres.), Escondido C. of C. (dir.). Office: Young Pontiac Cadillac Dealership 1515 Auto Park Way N Escondido CA 92029-2098

YOUNG, GORDON, elementary education educator; Tchr. Grandview H.S., Aurora, Colo. Recipient Tchr. Excellence award Internat. Tech. Edn. Assn., Colo., 1992. Office: Grandview H S 20500 E Rapaho Rd Aurora CO 80016

YOUNG, HENRY, executive director; Exec. dir. Dance Aspen, Inc., Colo. Office: Dance Aspen Inc PO Box 8745 Aspen CO 81612-8745

YOUNG, HOWARD THOMAS, foreign language educator; b. Cumberland, Md., Mar. 24, 1926; s. Samuel Phillip and Sarah Emmaline (Frederick) Y.; m. Carol Osborne, Oct. 5, 1949 (div. 1966); children: Laurie Margaret, Jennifer Anne; m. Edra Lee Airheart, May 23, 1981; 1 child, Timothy Howard B.S. summa cum laude, Columbia U., 1950, M.A., 1952, Ph.D., 1954. Lectr. Columbia U., N.Y.C., 1950-54; asst. prof. Romance langs. Pomona Coll., Claremont, Calif., 1954-60, assoc. prof., 1960-66, Smith prof. Romance langs., 1966-98, prof. emeritus, 1998—. Vis. prof. Middlebury Program in Spain, Madrid, 1986-87, U. Zaragoza, 1967-68, Columbia U., summer 2000; chief reader Spanish AP Ednl. Testing Service, Princeton, 1975-78, chmn. Spanish lang. devel. commn., 1976-79; mem. fgn. lang. adv. commn. Coll. Bd., N.Y.C., 1980-83; mem. West Coast selection commn. Mellon Fellowships for Humanities, Princeton, 1984-86, European selection com., 1987, 90; trans. cons. Smithsonian. Author: The Victorious Expression, 1964, Juan Ramón Jimènez, 1967, The Line in the Margin, 1980; editor: T.S. Eliot and Hispanic Modernity, 1995; contbr. London Times Higher Edn. Supplement; contbr. numerous articles and book revs. to profl. jours. Dir. NEH summer seminar for Sch. tchrs., 1993. Served with USNR, 1944-46, ETO Fellow Del Amo Found., 1960-61, NEH, 1975, 89-90; Fulbright fellow; 1967-68; Rockefeller Study Ctr. scholar, 1976 Mem. MLA, Assn. Tchrs. Spanish and Portuguese, Am. Comparative Lit. Assn., Acad. Am. Poets, Assn. Lit. Scholars and Critics. Home: 447 W Redlands Ave Claremont CA 91711-1638 Office: Pomona Coll Romance Lang Dept 550 Harvard Ave Claremont CA 91711-6380 E-mail: htyoung@pomona.edu

YOUNG, JACQUELINE EURN HAI, state legislator, consultant; b. Honolulu, May 20, 1934; d. Paul Bai and Martha (Cho) Y.; m. Harry Valentine Daniels, Dec. 25, 1954 (div. 1978); children: Paula, Harry, Nani, Laura; m. Daniel Anderson, Sept. 25, 1978 (div. 1984); m. Everett Kleinjans, Sept. 4, 1988 (div. 1998). BS in Speech Pathology, Audiology, U. Hawaii, 1969; MS in Edn., Spl. Edn., Old Dominion U., 1972; advanced cert., Loyola Coll., 1977; PhD in Communication, Women's Studies, Union Inst., 1989. Dir. dept. speech and hearing Md. Sch. for the Blind, Balt., 1975-77; dir. deaf-blind project Easter Seal Soc. Oahu, Hawaii,

1977-78; project dir. equal ednl. opportunity programs Hawaii State Dept. Edn., Honolulu, 1978-85, state ednl. specialist, 1978-90; state rep. dist. 20 Hawaii State Legislature, Honolulu, 1990-92, state rep. dist. 51, 1992-94; vice-speaker Hawaii Ho. of Reps., Honolulu. Apptd. to U.S. Dept. Def. Adv. Commn. on Women in the Svc.; cons. spl. edn. U.S. Dept. Edn., dept. edn. Guam, Am. Samoa, Ponape, Palau, Marshall Islands, 1977-85; cons. to orgns. on issues relating to workplace diversity; adj. prof. commn., anthopology, mgmt. Hawaii Pacific U.; dir. mktg. Am. Cancer Soc. Hawaii Pacific, 1985—, dir. mktg., 1999—. TV writer, host, producer, 1992—. 1st v.p. Nat. Women's Polit. Caucus, 1988-90; chair Hawaii Women's Polit. Caucus, 1987-89; bd. dirs. YWCA Oahu, Kalihi Palama Immigrant Svc. Ctr., Hawaii Dem. Movement, Family Peace Ctr.; appointee Honolulu County Com. on the Status of Women, 1986-87; mem. Adv. Coun. on Family Violence: campaign dir. Protect Our Constn., 1998; trustee St. Louis Sch., 1997-99. Recipient Outstanding Woman Leader award YWCA of Oahu, 1994, Pres.'s award Union Inst., 1993, Fellow of the Pacific award Hawaii-Pacific U., 1993, Headliner award Honolulu chpt. Women in Commn., 1993, Korean Am. Alliance Washington Spl. Recognition award, 1998, Hawaii Women Lawyers Disting. Svc. award, 1999, Disting. Equity Adv. award Hawaii chpt. Nat. Coalition for Sex Equity in Edn., 1998, NEA Mary Hatwood Futrell for advancing women's rights award, 1999, Friend of Social Work award Hawaii chpt. NASW, 1998, Allan Saunders award Hawaii chpt. ACLU, 1999; named one of Extraordinary Women Hawaii, Found. Hawaii Women's History, 2001. Home: 212 Luika Pl Kailua HI 96734-3237

YOUNG, JEFF, physicist, educator; Prof. U. B.C., Vancouver, Can. Recipient Gerhard Herzberg medal Can. Assn Physicists, 1994. Fellow Can. Inst. for Advanced Rsch. (dir. nanoelectronics program). Office: U BC Dept Physics and Astronomy Vancouver BC Canada V6T 1Z1 E-mail: young@physics.ubc.ca

YOUNG, JERRY WAYNE, college president; b. Newbern, Tenn., Apr. 14, 1938; s. William Wesson and Elvaura (Jones) Y.; m. Linda F. Yoder; 1 child, Jeffrey W. BS, U. Utah, 1961; MA, Ariz. State U., 1968; PhD, Kent State U., 1973. Commd. 2d lt. USMC, 1960, advance through grades to maj., 1968; instr. U. Utah, Salt Lake City, 1960-61; tchr., coach Yuma (Ariz.) High Sch., 1963-66; dir. student activities Cuyahoya Community Coll., Cleve., 1967-69; coord. student union Kent (Ohio) State U., 1969-70; dean students Allegany Community Coll., Cumberland, Md., 1971-77; dean Clark City Community Coll., Las Vegas, 1977-83; pres. Centralia (Wash.) Coll., 1983-86, Chaffey Coll., Rancho Cucamonga, Calif., 1986—. Contbr. articles to profl. jours. Bd. dirs. Baldy View United Way, Ontario, Calif., 1990—. Recipient Master Tchr. award Tempe Elem. Dist., 1967; Harvard U. Inst. for Edn. Mgmt. grantee, 1988. Mem. Am. Assn. Community and Jr. Colls., Assn. Calif. Coll. Adminstrs., Am. Assn. Univ. Adminstrs., Calif. Community Coll. Chief Exec. Officers, Rancho Cucamonga C. of C. (v.p. 1990—), Inland Empire Indsl. Rsch. Assn. (pres. 1990—), Western Region Accreditation Assn. (accreditation evaluator 1987—) Northwest Region Accreditation Assn. (accreditation evaluator 1980—). Avocations: jogging, camping, reading, writing, photography. Office: Chaffey Cmty Coll Office Pres 5885 Haven Ave Rancho Cucamonga CA 91737-3002

YOUNG, JOHN ALAN, electronics company executive; b. Nampa, Idaho, Apr. 24, 1932; s. Lloyd Arthur and Karen Eliza (Miller) Y.; m. Rosemary Murray, Aug. 1, 1954; children: Gregory, Peter, Diana. BSEE, Oreg. State U., 1953; MBA, Stanford U., 1958. Various mktg. and fin. positions Hewlett Packard Co. Inc., Palo Alto, Calif., 1958-63, gen. mgr. microwave divsn., 1963-68, v.p. electronic products group, 1968-74, exec. v.p., 1974-77, COO, 1977-78, pres., 1977-92, CEO, 1978-92; ret., 1992. Bd. dirs. Chevron Corp., Glaxo Smithkline Plc., Affymetrix, Inc., Ciphergen, Lucent Technologies, Perlegen, Fluidigm. Chmn. ann. fund Stanford U., 1966-73, nat. chmn. corp. gifts, 1973-77, mem. adv. coun. Grad. Sch. Bus., 1967-73, 75-80, Univ. trustee, 1977-87; bd. dirs. Mid-Peninsula Urban Coalition, 1971-80, co-chmn., 1983-85; chmn. Pres.'s Commn. on Indsl. Competitiveness, 1983-85, Nat. Jr. Achievement, 1983-84; pres. Found. for Malcolm Baldrige Nat. Quality Award; mem. Adv. Com. on Trade Policy and Negotiations, 1988-92. With USAF, 1954-56. Mem. Nat. Acad. Engring., Coun. on Competitiveness (founder, founding chair computer systems policy project 1986), Bus. Coun. (co-chair pres. com. of adcisors on sci. & tech. 1993—).

YOUNG, JOHN BYRON, retired lawyer; b. Bakersfield, Calif., Aug. 10, 1913; s. Lewis James and Gertrude Lorraine (Clark) Y.; m. Helen Beryl Stone, Dec. 26, 1937; children: Sally Jean, Patricia Helen, Lucia Robin. BA, UCLA, 1934; LLB, U. Calif., Berkeley, 1937. Pvt. practice law Hargreaves & Young, later Young Wooldridge, Bakersfield, 1937-40; dep. county counsel County of Kern, Bakersfield, 1940-42; dep. rationing atty. U.S. OPA, Bakersfield and Fresno, Calif., 1942; ptnr. firm Young Wooldridge and predecessors, Bakersfield, 1946-78, assoc. law firm, 1978-91. Bd. dirs., legal counsel Kern County Water Assn., Bakersfield, 1953-76. Mem., chmn. Kern County Com. Sch. Dist. Orgn., Bakersfield, 1950s and 60s; mem. Estate Planning Coun. of Bakersfield, 1960-76, pres., 1965-66. Capt. JAGC, U.S. Army, 1943-46. Mem. Kern County Bar Assn. (prs. 1948, Bench and Bar award 1978). Home: 13387 Barbados Way Del Mar CA 92014-3501 Office: Young Wooldridge 1800 30th St Fl 4 Bakersfield CA 93301-5298

YOUNG, LAI-SANG, mathematician, educator; Prof. math. UCLA. Recipient Ruth Lyttle Math. prize Am. Math. Soc., 1993. Office: U Calif Dept Math 405 Hilgard Ave Los Angeles CA 90095-9000

YOUNG, LAWRENCE, electrical engineering educator; b. Hull, Eng., July 5, 1925; arrived in Can., 1955; naturalized, 1972; s. Herbert and Dora Y.; m. Margaret Elisabeth Jane, Jan. 5, 1951. BA, Cambridge (Eng.) U., 1946, PhD, 1950, ScD, 1963. Asst. lectr. Imperial Coll., London, 1952-55; mem. research staff B.C. Research Council, 1955-63; assoc. prof. U. B.C., Vancouver, 1963-65, prof. dept. elec. engring., 1965-90, prof. emeritus, 1990—. Author: Anodic Oxide Films, 1961; contbr. articles to profl. jours. Recipient Callinan award Dielectrics div. Electrochemical Soc., 1983, Can. Electrochem. Gold medal, 1990. Fellow IEEE, Royal Soc. Can., Electrochem. Soc. Office: U BC Dept Elec Engring Vancouver BC Canada V6T 1W5 E-mail: youngl@interchange.ubc.ca

YOUNG, LIONEL WESLEY, radiologist; b. New Orleans, Mar. 14, 1932; s. Charles Henry and Ethel Elsie (Johnson) Y.; m. Florence Inez Brown, June 24, 1957; children: Tina Inez, Lionel Thomas, Owen Christopher. BS in Biology, St. Benedict's Coll., Atchison, Kans., 1953; MD, Howard U., 1957. Diplomate Am. Bd. Radiology. Intern Detroit Receiving Hosp., Wayne State Univ. Coll. of Medicine, 1957-58; resident Strong Meml. Hosp., U. Rochester (N.Y.) Med. Ctr., 1958-61; pediatric radiologist, assoc. prof. radiology and pediatrics U. Rochester Med. Ctr., 1965-75; prof. radiology and pediatrics U. Pitts., 1975-86; dir. radiology and pediatrics Children's Hosp. of Pitts., 1980-86; chmn. radiology Children's Hosp. Med. Ctr. of Akron (Ohio), 1986-91, Children's Hosp. and Northeastern Ohio U. Coll. Medicine, Rootstown, 1987-91; dir. Divsn. Pediat. Radiology Loma Linda (Calif.) U. Med. Ctr. and Children's Hosp., 1991—. Pres. Akron Pediatric Radiologists, 1986—. Lt. comdr. USN, 1961-63. Mem. Am. Coll. Radiology (mem. coun., steering com.), Soc. for Pediatric Radiology. Democrat. Roman Catholic. Avocation: music. Office: Divsn Pediatric Radiology Loma Linda U Childrens Hosp 11234 Anderson St Loma Linda CA 92354-2804

YOUNG, LOWELL SUNG-YI, medical administrator, educator; b. Honolulu, Dec. 5, 1938; AB, Princeton U., 1960; MD, Harvard U., 1964. Di;omate Am. Bd. Internal Medicine with subspecialty in infectious diseases. Intern, jr. asst. resident, sr. asst. resident med. divsn. Bellevue Hosp. and Meml. Hosp., N.Y.C., 1964-67; fellow in medicine Cornell U. Med. Coll., 1965-67; epidemic intelligence officer bacterial diseases br. Nat. Communicable Disease Ctr., Atlanta, 1967-69, chief spl. pathogens sect., 1968-69; spl. postdoctoral rsch. fellow Nat. Inst. Allergy and Infectious Diseases, 1969-70; rsch. fellow in medicine Meml. Hosp./Cornell U. Med. Coll., 1969-70; clin. asst. physicisn infectious disease svc. dept. medicine Meml. Hosp., 1970-72, assoc. dir. microbiology lab., 1971-72; instr. in medicine Cornell U. Med. Coll., 1970-72; asst. clinician Sloan-Kettering Inst. for Cancer Rsch., 1971-72; chief divsn. infectious disease Calif. Pacific Med. Ctr., San Francisco, 1985-99; dir. Kuzell Inst., San Francisco, 1985—. Adj. prof. pharmacy U. of Pacific, San Francisco, 1989—; mem. microbiology and invectious diseases adv. com. Nat. Inst. Allergy and Infectious Diseases, 1981-85, mem. allergy and immunology rsch. com., 1975-79; mem. staff Calif. Pacific Med. Ctr., Mt. Zion Hosp. and Med. Ctr., U. Calif., San Francisco; mem. sci. adv. bd. Am. Found. for AIDS Rsch. Mem. editl. bd. Infection, Infectious Diseases in Clin. Practice, Diagnostic Microbiology and Infectious Diseases, Antimicrobial Agts. and Chemotherapy, Infection and Immunity; contbr. numerous articles to profl. jours., chpts. to books. Recipient Alexander D. Langmuir prize Epidemic Intelligence Svc., 1970, Garrod medal Brit. Soc., 1992. Fellow ACP (mem. med. self-assessment com.), Infectious Diseases Soc. Am. (councillor 1983-85); mem. Am. Soc. for Clin. Investigation, Am. Fedn. for Clin. Rsch., Am. Soc. for Microbiology, Western Soc. for Clin. Rsch., Internat. Immunocompromised Host Soc., Brit. Soc. Antimicrobial Chemotherapy. Office: Kuzell Inst 2200 Webster St Ste 305 San Francisco CA 94115-1821 also: Calif Pacific Med Ctr 2100 Webster St Ste 326 San Francisco CA 94115-2378 E-mail: kiaid@cooper.cpmc.org

YOUNG, SCOTT THOMAS, business management educator; b. Oak Park, Ill., Dec. 28, 1949; s. Thomas Menzies and Grace (Butler) Y.; children: Reginald, Galen; m. Luciana Pagotto. BA, U. Ga., 1974; MBA, Ga. Coll., 1982; PhD, Ga. State U., 1987. Prof. U. Utah, Salt Lake City, 1987—, chmn. mgmt. dept., 1994-97, assoc. dean David Eccles Sch. Bus., 1997-99. Mgmt. cons. to numerous orgns.; lectr., speaker, cons. on ops., quality and project mgmt. Author: Managing Global Operations; contbr. numerous articles to profl. jours. With U.S. Army, 1971-73. Decorated Commendation medal; grantee Nat. Assn. Purchasing Mgmt., 1986. Mem. Decision Sci. Inst., Acad. Mgmt., Prodn. and Ops. Mgmt. Soc. Avocation: marathon running. Office: U Utah David Eccles Sch Bus Salt Lake City UT 84112 E-mail: mgtsty@business.utah.edu

YOUNG, STEVEN, professional football player; b. Salt Lake City, Oct. 11, 1961; JD, Brigham Young, 1993. With L.A. Express, USFL, 1984-85, Tampa Bay Buccaneers, 1985-87; quarterback San Francisco 49ers, 1987—; NFL MVP, 1992; NFL Player of the Year, 1994. Organized, manages the Forever Young Found. benefitting Bay Area & Utah youth-oriented charities. Davey O'Brien Award, 1983, All-America team quarterback, The Sporting News, 1983; Named NFL's Top-rated quarterback, 1991, named NFL MVP The Sporting News, 1992, NFL All-Pro team quarterback, The Sporting News, 1992, Bay Area Sports Hall of Fame Profl. Athlete of the Year, 1992, Superbowl MVP, 1994. Played in Pro Bowl 1992, 93; highest rated passer NFL, 1991-93. Office: San Francisco 49ers 4949 Centennial Blvd Santa Clara CA 95054-1229

YOUNG, WILLIAM D. chemical engineer; BS in Chem. Engring., Purdue U., D. in Engring. (hon.), 2000; MBA, Ind. U. Various positions in prodn. and process engring. Eli Lilly and Co.; various positions Genentech, Inc., 1980-99, COO; CEO, chmn. of bd. ViroLogic, Inc., San Francisco, 1999—. Mem. NAE. Office: ViroLogic Inc 270 E Grand Ave San Francisco CA 94080

YOUNGBAUER, STEVEN R. state legislator, laywer; b. Alma, Wis., Feb. 25, 1950; m. Echo Youngbauer; 1 child. BA, Winona State Coll., 1974; JD, U. Wyo., 1982. Bar: Wyo. Pvt. practice, 1982-86; gen. coun., atty., 1987-90; mgr. land, atty., 1990—; mem. Wyo. Senate, Dist. 23, Cheyenne, 1998—. Mem. Wyo. Environ. Quality Coun. (chairperson), Wyo. State Bar Assn., Wyo. Mining Assn., Wyo. Tax Payers Assn. Republican. Roman Catholic. Home: 4675 S Douglas Hwy Gillette WY 82718-6703 E-mail: youngbauer@vcn.com

YOUPA, DONALD GEORGE, broadcast executive; b. N.J. BA in Polit. Sci., Rutgers U., 1959. Exec. dir., v.p. Sears-Roebuck Found., Chgo.; v.p. devel. KCET, L.A., 1978-80, sr. v.p. mktg. and devel., 1980-87, exec. v.p., 1987-94, exec. v.p., COO, 1994—. Office: KCET 4401 Sunset Blvd Los Angeles CA 90027-6090 E-mail: dyoupa@kcet.org

YU, JEN, medical educator; b. Taipei, Taiwan, Jan. 23, 1943; came to U.S., 1969; s. Chin Chuan and Shiu Lan (Lin) Y.; m. Janet Chen, June 16, 1973; children: Benjamin, Christopher. MD, Nat. Taiwan U., 1968; PhD in Physiology, U. Pa., 1972. Diplomate Am. Bd. Phys. Medicine and Rehab. Intern Phila. Gen. Hosp., 1972-73; resident in phys. medicine and rehab. Hosps. of U. Pa., 1973-75; asst. prof. dept. phys. medicine and rehab. U. Pa. Sch. Medicine, Phila., 1975-76, U. Tex. Health Sci. Ctr., San Antonio, 1976-79, assoc. prof., 1979-81; prof. dept. phys. medicine and rehab. U. Calif. Irvine Coll. Medicine, 1981-82, prof., chmn. dept. phys. medicine and rehab., 1982—. Contbr. articles to profl. jours. Mem. Am. Acad. Phys. Medicine and Rehab., Am. Congress Rehab. Medicine, Assn. Acad. Physiatrists, Am. Assn. Anatomists, Soc. for Neurosci. Office: U Calif Irvine Med Ctr Dept Phys Medicine & Rehab 101 The City Dr Orange CA 92868-3201 E-mail: jyu@uci.edu

YUAN, ROBIN TSU-WANG, plastic surgeon; b. Boston, July 2, 1954; s. Robert Hsun-Piao and Grace I. (Chen) Y. AB, Harvard U., 1974, MD, 1978. Diplomate Am. Bd. Plastic Surgery. Resident in gen. surgery UCLA Med. Ctr., 1978-80, Cedars-Sinai Med. Ctr., L.A., 1980-81, 83-84; resident in plastic surgery U. Miami (Fla.)-Jackson Meml. Hosp., 1985-87; pvt. practice L.A., 1987—. Clin. instr. div. plastic surgery UCLA, 1987-98, asst. clin. prof. div. plastic surgery UCLA, 1998—; vice-chief div. plastic surgery Cedars-Sinai Med. Ctr., L.A., 1991—; pres., chief exec. officer, founder Family of Independent Reconstructive Surgery Teams (F.I.R.S.T.), 1990—; mem. adv. bd. Radiation Ctrs. Am., Inc. Author: Cheer Up...You're Only Half Dead!, Reflections at Mid-Life, 1996; contbr. numerous articles to med. jours. Mem. Am. Soc. Plastic and Reconstructive Surgery, Am. Cleft Palate Assn., Calif. Med. Assn. (del.), L.A. County Med. Assn. (bd. govs. dist. 1), Phi Lambda (co-mgr. 1991—). Avocations: tennis, skiing, golf, creative writing, violin. Office: 150 N Robertson Blvd Ste 315 Beverly Hills CA 90211-2145

YUE, AGNES KAU-WAH, otolaryngologist; b. Shanghai, Peoples Republic China, Dec. 1, 1947; came to U.S., 1967; d. Chen Kia and Nee Yuan (Ying0 ; m. Gerald Kumata, Sept. 25, 1982; children: Julie, Allison Benjamin. BA, Wellesley Coll., 1970; MD, Med. Coll. Pa., 1974; postgrad., Yale U., 1974-78. Intern Yale-New Haven Hosp., 1974-75, resident, 1975-78; fellow U. Tex. M.D. Anderson Cancer Ctr., Houston, 1978-79; asst. prof. U. Wash., Seattle, 1979-82; physician Pacific Med. Ctr., Seattle, 1979-90; pvt. practice Seattle, 1991—. Fellow Am. Acad. Otolaryngology, Am. Coll. Surgeons; mem. Northwest Acad. Otolaryngology. Avocations: sailing, opera, profl. voice, cooking. Office: 1801 NW Market St Ste 410 Seattle WA 98107-3909

YUE, ALFRED SHUI-CHOH, metallurgical engineer, educator; b. China, Nov. 12, 1920; s. Choy Noon-woo and Sze Man-hun (Tom) Y.; m. Virginia Chin-wen Tang, May 21, 1944; children: Mary, Raymond Yuan, John, Ling Tsao, David, Nancy Chang. B.S., Chao-tung U., 1942; M.S., Ill. Inst. Tech., 1950; Ph.D., Purdue U., 1956. Assoc. engr. Taiwan Aluminum Co., 1942-47; instr. Purdue U., 1952-56; research engr. Dow Chem. Co., Midland, Mich., 1956-62; sr. mem. Lockheed, Palo Alto Research Lab., 1962-69; now cons.; prof. engring. and applied sci. U. Calif., Los Angeles, 1969—. Hon. prof. Xian Jiao-tong U., China, 1980; cons. LTV Aerospace Co., Lockheed Missile & Space Co., Atlantic Richfield Co.; Sec.-gen. Chinese Culture Assn. in, U.S.A., 1967, also; bd. dirs. Chinese scholar to U.S.A. Fellow AIAA (assoc.); mem. AAAS, AIME, Am. Soc. Metals, Materials Rsch. Soc., Sigma Xi, Sigma Pi Sigma, Tau Beta Pi, Phi Tau Phi (pres. 1978-82) E-mail: yuealfred@aol.com

YUEN, HENRY C. consumer electronics manufacturing company executi; BS in Maths., U. Wisc.; D, Calif. Inst. Tech.; LLB, Loyola U. Rsch. scientist TRW Inc.; various faculty positions Calif. Inst. Tech., NYU; co-founder Gemstar Internat. Group Ltd., CEO, chmn. bd. dirs., 1999—. Contbr. articles to profl. jours. Recipient Nat. Entrepreneur of Yr. award Ernst & Young USA Today and NASDAQ, 1996, Disting. Alumni award Calif. Inst. Tech., 1999, Disting. Alumni award Loyola Law Sch., 1999. Office: Gemstar Internat Group Ltd 135 N Los Robles AveSte 800 Pasadena CA 91101

YUILLE, ALAN LODDON, physicist, researcher; BA in Math. with hons., Cambridge (Eng.) U., 1976, PhD in Applied Math., Physics, 1986. Rsch. assoc. Harvard U., Cambridge, Mass., 1986-88, asst. prof., 1988-92, assoc. prof., 1992-96; sr. rsch. scientist Smith-Kettlewell Eye Rsch. Inst., San Francisco, 1995—. Vis. scientist MIT, Cambridge, 1982-83, affiliate, 1986-88, Isaac Newton Inst. Math., Cambridge, 1993; lectr. Harvard U., Cambridge, 1986-87; Fesler-Lambert vis. prof. U. Minn., 1992; presenter in field. Author: (chpt.) Computer Vision: Theory and Industrial Applications, 1986, The Handbook of Brain Theory and Neural Networks, 1994; co-author: (chpt.) Image Understanding, 1985, 87, The Neuron as a Computational Unit, 1989, An Invitation to Cognitive Science, Vol. 2, 1990, Advances in Control Networks and Large-Scale Parallel-Distributed Processing Models, 1991, Computational Models of Visual Processing, 1991Active Vision, 1992, Bayesian Approaches to Perception, 1994, DIMACS: Partitioning Data Sest, 1994, Artificial Neural Networks with Applications in Speech and Vision, 1994 ; contbr. articles to Neural Computation, Neural Networks, Vision Rsch., Jour. Complexity, Jour. Optical Soc. Am., Jour. Math. Imaging Vision, Pattern Analysis Machine Intelligence, Jour. Theoretical Biology, Biological Cybernetics, Internat. Jour. Robotic Vision, Internat. Jour. Computer Image, Nature, Jour. Cognitive Neurosci., Neural Computation; editor Jour. Math. Imaging Vision. NATO fellow, 1981-82; Trinity Coll. scholar, 1974-78; recipient Rouse Ball prize, 1974-77, Raleigh Rsch. prize, 1979. Office: Smith Kettlewell Eye Rsch Inst 2232 Webster St San Francisco CA 94115-1821

YUKAWA, SUMIO, engineering consultant, researcher; b. Seattle; BS, MS, U. Mich., PhD in Metall. Engring., 1954. With GE; cons. Boulder. With U.S. Army, 194-47. Mem. ASME (Pressuve Vessel and Piping award 1998). Achievements include research on materials for steam and gas turbines and nuclear energy equipment. Office: 4925 Valkyrie Dr Boulder CO 80301-4360

YUKELSON, DANIEL M. marketing company executive; b. L.A., 1962; Degree, Calif. State U., Northridge, 1985. V.p. fin., CFO, sec. E4L, Inc., Encino, Calif.; sr. v.p., CFO Premiere Radio Networks, Inc., Sherman Oaks. Office: E4L Inc 15821 Ventura Blvd 5th Fl Encino CA 91436

YUND, MARY ALICE, biotechnology consultant; b. Xenia, Ohio, Feb. 12, 1943; d. John Edward and Ethel Louise Stallard; m. E. William Yund, June 11, 1966. BA, Knox Coll., 1965; PhD, Harvard U., 1970. Asst. rsch. geneticist U. Calif., Berkeley, 1975-88; pvt. practice cons. Berkeley, 1988-97; biotech. cons. Tech. Forecasters, Inc., Alameda, Calif., 1997—. Mem. devel. biology adv. panel NSF, Washington, 1983-87; vis. scientist NSF/ CSIRO U.S./ Australia Coop. Sci. Progam, North Ryde, Australia, 1980; co-chair women in Biosci. Conf., Stanford, Calif., 1993; organizer sci. seminar series and confs. in field. Contbr. articles, revs. to profl. jours., chpts. to books. Cons., counselor Bay Area Biosci. Ctr., Oakland, Calif., 1992—. Rsch. grantee NSF, NIH, 1975-86. Mem. AAAS, Genetics Soc. Am., Soc. for Developmental Biology, Am. Soc. Zoologists, Assn. for Women in Sci. (chpt. officer 1991—), Phi Beta Kappa, Sigma Xi. Achievements include first identification and characterization of ecdysteroid receptors. Office: 723 Woodhaven Rd Berkeley CA 94708-1540

YURIST, SVETLAN JOSEPH, mechanical engineer; b. Kharkov, USSR, Nov. 20, 1931; came to U.S., 1979, naturalized, 1985; s. Joseph A. and Rosalia S. (Zoilman) Y.; m. Imma Lea Erlikh, Oct. 11, 1960; 1 child, Eugene. MSME with honors, Poly. Inst. Odessa, USSR, 1954. Engr., designer Welding Equipment Plant, Novaya Utka, USSR, 1954-56; sr. tech. engr. Heavy Duty Automotive Crane Plant, Odessa, USSR, 1956-60, asst. chief metallugist, 1971-78; supr. rsch. lab. Inst. Spl. Methods in Foundry Industry, Odessa, 1960-66, project engr. sci. rsch., 1966-70; engr. designer Teledyne Cast Product, Pomona, Calif., 1979-81; sr. mech. engr. Walt Elliot Disney Enterprises, Glendale, 1981-83; foundry liaison engr. Pacific Pumps divsn. Dresser Industries, Inc., Huntington Park, 1984-86; casting engr. Superior Industries Internat., Inc., Van Nuys, 1986-89; mech. engr. TAMCO Steel, Ramcho Cucamonga, 1989-96. Contbr. reports, articles to collections All Union Confs. Spl. Methods in Foundry, USSR; USSR patentee permanent mold casting. Recipient award for design of automatic lines for casting electric motor parts USSR Ministry Machine Bldg. and Handtools Mfr., 1966, for equipment for permanent mold casting All Union Exhbn. of Nat. Econ. Achievements, 1966-70. Mem. Am. Foundrymen's Soc. Home: 1718 Downs St Oceanside CA 92054-6191 E-mail: siyurist@earthlink.net

ZABLE, WALTER JOSEPH, electronic products manufacturing company executive; b. Los Angeles, 1915. B.S., Coll. William and Mary, 1937; M.S. in Physics and Math., U. Fla., 1939. Electronics engr. Newport News Shipyard & Drydock Co., 1940-43; sr. devel. engr., Sperry Gyroscope Co., 1944-47; prior 1951 ITT Fed. Telecommunications Labs., Flight Research Co., Gen. Dynamics Corp., Convair div.; with Cubic Corp., San Diego, 1951— , chmn. bd., pres., chief exec. officer, also dir.; dir. First Nat. Bank. Mem. Nat. Assn. Mfrs. (dir.). Office: Cubic Corp 9333 Balboa Ave PO Box 85587 San Diego CA 92186-5587

ZADEH, LOTFI ASKER, engineering educator, educator; b. Feb. 4, 1921; came to U.S., 1944, naturalized, 1956; s. Rahim A. and Fania (Koriman) Asker; m. Fay Sand, Mar. 21, 1946; children: Stella, Norman. BSEE, U. Tehran, Iran, 1942; MSEE, MIT, 1946; PhD, Columbia U., 1949; DSc (hon.), Paul-Sabatier U., Toulouse, France, 1986, SUNY, , 1989. From instr. to assoc. prof. elec. engring. Columbia U., 1946-57; mem. Inst. Advanced Study, Princeton, N.J., 1956; prof. elec. engring. U. Calif., Berkeley, 1959-92, chmn. dept., 1963-68, prof. Grad. Sch., 1992—. Vis. prof. elec. engring. MIT, 1962, 68, vis. scientist IBM Rsch. Lab., San Jose, Calif., 1968, 73, 77; vis. scholar Artificial Intelligence Ctr., SRI Internat., Menlo Park, Calif., 1981; vis. mem. Ctr. for Study Lang. and Info., Stanford U., 1988. Author: (with C. A. Desoer) Linear System Theory, 1963, also articles; editor: (with F. Polak) System Theory, 1968; editor: Fuzzy Sets and Systems, Jour. Computer and Sys. Scis.; hon. editor Jour. Fuzzy Sys. and Artificial Intelligence; assoc. editor Jour. Math. Analysis Applications, Info. Scis., Networks; adv. editor: Data Knowledge and

Engring.; mem. editl. bd.: Applied Intelligence, Applied Math. Letters, Fuzzy Math., Computers and Structures, Jour. Optimization Theory and Application, Math. and Computer Modeling, Jour. Info. and Optimization Theory and Applications, Math. and Computer Modeling, Jour. Info. and Optimization Scis., Jour. Gen. Sys., Internat. Jour. Sys., Measurement and Decision, Future Generations Computer Sys., Internat. Jour. Expert Sys., Internat. jour. Pattern Recognition and Artificial Intelligence, Internat. Jour. Intelligent Sys., Japan Artificial Intelligence Newsletter, AI in Medicine, Internat. Jour. Approximate Reasoning, Math. and Statis. Methods, Internat. Jour. Neural, Parallel and Sci. Computations, Internat. Jour. Uncertainty, Fuzziness and Knowledge-Based Sys., Theory and Decision Libr., Neural, Parallel and Sci. Computations, Multiple-Valued Logic-an Internat. Jour.; mem. editl. adv. bd. Computers and Elec. Engring., Jour. Intelligent and Fuzzy Sys., Info. Sys., Cybernetics and Sys. Mem. U.S. commn. 6, Internat. Sci. Radio Union, 1960-63; mem. tech. adv. bd. U.S. Postal Svc. Recipient Congress award Internat. Congress on Applied Sys. Rsch. and Cybernetics, 1980, Outstanding Paper award Internat. Symposium on Multiple-Valued Logic, 1984, Honda prize Honda Found., 1989, Berkeley citation U. Calif., 1991, Rufus Oldenburger medal ASME, 1993, Grigore Moisil award for fundamental rsch. Romanian Soc. for Fuzzy Sys., 1993, Premier Best Paper award 2d Internat. Conf. on Fuzzy Theory and Tech. Duke U., 1993, Richard E. Bellman Control Heritage award Am. Coun. on Automatic Control, 1998, Info. Sci. award Assn. for Intelligent Machinery, 1998; Guggenheim fellow, 1967-68, NSF postdoctoral fellow, 1956-57, 62-63. Fellow IEEE (Edn. medal 1973, Centennial medal 1984, cert. appreciation 1988, Richard W. Hamming medal 1992, medal of honor 1995, J.P. Whol Career Achievement award 1997), AAAS, Am. Assn. for Artificial Intelligence, Assn. Computing Machinery, World Congress Cybernetics; mem. NAE, Am. Math. Soc., Soc. Engring. Sci. (Eringen medal, lectr. 1975), N. Am. Fuzzy Info. Processing Soc. (bd. dirs.), Internat. Fuzzy Sys. Assn., Biomed. Fuzzy Sys. Assn. Japan (hon. pres.), Internat. Assn. of Knowledge Engrs. (trustee). Home: 904 Mendocino Ave Berkeley CA 94707-1925 Office: U Calif Dept Computer Sci Berkeley CA 94720-0001

ZAFFARONI, ALEJANDRO C. biochemist, medical research company executive; b. Montevideo, Uruguay, Feb. 27, 1923; came to U.S., 1944; s. Carlos and Luisa (Alfaro) Z.; m. Lyda Russomanno, July 5, 1946; children— Alejandro A., Elisa B., U. Montevideo, 1943; Ph.D. in Biochemistry, U. Rochester, 1949; Doctorate (hon.), U. Republic, Montevideo, 1983; M.Divinity, Cen. Bapt. Seminary, 1987. Dir. biochem. research Syntex S.A., Mexico City, 1951-54, v.p., dir. research, 1954-56; exec. v.p., dir. Syntex Corp., Palo Alto, Calif., 1956-68; pres. Syntex Labs. Inc., Palo Alto, 1962-68, Syntex Research, Palo Alto, 1962-68; founder, co-chmn. ALZA Corp., Palo Alto, 1968—, also CEO, till 1998, founder, dir. emeritus, 1998-99, ret., 1999; founder, mem. policy bd. and exec. com. DNAX Research Inst. of Molecular and Cellular Biology, Inc., Palo Alto, Calif., 1980—, chmn., 1980-82; founder, chmn., chief exec. officer Affymax, N.V., Palo Alto, 1989—. Chmn. Internat. Psoriasis Research Found., Palo Alto; incorporator Neuroscis. Research Found. MIT, Brookline, Mass.; bd. govs. Weizmann Inst. Sci., Rehovot, Israel; mem. pharm. panel of com. on tech. and internat. econs. and trade issues Nat. Acad. Engring. Office of Fgn. Sec. and Assembly of Engring., Washington; hon. prof. biochemistry Nat. U. Mex., 1957, U. Montevideo, 1959 Contbr. numerous articles to profl. jours.; patentee in field Recipient Barren medal Barren Found., Chgo., 1974; Pres.'s award Weizmann Inst. Sci., 1978; Chem. Pioneer award Am. Inst. Chemists, Inc., 1979, National Medal of Technology, 1995. Fellow Am. Acad. Arts and Scis., Am. Pharm. Assn.; mem. NAE, AAAS, Am. Chem. Soc., Am. Found. Pharm. Edn., Am. Inst. Chemists, Inc., Am. Soc. Biol. Chemists, Inc., Am. Soc. Microbiology, Am. Soc. Pharmacology and Exptl. Therapeutics, Biomed. Engring. Soc., Calif. Pharmacists Assn., Internat. Pharm. Fedn., Internat. Soc. Chronobiology, Internat. Soc. Study of Biol. Rhythms, Soc. Exptl. Biology and Medicine, Sociedad Mexicana de Nutricion y Endocrinologia, Biochem. Soc. Eng., Endocrine Soc., Internat. Soc. Research in Biology of Reproduction, N.Y. Acad. Scis., Christian Legal Soc. (Mo. bd. dirs. 1973—), Tau Kappa Epsilon (internat. pres. 1953-57).

ZAFIROPOULO, ARTHUR, executive; Pres. Kayex; v.p. lab. elecs., founder, pres. Drytek; pres. internat. ops. Gen. Signal Semiconductor Equipment Groups; CEO, pres., chmn. Ultratech Stepper, San Jose, Calif., 1990—. Patentee in field. Office: 3050 Zanker Rd San Jose CA 95134-2126

ZAHARIA, ERIC STAFFORD, health facility administrator; b. Pomona, Calif., Aug. 24, 1948; s. Edgar A. and Dorothy (Stafford) Z.; m. Caryle Koentz, Dec. 23, 1967; children: Tye W., Tieg A. BA, Pomona Coll., 1970; MEd, U. Ariz.-Tucson, 1973; PhD, George Peabody Coll., 1978; postgrad., Govt. Execs. Inst. U. N.C., Chapel Hill, 1981. Mental retardation worker Ariz. Tng. Program, Tucson, 1970-71, unit dir., 1971-73; dir. residential svcs. Willmar State Hosp., (Minn.), 1973-76; rsch. asst. Inst. on Mental Retardation and Intellectual Devel., Nashville, 1976-78; dir. mental retardation program svcs. Dept. Mental Health/Mental Retardation, State of Tenn., Nashville, 1978-79; dir. Caswell Ctr., Kinston, N.C., 1979-86; program adminstr. Colo. Divsn. of Devel. Disabilities, Denver, 1986-90; dir. Utah divsn. Svcs. for People with Disabilities, Salt Lake City, 1990-95; ind. cons. Park City, Utah, 1995-2000; dir. Ariz. Divsn. Devel. Disabilities, Phoenix, 2000—. Mem. adj. faculty East Carolina U., Greenville, 1979-86; bd. dirs. Neuse Enterprises Inc., Kinston. Chmn. Big Bros./Sisters Kinston Inc., 1980-83; mem. N.C. Coalition for Community Svc., 1982-85. Mem. Am. Assn. Mental Retardation, Nat. Assn. Supts., Pub. Residential Facilities, Assn. Retarded Citizens, Kinston C. of C. (bd. dirs. 1983-86). Home: 1352 N Hibbert Mesa AZ 85201

ZAILLIAN, STEVEN, screenwriter, director; b. Calif., Jan. 30, 1953; BA, San Francisco State U., 1975. Scripts include: The Falcon and the Snowman, 1985, Awakenings, 1990 (Acad. award nominee for best adapted screenplay, 1990), Jack the Bear, 1993, Schindler's List, 1993 (Acad. award best adapted screenplay 1993); co-writer (with Donald Stewart and John Milius) Clear and Present Danger, 1994; scriptwriter, dir.: Searching for Bobby Fisher, 1993, A Civil Action, 1998.

ZAJAC, JOHN, semiconductor equipment company executive; b. N.Y.C., July 21, 1946; s. John Andrew and Catherine (Canepa) Z.; m. Vera Barbagallo, Jan. 13, 1973; children: Jennifer, Michelle. AAS, NYU, 1966; BEE, U. Ky., 1968. Project engr. B.C.D. Computing, N.Y.C., 1968-70; v.p. Beacon Systems, Commack, N.Y., 1970-73, E.T. Systems, Santa Clara, Calif., 1973-77; v.p. research and devel. Eaton Corp., Sunnyvale, 1977-81; pres. Semitech/Gen. Signal, Los Gatos, 1981-83; mgr. advanced product div. Tegal/Motorola Inc., Novato, 1983-86; v.p. research and devel. U.S.A. Inc., San Jose, 1986-94; staff scientist Mattson Tech., Fremont, 1994—. Author: The Delicate Balance, 1988, A Thief's Way to Heaven, 1999, Pyramids, Prophecy and 666, 2000; holder of 25 patents in field; guest TV and radio. Office: Mattson Tech 3550 W Warren Ave Fremont CA 94538-6499 E-mail: zajacjohn@aol.com

ZAJONC, ROBERT B(OLESLAW), psychology educator; b. Lodz, Poland, Nov. 23, 1923; came to U.S., 1949, naturalized, 1953; s. Mieczyslaw and Anna (Kwiatkowska) Z.; m. Donna Benson, June 20, 1953 (div. 1981); children: Peter Clifford, Michael Anton, Joseph Robert; m. Hazel Markus, May 25, 1982; 1 child, Krysia Courcelle Rose Ph.D., U. Mich., 1955; Dr. hon. causa, U. Louvain, 1984, U. Warsaw, 1989. Asst. prof. psychology U. Mich., 1955-60, assoc. prof., 1960-63, prof., 1963-94, Charles Horton Cooley Disting. prof. psychology, 1983-94, rsch. scientist Inst. for Social Rsch., 1960-83, dir., 1989-94; prof. psychology Stanford (Calif.) U., 199[illegible] Directeur d'etudes Maison des Sciences de L'Homme, Paris, 1985-86; vis. prof. U. Oxford, 1971-72. Author: Social Psychology: An Experimental Approach, 1965; editor: Animal Social Psychology, 1970; assoc. editor: Jour. Personality and Social Psychology, 1960-66. Guggenheim fellow, 1978-79, Fulbright fellow, 1962-63; recipient Disting. Prof. award of social sci., 1983. Fellow AAAS (co-recipient Psychol. prize 1976), APA (Disting. Sci. Contbrn. award 1978), Japan Soc. Promotion of Sci., N.Y. Acad. Scis.; mem. Soc. for Exptl. Social Psychology (Disting. Scientist award 1986), Polish Acad. Scis. (fgn.). Office: Stanford U Dept Psychology Jordan Hall Stanford CA 94305

ZAKHEIM, IRVING LEE, gift import company executive; b. L.A., Dec. 4, 1948; s. Benjamin David and Louise Victoria (deMayo) Z.; m. Angela Rae Long, Feb. 29, 1988; chidlren: Sara Rose, Robert Joseph, Mary Louise, Benjamin Charles. BA, Calif. State U., Northridge, 1972. Profl. baseball player Chgo. White Sox, 1971-73; ins. agt. Equitable Life, L.A., 1973-75; pres., CEO Zak Designs, Inc., L.A., 1976—, also chmn. bd., 1976—; pres. Patchwork Creations, Angeles City, Philippines, 1976-83. Mem. L.A. C. of C., L.A. City C. of C., Spokane Area C. of C., Indland N.W. World Trade Coun., Nat. Housewares Mfrs. Assn., Juvenile Products Mfrs. Assn., Nat. Bath, Bed and Linen Assn., Nat. Assn. Catalog Showroom Mfrs. Avocations: golf, tennis, running. Office: Zak Designs Inc 1604 S Garfield Rd Spokane WA 99224-9720

ZAKIAN, MICHAEL, museum director; Dir. Frederick R. Weisman Mus. Art, Malibu, Calif., 1994—. Office: The Frederick R Weisman Art Museum Pepperdine U 24255 Pacific Coast Hwy Malibu CA 90263

ZALL, PAUL MAXWELL, retired English language educator, consultant; b. Lowell, Mass., Aug. 3, 1922; s. Nathan and Bertha (Rubin) Z.; m. Elisabeth Weisz, June 21, 1948; children: Jonathan, Barnaby, Andrew. BA, Swarthmore Coll., 1948; AM, Harvard U., 1950, PhD, 1951. Teaching fellow Harvard U., 1950-51; instr. Cornell U., 1951-55, U. Oreg., 1955-56; research editor Boeing Co., 1956-57; asst. prof. Calif. State Coll., Los Angeles, 1957-61, asso. prof., 1961-64, prof. English, 1964-86; research scholar, cons. to library docents Huntington Library, San Marino, Calif., 1986-96; acting chmn. dept. Calif. State Coll., 1969-71. Cons. in report writing, proposal preparation and brochures to industry and govt. agys., 1957-99. Author: Elements of Technical Report Writing, 1962, Hundred Merry Tales, 1963, Nest of Ninnies, 1970, Literary Criticism of William Wordsworth, 1966, (with John Durham) Plain Style, 1967, Simple Cobler of Aggawam in America, 1969; (with J.R. Trevor) Proverb to Poem, 1970, Selected Satires of Peter Pindar, 1971, Comical Spirit of Seventy Six, 1976, Ben Franklin Laughing, 1980; (with J.A.L. Lemay) Autobiography of Benjamin Franklin, 1981; (with Leonard Franco) Practical Writing, 1978, Norton Critical Edition of Franklin's Autobiography, 1986, Abe Lincoln Laughing, 1983, 95; (with E. Birdsall) Descriptive Sketches, 1984, Mark Twain Laughing, 1985, Being Here, 1987, George Washington Laughing, 1989, Franklin's Autobiography: Model Life, 1989, Founding Mothers, 1991, Becoming American, 1993, 98, Lincoln's Legacy, 1994, Wit and Wisdom of the Founding Fathers, 1996, Blue and Gray Laughing, 1996, Lincoln on Lincoln, 1999, Dolley Madison, 2001, Franklin on Franklin, 2001. Pres. Friends of South Pasadena Library, 1967-70. Served with USAAF, 1942-45, ETO. Am. Philos. Soc. fellow, 1964, 66; John Carter Brown Libr. rsch. grantee, Huntington Libr. rsch. grantee, fellow, 1993. Home: 1911 Leman Ln South Pasadena CA 91030-4628 Office: Huntington Libr San Marino CA 91108 Fax: 626-449-5720

ZAMBRANO, OCTAVIO, professional soccer coach; b. Ecuador, Feb. 3, 1958; Student, Chapman Coll. Player L.A. Lazers, Major Indoor Soccer League; asst. coach Calif. Emperors, APSL, L.A. Salsa, APSL, L.A. Galaxy, 1996-97, interim head coach, 1997, head coach, 1998—. Head coach L.A. Salsa USISL team; founder A-League Orange County Zodiac; dir. Mission Viejo Soccer Acad. Led Salsa Under-19 squad to 1993 McGuire Cup finals. Office: c/o LA Galaxy 1640 S Sepulveda Blvd Ste 114 Los Angeles CA 90025-7510

ZANUCK, RICHARD DARRYL, motion picture company executive; b. Beverly Hills, Calif., Dec. 13, 1934; s. Darryl F. and Virginia (Fox) Z.; m. Lili Gentle; children: Virginia, Janet; m. Linda Harrison, Oct. 26, 1969; children: Harrison Richard, Dean Francis; m. Lili Fini, Sept. 23, 1978. Grad., Harvard Mil. Acad., 1952; B.A., Stanford, 1956. Story, prodn. asst. Darryl F. Zanuck Prodns., 1956, v.p., 1956-62; president's prodn. rep. 20th Century-Fox Studios, Beverly Hills, 1962-63, v.p. charge prodn., 1963-69, pres., 1969-71, dir., 1966-71; founder, pres., owner Zanuck Co., Beverly Hills, 1989—. Chmn. 20th Century-Fox Television, Inc.; sr. exec. v.p. Warner Bros., Inc., 1971-72; co-founder, pres. Zanuck/Brown Co., 1972-88. Producer: The Sting, 1973 (Acad. award), The Sugarland Express, 1974, Jaws, 1975, Jaws 2, 1978, The Island, 1980, Neighbors, 1982, The Verdict, 1983, Cocoon, 1985, Target, 1985, Cocoon, the Return, 1988, Driving Miss Daisy, 1989 (Acad. award, Irving G. Thalberg award 1991), Rush, 1991, Rich in Love, 1992, Clean Slate, 1993, Wild Bill, 1995, Mulholland Falls, 1996, Deep Impact, 1998. Nat. chmn. Fibrosis Assn., 1966-68; mem. organizing com. 1984 Olympics; trustee Harvard Sch. 2d lt. U.S. Army. Named Producer of Yr., Nat. Assn. Theatre Owners, 1974, '85, Producers Guild Am., 1989; recipient Irving Thalberg award, 1991, Lifetime Achievement award, Producers Guild Am., 1993. Mem. Acad. Motion Picture Arts and Scis. (bd. govs.), Screen Producers Guild, Phi Gamma Delta. Office: Zanuck Co 9465 Wilshire Blvd Ste 930 Beverly Hills CA 90212-2608

ZAPATA, FRANK, federal judge; b. 1944; AA, Ea. Ariz. Coll., 1964; BA, U. Ariz., 1966, JD, 1973. Staff atty. So. Ariz. Legal Aid, Inc., 1973-74; asst. fed. pub. defender Ariz., 1974-84; chief asst. fed. pub. defender, 1984-94; magistrate judge U.S. Dist. Ct. Ariz., 1994-96, apptd. dist. ct. judge, 1996. Tchr. Hayden-Winkelman Sch. Dist., 1967-69, Tucson Unified Sch. Dist., 1969-70; asst. adj. prof. U. Ariz. Coll. Law, 1988-90. Bd. dirs. Robles Meml. Found., 1980-90, Cath. Comty. Svcs., 1974-76; bd. dirs., v.p. So. Ariz. Legal Aid, Inc., 1987-93. With Ariz. Army N.G., 1967-73. Mem. FBA (Tucson chpt.), U.S. Magistrate Judges Assn., Ariz. State Bar Assn., Ariz. Minority Bar Assn., Pima County Bar Assn. (bd. dirs. nominating com.), U. Ariz. Alumni Assn. (bd. dirs. 1980), Delta Sigma Pi. Office: US Courthouse Rm 107 55 E Broadway Blvd Tucson AZ 85701-1719

ZAPEL, ARTHUR LEWIS, book publishing executive; b. Chgo., 1921; m. Janet Michel (dec.); children: Linda (dec.), Mark, Theodore, Michelle; m. Cynthia Rogers Pisor, 1986; stepchildren: Dawn, Anthony. BA in English, U. Wis., 1946. Writer, prodr. Westinghouse Radio Stas.; film writer Galbreath Studios, Ft. Wayne; creative dir. Kling Studios, Chgo., 1952-54; writer, prodr. TV commls. J. Walter Thompson Advt., Chgo., 1954-73, v.p. TV and radio prodn., 1954-73; founder, pres. Arthur Meriwether, Inc., 1973-83; pres. Meriwether Pub. Ltd., 1969-90, chmn., 1990-97. Pres. Westcliffe (Colo.) Ctr. for the Arts. Author: Sweet Uncertainty, 2000; illustrator: 'Twas the Night Before, The Jabberwock; created game A Can of Squirms; wrote plays for ednl. use in schs. and chs.; supr. editing and prodn. 2200 plays and musicals, 1970-99; exec. editor 192 books on theater skills for secular and religious use. Founding pres. Art Students League of Colorado Springs, 1992; past pres. Colo. Springs Symphony Coun.; past bd. dirs. Colorado Springs Opera Festival. Recipient numerous awards Freedoms Found., Valley Forge, Art Dirs. Club N.Y., Art Dirs. Chgo., Hollywood Advt., 1960-67, Gold Records Radio Ad Bur., 1959-60, XV Festival Internat. Du Film Publicitaire Venise, 1968, Gold Camera award U.S. Indsl. Film Festival, 1983, Dukane award, 1982, Gold award Houston Internat. Film Festival, 1984. Office: Meriwether Pub Ltd 885 Elkton Dr Colorado Springs CO 80907-3576 E-mail: merpcds@aol.com, alzart@aol.com

ZAPPA, GAIL, record producer; m. Frank Zappa (dec.); children: Moon, Dweezil, Ahmet, Diva. Recipient (with Frank Zappa) Best Recording Package-Boxed Grammy award for Frank Zappa's Civilization, Phaze III, 1996.

ZAPPE, JOHN PAUL, city editor, educator, newspaper executive; b. N.Y.C., July 30, 1952; s. John Paul and Carolyn (Pikor) Z.; m. Siobhan Bradshaw, May 30, 1982. JD, Syracuse (N.Y.) U., 1978. Reporter Poughkeepsie Jour., 1973-75, Nev. State Jour., Reno, 1979-80; prin. Am. Media Bold, Oakland, Calif., 1981-83; reporter Press-Telegram, Long Beach, 1983-88, city editor, 1988-97, webmaster PT Connect, 1995-97, mgr. new media, 1997-98; dir. new media Riverside (Calif.) Press-Enterprise, 1998-2000; v.p. new media L.A. Newspaper Group, Woodland Hills, Calif., 2000—. Tchr. Syracuse U., 1976-78, Calif. State U., 1985-87; cons. Am. Media Bold, 1981-83. Chmn. Local 69 Newspaper Guild, Long Beach, 1984-87. Mem. Investigative Editors and Reporters, NAA New Media Fedn. Office: LA Daily News 21221 Oxnard St Los Angeles CA 91367 E-mail: JZappe@LangNews.com

ZARANKA, WILLIAM F. academic administrator, author; b. Elizabeth, N.J., Dec. 22, 1944; s. William A. and Anne M. (Paulauska) Z.; m. Ruth Annalea Falchero; children: Jacob, Philip. BA, Upsala Coll., 1966; MA, Purdue U., 1968; PhD, U. Denver, 1974. Instr. Purdue U., West Lafayette, Ind., summer 1969; asst. prof. U. Pa., Phila., 1975-78; teaching fellow U. Denver, 1969-71, instr. English, 1969-71, 74-75, asst. prof., dir. creative writing, 1978-84, dean arts and humanities, 1984-89, provost, 1989—. Author: The Branx X Anthology of Poetry, 1981, The Brand X Anthology of Fiction, 1983, (poetry) A Mirror Driven through Nature, 1981, Blessing, 1986. Fellow Breadd Loaf Writers Conf., 1981. Roman Catholic. Avocation: astronomy. Office: U Denver Office of Provost 2199 S University Blvd Denver CO 80210-4711

ZARE, RICHARD NEIL, chemistry educator; b. Cleve., Nov. 19, 1939; s. Milton and Dorothy (Amdur) Z.; m. Susan Leigh Shively, Apr. 20, 1963; children: Bethany Jean, Bonnie Sue, Rachel Amdur. BA, Harvard, 1961; postgrad., U. Calif., Berkeley, 1961-63; PhD (NSF predoctoral fellow), Harvard, 1964; DS (hon.), U. Ariz., 1990, Northwestern U., 1993, ETH, Zürich, 1993, Columbia U., , 2000, State U. West Ga., 2001; DP (hon.), Uppsala (Sweden) U., 2000. Postdoctoral fellow Harvard, 1964; postdoctoral research asso. Joint Inst. for Lab. Astrophysics, 1964-65; asst. prof. chemistry Mass. Inst. Tech., 1965-66; asst. prof. dept. physics and astrophysics U. Colo., 1966-68, assoc. prof. physics and astrophysics, asso. prof. chemistry, 1968-69; prof. chemistry Columbia, 1969-77, Higgins prof. natural sci., 1975-77; prof. Stanford U., 1977—, Shell Disting. prof. chemistry, 1980-85, Marguerite Blake Wilbur prof. natural sci., 1987—, prof. physics, 1992—. Cons. Aeronomy Lab., NOAA, 1966-77, radio standards physics divsn. Nat. Bur. Standards, 1968-77, Lawrence Livermore Lab., U. Calif., 1974—, SRI, Internat., 1974—, Los Alamos Sci. Lab., U. Calif., 1975—; fellow adjoint Joint Inst. Lab. Astrophysics, U. Colo.; mem. IBM Sci. Adv. Com., 1977-92; chmn. commn. on phys. scis., math. and applications Nat. Rsch. Coun., 1992-95; chmn. bd. dirs. Annual Revs., Inc., 1995—; rschr. and author publs. on laser chemistry and chem. physics. Editor Chem. Physics Letters, 1982-85; contbr. and rschr. articles on laser chemistry and chem. physics to profl. jours. Recipient Fresenius award Phi Lambda Upsilon, 1974, Michael Polanyi medal, 1979, Nat. Medal Sci., 1983, Spectroscopy Soc. Pitts. award, 1983, Michelson-Morley award Case Inst. Tech. Case We. Res. U., 1986, ISCO award for Significant Contbns. to Instrumentation for Biochem. Separations, 1990, Ea. Analytical Symposium award, 1997, Exceptional Sci. Achievement award NASA, 1997, Space award Aviation Week and Space Tech., 1997, Disting. Svc. award Nat. Sci. Bd., 1998, Centennial medal Harvard U., Faraday medal Royal Soc. Chemistry, 2001, The Welch award, 1999; nonresident fellow Joint Inst. for Lab. Astrophysics, 1970—, Alfred P. Sloan fellow, 1967-69, Christensen fellow St. Catherine's Coll., Oxford U., 1982, fellow Stanford U., 1984-86; Bing Fellowship Tchg. award, 1996; named Calif. Scientist of Yr., 1997. Fellow AAAS, Calif. Acad. Scis. (hon.), Inst. of Physics; mem. NAS (mem. coun., Chem. Scis. award 1991), Am. Acad. Arts and Scis., Am. Phys. Soc. (Earle K. Plyler prize 1981, Irving Langmuir prize 1985, Arthur L. Scharlow prize in laser sci. 2000), Am. Chem. Soc. (Harrison Howe award Rochester chpt. 1985, Remsen award Md. chpt. 1985, Kirkwood award Yale U. chpt. 1986, Willard Gibbs medal Chgo. chpt. 1990, Peter Debye award in phys. chemistry 1991, Linus Pauling medal 1993, The Harvey prize 1993, Dannie-Heineman Preis 1993, Analytical Chemistry Divsn. award in chem. instrumentation 1995, Analytical Chemistry award 1998, G.M. Kosalapoff award 1998, E. Bright Wilson award in Spectroscopy, 1999, Charles Lathrop Parsons award 2001, Madison Marshall award 2001, Nobel Laureate Signature award 2000), Am. Philos. Soc., Chem. Soc. London, Royal Soc. London (fgn.), Phi Beta Kappa, Phi Beta Delta. Office: Stanford U Dept Chemistry Stanford CA 94305-5080

ZARELLI, JOSEPH, state legislator; m. Tani Zarelli; 4 children. AAS, Clark Coll. Mem. Wash. Senate, Dist. 18, Olympia, 1995—; mem. human svcs. and corrections com.; mem. edn. com.; mem. ways and means com. Foster parent Clark County, 1986—. With USN, 1982-89. Mem. Am. Soc. for Indsl. Security (Columbia River chpt.). Republican. Office: 203 Irving Newhouse Ofc Olympia WA 98504-0001

ZARINS, CHRISTOPHER KRISTAPS, surgery educator, vascular surgeon; b. Tukums, Latvia, Dec. 2, 1943; came to U.S., 1946; s. Richard A. and Maria (Rozenbergs) Z.; m. Zinta Zarins, July 8, 1967; children: Daina, Sascha, Karina. BA, Lehigh U., 1964; MD, Johns Hopkins U., 1968. Surgery residency U. Mich., Ann Arbor, 1968-74; asst. prof. surgery U. Chgo., 1976-79, assoc. prof. surgery, 1979-82, prof. surgery, 1983-93, chief of vascular surgery, 1978-93; prof. surgery, chmn. divsn. vascular surgery Stanford (Calif.) U., 1993—, acting chmn. dept. of surgery, 1995-97. Author: Essays In Surgery, 1986, Atlas of Vascular Surgery, 1988; editor Jour. of Surg. Rsch., 1982-95; contbr. articles to profl. jours. Pres. Latvian Med. Found., Boston, 1991. Lt. comdr. USN, 1974-76. Grantee NIH, NSF. Mem. Am. Surg. Soc., Soc. for Clin. Surgery, Soc. for Vascular Surgery (pres. 1998-99), Internat. Soc. for Cardiovascular Surgery, Soc. of Univ. Surgeons, Latvian Nat. Acad. of Scis., Latvian Vascular Surg. Soc. (pres. 1989), Soc. for Vascular Surgery (pres. 1998-99). Avocations: triathlons, skiing. Office: Stanford U Med Ctr Divsn Vascular Surgery 300 Pasteur Dr # H3630 Palo Alto CA 94304-2203

ZARO, BRAD A. research company executive, biologist; b. San Jose, Calif., Dec. 4, 1949; s. Raymond J. and Irene R. Z.; children: Amy C., Kristen E. BA in Zoology, San Jose State U., 1974, MA in Biology, 1981. Chemist, Dept. Drug Metabolism Syntex Rsch., Inc., Palo Alto, Calif., 1976-78, chemist II, Dept. Drug Metabolism, 1978-81, chemist III, Dept. Drug Metabolism, 1981-84, clin. rsch. assoc. I, Inst. of Clin. Medicine, 1984-85, clin. rsch. assoc. II, Inst. of Clin. Medicine, 1985-87, sen. clin. rsch. assoc., Inst. of Clin. Medicine, 1985-87; sen. clin. rsch. assoc. Triton Biosciences, Inc., Alameda, 1988, mgr. clin. trials, 1988; pres., CEO Clinimetrics Rsch. Assoc., Inc., San Jose, 1988—. Contbr. articles to scholarly jours. Mem. AAAS, Am. Coll. Clin. Pharmacology, Am. Soc. Pharmacognosy, Assn. Clin. Rsch. Profls., Drug Info. Assn. Democrat. Roman Catholic. Avocations: scuba diving, skiing, flying airplanes. Office: Clinimetrics Rsch Assocs 5285 Hellyer Ave San Jose CA 95138

ZAWACKI, BRUCE EDWIN, surgeon, educator, ethicist; b. Northampton, Mass., Dec. 6, 1935; BS, Coll. of Holy Cross, 1957; MD, Harvard U., 1961; MPH, U. So. Calif., 1980. Diplomate Am. Bd. Surgery. Gen. surgeon So. Calif. Permanente Med. Group, Panorama City, 1969-71; dir. burn ctr. L.A. County and U. So. Calif. Med. Ctr., L.A., 1971-98; assoc. prof. surgery U. So. Calif. Sch. Medicine, L.A., 1975-98, assoc. prof. emeritus,

1998—; assoc. prof. religion U. So. Calif. Sch. Religion, L.A., 1992-98; assoc. dir. for edn. Pacific Ctr. for Health Policy and Ethics, 1997-2000. Contbr. articles to profl. jours. Served to maj. U.S. Army, 1967-68. Mem. Am. Burn Assn. (2d v.p., bd. trustees 1992-93; Harvey Stuart Allen Disting. Svc. award 1996), Soc. for Health and Human Values, L.A. Surg. Soc., Internat. Soc. for Burn Injuries. Achievements include first to describe the natural history of reversible burn injury, the independence of burn hypermetabolism from evaporative water loss and an autonomous role for burn patients without precedent for survival.

ZEBROSKI, EDWIN LEOPOLD, safety engineer, consultant; b. Chgo., Apr. 1, 1921; s. Peter Paul and Sophie (Rydz) Z.; m. Gisela Karin Rudolph, Sept. 6, 1969; children: Lars, Zoe, Susan, Peggy. BS, U. Chgo., 1941; PhD, U. Calif., Berkeley, 1947. Registered prof. engr., Calif. Project engr. Gen. Electric Co., Schenectady, N.Y., 1947-53, mgr. devel. engring. San Jose, Calif., 1958-73; mgr. engring. SRI Internat., Menlo Park, 1954-58, dir. systems and materials dept., 1974-79; dir. nuclear safety analysis ctr. EPRI, Palo Alto, 1979-81; v.p. engring. INPO, Atlanta, 1981-83; chief nuclear scientist EPRI, 1983-88; dir. risk mgmt. svcs. APTECH Engring. Svcs., Sunnyvale, Calif., 1988-97. Vis. prof. Purdue U., West Lafayette, Ind., 1977-78; cons. OTA, Washington, 1980, 82-83, Dept. Energy, Washington, 1985-90, panels Nat. Rsch. Coun., 1990—, Electricite de France, 1986-87, Dept. Interior, Washington, 1987-89, EPRI, Palo Alto, 1988-98, Acad. Sci., USSR, 1987, Juelich Lab., Germany, 1988; mem. commn. engring. edn. NRC, Washington, 1970-73; mem. NAS-NRC Panel on Decision-Making in Govt. Agy., 1997-98; mem. NAS-NRC Panel on High Level Waste R&D, 2001; mem. DOE-Sandia Panel on Reliability, 2000—. Contbr. chpts. to books, numerous articles to profl. jours.; patentee in field. Pres. bd. Unitarian Ch., Palo Alto, 1967-68. Recipient Charles A. Coffin award Gen. Electric Co., Schenectady, 1954. Fellow AAAS, Am. Nuclear Soc. (bd. exec. com. 1969-71), Am. Inst. Chemists; mem. NAE (chmn. energy com. 1984-86, chmn. mem. com. 1986-87, policy com. 1995-96), Am. Phys. Soc., Soc. for Risk Analysis. Avocations: safety and risk management, decision analysis, music, writing. Office: ELGIS Consulting 1546 Plateau Ave Los Altos CA 94024-5320 E-mail: edzebroski@worldnet.att.net

ZEECK, DAVID, newspaper editor; Exec. editor The News Tribune, Tacoma. Office: The News Tribune 1950 South St Tacoma WA 98405

ZEFF, OPHELIA HOPE, lawyer; b. Oak Park, Ill., Aug. 19, 1934; d. Bernard Allen and Esther (Levinsohn) Gurvis; m. David Zeff, Dec. 29, 1957 (div. 1983); children: Sally Lyn Zeff Propper, Betsy Zeff Russell, Ellen, Adam; m. John Canterbury Davis, Sept. 18, 1987. BA, Calif. State U., 1956; JD, U. Pacific, 1975. Bar: Calif. 1975. Reporter Placerville (Calif.) Mountain Dem., 1956-57, Salinas Californian, 1957-59; corr. Modesto (Calif.) Bee, 1962-64; atty. ALRB, Sacramento, 1975-76, Yolo County Counsel, Woodland, Calif., 1976-78, Law Office of O.H. Zeff, Woodland, 1978-85; employee rels. officer Yolo County, 1985-87; ptnr. Littler, Mendelson, Fastiff, Tichy & Mathiason, Sacramento, 1987-98, Atkinson, Andelson, Loya, Ruud & Romo, Sacramento, 1998—. Mem. Vallejo (Calif.) Sch. Bd., 1971-74, pres., 1974; mem. Woodland Libr. Bd., 1982; v.p. LWV, Vallejo, 1972; mem. LWV, Sacramento, 1987—. Recipient Am. Jurisprudence Lawyer Coop. Pub., 1974. Mem. Sacramento County Bar, Sacramento Women Lawyers, Indsl. Rels. Assn. No. Calif., Traynor Soc. (life). Democrat. Jewish. Avocations: hiking, skiing, biking, reading, traveling. Office: Atkinson Andelson Loya Ruud & Romo 555 Capitol Mall Ste 645 Sacramento CA 95814-4502

ZEHR, CLYDE JAMES, religious organization administrator; b. Valley Ctr., Kans., Oct. 4, 1934; s. John Wesley and Anna Mae (Carithers) Z.; m. Leona Mae Zehr, Nov. 23, 1957; children: Karen Elaine, Mark Wesley. BS, U. Kans., 1957; ThM, Western Evang. Sem., Portland, Oreg., 1961; MBA, Seattle U., 1976. Ordained to ministry Evang. Meth. Ch., 1961. Structural engr. Boeing Co., Seattle, 1957-59; pastor Rockwood Evang. Meth. Ch., Portland, 1961-63; missionary OMS Internat., Seoul, Republic of Korea, 1964-80; dir. Christian Leadership Seminars, Kent, Wash., 1980-82; supt. N.W. dist. Evang. Meth. Ch., Kent, 1982-86, gen. supt. Wichita, Kans., 1986-94, N.W. dist. supt. Seattle, 1995—. Author: Study Notes on Leadership, 1982, The Innovator/Administrator Conflict, 1986, Focus on Effectiveness, 1990. Republican. Office: Evang Meth Ch NW Dist Office PO Box 75673 Seattle WA 98125-0673

ZEHR, NORMAN ROBERT, association administrator; b. Niagara Falls, N.Y., May 19, 1930; s. George Andrew and Ina Kate (Morrell) Z.; Engr. of Mines, Colo. Sch. Mines, 1952, M.S., 1956; m. Janet Hutchinson, Apr. 24, 1976; children— Jeannette Ann, Leslie. Sales trainee Ingersoll-Rand Co., N.Y.C., 1955 56, sales engr., Lima, Peru, 1956-64, regional mgr. mining and constrn. sales, Lima, Peru and N.Y.C., 1964-68, gen. sales mgr. Latin Am., N.Y.C., 1968-69, gen. mgr. Latin Am. ops., N.Y.C., 1969-71, v.p. Ingersoll Rand Internat., Woodcliff Lake, N.J., 1971-72, pres., 1972-83, v.p. Ingersoll-Rand Co., 1975-83; exec. dir. Colo. Sch. Mines Alumni Assn., 1984-95, ret. 1995. Served with AUS, 1952-54. Recipient Colo. Sch. Mines Disting. Achievement medal, 1977. Mem. AIME, Scabbard and Blade, Nat. Soc. Pershing Rifles, Mining Club, Sigma Nu.

ZEIGER, ROBERT S. allergist; b. Bklyn., July 31, 1942; s. Murray and Mildred (Oransky) Z.; m. Karen P. Zeiger, June 25, 1967; children: Joanna, Laurie. BA with honors, Tulane U., 1963; MD, PhD, SUNY, Bklyn., 1969. Diplomate Am. Bd. Pediatrics, Am. Bd. Allergy-Immunology. Intern pediatrics Harriet Lane Johns Hopkins Hosp., Balt., 1969-70; staff assoc. NIH, Bethesda, Md., 1970-72; resident pediatrics Boston Children's Hosp., 1972-73, allergy fellow, 1973-75; instr. Harvard Med. Sch., Boston, 1975-76; chief of allergy Kaiser Permanente, San Diego, 1976—; clin. assoc. prof. U. Calif., San Diego, 1980-87, clin. prof., 1987—. Editorial bd. Family Practice Survey, 1983-85, Jour. Allergy Clin. Immunology, 1985-91, Pediatric Allergy Immunology Jour., 1990—; author: Nasal Manifestations of Systemic Diseases, 1990; contbr. articles to profl. jours. Lt. comdr. USPHS, 1970-72. Phizer Honor scholar Phizer Corp., 1967-69, Charles A. Janeway scholar Harvard U., 1975; Hood Found. grantee, 1975-77. Fellow Am. Acad. Pediatrics, Am. Acad. Allergy Clin. Immunology (Travel award 1975), Phi Beta Kappa, Alpha Omega Alpha. Democrat. Avocations: tennis, travel, golf, cinema. Office: Kaiser Permanente 7060 Clairemont Mesa Blvd San Diego CA 92111-1003 also: U Calif San Diego Dept Pediat 9500 Gilmann Dr La Jolla CA 92093-0833

ZEITLIN, HERBERT ZAKARY, retired college president, real estate company executive; b. N.Y.C., Jan. 14, 1919; s. Leonard and Martha Josephine (Soff) Z.; m. Eugenia F. Pawlik, July 3, 1949; children: Mark Clyde, Joyce Therese Zeitlin Harris, Ann Victoria, Clare Katherine. BS, NYU, 1947, MA, 1949; EdD, Stanford U., 1956. Tchr. Mepham High Sch., Bellmore, N.Y., 1946-47, Nassau County Vocat. Edn. Extension Bd., Mineola; electronics instr., adj. faculty Mephan C.C., 1946-49; tchr., counselor, dir. testing Phoenix Union High Sch. and Coll. Dist., 1949-57; dean eve. coll., prin. high sch. Antelope Valley Union High Sch. and Coll. Dist., Lancaster, Calif., 1957-62; dean instrn. Southwestern Coll., Chula Vista, 1962-64; pres., supt. Triton Coll., River Grove, Ill., 1964-76; pres., dean West L.A. Coll., 1976-80; pres. Trident Consultants, L.A., mgmt. cons., 1976—; adj. faculty Ariz. State U., Flagstaff, 1953-55, No. Ill. U., DeKalb, 1971-76, U. Calif., Santa Barbara, 1979. Author: Turbulent Birth of Triton College: How a California Dean Overcomes Corruption in the Founding of a Community College in Chicagoland, 2001; editor in field. Pres. Antelope Valley Breeze & Sage, 1959-60, Bob Vivant Homeowners Assn., 1982-84; mayor Upper Woodland Hills, Calif. Served with USAAF, 1942-46. Recipient spl. commendation Chgo. Tribune, spl. commendation Richard Ogilvie, former gov. Ill.; Adminstr. of Yr. award Triton Coll. Faculty Assn., 1974; Spl. Achievement award for visionary accomplishment Ill. Sch. Adminstrs. Assn., 1976. Mem. Ariz. Vocat. Guidance Assn. (pres. 1951-52), Ariz. State Vocat. Assn. (pres. 1952-53), Antelope Valley Rotary (pres. 1962), Maywood Ill. Rotary (pres. 1972-73). Home: 20124 Phaeton Dr Woodland Hills CA 91364-5633 Office: Paramount Properties 21731 Ventura Blvd Woodland Hills CA 91364-1845

ZEITLIN, MARILYN AUDREY, museum director; b. Newark, July 14, 1941; d. Sidney M. and Theresa Feigenblatt) Litchfield; widowed; children: Charles C. Sweedler, Milo Sweedler. Student, Vanderbilt U., 1963-65; AB in Humanities, Harvard U., 1966, MA in Teaching of English, 1967; postgrad., Cornell U., 1971-74. Dir. Ctr. Gallery, Bucknell U., Lewisburg, Pa., 1975-78; Freedman Gallery, Albright Coll., Reading, 1978-81; Anderson Gallery, Va. Commonwealth U., Richmond, 1981-87; curator, acting co-dir. Contemporary Arts Mus., Houston, 1987-90; exec. dir. Washington Projects for the Arts, 1990-92; dir. Univ. Art Mus., Ariz. State U., Tempe, 1992—. Juror Dallas Mus. of Arts, McKnight Awards, Mpls.; grant evaluator IMS; grant evaluator, panelist NEH; lectr., cons. in field. Editor, contbr. essays to art publs. Bd. dirs. Cultural Alliance Washington; curator, commr. for U.S. for 1995 Venice Biennale. Samuel H. Kress fellow, 1972-73. Mem. Assn. Coll. and Univ. Mus. and Galleries (v.p. 1986-88), Am. Assn. Mus., Coll. Art Assn. (U.S. commr. Venice Biennale 1995). Office: Ariz State U Art Mus PO Box 872911 Tempe AZ 85287-2911

ZEKMAN, TERRI MARGARET, graphic designer; b. Chgo., Sept. 13, 1950; d. Theodore Nathan and Lois (Bernstein) Z.; m. Alan Daniels, Apr. 12, 1980; children: Jesse Logan, Dakota Caitlin. BFA, Washington U., St. Louis, 1971; postgrad, Art Inst. Chgo., 1974-75. Graphic designer (on retainer) greeting cards and related products Recycled Paper Products Co., Chgo., 1970—, Jillson Roberts, Inc., Calif.; apprenticed graphic designer Helmuth, Obata & Kassabaum, St. Louis, 1970-71; graphic designer Container Corp., Chgo., 1971; graphic designer, art dir., photographer Cuerden Advt. Design, Denver, 1971-74; art dir. D'Arcy, McManus & Masius Advt., Chgo., 1975-76; freelance graphic designer Chgo., 1976-77; art dir. Garfield Linn Advt., Chgo., 1977-78; graphic designer Keiser Design Group, Van Noy & Co., Los Angeles, 1978-79; owner and operator graphic design studio Los Angeles, 1979—. Art and photography tchr. Ctr. for Early Edn., L.A., 1996—, Buckley Sch., Sherman Oaks, 1996—; 3d grade tchr. asst., 1999—. Recipient cert. of merit St. Louis Outdoor Poster Contest, 1970, Denver Art Dirs. Club, 1973

ZELENOK, DAVID S. city official; BSCE, U.S. Air Force Acad.; MS in Engring., U. Tex. Civil engr. USAF, Washington, San Antonio, Austin; mem. faculty dept. civil engring. U.S. Air Force Acad.; county hwy. mgr. Pa. Dept. Transp.; city engr. Wichita Falls, Tex.; st. supt. City of Colorado Springs, Colo., 1987-90, transp. dir., 1990—. Office: Transp Dept City Adminstrn Bldg 30 S Nevada Ave Ste 405 Colorado Springs CO 80903-1802

ZELIKOW, HOWARD MONROE, management and financial consultant; b. Bklyn., Apr. 17, 1934; s. Herman and Mae (Rebell) Z.; m. Doris Brown, June 10, 1956 (div. Aug. 1987); children: Lori Ann Zelikow Florio, Daniel M.; m. Marcie Peskin Rosenblum, Dec. 12, 1987. BA, Dartmouth Coll., 1955; MBA, Amost Tuck Sch., 1956. Acct. Ernst & Ernst, N.Y.C., 1956-61; controller Kratter Corp., N.Y.C., 1961-64; mgr. J.H. Cohn, CPAs, Newark, 1964-65; ptnr. Zelikow & Rebell CPAs, N.Y.C., 1965-70; v.p. Oxbow Constrn. Corp., Port Washington, N.Y., 1970-76; exec. v.p., treas., chief fin. officer Progressive Ins. Cos., Mayfield Village, Ohio, 1976-87; prin. ZKA Assocs., Cleve., 1987-96; ptnr., mng. dir. Kayne Anderson Investment Mgmt., L.A., 1988—. Bd. dirs. The Right Start Inc., Westlake, Calif. Trustee Village of Great Neck Estates, Great Neck, N.Y., 1975-76. Mem. Hillcrest Club, Phi Beta Kappa. Jewish. Home: 10114 Empyrean Way Los Angeles CA 90067-3830 Office: Kayne Anderson Investment Mgmt 1800 Avenue Of The Stars Los Angeles CA 90067-4212

ZELLERBACH, WILLIAM JOSEPH, retired paper company executive; b. San Francisco, Sept. 15, 1920; s. Harold Lionel and Doris (Joseph) Z.; m. Margery Haber, Feb. 25, 1946; children: John William, Thomas Harold, Charles Ralph, Nancy. B.S., Wharton Sch., U. Pa., 1942; grad., Advanced Mgmt. Program, Harvard U., 1958. With Crown Zellerbach Corp. and subs., 1946-85; officer, dir. Crown Zellerbach Corp., 1960-85. Mem gen. adv. com. fgn. assistance programs AID, 1965-68; pres. Zellerbach Family Fund. Served as lt. USNR, 1942-46. Mem. Nat. Paper trade Assn. (pres. 1970) Clubs: Villa Taverna (San Francisco), Presidio Golf (San Francisco), Pacific Union (San Francisco), Commonwealth (San Francisco); Peninsula Country (San Mateo, Calif.). Office: 120 Montgomery St Ste 2000 San Francisco CA 94104-4323

ZELMANOWITZ, JULIUS MARTIN, mathematics educator, university administrator; b. N.Y.C., Feb. 20, 1941; s. Morris and Tillie (Holtz) Z.; m. Joan R. Traubel, June 24, 1962; 1 child, Dawn Michèle. AB, Harvard U., 1962; MS, U. Wis., 1963, PhD, 1966. Asst. prof. U. Calif., Santa Barbara, 1966-73, assoc. prof., 1973-77, prof. maths., 1977—, assoc. vice chancellor acad. affairs, 1985-87, assoc. vice chancellor acad. personnel, 1988-98; assoc. prof. Carnegie-Mellon U., Pitts., 1970-71; interim vice provost acad. initiatives U. Calif., 1999-2000, v.p. acad. initiatives, 2000—. Vis. asst. prof. UCLA, 1969-70, vis. assoc. prof. 1973-74; vis. prof. U. Rome, 1977, McGill U., Montreal, Quebec, 1982-83, 87-88, U. Munich, 1983, 88. Contbr. articles to profl. jours. Sr. rsch. grantee Italian Nat. Rsch. Coun., Rome, 1977, Palermo, 1988; named Milw. Prof. of Maths. The Technion, Haifa, Israel, 1979; Fulbright sr. fellow, Munich, 1983. Mem. Am. Math. Soc., Math. Assn. Am. Home: 2040 Franklin St # 1407 San Francisco CA 94109-2982 Office: Off Pres Acad Initiatives 1111 Franklin St Oakland CA 94607-5200 E-mail: julius.zelmanowit@ucop.edu

ZELON, LAURIE DEE, lawyer; b. Durham, N.C., Nov. 15, 1952; d. Irving and Doris Miriam (Baker) Z.; m. David L. George, Dec. 30, 1979; children: Jeremy, Daniel. BA in English with distinction, Cornell U., 1974; JD, Harvard U., 1977. Bar: Calif. 1977, U.S. Ct. Appeals (9th cir.) 1978, U.S. Supreme Ct. 1989. Assoc. Beardsley, Hufstedler & Kemble, L.A., 1977-81, Hufstedler, Miller, Carlson & Beardsley, L.A., 1981-82, ptnr., 1983-88, Hufstedler, Miller, Kaus & Beardsley, L.A., 1988-90, Hufstedler, Kaus & Ettinger, L.A., 1990-91, Morrison & Foerster, L.A., 1991-2000; judge L.A. Superior Ct., 2000—. Contbg. author: West's California Litigation Forms: Civil Procedure Before Trial, 1996; editor-in-chief Harvard Civil Rights and Civil Liberties Law Rev., 1976-77 Bd. dirs. N.Y. Civil Liberties Union, 1973-74. Mem. ABA (chmn. young lawyers divsn. pro bono project 1981-83, delivery and pro bono projects com. 1983-85, subgrant competition-subgrant monitoring project 1985-86, chair standing com. on lawyers pub. svc. responsibility 1987-90, chair law firm pro bono project 1989-91, standing com. legal aid and indigent defendants 1991-97, chmn. 1993-97, mem. ho. dels. 1993—, state del. 1998—, commn. on ethics 2000 1997—), Calif. Bar Assn. (bd. dirs. appellate project 1995-2000, chair commn. on access to justice 1997-99), L.A. County Bar Assn. (trustee 1989-91, v.p. 1992-93, sr. v.p. 1993-94, pres.-elect 1994-95, pres. 1995-96, fed. cts. and practices com. 1984-93, vice chmn. 1987-88, chmn. 1988-89, chmn. judiciary com. 1991-92, chmn. real estate litigation subsect. 1991-92), Women Lawyers Assn. L.A., Calif. Women Lawyers Assn. Democrat. Office: Los Angeles Superior Ct 111 N Hill St Los Angeles CA 90012-3117

ZEMPLENYI, TIBOR KAROL, cardiologist, educator; b. Part Lupča, Czechoslovakia, July 16, 1916; came to U.S., 1968, naturalized, 1974; s. David Dezider and Irene (Pollak) Z.; m. Hana Bendová, Aug. 13, 1952; 1 son, Jan. MD, Charles U., Prague, Czechoslovakia, 1946, Docent Habilit., 1966; CSc. (PhD), Czechoslovak Acad. Sci., 1960, DSc., 1964. Clin. asst. with dept medicine Prague Motol Clinic and Charles U., 1946-52; head atherosclerosis rsch. Inst. for Cardiovascular Rsch., Prague, 1952-68; assoc. prof. medicine Charles U., 1966-68, U. So. Calif., L.A., 1969-75, prof., 1975-92, prof. emeritus, 1992—. Attending physician L.A. County-U.So. Calif. Med. Ctr. Author: Enzyme Biochemistry of the Arterial Wall, 1968; editl. bd. Atherosclerosis, 1962-75, Cor et Vasa, 1993—; adv. bd. Advances in Lipid Rsch., 1963-66; contbr. articles to numerous profl. jours. WHO fellow for study in Sweden and Gt. Britain, 1959. Fellow Am. Heart Assn., Am. Coll. Cardiology; mem. Western Soc. for Clin. Rsch., Longevity Assn. (mem. sci. bd.), European Atherosclerosis Group, Italian Soc. for Atherosclerosis (hon.). Office: 3400 Loadstone Dr Sherman Oaks CA 91403-4512

ZENEV, IRENE LOUISE, museum curator; b. Albuquerque, Nov. 18, 1948; d. Stanley D. and Louise Marie (Risler) Z.; 1 child, Carson M. Bell. BA, U. N.Mex., 1971. Dir. Umpqua Valley Arts Assn., Roseburg, Oreg., 1978-82; edn. coord. Douglas County Mus., Roseburg, 1985-86, curator history, 1986-98; exhibits curator Benton County Mus., Philomath, Oreg., 1998—; editor Dispatch newsletter Oreg. Mus. Assn., 1995-98. Publs. rschr. Oreg. Mus. Assn., Portland, 1989-92. Reviewer The Roseburg News-Review, 1989-93. Chmn. Douglas County Oreg. Trail Sesquicentennial Celebration Com., 1991-93; mem. Oreg. Coun. for Humanities, 1997-2000, sec. bd., 1998-2000. Mem. Registrar's Com. Western Region (Oreg. state rep. 1995-99), Mus. Assessment Program Peer Reviewer, Am. Assn. Mus., 1997—. E-mail: Ilzenev@aol.com

ZENTMYER, GEORGE AUBREY, plant pathology educator; b. North Platte, Nebr., Aug. 9, 1913; s. George Aubrey and Mary Elizabeth (Strahorn) Z.; m. Dorothy Anne Dudley, May 24, 1941; children: Elizabeth Zentmyer Dossa, Jane Zentmyer Fernald, Susan Dudley. A.B., UCLA, 1935; M.S., U. Calif., 1936, Ph.D., 1938. Asst. forest pathologist U.S. Dept. Agr., San Francisco, 1937-40; asst. pathologist Conn. Agrl. Expt. Sta., New Haven, 1940-44; asst. plant pathologist to plant pathologist U. Calif., Riverside, 1944-62, prof. plant pathology, 1962—, prof. emeritus, 1981—, faculty rsch. lectr., 1964, chmn. dept., 1968-73, trustee, 1993-94. Cons. NSF, Trust Ty. of Pacific Islands, 1964, 66, Commonwealth of Australia Forest and Timber Bur., 1968, AID, Ghana and Nigeria, 1969, Govt. South Africa, 1980, Govt. Israel, 1983, Govt. Western Australia, 1983, Ministry Agriculture and U. Cordoba, Spain, 1989, Govt. Costa Rica, 1993; mem. NRC panels, 1968-73. Author: Plant Disease Development and Control, 1968, Recent Advances in Pest Control, 1957, Plant Pathology, An Advanced Treatise, 1977, The Soil-Root Interface, 1979, Phytophthora Cinnamomi and the Diseases it Causes, 1980, Phytophthora: Its Biology, Taxonomy, Ecology and Pathology, 1983, Ecology and Management of Soilborne Plant Pathogens, 1984, Compendium of Tropical Fruit Diseases, 1994; assoc. editor: Ann. Rev. of Phytopathology, 1971—, Jour. Phytopathology, 1951-54, internat. editl. bd. Internat. Jour. Pest Mgmt., 1990—, also jour. articles. Bd. dirs. Riverside YMCA, 1949-58, Friends of Mission Inn, 1981—, pres., 1991-93, Calif. Mus. Photography, 1988—; pres. Town and Gown Orgn., Riverside, 1962; bd. dirs. Riverside Hospice, 1982-85, pres., 1984-85; bd. dirs. Friends U. Calif. Riverside Botanic Garden, 1985-89, 91-95, pres., 1987-89; bd. trustees U. Calif. Riverside Found., 1993-94. Recipient award of honor Calif. Avocado Soc., 1954, spl. award of honor, 1981; recipient Emeritus Faculty award U. Calif., Riverside, 1991, UCLA Alumnus award, 1996; Guggenheim fellow, Australia, 1964-65, NATO sr. sci. fellow, Eng., 1971; NSF rsch. grantee, 1963, 68, 71, 74, 78; Bellagio scholar Rockefeller Found., 1985. Fellow AAAS (pres. Pacific div. 1974-75), Am. Phytopath. Soc. (pres. 1966, pres. Pacific eiv. 1955, found. bd. dirs. 1987—, v.p. 1991—, award of merit Caribbean div. 1972, award of distinction 1983, Lifetime Achievement award Pacific div. 1991), Explorers Club; mem. NAS, Mycol. Soc. Am., Am. Inst. Biol. Scis., Bot. Soc. Am., Internat. Avocado Soc. (hon.), Brit. Mycol. Soc., Australasian Plant Pathology Soc., Philippine Phytopath. Soc., Indian Phytopath. Soc., Assn. Tropical Biology, Internat. Soc. Plant Pathology (councilor 1973-78), Pacific Assn. Tropical Phytopathology, Internat. Avocado Soc. (hon.), Sigma Xi, Gamma Sigma Delta. Home: 5265 Chapala Dr # 212 Riverside CA 92507-5987

ZEPEDA, OFELIA, linguist, educator; b. Stanfield, Ariz., Mar. 24, 1954; BA, U. Ariz., 1980, MA, 1981, PhD, 1984. Tchr. O'odham and linguistics U. Ariz., 1979-92, assoc. prof. linguistics, 1992-98, full prof., 1998—. Tchr. O'odham and Pima, Am. Indian Lang. Devel. Inst., 1980—, co-dir., 1989—. Author: A Papago Grammar, 1983, Ocean Power: Poems From the Desert, 1995, Earth Movement, 1997; editor: Mat Hekid o Ju: When It Rains: Papago and Pima Poetry, 1982; co-editor: South Corner of Time, 1980; contbr.: Returning the Gift, 1994, Home Places, 1995; series editor Sun Tracks Fellow MacArthur, 1999—; grantee, NSF, 1986, NEH, 1992. Office: U Ariz Douglass Bldg Rm 222 Tucson AZ 85721-0001 E-mail: ofelia@u.arizona.edu

ZERELLA, JOSEPH T. retired pediatric surgeon; b. Youngstown, Ohio, Mar. 7, 1941; s. Atilio and Ann (Capuzello) Z.; m. Diana Isabelle Talbot, Aug. 5, 1967; children: Ann, Michael, Mark. BS, Northwestern U., 1962, MD, 1966. Diplomate Am. Bd. Surgery, Am. Bd. Pediatric Surgery. Intern Med. Coll. Wis., Milw., 1966-67, resident in surgery, 1967-68, 70-73; tng. fellow in pediatric surgery Children's Hosp. Med. Ctr., Cin., 1973-75; staff pediatric surgeon Phoenix Children's Hosp., 1975—; pvt. practice medicine, specializing in pediatric surgery Phoenix, 1975—. Mem. staff Good Samaritan Hosp., Phoenix, 1975— , sect. chief pediatric surgery, 1979— ; mem. staff St. Joseph's Hosp., Phoenix, 1975— , sect. chief pediatric surgery, 1980—. Contbr. articles to profl. jours. Served as capt. U.S. Army, 1968-70. Served as capt. USAR, 1968—70. Fellow ACS, Am. Acad. Pediatrics, Am. Pediatric Surg. Assn., Pacific Assn. Pediatric Surgeons. Roman Catholic. Office: Saguaro Childrens Surgery Ltd 1301 E Mcdowell Rd Ste 100 Phoenix AZ 85006-2605

ZERZAN, CHARLES JOSEPH, JR. retired gastroenterologist; b. Portland, Oreg., Dec. 1, 1921; s. Charles Joseph and Margaret Cecelia (Mahony) Z.; m. Joan Margaret Kathan, Feb. 7, 1948; children: Charles Joseph, Michael, Kathryn, Paul, Joan, Margaret, Terrance, Phillip, Thomas, Rose, Kevin, Gregory. BA, Wilamette U., 1948; MD, Marquette U., 1951. Diplomate Am. Bd. Internal Medicine. Commd. 2d lt. U.S. Army, 1940, advanced through grades to capt., 1945, ret., 1946, re-enlisted, 1951, advanced through grades to lt. col., M.C., 1965; intern Madigan Gen. Hosp., Ft. Lewis, Wash., 1951-52; resident in internal medicine Letterman Gen. Hosp., San Francisco, 1953-56, Walter Reed Gen. Hosp., San Francisco, 1960-61; chief of medicine Rodriquez Army Hosp., 1957-60, U.S. Army Hosp., Fort Gordon, Calif., 1962-65; chief gastroenterology Fitzsimmons Gen. Hosp., Denver, 1965-66; chief profl. svcs. U.S. Army Hosp., Ft. Carson, Colo., 1967-68; dir. continuing med. edn. U. Oreg., Portland, 1968-73; ptnr. Permanente Clinic, Portland, 1973-92, ret., 1992. Assoc. clin. prof. medicine U. Oreg., 1973-97; individual practice medicine, specializing in gastroenterology, Portland, 1968-92; staff Northwest Permanente, P.C., ret., 1992, dir., 1980-83. Decorated Legion of Merit, Army Commendation medal with oak leaf cluster; Meritorious Alumnus award Oreg. Health Scis. U., 1990. Fellow ACP; mem. Am. Gastroenterol. Assn., Oreg. Med. Assn. (del. Clackamas County), Ret. Officers Assn., China-Burma-India Vet. Assn., Burma Star Assn. Republican. Roman Catholic. Home and Office: 6364 SE Mcnary Rd Portland OR 97267-5119

ZEWAIL, AHMED HASSAN, chemistry and physics educator, editor, consultant; b. Damanhour, Egypt, Feb. 26, 1946; came to U.S., 1969, naturalized, 1982; s. Hassan A. Zewail and Rawhia Dar; m. Dema Zewail; children: Maha, Amani, Nabeel, Hani. BS, Alexandria U., Egypt, 1967, MS, 1969; PhD, U. Pa., 1974; MA (hon.), Oxford U., 1991; DS (hon.), Am. U., Cairo, 1993, Katholieke U., Leuven, Belgium, U. Pa., U. Lausanne, Switzerland, 1997; DU (hon.), Swinburne U., Australia, 1999; HDA Sc (hon.), Arab Acad. for Sci. and Tech., Egypt, 1999; HDASc (hon.), Alexandria U., Egypt, 1999; DSc (hon.), U. New Brunswick, Canada, 2000; Dhc (hon.), U. Rome, Italy, 2000, U. de Liège, Belgium, 2000. Teaching asst. U. Pa., Phila., 1969-70; IBM fellow U. Calif., Berkeley, 1974-76; asst. prof. chem. physics Calif. Inst. Tech., Pasadena, 1976-78, assoc. prof., 1978-82, prof., 1982-89, Linus Pauling prof. chem. physics, 1990-94, Linus Pauling prof. chemistry and prof. physics, 1995—, dir. NSF Lab. for Molecular Scis., 1996—. Cons. Xerox Corp., Webster, N.Y., 1977-80, ARCO Solar, Inc., Calif., 1978-81. Editor Laser Chemistry, 1980-85, Jour. Phyical Chemistry, 1985-90, Chem. Physics Letters, 1991—, Internat. Series Monographs on Chemistry, 1992—, Advances in Laser Spectroscopy Vol. I, 1977, Advances in Laser Chemistry Vol. III, 1978, Photochemistry and Photobiology, Vols. I and II, 1983, Ultrafast Phenomena VII, 1990, VIII, 1993, IX, 1994, The Chemical Bond: Structure and Dynamics, 1992, Femtochemistry-Ultrafst Dynamics of the Chemical Bond, Vols. I and II, 1994; contbr. numerous articles to sci. jours.; patentee in solar energy field. Recipient Tchr.-Scholar award Dreyfus Found., 1979-85, Alexander von Humboldt Sr. U.S. Scientist award, 1983, John Simon Guggenheim Meml. Found. award, 1987, King Faisal Internat. prize in sci., 1989, NASA award, 1991, 1st AMM Achievement award, 1991, Nobel Laureate Signature award, 1992, Carl Zeiss award, Cairo U. Medal and Shield of Honor, 1992, U. Qatar medal, 1993, Niles award of honor Bonner Chemiepreis, Germany, 1994, Order of Merit first class Egypt, Coll. de France medal Leonardo Da Vinci award of excellence, France, 1995, J.G. Kirwood medal Yale U., Peking U. medal, China, 1996, Robert A. Welch award in chemistry, Pitts. Spectroscopy award, 1997, Benjamin Franklin medal, Paul Karrer gold medal, Zurich, Roentgen prize, Germany, E.O. Lawrence award U.S. Govt., Merski award U. Nebr., Nobel Prize in Chemistry, 1999, Egypt Postage Stamp with portrait issued, 1999, Röntgen prize, Germany, 1999, Grand Collar of the Nile, Highest Award, Egypt, Order of Zayed, State United Arab Emirates; Ahmed Zewail fellow established U. Pa., Order of Cedar, Lebanon, Order of ISESCO, first class, Saudi Arabia, Order of Merit Tunisia, Insignia Pontifical Acad., Vatican, 2000. Mem. AAAS, NAS (Chem. Scis. award 1996), Am. Acad. Arts and Scis. (Royal Netherlands Acad. Arts and Scis. medal 1993), Am. Chem. Soc. (Buck-Whitney medal 1985, Harrison-Howe award 1989, Hoechst prize 1990, Peter Debye award, Linus Pauling medal 1997, 1st E.B. Wilson award 1997, William H. Nichols award 1998, Richard C. Tolman Medal award 1998), Am. Phil. Soc., Am. Phys. Soc. (Herbert P. Broida prize 1995), Pontifical Acad. Sci., Royal Danish Acad. Scis. and Letters, European Acad. Arts, Scis., and Humanities, Third World Acad. Scis., Sigma Xi (Earle K. Plyler prize 1993, Wolf prize 1993). Office: Calif Inst Tech Divsn Chemistry & Chem Engring Mail Code 127 72 Pasadena CA 91125-0001

ZHU, PETER CHAOQUAN, chemist; b. Jiashan, China, May 8, 1957; came to U.S., 1987; s. Sanguan and Mingbao (Shen) Z.; m. June Zhu, Aug. 7, 1998. BS, Jiangxi Coll. Chinese Medicine, Nanchang, China, 1981, MS, 1987; PhD, Miss. State U., 1993. Instr. Jiangxi Coll Chinese Medicine, Nanchang, China, 1981-85; rsch. scientist 1st Chem. Corp., Mississippi State, Miss., 1990-92; sr. rsch. chemist 3M Health Care, Tustin, Calif., 1994-99, Terumo Med. Corp., Tustin, 1999-2000; prin. scientist ASP, Johnson & Johnson, Irvine, Calif., 2000—. Adj. chemistry prof. Irvine Valley Coll., 1997—; cons. and rschr. in field. Postdoctoral fellow U. Calif., Santa Barbara, 1993-94. Mem. Am. Chem. Soc. (divsn. organic chemistry, divsn. polymer, divsn. medicinal chemistry, divsn. carbohydrate chemistry, divsn. analytical chemistry, divsn. environ. chemistry). Achievements include nanochemistry application, nanobeads chemistry, attachment chemistry, DNA attachment, new chemistry application in molecular biology; development of new chemistry of cyclic ketene acetals, including synthetic procedures and new reactions; invented pure monoacetylation of diols via cyclic ketene acetals; first cationically polymerized cyclic ketene acetals and obtained stable polymers and copolymers; developed new chemistry which led to a chemical oxygen sensor used for open-heart surgery, of new glucose and CO2 chemical sensor for medical use; invented several industrial processes of speciality chemicals; discovered a new silicone reaction; isolated one anti-cancer agent from a plant; development of a new preparative TLC methods, analytical methods of amine in organic and inorganic polymers, a synthetic procedure to introduce PhSe group. Avocations: walking, fishing, piano, pingpong. Office: ASP Biocides Rsch Johnson & Johnson 33 Technology Dr Irvine CA 92618 Fax: 949-450-6850. E-mail: pzhu1@aspus.jnj.com

ZIADEH, FARHAT J. Middle Eastern studies educator; b. Ramallah, Palestine, Apr. 8, 1917; s. Jacob and Nimeh Farah Z.; m. Suad Salem, July 24, 1949; children— Shireen, Susan, Rhonda, Deena, Reema. B.A., Am. U., Beirut, 1937; LL.B., U. London, 1940. Bar: Barrister-at-law Lincoln's Inn 1946. Instr. Princeton U., 1943-45, lectr. Oriental studies, 1948-54, asst. prof., 1954-58, asso. prof., 1958-66; magistrate Govt. of Palestine, 1947-48; editor Voice of Am., USIA, 1950-54; prof. U. Wash., Seattle, 1966—, prof., chmn. dept. Near Eastern lang. and lit., 1970-82, dir. Ctr. Arabic Study Abroad, 1983-89. Adj. prof. U. Wash. Law Sch., 1978-87, prof. emeritus, 1987— Author: Reader in Modern Literary Arabic, 1964, Lawyers, The Rule of Law and Liberalism in Modern Egypt, 1968, Property Law in the Arab World, 1979; contbr. articles to profl. jours. Mem. Middle East Studies Assn. (pres. 1979-80), Am. Oriental Soc. (past pres. western br.), Am. Research Center in Egypt (past bd. govs., exec. com.), Am. Assn. Tchrs. Arabic (past pres.) Eastern Orthodox. Office: Univ Wash Mid Eastern Studies Dept Seattle WA 98195-0001

ZIEGAUS, ALAN JAMES, public relations executive; b. Bremerton, Wash., May 8, 1948; s. Alan Moon and Dorothy (Lamont) Z.; m. Constance Jean Carver, 1972; children: Jennifer, Ashley. BJ, San Diego State U., 1970. Staff writer San Diego Tribune, 1972-77; exec. asst. San Diego City Council, 1977-78; v.p. Gable Agy., San Diego, 1978-80; pres. Stoorza, Ziegaus & Metzger, San Diego, 1980-2000. Mem. planning com. County San Diego, 1980-82; mem. sewage task force City of San Diego, 1986-88, civil svc. com., 1992—; trustee armed forces YMCA, San Diego, 1984—. Recipient Best Investigative Series award AP, 1975. Mem. San Diego Press Club (Best News Story award 1973). Home: Apt 3205 15606 Bernardo Center Dr San Diego CA 92127-1826 Office: Stoorza Ziegaus & Metzger 225 Broadway Fl 18 San Diego CA 92101-5005

ZIEGLER, JACK (DENMORE), cartoonist; b. N.Y.C., July 13, 1942; s. John Denmore and Kathleen Miriam (Clark) Z.; m. Jean Ann Rice, Apr. 20, 1968 (div. 1995); children: Jessica, Benjamin, Maxwell; m. Kelli Joseph, Aug. 1996. B.A. in Communication Arts, Fordham U., 1964. Free-lance cartoonist, N.Y.C., 1972—; cartoonist The New Yorker, N.Y.C., 1974—. Author: Hamburger Madness, 1978, Filthy Little Things, 1981, Marital Blitz, 1987, Celebrity Cartoons of the Rich and Famous, 1987, Worst Case Scenarios, 1990, Mr. Knocky, 1993, The Essential Jack Ziegler, 2000; illustrator: (children's books) Lily of the Forest, 1987, Flying Boy, 1988, Annie's Pet, 1989, Eli and the Dimplemeyers, 1994 (adult books) Waiting [illegible], The Joy of [illegible], That's Incurable!, 1994, Modern Superstitions, 1985, The No-Sex Handbook, 1990, There'll Be a Slight Delay, 1991, Byte Me!, 1996. Democrat.

ZIEGLER, R. W., JR. lawyer, consultant; b. Pitts. children: Caroline, Gretchen, Jeremy, Benjamin, Phoebe, Polly. Student, Carnegie Tech., U. Pitts.; JD, Duquesne U., 1972. Bar: Pa. 1972, Calif. 1981, U.S. Ct. Appeals (3d cir.) 1977, U.S. Dist. Ct. (we. dist.) Pa. 1972, U.S. Supreme Ct. 1977, U.S. Tax Ct. 1978, Calif. 1982, U.S. Dist. Ct. (no. dist.) Calif. 1982, U.S. Ct. Appeals (9th cir.) 1982. Ptnr. Ziegler & Ombres, Pitts., 1973-79; pres. Ziegler Ross Inc., San Francisco, 1979—. Lectr. for Bar Assns. Author: Law Practice Management; editor: Law Office Guide in Computing. Mem. ABA, Am. Mgmt. Assn., Pa. State Bar Assn., Calif. State Bar Assn. Office: 580 Market St Ste 500 San Francisco CA 94104-5413

ZIELINSKI, MELISSA L. museum director; BS, Coll. William an Mary, 1978; MS, N.C. State U., 1983. Park svc. ranger, interpreter Cape Hatteras Nat. Seashore, Buxton, N.C., 1980, 81; exhibits intern N.C. Mus. Natural Scis., Raleigh, 1980-81, 81-82, asst. curator pub. programs, 1984-92; vol. svcs. coord. N.C. State U., 1981-82, 82-83, lab. instr. vertebrate zoology lab., 1983; naturalist Durant Nature Park Raleigh (N.C.) Parks and Recreation Dept., 1983-84; mus. educator Humboldt State U. Natural History Mus., Arcata, Calif., 1992-93, dir., 1993—. Co-author, editor, illustrator vertebrate zoology lab. text, 1983-84. Sch. edn. program dir. Friends of the Dunes The Nature Conservancy, Arcata, Calif., 1993-94, mem. Mem. Am. Mus. Natural History, Nat. Assn. Interpretation, Nat. Marine Educators Assn., Guild of Natural Sci. Illustrators, Nat. Audubon Soc. Home: 1363 Mill Creek Rd Mckinleyville CA 95519-4448 Office: Humboldt State U Natural History Mus 1315 G St Arcata CA 95521-5820

ZIEMANN, G. PATRICK, bishop; b. Pasadena, Calif., Sept. 13, 1941; Attended, St. John's Coll. and St. John's Sem., Camarillo, Calif., Mt. St. Mary's Coll., L.A. Ordained priest Roman Cath., 1967. Titular bishop, aux. bishop Diocese Santa Rosa, Obba, 1986-92, bishop Santa Rosa, Calif., 1992—. Office: Diocese of Santa Rosa 320 10th St Santa Rosa CA 95401-5219

ZIEMER, RODGER EDMUND, electrical engineering educator, consultant; b. Sargeant, Minn., Aug. 22, 1937; s. Arnold Edmund and Ruth Ann (Rush) Z.; m. Sandra Lorann Person, June 23, 1960; children: Mark Edmund, Amy Lorann, Norma Jean, Sandra Lynn. B.S., U. Minn., 1960, M.S., 1962, Ph.D., 1965. Registered profl. engr., Mo. Research asst. U. Minn., Mpls., 1960-62, research assoc., 1962; prof. elec. engring. U. Mo., Rolla, 1968-83, U. Colo., Colorado Springs, 1984—, chmn. dept. elec. engring., 1984-93; program dir. comms. rsch. NSF, 1998-2001. Cons. Emerson Electric Co., St. Louis, 1972-84, Mid-Am. Regional Coun., Kansas City, Mo., 1974, Motorola, Inc., Scottsdale, Ariz., 1980-84, Martin Marietta, Orlando, 1980-81, TRW, Colorado Springs, summer, 1985, Sperry, Phoenix, 1986, Pericle Communications, summer, 1994, Motorola, Schaumburg, 1995, Scottsdale, 1996, Arlington Heights, 1997. Author: Principles of Communications, 1976, 2d edit., 1985, 3d edit., 1990, 4th edit., 1995, Signals and Systems, 1983, 2d edit., 1989, 3rd edit., 1993, 4th edit., 1998, Digital Communications and Spread Spectrum Systems, 1985, Introduction to Digital Communication, 1992, 2d edit., 2001, Introduction to Spread Spectrum Communications, 1995, Elements of Engineering Probability and Statistics, 1997; editor: IEEE Jour. on Selected Areas in Communications, 1989, 92, 95, IEEE Communications Mag., 1991. Served to capt. USAF, 1965-68. Scholar Western Electric, 1957-59; trainee NASA, 1962-65 Fellow IEEE (Third Millenium award 2000); mem. Am. Soc. Engring. Edn., Armed Forces Communications and Electronics Assn., Sigma Xi, Tau Beta Pi, Eta Kappa Nu Lutheran. Home: 8315 Pilot Ct Colorado Springs CO 80920-4412 Office: Univ Colo PO Box 7150 Colorado Springs CO 80933-7150 E-mail: ziemer@eas.uccs.edu

ZIERING, MICHAEL, medical products executive; b. 1957; V.p. adminstrn. Diagnostic Products Corp., pres., dir., COO, 1994-99, pres., COO, CEO, 1999—. Office: Diagnostic Products Corp 5700 W 96th St Los Angeles CA 90045-5544

ZIERING, SIGI, medical company executive; b. Kassel, Germany, Mar. 20, 1928; came to U.S., 1949; s. Isaac and Cilly (Frisch) Z.; m. Marilyn Brisman, June 14, 1953; children— Michael, Rosanne, Ira, Amy. B.A., Bklyn. Coll., 1953; M.A., Syracuse U., 1955, Ph.D., 1957. Sr. scientist Raytheon Co., Waltham, Mass., 1957-59; dept. head Allied Research, Boston, 1959-61; pres. Space Scis., Waltham, 1961-68; research dir. Whittaker Corp., Los Angeles, 1968-70; v.p. med. group Dynascis., Los Angeles, 1970-71; pres. Diagnostic Products, Los Angeles, 1972— , also dir. Contbr. articles to physics jours. Pres., Temple Beth Am., Los Angeles, 1979-80. Mem. Am. Phys. Soc., Am. Assn. Clin. Chemists. Office: Diagnostic Products Corp 5700 W 96th St Los Angeles CA 90045-5597

ZIERING, WILLIAM MARK, lawyer; b. New Britain, Conn., Feb. 4, 1931; s. Jacob Max and Esther (Freedman) Z.; m. Harriet Koskoff, Aug. 20, 1958 (div. Sept. 1993); 1 son, Benjamin. B.A., Yale U., 1952; J.D., Harvard U., 1955. Bar: Conn. 1955, Calif. 1962. Assoc. Koskoff & McMahon, Plainville, Conn., 1959-60; sr. trial atty. SEC, San Francisco, 1960-65; pvt. practice law San Francisco, 1965—; ptnr. Bremer & Ziering, 1972-77. Instr. Golden Gate U. Law Sch., San Francisco, 1968-75 Vice pres., bd. dirs. Calif. League Handicapped, 1972— . Served to comdr. USNR, 1955-58. Mem. ABA, Calif. Bar Assn., San Francisco Bar Assn. (past chmn. securities, corps. and banking), Navy League (dir.) Club: Commonwealth. Home: 440 Davis Ct Apt 620 San Francisco CA 94111-2418 Office: 4 Embarcadero Ctr Ste 3400 San Francisco CA 94111-4187

ZIFFREN, KENNETH, lawyer; b. Chgo., June 24, 1940; BA, Northwestern U., 1962; JD, UCLA, 1965. Bar; Calif. 1967. Law clerk to Chief Justice Warren, 1965-66; ptnr. Ziffren, Brittenham, Branca & Fischer, L.A. Mem. ABA, State Bar Calif., L.A. County Bar Assn., Beverly Hills Bar Assn., L.A. Copyright Soc. (pres. 1977-78). Office: Ziffren Brittenham Branca & Fischer 1801 Century Park W Los Angeles CA 90067-6406

ZIL, J. S. psychiatrist, physiologist; b. Chgo. s. Stephen Vincent and Marillyn Charlotte (Jackson) Z.; 1 child, Charlene-Elena. BS magna cum laude, U. Redlands, 1969; MD, U. Calif., San Diego, 1973; MPH, Yale U., 1977; JD with honors, Jefferson Coll., 1985. Med. clk. Clinica de Casa de Todos, Tijuana, Mexico, 1968—70; intern, resient in psychiatry and neurology U. Ariz., 1973-75; fellow in psychiatry, advanced fellow in social, cmty. and forensic psychiatry, Yale cmty. cons. to Conn. State Dept. Corrections Yale U., 1975-77, instr. psychiatry and physiology, 1976-77; instr. physiology U. Mass., 1976-77; unit chief Inpatient and Day Hosp. Conn. Mental Health Ctr. Yale-New Haven Hosp., Inc., 1975-76, unit chief, 1976-77; asst. prof. psychiatry U. Calif., San Francisco, 1977-82, assoc. prof. psychiatry and medicine, 1982-86, vice-chmn. dept. psychiatry, 1983-86; prof. natural sci. Calif. State U., 1985-87; assoc. prof. bioengring. U. Calif., Berkeley, San Francisco, 1982-92, clin. faculty Davis, 1991-99, legis. liaison Ctrl. Office Berkeley, 1988—. Chief psychiatry and neurology VA Med. Ctr., Calif., 1977-86, prin. investigator Sleep Rsch. & Physiology Lab., 1980-86; dir. dept. psychiatry and neurology U. Calif.-San Francisco, Ctrl. San Joaquin Valley Med. Edn. Program and Affiliated Hosps. and Clinics, 1983-86; chief psychiatrist State of Calif. Dept. Corrections, 1986-2000, chief forensic psychiatrist, 2000—; chmn. State of Calif. Inter-Agy. Tech. Adv. Com. on Mentally Ill Inmates & Parolees, 1986-92; mem. med. adv. com. Calif. State Pers. Bd., 1986-95; appointed councillor Calif. State Mental Health Plan, 1988-93; cons. Nat. Inst. Corrections, 1992-94; invited faculty contbr. and editor Am. Coll. Psychiatrist's Resident in Tng. Exam, 1981-86. Author: The Case of the Sleepwalking Rapist, 1992, Mentally Disordered Criminal Offenders, 5 vols., 1989, 2d edit., 1991, Suicide Prevention Handbook, 1987, 2d edit., 1992, 3d edit., 1996, 4th edit., 1996; contbg. author: The Measurement Mandate: On the Road to Performance Improvement in Health Care, 1993; co-author: Psychiatric Services in Jails and Prisons, 2d edit., 2000; assoc. editor Corrective and Social Psychiatry Jour., 1978-97, referee, 1980—, reviewer, 1981—; contbr. articles in field to profl. jours. Nat. Merit scholar, 1965; recipient Nat. Recognition award Bank of Am., 1965, Julian Lee Roberts award U. Redlands, 1969, Kendall award Internat. Symposium in Biochemistry Rsch., 1970, Campus-Wide Profl. Achievement award U. Redlands, 1994. Fellow Royal Soc. Health, Am. Assn. Social Psychiatry; mem. AAUP, APHA, Am. Psychiat. Assn., Am. Assn. Mental Health Profls. in Corrections (nat. pres. 1978-97), Nat. Coun. on Crime and Delinquency, Calif. Scholarship Fedn. (past pres.), Delta Alpha, Alpha Epsilon Delta. Office: PO Box 160208 Sacramento CA 95816-0208 E-mail: corrmentalhealth@aol.com

ZILLY, THOMAS SAMUEL, federal judge; b. Detroit, Jan. 1, 1935; s. George Samuel and Bernice M. (McWhinney) Z.; divorced; children: John, Peter, Paul, Luke; m. Jane Greller Noland, Oct. 8, 1988; stepchildren: Allison Noland, Jennifer Noland. BA, U. Mich., 1956; LLD, Cornell U., 1962. Bar: Wash. 1962, U.S. Ct. Appeals (9th cir.) 1962, U.S. Supreme Ct. 1976. Ptnr. Lane, Powell, Moss & Miller, Seattle, 1962-88; dist. judge U.S. Dist. Ct. (we. dist.) Wash., Seattle, 1988—. Judge pro tem Seattle Mcpl. Ct., 1972-80. Contbr. articles to profl. jours. Mem. Cen. Area Sch. Council, Seattle, 1969-70; scoutmaster Thunderbird Dist. council Boy Scouts Am. Seattle, 1976-84; bd. dirs. East Madison YMCA. Served to lt. (j.g.) USN, 1956-59. Recipient Tuahku Dist. Service to Youth award Boy Scouts Am., 1983. Mem. ABA, Wash. State Bar Assn., Seattle-King County Bar Assn. (treas. 1979-80, trustee 1980-83, sec. 1983-84, 2d v.p. 1984-85, 1st v.p. 1985-86, pres. 1986-87). Office: US Dist Ct 410 US Courthouse 1010 5th Ave Seattle WA 98104-1189

ZIMA, GORDON EVERETT, metallurgist; b. Mason City, Iowa, June 20, 1920; s. Albert Gordon and Agnes Elisabeth (Nolan) Z.; m. Phyllis Anne Main, July 10, 1942; children: Marguerite, Antonia, Paula. AB, Stanford U., 1942; MS, Calif. Inst. Tech., 1952, PhD, 1956. Sr. rsch. engr. Jet Propulsion Lab., Pasadena, Calif., 1946-50; sect. head propulsion Naval Ordnance Test Sta., Pasadena, 1950-55; sr. rsch. metallurgist Internat. Nickel Co., Bayonne, N.J., 1956-58; sr. rsch. specialist GE Hanford Atomic Products, Richland, Wash., 1958-62, Boeing Nuclear Power Divsn., Seattle, 1962-63; sr. rsch. engr. Lawrence Radiation Lab., Livermore, Calif., 1963-70; sr. devel. engr. Battelle Pacific NW Lab., Richland, 1974-83. Patentee on classified materials; contbr. articles to tech. jours including Am. Soc. Metals, Powder Metallurgy, Metal Progress of Am. Soc. Metallurgists. Author: (young readers book) Sun Birds and Evergreens, 1996. 1st lt. U.S. Army Air Corps, 1942-46 PTO. Mem. Sigma Xi, Phi Lamda Upsilon. Avocations: photography, fly fishing, golf, tennis, hiking. Home: 4675 San Anselmo Rd Atascadero CA 93422-2618

ZIMBALIST, EFREM, III, publishing company executive; s. Efrem Zimbalist Jr. BA in Econs., Harvard U., 1968, MBA, 1972. Sr. engagement mgr. McKinsey and Co., Inc., L.A., 1972-77; chmn., CEO, Correia Art Glass, Inc., 1977-92; asst. to group v.p. newspapers Times Mirror, N.Y.C., 1992-93, v.p. strategic devel., 1995; pres., CEO Times Mirror Mags., Inc., N.Y.C., 1995-99; exec. v.p. Times Mirror Co., N.Y.C., 1999; CEO and Chmn. Times Mirror Mags., Inc., N.Y.C., 1999—; CFO, Times Mirror Co., L.A., 1999—. Bd. dirs. Cheniere Energy; trustee Hartford Courant Founds. Mem. nat. coun. House Ear Inst.; chmn. emeritus bd. trustees Robert Louis Stevenson Sch. Officer M.I., U.S. Army, 1969-70, Vietnam. Office: Times Mirror Co Los Angeles CA 20053

ZIMBARDO, PHILIP GEORGE, psychologist, educator, writer; b. N.Y.C., Mar. 23, 1933; s. George and Margaret (Bisicchia) Z.; m. Christina Maslach, Aug. 10, 1972; children: Zara, Tanya; 1 son by previous marriage, Adam. AB, Bklyn. Coll., 1954; MS, Yale U., 1955, PhD, 1959; D (hon.), U. Peru, 1996; LHD in Clin. Psychology, Pacific Grad. Sch. Psychology, 1996, D (hon.), 1997, Nat. U. of San Martin, 1996, Nat. U. Peru, Thessalonoki, Greece, 1997, Aristotle U., 1998. Asst. prof. psychology Yale U., New Haven, 1959-61, NYU, N.Y.C., 1961-67; vis. assoc. prof. psychology Columbia U., N.Y.C., 1967-68; prof. psychology Stanford (Calif.) U., 1968—. Pres. P.G. Zimbardo, Inc., San Francisco. Author: Cognitive Control of Motivation, 1969, Canvassing for Peace, 1970, Psychology and Life, 16th edit., 2000, Shyness, What It Is, What To Do About It, 1977, Influencing Attitudes and Changing Behavior, rev. edit., 1977, The Shyness Workbook, 1979, A Parent's Guide to the Shy Child, 1981, reprinted, 1999, The Psychology of Attitude Change and Social Influence, 1991, Psychology, 3rd edit., 1999. Sr. project advisor Exploratorium, 1993; host, writer, gen. acad. advisor PBS-TV series Discovering Psychology, 1987-90. Ctr. for Advanced Study of Behavioral Scis. fellow, 1971; recipient Peace medal Tokyo Police Dept., 1972, City Medal of Honor, Salamanca, Spain, Disting. Tchr. award Am. Psychol. Found., 1975. Fellow APA (pres. 2002—, Presdl. citation Discovery Psychology series 1994, Tchg. award 1999); mem. Am. Psychol. Soc., AAUP, Internat. Congress Psychology, Western Psychol. Assn. (pres. 1983, 2000), Ea. Psychol. Assn., Calif. Psychol. Assn. (Disting. Contbn. to Rsch. award 1978), Soc. for Psychol. Study of Social Issues, Sigma Xi, Phi Beta Kappa, Psi Chi. Roman Catholic. Home: 25 Montclair Ter San Francisco CA 94109-1517 Office: Stanford U Psychology Dept Stanford CA 94305 E-mail: zim@psych.stanford.edu

ZIMENT, IRWIN, medical educator; b. England, 1936; MB BChir, Cambridge U., 1961. Intern, resident, England, 1961-64, USA, 1964-65; resident Bronx Mcpl. Hosp. Ctr., 1965-66; dir. respiratory therpay Harbor Gen. Hosp., Torrance, Calif., 1968-75; chief medicine Olive View-UCLA Med. Ctr., 1975—, med. dir., 1994-97; prof. medicine UCLA Sch. Medicine, 1980—. Contbr. articles to profl. jours. Infectious Disease fellow Wadsworth VA Hosp., L.A., 1966-68. Mem. Am. Thoracic Soc. (clin. problems assembly chmn. 1981-82 , resp. bd. med. advisors 1986-90), Am. Coll. Chest Physicians (mem. editl. bd.), Nat. Assn. Med. Dir. Respiratory Care (founding mem., vice pres. 1978, treas. 1979-81, bd. dirs. 1983-89, 98—), Calif Thoracic Soc. (pres. 1980-81, various coms. 1970-85), L.A. Lung Assn. (various coms. 1969-86). Office: Olive View UCLA Med Ctr Dept Med Rm 2B 182 14445 Olive View Dr Sylmar CA 91342-1437

ZIMET, CARL NORMAN, psychologist, educator; b. Vienna, Austria, June 3, 1925; came to U.S., 1943, naturalized, 1945; s. Leon and Gisela (Kosser) Z.; m. Sara F. Goodman, June 4, 1950; children: Andrew, Gregory. BA, Cornell U., 1949; PhD, Syracuse U., 1953; postdoctoral fellow, Standard U., 1953-55. Diplomate in clin. psychology Am. Bd. Profl. Psychology (trustee 1966-74). Instr., then asst. prof. psychology and psychiatry Yale U., 1955-63; mem. faculty U. Colo. Med. Center, 1963—, prof. clin. psychology, 1965—, head div., 1963—. Mem. Colo. Bd. Psychol. Examiners, 1966-72, Colo. Mental Health Planning Commn., 1964-66; mem. acad. adv. com. John F. Kennedy Child Devel. Center, U. Colo., 1966-68; chmn. Council for Nat. Register of Health Service Providers in Psychology, 1975-85, pres., mem. exec. bd. div. psychotherapy, 1970-89; chair exec. com. Assn. Psychol. Internship Ctrs., 1988-91. Bd. editors: Jour. Clin. Psychology, 1962-91, Jour. Clin. and Cons. Psychology, 1964-73, Psychotherapy, 1967—, Profl. Psychology, 1969-75. With USNR, 1943-46. Recipient Disting. Service award Colo. Psychol. Assn., 1976 Fellow APA (council reps. 1969-72, 73—, bd. dirs. 1985-88, Disting. award for profl. contbn. 1987, div. psychotherapy and div. clin. psychology), Soc. Personality Assessment (pres. 1975-76, bd. [illegible] Psychology (pres. 1993—), Denver Psychoanalytic (trustee 1968-71), Med. Sch. Profs. Psychology (pres. 1992-94). Home: 4325 E 6th Ave Denver CO 80220-4939 E-mail: Carl.Zimet@uchsc.edu

ZIMMER, GEORGE, men's apparel executive; CEO Men's Wearhouse, Fremont, Calif. Office: Mens Wearhouse 40650 Encyclopedia Cir Fremont CA 94538-2453

ZIMMER, LARRY WILLIAM, JR. sports announcer; b. New Orleans, Nov. 13, 1935; s. Lawrence W. Sr. and Theodora (Ahrens) Z.; m. Dawn M. Caillouet, June 4, 1955 (div. June 1972); children: Larry III, Tracey; m. Brigitte Bastian, Nov. 17, 1972. Student, La. State U., 1953-55; BJ, U. Mo., 1957. Sports dir. KFRU Radio, Columbia, Mo., 1960-66; asst. mgr. programming WAAM Radio, Ann Arbor, Mich., 1966-71; broadcaster football, basketball, 1966-70; sportscaster, sports dir. KOA Radio, Denver, 1971—; broadcaster Denver Broncos Football, 1971-96; broadcaster football, basketball Colo., 1971—; broadcaster Denver Rockets, 1972-74. Bd. mem. Colo. Ski Mus. and Hall of Fame, Vail, 1981—, Opera Colo., Denver, 1985—, Colo. chap. Nat. Football Found; adv. bd. Jefferson Co. Youth Advocacy Ctr. 1st lt. U.S. Army, 1958-60. Named Colo. Sportscaster of the Yr., Nat. Sportscasters and Sportswriters Assn., Salisbury, N.C., 1988, 90, 91, Broadcaster of the Yr., Colo. Broadcaster's Assn., Denver, 1995; recipient Powerade award for best radio/TV sports story of yr. Nat. Sportscasters and Sportswriters Assn., 2000. Avocations: skiing, jogging, opera. Office: KOA Radio 4695 S Monaco St Denver CO 80237-3403 E-mail: larryzimmer@clearchannel.com

ZIMMERER, KATHY LOUISE, university art gallery director; b. Whittier, Calif., Dec. 9, 1951; BA cum laude, U. Calif., Berkeley, 1974; MA, Williams Coll., 1976. From tour guide to curatorial asst. Sterling and Francine Clark Inst., Williamstown, Mass., 1975-76; spl. asst. dept. modern art L.A. County Mus. Art, 1976-77; mus. edn. fellow Fine Arts Mus. San Francisco, 1977-78; dir. coll. art gallery SUNY, New Paltz, 1978-80; cons. in field, 1980-81; dir. univ. art gallery Calif. State U., Dominguez Hills, 1982—. Project dir. Painted Light: California Impressionist Paintings from the Gardena H.S./L.A. Unified Sch. Dist., 1996—. Mem. Internat. Assn. Art Critics, Art Table. Office: Univ Art Gallery Calif State U 1000 E Victoria St Carson CA 90747-0001 E-mail: kzimmerer@cas.csudh.edu

ZIMMERMAN, BERNARD, judge; b. Munich, Fed. Republic Germany, May 31, 1946; came to U.S., 1949; s. Sam and Roza (Spodek) Z.; m. Grace L. Suarez, Oct. 23, 1976; children: Elizabeth, Adam, David, Dara Bylah. AB, U. Rochester, 1967; JD, U. Chgo., 1970. Bar: Calif. 1971, La. 1971, U.S. Supreme Ct. 1975, U.S. Dist. Ct. (no., ea., cen. and so. dists.) Calif., U.S. Dist. Ct. (ea. dist.) La., U.S. Ct. Appeals (9th cir.). Law. clk. chief judge U.S. Dist. Ct. (ea. dist.) La., New Orleans, 1970-71; asst. prof. law La. State U., Baton Rouge, 1971-72; ptnr. Pillsbury, Madison & Sutro, San Francisco, 1972-95; legal cons. 3d Constnl. Conv. Commonwealth of the No. Mariana Islands, Northern Mariana Islands, 1995; U.S. magistrate judge U.S. Dist. Ct. (no. dist.) Calif., 1995—. Dep. pub. defender City of San Francisco, 1975; arbitrator U.S. Dist. Ct., San Francisco, AAA; judge pro tem San Francisco Superior and Mcpl. Cts. Bd. dirs., mem. exec. com. San Francisco Lawyers' Com. on Urban Affairs, 1984-95, treas., 1987; mem. regional bd. Anti-Defamation League, 1989-95. Mem. Phi Beta Kappa. Democrat. Jewish. Club: Olympic (San Francisco). Office: 450 Golden Gate Ave San Francisco CA 94102-3661

ZIMMERMAN, EVERETT LEE, English educator, academic administrator; b. Lancaster, Pa., Dec. 9, 1936; s. Amos Wanner and Anna (Sensenig) Z.; m. Muriel Laden, Apr. 28, 1963, children: Andrew, Daniel. BA, Bob Jones U., 1958; MA, Temple U., 1961, PhD, 1966. Lectr. Temple U., Phila., 1961-62; instr. Rutgers U., Camden, N.J., 1962-66, asst. prof., 1966-69, U. Calif., Santa Barbara, 1969-72, assoc. prof., 1972-80, prof. English, 1980—, dean, 1988-89, provost, 1997—. Author: Defoe and the Novel, 1975, Swift's Narrative Satires, 1983, The Boundaries of Fiction, 1996; also articles. Dem. committeeman, Phila., 1965-66. Jr. Faculty fellow, 1971, Humanities Inst. fellow, 1975 U. Calif.; NEH grantee, 1986; Guggenheim fellow, 1989-90. Mem. MLA, Am. Soc. 18th Century Studies. Home: 1822 Prospect Ave Santa Barbara CA 93103-1950 Office: U Calif Coll Letters & Sci Office of Provost Santa Barbara CA 93106 E-mail: ezimmer@humanitas.UCSB.edu

ZIMMERMAN, GAIL MARIE, medical foundation executive; b. Fort Wayne, Ind., June 23, 1945; d. Albert Douglas and Aina Dorothy (Johnson) Z. BA, U. Puget Sound, 1967. Intelligence analyst CIA, Washington, 1970-72; research asst. Arthur Young & Co., Portland, Oreg., 1972-74; emergency med. service planner Marion-Polk-Yamhill Counties, Salem, 1975-76; health cons. Freedman Assocs., Portland, 1976-77; legis. asst. U.S. Senator Bob Packwood, Portland, 1977-78; exec. dir. Nat. Psoriasis Found., Portland, 1979—. Mem. dermatology panel U.S. Parmacopoeial Conv., 1985-94; lay rep. Nat. Inst. Arthritis, Musculoskeletal and Skin Disease, NIH, 1990-94. Founding bd. dirs. Nat. Abortion Rights Action League, Portland, 1977; pres. bd. dirs. Oreg. Common Cause, Portland, 1977-78 Mem. Internat. Fedn. Psoriasis Assn. (pres. 1995-2001, v.p. 2001—, chair 1995-2001, vice chair 2001—). Democrat Avocations: tennis; flute. Office: Nat Psoriasis Found 6600 SW 92nd Ave Ste 300 Portland OR 97223-7195 E-mail: gail@npfupa.org

ZIMMERMAN, HAROLD SAMUEL, retired state legislator, newspaper editor and publisher, state administrator; b. Valley City, N.D., June 1, 1923; s. Samuel Alwin and Lulu (Wylie) Z.; m. Julianne Williams, Sept. 12, 1946; children: Karen, Steven, Judi Jean (dec.). BA, U. Wash., 1947. News editor Sedro-Woolley (Wash.) Courier-Times, 1947-50; editor, pub. Advocate, Castle Rock, Wash., 1950-57; pub. Post-Record, Camas, 1957-80, assoc. pub., columnist, 1980; assoc. pub., columnist, dir. Eagle Publs., Camas, 1980-88. Mem. Wash. Ho. of Reps., 1967-80; mem. Wash. Senate, 1981-88, Wash. State Environ. Hearings Bd., Lacey, 1988-93. Mem. Grange, Lions, Kiwanis, Sigma Delta Chi, Sigma Chi. Republican. United Methodist. E-mail: hszim@aol.com

ZIMMERMAN, MICHAEL DAVID, lawyer; b. Chgo., Oct. 21, 1943; s. Elizabeth Porter; m. Lynne Mariani (dec. 1994); children: Evangeline Albright, Alessandra Mariani, Morgan Elisabeth; m. Diane Hamilton, 1998. BS, U. Utah, 1966, JD, 1969. Bar: Calif. 1971, Utah 1978. Law clk. to Chief Justice Warren Earl Burger U.S. Supreme Ct., Washington, 1969-70; assoc. O'Melveny & Myers, L.A., 1970-76; assoc. prof. law U. Utah, 1976-78, adj. prof. law, 1978-84, 89-93; of counsel Kruse, Landa, Zimmerman & Maycock, Salt Lake City, 1978-80; spl. counsel Gov. of Utah, Salt Lake City, 1978-80; ptnr. Watkiss & Campbell, Salt Lake City, 1980-84; assoc. justice Supreme Ct. Utah, Salt Lake City, 1984-93, 98-00, chief justice, 1994-98; atty., mediator, arbitrator, of counsel Snell & Wilmer, Salt Lake City, 2000—. Co-moderator Justice Soc. Program of Snowbird Inst. for Arts and Humanities, 1991, 92, 93, 94, 95, 97, 98; moderator, Tanner lecture panel dept. philosophy U. Utah, 1994; faculty Judging Sci. Program Duke U., 1992, 93; bd. dirs. Conf. of Chief Justices, 1995-98. Note editor: Utah Law Rev., 1968-69; contbr. numerous articles to legal publs. Mem. Project 2000, Coalition for Utah's Future, 1985-96; trustee Hubert and Eliza B. Michael Found., 1994-98, Rowland-Hall St. Mark's Sch., 1997—, Utah Mus. Natural History Found., 1997—; bd. dirs. Summit Inst. for Arts and Humanities, 1998—, chair, 1999—; bd. dirs. Hansen Planetarium, 1998—, Snowbird Inst. for Arts & Humanities, 1989-98, Deer Valley Inst. for Arts & Humanities, 1996-98; bd. dirs. Kanzeon Zen Ctr., 1999—, chair, 2000—; bd. dirs., chair Utah Coun. on Conflict Resolution, 1999—; mem. Pvt. Adjudication Ctr., Duke U., 2000—; co-dir., chair, Registry of Ind. Sci. and Tech. Advisors, 2000—. Named Utah State Bar Appellate Ct. Judge of Yr., 1988; recipient Excellence in Ethics award, Ctr. for Study of Ethics, 1994, Disting. Svc. award Utah State Bar, 1998, Individual Achievement award Downtown Alliance, 1998; participant Justice and Soc. Program of Aspen Inst. for Humanistic Studies, 1988, co-moderator, 1989. Fellow Am. Bar Found.; mem. ABA (faculty mem. appellate judges' seminar 1993), Am. Law Inst., Utah Bar Assn., Salt Lake County Bar Assn., Jud. Conf. U.S. (adv. com. civil rules 1985-91), Utah Jud. Coun. (supreme ct. rep. 1986-91, chair 1994-98), Am. Inns of Ct. VII, Am. Judicature Soc. (bd. dirs. 1995—), Order of Coif, Phi Kappa Phi. Office: Snell & Wilmer 15 West South Temple Ste 1200 Salt Lake City UT 84101

ZIMMERMAN, WILLIAM ROBERT, entrepreneur, engineering based manufacturing company executive; b. Cleve., May 11, 1927; s. Irving and Ella (Berger) Z.; m. Nancy Owen, 1963 (div. 1970); 1 child, Amanda; m. Eileen Samuelson, Nov. 11, 1979. BS, MIT, 1948, MS, 1949. Cons. Kurt Salmon Assocs., Washington, 1949-50, A.T. Kearney and Co., Chgo., 1950-52; mill mgr. Am. Envelope Co., West Carrollton, Ohio, 1952-56; exec. v.p. Avery Internat., Pasadena, Calif., 1956-67; pres. Swedlow, Inc., Garden Grove, 1967-73, Monogram Industries, Inc., Santa Monica, 1973-78. Bd. dirs. Avtel, Mojave, Calif., OSO Techs., Rancho Cucamonga, Calif., Monitor Products, Inc., Oceanside, Calif., Summa Industries, Fullerton, Calif. Pres. coun. Boy Scouts Am., Painesville, Ohio, 1957-62; exec. com. Jr. Achievement So. Calif., L.A., 1975-77; trustee Los Angeles County Mus. Nat. History, 1987-97, Harvey Mudd Coll., Claremont, Calif., 1983—. Republican. Clubs: Calif. (Los Angeles); Valley Hunt, Annendale (Pasadena). Avocations: tennis, jogging, golf. Office: Zimmerman Holdings Inc PO Box 3570 South Pasadena CA 91031-6570

ZIMMERMANN, JOHN PAUL, plastic surgeon; b. Milw., Mar. 9, 1945; s. Paul August and Edith Josephine (Tutsch) Z.; m. Bianca Maria Schaldach, June 13, 1970; cbildren: Veronica, Jean-Paul. BS in Biology, Chemistry, Marquette U., 1966; MD, Med. Coll. Wis., 1970. Diplomate Am Bd. Plastic Surgery. Internship surgery Stanford U. Sch. of Medicine, Calif., 1970-71, residency in gen. surgery, plastic & reconstructive surgery, 1974-79; flight surgeon USAF, 1971-73; fellowship head & neck surgery Roswell Park Meml. Cancer Inst., Buffalo, 1977; pvt. practice Napa, Calif., 1979—. Dir. Aesthetic Surgery Ctr. of Napa Valley, Calif., 1993—; clinical asst. prof. of plastic surgery Stanford U. Sch. of Medicine, Calif., 1993—; bd. dirs. Interplast, Palo Alto, Calif. (pres., bd. dirs. 1991-94, chmn. bd. dirs. 1994-95). Mem. Am. Soc. Plastic Surgeons, Am. Soc. Aesthetic Plastic Surgeons, Lipoplasty Soc., Calif. Soc. Plastic Surgeons (bd. dirs.), Calif. Med. Assn., Napa County Med. Assn. Republican. Roman Catholic. Avocations: sailing, golf, direct care of indigent patientsthrough Interplast. Office: Plastic Reconstructive Surgery Ctr 3443 Villa Ln Ste 10 Napa CA 94558-6417

ZIMRING, FRANKLIN E. law educator, lawyer; b. 1942; BA, Wayne State U., 1963; JD, U. Chgo., 1967. Bar: Calif. 1968. Asst. prof. U. Chgo., 1967-69, assoc. prof., 1969-72, prof., 1972-85; co-dir. Ctr. for Studies in Criminal Justice, 1973-75, dir., 1975-86; prof. law dir. Earl Warren Legal Inst., Univ. Calif., Berkeley, 1985—. Author: (with Newton) Firearms and Violence in American Life, 1969; The Changing Legal World of Adolescence, 1982; (with Hawkins): Deterrence, 1973, Capital Punishment and the American Agenda, 1986, The Scale of Imprisonment, 1991, The Search for Rational Drug Control, 1992, Incapacitation: Penal Confinement and the Restraint of Crime, 1995, Crime is Not the Problem, 1997, American Youth Violence, 1998, Punishment and Democracy, 2001. Mem. Am. Acad. Arts and Scis. Office: U Calif Earl Warren Legal Inst Boalt Hall Berkeley CA 94720 E-mail: zimring@law.berkeley.edu

ZINGALE, DONALD PAUL, academic administrator, educator; b. Bklyn., Aug. 3, 1946; s. Charles and Helen (Puglisi) Z. BS in Health, Phys. Edn., Bklyn. Coll., 1967; MS in Phys. Edn., U. Mass., 1969; PhD in Phys. Edn., Ohio State U., 1973; MSW, Calif. State U., Sacramento, 1984. Lic. clin. social worker, Calif.; lic. marriage and family counselor, Calif.; cert. health and phys. edn. instr. secondary schs., N.Y.C., N.Y.; cert. Alpine ski instr. Prof., assoc. dean health, human svcs. Calif. State U., Sacramento, 1973-93, assoc. v.p. rsch. and grad. studies, 1993-95; withColl. Health and Human Svcs. San Francisco U., 2000. Contbr. articles to profl. jours. and publs. Mem. APHA, Am. Assn. Health Physical Edn., Recreation, and Dance, Am. Assn. Higher Edn., Nat. Coun. U. Rsch. Adminstrs., Congress Faculty Assns., Profl. Ski Instrs. Am. Roman Catholic. Avocations: Alpine skiing, sailing, traveling, cooking, home renovation. Office: Coll Health & Human Svcs San Francisco State U 1600 Holloway Ave San Francisco CA 94132

ZINMAN, DAVID JOEL, conductor; b. N.Y.C., July 9, 1936; s. Samuel and Rachel Ilo (Samuels) Z.; m. Leslie Heyman (dec.); children: Paul Pierre, Rachel Linda; m. Mary Ingham, May 19, 1974; 1 child, Raphael. B.Mus., Oberlin (Ohio) Conservatory, 1958; M.A., U. Minn., 1961. Asst. to Pierre Monteux, 1961-64; guest condr. U.S. and Europe; music dir. Netherlands Chamber Orch., 1964-77, Rochester (N.Y.) Philharm. Orch., 1974-85; prin. guest condr. Rotterdam Philharm. Orch., 1977-79, chief condr., 1979-82; prin. guest condr., music dir. designate Balt. Symphony Orch., 1983-85, music dir., 1985-98, Tonhalle Orch., Zurich, Switzerland, 1995; music dir. designate Aspen (Colo.) Music Festival and Sch., 1997, music dir., 1998—. Adj. prof. Eastman Sch. Music, Rochester Rec. artist Phillips, Nonesuch, Decca/London, Decca/Argo, Angel/EMI, Telarc, Sony Classical. Recipient Grand Prix du Disque, 1967, 82, Edison award, 1967, 3 Grammy awards, 1990, Grammophone best selling record award, 1993, Grammophone award, 1994, Deutschen Schallplatten prize, George Peabody medal outstanding contbn. music in Am., 1996. Office: Aspen Music Festival & Sch 2 Music School Rd Aspen CO 81611-8500

ZINN, RAY, computer company executive; CEO Micrel, San Jose, Calif. Office: Micrel 1849 Fortune Dr San Jose CA 95131-1724

ZIPPIN, CALVIN, epidemiologist, educator; b. Albany, N.Y., July 17, 1926; s. Samuel and Jennie (Perkel) Z.; m. Patricia Jayne Schubert, Feb. 9, 1964; children: David Benjamin, Jennifer Dorothy. AB magna cum laude, SUNY, Albany, 1947; ScD, Johns Hopkins U., Balt., 1953. Rsch. asst. Sterling-Winthrop Rsch. Inst., Rensselaer, N.Y., 1947-50; instr. biostats. Sch. Pub. Health, U. Calif., Berkeley, 1953-55; asst. to full rsch. biostatistician Sch. Medicine U. Calif., San Francisco, 1955-67, asst. prof. preventive medicine, 1958-60; post doctoral fellow London Sch. Hygiene and Tropical Medicine, 1964-65; prof. epidemiology U. Calif., San Francisco, 1967-91, prof. emeritus, 1991—. Vis. assoc. prof. stats. Stanford U., 1962; adv. WHO, 1969—; vis research worker Middlesex Hosp. Med. Sch., London, 1975; various coms. Am. Cancer Soc. and Nat. Cancer Inst., 1956—; faculty adviser Regional Cancer Centre, Trivandrum, India, 1983—; cons., lectr., vis. prof. in field. Co-author book, book chpts.; author or co-author papers primarily on biometry and epidemiology of cancer; editorial advisor Jour. Stats. in Medicine, Boston, 1981-86. Mem., alt. mem. Dem. Ctrl. Com., Marin County, Calif., 1987-96. Recipient Disting. Alumnus award SUNY, Albany, 1969, also awards, fellowships and grants for work in cancer biometry and epidemiology. Fellow Am. Statis. Assn., Am. Coll. Epidemiology, Royal Statis. Soc. Gt. Britain; mem. Biometric Soc. (mem. internat. coun. 1978-81, pres. Western N.Am. region 1979-80), Calif. Cancer Registrars Assn. (hon.), Internat. Assn. Cancer Registries (hon.), B'nai B'rith (pres. Golden Gate lodge 1970-71, pres. Greater San Francisco Bay area coun. 1974-75), Phi Beta Kappa, Sigma Xi, Delta Omega. Office: Univ Calif Dept Epidemiology Biostats San Francisco CA 94143-0001 E-mail: czippin@itsa.ucsf.edu

ZIRIN, HAROLD, astronomer, educator; b. Boston, Oct. 7, 1929; s. Jack and Anna Zirin; m. Mary Noble Fleming, Apr. 20, 1957; children: Daniel Meyer, Dana Mary. AB, Harvard U., 1950, AM, 1951, PhD, 1952. Asst. phys. scientist RAND Corp., 1952-53; lectr. Harvard, 1953-55; research staff High Altitude Obs., Boulder, Colo., 1955-64; prof. astrophysics Calif. Inst. Tech., 1964-98, prof. emeritus, 1998—; staff mem. Hale Obs., 1964-80; chief astronomer Big Bear Solar Obs., 1969-80, dir., 1980-97; Disting. Rsch. Prof. N.J. Inst. Tech., 1996—. U.S.- USSR exchange scientist, 1960-61; vis. prof. Coll. de France, 1986, Japan Soc. P. Sci., 1992. Author: The Solar Atmosphere, 1966, Astrophysics of the Sun, 1987; co-translator: Five Billion Vodka Bottles to the Moon, 1991; adv. editor: Soviet Astronomy, 1965-69; editor Magnetic and Velocity Fields of Solar Active Regions. Trustee Polique Canyon Assn., 1977-90. Agassiz fellow, 1951-52; Sloan fellow, 1958-60; Guggenheim fellow, 1960-61 Mem. Am. Astron. Soc., Internat. Astron. Union, AURA (dir. 1977-83) Home: 1178 Sonoma Dr Altadena CA 91001-3150 Office: Calif Inst Tech 264 33 Pasadena CA 91125-0001 E-mail: hz@caltech.edu

ZIRKLE, LEWIS GREER, orthopedist; b. Pittsfield, Mass., July 23, 1940; s. Lewis Greer and Vivian (Shaw) Z.; m. Sara K. Zirkle, Aug. 24, 1963; children: Elizabeth, Molly, Julie. BS, Davidson Coll., 1962; MD, Duke U., 1966. Intern Duke U. Hosp., 1966-67, resident, 1968-73, U.S. Army, Shriner's Hosp., 1967-68; pvt. practice Richland, Wash., 1973—. Chmn. program in Vietnam, Orthopedics Overseas, 1992—; bd. dirs., pres. S.E. Asia helmet program, Surg. Implant Generations Network. Contbr. articles to profl. jours. Maj. U.S. Army, 1968-73. Recipient Kiwanis World Svc. medal, 1997; named Vol. of Yr., Orthopedics Overseas. Presbyterian. Avocations: reading, sports. Home: 2548 Harris Ave Richland WA 99352-1638 Office: NW Orthopedics 875 Swift Blvd Richland WA 99352-3592

ZIVE, GREGG WILLIAM, judge; b. Chgo., Aug. 9, 1945; s. Simon Louis and Betty Jane (Hansen) Z.; m. Franny Alice Forsman, Sept. 3, 1966; children: Joshua Carleton; m. Lu Ann Zive, June 9, 1974; 1 child, Dana Mary. BA in Journalism, U. Nev., 1967; JD magna cum laude, U. Notre Dame, 1973. Bar: Calif. 1973, Nev. 1976, U.S. Ct. Appeals (9th cir.), U.S. Supreme Ct. Assoc. Gray, Cary, Ames & Frye, San Diego, 1973-75, Breen, Young, Whitehead & Hoy, Reno, 1975-76; ptnr. Hale Lane, Peek, Dennison & Howard, Reno, 1977-90, Lionel, Sawyer & Collins, Reno, 1990-92, Bible, Hoy, Trachok, Wadhams & Zive, 1992-95; U.S. bankruptcy judge Dist. Nev., 1995—. Lectr. bus. law U. Nev., 1977—. Note and comment editor Notre Dame, 1972-73; contbr. articles to profl. jours. Bd. dirs. Washoe Youth Found., 1977-81, Jr. Achievement; commr. Washoe County Parks, 1988-95, chmn., 1990; trustee U. Nev., Reno Found., 1986-94, trustee emeritus, 1994—, chmn., 1993, exec. bd., 1991-96; bd. dirs. YMCA Sierra, 1989-95; mem. univ. legis. rels. com., 1986-95; dir. Friends of Libr., 1995—, v.p., 1998; mem. adv. com. Sparks Redevelopment Authority, 1992—; trustee Access to Justice Found., 1998—. 1st lt. U.S. Army, 1968-70. Mem. Calif. Bar Assn., State Nev. Bar Assn. (law related edn. com.), San Diego County Bar Assn., Washoe County Bar Assn. (exec. bd. 1987-93, pres. 1992-93), Nat. Conf. Bankruptcy Judges (bd. govs. 1998—), Am. Bankruptcy Inst., Master Inns Ct., Bruce Thompson Chpt., Am. Judicature Soc., Vol. Lawyers Washoe County (bd. dirs. 1991), Washoe Legal Svc. (bd. dirs. 1992-96, pres. 1996), Soc. Profl. Journalists, U. Nev. Alumni Assn. (coun. 1981-87, pres. 1986-87), Univ. Club (dir., past pres.).

ZLAKET, THOMAS A. state supreme court chief justice; b. May 30, 1941; AB in Polit. Sci., U. Notre Dame, 1962; LLB, U. Ariz., 1965. Bar: Ariz. 1965, U.S. Dist. Ct. Ariz. 1967, U.S. Ct. Appeals (9th cir.) 1969, Calif. 1976. Atty. Lesher Scruggs Rucker Kimble & Lindamood, Tucson, 1965-68, Maud & Zlaket, 1968-70, Estes Browning Maud and Zlaket, 1970-73, Slutes Estes Zlaket Sakrison & Wasley, 1973-82, Zlaket & Zlaket, 1982-92; judge pro tempore Pima County (Ariz.) Superior Ct., 1983—; justice Ariz. Supreme Ct., 1992, vice chief justice, 1996, chief justice, 1997. Fellow Am. Coll. Trial Lawyers, Am. Bar Found., Ariz. Bar Found.; mem. ABA, Pima County Bar Assn., Am. Bd. Trial Advocates, Ariz. Coll. Trial Advocacy, U. Ariz. Law Coll. Assn., Ariz. Law Rev. Assn. Office: Arizona Supreme Ct 1501 W Washington St Phoenix AZ 85007-3222

ZOBELL, CHARLES W. newspaper managing editor; b. Provo, Utah, Mar. 17, 1950; m. Marilyn M. Earl, May 5, 1978; children: David, Rebecca. BA in Comm., Brigham Young U., 1974. Reporter Las Vegas Rev.-Jour., 1975-78; dir. Office Intergovtl. Rels. City of Las Vegas, 1978-80; city editor Las Vegas Rev.-Jour., 1980-92, mng. editor, 1992—. Vol. rep. Mormon Ch., Argentina, 2 yrs. Office: Las Vegas Review Jour Donrey Med Grp PO Box 70 1111 W Bonanza Rd Las Vegas NV 89125

ZOHN, MARTIN STEVEN, lawyer; b. Denver, Oct. 22, 1947; s. William and Alice (Lewis) Z.; m. Carol Falender, June 6, 1980; children: David Joseph, Daniel Robert. BA, Ind. U., 1969; JD, Harvard U., 1972. Bar: Calif. 1972, Ind. 1973, U.S. Ct. Claims 1980, U.S. Supreme Ct. 1980, U.S. Ct. Appeals (9th cir.) 1981. Assoc. Cadick, Burns, Duck & Neighbors, Indpls., 1972-77, ptnr., 1977-80, Pacht, Ross, Warne, Bernhard & Sears, Inc., L.A., 1980-86, Shea & Gould, L.A., 1986-89, Proskauer Rose LLP, L.A., 1989—. Pres. Indpls. Settlements, Inc., 1977-79. Bd. dirs. Pub. Counsel, 2001—. Mem. Fin. Lawyers Conf., L.A. County Bar Assn. (exec. com. prejudgment remedies sect. 1985-92), Beverly Hills Bar Assn. (exec. com. bus. law sect. 1985-92), Phi Beta Kappa. E-mail. mzohn@proskauer.com

ZOHOURI, SAEED, electronics company executive; MS in Chemistry, Manchester U., Eng.; D in Chemistry, Stanford U. former chemistry instr. Razi U., Iran. Various positions to chief technology officer, pres. N.Am. Solectron Corp., Milpitas, Calif., 1980-99, sr. v.p., CEO, 1999—. Office: Solectron Corp 777 Gibraltar Dr Milpitas CA 95035

ZOOK, TOM, state senator; b. Miles City, Mont., Jan. 29, 1932; m. Isabel Zook. Diploma, Custer County H.S. Rancher; Rep. rep. dist. 3 Mont. Ho. of Reps., 1988-2000; Rep. senator dist. 2 Mont. State Senate, 2000—. Mem. adv. bd. Fed. Intermediate Credit Bank, Spokane; chair appropriations Mont. State Senate, joint appropriations subcom. on long-range planning. Mem. Miles City PCA; trustee Sch. Bd. With USN, 1951-55. Office: HC 40 Miles City MT 59301-9806 also: Capitol Station Helena MT 59620

ZORNES, MILFORD, artist; b. Camargo, Okla., Jan. 25, 1908; s. James Francis and Clara Delphine (Lindsay) Z.; m. Gloria Codd, 1935; 1 son, Franz Milford; m. Patricia Mary Palmer, Nov. 8, 1942; 1 dau., Maria Patricia. Student, Otis Art Inst., Los Angeles, 1929, Pomona Coll., , 1930-34. Instr. art Pomona Coll., 1946-50; art dir. Vortox and Padua Hills Theatre, Claremont, 1954-66. Exhibited, Calif. Watercolor Soc., Met. Mus., Am. Watercolor Soc., Corcoran Gallery, Bklyn. Mus., Denver Mus., Cleve. Mus., L.A. Mus., Brooks Gallery, London, Bombay Art Assn., Chgo. Art Inst., Butler Mus., Gallery Modern Masters, Washington, Santa Barbara (Calif.) Mus., Cin. Mus., Laguna (Calif.) Art Gallery, Oklahoma City Mus., Springville (Utah) Mus., Claremont (Calif.) Fine Arts, Anderson Art Gallery, Sunset Beach, Calif.; represented in permanent collections at L.A. Mus., White House Collection, Met. Mus., Pentagon Bldg., Butler Mus., UCLA, Nat. Acad., San Diego Mus., L.A. County Fair, Home Savs. and Loan Assn., L.A., Corcoran Gallery, Washington; mem. art com., Nat. Orange Show, San Bernardino, Calif., 1963-65; author: A Journey to Nicaragua, 1977, The California Style: California Watercolor Artists, 1925-1955, 1985; subject of book by Gordon McClelland: Milford Zornes, Hillcrest Press, 1991. Served with U.S. Army, 1943-45, CBI. Recipient Paul Prescott Barrow award Pomona Coll., 1987, David Prescott Burrows award, 1991, A Most Disting. Citizen award So. Utah State Coll., 1988, Am. Artist Achievement award Am. Artist Mag., 1994; named Nat. Academician. Mem. NAD, Am. Watercolor Soc., Southwestern Watercolor Soc., Watercolor West, Nat. Watercolor Soc., Utah Watercolor Soc. Address: 2136 Brescia Ave Claremont CA 91711-1804

ZSCHAU, MARILYN, singer; b. Chgo., Feb. 9, 1944; d. Edwin Arthur Eugene and Helen Elizabeth (Kelly) Z. BA in Radio, TV and Motion Pictures, U. N.C.; ed., Juilliard Sch. Music; opera theatre with Christopher West, voice with Florence Page Kimball, also studied with John Lester. Toured with Met. Nat. Co., 1965-66; debut, Vienna Volksoper, in Die Tote Stadt, 1967, Vienna Staatsoper, in Ariadne auf Naxos, 1971; with N.Y.C. Opera in La Fanciulla del West, 1978; debut Met. Opera, in La Boheme, 1985, La Scala, in Die Frau ohne Schatten, 1986, Royal Opera, Covent Garden in La Boheme, 1982; has toured and sung in many countries including S.Am. and Australia. Office: 4245 Wilshire Blvd Oakland CA 94602-3549

ZSIGMOND, VILMOS, cinematographer, director; b. Szeged, Hungary, June 16, 1930; came to U.S., 1957, naturalized, 1962; s. Vilmos and Bozena (Illichmann) Z.; children: Julia, Susi. MA, U. Film and Theater Arts, Budapest, Hungary, 1955. Free-lance cinematographer for numerous commls., also ednl., documentary and low-budget feature films, 1965-71; now dir., cinematographer on commls. (winner several nat. and internat. awards); feature films, 1971— ; films include McCabe and Mrs. Miller, 1971; Images, 1972, Deliverance, 1972, The Long Goodbye, 1973, Scarecrow, 1973, Cinderella Liberty, 1973, The Sugarland Express, 1974, Obsession, 1976, Close Encounters of the Third Kind, 1977 (Acad. award 1977), The Last Waltz, 1978, The Rose, 1978, The Deerhunter, 1978 (Acad. award nomination and Brit. Acad. award), Heavens Gate, 1979, The Border, 1980, Blow Out, 1980, Jinxed, 1981, Table for Five, 1982, The River, 1983 (Acad. award nomination), No Small Affair, 1984, Real Genius, 1985, Witches of Eastwick, 1986, Journey to Spirit Island, 1988, Fatman and Little Boy, 1989, Two Jakes, 1989, Bonfire of the Vanities, 1990, Stalin, 1991 (CableAce award, Direction of Photography and/or Lighting Direction in a Dramatic/Theatrical Special/Movie or Miniseries, ASC award, Emmy award), Sliver, 1992; dir. The Long Shadow, 1992, Intersection, 1993, Maverick, 1993, The Crossing Guard, 1994, Assassins, 1995, The Ghost and the Darkness, 1996 (ASC Award nomination), Fantasy for a New Age, 1997, Playing By Heart, 1998, The Body, 1999, The Mists of Avalon, 2000, Life as a House, 2001, (opera film) Bank Ban, 2001. Recipient lifetime achievement award Worldfest, Flagstaff, 1998. Mem. Acad. Motion Picture Arts and Scis., Dirs. Guild, Am. Soc. Cinematographers (lifetime achievement award 1998). Office: Feinstein & Berson 16255 Ventura Blvd Ste 625 Encino CA 91436-2418 E-mail: vzsigmond@home.com

ZUCKERKANDL, EMILE, molecular evolutionary biologist, scientific institute executive; b. Vienna, Austria, July 4, 1922; came to U.S., 1975; s. Frederic and Gertrude (Stekel) Z.; m. Jane Gammon Metz, June 2,1950 M.S., U. Ill., 1947; Ph.D., Sorbonne, Paris, 1959. Postdoctoral rsch. fellow Calif. Inst. Tech., Pasadena, 1959-64; rsch. dir. CNRS, Montpellier, France, 1967-80, dir. Ctr. Macromolecular Biochemistry France, 1965-75; pres. Linus Pauling Inst., Palo Alto, Calif., 1980-92, Inst. Molecular Med. Scis., Palo Alto, 1992—. Cons. in genetics Stanford U., 1963, vis. prof., 1964; vis. prof. U. Del., 1976 Contbg. author: Horizons in Biochemistry, 1962, Evolving Genes and Proteins, 1965; co-author: Genetique des Populations, 1976; editor Jour. Molecular Evolution, 1971-2000. Decorated Hon. Cross for Sci. and Art (Austria), Order of Merit (France). Fellow AAAS; mem. Societe de Chimie Biologique, Internat. Soc. Study Origin of Life, Internat. Soc. Molecular Evolution. Home: 565 Arastradero Rd Ph A Palo Alto CA 94306-4323 Office: Inst Molecular Med Scis PO Box 20452 Stanford CA 94309-0452

ZUFRYDEN, FRED S. academic administrator, marketing educator, researcher; b. Grenoble, France, June 13, 1943; came to U.S., 1956; s. Henri and Cecile (Frymer) Z.; m. Toby Marlene Levin, Dec. 24, 1967; 1 child, Ryan B.A. in Math., UCLA, 1965, M.B.A., 1966, Ph.D. in Bus. Adminstrn., 1971. Rsch. engr. mil. ops. and systems analysis group N.Am. Aviation, Inc., L.A., 1966-67; rsch. assoc. resources rsch. dept. Planning Rsch. Corp., L.A., 1967-68; ops. rsch. specialist data systems div. Litton Systems, Inc., L.A., 1968-70; asst. prof. dept. mgmt. scis. Sch. Bus. and Econs., U. Calif., Northridge, 1970-71; asst. prof. dept. mktg. Grad. Sch. Bus. U. So. Calif., L.A., 1971-75, assoc. prof., 1975-82, prof., 1982—, Ernst Hahn prof. mktg., 1991—, chmn. mktg. dept., 1987-90, rsch. dir. internat. bus. econs. and rsch. Grad. Sch. Bus., 1983—. Mem. editorial bd. Jour. Advt. Rsch., 1981—, Mktg. Sci., 1979—, Jour. Mktg., 1978—; mem. cons. and planning com. Mktg. Sci. Jour., 1979; referee Jour. Mktg. Rsch., Mgmt. Sci., Decision Sci., Jour. Internat. Rsch. in Mktg.; mem. abstract writing staff International Abstracts in Operations Rsch./Mgmt. Sci., 1973; contbr. articles to profl. jours. including Jour. Mktg. Rsch., Mktg. Sci., Jour. Operational Rsch. Soc., Mgmt. Sci., Decision Scis., Jour. Mktg., Jour. Advt. Rsch., Jour. Internat. Rsch. in Mktg., Jour. Royal Statis. Soc., Interfaces, Rsch. in Mktg., Jour. of Mktg. Rsch. Soc., Jour. of Bus., others Rsch. grantee U. So. Calif., 1973, 75, 76, 77, 78, A.C. Nielsen Co., 1988-90. Mem. Am. Mktg. Assn. (cert. recognition 1974), Ops. Rsch. Soc. Am., Inst. Mgmt. Sci., Omega Rho, Beta Gamma Sigma

ZUICHES, JAMES JOSEPH, academic administrator; b. Eau Claire, Wis., Mar. 24, 1943; s. William Homer and Bronnie Monica (Stich) Z.; m. Carol Ann Kurilo, Aug. 19, 1967; children:, James Daniel, Joseph Kurilo. BA in Philosophy, U. Portland, 1967; MS in Sociology, U. Wis., 1969, PhD in Sociology, 1973. Instr., asst. prof., assoc. prof. sociology Mich. State U., East Lansing, 1971-82, prof., 1982; assoc. program dir. in sociology NSF, Washington, 1979-80, program dir. in sociology, 1980-82; assoc. dir. rsch. Cornell U., Ithaca, N.Y., 1982-86; assoc. dean Coll. Agr. and Home Econs., Wash. State U., Pullman, 1986-94, dir. Agrl. Rsch. Ctr., 1986-94; program dir. food sys. and rural devel. W.K. Kellogg Found., Battle Creek, Mich., 1994-95; dean Coll. Agr. and Home Econs. Wash. State U., Pullman, 1995—. Mem. adv. subcom. NSF, 1977-79; sci. adv. com. USDA Nat. Rsch. Initiative, Washington, 1992-93; com. on future land grant univ. bd. on agr., NRC, Washington, 1994-96; pub. Wash. Land and People Mag., 1987-92. Co-editor: The Demography of Rural Life, 1993; contbr. articles to profl. jours. Pres., bd. dirs. Edgewood Village Children's Ctr., East Lansing, 1978-79. Recipient sustained superior performance award NSF, 1981; rsch. grantee NIMH, 1973, ERDA, 1978. Fellow AAAS; mem. Rural Sociol. Soc. (pres. 1992-93, editor 50th Anniversary Rsch. Series, 5 vols. 1988-93), Am. Sociol. Assn., Population Assn. Am. Roman Catholic. Avocations: skiing, swimming, hiking, reading.

ZUMWALT, ROGER CARL, hospital administrator; b. Eugene, Oreg., Oct. 26, 1943; s. Robert Walter and Jean Elaine (Adams) Z.; m. Sharon Marlene Ryan, Aug. 22, 1970; children: Kathryn Nicole Zumwalt Deweber, Timothy Robert. Student, Boise State U., 1963-65; BA, We. Oreg. U., 1969; postgrad., U. Iowa, 1969-71; MA cum laude, Oreg. State U., 1973. Adminstr. Coulee Cmty. Hosp., Grand Coulee, Wash., 1973-75, Eastmoreland Hosp., Portland, Oreg., 1975-81; exec. dir. Cmty. Hosp., Grand Junction, Colo., 1981-97; pres., healthcare cons. accreditation Zumwalt Consulting, Salem, Oreg., 1997—; dir. adminstrv. svcs. divsn. SAIF Corp., Salem, 1998—. Chmn., bd. dirs. Alphabet House Pediat. Rehab. and Edn., 1998-2000, Castle Rock Med. Group, Inc., Denver, 1998—, Castle Rock (Colo.) Med. Ctr., 1998—, Northwest Okla. Regional Med. Ctr., Cherokee, 2000—; speaker numerous local and nat. presentations, subjects including healthcare, hosp. mktg./success/costs, 1981-97; CEO Cmty. Med. Plz., 1984-97, Cmty. Health Care Providers Orgn., 1986-97, Cmty. Hosp. Found., 1988-97; guest lectr. Mesa Stae Coll., 1993-98, Colo. Christian Coll., 1996-98. Newspaper columnist, 1973-75; contbr. articles, presentations to profl. publs. Commr. Multnomah County Health Care Commn., Portland, 1978-81; health cons. Grant County Housing Auth., Grand Coulee, 1974-75; mem. pk. bd. City of Tigard, Oreg., 1976-78; caucus rep. Mesa County Rep. Party, Grand Junction, 1988; mem. adv. com., pres.'s office Mesa State Coll., Grand Junction, 1989; bd. dirs. Hospice of Grand Valley, Grand Junction, 1992-97, mem. devel. com., 1993-97, vice chmn. bd. dirs., 1994-97; bd. dirs. Grand Valley Hospice, 1992-96; com. mem. Salem Coalition on Youth Literacy, 2000—. Fellow Coll. Osteo. Healthcare Execs. (bd. dirs. 1985-88, pres. 1987, examiner 1989—, Disting. Svc. award 1989); mem. Am. Osteo. Healthcare Assn. (bd. dirs. 1987-98, treas. 1992-93, 1st v.p. 1994-95, 2d v.p. 1993-94, vice chairperson 1994-95, chmn. 1996-97, chairperson 1997-98, past chmn. 1998), Am. Osteo. Assn. (ex-officio mem. bd. dirs. 1996), Bur. Healthcare Facilities Accreditation (v.p. 1994, advisor 1995-98, accreditation cons. 1995—, accreditation surveyer 1978—, accreditation survey instr. 1994—), Joint Commn. on Am. Healthcare Orgn. (task force on small and rural hosps. 1994-98), Colo. Hosp. Assn. (bd. dirs. 1987-92), Mountain States Vol. Hosp. Assn. (bd. dirs. 1984-98, exec. com. 1991-98, v.p. 1993, vice chmn. bd. dirs. 1992-98), We. Coll. Ind. Practice Assn. (Medicine Mauls Measles com., fin. com. 1991-92), We. Colo. Health Care Alliance (bd. dirs. 1989-94, v.p. 1992, chmn. bd. dirs. 1993, past chmn. bd. dirs. 1994), Mesa County Mental Health Assn. (bd. dirs. 1988-89, 91-92), Grand Junction C. of C. (bd. dirs. 1991-93), Rotary (grand coolee Wash. 1973-75, Portland, Oreg. 1975-81, Grand Junction, Colo. 1981-98, Salem, Oreg. 1998—, chair fund raising com. 2000—, bd. dirs. 2001—), Masons, Shriners (pres. Grand Junction club 1989, bd. dirs. El Jebel 1986-90, 1st v.p. Western Colo. club 1989). Republican. Methodist. Avocations: golf, camping, fishing, hunting. Home: 413 NW Heather Ave Sublimity OR 97385-9818 Office: SAIF Corp 440 Church St SE PWB 2 Salem OR 97312-2000 Fax: 503-315-3086. E-mail: Roshzum@cs.com

ZUMWALT, ROSS EUGENE, forensic pathologist, educator; b. Goodrich, Mich., July 18, 1943; s. Paul Lawrence and Lila Ann (Birky) Z.; m. Theresa Ann Schar, Sept. 12, 1970 (div. Apr. 1988); children: Christopher Todd, Tenley Ann; m. Cheryl Lynn Willman, Sept. 4, 1988; 1 child, David Willman Zumwalt. BA, Wabash Coll., 1967; MD, U. Ill., 1971. Diplomate in anat. and forensic pathology Am. Bd. Pathology. Intern, resident in pathology Mary Bassett Hosp., Cooperstown, N.Y., 1971-73; resident in anat. and forensic pathology Southwestern Med. Sch., Dallas, 1973-76; asst. med. examiner Dallas County, Dallas, 1974-76; staff pathologist, dir. labs. Naval Regional Med. Ctr., Camp Lejeune, N.C., 1976-78; dep. coroner Cuyahoga County, Cleve., 1978-80, Hamilton County, Cin., 1980-86; assoc. prof. pathology U. Cin. Sch. Medicine, 1980-86; prof. pathology U. N.Mex. Sch. Medicine, Albuquerque, 1987—; chief med. investigator Office of Med. Investigator, Albuquerque, 1991—; pres. Am. Bd. of Pathology, Tampa, 2000-. Trustee Am. Bd. Pathology, Tampa, Fla., 1993—. Lt. comdr. USN, 1976-78. Fellow Am. Acad. Forensic Scis., Coll. Am. Pathologists; mem. AMA, Nat. Assn. Med. Examiners (bd. dirs. 1984-96, pres. 1995-96), Am. Soc. Clin. Pathologists, Am. and Can. Acad. Pathologists. Avocation: golf.

ZURZOLO, VINCENT P. federal judge; b. 1956; BA, U. Calif., San Diego, 1978; JD, U. Calif., Davis, 1982. With Greenberg, Glusker, Fields, Claman & Machtinger, L.A.; apptd. bankruptcy judge cen. dist. U.S. Dist. Ct. Calif., 1988. Mem. ABA, Nat. Conf. Bankruptcy Judges, Fin. Lawyers Conf., L.A. County Bar Assn. (bankruptcy com. of comml. law and bankruptcy sect.). Office: 1360 Roybal Federal Bldg 255 E Temple St Los Angeles CA 90012-3334

ZUSSY, NANCY LOUISE, librarian; b. Tampa, Fla., Mar. 4, 1947; d. John David and Patsy Ruth (Stone) Roche; m. R. Mark Allen, Dec. 20, 1986. BA in Edn., U. Fla., 1969; MLS, U. So. Fla., 1977, MS in Pub. Mgmt., 1980. Cert. librarian, Wash. Ednl. evaluator State of Ga., Atlanta, 1969-70; media specialist DeKalb County Schs., Decatur, Ga., 1970-71; researcher Ga. State Libr., Atlanta, 1971; asst. to dir. reference Clearwater (Fla.) Pub. Libr., 1972-78, dir. librs., 1978-81; dep. state libr. Wash. State Libr., Olympia, 1981-86, state libr., 1986—. Chmn. Consortium Automated Librs., Olympia, 1982-97; cons. various pub. librs., Wash. and other U.S. states, Uzbekistan, Russia, 1981—; exec. officer Wash. Libr. Network, 1986-90; v.p. WLN (non-profit orgn.), 1990-93. Contbr. articles to profl. jours. Treas. Thurston-Mason Community Mental Health Bd., Olympia, 1983-85, bd. dirs., 1982-85; mem. race com. Seafair Hydroplane Race, Seattle, 1986—, mem. milk carton derby team, 1994—, announcer, prodr. air show; co-chair Pub. Info. Access Policy Task Force, 1995-96; mem. Gov.'s Work Group on Comml. Access to Govt. Electronic Records, 1996-97; mem. K-20 Telecomms. Oversight and Policy Com., 1996—. Mem. ALA, Assn. Specialized and Coop. Libr. Agys. (legis. com. 1983-86, chmn.. 1985-87, vice chmn. state libr. agys. sect. 1985-86, chmn. 1986-87, chmn. govt. affairs com. Libr. Adminstrn. and Mgmt. Assn., 1986-87), Freedom To Read Found. (bd. dirs. 1987-91), Chief Officers of State Libr. Agys. (bd. dirs.-at-large 1987-90, v.p., pres.-elect 1990-92, pres. 1992-94), Wash. Libr. Assn. (co-founder legis. planning com. 1982—, fed. rels. coord. 1984—), Fla. Libr. Assn. (legis. and planning com. 1978-81), Pacific N.W. Libr. Assn., Rotary (bd. dirs. 1995-96), Phi Kappa Phi, Phi Beta Mu. Avocations: hiking, barbershop chorus/quartet, hydroplane boat racing, cross country skiing. Home: 716 Sherman St NW Olympia WA 98502-8801 Office: Wash State Libr PO Box 42460 Olympia WA 98504-2460

ZWAHLEN, FRED CASPER, JR. journalism educator; b. Portland, Oreg., Nov. 11, 1924; s. Fred and Katherine (Meyer) Z.; m. Grace Eleanor DeMoss, June 24, 1959; children: Molly, Skip. BA, Oreg. State U., 1949; MA, Stanford U., 1952. Reporter San Francisco News, 1949-50; acting editor Stanford Alumni Rev., Palo Alto, Calif., 1950; successively instr. journalism, news bur. asst., prof. journalism, chmn. journalism dept. Oreg. State U., Corvallis, 1950-91, prof. emeritus, 1991—. Swiss tour guide, 1991—; corres. Portland Oregonian, 1950-67. Author: (with others) Handbook of Photography, 1984, Two Centuries of Shadow Catchers, A History of Photography, 1996. Coord. E.E. Wilson Scholarship Fund, 1964—; active budget com. Corvallis Sch. Dist., 1979. Recipient Achievement award Sch. Journalism U. Oregon, 1988. Mem. Assn. for Edn. in Journalism and Mass Communications (conv. chmn. 1983, pres.' award 1988), Oreg. Newspaper Pubs. Assn. (hon. life 1998, bd. dirs. 1980-85, student loan fund named in his honor 1988), Soc. Profl. Journalists (nat. svc. citation 1988), Corvallis Country Club, Shriners, Masons, Elks, Moose, Eagles, Delta Tau Delta. Republican. Presbyterian. Avocations: photography, sightseeing, travel. Home: 240 SW 7th St Corvallis OR 97333-4551 E-mail: zwahlenf@ucs.orst.edu

ZWEIFEL, DONALD EDWIN, newspaper editor, lobbyist, consultant; b. L.A., Nov. 30, 1940; s. Robert Fredrick and Eugenia Bedford (White) Z.; m. Donna Jean Croslin; 1 son, Phillip Matthew. Student, Orange Coast Coll., 1963-67, 90-92, U. Calif., Irvine, 1968-70, Western State U. Coll. Law, , 1973, Irvine U. Coll. Law, 1974-75, Rancho Santiago Jr. Coll., 1988, Chapman U., 1989, 93-97; grad., Aviation Ground Sch., 1990; student, USAF Air U., 1994-95, 2000—. Cert. Student Pilot, 1989, registered lobbyist, Calif. State Legislature. Devel. tech. Hughes Aircraft, Newport Beach, Calif., 1963-64; co-founder Sta. KUCI-FM, Irvine, 1970; owner, mgr. Zweifel Jaguar Car Sales and Svc., Santa Ana, 1975-76; pres. Zweifel & Assocs. Inc., Santa Ana, 1977-86, Zweifel South Coast Exotic Cars, Orange, Calif., 1987-96, ret., 1996; assoc. editor Compliance News Pub. Co., Long Beach, 1998—. Co-author: Challenge 2000, Regaining the America's Cup, 1996; editor: (coll. textbook) The Dream Is Alive, Space Flight and Operations In Earth Orbit. Vol. emergency coord. emergency mgmt. div. Orange County Fire Authority, 1985-87, Navy Relief Soc., 1993, 1st lt. CAP Squadron 88 Group VII, 1993-95, sr. programs officer, 1993-94, asst. transp. officer Calif. Wing Hdqrs., 1994-95, Group VII Facilities officer, 1994-95, 2000—, squadron pers. officer, 1993-95, 2000—, Calif. wing rep. to Orange County Vol. Orgns. Active in Disaster, ARC, 1994-95, Calif. wing vol. Office Emergency Svcs., Calif., 1994-96, 2000—, grad. Squadron Leadership Sch., 1993, Wing Supply Officers Sch., 1995, squadron safety officer, pub. affairs officer, asst. aerospace edn. officer, 1998—; program coord. Young Astronaut Coun., 1989-90; cadet CAP, USAF auxiliary, Long Beach, Calif., 1953-59; mem. Orange County Homeless Issues Taskforce, 1994-95, 1997—, Orange County Homeless Svc. Providers for the Reuse of Marine Corps Air Sta., Tustin, Calif., 1994-95; mem. legis. com. Orange County Vets. Adv. Coun., 1998— (Certificate of Commendation 1998) Orange County, Mem. Am Vets post 18, mem. restoration adv. bd., chmn. Tech. Review subcom. Marine Corps Air Sta., El Toro, Calif., 1994—; apptd. to CalEPA DTSC Adv. Group Mil. Base Closure, 1995—, CalEPA Dept. Toxics & Substances Control Adv. Group pro-bono cons., Orange County Citizen's Adv. Commn. and El Toro Local Redevel. Authority, 1996—; vol. mediator Victim-Offender Reconciliation program, 1995-96; restoration adv. bd. MCAS Tustin, 1994—, El Toro, Calif., 2001. With Army N.G. (hon. discharge), 1958-59. Recipient 6 certs. achievement Fed. Emergency Mgmt. Agy., 1989-96, 2 certs. appreciation CAP, 2 certs commendation, 1994, cert. appreciation Southwest Divsn. Naval Facilities Engring. Commd., 2000, Meritorious Svc. award, Calif. State Assembly Restoration Adv. Bd. Assemblyman John Campbell, 2001. Mem. Air Force Assn. (vice-chmn. civilian recruitment Calif. state membership com. 1988-89, 90-91, v.p. membership, Gen. Doolittle chpt. bd. dirs. 1987-89, 90-92, Exceptional Svc. award Gen. Jimmy Doolittle chpt. 1988, 91, Calif. Meritorious Svc. award 1988, v.p. membership Gen. Curtis E. LeMay Orange County chpt. 2000—), Calif. Assn. for Aerospace Edn. (fellow), Marine Corps Hist. Found. (life), Aerospace Edn. Found. (Gen. Jimmy Doolittle fellow 1988, Gen. Ira Eaker fellow 1989, Pres.'s award 1988), U.S. Naval Inst., AIAA (Cert. of Appreciation 1989, L.A. chpt. hist. com. 1989), Gulf & Vietnam Vets. Strategic Studies Archives (cons., co-founder 1983—, dir.), Marine Corps League (assoc., capt. Heinsey detachment 2000—), U.S. Marine Corps Combat Correspondents Assn. (affiliate), Confederate Air Force (col. 1989, adj. 1st Composite Group detachment 1989), Orange County Peace Officers Assn. (assoc.), Free and Accepted Masons Orange Grove Lodge. Avocations: sailing, bicycle racing, traveling, flying. Home and Office: Gulf/Vietnam Vets Strategic & Environ Studies Archives 2110 Larkspur Dr Orange CA 92868-3423 E-mail: zweifel@earthlink.net

ZWEIG, GEORGE, physicist, neurobiologist; b. Moscow, May 20, 1937; came to U.S., 1938; s. Alfred and Rachael (Frölich) Z. BS in Math., U. Mich., 1959; PhD in Physics, Calif. Inst. Tech., 1963. NAS-NRC fellow European Orgn. for Nuclear Rsch., Geneva, 1963-64; asst. prof. physics Calif. Inst. Tech., Pasadena, 1964-66, assoc. prof., 1966-67, prof., 1967-83; staff mem. Los Alamos (N.Mex.) Nat. Lab., 1981-85, fellow, 1985—; founder, pres. Signition, Inc., Los Alamos, 1985—. Vis. prof. physics U. Wis., Madison, 1967-68; mem. Jason div. Inst. for Def. Analysis, Arlington, Va., 1965-72. Recipient MacArthur prize MacArthur Found., 1981, Disting. Alumnus award Calif. Inst. Tech., 1984; Alfred P. Sloan Found. fellow in physics, 1966-74, in neurobiology, 1974-78. Mem. IEEE, AAAS, NAS, Am. Math. Soc., Am. Phys. Soc., Assn. for Rsch. in Otolaryngology. Achievements include discovering quarks, 1963; creating continuous wavelet transform for signal processing, 1975, active model of coclear mechanics, 1987. Office: LANL MS B276 PO Box 1663 Los Alamos NM 87544-0600

ZWERDLING, ALEX, English educator; b. Breslau, Germany, June 21, 1932; came to U.S., 1941, naturalized, 1946; s. Norbert and Fanni (Alt) Z.; m. Florence Goldberg, Mar. 23, 1969; 1 son, Antony Daniel. B.A., Cornell U., 1953; postgrad. (Fulbright scholar), U. Munich, Germany, 1953-54; M.A., Princeton U., 1956, Ph.D., 1960. Instr. English Swarthmore Coll., 1957-61; asst. prof. English U. Calif., Berkeley, 1961-67, asso. prof., 1967-73, prof., 1973-86, prof. English, 1988—, chmn. grad. studies, 1985-86; univ. prof. George Washington U., 1986-88. Vis. prof. Northwestern U., 1977; dir. edn. abroad program U. Calif., London, 1996-98; mem. advanced placement exam. com. Ednl. Testing Svc., 1975-79; mem. fellowship panel Nat. Endowment for Humanities, 1977-82, 84-87, Nat. Humanities Ctr., 1989-90; fellow Ctr. for Advanced Study in Behavioral Scis., 1964-65. Author: Yeats and the Heroic Ideal, 1965, Orwell and the Left, 1974, Virginia Woolf and the Real World, 1986, Improvised Europeans: American Literary Expatriates and the Siege of London, 1998; mem. adv. com. PMLA, 1978-82. Am. Coun. Learned Socs. fellow, 1964-65; NEH fellow, 1973-74; Guggenheim fellow, 1977-78; Woodrow Wilson Ctr. fellow, 1991-92, fellow Nat. Humanities Ctr., 1992-93. Mem. MLA (chmn. 20th Century Brit. lit. div. 1969-70, 85-86) Office: U Calif Dept English Berkeley CA 94720-0001

ZWICK, BARRY STANLEY, newspaper editor, speechwriter; b. Cleve., July 21, 1942; s. Alvin Albert and Selma Davidovna (Makofsky) Z.; m. Roberta Joan Yaffe, Mar. 11, 1972; children: Natasha Yvette, Alexander Anatol. BA in Journalism, Ohio State U., 1963; MS in Journalism, Columbia U., 1965. Copy editor Phila. Inquirer, 1964; night news editor Detroit Free Press, 1965-67; West Coast editor L.A. Times/Washington Post News Svc, 1967-77; makeup editor L.A. Times, 1978—. Adj. prof. U. So. Calif., L.A., 1975-77. Author: Hollywood Tanning Secrets, 1980. NEH profl. journalism fellow Stanford U., 1977-78. Jewish. Avocations: photography, jet skiing, snowmobiling. Office: LA Times Times Mirror Sq Los Angeles CA 90012 E-mail: barryzwick@aol.com

ZWOYER, EUGENE MILTON, consulting engineering executive; b. Plainfield, N.J., Sept. 8, 1926; s. Paul Ellsworth and Marie Susan (Britt) Z.; m. Dorothy Lucille Seward, Feb. 23, 1946; children: Gregory, Jeffrey, Douglas. Student, U. Notre Dame, 1944, Mo. Valley Coll., 1944-45; BS, U. N.Mex., 1947; MS, Ill. Inst. Tech., 1949; PhD, U. Ill., 1953. Mem. faculty U. N.Mex., Albuquerque, 1948-71, prof. civil engring., dir. Eric Wang Civil Engring. Rsch. Facility, 1961-70; rsch. assoc. U. Ill., Urbana, 1951-53; owner, cons. engr. Eugene Zwoyer & Assocs., Albuquerque, 1954-72; exec. dir., sec. ASCE, N.Y.C., 1972-82; pres. Am. Assn. Engring. Socs., N.Y.C., 1982-84; exec. v.p. T.Y. Lin Internat., San Francisco, 1984-86, pres., 1986-89; owner Eugene Zwoyer Cons. Engr., 1989—; chief oper. officer, treas. Polar Molecular Corp., Saginaw, Mich., 1990, exec. v.p., 1991-92. Trustee Small Bus. Research Corp., 1976-80; trustee Engring. Info., Inc., 1981-84; internat. trustee People-to-People Internat. 1974-86; v.p. World Fedn. Engring. Orgns., 1982-85. Served to lt. (j.g.) USN, 1944-46. Named Outstanding Engr. of Yr. Albuquerque chpt. N.Mex Soc. Profl. Engrs., 1969, One Who Served the Best Interests of the Constrn. Industry, Engring. News Record, 1980; recipient Disting. Alumnus award the Civil Engring. Alumni Assn. at U. Ill., 1979, Disting. Alumnus award Engring. Coll. Alumni Assn., U. N.Mex., 1982, Can.-Am. Civil Engring. Amity award Am. Soc. Civil Engrs., 1988, Award for Outstanding Profl. Contbns. and Leadership Coll. Engring. U. N.Mex., 1989 Mem. AAAS, ASCE (dist. bd. dirs. 1968-71), NSPE, Am. Soc. Engring. Edn., Am. Concrete Inst., Nat. Acad. Code Adminstrn. (trustee, mem. exec. com. 1973-79), Engrs. Joint Coun. (bd. dirs. 1978-79), Engring. Soc. Commn. on Energy (bd. dirs. 1977-82), Sigma Xi, Sigma Tau, Chi Epsilon. Home and Office: 6363 Christie Ave Apt 1326 Emeryville CA 94608-1940

Professional Index

AGRICULTURE

UNITED STATES

CALIFORNIA

Camarillo
Barker, John William *agricultural property management*

Davis
Carter, Harold O. *agricultural economics educator*

Hayward
Gallo, Joseph E. *vintner*

Healdsburg
Merinoff, Herman I. *vintager, wine and spirits executive*

Modesto
Freedman, Louis *vintager executive*
Gallo, Ernest *vintner*

Pacific Palisades
Jennings, Marcella Grady *rancher, investor*

Sacramento
Wightman, Thomas Valentine *rancher, researcher*

San Diego
Foxley, William Coleman *cattleman*
Sentz, Dennis *chemical company executive*

San Francisco
Hills, Austin Edward *vineyard executive*

COLORADO

Denver
Decker, Peter Randolph *rancher, former state official*
McFarlane, Willis McKee *buffalo company executive*

Fort Collins
Heird, James C. *agricultural studies educator*

Kremmling
Lewis, Charles D. *rancher, consultant*

Springfield
Wessler, Melvin Dean *farmer, rancher*

HAWAII

Honolulu
Ching, Chauncey Tai Kin *agricultural economics educator*

Waialua
Singlehurst, Dona Geisenheyner *horse farm owner*

IDAHO

Twin Falls
Jones, Douglas Raymond *farming executive, state legislator*

MONTANA

Choteau
De Bruycker, Lloyd Henry *rancher, feedlot operator*

Pony
Anderson, Richard Ernest *agribusiness development consultant, rancher*

NEW MEXICO

Deming
White, Don William *rancher, minister*

Santa Fe
Jennings, Timothy Zeph *rancher, state legislator*

OREGON

Grants Pass
Miller, Richard Alan *agricultural consultant, hypnotherapist*

Medford
Smith, Robert F. (Bob Smith) *rancher, congressman*

WYOMING

Wheatland
Bunker, John Birkbeck *cattle rancher, retired sugar company executive*

CANADA

BRITISH COLUMBIA

Vancouver
Stephens, Tom *forest products company executive*

ADDRESS UNPUBLISHED

Hitchcock, Vernon Thomas *farmer, lawyer*
Johnson, Maurice Verner, Jr. *agricultural research and development executive*

ARCHITECTURE & DESIGN

UNITED STATES

ALASKA

Anchorage
Maynard, Kenneth Douglas *architect*

ARIZONA

Paradise Valley
Blumer, Harry Maynard *architect*

Phoenix
DeBartolo, Jack, Jr. *architect*
Hawkins, Jasper Stillwell, Jr. *architect*
Schiffner, Charles Robert *architect*
Winslow, Paul David *architect*

Scottsdale
Rutes, Walter Alan *architect*

Sedona
Iverson, Wayne Dahl *landscape architect, consultant*

Sonoita
Cook, William Howard *architect*

Tempe
Mc Sheffrey, Gerald Rainey *architect, educator, city planner*

Tucson
Breckenridge, Klindt Duncan *architect*
Gourley, Ronald Robert *architect, educator*
Hershberger, Robert Glen *architect, educator*
McConnell, Robert Eastwood *architect, educator*
Wallach, Leslie Rothaus *architect*

CALIFORNIA

Bakersfield
McAlister, Michael H. *architect*

Berkeley
Brocchini, Ronald Gene *architect*
Burger, Edmund Ganes *architect*
Cardwell, Kenneth Harvey *architect, educator*
Hester, Randolph Thompson, Jr. *landscape architect, educator*
Stoller, Claude *architect*

Burbank
Naidorf, Louis Murray *architect*

Corona Del Mar
Yeo, Ron *architect*

Costa Mesa
Dougherty, Betsey Olenick *architect*

Culver City
Moss, Eric Owen *architect*

Encino
Rance, Quentin E. *interior designer*

Fresno
Darden, Edwin Speight, Sr. *architect*
Patnaude, William Eugene *architect, writer*
Putman, Robert Dean *retired golf course architect*

Irvine
Kraemer, Kenneth Leo *architect, urban planner, educator*

La Jolla
Baesel, Stuart Oliver *architect*

Laguna Niguel
Axon, Donald Carlton *architect*
Robinson, Theodore Gould *landscape and golf course architect*

Long Beach
Perkowitz, Simon *architect*

Los Angeles
Bobrow, Michael Lawrence *architect*
Dworsky, Daniel Leonard *architect, educator*
Eisenshtat, Sidney Herbert *architect*
Holdsworth, Ray W. *architectural firm executive*
Kline, Lee B. *retired architect*
Krag, Olga *interior designer*
Maltzan, Michael Thomas *architect*
Man, Lawrence Kong *architect, graphic, furniture and fashion designer*
Moe, Stanley Allen *architect, consultant*
Myers, Barton *architect*
Nelson, Mark Bruce *interior designer*
Phelps, Barton Chase *architect, educator*

Mill Valley
D'Amico, Michael *architect, urban planner*

Montrose
Greenlaw, Roger Lee *interior designer*

Newport Beach
Bissell, George Arthur *architect*
Jacobs, Donald Paul *architect*
Richardson, Walter John *architect*

Novato
Thompson, Peter Layard Hailey, Sr. *landscape and golf course architect*

Oakland
Nicol, Robert Duncan *architect*

Orange
Shirvani, Hamid *architect, educator, author, administrator*

Oxnard
O'Connell, Hugh Mellen, Jr. *retired architect*

Palos Verdes Peninsula
Rester, George G. *architect, designer, painter, sculptor, showman*

Pasadena
Goei, Bernard Thwan-Poo (Bert Goei) *architectural and engineering firm executive*
Thomas, Joseph Fleshman *retired architect*

Redondo Beach
Shellhorn, Ruth Patricia *landscape architect*

Sacramento
Hallenbeck, Harry C. *architect*
Lionakis, George *architect*
Wasserman, Barry L(ee) *architect*

San Diego
Delawie, Homer Torrence *architect*
Henderson, John Drews *architect*
Holl, Walter John *architect, interior designer*
Livingston, Stanley C. *architect*
Paderewski, Sir Clarence Joseph *architect*
Wilson, Richard Allan *landscape architect*

San Francisco
Brown, Joseph E. *landscape architecture executive*
Bull, Henrik Helkand *architect*
Costa, Walter Henry *architect*
Del Campo, Martin Bernardelli *architect*
Dodge, Peter Hampton *architect*
Field, John Louis *architect*
Friedrichs, Edward Charles *architect*
Judd, Bruce Diven *architect*
Kriken, John Lund *architect*
Moris, Lamberto Giuliano *architect*
Raeber, John Arthur *architect, construction consultant*
Ream, James Terrill *architect, sculptor*
Thistlethwaite, David Richard *architect*
Valentine, William Edson *architect*
Werner, William Arno *architect*

San Jose
Kwock, Royal *architect*
Tanaka, Richard Koichi, Jr. *architect, planner*

San Luis Obispo
Deasy, Cornelius Michael *architect*
Fraser, Bruce Douglas, Jr. *architect, artist*
Hasslein, George Johann *architectural educator*

San Mateo
Castleberry, Arline Alrick *architect*

San Rafael
Badgley, John Roy *architect*
Clark, Charles Sutter *interior designer*

Santa Barbara
Kruger, Kenneth Charles *retired architect*

Santa Monica
Eizenberg, Julie *architect*
Gehry, Frank Owen *architect*
Koning, Hendrik *architect*

Santa Rosa
Gilger, Paul Douglass *architect*

Sausalito
Leefe, James Morrison *architect*

Seal Beach
Rossi, Mario Alexander *architect*

Sonoma
Allen, Rex Whitaker *retired architect*

Woodbridge, John Marshall *architect, urban planner*

South Pasadena
Girvigian, Raymond *architect*

COLORADO

Aspen
Alstrom, Sven Erik *architect*
Caudill, Samuel Jefferson *architect*
Ensign, Donald H. *landscape architect*

Colorado Springs
Phibbs, Harry Albert *interior designer, professional speaker, lecturer*

Denver
Abo, Ronald Kent *freelance/self-employed architect*
Anderson, John David *architect*
Brownson, Jacques Calmon *architect*
Dominick, Peter Hoyt, Jr. *architect*
Fuller, Robert Kenneth *architect, urban designer*
Havekost, Daniel John *architect*
Williams, John James, Jr. *architect*
Wirkler, Norman Edward *architectural, engineering, construction management firm executive*

Englewood
Eccles, Matthew Alan *landscape and golf course architect*

Fort Collins
Grandin, Temple *industrial designer, science educator*

Vail
Vosbeck, Robert Randall *architect*

HAWAII

Haiku
Riecke, Hans Heinrich *architect*

Honolulu
Botsai, Elmer Eugene *architect, educator, former university dean*
Cain, Raymond Frederick *landscape architect, planning company executive*
Hale, Nathan Robert *architect*
Hamada, Duane Takumi *architect*
Lau, Charles Kwok-Chiu *architect, architectural firm executive*
Yeh, Raymond Wei-Hwa *architect, educator*

Kaneohe
Fisette, Scott Michael *landscape and golf course architect*

IDAHO

Boise
Hunsucker, Wayne (Carl Wayne Hunsucker) *architectural firm executive, educator*

Sun Valley
Bryant, Woodrow Wesley *architect*

MONTANA

Bozeman
DeHaas, John Neff, Jr. *retired architecture educator*

Great Falls
Davidson, David Scott *architect*

NEVADA

Las Vegas
Marnell, Anthony Austin, II *architect*

NEW MEXICO

Albuquerque
Sabatini, William Quinn *architect*

Santa Fe
Leon, Bruno *architect, educator*

OREGON

Beaverton
Ivester, (Richard) Gavin *industrial designer*

Medford
Skelton, Douglas H. *architect*
Straus, David A. *architectural firm executive*

Portland
Frasca, Robert John *architect*
Gunsul, Brooks R. W. *architect*
Hacker, Thomas Owen *architect*

Kilbourn, Lee Ferris *architect, specifications writer*
Ritz, Richard Ellison *architect, architectural historian, writer*

Springfield
Lutes, Donald Henry *architect*

UTAH

Salt Lake City
Beall, Burtch W., Jr. *architect*
Brems, David Paul *architect*
Chong, Richard David *architect*
Christopher, James Walker *architect, educator*

WASHINGTON

Bainbridge Island
Bowden, William Darsie *retired interior designer*

Bellevue
Hoag, Paul Sterling *architect*

Kirkland
Steinmann, John Colburn *architect*

Mount Vernon
Hall, David Ramsay *architect*
Klein, Henry *architect*

Redmond
King, Indle Gifford *industrial designer, educator*
Sowder, Robert Robertson *architect*

Seattle
Bain, William James, Jr. *architect*
Bosworth, Thomas Lawrence *architect, educator*
Buursma, William F. *architect*
Hastings, L(ois) Jane *architect, educator*
Hinshaw, Mark Larson *architect, urban planner*
Jacobson, Phillip Lee *architect, educator*
Johnston, Norman John *architecture educator, department chairman*
Jonassen, James O. *architect*
Jones, Grant Richard *landscape architect, planner*
Kolb, Keith Robert *architect, educator*
Lovett, Wendell Harper *architect, educator*
Malcolm, Garold Dean *architect*
Meyer, C. Richard *architect*
Miles, Don Clifford *architect*
Morse, John Moore *architect, planner*
Olson, James William Park *architect*
Piven, Peter Anthony *architect, management consultant*

Tacoma
Liddle, Alan Curtis *retired architect*

CANADA

BRITISH COLUMBIA

Vancouver
Erickson, Arthur Charles *architect*
Oberlander, Cornelia Hahn *landscape architect*
Patkau, John *architect*
Patkau, Patricia Frances *architect, architecture educator*

SASKATCHEWAN

Saskatoon
Henry, Keith Douglas *architect*

ADDRESS UNPUBLISHED

Blair, Frederick David *interior designer*
Brotman, David Joel *retired architectural firm executive, consultant*
Budzinski, James Edward *interior designer*
Crowther, Richard Layton *architect, consultant, researcher, author, lecturer*
Dermanis, Paul Raymond *architect*
Dobbel, Rodger Francis *interior designer*
Gerou, Phillip Howard *architect*
Hooper, Roger Fellowes *architect, retired*
Kultermann, Udo *architectural and art historian, educator, author*
Moore, Richard Alan *landscape architect*
Odermatt, Robert Allen *architect*
Peters, Robert Woolsey *architect*
Siefer, Stuart B. *architect*
Thiel, Philip *design educator*
Tomasi, Donald Charles *architect*
Woerner, Robert Lester *landscape architect*

ARTS: LITERARY. *See also* COMMUNICATIONS MEDIA.

UNITED STATES

ALASKA

Anchorage
Strohmeyer, John *writer, former editor*
Thomas, Lowell, Jr. *writer, lecturer, former lieutenant governor, former state senator*

ARIZONA

Phoenix
[illegible] *poet, musician, retired social worker*
Ellison, Cyril Lee *literary agent, retired publisher*

Tempe
Raby, William Louis *writer, consultant*

Tucson
Kingsolver, Barbara Ellen *writer*
Young, Donald Allen *writer, consultant*

CALIFORNIA

Alamo
Reed, John Theodore *writer, publisher*

Arcadia
Sloane, Beverly LeBov *writer, consultant*

Berkeley
Brooke, Tal (Robert Taliaferro) *writer*
Dundes, Alan *writer, folklorist, educator*
Katzen, Mollie *writer, artist*
Kingston, Maxine Hong *writer, educator*
Meltzer, David *author, musician, educator*
Milosz, Czeslaw *poet, writer, educator*
Temko, Allan Bernard *writer*

Beverly Hills
Darabont, Frank *screenwriter, director*
Farrelly, Bobby *writer, producer, director*
Goldman, William *writer*
Mazursky, Paul *screenwriter, theatrical director and producer*
Schulian, John (Nielsen Schulian) *screenwriter, author*
Schulman, Tom *screenwriter*
Shepard, Sam (Samuel Shepard Rogers) *playwright, actor*
Towne, Robert *screenwriter*
Ward, David Schad *screenwriter, film director*

Burbank
Goldstein, Kenneth F. *entertainment executive, software executive*

Cayulos
Shahan, Sherry Jean *writer, educator*

Chino Hills
Sanders, Nancy Ida *writer*

Claremont
Mezey, Robert *poet, educator*
Tilden, Wesley Roderick *writer, retired computer programmer*
Wachtel, Albert *writer, educator*

Cromberg
Kolb, Ken Lloyd *writer*

Cypress
Edmonds, Ivy Gordon *writer*

Davis
Major, Clarence Lee *novelist, poet, educator*

Encino
Williamson, Kevin *writer, producer, director*

Escondido
Bowman, Raymond DeArmond, Sr. *writer, music critic*

Fresno
Levine, Philip *poet, retired educator*
Wayne, Kyra Petrovskaya *writer*

Garden Valley
Price, Lew Paxton *writer, engineer, scientist*

Georgetown
Lengyel, Cornel Adam (Cornel Adam) *writer*

Glendora
Phillips, Jill Meta *novelist, critic, astrologer*

Gualala
Alinder, Mary Street *writer, lecturer*

Hillsborough
Atwood, Mary Sanford *writer*

Irvine
Shusterman, Neal Douglas *writer, screenwriter*
Wolff, Geoffrey Ansell *novelist, critic, educator*

Julian
Rice, Earle (Wilmont), Jr. *writer*

Kensington
Littlejohn, David *writer*
Mc Cann, Cecile Nelken *writer, artist*

La Jolla
Antin, David *poet, critic*
Chopra, Deepak *writer*

Laguna Beach
Ghiselin, Brewster *author, English language educator emeritus*

Lodi
Schulz, Laura Janet *writer, retired secretary*

Long Beach
Dawson, Frances Emily *poet, nurse*

Los Angeles
Basil, Douglas Constantine *writer, educator*
Cohen, Leonard (Norman Cohen) *poet, novelist, musician, songwriter*
Fraser, Brad *playwright, theatrical director, screenwriter*
Highwater, Jamake *author, lecturer*
Lettich, Sheldon Bernard *director, screenwriter*
Messerli, Douglas *writer, publisher*
Quinn, Patricia K. *literary agent*
Rubin, Bruce Joel *screenwriter, director, producer*
Shapiro, Mel *playwright, director, drama educator*
Silverman, Treva *writer, producer, consultant*
Steel, Ronald Lewis *writer, historian, educator*
Westheimer, David Kaplan *novelist*

Oakland
Foley, Jack (John Wayne Harold Foley) *poet, writer, editor*

Palm Springs
Minahan, John English *writer*

Palo Alto
Drexler, Kim Eric *researcher, writer*

Petaluma
Hass, Robert L. *writer, educator*
Pronzini, Bill John (William Pronzini) *writer*

Playa Del Rey
McNeill, Daniel Richard *writer*

Rohnert Park
Haslam, Gerald William *writer, educator*

Sacramento
Robinson, Curtis John *educator, writer, marketer, consultant*

San Anselmo
Torbet, Laura *writer, artist, photographer, graphic designer*

San Diego
Boersma, June Elaine (Jalma Barrett) *writer, photographer*
Krull, Kathleen *juvenile fiction and nonfiction writer*
Lederer, Richard Henry *writer, educator, columnist*
Mahdavi, Kamal B. *writer, researcher*
Prescott, Lawrence Malcolm *medical and health science writer*
Sauer, David Andrew *writer, computer consultant*

San Francisco
Ferris, Russell James, II *freelance writer*
Turner, Tom *writer, editor*
Wayburn, Peggy (Cornelia Elliott Wayburn) *writer, editor*
Whalen, Philip Glenn *poet, novelist*

San Jose
Loventhal, Milton *writer, playwright, lyricist*
Singh, Loren Chan *technical writing specialist*

San Marino
Hull, Suzanne White *writer, retired administrator*

San Rafael
Turner, William Weyand *writer*

Santa Barbara
Bock, Russell Samuel *writer*
Carrel, Annette Felder *writer*
Jackson, Beverley Joy Jacobson *columnist, lecturer*

Santa Clara
Simmons, Janet Bryant *writer, publisher*

Sherman Oaks
Locke, Virginia Otis *writer*

Stanford
Conquest, (George)Robert (Acworth) *writer, historian, poet, critic, journalist*
Gardner, John William *writer, educator*
Steele, Shelby *writer, educator*
Wolff, Tobias (Jonathan Ansell Wolff) *writer*

Studio City
Shavelson, Melville *writer, theatrical producer and director*

West Hollywood
Grasshoff, Alex *writer, producer, director*

COLORADO

Boulder
Waldman, Anne Lesley *poet, performer, editor, publisher, educational administrator*

Colorado Springs
Dassanowsky, Robert von *educator, producer, writer, editor*
Hicks, David Earl *writer, inventor*
Whalin, W. Terry *writer, editor*
Yaffe, James *writer*

Denver
Dallas, Sandra *writer*
Ducker, Bruce *novelist, lawyer*
MacGregor, George Lescher, Jr. *freelance writer*
Nemiro, Beverly Mirium Anderson *author, educator*

HAWAII

Pahoa
Salat, Cristina *writer*

IDAHO

Sun Valley
Briley, John Richard *writer*

MONTANA

Bonner
Smith, Annick *writer, producer*

NEVADA

Henderson
Furimsky, Stephen, Jr. *freelance writer*

NEW MEXICO

Galisteo
Lippard, Lucy Rowland *writer, lecturer*

Las Cruces
Medoff, Mark Howard *playwright, screenwriter, novelist*

Portales
Williamson, Jack (John Stewart) *writer*

Ranchos De Taos
Dickey, Robert Preston *writer, educator, poet*

Santa Fe
Bergé, Carol *writer*
Tarn, Nathaniel *poet, translator, educator*

NEW YORK

New York
Hjortsberg, William Reinhold *writer*

OREGON

Grants Pass
Stafford, Patrick Purcell *poet, writer, management consultant*

Mcminnville
Kherdian, David *writer*

Newport
Kennedy, Richard Jerome *writer*

Pleasant Hill
Kesey, Ken *writer*

Portland
Rutsala, Vern A. *poet, English language educator, writer*

UTAH

Provo
Hart, Edward LeRoy *poet, educator*

Salt Lake City
Osherow, Jacqueline Sue *poet, English language educator*
Skurzynski, Gloria Joan *writer*

WASHINGTON

Bremerton
Hanf, James Alphonso *poet, government official*

Kirkland
Szablya, Helen Mary *writer, language professional, lecturer*

La Conner
Robbins, Thomas Eugene *writer*

Lynnwood
Bear, Gregory Dale *writer, illustrator*

Port Angeles
Muller, Willard C(hester) *writer*

Sammamish
Trask, Robert Riley Chauncey *author, lecturer, foundation executive*

Seattle
Kenney, Richard Laurence *poet, English language educator*
MacKenzie, Peter Sean *writer*
Mc Intyre, Vonda Neel *writer*
McHugh, Heather *poet*
Wagoner, David Russell *writer, educator*

Tacoma
Maynard, Steven Harry *writer*

WYOMING

Laramie
Boresi, Arthur Peter *writer, educator*

Pinedale
Barlow, John Perry *writer*

CANADA

BRITISH COLUMBIA

Chilliwack
Kinsella, William Patrick *writer, educator*

Vancouver
Bowering, George Harry *writer, English literature educator*

ADDRESS UNPUBLISHED

Avery, Stephen Neal *playwright, author*
Baird, Alan C. *screenwriter*
Baker, Lucinda *writer*
Barker, Clive *artist, screenwriter, director, producer, writer*
Berry, Richard Lewis *writer, magazine editor, lecturer, programmer*
Bower, Janet Esther *writer, educator*
[illegible]
Coonts, Stephen Paul *novelist*
Davidson, Mark *writer, educator*
Donnally, Patricia Broderick *writer*

Eglee, Charles Hamilton *television and movie writer, producer*
Farrelly, Peter John *screenwriter*
Fraser, Kathleen Joy *poet, creative writing educator*
Gottlieb, Sherry Gershon *author, editor*
Groening, Matthew *writer, cartoonist*
Haas, Charlie *screenwriter*
Herman, George Adam *retired writer*
Houze, Herbert George *writer*
Isbell, Harold M(ax) *writer, investor*
Krantz, Judith Tarcher *novelist*
Kushner, Tony *playwright*
Lawrence, Jerome *playwright, director, educator*
Lopez, Barry Holstun *writer*
Madsen, Susan Arrington *writer*
McMillan, Terry L. *writer, educator*
Mogel, Leonard Henry *writer*
Morrow, Barry Nelson *screenwriter, producer*
Pantaleo, Jack *writer, composer, social worker, harpist*
Parke, Marilyn Neils *writer*
Schenkkan, Robert Frederic *writer, actor*
Selby, Hubert, Jr. *writer*
Shagan, Steve *screenwriter, novelist, film producer*
Shearer, Harry Julius *screenwriter, director, actor*
Shindler, Merrill Karsh *writer, radio personality*
Skinner, Knute Rumsey *poet, English educator*
Stone, Oliver *screenwriter, director*
Zaillian, Steven *screenwriter, director*

ARTS: PERFORMING

UNITED STATES

ARIZONA

Flagstaff
Aurand, Charles Henry, Jr. *music educator, educator*

Mesa
Mason, Marshall W. *theater director, educator*

Phoenix
Aschaffenburg, Walter Eugene *composer, music educator*
Speers, David *opera company director*
Uthoff, Michael *dancer, choreographer, artistic director*

Scottsdale
Smith, Leonard Bingley *musician*
Wolfgang, Bonnie Arlene *musician, bassoonist*

Sedona
Gregory, James *retired actor*
Griffin, Jean (Alva Jean Griffin) *entertainer*
Rhines, Marie Louise *composer, violinist*

Sun City
Yestadt, James Francis *music director, conductor*

Tempe
Lombardi, Eugene Patsy *retired orchestra conductor, violinist, educator*
Nagrin, Daniel *dancer, educator, choreographer, lecturer, writer*

Tucson
Hanson, George *music director, conductor*
Roe, Charles Richard *baritone*
Seaman, Arlene Anna *retired musician, educator*

CALIFORNIA

Albany
Boris, Ruthanna *dancer, choreographer, dance therapist, educator*

Apple Valley
Beller, Gerald Stephen *professional magician, former insurance company executive*

Aptos
Swenson, Kathleen Susan *music and art educator*

Benicia
Cummings, Barton *musician*

Berkeley
Dresher, Paul Joseph *composer, music educator, performer*
Reid, Frances Evelyn Kroll *cinematographer, director, film company executive*

Beverly Hills
Allen, Debbie *actress, dancer, director, choreographer*
Ames, Edmund Dantes *singer, actor, producer*
Anders, Allison *film director, screenwriter*
Anderson, Louie *comedian*
Anka, Paul *singer, composer*
Bauer, Marty *talent agency executive*
Berkus, James *talent agent*
Bishop, Joey (Joseph Abraham Gottlieb) *comedian*
Blades, Ruben *singer, songwriter, composer*
Brockie, Pamela *motion picture executive*
Brokaw, Norman Robert *talent agency executive*
Burnham, John Ludwig *agent*
Carreras, José *tenor*
Casey, Sue (Suzanne Marguerite Philips) *actress, real estate broker*
Cher, (Cherilyn Sarkisian) *singer, actress*
Chritton, George A. *theater producer*
Columbus, Chris *film director, screenwriter*
Crawford, Cindy *model, actress*
Eastwood, Clint *actor, film director, former mayor*
Emmerich, Roland *director, producer, writer*
Foster, Lawrence *concert and opera conductor*
Gabler, Lee *talent agency executive*
Grey, Brad *producer, agent*
Griffin, Merv Edward *former entertainer, television producer, entrepreneur*
Guest, Christopher *actor, director, screenwriter*
Hanson, Curtis *director, writer*
Heston, Charlton (John Charlton Carter) *actor*
Hewitt, Jennifer Love *actress, singer*
Hill, Michael J. *film editor*
Hoy, William *film editor*
Hughes, John W. *film producer, screenwriter, film director*
Hurd, Gale Anne *film producer*
Hurley, Elizabeth *actress, model*
Huvane, Kevin *talent agent*
Idle, Eric *actor, screenwriter, producer, songwriter*
Ingels, Marty *theatrical agent, television and motion picture production executive*
Jackson, Janet Damita *singer, dancer*
Jordan, Glenn *director*
Josephson, Nancy *talent agent*
Kellman, Barnet Kramer *film, stage and television director*
Kerns, Joanna de Varona *actress, writer, director*
Kravitz, Lenny *singer, guitarist*
Leary, Denis *comedian*
Leder, Mimi *television director*
Limato, Edward Frank *talent agent*
Linkletter, Arthur Gordon *radio and television broadcaster*
Little, Rich (Richard Caruthers Little) *comedian, impressionist, actor*
Lopez, Jennifer *actress, dancer, singer*
Lourd, Bryan *talent agent*
Lovett, Richard *talent agency executive*
Mann, Michael K. *producer, director, writer*
Martin, Steve *comedian, actor*
Mischer, Donald Leo *television director and producer*
Nabors, James Thurston *actor, singer*
Nesmith, Michael *film producer, video specialist*
Neuwirth, Bebe *dancer, actress*
Nicita, Rick *agent*
O'Connor, David *talent agent*
Penderecki, Krzysztof *composer, conductor*
Ptak, John *talent agent*
Rafkin, Alan *television and film director*
Reese, Della (Deloreese Patricia Early) *singer, actress*
Reiser, Paul *actor, comedian*
Riley, Jack *actor, writer*
Rivers, Joan *entertainer*
Rosenberg, Philip *production designer*
Russell, Ken (Henry Kenneth Alfred Russell) *film and theatre director*
Shandling, Garry *comedian, scriptwriter, actor*
Short, Martin *actor, comedian*
Simpson, Michael *talent agent*
Sonnenfeld, Barry *director, cinematographer*
Spielberg, Steven *motion picture director, producer*
Streisand, Barbra Joan *singer, actress, director*
Swayze, Patrick *actor, dancer*
Thompson, Caroline Warner *film director, screenwriter*
Thompson, Larry Angelo *producer, lawyer, personal manager*
Trueba, Fernando *film director and producer, screenwriter*
Turlington, Christy *model*
Underwood, Ronald Brian *director, producer*
White, Betty *actress, comedienne*
Wiatt, James Anthony *theatrical agency executive*
Yorn, Rick *talent agent*

Box Canyon
Dolenz, Mickey (George Michael Dolenz) *singer, actor, television producer*

Burbank
Baker, Rick *make-up artist*
Berman, Bruce *entertainment company executive, television producer*
Clark, Dick *performer, producer*
Cole, Paula *pop singer, songwriter*
de Cordova, Frederick Timmins *television producer, director*
DeMent, Iris *vocalist, songwriter*
Ernst, Donald William *producer*
Fogerty, John Cameron *musician, composer*
Greene, Shecky *entertainer*
La Maina, Francis C. *performing company executive*
Lang, K. D. (Katherine Dawn Lang) *country music singer, composer*
Leno, Jay (James Douglas Muir Leno) *television personality, comedian, writer*
Mc Govern, Maureen Therese *entertainer*
Neill, Ve *make-up artist*
Petty, Tom *rock guitarist, band leader, composer*
Sajak, Pat *television game show host*
Snyder, David L. *film production designer*

Calabasas
Bernhard, Sandra *actress, comedienne, singer*
Isham, Mark *composer, jazz musician*

Carlsbad
Missett, Judi Sheppard *dancer, jazzercise company executive*

Carmel Valley
Meckel, Peter Timothy *arts administrator, educator*

Claremont
Herschensohn, Bruce *film director, writer*

Coronado
Neblett, Carol *soprano*

Culver City
Brooks, Mel *producer, director, writer, actor*
Devlin, Dean *producer, writer, actor*
Walsh, Thomas A. *production designer*

Dana Point
Camp, Joseph Shelton, Jr. *film producer, director, writer*

Davis
Swift, Richard G(ene) *composer, educator*

Del Mar
Ogdon, Wilbur (Will Ogdon) *composer, music educator*

Encino
Conway, Tim *comedian*
Zsigmond, Vilmos *cinematographer, director*

Fresno
Shmavonian, Gerald S. *film producer*

Fullerton
Duncan, Griff *music theater company executive*
Karson, Burton Lewis *musician, educator*

Glendale
Grillo, Leo *actor, photographer, animal rescuer*
Michelson, Lillian *motion picture researcher*
Sprosty, Joseph Patrick *producer, writer, weapons specialist*

Hollywood
Lewis, Huey (Hugh Anthony Cregg III) *singer, composer, bandleader*
Little Richard, (Richard Wayne Penniman) *recording artist, pianist, songwriter, minister*
Miles, Joanna *actress, playwright, director*
Salzman, David Elliot *entertainment industry executive*
Warren, Diane *song writer*

Irvine
Cohen, Robert Stephen *drama educator*
Ruyter, Nancy Lee Chalfa *dance educator*
Van Mason, Raymond *dancer, choreographer*

Kentfield
Halprin, Anna Schuman (Mrs. Lawrence Halprin) *dancer*

La Jolla
Davis, Anthony *composer, pianist, educator*
Reynolds, Roger Lee *composer, educator*

Long Beach
Wilcox, David Cornell *ballet company director*

Los Angeles
Banner, Bob *television producer, director*
Barker, Robert William *television personality*
Bell, Lee Phillip *television personality, television producer*
Bialosky, Marshall Howard *composer*
Borda, Deborah *symphony orchestra executive*
Burrows, James *television and motion picture director, producer*
Carlin, George Denis *comedian*
Cates, Gilbert *film, theater, television producer and director*
Charles, Ray *musician, composer, lyricist, arranger, conductor*
Cho, Margaret *comedian, actress*
Cole, Natalie Maria *singer*
Conner, Lindsay Andrew *screenwriter, producer*
Conniff, Ray *popular musician, conductor, composer, arranger*
Craig, Sidney Richard *theatrical agent*
Crockett, Donald Harold *composer, university educator*
D'Accone, Frank Anthony *music educator*
Davidson, Gordon *theatrical producer, director*
DuMont, James Kelton, Jr. *actor, producer*
Elrod, Lu *music educator, actress, author*
Englund, Robert *actor, director, producer*
Feinstein, Michael Jay *singer, pianist, musicologist, actor*
Fleischmann, Ernest Martin *music administrator*
Garofalo, Janeane *actress, comedienne*
Gibbons, Leeza *television talk show host, entertainment reporter*
Goldsmith, Jerry *composer*
Hart, Mary *television talk show host*
Hartke, Stephen Paul *composer, educator*
Hayes, Isaac *rhythm and blues singer, composer*
Helgeland, Brian *film director, writer, producer*
Hemion, Dwight Arlington *television producer, director*
Hirsch, Judd *actor*
Horovitz, Adam *recording artist*
Ice-T, (Tracy Marrow) *rap singer, actor*
Iglesias, Julio (Julio Jose Iglesias De La Cueva) *singer, songwriter*
Jones, Tom *singer*
Kelley, David E. *producer, writer*
Kovacs, Laszlo *cinematographer*
Lansing, Sherry Lee *motion picture production executive*
Lear, Norman Milton *producer, writer, director*
Leighton, Robert *film editor*
London, Andrew Barry *film editor*
Love, Courtney *singer, actress*
Lunden, Joan *television personality*
Maher, Bill *talk show host, comedian, producer*
Maldonado, Gregory Matthew *music director, educator*
Malick, Terrence (David Whitney II) *film director*
Malone, Nancy *actor, director, producer*
Marshall, Meryl *telecommunications executive, lawyer*
McQueen, Justice Ellis (L. Q. Jones) *actor, director*
Miller, Ann (Lucille Ann Collier) *actress, dancer, singer*
Milsome, Douglas *cinematographer*
Mirisch, Lawrence Alan *motion picture agent*
Mueller, Carl Richard *theater arts educator, author*
Newhart, Bob *entertainer*
Nilles, Laila Padorr *musician, record producer*
Norman, Marc *screenwriter, producer*
O'Day, Anita Belle Colton *entertainer, singer*
Perez, Rosie *actress*
Pettibon, Raymond *video artist*
Pickett, Wilson *vocalist, composer*
Presley, Priscilla *actress*
Rachins, Alan *actor, screenwriter*
Reid, Tim *actor, producer*
Rickles, Donald Jay *comedian, actor*
Sargent, Joseph Daniel *motion picture and television director*
Sayles, John Thomas *film director, writer, actor*
Schmidt, Arthur *film editor*
Tarantino, Quentin *film director, screenwriter*
Ullman, Tracey *actress, singer*
Urioste, Frank J. *film editor*
Van Dyke, Jerry *actor, comedian*
Waits, Thomas Alan *composer, actor, singer*
Williams, Paul Hamilton *composer, singer*
Winters, Barbara Jo *musician*
Yankovic, (Weird) Al *singer, satirist*

Menlo Park
Baez, Joan Chandos *folk singer*

Mountain View
Bobel, Mary *video development company financial executive*

North Hollywood
Grasso, Mary Ann *theater association executive*
Kantor, Igo *film and television producer*
Smothers, Tom *actor, singer*
Taravella, Rosie *actress, writer*

Oakland
DeFazio, Lynette Stevens *dancer, choreographer, educator, chiropractor, author, actress, musician*
Randle, Ellen Eugenia Foster *opera and classical singer, educator*
Zschau, Marilyn *singer*

Ojai
Cusumano, James Anthony *filmmaker, retired pharmaceutical company executive*

Pasadena
Horak, Jan-Christopher *film studies educator, curator*

Petaluma
Murphy, George *special effects expert*

Pleasant Hill
Jekowsky, Barry *conductor, music director*

Pleasanton
Goddard, John Wesley *cable television company executive*

Richmond
Lasseter, John P. *film director, computer animator*

Riverside
Adams, Byron *composer, conductor*

Sacramento
Nice, Carter *conductor, music director*

San Diego
Arova, Sonia *artistic director, ballet educator*
Campbell, Ian David *opera company director*
Flettner, Marianne *opera administrator*
Ward-Steinman, David *composer, music educator, pianist*

San Dimas
Peters, Joseph Donald *filmmaker*

San Francisco
Caniparoli, Val William *choreographer, dancer*
Cisneros, Evelyn *dancer*
Eilenberg, Lawrence Ira *theater educator, artistic director*
Festinger, Richard *music educator, composer*
George, Vance *conductor*
Getty, Gordon Peter *composer, philanthropist*
Hastings, Edward Walton *theater director*
Jacobus, Arthur *dance company administrator*
King, Alonzo *artistic director, choreographer*
LeBlanc, Tina *dancer*
Maffre, Muriel *ballet dancer*
Peterson, Wayne Turner *composer, pianist*
Pippin, Donald Ferrell *musician, director, conductor*
Runnicles, Donald *conductor*
Sheinfeld, David *composer*
Stowell, Christopher R. *dancer*
Talbot, Stephen Henderson *television producer, writer*
Tiano, Anthony Steven *television producer, book publishing executive*
Tomasson, Helgi *dancer, choreographer, dance company executive*
Van Dyck, Wendy *dancer*

San Jose
Dalis, Irene *mezzo-soprano, opera company administrator, music educator*
Grin, Leonid *conductor*
Near, Timothy *theater director*
Shuster, Diana *artistic director*

San Marino
Hicklin, Ronald Lee *music production company executive*

San Rafael
Lucas, George W., Jr. *film director, producer, screenwriter*
Sheldon, Gary *conductor, music director*

Santa Ana
St. Clair, Carl *conductor, music director*

Santa Barbara
Ben-Dor, Gisselle *conductor, musician*
Wayland, Newton Hart *conductor*

Santa Cruz
Winston, George *solo pianist, guitarist, harmonica player*

Santa Monica
Cameron, James *film director, screenwriter, producer*
Diamond, Neil Leslie *singer, composer*
Hersh, Kristin *vocalist, musician*
Kaminski, Janusz *cinematographer*
LaBelle, Patti *singer*
Pisano, A. Robert *entertainment company executive, lawyer*
Smith, Anna Deavere *actor, educator, playwright*
Suschitzky, Peter *cinematographer*
Vacano, Jost *cinematographer*

Santa Ynez
Harris, Richard A. *film editor*

Sebastopol
Snyder, Allegra Fuller *dance educator*

Sherman Oaks
Bergman, Alan *lyricist, writer*
Bergman, Marilyn Keith *lyricist, writer*
Gibbs, Antony (Tony) *film editor*
Hemsley, Sherman *comedian, actor*

Horner, James *composer*
Schlessinger, Laura *radio talk show host*
Tesh, John *television talk show host, musician*
Williams, John Towner *composer, conductor*

South Pasadena
White-Thomson, Ian Leonard *opera company administrator*

Stanford
Cohen, Albert *musician, educator*

Studio City
Barbera, Joseph *motion picture and television producer, cartoonist*
Barrett, Dorothy *performing arts administrator*
Duffield, Thomas Andrew *art director, production designer*
Johnston, Kristen *television personality*
Richman, Peter Mark *actor, painter, writer, producer*
Werner, Tom *television producer, professional baseball team executive*

Turlock
Klein, James Mikel *music educator, associate dean*

Universal City
Meyer, Ron *agent*
Midler, Bette *singer, entertainer, actress*

Universal Cty
Rapke, Jack *agent*

Upland
Robertson, Carey Jane *musician, educator*

Valley Vlg
Barkin, Elaine Radoff *composer, music educator*

Van Nuys
Morgan, Lanny *musician*

West Hollywood
Annakin, Kenneth Cooper *film director, writer*
Baker, Anita *singer*
Henley, Don *singer, drummer, songwriter*
Jaglom, Henry David *actor, director, writer*
Madonna, (Madonna Louise Veronica Ciccone) *singer, actress*
Seymour, Michael *production designer*
Shaye, Robert Kenneth *cinema company executive*
Stein, Benjamin J. *television personality, writer, lawyer, economist*

Woodland
Bryson, Peabo *vocalist, songwriter*

Woodland Hills
Levy, Norman *motion picture company executive*
Wester, Keith Albert *film and television recording engineer, real estate developer*

COLORADO

Aspen
Young, Henry *executive director*
Zinman, David Joel *conductor*

Boulder
Bernstein, Giora *artistic director*
Boydston, James Christopher *composer*
Brakhage, James Stanley *filmmaker, educator*
Duckworth, Guy *musician, pianist, educator*
Fink, Robert Russell *music theorist, former university dean*
Kuchar, Theodore *conductor, academic administrator, musician*
Lightfoot, William Carl *performing arts association executive, symphony musician*
Sable, Barbara Kinsey *former music educator*
Sarson, John Christopher *television producer, director, writer*
Symons, James Martin *theater and dance educator*

Colorado Springs
Bergman, Yaacov *performing company executive*

Denver
Allen, Keith W. *actor, singer, songwriter*
Alsop, Marin *conductor*
Ceci, Jesse Arthur *violinist*
Fredmann, Martin *ballet artistic director, educator, choreographer*
Robinson, Cleo Parker *artistic director*

Grand Junction
Gustafson, Kirk *performing company executive*

HAWAII

Honolulu
Moulin, Jane Ann Freeman *ethnomusicology educator, researcher*
Wong, Samuel *conductor*

IDAHO

Boise
Ogle, James *performing company executive*
Pimble, Toni *artistic director, choreographer, educator*

Idaho Falls
LoPiccolo, John *conductor, music director*

Pocatello
George, Thom Ritter *conductor, composer*
Stanek, Alan Edward *music educator, performer, administrator, retired*

Sandpoint
Kramer, Remi Thomas *film director*

MONTANA

Billings
Barnea, Uri N. *music director, conductor, composer, violinist*

Bozeman
Savery, Matthew *music conductor, director, educator*

Great Falls
Johnson, Gordon James *artistic director, conductor*

Missoula
Knowles, William Leroy (Bill Knowles) *television news producer, journalism educator*

NEVADA

Carson City
Bugli, David *conductor, arranger, composer*

Las Vegas
Castro, Joseph Armand *music director, pianist, composer, orchestrator*
Goulet, Robert Gerard *singer, actor*
Lewis, Jerry (Joseph Levitch) *comedian*
Sulich, Vassili *artistic director*
Wiemer, Robert Ernest *film and television producer, writer, director*

Reno
Daniels, Ronald Dale *conductor*

NEW MEXICO

Albuquerque
Evans, Bill (James William Evans) *dancer, choreographer, educator, arts administrator*

Santa Fe
Ballard, Louis Wayne *composer*
Crosby, John O'Hea *opera general director*
Gaddes, Richard *performing arts administrator*
Reggio, Godfrey *film director*
Rubenstein, Bernard *orchestra conductor*

NEW YORK

New York
Mansouri, Lotfollah (Lotfi Mansouri) *general director of opera company*
Nagano, Kent George *conductor*
Tilson Thomas, Michael *symphony conductor*

OHIO

Cleveland
Nahat, Dennis F. *artistic director, choreographer*

OREGON

Ashland
Hirschfeld, Gerald Joseph *cinematographer*
Shaw, Arthur E. *conductor*

Eugene
Bailey, Exine Margaret Anderson *soprano, educator*
Benson, Joan *musician, music educator*
Riley, Grannan *performing company executive*

Portland
Bailey, Robert C. *opera company executive*
Berentsen, Kurtis George *music educator, choral conductor*
Canfield, James *artistic director*
DePreist, James Anderson *conductor*
Huggett, Monica *performing company executive*
Leyden, Norman *conductor*

UTAH

Cedar City
Cook, Douglas Neilson *theater educator, producer, artistic director*

Provo
Woodbury, Lael Jay *theater educator*

Salt Lake City
Andrews, Donald L. *performing arts company executive*
Ewers, Anne *opera company director*
Grant, Raymond Thomas *arts administrator*
Morey, Charles Leonard, III *theatrical director*
Silverstein, Joseph Harry *conductor, musician*

WASHINGTON

Bremerton
Cottrell-Adkins, Leone *opera company director*

Friday Harbor
Waite, Ric *cinematographer*

Seattle
Anang, Kofi *artistic director, educator, dancer*
Card, Deborah Frances *orchestra administrator*
Forbes, David Craig *musician*
Jenkins, Speight *opera company executive, writer*
Jones, Samuel Leander *conductor*
Nishitani, Martha *dancer*
Russell, Francia *ballet director, educator*
Smith, Jeffrey L. (The Frugal Gourmet) *cooking expert, television personality, author*
Stowell, Kent *ballet director*
Thomas, Karen P. *composer, conductor*
Wolf, Hans *opera company director*

Snohomish
Philpott, Larry La Fayette *horn player*

Spokane
Bray, R(obert) Bruce *music educator*
Graham, Bill *opera company director*
Halvorson, Marjory *opera director*
Pugh, Kyle Mitchell, Jr. *musician, retired music educator*

CANADA

ALBERTA

Alberta
Nissinen, Mikko Pekka *dancer*

Calgary
Graf, Hans *conductor*
Monk, Allan James *baritone*
Raeburn, Andrew Harvey *performing arts association executive, record producer*

BRITISH COLUMBIA

Vancouver
Agler, David *conductor*
Raffi, (Raffi Cavoukian) *folksinger, children's entertainer*
Washburn, Jon *artistic director*
Wright, James W. *entertainment company executive*

Victoria
Devan, David *opera company director*
Vernon, Timothy *artistic director*

ENGLAND

London
Hemmings, Peter William *orchestra and opera administrator*

ADDRESS UNPUBLISHED

Adams, Bryan *vocalist, composer*
Alberts, David *artistic director, mime*
Baerwald, Susan Grad *television broadcasting company executive producer*
Bergen, Candice *actress, writer, photojournalist*
Bissell, James Dougal, III *motion picture production designer*
Brady, Mary Rolfes *music educator, educator*
Brosnan, Peter Lawrence *documentary filmmaker*
Crosby, Norman Lawrence *comedian*
Cunningham, Ron *choreographer, artistic director*
Debus, Eleanor Viola *retired business management company executive*
DeGeneres, Ellen *actress, comedian*
Elias, Rosalind *mezzo-soprano*
Elikann, Lawrence S. (Larry Elikann) *television and film director*
Epton, Gregg *performing company executive*
Fogelberg, Daniel Grayling *songwriter, singer*
Frankish, Brian Edward *film producer, director*
Fullenwider, Nancy Vrana *music composer, dance educator, pianist*
Goddard, James Russell *producer, writer, actor*
Goen, Bob *television show host*
Great, Don Charles *composer, music company executive*
Guttman, Irving Allen *opera stage director*
Harper, Richard Henry *film producer, director*
Holman, Bill *composer*
Huning, Devon Gray *actress, dancer, audiologist, veterinary technician, photographer, video producer and editor*
Issari, M(ohammad) Ali *film producer, writer, consultant*
Jarrett, Keith *pianist, composer*
Kaylan, Howard Lawrence *musical entertainer, composer*
Kåge, Jonas *ballet company artistic director*
Lewitzky, Bella *choreographer*
Little, Loren Everton *musician, ophthalmologist*
Marshall, Peter *actor, singer, game show host*
Mehta, Zubin *conductor, musician*
Muren, Dennis E. *visual effects director*
Myers, Mike *actor, writer*
Myerson, Alan *film and television director*
Neary, Patricia Elinor *ballet director*
Nichols, Mike *stage and film director*
O'Brien, Jack George *artistic director*
O'Hara, Catherine *actress, comedienne*
Pastreich, Peter *orchestra executive director*
Phillips, Michelle Gilliam *actress, author*
Poledouris, Basil K. *composer*
Poster, Steven Barry *cinematographer, photographer, publisher, digital imaging consultant*
Redgrave, Lynn *actress*
Roseanne, (Roseanne Barr) *actress, comedienne, producer, writer*
Sandrich, Jay H. *television director*
Seale, John Clement *director, cinematographer*
Seinfeld, Jerry *comedian*
Silvestri, Alan Anthony *film composer*
Smith, Irby Jay *film producer*
Strock, Herbert Leonard *motion picture producer, director, editor, writer*
Summers, Cathleen Ann *film producer*
Symmes, Daniel Leslie *technology executive, producer, director*
Taylor, Guy Watson *symphonic conductor*
Tinker, Mark Christian *producer, director*
Vallone, John Charles *motion picture production designer*
von Brandenstein, Patrizia *production designer*
Williamson, Laird *stage director, actor*
Yared, Gabriel *composer*

Zappa, Gail *record producer*

ARTS: VISUAL

UNITED STATES

ALASKA

Cordova
Bugbee-Jackson, Joan *sculptor, educator*

ARIZONA

Clarkdale
Eide, Joel S. *art consultant, appraiser*

Lake Montezuma
Burkee, Irvin *artist*

Mesa
Kaida, Tamarra *art and photography educator*

Phoenix
Herranen, Kathy *artist, graphic designer*

Prescott
Stasack, Edward Armen *artist*
Willoughby, James Russell *artist, writer*

Prescott Valley
Decil, Stella Walters (Del Decil) *artist*

Scottsdale
Heller, Jules *artist, writer, educator*
Lang, Margo Terzian *artist*
Pitcher, Helen Ione *advertising director*

Tucson
Kingery, William David *ceramics and anthropology educator*
Matthew, Neil Edward *artist, educator*

CALIFORNIA

Anaheim
Nelipovich, Sandra Grassi *artist*

Aptos
Woods, Gurdon Grant *sculptor*

Arcadia
Danziger, Louis *graphic designer, educator*

Arcata
Land-Weber, Ellen *photography educator*

Aromas
Nutzle, Futzie (Bruce John Kleinsmith) *artist, writer, cartoonist*

Berkeley
Genn, Nancy *artist*
Hartman, Robert Leroy *artist, educator*
Kasten, Karl Albert *painter, printmaker, educator*
Miyasaki, George Joji *artist*
Nanao, Kenjilo *artist, educator*
Simpson, David William *artist, educator*
Sussman, Wendy Rodriguez *artist, educator*

Beverly Hills
Rodkin, Loree *jewelry artist*

Bodega
Hedrick, Wally Bill *artist*

Bolinas
Okamura, Arthur Shinji *artist, educator, writer*

Carlsbad
Diaz, David *illustrator*

Carmel
Jacobs, Ralph, Jr. *artist*
Kenna, Michael *photographer*
Kennedy, John Edward *art dealer, appraiser, curator*

Carson
Hirsch, Gilah Yelin *artist, writer*

Claremont
Benjamin, Karl Stanley *art educator*
Blizzard, Alan *artist*
Casanova, Aldo John *sculptor*
Dunye, Cheryl *artist, film maker*
Zornes, Milford *artist*

Costa Mesa
Muller, Jerome Kenneth *photographer, art director, editor*

Culver City
Pittard, William Blackburn (Billy Pittard) *television graphic designer*

Cypress
Bloom, Julian *artist, editor*

Flintridge
Johnston, Oliver Martin, Jr. *animator*

Fresno
Stuart, Dorothy Mae *artist*

Greenbrae
Blatt, Morton Bernard *medical illustrator*

Irvine
Giannulli, Mossimo *designer, apparel business executive*

La Jolla
Silva, Ernest R. *visual arts educator, artist*

Lafayette
Shurtleff, Akiko Aoyagi *artist, consultant*

Larkspur
Napoles, Veronica Kleeman *graphic designer, consultant*

Long Beach
Viola, Bill *artist, writer*

Los Angeles
Byrd, Marc Robert *designer, florist*
Caroompas, Carole Jean *artist, educator*
Caryl, Naomi *artist*
Curran, Darryl Joseph *photographer, educator*
Galanos, James *retired fashion designer*
Hamilton, Patricia Rose *artist agent*
Hockney, David *artist*
Judge, Mike *animator*
Ketchum, Robert Glenn *photographer, print maker*
Park, Lee (Lee Parklee) *artist*
Pastor, Jennifer *sculptor*
Pederson, Con *animator*
Rankaitis, Susan *artist*
Stone, George *artist, art educator*
Wells, Annie *photographer*

Malibu
Bowman, Bruce *art educator, writer, artist*

Mckinleyville
Berry, Glenn *educator, artist*

Mendocino
de la Fuente, Lawrence Edward *artist*

Monrovia
Dobay, Susan Vilma *artist*

Monterey
Karsh, Yousuf *photographer*

Morgan Hill
Freimark, Robert (Bob Freimark) *artist*

Oakland
Gonzalez, Arthur Padilla *artist, educator*
Rath, Alan T. *sculptor*
Thompson, Mark Lee *art educator, sculptor*

Orinda
Epperson, Stella Marie *artist*

Oxnard
Sweet, Harvey *theatrical set designer, lighting designer*

Pacific Grove
Elinson, Henry David *artist, language educator*

Palm Desert
Moroles, Jesus Bautista *sculptor*

Pasadena
Pashgian, Margaret Helen *artist*
Sakoguchi, Ben *artist, retired art educator*

Phelan
Erwin, Joan Lenore *artist, educator*

Pinole
Gerbracht, Robert Thomas (Bob Gerbracht) *painter, educator*

Riverside
Bell, Helen Lavin *artist*

San Diego
Barone, Angela Maria *artist, researcher*

San Francisco
Adams, Mark *artist*
Beall, Dennis Ray *artist, educator*
Bechtle, Robert Alan *artist, educator*
Chin, Sue Soone Marian (Suchin Chin) *conceptual artist, portraitist, photographer, community affairs activist*
DeSoto, Lewis Damien *art educator*
Dickinson, Eleanor Creekmore *artist, educator*
Frey, Viola *sculptor, educator*
Hershman, Lynn Lester *artist*
Howard, David E. *artist*
Komenich, Kim *photographer*
Martin, Fred *artist, college administrator*
Mayeri, Beverly *artist, ceramic sculptor, educator*
McClintock, Jessica *fashion designer*
Piccolo, Richard Andrew *artist, educator*
Presniakov, Alexander *painter, sculptor, inventor*
Raciti, Cherie *artist*
Rascón, Armando *artist*
Stermer, Dugald Robert *designer, illustrator, writer, consultant*
Van Hoesen, Beth Marie *artist, printmaker*

San Jose
Estabrook, Reed *artist, educator*
Porter, John Paul *artist, educator*

San Luis Obispo
Dickerson, Colleen Bernice Patton *artist, educator*

San Pedro
Parkhurst, Violet Kinney *artist*

Santa Barbara
Eguchi, Yasu *artist*

Santa Cruz
Summers, Carol *artist*

Santa Monica
Jenkins, George *stage designer, film art director*
Schroeder, William Robert *graphic designer, actor, linguist*

Santa Rosa
Monk, Diana Charla *artist, stable owner*

Santa Ynez
Rymer, Ilona Suto *artist, retired educator*

Sausalito
Kuhlman, Walter Egel *artist, educator*

Sherman Oaks
Hoover, Richard *set designer*
Powell, Sandy *costume designer*
Weiss, Julie *costume designer*

Somis
Kehoe, Vincent Jeffré-Roux *photographer, author, cosmetic company executive*

South Pasadena
Askin, Walter Miller *artist, educator*

Stockton
Oak, Claire Morisset *artist, educator*

Temecula
Bouchard, Paul Eugene *artist*

Topanga
Millar, Robert *artist*

Venice
Chipman, Jack *artist*
Garabedian, Charles *artist*

West Covina
Shiershke, Nancy Fay *artist, educator, property manager*

West Hollywood
Chillida, Eduardo *sculptor*

COLORADO

Boulder
Chong, Albert Valentine *artist, educator*
Matthews, Eugene Edward *artist*

Colorado Springs
Goehring, Kenneth *artist*

Denver
Enright, Cynthia Lee *illustrator*
McElhinney, James Lancel *artist, educator*

Lake George
Norman, John Barstow, Jr. *designer, educator*

Littleton
Barnes, Cloyd Ray *sculptor, retired engineer*

Loveland
Bierbaum, Janith Marie *artist*

Snowmass Village
Beeman, Malinda Mary *artist, program administrator*

HAWAII

Lahaina
Sato, Tadashi *artist*

MONTANA

Livingston
Chatham, Russell *artist*

Missoula
Autio, Rudy *artist, educator*
Rippon, Thomas Michael *art educator, artist*

NEVADA

Henderson
Turner, Florence Frances *ceramist*

Las Vegas
Goldblatt, Hal Michael *photographer, accountant*

Reno
Goin, Peter Jackson *art educator*
High, Steven Samuel *art gallery official*
Newberg, Dorothy Beck (Mrs. William C. Newberg) *portrait artist*
Waddell, Theodore *painter*

NEW MEXICO

Albuquerque
Adams, Clinton *artist, historian*
Antreasian, Garo Zareh *artist, lithographer, art educator*
Barrow, Thomas Francis *artist, educator*
Barry, Steve *sculptor, educator*
Hahn, Betty *artist, photographer, educator*
Keating, David *photographer*
Witkin, Joel-Peter *photographer*

Belen
Chicago, Judy *artist*

Corrales
Eaton, Pauline *artist*

Rio Rancho
Qualley, Charles Albert *art educator, educator*

Santa Fe
Allen, Terry *artist*
Clift, William Brooks, III *photographer*

Taos
Martin, Agnes *artist*

OREGON

Applegate
Boyle, (Charles) Keith *artist, educator*

Ashland
Hay, Richard Laurence *theater set designer*

Cannon Beach
Greaver, Harry *artist*

Hillsboro
Hurley, Bruce Palmer *artist*

Newport
Gilhooly, David James, III *artist*

Portland
Lorenz, Nancy *artist*
Waddingham, John Alfred *artist, journalist*

UTAH

Smithfield
Rasmuson, Brent (Jacobsen) *photographer, graphic artist, lithographer*

WASHINGTON

Bainbridge Island
Carlson, Robert Michael *artist*

Battle Ground
Hansen, James Lee *sculptor*

Kent
Pierce, Danny Parcel *artist, educator*

Mercer Island
Steinhardt, Henry *photographer*

Ocean Park
Lee, Martha *artist, writer*

Olympia
Haseltine, James Lewis *artist, consultant*

Palouse
Duffy, Irene Karen *artist*

Seattle
Berger, Paul Eric *artist, photographer*
Blomdahl, Sonja *artist*
Chihuly, Dale Patrick *artist*
De Alessi, Ross Alan *lighting designer*
Du Pen, Everett George *sculptor, educator*
Farbanish, Thomas *sculptor*
Feldman, Roger Lawrence *artist, educator*
Gardiner, T(homas) Michael *artist*
Garvens, Ellen Jo *art educator, artist*
Govedare, Philip Bainbridge *artist, educator*
Spafford, Michael Charles *artist*
Washington, James Winston, Jr. *artist, sculptor*

Sequim
Belson, Patricia A. *artist*

WYOMING

Centennial
Russin, Robert Isaiah *sculptor, educator*

Cheyenne
Moore, Mary French (Muffy Moore) *potter, community activist*

Laramie
Reif, David (Frank David Reif) *artist, educator*

CANADA

ALBERTA

Calgary
Esler, John Kenneth *artist*

Edmonton
Jungkind, Walter *design educator, writer, consultant*

BRITISH COLUMBIA

Duncan
Hughes, Edward John *artist*

Salt Spring Island
Raginsky, Nina *artist*

Victoria
Harvey, Donald *artist, educator*

SASKATCHEWAN

Saskatoon
Bornstein, Eli *artist, sculptor*

SPAIN

Seville
Sanchez, Leonedes Monarrize Worthington (His Royal Highness Duke de Leonedes of Spain Sicily Greece) *fashion designer*

ADDRESS UNPUBLISHED

Bateman, Robert McLellan *artist*
Benton, Fletcher *sculptor*
Butterfield, Deborah Kay *sculptor*
Campbell, Demarest Lindsay *artist, designer, writer*
Colbert, Margaret Matthew *artist*
Cox, Pat *artist*
Dill, Laddie John *artist*
Dominguez, Eddie *artist*
Ewing, Edgar Louis *artist, educator*
Ferreira, Armando Thomas *sculptor, educator*
Gold, Betty Virginia *artist*
Hanson, Janice Crawford *artist, financial analyst*
Hughes, Michael Patrick *artist*
Jimenez, Luis Alfonso, Jr. *sculptor*
Lefranc, Margaret (Margaret Schoonover) *artist, illustrator, editor, writer*
Minami, Robert Yoshio *artist, graphic designer*
Misrach, Richard Laurence *photographer*
Nagatani, Patrick Allan Ryoichi *artist, art educator*
Nichols, Iris Jean *illustrator*
Scott, Deborah L. *costume designer*
Sturgen, Winston *photographer, printmaker, artist*
Turner, Bonese Collins *artist, educator*
Tyler, Richard *fashion designer*
Versch, Esther Marie *artist*
Yates, Steven A. *artist, curator*
Zekman, Terri Margaret *graphic designer*

ASSOCIATIONS AND ORGANIZATIONS. *See also* specific fields.

UNITED STATES

ALASKA

Anchorage
Jones, Jewel *social services administrator*
Jones, Mark Logan *educational association executive, educator*
O'Regan, Deborah *association executive, lawyer*
Wilkniss, Peter E. *foundation administrator, researcher*

ARIZONA

Dragoon
Woosley, Anne I. *cultural organization administrator*

Phoenix
Fleisher, Mark *political organization administrator*
Lloyd, Llyn Allan *association executive*
Minnaugh, Mike *political organization administrator*
Rodriguez, Leonard *foundation administrator*

Scottsdale
Jacobson, Frank Joel *cultural organization administrator*
Milanovich, Norma JoAnne *training and development company executive*
Mohraz, Judy Jolley *foundation administrator*
Muller, H(enry) Nicholas, III *foundation executive*
O'Meara, Sara *nonprofit organization executive*

Tucson
Johnson, Robert Bruce *company director*
Ross, Robert *health agency administrator*
Tirrell, John Albert *organization executive, consultant*

CALIFORNIA

Avila Beach
Dvora, Susan (Susan Bernstein) *non-profit organization professional*

Berkeley
Myers, Miles Alvin *educator, educational association administrator*

Beverly Hills
Davis, Bruce *cultural organization administrator*

Burbank
McGraw, John *political organization administrator*
Rawlinson, Joseph Eli *foundation executive, lawyer*

Canoga Park
Lederer, Marion Irvine *cultural administrator*

Claremont
Arnn, Larry Paul *former foundation executive, editor*
Pendleton, Othniel Alsop *fundraiser, clergyman*

Culver City
Netzel, Paul Arthur *fund raising management executive, consultant*

Encino
Baker, William Morris *cultural organization administrator*

Irvine
Fouste, Donna H. *association executive*

Keene
Rodriguez, Arturo Salvador *labor union official*

Long Beach
Muchmore, Don Moncrief *museum, foundation, educational, financial fund raising and public opinion consulting firm administrator, banker*
Patino, Douglas Xavier *foundation, government agency, and university administrator*

Los Altos
Orr, Susan Packard *business owner*
Wilbur, Colburn Sloan *foundation trustee, former executive*

Los Angeles
Ellsworth, Frank L. *non-profit executive*
Hubbs, Donald Harvey *foundation executive*
Kipke, Michele Diane *education and social services administrator, former hospital director*
Lindley, F(rancis) Haynes, Jr. *foundation executive, lawyer*
Mack, J. Curtis, II *civic organization administrator*
Munitz, Barry *foundation administrator*
Orsatti, Alfred Kendall *organization executive*
Poole, Robert William, Jr. *foundation executive*
Williams, Harold Marvin *foundation official, former government official, former university dean, former corporate executive*
Wilson, Gayle Ann *civic worker*

Menlo Park
Altman, Drew E. *foundation executive*
Nichols, William Ford, Jr. *foundation executive, business executive*
Pallotti, Marianne Marguerite *foundation administrator*
Shulman, Lee S. *foundation executive*

Modesto
Whiteside, Carol Gordon *foundation executive*

Mountain View
Bills, Robert Howard *political party executive*
Karp, Nathan *political activist*

Napa
Loar, Peggy Ann *foundation administrator, museum administrator*

Newbury Park
McCune, Sara Miller *foundation executive, publisher*

Newport Beach
Kallman, Burton Jay *foods association director*

Oakland
Carter, Mandy *professional organization administrator*
Hawkins, Robert B. *think tank executive*
Peck, Raymond Charles, Sr. *driver behavior research specialist and research consultant*

Orinda
Fisher, Robert Morton *foundation administrator, university administrator*

Pasadena
Staehle, Robert L. *foundation executive*

Redwood City
Postel, Mitchell Paul *association administrator*
Spangler, Nita Reifschneider *volunteer*

San Diego
Grosser, T.J. *administrator, developer, fundraiser*
Krejci, Robert Harry *non-profit organizations development consultant*
Sanders, Jerry *social services executive*

San Francisco
Clarey, Patricia *association executive*
Collins, Dennis Arthur *foundation executive*
Eastham, Thomas *foundation administrator*
Fuller, William P. *foundation administrator*
Giovinco, Joseph *nonprofit administrator, writer*
Grose, Andrew Peter *foundation executive*
Metz, Mary Seawell *foundation administrator, retired academic administrator*
Murdoch, Colin *cultural organization administrator*
Nee, D. Y. Bob *think tank executive, engineering consultant*
Newirth, Richard Scott *cultural organization administrator*
Pipes, Sally C. *think-tank executive*
Pope, Carl *professional society administrator*
Tobin, Gary Allan *cultural and community organization educator*

San Luis Obispo
Jamieson, James Bradshaw *foundation administrator*

Santa Ana
Reed, David Andrew *foundation executive*

Santa Clarita
Boyer, Carl, III *non-profit organization executive, former mayor, city official, secondary education educator*

Santa Monica
Greene, C. Michael *art association administrator*
Rich, Michael David *research corporation executive, lawyer*
Thomson, James Alan *research company executive*

South Lake Tahoe
Nason, Rochelle *conservation organization administrator*

Stanford
Lyman, Richard Wall *foundation and university executive, historian*

Stockton
Blodgett, Elsie Grace *association executive*

Studio City
Frumkin, Simon *political activist and columnist*

Tiburon
Burke, Kathleen J. *foundation administrator*

Universal City
Gumpel, Glenn J. *association executive*

COLORADO

Boulder
Brinkman, Paul Del(bert) *foundation executive, university administrator*

Colorado Springs
Killian, George Ernest *educational association administrator*
Miller, Zoya Dickins (Mrs. Hilliard Eve Miller Jr.) *civic worker*
Rochette, Edward Charles *association executive*

Denver
Beauprez, Bob *political organization administrator*
Groff, JoAnn *organization administrator*
Hogan, Curtis Jule *union executive, industrial relations consultant*
Knaus, Tim *political organization administrator*
Low, Merry Cook *civic worker*
Nelson, Bernard William *foundation executive, educator, physician*
Raughton, Jimmie Leonard *education consultant, public administrator, urban planner*

Englewood
Bryan, A(lonzo) J(ay) *retired service club official*

Greeley
Schrenk, Gary Dale *foundation executive*

Greenwood Village
Chesser, Al H. *union official*

Highlands Ranch
Massey, Leon R. (R.L. Massey) *professional association administrator*

Littleton
Keogh, Heidi Helen Dake *advocate*
Walker, Eljana M. du Vall *civic worker*

Snowmass
Lovins, L. Hunter *public policy institute executive*

HAWAII

Hawaii National Park
Nicholson, Marilyn Lee *arts administrator*

Honolulu
Blackfield, Cecilia Malik *civic volunteer, educator*
Morrison, Charles E. *think-tank executive*
Robinson, Robert Blacque *foundation administrator*
Schoenke, Marilyn Leilani *foundation administrator*

Wailuku
Lingle, Linda *political organization administrator, former mayor*

IDAHO

Boise
Boyce, Carolyn *political organization administrator*

MONTANA

Billings
Sample, Joseph Scanlon *foundation executive*

Helena
Denny, Matthew *political organization administrator*
Ream, Bob *political organization administrator*

Missoula
Kemmis, Daniel Orra *cultural organization administrator, author*

NEVADA

Carson City
Ayres, Janice Ruth *social service executive*

Henderson
Freyd, William Pattinson *fund raising executive, consultant*

Incline Village
Johnston, Bernard Fox *foundation executive, writer*

Las Vegas
Martin, Myron Gregory *foundation administrator*
Reid, Rory *political organization administrator*
Segerblom, Sharon B. *social services administrator*

Pahrump
Hersman, Marion Frank *professional administrator, lawyer*

NEW MEXICO

Albuquerque
Cole, Terri Lynn *organization administrator*
Dendahl, John *political organization administrator*
Denish, Diane D. *political organization administrator*

OREGON

Bend
Evers-Williams, Myrlie *cultural organization administrator*

Corvallis
Wilkins, Caroline Hanke *consumer agency administrator, political worker*

Lake Oswego
Miller, Barbara Stallcup *development consultant*

Portland
Collins, Maribeth Wilson *foundation president*
Edmunson, James L. *political organization administrator*
Hudson, Jerry E. *foundation administrator*
McClave, Donald Silsbee *professional society administrator*
Rooks, Charles S. *foundation administrator*

Salem
Atkinson, Perry *political organization administrator*
Corcoran, Anthony Austin *union organizer, state senator*

UTAH

Cedar City
Weaver, Max Kimball *social worker, consultant*

Logan
Iannoli, Joseph John, Jr. *university development executive*

Ogden
Davis, Lori *foundation executive*

Salt Lake City
Bishop, Rob *political party executive*
Bishop, Robert *political organization administrator*
Evans, Max Jay *historical society administrator*
Holbrook, Meghan Zanolli *fundraiser, public relations specialist, political organization chairman*
Julander, Paula Foil *health care and political consultant, state legislator*

WASHINGTON

Olympia
Olson, Steven Stanley *social service executive*

Redmond
Andrew, Jane Hayes *non-profit organization executive*

Seattle
Berendt, Paul *political party administrator*
Chapman, Bruce Kerry *institute executive*

Spokane
Falkner, James George, Sr. *foundation executive*

Tacoma
Garner, Carlene Ann *fundraising consultant*
Graybill, David Wesley *chamber of commerce executive*
Rieke, William Oliver *foundation director, medical educator, former university president*

WYOMING

Casper
Constantino, Becky *political organization administrator*

Cody
Coe, Margaret Louise Shaw *community service volunteer*

CANADA

ALBERTA

Calgary
Roberts, John Peter Lee *cultural advisor, administrator, educator, writer*

ADDRESS UNPUBLISHED

Becerra, Rosina Madeline *social welfare educator*
Boal, Dean *retired arts center administrator, educator*
Boysen, Thomas Cyril *educational association administrator*
Chassman, Leonard Fredric *labor union administrator, retired*
Conran, James Michael *consumer advocate, public policy consultant*
Eliot, Theodore Lyman, Jr. *international consultant*
Hammer, Susan W. *educational foundation executive, former mayor*
Himes, Diane Adele *buyer, fundraiser, actress, lobbyist*
Huerta, Dolores Fernandez *labor union administrator*
Mason, John E. *political association executive*
McMurray, Ron *political candidate, former political association executive*
Miller, Harriet Sanders *former art center director*
Peck, Robert David *educational foundation administrator*
Quehl, Gary Howard *consultant, association executive*
Ramo, Virginia M. Smith *civic worker*
Rice, Susan F. *fundraising consultant*
Ross, Charlotte Pack *social services administrator*
Stout, Elizabeth West *foundation administrator*
Swig, Roselyne Chroman *community consultant*
Toms, Justine Willis *educational organization executive*
Uhde, Larry Jackson *joint apprentice administrator*

Zehr, Norman Robert *association administrator*

ATHLETICS

UNITED STATES

ARIZONA

Phoenix
Bell, Jay Stuart *baseball player*
Bidwill, William V. *professional football executive*
Colangelo, Bryan *professional sports team executive*
Colangelo, Jerry John *professional sports team executive*
Fitzsimmons, Cotton (Lowell Cotton Fitzsimmons) *professional basketball executive, broadcaster, former coach*
Garagiola, Joe, Jr. *baseball team executive*
Gillom, Jennifer *professional basketball player*
Green, Travis *professional hockey player*
Hardaway, Penny (Anfernee Deon Hardaway) *professional basketball player*
Hemond, Roland A. *professional baseball team executive*
Johnson, Kevin Maurice *professional basketball player*
Johnson, Randy (Randall David Johnson) *professional baseball player*
Kidd, Jason *professional basketball player*
Miller, Cheryl DeAnn *professional basketball coach, broadcaster*
Plummer, Jason Steven (Jake) *professional football player*
Schilling, Curtis Montague *professional baseball player*
Showalter, Buck (William Nathaniel Showalter III) *major league baseball team manager*
Skiles, Scott *professional basketball coach*
Swann, Eric Jerrod *professional football player*
Timms, Michele *professional basketball player*
Tobin, Vincent Michael *professional football coach, former sports team executive*
Van Arsdale, Dick *professional basketball team executive*
Williams, Aeneas Demetrius *professional football player*
Williams, Matt (Matthew Derrick Williams) *professional baseball player*

Scottsdale
Burke, Richard T., Sr. *professional sports team executive*
Francis, Robert *professional hockey coach*
Gretzky, Wayne Douglas *retired hockey player, businessman*
Hebert, Guy *professional hockey player*
Roenick, Jeremy *professional hockey player*

Tempe
Moore, Rob *professional football player*
Snyder, Lester M. *sports association executive*

Tucson
Bonvicini, Joan M. *university women's basketball coach*
Case, Richard W. *sports association executive*
Kearney, Joseph Laurence *retired athletic conference administrator*

CALIFORNIA

Alameda
Brown, Timothy Donell *professional football player*
Davis, Allen *professional football team executive*
Gordon, Darrien X. Jamal *professional football player*
Gruden, Jon *professional football coach*
Herrera, John *professional football team executive*
Jett, James *professional football player*
Nedney, Joseph Thomas *professional football player*
Wisniewski, Stephen Adam *professional football player*

Anaheim
Collins, Terry *professional baseball manager*
DiSarcina, Gary Thomas *professional baseball player*
Hartsburg, Craig William *professional hockey coach*
Kariya, Paul *professional hockey player*
Salmon, Timothy James *professional baseball player*
Selanne, Teemu *professional hockey player*
Tavares, Tony *professional hockey and baseball leagues executive*
Vaughn, Mo (Maurice Samuel Vaughn) *professional baseball player*

Beverly Hills
Lott, Ronnie (Ronald Mandel Lott) *retired professional football player, television broadcaster*
Shoemaker, Bill (William Lee Shoemaker) *retired jockey, horse trainer*

Culver City
Johnson, Magic (Earvin Johnson) *professional sports team executive, former professional basketball coach*

Danville
Behring, Kenneth E. *professional sports team owner*

El Segundo
Sharman, William *professional basketball team executive*

Fountain Valley
Treadway-Dillmon, Linda Lee *athletic trainer, actress, stuntwoman*

Inglewood
Bryant, Kobe *professional basketball player*
Dixon, Tamecka *professional basketball player*
Jackson, Philip Douglas *professional basketball coach*
Kupchak, Mitchell *professional sports team executive*
Leslie, Lisa DeShaun *professional basketball player*
O'Neal, Shaquille Rashaun *professional basketball player*
Rice, Glen Anthony *professional basketball player*
Roski, Edward P., Jr. *professional sports team executive*
Smolinski, Bryan *professional hockey player*
Toler, Penny *former professional basketball player, sports team executive*

Irvine
Farrell, Dennis *sports association executive*

Los Angeles
Audette, Donald *professional hockey player*
Baylor, Elgin Gay *professional basketball team executive*
Brown, James Kevin *professional baseball player*
Dalis, Peter T. *athletic director*
Daly, Robert Anthony *professional baseball team executive, former film executive*
Fiset, Stephane *professional hockey player*
Ford, Chris *professional basketball coach*
Grudzielanek, Mark James *professional baseball player*
Hershiser, Orel Leonard, IV *professional baseball player*
Hundley, Todd Randolph *professional baseball player*
Johnson, Davey (David Allen Johnson) *professional baseball team manager*
Karros, Eric Peter *professional baseball player*
Lasorda, Thomas Charles (Tommy Lasorda) *professional baseball team manager*
Lavin, Stephen Michael *university basketball coach*
Leiweke, Timothy *sports executive, marketing professional*
Leyritz, James Joseph *professional baseball player*
Lipinski, Tara Kristen *professional figure skater*
Murray, Andy *professional hockey coach*
Olowokandi, Michael *professional basketball player*
Park, Chan Ho *professional baseball player*
Robitaille, Luc *professional hockey player*
Russell, Bill *professional baseball coach*
Scates, Allen Edward *professional volleyball coach*
Sheffield, Gary Antonian *professional baseball player*
Sherfy, Bradley Lloyd *professional golfer*
Simpson, O. J. (Orenthal James Simpson) *former professional football player, actor, sports commentator*
Sterling, Donald T. *professional basketball team executive*
White, Devon Markes *professional baseball player*
Zambrano, Octavio *professional soccer coach*

Marina Dl Rey
Banks, Ernest (Ernie Banks) *retired professional baseball player*

Menlo Park
Montana, Joseph C., Jr. *former professional football player*

Oakland
Appier, Kevin (Robert Kevin Appier) *professional baseball player*
Blaylock, Mookie (Daron Oshay Blaylock) *professional basketball player*
Bogues, Muggsy (Tyrone Curtis Bogues) *professional basketball player*
Carlesimo, P. J. (Peter J. Carlesimo) *former professional basketball coach*
Cohan, Christopher *professional sports team executive*
Giambi, Jason Gilbert *professional baseball player*
Hofmann, Ken *professional sports team executive*
Howe, Art (Arthur Henry Howe Jr.) *professional baseball manager*
Phillips, Keith Anthony (Tony) *professional baseball player*
Schott, Stephen C. *professional sports team executive*
St. Jean, Garry *professional basketball coach*
Starks, John Levell *professional basketball player*

Palm Springs
Jumonville, Felix Joseph, Jr. *physical education educator, realtor*

Pasadena
Cienfuegos, Mauricio *professional soccer player*
Del Prado, Sergio *professional soccer team executive*
Schmid, Sigi *professional soccer coach*

Sacramento
Adelman, Rick *professional basketball coach*
Allen, Sonny *professional basketball coach*
Bolton-Holifield, Alice Ruth *basketball player*
Byears, Latasha *professional basketball player*
Fox, Ned *professional sports team owner*
Hardmon, Lady *professional athlete*
Maloof, Gavin *professional sports team executive*
Maloof, Joseph *professional sports team executive*
Martin, Darrick David *professional basketball player*
Petrie, Geoff *professional basketball team executive*
Reynolds, Jerry Owen *sports team executive*
Webber, Chris, III (Mayce Edward Christopher Webber) *professional basketball player*
Williams, Jason *professional basketball player*
Williamson, Corliss *professional basketball player*

San Diego
Addis, Thomas Homer, III *professional golfer*
Bochy, Bruce *professional sports team manager, coach*
Boone, Bret Robert *professional baseball player*
Carney, John Michael *professional football player*
Gwynn, Anthony Keith (Tony Gwynn) *professional baseball player*
Harbaugh, James Joseph *professional football player*
Hoffman, Trevor William *professional baseball player*
Lucchino, Lawrence *sports team executive, lawyer*
Magadan, David Joseph *professional baseball player*
Moores, John *professional sports team executive*
Riley, Michael (Mike Riley) *professional football coach*
Seau, Junior (Tiana Seau Jr.) *professional football player*
Spanos, Dean A. *professional sports team executive, business executive*
Towers, Kevin *baseball team executive*

San Francisco
Baker, Dusty (Johnnie B. Baker Jr.) *professional baseball team manager*
Bonds, Barry Lamar *professional baseball player*
Cepeda, Orlando *retired professional baseball player*
Estes, Shawn *professional baseball player*
Hernandez, Livan Eisler *professional baseball player*
Kent, Jeffrey Franklin *professional baseball player*
Magowan, Peter Alden *professional baseball team executive, grocery chain executive*
McCovey, Willie Lee *former professional baseball player*
Nen, Robert Allen (Robb Nen) *professional baseball player*
Sabean, Brian R. *professional baseball team executive*

San Jose
Cerritos, Ronald *professional soccer player*
Damphousse, Vincent *professional hockey player*
McEnery, Tom *professional sports team executive*
Nolan, Owen *professional hockey player*
Osiander, Lothar *professional soccer coach*
Sutter, Darryl John *professional hockey coach*

Santa Clara
Chastain, Brandi Denise *professional soccer player*
DeBartolo-York, Denise *sports team executive*
Hearst, Garrison (Gerald Garrison Hearst) *professional football player*
Mariucci, Steve *professional football coach, former college coach*
Norton, Kenneth Howard, Jr. *professional football player*
Rice, Jerry Lee *professional football player*
Walsh, Bill *former professional football coach*
Young, Bryant Colby *football player*
Young, Steven *professional football player*

Stanford
Montgomery, Mike *university basketball coach*
Van Derveer, Tara *university athletic coach*

Stockton
Murphy, Jeremiah T. *professional sports team executive/constuction services*

Studio City
Hamilton, Scott Scovell *professional figure skater, former Olympic athlete*

Walnut Creek
Hallock, C. Wiles, Jr. *athletic official*
Hansen, Thomas Carter *college athletics conference commissioner*

COLORADO

Boulder
Neinas, Charles Merrill *athletic association executive*
Tharp, Richard *athletic director*

Colorado Springs
Bobek, Nicole *professional figure skater*
Buckner-Davis, Annett *professional volleyball player*
Corwin, Amber *figure skater*
Cutone, Kathaleen Kelly *figure skater, former skating judge, athletic representative*
D'Entremont, Amy *professional figure skater*
Evans, Janet *former Olympic swimmer*
Granato, Catherine (Cammi Granato) *professional hockey player*
Halber, Diane *professional figure skater*
Hughes, Sarah *figure skater*
Ina, Kyoko *professional figure skater*
Kwan, Karen *professional figure skater*
Kwan, Michelle *professional figure skater*
Murray, Ty (King of the Cowboys) *professional rodeo cowboy*
Nikodinov, Angela *professional figure skater, Olympic athlete*
Scherr, James Edwin *sports association executive*
Tueting, Sarah *professional hockey player*
Woolridge, Orlando *former professional basketball coach, Olympic coach*

Denver
Balboa, Marcelo *professional soccer player*
Bell, David Gus (Buddy Bell) *professional baseball manager*
Bourque, Ray *professional hockey player*
Bravo, Paul *professional soccer player*
D'Antoni, Mike *former professional basketball coach*
Deadmarsh, Adam *professional hockey player*
DiPoto, Jerry *professional baseball player*
Forsberg, Peter *professional hockey player*
Gebhard, Bob *professional baseball team executive*
Hartley, Bob *hockey coach*
Helton, Todd *professional baseball player*
Huskey, Robert Leon (Butch Huskey) *professional baseball player*
Issel, Daniel Paul *sports team executive, former professional basketball coach*
Jones, Popeye *professional basketball player*
Kroenke, E. Stanley *professional sports team executive, sports association administrator*
Leyland, James Richard *professional baseball team manager*
McDyess, Antonio *professional basketball player*
Myernick, Glenn *professional soccer coach*
Roy, Patrick *professional hockey player*
Sakic, Joseph Steve *professional hockey player*
Van Exel, Nickey Maxwell *professional basketball player*
Walker, Larry Kenneth Robert *professional baseball player*

Englewood
Beake, John *professional football team executive*
Bowlen, Pat(rick)(Dennis) *professional sports team executive, holding company executive, lawyer*
Carter, Dale Lavelle *professional football player*
Craw, Nicholas Wesson *motor sports association executive*
Davis, Terrell *professional football player*
Elam, Jason *professional football player*
Shanahan, Mike *professional football coach*
Smith, Neil *professional football player*

Fort Collins
Collen, Tom *women's basketball coach*
Weiser, Timothy L. *athletic director*

U S A F Academy
DeBerry, Fisher *college football coach*

MICHIGAN

Auburn Hills
Palmer, Wendy *professional basketball player*

MONTANA

Billings
Hahn, Woody *sports association executive*

NEVADA

Incline Village
Groebli, Werner Fritz (Mr. Frick) *professional ice skater, realtor*

NORTH CAROLINA

Charlotte
Cowens, David William (Dave Cowens) *professional basketball coach, insurance executive, retired professional basketball player*

OREGON

Eugene
Sisley, Becky Lynn *physical education educator*

Portland
Dunleavy, Michael Joseph *professional basketball coach*
Glickman, Harry *professional basketball team executive*
Hargrove, Linda *professional basketball coach*
Kolde, Bert *professional basketball team executive*
Pippen, Scottie *professional basketball player*
Smith, Steven Delano *professional basketball player*
Weinberg, Lawrence *professional basketball team owner*
Whitsitt, Robert James *professional basketball team executive*
Witherspoon, Sophia *professional basketball player*

UTAH

Murray
Witworth, Clark L. *sports team executive*

Park City
Kelly, Thomas J. *sports association executive*

Salt Lake City
Dydek, Malgorzata *professional basketball player*
Hlede, Korie *professional basketball player*
Hornacek, Jeffrey John *professional basketball player*
Howells, R. Tim *professional sports team executive*
Layden, Francis Patrick (Frank Layden) *professional basketball team executive, former coach*
Malone, Karl *professional basketball player*
Miller, Larry H. *professional sports team executive, automobile dealer*
Polynice, Olden *professional basketball player*
Russell, Bryon *basketball player*
Sloan, Jerry (Gerald Eugene Sloan) *professional basketball coach*
Stockton, John Houston *professional basketball player*

WASHINGTON

Kirkland
Brown, Chadwick Everett *professional football player*
Holmgren, Mike *professional football coach*
Kennedy, Cortez *professional football player*
Watters, Richard James *professional football player*

Seattle
Ackerley, Barry *professional basketball team executive, communications company executive*
Armstrong, Charles G. *professional baseball executive, lawyer*
Baker, Vincent Lamont *professional basketball player*
Buhner, Jay Campbell *professional baseball player*
Dunn, Lin *professional basketball coach*
Ellis, John W. *professional baseball team executive, utility company executive*
Henderson, Rickey Henley *professional baseball player*
Martinez, Edgar *professional baseball player*
Olerud, John Garrett *professional baseball player*
Payton, Gary Dwayne *professional basketball player*
Piniella, Louis Victor *professional baseball team manager*
Swift, William Charles *professional baseball player, Olympic athlete*
Walker, Walter Frederick *professional basketball team executive*
Westphal, Paul *professional basketball coach*

Spokane
Ueberroth, Peter Victor *former baseball commissioner*

CANADA

ALBERTA

Calgary
Bartlett, Grant A. *professional sports team executive*
Edwards, N. Murray *professional sports team owner*
Hay, Don *professional hockey coach*
Hay, William Charles *professional hockey team executive*
Hotchkiss, Harley N. *professional hockey team owner*

Edmonton
Lowe, Kevin Hugh *professional hockey coach, former professional hockey player*
MacTavish, Craig *professional hockey coach, former hockey player*
Sather, Glen Cameron *professional hockey team executive, coach*
Weight, Doug *professional hockey player*

BRITISH COLUMBIA

Vancouver
Abdul-Rahim, Shareef *professional basketball player*
Jackson, Stu *professional sports team executive, former university basketball coach*
McCaw, John E., Jr. *professional sports team executive*
Messier, Mark Douglas *professional hockey player*
Potvin, Felix *professional hockey player*

ADDRESS UNPUBLISHED

Abdul-Jabbar, Kareem (Lewis Ferdinand Alcindor) *retired professional basketball player, sports commentator*
Axelson, Joseph Allen *professional athletics executive, publisher*
Crawford, Marc *professional hockey coach*
Elway, John Albert *retired professional football player*
Hollandsworth, Todd Mathew *professional baseball player*
Lacroix, Pierre *professional sports team professional*
Malone, Kevin *sports team executive*
Olson, Lute *university athletic coach*
Rodriguez, Alexander Emmanuel *professional baseball player*
Schrempf, Detlef *professional basketball player*
Scioscia, Mike *professional baseball team manager*
Thomas, Jim *former professional basketball team executive*
Thompson, Craig Dean *sports association executive*
Wagner, Richard *athletics consultant, former baseball team executive*
West, Jerry Alan *professional basketball team executive*
Wooden, John Robert *former basketball coach*

BUSINESS. *See* **FINANCE: INDUSTRY.**

COMMUNICATIONS. *See* **COMMUNICATIONS MEDIA; INDUSTRY: SERVICE.**

COMMUNICATIONS MEDIA. *See also* ARTS: LITERARY.

UNITED STATES

ALASKA

Anchorage
Cowell, Fuller A. *newspaper publisher*
Dougherty, Patrick *editor*
Tobin, William Joseph *newspaper editor*

ARIZONA

Fountain Hills
Kinderwater, Joseph C. (Jack Kinderwater) *publishing company executive*

Gilbert
Kenney, Thomas Frederick *broadcasting executive*

Phoenix
Benson, Stephen R. *editorial cartoonist*
Early, Robert Joseph *magazine editor*
Edens, Gary Denton *broadcasting executive*
Elliott, Steve *newspaper editor*
Grafe, Warren Blair *cable television executive*
Gunty, Christopher James *newspaper editor*
Johnson, Pam *newspaper editor*
Leach, John F. *editor, journalism educator*
Miller, William *broadcast executive*
Moyer, Alan Dean *retired newspaper editor*
North, Patrick *broadcasting executive*
Oppedahl, John Fredrick *newspaper publisher, publishing executive*
Schatt, Paul *newspaper editor*
Stahl, Richard G. C. *journalist, editor*
Steckler, Phyllis Betty *publishing company executive*
Wallace, Julia Diane *newspaper editor*
Weber, Fredric G. *former broadcast executive*
Weil, Louis Arthur, III (Chip) *retired newspaper publishing executive*

Scottsdale
Everingham, Harry Towner *editor, publisher*
Fox, Kenneth L. *retired newspaper editor, writer*
Frischknecht, Lee Conrad *retired broadcasting executive*
McClay, Bob *broadcast executive*
Reidy, Richard Robert *publishing company executive*

Sedona
Chicorel, Marietta Eva *publishing company executive, consultant*

Tempe
Allen, Charles Raymond *television station executive*
Owens, Michael L. *radio station executive*

Tucson
Buel, Bobbie Jo *editor*
Davis, Cathy *publishing executive*
Martin, June Johnson Caldwell *journalist*

CALIFORNIA

Agoura Hills
Chagall, David *journalist, writer*
Fabregas, J. Robert *retail appearel executive*
Teresi, Joseph *publishing executive*

Alpine
Greenberg, Byron Stanley *newspaper and business executive, consultant*

Anaheim
Kelley, Lee *publishing executive*

Arcadia
Belnap, David F. *journalist*

Avila Beach
Kamm, Herbert *journalist*

Bakersfield
Beene, Richard Stuart *newspaper editor*
Jenner, Mike *newspaper editor*

Belmont
Carlson, Gary R. *publishing executive*

Belvedere Tiburon
Kramer, Lawrence Stephen *journalist*

Berkeley
Bagdikian, Ben Haig *journalist, emeritus university educator*
Clark, James Henry *publishing company executive*
Drechsel, Edwin Jared *retired magazine editor*
Lesser, Wendy *literary magazine editor, writer, consultant*
Witt, Melvin Sylvan *periodical editor, publisher*

Beverly Hills
Beck, Marilyn Mohr *columnist*
Berry, Nancy *recording industry executive*
Boyle, Barbara Dorman *motion picture company executive*
Bradshaw, Terry *sports announcer, former professional football player*
Corwin, Stanley Joel *book publisher*
Filosa, Gary Fairmont Randolph V., II *multimedia executive, financier*
Friedman, Robert Lee *film company executive*
Gerber, William Norman *motion picture executive*
Grazer, Brian *film company executive*
Grushow, Sandy *broadcast executive*
Hefner, Hugh Marston *editor-in-chief*
Heller, Paul Michael *film company executive, producer*
Lond, Harley Weldon *editor, publisher*
Mechanic, William M. *television and motion picture industry executive*
Rosenzweig, Richard Stuart *publishing company executive*
Rothman, Thomas Edgar *production executive*
Schneider, Charles Ivan *newspaper executive*
Zanuck, Richard Darryl *motion picture company executive*

Brisbane
Daniels, Caroline *publishing company executive*

Burbank
Altschul, David Edwin *record company executive, lawyer*
Brogliatti, Barbara Spencer *television and motion picture executive*
Disney, Roy Edward *broadcasting company executive*
Eisner, Michael Dammann *entertainment company executive*
Hashe, Janis Helene *editor*
Jonas, Tony *television executive*
Kellner, Jamie *broadcasting executive*
Lang, Laurie *entertainment company executive*
Letterie, Kathleen *broadcast executive*
Lieberfarb, Warren N. *broadcast executive*
Liss, Walter C., Jr. *television station executive*
Mestres, Ricardo A., III *motion picture company executive*
Robertson, Richard Trafton *entertainment company executive*
Roth, Joe *motion picture company executive*
Roth, Peter *broadcast executive*
Schneider, Peter *film company executive*
Schumacher, Thomas *film company executive*
Shriver, Maria Owings *news correspondent*
Staggs, Thomas *entertainment company executive*
Sweeney, Anne M. *cable television company executive*
Thyret, Russ *recording industry executive*
Wolper, David Lloyd *motion picture and television executive*

Burlingame
Mendelson, Lee M. *film company executive, writer, producer, director*

Camarillo
DePatie, David Hudson *motion picture company executive*
Doebler, Paul Dickerson *publishing management executive*

Carmel
Mollman, John Peter *book publisher, consultant electronic publishing*

Chatsworth
Faerber, Charles N. *editor*

Chula Vista
Blankfort, Lowell Arnold *newspaper publisher*

Corona Del Mar
Crump, Spencer *publishing company executive*

Costa Mesa
Jabbari, Ahmad *publishing executive*

Culver City
Calley, John *motion picture company executive, film producer*
Feingold, Benjamin S. *broadcast executive*
Fisher, Lucy J. *motion picture company executive*
Neufeld, Mace *film company executive*
Pascal, Amy *film company executive*
Wigan, Gareth *film company executive*

Del Mar
Faludi, Susan C. *journalist, scholarly writer*
Kaye, Peter Frederic *newspaper columnist*

El Cerrito
Doyle, William Thomas *retired newspaper editor*

El Segundo
Conrad, Paul Francis *editorial cartoonist*

Encino
Rawitch, Robert Joe *journalist, educator*
Rose, Doyle *broadcast executive*

Fall River Mills
Caldwell, Walter Edward *editor, small business owner*

Foster City
Rosenzweig, Fred *desktop publishing executive*

Frazier Park
Nelson, Harry *journalist, medical writer*

Fremont
Rockstroh, Dennis John *journalist, screenwriter*

Fresno
Lumbye, Betsy *editor*
Moyer, J. Keith *newspaper editor*
Waters, Charles R., Jr. *executive editor*

Glendale
Katzenberg, Jeffrey *motion picture studio executive*
Kaye, Jhani *radio station manager, owner production company*

Hollywood
Halperin, Stuart *entertainment company executive*
Perth, Rod *network entertainment executive*

Huntington Beach
De Massa, Jessie G. *media specialist*

Irvine
Lesonsky, Rieva *editor*
Power, Francis William *newspaper publisher*

La Canada
Paniccia, Patricia Lynn *journalist, writer, lawyer, educator*

La Jolla
Copley, David C. *newspaper publishing company executive*
Copley, Helen Kinney *newspaper publisher*
Freedman, Jonathan Borwick *journalist, writer, lecturer, educator*
Hall, TennieBee M. *editor*
Hallin, Daniel Clark *communications educator*
Harris, T. George *editor*
Hornaday, Aline Grandier *publisher, independent scholar*
Jones, Charlie *television sports announcer*

Linden
Smith, Donald Richard *editor, publisher*

Long Beach
Adler, Jeffrey D. *political consultant, public affairs consultant, crisis management expert*
Ruszkiewicz, Carolyn Mae *newspaper editor*

Los Altos
Miller, Ronald Grant *writer, critic*

Los Angeles
Archerd, Army (Armand Archerd) *columnist, television commentator*
Banks, Robin *broadcast executive*
Bart, Peter Benton *newspaper editor, film producer, novelist*
Bernstein, William *film company executive*
Berry, Stephen Joseph *reporter*
Bloomberg, Stu *broadcast executive*
Camron, Roxanne *retired magazine editor, consultant*
Carey, Chase *broadcast executive*
Carroll, John Sawyer *newspaper editor*
Chernin, Peter *motion picture company executive*
Churgin, Amy *publishing executive*
Clarke, Peter *communications and health educator*
Cross, Sue *newspaper editor*
Darling, Juanita Marie *correspondent*
Del Olmo, Frank *newspaper editor*
DeLuca, Michael *film company executive*
Delugach, Albert Lawrence *journalist*
Dolan, Mary Anne *journalist, columnist*
Duffy, Patrick *broadcast executive*
Dwyre, William Patrick *journalist, public speaker*
Field, Ted (Frederick Field) *film and record industry executive*
Firestone, Roy *sportscaster*
Firstenberg, Jean Picker *film institute executive*
Flanigan, James J(oseph) *journalist*
Garza, Oscar *newspaper editor*
Gauff, Lisa *broadcast journalist*
Groves, Martha *newspaper writer*
Hamlin, Doug *publishing executive*
Hart, John Lewis (Johnny Hart) *cartoonist*
Hiltzik, Michael *journalist*
Iovine, Jimmy *recording industry executive*
Israel, David *journalist, screenwriter, producer*
Jacobson, Sidney *editor*
Jones, Quincy *producer, composer, arranger, conductor, trumpeter*
Kallet, Judith S. *publishing executive*
King, Michael *syndicated programs distributing company executive*
Kleiner, Arnold Joel *television station executive*
Kraft, Scott Corey *correspondent*
Kristof, Kathy M. *journalist*
Laird, Jere Don *news reporter*
Lange, Tim *newspaper publishing executive*
Lazano, Monica *publishing executive*
Lazarus, Mell *cartoonist*
Levine, Jesse E. *publishing executive*
Lewis, Tommi *magazine editor*
Maltin, Leonard *television commentator, writer*
Mann, Wesley F. *newspaper editor*
Margulies, Lee *newspaper editor*
Masters, Lee *broadcast executive*
McCluggage, Kerry *television executive*
Miles, Jack (John Russiano) *journalist, educator*
Miller, Percy *record company executive*
Mottek, Frank *broadcaster, journalist*
Murphy, Philip Edward *broadcast executive*
Nagy, Bob *editor periodical*
Newcombe, Richard Sumner *newspaper syndicate executive*
O'Neil, William Scott *publishing executive*
O'Reilly, Richard Brooks *journalist*
Parisi, Paula Elizabeth *writer, photographer, editor*
Parks, Michael Christopher *journalist*
Paul, Charles S. *motion picture and television company executive*
Perenchio, Andrew Jerrold *film and television executive*
Petersen, Robert E. *magazine publishing executives*
Philips, Chuck *journalist*
Phillips, Geneva Ficker *academic editor*
Plate, Thomas Gordon *newspaper columnist, educator*
Press, Beth *publishing executive*
Puerner, John P. *newspaper publishing executive*
Ramirez, Michael P. *editorial cartoonist*
Reardon, John E. *broadcast executive*
Reich, Kenneth Irvin *journalist*
Rense, Paige *editor, publishing company executive*
Rosenberg, Howard Anthony *journalist*
Russell, James Brian *broadcast executive, media consultant*
Salmon, Beth Ann *magazine editor in chief*
Saltzman, Joseph *journalist, producer, educator*
Sarnoff, Thomas Warren *television executive*
Saylor, Mark Julian *newspaper editor*
Scott, Kelly *newspaper editor*
Scully, Vincent Edward *sports broadcaster*
Shapazian, Robert Michael *publishing executive*
Shaw, David Lyle *journalist, writer*
Shea, Fran *broadcast executive*
Shuster, Alvin *journalist, newspaper editor*
Sigband, Norman Bruce *management communication educator*
Sinay, Hershel David *publishing executive*
Sloan, L. Lawrence *publishing executive*
Smith, Gordon E. *publishing executive*
Sperling, Irene R. *publishing executive*
Spiegelman, Arthur *broadcast executive*
Spirtos, Maria *magazine publisher*
Steele, Bruce Carl *magazine editor*
Stern, Leonard Bernard *television and motion picture production company executive*
Thompson, Anne Kathleen *entertainment journalist*
Tobias, Anita *publishing executive*
Truman, James *magazine editor*
Tulsky, Fredric Neal *journalist*
Turner, Craig *journalist*
Valentine, Dean *broadcast executive*
Vargas, Diana Lisa *television station executive*
Ward, Leslie Allyson *journalist, editor*
Wardlow, Bill *record industry consultant, entertainer*
Wasserman, Steve *editor*
Wolinsky, Leo C. *newspaper editor*
Youpa, Donald George *broadcast executive*
Zappe, John Paul *city editor, educator, newspaper executive*
Zimbalist, Efrem, III *publishing company executive*
Zwick, Barry Stanley *newspaper editor, speechwriter*

Los Gatos
Meyers, Ann Elizabeth *sports broadcaster*

Marina Del Rey
Lindheim, Richard David *television company executive, university official*

Menlo Park
Bull, James Robert *publishing executive*
Crisp, Michael Graves *publishing executive*
Wright, Rosalie Muller *magazine and newspaper editor*

Mill Valley
Cohn, Bruce *film and television company executive*

Modesto
Vasche, Mark *newspaper editor*

Mountain View
Heins, John *publishing executive*

Newport Beach
Bryant, Thomas Lee *magazine editor*
Dean, Paul John *magazine editor*
McMahon, Brian *publishing executive*

North Hollywood
Powers, Melvin *publishing executive*

Oakland
Burt, Christopher Clinton *publishing company executive*
Conway, Nancy Ann *newspaper editor*
George, Donald Warner *online columnist and editor, freelance writer*
McKinney, Judson Thad *broadcast executive*
Schrag, Peter *editor, writer*

Oceanside
Howard, Robert Staples *newspaper publisher*

Orange
Fletcher, James Allen *video company executive*
Zweifel, Donald Edwin *newspaper editor, lobbyist, consultant*

Pacific Palisades
Price, Frank *motion picture and television company executive*

Pacifica
Cole, David Macaulay *journalist, consultant*

Palm Desert
Ayling, Henry Faithful *writer, editor, consultant*

Palm Springs
Browning, Norma Lee (Mrs. Russell Joyner Ogg) *journalist*
Mann, Zane Boyd *editor, publisher*

Palo Alto
Hamilton, David Mike *publishing company executive*

Pasadena
Spector, Phil *record company executive*

Paso Robles
Brown, Benjamin Andrew *journalist*

Rancho Palos Verdes
Hillinger, Charles *journalist, writer*

Redwood City
Hearst, William Randolph, III *newspaper publisher*

Riverside
McLaughlin, Leighton Bates, II *journalism educator, former newspaperman*
McQuern, Marcia Alice *newspaper publishing executive*
Opotowsky, Maurice Leon *newspaper editor*
Rodrigue, George P. *newspaper editor*
Sokolsky, Robert Lawrence *journalist, entertainment writer*

Sacramento
Baltake, Joe *film critic*
Endicott, William F. *journalist*
Glackin, William Charles *arts critic, editor*
Heaphy, Janis D. *newspaper executive*
Hendricks, Chris *publishing executive*
Knudson, Thomas Jeffery *journalist*
LaMont, Sanders Hickey *journalist*
Lundstrom, Marjie *newspaper editor and columnist*
McClatchy, James B. *newspaper publisher, editor*
Potts, Erwin Rea *newspaper executive*
Pruitt, Gary B. *newspaper executive*
Shaw, Eleanor Jane *newspaper editor*
Walsh, Denny Jay *reporter*
Walters, Daniel Raymond *political columnist*
Williams, Arthur Cozad *broadcasting executive*

San Bernardino
Reginald, Robert *administrator, writer, university librarian*

San Clemente
Stallknecht-Roberts, Clois Freda *publisher, publicist*

San Diego
Bell, Gene *newspaper publishing executive*
Brown, Darrell *broadcast executive*
Da Rosa, Alison *travel editor*
Glickenhaus, Mike *radio station executive*
Kaufman, Julian Mortimer *broadcasting company executive, consultant*
Klein, Herbert George *newspaper editor*
Krulak, Victor Harold *newspaper executive*
McCarthy, Kevin *broadcast executive*
Milner, Daniel Paul *publishing executive, composer, producer*
Morgan, Neil *writer, newspaper editor, lecturer, columnist*
Myrland, Doug *broadcast executive*
O'Loughlin, Joanie *broadcast executive*
Pincus, Robert Lawrence *art critic, cultural historian*
Quinn, Edward J. *broadcasting company executive*

Gwinn, Mary Ann *newspaper reporter*
Hartl, John George *film critic*
Henkel, Cathy *newspaper sports editor*
Hills, Regina J. *journalist*
Horsey, David *editorial cartoonist*
Johnson, Wayne Eaton *writer, editor, former drama critic*
Kelly, Carolyn Sue *newspaper executive*
Lacitis, Erik *journalist*
MacLeod, Alex *newspaper editor*
Nalder, Eric Christopher *investigative reporter*
Nash, Cynthia Jeanne *journalist*
Oglesby, Roger *publishing executive, editor*
Parks, Michael James *publisher, editor*
Pascal, Naomi Brenner *editor-in-chief, publishing executive*
Payne, Ancil Horace *retired broadcasting executive*
Rinearson, Peter Mark *journalist, writer, software developer*
Scott, Patrick *broadcast executive*
Sizemore, Herman Mason, Jr. *newspaper executive*
Smulyan, Jeffrey *radio station executive, owner pro baseball team*
Soden, John P. *publishing executive*
Stanton, Michael John *newspaper editor*
Steele, Cynthia *literary critic, translator, educator*
Turner, Wallace L. *reporter*

Spokane
Cowles, William Stacey *newspaper publisher*
Gray, Alfred Orren *retired journalism educator*
Kafentzis, John Charles *journalist, educator*
Kunkel, Richard Lester *public radio executive*
Peck, Christopher *newspaper editor*
Steele, Karen Dorn *journalist*

Tacoma
Brenner, Elizabeth (Betsy Brenner) *publishing executive*
Mladenich, Ronald E. *publishing executive*
Zeeck, David *newspaper editor*

Vancouver
Campbell, Scott *newspaper publishing company executive*

Vashon
Mann, Claud Prentiss, Jr. *retired television journalist, real estate agent*

WYOMING

Riverton
Peck, Robert A. *newspaper publisher, state legislator*

CANADA

ALBERTA

Calgary
Shaw, Jim, Jr. *broadcast executive*

Edmonton
Davis, Murdoch *editor-in-chief journal*
Hughes, Linda J. *newspaper publisher*
Stanway, Paul William *newspaper editor*

BRITISH COLUMBIA

Vancouver
Babick, Don *newspaper executive*
Yaffe, Barbara Marlene *journalist*

Victoria
Poole, Robert Anthony *journalist*
Tighe, James C. *publishing executive*

ADDRESS UNPUBLISHED

Adelson, Merv Lee *entertainment and communication industry executive*
Akiyama, Carol Lynn *motion picture industry executive*
Ambrose, Daniel Michael *publishing executive*
Anders, George Charles *journalist, writer*
Barry, Rick (Richard Francis Dennis Barry III) *sportscaster, retired professional basketball player, marketing professional*
Berkowitz, Steve *publishing company executive*
Bernheimer, Martin *music critic*
Blackstock, Joseph Robinson *newspaper editor*
Cardone, Bonnie Jean *freelance photojournalist*
Chaplin, George *newspaper editor*
Clark, Peter Bruce *newspaper executive*
Culp, Mildred Louise *corporate executive*
Curtin, David Stephen *newswriter*
Day, Anthony *book critic*
Denious, Sharon Marie *retired publisher periodical*
Dietrich, William Alan *writer, journalist*
Downing, Kathryn M. *newspaper publishing executive, lawyer*
Ewell, Miranda Juan *journalist*
Farnsworth, Elizabeth *broadcast journalist*
Fenwick, James Henry *editor*
Foster, Mary Christine *motion picture and television executive*
Franklin, Jon Daniel *writer, journalist, educator*
Gates, Susan Inez *magazine publisher*
Gray, Thomas Stephen *journalist, writer*
Grossinger, Richard Selig *publisher, writer, editor*
Guittar, Lee John *retired newspaper executive*
Hahn, Helene B. *motion picture company executive*
Jensen, Jack Michael *publishing executive*
Johnson, Carol Ann *editor*
Jones, Leonade Diane *media publishing company executive*
Joseph, Michael Thomas *broadcast consultant*
Kramer, Donovan Mershon, Sr. *newspaper publisher*
Levin, Robert Barry *motion picture company executive*
Lewis, Thomasine Elizabeth *magazine editor-in-chief*
Lloyd, Michael Jeffrey *recording producer*
Main, Robert Gail *communications educator, training consultant, television and film producer, former army officer*
Malott, Adele Renee *editor*
Manning, Richard Dale *writer*
Melody, Michael Edward *publishing company executive*
Might, Thomas Owen *newspaper company executive*
Miller, Carole Ann Lyons *editor, publisher, video and marketing specialist*
Peterson, Kevin Bruce *newspaper editor, publishing executive*
Read, Richard Eaton *newspaper reporter*
Reid-Bills, Mae *magazine editor, historian*
Ridder, Paul Anthony *newspaper executive*
Riggs, George E. *newspaper publishing executive*
Sackett, Susan Deanna *film and television production associate, writer*
Sapsowitz, Sidney H. *entertainment and media company executive*
Singer, Kurt Deutsch *news commentator, writer, publisher*
Smith, Martin Bernhard *journalist*
Stamper, Malcolm Theodore *publishing company executive*
Stennett, William Clinton (Clint Stennett) *radio and television station executive, state legislator*
Taylor, George Frederick *newspaper publisher, editor*
Vandenberg, Peter Ray *magazine publisher*
Voorhees, John Lloyd *columnist*
Weaver, Howard C. *newspaper executive*
Welsome, Eileen *journalist*
Whitesell, John Edwin *motion picture company executive*
Wright, Donald Franklin *retired newspaper executive*
Ziegler, Jack (Denmore) *cartoonist*

EDUCATION. For postsecondary education, *See also* specific fields.

UNITED STATES

ALASKA

Anchorage
Anthony, Susan *secondary education educator*
Bowie, Phyllis *secondary education educator*
Byrd, Milton Bruce *college president, former business executive*
Gorsuch, Edward Lee *chancellor*
Johnson, Daniel M. *provost*

Fairbanks
Alexander, Vera *dean, marine science educator*
Doran, Timothy Patrick *educational administrator*
Hamilton, Mark R. *academic administrator*
Lind, Marshall L. *academic administrator*
Reichardt, Paul Bernard *provost, chemistry educator*

Juneau
Pugh, John Robert *chancellor, former state health administrator*

ARIZONA

Arizona City
Donovan, Willard Patrick *retired elementary education educator*

Fort Huachuca
Adams, Frank *education specialist*

Glendale
Altersitz, Janet Kinahan *principal*

Mesa
Christiansen, Larry K. *college president*

Phoenix
Fitzgerald, Joan *principal*
Klor de Alva, Jorge *academic administrator*
Lovett, Clara Maria *university administrator, historian*

Prescott
Rheinish, Robert Kent *university administrator*

Scottsdale
Churchill, William DeLee *retired education educator, psychologist*
Hill, Louis Allen, Jr. *former university dean, consultant*

Sun Lakes
Johnson, Marian Ilene *education educator*

Tempe
Burnham, Clifford Wayne *educator*
Coor, Lattie Finch *university president*
Durand, Barbara *dean, nursing educator*
Forsyth, Ben Ralph *academic administrator, medical educator*
Thor, Linda Maria *college president*
White, Patricia Denise *dean, law educator*
Wills, J. Robert *academic administrator, drama educator, writer*

Tucson
Cate, Rodney Michael *academic administrator*
Eribes, Richard *dean*
Kaltenbach, C(arl) Colin *dean, educator*
Likins, Peter William *university administrator*
Massaro, Toni Marie *dean, law educator*
Stoffle, Carla Joy *university library dean*

CALIFORNIA

Alameda
Carter, Roberta Eccleston *therapist, counselor*
Sakamoto, Katsuyuki *retired college chancellor, psychology educator*

Anaheim
Jackson, David Robert *school system administrator*

Angwin
Maxwell, Donald Malcolm *college president, minister*

Aptos
Bohn, Ralph Carl *educational consultant, retired educator*

Arcadia
Baltz, Patricia Ann (Pann Baltz) *elementary education educator*

Arcata
Bowker, Lee Harrington *academic administrator*
McCrone, Alistair William *university president*

Azusa
Felix, Richard E. *academic administrator*
Liegler, Rosemary Menke *dean, nursing educator*

Bakersfield
Arciniega, Tomas Abel *university president*
Hefner, John *principal*
Saucier, Bonnie L. *dean, pediatrics nurse*

Bayside
Bank, Ron *principal*

Berkeley
Bender, Richard *university dean, architect, educator*
Berdahl, Robert Max *academic administrator, historian, educator*
Bowker, Albert Hosmer *retired university chancellor*
Cieslak, William *academic administrator*
Crandall, Keith C. *dean*
Freedman, Sarah Warshauer *education educator*
Glenny, Lyman Albert *retired education educator*
Hyatt, James Armstrong *university administrator*
Kay, Herma Hill *education educator*
Kerr, Clark *academic administrator emeritus*
Leonard, Thomas *dean, educator, librarian*
Merrill, Richard James *educational director*
Miles, Raymond Edward *former university dean, organizational behavior and industrial relations educator*
Ralston, Lenore Dale *academic policy and program analyst*
Schell, Orville *dean*
Tyson, Laura D'Andrea *dean, economist, educator*

Boulevard
Charles, Blanche *retired elementary education educator*

Brentwood
Groseclose, Wanda Westman *retired elementary school educator*

Burbank
Nielsen, Kenneth Ray *academic administrator*

Chico
Esteban, Manuel Antonio *university administrator, educator*

Chula Vista
Wyatt, Edith Elizabeth *elementary education educator*

Claremont
Alexander, John David, Jr. *college administrator*
Bekavac, Nancy Yavor *academic administrator, lawyer*
Douglass, Enid Hart *educational program director*
Fucaloro, Anthony Frank *dean*
Gann, Pamela Brooks *academic administrator*
Maguire, John David *academic administrator, educator, writer*
Platt, Joseph Beaven *former college president*
Riggs, Henry Earle *academic administrator, engineering management educator*
Stanley, Peter William *academic administrator*
Stark, Jack Lee *academic administrator, director*
Strauss, Jon Calvert *academic administrator*
Wettack, F. Sheldon *academic administrator*

Concord
Thall, Richard Vincent *school system administrator*

Culver City
Maxwell-Brogdon, Florence Morency *school administrator, educational adviser*

Davis
Grey, Robert Dean *academic administrator, biology educator*
Perschbacher, Rex Robert *dean, law educator*
Smiley, Robert Herschel *university dean*
Vanderhoef, Larry Neil *academic administrator*

Diamond Bar
Domeño, Eugene Timothy *elementary education educator, principal*

El Dorado Hills
Bartlett, Robert Watkins *education consultant, metallurgist*

Escondido
Sanders, Adrian Lionel *educational consultant*

Fair Oaks
Lemke, Herman Ernest Frederick, Jr. *retired elementary education educator, consultant*

Fairfield
Kirkorian, Donald George *retired college official, management consultant*

Fallbrook
Evans, Anthony Howard *university president*

Fountain Valley
Purdy, Leslie *community college president*

Fremont
Brown, David Richard *school system administrator, minister*
Lapiroff, Jerry *secondary school educator*

Fresno
Haak, Harold Howard *university president*
Klassen, Peter James *academic administrator, history educator*
Ortiz, John Michael *provost*
Stewart, Deborah Claire *dean*
Welty, John Donald *academic administrator*

Fullerton
Donoghue, Mildred Ransdorf *education educator*
Gordon, Milton Andrew *academic administrator*
Smith, Ephraim Philip *academic administrator, former university dean, educator*

Glendale
DeVincintis, Lani *adult education educator*
Whalen, Lucille *retired academic administrator*

Glendora
Schiele, Paul Ellsworth, Jr. *education business owner, writer*

Hayward
McCune, Ellis E. *retired university system chief administrator, higher education consultant*
Rees, Norma S. *academic administrator*

Huntington Beach
Yglesias, Kenneth Dale *college president*

Indian Wells
Trotter, F(rederick) Thomas *retired academic administrator*

Inglewood
Guzy, Marguerita Linnes *middle school education educator*

Irvine
Cesario, Thomas Charles *dean*
Cicerone, Ralph John *academic administrator, geophysicist*
Fleischer, Everly Borah *academic administrator*
Peltason, Jack Walter *foundation executive, educator*

La Jolla
Cavenee, Webster K. *director*
Chandler, Marsha *academic administrator, professor*
Dreilinger, Charles Lewis (Chips Dreilinger) *dean*
Dynes, Robert C. *academic administrator*
Frieman, Edward Allan *academic administrator, educator*
Lee, Jerry Carlton *university administrator*
Masys, Daniel Richard *medical school director*
Savoia, Maria Christina *associate dean*
Talke, Frank Eberhard *education educator*

La Verne
Morgan, Stephen Charles *academic administrator*

Lafayette
Fielding, Elizabeth Brown *education educator*

Loma Linda
King, Helen Emori *dean*
Klooster, Judson *academic administrator, dentistry educator*

Long Beach
Anatol, Karl W. E. *provost*
Culton, Paul Melvin *retired counselor, educator, interpreter*
Lathrop, Irvin Tunis *retired academic dean, educator*
Lauda, Donald Paul *university dean*
Maxson, Robert C. *university president*
McDonough, Patrick Dennis *academic administrator*
Reed, Charles Bass *chief academic administrator*

Los Angeles
Armstrong, Lloyd, Jr. *university official, physics educator*
Astin, Alexander William *education educator*
Bernstein, Leslie *dean*
Bice, Scott Haas *dean, lawyer, educator*
Carnesale, Albert *university chancellor*
Dewey, Donald Odell *dean, academic administrator*
Gothold, Stuart Eugene *school system administrator, educator*
Hayes, Robert Mayo *university dean, library and information science educator*
Hoi, Samuel Chuen-Tsung *art school president*
Hubbard, John Randolph *university president emeritus, history educator, diplomat*
Hume, Wyatt *university administrator*
Inocencio, E. Bing *college president*
Jackson, Kingsbury Temple *educational contract consultant*
Kelly, James J. *dean, social work educator*
Kleingartner, Archie *founding dean, educator*
Lieber, David Leo *university president*
Lim, Larry Kay *university official*
Lynch, Beverly Pfeifer *education and information studies educator*
Mandel, Joseph David *academic administrator, lawyer*
McCabe, Edward R. B. *academic administrator, educator, physician*
Merrifield, Donald Paul *university chancellor*
Mitchell, Theodore Reed *academic administrator*
Moore, Donald Walter *academic administrator, school librarian*
Mori, Allen Anthony *university dean, consultant, researcher*
Parks, Debora Ann *private school director*
Pierskalla, William Peter *university dean, management-engineering educator*

Polon, Linda Beth *elementary school educator, writer, illustrator*
Rodes, David Stuart *college program director*
Rosser, James Milton *academic administrator*
Sample, Steven Browning *university executive*
Shearer, Derek Norcross *international studies educator, diplomat, administrator*
Silverman, Leonard M. *university dean, electrical engineering educator*
Sloane, Robert Malcolm *university administrator*
Spangler, Mary *college president*
Steinberg, Warren Linnington *school principal*
Taylor, Leigh Herbert *college dean*
Varat, Jonathan D. *dean, law educator*
Wagner, William Gerard *university dean, physicist, consultant, information scientist, investment manager*
Wazzan, A(hmed) R(assem) Frank *engineering educator, dean*
Westerfield, Randolph W. *university dean, business educator*
Wexler, Robert *university administrator*
Wilkerson, LuAnn *dean*

Los Gatos
Dunham, Anne *educational institute director*

Malibu
Benton, Andrew Keith *university administrator, lawyer*
Phillips, Ronald Frank *retired academic administrator*

Merced
Tomlinson-Keasey, Carol Ann *university administrator*

Mill Valley
Mac Intyre, Donald John *college president*

Modesto
Bairey, Marie *principal*
Price, Robert William *school superintendent, consultant*

Moffett Field
Scott, Donald Michael *educator*

Monterey
Kadushin, Karen Donna *law school dean*

Monterey Park
Moreno, Ernest H. *college president*

Napa
Rada, Alexander *university official*

Northridge
Curzon, Susan Carol *university administrator*

Oakland
Anderson, Brother Timothy Mel *academic administrator*
Atkinson, Richard Chatham *university president*
Chook, Edward Kongyen *university administrator, disaster medicine educator*
Diaz, Sharon *education administrator*
Gomes, Wayne Reginald *academic administrator*
Holmgren, Janet L *college president*
King, C. Judson *academic administrator*
Rippel, Clarence W. *academic administrator*

Orange
Doti, James L. *academic administrator*
Hamilton, Harry Lemuel, Jr. *educator*

Orinda
Glasser, Charles Edward *university president*

Pacific Palisades
Georges, Robert Augustus *emeritus educator, researcher, writer*

Palo Alto
Bohrnstedt, George William *educational researcher*
Gong, Mamie Poggio *elementary education educator*

Pasadena
Baltimore, David *university president, microbiologist, educator*
Brown, David R. *former academic administrator*
Everhart, Thomas Eugene *retired university president, engineering educator*
Lingenfelter, Sherwood Galen *university provost, anthropology educator*
Oviatt, Larry Andrew *retired secondary school educator*
Pings, Cornelius John *educational consultant, director*
Stolper, Edward Manin *secondary education educator*

Pleasant Hill
Edelstein, Mark Gerson *college president*
Lundgren, Susan Elaine *counselor, educator*

Pleasanton
Lucas, Linda Lucille *dean*

Pomona
Demery, Dorothy Jean *secondary school educator*
Dishman, Rose Marie Rice *academic administrator, researcher*
Suzuki, Bob H. *university president*

Rancho Cucamonga
Young, Jerry Wayne *college president*

Redlands
Appleton, James Robert *university president, educator*

Redondo Beach
Marsee, Stuart (Earl) *educational consultant, retired*

Reseda
Anstad, Neil *director*

Riverside
Geraty, Lawrence Thomas *academic administrator, archaeologist*
Hendrick, Irving Guilford *education educator*
Yacoub, Ignatius I. *university dean*

Rohnert Park
Arminana, Ruben *academic administrator, educator*
Babula, William *university dean*

Sacramento
Gerth, Donald Rogers *university president*
Harris, Robert M. *college president*
O'Leary, Marion Hugh *university dean, chemist*
Reed-Graham, Lois L. *administrator, secondary education educator*
Silva, Joseph, Jr. *dean, medical educator*
Smith, Marie B. *college president*
Stuart, David R. *academic administrator*

San Diego
Alksne, John F. *dean*
Brose, Cathy *principal*
Castruita, Rudy *school system administrator*
Donley, Dennis Lee *school librarian*
Feinberg, Lawrence Bernard *university dean, psychologist*
Hayes, Alice Bourke *academic administrator, biologist, educator*
Hays, Garry D. *academic administrator*
Lauer, Jeanette Carol *college dean, history educator, writer*
Perrault, Jacques *educator*
Weber, Stephen Lewis *university president*

San Francisco
Albino, Judith Elaine Newsom *university president*
Boyden, Jaclyne Witte *university vice dean*
Corrigan, Robert Anthony *academic administrator*
Dullea, Charles W. *university chancellor emeritus, priest*
Goldstine, Stephen Joseph *college administrator*
Hall, Zach Winter *academic administrator*
Howatt, Sister Helen Clare *former human services director, former college library director*
Kane, Mary Kay *dean, law educator*
Kleinberg, David Lewis *education administrator*
Kozloff, Lloyd M. *university dean, educator, scientist*
Krevans, Julius Richard *university administrator, physician*
LaBelle, Thomas Jeffrey *academic administrator*
Lo, Bernard *education educator*
Lo Schiavo, John Joseph *university executive*
Naegele, Carl Joseph *university academic administrator, educator*
Stephens, Elisa *art college president, lawyer*
Torrey, Ella King *academic administrator*
Wara, Diane *dean*
Zingale, Donald Paul *academic administrator, educator*

San Jose
Bain, Linda L. *academic administrator*
Caret, Robert Laurent *university president*
Collett, Jennie *principal*
Cruz, B. Robert *academic administrator*
Okerlund, Arlene Naylor *university official*
Wiens, Beverly Jo *educator*

San Lorenzo
Glenn, Jerome T. *secondary school principal*

San Luis Obispo
Baker, Warren J(oseph) *university president*
Haile, Allen Cleveland *educator and administrator*

San Marcos
Lilly, Martin Stephen *university dean*

San Rafael
Fink, Joseph Richard *academic administrator*

Santa Ana
Barry, Mary H. *college official*
Beal, Dennis *academic administrator*
Moore, David Gene *academic administrator*
Wilson, Beth A. *college official*

Santa Barbara
Boyan, Norman J. *retired education educator*
O'Dowd, Donald Davy *retired university president*
Sinsheimer, Robert Louis *retired university chancellor and educator*
Sprecher, David A. *university administrator, mathematician*
Yang, Henry T. *university chancellor, educator*

Santa Clara
Locatelli, Paul Leo *academic administrator*
Shoup, Terry Emerson *university dean, engineering educator*

Santa Clarita
Lavine, Steven David *academic administrator*

Santa Cruz
Brothers, Cheryl Marianne Morris *school superintendent*
Greenwood, M. R. C. *college dean, biologist, nutrition educator*

Santa Monica
Robertson, Piedad F. *college president*

Santa Rosa
Christiansen, Peggy *principal*

Saratoga
Houston, Elizabeth Reece Manasco *correctional education consultant*

Signal Hill
Vandament, William Eugene *retired academic administrator*

Silverado
Mamer, James Michael *secondary education educator*

Simi Valley
Jackson, Thirston Henry, Jr. *retired adult education educator*

Stanford
Bridges, Edwin Maxwell *education educator*
Gross, Richard Edmund *education educator*
Henriksen, Thomas Hollinger *university official*
Kays, William Morrow *university administrator, mechanical engineer*
Kirst, Michael Weile *education educator, researcher*
Metzenberg, Robert L. *education educator*
Naimark, Norman M. *academic administrator*
Palm, Charles Gilman *university official*
Raisian, John *academic administrator, economist*
Rice, Condoleezza *academic administrator, political scientist*
Spence, Andrew Michael *dean, finance educator*
Stone, William Edward *academic administrator, consultant*
Strober, Myra Hoffenberg *education educator, consultant*
Veinott, Arthur Fales, Jr. *university educator*

Stockton
DeRicco, Lawrence Albert *college president emeritus*
Jantzen, J(ohn) Marc *retired education educator*
Sorby, Donald Lloyd *university dean*

Torrance
Kuc, Joseph A. *education educator, consultant*
Roney, Raymond G. *educator, publisher*

Tujunga
Mayer, George Roy *educator*

Turlock
Hughes, Marvalene *academic administrator*

Ventura
Renger, Marilyn Hanson *elementary education educator*

Victorville
Peterson, Leroy *retired secondary education educator*

Walnut Creek
Lilly, Luella Jean *academic administrator*

Weimar
Kerschner, Lee R(onald) *academic administrator, political science educator*

Whittier
Drake, E. Maylon *academic administrator*

Woodland Hills
Zeitlin, Herbert Zakary *retired college president, real estate company executive*

Yorba Linda
Lunde, Dolores Benitez *retired secondary education educator*

COLORADO

Aurora
Gibson, Elisabeth Jane *principal*
Hartenbach, David Lawrence *school system administrator*
Jarvis, Mary G. *principal*
Young, Gordon *elementary education educator*

Boulder
Anderson, Ronald Delaine *education educator*
Bruff, Harold Hastings *dean*
Buechner, John C. *academic administrator*
Byyny, Richard Lee *academic administrator, physician*
Dilley, Barbara Jean *college administrator, choreographer, educator*
Healy, James Bruce *cooking school administrator, writer*
Vigil, Daniel Agustin *academic administrator*
Williams, James Franklin, II *university dean, librarian*

Colorado Springs
Burnley, Kenneth Stephen *school system administrator*
Mohrman, KathrynJ *academic administrator*
Shade, Linda Bunnell *university chancellor*

Denver
Bosworth, Bruce Leighton *school administrator, educator, consultant*
Craine, Thomas Knowlton *non-profit administrator*
Fulginiti, Vincent *university dean*
Fulkerson, William Measey, Jr. *college president*
Grounds, Vernon Carl *seminary administrator*
Halgren, Lee A. *academic administrator*
Jarvis, Richard S. *academic administrator*
Kaplan, Sheila *academic administrator*
Messer, Donald Edward *theological school president, theology educator*
Palmreuter, Kenneth Richard Louis *principal*
Ritchie, Daniel Lee *academic administrator*
Vogel, Robert Lee *college administrator, clergyman*
Zaranka, William F. *academic administrator, author*

Durango
Jones, Joel Mackey *academic administrator*

Fort Collins
Baldwin, Lionel Vernon *retired university president*
Fotsch, Dan Robert *elementary education educator*
Harper, Judson Morse *university administrator, consultant, educator*
Jaros, Dean *university official*
Panik, Sharon McClain *primary education educator, writer*
Savage, Eldon Paul *retired environmental health educator*
Yates, Albert Carl *academic administrator, chemistry educator*

Golden
Bickart, Theodore Albert *university president emeritus*
Klug, John Joseph *secondary education educator, director of dramatics*
Mueller, William Martin *former academic administrator, metallurgical engineering educator*
Shea, Dion Warren Joseph *university official, fund raiser*
Truly, Richard H. *academic administrator, former federal agency administrator, former astronaut*

Grand Junction
Moberly, Linden Emery *educational administrator*

Greeley
Brown, Hank *university administrator, former senator*
Duff, William Leroy, Jr. *university dean emeritus, business educator*
Thompson, Paul N. *college president*

Lakewood
West, Marjorie Edith *former elementary education educator*

Littleton
Bush, Stanley Giltner *secondary school educator*
Lesh-Laurie, Georgia Elizabeth *university administrator, biology educator, researcher*
Rothenberg, Harvey David *educational administrator*

Westminster
Hartman, Susan P(atrice) *adult education administrator*

HAWAII

Honolulu
Gee, Chuck Yim *dean*
King, Arthur R., Jr. *education educator, researcher*
Mortimer, Kenneth P. *academic administrator*
Perkins, Frank Overton *university official, marine scientist*
Wright, Chatt Grandison *academic administrator*

Kailua
Tokumaru, Roberta *principal*

Kailua Kona
Diama, Benjamin *retired educator, artist, composer, writer*
Feaver, Douglas David *retired university dean, classics educator*
Malmstadt, Howard Vincent *university provost*

Pearl City
Lee, Kenneth *secondary education educator*

IDAHO

Boise
Andrus, Cecil Dale *academic administrator*
Griffin, Gloria Jean *elementary school educator*
Howard, Marilyn *school system administrator*
Kaupins, Gundars Egons *education educator*
Maloof, Giles Wilson *academic administrator, educator, author*
Ruch, Charles P. *academic administrator*

Caldwell
Hendren, Robert Lee, Jr. *academic administrator*

Moscow
Hatch, Charles R. *university dean*
Hendee, John Clare *university research educator*
Hoover, Robert Allan *university president*

Mountain Home
Graves, Karen Lee *high school counselor*

New Plymouth
Matthews-Burwell, Vicki *elementary education educator*

Pocatello
Bowen, Richard Lee *academic administrator, political science educator*
Sagness, Richard Lee *education educator, former academic dean*

ILLINOIS

Northbrook
Beljan, John Richard *university administrator, medical educator*

MONTANA

Billings
DeRosier, Arthur Henry, Jr. *college president*
Park, Janie C. *provost*

Bozeman
Acord, Lea *dean, nursing educator*

Dillon
Hulbert, Stephen Thompson *academic administrator*

Helena
Crofts, Richard A. *academic administrator*
Scott, Joyce Alaine *university official*

Lewistown
Edwards, Linda L. *former elementary education educator*

Missoula
Brown, Perry Joe *university dean*
Dennison, George Marshel *academic administrator*
Vogelsberg, Ross Timm *education educator, researcher*

NEVADA

Fallon
Plants, Walter Dale *elementary education educator, minister*

Henderson
Moore, Richard *academic administrator*

Las Vegas
Cram, Brian Manning *school system administrator*
Hair, Kittie Ellen *secondary educator*
Harter, Carol Clancey *university president, English language educator*
Morgan, Richard J. *dean, educator*
Phillips, Karen *secondary education educator*

Minden
Pyle, David *elementary education educator*
Tyndall, Gaye Lynn *secondary education educator*

Reno
Crowley, Joseph Neil *university president, political science educator*
Daugherty, Robert Melvin, Jr. *university dean, medical educator*
Perry, Jean Louise *dean*
Walen, Joanne Michele *secondary education educator, consultant*
Westfall, David Patrick *academic administrator, educator*

NEW MEXICO

Albuquerque
Anaya, Rudolfo *educator, writer*
Garcia, F. Chris *academic administrator, political science educator, public opinion researcher*
Gordon, William Charles *college administrator*
Graff, Pat Stuever *secondary education educator*
Hadley, William Melvin *college dean*
Lattman, Laurence Harold *retired academic administrator*

Las Cruces
Conroy, William B. *retired university administrator*
Thayer, Michael J. *secondary education educator*

Montezuma
Geier, Philip Otto, III *college president*

Portales
Byrnes, Lawrence William *dean*

Santa Fe
Cerny, Charlene Ann *director*

Socorro
Lopez, Daniel Heraldo *academic administrator*

NEW YORK

New York
Slaughter, John Brooks *former university administrator*

OREGON

Ashland
Kreisman, Arthur *higher education consultant, humanities educator emeritus*

Corvallis
Arnold, Roy Gary *academic administrator*
Byrne, John Vincent *higher education consultant*
Davis, John Rowland *university administrator*
Parker, Donald Fred *college dean, human resources management educator*
Risser, Paul Gillan *academic administrator, botanist*

Eugene
Cox, Joseph William *academic administrator*
Frohnmayer, David Braden *academic administrator*
Gall, Meredith Damien (Meredith Mark Damien Gall) *education educator, writer*
Moseley, John Travis *university administrator, research physicist*
Walker, Hill M. *educator*

Forest Grove
Singleton, Francis Seth *dean*

Hillsboro
Cleveland, Charles Sidney *secondary education educator*

Mcminnville
Bull, Vivian Ann *college president*

North Bend
de Sá e Silva, Elizabeth Anne *secondary school educator*

Oceanside
Wadlow, Joan Krueger *academic administrator*

Portland
Bartlett, Thomas Alva *educational administrator*
Bennett, Charles Leon *vocational and graphic arts educator*
Bloom, Joseph D. *medical educator, psychiatrist*
Johnson, David J. *educational center administrator*
Johnson, Thomas Floyd *former college president, educator*
Koblik, Steven S. *academic administrator*
Lawrence, Sally Clark *academic administrator*
Misener, Terry Richard *dean, nursing educator*
Mooney, Michael Joseph *college president*
Potempa, Kathleen *dean, nursing educator*
Shaff, Beverly Gerard *education administrator*
Sherrer, Charles David *college dean, clergyman*
Tyson, David T. *university president*
Walker, James Bradley *academic institution administrator*
Wiest, William Marvin *education educator, psychologist*

Roseburg
Tilson, Daniel *elementary education educator*

Sunriver
Schade, Wilbert Curtis *education administrator*

UTAH

Kaysville
Johnson, Charles N. *elementary education educator*

Logan
Emert, George Henry *academic administrator, biochemist*
McKell, Cyrus M. *retired college dean, plant physiologist*
Shaver, James Porter *education educator, university dean*

Ogden
Protzman, Grant Dale *university administrator, state legislator*
Thompson, Paul Harold *university president*

Orem
Romesburg, Kerry D. *university president, former state education administrator*

Provo
Bangerter, Vern *secondary education educator*
Bateman, Merrill Joseph *university president*
Densley, Colleen T. *elementary educator, curriculum specialist*
Fleming, Joseph Clifton, Jr. *dean, law educator*
Hansen, H. Reese *dean, educator*
Stahmann, Robert F. *education educator*

Salt Lake City
Bennion, John Warren *urban education educator*
Cannell, Cyndy Michelle *elementary school principal*
Christensen, Bruce LeRoy *former academic administrator, commercial broadcasting executive*
Drew, Clifford James *university administrator, special education and educational psychology educator*
Kim, Sung Wan *educator*
Machen, Bernard J. *academic administrator*
Markham, Reed B. *education educator, consultant*
Matsen, John Martin *academic administrator, pathologist*
McCleary, Lloyd E(verald) *education educator*
Miller, William Charles *college dean, architect*
Peterson, Chase N. *university president*
Stock, Peggy A(nn) *college president, educator*

Sandy
Sabey, J(ohn) Wayne *academic administrator, consultant*

West Jordan
Shepherd, Paul H. *elementary school educator*

WASHINGTON

Bellevue
Pastore, Michael Anthony *college administrator*

Bellingham
Morse, Karen Williams *academic administrator*

Centralia
Kirk, Henry Port *academic administrator*

Cheney
Jordan, Stephen M. *university president*

Chimacum
Hollenbeck, Dorothy Rose *special education educator*

Ellensburg
McIntyre, Jerilyn Sue *academic administrator*

Kirkland
Rich, Clayton *retired university official and educator*

Lacey
Spangler, David Robert *college administrator, engineer*

Lynnwood
Oharah, Jack *academic administrator*
Rocheleau, James Romig *retired university president*

Olympia
Bergeson, Teresa *state system administrator*

Pullman
Hatch, Lynda Sylvia *elementary and middle school education educator*
Lewis, Norman G. *academic administrator, researcher, consultant*
Rawlins, V. Lane *university president*

Richland
Piippo, Steve *educator*

Seattle
Abbott, Robert Dean *education scientist*
Baker, Roland Jerald *educator*
Banks, James Albert *educational research director, educator*
Carlson, Dale Arvid *university dean*
Debro, Julius *university dean, sociology educator*
Gardiner, John Jacob *leadership educator, writer, philosopher, speaker*
Gerberding, William Passavant *retired university president*
Gibaldi, Milo *dean*
Goodlad, John Inkster *education educator, writer*
Hegyvary, Sue Thomas *nursing school dean*
Huntsman, Lee *university provost, academic administrator*
Jennerich, Edward John *university official and dean*
Kelley, Lucille Marie Kindely *dean, psychosocial nurse*
McCormick, Richard Levis *academic administrator*
Plotnick, Robert David *educator, economic consultant*
Robertson, Paul B. *dean, dental educator*
Silver, Michael *school superintendent*
Stringer, William Jeremy *university official*
Sundborg, Father Stephen V. *academic administrator*
Terrell, W(illiam) Glenn *university president emeritus*
Tschernisch, Sergei P. *academic administrator*
Woods, Nancy Fugate *dean, women's health nurse*

Spanaway
Paris, Kathleen *secondary school educator*
Roberts-Dempsey, Patricia E. *secondary school educator*

Spokane
Hirsch, Anne *dean, nursing educator*
McManus, Patrick Francis *educator, writer*
Robinson, William P. *academic administrator, consultant, speaker*
Spitzer, Robert J. *academic administrator*

Tacoma
King, Gundar Julian *retired university dean*
Pierce, Susan Resneck *academic administrator, English language educator*

Toppenish
Ross, Kathleen Anne *college president*

Walla Walla
Cronin, Thomas Edward *academic administrator*

Yakima
Ullas, Yvonne L. *primary school educator*

WYOMING

Afton
Hoopes, Farrel G. *secondary education educator*

Centennial
Houston, Jane Hunt *retired educator*

Cheyenne
Rice, Wallace William *secondary education educator*
Weigner, Brent James *secondary education educator*

Jackson
Massy, William Francis *education educator, consultant*

Laramie
Dubois, Philip Leon *university administrator, political science educator*
McBride, Judith *elementary education educator*

Rock Springs
Kathka, David Arlin *director educational services*

Sheridan
Maier, Stephen John *college president*

CANADA

ALBERTA

Calgary
Neale, E(rnest) R(ichard) Ward *retired university official, consultant*
Rasporich, Anthony Walter *university dean*
Watanabe, Mamoru *former university dean, physician, researcher*
White, Terrence Harold *academic administrator, sociologist*

Edmonton
Adams, Peter Frederick *university president, civil engineer*
Tyrrell, D. Lorne J. *university dean*

BRITISH COLUMBIA

Kelowna
Muggeridge, Derek Brian *dean, engineering consultant*

Vancouver
Finnegan, Cyril Vincent *retired university dean, zoology educator*
Haycock, Kenneth Roy *educator, consultant, administrator*
Lusztig, Peter Alfred *university dean, educator*
McNeill, John Hugh *pharmaceutical sciences educator*
Webber, William Alexander *university administrator, physician*

Victoria
Strong, David F. *university administrator*
Welch, S(tephen) Anthony *university administrator, Islamic studies and arts educator*

SASKATCHEWAN

Regina Beach
Barber, Lloyd Ingram *retired university president*

Saskatoon
Knott, Douglas Ronald *college dean, agricultural sciences educator, researcher*
Popkin, David Richard *academic dean, obstetrician, gynecologist*

ADDRESS UNPUBLISHED

Backlar, Patricia *education educator*
Casper, Gerhard *academic administrator, law educator*
Cinque, Thomas Joseph *dean*
Cobb, Jewel Plummer *former college president, educator*
Copeland, Phillips Jerome *former academic administrator, former air force officer*
Cross, Kathryn Patricia *education educator*
Dobler, Donald William *retired college dean, consultant, corporate executive*
Dutson, Thayne R. *university dean*
Ellner, Carolyn Lipton *university dean, consultant*
Evans, Geraldine Ann *academic administrator*
Evans, James Handel *university administrator, architect, educator*
Fetters, Doris Ann *retired secondary education educator*
Frison, George Carr *education educator*
Frost, Everett Lloyd *anthropologist, academic administrator*
Gabel, Katherine *academic administrator*
Gray, Richard Moss *retired college president*
Harrigan, Rosanne Carol *dean, nursing educator*
Hegarty, George John *university president, English educator*
Hull, McAllister Hobart, Jr. *retired university administrator*
Jacobson, Eugene Donald *educator, administrator, researcher*
Jerrytone, Samuel Joseph *trade school executive*
Jervis, Jane Lise *college official, science historian*
Kormondy, Edward John *retired university chancellor, biology educator*
Krueger, Eugene Rex *academic program consultant*
Langworthy, William Clayton *college official*
Legington, Gloria R. *middle school educator*
Lynch, John Daniel *secondary education educator, state legislator*
Matera, Frances Lorine *elementary educator*
Matheson, Scott Milne, Jr. *dean, law educator*
Meyer, Robert Lee *secondary education educator*
Moore, Thomas David *academic administrator*
Munlu, Kamil Cemal *business educator, executive*
Perry, William James *educator, former federal official*
Rohwer, William D., Jr. *university dean*
Sanchez, Gilbert *retired academic administrator, microbiologist, researcher*
Sestini, Virgil Andrew *retired biology educator*
Sherratt, Gerald Robert *retired university president*
Shutler, Mary Elizabeth *academic administrator*
Skaggs, Bebe Rebecca Patten *college dean, clergywoman*
Smith, Samuel Howard *academic administrator, plant pathologist*
Stewart, John Wray Black *college dean*
Stewart, Lucille Marie *retirede special education coordinator*
Sullivan, Charles *university dean, educator, author*
Tarbi, William Rheinlander *secondary education educator, curriculum consultant, educational technology researcher*
Terada, Alice Masae *retired elementary school teacher, writer*
Tiedeman, David Valentine *education educator*
Tonjes, Marian Jeannette Benton *education educator*
Weller, Debra Anne *elementary educator*
Wilkening, Laurel Lynn *academic administrator, planetary scientist*
Williams, Lewis T. (Rusty Williams) *education educator*
Wilson, Robin Scott *university president, writer*
Wong, David Yue *academic administrator, physics educator*
Zufryden, Fred S. *academic administrator, marketing educator, researcher*
Zuiches, James Joseph *academic administrator*

ENGINEERING

UNITED STATES

ALASKA

Anchorage
Leman, Loren Dwight *civil engineer, state legislator*

Fairbanks
Woodall, David Monroe *research engineer, dean*

ARIZONA

Chandler
Meieran, Eugene Stuart *material scientist*
Myers, Gregory Edwin *aerospace engineer*

Flagstaff
Somerville, Mason Harold *mechanical engineering educator, university dean*

Glendale
Harris, Warren Lynn *development engineer*

Mesa
Rummel, Robert Wiland *aeronautical engineer, writer*

Paradise Valley
Ratkowski, Donald J. *mechanical engineer, consultant*
Russell, Paul Edgar *electrical engineering educator*

Phoenix
Burchard, John Kenneth *chemical engineer*
Freyermuth, Clifford L. *structural engineering consultant*
Fullmer, Steven Mark *systems engineer*
Morrison, John Haddow, Jr. *engineering company executive*
Nishioka, Teruo (Ted Nishioka) *electrical engineer*

Prescott
Bieniawski, Zdzislaw Tadeusz Richard *engineering educator emeritus, writer, consultant*
Hasbrook, A. Howard *safety engineer, consultant*
Kahne, Stephen James *systems engineer, educator, academic administrator, engineering executive*

Rio Verde
Jordan, Richard Charles *engineering executive*

Scottsdale
Cazier, Barry James *electrical engineer, software developer*
Fisher, John Richard *engineering consultant, former naval officer*
Kiehn, Mogens Hans *aviation engineer, consultant*

Sun City West
Woodruff, Neil Parker *agricultural engineer*

Tempe
Balanis, Constantine Apostle *electrical engineering educator*
Berman, Neil Sheldon *chemical engineering educator*
Carpenter, Ray Warren *materials scientist and engineer, educator*
Ferry, David Keane *electrical engineering educator*
Guilbeau, Eric J. *biomedical engineer, electrical engineer, educator*
Karady, George Gyorgy *electrical engineering educator, consultant*
Kaufman, Irving *retired engineering educator*
Mense, Allan Tate *research and development engineering executive*
Roberts, Peter Christopher Tudor *engineering executive*
Schroder, Dieter Karl *electrical engineering educator*
Shah, Jami J. *mechanical engineering educator, researcher*
Shaw, Milton Clayton *mechanical engineering educator*

Tucson
Arnell, Walter James William *mechanical engineering educator, consultant*
Buras, Nathan *hydrology and water resources educator*
Harrington, Roger Fuller *electrical engineering educator, consultant*
Hiskey, J. Brent *metallurgical engineer, educator*
Kerwin, William James *electrical engineering educator, consultant*
Kinney, Robert Bruce *mechanical engineering educator*
Prince, John Luther, III *engineering educator*
Slack, Donald Carl *agricultural engineer, educator*
Smerdon, Ernest Thomas *engineering educator*
Wyant, James Clair *engineering company executive, educator*

CALIFORNIA

Alpine
Roberts, Dwight Loren *engineering consultant, writer*

Alta Loma
Bordner, Gregory Wilson *chemical engineer*

Anaheim
Demarchi, Ernest Nicholas *aerospace engineering administrator*

Berkeley
Berger, Stanley Allan *mechanical and biomechanical engineering educator*
Birdsall, Charles Kennedy *electrical engineer*
Blanch, Harvey Warren *chemical engineering educator*
Bogy, David B(eauregard) *mechanical engineering educator*
Brodersen, Robert W. *engineering educator*
Cairns, Elton James *chemical engineering educator*
Chapman, Gary T. *aeronautics and astronautics scientist, educator*
Chopra, Anil Kumar *civil engineering educator*
Desoer, Charles Auguste *electrical engineer*
Dornfeld, David Alan *engineering educator*
Dubon, Oscar D., Jr. *engineering educator*
Fenves, Gregory L. *engineering educator*
Filippou, Filip C. *engineering educator*
Finnie, Iain *mechanical engineer, educator*
Frisch, Joseph *mechanical engineer, educator, consultant*
Fuerstenau, Douglas Winston *mineral engineering educator*
Garrison, William Louis *civil engineering educator*
Goldsmith, Werner *mechanical engineering educator*
Gray, Paul Russell *electrical engineering educator*
Grossman, Lawrence Morton *nuclear engineering educator*
Hodges, David Albert *electrical engineering educator*
Hsu, Chieh Su *applied mechanics engineering educator, researcher*
Hu, Chenming *electrical engineering educator*
Jewell, William Sylvester *engineering educator*
Kastenberg, William Edward *nuclear engineering and applied science educator*
Katz, Randy H. *electrical engineering, computer sciences educator*
Kuh, Ernest Shiu-Jen *electrical engineering educator*
Leitmann, George *mechanical engineering educator*
Lieberman, Michael A. *electrical engineer, educator*
May, Adolf Darlington *civil engineering educator*
Monismith, Carl Leroy *civil engineering educator*
Muller, Richard Stephen *electrical engineer, educator*
Neureuther, Andrew R. *engineering educator*
Newman, John Scott *chemical engineer, educator*
Oldham, William George *electrical engineering and computer science educator*
Ott, David Michael *engineering company executive*
Pagni, Patrick John *mechanical and fire safety engineering science educator*
Pask, Joseph Adam *ceramic engineering educator*
Pederson, Donald Oscar *electrical engineering educator*
Penzien, Joseph *structural engineering educator*
Pigford, Thomas Harrington *nuclear engineering educator*
Pister, Karl Stark *engineering educator*
Polak, Elijah *engineering educator, computer scientist*
Popov, Egor Paul *retired engineering educator*
Prausnitz, John Michael *chemical engineer, educator*
Schwarz, Steven Emanuel *electrical engineering educator, administrator*
Scordelis, Alexander Costicas *civil engineering educator*
Susskind, Charles *engineering educator, writer, publishing executive*
Tien, Chang-Lin *mechanical engineer, educator*
Varaiya, Pravin P. *electrical engineer*
Webster, William C. *engineering educator*
Whinnery, John Roy *electrical engineering educator*
White, Richard Manning *electrical engineering educator*
Wilson, Edward Lawrence *civil engineering educator, structural engineering consultant*
Zadeh, Lotfi Asker *engineering educator, educator*

Berry Creek
Miller, Joseph Arthur *retired manufacturing engineer, educator, consultant*

Brentwood
Rawson, Eric Gordon *optical engineer*

Camarillo
MacDonald, Norval (Woodrow) *safety engineer*

Campbell
Ross, Hugh Courtney *electrical engineer*

Carmichael
Hartman, Howard Levi *mining engineering educator, consultant*

Cerritos
Subramanya, Shiva *aerospace systems engineer*

Chatsworth
Levine, Arnold Milton *retired electrical engineer, documentary filmmaker*

Chico
Allen, Charles William *mechanical engineering educator*
Learned, Vincent Roy *electrical engineer, educator*

Chula Vista
Rusconi, Louis Joseph *marine engineer*

Claremont
Dym, Clive Lionel *engineering educator*
Molinder, John Irving *engineering educator, consultant*
Monson, James Edward *electrical engineer, educator*
Tanenbaum, Basil Samuel *engineering educator*

Compton
Wang, Charles Ping *engineering executive*

Concord
Crandall, Ira Carlton *consulting electrical engineer*

Corona
Blanche, Joe Advincula *aerospace engineer, consultant, educator*

Coronado
Crilly, Eugene Richard *engineering consultant*

Costa Mesa
Carpenter, Frank Charles, Jr. *retired electronics engineer*

Cupertino
Edson, William Alden *electrical engineer, researcher*

Davis
Akesson, Norman Berndt *agricultural engineer, emeritus educator*
Beadle, Charles Wilson *retired mechanical engineering educator*
Bower, Robert W. *electrical engineer*
Brandt, Harry *mechanical engineering educator*
Chancellor, William Joseph *agricultural engineering educator*
Cheney, James Addison *civil engineering educator*
Dorf, Richard Carl *electrical engineering and management educator*
Fridley, Robert Bruce *agricultural engineering educator*
Gates, Bruce Clark *chemical engineer, educator*
Ghausi, Mohammed Shuaib *electrical engineering educator, university dean*
Hakimi, S. Louis *electrical and computer engineering educator*
Krener, Arthur J. *systems engineering educator*
Krone, Ray Beyers *civil and environmental engineering educator, consultant*
Larock, Bruce Edward *civil engineering educator*
Laub, Alan John *engineering educator*
Levy, Bernard C. *electrical engineer, educator*
Wang, Shih-Ho *electrical engineer, educator*

El Segundo
Bauer, Jerome Leo, Jr. *chemical engineer*
Chang, I-Shih *aerospace engineer*

Emeryville
Catmull, Edwin E. *computer graphics engineer*
Fuchs, Renato *bioengineer*
Zwoyer, Eugene Milton *consulting engineering executive*

Encinitas
Morrow, Charles Tabor *aerospace consulting engineer*

Encino
Friedman, George Jerry *aerospace engineer, executive*
Knuth, Eldon Luverne *engineering educator*

Fair Oaks
Agerbek, Sven *mechanical engineer*

Foster City
Ham, Lee Edward *civil engineer*

Fountain Valley
Hosokawa, Koichi *engineering company executive*
Tu, John *engineering executive*

Fremont
Engelbart, Doug *engineering executive*
Wu, James Chen-Yuan *aerospace engineering educator*

Fresno
Brahma, Chandra Sekhar *civil engineering educator*
Leeland, Steven Brian *electronics engineer*

Fullerton
Tuazon, Jesus Ocampo *electrical engineer, educator, consultant*

Glendale
Knoop, Vern Thomas *civil engineer, consultant*

Greenbrae
Elder, Rex Alfred *civil engineer*

Hacienda Heights
Love, Daniel Joseph *consulting engineer*

Huntington Beach
Nichols, Mark Edward *aerospace engineer*

Indian Wells
Jorgensen, Gordon David *retired engineering company executive*

Irvine
Ang, Alfredo Hua-Sing *civil engineering educator*
Bershad, Neil Jeremy *electrical engineering educator*
Guymon, Gary LeRoy *civil engineering educator, consultant*
Liebeck, Robert H. *aerospace engineer*
Nicholas, Henry Thompson, III *communications engineering executive*
Samueli, Henry *electrical engineering educator, entrepreneur*
Sirignano, William Alfonso *aerospace and mechanical engineer, educator*
Sklansky, Jack *electrical and computer engineering educator, researcher*
Stubberud, Allen Roger *electrical engineering educator*
Ting, Albert Chia *bioengineering researcher*

La Canada Flintridge
Price, Humphrey Wallace *aerospace engineer*

La Jolla
Beyster, John Robert *engineering company executive*
Chang, William Shen Chie *electrical engineering educator*
Chien, Shu *physiology and bioengineering educator*
Conn, Robert William *engineering science educator*
Counts, Stanley Thomas *aerospace consultant, retired naval officer, retired electronics company executive*
Fung, Yuan-Cheng Bertram *bioengineering educator, writer*
Karin, Sidney *computer science and engineering educator*
Levy, Ralph *engineering executive, consultant*
Milstein, Laurence Bennett *electrical engineering educator, researcher*
Penner, Stanford Solomon *engineering educator*
Rudee, Mervyn Lea *engineering educator, researcher*
Rudolph, Walter Paul *engineering research company executive*
Schmid-Schoenbein, Geert Wilfried *biomedical engineer, educator*
Simnad, Massoud T. *engineering educator*
Sung, Kuo-Li Paul *bioengineering educator*
Williams, Forman Arthur *engineering science educator, combustion theorist*
Wolf, Jack Keil *electrical engineer, educator*

Laguna Hills
Hammond, R. Philip *chemical engineer*

Laguna Woods
Larson, Harry Thomas *electronics engineer, executive, consultant*
Sesonske, Alexander *nuclear and chemical engineer*

Livermore
Christensen, Richard Monson *mechanical engineer, materials engineer*
Hill, John Earl *mechanical engineer*
Johnson, Roy Ragnar *electrical engineer, researcher*
King, Ray John *electrical engineer, educator*

Lompoc
Means, James Andrew *engineer*

Long Beach
Dillon, Michael Earl *engineering executive, mechanical engineer, educator*
Elliott, John Gregory *aerospace design engineer*
Harsha, Philip Thomas *aerospace engineer*
Jager, Merle LeRoy *aerospace engineer*
Kumar, Rajendra *electrical engineering educator*
Robinson, Michael R. *aeronautical engineer*

Los Altos
Sharpe, Roland Leonard *engineering company executive, earthquake and structural engineering consultant*
Zebroski, Edwin Leopold *safety engineer, consultant*

Los Altos Hills
Fondahl, John Walker *civil engineering educator*

Los Angeles
Atluri, Satya N(adham) *aerospace engineering educator*
Breuer, Melvin Allen *electrical engineering educator*
Bucy, Richard Snowden *aerospace engineering and mathematics educator, consultant*
Cheng, Tsen-Chung *electrical engineering educator*
Crombie, Douglass Darnill *aerospace communications system engineer*
Dhir, Vijay K. *mechanical engineering educator*
Dorman, Albert A. *consulting engineer executive, architect*
Friedlander, Sheldon Kay *chemical engineering educator*
Hovanessian, Shahen Alexander *electrical engineer, educator, consultant*
Incaudo, Joseph August *engineering company executive*
Itoh, Tatsuo *engineering educator*
Jenniches, F. Suzanne *engineering executive*
Johnston, Roy G. *consulting structural engineer*
Ju, Jiann-Wen *mechanics educator, researcher*
Karplus, Walter J. *engineering educator*
King-Ning, Tu *materials science and engineering educator*
Klinger, Allen *engineering and applied science educator*
Kuehl, Hans Henry *electrical engineering educator*
Leal, George D. *engineering company executive*
Lin, Tung Hua *civil engineering educator*
MacKenzie, John Douglas *engineering educator*
Marmarelis, Vasilis Zissis *engineering educator, writer, consultant*
Martin, J(ohn) Edward *architectural engineer*
Maxworthy, Tony *mechanical and aerospace engineering educator*
Meecham, William Coryell *engineering educator*
Mendel, Jerry Marc *electrical engineering educator*
Muntz, Eric Phillip *aerospace and mechanical engineering and radiology educator, consultant*
Newman, Richard *engineering executive*
Nobe, Ken *chemical engineering educator*
O'Neill, Russell Richard *engineering educator*
Orchard, Henry John *electrical engineer*
Perrine, Richard Leroy *environmental engineering educator*
Philpott, Lindsey *civil engineer, researcher, educator*
Ramo, Simon *retired engineering executive*
Reed, Irving S. *electrical engineer*
Rubinstein, Moshe Fajwel *engineering educator*
Safonov, Michael George *electrical engineering educator, consultant*
Scholtz, Robert Arno *electrical engineering educator*
Settles, F. Stan, Jr. *engineering educator, manufacturing executive*
Shinozuka, Masanobu *civil engineer, educator*
Speyer, Jason Lee *aeronautical engineer, educator*
Udwadia, Firdaus Erach *engineering educator, consultant*
Urena-Alexiades, Jose Luis *electrical engineer*
Wagner, Christian Nikolaus Johann *materials engineering educator*
Weber, Charles L. *electrical engineering educator*
Welch, Lloyd Richard *electrical engineering educator, communications consultant*
Willner, Alan Eli *electrical engineer, educator*
Yablonovitch, Eli *electrical engineering educator*
Yeh, William Wen-Gong *civil engineering educator*
Yen, Teh Fu *civil and environmental engineering educator*

Los Gatos
Bell, Chester Gordon *computer engineering company executive*

Manhattan Beach
Ricardi, Leon Joseph *electrical engineer, researcher*

Menlo Park
Honey, Richard Churchill *retired electrical engineer*
Levenson, Milton *chemical engineer, consultant*
McCarthy, Roger Lee *mechanical engineer*
Montague, L. David *aerospace engineer*
Shah, Haresh Chandulal *civil engineering educator*
Stonebraker, Michael R. *electrical engineering & computer science educator*

Moffett Field
Erzberger, Heinz *aeronautical engineer*
Kerr, Andrew W. *aerodynamics researcher*
McCroskey, William James *aeronautical engineer*
Mikula, Julie *aerospace engineer*
Statler, Irving Carl *aerospace engineer*

Monarch Beach
Dougherty, Elmer Lloyd, Jr. *retired chemical engineering educator, consultant*

Monrovia
Edwards, Kenneth Neil *chemical engineering executive*
Mac Cready, Paul Beattie *aeronautical engineer*

Monterey
Butler, Jon Terry *computer engineering educator, researcher*
Marto, Paul James *retired mechanical engineering educator, consultant, researcher*
Sarpkaya, Turgut *mechanical engineering educator*

Mountain View
Chandramouli, Ramamurti *electrical engineer*
Johnson, Conor Deane *mechanical engineer*

Murphys
Moody, Frederick Jerome *mechanical engineer, consultant*

Northridge
Bekir, Nagwa Esmat *electrical engineer, educator, consultant*
Bradshaw, Richard Rotherwood *engineering executive*
Kiddoo, Robert James *engineering service company executive*
Torgow, Eugene N. *electrical engineer*

Oakland
Brown, Stephen Lawrence *environmental consultant*
Kavanaugh, Michael C. *environmental engineer*
King, Cary Judson, III *chemical engineer, educator, university official*
Vallerga, Bernard A. *engineering administrator*

Oceanside
Yurist, Svetlan Joseph *mechanical engineer*

Orange
Jones, Cleon Boyd *research engineer*
Monsees, James Eugene *engineering executive, consultant*

Orinda
Gilbert, Jerome B. *consulting environmental engineer*

Palm Desert
Hoglund, Richard Frank *research and technical executive*

Palo Alto
Chow, Winston *engineering research executive*
Culler, Floyd LeRoy, Jr. *chemical engineer*
Diffie, Whitfield *computer and communications engineer*
Giffard, Robin P. *computer engineer, industrial physicist*
Hodge, Philip Gibson, Jr. *mechanical and aerospace engineering educator*
Jeffries, Robin *computer engineer*
Quate, Calvin Forrest *engineering educator*
Swartz, James R. *chemical engineer, educator*
Taylor, John Joseph *nuclear engineer, researcher*

Palos Verdes Estates
Aro, Glenn Scott *environmental and safety executive*

Pasadena
Bower, Curtis A. *engineering executive*
Breckinridge, James Bernard *optical science engineer, program manager*
Bridges, William Bruce *electrical engineer, researcher, educator*
Carroll, William Jerome *civil engineer*
Cass, Glen Rowan *environmental engineer*
Cook, Richard A. *aerospace engineer*
Dallas, Saterios (Sam) *aerospace engineer, researcher, consultant*
Davis, Mark E. *chemical engineering educator*
Farr, Donald Eugene *engineering scientist*
Gavalas, George R. *chemical engineering educator*
Gould, Roy Walter *engineering educator*
Hall, William E. *engineering and construction company executive*
Hilbert, Robert S(aul) *optical engineer*
Hornung, Hans Georg *aeronautical engineering educator, science facility administrator*
Housner, George William *retired civil engineering educator, consultant*
Iwan, Wilfred Dean *mechanical engineer, educator*
Jacobs, Joseph John *engineering company executive*
Jennings, Paul Christian *civil engineering educator, academic administrator*
Knauss, Wolfgang Gustav *engineering educator*
Knowles, James Kenyon *applied mechanics educator*
Kornfield, Julia Ann *chemical engineering educator*
List, Ericson John *environmental engineering science educator, engineering consultant*
Manning, Robert M. *aerospace engineer*
Marble, Frank E(arl) *engineering educator*
Martin, Craig Lee *engineering company executive*
Middlebrook, Robert David *electronics educator*
Muirhead, Brian K. *aerospace engineer*
Otoshi, Tom Yasuo *electrical engineer, consultant*
Perez, Reinaldo Joseph *electrical engineer*
Poon, Peter Tin-Yau *engineer, physicist*
Presecan, Nicholas Lee *environmental and civil engineer, consultant*
Raichlen, Fredric *civil engineering educator, consultant*
Riveluni, Tomasso P. *engineer*
Roshko, Anatol *aeronautic engineer*
Sabersky, Rolf Heinrich *mechanical engineer*
Seinfeld, John Hersh *chemical engineering educator*
Simon, Marvin Kenneth *electrical engineer, consultant*
Smith, Michael Robert *electro-optical engineer, physicist*
Stewart, Homer Joseph *engineering educator*
Tolaney, Murli *environmental engineering executive*
Trussell, R(obert) Rhodes *environmental engineer*
Yamarone, Charles Anthony, Jr. *aerospace engineer, consultant*
Yariv, Amnon *electrical engineering educator, scientist*

Penn Valley
Throner, Guy Charles, Jr. *engineering executive, scientist, engineer, inventor, consultant*

Pleasanton
Rosen, Charles Abraham *electrical engineer, consultant*

Poway
Dean, Richard Anthony *mechanical engineer, engineering executive*

Rancho Mirage
Kramer, Gordon *mechanical engineer*

Rancho Palos Verdes
Raue, Jorg Emil *electrical engineer*

Richmond
Moehle, Jack P. *civil engineer, engineering executive*

Riverside
Beni, Gerardo *electrical and computer engineering educator, robotics scientist*
Hackwood, Susan *electrical and computer engineering educator*

Rodeo
Emmanuel, Jorge Agustin *chemical engineer, environmental consultant*

Rohnert Park
Lord, Harold Wilbur *electrical engineer, electronics consultant*

Rolling Hills Estates
Diaz-Zubieta, Agustin *nuclear engineer, engingeering executive*

Sacramento
Bezzone, Albert Paul *structural engineer*
Collins, William Leroy *telecommunications engineer*
Forsyth, Raymond Arthur *civil engineer, consultant*
Roberts, James E. *civil engineer*

San Bernardino
French, Kirby Allan *transportation engineer, computer programmer*

San Carlos
Symons, Robert Spencer *electronic engineer*

San Clemente
Cramer, Eugene Norman *nuclear power engineer, computer educator*
White, Stanley Archibald *research electrical engineer*

San Diego
Basso, Robert J. *manufacturing engineer, inventor*
Brown, Alan J. *electrical engineer*
Burke, Arthur Thomas *engineering consultant*
Chang, Daniel Haiming *engineering executive*
Conly, John Franklin *engineering educator, researcher*
Crook, Sean Paul *aerospace systems division director*
Evans, Ersel Arthur *consulting engineer executive*
Gupta, Madhu Sudan *electrical engineering educator*
Hanna, Nabil *biomedical engineer*
Marple, Stanley Lawrence, Jr. *electrical engineer, signal processing researcher*
Paget, John Arthur *mechanical engineer*
Slate, John Butler *biomedical engineer*
Tricoles, Gus Peter *electromagnetic engineer, physicist, consultant*
Viterbi, Andrew James *electrical engineering and computer science educator, business executive*

San Francisco
Abramson, Norman *retired electronics executive*
Bechtel, Riley Peart *engineering company executive*
Bechtel, Stephen Davison , Jr. *engineering company executive*
Burkey, Marcia B. *engineering executive*
Cheng, Wan-Lee *mechanical engineer, industrial technology educator*
Danziger, Bruce Edward *structural engineer*
Dolby, Ray Milton *engineering company executive, electrical engineer*
Gerwick, Ben Clifford, Jr. *construction engineer, educator*
Keller, Edward Lowell *electrical engineer, educator*
Koffel, Martin M. *engineering company executive*
Lin, Tung Yen *civil engineer, educator*
Shor, Samuel Wendell Williston *naval engineer*
Tang, Man-Chung *engineer, administrator*
Tank, Man-Chung *civil engineer*
Young, William D. *chemical engineer*

San Jose
Chamberlin, Donald Dean *computer engineer*
Contos, Paul Anthony *engineer, investment consultant*
Dennison, Ronald Walton *engineer*
Der Torossian, Papken *engineering executive*
Hill, Richard *egineering executive*
Hoff, Marcian Edward, Jr. *electronics engineer*
Kirk, Donald Evan *electrical engineering educator, dean*
Markle, David A. *optical engineer*
Thompson, David A. *electrical engineer*

San Luis Obispo
Hoffmann, Jon Arnold *aeronautical engineer, educator*

San Marcos
Purdy, Alan Harris *biomedical engineer*

San Pedro
Ellis, George Edwin, Jr. *chemical engineer*
McCarty, Frederick Briggs *electrical engineer, consultant*

San Rafael
Wright, Frederick Herman Greene, II *computer systems engineer*

Santa Ana
Amoroso, Frank *retired communication system engineer, consultant*

Santa Barbara
Chmelka, Bradley Floyd *chemical engineering educator*
Clarke, David R. *materials engineer*
Coldren, Larry Allen *engineering educator, consultant*
Fredrickson, Glenn Harold *chemical engineering and materials educator*
Hu, Evelyn Lynn *electrical and computer engineering educator*
Kokotovic, Petar V. *electrical and computer engineer, educator*
Kramer, Edward John *materials science and engineering educator*
Kroemer, Herbert *electrical engineering educator*
Lange, Frederick F. *materials engineer, educator*
Lawrance, Charles Holway *retired civil and sanitary engineer*
Lick, Wilbert James *mechanical engineering educator*
Mitra, Sanjit Kumar *electrical and computer engineering educator*
Odette, G. Robert *mechanical and environmental engineering educator*
Russell, Charles Roberts *chemical engineer*
Sensiper, Samuel *consulting electrical engineer*
Theofanous, Theo G. *engineering educator, consultant*
Tirrell, Matthew *chemical engineering, materials science educator*

Santa Clara
Chan, Shu-Park *electrical engineering educator*
Chen, Wai-Kai *electrical engineering and computer science educator, consultant*
Hoagland, Albert Smiley *electrical engineer, researcher*
Parden, Robert James *engineering educator, management consultant*
Wang, Huai-Liang William *mechanical engineer*
Weinberg, William Henry *chemical engineer, chemical physicist, educator*

Santa Cruz
Langdon, Glen George, Jr. *electrical engineer*

Santa Monica
Gritton, Eugene Charles *nuclear engineer, department chairman*
Kayton, Myron *engineering company executive*
Kummer, Wolfgang H. *freelance/self-employed electrical engineer*
Sherman, Zachary *civil and aerospace engineer, consultant*

Santa Rosa
Apfel, Joseph H. *optical engineer, research scientist*

Saratoga
Johnson, Noel Lars *biomedical engineer*

Sonoma
Sasaki, Y(asunaga) Tito *engineering executive*

South Pasadena
Glad, Dain Sturgis *aerospace engineer, consultant*
Kopp, Eugene Howard *electrical engineer*

Stanford
Aziz, Khalid *petroleum engineering educator*
Boudart, Michel *chemical engineer, chemist, educator, consultant*
Bracewell, Ronald Newbold *electrical engineering educator*
Bradshaw, Peter *engineering educator*
Bryson, Arthur Earl, Jr. *retired aerospace engineering educator*
Cannon, Robert Hamilton, Jr. *aerospace engineering educator*
Carlson, Robert Codner *industrial engineering educator*
Cox, Donald Clyde *electrical engineering educator*
Eshleman, Von Russel *electrical engineering educator*
Eustis, Robert Henry *mechanical engineer*
Franklin, Gene Farthing *engineering educator, consultant*
Gibbons, James Franklin *electrical engineering educator*
Goodman, Joseph Wilfred *electrical engineering educator*
Gray, Robert M(olten) *electrical engineering educator*
Harris, Stephen Ernest *electrical engineering and applied physics educator*
Herrmann, George *mechanical engineering educator*
Hesselink, Lambertus *electrical engineering and physics educator*
Hewett, Thomas Avery *petroleum engineer, educator*
Howard, H. Taylor *electrical engineer, educator*
Howard, Ronald A. *systems engineer, educator*
Hughes, Thomas J.R. *mechanical engineering educator, consultant*
Inan, Umran Savas *electrical engineering educator, researcher*
Jameson, Antony *aerospace engineering educator*
Journel, André G. *petroleum engineering educator*
Kailath, Thomas *electrical engineer, educator*
Kane, Thomas Reif *engineering educator*
Kelley, David M. *mechanical engineer, educator*
Kino, Gordon Stanley *electrical engineering educator*
Kitanidis, Peter K. *engineering educator*
Kruger, Charles Herman, Jr. *mechanical engineering educator*
Linvill, John Grimes *engineering educator*
Macovski, Albert *electrical engineering educator*
Madix, Robert James *chemical engineer, educator*
Mathews, Max V. *acoustical engineer, educator*
McCarty, Perry Lee *civil and environmental engineering educator*
Mitchell, Reginald Eugene *mechanical engineering educator*
Moin, Parviz *mechanical engineering educator*
Orr, Franklin Mattes, Jr. *petroleum engineering educator*
Ortolano, Leonard *civil engineering educator, water resources planner*
Ott, Wayne Robert *environmental engineer*
Parkinson, Bradford Wells *astronautical engineer, educator*
Paulson, Boyd Colton, Jr. *civil engineering educator*
Pease, Roger Fabian Wedgwood *electrical engineering educator*
Reynolds, William Craig *mechanical engineer, educator*
Roberts, Paul V. *civil and environmental engineering educator*
Siegman, Anthony Edward *electrical engineer, educator*
Springer, George Stephen *mechanical engineering educator*
Steele, Charles Richard *biomedical and mechanical engineering educator*
Street, Robert Lynnwood *civil, mechanical and environmental engineer*
Stuart, Andrew Mark *mechanical engineering educator*
Tyler, George Leonard *electrical engineering educator*
Van Dyke, Milton Denman *aeronautical engineering educator*
Vincenti, Walter Guido *aeronautical engineer, emeritus educator*
White, Robert Lee *electrical engineer, educator*

Sunnyvale
Kim, Wan Hee *electrical engineering educator, business executive*
Ma, Fengchow Clarence *agricultural engineering consultant*
Puckett, W. Greer *engineer*
Robbins, James Edward *electrical engineer*

Tarzana
Hansen, Robert Clinton *electrical engineering consultant*

Temecula
Minogue, Robert Brophy *retired nuclear engineer*

Thousand Oaks
Deisenroth, Clinton Wilbur *electrical engineer*
Krumm, Charles Ferdinand *electrical engineer*

Torrance
Bateman, Donald *aerospace engineer*
Gran, Robert *engineering company executive*
Mende, Howard Shigeharu *mechanical engineer*
Wylie, Richard Thornton *aerospace engineer*

Ventura
Gaynor, Joseph *chemical engineer, technical-management consultant*

Walnut Creek
Van Maerssen, Otto L. *aerospace engineer, consulting firm executive*

Westminster
Armstrong, Gene Lee *systems engineering consultant, retired aerospace company executive*

Yorba Linda
Porcello, Leonard Joseph *engineering research and development executive*

COLORADO

Arvada
Ferguson, Lloyd Elbert *retired manufacturing engineer*

Boulder
Avery, Susan Kathryn *electrical engineering educator, research administrator*
Born, George H. *aerospace engineer, educator*
Cathey, Wade Thomas *electrical engineering educator*
Corotis, Ross Barry *civil engineering educator, academic administrator*
Gupta, Kuldip Chand *electrical and computer engineering educator, researcher*
Hanna, William Johnson *electrical engineering educator*
Hauser, Ray Louis *research engineer, entrepreneur*
Hill, David Allan *electrical engineer*
Joy, Edward Bennett *electrical engineer, educator*
Lewin, Leonard *electrical engineering educator*
Mikulas, Martin M., Jr. *aerospace engineer, educator*
Reitsema, Harold James *aerospace engineer*
Rodriguez, Juan Alfonso *technology corporation executive*
Sani, Robert LeRoy *chemical engineering educator*
Seebass, Alfred Richard, III *aerospace engineer, educator, university dean*
Smith, Ernest Ketcham *electrical engineer*
Sodal, Ingvar Edmund *electrical engineer, scientist*
Timmerhaus, Klaus Dieter *chemical engineering educator*
Yukawa, Sumio *engineering consultant, researcher*

Colorado Springs
Chapman, Richard Cady *engineer*
James, Wayne Edward *electronic engineer*
Watts, Oliver Edward *engineering consultancy company executive*

Helstrom, Carl Wilhelm *electrical engineering educator*
Kahn, Irwin William *industrial engineer*
Krause, Keith Winston *quality engineer executive*
Liu, Young King *biomedical engineering educator*
Luenberger, David Gilbert *electrical engineer, educator*
Luthy, Richard Godfrey *environmental engineering educator*
Mason, John Latimer *engineering executive*
McCloskey, Thomas Henry *mechanical engineer, consultant*
McCraw, Leslie G. *retired engineering and construction company executive*
Mitzner, Kenneth Martin *electrical engineering consultant*
Morgan, James John *environmental engineering educator*
Nahman, Norris Stanley *electrical engineer*
Nielsen, Jakob *computer interface engineer*
Nordby, Gene Milo *engineering educator, educator*
Peters, Douglas Cameron *mining engineer, geologist*
Pratt, David Terry *engineering consultant*
Remer, Donald Sherwood *engineering educator, economist, consultant*
Rosa, Richard John *mechanical engineer, educator*
Salamon, Miklos Dezso Gyorgy *mining engineer, educator*
Savrun, Ender *engineering executive, researcher, engineer*
Shank, Maurice Edwin *aerospace engineering executive, consultant*
Siljak, Dragoslav D. *engineering educator, researcher*
Thomas, Frank Joseph *retired nuclear engineer*
Van Dreser, Merton Lawrence *ceramic engineer*
Vega, J. William *aerospace engineering executive, consultant*
Williams, Howard Walter *aerospace engineer, executive*
Williams, Ronald Oscar *systems engineer*
Willis, Selene Lowe *electrical engineer, software consultant*
Yeager, Kurt Eric *research institute official*
Yue, Alfred Shui-choh *metallurgical engineer, educator*

FINANCE: BANKING SERVICES. *See also* FINANCE: INVESTMENT SERVICES.

UNITED STATES

ALASKA

Anchorage
Cuddy, Daniel Hon *bank executive*
Rasmuson, Edward Bernard *banker*
Strutz, Richard *bank executive*

ARIZONA

Gilbert
Duran, Michael Carl *bank executive*

Phoenix
Bradley, Gilbert Francis *retired banker*
Welborn, R. Michael *bank executive*

Scottsdale
Garfield, Ernest *bank consultant*

CALIFORNIA

Aptos
Dobey, James Kenneth *banker*

Arcadia
Ulrich, Peter Henry *banker*

Beverly Hills
Benter, George H., Jr. *banker*
Goldsmith, Bram *banker*
Israel, Richard Stanley *investment banker*
Walker, William Tidd, Jr. *investment banker*

Burbank
DeMieri, Joseph L. *bank executive*
Miller, Clifford Albert *merchant banker, business consultant*

Fairfax
Delaney, Marion Patricia *bank executive*

Fresno
Smith, Richard Howard *banker*

Inglewood
Creighton, Norman P. *bank executive*
Mathis, Daniel R. *banking officer*

Irvine
Kuhn, Robert Lawrence *investment banker, corporate financier, strategist, author, educator*

La Mesa
Schmidt, James Craig *retired bank executive*

Lafayette
Dethero, J. Hambright *banker*

Laguna Hills
Pelton, Harold Marcel *mortgage broker*

Lake Arrowhead
Fitzgerald, John Charles, Jr. *investment banker*

Long Beach
Hancock, John Walker, III *banker*

Los Angeles
Badie, Ronald Peter *banker*
Brown, Kathleen *bank executive, lawyer*
Lenard, Michael Barry *merchant banker, lawyer*
Riordan, George Nickerson *investment banker*
Takakura, Tamio *bank official*
Willison, Bruce Gray *banker*
Wu, Li-Pei *banker*

Menlo Park
Cotsakos, Christos Michael *internet financial services company executive*
Schmidt, Chauncey Everett *banker*

Newport Beach
Frederick, Dolliver H. *merchant banker*
McAlister, Maurice L. *savings and loan association executive*
Woollatt, Paul G. *financial company executive*

Oakland
Judd, James Thurston *savings and loan executive*
Kettell, Russell Willard *banker*
Sandler, Herbert M. *retired savings and loan association executive*
Sandler, Marion Osher *retired savings and loan association executive*

Orinda
Trowbridge, Thomas, Jr. *mortgage banking company executive*

Pasadena
Patton, Richard Weston *retired mortgage company executive*
Vaughn, John Vernon *banker, industrialist*

San Diego
Kendrick, Ronald H. *banker*
Reinhard, Christopher John *merchant banking, venture capital executive*
Wiesler, James Ballard *retired banker*

San Francisco
August-deWilde, Katherine *banker*
Baumhefner, Clarence Herman *banker*
Bee, Robert Norman *banker*
Deily, Linnet Frazier *banker*
Dellas, Robert Dennis *investment banker*
Demarest, David Franklin, Jr. *banker, former government official*
Eckersley, Norman Chadwick *bank executive*
Ford, Gerald J. *bank executive*
Gillette, Frankie Jacobs *retired savings and loan executive, social worker, government administrator*
Hazen, Paul Mandeville *banker*
Hewitt, Conrad W. *bank executive*
Jacobs, Rodney L. *retired bank executive*
Johnson, Charles M. *former banker*
Kari, Ross *banking executive*
Kovacevich, Richard M. *bank executive*
Luikart, John Ford *investment banker*
Matthews, Gilbert Elliott *investment banker*
McGettigan, Charles Carroll, Jr. *investment banker*
Mehta, Shailesh J. *banker*
Ostler, Clyde W. *banker*
Peterson, Rudolph A. *banker*
Petrini, David J. *banking executive*
Rosenberg, Richard Morris *banker*
Shansby, John Gary *investment banker*
Trafton, Stephen J. *bank executive*
Warner, Harold Clay, Jr. *banker, investment management executive*
Webb, Carl B. *bank officer*

San Jose
Hall, Robert Emmett, Jr. *investment banker, realtor*

San Mateo
Douglass, Donald Robert *banker*

San Rafael
Djordjevich, Miroslav-Michael *bank executive*
Payne, David L. *bank executive*

Santa Barbara
Anderson, Donald Meredith *bank executive*
Tilton, David Lloyd *savings and loan association executive*

Santa Clara
Kamm, Barbara B. *bank executive*

Santa Monica
Heimbuch, Babette E. *bank executive*
Mortensen, William S. *banking executive*
Rampino, Louis J. *bank executive*
Weil, Leonard *banker*

Sherman Oaks
Montgomery, James Fischer *savings and loan association executive*

Turlock
Wallström, Wesley Donald *bank executive*

Walnut Creek
McGrath, Don John *banker*
Rhody, Ronald Edward *banker, communications executive*

COLORADO

Colorado Springs
Olin, Kent Oliver *banker*
Ostergard, Paul Michael *not for profit executive*

Denver
Childears, Linda *banker*
Fugate, Ivan Dee *banker, lawyer*
Grant, William West, III *banker*
Imhoff, Walter Francis *investment banker*
Malone, Robert Joseph *retired bank executive*
Nicholson, Will Faust, Jr. *bank holding company executive*

Englewood
Corboy, James McNally *investment banker*
Rosser, Edwin Michael *mortgage company executive*

Greenwood Village
Sims, Douglas D. *bank executive*

Highlands Ranch
Hoover, Gary Lynn *banker*

Lakewood
Orullian, B. LaRae *bank executive*

HAWAII

Honolulu
Dods, Walter Arthur, Jr. *bank executive*
Hoag, John Arthur *retired bank executive*
Johnson, Lawrence M. *banker*
Keir, Gerald Janes *banker*
Midkiff, Robert Richards *financial and trust company executive, consultant*
O'Neill, Michael E. *bank executive*
Wolff, Herbert Eric *banker, former army officer*

IDAHO

Ketchum
McElhinny, Wilson Dunbar *banker*

NEVADA

Las Vegas
Troidl, Richard John *banker*

Logandale
Smiley, Robert William, Jr. *investment banker*

Reno
Day, Kevin Thomas *banker, community services director*

NEW MEXICO

Rio Rancho
Truscio, James, Jr. *banker*

Santa Fe
Clyde, Larry Forbes *banker*
Dreisbach, John Gustave *investment banker*

OREGON

Portland
McKay, Laura L. *banker, consultant*

UTAH

Ogden
Browning, Roderick Hanson *banker*

Saint George
Beesley, H(orace) Brent *savings and loan executive*

Salt Lake City
Eccles, Spencer Fox *banker*
Simmons, Roy William *banker*

WASHINGTON

Bellevue
Davidson, Robert William *merchant banker*

Mercer Island
Spitzer, Jack J. *banker*

Seattle
Andrew, Lucius Archibald David, III *bank executive*
Arnold, Robert Morris *banker*
Campbell, Robert Hedgcock *investment banker, lawyer*
Faulstich, James R. *retired bank executive*
Fetters, Norman Craig , II *banker*
Green, Joshua, III *retired banker*
Helms, Luke *bank executive*
Killinger, Kerry Kent *bank executive*
Longbrake, William Arthur *bank executive*
Rice, Norman B. *bank executive, former mayor*
Wilson, S. Liane *bank executive*

Sequim
Laube, Roger Gustav *retired trust officer, financial consultant*

Spokane
Jones, D. Michael *banker*

WYOMING

Cheyenne
Knight, Robert Edward *banker*

CANADA

BRITISH COLUMBIA

Vancouver
Lyons, Terrence Allan *merchant banking, investment company executive*

ADDRESS UNPUBLISHED

Clark, Raymond Oakes *banker*
Cockrum, William Monroe, III *investment banker, consultant, educator*
Coleman, Lewis Waldo *bank executive*
Duval, Michael Raoul *investment banker*
Eaton, Curtis Howarth *banker, lawyer*
Giannini, Valerio Louis *investment banker*
Gilchrist, James Beardslee *banker*
Jensen, Edmund Paul *retired bank holding company executive*
Miracle, Robert Warren *retired banker*
Rank, Larry Gene *retired banker*
Ripper, Rita Jo (Jody Ripper) *strategic planner, researcher*
Skillern, Frank L., Jr. *bank executive*
Stephenson, Herman Howard *retired banker*
Taylor, David George *retired banker*
Winnowski, Thaddeus Richard (Ted Winnowski) *bank executive*

FINANCE: FINANCIAL SERVICES

UNITED STATES

ARIZONA

Peoria
Molinsky, Bert *tax consultant*

Phoenix
Campbell, Jon R. *financial services executive*
Castleberry, W. Thomas *financial company executive*
Daniel, James Richard *accountant, computer company financial executive*
Gibbs, William Harold *finance company executive*
Khan, Ahmed Mohiuddin *finance, insurance executive*
Richardson, Judy McEwen *education administrator, consultant, cartoonist*
Smith, Gordon *finance company executive*
Upson, Donald V. *financial executive, retired*

Scottsdale
Breyne, Matthew M. *finance company executive*
Cox, Mark Baker *financial executive*
Marszowski, Bruno A. *finance company executive*
Weil, John David *financial executive*

Sun City
Cortright, Inga Ann *accountant*

Tempe
Kaufman, Herbert Mark *finance educator*
Pany, Kurt Joseph *accounting educator, consultant*
Poe, Jerry B. *financial educator*

Tucson
Adelstone, Jeffrey Alan *accountant, tax law specialist, educator*
Brasswel, Kerry *tax accountant*
Hellon, Michael Thomas *tax consultant, political party official*
Nixon, Robert Obey, Sr. *business educator*

CALIFORNIA

Atherton
Barker, Robert Jeffery *financial executive*

Bakersfield
Bacon, Leonard Anthony *accounting educator*

Berkeley
Staubus, George Joseph *accounting educator*

Beverly Hills
Matzdorff, James Arthur *investment banker, financier*
McGagh, William Gilbert *financial consultant*
Widaman, Gregory Alan *financial executive, accountant*

Burbank
Gold, Stanley Phillip *diversified investments executive*
Murphy, Peter E. *corporate financial officer*
Shao, Shiu *financial executive*

Calabasas
Garcia, Carlos M. *financial services company executive*
Kurland, Stanford L. *financial lending company executive*
Mozilo, Angelo R. *diversified financial services company executive*

Camarillo
Smith, David Michael *financial planner*

Carmel
Bonfield, Andrew Joseph *tax practitioner*
Steele, Charles Glen *retired accountant*

Coronado
Allen, Charles Richard *retired financial executive*

Costa Mesa
Parnes, Andrew H. *financial executive*

Culver City
Richardson, John Edmon *marketing educator*

Dana Point
Kesselhaut, Arthur Melvyn *financial consultant*

Encino
Dor, Yoram *accountant, firm executive*

Fountain Valley
Penderghast, Thomas Frederick *business educator*

Fresno
Pinkerton, Richard LaDoyt *retired management educator*

Farrar, John Edson, II *business executive, consultant, investment adviser*
Franklin, William Emery *international business educator*
Hickson, Ernest Charles *financial executive*
Japha, Barbara *financial executive*
Larson, Mark Allan *financial executive*
Martin, Preston *financial services executive*
Norton, Karen Ann *accountant*
Palmer, Gary Andrew *portfolio manager*
Rauwerdink, William Jay *accountant*
Saunders, James Harwood *accountant*
Snyder, Alan Carhart *financial services executive*
Srinivasan, Venkataraman *marketing and management educator*
Turner, Henry Brown *finance executive*
Wachbrit, Jill Barrett *accountant, tax specialist*
Wall, M. Danny *financial services company executive*

FINANCE: INSURANCE

UNITED STATES

ALASKA

Anchorage
Trevithick, Ronald James *underwriter*

ARIZONA

Bullhead City
Shervheim, Lloyd Oliver *insurance company executive, lawyer*

Phoenix
Foley, William Patrick, II *title insurance company executive*

Scottsdale
Burr, Edward Benjamin *life insurance company executive, financial executive*
Prisbrey, Rex Prince *retired insurance agent, underwriter, consultant*
Tyner, Neal Edward *retired insurance company executive*

CALIFORNIA

Alhambra
Fried, Elaine June *insurance company executive*

Concord
Basconcillo, Lindy *insurance and financial services company executive*

Dana Point
Lang, George Frank *insurance executive, consultant, lawyer*

Encino
Parrott, Dennis Beecher *retired insurance executive*

Garden Grove
Williams, J(ohn) Tilman *insurance executive, real estate broker, city official*

Los Angeles
Faulwell, Gerald Edward *insurance company executive*
Gurash, John Thomas *insurance company executive*
Houston, Ivan James *insurance company executive*
Inman, James Russell *claims consultant*
Johnson, E. Eric *insurance executive*
Milgrim, Darrow A. *insurance broker, recreation consultant*
Winthrop, Kenneth Ray *insurance executive*

Newport Beach
Gerken, Walter Bland *insurance company executive*
Schafer, Glenns *insurance company executive*
Sutton, Thomas C. *insurance company executive*
Tran, Khanh T. *insurance company executive*

Palm Springs
Levine, Norman Gene *insurance company executive*

Pismo Beach
Brisbin, Robert Edward *insurance agency executive*

Rancho Cordova
Alenius, John Todd *retired insurance executive*

Sacramento
Whitehead, Ian *insurance company executive*

San Diego
Jeffers, Donald E. *retired insurance executive, consultant*

San Francisco
Drexler, Fred *insurance executive*
Lamberson, John Roger *insurance company executive*

Santa Ana
Kennedy, Donald Parker *title insurance company executive*

Santa Barbara
Evans, Thomas Edgar, Jr. *title insurance agency executive*
Stinson, Alan L. *insurance company executive*
Stone, Patrick F. *insurance company executive*

Santa Rosa
Farrell, Thomas Joseph *insurance company executive, consultant*

Sonoma
Bow, Stephen Tyler, Jr. *insurance and computer industry consultant*

Tarzana
Rinsch, Charles Emil *retired insurance company executive*

Thousand Oaks
Gregory, Calvin *insurance service executive*
Weinberg, D. Mark *health insurance company executive*

Vista
Fuhlrodt, Norman Theodore *retired insurance executive*

Woodland Hills
Erwin, Steven P. *insurance company executive*
Newman, Steven Harvey *insurance company executive, director*

COLORADO

Englewood
Conroy, Thomas Francis *insurance company consultant*
Hardy, Wayne Russell *insurance and investment broker*
Manley, Richard Walter *insurance executive*

Fort Collins
Schendel, Winfried George *insurance company executive*

Littleton
Moore, Dan Sterling *insurance executive, sales trainer*
Rotherham, Larry Charles *insurance executive*

HAWAII

Honolulu
Metcalf, Wayne C., III *insurance commissioner*

IDAHO

Nampa
Heidt, Raymond Joseph *insurance company executive*

Twin Falls
Lewis, Frederick Thomas *insurance company executive*

MONTANA

Whitefish
Hemp, Ralph Clyde *retired reinsurance company executive, consultant, arbitrator, umpire*

NEVADA

Reno
Delaney, William Francis, Jr. *reinsurance broker*

NEW MEXICO

Tucumcari
Woodard, Dorothy Marie *insurance broker*

OREGON

Hillsboro
Yates, Keith Lamar *retired insurance company executive*

Portland
Galbraith, John Robert *insurance company executive*
Timpe, Ronald E. *insurance company executive*

Tualatin
Chambers, Lois Irene *insurance automation consultant*

West Linn
Dunstan, Larry Kenneth *insurance company executive*

UTAH

Sandy
Macumber, John Paul *insurance company executive*

WASHINGTON

Kirkland
McDonald, Joseph Lee *insurance broker*

Mountlake Terrace
Dyer, Philip E. *insurance company executive*

Olympia
Neeld, Michael Earl *public affairs executive, communications specialist*
Senn, Deborah *insurance commissioner*

Seattle
Armstrong, Mary M. *insurance company executive*
Eigsti, Roger Harry *retired insurance company executive*
Pierson, Rodney *insurance company executive*

CANADA

ALBERTA

Calgary
Libin, Alvin G. *business executive*

ADDRESS UNPUBLISHED

Broome, Burton Edward *former insurance company executive*
Dackow, Orest Taras *insurance company executive*
Fibiger, John Andrew *life insurance company executive*
Mehdizadeh, Parviz *insurance company executive*
Morrill, Thomas Clyde *insurance company executive*
Porter, Dixie Lee *insurance company executive, consultant*

FINANCE: INVESTMENT SERVICES

UNITED STATES

ALASKA

Anchorage
Hickel, Walter Joseph *investment firm executive, forum administrator*

Juneau
Bushre, Peter Alvin *retired investment company executive*

ARIZONA

Phoenix
Stern, Richard David *investment company executive*

Tucson
Lomicka, William Henry *investor*

ARKANSAS

Little Rock
Heath, Richard Raymond *investment company executive, retired*

CALIFORNIA

Anaheim
Drew, Paul S. *entrepreneur*

Arcadia
Berkus, David William *venture capitalist*

Atherton
Sollman, George Henry *venture capitalist*

Benicia
Szabo, Peter John *investment company executive, financial planner, mining engineer, lawyer*

Beverly Hills
Dawson, Derek *investment company executive*
Evans, Louise *investor, retired psychologist, philanthropist*
Gambrell, Thomas Ross *investor, retired physician, surgeon*

Camarillo
Sullivan, Michael Evan *investment and management company executive*

Carmel
Hamilton, Beverly Lannquist *investment management professional*

Century City
Feiman, Thomas E. *investment manager*

Escondido
Allen, Donald Vail *investment executive, writer, concert pianist*

Fairfax
Ross, Sue *entrepreneur, author, fundraising executive*

Fresno
Armey, Douglas Richard *investment consultant*
Dauer, Donald Dean *investment executive*

Hollywood
Marshall, Conrad Joseph *entrepreneur*

Irvine
Jones, Joie Pierce *entrepreneur, acoustician, educator, writer, scientist*

La Jolla
Stone, Donald D. *investment and sales executive*

Livermore
[illegible] *business executive, educator*

Los Altos
Carsten, Jack Craig *venture capitalist*

Los Angeles
Angeloff, Dann Valentino *investment banking executive*
Baxter, Frank Edward *brokerage executive*
Binder, Gordon M. *venture capitalist*
Bradshaw, Carl John *investor, lawyer, consultant*
Clemmenson, Larry P. *investment company executive*
Gebhart, Carl Grant *security broker*
Gordy, Berry *entrepreneur, record company executive, motion picture executive*
Hurt, William Holman *investment management company executive*
Hurwitz, Lawrence Neal *investment banking company executive*
Jarrell, Leeann *investment company executive*
Larkin, Thomas Ernest, Jr. *investment management company executive*
Latzer, Richard Neal *investment company executive*
Mann, Nancy Louise (Nancy Louise Robbins) *entrepreneur*
Schmitz, Clarence T. *investment company executive*
Tennenbaum, Michael Ernest *private investor*

Menlo Park
Balkanski, Alexandre *investment company executive*
Fenton, Noel John *venture capitalist*
Lucas, Donald Leo *private investor*
Lynch, Charles Allen *investment executive, corporate director*
Roberts, George R. *investment banking company executive*
Walsh, William Desmond *investor*
Wolfson, Mark Alan *investor, business educator*

Mountain View
Briscoe, Lawrence Winton *brokerage house executive*
Crowley, Jerome Joseph, Jr. *investment company executive*

Napa
Strock, David Randolph *brokerage house executive*

Newport Beach
Thorp, Edward Oakley *investment management company executive*

Palm Desert
Krallinger, Joseph Charles *entrepreneur, business advisor, author*

Palo Alto
Berg, Olena *investment company executive, former federal official*
Breyer, James William *venture capitalist*
Collinson, Jeffrey Joseph *venture capitalist*

Palos Verdes Estates
Mennis, Edmund Addi *investment management consultant*

Pasadena
Arnott, Robert Douglas *investment company executive*
Baum, Dwight Crouse *investment banking executive*

Rancho Santa Fe
Kessler, A. D. *business, financial, investment and real estate advisor, consultant, lecturer, author, broadcaster, producer*

San Diego
Dunn, David Joseph *financial executive*
Koehler, John Edget *entrepreneur*

San Francisco
Buckner, John Knowles *investor*
Coughlan, John P. *investment company executive*
Dachs, Alan Mark *investment company executive*
Dunn, Patricia C. *investment company executive*
Dunn, Richard Joseph *retired investment counselor*
Gardner, James Harkins *venture capitalist*
Gund, George, III *financier, professional sports team executive*
Halliday, John Meech *investment company executive*
Hambrecht, William R. *retired venture capitalist*
Morgan, Christina *venture capital firm executive*
Pfau, George Harold, Jr. *stockbroker*
Pottruck, David Steven *brokerage house executive*
Rock, Arthur *venture capitalist*
Rosenberg, Claude Newman, Jr. *investment adviser*
Scheid, Steven L. *investment company executive*
Schwab, Charles R. *brokerage house executive*
Strock, James Martin *management consultant, author, negotiation expert*
Turner, Marshall C., Jr. *investment manager, consultant*
Turner, Ross James *investment corporation executive*
Weisel, Thomas W. *investment company executive*
Winblad, Ann *investment company executive*

San Rafael
Swanson, Janese *entrepreneur, technology company executive*

Santa Barbara
Bartlett, James Lowell, III *investment company executive*

Santa Monica
Unterman, Thomas *venture capitalist, lawyer*

Saratoga
Horn, Christian Friedrich *venture capital company executive*

Sausalito
Apatoff, Michael John *financial entrepreneur*

South Pasadena
Zimmerman, William Robert *entrepreneur, engineering based manufacturing company executive*

GOVERNMENT: AGENCY ADMINISTRATION

UNITED STATES

ADDRESS UNPUBLISHED

Adelman, Rodney Lee *federal agency administrator*
Anderson, Wayne Carl *public affairs officer, former corporate executive*
Bishop, C. Diane *state agency administrator, educator*
Brubaker, Crawford Francis, Jr. *federal agency official, aerospace consultant*
Bustamante, Tommy A. *protective services official*
De Herrera, Juan Abran (Age) *federal judicial security official*
Graham, Patrick J. *state agency administrator*
Guay, Gordon Hay *federal agency administrator, marketing educator, consultant*
Hedrick, Basil Calvin *state agency administrator, ethnohistorian, educator, museum and multicultural institutions consultant*
Shuman, Thomas Alan *protective services official, consultant*
Silva, Robert Owen *retired protective service official*

GOVERNMENT: EXECUTIVE ADMINISTRATION

UNITED STATES

ALASKA

Anchorage
Mystrom, Rick *mayor*

Fairbanks
Smith, Robert London, Sr. *commissioner, retired air force officer, political scientist, educator*

Juneau
Botelho, Bruce Manuel *state attorney general, mayor*
Knowles, Tony *governor*
Ulmer, Frances Ann *lieutenant governor*

ARIZONA

Chandler
Tibshraeny, Jay *mayor*

Glendale
Scruggs, Elaine M. *mayor*

Mesa
Brown, Wayne J. *mayor*

Phoenix
Bayless, Betsey *state official*
Curcio, Christopher Frank *city official*
DiCiccio, Sal *city official*
Hull, Jane Dee *governor, former state legislator*
Lyons, Lionel Dale *city official*
Miel, Vicky Ann *city official*
Napolitano, Janet Ann *state attorney general*
Noyes, Francie *state official*
Pettle, Cecile *city official*
Quayle, Dan (James Danforth Quayle) *former vice president United States, entrepreneur*
Rimsza, Skip *mayor*
Springer, Carol *state official*
West, Tony *former state official*

Scottsdale
Manross, Mary *mayor*

Tempe
Giuliano, Neil Gerard *mayor, former academic administrator*
Tambs, Lewis Arthur *diplomat, historian, educator*

Tucson
Crawford, Michael *city council*
Garza, Elizeo *director solid waste management, Tucson*
Ibarra, Jose *city council*
Leal, Steve *city council*
Meyerson, Ronald L. *city official*
Miller, Elizabeth Rodriguez *city official*
Scott, Shirley *city council*
Walkup, Robert E. *mayor*

CALIFORNIA

Anaheim
Daly, Tom *mayor*
Hill, Harry David *city official, human resources professional*
Jung, Charlene *city treasurer*

Aptos
Trounstine, Philip John *communications consultant*

Bakersfield
Price, Robert Otis *mayor*

Benicia
von Studnitz, Gilbert Alfred *state official*

Berkeley
Rice, Edward Earl *former government official, author*

Beverly Hills
Covitz, Carl D. *state official, real estate and investment executive*

Chula Vista
Horton, Shirley A. *mayor*

Coronado
Hostler, Charles Warren *former ambassador, international affairs consultant*

El Cajon
Pollock, Richard Edwin *former county official*

Felicity
Istel, Jacques Andre *mayor*

Fremont
Lydon, Daniel T. *city official*
Morrison, Gus (Angus Hugh Morrison) *mayor, engineer*
Perkins, Jan *municipal official*

Fresno
Patterson, James *mayor*

Fullerton
Sa, Julie *councilwoman*

Garden Grove
Broadwater, Bruce A. *mayor*

Hayward
Cooper, Roberta *mayor*

Huntington Beach
Garofalo, David *mayor*
Green, Peter *former mayor, biological sciences educator*

Irvine
Shea, Christina *mayor*

La Jolla
Lundine, Stanley Nelson *state government official, former congressman, lawyer*

Livermore
Brown, Cathie *city official*

Long Beach
Burroughs, Gary L. *city official*
O'Neill, Beverly Lewis *mayor, former college president*

Los Angeles
Adelman, Andrew A. *city manager*
Antonovich, Michael Dennis *county official*
Fong, Matthew Kipling *state official*
Galanter, Ruth *city official*
Hernandez, Mike *city official*
Howe, Con Edward *city manager*
Mattingly, Gary *city manager*
Morris, Sharon Hutson *city manager*
Nodal, Adolfo V. *city manager*
Reagan, Nancy Davis (Anne Francis Robbins) *volunteer, wife of former President of United States*
Reagan, Ronald Wilson *Fourtieth President of the United States*
Riordan, Richard J. *mayor*
Schnabel, Rockwell Anthony *ambassador*
Smith, Ann Delorise *municipal official*
Toman, Mary Ann *federal official*
Torres-Gil, Fernando M. *federal official, academic administrator*
Walston, Roderick Eugene *state government official*

Menlo Park
Lane, Laurence William, Jr. *retired ambassador, publisher*

Modesto
Sabatino, Carmen *mayor*

Moreno Valley
Stewart, Richard A. *mayor*

Oakland
Brown, Jerry (Edmund Gerald Brown Jr.) *mayor, former governor*
Chan, Wilma *county official*
Musgrove, George *city official*

Oceanside
Lyon, Richard *mayor emeritus, retired naval officer*

Ontario
Ovitt, Gary C. *mayor*

Oroville
Curry, William Sims *county official*

Oxnard
Lopez, Manuel M. *mayor*

Pasadena
Bogaard, William Joseph *mayor, lawyer, educator*

Penn Valley
Holmes, Genta Hawkins *diplomat*

Pomona
Cortez, Edward S. *mayor*

Rancho Mirage
Ford, Betty Bloomer (Elizabeth Ford) *former First Lady of United States, health facility executive*
Ford, Gerald Rudolph, Jr. *thirty eighth President of the United States*

Redlands
Hanson, Gerald Warner *retired county official*

Richmond
Corbin, Rosemary MacGowan *mayor*

Riverside
Loveridge, Ronald Oliver *mayor*

Sacramento
Burton, John *state official*
Bustamante, Cruz M. *state official*
Connell, Kathleen *state official*
Davis, Gray (Joseph Graham Davis) *governor*
Friery, Thomas P. *city treasurer*
Hodgkins, Francis Irving (Butch Hodgkins) *county official*
Jones, Bill *state official, rancher*
Lockyer, Bill *state attorney general*
Sequeira, Jim *city official*
Villaraigosa, Antonio R. *state official*
Yee, Jimmie R. *mayor*

Salinas
Wong, Walter Foo *county official*

San Bernardino
Lenz, Philip Joseph *municipal administrator*
Valles, Judith *mayor, former academic administrator*

San Diego
Golding, Susan *mayor*
Gwinn, Casey *city attorney San Diego, California*
Jacob, Dianne *county official*
Lungren, Daniel Edward *former state attorney general*
Roberts, Ron *county official*

San Francisco
Achtenberg, Roberta *former federal official*
Ammiano, Tom *county and municipal official*
Brown, Willie Lewis, Jr. *mayor, former state legislator, lawyer*
Frank, Anthony Melchior *federal official, former financial executive*
Hancock, Loni *mayor*
Islambouly, Hagar Abdel-Hamid *consul general*
Reilly, William Kane *former government official, educator, lawyer, conservationist*
Ward, Doris M. *county official*
Yaki, Michael J. *municipal official*

San Jose
Dando, Pat *city official*
Gonzales, Ron *mayor, former county supervisor*
McHugh, Peter *mayor*

Santa Ana
Pulido, Miguel Angel *mayor*
Williams, Cleveland *municipal or county official*

Santa Monica
Rice, Donald Blessing *business executive, former secretary of air force*

Seaside
Panetta, Leon Edward *federal official, former congressman*

Solana Beach
Gildred, Theodore E. *former diplomat, real estate developer*

South Gate
Mosby, Dorothea Susan *municipal official*

Stanford
Shultz, George Pratt *former government executive, economics educator*

Stockton
Giottonini, James B. *city official*
Meissner, Katherine Gong *city official*
Pinkerton, Steven James *city official*
Podesto, Gary *mayor*

Torrance
Hardison, Dee *mayor*

West Covina
Manners, Nancy *retired mayor*

Yuba City
Kemmerly, Jack Dale *retired state official, aviation consultant*

COLORADO

Aurora
Nicholas, Thomas Peter *municipal official*
Sheffield, Nancy *city agency administrator*
Tauer, Paul E. *mayor, educator*

Colorado Springs
Cousar, Ronny *city official*
Makepeace, Mary Lou *mayor*
Mullen, James Harry *city manager*
Swihart, James W., Jr. *diplomat*
Zelenok, David S. *city official*

Denver
Barnhart, Arthur L. *state official*
Brown, Keith Lapham *retired ambassador*
Cohen-Vader, Cheryl Denise *municipal official*
Davidson, Donetta *state official*
Frontera, Michael P. *municipal official*
Gallagher, Dennis Joseph *municipal official, state senator, educator*
Hackworth, Theodore James, Jr. *city official*
Moulton, Jennifer T. *city official, architect*
Owens, Bill *governor*
Palmer, Robert *state official*
Rogers, Joe *lieutenant governor*
Romer, Roy R. *former governor*
Rowe, Tina L. *government official*
Salazar, Kenneth L. *state attorney general*
Webb, Wellington E. *mayor*

Englewood
Kourlis, Thomas A. *state commissioner*

Lakewood
Burkholder, Steve *mayor*

Pueblo
Occhiato, Michael Anthony *city official*

Sterling
Gustafson, Randall Lee *city manager*

DISTRICT OF COLUMBIA

Washington
Norton, Gale Ann *secretary of the interior*

HAWAII

Camp H M Smith
Twining, Charles Haile *ambassador*

Honolulu
Anzai, Earl I. *state attorney general*
Bronster, Margery S *state attorney general*
Cayetano, Benjamin Jerome *governor, former state senator and representative*
Goto Sabas, Jennifer *state official*
Harris, Jeremy *mayor*
Hirono, Mazie Keiko *lieutenant governor*
Marks, Robert Arthur *lawyer, attorney general*
Mizuguchi, Norman *state official*
Say, Calvin *state official*
Wakatsuki, Lynn Y. *commissioner*

Lihue
Kusaka, Maryanne Winona *mayor*

Wailuku
Baker, Rosalyn Hester *county agency administrator, former state legislator*

IDAHO

Boise
Benham, James H. *state official*
Cenarrusa, Pete T. *state official*
Coles, H. Brent *mayor*
Gee, Gavin M. *state government official*
Hawkins, James Victor *former state official*
Kempthorne, Dirk Arthur *governor*
Lance, Alan George *state attorney general*
Riggs, Jack Timothy *lt governor, emergency physician*
Williams, J. D. *state controller*

Soda Springs
Clark, Trent L. *government public affairs manager*

MONTANA

Billings
Larsen, Richard Lee *former mayor and city manager, business, municipal and labor relations consultant, arbitrator*

Clancy
Ekanger, Laurie *retired state official*

Fairfield
Graf, Ervin Donald *municipal official*

Helena
Brown, Robert J. (Bob Brown) *secretary of state*
Cooney, Mike *state official*
Hutchinson, Donald Wilson *state commissioner*
Mazurek, Joseph P. *state attorney general, former state legislator*
O'Keefe, Mark David *state official*

NEVADA

Carson City
Guinn, Kenny C. *governor*
Heller, Dean *state official*
Hunt, Lorraine T. *lieutenant governor*
Krolicki, Brian Keith *state official*
Molasky-Arman, Alice Anne *state commissioner*
Walshaw, L. Scott *commissioner*

Henderson
Gibson, James B. *mayor*
McKinney, Sally Vitkus *state official*

Las Vegas
Augustine, Kathy Marie *state controller, state legislator, secondary education educator*
Goodman, Oscar Baylin *mayor, lawyer*
Hammargren, Lonnie *former lieutenant governor*
Rumbolz, Michael David *gaming control board chairman, lawyer*
Seale, Robert L. *former state treasurer, political organization chairman*

Reno
Griffin, Jeff *mayor*

NEW MEXICO

Albuquerque
Baca, Jim *mayor*
Baca Archulata, Margie *city clerk*
Darnell, Ray D. *city official*
Gonzales, Stephanie *state official*
Kotchian, Sarah Bruff *municipal official*
Ortiz y Pino, Gerald *municipal official*
Rael, Lawrence *city official*
Sedillo, Orlando Delano *city official*

Las Cruces
Smith, Ruben *mayor*

Santa Fe
Bradley, Walter D. *lieutenant governor, real estate broker*
Johnson, Gary Earl *governor*
Kinderwater, Diane *state official*
Madrid, Patricia A. *state attorney general, lawyer*
Montoya, Michael A. *state official, accountant*
Vigil-Giron, Rebecca *state official*

OREGON

Eugene
Bascom, Ruth F. *retired mayor*
Torrey, James D. *mayor, communications executive, consultant*

Lake Oswego
Campbell, Colin Harold *former mayor*

Portland
Burton, Mike *county official*
Church-Gaultier, Lorene Kemmerer *retired government official*
Katz, Vera *mayor, former college administrator, state legislator*
Stein, Beverly *county official*

Salem
Bradbury, William Chapman, III *state official*
Hill, Jim *state official*
Kitzhaber, John Albert *governor, physician, former state senator*
McMurdo, C(harles) Gregory *state official, lawyer*
Myers, Hardy *state attorney general, lawyer*
Swaim, Michael E. *mayor*
Wyatt, Bill *government staff*

UTAH

Ogden
Evans, Keith Edward *government official, researcher*

Salt Lake City
Alter, Edward T. *state treasurer*
Anderson, Ross Carl *mayor, lawyer*
Corradini, Deedee *mayor*
Foxley, Cecelia Harrison *commissioner*
Graham, Jan *state attorney general*
Leary, G. Edward *state commisioner*
Leavitt, Michael Okerlund *governor, insurance executive*
Shurtleff, Mark L. *state attorney general*
Stephens, Martin R. *state official*
Varela, Vicki *state official*
Walker, Olene S. *lieutenant governor*

West Valley City
Wright, Gearld Lewis *mayor, retired educator*

WASHINGTON

Edmonds
Thyden, James Eskel *diplomat, educator, lecturer*

Everett
Vaughn, Kathy *municipal official*

Olympia
Belcher, Jennifer Marion *state official, consultant*
Chopp, Frank *state official*
Gregoire, Christine O. *state attorney general*
Locke, Gary *governor*
Long, Marsha Tadano *state official*
Munro, Ralph Davies *state official*
Murphy, Michael Joseph *state official*
Owen, Bradley Scott *lieutenant governor*

Renton
Lowry, Mike *former governor, former congressman*

Seattle
Covington, Germaine Ward *municipal agency administrator*
Diers, James Alan *municipal official*
Knox, Venerria L. *city official*
Krochalis, Richard F. *municipal government official*
Nuxoll, Carla *federal official*
Schell, Paul E. S. *mayor*

Sequim
Huntley, James Robert *government official, international affairs scholar and consultant*

Spokane
Greenwood, Collette P. *municipal official, finance officer*
Kobluk, Michael Daniel *retired municipal official*
Pfister, Terri *city official*
Sciuchetti, Dale *municipal official*
Talbott, John *mayor*

Sumas
Hemry, Larry Harold *former federal agency official, writer, inventor*

Tacoma
Ebersole, Brian *mayor*
Luttropp, Peter C. *city official*
Sutherland, Douglass B. *former mayor, tent and awning company executive*
Vlasak, Walter Raymond *state official, human resource manager*

WYOMING

Cheyenne
Catchpole, Judy *state official*
Geringer, James E. *governor*
Lummis, Cynthia Marie *state treasurer, lawyer*
MacMillan, Hoke *state attorney general*
McBride, John P. *state commissioner*
Meyer, Joseph B. *state official, former academic administrator*
Ohman, Diana J. *state official, former school system administrator*
Rodekohr, Diane E. *state official*
Woodhouse, Gay Vanderpoel *state attorney general*

Laramie
Dickman, Francois Moussiegt *former foreign service officer, educator*

TERRITORIES OF THE UNITED STATES

GUAM

Agana
Bordallo, Madeleine Mary (Mrs. Ricardo Jerome Bordallo) *lieutenant governor*

NORTHERN MARIANA ISLANDS

Saipan
Soll, Herbert D. *attorney general of Northern Mariana Islands*

CANADA

ALBERTA

Calgary
Day, Stockwell Burt *government official*
McCrank, Michael Neil *government official*

BRITISH COLUMBIA

Kaleden
Siddon, Thomas Edward *Canadian government official, environmental consultant*

Sidney
Richards, Laura *government researcher*

Vancouver
Duncan, Mark *government official*
Harcourt, Michael Franklin *retired premier of Province of British Columbia, lawyer, educator*
Schroeter, Thomas G. *federal government official, geologist*

Victoria
Gardom, Garde Basil *lieutenant governor of British Columbia*
Penikett, Antony David John *Canadian government official*

SASKATCHEWAN

Regina
Atkinson, Patricia *government official*

Saskatoon
Blakeney, Allan Emrys *Canadian government official, lawyer*
Hewitt, William James *municipal official*
Romanow, Roy John *provincial government official, barrister, solicitor*

ADDRESS UNPUBLISHED

Allen, Edgar Burns *records management professional*
Batt, Philip E. *former governor*
Coop, Frederick Robert *retired city manager*
Daly, Paul Sylvester *mayor, retired academic administrator, management consultant*
Del Papa, Frankie Sue *state attorney general*
Dunford, David Joseph *foreign service officer, ambassador*
Edwards, Lydia Justice *state official*
Eu, March Fong *ambassador, former state official*
Ferraro, John *city official*
Hett, Joan Margaret *civic administrator*
Jones, Jan Laverty *mayor*
Maestrone, Frank Eusebio *diplomat*
Martz, Judy Helen *governor*
Miller, George *former mayor*
Nelson, Cynthia J. *city official*
Peña, Federico Fabian *retired federal official*
Pies, Ronald E. *retired city official*
Ritter, Russell Joseph *mayor, college official*
Rudin, Anne Noto *former mayor, nurse*
Schoettler, Gail Sinton *former state official*
Smith, Stanford Sidney *former state treasurer*
Wallach, Patricia *mayor, retired*
Wilson, Pete *former governor*

GOVERNMENT: LEGISLATIVE ADMINISTRATION

UNITED STATES

ALASKA

Anchorage
Bunde, Con *state legislator, communication educator*
Porter, Brian Stanley *state legislator*
Sturgulewski, Arliss *state legislator, director*

Homer
Phillips, Gail *state legislator*

Juneau
Adams, Albert *state legislator, management consultant*
Austerman, Alan *state senator*
Cowdery, John J. *state senator*
Davis, Bettye *state senator*
Donley, Dave *state legislator*
Ellis, Johnny *state legislator*
Green, Lyda N. *state legislator*
Halford, Rick *state legislator*
Hoffman, Lyman *state legislator*
Kelly, Pete *state legislator*
Kelly, Timothy Donahue *state legislator*
Kerttula, Beth *state legislator*
Lincoln, Georgianna *state legislator*
Mackie, Jerry *state legislator, business owner*
Miller, Mike *state legislator, small business owner*
Murkowski, Lisa *state legislator*
Olson, Donald *state senator*
Parnell, Sean *state legislator, lawyer*
Pearce, Drue *state legislator*
Phillips, Randy *state legislator, marketing professional*
Taylor, Robin L. *state legislator, lawyer*
Therriault, Gene *state senator*
Torgerson, John *state senator*
Torgeson, John *state senator*
Ward, Jerry *state legislator, real estate executive*
Wilken, Gary R. *state legislator*

North Pole
James, Jeannette Adeline *state legislator, accountant*

ARIZONA

Phoenix
Aguirre, Linda *state senator*
Arzberger, Gus *state legislator, retired farmer and rancher*
Arzberger, Marsha *state senator*
Bee, Keith A. *state legislator*
Bee, Tim *state senator*
Blanchard, Jay S. *state senator*
Bowers, Russell W. *state legislator, sculptor, painter*
Brown, Jack A. *state legislator, rancher, real estate broker*
Bundgaard, Scott *state legislator*
Burns, Brenda *state legislator*
Cirillo, Edward J. *state legislator, retired financial manager*
Cummiskey, Chris *state legislator*
Daniels, Lori S. *state legislator, insurance agent*
Day, Ann *state legislator*
Freestone, Thomas Lawrence *state legislator*
Gerard, Susan *state senator*
Gnant, Randall *state legislator*
Grace, Sue *state legislator*
Groscost, Jeff *state legislator, small business owner*
Guenther, Herb *state legislator, executive assistant*
Hamilton, Darden Cole *state legislator, flight test engineer*
Hartley, Mary *state legislator*
Hellon, Toni *state senator*
Huppenthal, John *state senator, planning analyst*
Jackson, Jack C. *state legislator, rancher, educator*
Lopez, Joe Eddie *state legislator*
Martin, Dean *state senator*
Mitchell, Harry E. *state legislator, former mayor, educator*
Petersen, David A. *state legislator, financial advisor*
Rios, Peter *state legislator, counselor*
Siebert, Dave *councilman*
Smith, Tom *state legislator, educator, military officer*
Solomon, Ruth *state legislator, teacher*
Soltero, Victor *state legislator*
Spitzer, Marc Lee *state legislator, lawyer*
Valadez, Ramon *state senator*
Wettaw, John *state legislator, chemistry educator*
Williams, A. Cody *councilman*
Wold, Kimberly G. *legislative staff member*

Scottsdale
Rudd, Eldon *retired congressman, political consultant*
Salmon, Matt *former congressman, communications company executive*

Tucson
Bartlett, David Carson *state legislator*
Marcus, Janet *former city council*
Richardson, Elaine *state legislator*

Window Rock
Henderson, James, Jr. *former state legislator, political consultant*

CALIFORNIA

Alamo
Baker, William P. (Bill Baker) *former congressman*

Arcadia
Margett, Bob G. *state legislator*

Campbell
Beyer, Casey K. *legislative staff member*

Fullerton
Ackerman, Richard C. *state legislator*

Garden Grove
Dornan, Robert Kenneth *former congressman*

Glendale
Moorhead, Carlos J. *former congressman*

Granada Hills
McClintock, Tom *state senator*
Smith, Greig Louis *deputy councilman*

Inglewood
Dymally, Mervyn Malcolm *retired congressman, international business executive*
Vincent, Edward *state legislator*

Long Beach
Karentte, Betty *state legislator*

Los Angeles
Chick, Laura *councilwoman*
Goldberg, Jackie *councilwoman*
Svorinich, Rudy, Jr. *councilman*
Walters, Rita *councilwoman*

Martinez
Torlakson, Tom A. *state senator*

Palm Desert
Battin, Jim F. *state legislator*

Pasadena
Scott, Jack A. *state senator*

Redondo Beach
Harman, Jane *congresswoman, lawyer*

Roseville
Oller, Thomas R. *state senator*

Sacramento
Alpert, Deirdre Whittleton (Dede Alpert) *state legislator*
Brulte, James L. *state legislator*
Costa, Jim *state senator*
Dunn, Joseph *state senator*
Escutia, Martha *state senator*
Figueroa, Liz *state senator*
Holmes, Robert Eugene *legislative staff member, journalist*
Hughes, Teresa P. *state legislator*
Johannessen, Maurice *state senator*
Johnson, Ross *state legislator*
Johnston, Patrick *state senator*
Kelley, David G. *state senator*
Knight, William J. (Pete Knight) *state legislator, retired air force officer*
Kuehl, Sheila James *state legislator*
Lewis, John R. *state legislator*
Machado, Michael John *state legislator, farmer*
McPherson, Bruce *state legislator*
Monteith, Dick *state legislator*
Morrow, Bill *state legislator*
Mountjoy, Richard *state legislator*
Murray, Kevin *state legislator*
O'Connell, Jack *state legislator*
Ortiz, Deborah V. *state legislator*
Peace, Steve *state legislator*
Perata, Don *state legislator*
Polanco, Richard G. *state senator*
Poochigian, Charles *state legislator*
Rainey, Richard K. *state legislator*
Romero, Gloria *state senator*
Speier, Jackie *state senator*
Torres, Art *state legislator*
Wright, Cathie *state legislator*

San Diego
McCarty, Judy *councilman*
Stallings, Valerie Aileen *retired councilwoman, consultant*
Stein, Greg *legislative staff member*
Wear, Byron *councilman*

San Jose
Sher, Byron D. *state legislator, law educator*
Vasconcellos, John *state legislator*

Santa Barbara
Jackson, Hanna Beth *state legislator*

Santa Rosa
Chesbro, Wesley *state senator*

Van Nuys
Alarcon, Richard *state legislator, former councilman*
Hertzberg, Robert M. *state legislator*

West Covina
Torres, Esteban Edward *former congressman, business executive*

COLORADO

Aurora
Hagedorn, Bob *state senator*
Takis, Stephanie *state senator*

Boulder
Tupa, Ron *state senator*

Colorado Springs
May, Ron *state senator*
McElhany, Andy *state senator*

Denver
Adkins, Jeanne M. *state legislator*
Anderson, Norma V. *state legislator*
Andrews, John *state legislator*
Arnold, Ken *state legislator*
Blickensderfer, Charles Thomas (Tom) *state legislator, lawyer*
Cairns, Bruce Earle *state senator*
Chlouber, Ken *state legislator*
Congrove, Jim *state legislator*
Dennis, Ginette E. (Gigi) *state legislator*
Dicks, Patricia K. *legislative staff member*
Dyer, Jim *state senator*
Epps, Mary Ellen *state legislator*
Evans, John *state legislator, lawyer, educator*
Feeley, Michael F. *state legislator*
Fitz-Gerald, Joan *state senator*
Gordon, Ken *state senator*
Hernandez, Robert Michael *state legislator, software engineer*
Hillman, Mark D. *state legislator*
Lacy, Elsie *state legislator*
Lamborn, Douglas L. *state legislator*
Linkhart, Douglas D. (Doug) *state legislator*
Martinez, Robert *state legislator*
Matsunaka, Stanley T. *state legislator*
Meiklejohn, Alvin J., Jr. *state legislator, lawyer, accountant*
Musgrave, Marilyn N. *state legislator*
Nichol, Alice J. *state legislator*
Owen, David Turner *state legislator, owner, operator*
Perlmutter, Edwin George (Ed) *state legislator*
Phillips, Terry *state legislator*
Powers, Ray Lloyd *state legislator, dairy farmer, rancher*
Reeves, Peggy *state legislator*
Rupert, Dorothy *state legislator*
Sullivant, Bryan Sterling *state legislator*
Tanner, Gloria Travis *state legislator*
Tate, Penfield *state senator*
Tebedo, MaryAnne *state legislator*
Teck, Ronald Jay *state legislator*
Thiebaut, William *state legislator, lawyer*
Wattenberg, Dave *state legislator, rancher*
Weddig, Frank O. *state legislator*
Wham, Dorothy Stonecipher *state legislator*
Windels, Sue *state senator*

Grand Junction
Bishop, Tilman Malcolm *state legislator, college administrator, retired*

Lakewood
Hanna, Deanna *state senator*

Steamboat Springs
Taylor, Jack *state senator*

DISTRICT OF COLUMBIA

Washington
Abercrombie, Neil *congressman*
Akaka, Daniel Kahikina *senator*
Allard, Wayne (A. Wayne Allard) *senator, veterinarian*
Baca, Joe *congressman*
Baird, Brian N. *congressman*
Becerra, Xavier *congressman, lawyer*
Bennett, Robert F. *senator*
Berkley, Shelley *congresswoman*
Berman, Howard Lawrence *congressman*
Bingaman, Jeff *senator*
Blumenauer, Earl *congressman*
Bono, Mary *congresswoman*
Boxer, Barbara *senator*
Burns, Conrad Ray *senator*
Calvert, Ken *congressman*
Campbell, Ben Nighthorse *senator*
Cannon, Christopher B. *congressman*
Capps, Lois Ragnhild Grimsrud *congresswoman, former school nurse*
Condit, Gary Adrian *congressman*
Cox, Christopher (Charles Cox) *congressman*
Craig, Larry Edwin *senator*
Crapo, Michael Dean *senator, former congressman, lawyer*
Cubin, Barbara Lynn *congresswoman, former state legislator*
Cunningham, Randy *congressman*
Davis, Susan A. *congresswoman*
DeFazio, Peter A. *congressman*
Dicks, Norman De Valois *congressman*
Domenici, Pete V. (Vichi Domenici) *senator*
Dooley, Calvin Millard *congressman*
Doolittle, John Taylor *congressman*
Dreier, David Timothy *congressman*
Dunn, Jennifer Blackburn *congresswoman*
Enzi, Michael Bradley *senator, accountant*
Eshoo, Anna Georges *congresswoman*
Faleomavaega, Eni Fa'auaa Hunkin *congressman*
Farr, Sam *congressman*
Feinstein, Dianne *senator*
Filner, Bob *congressman*
Flake, Jeff *congressman*
Gallegly, Elton William *congressman*
Gibbons, James Arthur *congressman*
Hansen, James Vear *congressman*
Hastings, Doc *congressman*
Hayworth, J(ohn) D(avid), Jr. *congressman, former sportscaster*
Hefley, Joel M. *congressman*
Herger, Wally W. *congressman*
Honda, Michael M. *congressman*
Hooley, Darlene *congresswoman, former county commissioner*
Horn, Stephen *congressman, political science educator*
Inouye, Daniel Ken *senator*
Inslee, Jay R. *congressman*
Issa, Darrell E. *congressman*
Kolbe, James Thomas *congressman*
Kyl, Jon L. *senator*
Lantos, Thomas Peter *congressman*
Lee, Barbara *congresswoman*
Lewis, Charles Jeremy (Jerry Lewis) *congressman*
Lofgren, Zoe *congresswoman*
Matsui, Robert Takeo *congressman*
McDermott, James A. *congressman, psychiatrist*
McInnis, Scott Steve *congressman, lawyer*
McKeon, Howard P. (Buck McKeon) *congressman, former mayor*
Millender-McDonald, Juanita *congresswoman, former school system administrator*
Miller, Gary G. *congressman*
Miller, George *congressman*
Mink, Patsy Takemoto *congresswoman*
Murkowski, Frank Hughes *senator*
Murray, Patty *senator*
Napolitano, Grace F. *congresswoman*
Nethercutt, George Rector, Jr. *congressman, lawyer*
Ose, Douglas *congressman*
Otter, Clement Leroy (Butch Otter) *congressman*
Pastor, Edward *congressman*
Pelosi, Nancy *congresswoman*
Pombo, Richard *congressman, rancher, farmer*
Radanovich, George P. *congressman*
Rehberg, Dennis R. *congressman*
Rohrabacher, Dana *congressman*
Roybal-Allard, Lucille *congresswoman*
Royce, Edward R. (Ed Royce) *congressman*
Sanchez, Loretta *congresswoman*
Schaffer, Robert (Bob Schaffer) *congressman*
Schiff, Adam Bennett *congressman, lawyer*
Shadegg, John B. *congressman*
Sherman, Brad James *congressman*
Simpson, Michael K. *congressman*
Skeen, Joseph Richard *congressman*
Smith, D. Adam *congressman*
Smith, Gordon Harold *senator*
Solis, Hilda Lucia *congresswoman, educational administrator*
Stark, Fortney Hillman (Pete Stark) *congressman*
Stevens, Theodore Fulton *senator*
Stump, Bob *congressman*
Tancredo, Thomas G. *congressman*
Thomas, Craig *senator*
Thomas, William Marshall *congressman*
Thompson, C. Michael *congressman*
Timmer, Barbara *United States Senate official, lawyer*
Udall, Mark *congressman*
Udall, Thomas (Tom Udall) *congressman*
Underwood, Robert Anacletus *congressman, university official*
Walden, Greg *congressman*
Waters, Maxine *congresswoman*
Watson, Diane Edith *congresswoman*
Wilson, Heather Ann *congresswoman*
Woolsey, Lynn *congresswoman*
Wu, David *congressman*
Wyden, Ron *senator*
Young, Donald E. *congressman*

HAWAII

Hilo
Ushijima, John Takeji *state legislator, lawyer*

Honolulu
Anderson, Whitney *state legislator*
Buen, Jan Yagi *state legislator*
Bunda, Robert *state legislator*
Cachola, Romy Munoz *state legislator*
Chumbley, Avery B. *state legislator*
Chun, Jonathan J. *state legislator*
Chun Oakland, Suzanne Nyuk Jun *state legislator*
English, J. Kalani *state senator*
Fasi, Frank Francis *state legislator*
Fukunaga, Carol A. *state legislator, lawyer*
Hanabusa, Colleen *state legislator, lawyer*
Hemmings, Fred *state senator*
Hogue, Bob *state senator*
Ige, David Y. *state legislator*
Ige, Marshall *state legislator*
Ihara, Les, Jr. *state legislator*
Inouye, Lorraine R. *state legislator*
Iwase, Randall Yoshio *former state legislator*
Kanno, Brian M. *state legislator, volunteer worker*
Kawamoto, Calvin Kazuo *state legislator*
Kim, Donna Mercado *state senator*
Kokubun, Russell *state senator*
Levin, Andrew *state legislator*
Matsunaga, Matthew Masao *state legislator, lawyer, accountant*
Matsuura, David M. *state legislator*
Menor, Ron *state legislator*
Nakata, Robert *state legislator*
Slom, Samuel M. *state legislator*
Takumi, Roy Mitsuo *state legislator*
Tam, Rod *state legislator*
Tanaka, Joe Sueo *state legislator*
Taniguchi, Brian T. *state senator*

Kailua
Young, Jacqueline Eurn Hai *state legislator, consultant*

Kapolei
Sakamoto, Norman Lloyd *state legislator, civil engineer*

IDAHO

Boise
Andreason, John C. *state legislator*
Black, Pete *retired state legislator, educator*
Boatright, Clyde A. *state legislator*
Branch, W. Ric *state legislator*
Bunderson, Harold R. *state legislator*
Cameron, Dean L. *state legislator*
Crow, Gordon F. *state legislator*
Danielson, Judith A. *state legislator*
Darrington, Denton C. *state legislator*
Deide, Darrel A. *state legislator*
Dunklin, Betsy D. *state legislator*
Frasure, Evan S. *state legislator*
Geddes, Robert L. *state legislator*
Hawkins, Stan *state legislator*
Keough, Shawn *state legislator*
Lee, Robert R. *state legislator*
McLaughlin, Marguerite P. *state legislator, logging company executive*
Newcomb, Bruce *state legislator, farmer, rancher*
Noh, Laird *state legislator*
Parry, Atwell J., Jr. *state legislator, retail executive*
Sandy, John A. *state legislator*
Stegner, Joe *state legislator*
Thorne, Jerrold L. *state legislator*
Twiggs, Jerry T. *state legislator*
Wheeler, Ralph I. (Moon) *state legislator, pharmacist*
Whitworth, A. Lin *state legislator*
Wood, Jeannine Kay *legislative staff member*

Coeur d'Alene
Goedde, John W. *state senator*

Glenns Ferry
King-Barrutia, Robbie L. *state senator*

Huston
Lodge, Patti Anne *state senator*

Idaho Falls
Davis, Bart McKay *state legislator, lawyer*
Richardson, Melvin Mark *state legislator, broadcast executive*

Jerome
Bell, Maxine Toolson *state legislator, librarian*

Kooskia
Brandt, R. Skipper *state senator*

Moscow
Schroeder, Gary Joseph *state legislator, business owner, writer*

Pingree
Williams, J. Stanley *state senator*

Terreton
Burtenshaw, Don M. *state senator*

MONTANA

Anaconda
McCarthy, Bea *state legislator*

Augusta
Cobb, John Richardson *state senator*

Belgrade
Hargrove, Don *state legislator*

Big Sandy
Tester, Jon *state legislator*

Big Timber
Grosfield, Lorents *state legislator*

Bigfork
Keenan, Bob *state legislator*

Billings
Bishop, Al *state legislator, retired lawyer*
Bohlinger, John C. *state legislator*
Crippin, Bruce D. *state legislator, real estate manager*
Johnson, Royal C. *state senator*
Keating, Thomas Francis *state legislator*
Sprague, Mike *state legislator*

Bozeman
Wells, Jack Moore *state legislator*

Butte
Harrington, Dan W. *state senator*
Shea, Debbie Bowman *state legislator*

Cascade
Mesaros, Kenneth Lee *state legislator, rancher*

Chinook
Jergeson, Greg *state legislator*

Choteau
Ekegren, E. Peter (Pete Ekegren) *state legislator*

Clancy
Grimes, Duane D. *state legislator*

Cut Bank
Roush, Glenn A. *state senator*

Dillon
Swysgood, Charles *state legislator*
Tash, Bill *state senator*

Glendive
Holden, Ric R. *state legislator, farmer, rancher*

Great Falls
Franklin, Eve *state legislator*
Ryan, Don *state legislator*
Wilson, Bill *state senator*

Hamilton
Berry, Dale E. *state legislator*

Hardin
Jabs, Reiny *state legislator, farmer, rancher*

Helena
Bartlett, Sue *state legislator*
Beck, Tom *state legislator, rancher*
Cocchiarella, Vicki Marshall *state legislator*
Cramer, Chuckie *legislative staff member*
Eck, Dorothy Fritz *state legislator*
Hanson, Marian W. *state legislator*
Mahlum, Dale Duane *state legislator, small business owner*
Mohl, Arnie *state legislator*
Toole, Kenneth R., Jr. *state senator*

Huntley
Glaser, William E. *state legislator*

Hysham
Cole, Mack *state legislator, rancher*

Kalispell
Harp, John G. *state legislator*
O'Neil, Jerry *state senator*

Laurel
Miller, Ken *state legislator*

Libby
Crismore, William *state legislator*

Lodge Grass
Pease, Gerald *state legislator*

Lustre
Toews, Daryl *state senator*

Medicine Lake
Nelson, Linda J. *state legislator*

Miles City
Devlin, Gerry *state legislator, farmer, rancher*
Zook, Tom *state senator*

Missoula
Ellingson, Jon Eric *state legislator*
Halligan, Mike *state legislator*
Williams, Pat *former congressman*

Moore
Hertel, John R. *state legislator, farmer, rancher*

Polson
Mercer, John A. *state legislator*

Proctor
Taylor, Mike A. *state legislator*

Red Lodge
Ellis, Alvin *state legislator, farmer, rancher*

Saint Regis
Stang, Barry *state legislator*

Sidney
McNutt, Walter L. *state legislator*

Stevensville
Thomas, Fred *state legislator*

Trout Creek
Elliott, Jim *state senator*

Whitefish
DePratu, Robert L. *state legislator*

Winifred
Butcher, Edward B. *state senator*

NEVADA

Carson City
Amodei, Mark E. *state legislator, lawyer*
McGinness, Mike W. *state legislator*
Neal, Joseph M., Jr. *state legislator*
O'Connell, Mary Ann *state legislator, business owner*
Rhoads, Dean Allan *state legislator, cattle rancher*
Tiffany, Sandra L. *state legislator*
Titus, Alice Cestandina (Dina Titus) *state legislator*
Washington, Maurice E. *state legislator*

Henderson
Porter, Jon Christopher *state legislator*

Las Vegas
Care, Terry *state legislator, lawyer*
Carlton, Maggie *state legislator*
Coffin, James Robert *state legislator, small business owner*
Ensign, John E. *senator, former congressman*
James, Mark A. *state legislator, lawyer*
O'Donnell, William Russell *state legislator*
Schneider, Michael A. *state legislator*
Wiener, Valerie *state senator, communications consultant, positioning strategist, author*

Minden
Jacobsen, Lawrence E. *state legislator*

North Las Vegas
Shaffer, Raymond C. *state legislator*

Reno
Raggio, William John *state legislator*
Townsend, Randolph J. *state legislator*

Sparks
Mathews, Bernice Martin *state legislator, small business owner*

Yerington
Dini, Joseph Edward, Jr. *state legislator*

NEW MEXICO

Albuquerque
Boitano, Mark L. *state legislator*
Carraro, Joseph John *state legislator, business owner, consultant*
Davis, William F. *state legislator*
Feldman, Dede *state legislator*
Gorham, Ramsay L. *state legislator*
Lopez, Linda M. *state legislator*
Maloof, Phillip J. *state legislator*
McGuire, Susan Grayson *legislative staff member*
Payne, William H. *state legislator, lawyer*
Robinson, Shannon *state legislator*
Romero, Richard M. *state legislator, educator*
Vernon, L. Skip *state legislator, lawyer*
Wilson, Sue *state legislator*

Belen
Sanchez, Michael Steven *state legislator, lawyer*

Bloomfield
Stockard, R. L. *state legislator*

Carlsbad
Kidd, Don *state legislator, bank executive*

Crownpoint
Tsosie, Leonard *state legislator, lawyer*

Cuervo
Lyons, Patrick Hiller *state legislator*

Deming
Smith, John Arthur *state legislator*

Dona Ana
Garcia, Mary Jane Madrid *state legislator*

Farmington
Kysar, Raymond L. *state legislator*

Grants
Fidel, Joseph A. *state legislator*

Hobbs
McKibben, Billy *state legislator*
Reagan, Gary Don *state legislator, lawyer*

Jal
Leavell, Carroll H. *state legislator*

Las Cruces
Rawson, Leonard Lee *state legislator, business executive*

Las Vegas
Campos, Pete *state legislator*

Los Alamos
Redmond, Bill *former congressman, minister*

Mesilla
Macias, Fernando *state legislator, lawyer*

Ojo Caliente
Rodarte, Arthur H. *state legislator*

Portales
Ingle, Cress Stuart *state legislator*

Questa
Cisneros, Carlos R. *state legislator*

Roswell
Adair, Rod *state legislator*
Casey, Barbara A. Perea *state legislator, school superintendent*

San Jose
Griego, Phil A. *state legislator*

Santa Fe
Altamirano, Ben D. *state legislator, merchant, insurance agent*
Aragon, Manny M. *state legislator*
Bailey, Shirley M. *state senator*
Cravens, Kent L. *state senator*
Howes, Gloria *state legislator*
Hurt, Allen V. *state senator*
Komadina, Steve *state senator*
Maes, Roman M., III *state legislator, lawyer*
Martinez, Richard C. *state senator*
Nava, Cynthia L. *state legislator*
Papen, Mary Kay *state senator*
Rainaldi, Lidio G. *state senator*
Rodriguez, Nancy *state legislator*
Sanchez, Bernadette M. *state senator*
Sanchez, Raymond G. [illegible]

Sharer, William E. *state senator*
Snyder, Helen Diane *state senator*

Tohatchi
Pinto, John *state legislator, educator*

Tularosa
Duran, Dianna J. *state legislator*

OREGON

Ashland
Hannon, Lenn L. *state legislator, insurance agent*

Beaverton
Deckert, Ryan P. *state senator*

Bend
Clarno, Beverly Ann *state legislator, farmer*
Cooley, Wes *former congressman*

Coos Bay
Messerle, Kenneth C. *state senator*

Eugene
Castillo, Susan *state legislator*
Hayden, Cedric L. *state legislator, dentist*

John Day
Ferrioli, Ted *state legislator*

Lake Oswego
Miller, Randy *state legislator, educator, lawyer*

Newberg
George, Gary *state legislator, farmer*

Pendleton
Nelson, David *state legislator, farmer, lawyer*

Portland
Hatfield, Mark Odom *former senator*
Lim, John K. *state senator, business executive*
Shields, Frank W. *state legislator*
Wilde, Thomas Andrew *state legislator, home remodeler, writer*

Salem
Adams, Brady *state legislator*
Atkinson, Jason A. *state senator*
Beyer, Lee Louis *state legislator*
Beyer, Roger *state senator*
Brown, Kate *state legislator*
Bryant, Neil *state legislator, lawyer*
Burdick, Ginny *state legislator*
Courtney, Peter C. *state legislator*
Derfler, Eugene L. *state legislator, real estate broker*
Dukes, Joan *state legislator*
Duncan, Verne Allen *state legislator, university dean*
Fisher, William G.E. *state legislator, rental investor, assisted living facility owner*
Harper, Steven V. *state senator*
Hartung, Thomas F. *state legislator*
Oakley, Carolyn Le *state legislator, small business owner*
Qutub, Eileen *state legislator, real estate appraiser*
Shannon, Marylin Linfoot *state legislator, educator*
Starr, Charles *state legislator, contractor, farmer*
Tarno, Veral *state legislator*
Trow, Clifford W. *state legislator*
Yih, Mae Dunn *state legislator*

Troutdale
Minnis, John Martin *state legislator, protective services official*

Welches
Metsger, Rick T. *state legislator*

UTAH

Benjamin
Muhlestein, Robert M. *state senator*

Bountiful
Burningham, Kim Richard *former state legislator*
Eastman, Dan R. *state legislator*

Brigham City
Knudson, Peter C. *state legislator, orthodontist*

Corinne
Ferry, Miles Yeoman *state legislator*

Draper
Stephenson, Howard A. *state legislator*

Elberta
Wright, Bill *state legislator*

Hooper
Hull, Joseph L. *state legislator*

Kaysville
Steele, David H. *state legislator*

Layton
Spencer, Terry R. *state legislator, lawyer*

Logan
Hillyard, Lyle William *state legislator, lawyer*

Midvale
Mansell, L. Alma *state legislator*

Moroni
Blackham, Leonard Moyle *state legislator*

Ogden
Allen, D. Edgar *state legislator*
Gladwell, David L. *state legislator*
Montgomery, Robert F. *state legislator, retired surgeon, cattle rancher*

Orem
Hellewell, Parley G. *state legislator*
Peterson, Craig Anton *former state legislator*

Plain City
Jenkins, Scott K. *state legislator*

Price
Dmitrich, Mike *state legislator*

Provo
Bramble, Curtis S. *state legislator*
Valentine, John Lester *state legislator, lawyer*

Riverton
Evans, R. Mont *state legislator*

Saint George
Hickman, John William *state legislator*

Salt Lake City
Black, Wilford Rex, Jr. *former state senator*
Bowen, Melanie *legislative staff administrator*
Carnahan, Orville Darrell *retired state legislator, retired college president*
Cook, Merrill A. *former congressman, explosives industry executive*
Evans, Beverly Ann *state legislator, school system administrator*
Garn, Edwin Jacob (Jake Garn) *former senator*
Greene, Enid *former congresswoman*
Hale, Karen *state legislator*
Martinez, Art L. *legislative staff member*
Mayne, Eddie P. *state legislator, former union official*
Minson, Dixie L. *legislative staff member*
Moore, Annette B. *legislative staff member*
Orton, William H. (Bill Orton) *former congressman, retired lawyer*
Peterson, Millie M. *state senator*
Poulton, L. Steven *state legislator*
Shepherd, Karen *former congresswoman*
Suazo, Pete *state legislator*
Walker, Carlene M. *state legislator*

Taylorsville
Waddoups, Michael G. *state legislator*

Tooele
Allen, Ronald Carl *state legislator, computer consulting executive, visual artist*

Veyo
Jones, Lorin V. *state senator*

West Bountiful
Beattie, Lane *state legislator*

West Jordan
Buttars, D. Chris *state legislator*

WASHINGTON

Everett
Nelson, Gary *councilman, electrical engineer*

Lake Stevens
Quigley, Kevin Walsh *former state legislator, lawyer*

Langley
Metcalf, Jack *former congressman, retired state senator*

Olympia
Ballard, Clyde *state legislator*
Bauer, Albert *state legislator, educator*
Brown, Lisa J. *state legislator, educator*
Carlson, Don M. *state senator*
Constatine, Dow *state senator*
Cook, Tony Michael *legislative staff member*
Costa, Jeralita *state legislator*
Deccio, Alexander A. *state legislator*
Eide, Tracey J. *state legislator*
Fairley, Darlene *state legislator*
Finkbeiner, William *state legislator*
Franklin, Rosa G. *state legislator, retired nurse*
Fraser, Karen *state legislator*
Gardner, Georgia Anne *state legislator*
Goings, Calvin *state legislator*
Hale, Patricia S. *state legislator*
Hargrove, James E. *state legislator*
Haugen, Mary Margaret *state legislator*
Heavey, Mike *state legislator, lawyer*
Hewitt, Mike *state senator*
Hochstatter, Harold *state legislator*
Honeyford, James D. *state legislator*
Horn, James A. *state legislator*
Jacobsen, Kenneth G. *state legislator*
Johnson, Stephen L. *state legislator, lawyer*
Kastama, Jim *state senator*
Kessler, Lynn Elizabeth *state legislator*
Kline, Adam *state legislator, lawyer*
Kohl-Welles, Jeanne Elizabeth *state legislator, sociologist, educator*
Long, Jeanine Hundley *state legislator*
Loveland, Valoria *state legislator*
McAuliffe, Rosemary *state legislator*
McCaslin, Robert L. *state legislator*
McDonald, Daniel Robert *state legislator*
Morton, Bob *state legislator*
Oke, Robert Eugene *state legislator*
Parlette, Linda Evans *state senator*
Patterson, Julia *state legislator*
Prentice, Margarita *state legislator, nurse*
Rasmussen, Marilyn *state legislator*
Regala, Debbie *state senator*
Roach, Pam *state legislator*
Rossi, Dino J. *state legislator, real estate broker*
Sellar, George L. *state legislator*
Sheahan, Larry L. *state legislator, lawyer*
Sheldon, Betti L. *state legislator*
Sheldon, Timothy *state legislator*
Snyder, Sid *state legislator, retail executive*
Spanel, Harriet Rosa Albertsen *state legislator*
Stevens, Val *state legislator*
Swecker, Dan *state legislator*
Thibaudeau, Patricia *state legislator*
Thomas, Brian Chester *state legislator, engineer*
West, James E. *state legislator*
Winsley, Shirley J. *state legislator, insurance agent*
Wojahn, R. Lorraine *state senator*
Zarelli, Joseph *state legislator*

Ritzville
Schoesler, Mark Gerald *state legislator, farmer*

Vancouver
Benton, Donald Mark *state legislator, political organization chairman*

WYOMING

Casper
Donley, Russell Lee, III *former state legislator*
Goodenough, Keith *state legislator*
Hawks, Bill *state legislator, oil company executive*

Cheyenne
Burton, R. Johnnie Medinger *state official, data processing executive, finance company executive*
Cathcart, Richard *state legislator*
Decaria, Ken *state legislator, educator*
Devin, Irene K. *state legislator, nurse*
Erb, Richard A. *state legislator, real estate executive*
Kunz, April Brimmer *state legislator, lawyer*
Mockler, Esther Jayne *state legislator*
Schiffer, John C. *state legislator*
Sessions, Kathryn L. *state legislator, educator*

Cody
Coe, Henry H. R. *state legislator*
Simpson, Alan Kooi *former senator, lawyer*

Douglas
Twiford, Jim *state legislator*

Etna
Roberts, Delaine *state legislator*

Gillette
Gilbertz, Larry E. *state legislator, entrepreneur*
Youngbauer, Steven R. *state legislator, laywer*

Green River
Harris, Mark O. *state legislator*

Greybull
Miller, Carroll S. *state legislator, dentist*

Jackson
Larson, Grant C. *state legislator*

Lagrange
Meier, Curt *state legislator, farmer, rancher*

Lander
Case, Cale *state legislator, economist*
Tipton, Harry Basil, Jr. *state legislator, physician*

Laramie
Hansen, Matilda *former state legislator*
Massie, Michael Anthony *state legislator, historian*
Maxfield, Peter C. *state legislator, law educator, lawyer*

Rawlins
Vasey, William Joseph *state legislator, college program director*

Rock Springs
Boggs, Tex *state legislator*
Job, Rae Lynn *state legislator*

Sheridan
Kinnison, Thomas *state legislator*

Upton
Barton, Billie L. *state legislator*

Worland
Geis, Gerald E. *state legislator, trucking company executive*
Fong, Hiram Leong *former senator*

CANADA

BRITISH COLUMBIA

Victoria
Boone, Lois Ruth *legislator*
Weisgerber, John Sylvester *provincial legislator*

ADDRESS UNPUBLISHED

Bilbray, Brian P. *former congressman*
Bilbray, James Hubert *former congressman, lawyer, consultant*
Browder, John Glen *former congressman, educator*
Campbell, Thomas J. *former congressman*
Chenoweth-Hage, Helen P. *former congresswoman*
Cunningham, George *state senator*
De Gette, Diana Louise *congresswoman, lawyer*
Gordly, Avel Louise *state legislator, community activist*
Hatch, Orrin Grant *senator*
Hayden, Tom *retired state senator*
Hickey, Winifred E(spy) *former state legislator, social worker*
Hill, Rick Allan *former congressman*
Hunter, Duncan Lee *congressman*
Ipsen, Grant Ruel *state legislator, insurance and investments professional*
Konnyu, Ernest Leslie *former congressman*
Leslie, Tim (Robert Leslie) *state legislator*
Martinez, Matthew Gilbert *former congressman*
McSorley, Cisco *state legislator, lawyer*
Nichols, Andrew Wilkinson *state legislator, public health physician, educator*
Nielson, Howard Curtis *state legislator, retired educator, former congressman*
Packard, Ronald C. *former congressman*
Pascoe, Patricia Hill *state legislator, writer*
Pettis-Roberson, Shirley McCumber *former congresswoman*
Reid, Harry *senator*
Russell, Newton Requa *retired state legislator*
Scott, Charles Kennard *state legislator, cattle rancher*
Sorensen, Sheila *state legislator*
Tauscher, Ellen O. *congresswoman*
Vucanovich, Barbara Farrell *former congresswoman*
Zimmerman, Harold Samuel *retired state legislator, newspaper editor and publisher, state administrator*

HEALTHCARE: DENTISTRY

UNITED STATES

ARIZONA

Tucson
Davis, Richard Calhoun *dentist*
Hawke, Robert Francis *dentist*
Nadler, George L. *orthodontist*

CALIFORNIA

Arcadia
Gamboa, George Charles *oral surgeon, educator*

Arcata
Hise, Mark Allen *dentist*

Loma Linda
Feller, Ralph Paul *dentist, educator*

Long Beach
Gehring, George Joseph, Jr. *dentist*

Los Angeles
Bertolami, Charles Nicholas *oral surgeon*
Dummett, Clifton Orrin *dentist, educator*
Evans, Caswell Alves, Jr. *dentist*

Manteca
Tonn, Elverne Meryl *pediatric dentist, dental benefits consultant, forensic odontologist*

Northridge
Logan, Lee Robert *orthodontist*

Pasadena
Mc Carthy, Frank Martin *oral surgeon, surgical sciences educator*

San Francisco
Braham, Raymond L. *pediatric dentistry educator*
Den Besten, Pamela Kay *biomedical researcher, dentist*
Dugoni, Arthur A. *orthodontics educator, university dean*
Greenspan, Deborah *dental educator*
Greenspan, John S. *dental and medical educator, scientist, administrator*
Khosla, Ved Mitter *oral and maxillofacial surgeon, educator*
Wirthlin, Milton Robert, Jr. *periodontist*

Vacaville
Dedeaux, Paul J. *orthodontist*

Whittier
Lowe, Oariona *dentist*

COLORADO

Boulder
Schaffer, Joel Lance *dentist*

Denver
Patterson, Daniel William *dentist*

HAWAII

Honolulu
Nishimura, Pete Hideo *oral surgeon*
Scheerer, Ernest William *dentist*

NEVADA

Las Vegas
Rawson, Raymond D. *dentist, state legislator*

WASHINGTON

Bellevue
Page, Roy Christopher *periodontist, scientist, educator*

Seattle
Dworkin, Samuel Franklin *dentist, psychologist*
Herring, Susan Weller *dental educator, oral anatomist*

Spokane
Kolsrud, Henry Gerald *dentist*

WYOMING

Casper
Keim, Michael Ray *dentist*

ADDRESS UNPUBLISHED

Geistfeld, Ronald Elwood *retired dental educator*
Herman, David Jay *orthodontist*

Newbrun, Ernest *oral biology and periodontology educator*

HEALTHCARE: HEALTH SERVICES

UNITED STATES

ARIZONA

Casa Grande
McGillicuddy, Joan Marie *psychotherapist, consultant*

Mesa
Boyd, Leona Potter *retired social worker*
Zaharia, Eric Stafford *health facility administrator*

Phoenix
Binnie, Nancy Catherine *retired nurse, educator*
Crews, James Cecil *hospital administrator*
Evans, Don A. *healthcare company executive*
Seiler, Steven Lawrence *health facility administrator*
Welliver, Charles Harold *hospital administrator*

Pima
Shafer, James Albert *health care administrator*

Scottsdale
Wesbury, Stuart Arnold, Jr. *health administration and policy educator*

Sedona
Catterton, Marianne Rose *occupational therapist*

Sonoita
Scott, William Coryell *medical executive*

Tucson
Bootman, J. Lyle *pharmacy educator, dean*
Shropshire, Donald Gray *hospital executive*

CALIFORNIA

Agoura Hills
Merchant, Roland Samuel, Sr. *hospital administrator, educator*

Arcadia
Anderson, Holly Geis *women's health facility administrator, commentator, educator*

Berkeley
Calloway, Doris Howes *nutrition educator*
Carpenter, Kenneth John *nutrition educator*
Cohn, Theodore Elliot *optometry educator, vision scientist*
Day, Lucille Lang *health facility administrator, educator, writer*
Enoch, Jay Martin *optometrist, educator*
Gilbert, Neil Robin *social work educator, writer, consultant*
Hafey, Joseph Michael *health association executive*
Holder, Harold D. *public health administrator, communications specialist, educator*
Lashof, Joyce Cohen *public health educator*
Margen, Sheldon *public health educator*
Tutashinda, Kweli (Brian P. Altheimer) *chiropractic physician, educator*

Burbank
Hartshorn, Terry O. *health facility administrator*

Chico
Ward, Chester Lawrence *physician, retired county health official, retired military officer*

Claremont
Martin, Jay Herbert *psychoanalyst, English educator*

Colton
Godager, Jane Ann *social worker*

Concord
Koffler, Herbert *health plan administrator, educator*

Costa Mesa
Graff, Cynthia Stamper *health care executive*

Culver City
Stoughton, W. Vickery *healthcare executive*

Davis
Fowler, William Mayo, Jr. *rehabilitation medicine physician*
King, Janet Carlson *nutrition educator, researcher*
Lewis, Jonathan *health care association administrator*
Schneeman, Barbara Olds *nutritionist, educator*
Stern, Judith Schneider *nutritionist, researcher, educator*
Turnlund, Judith Rae *nutritionist*

Downey
Diaz, Consuelo *health facility administrator*

El Monte
Glass, Jean Ann *special education services professional*

Emeryville
Greene, Albert Lawrence *healthcare executive*

Encino
Bekey, Shirley White *psychotherapist*

Fremont
Loarie, Thomas Merritt *healthcare executive*
Sahatjian, Manik *nurse, psychologist*

Fresno
Schroeder, Rita Molthen *retired chiropractor*

La Jolla
Grobstein, Ruth H. *health facility administrator*

Laguna Niguel
Smith, Leslie Roper *hospital and healthcare administrator*

Lake View Terrace
McCraven, Eva Stewart Mapes *health service administrator*

Long Beach
Mullins, Ruth Gladys *nurse*

Los Altos
McCreary, Deborah Dennis *oncology nurse*

Los Angeles
Andersen, Ronald Max *health services educator, researcher*
Boswell, James Douglas *medical research executive*
Bourque, Linda Anne Brookover *public health educator*
Cohn, Daniel Howard *laboratory director*
Cowan, Marie Jeanette *nurse, pathology and cardiology educator*
Dracup, Kathleen Anne *nursing educator*
Haughton, James Gray *medical facility administrator, municipal health department administrator, consultant, physician*
Horowitz, Ben *health facility administrator*
Karpf, Michael *health facility administrator*
Katzin, Carolyn Fernanda *nutritionist, consultant*
Noce, Walter William, Jr. *hospital administrator*
Priselac, Thomas M. *health facility administrator*
Roberts, Robert Winston *social work educator, dean*
Territo, Mary C. *health facility administrator, oncologist*
Thompson, Judith Kastrup *nursing researcher*
Utz, Sarah Winifred *nursing educator*
van Dam, Heiman *psychoanalyst*
Ver Steeg, Donna Lorraine Frank *nurse, sociologist, educator*
Whybrow, Peter Charles *psychiatrist, educator, author*

Malibu
Palacio, June Rose Payne *nutritional science educator*

Marina Del Rey
Nizze, Judith Anne *retired physician assistant*

Marysville
Myers, Elmer *social worker, psychiatrist*

Moraga
Allen, Richard Garrett *healthcare and education consultant*

Moreno Valley
Hadfield, Tomi Senger *hospital administrator*

Mount Shasta
Mariner, William Martin *chiropractor*

Napa
Lee, Margaret Anne *psychotherapist, social worker*
Sedlock, Joy *psychiatric social worker*

Newport Beach
Stephens, Michael Dean *hospital administrator*

Oakland
Caulfield, W. Harry *retired health care industry executive, physician*
Lawrence, David M. *health facility administrator*
Miller, Barry *research administrator, psychologist*

Orange
Brown, Lillian Eriksen *retired nursing administrator, consultant*

Oxnard
Dimitriadis, Andre C. *health care executive*

Palm Springs
Boyajian, Timothy Edward *public health officer, educator, consultant*

Palo Alto
Skeff, Kelley Michael *health facility administrator*

Rancho Mirage
Kiser, Roberta Katherine *medical records administrator, education educator*

Redlands
Coleman, Arlene Florence *retired nurse practitioner*

Richmond
Terrill, Karen Stapleton *retired medical planning consultant*

Riverside
Smith, Jeffry Alan *health administrator, physician, consultant*

Sacramento
Armacost, Mary Jane *healthcare company executive*
Friedman, Kenni *healthcare company official, councilwoman*
Johnson, Van R. *health facility administrator*
Woo, Sharon Y. *healthcare organization executive*

San Bernardino
Timmreck, Thomas C. *health sciences and health administration educator*

San Diego
Brokaw, Meredith A. *women's health care company director*
Colling, Kenneth Frank *retired hospital administrator*
Crawford, Debra P. *women's healthcare company executive*
Crawford, Randi *women's healthcare company executive*
Dubé, Susan E. *women's healthcare company executive*
Essex, Lauren S. *women's health care company executive*
Guthrie, Michael B. *health facility administrator*
Johnson, Wendy S. *women's healthcare company executive*
Martin, Julie *women's healthcare company executive*
Rodgers, Janet Ahalt *nursing educator, dean*
Rosen, Peter *health facility administrator, emergency physician, educator*
Schmidt, Terry Lane *health care executive*
Smith, Raymond Edward *retired health care administrator*
Steele, Dale F. *women's healthcare company executive*
Varga, Jeanne-Marie *women's healthcare company executive*

San Francisco
Auerback, Sandra Jean *social worker*
Chater, Shirley Sears *health educator*
Eng, Catherine *health care facility administrator, physician, medical educator*
Fetter, Trevor *healthcare industry executive*
Gortner, Susan Reichert *nursing educator*
Green, Robert Leonard *hospital management company executive*
Harrington, Charlene Ann *sociology and health policy educator*
Martinson, Ida Marie *nursing educator, nurse, physiologist*
Norbeck, Jane S. *nursing educator*
Smith, Cecilia May *hospital official*
Young, Lowell Sung-yi *medical administrator, educator*

San Jose
Cunnane, Patricia S. *medical facility administrator*
Lu, Nancy Chao *nutrition and food science educator*

San Mateo
Richens, Muriel Whittaker *marriage and family therapist, educator*
Schreiber, Andrew *psychotherapist*

San Rafael
Friesecke, Raymond Francis *health company executive*

Santa Ana
Bowlus, Brad A. *health science association administrator*
Folick, Jeffrey M. *healthcare systems company executive*
Lyons, Linda *health science association administrator*
Schub, Craig S. *health science association administrator*

Santa Barbara
Barbakow, Jeffrey C. *healthcare industry executive*
Dennis, David L. *healthcare executive*
Focht, Michael Harrison *health care industry executive*
Herlinger, Daniel Robert *hospital administrator*
Mackey, Thomas B. *health facility administrator*

Santa Clara
Goldstein, Jack *health science executive, microbiologist*

Santa Monica
Brook, Robert Henry *health services researcher, physician, educator*
Dillenberg, Jack *public health officer*
Epstein, Marsha Ann *public health administrator, physician*

Santa Ynez
Walker, Burton Leith *psychotherapist, engineering writer*

Sepulveda
Burton, Paul Floyd *social worker*

Sonoma
Markey, William Alan *health care administrator*

Stanford
Basch, Paul Frederick *international health educator, parasitologist*
Mc Namara, Joseph Donald *researcher, retired police chief, novelist*

Stockton
Matuszak, Alice Jean Boyer *pharmacy educator*

Thousand Oaks
Emerson, Alton Calvin *retired physical therapist*
Gaus, Clifton R. *healthcare executive*
Herman, Joan Elizabeth *healthcare company executive*
Schaeffer, Leonard David *healthcare executive*
Souza, Lawrence M. *health facility administrator*

Torrance
Thiry, Kent J. *health facility administrator*

Union City
Glueck, Mary Audrey *retired psychiatric and mental health nurse*

Vacaville
Dailey, Dawn Elaine *public health service official*

Woodland Hills
Costa, Maurice *health care company executive*
John Robert, Bruce *healthcare company executive*
Pettit, John W. *administrator*
Tellez, Cora *healthcare company executive*
Yates, Gary L. *marriage and family therapist*

COLORADO

Buena Vista
Herb, Edmund Michael *optometrist, educator*

Denver
Hand, Dale L. *pharmacist*
Jennett, Shirley Shimmick *home care management executive, nurse*
Kirkpatrick, Charles Harvey *physician, immunology researcher*
McDonnell, Barbara *health facility administrator*
Rael, Henry Sylvester, Sr. *retired health administrator, financial and management consultant*
Taussig, Lynn Max *healthcare administrator, pulmonologist, pediatrician, educator*

Fort Collins
Gubler, Duane J. *research scientist, administrator*
Schatz, Mona Claire Struhsaker *social worker, educator, consultant, researcher*

Grand Junction
Pantenburg, Michel *hospital administrator, health educator, holistic health coordinator*
Van Horn, O. Frank *retired counselor, consultant*

Parker
Haas, Bradley Dean *pharmacy director, clinical pharmacist, consultant*

Pueblo
Hawkins, Robert Lee *health facility administrator*

HAWAII

Hanalei
Snyder, Francine *psychotherapist, registered nurse, writer*

Honolulu
Fischer, Joel *social work educator*
Katz, Alan Roy *public health educator*
Lum, Jean Loui Jin *nursing educator*
Yokouchi, Kathy *nursing administrator*

Kaneohe
Au, Whitlow W.L. *acoustician*

Waipahu
Kuwabara, Dennis Matsuichi *optometrist*

IDAHO

Boise
Harper, Anthony *counselor, singer*

Hope
Meyers, Marlene O. *retired hospital administrator*

MONTANA

Helena
Wickham, Dianne *nursing administrator*

Missoula
Wemple, James Robert *psychotherapist*

NEVADA

Las Vegas
Francis, Timothy Duane *chiropractor*
Israel, Joan *social worker*
MacDonald, Erin E. *healthcare company executive*
Marlon, Anthony M. *healthcare company executive, cardiologist*
Michel, Mary Ann Kedzuf *nursing educator*

Reno
Graham, Denis David *marriage and family therapist, educational consultant*
Pinson, Larry Lee *pharmacist*

NEW MEXICO

Albuquerque
Mateju, Joseph Frank *hospital administrator*
Solomon, Arthur Charles *pharmacist*

Clovis
Rehorn, Lois M(arie) *nursing administrator*

Las Cruces
Welsh, Mary McAnaw *family mediator, educator*

Santa Fe
Melnick, Alice Jean (AJ Melnick) *counselor*

Truth Or Consequences
Rush, Domenica Marie *health facilities administrator*

OREGON

Corvallis
Oldfield, James Edmund *nutrition educator*

Lake Oswego
Tyler, Darlene Jasmer *retired dietitian*

Pendleton
Smiley, Richard Wayne *researcher*

Portland
Griffin, Sandra Lee *nursing administrator*
Goldfarb, Timothy Moore *hospital administrator*
Greenlick, Merwyn Ronald *health services researcher*
King, John G. *health service administrator*

Meighan, Stuart Spence *hospital consultant, internist, writer*
Pfeifer, Larry Alan *public health service coordinator*
Rooks, Judith Pence *midwifery, public health consultant*
Shireman, Joan Foster *social work educator*

Salem
Callahan, Marilyn Joy *social worker*
Zumwalt, Roger Carl *hospital administrator*

UTAH

Kaysville
Ashmead, Allez Morrill *speech, hearing, and language pathologist, orofacial myologist, consultant*

Salt Lake City
Jorgensen, Lou Ann Birkbeck *social worker*
Kelen, Joyce Arlene *social worker*
Lee, Glenn Richard *medical administrator, educator*
Mason, James Ostermann *public health administrator*
Melton, Arthur Richard *healthcare executive*
Wolf, Harold Herbert *pharmacy educator*

WASHINGTON

Bellevue
Edwards, Kirk Lewis *medical services company executive*

Bothell
McDonald, Michael Lee *clinic administrator, retired naval officer*

Everett
Crerand, Raymond F. *hospital administrator*

Everson
McGulpin, Elizabeth Jane *nurse*

Gig Harbor
Larson, Maureen Inez *rehabilitation consultant*

Olympia
Inverso, Marlene Joy *optometrist*

Poulsbo
Carle, Harry Lloyd *social worker*

Redmond
Kim, Jeong-Han *researcher*
Sasenick, Joseph Anthony *animal health and food safety company executive*

Seattle
Barnard, Kathryn Elaine *nursing educator, researcher*
Dorpat, Theodore Lorenz *psychoanalyst*
Ellis, Janice Rider *nursing educator, consultant*
Johnston, William Frederick *emergency services administrator*
Monsen, Elaine Ranker *nutritionist, educator, editor*
Perkin, Gordon Wesley *international health executive*
Perrin, Edward Burton *health services researcher, biostatistician, public health educator*
Peterson, Jane White *nursing educator, anthropologist*
Portuesi, Donna Rae *psychotherapist, consultant*
Prins, David *speech pathologist, educator*

Spanaway
Campbell, Thomas J. *chiropractor, legislator*

Spokane
Murphy, Mary Ann *human services administrator*
Robinson, Herbert Henry, III *educator, psychotherapist*

Yakima
Simonson, Susan Kay *hospital clinical care coordinator*

WYOMING

Bondurant
Ellwood, Paul Murdock, Jr. *health policy analyst, consultant*

Cheyenne
Dale, Marcia Lyn *nursing educator*
Nisbet, Toma A. *nursing administrator*

Hanna
Turner, Lillian Erna *retired nurse*

CANADA

ALBERTA

Edmonton
Fields, Anthony Lindsay Austin *health facility administrator, oncologist, educator*
Hislop, Mervyn Warren *health advocate administrator, psychologist*

BRITISH COLUMBIA

New Westminster
Fair, James Stanley *hospital administrator*

Vancouver
Gilbert, John Humphrey Victor *speech scientist, educator*
Riedel, Bernard Edward *retired pharmaceutical sciences educator*

ADDRESS UNPUBLISHED

Aehlert, Barbara June *health services executive*
Alton, N. Kirby *health facility administrator*
Anderson, Dorothy Fisher *social worker, psychotherapist*
Belles, Donald Arnold *pastoral therapist, mental health counselor*
Blumberg, Mark Stuart *health services consultant*
Brown, Barbara June *hospital and nursing administrator*
Callison, Nancy Fowler *nurse administrator*
Christiansen, David K. *hospital administrator*
Clayton, Paul Douglas *health care administrator*
Condry, Robert Stewart *retired hospital administrator*
Craig, Carol Mills *marriage, family and child counselor*
DeLapp, Tina Davis *nursing educator*
Devine, Percy, III *human services administrator*
Doi, Lois *psychiatric social worker*
Dreyfuss, John Alan *retired health facility administrator*
Eberhart, Gregory E. *pharmacist, registrar, administrator*
Ewell, Charles Muse *health care industry executive, consultant, publisher, educator*
Fehr, Lola Mae *health facility administrator*
Gengler, Sue Wong *health educator, evaluation consultant, speaker, trainer*
Grant, Richard Earl *medical and legal consultant*
Healy, Sonya Ainslie *retired health facility administrator*
Higgins, Ruth Ann *social worker, family therapist*
Hinton, James H. *healthcare services administrator*
Hofmann, Paul Bernard *healthcare consultant*
Howard, Mark J. *hospital administrator*
Hummel, Joseph William *retired hospital administrator*
Kerr, Frederick Hohmann *retired health care company executive*
MacPherson, Shirley *clinical therapist*
Markham, Richard Glover *research executive*
Mikel, Thomas Kelly, Jr. *laboratory administrator*
Poe, Laura *nursing educator, administrator*
Preszler, Sharon Marie *psychiatric home health nurse*
Rindone, Joseph Patrick *clinical pharmacist, educator*
Robinson, Gail Patricia *retired mental health counselor*
Sanders, Augusta Swann *retired nurse*
Scala, James *health care industry consultant, writer*
Schnabel, Gary A. *health facility administrator, director*
Stickles, Bonnie Jean *nurse*
Suber, Robin Hall *former medical and surgical nurse*
Tyler, Gail Madeleine *nurse*
Uris, Patricia Firme *health science association administrator*
Vohs, James Arthur *health care program executive*
Wiebe, Leonard Irving *radiopharmacist, educator*

HEALTHCARE: MEDICINE

UNITED STATES

ALASKA

Fairbanks
Bergeson, Marvin Ernest *pediatrician*

Valdez
Todd, Kathleen Gail *physician*

ARIZONA

Fountain Hills
Herzberger, Eugene E. *retired neurosurgeon*

Gilbert
Labovitz, Earl A. *allergist*

Mesa
Bunchman, Herbert Harry, II *plastic surgeon*
Fiorino, John Wayne *podiatrist*
Hagen, Nicholas Stewart *medical educator, consultant*

Paradise Valley
Lorenzen, Robert Frederick *ophthalmologist*

Phoenix
Ammon, John Richard *anesthesiologist*
Borel, James David *anesthesiologist*
Buffmire, Donald K. *internist*
Fishburne, John Ingram, Jr. *obstetrician/gynecologist, educator*
Goldberg, Morris *internist*
Holman, Paul David *plastic surgeon*
Lovett, William Lee *surgeon*
Reed, Wallace Allison *anesthesiologist*
Stern, Stanley *psychiatrist*
Teague, Robert Cole *physician*
Underwood, Paul Lester *cardiologist*
Zerella, Joseph T. *retired pediatric surgeon*

Scottsdale
Cawley, Leo Patrick *pathologist, immunologist*
Clement, Richard William *plastic and reconstructive surgeon*
Evans, Tommy Nicholas *obstetrician/gynecologist, educator*
Friedman, Shelly Arnold *cosmetic surgeon*
Kandell, Howard Noel *pediatrician*
Lewis, John Christopher *allergist*
Nadler, Henry Louis *pediatrician, geneticist, medical educator*
Orford, Robert Raymond *consulting physician*
Reznick, Richard Howard *pediatrician*
Sanderson, David R. *physician*

Sedona
Reno, Joseph Harry *retired orthopedic surgeon*

Shors, Clayton Marion *cardiologist*

Tempe
Anand, Suresh Chandra *physician*
Rowley, Beverley Davies *medical sociologist*
Schneller, Eugene Stuart *health administration and policy educator*

Tucson
Abrams, Herbert Kerman *physician, educator*
Alpert, Joseph Stephen *physician, educator*
Anderson, John Albert *physician*
Ben-Asher, M. David *physician*
Burrows, Benjamin *retired physician, educator*
Capp, Michael Paul *physician, educator*
Dalen, James Eugene *cardiologist, educator*
DeLuca, Dominick *medical educator, researcher*
Ewy, Gordon Allen *cardiologist, clinician, researcher, educator*
Harris, David Thomas *immunology educator*
Hess, Richard Neal *plastic surgeon*
Levenson, Alan Ira *psychiatrist, physician, educator*
Marcus, Frank Isadore *cardiologist, educator*
Martin, Loren Winston *allergist*
Nugent, Charles Arter *internist, educator*
Reinmuth, Oscar MacNaughton *physician, educator*
Smith, Josef Riley *internist*
Weil, Andrew Thomas *physician, educator*
Weinstein, Ronald S. *pathologist, educator*
Witte, Marlys Hearst *internist, educator*
Woolfenden, James Manning *nuclear medicine physician, educator*
Woosley, Raymond *pharmacology and medical educator*

CALIFORNIA

Agoura Hills
deCiutiis, Alfred Charles Maria *medical oncologist, television producer*
Havlicek, Michael *medical association administrator*

Alameda
Patterson, Lloyd Clifford *retired psychiatrist*
Whorton, M. Donald *occupational and environmental health physician, epidemiologist*

Bakersfield
Prunes, Fernando *plastic surgeon, educator*

Berkeley
Allison, James Patrick *immunology educator, medical association administrator*
Budinger, Thomas Francis *radiologist, educator*
Buffler, Patricia Ann *epidemiology educator, retired dean*
Diamond, Marian Cleeves *anatomy educator*
Duhl, Leonard *psychiatrist, educator*
Falkner, Frank Tardrew *physician, educator*
Grossman, Elmer Roy *pediatrician*
Shortell, Stephen Michael *health services researcher*
Syme, Sherman Leonard *epidemiology educator*
Tempelis, Constantine Harry *immunologist, educator*

Beverly Hills
Cambre, Athleo Louis, Jr. *plastic surgeon*
Dennis, Karen Marie *plastic surgeon*
Karpman, Harold Lew *cardiologist, educator, writer*
Klein, Arnold William *dermatologist*
Marshak, Harry *plastic surgeon*
Menkes, John Hans *pediatric neurologist*
Sciff, Stephen S. *ophthalmologist*
Semel, George Herbert *plastic surgeon*
Yuan, Robin Tsu-Wang *plastic surgeon*

Borrego Springs
Strong, John Oliver *plastic surgeon, educator*

Burbank
Renner, Andrew Ihor *surgeon*

Carlsbad
Bennett, C. Frank *molecular pharmacologist*
Colten, Harvey Radin *pediatrician, educator*

Carmichael
Wagner, Carruth John *physician*

Chula Vista
Cohen, Elaine Helena *pediatrician, pediatric cardiologist, educator*

Culver City
Rose, Margarete Erika *pathologist*

Davis
Cardiff, Robert Darrell *pathology educator*
Enders, Allen Coffin *anatomy educator*
Gardner, Murray Briggs *pathologist, educator*
Halsted, Charles Hopkinson *internist*
Hollinger, Mannfred Alan *pharmacologist, educator, toxicologist*
Jensen, Hanne Margrete *pathology educator*
Overstreet, James Wilkins *obstetrics and gynecology educator, administrator*
Plopper, Charles George *anatomist, cell biologist*
Richman, David Paul *neurologist, educator, researcher*
Schenker, Marc Benet *preventive medicine educator*
Stowell, Robert Eugene *pathologist, retired educator*
Williams, Hibbard Earl *medical educator, physician*

Del Mar
Dennish, George William, III *cardiologist*

Downey
Gong, Henry, Jr. *physician, researcher*
Perry, Jacquelin *orthopedic surgeon*
Shapiro, Richard Stanley *physician*

Duarte
Comings, David Edward *physician, medical genetics scientist*

El Dorado Hills
Sparks, Robert Dean *medical administrator, physician*

El Macero
Raventos, Antolin *radiology educator*

Emeryville
Hurst, Deborah *pediatric hematologist*

Encinitas
Jaffe, Charles J. *allergist*

Encino
Costea, Nicolas Vincent *physician, researcher*

Fontana
Resch, Charlotte Susanna *plastic surgeon*

Fremont
Behrens, M. Kathleen *medical researcher*
Maynard, Catherine *medical researcher*
Steinmetz, Seymour *pediatrician*

Fresno
Chandler, Bruce Frederick *internist*
Glassheim, Jeffrey Wayne *allergist, immunologist, pediatrician*
Holmes, Albert William, Jr. *physician*
Leigh, Hoyle *psychiatrist, educator, writer*
Patton, Jack Thomas *family practice physician*
Thompson, Leonard Russell *pediatrician*

Fullerton
Aston, Edward Ernest, IV *dermatologist*
Sugarman, Michael *physician, rheumatologist*

Gilroy
Grisez, James Louis *physician, plastic surgeon*

Glendale
Dent, Ernest DuBose, Jr. *pathologist*

Grass Valley
Ely, Parry Haines *dermatologist, educator*

Greenbrae
Cushing, Matthew *internist*
Levy, S. William *dermatologist, educator*
Parnell, Francis William, Jr. *otolaryngologist*

Gualala
Ring, Alice Ruth Bishop *retired physician*

Inglewood
Sukov, Richard Joel *radiologist*

Irvine
Connolly, John Earle *surgeon, educator*
Felton, Jean Spencer *physician*
Friedenberg, Richard Myron *radiology educator, physician*
George, Kattunilathu Oommen *physician, educator*
Gupta, Sudhir *immunologist, educator*
Hubbell, Floyd Allan *physician, educator*
Korc, Murray *endocrinologist*
Miledi, Ricardo *neurobiologist*
Quilligan, Edward James *obstetrician, gynecologist, educator*
Tobis, Jerome Sanford *physician*
van-den-Noort, Stanley *neurologist, educator*
Weinstein, Gerald D. *dermatology educator*

Jamul
Harwood, Ivan Richmond *retired pediatric pulmonologist*

La Crescenta
Riccardi, Vincent Michael *pediatrician, researcher, educator, entrepreneur*

La Jolla
Bailey, David Nelson *pathology educator, university official*
Barrett-Connor, Elizabeth Louise *epidemiologist, educator*
Beutler, Ernest *physician, research scientist*
Brown, Stuart I. *ophthalmologist, educator*
Covell, Ruth Marie *medical educator, medical school administrator*
Dalessio, Donald John *physician, neurologist, educator*
Dixon, Frank James *medical scientist, educator*
Edgington, Thomas S. *pathologist, educator, molecular biologist, vascular biologist*
Edwards, Charles Cornell *surgeon, research administrator*
Friedmann, Theodore *physician*
Garland, Cedric Frank *epidemiologist, educator*
Gill, Gordon N. *medical educator*
Gittes, Ruben Foster *urological surgeon*
Glass, Christopher Kevin *physician*
Hamburger, Robert N. *pediatrics educator, consultant*
Han, Jiahuai *medical researcher*
Hofmann, Alan Frederick *biomedical educator, researcher*
Holmes, Edward W. *physician, educator*
Horner, Anthony Adam *pediatrician, educator*
Jaffer, Adrian Michael *physician*
Judd, Lewis Lund *psychiatrist, educator*
Katzman, Robert *medical educator, neurologist*
Malhotra, Vivek *medical educator*
Mendoza, Stanley Atran *pediatric nephrologist, educator*
Nakamura, Robert Motoharu *pathologist*
Nyhan, William Leo *pediatrician, educator*
Pashler, Harold E. *psychologist, educator*
Rearden, Carole Ann *clinical pathologist, educator*
Resnik, Robert *medical educator*
Rosenfeld, Michael G. *medical educator*
Ruoslahti, Erkki *medical research administrator*
Schneider, Gerald L. *plastic surgeon*
Singer, Robert *plastic surgeon*
Smith, Richard Alan *neurologist, medical association administrator*
Spiegelberg, Hans Leonhard *medical educator*
Steinberg, Daniel *preventive medicine physician, educator*
Tan, Eng Meng *immunologist, biomedical scientist*

Taylor, Palmer W. *pharmacology educator*
Terry, Robert Davis *neuropathologist, educator*
Weigle, William Oliver *immunologist, educator*
Yen, Samuel S(how)-C(hih) *obstetrics and gynecology educator, reproductive endocrinologist*

La Mirada
Salinger, Charles *dermatologist*

La Quinta
Pitkin, Roy Macbeth *obstetrician, educator, retired*

Laguna Hills
Ierardi, Stephen John *physician*
Widyolar, Sheila Gayle *dermatologist*

Loma Linda
Bailey, Leonard Lee *surgeon*
Behrens, Berel Lyn *physician, academic and healthcare administrator*
Brandstater, Murray Everett *physiatrist*
Briggs, Burton A. *medical educator*
Bull, Brian Stanley *pathology educator, medical consultant, business executive*
Chan, Philip J. *medical educator*
Condon, Stanley Charles *gastroenterologist*
Hardesty, Robert Alan *plastic surgeon*
Hinshaw, David B., Jr. *radiologist*
Kirk, Gerald Arthur *nuclear radiologist*
Llaurado, Josep G. *nuclear medicine physician, scientist*
Mace, John Weldon *pediatrician*
Rendell-Baker, Leslie *anesthesiologist, educator*
Roberts, Walter Herbert Beatty *anatomist, educator*
Slater, James Munro *radiation oncologist*
Strother, Allen *biochemical pharmacologist, researcher*
Young, Lionel Wesley *radiologist*

Long Beach
Stemmer, Edward Alan *surgeon, educator*

Los Altos
Abrams, Arthur Jay *physician*
Castellino, Ronald Augustus Dietrich *radiologist, educator*

Los Angeles
Alkon, Ellen Skillen *physician*
Anderson, Gail V. *obstetrician/gynecologist*
Anderson, Kathryn D. *surgeon*
Ansell, Benjamin Jesse *physician*
Apt, Leonard *physician*
Aronowitz, Joel Alan *plastic and reconstructive surgeon*
Barrett, Cynthia Townsend *neonatologist*
Beart, Robert W., Jr. *surgeon, educator*
Becker, Donald Paul *surgeon, neurosurgeon*
Bernstein, Sol *cardiologist, educator*
Biles, John Alexander *pharmacology educator, chemistry educator*
Blahd, William Henry *physician*
Bluestone, David Allan *pediatrician*
Bondareff, William *psychiatry educator*
Borenstein, Daniel Bernard *psychiatrist, educator*
Braunstein, Glenn David *physician, educator*
Caprioli, Joseph *ophthalmologist*
Chandor, Stebbins Bryant *pathologist*
Cherry, James Donald *pediatrician*
Clemente, Carmine Domenic *anatomist, educator*
Cooper, Edwin Lowell *anatomy educator*
Corman, Marvin Leonard *surgeon, educator*
Dann, Francis Joseph *dermatologist, educator*
Danoff, Dudley Seth *surgeon, urologist*
Davidson, Ezra C., Jr. *physician, educator*
De Cherney, Alan Hersh *obstetrics and gynecology educator*
Detels, Roger *epidemiologist, physician, former university dean*
Dignam, William Joseph *obstetrician, gynecologist, educator*
Edgerton, Bradford Wheatly *plastic surgeon*
Enstrom, James Eugene *epidemiologist*
Ettenger, Robert Bruce *physician, nephrologist*
Fahey, John Leslie *immunologist*
Feig, Stephen Arthur *pediatrics educator, hematologist, oncologist*
Fielding, Jonathan E. *pediatrician*
Fish, Barbara *psychiatrist, educator*
Fleming, Arthur Wallace *physician, surgeon*
Fogelman, Alan Marcus *internist*
Fowler, Vincent R. *dermatologist*
Francis, Charles K. *medical educator*
Frasier, S. Douglas *medical educator*
Friedman, Nathan Baruch *medical educator*
Gale, Robert Peter *physician, scientist, researcher*
Geller, Stephen Arthur *pathologist, educator*
Giannotta, Steven Louis *neurosurgery educator*
Gonick, Harvey Craig *nephrologist, educator*
Gorney, Roderic *psychiatry educator*
Grody, Wayne William *physician*
Guze, Phyllis Arlene *internist, educator, academic administrator*
Haywood, L. Julian *physician, educator*
Hirsch, Anthony Terry *physician*
Holland, Gary Norman *ophthalmologist, educator*
Hollander, Daniel *gastroenterologist, medical educator*
Horwitz, David A. *physician, scientist, educator*
House, John William *otologist*
Ignarro, Louis J. *pharmacology educator*
Itabashi, Hideo Henry *neuropathologist*
Jacobson, Edwin James *medical educator*
Jadvar, Hossein *nuclear medicine physician, biomedical engineer*
Jalali, Behnaz *psychiatrist, educator*
Jelliffe, Roger Woodham *cardiologist, clinical pharmacologist*
Johnson, Cage Saul *hematologist, educator*
Jones, Neil Ford *surgeon, educator*
Jones, Peter Anthony *medical research administrator*
Kahn, Fredrick Henry *internist*
Kamil, Elaine Scheiner *pediatrician, educator*
Kaplan, Samuel *pediatric cardiologist*
Kaplowitz, Neil *physician, educator*
Katz, Ronald Lewis *physician, educator*
Kelly, Arthur Paul *physician*
Kleeman, Charles Richard *medical educator, nephrologist, researcher*
Koch, Richard *pediatrician, educator*
Korsch, Barbara M. *pediatrician*
Landing, Benjamin Harrison *pathologist, educator*
Levey, Gerald Saul *internist, educator*
Lewin, Klaus J. *pathologist, educator*
Lewis, Charles Edwin *epidemiologist, educator*
Liberman, Robert Paul *psychiatry educator, researcher, writer*
Lim, David Jong-Jai *otolaryngology educator, researcher*
Linde, Leonard M. *pediatric cardiologist*
Longmire, William Polk, Jr. *physician, surgeon*
Malcolm, Dawn Grace *family physician*
Marmor, Judd *psychiatrist, educator*
Mellinkoff, Sherman Mussoff *medical educator*
Miller, Timothy Alden *plastic and reconstructive surgeon*
Mishell, Daniel R., Jr. *obstetrician/gynecologist, educator*
Moss, Arthur J. *physician, educator*
Moxley, John Howard, III *internist*
Nathwani, Bharat Narottam *pathologist, consultant*
Newman, Anita Nadine *surgeon*
Noble, Ernest Pascal *pharmacologist, biochemist, educator*
Parker, Robert George *radiation oncology educator, academic administrator*
Parmelee, Arthur Hawley, Jr. *pediatric medical educator*
Pike, Malcolm Cecil *preventive medicine educator*
Rachelefsky, Gary Stuart *medical educator*
Rimoin, David Lawrence *physician, geneticist*
Ritvo, Edward Ross *psychiatrist*
Rotter, Jerome Israel *medical geneticist*
Roven, Alfred Nathan *surgeon*
Ryan, Stephen Joseph, Jr. *ophthalmology educator, university dean*
Sager, Philip Travis *academic physician, cardiac electrophysiologist*
Sawyer, Charles Henry *anatomist, educator*
Scheibel, Arnold Bernard *psychiatrist, educator, research director*
Schelbert, Heinrich Ruediger *nuclear medicine physician*
Schiff, Martin *physician, surgeon*
Schwabe, Arthur David *physician, educator*
Schwartz, William Benjamin *internist, educator*
Sherman, Randolph *plastic and reconstructive surgeon, educator*
Siegel, Michael Elliot *nuclear medicine physician, educator*
Siegel, Sheldon C. *pediatrician, allergist, immunologist*
Solomon, George Freeman *psychiatrist, educator*
Steckel, Richard J. *radiologist, academic administrator*
Stern, Walter Eugene *neurosurgeon, educator*
Stiehm, E. Richard *pediatrician, educator*
Straatsma, Bradley Ralph *ophthalmologist, educator*
Sullivan, Stuart Francis *anesthesiologist, educator*
Tabachnick, Norman Donald *psychiatrist, educator*
Tompkins, Ronald K. *surgeon*
Vredevoe, Donna Lou *research immunologist, microbiologist, educator*
Weiner, Leslie Philip *neurology educator, researcher*
Weinstein, Irwin Marshall *internist, hematologist*
Weiss, Martin Harvey *neurosurgeon, educator*
Wilkinson, Alan Herbert *nephrologist, medical educator*
Williams, Roberta Gay *pediatric cardiologist, educator*
Wilson, Miriam Geisendorfer *retired physician, educator*
Wilson, Myron Robert, Jr. *retired psychiatrist*
Withers, Hubert Rodney *radiotherapist, radiobiologist, educator*
Woodley, David Timothy *dermatology educator*
Yamamoto, Joe *psychiatrist, educator*

Los Gatos
Naughten, Robert Norman *pediatrician*

Malibu
Jenden, Donald James *pharmacologist, educator*

Menlo Park
Healy, Cynthia *pharmacologist, life scientist, researcher*
Hoffman, Thomas Edward *dermatologist*
Kovachy, Edward Miklos, Jr. *psychiatrist, consultant*
Speidel, John Joseph *physician, foundation officer*

Milpitas
Chiu, Peter Yee-Chew *physician*

Monterey
Black, Robert Lincoln *pediatrician, educator*
Lehr, Jeffrey Marvin *immunologist, allergist*

Moraga
Frey, William Rayburn *healthcare educator, consultant*

Mountain View
Abel, Elizabeth A. *dermatologist*
Lowen, Robert Marshall *plastic surgeon*
Warren, Richard Wayne *obstetrician/gynecologist*

Napa
Zimmermann, John Paul *plastic surgeon*

Newhall
Stein, Karl N. *plastic and reconstructive surgeon*

Newport Beach
Chiu, John Tang *physician*
Solmer, Richard *surgeon*

Oakland
Benton-Hardy, Lisa Renee *psychiatrist, educator*
Collen, Morris Frank *medical association administrator, physician*
Efron, Robert *retired neurology educator, research institute administrator*
Ng, Lawrence Ming-Loy *pediatrician*
Sharpton, Thomas *physician*

Oceanside
Curtin, Thomas Lee *ophthalmologist*

Orange
Achauer, Bruce Michael *plastic surgeon*
Anzel, Sanford Harold *orthopedic surgeon*
Armentrout, Steven Alexander *oncologist*
Barr, Ronald Jeffrey *dermatologist, pathologist*
Berk, Jack Edward *gastroenterologist, educator*
Crumley, Roger Lee *surgeon, educator*
DiSaia, Philip John *gynecologist, obstetrician, radiology educator*
Kim, Moon Hyun *endocrinologist, educator*
Lott, Ira Totz *pediatric neurologist*
MacArthur, Carol Jeanne *pediatric otolaryngology educator*
Morgan, Beverly Carver *pediatrician, educator*
Mosier, Harry David, Jr. *physician, educator*
Thompson, William Benbow, Jr. *obstetrician/gynecologist, educator*
Vaziri, Nosratola Dabir *internist, nephrologist, educator*
Wilson, Archie Fredric *medical educator*
Yu, Jen *medical educator*

Pacific Palisades
Beck, John Christian *physician, educator*
Claes, Daniel John *physician*
Love, Susan Margaret *surgeon, educator, writer*
Tourtellotte, Wallace William *neurologist, educator*

Palm Springs
Kern, Donald Michael *internist*
Weil, Max Harry *physician, medical educator, medical scientist*

Palo Alto
Amylon, Michael David *physician, educator*
Bensch, Klaus George *pathology educator*
Blessing-Moore, Joann Catherine *allergist*
Britton, M(elvin) C(reed), Jr. *physician, rheumatologist*
Chen, Stephen Shi-hua *pathologist, biochemist*
Cooke, John P. *cardiologist, medical educator, medical researcher*
Dafoe, Donald Cameron *surgeon, educator*
Daniels, John R. *oncologist, educator*
Dement, William Charles *medical researcher, medical educator*
Desai, Kavin Hirendra *pediatrician*
Donaldson, Sarah Susan *radiologist*
Farber, Eugene Mark *research institute administrator*
Farquhar, John William *physician, educator*
Fortmann, Stephen Paul *medical educator, researcher, epidemiologist*
Fries, James Franklin *internal medicine educator*
Goldstein, Mary Kane *physician*
Harris, Edward D., Jr. *physician*
Hays, Marguerite Thompson *nuclear medicine physician, educator*
Hentz, Vincent R. *surgeon*
Holman, Halsted Reid *medical educator, educator*
Hubert, Helen Betty *epidemiologist*
Jamison, Rex Lindsay *medical educator*
Jamplis, Robert Warren *surgeon, medical foundation executive*
Lane, Alfred Thomas *medical educator*
Linna, Timo Juhani *immunologist, researcher, educator*
Litt, Iris Figarsky *pediatrics educator*
Matthews, Zakee *psychiatrist, educator*
Melmon, Kenneth Lloyd *internist, biologist, pharmacologist, consultant*
Michie, Sara H. *pathologist, educator*
Schrier, Stanley Leonard *hematologist, educator*
Schurman, David Jay *orthopedic surgeon, educator*
Shuer, Lawrence Mendel *neurosurgery educator*
Strober, Samuel *immunologist, educator*
Tune, Bruce Malcolm *pediatrics educator, renal toxicologist*
Urquhart, John *medical researcher, educator*
Weston, Jane Sara *plastic surgeon, educator*
Winkleby, Marilyn A. *medical researcher*
Zarins, Christopher Kristaps *surgery educator, vascular surgeon*

Palos Verdes Peninsula
Thomas, Claudewell Sidney *psychiatry educator*

Panorama City
Bass, Harold Neal *pediatrician, medical geneticist*
Sue, Michael Alvin *allergist*

Pasadena
Glovsky, Myron Michael *medical educator*
Harvey, Joseph Paul, Jr. *orthopedist, educator*
Mathies, Allen Wray, Jr. *former pediatrician, hospital administrator*
Newman, Marjorie Yospin *psychiatrist*
Opel, William *medical research administrator*
Shaw, Anthony *physician, pediatric surgeon*
Yeager, Caroline Hale *radiologist, consultant*

Pinole
Harvey, Elinor B. *child psychiatrist*
Naughton, James Lee *internist*

Placerville
Bonser, Quentin *retired surgeon*

Pleasanton
Hisaka, Eric Toru *plastic surgeon*

Rancho Mirage
Cone, Lawrence Arthur *medical educator*

Redding
Renard, Ronald Lee *allergist*

Redlands
Adey, William Ross *physician*
Richardson, A(rthur) Leslie *former medical group consultant*
Skoog, William Arthur *former oncologist, educator*

Redwood City
Ellis, Eldon Eugene *surgeon*

Rescue
Frey, Charles Frederick [illegible]

Riverside
Bricker, Neal S. *physician, educator*

Childs, Donald Richard *pediatric endocrinologist*
Jung, Timothy Tae Kun *otolaryngologist*
Linaweaver, Walter Ellsworth, Jr. *physician*
Sparks, Dale Boyd *allergist, health facility administrator*
Stone, Herman Hull *internist*

Rllng Hls Est
Kline, Frank Menefee *psychiatrist*

Sacramento
Achtel, Robert Andrew *pediatric cardiologist*
Chapman, Michael William *orthopedist, educator*
Lilla, James A. *plastic surgeon*
Lim, Alan Young *plastic surgeon*
Lynch, Peter John *former dermatologist*
Nagy, Stephen Mears, Jr. *physician, allergist*
Reiber, Gregory Duane *forensic pathologist*
Rounds, Barbara Lynn *psychiatrist*
Sharma, Arjun Dutta *cardiologist*
Stevenson, Thomas Ray *plastic surgeon*
Styne, Dennis Michael *physician, educator*
Tung, Prabhas *plastic surgeon*
Wolfman, Earl Frank, Jr. *surgeon, educator*
Wolkov, Harvey Brian *radiation oncologist, researcher*
Zil, J. S. *psychiatrist, physiologist*

San Bernardino
De Haas, David Dana *emergency physician*
Gorenberg, Alan Eugene *physician*

San Bruno
Bradley, Charles William *podiatrist, educator*

San Clemente
Kim, Edward William *ophthalmic surgeon*

San Diego
Backer, Matthias, Jr. *obstetrician/gynecologist*
DeMaria, Anthony Nicholas *cardiologist, educator*
Ebbeling, William Leonard *physician*
Friedman, Paul Jay *radiologist, educator*
Goltz, Robert William *physician, educator*
Intriere, Anthony Donald *retired internist, gastroenterologist*
Isenberg, Jon Irwin *gastroenterologist, educator*
Jacoby, Irving *physician*
Jamieson, Stuart William *surgeon, educator*
Kaback, Michael *medical educator*
Kaplan, George Willard *urologist*
Kaweski, Susan *plastic surgeon, naval officer*
Kruggel, John Louis *plastic surgeon*
Leopold, George Robert *radiologist*
Lewis, Carson McLaughl *retired plastic surgeon*
Moossa, A. R. *surgery educator*
Neuman, Tom S. *emergency medical physician, educator*
O'Malley, Edward *psychiatrist, consultant*
Parthemore, Jacqueline Gail *internist, educator*
Pitt, William Alexander *cardiologist*
Radke, Jan Rodger *pulmonologist, physician executive*
Ray, Albert *family physician*
Reid, Robert Tilden *medical association administrator, internist*
Ross, John, Jr. *cardiologist, educator*
Scherger, Joseph E. *family physician, educator*
Schmidt, Joseph David *urologist*
Seagren, Stephen Linner *oncologist*
Silverstone, Leon Martin *neuroscientist, cardiologist, educator, researcher*
Van Gorder, Chris *medical executive*
Wallace, Helen Margaret *physician, educator*
Wasserman, Stephen Ira *physician, educator*
Yalam, Arnold Robert *allergist, immunologist, consultant*
Zeiger, Robert S. *allergist*

San Francisco
Amend, William John Conrad, Jr. *physician, educator*
Bainton, Dorothy Ford *pathology educator, researcher*
Barondes, Samuel Herbert *psychiatrist, educator*
Baxter, John Darling *physician, educator, health facility administrator*
Benet, Leslie Zachary *pharmacokineticist, educator*
Berger, Mitchel Stuart *neurosurgeon*
Bernstein, Harold Seth *pediatric cardiologist, molecular geneticist*
Bishop, John Michael *biomedical research scientist, educator*
Boles, Roger *otolaryngologist*
Bradford, David S. *surgeon*
Brown, Donald Malcolm *plastic surgeon*
Brown, Eric Joel *biomedical researcher, researcher*
Capozzi, Angelo *surgeon*
Castro, Joseph Ronald *retired oncology researcher, educator, physician*
Cheitlin, Melvin Donald *physician, educator*
Clever, Linda Hawes *physician*
Dawson, Chandler Robert *ophthalmologist, educator*
Debas, Haile T. *gastrointestinal surgeon, physiologist, educator*
Engleman, Ephraim Philip *rheumatologist*
Epstein, Charles Joseph *physician, medical geneticist, pediatrics and biochemistry educator*
Epstein, John Howard *dermatologist*
Erskine, John Morse *surgeon*
Fielder, David R. *medical research administrator*
Fields, Howard Lincoln *neurology and physiology educator*
Fishman, Robert Allen *neurologist, educator*
Frick, Oscar Lionel *physician, educator*
Fu, Karen King-Wah *radiation oncologist*
Gellin, Gerald Alan *dermatologist*
German, Donald Frederick *physician*
Goldberg, Robert Lewis *preventive and occupational medicine physician, internet executive*
Goode, Erica Tucker *internist*
Gooding, Charles Arthur *radiologist, physician, educator*
Gooding, Gretchen Ann Wagner *physician, educator*
Gradinger, Gilbert Paul *plastic surgeon*
Greenspan, Francis S. *physician*
Grossman, William *medical researcher, educator*
Grumbach, Melvin Malcolm *physician, educator*
Hanley, Frank L. *surgeon, educator*
Hauser, Stephen L. *medical educator*

Havel, Richard Joseph *physician, educator*
Heyman, Melvin Bernard *pediatric gastroenterologist*
Hinman, Frank, Jr. *urologist, educator*
Hoffman, Julien Ivor Ellis *pediatric cardiologist, educator*
Ikeda, Clyde Junichi *plastic and reconstructive surgeon*
Jablons, David M. *surgeon, educator*
Jaffe, Robert Benton *obstetrician, gynecologist, reproductive endocrinologist*
Kan, Yuet Wai *hematologist, educator*
Kaplan, Selna L. *medical educator*
Katzung, Bertram George *pharmacologist*
Kline, Howard Jay *cardiologist, educator*
Kramer, Steven G. *ophthalmologist, educator*
Lee, Philip Randolph *medical educator*
Low, Randall *internist, cardiologist*
Lucia, Marilyn Reed *physician*
Mason, Dean Towle *cardiologist*
Mathes, Stephen John *plastic and reconstructive surgeon, educator*
McAninch, Jack Weldon *urological surgeon, educator*
McNamara, Margaret M. *pediatrician*
Miller, Walter Luther *pediatrician, educator*
Myers, Howard Milton *pharmacologist, educator*
O'Connor, G(eorge) Richard *ophthalmologist*
Perkins, Herbert Asa *hematologist, educator*
Petrakis, Nicholas Louis *edidemiologist, medical researcher, educator*
Phillips, Theodore Locke *radiation oncologist, educator*
Piel, Carolyn Forman *pediatrician, educator*
Rabow, Michael Warren *physician, educator*
Rudolph, Abraham Morris *pediatrician, educator*
Schmid, Rudi (Rudolf Schmid) *internist, educator, scientist*
Schmidt, Robert Milton *physician, scientist, educator, administrator*
Schrock, Theodore R. *surgeon*
Seebach, Lydia Marie *physician*
Shapiro, Larry Jay *pediatrician, scientist, educator*
Shinefield, Henry Robert *pediatrician*
Smith, Lloyd Hollingsworth *physician*
Sokolow, Maurice *physician, educator*
Stamper, Robert Lewis *ophthalmologist, educator*
Steinman, John Francis *psychiatrist*
Terr, Lenore Cagen *psychiatrist, writer*
Thompson, Charlotte Ellis *pediatrician, educator, author*
Van Dyke, Craig *psychiatrist, director*
Volberding, Paul Arthur *academic physician*
Volpe, Peter Anthony *surgeon*
Washington, A. Eugene *medical educator*
Way, E(dward) Leong *pharmacologist, toxicologist, educator*
Wayburn, Edgar *internist, environmentalist*
Wescott, William Burnham *oral maxillofacial pathologist, educator*
Wilson, Charles B. *neurosurgeon, educator*
Wintroub, Bruce Urich *dermatologist, educator, researcher*
Wolff, Sheldon *radiobiologist, educator*
Zippin, Calvin *epidemiologist, educator*

San Gabriel
Terry, Roger *pathologist, consultant*

San Jose
Avakoff, Joseph Carnegie *medical and legal consultant*
Gale, Arnold David *pediatric neurologist, consultant*
Kramer, Richard Jay *gastroenterologist*
Nguyen, Thinh Van *internist*
Weeker, Ellis *emergency physician*

San Juan Capistrano
Fisher, Delbert Arthur *physician, educator*

San Marino
Sadun, Alfredo Arrigo *neuro-ophthalmologist, scientist, educator*

San Mateo
Bell, Leo S. *retired physician*
Kidera, George Jerome *former physician*
Van Kirk, John Ellsworth *retired cardiologist*
Wong, Otto *epidemiologist*

San Pablo
Woodruff, Kay Herrin *pathologist, educator*

San Ramon
Litman, Robert Barry *physician, writer, television and radio commentator*

Santa Ana
Myers, Marilyn Gladys *pediatric hematologist and oncologist*

Santa Barbara
Bischel, Margaret DeMeritt *physician, managed care consultant*
Enelow, Allen Jay *psychiatrist, educator*
Fisher, Steven Kay *neurobiology educator*
Formby, Bent Clark *immunologist*
Klakeg, Clayton Harold *cardiologist*
Kohn, Roger Alan *surgeon*
Liebhaber, Myron I. *allergist*
Prager, Elliot David *surgeon, educator*
Shackman, Daniel Robert *psychiatrist*

Santa Cruz
Pletsch, Marie Eleanor *plastic surgeon*
Shorenstein, Rosalind Greenberg *internist*

Santa Monica
Carr, Ruth Margaret *plastic surgeon*
Hoefflin, Steven M. *plastic surgeon*
Katz, Roger *pediatrician, educator*
Kawamoto, Henry K. *plastic surgeon*
McGuire, Michael Francis *plastic and reconstructive surgeon*
Resnick, Jeffrey I. *plastic surgeon*
Schultz, Victor M. *physician*
Singer, Frederick Raphael *medical researcher, educator*
Solomon, David Harris *geriatrician, educator*
Wells, Kenneth B. *medical educator*
Wilfert, Catherine M. *medical association administrator, medical educator*

Santa Paula
Edwards, Samuel Roger *internist*

Santa Rosa
Bozdech, Marek Jiri *physician, educator*
Leuty, Gerald Johnston *osteopathic physician and surgeon*
Trucker, Albert *plastic surgeon*

Santee
Yang, Hsin-Ming *immunologist*

Sherman Oaks
King, Peter D. *psychiatrist, educator, real estate developer*
Zemplenyi, Tibor Karol *cardiologist, educator*

South San Francisco
Blethen, Sandra Lee *pediatric endocrinologist*
Curd, John Gary *physician, scientist*
Dixit, Vishva M. *pathology educator*

Spring Valley
Long, David Michael, Jr. *biomedical researcher, cardiothoracic surgeon*

Stanford
Abrams, Herbert LeRoy *radiologist, educator*
Bauer, Eugene Andrew *dermatologist, educator*
Baylor, Denis Aristide *neurobiology educator*
Blaschke, Terrence Francis *medicine and molecular pharmacology educator*
Blau, Helen Margaret *molecular pharmacology educator*
Brown, J. Martin *oncologist, educator*
Carlson, Robert Wells *physician, educator*
Chase, Robert Arthur *surgeon, educator*
Cohen, Harvey Joel *pediatric hematology and oncology educator*
Egbert, Peter Roy *ophthalmologist, educator*
Fee, Willard Edward, Jr. *otolaryngologist*
Friedman, Gary David *epidemiologist*
Garber, Alan Michael *physician, educator, economist*
Glazer, Gary Mark *radiology educator*
Goldstein, Avram *pharmacology educator*
Goodman, Stuart B. *medical educator*
Hlatky, Mark Andrew *cardiologist, medical researcher*
Jacobs, Charlotte De Croes *medical educator, oncologist*
Jardetzky, Oleg *medical educator, researcher*
Mansour, Tag Eldin *pharmacologist, educator*
Mark, James B. D. *surgeon, educator*
Marmor, Michael Franklin *ophthalmologist, educator*
McDevitt, Hugh O'Neill *immunologist, educator*
McDougall, Iain Ross *nuclear medicine educator*
Merigan, Thomas Charles, Jr. *internist, medical researcher, educator*
Paffenbarger, Ralph Seal, Jr. *epidemiologist, educator*
Payne, Anita Hart *reproductive endocrinologist, researcher*
Polan, Mary Lake *obstetrics and gynecology educator*
Powers, Rebecca Ann *psychiatrist, health facility administrator*
Raffin, Thomas A. *physician*
Reitz, Bruce Arnold *cardiac surgeon, educator*
Rosenberg, Saul Allen *oncologist, educator*
Rubenstein, Edward *physician, educator*
Schatzberg, Alan Frederic *psychiatrist, researcher*
Schendel, Stephen Alfred *plastic surgery educator, craniofacial surgeon*
Shumway, Norman Edward *surgeon, educator*
Stamey, Thomas Alexander *urologist, educator*
Weissman, Irving L. *medical scientist*

Sylmar
Corry, Dalila Boudjellal *internist*
Tully, Susan Balsley *pediatrician, educator*
Ziment, Irwin *medical educator*

Tehachapi
Badgley, Theodore McBride *psychiatrist, neurologist*

Templeton
Abernathy, Shields B. *allergist, immunologist, internist*
Carey, James C., Jr. *plastic surgeon*

Thousand Oaks
Walker, Lorenzo Giles *surgeon, educator*

Tiburon
Kilgore, Eugene Sterling, Jr. *former surgeon*

Torrance
Algra, Ronald James *dermatologist*
Brasel, Jo Anne *pediatrician, educator*
Emmanouilides, George Christos *physician, educator*
Mehringer, Charles Mark *medical educator, educator*
Miller, Milton Howard *psychiatrist*
Myhre, Byron Arnold *pathologist, educator*
Narasimhan, Padma Mandyam *physician*
Stabile, Bruce Edward *surgeon*
Swerdloff, Ronald S. *medical educator, researcher*
Tabrisky, Joseph *radiologist, educator*
Tanaka, Kouichi Robert *hematologist, educator*

Ukiah
McClintock, Richard Polson *dermatologist*

Ventura
Abul-Haj, Suleiman Kahil *pathologist*
Karlsberg, Paul *neurosurgeon*
Villaveces, James Walter *allergist, immunologist*

Visalia
Riegel, Byron William *ophthalmologist, educator*

Walnut Creek
Cannon, Grace Bert *immunologist*
Carson, Jay Wilmer *pathologist, educator*
Sheen, Portia Yunn-ling *retired physician*

Watsonville
Alfaro, Felix Benjamin *physician*

West Los Angeles
Wasterlain, Claude Guy *neurologist*

Westlake Vlg
Pakula, Anita Susan *dermatologist*

Whittier
Prickett, David Clinton *physician*

Woodside
Blum, Richard Hosmer Adams *educator, writer*

COLORADO

Aurora
Battaglia, Frederick Camillo *physician*
Grainger, John R. *medical association administrator*
Nora, Audrey Hart *physician*

Basalt
Weill, Hans *medical educator*

Canon City
Mohr, Gary Alan *physician*

Colorado Springs
Anderson, Paul Nathaniel *oncologist, educator*
Simerville, James Jasper *pediatrician*
Todd, Harold Wade *retired association executive, retired air force officer*

Denver
Accurso, Frank Joseph *physician, educator*
Bunn, Paul A., Jr. *oncologist, educator*
Churchill, Mair Elisa Annabelle *medical educator*
Clayton, Mack Louis *surgeon, educator*
Cochran, John Howard *plastic and reconstructive surgeon*
Deitrich, Richard Adam *pharmacology educator*
Eickhoff, Theodore Carl *epidemiologist*
Fennessey, Paul Vincent *pediatrics and pharmacology educator, research administrator*
Gabow, Patricia Anne *internist*
Gibbs, Ronald Steven *obstetrician/gynecologist*
Golitz, Loren Eugene *dermatologist, pathologist, clinical administrator, educator*
Green, Larry Alton *physician, educator*
Greyson, Clifford Russell *internist*
Harken, Alden Hood *thoracic surgeon*
Harris, Robert Adron *pharmacologist*
Hoehn, Robert J. *plastic surgeon, educator*
Huang, Linda Chen *plastic surgeon*
Imber, Richard Joseph *physician, dermatologist*
Jafek, Bruce William *otolaryngologist, educator*
Johnson, Candice Elaine Brown *pediatrics educator*
Johnston, Richard Boles, Jr. *pediatrician, educator, biomedical researcher*
Jones, M. Douglas, Jr. *pediatrics educator*
Kauvar, Abraham J. *gastroenterologist, medical administrator*
Krugman, Richard David *pediatrician, university administrator, educator*
Larsen, Gary Loy *physician, researcher*
Lubeck, Marvin Jay *ophthalmologist*
Markovchick, Vincent J. *surgeon*
Martin, Richard Jay *medical educator*
McAtee, Patricia Anne Rooney *medical educator*
Moore, Ernest Eugene, Jr. *surgeon, educator*
Moore, George Eugene *surgeon*
Novins, Douglas K. *psychiatrist, educator*
Nutting, Paul Albert *medical educator, medical science administrator*
Petty, Thomas Lee *physician, educator*
Pomerantz, Marvin *thoracic surgeon*
Rainer, William Gerald *cardiac surgeon*
Repine, John Edward *internist, educator*
Rosenwasser, Lanny Jeffrey *allergist, immunologist*
Schiff, Donald Wilfred *pediatrician, educator*
Schrier, Robert William *physician, educator*
Shore, James H(enry) *psychiatrist*
Sujansky, Eva Borska *pediatrician, geneticist, educator*
Szefler, Stanley James *pediatrics and pharmacology educator*
Weatherley-White, Roy Christopher Anthony *surgeon, consultant*
Weston, William Lee *dermatologist*
Wiggs, Eugene Overbey *ophthalmologist, educator*

Fort Collins
Gillette, Edward LeRoy *radiation oncology educator*
Reif, John Steven *epidemiologist, veterinarian*
Roehrig, John T. *immunologist, educator*

Golden
Johnson, Mark Bernarr *preventive medicine physician*

Grand Junction
Janson, Richard Anthony *plastic surgeon*

Greeley
Cook, Donald E. *pediatrician, educator*
Jaouen, Richard Matthie *plastic surgeon*

Lakewood
Karlin, Joel Marvin *allergist*

Pueblo
Mou, Thomas William *physician, medical educator and consultant*

Silverthorne
Rutherford, Robert Barry *vascular surgeon*

Vail
Bevan, William Arnold, Jr. *emergency physician*

Wheat Ridge
Fleischaker, Gordon Henry, Jr. *pediatrician*
Hashimoto, Christine L. *physician*

HAWAII

Honolulu
Chesne, Edward Leonard *physician*
Chock, Clifford Yet-Chong *family practice physician*
Curb, Jess David *medical educator*
Goldstein, Sir Norman *dermatologist*
Hammar, Sherrel Leyton *medical educator, dean*
Hay-Roe, Victor *plastic surgeon*
Ho, Reginald Chi Shing *medical educator*
Ishii, Clyde Hideo *plastic surgeon*
Kane, Thomas Jay, III *orthopaedic surgeon, educator*
Lau, H. Lorrin *obstetrician/gynecologist, inventor*
Lee, Yeu-Tsu Margaret *surgeon, educator*
McCarthy, Laurence James *physician, pathologist*
Oda, Yoshio *physician, internist*
Parsa, Fereydoun Don *plastic surgeon*
Schatz, Irwin Jacob *cardiologist, educator*
Sharma, Santosh Devraj *obstetrician/gynecologist, educator*
Wallach, Stephen Joseph *cardiologist*

Mililani
Gardner, Sheryl Paige *gynecologist*

Waikoloa
Copman, Louis *radiologist*

IDAHO

Coeur D Alene
Strimas, John Howard *allergist, immunologist, pediatrician*

MONTANA

Billings
Glenn, Guy Charles *pathologist*

Bozeman
Pardue, A. Michael *retired plastic and reconstructive surgeon*
Quinn, Mark T. *medical educator*

Helena
Reynolds, James Francis, Jr. *physician*
Strickler, Jeffrey Harold *pediatrician*

Whitefish
Miller, Ronald Alfred *family physician*

NEVADA

Las Vegas
Canada, William H. *plastic surgeon*
McAnelly, Robert D. *physiatrist*
Merkin, Albert Charles *pediatrician, allergist*
Miller, Robert Harold *otolaryngologist, educator*
Moritz, Timothy Bovie *psychiatrist*
Shires, George Thomas *surgeon, educator*
Trigiano, Lucien Lewis *physician*
Weiss, Robert Michael *dermatologist*

Reno
Small, Elisabeth Chan *psychiatrist, educator*

NEW HAMPSHIRE

Grantham
Figley, Melvin Morgan *radiologist, physician, educator*

NEW MEXICO

Alamogordo
Ashdown, Franklin Donald *physician, composer*

Albuquerque
Alfidi, Ralph Joseph *radiologist, educator*
Baack, Bret Rolyn *plastic surgeon*
Chang, Barbara Karen *medical educator*
Cobb, John Candler *medical educator*
Crawford, Michael Howard *cardiologist, educator, researcher*
Heffron, Warren A. *medical educator, physician*
Hudson, Patrick A. *plastic surgeon*
King, Lowell Restell *pediatric urologist*
Knospe, William Herbert *medical educator*
Mason, William vanHorn *dermatologist*
Napolitano, Leonard Michael *anatomist, university administrator*
Omer, George Elbert, Jr. *orthopaedic surgeon, educator*
Roth, Paul B. *emergency medicine physician*
Saland, Linda Carol *anatomy educator, neuroscience researcher*
Smith, Edgar Benton *dermatologist*
Stevenson, James Richard *radiologist, lawyer*
Twigg, Nancy L. *nursing association administrator*
Uhlenhuth, Eberhard Henry *psychiatrist, educator*
Waitzkin, Howard Bruce *internist, sociologist, educator*
Wimer, Mark G. *healthcare management company executive*
Winslow, Walter William *psychiatrist, educator*

Chama
Moser, Robert Harlan *physician, educator, writer*

Farmington
Neidhart, James Allen *oncologist, educator*

Las Cruces
Jacobs, Kent Frederick *dermatologist*

Los Alamos
Smith, Fredrica Emrich *rheumatologist, internist*

Portales
Goodwin, Martin Brune *radiologist*

Santa Fe
Williams, Ralph Chester, Jr. *physician, educator*

OREGON

Ashland
Kirschner, Richard Michael *naturopathic physician, speaker, writer*

Corvallis
Steele, Robert Edwin *orthopedic surgeon*

Eugene
Biglan, Anthony *medical educator*
Loescher, Richard Alvin *gastroenterologist*
Roe, Thomas Leroy Willis *pediatrician*

Klamath Falls
Bohnen, Robert Frank *hematologist, oncologist, educator*
Novak, James F. *physician*

Lake Oswego
Thong, Tran *biomedical company executive*

Medford
Burket, John McVey *dermatologist*
Shekhar, Stephen S. *obstetrician/gynecologist*

Portland
Baker, Diane R.H. *dermatologist*
Barry, John Maynard *urologist*
Bennett, William Michael *internist, nephrologist, educator*
Benson, John Alexander, Jr. *physician, educator*
Berthelsdorf, Siegfried *psychiatrist*
Bouchard, Joan C. *nursing association administrator*
Campbell, John Richard *pediatric surgeon*
Connor, William Elliott *physician, educator*
Fraunfelder, Frederick Theodore *ophthalmologist, educator*
Greer, Monte Arnold *endocrinologist, educator*
Hutchens, Tyra Thornton *physician, educator*
Jacob, Stanley Wallace *surgeon, educator*
Julien, Robert Michael *anesthesiologist, writer*
Kendall, John Walker, Jr. *medical educator, researcher, university dean*
Kohler, Peter Ogden *physician, educator, university president*
Layman, Charles Donald *plastic surgeon*
Mozena, John Daniel *podiatrist*
Palmer, Earl A. *ophthalmologist, educator*
Patterson, James Randolph *physician*
Prendergast, William John *ophthalmologist*
Robertson, Joseph E., Jr. *ophthalmologist, educator*
Schmidt, Waldemar Adrian *pathologist, educator*
Scott, John D. *pharmacologist*
Stevens, Wendell Claire *retired anesthesiology educator*
Swan, Kenneth Carl *surgeon*
Taylor, Robert Brown *medical educator*
Vernon, Jack Allen *otolaryngology educator, laboratory administrator*
Zerzan, Charles Joseph, Jr. *retired gastroenterologist*
Zimmerman, Gail Marie *medical foundation executive*

Silverton
Centerwall, Willard Raymond *pediatrician, educator*

UTAH

Mapleton
Hillyard, Ira William *pharmacologist, educator*

Provo
Latta, George Haworth, III *neonatologist*

Salt Lake City
Abildskov, J. A. *cardiologist, educator*
Adashi, Eli Y. *obstetrician, gynecologist*
Bauer, A(ugust) Robert, Jr. *surgeon, educator*
Brandon, Kathryn Elizabeth Beck *pediatrician*
Carey, John Clayton *pediatrician, medical geneticist*
Carroll, Karen Colleen *physician, infectious disease educator, medical microbiologist*
Davis, Roy Kim *otolaryngologist, health facility administrator*
Dolcourt, John (Jack) Lawrence *pediatrician*
Fujinami, Robert Shin *neurology educator*
Goldstein, Michael L. *neurologist*
Grosser, Bernard Irving *psychiatry educator*
Lloyd, Ray Dix *health physicist*
Lyon, Joseph Lynn *physician, medical educator*
Moser, Royce, Jr. *physician, medical educator*
Nelson, John C. *obstetrician/gynecologist*
Nelson, Russell Marion *surgeon, educator*
Odell, William Douglas *endocrinologist, educator*
Petersen, Finn Bo *oncologist, educator*
Renzetti, Attilio David, Jr. *physician*
Stanford, Joseph Barney *medical educator, physician*
Thomas, David Snow *plastic surgeon*
Ward, John Robert *physician, educator*

WASHINGTON

Auburn
Sata, Lindbergh Saburo *psychiatrist, educator*

Bellevue
Phillips, Zaiga Alksnis *pediatrician*

Bellingham
Howe, Warren Billings *physician*
James, Helen Ann *plastic surgeon*
Wayne, Marvin Alan *emergency medicine physician*

Centralia
Miller, James McCalmont *pediatrician*

Clarkston
Chinchinian, Harry *pathologist, educator*

Clyde Hill
Condon, Robert Edward *surgeon, educator, consultant*

Everett
Valentine, Mark Conrad *dermatologist*

Issaquah
Barchet, Stephen *physician, former naval officer*

Kent
O'Bara, Kenneth J. *physician*

Kirkland
Barto, Deborah Ann *physician*
Dundas, Dennis Franklin *plastic surgeon*

Mazama
Hogness, John Rusten *physician, academic administrator*

Mercer Island
Coe, Robert Campbell *retired surgeon*

Olympia
Smith, Sherwood Paul *plastic surgeon*

Richland
Bair, William J. *radiation biologist*
Zirkle, Lewis Greer *orthopedist*

Seattle
Andrews, Robert Goff *pediatrician, medical educator*
Ansell, Julian S. *physician, retired urology educator*
Bornstein, Paul *physician, biochemist*
Bowden, Douglas McHose *neuropsychiatric scientist, educator, research center administrator*
Catterall, William A. *pharmacology, neurobiology educator*
Chatard, Peter Ralph Noel, Jr. *aesthetic plastic surgeon*
Clarren, Sterling Keith *pediatrician*
Clowes, Alexander Whitehill *surgeon, educator*
Couser, William Griffith *medical educator, academic administrator, nephrologist*
Cullen, Bruce F. *anesthesiologist*
Dale, David C. *physician, medical educator*
Dawson, Patricia Lucille *surgeon*
Dunner, David Louis *medical educator*
Eschbach, Joseph Wetherill *nephrology educator*
Eyre, David R. *orthopedics educator*
Fine, James Stephen *physician*
Fisher, Nancy Louise *pediatrician, medical geneticist, former nurse*
Gabbe, Steven Glenn *obstetrician/gynecologist, educator*
Geyman, John Payne *physician, educator*
Giblett, Eloise Rosalie *hematology educator*
Grayston, J. Thomas *medical and public health educator*
Guntheroth, Warren Gaden *pediatrician, educator*
Guralnick, Michael J. *medical research administrator*
Hazzard, William Russell *geriatrician, educator*
Holm, Vanja Adele *developmental pediatrician, educator*
Holmes, King Kennard *medical educator*
Hornbein, Thomas Frederic *anesthesiologist*
Hudson, Leonard Dean *physician*
Jonsen, Albert R(upert) *retired medical ethics educator*
Kahn, Steven Emanuel *medical educator*
Kalina, Robert Edward *opthalmologist, educator*
Klebanoff, Seymour Joseph *medical educator*
Larrabee, Wayne Fox, Jr. *plastic surgeon*
Maier, Ronald Vitt *surgeon*
Mankoff, David Abraham *nuclear medicine physician*
Martin, George M. *pathologist, gerontologist, educator*
Matsen, Frederick Albert, III *orthopedic educator*
Mayhew, Eric George *medical researcher, educator*
Merendino, K. Alvin *surgical educator*
Moore, Daniel Charles *internist*
Nelson, James Alonzo *radiologist, educator*
Ostrow, Jay Donald *gastroenterology educator, researcher*
Palmer, Jerry Philip *medical educator, researcher, internist*
Petersdorf, Robert George *physician, medical educator, academic administrator*
Phillips, William Robert *physician*
Ramsey, Paul Glenn *internist, dean*
Ravenholt, Reimert Thorolf *epidemiologist, researcher*
Risse, Guenter Bernhard *physician, historian, educator*
Ritchie, James L. *cardiologist*
Rivara, Frederick Peter *pediatrician, educator*
Rosenblatt, Roger Alan *physician, educator*
Shepard, Thomas Hill *physician, educator*
Simkin, Peter Anthony *internist, educator*
Stanford, Janet Lee *physician, epidemiologist*
Stenchever, Morton Albert *obstetrician/gynecologist, educator*
Stolov, Walter Charles *physician, rehabilitation educator, physiatrist*
Strandjord, Paul Edphil *physician, educator*
Strandness, Donald Eugene, Jr. *surgeon*
Su, Judy Ya Hwa Lin *pharmacologist*
Swanson, Phillip Dean *neurologist*
Tapper, David *pediatric surgeon*
Thomas, Edward Donnall *physician, researcher*
Todaro, George Joseph *pathologist, researcher*
Tucker, Gary Jay *physician, educator*
Weiss, Noel S. *epidemiologist*
Welk, Richard Andrew *plastic surgeon*
Winn, H. Richard *surgeon*
Yue, Agnes Kau-Wah *otolaryngologist*

Spokane
Bakker, Cornelis B. *psychiatrist, educator*
Cohen, Arnold Norman *gastroenterologist*
Lee, Hi Young *physician, acupuncturist*
Mielke, Clarence Harold, Jr. *hematologist*

Tacoma
Irish, Thomas Judson *plastic surgeon*
Verhey, Joseph William *psychiatrist, educator*
Wagonfeld, James B. *gastroenterologist*

Tracyton
Pliskow, Vita Sari *anesthesiologist*

University Place
Flemming, Stanley Lalit Kumar *family practice physician, mayor, state legislator*

Wenatchee
Gotthold, William Eugene *emergency physician*

WYOMING

Buffalo
Fehir, Kim Michele *oncologist, hematologist*

Casper
Bennion, Scott Desmond *physician*

Cheyenne
Flick, William Fredrick *surgeon*

Laramie
Kelley, Robert Otis *medical science educator*

CANADA

ALBERTA

Calgary
Lederis, Karolis Paul (Karl Lederis) *pharmacologist, educator, researcher*
Melvill-Jones, Geoffrey *internist, educator*
Smith, Eldon *cardiologist, physiology and biophysics educator*
ter Keurs, Henk E. D. J. *cardiologist, educator*

Edmonton
Cook, David Alastair *pharmacology educator*
Miller, Jack David R. *radiologist, physician, educator*

BRITISH COLUMBIA

Vancouver
Baird, Patricia Ann *physician, educator*
Chow, Anthony Wei-Chik *physician*
Doyle, Patrick John *otolaryngologist, department chairman*
Eaves, Allen Charles Edward *hematologist, medical agency administrator*
Friedman, Sydney M. *anatomy educator, medical researcher*
Hardwick, David Francis *pathologist, department chairman*
Knobloch, Ferdinand J. *psychiatrist, educator*
Levy, Julia *immunology educator, researcher*
McGeer, Edith Graef *neurological science educator*
Mizgala, Henry F. *physician, consultant, retired medical educator*
Rootman, Jack *ophthalmologist, surgeon, pathologist, oncologist, artist*
Roy, Chunilal *psychiatrist*
Slonecker, Charles Edward *anatomist, medical educator, writer*
Sutter, Morley Carman *medical scientist*
Tingle, Aubrey James *pediatric immunologist, research administrator*

Victoria
Mac Diarmid, William Donald *physician*

ADDRESS UNPUBLISHED

Aldrich, Franklin Dalton *research physician*
Altman, Adele Rosenhain *radiologist*
Appenzeller, Otto *neurologist, researcher*
Arenberg, Irving Kaufman Karchmer *surgeon, educator, entrepeneur*
Barbo, Dorothy Marie *obstetrician/gynecologist, educator*
Barricks, Michael Eli *retinal surgeon*
Benfield, John Richard *surgeon, educator*
Berg, Alfred Oren *epidemiology and family practice medicine educator*
Boddie, Lewis Franklin *obstetrics and gynecology educator*
Bonn, Ethel May *psychiatrist, educator*
Brown, James W. *gastroenterologist*
Buist, Neil Robertson MacKenzie *medical educator, medical administrator*
Carrison, Dale Mitchell *emergency medicine physician*
Chiu, Dorothy *retired pediatrician*
Cleaver, James Edward *radiologist, educator*
Clement, Douglas Bruce *medical educator*
Cline, Carolyn Joan *plastic and reconstructive surgeon*
Cooper, Allen David *medical researcher, educator*
Coppolillo, Henry Peter *psychiatrist*
Cozen, Lewis *orthopedic surgeon*
Date, Elaine Satomi *physiatrist, educator*
Davidson, Mayer B. *medical educator, researcher*
Day, Robert Winsor *preventive medicine physician, researcher*
DePalma, Ralph George *surgeon, educator*
Drake, Michael V. *ophthalmologist, educator, dean*
Dziewanowska, Zofia Elizabeth *neuropsychiatrist, pharmaceutical executive, researcher, educator*
Edwards, Bruce George *retired ophthalmologist, naval officer*
Erich, Louis Richard *physician*
Giem, Ross Nye, Jr. *surgeon*
Glaser, Robert Joy *retired physician, foundation executive*
Goldberg, Mark Arthur *neurologist*
Gross, Ruth Taubenhaus *former pediatrician*
Heiner, Douglas Cragun *pediatrician, educator, immunologist, allergist*
Hood, William Boyd, Jr. *cardiologist, educator*
Jarvik, Gail Pairitz *medical geneticist*
Kraft, George Howard *physician, educator*
Leighninger, David Scott *cardiovascular surgeon*
Mala, Theodore Anthony *physician, consultant*
Mathews, William Edward *neurological surgeon, educator*
Metzner, Richard Joel *psychiatrist, psychopharmacologist, educator*
Millikan, Clark Harold *physician*
Morgan, Stanley Charles *plastic and reconstructive surgeon*
Motto, Jerome Arthur *psychiatry educator*
Mountain, Clifton Fletcher *surgeon, educator*
Nelson, William Rankin *surgeon, educator*
Nora, James Jackson *physician, writer, educator*
Prusiner, Stanley Ben *neurology and biochemistry educator, researcher*
Ranney, Helen Margaret *physician, educator*
Rebhun, Joseph *allergist, immunologist, medical educator*
Renson, Jean Felix *retired psychiatry educator*
Rewcastle, Neill Barry *neuropathology educator*
Riker, William Kay *pharmacologist, educator*
Rippen, Helga Edith *pharmaceutical company administrator*
Roberts, Alan Silverman *orthopedic surgeon*
Ross, Russell *pathologist, educator*
Schauf, Victoria *pediatrician, educator, infectious diseases consultant*
Schneider, Calvin *physician*
Sewell, Robert Dalton *pediatrician*
Sher, Paul Phillip *pathologist*
Silverstein, Martin Elliot *surgeon, consultant, writer*
Simmons, Geoffrey Stuart *physician*
Stringham, Renée *physician*
Williams, Roger Stewart *neurologist*
Yarington, Charles Thomas, Jr. *surgeon, administrator*
Youmans, Julian Ray *neurosurgeon, educator*
Zawacki, Bruce Edwin *surgeon, educator, ethicist*
Zumwalt, Ross Eugene *forensic pathologist, educator*

HUMANITIES: LIBERAL STUDIES

UNITED STATES

ALASKA

Anchorage
Crawford, Ronald Merritt *history and geography educator*

Fairbanks
Krauss, Michael Edward *linguist*

ARIZONA

Flagstaff
Marcus, Karen Melissa *foreign language educator*

Green Valley
Dmytryshyn, Basil *historian, educator*

Lake Havasu City
Brydon, Ruth Vickery *history educator*

Phoenix
Cristiano, Marilyn Jean *speech communication educator*
Land, George A. *philosopher, writer, educator, consultant*
Maimon, Elaine Plaskow *English educator, university provost*

Scottsdale
Donaldson, Scott *English language educator, writer*

Tempe
Adelson, Roger Dean *history educator, editor, historian*
Iverson, Peter James *historian, educator*
MacKinnon, Stephen R. *Asian studies administrator, educator*
Ruiz, Vicki Lynn *history educator*

Tucson
Birkinbine, John, II *philatelist*
Dinnerstein, Leonard *historian, educator*
Furlow, Mary Beverley *English language educator*
Kleese, William Carl *genealogy research consultant, financial services representative*
Langendoen, Donald Terence *linguistics educator*
Schulz, Renate Adele *German studies and second language acquisition educator*
Tao, Chia-lin Pao *humanities educator*
Zepeda, Ofelia *linguist, educator*

CALIFORNIA

Atherton
Bales, Royal Eugene *philosophy educator*

Bakersfield
Kegley, Jacquelyn Ann *philosophy educator*

Berkeley
Alter, Robert Bernard *comparative literature educator, critic*
Anderson, William Scovil *classics educator*
Bronstein, Arthur J. *linguistics educator*
Christ, Carol Tecla *English educator, former academic administrator*
Costa, Gustavo *Italian studies educator*
Crews, Frederick Campbell *humanities educator, writer*
Davidson, Donald Herbert *philosophy educator*
Herr, Richard *history educator*
Karlinsky, Simon *language educator, writer*
Kay, Paul de Young *linguist*
Kerman, Joseph Wilfred *musicologist, critic*
Litwack, Leon Frank *historian, educator*
Long, Anthony Arthur *classics educator*
Middlekauff, Robert Lawrence *history educator, administrator*

Nagler, Michael Nicholas *classics and comparative literature educator*
Rauch, Irmengard *linguist, educator*
Selz, Peter Howard *art historian, educator*
Shannon, Thomas Frederic *German language educator*
Sloane, Thomas O. *speech educator*
Tracy, Robert (Edward) *English language educator, poetry translator*
Wakeman, Frederic Evans , Jr. *historian, educator*
Wang, William Shi-Yuan *linguistics educator*
Zwerdling, Alex *English educator*

Carmel
Chung, Kyung Cho *Korean specialist, educator, writer*

Chico
Moore, Brooke Noel *philosophy educator*

Claremont
Atlas, Jay David *philosopher, consultant, linguist*
Burns, Richard Dean *history educator, publisher, writer*
Davis, Nathaniel *humanities educator*
Elsbree, Langdon *English language educator*
Kucheman, Clark Arthur *philosophy and religious studies educator*
Lofgren, Charles Augustin *legal and constitutional historian, history educator*
Macaulay, Ronald Kerr Steven *linguistics educator, former college dean*
McKirahan, Richard Duncan *classics and philosophy educator*
Moss, Myra Ellen (Myra Moss Rolle) *philosophy educator*
Pinney, Thomas Clive *retired English language educator*
Roth, John King *philosopher, educator*
Sontag, Frederick Earl *philosophy educator*
Young, Howard Thomas *foreign language educator*

Davis
Hayden, John Olin *English literature educator, writer*
Hoffman, Michael Jerome *humanities educator, educator*
Waddington, Raymond Bruce, Jr. *English language educator*
Williamson, Alan Bacher *English literature educator, poet, writer*
Willis, Frank Roy *history educator*

El Cerrito
Kuo, Ping-chia *historian, educator*

Fresno
Clifton, Michael Edward *English language educator*
Genini, Ronald Walter *history educator, historian*

Glendale
de Grassi, Leonard *art historian, educator*

Irvine
Boyd, Carolyn Patricia *history educator*
Clark, Michael Phillip *English educator*
Key, Mary Ritchie (Mrs. Audley E. Patton) *linguist, writer, educator*
Kluger, Ruth *German language educator, editor*
Lillyman, William John *German language educator, academic administrator*
Mc Culloch, Samuel Clyde *history educator*
Sutton, Dana Ferrin *classics educator*
Wiener, Jon *history educator*

La Jolla
Bernstein, Michael Alan *history educator*
Langacker, Ronald Wayne *linguistics educator*
McDonald, Marianne *classicist*
Newmark, Leonard Daniel *linguistics educator*
Olafson, Frederick Arlan *philosophy educator*
Oreskes, Naomi *science historian*
Wesling, Donald Truman *English literature educator*
Wright, Andrew *English literature educator*

Long Beach
Lunderville, Gerald Paul *bilingual ESL/social studies educator*
Nguyen, Huong Tran *English language professional, federal agency official*

Los Angeles
Alkon, Paul Kent *English language educator*
Allen, Michael John Bridgman *English educator*
Alpers, Edward Alter *history educator*
Appleby, Joyce Oldham *historian, educator*
Bahr, Ehrhard *Germanic languages and literature educator*
Bauml, Franz Heinrich *German language educator*
Boime, Albert Isaac *art history educator*
Bradshaw, Murray Charles *musicologist, educator*
Cohen, S(tephen) Marshall *philosophy educator*
Davidson, Herbert Alan *Near Eastern languages and cultures educator*
Dumitrescu, Domnita *Spanish language educator, researcher*
Dyck, Andrew Roy *philologist, educator*
Fry, Michael Graham *historian, educator*
Hadda, Janet Ruth *Yiddish language educator, lay psychoanalyst*
Hovannisian, Richard G. *Armenian and Near East history educator*
Hundley, Norris Cecil, Jr. *history educator*
Kelly, Henry Ansgar *English language educator*
Kolve, V. A. *English literature educator*
Laird, David *humanities educator emeritus*
Levine, Philip *classics educator*
Löfstedt, Bengt Torkel Magnus *classics educator*
Mellor, Ronald John *history educator*
Miles, Richard Robert *art historian, writer*
Nakanishi, Don Toshiaki *Asian American studies educator, writer*
Ochs, Elinor *linguistics educator*
Rathbun, John Wilbert *American studies educator*
Rogger, Hans Jack *history educator*
Rouse, Richard Hunter *historian, educator*
Schaefer, William David *English language educator*
Schutz, John Adolph *historian, educator, former university dean*
Schwartz, Leon *foreign language educator*
See, Carolyn *English language educator, novelist, book critic*
Shideler, Ross Patrick *foreign language and comparative literature educator, writer, translator, poet*
Stockwell, Robert Paul *linguist, educator*
Toulmin, Stephen Edelston *humanities educator, educator*
Troy, Nancy J. *art history educator*
Weber, Eugen *historian, educator, writer*
Wills, John Elliot, Jr. *history educator, writer*
Wortham, Thomas Richard *English language educator*

Merced
Elliott, Gordon Jefferson *retired English language educator*

Northridge
Chen, Joseph Tao *historian, educator*

Palo Alto
Eitner, Lorenz Edwin Alfred *art historian, educator*

Pasadena
Elliot, David Clephan *historian, educator*
Kousser, J(oseph) Morgan *history educator*
Mandel, Oscar *literature educator, writer*

Riverside
Elliott, Emory Bernard *English language educator, educational administrator*
Fagundo, Ana Maria *creative writing and Spanish literature educator*
Ross, Delmer Gerrard *historian, educator*
Snyder, Henry Leonard *history educator, bibliographer*

Sacramento
Carr, Gerald Francis *German educator*
Meindl, Robert James *English language educator*

San Diego
Alcosser, Sandra Beth *English language educator, writer*
González-Trujillo, César Augusto *Chicano studies educator, writer*
Peterson, Richard Hermann *history educator, retired*

San Francisco
Cherny, Robert Wallace *history educator*
Needleman, Jacob *philosophy educator, writer*
Papakonstantino, Stacy *English language educator*

San Marcos
Christman, Albert Bernard *historian*
Tanner, John Douglas, Jr. *history educator, writer*

San Marino
Karlstrom, Paul Johnson *art historian*
Ridge, Martin *historian, educator*
Rolle, Andrew F. *historian, writer*
Steadman, John Marcellus, III *English educator*
Zall, Paul Maxwell *retired English language educator, consultant*

Santa Barbara
Brownlee, Wilson Elliot, Jr. *history educator*
Chafe, Wallace LeSeur *linguist, educator*
Collins, Robert Oakley *history educator*
Crawford, Donald Wesley *philosophy educator, university official*
Fingarette, Herbert *philosopher, educator*
Fleming, Brice Noel *retired philosophy educator*
Gunn, Giles Buckingham *English educator, religion educator*
Helgerson, Richard *English literature educator*
Hsu, Immanuel Chung Yueh *history educator*
McGee, James Sears *historian, educator*
Renehan, Robert Francis Xavier *Greek and Latin educator*
Rose, Mark Allen *humanities educator, educator*
Russell, Jeffrey Burton *historian, educator*
Wilkins, Burleigh Taylor *philosophy educator*
Zimmerman, Everett Lee *English educator, academic administrator*

Santa Clara
Meier, Matthias S(ebastian) *historian*

Santa Cruz
Lieberman, Fredric *ethnomusicologist, educator*
Stevens, Stanley David *local history researcher, retired librarian*
Suckiel, Ellen Kappy *philosophy educator*

Stanford
Baker, Keith Michael *history educator*
Carnochan, Walter Bliss *retired humanities educator*
Dekker, George Gilbert *literature educator, literary scholar, writer*
Dunlop, John Barrett *foreign language educator, research institution scholar*
Duus, Peter *history educator*
Fredrickson, George Marsh *history educator*
Gelpi, Albert Joseph *English educator, literary critic*
Giraud, Raymond Dorner *retired language professional*
Kennedy, David Michael *historian, educator*
Loftis, John (Clyde), Jr. *English language educator*
Lohnes, Walter F. W. *German language and literature educator*
Middlebrook, Diane Wood *English language educator*
Moravcsik, Julius Matthew *philosophy educator*
Newman-Gordon, Pauline *French language and literature educator*
Perloff, Marjorie Gabrielle *English and comparative literature educator*
Perry, John Richard *philosophy educator*
Robinson, Paul Arnold *historian, educator, writer*
Sheehan, James John *historian, educator*
Simons, Thomas W., Jr. *history educator*
Sorrentino, Gilbert *English language educator, novelist, poet*
Stansky, Peter David Lyman *historian*
Traugott, Elizabeth Closs *linguistics educator, researcher*

Stockton
Limbaugh, Ronald Hadley *retired history educator, history center director*

Torrance
Anderson, Marilyn Wheeler *English language educator*

COLORADO

Boulder
Frey, Julia Bloch *French language educator, art historian educator*
Hill, Boyd H., Jr. *medieval history educator*
Limerick, Patricia Nelson *history educator*
Main, Jackson Turner *history educator*
Rood, David S. *linguistics educator*
Taylor, Allan Ross *linguist, educator*

Colorado Springs
Cramer, Owen Carver *classics educator*
Hallenbeck, Kenneth Luster *numismatist*
Stavig, Mark Luther *English language educator*

Denver
Wetzel, Jodi (Joy Lynn Wetzel) *history and women's studies educator*

Fort Collins
Tremblay, William Andrew *English language educator*

Glenwood Springs
Walker, Robert Harris *historian, writer, editor*

Golden
Sneed, Joseph Donald *philosophy educator, writer*

Grand Junction
Fay, Abbott Eastman *history educator*

Greeley
Worley, Lloyd Douglas *English language educator*

Pueblo
Farwell, Hermon Waldo, Jr. *parliamentarian, educator, former speech communication educator*

HAWAII

Honolulu
Aung-Thwin, Michael Arthur *history educator*
Bender, Byron Wilbur *linguistics educator*
Dyen, Isidore *linguistic scientist, educator*
Hoffmann, Kathryn Ann *humanities educator*
Peterson, Barbara Ann Bennett *history educator, television personality*
Rapson, Richard L. *history educator*
Varley, Herbert Paul *Japanese language and cultural history educator*

IDAHO

Moscow
Harris, Robert Dalton *history educator, researcher, writer*

MONTANA

Missoula
Kittredge, William Alfred *humanities educator*

NEVADA

Las Vegas
Adams, Charles Lynford *English language educator*

NEW MEXICO

Albuquerque
Hutton, Paul Andrew *history educator, writer*
Peña, Juan José *interpreter*

Santa Fe
Maehl, William Henry *historian, university administrator, educational consultant*

OREGON

Eugene
Pascal, C(ecil) Bennett *classics educator*
Wickes, George *English literature educator, writer*

Port Orford
Drinnon, Richard *retired history educator*

Portland
Orloff, Chet *historian*
Steinman, Lisa Malinowski *English literature educator, writer*

TEXAS

Kingwood
Johnson, John J. *historian, educator*

UTAH

Logan
Milner, Clyde A., II *historian*

Paradise
Bremer, Ronald Allan *genealogist, editor*

Provo
Forster, Merlin Henry *foreign languages educator, writer, researcher*
Lyon, James Karl *German language educator*

Salt Lake City
Sillars, Malcolm Osgood *communication educator*

WASHINGTON

Bellingham
Whisenhunt, Donald Wayne *history educator*

Seattle
Adams, Hazard Simeon *English educator, writer*
Bozarth, George S. *historian, musicologist, pianist*
Burgess, Charles Orville *history educator*
Butow, Robert Joseph Charles *history educator*
Coburn, Robert Craig *philosopher, educator*
Coldewey, John Christopher *English literature educator*
Ellison, Herbert Jay *history educator*
Gerstenberger, Donna Lorine *humanities educator*
Harmon, Daniel Patrick *classics educator*
Heer, Nicholas Lawson *Arabist and Islamist educator*
Jones, Edward Louis *historian, educator*
Keyt, David *philosophy and classics educator*
Korg, Jacob *English literature educator*
Newmeyer, Frederick Jaret *linguist, educator*
Pressly, Thomas James *history educator*
Pyle, Kenneth Birger *historian, educator*
Webb, Eugene *English language educator*
Ziadeh, Farhat J. *Middle Eastern studies educator*

Spokane
Carriker, Robert Charles *history educator*
Kossel, Clifford George *retired philosophy educator, clergyman*

Walla Walla
Edwards, Glenn Thomas *history educator*

WYOMING

Cody
Garry, James B. *historian, naturalist, storyteller, writer*
Price, B. Byron *historian*

Laramie
Chisum, Emmett Dewain *historian, archeologist, researcher*
Hardy, Deborah Welles *history educator*
Nye, Eric William *English language and literature educator*

Sheridan
Goodwin, Doris Helen Kearns *history educator, writer*

CANADA

ALBERTA

Edmonton
McMaster, Juliet Sylvia *English language educator*

BRITISH COLUMBIA

Burnaby
Buitenhuis, Peter Martinus *language professional, educator*
Kitchen, John Martin *historian, educator*

Vancouver
Batts, Michael Stanley *German language educator*
Bentley, Thomas Roy *English language educator, writer, consultant*
Conway, John S. *history educator*
Overmyer, Daniel Lee *Asian studies educator*
Pacheco-Ransanz, Arsenio *Hispanic and Italian studies educator*
Saint-Jacques, Bernard *linguistics educator*
Unger, Richard Watson *history educator*

ADDRESS UNPUBLISHED

Attebery, Louie Wayne *English language educator, folklorist*
Bosmajian, Haig Aram *speech communication educator*
Bush, Sarah Lillian *historian*
Chaffee, Steven *communication educator*
Dunbar, Maurice Victor *English language educator*
Ellis, John Martin *German literature educator*
Ghymn, Esther Mikyung *English educator, writer*
Gilb, Corinne Lathrop *history educator*
Gillespie, Gerald Ernest Paul *comparative literature educator, writer*

Nix, Nancy Jean *librarian, designer*
Riasanovsky, Nicholas Valentine *historian, educator*
Vaz, Katherine Anne *English language educator, writer*

HUMANITIES: LIBRARIES

UNITED STATES

ALASKA

Anchorage
Rollins, Alden Milton *documents librarian*

Juneau
Crane, Karen R. *library director*
Schorr, Alan Edward *librarian, publisher*

ARIZONA

Scottsdale
Dalton, Phyllis Irene *library consultant*

Tucson
Griffen, Agnes Marthe *library administrator*
Laird, Wilbur David, Jr. *bookseller, editor*
Wolfe, William Jerome *librarian, English language educator*

CALIFORNIA

Anaheim
Miller, Jean Ruth *retired librarian*

Bakersfield
Duquette, Diane Rhea *library director*

Berkeley
Buckland, Michael Keeble *librarian, educator*
Danton, Joseph Periam *librarian, educator*
Harlan, Robert Dale *information studies educator, academic administrator*
Minudri, Regina Ursula *librarian, consultant*

Carlsbad
Lange, Clifford E. *librarian*

Chico
Moore, Everett LeRoy *library administrator*

Cupertino
Fletcher, Homer Lee *librarian*

Davis
Grossman, George Stefan *library director, law eductor*
Sharrow, Marilyn Jane *library administrator*

Fremont
Wood, Linda May *librarian*

Fresno
Gorman, Michael Joseph *library director, educator*
Kallenberg, John Kenneth *librarian*

Fullerton
Ayala, John *librarian, dean*

Huntington Beach
Hayden, Ron L. *library director*

La Jolla
Mirsky, Phyllis Simon *librarian*

La Mesa
Freeland, Robert Frederick *retired librarian*

Livermore
Love, Sandra Rae *information specialist*

Los Angeles
Bates, Marcia Jeanne *information scientist educator*
Brecht, Albert Odell *library and information technology administrator*
Chang, Henry Chung-Lien *library administrator*
Ciccone, Amy Navratil *art librarian*
Cuadra, Carlos Albert *information scientist, management executive*
Gilman, Nelson Jay *library director*
Helgeson, Duane Marcellus *retired librarian*
Kent, Susan *library director, consultant*
Patron, Susan Hall *librarian, writer*
Richardson, John Vinson, Jr. *library and information science educator*
Steele, Victoria Lee *librarian*
Sutherland, Michael Cruise *librarian*
Werner, Gloria S. *librarian*

Mission Hills
Weber, Francis Joseph *archivist, museum director*

Modesto
Kreissman, Starrett *librarian*

Monterey
Reneker, Maxine Hohman *librarian*

Mountain View
Michalko, James Paul *library association administrator*

Napa
Glaser, Edwin Victor *rare book dealer*

Newport Beach
Kienitz, LaDonna Trapp *librarian, city official*

North Hollywood
Schlosser, Anne Griffin *librarian*

Oakland
Hafter, Ruth Anne *library director, educator*
Woodbury, Marda Liggett *librarian, writer*

Pasadena
Buck, Anne Marie *library director, consultant*

Pollock Pines
Rickard, Margaret Lynn *library and grants consultant, former library director*

Redlands
Burgess, Larry Eugene *library director, history educator*
Musmann, Klaus *librarian*

Riverside
Auth, Judith *library director*

Sacramento
Gray, Walter P., III *archivist, consultant*
Killian, Richard M. *library director*
Starr, Kevin *librarian, educator*

San Bernardino
Burgess, Michael *library science educator, publisher*

San Diego
Sannwald, William Walter *librarian*

San Francisco
Cline, Fred Albert, Jr. *retired librarian, conservationist*

San Jose
Light, Jane Ellen *librarian*
Schmidt, Cyril James *librarian*
Woolls, Esther Blanche *library science educator*

San Marcos
Ciurczak, Alexis *librarian*

San Marino
Robertson, Mary Louise *archivist, historian*

Santa Ana
Adams, John M. *library director*
Richard, Robert John *library director*

Santa Barbara
Keator, Carol Lynne *library director*

Santa Clara
Hopkinson, Shirley Lois *library and information science educator*

Santa Clarita
Gardner, Frederick Boyce *library director*

Santa Cruz
Dyson, Allan Judge *librarian*

Santa Monica
Levin, Barry Raymond *rare book dealer*

Santa Rosa
Pearson, Roger Lee *library director*

Sebastopol
Sabsay, David *library consultant*

Stanford
Derksen, Charlotte Ruth Meynink *librarian*
Gold, Anne Marie *library director*
Keller, Michael Alan *librarian, educator, musicologist*

Stockton
Foster, Colleen *library director*

Thousand Oaks
Brogden, Stephen Richard *library administrator*

Torrance
Buckley, James W. *librarian*

Westminster
Gylseth, Doris (Lillian) Hanson *retired librarian*

Yorba Linda
Naulty, Susan Louise *archivist*

COLORADO

Aurora
Miller, Sarah Pearl *librarian*

Boulder
Gralapp, Marcelee Gayl *librarian*
O'Brien, Elmer John *librarian, educator*

Canon City
Cochran, Susan Mills *librarian*

Denver
Ashton, Rick James *librarian*
Garcia, June Marie *librarian*

Edwards
Chambers, Joan Louise *retired librarian, retired university educator and dean*

Englewood
Wynar, Bohdan Stephen *librarian, writer, editor*

Golden
Mathews, Anne Jones *library educator and administrator, consultant*

Lakewood
Knott, William Alan *library director, manager and building consultant*

HAWAII

Honolulu
Flynn, Joan Mayhew *librarian*
Spencer, Caroline *library director*

IDAHO

Boise
Bolles, Charles Avery *librarian*

Moscow
Force, Ronald Wayne *librarian*

MONTANA

Billings
Cochran, William Michael *librarian*

Helena
Fitzpatrick, Lois Ann *library administrator*
Schlesinger, Deborah Lee *librarian*

NEVADA

Carson City
Rocha, Guy Louis *archivist, historian*

Las Vegas
Hunsberger, Charles Wesley *library director*

NEW MEXICO

Albuquerque
Freeman, Patricia Elizabeth *library and education specialist*
Snell, Patricia Poldervaart *librarian, consultant*

Carlsbad
Regan, Muriel *librarian*

Santa Fe
Myers, R. David *library director, dean*

OREGON

Ashland
Gaulke, Mary Florence *library administrator*

Corvallis
Landers, Teresa Price *librarian*

Eugene
Edwards, Ralph M. *librarian*
Hildebrand, Carol Ilene *librarian*

Klamath Falls
Leonhardt, Thomas Wilburn *librarian, library director*

Portland
Cooper, Ginnie *library director*
Eshelman, William Robert *librarian, editor*
Morgan, James Earl *librarian, administrator*

Salem
Kenyon, Carleton Weller *librarian*
Oberg, Larry Reynold *librarian*
Turnbaugh, Roy Carroll *archivist*

UTAH

Logan
Anderson, Janet Alm *librarian*

Orem
Hall, Blaine Hill *retired librarian*

Provo
Jensen, Richard Dennis *librarian*

Salt Lake City
Buttars, Gerald Anderson *librarian*
Morrison, David Lee *librarian, educator*

WASHINGTON

Olympia
Zussy, Nancy Louise *librarian*

Port Townsend
Hiatt, Peter *retired librarian studies educator*

Seattle
Blase, Nancy Gross *librarian*
Boylan, Merle Nelson *librarian, educator*
Fidel, Raya *library science educator*
Stroup, Elizabeth Faye *librarian*

Spokane
Burr, Robert Lyndon *information services specialist*
George, Aubrey Westmoreland *library director*
Wirt, Michael James *library director*

Tacoma
Crisman, Mary Frances Borden *librarian*

Walla Walla
Yaple, Henry Mack *library director*

WYOMING

Casper
Cottam, Keith M. *librarian, educator, administrator*

CANADA

ALBERTA

Calgary
MacDonald, Alan Hugh *librarian, university administrator*

Lethbridge
Rand, Duncan Dawson *librarian, retired*

BRITISH COLUMBIA

Vancouver
Aalto, Madeleine *library director*

Victoria
Richards, Vincent Philip Haslewood *retired librarian*

SASKATCHEWAN

Regina
Powell, Trevor John David *archivist*

Saskatoon
Kennedy, Marjorie Ellen *librarian*

ADDRESS UNPUBLISHED

Anderson, Herschel Vincent *retired librarian*
Anderson, Rachael Keller *retired library administrator*
Baker, Zachary Moshe *librarian*
Curley, Elmer Frank *librarian*
Gould, Martha Bernice *retired librarian*
Gregor, Dorothy Deborah *librarian*
Johnson, Wayne Harold *librarian, county official*
Nelson, Helen Martha *retired library director*
Pierik, Marilyn Anne *retired librarian, piano teacher*
Wolf, Cynthia Tribelhorn *librarian, library educator*

HUMANITIES: MUSEUMS

UNITED STATES

ALASKA

Anchorage
Spencer, Ted M. *museum director*
Wolf, Patricia B. *museum director*

Denali National Park
Martin, Steve *national park service officer*

Fairbanks
Jonaitis, Aldona Claire *museum administrator, art historian*

Juneau
Kato, Bruce *curator*

ARIZONA

Bisbee
Gustavson, Carrie *museum director*

Flagstaff
Fox, Michael J. *museum director*

Ganado
Chamberlin, Ed *curator*

Mesa
Mead, Tray C. *museum director*

Petrified Forest Natl Park
Hillickson, Michele *national parks service administrator*

Phoenix
Ballinger, James K. *art museum executive*
Carman, Michael Dennis *museum director*
Johnson, Mary *museum director*
Lidman, Roger Wayne *museum director*

Tempe
Zeitlin, Marilyn Audrey *museum director*

Tonalea
Francisco, Irving *national monument administrator*

Tucson
Brown, Don *museum director*
Daley, Richard Halbert *museum director*
Yassin, Robert Alan *museum administrator, curator*

CALIFORNIA

Arcata
Zielinski, Melissa L. *museum director*

Bakersfield
Enriquez, Carola Rupert *museum director*
Meyer, Charles G. *museum director*

Berkeley
Baas, Jacquelynn *museum consultant, art historian*
Benedict, Burton *retired museum director, anthropology educator*

INDUSTRY: MANUFACTURING. *See also* FINANCE: FINANCIAL SERVICES.

UNITED STATES

Atherton
Goodman, Sam Richard *electronics company executive*

Bakersfield
Akers, Tom, Jr. *cotton broker, consultant*
Grimm, Bob *food products executive*
Lundquist, Gene Alan *cotton company executive*

Belmont
Endriz, John Guiry *electronics executive, consultant*

Berkeley
Castello, John L. *pharmaceutical executive*
Maxwell, Jennifer *food products executive*
Simpson, Barclay *manufacturing company executive*

Beverly Hills
Borgnine, Tova *cosmetic executive*
Colburn, Richard Dunton *business executive*
Korn, Lester Bernard *business executive, diplomat*
Leong, Margaret *construction executive*
Mohajer, Dineh *cosmetics company executive*
Susaki, John *construction executive*
Winthrop, John *wines and spirits company executive*

Brea
Nelson, Maurice S., Jr. *metal products company executive*

Buena Park
Okamura, Hideo *manufacturing executive*

Burbank
Raulinaitis, Pranas Algis *electronics executive, consultant*

Calabasas
Cohen, William *construction executive*
Laney, Michael L. *manufacturing executive*
Sperber, Burton S. *construction executive*

Camarillo
Boskovich, George, Jr. *food products executive*
Cleary, Thomas Charles *technology company executive*
Denmark, Bernhardt *manufacturing executive*
Weiss, Carl *aerospace company executive*

Campbell
Crawford, Curtis J. *computer and electronics company executive*

Carlsbad
Anderson, Paul Irving *management executive*
Callaway, Ely Reeves, Jr. *golf club manufacturer*
Crooke, Stanley Thomas *pharmaceutical company executive*
Hammes, Michael Noel *automotive company executive*
Mulford, Rand Perry *business executive*
Randall, William B. *manufacturing company executive*

Carmel
Alich, John Arthur, Jr. *manufacturing company executive*

Carmel Valley
Kasson, James Matthews *electronics executive*

Carson
Bensussen, Gale *health products company executive*
Eischeid, Theodore J. *toy company executive, lawyer*

Castro Valley
Thorburn, Lisa A. *acoustical consulting company executive*

Coachella
Barker, Douglas P. *food products executive*

Colton
Smith, Phillip J. *food products executive*

Compton
Joseph, Ezekiel (Ed Joseph) *manufacturing company executive*

Coronado
Dalton, Matt *retired foundry executive*
Sack, Edgar Albert *electronics company executive*

Costa Mesa
Brady, John Patrick, Jr. *electronics educator, consultant*
Halvorsen, Clay A. *construction executive*
Hazewinkel, Van *manufacturing executive*
Lerner, Sandy *cosmetics executive*
Panic, Milan *pharmaceutical and health products company executive*
Scarborough, Stephen J. *construction executive*
Svendsen, Arthur E. *construction executive*

Covina
Fillius, Milton Franklin, Jr. *food products company executive*

Culver City
Leve, Alan Donald *electronic materials manufacturing company owner, executive*

Cupertino
Burg, John Parker *signal processing executive*
Mathias, Leslie Michael *electronic manufacturing company executive*

Dana Point
Wong, Wallace *medical supplies company executive, real estate investor*

Danville
Amon, William Frederick, Jr. *biotechnology company executive*

Del Mar
Cooper, Martin *electronics company executive*

Delano
Caratan, Anton G. *food products executive*
Caratan, George *food products executive*

Duarte
Bres, Philip Wayne *automotive executive*

Dublin
Whetten, John D. *food products executive*

El Segundo
Connelly, Thomas *construction executive*
Eckert, Robert A. *manufacturing company executive*
Knapp, Evan *construction executive*
Lidow, Eric *electrical parts manufacturing company executive*
Luzuriaga, Francesca *former manufacturing executive*
Manchester, Craig *construction executive*
Mansour, Ned *manufacturing company executive*
Rosenfield, Gene *construction executive*
Steffensen, Dwight A. *medical products and data processing services executive*

Emeryville
Lance, Sean P. *pharmaceutical executive*
McEachern, Alexander *electronics company executive*
Nady, John *electronics company executive*
Penhoet, Edward *biochemicals company executive*

Encinitas
Bartok, Michelle *cosmetic company executive*

Escalon
Barton, Gerald Lee *farming company executive*

Foster City
Bischofberger, Norbert W. *medical products company executive*
Inouye, Michael K. *medical products company executive*
Martin, John C. *medical products executive*
McManus, Dana C. *construction company executive*
Perry, Mark L. *medical products executive*
Rudolph, John *construction executive*

Fremont
Blair, Robert L. *technology company executive*
Chan, Fred S.L. *electronics company executive*
Chuang, Kevin *electronics manufacturing executive*
Ciffone, Donald *electronics company executive*
Conlisk, Raimon L. *high technology management consulting executive*
Guire, Ronald W. *electronics company executive*
Hsu, Gerald C. *electrical company executive*
Huang, Robert *electronics manufacturing executive*
Rugge, Henry Ferdinand *medical products executive*
Shah, Ajay *electronics company executive*
Wang, Stanley *electronics executive*
Wolf, Hans Abraham *retired pharmaceutical company executive*
Zajac, John *semiconductor equipment company executive*
Zimmer, George *men's apparel executive*

Fresno
Baloian, Edward *food products executive*
Baloian, Timothy *food products executive*
Emigh, Mike *agricultural products company executive*

Fullerton
Miller, Arnold *electronics executive*
Wareham, John L. *electronics executive*

Gardena
Kanner, Edwin Benjamin *electrical manufacturing company executive*

Glendora
Cahn, David Stephen *cement company executive*

Greenfield
Munoz, John Joseph *retired transportation company executive*

Hayward
Casamento, Charles Joseph *pharmaceutical industry executive*
Minzner, Dean Frederick *aviation company executive*
Pinckert, Warren, II *pharmaceutical executive*

Hillsborough
Keller, John Francis *retired wine company executive, mayor*
Schapiro, George A. *electronics company executive*

Hollywood
Parks, Robert Myers *appliance manufacturing company executive*

Irvine
Alspach, Philip Halliday *manufacturing company executive*
Asura, John F. *paper company executive*
Beckman, Arnold Orville *analytical instrument manufacturing company executive*
Click, James H. *automotive executive*
Copeland, Lawrence R. *construction company executive*
Haggerty, Charles A. *former electronics executive*
Kabel, Steve *home construction company executive*
Laidlaw, Victor D. *construction executive*
Mussey, Joseph Arthur *health and medical product executive*
Olson, Gene L. *food products executive*
Pyott, David Edmund Ian *pharmaceutical executive*
Salesky, William Jeffrey *corporate executive*

Stelmar, Wayne J. *chief financial officer home building company*
Werner, David A. *paper company executive*
Wetterau, Mark S. *food products/distributor executive*
Williams, James E. *food products manufacturing company executive*

Jackson
Halvorson, William *former automotive executive*

La Jolla
Drake, Hudson Billings *aerospace and electronics company executive*
Stevens, Paul Irving *manufacturing company executive*
Todd, Harry Williams *aircraft propulsion system company executive*

La Puente
Hitchcock, Fritz *automotive company executive*

Lafayette
Lewis, Sheldon Noah *technology consultant*

Laguna Hills
Rossiter, Bryant William *chemistry consultant*

Livermore
Bennett, Alan Jerome *electronics executive, physicist*

Livingston
Fox, Robert August *food company executive*

Lodi
Elkins, Carl *food products executive*

Lompoc
Bongiorno, James William *electronics company executive*

Long Beach
Berenato, Joseph C. *manufacturing company executive*
Heiser, James S. *manufacturing company executive*

Los Altos
Kao, Cheng Chi *electronics executive*

Los Angeles
Adler, Fred Peter *retired electronics company executive*
Aroesty, Sidney A. *medical diagnostic manufacturing company executive*
Ash, Roy Lawrence *business executive*
Campion, Robert Thomas *manufacturing company executive*
Davidson, Robert C., Jr. *manufacturing executive*
Forester, Bernard I. *recreational equipment company executive*
Gerstell, A. Frederick *aggregates, asphalt and concrete manufacturing executive*
Hannah, David H. *metal products executive*
Henn, Michael *financial executive, home building company*
Iacocca, Lee (Lido Anthony Iacocca) *former automotive manufacturing executive, venture capitalist*
Irani, Ray R. *oil, gas and chemical company executive*
Jones, Jerve Maldwyn *construction company executive*
Karatz, Bruce E. *business executive*
Karges, William A., III *food company executive*
Little, Carole *women's apparel company executive*
Lobell, Jeanine *cosmetics company executive*
Mager, Artur *retired aerospace company executive, consultant*
Mall, William John, Jr. *aerospace executive, retired Air Force general*
Marciano, Maurice *apparel executive*
Mullen, John H. *corporate executive*
Nafilyan, Guy *vice president home building corporation*
Perkins, William Clinton *company executive*
Ramer, Lawrence Jerome *corporation executive*
Roche, James G. *electronics executive*
Rodstein, Richard M. *apparel executive*
Ruth, Craig *business executive*
Segil, Larraine Diane *materials company executive*
Spindler, Paul *corporate executive, consultant*
Tamkin, S. Jerome *business executive, consultant*
Wyatt, James Luther *drapery hardware company executive*
Ziering, Michael *medical products executive*
Ziering, Sigi *medical company executive*

Malibu
Berman, Stephen G. *toy manufacturing executive*
Smith, George Foster *retired aerospace company executive*

Mckinleyville
Thueson, David Orel *pharmaceutical executive, researcher, educator, writer*

Menlo Park
Bremser, George, Jr. *electronics company executive*
Carlson, Curtis R. *electronics research industry executive*
Evans, Bob Overton *electronics executive, director*
Jackson, Jeanne Pellegren *apparel executive*
Kalinske, Thomas J. *education, video game and toy company executive*
Kaplan, Jerry (S. Jerrold Kaplan) *electronics company executive*
Pausa, Clements Edward *electronics company executive*
Saifer, Mark Gary Pierce *pharmaceutical executive*
Taft, David Dakin *chemical executive*
Westcott, Brian John *manufacturing executive*

Mill Valley
Bitting, William *manufacturing executive*

Milpitas
Brown, Michael A. *computer hardware company executive*
Cannon, Michael R. *manufacturing executive*
Coghlan, Paul *electronics executive*
Forsyth, G. Fred *electronics company executive*
Granchelli, Ralph S. *company executive*
Gray, Bruce *computer and electronics company executive*
Nishimura, Koichi *electronics manufacturing company executive*
Perez, Daniel *electronics company executive*
Stephens, Bob *electronic executive*
Watkins, William D. *technology company executive*
Zohouri, Saeed *electronics company executive*

Modesto
Riesenbeck, Ronald *supermarket executive*
Youga, Tony *winery executive*

Monterey
Meyers, Gerald A. *metal products executive*

Moorpark
Kavli, Fred *manufacturing executive*

Mountain View
Castor, Jon Stuart *electronics company executive*
de Geus, Aart J. *computer software company executive*
Levy, Ricardo Benjamin *chemical company executive*
Neil, Gary Lawrence *pharmaceutical company research executive, biochemical pharmacologist*
Smith, Lonnie Max *diversified industries executive*

Newark
Mueller, Nancy *food products executive*

Newport Beach
Crean, John C. *retired housing and recreational vehicles manufacturing company executive*
Johnson, William Stanley *metal distribution company executive*
Jones, Roger Wayne *electronics executive*
Lyon, William *builder*
Miller, Charles Dale *self-adhesive materials company executive*
Siegel, David M. *construction executive*

Norco
Eisen, Hilda *food products executive*

North Hills
Boeckmann, Herbert F., II *automotive executive*

Oakland
Cronk, William F., III *food products executive*
Kahn, Timothy F. *food products company executive*
Rogers, T. Gary *food products company executive*
Sullivan, G. Craig *household products executive*

Orange
Dimick, Neil Francis *medical products wholesale executive*
Hamann, Dennis *food products executive*
Kaempen, Charles Edward *manufacturing company executive*

Orinda
Graber, William Raymond *pharmaceutical executive*

Oxnard
Gill, David *food products executive*
Poole, Henry Joe, Jr. *business executive*

Palo Alto
Balzhiser, Richard Earl *research and development company executive*
Couder, Alain *personal computer manufacturing company executive*
DeLustro, Frank Anthony *biomedical company executive, research immunologist*
Early, James Michael *electronics research consultant*
Kung, Frank F. *biotechnology and life sciences investor, venture capitalist*
Saldich, Robert Joseph *electronics company executive*
Staprans, Armand *electronics executive*
Sweitzer, Michael Cook *healthcare product executive*
Whitfield, Roy A. *pharmaceutical executive*
Winfield, Roy A. *pharmaceutical company executive*

Palos Verdes Estates
Mackenbach, Frederick W. *welding products manufacturing company executive*

Palos Verdes Peninsula
Thomas, Hayward *manufacturing company executive*
Wilson, Theodore Henry *retired electronics company executive, aerospace engineer*

Pasadena
Marlen, James S. *chemical, plastics and building materials manufacturing company executive*
McNulty, James F. *export company executive*
Neal, Philip Mark *diversified manufacturing executive*
Smith, Howard Russell *manufacturing company executive*
Tollenaere, Lawrence Robert *retired industrial products company executive*
Watson, Noel G. *construction executive*
Weiswasser, Stephen *electronics manufacturing executive*
Yuen, Henry C. *consumer electronics manufacturing company executi*

Pebble Beach
Rivette, Gerard Bertram *manufacturing company executive*

Pico Rivera
Collanton, Greg *manufacturing executive, controller*

Cowan, Richard *manufacturing executive*

Pleasanton
Bond, David F. *food products executive*
Ching, David T. *food products executive*
Magelitz, Larry L. *construction company executive*
Sundgren, Donald E. *construction executive*
Weiss, Robert Stephen *medical manufacturing company financial executive*

Pomona
Brown, Ronald G. *automotive company executive*
Hogarty, Charles J. *automotive executive*

Poway
Aschenbrenner, Frank Aloysious *former diversified manufacturing company executive*
Barnhart, Douglas Edward *construction company executive*

Rancho Cordova
Martin, Rafael M., Sr. *construction company executive*
Warnking, Reinhard Johannes *medical device company executive*

Rancho Mirage
Foster, David Ramsey *soap company executive*
Greenbaum, James Richard *liquor distributing company executive, real estate developer*

Redding
Emerson, Mark *lumber company executive*
Emerson, Red *lumber company executive*
Emmerson, Mark *paper/lumber company executive*
Emmerson, Red *sawmill owner*

Redondo Beach
Dockstader, Jack Lee *retired electronics executive*
Kagiwada, Reynold Shigeru *advanced technology manager*
Sabin, Jack Charles *engineering and construction firm executive*

Redwood City
Bramson, Edward J. *electronics corporation executive, financial executive*
Hanf, Michael W. *construction executive*
Hawkins, Trip *electronics company executive*
Nosler, Peter Cole *construction company executive*
Piraino, James V. *construction executive*
Wang, Chen Chi *electronics company, real estate, finance company, investment services, and international trade executive*
Williams, Duston *electronics company executive*

Richmond
Freiman, Paul E. *pharmaceutical company executive*

Riverside
Kummer, Glenn F. *manufactured housing executive*
Parks, Richard E. *manufacturing executive*

Sacramento
Baccigaluppi, Roger John *agricultural company executive*
Lucchetti, David J. *manufacturing executive*

Salinas
Drever, Mark *food products executive*
Esquivel, Joe G. *food products executive*
Esquivel, Mary *agricultural products company executive*
Taylor, Steven Bruce *agriculture company executive*

San Carlos
Cross, Elizabeth *apparel manufacturing company executive*

San Clemente
Clark, Earnest Hubert, Jr. *tool company executive*

San Diego
Adams, William B. *chemical company executive*
Baird, Mellon Campbell, Jr. *electronics industry executive*
Casey, Nancy J. *women's healthcare company executive*
Darmstandler, Harry Max *real estate executive, retired air force officer*
Devine, Brian Kiernan *pet food and supplies company executive*
Duddles, Charles Weller *food company executive*
Gelwix, Max D. *chemical company executive*
Jennings, Jackie *construction executive, contractor*
Lewis, Alan James *pharmaceutical executive, pharmacologist*
Maier, Paul Victor *pharmaceutical executive*
Nassif, Thomas Anthony *business executive, former ambassador*
Price, Robert E. *manufacturing company executive*
Ray, Gene Wells *industrial executive*
Roth, Duane J. *pharmaceutical executive*
Shaffer, Oren George *former manufacturing company executive*
Spanos, Alexander Gus *construction executive, professional sports team executive*
Weitzen, Jeffrey *computer manufacturing company executive*
Zable, Walter Joseph *electronic products manufacturing company executive*

San Francisco
Callahan, Darry W. *energy company executive*
Chiasson, William B. *apparel executive*
Chiaverini, John Edward *construction company executive*
Grubb, David H. *construction company executive*
Haas, Robert Douglas *apparel manufacturing company executive*
Hammergren, John H. *pharmaceutical company executive*
Hawkins, Richard *pharmaceutical and cosmetics company executive*
Hull, Cordell William *business executive*
Jewett, George Frederick, Jr. *forest products company executive*
Keogh, Keith *food company executive*
Kreitzberg, Fred Charles *construction management company executive*
Lonergan, Kevin M. *retail apparel company executive*
Mahoney, David L. *pharmaceutical wholesale and healthcare management company executive*
Marineau, Philip Albert *apparel executive*
Merrill, Harvie Martin *manufacturing executive, director*
Meyers, David L. *food products executive*
Ming, Jenny *retail apparel company executive*
Newman, Francis A. *medical device company executive*
Pilot, Ken *retail apparel company executive*
Proctor, Georganne C. *company executive*
Pulido, Mark A. *pharmaceutical and cosmetics company executive*
Seelenfreund, Alan *pharmaceutical company executive*
Thacher, Carter Pomeroy *diversified manufacturing company executive*
Tompkins, Susie *apparel company executive, creative director*
Tully, Herbert Bullard *chemical manufacturing executive*
Wertheimer, Robert E. *paper company executive*
Wilson, John B. *clothing company executive*
Wolford, Richard *food products executive*
Zellerbach, William Joseph *retired paper company executive*

San Jose
Abbe, Charles J. *manufacturing company executive*
Ackel, Rick R. *electronics manufacturing executive*
Bell, W. Donald *electronics company executive*
Bingham, H. Raymond *software company executive*
Carrekea, James *electronics company executive*
Cartwright, Peter *electronics company executive*
Dickerson, Gary E. *electronics executive*
Faggin, Federico *electronics executive*
Fry, David *electronics executive*
Fry, John *electronics executive*
Furr, Randy W. *electronics manufacturing executive*
Jacobson, Raymond Earl *electronics company entrepreneur and executive*
Kalkhoven, Kevin N. *electronics company executive*
Kispert, John H. *tool manufacturing executive*
Kissner, Charles D. *electrical company executive*
Madrid, Don *electronics executive*
Marks, Michael E. *electronics company executive*
Muller, Anthony Richard *electronics company executive*
Perlegos, George *electronic executive*
Rodgers, Thomas J. *electronics executive*
Rosendin, Raymond Joseph *electrical contracting company executive*
Schroeder, Kenneth L. *electronics executive*
Schroeder, William John *electronics executive*
Scifres, Donald Ray *semiconductor laser, fiber optics and electronics company executive*
Smith, Rodney *electronics executive*
Steinberg, Charles Allan *electronics manufacturing company executive*
Straus, Jozef *manufacturing company executive*
Thomsen, Carl *electronics company executive*
Wozniak, Curtis S. *electronics company executive*

San Marcos
Page, Leslie Andrew *disinfectant manufacturing company executive*

San Mateo
Graham, Howard Holmes *financial executive*
Halperin, Robert Milton *retired electrical machinery company executive*
Mishelevich, David Jacob *medical company executive, consultant*
Rollo, F. David *hospital management company executive, health care educator*

San Rafael
Neuburger, Karen *apparel executive*

San Ramon
Bruns, George H. *electronics executive*
Cosmez, Mark H., II *electronics executive*
Mariotta, Claudio *electronics executive*
Stabbert, Frederick Joseph *paper company executive*

Sanger
Albertson, David *food products executive*

Santa Ana
Baugh, Coy Franklin *corporate executive*
Falstrup, Asger *electronics company executive*
Murai, Kevin *electronics company executive*
Phanstiel, Howard G. *health care system executive*

Santa Anna
Scott, Gregory W. *health care company executive*

Santa Barbara
Prindle, William Roscoe *retired glass company executive, consultant*

Santa Clara
Burkett, Marvin *personal computer manufacturing company executive*
Carey, D. John *electronics executive*
Fodor, Stephen P. A. *chemical company executive*
Grove, Andrew S. *electronics company executive*
Halla, Brian L. *electronics company executive*
Larson, William *electrical company executive*
Lee, Jimmy S.M. *electronic executive*
Logan, Mark Byron *optics corporation executive*
Maydan, Dan *chemical company executive*
Moore, Gordon E. *electronics company executive*
Morgan, James C. *electronics executive*
Somekh, Sasson *chemical company executive*
Wang, David N.K. *chemical company executive*

Santa Maria
Ardantz, Henri *agricultural products executive*
Ferini, Robert Pat *agricultural products company executive*

Santa Monica
Hardin, Wayne *automotive executive*

Santa Paula
Dillard, Michael L. *food products company executive*

Saratoga
Houston, Joseph Brantley, Jr. *optical instrument company executive*
Reagan, Joseph Bernard *retired aerospace executive, management consultant*

Sausalito
Katz, Bruce R. *company executive*

Simi Valley
Mow, William *apparel executive*
Weiser, Paul David *manufacturing company executive*

Solana Beach
Arledge, Charles Stone *former aerospace executive, entrepreneur*
Brody, Arthur *industrial executive*
Derbes, Daniel William *manufacturing executive*

South San Francisco
Hellman, Susan D. *medical products manufacturing executive*
Walker, John P. *pharmaceutical executive*

Sun Valley
Kamins, Philip E. *diversified manufacturing company executive*

Sunnyvale
Bachman, Brian Richard *former electronics executive*
Bowman, A. Blaine *electronics company executive*
Evans, Barton, Jr. *analytical instrument company executive*
Lewis, John Clark, Jr. *retired manufacturing company executive*
McCollam, Craig A. *business executive*
Ng, Betty *electronics executive*
Simon, Ralph E. *electronics executive*
Yancey, Gary *electronics company executive*

Tarzana
Firestone, Morton H. *business management executive*

Thousand Oaks
Colburn, Keith W. *electronics executive*
Falberg, Kathryn E. *pharmaceutical executive*
Sharer, Kevin W. *healthcare products company executive*

Torrance
Edelbrock, O. Victor *automotive part manfacturing executive*
Feles, Aristedes *automotive parts manfacturing executive*
Thompson, Jeffrey L. *automotive parts manfacturing executive*

Turlock
Arias, Joe *agricultural products company executive*

Tustin
Hester, Norman Eric *chemical company technical executive, chemist*

Upland
Goodman, John M. *construction executive*

Valencia
House, David L. *electronics components company executive*

Vallejo
Womack, Thomas Houston *manufacturing company executive*

Walnut
Brock, Mark *construction company executive*
Humphreys, Roy *construction executive*
Shea, John F. *construction executive, contractor*
Shontere, James G. *construction executive*

Walnut Creek
Roath, Stephen D. *pharmaceutical company executive*
Shastid, Jon Barton *wine company executive*

Watsonville
Barton, William E. *construction company executive*
Costanzo, Patrick M. *construction executive*
Dorey, William G. *construction company executive*
Franich, Steven *automotive company executive*
Repass, Randy *electrical company executive*
Solari, R. C. *retired heavy construction company executive*
Watts, David H. *construction company executive*

West Sacramento
Teel, Michael J. *supermarket chain executive*

Westlake Village
Kay, Kenneth Jeffrey *food products company executive*
Lullo, Thomas A. *electronics executive*
Nichols, Steven *shoe and clothing manufacturing executive*
Powlick, George *shoe and clothing manufacturing executive*
Tate, John William *food products executive*

Westlake Vlg
DeLorenzo, David A. *food products executive*

Woodland Hills
Brandenberg, Frank G. *electronics executive*
Brann, Alton Joseph *manufacturing company executive*
Brown, Michael R. *defense industry executive*
Dreier, R. Chad *construction and mortgage company executive*
Frame, Larry A. *electronics executive*
Gellert, Jay M. *health/medical products executive*
Halamandaris, Harry *aerospace executive*
Hoch, Orion Lindel *corporate executive*
Morishita, Akihiko *trading company executive*

Woodside
Gates, Milo Sedgwick *retired construction company executive*

Yorba Linda
Forth, Kevin Bernard *beverage distributing industry consultant*

COLORADO

Boulder
Clark, Melvin Eugene *chemical company executive*
Daughenbaugh, Randall Jay *retired chemical company executive, consultant*

Breckenridge
Ehrhorn, Richard William *electronics company executive*

Broomfield
Hoover, R. David *manufacturing executive*
Midgett, Leon A. *manufacturing executive*

Colorado Springs
Cimino, Jay *automotive company executive*

Denver
Alvarado, Linda G. *construction company executive*
Ells, Steve *food company executive*
Gates, Charles Cassius *rubber company executive*
Henry, Charles L. (Jerry) *manufacturing executive*
Hohner, Kenneth Dwayne *retired fodder company executive*
Klump, Ron *food products executive*
Leprino, James G. *food products executive*
Livingston, Johnston Redmond *manufacturing executive*
Marcum, Walter Phillip *manufacturing executive*
Martin, J. Landis *manufacturing company executive, lawyer*
Mizel, Larry A. *housing construction company executive*
Nields, Morgan Wesson *medical supply company executive*
Reidy, Mike *food products executive*
Shreve, Theodore Norris *construction company executive*

Englewood
Appel, Joel *household cleaner manufacturing executive*
Betker, Mark Alan *manufacturing executive*
Chavez, Lloyd G. *automotive executive*
Mahoney, Gerald Francis *manufacturing company executive*
McVey, Larry *household cleaner manufacturing executive*
Reese, Monte Nelson *agricultural association executive*
Saliba, Jacob *manufacturing executive*

Fort Collins
Bethune, David Ross *pharmaceutical executive*
Newlin, Douglas Randal *lead information engineer*

Golden
Coors, Jeffrey H. *technology manufacturing executive*
Coors, William K. *brewery executive*

Greeley
Carrico, Stephen J. *construction company executive*
Morgensen, Jerry Lynn *construction company executive*

Lakewood
Heath, Gary Brian *manufacturing firm executive, engineer*
Rosa, Fredric David *construction company executive*

Littleton
Dixon, Terry *automotive executive*

Lone Tree
Bauer, Randy Mark *management training firm executive*

Longmont
Breuer, Werner Alfred *retired plastics company executive*
Marcy, Charles Frederick *food company executive*

Louisville
Kenney, Belinda Jill Forseman *technology company executive*

Snowmass Village
Mattis, Louis Price *pharmaceutical and consumer products company executive*

Wellington
Grant, Lewis O. *agricultural products executive, meteorology educator*

HAWAII

Honolulu
Andrasick, James Stephen *agribusiness company executive*
Couch, John Charles *retired diversified company executive*
Goth, Harvey L. *construction company executive*
Schuler, James K. *construction executive*

Usui, Leslie Raymond *retired clothing executive*

Papaikou
Buyers, John William Amerman *agribusiness and specialty foods company executive*

IDAHO

Boise
Aiton, John W. *manufacturing executive*
Appleton, Steven R. *electronics executive*
Beebe, Stephen A. *agricultural products company executive*
Bender, John C. *paper company executive*
Crumley, Theodore *paper lumber company executive*
Groce, Augustus Ben *paper company executive*
Harad, George Jay *manufacturing company executive*
Hawkins, Jay L. *electronics executive*
Lewis, Roderic W. *technology company executive, lawyer*
Littman, Irving *forest products company executive*
Miller, Jon Hamilton *forest products company executive*
Mogensen, Dennis *agricultural products company executive*
Washington, Dennis R. *contracting company executive*

Hayden Lake
Wogsland, James Willard *retired heavy machinery manufacturing executive*

Salmon
Snook, Quinton *construction company executive*

ILLINOIS

Lake Forest
Hammar, Lester Everett *health care manufacturing executive, retired*

MONTANA

Great Falls
Semenza, Dirk A. *metal fabrication executive*
Sletten, John Robert *construction company executive*

Helena
Warren, Christopher Charles *electronics executive*

Missoula
Washington, Dennis *construction executive*

NEVADA

Carson City
Burns, Dan W. *manufacturing company executive*

Las Vegas
Adcock, Corey J. *construction executive*
Jones, Fletcher, Jr. *automotive company executive*
Kaiser, Glen David *construction company executive*
Peck, Gaillard Ray, Jr. *defense contractor, aerospace and business consultant, business owner*
Strahan, Julia Celestine *electronics company executive*
Swanson, Kurt *metal fabricating company executive*

Sparks
Kramer, Gordon Edward *manufacturing executive*

NEW JERSEY

Princeton
Mario, Ernest *pharmaceutical company executive*

NEW MEXICO

Albuquerque
Collins, Julie *healthcare organization executive*
Friberg, George Joseph *electronics company executive*
Golleher, George *food company executive*
King, James Nedwed *construction company executive, lawyer*
Pohl, Elizabeth *contracting company executive*
Stamm, Robert Jenne *building contractor, construction company executive*
Turner, Andrew L. *healthcare management company executive*
Woltil, Robert D. *healthcare management company executive*

Carlsbad
Watts, Marvin Lee *minerals company executive, chemist, educator*

Estancia
Swenka, Arthur John *retired food products executive*

Santa Fe
Odell, John H. *construction company executive*
Robinson, Charles Wesley *energy company executive*

OREGON

Beaverton
Barnes, Keith Lee *electronics executive*
Blair, Donald W. *shoe manufacturing company executive*
[illegible], Thomas [illegible] *apparel executive*
Donahue, Richard King *athletic apparel executive, lawyer*
Harold, Robert *apparel executive*
Knight, Philip H(ampson) *shoe manufacturing company executive*
Meyer, Jerome J. *diversified technology company executive*
Slade, Colin L. *electronics manufacturing executive*
Wills, Richard H. *electronics manufacturing executive*

Bend
Babcock, Walter Christian, Jr. *membrane company executive*

Forest Grove
Coleman, Deborah Ann *electronics company executive*

Gladstone
Thomason, Scott *automobile executive*

Hood River
Garcia, David *agricultural products executive*
Girardelli, Ronald K. *food products executive*

Klamath Falls
Hoggarth, Karen *lumber company executive*
Wendt, Richard L. *manufacturing executive*

Medford
Heimann, M.L. "Dick" *auto dealership executive*

Portland
Boyle, Gertrude *sportswear company executive*
Cassard, Christopher D. *lumber company executive*
Dooley, James T. *electronic manfacturing executive*
Drinkward, Cecil W. *construction company executive*
Flowerree, Robert Edmund *retired forest products company executive*
Gast, Nancy Lou *retired chemical company executive*
Hawley, Greg W. *paper company executive*
Kinnune, William P. *forest products executive*
McDougall, Duane C. *manufacturing executive*
McKennon, Keith Robert *chemical company executive*
Pamplin, Robert Boisseau, Jr. *manufacturing company executive, minister, writer*
Pamplin, Robert Boisseau, Sr. *retired textile manufacturing executive*
Russell, Marjorie Rose *manufacturing company executive*
Steinfeld, Ray, Jr. *food products executive*
Stott, Peter Walter *forest products company executive*
Swindells, William, Jr. *lumber and paper company executive*
Thurston, George R. *lumber company executive*
VanLuvanee, Donald Robert *electronics executive*
Watkins, Charles Reynolds *medical equipment company executive*
Whitsell, Helen Jo *lumber executive*

Springfield
Detlefsen, William David, Jr. *chemicals executive*

UTAH

Heber City
Day, Gerald W. *wholesale grocery company executive*

Logan
Wheeler, Dolores *food products executive*

Ogden
Nickerson, Guy Robert *lumber company executive*

Provo
Newitt, Jay *construction management educator*
Raney, Dennis R. *computer hardware company executive*

Salt Lake City
Beck, Teresa *supermarket executive*
Clark, Jeffrey Raphiel *research and development company executive*
Esplin, Kimo *chemical company executive*
Gregory, Herold La Mar *chemical company administrator*
Hembree, James D. *retired chemical company executive*
Horan, John J. *pharmaceutical company executive*
Huntsman, Jon Meade *chemical company executive*
Huntsman, Peter R. *chemicals executive*
Norton, Delmar Lynn *candy company executive*
Oyler, James Russell, Jr. *manufacturing executive*
Steiner, Richard Russell *textile & apparel company executive*
Wilson, James Rigg *aircraft manufacturing company executive*

Vineyard
Brown, Birchel S. *steel products company executive*
Cannon, Joseph A. *steel products company executive*
Johnsen, Ken C. *steel products company executive*
Wanlass, Dennis L. *manufacturing executive*

West Jordan
Bland, Dorothy Ann *construction executive, real estate agent*

WASHINGTON

Bellevue
Cremin, Robert W. *manufacturing executive*
George, Robert D. *technology corporation executive*
Hovind, David J. *manufacturing company executive*
Pigott, Charles McGee *transportation equipment manufacturing executive*
Pigott, Mark C. *automotive executive*
Tembreull, Michael A. *automotive executive*
Young, Frank Nolan, Jr. *commercial building contracting company executive*

Bellingham
Haggen, Donald E. *food products executive*
Henley, Dale C. *grocery company executive*

Bothell
Stein, Michael A. *pharmaceutical executive*

Coupeville
Thom, Richard David *retired aerospace executive*

Eastsound
Anders, William Alison *aerospace and defense manufacturing executive*

Everett
Helsell, Robert M. *construction executive*

Federal Way
Hogans, Mack L. *paper company executive*
Rogel, Steven R. *forest products company executive*

Gig Harbor
Stover, Miles Ronald *manufacturing executive*

Hoquiam
Lamb, Isabelle Smith *manufacturing company executive*

Kent
Hebeler, Henry Koester *retired aerospace and electronics executive*

Kirkland
Kozloff, Benett *food products executive*
Witte, Peggy *metal products executive*

Lake Stevens
Durden, Rome L. *aircraft manufacturing company executive*

Longview
Wollenberg, Richard Peter *paper manufacturing company executive*

Manson
Stager, Donald K. *retired construction company executive*

Puyallup
Absher, Dan *construction executive*

Redmond
Hatlen, Joel S. *electronics manufacturing executive*
Hume, Frederick Raymond *electronics company executive*

Renton
Huck, Larry Ralph *manufacturing executive, sales consultant*

Seattle
Albrecht, Richard Raymond *retired airplane manufacturing executive, lawyer*
Behnke, Carl Gilbert *beverage franchise executive*
Bundrant, Charles H. *food products executive*
Gillis, Steven *biotechnology company executive*
Lincoln, Howard *manufacturing company and sports team executive*
Lowber, Stephen Scott *financial executive*
Mennella, Vincent Alfred *automotive manufacturing and airplane company executive*
Moseley, Colin *lumber company executive*
Pollnow, C. *lumber company executive*
Schoenfeld, Walter Edwin *manufacturing company executive*
Shrontz, Frank Anderson *airplane manufacturing executive*
Stonecipher, Harry Curtis *manufacturing company executive*

Spokane
Hiller, Stanley, Jr. *manufacturing company executive*
Paulson, Richard L. *paper and wood products executive*
Siegel, L. Pendleton *paper and wood products executive*
Siegel, Louis Pendleton *forest products executive*
Tarr, Gregory L. *health and medical products company executive*

Tacoma
Corbin, William R. *wood products executive*
Gaynor, C.W. *paper company executive*
Hanson, Richard E. *paper company executive*
Tash, Graham Andrew, Jr. *automobile retail company executive*
Weyerhaeuser, George H., Jr. *paper manufacturing company executive*

Tukwila
Harnish, John J. *manufacturing executive*

Vancouver
Berglund, Carl Neil *electronics company executive*

Wenatchee
Birdsall, Brian *food products executive*
Chandler, Allen *food products executive*

Yakima
Long, David R. *food products executive*

WYOMING

Jackson
Gordon, Stephen Maurice *manufacturing company executive, rancher*

CANADA

ALBERTA

Calgary
Holman, J(ohn) Leonard *retired manufacturing corporation executive*
Jenkins, Kevin J. *technology and industrial company executive*
Newall, James Edward Malcolm *manufacturing company executive*

Edmonton
Stollery, Robert *construction company executive*

BRITISH COLUMBIA

Annacis Island
Brackhaus, Karl H. *technology company executive*

Vancouver
Bentley, Peter John Gerald *forest industry company executive*

SASKATCHEWAN

Regina
Phillips, Roger *steel company executive*

Saskatoon
Steck, Warren Franklin *retired chemical company executive, biochemist*

ADDRESS UNPUBLISHED

Azarnoff, Daniel Lester *pharmaceutical company consultant*
Baker, Charles DeWitt *research and development company executive*
Barca, George Gino *winery executive, financial investor*
Bennett, Paul Grover *agribusiness executive*
Bertiger, Bary *electronics executive*
Bos, John Arthur *retired aircraft manufacturing executive*
Broadhurst, Norman Neil *food products executive*
Butler, Jack Fairchild *semiconductors company executive*
Campbell, Richard Alden *electronics company executive*
Chaykin, Robert Leroy *manufacturing and marketing executive*
Chu, James *computer display equipment manufacturing executive*
Crawford, James Dee *chemical distribution executive*
Cutter, David Lee *pharmaceutical company executive*
Dion, Philip Joseph *consumer products and services executive, real estate and construction company executive*
Eriksen, Otto Louis *retired manufacturing company executive*
Fitch, Robert McLellan *business and technology consultant*
Fogg, Richard Lloyd *food products company executive*
Fritz, Rene Eugene, Jr. *manufacturing executive*
Garruto, John Anthony *cosmetics executive*
Gary, James Frederick *business and energy advising company executive*
Goldberg, Lee Winicki *furniture company executive*
Gorman, Michael Stephen *construction executive*
Gulcher, Robert Harry *aircraft company executive*
Gurney, Daniel Sexton *race car manufacturing company executive, racing team executive*
Halle, Bruce T. *automotive products company executive*
Hanson, Larry Keith *plastics company executive*
Hausman, Arthur Herbert *electronics company executive*
Herbert, Gavin Shearer *health care products company executive*
Hind, Harry William *pharmaceutical company executive*
Hirsch, Horst Eberhard *business consultant*
Kapcsandy, Louis Endre *building construction and manufacturing executive, chemical engineering consultant*
Kern, Irving John *retired food company executive*
Krueger, Kenneth John *corporate executive, nutritionist, educator*
Larsen, Weldon *company executive*
Madden, Richard Blaine *forest products executive*
Maughan, Rex *natural healthcare products company executive*
McCann, Jack Arland *former construction and mining equipment company executive*
Parker, Pam *apparel manufacturing company executive*
Pedhirney, Gayland *food products company executive*
Perrish, Albert *retired steel company executive*
Platt, Lewis Emmett *retired electronics company executive*
Price, Tom *automotive sales executive*
Richard, Edward H. *manufacturing company executive, former municipal government official*
Saute, Robert Emile *drug and cosmetic consultant*
Shapiro, Barry *toy company executive*
Sissel, George Allen *manufacturing executive, lawyer*
Smith, Charles Conard *refractory company executive*
Smith, James Alexander *metal processing executive*
Solloway, C. Robert *retired forest products company executive*
Stern, Arthur Paul *electronics company executive*
Stivers, William Charles *forest [illegible] executive*
Tutor, Ronald N. *construction company executive*
Watkins, Dean Allen *electronics executive, educator*

Weiss, Max Tibor *retired aerospace company executive*
Wiedow, Carl Paul *electromechanical and geophysical instruments company executive*
Wolff, Brian Richard *metal manufacturing company executive*
Young, John Alan *electronics company executive*

INDUSTRY: SERVICE

UNITED STATES

ALASKA

Anchorage
Brady, Carl Franklin *retired aircraft charter company executive*
Lowber, John M. *communications executive*

Juneau
Elton, Kim Steven *state legislator, pollster*
King, Robert Wilson *public relations specialist*

ARIZONA

Cave Creek
O'Reilly, Thomas Eugene *human resources consultant, retired*

Chandler
Brunello-McCay, Rosanne *sales executive*
Guinouard, Philip Andre *restaurant executive*

Cortaro
Fossland, Joeann Jones *professional speaker, personal coach*

Flagstaff
Evans, Ronald Allen *lodging chain executive*

Glendale
Baum, Phyllis Gardner *travel management consultant*

Green Valley
Ragan, James Thomas *communications executive*

Mesa
Johnson, Doug *advertising and public relations executive*
Murphy, Edward Francis *executive*

Paradise Valley
Hazard, Robert Culver, Jr. *hotel executive*

Payson
Hegarty, Christopher Joseph *management and financial consultant*

Peoria
Saunders, James *management and training consultant*

Phoenix
Armstrong, Nelson William, Jr. *gaming company executive*
Bohannon, Robert H. *diversified services company executive*
Drain, Albert Sterling *business management consultant*
Gall, Donald Alan *data processing executive*
Genrich, Mark L. *public relations executive*
Highet, Mac *travel company executive*
Holmes, Gregg *communications executive*
Lemon, Leslie Gene *retired diversified services company executive*
Lyon, Russ *executive*
Rubeli, Paul E. *gaming company executive*
Simpson, Charles Robert *marketing professional*
Snell, Richard *holding company executive*
Subach, James Alan *information systems company executive, consultant*
Teets, John William *retired diversified company executive*
Travers, Paul *company executive*
Ward, Rob *company executive*

Prescott
Palmer, Robert Arthur *private investigator*

Scottsdale
Baum, Herbert Merrill *consumer products company executive*
Blinder, Martin S. *business consultant, art dealer*
Grier, James Edward *hotel company executive, lawyer*
Gwinn, Mary Dolores *business developer, philosopher, writer, speaker*
Millon, Jean-Pierre *health care executive*
O'Donnell, William Thomas *management consultant*
Siburg, Dan *marketing professional*
Swanson, Robert Killen *management consultant*
Tierney, Jack *consumer products company executive*
Van Weelden, Thomas H. *waste industry company executive*

Sedona
Wolfe, Al *marketing and advertising consultant*

Sun City West
Stevens, George Richard *business consultant, public policy commentator*
Suttles, Virginia Grant *advertising executive*

Tempe
Andrews, John H. *communications executive*
Koziol, Christopher J. *communications executive*
McKeever, Jeffrey D. *computer company executive*
Ward, Richard *computer company executive*

Tucson
Barton, Stanley Faulkner *management consultant*
Bergamo, Ron *marketing executive*
Eberhardt, Marty Lampert *botanical garden administrator*
Sarlat, Gladys *public relations consultant*
Willert, Sister St. Joan *health care corporation executive*

CALIFORNIA

Agoura Hills
Goodall, Stephen C. *marketing professional*
Gressak, Anthony Raymond, Jr. *sales executive*
Powers, J. D., III *marketing executive*

Alamo
da Roza, Victoria Cecilia *human resources administrator*
Whalen, John Sydney *management consultant*

Aliso Viejo
Grigsby, Frederick J., Jr. *human resources executive*
Harder, Wendy Wetzel *communications executive*
Rollans, James O. *service company executive*

Anaheim
Kallay, Michael Frank, II *medical devices company official*
Noorda, Raymond J. *computer software company executive*
Puzder, Andrew F. *restaurant executive, lawyer*

Atherton
Baran, Paul *computer executive*
Phipps, Allen Mayhew *management consultant*

Baldwin Park
Snyder, Esther *food service executive*

Belvedere Tiburon
Denton, Charles Mandaville *corporate consultant*

Berkeley
Chamberlain, Bob *computer company executive*
Edwards, Susan M. *hotel executive*
Poulos-Woolley, Paige M. *public relations executive*
Thomas, Lisa *food service executive*
Wilton, Peter Campbell *marketing educator*

Beverly Hills
Annunziata, Robert *fiber optics company executive*
Carlson, Gary Lee *public relations executive, director, producer*
Casey, Thomas J. *communications company executive, lawyer*
Cohrs, Dan *fiber optics company executive*
David, Clive *event planning executive*
Fickinger, Wayne Joseph *communications executive*
Hilton, Barron *hotel executive*
Huckestein, Dieter H. *hotel company executive*
Kingsley, Patricia *public relations executive*
Lee, David *fiber optics company executive*
Nyman, Michael S. *company executive*
Ovitz, Michael S. *communications executive*
Riess, Gordon Sanderson *management consultant*
Scanlon, John M. (Jack) *fiber optics company executive*
Shepard, Kathryn Irene *public relations executive*
Toffel, Alvin Eugene *corporate executive, business and governmental consultant*
Winnick, Gary *fiber optics company executive*

Brea
Streeter, Stephanie Anne *executive*

Brisbane
Hamilton, Judith Hall *computer company executive*

Burbank
Cohen, Valerie A. *entertainment company executive*
Cook, Richard W. *motion picture company executive*
Margol, Irving *personnel consultant*

Camarillo
Cobb, Roy Lampkin, Jr. *retired computer sciences corporation executive*

Cambria
Morse, Richard Jay *human resources and organizational development consultant, manufacturers' representative company executive*

Campbell
Roberts, George P. *computer company executive*

Carlsbad
Hale, David Fredrick *health care company executive*
Lambert, James L. *data storage systems company executive*

Carmel
Creighton, John Wallis, Jr. *novelist, publisher, former management educator, consultant*
Krugman, Stanley Lee *international management consultant*
Smith, Gordon Paul *management consulting company executive*

Carpinteria
Lopker, Pamela *technology industry executive*
Morgan, Alfred Vance *management consulting company executive*

Chino Hills
Burge, Willard, Jr. *software company executive*

Chula Vista
Ortiz, Antonio Ignacio *public relations executive*

Compton
Beauchamp, Patrick L. *distributing company executive*
Janeway, Barbara *public relations executive*

Concord
Travers, Judith Lynnette *human resources executive*

Corona
Garcia, Monicae *communications equipment company executive*

Corte Madera
Mindel, Laurence Brisker *restaurateur*

Costa Mesa
Cox, Fred B. *software company executive*
Gimple, W. Thomas *sales executive*
Paine, David M. *public relations executive*

Culver City
Berland, James Fred *software company executive*
Boonshaft, Hope Judith *public relations executive*
Dutt, Birendra *research specialist*

Cupertino
Anderson, Fred D. *computer company executive*
Cook, Timothy D. *computer company executive*
Dalrymple, Cheryl *former online information company executive*
Devlin, Mike *software company executive*
Hall, Brenda *human resources executive*
Heinen, Nancy R. *computer company executive*
Mandich, Mitchell *computer company executive*
Mattathil, George Paul *communications specialist, consultant*
Rubinstein, Jonathan *computer company executive*

Daly City
Hargrave, Sarah Quesenberry *consulting company executive*

Dana Point
Mardian, Robert Charles, Jr. *restaurateur*

Del Mar
Comrie, Sandra Melton *human resource executive*

El Cajon
Silverberg, Lewis Henry *legal consultant*

El Dorado Hills
Davies, William Ralph *service executive*

El Segundo
Autolitano, Astrid *consumer products executive*
Cordner, Tom *advertising executive*
Farr, Kevin M. *consumer products executive*
Honeycutt, Van B. *computer services company executive*
Jenson, Timothy N. *computer software and services executive*
Katz, Lew *advertising executive*
Level, Leon Jules *information services executive*

Encinitas
Deuble, John L., Jr. *environmental science and engineering services consultant*

Encino
Greenberg, Allan *advertising and marketing research consultant*
La Cagnina, Victor S. *company executive*
Laba, Marvin *management consultant*
Lehman, Stephen C. *direct response programming executive*
Weiss, Eric R. *direct response programming executive*
Yukelson, Daniel M. *marketing company executive*

Escondido
Daniels, Richard Martin *public relations executive*
Mogul, Leslie Anne *business development and marketing consultant*

Exeter
Duncan, James Daniel *paper distribution company executive*

Fair Oaks
Nolan, Mark Gregory *advertising executive*

Fort Bragg
Galli, Darrell Joseph *management consultant*

Foster City
Avida, Dan *printing company executive*
Gecht, Guy *publishing company executive*
McHenry, Julie *communications executive*
Miller, Jon Philip *marketing professional, pharmaceutical executive*
Shaheen, George T. *management consultant*
Wilson, Lerry *public relations executive*

Fountain Valley
Lonegan, Thomas Lee *retired restaurant corporation executive*

Fremont
Bagley, James W. *research company executive*
Hackworth, Michael L. *electronics company executive*
Liang, Marcel *corporate executive*
Parikh, Mihir *executive*
Schauer, Ronald L. *executive*
Weinstein, Marta *packaging services company executive*

Fresno
Ganulin, Judy *public relations professional*
Levy, Joseph William *department stores executive*

Glendale
Dohring, Doug *marketing executive*
Dohring, Laurie *marketing executive*
Herzer, Richard Kimball *franchising company executive*
Misa, Kenneth Franklin *management consultant*

Half Moon Bay
Fennell, Diane Marie *marketing executive, process engineer*

Hillsborough
Westerfield, Putney *management consulting executive*

Irvine
Albright, William Alexander, Jr. *pharmaceutical company executive*
Alcone, Matt *advertising executive*
Hopp, Terry A. *computer company executive*
Jordan, Michelle Henrietta *public relations company executive*
Leber, Mike *advertising executive*
Maybay, Duane Charles *recycling systems executive*
Oliver, Travis *advertising agency executive*
Probert, William B. *sales executive*
Seller, Gregory Erol *marketing executive, writer, consultant*
Vidovich, Mark A. *paper products executive*

Jackson
Halvorson, Frank Elsworth *sales executive*

La Jolla
Bardwick, Judith Marcia *management consultant*
Bavasi, Peter Joseph *sports management executive*
Craig, Jenny *weight management executive*
Kelly, James S. *personal care industry executive*
Morse, Jack Hatton *management consultant*
Wertheim, Robert Halley *national security consultant*

La Puente
Sheridan, Christopher Frederick *human resources executive*

La Quinta
Peden, Lynn Ellen *marketing executive*

Laguna Beach
Arnold, John David *management counselor, catalyst*
Taylor, James Walter *business and management educator*

Laguna Hills
Miller, Eldon Earl *corporate business publications consultant, retired manufacturing company executive*

Laguna Niguel
Greenberg, Lenore *public relations professional*
Kursewicz, Lee Z. *marketing consultant*

Lake Forest
Earhart, Donald Marion *management consultant, health care company executive*

Livermore
Williams, David Michael *manufacturing executive*

Long Beach
Nussbaum, Luther James *computer company executive*

Los Alamitos
Caplan, Karen B. *company executive*

Los Altos
Esber, Edward Michael, Jr. *software company executive*
Heymann, Stephen *marketing management consultant*
Lynch, Daniel C. *multimedia executive*

Los Angeles
Anderson, Herbert W. *consumer products company executive*
Bender, Dean *public relations executive*
Bloch, Paul *public relations executive*
Bohle, Sue *public relations executive*
Brumfield, Jack *communications executive*
Burghdorf, Roger *business executive*
Burkle, Ronald W. *former food service executive, business investor*
Clow, Lee *advertising agency executive*
Cooke, John F. *entertainment company executive*
Crisci, Mathew G. *marketing executive, writer*
Crosby, Peter Alan *management consultant*
Doll, Lynne Marie *public relations agency executive*
Emerson, Barry D. *computer company executive*
Farrell, Joseph *movie market analyst, producer, entertainment research company executive, writer, sculptor, designer*
Fenimore, George Wiley *management consultant*
Ferry, Richard Michael *executive search firm executive*
Fils, Elliott *advertising executive*
Fishman, Arnie *marketing executive, consultant, film producer*
Gibbon, Tim *communications executive*
Gottfried, Ira Sidney *management consulting executive*
Greene, Alvin *service company executive, management consultant*
Hale, Kaycee *research marketing professional*
Hansen, Alexander E. *advertising agency executive*
Hartsough, Gayla Anne Kraetsch *management consultant*
Hateley, J. Michael *human resources executive*
Helper, Lee *strategic business marketing and marketing communications consultant*
Hill, Bonnie Guiton *company executive*
Hodal, Melanie *public relations executive*
Hofert, Jack *consulting company executive, lawyer*
Hollinger, William R. *controller home builder company*
Holt, Dennis F. *media buying company executive*
Humphreys, Robert Lee *advertising executive*
Hunt, Dennis *public relations executive*
Irwin-Hentschel, Noël *travel company executive*
Klein, Jim *company executive*
Kline, Richard Stephen *public relations executive*
Krueger, Robert William *management consultant*
Leahy, T. Liam *business development, technology investor*
Leibert, Richard William *special events producer*
Levine, Michael *public relations executive, writer*
Lewis, Randall *home building company executive*

Litewka, Albert Bernard *communications and publishing company executive*
Logan, Nancy Jane *broadcast sales and marketing executive*
Mamer, John William *business educator*
Miller, Bruce *advertising executive*
Nadler, Gerald *management consultant, educator*
Pondel, Roger S. *public relations executive*
Poole, Christopher K. *computer company executive*
Proper, Mary *advertising executive*
Puck, Wolfgang *executive chef*
Resnick, Lynda *art company executive*
Rice, Regina Kelly *marketing executive*
Rogers, Ronald *public relations executive*
Sackman, Dave *marketing executive*
Santiago, Mike *communications executive*
Silverman, Bruce Gary *advertising executive*
Silverton, Nancy *food service executive*
Spofford, Robert Houston *advertising agency executive*
Stanton, Lewis Harris *Internet learning company executive*
Suissa, David *advertising executive*
Tardio, Thomas A. *public relations executive*
Tatum, Jackie *former parks and recreation manager, municipal official*
Tomash, Erwin *retired computer equipment company executive*
Williams, Carlton L. *communications executive*
Winkler, Howard Leslie *business, finance, government relations consultant*
Zelikow, Howard Monroe *management and financial consultant*

Malibu
Tellem, Susan Mary *public relations executive*

Manhattan Beach
Deutsch, Barry Joseph *consulting and management development company executive*
Triplett, Arlene Ann *management consultant*

Marina Del Rey
Gold, Carol Sapin *international management consultant, speaker*

Menlo Park
Alsop, Stewart *communications executive*
Fenner, Peter David *communications executive*
Kashnow, Richard A. *executive*
Kurtzig, Sandra L. *software company executive*
Kvamme, Mark D. *marketing professional*
Richards, Stephen C. *corporate development executive*
Saffo, Paul *communications executive*

Mill Valley
Baker, Malcolm *marketing executive*

Millbrae
Mank, Edward Warren *marketing professional*

Milpitas
Corrigan, Wilfred J. *data processing and computer company executive*
Francis, Curt *computer company executive*
Gannon, John *computer company executive*
Levy, Kenneth *executive*
Rabbat, Guy *electronics company executive, inventor*
Swanson, Robert H. Jr. *consumer products company executive*
Yansouni, Cyril J. *computer company executive*

Mission Viejo
Dillon, Francis Patrick *human resources executive, financial, insurance and tax consultant*

Monrovia
Jemelian, John Nazar *management consultant*

Morgan Hill
Locklin, Paul G. *executive*
McGuire, Thomas Roger *distribution company executive*

Mountain View
Baker, Mari Jean *marketing director*
Barksdale, James Love *communications company executive*
Belluzzo, Richard E. *former computer company executive*
Bennett, Stephen M. *computer company executive*
Boyd, Dean Weldon *management consultant*
Drexler, Jerome *technology company executive*
Edsell, Patrick L. *computer company executive*
Garlick, Larry *executive*
Gomo, Steven J. *technical communications product company executive*
Harris, Bill H. *computer software company executive*
Kelly, William M. *former computer company executive*
Leslie, Mark *software company executive*
Livermore, Ann M. *computer company executive*
Otus, Simone *public relations executive*
Polese, Kim *software company executive*
Qureishi, A. Salam *computer software and services company executive*

Newport Beach
Cable, Wade H. *executive*
de Garcia, Lucia *marketing professional*
Gellman, Gloria Gae Seeburger Schick *marketing professional*
Lipson, Melvin Alan *technology and business management consultant*
Shonk, Albert Davenport, Jr. *advertising executive*
Spisak, John Francis *environmental company executive*

Novato
Fraser, Margot *consumer products company executive*
Guadarrama, Belinda *executive*

Oakland
Crane, Robert Meredith *health care executive*
Ejabat, Mory *communications executive*
Howard, Bradford Reuel *travel company executive*
Johnston, Gerald E. *manufacturing company executive*

Potash, Jeremy Warner *public relations executive*
Warrick, Brooke *marketing executive*

Oildale
Gallagher, Joseph Francis *marketing executive*

Orange
Scherman, Carol E. *human resources professional*

Orinda
Somerset, Harold Richard *retired business executive*

Palm Desert
Gaetano, Joy M. *human resources executive*
Stanczak, Stephen Phillip *environmental services administrator, lawyer*

Palm Springs
Arnold, Stanley Norman *manufacturing consultant*
Scott, Walter, Jr. *business consultant*
Seale, Robert McMillan *office services company executive*

Palo Alto
Allen, Louis Alexander *management consultant*
Barnholt, Edward W. *computer company executive*
Barrett, Ronald W. *executive*
Bowick, Susan D. *computer company executive*
Colligan, John C. (Bud Colligan) *multimedia company executive*
Dower, William J. *research company executive*
Fiorina, Carleton S. (Carly . Fiorina) *computer company executive*
Hamilton, Joe *communications company executive*
Joy, Bill *computer company executive*
Lehman, Michael Evans *computer company executive*
Levinson, Kathy *multimedia executive*
McNealy, Scott G. *computer company executive*
Morris, Michael H. *computer company executive*
Oshman, M. Kenneth *computer company executive*
Ticknor, Carolyn M. *computer company executive*
Waller, Peter William *public affairs executive*
Wayman, Robert Paul *computer company executive*
Willem, Karen J. *business software company financial executive*

Pasadena
Caine, Stephen Howard *data processing executive*
Caldwell, Kim A. *company executive*
Dayton, Sky *communications company executive*
Nackel, John George *technology executive*
Ott, George William, Jr. *management consulting executive*
Scarborough, Dean A. *consumer product company executive*
Watkins, John Francis *management consultant*

Pico Rivera
Luevano, Fred, Jr. *computer systems executive*

Piedmont
Hurley, Morris Elmer, Jr. *management consultant*

Playa Del Rey
Coots, Laurie *advertising executive*
Kuperman, Robert Ian *advertising agency executive*
Weir, Alexander, Jr. *utility consultant, inventor*

Pleasanton
Burd, Steve *food service executive*
Conway, Craig *computer software executive*
Smith, Gary *marketing executive*

Rancho Mirage
Abel, Michael L. *marketing executive*
Vivian, Linda Bradt *sales and public relations executive*

Rancho Palos Verdes
Rubenstein, Leonard Samuel *communications executive, ceramist, painter, sculptor, photographer*

Rancho Santa Fe
Baker, Charles Lynn *management consultant*
LaBonté, C(larence) Joseph *financial and marketing executive*
Matthews, Leonard Sarver *advertising and marketing executive*
Schirra, Walter Marty, Jr. *business consultant, former astronaut*

Redwood City
Bell, George *media executive*
Bloom, Gary L. *database company executive*
Cook, Paul Maxwell *technology company executive*
Feld, Donald H. *network consultant*
Henley, Jeffrey O. *computer software company executive*
Jermoluk, Thomas A. *computer company executive*
Lane, Raymond J. *software systems consulting company executive*
Rohde, James Vincent *software systems company executive*
Stone, Herbert Allen *management consultant*

Redwood Shores
Ellison, Lawrence J. *computer software company executive*

Reseda
Brooks, Robert Eugene *management consultant*

Richmond
Jobs, Steven Paul *computer corporation executive*

Riverside
Smith, Mallory S. *business executive*

Sacramento
Lucas, Donna *communications executive*
McElroy, Leo Francis *communications consultant, journalist*
Swatt, Stephen Benton *communications executive, consultant*

Salinas
Jeffries, Russell Morden *communications company official*

San Bruno
Howley, Peter Anthony *communications executive*

San Carlos
Kertzman, Mitchell E. *software company executive*

San Clemente
Alter, Robert A. *hotel executive*
Stenzel, William A. *consulting services executive*

San Diego
Adams, Loretta *marketing executive*
Antone, Douglas R. *corporate executive*
Bellamy, Paul *communications executive*
Berger, Newell James, Jr. *retired security professional*
Bradley, R. Todd *computer company executive*
DePinto, David J. *public relations executive*
Epstein, Daniel J. *management consultant*
Forrester, Brad *management consultant*
Gilbertson, Oswald Irving *marketing executive*
Goodall, Jackson Wallace, Jr. *restaurant company executive*
Jacobs, Irwin Mark *communications executive*
Jones, Ronald H. *computer information systems executive*
Nelson, Craig Alan *management consultant*
North, Robert L. *computer software executvie*
Nugent, Robert J., Jr. *fast food company executive*
Partida, Gilbert A. *executive*
Robino, David J. *computer company executive*
Stoorza Gill, Gail *corporate professional*
Tillinghast, Charles Carpenter, III *marketing company executive*
Todd, John J. *computer company executive*
Waitt, Ted W. *computer company executive*
Warner, John Hilliard, Jr. *technical services, military and commercial systems and software company executive*
Ziegaus, Alan James *public relations executive*

San Francisco
Bancel, Marilyn *fund raising management consultant*
Bianchi, Carisa *advertising company executive*
Blanc, Maureen *public relations executive*
Boehlke, Christine *public relations executive*
Boehlke, William Fredrick *public relations executive, consultant*
Bonnie, Shelby W. *computer company executive*
Brinkley, Susan *executive pastry chef*
Butenhoff, Susan *public relations executive*
Colton, Roy Charles *management consultant*
D'Errico, Didi *public relations executive*
DiStefano, Tony E. *communications executive*
Eckstut, Michael Kauder *management consultant*
Everett-Thorp, Kate *digital marketing executive*
Goldberg, Fred Sellmann *advertising executive*
Goodby, Jeffrey *advertising agency executive*
Gordon, Judith *communications consultant, writer*
Green, Bartley Crocker *advertising executive*
Haas, Peter E., Sr. *apparel company executive*
Hara, George *software company executive*
Harlan, Neil Eugene *retired healthcare company executive*
Hazen, Don *communications executive*
Hearon, Reed *chef*
Hernandez, Aileen C(larke) *urban consultant*
Heynes, Aedhmar *public relations executive*
Holmes, Irvin R., Jr. *marketing professional*
Horne, Grant Nelson *public relations consultant*
Johnson, Camille *media executive*
Kahle, Brewster *communications executive*
Kamer, Larry *public relations executive*
Kelly, Alan *public relations executive*
Kielarowski, Henry Edward *marketing executive*
Kimpton, Bill *hotel executive*
Kurtz, Larry *corporate communications executive*
Landis, Richard Gordon *retired food company executive*
LaTour, Thomas W. *hotel executive*
Leondakis, Niki Anna *food service executive*
Maneatis, George A. *retired utility company executive*
Marshall, Scott *advertising agency executive*
Massaro, Mike *advertising executive*
McEvoy, Nan Tucker *publishing company executive, olive rancher*
Minor, Halsey *multimedia company executive*
Muegge, Lyn *advertising executive*
Murphy, Kathleen Anne Foley *advertising agency executive*
Nelson, Jonathan *computer communications company executive*
O'Rourke, Dennis *advertising executive*
Owades, Ruth Markowitz *marketing company executive*
Probert, Colin *advertising executive*
Riney, Hal Patrick *advertising executive*
Rosenfield, Ruth *advertising executive*
Shorenstein, Douglas W. *corporate executive*
Slipsager, Henrik C. *human resources specialist*
Sproul, John Allan *retired public utility executive*
Steel, Jon *advertising executive*
Suiter, Thomas *advertising executive*
Torme, Margaret Anne *public relations executive, communications consultant*
Wernick, Sandra Margot *advertising and public relations executive*
Wilbur, Brayton, Jr. *distribution company executive*
Winkler, Agnieszka M. *Internet executive*

San Jose
Baab, Carlton *advertising executive*
Bengier, Gary T. *online company executive*
Carter, Larry R. *computer company executive*
Chambers, John T. *computer company executive*
Chen, Tu *computer executive*
Daichendt, Gary J. *executive sales professional*
Estrin, Judith *computer company executive*
Hawley, Kimra *software company executive*
Highlander, Richard William *communications executive*
Hutcheson, Jerry Dee *manufacturing company executive*
Nguyen, Lam Duc *business executive, consultant*
Raghavan, Asuri *executive*
Roberts, Lawrence Gilman *telecommunications company executive*

Roelandts, Willem P. *computer company executive*
Rostoker, Michael David *former micro-electronics company executive, lawyer*
Scott, Edward William, Jr. *computer software company executive*
Skoll, Jeffrey *Internet company executive*
Swette, Brian T. *online computer executive*
Warnock, John Edward *computer company executive*
Weinhardt, J. W. *computer company executive*
Whitman, Margaret, C *internet executive*
Williams, Jouston L. *service industry executive*
Witter, Dean, III *computer company executive*
Zafiropoulo, Arthur *executive*
Zinn, Ray *computer company executive*

San Juan Capistrano
McIntosh, L(orne) William *marketing executive*

San Luis Obispo
DuFresne, Armand Frederick *management and engineering consultant*

San Marcos
Huff, Dale Eugene *retired environmental services executive*

San Mateo
Siebel, Thomas M. *executive*

San Rafael
Bartz, Carol *software company executive*
Evenhuis, Henk J. *research company executive*
Kennedy, James Waite *management consultant, writer*
Thompson, John William *international management consultant*

San Ramon
Shapiro, Fania *computer company executive*

Santa Ana
Boynton, William Lewis *retired electronic manufacturing company official*
Foster, Kent B. *computer technology company executive*
Grainger, Michael J. *data processing executive*
Holtz, Joseph Norman *marketing executive*

Santa Barbara
Adizes, Ichak *management consultant, writer*
Emmons, Robert John *corporate executive*
McKee, Kathryn Dian Grant *human resources consultant*

Santa Clara
Barrett, Craig R. *computer company executive*
Benhamou, Eric A. *computer company executive*
Bryant, Andy D. *computer company executive*
Carter, Dennis Lee *marketing professional*
Claflin, Bruce *communications company executive*
Couillaud, Bernard J. *executive*
Ellis, Carlene *computer company executive*
Filo, David *computer communications executive*
Floyd, Shelly L. *computer company executive*
Hart, John H. *communications professional*
Hathcock, Bonita Catherine *telecommunications company executive*
Holdt, Terry *computer company executive*
Koogle, Timothy K. *communications executive*
Lin, Frank C. *computer company executive*
Luongo, John R. *executive*
Moore, Bruce *executive*
Morris, Sandra K. *computer company executive*
Murray, Patricia *computer company executive*
Otellini, Paul S. *communications executive*
Parker, Gerhard H. *communications professional*
Perham, Len *communications executive*
Pollace, Pamela L. *public relations executive*
Rescoe, Michael E. *computer company executive*
Roberts, Janice *marketing professional*
Rudolph, Ronald Alvin *human resources executive*
Vincent, David Ridgely *management consulting executive*
Yang, Jerry *online computer services executive*

Santa Cruz
Michels, Doug *computer company executive*

Santa Fe Springs
Hammond, Judy McLain *business services executive*

Santa Monica
Bachrach, Charles Lewis *advertising agency executive*
Biondi, Frank J., Jr. *entertainment company executive*
Hagelstein, William C. *advertising executive*
Hutton, Fiona S. *communications executive*
Katinsky, Steven *communications company executive*
Kessler, Robert Allen *data processing executive*
Mancuso, Vince *advertising executive*
Patel, Chandra Kumar Naranbhai *communications company executive, educator, researcher, entrepreneur*
Postaer, Larry *advertising executive*
Price, David *golf courses facilities executive*
Remsing, Dennis *advertising agency executive*
Roberts, Kevin *recreational facility executive*
Rubin, Gerrold Robert *advertising executive*
Ryan, Jane Frances *corporate communications executive*
Siegel, Mace *company executive*
Williams, Kathleen *advertising executive*

Santa Rosa
Cavanagh, John Charles *advertising agency executive*
Schudel, Hansjoerg *international business consultant*

Santa Ynez
Palola, Harry Joel *international affairs executive, consultant*

Scotts Valley
Luczo, Stephen J. *computer equipment company executive*
Pope, Charles C. *data processing executive*
Shugart, Alan F. *retired electronic computing equipment company executive*

WASHINGTON

Anacortes
Spaulding, John Pierson *public relations executive, marine consultant*

Bellevue
Evans, Robert Vincent *sales and marketing executive*
Myhrvold, Nathan *technology executive*
O'Byrne, Michael *management consultant*
Otterholt, Barry L. *technology management consultant*
Pool, David *software executive*
Pritt, Frank W. *computer company executive*

Centralia
Bates, Charles Walter *human resources executive, lawyer*

Federal Way
Dooley, James H. *product company executive*
Muzyka-McGuire, Amy *marketing professional, nutrition consultant*

Gig Harbor
Robinson, James William *retired management consultant*

Kent
Cheung, John B. *research and development executive*

Kirkland
Ladd, James Roger *international business executive and consultant*

Liberty Lake
Williams, Judi *communications executive*

Littlerock
Gunderson, Cleon Henry *management consultant corporation executive*

Mercer Island
Herres, Phillip Benjamin *computer software executive*

Mountlake Terrace
Kallshian, Jan *electronics manufacturing company executive*
Thompson, David C. *electronics manufacturing company executive*

Oak Harbor
Meaux, Alan Douglas *facilities technician, sculptor*

Olympia
Marcelynas, Richard Chadwick *management consultant*
Weese, Bruce Eric *pharmaceutical sales executive*

Port Angeles
Smithson, Michael *parks director*

Redmond
Ballmer, Steve *software company executive*
Barton, Richard N. *computer company executive*
Connors, John G. *computer company executive*
Gates, Bill (III William Henry Gates) *software company executive*
Gyani, Mohan *communications company executive*
Herbold, Robert J. *software company executive*
Maffei, Greg *computer company executive*
Mathews, Mich *computer company executive*

Renton
Pugh, Donald E. *industry executive*
Raden, Gary *business executive*

Seattle
Beetham, Stanley Williams *management consultant*
Bezos, Jeffrey P. *multimedia executive*
Bianco, James A. *research and development executive*
Burns, Michael Joseph *operations and sales-marketing executive*
Dagnon, James Bernard *human resources executive*
Dederer, Michael Eugene *public relations company executive*
Duryee, David Anthony *management consultant*
Eastham, John D. *business executive*
Elgin, Ron Alan *advertising executive*
Glaser, Rob *communications company executive*
Griffin, William Ray *consulting and publishing company executive*
Hopson, Andy *public relations executive*
Hough, John Dennis *public relations executive*
Howell, R. Scott *industry executive*
Komen, Richard B. *food service executive*
Kraft, Donald Bowman *advertising agency executive*
MacDonald, Andrew Stephen *management consulting firm executive*
McConnell, J. Daniel *sports marketing professional*
McReynolds, Neil Lawrence *management consultant*
Miyata, Keijiro *culinary arts educator*
Rowe, Katherine L. *computer company executive*
Ruckelshaus, William Doyle *investment group executive*
von Bargen, Sally *stock image photography company executive*
Walker, Douglas *computer developement company executive*
Yamin, John *food service executive*

Snoqualmie
Giuliani, David *personal care products company executive*
Stull, Mike *personal care industry executive*

Spokane
Geraghty, John Vincent *public relations consultant*
[illegible], Ronald T. *computer company executive*
Oehlke, Jack W. *computer company executive*
Woodard, Alva Abe *business consultant*

Tacoma
Hudson, Edward Voyle *linen supply company executive*
Licens, Lila Louise *administrative assistant*
Robinson, Richard Allen, Jr. *human resources development trainer, consultant*

Vancouver
Braden, Robert *communications company executive*
Cook, Brian R. *corporate professional*
Graf, Rudy J. *communications company executive*
Ogden, Valeria Munson *management consultant, state representative*
Rice, Rod W. *corporate executive*
Smith, Milton Ray *computer company executive, lawyer*
Tau, Leonard *communications company executive*

Woodinville
Love, Keith Sinclair *communications executive*

Yakima
Shields, William *printing company executive*

WYOMING

Fort Laramie
Mack, James A. *parks director*

CANADA

ALBERTA

Calgary
Hume, James Borden *corporate professional, foundation executive*
Shaw, J.R. *communications executive*

BRITISH COLUMBIA

Burnaby
Rasul, Firoz *business executive*

North Vancouver
Francis, Norm *computer software executive, accountant*

Vancouver
Anderson, Norman *management consultant*
Campbell, Bruce Alan *market research consultant*
Collins, Mary *management consultant, former Canadian legislator*
Cormier, Jean G. *communications company executive*
O'Neill, John *hotel executive*
O'Neill, Rob *hotel executive*
Saywell, William George Gabriel *business development and management consultant*

Victoria
Nuttall, Richard Norris *management consultant, physician*

SASKATCHEWAN

Regina
Clayton, Raymond Edward *government official*

ADDRESS UNPUBLISHED

Albertine, Anne *corporate chef*
Allan, James S. *sales professional*
Allen, Paul G. *computer executive, professional sports team owner*
Anderegg, Karen Klok *business executive*
Barad, Jill Elikann *family products company executive*
Barca, Kathleen *marketing executive*
Barger, William James *management consultant, educator*
Barton, Peter Richard, III *communications executive*
Becerra, Octavio *corporate executive chef*
Blaine, Davis Robert *investment banker, valuation consultant executive*
Borda, Richard Joseph *management consultant*
Braden, George Walter, II (Baron of Carrigaline) *company executive*
Brun, Margaret Ann Charlene *semiconductor industry buyer, planner*
Buck, Linda Dee *executive recruiting company executive*
Buras-Elsen, Brenda Allynn *retired public affairs executive*
Chamberlain, William Edwin, Jr. *management consultant*
Collins, Russell Ambrose *retired advertising executive, creative director*
Crosson, John Albert *advertising executive*
Cunningham, Andrea Lee *public relations executive*
Davis, J. Steve *advertising agency executive*
deWilde, David Michael *executive search consultant, financial services executive, lawyer*
Doan, Mary Frances *advertising executive*
Dolich, Andrew Bruce *sports marketing executive*
Dowie, Ian James *management consultant*
Duke, William Edward *public affairs executive*
Dwan, Dennis Edwin *broadcast executive, photographer*
Ecton, Donna R. *business executive*
Eddy, David Maxon *health policy and management administrator*
Ellis, Robert Harry *retired television executive, university administrator*
Erb, Richard Louis Lundin *resort and hotel executive*
[illegible]
Flagg, Norman Lee *retired advertising executive*
Gilbertson, Robert G. *computer company executive*
Glatzer, Robert Anthony *marketing and sales executive*
Grindal, Mary Ann *former sales professional*
Grody, Mark Stephen *public relations executive*
Hall, Adrienne A. *international marketing executive, venture capitalist consultant*
Hapka, Catherine M. *Internet executive*
Harris, Robert Norman *advertising and communications educator*
Hayes, Janet Gray *retired business manager, former mayor*
Henry, Philip Lawrence *marketing professional*
Hickerson, Glenn Lindsey *leasing company executive*
Holzman, D. Keith *management consultant, record company executive, producer, arts consultant*
Joffe, Barbara Lynne *computer management professional, computer artist*
Jordan, Jeffrey Guy *marketing and marketing research consultant*
Karalis, John Peter *computer company executive, lawyer*
Kelleher, Richard Cornelius *marketing and communications executive*
Kennedy, Debra Joyce *marketing professional*
Lampert, Eleanor Verna *retired human resources specialist*
Lavidge, Robert James *marketing research executive*
Lee, Richard Kenneth *software company executive*
Lowy, Peter *executive*
Matthew, Lyn *sales and marketing executive consultant*
McCaw, Craig O. *communications executive*
McVeigh-Pettigrew, Sharon Christine *communications consultant*
Morrison, David Fred *software company executive*
Noolan, Julie Anne Carroll *management consultant*
Olson, Dale C. *public relations executive*
Parenti, Kathy Ann *sales professional*
Patterson, Dennis Joseph *management consultant*
Petty, George Kibbe *communications executive*
Rasor, Dina Lynn *investigator, journalist*
Reis, C. Dale *company executive*
Russell, Carol Ann *personnel service company executive*
Savage, Neve Richard *marketing executive*
Scaglione, Cecil Frank *marketing executive, publisher*
Selvin, Neil *computer company executive*
Smith, Thomas Winston *cotton marketing executive*
Smyth, Cornelius Edmonston *retired hotel executive*
Sollender, Joel David *management consultant, financial executive*
Spoor, James Edward *human resources executive, entrepreneur*
Stevens, Berton Louis, Jr. *data processing manager*
Stewart, Richard Alfred *business executive*
Terry, Richard Frank *data transcriber*
Thompson, Craig Snover *corporate communications executive*
Tipton, Gary Lee *retired services company executive*
Tooley, Charles Frederick *communications executive, consultant*
Walker, Henry Gilbert *health care executive, consultant*
Wasserman, Anthony Ira *software company executive, educator*
White, Bonnie Yvonne *management consultant, retired educator*
White, Loray Betty *TV talk show host, writer, producer, singer, actress, director*
Williams, Harry Edward *management consultant, management consultant, consultant*
Winsor, David John *cost consultant*
Yocam, Delbert Wayne *retired software products company executive*

INDUSTRY: TRADE

UNITED STATES

ALASKA

Anchorage
Schnell, Roger Thomas *business owner, retired state official and career officer*

Denali Park
Swenson, Richard Allen *business owner, animal trainer*

ARIZONA

Chandler
Anderson, Darl *retail executive*
Basha, Edward N., Jr. *grocery chain owner*
Fowler, Reggie *retail executive*

Phoenix
Francis, Philip L. *retail executive*

Sun City
Thompson, Betty Jane *small business owner*

CALIFORNIA

Aliso Viejo
Purdy, Alan MacGregor *financial executive*

Arcadia
Stangeland, Roger Earl *retail chain store executive*

Beverly Hills
Carter, William B. *global development company official*

Burbank
Wise, Woodrow Wilson, Jr. *retired small business owner*

Burlingame
Moldaw, Stuart G. *venture capitalist, retail clothing stores executive*

Cathedral City
Jackman, Robert Alan *retail executive*

City Of Commerce
Lynch, Martin Andrew *retail company executive*

Colton
Brown, Jack H. *supermarket company executive*

Commerce
Martin, Richard J. *food wholesale executive*
Plamann, Alfred A. *wholesale distribution executive*

Danville
Ritchey, Samuel Donley, Jr. *retired retail store executive*

El Segundo
King, Sharon Marie *consulting company executive*

Escondido
Young, Gladys *business owner*

Fremont
Lane, Eric Jay *retail executive*
Liang, Christine *import company executive*

Fresno
Blum, Gerald Henry *department store executive*

Goleta
Winslow, Norman Eldon *business executive*

Hollywood
Lore, Linda *retail executive*

Irvine
Massengill, Matthew H. *retail company executive*

Lafayette
Brown, William E. *retail executive*

Los Angeles
Hawley, Philip Metschan *retired retail executive, consultant*
Roeder, Richard Kenneth *business owner, lawyer*
Sinay, Joseph *retail executive*
Williams, Theodore Earle *retired industrial distribution company executive*

Modesto
Piccinini, Robert M. *grocery store chain executive*

Newark
Balmuth, Michael A. *retail executive*
Ferber, Norman Alan *retail executive*

Newport Beach
Peets, Terry R. *retail executive*

Orange
Andrews, Charles *wholesale distribution executive*
Underwood, Vernon O., Jr. *grocery stores executive*

Palo Alto
Carey, Theresa Wilkinson *small business owner, writer, editor*

Pleasanton
Plaisance, Melissa *retail executive*

San Francisco
Draper, William Henry, III *business executive*
Drexler, Millard S. *retail executive*
Fisher, Donald G. *casual apparel chain stores executive*
Fisher, Robert *retail executive*
Kircher, Matt *retail executive*
Kunz, Heidi *retail store executive*
Lester, W. Howard *retail executive*
Majeske, Mark T. *retail sales professional*
Ullman, Myron Edward, III *retail executive*

San Jose
Finnigan, Robert Emmet *business owner*

South San Francisco
Allen, Robert A *wholesale distribution executive*
Korman, Leo *wholesale distribution executive*
Mertens, Lynne G. *retail executive*

Thousand Oaks
Calborn, Keith W. *wholesale distribution executive*

Walnut Creek
Long, Robert Merrill *retail drug company executive*
McCann, Steven *retail executive*

West Sacramento
Searson, Dee *retail products executive*
Solomon, Russell M. *retail products executive*
Teel, Joyce Raley *supermarket and drugstore retail executive*

Woodland Hills
Weider, Joseph *wholesale distribution executive*

COLORADO

Aurora
Reynolds, Robert Harrison *retired export company executive*

Broomfield
King, Robert *retail company executive*

Colorado Springs
[illegible]

Denver
Cashman, Michael Richard *small business owner*
Hendrickson, Thomas T. *retail executive*
McCaghren, Michael *retail executive*
Morton, John Douglas *retail executive*
Vigil, Jeffrey L. *infant and child products manufacturing executive*

Loveland
Rodman, Alpine C. *arts and crafts company executive*
Rodman, Sue A. *wholesale company executive, artist, writer*

DISTRICT OF COLUMBIA

Washington
Kimmitt, Robert Michael *executive, banker, diplomat*

IDAHO

Boise
Long, William D. *grocery store executive*
Lynch, Peter L. *supermarket/drug store executive*
Michael, Gary G. *retail supermarket and drug chain executive*
Olson, A. Craig *retail executive*
Piva, Gary *retail grocery executive*

MONTANA

Helena
Brown, Jan Whitney *small business owner*

NEW MEXICO

Carlsbad
Queen, Dorothy *distribution company executive*

OREGON

Burns
Timms, Eugene Dale *wholesale business owner, state senator*

Klamath Falls
Pastega, Richard Louis *retired retail specialist*

Medford
De Boer, Jeffrey B. *auto dealership executive*
De Boer, Sydney B. *auto dealership executive*

Myrtle Creek
Shirtcliff, John Delzell *business owner, oil jobber*

Portland
Greenstein, Merle Edward *import and export company executive*
Maletis, Ed *distribution executive*
Tomjack, T.J. *wholesale distribution executive*

Prineville
Wick, Philip *wholesale distribution executive*

Salem
Snodgrass, Lynn *small business owner, state legislator*

UTAH

Logan
Watterson, Scott *home fitness equipment manufacturer*

Salt Lake City
Fields, Debbi *cookie franchise executive*
Miller, Lorraine *business owner*

WASHINGTON

Bellingham
Cole, Craig W. *grocery chain executive*

Issaquah
Brotman, Jeffrey H. *variety stores executive*
Galanti, Richard A. *wholesale business executive*
Sinegal, James D. *wholesale distribution executive*
Wendling, Louise *wholesale distribution executive*

Redmond
Brakken, William *home improvement retail executive*

Seattle
Bridge, Herbert Marvin *jewelry executive*
Cottle, Gail Ann *retail executive*
Fix, Wilbur James *department store executive*
Leale, Olivia Mason *import marketing company executive*
Moriguchi, Tomio *gift and grocery store executive*
Nordstrom, Blake W. *retail executive*
Nordstrom, Bruce A. *department store executive*
Nordstrom, John N. *department store executive*
Stewart, Thomas J. *wholesale distribution executive*

Spokane
Sines, Randy Dwain *business executive*
Swanson, Dale Charles *small business owner, industrial engineer*
Zakheim, Irving Lee *gift import company executive*

Tacoma
Gozon, Richard C. *paper distribution executive*

Yakima
Newland, Ruth Laura *small business owner*

WYOMING

Jackson
Law, Clarene Alta *innkeeper, state legislator*

ADDRESS UNPUBLISHED

Biagi, Richard Charles *retail executive, real estate consultant*
Brewer, Stanley R. *wholesale distribution consultant*
Busch, Joyce Ida *small business owner*
Chevalier, Paul Edward *retired retail executive, lawyer*
Day, John Denton *retired company executive, cattle and horse rancher, breeder, trainer, wrangler, actor, educator*
Edwards, Patricia Burr *small business owner, counselor, consultant*
Folkman, David H. *retail, wholesale and consumer products consultant*
Goldman, Gerald Hillis *beverage distribution company executive*
Martini, Robert Edward *wholesale pharmaceutical and medical supplies company executive*
Nagel, Daryl David *retail executive*
Samson, Alvin *former distributing company executive, consultant*
Williams, Leona Rae *lingerie shop owner, consultant*

INDUSTRY: TRANSPORTATION

UNITED STATES

ALASKA

Anchorage
Bowers, Paul D. *transportation company executive*
Sullivan, George Murray *transportation consultant, former mayor*

Fairbanks
Ruff, Doyle C. *airport manager*

Ketchikan
Miller, David C. *airport manager*

ARIZONA

Bullhead City
Bettendorf, Jerry *retired airport administrator*
Hicks, Norm *airport authority executive*

Grand Canyon
Bryant, Leland Marshal *business and nonprofit executive*

Phoenix
Amoako, James Kwaku *transportation services executive, financial analyst*
Johnson, Robert D. *aerospace transportation executive*
Knight, Gary J. *transportation executive*
Knight, Kevin P. *transportation executive*
Krietor, David *airport authority executive*
Moyes, Jerry C. *transportation executive*
Solomon, John Davis *aviation executive*

Tucson
Burg, Walter A. *airport terminal executive*

CALIFORNIA

Camarillo
McConnel, Richard Appleton *aerospace company official*

Edwards
Brand, Vance Devoe *astronaut*

Encino
Aaronson, Robert Jay *aviation executive*
Gasich, Welko Elton *retired aerospace executive, management consultant*

Gilroy
Borton, George Robert *retired airline captain*

Hawthorne
Hunt, Brian L. *program manager*

Hermosa Beach
Kokalj, James Edward *retired aerospace administrator*

Long Beach
Anderson, Gerald Verne *retired aerospace company executive*
Myers, John Wescott *aviation executive*

Los Angeles
Anderson, Roy Arnold *aerospace company executive*
Bruce, William A. *airport executive*
Gross, Ken *transportation executive*
Kennard, Lydia H. *airport terminal executive*
Knowles, Marie L. *transportation executive*
Kresa, Kent *aerospace executive*
Myers, Albert F. *transportation executive*
Park, Sam-Koo *transportation executive*
Waugh, Richard B., Jr. *aircraft company executive, lawyer*

Los Osos
Moore, Walter Dengel *rapid transit system professional*

Menlo Park
O'Brien, Raymond Francis *transportation executive*

Newbury Park
Lindsey, Joanne M. *flight attendant, poet*

Oakland
Crowley, Thomas B., Jr. *water transportation executive*
Rhein, Timothy J. *retired transportation company executive*
Wade, Bill *airport executive*

Ontario
Drinkwater, Peter Loftus *airport executive*

Palo Alto
Berry, Robert Emanuel *aerospace company executive*
Detter, Gerald L. *transportation company executive*
Moffitt, Donald Eugene *transportation company executive*
Ratnathicam, Chutta *transportation company executive*

Ramona
Hoffman, Wayne Melvin *retired airline official*

Ranchero Cordova
Hall, Terry *air transportation executive*

Redwood City
Foley, Patrick *air courier company executive*
Smartt, Bill *air courier company executive*
Waller, Stephen *air transportation executive*

Sacramento
Hally, Terry L. *aerospace executive*
Wolfe, Robert A. *aerospace executive*

San Diego
Bowens, Thella *senior aviation director*

San Francisco
Anschutz, Philip F. *transportation executive, communications executive*
Dutt, Ronald F. *transportation executive*
Freitag, Peter Roy *transportation specialist*
Fritz, Lynn C. *transportation executive*
Guinasso, Victor *delivery service executive*
Martin, John L. *airport executive*
Napier, Graham R.F. *transportation executive*

San Jose
Tonseth, Ralph G. *airport executive*

San Mateo
Trabitz, Eugene Leonard *aerospace company executive*

San Pedro
Keller, Larry Alan *water transportation executive*

Santa Ana
Bailey, Don Matthew *aerospace and electronics company executive*
Dean, William Evans *aerospace industry executive*

Sherman Oaks
Caren, Robert Poston *aerospace company executive*

Stockton
Biddle, Donald Ray *aerospace company executive*
DeAngelis, Dan *transportation executive*

Torrance
Savitz, Maxine Lazarus *aerospace company executive*

COLORADO

Denver
Baumgartner, Bruce *airport administrator*
McMorris, Jerry *transportation company executive, sports team executive*

HAWAII

Honolulu
Pfeiffer, Robert John *business executive*

IDAHO

Boise
Ilett, Frank, Jr. *trucking company executive, educator*

Idaho Falls
Thorsen, James Hugh *retired aviation director, airport manager, retired*

NEVADA

Las Vegas
Walker, Randall H. *air transportation executive*

Reno
Horton, Gary Bruce *transportation company executive*
Shoen, Edward Joseph *transportation and insurance companies executive*
White, Robert C. *air transportation executive*

NEW MEXICO

Albuquerque
Weh, Allen Edward *airline executive*

Holloman Air Force Base
Klause, Klaus J. *aircraft company executive*

OKLAHOMA

Grove
Trippensee, Gary Alan *aerospace executive, retired*

OREGON

Mcminnville
Lane, Larry K. *air industry service executive*

Portland
Brockley, John P. *airport terminal executive*
Cheston, Michael Galloway *airport executive*

UTAH

North Salt Lake
Bouley, Joseph Richard *pilot*

Orem
Snow, Marlon O. *trucking executive, state agency administrator*

West Valley City
Simon, Richard D. *transportation executive*

WASHINGTON

Kirkland
Clarkson, Lawrence William *airplane company executive*

Seattle
Albaugh, James F. *aerospace transportation executive*
Brazier, Robert G. *transportation executive*
Cella, John J. *freight company executive*
Cline, Robert Stanley *air freight company executive*
Condit, Philip Murray *aerospace executive, engineer*
Freudenberger, Kent W. *freight company executive*
Givan, Boyd Eugene *aircraft company executive*
Grinstein, Gerald *transportation executive*
Kelley, John F. *airline executive*
Kelly, John F. *air transportation executive*
Lindsey, Gina Marie *airport executive*
Rose, Peter J. *delivery service executive*
Schmidt, Peter Gustav *shipbuilding industry executive*
Sears, William M. *aerospace transportation executive*
Smith, F. D. (Ricky Smith) *rail transporation executive*
Warner, John D. *aerospace company executive*

Spokane
Ueberroth, John A. *air transportation executive*

Vancouver
Blake, Patrick H. *trucking executive*

WYOMING

Worland
Woods, Lawrence Milton *airline company executive*

CANADA

ALBERTA

Calgary
Caron, Ernie Matthew *airport executive*
McCaig, Jeffrey James *transportation company executive*

Edmonton
Marcotte, Brian *transportation executive*

BRITISH COLUMBIA

Sidney
Paquette, Richard *airport executive*

ADDRESS UNPUBLISHED

Butterfield, Alexander Porter *former business executive, government official*
Cook, Stephen Champlin *retired shipping company executive*
Deets, Dwain Aaron *retired aerospace technology executive*
Kerbs, Wayne Allan *transportation executive*
Quesnel, Gregory L. *transportation company executive*
Roberts, Linda *truck transportation services company executive*

INDUSTRY: UTILITIES, ENERGY, RESOURCES

UNITED STATES

ALASKA

Anchorage
Duncan, Ronald A. *telecommunications company executive*
Thompson, J. Ken *gas, oil industry executive*
Walp, Robert M. *communications carrier and internet/cable providerexecutive*

Fairbanks
Beistline, Earl Hoover *mining consultant*

ARIZONA

Carefree
Birkelbach, Albert Ottmar *retired oil company executive*

Phoenix
De Michele, O. Mark *utility company executive*
Huffman, Edgar Joseph *oil company executive*
Post, William Joseph *utility executive*
Yearley, Douglas Cain *mining and manufacturing company executive*

Prescott
Bennett, Kenneth R. *oil company executive, state legislator*

Scottsdale
Bullerdick, Kim H. *petroleum executive*
Holliger, Fred Lee *oil company executive*

Tempe
Clevenger, Jeffrey Griswold *mining company executive*

Tucson
Jamison, Harrison Clyde *former oil company executive, petroleum exploration consultant*
Kissinger, Karen G. *energy executive*
Nelson, Dennis R. *energy executive*
Peeler, Stuart Thorne *petroleum industry executive and independent oil operator*
Peters, Charles William *research and development company manager*

CALIFORNIA

Anaheim
Fenton, Donald Mason *retired oil company executive*

Brea
Stegemeier, Richard Joseph *oil company executive*

Camarillo
MacAlister, Robert Stuart *oil company executive*

Carpinteria
McIntyre, Bruce Martin *oil company executive*

El Segundo
Beach, Roger C. *retired oil company executive*
Fisher, Thomas E. *energy company executive*
Imle, John F., Jr. *oil company executive*
Williamson, Charles R. *energy company executive*

Folsom
Regan, William Joseph, Jr. *energy company executive*

Hillsborough
Quigley, Philip J. *retired telecommunications industry executive*

Huntington Beach
Schaffner-Irvin, Kristen *oil executive*

Irvine
Fohrer, Alan J. *utilities company executive*

La Jolla
Trujillo, Solomon D. *telecommunications executive*

Los Angeles
Bowlin, Michael Ray *oil company executive*
Chazen, Stephen I. *oil company executive*
Davis, Marvin *petroleum company executive, entrepreneur*
Foley, John V. *water company executive*
Glickman, David *telecommunications industry executive*
Greenberg, Kate *telecommunications industry executive*
Laurance, Dale R. *oil company executive*
Thelander, Beverly *oil company executive*
Van Horne, R. Richard *oil company executive*
Wiley, Michael E. *gas and oil executive*

Martinez
Meyer, Jarold Alan *oil company research executive*

Mill Valley
Premo, Paul Mark *oil company executive*

Pacific Palisades
Middleton, James Arthur *oil and gas company executive*
Mulryan, Henry Trist *mineral company executive, consultant*

Palo Alto
Glauthier, T. J. *non-profit CEO*

Palos Verdes Peninsula
Christie, Hans Frederick *retired utility company subsidiaries executive, consultant*

Piedmont
Willrich, Mason *energy industry executive*

Rosemead
Bryson, John E. *utilities company executive*
Bushey, Richard Kenneth *utility executive*
Craver, Theodore F., Sr. *utilites/energy executive*

Sacramento
Wickland, J. Al, Jr. *petroleum product executive, real estate executive*

San Diego
Altman, Steven *telecommunications executive*
Baum, Stephen L. *utilities company executive*
Farman, Richard Donald *energy company executive*
Felsinger, Donald E. *utilities corporation executive*
Guiles, Edwin A. *utilities company executive*
Roper, William Alford, Jr. *diversified technology services company executive*
Schmale, Neal E. *utilites company executive*
Sulpizio, Richard *communications company executive*
Thornley, Anthony S. *telecommunications company executive*

San Francisco
Bonney, John Dennis *retired oil company executive*
Caccamo, Aldo M. *oil industry executive*
Clarke, Richard Alan *electric and gas utility company executive, lawyer*
Darbee, Peter A. *electric power company executive*
Derr, Kenneth T. *retired oil company executive*
Ginn, Sam L. *telephone company executive*
Glynn, Robert D., Jr. *electric power and gas industry executive*
High, Thomas W. *energy services executive*
Iribe, P. Chrisman *utilities executive*
Klitten, Martin R. *oil industry executive*
Lerdal, Mark D. *energy company executive*
Maddox, Lyn E. *utilities company executive*
Matzke, Richard H. *oil industry executive*
O'Reilly, David J. *oil company executive*
Politan, Nicholas *energy company executive*
Sullivan, James N. *retired oil industry executive*
Watson, John S. *oil company executive*

San Jose
Foy, Robert W(illard) *water service company executive*
Wall, James Edward *telecommunications, petroleum and pharmaceutical executive*

San Ramon
Carter, George Kent *oil company executive*
Hickson, Robin Julian *mining company executive*
Robertson, Peter James *oil company executive*
Woertz, Patricia A. *petroleum industry executive*

Santa Barbara
Casey, Mary A. *telecommunications company executive*
Enos, Kelly D. *telecommunications company financial executive*

South Pasadena
Finnell, Michael Hartman *corporate executive*

Turlock
Williams, Delwyn Charles *telephone company executive*

COLORADO

Denver
Anderson, Donald H. *gas industry executive*
Cambre, Ronald C. *mining executive*
Dietler, Cortlandt S. *oil company executive*
Hamilton, Frederic Crawford *oil company executive*
Kleeman, Michael Jeffrey *business strategist and environmentalist*
Lewis, Jerome A. *petroleum company executive, investment banker*
Macey, William Blackmore *oil company executive*
Mohebbi, Afshin *telecommunications industry executive*
Murdy, Wayne William *mining company executive, financial officer*
Norman, John Edward *petroleum landman*
Outlaw, Lanny F. *gas company executive*
Robertson, Monroe Wayne, Jr. *oil company executive*
Roellig, Mark D. *telecommunications industry executive, lawyer*
Spies, Allan *telecommunications executive*
Thompson, Lohren Matthew *oil company executive*
Trueblood, Harry Albert, Jr. *oil company executive*
Wilks, Lewis O. *telecommunications company executive*

Durango
Thurston, William Richardson *oil and gas industry executive, geologist*

Englewood
Leclerc, Robert L. *mining company executive*
Malone, John C. *telecommunications executive*
Somers, Daniel E. *telecommunications industry executive*

Lakewood
Hall, Larry D. *energy company executive, lawyer*

Littleton
Haley, John David *petroleum consulting company executive*

Loveland
Bierbaum, J. Armin *petroleum company executive, consultant*

HAWAII

Honolulu
Clarke, Robert F. *utilities company executive*

Kaneohe
Amioka, Wallace Shuzo *retired petroleum company executive*

IDAHO

Coeur D Alene
Wheeler, Dennis Earl *mining company executive, lawyer*

Mountain Home
Hiddleston, Ronal Eugene *drilling and pump company executive*

MONTANA

Billings
Reed, Kenneth G. *petroleum company executive*

Butte
Burke, John James *utility executive*
Mc Elwain, Joseph Arthur *retired power company executive*
Pederson, Jerold P. *diversified utilities executive*

NEVADA

Las Vegas
Laub, William Murray *retired utility executive*

Reno
Busig, Rick Harold *mining executive*

Winnemucca
Hesse, Martha O. *natural gas company executive*

NEW MEXICO

Albuquerque
Gorham, Frank DeVore, Jr. *petroleum company executive*

Hobbs
Garey, Donald Lee *pipeline and oil company executive*

Roswell
Anderson, Donald Bernard *oil company executive*
Robinson, Mark Leighton *oil company executive, petroleum geologist, horse farm owner*

OREGON

Portland
Bacon, Vicky Lee *lighting services executive*
Bolender, David Francis *utility company executive*
Frisbee, Don Calvin *retired utilities executive*
Jungers, Francis *oil consultant*
Lorenzini, Paul Gilbert *electric power industry executive*
Reiten, Richard G. *natural gas industry executive*

UTAH

Brigham City
Adams, J. Phillip *oil industry executive*
Brown, Paul F *oil industry executive*

Salt Lake City
Barlow, Charles *oil company executive*
Cash, R(oy) Don *gas and petroleum company executive*
Holding, R(obert) E(arl) *oil company executive*
Losse, John William, Jr. *mining company executive*

WASHINGTON

Bellevue
Groten, Barnet *energy company executive*
Weaver, William Schildecker *electric power industry executive*

Richland
Wright, Malcolm Sturtevant *nuclear facility manager, retired career officer*

Seattle
Beighle, Douglas Paul *electric power industry executive, retired*

Spokane
Eliassen, Jon Eric *utility company executive*
Ely, Gary G. *utilities company executive*
Fukai, Robert D. *energy executive*
Matthews, Thomas M. *utilities company executive*
Matthews, Thomas Michael *energy company executive*
Meyer, David J. *energy executive, lawyer*

Tacoma
Temple, Thomas C. *oil company executive*

WYOMING

Casper
Stroock, Thomas Frank *oil and gas company executive*

Riverton
Bebout, Eli Daniel *oil executive*

CANADA

ALBERTA

Calgary
Anderson, J.C. *oil and gas exploration company executive*
Auchinleck, Richard H. *exploration company executive*
Baldwin, Douglas Daniel *pipeline company executive*
Faithfull, Timothy William *petroleum industry executive*
George, Richard Lee *oil company executive*
Gish, Norman Richard *energy industry executive*
Haskayne, Richard Francis *petroleum company executive*
Horton, William Russell *retired utility company executive*
Little, Brian Frederick *oil company executive*
MacNeill, Brian F. *retired oil and natural gas company executive*
Maier, Gerald James *corporate executive*
Mc Kee, John Angus *oil company executive*
McIntyre, Norman F. *petroleum industry executive*
McKinnon, F(rancis) A(rthur) Richard *utility executive*
Morgan, Gwyn *oil and gas executive*
O'Brien, David Peter *business executive*
Pick, Michael Claude *international exploration consultant*
Seaman, Daryl Kenneth *oil company executive*
Southern, Ronald D. *diversified corporation executive*
Stanford, James M. *oil company executive*
Travis, Vance Kenneth *petroleum business executive*
Wagner, Norman Ernest *corporate education executive*

Fort McMurray
Carter, James E. *mining company executive*

Red Deer
Donald, Jack C. *oil company executive*

BRITISH COLUMBIA

Vancouver
Keevil, Norman Bell *mining executive*
Phelps, Michael Everett Joseph *energy company executive*
Willson, John Michael *retired mining company executive*
Wilson, Graham McGregor *energy company executive*

ONTARIO

Toronto
Ward, Milton Hawkins *former mining company executive*

ADDRESS UNPUBLISHED

Arlidge, John Walter *retired utility company executive*
Ataie, Ata Jennati *oil products marketing executive*
Bruce, James Edmund *retired utility company executive*
Childers, Charles Eugene *mining company executive*
Conger, Harry Milton *mining company executive*
Eltringham, Thomas James Gyger *telecommunications professional*
Fagin, David Kyle *natural resources executive*
Gundersen, Wayne Campbell *management consultant, oil and gas consultant*
Gurian, Mal *telecommunications executive*
Huffman, James Thomas William *oil exploration company executive*
Land, Kenneth Dean *test and balance agency executive, energy and environmental consultant*
Littlefield, Edmund Wattis *mining company executive*
Mc Duffie, Malcolm *oil company executive*
McCready, Kenneth Frank *past electric utility executive*
Orden, Ted *gasoline service stations executive*
Ormasa, John *retired utility executive, lawyer*
Osterhoff, James Marvin *retired telecommunications company executive*
Pierce, Robert Lorne *petrochemical, oil and gas company executive*
Rendu, Jean-Michel Marie *mining executive*
Sanders, Charles Franklin *management and engineering consultant*
Soregaroli, A(rthur) E(arl) *mining company executive, geologist*
Taylor, Leslie George *mining and financial company executive*
Thompson, Jack Edward *mining company executive*
Watson, George W. *energy company executive*
Wood, Willis Bowne, Jr. *retired utility holding company executive*

INFORMATION TECHNOLOGY. *See also* SCIENCE: MATHEMATICS AND COMPUTER SCIENCE.

UNITED STATES

ARIZONA

Tempe
Crown, Timothy A. *computer technology company executive*
Martin, Charles *chief information officer*
Stott, Brian *software company executive, consultant*

CALIFORNIA

Altadena
Fairbanks, Mary Kathleen *data analyst, researcher*

Burlingame
Garnett, Katrina A. *information technology executive*

INTERNET *See* INFORMATION TECHNOLOGY

LAW: JUDICIAL ADMINISTRATION

UNITED STATES

Moon, Ronald T. Y. *state supreme court chief justice*
Nakayama, Paula Aiko *state supreme court justice*
Pence, Martin *retired federal judge*
Ramil, Mario R. *state supreme court justice*
Watanabe, Corinne Kaoru Amemiya *judge, state official, lawyer*
Yamashita, Francis Isami *magistrate judge*

IDAHO

Boise
Boyle, Larry Monroe *federal judge*
Kidwell, Wayne L. *state supreme court justice*
Lodge, Edward James *federal judge*
McDevitt, Charles Francis *retired state supreme court justice, lawyer*
Nelson, Thomas G. *federal judge*
Pappas, Jim D. *federal bankruptcy judge*
Silak, Cathy R. *former state supreme court justice*
Trott, Stephen Spangler *federal judge, musician*
Walters, Jesse Raymond, Jr. *state supreme court justice*
Williams, Mikel Howard *magistrate judge*
Winmill, B. Lynn *judge*

MONTANA

Billings
Fagg, Russell *judge, lawyer*
Shanstrom, Jack D. *federal judge*
Thomas, Sidney R. *federal judge*

Circle
McDonough, Russell Charles *retired state supreme court justice*

Helena
Gray, Karla Marie *state supreme court chief justice*
Harrison, John Conway *state supreme court justice*
Hunt, William E., Sr. *state supreme court justice*
Leaphart, W. William *state supreme court justice*
Lovell, Charles C. *federal judge*
Nelson, James C *state supreme court justice*
Regnier, James *state supreme court justice*
Trieweiler, Terry Nicholas *state supreme court justice*

Missoula
Erickson, Leif B. *federal judge*

Polson
Turnage, Jean Allen *retired state supreme court chief justice*

NEVADA

Carson City
Agosti, Deborah Ann *state supreme court justice*
Gunderson, Elmer Millard *state supreme court justice, law educator*
Leavitt, Myron E. *state supreme court justice*
Maupin, A. William *state supreme court justice*
Rose, Robert E(dgar) *state supreme court chief justice*
Springer, Charles Edward *retired state supreme court chief justice*
Young, C. Clifton *state supreme court justice*

Las Vegas
Becker, Nancy Anne *state supreme court justice*
George, Lloyd D. *federal judge*
Hunt, Roger Lee *judge*
Johnston, Robert Jake *federal magistrate judge*
Pro, Philip Martin *judge*
Steffen, Thomas Lee *former state supreme court justice, lawyer*

Reno
Brunetti, Melvin T. *federal judge*
Goldwater, Bert M. *federal judge*
Hagen, David Warner *judge*
Hug, Procter Ralph, Jr. *federal judge*
McKibben, Howard D. *federal judge*
McQuaid, Robert A., Jr. *federal judge*
Reed, Edward Cornelius, Jr. *federal judge*

NEW MEXICO

Albuquerque
Black, Bruce D. *judge*
Conway, John E. *federal judge*
DeGiacomo, Robert J. *federal judge*
Garcia, Lorenzo F. *federal judge*
Hansen, Curtis LeRoy *federal judge*
Parker, James Aubrey *federal judge*
Puglisi, Richard Lawrence *federal judge*
Svet, Don J. *federal judge*

Clovis
Tharp, Fred C., Jr. *federal judge, lawyer*

Gallup
Ionta, Robert W. *federal judge, lawyer*

Las Cruces
Bratton, Howard Calvin *federal judge*
Galvan, Joe H. *federal judge*
Smith, Leslie C. *federal judge*

Roswell
Baldock, Bobby Ray *federal judge*

Santa Fe
Baca, Joseph Francis *state supreme court justice*
Franchini, Gene Edward *state supreme court justice*
Kelly, Paul Joseph, Jr. *judge*
Maes, Petra Jimenez *state supreme court justice*
Minzner, Pamela Burgy *state supreme court justice*
[illegible] *state supreme court chief justice*
Vazquez, Martha Alicia *judge*
Yalman, Ann *judge, lawyer*

OREGON

Eugene
Coffin, Thomas M. *federal magistrate judge*
Hogan, Michael R(obert) *judge*
Radcliffe, Albert E. *judge*

Medford
Cooney, John P. *judge*

Pendleton
Bloom, Stephen Michael *magistrate judge, lawyer*

Portland
Beatty, John Cabeen , Jr. *judge*
Dunn, Randall L. *federal judge*
Frye, Helen Jackson *federal judge*
Graber, Susan P. *federal judge*
Haggerty, Ancer Lee *judge*
Higdon, Polly Susanne *federal judge*
Jones, Robert Edward *federal judge*
Kulongoski, Theodore Ralph *state supreme court justice*
Leavy, Edward *federal judge*
Marsh, Malcolm F. *federal judge*
O'Scannlain, Diarmuid Fionntain *judge*
Panner, Owen M. *federal judge*
Redden, James Anthony *federal judge*
Skopil, Otto Richard, Jr. *federal judge*
Stewart, Janice Mae *judge*
Unis, Richard L. *judge*
Van Hoomissen, George Albert *state supreme court justice*

Salem
Carson, Wallace Preston, Jr. *state supreme court chief justice*
Durham, Robert Donald, Jr. *state supreme court justice*
Leeson, Susan M. *state supreme court judge*
Linde, Hans Arthur *state supreme court justice*
Peterson, Edwin J. *retired supreme court justice, law educator*
Riggs, R. William *state supreme court judge*

UTAH

Monticello
Redd, F. Bennion *federal magistrate*

Provo
Schofield, Anthony Wayne *judge*

Saint George
Nuffer, David O. *federal judge*

Salt Lake City
Anderson, Stephen Hale *federal judge*
Benson, Dee Vance *federal judge*
Boyce, Ronald N. *federal judge*
Campbell, Tena *judge*
Clark, Glen Edward *judge*
Durham, Christine Meaders *state supreme court justice*
Durrant, Matthew B. *state judge*
Greene, John Thomas *judge*
Hall, Gordon R. *retired state supreme court chief justice*
Howe, Richard Cuddy *state supreme court chief justice*
Jenkins, Bruce Sterling *federal judge*
McKay, Monroe Gunn *federal judge*
Murphy, Michael R. *federal judge*
Russon, Leonard H. *state supreme court justice*
Sam, David *federal judge*
Wilkins, Michael Jon *state supreme court justice*
Winder, David Kent *federal judge*

WASHINGTON

Olympia
Alexander, Gerry L. *state supreme court chief justice*
Bridge, Bobbe J. *state supreme court justice*
Durham, Barbara *retired state supreme court justice*
Guy, Richard P. *retired state supreme court justice*
Ireland, Faith *state supreme court justice*
Johnson, Charles William *state supreme court justice*
Kite, Marilyn S. *state supreme court justice, lawyer*
Sanders, Richard Browning *state supreme court justice*
Smith, Charles Z. *state supreme court justice*

Seattle
Beezer, Robert Renaut *federal judge*
Brandt, Philip H. *federal judge*
Coughenour, John Clare *federal judge*
Dimmick, Carolyn Reaber *federal judge*
Dwyer, William L. *federal judge*
Farris, Jerome *federal judge*
Fletcher, Betty Binns *federal judge*
Glover, Thomas T. *federal judge*
Gould, Ronald Murray *judge*
Mc Govern, Walter T. *federal judge*
Overstreet, Karen A. *federal judge*
Pekelis, Rosselle *judge*
Rothstein, Barbara Jacobs *federal judge*
Steiner, Samuel J. *judge*
Tallman, Richard C. *federal judge, lawyer*
Weinberg, John Lee *federal judge*
Wilson, David Eugene *former magistrate judge, lawyer*
Wright, Eugene Allen *federal judge*
Zilly, Thomas Samuel *federal judge*

Spokane
Imbrogno, Cynthia *magistrate judge*
Nielsen, William Fremming *federal judge*
Quackenbush, Justin Lowe *federal judge*
Van Sickle, Frederick L. *federal judge*
Whaley, Robert Hamilton *judge*
Williams, Patricia C. *federal judge*

Tacoma
[illegible]
Bryan, Robert J. *federal judge*
Burgess, Franklin Douglas *judge*
Snyder, Paul *federal judge*

Yakima
McDonald, Alan Angus *federal judge*
Suko, Lonny Ray *judge*

WYOMING

Casper
Downes, William F. *judge*

Cheyenne
Brimmer, Clarence Addison *federal judge*
Brorby, Wade *federal judge*
Golden, T. Michael *state supreme court justice*
Hill, William U. *state supreme court justice*
Johnson, Alan Bond *federal judge*
Lehman, Larry L. *state supreme court justice*
McNiff, Peter J. *federal judge*
Taylor, William Al *state supreme court justice*
Thomas, Richard Van *state supreme court justice*

Cody
Patrick, H. Hunter *judge*

Green River
Marty, Lawrence A. *magistrate*

Jackson
Bommer, Timothy J *magistrate judge, lawyer*

Lander
Gist, Richard D. *federal judge*

Sheridan
Connor, Robert W., Jr. *federal judge*

Yellowstone National Park
Cole, Stephen E. *magistrate judge*

MILITARY ADDRESSES OF THE UNITED STATES

PACIFIC

APO
Faucher, David F. *federal judge*

CANADA

ALBERTA

Edmonton
Fraser, Catherine Anne *Canadian chief justice*

BRITISH COLUMBIA

Vancouver
Lysyk, Kenneth Martin *judge*
McEachern, Allan *Canadian justice*

SASKATCHEWAN

Regina
Bayda, Edward Dmytro *judge*

ADDRESS UNPUBLISHED

Aiken, Ann L. *federal judge*
Allred, Clark B. *judge*
Barrett, James Emmett *federal judge*
Bedsworth, William W. *judge*
Boren, Roger W. *judge*
Boulden, Judith Ann *judge*
Brennan, Joan Stevenson *federal judge*
Brooks, Ruben B. *judge*
Burke, Edmond Wayne *retired judge, lawyer*
Dela Cruz, Jose Santos *retired state supreme court justice*
Dolliver, James Morgan *retired state supreme court justice*
Fadeley, Edward Norman *retired state supreme court justice*
Gillette, W. Michael *state supreme court justice*
Gold, Arnold Henry *judge*
Hawkins, Michael Daly *federal judge*
Johnson, Byron Jerald *retired state supreme court judge*
Macy, Richard J. *retired state supreme court justice*
Madsen, Barbara A *state supreme court justice*
Matthews, Warren Wayne *state supreme court justice*
McKee, Roger Curtis *retired federal judge*
Moore, Daniel Alton, Jr. *retired state supreme court justice*
Reinhardt, Stephen Roy *federal judge*
Schroeder, Gerald Frank *state supreme court justice*
Shearing, Miriam *state supreme court justice*
Shubb, William Barnet *judge*
Stewart, Isaac Daniel, Jr. *retired state supreme court justice*
Talmadge, Philip Albert *state supreme court justice, former state senator*
Trout, Linda Copple *state supreme court chief justice*
Utter, Robert French *retired state supreme court justice*
Weber, Fred J. *retired state supreme court justice*

Zive, Gregg William *judge*

LAW: LAW PRACTICE AND ADMINISTRATION

UNITED STATES

ALASKA

Anchorage
Bundy, Robert Charles *prosecutor*
De Lisio, Stephen Scott *lawyer, director*
Edwards, George Kent *lawyer*
Greenstein, Marla Nan *lawyer*
Oesting, David W. *lawyer*
Reeves, James N. *lawyer*
Roberts, John Derham *lawyer*
Willard-Jones, Donna C. *lawyer*

Bethel
Cooke, Christopher Robert *former state judge, lawyer*

Fairbanks
Schendel, William Burnett *lawyer*

Juneau
Cole, Charles Edward *lawyer, former state attorney general*
Collins, Patricia A. *lawyer, judge*

Kodiak
Jamin, Matthew Daniel *lawyer, magistrate judge*

Salcha
Rice, Julian Casavant *lawyer*

ARIZONA

Eloy
O'Leary, Thomas Michael *lawyer*

Flagstaff
Verkamp, John *lawyer, state legislator*

Gilbert
Handy, Robert Maxwell *lawyer*

Kingman
Basinger, Richard Lee *lawyer*

Nogales
Castro, Raul Hector *lawyer, former ambassador, former governor*

Phoenix
Allen, Robert Eugene Barton *lawyer*
Alsentzer, William James, Jr. *lawyer*
Bain, C. Randall *lawyer*
Baker, William Dunlap *lawyer*
Bakker, Thomas Gordon *lawyer*
Begam, Robert George *lawyer*
Beggs, Harry Mark *lawyer*
Birk, David R. *lawyer*
Bivens, Donald Wayne *lawyer, judge*
Blanchard, Charles Alan *lawyer, former state senator*
Bouma, John Jacob *lawyer*
Burke, Timothy John *lawyer*
Cohen, Jon Stephan *lawyer*
Colburn, Donald D. *lawyer*
Cole, George Thomas *lawyer*
Colton, David S. *lawyer, company executive*
Comus, Louis Francis, Jr. *lawyer*
Cooledge, Richard Calvin *lawyer*
Coppersmith, Sam *lawyer*
Crockett, Clyll Webb *lawyer*
Daughton, Donald *lawyer*
Davies, David George *lawyer, educator*
Dawson, John Joseph *lawyer*
Deeny, Robert Joseph *lawyer*
Derouin, James Gilbert *lawyer*
Everroad, John David *lawyer*
Fennelly, Jane Corey *lawyer*
Fenzl, Terry Earle *lawyer*
Fine, Charles Leon *lawyer*
Frank, John Paul *lawyer, writer*
Gaffney, Donald Lee *lawyer*
Gallagher, Michael L. *lawyer*
Gilbert, Donald Roy *lawyer*
Griller, Gordon Moore *legal administrator*
Halpern, Barry David *lawyer*
Hammond, Larry Austin *lawyer*
Harrison, Mark Isaac *lawyer*
Hayden, William Robert *lawyer*
Hicks, William Albert, III *lawyer*
Hirsch, Steven A. *lawyer*
Hoecker, Thomas Ralph *lawyer*
Holden, Michael John *lawyer*
Hoxie, Joel P. *lawyer*
Huntwork, James Roden *lawyer*
Jacobson, Edward (Julian Edward Jacobson) *lawyer*
James, Charles E., Jr. *lawyer*
Jirauch, Charles W. *lawyer*
Johns, Michael A. *prosecutor*
Klausner, Jack Daniel *lawyer*
Klein, R. Kent *lawyer*
Knoller, Guy David *lawyer*
Koester, Berthold Karl *lawyer, law educator, retired honorary German consul*
Kreutzberg, David W. *lawyer*
Kurn, Neal *lawyer*
Lowry, Edward Francis, Jr. *lawyer*
Lundin, John E. *lawyer*
MacDonnell, Philip J. *lawyer*
Madden, Paul Robert *lawyer, director*
Martori, Joseph Peter *lawyer*
May, Bruce Barnett *lawyer*
Mc Clennen, Louis *lawyer, educator*
McDougall, Roderick Gregory *lawyer*
McRae, Hamilton Eugene, III *lawyer*
Merritt, Nancy-Jo *lawyer*
Meschkow, Jordan M. *lawyer*
Meyerson, Bruce Elliot *lawyer*
Miller, Louis Rice *lawyer*
Moya, Patrick Robert *lawyer*

Olsen, Alfred Jon *lawyer*
Platt, Warren E. *lawyer*
Rathwell, Peter John *lawyer*
Refo, Patricia Lee *lawyer*
Rivera, Jose de Jesus *lawyer*
Rose, Scott A. *lawyer*
Rudolph, Gilbert Lawrence *lawyer*
Savage, Stephen Michael *lawyer*
Sherk, Kenneth John *lawyer*
Silverman, Alan Henry *lawyer*
Stahl, Louis A. *lawyer*
Storey, Norman C. *lawyer*
Thompson, Terence William *lawyer*
Udall, Calvin Hunt *lawyer*
Walker, Richard K. *lawyer*
Wall, Donald Arthur *lawyer*
Wheeler, Steven M. *lawyer*
Whisler, James Steven *lawyer, mining and manufacturing executive*
Williams, Quinn Patrick *lawyer*
Winthrop, Lawrence Fredrick *lawyer*
Wolf, G. Van Velsor, Jr. *lawyer*
Woods, Grant *lawyer, former state attorney general*
Woolf, Michael E. *lawyer*
Yarnell, Michael Allan *lawyer*

Rio Rico
Ryan, John Duncan *lawyer*

Scottsdale
Howard, William Matthew *arbitrator, writer, lawyer*
Inman, William Peter *lawyer*
Krupp, Clarence William *lawyer, personnel and hospital administrator*
Marks, Merton Eleazer *lawyer*
Peshkin, Samuel David *lawyer*

Sun City
Treece, James Lyle *lawyer*

Tempe
Goldberg, David Theo *law educator, writer*
Jennings, Marianne Moody *lawyer, educator*
Matheson, Alan Adams *law educator*
Schatzki, George *law educator*
Spritzer, Ralph Simon *lawyer, educator*

Tucson
Boswell, Susan G. *lawyer*
Dobbs, Dan Byron *lawyer, educator*
Froman, Sandra Sue *lawyer*
Gantz, David Alfred *lawyer, university official*
Kimble, William Earl *lawyer*
Kozolchyk, Boris *law educator, consultant*
Lesher, Robert Overton *lawyer*
Mc Donald, John Richard *lawyer*
Meehan, Michael Joseph *lawyer*
Morrow, James Franklin *lawyer*
Pace, Thomas M. *lawyer*
Robinson, Bernard Leo *retired lawyer*
Samet, Dee-Dee *lawyer*
Schorr, S. L. *lawyer*
Simmons, Sarah R. *lawyer*
Strong, John William *lawyer, educator*
Tindall, Robert Emmett *lawyer, educator*

CALIFORNIA

Alamo
Madden, Palmer Brown *lawyer*

Aliso Viejo
Fisher, Lawrence N. *lawyer*

Angels Camp
Arkin, Michael Barry *lawyer, arbitrator, writer*

Arcadia
Mc Cormack, Francis Xavier *lawyer, former oil company executive*

Auburn
Henry, Karen Hawley *lawyer*

Bakersfield
Kind, Kenneth Wayne *lawyer, real estate broker*
Martin, George Francis *lawyer*
Young, John Byron *retired lawyer*

Belvedere Tiburon
Obninsky, Victor Peter *lawyer*

Berkeley
Barton, Babette B. *lawyer, educator*
Berring, Robert Charles, Jr. *law educator, law librarian, former dean*
Buxbaum, Richard M. *law educator, lawyer*
Choper, Jesse Herbert *law educator, university dean*
Eisenberg, Melvin A. *law educator*
Feeley, Malcolm M. *law educator, political scientist*
Feller, David E. *law educator, arbitrator*
Goldsmith, Donald William *lawyer, astronomer, writer*
Gordley, James Russell *law educator*
Halbach, Edward Christian, Jr. *law educator, educator*
Haley, George Patrick *lawyer*
Kadish, Sanford Harold *law educator*
Kagan, Robert Allen *law educator*
McNulty, John Kent *lawyer, educator*
Messinger, Sheldon L(eopold) *law educator*
Mishkin, Paul J. *lawyer, educator*
Moran, Rachel *lawyer, educator*
Peterson, Andrea Lenore *law educator*
Petty, George Oliver *lawyer*
Post, Robert Charles *law educator*
Samuelson, Pamela Ann *law educator*
Scheiber, Harry N. *law educator*
Shapiro, Martin *law educator*
Sorensen, Linda *lawyer*
Zimring, Franklin E. *law educator, lawyer*

Beverly Hills
Bloom, Jacob A. *lawyer*
Brown, Hermione Kopp *lawyer*
Burns, Marvin Gerald *lawyer*
Cook, Melanie *lawyer*
Hansen, Tom *lawyer*
Heinke, Rex S. *lawyer*
Hergott, Alan *lawyer*
Hogan, Steven L. *lawyer*
Jacobson, Craig *lawyer*
Jaffe, F. Filmore *lawyer, retired judge*
Ramer, Bruce M. *lawyer*
Rosky, Burton Seymour *lawyer*
Russell, Irwin Emanuel *lawyer*
Schiff, Gunther Hans *lawyer*
Shire, Harold Raymond *law educator, writer, scientist*
Sobelle, Richard E. *lawyer*

Burbank
Braverman, Alan N. *lawyer*
Cunningham, Robert D. *lawyer*
Davis, J. Alan *lawyer, writer*
Litvack, Sanford Martin *lawyer*
Meisinger, Louis M. *lawyer*

Burlingame
Cotchett, Joseph Winters *lawyer, author*

Carlsbad
McCracken, Steven Carl *lawyer*

Carmel
Robinson, John Minor *lawyer, retired business executive*

Chatsworth
Klein, Jeffrey S. *lawyer, media executive*
Weinman, Glenn Alan *lawyer*

Chino
Determan, John David *lawyer*

City Industry
Churchill, James Allen *lawyer, director*

Claremont
Ansell, Edward Orin *lawyer*

Coalinga
Frame, Ted Ronald *lawyer*

Corona
Everett, Pamela Irene *legal management company executive, educator*

Corte Madera
Gordon, Robert Eugene *lawyer*

Costa Mesa
Anderson, Jon David *lawyer*
Barclay, John Allen *lawyer*
Currie, Robert Emil *lawyer*
Daniels, James Walter *lawyer*
Frieden, Clifford E. *lawyer*
Guilford, Andrew John *lawyer*
Hamilton, James William *lawyer*
Hay, Howard Clinton *lawyer*
Jones, H(arold) Gilbert, Jr. *lawyer*
Oderman, Jeffrey M. *lawyer*
Reveal, Ernest Ira, III *lawyer*
Tanner, R. Marshall *lawyer*
Tennyson, Peter Joseph *lawyer*
Thurston, Morris Ashcroft *lawyer*

Davis
Bartosic, Florian *law educator, lawyer, arbitrator*
Bruch, Carol Sophie *lawyer, educator*
Imwinkelried, Edward John *law educator*
Wolk, Bruce Alan *law educator*
Wydick, Richard Crews *lawyer, educator*

Del Mar
Seitman, John Michael *lawyer, arbitrator, mediator*

El Cerrito
Garbarino, Joseph William *labor arbitrator, economics and business educator*

El Segundo
Codon, Dennis P. *lawyer*
Fisk, Hayward D. *lawyer*
Hunter, Larry Dean *lawyer*
Thomas, Timothy R. *lawyer*
Willis, Judy Ann *lawyer*

Emeryville
Arguedas, Cristina C. *lawyer*
Howe, Drayton Ford, Jr. *lawyer*

Encinitas
Wigmore, John Grant *lawyer*

Encino
Kaufman, Albert I. *lawyer*
Lombardini, Carol Ann *lawyer*

Foster City
Jeffrey, John Orval *lawyer*
Lonnquist, George Eric *lawyer*

Fresno
Palmer, Samuel Copeland, III *lawyer*

Fullerton
Goldstein, Edward David *lawyer, former glass company executive*
Moerbeek, Stanley Leonard *lawyer*

Glendale
Davidson, Suzanne Mouron *lawyer*
Fink, Richard A. *lawyer*
Hoffman, Donald M. *lawyer*
Kazanjian, Phillip Carl *lawyer, business executive*
MacDonald, Kirk Stewart *lawyer*
Martinetti, Ronald Anthony *lawyer*
Scott, A. Timothy *lawyer, business executive*
Simpson, Allyson Bilich *lawyer*
Stack, Kevin J. *lawyer*

Granada Hills
McLaughlin, Joseph Mailey *lawyer*

Granite Bay
Holtz, Sara *lawyer, consultant*

Greenbrae
Bonapart, Alan David *lawyer*

Half Moon Bay
Lambert, Frederick William *lawyer, educator*

Healdsburg
Kemp, Alson Remington, Jr. *lawyer, former law educator*

Irvine
Bastiaanse, Gerard C. *lawyer*
Beard, Ronald Stratton *lawyer*
Cahill, Richard Frederick *lawyer*
Clark, Karen Heath *lawyer*
Goldstein, Michael Gerald *lawyer, director*
Jansen, Allan W. *lawyer*
Jeffers, Michael Bogue *lawyer*
Marshall, Ellen Ruth *lawyer*
Ristau, Kenneth Eugene, Jr. *lawyer*
Williams, Lowell Craig *lawyer, employee relations executive*
Wintrode, Ralph Charles *lawyer*

La Canada Flintridge
Costello, Francis William *lawyer*

La Jolla
Karlen, Peter Hurd *lawyer, writer*
Kirchheimer, Arthur E(dward) *lawyer, business executive*
Siegan, Bernard Herbert *lawyer, educator*

Laguna Hills
Reinglass, Michelle Annette *lawyer*

Larkspur
Greenberg, Myron Silver *lawyer*
Ratner, David Louis *retired law educator*
Saxe, Steven Louis *lawyer*

Long Beach
Deukmejian, George *lawyer, former governor*
Helwick, Christine *lawyer*
Taylor, Reese Hale, Jr. *lawyer, former government administrator*
Wise, George Edward *lawyer*

Los Angeles
Abrams, Norman *law educator, university administrator*
Adamek, Charles Andrew *lawyer*
Adams, Thomas Merritt *lawyer*
Adell, Hirsch *lawyer*
Adler, Erwin Ellery *lawyer*
Adler, Michael I. *lawyer*
Alden, John W. *lawyer*
Allred, Gloria Rachel *lawyer*
Angel, Arthur Ronald *lawyer, consultant*
Apfel, Gary *lawyer*
April, Rand Scott *lawyer*
Arnold, Dennis B. *lawyer*
Bakaly, Charles George, Jr. *lawyer, mediator*
Barrett, Jane Hayes *lawyer*
Barton, Alan Joel *lawyer*
Barza, Harold A. *lawyer*
Basile, Paul Louis, Jr. *lawyer*
Bauman, Stephen Adrian *lawyer*
Baumann, Richard Gordon *lawyer*
Belleville, Philip Frederick *lawyer*
Bender, Charles William *lawyer*
Bendix, Helen Irene *lawyer*
Bennett, Fred Gilbert *lawyer*
Bernacchi, Richard Lloyd *lawyer*
Bernhard, Herbert Ashley *lawyer*
Biederman, Donald Ellis *lawyer*
Bishop, Sidney Willard *lawyer*
Black, Donna Ruth *lawyer*
Blencowe, Paul Sherwood *lawyer, private investor*
Blumberg, Grace Ganz *law educator, lawyer*
Bodkin, Henry Grattan, Jr. *lawyer*
Bogen, Andrew E. *lawyer*
Bomes, Stephen D. *lawyer*
Bonesteel, Michael John *lawyer*
Bonner, Robert Cleve *lawyer*
Bosl, Phillip L. *lawyer*
Boxer, Lester *lawyer*
Bradley, Lawrence D., Jr. *lawyer*
Branca, John Gregory *lawyer, consultant*
Brandler, Jonathan M. *lawyer*
Braun, David A(dlai) *lawyer*
Bressan, Paul Louis *lawyer*
Brian, Brad D. *lawyer*
Bridges, B. Ried *lawyer*
Brittenham, Skip *lawyer*
Broussard, Thomas Rollins *lawyer*
Burch, Robert Dale *lawyer*
Burdge, Richard James, Jr. *lawyer*
Butler, James Robertson, Jr. *lawyer*
Byrd, Christine Waterman Swent *lawyer*
Byrne, Jerome Camillus *lawyer*
Capron, Alexander Morgan *lawyer, educator*
Carlson, Robert Edwin *lawyer*
Carr, Willard Zeller, Jr. *lawyer*
Cartwright, Brian Grant *lawyer*
Castro, Leonard Edward *lawyer*
Cathcart, David Arthur *lawyer*
Chiate, Kenneth Reed *lawyer*
Christol, Carl Q(uimby) *lawyer, political science educator*
Christopher, Warren *lawyer, former government official*
Chu, Morgan *lawyer*
Clark, Marcia Rachel *former prosecutor*
Cleary, William Joseph, Jr. *lawyer*
Cochran, Johnnie L., Jr. *lawyer*
Cohan, John Robert *retired lawyer*
Cohen, Cynthia Marylyn *lawyer*
Cole, William L. *lawyer*
Collier, Charles Arthur, Jr. *lawyer*
Collins, Michael K. *lawyer*
Daniels, John Peter *lawyer*
Darby, G(eorge) Harrison *lawyer*
Darden, Christopher A. *lawyer, actor, writer*
De Brier, Donald Paul *lawyer*
de Castro, Hugo Daniel *lawyer*
Decker, Richard Jeffrey *lawyer*
DeLuce, Richard David *lawyer*
Demoff, Marvin Alan *lawyer*
Denham, Robert Edwin *lawyer, investment company executive*
Diamond, Stanley Jay *lawyer*
Dickson, Robert Lee *lawyer*
Dinel, Richard Henry *lawyer*
Donovan, John Arthur *lawyer*
Douglas, Joel Bruce *lawyer*
Dudziak, Mary Louise *law educator, lecturer*
Emanuel, William Joseph *lawyer*
English, Stephen Raymond *lawyer*
Etra, Donald *lawyer*
Faal, Edi M. O. *lawyer*
Fairbank, Robert Harold *lawyer*
Farmer, Robert Lindsay *lawyer*
Farrar, Stanley F. *lawyer*
Fenning, Lisa Hill *lawyer, mediator, former federal judge*
Field, Richard Clark *lawyer*
Fields, Bertram Harris *lawyer*
Follick, Edwin Duane *law educator, chiropractic physician*
Ford, Donald Hainline *lawyer*
Frackman, Russell Jay *lawyer*
Fragner, Matthew Charles *lawyer*
Francis, Merrill Richard *lawyer*
Friedman, Alan E. *lawyer*
Frimmer, Paul Norman *lawyer*
Gallo, Jon Joseph *lawyer*
Garcetti, Gilbert I. *prosecutor*
Gebb, Sheldon Alexander *lawyer*
Gentile, Joseph F. *lawyer, educator*
Gest, Howard David *lawyer*
Girard, Robert David *lawyer*
Gitt, Cynthia E. *lawyer*
Glazer, Michael *lawyer*
Golay, Frank H., Jr. *lawyer*
Goldman, Allan Bailey *lawyer*
Goldman, Benjamin Edward *lawyer*
Goodman, Max A. *lawyer, educator*
Gordon, David Eliot *lawyer*
Gorman, Joseph Gregory, Jr. *lawyer*
Gould, David *lawyer*
Graubart, Jeffrey Lowell *lawyer*
Grausam, Jeffrey Leonard *lawyer*
Green, William Porter *lawyer*
Griffey, Linda Boyd *lawyer*
Grobe, Charles Stephen *lawyer, accountant*
Gross, Allen Jeffrey *lawyer*
Grosz, Philip J. *lawyer*
Gurfein, Peter J. *lawyer*
Hahn, Elliott Julius *lawyer*
Hahn, James Kenneth *lawyer*
Halkett, Alan Neilson *lawyer*
Hansell, Dean *lawyer*
Hanson, John J. *lawyer*
Havel, Richard W. *lawyer*
Hayutin, David Lionel *lawyer*
Hemminger, Pamela Lynn *lawyer*
Hernandez, Antonia *lawyer*
Heyler, Grover Ross *retired lawyer*
Hieronymus, Edward Whittlesey *lawyer*
Hight, B. Boyd *lawyer*
Hirsch, Barry L. *lawyer*
Holliday, Thomas Edgar *lawyer*
Holtzman, Robert Arthur *lawyer*
Howard, Nancy E. *lawyer*
Hudson, Jeffrey Reid *lawyer*
Hufstedler, Seth Martin *lawyer*
Hufstedler, Shirley Mount (Mrs. Seth M. Hufstedler) *lawyer, former federal judge*
Hyman, Milton Bernard *lawyer*
Iamele, Richard Thomas *law librarian*
Irwin, Philip Donnan *lawyer*
James, William J. *lawyer*
Johnson, Jonathan Edwin, II *lawyer*
Jordan, Robert Leon *lawyer, educator*
Kaplowitz, Karen (Jill) *lawyer, business consultant*
Karst, Kenneth Leslie *law educator*
Kiekhofer, William Henry *lawyer*
Kindel, James Horace, Jr. *lawyer*
Kirwan, R. DeWitt *lawyer*
Kleinberg, Marvin H. *lawyer*
Klinger, Marilyn Sydney *lawyer*
Klowden, Michael Louis *lawyer*
Kuechle, John Merrill *lawyer*
Kupietzky, Moshe J. *lawyer*
Lambert, Thomas P. *lawyer*
Lappen, Chester I. *lawyer*
Latham, Joseph Al, Jr. *lawyer*
Lauchengco, Jose Yujuico, Jr. *lawyer*
Le Berthon, Adam *lawyer*
Le Sage, Bernard E. *lawyer*
Leibow, Ronald Louis *lawyer*
Lesser, Joan L. *lawyer*
Letwin, Leon *law educator*
Leung, Frankie Fook-Lun *lawyer*
Levine, C. Bruce *lawyer*
Lindholm, Dwight Henry *lawyer*
Link, George Hamilton *lawyer*
Lipsig, Ethan *lawyer*
Long, Gregory Alan *lawyer*
Lurvey, Ira Harold *lawyer*
Lynch, Patrick *lawyer*
MacLaughlin, Francis Joseph *lawyer*
Mancino, Douglas Michael *lawyer*
Mason, Cheryl White *lawyer*
Mayorkas, Alejandro *prosecutor*
McAniff, Edward John *lawyer*
McDermott, John E. *lawyer*
McKnight, Frederick L. *lawyer*
McLane, Frederick Berg *lawyer*
Metzger, Robert Streicher *lawyer*
Meyer, Michael Edwin *lawyer*
Millard, Neal Steven *lawyer*
Miller, Milton Allen *lawyer*
Mintz, Marshall Gary *lawyer*
Mitchell, Briane Nelson *lawyer*
Molleur, Richard Raymond *lawyer*
Moloney, Stephen Michael *lawyer*
Mosk, Richard Mitchell *lawyer*
Moskowitz, Joel Steven *lawyer*
Muhlbach, Robert Arthur *lawyer*
Neely, Sally Schultz *lawyer*
Neiter, Gerald Irving *lawyer*
Nelson, Grant Steel *lawyer, educator*
Newman, David Wheeler *lawyer*
Nicholas, William Richard *lawyer*
Niemeth, Charles Frederick *lawyer*
Niles, John Gilbert *lawyer*
Nocas, Andrew James *lawyer*
Nochimson, David *lawyer*
O'Connell, Kevin *lawyer*
O'Donnell, Pierce Henry *lawyer*
O'Leary, Prentice L. *lawyer*
Oliver, Dale Hugh *lawyer*
Olsen, Frances Elisabeth *law educator, theorist*
Ordin, Andrea Sheridan *lawyer*
Owen, Michael Lee *lawyer*
Pachino, Barton P. *lawyer*
Palmer, Robert L. *lawyer*
Papiano, Neil Leo *lawyer*
Parsky, Gerald Lawrence *lawyer*
Pascotto, Alvaro *lawyer*
Pasich, Kirk Alan *lawyer*
Peck, Austin H., Jr. *lawyer*
Pedersen, Norman A. *lawyer*
Perlis, Michael Fredrick *lawyer*

Perry, Ralph Barton, III *lawyer*
Peters, Aulana Louise *lawyer, former government agency commissioner*
Peters, Richard T. *lawyer*
Pieper, Darold D. *lawyer*
Pircher, Leo Joseph *lawyer, director*
Poindexter, William Mersereau *lawyer*
Polley, Terry Lee *lawyer*
Pollock, John Phleger *lawyer*
Power, John Bruce *lawyer*
Preble, Laurence George *lawyer*
Preonas, George Elias *lawyer*
Present, Sanford Calvin *lawyer, educator, writer*
Pugsley, Robert Adrian *law educator*
Rabinovitz, Joel *lawyer, educator*
Raeder, Myrna Sharon *lawyer, educator*
Rappeport, Ira J. *lawyer*
Rath, Howard Grant, Jr. *lawyer*
Ray, Gilbert T. *lawyer*
Reeves, Barbara Ann *lawyer*
Renwick, Edward S. *lawyer*
Reynoso, Cruz *lawyer, educator*
Ring, Michael Wilson *lawyer*
Robertson, Hugh Duff *lawyer*
Roney, John Harvey *lawyer, consultant*
Rosenthal, Sol *lawyer*
Rosett, Arthur Irwin *lawyer, educator*
Rothenberg, Alan I. *lawyer, professional sports association executive*
Samet, Jack I. *lawyer*
Saxe, Deborah Crandall *lawyer*
Schmidt, Karl A. *lawyer*
Schulman, Robert S. *lawyer*
Scoular, Robert Frank *lawyer*
Shacter, David Mervyn *lawyer*
Shanks, Patricia L. *lawyer*
Shapiro, Marvin Seymour *lawyer*
Shapiro, Robert *lawyer*
Shartin, Stacy D. *lawyer*
Sheehan, Lawrence James *lawyer*
Shortz, Richard Alan *lawyer*
Shultz, John David *lawyer*
Simmons, Richard J. *lawyer*
Sinclitico, Dennis J. *lawyer*
Slavitt, Earl Benton *lawyer*
Smith, Gregory R. *lawyer*
Stamm, Alan *lawyer*
Stashower, Arthur L. *lawyer*
Stephens, George Edward, Jr. *lawyer*
Stone, Lawrence Maurice *lawyer, educator*
Stromberg, Ross Ernest *lawyer*
Sullivan, Peter Meredith *lawyer*
Tan, William Lew *lawyer*
Tarr, Ralph William *lawyer, former federal government official*
Taylor, Minna *lawyer*
Teele, Cynthia Lombard *lawyer*
Title, Gail Migdal *lawyer*
Tobisman, Stuart Paul *lawyer*
Treister, George Marvin *lawyer*
Trimble, Phillip Richard *law educator*
Troy, Joseph Freed *lawyer*
Trygstad, Lawrence Benson *lawyer*
Ukropina, James R. *lawyer*
Valerio Barrad, Catherine M. *lawyer*
Van de Kamp, John Kalar *lawyer*
Vanderet, Robert Charles *lawyer*
Varner, Carlton A. *lawyer*
Vaughn, William Weaver *lawyer*
Victorino, Louis D. *lawyer*
Volpert, Richard Sidney *lawyer*
von Kalinowski, Julian Onesime *lawyer*
Wagner, Darryl William *lawyer*
Walcher, Alan Ernest *lawyer*
Wallock, Terrence J. *lawyer*
Wasserman, William Phillip *lawyer*
Wayte, Alan (Paul Wayte) *lawyer*
Weatherup, Roy Garfield *lawyer*
Weinstock, Harold *lawyer*
Weiss, Walter Stanley *lawyer*
Wessling, Robert Bruce *lawyer*
White, Robert Joel *lawyer*
Williams, Donald Clyde *lawyer*
Williams, Richard Thomas *lawyer*
Wine, Mark Philip *lawyer*
Winterman, Craig L. *lawyer*
Wolfen, Werner F. *lawyer*
Woodland, Irwin Francis *lawyer*
Wright, Kenneth Brooks *lawyer*
Yamaguchi, Colleen S. *lawyer*
York, Gary Alan *lawyer*
Zelon, Laurie Dee *lawyer*
Ziffren, Kenneth *lawyer*

Marina Dl Rey
Orr, Ronald Stewart *lawyer*

Martinez
Bray, Absalom Francis, Jr. *lawyer*

Menlo Park
Bader, W(illiam) Reece *lawyer*
Brest, Paul A. *law educator*
Ehrlich, Thomas *law educator, educator*
Haslam, Robert Thomas, III *lawyer*
Kaufman, Christopher Lee *lawyer*
Kelly, Daniel Grady, Jr. *lawyer*
Kirk, Cassius Lamb, Jr. *retired lawyer, investor*
Madison, James Raymond *lawyer*
McLain, Christopher M. *lawyer*
Mendelson, Alan Charles *lawyer*
Millard, Richard Steven *lawyer*
Scholes, Myron S. *law educator, finance educator*
Taylor, Robert P. *lawyer*

Mill Valley
Nemir, Donald Philip *lawyer*

Millbrae
Lande, James Avra *lawyer*
Rosenthal, Herbert Marshall *lawyer*

Milpitas
Kryder, Andrew *lawyer*

Mission Viejo
Sessions, Don David *lawyer*

Modesto
Owens, Jack Byron *lawyer*

Monte Sereno
Allan, Lionel Manning *lawyer*

Monterey
Davis, Craig Alphin *lawyer, manufacturing company executive*
Fenton, Lewis Lowry *lawyer*

Newport Beach
Adams, William Gillette *lawyer*
Allen, Russell G. *lawyer*
Baskin, Scott David *lawyer*
Caldwell, Courtney Lynn *lawyer, real estate consultant*
Carmichael, David Richard *lawyer*
Clark, Thomas P., Jr. *lawyer*
Harlan, Nancy Margaret *lawyer*
Johnson, Thomas Webber, Jr. *lawyer*
Katayama, Arthur Shoji *lawyer*
Mallory, Frank Linus *lawyer*
Martens, Don Walter *lawyer*
Pepe, Stephen Phillip *lawyer*
Phillips, Layn R. *lawyer*
Schnapp, Roger Herbert *lawyer, consultant*
Wagner, John Leo *lawyer, former magistrate judge*
Wentworth, Theodore Sumner *lawyer*

North Hollywood
Kreger, Melvin Joseph *lawyer*

Oak Park
Vinson, William Theodore *lawyer, diversified corporation executive*

Oakland
Allen, Jeffrey Michael *lawyer*
Boven, Douglas George *lawyer*
Bryant, Arthur H. *lawyer*
Johnson, Kenneth F. *lawyer*
Leslie, Robert Lorne *lawyer*
Miller, Kirk Edward *lawyer, health foundation executive*
Miller, Thomas Robbins *lawyer, publisher*
O'Connor, Paul Daniel *lawyer*
Quinby, William Albert *lawyer, mediator, arbitrator*
Roster, Michael *lawyer*
Skaff, Andrew Joseph *lawyer, public utilities, energy and transportation executive*
Wallis, Eric G. *lawyer*
West, Natalie Elsa *lawyer*
Wood, James Michael *lawyer*

Orange
Sawdei, Milan A. *lawyer*

Orinda
Roethe, James Norton *lawyer*

Oxnard
O'Hearn, Michael John *lawyer*

Pacific Palisades
Cale, Charles Griffin *lawyer, private investor*
Flattery, Thomas Long *lawyer, legal administrator*
Sevilla, Stanley *lawyer*
Verrone, Patric Miller *lawyer, writer*

Palm Springs
Dupree, Stanley M. *lawyer*

Palo Alto
Bates, William, III *lawyer*
Benton, Lee F. *lawyer*
Bradley, Donald Edward *lawyer*
Brigham, Samuel Townsend Jack, III *lawyer*
Climan, Richard Elliot *lawyer*
Deaktor, Darryl Barnett *lawyer*
Dwyer, John Charles *lawyer*
Furbush, David Malcolm *lawyer*
Herbst, David W. *lawyer*
Jackson, Cynthia L. *lawyer*
Kleinberg, James P. *lawyer*
Lacovara, Michael *lawyer*
Laurie, Ronald Sheldon *lawyer*
Lesser, Henry *lawyer*
Massey, Henry P., Jr. *lawyer*
Newcombe, George Michael *lawyer*
Nordlund, Donald Craig *lawyer*
Nycum, Susan Hubbell *lawyer*
O'Rourke, C. Larry *lawyer*
Pasahow, Lynn H(arold) *lawyer*
Patterson, Robert Edward *lawyer*
Phair, Joseph Baschon *lawyer*
Rinsky, Arthur C. *lawyer*
Smith, Glenn A. *lawyer*
Tanner, Douglas Alan *lawyer*
Taylor, Barry E. *lawyer*
Tiffany, Joseph Raymond, II *lawyer*
Van Atta, David Murray *lawyer*
Weithorn, Stanley Stephen *lawyer*
Wheeler, Raymond Louis *lawyer*

Palos Verdes Estates
Blackman, Lee L. *lawyer*
Pierno, Anthony Robert *lawyer*
Toftness, Cecil Gillman *lawyer, consultant*

Pasadena
Calleton, Theodore Edward *lawyer, educator*
D'Angelo, Robert William *lawyer*
Davis, Edmond Ray *lawyer*
Haight, James Theron *lawyer, corporate executive*
Hunt, Gordon *lawyer*
Koelzer, George Joseph *lawyer*
Logan, Francis Dummer *lawyer*
Mueth, Joseph Edward *lawyer*
Myers, R(alph) Chandler *lawyer*
Tanner, Dee Boshard *retired lawyer*
van Schoonenberg, Robert G. *lawyer*
Weiswasser, Stephen Anthony *lawyer, broadcast executive*
Wyatt, Joseph Lucian, Jr. *lawyer, writer*
Yohalem, Harry Morton *lawyer*

Paso Robles
Knecht, James Herbert *lawyer*

Petaluma
Paul, Amy *lawyer*

Pittsburg
Williscroft-Barcus, Beverly Ruth *lawyer*

Pleasanton
Beck, Edward William *lawyer*
Fine, Marjorie Lynn *lawyer*
Oder, Kenneth William *lawyer*
Ross, Michael Charles *lawyer*

Point Richmond
Edginton, John Arthur *lawyer*

Rancho Mirage
Goldie, Ray Robert *lawyer*

Rancho Santa Margarita
Curtis, John Joseph *lawyer*

Redondo Beach
Oh, Angela E. *lawyer*

Redwood City
Cooperman, Daniel *lawyer*
Tight, Dexter Corwin *lawyer*
Wilhelm, Robert Oscar *lawyer, civil engineer, developer*

Richmond
Quenneville, Kathleen *lawyer*

Riverside
Darling, Scott Edward *lawyer*
Lear, William H. *lawyer*
Marlatt, Michael James *lawyer*
Yamamoto, Stanly Tokio *prosecutor*

Rosemead
Danner, Bryant Craig *lawyer*

Sacramento
Blake, D. Steven *lawyer*
Bowen, Debra Lynn *lawyer, state legislator*
Brookman, Anthony Raymond *lawyer*
Burton, Randall James *lawyer*
Day, James McAdam, Jr. *lawyer*
Friedman, Morton Lee *lawyer*
Gillan, Kayla J. *lawyer*
Goode, Barry Paul *lawyer*
Lesch, Barry M. *lawyer*
Rich, Ben Arthur *lawyer, educator*
Robbins, Stephen J. M. *lawyer*
Seave, Paul L. *prosecutor*
Stevens, Charles J. *lawyer, former prosecutor*
Twiss, Robert Manning *prosecutor*
Zeff, Ophelia Hope *lawyer*

San Bernardino
Stout, Dennis Lee *prosecutor*

San Diego
Adelman, Marc D. *lawyer*
Andreos, George Phillip *lawyer*
Boggs, William S. *lawyer*
Brooks, John White *lawyer*
Buzunis, Constantine Dino *lawyer*
Conte, Mario G., Jr. *lawyer*
Copeland, Robert Glenn *lawyer*
Corbett, Luke Robinson *lawyer*
Damoose, George Lynn *lawyer*
Dorne, David J. *lawyer*
Dyer, Charles Richard *law librarian, law educator*
Guinn, Stanley Willis *lawyer*
Hofflund, Paul *lawyer*
Hutcheson, J(ames) Sterling *lawyer*
Kripke, Kenneth Norman *retired lawyer*
Lathrop, Mitchell Lee *lawyer*
LeBeau, Charles Paul *lawyer*
Mayer, James Hock *mediator, lawyer*
McClellan, Craig Rene *lawyer*
McDermott, Thomas John, Jr. *lawyer*
McGinnis, Robert E. *lawyer*
Meyer, Paul I. *lawyer*
Mittermiller, James Joseph *lawyer*
Morris, Grant Harold *law educator*
Morris, Sandra Joan *lawyer*
O'Malley, James Terence *lawyer*
Pray, Ralph Marble, III *lawyer*
Pugh, Richard Crawford *lawyer*
Root, George L., Jr. *lawyer*
Ross, Terry D. *lawyer*
Samuelson, Derrick William *lawyer*
Schoville, Dennis A(rnold) *lawyer*
Schuck, Carl Joseph *lawyer*
Scott, Douglas Edward *lawyer*
Shearer, William Kennedy *lawyer, publisher*
Shippey, Sandra Lee *lawyer*
Smith, Steven Ray *law educator*
Snyder, David Richard *lawyer*
St. George, William Ross *lawyer, retired naval officer, consultant*
Sterrett, James Kelley, II *lawyer*
Stiska, John Charles *lawyer*
Sullivan, William Francis *lawyer*
Vega, Gregory A. *prosecutor*
Weaver, Michael James *lawyer*

San Francisco
Adams, Dirk Standley *lawyer*
Alderman, William Fields *lawyer*
Alexander, Robert C. *lawyer*
Allen, Jose R. *lawyer*
Andrews, David Ralph *lawyer*
Arbuthnot, Robert Murray *lawyer*
Baker, Cameron *lawyer*
Bancroft, James Ramsey *lawyer, business executive*
Barbagelata, Robert Dominic *lawyer*
Barber, James P. *lawyer*
Bauch, Thomas Jay *financial/investment advisor, lawyer, educator, former apparel company executive*
Baxter, Ralph H., Jr. *lawyer*
Bedford, Daniel Ross *lawyer*
Bellardo, Brian *lawyer*
Benvenutti, Peter J. *lawyer*
Bookin, Daniel Henry *lawyer*
Booth, Forrest *lawyer*
Borowsky, Philip *lawyer*
Boucher, Harold Irving *retired lawyer*
Boyd, William Sprott *lawyer*
Bridges, Robert Lysle *retired lawyer*
Briscoe, John *lawyer*
Brown, Donald Wesley *lawyer*
Brown, Geoffrey Francis *public defender, lawyer*
Bruen, James A. *lawyer*
Buccieri, Shirley H. *lawyer*
Burns, Brian Patrick *lawyer, business executive*
Bushnell, Roderick Paul *lawyer*
Cabraser, Elizabeth Joan *lawyer*
Campbell, Scott Robert *lawyer, former food company executive*
Carlson, John Earl *lawyer*
Carter, John Douglas *lawyer*
Cartmell, Nathaniel Madison, III *lawyer*
Chao, Cedric C. *lawyer*
Cheatham, Robert William *lawyer*
Clopton, Karen Valentia *lawyer, president civil services commission*
Coffin, Judy Sue *lawyer*
Coleman, Thomas Young *lawyer*
Collas, Juan Garduño, Jr. *lawyer*
Coombe, George William, Jr. *lawyer, retired banker*
Corcoran, Maureen Elizabeth *lawyer*
Crawford, Roy Edgington, III *lawyer*
Cumming, George Anderson, Jr. *lawyer*
Danoff, Eric Michael *lawyer*
Davis, Roger Lewis *lawyer*
Dell, Robert Michael *lawyer*
DeMuro, Paul Robert *lawyer*
Diamond, Philip Ernest *lawyer*
Diekmann, Gilmore Frederick, Jr. *lawyer*
Dunne, Kevin Joseph *lawyer*
Edwards, Robin Morse *lawyer*
Ericson, Bruce Alan *lawyer*
Fergus, Gary Scott *lawyer*
Fogel, Paul David *lawyer*
Folberg, Harold Jay *lawyer, mediator, educator, university dean*
Foster, David Scott *lawyer*
Freeman, Tom M. *lawyer*
Freud, Nicholas S. *lawyer*
Friedman, K. Bruce *lawyer*
Friese, Robert Charles *lawyer*
Furth, Frederick Paul *lawyer*
Gaither, James C. *lawyer*
Garvey, Joanne Marie *lawyer*
Gibson, Virginia Lee *lawyer*
Gill, Margaret Gaskins *lawyer*
Gowdy, Franklin Brockway *lawyer*
Gresham, Zane Oliver *lawyer*
Guggenhime, Richard Johnson *lawyer*
Gust, Anne Baldwin *lawyer*
Haas, Raymond P. *lawyer*
Hall, Paul J. *lawyer*
Halloran, Michael James *lawyer*
Hanschen, Peter Walter *lawyer*
Heafey, Edwin Austin, Jr. *lawyer*
Heilbron, David M(ichael) *lawyer*
Hendrick, James T. *lawyer*
Heng, Donald James, Jr. *lawyer*
Henson, Ray David *law educator, consultant*
Hinman, Harvey DeForest *lawyer*
Hisert, George A. *lawyer*
Hofmann, John Richard, Jr. *retired lawyer*
Holden, Frederick Douglass, Jr. *lawyer*
Homer, Barry Wayne *lawyer*
Hudner, Philip *lawyer, rancher*
Hudson, Mark Woodbridge *lawyer*
Hunt, James L. *lawyer*
Hunter, William Dennis *lawyer*
Irwin, William Rankin *retired lawyer*
Johnson, Martin Wayne *lawyer*
Jones, J. Sorton *lawyer*
Joseph, Allan Jay *lawyer*
Jung, David Joseph *law educator*
Kallgren, Edward Eugene *lawyer*
Kaplan, Alvin Irving *lawyer, adjudicator, investigator*
Kasanin, Mark Owen *lawyer*
Kelly, J. Michael *lawyer*
Kennedy, Raoul Dion *lawyer*
Kern, John McDougall *lawyer*
Kimport, David Lloyd *lawyer*
Knapp, Charles Lincoln *law educator*
Knebel, Jack Gillen *lawyer*
Knutzen, Martha Lorraine *lawyer*
Koeppel, John A. *lawyer*
Kuhl, Paul Beach *lawyer*
Ladar, Jerrold Morton *lawyer*
Lane, Fielding H. *lawyer*
Larson, John William *lawyer*
Lasky, Moses *lawyer*
Lee, Richard Diebold *law educator, legal publisher, consultant*
Leshy, John David *lawyer, legal educator, government official*
Levit, Victor Bert *lawyer, foreign representative, civic worker*
Libbin, Anne Edna *lawyer*
Lindstrom, Gregory P. *lawyer*
Livsey, Robert Callister *lawyer*
Loeb, Ronald Marvin *lawyer*
Lopes, James Louis *lawyer*
MacGowan, Eugenia *lawyer*
Mann, Bruce Alan *lawyer, investment banker*
Marchant, David Judson *lawyer*
Marshall, Raymond Charles *lawyer*
Martel, John Sheldon *lawyer, writer*
Mattes, Martin Anthony *lawyer*
Mc Laughlin, Jerome Michael *lawyer, shipping company executive*
McElhinny, Harold John *lawyer*
McGuckin, John Hugh, Jr. *lawyer*
McKelvey, Judith Grant *lawyer, educator, university dean*
McNally, Thomas Charles, III *lawyer*
Metzler, Roger James, Jr. *lawyer*
Meyerson, Ivan D. *lawyer, holding company executive*
Miles, Donald F. *lawyer*
Miller, William Napier Cripps *lawyer*
Minnick, Malcolm David *lawyer*
Mitchell, Bruce Tyson *lawyer*
Mueller, Robert Swan, III *lawyer, former federal official*
Musfelt, Duane Clark *lawyer*
Musser, Sandra G. *retired lawyer*
Odgers, Richard William *lawyer*
Offer, Stuart Jay *lawyer*
Olejko, Mitchell J. *lawyer*
Olson, Walter Gilbert *lawyer*
Penskar, Mark Howard *lawyer*
Phillips, Steve *lawyer, school system administrator, columnist*
Pickett, Donn Philip *lawyer*
Popofsky, Melvin Laurence *lawyer*
Preuss, Charles Frederick *lawyer*
Ragan, Charles Ransom *lawyer*
Ramey, Drucilla Stender *legal association executive*
Raven, Robert Dunbar *lawyer*
Reding, John Anthony *lawyer*
Reese, John Robert *lawyer*
Rembe, Toni *lawyer, director*
Renfrew, Charles Byron *lawyer*
Richards, Norman Blanchard *lawyer*
Riley, William L. *lawyer*
Rogan, Richard A. *lawyer*
Roman, Stan G. *lawyer*
Roosevelt, Michael A. *lawyer*
Rosch, John Thomas *lawyer*

Las Vegas
Arum, Robert *lawyer, sports events promoter*
Bryan, Richard H. *lawyer, educator, former senator*
Curran, William P. *lawyer*
Faiss, Robert Dean *lawyer*
Goldberg, Aubrey *lawyer*
Gray, Patricia Joyce *legal administration*
Havemann, Michael R. *legal administration*
Kennedy, Dennis L. *lawyer*
Landreth, Kathryn E. *prosecutor*
Miller, Robert Joseph *lawyer, former governor*
Pray, Donald Eugene *lawyer*
Solomon, Jack Avrum *lawyer, automotive distributor, art dealer*
Solomon, Mark A. *lawyer*

Reno
Guild, Clark Joseph, Jr. *lawyer*
Hibbs, Loyal Robert *lawyer*
Jeannes, Charles A. *lawyer*
Pagni, Albert Frank *lawyer*

NEW MEXICO

Albuquerque
Addis, Richard Barton *lawyer*
Bardacke, Paul Gregory *lawyer, former attorney general*
Baum, Marsha Lynn *law educator*
Cargo, David Francis *lawyer*
Chavez, Martin Joseph *lawyer, former mayor*
Farmer, Terry D(wayne) *lawyer*
Hart, Frederick Michael *law educator*
Kelly, John J. *former prosecutor*
Miller, Ranne B. *lawyer*
Murphy, Robert F. *lawyer*
Paster, Janice Dubinsky *lawyer, former state legislator*
Roehl, Jerrald J. *lawyer*
Sisk, Daniel Arthur *lawyer*
Slade, Lynn Heyer *lawyer*
Thompson, Rufus E. *lawyer*
Thornton, J. Duke *lawyer*
White, Robert Milton *lawyer*

Clovis
Doerr, Stephen *lawyer*

Las Cruces
Lindley, Jearl Ray *lawyer*
Lutz, William Lan *lawyer*

Roswell
Kraft, Richard Lee *lawyer*
Olson, Richard Earl *lawyer, state legislator*

Santa Fe
Besing, Ray Gilbert *lawyer, writer*
Brannen, Jeffrey Richard *lawyer*
Culbert, Peter V. *lawyer*
Dodds, Robert James, III *lawyer*
Johnson, Reverdy *lawyer*
Pound, John Bennett *lawyer*
Stevens, Ron A. *lawyer, public interest organization executive*

Silver City
Foy, Thomas Paul *lawyer, retired state legislator, retired banker*

OHIO

Beavercreek
Richardson, Arthur Wilhelm *lawyer*

OREGON

Beaverton
Stewart, Lindsay D. *lawyer*

Bend
Achterman, Gail Louise *lawyer*

Eugene
Aldave, Barbara Bader *law educator, lawyer*
Clark, Chapin DeWitt *law educator*
Scoles, Eugene Francis *law educator, lawyer*

Gleneden Beach
Arant, Eugene Wesley *lawyer*

Medford
O'Connor, Karl William (Goodyear Johnson) *lawyer*

Newport
Strever, Kevin Kirk *lawyer*

Pendleton
Rew, Lawrence Boyd *lawyer*

Portland
Abrams, Marc *lawyer, state political party executive*
Abravanel, Allan Ray *lawyer*
Anderson, Herbert Hatfield *lawyer, farmer*
Arthur, Michael Elbert *lawyer, financial advisor*
Balmer, Thomas Ancil *lawyer*
Bernstine, Daniel O'Neal *law educator, university president*
Brenneman, Delbert Jay *lawyer*
Brown, David W. *lawyer*
Cable, John Franklin *lawyer*
Canaday, Richard A. *lawyer*
Chapman, Matthew William *lawyer*
Cooke, Roger Anthony *retired lawyer*
Crowell, John B., Jr. *lawyer, former government official*
Culpepper, David Charles *lawyer*
Dailey, Dianne K. *lawyer*
Deering, Thomas Phillips *lawyer*
Dotten, Michael Chester *lawyer*
English, Stephen Francis *lawyer*
Epstein, Edward Louis *lawyer*
Fell, James Frederick *lawyer*
Feuerstein, Howard M. *lawyer*
Foley, Ridgway Knight, Jr. *lawyer, writer*
Franzke, Richard Albert *lawyer*
Froebe, Gerald Allen *lawyer*
Georges, Maurice Ostrow *retired lawyer*
Glasgow, William Jacob *lawyer, venture capitalist, business executive*
Greene, Herbert Bruce *lawyer, investor*
Grossmann, Ronald Stanyer *lawyer*
Hart, John Edward *lawyer*
Helmer, M(artha) Christie *lawyer*
Hennings, Laury H. *lawyer*
Hinkle, Charles Frederick *lawyer, clergyman, educator*
Holman, Donald Reid *lawyer*
Jarvis, Peter R. *lawyer*
Johansen, Judith A. *lawyer*
Johnson, Alexander Charles *lawyer, electrical engineer*
Johnson, Mark Andrew *lawyer*
Jolles, Bernard *lawyer*
Josephson, Richard Carl *lawyer*
Kanter, Stephen *law educator, dean*
Kennedy, Jack Leland *lawyer*
Kester, Randall Blair *lawyer*
Knoll, James Lewis *lawyer*
Larpenteur, James Albert, Jr. *lawyer*
Leedy, Robert Allan, Sr. *retired lawyer*
Lewis, Charles S., III *lawyer*
Livingston, Louis Bayer *lawyer*
Love, William Edward *lawyer*
Luedtke, Roger A. *lawyer*
Lusky, John Anderson *lawyer*
Maloney, Robert E., Jr. *lawyer*
Matarazzo, Harris Starr *lawyer*
Miller, William Richey, Jr. *lawyer*
Mowe, Gregory Robert *lawyer*
Nash, Frank Erwin *lawyer*
Nicolai, Thomas R. *lawyer*
Norby, Mark Alan *lawyer*
Nunn, Robert Warne *lawyer*
Olson, Kristine *prosecutor*
Purcell, John F. *lawyer*
Rawlinson, Dennis Patrick *lawyer*
Richardson, Campbell *retired lawyer*
Richter, Peter Christian *lawyer*
Rosen, Steven O. *lawyer*
Rosenbaum, Lois Omenn *lawyer*
Rubin, Bruce Alan *lawyer*
Sand, Thomas Charles *lawyer*
Schreck, George Charles *lawyer*
Schuster, Philip Frederick , II *lawyer, writer*
Shellan, Ronald A. *lawyer*
Simpson, Robert Glenn *lawyer*
Sokol, Jan D. *lawyer*
Stewart, Milton Roy *lawyer*
Stone, Richard James *lawyer*
Sullivan, Edward Joseph *lawyer, educator*
Tomlinson, William M. *lawyer*
Van Valkenburg, Edgar Walter *lawyer*
Waggoner, James Clyde *lawyer*
Weaver, Delbert Allen *lawyer*
Westwood, James Nicholson *lawyer*
Whinston, Arthur Lewis *lawyer*
White, Douglas James, Jr. *lawyer*
Wilson, Owen Meredith, Jr. *lawyer*
Wood, Marcus Andrew *lawyer*
Wyse, William Walker *lawyer, real estate executive*

Salem
Bailey, Henry John, III *retired lawyer, educator*
Breen, Richard F., Jr. *law librarian, lawyer, educator*
Haselton, Rick Thomas *lawyer*
Mannix, Kevin Leese *lawyer*

UTAH

Logan
Jenkins, James C. *lawyer*

Provo
Lund, Steven Jay *lawyer*
Thomas, David Albert *law educator, director*

Salt Lake City
Adams, Joseph Keith *lawyer*
Anderson, Kent Taylor *lawyer*
Baldwin, John *legal association administrator, lawyer*
Baucom, Sidney George *lawyer*
Berman, Daniel Lewis *lawyer*
Brown, Charles R. *lawyer*
Buchi, Mark Keith *lawyer*
Christensen, Ray Richards *lawyer*
Clark, Scott H. *lawyer*
Cornaby, Kay Sterling *lawyer, former state senator*
Curtis, LeGrand R., Jr. *lawyer*
Detton, David K. *lawyer*
Hedger, Cecil Raymond *lawyer*
Holbrook, Donald Benson *lawyer*
Holtkamp, James Arnold *lawyer, educator*
Kirkham, John Spencer *lawyer, director*
Lehman, Mark Edwards *lawyer*
Leta, David Edward *lawyer*
Livsey, Herbert C. *lawyer*
Mabey, Ralph R. *lawyer*
Manning, Brent V. *lawyer*
Matsumori, Douglas *lawyer*
McCoy, Harry E., II *lawyer*
McIntosh, Terrie Tuckett *lawyer*
Mock, Henry Byron *lawyer, writer, consultant*
Mooney, Jerome Henri *lawyer*
Moore, James R. *lawyer*
Nielsen, Greg Ross *lawyer*
Oaks, Dallin Harris *lawyer, church official*
Ockey, Ronald J. *lawyer*
Rasmussen, Thomas Val, Jr. *lawyer, small business owner*
Reeder, F. Robert *lawyer*
Roberts, Jack Earl *lawyer, ski resort operator, wood products company executive, real estate developer*
Schwendiman, Dave J. *prosecutor*
Shea, Patrick A. *lawyer, educator*
Smith, Janet Hugie *lawyer*
Wadsworth, Harold Wayne *lawyer*
Wangsgard, Chris Prince *lawyer*
Warner, Paul M. *prosecutor*
West, Stephen Allan *lawyer*
Wikstrom, Francis M. *lawyer*
Zimmerman, Michael David *lawyer*

WASHINGTON

Bellevue
Medved, Robert Allen *lawyer*
Morie, G. Glen *lawyer, manufacturing company executive*
Sebris, Robert, Jr. *lawyer*

Colfax
Webster, Ronald B. *lawyer*

Everett
Fitzpatrick, Thomas Mark *lawyer*

Friday Harbor
Gonser, Thomas Howard *lawyer, former bar association executive*

Issaquah
Benoliel, Joel *lawyer*
Oles, Stuart Gregory *lawyer*

Olympia
Norwood, Deborah Anne *law librarian*
Walker, Francis Joseph *lawyer*

Redmond
Burt, Thomas William *lawyer*
Neukom, William H. *lawyer*

Seattle
Alkire, John D. *lawyer, mediator, arbitrator*
Anderson, Peter MacArthur *lawyer*
Andreasen, Steven W. *lawyer*
Andrews, J. David *lawyer*
Barnes, Susan Lewis *lawyer*
Birmingham, Richard Joseph *lawyer*
Black, W. L. Rivers, III *lawyer*
Blair, M. Wayne *lawyer*
Blais, Robert Howard *lawyer*
Blom, Daniel Charles *lawyer, investor*
Blumenfeld, Charles Raban *lawyer*
Boeder, Thomas L. *lawyer*
Boman, Marc Allen *lawyer*
Bridge, Jonathan Joseph *lawyer, retail executive*
Burke, William Thomas *law educator, lawyer*
Burkhart, William Henry *lawyer*
Cavanaugh, Michael Everett *lawyer, arbitrator, mediator*
Chapman, Fay L. *lawyer*
Char, Patricia Helen *lawyer*
Claflin, Arthur Cary *lawyer*
Clinton, Richard M. *lawyer*
Comfort, Robert Dennis *lawyer*
Cross, Bruce Michael *lawyer*
Cross, Harry Maybury *retired law educator, consultant*
Cullen, Jack Joseph *lawyer*
Cunningham, Joel Dean *lawyer*
Davis, John MacDougall *lawyer*
DeVore, Paul Cameron *lawyer*
Diggs, Bradley C. *lawyer*
Dolan, Andrew Kevin *lawyer*
Ellis, James Reed *lawyer*
Freedman, Bart Joseph *lawyer*
Gandara, Daniel *lawyer*
Giles, Robert Edward, Jr. *lawyer*
Gittinger, D. Wayne *lawyer*
Glover, Karen E. *lawyer*
Goeltz, Thomas A. *lawyer*
Gores, Thomas C. *lawyer*
Gorton, Slade *attorney, former senator*
Graham, Stephen Michael *lawyer*
Gray, Marvin Lee, Jr. *lawyer*
Greenan, Thomas J. *lawyer*
Gustafson, Alice Fairleigh *lawyer*
Guy, Andrew A. *lawyer*
Haman, Raymond William *lawyer*
Hamilton, Steven G. *lawyer*
Hansen, Wayne W. *lawyer*
Hazelton, Penny Ann *law librarian, educator*
Hermsen, James R. *lawyer*
Hilpert, Edward Theodore, Jr. *lawyer*
Holtan, Ramer B., Jr. *lawyer*
Hopp, Richard A. *lawyer*
Huff, Gary D. *lawyer*
Huston, John Charles *law educator*
Hutcheson, Mark Andrew *lawyer*
Isaki, Lucy Power Slyngstad *lawyer*
Israel, Allen D. *lawyer*
Jackson, Dillon Edward *lawyer*
Jaffe, Robert Stanley *lawyer*
Johnson, Bruce Edward Humble *lawyer*
Judson, C(harles) James (Jim Judson) *lawyer*
Kane, Alan Henry *lawyer*
Kane, Christopher *lawyer*
Kaplan, Barry Martin *lawyer*
Katz, Charles J., Jr. *lawyer*
Keegan, John E. *lawyer*
Kellogg, Kenyon P. *lawyer*
Kelly, Kevin Francis *lawyer*
Klein, Otto George, III *lawyer*
Koehler, Reginald Stafford, III *lawyer*
Kuhrau, Edward W. *lawyer*
Leitzell, Terry Lee *lawyer*
Lemly, Thomas Adger *lawyer*
Loftus, Thomas Daniel *lawyer*
Maleng, Norm *prosecutor*
McCann, Richard Eugene *lawyer*
McKay, Michael Dennis *lawyer*
Mussehl, Robert Clarence *lawyer*
Nellermoe, Leslie Carol *lawyer*
Niemi, Janice *retired lawyer, former state legislator*
Noble, Phillip D. *lawyer*
Oehler, Richard William *lawyer*
Olsen, Harold Fremont *lawyer*
Palm, Gerald Albert *lawyer*
Palmer, Douglas S., Jr. *lawyer*
Parker, Omar Sigmund, Jr. *lawyer*
Parks, Patricia Jean *lawyer*
Parsons, A. Peter *lawyer*
Petrie, Gregory Steven *lawyer*
Pettigrew, Edward W. *lawyer*
Pflaumer, Katrina C. *lawyer*
Prentke, Richard Ottesen *lawyer*
Price, John Richard *lawyer, law educator*
Pritchard, Llewelyn G. *lawyer*
Pym, Bruce Michael *lawyer*
Redman, Eric *lawyer*
Rieke, Paul Victor *lawyer*
Ritter, Daniel Benjamin *lawyer*
Ruddy, James W. *lawyer*
Rummage, Stephen Michael *lawyer*
Sandler, Michael David *lawyer*
Sandman, Irvin W(illis) *lawyer*
Schneidler, Jon Gordon *lawyer*
Sidran, Mark Harris *lawyer*
Soltys, John Joseph *lawyer*
Spitzer, Hugh D. *lawyer*
Squires, William Randolph, III *lawyer*
Steers, George W. *lawyer*
Stoebuck, William Brees *law educator*
Sweeney, David Brian *lawyer*
Thorne, David W. *lawyer*
Thorson, Lee A. *lawyer*
Treiger, Irwin Louis *lawyer*
Tune, James Fulcher *lawyer*
Veblen, John Elvidge *lawyer*
Vestal, Josephine Burnet *lawyer*
Wagner, Patricia Hamm *lawyer*
Wagoner, David Everett *lawyer*
Wechsler, Mary Heyrman *lawyer*
Wells, Christopher Brian *lawyer*
Whalen, Jerome Demaris *lawyer*
White, Rick *lawyer, former congressman*
Whitford, Joseph Peter *lawyer*
Williams, J. Vernon *lawyer*

Spokane
Clarke, Judy *lawyer*
Connelly, James P. *prosecutor*
Eymann, Richard Charles *lawyer*
Koegen, Roy Jerome *lawyer*

Tacoma
Gordon, Joseph Harold *lawyer*
Graves, Ray *lawyer*
Holt, William E. *lawyer*
Miller, Judson Frederick *lawyer, former military officer*
Waldo, James Chandler *lawyer*

Vancouver
Kleweno, Gilbert H. *lawyer*

Wenatchee
Foreman, Dale Melvin *lawyer, state official*

Yakima
Larson, Paul Martin *lawyer*

WYOMING

Buffalo
Kirven, Timothy J. *lawyer*

Cheyenne
Freudenthal, David D. *prosecutor*
Freudenthal, Steven Franklin *lawyer, political organization chairman*
Hanes, John Grier *lawyer, state legislator*
Palma, Jack D. *lawyer*
Scorsine, John Magnus *lawyer*

Cody
Housel, Jerry Winters *lawyer*

Jackson
Spence, Gerald Leonard *lawyer, writer*

Laramie
Kinney, Lisa Frances *lawyer*
Smith, Thomas Shore *lawyer*

Riverton
Girard, Nettabell *lawyer*

TERRITORIES OF THE UNITED STATES

GUAM

Agana
Black, Frederick A. *prosecutor*

CANADA

ALBERTA

Calgary
Hughes, Margaret Eileen *law educator, former dean*
Lougheed, Peter *lawyer, former Canadian official*

Edmonton
Patrick, Lynn Allen *lawyer, corporate governance and land development*

BRITISH COLUMBIA

Vancouver
Bonner, Robert William *lawyer, director*
Head, Ivan Leigh *law educator*
Ladner, Thomas E. *lawyer*
Peterson, Leslie Raymond *barrister*

Victoria
Partridge, Bruce James *lawyer, educator, writer*

SASKATCHEWAN

Regina
MacKay, Harold Hugh *lawyer*

Saskatoon
Ish, Daniel Russell *law educator, academic administrator*

JAPAN

Tokyo
Fehrman, Burton H. *lawyer*

Greenbrae
Burger, Eugene J. *property manager*

Healdsburg
Brunner, Howard William *professional land surveyor*

Irvine
Chronley, James Andrew *real estate executive*
Stack, Geoffrey Lawrence *real estate developer*
Webb, H. Lawrence *real estate executive*

La Jolla
Foley, L(ewis) Michael *real estate executive*
Ripley, Stuart McKinnon *real estate consultant*

Laguna Beach
Hanauer, Joe Franklin *real estate executive*

Laguna Niguel
York, James Orison *real estate executive*

Long Beach
McGann, John Milton *real estate executive*

Los Alamitos
Spiegel, Marilyn Harriet *real estate executive*

Los Altos
Getreu, Sanford *city planner*

Los Angeles
Abernethy, Robert John *real estate developer*
Bergman, Nancy Palm *real estate investment company executive*
Green, Richard E. *real estate company executive*
Levy, Alan David *real estate executive*
Linsk, Michael Stephen *real estate executive*
Mezger, Jeffrey T. *real estate company executive*
Nelson, James Augustus, II *real estate executive, architect, banker*

Lynwood
Dove, Donald Augustine *city planner, educator*

Manhattan Beach
Schoenfeld, Lawrence Jon *real estate developer, asset lender*

Menlo Park
Fischer, Michael Ludwig *environmental executive*

Newport Beach
Bren, Donald L. *real estate company executive*
Kenney, William John, Jr. *real estate development executive*
Matteucci, Dominick Vincent *real estate developer*

Palmdale
Anderson, R(obert) Gregg *real estate company executive*

Pasadena
Crowley, John Crane *real estate developer*

Placerville
Craib, Kenneth Bryden *resource development executive, physicist, economist*

Rancho Cucamonga
Previtti, James P. *real estate executive*

Rolling Hills Estates
Allbee, Sandra Moll *real estate broker*

Sacramento
Lukenbill, Gregg *real estate developer, sports promoter*

San Bruno
Williams, Barry Lawson *real estate executive*

San Diego
Mc Comic, Robert Barry *real estate development company executive, lawyer*
Sabin, Gary B. *real estate executive*
Wagmen, Lee H. *real estate executive*

San Francisco
Colwell, Kent Leigh *real estate counselor, investor*
Freund, Fredric S. *real estate broker, property manager*
Shorenstein, Walter Herbert *commercial real estate development company executive*

San Jose
Bracken, Thomas Robert James *real estate investment executive*
Rothblatt, Donald Noah *urban and regional planner, educator*

San Marcos
DeMarco, Ralph John *real estate developer*

San Rafael
Roulac, Stephen E. *real estate consultant*

Santa Barbara
Arnold, Michael Neal *real property appraiser, consultant*

Santa Cruz
Dilbeck, Charles Stevens, Jr. *real estate company executive*

Santa Monica
Anderson, Dana K. *real estate company executive*
Coppola, Arthur M. *real estate company executive, lawyer*

Tracy
Nevin, David Wright *real estate broker, mortgage broker*

Upland
Lewis, Goldy Sarah *real estate developer, corporation executive*

Valencia
Cusamano, Gary M. *real estate executive*
Dierckman, Thomas E. *land use planner*
Lee, Thomas L. *real estate executive*
Mork, Stuart R. *chief financial officer land and farming company*
Schmidt, Stephen C. *vice president, residential community development*

Vista
Cavanaugh, Kenneth Clinton *retired housing consultant*

Walnut
Satterfield, Buddy *real estate development executive*
Selva, Bert *real estate development executive*
Thomas, Les *real estate development executive*
Varker, Bruce *real estate development executive*

West Hills
Struhl, Stanley Frederick *real estate developer*

Yorba Linda
Vilardi, Agnes Francine *real estate broker*

COLORADO

Aurora
Lochmiller, Kurtis L. *real estate entrepreneur*

Boulder
Morris, John Theodore *planning official*
Stepanek, Joseph Edward *industrial development consultant*

Denver
Mandarich, David D. *real estate corporation executive*
Mugler, Larry George *regional planner*
Reece, Paris G. *chief financial officer home building company*

Englewood
Sellers, Robert Scot *real estate developer*

Grand Junction
Nelson, Paul William *real estate broker*

Greenwood Village
Staky, Richard *real estate development company executive*

Vail
Kelton, Arthur Marvin, Jr. *real estate developer*

HAWAII

Honolulu
Jones, Michael T. *real estate development executive*
Jones, Pamela S. *real estate development executive*
Oyler, David L. *real estate development executive*

Mililani
Olsen, Harris Leland *real estate and international business executive, educator, diplomat*

IDAHO

Boise
Fery, John Bruce *former real estate property manager*
Reuling, Michael Frederick *supermarket company, real estate executive*

Idaho Falls
Thorsen, Nancy Dain *real estate broker*

NEVADA

Las Vegas
Canarelli, Lawrence D. *real estate developer*
Pulliam, Francine Sarno *real estate broker, real estate developer*

Reno
Davenport, Janet Lee *real estate agent, small business owner*

NEW MEXICO

Albuquerque
Stahl, Jack Leland *real estate company executive*
Tinnin, Thomas Peck *real estate professional*

OREGON

Portland
Dickinson, Janet Mae Webster *relocation consulting executive*

Springfield
Davis, George Donald *executive land use policy consultant*

UTAH

Midvale
Teerlink, J(oseph) Leland *real estate developer*

Salt Lake City
Frazier, G. Rex *real estate executive*
Price, John *real estate executive*

WASHINGTON

Federal Way
McMichael, J(ack) Richard *real estate developer*

Rollingbay
Morris, Donald Charles *commercial real estate mergers and acquisitions*

Seattle
Sasaki, Tsutomu (Tom Sasaki) *real estate company executive, international trading company executive, consultant*

Tacoma
Nitta, Jeffrey W. *real estate executive*

CANADA

ALBERTA

Calgary
Milavsky, Harold Phillip *real estate executive*

BRITISH COLUMBIA

Vancouver
Goldberg, Michael Arthur *land policy and planning educator*

ADDRESS UNPUBLISHED

Beck, John Roland *environmental consultant*
Dickey, Robert Marvin (Rick Dickey) *property manager*
Fetterly, Lynn Lawrence *real estate broker, developer*
Fredericks, Patricia Ann *real estate executive*
Maguire, Robert Francis, III *real estate investor*
Malcuria, Sherry JoAnne *real estate company executive, interior designer*
Meyer, Daniel Kramer *real estate executive*
Mohamed, Joseph, Sr. *real estate broker, farmer*
Woods, Sandra Kay *real estate executive*

RELIGION

UNITED STATES

ALASKA

Anchorage
Fleming, Carolyn Elizabeth *religious organization administrator, interior designer*
Hurley, Francis T. *archbishop*
Schwietz, Roger L. *bishop*

ARIZONA

Arizona City
Ross, Lanson Clifford, Jr. *religious studies educator, writer*

Duncan
Ouzts, Eugene Thomas *minister, secondary education educator*

Paradise Valley
Sapp, Donald Gene *retired minister*

Phoenix
Dew, William Waldo, Jr. *bishop*
King, Felton *bishop*
Kuzma, George Martin *bishop*
O'Brien, Thomas Joseph *bishop*

Scottsdale
Mc Knight, William Warren, Jr. *publisher*

Tucson
Moreno, Manuel D. *bishop*

CALIFORNIA

Acton
Butman, Harry Raymond *clergyman, writer*

Alhambra
Duke, Donald Norman *publisher*

Anaheim
Nguyen, Tai Anh *minister*

Barstow
Jones, Nathaniel B., Jr. *bishop*

Berkeley
Mudge, Lewis Seymour *theologian, educator, university dean*

Castro Valley
Morrison, Glenn Leslie *minister*

Chino Hills
Nash, Sylvia Dotseth *religious organization executive, consultant*

Claremont
Sanders, James Alvin *minister, religious studies educator*

Costa Mesa
Williams, William Corey *theology educator, consultant*

Davis
[illegible]

Del Mar
Randall, Chandler Corydon *church rector*

Duarte
Driskill, James Lawrence *minister*

Elk Grove
Vang, Timothy Teng *religious organization administrator*

Fresno
Steinbock, John Thomas *bishop*

Fullerton
Kim, Sang Koo *pastor, educator*

Garden Grove
Schuller, Robert Harold *clergyman, author*

Glendora
Richey, Everett Eldon *religious studies educator*

Hollywood
Adjenian, Robert *publisher*

La Jolla
Freedman, David Noel *religious studies educator*

Laguna Hills
Wheatley, Melvin Ernest, Jr. *retired bishop*

Laguna Woods
Faw, Duane Leslie *lay worker, law educator, retired career officer, writer*

Lancaster
Runner, George Cyril, Jr. *minister, educational administrator*

Long Beach
Findley, John A., Jr. *publisher*

Los Alamitos
Booth, John Nicholls *minister, writer, photographer*

Los Angeles
Anderson, Robert Marshall *retired bishop*
Berenbaum, Michael Gary *theology educator*
Berg, Philip *religious organization administrator*
Borsch, Frederick Houk *bishop*
Boyd, Malcolm *minister, spiritual writer*
Breuer, Stephen Ernest *religious organization administrator*
Chedid, John G. *bishop*
Fitzgerald, Tikhon (Lee R. H. Fitzgerald) *bishop*
Mahony, Cardinal Roger Michael *archbishop*
Mc Pherson, Rolf Kennedy *clergyman, religious organization administrator*
Milligan, Sister Mary *theology educator, religious consultant*
O'Connor, Kevin Thomas *religious organization administrator*
Ogilvie, Lloyd John *clergyman*
Phillips, Keith Wendall *minister*
Setian, Nerses Mikail *retired bishop*
Ward, John J. *bishop*
Williams, Ronald Dean *minister, religious organization administrator*
Wolf, Alfred *rabbi*
Wooten, Cecil Aaron *religious organization administrator*

Malibu
Wilson, John Francis *religious studies educator, archaeologist*

Mill Valley
Crews, William Odell, Jr. *religious organization administrator*

Monterey
Ryan, Sylvester D. *bishop*
Shimpfky, Richard Lester *bishop*

Moreno Valley
Kari, Daven Michael *religious studies educator*

North Hollywood
Koran, Dennis Howard *publisher*

Oakland
Benham, Priscilla Carla *religious studies educator, college president*
Cummins, John Stephen *bishop*
Jakubowsky, Frank Raymond *religious writer*
Patten, Bebe Harrison *minister, chancellor*
Schomer, Howard *retired clergyman, educator, social policy consultant*

Orange
Brown, Tod David *bishop*
Mc Farland, Norman Francis *bishop*

Palm Springs
Jones, Milton Wakefield *publisher*

Pasadena
Sano, Roy I. *bishop*
Torres, Ralph Chon *minister*

Pittsburg
Schmalenberger, Jerry Lew *pastor, religious studies educator*

Pleasanton
Ice, Richard Eugene *retired minister, retirement housing company executive*

Portola Valley
Garsh, Thomas Burton *publisher*

Reedley
Dick, Henry Henry *minister*

Sacramento
Cole, Glen David *minister*
Garcia, Richard J. *bishop*
Quinn, Francis A. *bishop*
Weigand, William Keith *bishop*

San Bernardino
Barnes, Gerald R. *bishop*
Burgess, Mary Alice (Mary Alice Wickizer) *publisher*

SCIENCE: LIFE SCIENCE

UNITED STATES

Kofranek, Anton Miles *floriculturist, educator*
Meyer, Margaret Eleanor *microbiologist, educator*
Moyle, Peter Briggs *fisheries and biology educator*
Murphy, Frederick Augustus *virologist, researcher*
Murphy, Terence Martin *biology educator*
Qualset, Calvin O. *plant genetics and agronomy educator*
Rappaport, Lawrence *plant physiology and horticulture educator*
Rhode, Edward Albert *veterinary medicine educator, veterinary cardiologist*
Rick, Charles Madeira, Jr. *geneticist, educator*
Rost, Thomas Lowell *plant biology educator*
Rowhani, Adib *plant pathologist*
Schoener, Thomas William *zoology educator, researcher*
Sillman, Arnold Joel *physiologist, educator*
Steffey, Eugene Paul *veterinary medicine educator*
Uyemoto, Jerry Kazumitsu *plant pathologist, educator*
Van Alfen, Neal K. *plant pathologist*
Vermeij, Geerat Jacobus *marine biologist, educator*
Watt, Kenneth Edmund Ferguson *zoology educator*
Williams, William Arnold *agronomy educator*

Del Mar
Farquhar, Marilyn Gist *cell biology and pathology educator*

Duarte
Vaughn, James English, Jr. *neurobiologist*

Encinitas
Duval, Julian J. *arboretum administrator*

Foster City
Baselt, Randall Clint *toxicologist*

Fremont
White, Raymond Leslie *geneticist*

Fullerton
Dickson, Kathryn *science educator*
Jones, Claris Eugene, Jr. *botanist, educator*

Gilroy
Barham, Warren Sandusky *horticulturist*

Hopland
Jones, Milton Bennion *retired agronomist, educator*

Irvine
Allen, Douglas D. *horticulture and products company executive*
Ayala, Francisco José *geneticist, educator*
Bryant, Peter James *biologist, educator*
Fan, Hung Y. *virology educator, consultant*
Fitch, Walter M(onroe) *molecular biologist, educator, evolutionist*
Lawton, Michael James *entomologist, pest management specialist*
Lenhoff, Howard Maer *biological sciences educator, academic administrator, activist*
Silverman, Paul Hyman *science administrator, former university official*
Steward, Oswald *neuroscience educator, researcher*
Thigpen, Stephen P. *horticulture products company executive*

Kelseyville
Sandmeyer, E. E. *toxicologist, consultant*

La Jolla
Alvariño De Leira, Angeles (Angeles Alvariño) *biologist, oceanographer*
Bloom, Floyd Elliott *physician, research scientist*
Brooks, Charles Lee, III *computational biophysicist, educator*
Chrispeels, Maarten Jan *biology educator*
Guillemin, Roger C. L. *physiologist*
Helinski, Donald Raymond *biologist, educator*
Hunter, Tony (Anthony Rex Hunter) *molecular biologist, educator*
Knowlton, Nancy *biologist*
Lewin, Ralph Arnold *biologist*
Richman, Douglas Daniel *medical virologist, educator, internist*
Schroeder, Julian Ivan *biology educator*
Thal, Leon Joel *neuroscientist*
Vacquier, Victor Dimitri *biology educator*
West, John Burnard *physiologist, physician, educator*
Wilkie, Donald Walter *biologist, aquarium museum director*
Wilson, Ian Andrew *molecular biology educator*
Wong-Staal, Flossie *geneticist, medical educator*

Laguna Niguel
Coleman, Roger Dixon *bacteriologist*

Loma Linda
Longo, Lawrence Daniel *physiologist, obstetrician-gynecologist*
Taylor, Barry Llewellyn *microbiologist, educator*

Long Beach
Iliff, Warren Jolidon *zoo administrator*

Los Alamitos
Aberman, Harold Mark *veterinarian*

Los Angeles
Baker, Robert Frank *molecular biologist, educator*
Birren, James Emmett *university research center executive*
Bok, Dean *cell biologist, educator*
Bottjer, David John *earth scientist, biologist, educator*
Chen, Irvin Shao Yu *microbiologist, educator*
Craft, Cheryl Mae *neurobiologist, anatomist, researcher*
Diamond, Jared Mason *biologist*
Eisenberg, David Samuel *molecular biologist, educator*
Finch, Caleb Ellicott *neurobiologist, educator*
[illegible] *microbiology educator*
Gilman, John Joseph *research scientist*
Gordon, Malcolm Stephen *biology educator*

Grinnell, Alan Dale *neurobiologist, educator, researcher*
Kadner, Carl George *biology educator emeritus*
Mockary, Peter Ernest *clinical laboratory scientist, researcher, medical writer*
Phinney, Bernard O. *research scientist, educator*
Schopf, James William *paleobiologist*
Sonnenschein, Ralph Robert *physiologist*
Szego, Clara Marian *cell biologist, educator*
Tobin, Allan Joshua *biologist*
Villablanca, Jaime Rolando *medical neuroscientist, educator*
Wright, Ernest Marshall *physiologist, consultant*
Yang, Yang *science educator*

Madera
Curry, Cynthia J. R. *geneticist*

Menlo Park
Crane, Hewitt David *science advisor*
Jorgensen, Paul J. *research company executive*

Mentone
Halstead, Bruce Walter *biotoxicologist*

Moffett Field
Dalton, Bonnie *life science administrator*
Greenleaf, John Edward *research physiologist*
Gundy-Burlet, Karen *research scientist*
Kittel, Peter *research scientist*
McDonald, Henry (Harry McDonald) *research center administrator*
Morrison, David *science administrator, researcher*

Monrovia
Kimnach, Myron William *botanist, horticulturist, consultant*

Monterey
Packard, Julie *aquarium administrator*

Mountain View
Klein, Harold Paul *microbiologist*
Larrick, James William *science administrator*
Mansfield, Elaine Schultz *molecular geneticist, automation specialist*
Pierson, Thomas *scientific institute administrator*

Northridge
Sparling, Mary Lee *biology educator*

Oakland
Collins, James Francis *toxicologist*
Earle, Sylvia Alice *research biologist, oceanographer*
Parrott, Joel J. *zoo director*

Pacific Grove
Epel, David *biologist, educator*

Palm Desert
Sausman, Karen *zoological park administrator*

Palmdale
Smith, Maureen McBride *laboratory administrator*

Palo Alto
Anderson, Charles Arthur *former research institute administrator*
Botstein, David *geneticist, educator*
Briggs, Winslow Russell *plant biologist, educator*
Johnson, Noble Marshall *research scientist*
Pake, George Edward *research executive, physicist*
Tsien, Richard Winyu *biology educator*
Wrighton, Nicholas C. *research scientist*

Parlier
Michailides, Themis J. *plant pathology educator*

Pasadena
Abelson, John Norman *biology educator*
Attardi, Giuseppe M. *biology educator*
Beer, Reinhard *atmospheric scientist*
Davidson, Eric Harris *molecular and developmental biologist, educator*
Horowitz, Norman Harold *biologist, emeritus educator*
Konishi, Masakazu *neurobiologist, educator*
Lewis, Edward B. *biology educator*
Meyerowitz, Elliot Martin *biologist, educator*
North, Wheeler James *marine ecologist, educator*
Owen, Ray David *biology educator*
Revel, Jean-Paul *biology educator*
Tirrell, David A. *research scientist, educator*
Varshavsky, Alexander Jacob *molecular biologist*

Pomona
Keating, Eugene Kneeland *animal scientist, educator*

Redwood City
Neville, Roy Gerald *scientist, chemical management and environmental consultant*

Richmond
Beall, Frank Carroll *science director and educator*

Riverside
Bartnicki-Garcia, Salomon *microbiologist, educator*
Clegg, Michael Tran *genetics educator, researcher*
Erwin, Donald Carroll *plant pathology educator*
Hall, Anthony Elmitt *crop ecologist*
Keen, Noel Thomas *plant pathology educator*
Moore, John Alexander *biologist*
Page, Albert Lee *soil science educator, researcher*
Sherman, Irwin William *biological sciences educator*
Spencer, William Franklin, Sr. *soil scientist, researcher*
Van Gundy, Seymour Dean *nematologist, plant pathologist, educator*
Zentmyer, George Aubrey *plant pathology educator*

Sacramento
Booze, Thomas Franklin *toxicologist*

San Diego
Archibald, James David *biology educator, paleontologist*

Bernstein, Sanford Irwin *biology educator*
Bieler, Charles Linford *zoo executive director emeritus, former development director*
Chory, Joanne *plant biologist*
Crick, Francis Harry Compton *science educator, researcher*
Dolan, James Michael, Jr. *zoological park administrator*
Eckhart, Walter *molecular biologist, educator*
Heinemann, Stephen F. *molecular neurobiologist educator*
Hemmingsen, Barbara Bruff *microbiology educator*
McGraw, Donald Jesse *biologist, science historian, writer*
Myers, Douglas George *zoological society administrator*
Risser, Arthur Crane, Jr. *zoo administrator*
Schaechter, Moselio *microbiology educator*
Sejnowski, Terrence Joseph *science educator*
Taylor, Tony S. *research scientist*
Thomas, Charles Allen, Jr. *molecular biologist, educator*

San Francisco
Anderson, David E. *zoological park administrator*
Blackburn, Elizabeth Helen *molecular biologist*
Borson, Daniel Benjamin *physiology educator, inventor, researcher, lawyer*
Cape, Ronald Elliot *retired biotechnology company executive*
Clements, John Allen *physiologist*
Dallman, Mary F. *physiology educator*
Desjardin, Dennis E. *plant pathologist, educator*
Furst, Arthur *toxicologist, educator*
Ganong, William F(rancis) *physiologist, physician*
Handler, Evelyn *science administrator*
Herskowitz, Ira *educator, molecular geneticist*
Heyneman, Donald *parasitology and tropical medicine educator*
Lyon, David William *research executive*
Ralston, Henry James, III *neurobiologist, anatomist, educator*
Werb, Zena *cell biologist, educator*
Wyse, Roger Earl *physiologist, department chairman*
Yamamoto, Keith Robert *molecular biologist, educator*

San Jose
Taylor, Kendrick Jay *microbiologist*
Weller, Dieter M. *botanist, researcher*
Zaro, Brad A. *research company executive, biologist*

San Juan Capistrano
White, Beverly Jane *cytogeneticist*

San Mateo
Cooper-Smith, Jeffrey Paul *botanic garden administrator*

Santa Ana
Glazier, Ron *zoological park administrator*

Santa Barbara
Badash, Lawrence *science history educator*
Christman, Arthur Castner, Jr. *scientific advisor*
Schneider, Edward Lee *botanic garden administrator*
Tucker, Shirley Lois Cotter *botany educator, researcher*

Santa Cruz
Beevers, Harry *biologist, educator*
Dasmann, Raymond Fredric *ecologist*
Griggs, Gary Bruce *science administrator, oceanographer, geologist, educator*
Langenheim, Jean Harmon *biology educator*

Santa Monica
Augenstein, Bruno W. *research scientist, researcher*
Shubert, Gustave Harry *research executive, consultant, social scientist*

Santee
Morris, John David *research institute administrator, geology educator*

South San Francisco
Gerritsen, Mary Ellen *vascular and cell biologist*
Levinson, Arthur David *molecular biologist*

Stanford
Atkin, J. Myron *science educator*
Brown, Patrick O. *molecular biologist, educator*
Campbell, Allan McCulloch *bacteriology educator*
Cohen, Stanley Norman *geneticist, educator*
Cork, Linda Katherine *veterinary pathologist, educator*
Cox, David R. *geneticist, educator*
Davis, Mark M. *microbiologist, educator*
Davis, Ronald Wayne *genetics researcher, biochemistry educator*
Ehrlich, Anne Howland *research biologist*
Ehrlich, Paul Ralph *biology educator*
Elliott, David Duncan, III *science research company executive*
Falkow, Stanley *microbiologist, educator*
Francke, Uta *medical geneticist, genetics researcher, educator*
Hanawalt, Philip Courtland *biology educator, researcher*
Kendig, Joan Johnston *neurobiology educator*
Long, Sharon Rugel *molecular biologist, plant biology educator*
Mooney, Harold Alfred *plant ecologist*
Scheller, Richard H. *molecular and cellular physiology educator*
Scott, Matthew Peter *biology educator*
Shapiro, Lucille *molecular biology educator*
Shooter, Eric Manvers *neurobiology educator, consultant*
Simoni, Robert D. *biology educator*
Somerville, Chris *plant biologist, educator*
Spudich, James A. *biology educator*
Yanofsky, Charles *biology educator*
Zuckerkandl, Emile *molecular evolutionary biologist, scientific institute executive*

Stockton
Magness, Rhonda Ann *microbiologist*

McNeal, Dale William, Jr. *biological sciences educator*

The Sea Ranch
Hayflick, Leonard *microbiologist, cell biologist, gerontologist, educator, writer*

Thousand Oaks
Malmuth, Norman David *research scientist, program manager*

Tulare
Vickrey, Herta Miller *microbiologist*

Woodland Hills
Fox, Stuart Ira *physiologist*

COLORADO

Arvada
Dotson, Gerald Richard *retired biology educator*

Boulder
Armstrong, David Michael *biology educator*
Breed, Michael Dallam *environmental, population, organismic biology educator*
Clifford, Steven Francis *science research director*
De Fries, John Clarence *behavioral genetics educator, researcher*
Dubin, Mark William *educator, neuroscientist*
Hanley, Howard James Mason *research scientist*
Knoelker, Michael *science observatory director*
Mc Intosh, J(ohn) Richard *biologist, educator*
Meier, Mark Frederick *research scientist, glaciologist, educator*
Prescott, David Marshall *biology educator*
Roble, Raymond Gerald *science administrator*
Serafin, Robert Joseph *science center administrator, electrical engineer*
Staehelin, Lucas Andrew *cell biology educator*
Thomas, Gary Edward *science educator, researcher*
Wood, William Barry, III *biologist, educator*

Brush
Gabriel, Donald Eugene *science educator*

Carbondale
Cowgill, Ursula Moser *biologist, educator, environmental consultant*

Colorado Springs
Bybee, Rodger Wayne *science education administrator*
Cameron, Paul Drummond *research facility administrator*
Comes, Robert George *research scientist*
Engfer, Susan Marvel *zoological park executive*

Denver
Freiheit, Clayton Fredric *zoo director*
Hildebrand, Verna Lee *human ecology educator*
Holmes, Randall Kent *microbiology educator, physician, university administrator*
LaMendola, Walter Franklin *technology educator, business executive*
Pfenninger, Karl H. *cell biology and neuroscience educator*
Puck, Theodore Thomas *geneticist, biophysicist, educator*

Estes Park
Jones, A. Durand *park administrator*

Fort Collins
Benjamin, Stephen Alfred *veterinary medicine educator, environmental pathologist, researcher*
Burns, Denver P. *forestry research administrator*
Follett, Ronald Francis *soil scientist*
Grieve, Robert Burton *parasitologist, educator*
Halvorson, Ardell David *soil scientist, researcher*
Keim, Wayne Franklin *retired genetics educator, plant geneticist*
Mortvedt, John Jacob *soil scientist, researcher*
Niswender, Gordon Dean *physiologist, educator*
Peterson, Gary Andrew *agronomics researcher*
Quick, James S. *geneticist, plant breeder*
Roos, Eric Eugene *plant physiologist*
Seidel, George Elias, Jr. *animal scientist, educator*
Shands, Henry Lee *plant geneticist, administrator*
Smith, Ralph Earl *virologist*

Highlands Ranch
Brierley, James Alan *biohydrometallurgy consultant*

Littleton
Vail, Charles Daniel *veterinarian, consultant*

Longmont
Dierks, Richard Ernest *veterinarian, educational administrator*

HAWAII

Aiea
Munechika, Ken Kenji *research center administrator*

Honolulu
Abbott, Isabella Aiona *retired biology educator*
Carson, Hampton Lawrence *geneticist, educator*
Donlon, Timothy A. *cytogeneticist*
Fok, Agnes Kwan *cell biologist, educator*
Fujioka, Roger Sadao *microbiologist, researcher*
Kamemoto, Fred Isamu *zoologist, educator*
Kamemoto, Haruyuki *horticulture educator*
Kay, Elizabeth Alison *zoology educator*
Mandel, Morton *molecular biologist*
Redman, Ken *zoo officer*
Sagawa, Yoneo *horticulturist, educator*

[illegible]
Cox, Paul Alan *ethnobotanist, educator*

Kamuela
[illegible] D. *national historic site official*

Tripler Army Medical Center
Uyehara, Catherine Fay Takako (Yamauchi) *physiologist, educator, pharmacologist*

IDAHO

Moscow
Scott, James Michael *research biologist*

Sun Valley
Ring, Terry William *company executive, environmentalist*

Twin Falls
Burton, Lawrence DeVere *agriculturist, educator*

ILLINOIS

Champaign
Smarr, Larry Lee *science administrator, educator, astrophysicist*

MARYLAND

Bethesda
Rubin, Gerald Mayer *molecular biologist, biochemistry educator*

MISSOURI

Lees Summit
Hubbard, Harold Mead *independent consultant*

MONTANA

Arlee
MacFarland, Craig George *natural resource management professional*

Bozeman
Costerton, John William Fisher *microbiologist*
Hovin, Arne William *agronomist, educator*
Lavin, Matthew T. *horticultural educator*
Patten, Duncan Theunissen *ecologist educator*
Todd, Kenneth S., Jr. *parasitologist, educator*

Butte
Peoples, Donald R. *research scientist*

Hamilton
Garon, Claude Francis *laboratory administrator, researcher*

Helena
Johnson, John Philip *geneticist, researcher*

Missoula
Craighead, John Johnson *wildlife biologist*
Thomas, Jack Ward *wildlife biologist*

Polson
Stanford, Jack Arthur *biological station administrator*

NEVADA

Las Vegas
Hess, John Warren *scientific institute administrator, educator*

Reno
Bohmont, Dale Wendell *agricultural consultant*
Gifford, Gerald Frederic *retired science educator*
Smith, Aaron *retired research director, clinical psychologist*

NEW MEXICO

Albuquerque
Goldstein, Barry Bruce *biologist, food company executive, lawyer*
Henderson, Rogene Faulkner *toxicologist, researcher*
Hsi, David Ching Heng *plant pathologist and geneticist, educator*

Alto
Thrasher, Jack Dwayne *toxicologist, researcher, consultant*

Las Cruces
McElyea, Ulysses, Jr. *veterinarian*

Los Alamos
Browne, John Charles *national research laboratory executive, physics researcher*
Gregg, Charles Thornton *research company executive*
Wallace, Terry Charles, Sr. *retired technical administrator, researcher*

Santa Fe
Moore, Jay Winston *director cytogenetics laboratory*

OREGON

Beaverton
Machida, Curtis A. *research molecular neurobiologist, educator*

Corvallis
Castellano, Michael Angelo *research forester*
Castle, Emery Neal *agricultural and resource economist, educator*
Chambers, Kenton Lee *botany educator*
Dougherty, William G. *microbiologist, educator*
Frakes, Rodney Vance *plant geneticist, educator*
Johnson, Kenneth Bjorn *botany and plant pathology educator*
Loper, Joyce E. *plant pathologist, educator*
Lubchenco, Jane *marine biologist, educator*
Moore, Thomas Carrol *botanist, retired educator*
Morita, Richard Yukio *microbiology and oceanography educator*
Pinkerton, John N. *plant pathologist*
Stone, Jeffrey Kyle *mycologist, educator*
Westwood, Melvin Neil *horticulturist, pomologist*

Eugene
Matthews, Brian W. *molecular biology educator*
Stahl, Franklin William *biology educator*
Wessells, Norman Keith *biologist, educator, university administrator*

Mcminnville
Roberts, Michael Foster *biology educator*

Newport
Weber, Lavern John *marine science administrator, educator*

Pendleton
Klepper, Elizabeth Lee *physiologist*

Portland
Barmack, Neal Herbert *neuroscientist*
Bhagwan, Sudhir *computer industry and research executive, consultant*
Gillette, Richard Gareth *neurophysiology educator, researcher*
Hagenstein, William David *forester, consultant*
Spencer, Peter Simner *neurotoxicologist*
Stafford, Helen Adele *retired biology educator*
Vecchio, Tony *zoological park administrator*

Talent
MacMillen, Richard Edward *biological sciences educator, researcher*

TEXAS

San Antonio
McComas, David John *science administrator, space physicist*

UTAH

Logan
Dobrowolski, James Phillip *agriculturist, educator*
Malechek, John Charles *ecology and range science educator*
Rasmussen, Harry Paul *horticulture and landscape educator*

Provo
McArthur, Eldon Durant *geneticist, researcher*
Smith, H(oward) Duane *zoology educator*

Salt Lake City
Capecchi, Mario Renato *geneticist, educator*
Dinsmore, Craig *zoo director*
Emerson, Sharon B. *biology researcher and educator*
Johnson, Stephen Charles *exercise physiology and sport science educator*
Opitz, John Marius *clinical geneticist, pediatrician*
Roth, John Roger *geneticist, biology educator*
Warner, Homer R. *physiologist, educator*

WASHINGTON

Bellingham
Ross, June Rosa Pitt *biologist, educator*

Eatonville
Geddes, Gary Lee *wildlife park director*

Friday Harbor
Brookbank, John W(arren) *retired microbiology educator*

Pullman
Carlson, James Roy *animal science educator*
Carrington, James C. *botanist, educator*
Henson, James Bond *veterinary pathologist*
Hosick, Howard Lawrence *cell biology educator, academic administrator*
Thomashow, Linda Suzanne *microbiologist*

Richland
Chikalla, Thomas David *retired science facility administrator*

Seattle
Bassingthwaighte, James Bucklin *physiologist, educator, medical researcher*
Boersma, P. Dee *zoology educator*
Brownstein, Barbara Lavin *geneticist, educator, university official*
Buffington, John Douglas *ecologist*
Byers, Peter H. *geneticist*
Daniel, Thomas L. *zoology educator*
Disteche, Christine M. *geneticist*
Evans, Charles Albert *microbiology educator*
Gottschling, Daniel E. *molecular research biologist*
Hartwell, Leland Harrison *geneticist, educator*
Hendrickson, Anita Elizabeth *biology educator*
Hille, Bertil *physiology educator*
Hood, Leroy Edward *molecular biologist, educator*
Karr, James Richard *ecologist, educator, research director*
King, Mary-Claire *geneticist, educator*
Kohn, Alan J. *zoology educator*
Kruckeberg, Arthur Rice *botanist, educator*
Kuhl, Patricia K. *science educator, educator*
Miller, Robert Carmi, Jr. *microbiology educator, university administrator*
Motulsky, Arno Gunther *geneticist, physician, educator*
Nester, Eugene William *microbiology educator*
Olstad, Roger Gale *science educator*
Orians, Gordon Howell *biology educator*
Riddiford, Lynn Moorhead *zoologist, educator*
Smith, Orville Auverne *physiology educator*
Stuart, Kenneth D. *plant research administrator, microbiologist*
Towne, David L. *zoological park administrator*
Tukey, Harold Bradford, Jr. *horticulture educator*
Woods, James Sterrett *toxicologist*
Wooster, Warren S(criver) *marine science educator*
Wott, John Arthur *arboretum and botanical garden executive, horticulture educator*

Wenatchee
Elfving, Don C. *horticulturist*
Schrader, Lawrence Edwin *plant physiologist, educator*

WYOMING

Cheyenne
Schuman, Gerald Eugene *soil scientist, researcher*

Laramie
Lewis, Randolph Vance *molecular biologist, researcher*

Moose
Craighead, Frank Cooper, Jr. *ecologist*

CANADA

ALBERTA

Calgary
Johnson, Edward Arnold *ecologist, educator*
Jones, Geoffrey Melvill *physiology research educator*
Stell, William Kenyon *neuroscientist, educator*

Edmonton
Christian, Ralph Gordon *agricultural research administrator*
Cossins, Edwin Albert *biology educator, academic administrator*
Hiruki, Chuji *plant virologist, science educator*
Kalra, Yash Pal *soil chemist*
Schindler, David William *research scientist, educator*

Lethbridge
Cho, Hyun Ju *veterinary research scientist*
Johnson, Daniel Lloyd *entomologist, biogeographer, educator*
Lysyk, Timothy James *livestock insect population ecologist, researcher*

BRITISH COLUMBIA

Bamfield
Druehl, Louis Dix *biology educator*

Burnaby
Borden, John Harvey *entomologist, educator*
Brandhorst, Bruce Peter *biology educator*
Roitberg, Bernard David *biology educator*

Kelowna
Beaton, James Duncan *soil scientist*

Penticton
Landecker, Tom L. *research center director*

Sidney
Bigelow, Margaret Elizabeth Barr (M.E. Barr) *mycology educator*
Kendrick, William Bryce *biology educator, writer, publisher*

Summerland
Looney, Norman Earl *pomologist, plant physiologist*

Vancouver
Blair, Robert *animal science administrator, educator, researcher*
Grand, Tamara C. *zoology researcher*
Hochachka, Peter William *biology educator*
Jones, David Robert *zoology educator*
Lavkulich, Leslie Michael *soil science educator*
Lindsey, Casimir Charles *zoologist, educator*
Newman, Murray Arthur *aquarium administrator*
Phillips, Anthony George *neurobiology educator*
Phillips, John Edward *zoologist, educator*
Pitcher, Tony John *fishery science educator, writer*
Rennie, Paul Steven *research scientist*
Shaw, Michael *biologist, educator*
Suzuki, David Takayoshi *geneticist, science broadcaster*
Wellington, William George *entomologist, ecologist, educator*

Victoria
Turpin, David Howard *biologist, educator*

West Vancouver
Donaldson, Edward Mossop *research scientist, aquaculture consultant*

SASKATCHEWAN

Regina
Devine, D. Grant *agriculturalist*
Sonntag, Bernard H. *agrologist, public service executive*

Saskatoon
Babiuk, Lorne Alan *virologist, immunologist, research administrator*
Furtan, William Hartley *director scientific organization*
Harvey, Bryan Laurence *crop science educator*
Huang, Pan Ming *soil science educator*
Kaminskyj, Susan Gail Willets *fungal research biologist*
Kartha, Kutty Krishnan *plant pathologist*
Patience, John Francis *research scientist*
St. Arnaud, Roland *soil scientist*

HONG KONG

Kowloon
Randall, David John *physiologist, zoologist, educator*

ITALY

Milan
Dulbecco, Renato *biologist, educator*

ADDRESS UNPUBLISHED

Bautista, Anthony Hernandez *biomedical company executive*
Bishop, William Peter *research scientist*
Block, Barbara Ann *biology educator*
Brattstrom, Bayard Holmes *biology educator*
Bucalo, Louis Randall *biotechnology executive*
Bullock, Theodore Holmes *biologist, educator*
Carter, David LaVere *soil scientist, researcher, consultant*
Coyle, Marie Bridget *retired microbiology educator, laboratory director*
De Antoni, Edward Paul *cancer control research scientist*
Farkas, Daniel Frederick *food science and technology educator*
Gennaro, Antonio L. *biology educator*
Goldstein, Walter Elliott *biotechnology executive*
Herz, Michael Joseph *marine environmental scientist*
Iacono, James Michael *research center administrator, nutrition educator*
Kolb, James A. *science association director, writer*
Koller, Loren D. *veterinary medicine educator*
March, Beryl Elizabeth *animal scientist, educator*
Palade, George Emil *biologist, educator*
Peter, Richard Ector *zoology educator*
Roeller, Herbert Alfred *biology and medical scientist, educator*
Rogers, Jack David *plant pathologist, educator*
Simon, Melvin I. *molecular biologist, educator*
Southwick, Charles Henry *zoologist, educator*
Stark, Nellie May *forest ecology educator*
Stickney, Robert Roy *fisheries educator*
Talmage, David Wilson *microbiology and medical educator, physician, former university administrator*
Witte, Owen Neil *microbiologist, molecular biologist, educator*

SCIENCE: MATHEMATICS AND COMPUTER SCIENCE *.See also* INFORMATION TECHNOLOGY.

UNITED STATES

ARIZONA

Fort Huachuca
Clark, Brian Thomas *mathematical statistician, operations research analyst*

Phoenix
Doto, Irene Louise *statistician*

Sierra Vista
Sizemore, Nicky Lee *computer scientist*

Tempe
Smith, Harvey Alvin *mathematics educator, consultant*
Yau, Stephen Sik-sang *computer science and engineering educator, computer scientist, researcher*

Tucson
Willoughby, Stephen Schuyler *mathematics educator*

CALIFORNIA

Berkeley
Arveson, William Barnes *mathematics educator*
Bailey, David H. *computer scientist*
Bergman, George Mark *mathematician, educator*
Bickel, Peter John *statistician, educator*
Borcherds, Richard Ewen *mathematics educator*
Chern, Shiing-Shen *mathematics educator*
Chorin, Alexandre Joel *mathematician, educator*
Cooper, William Secord *information science educator*
Demmel, James W. *computer science educator*
Freedman, David Amiel *statistics educator, consultant*
Jones, Frederick Randal *mathematician, educator*
Kaplansky, Irving *mathematician, educator, research institute director*
Karp, Richard Manning *computer sciences educator*
Lehmann, Erich Leo *statistics educator*
McKusick, Marshall Kirk *computer scientist*
Osserman, Robert *mathematician, educator, writer*
Patterson, David Andrew *computer scientist, educator, consultant*
Ratner, Marina *mathematician, educator, researcher*
Smith, Alan Jay *computer science educator, consultant*
Séquin, Carlo H. *computer science educator*
Tarter, Michael Ernest *biostatistician, educator*
Thomas, Paul Emery *mathematics educator*
Vojta, Paul Alan *mathematics educator*

Wolf, Joseph Albert *mathematician, educator*
Xie, Ganquan *mathematician, computational geophysical scientist, educator*

Camarillo
Vannix, C(ecil) Robert *programmer, systems analyst*

Carson
Kowalski, Kazimierz *computer science educator, researcher*

Chatsworth
Ulin, Samuel Alexander *computer systems developer*

Claremont
Coleman, Courtney Stafford *mathematician, educator*
Henriksen, Melvin *mathematician, educator*

Davis
Olsson, Ronald Arthur *computer science educator*
Thurston, William Paul *mathematician*

El Segundo
Woike, Lynne Ann *computer scientist*

Elk Grove
McDavid, Douglas Warren *systems consultant*

Encinitas
Burgin, George Hans *computer scientist, educator*

Glendale
Kay, Alan *computer scientist*

Hayward
Sabharwal, Ranjit Singh *mathematician*

Irvine
Hoffman, Donald David *cognitive and computer science educator*
Juberg, Richard Kent *mathematician, educator*
Saari, Donald Gene *mathematician, economist*

La Jolla
Goguen, Joseph Amadee *computer science educator*
Graham, Ronald Lewis *mathematician*
Halkin, Hubert *mathematics educator, research mathematician*
Rosen, Judah Ben *computer scientist*
Rosenblatt, Murray *mathematics educator*
Terras, Audrey Anne *mathematics educator*
Wulbert, Daniel Eliot *mathematician, educator*

Los Angeles
Afifi, Abdelmonem A. *biostatistics educator, academic dean*
Arbib, Michael Anthony *neuroscientist, educator, computer scientist*
Bekey, George Albert *computer scientist, educator, engineer*
Boehm, Barry William *computer science educator*
Chacko, George Kuttickal *systems science educator, consultant*
Delaney, Matthew Sylvester *mathematics educator, academic administrator*
Estrin, Gerald *computer scientist, engineering educator, academic administrator*
Golomb, Solomon Wolf *mathematician, electrical engineer, educator, university official*
Gordon, Basil *mathematics educator*
Greenberger, Martin *technologist, information scientist, educator*
Harris, Theodore Edward *mathematician, educator*
Jacobsen, Laren *programmer, analyst*
Kalaba, Robert Edwin *applied mathematician*
Kleinrock, Leonard *computer scientist*
Pearl, Judea *computer scientist, educator*
Petak, William John *systems management educator*
Port, Sidney Charles *mathematician, educator*
Roberts, Paul Harry *mathematics educator*
Waterman, Michael Spencer *mathematics educator, biology educator*
Young, Lai-Sang *mathematician, educator*

Menlo Park
Chui, Charles K. *mathematics educator*
Neumann, Peter Gabriel *computer scientist*

Milpitas
Wheeler, William Roy *technical advisor*

Moss Landing
Lange, Lester Henry *mathematics educator*

Mountain View
Kolarov, Krasimir Dobromirov *computer scientist, researcher*
Shah, Girish Popatlal *information technology consultant*
Vrolyk, John R. *computer systems company executive*

Oakland
Zelmanowitz, Julius Martin *mathematics educator, university administrator*

Palo Alto
Beretta, Giordano Bruno *computer scientist, researcher*
Borg, Anita *computer scientist*
Green, Cordell *computer scientist, educator*
Lamport, Leslie B. *computer scientist*
Martin, Roger John *computer scientist*
Sutherland, Ivan E. *computer scientist*

Pasadena
Franklin, Joel Nicholas *mathematician, educator*
Keller, Herbert Bishop *mathematics educator*
Marsden, Jerrold Eldon *mathematician, educator, engineer*
Mead, Carver Andress *computer science educator*
Saffman, Philip G. *mathematician, educator*
Todd, John *mathematician, educator*
Whitham, Gerald Beresford *mathematics educator*

Pomona
Bernau, Simon John *mathematics educator*

Portola Valley
Kuo, Franklin F. *computer scientist, electrical engineer*

Riverside
Ratliff, Louis Jackson, Jr. *mathematics educator*

San Diego
Hales, Alfred Washington *mathematics educator, consultant*
Legrand, Shawn Pierre *computer systems programmer*
Willerding, Margaret Frances *mathematician, educator*

San Francisco
Cruse, Allan Baird *mathematician, computer scientist, educator*
Gray, James N. *computer scientist*
Leung, Kason Kai Ching *computer specialist*

San Gabriel
Kettemborough, Clifford Russell *computer scientist, consultant, manager*

Santa Barbara
Johnsen, Eugene Carlyle *mathematician and educator*
Minc, Henryk *mathematics educator*
Newman, Morris *mathematician, educator*
Simons, Stephen *mathematics educator, researcher*

Santa Clara
Halmos, Paul Richard *mathematician, educator*

Santa Cruz
Huskey, Harry Douglas *information and computer science educator*

Santa Monica
Ware, Willis Howard *computer scientist*

Stanford
Anderson, Theodore Wilbur *statistics educator*
Brown, Byron William, Jr. *biostatistician, educator*
Cohen, Paul Joseph *mathematician*
Cover, Thomas M. *statistician, electrical engineer, educator*
Dantzig, George Bernard *applied mathematics educator*
Efron, Bradley *mathematics educator*
Feigenbaum, Edward Albert *computer science educator*
Hanrahan, Patrick M. *computer scientist*
Karlin, Samuel *mathematics educator, researcher*
Keller, Joseph Bishop *mathematician, educator*
Knuth, Donald Ervin *computer sciences educator*
McCarthy, John *computer scientist, educator*
Moses, Lincoln E. *statistician, educator*
Olshen, Richard A. *statistician, educator*
Ornstein, Donald Samuel *mathematician, educator*
Rubin, Karl Cooper *mathematics educator*
Schoen, Richard Melvin *mathematics educator, researcher*
Ullman, Jeffrey David *computer science educator*

Stockton
Landre, Debra Ann *mathematics educator*

Westlake Village
Munson, John Backus *computer systems consultant, retired computer engineering company executive*

Woodland Hills
Stratton, Gregory Alexander *computer specialist, administrator, mayor*

COLORADO

Boulder
Beylkin, Gregory *mathematician*
Crow, Edwin Louis *mathematical statistician, consultant*
Glover, Fred William *artificial intelligence and optimization research director, educator*
Monarchi, David Edward *management scientist, information scientist, educator*
Mycielski, Jan *mathematician, educator*

Colorado Springs
Simmons, George Finlay *mathematics educator*

Denver
Cutter, Gary Raymond *biostatistician*
Kushner, Todd Roger *computer scientist, software engineer*

Fort Collins
Anderson, Charles William *computer science educator*
Mielke, Paul William, Jr. *statistician, consultant*

HAWAII

Hilo
Gersting, Judith Lee *computer science educator, researcher*

Honolulu
Swanson, Richard William *retired statistician*

IDAHO

Moscow
Bobisud, Larry Eugene *mathematics educator*
Goetschel, Roy Hartzell, Jr. *mathematician, researcher*

NEVADA

Las Vegas
Blattner, Meera McCuaig *computer science educator*

Yerington
Price, Thomas Munro *computer consultant*

NEW MEXICO

Albuquerque
Bell, Stoughton *computer scientist, mathematician, educator*
Sobolewski, John Stephen *computer scientist, consultant*

Belen
Gutjahr, Allan Leo *mathematics educator, researcher*

Jemez Springs
Sigler, Marjorie Diane *computer programming executive, analyst*

Las Cruces
Harary, Frank *mathematician, computer scientist, educator*

OREGON

Corvallis
Parks, Harold Raymond *mathematician, educator*

Eugene
Andrews, Fred Charles *mathematics educator*

Portland
Ahuja, Jagdish Chand *mathematics educator*
Hall, Howard Pickering *engineering and mathematics educator*
Maier, David Eugene *computer science educator*

UTAH

Orem
Moore, Hal G. *mathematician, educator*

Salt Lake City
Horn, Susan Dadakis *statistics educator*

WASHINGTON

Ellensburg
Comstock, Dale Robert *mathematics educator*

Pullman
Hildebrandt, Darlene Myers *retired information scientist*
Kallaher, Michael Joseph *mathematics educator*

Redmond
Blinn, James F. *computer scientist*
Freedman, Michael Hartley *mathematician, educator*
Kimmich, Jon Bradford *computer science program executive*

Richland
Cochran, James Alan *mathematics educator*

Seattle
Breslow, Norman Edward *biostatistics educator, researcher*
Criminale, William Oliver, Jr. *applied mathematics educator*
Klee, Victor La Rue *mathematician, educator*
Lee, John Marshall *mathematics educator*
Michael, Ernest Arthur *mathematics educator*
Nijenhuis, Albert *mathematician, educator*
O'Malley, Robert Edmund, Jr. *mathematics educator*
Pyke, Ronald *mathematics educator*
Segal, Jack *mathematics educator*

Yakima
Jongeward, George Ronald *retired systems analyst*

CANADA

ALBERTA

Edmonton
Davis, Wayne Alton *computer science educator*

BRITISH COLUMBIA

Burnaby
Borwein, Peter Benjamin *mathematician*

Vancouver
Boyd, David William *mathematician, educator*
Clark, Colin Whitcomb *mathematics educator*
Feldman, Joel Shalom *mathematician*
Granirer, Edmond Ernest *mathematician, educator*
Miura, Robert Mitsuru *mathematician, researcher, educator*
Seymour, Brian Richard *mathematics educator, researcher*
Sion, Maurice *mathematics educator*
Swanson, Charles Andrew *mathematics educator*

Victoria
Manning, Eric *computer science and engineering educator, university dean, researcher*

SASKATCHEWAN

Regina
Symes, Lawrence Richard *computer science educator, university dean*

ADDRESS UNPUBLISHED

Basch, Reva *information services company executive*
Borwein, Jonathan Michael *mathematics educator*
Chacon, Michael Ernest *directory services and eBusiness specialist*
Geschke, Charles M. *computer scientist, computer company executive*
Greever, Margaret Quarles *retired mathematics educator*
Holland, Michael James *computer services administrator*
Hoppensteadt, Frank Charles *educator, mathematician, university administrator*
Lerner, Vladimir Semion *computer scientist, educator*
Mints, Grigori Efroim *mathematics specialist*
Natsuyama, Harriet Hatsune *mathematician, educator*
Norman, E. Gladys *business computer educator, consultant*
Suppes, Patrick *statistics, education, philosophy and psychology educator*
Winder, Robert Owen *mathematician, computer engineer, geophysicist*

SCIENCE: PHYSICAL SCIENCE

UNITED STATES

ALASKA

Anchorage
Ennis, William Lee *physics educator*

Fairbanks
Duffy, Lawrence Kevin *biochemist, educator*
Eichelberger, John Charles *volcanologist, educator*
Fathauer, Theodore Frederick *meteorologist*
Fischer, Robert Edward *meteorologist*
Lingle, Craig Stanley *glaciologist, educator*
Roederer, Juan Gualterio *physics educator*
Weller, Gunter Ernst *geophysics educator*

ARIZONA

Amado
Criswell, Stephen *astronomer*

Flagstaff
Colbert, Edwin Harris *paleontologist, museum curator*
Millis, Robert Lowell *astronomer*
Shoemaker, Carolyn Spellmann *planetary astronomer*

Green Valley
Bates, Charles Carpenter *oceanographer*

Oracle
Garmany, Catharine Doremus *astronomer*

Phoenix
Grinell, Sheila *science center administrator*

Rio Rico
Lowell, J(ames) David *geological consultant, cattle rancher*

Scottsdale
Hockmuth, Joseph Frank *physicist, psychotherapist*

Tempe
Bauer, Ernst Georg *physicist, educator*
Blankenship, Robert Eugene *biochemistry educator*
Buseck, Peter R. *geochemistry educator*
Cowley, John Maxwell *physics educator*
Glick, Milton Don *chemist, university administrator*
Goronkin, Herbert *physicist*
Herald, Cherry Lou *research educator, research director*
Juvet, Richard Spalding, Jr. *chemistry educator*
Mahajan, Subhash *electronic materials educator*
McMillan, Paul Francis *chemistry educator*
Moore, Carleton Bryant *geochemistry educator*
Nigam, Bishan Perkash *physics educator*
Pettit, George Robert *chemistry educator, cancer researcher*
Picraux, Samuel Thomas *applied science and physics researcher*
Quadt, Raymond Adolph *metallurgist, cement company executive*
Smith, David John *physicist, educator*
Vandenberg, Edwin James *chemist, educator*

Tucson
Angel, James Roger Prior *astronomer*
Barrett, Bruce Richard *physics educator*
Bloembergen, Nicolaas *physicist, educator*
Broadfoot, Albert Lyle *physicist*
Crawford, David L. *astronomer*
Davies, Roger *geoscience educator*
Davis, Stanley Nelson *hydrologist, educator*
De Young, David Spencer *astrophysicist, educator*
Dessler, Alexander Jack *astrophysicist, educator*
Dodd, Charles Gardner *physical chemist*
Drake, Michael J. *meteoriticist, planetary scientist, educator*
Fang, Li-Zhi *physicist, educator*
Foltz, Craig B. *astronomer, educator*
Girardeau, Marvin Denham *physics educator*
Green, Richard Frederick *astronomer*
Hall, Henry Kingston, Jr. *chemistry educator*
Hartmann, William Kenneth *astronomy scientist*
Haynes, Caleb Vance, Jr. *geology and archaeology educator*
Hill, Henry Allen *physicist, educator*
Hoffmann, William Frederick *astronomer*
Howard, Robert Franklin *observatory administrator, astronomer*

Hubbard, William Bogel *planetary sciences educator*
Hunten, Donald Mount *planetary scientist, educator*
Jackson, Kenneth Arthur *physicist, researcher*
Karkoschka, Erich *planetary science researcher, writer*
Kessler, John Otto *physicist, educator*
Krider, E. Philip *atmospheric scientist, educator*
Lamb, Willis Eugene, Jr. *physicist, educator*
Law, John Harold *biochemistry educator*
Lunine, Jonathan Irving *planetary scientist, educator*
Macleod, Hugh Angus McIntosh *optical science educator, physicist, consultant*
Malhotra, Renu *scientist*
Marcialis, Robert Louis *planetary astronomer*
McEwen, Alfred Sherman *planetary geologist*
Parmenter, Robert Haley *physics educator*
Powell, Richard C. *physicist, educator, researcher*
Roemer, Elizabeth *astronomer, educator*
Schaefer, John Paul *chemist, corporate executive*
Scotti, James Vernon *astronomer*
Sprague, Ann Louise *space scientist*
Strittmatter, Peter Albert *astronomer, educator*
Swalin, Richard Arthur *scientist, company executive*
Tifft, William Grant *astronomer, educator*
Titley, Spencer Rowe *geology educator*
Willis, Clifford Leon *geologist*
Wolff, Sidney Carne *astronomer, observatory administrator*

CALIFORNIA

Atascadero
Zima, Gordon Everett *metallurgist*

Atherton
Coleman, Robert Griffin *geology educator*
Fried, John H. *chemist*
Gill, Stephen Paschall *retired physicist, mathematician*

Azusa
Kostoulas, Ioannis Georgiou *physicist*

Bakersfield
Dorer, Fred Harold *retired chemistry educator*

Bellflower
Martin, Melissa Carol *radiological physicist*

Berkeley
Alper, Mark D. *biochemist*
Attwood, David Thomas *physicist, educator*
Barnett, R(alph) Michael *theoretical physicist, educational agency administrator*
Bartlett, Neil *chemist, emeritus educator*
Benson, Sally M. *atmospheric scientist*
Bergman, Robert George *chemist, educator*
Berry, William Benjamin Newell *geologist, educator, former museum administrator*
Bertozzi, Carolyn R. *chemistry educator*
Blitz, Leo *astronomer, educator*
Bragg, Robert Henry *physicist, educator*
Carmichael, Ian Stuart Edward *geologist, educator*
Cerny, Joseph, III *chemistry educator, scientific laboratory administrator, university dean and official*
Chamberlain, Owen *nuclear physicist*
Chamberlin, Michael John *biochemistry educator*
Chew, Geoffrey Foucar *physicist*
Clarke, John *physics educator*
Cohen, Marvin Lou *physics educator*
Diamond, Richard Martin *nuclear chemist*
Ellman, Jonathon Anthony *chemist*
Fleming, Graham Richard *chemistry educator*
Fowler, Thomas Kenneth *physicist*
Fréchet, Jean Marie Joseph *chemistry educator*
Gaillard, Mary Katharine *physics educator*
Glaser, Donald Arthur *physicist*
Goldhaber, Gerson *physicist, educator*
Hahn, Erwin Louis *physicist, educator*
Haller, Eugene Ernest *materials scientist, educator*
Heathcock, Clayton Howell *chemistry educator, researcher*
Heiles, Carl Eugene *astronomer, educator*
Helmholz, August Carl *physicist, educator emeritus*
Hoffman, Darleane Christian *chemistry educator*
Jeanloz, Raymond *geophysicist, educator*
Johnston, Harold S(ledge) *chemistry educator*
Kahn, Steven Michael *astrophysicist, educator*
Kerth, Leroy T. *physics educator*
Kikuchi, Ryoichi *physics educator*
King, Ivan Robert *astronomy educator*
Kittel, Charles *physicist, educator emeritus*
Klinman, Judith Pollock *biochemist, educator*
Koshland, Daniel Edward, Jr. *biochemist, educator*
Leemans, Wim Pieter *physicist*
Leopold, Luna Bergere *geology educator*
Lester, William Alexander, Jr. *chemist, educator*
Lin, Robert Peichung *physicist, educator, researcher*
Linn, Stuart Michael *biochemist, educator*
Lipps, Jere Henry *paleontology educator*
Louie, Steven Gwon Sheng *physics educator, researcher*
Mandelstam, Stanley *physicist*
Marg, Elwin *physiological optics, optometry educator*
McKee, Christopher Fulton *astrophysics and astronomy educator*
Miller, William Hughes *theoretical chemist, educator*
Nygren, David Robert *physicist, researcher*
Pavlath, Attila Endre *research chemist*
Perez-Mendez, Victor *physics educator*
Perry, Dale Lynn *chemist*
Pines, Alexander *chemistry educator, researcher, consultant*
Rasmussen, John Oscar *nuclear scientist, researcher*
Raymond, Kenneth Norman *chemistry educator, research chemist*
Ritchie, Robert Oliver *materials science educator*
Rosenblatt, Gerd Matthew *chemist*
Saykally, Richard James *chemistry educator*
Sessler, Andrew Marienhoff *physicist*
Shen, Yuen-Ron *physics educator*
Shu, Frank Hsia-San *astronomy educator, researcher, writer*
Shugart, Howard Alan *physicist, educator*
Smith, Kirk Robert *environmental health sciences educator, researcher*
Smith, Neville Vincent *physicist*
Smoot, George Fitzgerald, III *astrophysicist*
Somorjai, Gabor Arpad *chemist, educator*
Spinrad, Hyron *astronomer*
Stacy, Angelica M. *chemistry educator*
Steiner, Herbert Max *physics educator*
Strauss, Herbert Leopold *chemistry educator*
Streitwieser, Andrew, Jr. *chemistry educator*
Thomas, Gareth *metallurgy educator*
Thompson, Anthony Wayne *metallurgist, educator, consultant*
Tjian, Robert Tse Nan *biochemistry educator, biology researcher, virology researcher*
Townes, Charles Hard *physics educator*
Trilling, George Henry *physicist, educator*
Valentine, James William *paleobiology educator, writer*
Wurtele, Morton Gaither *meteorologist, educator*

Canyon Lake
Schilling, Frederick Augustus, Jr. *geologist, consultant*

Carlsbad
Smith, Warren James *optical scientist, consultant, lecturer*

China Lake
Bennett, Jean Louise McPherson *physicist, research scientist*

Chino
Koestel, Mark Alfred *geologist, photographer*

Chula Vista
Wolk, Martin *physicist, electronics engineer*

Claremont
Helliwell, Thomas McCaffree *physicist, educator*
Kubota, Mitsuru *chemistry educator*
Pinnell, Robert Peyton *chemistry educator*

Concord
Hearst, John Eugene *chemistry educator, researcher, consultant*

Corona Del Mar
Britten, Roy John *biophysicist*

Dana Point
Parker, John Marchbank *consulting geologist*

Davis
Black, Arthur Leo *biochemistry educator*
Cahill, Thomas Andrew *physicist, educator*
Conn, Eric Edward *plant biochemist*
Day, Howard Wilman *geology educator*
Feeney, Robert Earl *research biochemist*
Hedrick, Jerry Leo *biochemistry and biophysics educator*
Jungerman, John Albert *physics educator*
Mukherjee, Amiya K *metallurgy and materials science educator*
Nash, Charles Presley *chemistry educator*
Stumpf, Paul Karl *biochemistry educator emeritus*
Troy, Frederic Arthur, II *medical biochemistry educator*
Volman, David Herschel *chemistry educator*
Wooten, Frederick (Oliver) *applied science educator*

El Granada
Heere, Karen R. *astrophysicist*

Emeryville
Masri, Merle Sid *biochemist, consultant*

Encinitas
Mullis, Kary Banks *biochemist*

Encino
Hawthorne, Marion Frederick *chemistry educator*
Lauer, George *environmental consultant*
Phelps, Michael Edward *biophysics educator*

Fresno
Gump, Barry Hemphill *chemistry and food science educator*
Kauffman, George Bernard *chemistry educator*

Fullerton
Shapiro, Mark Howard *physicist, educator, academic dean, consultant*

Grass Valley
Bennison, Allan Parnell *geological consultant*

Hayward
Hirschfeld, Sue Ellen *geological sciences educator*

Hollister
Smith, George Larry *analytical and environmental chemist*

Irvine
Bander, Myron *physics educator, university dean*
Benford, Gregory Albert *physicist, writer*
Bradshaw, Ralph Alden *biochemistry educator*
Cho, Zang Hee *physics educator*
Clark, Bruce Robert *geology consultant*
Knight, Patricia Marie *optics researcher*
Maradudin, Alexei A. *physics educator*
McLaughlin, Calvin Sturgis *biochemistry educator*
Nalcioglu, Orhan *physics educator, radiological sciences educator*
Nomura, Masayasu *biological chemistry educator*
Nowick, James S. *chemistry educator*
Overman, Larry Eugene *chemistry educator*
Phalen, Robert Franklynn *environmental scientist*
Rowland, Frank Sherwood *chemistry educator*
Rynn, Nathan *physics educator, consultant*
White, Stephen Halley *biophysicist, educator*
Zhu, Peter Chaoquan *chemist*

La Canada Flintridge
Baines, Kevin Hays *planetary scientist, astronomer*

La Jolla
Abarbanel, Henry Don Isaac *physicist, academic administrator*
Andre, Michael Paul *physicist, educator*
Arnold, James Richard *chemist, educator*
Asmus, John Fredrich *physicist*
Backus, George Edward *theoretical geophysicist*
Benson, Andrew Alm *biochemistry educator*
Berger, Wolfgang H. *oceanographer, marine geologist*
Boger, Dale L. *chemistry educator*
Buckingham, Michael John *oceanography educator*
Burbidge, E. Margaret *astronomer, educator*
Burbidge, Geoffrey *astrophysicist, educator*
Continetti, Robert E. *chemistry educator*
Cox, Charles Shipley *oceanography researcher, educator*
Cunningham, Bruce Arthur *biochemist, educator*
Doolittle, Russell Francis *biochemist, educator*
Driscoll, Charles Frederick *physics educator*
Edelman, Gerald Maurice *biochemist, neuroscientist, educator*
Engvall, Eva *biochemist*
Feher, George *physics and biophysics scientist, educator*
Fisher, Frederick Hendrick *oceanographer emeritus*
Geiduschek, E(rnest) Peter *biophysics and molecular biology educator*
Gilbert, James Freeman *geophysics educator*
Goodman, Murray *chemistry educator*
Itano, Harvey Akio *biochemistry educator*
Janda, Kim D. *chemist, educator*
Joyce, Gerald Francis *biochemist, educator*
Kadonaga, James Takuro *biochemist*
Kearns, David Richard *chemistry educator*
Keeling, Charles David *oceanography educator*
Kolodner, Richard David *biochemist, educator*
Lal, Devendra *nuclear geophysics educator*
Lauer, James Lothar *physicist, educator*
Lerner, Richard Alan *chemistry educator, scientist*
Maple, M. Brian *physics educator*
McCammon, James Andrew *chemistry educator*
McIlwain, Carl Edwin *physicist*
Miller, Stanley Lloyd *chemistry and biochemistry educator*
Munk, Walter Heinrich *geophysics educator*
Nicolaou, K. C. *chemistry educator*
O'Neil, Thomas Michael *physicist, educator*
Orcutt, John Arthur *geophysicist, researcher*
Patton, Stuart *biochemist, educator*
Peterson, Laurence E. *physics educator*
Rebek, Julius, Jr. *chemistry educator, consultant*
Ride, Sally Kristen *physics educator, scientist, former astronaut*
Rosenbluth, Marshall Nicholas *physicist, educator*
Rotenberg, Manuel *physics educator*
Schimmel, Paul Reinhard *biochemist, biophysicist, educator*
Sclater, John George *geophysics educator*
Seegmiller, Jarvis Edwin *biochemist, educator*
Sham, Lu Jeu *physics educator*
Sharpless, K. Barry *chemist, educator*
Shuler, Kurt Egon *chemist, educator*
Siegel, Jay Steven *chemistry educator*
Somerville, Richard Chapin James *atmospheric scientist, educator*
Spiess, Fred Noel *oceanographer, educator*
Thiemens, Mark H. *chemistry educator*
Tietz, Norbert Wolfgang *clinical chemistry educator, administrator*
Tsien, Roger Yonchien *chemist, cell biologist*
Van Lint, Victor Anton Jacobus *physicist*
Verma, Inder M. *biochemist*
Watson, Kenneth Marshall *physics educator*
Wolynes, Peter Guy *chemistry researcher, educator*
Wong, Chi-Huey *chemistry educator*
York, Herbert Frank *physics educator, government official*

Livermore
Alder, Berni Julian *physicist, researcher*
Bjorkholm, John Ernst *physicist*
Campbell, Edward Michael *research physicist, science administrator*
Cauble, Robert C. *research scientist*
Celliers, Peter H. *physicist*
Collins, Gilbert Wilson *physicist*
Cook, Robert Crossland *research chemist*
Da Silva, Luis B. *scientist*
Haan, Steven William *physics researcher*
Hooper, Edwin Bickford *physicist*
Hulet, Ervin Kenneth *retired nuclear chemist*
Kidder, Ray Edward *physicist, consultant*
Kilkenny, Joseph David *physics researcher*
Kirkwood, Robert Keith *applied physicist*
Leith, Cecil Eldon, Jr. *retired physicist*
Lindl, John D. *physicist*
Max, Claire Ellen *physicist*
Nuckolls, John Hopkins *physicist, researcher*
Remington, Bruce A. *physics researcher*
Santer, Benjamin *atmospheric scientist, meteorologist*
Schock, Robert Norman *geophysicist*
Shotts, Wayne J. *nuclear scientist, federal agency administrator*
Spiller, Eberhard Adolf *physicist, researcher*
Tarter, Curtis Bruce *physicist, science administrator*
Wallace, Russell John *physicist*
Weber, Stephen Vance *physics researcher, astrophysicist*
Wong, Joe *physical chemist*

Loma Linda
Slattery, Charles Wilbur *biochemistry educator*
Wilcox, Ronald Bruce *biochemistry educator, researcher*

Long Beach
Bauer, Roger Duane *chemistry educator, science consultant*

Los Altos
Fraknoi, Andrew *astronomy educator, astronomical society executive*
Hahn, Harold Thomas *physical chemist, chemical engineer*

Los Angeles
Adamson, Arthur Wilson *chemistry educator*
Aller, Lawrence Hugh *astronomy educator, researcher*
Allerton, Samuel Ellsworth *biochemist*
Anderson, W. French *biochemist, physician*
Benson, Sidney William *chemistry researcher*
Bhaumik, Mani Lal *physicist*
Bird, Peter *geology educator*
Boado, Ruben Jose *biochemist*
Boyer, Paul D. *biochemist, educator*
Braginsky, Stanislav Iosifovich *physicist, geophysicist, researcher*
Byers, Nina *physics educator*
Campbell, Kenneth Eugene, Jr. *vertebrate paleontologist, ornithologist*
Carter, Emily Ann *physical chemist, researcher, educator*
Chapman, Orville Lamar *chemist, educator*
Chen, Francis F. *physics and engineering educator*
Chester, Marvin *physics educator*
Clarke, Steven Gerard *chemistry educator*
Coleman, Charles Clyde *physicist, educator*
Coleman, Paul Jerome, Jr. *physicist, educator*
Cornwall, John Michael *physics educator, consultant, researcher*
Coroniti, Ferdinand Vincent *physics educator, consultant*
Dawson, John Myrick *physics educator*
Dows, David Alan *chemistry educator*
Dunn, Arnold Samuel *biochemistry educator*
Dunn, Bruce Sidney *materials science educator*
Fischer, Alfred George *geology educator*
Foote, Christopher Spencer *chemist, educator*
Fried, Burton David *physicist, educator*
Ganas, Perry Spiros *physicist*
Ghez, Andrea Mia *astronomy and physics educator*
Ghil, Michael *atmospheric scientist, geophysicist*
Hall, Clarence Albert, Jr. *geologist, educator*
Haw, James F. *organic chemist*
Heath, James R. *chemistry educator*
Houk, Kendall Newcomb *chemistry educator*
Jaffe, Sigmund *chemist, educator*
Jordan, Thomas Hillman *geophysicist, educator*
Joshi, Chandrashekhar Janardan *physics educator*
Jung, Michael Ernest *chemistry educator*
Kaesz, Herbert David *chemistry educator*
Kaplan, Isaac Raymond *chemistry educator, corporate executive*
Kedes, Laurence H. *biochemistry educator, physician, researcher*
Kivelson, Daniel *chemistry educator*
Kivelson, Margaret Galland *physicist*
Knopoff, Leon *geophysics educator*
Koga, Rokutaro (Rocky) (Rocky Koga) *physicist*
Krupp, Edwin Charles *astronomer*
Levine, Raphael David *chemistry educator*
Lieber, Michael Randall *biochemist, educator*
Liou, Kuo-Nan *atmospheric sciences educator, researcher*
Maki, Kazumi *physicist, educator*
Markland, Francis Swaby, Jr. *biochemist, educator*
Neufeld, Elizabeth Fondal *biochemist, educator*
Olah, George Andrew *chemist, educator*
Onak, Thomas Philip *chemistry educator*
Paulson, Donald Robert *chemistry educator*
Reiss, Howard *chemistry educator*
Roberts, Sidney *biological chemist*
Scott, Robert Lane *chemist, educator*
Smith, Emil L. *biochemist, consultant*
Smith, William Ray *former biophysicist, former engineer*
Stellwagen, Robert Harwood *biochemistry educator*
Stoddart, J. Fraser *chemistry educator*
Szwarc, Michael *polymer scientist*
Taylor, Howard S. *chemistry and physics educator, research physicist*
Thorne, Richard Mansergh *physicist*
Trimble, Stanley Wayne *hydrology and geography educator*
Ufimtsev, Pyotr Yakovlevich *physicist, electrical engineer, educator*
Vidale, John Emilio *geologist*
Walker, Raymond John *physicist*
Whitten, Charles Alexander, Jr. *physics educator*
Wittry, David Beryle *physicist, educator*
Wong, Alfred Yiu-fai *physics educator*
Woodruff, Fay *paleoceanographer, geological researcher*
Wudl, Fred *chemistry educator*

Los Osos
Topp, Alphonso Axel, Jr. *environmental scientist, consultant*

Malibu
Margerum, J(ohn) David *chemist, researcher*
Pepper, David M. *physicist, educator, writer, inventor*

Marina
Shane, William Whitney *astronomer*

Menlo Park
Bukry, John David *geologist*
Carr, Michael Harold *geologist*
Dieterich, James H. *geologist*
Drell, Sidney David *physicist, educator*
Funkhouser, Lawrence William *retired geologist*
Lachenbruch, Arthur Herold *geophysicist, researcher*
Penzias, Arno Allan *astrophysicist, technology consultant, research scientist, information systems specialist*
Taylor, Richard Edward *physicist, educator*

Moffett Field
Holton, Emily *physicist*
Lissauer, Jack Jonathan *astronomy educator*
Pendleton, Yvonne *astrophysicist*
Ragent, Boris *physicist*
Seiff, Alvin *planetary, atmospheric and aerodynamics scientist*

Monrovia
Andary, Thomas Joseph *biochemist, researcher*

Montecito
Wheelon, Albert Dewell *physicist*

Monterey
Collins, Curtis Allan *oceanographer*

Shull, Harrison *chemist, educator*
Turner, Robert Elwood *physicist*

Morgan Hill
Kuster, Robert Kenneth *former scientist*

Moss Landing
Brewer, Peter George *ocean geochemist*
Clague, David A. *geologist*
Coale, Kenneth Hamilton *biogeochemist, educator*

Mountain View
Drake, Frank Donald *radio astronomer, educator*

Murietta
Lake, Bruce Meno *applied physicist*

Northridge
Smathers, James Burton *medical physicist, educator*

Oak Park
Caldwell, Stratton Franklin *kinesiology educator*

Oakland
Ames, Bruce N(athan) *biochemist, molecular biologist*
Linford, Rulon Kesler *physicist, engineer*

Oceanside
L'Annunziata, Michael Frank *chemist, consultant*

Orange
Korb, Lawrence John *metallurgist*

Oroville
Sincoff, Steven Lawrence *chemistry educator*

Pacific Grove
Lindstrom, Kris Peter *environmental consultant*

Pacific Palisades
Csendes, Ernest *chemist, corporate and financial executive*

Palo Alto
Breiner, Sheldon *geophysics educator, business executive*
Cohen, Karl Paley *nuclear energy consultant*
Cutler, Leonard Samuel *physicist*
Eng, Lawrence Fook *biochemistry educator, neurochemist*
Ernst, Wallace Gary *geology educator*
Flory, Curt Alan *research physicist*
Haisch, Bernard Michael *astronomer, researcher*
Loewenstein, Walter Bernard *nuclear power technologist*
Palmer, Robert Brian *physicist*
Sleep, Norman H. *geophysics educator*
Street, Robert A. *research physicist*
Theeuwes, Felix *physical chemist*

Paradise
Wilder, James D. *geology and mining administrator*

Pasadena
Ahrens, Thomas J. *geophysicist*
Albee, Arden Leroy *geologist, educator*
Allen, Clarence Roderic *geologist, educator*
Anderson, Don Lynn *geophysicist, educator*
Anson, Fred Colvig *chemistry educator*
Babcock, Horace W. *retired astronomer*
Baldeschwieler, John Dickson *chemist, educator*
Barnes, Charles Andrew *physicist, educator*
Beauchamp, Jesse Lee (Jack Beauchamp) *chemistry educator*
Bejczy, Antal Károly *research scientist, research facility administrator*
Bercaw, John Edward *chemistry educator, consultant*
Blandford, Roger David *astronomy educator*
Boehm, Felix Hans *physicist, educator*
Buratti, Bonnie J. *aerospace scientist*
Chahine, Moustafa Toufic *atmospheric scientist*
Chan, Sunney Ignatius *chemist, educator*
Cohen, Marshall Harris *astronomer, educator*
Crisp, David *atmospheric physicist, research scientist*
Culick, Fred Ellsworth Clow *physics and engineering educator*
Davidson, Norman Ralph *biochemistry educator*
Dervan, Peter Brendan *chemistry educator*
Dougherty, Dennis A. *chemistry educator*
Dressler, Alan Michael *astronomer*
Duxbury, Thomas Carl *planetary scientist*
Epstein, Samuel *geologist, educator*
Farley, Kenneth A. *geochemist, educator*
Ferber, Robert Rudolf *physics researcher, educator, science administrator*
Frautschi, Steven Clark *physicist, educator*
Fu, Lee-Lueng *oceanographer*
Goldreich, Peter Martin *astrophysics and planetary physics educator*
Goodstein, David Louis *physics educator*
Gray, Harry Barkus *chemistry educator*
Grubbs, Robert Howard *chemistry educator*
Gurnis, Michael Christopher *geological sciences educator*
Heindl, Clifford Joseph *physicist, researcher*
Helin, Eleanor Francis *astronomer, geologist*
Helmberger, Donald Vincent *geophysical educator, researcher*
Hitlin, David George *physicist, educator*
Ingersoll, Andrew Perry *planetary science educator*
Jastrow, Robert *physicist, educator*
Johnson, William Lewis *materials science educator*
Kanamori, Hiroo *geophysics educator*
Koonin, Steven Elliot *physicist, educator, academic administrator*
Lewis, Nathan Saul *chemistry educator*
Lopes, Rosaly Mutel Crocce *astronomer, planetary geologist*
Marcus, Rudolph Arthur *chemist, educator*
Matijevic, Jacob R. *aerospace scientist*
Mc Koy, Basil Vincent Charles *theoretical chemist, educator*
McGill, Thomas Conley *physics educator*
Neugebauer, Gerry *retired astrophysicist, educator*
[illegible]
Oemler, Augustus, Jr. *astronomer, educator*
Phinney, E. Sterl, III *astrophysicist*

Roberts, John D. *chemist, educator*
Sandage, Allan Rex *astronomer*
Sargent, Wallace Leslie William *astronomer, educator*
Schmidt, Maarten *astronomy educator*
Schwarz, John Henry *theoretical physicist, educator*
Sekanina, Zdenek *astronomer*
Sharp, Robert Phillip *geology educator, researcher*
Smith, Edward John *geophysicist, physicist*
Spilker, Linda Joyce *aerospace scientist*
Stevenson, David John *planetary scientist, educator*
Stone, Edward Carroll *physicist, educator*
Thorne, Kip Stephen *physicist, educator*
Tombrello, Thomas Anthony, Jr. *physics educator, consultant*
Vogt, Rochus Eugen *physicist, educator*
Wasserburg, Gerald Joseph *geology and geophysics educator*
Westphal, James Adolph *planetary science educator*
Yeomans, Donald Keith *astronomer*
Zewail, Ahmed Hassan *chemistry and physics educator, editor, consultant*
Zirin, Harold *astronomer, educator*

Pomona
Bidlack, Wayne Ross *nutritional biochemist, toxicologist, food scientist*

Redondo Beach
Foster, John Stuart, Jr. *physicist, former defense industry executive*

Redwood City
Nacht, Sergio *biochemist*

Richmond
Thomas, John Richard *retired chemist*

Riverside
Green, Harry Western, II *geology-geophysics educator*
Orbach, Raymond Lee *physicist, educator*
Rabenstein, Dallas Leroy *chemistry educator*

Sacramento
Rosenfeld, Arthur H. *physics educator, research director*

San Diego
Bussard, Robert William *physicist*
Cantor, Charles Robert *biochemistry educator*
Cobble, James Wikle *chemistry educator*
Gastil, Russell Gordon *geologist, educator*
Greene, John M. *physicist*
Kraus, Pansy Daegling *gemology consultant, editor, writer*
Lao, Lang Li *nuclear fusion research physicist*
Mohan, Chandra *research biochemistry educator*
Morgan, Mark Quenten *astrophysics educator*
Pincus, Howard Jonah *geologist, engineer, educator*
Shneour, Elie Alexis *biochemist, researcher*
Springer, Wayne Richard *healthcare system official, research biochemist*
Stambaugh, Ronald Dennis *physicist, researcher*
Strait, Edward J. *research physicist*

San Francisco
Burlingame, Alma Lyman *chemist, educator*
Cluff, Lloyd Sterling *earthquake geologist*
Dickinson, Wade *physicist, oil and gas company executive, educator*
Goldstein, David Baird *energy program director, physicist*
Grodsky, Gerold Morton *biochemistry educator*
Gross, Carol A. *biochemist, educator*
James, Thomas Larry *chemistry educator*
Kelly, Regis Baker *biochemistry educator, biophysics educator*
Kollman, Peter A. *chemistry educator*
Landahl, Herbert Daniel *biophysicist, mathematical biologist, researcher, consultant*
Mandra, York T. *geology educator*
Nguyen, Ann Cac Khue *pharmaceutical and medicinal chemist*
Yuille, Alan Loddon *physicist, researcher*

San Jose
Daffom, Geoffrey Alan *biochemist*
Eigler, Donald Mark *physicist*
Forster, Julian *physicist, consultant*
Gruber, John Balsbaugh *physics educator, university administrator*
Ito, Hiroshi *research chemist*
Lau, John Hon Shing *electronics scientist*
Lutz, Chris P. *research physicist*
Mee, C(harles) Denis *physicist*
Neptune, John Addison *chemistry educator, consultant*
Parkin, Stuart Stephen Papworth *materials scientist*
Russell, Thomas Paul *physicist*

San Leandro
Stallings, Charles Henry *physicist*

San Mateo
Holmes, John Richard *physicist, educator*

San Pedro
Simmons, William *physicist, retired aerospace research executive*

Santa Barbara
Ahlers, Guenter *physicist, educator*
Atwater, Tanya Maria *marine geophysicist, educator*
Bowers, Michael Thomas *chemistry educator*
Bruice, Thomas C. *chemist, educator*
Buratto, Steven K. *chemistry educator*
Clarke, Peter J. *physicist, technology executive*
Crowell, John C(hambers) *geology educator, researcher*
Dudziak, Walter Francis *physicist*
Dunne, Thomas *geology educator*
Fisher, Matthew P. A. *physicist*
Ford, Peter C. *chemistry educator*
Gossard, Arthur Charles *physicist, researcher*
Gutsche, Steven Lyle *physicist*
Heeger, Alan Jay *physicist, educator*

Hubbard, Arthur Thornton *chemistry educator, electro-surface chemist*
Kohn, Walter *educator, physicist*
Langer, James Stephen *physicist, educator*
Luyendyk, Bruce Peter *geophysicist, educator, institution administrator*
Macdonald, Ken Craig *geophysicist*
Morse, Daniel E. *biochemistry educator, science administrator*
Peale, Stanton Jerrold *physics educator*
Pilgeram, Laurence Oscar *biochemist*
Scalapino, Douglas James *physics educator*
Tilton, George Robert *geochemistry educator*
White, Robert Stephen *physics educator*
Wilson, Leslie *biochemist, cell biologist, biology educator*

Santa Cruz
Bunnett, Joseph Frederick *chemist, educator*
Faber, Sandra Moore *astronomer, educator*
Heusch, Clemens August *physicist, educator*
Kraft, Robert Paul *astronomer, educator*
Lay, Thorne *geosciences educator*
Miller, Joseph S. *astronomy researcher*
Nelson, Jerry Earl *astrophysics educator*
Osterbrock, Donald E(dward) *astronomy educator*
Silver, Mary Wilcox *oceanography educator*
Williams, Quentin Christopher *geophysicist, educator*
Wipke, W. Todd *chemistry educator*

Santa Maria
Ellis, Emory Leon *former biochemist*

Santa Monica
Intriligator, Devrie Shapiro *physicist*
Park, Edward Cahill, Jr. *retired physicist*

South San Francisco
Canova-Davis, Eleanor *biochemist, researcher*

Stanford
Allen, Matthew Arnold *physicist*
Andersen, Hans Christian *chemistry educator*
Baldwin, Robert Lesh *biochemist, educator*
Berg, Paul *biochemist, educator*
Bienenstock, Arthur Irwin *physicist, educator, government official*
Boxer, Steven G. *physical chemistry educator*
Brauman, John I. *chemist, educator*
Bravman, John Cole *materials scientist, educator*
Brünger, Axel Thomas *biophysicist, researcher, educator*
Bube, Richard Howard *materials scientist, educator*
Byer, Robert Louis *applied physics educator, university dean*
Chu, Steven *physics educator*
Collman, James Paddock *chemistry educator*
Djerassi, Carl *chemist, educator, writer*
Dorfan, Jonathan Mannie *physicist, educator*
Fejer, Martin M. *physics educator*
Fetter, Alexander Lees *theoretical physicist, educator*
Flinn, Paul Anthony *materials scientist*
Harbaugh, John Warvelle *geologist, educator*
Harrison, Walter Ashley *physicist, educator*
Herring, William Conyers *physicist, emeritus educator*
Kallosh, Renata *physics educator*
Kool, Eric T. *chemist, educator*
Kornberg, Arthur *biochemist, educator*
Kornberg, Roger David *biochemist, structural biologist*
Kovach, Robert Louis *geophysics educator*
Krauskopf, Konrad Bates *geology educator*
Laughlin, Robert B. *physics educator*
Lehman, I. Robert *biochemist, educator*
Levinthal, Elliott Charles *physicist, educator*
Little, William Arthur *physicist, educator*
Matson, Pamela Anne *environmental science educator*
McConnell, Harden Marsden *biophysical chemistry researcher, chemistry educator*
Osheroff, Douglas Dean *physicist, researcher*
Panofsky, Wolfgang Kurt Hermann *physicist, educator*
Perl, Martin Lewis *physicist, engineer, educator*
Richter, Burton *physicist, educator*
Ross, John *physical chemist, educator*
Schneider, Stephen Henry *climatologist, environmental policy analyst, researcher*
Shaw, Herbert John *physics educator emeritus*
Spicer, William Edward, III *physicist, educator, engineer*
Stryer, Lubert *biochemist, educator*
Sturrock, Peter Andrew *space science and astrophysics educator*
Susskind, Leonard *physicist, educator*
Taube, Henry *chemistry educator*
Teller, Edward *physicist*
Thompson, George Albert *geophysics educator*
Trost, Barry Martin *chemist, educator*
Wagoner, Robert Vernon *astrophysicist, educator*
Walt, Martin *physicist, consulting educator*
Waymouth, Robert *chemistry educator*
Wender, Paul Anthony *chemistry educator*
Wojcicki, Stanley George *physicist, educator*
Zare, Richard Neil *chemistry educator*

Sunnyvale
Armistead, Robert Ashby, Jr. *scientific research company executive*

Torrance
Manasson, Vladimir Alexandrovich *physicist*
Rogers, Howard H. *chemist*

COLORADO

Boulder
Albritton, Daniel Lee *atmospheric scientist*
Alldredge, Leroy Romney *retired geophysicist*
Anderson, Dana Z. *physics educator*
Bartlett, David Farnham *physics educator*
Begelman, Mitchell Craig *astrophysicist, educator, writer*
Calvert, Jack George *atmospheric chemist, educator*
[illegible] *meteorologist, consultant*
Clark, Alan Fred *physicist*
Conti, Peter Selby *astronomy educator*

Cornell, Eric Allin *physics educator*
Cristol, Stanley Jerome *chemistry educator*
Dryer, Murray *physicist, educator*
Dunn, Gordon Harold *physicist, researcher*
Faller, James Elliot *physicist, educator*
Ferguson, Eldon Earl *retired physicist*
Fleming, Rex James *meteorologist*
Garstang, Roy Henry *astrophysicist, educator*
Hall, John Lewis *physicist, researcher*
Hermann, Allen Max *physics educator*
Hildner, Ernest Gotthold, III *solar physicist, science administrator*
Holzer, Thomas E. *physicist*
Joselyn, Jo Ann *space scientist*
Kapteyn, Henry Cornelius *physics and engineering educator*
King, Edward Louis *retired chemistry educator*
Koch, Tad Harbison *chemistry educator, researcher*
Lally, Vincent Edward *atmospheric scientist*
LeMone, Margaret Anne *atmospheric scientist*
Leone, Stephen Robert *chemical physicist, educator*
Lineberger, William Carl *chemistry educator*
Little, Charles Gordon *radiophysicist*
Low, Boon Chye *physicist*
McCray, Richard Alan *astrophysicist, educator*
Miller, Harold William *nuclear geochemist*
Norcross, David Warren *physicist, researcher*
Peterson, Roy Jerome *physics educator*
Phelps, Arthur Van Rensselaer *physicist, consultant*
Ravishankara, Akkihebal R. *chemist*
Robinson, Peter *paleontology educator, consultant*
Roellig, Leonard Oscar *physics educator*
Schneider, Nicholas McCord *planetary scientist, educator, textbook author*
Snow, Theodore Peck *astrophysics educator*
Tatarskii, Valerian Il'Ich *physics researcher*
Tolbert, Margaret A. *geochemistry educator*
Trenberth, Kevin Edward *atmospheric scientist*
Washington, Warren Morton *meteorologist*
Webster, Peter John *meteorology educator*
Wieman, Carl E. *physics educator*

Colorado Springs
Corry, Charles Elmo *geophysicist, consultant*
Hoffman, John Raleigh *physicist*
Schwartz, Donald *chemistry educator*

Denver
Chappell, Willard Ray *physics educator, environmental scientist*
Cobban, William Aubrey *paleontologist*
Eaton, Gareth Richard *chemistry educator, university dean*
Foster, Norman Holland *geologist*
Hetzel, Fredrick William *biophysicist, educator*
Iona, Mario *retired physics educator*
Landon, Susan Melinda *petroleum geologist*
McCord, Joe Milton *biochemist, educator*
Mullineaux, Donal Ray *geologist*
Neumann, Herschel *physics educator*
Smith, Dwight Morrell *chemistry educator*
Stedman, Donald Hugh *chemist, educator*
Weihaupt, John George *geosciences educator, scientist, university administrator*

Fort Collins
Bamburg, James Robert *biochemistry educator*
Bernstein, Elliot Roy *chemistry educator*
Fixman, Marshall *chemist, educator*
Gray, William Mason *meteorologist, atmospheric science educator*
Ladanyi, Branka Maria *chemist, educator*
Meyers, Albert Irving *chemistry educator*
Mosier, Arvin Ray *chemist, researcher*
Patton, Carl Elliott *physics educator*
Vonder Haar, Thomas H. *meteorology educator*
Woolhiser, David Arthur *hydrologist*

Golden
Edwards, Glen R. *metallurgist*
Kennedy, George Hunt *chemistry educator*
Krauss, George *metallurgist*
Tilton, John Elvin *mineral economics educator*
Weimer, Robert Jay *geology educator, energy consultant, civic leader*
White, James Edward *geophysicist, educator*

Littleton
Sydansk, Robert Dunn *chemist, petroleum engineer*

Snowmass
Lovins, Amory Bloch *physicist, energy consultant*

HAWAII

Hawaii National Park
Swanson, Donald Alan *geologist*

Hilo
Griep, David Michael *astronomical scientist, researcher*

Honolulu
Bercovici, David Anthony Leonardo *geophysics educator, researcher*
Hawke, Bernard Ray *planetary scientist*
Helsley, Charles Everett *geologist, geophysicist*
Herbig, George Howard *astronomer, educator*
Ihrig, Judson La Moure *chemist*
Kaiser, Nicholas *physicist, educator*
Keil, Klaus *geology educator, consultant*
Raleigh, Cecil Baring *geophysicist*
Scheuer, Paul Josef *chemistry educator*
Sharma, Shiv Kumar *geophysicist*

IDAHO

McCall
Hamilton, Charles Howard *metallurgy educator*

Moscow
Bitterwolf, Thomas Edwin [illegible]
Miller, Maynard Malcolm *geologist, educator, research institute director, explorer, legislator*
Shreeve, Jean'ne Marie *chemist, educator*
Stumpf, Bernhard Josef *physicist*

MONTANA

Bozeman
Grieco, Paul Anthony *chemistry educator*
Horner, John Robert *paleontologist, researcher*
Jacobsen, Jeffrey Scott *environmental scientist*
Lapeyre, Gerald J. *physics educator, researcher*
Mertz, Edwin Theodore *retired biochemist, emeritus educator*
Moak, David *geologist*

Missoula
Osterheld, R(obert) Keith *chemistry educator*

NEVADA

Carson City
Crawford, John Edward *geologist, scientist*
Holmes, Richard Brooks *mathematical physicist*

Las Vegas
Barth, Delbert Sylvester *environmental studies educator*

Reno
Johnson, Arthur William, Jr. *planetarium executive*
Leipper, Dale Frederick *physical oceanographer, meteorologist, educator*
Livermore, John S. *geologist*
Price, Jonathan G. *geologist*

NEW MEXICO

Albuquerque
Beckel, Charles Leroy *physics educator*
Campana, Michael Emerson *hydrogeology and hydrology educator, researcher*
Cramer, James Dale *physicist, scientific company executive*
Feibelman, Peter Julian *physicist*
Loehman, Ronald Ernest *materials scientist*
Loftfield, Robert Berner *biochemistry educator*
Mattox, Donald *metallurgist, materials scientist, physicist*
Robinson, Charles Paul *nuclear physicist, diplomat, business executive*
Romig, Alton Dale, Jr. *materials scientist, educator*
Scully, Marlan Orvil *physics educator*
Van Devender, J. Pace *physical scientist, management consultant*

Las Cruces
Kemp, John Daniel *biochemist, educator*
Walterbos, René Antonius *astronomer*

Los Alamos
Becker, Stephen A. *physicist, designer*
Bell, George Irving *biophysics researcher*
Campbell, Mary Stinecipher *research chemist, educator*
Colgate, Stirling Auchincloss *physicist*
Engelhardt, Albert George *physicist*
George, Timothy G. *metallurgist*
Gibson, Benjamin Franklin *physicist*
Grilly, Edward Rogers *physicist*
Hakkila, Eero Arnold *retired nuclear safeguards technology chemist*
Hansen, Glen Arthur *scientist, researcher*
Hirt, Cyril William *physicist*
Johnson, Mikkel Borlaug *physicist*
Judd, O'Dean P. *physicist*
Keller, Richard Allen *chemist*
Kubas, Gregory Joseph *research chemist*
Maloy, Stuart *materials scientist, engineer*
Mihalas, Dimitri Manuel *astrophysicist, educator*
Mitchell, Terence Edward *materials scientist*
Moss, Joel M. *physicist*
Nix, James Rayford *nuclear physicist, consultant*
Pack, Russell T. *theoretical chemist*
Press, William Henry *astrophysicist, computer scientist*
Pynn, Roger *physicist*
Reynders, John Van Wicheren *computational physicist*
Rosen, Louis *physicist*
Selden, Robert Wentworth *physicist, science advisor*
Smith, James Lawrence *research physicist*
Terrell, James (Nelson James Terrell) *physicist*
Wahl, Arthur Charles *retired chemistry educator*
WoldeGabriel, Giday *research geologist*
Zweig, George *physicist, neurobiologist*

Los Lunas
Seiler, Fritz Arnold *physicist*

Santa Fe
Cowan, George Arthur *chemist, bank executive, director*
Fisher, Robert Alan *laser physicist*
Gell-Mann, Murray *theoretical physicist, educator*
Giovanielli, Damon Vincent *physicist, consulting company executive*
Jones, Walter Harrison *chemist, educator*
Lee, David Mallin *physicist*
Montgomery, Michael Davis *physics/astrophysics company executive, consultant*
Schoenborn, Benno P. *biophysicist, educator*
Whitten, David George *chemistry educator*

Socorro
Chapin, Charles E. *geologist, mineralogist*

Sunspot
Altrock, Richard Charles *astrophysicist*
Beckers, Jacques Maurice *astrophysicist*
Dunn, Richard Bradner *retired solar astronomer*
Keil, Stephen Lesley *astrophysicist*

OREGON

Albany
Dooley, George Joseph, III *metallurgist*

Ashland
Abrahams, Sidney Cyril *physicist, crystallographer*
Addicott, Warren Oliver *retired geologist, educator*

Beaverton
Pankow, James F. *environmental science and engineering educator*

Corvallis
Baird, William McKenzie *chemical carcinogenesis researcher, biochemistry educator*
Dalrymple, Gary Brent *research geologist*
Drake, Charles Whitney *physicist*
Evans, Harold J. *plant physiologist, biochemist, educator*
Huyer, Adriana *oceanographer, educator*
Karplus, Paul Andrew *biochemistry educator*
Sleight, Arthur William *chemist, educator*
Thomas, Thomas Darrah *chemistry educator*
Van Holde, Kensal Edward *biochemistry educator*
Whanger, Philip Daniel *biochemistry educator and researcher, nutrition educator*
Yeats, Robert Sheppard *geologist, educator*

Eugene
Crasemann, Bernd *physicist, educator*
Donnelly, Russell James *physicist, educator*
Griffith, Osbie Hayes *chemistry educator*
Hutchison, James E. *chemistry educator*
Mazo, Robert Marc *chemistry educator, retired*
Peticolas, Warner Leland *retired physical chemistry educator*
Retallack, Gregory John *geologist, educator*
Schellman, John A. *chemistry educator*
von Hippel, Peter Hans *chemistry educator, molecular biology researcher*

Medford
Bouquet, Francis Lester *physicist*

Portland
Weeks, Wilford Frank *retired geophysics educator, glaciologist*

UTAH

Brigham City
Fife, Dennis Jensen *chemistry educator, career officer*

Logan
Aust, Steven Douglas *biochemistry, biotechnology and toxicology educator*
Scouten, William Henry *chemistry educator, academic administrator*
Steed, Allan J. *physical science research administrator*

Provo
Bradshaw, Jerald Sherwin *chemistry educator, researcher*
Hall, Howard Tracy *chemist*
Henderson, Douglas James *physicist, chemist, researcher*
Izatt, Reed M. *chemistry researcher*

Salt Lake City
Allison, Merle Lee *geologist*
Anspaugh, Lynn Richard *research biophysicist*
Callender, Jonathan Ferris *environmental geologist, resource planner*
Dick, Bertram Gale, Jr. *physics educator*
Kenison, Lynn T. *chemist*
Miller, Jan Dean *metallurgy educator*
Parry, Robert Walter *chemistry educator*
Poulter, Charles Dale *chemist, educator, consultant*
Stang, Peter John *organic chemist*
Straight, Richard Coleman *photobiologist, natural philosopher*
Wall, Lloyd L. *geological engineer*
Wan, Rong-Yu *metallurgist*

WASHINGTON

Bellevue
Delisi, Donald Paul *geophysicist, fluid mechanic*

Bellingham
Morse, Joseph Grant *chemistry educator*

Clinton
Forward, Robert L(ull) *physicist, businessman, consultant, writer*

Coupeville
Eaton, Gordon Pryor *geologist, consultant*

Edmonds
Galster, Richard W. *engineering geologist*

Ellensburg
Rosell, Sharon Lynn *physics and chemistry educator, researcher*

Friday Harbor
Agosta, William Carleton *chemist, educator*

Lopez Island
Whetten, John Theodore *geologist, researcher*

Port Ludlow
Dunning, Kenneth Laverne *research physicist*

Pullman
Crosby, Glenn Arthur *chemistry educator*
Gupta, Yogendra M. *physicist, educator*
Ryan, Clarence Augustine, Jr. *biochemistry educator*

Richland
Bevelacqua, Joseph John *physicist, researcher*
Bush, Spencer Harrison *metallurgist, consultant*
Dunning, Thom H., Jr. *environmental molecular science executive*
Fruchter, Jonathan Sewell *research scientist, geochemist*
Moore, Emmett Burris, Jr. *physical chemist, educator*

Seattle
Andersen, Niels Hjorth *chemistry educator, biophysics researcher, consultant*
Arons, Arnold Boris *physicist, educator*
Banse, Karl *retired oceanography educator*
Baum, William Alvin *astronomer, educator*
Bernard, Eddie Nolan *oceanographer*
Bichsel, Hans *physicist, consultant, researcher*
Borden, Weston Thatcher *chemistry educator*
Brown, Lowell Severt *physicist, educator*
Brownlee, Donald Eugene, II *astronomer, educator*
Charlson, Robert Jay *atmospheric sciences educator, scientist*
Christian, Gary Dale *chemistry educator*
Cramer, John Gleason, Jr. *physics educator, experimental physicist*
Creager, Joe Scott *geology and oceanography educator*
Dalton, Larry Raymond *chemistry educator, researcher, consultant*
Davie, Earl Warren *biochemistry educator*
Dehmelt, Hans Georg *physicist, educator*
El-Moslimany, Ann Paxton *paleoecologist, educator, writer*
Engel, Thomas *chemistry educator*
Evans, Bernard William *geologist, educator*
Fischer, Edmond Henri *biochemistry educator*
Floss, Heinz G. *chemistry educator, scientist*
Fortson, Edward Norval *physics educator*
Gouterman, Martin Paul *chemistry educator*
Gregory, Norman Wayne *chemistry educator, researcher*
Halver, John Emil *nutritional biochemist*
Heath, George Ross *oceanographer*
Henley, Ernest Mark *physics educator, university dean emeritus*
Hodge, Paul William *astronomer, educator*
Hogan, Craig J. *astronomer, educator*
Ingalls, Robert Lynn *physicist, educator*
Krebs, Edwin Gerhard *biochemistry educator*
Kwiram, Alvin L. *physical chemistry educator, university official*
Lingafelter, Edward Clay, Jr. *chemistry educator*
Lord, Jere Johns *retired physics educator*
Lubatti, Henry Joseph *physicist, educator*
Malins, Donald Clive *biochemistry, researcher*
Mallory, V(irgil) Standish *geologist, educator*
Neurath, Hans *biochemist, educator*
Olmstead, Marjorie Ann *physics educator*
Pocker, Yeshayau *chemistry, biochemistry educator*
Porter, Stephen Cummings *geologist, educator*
Reed, Richard John *retired meteorology educator*
Reinhardt, William Parker *chemical physicist, educator*
Rhines, Peter Broomell *oceanographer, atmospheric scientist*
Robertson, Robert Graham Hamish *physicist*
Stern, Edward Abraham *physics educator*
Stubbs, Christopher W. *physics educator*
Szkody, Paula *astronomy educator, researcher*
Thouless, David James *physicist, educator*
Varanasi, Usha *environmental scientist*
Wallerstein, George *astronomer, educator*
Walsh, Kenneth Andrew *biochemist*
Weitkamp, William George *retired nuclear physicist*
Wilets, Lawrence *physics educator*

Tacoma
Harding, Karen Elaine *chemistry educator*

WYOMING

Casper
Ptasynski, Harry *geologist, oil producer*
Wold, John Schiller *geologist, former congressman*

Laramie
Borgman, Leon E. *geologist*
Johnson, Paul E. *astronomer, educator*
Meyer, Edmond Gerald *energy and natural resources educator, resources scientist, entrepreneur, former chemistry educator, university administrator*
Roark, Terry Paul *astronomer, educator*

CANADA

ALBERTA

Calgary
Campbell, Finley Alexander *geologist, consultant*
Carsted, Douglas J. *geologist*
Chipperfield, John *geologist*
Goren, Howard Joseph *biochemistry educator*
Hicks, R.B. *astronomer, educator*
Hyne, James Bissett *chemistry educator, industrial scientist, consultant*
Milone, Eugene Frank *astronomer, educator*
Mossop, Grant Dilworth *geologist, researcher*
Nigg, Benno Maurus *biomechanics educator, researcher*
Nowlan, Godfrey S. *geologist*
Sreenivasan, Sreenivasa Ranga *physicist, educator*
Walker, Roger Geoffrey *geology educator, consultant*

Drumheller
Currie, Philip John *research paleontologist, museum curator*

Edmonton
Freeman, Gordon Russel *chemistry educator*
Gough, Denis Ian *geophysics educator*
Harris, Walter Edgar *chemistry educator*
Hodges, Robert Stanley *biochemist, educator, researcher in biotechnology*
Kay, Cyril Max *biochemist, educator*
Khanna, Faqir Chand *physics educator*
Kratochvil, Byron George *chemistry educator, researcher*
Rostoker, Gordon *physicist, educator*
Rutter, Nathaniel Westlund *geologist, educator*
Stelck, Charles Richard *geology educator*

BRITISH COLUMBIA

Burnaby
Thewalt, Michael L. W. *physics educator*
Wainwright, David Stanley *intellectual property professional*

Penticton
Higgs, Lloyd Albert *astronomer, observatory administrator*

Vancouver
Affleck, Ian Keith *physics educator*
Bloom, Myer *physicist, educator*
Comisarow, Melvin B. *chemist, educator*
Hardy, Walter Newbold *physics educator, researcher*
Maiman, Theodore Harold *physicist, researcher*
Ozier, Irving *physicist, educator*
Pincock, Richard Earl *chemistry educator*
Russell, Richard Doncaster *geophysicist, educator, geoscientist*
Sinclair, Alastair James *geology educator*
Snider, Robert F. *chemistry educator, researcher*
Stewart, Ross *chemistry educator*
Tiedje, Tom *physics and astronomy educator*
Unruh, William G. *physics educator, researcher*
Vogt, Erich Wolfgang *physicist, academic administrator*
Walker, Gordon Arthur Hunter *astronomy educator*
Wheeler, John Oliver *geologist*
Withers, Stephen George *chemistry educator*
Young, Jeff *physicist, educator*

Victoria
Batten, Alan Henry *astronomer*
Best, Melvyn Edward *geophysicist*
Hesser, James Edward *astronomy researcher*
Hutchings, John Barrie *astronomer, researcher*
Israel, Werner *physics educator*
Morton, Donald Charles *astronomer*
Picciotto, Charles Edward *astronomer, educator*
Stetson, Peter Brailey *astronomer*
Wiles, David McKeen *chemist*

West Vancouver
Wynne-Edwards, Hugh Robert *geologist, educator, entrepreneur*

SASKATCHEWAN

Regina
Kybett, Brian David *chemist*

Saskatoon
Bancroft, George Michael *chemical physicist, educator*
Hirose, Akira *physics educator, researcher*
Kupsch, Walter Oscar *geologist*

TAIWAN

Taipei
Lee, Yuan Tseh *chemistry educator*

ADDRESS UNPUBLISHED

Akasofu, Syun-Ichi *geophysicist, educator*
Baker, Daniel Neil *physicist*
Baldwin, George Curriden *physicist, educator*
Ball, Lawrence *retired physical scientist*
Behrendt, John Charles *geophysicist researcher, writer*
Boyer, Herbert Wayne *retired biochemist*
Cahn, Robert Nathan *physicist*
Chemla, Daniel S. *physics educator*
Christoffersen, Ralph Earl *chemist, researcher*
Dixon, Gordon Henry *biochemist, educator*
Eck, Robert Edwin *physicist*
Frauenfelder, Hans *physicist, educator*
Friedlander, Charles Douglas *space consultant*
Gardner, Wilford Robert *physicist, educator*
Getting, Ivan Alexander *physicist, former aerospace company executive*
Goldberger, Marvin Leonard *physicist, educator*
Hatcher, Herbert John *biochemist, microbiologist*
Ho, Chih-Ming *physicist, educator*
Horton, Robert Carlton *geologist*
Ingle, James Chesney, Jr. *geology educator*
Jarmie, Nelson *physicist, consultant*
Jones, Thornton Keith *research chemist*
Kamen, Martin David *physical biochemist*
Kanes, William Henry *geology educator, research center administrator*
Kennel, Charles Frederick *physics educator, government official, academic administrator*
Kraichnan, Robert Harry *theoretical physicist, consultant*
Kustin, Kenneth *chemist*
Levenson, Marc David *optics and lasers specialist, scientist, editor*
Lillegraven, Jason Arthur *paleontologist, educator*
Lloyd, Joseph Wesley *physicist, researcher*
Maglich, Bogdan Castle *physicist*
Mauzy, Michael Philip *environmental consultant, chemical engineer*
Noyes, H(enry) Pierre *physicist*
Olsen, Clifford Wayne *retired physical chemist, consultant*
Portis, Alan Mark *physicist, educator*
Price, Clifford Warren *retired metallurgist, researcher*
Proctor, Richard J. *geologist, consultant*
Richards, Paul Linford *physics educator, researcher*
Rosenkilde, Carl Edward *physicist*
Rychnovsky, Scott Douglas *chemist, educator*
Shariff, Asghar J. *geologist*
Sharon, Timothy Michael *physicist*
Sheffield, Richard Lee *physicist*
Shirley, David Arthur *chemistry educator, science administrator*
Solomon, Susan *chemist, scientist*
Taylor, Hugh Pettingill, Jr. *geologist, educator*
Tedford, Charles Franklin *biophysicist*
Wolff, Manfred Ernst *medicinal chemist, pharmaceutical company executive*

Woodruff, Truman O(wen) *physicist, emeritus educator*
Yates, David John C. *chemist, researcher*
Zaffaroni, Alejandro C. *biochemist, medical research company executive*

SOCIAL SCIENCE

UNITED STATES

ALASKA

Anchorage
Henderson, Karen Sue *psychologist*

ARIZONA

Flagstaff
McDonald, Craydon Dean *psychologist*

Phoenix
Cheifetz, Lorna Gale *psychologist*

Sacaton
Stephenson, Larry Kirk *stategic planner, management, geography educator*

Scottsdale
Kizziar, Janet Wright *psychologist, writer, lecturer*

Tempe
Alisky, Marvin Howard *political science educator*
Balling, Robert C., Jr. *geography educator*
Gordon, Leonard *sociology educator*
Guinouard, Donald Edgar *psychologist*
Johanson, Donald Carl *physical anthropologist*
Lounsbury, John Frederick *geographer, educator*
Melnick, Rob *research administrator*
O'Neil, Michael Joseph *opinion survey executive, marketing consultant*
Simon, Sheldon Weiss *political science educator*
Uttal, William R(eichenstein) *psychology and engineering educator, research scientist*

Tucson
Beach, Lee Roy *psychologist, educator, academic administrator*
Block, Michael Kent *economics and law educator, public policy association executive, former government official, consultant*
Brainerd, Charles J(on) *experimental psychologist, applied mathematician, educator*
Clarke, James Weston *political science educator, writer*
Done, Robert Stacy *educator, consultant*
Marshall, Robert Herman *economics educator*
Mishler, William, II *political science educator*
Smith, David Wayne *psychologist, educator*
Smith, Vernon Lomax *economist, researcher*
Soren, David *archaeology educator, cinema author*
Stini, William Arthur *anthropologist, educator*
Stubblefield, Thomas Mason *agricultural economist, educator*
Thompson, Raymond Harris *retired anthropologist, educator*
Volgy, Thomas John *political science educator, organization official*
Wahlke, John Charles *political science educator*
Whiting, Allen Suess *political science educator, writer, consultant*

West Sedona
Eggert, Robert John, Sr. *economist*

CALIFORNIA

Apple Valley
Fisher, Weston Joseph *economist*

Arcata
Emenhiser, JeDon Allen *political science educator, academic administrator*

Berkeley
Adelman, Irma Glicman *economics educator*
Alhadeff, David Albert *economics educator*
Auerbach, Alan Jeffrey *economist, educator*
Baumrind, Diana *research psychologist*
Bellah, Robert Neelly *sociologist, educator*
Brandes, Stanley Howard *anthropology educator, writer*
Breslauer, George William *political science educator*
Cheit, Earl Frank *economist, educator*
Clark, John Desmond *anthropology educator*
Colson, Elizabeth Florence *anthropologist*
Gilbert, Richard Joseph *economics educator*
Hafter, Ervin R. *psychology educator*
Howell, Francis Clark *anthropologist, educator*
Ivry, Richard *psychology educator*
Jensen, Arthur Robert *psychology educator*
Joyce, Rosemary Alexandria *anthropology educator*
Kirch, Patrick Vinton *anthropology educator, archaeologist*
Lambert, Nadine Murphy *psychologist, educator*
Landau, Martin *political science educator*
Lazarus, Richard Stanley *psychology educator*
Lee, Ronald Demos *demographer, economist, educator*
Luker, Kristin *sociology educator*
Maisel, Sherman Joseph *economist, educator*
Maslach, Christina *psychology educator*
McFadden, Daniel Little *economics educator*
Muir, William Ker, Jr. *political science educator*
Quigley, John Michael *economist, educator*
Ranney, Austin (Joseph Ranney) *political science educator*
Rausser, Gordon C(lyde) *agricultural and resource economics educator*
Rosenzweig, Mark Richard *psychology educator*
Sarich, Vincent M. *anthropologist, educator*
Smolensky, Eugene *economics educator*
Sulloway, Frank Jones *psychologist, historian*
Varian, Hal Ronald *economics educator*
Wilensky, Harold L. *political science and industrial relations educator*
Williamson, Oliver Eaton *economics and law educator*
Wolfinger, Raymond Edwin *political science educator*

Carpinteria
Wheeler, John Harvey *political scientist, writer*

Carson
Palmer, Beverly Blazey *psychologist, educator*

Chico
Farrer, Claire Anne Rafferty *anthropologist, folklorist, educator*
McNall, Scott Grant *sociology educator*
Smith, Valene *anthropology educator*

Claremont
Bjork, Gordon Carl *economist, educator*
Leeb, Charles Samuel *clinical psychologist*
Pachon, Harry Peter *politics educator*
Rossum, Ralph Arthur *political science educator*

Corona Del Mar
Davis, Arthur David *psychology educator, musician*

Davis
Cohen, Lawrence Edward *sociology educator, criminologist*
Groth, Alexander Jacob *political science educator*
Jett, Stephen Clinton *geography and textiles educator, researcher*
Krubitzer, Leah *psychology educator, neuroscientist*
MacCannell, Dean *anthropology educator*
Mason, William A(lvin) *psychologist, educator, researcher*
McHenry, Henry Malcolm *anthropologist, educator*
Musolf, Lloyd Daryl *political science educator, institute administrator*
Owings, Donald Henry *psychology educator*
Skinner, G(eorge) William *anthropologist, educator*
Smith, Michael Peter *social science educator, researcher*
Spindler, George Dearborn *anthropologist, educator, writer, editor*
Sumner, Daniel Alan *economist, educator*
Wegge, Leon Louis François *retired economics educator*

El Cerrito
Conti, Isabella *psychologist, consultant*

Fresno
Dackawich, S. John *sociology educator*
O'Brien, John Conway *economist, educator, writer*
O'Connor, Kevin John *psychologist, educator*

Fullerton
Hershey, Gerald Lee *psychologist, educator*
Kaisch, Kenneth Burton *psychologist, priest*

Hayward
Meyer, Ann Jane *human development educator*
Whalen, Thomas Earl *psychology educator*

Hollywood
Fisher, Joel Marshall *political scientist, legal consultant, educator*

Irvine
Bean, Frank D(awson) *sociology and demography educator*
Burton, Michael Ladd *anthropology educator*
Danziger, James Norris *political science educator*
Freeman, Linton Clarke *sociology educator*
Greenberger, Ellen *psychologist, educator*
Huff, C(larence) Ronald *public policy and criminology educator*
Lave, Charles Arthur *economics educator*
Luce, R(obert) Duncan *psychology educator*
Margolis, Julius *economist, educator*
Mc Gaugh, James Lafayette *psychobiologist*
Schonfeld, William Rost *political science educator, researcher*
Sperling, George *cognitive scientist, educator*
Treas, Judith Kay *sociology educator*
White, Douglas Richie *anthropology educator*

Kenwood
Podboy, John Watts *clinical, forensic psychologist*

La Jolla
Attiyeh, Richard Eugene *economics educator*
Cain, William Stanley *experimental psychologist, educator, researcher*
Coburn, Marjorie Foster *psychologist, educator*
Farson, Richard Evans *psychologist*
Harris, Philip Robert *management and space psychologist*
Kaplan, Robert Malcolm *health researcher, educator*
Lane, Sylvia *economist, educator*
Lupia, Arthur W. *political science educator*
Mandler, George *psychologist, educator*
Mandler, Jean Matter *psychologist, educator*
Pratt, George Janes, Jr. *psychologist, author*
Smith, Peter Hopkinson *political scientist, consultant, writer*
Spiro, Melford Elliot *anthropology educator*
Starr, Ross Marc *economist, educator*

Larkspur
Saxton, Lloyd *psychologist, writer*

Los Altos
Haines, Richard Foster *retired psychologist*

Los Angeles
Anawalt, Patricia Rieff *anthropologist, researcher*
Anderson, Austin Gilman *economics research company consultant*
Arnold, Jeanne Eloise *anthropologist, archaeologist, educator*
Basch, Darlene Chakin *clinical social worker*
Bennett, Charles Franklin, Jr. *biogeographer, educator*
Brubaker, William Rogers *sociology educator*
Burns, Marcelline *psychologist, researcher*
Butterworth, Robert Roman *psychologist, researcher, media therapist*
Cerrell, Joseph Robert *political scientist, public relations consultant*
Champagne, Duane Willard *sociology educator*
Clark, Burton Robert *sociologist, educator*
Coombs, Robert Holman *behavioral scientist, medical educator, therapist, writer*
Darby, Michael Rucker *economist, educator*
Dekmejian, Richard Hrair *political science educator*
Demsetz, Harold *economist, educator*
Ellickson, Bryan Carl *economics educator*
Fanselow, Michael Scott *psychology educator*
Forness, Steven Robert *educational psychologist*
Goldstein, Michael Saul *sociologist*
Hoffenberg, Marvin *political science educator, consultant*
Intriligator, Michael David *economist, educator*
Jamison, Dean Tecumseh *economist*
Kelley, Harold Harding *psychology educator*
Klein, Benjamin *economics educator, consultant*
La Force, James Clayburn, Jr. *economist, educator*
Leijonhufvud, Axel Stig Bengt *economics educator*
Levine, Robert Arthur *economist, policy writer*
Lowenthal, Abraham Frederic *international relations educator*
Lyman, John *psychology and engineering educator*
Malamuth, Neil Moshe *psychology and communication educator*
Michael, William Burton *psychologist, educator*
Morgner, Aurelius *economist, educator*
Nelson, Howard Joseph *geographer, educator*
Nilles, John Mathias (Jack Nilles) *futurist*
Orme, Antony Ronald *geography educator*
Phinney, Jean Swift *psychology educator*
Raven, Bertram H(erbert) *psychology educator*
Sears, David O'Keefe *psychology educator*
Seeman, Melvin *sociologist, educator*
Sklar, Richard Lawrence *political science educator*
Strack, Stephen Naylor *psychologist*
Thompson, Richard Frederick *psychologist, neuroscientist, educator*
Totten, George Oakley, III *political science educator*
Turner, Ralph Herbert *sociologist, educator*
Williams, Robert Martin *economist, consultant*
Wittrock, Merlin Carl *educational psychologist*
Wong, James Bok *economist, engineer, technologist*
Wood, Nancy Elizabeth *psychologist, educator*
Álvarez, Rodolfo *sociology educator, consultant*

Menlo Park
Clair, Theodore Nat *educational psychologist*

Modesto
Berry, John Charles *clinical psychologist, educational administrator*

Moffett Field
Clearwater, Yvonne A. *psychologist*
Cohen, Malcolm Martin *psychologist, researcher*

Monterey
Kennedy-Minott, Rodney *international relations educator, former ambassador*

Mountain View
Bishop, Robert R. *economist*

Northridge
Reagan, Janet Thompson *psychologist, educator*

Oakland
Chodorow, Nancy Julia *sociology educator*
Farrell, Kenneth Royden *economist*
Nebelkopf, Ethan *psychologist*

Oroville
Shelton, Joel Edward *clinical psychologist*

Pacific Palisades
Longaker, Richard Pancoast *political science educator emeritus*

Palo Alto
Calvin, Allen David *psychologist, educator*
Flanagan, Robert Joseph *economics educator*
Moos, Rudolf H. *psychologist, researcher*
Rosaldo, Renato Ignacio, Jr. *cultural anthropology educator*
Scitovsky, Anne Aickelin *economist, researcher*

Pasadena
Balswick, Jack Orville *social science educator*
Davis, Lance Edwin *economics educator*
Horner, Althea Jane *psychologist*
Ledyard, John Odell *economics educator, consultant*
Munger, Edwin Stanton *political geography educator*
Plott, Charles Raymond *economics educator*
Scudder, Thayer *anthropologist, educator*

Placentia
Gobar, Alfred Julian *economic consultant, educator*

Pleasant Hill
Richard, Robert Carter *psychologist*

Pomona
Garrity, Rodman Fox *psychologist, educator*

Rancho Santa Margarita
Aguilera, Donna Conant *psychologist, researcher*

Redlands
Dangermond, Jack *geographer*

Redondo Beach
Naples, Caesar Joseph *law and public policy educator, lawyer, consultant*

Riverside
Adrian, Charles Raymond *political science educator*
Griffin, Keith Broadwell *economics educator*
Ham, Gary Martin *psychologist*
Petrinovich, Lewis Franklin *psychology educator*
Rosenthal, Robert *psychology educator*
Turk, Austin Theodore *sociology educator*
Warren, David Hardy *psychology educator*

Rolling Hills
Castor, Wilbur Wright *futurist, writer, consultant*

Sacramento
Bennett, Lawrence Allen *psychologist, criminal justice researcher*
Majesty, Melvin Sidney *psychologist, consultant*
Newland, Chester Albert *public administration educator*

San Carlos
Burgess, Leonard Randolph *business administration and economics educator, writer*

San Diego
Bales, Robert Freed *social psychologist, educator*
Gazell, James Albert *public administration educator*
Getis, Arthur *geography educator*
Kiesler, Charles Adolphus *psychologist, academic administrator*
Lewis, Shirley Jeane *psychology educator*
Madhavan, Murugappa Chettiar *economics educator, international consultant*
Sutton, L. Paul *criminal justice educator*
Weeks, John Robert *geographer, sociology educator*

San Francisco
Adler, Nancy Elinor *psychologist, educator*
Butz, Otto William *political science educator*
Estes, Carroll Lynn *sociologist, educator*
Luft, Harold S. *health economist*
Marston, Michael *urban economist, asset management executive*
Rice, Dorothy Pechman (Mrs. John Donald Rice) *medical economist*

San Jose
McDowell, Jennifer *sociologist, composer, playwright, publisher*
Pellegrini, Robert J. *psychology educator*
Voth, Alden H. *political science educator*

San Rafael
Tosti, Donald Thomas *psychologist, consultant*

Santa Barbara
Aigner, Dennis John *economics educator, consultant*
Beutler, Larry Edward *psychology educator*
Comanor, William S. *economist, educator*
Davidson, Roger H(arry) *political scientist, educator*
Erasmus, Charles John *anthropologist, educator*
Ford, Anabel *research anthropologist, archaeologist*
Goodchild, Michael *geographer, educator*
Jochim, Michael Allan *archaeologist*
Kendler, Howard H(arvard) *psychologist, educator*
Mayer, Richard Edwin *psychology educator*

Santa Cruz
Tharp, Roland George *psychology, education educator*

Santa Monica
Smith, James Patrick *economist*
Wolf, Charles, Jr. *economist, educator*

Simi Valley
Whitley, David Scott *archaeologist*

Stanford
Abramovitz, Moses *economist, educator*
Almond, Gabriel Abraham *political science educator*
Amemiya, Takeshi *economist, statistician*
Anderson, Martin Carl *economist*
Arrow, Kenneth Joseph *economist, educator*
Bandura, Albert *psychologist, educator*
Bunzel, John Harvey *political science educator, researcher*
Carlsmith, James Merrill *psychologist, educator*
Damon, William Van Buren *developmental psychologist, educator, writer*
Enthoven, Alain Charles *economist, educator*
Fishman, Joshua Aaron *sociolinguist, educator*
Friedman, Milton *economist, educator, writer*
Fuchs, Victor Robert *economics educator*
George, Alexander Lawrence *political scientist, educator*
Greif, Avner *economics educator*
Hall, Robert Ernest *economics educator*
Harris, Donald J. *economics educator*
Hickman, Bert George, Jr. *economist, educator*
Hilgard, Ernest Ropiequet *psychologist*
Holloway, David James *political science educator*
Howell, James Edwin *economist, educator*
Inkeles, Alex *sociology educator*
Johnston, Bruce Foster *economics educator*
Kreps, David Marc *economist, educator*
Krueger, Anne O. *economics educator*
Krumboltz, John Dwight *psychologist, educator*
Kurz, Mordecai *economics educator*
Laitin, David Dennis *political science educator*
Lau, Lawrence Juen-Yee *economics educator, consultant*
Lazear, Edward Paul *economics and labor relations educator, researcher*
Lepper, Mark Roger *psychology educator*
Lewis, John Wilson *political science educator*
Maccoby, Eleanor Emmons *psychology educator*
Manley, John Frederick *political scientist, educator*
March, James Gardner *social scientist, educator*
Mc Lure, Charles E., Jr. *economist, consultant*
Meier, Gerald Marvin *economics educator*
Noll, Roger Gordon *economist, educator*
North, Robert Carver *political science educator*
Paul, Benjamin David *anthropologist, educator*
Rakove, Jack Norman *history educator*
Reynolds, Clark Winton *economist, educator*

Roberts, Donald John *economics and business educator, consultant*
Rowen, Henry Stanislaus *economics educator*
Scott, W(illiam) Richard *sociology educator*
Shepard, Roger Newland *psychologist, educator*
Solomon, Ezra *economist, educator*
Triska, Jan Francis *retired political science educator*
Van Horne, James Carter *economist, educator*
Zajonc, Robert B(oleslaw) *psychology educator*
Zimbardo, Philip George *psychologist, educator, writer*

Sylmar
Yguado, Alex Rocco *economics educator*

Turlock
Ahlem, Lloyd Harold *psychologist*

Walnut Creek
Keith, Bruce Edgar *political analyst, genealogist*

Woodland Hills
Nierenberg, Norman *urban land economist, retired state official*

COLORADO

Aspen
Manosevitz, Martin *psychologist*

Boulder
Borysenko, Joan *psychologist, biologist*
Bourne, Lyle Eugene, Jr. *psychology educator*
Greenberg, Edward Seymour *political science educator, writer*
Greene, David Lee *physical anthropologist, educator*
Healy, Alice Fenvessy *psychology educator, researcher*
Jessor, Richard *psychologist, educator*
Kintsch, Walter *psychology educator, director*

Denver
Cortese, Charles Franklin *sociologist, educator, planning consultant*
Mendelsohn, Harold *sociologist, educator*
Nelson, Sarah Milledge *archaeology educator*
Purcell, Kenneth *psychology educator, university dean*
Zimet, Carl Norman *psychologist, educator*

Englewood
Hendrick, Hal Wilmans *human factors educator*
PiLand, Neill Finnes *health services economist, researcher*

Estes Park
Moore, Omar Khayyam *experimental sociologist*

Fort Collins
Bennett, Thomas LeRoy, Jr. *clinical neuropsychology educator*
Berry, Kenneth J. *sociology educator*
Eitzen, David Stanley *sociologist, educator*
Sunn, Richard Michael *psychologist*

Golden
Petrick, Alfred, Jr. *mineral economics educator, consultant*
Woolsey, Robert Eugene Donald *mineral economics, mathematics and business administration educator*

Littleton
Lohman, Loretta Cecelia *social scientist, consultant*

Pine
Jones, David Milton *economist, educator*

DISTRICT OF COLUMBIA

Washington
Taylor, John Brian *economist, educator*

HAWAII

Honolulu
Bitterman, Morton Edward *psychologist, educator*
Cho, Lee-Jay *social scientist, demographer*
Fullmer, Daniel Warren *former psychologist, educator*
Hatfield, Elaine Catherine *psychology educator*
Jordan, Amos Azariah, Jr. *foreign affairs educator, retired army officer*
Kuroda, Yasumasa *political science educator, researcher*
Mark, Shelley Muin *economist, educator, government official*
Suh, Dae-Sook *political science educator*

IDAHO

Boise
Overgaard, Willard Michele *retired political scientist, jurisprudent*

Caldwell
Lonergan, Wallace Gunn *economics educator, management consultant*

Sandpoint
Glock, Charles Young *sociologist, writer*

MONTANA

Bozeman
Gray, Philip Howard *former psychologist, writer*
Spencer, Robert C. *retired political science educator*
Stroup, Richard Lyndell *economics educator, writer*

Missoula
Lopach, James Joseph *political science educator*
Power, Thomas Michael *economist, educator*
Watkins, John Goodrich *psychologist, educator*
Wollersheim, Janet Puccinelli *psychology educator*

NEVADA

Las Vegas
Beck, Colleen Marguerite *archaeologist*
Goodall, Leonard Edwin *public administration educator*
Weeks, Gerald *psychology educator*

Reno
Chapman, Samuel Greeley *political science educator, criminologist*
Cummings, Nicholas Andrew *psychologist*
Haynes, Gary Anthony *archaeologist*
Hoadley, Walter Evans *economist, financial executive, lay worker*
Larwood, Laurie *psychologist*
Lemire, David Stephen *school psychologist, educator*
Webster, Michael Anderson *experimental psychologist*
Weinberg, Leonard Burton *political scientist*

NEW MEXICO

Albuquerque
Basso, Keith Hamilton *cultural anthropologist, linguist, educator*
Condie, Carol Joy *anthropologist, research facility administrator*
Elliott, Charles Harold *clinical psychologist*
Gordon, Larry Jean *political science educator, public health administrator*
Harris, Fred R. *political science educator, former senator*
Heady, Ferrel *retired political science educator*
May, Philip Alan *sociology educator*
Schwerin, Karl Henry *anthropology educator, researcher*
Sickels, Robert Judd *political science educator*
Stuart, David Edward *anthropologist, writer, educator*

Corrales
Adams, James Frederick *psychologist, educational administrator*

Las Cruces
Roscoe, Stanley Nelson *psychologist, aeronautical engineer*

Las Vegas
Riley, Carroll Lavern *anthropology educator*

Santa Fe
Anderson, Duane *anthropologist*
Williams, Stephen *anthropologist, educator*

Silver City
French, Laurence Armand *social science educator, psychology educator*

OREGON

Ashland
Houston, John Albert *political science educator*

Beaverton
Ricks, Mary F(rances) *archaeologist, anthropologist, consultant*

Corvallis
Gillis, John Simon *psychologist, educator*
Harter, Lafayette George, Jr. *economics educator emeritus*

Eugene
Aikens, C(lyde) Melvin *anthropology educator, archaeologist*
Davis, Richard Malone *economics educator*
Freyd, Jennifer Joy *psychology educator*
Khang, Chulsoon *economics educator*
Littman, Richard Anton *psychologist, educator*

Monmouth
Shay, Roshani Cari *political science educator*

Newberg
Adams, Wayne Verdun *pediatric psychologist, educator*

Pendleton
Reeder, Clinton Bruce *economist, public policy consultant, farmer*

Portland
Blodgett, Forrest Clinton *economics educator*
Davis, James Allan *gerontologist, educator*
Kristof, Ladis Kris Donabed *political scientist, writer*
Matarazzo, Joseph Dominic *psychologist, educator*
Wiens, Arthur Nicholai *psychology educator*

Salem
Warnath, Maxine Ammer *organizational psychologist, mediator*

White City
Moore, Charles August, Jr. *psychologist*

TEXAS

Bedford
Hoston, Germaine Annette *political science educator*

UTAH

Logan
Fifield, Marvin G. *psychologist, educator*
Roberts, Richard N. *psychologist*

North Salt Lake
Barden, Robert Christopher *lawyer, psychologist, educator, legislative analyst, speaker, writer*

Provo
Bahr, Howard Miner *sociologist, educator*
Fry, Earl Howard *political scientist, educator*
Hawkins, Alan J. *family life educator, researcher*
Kunz, Phillip Ray *sociologist, educator*
Porter, Blaine Robert Milton *sociology and psychology educator*

Salt Lake City
Benjamin, Lorna Smith *psychologist*
Giles, Gerald Lynn *psychology, learning enhancement, computer educator*
Harpending, Henry Cosad *anthropologist, educator*
Kumpfer, Karol Linda *research psychologist*
Lease, Ronald Charles *financial economics educator*

Sandy
Smith, Willard Grant *psychologist, educator*

VIRGINIA

Alexandria
Carleson, Robert Bazil *public policy consultant, corporation executive*

WASHINGTON

Bellevue
Akutagawa, Donald *psychologist, educator*

Bellingham
Burdge, Rabel James *sociology educator*

Ellensburg
Jacobs, Robert Cooper *political scientist, consultant*

Friday Harbor
MacGinitie, Walter Harold *psychologist, educator*

La Conner
Knopf, Kenyon Alfred *economist, educator*

Port Angeles
Osborne, Richard Hazelet *anthropology and medical genetics educator*

Pullman
Dillman, Donald Andrew *sociologist, educator, survey methodologist*
McSweeney, Frances Kaye *psychology educator*
Warner, Dennis Allan *psychology educator*

Richland
Roop, Joseph McLeod *economist*

Seattle
Beyers, William Bjorn *geography educator*
Borgatta, Edgar F. *social psychologist, educator*
Chirot, Daniel *sociology and international studies educator*
Donovan, Dennis Michael *psychologist, researcher*
Gross, Edward *retired sociologist, educator, lawyer*
Hirschman, Charles, Jr. *sociologist, educator*
Matthews, Donald Rowe *political scientist, educator*
Morrill, Richard Leland *geographer, educator*
Olson, David John *political science educator*
Patrick, Donald Lee *social scientist, health services researcher*
Turnovsky, Stephen John *economics educator*
van den Berghe, Pierre Louis *sociologist, anthropologist*
Wolfle, Dael Lee *public affairs educator*

Spokane
Novak, Terry Lee *public administration educator*

University Place
Bourgaize, Robert G. *economist*

WYOMING

Laramie
Allen, John Logan *geographer, department chairman*
Chai, Winberg *political science educator*
Crocker, Thomas Dunstan *economics educator*
Gill, George Wilhelm *anthropologist*

Powell
Brophy, Dennis Richard *psychology and philosophy educator, administrator, clergyman*

CANADA

ALBERTA

Calgary
Stebbins, Robert Alan *sociology educator*

Edmonton
Freeman, Milton Malcolm Roland *anthropology educator*
Krotki, Karol Jozef *sociology educator, demographer*
Lechelt, Eugene Carl *psychology educator*

BRITISH COLUMBIA

Burnaby
Brantingham, Paul Jeffrey *criminology educator*
Copes, Parzival *economist, researcher*
Hayter, Roger *geographer educator*
Kimura, Doreen *psychology educator, researcher*

Vancouver
Aberle, David Friend *anthropologist, educator*
Cynader, Max Sigmund *psychology, physiology, brain research educator, researcher*
Elkins, David J. *political science educator*
Ericson, Richard Victor *social science-law educator, university official*
Feaver, George Arthur *political science educator*
Holsti, Kalevi Jacque *political scientist, educator*
Kesselman, Jonathan Rhys *economics educator, public policy researcher*
Langdon, Frank Corriston *political science educator, researcher*
Laponce, Jean Antoine *political scientist, educator*
Lipsey, Richard George *economist, educator*
Marchak, Maureen Patricia *anthropology and sociology educator*
McGee, Terry *geography educator*
Robinson, John Lewis *geography educator*
Shearer, Ronald Alexander *economics educator*
Suedfeld, Peter *psychologist, educator*
Tees, Richard Chisholm *psychology educator, researcher*

Victoria
Barber, Clarence Lyle *economics educator*

SASKATCHEWAN

Saskatoon
Randhawa, Bikkar Singh *psychologist, educator*

ENGLAND

Guildford
Yamamoto, Kaoru *retired psychology and education educator*

ADDRESS UNPUBLISHED

Aiken, Lewis Roscoe, Jr. *psychologist, educator*
Alker, Hayward Rose *political science educator*
Archer, Stephen Hunt *economist, educator*
Benbow, Richard Addison *psychological counselor*
Bergin, Allen Eric *clinical psychologist, educator*
Bonnell, Victoria Eileen *sociologist, educator*
Bracey, Earnest Norton *political science educator*
Debreu, Gerard *economics and mathematics educator*
Finnberg, Elaine Agnes *psychologist, editor*
Hirsch, Walter *economist, researcher*
Holmes, Paul Luther *political scientist, educational consultant*
Kendrick, Budd Leroy *psychologist*
Kohan, Dennis Lynn *international trade educator, consultant*
Lewis, Robert Turner *former psychologist*
McDonald, Michael Brian *economist, consultant*
Pearson, Richard Joseph *archaeologist, educator*
Pilisuk, Marc *community psychology educator*
Risley, Todd Robert *psychologist, educator*
Schubert, Glendon *political scientist, educator*
Sebastian, Peter *international affairs consultant, former ambassador*
Sharpe, William Forsyth *economics educator*
Smelser, Neil Joseph *sociologist*
Spinweber, Cheryl Lynn *psychologist, sleep specialist*
Textor, Robert Bayard *cultural anthropology writer, consultant, educator*
Tonello-Stuart, Enrica Maria *political economist*
Werner-Jacobsen, Emmy Elisabeth *developmental psychologist*